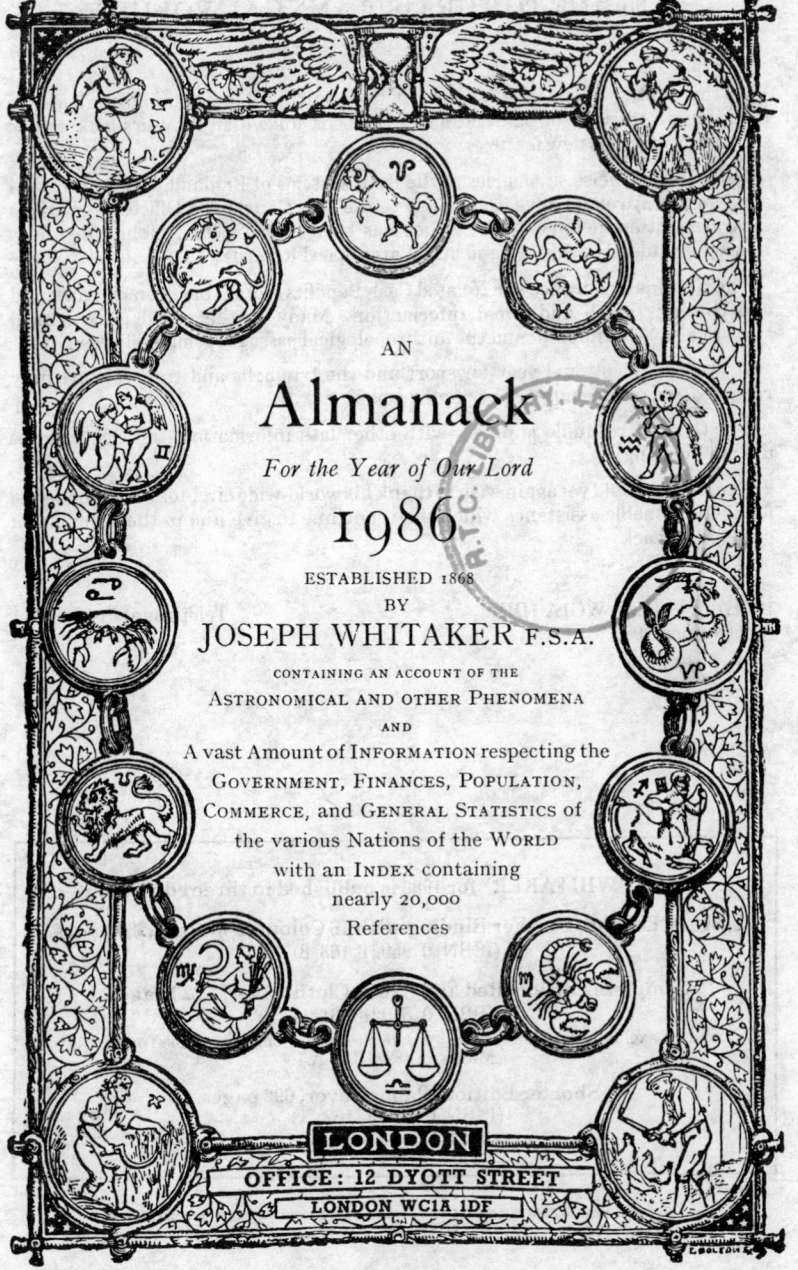

AN

Almanack

For the Year of Our Lord

1986

ESTABLISHED 1868

BY

JOSEPH WHITAKER F.S.A.

CONTAINING AN ACCOUNT OF THE

ASTRONOMICAL AND OTHER PHENOMENA

AND

A vast Amount of INFORMATION respecting the
GOVERNMENT, FINANCES, POPULATION,
COMMERCE, and GENERAL STATISTICS of
the various Nations of the WORLD
with an INDEX containing
nearly 20,000
References

LONDON

OFFICE: 12 DYOTT STREET
LONDON WC1A 1DF

PREFACE TO THE 118TH ANNUAL VOLUME
(1986)

In this 118th volume of WHITAKER it has continued to be the Editor's aim to maintain all those essential sections of the book for which its users look, but to seek also to present new features.

Useful and concise summaries of the legal systems of England, Wales, Scotland and Northern Ireland have been added to the Law Courts and Offices pages and a separate section devoted to the Police has been introduced. Among other new items is a detailed listing of Land and Water Speed Records.

The National Insurance and Related Cash Benefits section has been restructured and contains much additional information. Many of the world geographical statistics have been recast and the anthropological passages completely rewritten.

It was an exceptional year for sport and the triumphs and tragedies are duly recorded and commemorated by photographs.

The Cabinet reshuffle is noted, with other late information, in "Occurrences during Printing".

The Editor would yet again wish to thank his world-wide circle of correspondents, for the invaluable assistance which they continue to give him in the compilation of the Almanack.

12 Dyott Street, WC1A 1DF   Telephone: 01-836 8911
October, 1985

Note—"WHITAKER" for 1986 is published in three editions:

Library Edition, Leather Binding with 16 Coloured Maps, 1,220 pages.
(ISBN 0 85021 163 8)

Complete Edition, Red and Green Cloth Cover, 1,220 pages.
(ISBN 0 85021 161 1)
(Distributed exclusively in the U.S.A. by Gale Research Company, Book Tower, Detroit, Michigan 48226, U.S.A.)

Shorter Edition, Paper Cover, 692 pages.
(ISBN 0 85021 162 X)
© 1985 J. Whitaker & Sons, Ltd.

TYPESET BY CCC; PRINTED AND BOUND IN GREAT BRITAIN BY WILLIAM CLOWES LIMITED
BECCLES AND LONDON

TABLE OF CONTENTS

And in "Complete Edition" and "Library Edition"

INDEX

Pages 693–1236 are omitted from the Shorter *Edition*

Pages 693–1236 *are omitted from the* Shorter Edition

Pages 693–1236 are omitted from the Shorter Edition

Pages 693–1236 are omitted from the Shorter Edition

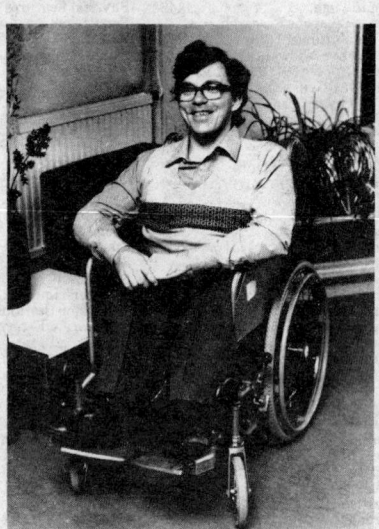

Pages 693–1236 are omitted from the Shorter Edition

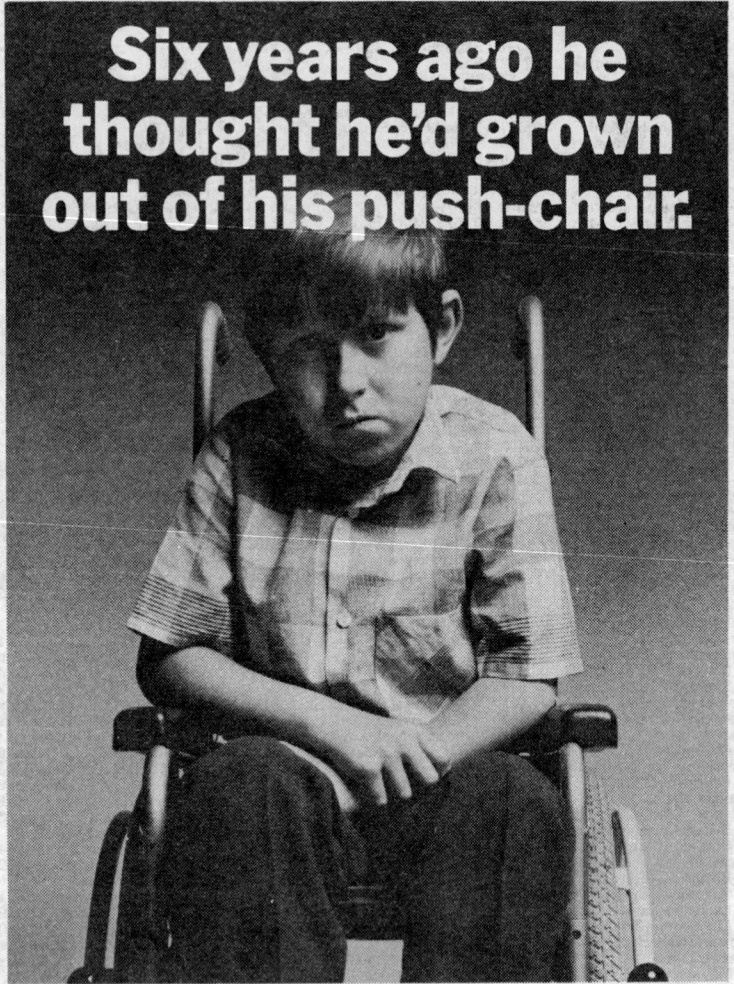

Six years ago he thought he'd grown out of his push-chair.

David has muscular dystrophy.

In its severest form, this cruel, muscle-wasting disease is fatal. Affecting little boys, it impairs their progress the moment they start to walk. In their teens, it halts it altogether. What a waste.

MUSCULAR DYSTROPHY

35 Macaulay Road, London SW4 0QP. Reg. Charity No. 205395.

"Would you like to be growing up today?"

Growing up is more depressing and difficult today than ever before. Housing conditions are often appalling, recreational facilities are often lacking; many young people are homeless while others live in unhappy homes. For most, secondary education sends them out ill-prepared for adult life and work. Worst of all is the extent of unemployment facing school-leavers.

In these circumstances, it is hardly surprising that some young people end up in trouble with the law.

The Rainer Foundation is the only national charity concentrating exclusively on these important problems of adolescence. Our pioneering projects help many hundreds of young people every year to find their feet. In our early days as the 'London Police Court Mission' one of our first tasks was the establishment of the Probation Service.

But we are seriously short of funds and must ask for your support — by covenant, legacy or donation. Your help will give someone a chance in life. "

The Rt. Hon. Lord Hunt of Llanfair Waterdine; President of the Rainer Foundation

Patron – HRH Prince Philip, Duke of Edinburgh.

The Rainer Foundation (Reg. Charity 213133), Attn. Christopher Naylor, 89a Blackheath Hill, London SE10 8TJ; 01 691 3124

Pages 693–1236 are omitted from the Shorter Edition

The Book Trade Benevolent Society

The Book Trade can take pride in its own charity, the Book Trade Benevolent Society: pride in its generous support of the Society and in the fine work done by the Society since it began well over 100 years ago.

The support which is offered by the Society is twofold. Some 40 people live at The Retreat, at Kings Langley in Hertfordshire, where the executive secretary, Mrs Ann Brown is permanently based. And, through its relief committee, the Society finds and helps, with advice and finance, retired book trade people with a wide range of worries.

Much valuable time is given by active members of the trade to the Society, but there is a continuing need to raise more money; The Retreat alone has running costs of over £50,000 a year.

Bookrest, the fund-raising and publicity arm of the BTBS under the chairmanship of Viscount Macmillan of Ovenden, offers events to suit all tastes, as an important addition to the donations and covenants which help to finance the Society. In 1985, Bookrest's activities included the Bookrest Walk, a Book Sale, a Pro-Am Golf Tournament and a Christmas Carol Service at St. Martin-in-the-Fields. But whilst Bookrest works hard to raise funds, and the Society receives so much generous help, more is always welcomed – and needed.

Your Charity - At Your Service

The Book Trade Benevolent Society, Dillon Lodge, The Retreat, Kings Langley, Herts WD4 8LT.

Pages 693–1236 are omitted from the Shorter Edition

Pages 693–1236 are omitted from the Shorter Edition

Pages 693–1236 are omitted from the **Shorter Edition**

Pages 693–1236 are omitted from the Shorter Edition

Pages 693–1236 are omitted from the Shorter Edition

Pages 693–1236 are omitted from the Shorter Edition

Pages 693–1236 are omitted from the Shorter Edition

Pages 693–1236 are omitted from the Shorter Edition

Pages 693–1236 *are omitted from the* Shorter Edition

Pages 693–1236 are omitted from the Shorter Edition

Pages 693–1236 are omitted from the Shorter Edition

Pages 693–1236 are omitted from the Shorter Edition

Pages 693–1236 are omitted from the **Shorter** *Edition*

Pages 693–1236 are omitted from the Shorter Edition

Pages 693–1236 are omitted from the Shorter Edition

Pages 693–1236 are omitted from the Shorter Edition

Pages 693–1236 are omitted from the Shorter Edition

Pages 693–1236 are omitted from the Shorter Edition

Pages 693–1236 are omitted from the Shorter Edition

Pages 693–1236 are omitted from the Shorter Edition

Pages 693–1236 are omitted from the Shorter *Edition*

Pages 693–1236 are omitted from the Shorter Edition

Pages 693–1236 are omitted from the Shorter Edition

Pages 693–1236 are omitted from the Shorter Edition

Pages 693–1236 are omitted from the Shorter Edition

Pages 693–1236 *are omitted from the* Shorter Edition

Pages 693–1236 are omitted from the Shorter Edition

Pages 693–1236 *are omitted from the* Shorter Edition

Pages 693–1236 are omitted from the Shorter *Edition*

Pages 693–1236 are omitted from the Shorter Edition

Pages 693–1236 are omitted from the Shorter Edition

Pages 693–1236 are omitted from the Shorter *Edition*

Pages 693–1236 are omitted from the Shorter Edition

Pages 693–1236 are omitted from the Shorter Edition

Pages 693–1236 *are omitted from the* Shorter Edition

Pages 693–1236 *are omitted from the* Shorter Edition

The Book Trade Benevolent Society

The Book Trade can take pride in its own charity, the Book Trade Benevolent Society: pride in its generous support of the Society and in the fine work done by the Society since it began well over 100 years ago.

The support which is offered by the Society is twofold. Some 40 people live at The Retreat, at Kings Langley in Hertfordshire, where the executive secretary, Mrs Ann Brown is permanently based. And, through its relief committee, the Society finds and helps, with advice and finance, retired book trade people with a wide range of worries.

Much valuable time is given by active members of the trade to the Society, but there is a continuing need to raise more money; The Retreat alone has running costs of over £50,000 a year.

Bookrest, the fund-raising and publicity arm of the BTBS under the chairmanship of Viscount Macmillan of Ovenden, offers events to suit all tastes, as an important addition to the donations and covenants which help to finance the Society. In 1985, Bookrest's activities included the Bookrest Walk, a Book Sale, a Pro-Am Golf Tournament and a Christmas Carol Service at St. Martin-in-the-Fields. But whilst Bookrest works hard to raise funds, and the Society receives so much generous help, more is always welcomed – and needed.

Your Charity – At Your Service

The Book Trade Benevolent Society, Dillon Lodge, The Retreat, Kings Langley, Herts WD4 8LT.

Pages 693–1236 *are omitted from the* Shorter Edition

Pages 693-1236 *are omitted from the* Shorter Edition

OCCURRENCES DURING PRINTING

EVENTS

Sept. 1. Mr. Robert Maxwell, publisher of Mirror Group Newspapers, reversed his decision to stop all printing at the group's London headquarters. **2.** Mrs. Thatcher announced her Government reshuffle (*see below*); Mr. Norman Tebbit became Conservative Party chairman and on the following day, Mr. Jeffrey Archer was appointed deputy chairman. England regained the Ashes after winning the Test series against Australia by three matches to one. **3.** T.U.C. in Blackpool voted to support miners' union demand that a future Labour government must reimburse fines imposed on the union during the pit strike. **9.** Two Asians died in riots in the Handsworth area of Birmingham; the Home Secretary was stoned when he visited the district. President Reagan announced limited economic sanctions against South Africa. **11.** President Botha stated that the South African Government was willing to restore citizenship to blacks in homelands. **12.** Britain ordered 25 Soviet spies to leave the country following the defection of Mr. Oleg Gordievsky, the KGB chief in London; tit-for-tat expulsions followed. **13.** The annual rate of inflation dropped in August to 6·2 per cent. **15.** Europe won the Ryder Cup. **19.** A severe earthquake hit Mexico City and western Mexico, causing thousands of deaths and devastation. **28.** Rioting erupted in Brixton with widespread burning and looting after a black woman was shot and seriously wounded during a police raid on her home. **30.** Alderman William Davis was elected next Lord Mayor of London.

Oct. 1. At the Labour conference in Bournemouth, Mr. Kinnock, the party leader, attacked the Militant Tendency members of Liverpool city council; on the following day, conference carried an N.U.M. resolution urging a future Labour government to reimburse the union for fines imposed on it during the pit strike. **6.** A policeman was hacked to death and others shot at in a huge riot by hundreds of black youths in Tottenham; 223 police and 20 civilians were injured; the riot followed the death of a West Indian woman who collapsed as police searched her house. **7.** An Italian cruise liner with 454 people aboard was seized off the Egyptian coast by Palestinian hijackers.

OBITUARIES

Sept. 1. Baroness Sharp, at the age of 82. **10.** Jock Stein, Scotland's football manager, aged 62. **17.** Laura Ashley, fashion designer, at the age of 60. **22.** Dickie Henderson, comedian, aged 62. **30.** Simone Signoret, French actress, at the age of 64. **Oct. 2.** Rock Hudson, film actor, aged 59.

THE CABINET
(Following Sept. reshuffle)

Prime Minister, First Lord of the Treasury, Minister for the Civil Service, Mrs. Margaret Thatcher.
Lord President of the Council and Leader of the Lords, The Viscount Whitelaw.
Lord Chancellor, The Lord Hailsham of St. Marylebone.
Foreign and Commonwealth Secretary, Sir Geoffrey Howe.
Trade and Industry Secretary, Leon Brittan.
Chancellor of the Exchequer, Nigel Lawson.
Home Secretary, Douglas Hurd.
Education Secretary, Sir Keith Joseph.
Energy Secretary, Peter Walker.
Defence Secretary, Michael Heseltine.
Scottish Secretary, George Younger.
Welsh Secretary, Nicholas Edwards.
Lord Privy Seal and Leader of the Commons, John Biffen.
Social Services Secretary, Norman Fowler.
Chancellor of the Duchy of Lancaster, Norman Tebbit.
Northern Ireland Secretary, Tom King.
Minister of Agriculture, Fisheries and Food, Michael Jopling.
Transport Secretary, Nicholas Ridley.
Employment Secretary, The Lord Young of Graffham.
Environment Secretary, Kenneth Baker.
Paymaster-General, Kenneth Clarke.
Chief Secretary to the Treasury, John MacGregor.

ELEMENTS

Element	Symbol	Atomic Number	Element	Symbol	Atomic Number	Element	Symbol	Atomic Number
Actinium	Ac	89	Hafnium	Hf	72	Promethium	Pm	61
Aluminium	Al	13	Helium	He	2	Protactinium	Pa	91
Americium	Am	95	Holmium	Ho	67	Radium	Ra	88
Antimony	Sb	51	Hydrogen	H	1	Radon	Rn	86
Argon	Ar	18	Indium	In	49	Rhenium	Re	75
Arsenic	As	33	Iodine	I	53	Rhodium	Rh	45
Astatine	At	85	Iridium	Ir	77	Rubidium	Rb	37
Barium	Ba	56	Iron	Fe	26	Ruthenium	Ru	44
Berkelium	Bk	97	Krypton	Kr	36	Samarium	Sm	62
Beryllium	Be	4	Lanthanum	La	57	Scandium	Sc	21
Bismuth	Bi	83	Lawrencium	Lr	103	Selenium	Se	34
Boron	B	5	Lead	Pb	82	Silicon	Si	14
Bromine	Br	35	Lithium	Li	3	Silver	Ag	47
Cadmium	Cd	48	Lutetium	Lu	71	Sodium	Na	11
Caesium	Cs	55	Magnesium	Mg	12	Strontium	Sr	38
Calcium	Ca	20	Manganese	Mn	25	Sulphur	S	16
Californium	Cf	98	Mendelevium	Md	101	Tantalum	Ta	73
Carbon	C	6	Mercury	Hg	80	Technetium	Tc	43
Cerium	Ce	58	Molybdenum	Mo	42	Tellurium	Te	52
Chlorine	Cl	17	Neodymium	Nd	60	Terbium	Tb	65
Chromium	Cr	24	Neon	Ne	10	Thallium	Tl	81
Cobalt	Co	27	Neptunium	Np	93	Thorium	Th	90
Copper	Cu	29	Nickel	Ni	28	Thulium	Tm	69
Curium	Cm	96	Niobium	Nb	41	Tin	Sn	50
Dysprosium	Dy	66	Nitrogen	N	7	Titanium	Ti	22
Einsteinium	Es	99	Nobelium	No	102	Tungsten	W	74
Erbium	Er	68	Osmium	Os	76	(Wolfram)		
Europium	Eu	63	Oxygen	O	8	Uranium	U	92
Fermium	Fm	100	Palladium	Pd	46	Vanadium	V	23
Flourine	F	9	Phosphorus	P	15	Xenon	Xe	54
Francium	Fr	87	Platinum	Pt	78	Ytterbium	Yb	70
Gadolinium	Gd	64	Plutonium	Pu	94	Yttrium	Y	39
Gallium	Ga	31	Polonium	Po	84	Zinc	Zn	30
Germanium	Ge	32	Potassium	K	19	Zirconium	Zr	40
Gold	Au	79	Praseodymium	Pr	59			

ROMAN EMPERORS

[The *First Triumvirate* (Julius Cæsar, Pompey and Crassus) 60–53 B.C.]

The Twelve Cæsars

I. Caius JULIUS CÆSAR, *born* A.U.C. 651 (102 B.C.); *Dictator* A.U.C. 705 (48 B.C.); *Assassinated* A.U.C. 709 (44 B.C.).

[The *Second Triumvirate* (Octavian, Antony and Lepidus) 44–31 B.C.]

II. Caius Julius Cæsar Octavianus AUGUSTUS, *born* 63 B.C.; *Emperor* 27 B.C.; *Died* A.D. 14.
III. Claudius Nero Cæsar TIBERIUS, *born* 24 B.C.; *Emperor* A.D. 14; *Died* A.D. 37.
IV. Caius Cæsar CALIGULA, *born* A.D. 12; *Emperor* A.D. 37; *Assassinated* A.D. 41.
V. Tiberius Drusus CLAUDIUS, *born* 10 B.C.; *Emperor* A.D. 41; *Assassinated* A.D. 54.
VI. Claudius NERO, *born* A.D. 37; *Emperor* A.D. 54; *Suicide* A.D. 68.
VII. Servius Sulpicius GALBA, *born* 3 B.C.; *Emperor* A.D. 68; *Assassinated* A.D. 69.
VIII. Marcus Salvius OTHO, *born* A.D. 32; *Emperor* A.D. 69; *Suicide* A.D. 69.
IX. AULUS VITELLIUS, *born* A.D. 15; *Emperor* A.D. 69; *Assassinated* A.D. 69.
X. Titus Flavius VESPASIAN, *born* A.D. 9; *Emperor* A.D. 69; *Died* A.D.79.
XI. Flavius Sabinus Vespasianus TITUS, *born* A.D. 48; *Emperor* A.D. 79; *Died* A.D. 81.
XII. Titus Flavius DOMITIAN, *born* A.D. 52; *Emperor* A.D. 81; *Assassinated* A.D. 96.

WEDDING ANNIVERSARIES

First	Cotton	Twentieth	China
Second	Paper	Twenty-Fifth	Silver
Third	Leather	Thirtieth	Pearl
Fourth	Fruit and Flower	Thirty-Fifth	Coral
Fifth	Wood	Fortieth	Ruby
Sixth	Sugar	Forty-Fifth	Sapphire
Seventh	Wool	Fiftieth	Gold
Tenth	Tin	Sixtieth	Diamond
Twelfth	Silk and Fine Linen	Seventieth	Platinum
Fifteenth	Crystal		

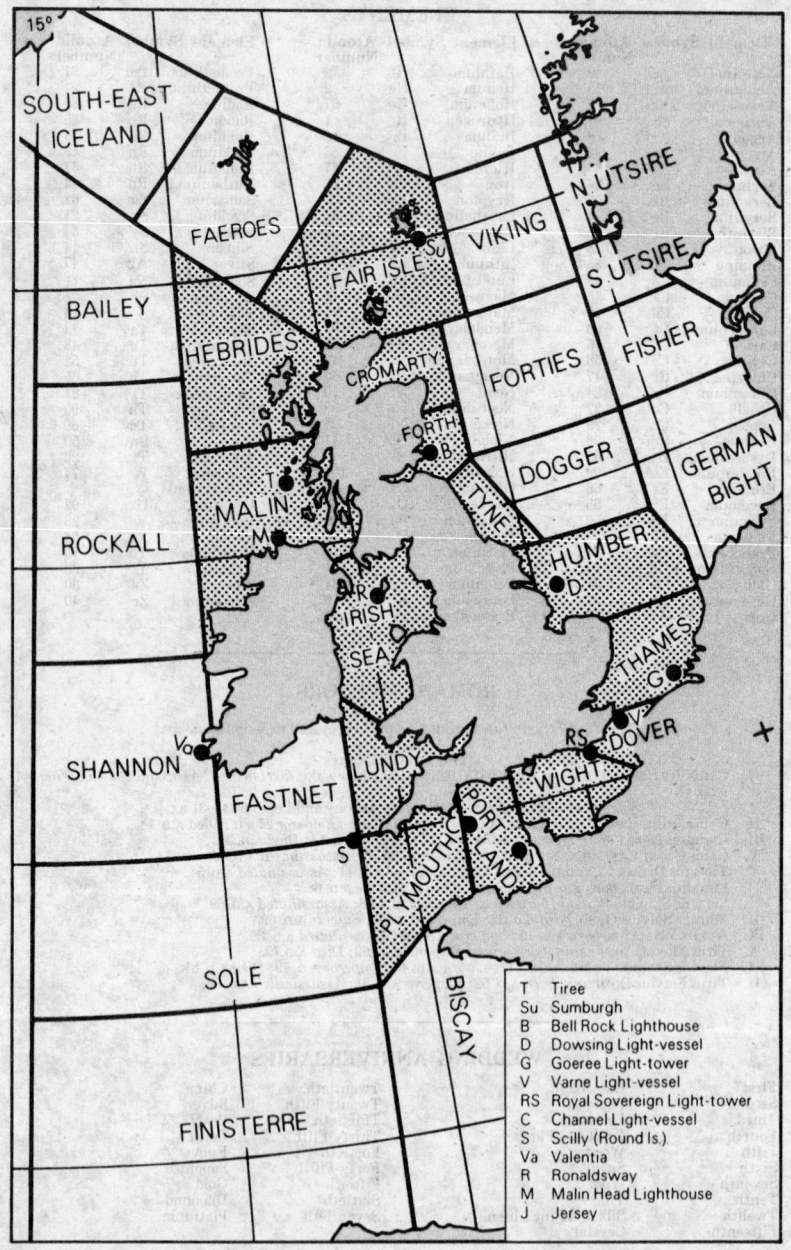

T	Tiree
Su	Sumburgh
B	Bell Rock Lighthouse
D	Dowsing Light-vessel
G	Goeree Light-tower
V	Varne Light-vessel
RS	Royal Sovereign Light-tower
C	Channel Light-vessel
S	Scilly (Round Is.)
Va	Valentia
R	Ronaldsway
M	Malin Head Lighthouse
J	Jersey

SYMBOLS FOR CORRECTING PROOFS

Supplied by WILLIAM CLOWES LTD, Beccles, Suffolk, Printers of "WHITAKER"

Letter(s) or word(s) requiring alteration should be struck through IN INK in the text and the substitution should be written in the nearest margin followed by / (the symbol used to denote that the marginal mark is concluded). Insertions should be indicated by / or ∧ at the conclusion of the marginal mark *and* at the desired place in the text.

Alteration required	Mark in margin	Mark in text	Alteration required	Mark in margin	Mark in text
Delete (take out)	*(symbol)* or *(symbol)*	/ or ——— Vertical stroke to delete one or two letters; horizontal line to delete more	Take letter(s) or word(s) from beginning of one line to end of preceding line	*back* or *take back*	*(bracket symbol)*
Delete and close up	*(symbol)* or *(symbol)*	Strike out letter(s) not required and add "close up" mark above and below	Begin a new paragraph	*n. p.*	before first word of new paragraph
Close up: delete space between letters	*(symbol)*	linking letters or words	No new para. here or run on previous matter with later matter	*run on*	between paras. or other matter
Use ligature (fi, fl, ffl, etc.) or diphthong (æ, œ)	*enclosing ligature or diphthong required*	enclosing letters to be altered	Spell out in full the abbreviation, contraction, or figure	*spell out*	Encircle words, etc., or figures concerned
Insert space between letters or words	# ∧	∧	Insert omitted portion of copy	*out - see copy*	∧ Attach the relevant copy to the proof, indicating omitted portion
Leave as printed (i.e. a cancellation of previous marking)	*stet*	.... under letter(s) or word(s) crossed out but to be retained	Inserted or substituted letter(s), figure(s), or sign(s) under which this is placed to be superscript (i.e. high alignment)[1]	*(symbol)* *(see footnote)*	∧ for insertions For substitutions encircle letter(s). figure(s). or sign(s) to be altered
Invert type (of letter(s) upside down)	*(symbol)*	Encircle letter(s) to be altered	Inserted or substituted letter(s), figure(s), or sign(s) over which this is placed to be subscript (low alignment)[2]	*(symbol)* *(see footnote)*	∧ for insertions For substitutions encircle letter(s), figure(s), etc., to be altered
"Battered" letter(s) to be replaced by similar but undamaged characters	×	Encircle letter(s) or word(s) to be replaced and write the correct letter(s) in the margin			
Push down space or "high" letter(s) or word(s)	*(symbol)*	Encircle space, letter(s), or word(s) affected	Change to lower case	*l. c.*	Encircle letter(s) to be altered
Transpose	*tr.* or *trs.*	*(symbol)* between letters or words, numbered when necessary	Replace "wrong fount" by letter(s) of correct fount	*w. f.*	Encircle letter(s) or word(s) to be altered
Take letter(s) or word(s) from end of one line to beginning of next line	*take over* or *over*	*(bracket symbol)*	Change to capital letters	*caps.*	≡ under letter(s) or word(s) to be altered
			Change to small capitals	*s. c.*	═ under letter(s) or word(s) to be altered

(symbol) indicates a superior (superscript) figure one   *(symbol)* indicates an inferior (subscript) figure two

Alteration required	Mark in margin	Mark in text	Alteration required	Mark in margin	Mark in text
Use capital letters for initial letter(s) (as desired) and small capitals for rest of word(s)	*caps* & *s.c.*	≡ under initial letter(s) and ≡ under the remainder of the word(s)	Move lines to the left	⌐⌐	at right side of group of lines to be moved (indicating approx. position)
Change to bold type	*bold*	∿ Draw wavy line under letter(s) or word(s) to be altered	Move portion of matter so that it is positioned as indicated	[ ]	[ ] at limits of required position
Change to roman type	*rom.*	Encircle letter(s) or word(s) to be altered	Raise lines	*raise*	⤒ over lines to be raised
Change to italic type	*italic*	⎯ Draw this straight line under letter(s) or word(s) to be altered	Lower lines	*lower*	⤓ under lines to be lowered
			Correct the vertical alignment	‖	‖
Letter(s) or word(s) to be underlined	*underline*	under letter(s), word(s), etc., to be underlined	Straighten lines	≡	through lines to be straightened
Equalize space between words	*eq. #*	⌐ between words	Insert parentheses (round-shaped brackets)	(/) or c|)|	⅄ ⅄ ⅄
Reduce space	*less #*	⌐ between words	Insert [square] brackets	[/] or [|]|	⅄ ⅄ ⅄
Space to be inserted between lines or paragraphs	# >	*Amount of space should be indicated*	Insert hyphen	ⵜ/	⅄
To be placed in centre of line, etc.	*centre*	Position to be indicated by ⌐ ⌐	Insert en (= half-em) rule (*see above*)	en/	⅄
Indent one en (approx. space occupied by n of type in use)	en ☐⅄	indicating approximate position	Insert one-em rule (*see above*)	em/	⅄
Indent one em (approx. space occupied by M of type in use)	em ☐⅄	Ditto	Insert two-em rule (*see above*)	2em/	⅄
Indent two ems (approx. space occupied by MM of type in use)	☐☐⅄	Ditto	Insert apostrophe	⸲	⅄
Move to the left	⌐	Ditto	Insert single quotation marks	⸲ ⸲	⅄ ⅄
Move to the right	⌐	Ditto	Insert double quotation marks	⸳⸳ ⸳⸳	⅄ ⅄
Move lines to the right	⌐	at left side of group of lines to be moved (indicating approx. position)	Insert ellipsis	••• /	⅄
			Insert leader (*visual guide to alignment in contents pages, etc.*)	⊙⊙⊙ ⊙⊙ ⊙	⅄ (three, two, or one dot)
			Insert shilling stroke (oblique)	Ⓛ	⅄

| *Punctuation* | ⸲⅄ | ⸳/ | ⸲⅄ | ⸳/ | ⊙ | ⊙ | ?⅄ | ?/ | !⅄ | !/ |

FOREIGN EXCHANGE RATES

Country	Denomination	1939 Average Rate to £ (approx.)	16 September, 1985 Middle Rate
A. London Market Rates			
Austria	*Schilling*	—	27·2295
Belgium	*Franc*	26·49 *Belgas*	78·15
Canada	*Canadian Dollar*	4·545	1·8445
Denmark	*Krone*	22·26	14·0075
Finland	*Markka*	217¼	8·2125
France	*Franc*	176·10	11·8015
Germany (West)	*Deutsche Mark*		3·8710
Greece	*Drachma*	545	187·00
Italy	*Lira*	85	2,588·0
Japan	*Yen*	½d	323·90
Netherlands	*Guilder*	8·34	4·3480
Netherlands (Antilles)	*Antillian Guilder*	8·34	2·41
Norway	*Krone*	19·45	11·3415
Portugal	*Escudo*	110·07	234·35
Spain	*Peseta*	42·45	229·45
Sweden	*Krona*	18·59	11·3750
Switzerland	*Franc*	19·87	3·1980
U.S.A......................	*Dollar*	4·485	1·3430
B. Former Scheduled Territories			
Australia...................	*Australian Dollar*	A£1·2525	1·9765
Bahamas	*Bahamas Dollar*	—	1·3430
Barbados	*Barbados Dollar*	—	2·6730
Belize	*Belize Dollar*	—	2·66
Bermuda	*Bermuda Dollar*	—	1·3325
Cyprus....................	*Cyprus £*	—	0·801
Ghana	*New Cedi*	—	76·2660
Hong Kong	*Hong Kong Dollar*	—	10·5025
Iceland....................	*Krona*	—	56·5580
India......................	*Rupee*	13·38	16·46
Jamaica	*Jamaica Dollar*	—	7·61
Jordan	*Dinar*	Par	0·5235
Kenya	*Shilling*	—	23·00
Kuwait	*Dinar*	—	0·1075
Libya	*Dinar*	—	0·3935
Malawi....................	*Kwacha*	—	2·3680
Malaysia	*Ringitt*	8·571	3·3510
Malta	*Maltese £*	—	0·618
New Zealand...............	*New Zealand Dollar*	£1·2425	2·5630
Nigeria	*Naira*	—	1·2631
Pakistan	*Rupee*	—	21·35
South Africa...............	*Rand*	S.A.£1	3·28
Sri Lanka	*Rupee*	13·38 (Ceylon Rs.)	36·1750
Tanzania	*Shilling*	—	22·9750
Trinidad	*Trinidad and Tobago $*	—	3·20
Uganda	*Shilling*	—	797·50
Yemen	*Riyal*	—	9·33
Zambia....................	*Kwacha*	—	3·00
C. Other Rates			
Algeria....................	*Dinar*	—	6·70
Argentina	*Austral*	19	1·0640
Bolivia	*Peso*	141·50	99,675·0
Brazil	*Cruzeiro*	82	9,914·5
Bulgaria	*Lev*	375	1·4145
Burma	*Kyat*	13·38	11·4514
Chile......................	*Peso*	116½	231·02
China	*Renminbi Yuan*	4½	3·9667
Colombia	*Peso*	7·59	200·98
Costa Rica	*Colon*	25·16	68·71
Cuba	*Peso*	4·386	1·2375
Czechoslovakia	*Koruna*	—	9·20
Ecuador	*Sucre*	66	128·44
Egypt	*Egyptian £*	97½ (per £100 London)	1·1039
Ethiopia...................	*Ethiopian Dollar*	—	2·7550
Germany (East)	*Ostmark*	—	3·8710

Country	Denomination	1939 Average Rate to £ (approx.)	16 September, 1985 Middle Rate
Guatemala	*Quetzel*	4·386	1·3430
Guinea Republic	*Syli*	—	32·40
Haiti	*Gourde*	22·4	6·65
Honduras Republic	*Lempira*	8¼	2·67
Hungary	*Forint*	20¼	66·9855
Indonesia	*Rupiah*	—	1,492·47
Iran	*Rial*	80·50 (Persian)	121·00
Iraq	*Dinar*	Par	0·4141
Israel	*Israel £*	Par	1,975·00
Lebanon	*Lebanese £*	9·65	24·82
Malagasy Republic	*M. G. Franc*	17 (F. Fr.)	788·00
Mexico	*Peso*	—	510·35
Morocco	*Dirham*	176·10 (F. Fr.)	14·00
Nicaragua	*Cordoba*	24	37·10
Paraguay	*Guarani*	—	318·00
Peoples Democratic Republic of Vietnam	*Dong*	—	131·25
Peru	*Sol*	24¼	18,536·5
Philippines	*Peso*	—	23·70
Poland	*Zloty*	23¼	203·49
Romania	*Leu*	655	5·71
Salvador, El	*Colon*	11·20	3·33
Saudi Arabia	*Riyal*	—	4·9040
Sudan	*Sudan £*	97¼ (per 100)	3·32
Syria	*Syrian £*	—	9·00
Thailand	*Baht*	10·91	36·1750
Tunisia	*Tunisian Dinar*	—	1·1010
Turkey	*Turkish Lira*	—	726·52
Uruguay	*New Peso*	9	138·77
U.S.S.R.	*Rouble*	23·75	1·13
Venezuela	*Bolivar*	14·15	19·6755
Yugoslavia	*New Y Dinar*	197¼ (YD)	397·1586
Zaire Republic	*Zaire*	—	71·0054

BUCHAN'S WEATHER PERIODS OR RECURRENCES OF WEATHER

Dr. Alexander Buchan, f.r.s., Secretary of the Scottish Meteorological Society, published in 1867 a paper in the Journal of that Society entitled "Interruptions in the regular rise and fall of temperature in the course of the year". Buchan gave six cold periods and three warm periods, based on his examination of the mean daily temperature as recorded at stations in Scotland covering long periods. The cold periods were February 7–14, April 11–14, May 9–14, June 29–July 4, August 6–11, November 6–13, and the warm periods July 12–15, August 12–15, and December 3–14. This early work aroused considerable interest later. It should be noted, however, that Buchan claimed no more than the existence of tendencies for short spells of relatively cold and warm weather to occur at certain times of the year.

In recent years these smaller fluctuations of weather super-imposed on the normal seasonal changes have been examined from the aspect of tendencies to stormy or anticyclonic spells over the British Isles and have been referred to as "singularities". Stormy periods are relatively warm in winter and cool in summer. The following tendencies have been given:—Jan. 5–17 stormy; Jan. 18–24 anticyclonic; Jan. 24–Feb. 1 stormy; Feb. 8–16 anticyclonic; Feb. 21–25 cold; Feb. 26–Mar. 9 stormy; Mar. 12–19 anticyclonic; Mar. 24–31 stormy; April 10–15 stormy; April 23–26 unsettled; June 1–21 summer monsoon; July 10–24 warm; Aug. 20–30 stormy; Sept. 1–17 anticyclonic; Sept. 17–24 stormy; Sept. 24–Oct. 4 anticyclonic; Oct. 5–12 stormy; Oct. 16–20 anticyclonic; Oct. 24–Nov. 13 stormy; Nov. 15–21 anticyclonic; Nov. 24–Dec. 14 stormy; Dec. 18–24 anticyclonic; Dec. 25–Jan. 1 stormy.

ABBREVIATIONS

Ψ = Seaport.

A

A.—Associate of.
A.A.—Automobile Association; Anti-Aircraft.
A.A.A.—Amateur Athletic Association.
A. and M.—(Hymns) Ancient and Modern.
A.B.—Able-bodied seaman.
A.B.A.—Amateur Boxing Association.
abbrev.—abbreviation.
A.B.M.—Anti-ballistic missile defence system.
Abr.—abridged.
a.c.—alternating current.
a/c.—accounts.
A.C.—Companion, Order of Australia; Aircraftman.
A.C.A.S.—Advisory, Conciliation and Arbitration Service.
A.C.T.—Australian Capital Territory.
A.C.T.T.—Association of Cinematograph, Television and Allied Technicians.
A.C.U.—Association of Commonwealth Universities.
ad(vert)—advertisement.
A.D.—(*Anno Domini*) In the year of our Lord.
A.D.C.—Aide-de-Camp.
A.D.C. (P).—Personal A.D.C. to The Queen.
adj.—adjective.
Adjt.—Adjutant.
Ad lib.—(*ad libitum*) at pleasure.
Adm.—Admiral; Admission.
adv.—adverb.
A.E.—Air Efficiency Award.
A.E.A.—Atomic Energy Authority.
A.E.M.—Air Efficiency Medal.
A.E.R.E.—Atomic Energy Research Establishment.
A.F.C.—Air Force Cross; Association Football Club.
A.F.M.—Air Force Medal.
A.F.V.—Armoured fighting vehicle.
A.G.—Adjutant-General.
A.H.—(*Anno Hegirae*) In the year of the Hegira.
A.I.D.S.—Acquired Immune Deficiency Syndrome.
alt.—altitude.
a.m.—(*ante meridiem*) before noon.
A.M.—(*Anno mundi*) In the year of the world.
A.M.D.G.—(*Ad majorem Dei gloriam*) To the greater glory of God.
amp.—ampere.
A.N.C.—African National Congress.
anon.—anonymous.
A.N.Z.A.C.—Australian and New Zealand Army Corps.
A.O.—Officer, Order of Australia.
A.O.C.—Air Officer Commanding.
A.P.T.—Advanced Passenger Train.
A.R.C.—Agricultural Research Council.
A.S.—Anglo-Saxon.

A.S.A.—Amateur Swimming Association.
A.S.B.—Alternative Service Book.
A.S.E.A.N.—Association of South East Asia Nations.
A.S.H.—Action on Smoking and Health.
A.S.L.E.F.—Associated Society of Locomotive Engineers and Firemen.
A.S.L.I.B.—Association for Information Management (*formerly* Association of Special Libraries and Information Bureaux).
A.S.T.M.S.—Association of Scientific, Technical and Managerial Staffs.
A.T.C.—Air Training Corps.
A.U.C.—(*ab urbe condita*) In the year from the foundation of Rome; (*anno urbis conditae*) In the year of the founding of the city.
A.U.E.W.—Amalgamated Union of Engineering Workers.
A.U.T.—Association of University Teachers.
A.V.—Authorized Version.
A.V.R.—Army Volunteer Reserve.
A.W.O.L.—Absent without leave.

B

b.—born; bowled.
B.A.—Bachelor of Arts.
B.A.A.—British Astronomical Association; British Airports Authority.
B. Acc.—Bachelor of Accountancy.
B.A.F.—British Athletic Federation.
B.A.F.T.A.—British Academy of Film and Television Arts.
B.A.O.R.—British Army of the Rhine.
B. Arch.—Bachelor of Architecture.
B.A.S.—British Antarctic Survey.
B.B.—Boys' Brigade.
B.B.C.—British Broadcasting Corporation.
B.C.—Before Christ; British Columbia.
B. Ch. (or Ch.B.)—Bachelor of Surgery.
B.C.L.—*do*, of Civil Law.
B. Com.—*do*, of Commerce.
B.D.—*do*, of Divinity.
B.D.A.—British Dental Association.
B.D.S. (or B.Ch.D.)—Bachelor of Dental Surgery.
B. Ed.—*do*, of Education.
B.E.M.—British Empire Medal.
B. Eng.—Bachelor of Engineering.
B.F.I.—British Film Institute.
B.F.P.O.—British Forces Post Office.
B.I.M.—British Institute of Management.
B.L.A.I.S.E.—British Library Automated Information Service.
B. Litt.—Bachelor of Literature *or* of Letters.

B.M.—*do*, of Medicine; British Museum.
B.M.A.—British Medical Association.
B.M.C.—British Motor Corporation.
B. Mus.—Bachelor of Music.
B.O.T.B.—British Overseas Trade Board.
Bp.—Bishop.
B. Pharm.—Bachelor of Pharmacy.
B. Phil.—*do*, of Philosophy.
Br. (*or* Brit.)—British.
B.R.—British Rail.
B.R.C.S.—British Red Cross Society.
Brig.—Brigadier.
B.Sc.—Bachelor of Science.
B.S.C.—British Steel Corporation.
B.S.I.—British Standards Institution.
B.S.T.—British Summer Time.
Bt. (*or* Bart.)—Baronet.
B.T.G.—British Technology Group.
B. Th.—Bachelor of Theology.
B.t.u.—British thermal unit.
B.U.P.A.—British United Provident Association.
B.V.M.—Blessed Virgin Mary.
B.V.M.S.—Bachelor of Veterinary Medicine and Surgery.
B.W.B.—British Waterways Board.

C

c.—(*circa*) about.
C.—Celsius; Centigrade.
C. (*or* Con.)—Conservative.
C.A.—Chartered Accountant (*Scottish Institute*).
C.A.A.—Civil Aviation Authority.
C.A.B.—Citizens' Advice Bureau.
Cantab.—(of) Cambridge.
Cantuar.—of Canterbury (*Archbishop*).
C.A.P.—Common Agricultural Policy.
Capt.—Captain.
Caricom—Caribbean Community and Common Market.
Carliol.—of Carlisle (*Bishop*).
C.A.S.—Chief of Air Staff.
C.B.—Companion, Order of the Bath.
C.B.E.—Commander, Order of the British Empire.
C.B.I.—Confederation of British Industry.
cc.—cubic centimetres.
C.C.—County Council; County Councillor; Chamber of Commerce.
C.C.C.—County Cricket Club.
C. Chem.—Chartered Chemist.
C.D.—Civil Defence.
Cdr.—Commander.
Cdre.—Commodore.
C.E.—Civil Engineer.
C.E.G.B.—Central Electricity Generating Board.
C. Eng.—Chartered Engineer.
C.E.N.T.O.—Central Treaty Organization.
C.E.T.—Common External Tariff; Central European Time.

Cestr.—of Chester (*Bishop*).

cf.—confer; compare.

C.F.—Chaplain to the Forces.

C.G.M.—Conspicuous Gallantry Medal.

C.G.S.—Chief of General Staff; Centimetre-gramme-second (system).

C.H.—Companion of Honour.

Ch.B./M.—Bachelor/Master of Surgery.

C.I.—The Imperial Order of the Crown of India; Channel Islands.

C.I.A.—Central Intelligence Agency.

C.I.D.—Criminal Investigation Department.

C.I.E.—Companion, Order of the Indian Empire.

c.i.f.—cost, insurance and freight.

C.-in-C.—Commander-in-Chief.

C.I.P.F.A.—Chartered Institute of Public Finance and Accountancy.

Cicestr.—of Chichester (*Bishop*).

C.L. (*or* C. Litt.)—Companion of Literature.

C.M.—(*Chirurgiae Magister*) Master of Surgery.

C.M.G.—Companion, Order of St. Michael and St. George.

C.M.S.—Church Missionary Society.

C.N.A.A.—Council for National Academic Awards.

C.N.D.—Campaign for Nuclear Disarmament.

c/o—care of.

C.O.—Commanding Officer; Conscientious Objector.

C.O.D.—Cash on delivery.

C. of E.—Church of England.

C.O.H.S.E.—Confederation of Health Service Employees.

C.O.I.—Central Office of Information.

Col.—Colonel.

Comecon.—Council for Mutual Economic Assistance (East European).

C.P.—Communist Party.

Cpl.—Corporal.

C.P.R.E.—Council for the Protection of Rural England.

C.R.E.—Council for Racial Equality.

C.S.E.—Certificate of Secondary Education.

C.S.I.—Companion, Order of the Star of India.

C.T.—Civic Trust.

C.T.C.—Cyclists' Touring Club.

C.V.O.—Commander, Royal Victorian Order.

cwt.—hundredweight.

D

d.—(*denarius*) penny.

D.B.E.—Dame Commander, Order of the British Empire.

d.c.—direct current.

D.C.—District of Columbia.

D.C.B.—Dame Commander, Order of the Bath.

D. Ch.—(*Doctor Chirurgiae*) Doctor of Surgery.

D.C.L.—Doctor of Civil Law.

D.C.M.—Distinguished Conduct Medal.

D.C.M.G.—Dame Commander, Order of St. Michael and St. George.

D.C.V.O.—Dame Commander, Royal Victorian Order.

D.D.—Doctor of Divinity.

D.D.S.—*do*, of Dental Surgery.

D.D.T.—dichlorodiphenyl-trichloroethane (insecticide).

del.—(*delineavit*) he/she drew it.

D.E.S.—Department of Education and Science.

D.F.C.—Distinguished Flying Cross.

D.F.M.—Distinguished Flying Medal.

D.G.—(*Dei gratia*) By the grace of God; Director-General.

D.H.Q.—District Headquarters.

D.H.S.S.—Department of Health and Social Security.

Dip. Ed.—Diploma in Education.

Dip. H. E.—Diploma in Higher Education.

Dip. Tech.—Diploma in Technology.

D.J.—Disc jockey.

D.L.—Deputy-Lieutenant.

D. Litt.—Doctor of Letters *or* of Literature.

D. Mus.—*do*, of Music.

D.N.A.—deoxyribonucleic acid.

D.N.B.—Dictionary of National Biography.

Do.—(*ditto*) the same.

D.o.E.—Department of the Environment.

D.O.M.—(*Dominus Omnium Magister*) God the Master of All.

D. Phil.—Doctor of Philosophy.

D.P.P.—Director of Public Prosecutions.

Dr.—Doctor.

D.Sc.—Doctor of Science.

D.S.C.—Distinguished Service Cross.

D.S.M.—Distinguished Service Medal.

D.S.O.—Companion, Distinguished Service Order.

D.Th.—Doctor of Theology.

Dunelm.—of Durham.

D.V.—(*Deo volente*) God willing.

E

E. (*or* O.E.)—Errors and omissions excepted.

Ebor.—of York (*Archbishop*).

E.C.—European Community; Electricity Council.

E.C.G.—Electrocardiograph.

E.C.S.C.—European Coal and Steel Community.

E.C.T.U.—European Confederation of Trade Unions.

E.D.—Efficiency Decoration.

E.E.C.—European Economic Community.

E.E.G.—Electroencephalograph.

E.F.T.A.—European Free Trade Association.

e.g.—(*exempli gratia*) for the sake of example.

Elien.—of Ely (*Bishop*).

E.M.S.—European Monetary System.

E.N.E.A.—European Nuclear Energy Agency.

E.R.—Elizabeth Regina.

E.R.D.—Emergency Reserve Decoration.

E.R.N.I.E.—Electronic random number indicator equipment.

E.S.A.—European Space Agency.

E.S.P.—Extra-sensory perception.

E.S.R.C.—Economic and Social Research Council.

et al.—(*et alibi*) and elsewhere; (*et alii*) and others.

etc.—(*et cetera*) and the other things.

et seq.—(*et sequentia*) and the following.

Euratom—European Atomic Energy Commission.

ex lib.—(*ex libris*) from the books of.

Exon.—of Exeter (*Bishop*).

F

f (ff)—and the following page(s).

F.—Fahrenheit; Fellow of.

F.A.—Football Association.

F.A.N.Y.—First Aid Nursing Yeomanry.

F.A.O.—Food and Agriculture Organization.

F.B.A.—Fellow of British Academy.

F.B.A.A.—*do*, of the British Association of Accountants.

F.B.I.—Federal Bureau of Investigation.

F.B.I.M.—Fellow of the British Institute of Management.

F.B.S.—*do*, of Botanical Society.

F.C.A.—*do*, of Institute of Chartered Accountants (of England and Wales).

F.C.C.A.—*do*, of Association of Certified Accountants.

F.C.G.I.—*do*, of City and Guilds Institute.

F.C.I.A.—*do*, of Corporation of Insurance Agents.

F.C.I.B.—*do*, of Corporation of Insurance Brokers.

F.C.I.B.S.—*do*, of Chartered Institution of Building-Services Engineers.

F.C.I.I.—*do*, of Chartered Insurance Institute.

F.C.I.S.—*do*, of Chartered Institute of Secretaries and Administrators.

F.C.I.T.—*do*, of Chartered Institute of Transport.

F.C.M.A.—*do*, of Institute of Cost and Management Accountants.

F.C.O.—Foreign and Commonwealth Office.

fcp.—foolscap.

F.C.P.—Fellow of the College of Preceptors.

F.D.—(*Fidei Defensor*) Defender of the Faith.

fec.—(*fecit*) he did it/made it.

F.F.A.S.—Fellow of the Faculty of Architects and Surveyors.

F.F.R.—*do*, of Faculty of Radiologists.

F.G.S.—*do*, of Geological Society.

F.H.—Fire hydrant.

F.H.S.—Fellow of the Heraldry Society.

F.I.A.—*do*, of Institute of Actuaries.

F.I.Arb.—*do*, of Institute of Arbitrators.

F.I.B.—*do*, of Institute of Bankers.

F.I.C.E.—*do*, of Institution of Civil Engineers.

F.I.C.S.—*do*, of Institution of Chartered Shipbrokers.

F.I.E.E.—*do*, of Institution of Electrical Engineers.

F.I.M.—*do*, of Institution of Metallurgists.

F.Inst.F.—*do*, of the Institute of Fuel.

F.Inst.P.—*do*, of Institute of Physics.

F.I.Q.S.—*do*, of Institute of Quantity Surveyors.

F.I.R.E.—*do*, of Institute of Radio Engineers.

F.I.S.—*do*, of Institute of Statisticians; Family Income Supplement.

F.J.I.—*do*, of Institute of Journalists.

fl.—(*floruit*) he/she flourished.

F.L.A.—Fellow of Library Assoc.

F.L.S.—*do*, of Linnean Society.

F.M.—Field Marshal.

fo.—folio.

F.O.—Flying Officer.

f.o.b.—free on board.

F.P.A.—Family Planning Assoc.

F.Ph.S.—Fellow of the Philosophical Society.

F.P.S.—*do*, of Pharmaceutical Society.

F.R.A.D.—*do*, of Royal Academy of Dancing.

F.R.A.I.—*do*, of Royal Anthropological Institute.

F.R.A.M.—*do*, of Royal Academy of Music.

F.R.A.S.—*do*, of Royal Astronomical Society.

F.R.Ae.S.—*do*, of Royal Aeronautical Society.

F.R.B.S.—*do*, of Royal Society of British Sculptors.

F.R.C.M.—*do*, of Royal College of Music.

F.R.C.O.—*do*, of Royal College of Organists.

F.R.C.O.G.—*do*, of Royal College of Obstetricians and Gynaecologists.

F.R.C.P., (Ed.), (I.)—*do*, of Royal College of Physicians (in Edinburgh), (of Ireland).

F.R.C.P.S.G.—*do*, of Royal College of Physicians and Surgeons of Glasgow.

F.R.C.S., (Ed.), (I.)—*do*, of Royal College of Surgeons (in Edinburgh), (of Ireland).

F.R.C.V.S.—*do*, of Royal College of Veterinary Surgeons.

F.R.Econ.S.—*do*, of Royal Economic Society.

F.R.G.S.—*do*, of Royal Geographical Society.

F.R.H.S.—*do*, of Royal Horticultural Society.

F.R.Hist.S.—*do*, of the Royal Historical Society.

F.R.I.B.A.—*do*, of Royal Institute of British Architects.

F.R.I.C.S.—*do*, of Royal Institution of Chartered Surveyors.

F.R.M.S.—*do*, of Royal Microscopical Society.

F.R.Met.S.—*do*, of Royal Meteorological Society.

F.R.N.S.—*do*, of Royal Numismatic Society.

F.R.P.S.—*do*, of Royal Photographic Society.

F.R.S.—*do*, of Royal Society.

F.R.S.A.—*do*, of Royal Society of Arts.

F.R.S.C.—*do*, of Royal Society of Chemistry.

F.R.S.E.—*do*, of Royal Society of Edinburgh.

F.R.S.L.—*do*, of Royal Society of Literature.

F.R.T.P.I.—*do*, of Royal Town Planning Institute.

F.S.A.—*do*, of Society of Antiquaries.

F.S.S.—*do*, of Statistical Society.

F.S.V.A.—*do*, of Society of Valuers and Auctioneers.

F.T.—*Financial Times*.

F.T.I.—Fellow of the Textile Institute.

F.T.I.I.—*do*, of the Taxation Institute Inc.

F.Z.S.—*do*, of Zoological Society.

G

G.A.T.T.—General Agreement on Tariffs and Trade.

G.B.E.—Knight/Dame Grand Cross, Order of the British Empire.

G.C.—George Cross.

G.C.B.—Knight/Dame Grand Cross, Order of the Bath.

G.C.E.—General Certificate of Education.

G.C.H.Q.—Government Communications Headquarters.

G.C.I.E.—Knight Grand Commander, Order of the Indian Empire.

G.C.M.G.—Knight/Dame Grand Cross, Order of St. Michael and St. George.

G.C.S.I.—Knight Grand Commander, Order of the Star of India.

G.C.V.O.—Knight/Dame Grand Cross, Royal Victorian Order.

G.D.I.—Gross domestic income.

G.D.P.—Gross domestic product.

G.D.R.—German Democratic Republic (E. Germany).

Gen.—General.

G.H.Q.—General Headquarters.

Gib.—Gibraltar.

G.M.—George Medal.

G.M.T.—Greenwich Mean Time.

G.N.P.—Gross national product.

G.O.C.—General Officer Commanding.

G.P.—General Practitioner.

Gp. Capt.—Group Captain.

G.S.O.—General Staff Officer.

H

H.A.C.—Honourable Artillery Company.

H.B.M.—Her Britannic Majesty('s).

H.C.F.—Highest common factor.

H.E.—His Excellency; His Eminence; high explosive.

H.H.—His/Her Highness.

H.I.M.—His/Her Imperial Majesty.

H.J.S.—(*hic jacet sepultus*) here lies buried.

H.M.—His/Her Majesty.

H.M.A.S.—Her Majesty's Australian Ship.

H.M.C.—Headmasters' Conference.

H.M.I.—Her Majesty's Inspector.

H.M.L.—Her Majesty's Lieutenant.

H.M.S.—Her Majesty's Ship.

H.M.S.O.—Her Majesty's Stationery Office.

H.N.C.—Higher National Certificate.

H.N.D.—Higher National Diploma.

Hon.—Honourable; Honorary.

h.p.—horse power.

H.P.—Hire purchase.

H.Q.—Headquarters.

H.R.H.—His/Her Royal Highness.

H.S.E.—(*hic sepultus est*) here lies buried. *cf.* H.J.S.

H.T.R.—High temperature reactor.

H.W.M.—High water mark.

I

I.A.A.S.—Incorporated Association of Architects and Surveyors.

I.A.E.A.—International Atomic Energy Agency.

I.A.T.A.—International Air Transport Association.

I.B.A.—Independent Broadcasting Authority.

Ibid.—(*ibidem*) in the same place.

I.B.R.D.—International Bank for Reconstruction and Development.

I.C.A.O.—International Civil Aviation Organization.

I.C.B.M.—Inter-continental ballistic missile.

I.C.I.—Imperial Chemical Industries.

I.C.J.—International Court of Justice.

I.C.R.C.—International Committee of the Red Cross.

I.C.T.—International Computers and Tabulators.

Id.—(*idem*) the same.

i.e.—(*id est*) that is.

I.E.A.—International Energy Agency.

I.F.C.—International Finance Corporation.

I.H.S.—(*Iesus Hominum Salvator*) Jesus the Saviour of Mankind; originally, these were the Greek capital letters, I H Σ.

I.L.E.A.—Inner London Education Authority.

I.L.O.—International Labour Organization.

I.M.C.O.—Inter-Governmental Maritime Consultative Organization.

I.M.F.—International Monetary Fund.

Inc.—Incorporated.

Incog.—(*incognito*) unknown, unrecognized.

I.N.L.A.—Irish National Liberation Army.

In loc.—(*in loco*) in its place.

I.N.R.I.—(*Iesus Nazarenus Rex Iudaeorum*) Jesus of Nazareth, King of the Jews.

Inst.—(*instant*) current month.

Intelsat—International Telecommunications Satellite Consortium.

Interpol—International Criminal Police Commission.

I.O.M.—Isle of Man.

I.O.U.—I owe you.

I.O.W.—Isle of Wight.

I.Q.—Intelligence quotient.

I.R.A.—Irish Republican Army.

I.R.C.—International Red Cross.

I.S.B.N.—International Standard Book Number.

I.S.O.—Imperial Service Order.

I.T.U.—International Telecommunication Union.

I.T.V.—Independent Television.

J

J.—Judge.

J.P.—Justice of the Peace.

K

K.—Köchel numeration (of Mozart's works).

K.A.N.U.—Kenyan African National Union.

K.B.E.—Knight Commander, Order of the British Empire.

K.C.B.—*do*, Order of the Bath.

K.C.I.E.—*do*, Order of the Indian Empire.

K.C.M.G.—*do*, Order of St. Michael and St. George.

K.C.S.I.—*do*, Order of the Star of India.

K.C.V.O.—*do*, Royal Victorian Order.

K.G.—Knight of the Garter.

K.G.B.—Soviet State Security Service.

K.K.K.—Ku Klux Klan.

k.o.—knock out (boxing).

K.P.—Knight, Order of St. Patrick.

K.St.J.—Knight, Order of St. John of Jerusalem.

Kt.—Knight.

K.T.—Knight, Order of the Thistle.

K.V.—Kilovolt.

K.W.—Kilowatt.

K.W.h.—Kilowatt hour.

L

L. (*or* Lib.)—Liberal.

Lab.—Labour.

Lat.—Latitude.

L.A.M.D.A.—London Academy of Music and Dramatic Art.

lb.—(*libra*) pound weight.

l.b.w.—leg before wicket.

l.c.—lower case (*printing*).

L.C.J.—Lord Chief Justice.

L.C.M.—Least common multiple.

L.C.P.—Licentiate of College of Preceptors.

L.D.S.—*do*, in Dental Surgery.

L.E.A.—Local Education Authority.

L.H.D.—(*Litterarum Humaniorum Doctor*) Doctor of Humane Letters.

Lic. Med.—Licentiate in Medicine.

Lic. S.—*do*, in Surgery.

Lit.—Literary.

Lit. Hum.—(*Litterae Humaniores*) study of the classics.

Litt. D.—Doctor of Letters.

L.J.—Lord Justice.

LL.B.—Bachelor of Laws; LL.D.—Doctor of Laws; LL.M.—Master of Laws.

L.M.—Licentiate in Midwifery.

L.M.S.S.A.—*do*, in Medicine and Surgery, Society of Apothecaries.

loc. cit.—(*loco citato*) in the place cited.

log.—logarithm.

Londin.—of London (*Bishop*).

L.R.A.D.—Licentiate of the Royal Academy of Dancing.

L.R.A.M.—*do*, of the Royal Academy of Music.

L.R.C.P., (Ed.)—*do*, of the Royal College of Physicians, (of Edinburgh).

L.R.C.S., (Ed.)—*do*, of the Royal College of Surgeons, (of Edinburgh).

L.R.C.P.S.G.—*do*, of the Royal College of Physicians and Surgeons of Glasgow.

L.R.C.V.S.—*do*, of Royal College of Veterinary Surgeons.

L.S.—(*loco sigilli*) place of the seal.

L.S.A.—Licentiate of Society of Apothecaries.

L.s.d.—(*Librae, solidi, denarii*) £, shillings and pence.

L.S.E.—London School of Economics.

L.S.O.—London Symphony Orchestra.

Lt.—Lieutenant.

L.T.A.—Lawn Tennis Association.

Ltd.—Limited liability.

L.Th.—Licentiate in Theology.

L.T.M.—*do*, of Tropical Medicine.

L.W.M.—Low water mark.

M

M.—Member of; Monsieur.

M.A.—Master of Arts.

M.A.F.F.—Ministry of Agriculture, Fisheries and Food.

Maj.—Major.

max.—maximum.

M.B./D.—Bachelor/Doctor of Medicine.

M.B.E.—Member, Order of the British Empire.

M.C.—Master of Ceremonies; Military Cross.

M.C.C.—Marylebone Cricket Club.

M.Ch.(D.)—Master of (Dental) Surgery.

M.D.S.—*do*, of Dental Surgery.

M.E.—Middle English.

M.E.C.—Member of Executive Council.

M.Ed.—Master of Education.

mega—one million times.

M.E.P.—Member of the European Parliament.

M.F.H.—Master of Foxhounds.

Mgr.—Monsignor.

M.I.—Military Intelligence.

micro—one-millionth part.

milli—one-thousandth part.

min.—minimum.

M.L.A.—Member of Legislative Assembly.

M.L.C.—Member of Legislative Council.

Mlle.—Mademoiselle.

M.L.R.—Minimum lending rate.

M.M.—Military Medal.

Mme.—Madame.

M.N.—Merchant Navy.

M.O.—Medical Officer/Orderly.

M.O.D.—Ministry of Defence.

M.O.T.—Ministry of Transport.

M.P.—Member of Parliament; Military Police.

m.p.h.—miles per hour.

M.R.—Master of the Rolls.

M.R.C.—Medical Research Council.

M.S.—Master of Surgery; Manuscript (pl. MSS).

M.Sc.—*do*, of Science.

M.T.B.—Motor Torpedo Boat.

M.Th.—Master of Theology.

Mus. B./D.—Bachelor/Doctor of Music.

M.V.—million volts (*or* megavolts); Merchant Vessel; Motor Vessel.

M.V.O.—Member, Royal Victorian Order.

M.W.—million watts (*or* megawatts).

N

N.A.A.F.I.—Navy Army and Air Force Institutes.

N.A.B.M.—National Association of British Manufacturers.

N.A.L.G.O.—National and Local Government Officers Association.

N.A.S.A.—National Aeronautics and Space Administration.

N.A.T.O.—North Atlantic Treaty Organization.

N.B.—(*Nota bene*) note well; New Brunswick.

N.C.B.—National Coal Board.

N.C.O.—Non-commissioned Officer.

n.d.—no date (*of books*).

N.E.B.—New English Bible.

N.E.D.C.—National Economic Development Council.

Nem. con.—(*Nemine contradicente*) no one contradicting.

N.E.R.C.—Natural Environment Research Council.

N.F.T.—National Film Theatre.

N.G.A.—National Graphical Association.

N.H.S.—National Health Service.

N.I.—Northern Ireland.

No.—(*numero*) number.

Non seq.—(*Non sequitur*) it does not follow.

Norvic.—of Norwich (*Bishop*).

N.P.—Notary Public.

N.R.A.—National Rifle Assoc.
N.S.—New Style (calendar); Nova Scotia.
N.S.P.C.C.—National Society for the Prevention of Cruelty to Children.
N.S.W.—New South Wales.
N.T.—National Theatre; New Testament.
N.U.J.—National Union of Journalists.
N.U.M.—*do*, of Mineworkers.
N.U.P.E.—*do*, of Public Employees.
N.U.R.—*do*, of Railwaymen.
N.U.S.—*do*, of Seamen; *do*, of Students.
N.U.T.—*do*, of Teachers.
N.W.T.—Northwest Territory.
N.Y.—New York.
N.Z.—New Zealand.

O

O. and M.—Organization and method.
O.A.P.E.C.—Organization of Arab Petroleum Exporting Countries.
O.A.S.—Organization of American States.
O.A.U.—Organization of African Unity.
Ob. (*or* obit.)—died.
O.B.E.—Officer, Order of the British Empire.
O.C.—Officer Commanding.
O.E.—Old English.
O.E.C.D.—Organization for Economic Co-operation and Development.
O.E.D.—Oxford English Dictionary.
O.F.M.—Order of Friars Minor (Franciscans).
O.H.M.S.—On Her Majesty's Service.
O.M.—Order of Merit.
O.P.—Order of Preachers (Dominicans); opposite prompt side (of theatre); out of print (of books).
op.—(*opus*) work.
op. cit.—(*opere citato*) in the work cited.
O.P.C.S.—Office of Population Censuses and Surveys.
O.P.E.C.—Organization of Petroleum Exporting Countries.
O.S.—Old Style (calendar).
O.S.A.—Order of St. Augustine.
O.S.B.—Order of St. Benedict.
O. St. J.—Officer, Order of St. John of Jerusalem.
O.T.—Old Testament.
O.T.C.—Officer Training Corps.
Oxon.—(of) Oxford; Oxfordshire.
Oz.—ounce.

P

P.A.—Press Association.
p.c.—per cent.
P.C.—Privy Counsellor; Police Constable.
P.D.S.A.—People's Dispensary for Sick Animals.
P.E.—Physical Education.
Petriburg—of Peterborough (*Bishop*).
Ph.D.—Doctor of Philosophy.

pinx(it)—he/she painted it.
P.L.A.—Port of London Authority.
P.L.C.—Public Limited Company.
P.L.O.—Palestine Liberation Organization.
p.m.—(*post meridiem*) afternoon.
P.M.—Prime Minister.
P.M.R.A.F.N.S.—Princess Mary's Royal Air Force Nursing Service.
P.O.—Post Office; Postal Order; Petty Officer; Pilot Officer.
P. & O.—Peninsular and Oriental Steamship Co.
P.O.U.N.C.—Post Office Users' National Council.
P.O.W.—Prisoner of War.
p.p. (*or* per pro)—(*per procurationem*) by proxy.
P.P.S.—Parliamentary Private Secretary.
P.R.—Proportional Representation; Public Relations.
P.R.A.—President of the Royal Academy.
Pro tem.—(*pro tempore*) for the time being.
P.R.S.—President of the Royal Society.
P.R.S.E.—*do*, of Edinburgh.
Prox.—(*proximo*) next month.
Ps.—Psalm.
P.S.—(*Post scriptum*) postscript.
P.S.B.R.—Public sector borrowing requirement.
Pte.—Private.
P.T.O.—Please turn over.

Q

Q.A.R.(A.)N.C.—Queen Alexandra's Royal (Army) Nursing Corps.
Q.A.R.N.N.S.—Queen Alexandra's Royal Naval Nursing Service.
Q.B.—Queen's Bench.
Q.C.—Queen's Counsel.
Q.e.d.—(*quod erat demonstrandum*) which was to be proved.
Q.G.M.—Queen's Gallantry Medal.
Q.H.C.—Honorary Chaplain to the Queen.
Q.H.D.S.—Honorary Dental Surgeon to the Queen.
Q.H.N.S.—Honorary Nursing Sister to the Queen.
Q.H.P.—Honorary Physician to the Queen.
Q.H.S.—Honorary Surgeon to the Queen.
Q.M.G.—Quartermaster General.
Q.P.M.—Queen's Police Medal.
Q.S.—Quarter Sessions.
Q.S.O.—Quasi-stellar object (quasar).
Q.S.S.s—Quasi-stellar radio sources (quasar).
q.v.—(*quod vide*) which see.

R

R.—(*Rex*) King; (*Regina*) Queen.
R.A.—Royal Artillery; Royal Academy/Academician.
R.A.C.—Royal Armoured Corps; Royal Automobile Club.
R.A.D.A.—Royal Academy of Dramatic Art.

R.A.D.C.—Royal Army Dental Corps.
R.A.E.—Royal Aircraft Establishment.
R.A.E.C.—Royal Army Education Corps.
R.Ae.S.—Royal Aeronautical Society.
R.A.F.—Royal Air Force.
R.A.M.—Royal Academy of Music.
R.A.M.C.—Royal Army Medical Corps.
R.A.N.—Royal Australian Navy.
R. and D.—Research and Development.
R.A.O.C.—Royal Army Ordnance Corps.
R.A.P.C.—Royal Army Pay Corps.
R.A.V.C.—Royal Army Veterinary Corps.
R.B.A.—Royal Society of British Artists.
R.B.S.—Royal Society of British Sculptors.
R.C.—Roman Catholic; Red Cross.
R.C.M.—Royal College of Music.
R.C.N.—Royal Canadian Navy.
R.C.N.C.—Royal Corps of Naval Constructors.
R.C.T.—Royal Corps of Transport.
R.D.—Naval Reserve Decoration; Rural Dean; refer to drawer (*banking*).
R.D.I.—Designer for Industry of the Royal Society of Arts.
R.E.—Royal Engineers.
R.E.M.E.—Royal Electrical and Mechanical Engineers.
Rep.—Republican; Representative.
Rev.—Reverend.
R.G.N.—Registered General Nurse.
R.G.S.—Royal Geographical Society.
R.H.S.—Royal Horticultural Society; Royal Humane Society.
R.I.—Royal Institution; Royal Institute of Painters in Watercolours; Rhode Island.
R.I.A.—Royal Irish Academy.
R.I.B.A.—Royal Institute of British Architects.
R.I.P.—(*Requiescat in pace*) May he/she rest in peace.
R.L.—Rugby League.
R.M.—Royal Marines.
R.M.A.—Royal Military Academy.
R.M.S.—Royal Mail Steamer.
R.N.—Royal Navy.
R.N.I.B.—Royal National Institute for the Blind.
R.N.L.I.—Royal National Lifeboat Institution.
R.N.R.—Royal Naval Reserve.
R.N.V.R.—Royal Naval Volunteer Reserve.
R.N.Z.N.—Royal New Zealand Navy.
Ro.—(*Recto*) on the right-hand page.
R.O.C.—Royal Observer Corps.
Roffen.—of Rochester (*Bishop*).
R.O.I.—Royal Institute of Oil Painters.
Ro. S.P.A.—Royal Society for the Prevention of Accidents.

R.P.—Royal Society of Portrait Painters.

r.p.m.—revolutions per minute.

R.R.C.—Lady of Royal Red Cross.

R.R.E.—Royal Radar Establishment.

R.S.A.—Royal Society of Arts; Royal Scottish Academician; Republic of South Africa.

R.S.C.—Royal Shakespeare Company.

R.S.E.—Royal Society of Edinburgh.

R.S.M.—Regimental Sergeant Major.

R.S.P.B.—Royal Society for the Protection of Birds.

R.S.P.C.A.—Royal Society for the Prevention of Cruelty to Animals.

R.S.V.P.—(*Respondez s'il vous plait*) Answer, if you please.

R.S.W.—Royal Scottish Society of Painters in Watercolours.

R.T.P.I.—Royal Town Planning Institute.

R.U.—Rugby Union.

R.U.C.—Royal Ulster Constabulary.

R.V.—Revised Version (of Bible).

R.W.S.—Royal Water Colour Society.

R.Y.S.—Royal Yacht Squadron.

S

s.—(*solidus*) shilling.

S.A.—Salvation Army; Sex Appeal; South Africa; South America; South Australia.

Salop.—Shropshire.

S.A.L.T.—Strategic Arms Limitation Treaty.

Sarum.—of Salisbury (*Bishop*).

S.A.S.—Special Air Service Regiment.

S.B.S.—Special Boat Squadron.

Sc.D.—Doctor of Science.

S.C.M.—State Certified Midwife.

S.D.P.—Social Democratic Party.

S.D.L.P.—Social Democratic and Labour Party (N. Ireland).

S.E.A.T.O.—South East Asia Treaty Organization.

S.E.N.—State Enrolled Nurse.

S.E.R.C.—Science and Engineering Research Council.

S.H.A.P.E.—Supreme Headquarters, Allied Powers, Europe.

S.I.—(*Système International d'Unités*) International System of Units; Statutory Instruments.

Sic.—So written.

Sig.—Signalman.

S.J.—Society of Jesus (Jesuits).

S.N.P.—Scottish National Party.

S.O.G.A.T.—Society of Graphical and Allied Trades.

S.O.S.—Save Our Souls (distress signal).

s.p.—(*sine prole*) without issue.

S.P.C.K.—Society for the Promotion of Christian Knowledge.

sp.gr.—specific gravity.

S.P.Q.R.—(*Senatus Propulusque Romanus*) The Senate and People of Rome.

Sqn. Ldr.—Squadron Leader.

S.R.N.—State Registered Nurse.

SS.—Saints.

S.S.—Steamship.

S.S.A.F.A.—Soldiers', Sailors', and Airmen's Families Association.

S.S.C.—Solicitor before Supreme Court (Scotland).

S.S.F.—Society of St. Francis.

St.—Saint; Street.

S.T.A.R.—Satellites for Telecommunications, Applications and Research.

Stet.—Let it stand.

S.T.D.—Subscriber Trunk Dialling.

s.t.p.—Standard temperature and pressure.

S.T.P.—(*Sacrae Theologiae Professor*) Doctor of Divinity.

Sub Lt.—Sub-Lieutenant.

S.W.A.P.O.—South West Africa People's Organization.

T

T.A.—Territorial Army.

T.B.—Tuberculosis.

T.C.C.B.—Test and County Cricket Board.

T.D.—Territorial Decoration.

temp.—temperature; temporary employee.

T.E.S.—*Times Education Supplement.*

T.G.W.U.—Transport and General Workers Union.

T.L.S.—*Times Literary Supplement.*

T.N.T.—trinitrotoluene (explosive).

Toc. H.—Talbot House.

tr.—transpose (*printing*).

Truron—of Truro (*Bishop*).

T.T.—Teetotal; Tubercular tested.

T.U.C.—Trades Union Congress.

T.V.—Television.

U

U.—Unionist.

U.A.E.—United Arab Emirates.

u.c.—upper case (*printing*).

U.C.C.A.—University Central Council on Admissions.

U.C.L.—University College, London.

U.D.I.—Unilateral Declaration of Independence.

U.D.R.—Ulster Defence Regiment.

U.F.O.—Unidentified flying object.

U.G.C.—University Grants Committee.

u.h.f.—ultra-high frequency.

U.K.—United Kingdom.

U.K.A.E.A.—United Kingdom Atomic Energy Authority.

Ult.—(*ultimo*) in the preceding month.

U.N.E.S.C.O.—United Nations Educational, Scientific and Cultural Organization.

U.N.I.C.E.F.—United Nations International Children's Emergency Fund.

Unita.—National Union for the Total Independence of Angola.

U.N.O.—United Nations Organization.

U.P.U.—Universal Postal Union.

U.S. (*or* U.S.A.)—United States (of America).

U.S.P.G.—United Society for the Propagation of the Gospel.

U.S.S.R.—Union of Soviet Socialist Republics.

U.U.—Ulster Unionist.

V

v.—(*versus*) against.

V.—Volt.

V.A.—Vicar Apostolic; Victoria and Albert Order.

V. and A.—Victoria and Albert Museum.

V.A.D.—Voluntary Aid Detachment.

V.A.T.—Value added tax.

V.C.—Victoria Cross.

V.D.—Volunteer Officers' Decoration; venereal disease.

V.D.U.—Visual display unit.

Ven.—Venerable.

Verb. sap.—(*Verbum sapienti satis est*) A word to the wise is enough.

v.h.f.—very high frequency.

V.I.P.—Very important person.

Viz.—(*videlicet*) namely.

Vo.—(*Verso*) on the left-hand page.

V.R.D.—Volunteer Reserve Decoration.

V.S.O.—Voluntary Service Overseas.

V.T.O.L.—Vertical take-off and landing (*aircraft*).

W

W.C.C.—World Council of Churches.

W.E.U.—Western European Union.

W.H.O.—World Health Organization.

W.I.—West Indies; Women's Institutes.

Winton.—of Winchester (*Bishop*).

W.M.O.—World Meteorological Organization.

W.O.—Warrant Officer.

W.R.A.C.—Women's Royal Army Corps.

W.R.A.F.—Women's Royal Air Force.

W.R.N.S.—Women's Royal Naval Service.

W.R.V.S.—Women's Royal Voluntary Service.

W.S.—Writer to the Signet.

Y

Y.H.A.—Youth Hostels Assoc.

Y.M.C.A.—Young Men's Christian Association.

Y.W.C.A.—Young Women's Christian Association.

Z

Z.A.N.U.—Zimbabwe African National Union.

Z.A.P.U.—Zimbabwe African People's Union.

BEING THE SECOND YEAR AFTER BISSEXTILE OR LEAP YEAR

Golden Number	.. .. ..	XI
Epact ..	.. .. ..	19
Dominical Letter	.. .. ..	E
Solar Cycle	.. .. ..	7
Roman Indiction	.. .. ..	9
Julian Period	.. .. ..	6699
Julian Day, Jan. 1 (begins at noon)	..	2,446,432
New Year's Day (Wednesday)	..	Jan. 1
Septuagesima Sunday	.. ..	„ 26
Australia Day	.. .. ..	„ 26
Accession of Queen Elizabeth II	..	Feb. 6
New Zealand Day	.. ..	„ 6
Chinese New Year (Tiger)	..	„ 9
Ash Wednesday	.. ..	„ 12
Prince Andrew's Birthday (1960)	..	„ 19
St. David's Day	.. ..	Mar. 1
Prince Edward's Birthday (1964)	..	„ 10
Commonwealth Day	.. ..	„ 10
St. Patrick's Day	.. ..	„ 17
Good Friday	.. .. ..	„ 28
Easter Day	.. .. ..	„ 30
Birthday of Queen Elizabeth II ..		Apr. 21
St. George's Day	.. ..	„ 23

Passover, first day	.. .. ..	„ 24
Ascension Day ..	.. ..	May 8
Ramadam, first day	.. ..	„ 10
Whit Sunday ..	.. ..	„ 18
Trinity Sunday	.. ..	„ 25
Corpus Christi ..	.. ..	„ 29
Duke of Edinburgh's Birthday (1921)	..	June 10
Queen's Official Birthday	..	„ 14
Prince William of Wales's Birthday (1982)		„ 21
Princess of Wales's Birthday (1961)	..	July 1
National Day Canada (1867)	..	„ 1
The Queen Mother's Birthday (1900)	..	Aug. 4
Princess Anne's Birthday (1950)	..	„ 15
Islamic New Year (1407)	..	Sept. 6
Jewish New Year (5747)	..	Oct. 4
Day of Atonement (Yom Kippur)	..	„ 13
Remembrance Sunday ..	..	Nov. 9
Prince of Wales's Birthday (1948)	..	„ 14
St. Andrew's Day	.. ..	„ 30
First Sunday in Advent	..	„ 30
Christmas Day ..	.. ..	Dec. 25

Spring Equinox	Sun enters Sign Aries	March 20d 22h	
Summer Solstice	„ „ „ Cancer ..	June 21d 16h	G.M.T.
Autumn Equinox	„ „ „ Libra	Sept. 23d 08h	
Winter Solstice	„ „ „ Capricornus ..	Dec. 22d 04h	

CALENDAR FOR THE YEAR 1986

	January							*April*							*July*							*October*				
Su.	.. — 5 12 19 26						Su.	.. — 6 13 20 27						Su.	.. — 6 13 20 27						Su.	.. — 5 12 19 26				
M.	.. — 6 13 20 27						M.	.. — 7 14 21 28						M.	.. — 7 14 21 28						M.	.. — 6 13 20 27				
Tu.	.. — 7 14 21 28						Tu.	.. 1 8 15 22 29						Tu.	.. 1 8 15 22 29						Tu.	.. — 7 14 21 28				
W.	.. 1 8 15 22 29						W.	.. 2 9 16 23 30						W.	.. 2 9 16 23 30						W.	.. 1 8 15 22 29				
Th.	.. 2 9 16 23 30						Th.	.. 3 10 17 24 —						Th.	.. 3 10 17 24 31						Th.	.. 2 9 16 23 30				
F.	.. 3 10 17 24 31						F.	.. 4 11 18 25 —						F.	.. 4 11 18 25 —						F.	.. 3 10 17 24 31				
S.	.. 4 11 18 25 —						S.	.. 5 12 19 26 —						S.	.. 5 12 19 26 —						S.	.. 4 11 18 25 —				
	February							*May*							*August*							*November*				
Su.	.. — 2 9 16 23						Su.	.. — 4 11 18 25						Su.	.. — 3 10 17 24 31						Su.	.. — 2 9 16 23 30				
M.	.. — 3 10 17 24						M.	.. — 5 12 19 26						M.	.. — 4 11 18 25 —						M.	.. — 3 10 17 24 —				
Tu.	.. — 4 11 18 25						Tu.	.. — 6 13 20 27						Tu.	.. — 5 12 19 26 —						Tu.	.. — 4 11 18 25 —				
W.	.. — 5 12 19 26						W.	.. — 7 14 21 28						W.	.. — 6 13 20 27 —						W.	.. — 5 12 19 26 —				
Th.	.. — 6 13 20 27						Th.	.. 1 8 15 22 29						Th.	.. — 7 14 21 28 —						Th.	.. — 6 13 20 27 —				
F.	.. — 7 14 21 28						F.	.. 2 9 16 23 30						F.	.. 1 8 15 22 29 —						F.	.. — 7 14 21 28 —				
S.	.. 1 8 15 22 —						S.	.. 3 10 17 24 31						S.	.. 2 9 16 23 30 —						S.	.. 1 8 15 22 29 —				
	March							*June*							*September*							*December*				
Su.	.. — 2 9 16 23 30						Su.	.. 1 8 15 22 29						Su.	.. — 7 14 21 28						Su.	.. — 7 14 21 28				
M.	.. — 3 10 17 24 31						M.	.. 2 9 16 23 30						M.	.. 1 8 15 22 29						M.	.. 1 8 15 22 29				
Tu.	.. — 4 11 18 25 —						Tu.	.. 3 10 17 24 —						Tu.	.. 2 9 16 23 30						Tu.	.. 2 9 16 23 30				
W.	.. — 5 12 19 26 —						W.	.. 4 11 18 25 —						W.	.. 3 10 17 24 —						W.	.. 3 10 17 24 31				
Th.	.. — 6 13 20 27 —						Th.	.. 5 12 19 26 —						Th.	.. 4 11 18 25 —						Th.	.. 4 11 18 25 —				
F.	.. — 7 14 21 28 —						F.	.. 6 13 20 27 —						F.	.. 5 12 19 26 —						F.	.. 5 12 19 26 —				
S.	.. 1 8 15 22 29 —						S.	.. 7 14 21 28 —						S.	.. 6 13 20 27 —						S.	.. 6 13 20 27 —				

PUBLIC HOLIDAYS

BANK HOLIDAYS IN ENGLAND, WALES, NORTHERN IRELAND AND THE CHANNEL ISLANDS ARE (1986):— Jan. 1; March 31; May 5; May 26; Aug. 25 and Dec. 26.

Liberation Day (May 9) is a bank and public holiday in the Channel Islands.

Banks are also closed on Good Friday and Christmas Day and on all Saturdays.

The Stock Exchange is closed on Bank Holidays, Good Friday, Christmas Day and New Year's Day; and on Saturdays throughout the year.

Custom House and Docks, as *Banks*; with the Queen's Birthday (when decreed).

Excise and Stamp Offices, as Banks; with Whit Tuesday and Coronation Day, if and when decreed.

Law Offices.—Good Friday, Easter Monday and Tuesday, Spring Bank Holiday (*see* col. 1), Christmas Day, and first week-day after Christmas.

BANK HOLIDAYS IN SCOTLAND ARE (1986):—Jan. 1 and 2; May 5 and 26; Aug. 4; Dec. 26.

Banks in Scotland are also closed on Good Friday, Christmas Day and on Saturdays.

Scotland has special *Term* (*Quarter*) *Days*:—Candlemas, Feb. 2; Whitsunday, May 15 (fixed date); Lammas, Aug. 1; and Martinmas, Nov. 11; the *Removal Terms* are May 28 and Nov. 28.

Month	Week	*Janus*, god of the portal, facing two ways, past and future. Sun's Longitude 300° ≈ 20ᵈ 09ʰ

Janus, god of the portal, facing two ways, past and future.

Sun's Longitude 300° ≈ 20^d 09^h

1	W.	**Circumcision.** E. M. Forster b. 1879.
2	Th.	Sir Michael Tippett b. 1905.
3	F.	Clement Attlee b. 1883. Herbert Morrison b. 1888.
4	S.	Albert Camus d. 1960. T. S. Eliot d. 1965.
5	☉	**2nd S. after Christmas.** Edward the Confessor d. 1066.
6	M.	**Epiphany.** Twelfth Day.
7	Tu.	First Balloon Crossing of English Channel 1785.
8	W.	Galileo d. 1642. Wilkie Collins b. 1824.
9	Th.	Napoleon III d. 1873.
10	F.	Archbishop Laud beheaded 1645.
11	S.	HILARY LAW SITTINGS BEGIN.
12	☉	**1st S. after Epiphany.** Edmund Burke b. 1729.
13	M.	Plow Monday. Edmund Spenser d. 1599.
14	Tu.	Edmund Halley d. 1742. Lewis Carroll d. 1898.
15	W.	Martin Luther King b. 1929.
16	Th.	Coruña 1809. Amilcare Ponchielli d. 1886.**
17	F.	Benjamin Franklin b. 1706. Lloyd George b. 1863.
18	S.	A. A. Milne b. 1882. Rudyard Kipling d. 1936.
19	☉	**2nd S. after Epiphany.** James Watt b. 1736.
20	M.	George V d. 1936.
21	Tu.	Louis XVI guillotined 1793.
22	W.	Francis Bacon b. 1561. Lord Byron b. 1788.
23	Th.	Edouard Manet b. 1832. Dame Clara Butt d. 1936.
24	F.	Sir Winston Churchill d. 1965.
25	S.	**Conversion of St. Paul.** Robert Burns b. 1759.
26	☉	**9th S. before Easter.** Gen. Gordon d. 1885.
27	M.	Mozart b. 1756. Verdi d. 1901.
28	Tu.	Charlemagne d. 814. Artur Rubinstein b. 1887.
29	W.	First successful petrol-driven car patented 1886.**
30	Th.	Charles I exec. 1649. Gandhi assass. 1948.
31	F.	Franz Schubert b. 1797. Anna Pavlova b. 1885.

PHENOMENA

January 2^d 05^h Earth at Perihelion (147,000,000 kilometres).

6^d 01^h Mars in conjunction with the Moon. Mars 1°·7 N.

7^d 14^h Saturn in conjunction with the Moon. Saturn 4° N.

12^d 14^h Jupiter in conjunction with the Moon. Jupiter 4° N.

19^d 16^h Venus in superior conjunction.

CONSTELLATIONS

The following constellations are near the meridian at

	d	h		d	h
Dec.	1	24	Dec.	16	23
Jan.	1	22	Jan.	16	21
Feb.	1	20	Feb.	15	19

Draco (below the Pole), Ursa Minor (below the Pole), Camelopardus, Perseus, Auriga, Taurus, Orion, Eridanus and Lepus.

MINIMA OF ALGOL

d	h	d	h
2	9	19	14
5	6	22	11
8	3	25	8
10	23	28	4
13	20	31	1
16	17		

PHASES OF THE MOON

	d	h	m
☾ Last Quarter	3	19	47
● New Moon	10	12	22
☽ First Quarter	17	22	13
○ Full Moon	26	00	31

	d	h
Perigee (363,300 kilometres)	8	07
Apogee (404,720 „)	20	01

Mean Longitude of Ascending Node on January 1, 36°.

MONTHLY NOTES

Jan.   1. Bank Holiday in England, Scotland, Wales and Northern Ireland.

     2. Bank Holiday, Scotland.

     26. Australia Day. Republic Day, India.

     **Centenary

	\multicolumn{7}{c}{THE SUN s.d. 16′·3}							Transit
Day	Right Ascension	Dec. −	Equation of Time	\multicolumn{2}{c}{Rise}		Transit	\multicolumn{2}{c}{Set}	Sidereal Time	of First Point of Aries
				52°	56°		52°	56°		

Day	Right Ascension (h m s)	Dec. − (° ′)	Equation of Time (m s)	Rise 52° (h m)	Rise 56° (h m)	Transit (h m)	Set 52° (h m)	Set 56° (h m)	Sidereal Time (h m s)	Transit of First Point of Aries (h m s)
1	18 44 40	23 03	− 3 16	8 08	8 32	12 04	15 59	15 36	6 41 24	17 15 45
2	18 49 05	22 58	− 3 44	8 08	8 32	12 04	16 00	15 37	6 45 21	17 11 49
3	18 53 29	22 52	− 4 12	8 08	8 31	12 04	16 01	15 38	6 49 17	17 07 53
4	18 57 54	22 47	− 4 40	8 08	8 31	12 05	16 02	15 39	6 53 14	17 03 57
5	19 02 17	22 40	− 5 07	8 08	8 30	12 05	16 03	15 41	6 57 10	17 00 02
6	19 06 41	22 33	− 5 34	8 07	8 30	12 06	16 04	15 42	7 01 07	16 56 06
7	19 11 04	22 26	− 6 01	8 07	8 29	12 06	16 06	15 44	7 05 03	16 52 10
8	19 15 26	22 19	− 6 27	8 07	8 29	12 07	16 07	15 45	7 09 00	16 48 14
9	19 19 48	22 11	− 6 52	8 06	8 28	12 07	16 08	15 47	7 12 57	16 44 18
10	19 24 10	22 02	− 7 17	8 06	8 27	12 07	16 10	15 48	7 16 53	16 40 22
11	19 28 31	21 53	− 7 41	8 05	8 26	12 08	16 11	15 50	7 20 50	16 36 26
12	19 32 51	21 44	− 8 05	8 04	8 26	12 08	16 12	15 52	7 24 46	16 32 30
13	19 37 11	21 34	− 8 28	8 04	8 25	12 09	16 14	15 53	7 28 43	16 28 34
14	19 41 30	21 24	− 8 51	8 03	8 24	12 09	16 16	15 55	7 32 39	16 24 38
15	19 45 49	21 13	− 9 13	8 02	8 23	12 09	16 17	15 57	7 36 36	16 20 42
16	19 50 07	21 02	− 9 34	8 01	8 22	12 10	16 19	15 59	7 40 32	16 16 47
17	19 54 24	20 51	− 9 55	8 00	8 20	12 10	16 20	16 00	7 44 29	16 12 51
18	19 58 40	20 39	−10 15	8 00	8 19	12 10	16 22	16 02	7 48 26	16 08 55
19	20 02 56	20 27	−10 34	7 59	8 18	12 11	16 24	16 04	7 52 22	16 04 59
20	20 07 11	20 14	−10 52	7 58	8 16	12 11	16 25	16 06	7 56 19	16 01 03
21	20 11 25	20 01	−11 10	7 56	8 15	12 11	16 27	16 08	8 00 15	15 57 07
22	20 15 38	19 48	−11 26	7 55	8 14	12 12	16 29	16 10	8 04 12	15 53 11
23	20 19 51	19 34	−11 42	7 54	8 12	12 12	16 30	16 12	8 08 08	15 49 15
24	20 24 03	19 20	−11 58	7 53	8 10	12 12	16 32	16 15	8 12 05	15 45 19
25	20 28 14	19 05	−12 12	7 52	8 09	12 12	16 34	16 17	8 16 02	15 41 23
26	20 32 24	18 51	−12 26	7 50	8 07	12 13	16 36	16 19	8 19 58	15 37 27
27	20 36 33	18 35	−12 39	7 49	8 06	12 13	16 38	16 21	8 23 55	15 33 31
28	20 40 42	18 20	−12 51	7 48	8 04	12 13	16 39	16 23	8 27 51	15 29 36
29	20 44 50	18 04	−13 02	7 46	8 02	12 13	16 41	16 25	8 31 48	15 25 40
30	20 48 57	17 48	−13 13	7 45	8 00	12 13	16 43	16 27	8 35 44	15 21 44
31	20 53 03	17 32	−13 22	7 43	7 59	12 13	16 45	16 29	8 39 41	15 17 48

Duration of Civil (C), Nautical (N), and Astronomical (A), Twilight (in minutes)

Lat.	\multicolumn{3}{c}{Jan. 1}			\multicolumn{3}{c}{Jan. 11}			\multicolumn{3}{c}{Jan. 21}			\multicolumn{3}{c}{Jan. 31}		
°	C	N	A	C	N	A	C	N	A	C	N	A
52	41	84	125	40	82	123	38	80	120	37	78	117
56	47	96	141	45	93	138	43	90	134	41	87	130

ASTRONOMICAL NOTES

MERCURY is unsuitably placed for observation throughout the month.

VENUS is too close to the Sun for observation, superior conjunction occurring on the 19th.

MARS, magnitude +1·4, is a morning object, visible low in the south-eastern sky for several hours before fading in the morning twilight. The old crescent Moon passes south of the planet on the morning of the 6th. Mars is in the constellation of Libra. Mars has a slightly reddish tint which is a help in indentification.

JUPITER, magnitude −1·6, is an evening object, visible low in the south-western sky for a short while in the early evening, becoming a difficult object by the end of the month. The crescent Moon will be near the planet on the evening of the 12th.

SATURN, magnitude +0·8, is visible in the morn-ings, low in the south-eastern sky before twilight inhibits observation. By the end of the month Saturn is visible soon after 04ʰ. On the morning of the 7th the old crescent Moon will be seen approaching the planet. Saturn is in the constellation of Scorpius. Titan, Saturn's largest satellite, is of magnitude +8·5, and thus visible in small telescopes.

COMET HALLEY should still be visible in the early evenings low in the south-western sky but it is moving south and getting closer to the Sun and will probably still need some optical aid for its detection. Its position can be found from the following ephemeris.

Date	R.A. h m	Dec. ° ′
Jan. 0	22 17·5	− 2 18
Jan. 10	21 55·8	− 4 28
Jan. 20	21 37·8	− 6 17
Jan. 30	21 20·2	− 8 11

THE MOON

Day	R.A.	Dec.	Hor. Par.	Semi-diam.	Sun's Co-long.	P.A. of Bright Limb	Phase	Age	Rise 52°	Rise 56°	Tran-sit	Set 52°	Set 56°
	h m	°	′	′	°	°		d	h m	h m	h m	h m	h m
1	10 34	+13·8	57·0	15·5	151	109	79	20·0	21 50	21 42	4 01	11 12	11 21
2	11 23	+ 8·1	57·6	15·7	163	112	70	21·0	23 10	23 09	4 47	11 25	11 29
3	12 11	+ 1·9	58·2	15·8	175	113	59	22·0	..	..	5 32	11 37	11 36
4	13 00	− 4·4	58·8	16·0	187	113	48	23·0	0 33	0 37	6 19	11 50	11 43
5	13 51	−10·7	59·3	16·2	199	111	37	24·0	1 58	2 08	7 08	12 04	11 52
6	14 45	−16·6	59·8	16·3	211	107	26	25·0	3 27	3 44	8 01	12 23	12 04
7	15 42	−21·6	60·2	16·4	223	101	17	26·0	4 59	5 24	8 59	12 49	12 23
8	16 44	−25·3	60·3	16·4	236	93	9	27·0	6 28	7 02	10 01	13 28	12 54
9	17 50	−27·3	60·3	16·4	248	81	3	28·0	7 47	8 24	11 06	14 24	13 47
10	18 56	−27·4	60·0	16·4	260	51	1	29·0	8 46	9 21	12 10	15 39	15 05
11	20 00	−25·6	59·5	16·2	272	296	1	0·5	9 26	9 54	13 11	17 05	16 38
12	21 01	−22·2	58·8	16·0	284	267	3	1·5	9 53	10 13	14 07	18 32	18 13
13	21 56	−17·6	58·0	15·8	297	257	8	2·5	10 12	10 26	14 57	19 56	19 44
14	22 47	−12·3	57·1	15·6	309	252	15	3·5	10 26	10 34	15 43	21 15	21 08
15	23 34	− 6·6	56·3	15·3	321	249	23	4·5	10 37	10 41	16 26	22 30	22 29
16	0 19	− 0·8	55·6	15·1	333	248	32	5·5	10 48	10 47	17 07	23 42	23 46
17	1 03	+ 4·9	55·0	15·0	345	248	41	6·5	10 59	10 53	17 48	..	..
18	1 46	+10·3	54·5	14·9	357	249	51	7·5	11 10	10 59	18 29	0 54	1 03
19	2 31	+15·3	54·3	14·8	10	252	60	8·5	11 24	11 08	19 12	2 06	2 21
20	3 17	+19·7	54·2	14·8	22	256	69	9·5	11 41	11 19	19 57	3 18	3 39
21	4 05	+23·3	54·2	14·8	34	261	77	10·5	12 05	11 37	20 46	4 31	4 58
22	4 57	+25·9	54·5	14·8	46	267	85	11·5	12 37	12 04	21 37	5 41	6 14
23	5 50	+27·4	54·8	14·9	58	275	91	12·5	13 23	12 46	22 30	6 44	7 20
24	6 46	+27·6	55·2	15·1	70	285	96	13·5	14 23	13 48	23 24	7 35	8 10
25	7 42	+26·4	55·7	15·2	82	302	99	14·5	15 35	15 05	..	8 14	8 44
26	8 37	+23·7	56·2	15·3	95	191	100	15·5	16 54	16 32	0 17	8 42	9 05
27	9 30	+19·9	56·8	15·5	107	86	99	16·5	18 16	18 00	1 08	9 03	9 20
28	10 22	+15·0	57·3	15·6	119	101	96	17·5	19 38	19 29	1 58	9 19	9 30
29	11 11	+ 9·3	57·7	15·7	131	108	90	18·5	20 59	20 56	2 45	9 32	9 38
30	12 00	+ 3·1	58·1	15·8	143	111	83	19·5	22 21	22 24	3 31	9 44	9 45
31	12 49	− 3·3	58·5	15·9	155	112	74	20·5	23 45	23 54	4 17	9 57	9 52

MERCURY ☿

Day	R.A.	Dec. −	Diam.	Phase	Tran-sit		Day	R.A.	Dec. −	Diam.	Phase	Tran-sit	
	h m	°	″		h m			h m	°	″		h m	
1	17 29	23·0	5	87	10 49		16	19 08	23·9	5	96	11 29	
4	17 48	23·5	5	90	10 56	Mercury is too	19	19 29	23·5	5	97	11 38	Mercury is too
7	18 07	23·9	5	92	11 04	close to the	22	19 49	22·9	5	98	11 47	close to the
10	18 27	24·1	5	94	11 12	Sun for	25	20 10	22·1	5	99	11 56	Sun for
13	18 47	24·1	5	95	11 20	observation	28	20 31	21·0	5	99	12 05	observation
16	19 08	23·9	5	96	11 29		31	20 52	19·7	5	100	12 14	

VENUS ♀   MARS ♂

Day	R.A.	Dec. −	Diam.	Phase	Tran-sit		Day	R.A.	Dec. −	Diam.	Phase	Tran-sit	5° high. 52°	5° high. 56°
	h m	°	″		h m			h m	°	″		h m	h m	h m
1	18 25	23·6	10	100	11 45		1	14 34	14·0	5	93	7 52	3 43	4 01
6	18 53	23·4	10	100	11 52		6	14 46	15·0	5	92	7 44	3 42	4 00
11	19 20	22·9	10	100	12 00	Venus is too	11	14 58	15·9	5	92	7 37	3 40	4 00
16	19 47	22·0	10	100	12 07	close to the	16	15 10	16·8	5	92	7 29	3 38	4 00
21	20 14	20·9	10	100	12 14	Sun for	21	15 22	17·6	5	91	7 21	3 36	3 59
26	20 40	19·6	10	100	12 20	observation	26	15 34	18·3	6	91	7 14	3 34	3 58
31	21 05	18·0	10	100	12 26		31	15 46	19·1	6	91	7 06	3 32	3 57

SUNRISE AND SUNSET

Day	London a.m. h m	London p.m. h m	Bristol a.m. h m	Bristol p.m. h m	Birmingham a.m. h m	Birmingham p.m. h m	Manchester a.m. h m	Manchester p.m. h m	Newcastle a.m. h m	Newcastle p.m. h m	Glasgow a.m. h m	Glasgow p.m. h m	Belfast a.m. h m	Belfast p.m. h m
1	8 06	4 01	8 16	4 12	8 18	4 03	8 25	4 00	8 31	3 48	8 48	3 54	8 47	4 08
2	8 06	4 02	8 16	4 13	8 18	4 04	8 25	4 01	8 31	3 49	8 48	3 55	8 47	4 09
3	8 06	4 03	8 16	4 14	8 18	4 05	8 25	4 02	8 31	3 50	8 47	3 56	8 47	4 10
4	8 06	4 05	8 16	4 15	8 18	4 06	8 25	4 03	8 31	3 51	8 47	3 57	8 47	4 11
5	8 06	4 06	8 15	4 16	8 17	4 08	8 24	4 05	8 30	3 53	8 46	3 59	8 46	4 13
6	8 05	4 07	8 15	4 17	8 17	4 09	8 24	4 06	8 30	3 54	8 46	4 00	8 46	4 14
7	8 05	4 08	8 15	4 19	8 17	4 10	8 24	4 07	8 29	3 56	8 45	4 02	8 45	4 16
8	8 05	4 09	8 15	4 20	8 16	4 12	8 23	4 09	8 29	3 57	8 45	4 03	8 45	4 17
9	8 04	4 10	8 14	4 21	8 15	4 13	8 22	4 10	8 28	3 59	8 44	4 05	8 44	4 19
10	8 04	4 12	8 13	4 23	8 15	4 15	8 22	4 12	8 27	4 00	8 43	4 06	8 43	4 20
11	8 03	4 13	8 13	4 24	8 14	4 16	8 21	4 13	8 26	4 02	8 42	4 08	8 42	4 22
12	8 02	4 14	8 12	4 25	8 13	4 17	8 20	4 14	8 26	4 04	8 42	4 10	8 42	4 24
13	8 02	4 16	8 12	4 27	8 13	4 19	8 20	4 16	8 25	4 05	8 41	4 11	8 41	4 25
14	8 01	4 18	8 11	4 28	8 12	4 21	8 19	4 18	8 24	4 07	8 40	4 13	8 40	4 27
15	8 00	4 19	8 10	4 30	8 11	4 22	8 18	4 19	8 23	4 09	8 39	4 15	8 39	4 29
16	7 59	4 21	8 09	4 31	8 10	4 24	8 17	4 21	8 22	4 10	8 38	4 17	8 38	4 30
17	7 58	4 22	8 08	4 33	8 09	4 25	8 16	4 22	8 21	4 12	8 36	4 19	8 37	4 32
18	7 58	4 24	8 08	4 34	8 09	4 27	8 16	4 24	8 20	4 14	8 35	4 20	8 36	4 34
19	7 57	4 26	8 07	4 36	8 08	4 29	8 14	4 26	8 18	4 16	8 34	4 22	8 34	4 36
20	7 56	4 27	8 06	4 37	8 07	4 30	8 13	4 27	8 17	4 17	8 32	4 24	8 33	4 37
21	7 54	4 29	8 04	4 39	8 05	4 32	8 12	4 29	8 16	4 19	8 31	4 26	8 32	4 39
22	7 53	4 31	8 03	4 41	8 04	4 34	8 11	4 31	8 15	4 21	8 30	4 28	8 31	4 41
23	7 52	4 32	8 02	4 42	8 03	4 35	8 09	4 33	8 13	4 23	8 28	4 30	8 29	4 43
24	7 51	4 34	8 01	4 44	8 02	4 37	8 08	4 35	8 11	4 26	8 26	4 33	8 28	4 45
25	7 50	4 36	8 00	4 46	8 01	4 39	8 07	4 37	8 10	4 28	8 25	4 35	8 27	4 47
26	7 48	4 38	7 58	4 48	7 59	4 41	8 05	4 39	8 08	4 30	8 23	4 37	8 25	4 49
27	7 47	4 40	7 57	4 50	7 58	4 43	8 04	4 41	8 07	4 32	8 22	4 39	8 24	4 51
28	7 46	4 41	7 56	4 51	7 57	4 44	8 02	4 43	8 05	4 34	8 20	4 41	8 22	4 53
29	7 44	4 43	7 54	4 53	7 55	4 46	8 01	4 45	8 04	4 36	8 18	4 43	8 20	4 55
30	7 43	4 45	7 53	4 55	7 54	4 48	7 59	4 47	8 02	4 38	8 16	4 45	8 18	4 57
31	7 41	4 47	7 51	4 57	7 52	4 50	7 57	4 49	8 00	4 40	8 15	4 47	8 17	4 59

JUPITER ♃   SATURN ♄

Day	JUPITER R.A. h m	JUPITER Dec. − °	JUPITER Transit h m	JUPITER 5° high 52° h m	JUPITER 5° high 56° h m	SATURN R.A. h m	SATURN Dec. − °	SATURN Transit h m	SATURN 5° high 52° h m	SATURN 5° high 56° h m
1	21 24	16·1	14 40	18 36	18 16	16 14	19·4	9 31	6 00	6 26
11	21 32	15·4	14 10	18 10	17 50	16 18	19·6	8 56	5 26	5 52
21	21 41	14·7	13 39	17 44	17 26	16 22	19·7	8 21	4 51	5 18
31	21 50	13·9	13 09	17 19	17 01	16 26	19·8	7 45	4 16	4 43

Equatorial diameter of Jupiter 33″; of Saturn 16″.   Diameters of Saturn's rings 35″ and 15″.

URANUS ♅   NEPTUNE ♆

Day	URANUS R.A. h m	URANUS Dec. − ° ′	URANUS Transit h m		NEPTUNE R.A. h m	NEPTUNE Dec. − ° ′	NEPTUNE Transit h m	
1	17 14·3	23 05	10 31	Uranus is too close to the Sun for observation	18 15·5	22 20	11 32	Neptune is too close to the Sun for observation
11	17 16·8	23 08	9 54		18 17·1	22 19	10 55	
21	17 19·0	23 10	9 17		18 18·7	22 19	10 17	
31	17 21·1	23 12	8 40		18 20·1	22 18	9 39	

Diameter 4″   Diameter 2″

Februa, Roman festival of Purification

Sun's Longitude 330° ♓ 18^{d} 23^{h}

Day of Month	Day of Week	
1	S.	Mary Shelley d. 1851. Dame Clara Butt b. 1873.
2	S	**8th S. before Easter. Purification.**
3	M.	Felix Mendelssohn b. 1809. Walter Bagehot b. 1826.
4	Tu.	Charles Lindbergh b. 1902.
5	W.	Sir Robert Peel b. 1788. Admiral Lord Fraser b. 1888.
6	Th.	QUEEN'S ACCESSION 1952. Ronald Reagan b. 1911.
7	F.	Sir Thomas More b. 1478. Charles Dickens b. 1812.
8	S.	Mary, Queen of Scots exec. 1587.
9	S	**7th S. before Easter.**
10	M.	Charles Lamb b. 1775. Pushkin d. 1837.
11	Tu.	SHROVE TUESDAY. Thomas Edison b. 1847.
12	W.	**Ash Wednesday.** Charles Darwin b. 1809.
13	Th.	Massacre of Glencoe 1692.
14	F.	VALENTINE'S DAY. Capt. Cook killed 1779.
15	S.	Galileo b. 1564. Sir Ernest Shackleton b. 1874.
16	S	**1st S. in Lent.** Admiral Coligny b. 1519.
17	M.	Moliere d. 1673. Heinrich Heine d. 1856.
18	Tu.	Mary I b. 1516. Martin Luther d. 1546.
19	W.	PRINCE ANDREW b. 1960. David Garrick b. 1717.
20	Th.	Dame Marie Rambert b. 1888.
21	F.	Card. Newman b. 1801. W. H. Auden b. 1907.
22	S.	George Washington b. 1732. Schopenhauer b. 1788.
23	S.	**2nd S. in Lent.** George Frederick Handel b. 1685.
24	M.	Wilhelm Grimm b. 1786.**
25	Tu.	Pierre Renoir b. 1841. Enrico Caruso b. 1873.
26	W.	Victor Hugo b. 1802.
27	Th.	Longfellow b. 1807. John Steinbeck b. 1902.
28	F.	Montaigne b. 1533. Henry James d. 1916.

PHENOMENA

February 1^{d} 01^{h} Mercury in superior conjunction.

3^{d} 12^{h} Mars in conjunction with the Moon. Mars 3° N.

4^{d} 01^{h} Saturn in conjunction with the Moon. Saturn 5° N.

18^{d} 00^{h} Mars in conjunction with Saturn. Mars 1°·3 S.

18^{d} 10^{h} Jupiter in conjunction with the Sun.

28^{d} 16^{h} Mercury at greatest eastern elogation (18°).

CONSTELLATIONS

The following constellations are near the meridian at

	d	h		d	h
Jan.	1	24	Jan.	16	23
Feb.	1	22	Feb.	15	21
Mar.	1	20	Mar.	16	19

Draco (below the Pole), Camelopardus, Auriga, Taurus, Gemini, Orion, Canis Minor, Monoceros, Lepus, Canis Major and Puppis.

MINIMA OF ALGOL

d	h	d	h
2	22	17	6
5	19	20	3
8	16	23	0
11	12	25	21
14	9	28	17

PHASES OF THE MOON

	d	h	m
☾ Last Quarter	2	04	41
● New Moon	9	00	55
☽ First Quarter	16	19	55
○ Full Moon	24	15	02

	d	h
Perigee (368,820 kilometres)	4	16
Apogee (404,260 „)	16	22

Mean Longitude of Ascending Node on February 1, 34°.

MONTHLY NOTES

Feb. 1. Pheasant and partridge shooting ends.
6. National Day, New Zealand.
9. Chinese New Year (Year of the Tiger).
12. First Day of Lent.

QUARTER DAYS (England, Wales and Northern Ireland)

Lady Day . . . . . March 25 — *Michaelmas* . . September 29
Midsummer . . June 24 — *Christmas* . . . . December 25

SCOTTISH TERM DAYS

Candlemas . . . February 2 — *Lammas* . . . . . . August 1
Whitsunday . . May 15 — *Martinmas* . . . November 11

Removal Terms are May 28 and November 28.

**Centenary

Day	THE SUN s.d. 16'·2								Sidereal Time	Transit of First Point of Aries
	Right Ascension	Dec. −	Equation of Time	Rise		Transit	Set			
				52°	56°		52°	56°		
	h m s	° '	m s	h m	h m	h m	h m	h m	h m s	h m s
1	20 57 08	17 15	−13 31	7 42	7 57	12 14	16 47	16 32	8 43 37	15 13 52
2	21 01 13	16 58	−13 39	7 40	7 55	12 14	16 48	16 34	8 47 34	15 09 56
3	21 05 17	16 40	−13 46	7 38	7 53	12 14	16 50	16 36	8 51 30	15 06 00
4	21 09 20	16 23	−13 53	7 37	7 51	12 14	16 52	16 38	8 55 27	15 02 04
5	21 13 22	16 05	−13 59	7 35	7 49	12 14	16 54	16 40	8 59 24	14 58 08
6	21 17 24	15 46	−14 04	7 33	7 47	12 14	16 56	16 42	9 03 20	14 54 12
7	21 21 24	15 28	−14 08	7 32	7 45	12 14	16 58	16 45	9 07 17	14 50 17
8	21 25 24	15 09	−14 11	7 30	7 43	12 14	17 00	16 47	9 11 13	14 46 21
9	21 29 23	14 50	−14 13	7 28	7 41	12 14	17 02	16 49	9 15 10	14 42 25
10	21 33 21	14 31	−14 15	7 26	7 39	12 14	17 03	16 51	9 19 06	14 38 29
11	21 37 19	14 11	−14 16	7 24	7 36	12 14	17 05	16 53	9 23 03	14 34 33
12	21 41 16	13 52	−14 16	7 23	7 34	12 14	17 07	16 56	9 27 00	14 30 37
13	21 45 12	13 32	−14 16	7 21	7 32	12 14	17 09	16 58	9 30 56	14 26 41
14	21 49 07	13 12	−14 14	7 19	7 30	12 14	17 11	17 00	9 34 53	14 22 45
15	21 53 01	12 51	−14 12	7 17	7 28	12 14	17 13	17 02	9 38 49	14 18 49
16	21 56 55	12 31	−14 09	7 15	7 25	12 14	17 14	17 04	9 42 46	14 14 53
17	22 00 48	12 10	−14 06	7 13	7 23	12 14	17 16	17 07	9 46 42	14 10 57
18	22 04 40	11 49	−14 01	7 11	7 21	12 14	17 18	17 09	9 50 39	14 07 02
19	22 08 32	11 28	−13 56	7 09	7 18	12 14	17 20	17 11	9 54 35	14 03 06
20	22 12 22	11 06	−13 51	7 07	7 16	12 14	17 22	17 13	9 58 32	13 59 10
21	22 16 12	10 45	−13 44	7 05	7 14	12 14	17 24	17 15	10 02 29	13 55 14
22	22 20 02	10 23	−13 37	7 03	7 11	12 14	17 26	17 18	10 06 25	13 51 18
23	22 23 51	10 01	−13 29	7 01	7 09	12 13	17 27	17 20	10 10 22	13 47 22
24	22 27 39	9 39	−13 21	6 59	7 06	12 13	17 29	17 22	10 14 18	13 43 26
25	22 31 27	9 17	−13 12	6 56	7 04	12 13	17 31	17 24	10 18 15	13 39 30
26	22 35 14	8 55	−13 02	6 54	7 01	12 13	17 33	17 26	10 22 11	13 35 34
27	22 39 00	8 32	−12 52	6 52	6 59	12 13	17 35	17 28	10 26 08	13 31 38
28	22 42 46	8 10	−12 42	6 50	6 56	12 13	17 36	17 30	10 30 04	13 27 42

Duration of Civil (C), Nautical (N), and Astronomical (A), Twilight (in minutes)

Lat. °	Feb. 1			Feb. 11			Feb. 21			Feb. 28		
	C	N	A	C	N	A	C	N	A	C	N	A
52	37	77	117	35	75	114	34	74	113	34	73	112
56	41	86	130	39	83	126	38	81	125	38	81	124

ASTRONOMICAL NOTES

MERCURY is unsuitably placed for observation at first since superior conjunction occurs on the 1st. However, for the last week of February it is visible as an evening object (magnitude −1·0 to −0·1), attaining greatest eastern elongation on the last day of the month. It may be seen low above the W.S.W. horizon around the time of end of civil twilight. For observers in the northern hemisphere this is the most favourable evening apparition of the year.

VENUS is too close to the Sun for observation for the first three weeks of February. Thereafter a keen-sighted observer might be able to glimpse the planet immediately after sunset, about 5° above the W.S.W. horizon. Do not confuse Venus with Mercury: Venus is about 3 magnitudes brighter than Mercury and is closer to the Sun.

MARS, magnitude +1·1, continues to be visible in the south-eastern sky in the mornings. During the month Mars passes from Libra, through Scorpius and into Ophiuchus, passing 5° N. of Antares on the morning of the 17th, while less than a day later it passes 1°·3 S. of Saturn. The old crescent Moon is near the planet on the morning of the 3rd.

JUPITER may only be glimpsed with difficulty at the beginning of the month, low above the south-western horizon at the end of evening civil twilight. Thereafter it is too close to the Sun for observation, conjunction occurring on the 18th.

SATURN magnitude +0·7, continues to be visible low in the south-eastern sky, in the mornings. Saturn passes 7° N. of Antares on the 10th.

ZODIACAL LIGHT. The evening cone may be observed in the western sky after the end of twilight from the beginning of the month to the 10th and again after the 25th. This faint phenomenon is only visible under good conditions, in the absence of both moonlight and artificial lighting.

THE MOON

Day	R.A.	Dec.	Hor. Par.	Semi-diam.	Sun's Co-long.	P.A. of Bright Limb	Phase	Age	Rise 52°	Rise 56°	Transit	Set 52°	Set 56°
	h m	°	′	′	°	°		d	h m	h m	h m	h m	h m
1	13 39	− 9·6	58·8	16·0	167	111	63	21·5	..	..	5 05	10 10	10 00
2	14 31	−15·5	59·1	16·1	180	108	52	22·5	1 11	1 27	5 56	10 27	10 10
3	15 26	−20·6	59·3	16·2	192	104	41	23·5	2 40	3 03	6 50	10 49	10 25
4	16 25	−24·6	59·4	16·2	204	98	30	24·5	4 09	4 40	7 49	11 22	10 50
5	17 28	−27·1	59·4	16·2	216	90	20	25·5	5 30	6 07	8 51	12 09	11 32
6	18 32	−27·8	59·3	16·2	228	81	12	26·5	6 35	7 12	9 54	13 15	12 38
7	19 36	−26·6	59·1	16·1	240	71	5	27·5	7 21	7 53	10 55	14 36	14 05
8	20 37	−23·8	58·7	16·0	253	55	2	28·5	7 53	8 17	11 52	16 02	15 40
9	21 34	−19·6	58·2	15·8	265	167	0	29·5	8 14	8 31	12 45	17 28	17 13
10	22 26	−14·4	57·5	15·7	277	268	1	1·0	8 30	8 41	13 33	18 50	18 41
11	23 15	− 8·7	56·8	15·5	289	255	5	2·0	8 43	8 48	14 18	20 08	20 05
12	0 02	− 2·8	56·1	15·3	301	250	10	3·0	8 54	8 55	15 00	21 23	21 25
13	0 46	+ 3·1	55·5	15·1	314	249	17	4·0	9 04	9 00	15 42	22 36	22 43
14	1 30	+ 8·7	55·0	15·0	326	249	24	5·0	9 15	9 06	16 23	23 49	..
15	2 15	+13·9	54·6	14·9	338	251	33	6·0	9 28	9 14	17 06	..	0 02
16	3 01	+18·5	54·3	14·8	350	254	42	7·0	9 44	9 24	17 50	1 02	1 21
17	3 48	+22·4	54·2	14·8	2	258	52	8·0	10 04	9 38	18 38	2 15	2 40
18	4 39	+25·4	54·3	14·8	14	263	61	9·0	10 33	10 01	19 27	3 26	3 58
19	5 31	+27·3	54·6	14·9	27	269	70	10·0	11 12	10 36	20 20	4 32	5 08
20	6 26	+27·9	55·0	15·0	39	276	78	11·0	12 06	11 29	21 13	5 28	6 05
21	7 22	+27·1	55·6	15·1	51	283	86	12·0	13 14	12 41	22 07	6 11	6 44
22	8 17	+24·9	56·2	15·3	63	291	92	13·0	14 31	14 06	22 59	6 43	7 10
23	9 11	+21·4	56·9	15·5	75	300	97	14·0	15 54	15 35	23 50	7 07	7 27
24	10 04	+16·7	57·5	15·7	87	320	99	15·0	17 17	17 06	..	7 24	7 38
25	10 55	+11·1	58·2	15·8	99	73	100	16·0	18 41	18 36	0 38	7 39	7 46
26	11 45	+ 4·9	58·7	16·0	112	104	98	17·0	20 05	20 06	1 26	7 51	7 54
27	12 35	− 1·7	59·0	16·1	124	110	93	18·0	21 31	21 37	2 13	8 04	8 00
28	13 26	− 8·2	59·3	16·2	136	111	86	19·0	22 58	23 12	3 02	8 17	8 08

MERCURY ☿

Day	R.A.	Dec. −	Diam.	Phase	Transit		Day	R.A.	Dec. −	Diam.	Phase	Transit	5° high 52°	5° high 56°
	h m	°	″		h m			h m	°	″		h m	h m	h m
1	20 59	19·3	5	100	12 17		16	22 43	−9·3	5	90	13 01	17 43	17 31
4	21 20	17·7	5	100	12 27	Mercury is too	19	23 02	−6·8	6	84	13 08	18 03	17 55
7	21 41	15·9	5	99	12 36	close to the Sun for	22	23 19	−4·3	6	75	13 14	18 22	18 16
10	22 02	13·9	5	97	12 45	observation	25	23 35	−2·0	7	64	13 17	18 37	18 33
13	22 23	11·7	5	95	12 53		28	23 47	+0·2	7	51	13 17	18 48	18 45
16	22 43	9·3	5	90	13 01		31	23 56	+1·9	7	37	13 13	18 51	18 50

VENUS ♀   MARS ♂

Day	R.A.	Dec. −	Diam.	Phase	Transit		Day	R.A.	Dec. −	Diam.	Phase	Transit	5° high 52°	5° high 56°
	h m	°	″		h m			h m	°	″		h m	h m	h m
1	21 11	17·6	10	100	12 28		1	15 49	19·2	6	91	7 05	3 31	3 57
6	21 36	15·8	10	100	12 33	Venus is too	6	16 01	19·9	6	90	6 57	3 29	3 56
11	22 00	13·7	10	100	12 38	close to the Sun for	11	16 13	20·5	6	90	6 50	3 26	3 54
16	22 24	11·5	10	99	12 42	observation	16	16 25	21·0	6	90	6 42	3 23	3 52
21	22 48	9·2	10	99	12 46		21	16 38	21·5	7	89	6 35	3 19	3 50
26	23 11	6·8	10	99	12 49		26	16 50	21·9	7	89	6 27	3 15	3 47
31	23 34	4·3	10	99	12 52		31	17 02	22·3	7	89	6 19	3 11	3 44

SUNRISE AND SUNSET

Day	London a.m. h m	London p.m. h m	Bristol a.m. h m	Bristol p.m. h m	Birmingham a.m. h m	Birmingham p.m. h m	Manchester a.m. h m	Manchester p.m. h m	Newcastle a.m. h m	Newcastle p.m. h m	Glasgow a.m. h m	Glasgow p.m. h m	Belfast a.m. h m	Belfast p.m. h m
1	7 40	4 49	7 50	4 59	7 51	4 52	7 56	4 51	7 59	4 42	8 13	4 50	8 15	5 02
2	7 39	4 52	7 48	5 00	7 49	4 54	7 54	4 53	7 57	4 44	8 11	4 52	8 13	5 04
3	7 37	4 52	7 46	5 02	7 47	4 56	7 52	4 55	7 55	4 46	8 09	4 54	8 11	5 06
4	7 36	4 54	7 45	5 04	7 46	4 58	7 51	4 57	7 53	4 48	8 07	4 56	8 10	5 08
5	7 34	4 56	7 43	5 06	7 44	5 00	7 49	4 59	7 51	4 50	8 05	4 58	8 08	5 10
6	7 32	4 58	7 42	5 08	7 42	5 02	7 47	5 01	7 49	4 52	8 03	5 00	8 06	5 12
7	7 31	4 59	7 40	5 09	7 40	5 04	7 45	5 03	7 47	4 55	8 01	5 03	8 04	5 14
8	7 29	5 01	7 38	5 11	7 38	5 06	7 43	5 05	7 45	4 57	7 59	5 05	8 02	5 16
9	7 27	5 03	7 37	5 13	7 36	5 08	7 41	5 07	7 43	4 59	7 57	5 07	8 00	5 18
10	7 25	5 04	7 35	5 14	7 34	5 09	7 39	5 08	7 41	5 01	7 55	5 09	7 58	5 20
11	7 23	5 06	7 33	5 16	7 32	5 11	7 37	5 10	7 39	5 03	7 53	5 11	7 56	5 22
12	7 22	5 08	7 32	5 18	7 31	5 13	7 36	5 12	7 37	5 05	7 51	5 13	7 54	5 24
13	7 20	5 10	7 30	5 20	7 29	5 15	7 34	5 14	7 35	5 07	7 49	5 15	7 52	5 26
14	7 18	5 12	7 28	5 22	7 27	5 17	7 32	5 16	7 33	5 09	7 47	5 17	7 50	5 28
15	7 16	5 14	7 26	5 24	7 25	5 19	7 30	5 18	7 31	5 11	7 45	5 19	7 48	5 30
16	7 14	5 15	7 24	5 25	7 23	5 20	7 28	5 20	7 28	5 13	7 42	5 21	7 46	5 32
17	7 12	5 17	7 22	5 27	7 21	5 22	7 26	5 22	7 26	5 16	7 40	5 24	7 44	5 34
18	7 10	5 19	7 20	5 29	7 19	5 24	7 24	5 24	7 24	5 18	7 38	5 26	7 42	5 36
19	7 08	5 21	7 18	5 31	7 17	5 26	7 21	5 26	7 21	5 20	7 35	5 28	7 39	5 38
20	7 06	5 23	7 16	5 33	7 15	5 28	7 19	5 28	7 19	5 22	7 33	5 30	7 37	5 40
21	7 04	5 25	7 14	5 35	7 13	5 30	7 17	5 30	7 17	5 24	7 31	5 32	7 35	5 42
22	7 02	5 27	7 12	5 37	7 11	5 32	7 15	5 32	7 15	5 26	7 28	5 35	7 32	5 45
23	7 00	5 28	7 10	5 38	7 09	5 33	7 12	5 34	7 12	5 28	7 26	5 37	7 30	5 47
24	6 58	5 30	7 07	5 40	7 07	5 35	7 10	5 36	7 10	5 30	7 23	5 39	7 27	5 49
25	6 55	5 32	7 05	5 42	7 04	5 37	7 08	5 38	7 08	5 32	7 21	5 41	7 25	5 51
26	6 53	5 34	7 03	5 44	7 02	5 39	7 06	5 40	7 05	5 34	7 18	5 43	7 23	5 53
27	6 51	5 36	7 01	5 46	7 00	5 41	7 03	5 42	7 03	5 36	7 16	5 45	7 20	5 55
28	6 49	5 37	6 59	5 47	6 58	5 43	7 01	5 44	7 00	5 38	7 13	5 47	7 18	5 57

	JUPITER ♃				SATURN ♄			5° high.	
Day	R.A.	Dec. —	Transit		R.A.	Dec. —	Transit	52°	56°
	h m	°	h m		h m	°	h m	h m	h m
1	21 51	13·9	13 06	Jupiter is too	16 26	19·8	7 41	4 13	4 39
11	22 01	13·0	12 36	close to the	16 29	19·9	7 05	3 37	4 04
21	22 10	12·2	12 06	Sun for	16 31	20·0	6 27	3 00	3 27
31	22 19	11·4	11 36	observation	16 32	20·0	5 50	2 22	2 49

Equatorial diameter of Jupiter 33″; of Saturn 16″. Diameters of Saturn's rings 37″ and 16″.

	URANUS ♅			10° high.		NEPTUNE ♆			10° high.	
Day	R.A.	Dec. —	Transit	52°	56°	R.A.	Dec. —	Transit	52°	56°
	h m	° ′	h m	h m	h m	h m	° ′	h m	h m	h m
1	17 21·3	23 12	8 36	6 32	7 44	18 20·2	22 18	9 35	7 20	8 18
11	17 23·0	23 14	7 59	5 55	7 07	18 21·5	22 17	8 57	6 42	7 40
21	17 24·5	23 16	7 21	5 17	6 30	18 22·7	22 16	8 19	6 03	7 01
31	17 25·6	23 17	6 43	4 39	5 52	18 23·6	22 15	7 40	5 25	6 22

Diameter 4″   Diameter 2″

Month	Week		
		Mars, Roman god of battle	
		Sun's Longitude 0° ♈ 20ᵈ 22ʰ	
1	S.	**St. David.** Frederic Chopin b. 1810.	
2	♄.	**3nd S. in Lent.** Cardinal Hume b. 1923.	
3	M.	William Macready b. 1793. Sir Henry Wood b. 1869	
4	Tu.	Antonio Vivaldi b. 1678. R.N.L.I. founded 1824.	
5	W.	Henry II b. 1133. Gerardus Mercator b. 1512.	
6	Th.	Michaelangelo b. 1475. Louisa M. Alcott d. 1888.	
7	F.	Sir John Herschel b. 1792. Maurice Ravel b. 1875.	
8	S.	Outbreak of Russian Revolution 1917.	
9	♄.	**4th S. in Lent.** William Cobbett b. 1763.	
10	M.	Prince Edward b. 1964. First Cruft's Dog Show 1886.**	
11	Tu.	William Huskisson b. 1770. Earl Beatty d. 1936.	
12	W.	d'Annunzio b. 1864. Nijinsky b. 1890.	
13	Th.	Joseph Priestley b. 1733. Sir Hugh Walpole b. 1884.	
14	F.	Johann Strauss b. 1804. Albert Einstein b. 1879.	
15	S.	Julius Caesar d. 44 B.C. Lord Melbourne b. 1779.	
16	♄	**5th S. in Lent.** Georg Simon Ohm b. 1787.	
17	M.	**St. Patrick.** Edmund Kean b. 1787.	
18	Tu.	Rimsky-Korsakov b. 1844. Wilfred Owen b. 1893.	
19	W.	**St. Joseph of Nazareth.** Livingstone b. 1813.	
20	Th.	Napoleon II b. 1811. Henrik Ibsen b. 1828.	
21	F.	Archbp Cranmer exec. 1556. J. S. Bach b. 1685.	
22	S.	Sir Anthony van Dyck b. 1599.	
23	♄.	**Palm Sunday.** Sir Roger Bannister b. 1929.	
24	M.	Elizabeth I d. 1603. Queen Mary d. 1953.	
25	Tu.	Arturo Toscanini b. 1867. Belá Bartok b. 1881.	
26	W.	Hilary Law Sittings End. Beethoven d. 1827.	
27	Th.	Maundy Thursday. James I d. 1625.	
28	F.	**Good Friday.** Neil Kinnock b. 1942.	
29	S.	Towton Field 1461. Charles Wesley d. 1788.	
30	♄.	**Easter Day.** Goya b. 1746. van Gogh b. 1853.	
31	M.	Andrew Marvell b. 1611. Haydn b. 1732.	

PHENOMENA

March 3ᵈ 08ʰ Saturn in conjunction with the Moon. Saturn 5° N.

3ᵈ 20ʰ Mars in conjunction with the Moon. Mars 4° N.

8ᵈ 13ʰ Mercury in conjunction with Venus. Mercury 5° N.

11ᵈ 15ʰ Venus in conjunction with the Moon. Venus 1°·3 N.

16ᵈ 20ʰ Mercury in inferior conjunction.

20ᵈ 22ʰ Equinox.

30ᵈ 15ʰ Saturn in conjunction with the Moon. Saturn 5° N.

CONSTELLATIONS

The following are near the meridian at

	d	h		d	h
Feb.	1	24	Feb.	15	23
Mar.	1	22	Mar.	16	21
Apr.	1	20	Apr.	15	19

Cepheus (below the Pole), Camelopardus, Lynx, Gemini, Cancer, Leo, Canis Minor, Hydra, Monoceros, Canis Major and Puppis.

MINIMA OF ALGOL

d	h	d	h
3	14	17	22
6	11	20	19
9	8	23	16
12	5	26	13
15	1	29	9

PHASES OF THE MOON

	d	h	m
☾ Last Quarter.......	3	12	17
● New Moon..........	10	14	52
☽ First Quarter	18	16	39
○ Full Moon	26	03	02

	d	h
Perigee (369,170 kilometres)	1	10
Apogee (404,610 „)	16	19
Perigee (363,960 „)	28	14
Mean Longitude of Ascending Node on March 1, 33°.		

Summer Time in 1986 (*see* p. 142).—Begins: March 30ᵈ at 01ʰ G.M.T.
Ends: October 26ᵈ 01ʰ G.M.T.

MONTHLY NOTES

Mar.
10. Commonwealth Day.
17. Bank Holiday in Northern Ireland.
25. Lady Day. Quarter Day.
29. Lent ends at midnight.
31. Bank Holiday, England, Wales and Northern Ireland.
31. Financial Year 1985–86 ends.

**Centenary

Day	Right Ascension	Dec.	Equation of Time	Rise 52°	Rise 56°	Transit	Set 52°	Set 56°	Sidereal Time	Transit of First Point of Aries
	h m s	° ′	m s	h m	h m	h m	h m	h m	h m s	h m s
1	22 46 31	− 7 47	−12 31	6 48	6 54	12 12	17 38	17 32	10 34 01	13 23 47
2	22 50 16	− 7 24	−12 19	6 46	6 51	12 12	17 40	17 35	10 37 57	13 19 51
3	22 54 01	− 7 01	−12 07	6 43	6 49	12 12	17 42	17 37	10 41 54	13 15 55
4	22 57 45	− 6 38	−11 54	6 41	6 46	12 12	17 44	17 39	10 45 51	13 11 59
5	23 01 28	− 6 15	−11 41	6 39	6 44	12 12	17 45	17 41	10 49 47	13 08 03
6	23 05 11	− 5 52	−11 28	6 37	6 41	12 11	17 47	17 43	10 53 44	13 04 07
7	23 08 54	− 5 29	−11 14	6 34	6 39	12 11	17 49	17 45	10 57 40	13 00 11
8	23 12 36	− 5 05	−10 59	6 32	6 36	12 11	17 51	17 47	11 01 37	12 56 15
9	23 16 18	− 4 42	−10 45	6 30	6 33	12 11	17 52	17 49	11 05 33	12 52 19
10	23 20 00	− 4 18	−10 30	6 28	6 31	12 10	17 54	17 51	11 09 30	12 48 23
11	23 23 41	− 3 55	−10 14	6 25	6 28	12 10	17 56	17 54	11 13 26	12 44 27
12	23 27 22	− 3 31	− 9 59	6 23	6 26	12 10	17 58	17 56	11 17 23	12 40 32
13	23 31 02	− 3 08	− 9 43	6 21	6 23	12 10	18 00	17 58	11 21 20	12 36 36
14	23 34 42	− 2 44	− 9 26	6 19	6 21	12 09	18 01	18 00	11 25 16	12 32 40
15	23 38 22	− 2 20	− 9 10	6 16	6 18	12 09	18 03	18 02	11 29 13	12 28 44
16	23 42 02	− 1 57	− 8 53	6 14	6 15	12 09	18 05	18 04	11 33 09	12 24 48
17	23 45 42	− 1 33	− 8 36	6 12	6 13	12 08	18 07	18 06	11 37 06	12 20 52
18	23 49 21	− 1 09	− 8 19	6 09	6 10	12 08	18 08	18 08	11 41 02	12 16 56
19	23 53 00	− 0 46	− 8 01	6 07	6 07	12 08	18 10	18 10	11 44 59	12 13 00
20	23 56 39	− 0 22	− 7 44	6 05	6 05	12 08	18 12	18 12	11 48 55	12 09 04
21	00 00 18	+ 0 02	− 7 26	6 02	6 02	12 07	18 14	18 14	11 52 52	12 05 08
22	00 03 56	+ 0 26	− 7 08	6 00	5 59	12 07	18 15	18 16	11 56 49	12 01 12
23	00 07 35	+ 0 49	− 6 50	5 58	5 57	12 07	18 17	18 18	12 00 45	11 57 17
24	00 11 13	+ 1 13	− 6 32	5 56	5 54	12 06	18 19	18 20	12 04 42	11 53 21
25	00 14 51	+ 1 37	− 6 13	5 53	5 52	12 06	18 20	18 22	12 08 38	11 49 25
26	00 18 30	+ 2 00	− 5 55	5 51	5 49	12 06	18 22	18 24	12 12 35	11 45 29
27	00 22 08	+ 2 24	− 5 37	5 48	5 46	12 06	18 24	18 26	12 16 31	11 41 33
28	00 25 46	+ 2 47	− 5 19	5 46	5 43	12 05	18 25	18 28	12 20 28	11 37 37
29	00 29 25	+ 3 11	− 5 00	5 44	5 41	12 05	18 27	18 30	12 24 24	11 33 41
30	00 33 03	+ 3 34	− 4 42	5 42	5 38	12 05	18 29	18 32	12 28 21	11 29 45
31	00 36 41	+ 3 57	− 4 24	5 39	5 36	12 04	18 30	18 34	12 32 18	11 25 49

THE SUN   s.d. 16′·1

Duration of Civil (C), Nautical (N), and Astronomical (A), Twilight (in minutes)

Lat. °	Mar. 1 C	Mar. 1 N	Mar. 1 A	Mar. 11 C	Mar. 11 N	Mar. 11 A	Mar. 21 C	Mar. 21 N	Mar. 21 A	Mar. 31 C	Mar. 31 N	Mar. 31 A
52	34	73	112	34	73	113	34	74	116	34	76	120
56	38	81	124	37	80	125	37	82	129	38	84	136

ASTRONOMICAL NOTES

MERCURY, its magnitude fading rapidly from − 0·1 to + 1·7, may be seen in the evenings for the first ten days of the month, low above the W.S.W. horizon at the end of civil twilight. Thereafter it is too close to the Sun for observation, inferior conjunction occurring on the 16th.

VENUS is visible in the evenings, magnitude − 3·4, low in the western sky after sunset. The thin crescent Moon, only about 28 hours old may be detected only a couple of degrees to the left of Venus, on the evening of the 11th, with Mercury 6 degrees away in the opposite direction.

MARS, is a morning object, its magnitude brightening during the month from + 0·9 to + 0·3. Towards the end of the month Mars moves from Ophiuchus into Sagittarius.

JUPITER is unsuitably placed for observation.

SATURN, magnitude + 0·6, is a morning object low in the south-eastern and southern sky. The Moon, near Last Quarter, will be seen approaching Saturn on the mornings of the 3rd and the 30th.

ZODIACAL LIGHT. The evening cone may be observed in the western sky after the end of twilight from the beginning of the month to the 11th and again after the 25th.

HALLEY'S COMET is now a morning object, low on the south-eastern horizon but a difficult object in the twilight, and still probably needing a low powered telescope for its detection. Positions are:—

Date	R.A. h m	Dec. ° ′
Mar. 1	20 26·5	− 16 19
Mar. 11	20 07·5	− 20 27
Mar. 21	19 38·5	− 26 43
Mar. 31	18 32·6	− 37 25

THE MOON

Day	R.A.	Dec.	Hor. Par.	Semi-diam.	Sun's Co-long.	P.A. of Bright Limb	Phase	Age	Rise 52°	Rise 56°	Tran-sit	Set 52°	Set 56°
	h m	°	′	′	°	°		d	h m	h m	h m	h m	h m
1	14 18	−14·4	59·4	16·2	148	110	77	20·0	..	..	3 52	8 32	8 17
2	15 13	−19·8	59·4	16·2	160	106	67	21·0	0 28	0 49	4 46	8 53	8 30
3	16 12	−24·1	59·3	16·2	172	101	56	22·0	1 57	2 26	5 43	9 21	8 51
4	17 13	−26·9	59·1	16·1	185	94	45	23·0	3 21	3 57	6 44	10 03	9 26
5	18 16	−28·0	58·8	16·0	197	87	34	24·0	4 30	5 08	7 45	11 02	10 23
6	19 19	−27·3	58·5	15·9	209	79	23	25·0	5 21	5 55	8 46	12 17	11 43
7	20 19	−24·9	58·2	15·8	221	72	15	26·0	5 56	6 23	9 43	13 40	13 14
8	21 16	−21·1	57·7	15·7	233	65	8	27·0	6 19	6 39	10 37	15 05	14 47
9	22 09	−16·3	57·3	15·6	246	57	3	28·0	6 36	6 50	11 25	16 28	16 16
10	22 58	−10·8	56·8	15·5	258	40	1	29·0	6 50	6 57	12 11	17 47	17 41
11	23 45	− 4·9	56·2	15·3	270	280	0	0·4	7 01	7 03	12 54	19 03	19 03
12	0 30	+ 1·0	55·7	15·2	282	254	2	1·4	7 11	7 09	13 36	20 17	20 22
13	1 14	+ 6·9	55·2	15·0	294	250	6	2·4	7 22	7 15	14 17	21 31	21 41
14	1 59	+12·3	54·8	14·9	307	250	11	3·4	7 33	7 21	15 00	22 44	23 01
15	2 45	+17·2	54·4	14·8	319	252	18	4·4	7 47	7 30	15 44	23 58	..
16	3 32	+21·4	54·2	14·8	331	255	26	5·4	8 06	7 42	16 30	..	0 21
17	4 21	+24·7	54·2	14·8	343	259	34	6·4	8 30	8 00	17 18	1 11	1 41
18	5 13	+27·0	54·3	14·8	355	265	44	7·4	9 04	8 29	18 09	2 20	2 55
19	6 07	+28·0	54·6	14·9	7	271	53	8·4	9 51	9 14	19 02	3 20	3 57
20	7 01	+27·7	55·1	15·0	20	277	63	9·4	10 53	10 17	19 55	4 08	4 43
21	7 56	+26·1	55·7	15·2	32	284	72	10·4	12 05	11 36	20 47	4 43	5 13
22	8 50	+23·1	56·4	15·4	44	290	80	11·4	13 26	13 04	21 38	5 10	5 33
23	9 43	+18·8	57·2	15·6	56	295	88	12·4	14 49	14 34	22 27	5 29	5 46
24	10 35	+13·5	58·1	15·8	68	300	94	13·4	16 13	16 05	23 15	5 44	5 55
25	11 26	+ 7·5	58·8	16·0	80	306	98	14·4	17 39	17 37	..	5 58	6 02
26	12 16	+ 0·8	59·5	16·2	93	348	100	15·4	19 06	19 10	0 04	6 10	6 09
27	13 07	− 5·9	60·0	16·3	105	107	99	16·4	20 35	20 46	0 53	6 23	6 16
28	14 00	−12·5	60·2	16·4	117	111	95	17·4	22 07	22 25	1 44	6 37	6 24
29	14 56	−18·4	60·2	16·4	129	109	89	18·4	23 40	..	2 38	6 56	6 36
30	15 56	−23·2	60·0	16·4	141	104	80	19·4	..	0 07	3 36	7 22	6 54
31	16 58	−26·5	59·7	16·3	153	98	70	20·4	1 09	1 44	4 37	7 59	7 24

MERCURY ☿

Day	R.A.	Dec. +	Diam.	Phase	Tran-sit	5° high. 52°	5° high. 56°	Day	R.A.	Dec.	Diam.	Phase	Tran-sit	
	h m	°	″		h m	h m	h m		h m	°	″		h m	
1	23 51	0·8	7	46	13 16	18 50	18 47	16	23 42	+1·9	11	1	12 05	
4	23 58	2·3	8	33	13 10	18 51	18 50	19	23 33	+0·5	11	1	11 44	Mercury is too
7	0 00	3·2	9	20	13 00	18 44	18 43	22	23 24	−1·1	11	5	11 24	close to the
10	23 58	3·5	10	10	12 45	18 29	18 28	25	23 18	−2·6	11	10	11 07	Sun for
13	23 51	3·0	10	4	12 26	18 06	18 05	28	23 15	−3·7	10	16	10 53	observation
16	23 42	1·9	11	1	12 05	17 39	17 37	31	23 15	−4·5	10	23	10 41	

VENUS ♀ / MARS ♂

Day	R.A.	Dec.	Diam.	Phase	Tran-sit	5° high. 52°	5° high. 56°	Day	R.A.	Dec. −	Diam.	Phase	Tran-sit	5° high. 52°	5° high. 56°
	h m	°	″		h m	h m	h m		h m	°	″		h m	h m	h m
1	23 25	−5·3	10	99	12 51	17 53	17 45	1	16 57	22·2	7	89	6 23	3 12	3 45
6	23 48	−2·8	10	98	12 54	18 09	18 04	6	17 09	22·5	7	89	6 15	3 08	3 41
11	0 10	−0·2	10	98	12 57	18 26	18 23	11	17 21	22·8	8	89	6 07	3 02	3 37
16	0 33	+2·3	10	97	13 00	18 42	18 41	16	17 32	23·1	8	89	5 59	2 57	3 32
21	0 56	+4·9	10	97	13 03	18 58	18 59	21	17 44	23·3	8	89	5 51	2 50	3 26
26	1 19	+7·4	10	96	13 06	19 14	19 17	26	17 55	23·4	9	89	5 42	2 43	3 20
31	1 42	+9·8	10	96	13 10	19 30	19 35	31	18 06	23·5	9	89	5 34	2 35	3 12

SUNRISE AND SUNSET

Day	London a.m.	London p.m.	Bristol a.m.	Bristol p.m.	Birmingham a.m.	Birmingham p.m.	Manchester a.m.	Manchester p.m.	Newcastle a.m.	Newcastle p.m.	Glasgow a.m.	Glasgow p.m.	Belfast a.m.	Belfast p.m.
	h m	h m	h m	h m	h m	h m	h m	h m	h m	h m	h m	h m	h m	h m
1	6 47	5 39	6 57	5 49	6 56	5 45	6 59	5 46	6 58	5 40	7 11	5 49	7 16	5 59
2	6 45	5 41	6 55	5 51	6 53	5 47	6 56	5 48	6 55	5 42	7 08	5 52	7 13	6 01
3	6 43	5 43	6 52	5 53	6 51	5 48	6 54	5 49	6 53	5 44	7 06	5 54	7 11	6 02
4	6 41	5 45	6 50	5 55	6 49	5 50	6 52	5 51	6 51	5 46	7 03	5 56	7 09	6 04
5	6 39	5 46	6 48	5 56	6 46	5 52	6 49	5 53	6 48	5 48	7 01	5 58	7 06	6 06
6	6 37	5 48	6 46	5 58	6 44	5 54	6 47	5 55	6 46	5 50	6 58	6 00	7 04	6 08
7	6 34	5 50	6 44	6 00	6 41	5 56	6 44	5 57	6 43	5 52	6 56	6 02	7 01	6 10
8	6 32	5 51	6 42	6 01	6 39	5 58	6 42	5 59	6 41	5 54	6 53	6 04	6 59	6 12
9	6 30	5 53	6 40	6 03	6 37	5 59	6 40	6 00	6 38	5 56	6 50	6 06	6 56	6 14
10	6 28	5 55	6 37	6 05	6 35	6 01	6 38	6 02	6 36	5 58	6 48	6 08	6 54	6 16
11	6 25	5 56	6 35	6 06	6 32	6 03	6 35	6 04	6 33	6 01	6 45	6 11	6 51	6 19
12	6 23	5 58	6 33	6 08	6 30	6 05	6 33	6 06	6 31	6 03	6 43	6 13	6 49	6 21
13	6 21	6 00	6 31	6 10	6 28	6 07	6 31	6 08	6 28	6 05	6 40	6 15	6 46	6 23
14	6 19	6 01	6 29	6 11	6 26	6 08	6 29	6 10	6 26	6 07	6 38	6 17	6 44	6 25
15	6 16	6 03	6 26	6 13	6 23	6 10	6 26	6 11	6 23	6 08	6 35	6 19	6 41	6 26
16	6 14	6 05	6 24	6 15	6 21	6 12	6 24	6 13	6 21	6 10	6 32	6 21	6 39	6 28
17	6 12	6 07	6 22	6 17	6 19	6 14	6 21	6 15	6 18	6 12	6 30	6 23	6 36	6 30
18	6 09	6 08	6 19	6 18	6 16	6 15	6 19	6 17	6 16	6 14	6 27	6 25	6 34	6 32
19	6 07	6 10	6 17	6 20	6 14	6 17	6 16	6 19	6 13	6 16	6 24	6 27	6 31	6 34
20	6 05	6 12	6 15	6 22	6 12	6 19	6 14	6 21	6 11	6 18	6 22	6 29	6 29	6 36
21	6 02	6 14	6 12	6 24	6 09	6 21	6 11	6 23	6 08	6 20	6 19	6 31	6 26	6 38
22	6 00	6 15	6 10	6 25	6 07	6 22	6 09	6 25	6 06	6 22	6 16	6 33	6 24	6 40
23	5 58	6 17	6 08	6 27	6 05	6 24	6 06	6 27	6 03	6 24	6 14	6 35	6 21	6 42
24	5 56	6 19	6 06	6 29	6 02	6 26	6 04	6 28	6 01	6 25	6 11	6 37	6 19	6 43
25	5 53	6 20	6 03	6 30	6 00	6 27	6 01	6 30	5 58	6 27	6 09	6 39	6 16	6 45
26	5 51	6 22	6 01	6 32	5 58	6 29	5 59	6 32	5 56	6 29	6 06	6 41	6 14	6 47
27	5 49	6 24	5 59	6 34	5 55	6 31	5 56	6 34	5 53	6 31	6 03	6 43	6 11	6 49
28	5 46	6 25	5 56	6 35	5 53	6 32	5 54	6 35	5 50	6 33	6 00	6 45	6 08	6 51
29	5 44	6 27	5 54	6 37	5 51	6 34	5 52	6 37	5 48	6 35	5 58	6 47	6 06	6 53
30	5 42	6 29	5 52	6 38	5 49	6 36	5 50	6 39	5 45	6 37	5 55	6 49	6 03	6 55
31	5 40	6 30	5 50	6 40	5 46	6 37	5 47	6 40	5 43	6 39	5 53	6 51	6 01	6 57

JUPITER ♃ / SATURN ♄

Day	R.A.	Dec. −	Transit		R.A.	Dec. −	Transit	5° high. 52°	5° high. 56°
	h m	°	h m		h m	°	h m	h m	h m
1	22 17	11·5	11 42	Jupiter is too	16 32	20·0	5 57	2 30	2 57
11	22 26	10·7	11 11	close to the	16 33	20·0	5 19	1 52	2 19
21	22 35	9·9	10 41	Sun for	16 33	20·0	4 40	1 12	1 39
31	22 44	9·0	10 10	observation	16 33	19·9	4 00	0 32	0 59

Equatorial diameter of Jupiter 33″; of Saturn 17″. Diameters of Saturn's rings 39″ and 17″.

URANUS ♅ / NEPTUNE ♆

Day	R.A.	Dec. −	Transit	10° high. 52°	10° high. 56°	R.A.	Dec. −	Transit	10° high. 52°	10° high. 56°
	h m	° ′	h m	h m	h m	h m	° ′	h m	h m	h m
1	17 25·4	23 16	6 50	4 47	6 00	18 23·4	22 16	7 48	5 32	6 30
11	17 26·2	23 17	6 12	4 08	5 22	18 24·2	22 15	7 10	4 54	5 51
21	17 26·7	23 18	5 33	3 30	4 43	18 24·7	22 14	6 31	4 15	5 12
31	17 26·7	23 18	4 54	2 50	4 04	18 25·0	22 14	5 52	3 36	4 33

Diameter 4″   Diameter 2″

Month	Week	

Aperire, to open. Earth opens to receive seed.
Sun's Longitude 30° ♉ 20ᵈ 09ʰ

1	Tu.	William Harvey b. 1578. Bismark b. 1815
2	W.	Charlemagne b. 742. Copenhagen 1801.
3	Th.	George Herbert b. 1593. Brahms d. 1897.
4	F.	Martin Luther King d. 1968.
5	S.	Thomas Hobbes b. 1588. Joseph Lister b. 1827.
6	☞.	**1st S. after Easter.** Low Sunday.
7	M.	**Annunciation.** William Wordsworth b. 1770.
8	Tu.	EASTER LAW SITTINGS BEGIN. Richard I d. 1199.
9	W.	Lenin b. 1870. Edward Thomas d. 1917.
10	Th.	William Hazlitt b. 1778. Gen. William Booth b. 1829.
11	F.	Treaty of Utrecht 1713. U.S. Civil War starts 1861.
12	S.	First manned space flight 1961.
13	☞.	**2nd S. after Easter.** Samuel Beckett b. 1906.
14	M.	Handel d. 1759. Sir John Gielgud b. 1904.
15	Tu.	Henry James b. 1843. Matthew Arnold d. 1888.
16	W.	Culloden 1746. Charlie Chaplin b. 1889.
17	Th.	Diet of Worms 1521. Edward Gibbon b. 1737.
18	F.	John Foxe d. 1587. Judge Jeffreys d. 1689.
19	S.	David Ricardo b. 1772. Lexington 1775.
20	☞.	**3rd S. after Easter.** Adolf Hitler b. 1889.
21	M.	QUEEN ELIZABETH II b. 1926. Henry VII d. 1507.
22	Tu.	Immanuel Kant b. 1724. Yehudi Menuhin b. 1916.
23	W.	**St. George.** Shakespeare b. 1564; d. 1616.
24	Th.	Edmund Cartwright b. 1743. Anthony Trollope b.1815.
25	F.	**St. Mark.** Oliver Cromwell b. 1599.
26	S.	David Hume b. 1711. Alfred Krupp b. 1812.
27	☞.	**4th S. after Easter.** Samuel Morse b. 1791.
28	M.	Edward IV b. 1442. Mutiny on the *Bounty* 1789.
29	Tu.	Sir Thomas Beecham b. 1879. Sir Malcolm Sargent b. 1895.
30	W.	Mary II b. 1662. A. E. Housman d. 1936.

PHENOMENA

April 1ᵈ 03ʰ Mars in conjunction with the Moon. Mars 5° N.

6ᵈ 02ʰ Jupiter in conjunction with the Moon. Jupiter 3° N.

6ᵈ 21ʰ Mercury in conjunction with the Moon. Mercury 2° N.

11ᵈ 02ʰ Venus in conjunction with the Moon. Venus 1°·3 S.

13ᵈ 15ʰ Mercury at greatest western elongation (28°).

26ᵈ 21ʰ Saturn in conjunction with the Moon. Saturn 5° N.

29ᵈ 06ʰ Mars in conjunction with the Moon. Mars 4° N.

CONSTELLATIONS

The following constellations are near the meridian at

	d	h		d	h
Mar.	1	24	Mar.	16	23
Apr.	1	22	Apr.	15	21
May	1	20	May	16	19

Cepheus (below the Pole), Cassiopeia (below the Pole), Ursa Major, Leo Minor, Leo, Sextans, Hydra and Crater.

MINIMA OF ALGOL

d	h		d	h
1	6		18	11
4	3		21	8
7	0		24	5
9	21		27	2
12	18		29	22
15	14			

PHASES OF THE MOON

	d	h	m
☾ Last Quarter	1	19	30
● New Moon	9	06	08
☽ First Quarter	17	10	35
○ Full Moon	24	12	46

	d	h
Apogee (405,520 kilometres)	13	12
Perigee (359,350 ,,)	25	18

Mean Longitude of Ascending Node on April 1, 31°.

See note on *Summer Time*, p. 98.

MONTHLY NOTES

April 5. Income Tax Year (1985–86) ends.

24. First day of Passover.

Day	THE SUN s.d. 16′·0								Sidereal Time	Transit of First Point of Aries
	Right Ascension	Dec. +	Equation of Time	Rise		Transit	Set			
				52°	56°		52°	56°		
	h m s	° ′	m s	h m	h m	h m	h m	h m	h m s	h m s
1	0 40 20	4 20	− 4 06	5 37	5 33	12 04	18 32	18 36	12 36 14	11 21 53
2	0 43 59	4 44	− 3 48	5 35	5 30	12 04	18 34	18 39	12 40 11	11 17 57
3	0 47 37	5 07	− 3 30	5 32	5 28	12 03	18 36	18 41	12 44 07	11 14 02
4	0 51 16	5 30	− 3 13	5 30	5 25	12 03	18 37	18 43	12 48 04	11 10 06
5	0 54 55	5 53	− 2 55	5 28	5 22	12 03	18 39	18 45	12 52 00	11 06 10
6	0 58 35	6 15	− 2 38	5 26	5 20	12 03	18 41	18 47	12 55 57	11 02 14
7	1 02 14	6 38	− 2 21	5 23	5 17	12 02	18 42	18 49	12 59 53	10 58 18
8	1 05 54	7 01	− 2 04	5 21	5 15	12 02	18 44	18 51	13 03 50	10 54 22
9	1 09 34	7 23	− 1 47	5 19	5 12	12 02	18 46	18 53	13 07 47	10 50 26
10	1 13 14	7 45	− 1 31	5 16	5 10	12 01	18 48	18 55	13 11 43	10 46 30
11	1 16 54	8 08	− 1 15	5 14	5 07	12 01	18 49	18 57	13 15 40	10 42 34
12	1 20 35	8 30	− 0 59	5 12	5 04	12 01	18 51	18 59	13 19 36	10 38 38
13	1 24 16	8 52	− 0 44	5 10	5 02	12 01	18 53	19 01	13 23 33	10 34 42
14	1 27 57	9 13	− 0 28	5 07	4 59	12 00	18 54	19 03	13 27 29	10 30 47
15	1 31 39	9 35	− 0 13	5 05	4 57	12 00	18 56	19 05	13 31 26	10 26 51
16	1 35 21	9 56	+ 0 03	5 03	4 54	12 00	18 58	19 07	13 35 22	10 22 55
17	1 39 03	10 18	+ 0 15	5 01	4 52	12 00	19 00	19 09	13 39 19	10 18 59
18	1 42 46	10 39	+ 0 29	4 59	4 49	11 59	19 01	19 11	13 43 16	10 15 03
19	1 46 29	11 00	+ 0 43	4 56	4 47	11 59	19 03	19 13	13 47 12	10 11 07
20	1 50 12	11 21	+ 0 56	4 54	4 44	11 59	19 05	19 15	13 51 09	10 07 11
21	1 53 56	11 41	+ 1 09	4 52	4 42	11 59	19 06	19 17	13 55 05	10 03 15
22	1 57 40	12 01	+ 1 21	4 50	4 39	11 59	19 08	19 19	13 59 02	9 59 23
23	2 01 25	12 22	+ 1 33	4 48	4 37	11 58	19 10	19 21	14 02 58	9 55 23
24	2 05 10	12 42	+ 1 44	4 46	4 34	11 58	19 11	19 23	14 06 55	9 51 27
25	2 08 56	13 01	+ 1 55	4 44	4 32	11 58	19 13	19 25	14 10 51	9 47 31
26	2 12 42	13 21	+ 2 06	4 42	4 30	11 58	19 15	19 27	14 14 48	9 43 36
27	2 16 28	13 40	+ 2 16	4 40	4 27	11 58	19 16	19 29	14 18 45	9 39 40
28	2 20 16	13 59	+ 2 25	4 38	4 25	11 58	19 18	19 31	14 22 41	9 35 44
29	2 24 03	14 18	+ 2 34	4 36	4 22	11 57	19 20	19 33	14 26 38	9 31 48
30	2 27 51	14 37	+ 2 43	4 34	4 20	11 57	19 22	19 35	14 30 34	9 27 52

Duration of Civil (C), Nautical (N), and Astronomical (A), Twilight (in minutes)

Lat. °	Apr. 1			Apr. 11			Apr. 21			Apr. 30		
	C	N	A	C	N	A	C	N	A	C	N	A
52	34	76	121	35	79	128	37	84	138	39	89	152
56	38	85	137	40	90	148	42	96	167	44	105	200

ASTRONOMICAL NOTES

MERCURY is too close to the Sun for observation throughout the month.

VENUS, magnitude − 3·3, is visible for a short while in the evenings, low in the western sky after sunset. The thin crescent Moon, only 1½ days old, will be seen approaching Venus on the evening of the 10th.

MARS continues to brighten as it moves closer to the Earth, its magnitude increasing from + 0·3 to − 0·4 during the month. It continues to be visible low in the south-eastern sky in the mornings. The Moon, near Last Quarter, passes south of Mars on the mornings of the 1st and the 29th. Mars is in the constellation of Sagittarius.

JUPITER is unsuitably placed for observation at first but gradually becomes a morning object, magnitude − 1·6, during the last week of the month, low above the E.S.E. horizon before dawn.

SATURN, magnitude + 0·4, is a morning object, becoming visible soon after midnight at the beginning of April. The gibbous Moon will be seen near the planet on the night of 26th–27th.

ECLIPSE. A partial eclipse of the Sun occurs on the 9th. See page 148 for details.

ECLIPSE. A total eclipse of the Moon on the 24th. See page 148 for details.

THE MOON

Day	R.A.	Dec.	Hor. Par.	Semi-diam.	Sun's Co-long.	P.A. of Bright Limb	Phase	Age	Rise 52°	Rise 56°	Transit	Set 52°	Set 56°
	h m	°	'	'	°	°		d	h m	h m	h m	h m	h m
1	18 02	−28·0	59·2	16·1	166	91	59	21·4	2 25	3 04	5 39	8 53	8 14
2	19 05	−27·7	58·7	16·0	178	83	48	22·4	3 22	3 58	6 41	10 04	9 29
3	20 06	−25·7	58·1	15·8	190	77	37	23·4	4 00	4 30	7 39	11 26	10 57
4	21 03	−22·2	57·6	15·7	202	71	27	24·4	4 26	4 48	8 33	12 50	12 29
5	21 56	−17·7	57·0	15·5	214	66	18	25·4	4 44	5 00	9 22	14 13	13 59
6	22 45	−12·4	56·5	15·4	227	63	11	26·4	4 58	5 08	10 08	15 31	15 24
7	23 32	− 6·7	56·0	15·3	239	60	5	27·4	5 09	5 14	10 51	16 47	16 45
8	0 17	− 0·7	55·6	15·1	251	58	2	28·4	5 20	5 19	11 32	18 01	18 04
9	1 01	+ 5·1	55·1	15·0	263	44	0	29·4	5 30	5 25	12 13	19 15	19 23
10	1 45	+10·7	54·8	14·9	276	250	1	0·7	5 41	5 30	12 55	20 28	20 42
11	2 30	+15·8	54·4	14·8	288	249	3	1·7	5 54	5 38	13 39	21 42	22 03
12	3 17	+20·2	54·2	14·8	300	252	7	2·7	6 10	5 48	14 24	22 56	23 23
13	4 06	+23·9	54·1	14·7	312	256	13	3·7	6 31	6 03	15 12	··	··
14	4 57	+26·5	54·1	14·7	324	261	19	4·7	7 01	6 27	16 02	0 07	0 40
15	5 49	+27·9	54·2	14·8	337	267	27	5·7	7 43	7 05	16 53	1 11	1 48
16	6 43	+28·0	54·5	14·9	349	273	36	6·7	8 38	8 00	17 45	2 03	2 40
17	7 38	+26·9	55·0	15·0	1	279	46	7·7	9 45	9 13	18 37	2 43	3 16
18	8 31	+24·4	55·6	15·2	13	285	56	8·7	11 01	10 36	19 27	3 12	3 38
19	9 23	+20·7	56·4	15·4	25	290	66	9·7	12 21	12 03	20 16	3 33	3 53
20	10 14	+15·9	57·3	15·6	38	294	75	10·7	13 43	13 32	21 04	3 50	4 03
21	11 04	+10·2	58·2	15·9	50	296	84	11·7	15 07	15 02	21 51	4 03	4 11
22	11 54	+ 3·8	59·1	16·1	62	298	91	12·7	16 33	16 33	22 39	4 16	4 18
23	12 45	− 3·0	59·9	16·3	74	297	97	13·7	18 01	18 09	23 29	4 28	4 24
24	13 37	− 9·8	60·6	16·5	86	294	100	14·7	19 34	19 48	··	4 41	4 32
25	14 33	−16·1	60·9	16·6	98	117	100	15·7	21 10	21 33	0 23	4 58	4 42
26	15 33	−21·5	61·0	16·6	111	110	97	16·7	22 45	23 17	1 21	5 21	4 57
27	16 36	−25·6	60·8	16·6	123	103	91	17·7	··	··	2 23	5 54	5 21
28	17 42	−27·8	60·3	16·4	135	96	83	18·7	0 10	0 49	3 28	6 43	6 04
29	18 47	−28·0	59·7	16·3	147	88	73	19·7	1 17	1 55	4 32	7 51	7 13
30	19 51	−26·4	58·9	16·1	159	81	63	20·7	2 02	2 34	5 33	9 12	8 40

MERCURY ☿

Day	R.A.	Dec. −	Diam.	Phase	Transit		Day	R.A.	Dec.	Diam.	Phase	Transit	
	h m	°	″		h m			h m	°	″		h m	
1	23 16	4·7	10	25	10 38		16	23 57	−2·9	7	51	10 22	
4	23 20	5·0	9	31	10 31	Mercury is too	19	0 11	−1·7	7	55	10 24	Mercury is too
7	23 27	4·9	9	36	10 26	close to the	22	0 25	−0·3	7	60	10 26	close to the
10	23 35	4·5	8	42	10 23	Sun for	25	0 40	+1·3	6	64	10 30	Sun for
13	23 46	3·8	8	47	10 22	observation	28	0 56	+3·1	6	68	10 34	observation
16	23 57	2·9	7	51	10 22		31	1 13	+5·0	6	72	10 40	

VENUS ♀

Day	R.A.	Dec. +	Diam.	Phase	Transit	5° high. 52°	5° high. 56°
	h m	°	″		h m	h m	h m
1	1 46	10·3	10	96	13 10	19 33	19 38
6	2 10	12·6	10	95	13 14	19 49	19 56
11	2 33	14·8	11	94	13 18	20 05	20 14
16	2 57	16·9	11	93	13 22	20 20	20 32
21	3 22	18·7	11	92	13 27	20 35	20 49
26	3 47	20·4	11	91	13 33	20 50	21 05
31	4 12	21·8	11	90	13 38	21 05	21 21

MARS ♂

Day	R.A.	Dec. −	Diam.	Phase	Transit	5° high. 52°	5° high. 56°
	h m	°	″		h m	h m	h m
1	18 08	23·6	9	89	5 32	2 34	3 11
6	18 19	23·6	10	89	5 23	2 25	3 03
11	18 29	23·7	10	89	5 13	2 16	2 54
16	18 39	23·7	10	89	5 03	2 07	2 45
21	18 49	23·7	11	89	4 53	1 57	2 34
26	18 58	23·7	11	89	4 42	1 46	2 24
31	19 06	23·7	12	90	4 31	1 35	2 12

Day	\multicolumn{14}{c}{SUNRISE AND SUNSET}

	\multicolumn{2}{c}{London}	\multicolumn{2}{c}{Bristol}	\multicolumn{2}{c}{Birmingham}	\multicolumn{2}{c}{Manchester}	\multicolumn{2}{c}{Newcastle}	\multicolumn{2}{c}{Glasgow}	\multicolumn{2}{c}{Belfast}
	a.m.	p.m.	a.m.	p.m.	a.m.	p.m.	a.m.	p.m.	a.m.	p.m.	a.m.	p.m.	a.m.	p.m.
	h m	h m	h m	h m	h m	h m	h m	h m	h m	h m	h m	h m	h m	h m
1	5 38	6 32	5 48	6 41	5 44	6 39	5 45	6 42	5 40	6 41	5 50	6 53	5 58	6 59
2	5 36	6 34	5 46	6 43	5 42	6 41	5 43	6 44	5 38	6 43	5 47	6 56	5 56	7 01
3	5 33	6 36	5 43	6 45	5 39	6 43	5 40	6 46	5 35	6 45	5 45	6 58	5 53	7 03
4	5 31	6 37	5 41	6 46	5 37	6 45	5 38	6 48	5 33	6 47	5 42	7 00	5 51	7 05
5	5 29	6 39	5 39	6 48	5 34	6 47	5 35	6 50	5 30	6 49	5 39	7 02	5 48	7 07
6	5 27	6 40	5 37	6 50	5 32	6 49	5 33	6 52	5 28	6 51	5 37	7 04	5 46	7 09
7	5 24	6 42	5 34	6 51	5 29	6 50	5 30	6 54	5 25	6 53	5 34	7 06	5 43	7 11
8	5 22	6 43	5 32	6 53	5 27	6 52	5 28	6 55	5 23	6 55	5 32	7 08	5 41	7 12
9	5 20	6 45	5 30	6 55	5 25	6 54	5 26	6 57	5 20	6 57	5 29	7 10	5 39	7 14
10	5 17	6 47	5 27	6 57	5 22	6 56	5 23	6 59	5 18	6 59	5 27	7 12	5 36	7 16
11	5 15	6 48	5 25	6 58	5 20	6 57	5 21	7 01	5 15	7 01	5 24	7 14	5 34	7 18
12	5 13	6 50	5 23	7 00	5 18	6 59	5 18	7 03	5 12	7 03	5 21	7 16	5 31	7 20
13	5 11	6 52	5 21	7 02	5 16	7 01	5 16	7 04	5 10	7 04	5 19	7 18	5 29	7 22
14	5 08	6 53	5 18	7 03	5 13	7 02	5 14	7 06	5 08	7 06	5 16	7 20	5 26	7 24
15	5 06	6 55	5 16	7 05	5 11	7 04	5 11	7 08	5 05	7 08	5 14	7 22	5 24	7 26
16	5 04	6 57	5 14	7 07	5 09	7 06	5 09	7 10	5 03	7 10	5 11	7 24	5 21	7 28
17	5 02	6 59	5 12	7 09	5 07	7 08	5 07	7 12	5 01	7 12	5 09	7 26	5 19	7 30
18	5 00	7 00	5 10	7 10	5 05	7 09	5 04	7 14	4 58	7 14	5 06	7 28	5 16	7 32
19	4 57	7 02	5 07	7 12	5 02	7 11	5 02	7 16	4 56	7 16	5 04	7 30	5 14	7 34
20	4 55	7 04	5 05	7 14	5 00	7 13	5 00	7 18	4 53	7 18	5 01	7 32	5 12	7 36
21	4 53	7 05	5 03	7 15	4 58	7 14	4 57	7 19	4 51	7 20	4 59	7 34	5 09	7 37
22	4 51	7 07	5 01	7 17	4 56	7 16	4 55	7 21	4 48	7 22	4 56	7 36	5 07	7 39
23	4 49	7 09	4 59	7 19	4 54	7 18	4 53	7 23	4 46	7 24	4 54	7 38	5 05	7 41
24	4 47	7 10	4 57	7 20	4 52	7 19	4 51	7 24	4 43	7 26	4 51	7 40	5 02	7 43
25	4 45	7 12	4 55	7 22	4 50	7 21	4 49	7 26	4 41	7 28	4 49	7 42	5 00	7 45
26	4 43	7 14	4 53	7 24	4 48	7 23	4 47	7 28	4 39	7 30	4 47	7 44	4 58	7 47
27	4 41	7 15	4 51	7 25	4 46	7 25	4 45	7 30	4 37	7 32	4 45	7 46	4 56	7 49
28	4 40	7 17	4 50	7 27	4 44	7 26	4 43	7 31	4 35	7 33	4 43	7 47	4 54	7 50
29	4 38	7 19	4 48	7 28	4 42	7 28	4 41	7 33	4 32	7 35	4 40	7 49	4 52	7 52
30	4 36	7 21	4 46	7 30	4 39	7 30	4 38	7 35	4 30	7 37	4 38	7 51	4 49	7 54

	\multicolumn{5}{c}{JUPITER ♃}	\multicolumn{5}{c}{SATURN ♄}
Day	R.A.	Dec. −	Transit	\multicolumn{2}{c}{5° high.}	R.A.	Dec. −	Transit	\multicolumn{2}{c}{5° high.}
				52°	56°				52°	56°
	h m	°	h m	h m	h m	h m	°	h m	h m	h m
1	22 44	9·0	10 07	5 28	5 40	16 33	19·9	3 56	0 28	0 55
11	22 53	8·2	9 36	4 52	5 03	16 32	19·9	3 15	23 43	0 14
21	23 00	7·4	9 04	4 17	4 26	16 30	19·8	2 34	23 01	23 28
31	23 08	6·7	8 32	3 41	3 50	16 28	19·7	1 53	22 19	22 45

Equatorial diameter of Jupiter 34″; of Saturn 18″. Diameters of Saturn's rings 41″ and 18″.

	\multicolumn{5}{c}{URANUS ♅}	\multicolumn{5}{c}{NEPTUNE ♆}
Day	R.A.	Dec.	Transit	\multicolumn{2}{c}{10° high.}	R.A.	Dec.	Transit	\multicolumn{2}{c}{10° high.}
				52°	56°				52°	56°
	h m	° ′	h m	h m	h m	h m	° ′	h m	h m	h m
1	17 26·7	23 18	4 50	2 47	4 00	18 25·1	22 14	5 48	3 32	4 29
11	17 26·4	23 18	4 10	2 07	3 20	18 25·1	22 13	5 09	2 52	3 50
21	17 25·7	23 17	3 30	1 27	2 40	18 24·9	22 13	4 29	2 13	3 10
31	17 24·7	23 17	2 50	0 46	1 59	18 24·5	22 13	3 49	1 33	2 31

Diameter 4″   Diameter 2″

DAY OF		
Month	Week	

Maia, goddess of growth and increase.

Sun's Longitude 60° II 21ᵈ 08ʰ

1	Th.	**SS. Philip and James.**
2	F.	da Vinci d. 1519. Catherine the Great b. 1729.
3	S.	Nicolo Machiavelli b. 1469. D'Oyly Carte b. 1844.
4	☙.	**5th S. after Easter. Rogation Sunday.**
5	M.	Kierkegaard b. 1813. Karl Marx b. 1818.
6	Tu.	Robespierre b. 1758. Sigmund Freud b. 1856.
7	W.	Robert Browning b. 1812. Johannes Brahms b. 1833.
8	Th.	**Ascension Day.** V.E. Day 1945.
9	F.	Schiller d. 1805. J. M. Barrie b. 1860.
10	S.	Sir Henry Morton Stanley d. 1904.
11	☙.	**S. after Ascension.** Spencer Perceval assass. 1812.
12	M.	Edward Lear b. 1812. Florence Nightingale b. 1820.
13	Tu.	Sir Arthur Sullivan b. 1842.
14	W.	**St. Matthias.** Gabriel Fahrenheit b. 1686.**
15	Th.	Emily Dickinson d. 1886.** Edwin Muir b. 1887.
16	F.	John Sell Cotman b. 1782. H. E. Bates b. 1905.
17	S.	Edward Jenner b. 1749. Erik Satie b. 1866.
18	☙.	**Pentecost. Whit Sunday.** Pope John Paul II b. 1920.
19	M.	Anne Boleyn exec. 1536. Gladstone d. 1898.
20	Tu.	Balzac b. 1799. G. K. Chesterton b. 1874.
21	W.	Albrecht Dürer b. 1471. Alexander Pope b. 1688.
22	Th.	Richard Wagner b. 1813. Conan Doyle b. 1859.
23	F.	EASTER LAW SITTINGS END. Leopold von Ranke d. 1886.**
24	S.	Copernicus d. 1543. Victoria I b. 1819.
25	☙.	**Trinity Sunday.**
26	M.	Marlborough b. 1650. Sinking of *Bismark* 1941.
27	Tu.	Arnold Bennett b. 1867. Isadora Duncan b. 1878.
28	W.	William Pitt the Younger b. 1759.
29	Th.	Charles II b. 1630. Restoration Day 1660.
30	F.	Joan of Arc burned 1431.
31	S.	Walt Whitman b. 1819. Jutland 1916.

** Centenary

PHENOMENA

May 3ᵈ 18ʰ Jupiter in conjunction with the Moon. Jupiter 3° N.

7ᵈ 11ʰ Mercury in conjunction with the Moon. Mercury 2° S.

11ᵈ 11ʰ Venus in conjunction with the Moon. Venus 3° S.

23ᵈ 01ʰ Mercury in superior conjunction.

24ᵈ 05ʰ Saturn in conjunction with the Moon. Saturn 5° N.

27ᵈ 03ʰ Mars in conjunction with the Moon. Mars 3° N.

28ᵈ 01ʰ Saturn at opposition.

31ᵈ 08ʰ Jupiter in conjunction with the Moon. Jupiter 2° N.

CONSTELLATIONS

The following constellations are near the meridian at

	d h		d h
Apr.	1 24	Apr.	15 23
May	1 22	May	16 21
June	1 20	June	15 19

Cepheus (below the Pole), Cassiopeia (below the Pole), Ursa Minor, Ursa Major, Canes Venatici, Coma Berenices, Bootes, Leo, Virgo, Crater, Corvus, and Hydra.

ALGOL

ALGOL is inconveniently situated for observation during May.

PHASES OF THE MOON			
		d	h m
☾ Last Quarter		1	03 22
● New Moon		8	22 10
☽ First Quarter		17	01 00
○ Full Moon		23	20 45
☾ Last Quarter		30	12 55
		d	h
Apogee (406,330 kilometres)		10	23
Perigee (357,100 „)		24	03

Mean Longitude of Ascending Node on May 1, 29°.

See note on *Summer Time*, p. 98.

MONTHLY NOTES

May
3. Greek Orthodox Easter.
5. Bank Holiday, England, Wales, N. Ireland and Scotland.
9. Liberation Day, Channel Islands.
10. First Day of Ramadân.
15. Whitsunday (Scotland). Scottish Term Day.
26. Bank Holiday, England, Wales, N. Ireland and Scotland.
28. Removal Day, Scotland.

** Centenary.

Day	Right Ascension	Dec. +	Equation of Time	Rise 52°	Rise 56°	Transit	Set 52°	Set 56°	Sidereal Time	Transit of First Point of Aries
	h m s	° ′	m s	h m	h m	h m	h m	h m	h m s	h m s
1	2 31 40	14 55	+ 2 51	4 32	4 18	11 57	19 23	19 37	14 34 31	9 23 56
2	2 35 29	15 13	+ 2 58	4 30	4 16	11 57	19 25	19 39	14 38 27	9 20 00
3	2 39 19	15 31	+ 3 05	4 28	4 13	11 57	19 26	19 41	14 42 24	9 16 04
4	2 43 09	15 49	+ 3 11	4 26	4 11	11 57	19 28	19 43	14 46 20	9 12 08
5	2 47 00	16 06	+ 3 17	4 24	4 09	11 57	19 30	19 45	14 50 17	9 08 12
6	2 50 52	16 24	+ 3 22	4 22	4 07	11 57	19 32	19 47	14 54 14	9 04 16
7	2 54 44	16 40	+ 3 26	4 21	4 05	11 57	19 33	19 49	14 58 10	9 00 21
8	2 58 36	16 57	+ 3 30	4 19	4 03	11 56	19 35	19 51	15 02 07	8 56 25
9	3 02 29	17 13	+ 3 34	4 17	4 00	11 56	19 36	19 53	15 06 03	8 52 29
10	3 06 23	17 29	+ 3 36	4 16	3 58	11 56	19 38	19 55	15 10 00	8 48 33
11	3 10 18	17 45	+ 3 39	4 14	3 56	11 56	19 40	19 57	15 13 56	8 44 37
12	3 14 12	18 00	+ 3 40	4 12	3 54	11 56	19 41	19 59	15 17 53	8 40 41
13	3 18 08	18 15	+ 3 41	4 10	3 52	11 56	19 43	20 01	15 21 49	8 36 45
14	3 22 04	18 30	+ 3 42	4 09	3 51	11 56	19 44	20 03	15 25 46	8 32 49
15	3 26 01	18 45	+ 3 42	4 07	3 49	11 56	19 46	20 05	15 29 43	8 28 53
16	3 29 58	18 59	+ 3 41	4 06	3 47	11 56	19 48	20 07	15 33 39	8 24 57
17	3 33 55	19 13	+ 3 40	4 04	3 45	11 56	19 49	20 08	15 37 36	8 21 01
18	3 37 54	19 26	+ 3 38	4 03	3 43	11 56	19 51	20 10	15 41 32	8 17 06
19	3 41 52	19 40	+ 3 36	4 01	3 42	11 56	19 52	20 12	15 45 29	8 13 10
20	3 45 52	19 52	+ 3 33	4 00	3 40	11 56	19 54	20 14	15 49 25	8 09 14
21	3 49 51	20 05	+ 3 30	3 59	3 38	11 57	19 55	20 16	15 53 22	8 05 18
22	3 53 52	20 17	+ 3 26	3 57	3 36	11 57	19 56	20 17	15 57 18	8 01 22
23	3 57 53	20 29	+ 3 22	3 56	3 35	11 57	19 58	20 19	16 01 15	7 57 26
24	4 01 54	20 40	+ 3 17	3 55	3 33	11 57	19 59	20 21	16 05 12	7 53 30
25	4 05 56	20 51	+ 3 12	3 54	3 32	11 57	20 00	20 22	16 09 08	7 49 34
26	4 09 58	21 02	+ 3 06	3 52	3 30	11 57	20 02	20 24	16 13 05	7 45 38
27	4 14 01	21 13	+ 3 00	3 51	3 29	11 57	20 03	20 26	16 17 01	7 41 42
28	4 18 05	21 23	+ 2 53	3 50	3 28	11 57	20 04	20 27	16 20 58	7 37 46
29	4 22 09	21 32	+ 2 46	3 49	3 26	11 57	20 06	20 29	16 24 54	7 33 51
30	4 26 13	21 42	+ 2 38	3 48	3 25	11 57	20 07	20 30	16 28 51	7 29 55
31	4 30 18	21 51	+ 2 30	3 47	3 24	11 58	20 08	20 32	16 32 47	7 25 59

THE SUN   s.d. 15′·8

Duration of Civil (C), Nautical (N), and Astronomical (A), Twilight (in minutes)

Lat. °	May 1 C	May 1 N	May 1 A	May 11 C	May 11 N	May 11 A	May 21 C	May 21 N	May 21 A	May 31 C	May 31 N	May 31 A
52	39	90	154	41	97	179	44	106	T.A.N.	46	116	T.A.N.
56	45	106	209	49	121	T.A.N.	53	143	T.A.N.	57	T.A.N.	T.A.N.

ASTRONOMICAL NOTES

MERCURY is unsuitably placed for observation throughout May, superior conjunction occurring on the 23rd.

VENUS is a brilliant object, magnitude −3·4, visible in the western sky in the evenings for nearly two hours after sunset. The thin crescent Moon will be near the planet on the evening of the 11th. Venus passes 6° N. of Aldebaran on the 5th.

MARS, magnitude −0·4 to −1·3, continues to be visible as a morning object, low in the south-eastern sky, in the constellation of Sagittarius. By the end of the month the planet is visible shortly after midnight. The gibbous Moon passes 3° S. of Mars on the morning of the 27th.

JUPITER, magnitude −1·8, is a morning object, though only visible in the south-eastern sky for a short while before dawn. Jupiter is in the constellation of Aquarius, where it remains throughout the year. The old crescent Moon is near Jupiter on the mornings of the 3rd and 4th and again on the 31st.

SATURN, magnitude +0·2, reaches opposition on the 28th and thus is visible throughout the hours of darkness. On the morning of the 24th the Full Moon passes 5° S. of the planet. Saturn is on the borders of Scorpius and Ophiuchus. Even in a small telescope the Rings of Saturn are a beautiful sight and they are now well open, after the Earth's last passage through the ring plane early in 1980.

THE MOON

Day	R.A.	Dec.	Hor. Par.	Semi-diam.	Sun's Co-long.	P.A. of Bright Limb	Phase	Age	Rise 52°	Rise 56°	Transit	Set 52°	Set 56°
	h m	°	′	′	°	°		d	h m	h m	h m	h m	h m
1	20 50	−23·2	58·1	15·8	172	75	52	21·7	2 32	2 56	6 29	10 37	10 14
2	21 44	−18·8	57·4	15·6	184	70	41	22·7	2 52	3 10	7 20	12 01	11 45
3	22 34	−13·6	56·7	15·4	196	66	31	23·7	3 07	3 18	8 07	13 20	13 11
4	23 21	− 8·0	56·0	15·3	208	64	22	24·7	3 19	3 25	8 50	14 36	14 32
5	0 06	− 2·2	55·5	15·1	220	64	14	25·7	3 29	3 30	9 32	15 50	15 51
6	0 50	+ 3·6	55·0	15·0	233	65	8	26·7	3 39	3 35	10 12	17 03	17 09
7	1 33	+ 9·2	54·7	14·9	245	67	3	27·7	3 49	3 41	10 53	18 15	18 28
8	2 18	+14·5	54·4	14·8	257	74	1	28·7	4 01	3 48	11 36	19 29	19 47
9	3 04	+19·1	54·1	14·8	269	190	0	0·1	4 16	3 57	12 20	20 43	21 08
10	3 52	+22·9	54·0	14·7	282	245	1	1·1	4 36	4 10	13 07	21 55	22 26
11	4 42	+25·8	54·0	14·7	294	254	4	2·1	5 02	4 31	13 56	23 02	23 38
12	5 35	+27·6	54·0	14·7	306	261	8	3·1	5 39	5 03	14 47	23 58	..
13	6 28	+28·1	54·2	14·8	318	268	14	4·1	6 29	5 52	15 39	..	0 36
14	7 22	+27·3	54·5	14·9	331	275	22	5·1	7 32	6 58	16 30	0 42	1 16
15	8 15	+25·2	54·9	15·0	343	281	30	6·1	8 44	8 16	17 20	1 14	1 43
16	9 07	+21·9	55·5	15·1	355	286	40	7·1	10 01	9 40	18 08	1 38	2 00
17	9 57	+17·5	56·3	15·3	7	290	50	8·1	11 21	11 06	18 55	1 55	2 11
18	10 46	+12·3	57·1	15·6	19	293	60	9·1	12 41	12 33	19 41	2 09	2 19
19	11 34	+ 6·3	58·1	15·8	32	295	70	10·1	14 03	14 01	20 27	2 22	2 26
20	12 23	− 0·2	59·0	16·1	44	295	80	11·1	15 28	15 32	21 15	2 33	2 32
21	13 14	− 6·8	59·9	16·3	56	293	88	12·1	16 57	17 07	22 06	2 46	2 39
22	14 08	−13·3	60·7	16·5	68	289	95	13·1	18 31	18 49	23 02	3 00	2 48
23	15 05	−19·2	61·2	16·7	80	278	99	14·1	20 08	20 35	..	3 20	3 00
24	16 08	−24·0	61·4	16·7	93	158	100	15·1	21 42	22 17	0 03	3 47	3 19
25	17 14	−27·0	61·3	16·7	105	108	98	16·1	23 00	23 39	1 08	4 29	3 53
26	18 22	−28·1	60·8	16·6	117	96	93	17·1	23 56	..	2 15	5 30	4 51
27	19 29	−27·1	60·2	16·4	129	87	86	18·1	..	0 31	3 20	6 49	6 15
28	20 31	−24·2	59·3	16·2	141	79	77	19·1	0 33	1 00	4 20	8 17	7 51
29	21 29	−20·1	58·4	15·9	154	73	66	20·1	0 57	1 17	5 15	9 45	9 26
30	22 21	−15·0	57·5	15·7	166	69	56	21·1	1 14	1 27	6 04	11 07	10 56
31	23 10	− 9·3	56·6	15·4	178	67	45	22·1	1 27	1 35	6 49	12 25	12 20

MERCURY ☿

Day	R.A.	Dec. +	Diam.	Phase	Transit		Day	R.A.	Dec. +	Diam.	Phase	Transit	
	h m	°	″		h m			h m	°	″		h m	
1	1 13	5·0	6	72	10 40		16	2 57	16·0	5	95	11 25	
4	1 32	7·0	6	77	10 46	Mercury is too	19	3 22	18·2	5	98	11 39	Mercury is too
7	1 51	9·2	6	81	10 54	close to the	22	3 48	20·2	5	100	11 53	close to the
10	2 12	11·4	5	86	11 03	Sun for	25	4 15	22·0	5	99	12 09	Sun for
13	2 34	13·7	5	91	11 14	observation	28	4 43	23·5	5	97	12 25	observation
16	2 57	16·0	5	95	11 25		31	5 11	24·5	5	92	12 41	

VENUS ♀   MARS ♂

Day	R.A.	Dec. +	Diam.	Phase	Transit	5° high. 52°	5° high. 56°	Day	R.A.	Dec. −	Diam.	Phase	Transit	5° high. 52°	5° high. 56°
	h m	°	″		h m	h m	h m		h m	°	″		h m	h m	h m
1	4 12	21·8	11	90	13 38	21 05	21 21	1	19 06	23·7	12	90	4 31	1 35	2 12
6	4 38	23·0	11	89	13 44	21 18	21 36	6	19 14	23·7	13	90	4 19	1 23	2 01
11	5 04	23·9	12	88	13 51	21 30	21 49	11	19 21	23·8	13	91	4 06	1 10	1 48
16	5 30	24·6	12	87	13 58	21 40	22 00	16	19 27	23·8	14	91	3 53	0 58	1 36
21	5 57	24·9	12	86	14 04	21 49	22 10	21	19 32	23·9	15	92	3 38	0 44	1 23
26	6 23	25·0	12	84	14 11	21 56	22 16	26	19 37	24·1	16	93	3 23	0 30	1 09
31	6 50	24·7	12	83	14 18	22 00¹	22 20	31	19 40	24·3	17	94	3 06	0 16	0 56

SUNRISE AND SUNSET

Day	London a.m. h m	London p.m. h m	Bristol a.m. h m	Bristol p.m. h m	Birmingham a.m. h m	Birmingham p.m. h m	Manchester a.m. h m	Manchester p.m. h m	Newcastle a.m. h m	Newcastle p.m. h m	Glasgow a.m. h m	Glasgow p.m. h m	Belfast a.m. h m	Belfast p.m. h m
1	4 34	7 22	4 44	7 31	4 37	7 32	4 36	7 37	4 28	7 39	4 36	7 53	4 47	7 56
2	4 32	7 24	4 42	7 33	4 35	7 34	4 34	7 39	4 26	7 41	4 34	7 55	4 45	7 58
3	4 30	7 25	4 40	7 34	4 33	7 35	4 32	7 41	4 23	7 43	4 31	7 57	4 43	8 00
4	4 28	7 27	4 38	7 36	4 31	7 37	4 30	7 43	4 21	7 45	4 29	7 59	4 41	8 02
5	4 26	7 28	4 36	7 38	4 29	7 39	4 28	7 44	4 19	7 47	4 27	8 01	4 39	8 03
6	4 24	7 30	4 34	7 40	4 27	7 41	4 26	7 46	4 17	7 49	4 25	8 03	4 37	8 05
7	4 23	7 31	4 33	7 41	4 26	7 42	4 24	7 48	4 15	7 51	4 23	8 05	4 35	8 07
8	4 21	7 33	4 31	7 43	4 24	7 44	4 22	7 50	4 13	7 53	4 21	8 07	4 33	8 09
9	4 19	7 34	4 29	7 44	4 22	7 45	4 20	7 51	4 11	7 54	4 18	8 09	4 30	8 11
10	4 18	7 36	4 28	7 46	4 21	7 47	4 18	7 53	4 09	7 56	4 16	8 11	4 28	8 13
11	4 16	7 38	4 26	7 48	4 19	7 49	4 17	7 55	4 07	7 58	4 14	8 13	4 27	8 15
12	4 14	7 39	4 24	7 49	4 17	7 50	4 15	7 57	4 05	8 00	4 12	8 15	4 25	8 17
13	4 12	7 41	4 22	7 51	4 15	7 52	4 13	7 58	4 03	8 02	4 10	8 17	4 23	8 18
14	4 11	7 42	4 21	7 52	4 14	7 53	4 11	8 00	4 02	8 04	4 09	8 19	4 21	8 20
15	4 09	7 44	4 19	7 54	4 12	7 55	4 09	8 02	4 00	8 06	4 07	8 21	4 19	8 22
16	4 08	7 46	4 18	7 56	4 11	7 57	4 08	8 03	3 58	8 07	4 05	8 23	4 18	8 23
17	4 06	7 47	4 16	7 57	4 09	7 58	4 06	8 05	3 56	8 09	4 03	8 24	4 16	8 25
18	4 05	7 49	4 15	7 59	4 08	8 00	4 05	8 07	3 55	8 11	4 01	8 26	4 15	8 27
19	4 03	7 50	4 14	8 00	4 06	8 01	4 03	8 08	3 53	8 12	4 00	8 28	4 13	8 28
20	4 02	7 52	4 13	8 02	4 05	8 03	4 02	8 10	3 51	8 14	3 58	8 30	4 11	8 30
21	4 01	7 53	4 11	8 03	4 04	8 04	4 01	8 11	3 50	8 16	3 56	8 32	4 10	8 32
22	3 59	7 54	4 10	8 04	4 02	8 05	3 59	8 12	3 48	8 17	3 54	8 33	4 08	8 33
23	3 58	7 56	4 09	8 06	4 01	8 07	3 58	8 14	3 47	8 19	3 53	8 35	4 07	8 35
24	3 57	7 57	4 08	8 07	4 00	8 08	3 57	8 15	3 45	8 21	3 51	8 37	4 05	8 37
25	3 56	7 58	4 07	8 08	3 59	8 10	3 56	8 17	3 44	8 22	3 50	8 38	4 04	8 38
26	3 55	8 00	4 05	8 09	3 57	8 11	3 54	8 18	3 42	8 24	3 48	8 40	4 02	8 40
27	3 54	8 01	4 04	8 11	3 56	8 13	3 53	8 20	3 41	8 26	3 47	8 42	4 01	8 42
28	3 53	8 02	4 03	8 12	3 55	8 14	3 52	8 21	3 40	8 27	3 46	8 43	4 00	8 43
29	3 52	8 04	4 02	8 13	3 54	8 15	3 51	8 22	3 39	8 28	3 44	8 45	3 59	8 44
30	3 51	8 05	4 01	8 14	3 53	8 17	3 50	8 24	3 38	8 30	3 43	8 46	3 58	8 46
31	3 50	8 06	4 00	8 15	3 51	8 18	3 48	8 25	3 36	8 31	3 42	8 48	3 56	8 47

JUPITER ♃ / SATURN ♄

Day	JUPITER R.A. h m	JUPITER Dec. − °	JUPITER Transit h m	JUPITER 5° high 52° h m	JUPITER 5° high 56° h m	SATURN R.A. h m	SATURN Dec. − °	SATURN Transit h m	SATURN 5° high 52° h m	SATURN 5° high 56° h m
1	23 08	6·7	8 32	3 41	3 50	16 28	19·7	1 53	22 19	22 45
11	23 14	6·0	7 59	3 04	3 13	16 25	19·6	1 11	21 36	22 02
21	23 20	5·4	7 26	2 28	2 36	16 22	19·5	0 28	20 53	21 19
31	23 25	4·9	6 51	1 51	1 58	16 19	19·3	23 42	20 10	20 35

Equatorial diameter of Jupiter 37″; of Saturn 18″.   Diameters of Saturn's rings 42″ and 18″.

URANUS ♅ / NEPTUNE ♆

Day	URANUS R.A. h m	URANUS Dec. − ° ′	URANUS Transit h m	URANUS 10° high 52° h m	URANUS 10° high 56° h m	NEPTUNE R.A. h m	NEPTUNE Dec. − ° ′	NEPTUNE Transit h m	NEPTUNE 10° high 52° h m	NEPTUNE 10° high 56° h m
1	17 24·7	23 17	2 50	0 46	1 59	18 24·5	22 13	3 49	1 33	2 31
11	17 23·4	23 16	2 09	0 05	1 18	18 23·9	22 14	3 09	0 53	1 51
21	17 21·8	23 14	1 28	23 20	0 37	18 23·0	22 14	2 29	0 13	1 11
31	17 20·2	23 13	0 47	22 39	23 51	18 22·1	22 14	1 49	23 29	0 31

Diameter 4″.   Diameter 2″.

DAY OF		
Month	Week	

Junius, Roman *gens* (family).

Sun's Longitude 90° ♋ 21ᵈ 16ʰ

1	♋.	**1st S. after Trinity.** Glorious First of June 1794.
2	M.	CORONATION DAY 1953. Elgar b. 1857.
3	Tu.	TRINITY LAW SITTINGS BEGIN.
4	W.	George III b. 1738. Kaiser Wilhelm II d. 1941.
5	Th.	Igor Stravinsky b. 1882. Lord Kitchener d. 1916.
6	F.	Pushkin b. 1799 N.S. D-Day 1944.
7	S.	Beau Brummell b. 1778. Paul Gauguin b. 1848.
8	♋.	**2nd S. after Trinity.** Robert Schumann b. 1810.
9	M.	George Stephenson b. 1781. Charles Dickens d. 1870.
10	Tu.	DUKE OF EDINBURGH b. 1921.
11	W.	**St. Barnabas.** John Constable b. 1776.
12	Th.	Charles Kingsley b. 1819.
13	F.	Fanny Burney b. 1752. W. B. Yeats b. 1865.
14	S.	Naseby 1645. Harriet Beecher Stowe b. 1811.
15	♋.	**3rd S. after Trinity.** Edvard Grieg b. 1843.
16	M.	Marlborough d. 1722. Quatre Bras 1815.
17	Tu.	Edward I b. 1239. John Wesley b. 1703.
18	W.	Waterloo 1815. Capt. M. Webb b. 1848.
19	Th.	James I b. 1566. Blaise Pascal b. 1623.
20	F.	Black Hole of Calcutta 1756.
21	S.	PRINCE WILLIAM OF WALES b. 1982.
22	♋.	**4th S. after Trinity.** Anzio landings 1944.
23	M.	Plassey 1757. Duke of Windsor b. 1894.
24	Tu.	**St. John Baptist.** Bannockburn 1314.
25	W.	Earl Mountbatten of Burma b. 1900.
26	Th.	George IV d. 1830. U.N. Charter signed 1945.
27	F.	Charles Parnell b. 1846. Helen Keller b. 1880.
28	S.	Henry VIII b. 1491. Rousseau b. 1712.
29	♋.	**5th S. after Trinity. St. Peter.**
30	M.	John Gay b. 1685.

PHENOMENA

June 9ᵈ 06ʰ Mercury in conjunction with the Moon. Mercury 3° S.

10ᵈ 16ʰ Venus in conjunction with the Moon. Venus 3° S.

11ᵈ 15ʰ Uranus at opposition.

20ᵈ 13ʰ Saturn in conjunction with the Moon. Saturn 5° N.

21ᵈ 16ʰ Summer Solstice.

23ᵈ 13ʰ Mars in conjunction with the Moon. Mars 0°·5 N.

25ᵈ 20ʰ Mercury at greatest eastern elongation (25°).

26ᵈ 08ʰ Neptune at opposition.

27ᵈ 20ʰ Jupiter in conjunction with the Moon. Jupiter 1°·9 N.

CONSTELLATIONS

The following constellations are near the meridian at

	d	h		d	h
May	1	24	May 16	23
June	1	22	June 15	21
July	1	20	July 16	19

Cassiopeia (below the Pole), Ursa Minor, Draco, Ursa Major, Canes Venatici, Bootes, Corona, Serpens, Virgo and Libra.

ALGOL

ALGOL is inconveniently situated for observation during June.

PHASES OF THE MOON

	d	h	m
● New Moon	7	14	00
☽ First Quarter	15	12	00
○ Full Moon	22	03	42
☾ Last Quarter	29	00	53

	d	h
Apogee (406,560 kilometres)	7	02
Perigee (357,670 ,,)	21	13

Mean Longitude of Ascending Node on June 1, 28°.

See note on *Summer Time*, p. 98.

MONTHLY NOTES

June 13. Jewish Feast of Weeks begins.

14. Queen's Official Birthday.

21. Longest day.

24. Midsummer Day. Quarter Day.

Day	Right Ascension	Dec. +	Equation of Time	Rise 52°	Rise 56°	Transit	Set 52°	Set 56°	Sidereal Time	Transit of First Point of Aries
	h m s	° '	m s	h m	h m	h m	h m	h m	h m s	h m s
1	4 34 23	21 59	+ 2 21	3 46	3 23	11 58	20 09	20 33	16 36 44	7 22 03
2	4 38 29	22 07	+ 2 12	3 46	3 22	11 58	20 10	20 34	16 40 41	7 18 07
3	4 42 35	22 15	+ 2 02	3 45	3 21	11 58	20 11	20 36	16 44 37	7 14 11
4	4 46 41	22 22	+ 1 52	3 44	3 20	11 58	20 12	20 37	16 48 34	7 10 15
5	4 50 48	22 29	+ 1 42	3 43	3 19	11 58	20 13	20 38	16 52 30	7 06 19
6	4 54 55	22 36	+ 1 31	3 43	3 18	11 59	20 14	20 39	16 56 27	7 02 23
7	4 59 03	22 42	+ 1 20	3 42	3 17	11 59	20 15	20 40	17 00 23	6 58 27
8	5 03 10	22 48	+ 1 09	3 42	3 16	11 59	20 16	20 42	17 04 20	6 54 31
9	5 07 19	22 53	+ 0 58	3 41	3 16	11 59	20 17	20 43	17 08 16	6 50 36
10	5 11 27	22 58	+ 0 46	3 41	3 15	11 59	20 18	20 44	17 12 13	6 46 40
11	5 15 35	23 03	+ 0 34	3 40	3 14	11 59	20 19	20 44	17 16 10	6 42 44
12	5 19 44	23 07	+ 0 22	3 40	3 14	12 00	20 19	20 45	17 20 06	6 38 48
13	5 23 53	23 11	+ 0 09	3 40	3 14	12 00	20 20	20 46	17 24 03	6 34 52
14	5 28 02	23 14	− 0 03	3 40	3 13	12 00	20 21	20 47	17 27 59	6 30 56
15	5 32 11	23 17	− 0 16	3 39	3 13	12 00	20 21	20 48	17 31 56	6 27 00
16	5 36 21	23 20	− 0 29	3 39	3 13	12 01	20 22	20 48	17 35 52	6 23 04
17	5 40 30	23 22	− 0 42	3 39	3 13	12 01	20 22	20 49	17 39 49	6 19 08
18	5 44 40	23 24	− 0 54	3 39	3 12	12 01	20 23	20 49	17 43 45	6 15 12
19	5 48 49	23 25	− 1 07	3 39	3 12	12 01	20 23	20 50	17 47 42	6 11 16
20	5 52 59	23 26	− 1 20	3 39	3 13	12 01	20 23	20 50	17 51 39	6 07 21
21	5 57 08	23 26	− 1 33	3 39	3 13	12 02	20 24	20 50	17 55 35	6 03 25
22	6 01 18	23 27	− 1 46	3 39	3 13	12 02	20 24	20 50	17 59 32	5 59 29
23	6 05 27	23 26	− 1 59	3 40	3 13	12 02	20 24	20 51	18 03 28	5 55 33
24	6 09 37	23 25	− 2 12	3 40	3 13	12 02	20 24	20 51	18 07 25	5 51 37
25	6 13 46	23 24	− 2 25	3 40	3 14	12 03	20 24	20 51	18 11 21	5 47 41
26	6 17 55	23 23	− 2 38	3 41	3 14	12 03	20 24	20 51	18 15 18	5 43 45
27	6 22 04	23 21	− 2 50	3 41	3 15	12 03	20 24	20 50	18 19 15	5 39 49
28	6 26 13	23 18	− 3 03	3 42	3 15	12 03	20 24	20 50	18 23 11	5 35 53
29	6 30 22	23 16	− 3 15	3 42	3 16	12 03	20 24	20 50	18 27 08	5 31 57
30	6 34 31	23 12	− 3 27	3 43	3 17	12 04	20 24	20 50	18 31 04	5 28 01

Duration of Civil (C), Nautical (N), and Astronomical (A), Twilight (in minutes)

Lat. °	June 1 C	N	A	June 11 C	N	A	June 21 C	N	A	June 30 C	N	A
52	47	117	T.A.N.	48	125	T.A.N.	49	128	T.A.N.	49	125	T.A.N.
56	58	T.A.N.	T.A.N.	61	T.A.N.	T.A.N.	63	T.A.N.	T.A.N.	62	T.A.N.	T.A.N.

ASTRONOMICAL NOTES

MERCURY is at greatest eastern elongation on the 25th and thus theoretically visible as an evening object around the middle of the month. The long twilight will hinder observation somewhat but under good conditions Mercury should be glimpsed low above the W.N.W. horizon at about the time of end of evening civil twilight. Mercury will be about magnitude 0.

VENUS, magnitude −3·5, is visible in the western sky in the evenings. Although it is continuing to increase its eastern elongation from the Sun the period available for observation actually decreases slightly during the month because it is moving southward in declination and also because the Sun is setting about a quarter-of-an-hour later at the end of the month than it is at the beginning. The 3-day old Moon will be seen near Venus on the evening of the 10th.

MARS, magnitude −1·3 to −2·2, continues to be visible as a morning object, low in the south-eastern sky. Mars is moving slowly in Sagittarius, reaching its first stationary point on the 10th.

JUPITER, magnitude −2·0, is a morning object in the south-eastern sky.

SATURN, magnitude +0·3, is visible for the greater part of the night, low in the southern sky. By the end of the month it is too low on the south-western horizon after about 01ʰ. The gibbous Moon is near the planet on the evening of the 20th.

URANUS is at opposition on the 11th, in the southern part of Ophiuchus. Uranus is barely visible to the naked-eye since its magnitude is +5·8 but it is readily located with only small optical aid.

NEPTUNE is at opposition on the 26th, in the western part of Sagittarius. It is not visible to the naked-eye since its magnitude is +7·7.

THE MOON

Day	R.A.	Dec.	Hor. Par.	Semi-diam.	Sun's Co-long.	P.A. of Bright Limb	Phase	Age	Rise 52°	Rise 56°	Transit	Set 52°	Set 56°
	h m	°	′	′	°	°		d	h m	h m	h m	h m	h m
1	23 55	− 3·5	55·9	15·2	190	66	35	23·1	1 38	1 41	7 31	13 40	13 40
2	0 39	+ 2·4	55·3	15·1	202	66	26	24·1	1 48	1 46	8 12	14 53	14 58
3	1 23	+ 8·0	54·8	14·9	215	68	18	25·1	1 58	1 51	8 53	16 05	16 16
4	2 07	+13·3	54·4	14·8	227	71	11	26·1	2 10	1 58	9 35	17 18	17 34
5	2 52	+18·0	54·1	14·8	239	76	6	27·1	2 23	2 06	10 18	18 32	18 54
6	3 40	+22·1	54·0	14·7	251	85	2	28·1	2 41	2 18	11 04	19 45	20 14
7	4 30	+25·2	53·9	14·7	264	109	0	29·1	3 05	2 36	11 53	20 53	21 28
8	5 22	+27·2	54·0	14·7	276	224	0	0·4	3 39	3 04	12 43	21 53	22 31
9	6 15	+28·0	54·1	14·7	288	255	2	1·4	4 25	3 48	13 35	22 41	23 17
10	7 09	+27·5	54·3	14·8˙	300	267	5	2·4	5 24	4 49	14 27	23 16	23 47
11	8 02	+25·7	54·6	14·9	313	275	11	3·4	6 34	6 04	15 17	23 42	..
12	8 54	+22·7	55·1	15·0	325	282	17	4·4	7 49	7 26	16 05	..	0 06
13	9 44	+18·6	55·6	15·1	337	287	25	5·4	9 06	8 50	16 51	0 01	0 19
14	10 32	+13·7	56·2	15·3	349	290	35	6·4	10 25	10 14	17 36	0 16	0 28
15	11 19	+ 8·0	57·0	15·5	1	293	45	7·4	11 43	11 39	18 20	0 28	0 35
16	12 07	+ 1·9	57·8	15·8	14	294	55	8·4	13 04	13 05	19 06	0 40	0 41
17	12 55	− 4·5	58·7	16·0	26	293	66	9·4	14 28	14 35	19 54	0 51	0 47
18	13 46	−10·9	59·6	16·2	38	291	77	10·4	15 56	16 11	20 45	1 04	0 54
19	14 40	−16·9	60·4	16·4	50	286	86	11·4	17 30	17 53	21 42	1 21	1 04
20	15 39	−22·1	60·9	16·6	63	279	93	12·4	19 06	19 37	22 45	1 43	1 19
21	16 44	−25·9	61·3	16·7	75	266	98	13·4	20 33	21 11	23 52	2 17	1 44
22	17 51	−27·8	61·3	16·7	87	208	100	14·4	21 41	22 19	..	3 08	2 29
23	19 00	−27·7	61·0	16·6	99	106	99	15·4	22 28	22 59	0 59	4 20	3 43
24	20 06	−25·5	60·4	16·4	111	88	95	16·4	22 58	23 21	2 04	5 47	5 17
25	21 07	−21·6	59·6	16·2	123	79	88	17·4	23 18	23 34	3 03	7 19	6 57
26	22 03	−16·7	58·6	16·0	136	73	80	18·4	23 33	23 43	3 56	8 46	8 32
27	22 54	−11·0	57·7	15·7	148	69	71	19·4	23 45	23 49	4 44	10 09	10 01
28	23 42	− 5·0	56·8	15·5	160	67	61	20·4	23 56	23 55	5 28	11 26	11 25
29	0 27	+ 0·9	55·9	15·2	172	67	51	21·4	..	..	6 10	12 41	12 44
30	1 11	+ 6·7	55·3	15·1	185	68	41	22·4	0 06	0 00	6 51	13 54	14 03

MERCURY ☿

Day	R.A.	Dec. +	Diam.	Phase	Transit	Day	R.A.	Dec. +	Diam.	Phase	Transit	5° high 52°	5° high 56°
	h m	°	″		h m			h m	°	″		h m	h m	h m
1	5 20	24·8	5	90	12 46	16	7 16	24·1	7	58	13 42	21 20	21 39
4	5 46	25·3	6	84	13 00	19	7 34	23·2	7	52	13 47	21 19	21 37
7	6 12	25·5	6	77	13 14	22	7 50	22·2	8	46	13 51	21 15	21 32
10	6 35	25·3	6	70	13 25	25	8 03	21·1	8	41	13 52	21 09	21 24
13	6 57	24·8	6	64	13 34	28	8 14	19·9	8	36	13 50	21 01	21 15
16	7 16	24·1	7	58	13 42	31	8 22	18·8	9	31	13 47	20 51	21 03

Mercury is too close to the Sun for observation

VENUS ♀

Day	R.A.	Dec. +	Diam.	Phase	Transit	5° high 52°	5° high 56°
	h m	°	″		h m	h m	h m
1	6 55	24·6	13	83	14 19	22 01	22 21
6	7 21	24·0	13	81	14 25	22 03	22 22
11	7 47	23·1	13	80	14 31	22 03	22 21
16	8 12	22·0	14	78	14 36	22 01	22 17
21	8 36	20·6	14	77	14 41	21 57	22 12
26	9 00	19·0	14	75	14 45	21 51	22 04
31	9 23	17·2	15	73	14 48	21 44	21 55

MARS ♂

Day	R.A.	Dec. −	Diam.	Phase	Transit	5° high 52°	5° high 56°
	h m	°	″		h m	h m	h m
1	19 40	24·4	17	94	3 03	0 13	0 53
6	19 42	24·6	18	95	2 45	23 54	0 39
11	19 42	25·0	19	96	2 26	23 38	0 25
16	19 41	25·4	20	97	2 05	23 22	0 10
21	19 39	25·9	21	98	1 43	23 04	23 53
26	19 36	26·4	21	99	1 20	22 46	23 39
31	19 31	26·9	22	99	0 56	22 27	23 24

SUNRISE AND SUNSET

Day	London a.m. h m	London p.m. h m	Bristol a.m. h m	Bristol p.m. h m	Birmingham a.m. h m	Birmingham p.m. h m	Manchester a.m. h m	Manchester p.m. h m	Newcastle a.m. h m	Newcastle p.m. h m	Glasgow a.m. h m	Glasgow p.m. h m	Belfast a.m. h m	Belfast p.m. h m
1	3 49	8 07	3 59	8 16	3 50	8 19	3 47	8 26	3 35	8 32	3 41	8 49	3 55	8 48
2	3 49	8 08	3 59	8 17	3 50	8 20	3 46	8 27	3 34	8 33	3 40	8 50	3 54	8 49
3	3 48	8 09	3 58	8 18	3 49	8 21	3 45	8 29	3 33	8 35	3 39	8 52	3 53	8 51
4	3 47	8 10	3 57	8 19	3 48	8 22	3 45	8 30	3 33	8 36	3 38	8 53	3 53	8 52
5	3 46	8 11	3 56	8 20	3 47	8 23	3 44	8 31	3 32	8 37	3 37	8 54	3 52	8 53
6	3 46	8 12	3 56	8 21	3 47	8 24	3 43	8 32	3 31	8 38	3 36	8 55	3 51	8 54
7	3 45	8 13	3 55	8 22	3 46	8 25	3 42	8 33	3 30	8 39	3 35	8 56	3 50	8 55
8	3 45	8 14	3 55	8 23	3 46	8 26	3 42	8 34	3 29	8 41	3 34	8 58	3 50	8 56
9	3 44	8 14	3 54	8 24	3 45	8 27	3 41	8 35	3 29	8 42	3 34	8 59	3 49	8 57
10	3 44	8 15	3 54	8 25	3 45	8 28	3 41	8 36	3 28	8 43	3 33	9 00	3 49	8 58
11	3 43	8 16	3 53	8 26	3 44	8 29	3 40	8 36	3 27	8 43	3 32	9 00	3 48	8 58
12	3 43	8 17	3 53	8 26	3 44	8 29	3 40	8 37	3 27	8 44	3 32	9 01	3 48	8 59
13	3 43	8 17	3 53	8 27	3 44	8 30	3 40	8 38	3 27	8 45	3 32	9 02	3 48	9 00
14	3 43	8 18	3 53	8 28	3 44	8 31	3 39	8 39	3 26	8 46	3 31	9 03	3 47	9 01
15	3 42	8 18	3 52	8 28	3 43	8 31	3 39	8 39	3 26	8 46	3 31	9 04	3 47	9 01
16	3 42	8 19	3 52	8 29	3 43	8 32	3 39	8 40	3 26	8 47	3 31	9 04	3 47	9 02
17	3 42	8 19	3 52	8 29	3 43	8 32	3 39	8 40	3 26	8 47	3 31	9 05	3 47	9 02
18	3 42	8 20	3 52	8 30	3 43	8 33	3 39	8 41	3 26	8 48	3 30	9 05	3 47	9 03
19	3 42	8 20	3 52	8 30	3 43	8 33	3 39	8 41	3 26	8 48	3 30	9 06	3 47	9 03
20	3 42	8 20	3 52	8 30	3 43	8 33	3 39	8 42	3 26	8 49	3 31	9 06	3 47	9 04
21	3 42	8 21	3 52	8 31	3 43	8 34	3 39	8 42	3 26	8 49	3 31	9 06	3 47	9 04
22	3 42	8 21	3 52	8 31	3 43	8 34	3 39	8 42	3 26	8 49	3 31	9 06	3 47	9 04
23	3 43	8 21	3 53	8 31	3 44	8 34	3 40	8 42	3 26	8 49	3 31	9 07	3 47	9 04
24	3 43	8 21	3 53	8 31	3 44	8 34	3 40	8 42	3 27	8 49	3 31	9 07	3 48	9 04
25	3 43	8 21	3 53	8 31	3 44	8 34	3 40	8 42	3 27	8 49	3 32	9 07	3 48	9 04
26	3 44	8 21	3 54	8 31	3 45	8 34	3 40	8 42	3 27	8 49	3 32	9 07	3 49	9 04
27	3 44	8 21	3 54	8 31	3 45	8 34	3 41	8 42	3 28	8 49	3 33	9 06	3 49	9 04
28	3 45	8 21	3 55	8 31	3 46	8 34	3 41	8 42	3 28	8 49	3 33	9 06	3 49	9 04
29	3 45	8 21	3 55	8 31	3 46	8 34	3 42	8 42	3 29	8 49	3 34	9 06	3 50	9 04
30	3 46	8 21	3 56	8 31	3 47	8 34	3 43	8 42	3 30	8 49	3 35	9 06	3 51	9 04

		JUPITER ♃						SATURN ♄			
Day	R.A.	Dec. −	Transit	5° high. 52°	5° high. 56°	R.A.	Dec. −	Transit	5° high. 52°	5° high. 56°
	h m	°	h m	h m	h m	h m	°	h m	h m	h m
1	23 26	4·9	6 48	1 47	1 54	16 18	19·3	23 38	3 14	2 48
11	23 30	4·5	6 13	1 10	1 17	16 15	19·2	22 55	2 32	2 07
21	23 33	4·2	5 36	0 32	0 39	16 13	19·1	22 13	1 51	1 26
31	23 35	4·1	4 59	23 50	0 01	16 10	19·0	21 31	1 10	0 45

Equatorial diameter of Jupiter 41″; of Saturn 18″. Diameters of Saturn's rings 42″ and 18″.

		URANUS ♅						NEPTUNE ♆			
Day	R.A.	Dec. −	Transit	10° high. 52°	10° high. 56°	R.A.	Dec. −	Transit	10° high. 52°	10° high. 56°
	h m	° ′	h m	h m	h m	h m	° ′	h m	h m	h m
1	17 20·0	23 13	0 43	2 47	1 36	18 22·0	22 14	1 45	23 25	0 26
11	17 18·2	23 11	0 02	2 07	0 55	18 20·9	22 15	1 05	22 45	23 42
21	17 16·4	23 09	23 17	1 26	0 15	18 19·8	22 15	0 24	22 04	23 02
31	17 14·7	23 08	22 36	0 45	23 31	18 18·6	22 16	23 40	21 24	22 22

Diameter 4″   Diameter 2″

DAY OF		*Julius* Caesar, formerly *Quintilis*, 5th month (from March). *Sun's Longitude* 120° ♌ 23ᵈ 03ʰ
Month	Week	
1	Tu.	PRINCESS OF WALES b. 1961.
2	W.	Archbp. Cranmer b. 1489. Marston Moor 1644.
3	Th.	**St. Thomas.** Leoš Janáček b. 1854.
4	F.	INDEPENDENCE DAY, U.S.A., 1776.
5	S.	Cecil Rhodes b. 1853. Jean Cocteau b. 1889.
6	♄.	**6th S. after Trinity.** Sedgemoor 1685.
7	M.	Gustave Mahler b. 1860.
8	Tu.	Percy Bysshe Shelley drowned 1822.
9	W.	Mrs. Ann Radcliffe b. 1764.
10	Th.	John Calvin b. 1509. George Stubbs d. 1806.
11	F.	Robert the Bruce b. 1274. Courtrai 1302.
12	S.	Julius Caesar b. 102 B.C.
13	♄.	**7th S. after Trinity.** Jean Paul Marat d. 1793.
14	M.	FÊTE NATIONALE, FRANCE . Alfred Krupp d. 1887.
15	Tu.	ST. SWITHIN'S DAY. Rembrandt b. 1606.
16	W.	Sir Joshua Reynolds b. 1723. Amundsen b. 1872.
17	Th.	Isaac Watts b. 1674. Charlotte Corday d. 1793.
18	F.	Jane Austen d. 1817. Dr. W. G . Grace b. 1848.
19	S.	*Mary Rose* sank 1545. Edgar Degas b. 1834.
20	♄.	**8th S. after Trinity.** Petrarch b. 1304.
21	M.	First Men on Moon 1969.
22	Tu.	**St. Mary Magdalene.** Gregor Mendel b. 1822.
23	W.	Sir Arthur Whitton Brown b. 1886.**
24	Th.	Simón Bolivár b. 1783. Dumas (père) b. 1802.
25	F.	**St. James.** First Cross Channel Flight 1909.
26	S.	G. B. Shaw b. 1856. C. G. Jung b. 1875.
27	♄.	**9th S. after Trinity.** Hilaire Belloc b. 1870.
28	M.	First potatoes arrive in Britain 1586**.
29	Tu.	Defeat of Spanish Armada 1588.
30	W.	Emily Brontë b. 1818. Henry Moore b. 1898.
31	Th.	TRINITY LAW SITTINGS END. Franz Liszt d. 1886.**

PHENOMENA

July 5ᵈ 10ʰ Earth at aphelion (152,000,000 kilometres).

8ᵈ 20ʰ Mercury in conjunction with the Moon. Mercury 8° S.

10ᵈ 05ʰ Mars at opposition.

10ᵈ 17ʰ Venus in conjunction with the Moon. Venus 3° S.

17ᵈ 20ʰ Saturn in conjunction with the Moon. Saturn 5° N.

20ᵈ 13ʰ Mars in conjunction with the Moon. Mars 0°·9 S.

23ᵈ 11ʰ Mercury in inferior conjunction.

25ᵈ 06ʰ Jupiter in conjunction with the Moon. Jupiter 1°·5 N.

CONSTELLATIONS

The following constellations are near the meridian at

	d h		d h
June	1 24	June 15	23
July	1 22	July 16	21
Aug.	1 20	Aug. 16	19

Ursa Minor, Draco, Corona, Hercules, Lyra, Serpens, Ophiuchus, Libra, Scorpius and Sagittarius.

MINIMA OF ALGOL

d	h	d	h
2	0	19	5
4	21	22	2
7	18	24	23
10	15	27	20
13	12	30	17
16	8		

PHASES OF THE MOON

	d	h	m
● New Moon.........	7	04	55
☽ First Quarter	14	20	10
○ Full Moon	21	10	40
☾ Last Quarter.......	28	15	34

	d	h
Apogee (406,100 kilometres)	4	08
Perigee (360,850 „)	19	20
Apogee (405,170 „)	31	21

Mean Longitude of Ascending Node on July 1, 26°

See note on *Summer Time*, p. 98.

MONTHLY NOTES

July 1. National Day, Canada.

3. Dog Days begin (end Aug. 15).

5. Tynwald Day, Isle of Man.

12. Bank holiday, Northern Ireland.

** Centenary.

Day	Right Ascension	Dec. +	Equation of Time	Rise 52°	Rise 56°	Transit	Set 52°	Set 56°	Sidereal Time	Transit of First Point of Aries
	h m s	° ′	m s	h m	h m	h m	h m	h m	h m s	h m s
1	6 38 39	23 09	−3 39	3 43	3 17	12 04	20 23	20 49	18 35 01	5 24 06
2	6 42 48	23 05	−3 50	3 44	3 18	12 04	20 23	20 49	18 38 57	5 20 10
3	6 46 55	23 00	−4 02	3 45	3 19	12 04	20 22	20 48	18 42 54	5 16 14
4	6 51 03	22 55	−4 13	3 46	3 20	12 04	20 22	20 48	18 46 50	5 12 18
5	6 55 11	22 50	−4 24	3 46	3 21	12 04	20 22	20 47	18 50 47	5 08 22
6	6 59 18	22 45	−4 34	3 47	3 22	12 05	20 21	20 46	18 54 44	5 04 26
7	7 03 24	22 39	−4 45	3 48	3 23	12 05	20 20	20 46	18 58 40	5 00 30
8	7 07 31	22 32	−4 54	3 49	3 24	12 05	20 20	20 45	19 02 37	4 56 34
9	7 11 37	22 25	−5 04	3 50	3 25	12 05	20 19	20 44	19 06 33	4 52 38
10	7 15 42	22 18	−5 13	3 51	3 26	12 05	20 18	20 43	19 10 30	4 48 42
11	7 19 47	22 11	−5 21	3 52	3 28	12 05	20 18	20 42	19 14 26	4 44 46
12	7 23 52	22 03	−5 29	3 53	3 29	12 06	20 17	20 41	19 18 23	4 40 51
13	7 27 56	21 54	−5 37	3 54	3 30	12 06	20 16	20 40	19 22 19	4 36 55
14	7 32 00	21 46	−5 44	3 55	3 32	12 06	20 15	20 39	19 26 16	4 32 59
15	7 36 03	21 37	−5 51	3 57	3 33	12 06	20 14	20 37	19 30 13	4 29 03
16	7 40 06	21 27	−5 57	3 58	3 35	12 06	20 13	20 36	19 34 09	4 25 07
17	7 44 08	21 17	−6 03	3 59	3 36	12 06	20 12	20 35	19 38 06	4 21 11
18	7 48 10	21 07	−6 08	4 00	3 38	12 06	20 11	20 33	19 42 02	4 17 15
19	7 52 11	20 57	−6 12	4 02	3 39	12 06	20 10	20 32	19 45 59	4 13 19
20	7 56 11	20 46	−6 16	4 03	3 41	12 06	20 09	20 30	19 49 55	4 09 23
21	8 00 11	20 34	−6 20	4 04	3 43	12 06	20 07	20 29	19 53 52	4 05 27
22	8 04 11	20 23	−6 23	4 06	3 44	12 06	20 06	20 27	19 57 49	4 01 31
23	8 08 10	20 11	−6 25	4 07	3 46	12 06	20 05	20 26	20 01 45	3 57 36
24	8 12 08	19 59	−6 27	4 08	3 48	12 06	20 04	20 24	20 05 42	3 53 40
25	8 16 06	19 46	−6 28	4 10	3 49	12 06	20 02	20 22	20 09 38	3 49 44
26	8 20 03	19 33	−6 28	4 11	3 51	12 06	20 01	20 21	20 13 35	3 45 48
27	8 23 59	19 20	−6 28	4 12	3 53	12 06	19 59	20 19	20 17 31	3 41 52
28	8 27 55	19 06	−6 28	4 14	3 54	12 06	19 58	20 17	20 21 28	3 37 56
29	8 31 51	18 53	−6 26	4 16	3 56	12 06	19 56	20 15	20 25 24	3 34 00
30	8 35 45	18 38	−6 25	4 17	3 58	12 06	19 55	20 13	20 29 21	3 30 04
31	8 39 40	18 24	−6 22	4 19	4 00	12 06	19 53	20 11	20 33 17	3 26 08

Duration of Civil (C), Nautical (N), and Astronomical (A), Twilight (in minutes)

Lat. °	July 1 C	N	A	July 11 C	N	A	July 21 C	N	A	July 31 C	N	A
52	48	124	T.A.N.	46	116	T.A.N.	44	107	T.A.N.	41	98	180
56	61	T.A.N.	T.A.N.	58	T.A.N.	T.A.N.	53	144	T.A.N.	49	122	T.A.N.

ASTRONOMICAL NOTES

MERCURY is unsuitably placed for observation throughout the month, inferior conjunction occurring on the 23rd.

VENUS, magnitude −3·6, continues to be visible low in the western sky in the evenings after sunset. The crescent Moon passes 3° N. of Venus on the 10th while Venus itself is passing N. of Regulus.

MARS, magnitude −2·4, reaches opposition on the 10th and is thus visible throughout the hours of darkness. Mars is in Sagittarius and clearly the brightest object in the southern sky. The Full Moon will be seen near Mars on the 20th. Because of the eccentricity of its orbit closest approach to the Earth (61 million kilometres) does not occur until the 16th, six days after opposition.

JUPITER, magnitude −2·2, continues to be visible as a morning object, in the south-eastern sky, and is now above the horizon before midnight. On the morning of the 25th the gibbous Moon will be seen approaching the planet, passing 2° S. of it after sunrise.

SATURN continues to be visible in the evenings, in the south western sky. Its magnitude is +0·5. The gibbous Moon passes 5° S. of Saturn on the evening of the 17th.

TWILIGHT. Reference to the section just above these notes shows that astronomical twilight last all night for some time around the summer solstice (i.e. in June and July), even in southern England. Under these conditions the sky never gets completely dark since the Sun is always less than 18° below the horizon.

THE MOON

Day	R.A.	Dec.	Hor. Par.	Semi-diam.	Sun's Co-long.	P.A. of Bright Limb	Phase	Age	Rise 52°	Rise 56°	Tran-sit	Set 52°	Set 56°
	h m	°	′	′	°	°		d	h m	h m	h m	h m	h m
1	1 55	+12·1	54·7	14·9	197	70	31	23·4	0 17	0 07	7 33	15 07	15 22
2	2 40	+17·0	54·3	14·8	209	73	23	24·4	0 30	0 14	8 16	16 21	16 41
3	3 27	+21·2	54·1	14·7	221	78	15	·25·4	0 46	0 25	9 01	17 34	18 01
4	4 17	+24·6	54·0	14·7	233	85	9	26·4	1 09	0 41	9 49	18 44	19 18
5	5 08	+26·9	54·0	14·7	246	94	5	27·4	1 39	1 05	10 39	19 47	20 24
6	6 01	+27·9	54·1	14·8	258	108	2	28·4	2 21	1 44	11 31	20 39	21 16
7	6 56	+27·7	54·4	14·8	270	160	0	29·4	3 17	2 41	12 23	21 18	21 50
8	7 49	+26·2	54·6	14·9	282	251	1	0·8	4 24	3 53	13 14	21 46	22 12
9	8 42	+23·4	55·0	15·0	295	272	3	1·8	5 39	5 14	14 03	22 07	22 26
10	9 32	+19·5	55·4	15·1	307	281	8	2·8	6 56	6 38	14 49	22 23	22 36
11	10 21	+14·7	55·9	15·2	319	287	14	3·8	8 14	8 02	15 34	22 36	22 44
12	11 08	+ 9·2	56·5	15·4	331	291	21	4·8	9 32	9 26	16 18	22 47	22 50
13	11 54	+ 3·2	57·1	15·6	344	292	31	5·8	10 50	10 50	17 03	22 58	22 56
14	12 41	− 3·0	57·8	15·7	356	293	41	6·8	12 11	12 16	17 48	23 10	23 02
15	13 30	− 9·3	58·5	15·9	8	292	52	7·8	13 35	13 47	18 37	23 24	23 11
16	14 22	−15·3	59·2	16·1	20	289	63	8·8	15 03	15 23	19 29	23 43	23 22
17	15 17	−20·6	59·8	16·3	33	284	74	9·8	16 36	17 03	20 27	..	23 41
18	16 18	−24·8	60·4	16·4	45	277	83	10·8	18 05	18 41	21 31	0 10	..
19	17 23	−27·4	60·7	16·5	57	268	91	11·8	19 22	20 01	22 37	0 51	0 15
20	18 31	−28·0	60·8	16·6	69	254	97	12·8	20 18	20 53	23 43	1 53	1 14
21	19 38	−26·6	60·6	16·5	81	222	100	13·8	20 56	21 22	..	3 14	2 40
22	20 41	−23·4	60·1	16·4	94	108	99	14·8	21 20	21 39	0 45	4 45	4 20
23	21 40	−18·7	59·4	16·2	106	82	96	15·8	21 37	21 50	1 42	6 17	5 59
24	22 34	−13·1	58·6	16·0	118	74	91	16·8	21 51	21 57	2 33	7 44	7 34
25	23 24	− 7·1	57·7	15·7	130	70	84	17·8	22 02	22 03	3 20	9 06	9 02
26	0 11	− 0·9	56·8	15·5	142	68	76	18·8	22 12	22 09	4 04	10 24	10 25
27	0 56	+ 5·1	56·0	15·3	155	68	66	19·8	22 23	22 15	4 47	11 39	11 46
28	1 41	+10·8	55·3	15·1	167	69	56	20·8	22 36	22 22	5 29	12 53	13 06
29	2 27	+15·9	54·8	14·9	179	72	47	21·8	22 51	22 31	6 12	14 08	14 26
30	3 13	+20·3	54·4	14·8	191	75	37	22·8	23 11	22 45	6 57	15 22	15 47
31	4 02	+23·9	54·2	14·8	203	80	28	23·8	23 38	23 06	7 44	16 34	17 05

MERCURY ☿

Day	R.A.	Dec. +	Diam.	Phase	Tran-sit		Day	R.A.	Dec. +	Diam.	Phase	Tran-sit	
	h m	°	″		h m			h m	°	″		h m	
1	8 22	18·8	9	31	13 47		16	8 25	15·0	11	6	12 48	
4	8 28	17·7	10	25	13 40	Mercury is too	19	8 18	14·9	11	3	12 29	Mercury is too
7	8 32	16·8	10	20	13 31	close to the	22	8 10	15·1	11	1	12 09	close to the
10	8 32	15·9	11	15	13 19	Sun for	25	8 01	15·5	11	1	11 49	Sun for
13	8 30	15·3	11	10	13 05	observation	28	7 54	16·1	11	3	11 30	observation
16	8 25	15·0	11	6	12 48		31	7 49	16·7	10	8	11 14	

VENUS ♀ / MARS ♂

Day	R.A.	Dec. +	Diam.	Phase	Tran-sit	5° high. 52°	5° high. 56°	Day	R.A.	Dec. −	Diam.	Phase	Tran-sit	5° high. 52°	5° high. 56°
	h m	°	″		h m	h m	h m		h m	°	″		h m	h m	h m
1	9 23	17·2	15	73	14 48	21 44	21 55	1	19 31	26·9	22	99	0 56	3 20	2 24
6	9 46	15·3	15	72	14 51	21 36	21 45	6	19 25	27·4	23	100	0 30	2 49	1 48
11	10 08	13·2	16	70	14 53	21 27	21 34	11	19 19	27·8	23	100	0 04	2 17	1 11
16	10 29	10·9	16	68	14 55	21 16	21 22	16	19 13	28·2	23	100	23 33	1 47	0 34
21	10 50	8·6	17	66	14 56	21 05	21 09	21	19 06	28·4	23	99	23 08	1 18	23 51
26	11 10	6·2	18	64	14 56	20 53	20 55	26	19 01	28·6	23	98	22 43	0 50	23 19
31	11 30	3·7	19	62	14 56	20 41	20 40	31	18 57	28·7	22	97	22 19	0 25	22 52

SUNRISE AND SUNSET

Day	London a.m. h m	London p.m. h m	Bristol a.m. h m	Bristol p.m. h m	Birmingham a.m. h m	Birmingham p.m. h m	Manchester a.m. h m	Manchester p.m. h m	Newcastle a.m. h m	Newcastle p.m. h m	Glasgow a.m. h m	Glasgow p.m. h m	Belfast a.m. h m	Belfast p.m. h m
1	3 46	8 21	3 56	8 30	3 47	8 33	3 43	8 41	3 30	8 48	3 35	9 05	3 51	9 03
2	3 47	8 20	3 57	8 30	3 48	8 33	3 44	8 41	3 31	8 48	3 36	9 05	3 52	9 03
3	3 48	8 20	3 58	8 29	3 49	8 32	3 45	8 40	3 32	8 47	3 37	9 04	3 53	9 02
4	3 49	8 20	3 59	8 29	3 50	8 32	3 46	8 40	3 33	8 47	3 38	9 04	3 54	9 02
5	3 49	8 20	3 59	8 29	3 50	8 32	3 47	8 39	3 34	8 46	3 39	9 03	3 55	9 01
6	3 50	8 19	4 00	8 28	3 51	8 31	3 48	8 39	3 35	8 45	3 40	9 02	3 56	9 01
7	3 51	8 18	4 01	8 27	3 52	8 30	3 49	8 38	3 36	8 45	3 41	9 02	3 57	9 00
8	3 52	8 18	4 02	8 27	3 53	8 30	3 50	8 38	3 37	8 44	3 42	9 01	3 58	9 00
9	3 53	8 17	4 03	8 26	3 54	8 29	3 51	8 37	3 38	8 43	3 43	9 00	3 59	8 59
10	3 54	8 16	4 04	8 25	3 55	8 28	3 52	8 36	3 39	8 42	3 44	8 59	4 00	8 58
11	3 55	8 16	4 05	8 25	3 56	8 28	3 53	8 35	3 41	8 41	3 46	8 58	4 01	8 57
12	3 56	8 15	4 06	8 24	3 57	8 27	3 54	8 34	3 42	8 40	3 47	8 57	4 02	8 56
13	3 57	8 14	4 07	8 23	3 58	8 26	3 55	8 33	3 43	8 39	3 48	8 56	4 03	8 55
14	3 58	8 13	4 08	8 22	3 59	8 25	3 56	8 32	3 44	8 38	3 50	8 55	4 04	8 54
15	3 59	8 12	4 10	8 22	4 01	8 24	3 58	8 31	3 46	8 37	3 51	8 53	4 06	8 53
16	4 00	8 11	4 11	8 21	4 02	8 23	3 59	8 30	3 47	8 36	3 53	8 52	4 07	8 52
17	4 01	8 10	4 12	8 20	4 03	8 22	4 00	8 29	3 48	8 35	3 54	8 51	4 08	8 51
18	4 03	8 09	4 13	8 19	4 05	8 21	4 02	8 28	3 50	8 33	3 56	8 49	4 10	8 49
19	4 04	8 08	4 15	8 18	4 06	8 19	4 03	8 26	3 51	8 32	3 57	8 48	4 11	8 48
20	4 05	8 07	4 16	8 17	4 08	8 18	4 05	8 25	3 53	8 30	3 59	8 46	4 13	8 46
21	4 06	8 05	4 17	8 15	4 09	8 17	4 06	8 24	3 55	8 29	4 01	8 45	4 15	8 45
22	4 08	8 04	4 18	8 14	4 11	8 15	4 08	8 22	3 56	8 27	4 02	8 43	4 16	8 43
23	4 09	8 03	4 20	8 13	4 12	8 14	4 09	8 21	3 58	8 26	4 04	8 42	4 18	8 42
24	4 10	8 02	4 21	8 12	4 13	8 13	4 10	8 20	4 00	8 24	4 06	8 40	4 20	8 40
25	4 12	8 00	4 22	8 10	4 15	8 11	4 12	8 18	4 01	8 23	4 07	8 38	4 21	8 39
26	4 13	7 59	4 24	8 09	4 16	8 10	4 13	8 17	4 03	8 21	4 09	8 37	4 23	8 37
27	4 14	7 57	4 25	8 07	4 17	8 08	4 14	8 15	4 04	8 19	4 11	8 35	4 24	8 35
28	4 16	7 56	4 26	8 06	4 19	8 07	4 16	8 14	4 06	8 18	4 12	8 33	4 26	8 34
29	4 18	7 54	4 28	8 04	4 21	8 05	4 18	8 12	4 08	8 16	4 14	8 31	4 28	8 32
30	4 19	7 53	4 29	8 03	4 22	8 04	4 19	8 10	4 09	8 14	4 16	8 29	4 29	8 30
31	4 21	7 51	4 31	8 01	4 24	8 02	4 21	8 09	4 11	8 12	4 18	8 27	4 31	8 29

JUPITER ♃ / SATURN ♄

Day	JUPITER R.A. h m	JUPITER Dec. − °	JUPITER Transit h m	JUPITER 5° high. 52° h m	JUPITER 5° high. 56° h m	SATURN R.A. h m	SATURN Dec. − °	SATURN Transit h m	SATURN 5° high. 52° h m	SATURN 5° high. 56° h m
1	23 35	4·1	4 59	23 50	0 01	16 10	19·0	21 31	1 10	0 45
11	23 36	4·0	4 21	23 11	23 18	16 08	19·0	20 50	0 29	0 04
21	23 35	4·1	3 41	22 32	22 39	16 07	19·0	20 09	23 44	23 19
31	23 34	4·3	3 00	21 52	21 59	16 06	19·0	19 29	23 04	22 39

Equatorial diameter of Jupiter 45″; of Saturn 18″.   Diameters of Saturn's rings 41″ and 17″.

URANUS ♅ / NEPTUNE ♆

Day	URANUS R.A. h m	URANUS Dec. − ° ′	URANUS Transit h m	URANUS 10° high. 52° h m	URANUS 10° high. 56° h m	NEPTUNE R.A. h m	NEPTUNE Dec. − ° ′	NEPTUNE Transit h m	NEPTUNE 10° high. 52° h m	NEPTUNE 10° high. 56° h m
1	17 14·7	23 08	22 36	0 45	23 31	18 18·6	22 16	23 40	1 59	1 01
11	17 13·2	23 06	21 55	0 05	22 51	18 17·5	22 17	22 59	1 19	0 21
21	17 11·8	23 05	21 14	23 20	22 11	18 16·4	22 17	22 19	0 38	23 36
31	17 10·7	23 03	20 34	22 40	21 32	18 15·4	22 18	21 38	23 54	22 56

Diameter 4″   Diameter 2″

Julius Caesar *Augustus*, formerly *Sextilis*, 6th month (from March).

Sun's Longitude 150° ♍ $23^{d}\ 10^{h}$

Day of Month	Day of Week	
1	F.	Minden 1754. The Nile 1798.
2	S.	William II (Rufus) d. 1100. Gainsborough d. 1788.
3	𝕾.	**10th S. after Trinity.** Rupert Brooke b. 1887.
4	M.	QUEEN ELIZABETH THE QUEEN MOTHER b. 1900.
5	Tu.	Guy de Maupassant b. 1850.
6	W.	**Transfiguration.** First atomic bomb dropped 1945.
7	Th.	Admiral Robert Blake d. 1657.
8	F.	Great Train Robbery 1963.
9	S.	Izaak Walton b. 1593. Thomas Telford b. 1757.
10	𝕾.	**11th S. after Trinity.** Otterburn 1388.
11	M.	Battle of Britain began 1940.
12	Tu.	George IV b. 1762. Robert Southey b. 1774.
13	W.	Blenheim 1704. John Logie Baird b 1888.
14	Th.	John Galsworthy b. 1867. Japan surrenders 1945.
15	F.	PRINCESS ANNE b. 1950. T. E. Shaw b. 1888.
16	S.	Peterloo Massacre 1819.
17	𝕾.	**12th S. after Trinity.** Frederick the Great d. 1786.**
18	M.	Honoré de Balzac d. 1850.
19	Tu.	John Dryden b 1631. Garcia Lorca d. 1936.
20	W.	Gen. William Booth d. 1912. Trotsky assass. 1940.
21	Th.	PRINCESS MARGARET b. 1930.
22	F.	Bosworth Field 1485. Claude Debussy b. 1862.
23	S.	William Wallace exec. 1305.
24	𝕾.	**13th S. after Trinity. St. Bartholomew.**
25	M.	Liberation of Paris 1944.
26	Tu.	Crecy 1346. Prince Albert b. 1819.
27	W.	Earl Mountbatten of Burma killed 1979.
28	Th.	Johann von Goethe b. 1749. Tolstoy b. 1828.
29	F.	John Locke b. 1632. Eamon de Valera d. 1975.
30	S.	Mary Shelley b. 1797. Lord Rutherford b. 1871.
31	𝕾.	**14th S. after Trinity.** Henry V d. 1422.

PHENOMENA

August $4^{d}\ 06^{h}$ Mercury in conjunction with the Moon. Mercury 8° S.

$9^{d}\ 11^{h}$ Venus in conjunction with the Moon. Venus 2° S.

$11^{d}\ 16^{h}$ Mercury at greatest western elongation (19°).

$14^{d}\ 02^{h}$ Saturn in conjunction with the Moon. Saturn 5° N.

$16^{d}\ 16^{h}$ Mars in conjunction with the Moon. Mars 0°·5 S.

$21^{d}\ 11^{h}$ Jupiter in conjunction with the Moon. Jupiter 1°·4 N.

$27^{d}\ 09^{h}$ Venus at greatest eastern elongation (46°).

CONSTELLATIONS

The following constellations are near the meridian at

	d	h		d	h
July	1	24	July	16	23
Aug.	1	22	Aug.	16	21
Sept.	1	20	Sept.	15	19

Draco, Hercules, Lyra, Cygnus, Sagitta, Ophiuchus, Serpens, Aquila and Sagittarius.

MINIMA OF ALGOL

d	h	d	h
2	13	19	18
5	10	22	15
8	7	25	12
11	4	28	9
14	1	31	6
16	21		

PHASES OF THE MOON

	d	h	m
● New Moon	5	18	36
☽ First Quarter	13	02	21
○ Full Moon	19	18	54
☾ Last Quarter	27	08	38

	d	h
Perigee (365,720 kilometres)	16	17
Apogee (404,380 „)	28	15

Mean Longitude of Ascending Node on August 1, 25°.

See note on *Summer Time*, p. 98.

MONTHLY NOTES

Aug. 1. Lammas. Scottish Term Day.
4. Bank Holiday, Scotland.
12. Grouse shooting begins.
25. Bank and General Holiday, England, Wales and N. Ireland.

**Centenary.

Day	Right Ascension	Dec. +	Equation of Time	Rise 52°	Rise 56°	Transit	Set 52°	Set 56°	Sidereal Time	Transit of First Point of Aries
	h m s	° '	m s	h m	h m	h m	h m	h m	h m s	h m s
1	8 43 33	18 09	− 6 19	4 20	4 02	12 06	19 51	20 09	20 37 14	3 22 12
2	8 47 26	17 54	− 6 16	4 22	4 04	12 06	19 50	20 07	20 41 11	3 18 16
3	8 51 19	17 39	− 6 12	4 23	4 06	12 06	19 48	20 05	20 45 07	3 14 21
4	8 55 11	17 23	− 6 07	4 25	4 07	12 06	19 46	20 03	20 49 04	3 10 25
5	8 59 02	17 07	− 6 02	4 26	4 09	12 06	19 45	20 01	20 53 00	3 06 29
6	9 02 52	16 51	− 5 56	4 28	4 11	12 06	19 43	19 59	20 56 57	3 02 33
7	9 06 43	16 34	− 5 49	4 30	4 13	12 06	19 41	19 57	21 00 53	2 58 37
8	9 10 32	16 17	− 5 42	4 31	4 15	12 06	19 39	19 55	21 04 50	2 54 41
9	9 14 21	16 00	− 5 34	4 33	4 17	12 06	19 37	19 52	21 08 47	2 50 45
10	9 18 09	15 43	− 5 26	4 34	4 19	12 05	19 35	19 50	21 12 43	2 46 49
11	9 21 57	15 25	− 5 17	4 36	4 21	12 05	19 33	19 48	21 16 40	2 42 53
12	9 25 44	15 08	− 5 08	4 38	4 23	12 05	19 32	19 46	21 20 36	2 38 57
13	9 29 30	14 50	− 4 58	4 39	4 25	12 05	19 30	19 44	21 24 33	2 35 01
14	9 33 16	14 31	− 4 47	4 41	4 27	12 05	19 28	19 41	21 28 29	2 31 06
15	9 37 01	14 13	− 4 36	4 42	4 29	12 05	19 26	19 39	21 32 26	2 27 10
16	9 40 46	13 54	− 4 24	4 44	4 31	12 04	19 24	19 37	21 36 22	2 23 14
17	9 44 31	13 35	− 4 12	4 46	4 33	12 04	19 22	19 34	21 40 19	2 19 18
18	9 48 14	13 16	− 3 59	4 47	4 35	12 04	19 20	19 32	21 44 16	2 15 22
19	9 51 57	12 57	− 3 46	4 49	4 37	12 04	19 18	19 29	21 48 12	2 11 26
20	9 55 40	12 37	− 3 32	4 50	4 39	12 03	19 15	19 27	21 52 09	2 07 30
21	9 59 22	12 17	− 3 17	4 52	4 41	12 03	19 13	19 24	21 56 05	2 03 34
22	10 03 04	11 57	− 3 03	4 54	4 43	12 03	19 11	19 22	22 00 02	1 59 38
23	10 06 45	11 37	− 2 47	4 55	4 44	12 03	19 09	19 20	22 03 58	1 55 42
24	10 10 26	11 17	− 2 32	4 57	4 46	12 02	19 07	19 17	22 07 55	1 51 46
25	10 14 07	10 56	− 2 16	4 59	4 48	12 02	19 05	19 15	22 11 51	1 47 51
26	10 17 47	10 36	− 1 59	5 00	4 50	12 02	19 02	19 12	22 15 48	1 43 55
27	10 21 27	10 15	− 1 42	5 02	4 52	12 02	19 00	19 10	22 19 44	1 39 59
28	10 25 06	9 54	− 1 25	5 04	4 54	12 01	18 58	19 07	22 23 41	1 36 03
29	10 28 45	9 33	− 1 07	5 05	4 56	12 01	18 56	19 05	22 27 38	1 32 07
30	10 32 23	9 11	− 0 49	5 07	4 58	12 01	18 54	19 02	22 31 34	1 28 11
31	10 36 02	8 50	− 0 31	5 08	5 00	12 00	18 52	18 59	22 35 31	1 24 15

Duration of Civil (C), Nautical (N), and Astronomical (A), Twilight (in minutes)

Lat. °	Aug. 1			Aug. 11			Aug. 21			Aug. 31		
	C	N	A	C	N	A	C	N	A	C	N	A
52	41	97	177	39	89	153	37	83	138	35	79	127
56	48	120	T.A.N.	45	106	205	42	96	166	40	89	147

ASTRONOMICAL NOTES

MERCURY , magnitude +0·8 to −0·8, is a morning object during the middle two weeks of the month, low above the eastern horizon at the time of beginning of morning civil twilight.

VENUS is visible low in the western sky after sunset, magnitude −3·9. Although greatest eastern elongation occurs on the 27th Venus is only visible for a short while after sunset. The thin crescent Moon will be seen near Venus on the evenings of the 8th and 9th. On the last day of the month Venus passes 0°·5 S. of Spica.

MARS, just past opposition, is now fading, its magnitude changing from −2·2 to −1·4 during the month. Mars is still in Sagittarius, reaching its second stationary point on the 12th. Mars is no longer visible after midnight, except at the beginning of the month. The gibbous Moon is near Mars on the 16th.

JUPITER is a brilliant object in the sky for most of the night, being visible as early as 20ʰ by the end of the month. Its magnitude is −2·4. The gibbous Moon makes another close approach to the planet on the morning of the 21st.

SATURN, magnitude +0·7, is visible low in the south-western sky in the evenings, though by the end of the month it is no longer visible after 21ʰ.

METEORS. The maximum of the famous Perseid meteor shower occurs during the night of August 12–13. Conditions for observing are favourable since the Moon sets before 22ʰ.

THE MOON

Day	R.A.	Dec.	Hor. Par.	Semi-diam.	Sun's Co-long.	P.A. of Bright Limb	Phase	Age	Rise 52°	Rise 56°	Tran-sit	Set 52°	Set 56°
	h m	°	′	′	°	°		d	h m	h m	h m	h m	h m
1	4 53	+26·5	54·1	14·7	216	86	20	24·8	..	23 39	8 33	17 40	18 16
2	5 46	+27·9	54·2	14·8	228	94	13	25·8	0 16	..	9 25	18 35	19 13
3	6 40	+28·0	54·4	14·8	240	102	8	26·8	1 08	0 30	10 17	19 18	19 53
4	7 35	+26·7	54·7	14·9	252	113	3	27·8	2 12	1 38	11 09	19 50	20 18
5	8 28	+24·2	55·1	15·0	265	133	1	28·8	3 25	2 58	11 59	20 13	20 34
6	9 19	+20·5	55·6	15·1	277	227	0	0·2	4 43	4 23	12 47	20 30	20 45
7	10 09	+15·8	56·0	15·3	289	275	2	1·2	6 02	5 49	13 33	20 44	20 53
8	10 57	+10·4	56·5	15·4	301	286	5	2·2	7 21	7 14	14 17	20 55	20 59
9	11 43	+ 4·4	57·0	15·5	314	290	11	3·2	8 40	8 38	15 02	21 06	21 05
10	12 30	− 1·8	57·5	15·7	326	292	18	4·2	10 00	10 04	15 46	21 17	21 11
11	13 18	− 8·1	58·0	15·8	338	292	27	5·2	11 22	11 32	16 33	21 30	21 18
12	14 09	−14·1	58·5	15·9	350	290	38	6·2	12 48	13 05	17 24	21 47	21 28
13	15 02	−19·5	59·0	16·1	2	286	49	7·2	14 17	14 42	18 18	22 10	21 44
14	16 00	−23·9	59·4	16·2	15	281	60	8·2	15 46	16 19	19 18	22 44	22 10
15	17 02	−26·9	59·7	16·3	27	274	71	9·2	17 06	17 45	20 21	23 35	22 56
16	18 07	−28·2	59·9	16·3	39	266	81	10·2	18 09	18 47	21 26	..	..
17	19 13	−27·5	59·9	16·3	51	256	89	11·2	18 53	19 23	22 29	0 47	0 09
18	20 17	−24·9	59·8	16·3	64	246	96	12·2	19 21	19 44	23 27	2 13	1 44
19	21 17	−20·7	59·4	16·2	76	229	99	13·2	19 41	19 56	..	3 45	3 24
20	22 12	−15·4	58·9	16·1	88	125	100	14·2	19 56	20 05	0 21	5 14	5 01
21	23 04	− 9·5	58·2	15·9	100	78	98	15·2	20 08	20 11	1 10	6 39	6 32
22	23 52	− 3·2	57·5	15·7	112	71	94	16·2	20 19	20 17	1 56	8 00	7 59
23	0 39	+ 3·0	56·7	15·5	124	68	88	17·2	20 29	20 22	2 40	9 18	9 23
24	1 25	+ 9·0	56·0	15·3	137	68	81	18·2	20 41	20 29	3 23	10 35	10 45
25	2 11	+14·4	55·3	15·1	149	70	72	19·2	20 55	20 37	4 06	11 50	12 07
26	2 58	+19·2	54·8	14·9	161	73	63	20·2	21 13	20 49	4 51	13 06	13 29
27	3 46	+23·1	54·4	14·8	173	77	54	21·2	21 37	21 06	5 37	14 20	14 49
28	4 37	+26·0	54·3	14·8	185	82	44	22·2	22 10	21 34	6 26	15 29	16 05
29	5 29	+27·8	54·2	14·8	198	88	35	23·2	22 56	22 18	7 17	16 29	17 07
30	6 23	+28·3	54·4	14·8	210	95	26	24·2	23 56	23 20	8 09	17 17	17 53
31	7 17	+27·4	54·7	14·9	222	102	18	25·2	..	..	9 01	17 52	18 23

MERCURY ☿

Day	R.A.	Dec. +	Diam.	Phase	Tran-sit	5° high. 52°	5° high. 56°	Day	R.A.	Dec. +	Diam.	Phase	Tran-sit	5° high. 52°	5° high. 56°
	h m	°			h m	h m	h m		h m	°			h m	h m	h m
1	7 49	17·0	10	10	11 09	4 14	4 03	16	8 28	18·9	7	57	10 53	3 46	3 32
4	7 48	17·7	9	16	10 58	3 58	3 47	19	8 47	18·4	6	69	11 01	3 56	3 43
7	7 52	18·3	9	25	10 51	3 47	3 35	22	9 09	17·5	6	79	11 10	4 11	3 59
10	8 00	18·8	8	34	10 48	3 41	3 28	25	9 31	16·1	5	88	11 21	4 29	4 19
13	8 13	19·0	7	46	10 48	3 41	3 27	28	9 54	14·5	5	94	11 33	4 50	4 41
16	8 28	18·9	7	57	10 53	3 46	3 32	31	10 17	12·5	5	97	11 44	5 11	5 04

VENUS ♀

Day	R.A.	Dec.	Diam.	Phase	Tran-sit	5° high. 52°	5° high. 56°
	h m	°	″		h m	h m	h m
1	11 33	+ 3·2	19	61	14 56	20 38	20 37
6	11 53	+ 0·7	20	59	14 56	20 25	20 22
11	12 11	− 1·8	21	57	14 55	20 11	20 06
16	12 30	− 4·2	22	54	14 53	19 56	19 49
21	12 48	− 6·7	23	52	14 51	19 41	19 32
26	13 05	− 9·0	24	49	14 49	19 26	19 14
31	13 22	−11·3	26	47	14 47	19 10	18 55

MARS ♂

Day	R.A.	Dec. −	Diam.	Phase	Tran-sit	5° high. 52°	5° high. 56°
	h m	°	″		h m	h m	h m
1	18 56	28·7	22	97	22 14	0 20	22 47
6	18 53	28·7	22	96	21 52	23 54	22 27
11	18 52	28·6	21	95	21 32	23 35	22 12
16	18 52	28·4	20	94	21 13	23 18	22 00
21	18 54	28·2	19	93	20 55	23 04	21 51
26	18 57	27·9	19	91	20 39	22 51	21 44
31	19 02	27·6	18	90	20 24	22 41	21 38

SUNRISE AND SUNSET

Day	London a.m.	London p.m.	Bristol a.m.	Bristol p.m.	Birmingham a.m.	Birmingham p.m.	Manchester a.m.	Manchester p.m.	Newcastle a.m.	Newcastle p.m.	Glasgow a.m.	Glasgow p.m.	Belfast a.m.	Belfast p.m.
	h m	h m	h m	h m	h m	h m	h m	h m	h m	h m	h m	h m	h m	h m
1	4 22	7 49	4 32	7 59	4 25	8 00	4 23	8 07	4 13	8 10	4 20	8 25	4 33	8 27
2	4 24	7 48	4 34	7 58	4 27	7 59	4 24	8 05	4 15	8 08	4 22	8 23	4 34	8 25
3	4 25	7 46	4 35	7 56	4 28	7 57	4 26	8 03	4 17	8 06	4 24	8 21	4 36	8 23
4	4 27	7 44	4 37	7 54	4 30	7 55	4 28	8 01	4 18	8 04	4 25	8 19	4 38	8 21
5	4 28	7 43	4 38	7 53	4 31	7 54	4 29	7 59	4 20	8 02	4 27	8 17	4 39	8 19
6	4 30	7 41	4 40	7 51	4 33	7 52	4 31	7 57	4 22	8 00	4 29	8 15	4 41	8 17
7	4 32	7 39	4 42	7 49	4 35	7 50	4 33	7 55	4 24	7 58	4 31	8 13	4 43	8 15
8	4 33	7 37	4 43	7 47	4 36	7 48	4 35	7 53	4 26	7 56	4 33	8 11	4 45	8 13
9	4 35	7 36	4 45	7 45	4 38	7 46	4 36	7 51	4 27	7 54	4 35	8 08	4 47	8 10
10	4 36	7 34	4 46	7 43	4 39	7 44	4 38	7 49	4 29	7 52	4 37	8 06	4 49	8 08
11	4 38	7 32	4 48	7 41	4 41	7 42	4 40	7 47	4 31	7 50	4 39	8 04	4 51	8 06
12	4 40	7 30	4 50	7 40	4 43	7 40	4 42	7 45	4 33	7 48	4 41	8 02	4 53	8 04
13	4 41	7 29	4 51	7 38	4 44	7 38	4 43	7 43	4 35	7 46	4 43	8 00	4 54	8 02
14	4 42	7 27	4 52	7 36	4 46	7 36	4 45	7 41	4 37	7 43	4 45	7 57	4 56	8 00
15	4 44	7 25	4 54	7 34	4 48	7 34	4 47	7 39	4 39	7 41	4 47	7 55	4 58	7 58
16	4 46	7 23	4 56	7 32	4 50	7 32	4 49	7 37	4 41	7 39	4 49	7 53	5 00	7 56
17	4 47	7 21	4 57	7 30	4 52	7 30	4 51	7 35	4 43	7 37	4 51	7 51	5 02	7 54
18	4 48	7 19	4 58	7 28	4 53	7 28	4 52	7 33	4 44	7 34	4 52	7 48	5 03	7 51
19	4 50	7 17	5 00	7 26	4 55	7 26	4 54	7 31	4 46	7 32	4 54	7 46	5 05	7 49
20	4 52	7 14	5 02	7 24	4 56	7 23	4 55	7 28	4 48	7 30	4 56	7 44	5 07	7 47
21	4 53	7 12	5 03	7 22	4 58	7 21	4 57	7 26	4 50	7 27	4 58	7 41	5 09	7 44
22	4 55	7 10	5 05	7 20	5 00	7 19	4 59	7 24	4 52	7 25	5 00	7 39	5 10	7 42
23	4 56	7 08	5 06	7 18	5 01	7 17	5 00	7 22	4 53	7 23	5 01	7 37	5 12	7 40
24	4 58	7 06	5 08	7 16	5 03	7 15	5 02	7 20	4 55	7 20	5 03	7 34	5 14	7 38
25	5 00	7 04	5 10	7 14	5 05	7 13	5 04	7 17	4 57	7 18	5 05	7 32	5 16	7 35
26	5 01	7 01	5 11	7 11	5 06	7 10	5 06	7 15	4 59	7 15	5 07	7 29	5 18	7 33
27	5 03	6 59	5 13	7 09	5 08	7 08	5 07	7 13	5 01	7 13	5 09	7 27	5 19	7 31
28	5 05	6 57	5 15	7 07	5 10	7 06	5 09	7 10	5 03	7 10	5 11	7 24	5 21	7 28
29	5 06	6 55	5 16	7 05	5 12	7 04	5 11	7 08	5 05	7 08	5 13	7 22	5 23	7 26
30	5 08	6 53	5 18	7 03	5 13	7 02	5 13	7 06	5 07	7 06	5 15	7 19	5 25	7 23
31	5 09	6 51	5 19	7 01	5 14	7 00	5 14	7 03	5 08	7 03	5 17	7 16	5 27	7 20

JUPITER ♃ / SATURN ♄

Day	Jupiter R.A.	Jupiter Dec. −	Jupiter Transit	Jupiter 5° high 52°	Jupiter 5° high 56°	Saturn R.A.	Saturn Dec.	Saturn Transit	Saturn 5° high 52°	Saturn 5° high 56°
	h m	°	h m	h m	h m	h m	°	h m	h m	h m
1	23 34	4·3	2 56	21 48	21 55	16 06	19·0	19 25	23 00	22 35
11	23 31	4·7	2 14	21 08	21 15	16 06	19·0	18 46	22 21	21 55
21	23 27	5·1	1 31	20 27	20 35	16 06	19·1	18 07	21 41	21 16
31	23 23	5·6	0 47	19 46	19 54	16 07	19·2	17 29	21 03	20 37

Equatorial diameter of Jupiter 48″; of Saturn 17″.   Diameters of Saturn's rings 39″ and 16″.

URANUS ♅ / NEPTUNE ♆

Day	Uranus R.A.	Uranus Dec. −	Uranus Transit	Uranus 10° high 52°	Uranus 10° high 56°	Neptune R.A.	Neptune Dec. −	Neptune Transit	Neptune 10° high 52°	Neptune 10° high 56°
	h m	° ′	h m	h m	h m	h m	° ′	h m	h m	h m
1	17 10·6	23 03	20 30	22 36	21 28	18 15·3	22 18	21 34	23 50	22 52
11	17 09·8	23 02	19 50	21 56	20 48	18 14·5	22 19	20 54	23 10	22 11
21	17 09·4	23 02	19 10	21 17	20 08	18 13·8	22 19	20 14	22 29	21 31
31	17 09·3	23 02	18 31	20 37	19 29	18 13·4	22 20	19 35	21 50	20 51

Diameter 4″   Diameter 2″

DAY OF		
Month	Week	

Septem (seven), 7th month of Roman (pre-Julian) Calendar.

Sun's Longitude 180° ≏ 23^d 08^h

1	M.	Edward Alleyn b. 1566. 'Gentleman Jim' Corbett b. 1866.
2	Tu.	Fire of London starts 1666. Omdurman 1898.
3	W.	Worcester 1651. World War II began 1939.
4	Th.	Surrender of Geronimo 1886.**
5	F.	Louis XIV b. 1638.
6	S.	*Mayflower* sails from Plymouth 1620.
7	⊛.	**15th S. after Trinity.** Elizabeth I b. 1533.
8	M.	**Blessed Virgin Mary.** Richard I b. 1157.
9	Tu.	William the Conqueror d. 1087. Flodden 1513.
10	W.	Treaty of St. Germain 1919.
11	Th.	Malplaquet 1709. D. H. Lawrence b. 1885.
12	F.	H. H. Asquith b. 1852. Maurice Chevalier b. 1888.
13	S.	William Cecil b. 1520. Quebec 1759.
14	⊛.	**16th S. after Trinity.** Dante d. 1321.
15	M.	PRINCE HENRY OF WALES b. 1984. BATTLE OF BRITAIN DAY.
16	Tu.	Henry V b. 1387. Fire of Moscow 1812.
17	W.	James II d. 1701. W. Savage Landor d. 1864.
18	Th.	Dr. Samuel Johnson b. 1709.
19	F.	Poitiers 1356. Sir Francis Chichester b. 1901.
20	S.	Mungo Park b. 1771. Valmy 1792.
21	⊛.	**17th S. after Trinity. St. Matthew.**
22	M.	Zutphen 1586.** Michael Faraday b. 1791.
23	Tu.	Wilkie Collins d. 1889. Sigmund Freud d. 1939.
24	W.	Horace Walpole b. 1717. A. P. Herbert b. 1890.
25	Th.	Stamford Bridge 1066. Shostakovitch b. 1906.
26	F.	Sir Barnes Wallis b. 1887. T. S. Eliot b. 1888.
27	S.	Edward II d. 1327. Bossuet b. 1627.
28	⊛.	**18th S. after Trinity.** Caravaggio b. 1573.
29	M.	**St. Michael and All Angels.** Nelson b. 1758.
30	Tu.	Pierre Corneille b. 1684. Lord Raglan b. 1788.

PHENOMENA

September 5^d 18^h Mercury in superior conjunction.

7^d 20^h Venus in conjunction with the Moon. Venus 3° S.

10^d 09^h Saturn in conjunction with the Moon. Saturn 5° N.

10^d 21^h Jupiter at opposition.

13^d 10^h Mars in conjunction with the Moon. Mars 0°·9 N.

17^d 14^h Jupiter in conjunction with the Moon. Jupiter 1°·6 N.

23^d 08^h Equinox.

CONSTELLATIONS

The following constellations are near the meridian at

	d	h		d	h
Aug.	1	24	Aug.	16	23
Sept.	1	22	Sept.	15	21
Oct.	1	20	Oct.	16	19

Draco, Cepheus, Lyra, Cygnus, Vulpecula, Sagitta, Delphinus, Equuleus, Aquila, Aquarius and Capricornus.

MINIMA OF ALGOL

d	h	d	h
3	2	17	10
5	23	20	7
8	20	23	4
11	17	26	1
14	14	28	22

PHASES OF THE MOON

		d	h	m
●	New Moon	4	07	10
☽	First Quarter	11	07	41
○	Full Moon	18	05	34
☾	Last Quarter	26	03	17

		d	h
Perigee (369,820 kilometres)		12	00
Apogee (404,330 ,,)		25	10

Mean Longitude of Ascending Node on September 1, 23°.

See note on *Summer Time*, p. 98.

MONTHLY NOTES

Sept. 1. Partridge shooting begins.

      6. Islamic New Year (A.H. 1407).

     29. Michaelmas. Quarter day.

** Centenary.

Day	Right Ascension	Dec.	Equation of Time	Rise 52°	Rise 56°	Transit	Set 52°	Set 56°	Sidereal Time	Transit of First Point of Aries
	h m s	° ′	m s	h m	h m	h m	h m	h m	h m s	h m s
1	10 39 40	+8 28	− 0 13	5 10	5 02	12 00	18 49	18 57	22 39 27	1 20 19
2	10 43 17	+8 06	+ 0 06	5 12	5 04	12 00	18 47	18 54	22 43 24	1 16 23
3	10 46 55	+7 45	+ 0 25	5 13	5 06	11 59	18 45	18 52	22 47 20	1 12 27
4	10 50 32	+7 23	+ 0 45	5 15	5 08	11 59	18 42	18 49	22 51 17	1 08 31
5	10 54 09	+7 00	+ 1 05	5 16	5 10	11 59	18 40	18 46	22 55 13	1 04 36
6	10 57 45	+6 38	+ 1 24	5 18	5 12	11 58	18 38	18 44	22 59 10	1 00 40
7	11 01 22	+6 16	+ 1 45	5 20	5 14	11 58	18 36	18 41	23 03 07	0 56 44
8	11 04 58	+5 53	+ 2 05	5 22	5 16	11 58	18 33	18 39	23 07 03	0 52 48
9	11 08 34	+5 31	+ 2 26	5 23	5 18	11 57	18 31	18 36	23 11 00	0 48 52
10	11 12 10	+5 08	+ 2 46	5 25	5 20	11 57	18 28	18 33	23 14 56	0 44 56
11	11 15 45	+4 45	+ 3 07	5 26	5 22	11 57	18 26	18 31	23 18 53	0 41 00
12	11 19 21	+4 23	+ 3 28	5 28	5 24	11 56	18 24	18 28	23 22 49	0 37 04
13	11 22 56	+4 00	+ 3 49	5 30	5 26	11 56	18 22	18 25	23 26 46	0 33 08
14	11 26 32	+3 37	+ 4 11	5 31	5 28	11 56	18 19	18 23	23 30 42	0 29 12
15	11 30 07	+3 14	+ 4 32	5 33	5 30	11 55	18 17	18 20	23 34 39	0 25 16
16	11 33 42	+2 51	+ 4 53	5 35	5 32	11 55	18 15	18 17	23 38 36	0 21 21
17	11 37 17	+2 27	+ 5 15	5 36	5 34	11 55	18 12	18 15	23 42 32	0 17 25
18	11 40 52	+2 04	+ 5 36	5 38	5 36	11 54	18 10	18 12	23 46 29	0 13 29
19	11 44 27	+1 41	+ 5 58	5 40	5 38	11 54	18 08	18 09	23 50 25	0 09 33
20	11 48 02	+1 18	+ 6 19	5 41	5 39	11 54	18 05	18 07	23 54 22	0 05 37
21	11 51 38	+0 54	+ 6 41	5 43	5 41	11 53	18 03	18 04	23 58 18	{ 0 01 41 / 23 57 45
22	11 55 13	+0 31	+ 7 02	5 44	5 43	11 53	18 00	18 01	0 02 15	23 53 49
23	11 58 48	+0 08	+ 7 23	5 46	5 45	11 52	17 58	17 59	0 06 11	23 49 53
24	12 02 24	−0 16	+ 7 44	5 48	5 47	11 52	17 56	17 56	0 10 08	23 45 57
25	12 05 59	−0 39	+ 8 05	5 49	5 49	11 52	17 54	17 53	0 14 05	23 42 01
26	12 09 35	−1 02	+ 8 26	5 51	5 51	11 51	17 51	17 51	0 18 01	23 38 06
27	12 13 11	−1 26	+ 8 46	5 53	5 53	11 51	17 49	17 48	0 21 58	23 34 10
28	12 16 47	−1 49	+ 9 07	5 54	5 55	11 51	17 46	17 45	0 25 54	23 30 14
29	12 20 24	−2 12	+ 9 27	5 56	5 57	11 50	17 44	17 43	0 29 51	23 26 18
30	12 24 01	−2 36	+ 9 47	5 58	5 59	11 50	17 42	17 40	0 33 47	23 22 22

THE SUN   s.d. 15′·9

Duration of Civil (C), Nautical (N), and Astronomical (A), Twilight (in minutes)

Lat. °	Sept. 1 C	N	A	Sept. 11 C	N	A	Sept. 21 C	N	A	Sept. 30 C	N	A
52	35	79	127	34	76	120	34	74	115	34	73	113
56	39	89	146	38	84	135	37	82	129	37	80	126

ASTRONOMICAL NOTES

MERCURY is unsuitably placed for observation throughout the month, superior conjunction occuring on the 5th.

VENUS is a magnificent object in the early evenings for a short while after sunset, its magnitude being −4·2. The thin crescent Moon passes 3° N. of the planet on the evening of the 7th. Venus gets too close to the Sun for observation by the middle of the month.

MARS, magnitude −1, continues to be visible in the south-western skies in the evenings, still in the constellation of Sagittarius. The gibbous Moon is near Mars on the evenings of the 12th and 13th.

JUPITER, magnitude −2·4, reaches opposition on the 10th and thus is observable throughout the hours of darkness. The Full Moon is near the planet on the 17th.

SATURN, magnitude +0·8, is still visible low above the south-western horizon in the early evening, but is now approaching the end of its period of visibility.

ZODIACAL LIGHT. The morning cone may be seen stretching up from the eastern horizon before the beginning of morning twilight from the 3rd to the 16th.

THE MOON

Day	R.A.	Dec.	Hor. Par.	Semi-diam.	Sun's Co-long.	P.A. of Bright Limb	Phase	Age	Rise 52°	Rise 56°	Tran-sit	Set 52°	Set 56°
	h m	°	′	′	°	°		d	h m	h m	h m	h m	h m
1	8 11	+25·3	55·1	15·0	234	109	11	26·2	1 07	0 37	9 52	18 18	18 42
2	9 03	+21·9	55·6	15·2	247	116	6	27·2	2 24	2 02	10 41	18 36	18 54
3	9 53	+17·4	56·2	15·3	259	125	2	28·2	3 41	3 28	11 28	18 51	19 03
4	10 42	+12·1	56·8	15·5	271	156	0	29·2	5 05	4 55	12 14	19 03	19 09
5	11 30	+ 6·1	57·3	15·6	283	276	1	0·7	6 25	6 21	12 59	19 14	19 15
6	12 18	− 0·3	57·8	15·8	296	289	3	1·7	7 46	7 48	13 44	19 25	19 21
7	13 06	− 6·7	58·3	15·9	308	292	8	2·7	9 09	9 17	14 31	19 38	19 27
8	13 56	−12·9	58·7	16·0	320	291	16	3·7	10 35	10 50	15 21	19 53	19 36
9	14 50	−18·5	58·9	16·1	332	288	25	4·7	12 04	12 27	16 14	20 13	19 49
10	15 47	−23·2	59·1	16·1	344	284	35	5·7	13 34	14 05	17 12	20 43	20 11
11	16 47	−26·6	59·3	16·1	357	278	46	6·7	14 56	15 35	18 13	21 27	20 49
12	17 51	−28·2	59·3	16·2	9	270	58	7·7	16 04	16 43	19 16	22 31	21 52
13	18 55	−28·0	59·3	16·1	21	263	69	8·7	16 52	17 26	20 18	23 51	23 18
14	19 58	−26·0	59·1	16·1	33	255	79	9·7	17 24	17 50	21 17	. .	. .
15	20 58	−22·3	58·9	16·0	45	248	87	10·7	17 46	18 04	22 11	1 20	0 55
16	21 53	−17·4	58·5	16·0	58	242	94	11·7	18 02	18 14	23 01	2 49	2 32
17	22 45	−11·7	58·1	15·8	70	235	98	12·7	18 15	18 21	23 47	4 14	4 05
18	23 34	− 5·5	57·5	15·7	82	205	100	13·7	18 25	18 26	. .	5 36	5 33
19	0 21	+ 0·8	56·9	15·5	94	75	99	14·7	18 36	18 31	0 32	6 55	6 57
20	1 07	+ 6·9	56·3	15·3	106	68	97	15·7	18 47	18 37	1 15	8 13	8 21
21	1 53	+12·6	55·7	15·2	118	70	92	16·7	19 00	18 44	1 59	9 30	9 44
22	2 40	+17·7	55·2	15·0	131	70	86	17·7	19 16	18 54	2 43	10 47	11 07
23	3 29	+22·0	54·7	14·9	143	74	78	18·7	19 37	19 09	3 30	12 03	12 30
24	4 19	+25·3	54·4	14·8	155	79	70	19·7	20 06	19 32	4 18	13 15	13 49
25	5 12	+27·5	54·2	14·8	167	84	61	20·7	20 47	20 08	5 08	14 19	14 58
26	6 05	+28·4	54·3	14·8	179	90	51	21·7	21 41	21 03	6 00	15 12	15 50
27	6 59	+28·0	54·4	14·8	192	97	42	22·7	22 47	22 14	6 51	15 52	16 26
28	7 52	+26·3	54·8	14·9	204	103	33	23·7	. .	23 36	7 42	16 21	16 48
29	8 45	+23·3	55·3	15·1	216	108	24	24·7	0 02	. .	8 32	16 41	17 02
30	9 35	+19·2	55·9	15·2	228	113	16	25·7	1 21	1 02	9 19	16 57	17 12

MERCURY ☿

Day	R.A.	Dec. +	Diam.	Phase	Tran-sit		Day	R.A.	Dec.	Diam.	Phase	Tran-sit	
	h m	°	″		h m			h m	°	″		h m	
1	10 25	11·8	5	98	11 47		16	12 07	+ 0·2	5	97	12 30	
4	10 47	9·6	5	100	11 57	Mercury is too	19	12 25	− 2·1	5	95	12 36	Mercury is too
7	11 08	7·3	5	100	12 07	close to the	22	12 43	− 4·4	5	93	12 42	close to the
10	11 29	5·0	5	99	12 15	Sun for	25	13 00	− 6·5	5	91	12 47	Sun for
13	11 48	2·6	5	98	12 23	observation	28	13 17	− 8·7	5	89	12 52	observation
16	12 07	0·2	5	97	12 30		31	13 34	−10·7	5	87	12 57	

VENUS ♀ / MARS ♂

Day	R.A.	Dec. −	Diam.	Phase	Tran-sit	5° high. 52°	5° high. 56°	Day	R.A.	Dec. −	Diam.	Phase	Tran-sit	5° high. 52°	5° high. 56°
	h m	°	″		h m	h m	h m		h m	°	″		h m	h m	h m
1	13 26	11·8	26	46	14 46	19 07	18 52	1	19 03	27·5	18	90	20 21	22 39	21 37
6	13 42	14·0	28	43	14 43	18 50	18 32	6	19 09	27·1	17	89	20 08	22 30	21 32
11	13 58	16·0	29	40	14 39	18 33	18 12	11	19 16	26·7	16	89	19 56	22 23	21 29
16	14 13	17·9	31	37	14 34	18 15	17 51	16	19 25	26·2	15	88	19 44	22 17	21 27
21	14 27	19·6	34	33	14 28	17 56	17 29	21	19 34	25·7	15	87	19 34	22 12	21 26
26	14 39	21·1	37	30	14 20	17 37	17 07	26	19 44	25·1	14	87	19 24	22 09	21 25
31	14 49	22·4	40	26	14 10	17 17	16 43	31	19 54	24·4	14	86	19 15	22 06	21 26

Day	SUNRISE AND SUNSET													
	London		Bristol		Birmingham		Manchester		Newcastle		Glasgow		Belfast	
	a.m.	p.m.	a.m.	p.m.	a.m.	p.m.	a.m.	p.m.	a.m.	p.m.	a.m.	p.m.	a.m.	p.m.
	h m	h m	h m	h m	h m	h m	h m	h m	h m	h m	h m	h m	h m	h m
1	5 11	6 48	5 21	6 58	5 16	6 57	5 16	7 01	5 10	7 01	5 19	7 14	5 29	7 18
2	5 13	6 46	5 23	6 56	5 18	6 55	5 18	6 58	5 12	6 58	5 21	7 11	5 31	7 15
3	5 14	6 44	5 24	6 54	5 19	6 53	5 20	6 56	5 14	6 56	5 23	7 09	5 33	7 13
4	5 16	6 42	5 26	6 51	5 21	6 50	5 22	6 54	5 16	6 53	5 25	7 06	5 35	7 11
5	5 17	6 39	5 27	6 49	5 22	6 48	5 23	6 51	5 18	6 50	5 27	7 03	5 36	7 08
6	5 19	6 37	5 29	6 47	5 24	6 46	5 25	6 49	5 20	6 48	5 29	7 01	5 38	7 06
7	5 21	6 35	5 31	6 45	5 26	6 43	5 27	6 46	5 22	6 45	5 31	6 58	5 40	7 03
8	5 23	6 33	5 33	6 42	5 28	6 41	5 29	6 44	5 24	6 43	5 33	6 56	5 42	7 01
9	5 24	6 31	5 34	6 40	5 30	6 38	5 31	6 41	5 26	6 40	5 35	6 53	5 44	6 58
10	5 26	6 28	5 36	6 37	5 31	6 36	5 32	6 39	5 27	6 38	5 37	6 50	5 45	6 56
11	5 27	6 26	5 37	6 35	5 33	6 33	5 34	6 36	5 29	6 35	5 39	6 48	5 47	6 53
12	5 29	6 24	5 39	6 33	5 35	6 31	5 36	6 34	5 31	6 33	5 41	6 45	5 49	6 51
13	5 30	6 22	5 40	6 31	5 37	6 29	5 38	6 32	5 33	6 30	5 43	6 42	5 51	6 48
14	5 32	6 19	5 42	6 29	5 38	6 26	5 39	6 29	5 35	6 28	5 45	6 40	5 53	6 46
15	5 33	6 17	5 43	6 27	5 40	6 24	5 41	6 27	5 37	6 25	5 47	6 37	5 55	6 43
16	5 35	6 15	5 45	6 24	5 42	6 22	5 43	6 25	5 39	6 22	5 49	6 34	5 57	6 40
17	5 36	6 12	5 46	6 22	5 43	6 19	5 44	6 22	5 41	6 20	5 51	6 32	5 59	6 38
18	5 38	6 10	5 48	6 20	5 45	6 17	5 46	6 20	5 43	6 17	5 53	6 29	6 01	6 35
19	5 40	6 08	5 50	6 18	5 47	6 15	5 48	6 17	5 44	6 14	5 55	6 26	6 02	6 32
20	5 41	6 05	5 51	6 15	5 48	6 12	5 49	6 15	5 46	6 12	5 56	6 24	6 04	6 30
21	5 43	6 03	5 53	6 13	5 50	6 10	5 51	6 12	5 48	6 09	5 58	6 21	6 06	6 27
22	5 44	6 00	5 54	6 10	5 51	6 07	5 53	6 10	5 50	6 07	6 00	6 18	6 08	6 25
23	5 46	5 58	5 56	6 08	5 53	6 05	5 55	6 07	5 52	6 04	6 02	6 16	6 10	6 22
24	5 48	5 56	5 58	6 06	5 55	6 03	5 56	6 05	5 53	6 02	6 04	6 13	6 11	6 20
25	5 49	5 54	5 59	6 04	5 56	6 01	5 58	6 02	5 55	5 59	6 06	6 10	6 13	6 17
26	5 51	5 51	6 01	6 01	5 58	5 58	6 00	6 00	5 57	5 57	6 08	6 08	6 15	6 15
27	5 53	5 49	6 03	5 59	6 00	5 56	6 02	5 57	5 59	5 54	6 10	6 05	6 17	6 12
28	5 54	5 46	6 04	5 56	6 01	5 53	6 04	5 55	6 01	5 52	6 12	6 02	6 19	6 10
29	5 56	5 44	6 06	5 54	6 03	5 51	6 05	5 52	6 02	5 49	6 14	6 00	6 20	6 07
30	5 58	5 42	6 08	5 52	6 05	5 49	6 07	5 50	6 04	5 47	6 16	5 57	6 22	6 05

JUPITER ♃   SATURN ♄

Day	R.A.	Dec. −	Transit	5° high.		R.A.	Dec. −	Transit	5° high.	
				52°	56°				52°	56°
	h m	°	h m	h m	h m	h m	°	h m	h m	h m
1	23 23	5·7	0 43	5 39	5 31	16 08	19·2	17 25	20 59	20 33
11	23 18	6·2	23 54	4 53	4 44	16 09	19·3	16 48	20 20	19 55
21	23 13	6·7	23 10	4 06	3 56	16 12	19·4	16 11	19 43	19 17
31	23 08	7·2	22 27	3 19	3 10	16 15	19·6	15 35	19 05	18 39

Equatorial diameter of Jupiter 50″; of Saturn 16″. Diameters of Saturn's rings 37″ and 16″.

URANUS ♅   NEPTUNE ♆

Day	R.A.	Dec. −	Transit		R.A.	Dec. −	Transit	10° high.	
								52°	56°
	h m	° ′	h m		h m	°	h m	h m	h m
1	17 9·4	23 02	18 27	Uranus is	18 13·4	22 20	19 31	21 46	20 47
11	17 9·7	23 02	17 48	too close to	18 13·2	22 20	18 51	21 06	20 07
21	17 10·4	23 03	17 09	the Sun for	18 13·2	22 21	18 12	20 27	19 28
31	17 11·5	23 05	16 31	observation	18 13·5	22 21	17 33	19 48	18 49
	Diameter 4″				Diameter 2″				

DAY OF		
Month	**Week**	

Octo (eight), 8th month
of Roman (pre-Julian)
Calendar.

Sun's Longitude 210° ♏ 23ᵈ 17ʰ

1	W.	MICHAELMAS LAW SITTINGS BEGIN.
2	Th.	Mahatma Gandhi b. 1869. Archbp. Runcie b. 1921.
3	F.	Eleanora Duse b. 1858. William Morris d. 1896.
4	S.	Rembrandt d. 1669.
5	☉.	**19th S. after Trinity.** R101 disaster 1930.
6	M.	William Tyndale exec. 1536. Jenny Lind b. 1820
7	Tu.	Archbp. Laud b. 1573. Edgar Allen Poe d. 1849.
8	W.	Henry Fielding d. 1754. Earl Attlee d. 1967.
9	Th.	Saint-Saëns b. 1835. Alfred Dreyfus b. 1859.
10	F.	Giuseppe Verdi b. 1813. Fridtjof Nansen b. 1861.
11	S.	Camperdown 1797. Jean Cocteau d. 1963.
12	☉.	**20th S. after Trinity.** Edward VI b. 1537.
13	M.	Lillie Langtry b. 1852. Margaret Thatcher b. 1925.
14	Tu.	Hastings 1066. Katherine Mansfield b. 1888.
15	W.	Nietzsche b. 1844. P. G. Wodehouse b. 1882.
16	Th.	Oscar Wilde b. 1856. David Ben-Gurion b. 1886.**
17	F.	Sir Philip Sidney d. 1586.** Saratoga 1777.
18	S.	**St. Luke.** Canaletto b. 1697.
19	☉.	**21st S. after Trinity.** John I d. 1216.
20	M.	Sir Christopher Wren b. 1632. Lord Palmerston b. 1784.
21	Tu.	S. T. Coleridge b. 1772. Trafalgar 1805.
22	W.	Franz Liszt b. 1811. Sarah Bernhardt b. 1844.
23	Th.	Edgehill 1642. El Alamein 1942.
24	F.	Peace of Westphalia 1648.
25	S.	Agincourt 1415. Balaclava 1854.
26	☉.	**22nd S. after Trinity.** Trotsky b. 1879.
27	M.	Capt. Cook b. 1728. Dylan Thomas b. 1914.
28	Tu.	**SS. Simon and Jude.** Statue of Liberty unveiled 1886.**
29	W.	Sir Walter Raleigh exec. 1618.
30	Th.	R. B. Sheridan b. 1751. Ezra Pound b. 1885.
31	F.	Hallowmass Eve. Chiang Kai Shek b. 1887.

PHENOMENA

October 1ᵈ 10ʰ Venus at greatest brilliancy.

5ᵈ 07ʰ Mercury in conjunction with the Moon. Mercury 0°·4 S.

6ᵈ 10ʰ Venus in conjunction with the Moon. Venus 4° S.

7ᵈ 18ʰ Saturn in conjunction with the Moon. Saturn 5° N.

11ᵈ 13ʰ Mars in conjunction with the Moon. Mars 2° N.

14ᵈ 16ʰ Jupiter in conjunction with the Moon. Jupiter 1°·9 N.

18ᵈ 14ʰ Mercury in conjunction with Venus. Mercury 4° N.

21ᵈ 22ʰ Mercury at greatest eastern elongation (24°).

CONSTELLATIONS

The following constellations are near the meridian at

	d	h		d	h
Sept. 1	24		Sept. 15	23	
Oct. 1	22		Oct. 16	21	
Nov. 1	20		Nov. 15	19	

Ursa Major (below the Pole), Cepheus, Cassiopeia, Cygnus, Lacerta, Andromeda, Pegasus, Capricornus, Aquarius and Piscis Austrinus.

MINIMA OF ALGOL

d	h	d	h
1	18	18	23
4	15	21	20
7	12	24	17
10	9	27	14
13	6	30	11
16	3		

PHASES OF THE MOON

	d	h	m
● New Moon	3	18	55
☽ First Quarter	10	13	28
○ Full Moon	17	19	22
☾ Last Quarter	25	22	26

	d	h
Perigee (367,200 kilometres)	7	10
Apogee (405,070　„　)	23	06

Mean Longitude of Ascending Node on October 1, 21°.

MONTHLY NOTES

Oct.　1. Pheasant shooting begins.

4. Jewish New Year (A.M. 5747).

13. Jewish Day of Atonement (Yom Kippur).

18. First Day of Tabernacles.

26. *Summer Time* ends at 01ʰ G.M.T.

**Centenary.

Day	Right Ascension	Dec. −	Equation of Time	Rise 52°	Rise 56°	Transit	Set 52°	Set 56°	Sidereal Time	Transit of First Point of Aries
	h m s	° ′	m s	h m	h m	h m	h m	h m	h m s	h m s
1	12 27 38	2 59	+10 06	5 59	6 01	11 50	17 40	17 38	0 37 44	23 18 26
2	12 31 15	3 22	+10 25	6 01	6 03	11 49	17 37	17 35	0 41 40	23 14 30
3	12 34 52	3 46	+10 44	6 03	6 05	11 49	17 35	17 32	0 45 37	23 10 34
4	12 38 30	4 09	+11 03	6 04	6 07	11 49	17 33	17 30	0 49 34	23 06 38
5	12 42 09	4 32	+11 21	6 06	6 09	11 49	17 30	17 27	0 53 30	23 02 42
6	12 45 47	4 55	+11 39	6 08	6 11	11 48	17 28	17 24	0 57 27	22 58 46
7	12 49 26	5 18	+11 57	6 09	6 13	11 48	17 26	17 22	1 01 23	22 54 51
8	12 53 05	5 41	+12 14	6 11	6 15	11 48	17 24	17 19	1 05 20	22 50 55
9	12 56 45	6 04	+12 31	6 13	6 17	11 47	17 22	17 19	1 09 16	22 46 59
10	13 00 25	6 27	+12 47	6 14	6 19	11 47	17 19	17 14	1 13 13	22 43 03
11	13 04 06	6 50	+13 03	6 16	6 21	11 47	17 17	17 12	1 17 09	22 39 07
12	13 07 47	7 12	+13 19	6 18	6 23	11 47	17 14	17 09	1 21 06	22 35 11
13	13 11 28	7 35	+13 34	6 20	6 25	11 46	17 12	17 07	1 25 03	22 31 15
14	13 15 10	7 57	+13 48	6 21	6 27	11 46	17 10	17 04	1 28 59	22 27 19
15	13 18 53	8 20	+14 02	6 23	6 29	11 46	17 08	17 02	1 32 56	22 23 23
16	13 22 36	8 42	+14 16	6 25	6 31	11 46	17 06	16 59	1 36 52	22 19 27
17	13 26 20	9 04	+14 29	6 27	6 33	11 45	17 04	16 56	1 40 49	22 15 31
18	13 30 04	9 26	+14 41	6 28	6 36	11 45	17 01	16 54	1 44 45	22 11 36
19	13 33 49	9 48	+14 53	6 30	6 38	11 45	16 59	16 52	1 48 42	22 07 40
20	13 37 34	10 09	+15 04	6 32	6 40	11 45	16 57	16 49	1 52 38	22 03 44
21	13 41 20	10 31	+15 15	6 34	6 42	11 45	16 55	16 47	1 56 35	21 59 48
22	13 45 07	10 52	+15 24	6 35	6 44	11 45	16 53	16 44	2 00 32	21 55 52
23	13 48 54	11 13	+15 33	6 37	6 46	11 44	16 51	16 42	2 04 28	21 51 56
24	13 52 43	11 34	+15 42	6 39	6 48	11 44	16 49	16 40	2 08 25	21 48 00
25	13 56 31	11 55	+15 50	6 41	6 50	11 44	16 47	16 37	2 12 21	21 44 04
26	14 00 21	12 16	+15 57	6 42	6 52	11 44	16 45	16 35	2 16 18	21 40 08
27	14 04 11	12 36	+16 03	6 44	6 54	11 44	16 43	16 32	2 20 14	21 36 12
28	14 08 02	12 57	+16 09	6 46	6 57	11 44	16 41	16 30	2 24 11	21 32 16
29	14 11 54	13 17	+16 14	6 48	6 59	11 44	16 39	16 28	2 28 07	21 28 21
30	14 15 47	13 37	+16 17	6 50	7 01	11 44	16 37	16 26	2 32 04	21 24 25
31	14 19 40	13 56	+16 20	6 51	7 03	11 44	16 35	16 23	2 36 01	21 20 29

Duration of Civil (C), Nautical (N), and Astronomical (A), Twilight (in minutes)

Lat. °	Oct. 1 C	N	A	Oct. 11 C	N	A	Oct. 21 C	N	A	Oct. 31 C	N	A
52	34	73	113	34	73	112	34	74	113	36	75	114
56	37	80	125	37	80	124	38	81	124	40	83	126

ASTRONOMICAL NOTES

MERCURY is unsuitably placed for observation throughout October.

VENUS is unsuitably placed for observation. Although it is still almost 40° from the Sun at the beginning of the month its low declination (−23°) completely nullifies this apparently favourable elongation as seen from the latitudes of the British Isles.

MARS, magnitude −0·5, is now two magnitudes fainter than when at opposition in July. It is still visible low in the south-western sky in the evenings. During October Mars moves from Sagittarius into Capricornus. The Moon, near First Quarter, is near Mars on the evenings of the 10th and 11th.

JUPITER, magnitude −2·3, is a brilliant object in the southern skies for the greater part of the night,

though by the end of the month it is not visible after 01ʰ. The gibbous Moon is near the planet on the 14th, passing 2° S. of it shortly before sunset. The four Galilean satellites are readily observable with any small telescope, or even a good pair of binoculars provided that they are held rigidly.

SATURN, magnitude +0·8, may still be glimpsed for a short while in the early evenings low above the south-western horizon, early in the month: thereafter it disappears from view in the twilight.

ECLIPSE. An annular-total eclipse of the Sun occurs on the 3rd. See page 148 for details.

ECLIPSE. A total eclipse of the Moon occurs on the 17th, visible from the British Isles. See page 148 for details.

THE MOON

Day	R.A.	Dec.	Hor. Par.	Semi-diam.	Sun's Co-long.	P.A. of Bright Limb	Phase	Age	Rise 52°	Rise 56°	Transit	Set 52°	Set 56°
	h m	°	′	′	°	°		d	h m	h m	h m	h m	h m
1	10 25	+14·2	56·7	15·4	240	117	9	26·7	2 41	2 28	10 06	17 10	17 19
2	11 13	+ 8·4	57·4	15·6	253	120	4	27·7	4 02	3 55	10 51	17 22	17 25
3	12 01	+ 2·0	58·1	15·8	265	124	1	28·7	5 23	5 23	11 37	17 33	17 30
4	12 50	− 4·6	58·7	16·0	277	278	0	0·2	6 47	6 53	12 24	17 45	17 37
5	13 40	−11·1	59·2	16·1	289	293	2	1·2	8 15	8 27	13 14	17 59	17 44
6	14 34	−17·1	59·6	16·2	302	292	6	2·2	9 45	10 06	14 07	18 17	17 56
7	15 31	−22·2	59·7	16·3	314	287	13	3·2	11 18	11 47	15 05	18 44	18 14
8	16 32	−26·0	59·7	16·3	326	281	22	4·2	12 46	13 23	16 07	19 24	18 46
9	17 36	−28·1	59·5	16·2	338	274	32	5·2	13 59	14 40	17 10	20 22	19 41
10	18 41	−28·3	59·3	16·2	350	267	44	6·2	14 53	15 29	18 13	21 38	21 02
11	19 44	−26·7	58·9	16·1	2	259	55	7·2	15 29	15 57	19 12	23 04	22 36
12	20 44	−23·4	58·6	16·0	15	253	66	8·2	15 53	16 14	20 06	. .	. .
13	21 39	−18·9	58·1	15·8	27	248	76	9·2	16 10	16 24	20 56	0 31	0 12
14	22 31	−13·4	57·7	15·7	39	245	85	10·2	16 23	16 31	21 43	1 56	1 44
15	23 20	− 7·5	57·2	15·6	51	243	92	11·2	16 34	16 36	22 27	3 18	3 12
16	0 06	− 1·3	56·7	15·5	63	242	97	12·2	16 44	16 41	23 10	4 36	4 36
17	0 52	+ 4·9	56·2	15·3	76	243	99	13·2	16 54	16 47	23 53	5 54	5 59
18	1 38	+10·7	55·7	15·2	88	56	100	14·2	17 06	16 53	. .	7 10	7 21
19	2 24	+16·1	55·3	15·1	100	65	99	15·2	17 20	17 02	0 37	8 27	8 45
20	3 12	+20·7	54·8	14·9	112	69	95	16·2	17 39	17 14	1 22	9 44	10 08
21	4 02	+24·3	54·5	14·8	124	74	90	17·2	18 05	17 33	2 10	10 58	11 30
22	4 54	+26·9	54·2	14·8	136	80	84	18·2	18 41	18 03	3 00	12 07	12 44
23	5 47	+28·2	54·1	14·8	148	86	77	19·2	19 29	18 50	3 51	13 05	13 44
24	6 41	+28·3	54·2	14·8	161	92	68	20·2	20 31	19 55	4 42	13 49	14 25
25	7 34	+27·0	54·4	14·8	173	98	59	21·2	21 41	21 12	5 33	14 22	14 52
26	8 26	+24·5	54·8	14·9	185	104	50	22·2	22 57	22 35	6 23	14 45	15 09
27	9 17	+20·9	55·3	15·1	197	109	40	23·2	. .	. .	7 10	15 03	15 20
28	10 06	+16·2	56·0	15·3	209	112	30	24·2	0 16	0 00	7 56	15 16	15 28
29	10 53	+10·8	56·8	15·5	222	115	21	25·2	1 35	1 25	8 41	15 28	15 34
30	11 41	+ 4·7	57·7	15·7	234	116	13	26·2	2 55	2 52	9 26	15 39	15 39
31	12 29	− 1·8	58·6	16·0	246	115	7	27·2	4 17	4 20	10 12	15 50	15 45

MERCURY ☿

Day	R.A.	Dec. −	Diam.	Phase	Transit		Day	R.A.	Dec. −	Diam.	Phase	Transit	
	h m	°	″		h m			h m	°	″		h m	
1	13 34	10·7	5	87	12 57		16	14 51	19·0	6	72	13 15	
4	13 50	12·6	5	84	13 01	Mercury is too	19	15 05	20·2	6	68	13 16	Mercury is too
7	14 06	14·4	5	82	13 05	close to the	22	15 18	21·2	7	62	13 17	close to the
10	14 21	16·1	6	79	13 09	Sun for	25	15 29	22·0	7	56	13 16	Sun for
13	14 36	17·6	6	76	13 12	observation	28	15 38	22·5	8	48	13 13	observation
16	14 51	19·0	6	72	13 15		31	15 44	22·7	8	39	13 06	

VENUS ♀   MARS ♂

Day	R.A.	Dec. −	Diam.	Phase	Transit	5° high 52°	5° high 56°	Day	R.A.	Dec. +	Diam.	Phase	Transit	5° high 52°	5° high 56°
	h m	°	″		h m	h m	h m		h m	°	″		h m	h m	h m
1	14 49	22·4	40	26	14 10	17 17	16 43	1	19 54	24·4	14	86	19 15	22 06	21 26
6	14 57	23·4	43	22	13 58	16 56	16 19	6	20 05	23·7	13	86	19 06	22 04	21 27
11	15 02	24·1	47	18	13 43	16 35	15 55	11	20 16	22·9	12	86	18 58	22 03	21 28
16	15 04	24·5	51	13	13 25	16 14	15 33	16	20 28	22·1	12	85	18 50	22 02	21 30
21	15 01	24·3	55	8	13 02	15 53	15 14	21	20 40	21·1	11	85	18 42	22 02	21 33
26	14 55	23·6	58	4	12 36	15 34	14 57	26	20 52	20·2	11	85	18 35	22 02	21 35
31	14 46	22·4	61	1	12 07	15 17	14 44	31	21 04	19·1	11	85	18 27	22 03	21 38

SUNRISE AND SUNSET

Day	London a.m. h m	London p.m. h m	Bristol a.m. h m	Bristol p.m. h m	Birmingham a.m. h m	Birmingham p.m. h m	Manchester a.m. h m	Manchester p.m. h m	Newcastle a.m. h m	Newcastle p.m. h m	Glasgow a.m. h m	Glasgow p.m. h m	Belfast a.m. h m	Belfast p.m. h m
1	5 59	5 40	6 09	5 50	6 06	5 47	6 09	5 48	6 06	5 45	6 18	5 55	6 24	6 03
2	6 01	5 37	6 11	5 47	6 08	5 44	6 11	5 45	6 08	5 42	6 20	5 52	6 26	6 00
3	6 03	5 35	6 13	5 45	6 10	5 42	6 13	5 43	6 10	5 39	6 22	5 49	6 28	5 57
4	6 04	5 33	6 14	5 43	6 11	5 40	6 14	5 41	6 12	5 37	6 24	5 47	6 30	5 55
5	6 06	5 31	6 16	5 41	6 13	5 37	6 16	5 38	6 14	5 34	6 26	5 44	6 32	5 52
6	6 08	5 29	6 17	5 39	6 15	5 35	6 18	5 36	6 16	5 31	6 28	5 41	6 34	5 49
7	6 09	5 26	6 19	5 36	6 16	5 33	6 19	5 34	6 18	5 29	6 30	5 39	6 36	5 47
8	6 11	5 24	6 20	5 34	6 18	5 30	6 21	5 31	6 20	5 26	6 32	5 36	6 38	5 44
9	6 13	5 22	6 22	5 32	6 20	5 28	6 23	5 29	6 22	5 24	6 34	5 34	6 40	5 42
10	6 14	5 20	6 23	5 30	6 22	5 26	6 25	5 27	6 24	5 22	6 36	5 31	6 42	5 40
11	6 16	5 18	6 25	5 28	6 24	5 23	6 27	5 24	6 26	5 19	6 38	5 29	6 44	5 37
12	6 18	5 15	6 27	5 25	6 25	5 21	6 28	5 22	6 27	5 17	6 40	5 26	6 45	5 35
13	6 19	5 13	6 29	5 23	6 27	5 19	6 30	5 20	6 29	5 15	6 42	5 24	6 47	5 33
14	6 21	5 11	6 30	5 21	6 29	5 16	6 32	5 17	6 31	5 12	6 44	5 21	6 49	5 30
15	6 22	5 09	6 32	5 19	6 31	5 14	6 34	5 15	6 33	5 10	6 46	5 19	6 51	5 28
16	6 24	5 07	6 34	5 17	6 33	5 12	6 36	5 12	6 35	5 07	6 48	5 16	6 53	5 25
17	6 26	5 05	6 36	5 15	6 35	5 10	6 38	5 10	6 37	5 04	6 50	5 13	6 55	5 23
18	6 27	5 02	6 37	5 12	6 36	5 07	6 40	5 08	6 40	5 02	6 53	5 11	6 57	5 21
19	6 29	5 00	6 39	5 10	6 38	5 05	6 42	5 06	6 42	5 00	6 55	5 09	6 59	5 19
20	6 31	4 58	6 41	5 08	6 40	5 03	6 44	5 03	6 44	4 57	6 57	5 06	7 01	5 16
21	6 33	4 56	6 43	5 06	6 42	5 01	6 46	5 01	6 46	4 55	6 59	5 04	7 03	5 14
22	6 34	4 54	6 44	5 04	6 43	4 59	6 47	4 59	6 47	4 53	7 01	5 01	7 05	5 11
23	6 36	4 52	6 46	5 02	6 45	4 57	6 49	4 56	6 49	4 50	7 03	4 59	7 07	5 09
24	6 38	4 50	6 48	5 00	6 47	4 55	6 51	4 54	6 51	4 48	7 05	4 57	7 09	5 07
25	6 40	4 48	6 50	4 58	6 49	4 53	6 53	4 52	6 53	4 46	7 07	4 54	7 11	5 04
26	6 41	4 46	6 51	4 56	6 50	4 51	6 55	4 50	6 55	4 44	7 09	4 52	7 13	5 02
27	6 43	4 44	6 53	4 54	6 52	4 49	6 57	4 48	6 57	4 41	7 11	4 49	7 15	5 00
28	6 45	4 42	6 55	4 52	6 54	4 47	6 59	4 46	7 00	4 39	7 14	4 47	7 17	4 58
29	6 47	4 40	6 57	4 50	6 56	4 45	7 01	4 44	7 02	4 37	7 16	4 45	7 19	4 56
30	6 49	4 38	6 59	4 48	6 58	4 43	7 03	4 42	7 04	4 35	7 18	4 43	7 21	4 54
31	6 51	4 36	7 00	4 46	6 59	4 41	7 04	4 40	7 06	4 33	7 20	4 41	7 23	4 52

JUPITER ♃   SATURN ♄

Day	R.A. h m	Dec. − °	Transit h m	5° high 52° h m	5° high 56° h m	R.A. h m	Dec. − °	Transit h m	
1	23 08	7·2	22 27	3 19	3 10	16 15	19·6	15 35	Saturn is too
11	23 04	7·6	21 43	2 34	2 24	16 19	19·8	14 59	close to the Sun
21	23 02	7·8	21 01	1 50	1 40	16 23	20·0	14 24	for observation
31	23 00	8·0	20 20	1 09	0 58	16 27	20·2	13 49	

Equatorial diameter of Jupiter 47″; of Saturn 15″. Diameters of Saturn's rings 35″ and 15″.

URANUS ♅   NEPTUNE ♆

Day	R.A. h m	Dec. − ° ′	Transit h m		R.A. h m	Dec. ° ′	Transit h m	
1	17 11·5	23 05	16 31	Uranus is too	18 13·5	22 21	17 33	Neptune is too
11	17 12·9	23 06	15 53	close to the Sun	18 14·0	22 21	16 54	close to the Sun
21	17 14·6	23 08	15 16	for observation	18 14·7	22 22	16 15	for observation
31	17 16·6	23 10	14 38		18 15·6	22 22	15 37	

Diameter 4″   Diameter 2″

Month	Week	*Novem* (nine), 9th month of Roman (pre-Julian) Calendar. *Sun's Longitude* 240° ♐ 22ᵈ 15ʰ

Novem (nine), 9th month of Roman (pre-Julian) Calendar.

Sun's Longitude 240° ♐ 22ᵈ 15ʰ

1	S.	**All Saints.** L. S. Lowry b. 1887.
2	♋.	**23rd S. after Trinity. All Souls.**
3	M.	Henry Ireton b. 1611. Henri Matisse d. 1954.
4	Tu.	Mendelssohn d. 1847. Wilfred Owen d. 1918.
5	W.	Guy Fawkes Night (1605). Inkerman 1854.
6	Th.	Peter Tchaikovsky d. 1893.
7	F.	Marie Curie b. 1867. October Revolution 1917.
8	S.	Edmund Halley b. 1656. Fred Archer d. 1886.**
9	♋.	**24th S. after Trinity.** Edward VII b. 1841.
10	M.	Martin Luther b. 1483. Schiller b. 1759.
11	Tu.	ARMISTICE DAY 1918. Prince of Condé d. 1686.**
12	W.	Mrs. Gaskell d. 1865. *Tirpitz* sunk 1944.
13	Th.	Edward III b. 1312. R. L. Stevenson b. 1850.
14	F.	PRINCE OF WALES b. 1948. Nehru b. 1889.
15	S.	W. F. Herschel b. 1738. Christoph Gluck d. 1787.
16	♋.	**25th S. after Trinity.** Henry III d. 1272.
17	M.	Viscount Montgomery of Alamein b. 1887.
18	Tu.	Carl von Weber b. 1786.** Chester A. Arthur d. 1886.**
19	W.	Charles I b. 1600. Franz Schubert d. 1828.
20	Th.	QUEEN'S WEDDING DAY 1947. Chatterton b. 1752.
21	F.	Voltaire b. 1694. André Gide b. 1869.
22	S.	George Eliot b. 1819. J. F. Kennedy assass. 1963.
23	♋.	**26th S. after Trinity.** Thomas Tallis d. 1585.
24	M.	Laurence Sterne b. 1713. Grace Darling b. 1815.
25	Tu.	Charles Kemble b. 1775. Andrew Carnegie b. 1835.
26	W	William Cowper b. 1731. Coventry Patmore d. 1896.
27	Th.	Anders Celsius b. 1701. Fanny Kemble b. 1809.
28	F.	William Blake b. 1757. Friedrich Engels b. 1820.
29	S.	Donizetti b. 1798. Louisa M. Alcott b. 1832.
30	♋.	**Advent Sunday.** Sir Winston Churchill b. 1874.

PHENOMENA

November 3ᵈ 14ʰ Mercury in conjunction with the Moon. Mercury 0°·8 N.

4ᵈ 07ʰ Saturn in conjunction with the Moon. Saturn 6° N.

5ᵈ 10ʰ Venus in inferior conjunction.

9ᵈ 00ʰ Mars in conjunction with the Moon. Mars 3° N.

10ᵈ 19ʰ Jupiter in conjunction with the Moon. Jupiter 2° N.

13ᵈ 04ʰ Mercury in inferior conjunction.

29ᵈ 11ʰ Venus in conjunction with the Moon. Venus 2° N.

30ᵈ 03ʰ Mercury at greatest western elongation (20°).

30ᵈ 09ʰ Mercury in conjunction with the Moon. Mercury 5° N.

CONSTELLATIONS

The following constellations are near the meridian at

	d h		d h
Oct. 1	24	Oct. 16	23
Nov. 1	22	Nov. 15	21
Dec. 1	20	Dec. 16	19

Ursa Major (below the Pole), Cepheus Cassiopeia, Andromeda, Pegasus, Pisces, Aquarius and Cetus.

MINIMA OF ALGOL

d	h	d	h
2	7	16	16
5	4	19	12
8	1	22	9
10	22	25	6
13	19	28	3

PHASES OF THE MOON

	d	h	m
● New Moon	2	06	02
☽ First Quarter	8	21	11
○ Full Moon	16	12	12
☾ Last Quarter	24	16	50

	d	h
Perigee (361,820 kilometres)	4	03
Apogee (406,030 „)	19	22

Mean Longitude of Ascending Node on November 1, 20°.

MONTHLY NOTES

Nov. 1. Fox-hunting begins.

    8. Lord Mayor's Show.

    9. Remembrance Sunday.

  11. Martinmas. Scottish Term Day.

  28. Removal Day, Scotland.

** Centenary.

Day	THE SUN s.d. 16′·2 Right Ascension	Dec. −	Equation of Time	Rise 52°	Rise 56°	Transit	Set 52°	Set 56°	Sidereal Time	Transit of First Point of Aries
	h m s	° ′	m s	h m	h m	h m	h m	h m	h m s	h m s
1	14 23 34	14 16	+16 23	6 53	7 05	11 44	16 33	16 21	2 39 57	21 16 33
2	14 27 29	14 35	+16 24	6 55	7 07	11 44	16 31	16 19	2 43 54	21 12 37
3	14 31 25	14 54	+16 25	6 57	7 09	11 44	16 30	16 17	2 47 50	21 08 41
4	14 35 22	15 13	+16 25	6 59	7 11	11 44	16 28	16 15	2 51 47	21 04 45
5	14 39 19	15 31	+16 24	7 00	7 14	11 44	16 26	16 13	2 55 43	21 00 49
6	14 43 17	15 50	+16 22	7 02	7 16	11 44	16 24	16 11	2 59 40	20 56 53
7	14 47 16	16 08	+16 20	7 04	7 18	11 44	16 23	16 09	3 03 36	20 52 57
8	14 51 16	16 25	+16 17	7 06	7 20	11 44	16 21	16 07	3 07 33	20 49 01
9	14 55 17	16 43	+16 13	7 08	7 22	11 44	16 19	16 05	3 11 30	20 45 06
10	14 59 18	17 00	+16 08	7 10	7 24	11 44	16 18	16 03	3 15 26	20 41 10
11	15 03 21	17 17	+16 02	7 11	7 26	11 44	16 16	16 01	3 19 23	20 37 14
12	15 07 24	17 33	+15 55	7 13	7 28	11 44	16 14	15 59	3 23 19	20 33 18
13	15 11 28	17 50	+15 48	7 15	7 30	11 44	16 13	15 57	3 27 16	20 29 22
14	15 15 33	18 06	+15 40	7 17	7 33	11 44	16 11	15 55	3 31 12	20 25 26
15	15 19 38	18 21	+15 30	7 18	7 35	11 45	16 10	15 54	3 35 09	20 21 30
16	15 23 45	18 36	+15 21	7 20	7 37	11 45	16 09	15 52	3 39 05	20 17 34
17	15 27 52	18 51	+15 10	7 22	7 39	11 45	16 07	15 50	3 43 02	20 13 38
18	15 32 00	19 06	+14 58	7 24	7 41	11 45	16 06	15 48	3 46 59	20 09 42
19	15 36 09	19 20	+14 46	7 25	7 43	11 45	16 05	15 47	3 50 55	20 05 46
20	15 40 19	19 34	+14 32	7 27	7 45	11 46	16 03	15 45	3 54 52	20 01 51
21	15 44 30	19 48	+14 18	7 29	7 47	11 46	16 02	15 44	3 58 48	19 57 55
22	15 48 41	20 01	+14 03	7 30	7 49	11 46	16 01	15 42	4 02 45	19 53 59
23	15 52 54	20 14	+13 48	7 32	7 51	11 46	16 00	15 41	4 06 41	19 50 03
24	15 57 07	20 27	+13 31	7 34	7 53	11 47	15 59	15 40	4 10 38	19 46 07
25	16 01 21	20 39	+13 14	7 35	7 55	11 47	15 58	15 38	4 14 34	19 42 11
26	16 05 35	20 51	+12 55	7 37	7 56	11 47	15 57	15 37	4 18 31	19 38 15
27	16 09 51	21 02	+12 37	7 38	7 58	11 48	15 56	15 36	4 22 28	19 34 19
28	16 14 07	21 13	+12 17	7 40	8 00	11 48	15 55	15 35	4 26 24	19 30 23
29	16 18 24	21 23	+11 57	7 42	8 02	11 48	15 54	15 34	4 30 21	19 26 27
30	16 22 42	21 34	+11 35	7 43	8 04	11 49	15 54	15 33	4 34 17	19 22 31

Duration of Civil (C), Nautical (N), and Astronomical (A), Twilight (in minutes)

Lat.	Nov. 1 C	Nov. 1 N	Nov. 1 A	Nov. 11 C	Nov. 11 N	Nov. 11 A	Nov. 21 C	Nov. 21 N	Nov. 21 A	Nov. 30 C	Nov. 30 N	Nov. 30 A
°												
52	36	75	115	37	78	117	38	80	120	39	82	123
56	40	84	127	41	87	130	43	90	134	45	93	137

ASTRONOMICAL NOTES

MERCURY is unsuitably placed for observation at first, inferior conjunction (and an actual transit across the face of the Sun) occurring on the 13th. During the last ten days of the month the planet is visible as a morning object, magnitude +1·0 to −0·2, low above the S.E. horizon at the time of beginning of morning civil twilight.

VENUS is unsuitably placed for observation at first, inferior conjunction occurring on the 5th. However, just before the middle of the month Venus has become visible low above the south-eastern horizon before dawn. Venus is of magnitude −4. The old crescent Moon will be seen approaching Venus on the morning of the 29th.

MARS, magnitude +0·1, continues to be visible in the evening sky, low in the south-west. Although it is 10° nearer to the Sun at the end of the month as compared with the beginning, the period of time available for observation increases as the planet moves northward in declination. On the evening of the 8th the crescent Moon will be seen approaching the planet. During the month Mars moves from Capricornus to Aquarius.

JUPITER, magnitude −2·2, is an evening object, low in the south and south-western sky. It is still in the constellation of Aquarius. On the evening of the 10th the gibbous Moon passes 2° S. of Jupiter.

SATURN is unsuitably placed for observation.

TRANSIT. There is a transit of Mercury across the disc of the Sun on the 13th. See page 148 for details.

THE MOON

Day	R.A.	Dec.	Hor. Par.	Semi-diam.	Sun's Co-long.	P.A. of Bright Limb	Phase	Age	Rise 52°	Rise 56°	Tran-sit	Set 52°	Set 56°
	h m	°	′	′	°	°		d	h m	h m	h m	h m	h m
1	13 19	− 8·4	59·4	16·2	258	112	2	28·2	5 44	5 53	11 01	16 03	15 52
2	14 12	−14·8	60·0	16·4	270	88	0	29·2	7 15	7 31	11 54	16 20	16 02
3	15 09	−20·4	60·4	16·5	283	300	1	0·7	8 50	9 14	12 52	16 44	16 17
4	16 11	−24·8	60·6	16·5	295	289	4	1·7	10 23	10 57	13 54	17 19	16 44
5	17 16	−27·6	60·5	16·5	307	280	11	2·7	11 46	12 26	15 00	18 11	17 31
6	18 23	−28·4	60·2	16·4	319	272	19	3·7	12 49	13 28	16 05	19 24	18 46
7	19 28	−27·2	59·7	16·3	331	264	29	4·7	13 31	14 02	17 06	20 49	20 19
8	20 30	−24·2	59·1	16·1	344	257	40	5·7	13 59	14 22	18 03	22 18	21 56
9	21 27	−19·9	58·4	15·9	356	252	51	6·7	14 18	14 33	18 54	23 44	23 30
10	22 20	−14·7	57·8	15·7	8	248	62	7·7	14 31	14 41	19 41	··	··
11	23 08	− 8·9	57·1	15·6	20	246	72	8·7	14 43	14 47	20 25	1 06	0 58
12	23 55	− 2·8	56·6	15·4	32	245	81	9·7	14 53	14 52	21 08	2 24	2 22
13	0 40	+ 3·3	56·0	15·3	44	246	88	10·7	15 03	14 57	21 50	3 40	3 44
14	1 25	+ 9·2	55·5	15·1	57	249	94	11·7	15 14	15 03	22 33	4 56	5 05
15	2 11	+14·6	55·1	15·0	69	255	98	12·7	15 27	15 11	23 18	6 11	6 27
16	2 58	+19·4	54·8	14·9	81	276	100	13·7	15 44	15 21	··	7 28	7 49
17	3 47	+23·3	54·4	14·8	93	46	100	14·7	16 07	15 38	0 04	8 43	9 12
18	4 39	+26·2	54·2	14·8	105	69	98	15·7	16 39	16 04	0 53	9 54	10 29
19	5 31	+27·9	54·1	14·7	117	78	94	16·7	17 23	16 44	1 44	10 56	11 35
20	6 25	+28·3	54·0	14·7	129	86	89	17·7	18 20	17 43	2 36	11 46	12 23
21	7 18	+27·4	54·1	14·7	142	93	83	18·7	19 27	18 55	3 27	12 22	12 54
22	8 10	+25·3	54·3	14·8	154	100	75	19·7	20 40	20 15	4 16	12 48	13 14
23	9 01	+22·0	54·7	14·9	166	105	66	20·7	21 56	21 38	5 03	13 08	13 27
24	9 49	+17·8	55·2	15·0	178	109	57	21·7	23 13	23 01	5 49	13 22	13 36
25	10 36	+12·7	55·9	15·2	190	112	47	22·7	··	··	6 33	13 34	13 42
26	11 22	+ 7·0	56·7	15·4	202	114	37	23·7	0 30	0 24	7 16	13 45	13 48
27	12 09	+ 0·8	57·6	15·7	215	114	27	24·7	1 49	1 48	8 01	13 56	13 53
28	12 57	− 5·6	58·6	16·0	227	113	18	25·7	3 11	3 16	8 47	14 08	14 00
29	13 48	−12·0	59·5	16·2	239	110	10	26·7	4 38	4 50	9 37	14 22	14 08
30	14 43	−18·0	60·4	16·4	251	103	4	27·7	6 10	6 31	10 32	14 42	14 20

MERCURY ☿

Day	R.A.	Dec. −	Diam.	Phase	Tran-sit		Day	R.A.	Dec. −	Diam.	Phase	Tran-sit	5° high 52°	5° high 56°
	h m	°	″		h m			h m	°	″		h m	h m	h m
1	15 45	22·7	8	35	13 03		16	14 59	15·9	10	3	11 16	7 19	7 39
4	15 45	22·3	9	24	12 50	Mercury is too	19	14 49	14·3	9	14	10 55	6 49	7 06
7	15 39	21·3	9	13	12 32	close to the	22	14 45	13·6	8	27	10 41	6 30	6 46
10	15 28	19·8	10	4	12 08	Sun for	25	14 48	13·6	8	41	10 33	6 21	6 38
13	15 13	17·9	10	0	11 42	observation	28	14 55	14·1	7	54	10 29	6 21	6 39
16	14 59	15·9	10	3	11 16		31	15 07	15·1	7	64	10 29	6 27	6 46

VENUS ♀

Day	R.A.	Dec. −	Diam.	Phase	Tran-sit	5° high. 52°	5° high. 56°
	h m	°	″		h m	h m	h m
1	14 44	22·1	61	1	12 01	8 50	9 21
6	14 33	20·3	62	0	11 31	8 05	8 32
11	14 23	18·2	61	1	11 01	7 20	7 43
16	14 15	16·2	59	3	10 34	6 39	6 59
21	14 11	14·5	56	9	10 10	6 05	6 22
26	14 10	13·3	52	12	9 50	5 37	5 53
31	14 14	12·5	48	17	9 34	5 16	5 31

MARS ♂

Day	R.A.	Dec. −	Diam.	Phase	Tran-sit	5° high. 52°	5° high. 56°
	h m	°	″		h m	h m	h m
1	21 07	18·9	11	85	18 26	22 03	21 38
6	21 19	17·8	10	85	18 19	22 04	21 41
11	21 32	16·6	10	85	18 12	22 05	21 44
16	21 45	15·4	9	85	18 05	22 06	21 47
21	21 57	14·1	9	86	17 58	22 07	21 50
26	22 10	12·8	9	86	17 51	22 08	21 53
31	22 23	11·5	8	86	17 44	22 10	21 56

SUNRISE AND SUNSET

Day	London a.m. h m	London p.m. h m	Bristol a.m. h m	Bristol p.m. h m	Birmingham a.m. h m	Birmingham p.m. h m	Manchester a.m. h m	Manchester p.m. h m	Newcastle a.m. h m	Newcastle p.m. h m	Glasgow a.m. h m	Glasgow p.m. h m	Belfast a.m. h m	Belfast p.m. h m
1	6 52	4 34	7 02	4 44	7 01	4 39	7 06	4 38	7 08	4 31	7 22	4 39	7 25	4 50
2	6 54	4 33	7 04	4 43	7 03	4 37	7 08	4 36	7 10	4 29	7 24	4 37	7 27	4 48
3	6 56	4 31	7 06	4 41	7 05	4 36	7 10	4 35	7 12	4 27	7 26	4 35	7 29	4 46
4	6 58	4 29	7 07	4 39	7 07	4 34	7 12	4 33	7 14	4 25	7 28	4 33	7 31	4 44
5	6 59	4 28	7 09	4 38	7 09	4 32	7 14	4 31	7 16	4 23	7 30	4 31	7 33	4 42
6	7 01	4 26	7 10	4 36	7 11	4 30	7 16	4 29	7 18	4 21	7 32	4 29	7 35	4 40
7	7 03	4 24	7 12	4 34	7 13	4 28	7 18	4 27	7 20	4 19	7 34	4 27	7 37	4 38
8	7 05	4 23	7 14	4 33	7 15	4 26	7 20	4 25	7 22	4 17	7 36	4 25	7 39	4 36
9	7 07	4 21	7 16	4 31	7 16	4 24	7 21	4 23	7 24	4 15	7 38	4 23	7 40	4 34
10	7 08	4 20	7 18	4 30	7 18	4 23	7 23	4 22	7 26	4 13	7 40	4 21	7 42	4 33
11	7 10	4 18	7 19	4 28	7 20	4 21	7 25	4 20	7 28	4 11	7 42	4 19	7 44	4 31
12	7 11	4 16	7 21	4 26	7 22	4 19	7 27	4 18	7 30	4 09	7 44	4 17	7 46	4 29
13	7 13	4 15	7 23	4 25	7 24	4 18	7 29	4 17	7 32	4 08	7 46	4 15	7 48	4 27
14	7 15	4 13	7 25	4 23	7 26	4 16	7 31	4 15	7 34	4 06	7 49	4 13	7 51	4 25
15	7 16	4 12	7 26	4 22	7 27	4 15	7 33	4 13	7 36	4 04	7 51	4 12	7 53	4 24
16	7 18	4 11	7 28	4 21	7 29	4 14	7 35	4 12	7 38	4 03	7 53	4 10	7 55	4 22
17	7 20	4 09	7 30	4 19	7 31	4 12	7 37	4 10	7 40	4 01	7 55	4 08	7 57	4 20
18	7 22	4 08	7 32	4 18	7 33	4 11	7 39	4 09	7 42	3 59	7 57	4 06	7 59	4 19
19	7 23	4 07	7 33	4 17	7 34	4 10	7 41	4 07	7 44	3 58	7 59	4 05	8 01	4 17
20	7 25	4 05	7 35	4 15	7 36	4 08	7 43	4 06	7 46	3 56	8 01	4 03	8 03	4 16
21	7 27	4 04	7 37	4 14	7 38	4 07	7 44	4 05	7 48	3 55	8 03	4 02	8 04	4 15
22	7 28	4 03	7 38	4 13	7 39	4 06	7 46	4 03	7 50	3 53	8 05	4 00	8 06	4 13
23	7 30	4 02	7 40	4 12	7 41	4 05	7 48	4 02	7 52	3 52	8 07	3 59	8 08	4 12
24	7 32	4 01	7 42	4 11	7 43	4 04	7 50	4 01	7 54	3 51	8 09	3 58	8 10	4 11
25	7 33	4 00	7 43	4 10	7 44	4 03	7 51	4 00	7 55	3 50	8 11	3 56	8 11	4 10
26	7 35	3 59	7 45	4 09	7 46	4 02	7 53	3 59	7 57	3 49	8 12	3 55	8 13	4 09
27	7 36	3 58	7 46	4 08	7 47	4 01	7 54	3 58	7 59	3 48	8 14	3 54	8 15	4 08
28	7 38	3 57	7 48	4 08	7 49	4 00	7 56	3 57	8 01	3 47	8 16	3 53	8 17	4 07
29	7 40	3 56	7 50	4 07	7 51	3 59	7 58	3 56	8 02	3 46	8 18	3 52	8 18	4 06
30	7 41	3 56	7 51	4 06	7 52	3 58	7 59	3 56	8 04	3 45	8 20	3 51	8 20	4 05

		JUPITER ♃						SATURN ♄			
Day	R.A.	Dec. −	Transit	5° high.		R.A.	Dec. −	Transit			
				52°	56°						
	h m	°	h m	h m	h m	h m	°	h m			
1	23 00	8·0	20 16	1 04	0 54	16 27	20·2	13 45	Saturn is		
11	22 59	8·0	19 37	0 25	0 14	16 32	20·4	13 11	too close to		
21	23 00	7·8	18 59	23 43	23 33	16 37	20·5	12 36	the Sun for		
31	23 02	7·6	18 21	23 08	22 58	16 42	20·7	12 02	observation		

Equatorial diameter of Jupiter 44″; of Saturn 15″. Diameters of Saturn's rings 34″ and 15″.

		URANUS ♅				NEPTUNE ♆			
Day	R.A.	Dec. ° ′	Transit		R.A.	Dec. ° ′	Transit		
	h m	° ′	h m		h m	° ′	h m		
1	17 16·8	23 11	14 35	Uranus is too	18 15·7	22 22	15 33	Neptune is too	
11	17 19·0	23 13	13 58	close to the Sun	18 16·9	22 22	14 55	close to the Sun	
21	17 21·4	23 15	13 21	for observation	18 18·2	22 21	14 17	for observation	
31	17 24·0	23 18	12 44		18 19·6	22 21	13 39		

Diameter 4″   Diameter 2″

DAY OF		
Month	Week	

Decem (ten), 10th month
of Roman (pre-Julian)
Calendar.

Sun's Longitude 27° ♑ 22ᵈ 04ʰ

1	M.	**St. Andrew.** Edmund Campion exec. 1581.
2	Tu.	Austerlitz 1805. John Brown exec. 1859.
3	W.	Joseph Conrad b. 1857. Anton Webern b. 1883.
4	Th.	Thomas Carlyle b. 1795. Benjamin Britten d. 1976.
5	F.	Mozart d. 1791. Claude Monet d. 1926.
6	S.	Henry VI b. 1421. Warren Hastings b. 1732.
7	☉.	**2nd S. in Advent.** Pearl Harbour 1941.
8	M.	Mary, Queen of Scots b. 1542. Sibelius b. 1865.
9	Tu.	John Milton b. 1608. Joseph Stalin b. 1879.
10	W.	Abdication of Edward VIII 1936.
11	Th.	Llywelyn ap Gruffydd d. 1282. Berlioz b. 1803.
12	F.	Gustave Flaubert b. 1821. Robert Browning d. 1889.
13	S.	Dr. Samuel Johnson d. 1784.
14	☉.	**3rd S. in Advent.** Prince Albert d. 1861.
15	M.	Jan Vermeer d. 1675. Izaak Walton d. 1683.
16	Tu.	Beethoven b. 1770. Jane Austen b. 1775.
17	W.	First flight by Wright brothers 1903.
18	Th.	Charles Wesley b. 1707.
19	F.	Emily Brontë d. 1848. J. M. W. Turner d. 1851.
20	S.	Leopold von Ranke b. 1795. Sir Robert Menzies b. 1894.
21	☉.	**4th S. in Advent.** MICHAELMAS LAW SITTINGS END.
22	M.	Giacomo Puccini b. 1858. George Eliot d. 1880.
23	Tu.	Roger Ascham d. 1568. Richard Arkwright b. 1732.
24	W.	CHRISTMAS EVE. John I b. 1167.
25	Th.	**Christmas Day.**
26	F.	**St. Stephen.** Thomas Gray b. 1716.
27	S.	**St. John.** Louis Pasteur b. 1822.
28	☉.	**1st S. after Christmas.**
29	M.	**Holy Innocents Day.** Thomas à Beckett d. 1170.
30	Tu.	Rudyard Kipling b. 1865. Pablo Casals b. 1876.
31	W.	The Young Pretender b. 1720. Matisse b. 1869.

PHENOMENA

December 4ᵈ 16ʰ Saturn in conjunction with the Sun.

7ᵈ 16ʰ Mars in conjunction with the Moon. Mars 3° N.

8ᵈ 04ʰ Jupiter in conjunction with the Moon. Jupiter 1°·8 N.

11ᵈ 20ʰ Venus at greatest brilliancy.

19ᵈ 07ʰ Mars in conjunction with Jupiter. Mars 0°·5 N.

19ᵈ 15ʰ Mercury in conjunction with Saturn. Mercury 1°·3 S.

22ᵈ 04ʰ Winter Solstice.

28ᵈ 01ʰ Venus in conjunction with Moon. Venus 7° N.

29ᵈ 15ʰ Saturn in conjunction with the Moon. Saturn 6° N.

CONSTELLATIONS

The following constellations are near the meridian at

	d	h		d	h
Nov.	1	24	Nov.	15	23
Dec.	1	22	Dec.	16	21
Jan.	1	20	Jan.	16	19

Ursa Major (below the Pole), Ursa Minor (below the Pole), Cassiopeia, Andromeda, Perseus, Triangulum, Aries, Taurus, Cetus and Eridanus.

MINIMA OF ALGOL

d	h	d	h
1	0	18	5
3	20	21	1
6	17	23	22
9	14	26	19
12	11	29	16
15	8		

PHASES OF THE MOON

	d	h	m
● New Moon.........	1	16	43
☽ First Quarter	8	08	01
○ Full Moon	16	07	04
☾ Last Quarter.......	24	09	17
● New Moon.........	31	03	10

	d	h
Perigee (357,740 kilometres)	2	11
Apogee (406,510 ,,)	17	05
Perigee (356,620 ,,)	30	23

Mean Longitude of Ascending Node on December 1, 18°.

MONTHLY NOTES

Dec. 10. Grouse shooting ends.

22. Shortest day.

25. Quarter day.

26. General Holiday, England, Wales, N. Ireland and Scotland.

31. Various licences expire.

Day	Right Ascension	Dec. —	Equation of Time	Rise 52°	Rise 56°	Transit	Set 52°	Set 56°	Sidereal Time	Transit of First Point of Aries
	h m s	° ′	m s	h m	h m	h m	h m	h m	h m s	h m s
1	16 27 00	21 43	+11 14	7 44	8 05	11 49	15 53	15 32	4 38 14	19 18 36
2	16 31 19	21 53	+10 51	7 46	8 07	11 49	15 52	15 31	4 42 10	19 14 40
3	16 35 39	22 02	+10 28	7 47	8 09	11 50	15 52	15 30	4 46 07	19 10 44
4	16 39 59	22 10	+10 04	7 49	8 10	11 50	15 51	15 29	4 50 03	19 06 48
5	16 44 20	22 18	+ 9 40	7 50	8 12	11 51	15 50	15 28	4 54 00	19 02 52
6	16 48 41	22 26	+ 9 15	7 51	8 13	11 51	15 50	15 28	4 57 57	18 58 56
7	16 53 03	22 33	+ 8 50	7 53	8 15	11 51	15 50	15 27	5 01 53	18 55 00
8	16 57 25	22 40	+ 8 24	7 54	8 16	11 52	15 49	15 27	5 05 50	18 51 04
9	17 01 48	22 46	+ 7 58	7 55	8 18	11 52	15 49	15 26	5 09 46	18 47 08
10	17 06 12	22 52	+ 7 31	7 56	8 19	11 53	15 49	15 26	5 13 43	18 43 12
11	17 10 35	22 57	+ 7 04	7 57	8 20	11 53	15 49	15 26	5 17 39	18 39 16
12	17 14 59	23 02	+ 6 36	7 58	8 21	11 54	15 48	15 25	5 21 36	18 35 20
13	17 19 24	23 07	+ 6 09	7 59	8 23	11 54	15 48	15 25	5 25 32	18 31 25
14	17 23 49	23 11	+ 5 40	8 00	8 24	11 55	15 48	15 25	5 29 29	18 27 29
15	17 28 14	23 15	+ 5 12	8 01	8 25	11 55	15 48	15 25	5 33 26	18 23 33
16	17 32 39	23 18	+ 4 43	8 02	8 26	11 56	15 49	15 25	5 37 22	18 19 37
17	17 37 05	23 20	+ 4 14	8 03	8 26	11 56	15 49	15 25	5 41 19	18 15 41
18	17 41 30	23 22	+ 3 45	8 04	8 27	11 56	15 49	15 25	5 45 15	18 11 45
19	17 45 56	23 24	+ 3 15	8 04	8 28	11 57	15 49	15 26	5 49 12	18 07 49
20	17 50 22	23 25	+ 2 46	8 05	8 29	11 57	15 50	15 26	5 53 08	18 03 53
21	17 54 49	23 26	+ 2 16	8 06	8 30	11 58	15 50	15 26	5 57 05	17 59 57
22	17 59 15	23 27	+ 1 46	8 06	8 30	11 58	15 51	15 27	6 01 02	17 56 01
23	18 03 41	23 26	+ 1 16	8 07	8 30	11 59	15 51	15 27	6 04 58	17 52 05
24	18 08 08	23 26	+ 0 47	8 07	8 31	11 59	15 52	15 28	6 08 55	17 48 10
25	18 12 34	23 25	+ 0 17	8 08	8 31	12 00	15 52	15 29	6 12 51	17 44 14
26	18 17 01	23 23	− 0 13	8 08	8 32	12 00	15 53	15 29	6 16 48	17 40 18
27	18 21 27	23 21	− 0 43	8 08	8 32	12 01	15 54	15 30	6 20 44	17 36 22
28	18 25 53	23 19	− 1 12	8 08	8 32	12 01	15 55	15 31	6 24 41	17 32 26
29	18 30 19	23 16	− 1 42	8 09	8 32	12 02	15 56	15 32	6 28 37	17 28 30
30	18 34 45	23 12	− 2 11	8 09	8 32	12 02	15 57	15 33	6 32 34	17 24 34
31	18 39 11	23 08	− 2 40	8 09	8 32	12 03	15 58	15 34	6 36 31	17 20 38

Duration of Civil (C), Nautical (N), and Astronomical (A), Twilight (in minutes)

Lat. °	Dec. 1 C	N	A	Dec. 11 C	N	A	Dec. 21 C	N	A	Dec. 31 C	N	A
52	40	82	123	41	84	125	41	85	126	41	84	125
56	45	93	138	47	96	141	47	97	142	47	96	141

ASTRONOMICAL NOTES

MERCURY continues to be visible in the mornings for the first two weeks of the month, magnitude −0·5. It may be glimpsed low above the S.E. horizon at the beginning of morning civil twilight. For the remainder of the month it is unsuitably placed for observation.

VENUS is a brilliant object, magnitude −4·4, dominating the south-eastern sky for several hours before dawn. On the morning of the 28th the waning crescent Moon will have passed 7° S. of Venus about seven hours before the Sun rises and observers who enjoy detecting Venus in daylight can use the Moon as a guide on that morning. Observers with telescopes will notice that the phase of Venus increases noticeably during the month.

MARS, magnitude +0·5, is still visible in the south-western skies in the evenings until about 22ʰ. On the 19th Mars passes only $\frac{1}{4}$° N. of Jupiter. On the evening of the 7th the waxing crescent Moon will be seen near the planet. Towards the end of the month Mars passes from Aquarius into Pisces.

JUPITER, magnitude −2·0, continues to be visible in the evenings, crossing the meridian around sunset towards the end of the month. The Moon, around First Quarter, is near the planet on the evenings of the 7th and 8th.

SATURN is in conjunction on the 4th and thus unsuitably placed for observation.

METEORS. The maximum of the well-known Geminid meteor shower occurs during the night of the 13th–14th. Conditions for observation are rather unfavourable since the gibbous Moon is above the horizon until the beginning of morning astronomical twilight.

THE MOON

Day	R.A.	Dec.	Hor. Par.	Semi-diam.	Sun's Co-long.	P.A. of Bright Limb	Phase	Age	Rise 52°	Rise 56°	Transit	Set 52°	Set 56°
	h m	°	′	′	°	°		d	h m	h m	h m	h m	h m
1	15 43	−23·0	61·0	16·6	263	85	1	28·7	7 47	8 16	11 33	15 11	14 40
2	16 48	−26·6	61·3	16·7	275	321	0	0·3	9 19	9 56	12 39	15 55	15 17
3	17 56	−28·2	61·2	16·7	288	284	3	1·3	10 34	11 14	13 47	17 01	16 22
4	19 04	−27·7	60·9	16·6	300	272	8	2·3	11 27	12 01	14 53	18 26	17 53
5	20 10	−25·2	60·3	16·4	312	262	16	3·3	12 01	12 26	15 54	19 58	19 33
6	21 10	−21·2	59·5	16·2	324	256	25	4·3	12 23	12 41	16 49	21 28	21 12
7	22 06	−16·0	58·7	16·0	336	251	36	5·3	12 39	12 50	17 39	22 53	22 44
8	22 56	−10·2	57·8	15·8	349	248	47	6·3	12 51	12 57	18 24	..	..
9	23 44	− 4·1	57·0	15·5	1	246	57	7·3	13 01	13 02	19 07	0 13	0 10
10	0 29	+ 2·0	56·3	15·3	13	246	67	8·3	13 11	13 07	19 49	1 30	1 32
11	1 14	+ 7·9	55·6	15·2	25	248	76	9·3	13 22	13 13	20 32	2 45	2 53
12	1 59	+13·4	55·1	15·0	37	251	84	10·3	13 35	13 20	21 15	4 00	4 13
13	2 46	+18·3	54·7	14·9	49	256	90	11·3	13 50	13 29	22 01	5 16	5 35
14	3 34	+22·4	54·4	14·8	61	263	95	12·3	14 11	13 44	22 49	6 31	6 57
15	4 25	+25·5	54·1	14·8	74	276	98	13·3	14 40	14 06	23 39	7 43	8 16
16	5 17	+27·5	54·0	14·7	86	320	100	14·3	15 20	14 42	..	8 48	9 26
17	6 11	+28·2	53·9	14·7	98	59	99	15·3	16 12	15 35	0 31	9 42	10 20
18	7 04	+27·7	54·0	14·7	110	82	97	16·3	17 17	16 44	1 22	10 22	10 56
19	7 57	+25·8	54·1	14·7	122	93	93	17·3	18 29	18 02	2 12	10 51	11 19
20	8 47	+22·8	54·3	14·8	134	100	88	18·3	19 43	19 23	3 00	11 13	11 34
21	9 36	+18·8	54·7	14·9	146	105	81	19·3	20 59	20 45	3 45	11 28	11 44
22	10 22	+14·0	55·1	15·0	159	109	73	20·3	22 14	22 06	4 29	11 41	11 51
23	11 08	+ 8·6	55·7	15·2	171	112	64	21·3	23 29	23 27	5 12	11 52	11 56
24	11 53	+ 2·7	56·5	15·4	183	113	54	22·3	..	..	5 54	12 02	12 02
25	12 39	− 3·5	57·3	15·6	195	113	44	23·3	0 47	0 50	6 38	12 13	12 07
26	13 27	− 9·7	58·3	15·9	207	112	33	24·3	2 08	2 18	7 24	12 25	12 14
27	14 18	−15·6	59·2	16·1	219	108	23	25·3	3 35	3 51	8 15	12 41	12 24
28	15 14	−21·0	60·1	16·4	231	102	14	26·3	5 07	5 32	9 11	13 04	12 39
29	16 16	−25·2	60·8	16·6	244	94	7	27·3	6 41	7 15	10 14	13 40	13 05
30	17 23	−27·7	61·3	16·7	256	79	2	28·3	8 07	8 46	11 21	14 34	13 55
31	18 32	−28·2	61·5	16·8	268	18	0	29·3	9 12	9 50	12 30	15 52	15 15

MERCURY ☿

Day	R.A.	Dec. −	Diam.	Phase	Transit	5° high 52°	5° high 56°	Day	R.A.	Dec. −	Diam.	Phase	Transit	
	h m	°	″		h m	h m	h m		h m	°	″		h m	
1	15 07	15·1	7	64	10 29	6 27	6 46	16	16 28	21·1	5	90	10 52	
4	15 20	16·3	6	72	10 31	6 37	6 58	19	16 47	22·1	5	93	10 59	Mercury is too
7	15 36	17·5	6	79	10 34	6 49	7 12	22	17 07	23·0	5	95	11 07	close to the
10	15 52	18·8	6	84	10 39	7 03	7 29	25	17 26	23·7	5	96	11 15	Sun for
13	16 10	20·0	5	87	10 45	7 18	7 46	28	17 47	24·2	5	97	11 23	observation
16	16 28	21·1	5	90	10 52	7 34	8 04	31	18 07	24·5	5	98	11 32	

VENUS ♀   MARS ♂

Day	R.A.	Dec. −	Diam.	Phase	Transit	5° high 52°	5° high 56°	Day	R.A.	Dec. −	Diam.	Phase	Transit	5° high 52°	5° high 56°
	h m	°	″		h m	h m	h m		h m	°	″		h m	h m	h m
1	14 14	12·5	48	17	9 34	5 16	5 31	1	22 23	11·5	8	86	17 44	22 10	21 56
6	14 20	12·2	44	21	9 21	5 01	5 16	6	22 36	10·1	8	86	17 37	22 11	21 58
11	14 29	12·2	41	26	9 11	4 51	5 06	11	22 48	8·7	8	86	17 30	22 12	22 01
16	14 41	12·6	38	30	9 03	4 46	5 01	16	23 01	7·2	8	87	17 23	22 13	22 03
21	14 55	13·3	35	34	8 57	4 44	5 00	21	23 14	5·8	7	87	17 16	22 14	22 06
26	15 10	14·1	32	37	8 53	4 45	5 02	26	23 26	4·3	7	87	17 08	22 15	22 08
31	15 27	15·0	30	41	8 50	4 48	5 07	31	23 39	2·8	7	88	17 01	22 15	22 09

SUNRISE AND SUNSET

Day	London a.m. h m	London p.m. h m	Bristol a.m. h m	Bristol p.m. h m	Birmingham a.m. h m	Birmingham p.m. h m	Manchester a.m. h m	Manchester p.m. h m	Newcastle a.m. h m	Newcastle p.m. h m	Glasgow a.m. h m	Glasgow p.m. h m	Belfast a.m. h m	Belfast p.m. h m
1	7 42	3 55	7 52	4 06	7 53	3 58	8 00	3 55	8 05	3 44	8 21	3 50	8 21	4 04
2	7 44	3 54	7 54	4 05	7 55	3 57	8 02	3 54	8 07	3 43	8 23	3 49	8 23	4 03
3	7 45	3 54	7 55	4 05	7 56	3 56	8 03	3 53	8 09	3 42	8 25	3 48	8 25	4 02
4	7 47	3 53	7 57	4 04	7 58	3 56	8 05	3 53	8 10	3 41	8 26	3 47	8 26	4 01
5	7 48	3 53	7 58	4 03	7 59	3 55	8 06	3 52	8 12	3 40	8 28	3 46	8 28	4 00
6	7 49	3 52	7 59	4 03	8 01	3 55	8 08	3 52	8 13	3 40	8 29	3 46	8 29	4 00
7	7 51	3 52	8 00	4 03	8 02	3 54	8 09	3 51	8 15	3 39	8 31	3 45	8 31	3 59
8	7 52	3 52	8 01	4 02	8 03	3 54	8 10	3 51	8 16	3 39	8 32	3 45	8 32	3 59
9	7 53	3 51	8 03	4 02	8 05	3 53	8 12	3 50	8 18	3 38	8 34	3 44	8 34	3 58
10	7 54	3 51	8 04	4 02	8 06	3 53	8 13	3 50	8 19	3 38	8 35	3 44	8 35	3 58
11	7 55	3 51	8 05	4 02	8 07	3 53	8 14	3 50	8 20	3 38	8 36	3 44	8 36	3 58
12	7 56	3 51	8 06	4 01	8 08	3 53	8 15	3 50	8 21	3 38	8 37	3 43	8 37	3 58
13	7 57	3 51	8 07	4 01	8 09	3 53	8 16	3 50	8 22	3 38	8 39	3 43	8 38	3 58
14	7 58	3 51	8 07	4 01	8 10	3 53	8 17	3 50	8 23	3 38	8 40	3 43	8 39	3 58
15	7 59	3 51	8 08	4 01	8 11	3 53	8 18	3 50	8 24	3 38	8 41	3 43	8 40	3 58
16	8 00	3 51	8 09	4 02	8 12	3 53	8 19	3 50	8 25	3 38	8 42	3 43	8 41	3 58
17	8 01	3 52	8 10	4 02	8 13	3 53	8 20	3 50	8 26	3 38	8 42	3 43	8 42	3 58
18	8 02	3 52	8 11	4 02	8 14	3 53	8 21	3 50	8 27	3 38	8 43	3 43	8 43	3 58
19	8 02	3 52	8 11	4 02	8 14	3 53	8 21	3 50	8 27	3 38	8 44	3 44	8 43	3 58
20	8 03	3 53	8 12	4 03	8 15	3 54	8 22	3 51	8 28	3 39	8 45	3 44	8 44	3 59
21	8 04	3 53	8 13	4 03	8 16	3 54	8 23	3 51	8 29	3 39	8 46	3 44	8 45	3 59
22	8 04	3 54	8 13	4 04	8 16	3 55	8 23	3 52	8 29	3 40	8 46	3 45	8 45	4 00
23	8 05	3 54	8 14	4 04	8 17	3 55	8 24	3 52	8 30	3 40	8 46	3 45	8 46	4 00
24	8 05	3 55	8 14	4 05	8 17	3 56	8 24	3 53	8 30	3 41	8 47	3 46	8 46	4 01
25	8 06	3 55	8 15	4 05	8 18	3 56	8 25	3 53	8 31	3 41	8 47	3 47	8 47	4 01
26	8 06	3 56	8 15	4 06	8 18	3 57	8 25	3 54	8 31	3 42	8 48	3 47	8 47	4 02
27	8 06	3 57	8 15	4 07	8 18	3 58	8 25	3 55	8 31	3 43	8 48	3 48	8 47	4 03
28	8 06	3 57	8 15	4 08	8 18	3 59	8 25	3 56	8 31	3 44	8 48	3 49	8 47	4 04
29	8 07	3 58	8 16	4 09	8 19	4 00	8 26	3 56	8 32	3 44	8 48	3 50	8 48	4 04
30	8 07	3 59	8 16	4 10	8 19	4 01	8 26	3 57	8 32	3 45	8 48	3 51	8 48	4 05
31	8 07	4 00	8 16	4 11	8 19	4 02	8 26	3 58	8 32	3 46	8 48	3 52	8 48	4 06

JUPITER ♃ / SATURN ♄

Day	R.A. h m	Dec. − °	Transit h m	5° high. 52° h m	5° high. 56° h m	R.A. h m	Dec. °	Transit h m	
1	23 02	7·6	18 21	23 08	22 58	16 42	20·7	12 02	Saturn is
11	23 06	7·2	17 45	22 34	22 25	16 47	20·9	11 28	too close to
21	23 10	6·7	17 11	22 02	21 53	16 52	21·0	10 53	the Sun for
31	23 15	6·1	16 37	21 31	21 23	16 57	21·2	10 19	observation

Equatorial diameter of Jupiter 39″; of Saturn 15″. Diameters of Saturn's rings 34″ and 15″.

URANUS ♅ / NEPTUNE ♆

Day	R.A. h m	Dec. − ° ′	Transit h m		R.A. h m	Dec. ° ′	Transit h m	
1	17 24·0	23 18	12 44	Uranus is too	18 19·6	22 21	13 39	Neptune is too
11	17 26·6	23 20	12 07	close to the Sun	18 21·2	22 20	13 02	close to the Sun
21	17 29·2	23 22	11 30	for observation	18 22·8	22 20	12 24	for observation
31	17 31·8	23 24	10 54		18 24·4	22 19	11 46	

Diameter 4″   Diameter 2″

INTRODUCTION TO ASTRONOMICAL SECTION

GENERAL

The astronomical data are given in a form suitable for those who practise naked-eye astronomy or use small telescopes. No attempt has been made to replace the *Astronomical Almanac* for professional astronomers. Positions of the heavenly bodies are given only to the degree of accuracy required by amateur astronomers for setting telescopes, or for plotting on celestial globes or star atlases. Where intermediate positions are required, linear interpolation may be employed.

All data are, unless otherwise stated, for 0ʰ G.M.T., *i.e.* at the midnight at the beginning of the day named.

(*See notes on British Summer Time, p. 142*).

Definitions of the terms used cannot be given in an ephemeris of this nature. They must be sought in astronomical literature and text-books. Probably the best source for the amateur is Norton's *Star Atlas* (Gall and Inglis, 16th edition, 1973; £4·50), which contains an excellent introduction to observational astronomy, and the finest series of star maps yet produced for showing stars visible to the naked eye. Certain more extended ephemerides are available in the British Astronomical Association Handbook, an annual very popular among amateur astronomers. (Secretary: Burlington House, Piccadilly, London, W.1.)

A special feature has been made of the times when the various heavenly bodies are visible in the British Isles. Since two columns, calculated for latitudes 52° and 56°, are devoted to risings and settings, the range 50° to 58° can be covered by interpolation and extrapolation. The times given in these columns are G.M.T.'s for the meridian of Greenwich. An observer west of this meridian must add his longitude (in time) and vice versa.

In accordance with the usual convention in astronomy, + and − indicate respectively north and south latitudes or declinations.

FIRST PAGE OF EACH MONTH

The Zodiacal signs through which the Sun is passing during each month are illustrated. The date of transition from one sign to the next, to the nearest hour, is also given.

The FASTS AND FESTIVALS in black-letter type are those so given in the Prayer Book.

Under the heading PHENOMENA will be found particulars of the more important conjunctions of the Sun, Moon and planets with each other, and also the dates of eclipses and other astronomical phenomena of special interest.

The CONSTELLATIONS listed each month are those that are near the meridian at the beginning of the month at 22ʰ local mean time. Allowance must be made for Summer Time if necessary. The fact that any star crosses the meridian 4ᵐ earlier each night or 2ʰ earlier each month may be used, in conjunction with the lists given each month, to find what constellations are favourably placed at any moment. The table preceding the list of constellations may be extended indefinitely at the rate just quoted.

Times of MINIMA OF ALGOL are approximate times of the middle of the period of diminished light.

The Principal PHASES OF THE MOON are the G.M.T.'s when the difference between the longitude of the Moon and that of the Sun is 0°, 90°, 180° or 270°. The times of perigee and apogee are those when the Moon is nearest to, and farthest from, the Earth, respectively. The nodes or points of intersection of the Moon's orbit and the ecliptic make a complete retrograde circuit of the ecliptic in about 19 years. From a knowledge of the longitude of the ascending node and the inclination, whose value does not vary much from 5°, the path of the Moon among the stars may be plotted on a celestial globe or star atlas.

The MONTHLY NOTES are self-explanatory.

SECOND PAGE OF EACH MONTH

The Sun's semi-diameter, in arc, is given once a month.

The right ascension given is that of the true Sun. The right ascension of the mean Sun is obtained by applying the equation of time, with the sign given, to the right ascension of the true Sun, or, more easily, by applying 12ʰ to the column Sidereal Time. The direction in which the equation of time has to be applied in different problems is a frequent source of confusion and error. Apparent Solar Time is equal to the Mean Solar Time plus the Equation of Time. For example at noon on Aug. 8 the Equation of Time is −5ᵐ 38ˢ and thus at 12ʰ Mean Time on that day the Apparent Time is 12ʰ − 5ᵐ 38ˢ = 11ʰ 54ᵐ 22ˢ.

The Greenwich Sidereal Time at 0ʰ and the Transit of the First Point of Aries (which is really the mean time when the sidereal time is 0ʰ) are used for converting mean time to sidereal time and vice versa.

The G.M.T. of transit of the Sun at Greenwich may also be taken as the L.M.T. of transit in any longitude. It is independent of latitude. The G.M.T. of transit in any longitude is obtained by adding the longitude to the time given if west, and vice versa.

The legal importance of SUNRISE and SUNSET is that the Road Traffic Act, 1956, defines Lighting-up Time for vehicles as being from half an hour after sunset to half an hour before sunrise throughout the year. In all laws and regulations "sunset" refers to the local sunset, i.e. the time at which the Sun sets at the place in question. This common-sense interpretation has been upheld by legal tribunals. Thus the necessity for providing for different latitudes and longitudes, as already described, is evident.

The times of SUNRISE and SUNSET are those when the Sun's upper limb, as affected by refraction is on the true horizon of an observer at sea-level. Assuming the mean refraction to be 34′, and the Sun's semi-diameter to be 16′, the time given is that when the true zenith distance of the Sun's centre is 90° + 34′ + 16′ or 90° 50′, or, in other words, when the depression of the Sun's centre below the true horizon is 50′. The upper limb is then 34′ below the true horizon, but is brought there by refraction. It is true, of course, that an observer on a ship might see the Sun for a minute or so longer, because of the dip of the horizon, while another viewing the sunset over hills or mountains would record an earlier time. Nevertheless, the moment when the true zenith distance of the Sun's centre is 90° 50′ is a precise time dependent only on the latitude and longitude of the place, and independent of its altitude above sea-level, the contour of its horizon, the vagaries of refraction or the small seasonal change in the Sun's semi-diameter; this moment is suitable in every way as a definition of sunset (or sunrise) for all statutory purposes.

It is well known that light reaches us before sunrise and also continues to reach us for some time after sunset. The interval between darkness and sunrise or sunset and darkness is called twilight. Astronomically speaking, twilight is considered to begin or end when the Sun's centre is 18° below the horizon, as no light from the Sun can then reach the observer. As thus defined twilight may last several hours; in high latitudes at the summer solstice the depression of 18° is not reached, and twilight lasts from sunset to sunrise.

The need for some sub-division of twilight was met some years ago by dividing the gathering darkness into four steps.

(1) *Sunrise or Sunset,* defined as above.

(2) *Civil twilight,* which begins or ends when the Sun's centre is 6° below the horizon. This marks the time when operations requiring daylight may commence or must cease. In England it varies from about 30 to 60 minutes after sunset and the same interval before sunrise.

(3) *Nautical twilight,* which begins or ends when the Sun's centre is 12° below the horizon. This marks the time when it is, to all intent and purposes, completely dark.

(4) *Astronomical twilight,* which begins or ends when the Sun's centre is 18° below the horizon. This marks theoretical perfect darkness. It is of little practical importance, especially if nautical twilight is tabulated.

To assist observers the durations of civil, nautical and astronomical twilights are given at intervals of ten days. The beginning of a particular twilight is found by subtracting the duration from the time of sunrise, while the end is found by adding the duration to the time of sunset. Thus the beginning of astronomical twilight in latitude 52°, on the Greenwich meridian, on March 11 is found as $06^h 25^m - 113^m = 04^h 32^m$ and similarly the end of civil twilight as $17^h 56^m + 34^m = 18^h 30^m$.

The letters T.A.N. are printed when twilight lasts all night.

Lighting-up time is a crude attempt to approximate to civil twilight over the British Isles.

Under the heading ASTRONOMICAL NOTES will be found notes describing the position and visibility of all the planets and also of other phenomena; these are intended to guide naked-eye observers, or those using small telescopes.

THIRD PAGE OF EACH MONTH

The Moon moves so rapidly among the stars that its position is given only to the degree of accuracy that permits linear interpolation. The right ascension and declination are geocentric, i.e. for an imaginary observer at the centre of the Earth. To an observer on the surface of the Earth the position is always different, as the altitude is always less on account of parallax which may reach 1°.

The lunar terminator is the line separating the bright from the dark part of the Moon's disk. Apart from irregularities of the lunar surface, the terminator is elliptical, because it is a circle seen in projection. It becomes the full circle forming the limb, or edge, of the Moon at New and Full Moon. The selenographic longitude of the terminator is measured from the mean centre of the visible disk, which may differ from the visible centre by as much as 8°, because of libration.

Instead of the longitude of the terminator the Sun's selenographic colongitude is tabulated. It is numerically equal to the selenographic longitude of the morning terminator, measured eastward from the mean centre of the disk. Thus its value is approximately 270° at New Moon, 360° at First Quarter, 90° at Full Moon and 180° at Last Quarter.

The Position Angle of the Bright Limb is the position angle of the midpoint of the illuminated limb, measured eastward from the north point on the disk. The column PHASE shows the percentage of the area of the Moon's disk illuminated; this is also the illuminated percentage of the diameter at right angles to the line of cusps. The terminator is a semi-ellipse whose major axis is the line of cusps, and whose semi-minor axis is determined by the tabulated percentage; from New Moon to Full Moon the east limb is dark, and vice versa.

The times given as moonrise and moonset are those when the upper limb of the Moon is on the horizon of an observer at sea-level. The Sun's horizontal parallax is about 9″, and is negligible when considering sunrise and sunset, but that of the Moon averages about 57′. Hence the computed time represents the moment when the true zenith distance of the Moon is 90° 50′ (as for the Sun) minus the horizontal parallax. The time required for the Sun or Moon to rise or set is about four minutes (except in high latitudes).

The tables have been constructed for the meridian of Greenwich, and for latitudes 52° and 56°. They give Greenwich Mean Time (G.M.T.) throughout the year. To obtain the G.M.T. of the phenomenon as seen from any other latitude and longitude, first interpolate or extrapolate for latitude by the usual rules of proportion. To the time thus found the longitude (expressed in time) is to be *added* if west (as it usually is in Great Britain) or *subtracted* if east. If the longitude is expressed in degrees and minutes of arc, it must be converted to time at the rate of 1° = 4^m and 15′ = 1^m.

The G.M.T. of transit of the Moon over the meridian of Greenwich is given: these times are independent of latitude, but must be corrected for longitude. For places in the British Isles it suffices to add the longitude if west, and vice versa. For more remote places a further correction is necessary because of the rapid movement of the Moon relative to the stars. The entire correction is conveniently determined by first finding the west longitude λ of the place. If the place is in west longitude, λ is the ordinary west longitude; if the place is in east longitude λ is the complement to 24^h (or $360°$) of the longitude and will be greater than 12^h (or $180°$). The correction then consists of two positive portions, namely λ and the fraction λ/24 (or λ°/360) multiplied by the difference between consecutive transits. Thus for Sydney, N.S.W., the longitude is $10^h 05^m$ east, so λ = $13^h 55^m$ and the fraction λ/24 is 0·58. The transit on the local date 1986 September 25 is found as follows:

	d	h	m
G.M.T. of transit at Greenwich .....Sept	24	04	18
λ		13	55
0·58 × ($5^h 08^m - 4^h 18^m$)			29
G.M.T. of transit at Sydney	24	18	42
Corr. to N.S.W. Standard Time		10	00
Local standard time of transit	25	04	42

It is evident of course, that for any given place the quantities λ and the correction to local standard time may be combined permanently, being here $23^h 55^m$.

Positions of Mercury are given for every third day, and those of Venus and Mars for every fifth day; they may be interpolated linearly. The column PHASE shows the illuminated percentage of the disk. In the case of the inner planets this approaches 100 at superior conjunction and 0 at inferior conjunction. When the phase is less than 50 the planet is crescent-shaped or horned; for greater phases it is gibbous. In the case of the exterior planet Mars, the phase approaches 100 at conjunction and opposition, and is a minimum at the quadratures.

Since the planets cannot be seen when on the horizon, the actual times of rising and setting are not given; instead, the time when the planet has an apparent altitude of 5° has been tabulated. If the time of transit is between 00^h and 12^h the time refers to an altitude of 5° above the eastern horizon: if between 12^h and 24^h, to the western horizon. The phenomenon tabulated is the one that occurs between sunset and sunrise; unimportant exceptions to these rules may occur because changes are not made during a month, except in the case of Mercury. The times given may be interpolated for latitude and corrected for longitude as in the case of the Sun and Moon.

The G.M.T. at which the planet transits the Greenwich meridian is also given. The times of transit are to be corrected to local meridians in the usual way, as already described.

PAGE FOUR OF EACH MONTH

The G.M.T.'s of Sunrise and Sunset may be used not only for these phenomena, but also for Lighting-up Times, which, under the Road Traffic Act, 1956, are from half an hour after sunset to half an hour before sunrise throughout the year.

The particulars for the four outer planets resemble those for the planets on Page III of each month, except that, under Uranus and Neptune, times when the planet is 10° high instead of 5° high are given;

this is because of the inferior brightness of these planets. The polar diameter of Jupiter is about 3" less than the equatorial diameter, while that of Saturn is about 2" less. The diameters given for the rings of Saturn are those of the major axis (in the plane of the planet's equator) and the minor axis respectively. The former has a small seasonal change due to the slightly varying distance of the Earth from Saturn, but the latter varies from zero when the Earth passes through the ring plane every 15 years to its maximum opening half-way between these periods. The rings were open at their widest extent in the middle of 1973.

TIME

From the earliest ages, the natural division of time into recurring periods of day and night has provided the practical time scale for the everyday activities of mankind. Indeed, if any alternative means of time measurement is adopted, it must be capable of adjustment so as to remain in general agreement with the natural time scale defined by the diurnal rotation of the Earth on its axis. Ideally the rotation should be measured against a fixed frame of reference; in practice it must be measured against the background provided by the celestial bodies. If the Sun is chosen as the reference point, we obtain Apparent Solar Time, which is the time indicated by a sundial. It is not a uniform time, but is subject to variations which amount to as much as a quarter of an hour in each direction. Such wide variations cannot be tolerated in a practical time scale, and this has led to the concept of Mean Solar Time in which all the days are exactly the same length and equal to the average length of the Apparent Solar Day.

The positions of the stars in the sky are specified in relation to a fictitious reference point in the sky known as the First Point of Aries (or the Vernal Equinox). It is therefore convenient to adopt this same reference point when considering the rotation of the Earth against the background of the stars. The time scale so obtained is known as Apparent Sidereal Time.

Greenwich Mean Time

The daily rotation of the Earth on its axis causes the Sun and the other heavenly bodies to appear to cross the sky from East to West. It is convenient to represent this relative motion as if the Sun really performed a daily circuit around a fixed Earth. Noon in Apparent Solar Time may then be defined as the time at which the Sun transits across the observer's meridian. In Mean Solar Time, noon is similarly defined by the meridian transit of a fictitious Mean Sun moving uniformly in the sky with the same average speed as the true Sun. Mean Solar Time observed on the meridian of the transit circle telescope of the Royal Observatory at Greenwich is called Greenwich Mean Time (G.M.T.). The mean solar day is divided into 24 hours and, for astronomical and other scientific purposes, these are numbered 0 to 23, commencing at midnight. Civil time is usually reckoned in two periods of 12 hours, designated a.m. (before noon) and p.m. (after noon).

Universal Time

Before 1925 January 1 G.M.T. was reckoned in 24 hours commencing at noon: since that date it has been reckoned from midnight. In view of the risk of confusion in the use of the designation G.M.T. before and after 1925, the International Astronomical Union recommended in 1928 that astronomers should, for the present, employ the term Universal Time, U.T. (or Weltzeit, W.Z.) to denote G.M.T. measured from Greenwich Mean Midnight.

In precision work it has now become necessary to take account of small variations, hitherto negligible, in Universal Time. These arise from small irregularities in the rotation of the Earth. Observed astronomical time is designated U.T.0. Observed time corrected for the effects of the motion of the poles (giving rise to a "wandering" in longitude) is designated U.T.1. There is also a seasonal fluctuation in the rate of rotation of the Earth arising from meteorological causes, often called the annual fluctuation. U.T.1 corrected for this effect is designated U.T.2 and provides a time scale free from short-period fluctuations. It is still subject to small secular and irregular changes.

Apparent Solar Time

As has been mentioned, the time shown by a sundial is called Apparent Solar Time. It differs from Mean Solar Time by an amount known as the Equation of Time, which is the total effect of two causes which make the length of the apparent solar day non-uniform. One cause of variation is that the orbit of the Earth is not a circle, but an ellipse, having the Sun at one focus. As a consequence, the angular speed of the Earth in its orbit is not constant; it is greatest at the beginning of January when the Earth is nearest the Sun. The other cause is due to the obliquity of the ecliptic; the plane of the equator (which is at right-angles to the axis of rotation of the Earth) does not coincide with the ecliptic (the plane defined by the apparent annual motion of the Sun around the celestial sphere) but is inclined to it at an angle of $23° 26'$. As a result, the apparent solar day is shorter than average at the equinoxes and longer at the solstices. From the combined effects of the components due to obliquity and eccentricity, the equation of time reaches its maximum values in February (-14 mins.) and early November ($+16$ mins.). It has a zero value on four dates during the year, and it is only on these dates (approx. April 15, June 14, Sept. 1, and Dec. 25) that a sundial shows Mean Solar Time.

Sidereal Time

A sidereal day is the duration of a complete rotation of the Earth with reference to the First Point of Aries. The term sidereal (or "star") time is perhaps a little misleading since the time scale so defined is not exactly the same as that which would be defined by successive transits of a selected star, as there is a small progressive motion between the stars and the First Point of Aries due to the precession of the Earth's axis. This makes the length of the sidereal day shorter than the true period of rotation by 0·008 seconds. Superimposed on this steady precessional motion are small oscillations called nutation, giving rise to fluctuations in apparent sidereal time amounting to as much as 1·2 seconds. It is therefore customary to employ Mean Sidereal Time, from which these fluctuations have been removed. The conversion of G.M.T. to Greenwich sidereal time (G.S.T.) may be performed by adding the value of the G.S.T. at 0^h on the day in question (page II of each month) to the G.M.T. converted to sidereal time using the table on p. 146.

Example. To find the G.S.T. at August $8^d 02^h 41^m 11^s$ G.M.T.

					h	m	s
G.S.T. at 0^h	..	..	..	..	21	04	50
G.M.T.	..	..	..	..	2	41	11
Acceleration for 2^h	..	..	..				20
„ „ $41^m 11^s$	..	..					7
Sum = G.S.T. =	..	..	..		23	46	28

If the observer is not on the Greenwich meridian then his longitude, measured positively westwards from Greenwich, must be subtracted from the G.S.T. to obtain Local Sidereal Time (L.S.T.). Thus, in the above example, an observer 5^h east of Greenwich, or 19^h west, would find his L.S.T. as $4^h 46^m 28^s$.

Terrestrial Dynamical Time

In the study of the motions of the Sun, Moon and planets, observations taken over an extended period are used in the preparation of tables giving the apparent position of the body each day. A table of this sort is known as an ephemeris, and may be used in the comparison of current observations with tabulated positions. A detailed examination of the observations made over the past 300 years shows that the Sun, Moon and planets appear to depart from their predicted positions by amounts proportional to their mean motions. The only satisfactory explanation is that the time scale to which the observations were referred was not uniform as had been supposed. Since the time scale was based on the rotation of the Earth, it follows that this rotation is subject to irregularities. The fact that the discrepancies between the observed and ephemeris positions were proportional to the mean motions of the bodies made it possible to secure agreement by substituting a revised time scale and recomputing the ephemeris positions. The time scale which brings the ephemeris into agreement with the observations has been named Terrestrial Dynamical Time (T.D.T.), formerly known as Ephemeris Time.

The new unit of time has been defined in terms of the apparent annual motion of the Sun. Thus the second is now defined in terms of the annual motion of the Earth in its orbit around the Sun ($1/31556925·9747$ of the Tropical Year for 1900 January $0^d 12^h$ T.D.T.) instead of in terms of the diurnal rotation of the Earth on its axis ($1/86\,400$ of the Mean Solar Day). In many branches of scientific work other than astronomy there has been a demand for a unit of time that is invariable, and the second of Ephemeris time was adopted by the Comité International des Poids et Mésures in 1956. The length of the unit has been chosen to provide general agreement with U.T. throughout the 19th and 20th centuries. During 1986 the estimated difference E.T.$-$U.T. is 55 seconds. The precise determination of T.D.T. from astronomical observations is a lengthy process, as the accuracy with which a single observation of the Sun can be made is far less than that obtainable in, for instance, a comparison between clocks. It is therefore necessary to average the observations over an extended period. Largely on account of its faster motion, the position of the Moon may be observed with greater accuracy, and a close approximation to Terrestrial Dynamical Time may be obtained by comparing observations of the moon with its ephemeris position. Even in this case, however, the requisite standard of accuracy can only be achieved by averaging over a number of years.

Atomic Time

The fundamental standards of time and frequency must be defined in terms of a periodic motion adequately uniform, enduring and susceptible of measurement. This has led in the past to the adoption of standards based on the observed motions in the Solar System. Recent progress has made it possible to consider the use of other natural standards, such as atomic or molecular oscillations. The oscillations so far employed are not in fact continuous periodic motions such as the revolution of the electrons in their orbits around the nuclei. The continuous oscillations are generated in an electrical circuit, the frequency of which is then compared or brought into coincidence with the frequency characteristic of the absorption or emission by the atoms or molecules when they change between two selected energy levels. At the National Physical Laboratory regular comparisons have been made since the middle of 1955 between quartz clocks of high stability and a frequency defined by atoms of caesium. The standard has proved of great value in the precise calibration of frequencies and time intervals: it has also been possible to build up a scale of "atomic time" by using continuously-running quartz clocks calibrated in terms of the caesium frequency standard.

Radio Time Signals

The establishment of a uniform time system by the assessment of the performance of standard clocks in terms of astronomical observations is the work of a national observatory, and standard time is then made generally available by means of radio time signals. In the United Kingdom, the Royal Greenwich Observatory is responsible for the legal standard of time, and controls the "6-pips" radio signals emitted by the British Broadcasting Corporation. Signals by land line from the Observatory correct the Post Office Speaking Clock, TIM.

For survey and scientific purposes in which the highest accuracy is required, special signals are transmitted from the Post Office Radio Station at Rugby. The International Signals, consisting of a five-minute series of pips, one-tenth of a second long, with the pips at the minutes lengthened for identification, are radiated at 02.54–03.00, 08.54–09.00, 14.54–15.00, 20.54–21.00 from GBR (16 kHz) and associated H.F. transmitters. The seconds pulses superposed on the MSF standard frequency transmissions, which

consists of five cycles of a 1,000 c.p.s. tone, are derived from the same master control at the transmitting station, and are radiated for ten minutes in each quarter-hour on $2\frac{1}{2}$, 5, and 10 MHz for 24 hours per day, and continuously on 60 kHz. The carrier frequencies of all the MSF transmissions, and of GBR, are closely controlled, and measured regularly at the National Physical Laboratory in terms of the caesium atomic resonance.

The Coordinated Universal Time (U.T.C.) system standard frequency emissions and radio time signals are broadcast on MSF, GBR, and by other national transmitters, eg. by WWV and WWVH in the U.S.A. in conformity with the International Atomic Time Scale in which the time intervals between pips correspond exactly to the seconds defined as follows: "The second is the duration of 9 192 631 770 periods of the radiation corresponding to the transition between the 2 hyperfine levels of the ground state of the caesium 133 atom."

As the rate of rotation of the Earth is variable the time signals will be adjusted by the introduction of a leap second when necessary in order that UTC shall not depart from UT by more than $0^s.9$. For convenience it has been decided to introduce leap seconds, when necessary, on the last second of a month preferably on 31 Dec. and/or 30 June. In the case of a positive leap second $23^h\ 59^m\ 60^s$ will be followed one second later by $0^h\ 00^m\ 00^s$ of the first day of the month. In the case of a negative leap second (required if the Earth were to have a sudden change of rate and begin to gain relative to UTC) $23^h\ 59^m\ 58^s$ will be followed one second later by $0^h\ 00^m\ 00^s$ of the first day of the month.

From 1972 Jan. 1 the six pips on the BBC have consisted of 5 short pips from second 55 to second 59 followed by one lengthened pip, the start of which indicates the exact minute.

SUMMER TIME

In the United Kingdom, in 1986, Summer Time, one hour in advance of G.M.T. will be in force from March $30^d\ 01^h$ to October $26^d\ 01^h$.

Variations from the standard time of some countries occurs during part of the year: they are decided annually and are usually referred to as Summer Time or Daylight Saving Time. These variations occur in:

The Commonwealth.—Parts of Australia; Bahamas; Canada; Channel Islands; Gibraltar; Hong Kong; New Zealand; Bermuda; Malta.

Foreign Countries.—Albania; Argentina; Austria; Brazil; Bulgaria; Canary Is.; Chile; parts of China; Corsica; Costa Rica; Cuba; Cyprus Ercan; Cyprus Larnaca; Czechoslovakia; Denmark; Dominican Republic; Egypt; Faroe; Finland; France; Germany; Greece; Guatemala; Haiti; Hungary; Iceland; Iraq; Israel; Italy; Libya; Macau; Madeira; Mexico; Mongolia; Norway; Peru; Pescadores Is.; Poland; Portugal; Romania; Sicily; Sudan; Sweden; Switzerland; Taiwan; Turkey; Uruguay; parts of U.S.A.; U.S.S.R; Yugoslavia.

In the Dominican Republic, the Irish Republic, and Paraguay, the variation occurs in winter and is called Winter Time.

STANDARD TIME

In the year 1880 it was enacted by statute that the word "time", when it occurred in any legal document relating to Great Britain, was to be interpreted, unless otherwise specifically stated, as the Mean Time of the Greenwich meridian.* Since the year 1883 the system of Standard Time by Zones has been gradually accepted, and now almost throughout the world a Standard Time which differs from that of Greenwich by an integral number of hours, either fast or slow, is used.

The large territories of the United States, Canada and U.S.S.R. are divided into zones approximately $7\frac{1}{2}°$ on either side of central meridians. The important ones are given below; there are in addition zones from 5 to 13 hours fast in the U.S.S.R. centred at 60° E. to 180° E.

Central-European	Hungary, Switzerland, Italy, Czechoslovakia, Yugoslavia, Albania, Tunisia, Nigeria, Malta, Sicily, Central African Republic, Cameroon Republic, Zaire, Angola, Spitsbergen, Benin, Corsica, Sardinia, Portugal, Niger, Irish Republic, Gibraltar.
Greenwich Time	The United Kingdom, Faroe, Channel Is., Iceland, Mauritania, Sierra Leone, Ivory Coast, Ifni, Ghana, Principe I., St. Helena, Gambia, Canary Is., Ascension I., Tangier, São Tomé, Rio de Oro, Madeira, Mali, Senegal, Liberia, Guinea Bissau, Algeria.

Fast on Greenwich Time

12 hrs. F ... Fiji, Kiribati Republic, New Zealand, Marshall Is., Caroline Is. (east of 160° E.), Nauru I.

$11\frac{1}{2}$,, F ... Norfolk I.

11 ,, F ... New Caledonia, Santa Cruz and Solomon Is., Ponape, Sakhalin, Republic of Vanuatu, Caroline Is. (150°E. to 160°E.).

10 ,, F ... Victoria, N.S.W. (except Broken Hill Area), Queensland, Tasmania, Admiralty Islds., Australian Capital Territory, Mariana Islds, Caroline Is. (135°E. to 150°E.), Truk.

$9\frac{1}{2}$,, F ... South Australia, Northern Territory of Australia, N.S.W. (Broken Hill Area).

9 ,, F ... Japan, Schouten Islds., Kurile Islds., Manchuria, Korea, Irian Jaya, Caroline Is. (west of 135°E.).

$8\frac{1}{2}$,, F ... Molucca Islds.

8 ,, F ... China (coast), Hong Kong, Philippine Is., Macau, Timor, Western Australia, Sulawesi (Celebes), Kalimantan†, Taiwan, Pescadores Islds, Malaysia.

7 ,, F ... Sumatra, Java, Christmas I. (Indian Ocean), Thailand, Kampuchea, Laos, Vietnam.

$6\frac{1}{2}$,, F ... Burma, Cocos-Keeling Islds.

6 ,, F ... Bangladesh, Chagos Archipelago.

$5\frac{1}{2}$,, F ... India, Sri Lanka, Laccadive Islds., Andaman and Nicobar Islds.

5 ,, F ... Pakistan.

4 ,, F ... Mauritius, Seychelles, Réunion, U.S.S.R., 40° E. to 52° 30′ E, United Arab Emirates.

$3\frac{1}{2}$,, F ... Iran.

3 ,, F ... U.S.S.R. west of 40° E., Iraq, Ethiopia, Yemen (Dem. Repub.), Socotra I., Somali Republic, Comoro Islds., Madagascar, Uganda, Kenya, Tanzania, Bahrain, Syria.

2 ,, F ... Greece, Bulgaria, Romania, Finland, Israel, Jordan, Egypt, Zimbabwe, Malawi, South Africa, Mozambique, Sudan, Burundi, Rwanda, Crete, Lebanon, Libya, Zambia, Botswana, Lesotho, Cyprus, Turkey. *(E. European)*

1 hr. F ... Sweden, Norway, Denmark, Netherlands, Belgium, Germany, France, Luxemburg, Spain, Monaco, Balearic Islds., Poland, Austria, Morocco.

Slow on Greenwich time

1 hr. S ... Azores, Cape Verde Is.

2 hrs. S ... Fernando Noronha I., South Georgia.

3 ,, S ... Greenland (excluding Thule), Eastern Brazil, Argentina, Uruguay, French Guiana, Guyana.

$3\frac{1}{2}$,, S ... Newfoundland, Suriname.

4 ,, S ... Canada east of 68° W., Greenland (Thule Area), Puerto Rico, Lesser Antilles, Central Brazil, Falkland Islds., Paraguay, Bermuda, Bolivia, Chile, Curaçao I., Venezuela, Labrador, Dominican Republic. *(Atlantic)*

5 hrs. S ... Canada from 68° W. to 85° W. (north) or 90° W. (south), Eastern States of U.S.A., Jamaica, Bahama Islds., Haiti, Peru, Panama, W. Brazil, Colombia, Cayman Is., Ecuador, Cuba. *(Eastern)*

6 hrs. S ... Central parts of U.S.A., Canada from 85° W. to 102° W., Costa Rica, Salvador, Honduras, part of Mexico, Guatemala, Nicaragua. *(Central)*

7 hrs. S ... Canada from 102° W. to 120° W., Mountain States of U.S.A., part of Mexico. *(Mountain)*

8 hrs. S ... Canada west of 120° W., Alaska (southeast coast), Western States of U.S.A., part of Mexico, Yukon (east of 138° W.). *(Pacific)*

9 hrs. S ... Alaska E. of W. 169°·5, Yukon (west of 138° W.).

10 ,, S ... Low Archipelago, Austral and Society Islds., Hawaii, Fanning I., Christmas Islds. (Pacific Ocean), Aleutian Islds. (W. of W. 169°·5).

11 ,, S ... Alaska (west coast), Samoa, Midway Islds.

In the Tonga Islands the time 13*h* fast and in Chatham Is. 12*h* 45*m* fast on Greenwich is used, as the Date line is to the East of them.

THE DATE OR CALENDAR LINE

The line where the change of date occurs is a modification of the 180th meridian, and is drawn so as to include islands of any one group on the same side of the line, or for political reasons. It is indicated by joining up the following nine points:

Lat.	Long.	Lat.	Long.	Lat.	Long.
60° S.	180°	15° S.	$172\frac{1}{2}°$ W.	53° N.	170° E.
51° S.	180°	5° S.	180°	$65\frac{1}{2}°$ N.	169° W.
45° S.	$172\frac{1}{2}°$ W.	48° N.	180°	75° N.	180°

---

* Summer Time is the "legal" time during the period in which its use is ordained. † *Formerly* Indonesian Borneo.

RISING AND SETTING TIMES

Table 1. Hour Angle

Dec.	Latitude and Declination of Opposite Signs						0°	Latitude and Declination of Same Signs					
	50°	45°	40°	30°	20°	10°	0°	10°	20°	30°	40°	45°	50°
°	h m	h m	h m	h m	h m	h m	h m	h m	h m	h m	h m	h m	h m
0	6 00	6 00	6 00	6 00	6 00	6 00	6 00	6 00	6 00	6 00	6 00	6 00	6 00
1	5 55	5 56	5 57	5 58	5 59	5 59	6 00	6 01	6 01	6 02	6 03	6 04	6 05
2	5 50	5 52	5 53	5 55	5 57	5 58	6 00	6 02	6 03	6 05	6 07	6 08	6 10
3	5 45	5 48	5 50	5 53	5 56	5 58	6 00	6 02	6 04	6 07	6 10	6 12	6 15
4	5 40	5 44	5 46	5 51	5 54	5 57	6 00	6 03	6 06	6 09	6 14	6 16	6 20
5	5 36	5 40	5 43	5 48	5 52	5 56	6 00	6 04	6 08	6 12	6 17	6 20	6 24
6	5 31	5 36	5 39	5 46	5 51	5 56	6 00	6 04	6 09	6 14	6 21	6 24	6 29
7	5 26	5 32	5 36	5 44	5 50	5 55	6 00	6 05	6 10	6 16	6 24	6 28	6 34
8	5 21	5 27	5 33	5 41	5 48	5 54	6 00	6 06	6 12	6 19	6 27	6 33	6 39
9	5 16	5 23	5 29	5 39	5 47	5 53	6 00	6 07	6 13	6 21	6 31	6 37	6 44
10	5 11	5 19	5 26	5 37	5 45	5 53	6 00	6 07	6 15	6 23	6 34	6 41	6 49
11	5 06	5 15	5 22	5 34	5 44	5 52	6 00	6 08	6 16	6 26	6 38	6 45	6 54
12	5 01	5 11	5 19	5 32	5 42	5 51	6 00	6 09	6 18	6 28	6 41	6 49	6 59
13	4 56	5 06	5 15	5 29	5 40	5 51	6 00	6 09	6 20	6 31	6 45	6 54	7 04
14	4 51	5 02	5 12	5 27	5 39	5 50	6 00	6 10	6 21	6 33	6 48	6 58	7 09
15	4 46	4 58	5 08	5 24	5 38	5 49	6 00	6 11	6 22	6 36	6 52	7 02	7 14
16	4 40	4 53	5 04	5 22	5 36	5 48	6 00	6 12	6 24	6 38	6 56	7 07	7 20
17	4 35	4 49	5 00	5 19	5 35	5 48	6 00	6 12	6 25	6 41	7 00	7 11	7 25
18	4 29	4 44	4 57	5 17	5 33	5 47	6 00	6 13	6 27	6 43	7 03	7 16	7 31
19	4 23	4 39	4 53	5 14	5 31	5 46	6 00	6 14	6 29	6 46	7 07	7 21	7 37
20	4 17	4 35	4 49	5 11	5 30	5 45	6 00	6 15	6 30	6 49	7 11	7 25	7 43
21	4 11	4 30	4 44	5 09	5 28	5 44	6 00	6 16	6 32	6 51	7 16	7 30	7 49
22	4 04	4 25	4 40	5 06	5 26	5 44	6 00	6 16	6 34	6 54	7 20	7 35	7 56
23	3 58	4 19	4 36	5 03	5 24	5 43	6 00	6 17	6 36	6 57	7 24	7 41	8 02
24	3 52	4 14	4 32	5 00	5 23	5 42	6 00	6 18	6 37	7 00	7 28	7 46	8 08
25	3 45	4 09	4 28	4 58	5 21	5 41	6 00	6 19	6 39	7 02	7 32	7 51	8 15
26	3 38	4 03	4 24	4 55	5 19	5 40	6 00	6 20	6 41	7 05	7 36	7 57	8 22
27	3 30	3 57	4 19	4 52	5 17	5 39	6 00	6 21	6 43	7 08	7 41	8 03	8 30
28	3 23	3 51	4 14	4 48	5 15	5 38	6 00	6 22	6 45	7 12	7 46	8 09	8 37
29	3 15	3 45	4 09	4 45	5 14	5 38	6 00	6 22	6 46	7 15	7 51	8 15	8 45

SUNRISE AND SUNSET

The local mean time of sunrise or sunset (as defined on page 138) may be found by determining the appropriate hour angle from the table above and applying it to the time of transit given in the ephemeris for each month. The hour angle is negative for sunrise and positive for sunset. A small correction to the hour angle, which always has the effect of increasing it numerically, is necessary to allow for the Sun's semi-diameter (16′) and for refraction (34′). This correction may be obtained from Table 2. The resulting local mean time may be converted into the standard time of the country by taking the difference between the longitude of the standard meridian of the country and that of the place, and adding it to the local mean time if the place is west of the standard meridian, and subtracting it if the place is east of the standard meridian.

Example.—Required the N.Z. Mean Time (12ʰ fast on G.M.T.) of sunset on May 24 at Auckland. The latitude is 36° 50′ south (or minus) and the longitude 11ʰ 39ᵐ east. Taking the declination as +20°·7, we find

		h	m
Tabular entry for 30° Lat. and Dec. 20°, opposite signs	+	5	11
Proportional part for 6° 50′ of Lat.	−		15
Proportional part for 0°·7 of Dec.	−		3
Correction (Table 2)	+		6
Hour angle		4	59
Sun transits		11	57
Longitudinal correction	+		21
N.Z. Mean Time		17	17

Table 2. Correction for Refraction and Semi-Diameter

Latitude	Declination			
	0°	10°	20°	29°
°	m	m	m	m
0	3	3	4	4
20	4	4	4	4
30	4	4	4	5
40	4	4	5	6
50	5	5	6	8

MOONRISE AND MOONSET

It is possible to calculate the times of moonrise and moonset using Table 1 though the method is more complicated because the apparent motion of the Moon is much more rapid than that of the Sun.

Table 3. Longitude Correction

X \ A	40^m	45^m	50^m	55^m	60^m	65^m	70^m
h	m	m	m	m	m	m	m
1	2	2	2	2	3	3	3
2	3	4	4	5	5	5	6
3	5	6	6	7	8	8	9
4	7	8	8	9	10	11	12
5	8	9	10	11	13	14	15
6	10	11	13	14	15	16	18
7	12	13	15	16	18	19	20
8	13	15	17	18	20	22	23
9	15	17	19	21	23	24	26
10	17	19	21	23	25	27	29
11	18	21	23	25	28	30	32
12	20	23	25	28	30	33	35
13	22	24	27	30	33	35	38
14	23	26	29	32	35	38	41
15	25	28	31	34	38	41	44
16	27	30	33	37	40	43	47
17	28	32	35	39	43	46	50
18	30	34	38	41	45	49	53
19	32	36	40	44	48	51	55
20	33	38	42	46	50	54	58
21	35	39	44	48	53	57	61
22	37	41	46	50	55	60	64
23	38	43	48	53	58	62	67
24	40	45	50	55	60	65	70

Notation

φ = latitude of observer
λ = longitude of observer (measured positively towards the west)
T_{-1} = time of transit of Moon on previous day
T_0 = time of transit of Moon on day in question
T_1 = time of transit of Moon on following day
δ_0 = approximate declination of Moon
δ_R = declination of Moon at moonrise
δ_S = declination of Moon at moonset
h_0 = approximate hour angle of Moon
h_R = hour angle of Moon at moonrise
h_S = hour angle of Moon at moonset
t_R = time of moonrise
t_S = time of moonset

The parallax of the Moon, about 57′, is near to the sum of the semi-diameter and refraction but has the opposite effect on these times. It is thus convenient to neglect all three quantities in the method outlined below.

Method

1. With arguments φ, δ_0 enter Table 1 on p. 144 to determine h_0 where h_0 is negative for moonrise and positive for moonset.

2. Form approximate times from
$$t_R = T_0 + \lambda + h_0$$
$$t_S = T_0 + \lambda + h_0$$

3. Determine δ_R, δ_S for times t_R, t_S respectively.

4. Re-enter Table 1 on p. 144 with—
   (a) arguments φ, δ_R to determine h_R
   (b) arguments φ, δ_S to determine h_S

5. Form $t_R = T_0 + \lambda + h_R + AX$
$$t_S = T_0 + \lambda + h_S + AX$$

where $A = (\lambda + h)$

$$X = (T_0 - T_{-1}) \quad \text{if} (\lambda + h) \quad \text{is negative}$$
and $$X = (T_1 - T_0) \quad \text{if} (\lambda + h) \quad \text{is positive}$$

AX is the respondent in Table 3.

Example.—To find the times of moonrise and moonset at Vancouver ($\varphi = +49°$, $\lambda = +8^h 12^m$) on 1986 January 6. The starting data (from p. 92) are

$$\begin{array}{lll} & h & m \\ T_{-1} & = 7 & 08 \\ T_0 & = 8 & 01 \\ T_1 & = 8 & 59 \\ \delta & = -17° \end{array}$$

1. $h_0 = 4^h 38^m$
2. Approximate values
$$\begin{aligned} t_R & = 6^d 08^h 01^m + 8^h 12^m + (-4^h 38^m) \\ & = 6^d 11^h 35^m \\ t_S & = 6^d 08^h 01^m + 8^h 12^m + (+4^h 38^m) \\ & = 6^d 20^h 51^m \end{aligned}$$
3. $\delta_R = -19°\cdot0$
   $\delta_S = -20°\cdot9$
4. $h_R = -4^h 26^m$
   $h_S = +4^h 16^m$
5. $t_R = 6^d 08^h 01^m + 8^h 12^m + (-4^h 26^m) + 9^m$
   $= 6^d 11^h 56^m$
   $t_S = 6^d 08^h 01^m + 8^h 12^m + (+4^h 16^m) + 31^m$
   $= 6^d 21^h 00^m$

To get the L.M.T. of the phenomenon the longitude is subtracted from the G.M.T. thus
Moonrise $= 6^d 11^h 56^m - 8^h 12^m = 6^d 03^h 44^m$
Moonset $= 6^d 21^h 00^m - 8^h 12^m = 6^d 12^h 48^m$

ASTRONOMICAL CONSTANTS

Solar Parallax	8″·794
Precession for the year 1986	50″·288
„ in R.A.	3ˢ·075
„ in Declination	20″·044
Constant of Nutation	9″·202
Constant of Aberration	20″·496
Mean Obliquity of Ecliptic (1986)	23° 26′ 28″
Moon's Equatorial Hor. Parallax	57′ 02″·70
Velocity of Light in vacuo *per sec*	299792·5 km.
Solar motion *per sec*	20·0 km.
Equatorial radius of the Earth	6378·140 km.
Polar radius of the Earth	6356·755 km.

North Galactic Pole } R.A. $12^h 49^m$ (1950·0).
(I.A.U. *Standard*). } Dec. 27°·4 N.
Solar Apex ... R.A. $18^h 06^m$ Dec. + 30°

Length of Year...Tropical	365·24220	
(*In Mean*	Sidereal	365·25636
Solar Days)	Anomalistic	365·25964
	(*Perihelion to Perihelion*)	
	Eclipse	346·6200

		d h m s
Length of Month	New Moon to New	29 12 44 02·9
(*Mean Values*)	Sidereal	27 07 43 11·5
	Anomalistic	27 13 18 33·2
	(*Perigee to Perigee*)	

MEAN AND SIDEREAL TIME

Acceleration				Retardation				MEAN REFRACTION	
h m s	h m s	m s s		h m s	h m s	m s s		Alt. Ref.	Alt. Ref.
1 0 10	13 2 08	0 00	0	1 0 10	13 2 08	0 00	0	° ′ ′	° ′ ′
2 0 20	14 2 18	3 02	0	2 0 20	14 2 18	3 03	1	1 20 21	4 30 10
3 0 30	15 2 28	9 07	1	3 0 29	15 2 27	9 09	2	1 30 20	5 06 9
4 0 39	16 2 38	15 13	2	4 0 39	16 2 37	15 15	3	1 41 19	5 50 8
		21 18	3			21 21		1 52 18	6 44 7
5 0 49	17 2 48	27 23	4	5 0 49	17 2 47	27 28	4	2 05 17	7 54 6
6 0 59	18 2 57	33 28	5	6 0 59	18 2 57	33 34	5	2 19 16	9 27 5
7 1 09	19 3 07	39 34	6	7 1 09	19 3 07	39 40	6	2 35 15	11 39 4
8 1 19	20 3 17	45 39	7	8 1 19	20 3 17	45 46	7	2 52 14	15 00 3
9 1 29	21 3 27	51 44	8	9 1 28	21 3 26	51 53	8	3 12 13	20 42 2
		57 49	9			57 59		3 34 12	32 20 1
10 1 39	22 3 37	60 00	10	10 1 38	22 3 36	60 00	10	4 00 11	62 17 0
11 1 48	23 3 47			11 1 48	23 3 46			4 30	90 00
12 1 58	24 3 57			12 1 58	24 3 56				

The length of a sidereal day in mean time is $23^h 56^m 04^s\cdot09$. Hence 1^h M.T. $= 1^h + 9^s\cdot86$ S.T. and 1^h S.T. $= 1^h - 9^s\cdot83$ M.T.

To convert an interval of mean time to the corresponding interval of sidereal time, enter the acceleration table with the given mean time (taking the hours and the minutes and seconds separately) and add the acceleration obtained to the given mean time. To convert an interval of sidereal time to the corresponding interval of mean time, take out the retardation for the given sidereal time and subtract.

The columns for the minutes and seconds of the argument are in the form known as Critical Tables. To use these tables, find in the appropriate left-hand column the two entries between which the given number of minutes and seconds lies; the quantity in the right-hand column between these two entries is the required acceleration or retardation. Thus the acceleration for $11^m 26^s$ (which lies between the entries $9^m 07^s$ and $15^m 13^s$) is 2^s. If the given number of minutes and seconds is a tabular entry, the required acceleration or retardation is the entry in the right-hand column *above* the given tabular entry; e.g. the retardation for $45^m 46^s$ is 7^s.

Example.—Convert $14^h 27^m 35^s$ from S.T. to M.T.

	h m s
Given S.T.	14 27 35
Retardation for 14^h	2 18
Retardation for $27^m 35^s$	5
Corresponding M.T.	14 25 12

For further explanation, see p. 141.
The refraction table is also in the form of a critical table.

THE SUMMER TIME ACTS

In 1916 an Act ordained that during a defined period of that year the legal time for general purposes in Great Britain should be one hour in advance of Greenwich Mean Time. The practice was stabilized (until the war) by the *Summer Time Acts*, 1922 to 1925, which enacted that "For the purposes of this Act, the period of summer time shall be taken to be the period beginning at two o'clock, Greenwich Mean Time, in the morning of the next day following the third Saturday in April, or, if that day be Easter Day, the day next following the second Saturday in April and ending at two o'clock, Greenwich Mean Time, in the morning of the day next following the first Saturday in October."

During the Second World War the duration of Summer Time was extended and in the years 1941–45 and in 1947, Double Summer Time (2 hrs. in advance of Greenwich Mean Time) was in force. Summer Time was extended in each year from 1948 to 1952 and again in 1961–1964, by Order in Council.

The duration of Summer Time during the last few years is given in the following table.

1960 Apr. 10—Oct. 2	1975 Mar. 16—Oct. 26
1961 Mar. 26—Oct. 29	1976 Mar. 21—Oct. 24
1962 Mar. 25—Oct. 28	1977 Mar. 20—Oct. 23
1963 Mar. 31—Oct. 27	1978 Mar. 19—Oct. 29
1964 Mar. 22—Oct. 25	1979 Mar. 18—Oct. 28
1965 Mar. 21—Oct. 24	1980 Mar. 16—Oct. 26
1966 Mar. 20—Oct. 23	1981 Mar. 29—Oct. 25
1967 Mar. 19—Oct. 29	1982 Mar. 28—Oct. 24
1968 Feb. 18—Oct. 27	1983 Mar. 27—Oct. 23
1972 Mar. 19—Oct. 29	1984 Mar. 25—Oct. 28
1973 Mar. 18—Oct. 28	1985 Mar. 31—Oct. 27
1974 Mar. 17—Oct. 27	

(British Standard Time, also one hour ahead of G.M.T., was kept between 1968 Oct. 27–1971 Oct. 31.) In 1986 Summer Time will be in force from March 30 to October 26.

ASTRONOMERS ROYAL

John Flamsteed, first Astronomer Royal	1675–1719	Sir William Henry Mahoney Christie	1881–1910
Edmund Halley	1720–1742	Sir Frank Watson Dyson	1910–1933
James Bradley	1742–1762	Sir Harold Spencer Jones	1933–1955
Nathaniel Bliss	1762–1764	Sir Richard van der Riet Woolley	1955–1971
Nevil Maskelyne	1765–1811	Sir Martin Ryle	1972–1982
John Pond	1811–1835	Prof. F. Graham Smith	1982–
Sir George Biddell Airy	1835–1881		

PHENOMENA OF JUPITER'S SATELLITES, 1986

G.M.T. Sat. Phen.

January

d	h	m	Sat	Phen
3	18	31	II	Sh.E.
4	18	48	III	Sh.E.
7	17	04	I	Sh.E.
10	18	15	II	Sh.I.
22	18	03	I	Ec.R.

June

d	h	m	Sat	Phen
4	03	25	III	Sh.I.
7	03	29	I	Sh.E.
9	01	21	II	Sh.I.
14	03	07	I	Sh.I.
19	02	01	IV	Ec.R.
22	01	20	III	Ec.D.
22	02	19	I	Ec.D.
23	01	44	I	Sh.I.
25	00	45	II	Ec.D.
30	01	23	I	Sh.I.
30	03	38	I	Sh.E.

July

d	h	m	Sat	Phen
2	03	20	II	Ec.D.
4	01	17	II	Sh.E.
7	03	17	I	Sh.I.
8	00	36	I	Ec.D.
9	00	00	I	Sh.E.
10	02	52	III	Sh.I.
11	01	05	II	Sh.I.
14	01	25	IV	Sh.I.
15	02	30	I	Ec.D.
15	23	39	I	Sh.I.
16	01	54	I	Sh.E.
17	03	26	III	Sh.I.
18	03	41	II	Sh.I.
23	01	32	I	Sh.I.
23	03	48	I	Sh.E.
23	22	52	I	Ec.D.
27	00	24	II	Ec.D.
28	00	49	III	Ec.R.
28	22	22	II	Sh.E.
30	03	26	I	Sh.I.
30	23	14	IV	Sh.E.
31	00	46	I	Ec.D.

August

d	h	m	Sat	Phen
1	00	11	I	Sh.E.
3	03	00	II	Ec.D.
4	01	24	III	Ec.D.
4	22	11	I	Sh.I.
5	00	58	II	Sh.E.
7	02	41	I	Ec.D.
7	23	49	I	Sh.E.
8	02	05	I	Sh.E.
12	00	47	II	Sh.I.
12	03	33	II	Sh.E.
14	04	35	I	Ec.D.

G.M.T. Sat. Phen.

August

d	h	m	Sat	Phen
14	22	51	III	Sh.E.
15	01	43	I	Sh.I.
15	03	59	I	Sh.E.
15	23	03	I	Ec.D.
16	22	28	I	Sh.I.
19	03	22	II	Sh.I.
20	21	31	II	Ec.D.
21	23	28	III	Sh.I.
22	02	52	III	Sh.I.
22	03	37	I	Sh.I.
23	00	58	I	Ec.D.
23	22	06	I	Sh.I.
24	00	22	I	Sh.E.
24	23	04	IV	Ec.D.
25	02	24	IV	Ec.R.
28	00	07	II	Ec.D.
29	03	30	III	Sh.I.
29	22	02	II	Sh.E.
30	02	52	I	Sh.I.
31	00	01	I	Sh.I.
31	02	17	I	Sh.E.
31	21	21	I	Ec.D.

September

d	h	m	Sat	Phen
1	20	46	I	Sh.E.
4	02	45	II	Ec.D.
5	21	52	II	Sh.I.
6	00	37	II	Sh.E.
6	04	47	I	Ec.D.
7	01	55	I	Sh.E.
7	04	12	I	Sh.E.
7	23	15	I	Sh.I.
8	20	24	I	Sh.I.
8	21	28	III	Ec.D.
8	22	40	I	Sh.E.
10	20	31	IV	Ec.R.
13	00	28	II	Sh.I.
13	03	13	II	Sh.I.
14	03	50	I	Sh.I.
14	21	28	I	Ec.R.
15	03	26	I	Sh.I.
15	22	19	I	Sh.E.
16	00	35	I	Sh.E.
16	21	54	I	Sh.E.
17	19	04	I	Sh.E.
19	02	40	IV	Sh.I.
20	03	04	III	Sh.I.
22	00	06	II	Ec.R.
23	00	14	I	Sh.I.
23	02	30	I	Sh.E.
23	19	06	II	Sh.E.

G.M.T. Sat. Phen.

September

d	h	m	Sat	Phen
23	23	49	I	Ec.R.
24	18	43	I	Sh.I.
24	20	59	I	Sh.E.
26	19	36	III	Sh.I.
26	22	56	III	Sh.E.
29	02	44	II	Ec.R.
30	02	10	I	Sh.I.
30	18	57	II	Sh.I.
30	21	41	II	Sh.E.

October

d	h	m	Sat	Phen
1	01	44	I	Ec.R.
1	20	38	I	Sh.I.
1	22	54	I	Sh.E.
2	20	12	I	Ec.R.
3	23	38	III	Sh.I.
4	02	57	III	Sh.E.
5	21	03	IV	Sh.I.
5	23	50	IV	Sh.E.
7	21	33	II	Sh.I.
8	00	16	II	Sh.E.
8	22	34	I	Sh.I.
9	00	50	I	Sh.E.
9	18	41	II	Ec.R.
9	22	07	I	Ec.R.
10	19	19	I	Sh.E.
14	20	56	III	Ec.R.
15	00	09	II	Sh.I.
16	00	30	I	Sh.I.
16	21	19	II	Ec.R.
17	00	02	I	Ec.R.
17	18	59	I	Sh.I.
17	21	14	I	Sh.E.
18	18	31	I	Ec.R.
21	21	39	III	Ec.D.
22	00	57	III	Ec.R.
22	17	59	IV	Sh.E.
22	23	58	II	Ec.R.
24	20	54	I	Sh.I.
24	23	10	I	Sh.E.
25	18	45	II	Sh.E.
25	20	26	I	Ec.R.
26	17	38	I	Sh.E.
31	00	19	IV	Ec.D.
31	22	50	I	Sh.I.

November

d	h	m	Sat	Phen
1	18	39	II	Sh.I.
1	19	03	III	Sh.E.
1	21	20	II	Sh.E.
1	22	21	I	Ec.R.
2	17	19	I	Sh.I.

G.M.T. Sat. Phen.

November

d	h	m	Sat	Phen
2	19	34	I	Sh.E.
8	19	50	III	Sh.I.
8	21	15	II	Sh.I.
8	23	04	III	Sh.E.
8	23	56	II	Sh.E.
9	00	16	I	Ec.R.
9	19	15	I	Sh.I.
9	21	30	I	Sh.E.
10	18	35	II	Ec.R.
10	18	45	I	Ec.R.
15	23	51	II	Sh.I.
15	23	53	III	Sh.I.
16	18	42	IV	Ec.D.
16	20	58	IV	Ec.R.
16	21	11	II	Sh.I.
16	23	26	I	Sh.E.
17	20	41	I	Ec.R.
17	21	14	II	Ec.R.
18	17	55	I	Sh.E.
19	17	03	III	Ec.R.
23	23	07	I	Sh.I.
24	22	36	I	Ec.R.
25	19	51	I	Sh.E.
26	17	05	I	Ec.R.
26	17	51	III	Ec.D.
26	18	25	III	Sh.E.
26	21	05	III	Ec.R.

December

d	h	m	Sat	Phen
2	19	32	I	Sh.I.
2	21	47	I	Sh.E.
3	18	22	II	Sh.I.
3	19	00	I	Ec.R.
3	21	01	II	Sh.E.
3	21	53	III	Ec.D.
9	21	29	I	Sh.I.
10	20	55	I	Ec.R.
10	20	58	II	Sh.I.
11	18	12	I	Sh.E.
12	18	29	II	Ec.R.
14	19	13	III	Sh.E.
18	17	54	I	Sh.I.
18	20	08	I	Sh.E.
19	17	20	I	Ec.R.
19	21	08	II	Sh.I.
21	20	07	III	Sh.I.
25	19	50	I	Sh.I.
26	19	15	I	Ec.R.
28	17	21	IV	Sh.I.
28	18	07	II	Sh.E.
28	18	25	IV	Sh.E.

Jupiter's satellites transit across the disk from east to west, and pass behind the disk from west to east. The shadows that they cast also transit across the disk. With the exception at times of Satellite IV, the satellites also pass through the shadow of the planet, i.e. they are eclipsed. Just before opposition the satellite disappears in the shadow to the west of the planet, and reappears from occultation on the east limb. Immediately after opposition the satellite is occulted at the west limb, and reappears from eclipse to the east of the planet. At times approximately two to four months before and after opposition, both phases of eclipses of Satellite III may be seen. When Satellite IV is eclipsed, both phases may be seen.

The list of phenomena gives most of the eclipses and shadow transits visible in the British Isles under favourable conditions.

Ec.	= Eclipse	R	= Reappearance
Sh.	= Shadow transit	I	= Ingress
D	= Disappearance	E	= Egress

CELESTIAL PHENOMENA FOR OBSERVATION IN 1986

ECLIPSES, 1986

There will be four eclipses during 1986, two of the Sun and two of the Moon. *Penumbral eclipses are not mentioned in this section as they are difficult to observe.*

1. A partial eclipse of the Sun on April 9 is visible from the south-eastern part of Indonesia, Australia, New Guinea, South Island of New Zealand, the southern part of the Indian Ocean and part of Antarctica. The eclipse begins at 04ʰ 10ᵐ and ends at 08ʰ 32ᵐ. At the time of maximum eclipse 0·82 of the Sun's diameter is obscured.

2. A total eclipse of the Moon on April 24 is visible from the western part of North America, the Pacific Ocean, Antarctica, Australasia, Indonesia, the Philippine Islands, Japan, the eastern part of Asia and the eastern part of the Indian Ocean. The eclipse begins at 11ʰ 04ᵐ and ends at 14ʰ 22ᵐ. Totality lasts from 12ʰ 11ᵐ to 13ʰ 15ᵐ.

3. An annular-total eclipse of the Sun on October 3. The path of the annular-total phase begins between Greenland and Iceland and ends to the south of Iceland. The partial phase is visible from the extreme north-eastern part of Asia, North America except the extreme south-western part, the arctic regions, Greenland, Iceland, the North Atlantic Ocean except the eastern part and the northern part of South America. The eclipse begins at 16ʰ 57ᵐ and ends at 21ʰ 13ᵐ; the annular phase begins at 18ʰ 56ᵐ and ends at 19ʰ 15ᵐ; the total phase begins at 19ʰ 05ᵐ and ends at 19ʰ 08ᵐ. The maximum duration of the annular phase is 2ˢ·6; the maximum duration of the total phase is 0ˢ·3.

4. A total eclipse of the Moon on October 17 is visible from Australia, New Guinea, Indonesia, the Philippine Islands, Japan, Asia, the Indian Ocean, Africa, Europe (including the British Isles), the eastern part of the Atlantic Ocean, Iceland, the eastern part of Greenland and the arctic regions. The eclipse begins at 17ʰ 30ᵐ and ends at 21ʰ 06ᵐ. Totality lasts from 18ʰ 41ᵐ to 19ʰ 55ᵐ.

TRANSIT, 1986

There will be a transit of Mercury across the disk of the Sun on November 13, visible from Australasia, Asia, part of Antarctica, Africa (except N.W.), and E. Europe. Ingress occurs at 01ʰ 43ᵐ–45ᵐ and egress at 06ʰ 29ᵐ–31ᵐ.

LUNAR OCCULTATIONS

Observations of the times of these occultations are made by both amateur and professional astronomers. Such observations are later analysed to yield accurate positions of the Moon: this is one method of determining the difference between ephemeris time and universal time.

Many of the observations made by amateurs are obtained with the use of a stop-watch which is compared with a time signal immediately after the observation. Thus an accuracy of about one-fifth of a second is obtainable, though the observer's personal equation may amount to one-third or one-half of a second.

The list on the opposite page includes most of the occultations visible under favourable conditions in the British Isles. No occultation is included unless the star is at least 10° above the horizon and the Sun sufficiently far below the horizon to permit the star to be seen with the naked eye or in a small telescope. The altitude limit is reduced from 10° to 2° for stars and planets brighter than magnitude 2·0 and such occultations are also predicted in daylight.

The column Phase shows whether a disappearance (1) or reappearance (2) is to be observed. The column headed "El. of Moon" gives the elongation of the Moon from the Sun, in degrees. The elongation increases from 0° at New Moon to 180° at Full Moon and on to 360° (or 0°) at New Moon again. Times and position angles (P), reckoned from the north point in the direction north, east, south, west, are given for Greenwich (Lat. 51° 30′, Long. 0°) and Edinburgh (Lat. 56° 00′, Long. 3° 12′ west).

The coefficients a and b are the variations in the G.M.T. for each degree of longitude (positive to the west) and latitude (positive to the north) respectively: they enable approximate times (to within about 1ᵐ generally) to be found for any point in the British Isles. If the point of observation is $\Delta\lambda$ degrees west and $\Delta\phi$ degrees north, the approximate time is found by adding $a.\Delta\lambda + b.\Delta\phi$ to the given G.M.T.

As an illustration the disappearance of z.c. 3419 on October 14 at Liverpool will be found from both Greenwich and Edinburgh.

	Greenwich	Edinburgh
	°	°
Longitude	0·0	+3·2
Long. of Liverpool	+3·0	+3·0
$\Delta\lambda$	+3·0	−0·2
Latitude	+51·5	+56·0
Lat. of Liverpool	+53·4	+53·4
$\Delta\phi$	+1·9	−2·6
	h m	h m
G.M.T.	20 57·5	20 52·3
$a.\Delta\lambda$	−7·2	+0·3
$b.\Delta\phi$	−0·2	−1·3
	20 50·1	20 51·3

If the occultation is given for one station but not the other, the reason for the suppression is given by the following code.

N = star not occulted.
A = star's altitude less than 10° (2° for bright stars and planets).
S = Sun not sufficiently below the horizon.
G = occultation is of very short duration.

It will be noticed that in some cases the coefficients a and b are not given: this is because the occultation is so short that prediction for other places by means of these coefficients would not be reliable.

LUNAR OCCULTATIONS, 1986

Date	Z.C. No.	Mag.	Phase	El. of Moon	GREENWICH U.T.	a	b	P	EDINBURGH U.T.	a	b	P
				°	h m	m	m	°	h m	m	m	°
Jan. 19	467	6·7	D.D.	112	22 27·2	−1·1	−1·1	80	22 20·2	−1·0	−0·5	65
20	582	5·8	D.D.	121	19 10·1	−0·1	4·4	7	N			
22	849	6·5	D.D.	142	S				17 12·7	−0·3	1·9	74
Feb. 15	429	6·9	D.D.	80	21 22·5	−0·8	0·5	35	21 24·3	−0·8	1·7	15
19	844	5·7	D.D.	115	3 02·1	..	..	24	3 02·6	..	..	12
19	958	6·7	D.D.	123	N				19 47·7	−1·7	−2·7	143
20	1088	5·6	D.D.	133	17 54·8	−1·1	0·8	107	17 56·8	−0·8	1·4	92
20	1105	6·5	D.D.	135	21 17·0	−1·5	−1·6	127	21 07·3	−1·4	−0·7	112
20	1108	6·9	D.D.	135	22 38·6	−1·7	0·0	73	22 34·9	−1·6	0·8	59
22	1251	5·9	D.D.	148	1 36·1	−0·5	−2·0	124	1 25·4	−0·6	−1·9	119
28	1945	5·4	R.D.	226	3 49·0	−1·8	−0·4	267	3 42·3	−1·5	−0·2	269
Mar. 3	2349	3·1	R.D.	265	3 16·4	−1·7	1·7	244	A			
13	272	5·9	D.D.	37	20 08·6	−0·3	0·1	35	20 09·5	−0·4	0·9	18
17	762	6·6	D.D.	81	20 51·3	−1·3	0·0	52	20 48·8	−1·3	0·8	37
17	780	6·8	D.D.	82	24 01·5	−0·2	−0·8	56	23 57·2	−0·3	−0·8	49
18	906	6·8	D.D.	92	21 21·3	..	..	156	21 02·3	−0·6	−3·3	138
18	909	6·1	D.D.	92	21 30·8	−1·2	−0·8	72	21 24·1	−1·2	−0·4	62
21	1211	6·2	D.D.	117	2 40·4	0·1	−1·4	84	2 34·2	0·0	−1·5	82
Apr. 11	457	6·5	D.D.	29	20 06·6	0·6	−3·2	130	19 54·9	0·2	−2·5	115
15	1013	6·9	D.D.	73	N				21 20·1	..	..	171
19	1393	6·7	D.D.	108	0 58·8	−0·3	−1·5	83	0 50·6	−0·4	−1·6	82
May 13	1105	6·5	D.D.	55	21 56·6	0·1	−1·6	101	21 49·3	0·0	−1·7	98
19	1772	4·0	D.D.	126	22 07·6	−1·0	−1·4	130	21 58·6	−0·9	−1·2	129
Jun. 19	2227	5·8	D.D.	149	23 05·3	−1·1	−1·0	139	22 58·1	−1·0	−0·7	138
19	2235	6·2	D.D.	149	23 43·9	−1·2	−1·1	114	A			
Sep. 10	2366	1·2	D.D.	81	16 05·5	−2·3	1·4	50	16 05·0	..	..	47
10	2366	1·2	R.B.	82	16 43·5	−0·5	−0·9	347	16 39·3	..	..	349
14	3052	6·2	D.D.	137	21 17·8	−1·9	−0·2	108	A			
15	3202	6·1	D.D.	151	22 30·3	−1·7	−0·1	89	22 25·5	−1·3	0·1	80
Oct. 11	2998	6·2	D.D.	106	18 46·5	−1·2	0·6	45	A			
12	3158	5·8	D.D.	120	21 40·0	−1·1	−0·3	66	21 35·8	−0·9	−0·2	55
12	3164	4·7	D.D.	121	23 35·8	..	..	356	N			
14	3419	4·5	D.D.	145	20 57·5	−2·4	−0·1	110	20 52·3	−1·7	0·5	98
15	3535	5·2	D.D.	157	19 59·5	−1·5	1·2	96	20 01·2	−1·1	1·4	89
19	465	4·5	R.D.	204	22 39·6	−0·2	2·7	202	22 49·9	−0·4	2·3	214
20	486	5·2	R.D.	208	5 26·4	−0·7	−2·3	287	5 11·2	−0·7	−3·7	306
23	890	4·5	R.D.	239	N				1 55·2	−0·3	4·5	202
Nov. 8	3102	6·9	D.D.	88	17 24·0	−2·0	0·0	113	17 19·4	−1·5	0·4	106
9	3265	6·6	D.D.	103	21 43·2	−0·6	−0·2	48	21 41·3	−0·4	0·0	34
20	1008	5·1	R.D.	221	5 05·5	−0·5	−3·6	327	4 44·2	..	..	347
25	1576	5·3	R.D.	277	S				7 00·5	−1·0	−1·2	311
Dec. 6	3202	6·1	D.D.	69	N				16 58·1	..	..	125
10	153	6·2	D.D.	118	17 22·1	−2·0	0·9	110	17 22·0	−1·3	1·3	98
11	180	5·6	D.D.	122	0 10·2	−0·5	0·3	35	0 11·8	−0·4	1·1	16
11	181	6·5	D.D.	122	0 11·1	−0·5	0·3	36	0 12·6	−0·4	1·1	16
12	299	6·3	D.D.	134	2 10·7	−0·4	0·0	38	2 10·8	−0·5	0·7	21
12	402	6·5	D.D.	143	22 50·8	−1·3	0·5	57	22 50·5	−1·0	1·1	41
13	415	6·0	D.D.	145	1 43·6	−0·8	0·3	38	1 44·1	−0·8	1·2	20
13	487	5·3	D.D.	151	16 21·5	0·1	1·9	59	16 30·4	0·1	1·9	53
13	492	5·9	D.D.	152	17 09·8	−0·4	1·7	86	17 16·7	−0·3	1·8	79

MEAN PLACES OF STARS, 1986·5

Name	Mag.	R.A.	Dec.	Spectrum
		h m	° ′	
α Andromedæ *Alpheratz*	2·1	0 07·7	+29 01	A0*p*
β Cassiopeiæ *Caph*	2·3	0 08·5	+59 05	F5
γ Pegasi *Algenib*	2·8	0 12·5	+15 07	B2
α Phœnicis	2·4	0 25·6	−42 23	K0
α Cassiopeiæ *Schedar*	2·2	0 39·7	+56 28	K0
β Ceti *Diphda*	2·0	0 42·9	−18 04	K0
γ Cassiopeiæ*	Var.	0 55·9	+60 39	B0*p*
β Andromedæ *Mirach*	2·1	1 09·0	+35 33	M0
δ Cassiopeiæ	2·7	1 24·9	+60 10	A5
α Eridani *Achernar*	0·5	1 37·2	−57 18	B5
β Arietis *Sheratan*	2·6	1 53·9	+20 45	A5
γ Andromedæ *Almak*	2·3	2 03·1	+42 16	K0
α Arietis *Hamal*	2·0	2 06·4	+23 24	K2
α Ursæ Minoris *Polaris*	2·0	2 17·8	+89 12	F8
β Persei *Algol**	Var.	3 07·3	+40 54	B8
α Persei *Mirfak*	1·8	3 23·4	+49 49	F5
η Tauri *Alcyone*	2·9	3 46·7	+24 04	B5*p*
α Tauri *Aldebaran*	0·9	4 35·1	+16 29	K5
β Orionis *Rigel*	0·1	5 13·9	− 8 13	B8*p*
α Aurigæ *Capella*	0·1	5 15·7	+45 59	G0
γ Orionis *Bellatrix*	1·6	5 24·4	+ 6 20	B2
β Tauri *Elnath*	1·7	5 25·4	+28 36	B8
δ Orionis	2·2	5 31·3	− 0 19	B0
α Leporis	2·6	5 32·1	−17 50	F0
ε Orionis	1·7	5 35·5	− 1 13	B0
ζ Orionis	1·8	5 40·1	− 1 57	B0
κ Orionis	2·1	5 47·1	− 9 40	B0.
α Orionis *Betelgeuse**	Var.	5 54·4	+ 7 24	M0
β Aurigæ *Menkalinan*	1·9	5 58·5	+44 57	A0*p*
β Canis Majoris *Mirzam*	2·0	6 22·1	−17 57	B1
α Carinæ *Canopus*	−0·7	6 23·7	−52 41	F0
γ Geminorum *Alhena*	1·9	6 36·9	+16 25	A0
α Canis Majoris *Sirius*	−1·5	6 44·6	−16 42	A0
ε Canis Majoris	1·5	6 58·1	−28 57	B1
δ Canis Majoris	1·9	7 07·8	−26 22	F8*p*
α Geminorum *Castor*	1·6	7 33·7	+31 55	A0
α Canis Minoris *Procyon*	0·4	7 38·6	+ 5 16	F5
β Geminorum *Pollux*	1·1	7 44·5	+28 04	K0
ζ Puppis	2·3	8 03·1	−39 58	Od
γ Velorum	1·8	8 09·1	−47 18	Oa*p*
ε Carinæ	1·9	8 22·2	−59 28	K0
δ Velorum	2·0	8 44·3	−54 40	A0
λ Velorum *Suhail*	2·2	9 07·5	−43 23	K5
β Carinæ	1·7	9 13·1	−69 40	A0
ι Carinæ	2·2	9 16·7	−59 13	F0
α Hydræ *Alphard*	2·0	9 26·9	− 8 36	K2
α Leonis *Regulus*	1·3	10 07·7	+12 02	B8
γ Leonis *Algeiba*	1·9	10 19·2	+19 55	K0
β Ursæ Majoris *Merak*	2·4	11 01·0	+56 27	A0
α Ursæ Majoris *Dubhe*	1·8	11 02·9	+61 49	K0

* γ Cassiopeiæ, 1985 mag. 2·6.   β Persei, mag. 2·2 to 3·2.
  α Orionis, mag. 0·1 to 1·2.

The positions of heavenly bodies on the celestial sphere are defined by two co-ordinates, right ascension and declination, which are analogous to longitude and latitude on the surface of the Earth. If we imagine the plane of the terrestrial equator extended indefinitely, it will cut the celestial sphere in a great circle known as the celestial equator. Similarly the plane of the Earth's orbit, when extended, cuts in the great circle called the ecliptic. The two intersections of these circles are known as the First Point of Aries and the First Point of Libra. If from any star a perpendicular be drawn to the celestial equator, the length of this perpendicular is the star's declination. The arc, measured eastwards along the equator from the First Point of Aries to the foot of this perpendicular, is the right ascension. An alternative definition of right ascension is that it is the angle at the celestial pole (where the Earth's axis, if prolonged, would meet the sphere) between the great circles to the First Point of Aries and to the star.

The plane of the Earth's equator has a slow movement, so that our reference system for right ascension and declination is not fixed. The consequent alteration in these quantities from year to year is called precession. In right ascension it is an increase of about 3ˢ a year for equatorial stars, and larger or smaller changes in either direction for stars near the poles, depending on the right ascension of the star. In declination it varies between +20″ and −20″ according to the right ascension of the star.

A star or other body crosses the meridian when the sidereal time is equal to its right ascension. The altitude is then a maximum, and may be deduced by remembering that the altitude of the elevated pole is numerically equal to the latitude, while that of the equator at its intersection with the meridian is equal to the co-latitude, or complement of the latitude.

MEAN PLACES OF STARS, 1986·5

NAME	Mag.	R.A.	Dec.	Spectrum
		h m	° ′	
δ Leonis	2·6	11 13·4	+20 36	A3
β Leonis *Denebola*	2·1	11 48·4	+14 39	A2
γ Ursæ Majoris *Phecda*	2·4	11 53·1	+53 46	A0
γ Corvi	2·6	12 15·1	−17 28	B8
α Crucis	1·0°	12 25·8	−63 01	B1
γ Crucis	1·6	12 30·4	−57 02	M3
γ Centauri	2·2	12 40·8	−48 53	A0
γ Virginis	2·7	12 41·0	− 1 23	F0
β Crucis	1·3	12 46·9	−59 37	B1
ε Ursæ Majoris *Alioth*	1·8	12 53·4	+56 02	A0*p*
α Canum Venaticorum	2·9	12 55·4	+38 23	A0*p*
ζ Ursæ Majoris *Mizar*	2·1	13 23·4	+55 00	A2*p*
α Virginis *Spica*	1·0	13 24·5	−11 05	B2
η Ursæ Majoris *Alkaid*	1·9	13 47·0	+49 23	B3
β Centauri *Hadar*	0·6	14 02·9	−60 19	B1
θ Centauri	2·1	14 05·9	−36 18	K0
α Bootis *Arcturus*	0·0	14 15·0	+19 15	K0
α Centauri *Rigil Kent*	0·1	14 38·7	−60 47	G0
ε Bootis	2·4	14 44·4	+27 08	K0
β Ursæ Minoris *Kochab*	2·1	14 50·7	+74 13	K5
α Coronæ Borealis *Alphecca* ..	2·2	15 34·1	+26 46	A0
δ Scorpii	2·3	15 59·5	−22 35	B0
β Scorpii	2·6	16 04·7	−19 46	B1
α Scorpii *Antares*	1·0	16 28·6	−26 24	M0
α Trianguli Australis.........	1·9	16 47·2	−69 00	K2
ε Scorpii	2·3	16 49·3	−34 16	K0
α Herculis*	Var.	17 14·0	+14 24	M3
λ Scorpii	1·6	17 32·7	−37 06	B2
α Ophiuchi *Rasalhague*	2·1	17 34·3	+12 34	A5
θ Scorpii	1·9	17 36·3	−42 59	F0
κ Scorpii	2·4	17 41·6	−39 01	B2
γ Draconis	2·2	17 56·3	+51 29	K5
ε Sagittarii *Kaus Australis* ...	1·9	18 23·3	−34 24	A0
α Lyræ *Vega*	0·0	18 36·5	+38 46	A0
σ Sagittarii................	2·0	18 54·4	−26 19	B3
β Cygni *Albireo*	3·1	19 30·2	+27 56	K0
α Aquilæ *Altair*	0·8	19 50·1	+ 8 50	A5
α Capricorni	3·8	20 17·3	−12 35	G5
γ Cygni	2·2	20 21·7	+40 13	F8*p*
α Pavonis	1·9	20 24·6	−56 47	B3
α Cygni *Deneb*	1·3	20 41·0	+45 14	A2*p*
α Cephei *Alderamin*	2·4	21 18·3	+62 32	A5
ε Pegasi..................	2·4	21 43·5	+ 9 49	K0
δ Capricorni	2·9	21 46·3	−16 11	A5
α Gruis	1·7	22 07·4	−47 02	B5
δ Cephei*	3·7	22 28·7	+58 21	*
β Gruis	2·1	22 41·9	−46 57	M3
α Piscis Austrini *Fomalhaut* ..	1·2	22 56·9	−29 42	A3
β Pegasi *Scheat*	2·4	23 03·1	+28 01	M0
α Pegasi *Markab*	2·5	23 04·1	+15 08	A0

* α Herculis, mag. 3·1 to 3·9.

δ Cephei, mag. 3·7 to 4·4, Spectrum F5 to G0.

Thus in London (Lat. 51° 30′) the meridian altitude of *Sirius* is found as follows:

		°	′
Altitude of equator		38	30
Declination south		16	42
Difference		21	48

The altitude of *Capella* (Dec. +45° 59′) at lower transit is:

Altitude of pole	51	30
Polar distance of star	44	01
Difference	7	29

The brightness of a heavenly body is denoted by its magnitude. Omitting the exceptionally bright stars *Sirius* and *Canopus*, the twenty brightest stars are of the first magnitude, while the faintest stars visible to the naked eye are of the sixth magnitude. The magnitude scale is a precise one, as a difference of five magnitudes represents a ratio of 100 to 1 in brightness. Typical second magnitude stars are *Polaris* and the stars in the Belt of Orion. The scale is most easily fixed in memory by comparing the stars with Norton's *Star Atlas* (see page 138). The stars *Sirius* and *Canopus* and the planets Venus and Jupiter are so bright that their magnitudes are expressed by negative numbers. A small telescope will show stars down to the ninth or tenth magnitude, while stars fainter than the twentieth magnitude may be photographed by long exposures with the largest telescopes.

Some of the astronomical information in this ALMANACK has been taken from *Astronomical Phenomena*, and is published here by arrangement with, and with the permission of, the Controller of H.M. Stationery Office.

ELEMENTS OF THE SOLAR SYSTEM

Orb	Mean Distance from Sun		Sidereal Period	Synodic Period	Inclination of Orbit to Ecliptic	Diameter	Mass compared with Earth	Period of Rotation on Axis
	Radii of Earth's Orbit	Millions of kilometres						
			y d	Days	° '	km.		d h m
Sun	0·39	...	...	...	...	1,392,000	332,948	25 09
Mercury	0·39	58	88	116	7 00	4,880	0·055	59
Venus	0·72	108	225	584	3 24	12,100	0·815	243
Earth	1·00	150	1 0	...	...	12,756eq.	1·00	23 56
Mars	1·52	228	1 322	780	1 51	6,790	0·107	24 37
Jupiter	5·20	778	11 315	399	1 18	142,800eq. 134,200p.	318	9 50 9 56
Saturn	9·54	1427	29 167	378	2 29	120,000eq. 108,000p.	95	10 14 10 38
Uranus	19·19	2870	84 6	370	0 46	52,000	14·6	16—28
Neptune	30·07	4497	164 288	367	1 46	48,400	17·2	18—20
Pluto	39·46	5950	247 255	367	17 09	3,000?	0·01	6 09

THE SATELLITES

Name	Star Mag.	Mean distance from Primary	Sidereal Period of Revolution	Name	Star mag.	Mean distance from Primary	Sidereal Period of Revolution
Earth		km.	d h m	*Saturn*		km.	d h m
Moon	—	384,400	27 07 43	Mimas	12	186,000	22 37
				Enceladus	12	238,000	1 08 53
				Tethys	11	295,000	1 21 18
Mars				Dione	11	378,000	2 17 41
Phobos	11	9,400	7 39	Rhea	10	527,000	4 12 25
Deimos	12	23,500	1 06 18	Titan	8½	1,222,000	15 22 42
				Hyperion	14	1,483,000	21 06 38
Jupiter				Iapetus	11	3,560,000	79 07 56
V. Amalthea	13	181,000	11 57	Phoebe	16	12,950,000	550
I. Io	5½	422,000	1 18 28				
II. Europa	5½	671,000	3 13 14	*Uranus*			
III. Ganymede ...	5	1,070,000	7 03 43	Miranda	17	130,000	1 10 00
IV. Callisto	6	1,883,000	16 16 32	Ariel	14	192,000	2 12 29
XIII. Leda	20	11,000,000	240	Umbriel	15	267,000	4 03 28
VI. Himalia	14	11,480,000	251	Titania	14	438,000	8 16 56
X. Lysithea	19	11,720,000	259	Oberon	14	586,000	13 11 07
VII. Elara	16	11,740,000	260	*Neptune*			
XII. Ananke	19	21,200,000	631	Triton	13½	355,000	5 21 03
XI. Carme	18	22,600,000	692	Nereid	19	5,562,000	359 10 00
VIII. Pasiphae	19	23,500,000	744	*Pluto*			
IX. Sinope	18	23,600,000	758	Charon	17	20,000	6 09 22

THE EARTH

The shape of the Earth is that of an oblate spheroid or solid of revolution whose meridian sections are ellipses not differing much from circles, whilst the sections at right angles are circles. The length of the equatorial axis is about 12,756 kilometres, and that of the polar axis is 12,714 kilometres. The mean density of the Earth is 5·5 times that of water, although that of the surface layer is less. The Earth and Moon revolve about their common centre of gravity in a lunar month; this centre in turn revolves round the Sun in a plane known as the ecliptic, that passes through the Sun's centre. The Earth's equator is inclined to this plane at an angle of 23½°. This tilt is the cause of the seasons. In mid-latitudes, and when the Sun is high above the Equator, not only does the high noon altitude make the days longer, but the Sun's rays fall more directly on the Earth's surface; these effects combine to produce summer. In equatorial regions the noon altitude is large throughout the year, and there is little variation in the length of the day. In higher latitudes the noon altitude is lower, and the days in summer are appreciably longer than those in winter.

The average velocity of the Earth in its orbit is 30 kilometres a second. It makes a complete rotation on its axis in about 23h 56m of mean time, which is the sidereal day. Because of its annual revolution round the Sun, the rotation with respect to the Sun, or the solar day, is more than this by about four minutes (*see* p. 140). The extremity of the axis of rotation, or the North Pole of the Earth, is not rigidly fixed, but wanders over an area roughly 20 metres in diameter.

TERRESTRIAL MAGNETISM

A magnetic compass points along the horizontal component of a magnetic line of force. These directions converge on the "magnetic dip-poles". At these poles a freely suspended magnetized needle would become vertical. Not only do the positions of these poles change with time, but their exact location is ill-defined, particularly so in the case of the north dip-pole where the lines of force, on the north side of it, instead of converging radially, tend to bunch into a channel. Although it is therefore unrealistic to attempt to specify the locations of the dip-poles exactly, the present adopted positions are 77°·5 N., 102°·6 W. and 65°·2 S., 139°·4 E. The two magnetic dip-poles are thus not antipodal, the line joining them passing the centre of the Earth at a distance of about 1,200 kilometres. The distances of the magnetic dip-poles from the north and south geographical poles are about 1,400 and 2,700 kilometres respectively.

There is also a "magnetic equator", at all points of which the vertical force is zero and a magnetized needle remains horizontal. This line runs between 2° and 10° north of the geographical equator in the eastern hemisphere, turns sharply south off the West African coast, and crosses South America through Brazil, Bolivia and Peru; it recrosses the geographical equator in mid-Pacific.

Reference has already been made to secular changes in the Earth's field. The following table indicates the changes in magnetic declination (or variation of the compass). Similar, though much smaller, changes have occurred in "dip" or magnetic inclination. Secular changes differ throughout the world. Although the London observations strongly suggest a cycle of several hundred years, an exact repetition is unlikely.

London				Greenwich		
1580	11°	15′	E.	1850	22°	24′ W.
1622	5	56	E.	1900	16	29 W.
1665	1	22	W.	1925	13	10 W.
1730	13	00	W.	1950	9	07 W.
1773	21	09	W.	1975	6	39 W.

In order that up-to-date information on the variation of the compass may be available, many governments publish magnetic charts on which there are lines (called isogonic) passing through all places at which specified values of declination will be found at the date of the chart.

In the British Isles, isogonic lines now run approximately north-east to south-west. Though there are considerable local deviations due to geographical causes, a rough value of magnetic declination may be obtained by assuming that at 50° N. on the meridian of Greenwich, the value in 1986 is 4° 29′ west and allowing an increase of 17′ for each degree of latitude northwards and one of 30′ for each degree of longitude westwards. For example, at 53° N., 5° W., declination will be about 4° 29′ + 51′ + 150′, i.e. 7° 50′ west. The average annual change at the present time is about 9½′ decrease.

The number of magnetic observatories now approaches 200—widely scattered over the globe. There are three in Great Britain maintained by the Government: at Hartland, North Devon, at Eskdalemuir in Dumfriesshire, Scotland, and at Lerwick, Shetland Islands. Some recent annual mean values of the magnetic elements for Hartland are given below.

The normal worldwide terrestrial magnetic field corresponds approximately to that of a very strong small bar magnet near the centre of the Earth but with appreciable smooth spatial departures. The origin and slow secular change of the normal field is not yet fully understood but is generally ascribed to electric currents associated with fluid motions within the Earth's core. Superposed on the normal field are local and regional anomalies whose magnitudes may in places exceed that of the normal field; these are due to the influence of mineral deposits in the Earth's crust. A small proportion of the field is of external origin, mostly associated with electric currents in the ionosphere. The configuration of the external field and the ionization of the atmosphere depend on the incident particle and radiation flux. There are, therefore, short-term and non-periodic as well as diurnal, 27-day, seasonal and 11-year periodic changes in the magnetic field, dependent upon the position of the Sun and the degree of solar activity.

Year	Declina-tion West	Dip or Inclina-tion	Hori-zontal Force	Vertical Force
	° ′	° ′	oersted	oersted
1950	11 06	66 54	0·1848	0·4334
1955	10 30	66 49	0·1859	0·4340
1960	9 59	66 44	0·1871	0·4350
1965	9 30	66 34	0·1887	0·4354
1970	9 06	66 26	0·1903	0·4364
1975	8 32	66 17	0·1921	0·4373
1980	7 44	66 10	0·1933	0·4377
1984	7 06	66 09	0·1937	0·4379

Magnetic Storms. Occasionally—sometimes with great suddenness—the Earth's magnetic field is subject for several hours to marked disturbance. In extreme cases, departures in field intensity as much as one tenth the normal value are experienced. In many instances, such disturbances are accompanied by widespread displays of aurorae, marked changes in the incidence of cosmic rays, an increase in the reception of "noise" from the Sun at radio frequencies together with rapid changes in the ionosphere and induced electric currents within the earth which adversely affect radio and telegraphic communications. The disturbances are generally ascribed to flux changes in the stream of neutral and ionized particles which emanates from the Sun and through which the Earth is continuously passing. Some of these changes are associated with visible eruptions on the Sun, usually in the region of sun-spots. There is a marked tendency for disturbances to recur after intervals of about 27 days, the apparent period of rotation of the Sun on its axis, which is consistent with the sources being located on particular areas of the Sun.

Artificial Satellites Launched in 1983–4

Desig-nation	Satellite	Launch date	i	P	e	Perigee height (km)
1983–		1983	°	m		
96	Cosmos 1498, rocket, engine	September 14	82·3	89·9	0·001	261
97	Cosmos 1499, rocket, engine	September 17	72·8	92·3	0·004	357
98	Galaxy 2	September 22	0·1	1436·3	0·001	35,770
99	Cosmos 1500, rocket	September 28	82·5	97·8	0·002	635
100	Ekran 11, launcher rocket, launcher, rocket	September 29	0·4	1,435·6	0·000	35,768
101	Cosmos 1501, rocket	September 30	82·9	94·5	0·003	468
102	Cosmos 1502, rocket	October 5	65·8	92·3	0·003	369
103	Cosmos 1503, rocket	October 12	74·0	100·9	0·001	790
104	Cosmos 1504, rocket	October 14	64·9	89·3	0·010	173
105	Intelsat 5 F-7, Ariane 1-07	October 19	0·5	1,433·3	0·005	35,513
106	Progress 18, rocket	October 20	51·6	91·2	0·001	329
107	Cosmos 1505, rocket, engine	October 21	72·9	92·3	0·004	358
108	Cosmos 1506, rocket	October 26	82·9	104·8	0·004	953
109	Meteor 2-10	October 28	81·2	101·4	0·009	754
110	Cosmos 1507, rocket	October 29	65·1	93·3	0·001	435
111	Cosmos 1508, rocket	November 11	82·9	109·1	0·104	400
112	Cosmos 1509, rocket, engine	November 17	72·9	89·7	0·005	227
113	DMSP 2-02	November 18	98·7	101·4	0·001	816
114	Molniya 1-59, launcher, launcher rocket, rocket	November 23	62·8	702·2	0·739	442
115	Cosmos 1510, rocket	November 24	73·6	116·1	0·003	1,481
116	STS 9	November 28	57·0	89·4	0·001	239
117	Cosmos 1511, rocket	November 30	67·1	89·7	0·013	172
118	Gorizont 8, launcher rocket, launcher, rocket	November 30	1·4	1,436·2	0·002	35,718
119	Cosmos 1512, rocket, engine	December 7	72·9	92·3	0·005	356
120	Cosmos 1513, rocket	December 8	82·9	104·9	0·004	963
121	Cosmos 1514, rocket	December 14	82·3	89·3	0·003	215
122	Cosmos 1515, rocket	December 15	82·5	97·8	0·002	638
123	Molniya 3-22, launcher rocket, launcher, rocket	December 21	62·8	736·0	0·741	618
124	Cosmos 1516, rocket	December 27	64·9	89·2	0·006	197
125	Cosmos 1517, rocket	December 27	50·7	88·4	0·003	180
126	Cosmos 1518, launcher rocket, launcher, rocket	December 28	62·9	709·2	0·736	585
127	Cosmos 1519, 1520, 1521	December 29	64·7	673·8	0·002	19,026
1984–		1984				
01	Cosmos 1522–1529, rocket	January 5	74·0	115·5	0·002	1,463
02	Cosmos 1530, rocket, engine	January 11	72·8	92·3	0·004	357
03	Cosmos 1531, rocket	January 11	82·9	105·1	0·002	985
04	Cosmos 1532, rocket	January 13	67·1	89·7	0·014	166
05	Yuri 2A	January 23	0·4	1,431·1	0·008	35,359
06	Cosmos 1533, rocket, engine	January 26	70·4	92·2	0·005	349
07	Cosmos 1534, rocket	January 26	65·8	94·5	0·003	469
08	China 14, rocket	January 29	36·0	160·7	0·312	362
09	DSCS 3-02	January 31				
10	Cosmos 1535, rocket	February 2	83·0	104·9	0·004	958
11	STS-41B, Westar 6, IRT, Palapa 4	February 3	28·5	90·0	0·001	275
12	NOSS 6, rocket	February 5	63·4	107·5	0·005	1,072
13	Cosmos 1536, rocket	February 8	82·5	97·8	0·002	636
14	Soyuz, rocket	February 8	51·6	90·1	0·001	282
15	Ohzora, rocket	February 14	74·6	97·2	0·038	357
16	Raduga 14, launcher rocket, launcher, rocket	February 15	1·2	1,436·0	0·001	35,766
17	Cosmos 1537, rocket, engine	February 16	82·3	89·4	0·005	209
18	Progress 19, rocket	February 21	51·6	90·1	0·000	282
19	Cosmos 1538, rocket	February 21	74·0	100·7	0·003	772

Artificial Satellites Launched in 1984—(cont.)

Desig-nation	Satellite	Launch date	i	P	e	Perigee height (km)
1984–		1984	°	m		
20	Cosmos 1539, rocket	February 28	67·1	89·6	0·013	168
21	Landsat 5, UOSAT 2	March 1	98·2	98·6	0·001	679
22	Cosmos 1540, launcher rocket, launcher, rocket	March 2	1·4	1,435·6	0·001	35,729
23	Intelsat 5 F-8, Ariane 1-08	March 5	0·4	1,436·0	0·003	35,679
24	Cosmos 1541, launcher rocket, launcher, rocket	March 6	62·9	717·6	0·737	600
25	Cosmos 1542, rocket, engine	March 7	70·3	92·2	0·005	350
26	Cosmos 1543, rocket	March 10	62·8	90·6	0·013	217
27	Cosmos 1544, rocket	March 15	82·5	97·7	0·002	635
28	Ekran 12, launcher rocket, launcher, rocket	March 16	0·0	1,423·3	0·001	35,485
29	Molniya 1-60, launcher rocket, launcher, rocket	March 16	62·9	734·9	0·740	623
30	Cosmos 1545, rocket, engine	March 21	72·8	90·9	0·012	236
31	Cosmos 1546, launcher rocket, launcher, rocket	March 29	1·3	1,451·7	0·001	36,071
32	Soyuz T-11, rocket	April 3	51·6	90·3	0·001	286
33	Cosmos 1547, launcher rocket, launcher, rocket	April 4	62·9	717·6	0·737	597
34	STS-41C, LDEF 1	April 6	28·5	94·3	0·000	494
35	China 15, rocket	April 8	0·7	1,444·5	0·010	35,520
36	Cosmos 1548, rocket	April 10	67·1	89·5	0·012	165
37	?	April 14	1·3	1,423·0	0·000	35,530
38	Progress 20, rocket	April 15	51·6	89·5	0·002	236
39	?	April 17	96·4	88·9	0·014	127
40	Cosmos 1549, rocket, engine	April 19	72·9	92·3	0·004	359
41	Gorizont 9, launcher rocket, launcher, rocket	April 22	1·5	1,436·0	0·000	35,784
42	Progress 21, rocket	May 7	51·6	89·6	0·003	243
43	Cosmos 1550, rocket	May 11	83·0	105·0	0·002	978
44	Cosmos 1551, rocket, engine	May 11	72·9	89·2	0·003	212
45	Cosmos 1552, rocket	May 14	64·9	89·4	0·010	181
46	Cosmos 1553, rocket	May 17	82·9	104·9	0·003	965
47	Cosmos 1554–1556, launcher rocket, launcher	May 19	64·8	676·1	0·001	19,125
48	Cosmos 1557, rocket, engine	May 22	82·3	89·1	0·003	213
49	Spacenet 1, Ariane 1-09	May 23	0·0	1,442·4	0·008	35,564
50	Cosmos 1558, rocket	May 25	67·2	89·5	0·012	169
51	Progress 22, rocket	May 28	51·6	90·7	0·003	290
52	Cosmos 1559–1566, rocket	May 28	74·0	115·8	0·003	1,472
53	Cosmos 1567, rocket	May 30	65·0	93·3	0·001	432
54	Cosmos 1568, rocket, engine	June 1	72·8	92·3	0·004	357
55	Cosmos 1569, launcher rocket, launcher, rocket	June 6	62·9	717·7	0·738	589
56	Cosmos 1570, rocket	June 8	74·1	100·9	0·001	791
57	Intelsat 5F-9, rocket	June 9	28·7	99·1	0·070	220
58	Cosmos 1571, rocket, engine	June 11	70·0	92·2	0·005	348
59	Navstar 9, rocket	June 13	62·5	729·6	0·006	20,318
60	Cosmos 1572, rocket, engine	June 15	82·3	89·9	0·001	261
61	Cosmos 1573, rocket, engine	June 19	72·9	89·9	0·006	232
62	Cosmos 1574, rocket	June 21	83·0	104·9	0·003	971
63	Raduga 15, launcher rocket, launcher, rocket	June 22	1·0	1,423·2	0·001	35,516
64	Cosmos 1575, rocket, engine	June 22	82·3	89·9	0·001	259
65	?	June 25	96·4	88·8	0·007	170
66	Cosmos 1576, rocket	June 26	67·1	89·7	0·014	169
67	Cosmos 1577, rocket	June 27	83·0	104·8	0·004	960
68	Cosmos 1578, rocket	June 28	50·7	104·4	0·092	295
69	Cosmos 1579, rocket, platform	June 29	65·0	89·6	0·001	251

Artificial Satellites Launched in 1984—(*cont.*)

Desig-nation	Satellite	Launch date	i	P	e	Perigee height (km)
1984–		1984	°	m		
70	Cosmos 1580, rocket, engine	June 29	62·8	89·5	0·003	229
71	Cosmos, 1581, launcher rocket, launcher, rocket	July 3	63·0	717·6	0·736	626
72	Meteor 2–11, rocket	July 5	82·5	104·1	0·001	945
73	Soyuz T-12, rocket	July 17	51·6	91·3	0·002	333
74	Cosmos 1582, rocket, engine	July 19	82·3	89·9	0·002	255
75	Cosmos 1583, rocket, engine	July 24	72·9	92·3	0·004	357
76	Cosmos 1584, rocket, engine	July 27	82·3	90·0	0·014	182
77	Cosmos 1585, rocket	July 31	64·7	89·2	0·009	174
78	Gorizont 10, launcher rocket, launcher, rocket	August 1	1·4	1,435·5	0·001	35,726
79	Cosmos 1586, launcher rocket, launcher, rocket	August 2	63·0	717·6	0·737	609
80	Himawari 3, rocket	August 2	1·9	1,450·2	0·007	35,783
81	ECS 2, Telecom 1A, Ariane 3-01	August 4	0·2	1,430·3	0·003	35,534
82	Cosmos 1587, rocket, engine	August 6	72·9	90·2	0·013	197
83	Cosmos 1588, rocket	August 7	65·0	93·3	0·001	429
84	Cosmos 1589, rocket	August 8	82·6	116·0	0·001	1,496
85	Molniya 1–61, launcher rocket, launcher, rocket	August 10	62·9	735·4	0·748	424
86	Progress 23, rocket	August 14	51·6	91·0	0·005	292
87	Cosmos 1590, rocket, engine	August 16	82·3	89·9	0·001	263
88	CCE 1, IRM 1, UKS 1	August 16	4·8	938·6	0·764	1,113
89	Molniya 1–62, launcher rocket, launcher, rocket	August 24	62·8	717·8	0·743	455
90	Ekran 13, launcher rocket, launcher, rocket	August 24	0·4	1,436·2	0·000	35,775
91	SDS 9, rocket	August 28	63·3	703·8	0·742	380
92	Cosmos 1591, rocket, engine	August 30	82·3	89·9	0·001	262
93	STS-41D, SBS 4, Leasat 2, Telstar 3C	August 30	28·5	90·4	0·001	295
94	Cosmos 1592, rocket, engine	September 4	72·9	89·7	0·005	226
95	Cosmos 1593–1595, launcher rocket, launcher, rocket	September 4	64·8	675·7	0·002	19,089
96	Cosmos 1596, launcher rocket, launcher, rocket	September 7	62·9	717·4	0·737	615
97	Navstar 10, rocket	September 8	63·2	730·6	0·008	20,271
98	China 16, rocket	September 12	67·9	90·2	0·017	175
99	Cosmos 1597, rocket, capsule	September 13	82·3	89·1	0·002	213
100	Cosmos 1598, rocket	September 13	82·9	105·0	0·003	972
101	Galaxy 3	September 21	0·2	1,449·4	0·007	35,753
102	Cosmos 1599, rocket	September 25	67·1	89·6	0·011	180
103	Cosmos 1600, rocket, engine	September 27	70·0	92·2	0·005	349
104	Cosmos 1601, rocket	September 27	65·8	94·5	0·003	475
105	Cosmos 1602, rocket	September 28	82·5	97·8	0·002	636
106	Cosmos 1603, rocket, launcher rocket, launcher	September 28	71·0	102·0	0·000	851
107	Cosmos 1604, launcher rocket, launcher, rocket	October 4	62·9	717·1	0·737	604
108	STS-41G, ERBS	October 5	57·0	91·5	0·001	345
109	Cosmos 1605, rocket	October 11	82·9	104·9	0·005	953
110	Nova 2, rocket	October 12	90·1	109·0	0·003	1,159
111	Cosmos 1606, rocket	October 18	82·5	97·7	0·002	633
112	Cosmos 1607, rocket, platform	October 31	65·0	89·6	0·001	251
113	STS-51A, Telesat 8, Leasat 1	November 8	28·5	90·5	0·001	304
114	Spacenet 2, Marecs 2, Ariane 3-02	November 10	0·1	1,441·7	0·009	35,520
115	NATO 3D	November 14	6·0	1,428·0	0·009	35,253

SATELLITE ORBITS

To consider the orbit of an artificial satellite it is best to imagine that one is looking at the Earth from a distant point in space. The Earth would then be seen to be rotating about its axis inside the orbit described by the rapidly revolving satellite. The inclination of a satellite orbit to the Earth's equator (which generally remains almost constant throughout the satellite's lifetime) gives at once the maximum range of latitudes over which the satellite passes. Thus a satellite whose orbit has an inclination of 53° will pass overhead all latitudes between S. 53° and N. 53°, but would never be seen in the zenith of any place nearer the poles than these latitudes. If we consider a particular place on the earth, whose latitude is less than the inclination of the satellite's orbit then the Earth's rotation carries this place under first the northbound part of the orbit and then, later on, under the southbound position of the orbit, these two occurrences being always less than 12 hours apart for satellites moving in direct orbits (*i.e.* to the east). For satellites in retrograde orbits the words "northbound" and "southbound" should be interchanged in the preceding statement. As the value of the latitude of the observer increases and approaches the value of the inclination of the orbit, so this interval gets shorter until (when the latitude is equal to the inclination) only one overhead passage occurs each day.

SATELLITE LAUNCHINGS

Apart from their names, *e.g.* Cosmos 6 Rocket or Injun 3, the satellites are also classified according to their date of launch. Thus 1961 α refers to the launching of Samos 2. The next satellite launching was 1961 β and so on. A number following the Greek letter is intended to indicate the relative brightness of the satellites put in orbit. From the beginning of 1963 the Greek letters are replaced by numbers and the numbers by roman letters *e.g.* 1963–01A. In this table are given the designation and names of the main objects in orbit (in the order A, B, C ... etc.), the launch date and some initial orbital data. These are the inclination to the equator (*i*), the nodal period of revolution (*P*), the eccentricity, *e*, and the perigee height.

OBSERVATION OF SATELLITES

The regression of the orbit around the Earth causes alternate periods of visibility and invisibility, though this is of little concern to the radio or radar observer. To the visual observer the following cycle of events normally occurs (though the cycle may start in any position): invisibility, morning observations before dawn, invisibility, evening observations after dusk, invisibility, morning observations before dawn, and so on. With reasonably high satellites and for observers in high latitudes around the summer solstice the evening observations follow the morning observations without interruption as sunlight passing over the polar regions can still illuminate satellites which are passing over temperate latitudes at local midnight. At the moment all satellites rely on sunlight to make them visible though a satellite with a flashing light has been suggested for a future launching. The observer must be in darkness or twilight in order to make any useful observations and the durations of twilight and the sunrise, sunset times given on page II of each month will be a useful guide.

Some of the satellites are visible to the naked eye and much interest has been aroused by the spectacle of a bright satellite disappearing into the Earth's shadow. The event is even more fascinating telescopically as the disappearance occurs gradually as the satellite traverses the Earth's penumbral shadow, and during the last few seconds before the eclipse is complete the satellite may change colour (under suitable atmospheric conditions) from yellow to red. This is because the last rays of sunlight are refracted through the denser layers of our atmosphere before striking the satellite.

Some satellites rotate about one or more axes so that a periodic variation in brightness is observed. This was particularly noticeable in several of the U.S.S.R. satellites.

Satellite research has already provided some interesting results. Among them may be mentioned a revised value of the Earth's oblateness, 1/298·2, and the discovery of the Van Allen radiation belts.

ROYAL OBSERVATORIES

Royal Greenwich Observatory
Herstmonceux, East Sussex, BN27 1RP
[0323 833171]

The Royal Observatory was founded at Greenwich by Charles II in 1675. Because of smog and light pollution, the Observatory was moved to Herstmonceux in East Sussex after the Second World War. The traditional work in positional astronomy and the determination of time remain as activities of the Observatory. The well-known "Greenwich 6 pips" are sent from Herstmonceux to the B.B.C. by land line. The rate of rotation of the Earth and other geophysical parameters are monitored by the satellite laser ranging telescope. Various almanacs and other astronomical data are prepared by H.M. Nautical Almanac Office, which is part of the Royal Greenwich Observatory. However, as an establishment of the Science and Engineering Research Council, the main task of the Observatory now is the provision of facilities for research in optical astronomy for astronomers in the universities. In particular, this involves the provision and running of the Isaac Newton group of telescopes with its associated instrumentation at the Roque de los Muchachos Observatory on the island of La Palma in the Canary Islands. This group comprises the Isaac Newton 2·5 m and the 1·0 m Jacobus Kapteyn telescopes which are already operating, and the William Herschel Telescope 4·2 m which will be commissioned shortly. The running of these is shared with the Netherlands, and, in the case of the Jacobus Kapteyn telescope, with Eire also. At Herstmonceux, there are facilities for the processing of astronomical data obtained from the telescopes on La Palma and elsewhere; these include a node of the STARLINK computing network. *Director*, Prof. A. Boksenberg, F.R.S.

Royal Observatory
Blackford Hill, Edinburgh

The Observatory was founded by the Astronomical Institution in 1818 and its Royal Charter dates from 1822. It is now responsible for some major national astronomical facilities funded by the Science and Engineering Research Council, including a 1·2 m Schmidt telescope in Australia, a 3·8 m infrared telescope in Hawaii and COSMOS, a fast automatic plate measuring machine. The Observatory is also part of the U.K. Starlink network for astronomical image and data processing. The Observatory specializes in the development of advanced technologies and the application of these to studies of the properties of matter in extreme environments in space. *Director and Astronomer Royal for Scotland,* Prof. M. S. Longair.

WEATHER IN THE UNITED KINGDOM, 1984-1985

(1984) July—Rainfall totals were below normal everywhere and the drought caused concern throughout the month with the use of water being restricted in many areas. In Glasgow (Strathclyde) it was the driest July since records began there in the middle of the last century. There were however frequent thunderstorms especially on the 2nd, from the 8th to the 15th, from the 22nd to the 25th and on the 30th. On the 9th lightning caused a fire which destroyed the roof of the 13th-century transept of York Minster. On the 11th there was considerable flooding near Carrickfergus (Co. Antrim) and two cricketers were thrown to the ground when lightning struck the pitch at Wolverhampton (West Midlands). On the 22nd there were thunderstorms over Norfolk and the Thames Valley when 21 mm. (0·79 ins.) of rain fell in one hour at Maidenhead (Berkshire) with hailstones up to 14 mm. (0·55 ins.) in diameter. In a severe thunderstorm on the 23rd the Bracknell (Berkshire) area had 43 mm. (1·69 ins.) in 48 minutes, 20 mm. (0·79 ins.) of which fell in 15 minutes. Hailstones in this storm were 10 to 20 mm. (0·4 to 0·8 ins.) in diameter and caused considerable damage. On the 24th 91·5 mm. (3·6 ins.) of rain fell at Hayling Island (Hampshire). Fog occurred frequently overnight particularly during the second half of the month when it became widespread. On the 21st a well developed dust-devil covered roofs and gardens at Velindre (Powys) with straw. Another dust-devil was reported at Towy Castle (Dyfed) on the 23rd and a whirlwind carried debris to a height of 50 to 60 metres (164 to 197 feet) at Bramham (West Yorkshire) on the 25th. Monthly mean temperatures were about 1°C. (1·8°F.) above average nearly everywhere in the United Kingdom except for parts of East Anglia where they were just below normal. At places in central Scotland temperatures were about 2°C. (3·6°F.) above average. The 8th was the warmest day since August 1983 with temperatures of over 26°C. (78·8°F.) in many places. At London (Heathrow) the temperature rose to 31·7°C. (89·1°F.). The heat cracked the westbound carriageway of the M40 motorway at Stokenchurch (Buckinghamshire) and caused the closure of one lane. The last four days of the month were again very warm with temperatures of 30°C. (86°F.) in parts of southeast England and the Channel Islands. Monthly sunshine totals were above normal nearly everywhere with over 150 per cent. of average being recorded in most of Wales, the west Midlands and parts of northeast England. 175 per cent. of average was recorded in parts of Co. Down, mid and north Wales.

August—Rainfall totals were again below normal everywhere and what rain there was did not raise the levels of the reservoirs in the areas suffering from an acute shortage of water. The period February to August was the driest since 1976 and the third driest this century. There were scattered thunderstorms during the first week in many areas and thunderstorms covered much of central Wales and southeast England between the 13th and 16th. Lightning wrecked a signal box at Westbury (Wiltshire) causing a two-hour delay to trains on the 15th. On the 20th there were further thunderstorms over Cornwall and the Scilly Isles extending on the 21st to most of Devon and on the 22nd to eastern and central southern England. On the 21st lightning damaged pumping stations, cut electricity supplies and telephone cables affecting thousands of households, struck houses, disrupted police communications and brought half a ton of masonry down at the Newton Abbot (Devon) railway station. On the 1st Milford Haven (Dyfed) had 46 mm. (1·81 ins.) of rain and on the 15th Wisley (Surrey) had 54 mm. (2·13 ins.) and Writtle (Essex)

had 49 mm. (1·93 ins.). There was extensive overnight fog during the month which was most widespread between the 13th and 17th and the 22nd and 28th. On the 22nd a whirlwind at Gotham near Nottingham ripped off roofs, uprooted trees and smashed some garages while on the 13th a dust-devil was reported at Jersey (Channel Islands). Winds were mostly light after the first week and Cowes Week Regatta in the Isle of Wight was a non event when 20 out of 25 races were abandoned for lack of wind. Monthly mean temperatures were above average everywhere. Most of the Midlands, Wales and parts of central southern England had temperatures more than 2°C. (3·6°F.) above average. Elsewhere temperatures were generally around 1·5°C. (2·7°F.) above average. The temperature reached 31·7°C. (89·1°F.) at St. Helier (Channel Islands) on the 20th. Also on the 20th the temperature reached 28·4°C. (83·1°F.) at Aviemore (Highland), 29·2°C. (84·6°F.) at Abbotsinch (Strathclyde), 28·8°C. (83·8°F.) at Madley (Hereford) and 28·3°C. (82·9°F.) at Hurn (Dorset). Monthly sunshine totals were above average everywhere except in parts of Devon, east Sussex, Kent and the western half of Northern Ireland where totals were just below average. Onich (Highland) had 154 per cent. of average. On the 11th 15·3 hours of sunshine were recorded at Morecambe (Lancashire) and on the 19th and 20th between 10 and 13 hours were recorded each day almost everywhere in the United Kingdom.

September—Rainfall totals were mostly above average and were between 140 and 200 per cent. of average in many places. Totals were below average in places on the south coast of England and isolated places on the Scottish border and east Essex. 92·5 mm. (3·64 ins.) of rain fell at Lochaline (Highland) on the 2nd. On the 3rd unsettled weather covered the whole Kingdom and heavy rain fell over Wales and northern England where Scamston Hall (North Yorkshire) had 71·1 mm. (2·8 ins.). On the 9th gales occurred in coastal areas and a boy was swept into the sea and drowned at Tintagel (Cornwall). There was rain followed by thunderstorms in all areas on the 8th and rain was widespread on the 13th. Falls were heavy in the north and west and 58 mm. (2·28 ins.) fell at Honister Pass (Cumbria). There were thunderstorms in the south and east on the 14th. The 19th and 20th were especially wet over Wales and the southern half of England. Rhoose (South Glamorgan) had 78 mm. (3·07 ins.) of rain in the 2 days, three quarters of its September average. Torrential rain, gales and huge waves caused havoc along the south coast of England on the 20th. There were widespread thunderstorms in England and Wales between the 21st and 24th and a boy was killed by lightning in Bedford on the 24th. There was further prolonged rain in southwest England and west Wales on the 27th and 28th with 51 mm. (2·01 ins.) falling at Tenby (Dyfed) and Aberporth (Dyfed) on the 27th. Fog occurred over large areas on the 13th and 16th. Monthly mean temperatures were mostly near normal in England and Wales except for the Kent coast. They were much below normal in Northern Ireland and Scotland. The temperatures rose to 29·1°C. (84·38°F.) at St. Helier (Channel Islands) on the 2nd but only reached 17°C. (62·6°F.) at the same place on the 5th. On the 6th the temperature fell to −3·1°C. (26·42°F.) at St. Harmon (Powys). On the 22nd the temperature only reached 8°C. (46·4°F.) at Aviemore (Highland) and on the 23rd London had its coldest day in September for 6 years. Sunshine totals were below normal everywhere which contrasted with the sunny and warm summer. 12·7 hours of sunshine were recorded at Cape Wrath (Highland) on the 1st but in southeast England the sunniest day was the 26th with 9 hours of sunshine.

October—Rainfall totals were near or above average except down the east coast of England and the Channel Islands where they were below normal. Thunderstorms were widely reported on the 2nd and 3rd and many places had heavy rain particularly in the south and west of England and Wales. Hail was also frequent and Anvil Green (Kent) received 72 mm. (2·83 ins.) of rain on the 2nd. On the 4th a whirlwind caused considerable damage in Hereford and on the 5th there was heavy rain and thunderstorms in southeast England and East Anglia. There was flooding in places in Suffolk, Essex and southwest London. In London it was the wettest day of the year so far. At Ewell (Surrey) 43 mm. (1·69 ins) fell of which 28 mm. (1·1 ins.) fell in 75 minutes. There was widespread rain everywhere on the 17th and 18th and at Sloy (Strathclyde) 80 mm. (3·15 ins.) fell in the two days. There were gales in many areas on the 18th causing a great deal of damage. A gust of 100 kts. (115 mph.) was recorded at Pendennis Point (Cornwall) and Great Dun Fell (Lancashire) recorded 94 kts. (108 mph.). A tornado damaged houses at Tuffley (Gloucestershire). Further heavy rain with hail and thunder affected much of the Kingdom on the 19th and 20th followed by widespread rain everywhere on the 21st and 22nd. At Cilfynydd (Mid-Glamorgan) 76 mm. (2·99 ins.) fell between the evening of the 21st and the evening of the 22nd. There was further rain in southern and western areas of England and Wales on the 24th. On the 31st 75 mm. (2·95 ins.) of rain fell at Prabost (Isle of Skye). Monthly mean temperatures were a little above average over England and Wales but a little below average over Scotland. On the 2nd the temperature fell to −3·7°C. (25·34°F.) at Aviemore (Highland) but on the 8th the temperature at Finningley (South Yorkshire) reached 21·2°C. (70·16°F.). On the 5th 20·5°C. (68·9°F.) was recorded at Glenlivet (Grampian) but on the 26th the maximum temperature at Glenlivet was only 7°C. (44·6°F.). On the 27th the temperature fell to −3·7°C. (25·34°F.) at Liphook (Hampshire). Sunshine totals were a little below average in southern England, northwest England and parts of east Scotland but generally totals were above normal. Lerwick (Shetland) received 153 per cent. of the normal amount for the month. 9·9 hours of sunshine were recorded at Penzance (Cornwall) on the 6th and at Hartland (Devon) on the 15th.

November—Rainfall totals were well above average everywhere except Northern Ireland, the Shetlands and small coastal parts of Norfolk and Kent. Dyce (Grampian) had more than three times the normal amount. At both Aberdeen (Grampian) and Sunderland (Tyne & Wear) it was the wettest month for at least 100 years. In the east the month started dry but in the west it started as it was to continue, wet and windy. Rain spread eastwards on the 2nd and by the 3rd it was very wet in northern England, southern, central and eastern Scotland. There was some particularly heavy falls causing flooding. At Hungry Snout (Borders) 110·2 mm. (4·34 ins.) fell on the 3rd. In some places the rain turned to sleet and snow with some thunder. Many places in northern England had more than 30 mm. (1·18 ins.) on the 2nd with similar amounts falling in southern and eastern Scotland and over the Pennines on the 3rd. From the 7th to 10th a belt of rain moved across the Kingdom and gave about 25 mm. (1 in.) of rain first in the southwest of England, then Wales and later in Scotland. On the 15th overnight fog persisted all day in much of central and eastern England, Wales and Northern Ireland. This fog did not clear in parts of the Midlands and northwest England until late on the 16th. There was heavy rain around the Moray Firth (Highland) on the 19th and this was the 6th successive day at Dyce (Grampian) with a total of more than 13 mm. (0·5 ins.).

The 6-day total of 115 mm. (4·5 ins.) exceeded the monthly average by 30 per cent. During the last 10 days of the month it was very wet over England and Wales and the west of Scotland where Fort William (Highland) received 75 per cent. of the month's total during this period. On the 21st 60·5 mm. (2·38 ins.) fell at Cilfynydd (Mid-Glamorgan), this being only a part of the 150 mm. (6 ins.) which fell at Cilfynydd during the 5 days 20th to 24th. Monthly mean temperatures were near or a little above average everywhere. On the 1st the temperature rose to 19·1°C. (66·38°F.) in London but on the 6th it fell to −8·7°C. (16·34°F.) at Tummel Bridge (Tayside). The maximum at Tummel Bridge on this day was only 0·2°C. (32·36°F.). Sunshine totals were mostly below normal except for coastal areas of northwest Scotland and parts of southern England. 9·1 hours of sunshine were recorded at Portland Bill (Dorset) on the 3rd. The Autumn period (September–November) was a wet season over most of the country with only Northern Ireland having below average rainfall for the period. Temperatures were mostly near or slightly above normal for the period and sunshine totals were mostly near or slightly below normal.

December—Rainfall totals were above average in most of Scotland, western areas of England and Wales and the south of England. Elsewhere totals were below average. At Newcastle (Tyne & Wear) only 38 per cent. of the normal amount fell during the month. The month started rather wet over much of the Kingdom and by the 3rd there was rain in all western areas and on the 4th a belt of rain crossed the whole of the United Kingdom. The 6th and 7th were mostly dry over England and Wales but 87 mm. (3·43 ins.) fell at Sloy (Strathclyde) on the 6th and 56 mm. (2·2 ins.) at Fort William (Highland) on the 7th. Most of the Kingdom had some rain on the 8th but by the end of the 10th it was generally dry everywhere. On the night of the 10th/11th dense fog was widespread over England and Wales and persisted in many areas for the next two days. From the 13th and for the next 12 days it was unsettled everywhere and precipitation became wintry. On the 17th snow was widespread over northern England and Scotland and roads were blocked for a time over the Pennines. There were several reports of prolonged heavy rain over northern Scotland on the 17th and 59·4 mm. (2·34 ins.) fell at Fraserburgh (Grampian) while 53 mm. (2·09 ins.) fell at Kirkwall (Orkney) and 43 mm. (1·69 ins.) fell at Aberdeen (Grampian). Wintry showers continued in Scotland and Northern Ireland at times but in the south mild, unsettled weather continued until Christmas when a belt of rain crossed the whole of the United Kingdom to be followed by sleet and hail showers as far south as the Chilterns. After this fog was fairly widespread overnight and persisted all day in some places. The last few days were generally unsettled with rain and drizzle at times. Monthly mean temperatures were above normal everywhere. On the 13th the temperature rose to 17·1°C. (62·78°F.) at Cape Wrath (Highland). Although it was generally a mild month overnight frost was widespread at times particularly on the night of the 10th/11th and after Christmas and it persisted all day in some places. On the 27th the maximum temperature at Glasgow (Abbotsinch) Airport (Strathclyde) was only −3·8°C. (25·16°F.). The minimum temperature at Abbotsinch on this day was −9·4°C. (15·08°F.). Sunshine totals were above average except in a few scattered places but even so there were long periods of complete cloud cover. At Guernsey (Channel Islands) 7·7 hours of sunshine were recorded on the 7th.

Year (1984)—For the year as a whole rainfall totals were a little above average in Scotland and East Anglia and near normal elsewhere. Annual mean temperatures were slightly above normal and sunshine totals were below average in northern and central Scotland and a few places on the south and southeast coasts of England but above average in remaining areas. January was a very wet month, cold and rather dull in the north and west but very sunny and rather warm in the south and east. It was the wettest January since 1948 in England and Wales and the 5th was the wettest day this century. The month was very windy with blizzards in the north and much gale damage in Northern Ireland and Scotland. A tornado damaged 100 houses in Doncaster on the 14th and a cargo ship sank near Guernsey on the 24th with a loss of 17 lives. A tornado caused damage in Teignmouth on the 26th. In London it was the sunniest January since 1929. February brought very variable rainfall with southwest Scotland and Northern Ireland being wet and southeast England dry. On the 4th gales caused much damage and travel was badly disrupted. Fog affected nearly all areas mid-month and by the 16th only the Hebrides had more than one hour of sunshine. The winter period (December to February) was generally wet or very wet and dull in the north and west. March also brought variable rainfall with more then twice the normal amount in southeast Scotland and northeast England but less than 50 per cent. of normal in south Wales and southeast England. This was a windy month, rather cold and very dull. Only southwest Cornwall had average sunshine and many places had less than half the normal amount. April was an exceptionally dry month with some southern areas of England receiving less than 5 per cent. of the normal rainfall. Only northwest Scotland had near normal amounts. Generally it was the driest April for 27 years. The last 10 days of the month were exceptionally sunny with over 12 hours sunshine per day in many places. London had its sunniest April since 1881. May was very wet in the southeast but exceptionally dry in the north. Eskdalemuir (Dumfries & Galloway) had a total of only 4 mm. (0·16 ins.) for the whole month. It was generally rather cold, dull in the south but with average sunshine in the north. The spring period (March to May) gave southwest Scotland its driest spring this century, in Glasgow the driest since 1869. June had generally below average rainfall. It was especially dry in southwest England where Penzance (Cornwall) had only 3·6 mm. (0·14 ins.) for the whole month. There were some severe thunderstorms and two boys were killed by lightning in St. Albans on the 17th. On the 20th there was considerable flooding in East Anglia with lightning damage. Temperatures were near normal and it was sunny in the south but dull in the north. July was a dry month with many places having less than a quarter of the average rainfall. It was the 5th driest July over England and Wales this century. There were some severe thunderstorms and York Minster was very badly damaged by lightning on the 9th. Hailstones 20 mm. (0·8 ins.) in diameter caused damage in Bracknell on the 23rd. Temperatures were generally above average and sunshine totals were well above average. August was another dry month with some severe thunderstorms. A whirlwind on the 2nd ripped off roofs, uprooted trees and smashed garages near Nottingham and lightning wrecked a railway signal box at Westbury on the 15th. Lightning caused much damage in Devon on the 21st and thousands of homes were without electricity or telephones. Masonry crashed down at Newton Abbot railway station. Early morning fog was more frequent than usual and Cowes Regatta was abandoned for lack of wind. Both temperatures and sunshine totals were above normal in most areas. The summer period (June to August) was warm, sunny and dry. Glasgow had only a third of its normal rainfall. September was a rather wet month

with rainfall being well above average in most areas. There were widespread thunderstorms. Temperatures were mostly near normal and sunshine totals were well below normal. October had near or above average rainfall in most areas and the 5th was particularly wet in southeast England and East Anglia. In London this was the wettest day of the year so far. A whirlwind caused considerable damage in Hereford on the 4th. Temperatures were a little above normal in the north but a little below in the south. Sunshine was generally near normal. November was a very wet month with rainfall totals well above average. It was especially wet in northeast England and east Scotland. Aberdeen and Sunderland had their wettest month for at least 100 years. Floods occurred in northern areas. Temperatures were near normal and sunshine totals were mostly below normal. The Autumn period (September–November) brought above average rainfall especially in eastern Scotland. December was very dry in northeast England, dry in East Anglia and central England but near normal elsewhere. Fog was very dense and widespread at times and slow to clear. It was a warm month with above average temperatures and above average sunshine in most places.

(1985) January—Rainfall totals were above average down the east coast and a few inland places in the east but otherwise totals were below average. Snow showers at the beginning of the month became steady snow over Kent on the 4th and 12 cms. (4·72 ins.) fell near Ramsgate. By the 5th snow had spread to much of England and southern Scotland. There was more snow in eastern England on the 6th and showers continued there until the 13th when a belt of snow moved across most of the Kingdom. On the 14th another belt of snow moved from north to south and falls were heavy. There was more heavy snow in East Anglia and Kent on the 15th and by the morning of the 16th everywhere but Shetland, Orkney and western Scotland was under a blanket of snow. Much of Kent and east Sussex had over 15 cms. (5·91 ins.) of snow cover. More general snow fell in southwest England and south Wales on the 17th and 18th with depths up to 20 cms. (7·87 ins.). Between the 20th and 22nd there was a general thaw over southern England but Scotland and northern England had further heavy snow on the 22nd with gale force winds creating blizzards. Aviemore (Highland) had 50 cms. (19·69 ins.) of level snow by the end of the day. The last five days of the month brought rain to most of England and Wales and a general thaw set in. On the 27th 28 mm. (1·5 ins.) of rain fell at Bastreet (Cornwall). Monthly mean temperatures were below average everywhere and in England and Wales generally it was the coldest month since 1979 but in the southeast it was the coldest since 1963. During the first fortnight the temperatures in southeast England were 5°C. (9°F.) below normal and over England and Wales generally temperatures were below freezing for much of this time. On the 5th the temperature was below −4°C. (24·8°F.) all day at Anvil Green (Kent) and it was the coldest day in England and Wales for 10 months. On the 8th the temperature fell to −15·6°C. (3·92°F.) at Jubilee Corner (Kent). In London the 16th was the coldest January day since 1963 and at Heathrow the temperature never rose above −4·7°C. (23·54°F.). At the Weather Centre in central London the maximum was −3·2°C. (26·24°F.). On the 17th the temperature fell to −14·9°C. (5·18°F.) at Elmdon (West Midlands). On the 25th the maximum temperature at Aviemore (Highland) was −8·9°C. (15·98°F.) and on the 27th the minimum at Aviemore was −22·4°C. (−8·32°F.). As a contrast the maximum temperature at Torquay (Devon) on the 31st was 12·7°C. (54·86°F.). Sunshine totals, in spite of the wintry weather, were near or above average everywhere except on the east coast of England and the north coast of Scotland. The Western Isles of Scotland were especially sunny. On the 5th 7·7 hours of sunshine were recorded at Jersey (Channel Islands).

February—Rainfall totals were well below normal everywhere and it was very dry in eastern England where Finningley (South Yorkshire) recorded only 1 mm. (0·04 ins.) of rain for the whole month. Less than 10 per cent. of normal fell in most of Yorkshire and Lincolnshire. There was heavy rain over much of southern areas on the 6th, 7th and 8th, the heaviest being in southern Wales and southwest England where 35·6 mm. (1·40 ins.) fell at Cardiff (Rhoose) Airport on the 6th and almost as much at St. Mary's (Scilly Isles) on the 7th and at Teignmouth (Devon) on the 8th. On the 9th snow fell over the Midlands, much of Wales and southern England and by mid-day over 20 cms. (7·87 ins.) had accumulated in central Wales and the Midlands. Elmdon (West Midlands) had 28 cms. (11·02 ins.) of level snow. There was considerable drifting in strong winds and many roads were blocked. From the 10th to 13th rain near the coast of southwest England quickly turned to snow inland and with gale force winds southwest England had a period of very severe weather. There were moderate to heavy falls of rain in Scotland on the 18th and 19th. Freezing fog, which had been patchy since the 17th became widespread on the 20th and persisted all day on the 20th and 21st in eastern England and the Midlands. The last week of the month was windy and unsettled over Scotland and Northern Ireland but in England and Wales it was a quiet period with only light winds, hazy sunshine by day and fog by night. Along the south and east coasts the fog lasted all day. Monthly mean temperatures were near normal in Scotland and Northern Ireland but below normal in England and Wales. The southeast and East Anglia were especially cold. On the 10th the temperature rose to only −5·8°C. (21·56°F.) at Cwmbargoed (Mid-Glamorgan) and on the 13th it fell to −15·1°C. (4·82°F.) at Aviemore (Highland). On the 28th the temperature rose to 15·6°C. (60·08°F.) at Valley (Anglesey). Sunshine totals were near or above normal everywhere and it was very sunny in central England where Nottingham had 163 per cent. of the normal amount. On the 23rd 9·8 hours of sunshine were recorded at Guernsey (Channel Islands) and on the 24th 9·8 hours were recorded at Tenby (Dyfed) and The Lizard (Cornwall). The Winter period (December to February) produced about 75 per cent. of the normal rainfall over the Kingdom as a whole. Over England and Wales and Northern Ireland temperatures for the period were about 1°C. (1·8°F.) below normal but they were near normal over Scotland. Sunshine totals were a little above normal everywhere.

March—Rainfall totals were very variable but in general they were near or above average everywhere except central England and the Isle of Man where they were a little below normal. There was rain and snow in the Midlands on the 1st and in western areas on the 2nd. On the 3rd and 4th there were gales on western coasts with outbreaks of heavy rain. On the 3rd 49 mm. (1·93 ins.) of rain fell at Trawsfynydd (Gwynedd). There was rain in places on the 7th. There was widespread morning fog on the 8th, 9th and 10th. There were showers everywhere on the 10th and on the 13th, after a belt of heavy rain, there were strong winds and widespread snow showers which persisted overnight in many places. By the morning of the 15th snow covered Scotland and the higher ground of England and Wales. More continuous snow fell in parts of Wales, the Midlands and central southern England on the 16th and in Hum-

berside and Lincolnshire that night. The wind decreased on the 17th and from then to the 20th there were freezing fog patches in the mornings in central and eastern areas. The 20th started a period of unsettled weather in all areas although the north was mostly dry until the 23rd. Many places in Cornwall had over 20 mm. (0·79 ins.) of rain on the 20th and places further inland had a good deal of snow during that night before it turned to rain again. On the 25th and 26th there was general rain over southern areas but much of central and northern England and northern Wales remained dry and Scotland continued to have wintry showers. On the 29th and 30th rain fell over much of the Kingdom but over Scotland the rain was preceded by a belt of heavy snow which led to considerable accumulations in the Edinburgh and Tayside areas. 12 cms. (4·72 ins.) at Turnhouse (Lothian) by the morning of the 30th. The last day of the month brought wet and blustery weather to southern areas. Monthly mean temperatures were below normal everywhere. The south and east of England were the coldest areas with temperatures up to 1·5°C. (2·7°F.) below normal. The 13th to 20th period was very cold generally with only the southwest of England having reasonable temperatures. At Upavon (Wiltshire) the temperature never rose above 1°C. (33·8°F.) on the 16th and at Aviemore (Highland) the temperature fell to −15·2°C. (4·64°F.) on the 18th. On the 28th the maximum temperature at Lerwick (Shetland) was −1·6°C. (29·12°F.) and by contrast on the 30th the maximum at Finningley (South Yorkshire) was 17·1°C. (62·78°F.). Sunshine totals were mostly near or above normal with the extreme northwest and southwest of the Kingdom being the dullest. 11·2 hours of sunshine were recorded at Douglas (Isle of Man) on the 25th.

April—Rainfall was above average everywhere except for parts of southern England. Scotland was very wet with a few places having nearly twice the normal amount of rain. April started with generally unsettled weather. The 9th and 10th were showery and on the 10th 50·5 mm. (1·99 ins.) of rain fell at Nantmor (Gwynedd). During the 11th coastal areas of England and Wales had winds of gale force 8 and above. Several places in Cornwall recorded gusts of 67 kts. (77·2 mph.). This was also one of the wettest days with many places in southern Scotland and northern and central England and Wales having over 20 mm. (0·79 ins.) of rain. On the 12th rain fell over most areas but was heaviest in Scotland where Fort William (Highland) had 23 mm. (0·91 ins.) in 24 hours with most of it falling overnight on the 12th/13th. Showery weather covered all areas until the 16th. There was a little rain on the 26th and on the 27th there were frequent snow and hail showers particularly near the east coast and over high ground. The month ended with unsettled weather. Monthly mean temperatures were near normal everywhere in Scotland but above average in England and Wales. On the 3rd the temperature at Cromer (Norfolk) rose to 20·2°C. (68·36°F.) this being the first time the temperature in the United Kingdom had reached 20°C. (68°F.) since October 1984. There were some remarkable temperature changes during the month. On the 20th temperatures were 10°C. (18°F.) lower in many places in England and Wales than temperatures on the 19th. At London Weather Centre the difference was 12°C. (21·6°F.). On the 27th, also at London Weather Centre, the temperature fell nearly 6°C. (10·8°F) in one hour during a shower. On the 19th the temperature rose to 21·4°C. (70·52°F.) in London but on the 25th the maximum at Lerwick (Shetland) and at Foula (Shetland) was only 2°C. (35·6°F.). The minimum temperature at St. Harmon (Powys) on the 26th was −7°C. (19·4°F.) and on the 28th the maximum at Salsburgh (Strathclyde) was 2°C. (35·6°F.). Sunshine totals were below normal everywhere except in parts of southern England where they were near or slightly above normal. On the 17th southern England, Wales and much of Scotland were very sunny with more than 10 hours of bright sunshine in many places and 13 hours in the Channel Islands. On the 19th 13·6 hours of sunshine were recorded at Worthing (Sussex).

May—Rainfall totals were mostly near or above normal apart from in a narrow strip along the south coast of England and the southwest coast of Wales where totals were only about 50 per cent. of normal. On the 5th there was rain over Wales and western England and on the 8th there was rain in eastern areas when 33 mm. (1·3 ins.) fell at Whitby (North Yorkshire). There was rain over northern and eastern areas on the 6th and 7th. There was thundery rain in the south and east on the 12th and on the 14th there was widespread thundery rain, heavy at times, and a number of places in eastern England had over 20 mm. (0·79 ins.) in a few hours. Leeming (North Yorkshire) had 39 mm. (1·54 ins.). Only Shetland and southwest England remained dry. There was rain, sometimes thundery, in Scotland and north and east England on the 17th and 18th. On the 20th and 21st there was some heavy thundery rain in southern areas and the 23rd and 24th were wet days over Northern Ireland, Scotland and northern England. On the 20th 58·1 mm. (2·3 ins.) of rain fell at Brize Norton (Oxfordshire). The 25th and 26th brought two wet days to Northern Ireland and Corgary (Co. Fermanagh) had over 80 mm. (3·15 ins.) during the 48 hours. On the 25th thunderstorms with heavy rain developed over southwest England and gradually extended northwards and eastwards on the 26th. Over East Anglia some of these storms were violent with large hail, squalls and a marked drop in temperature. At Stansted (Essex) the temperature fell 10°C. (18°F.) in one hour. After thick fog overnight in many places further thunderstorms developed over East Anglia and southeast England. The rest of the Kingdom also had a wet Bank Holiday as a belt of rain moved eastwards. The month ended warm, sunny and dry. Monthly mean temperatures were mostly near or a little below normal. On the 3rd the temperature fell to −4·6°C. (23·72°F.) at St. Harmon (Powys) and only rose to 5·1°C. (41·18°F.) at Binbrook (Lincolnshire). On the 17th temperatures reached 23°C. (73·4°F.) in Hampshire and on the 26th 24·5°C. (76·1°F.) was recorded at Norwich Weather Centre. Sunshine totals were mostly a little below

normal in spite of some long spells of unbroken sunshine at the end of the month. On the 29th 16·6 hours of sunshine were recorded at Leuchars (Fife). The Spring period (March to May) was a very average season with mean temperatures just below normal, rainfall a little above normal and sunshine totals a little below normal.

June—Rainfall totals were well above average in most places with the exception of the western islands of Scotland and Shetland where they were well below average. In East Anglia totals were up to 3 times the normal amount and in England and Wales generally it was the wettest June since 1982. The dry, warm and very sunny end to May continued into June so the first three days were dry but on the 4th thunder storms affected southern areas and moved north into central England and Wales. An extensive area of storms crossed the Midlands, London and East Anglia. Heavy rain and thunderstorms affected southern areas on the 5th and 6th and at Hadley (Hereford & Worcester) 79 mm. (3·11 ins.) fell in the two days, 51·6 mm. (2·03 ins.) of which fell on the 5th. By the end of the first week many places had already received their average amount for the month. On the 8th rain affected western areas and moved eastwards to give periods of rain everywhere during the next 4 days. On the 11th the rain was widespread and heavy in many places especially in north Wales where Trawsfynydd (Gwynedd) had 41 mm. (1·61 ins.). Parts of north Wales had a very wet day on the 17th. The 18th was drier but with rain in East Anglia. The south of England had a wet day on the 19th. Early morning fog affected large areas on the 19th and 20th as it did on the 26th. On the 20th and 21st many places in southwest England had over 50 mm. (1·97 ins.) of rain and Bristol (Avon) had 54 mm. (2·13 ins.) in 36 hours. The whole of the Kingdom was rather wet during the next 4 days. The last few days were drier but there was rain in places even then. Monthly mean temperatures were below normal everywhere and in England and Wales it was the coldest June since 1977. On the 3rd the temperature rose to 26·8°C. (80·24°F.) at Southampton (Hampshire) but the highest temperature at Fylingdales (North Yorkshire) on the 6th was only 8°C. (46·4°F.). The temperature fell to −4·0°C. (24·8°F.) at St. Harmon (Powys). Sunshine totals were mostly below normal but were above normal around northern coasts, the Western Isles and Northern Ireland. On the 2nd 16 hours of sunshine were recorded at Prabost (Isle of Skye), Eskmeals (Cumbria) and at Carlisle (Cumbria).

AVERAGE AND GENERAL VALUES, 1983–1985 (June)

Month	Rainfall (mm.)				Temperature (°C.)				Bright Sunshine (hrs. per day)			
	Aver. 1941–1970	1983	1984	1985	Aver. 1941–1970	1983	1984	1985	Aver. 1941–1970	1983	1984	1985
England and Wales												
January	86	92	144	72	4.0	7.0	3.8	1.0	1.6	1.6	2.2	1.7
February	65	42	57	29	4.2	2.6	3.5	2.3	2.4	2.7	2.2	2.9
March	59	67	59	66	6.2	7.0	4.6	4.6	3.7	2.8	2.1	3.8
April	58	108	11	70	8.8	7.3	8.5	8.3	5.3	4.7	7.4	4.6
May	67	117	59	65	11.6	10.6	10.1	10.6	6.3	4.3	5.6	5.5
June	61	37	43	94	14.7	14.6	14.7	12.5	6.8	5.8	7.0	5.9
July	73	40	27	—	16.3	19.2	16.6	—	5.9	7.4	7.9	—
August	90	33	57	—	16.1	17.6	17.8	—	5.5	6.9	6.5	—
September	83	101	116	—	14.3	14.2	14.1	—	4.4	3.7	3.8	—
October	83	78	100	—	11.2	11.0	11.7	—	3.3	3.6	3.3	—
November	97	53	145	—	7.2	8.1	8.7	—	1.9	1.5	1.8	—
December	90	111	81	—	5.1	6.3	5.7	—	1.5	1.6	1.8	—
YEAR	912	879	899	—	10.0	10.4	10.0	—	4.0	3.9	4.0	—
Scotland												
January	137	220	223	85	3.5	5.6	1.5	1.3	1.4	1.0	1.2	1.6
February	104	59	104	47	3.7	2.7	2.8	2.8	2.5	2.4	1.6	2.7
March	92	149	119	95	5.4	6.2	4.1	3.7	3.4	2.2	2.2	3.3
April	90	74	54	111	7.5	5.8	7.2	6.7	5.0	4.4	6.0	3.9
May	91	115	23	73	9.9	9.0	9.1	9.2	5.7	3.7	6.7	5.4
June	92	86	66	84	12.7	12.2	12.5	11.0	5.5	4.8	5.5	5.5
July	112	43	55	—	14.1	16.0	14.6	—	4.8	5.9	5.5	—
August	129	51	50	—	14.0	15.5	15.5	—	4.5	5.0	4.7	—
September	137	172	166	—	12.5	13.3	11.8	—	3.7	2.9	2.8	—
October	149	230	216	—	9.9	9.4	9.8	—	2.7	2.4	2.5	—
November	142	49	233	—	6.3	7.3	7.6	—	1.7	1.5	1.2	—
December	156	208	166	—	4.6	6.1	5.7	—	1.1	0.8	1.0	—
YEAR	1431	1456	1475	—	8.7	9.1	8.5	—	3.5	3.1	3.3	—

TEMPERATURE AND RAINFALL RECORDS

WORLD: The maximum air temperature recorded is 57.8°C. (136°F.) at San Louis, Mexico on August 11, 1933; the minimum air temperature recorded is −89.2°C. (−128.56°F.) at Vostok, Antarctica on July 21, 1983. The greatest rainfall recorded in one day is 1870 mm. (73.62 ins.) at Cilaos, Isle de Réunion on March 16, 1952; the greatest rainfall in one calendar month is 9,300 mm. (366.14 ins.) at Cherrapunji, Assam in July 1861, the greatest annual total being 22,990 mm. (905.12 ins.) also at Cherrapunji in 1861.

UNITED KINGDOM: The maximum air temperature recorded is 38.1°C. (100.5°F.) at Tonbridge, Kent on July 22 1868; the minimum air temperature recorded is −27.2°C. (−17°F.) at Braemar (Grampian) on February 11, 1895 and 10th January 1982. The greatest rainfall recorded in one day is 280 mm. (11 ins.) at Martinstown, Dorset on July 18, 1955. The greatest annual total is 6,528 mm. (257 ins.) at Sprinkling Tarn, Cumbria in 1954.

WIND FORCE MEASURES

The *Beaufort Scale* of wind force has been accepted internationally and is used in communicating weather conditions. Devised originally by Admiral Sir Francis Beaufort in 1805, it now consists of the numbers 0–17, each representing a certain strength or velocity of wind at 10 m. (33 ft.) above ground in the open.

Scale No.	Wind Force	M.p.h.	Knots	Scale No.	Wind Force	M.p.h.	Knots
0	Calm	1	1	9	Strong gale	47–54	41–47
1	Light air	1–3	1–3	10	Whole gale	55–63	48–55
2	Slight breeze	4–7	4–6	11	Storm	64–72	56–63
3	Gentle breeze	8–12	7–10	12	Hurricane	73–82	64–71
4	Moderate breeze	13–18	11–16	13	—	83–92	72–80
5	Fresh breeze	19–24	17–21	14	—	93–103	81–89
6	Strong breeze	25–31	22–27	15	—	104–114	90–99
7	High wind	32–38	28–33	16	—	115–125	100–108
8	Gale	39–46	34–40	17	—	126–136	109–118

TEMPERATURE, RAINFALL AND SUNSHINE
IN THE UNITED KINGDOM

The following table gives mean air temperature (°C.), total monthly rainfall (mm.) and mean daily bright sunshine (hrs.) at a representative selection of climatological reporting stations in the United Kingdom during the year July 1984 to June 1985 and the calendar year 1984. The heights (m.) of the reporting stations above mean sea level are also given.

| | | 1984 | | | | | | | | | | | |
| | Ht. in mtrs. | July | | | August | | | September | | | October | | |
Station		Temp. °C.	Rain mm.	Sun hrs.	Temp. °C.	Rain mm.	Sun hrs.	Temp. °C.	Rain mm.	Sun hrs.	Temp. °C.	Rain mm.	Sun hrs.
Aberdeen (Dyce) .	65	15·2	68	5·1	14·7	16	5·2	10·9	106	3·1	8·8	99	3·3
Aberporth	134	15·4	38	9·2	16·5	41	6·0	13·4	154	4·2	11·0	95	3·5
Aldergrove	68	15·6	64	6·4	16·1	49	5·1	12·3	91	3·3	9·9	82	3·1
Aspatria	61	15·6	39	8·6	15·8	82	6·8	12·2	149	3·2	11·4	122	2·7
Bala	163	14·7	20	8·2	16·1	94	5·9	12·7	149	3·0	9·8	195	2·6
Birmingham (Elmdon)	98	16·7	26	9·0	17·5	55	6·8	13·7	93	3·7	10·8	51	3·4
Boulmer.........	23	14·9	26	6·7	14·9	44	6·0	12·5	97	3·7	10·5	45	4·6
Bournemouth (Hurn)	10	16·3	14	8·9	17·4	15	6·5	14·3	55	4·0	11·3	91	2·8
Bradford	134	16·3	15	—	16·9	50	—	12·7	132	—	10·7	106	—
Braemar	339	14·5	30	6·7	14·1	16	5·5	9·6	105	2·5	7·3	109	2·1
Buxton	307	15·1	29	7·6	15·5	61	6·1	11·3	181	3·0	9·1	135	2·9
Cambridge.......	24	16·7	15	6·9	18·0	61	6·4	14·0	113	3·5	11·6	49	3·7
Cardiff	9	17·8	15	8·5	18·5	47	6·3	14·7	149	4·7	12·1	148	2·7
Cheltenham	65	18·2	10	—	18·2	44	6·8	14·3	121	3·9	11·4	63	3·2
Clacton-on-Sea...	16	16·5	27	6·2	17·9	29	7·5	14·4	54	3·4	12·1	50	3·9
Douglas	85	15·2	25	9·3	16·0	67	7·1	12·5	131	4·2	10·7	140	3·0
Dumfries	49	16·1	26	6·5	16·1	45	5·8	12·2	103	3·2	10·3	157	2·3
Dundee	45	16·3	32	6·8	16·3	13	5·3	12·1	93	3·3	9·7	83	2·5
Durham	102	15·7	21	6·5	15·9	56	5·3	12·7	96	3·3	10·5	40	4·1
East Malling	33	16·7	30	6·4	17·9	16	6·2	14·1	59	3·0	11·6	76	2·9
Edinburgh.......	134	16·3	37	7·7	15·7	29	6·2	12·1	83	3·3	9·9	83	3·2
Glasgow.........	107	16·5	10	6·5	16·0	47	5·3	11·5	129	2·8	9·4	161	2·4
Gogerddan	31	15·9	26	9·1	16·9	58	6·6	13·6	203	3·4	11·5	132	3·0
Hastings	45	16·7	46	8·0	17·2	23	5·8	14·7	65	3·9	12·7	86	3·7
Hull	2	16·7	34	—	17·6	81	—	14·2	80	—	11·7	42	—
Inverness	4	15·8	21	5·0	16·1	22	5·0	11·3	94	2·8	9·8	91	2·9
Leeming	32	16·3	9	6·8	16·7	34	6·1	13·3	95	3·2	10·7	67	3·4
Lerwick	82	11·9	35	2·3	12·7	34	5·8	10·3	147	2·3	8·5	173	3·1
London (Heathrow)	25	18·5	19	7·5	19·3	28	6·5	14·8	73	3·3	12·1	83	2·9
Long Ashton.....	51	17·5	25	8·9	18·0	72	6·4	14·5	128	4·6	11·7	91	3·1
Lowestoft	25	15·9	33	5·4	17·1	37	7·2	14·2	90	3·5	11·8	39	3·1
Manchester (Ringway)....	75	16·9	13	8·2	18·0	43	6·8	13·4	140	3·3	11·1	97	3·0
Margate........	16	17·3	21	6·8	18·1	27	—	14·9	60	—	12·5	78	—
Melbury.........	143	15·3	40	8·8	16·1	82	5·9	13·2	201	4·0	10·7	181	2·7
Morecambe	7	16·5	17	8·6	17·5	56	7·1	13·3	163	3·5	11·0	125	2·7
Nottingham (Watnall)......	117	16·9	18	7·6	17·6	83	7·1	13·5	86	3·5	10·5	51	3·3
Oxford	63	18·1	14	8·1	18·6	33	6·5	14·5	91	3·3	11·8	54	2·9
Penzance........	19	16·8	48	9·2	17·5	37	7·5	15·1	120	6·5	12·5	107	3·7
Plymouth	27	16·7	28	8·9	17·5	53	6·2	14·7	106	5·1	12·1	110	3·3
Prestwick	16	15·1	36	8·1	15·9	36	6·5	12·0	144	3·4	10·1	202	2·6
St. Mawgan......	103	16·7	53	9·3	17·3	43	7·0	14·3	114	5·1	11·9	97	3·6
Scarborough.....	52	15·7	23	6·6	16·0	51	6·5	13·5	107	3·6	11·1	53	3·8
Shanklin........	55	16·3	29	8·9	17·2	20	7·3	14·7	69	4·5	12·3	107	2·9
Shawbury	72	16·1	21	9·0	17·1	59	6·3	13·5	92	4·2	10·5	54	3·6
Sheffield........	131	17·2	13	8·3	17·5	82	5·9	13·5	118	2·9	11·0	83	2·4
Shoeburyness	2	16·7	21	6·9	17·6	47	6·9	14·7	46	3·5	12·2	74	3·9
Skegness	5	16·3	21	6·8	17·0	42	8·7	14·1	99	4·2	11·5	35	3·4
Southampton	3	17·8	29	8·5	18·6	23	6·7	14·9	63	4·1	12·3	96	2·7
Stornoway	15	13·5	75	2·4	14·1	32	5·2	10·7	119	2·5	8·9	167	2·9
Tenby	5	15·9	26	9·9	16·6	50	6·4	13·6	194	4·8	11·5	154	2·7
Tiree...........	9	13·9	38	5·1	14·9	57	5·9	12·0	149	3·6	10·1	238	2·5
Torbay	8	16·9	28	9·2	17·7	71	6·6	14·9	72	5·5	12·3	92	3·2
Trawscoed......	63	15·3	44	9·0	16·6	58	6·5	13·5	186	3·8	10·9	144	3·6
Waddington	68	16·5	17	7·3	17·3	90	7·1	13·5	81	3·5	10·9	35	3·9
Weymouth	21	16·4	16	9·2	17·6	33	6·6	14·9	64	4·8	12·5	60	3·1
Worthing	2	16·3	39	8·4	17·2	21	6·2	14·5	70	4·3	11·9	102	3·3

TEMPERATURE, RAINFALL AND SUNSHINE IN THE UNITED KINGDOM—*contd.*

Mean Temperature of the air (°C.), Rainfall (mm.) and Bright Sunshine (as mean hours per day) at a representative selection of reporting stations during the year July 1984 to June 1985. Fuller details of the weather are given in the *Monthly Weather Report* published by the Meteorological Office.

| | 1984 | | | | | | | | | 1985 | | | | | |
| | November | | | December | | | Year | | | January | | | February | | |
Station	Temp. °C.	Rain mm.	Sun hrs.	Temp. °C.	Rain mm.	Sun hrs.	Temp. °C.	Rain mm.	Sun hrs.	Temp. °C.	Rain mm.	Sun hrs.	Temp. °C.	Rain mm.	Sun hrs.
Aberdeen (Dyce)	6·9	268	1·1	5·3	119	1·5	8·1	1052	3·6	1·7	82	1·9	3·1	14	3·3
Aberporth	8·1	145	1·8	6·3	134	1·5	7·9	853	4·5	2·3	71	2·8	3·9	30	3·5
Aldergrove	5·7	67	1·6	5·3	100	1·0	9·1	848	3·8	0·9	57	1·7	3·9	30	2·7
Aspatria	7·4	134	1·5	5·4	97	1·1	9·2	914	4·2	0·6	35	1·5	2·3	12	3·2
Bala	6·9	213	1·1	4·6	104	1·1	8·7	1217	3·7	0·1	58	1·0	2·5	25	2·9
Birmingham (Elmdon)	7·5	124	1·3	4·7	41	2·0	9·5	681	4·2	0·6	40	1·7	1·0	42	3·0
Boulmer	7·7	163	1·7	5·0	39	1·9	8·5	675	4·2	2·2	92	1·5	3·0	15	2·7
Bournemouth (Hurn)	8·3	147	2·0	5·7	100	2·0	10·1	794	4·8	0·7	81	2·6	2·9	45	2·9
Bradford	7·5	156	—	4·7	46	—	9·1	887	—	—	84	—	2·9	7	—
Braemar	4·5	244	0·5	2·7	77	0·6	6·7	1126	3·3	−1·8	117	0·8	0·4	19	2·6
Buxton	6·3	185	1·4	3·7	86	1·3	7·9	1224	—	−0·2	114	1·1	0·8	13	2·7
Cambridge	8·5	88	1·6	5·5	35	2·2	9·9	630	4·2	0·6	37	1·3	1·5	15	2·8
Cardiff	8·7	218	1·4	6·3	115	1·6	10·9	1093	4·5	2·3	88	2·3	3·9	69	2·6
Cheltenham	8·3	121	1·8	5·7	50	2·2	10·3	701	—	0·7	33	1·6	2·7	42	3·3
Clacton-on-Sea	9·5	53	2·3	6·1	45	2·3	10·1	554	4·4	0·6	91	1·7	2·3	8	2·7
Douglas	8·1	196	1·5	6·9	129	1·1	9·6	1085	4·5	3·7	88	1·9	3·8	46	1·8
Dumfries	7·4	183	1·3	5·1	109	0·8	9·2	986	3·6	1·0	55	1·6	2·3	13	2·1
Dundee	7·3	182	1·2	5·3	54	1·6	9·1	790	3·8	1·5	72	2·0	3·3	7	2·3
Durham	7·3	134	1·9	4·3	24	1·3	8·8	616	3·8	0·9	82	1·2	2·1	6	2·7
East Malling	9·1	87	2·2	5·3	70	1·7	10·2	659	4·1	0·3	61	1·4	2·3	20	3·1
Edinburgh	6·7	161	1·5	5·1	45	1·7	8·8	762	4·1	1·0	38	1·6	3·1	10	3·2
Glasgow	6·7	176	1·1	4·7	102	0·7	8·9	986	3·3	0·5	43	1·6	2·7	14	2·4
Gogerddan	8·2	177	1·6	6·4	148	1·5	9·5	1037	4·3	1·3	61	2·0	4·0	49	3·5
Hastings	10·3	134	—	7·3	105	—	10·7	813	—	1·1	152	1·8	2·9	41	3·7
Hull	8·4	104	—	5·9	35	—	9·9	708	—	1·7	80	—	2·9	5	—
Inverness	7·0	139	1·3	5·5	45	1·6	9·0	583	3·3	1·5	17	1·3	2·9	9	3·6
Leeming	7·5	99	1·7	4·4	30	1·3	9·2	595	3·9	0·8	61	1·4	2·1	3	2·4
Lerwick	6·5	110	0·7	5·8	123	0·2	7·3	1085	2·6	2·1	119	1·1	3·1	70	1·9
London (Heathrow)	9·3	70	2·5	5·7	57	1·6	10·9	641	4·3	1·2	41	1·5	3·2	30	2·8
Long Ashton	8·3	134	1·5	5·9	87	1·4	10·4	911	4·6	1·3	69	1·7	2·7	52	3·0
Lowestoft	9·3	65	1·6	5·5	56	1·8	9·6	615	3·8	0·9	62	1·1	2·0	7	2·9
Manchester (Ringway)	7·9	121	1·6	5·5	49	1·9	9·9	743	4·1	1·2	55	1·5	2·9	10	2·9
Margate	10·5	71	—	6·9	61	—	10·5	592	—	1·3	72	—	2·9	7	—
Melbury	8·3	236	2·0	6·0	172	1·6	9·5	1416	4·5	1·7	112	2·1	3·8	43	2·7
Morecambe	8·3	164	1·4	5·9	107	1·4	9·9	978	4·2	1·5	69	1·5	2·9	35	2·5
Nottingham (Watnall)	7·5	103	1·3	4·7	41	1·9	9·4	716	4·2	0·7	56	1·7	1·9	13	3·0
Oxford	8·7	102	1·8	5·5	45	1·9	10·5	609	4·3	1·1	44	1·7	2·5	35	2·8
Penzance	9·7	167	2·4	8·1	133	2·3	11·3	1071	5·5	3·9	117	2·5	6·7	79	3·0
Plymouth	8·9	191	2·0	7·9	85	1·8	8·9	976	5·1	3·2	117	2·8	5·5	44	2·8
Prestwick	7·6	128	1·8	5·7	95	1·1	9·2	958	4·1	0·7	36	1·7	3·5	12	3·8
St. Mawgan	8·7	192	2·1	7·5	108	2·3	10·6	975	5·0	2·9	95	2·9	5·5	27	2·7
Scarborough	8·3	109	1·5	5·1	24	1·7	9·1	633	4·1	2·3	78	0·9	3·1	1	2·3
Shanklin	9·6	112	2·1	7·0	113	2·1	10·6	806	5·0	1·7	68	2·1	3·2	68	2·4
Shawbury	7·3	135	1·7	4·7	55	1·9	9·3	652	4·2	0·6	32	1·7	1·5	39	2·5
Sheffield	7·7	125	1·1	5·1	48	1·3	9·7	867	3·8	1·5	73	1·1	2·7	5	2·2
Shoeburyness	9·7	66	2·7	6·2	32	2·1	10·2	511	4·5	0·7	55	1·7	2·5	11	2·8
Skegness	8·3	81	1·6	5·2	45	1·9	9·5	610	3·9	1·5	66	1·4	2·5	4	2·4
Southampton	9·2	132	2·1	6·3	109	1·8	11·1	804	4·6	1·5	71	2·1	3·3	36	3·2
Stornoway	7·0	140	1·3	6·1	107	1·2	8·4	1072	3·2	3·1	80	1·7	4·3	42	3·0
Tenby	8·1	203	2·1	6·1	156	1·8	10·1	1099	5·0	2·3	70	3·2	3·8	49	3·9
Tiree	7·4	144	1·9	6·9	149	0·9	9·1	1256	3·7	2·8	66	2·3	4·7	36	2·5
Torbay	9·3	192	2·3	7·1	62	2·3	11·0	873	5·2	3·0	108	2·5	5·1	54	1·6
Trawscoed	7·7	197	1·7	5·9	169	1·4	9·5	1167	4·3	0·9	58	1·7	—	—	—
Waddington	7·5	95	1·7	4·7	47	2·0	9·3	661	4·3	0·7	56	1·5	2·0	3	3·1
Weymouth	9·7	146	2·2	7·5	103	2·1	10·9	725	4·9	2·0	71	2·5	3·9	40	2·2
Worthing	9·8	111	2·6	6·5	97	2·1	10·4	760	4·8	1·3	53	2·1	2·5	35	—

TEMPERATURE, RAINFALL AND SUNSHINE IN THE UNITED KINGDOM—*contd.*

Mean Temperature of the air (°C.), Rainfall (mm.) and Bright Sunshine (as mean hours per day) at a representative selection of reporting stations during the year July 1984 to June 1985. Fuller details of the weather are given in the *Monthly Weather Report* published by the Meteorological Office.

| | 1985 | | | | | | | | | | | |
| | March | | | April | | | May | | | June | | |
Station	Temp. °C.	Rain mm.	Sun hrs.	Temp. °C.	Rain mm.	Sun hrs.	Temp. °C.	Rain mm.	Sun hrs.	Temp. °C.	Rain mm.	Sun hrs.
Aberdeen (Dyce)	3·9	90	3·7	6·7	80	3·9	9·1	91	5·4	10·9	84	5·9
Aberporth	4·9	67	4·7	8·1	62	4·6	10·1	29	6·2	11·7	104	6·2
Aldergrove	4·5	59	3·2	8·1	56	4·3	9·9	67	5·1	12·2	56	6·3
Aspatria	4·4	75	4·3	7·6	71	3·5	10·3	49	5·8	11·8	54	6·6
Bala	3·7	86	2·9	7·6	100	3·5	9·6	62	4·9	11·1	102	4·9
Birmingham (Elmdon)	4·4	32	3·4	8·2	64	4·1	10·5	60	5·2	12·5	103	5·1
Boulmer	4·3	63	4·0	7·1	57	4·3	9·1	88	4·7	10·9	61	6·3
Bournemouth (Hurn)	4·5	59	3·8	8·7	46	5·2	11·6	37	6·3	13·5	62	6·4
Bradford	—	55	—	—	80	—	—	—	—	—	—	—
Braemar	1·5	60	2·2	5·7	68	3·8	7·9	70	4·4	9·5	85	5·1
Buxton.............	2·9	86	—	6·3	145	—	9·0	72	—	10·4	99	—
Cambridge..........	—	46	3·1	—	31	4·6	—	49	2·3	—	107	4·8
Cardiff	5·7	79	3·8	9·5	66	4·7	12·1	44	5·8	13·7	157	5·1
Cheltenham	5·1	73	3·6	8·9	60	4·7	11·3	90	6·5	13·0	145	5·5
Clacton-on-Sea	4·3	54	3·5	8·5	37	5·1	10·9	52	5·4	13·6	89	6·0
Douglas	4·9	54	4·7	7·6	94	4·3	10·0	52	5·3	11·9	61	7·5
Dumfries	4·1	72	3·6	7·4	65	3·5	10·2	60	5·3	11·5	60	5·4
Dundee	4·5	76	2·6	7·6	60	4·0	10·0	74	5·5	11·9	62	5·6
Durham	4·1	62	4·1	7·5	75	3·8	9·7	64	4·1	11·4	35	5·1
East Malling	5·1	48	3·1	9·4	37	4·9	11·5	52	4·9	13·9	67	5·2
Edinburgh..........	3·9	86	3·3	7·7	70	4·5	6·9	50	5·0	—	—	—
Glasgow............	4·3	77	2·9	7·7	64	3·5	10·7	54	4·5	11·9	69	5·2
Gogerddan	5·3	66	3·8	8·5	93	4·1	10·7	65	5·5	12·3	137	6·1
Hastings	5·1	59	3·9	9·0	34	5·8	12·2	59	5·8	14·0	44	6·2
Hull	5·3	42	—	8·7	66	—	10·5	91	—	12·9	53	—
Inverness	4·5	41	3·5	7·2	50	3·7	9·9	59	4·2	11·9	73	4·1
Leeming............	4·3	48	4·0	8·1	59	3·9	10·3	89	4·7	12·1	32	5·6
Lerwick	3·3	94	3·1	4·9	147	3·7	7·3	57	4·6	9·5	15	4·3
London (Heathrow)	5·3	34	3·4	9·7	33	5·3	12·3	65	5·3	14·2	89	5·6
Long Ashton	5·3	63	3·9	8·9	46	5·0	11·3	65	6·1	13·1	130	6·1
Lowestoft	4·5	34	3·5	8·2	60	4·4	9·9	65	4·7	12·8	123	4·7
Manchester (Ringway)	4·7	57	3·6	8·3	77	3·8	11·3	72	5·1	12·7	70	6·3
Margate............	5·1	51	—	9·3	29	—	11·0	54	—	13·9	59	—
Melbury............	5·1	86	4·5	8·3	110	4·7	10·1	78	6·9	12·3	136	6·4
Morecambe	4·9	59	4·3	8·1	90	3·4	11·7	47	6·3	12·8	51	6·7
Nottingham (Watnall).........	4·3	42	3·2	8·1	50	3·5	10·7	76	4·9	12·2	88	5·7
Oxford	5·1	37	3·6	9·1	33	4·6	11·5	81	5·7	13·3	123	5·5
Penzance	7·2	135	4·7	9·7	94	6·9	11·9	60	6·9	13·7	86	6·5
Plymouth	6·3	97	4·3	9·3	67	5·7	11·9	43	7·4	13·7	67	6·6
Prestwick	4·5	69	4·0	7·9	50	4·5	10·1	37	5·9	11·7	65	7·4
St. Mawgan.........	6·0	97	4·7	9·0	76	6·1	11·1	47	7·2	13·1	76	6·7
Scarborough	4·9	71	3·7	7·9	73	4·0	9·7	64	4·7	11·8	60	6·4
Shanklin	5·1	65	4·6	—	—	—	11·5	48	7·4	13·2	58	6·3
Shawbury	4·1	72	3·4	8·0	61	4·2	10·5	64	5·9	12·1	93	5·9
Sheffield	5·0	49	3·4	8·2	69	3·7	10·6	63	4·5	12·7	77	6·0
Shoeburyness	4·9	38	3·6	9·7	24	—	10·7	37	—	14·1	77	—
Skegness	4·7	59	3·8	8·5	40	3·0	9·9	50	4·5	12·3	85	5·4
Southampton	5·4	57	3·9	9·3	42	6·0	12·3	35	6·5	14·1	59	6·0
Stornoway	4·3	95	3·7	6·9	111	4·2	8·5	53	7·1	10·4	62	5·5
Tenby..............	5·2	91	4·6	8·3	59	5·0	10·3	48	6·6	12·7	119	6·4
Tiree...............	4·8	61	3·5	7·5	98	5·0	9·5	48	7·4	11·3	24	7·5
Torbay	6·1	115	4·3	9·5	60	5·5	12·0	60	7·1	14·0	38	6·5
Trawscoed	4·3	70	3·5	7·6	109	4·0	9·9	56	5·6	11·6	122	6·3
Waddington	4·3	48	4·0	8·1	44	3·9	10·3	71	4·8	12·3	104	5·6
Weymouth	5·6	59	4·5	8·9	35	5·9	11·7	27	7·4	13·5	37	6·4
Worthing	4·7	63	4·2	8·7	35	6·2	12·1	47	6·9	13·9	49	6·5

Weather Record, July, 1984

Day	Temperature Max. °C.	Min. °C.	Wind Speed knots	Rainfall mm.	Sunshine hrs.
1	21.9	10.4	4.7	0.0	5.3
2	18.1	10.9	6.5	0.1	6.6
3	22.0	8.5	3.7	0.0	12.3
4	22.5	9.7	2.9	0.0	11.7
5	26.1	12.0	3.7	0.0	13.4
6	27.7	12.4	3.6	0.0	13.5
7	28.2	13.6	4.5	0.0	13.8
8	31.7	15.5	7.3	0.0	11.9
9	22.2	14.5	6.2	0.6	1.7
10	24.4	14.3	9.3	0.0	12.2
11	23.3	13.2	6.0	0.0	5.3
12	20.1	13.6	9.5	5.8	1.6
13	21.9	12.5	7.3	1.3	5.5
14	19.9	14.1	6.0	0.9	0.5
15	18.9	11.2	6.6	5.1	7.3
16	21.2	10.5	4.1	0.0	9.7
17	23.4	10.2	2.7	0.0	8.3
18	24.5	16.0	3.9	0.1	4.1
19	21.2	14.2	5.7	0.0	4.9
20	20.2	12.3	3.3	0.0	2.6
21	27.3	11.2	4.8	0.0	9.2
22	25.8	14.2	5.5	1.6	5.1
23	26.8	14.0	5.7	0.0	9.6
24	23.5	12.8	8.8	0.2	6.1
25	19.3	12.6	4.3	2.3	0.9
26	24.3	11.6	3.8	0.0	5.3
27	30.6	12.5	5.3	0.0	6.1
28	30.6	15.7	7.0	0.0	13.9
29	28.4	12.6	5.4	0.0	11.9
30	28.9	18.0	4.3	1.2	5.3
31	25.5	16.2	6.1	0.0	6.9
Total	—	—	—	19.2	232.5
Mean	24.2	12.9	5.5	—	—
Temp. °F.	72.3	55.2	—	—	—
Average	22.0	12.8	8.2	58.0	181.0

Weather Record, August, 1984

Temperature Max. °C.	Min. °C.	Wind Speed knots	Rainfall mm.	Sunshine hrs.	Day
25.3	11.5	6.0	1.9	11.9	1
22.2	14.6	9.5	0.9	4.7	2
22.8	16.0	6.5	10.6	8.7	3
19.8	14.1	5.1	2.6	2.9	4
19.8	13.5	5.6	0.0	4.3	5
22.8	9.5	4.4	0.2	9.7	6
19.5	14.6	5.7	0.6	4.4	7
21.5	11.4	5.8	0.0	3.3	8
24.0	12.6	5.5	0.0	10.4	9
19.8	13.3	6.5	0.0	2.3	10
23.1	8.5	3.0	0.0	12.0	11
23.6	11.0	4.2	0.0	8.5	12
24.5	16.0	4.4	0.0	4.3	13
26.5	14.8	3.2	0.0	5.8	14
26.2	14.7	3.5	9.1	6.5	15
24.9	13.9	3.7	0.0	4.4	16
24.3	14.0	3.5	0.0	6.2	17
25.9	12.9	3.3	0.0	8.5	18
28.8	13.5	4.0	0.0	11.5	19
29.7	14.3	7.0	0.0	11.7	20
29.8	17.3	8.4	0.0	11.0	21
23.9	17.2	2.8	0.0	1.6	22
27.0	14.5	5.3	0.0	2.7	23
23.9	17.7	4.2	0.8	0.1	24
23.7	16.3	4.9	1.1	6.7	25
23.5	13.3	2.9	0.0	5.7	26
26.5	14.5	2.5	0.0	5.0	27
26.2	15.2	4.7	0.0	7.7	28
26.3	14.3	6.9	0.0	5.3	29
26.9	16.8	8.7	0.0	6.9	30
25.0	18.2	9.8	0.0	6.4	31
—	—	—	27.8	201.1	.. Total
24.4	14.2	5.2	—	—	.. Mean
75.9	57.6	—	—	—	Temp. °F.
21.5	12.5	8.0	65.0	170.0	Average

Weather Record, September, 1984

Day	Temperature Max. °C.	Min. °C.	Wind Speed knots	Rainfall mm.	Sunshine hrs.
1	24.4	15.9	6.3	0.0	4.7
2	25.3	12.4	4.3	0.0	7.1
3	25.4	16.5	11.3	3.3	7.4
4	16.3	14.4	9.3	0.0	0.3
5	16.6	6.7	7.1	0.0	6.3
6	17.4	9.7	5.2	0.0	0.8
7	16.6	9.0	3.3	0.0	1.3
8	19.4	9.2	5.9	0.1	1.8
9	21.2	13.5	11.7	4.5	3.9
10	16.8	10.3	8.3	0.0	0.8
11	22.1	10.2	6.6	0.0	1.5
12	22.4	11.7	3.4	0.0	1.6
13	21.5	12.6	5.2	4.3	2.5
14	19.0	14.4	5.7	2.5	2.8
15	17.2	13.1	7.0	0.0	2.9
16	18.6	13.4	2.5	1.4	0.0
17	16.0	13.0	4.4	4.5	0.1
18	18.1	9.3	4.9	0.0	5.4
19	18.4	11.9	6.5	13.2	2.0
20	17.6	12.2	6.5	21.8	1.0
21	15.2	8.0	8.4	6.5	6.2
22	16.7	9.0	5.6	0.2	5.4
23	12.7	7.5	6.2	0.5	1.1
24	13.6	8.4	6.5	1.7	1.9
25	16.0	5.8	5.5	0.0	2.0
26	17.6	6.4	2.4	0.0	9.0
27	18.1	8.0	5.6	0.0	0.1
28	20.5	13.2	6.2	6.0	4.7
29	19.2	13.5	5.6	2.9	7.8
30	17.0	11.8	6.7	0.0	5.4
31					
Total	—	—	—	73.4	97.8
Mean	18.6	11.0	6.1	—	—
Temp. °F.	65.5	51.8			
Average	19.1	10.8	7.9	52.0	142.0

Weather Record, October, 1984

Temperature Max. °C.	Min. °C.	Wind Speed knots	Rainfall mm.	Sunshine hrs.	Day
16.4	4.8	2.3	0.0	6.9	1
15.7	6.5	5.2	7.8	3.6	2
15.1	7.6	6.5	0.5	3.1	3
16.1	6.7	8.0	2.1	6.6	4
13.4	10.3	10.8	36.0	0.0	5
14.5	7.1	7.2	0.0	6.4	6
15.0	4.8	5.0	0.9	0.5	7
19.8	9.7	8.1	0.0	0.7	8
17.8	14.2	4.3	5.9	0.3	9
14.9	11.2	2.3	0.2	0.0	10
17.0	5.1	3.6	0.0	6.3	11
17.9	8.6	3.3	0.0	6.3	12
15.4	8.6	6.0	0.0	0.1	13
18.8	9.5	3.6	0.0	9.1	14
14.3	6.9	2.6	0.0	0.1	15
15.5	11.1	4.5	0.0	0.0	16
14.4	11.5	5.4	2.5	0.1	17
15.4	12.1	13.6	1.5	3.5	18
15.0	11.7	11.4	3.7	0.1	19
13.9	8.5	11.5	0.0	8.2	20
15.8	4.7	6.1	5.8	4.3	21
16.6	8.1	12.9	5.5	0.0	22
13.9	10.6	5.5	0.0	2.6	23
15.8	6.2	9.3	8.1	0.0	24
11.4	11.6	0.0	1.9	0.0	25
12.0	4.6	4.4	0.0	4.3	26
13.5	0.6	2.9	1.0	7.6	27
16.3	1.1	6.9	1.3	0.0	28
18.4	11.3	8.7	0.0	0.3	29
18.4	13.4	4.9	0.0	4.5	30
17.6	12.1	3.9	0.0	3.8	31
—	—	—	82.8	91.2	Total
15.8	8.4	6.5			Mean
60.4	47.1				Temp. °F.
15.1	7.8	7.8	57.0	105.0	Average

Entries of Maximum Temperature cover the day period 9–21 h.; Minimum Temperature the night period 21–9 h. entered to the day of reading; Rainfall is for the 24 hours commencing at 9 h. on the day of entry; Sunshine is for the 24 hours 0–24 h.; Mean Wind Speed is 10 metres above the ground. 100 knots = 115·1 m.p.h.; 100 mm. = 3·94 ins.; °F. = 9/5°C. + 32.

Averages are for the period 1941–1970 except for mean wind speed which is for 1961–1980.

Weather Record, November, 1984

Day	Temperature Max. °C.	Min. °C.	Wind Speed knots	Rain-fall mm.	Sun-shine hrs.
1	18.3	10.5	9.0	0.0	7.3
2	17.3	11.0	8.2	7.8	4.1
3	11.9	5.8	9.9	0.2	8.1
4	11.2	4.5	6.2	0.0	5.5
5	9.0	6.0	5.6	6.0	1.0
6	11.0	6.2	4.9	0.9	0.0
7	13.9	6.9	6.1	0.6	2.5
8	16.0	9.7	10.3	1.8	1.7
9	15.6	8.6	7.0	0.7	0.5
10	14.3	9.8	3.3	0.0	6.6
11	15.0	5.7	6.1	0.0	0.4
12	15.7	10.2	8.3	6.8	0.6
13	11.0	8.1	5.9	0.1	0.0
14	12.3	8.5	7.5	0.0	0.8
15	4.5	1.4	3.2	0.0	0.0
16	7.9	1.6	7.9	7.6	0.0
17	6.6	3.3	6.1	0.8	0.0
18	8.5	5.0	3.3	0.2	3.2
19	8.7	5.0	4.3	0.0	4.5
20	11.9	0.9	5.3	4.4	3.1
21	13.4	3.5	11.9	7.5	4.3
22	12.7	8.3	11.8	11.8	0.0
23	14.7	8.2	18.2	4.6	0.4
24	12.9	8.0	12.9	0.7	3.5
25	10.2	5.9	5.7	1.2	2.7
26	9.5	0.9	4.6	0.0	7.5
27	11.8	1.7	13.3	0.4	0.0
28	13.6	9.3	10.9	1.4	4.1
29	12.5	9.7	9.3	0.2	0.1
30	13.7	8.0	10.9	4.1	2.9
31					
Total	—	—	—	69.8	75.4
Mean	12.2	6.4	7.9	—	—
Temp. °F.	54.0	43.5	—	—	—
Average	9.9	4.5	8.9	63.0	61.0

Weather Record, December, 1984

Temperature Max. °C.	Min. °C.	Wind Speed knots	Rain-fall mm.	Sun-shine hrs.	Day
13.6	8.8	6.8	0.4	0.7	1
9.1	6.6	5.4	6.0	0.0	2
10.1	5.0	8.5	1.9	0.0	3
11.2	6.7	3.7	0.4	0.5	4
11.5	9.0	7.4	9.8	0.0	5
9.5	6.2	4.3	0.0	3.3	6
11.4	4.8	5.0	0.0	4.5	7
9.7	2.5	2.7	0.7	0.2	8
9.0	2.8	3.1	0.0	6.3	9
7.8	1.7	3.0	0.1	3.1	10
5.1	-0.3	2.4	0.1	0.0	11
7.5	0.0	2.8	0.0	1.3	12
9.0	3.0	5.5	4.8	0.0	13
9.1	3.4	6.5	0.9	1.0	14
8.0	2.6	2.3	9.4	3.4	15
6.7	1.3	3.8	2.6	0.2	16
9.7	1.0	6.1	1.5	0.0	17
8.9	-1.5	5.5	1.0	5.5	18
11.2	-0.3	8.4	1.6	1.3	19
12.3	8.0	7.3	0.2	0.0	20
7.6	1.5	5.4	0.0	5.5	21
10.5	1.7	5.9	3.1	0.0	22
12.6	3.5	7.6	0.9	0.0	23
8.6	7.9	10.4	0.9	0.4	24
7.5	-1.0	4.7	4.1	0.5	25
4.5	-0.8	4.1	0.0	5.5	26
4.5	-0.2	4.1	0.0	4.4	27
3.0	0.4	2.0	0.0	0.3	28
5.7	-1.6	2.4	5.1	0.1	29
7.0	-1.3	3.5	1.2	0.0	30
8.6	5.6	4.2	0.0	1.3	31
—	—	—	56.7	49.3	Total
8.7	2.8	5.0	—	—	Mean
47.7	37.0	—	—	—	Temp. °F.
7.1	2.5	7.0	54.0	45.0	Average

Weather Record, January, 1985

Day	Temperature Max. °C.	Min. °C.	Wind Speed knots	Rain-fall mm.	Sun-shine hrs.
1	5.4	2.7	9.5	0.0	4.4
2	3.6	0.7	5.2	0.0	3.0
3	3.4	0.6	4.7	0.0	0.0
4	3.5	-0.6	5.0	0.2	1.0
5	0.3	-2.7	5.5	2.0	3.7
6	3.6	-5.1	8.9	1.0	1.4
7	-1.7	-4.5	7.3	0.0	5.0
8	-1.0	-7.1	2.9	0.0	0.0
9	2.2	-4.6	3.5	0.0	0.9
10	3.5	-3.9	3.6	0.0	0.3
11	2.7	-2.5	2.7	0.0	0.9
12	4.1	-2.8	3.4	0.9	2.1
13	-0.6	-2.0	6.2	0.1	0.0
14	0.9	-3.6	8.6	0.4	0.0
15	-1.2	-3.3	7.8	0.1	2.7
16	-4.0	-6.5	4.3	0.0	0.0
17	0.6	-7.7	9.6	0.0	2.1
18	2.0	-8.0	8.8	0.0	0.0
19	1.8	0.0	3.0	0.0	0.0
20	6.6	-0.4	7.3	5.8	0.0
21	10.1	0.7	11.4	7.7	0.0
22	5.0	0.8	8.6	0.0	7.5
23	4.0	-0.8	5.4	0.0	6.4
24	8.2	-2.8	8.6	4.0	0.1
25	7.7	0.2	5.1	11.8	0.0
26	4.6	3.5	6.5	0.3	0.0
27	6.1	-4.6	7.1	1.5	0.0
28	9.8	-2.0	8.5	1.5	2.9
29	11.4	2.9	6.7	3.5	0.0
30	10.9	2.4	7.2	0.5	1.1
31	11.7	4.2	11.9	0.0	1.3
Total	—	—	—	41.3	46.8
Mean	4.1	-1.7	6.6	—	—
Temp. °F.	39.4	28.9	—	—	—
Average	6.1	1.4	8.6	52.0	48.0

Weather Record, February, 1985

Temperature Max. °C.	Min. °C.	Wind Speed knots	Rain-fall mm.	Sun-shine hrs.	Day
13.3	8.7	11.1	0.0	2.3	1
12.7	6.7	5.6	0.0	1.8	2
10.5	6.2	3.8	0.1	0.0	3
10.7	7.9	3.8	0.0	1.2	4
8.8	1.5	3.5	0.0	3.3	5
11.6	2.8	3.4	2.1	0.4	6
4.4	4.2	11.1	5.7	0.0	7
3.3	3.0	10.7	13.6	0.0	8
0.0	-0.5	11.3	4.2	0.0	9
-1.8	-3.3	18.7	0.0	6.3	10
-0.5	-4.6	16.1	0.0	8.1	11
0.5	-5.6	10.8	0.0	7.6	12
-1.0	-7.2	4.0	0.0	0.1	13
2.0	-7.0	8.0	0.0	3.9	14
-0.2	-3.6	14.4	0.0	4.2	15
3.7	-4.6	7.2	0.0	8.5	16
4.7	-2.3	8.3	0.0	5.6	17
4.1	-2.3	6.5	0.0	7.3	18
4.0	-6.4	4.5	0.0	3.8	19
5.3	-3.0	2.7	0.1	0.0	20
4.9	1.6	1.7	0.0	0.0	21
4.8	2.2	4.3	0.0	0.0	22
11.6	0.5	5.8	0.0	5.0	23
14.0	1.4	2.7	0.0	6.7	24
11.1	0.9	3.3	0.0	0.0	25
12.7	-0.3	2.1	0.1	1.8	26
12.1	1.9	1.8	0.0	0.4	27
8.2	4.6	6.8	3.9	0.0	28
					29
					30
					31
—	—	—	29.8	78.3	Total
6.3	0.1	6.9	—	—	Mean
43.3	32.2	—	—	—	Temp. °F.
7.0	1.5	9.3	39.0	65.0	Average

Weather Record, March, 1985

Day	Max. °C.	Min. °C.	Wind Speed knots	Rain-fall mm.	Sun-shine hrs.
1	11.7	2.0	7.5	1.9	2.0
2	9.2	0.7	5.6	1.3	1.6
3	9.6	4.8	8.5	3.6	0.0
4	9.8	3.8	7.1	0.0	3.5
5	11.2	−1.0	2.5	0.0	9.2
6	11.7	−1.6	4.2	1.4	8.9
7	10.4	1.4	4.0	0.1	0.2
8	12.4	0.6	3.3	0.0	6.0
9	10.9	2.8	3.3	0.0	1.7
10	12.6	3.7	6.9	0.2	2.2
11	9.9	2.8	8.4	0.0	8.0
12	11.1	−1.1	2.5	0.0	9.8
13	8.3	−1.5	3.3	0.1	0.0
14	9.1	1.1	6.9	0.0	4.4
15	6.2	−1.5	4.4	4.6	2.7
16	5.8	−1.5	6.7	0.5	3.9
17	6.0	−2.4	5.3	0.1	2.2
18	7.5	−2.0	3.5	0.0	10.2
19	4.9	−1.5	5.2	0.0	4.6
20	4.5	−3.4	5.6	0.0	4.7
21	6.9	−1.8	9.9	2.9	0.0
22	9.6	1.8	6.8	2.1	0.8
23	7.8	4.9	5.7	0.1	0.6
24	11.5	4.3	7.2	0.1	3.2
25	9.7	0.4	6.5	1.1	0.1
26	5.8	4.2	8.0	11.0	0.0
27	8.5	2.2	7.5	0.1	2.5
28	10.1	−2.3	9.1	0.0	5.6
29	10.0	4.0	13.3	0.7	0.0
30	12.0	7.4	15.1	0.1	0.0
31	16.0	8.4	11.3	2.1	6.6
Total	—	—	—	34.1	105.2
Mean	9.4	1.3	6.6		
Temp. °F.	48.9	34.3	—	—	—
Average	10.3	2.7	9.5	39.0	117.0

Weather Record, April, 1985

Max. °C.	Min. °C.	Wind Speed knots	Rain-fall mm.	Sun-shine hrs.	Day
17.6	8.5	17.1	0.3	1.7	1
16.3	8.5	11.3	0.0	6.2	2
18.6	11.1	11.2	0.8	4.2	3
17.2	9.5	8.7	0.3	0.4	4
12.8	8.8	6.3	0.4	0.1	5
14.7	7.0	5.6	1.2	3.3	6
14.0	5.4	10.5	8.1	0.8	7
12.5	7.5	12.9	0.2	1.6	8
14.5	2.3	5.1	0.1	9.2	9
13.6	4.2	4.7	3.5	6.4	10
11.4	5.4	14.6	5.0	0.3	11
12.7	5.0	14.2	0.4	7.5	12
12.4	5.9	15.2	0.7	7.3	13
12.8	7.0	13.9	0.0	6.1	14
13.7	1.7	5.7	0.0	3.5	15
17.6	7.4	6.4	0.0	7.0	16
16.0	6.8	4.7	0.0	12.0	17
18.6	6.5	6.3	0.0	9.5	18
20.2	5.4	5.6	0.0	10.6	19
8.6	7.1	7.3	6.3	2.0	20
11.4	−0.1	7.4	0.0	4.3	21
15.1	5.4	12.9	0.1	9.4	22
11.5	4.6	13.3	0.0	7.0	23
13.1	0.3	6.0	0.0	13.1	24
9.6	5.2	7.3	0.0	0.3	25
12.6	−2.0	7.0	0.0	9.3	26
11.6	5.5	10.7	1.4	1.6	27
11.0	−1.3	8.0	2.6	8.5	28
12.6	3.0	4.2	1.9	0.1	29
16.8	6.6	8.0	0.0	4.2	30
					31
—	—	—	33.3	157.5	Total
14.0	5.3	9.1			Mean
57.2	41.5	—	—	—	Temp. °F.
13.8	5.0	8.3	40.0	136.0	Average

Weather Record, May, 1985

Day	Max. °C.	Min. °C.	Wind Speed knots	Rain-fall mm.	Sun-shine hrs.
1	13.4	6.0	8.6	0.0	6.8
2	13.5	6.4	6.7	0.0	8.8
3	10.4	7.5	5.3	0.1	0.5
4	13.3	6.3	3.0	0.0	1.1
5	12.9	5.6	8.3	0.0	3.7
6	17.0	4.4	5.7	0.0	11.7
7	19.1	6.9	9.5	0.0	8.3
8	15.1	9.9	8.1	0.0	1.0
9	15.9	7.4	6.7	0.0	5.2
10	13.0	3.7	6.0	0.0	0.9
11	9.6	7.2	10.3	0.0	0.0
12	12.7	5.9	11.6	3.5	0.0
13	14.5	7.4	7.5	0.4	2.4
14	11.8	8.0	5.0	35.4	0.0
15	16.3	5.9	5.9	0.0	1.9
16	20.8	5.7	3.4	0.0	11.7
17	21.4	9.2	5.3	0.0	7.8
18	21.3	9.5	3.5	0.0	6.2
19	15.8	10.5	4.9	0.1	0.0
20	19.8	9.9	6.7	0.0	2.1
21	16.4	12.1	5.2	14.6	3.8
22	15.0	10.2	5.5	0.0	2.1
23	15.8	8.9	5.4	0.0	3.3
24	16.9	9.8	11.4	0.3	4.9
25	19.6	10.7	8.2	1.4	5.1
26	20.8	13.2	5.6	3.9	5.9
27	18.1	11.8	4.7	5.0	1.2
28	18.6	9.4	6.2	0.0	13.3
29	19.6	8.8	7.5	0.0	14.9
30	19.1	6.5	9.7	0.0	15.7
31	19.7	6.6	8.8	0.0	13.4
Total	—	—	—	64.7	163.7
Mean	16.4	8.2	6.8		
Temp. °F.	61.5	46.8	—	—	—
Average	17.2	7.7	8.5	50.0	191.0

Weather Record, June, 1985

Max. °C.	Min. °C.	Wind Speed knots	Rain-fall mm.	Sun-shine hrs.	Day
22.0	6.2	7.8	0.0	15.0	1
23.5	9.4	9.1	0.0	14.9	2
25.0	10.4	8.8	0.9	14.2	3
24.3	11.2	5.3	8.2	3.6	4
20.4	14.0	4.6	14.8	0.8	5
14.2	11.7	6.0	12.9	0.0	6
12.5	7.3	7.8	1.6	0.9	7
15.7	3.9	7.0	1.1	8.9	8
18.0	9.8	10.1	0.4	7.1	9
17.0	8.6	7.2	0.3	7.5	10
16.4	10.0	9.3	10.9	0.2	11
16.6	10.0	12.9	0.1	11.6	12
16.7	8.5	4.7	4.1	1.0	13
16.4	9.2	6.0	0.0	10.7	14
17.8	5.4	4.5	0.0	11.0	15
17.9	10.0	3.7	0.0	5.5	16
19.5	7.9	5.9	0.1	8.6	17
17.5	10.6	3.8	0.0	1.5	18
19.7	12.0	4.6	0.0	3.0	19
20.1	11.0	3.5	8.1	8.6	20
16.0	10.7	8.9	3.1	0.6	21
16.6	12.2	10.7	6.6	0.3	22
19.1	11.0	7.1	2.6	5.0	23
18.2	12.7	3.6	2.3	1.6	24
15.9	8.3	3.6	8.2	2.1	25
18.2	9.7	3.8	0.8	5.1	26
18.8	10.5	6.3	0.0	6.2	27
17.9	9.7	7.1	1.7	1.7	28
21.1	13.0	6.8	0.1	4.2	29
21.7	12.6	4.7	0.0	5.8	30
					31
—	—	—	88.9	167.2	Total
18.5	9.9	6.5			Mean
65.3	49.8	—	—	—	Temp. °F.
20.7	10.9	8.4	48.0	216.0	Average

TIDAL CONSTANTS

THE TIME OF HIGH WATER *at the undermentioned Ports and Places may be* approximately *found by taking the appropriate Time of High Water at the* Standard Port (*as shown on pp.* 172, 173, *etc.) and* adding thereto *the quantities annexed. The columns headed* "Springs" *and* "Neaps" *show the height of the tide above datum for Mean High Water Springs and Mean High Water Neaps respectively.*

Tidal data is no longer available for a number of places which formerly appeared in the list below. These places (with the name of the substitute now recorded) are: *Air Point* (Mostyn Quay); *Ardrishaig* (East Loch Tarbert); *Arisaig* (Loch Moidart); *Ayr Pt.,* I.o.M. (Peel); *Beachy Head* (Eastbourne); *Beaumaris* (Menai Bridge); *Brieile* (Scheveningen); *Broughty Ferry* (Newburgh); *Burryport* (Whiteford Lighthouse); *Caen* (Cayeux); *Caernarvon* (Llanddwyn Isld.); *Dumbarton* (Bowling); *Fareham* (Itchenor); *Fifeness* (Anstruther Easter); *Glasson Dock* (Tarn Pt.); *Gravesend* (Tilbury); *Greenwich* (R. Albert Dock); *Hythe* (Totland Bay); *Lancaster* (Duddon Bar); *Lynmouth* (Porlock Bay); *Nash Pt.* (Chepstow); *Needles Pt.* (Freshwater Bay); *Neath* (Porthcawl); *Nore Lt.* (Chatham); *Port Harrington* (Hestan Islet); *Portishead* (Avonmouth); *St. Agnes* (Coverack); *St. Mary's* (Sennen Cove); *Start Pt.* (Lulworth Cove); *Stockton* (Seaham); *Sutton Bridge* (Blacktoft); *Torbay* (Torquay); *Worms Head* (Ferryside); *Honfleur Harbour* (Duclair).

Port		Diff.	Springs	Neaps	Port		Diff.	Springs	Neaps
		h.m.	metres	metres			h.m.	metres	metres
Aberdeen	Leith	−1 19	4·3	3·4	Coverack	Avonmouth	−2 02	5·3	4·2
Aberdovey	Liverpool	−3 00	5·0	3·5	Cowes	London	−2 23	4·2	3·5
Aberystwyth	Liverpool	−3 30	5·0	3·5	Cromarty	Leith	−2 56	4·3	3·4
Aldeburgh	London	−3 05	2·8	2·7	Cromer	Hull	+0 35	5·3	4·2
Alderney	London	+5 33	6·3	4·7	Dartmouth	London	+4 32	4·8	3·6
Alloa	Leith	+0 47	5·6	4·2	Deal	London	−2 37	6·1	5·0
Amlwch	Liverpool	−0 33	7·3	5·8	Devonport (see Plymouth)				
Anstruther Easter	Leith	−0 22	5·5	4·4	Dieppe	London	−3 03	9·3	7·2
Antwerp	London	+0 50	5·6	4·3	Dingle Hbr.	Liverpool	+5 33	3·8	2·9
Appledore	Avonmouth	−1 15	7·5	5·2	Donegal Hbr.	Liverpool	−5 24	3·9	3·0
Arbroath	Leith	−0 33	5·0	4·1	Douglas	Liverpool	−0 04	6·9	5·4
Ardrossan	Greenock	−0 15	3·2	2·7	Dover	London	−2 52	6·7	5·3
†Arundel	London	−1 43	3·1	2·2	Duclair	London	−1 13	7·7	6·5
Avonmouth	A'mouth	0 00	13·2	10·0	Duddon Bar	Liverpool	+0 03	8·5	6·6
Ayr	Greenock	−0 25	3·0	2·6	Dunbar	Leith	−0 07	5·2	4·2
Ballycotton	Avonmouth	−1 47	4·1	3·3	Dundalk (Sldr's Pt)	L'pool	+0 22	5·1	4·2
Banff	Leith	−2 44	3·5	2·8	Dundee	Leith	+0 11	5·3	4·3
Bantry	Liverpool	+5 54	3·4	2·6	Dungeness	London	−3 04	7·7	5·8
Bardsey Island	Liverpool	−3 18	4·5	3·3	Dunkirk	London	−1 54	5·8	4·8
Barmouth	Liverpool	−2 57	5·0	3·5	Eastbourne	London	−2 50	7·3	5·6
Barnstaple	Avonmouth	−1 00	4·1	1·4	East Loch Tarbert	G'nock	+0 05	3·4	2·9
Barrow	Liverpool	+0 15	9·1	7·1	Exmouth Dock	London	+4 55	4·0	2·8
Barry	Avonmouth	−0 22	11·4	8·7	Eyemouth	Leith	−0 20	4·7	3·7
Belfast	London	−2 45	3·5	3·0	Falmouth	London	+3 35	5·3	4·2
Berwick	Leith	−0 02	4·7	3·8	Ferryside	Avonmouth	−0 58	6·7	4·5
Bideford	Avonmouth	−1 15	5·9	3·6	Filey Bay	Leith	+1 50	5·8	4·9
Blacktoft	Hull	+0 31	5·7	3·9	Fishguard	Liverpool	−4 00	4·8	3·4
Blakeney	Hull	+0 29	3·1	2·1	Flushing	London	−0 40	4·9	4·0
Blyth	Leith	+0 50	5·0	3·9	Folkestone	London	−3 04	7·1	5·7
Boscastle	Avonmouth	−1 20	7·3	5·6	Formby	Liverpool	−0 21	9·0	7·3
Boulogne	London	−2 44	8·9	7·2	Fowey	London	+3 53	5·4	4·3
Bovisand Pier	London	+3 55	5·3	4·3	Fraserburgh	Leith	−2 19	3·9	3·1
Bowling	Greenock	+0 15	4·0	3·4	*Freshwater Bay	London	−4 33	2·6	2·3
Brest	London	+2 28	7·5	5·9	Galway	Liverpool	−6 08	5·1	3·9
Bridgewater	Avonmouth	−0 22	4·6	1·9	Glasgow	Greenock	+0 20	4·7	4·1
Bridlington	Leith	+2 03	6·1	4·7	Goole	Hull	+0 59	5·7	3·7
Bridport	London	+4 37	4·1	3·0	Gorleston	London	−5 00	2·4	2·0
Brighton	London	−2 50	6·5	5·1	Granton	Leith	0 00	5·6	4·5
Buckie	Leith	−2 56	4·1	3·2	Granville	London	+4 32	12·8	9·6
Bude Haven	Avonmouth	−1 33	7·7	5·8	Grimsby	Hull	−0 28	7·0	5·6
Bull Sand Fort	Hull	−0 46	6·9	5·5	Hartlepool	Leith	+0 58	5·1	4·0
Burntisland	Leith	0 00	5·6	4·5	Harwich	London	−2 02	4·0	3·4
Calais	London	−2 04	7·2	6·0	Hastings	London	−2 57	7·5	5·8
Campbeltown	Greenock	+0 07	2·9	2·6	Haverfordwest	Liverpool	−4 50	5·2	0·3
Cape Cornwall	A'mouth	−2 30	6·0	4·3	Hestan Islet	Liverpool	+0 25	8·3	6·3
Cardiff	Avonmouth	−0 15	12·2	9·4	Hilbre Island	Liverpool	−0 16	9·0	7·2
Cardigan, Port	Liverpool	−3 37	4·7	3·4	Holyhead	Liverpool	−0 48	5·7	4·5
Carmarthen	Avonmouth	−0 48	2·6	0·4	Hook of Holland	London	−0 01	2·3	1·8
Cayeux	London	−2 55	10·2	7·9	*Hurst Point	London	−3 38	2·7	2·3
Chatham (N.Lock)	London	−1 10	6·0	4·9	Ijmuiden	London	+1 09	2·0	1·7
Chepstow	Avonmouth	+0 20	No Data		Ilfracombe	Avonmouth	−1 10	9·2	6·9
Cherbourg	London	−6 00	6·3	5·0	Inveraray	Greenock	+0 11	3·3	3·0
Chester	Liverpool	+1 05	4·0	2·0	Invergordon	Leith	−2 49	4·4	3·5
Chichester Hbr.	London	−2 25	4·9	4·0	Ipswich	London	−1 42	4·2	3·4
*Christchurch Hbr.	L'don	−4 53	1·8	1·4	Itchenor	London	−2 16	5·1	4·0
Cobh	Liverpool	−5 56	4·1	3·3	Kinsale	Liverpool	−6 08	4·0	3·2

† Very Approximate. * 1st H.W. (Springs).

Port	Diff.	Springs	Neaps		Port	Diff.	Springs	Neaps
	h.m.	metres	metres			h.m.	metres	metres
Kirkcudbright . *Liverpool*	+0 15	7·5	5·9		Ramsgate...... *London*	−2 32	4·9	3·8
Kirkwall .... *Leith*	−4 15	2·9	2·2		†Rosslare...... *Liverpool*	−5 23	1·9	1·4
Lamlash...... *Greenock*	−0 26	3·2	2·7		Rosyth .... *Leith*	+0 07	5·8	4·7
Le Havre ...... *London*	−3 55	7·8	6·5		Ryde .... *London*	−2 23	4·5	3·7
Lerwick .... *Leith*	−3 49	2·2	1·6		St. Anne's ..... *Liverpool*	−0 04	9·3	7·1
Limerick Dock .. *Leith*	−4 24	5·9	4·5		St. Helier ...... *London*	+4 48	11·1	8·1
Littlehampton .. *London*	−2 38	5·7	4·6		St. Ives ...... *Avonmouth*	−1 55	6·6	4·9
Lizard Point .. *London*	−2 17	5·3	4·2		St. Malo ...... *London*	+4 27	12·1	9·1
Llanddwyn Island *L'pool*	−1 53	5·0	4·0		St. Peter Port .. *London*	+4 54	9·0	6·7
Llanelli ..... *Avonmouth*	−0 56	7·8	5·8		Salcombe ...... *London*	+4 10	5·3	4·1
Loch Long .... *Greenock*	+6 02	4·8	3·5		Saltash......... *London*	+4 14	5·6	4·4
Loch Moidart .. *Greenock*	+6 02	4·8	3·5		Scarborough...... *Leith*	+1 33	5·7	4·6
Londonderry ... *London*	−5 37	2·7	2·0		Scheveningen... *London*	+0 29	2·1	1·8
Looe .... *London*	+3 55	5·4	4·2		Scrabster ...... *Leith*	+6 04	5·0	3·7
Lossiemouth...... *Leith*	−3 01	4·1	3·2		Seaham .... *Leith*	+0 53	5·2	4·1
Lowestoft ...... *London*	−4 25	2·4	2·1		Selsey Bill ...... *London*	−2 28	5·3	4·4
Lulworth Cove.. *London*	+5 00	2·3	1·5		Sennen Cove . *Avonmouth*	−2 30	6·1	4·8
Lundy Island *Avonmouth*	−1 23	8·0	5·9		Sharpness Dock . *A'mouth*	+0 42	9·3	5·8
Lyme Regis ..... *London*	+4 55	4·3	3·1		Sheerness ...... *London*	−1 16	5·7	4·8
*Lymington .... *London*	−3 33	3·0	2·6		Shoreham ...... *London*	−2 43	6·2	5·0
Margate........ *London*	−1 52	4·8	3·9		Silloth ...... *Liverpool*	+0 35	9·2	7·1
Maryport...... *London*	+0 24	8·6	6·6		Southampton ... *London*	−2 52	4·5	3·7
Menai Bridge .. *Liverpool*	−0 28	7·4	5·9		Southend....... *London*	−1 22	5·7	4·8
Mevagissey ..... *London*	+3 53	5·4	4·3		Southwold...... *London*	−3 50	2·5	2·2
Middlesbrough ..... *Leith*	+1 09	5·6	4·5		Spurn Head (see Bull Sand Fort)			
Milford Haven . *Liverpool*	−5 07	7·0	5·2		Stirling........... *Leith*	+1 13	2·9	1·6
Minehead .. *Avonmouth*	−0 40	10·6	8·1		Stonehaven....... *Leith*	−1 09	4·5	3·6
Montrose.......... *Leith*	−0 19	4·8	3·9		Stornoway ... *Liverpool*	−4 15	4·8	3·7
Morecambe .... *Liverpool*	+0 01	9·5	7·6		Stranraer ...... *Greenock*	−0 20	3·0	2·5
Mostyn Quay .. *Liverpool*	−0 17	8·5	6·7		Stromness ...... *Leith*	−5 24	3·4	2·6
Newburgh......... *Leith*	+0 48	4·1	3·0		Sunderland....... *Leith*	+0 51	5·2	4·2
Newcastle on Tyne . *Leith*	+0 54	5·3	4·1		*Swanage ...... *London*	−5 13	2·0	1·4
Newhaven...... *London*	−2 48	6·6	5·2		Swansea......... *Bristol*	−0 49	9·6	7·3
Newport (Gwent)*A'mouth*	−0 15	12·1	9·0		Tarn Point ..... *Liverpool*	+0 05	8·3	6·4
Newquay .... *Avonmouth*	−1 58	7·0	5·3		Tay River (Bar) .... *Leith*	−0 21	5·2	4·2
New Quay (Card.) . *L'pool*	−3 30	4·9	3·4		Tees R. (Ent.) ...... *Leith*	+1 08	5·5	4·3
North Shields ...... *Leith*	+0 51	5·0	3·9		Teignmouth ... *London*	+4 37	4·8	3·6
North Sunderland .. *Leith*	+0 05	4·8	3·7		Tenby .... *Avonmouth*	−1 05	8·4	6·3
Oban........... *Greenock*	+5 47	4·0	2·9		Tilbury......... *London*	−0 49	6·5	5·4
Old Lynn Road ..... *Hull*	+0 05	7·3	5·8		Tobermory .... *Liverpool*	−5 12	4·4	3·3
Orfordness ..... *London*	−2 50	2·8	2·7		Torquay........ *London*	+4 40	4·9	3·7
Ostend .... *London*	−1 32	5·1	4·2		*Totland Bay ... *London*	−3 53	2·7	2·3
Padstow..... *Avonmouth*	−1 45	7·3	5·6		Troon .... *Greenock*	−0 25	3·2	2·7
Peel......... *Liverpool*	−0 02	5·3	4·2		Truro .... *London*	+3 43	5·3	4·2
Pembroke Dock *Liverpool*	−5 07	7·0	5·2		Tyne River (Ent.)... *Leith*	+0 56	5·1	3·9
Penzance ... *Avonmouth*	−2 24	5·6	4·4		Ushant......... *London*	+2 30	7·5	5·8
Peterhead .... *Leith*	−1 59	3·8	3·1		Valentia Hbr... *Liverpool*	+5 31	3·8	3·0
Plymouth ...... *London*	+4 05	5·5	4·4		Walton-on-Naze . *London*	−2 10	4·2	3·4
Plymouth Breakwater (see Bovisand Pier)					Waterford Hbr . *Liverpool*	−4 59	4·5	3·6
*Poole (Entrance) *London*	−5 03	2·0	1·6		Weston S. Mare . *A'mouth*	−0 25	12·0	9·0
Porlock Bay . *Avonmouth*	−0 50	10·2	7·8		†Wexford Hbr .. *Liverpool*	−5 03	1·7	1·4
Porthcawl ... *Avonmouth*	−0 53	9·9	7·5		Whitby............ *Leith*	+1 22	5·4	4·3
Portmadoc..... *Liverpool*	−2 45	5·1	3·4		Whitehaven ... *Liverpool*	+0 10	8·0	6·3
Portland ...... *London*	+5 10	2·1	1·4		Wick............ *Leith*	−3 26	3·4	2·7
Portpatrick .. *Liverpool*	+0 22	3·8	3·0		Wisbech Cut ...... *Hull*	+0 01	7·0	5·1
Portsmouth..... *London*	−2 23	4·7	3·8		Woolwich ...... *London*	−0 22	7·0	5·9
Port Talbot .. *Avonmouth*	−0 53	9·6	7·3		Workington ... *Liverpool*	+0 20	8·2	6·4
Preston ...... *Liverpool*	0 00	5·4	3·5		Worthing ...... *London*	−2 36	6·1	4·8
Pwllheli .... *Liverpool*	−3 07	5·0	3·4		Yarmouth Roads *London* (*see* Gorleston)			
R.A. Dock (see Woolwich)					*Yarmth.(I.O.W.) *London*	−3 28	3·1	2·5
Ramsey (I.O.M.) *Liverpool*	+0 04	7·3	5·8		Youghal...... *Liverpool*	−5 50	4·1	3·3

† Very Approximate.   * 1st H.W. (Springs).

EXAMPLE.—Required times of high water at Stranraer on *January* 2, 1986:—

(a) *Morning Tide.*
Appropriate time of high
water at *Greenock* .... 0412 hrs. (*Jan.* 2)
Tidal difference .... −0020 hrs.

(b) *Afternoon Tide.*
Appropriate time of high
water at *Greenock* .... 1604 hrs. (*Jan* 2).
Tidal difference .... −0020 hrs.

H.W at *Stranraer* ... 0352 hrs.   H.W. at *Stranraer* .. 1544 hrs.

Tidal predictions (pp. 172–183) for London Bridge, Liverpool, Avonmouth, Hull, Dún Laoghaire and Leith are computed by the Institute of Oceanographic Sciences, copyright reserved. Those for Greenock have been supplied by the Hydrographer of the Navy and are crown copyright.

JANUARY, 1986

High Water at the undermentioned Places (G.M.T.*)—

Day of Month	Day of Week	London Bridge †3·20 m. below Mn. h.m.	Ht. m.	Aft. h.m.	Ht. m.	Liverpool †4·93 m. below Mn. h.m.	Ht. m.	Aft. h.m.	Ht. m.	Avonmouth †6·50 m. below Mn. h.m.	Ht. m.	Aft. h.m.	Ht. m.	Hull (Albert Dock) †3·90 m. below Mn. h.m.	Ht. m.	Aft. h.m.	Ht. m.	Greenock †1·62 m. below Mn. h.m.	Ht. m.	Aft. h.m.	Ht. m.	Leith †2·90 m. below Mn. h.m.	Ht. m.	Aft. h.m.	Ht. m.	Dun Laoghaire ‡0·20 m. above Mn. h.m.	Ht. m.	Aft. h.m.	Ht. m.
1	W	441	6·6	1712	6·8	2 2	8·5	1418	8·7	10 9	12·1	2235	11·7	925	6·8	2129	6·8	330	3·1	1518	3·7	541	5·0	18 1	5·1	228	3·6	1445	4·0
2	Th	518	6·5	1754	6·6	247	8·3	15 4	8·5	1052	11·9	2319	11·5	1010	6·6	2213	6·7	412	3·1	16 4	3·7	629	4·9	1849	5·0	317	3·5	1535	3·9
3	F	558	6·4	1842	6·4	336	8·1	1555	8·4	1140	11·7		11·4	1059	6·4	23 4	6·6	456	3·1	1654	3·6	722	4·8	1940	4·9	413	3·5	1631	3·8
4	Sa	646	6·2	1941	6·2	433	7·9	1655	8·2	0 8	10·9	1235	11·1	1157	6·3			545	3·1	1750	3·5	817	4·7	2037	4·9	516	3·5	1735	3·8
5	Su	751	6·1	2053	6·2	539	7·9	18 3	8·2	112	10·8	1345	11·2	0 5	6·5	13 6	6·3	647	3·1	1858	3·4	919	4·7	2139	4·9	624	3·6	1845	3·7
6	M	910	6·1	22 6	6·2	650	8·0	1916	8·5	232	10·8	1616	11·2	119	6·5	1416	6·6	8 8	3·1	2014	3·4	1024	4·9	2249	5·1	730	3·6	1954	3·8
7	Tu	1026	6·3	2315	6·5	758	8·2	2026	8·8	348	11·1	1723	12·0	232	6·6	1525	6·6	919	3·2	2126	3·4	1129	5·0	2356	5·1	828	3·7	2055	3·8
8	W	1137	6·4			9 1	8·6	2128	9·0	454	11·8	1824	12·4	345	6·8	1628	6·8	1016	3·3	2229	3·4			1231	5·1	921	3·8	2151	3·9
9	Th	017	6·4	1241	6·6	957	9·0	2226	9·2	556	12·3	1917	12·7	454	7·0	1723	7·1	11 8	3·4	2328	3·4	059	5·3	1326	5·1	10 8	4·1	2243	4·0
10	F	113	6·5	1337	6·7	1049	9·3	2318	—	650	13·0	20 6	12·8	553	7·2	1812	7·3	1157	3·6			156	5·5	1419	5·5	1053	4·1	2331	4·0
11	Sa	2 2	6·6	1427	6·9	1139	9·5		9·6	740	13·0	2050	12·8	645	7·3	1856	7·4	025	3·6	1247	3·7	250	5·6	1553	5·5	1141	4·2		
12	Su	249	6·8	1515	7·2	0 7	9·3	1225	9·5	826	13·1	2131	12·8	733	7·1	1938	7·5	119	3·4	1334	3·8	339	5·5	1638	5·6	021	3·9	1229	4·2
13	M	332	7·0	1604	7·3	052	8·9	13 9	9·3	9 8	12·9	2210	12·6	816	6·9	2018	7·5	2 9	3·3	1419	3·8	425	5·5	1723	5·6	1 8	3·9	1317	4·2
14	Tu	413	7·0	1644	7·3	135	8·9	1351	9·0	949	12·8	2247	12·2	857	6·7	2057	7·1	255	3·3	15 1	3·5	510	5·1	18 9	5·4	157	3·8	14 6	4·2
15	W	454	6·9	1725	7·2	215	8·6	1432	8·6	1027	12·3	2322	12·2	936	6·5	2136	7·1	337	3·2	1542	3·5	555	4·9	1856	5·1	246	3·5	1454	4·0
16	Th	532	6·6	1809	6·9	256	8·3	1512	8·1	11 5	11·8		11·3	1016	6·4	2216	6·7	416	3·2	1623	3·3	642	4·6	1941	4·9	338	3·3	1545	3·8
17	F	611	6·4	1849	6·5	336	7·5	1556	7·5	1143	11·4			1065	6·1	2259	6·7	454	3·0	17 8	3·3	730	4·4	2029	4·6	432	3·2	1639	3·6
18	Sa	655	6·1	1938	6·0	423	7·1	1647	7·3	0 0	11·0	1228	10·9	1142	5·9	2353	5·6	536	3·0	18 0	3·1	819	4·3	2125	4·5	535	3·2	1741	3·4
19	Su	751	5·8	2036	5·7	519	7·1	1747	7·3	048	10·4	1324	10·4	1 2	6·0	1241	5·6	625	2·9	19 4	3·0	913	4·4	2231	4·5	640	3·2	1849	3·3
20	M	856	5·6	2136	5·6	629	7·3	19 0	7·6	149	10·3	1432	10·2	219	5·9	1348	6·0	728	2·9	2019	2·9	1015	4·4	2338	4·7	741	3·3	1954	3·3
21	Tu	10 2	5·6	2240	5·8	744	7·5	2011	8·0	3 1	10·0	1543	10·3	332	6·1	1510	5·9	841	3·0	2128	3·0	1121	4·5	1219	5·1	834	3·5	2048	3·3
22	W	1111	5·7	2342	5·9	846	7·9	2110	8·3	416	10·3	1654	10·7	433	6·1	1610	5·8	942	3·2	2227	3·0			1311	5·2	919	3·8	2135	3·4
23	Th	032	6·2	1211	5·9	935	8·3	2157	8·6	520	11·5	1750	11·2	520	6·6	1657	6·1	1031	3·3	2316	3·1	038	4·8	1355	5·3	959	3·9	2215	3·5
24	F	117	6·4	1257	6·2	1017	8·7	2238	8·9	610	11·9	1835	12·0	6 1	6·8	1737	6·6	1112	3·1			129	4·8	1434	5·4	1035	3·7	2253	3·6
25	Sa	159	6·7	1341	6·5	1057	8·9	2316	—	650	12·2	1916	12·0	639	7·0	1814	6·8	0 1	3·1	1150	3·4	213	5·0	1510	5·4	1110	3·8	2330	3·7
26	Su	240	6·9	1423	6·8	1133	9·0	2354	—	728	12·6	1952	12·5	714	7·2	1848	7·0	043	3·0	1227	3·4	251	5·2	1544	5·4	1147	3·8		
27	M	318	7·0	15 3	7·0	031	9·0	1210	9·0	8 5	12·9	2029	12·8	751	7·2	1923	7·3	123	3·0	13 6	3·6	328	5·3	1619	5·4	0 6	3·7	1222	4·1
28	Tu	355	7·0	1542	7·2	1 9	9·0	1246	9·3	842	12·9	2142	12·7	829	7·2	1958	7·4	2 1	3·1	1345	3·6	4 2	5·3	1657	5·4	044	3·7	13 0	4·1
29	W	428	7·0	1619	7·1	057	9·3	1324	9·3	919	13·1	2220	12·8	9 7	7·0	2034	7·4	239	3·2	1425	3·8	439	5·3	1739	5·4	123	3·8	1339	4·1
30	Th	5 2	6·8	1657	7·0	147	9·0	14 2	9·2	957	13·2	2220	12·7	9 7	7·0	2112	7·4	316	3·3	15 8	3·8	519	5·3	1739	5·4	2 4	3·8	1421	4·1
31	F	5 2	6·8	1734	6·8	226	8·8	1442	9·0	1037	12·9	2259	12·3	948	7·0	2152	7·2	354	3·3	1548	3·8	6 4	5·1	1824	5·3	250	3·7	15 7	4·1

*All times shown are Greenwich Mean Time.   †Difference of height in metres from Ordnance Datum (Newlyn).   ‡Difference of height in metres from Ordnance Datum (Dublin).

FEBRUARY, 1986

High Water at the undermentioned Places (G.M.T.*)—

Datum of Predictions (†Difference of height in metres from Ordnance Datum (Newlyn); ‡from Ordnance Datum (Dublin)):
London Bridge 3·20 m. below · Liverpool 4·93 m. below · Avonmouth 6·50 m. below · Hull (Albert Dock) 3·90 m. below · Greenock 1·62 m. below · Leith 2·90 m. below · Dun Laoghaire 0·20 m. above

Day of Month	Day of Week	London Bridge Mn.	Ht.	Aft.	Ht.	Liverpool Mn.	Ht.	Aft.	Ht.	Avonmouth Mn.	Ht.	Aft.	Ht.	Hull (Albert Dock) Mn.	Ht.	Aft.	Ht.	Greenock Mn.	Ht.	Aft.	Ht.	Leith Mn.	Ht.	Aft.	Ht.	Dun Laoghaire Mn.	Ht.	Aft.	Ht.
1	Sa	539	6·7	1817	6·5	310	8·6	1527	8·8	1118	12·3	2342	11·6	1030	7·0	2238	6·8	432	3·3	1634	3·7	651	5·0	1911	5·1	339	3·6	16 0	3·9
2	Su	619	6·5	19 7	6·2	357	8·2	1620	8·4			12 4	11·6	1119	6·7	2333	6·5	513	3·1	1725	3·6	743	4·8	20 4	5·0	436	3·5	17 2	3·7
3	M	714	6·3	2012	6·1	458	7·8	1727	7·9	034	10·9	13 6	10·4			1222	6·4	6 3	3·0	1827	3·4	842	4·7	21 9	4·8	545	3·4	1818	3·6
4	Tu	833	6·1	2131	6·0	615	7·6	1853	7·7	152	10·3	1432	10·4	045	6·4	1341	6·4	714	3·0	1943	3·2	954	4·6	2231	4·8	659	3·4	1939	3·5
5	W	10 0	6·1	2249	6·1	738	7·8	2018	7·9	321	10·4	1557	10·6	212	6·1	15 5	6·4	851	3·0			1113	4·7	2352	4·9	810	3·5	2050	3·6
6	Th	1126	6·2			851	8·2	2128	8·3	440	10·9	1715	11·1	345	6·3	1619	6·7	10 6	3·1	2228	3·1			1224	4·9	911	3·7	2152	3·7
7	F	0 3	6·3	1236	6·5	953	8·7	2226	8·7	547	11·7	1819	11·8	458	6·7	1715	6·9	11 3	3·3	2331	3·1	1 0	5·1	1324	5·1	10 5	3·8	2244	3·8
8	Sa	1 3	6·5	1333	6·7	1045	9·1	2313	9·1	643	12·4	1912	12·4	553	7·0	18 1	7·0	1154	3·5			157	5·3	1415	5·4	1052	4·0	2330	3·8
9	Su	154	6·6	1422	7·0	1130	9·5	2357	9·5	730	12·9	1954	12·8	639	7·1	1842	7·1	026	3·5	1241	3·6	246	5·5	1458	5·6	1136	4·1		
10	M	237	6·8	15 4	7·2	1212	9·6			812	13·2	2033	13·0	720	7·2	1920	7·2	114	3·3	1326	3·7	328	5·5	1539	5·6	012	3·9	1219	4·2
11	Tu	317	7·0	1543	7·3	036	9·2	1250	9·6	850	13·3	2110	13·0	757	7·2	1955	7·3	159	3·3	14 8	3·8	4 7	5·3	1617	5·5	053	3·8	13 0	4·2
12	W	353	7·1	1621	7·2	112	9·1	1326	9·4	925	13·3	2143	12·8	832	7·1	2032	7·3	237	3·3	1446	3·8	446	5·3	1656	5·3	133	3·7	1342	4·1
13	Th	428	7·0	1657	7·0	145	8·8	1359	9·1	959	13·0	2213	12·5	9 4	7·1	21 5	7·1	312	3·3	1520	3·8	523	4·9	1735	5·0	211	3·7	1422	4·0
14	F	5 1	6·9	1730	6·7	216	8·5	1433	8·7	1030	12·5	2242	11·9	936	6·9	2141	6·9	343	3·3	1554	3·5	612	4·8	1813	4·8	252	3·5	15 3	4·0
15	Sa	533	6·6	18 5	6·4	250	8·2	1510	8·3	11 1	11·9	2312	11·3	10 9	6·7	2219	6·6	413	3·3	1631	3·4	641	4·5	1852	4·5	335	3·4	1547	3·6
16	Su	611	6·3	1845	6·1	326	7·7	1550	7·9	1134	11·1	2346	10·6	1044	6·4	23 1	6·2	447	3·2	1714	3·2	721	4·3	1932	4·3	424	3·3	1638	3·3
17	M	659	6·0	1934	5·8	412	7·3	1644	7·2			1217	10·3	1127	6·1	2358	5·8	527	3·0	18 7	2·9	8 7	4·1	2023	4·3	524	3·0	1742	3·1
18	Tu	758	5·6	2033	5·5	515	6·8	18 0	6·8	032	9·8	1317	9·5			1238	5·5	617	2·9	1912	2·8	9 7	4·2	2133	4·2	638	3·1	19 2	3·1
19	W	9 7	5·3	2138	5·4	646	6·7	1933	6·8	147	9·3	1447	9·2	127	5·6	1528	5·6	720	2·9	2041	2·8	1028	4·3	23 0	4·3	748	3·1	2014	3·1
20	Th	1020	5·3	2251	5·5	813	7·0	2047	7·3	327	9·3	1620	9·6	254	5·6	1630	5·8	844	3·0	22 5	2·9	1148	4·5			845	3·3	2111	3·3
21	F	1142	5·6			912	7·6	2139	7·8	449	10·0	1725	10·5	410	5·8	1715	6·1	957	3·0	23 2	2·9	014	4·6	1247	4·6	931	3·5	2156	3·5
22	Sa	0 4	5·8	1236	6·0	957	8·1	2220	8·4	543	11·1	1811	11·3	5 2	6·1	1751	6·6	1047	3·3	2347	3·0	110	4·9	1335	4·9	1011	3·7	2235	3·6
23	Su	056	6·3	1321	6·5	1037	8·7	2258	8·8	627	11·8	1852	12·0	543	6·5	1827	7·0	1129	3·3			154	5·2	1414	5·1	1049	3·9	2310	3·8
24	M	140	6·7	14 2	7·0	1113	9·1	2334	9·1	7 6	12·5	1931	12·6	619	6·9	19 2	7·3	027	3·2	12 9	3·4	232	5·4	1447	5·4	1124	4·1	2345	3·9
25	Tu	219	7·1	1443	7·3	1150	9·4			744	13·0	20 9	13·2	655	7·3	1937	7·6	1 5	3·0	1250	3·6	3 6	5·5	1520	5·6	1159	4·2		
26	W	257	7·3	1521	7·5	011	9·4	1227	9·6	822	13·5	2046	13·5	730	7·6	2012	7·8	143	3·1	1330	3·7	339	5·7	1555	5·7	021	3·9	1236	4·3
27	Th	332	7·3	1557	7·5	048	9·5	13 3	9·7	9 0	13·9	2122	13·6	8 6	7·8	2050	7·9	219	3·2	1411	3·8	416	5·7	1633	5·7	057	4·0	1315	4·3
28	F	4 6	7·3	1634	7·2	124	9·4	1341	9·6	938	13·8	22 0	13·3	843	7·8	2128	7·8	255	3·3	1450	3·9	455	5·5	1715	5·6	137	4·0	1357	4·3

*All times shown are Greenwich Mean Time. †Difference of height in metres from Ordnance Datum (Newlyn).
‡Difference of height in metres from Ordnance Datum (Dublin).

MARCH, 1986

High Water at the undermentioned Places (G.M.T.*)—

Day of Month	Day of Week	London Bridge †Datum 3·20 m. below				Liverpool †Datum 4·93 m. below				Avonmouth †Datum 6·50 m. below				Hull (Albert Dock) †Datum 3·90 m. below				Greenock †Datum 1·62 m. below				Leith †Datum 2·90 m. below				Dun Laoghaire ‡Datum 0·20 m. above			
		Mn.	Ht.	Aft.	Ht.	Mn.	Ht.	Aft.	Ht.	Mn.	Ht.	Aft.	Ht.	Mn.	Ht.	Aft.	Ht.	Mn.	Ht.	Aft.	Ht.	Mn.	Ht.	Aft.	Ht.	Mn.	Ht.	Aft.	Ht.
1	Sa	441	7·1	1712	6·9	204	9·2	1419	9·3	1016	13·3	2237	12·6	921	7·3	2131	7·5	329	3·4	1532	3·9	538	5·3	1759	5·5	220	3·9	1443	4·1
2	Su	518	6·9	1751	6·5	243	8·9	1503	8·9	1055	12·4	2316	11·6	1003	7·1	2217	7·1	405	3·4	1616	3·9	625	5·2	1847	5·2	308	3·7	1536	3·9
3	M	610	6·6	1838	6·2	331	8·4	1555	8·3	1139	11·3			1051	6·5	2313	6·6	445	3·4	1706	3·7	716	4·8	1944	4·8	404	3·6	1640	3·7
4	Tu	656	6·2	1941	5·9	431	7·8	1708	7·6	003	10·6	1238	10·3	1151	6·1			531	3·2	1804	3·4	816	4·6	2057	4·6	514	3·4	1740	3·4
5	W	815	6·0	2100	5·8	556	7·4	1846	7·3	124	9·8	1411	9·9	031	6·2	1316	5·8	632	3·0	1921	3·2	935	4·4	2230	4·4	637	3·3	1834	3·4
6	Th	946	5·9	2228	5·9	730	7·5	2019	7·6	300	9·8	1545	9·8	218	6·0	1454	6·0	830	2·9	2119	2·9	1108	4·5	2355	4·5	758	3·6	2051	3·5
7	F	1116	6·2	2349	6·2	946	8·0	2128	8·2	430	10·5	1709	10·8	353	6·2	1610	6·3	1006	3·0	2334	3·0			1222	4·8	904	3·6	2153	3·6
8	Sa	050	6·5	1321	7·0	1034	8·6	2219	8·7	539	11·5	1810	11·7	458	6·6	1744	6·9	1111	3·2			058	5·0	1318	5·1	959	3·8	2242	3·8
9	Su	138	6·8	1406	7·0	1115	9·1	2301	9·0	631	12·3	1856	12·4	546	6·9	1821	7·2	018	3·5	1229	3·5	149	5·5	1405	5·5	1044	4·0	2320	3·8
10	M	219	7·1	1446	7·3	1151	9·4	2337	9·2	713	12·9	1934	12·9	624	7·1	1856	7·5	059	3·6	1348	3·6	233	5·5	1444	5·6	1124	4·1	2357	4·2
11	Tu	256	7·1	1521	7·3	011	9·6	1225	9·5	751	13·1	2009	13·1	657	7·2	1930	7·8	136	3·6	1422	3·6	311	5·4	1517	5·5	029	3·8	1237	4·1
12	W	328	7·1	1553	7·2	042	9·2	1256	9·4	825	13·4	2043	13·3	730	7·2	2004	7·8	210	3·6	1452	3·4	344	5·3	1551	5·4	103	3·7	1313	4·1
13	Th	359	7·0	1623	7·0	112	9·1	1327	9·1	857	13·5	2112	13·3	801	7·1	2037	7·5	239	3·3	1523	3·3	416	5·3	1624	5·3	136	3·7	1349	3·9
14	F	427	6·9	1651	6·8	140	8·7	1358	8·8	928	13·3	2141	12·9	900	6·9	2110	7·1	305	3·3	1556	3·3	448	5·1	1658	5·1	210	3·6	1425	3·7
15	Sa	456	6·7	1722	6·6	240	8·4	1429	8·4	956	12·7	2206	12·3	928	6·6	2143	6·7	332	3·3	1635	3·1	522	4·9	1734	4·9	247	3·4	1504	3·5
16	Su	534	6·5	1757	6·3	332	7·9	1504	8·0	1023	12·0	2231	11·5	957	6·3	2220	6·2	404	3·1	1722	3·0	556	4·7	1818	4·7	329	3·3	1549	3·3
17	M	617	6·1	1838	5·9	413	7·5	1550	7·5	1051	11·0	2257	10·6	1031	5·9	2306	5·7	442	3·1	1818	3·1	630	4·5	1847	4·5	421	3·1	1647	3·1
18	Tu	707	5·7	1928	5·5	544	6·9	1704	7·0	1122	10·0	2330	9·6	1122	5·5	2349	5·3	528	2·9	1939	2·9	714	4·3	1939	4·3	530	3·1	1810	3·0
19	W	812	5·3	2036	5·3	731	6·8	1850	6·6			1207	8·9			1213		624	2·7	2144	2·7	812	4·0	2051	4·1	654	3·1	1937	3·0
20	Th	932	5·5	2233	5·5	840	7·5	2016	7·1	028	8·9	1326	8·6	032	5·4	1310	5·4	737	2·9	2241	3·0	1115	4·2	2223	4·0	803	3·5	2041	3·2
21	F	1104	5·5	2332	6·2	928	8·1	2110	8·4	211	8·7	1531	8·9	216	5·4	1443	5·5	914	3·0	2322	2·9	039	4·6	2341	4·2	857	3·7	2127	3·5
22	Sa	027	6·2	1253	6·7	1007	8·7	2152	9·3	404	9·5	1645	10·0	336	6·2	1552	6·9	1016	3·1	2358	3·0	124	5·3	1213	4·8	939	3·9	2207	3·7
23	Su	110	6·7	1335	7·1	1045	9·3	2230	9·6	505	10·7	1736	11·2	433	6·9	1641	7·4	1111	3·5			202	5·6	1311	5·3	1019	4·1	2243	3·9
24	M	149	7·1	1415	7·4	1123	9·6	2344	9·8	553	11·8	1821	12·0	516	7·1	1722	7·7	1145	3·1			237	5·7	1341	5·4	1055	4·3	2317	4·0
25	Tu	227	7·4	1454	7·5	022	9·7	1201	9·9	636	12·7	1913	13·0	553	7·5	1758	8·0	036	3·6	1228	3·1	348	5·6	1417	5·7	1131		2352	4·1
26	W	304	7·5	1531	7·5	102	9·7	1239	9·9	719	13·4	1944	13·6	628	7·7	1834	7·8	114	3·8	1310	3·5	429	5·7	1451	5·6			1250	4·3
27	Th	341	7·5	1610	7·3	141	9·4	1319	9·4	758	13·9	2022	13·9	740	7·8	2010	8·0	152	3·3	1352	3·8	514	5·6	1527	5·8	029	4·1	1336	4·3
28	F	420	7·3	1649	7·0	223	9·0	1447	8·8	837	14·1	2101	13·9	818	7·6	2029	7·8	228	3·4	1432	3·8	603	5·4	1652	5·9	110	4·1	1424	4·3
29	Sa	502	7·0	1732	7·0					917	13·9	2139	13·4	857	7·4	2114	7·5	303	3·5	1515	3·6			1740	5·5	154	4·0	1521	4·1
30	Su									957	13·1	2219	12·5	939	7·0	2224	6·9	340	3·8	1600	3·6			1833	5·2	245	3·8		
31	M									1038	12·1	2259	11·4																

*All times shown are Greenwich Mean Time.   †Difference of height in metres from Ordnance Datum (Newlyn).   ‡Difference of height in metres from Ordnance Datum (Dublin).

APRIL, 1986

High Water at the undermentioned Places (G.M.T.*)—

| Day of Month | Day of Week | LONDON BRIDGE †Datum of Predictions 3·20 m. below | | | | LIVERPOOL †Datum of Predictions 4·93 m. below | | | | AVONMOUTH †Datum of Predictions 6·50 m. below | | | | HULL (Albert Dock) †Datum of Predictions 3·90 m. below | | | | GREENOCK †Datum of Predictions 1·62 m. below | | | | LEITH †Datum of Predictions 2·90 m. below | | | | DUN LAOGHAIRE ‡Datum of Predictions 0·20 m. above | | | |
		Mn. h.m.	Ht. m.	Aft. h.m.	Ht. m.	Mn. h.m.	Ht. m.	Aft. h.m.	Ht. m.	Mn. h.m.	Ht. m.	Aft. h.m.	Ht. m.	Mn. h.m.	Ht. m.	Aft. h.m.	Ht. m.	Mn. h.m.	Ht. m.	Aft. h.m.	Ht. m.	Mn. h.m.	Ht. m.	Aft. h.m.	Ht. m.	Mn. h.m.	Ht. m.	Aft. h.m.	Ht. m.
1	Tu	551	6·6	1821	6·1	312	8·4	1545	8·0	1126	10·8	2353	10·3	1030	6·5	23 6	6·4	421	3·4	1651	3·3	656	4·8	1936	4·8	342	3·6	1631	3·5
2	W	653	6·2	1923	5·7	417	7·8	17 5	7·4	—		1231	9·8	1133	5·9	—		5 7	3·0	1749	3·0	8 2	4·5	2055	4·6	453	3·4	1757	3·3
3	Th	8 9	6·0	2039	5·7	546	7·4	1845	7·2	113	9·6	1357	9·4	034	5·8	13 0	5·8	6 6	2·9	1913	2·8	926	4·4	2227	4·6	620	3·4	1930	3·3
4	F	934	6·0	22 6	6·0	719	7·6	2012	7·6	243	9·7	1531	9·5	227	5·8	1442	5·9	813	2·8	2134	2·7	1056	4·5	2344	4·8	744	3·4	2045	3·5
5	Sa	11 1	6·3	2329	6·2	833	8·1	2112	8·2	412	10·5	1651	10·7	348	6·2	1550	6·4	955	2·9	2238	2·9	—		12 7	4·8	851	3·6	2141	3·6
6	Su	029	6·6	12 8	6·8	927	8·6	2159	8·6	518	11·5	1747	11·7	444	6·5	1641	6·8	1046	3·1	2319	3·0	043	5·1	13 0	5·1	945	3·8	2225	3·8
7	M	116	6·9	1344	7·2	1012	9·0	2237	8·9	6 7	12·3	1831	12·3	526	6·8	1720	7·1	1127	3·3	2355	3·1	130	5·2	1343	5·3	1028	4·0	23 0	3·8
8	Tu	157	7·0	1422	7·3	1049	9·2	2311	9·0	648	12·8	19 7	12·8	6 0	7·1	1756	7·2	12 7	3·4	—		2 9	5·3	1419	5·4	11 5	4·0	2333	3·8
9	W	230	7·0	1454	7·3	1123	9·3	2342	9·1	724	13·1	1941	13·1	631	7·1	1829	7·4	030	3·4	1245	3·5	243	5·4	1451	5·5	1140	4·0	—	
10	Th	3 1	7·0	1522	7·2	1156	9·3	—		757	13·3	2013	13·2	7 0	7·2	19 3	7·6	1 3	3·2	1321	3·5	314	5·3	1523	5·5	0 2	3·8	1212	4·0
11	F	328	6·9	1549	7·0	011	9·3	1227	9·2	829	13·3	2042	13·1	728	7·2	1938	7·5	134	3·3	1353	3·5	344	5·3	1552	5·4	030	3·8	1244	3·9
12	Sa	357	6·8	1614	6·9	1 7	9·1	1256	9·0	858	13·1	2110	12·8	758	7·1	2011	7·3	2 1	3·3	1422	3·4	414	5·2	1626	5·2	1 1	3·7	1317	3·9
13	Su	428	6·6	1645	6·8	137	8·9	1327	8·7	927	12·5	2135	12·3	826	6·9	2043	7·0	226	3·3	1452	3·3	441	5·0	1659	5·0	133	3·6	1353	3·8
14	M	5 5	6·5	1719	6·6	2 8	8·5	1358	8·5	953	11·7	2159	11·5	853	6·6	2115	6·5	254	3·2	1525	3·2	516	4·8	1735	4·8	210	3·5	1432	3·6
15	Tu	546	6·3	1758	6·4	246	8·1	1433	8·1	1019	10·9	2223	10·5	921	6·3	2150	6·0	326	3·1	16 4	3·0	553	4·6	1816	4·5	252	3·4	1517	3·4
16	W	632	6·0	1843	6·1	336	7·7	1518	7·7	1047	9·9	2254	9·8	952	5·6	2237	5·6	4 5	3·1	1648	3·0	637	4·3	1911	4·3	340	3·3	1613	3·2
17	Th	728	5·6	1942	5·7	457	7·2	1626	7·3	1129	9·2	2350	8·8	1040	5·6	2350	5·3	450	3·1	1740	2·7	735	4·2	2021	4·1	443	3·2	1727	3·1
18	F	846	5·4	2112	5·4	635	6·8	18 1	6·7	—		1238	8·8	135	5·4	1357	5·4	543	3·0	1848	2·6	851	4·1	2143	4·1	559	3·2	1852	3·1
19	Sa	1016	5·7	2245	5·6	751	7·0	1927	6·7	114	9·0	1422	9·0	251	5·8	15 5	5·5	648	2·9	21 0	2·7	1014	4·5	2258	4·7	713	3·3	20 0	3·1
20	Su	1125	6·2	2346	6·2	929	7·5	2027	7·1	3 4	9·6	1553	10·0	350	6·3	1559	5·9	819	2·9	22 3	2·8	1123	4·5	2356	4·8	813	3·5	2051	3·5
21	M	—		13 3	6·7	1012	8·2	2114	7·8	419	10·8	1654	11·3	438	6·8	1644	6·5	934	3·1	2243	3·0	—		1217	4·8	9 1	3·7	2132	3·7
22	Tu	035	6·7	1345	7·1	1054	9·0	2156	8·7	515	12·0	1746	12·4	519	7·2	1725	7·0	1025	3·5	2321	3·1	044	5·0	1311	5·2	944	4·0	22 9	3·9
23	W	117	7·1	1426	7·4	1134	9·3	2237	9·3	6 4	12·9	1832	13·2	558	7·5	18 5	7·4	1112	3·5	—		124	5·3	1341	5·5	1023	4·1	2246	4·1
24	Th	158	7·3	15 5	7·5	—		2316	9·9	650	13·7	1917	13·7	636	7·6	1846	7·7	0 0	3·6	1159	3·6	2 2	5·5	1419	5·7	11 3	4·2	2323	4·2
25	F	237	7·5	1548	7·5	039	9·7	2357	9·7	734	13·9	1959	13·9	716	7·7	1930	7·9	040	3·7	1245	3·7	241	5·7	15 2	5·9	1144	4·2	—	
26	Sa	319	7·5	1633	7·3	123	9·7	1218	9·7	818	13·9	2040	13·5	755	7·5	2016	7·6	121	3·7	1330	3·6	322	5·7	1545	5·9	0 2	4·2	1229	4·3
27	Su	4 4	7·4	1719	6·9	2 9	9·8	13 2	9·9	9 0	13·5	2122	12·7	839	7·3	2115	7·2	159	3·6	1415	3·6	4 6	5·6	1634	5·7	044	4·1	1317	4·1
28	M	455	6·9	1812	6·5	3 4	9·6	1348	9·8	945	12·7	22 7	12·3	925	6·9	22 2	6·7	237	3·5	15 0	3·6	455	5·5	1727	5·6	133	4·1	1411	4·0
29	Tu	550	6·7	—		4 4	9·7	1440	9·6	1031	11·7	2255	11·2	1017	6·5	23 8	6·2	318	3·6	1548	3·5	547	5·1	1825	5·1	225	3·9	1511	3·7
30	W	—		—		—		1542	8·4	1125	10·6	2353	10·3	—		—		4 1	3·2	1640	3·2	645	4·8	1930	4·8	328	3·7	1624	3·5

* All times shown are Greenwich Mean Time. †Difference of height in metres from Ordnance Datum (Newlyn). ‡Difference of height in metres from Ordnance Datum (Dublin).

MAY, 1986

High Water at the undermentioned Places (G.M.T.*)—

Day of Month	Day of Week	LONDON BRIDGE †Datum of Predictions 3.20 m. below — Mn. h.m	Ht. m	Aft. h.m	Ht. m	LIVERPOOL †Datum 4.93 m. below — Mn. h.m	Ht. m	Aft. h.m	Ht. m	AVONMOUTH †Datum 6.50 m. below — Mn. h.m	Ht. m	Aft. h.m	Ht. m	HULL (Albert Dock) †Datum 3.90 m. below — Mn. h.m	Ht. m	Aft. h.m	Ht. m	GREENOCK †Datum 1.62 m. below — Mn. h.m	Ht. m	Aft. h.m	Ht. m	LEITH †Datum 2.90 m. below — Mn. h.m	Ht. m	Aft. h.m	Ht. m	DUN LAOGHAIRE ‡Datum 0.20 m. above — Mn. h.m	Ht. m	Aft. h.m	Ht. m
1	Th	652	6.3	1912	5.9	410	7.9	17 1	7.5	—	—	1227	9.8	1120	6.2	1241	6.0	450	3.2	1740	2.9	752	4.6	2046	4.7	439	3.6	1749	3.3
2	F	759	6.1	2018	5.8	530	7.7	1828	7.4	1 2	9.9	1338	9.6	038	5.8	1412	6.1	551	2.9	1910	2.6	9 9	4.6	2317	4.8	6 2	3.5	1915	3.4
3	Sa	914	6.1	2136	5.8	652	7.8	1944	7.7	218	10.0	1458	9.9	213	5.9	1519	6.4	742	2.8	2113	2.7	1030	4.6	—	—	722	3.5	2023	3.5
4	Su	1034	6.1	2259	6.1	8 1	8.1	2042	8.4	338	10.6	1616	10.7	322	6.1	1610	6.7	1012	3.0	22 7	2.8	1137	4.8	1229	5.0	828	3.7	2116	3.6
5	M	1142	6.3	—	—	856	8.4	2128	8.6	444	11.5	1712	11.5	416	6.4	1652	6.9	1135	3.2	2245	2.9	012	5.0	1311	5.2	921	3.8	2158	3.7
6	Tu	0 0	6.7	1234	7.0	941	8.7	2240	8.8	534	12.1	1757	12.1	457	6.6	1729	7.1	1214	3.3	2320	3.0	058	5.1	1348	5.3	10 3	3.8	2233	3.8
7	W	048	6.5	1316	7.1	1019	8.9	2312	8.9	617	12.5	1835	12.5	530	6.8	18 4	7.2	026	3.2	2354	3.1	137	5.2	1422	5.3	1040	3.9	23 3	3.8
8	Th	128	6.9	1352	7.1	1054	8.9	2342	8.9	655	12.7	1912	12.7	6 1	6.9	1841	7.1	057	3.3	—	—	212	5.2	1454	5.2	1113	3.8	2333	3.8
9	F	2 2	6.9	1425	7.0	1126	8.9	—	—	728	12.8	1944	12.8	631	7.0	1916	7.0	125	3.3	1251	3.2	242	5.2	1527	5.1	1145	3.8	—	—
10	Sa	233	6.8	1451	6.9	1158	8.8	1231	8.7	8 1	12.8	2013	12.8	7 0	7.0	1949	7.0	152	3.4	1323	3.3	313	5.1	16 0	5.0	0 1	3.8	1218	3.7
11	Su	3 1	6.8	1518	6.8	012	8.7	13 3	8.5	832	12.5	2042	12.5	730	6.9	2022	6.9	221	3.4	1355	3.2	343	5.0	1635	4.8	032	3.7	1251	3.6
12	M	332	6.7	1546	6.7	042	8.5	1337	8.3	9 1	12.0	2110	11.9	827	6.8	2057	6.8	255	3.3	1427	3.2	414	4.7	1716	4.5	1 6	3.7	1329	3.5
13	Tu	4 6	6.6	1617	6.6	113	8.2	1415	7.9	929	11.5	2136	11.2	934	6.3	2136	6.3	334	3.1	15 1	3.1	450	4.5	1759	4.4	144	3.6	1355	3.2
14	W	444	6.5	1652	6.5	148	8.1	15 1	7.5	959	10.7	22 6	10.6	1023	6.1	2224	6.0	420	3.1	1541	3.0	529	4.4	1852	4.3	225	3.5	1454	3.2
15	Th	523	6.4	1732	6.3	227	7.9	16 2	7.2	1033	10.1	2237	9.9	1134	5.8	2327	5.8	5 1	3.0	1625	3.0	615	4.3	1953	4.3	314	3.4	1549	3.1
16	F	618	6.2	1815	6.0	318	7.5	1716	7.1	1116	9.7	2337	9.7	050	5.6	13 4	5.7	610	3.0	1714	2.9	711	4.4	21 1	4.3	4 9	3.4	1653	3.1
17	Sa	710	5.8	1910	5.7	426	7.3	1832	7.9	049	9.9	1218	10.4	2 2	5.9	1415	6.3	710	3.2	1812	2.8	814	4.4	22 6	4.5	511	3.4	18 6	3.3
18	Su	813	5.7	2025	5.6	543	7.7	1937	8.5	215	10.3	1337	11.4	3 3	6.3	1541	6.9	826	3.2	1945	2.7	922	4.6	23 6	4.7	621	3.6	1913	3.5
19	M	924	5.6	2152	5.7	655	8.2	2032	8.9	332	11.2	15 4	12.3	356	6.7	1654	7.4	945	3.4	21 8	2.8	1028	4.8	2359	5.2	726	3.7	2005	3.7
20	Tu	1035	5.8	2311	6.0	757	8.6	2119	9.2	435	12.1	1612	13.0	445	7.1	1742	7.5	1038	3.4	2157	2.8	1126	5.2	—	—	821	3.9	2055	3.9
21	W	1144	6.2	2356	6.6	849	9.0	22 6	9.5	532	13.0	1711	13.4	530	7.3	1831	7.6	1129	3.5	2241	3.0	046	5.2	1218	5.4	9 9	3.9	2137	4.0
22	Th	0 9	6.9	1232	7.0	938	9.2	2257	9.6	624	13.4	1852	13.5	614	7.5	1921	7.6	1218	3.4	2324	3.1	129	5.4	13 5	5.6	953	4.1	2216	4.1
23	F	045	7.1	1319	7.1	1026	9.5	2337	9.7	713	13.6	1940	13.9	657	7.6	2012	7.5	108	3.6	1220	3.3	213	5.6	1353	5.7	1037	4.1	2256	4.1
24	Sa	131	7.2	1402	7.2	1113	9.7	—	—	8 2	13.5	2026	13.6	741	7.5	2104	7.0	052	3.6	1311	3.5	259	5.7	1440	5.8	1123	4.1	2338	4.1
25	Su	218	7.3	1447	7.2	024	9.6	1250	9.6	850	13.4	2112	13.3	827	7.2	23 1	6.6	135	3.6	1450	3.4	348	5.6	1531	5.7	026	4.2	1213	4.1
26	M	3 5	7.2	1532	7.1	2 2	9.4	1341	9.4	938	13.4	2251	12.9	915	7.0	2355	6.2	218	3.5	1540	3.4	439	5.4	1624	5.4	117	4.1	13 6	4.1
27	Tu	357	7.3	1621	7.0	112	9.1	1436	9.0	1027	12.9	2343	12.3	10 6	6.7	12 8	7.0	348	3.4	1633	3.2	535	5.4	1720	5.4	214	4.0	14 3	3.8
28	W	451	7.3	1711	7.0	2 2	8.7	1535	8.5	1118	12.4	—	—	11 2	6.5	1252	6.6	438	3.3	1730	3.0	633	5.2	1817	5.2	314	3.9	15 4	3.7
29	Th	546	6.9	1811	6.9	257	8.5	1640	8.1	—	—	1211	11.7	017	6.5	2340	6.3	536	3.2	1842	2.9	734	5.0	1918	4.9	421	3.7	1611	3.5
30	F	641	6.6	1855	6.6	357	8.3	1750	7.7	041	11.2	13 9	11.1	108	6.4	—	—	636	3.1	1942	2.8	840	4.7	2023	4.7	535	3.7	1727	3.4
31	Sa	738	6.3	1951	6.3	5 2	8.0	1853	7.5	—	—	—	—	149	6.3	1229	6.3	740	3.1	1842	2.7	940	4.7	2131	4.7	635	3.6	1844	3.4

* All times shown are Greenwich Mean Time.   †Difference of height in metres from Ordnance Datum (Newlyn).   ‡Difference of height in metres from Ordnance Datum (Dublin).

JUNE, 1986

High Water at the undermentioned Places (G.M.T.*)—

Datum of Predictions: London Bridge 3·20 m. below; Liverpool 4·93 m. below; Avonmouth 6·50 m. below; Hull (Albert Dock) 3·90 m. below; Greenock 1·62 m. below; Leith 2·90 m. below; Dun Laoghaire 0·20 m. above.

Day of Month	Day of Week	London Bridge Mn. h.m.	Ht. m.	Aft. h.m.	Ht. m.	Liverpool Mn. h.m.	Ht. m.	Aft. h.m.	Ht. m.	Avonmouth Mn. h.m.	Ht. m.	Aft. h.m.	Ht. m.	Hull Mn. h.m.	Ht. m.	Aft. h.m.	Ht. m.	Greenock Mn. h.m.	Ht. m.	Aft. h.m.	Ht. m.	Leith Mn. h.m.	Ht. m.	Aft. h.m.	Ht. m.	Dun Laoghaire Mn. h.m.	Ht. m.	Aft. h.m.	Ht. m.
1	Su	843	6·2	2058	5·9	611	7·9	19 0	7·6	142	10·5	1413	10·3	135	5·9	1324	6·3	658	2·9	2015	2·6	948	4·7	2236	4·7	649	3·6	1948	3·4
2	M	956	6·2	2216	6·0	717	7·9	1959	7·8	250	10·7	1522	10·6	242	6·0	1436	6·4	827	2·8	2117	2·7	1053	4·8	2333	4·8	754	3·6	2042	3·5
3	Tu	11 5	6·4	2323	6·3	815	8·1	2049	8·0	356	11·2	1626	11·6	335	6·2	1532	6·6	928	3·0	2203	2·9	1149	4·9			848	3·7	2126	3·6
4	W	1158	6·6			9 4	8·3	2131	8·3	454	11·6	1718	12·0	420	6·3	1620	6·6	1016	3·0	2241	3·1	020	4·9	1236	5·0	934	3·7	22 3	3·7
5	Th	015	6·5	1243	6·7	946	8·4	22 9	8·5	542	12·0	18 1	12·2	458	6·5	1704	6·7	11 0	3·1	2317	3·1	1 3	5·0	1317	5·1	1014	3·7	2236	3·7
6	F	057	6·6	1321	6·7	1026	8·5	2244	8·6	624	12·2	1841	12·3	533	6·7	1744	6·8	1142	3·1	2352	3·2	141	5·0	1355	5·1	1050	3·7	23 6	3·7
7	Sa	134	6·6	1354	6·6	11 2	8·6	2318	8·7	7 3	12·3	1917	12·3	6 7	6·8	1822	6·8	1222	3·1			215	5·0	1433	5·1	1121	3·6	2337	3·7
8	Su	2 8	6·6	1425	6·7	1137	8·6			738	12·2	1951	12·2	638	6·8	1859	6·7	055	3·3	13 0	3·0	249	5·0	1510	5·1	1157	3·5		
9	M	242	6·6	1456	6·6	025	8·7	1211	8·7	812	12·0	2022	12·0	7 9	6·8	1934	6·6	126	3·3	1336	2·9	322	5·0	1546	5·0	011	3·7	1232	3·5
10	Tu	317	6·6	1528	6·5	1 0	8·6	1246	8·6	844	11·7	2053	11·7	740	6·7	20 9	6·6	158	3·3	1412	2·8	357	5·0	1624	5·0	046	3·7	1310	3·6
11	W	353	6·6	16 3	6·6	131	8·6	1324	8·4	917	11·3	2125	11·4	813	6·6	2047	6·5	233	3·3	1448	2·8	433	4·9	17 3	4·9	125	3·7	1352	3·7
12	Th	431	6·5	1640	6·6	216	8·2	14 4	8·2	950	11·0	2241	11·0	849	6·5	2129	6·3	313	3·3	1527	2·8	513	4·8	1746	4·8	2 6	3·7	1436	3·7
13	F	511	6·5	1716	6·5	3 3	8·2	1447	8·0	1027	10·8	2329	10·9	929	6·3	2214	6·2	356	3·3	16 9	2·8	557	4·7	1834	4·7	250	3·6	1524	3·6
14	Sa	553	6·3	1757	6·4	358	7·9	1538	7·9	11 9	10·6			1014	6·1	23 5	6·0	445	3·3	1653	2·8	647	4·7	1924	4·6	339	3·6	1618	3·6
15	Su	639	6·1	1843	6·3	458	7·7	1637	7·7	025	10·8	13 2	10·5	11 9	6·1			538	3·2	1742	2·8	740	4·6	2020	4·6	433	3·6	1720	3·5
16	M	735	6·1	1944	6·1	6 4	8·0	1743	7·7	134	10·9	1534	11·3	0 5	6·0	1215	6·0	643	3·2	1843	2·8	837	4·6	2119	4·6	535	3·6	1826	3·7
17	Tu	844	6·1	21 1	6·1	710	8·6	1849	8·0	251	10·9	1638	11·8	113	6·1	1324	6·2	757	3·2	20 3	2·9	937	4·7	2219	4·7	640	3·6	1927	3·6
18	W	957	6·2	2216	6·1	812	8·6	1951	8·3	4 2	11·8	1737	12·3	216	6·3	1429	6·4	9 6	3·3	2110	3·1	1039	4·8	2317	4·9	743	3·8	2020	3·6
19	Th	11 4	6·5	2320	6·2	911	8·6	2049	8·6	5 4	12·3	1834	12·7	317	6·5	1531	6·6	10 7	3·3	2234	3·2	1140	4·9			840	3·9	21 8	3·8
20	F			12 3	6·5	10 6	9·2	2142	8·9	6 3	12·8	1927	12·8	414	6·8	1631	6·8	11 5	3·5	2343	3·3	012	5·1	1239	5·1	931	3·9	2153	3·9
21	Sa	019	6·6	1256	6·6	1059	9·3	2234	9·2	7 0	12·8	2016	13·1	5 8	7·0	1730	7·0	12 2	3·6			1 5	5·2	1337	5·3	1022	4·0	2237	4·0
22	Su	116	6·7	1347	6·7	1153	9·4	2325	9·3	754	12·8	21 4	12·9	558	7·2	1827	7·2	032	3·6	1258	3·3	156	5·3	1431	5·4	1112	4·0	2323	4·1
23	M	2 0	6·8	1434	6·7			1243	9·5	843	12·5	2150	12·6	646	7·2	1919	7·3	121	3·6	1352	3·2	248	5·3	1524	5·6	013	4·2	12 4	4·1
24	Tu	3 0	6·9	1524	6·9	014	9·5	1334	9·5	931	12·2	2237	12·1	731	7·4	20 9	7·3	2 7	3·6	1444	3·1	337	5·5	1617	5·6	1 6	4·2	1257	4·2
25	W	352	7·1	1610	7·3	1 5	9·5	1423	9·3	1016	12·0	2322	11·6	816	7·3	2058	7·1	253	3·6	1534	3·0	429	5·5	1710	5·5	2 1	4·1	1353	4·1
26	Th	441	7·3	1658	7·3	152	9·3	1512	9·0	11 1	11·5			9 1	7·1	2148	7·0	338	3·6	1622	3·0	521	5·5	18 2	5·3	257	4·0	1450	4·0
27	F	530	7·1	1743	7·1	242	9·3	16 4	8·7			1231	10·7	948	7·1	2238	6·8	424	3·5	1709	2·9	614	5·2	1856	4·8	357	3·9	1549	3·9
28	Sa	619	7·0	1828	6·8	331	8·7	1659	8·3	0 8	11·1	1323	10·5	1035	6·8	2333	6·4	514	3·3	1759	2·8	7 3	5·0	1950	4·8	5 0	3·7	1653	3·7
29	Su	7 9	6·5	1917	6·5	423	8·3	18 1	7·4	059	11·2			1127	6·6			614	3·0	1859	3·0	8 3	4·8	2047	4·7	6 7	3·6	18 0	3·4
30	M	8 2	6·2	2013	6·2	520	7·9							035	5·9	1229	6·4							2146	4·6			19 5	3·3

*All times shown are Greenwich Mean Time. †Difference of height in metres from Ordnance Datum (Newlyn). ‡Difference of height in metres from Ordnance Datum (Dublin).

JULY, 1986

High Water at the undermentioned Places (G.M.T.*)—

Day of Month	Day of Week	LONDON BRIDGE †Datum of Predictions 3·20 m. below Mn.	Ht.	Aft.	Ht.	LIVERPOOL †Datum of Predictions 4·93 m. below Mn.	Ht.	Aft.	Ht.	AVONMOUTH †Datum of Predictions 6·50 m. below Mn.	Ht.	Aft.	Ht.	HULL (Albert Dock) †Datum of Predictions 3·90 m. below Mn.	Ht.	Aft.	Ht.	GREENOCK †Datum of Predictions 1·62 m. below Mn.	Ht.	Aft.	Ht.	LEITH †Datum of Predictions 2·90 m. below Mn.	Ht.	Aft.	Ht.	DUN LAOGHAIRE ‡Datum of Predictions 0·20 m. above Mn.	Ht.	Aft.	Ht.
1	Tu	9 4	6·2	2119	6·0	622	7·7	19 6	7·4	155	10·8	1422	10·5	140	5·8	1340	6·2	725	2·8	20 7	2·7	10 0	4·6	2244	4·6	713	3·5	20 2	3·4
2	W	1012	6·0	2233	5·9	727	7·6	20 6	7·6	258	10·8	1528	10·6	242	5·9	1447	6·2	836	2·8	2109	2·8	11 1	4·6	2340	4·6	813	3·5	2050	3·5
3	Th	1116	6·1	2337	6·0	826	7·7	2058	7·8	4 4	10·9	1633	11·0	336	6·0	1549	6·2	936	2·8	22 0	2·8	1158	4·7			9 4	3·5	2132	3·5
4	F			12 7	6·1	918	7·9	2143	8·1	5 5	11·2	1729	11·4	426	6·2	1642	6·3	1029	2·9	2243	2·9	030	4·7	1249	4·8	949	3·5	22 9	3·6
5	Sa	027	6·2	1250	6·3	10 3	8·1	2224	8·4	557	11·5	1817	11·7	5 9	6·4	1729	6·4	1117	2·9	2323	3·0	114	4·7	1336	4·9	1028	3·5	2244	3·7
6	Su	110	6·3	1327	6·4	1044	8·3	23 2	8·6	642	11·8	1857	11·9	547	6·5	1810	6·5	12 2	2·9	2359	3·1	156	4·8	1420	5·0	11 3	3·5	2317	3·8
7	M	148	6·4	14 5	6·6	1122	8·4	2337	8·7	723	11·8	1934	11·9	621	6·6	1848	6·5	1244	2·9			233	4·9	1459	5·1	1138	3·5	2352	3·8
8	Tu	227	6·5	1442	6·7	1158	8·5			758	11·7	20 8	11·9	655	6·7	1923	6·6	033	3·2	1324	2·8	3 9	4·9	1536	5·1			1215	3·5
9	W	3 5	6·6	1519	6·7	012	8·8	1235	8·6	832	11·7	2042	12·0	727	6·7	1958	6·6	1 8	3·3	14 2	2·7	344	5·1	1611	5·1	029	3·8	1251	3·5
10	Th	343	6·7	1556	6·7	049	8·8	1312	8·5	9 5	11·8	2117	12·1	8 2	6·8	2034	6·6	142	3·3	1438	2·7	419	5·1	1647	5·0	1 6	3·9	1332	3·5
11	F	420	6·8	1630	6·7	126	8·8	1348	8·3	941	11·8	2153	12·0	839	6·9	2114	6·8	218	3·4	1515	2·8	457	5·1	1727	5·0	144	3·9	1413	3·5
12	Sa	457	6·7	17 4	6·6	2 4	8·7	1429	8·3	1017	11·8	2231	11·5	917	6·8	2155	6·6	257	3·4	1551	2·9	538	5·1	18 9	4·9	225	3·9	1456	3·5
13	Su	534	6·6	1737	6·4	243	8·6	1511	8·0	1055	11·6	2312	11·5	957	6·7	2238	6·5	338	3·4	1630	2·9	622	5·0	1854	4·7	310	3·9	1545	3·5
14	M	615	6·5	1817	6·2	328	8·4	16 0	8·0	1137	11·3	2358	10·7	1041	6·5	2326	6·3	422	3·4	1712	3·0	7 9	5·0	1944	4·7	359	3·8	1640	3·5
15	Tu	7 3	6·3	19 6	6·1	419	8·1	1658	7·9			1228	10·7	1134	6·4			512	3·3	18 3	2·9	759	4·9	2038	4·7	456	3·7	1742	3·5
16	W	8 4	6·1	2015	6·1	520	8·1	18 7	7·9	056	11·1	1337	10·8	025	6·4	1241	6·3	610	3·2	19 3	2·9	857	4·9	2139	4·7	6 3	3·6	1848	3·5
17	Th	917	6·1	2136	6·2	632	8·0	1919	8·0	213	11·0	15 0	10·8	134	6·2	1354	6·3	718	3·2	2024	2·9	10 4	4·8	2245	4·7	713	3·6	1950	3·6
18	F	1030	6·2	2254	6·3	748	8·2	2026	8·3	332	11·0	1614	11·2	244	6·3	1511	6·5	836	3·3	2137	3·0	1119	4·8	2353	4·8	820	3·7	2047	3·7
19	Sa	1140	6·3			857	8·5	2128	8·7	444	11·4	1722	11·8	355	6·5	1627	6·8	948	3·4	2236	3·1	1230	5·1			921	3·7	2138	3·9
20	Su	0 7	6·4	1243	6·6	955	8·8	2226	9·1	553	11·9	1824	12·3	457	6·8	1732	7·2	1054	3·4	2331	3·3	055	5·1	1334	5·1	11 7	3·9	2228	4·0
21	M	110	6·6	1338	6·8	1055	9·1	2318	9·4	655	12·6	1919	13·1	549	7·1	1827	7·5	1156	3·4			151	5·3	1430	5·3	1159	3·9	2316	4·1
22	Tu	2 5	6·8	1427	7·1	1147	9·3			747	12·8	20 6	13·2	635	7·5	1914	7·5	023	3·4	1254	3·1	241	5·5	1521	5·6	054	4·3	1247	3·9
23	W	254	7·1	1512	7·3	050	9·6	1234	9·3	833	12·8	2051	13·0	719	7·6	1959	7·5	2 0	3·5	1348	3·1	328	5·6	1610	5·6	144	4·2	1357	3·8
24	Th	341	7·3	1556	7·3	134	9·5	1319	9·2	915	12·8	2134	13·0	759	7·6	2042	7·3	244	3·6	1437	3·1	414	5·6	1654	5·5	235	4·1	1425	3·8
25	F	426	7·3	1637	7·2	215	9·3	1359	8·9	956	12·6	2213	12·7	840	7·6	2124	6·9	325	3·6	1520	3·1	5 0	5·6	1739	5·3	324	4·0	1515	3·6
26	Sa	5 8	7·2	1716	7·1	256	8·9	1440	8·6	1034	12·3	2251	12·3	921	7·5	22 3	6·6	4 5	3·6	1559	3·0	547	5·4	1825	5·1	417	4·0	16 9	3·5
27	Su	550	6·9	1756	6·8	338	8·4	1521	8·2	11 9	11·7	2329	11·7	10 2	6·8	2244	6·3	446	3·3	1636	3·0	635	5·3	1913	4·8	457	3·8	17 7	3·4
28	M	631	6·5	1836	6·4	426	7·9	16 4	7·7	1146	11·2			1047	6·8	2327	6·0	533	3·1	1714	2·9	721	4·9	20 0	4·6	517	3·6	1811	3·3
29	Tu	716	6·2	1926	6·2	523	7·4	1655	7·3	010	11·2	1227	10·7	1137	6·4			629	2·8	1758	2·8	810	4·7	2051	4·4	626	3·4	1916	3·3
30	W	8 8	5·9	2027	5·9	635	7·1	18 1	7·1	057	10·6	1320	10·2	024	5·8	1243	6·0	739	2·7	1851	2·8	9 4	4·5	2150	4·4	736	3·3	2013	3·3
31	Th	9 8	5·7	2135	5·7			1920	7·1	2 1	10·2	1430	10·0	131	5·7	1359	5·9			1959	2·7	1010	4·4	2257	4·4				

*All times shown are Greenwich Mean Time.   †Difference of height in metres from Ordnance Datum (Newlyn).
‡Difference of height in metres from Ordnance Datum (Dublin).

AUGUST, 1986

High Water at the undermentioned Places (G.M.T.*)—

Day of Month	Day of Week	LONDON BRIDGE †Datum of Predictions 3·20 m. below Mn.	Ht.	Aft.	Ht.	LIVERPOOL †Datum of Predictions 4·93 m. below Mn.	Ht.	Aft.	Ht.	AVONMOUTH †Datum of Predictions 6·50 m. below Mn.	Ht.	Aft.	Ht.	HULL (Albert Dock) †Datum of Predictions 3·90 m. below Mn.	Ht.	Aft.	Ht.	GREENOCK †Datum of Predictions 1·62 m. below Mn.	Ht.	Aft.	Ht.	LEITH †Datum of Predictions 2·90 m. below Mn.	Ht.	Aft.	Ht.	DUN LAOGHAIRE †Datum of Predictions 0·20 m. above Mn.	Ht.	Aft.	Ht.
1	F	1014	5·7	2252	5·6	752	7·2	2029	7·4	315	10·0	1550	10·1	244	5·7	1518	5·8	857	2·7	2114	2·8	1122	4·4	1227	4·5	837	3·3	21 2	3·5
2	Sa	1126	5·8			857	7·5	2124	7·6	435	10·3	17 4	10·6	352	5·9	1626	5·9	10 5	2·8	2213	2·9	0 5	4·5	1322	4·6	926	3·4	2145	3·6
3	Su	0 1	5·8	1222	6·0	948	7·9	2207	7·8	537	10·8	1757	11·2	445	6·2	1716	6·2	11 2	2·8	2259	3·0	140	4·6	14 6	4·8	10 8	3·4	2222	3·7
4	M	050	6·0	13 7	6·2	1030	8·2	2247	8·3	624	11·3	1839	11·6	529	6·5	1757	6·4	1150	2·8	2339	3·1	219	4·8	1445	5·0	1046	3·5	2258	3·8
5	Tu	131	6·3	1347	6·5	11 8	8·5	2323	8·6	7 4	11·6	1916	11·9	6 4	6·6	1834	6·6	1233	3·2			253	5·0	1520	5·2	1120	3·6	2331	3·9
6	W	211	6·6	1426	6·8	1143	8·7	2357	8·9	740	11·9	1951	12·2	638	6·9	1940	6·9	016	3·2	1312	2·7	326	5·3	1553	5·3	1154	3·7		
7	Th	249	6·9	15 4	6·9			1217	9·1	813	12·4	2025	12·5	710	7·1	19 6	7·2	053	3·3	1348	2·7	359	5·4	1626	5·3	0 6	4·1	1229	3·8
8	F	325	7·0	1538	7·0	032	9·2	1252	9·0	849	12·6	21 0	12·8	744	7·3	2015	7·3	128	3·4	1423	2·8	434	5·4	17 4	5·1	042	4·1	13 4	3·8
9	Sa	4 2	7·1	1612	6·9	1 6	9·1	1327	8·9	922	12·6	2135	12·9	818	7·3	2050	7·3	2 4	3·5	1456	2·9	513	5·3	1744	5·1	118	4·1	1343	3·8
10	Su	435	7·0	1642	6·9	141	9·0	14 4	8·8	957	12·6	2212	12·8	854	7·2	2128	7·2	242	3·6	1529	3·0	554	5·3	1826	5·0	157	4·1	1424	3·7
11	M	511	6·8	1715	6·7	218	8·8	1443	8·6	1033	11·6	2249	12·3	932	7·1	2251	6·9	321	3·6	16 4	3·1	639	5·1	1912	4·7	240	4·1	1510	3·6
12	Tu	549	6·5	1750	6·5	257	8·5	1527	8·3	1111	11·3	2330	11·6	1013	6·9	2346	6·8	4 4	3·5	1728	3·1	729	4·8	20 6	4·6	329	4·0	16 1	3·5
13	W	631	6·2	1835	6·3	345	8·0	1620	7·7	1153	10·8			11 4	6·6			451	3·3	1823	2·9	830	4·7	2229	4·6	425	3·8	1816	3·7
14	Th	726	6·0	1941	6·1	445	7·7	1732	7·7	019	10·2	1256	10·3	059	6·0	1334	6·3	546	3·1	1944	2·9	948	4·7	2347	4·7	535	3·6	1929	3·9
15	F	840	5·9	2112	6·0	6 8	7·7	1859	8·0	312	10·5	1434	10·5	225	6·3	1514	6·1	652	2·9	2124	3·1			1233	5·0	656	3·5	2035	4·1
16	Sa	10 3	5·9	2241	6·1	740	8·1	2018	8·6	438	10·7	1559	11·4	346	6·7	1633	6·5	819	2·9	2234	3·0	052	5·0	1334	5·2	814	3·6	2132	4·2
17	Su	1125	6·1			857	8·6	2125	9·0	551	11·5	1715	12·4	448	7·0	1732	7·1	949	2·9	2328	3·2	146	5·5	1426	5·5	922	3·7	2222	4·3
18	M	0 3	6·4	1234	6·4	959	9·3	2220	9·5	649	12·3	1818	12·9	537	7·3	1819	7·3	1059	3·0			233	5·7	1511	5·6	1016	3·8	23 9	4·0
19	Tu	1 6	6·7	1328	6·8	1051	9·3	23 8	9·4	735	13·0	1952	13·5	619	7·5	19 2	7·5	019	3·5	1250	3·5	314	5·6	1551	5·6	11 6	3·9	2354	3·9
20	W	158	7·0	1415	6·8	1136	9·8	2350	9·4	815	13·1	2032	13·7	659	7·7	1940	7·7	1 5	3·6	1337	3·6	354	5·2	1631	5·3	1150	4·0		
21	Th	243	7·2	1457	7·0			1253	9·7	853	13·1	21 8	13·2	737	7·7	2015	7·7	149	3·6	1418	3·6	434	4·9	1711	5·3	037	4·4	1232	3·9
22	F	325	7·3	1535	7·1	031	9·7	1328	8·9	928	12·2	2143	13·1	813	7·9	2050	7·5	229	3·5	1454	3·5	515	4·6	1750	4·8	120	4·3	1311	3·7
23	Sa	4 3	7·3	1612	7·0	1 9	9·5	14 2	8·7	10 0	12·2	2217	12·7	851	7·9	2124	7·1	3 5	3·1	1527	3·3	558	4·2	1831	4·4	2 3	4·2	1353	3·6
24	Su	440	7·1	1645	7·0	144	8·9	1436	8·3	1031	11·5	2248	12·0	929	7·7	2157	6·8	338	3·0	1557	3·2	638	4·2	1913	4·2	247	4·0	1436	3·4
25	M	513	6·8	1719	6·8	218	8·4	1512	7·9	11 1	10·7	2320	11·2	10 7	7·3	2234	6·2	414	2·9	1631	3·1	721	4·2	1913	4·4	333	3·7	1520	3·3
26	Tu	549	6·5	1756	6·5	254	7·8	1556	7·4	1132	10·3			1049	6·8	2316	5·7	455	2·9	1710	3·0	811		1956		426	3·5	16 9	3·3
27	W	625	6·2	1839	6·1	335	7·2	1658	6·9	0 0	9·0	1214	9·9	1049	6·2	1316	5·4	545	2·9	1757	2·9	921		2053		531	3·3	1821	3·4
28	Th	712	5·9	1937	5·7	427	6·8	1831	6·7	055	9·4	1323	9·2	022	5·7	1449	5·4	646	2·7	1856	2·8	1048		2330		652	3·3	1932	3·6
29	F	8 9	5·5	2046	5·4	543	6·8	21 3	7·1	226	9·0	1512	9·1	149	5·4	16 6	5·4	815	2·6	2014	2·7			12 4		8 7	3·2	2030	
30	Sa	917	5·4	22 6	5·4	723	7·2			413	9·4	1642	9·9	315	5·6		5·7	951	2·6	2139	2·8					9 2	3·3	2118	
31	Su	1040	5·4	2336	5·4	839	7·7																						

*All times shown are Greenwich Mean Time. †Difference of height in metres from Ordnance Datum (Newlyn). ‡Difference of height in metres from Ordnance Datum (Dublin).

SEPTEMBER, 1986

High Water at the undermentioned Places (G.M.T.*)—

Day of Week	Day of Month	London Bridge †Datum of Predictions 3·20 m. below Mn. (h.m.)	Ht. (m.)	Aft. (h.m.)	Ht. (m.)	Liverpool †Datum 4·93 m. below Mn. (h.m.)	Ht. (m.)	Aft. (h.m.)	Ht. (m.)	Avonmouth †Datum 6·50 m. below Mn. (h.m.)	Ht. (m.)	Aft. (h.m.)	Ht. (m.)	Hull (Albert Dock) †Datum 3·90 m. below Mn. (h.m.)	Ht. (m.)	Aft. (h.m.)	Ht. (m.)	Greenock †Datum 1·62 m. below Mn. (h.m.)	Ht. (m.)	Aft. (h.m.)	Ht. (m.)	Leith †Datum 2·90 m. below Mn. (h.m.)	Ht. (m.)	Aft. (h.m.)	Ht. (m.)	Dun Laoghaire ‡Datum 0·20 m. above Mn. (h.m.)	Ht. (m.)	Aft. (h.m.)	Ht. (m.)
M	1	1156	5·7	—	—	929	8·2	2148	8·7	515	10·2	1733	10·8	419	6·1	1657	6·1	1051	2·7	2235	3·0	031	4·5	13 1	4·6	945	3·5	2156	3·8
Tu	2	027	6·0	1243	6·2	1010	8·3	2224	8·7	558	11·1	1812	11·6	5 4	6·5	1736	6·5	1135	2·8	2316	3·1	119	4·7	1344	4·9	1022	3·7	2232	4·0
W	3	1 7	6·4	1324	6·6	1045	8·7	2259	9·1	638	12·3	1849	12·2	540	6·9	1810	7·1	1212	2·8	2355	3·2	156	5·0	1422	5·1	1055	3·8	23 5	4·1
Th	4	147	6·8	14 1	6·9	1119	9·0	2333	9·4	713	12·7	1926	12·7	612	7·2	1842	7·4	1247	2·8	—	—	230	5·3	1455	5·4	1127	3·9	2338	4·2
F	5	223	7·1	1437	7·2	1153	9·2	—	—	749	13·0	20 1	13·2	645	7·4	1913	7·4	032	3·3	1322	2·9	3 0	5·5	1526	5·5	—	—	12 1	4·0
Sa	6	3 0	7·3	1511	7·3	0 7	9·5	1227	9·4	825	13·1	2037	13·5	717	7·6	1947	7·5	111	3·4	1356	2·9	332	5·6	16 0	5·5	013	4·3	1235	4·1
Su	7	335	7·3	1543	7·3	041	9·6	13 2	9·6	934	13·1	2112	13·5	752	7·6	2022	7·6	148	3·6	1430	3·1	4 7	5·6	1636	5·5	050	4·3	1311	4·1
M	8	410	7·2	1617	7·1	116	9·5	1337	9·5	10 9	12·5	2149	13·1	827	7·3	2057	7·3	225	3·6	1459	3·2	447	5·6	1717	5·3	130	4·3	1353	4·1
Tu	9	445	6·9	1651	6·9	152	9·3	1415	9·3	1127	10·6	2227	11·3	9 5	7·0	2136	6·9	3 4	3·7	1539	3·3	530	5·5	1759	5·1	213	4·2	1439	3·9
W	10	522	6·6	1730	6·6	232	8·9	1458	8·9	—	—	2358	10·3	949	6·6	2220	6·1	347	3·6	17 3	3·3	616	5·2	1847	4·9	3 4	4·0	1531	3·8
Th	11	604	6·1	1819	6·2	321	8·3	1555	8·3	1153	9·5	1238	10·3	1042	6·5	2316	5·8	435	3·4	1766	—	711	4·9	1944	4·7	4 4	3·8	1635	3·6
F	12	657	5·8	1931	5·8	427	7·7	1713	7·7	127	9·5	1420	9·6	1153	5·8	—	—	530	3·2	1917	—	821	4·7	2056	4·5	521	3·5	1753	3·5
Sa	13	816	5·6	—	—	744	7·5	1850	7·5	3 5	10·5	1552	9·6	035	5·8	1341	6·3	637	2·9	2127	—	951	4·6	2226	4·5	654	3·5	1916	3·6
Su	14	945	5·8	—	—	858	8·1	2015	8·0	437	11·7	17 9	11·4	218	6·3	1525	6·6	827	2·7	2233	—	1121	4·7	2346	4·8	817	3·6	2030	3·7
M	15	1112	6·1	—	—	952	8·7	2118	8·7	543	13·0	18 5	12·4	339	6·8	1634	7·0	10 7	2·8	2322	—	—	—	1231	5·0	924	3·7	2127	4·0
Tu	16	055	7·0	1313	—	1037	9·2	22 7	9·3	634	13·4	1852	13·3	437	7·2	1725	7·2	11 5	2·9	1232	3·0	047	5·1	1326	5·3	1012	3·9	2215	4·2
W	17	142	7·4	1357	—	1115	9·4	2249	9·6	751	13·4	1930	13·6	520	7·8	18 4	7·3	1150	3·0	1311	3·1	136	5·4	1412	5·5	1055	4·0	2258	4·3
Th	18	225	7·2	1436	—	1151	9·4	2329	9·8	825	13·4	20 6	13·6	558	7·9	1839	7·8	0 6	3·4	1348	3·2	217	5·6	1452	5·6	1133	4·1	2337	4·4
F	19	3 3	7·4	1511	—	0 4	9·6	1224	9·6	857	13·0	2040	13·4	634	7·9	1912	7·9	050	3·6	1420	3·3	254	5·7	1527	5·6	—	—	12 8	4·1
Sa	20	336	7·2	1542	—	038	9·8	1255	9·6	927	12·8	2112	13·4	710	7·6	1944	7·6	130	3·6	1449	3·3	329	5·7	16 2	5·5	015	4·4	1242	4·0
Su	21	4 7	7·0	1613	—	110	9·3	1326	9·3	955	11·5	2143	12·8	747	7·2	2016	7·0	2 6	3·5	1518	3·2	4 4	5·6	1637	5·3	053	4·3	1317	4·0
M	22	435	6·8	1644	—	141	8·9	1355	8·9	1020	10·6	2212	12·0	822	6·6	2047	6·3	238	3·5	1550	3·1	441	5·4	1712	5·1	132	4·1	1354	3·8
Tu	23	5 5	6·5	1718	—	215	8·4	1427	8·4	1045	9·6	2238	11·0	857	6·0	2117	5·5	3 9	3·3	1628	3·0	518	5·2	1748	4·8	210	3·9	1435	3·7
W	24	539	6·1	18 0	—	251	7·8	15 2	7·8	1118	—	2353	9·9	932	5·5	2145	5·1	343	3·1	1715	2·9	556	4·9	1825	4·6	253	3·7	1518	3·5
Th	25	619	5·9	1852	—	339	6·6	16 2	7·0	—	—	1212	9·0	10 9	5·2	2217	5·2	421	2·8	18 9	2·8	639	4·6	19 7	4·4	340	3·4	1611	3·4
F	26	712	5·5	1958	—	452	6·6	1736	6·7	110	8·3	14 6	8·8	1055	5·4	23 6	5·6	5 8	2·7	1918	2·7	731	4·3	20 3	4·2	440	3·2	1720	3·3
Sa	27	822	5·2	2122	—	645	7·1	1924	7·6	331	8·6	16 0	8·4	055	5·2	1227	6·1	6 4	2·6	1918	2·6	843	4·1	2121	4·1	6 3	3·1	1840	3·3
Su	28	955	5·2	2254	—	8 9	7·8	2029	8·2	435	9·7	1654	9·3	227	5·4	14 8	5·2	727	2·6	2053	2·8	1012	4·1	2247	4·2	730	3·2	1948	3·3
M	29	1119	5·6	2351	—	9 0	7·8	2114	8·2	—	—	—	—	339	5·9	1532	5·6	932	2·6	2053	2·8	1129	4·3	2354	4·5	830	3·4	2041	3·6
Tu	30	—	—	—	—	—	—	—	—	435	—	1654	—	—	—	1626	—	1028	2·8	22 0	3·0	—	—	1225	—	914	3·6	2122	3·9

*All times shown are Greenwich Mean Time.   †Difference of height in metres from Ordnance Datum (Newlyn).   ‡Difference of height in metres from Ordnance Datum (Dublin).

OCTOBER, 1986

High Water at the undermentioned Places (G.M.T.*)—

Day of Month	Day of Week	London Bridge †Datum of Predictions 3·20 m. below				Liverpool †Datum of Predictions 4·93 m. below				Avonmouth †Datum of Predictions 6·50 m. below				Hull (Albert Dock) †Datum of Predictions 3·90 m. below				Greenock †Datum of Predictions 1·62 m. below				Leith †Datum of Predictions 2·90 m. below				Dun Laoghaire ‡Datum of Predictions 0·20 m. above			
		Mn. h.m.	Ht. m.	Aft. h.m.	Ht. m.	Mn. h.m.	Ht. m.	Aft. h.m.	Ht. m.	Mn. h.m.	Ht. m.	Aft. h.m.	Ht. m.	Mn. h.m.	Ht. m.	Aft. h.m.	Ht. m.	Mn. h.m.	Ht. m.	Aft. h.m.	Ht. m.	Mn. h.m.	Ht. m.	Aft. h.m.	Ht. m.	Mn. h.m.	Ht. m.	Aft. h.m.	Ht. m.
1	W	035		1210	6·1	938	8·4	2152	8·8	520	11·6	1736	11·6	428	6·5	1714	6·6	11 5	2·9	2245	3·2	043	4·8	1310	4·9	951	3·8	2159	4·1
2	Th	114	6·5	1252	6·9	1013	8·8	2227	9·2	6 3	11·9	1817	11·9	542	7·3	1737	7·3	1138	2·9	2326	3·3	121	5·1	1349	5·2	1023	4·1	2233	4·2
3	F	152	6·9	1328	7·0	1047	9·2	23 1	9·6	642	12·6	1856	13·1	615	7·7	1811	7·6	1213	3·0	1249	3·1	156	5·4	1422	5·5	1056	4·2	23 7	4·4
4	Sa	230	7·2	14 5	7·3	1122	9·5	2337	9·8	720	13·2	1934	13·6	650	7·7	1843	7·6	0 6	3·6	1324	3·2	228	5·8	1531	5·6	1128	4·2	2344	4·3
5	Su	3 5	7·4	1440	7·4	1158	9·6			758	13·5	2012	13·8	726	7·6	1919	7·6	046	3·6	14 0	3·4	3 3	5·8	1652	5·7	022	4·4	12 4	4·3
6	M	342	7·4	1515	7·5	012	9·8	1235	9·6	834	13·6	2051	13·6	8 5	7·6	1954	7·3	126	3·7	1436	3·5	341	5·8	1737	5·6	1 4	4·2	1242	4·2
7	Tu	421	7·3	1553	7·4	050	9·7	1313	9·4	912	13·2	2129	13·1	847	6·9	2030	7·0	2 7	3·7	1515	3·5	423	5·7	1830	5·5	153	4·0	1325	4·1
8	W	5 2	6·9	1634	7·1	131	9·4	1354	9·0	950	12·5	2212	12·1	935	6·4	2111	6·1	249	3·6	1556	3·4	510	5·5	1933	4·9	247	3·7	1413	3·9
9	Th	549	6·5	1722	6·6	216	8·8	1442	8·5	1031	11·4	2257	10·9	1034	5·8	2159	5·8	334	3·6	1644	3·3	6 2	5·2	2051	4·7	353	3·5	15 8	3·7
10	F	648	5·7	1819	6·2	310	8·2	1542	8·0	1123	10·4			1154	5·8	2258		424	3·3	1739	3·0	7 5	4·9	2219	4·6	516	3·6	1616	3·6
11	Sa	8 5	5·1	1934	5·9	426	7·5	17 6	7·7	0 0	9·9	1241	9·6	019	5·8	1354	5·4	520	3·1	19 6	2·8	822	4·6	2219	4·7	652	3·5	1739	3·7
12	Su	928	5·6	2057	5·9	6 5	7·6	1841	8·2	123	9·4	14 9	9·7	321	5·2	1519	5·9	633	2·7	2120	2·8	950	4·6	1214	5·2	811	3·6	2017	3·8
13	M	1052	6·2	2223	6·2	737	7·6	1959	8·2	254	9·7	1651	10·4	416	5·2	1620	6·4	852	2·7	2333	3·1	1112	5·2	1348	5·5	911	3·8	2114	4·0
14	Tu			2337	6·7	843	8·0	2058	8·8	421	11·8	1743	12·5	458	5·8	1742	7·0	10 7	2·9	23 2	3·4	1214	5·4	1426	5·5	958	4·0	2114	4·2
15	W			12 0	7·2	932	8·7	2145	9·2	522	12·6	1827	13·1	534	6·8	1812	7·5	1050	3·1	2344		13 6	5·6	15 0	5·4	1036	4·1	2240	4·3
16	Th	034	7·2	1211	7·2	1049	8·7	2226	9·5	6 8	13·3	19 4	13·5	610	7·2	1842	7·7	1127	3·1	1238		1348	5·6	1531	5·1	1141	4·1	2316	4·2
17	F	121	7·4	1334	7·0	1122	8·9	23 2	9·6	648	13·3	1940	13·2	645	7·5	1913	7·7	12 3	3·1	1312		1426	5·6	16 4	5·0	1141	4·1	2351	4·1
18	Sa	2 1	7·1	1411	6·7	1154	9·0	2336	9·5	723	13·2	2012	12·6	721	7·7	1944	7·5	025	3·5	1344		15 0	5·5	1636	5·0	025		1212	4·1
19	Su	236	6·9	1443	6·9	0 8	9·1	1224	9·1	755	12·3	2044	11·7	757	7·7	2012	7·3	103	3·5	1412		1531	5·3	1710	4·7	1 9	4·1	1244	4·0
20	M	3 7	6·7	1514	6·7	039	9·0	1253	8·9	827	12·3	2112		830	7·3	2040	6·7	138	3·5	1441		16 4	5·3	1746	4·7	137	3·8	1318	3·9
21	Tu	334	6·5	1542	6·5	144	8·7	1323	8·6	856	11·7	2141	11·7	9 3	6·9	21 5	6·3	211	3·4	1514		1636	5·1	1830	4·8	218	3·4	1356	3·8
22	W	4 0	6·7	1614	6·7	219	7·8	1355	7·7	922	10·5	22 7	9·8	938	6·0	2135	6·0	241	3·3	1553		1710	4·9	1927	4·5	313	3·1	1439	3·6
23	Th	428	6·5	1649	6·5	3 4	7·3	1432	7·7	948	9·7	2235	9·0	1021	5·5	2217	5·6	315	3·0	1639		1746	4·7	1830	4·6	413	3·1	1629	3·5
24	F	5 1	6·0	1729	6·0	410	6·7	1522	6·9	1012	9·0	2313	8·7	1133	5·5	2342	6·1	353	3·0	1731		1830	4·7	1927	4·6	513	3·4	1741	3·4
25	Sa	539	6·0	1817	6·0	546	6·7	1641	7·0	1041	8·5			134	6·0	1316	6·6	438	2·9	1834		1927	4·4	2037	4·4	637	3·1	1854	3·4
26	Su	625	6·2	1913	6·2	714	6·8	1819	7·5	1130	8·6	1250	9·3	244	6·4	1434	6·6	530	2·7	1957		2037	4·4	2153	4·3	744	3·4	1954	3·5
27	M	724	5·7	2030	5·7	811	7·1	1934	8·1	017	9·6	1451	10·5	339	5·9	1535	6·1	637	2·6	2113		2153	4·7	2354	4·8	834	3·6	2041	3·7
28	Tu	856	5·3	2156	5·3	856	8·3	2026	8·7	2 8	10·8	1559	11·7	424	6·4	1620	6·6	845	2·8	22 5		23 1	4·8	1227	5·0	914	3·9	2124	3·9
29	W	1026	5·2	23 4	5·2	935	8·8	21 8	9·2	336	12·0	1652	12·6	339	6·6	1659	6·6	945	2·8	2250		1039		13 7	5·3	951	4·1	22 0	4·3
30	Th	1125	6·1	2356	6·1			2149		433		1739						1022	3·0			1138	4·7						
31	F			1211						522								1058	3·1			037	5·1	13 7	5·3				

NOVEMBER, 1986

High Water at the undermentioned Places (G.M.T.*)—

Datum of Predictions: London Bridge 3·20 m. below; Liverpool 4·93 m. below; Avonmouth 6·50 m. below; Hull (Albert Dock) 3·90 m. below; Greenock 1·62 m. below; Leith 2·90 m. below; Dun Laoghaire 0·20 m. above.

Day of Month	Day of Week	LONDON BRIDGE Mn.	Ht.	Aft.	Ht.	LIVERPOOL Mn.	Ht.	Aft.	Ht.	AVONMOUTH Mn.	Ht.	Aft.	Ht.	HULL (Albert Dock) Mn.	Ht.	Aft.	Ht.	GREENOCK Mn.	Ht.	Aft.	Ht.	LEITH Mn.	Ht.	Aft.	Ht.	DUN LAOGHAIRE Mn.	Ht.	Aft.	Ht.
1	Sa	039	6·9	1253	7·0	1013	9·3	2228	9·6	6 8	12·8	1825	13·3	5 5	7·3	1737	7·4	1134	3·2	2335	3·6	117	5·4	1345	5·5	1025	4·2	2239	4·4
2	Su	121	7·2	1333	7·2	1051	9·6	23 8	9·8	652	13·4	1910	13·7	625	7·6	1814	7·6	1213	3·3	1253	3·4	155	5·7	1423	5·6	1059	4·3	2317	4·4
3	M	2 1	7·3	1412	7·3	1132	9·6	2350	9·8	734	13·6	1951	13·7	7 5	7·7	1852	7·6	020	3·7	1332	3·6	235	5·8	15 2	5·7	1137	4·3	2359	4·3
4	Tu	240	7·3	1453	7·4			1212	9·7	815	13·6	2034	13·5	751	7·6	1931	7·3	1 5	3·7	1413	3·6	318	5·8	1544	5·7	047	4·1	1303	4·2
5	W	321	7·2	1538	7·2	032	9·7	1255	9·5	857	13·4	2119	13·2	840	7·6	2012	7·3	150	3·7	1455	3·6	4 6	5·8	1631	5·5	139	3·9	1356	4·0
6	Th	4 4	7·0	1627	7·0	119	9·3	1341	9·2	942	12·4	22 6	11·9	932	6·8	2057	7·0	237	3·6	1541	3·6	457	5·5	1723	5·3	239	3·7	1454	3·8
7	F	452	6·6	1722	6·8	2 9	8·7	1434	8·7	1031	11·5	2259	10·9	1034	5·9	2146	6·7	326	3·5	1630	3·4	555	5·2	1820	5·0	347	3·5	16 3	3·8
8	Sa	544	6·2	1822	6·4	310	8·1	1538	8·2	1127	10·7			1154		2245	6·3	418	3·3	1729	3·2	7 2	5·0	1925	4·8	516	3·5	1721	3·9
9	Su	643	5·9	1930	6·2	424	7·6	1655	7·9	0 0	10·2	1234	10·2			2358	6·1	516	3·0	1855	3·0	814	4·8	2037	4·7	637	3·6	1844	3·9
10	M	749	5·8	2040	6·2	549	7·5	1815	8·0	1 9	9·9	1347	10·0	131	6·2	1337	5·9	632	2·8	2047	3·0	932	4·8	2153	4·8	751	3·9	1956	4·0
11	Tu	9 3	5·9	2159	6·3	7 6	7·7	1928	8·2	225	10·1	1515	10·7	247	6·5	1453	6·2	833	2·8	2147	3·1	1044	4·9	23 4	4·9	848	3·9	2051	4·1
12	W	1023	6·2	2311	6·7	812	8·1	2027	8·6	345	10·6	1616	11·6	430	6·8	1550	6·5	938	2·9	2233	3·1	1146	5·1			932	4·0	2138	4·1
13	Th	1130	6·6			909	8·5	2115	8·9	447	11·6	1711	12·3	5 9	7·0	1635	6·9	1019	3·1	2315	3·4	0 0	5·3	1235	5·3	1012	4·0	2219	4·1
14	F	0 7	7·0	1224	7·0	943	8·9	2156	9·1	534	12·3	1756	12·7	547	7·2	1712	7·0	1130	3·1	2355	3·4	046	5·4	1318	5·4	1046	4·0	2255	4·0
15	Sa	053	7·1	13 7	7·3	1021	8·9	2234	9·1	617	12·7	1835	12·9	624	7·3	1744	7·1	12 4	3·3	1238	3·5	125	5·4	1356	5·4	1116	4·0	2328	4·0
16	Su	133	7·1	1344	7·1	1055	9·0	23 9	9·0	653	12·9	1912	13·0	7 2	7·4	1815	7·1	035	3·4	13 9	3·5	2 2	5·4	1431	5·3	1147	4·0		
17	M	2 8	7·1	1418	7·0	1126	9·0	2343	9·0	728	13·1	1947	13·0	737	7·1	1846	7·0	111	3·4	1340	3·5	238	5·3	1504	5·2	0 2	3·9	1218	3·9
18	Tu	237	7·0	1449	6·9	1157	9·0			8 1	13·0	2019	12·7	811	6·9	1917	6·9	146	3·2	1411	3·5	312	5·2	1535	5·2	036	3·6	1253	3·8
19	W	3 4	6·8	1519	6·8	015	8·8	1228	8·8	830	12·6	2050	12·2	844	6·7	1945	6·7	219	3·1	1445	3·3	347	5·1	16 8	5·1	113	3·5	1330	3·7
20	Th	332	6·7	1553	6·7	048	8·6	13 0	8·6	858	12·1	2119	11·5	921	6·4	2012	6·5	254	3·1	1524	3·3	423	5·0	1643	5·0	153	3·5	1411	3·6
21	F	4 3	6·6	1630	6·5	123	8·4	1334	8·5	925	11·0	2148	10·8	10 6	5·8	2042	6·0	332	3·0	16 9	3·3	5 3	4·9	1721	4·6	238	3·3	1457	3·5
22	Sa	437	6·4	17 9	6·3	159	7·9	1412	8·0	955	10·5	2220	10·2	11 2	5·5	2117	5·6	415	2·9	1657	3·2	546	4·7	1856	4·5	329	3·3	1549	3·6
23	Su	515	6·2	1753	6·1	243	7·5	1450	7·7	1028	9·9	2258	9·9			2134	5·6	5 1	2·8	1753	3·2	637	4·5	1955	4·4	429	3·4	1649	3·6
24	M	557	5·9	1842	5·9	338	7·2	16 0	7·4	1115	9·5			029	5·7	1217	5·7	556	2·8	2018	3·1	734	4·4	2057	4·5	539	3·4	1755	3·7
25	Tu	648	5·7	1942	5·7	448	7·0	1713	7·3	1 2	9·4	1340	9·4	145	5·9	1331	6·1	713	2·8	2121	3·4	838	4·5	2259	4·6	647	3·6	1859	3·8
26	W	754	5·6	2057	5·8	6 4	7·2	1825	7·6	233	9·9	15 4	10·7	246	6·3	1434	6·9	839	2·9	2215	3·4	942	4·5	2351	5·1	746	3·7	1957	4·0
27	Th	919	5·6	2210	6·0	710	7·4	1928	8·0	343	10·8	16 7	11·6	339	6·7	1531	6·7	932	3·0	23 5	3·5	1042	4·7			834	3·8	2047	4·1
28	F	1031	6·0	2311	6·4	8 5	8·1	2022	8·5	442	11·8	17 4	12·4	430	7·1	1620	7·1	1015	3·2			1137	4·9			916	4·0	2131	4·2
29	Sa	1129	6·4			854	8·7	2111	9·0	536	12·6	1757	13·0			17 6	7·2	1058	3·3			040	5·3	1225	5·2	956	4·1	2214	
30	Su	0 4	6·8	1219	6·8	941	9·1	2159	9·4															1311	5·4				

*All times shown are Greenwich Mean Time.   †Difference of height in metres from Ordnance Datum (Newlyn).
‡Difference of height in metres from Ordnance Datum (Dublin).
†Difference of height in metres from Ordnance Datum.
‡Difference of height in metres from Ordnance Datum (Dublin).

DECEMBER, 1986

High Water at the undermentioned Places (G.M.T.*)—

Day of Month	Day of Week	London Bridge †Datum 3.20 m below				Liverpool †Datum 4.93 m below				Avonmouth †Datum 6.50 m below				Hull (Albert Dock) †Datum 3.90 m below				Greenock †Datum 1.62 m below				Leith †Datum 2.90 m below				Dun Laoghaire †Datum 0.20 m above			
		Mn. h.m.	Ht.	Aft. h.m.	Ht.	Mn. h.m.	Ht.	Aft. h.m.	Ht.	Mn. h.m.	Ht.	Aft. h.m.	Ht.	Mn. h.m.	Ht.	Aft. h.m.	Ht.	Mn. h.m.	Ht.	Aft. h.m.	Ht.	Mn. h.m.	Ht.	Aft. h.m.	Ht.	Mn. h.m.	Ht.	Aft. h.m.	Ht.
1	M	052	7.0	13 6	7.0	1026	9.5	2247	9.6	627	13.1	1848	13.3	519	7.4	1750	7.4	1141	3.4	2357	3.7	127	5.5	1356	5.5	1035	4.2	2258	4.3
2	Tu	137	7.0	1352	7.2	1111	9.7	2334	9.6	714	13.4	1937	13.4	6 8	7.5	1834	7.5	1226	3.6			215	5.7	1440	5.7	1116	4.3	2345	4.2
3	W	222	7.1	1442	7.3	1157	9.7			8 2	13.4	2026	13.5	657	7.6	1917	7.5	048	3.7	1311	3.7	3 5	5.8	1528	5.7	036	4.1	1250	4.3
4	Th	3 7	7.1	1532	7.4	024	9.5	1245	9.6	850	13.2	2115	13.3	748	7.6	20 2	7.4	138	3.6	1356	3.8	357	5.7	1619	5.6	132	4.0	1344	4.3
5	F	356	7.0	1624	7.3	114	9.2	1335	9.3	938	12.9	22 4	12.8	839	7.3	2049	7.2	230	3.5	1442	3.7	451	5.6	1712	5.4	229	3.8	1443	4.3
6	Sa	445	6.8	1719	7.1	2 8	8.8	1429	9.0	1027	12.1	2254	11.5	931	6.9	2136	7.0	321	3.4	1530	3.6	548	5.3	18 9	5.2	336	3.7	1546	4.1
7	Su	536	6.6	1814	6.8	3 4	8.4	1527	8.6	1119	11.5			1027	6.5	2228	6.8	413	3.3	1621	3.4	647	5.1	19 8	5.1	447	3.5	1656	3.9
8	M	629	6.3	1912	6.5	4 6	8.0	1628	8.3	041	10.6	1212	11.5	1133	6.5			5 9	3.1	1717	3.1	751	4.9	2011	4.9	6 4	3.5	1811	4.0
9	Tu	724	6.1	2013	6.3	513	7.7	1736	8.1	142	10.5	1313	10.8	042	6.4	1256	6.0	611	2.9	1827	3.1	857	4.8	2116	4.8	715	3.6	1923	3.9
10	W	827	6.0	2122	6.2	624	7.6	1843	8.1	255	10.7	1418	10.9	158	6.5	14 6	6.4	733	2.9	1954	3.1	10 4	4.8	2222	4.8	814	3.7	2023	3.9
11	Th	941	6.1	2233	6.3	730	7.8	1947	8.2	359	11.1	1528	11.2	3 3	6.6	15 7	6.5	846	3.0	21 4	3.2	11 6	4.9	2322	4.9	9 4	3.8	2115	3.8
12	F	1054	6.3	2333	6.6	825	8.0	2042	8.3	455	11.6	1630	12.0	357	6.7	1557	6.7	937	3.0	2158	3.3	013	5.1	12 0	5.0	946	3.8	2159	3.8
13	Sa	1151	6.5			912	8.2	2128	8.4	544	12.2	1722	12.4	445	6.8	1641	6.8	1019	3.1	2245	3.4	059	5.1	1246	5.0	1023	3.9	2237	3.8
14	Su	024	6.7	1239	6.6	953	8.5	2210	8.6	627	12.4	18 7	12.9	530	6.8	1719	6.9	1057	3.3	2329	3.5	142	5.1	1327	5.1	1056	3.9	2312	3.8
15	M	1 4	6.8	1320	6.7	11 6	8.8	2248	8.6	7 4	12.5	1927	12.2	611	6.7	1754	6.9	1135	3.3			221	5.2	14 4	5.2	1128		2345	3.8
16	Tu	141	6.8	1357	6.7	1140	8.8	2325	8.6	813	12.0	20 2	12.6	648	6.7	1828	6.8	012	3.4	1210	3.5	259	5.1	1444	5.2	019	3.6	1235	3.9
17	W	213	6.8	1432	6.7	0 0	8.6	1214	8.8	844	11.7	2036	12.2	723	6.7	1859	6.7	052	3.3	1244	3.5	334	5.1	1518	5.0	056	3.6	1311	3.9
18	Th	244	6.8	15 7	6.7	035	8.7	1248	8.7	914	11.5	21 7	11.6	757	6.6	1927	6.7	130	3.1	1317	3.4	4 9	5.0	1551	4.9	133	3.5	1350	3.9
19	F	317	6.6	1542	6.6	110	8.6	1323	8.6	946	11.2	2138	11.3	832	6.5	1958	6.5	2 6	3.1	1350	3.4	447	4.9	1626	4.8	214	3.4	1429	3.9
20	Sa	350	6.6	1620	6.6	147	8.4	1359	8.4	1023	11.0	2210	11.0	910	6.3	2032	6.3	243	3.0	1425	3.4	526	4.8	17 2	4.7	259	3.4	1514	3.8
21	Su	426	6.5	1657	6.5	226	8.2	1440	8.2	1151	10.9	2247	10.8	950	6.0	21 8	6.1	318	3.0	15 2	3.4	6 9	4.7	1743	4.7	349	3.3	16 3	3.8
22	M	5 1	6.4	1734	6.4	310	8.0	1527	8.0	1151	10.7	2329	10.6	1035	6.2	2150	6.0	355	3.0	1543	3.4	658	4.6	1827	4.6	446	3.4	17 0	3.8
23	Tu	537	6.2	1817	6.3	4 6	7.8	1619	7.8	021	10.3	1250	10.7	1127	6.0	2237	6.2	435	3.0	1628	3.5	750	4.5	1915	4.6	550	3.5	18 6	3.7
24	W	618	6.1	19 4	6.1	510	7.6	1723	7.6	131	10.7	14 8	11.3	042	6.2	2334	6.6	518	3.0	1718	3.5	847	4.6	20 7	4.8	655	3.6	1912	3.7
25	Th	7 7	5.9	20 5	6.0	610	7.6	1831	7.8	256	11.3	1525	11.8	152	6.6	1229		6 9	3.0	1818	3.5	947	4.8	21 4	4.9	754	3.8	2013	3.7
26	F	816	5.9	2118	6.0	716	7.9	1940	8.2	4 6	11.8	1634	12.6	258	6.8	1337	6.8	717	3.1	1926	3.4	1049	4.8	21 6	5.2	847	3.8	2159	3.7
27	Sa	936	5.9	2228	6.2	819	8.3	2042	8.6	5 9	12.3	1734	12.7	4 3	6.8	1443	6.9	834	3.2	2038	3.5	1149	5.1	2310	5.4	932	4.0	2250	3.8
28	Su	1048	6.2	2332	6.5	915	8.8	2139	8.9	6 8	12.6	1835	13.1	5 9	7.1	1545	6.9	936	3.4	2143	3.5	013	5.2	1246	5.5	1018	4.1	2340	3.9
29	M	1151	6.5			10 9	9.2	2234	9.2	7 3	13.1	1930	13.0	6 3	7.3	1642	7.4	1028	3.5	2242	3.5	112	5.5	1339		11 3	4.2		4.0
30	Tu	029	6.6	1250	6.7	1059	9.5	2327	9.4							1734	6.9	1119	3.5	2340	3.6	2 7		1429					4.0
31	W	123	6.7	1345	6.9											1824	7.4	12 9	3.6										

*All times shown are Greenwich Mean Time. †Difference of height in metres from Ordnance Datum (Newlyn).
‡Difference of height in metres from Ordnance Datum (Dublin).

CHRONOLOGICAL NOTES

TIME MEASURES

Kelvin (1883) estimated the age of the earth's crust at 20–400 million years. Study of radio-activity has since shown cooling to have been slower. Holmes and others gave 1,500–2,000 million years as the age of the oldest known rocks. Jeffreys suggests an age not exceeding 8,000 million years for the separate existence of the earth, which, probably with other related planets, separated from the sun after a star-collision. Very early rocks, almost without traces of fossils, are variously named in North America and Europe and account for a period down to about 5,000 million years ago.

PALÆOZOIC (Old Animal Life) PERIODS include:—
Cambrian, Ordovician and Silurian rocks, all named from Wales (Cambria, Ordovices, Silures, the two latter ancient Celtic peoples). These rocks account for about 200 million years and there then followed a major phase of mountain-building, called Caledonian because studied early in Scotland, characterized by N.E.–S.W. lines of hills and valleys in several areas.
Devonian, including the Old Red Sandstone.
Carboniferous, including Mountain Limestone, Millstone Grit and Coal Measures.
These rocks account for about 100 million years and then there followed a major phase of mountain-building called Hercyian because widespread in W. Germany and adjacent areas. In Britain there are E.–W. lines of hills and valleys, and some N.–S.

MESOZOIC (Middle Forms of Life) PERIODS include:—
Permian rocks, widespread in Perm district, U.S.S.R. Triassic, including New Red Sandstone. Jurassic, important in the Jura Mts. Cretaceous, including the Greensands and the Chalk of England. In the Mesozoic, modern large land groups of animals, reptiles, birds and mammals first appear, but almost no modern genera or species of animals are known.

CAINOZOIC or CENOZOIC (Recent forms of Life) PERIODS include:—
Eocene. A few existing genera or species. Oligocene. A minority of existing forms. Miocene. Approach to a balance of existing and extinct forms. Pliocene. A majority of existing forms. Pleistocene. A very large majority of existing forms. Holocene. Existing forms only, save for a few exterminated by man. In the last 50 million years, from the Miocene through the Pliocene, the Alpine-Himalayan and the circum-Pacific phases of mountain building reached their climax.

During the Pleistocene period ice sheets repeatedly locked up masses of water as land ice, its weight depressed the land, but the locking up of water lowered sea-level by 100–200 metres. Milankovitch has worked out variations of radiation theoretically receivable from the sun and has reached conclusions not very markedly different as to the dates from those of Penck who studied sediments, and both can fit into Deperet's scheme based on study of river terraces. Milankovitch gives 600,000 years for the Pleistocene.

Phases of the Pleistocene:—
(a) Early Glaciations (probably 2), Gunz glaciations of Penck's Alpine series. About 600 to 500 thousand years ago.
(b) An interglacial phase with high sea level, Milazzian terraces (of Deperet's series) around the Mediterranean. About 500,000 years ago.
(c) A second pair of Glaciations, the Mindel of Penck's series. About 500 to rather before 400 thousand years ago.

(d) A long interglacial phase with high sea level, but less high than during (b). Tyrrhenian terraces around the Mediterranean. From about 400 to about 200 thousand years ago.
(e) The penultimate series of glaciations (probably 3), the Riss of Penck's series. About 200 to 150 thousand years ago.
(f) An interglacial phase with fairly high sea level, less high than during (d). Monastirian terraces around the Mediterranean. From about 150 to about 120 thousand years ago.
(g) The ultimate series of glaciations (probably 3, preceded perhaps by a cool phase), the Wurm of Penck's series. From about 115 to rather more than 20 thousand years ago.
(h) The last glacial retreat merging into the Holocene period about 10,000 or 8,000 years ago.

EARLY MAN

The starting point for any consideration of the history of man must be the fact that all members of the human race belong to one species of animal, i.e. homo sapiens, the definition of a species being in biological terms that all its members can interbreed. As a species of mammal it is possible to group man with other similar types, known as the primates, amongst which will be found a sub-group, the apes, which includes, in addition to man, the chimpanzees, gorillas, orang-utans and gibbons, all of which lack a tail, have shoulder blades at the back, and a Y-shaped chewing pattern on the surface of their molars, as well as showing the more general primate characteristics of four incisors, a thumb which is able to touch the fingers of the same hand, and finger and toe nails instead of claws. Taking into account all the factors available to scientific study, it appears that human beings have chimpanzees and gorillas as their nearest relatives in the animal world.

However, there remains the possibility that there once lived, now extinct, creatures which were in fact closer to modern man than the chimpanzees and gorillas. To decide whether or not this is the case it is necessary to consider the fossil evidence to see if any other extinct ape-like forms shared with modern man the characteristics of having flat faces (that is the absence of a pronounced muzzle), being bipedal, and possessing large brains. There are two broad groups of extinct apes recognised by specialists. First the ramapithecines, the remains of which, mainly jaw fragments, have been found in East Africa, Asia, and Turkey. They lived about 14 to 8 million years ago and from the evidence of their teeth, it seems they chewed more in the manner of modern man than that of the other presently living apes. The second group, the australopithecines, have left much more numerous remains amongst which sub-groups may be detected, although the geographic spread is limited to South and East Africa. Living between 5 and 1·5 million years ago, they were closer relatives of modern man to the extent that they walked upright, did not have an extensive muzzle, and had similar types of pre-molars. The first australopithecine remains were recognised at Taung in South Africa in 1924, and of subsequent discoveries, which include those at the famous site of Olduvai Gorge in Tanzania, perhaps the most impressive was made at Hadar in Ethiopia in 1974 when about half a skeleton, known as "Lucy" was found.

Also in East Africa, between 2 million and 1·5 million years ago, lived a hominid group which not only walked up-right, had a flat face, and a large brain case, but also made simple pebble and flake stone tools. These habilines on present evidence seem to have been the first people to make tools, however crude; this facility is related to the larger brain size and human beings are the only animals to make implements to be used in other processes. These early pebble tool users, because of their distinctive characteristics, have been grouped as a separate sub-species, now extinct, of the genus *homo*, and are known as *homo habilis*.

The use of fire, again a human characteristic, is associated with another group of extinct hominids whose remains, about a million years old, are found in South and East Africa, China, Indonesia, North Africa and Europe; no doubt the mastery of the techniques of making fire helped the colonisation of the colder northern areas and particular mention may be made in this respect of the important European site of Vertesszollos in Hungary. *Homo erectus* is the name given to this group of fossils and it now includes a number of famous individual discoveries from earlier decades, for example, Solo Man, Heidelberg Man, and especially Peking Man who lived at the cave site at Choukoutien, which has yielded evidence of fire and burnt bone.

The well known group, Neanderthal Man, or *homo sapiens neandertalensis*, is an extinct form of modern man who lived between about 100,000 and 40,000 years ago, thus spanning the last Ice Age, and indeed its ability to adapt to the cold climate on the edge of the ice sheets is one of its characteristic features, the remains being only found in Europe, Asia and the Middle East. Complete neandertal skeletons were found with evidence of tool-making and the use of fire. Distinguished by very large brains, it seems that neanderthal man was the first to develop recognisable social customs, especially deliberate burial rites. Why the neanderthalers became extinct is not clear, but it may be not unconnected with the climatic changes which occurred at the end of the Ice Ages which, would, of course, have seriously affected their food supplies; it may be that they became too specialised for their own good.

It is appropriate to mention the only known human fossil remains found in England, the Swanscombe skull, and to make the point that some specialists see Swanscombe Man (or rather, probably woman) as a neanderthaler. Others group these remains together with the Steinheim skull from Germany seeing both as a separate sub-species, *homo-sapiens steinheimenses*. Unfortunately there is just too little evidence as yet on which to form a final judgment.

Modern man, *homo sapiens sapiens*, the surviving sub-species of *homo sapiens* had evolved to our present physical condition and had colonised much of the world by about 30,000 years ago. There are many previously distinguished individual specimens, for example Cromagnon Man, which may now be grouped together as *homo sapiens sapiens*. It is appropriate to note that it was Modern Man who spread to the New World by crossing the landbridge between Siberia and Alaska and thence moved south through North and into South America. Equally it is Modern Man who over the last 30,000 years has been responsible for the major developments in technology, art and civilisation generally.

It may be remarked that one of the problems for those studying fossil man is the lack in many cases of sufficient quantities of fossil bone for analysis. It is of course important that theories should be tested against evidence, and not the evidence made to fit the theory; the celebrated Piltdown hoax is perhaps the best known example of "fossils" being forged to fit what where then seen in some quarters as the correct theory of man's evolution.

HUMAN CULTURAL DEVELOPMENT

It was perhaps inevitable that, given the Eurocentric bias of the early archaeologists, there should be an emphasis on looking for a starting point for the development of cultural ideas and clear lines of transmission, especially by migration, trade and warfare, in Europe and the Near East. In historical terms the Three Age System, whereby pre-history was divided into a Stone Age, Bronze Age, and Iron Age was devised by Christian Thomsen, Curator of the National Museum of Denmark in the early nineteenth century to facilitate the classification of the Museum's collections. The descriptive adjectives referred, of course, to the materials from which the implements and weapons were made, thereby coming to be taken as the dominant features of the societies to which they related. Despite achieving great popularity, indeed the refinement of the Three Age System came to dominate archaeological thought and still remains a generally accepted concept in the popular mind, it has come to be seen by archaeologists as an increasingly inadequate model for human development.

For example, commonsense alone came to suggest that there were no complete breaks between one so-called "Age" and another, any more than contemporaries would have regarded 1485 as a complete break between medieval and modern English history. Secondly, the Three Age System could not be applied universally in that for some areas it was necessary to insert a Copper Age, while in Africa south of the Sahara there would seem to be no Bronze Age at all; in Australia, Old Stone Age societies survived, while in South America, New Stone Age communities existed into modern times. As archaeologists in Europe came to appreciate the civilisations in other parts of the world it was clear that a Eurocentric theory of human development would not suffice.

If one takes the concept of the "Neolithic Revolution" associated with the domestication of plants and animals, a development of particular importance in the human cultural pattern as it reflected change from the more primitive hunter/gatherer economies to a more settled agricultural way of life and therefore, so the argument goes, in due course, allowed the development of urban civilisation. However, it can no longer be argued that this "Revolution" took place only in one area from which all development stemmed. It may well be that the cultivation of wheat and barley was first undertaken, together with the domestication of cattle and goats/sheep in the Fertile Crescent, but there is evidence that rice was first deliberately planted and pigs domesticated in South East Asia; maize first cultivated in Central America and llamas first domesticated in South America. Therefore increasingly in recent years it has come to be realised that cultural changes can take place independently of each other in different parts of the World at different rates and different times; there is no need therefore to apply a general diffusionist theory.

While it is clear that scholars will continue to study the particular societies which interest them, nevertheless it is also apparent that it may indeed be possible to obtain a reliable chronological framework, in absolute terms of years, against which the cultural development of any particular area may be set. The development and refinement of radio-carbon dating and other scientific methods of producing absolute chronologies is enabling the cross-referencing of societies to be undertaken; as the techniques of dating become more rigorous in application and the number of scientifically obtained dates increases, then the attainment of an absolute chronology becomes a reality for prehistoric societies throughout the World.

TIME MEASUREMENT AND CALENDARS

MEASUREMENTS OF TIME

Measurements of Time.—These are based on the time taken by the earth to rotate on its axis (*Day*); by the moon to revolve round the earth (*Month*); and by the earth to revolve round the sun (*Year*). From these, which are not commensurable, certain average or mean intervals have been adopted for ordinary use.

The Day begins at midnight and is divided into 24 hours of 60 minutes, each of 60 seconds. The hours are counted from midnight up to 12 noon (when the sun crosses the meridian), and these hours are designated A.M. (*ante meridiem*); and again from noon up to 12 at midnight, which hours are designated P.M. (*post meridiem*), except when the *Twenty-four Hour* reckoning is employed. The 24-hour reckoning ignores A.M. and P.M., and the hours are numbered 0 to 23 from midnight to midnight.

Colloquially the 24 hours are divided into *day* and *night*, day being the time while the sun is above the horizon (including the four stages of twilight defined on p. 139). Day is subdivided further into *morning*, the early part of daytime, ending at noon; *afternoon* from noon to 6 p.m. and *evening*, which may be said to extend from 6 p.m. until midnight. *Night*, the dark period between day and day, begins at the close of Astronomical Twilight (*see* p. 139) and extends beyond midnight to sunrise the next day.

The names of the Days—Sunday, Monday, Tuesday (Tiw = God of War), Wednesday (Woden or Odin), Thursday (Thor), Friday (Frig = wife of Odin), and Saturday—are derived from Old English translations or adaptions of the Roman titles (Sol, Luna, Mars, Mercurius, Jupiter, Venus and Saturnius).

The Week is a period of 7 days.

The Month in the ordinary calendar is approximately the twelfth part of a year, but the lengths of the different months vary from 28 (or 29) days to 31.

The Year.—The *Equinoctial or Tropical Year* is the time that the earth takes to revolve round the sun from equinox to equinox, or 365·2422 mean solar days. The *Calendar Year* consists of 365 days, but a year the date of which is divisible by 4, without remainder, is called *bissextile* (see Roman Calendar) or *Leap Year* and consists of 366 days, one day being added to the month February, so that a date "leaps over" a day of the week. The last year of a century is not a leap year unless its number is divisable by 400 (*e.g.* the years 1800 and 1900 had only 365 days).

The Solstice.—A Solstice is the point in the Tropical Year at which the Sun attains its greatest distance, north or south, from the Equator. In the northern hemisphere the greatest distance north of the Equator is the Summer Solstice and the greatest distance south is the Winter Solstice.

The Summer Solstice is also the *Longest Day*, measured from sunrise to sunset. At the Solstice the Sun, reaching its greatest northern declination, appears to stand still, the times of sunrise and sunset and the consequent length of the day showing no variation for several days together, before and after the longest day (June 21 or 22). For the remainder of this century the longest day will fall each year on June 21.

The date of the Solstice varies according to locality. If the Solstice falls on June 21 late in the day by Greenwich time, that day will be the longest of the year at Greenwich even though it may be by only a second of time or a fraction thereof, but it will be on June 22, local date, in Japan, and so June 22 will be the longest day there and at places in Eastern longitudes.

Leaving aside the question of locality, the date of the Solstice is also affected by the length of the Tropical Year, which is 365¼ days less about 11 minutes. If a Solstice happens late on June 21 in one year, it will be nearly six hours later in the next, *i.e.* early on June 22, and that will be the longest day. This delay of the Solstice is not permitted to continue because the extra day in Leap Year brings it back a day in the Calendar.

However, because of the 11 minutes above mentioned the additional day in Leap Year brings the Solstice back too far by 44 minutes, and the time of the Solstice in the Calendar is earlier as the century progresses. (In the year 2000 the Summer Solstice reaches its earliest date for 100 years, *i.e.*, June 21^d 02^h.) To remedy this the last year of a century is in most cases not a Leap Year, and the omission of the extra day puts the date of the Solstice later by about six hours too much, compensation for which is made by making the fourth centennial year a Leap Year.

Similar considerations apply to the day of the Winter Solstice, or the *Shortest Day* of the year. For the remainder of this century the shortest day will fall on Dec. 21 in two years of four and on Dec. 22 in the remaining two years. In the year 2000 the Winter Solstice reaches its earliest date, *i.e.*, Dec. 21^d 13^h. The difference due to locality also prevails in the same sense as for the longest day.

At Greenwich the Sun sets at its earliest by the clock about ten days before the shortest day, which is a circumstance that may require explanation. The daily change in the time of sunset is due in the first place to the Sun's movement southwards at this time of the year, which diminishes the interval between the Sun's transit, and its setting, and, secondly, because of the daily decrease of the Equation of Time which causes the time of Apparent noon to be continuously later, day by day, and so in a measure counteracts the first effect. The rates of change of these two quantities are not equal, nor are they uniform, but are such that their combination causes the date of earliest sunset to be Dec. 12 or 13 at Greenwich. In more southerly latitudes the effect of the movement of the Sun is less, and the change in the time of sunset depends on that of the Equation of Time to a greater degree, and the date of earliest sunset is earlier than it is at Greenwich.

The Equinox is the point at which the Sun crosses the Equator and day and night are of equal length all over the world. This occurs in March (Vernal Equinox—about March 21) and September (Autumnal Equinox—about September 21).

The Historical Year.—Before the year 1752, two Calendar systems were in use in England. The Civil or Legal Year began on March 25, while the Historical Year began on January 1. Thus the Civil or Legal date 1658 March 24, was the same day as 1659 March 24 Historical; and a date in that portion of the year is written as: March 24 165⅞, the lower figure showing the Historical year.

The New Year.—In England in the seventh century, and as late as the thirteenth, the year was reckoned from Christmas Day, but in the twelfth century the Anglican Church began the year with the Feast of The Annunciation of the Blessed Virgin (Lady Day) on March 25 and this practice was adopted generally in the fourteenth century. The Civil or Legal year in the British Dominions (exclusive of Scotland) began with "Lady Day" until 1751. But in and since 1752 the civil year has begun with Jan. 1. Certain dividends are still paid by the Bank of England on dates based on Old Style. New Year's Day in *Scotland* was changed from March 25 to Jan. 1 in 1600.

On the Continent of Europe Jan. 1 was adopted as

the first day of the year by Venice in 1522, Germany in 1544, Spain, Portugal, and the Roman Catholic Netherlands in 1556, Prussia, Denmark and Sweden in 1559, France 1564, Lorraine 1579, Protestant Netherlands 1583, Russia 1725, and Tuscany 1751.

The Masonic Year.—Two dates are quoted in warrants, dispensations etc., issued by the United Grand Lodge of England, those for the current year being expressed as *Anno Domini* 1986—*Anno Lucis* 5986. This *Year of Light* is based on the Book of Genesis 1: 3, the 4000 year difference being derived from *Ussher's Notation*, published in 1654, which place the Creation of the World in 4,000 B.C.

Regnal Years.—These are the years of a sovereign's reign, and each begins on the anniversary of his or her accession: *e.g.* Regnal year 35 of the present Queen began on Feb. 6, 1986. The system was used for dating Acts of Parliament until 1962. Since 1962 Acts of Parliament have been dated by the calendar year. The *Summer Time Act* of 1925, for example, is quoted as 15 and 16 Geo. V. c. 64, because it became law in the session which extended over part of both of these regnal years. The regnal years of Edward VII began on January 22, which was the day of Queen Victoria's death in 1901, so that Acts passed in that reign are, in general, quoted with only one year number, but year 10 of the series ended on May 6, 1910, being the day on which King Edward died, and Acts of the Parliamentary Session 1910 are headed 10 Edw. VII. and 1 Geo. V.; Acts passed in 1936 were dated 1 Edw. VIII. and 1 Geo. VI.; Acts passed in 1952 were dated 16 Geo. VI. and 1 Elizabeth II.

Lord Mayor's Day.—The Lord Mayor of London was previously elected on the Feast of St. Simon and St. Jude (Oct. 28), and from the time of Edward I, at least, was presented to the King or to the Barons of the Exchequer on the following day, except that day be a Sunday. The day of election was altered to Oct. 16 in 1346, and after some further changes was fixed for Michaelmas Day in 1546, but the ceremonies of admittance and swearing-in of the Lord Mayor continued to take place on Oct. 28 and 29 respectively until 1751. In 1752, at the reform of the Calendar (*see* page 188), the Lord Mayor was continued in office until Nov. 8, the "New Style" equivalent of Oct. 28. The Lord Mayor is now presented to the Lord Chief Justice at the Royal Courts of Justice on the second Saturday in November to make the final declaration of office, having been sworn in at Guildhall on the preceding day.

Dog Days.—The days about the heliacal rising of the Dog Star, noted from ancient times as the hottest and most unwholesome period of the year in the Northern Hemisphere. Their incidence has been variously calculated as depending on the Greater or Lesser Dog Star (Sirius or Procyon) and their duration has been reckoned as from 30 to 54 days. A generally accepted period is from July 3 to Aug. 15.

Metonic (Lunar, or Minor) **Cycle.**—In the year 432 B.C. Meton, an Athenian astronomer, found that 235 Lunations are very nearly, though not exactly equal in duration to 19 Solar Years, and, hence, after 19 years the Phases of the Moon recur on the same days of the month (nearly). The dates of Full Moon in a cycle of nineteen years were inscribed in *figures of gold* on public monuments in Athens, and the number showing the position of a year in the Cycle is called the **Golden Number** of that year.

Solar (or Major) **Cycle.**—A period of twenty-eight years, in any corresponding year of which the days of the week recur on the same day of the month.

Julian Period.—Proposed by Joseph Scaliger in 1582. The period is 7980 Julian years, and its first year coincides with the year 4713 B.C. 7980 is the product of the number of years in the Solar Cycle, the Metonic Cycle and the cycle of the Roman Indication ($28 \times 19 \times 15$).

Roman Indication.—A period of fifteen years, instituted for fiscal purposes about A.D. 300.

Epact.—The age of the calendar Moon, diminished by one day, on January 1, in the ecclesiastical lunar calendar.

THE FOUR SEASONS

Spring, the first season of the year, is defined astronomically to begin in the *Northern Hemisphere* at the Vernal Equinox when the Sun enters the sign Aries and to terminate at the Summer Solstice. In *Great Britain*, Spring in popular parlance comprises the months of February, March and April. In the *Southern Hemisphere* Spring corresponds with Autumn in the Northern Hemisphere.

Summer, the second and warmest season, begins astronomically at the Summer Solstice when the Sun enters the sign of Cancer. Summer terminates at the Autumnal Equinox. In popular parlance Summer in *Great Britain* includes the months of May, June, July and August, Midsummer Day being June 24.

Autumn, the third season, begins astronomically at the Autumnal Equinox when the Sun enters the sign Libra and ends at the Winter Solstice. In *Great Britain* it is popularly held to include the months of September and October. A warm period sometimes occurs round about St. Luke's Day (Oct. 18) and is known as "St. Luke's Summer." In the *Southern Hemisphere* it corresponds with Spring of the Northern.

Winter, the fourth and coldest season, begins astronomically at the Winter Solstice when the Sun enters the sign of Capricornus, and ends at the Vernal Equinox. In *Great Britain* the season is popularly held to comprise the months of November, December and January, mid-winter being marked by the Shortest Day. A warm period sometimes occurs round about Martinmas (Nov. 11) and is known as "St. Martin's Summer." In the *Southern Hemisphere* it corresponds with Summer of the Northern.

THE CHRISTIAN CALENDAR

In the Christian chronological system the years are distinguished by cardinal numbers before or after the Incarnation, the period being denoted by the letters B.C. (Before Christ) or, more rarely, A.C. (*Ante Christum*), and A.D. (*Annus Domini*). The correlative dates of the epoch are the 4th year of the 194th Olympiad, the 753rd year from the Foundation of Rome, A.M. 3761 (Jewish Chronology), and the 4714th year of the Julian Period.

The system was introduced into Italy in the sixth century, and though first used in France in the seventh it was not universally established there until about the eighth century. It has been said that the system was introduced into England by St. Augustine (A.D. 596), but was probably not generally used until some centuries later. It was ordered to be used by the Bishops at the Council of Chelsea, A.D. 816. The actual date of the birth of Christ is somewhat uncertain.

The Julian Calendar.—In the Julian Calendar all the centennial years were Leap Years, and for this reason towards the close of the sixteenth century there was a difference of 10 days between the tropical and calendar years; the equinox fell on March 11 of the Calendar, whereas at the time of the Council of Nicaea, A.D. 325, it had fallen on March 21. In 1582 Pope Gregory ordained that Oct. 5th should be called Oct. 15th and that of the end-century years only the fourth should be a Leap Year (*see* p. 186).

The Gregorian Calendar was adopted by Italy, France, Spain, and Portugal in 1582; by Prussia, the German Roman Catholic States, Switzerland, Holland, and Flanders on Jan. 1, 1583, Poland 1586, Hungary 1587, the German and Netherland Protestant States and Denmark 1700, Sweden (gradually) by the omission of eleven leap days, 1700–1740; Great Britain and her Dominions (including the North American Colonies) in 1752, by the omission of eleven days (Sept. 3 being reckoned as Sept. 14). Japan adopted the calendar in 1872, China in 1912, Bulgaria in 1915, Turkey and Soviet Russia in 1918, Yugoslavia and Rumania in 1919, and Greece in February, 1923.

In the same year that the change was made in England from the Julian to the Gregorian Calendar, the beginning of the new year was also changed from March 25 to January 1 (*see* p. 186).

The Orthodox Churches.—Some Orthodox Churches still use the Julian reckoning, but the majority of Greek Churches and the Rumanian Orthodox Church have adopted a modified "New Calendar", observing the Gregorian Calendar for fixed feasts and the Julian for movable feasts.

The Orthodox Church year begins on September 1. There are four fast periods, and in addition to Pascha (Easter), twelve great feasts, as well as numerous commemorations of the Saints of the Old and New Testaments throughout the year.

The Dominical Letter is one of the letters A–G which are used to denote the Sundays in successive years. If the first day of the year is a Sunday the letter is A; if the second, B; the third, C; and so on. Leap year requires two letters, the first for Jan. 1—Feb. 29, the second for March 1—Dec. 31.

Epiphany.—The Feast of the Epiphany, commemorating the manifestation of Christ, later became associated with the offering of gifts by the Magi. The day was of exceptional importance from the time of the Council of Nicaea (A.D. 325) as the primate of Alexandria was charged at every Epiphany Feast with the announcement in a letter to the Churches of the date of the forthcoming Easter. The day was of considerable importance in Britain as it influenced dates, ecclesiastical and lay, *e.g.* **Plow Monday**, when

work was resumed in the fields, falls upon the Monday in the first full week after the Epiphany.

Lent.—The Teutonic word *Lent*, which denotes the Fast preceding Easter, originally meant no more than the Spring season; but from Anglo-Saxon times, at least, it has been used as the equivalent of the more significant Latin term **Quadragesima**, meaning the "Forty Days" or, more literally, the fortieth day. As early as the fifth century some of the Fathers of the Church put forward the view that the forty days Fast is of Apostolic origin, but this is not supported or believed by modern scholars; and it appears to some that it dates from the early years of the fourth century. There is some suggestion that the Fast was kept originally for only forty hours. **Ash Wednesday** is the first day of Lent, which ends at midnight before Easter Day.

Sexagesima and Septuagesima.—It has been suggested that the unmeaning application of the names *Sexagesima* and *Septuagesima* to the second and third Sundays before Lent was made by analogy with the names *Quadragesima* and *Quinquagesima*. Another less likely conjecture is that *Septuagesima* means the seventh day before the Octave of Easter. It is not certain whether the name *Quinquagesima* is due to the fact that the Sunday in question is the fiftieth day before Easter (reckoned inclusive) or was simply formed on the analogy of *Quadragesima* (*New English Dictionary*).

Palm Sunday, the Sunday before Easter and the beginning of Holy Week, commemorates the triumphal entry of Christ into Jerusalem and is celebrated in Britain (when palm is not available) by branches of willow gathered for use in the decoration of churches on that day.

Maundy Thursday, the day before Good Friday, the name itself being a corruption of *dies mandati* (day of the mandate) when Christ washed the feet of the disciples and gave them the mandate to love one another.

Easter-Day is the first Sunday after the full moon which happens upon, or next after, the 21st day of March; and if the full moon happens upon a Sunday, Easter-Day is the Sunday after. This definition is contained in an Act of Parliament (24 Geo. II., cap. 23), and explanation is given in the preamble to the Act that the day of Full Moon depends on certain tables that have been prepared. These are the tables whose essential points are given in the early pages of the Book of Common Prayer. The Moon referred to is not the real Moon of the heavens, but a hypothetical Moon on whose "Full" the date of Easter depends, and the lunations of this "Calendar" Moon consist of twenty-nine and thirty days alternately with certain necessary modifications to make the date of its Full agree as nearly as possible with that of the real Moon, which is known as the **Paschal Full Moon**. As at present ordained, Easter falls on one of 35 days—(March 22–April 25).

A Fixed Easter.—On June 15, 1928, the House of Commons agreed to a motion for the third reading of the Bill that Easter Day shall, in the Calendar year next but one after the commencement of the Act and in all subsequent years, be *the first Sunday after the second Saturday in April*. Easter would thus fall between April 9 and 15, both inclusive—that is, on the second or third Sunday in April. A clause in the Bill provided that before it shall come into operation regard shall be had to any opinion expressed officially by the various Christian Churches. Efforts by the World Council of Churches to secure a unanimous choice of date for Easter by its 239 member Churches have so far been unsuccessful.

Holy Days and Saints Days were the normal factors in early times for settling the dates of future and recurrent appointments, *e.g.* the **Quarter Days** in England and Wales are the Feast of the Nativity, the Feast of the Annunciation, the Feast of St. John the Baptist and the Feast of St. Michael and All the Holy Angels, while **Term Days** in Scotland are Candlemas (Feast of the Purification), Whitsunday (a fixed date), Lammas (Loaf Mass) and Martinmas (St. Martin's Day). **Law Sittings** in England and Wales commence on the Feast of St. Hilary and the term which begins on Old Michaelmas Day ends on the former feast of St. Thomas the Apostle.

The number of Saints commemorated in the Calendar of the Book of Common Prayer is 73, but (with the exception of All Saint's Day) "days" are appointed only for those whose names are mentioned in the Bible. **Red Letter Days** (*see also* p. 225) were Holy Days and Saints Days indicated in early ecclesiastical calendars by letters printed in red ink. The days to be distinguished in this way were finally approved at the Council of Nicaea, A.D. 325, and special services are set apart for them in the Book of Common Prayer.

Rogation Days.—These are the Monday, Tuesday and Wednesday preceding Ascension Day, "Holy Thursday", and in the fifth century were ordered by the Church to be observed as Public Fasts with solemn processions and supplications. The processions were discontinued as religious observances at the Reformation, but survive in the ceremony known as "Beating the Parish Bounds".

Ascension Day is forty days after Easter Day.

Ember Days.—The Ember Days at the Four Seasons are the Wednesday, Friday and Saturday before (1) the Third Sunday in Advent, (2) the Second Sunday in Lent, and (3) the Sundays nearest to the Festivals of St. Peter, and St. Michael and All Angels.

Whit Sunday (or Pentecost) is seven weeks after Easter Day. It is generally said that this name is a variant of White Sunday, and was so called from the albs or white robes of the newly baptized, but other derivations have been suggested. In the Roman Catholic Church Sundays are reckoned "after Pentecost".

Trinity Sunday is eight weeks after Easter Day, on the Sunday following Whit Sunday, and subsequent Sundays are reckoned in the Church of England as "after Trinity".

Thomas Becket (1118–1170) was consecrated Archbishop of Canterbury on the Sunday after Whit Sunday and his first act was to ordain that the day of his consecration should be held as a new festival in honour of the Holy Trinity. The observance thus originated spread from Canterbury throughout the whole of Christendom.

Advent Sunday is the Sunday nearest to St. Andrew's Day, Nov. 30, which allows three Sundays between Advent and Christmas Day in all cases. The Sunday preceding Advent is the 27th after Trinity if Easter falls on one of the days, March 22–26 inclusive. It is the 22nd after Trinity when Easter Day is on April 24 or 25. If the date of Easter were determined as proposed (*see Fixed Easter*) there would generally be 24 Sundays after Trinity, the number being 25 only in the years when Easter fell on April 9. With a Fixed Easter there would never be a sixth Sunday after Epiphany. There would be a fifth Sunday when Easter Day fell on April 15 or April 14, the year being a leap year.

A TABLE OF THE MOVABLE FEASTS TO THE YEAR 2000

Year	Ash Wednesday	Easter	Ascension	Whit Sunday	Sundays after Trinity	Advent
1980	Feb. 20	April 6	May 15	May 25	xxv	Nov. 30
1981	March 4	April 19	May 28	June 7	xxiii	Nov. 29
1982	Feb. 24	April 11	May 20	May 30	xxiv	Nov. 28
1983	Feb. 16	April 3	May 12	May 22	xxv	Nov. 27
1984	March 7	April 22	May 31	June 10	xxiii	Dec. 2
1985	Feb. 20	April 7	May 16	May 26	xxv	Dec. 1
1986	Feb. 12	March 30	May 8	May 18	xxvi	Nov. 30
1987	March 4	April 19	May 28	June 7	xxiii	Nov. 29
1988	Feb. 17	April 3	May 12	May 22	xxv	Nov. 27
1989	Feb. 8	March 26	May 4	May 14	xxvii	Dec. 3
1990	Feb. 28	April 15	May 24	June 3	xxiv	Dec. 2
1991	Feb. 13	March 31	May 9	May 19	xxvi	Dec. 1
1992	March 4	April 19	May 28	June 7	xxiii	Nov. 29
1993	Feb. 24	April 11	May 20	May 30	xxiv	Nov. 28
1994	Feb. 16	April 3	May 12	May 22	xxv	Nov. 27
1995	March 1	April 16	May 25	June 4	xxiv	Dec. 3
1996	Feb. 21	April 7	May 16	May 26	xxv	Dec. 1
1997	Feb. 12	March 30	May 8	May 18	xxvi	Nov. 30
1998	Feb. 25	April 12	May 21	May 31	xxiv	Nov. 29
1999	Feb. 17	April 4	May 13	May 23	xxv	Nov. 28
2000	March 8	April 23	June 1	June 11	xxiii	Dec. 3

NOTES CONCERNING TABLE OF MOVABLE FEASTS

Ash Wednesday (first day in *Lent*) can fall at earliest on February 4 and at latest on March 10.
Easter Day can fall at earliest on March 22 and at latest on April 25.
Ascension Day can fall at earliest on April 30 and at latest on June 3.
Whit Sunday can fall at earliest on May 10 and at latest on June 13.
Rogation Sunday is the Sunday next before *Holy Thursday* (Ascension Day).
Trinity Sunday is the Sunday next after *Whit Sunday*.
Corpus Christi falls on the Thursday next after *Trinity Sunday*.
There are not less than xxii and not more than xxvii *Sundays after Trinity*.
Advent Sunday is the Sunday nearest to November 30.

A TABLE OF EASTER DAYS AND SUNDAY LETTERS, 1500 TO 2025

		1500—1599	1600—1699	1700—1799	1800—1899	1900—1999	2000—2025
d	Mar. 22	1573	1668	1761	1818		
e	„ 23	1505-16	1600	1788	1845-56	1913	2008
f	„ 24		1611-95	1706-99		1940	
g	„ 25	1543-54	1627-38-49	1722-33-44	1883-94	1951	
A	„ 26	1559-70-81-92	1654-65-76	1749-58-69-80	1815-26-37	1967-78-89	
b	Mar. 27	1502-13-24-97	1608-87-92	1785-96	1842-53-64	1910-21-32	2005-16
c	„ 28	1529-35-40	1619-24-30	1703-14-25	1869-75-80	1937-48	
d	„ 29	1551-62	1635-46-57	1719-30-41-52	1807-12-91	1959-64-70	
e	„ 30	1567-78-89	1651-62-73-84	1746-55-66-77	1823-34	1902-75-86-97	
f	„ 31	1510-21-32-83-94	1605-16-78-89	1700-71-82-93	1839-50-61-72	1907-18-29-91	2002-13-24
g	April 1	1526-37-48	1621-32	1711-16	1804-66-77-88	1923-34-45-56	2018
A	„ 2	1553-64	1643-48	1727-38-52(NS)	1809-20-93-99	1961-72	
b	„ 3	1575-80-86	1659-70-81	1743-63-68-74	1825-31-36	1904-83-88-94	
c	„ 4	1507-18-91	1602-13-75-86-97	1708-79-90	1847-58	1915-20-26-99	2010-21
d	„ 5	1523-34-45-56	1607-18-29-40	1702-13-24-95	1801-63-74-85-96	1931-42-53	2015
e	April 6	1539-50-61-72	1634-45-56	1729-35-40-60	1806-17-28-90	1947-58-69-80	
f	„ 7	1504-77-88	1667-72	1751-65-76	1822-33-44	1901-12-85-96	
g	„ 8	1509-15-20-99	1604-10-83-94	1705-87-92-98	1849-55-60	1917-28	2007-12
A	„ 9	1531-42	1615-26-37-99	1710-21-32	1871-82	1939-44-50	2023
b	„ 10	1547-58-69	1631-42-53-64	1726-37-48-57	1803-14-87-98	1955-66-77	
c	April 11	1501-12-63-74-85-96	1658-69-80	1762-73-84	1819-30-41-52	1909-71-82-93	2004
d	„ 12	1506-17-28	1601-12-91-96	1789	1846-57-68	1903-14-25-36-98	2009-20
e	„ 13	1533-44	1623-28	1707-18	1800-73-79-84	1941-52	
f	„ 14	1555-60	1639-50-61	1723-34-45-54	1805-11-16-95	1963-68-74	
g	„ 15	1571-82-93	1655-66-77-88	1750-59-70-81	1827-38	1900-06-79-90	2001
A	April 16	1503-14-25-36-87-98	1609-20-82-93	1704-75-86-97	1843-54-65-76	1911-22-33-95	2006-17
b	„ 17	1530-41-52	1625-36	1715-20	1808-70-81-92	1927-38-49-60	2022
c	„ 18	1557-68	1647-52	1731-42-56	1802-13-24-97	1954-65-76	
d	„ 19	1500-79-84-90	1663-74-85	1747-67-72-78	1829-35-40	1908-81-87-92	
e	„ 20	1511-22-95	1606-17-79-90	1701-12-83-94	1851-62	1919-24-30	2003-14-25
f	April 21	1527-38-49	1622-33-44	1717-28	1867-78-89	1935-46-57	2019
g	„ 22	1565-76	1660	1739-53-64	1810-21-32	1962-73-84	
A	„ 23	1508	1671		1848	1905-16	2000
b	„ 24	1519	1603-14-98	1709-91	1859		2011
c	„ 25	1546	1641	1736	1886	1943	

THE JEWISH CALENDAR

Origin.—The story in the Book of Genesis that the Flood began on the seventeenth day of the second month; that after the end of 150 days the waters were abated; and that on the seventeenth day of the seventh month the Ark rested on Mount Ararat, indicates a calendar of some kind and that the writers recognized 30 days as the length of a lunation. There is other mention of months by their original numbers in the Book of Genesis and in establishing the rite of the Passover Moses spoke of *Abib* as the month when the Israelites came out from Egypt and Abib was to be the first month of the year. In the first Book of Kings three months are mentioned by name, Zif the second month, Ethanim the seventh and Bul the eighth, but these are not names now in use. After the Dispersion, Jewish communities were left in considerable doubt as to the times of Fasts and Festivals, and this led to the formation of the Jewish Calendar as used to-day, which, it is said, was done in A.D. 358 by Rabbi Hillel II, a descendant of Gamaliel—though some assert that it did not happen until much later. This calendar is luni-solar, and is based on the lengths of the lunation and of the tropical year as found by Hipparchus (*Circ.* 120 B.C.)

which differ little from those adopted at the present day. The year 5746 A.D. (1985–86) is the 8th year of the 303rd *Metonic* (Minor or Lunar) *Cycle* of 19 years and the 6th year of the 206th *Solar* (or Major) *Cycle* of 28 years since the Era of the Creation, which the Jews hold to have occurred at the time of the Autumnal Equinox in the year known in the Christian Calendar as 3760 B.C. (954 of the Julian Period) and the epoch or starting point of Jewish Chronology corresponds to Oct. 7, 3761 B.C. At the beginning of each Solar Cycle the *Teku ah* of Nisan (the vernal equinox) returns to the same day and to the same hour.

The hour is divided into 1080 *minims* and the month between one new moon and the next is reckoned as 29 days, 12 hours, 793 minims. The normal calendar year, called a Common Regular year, consists of 12 months of 30 days and 29 days alternately. Since 12 months such as these comprise only 354 days, in order that each of them shall not diverge greatly from an average place in the solar year, a thirteenth month is occasionally added after the fifth month of the Civil year (which commences on the first day of the month Tishri), or as the penultimate month of the Ecclesiastical (which commences on the first day of month Nisan), the years when this happens being called Embolismic. Of the 19 years that form a Metonic cycle, 7 are embolismic; they occur at places in the cycle indicated by the numbers 3, 6, 8, 11, 14, 17, 19, these places being chosen so that the accumulated excesses of the solar years should be as small as possible. The first of each month is called the day of New Moon, though it is not necessarily the day of astronomical New Moon, that being the day on which conjunction of Sun and Moon occurs, but there is generally a difference of a day or two. In practice, in a month which follows one of 30 days, the day preceding its first day is also observed as a day of New Moon. The dates in the Christian calendar of the first days of the months depend on that of the first of Tishri, which therefore controls the dates of fasts and festivals in the Jewish year. For certain ceremonial reasons connected with these, the first of Tishri must not fall on a Sunday, Wednesday or Friday, and if this should happen as the result of the computation it is postponed to the next day in the Christian calendar. Also, if the New Moon of Tishri falls on any day of the week at noon or later than noon, then the following day is to be taken for the celebration of that New Moon and is Tishri 1, provided that it is not one of the forbidden days, in which case there is a further postponement of a day. These rules and others have been considered in detail, and finally a calendar scheme has been drawn up in which a Jewish year is of one of the following six types: Common Deficient (353 days), Common Regular (354 days), Common Abundant (355 days), Embolismic Deficient (383 days), Embolismic Regular (384 days), or Embolismic Abundant (385 days).

The Regular year has an alternation of 30 and 29 days. In an Abundant year, whether Common or Embolismic, Marcheshvan, the second month of the Civil year, has 30 days instead of 29; in Deficient years Kislev, the third month, has 29 instead of 30. The additional month in Embolismic years which is called Adar I., and precedes the month called Adar in Common years and Adar II., or Ve-Adar, in Embolismic, always has 30 days, but neither this, nor the other variations mentioned, is allowed to change the number of days in the other months which still follow the alternation of the normal twelve. In Embolismic years the month intercalated precedes Adar and usurps its name, but the usual Adar festivals are kept in Ve-Adar.

These are the main features of the Jewish Calendar which must be considered permanent, because as a Jewish law it cannot be altered except by a great Synhedrion.

The Jewish day begins between sunset and nightfall. The time used is that of the meridian of Jerusalem, which is 2h. 21m. in advance of Greenwich Mean Time. Rules for the beginning of Sabbaths and Festivals were laid down for the latitude of London in the eighteenth century and hours for nightfall are now fixed annually by the Chief Rabbi.

Jewish Calendar 5746–47

Jewish Month				A.M. 5746				A.M. 5747	
Tishri	1 ..	..	..	1985 September	16	..	..	1986 October	4
Marcheshvan	1 ..	..	..	October	16	..	..	November	3
Kislev	1 ..	..	..	November	14	..	..	December	3
Tebet	1 ..	..	..	December	13	..	..	1987 January	2
Shebat	1 ..	..	..	1986 January	11	..	..	January	31
Adar	1 ..	..	..	February	10	..	..	March	2
Ve-Adar	1 ..	..	..	March	12				
Nisan	1 ..	..	..	April	10	..	..	March	31
Iyar	1 ..	..	..	May	10	..	..	April	30
Sivan	1 ..	..	..	June	8	..	..	May	29
Tammuz	1 ..	..	..	July	8	..	..	June	28
Ab	1 ..	..	..	August	6	..	..	July	27
Elul	1 ..	..	..	September	5	..	..	August	26

A.M. 5746 (746) is an Embolismic Deficient Year of 13 months, 52 Sabbaths and 383 days. A.M. 5747 (747) is a Common Abundant Year of 12 months, 51 Sabbaths and 355 days.

Jewish Fasts and Festivals

Tishri	1	Rosh Hoshanah (New Year).	*Tebet*	10	Fast of Tebet.
,,	3	*Fast of Gedaliah.	*Adar*	13	§Fast of Esther.
,,	10	Yom Kippur (Day of Atonement).	,,	14	Purim.
,,	15–22	Succoth (Feast of Tabernacles).	,,	15	Shushan Purim.
,,	21	Hoshana Rabba.	*Nisan*	15–21	Passover.
,,	22	Solemn Assembly.	*Sivan*	6 and 7	Shavuot (Pentecost or Feast of Weeks).
,,	23	Rejoicing of the Law.	*Tammuz*	17	*Fast of Tammuz.
Kislev	25	Dedication of the Temple	*Ab*	9	*Fast of Ab.

NOTES.—* If these dates fall on the Sabbath the Fast is kept on the following day.

§ This fast is observed on Adar 11 (or Ve-Adar 11 in Embolismic years) if Adar 13 falls on a Sabbath.

THE ROMAN CALENDAR

Roman historians adopted as an epoch the Foundation of Rome, which is believed to have happened in the year 753 B.C., and the ordinal number of the years in Roman reckoning is followed by the letters A.U.C. (*Ab Urbe Condita*), so that the year 1986 is 2739 A.U.C. (MMDCCXXXIX). The Calendar that we know has developed from one established by Romulus, who is said to have used a year of 304 days divided into ten months, beginning with March, to which Numa added January and February, making the year consist of 12 months of 30 and 29 days alternately, with an additional day so that the total was 355. It is also said that Numa ordered an intercalary month of 22 or 23 days in alternate years, making 90 days in eight years, to be inserted after Feb. 23, but there is some doubt as to the origination and the details of the intercalation in the Roman Calendar, though it is certain that some scheme of this kind was inaugurated and not fully carried out, for in the year 46 B.C. Julius Cæsar, who was then Pontifex Maximus, found that the Calendar had been allowed to fall into some confusion. He therefore sought the help of the Egyptian astronomer Sosigenes, which led to the construction and adoption (45 B.C.) of the Julian Calendar, and, by a slight alteration, to the Gregorian now in use. The year 46 B.C. was made to consist of 445 days, and is called the *Year of Confusion*. In the Roman (Julian) Calendar the days of the month were counted backwards from three fixed points, or days, and an intervening day was said to be so many days *before* the next coming point, the first *and* last being counted. These three points were (1) the Kalends; (2) the Nones; and (3) the Ides. Their positions in the months and the method of counting from them will be seen in the table below. The year containing 366 days was called *bissextillis annus*, as it had a doubled sixth day (*bissextus dies*) before the March Kalends on Feb. 24—*ante diem sextum Kalendas Martias*, or VI Kal. Mart.

Present Days of the Month	March, May, July, October have thirty-one days	January, August, December have thirty-one days	April, June, September, November have thirty days	February has twenty-eight days, and in Leap Year twenty-nine
1	Kalendis.	Kalendis.	Kalendis.	Kalendis.
2	VI.⎱	IV.⎱ Ante	IV.⎱ Ante	IV.⎱ Ante
3	V.⎰ Ante	III.⎰ Nonas.	III.⎰ Nonas.	III.⎰ Nonas.
4	IV.⎰ Nonas.	Pridie Nonas.	Pridie Nonas.	Pridie Nonas.
5	III.⎰	Nonis.	Nonis.	Nonis.
6	Pridie Nonas.	VIII.⎱	VIII.⎱	VIII.⎱
7	Nonis.	VII.	VII.	VII.
8	VIII.⎱	VI. ⎰ Ante	VI. ⎰ Ante.	VI. ⎰ Ante
9	VII.	V. ⎰ Idus.	V. ⎰ Idus.	V. ⎰ Idus.
10	VI. ⎰ Ante	IV.	IV.	IV.
11	V. ⎰ Idus.	III.⎰	III.⎰	III.⎰
12	IV.⎰	Pridie Idus.	Pridie Idus.	Pridie Idus.
13	III.⎰	Idibus.	Idibus.	Idibus.
14	Pridie Idus.	XIX.⎱	XVIII.⎱	XVI.⎱
15	Idibus.	XVIII.	XVII.	XV.
16	XVII.⎱	XVII.	XVI.	XIV.
17	XVI.	XVI.	XV.	XIII.
18	XV.	XV.	XIV.	XII.
19	XIV. ⎰ (of the month	XIV. ⎰ (of the month	XIII. ⎰ (of the Month	XI.
20	XIII. ⎰ following).	XIII. ⎰ following).	XII. ⎰ following).	X. ⎰ Ante Kalendas Martias.
21	XII.	XII.	XI.	IX.
22	XI. ⎰ Ante Kalendas	XI. ⎰ Ante Kalendas	X. ⎰ Ante Kalendas	VIII.
23	X.	X.	IX.	VII.
24	IX.	IX.	VIII.	VI.⎰
25	VIII.	VIII.	VII.	V.
26	VII.	VII.	VI.	IV.
27	VI.	VI.	V.	III.⎰
28	V.	V.	IV.	Pridie Kalendas Martias.
29	IV.	IV.⎰	III.⎰	
30	III.⎰		Pridie Kalendas (of the month following).	
31	Pridie Kalendas (of the month following).	Pridie Kalendas (of the month following).		

ROMAN NUMERALS

1	I	9	IX	17	XVII	70	LXX
2	II	10	X	18	XVIII	80	LXXX
3	III	11	XI	19	XIX	90	XC
4	IV	12	XII	20	XX	100	C
5	V	13	XIII	30	XXX	200	CC
6	VI	14	XIV	40	XL	300	CCC
7	VII	15	XV	50	L	400	CD
8	VIII	16	XVI	60	LX	500	D

600	DC
700	DCC
800	DCCC
900	CM
1000	M
1500	MD
1900	MCM
2000	MM

Other Examples: 43 = XLIII; 66 = LXVI; 98 = XCVIII.
339 = CCCXXXIX; 619 = DCXIX; 988 = CMLXXXVIII; 996 = CMXCVI.
1674 = MDCLXXIV; 1962 = MCMLXII.

A bar placed over a numeral has the effect of multiplying the number by 1,000, *e.g.*:

6,000 = V̄I; 16,000 = X̄V̄I; 160,000 = C̄LX; 666,000 = D̄C̄L̄X̄V̄I.

THE MOSLEM CALENDAR

The basic date of the Moslem Calendar is the *Hejira*, or Flight of Muhammad from Mecca to Medina, the corresponding date of which is A.D. 622, July 16, in the Julian Calendar. Hejira years are used principally in Iran, Turkey, Arabia, Egypt, in certain parts of India and in Malaya. The system was adopted about A.D. 632, commencing from the first day of the month preceding the Hejira. The years are purely lunar and consist of 12 months containing in alternate sequence 30 or 29 days, with the intercalation of one day at the end of the 12th month at stated intervals in each cycle of 30 years, the object of the intercalation being to reconcile the date of the first of the month with the date of the actual New Moon. Some adherents still take the date of the evening of the first visibility of the crescent as that of the first of the month. In each cycle of 30 years 19 are common and contain 354 days and 11 are intercalary (355 days), the latter being called *kabishah*.

The mean length of the Hejira year is 354 days, 8 hours, 48 minutes and the period of mean lunation is 29 days, 12 hours, 44 minutes.

To ascertain if a Hejira year is common or *kabishah* divide it by 30; the quotient gives the number of completed cycles and the remainder shows the place of the year in the current cycle. If the remainder is 2, 5, 7, 10, 13, 16, 18, 21, 24, 26 or 29 the year is *kabishah* and consists of 355 days.

Hejira year A.H. 1406 (remainder 26) is a *Kabishah* year; A.H. 1407 (remainder 27) is a common year.

Hejira Years 1406 and 1407

Name and Length of Month	A.H. 1406		A.H. 1407	
Muharram (30)	1985 Sept.	16	1986 Sept.	6
Safar (29)	Oct.	16	Oct.	6
Rabìa I (30)	Nov.	14	Nov.	4
Rabìa II (29)	Dec.	14	Dec.	4
Jumâda I (30)	1986 Jan.	12	1987 Jan.	2
Jumâda II (29)	Feb.	11	Feb.	1
Rajab (30)	Mar.	12	Mar.	2
Shaabân (29)	April	11	April	1
Ramadân (30)	May	10	April	30
Shawwâl (29)	June	9	May	30
Dhù'l-Qa'da (30)	July	8	June	28
Dhù'l-Hijja (29 or 30)	Aug.	7	July	28

OTHER EPOCHS AND CALENDARS

China.—Until the year A.D. 1911 a Lunar Calendar was in force in China, but with the establishment of the Republic the Government adopted the Gregorian Calendar, and the new and old systems were used simultaneously by the people for several years. Since 1930 the publication and use of the old Calendar have been banned by the Government, and an official Chinese Calendar, corresponding with the European or Western system, is compiled, but the old Lunar Calendar is still in use to some extent in China. The old Chinese Calendar, with a cycle of 60 years, is still in use in Tibet, Hong Kong, Singapore, Malaysia and elsewhere in South-East Asia.

Ethiopia.—In the Coptic Calendar, which is used by part of the population of Egypt and Ethiopia, the year is made up of 12 months of 30 days each, followed, in general, by 5 complementary days. Every fourth year is an Intercalary or Leap year and in these years there are 6 complementary days. The Intercalary year of the Coptic Calendar immediately precedes the Leap year of the Julian Calendar. The Era is that of Diocletian or the Martyrs, the origin of which is fixed at A.D. 284, Aug. 29 (Julian date).

Greece.—Ancient Greek chronology was reckoned in *Olympiads*, cycles of 4 years corresponding with the periodic Olympic Games held on the plain of Olympia in Elis once in 4 years, the intervening years being the first, second, etc., of the Olympiad which received the name of the victor at the Games. The first recorded Olympiad is that of Choroebus, 776 B.C.

India.—In addition to the Moslem reckoning there are six eras used in India. The principal astronomical system was the *Kaliyuga Era*, which appears to have been adopted in the fourth century A.D. It began on Feb. 18, 3102 B.C. The chronological system of Northern India, known as the *Vikrama Samvat Era*, prevalent in Western India, began on Feb. 23, 57 B.C. The year A.D. 1986 is, therefore, the year 2043 of the Vikrama Era.

The *Saka Era* of Southern India dating from March 3, A.D. 78, was declared the uniform national calendar of the Republic of India with effect from March 22, 1957, to be used concurrently with the Gregorian Calendar. As revised, the year of the new *Saka Era*

begins at the spring equinox, with five successive months of 31 days and seven of 30 days in ordinary years; six months of each length in leap years. The year A.D. 1986 is 1908 of the revised *Saka Era*.

In the Hills, the *Saptarshi Era* dates from the moment when the Saptarshi, or saints, were translated and became the stars of the Great Bear in 3076 B.C.

The *Buddhists* reckoned from the death of Buddha in 543 B.C. (the actual date being 487 B.C.); and the epoch of the *Jains* was the death of Vardhamana, the founder of their faith, in 527 B.C.

Iran.—The chronology of Iran (Persia) is the Era of Hejira, which began on A.D. 622, July 16. The *Zoroastrian Calendar* was used in pre-Moslem days and is still employed by Zoroastrians in Iran and India (Parsees) with era beginning A.D. 632, June 16.

Japan.—The Japanese Calendar is the Gregorian, and is essentially the same as that in use by Western nations, the years, months and weeks being of the same length and beginning on the same days as those of the Western Calendar. The numeration of the years is different, for Japanese chronology is based on a system of epochs or periods, each of which begins at the accession of an Emperor or other important occurrence, the method being not unlike the former British system of Regnal years, but differing from it in the particular that each year of a period closes on Dec. 31. The Japanese scheme begins about A.D. 650 and the three latest epochs are defined by the reigns of Emperors, whose actual names are not necessarily used:

Epoch Meiji from 1868 Oct. 13 to 1912 July 31

    ,,   Taishō ,, 1912 Aug. 1 to 1926 Dec. 25

    ,,   Shōwa ,, 1926 Dec. 26

Hence the year Shōwa 61 begins 1986 Jan. 1. The months are not named. They are known as First Month, Second Month, etc., first month being the equivalent to January. The days of the week are Nichiyōbi (Sun-day), Getsuyōbi (Moon-day), Kayōbi (Fire-day), Suiyōbi (Water-day), Mokuyōbi (Wood-day), Kinyōbi (Metal-day), Doyōbi (Earth-day).

EASY REFERENCE CALENDAR [1986

for any year between 1770 and 2025 together with the dates of Easter in each of those years
TO SELECT THE CORRECT CALENDAR FOR ANY YEAR consult the INDEX below

INDEX TO CALENDARS

Year		Year		Year		Year		Year		Year	
1770	C	1813	K	1856	F*	1899	A	1942	I	1984	B*
1771	E	1814	M	1857	I	1900	C	1943	K	1985	E
1772	H*	1815	A	1858	K	1901	E	1944	N*	1986	G
1773	K	1816	D*	1859	M	1902	G	1945	C	1987	I
1774	M	1817	G	1860	B*	1903	I	1946	E	1988	L*
1775	A	1818	I	1861	E	1904	L*	1947	G	1989	A
1776	D*	1819	K	1862	G	1905	A	1948	J*	1990	C
1777	G	1820	N*	1863	I	1906	C	1949	M	1991	E
1778	I	1821	C	1864	L*	1907	E	1950	A	1992	H*
1779	K	1822	E	1865	A	1908	H*	1951	C	1993	K
1780	N*	1823	G	1866	C	1909	K	1952	F*	1994	M
1781	C	1824	J*	1867	E	1910	M	1953	I	1995	A
1782	E	1825	M	1868	H*	1911	A	1954	K	1996	D*
1783	G	1826	A	1869	K	1912	D*	1955	M	1997	G
1784	J*	1827	C	1870	M	1913	G	1956	B*	1998	I
1785	M	1828	F*	1871	A	1914	I	1957	E	1999	K
1786	A	1829	I	1872	D*	1915	K	1958	G	2000	N*
1787	C	1830	K	1873	G	1916	N*	1959	I	2001	C
1788	F*	1831	M	1874	I	1917	C	1960	L*	2002	E
1789	I	1832	B*	1875	K	1918	E	1961	A	2003	G
1790	K	1833	E	1876	N*	1919	G	1962	C	2004	J*
1791	M	1834	G	1877	C	1920	J*	1963	E	2005	A
1792	B*	1835	I	1878	E	1921	M	1964	H*	2006	C
1793	E	1836	L*	1879	G	1922	A	1965	K	2007	C
1794	G	1837	A	1880	J*	1923	C	1966	M	2008	F*
1795	I	1838	C	1881	M	1924	F*	1967	A	2009	I
1796	L*	1839	E	1882	A	1925	I	1968	D*	2010	K
1797	A	1840	H*	1883	C	1926	K	1969	G	2011	M
1798	C	1841	K	1884	F*	1927	M	1970	I	2012	B*
1799	E	1842	M	1885	I	1928	B*	1971	K	2013	E
1800	G	1843	A	1886	K	1929	E	1972	N*	2014	G
1801	I	1844	D*	1887	M	1930	G	1973	C	2015	I
1802	K	1845	G	1888	B*	1931	I	1974	E	2016	L*
1803	M	1846	I	1889	E	1932	L*	1975	G	2017	A
1804	B*	1847	K	1890	G	1933	A	1976	J*	2018	C
1805	E	1848	N*	1891	I	1934	C	1977	M	2019	E
1806	G	1849	C	1892	L*	1935	E	1978	A	2020	H*
1807	I	1850	E	1893	A	1936	H*	1979	C	2021	K
1808	L*	1851	G	1894	C	1937	K	1980	F*	2022	M
1809	C	1852	J*	1895	E	1938	M	1981	I	2023	A
1810	C	1853	M	1896	H*	1939	A	1982	K	2024	D*
1811	E	1854	A	1897	K	1940	D*	1983	M	2025	G
1812	H*	1855	C	1898	M	1941	G				

* Leap Year

A

January
```
Su. ..  1  8 15 22 29
M. ..   2  9 16 23 30
Tu. ..  3 10 17 24 31
W. ..   4 11 18 25
Th. ..  5 12 19 26
F. ..   6 13 20 27
S. ..   7 14 21 28
```

May
```
Su ...     7 14 21 28
M. ..   1  8 15 22 29
Tu. ..  2  9 16 23 30
W. ..   3 10 17 24 31
Th. ..  4 11 18 25
F. ..   5 12 19 26
S. ..   6 13 20 27
```

September
```
Su. ..  3 10 17 24
M. ..   4 11 18 25
Tu. ..  5 12 19 26
W. ..   6 13 20 27
Th. ..  7 14 21 28
F. ..   1  8 15 22 29
S. ..   2  9 16 23 30
```

February
```
Su. ..  5 12 19 26
M. ..   6 13 20 27
Tu. ..  7 14 21 28
W. ..   1  8 15 22
Th. ..  2  9 16 23
F. ..   3 10 17 24
S. ..   4 11 18 25
```

June
```
Su. ..  4 11 18 25
M. ..   5 12 19 26
Tu. ..  6 13 20 27
W. ..   7 14 21 28
Th. ..  1  8 15 22 29
F. ..   2  9 16 23 30
S. ..   3 10 17 24
```

October
```
Su. ..  1  8 15 22 29
M. ..   2  9 16 23 30
Tu. ..  3 10 17 24 31
W. ..   4 11 18 25
Th. ..  5 12 19 26
F. ..   6 13 20 27
S. ..   7 14 21 28
```

March
```
Su. ..  5 12 19 26
M. ..   6 13 20 27
Tu. ..  7 14 21 28
W. ..   1  8 15 22 29
Th. ..  2  9 16 23 30
F. ..   3 10 17 24 31
S. ..   4 11 18 25
```

July
```
Su. ..  2  9 16 23 30
M. ..   3 10 17 24 31
Tu. ..  4 11 18 25
W. ..   5 12 19 26
Th. ..  6 13 20 27
F. ..   7 14 21 28
S. ..   1  8 15 22 29
```

November
```
Su. ..  5 12 19 26
M. ..   6 13 20 27
Tu. ..  7 14 21 28
W. ..   1  8 15 22 29
Th. ..  2  9 16 23 30
F. ..   3 10 17 24
S. ..   4 11 18 25
```

April
```
Su. ..  2  9 16 23 30
M. ..   3 10 17 24
Tu. ..  4 11 18 25
W. ..   5 12 19 26
Th. ..  6 13 20 27
F. ..   7 14 21 28
S. ..   1  8 15 22 29
```

August
```
Su. ..  6 13 20 27
M. ..   7 14 21 28
Tu. ..  1  8 15 22 29
W. ..   2  9 16 23 30
Th. ..  3 10 17 24 31
F. ..   4 11 18 25
S. ..   5 12 19 26
```

December
```
Su. ..  3 10 17 24 31
M. ..   4 11 18 25
Tu. ..  5 12 19 26
W. ..   6 13 20 27
Th. ..  7 14 21 28
F. ..   1  8 15 22 29
S. ..   2  9 16 23 30
```

B (Leap year)

January
```
Su. ..  1  8 15 22 29
M. ..   2  9 16 23 30
Tu. ..  3 10 17 24 31
W. ..   4 11 18 25
Th. ..  5 12 19 26
F. ..   6 13 20 27
S. ..   7 14 21 28
```

May
```
Su. ..  6 13 20 27
M. ..   7 14 21 28
Tu. ..  1  8 15 22 29
W. ..   2  9 16 23 30
Th. ..  3 10 17 24 31
F. ..   4 11 18 25
S. ..   5 12 19 26
```

September
```
Su. ..  2  9 16 23 30
M. ..   3 10 17 24
Tu. ..  4 11 18 25
W. ..   5 12 19 26
Th. ..  6 13 20 27
F. ..   7 14 21 28
S. ..   1  8 15 22 29
```

February
```
Su. ..  5 12 19 26
M. ..   6 13 20 27
Tu ..   7 14 21 28
W. ..   1  8 15 22 29
Th. ..  2  9 16 23
F. ..   3 10 17 24
S. ..   4 11 18 25
```

June
```
Su. ..  3 10 17 24
M. ..   4 11 18 25
Tu. ..  5 12 19 26
W. ..   6 13 20 27
Th. ..  7 14 21 28
F. ..   1  8 15 22 29
S. ..   2  9 16 23 30
```

October
```
Su. ..  7 14 21 28
M. ..   1  8 15 22 29
Tu. ..  2  9 16 23 30
W. ..   3 10 17 24 31
Th. ..  4 11 18 25
F. ..   5 12 19 26
S. ..   6 13 20 27
```

March
```
Su. ..  4 11 18 25
M. ..   5 12 19 26
Tu. ..  6 13 20 27
W. ..   7 14 21 28
Th. ..  1  8 15 22 29
F. ..   2  9 16 23 30
S. ..   3 10 17 24 31
```

July
```
Su. ..  1  8 15 22 29
M. ..   2  9 16 23 30
Tu. ..  3 10 17 24 31
W. ..   4 11 18 25
Th. ..  5 12 19 26
F. ..   6 13 20 27
S. ..   7 14 21 28
```

November
```
Su. ..  4 11 18 25
M. ..   5 12 19 26
Tu. ..  6 13 20 27
W. ..   7 14 21 28
Th. ..  1  8 15 22 29
F. ..   2  9 16 23 30
S. ..   3 10 17 24
```

April
```
Su. ..  1  8 15 22 29
M. ..   2  9 16 23 30
Tu. ..  3 10 17 24
W. ..   4 11 18 25
Th. ..  5 12 19 26
F. ..   6 13 20 27
S. ..   7 14 21 28
```

August
```
Su. ..  5 12 19 26
M. ..   6 13 20 27
Tu. ..  7 14 21 28
W. ..   1  8 15 22 29
Th. ..  2  9 16 23 30
F. ..   3 10 17 24 31
S. ..   4 11 18 25
```

December
```
Su. ..  2  9 16 23 30
M. ..   3 10 17 24 31
Tu. ..  4 11 18 25
W. ..   5 12 19 26
Th. ..  6 13 20 27
F. ..   7 14 21 28
S. ..   1  8 15 22 29
```

Easter Days

March 26.	1815	1826	1837	1967	1978	1989.
April 2.	1809	1893	1899	1961.		
April 9.	1871	1882	1939	1950	2023.	
April 16.	1775	1786	1797	1843	1854	1865	1911
April 23.	1905.	[1922	1933	1995	2006	2017.

Easter Days

April 1.	1804	1888	1956.
April 8.	1792	1860	1928	2012.
April 22.	1832	1984.	

C

Day	January	May	September
Su	7 14 21 28	6 13 20 27	2 9 16 23 30
M	1 8 15 22 29	7 14 21 28	3 10 17 24
Tu	2 9 16 23 30	1 8 15 22 29	4 11 18 25
W	3 10 17 24 31	2 9 16 23 30	5 12 19 26
Th	4 11 18 25	3 10 17 24 31	6 13 20 27
F	5 12 19 26	4 11 18 25	7 14 21 28
S	6 13 20 27	5 12 19 26	1 8 15 22 29

Day	February	June	October
Su	4 11 18 25	3 10 17 24	7 14 21 28
M	5 12 19 26	4 11 18 25	1 8 15 22 29
Tu	6 13 20 27	5 12 19 26	2 9 16 23 30
W	7 14 21 28	6 13 20 27	3 10 17 24 31
Th	1 8 15 22	7 14 21 28	4 11 18 25
F	2 9 16 23	1 8 15 22 29	5 12 19 26
S	3 10 17 24	2 9 16 23 30	6 13 20 27

Day	March	July	November
Su	4 11 18 25	1 8 15 22 29	4 11 18 25
M	5 12 19 26	2 9 16 23 30	5 12 19 26
Tu	6 13 20 27	3 10 17 24 31	6 13 20 27
W	7 14 21 28	4 11 18 25	7 14 21 28
Th	1 8 15 22 29	5 12 19 26	1 8 15 22 29
F	2 9 16 23 30	6 13 20 27	2 9 16 23 30
S	3 10 17 24 31	7 14 21 28	3 10 17 24

Day	April	August	December
Su	8 15 22 29	12 19 26	2 9 16 23 30
M	2 9 16 23 30	6 13 20 27	3 10 17 24 31
Tu	3 10 17 24	7 14 21 28	4 11 18 25
W	4 11 18 25	1 8 15 22 29	5 12 19 26
Th	5 12 19 26	2 9 16 23 30	6 13 20 27
F	6 13 20 27	3 10 17 24 31	7 14 21 28
S	7 14 21 28	4 11 18 25	1 8 15 22 29

Easter Days

March 25.	1883	1894	1951.		
April 1.	1866	1877	1923	1934 1945	2018.
April 8.	1787	1798	1849	1855 1900	2007.
April 15.	1770	1781	1827	1838 1900 1906	1979
April 22.	1810	1821	1962	1973.	[1990 2001.

D (Leap year)

Day	January	May	September
Su	7 14 21 28	5 12 19 26	1 8 15 22 29
M	1 8 15 22 29	6 13 20 27	2 9 16 23 30
Tu	2 9 16 23 30	7 14 21 28	3 10 17 24
W	3 10 17 24 31	1 8 15 22 29	4 11 18 25
Th	4 11 18 25	2 9 16 23 30	5 12 19 26
F	5 12 19 26	3 10 17 24 31	6 13 20 27
S	6 13 20 27	4 11 18 25	7 14 21 28

Day	February	June	October
Su	4 11 18 25	2 9 16 23 30	6 13 20 27
M	5 12 19 26	3 10 17 24	7 14 21 28
Tu	6 13 20 27	4 11 18 25	1 8 15 22 29
W	7 14 21 28	5 12 19 26	2 9 16 23 30
Th	1 8 15 22 29	6 13 20 27	3 10 17 24 31
F	2 9 16 23	7 14 21 28	4 11 18 25
S	3 10 17 24	1 8 15 22 29	5 12 19 26

Day	March	July	November
Su	3 10 17 24 31	7 14 21 28	3 10 17 24
M	4 11 18 25	1 8 15 22 29	4 11 18 25
Tu	5 12 19 26	2 9 16 23 30	5 12 19 26
W	6 13 20 27	3 10 17 24 31	6 13 20 27
Th	7 14 21 28	4 11 18 25	7 14 21 28
F	1 8 15 22 29	5 12 19 26	1 8 15 22 29
S	2 9 16 23 30	6 13 20 27	2 9 16 23 30

Day	April	August	December
Su	7 14 21 28	4 11 18 25	1 8 15 22 29
M	1 8 15 22 29	5 12 19 26	2 9 16 23 30
Tu	2 9 16 23 30	6 13 20 27	3 10 17 24 31
W	3 10 17 24	7 14 21 28	4 11 18 25
Th	4 11 18 25	1 8 15 22 29	5 12 19 26
F	5 12 19 26	2 9 16 23 30	6 13 20 27
S	6 13 20 27	3 10 17 24 31	7 14 21 28

Easter Days

March 24.	1940.			
March 31.	1872	2024.		
April 7.	1776	1844	1912	1996.
April 14.	1816	1968.		

E

Day	January	May	September
Su	6 13 20 27	5 12 19 26	1 8 15 22 29
M	7 14 21 28	6 13 20 27	2 9 16 23 30
Tu	1 8 15 22 29	7 14 21 28	3 10 17 24
W	2 9 16 23 30	1 8 15 22 29	4 11 18 25
Th	3 10 17 24 31	2 9 16 23 30	5 12 19 26
F	4 11 18 25	3 10 17 24 31	6 13 20 27
S	5 12 19 26	4 11 18 25	7 14 21 28

Day	February	June	October
Su	3 10 17 24	2 9 16 23 30	6 13 20 27
M	4 11 18 25	3 10 17 24	7 14 21 28
Tu	5 12 19 26	4 11 18 25	1 8 15 22 29
W	6 13 20 27	5 12 19 26	2 9 16 23 30
Th	7 14 21 28	6 13 20 27	3 10 17 24 31
F	1 8 15 22	7 14 21 28	4 11 18 25
S	2 9 16 23	1 8 15 22 29	5 12 19 26

Day	March	July	November
Su	3 10 17 24 31	7 14 21 28	3 10 17 24
M	4 11 18 25	1 8 15 22 29	4 11 18 25
Tu	5 12 19 26	2 9 16 23 30	5 12 19 26
W	6 13 20 27	3 10 17 24 31	6 13 20 27
Th	7 14 21 28	4 11 18 25	7 14 21 28
F	1 8 15 22 29	5 12 19 26	1 8 15 22 29
S	2 9 16 23 30	6 13 20 27	2 9 16 23 30

Day	April	August	December
Su	7 14 21 28	4 11 18 25	1 8 15 22 29
M	1 8 15 22 29	5 12 19 26	2 9 16 23 30
Tu	2 9 16 23 30	6 13 20 27	3 10 17 24 31
W	3 10 17 24	7 14 21 28	4 11 18 25
Th	4 11 18 25	1 8 15 22 29	5 12 19 26
F	5 12 19 26	2 9 16 23 30	6 13 20 27
S	6 13 20 27	3 10 17 24 31	7 14 21 28

Easter Days

March 24.	1799.		[1918	1929	1991 2002	2013.
March 31.	1771	1782	1793	1839 1850	1861	1907
April 7.	1822	1833	1901	1985.		
April 14.	1805	1811	1895	1963	1974.	
April 21.	1867	1878	1889	1935 1946	1957	2019.

F (Leap year)

Day	January	May	September
Su	6 13 20 27	4 11 18 25	7 14 21 28
M	7 14 21 28	5 12 19 26	1 8 15 22 29
Tu	1 8 15 22 29	6 13 20 27	2 9 16 23 30
W	2 9 16 23 30	7 14 21 28	3 10 17 24
Th	3 10 17 24 31	1 8 15 22 29	4 11 18 25
F	4 11 18 25	2 9 16 23 30	5 12 19 26
S	5 12 19 26	3 10 17 24 31	6 13 20 27

Day	February	June	October
Su	3 10 17 24	1 8 15 22 29	5 12 19 26
M	4 11 18 25	2 9 16 23 30	6 13 20 27
Tu	5 12 19 26	3 10 17 24	7 14 21 28
W	6 13 20 27	4 11 18 25	1 8 15 22 29
Th	7 14 21 28	5 12 19 26	2 9 16 23 30
F	1 8 15 22 29	6 13 20 27	3 10 17 24 31
S	2 9 16 23	7 14 21 28	4 11 18 25

Day	March	July	November
Su	2 9 16 23 30	6 13 20 27	2 9 16 23 30
M	3 10 17 24 31	7 14 21 28	3 10 17 24
Tu	4 11 18 25	1 8 15 22 29	4 11 18 25
W	5 12 19 26	2 9 16 23 30	5 12 19 26
Th	6 13 20 27	3 10 17 24 31	6 13 20 27
F	7 14 21 28	4 11 18 25	7 14 21 28
S	1 8 15 22 29	5 12 19 26	1 8 15 22 29

Day	April	August	December
Su	6 13 20 27	3 10 17 24 31	7 14 21 28
M	7 14 21 28	4 11 18 25	1 8 15 22 29
Tu	1 8 15 22 29	5 12 19 26	2 9 16 23 30
W	2 9 16 23 30	6 13 20 27	3 10 17 24 31
Th	3 10 17 24	7 14 21 28	4 11 18 25
F	4 11 18 25	1 8 15 22 29	5 12 19 26
S	5 12 19 26	2 9 16 23 30	6 13 20 27

Easter Days

March 23.	1788	1856	2008.
April 6.	1828	1980.	
April 13.	1884	1952.	
April 20.	1924.		

G

	January	May	September
Su.	5 12 19 26	4 11 18 25	7 14 21 28
M.	6 13 20 27	5 12 19 26	1 8 15 22 29
Tu.	7 14 21 28	6 13 20 27	2 9 16 23 30
W.	1 8 15 22 29	7 14 21 28	3 10 17 24
Th.	2 9 16 23 30	1 8 15 22 29	4 11 18 25
F.	3 10 17 24 31	2 9 16 23 30	5 12 19 26
S.	4 11 18 25	3 10 17 24 31	6 13 20 27

	February	June	October
Su.	2 9 16 23	1 8 15 22 29	5 12 19 26
M.	3 10 17 24	2 9 16 23 30	6 13 20 27
Tu.	4 11 18 25	3 10 17 24	7 14 21 28
W.	5 12 19 26	4 11 18 25	1 8 15 22 29
Th.	6 13 20 27	5 12 19 26	2 9 16 23 30
F.	7 14 21 28	6 13 20 27	3 10 17 24 31
S.	1 8 15 22	7 14 21 28	4 11 18 25

	March	July	November
Su.	2 9 16 23 30	6 13 20 27	2 9 16 23 30
M.	3 10 17 24 31	7 14 21 28	3 10 17 24
Tu.	4 11 18 25	1 8 15 22 29	4 11 18 25
W.	5 12 19 26	2 9 16 23 30	5 12 19 26
Th.	6 13 20 27	3 10 17 24 31	6 13 20 27
F.	7 14 21 28	4 11 18 25	7 14 21 28
S.	1 8 15 22 29	5 12 19 26	1 8 15 22 29

	April	August	December
Su.	6 13 20 27	3 10 17 24 31	7 14 21 28
M.	7 14 21 28	4 11 18 25	1 8 15 22 29
Tu.	1 8 15 22 29	5 12 19 26	2 9 16 23 30
W.	2 9 16 23 30	6 13 20 27	3 10 17 24 31
Th.	3 10 17 24	7 14 21 28	4 11 18 25
F.	4 11 18 25	1 8 15 22 29	5 12 19 26
S.	5 12 19 26	2 9 16 23 30	6 13 20 27

Easter Days

March 23.	1845	1913.				
March 30.	1777	1823	1834	1902	1975	1986 1997.
April 6	1806	1817	1890	1947	1958	1969.
April 13.	1800	1873	1879	1941		[2014 2025.
April 20.	1783	1794	1851	1862	1919	1930 2003

H (Leap year)

	January	May	September
Su.	5 12 19 26	3 10 17 24 31	6 13 20 27
M.	6 13 20 27	4 11 18 25	7 14 21 28
Tu.	7 14 21 28	5 12 19 26	1 8 15 22 29
W.	1 8 15 22 29	6 13 20 27	2 9 16 23 30
Th.	2 9 16 23 30	7 14 21 28	3 10 17 24
F.	3 10 17 24 31	1 8 15 22 29	4 11 18 25
S.	4 11 18 25	2 9 16 23 30	5 12 19 26

	February	June	October
Su.	2 9 16 23	7 14 21 28	4 11 18 25
M.	3 10 17 24	1 8 15 22 29	5 12 19 26
Tu.	4 11 18 25	2 9 16 23 30	6 13 20 27
W.	5 12 19 26	3 10 17 24	7 14 21 28
Th.	6 13 20 27	4 11 18 25	1 8 15 22 29
F.	7 14 21 28	5 12 19 26	2 9 16 23 30
S.	1 8 15 22 29	6 13 20 27	3 10 17 24 31

	March	July	November
Su.	1 8 15 22 29	5 12 19 26	1 8 15 22 29
M.	2 9 16 23 30	6 13 20 27	2 9 16 23 30
Tu.	3 10 17 24 31	7 14 21 28	3 10 17 24
W.	4 11 18 25	1 8 15 22 29	4 11 18 25
Th.	5 12 19 26	2 9 16 23 30	5 12 19 26
F.	6 13 20 27	3 10 17 24 31	6 13 20 27
S.	7 14 21 28	4 11 18 25	7 14 21 28

	April	August	December
Su.	5 12 19 26	2 9 16 23 30	6 13 20 27
M.	6 13 20 27	3 10 17 24 31	7 14 21 28
Tu.	7 14 21 28	4 11 18 25	1 8 15 22 29
W.	1 8 15 22 29	5 12 19 26	2 9 16 23 30
Th.	2 9 16 23 30	6 13 20 27	3 10 17 24 31
F.	3 10 17 24	7 14 21 28	4 11 18 25
S.	4 11 18 25	8 15 22 29	5 12 19 26

Easter Days

March 29.	1812	1964.	
April 5	1896.		
April 12.	1868	1936	2020.
April 19.	1772	1840	1908 1992.

I

	January	May	September
Su.	4 11 18 25	3 10 17 24 31	6 13 20 27
M.	5 12 19 26	4 11 18 25	7 14 21 28
Tu.	6 13 20 27	5 12 19 26	1 8 15 22 29
W.	7 14 21 28	6 13 20 27	2 9 16 23 30
Th.	1 8 15 22 29	7 14 21 28	3 10 17 24
F.	2 9 16 23 30	1 8 15 22 29	4 11 18 25
S.	3 10 17 24 31	2 9 16 23 30	5 12 19 26

	February	June	October
Su.	1 8 15 22	7 14 21 28	4 11 18 25
M.	2 9 16 23	1 8 15 22 29	5 12 19 26
Tu.	3 10 17 24	2 9 16 23 30	6 13 20 27
W.	4 11 18 25	3 10 17 24	7 14 21 28
Th.	5 12 19 26	4 11 18 25	1 8 15 22 29
F.	6 13 20 27	5 12 19 26	2 9 16 23 30
S.	7 14 21 28	6 13 20 27	3 10 17 24 31

	March	July	November
Su.	1 8 15 22 29	5 12 19 26	1 8 15 22 29
M.	2 9 16 23 30	6 13 20 27	2 9 16 23 30
Tu.	3 10 17 24 31	7 14 21 28	3 10 17 24
W.	4 11 18 25	1 8 15 22 29	4 11 18 25
Th.	5 12 19 26	2 9 16 23 30	5 12 19 26
F.	6 13 20 27	3 10 17 24 31	6 13 20 27
S.	7 14 21 28	4 11 18 25	7 14 21 28

	April	August	December
Su.	5 12 19 26	2 9 16 23 30	6 13 20 27
M.	6 13 20 27	3 10 17 24 31	7 14 21 28
Tu.	7 14 21 28	4 11 18 25	1 8 15 22 29
W.	1 8 15 22 29	5 12 19 26	2 9 16 23 30
Th.	2 9 16 23 30	6 13 20 27	3 10 17 24 31
F.	3 10 17 24	7 14 21 28	4 11 18 25
S.	4 11 18 25	1 8 15 22 29	5 12 19 26

Easter Days

March 22.	1818.					
March 29.	1807	1891	1959	1970.		[1953 2015.
April 5.	1795	1801	1863	1874	1885	1931 1942
April 12.	1789	1846	1857	1903	1914	1925 1998
April 19.	1778	1829	1835	1981	1987.	[2009.

J (Leap year)

	January	May	September
Su.	4 11 18 25	2 9 16 23 30	5 12 19 26
M.	5 12 19 26	3 10 17 24 31	6 13 20 27
Tu.	6 13 20 27	4 11 18 25	7 14 21 28
W.	7 14 21 28	5 12 19 26	1 8 15 22 29
Th.	1 8 15 22 29	6 13 20 27	2 9 16 23 30
F.	2 9 16 23 30	7 14 21 28	3 10 17 24
S.	3 10 17 24 31	1 8 15 22 29	4 11 18 25

	February	June	October
Su.	1 8 15 22 29	6 13 20 27	3 10 17 24 31
M.	2 9 16 23	7 14 21 28	4 11 18 25
Tu.	3 10 17 24	1 8 15 22 29	5 12 19 26
W.	4 11 18 25	2 9 16 23 30	6 13 20 27
Th.	5 12 19 26	3 10 17 24	7 14 21 28
F.	6 13 20 27	4 11 18 25	1 8 15 22 29
S.	7 14 21 28	5 12 19 26	2 9 16 23 30

	March	July	November
Su.	7 14 21 28	4 11 18 25	7 14 21 28
M.	1 8 15 22 29	5 12 19 26	1 8 15 22 29
Tu.	2 9 16 23 30	6 13 20 27	2 9 16 23 30
W.	3 10 17 24 31	7 14 21 28	3 10 17 24
Th.	4 11 18 25	1 8 15 22 29	4 11 18 25
F.	5 12 19 26	2 9 16 23 30	5 12 19 26
S.	6 13 20 27	3 10 17 24 31	6 13 20 27

	April	August	December
Su.	4 11 18 25	1 8 15 22 29	5 12 19 26
M.	5 12 19 26	2 9 16 23 30	6 13 20 27
Tu.	6 13 20 27	3 10 17 24 31	7 14 21 28
W.	7 14 21 28	4 11 18 25	1 8 15 22 29
Th.	1 8 15 22 29	5 12 19 26	2 9 16 23 30
F.	2 9 16 23 30	6 13 20 27	3 10 17 24 31
S.	3 10 17 24	7 14 21 28	4 11 18 25

Easter Days

March 28.	1880	1948.	
April 4.	1920.		
April 11.	1784	1852	2004.
April 18.	1824	1976.	

K

	January	May	September
Su.	3 10 17 24 31	2 9 16 23 30	5 12 19 26
M.	4 11 18 25	3 10 17 24 31	6 13 20 27
Tu.	5 12 19 26	4 11 18 25	7 14 21 28
W.	6 13 20 27	5 12 19 26	1 8 15 22 29
Th.	7 14 21 28	6 13 20 27	2 9 16 23 30
F.	1 8 15 22 29	7 14 21 28	3 10 17 24
S.	2 9 16 23 30	1 8 15 22 29	4 11 18 25

	February	June	October
Su.	7 14 21 28	6 13 20 27	3 10 17 24 31
M.	1 8 15 22	7 14 21 28	4 11 18 25
Tu.	2 9 16 23	1 8 15 22 29	5 12 19 26
W.	3 10 17 24	2 9 16 23 30	6 13 20 27
Th.	4 11 18 25	3 10 17 24	7 14 21 28
F.	5 12 19 26	4 11 18 25	1 8 15 22 29
S.	6 13 20 27	5 12 19 26	2 9 16 23 30

	March	July	November
Su.	7 14 21 28	4 11 18 25	7 14 21 28
M.	1 8 15 22 29	5 12 19 26	1 8 15 22 29
Tu.	2 9 16 23 30	6 13 20 27	2 9 16 23 30
W.	3 10 17 24 31	7 14 21 28	3 10 17 24
Th.	4 11 18 25	1 8 15 22 29	4 11 18 25
F.	5 12 19 26	2 9 16 23 30	5 12 19 26
S.	6 13 20 27	3 10 17 24 31	6 13 20 27

	April	August	December
Su.	4 11 18 25	1 8 15 22 29	5 12 19 26
M.	5 12 19 26	2 9 16 23 30	6 13 20 27
Tu.	6 13 20 27	3 10 17 24 31	7 14 21 28
W.	7 14 21 28	4 11 18 25	1 8 15 22 29
Th.	1 8 15 22 29	5 12 19 26	2 9 16 23 30
F.	2 9 16 23 30	6 13 20 27	3 10 17 24 31
S.	3 10 17 24	7 14 21 28	4 11 18 25

Easter Days

March 28.	1869 1875 1937.	[2010 2021.
April 4.	1779 1790 1847 1858 1915 1926 1999	
April 11.	1773 1819 1830 1841 1909 1971 1982	
April 18.	1802 1813 1897 1954 1965.	
April 25.	1886 1943.	[1993.

L (Leap year)

	January	May	September
Su.	3 10 17 24 31	1 8 15 22 29	4 11 18 25
M.	4 11 18 25	2 9 16 23 30	5 12 19 26
Tu.	5 12 19 26	3 10 17 24 31	6 13 20 27
W.	6 13 20 27	4 11 18 25	7 14 21 28
Th.	7 14 21 28	5 12 19 26	1 8 15 22 29
F.	1 8 15 22 29	6 13 20 27	2 9 16 23 30
S.	2 9 16 23 30	7 14 21 28	3 10 17 24

	February	June	October
Su.	7 14 21 28	5 12 19 26	2 9 16 23 30
M.	1 8 15 22 29	6 13 20 27	3 10 17 24 31
Tu.	2 9 16 23	7 14 21 28	4 11 18 25
W.	3 10 17 24	1 8 15 22 29	5 12 19 26
Th.	4 11 18 25	2 9 16 23 30	6 13 20 27
F.	5 12 19 26	3 10 17 24	7 14 21 28
S.	6 13 20 27	4 11 18 25	1 8 15 22 29

	March	July	November
Su.	6 13 20 27	3 10 17 24 31	6 13 20 27
M.	7 14 21 28	4 11 18 25	7 14 21 28
Tu.	1 8 15 22 29	5 12 19 26	1 8 15 22 29
W.	2 9 16 23 30	6 13 20 27	2 9 16 23 30
Th.	3 10 17 24 31	7 14 21 28	3 10 17 24
F.	4 11 18 25	1 8 15 22 29	4 11 18 25
S.	5 12 19 26	2 9 16 23 30	5 12 19 26

	April	August	December
Su.	3 10 17 24	7 14 21 28	4 11 18 25
M.	4 11 18 25	1 8 15 22 29	5 12 19 26
Tu.	5 12 19 26	2 9 16 23 30	6 13 20 27
W.	6 13 20 27	3 10 17 24 31	7 14 21 28
Th.	7 14 21 28	4 11 18 25	1 8 15 22 29
F.	1 8 15 22 29	5 12 19 26	2 9 16 23 30
S.	2 9 16 23 30	6 13 20 27	3 10 17 24 31

Easter Days

March 27.	1796 1864 1932 2016.
April 3.	1836 1904 1988.
April 17.	1808 1892 1960.

M

	January	May	September
Su.	2 9 16 23 30	1 8 15 22 29	4 11 18 25
M.	3 10 17 24 31	2 9 16 23 30	5 12 19 26
Tu.	4 11 18 25	3 10 17 24 31	6 13 20 27
W.	5 12 19 26	4 11 18 25	7 14 21 28
Th.	6 13 20 27	5 12 19 26	1 8 15 22 29
F.	7 14 21 28	6 13 20 27	2 9 16 23 30
S.	1 8 15 22 29	7 14 21 28	3 10 17 24

	February	June	October
Su.	6 13 20 27	5 12 19 26	2 9 16 23 30
M.	7 14 21 28	6 13 20 27	3 10 17 24 31
Tu.	1 8 15 22	7 14 21 28	4 11 18 25
W.	2 9 16 23	1 8 15 22 29	5 12 19 26
Th.	3 10 17 24	2 9 16 23 30	6 13 20 27
F.	4 11 18 25	3 10 17 24	7 14 21 28
S.	5 12 19 26	4 11 18 25	1 8 15 22 29

	March	July	November
Su.	6 13 20 27	3 10 17 24 31	6 13 20 27
M.	7 14 21 28	4 11 18 25	7 14 21 28
Tu.	1 8 15 22 29	5 12 19 26	1 8 15 22 29
W.	2 9 16 23 30	6 13 20 27	2 9 16 23 30
Th.	3 10 17 24 31	7 14 21 28	3 10 17 24
F.	4 11 18 25	1 8 15 22 29	4 11 18 25
S.	5 12 19 26	2 9 16 23 30	5 12 19 26

	April	August	December
Su.	3 10 17 24	7 14 21 28	4 11 18 25
M.	4 11 18 25	1 8 15 22 29	5 12 19 26
Tu.	5 12 19 26	2 9 16 23 30	6 13 20 27
W.	6 13 20 27	3 10 17 24 31	7 14 21 28
Th.	7 14 21 28	4 11 18 25	1 8 15 22 29
F.	1 8 15 22 29	5 12 19 26	2 9 16 23 30
S.	2 9 16 23 30	6 13 20 27	3 10 17 24 31

Easter Days

March 27.	1785 1842 1853 1910 1921 2005.
April 3.	1774 1825 1831 1983 1994.
April 10.	1803 1814 1887 1898 1955 1966 1977.
April 17.	1870 1881 1927 1938 1949 2022.
April 24.	1791 1859 2011.

N (Leap year)

	January	May	September
Su.	2 9 16 23 30	7 14 21 28	3 10 17 24
M.	3 10 17 24 31	1 8 15 22 29	4 11 18 25
Tu.	4 11 18 25	2 9 16 23 30	5 12 19 26
W.	5 12 19 26	3 10 17 24 31	6 13 20 27
Th.	6 13 20 27	4 11 18 25	7 14 21 28
F.	7 14 21 28	5 12 19 26	1 8 15 22 29
S.	1 8 15 22 29	6 13 20 27	2 9 16 23 30

	February	June	October
Su.	6 13 20 27	4 11 18 25	1 8 15 22 29
M.	7 14 21 28	5 12 19 26	2 9 16 23 30
Tu.	1 8 15 22 29	6 13 20 27	3 10 17 24 31
W.	2 9 16 23	7 14 21 28	4 11 18 25
Th.	3 10 17 24	1 8 15 22 29	5 12 19 26
F.	4 11 18 25	2 9 16 23 30	6 13 20 27
S.	5 12 19 26	3 10 17 24	7 14 21 28

	March	July	November
Su.	5 12 19 26	2 9 16 23 30	5 12 19 26
M.	6 13 20 27	3 10 17 24 31	6 13 20 27
Tu.	7 14 21 28	4 11 18 25	7 14 21 28
W.	1 8 15 22 29	5 12 19 26	1 8 15 22 29
Th.	2 9 16 23 30	6 13 20 27	2 9 16 23 30
F.	3 10 17 24 31	7 14 21 28	3 10 17 24
S.	4 11 18 25	1 8 15 22 29	4 11 18 25

	April	August	December
Su.	2 9 16 23 30	6 13 20 27	3 10 17 24 31
M.	3 10 17 24	7 14 21 28	4 11 18 25
Tu.	4 11 18 25	1 8 15 22 29	5 12 19 26
W.	5 12 19 26	2 9 16 23 30	6 13 20 27
Th.	6 13 20 27	3 10 17 24 31	7 14 21 28
F.	7 14 21 28	4 11 18 25	1 8 15 22 29
S.	1 8 15 22 29	5 12 19 26	2 9 16 23 30

Easter Days

March 26.	1780.
April 2.	1820 1972.
April 9.	1944.
April 16.	1876.
April 23.	1848 1916 2000.

The World

The **Superficial Area** of the Earth is estimated to be 196,836,000 square miles, of which 55,786,000 square miles are Land and 141,050,000 square miles Water. The **Diameter** of the Earth at the Equator is 7,926¼ English miles, and at the Poles 7,900 English miles. The Equatorial **Circumference** is 24,901·8 English miles, divided into 360 Degrees of Longitude, each of 69·17 English (or 60 Geographical) miles; these Degrees are measured from the Meridian of Greenwich, and numbered East and West of that point to meet in the Antipodes at the 180th Degree. Distance North and South of the Equator is marked by Parallels of Latitude, which proceed from zero (at the Equator) to 90° at the Poles.

The velocity of a given point of the Earth's surface at the Equator exceeds 1,000 miles an hour (24,901·8 miles in 24 hours); the Earth's velocity in its orbit round the Sun is about 66,600 miles an hour (584,000,000 miles in 365¼ days). The Earth is distant from the Sun 93,000,000 miles, on the average.

AREA AND POPULATION

The total population of the world in mid-1983, was estimated at 4,684,000,000 compared with 3,003,000,000 in 1960 and 2,070,000,000 in 1930.

Continent, etc.	Area		Estimated Population, mid-1983
	Sq. miles '000	Sq. km. '000	
Europe[1]	1,906	4,937	489,000,000
Asia[2]	10,647	27,576	2,731,000,000
U.S.S.R.	8,649	22,402	272,000,000
Africa	11,710	30,330	521,000,000
North America[3]	8,307	21,515	259,000,000
Latin America[4]	7,941	20,566	388,000,000
Oceania	3,286	8,510	24,000,000
Total	52,446	135,836	4,684,000,000

[1] Includes European Turkey, excludes U.S.S.R.
[2] Excludes U.S.S.R.
[3] Includes Hawaii.
[4] Mexico and the remainder of the Americas south of the U.S.A.

Source: *U.N. Demographic Yearbook 1983*.

A United Nations report (*The Future Growth of World Population*) in 1958, pointed out that the population of the world had increased since the beginning of the 20th Century at an unprecedented rate: in 1850 it was estimated at 1,094,000,000 and in 1900 at 1,550,000,000, an increase of 42 per cent in 50 years. By 1925 it had risen to 1,907,000,000—23 per cent in 25 years—and by 1950 it had reached 2,500,000,000, an increase of 31 per cent in 25 years. Levels of population and the trend in distribution of the population by continents as forecast for the year 2000 were:—

[millions]

Continent, etc.	2000	
	Estimated Population	Per cent
Europe (including U.S.S.R.)	947	15·1
Asia (excluding U.S.S.R.)	3,870	61·8
Africa	517	8·2
N. America	312	5·0
Latin America†	592	9·4
Oceania	29	0·5
World	6,267	100

† Mexico and the remainder of America south of U.S.A.

THE CONTINENTS

Europe (including European Russia) forms about one-fourteenth of the land surface of the globe. Its length from the North Cape, 71° 12′ N., to Cape Matapan, in the south of Greece, 36° 23′ N., is about 2,400 miles, and its breadth from Cape St. Vincent to the Urals is about 3,300 miles. The boundary between Europe and Asia is the Urals in the north, while in the south-east it follows the valley of the Manych, north of the Caucasus.

Asia (including Asiatic Russia) extends over nearly one-third of the land surface of the globe. The distance between its extreme longitudes, the west coast of Asia Minor (26° E.) and the East Cape (170° W.), is 6,000 miles. The extreme latitudes, Cape Chelyuskin (78° 30″ N.) and Cape Bulus (76 miles north of the Equator), are 5,350 miles apart. Asia is bounded by the ocean on all sides except the west, where the isthmus of Suez connects it with Africa. The land boundary between Europe and Asia is formed on the west mainly by the Ural Mountains, the Ural River and in the south-west the valley of the Manych, which stretches from the Caspian Sea to the mouth of the Don. The islands of the archipelago which lie in the south-east between the continents of Asia and Australia may be divided into two groups by a line passing east of Timor, Timor Laut, the Kei Islands and the Moluccas.

Africa is about three times the area of Europe. Its extreme longitudes are 17° W. at Cape Verde and 51° 27′ 52″ E. at Ras Hafun. The extreme latitudes are Cape Blanco in 37° N. and Cape Agulhas in 35° S., at a distance of about 5,000 miles. It is surrounded by seas on all sides, except in the narrow isthmus of Suez, through which is cut the Suez Canal.

North America, including Mexico, is a little less than twice the size of Europe. Its extreme longitudes extend from a little west of 170° W. to 52½° W. in the east of Newfoundland, and its extreme latitudes from about 80° N. lat. to 15° N. lat. in the south of Mexico. It is surrounded by seas on all sides except in the south, where it joins the isthmian States of *Central America*, which have an area of about 200,000 square miles. The area of the *West Indies* is about 65,000 square miles, a little more than half that of the United Kingdom. They extend from about 27° N. latitude to 10° N. latitude.

South America is a little more than 1¾ times the size of Europe. The extreme longitudes are Cape Branco 35° W. and Punta Parina 81° W., and the extreme latitudes, Punta Gallinas, 12½° N. and Cape Horn 56° S. South America is surrounded by the ocean, except where it is joined to Central America by the narrow isthmus through which is cut the Panama Canal.

Oceania extends over an area 1½ times the size of Europe, from Australia (in the West) to the most easterly islands of Polynesia, and from New Zealand (in the south) to the Sandwich Islands (Hawaii) in the north.

Countries and Their Capitals

The appended tables of area and population are based on such information as is immediately available.

With regard to areas it will be realized that no complete survey of many countries has yet been either achieved or even undertaken and that consequently accurate area figures are not available.

The populations given hereunder are derived from various sources; some have as their basis an authenticated census; some are official and some are unofficial estimates. In certain cases where later information becomes available during printing the new figures are given in the overseas sections of the ALMANACK. What has been said about the survey of many of the world's countries applies equally to the question of census.

AFRICA

Country	Area Sq. Miles	Population	Capital	Population of Capital
Algeria	855,200	20,200,000	Algiers	3,250,000
Angola	488,000	7,100,000	Ψ Luanda	1,000,000
Benin	47,000	3,338,240*	Ψ Porto Novo	104,000
Botswana	220,000	937,000	Gaborone	79,400
Burkina Faso	100,000	6,660,000	Ouagadougou	200,000
Burundi	10,747	4,480,000	Bujumbura	150,000
Cameroon	475,400†	8,320,000	Yaoundé	522,000
Cape Verde Islands	1,516	296,093	Ψ Praia	6,000
Central African Republic	234,000	2,470,000	Bangui	350,000
Chad	488,000	4,000,000	Ndjaména	150,000
Comoros	800	378,000	Moroni	..
Congo	129,960	1,700,000	Brazzaville	500,000
Djibouti	9,000	330,000	Ψ Djibouti	150,000
Egypt	385,110	47,000,000	Cairo	11,500,000
Equatorial Guinea	28,000†	300,000	Ψ Malabo	9,000
Ethiopia	400,000	42,000,000	Addis Ababa	1,300,000
Gabon	101,400	1,200,000	Ψ Libreville	251,000
Gambia	4,003	700,000*	Ψ Banjul	45,000*
Ghana	92,100	12,205,574*	Ψ Accra	1,420,066*
Guinea	96,865	6,412,000	Ψ Conakry	655,000
Guinea-Bissau	14,000	920,000	Ψ Bissau	..
Ivory Coast	127,000	9,924,000	Ψ Abidjan	2,000,000
Kenya	224,960	17,000,000	Nairobi	1,000,000
Lesotho	11,716	1,204,000	Maseru	277,307
Liberia	43,000	2,110,000	Ψ Monrovia	300,000
Libya	810,000	3,300,000	Ψ Tripoli	1,000,000
Madagascar	228,000	9,230,000	Antananarivo	800,000
Malawi	45,747	6,270,000	Lilongwe	102,924*
Mali	465,000	7,340,000	Bamako	600,000
Mauritania	419,000	1,730,000	Nouakchott	500,000
Mauritius, etc.	805	1,000,432*	Ψ Port Louis	133,702
Mayotte	144	50,400	Dzaoudzi	4,147
Morocco	180,000	20,419,555	Ψ Rabat	518,616
Western Sahara	125,000	63,000	Villa Cisneros	250
Mozambique	297,657	12,600,000	Ψ Maputo	850,000
Namibia	318,261	1,039,400	Windhoek	61,260
Niger	459,000	6,170,000	Niamey	343,600
Nigeria	356,669	82,390,000	Ψ Lagos	3,000,000
Réunion	969	515,814	St. Denis	109,072
Rwanda	10,169	5,110,000	Kigali	7,000
St. Helena	47	5,895	Ψ Jamestown	1,516
Ascension	38	1,708	Ψ Georgetown	..
Tristan da Cunha	45	295	Ψ Edinburgh	..
Sao Tomé & Príncipe	372	115,000	Ψ São Tomé	3,187
Senegal	77,814	5,661,000	Ψ Dakar	1,000,000
Seychelles	171	65,032	Ψ Victoria	24,733
Sierra Leone	27,925	3,670,000	Ψ Freetown	274,000*
Somalia	246,000	5,000,000	Ψ Mogadishu	600,000
South Africa	1,130,422†	31,010,000	{ Pretoria	528,407
			{ Ψ Cape Town	1,107,764
Spanish Presidios:—				
Ceuta	5	65,264	..	..
Melilla	72	53,593	..	..
Sudan	967,500	19,500,000	Khartoum	194,000
Swaziland	6,782	600,000	Mbabane	30,000
Tanzania	362,820	17,551,925*	Ψ Dar-es-Salaam	757,346
Togo	21,000	2,470,000	Lomé	247,000
Tunisia	63,380	6,966,173	Ψ Tunis	1,394,749
Uganda	91,000	12,600,000	Kampala	400,000
Zaire	905,582	29,950,000	Kinshasa	2,500,000
Zambia	290,587	6,050,000	Lusaka	641,000
Zimbabwe	150,820	7,966,000	Harare	656,000

* Latest census result.   † Sq. km.   Ψ Seaport.

AMERICA

Country	Area Sq. Miles	Population	Capital	Population of Capital
North America				
Canada.................	3,851,809	25,318,000	Ottawa	756,600*
Alberta...............	255,000	2,358,000	Edmonton..........	683,000
British Columbia......	366,000	2,865,100	Ψ Victoria	242,000
Manitoba.............	251,000	1,057,400	Winnipeg	584,842
New Brunswick	28,000	717,200	Ψ Fredericton	64,439
Newfoundland	156,000	567,681*	Ψ St. John's	154,820
Nova Scotia...........	21,425	878,300	Ψ Halifax	176,871
Ontario	412,000	8,625,107*	Toronto...........	2,131,159
Prince Edward Island .	2,184	123,700	Ψ Charlottetown.....	15,282*
Quebec..............	594,860	6,510,100	Ψ Quebec	163,800
Saskatchewan	251,700	1,016,400	Regina	172,340
Yukon Territory.......	207,000	23,153*	Whitehorse	14,814
Northwest Territories ..	1,305,000	45,741*	Yellowknife	9,483
Mexico	761,604	67,383,000*	Mexico City	16,000,000
St. Pierre and Miquelon..	93	6,041	Ψ St. Pierre	..
United States	3,536,855	231,106,727	Washington, D.C. ...	633,425
Central America and the West Indies				
Anguilla	35	7,000	The Valley	500
Antigua and Barbuda....	170	78,000	Ψ St. John's	22,000
Bahamas	5,380	237,090*	Ψ Nassau............	135,437*
Barbados	166	252,000*	Ψ Bridgetown	7,466
Belize	8,867	148,300	Belmopan	2,935
Bermuda	21	57,237	Ψ Hamilton	1,617
Cayman Islands	100	18,750	Ψ George Town	8,200
Costa Rica	19,653	2,276,676	San José	808,919
Cuba..................	44,178	10,042,800	Ψ Havana	1,924,886
Dominica	290	74,069*	Ψ Roseau..........	8,346*
Dominican Republic	19,322	5,647,977*	Ψ Santo Domingo	1,550,739*
Grenada...............	133	110,410	Ψ St. George's	7,500
Guadeloupe.............	657	328,400	Ψ Pointe a Pitre	15,778
Guatemala	42,042	7,932,000	Guatemala	1,180,000
Haiti..................	10,700	6,009,000	Ψ Port au Prince	1,000,000
Honduras	43,278	3,600,000	Tegucigalpa	533,600
Jamaica	4,244	265,400	Ψ Kingston	662,501
Martinique	427	328,566	Ψ Fort de France	100,576
Montserrat	39	11,793	Ψ Plymouth	1,623
Netherlands Antilles	394	253,234	Ψ Willemstad	154,928
Nicaragua	57,145	3,200,000	Managua..........	615,000
Panama	32,537	2,040,000	Ψ Panama City	418,000
Puerto Rico.............	3,459	3,196,520	Ψ San Juan........	518,700
St. Kitts-Nevis	101	44,404*	Ψ Basseterre	15,000
St. Lucia	238	134,000	Ψ Castries	50,798
St. Vincent	133	127,883	Ψ Kingstown	33,694
El Salvador	8,200	4,950,000	San Salvador	425,119
Trinidad and Tobago	1,980	1,055,800	Ψ Port of Spain	59,800
Turks and Caicos Islds ...	192	7,436	Ψ Grand Turk	3,146
Virgin Islands:—				
British	59	12,034*	Ψ Road Town	2,479
U.S..................	133	96,569	Ψ Charlotte Amalie ..	11,000
South America				
Argentina	1,079,965	27,862,771*	Ψ Buenos Aires	9,677,200*
Bolivia	415,000	6,000,000	La Paz	654,700
Brazil.................	3,289,440	119,098,922*	Brasilia	1,176,748*
Chile..................	290,000	11,000,000	Santiago	4,000,000
Colombia	440,000	27,900,000	Bogotá...........	5,000,000
Ecuador	226,000	8,000,000	Quito	800,000
Falkland Islands	4,700	1,813	Ψ Stanley	1,050
Guiana, *French*	35,135	73,022	Ψ Cayenne	38,135
Guyana	83,000	793,000	Ψ Georgetown	185,000
Paraguay...............	157,000	3,477,000	Ψ Asunción	708,000
Peru	531,000	18,790,000	Lima	3,595,000
Surinam	63,250	410,000	Ψ Paramaribo	110,000
Uruguay...............	72,172	3,012,146	Ψ Montevideo	1,355,312
Venezuela..............	353,894	17,257,000	Caracas	3,507,800

* Latest census result.   Ψ Seaport.

ASIA

The expressions "The Near East," "The Middle East" and "The Far East" often appear in the Press of English-speaking countries, but have no definite boundaries. The following limits have been suggested:— *Near East* (Turkey to Iran) 25°–60° E. long., *Middle East* (Baluchistan to Burma) 60°–100° E. long., *Far East* (Thailand to Japan) 100°–160° E. long.

Country	Area Sq. Miles	Population	Capital	Population of Capital
Afghanistan	250,000	16,790,000	Kabul.............	2,000,000
Bahrain	231	350,798*	Ψ Manama	121,986*
Bangladesh	55,126	94,700,000	Dhaka	4,023,000
Bhutan	18,000	1,400,000	Thimphu	..
Brunei	2,226	214,000	Ψ Bandar Seri Begawan	58,000
Burma	262,000	35,313,905*	Ψ Rangoon	2,458,712*
Cambodia	70,000	6,000,000	Ψ Phnom Penh	..
China	3,700,000	1,008,175,288*	Peking	9,230,687*
Taiwan	13,800	18,270,749*	Taipei	2,196,237
Tibet................	463,000	1,892,392	Lhasa	..
Hong Kong	404	5,397,500	Ψ Victoria	767,000
India..................	1,261,816	685,184,692*	Delhi	6,220,000*
Indonesia	735,000	153,030,000	Ψ Jakarta	6,503,449
Iran (Persia)	628,000	42,000,000	Tehran	10,000,000
Iraq...................	172,000	14,000,000	Baghdad	3,205,645
Israel	7,992	4,148,500	Jerusalem	472,900
Japan	142,812	119,430,000	Tokyo	11,806,729
Jordan	37,700	2,495,000	Amman	744,000
Korea:—				
North Korea	48,000	20,000,000	Pyongyang	1,500,000
South Korea	38,500	42,000,000	Seoul	8,367,000
Kuwait	7,500	1,786,616	Ψ Kuwait	400,000
Laos	90,000	3,900,000	Vientiane	90,000
Lebanon................	4,300	2,740,000	Ψ Beirut	702,000
Macau	6	261,680	Ψ Macau	157,175
Malaysia	130,000	13,435,588*	Kuala Lumpur	937,875*
Johore	7,330	1,601,504*	Johore Bahru	..
Kedah	3,640	1,102,200*	Alor Star	..
Kelantan	5,765	877,575	Koto Bahru	..
Malacca..............	640	453,153*	Ψ Malacca	..
Negri Sembilan	2,570	563,955*	Seremban	..
Pahang	13,900	770,644*	Kuantan	..
Penang...............	400	911,586*	Ψ George Town	234,930
Perak	8,100	1,762,288*	Ipoh	125,776
Perlis	310	147,726*	Kangar	..
Sabah................	29,000	1,002,608*	Kota Kinabalu.....	41,830
Sarawak	48,000	1,294,753*	Ψ Kuching	63,491
Selangor	3,166	1,467,441*	Shah Alam	451,810
Trengganu	5,000	406,000	Kuala Trengganu ...	..
Maldives	115	160,200	Ψ Malé..............	37,000
Mongolia	600,000	1,866,300	Ulan Bator	480,000
Nepal	54,362	16,000,000	Kathmandu	235,000
Oman	120,000	850,000	Ψ Muscat	30,000
Pakistan	310,403	83,780,000	Islamabad	250,000
Philippines	114,834	54,400,000	Ψ Manila	5,925,884
Qatar	4,000	250,000	Doha	200,000
Saudi Arabia	927,000	9,160,000	Riyadh	1,000,000
Singapore	226	2,544,400		..
Sri Lanka	25,332	14,800,001*	Ψ Colombo	585,776
Syria..................	70,800	10,400,000	Damascus	2,250,000
Thailand	198,247	50,583,105	Ψ Bangkok	5,174,682
Turkey.................	285,000	45,217,556	Ankara	3,196,460
United Arab Emirates ...	32,000	1,300,000		..
U.S.S.R. (Asia)				
R.S.F.S.R. (Asia)	*See* Europe			
Armenia	11,300	3,267,000	Erevan	1,114,000
Azerbaidjan	33,436	6,506,000	Ψ Baku	1,661,000
Georgia	27,000	5,167,000	Tbilisi	1,140,000
Turkmenistan.........	188,400	3,118,000	Ashkhabad	346,000
Uzbekistan	157,000	17,498,000	Tashkent	1,986,000
Tadjikstan	54,000	4,365,000	Dushanbe	539,000
Kazakhstan	1,065,000	15,648,000	Alma Ata	1,046,000
Kirghizia	77,000	3,886,000	Frunze.............	590,000
Vietnam	129,000	60,000,000	Hanoi.............	925,000
Yemen A.R.............	75,000	8,556,974	Sana'a	277,817
Yemen P.D.R............	112,000	2,030,000	Ψ Aden	270,000

Ψ Seaport.   * Latest census report.

EUROPE AND THE MEDITERRANEAN

Country	Area Sq. Miles	Population	Capital	Population of Capital
Albania	10,700	2,752,300	Tirana	200,000
Andorra	190	41,600	Andorra La Vella	16,000
Austria	32,376	7,551,800	Vienna	1,531,346
Belgium	11,781	9,863,374	Brussels	1,000,221
Bulgaria	43,000	8,929,000	Sofia	1,082,315
Cyprus	3,572	650,000	Nicosia	233,500
Czechoslovakia	49,400	15,280,148	Prague	1,191,125
Denmark	17,000	5,116,464	Ψ Copenhagen	575,217
Finland	130,165	4,844,000	Ψ Helsinki	482,800
France	213,000	54,832,000	Paris	8,707,000
Germany:—				
Federal Republic of Germany‡	96,011	61,049,000	Bonn	292,900
German Democratic Republic	41,768	16,740,000	East Berlin	1,166,641
Gibraltar	2	28,719*	Ψ Gibraltar	..
Greece	51,182	9,740,417*	Athens	3,027,331*
Hungary	36,000	10,710,000	Budapest	2,093,000
Iceland	40,500	240,122	Ψ Reykjavik	88,505
Irish Republic	26,600	3,443,405*	Ψ Dublin	525,882*
Italy	131,000	57,080,498	Rome	2,826,733
Liechtenstein	62	26,680	Vaduz	4,872
Luxembourg	999	365,500	Luxemburg	78,900
Malta and Gozo	121	341,000	Ψ Valletta	14,042
Monaco	⅜	28,000	Monaco-ville	1,443
Netherlands	13,500	14,394,589	Amsterdam	687,397
Norway	°386,308	4,145,845	Ψ Oslo	448,747
Poland	121,000	36,400,000*	Warsaw	1,572,000
Portugal§	34,000	10,030,000	Ψ Lisbon	1,707,500
Romania	°237,500	22,480,000	Bucharest	1,960,097
San Marino	23	22,361	San Marino	..
Spain	196,700	37,833,863	Madrid	3,188,297
Sweden	173,436	8,330,573	Ψ Stockholm	1,409,048
Switzerland	15,950	6,482,000	Berne	145,700
The United Kingdom†	93,026	55,776,422*	Ψ London	6,696,008*
England	50,053	46,362,836*		
Wales	7,969	2,791,851*	Ψ Cardiff	281,300
Scotland	29,798	5,130,735*	Ψ Edinburgh	446,361
Northern Ireland	5,206	1,491,000*	Ψ Belfast	297,862*
U.S.S.R. (Europe)		214,397,000		
R.S.F.S.R.	6,593,391	142,117,000	Moscow	8,537,000
Ukraine	252,046	50,667,000	Kiev	2,409,000
Belorussia	80,300	9,878,000	Minsk	1,442,000
Moldavia	13,912	4,080,000	Kishinev	605,000
Estonia	17,413	1,518,000	Ψ Tallinn	458,000
Latvia	24,695	2,587,000	Ψ Riga	875,000
Lithuania	26,173	3,539,000	Vilnius	535,000
Vatican City State	109 *acres*	731	Vatican City	..
Yugoslavia	98,725	22,800,000	Belgrade	1,455,000

† *Land* areas are shown for U.K. and parts (*total* area of U.K., 94,216 sq. miles). ‡ Data include West Berlin. § Data include Madeira (314 sq. miles) and the Azores (922 sq. miles). Ψ Seaport. ° sq. kilometres. * Latest census report.

THE SEVEN WONDERS OF THE WORLD

I. The Pyramids of Egypt.—From Gizeh (near Cairo) to a southern limit 60 miles distant. The oldest is that of Zoser, at Saqqara, built about 2,700 B.C. The Great Pyramid of Cheops covers more than 12 acres and was originally 481 ft. in height and 756 × 756 ft. at the base.

II. The Hanging Gardens of Babylon.—Adjoining Nebuchadnezzar's palace, 60 miles south of Baghdad. Terraced gardens, ranging from 75 to 300 ft. above ground level, watered from storage tanks on the highest terrace.

III. The Tomb of Mausolus.—At Halicarnassus, in Asia Minor. Built by the widowed Queen Artemisia about 350 B.C. The memorial originated the term mausoleum.

IV. The Temple of Diana at Ephesus.—Ionic temple erected about 350 B.C. in honour of the goddess and burned by the Goths in A.D. 262.

V. The Colossus of Rhodes.—A bronze statue of Apollo, set up about 280 B.C. According to legend it stood at the harbour entrance of the seaport of Rhodes.

VI. The Statue of Jupiter Olympus.—At Olympia in the plain of Elis, constructed of marble inlaid with ivory and gold by the sculptor Phidias, about 430 B.C.

VII. The Pharos of Alexandria.—A marble watch tower and lighthouse on the island of Pharos in the harbour of Alexandria.

OCEANIA

Country	Area Sq. Miles	Population	Capital	Population of Capital
Australia	2,968,000	..	Canberra	..
New South Wales	309,000	5,436,900	Ψ Sydney	3,335,250
Queensland	667,000	2,505,300	Ψ Brisbane	1,145,410
South Australia	380,070	1,353,000	Adelaide	978,940
Tasmania	26,383	433,300	Ψ Hobart	128,603*
Victoria	87,884	4,075,900	Ψ Melbourne	2,888,400
Western Australia	975,920	1,382,468	Perth	982,570
Northern Territory	520,280	126,300*	Ψ Darwin	63,404
Norfolk Island	13	1,849	Ψ Kingston	..
Fiji	7,072	677,481	Ψ Suva	71,000
French Polynesia	1,522	168,000	Ψ Papeete	15,220
Kiribati	264	63,800*	Tarawa	24,400
Guam	209	105,979	Agaña	..
Mariana, Caroline and Marshall Islands†	687	133,442	Saipan	..
Nauru	8	8,042*	Ψ Nauru	..
New Caledonia	7,374	145,000	Ψ Noumea	12,000
New Zealand	103,736	3,265,500	Ψ Wellington	342,400
Cook Islands	200	{ 17,400	Avarua	..
Niue		{ 3,002	Alofi	956
Ross Dependency	175,000	..	..	..
Papua New Guinea	178,260	3,160,000	Ψ Port Moresby	139,300
Pitcairn Islands	1·75	61	..	..
Samoa:—				
Eastern	76	32,297	Ψ Fagatogo	..
Western	1,097	158,130*	Ψ Apia	33,100*
Solomon Islands	11,500	244,000	Ψ Honiara	18,346
Tonga, etc.	288	98,000	Ψ Nuku'alofa	21,000
Tuvalu	10	8,364	Ψ Funafuti	2,120
Vanuatu	6,050	112,596*	Ψ Vila	14,801*
Wallis and Futuna Is.	106	12,400	Mata-Utu	..

† Trust Territory of the Pacific Islands.   Ψ Seaport.   * Latest census result.

THE LARGEST CITIES OF THE WORLD

Ψ = Seaport	Population	Ψ = Seaport	Population
Mexico City, Mexico	16,000,000	São Paulo, Brazil	8,490,763
Ψ Shanghai, China	11,859,000	Seoul, Korea	8,367,000
Tokyo, Japan	11,806,729	Ψ Bombay, India	8,300,000
Cairo, Egypt	11,500,000	Tianjin, China	7,390,000
Paris, France	10,073,059	Ψ New York, U.S.A.	7,071,030
Tehran, Iran	10,000,000	Ψ Surabaya, Indonesia	7,027,913
Ψ Buenos Aires, Argentina	9,677,200	Ψ London, U.K.	6,776,000
Peking, China	9,230,687	Ψ Jakarta, Indonesia	6,503,449
Ψ Calcutta, India	9,200,000	Delhi, India	6,220,000
Moscow, U.S.S.R.	8,537,000	Chiongqing, China	6,200,000

WORLD GEOGRAPHICAL STATISTICS

North America
River	Mississippi–Missouri– Red Rock	3,741 miles
Lake	Superior	31,000 sq miles
Mountain	McKinley	20,320 ft
Waterfall	Yosemite, California	2,425 ft

South America
River	Amazon	4,007 miles
Lake	Titicaca	3,205 sq miles
Mountain	Aconcagua	22,834 ft
Waterfall	Angel, Venezuela	3,212 ft

Africa
River	Nile	4,145 miles
Lake	Victoria	26,800 sq miles
Mountain	Kilimanjaro	19,340 ft
Waterfall	Tugela, Natal	3,110 ft

Europe
River	Volga, USSR	2,293 miles
Lake	Ladoga, USSR	6,826 sq miles
Mountain	Elbruz, Caucasus	18,481 ft
Waterfall	Utigardd, Norway	2,625 ft

Asia
River	Yenisei, Mongolia– USSR	3,442 miles
Lake	Aral Sea, USSR	25,500 sq miles
Mountain	Everest	29,028 ft
Waterfall	Gersoppa, India	830 ft

Oceania
River	Murray-Darling, Australia	2,350 miles
Lake	Eyre, Australia	3,700 sq miles
Mountain	Cook, New Zealand	12,349 ft
Waterfall	Sutherland, New Zealand	1,904 ft

OCEAN AREAS AND DEPTHS

Oceans

Name	Area of Basin (sq. miles)	Greatest Depth (feet)	
Pacific	63,800,000	Mariana Trench,	36,198
Atlantic.......	31,830,000	Milwaukee Deep	30,238
Indian	28,360,000	Java Trench	25,344
Arctic.........	5,500,000	....	18,050

Seas

Name	Area of Basin (sq. miles)	Greatest Depth (feet)	
South China ...	1,148,500	....	16,452
Caribbean[(1)] ...	1,020,000	Cayman Trench,	25,216

Seas

Name	Area of Basin (sq. miles)	Greatest Depth (feet)	
Mediterranean[(2)]	966,750	Ionian Basin,	16,801
Bering	875,750	....	13,442
Gulf of Mexico .	590,000	Sigsbee Deep,	17,070
Okhotsk........	589,800	Kuril Trough,	11,069
East China	482,300	Okinawa Trench,	8,914
Hudson Bay ...	475,800	....	c. 1,500
Japan	389,000	....	12,276
Andaman	308,000	....	14,500
North Sea	222,125	Skaggerak,	2,400
Banda Sea	180,000	Weber Basin,	24,400
Black Sea (and Sea of Azov) .	178,500	....	7,257
Red Sea	169,000	....	8,984

[(1)] Excluding the Gulf of Mexico.
[(2)] Excluding the Black Sea.

PRINCIPAL LAND AREAS OF THE WORLD BELOW SEA LEVEL
(With approx. greatest depth in feet below Mean Sea Level.)

Europe: Netherlands coastal areas (15).
Asia: Jordan Valley, Dead Sea (1290)*.
  China: Sinkiang, Turfan Basin (980).
  U.S.S.R.–Iran: Caspian Sea (85)*.
  Arabia: Trucial Oman-U.A.E. (70).
Africa: Libyan Desert Depressions:—
  Qattara (440), Faiyum (150).
  Wadi Ryan (140), Sittra (110).

Africa: Libyan Desert Depressions (*continued*)—
  Areg (80), Wadi Natrun (75).
  Melfa (60), Siwa (55), Bahrain (50).
  Eritrea: Salt Plains depression (385).
  Algeria-Tunisia: Shott Melghir and El Gharsa (90)*.
America: Death Valley (275), Salton Sea (245)*.
Australia: Lake Eyre (40).

* Water surface

PRINCIPAL HEIGHTS ABOVE SEA LEVEL

	Feet
Europe: Alps—Mont Blanc	15,771
England: Scafell Pike....................	3,210
Wales: Snowdon	3,560
Scotland: Ben Nevis	4,406
Ireland: Carrantuohill..................	3,414
Asia: Everest	29,028
Africa: Kilimanjaro	19,340
North America: McKinley	20,320

	Feet
South America: Aconcagua	22,834
Australia: Kosciusko	7,316
New Zealand: Cook	12,349
Oceania: Jayakusumu[(1)]	16,500
Antarctica: Vinson Massif	16,864

[(1)] Variously known as Ngga Pulu, Carstensz Pyramid, Puntjak Sukarno.

THE ARCTIC OCEAN

The Arctic Ocean consists of a deep sea over 2,000 fathoms, on the southern margin of which there is a broad continental shelf with numerous islands. Into this deeper sea there is only one broad channel, about 700 miles, between Greenland and Scandinavia. Bering Strait is only 49 miles wide and 27 fathoms deep. The southern boundary of the Arctic Ocean is the Wyville-Thomson and Faeroe-Icelandic submarine ridge, which separates the North Atlantic from the Norwegian and Greenland Seas. The Norwegian Deep lies between Norway and Jan Mayen and Iceland; it exceeds 1,500 fathoms. The Greenland Deep, of similar depth, lies between Spitsbergen and Greenland. These two depressions are separated by a somewhat deeply submerged ridge from the east of Jan Mayen to Bear Island, south of Spitsbergen. A shallow ridge from the north-west of Spitsbergen to Greenland separates the Greenland Sea from the deep North Polar Basin. This extends from the north of Spitsbergen and Franz Josef Land to the north of the New Siberia Islands and of the North American Arctic Archipelago. Another more shallow depression is Baffin Bay, less than 1,000 fathoms. This is separated from the North Atlantic by a submarine ridge. Barent's Sea, between Spitsbergen, Norway and Novaya Zemlya, and the Kara Sea, between Novaya Zemlya and the Siberian coast, are respectively below 200 and 100 fathoms. The total area of the Arctic Sea is about 5·5 million square miles, of which 2·3 million square miles are probably covered with floating ice.

THE WORLD'S LAKES

The areas of some of these lakes are subject to seasonal variation.

Name	Locality	Length (Miles)	Area (Sq. Miles)	Name	Locality	Length (Miles)	Area (Sq. Miles)
Caspian Sea	Asia	760	143,000	Balkhash	U.S.S.R.	376	6,700
Superior	North America	383	31,800	Nettilling	Baffin Island	120	5,000
Victoria	Africa	210	26,800	Amadjuak	Baffin Island	75	4,000
Aral	U.S.S.R.	280	25,500	Bangweulu[1]	Africa	150	3,800 (max)
Huron	North America	206	23,100				
Michigan	North America	321	22,300	Onega	U.S.S.R.	145	3,753
Tanganyika	Africa	430	12,700	Eyre[1]	Australia	130	3,700
Great Bear	Canada	200	12,275	Titicaca	South America	110	3,205
Baikal	U.S.S.R.	395	12,200	Nicaragua	Nicaragua	110	3,190
Malawi	Africa	363	11,430	Athabasca	Canada	208	3,120
Great Slave	Canada	300	11,030	Gairdner	Australia	100	3,000
Erie	North America	241	9,910	Turkana			
Winnipeg	Canada	264	9,465	(Rudolf)	Africa	154	2,473
Chad[1]	Africa	175	9,000 (max)	Reindeer	Canada	152	2,467
Ontario	North America	193	7,550	Issyk-Kul	U.S.S.R.	115	2,445
Ladoga	U.S.S.R.	136	6,826	Koko-Nor[1]	China	68	2,300 (max)

[1] Area varies considerably according to season.

VOLCANOES OF THE WORLD

ACTIVE

Volcano	Locality	Height in Feet	Volcano	Locality	Height in Feet
Antofalla	Argentina	21,162	Nyamuragira	Zaire	10,150
Guallatiri	Chile	19,882	Mt. St. Helens	Cascade Range, U.S.A.	9,677
Cotopaxi	Ecuador	19,347	Tambora	Indonesia	9,351
Kluchevskaya	U.S.S.R.	15,913	Villarica	Chile	9,325
Mt Wrangell	Alaska	14,000	Ruapehu	New Zealand	9,175
Muana Loa	Hawaii	13,680	Paricutin	Mexico	9,100
Cameroon	Cameroon	13,350	Asama	Japan	8,340
Erebus	Antarctica	12,450	Ngauruhoe	New Zealand	7,515
Nyiragongo	Zaire	11,385	Hecla	Iceland	4,747
Iliamna	Aleutian Range, U.S.A.	11,000	Vesuvius	Italy	4,198
Etna	Sicily	10,853	Kilauea	Hawaii	4,077
Chillan	Chile	10,500	Stromboli	Lipari Is. Italy	3,038

DORMANT

Llullaillaco	Chile	22,057	Haleakala	Hawaii	10,022
Cayembe	Ecuador	18,982	The Peak	Tristan da Cunha	6,760
Demavend	Iran	18,384	Tongariro	New Zealand	6,458
Popocateptl	Mexico	17,887	Pelée	Martinique	4,800
Pico de Teide	Tenerife	12,198	Soufrière	St Vincent Is., W.I.	4,200
Semerou	Java	12,060			

BELIEVED EXTINCT

Aconcagua	Andes	22,834	Antisana	Ecuador	18,713
Chimborazo	Ecuador	20,561	Citlaltepetl	Mexico	18,700
Kilimanjaro	Tanzania	19,340	Elbruz	Caucasus	18,481

THE HIGHEST MOUNTAINS

The following list contains some of the principal peaks of such ranges as the Himalayas and the Andes, and the highest mountains in other ranges.

Name	Range or Country	Height in Feet	Name	Range or Country	Height in Feet
Everest	Himalayas	29,028	Llullaillaco	Andes	22,057
K 2	Karakoram	28,250	Sajama	Andes	21,463
Kanchenjunga	Himalayas	28,208	Illimani	Andes	21,200
Makalu I	Himalayas	27,824	Chimborazo	Andes	20,561
Dhaulagiri	Himalayas	26,810	McKinley	Alaska	20,320
Nanga Parbat	Himalayas	26,660	Logan	Yukon	19,850
Annapurna	Himalayas	26,504	Cotopaxi	Andes	19,347
Nanda Devi	Himalayas	25,646	Kilimanjaro	Tanzania	19,340
Kamet	Himalayas	25,446	Citlaltepetl	Sierra Madre	18,700
Namcha Barwa	China	25,445	Elbruz	Caucasus	18,481
Minya Konka	China	24,890	St. Elias	Alaska	18,008
Communism Peak	Pamirs	24,590	Popocateptl	Mexico	17,887
Pobedy Peak	Tian Shan	24,406	Foraker	Alaska	17,395
Lenin Peak	Pamirs	23,406	Lucania	Yukon	17,150
Aconcagua	Andes	22,834	Kenya	Kenya	17,058
Ojos del Salado	Andes	22,588	Ararat	Armenia	16,945
Bonete	Andes	22,545	Vinson Massif	Antarctica	16,864
Huascaran	Andes	22,204	Mont Blanc	Alps	15,771

THE LONGEST RIVERS

River	Outflow	Length in Miles
Nile	Mediterranean	4,145
Amazon	Atlantic	4,007
Mississippi-Missouri-Red Rock	Gulf of Mexico	3,741
Yenisei	Arctic	3,442
Yangtze	North Pacific	3,436
Ob-Irtysh	Arctic	3,362
Hwang-ho (Yellow River)	North Pacific	3,000
Zaire (Congo)	Atlantic	2,920
Lena	Arctic	2,734
Amur	North Pacific	2,700
Mackenzie-Peace	Beaufort Sea	2,635
Mekong	China Sea	2,600
Niger	Gulf of Guinea	2,600
Rio de la Plata-Parana	Atlantic	2,485
Murray-Darling	Southern Ocean	2,350
Volga	Caspian Sea	2,293
Zambezi	Indian Ocean	2,200
Madeira	(1)	2,100
Purus (Coxiuara)	(1)	2,000
Yukon	Bering Sea	1,979
St. Lawrence	Gulf of St. Lawrence	1,945
Rio Grande del Norte	Gulf of Mexico	1,885
Ganges-Brahmaputra	Bay of Bengal	1,800
São Francisco	Atlantic	1,800
Indus	Arabian Sea	1,790
Danube	Black Sea	1,770
Salween (No Chiang)	Gulf of Martaban	1,750
Tigris-Euphrates	Persian Gulf	1,700
Tocantins	Pará River	1,700
Orinoco	Atlantic	1,700
Severn	Bristol Channel	220
Thames	North Sea	215

(1) Tributaries of the Amazon.

SOME FAMOUS BRIDGES

Among the outstanding *suspension bridges* of the World are the Verrazano Narrows Bridge, New York (main span, 4,260 ft.); the Golden Gate Bridge, San Francisco (4,200 ft.); Mackinac Bridge, Michigan (3,800 ft.); Bosporus, Turkey (3,523 ft.); George Washington Bridge, New York (3,500 ft.); the Ponte 25 April (Tagus Bridge), Portugal (3,323 ft.); Forth Road Bridge, Scotland (3,300 ft.); Severn Bridge, England (3,240 ft.); Tacoma Bridge, Washington, U.S.A. (2,800 ft.); Orinoco Bridge, Venezuela (2,336 ft.) and the Kanmon Bridge, Japan (2,336 ft.). Lengths shown above are all those of the main or longest span. The Humber Bridge was opened in 1981 and has the longest single central span, 4,626 ft., of any suspension bridge in the world.

The Transbay Bridge (*suspension and cantilever*), crossing San Francisco Bay from Oakland to San Francisco is 7¼ miles long, with spans of 2,310 ft. each.

Among important *steel arch* bridges are the New River Gorge Bridge, Virginia, U.S.A. (1,700 ft); the Bayonne Bridge, from New Jersey to Staten Island, U.S.A. (1,652 ft.); Sydney Harbour Bridge, Australia (1,650 ft.); the Runcorn-Widnes Bridge, England (1,082 ft.); and the Glen Canyon Bridge over the Colorado River, U.S.A. (1,028 ft.). Major *concrete trestle* bridges include the Lake Pontchartrain Causeway, U.S.A. of 2,170 spans extending 23·87 miles and the Oosterscheldebrug, Netherlands, 3·12 miles long. Gladesville Bridge, Sydney, Australia, is a *concrete arch* bridge of 1,000 ft. span. The Tay Bridge in Scotland is a *steel box girder* bridge supported on twin piers (42 spans), 7,365 ft long.

The Chesapeake Bay Bridge-Tunnel (17·6 miles long) joining Cape Charles, Virginia, to Chesapeake Beach has 12·5 miles of *concrete trestle* bridge.

THE LARGEST ISLANDS

Name of Island	Ocean	Area in Sq. Miles
Greenland	Arctic	840,000
New Guinea	Pacific	300,000
Borneo	Pacific	280,100
Madagascar	Indian	227,800
Baffin Island	Arctic	183,810
Sumatra	Indian	182,860
Honshu	Pacific	88,031
Great Britain(1)	Atlantic	84,186
Victoria Island	Arctic	81,930
Ellesmere Island	Arctic	75,767

Name of Island	Ocean	Area in Sq. Miles
Celebes (Sulawesi)	Indian	72,987
South Island, N.Z.	Pacific	58,093
Java (Indian)	Indian	48,763
North Island, N.Z.	Pacific	44,281
Cuba	Atlantic	44,217
Newfoundland	Atlantic	43,359
Luzon	Pacific	40,420
Iceland	Atlantic	39,769
Mindanao	Pacific	36,381
Ireland	Atlantic	32,595

(1) Mainland only.

GREAT SHIP CANALS OF THE WORLD

Canal	Opened	Length, miles	Depth (ft.)†	Width (ft.)†
North Sea (Netherlands)	1876	14½	43	148
Corinth (Greece)	1893	4	26	72
Kiel (Germany)	1895	61	31	132
Manchester (England)	1894	35½	30	120
Panama	1914	50½	45	300
Suez (Egypt)	1869	100	42	197
Terneuzen-Ghent (Netherlands–Belgium)	1895	18½	38	102
St. Lawrence Seaway (Canada)	1959	378*	27	200

† Of largest vessels permitted.   * Includes Lake Ontario and Welland Canal.

INLAND WATERWAYS.—The British Waterways Board are the navigational authority for nearly 2,000 miles of canals and river navigations in England, Scotland and Wales. Some 340 miles are maintained and are being developed as commercial waterways for use by freight-carrying vessels, and another 1,200 miles are being developed for boating, fishing and other amenities. Over a third has now been restored to full navigational use and other stretches are available to small boats. The Manchester Ship Canal, Bridgewater Canal, Rochdale Canal, River Thames and Fenland Waterways are among those which are the responsibility of other authorities.

WATERFALLS OF THE WORLD

		Total height ft.	Greatest single drop ft.
Angel	Venezuela	3,212	2,648
Tugela	S. Africa	3,110	1,350
Utigard	Norway	2,625	1,970
Mongefossen	Norway	2,540	
Yosemite	California, U.S.A.	2,425	1,430
Mardalsfoss	Norway	2,154	974
Tyssestregone	Norway	2,120	948
Kukenaam	Venezuela	2,000	
Sutherland	New Zealand	1,904	815
Takkakaw	Canada	1,650	1,200
Ribbon	California, U.S.A.	1,612	1,612
King George VI	Guyana	1,600	
Wollomombi	Australia	1,580	1,100
Roraima	Guyana	1,500	
Gavarnie	France	1,385	

		Total height ft.	Greatest single drop ft.
BRITISH ISLES			
Eas Coul Aulin	Scotland	658	
Caldron Snout*	England	450	
Powerscourt	Ireland	350	
Pistyll Rhaeadr	Wales	300	

* Cataracts—no sheer drop.

		Width yd.
Khone Cataracts	Laos	11,667
Guayra	Brazil	5,300
Victoria	Zimbabwe-Zambia	1,534
Niagara	Canada–U.S.A.	1,200

LONGEST RAILWAY TUNNELS

E.R. = Eastern Region; L.M.R. = London Midland Region;
S.R. = Southern Region; W.R. = Western Region

United Kingdom

		Miles	Yards
Severn	W.R.	4	484
Totley	E.R.	3	950
Standedge	E.R.	3	66
Sodbury	W.R.	2	924
Disley	L.M.R.	2	346
Ffestiniog	L.M.R.	2	338
Bramhope	E.R.	2	241
Cowburn	L.M.R.	2	182
Sevenoaks	S.R.	1	1693
Morley	E.R.	1	1609
Box	W.R.	1	1452
Dove Holes	L.M.R.	1	1224
Littleborough (Summit)	L.M.R.	1	1125
Anderston	S.R.	1	1010
Ponsbourne	E.R.	1	924
Bleamoor	L.M.R.	1	869
Polhill	S.R.	1	851
Queensbury	E.R.	1	741
Kilsby	L.M.R.	1	666
Lydden	S.R.	1	609
Strood	S.R.	1	569
Oxted	S.R.	1	501
Clayton	S.R.	1	499
Penge	S.R.	1	381
Merstham New (Quarry)	S.R.	1	353
Greenock	Scottish Region	1	351

		Miles	Yards
Bradway	E.R.	1	267
Sough	L.M.R.	1	255
Watford, New	L.M.R.	1	230
Llangyfelach	W.R.	1	193
Caerphilly	W.R.	1	173
Abbot's Cliff	S.R.	1	182
Halton	L.M.R.	1	176
Corby	L.M.R.	1	160
Wenvoe	W.R.	1	107
Sapperton	W.R.	1	100
Wymington	L.M.R.	1	100

The London Underground *Northern Line* between Morden and East Finchley by the City Branch serves 25 stations and uses tunnels totalling 17¼ miles in length).

The World

		Miles	Yards
Simplon	Switzerland–Italy	12	560
Apennine	Italy	11	880
St. Gotthard	Switzerland	9	550
Lötschberg	Switzerland	9	130
Mont Cenis	Italy	8	870
Cascade	United States	7	1410
Arlberg	Austria	6	650
Moffat	United States	6	200
Shimizu	Japan	6	70

DISTANCE OF THE HORIZON

The limit of distance to which one can see varies with the height of the spectator. The greatest distance at which an object on the surface of the sea, or of a level plain, can be seen by a person whose eyes are at a height of five feet from the same level is nearly three miles. At a height of 20 feet the range is increased to nearly six miles, and an approximate rule for finding the range of vision for small heights is to increase the square root of the number of feet that the eye is above the level surface by a third of itself, the result being the distance of the horizon in miles, but is slightly in excess of that in the table below, which is computed by a more precise formula. The table may be used conversely to show the distance of an object of given height that is just visible from a point in the surface of the earth or sea. Refraction is taken into account both in the approximate rule and in the Table.

At a height of	the range is	At a height of	the range is	At a height of	the range is
5 ft.	2·9 miles	500 ft.	29·5 miles	4,000 ft.	83·3 miles
20 ft.	5·9 „	1,000 ft.	41·6 „	5,000 „	93·1 „
50 „	9·3 „	2,000 „	58·9 „	20,000 „	186·2 „
100 „	13·2 „	3,000 „	72·1 „		

CONTROL OF IMMIGRATION STATISTICS 1984

The following table shows the statistics of people accepted for settlement, the main measure of immigration of persons subject to immigration control. They comprise people accepted for settlement on arrival at the ports, and people accepted for settlement on removal of time limit. The latter are people initially admitted to the country subject to a time limit which was subsequently removed on application to the Home Office.

ACCEPTANCES FOR SETTLEMENT BY NATIONALITY 1984

Geographical region and nationality	Total	Men	Women	Children
All Nationalities	50,950	14,940	24,650	11,360
Europe				
European Community				
Belgium	120	30	70	20
Denmark	140	30	80	20
France	590	170	350	60
Germany (Federal Rep.)	640	160	400	70
Greece	220	150	60	20
Italy	520	270	210	50
Luxembourg	†	—	†	—
Netherlands	540	190	260	80
European Community	2,770	1,010	1,440	320
Other Western Europe				
Austria	140	40	80	20
Cyprus	470	250	180	40
Finland	100	10	90	10
Malta	210	110	80	10
Norway	210	50	100	60
Portugal	230	60	130	40
Spain	530	160	300	70
Sweden	400	80	220	100
Switzerland	180	40	120	20
Turkey	530	250	170	110
Yugoslavia	130	50	60	20
Other Western Europe	3,130	1,100	1,540	480
Eastern Europe				
Bulgaria	10	†	†	†
Czechoslavakia	30	†	20	†
German Democratic Republic	10	†	10	†
Hungary	40	10	30	†
Poland	310	40	240	30
Romania	20	†	10	†
USSR	50	†	30	20
Eastern Europe	470	70	340	60
Europe	6,370	2,180	3,320	870
Americas				
Argentina	40	20	20	10
Barbados	50	20	20	10
Brazil	190	30	100	60
Canada	1,400	520	680	200
Chile	60	20	30	10
Colombia	140	10	110	20
Cuba	†	†	†	†
Guyana	190	40	110	40
Jamaica	290	60	160	70
Mexico	70	20	40	10
Peru	60	10	40	10
Trinidad and Tobago	150	30	80	30
U.S.A.	3,750	1,120	1,710	920
Uruguay	†	†	†	—
Venezuela	50	10	20	10
Americas	6,440	1,920	3,120	1,400
Africa				
Algeria	60	50	10	—
Egypt	350	210	100	40
Ethiopia	40	10	20	10
Ghana	690	180	390	120
Kenya	610	140	260	210
Libya	70	40	10	20
Mauritius	470	190	250	30
Morocco	130	40	70	20
Nigeria	320	140	120	60

† Negligible.

ACCEPTANCES FOR SETTLEMENT BY NATIONALITY 1983—*Continued*

Geographical region and nationality	Total	Men	Women	Children
Sierra Leone	80	30	40	20
Somalia	20	10	10	†
South Africa	690	220	310	160
Sudan	50	30	10	10
Tanzania	300	80	140	80
Tunisia	60	30	20	10
Uganda	40	20	20	10
Zambia	110	30	40	40
Zimbabwe	280	100	110	70
Africa	4,380	1,540	1,930	910
Asia				
Indian sub-continent				
Bangladesh	4,180	240	1,430	2,510
India	5,140	1,210	3,150	780
Pakistan	5,510	770	2,910	1,830
Indian sub-continent	14,840	2,220	7,490	5,130
Middle East				
Iran	1,670	950	460	260
Iraq	400	220	100	70
Israel	290	120	120	50
Jordan	120	70	30	20
Kuwait	10	10	†	†
Lebanon	260	110	80	70
Saudi Arabia	50	20	10	20
Syria	70	40	20	10
Middle East	2,870	1,540	830	500
Remainder of Asia				
China	140	20	100	10
Indonesia	60	20	40	10
Japan	1,100	300	410	380
Malaysia	680	210	440	40
Philippines	630	40	470	120
Singapore	160	30	120	20
Sri Lanka	760	310	330	120
Thailand	300	30	220	50
BDTC Hong Kong	1,040	330	400	310
Remainder of Asia	4,860	1,270	2,520	1,060
Asia	22,560	5,030	10,850	6,690
Australasia				
Australia	3,590	1,400	1,930	260
New Zealand	2,460	1,020	1,330	110
Australasia	6,040	2,420	3,260	370
British Overseas citizens	2,690	1,160	1,060	470
Other countries not elsewhere specified	860	200	410	240
Stateless*	1,600	490	700	400
All Nationalities	50,950	14,940	24,650	11,360
Foreign	24,230	7,040	11,610	5,580
Commonwealth	26,720	7,900	13,040	5,780
Old Commonwealth	7,440	2,930	3,940	570
New Commonwealth and Pakistan	24,800	5,740	12,010	7,040
Foreign excluding Pakistan	18,720	6,270	8,700	3,750

*Includes refugees from south-east Asia.   † Negligible.

EMIGRANTS FROM THE UNITED KINGDOM (Thousands)

	Total			Professional			Manual and Clerical			Not gainfully employed†		
	Persons	Males	Females	Persons	Males	Females	Persons	Males	Females	Persons	Males	Females
1977	209	117	91	66	49	17	62	39	23	81	30	51
1978	192	108	85	56	39	16	56	36	20	81	33	48
1979	189	106	82	58	43	15	52	30	22	79	34	45
1980	229	134	95	65	49	16	62	42	20	102	43	59
1981	233	133	100	67	50	17	60	38	22	105	44	61
1982	259	135	124	67	48	19	66	37	29	126	50	76
1983	185	90	95	51	32	18	36	19	16	99	38	60

†Includes housewives, students, children and retired persons.

ENGLISH KINGS AND QUEENS A.D. 827 TO 1603

Name	DYNASTY	MARRIED	Access.	Died	Age	Rgnd. Yrs.
	Saxons and Danes					
EGBERT	King of Wessex and all England		827	839	—	12
ETHELWULF	Son of Egbert		839	858	—	19
ETHELBALD	Son of Ethelwulf		858	860	—	2
ETHELBERT	Son of Ethelwulf		858	866	—	8
ETHELRED	Son of Ethelwulf		866	871	—	5
ALFRED THE GREAT	Son of Ethelwulf	Ealhswith of Gaini	871	899	52	28
EDWARD THE ELDER	Son of Alfred the Great	1, Egwyn; 2, Elfed; 3, Eadgifu	899	925	55	26
ATHELSTAN	Eldest son of Edward the Elder (by 1)		925	940	45	15
EDMUND	Third son of Edward the Elder (by 3)	1, Elgifu; 2, Ethelfled	940	946	25	6
EDRED	Fourth son of Edward the Elder (by 3)		946	955	32	9
EDWY	Son of Edmund (by 1)	1, Ethelfled; 2, Elfthryth	955	959	18	3
EDGAR	Second son of Edmund (by 1)		959	975	32	17
EDWARD THE MARTYR	Son of Edgar (by 1)		975	978	17	4
ETHELRED II	Younger son of Edgar (by 2)	1, Elfgifu; 2, Emma, dau. of Richard, Duke of Normandy	978	1016	48	37
EDMUND IRONSIDE	Eldest son of Ethelred II (by 1)	1, Elfgifu of Deira; 2, Emma, widow of Ethelred II	1016	1016	27	0
CANUTE THE DANE	By conquest and election		1017	1035	40	18
HAROLD I	Son of Canute (by 1)		1035	1040	—	5
HARDICANUTE	Son of Canute (by 2)		1040	1042	24	2
EDWARD THE CONFESSOR	Son of Ethelred II (by 2)	Edith, dau. of Earl Godwin	1042	1066	62	24
HAROLD II	Son of Earl Godwin		1066	1066	44	0
	The House of Normandy					
WILLIAM I	Obtained the Crown by Conquest	Matilda, dau. of Baldwin, Count of Flanders	1066	1087	60	21
WILLIAM II	Third son of William I	(Died unmarried)	1087	1100	43	13
HENRY I	Youngest son of William I	1st Matilda, dau. of Malcolm Canmore, K. of Scotland; 2nd Adelicia, dau. of Godfrey, D. of Louvaine	1100	1135	67	35
STEPHEN	Third son of Stephen, Count of Blois, by Adela, fourth dau. of William I.	Matilda, dau. of Eustace, Count of Boulogne	1135	1154	50	19
	The House of Plantagenet					
HENRY II	Son of Geoffrey Plantagenet by Matilda, only dau. of Henry I; his grandmother, Matilda of Scotland, was a lineal descendant of Alfred and Egbert.	Eleanor, dau. of Guienne and divorced Queen of Louis VII of France	1154	1189	56	35
RICHARD I	Eldest surviving son of Henry II	Berengaria, dau. of Sancho VI, K. of Navarre	1189	1199	42	10
JOHN	Sixth and youngest son of Henry II	1st Avisa, dau. of E. of Gloucester, divorced upon grounds of consanguinity; 2nd Isabella dau. of Aymer, count of Angoulême	1199	1216	50	17
HENRY III	Elder son of John	Eleanor, dau. of Raymond, Count of Provence	1216	1272	65	56
EDWARD I	Eldest surviving son of Henry III	1st Eleanor, dau. of Ferdinand III, K. of Castile; 2nd Margaret, dau. of Philip III, the Hardy, K. of France	1272	1307	68	35
EDWARD II	Eldest surviving son of Edward I	Isabella, dau. of Philip IV, the Fair, K. of France	1307	1327	43	20

Name	DYNASTY	MARRIED	Access.	Died	Age	Rgnd.
EDWARD III	Eldest son of Edward II	Philippa, dau. of William, Count of Holland and Hainault.	1327	1377	65	Yrs. 50
RICHARD II	Son of the Black Prince, eldest son of Edward III	1st Anne, dau. of Emp. Charles IV; 2nd Isabel, dau. of Charles VI of France.	1377	dep. 1399 (d. 1400)	34	22
	The House of Lancaster					
HENRY IV	Son of John of Gaunt, 4th son of Edward III	1st Mary de Bohun, dau. of the E. of Hereford; 2nd Joanna of Navarre, widow of John de Montfort, D. of Brittany.	1399	1413	47	13
HENRY V	Eldest surviving son of Henry IV	Katherine, dau. of Charles VI, K. of France	1413	1422	34	9
HENRY VI	Only son of Henry V (died 1471)	Margaret of Anjou, dau. of René, D. of Anjou	1422	dep. 1461	49	39
	The House of York					
EDWARD IV	Son of Richard, grandson of Edmund, fifth son of Edward III; and of Anne, great-grand-daughter of Lionel, third son of Edward III	Elizabeth Widvile (or Woodville), dau. of Sir Richard Widvile and widow of Sir John Grey of Groby.	1461	1483	41	22
EDWARD V	Eldest son of Edward IV	(Died unmarried)	1483	1483	13	75 days 2
RICHARD III	Younger brother of Edward IV	Anne, dau. of the E. of Warwick, and widow of Edward, Prince of Wales, s. of Henry VI	1483	1485	32	2
	The House of Tudor					
HENRY VII	Son of Edmund, eldest son of Owen Tudor, Katherine, widow of Henry V; his mother, Margaret Beaufort, was great-grand-daughter of John of Gaunt	Elizabeth, dau. of Edward IV	1485	1509	53	24
HENRY VIII	Only surviving son of Henry VII	1st Katherine of Aragon, widow of his elder brother Arthur, (divorced); 2nd Anne, dau. of Sir Thomas Boleyn, (beheaded); 3rd Jane, dau. of Sir John Seymour, (died in childbirth of a son, aft. Edward VI); 4th Anne, sister of William, D. of Cleves, (divorced); 5th Catherine Howard, niece of the Duke of Norfolk, (beheaded); 6th Catherine, dau. of Sir Thomas Parr and widow of Edward Nevill, Lord Latimer.	1509	1547	56	38
EDWARD VI	Son of Henry VIII by Jane Seymour	(Died unmarried)	1547	1553	16	6
JANE	Grand-daughter of Mary, younger sister of Henry VIII, (beheaded Feb. 12, 1554)	Lord Guildford Dudley	1553	1554	17	14 days
MARY I	Daughter of Henry VIII by Katherine of Aragon	Philip II of Spain	1553	1558	43	5
ELIZABETH I	Daughter of Henry VIII by Anne Boleyn	(Died unmarried)	1558	1603	69	44

BRITISH KINGS AND QUEENS FROM 1603

Name	DYNASTY	MARRIED	Access.	Died	Age	Rgnd.
						Yrs.
JAMES I (VI OF SCOT.)	*The House of Stuart* Son of Mary, Queen of Scots, grand-daughter of James IV, and Margaret, daughter of Henry VII.	Anne, dau. of Frederick II of Denmark	1603	1625	59	22
CHARLES I	Only surviving son of James I	Henrietta-Maria, dau. of Henry IV of France	1625	Beh. 1649	48	24
	Oliver Cromwell, Lord Protector, 1653—8; Richard Cromwell, Lord Protector, 1658—9					
	Commonwealth declared May 19, 1649					
CHARLES II	Eldest son of Charles I (restored 1660)	The Infanta Catharine of Portugal, dau. of John IV and sister of Alphonso VI.	1649	1685	55	36
JAMES II (VII OF SCOT.)	Second son of Charles I (Interregnum, Dec. 11, 1688—Feb. 13, 1689)	1st Lady Anne Hyde, dau. of Edward, E. of Clarendon, who died before James ascended the throne; 2nd Mary Beatrice Eleanor d'Este, dau. of Alphonso, D. of Modena.	1685	Dep. 1688 Dec. 1701	68	3
WILLIAM III and MARY II	Son of William Prince of Orange and grand-son of Charles I Eldest Daughter of James II		1689	{1702 1694	51 33	13 6
ANNE	Second daughter of James II	Prince George of Denmark	1702	1714	49	12
GEORGE I	*The House of Hanover* Son of Elector of Hanover, by Sophia, daughter of Elizabeth, daughter of James I	Sophia, dau. of George William, D. of Celle.	1714	1727	67	13
GEORGE II	Only son of George I	Wilhelmina Caroline, dau. of John Frederick, Margrave of Brandenburg-Anspach.	1727	1760	77	33
GEORGE III	Grandson of George II	Charlotte Sophia, dau. of Charles Lewis Frederick, D. of Mecklenburg-Strelitz	1760	1820	81	59
GEORGE IV	Eldest son of George III (Regent from February 5, 1811)	Caroline, dau. of Charles William Ferdinand, D. of Brunswick-Wolfenbuttel,	1820	1830	67	10
WILLIAM IV	Third son of George III	Adelaide, dau. of George Frederick Charles, D. of Saxe-Meiningen.	1830	1837	71	7
VICTORIA	Daughter of Edward, 4th son of George III	Francis Albert Augustus Charles Emmanuel, D. of Saxe, Pr. of Saxe-Cobourg and Gotha.	1837	1901	81	63
EDWARD VII	*The House of Saxe-Coburg* Eldest son of Victoria	Princess Alexandra of Denmark	1901	1910	68	9
GEORGE V	*The House of Windsor* Surviving son of Edward VII	H.S.H. Princess Victoria Mary of Teck	1910	1936	70	25
EDWARD VIII	Eldest son of George V (abdicated 1936)	(Mrs. Wallis Warfield, June 3, 1937.)	1936	1972	77	325 days
GEORGE VI	Second son of George V	The Lady Elizabeth Angela Marguerite, dau. of the 14th Earl of Strathmore and Kinghorne (HER MAJESTY QUEEN ELIZABETH THE QUEEN MOTHER).	1936	1952	56	15
ELIZABETH II	Elder daughter of George VI	Philip, son of Prince Andrew of Greece (H.R.H. THE DUKE OF EDINBURGH).	1952	WHOM GOD PRESERVE.		

SCOTTISH KINGS AND QUEENS A.D. 1057 to 1603

SOVEREIGN	MARRIED	Access.	Died
MALCOLM III (CANMORE) — Son of Duncan I	1st Ingibiorg, widow of Thorfinn, Earl of Orkney; 2nd Margaret, sister of Edgar the Atheling.	1057	1093
DONALD BÁN — Brother of Malcolm Canmore		1093	—
DUNCAN II — Son of Malcolm Canmore, by first marriage		1094	1094
DONALD BÁN (Restored) — Son of Malcolm Canmore, by second marriage		1094	1097
EDGAR — Son of Malcolm Canmore	Died unmarried	1097	1107
ALEXANDER I — Son of Malcolm Canmore	Sybilla, natural daughter of Henry I of England	1107	1124
DAVID I — Son of Malcolm Canmore	Matilda, daughter of Waltheof, Earl of Northumbria ... widow of Simon, Earl of Northampton	1124	1153
MALCOLM IV (THE MAIDEN) — Son of Henry, eldest son of David I	Died unmarried	1153	1165
WILLIAM I (THE LION) — Brother of Malcolm the Maiden	Ermengarde, daughter of Richard, Viscount of Beaumont	1165	1214
ALEXANDER II — Son of William the Lion	1st Joanna, daughter of King John; 2nd Mary, daughter of Ingelram de Coucy (*Picardy*)	1214	1249
ALEXANDER III — Son of Alexander II, by second marriage	1st Margaret, daughter of Henry III of England; 2nd Joleta, daughter of the Count de Dreux	1249	1286
MARGARET, MAID OF NORWAY — Daughter of Eric II of Norway, grand-daughter of Alexander III.	Died unmarried	1286	1290
JOHN BALIOL — Grandson of eldest daughter of David, Earl of Huntingdon, brother of William the Lion		1292	1296
ROBERT I (BRUCE) — Great-grandson of 2nd daughter of David, Earl of Huntingdon, brother of William the Lion	1st Isabella, daughter of Donald, Earl of Mar; 2nd Elizabeth de Burgh, sister of Earl of Ulster.	1306	1329
DAVID II — Son of Robert I, by second marriage	1st Joanna, daughter of Edward II of England; 2nd Margaret, widow of Sir John Logie (divorced, 1369).	1329	1371
ROBERT II (STEWART) — Son of Marjorie, daughter of Robert I by first marriage, and Walter the Steward.	1st Elizabeth, dau. of Sir Robert Mure (or More) of Rowallan; 2nd Euphemia, dau. of Hugh, Earl of Ross, widow of John, Earl of Moray.	1371	1390
ROBERT III — (John, Earl of Carrick) son of Robert II	Annabella, daughter of Sir John Drummond of Stobhall, niece of Margaret Logie.	1390	1406
JAMES I — Son of Robert III	Jane Beaufort, daughter of John, Earl of Somerset, 4th son of John of Gaunt and grandson of Edward III of England.	1406	1437
JAMES II — Son of James I	Mary, daughter of Arnold, Duke of Gueldres	1437	1460
JAMES III — Eldest son of James II	Margaret, daughter of Christian I of Denmark, Norway and Sweden.	1460	1488
JAMES IV — Eldest son of James III	Margaret Tudor, daughter of Henry VII	1488	1513
JAMES V — Son of James IV	1st Madeleine, daughter of Francis I of France; 2nd Mary of Lorraine, daughter of Duc de Guise, widow of Duc de Longueville.	1513	1542
MARY — Daughter of James V, by second marriage	1st Francis, Dauphin of France; 2nd Henry, Lord Darnley; 3rd James, Earl of Bothwell	1542	1587
JAMES VI (Ascended the Throne of England 1603) — Son of Mary, by second marriage	Anne, daughter of Frederick II of Denmark	1567	1625

WELSH SOVEREIGNS AND PRINCES

WALES was ruled by Sovereign Princes from the "earliest times" until the death of Llywelyn in 1282. The first English Prince of Wales was the son of Edward I, and was born in Caernarvon town on April 25, 1284. According to a discredited legend, he was presented to the Welsh chieftains as their Prince, in fulfilment of a promise that they should have a Prince who "could not speak a word of English" and should be native born. This son, who afterwards became Edward II, was created "Prince of Wales and Earl of Chester" at the famous Lincoln Parliament on February 7, 1301. The title Prince of Wales is borne after individual conferment and is not inherited at birth; it was conferred on Prince Charles by Her Majesty the Queen on July 26, 1958. He was invested at Caernarvon on July 1, 1969.

Independent Princes, A.D. 844 to 1282

Rhodri the Great	844–878
Anarawd, son of Rhodri	878–916
Hywel Dda, the Good	916–950
Iago ab Idwal (or Ieuaf)	950–979
Hywel ab Ieuaf, the Bad	979–985
Cadwallon, his brother	985–986
Maredudd ab Owain ap Hywel Dda	986–999
Cynan ap Hywel ab Ieuaf	999–1008
Llywelyn ap Seisyll	1018–1023
Iago ab Idwal ap Meurig	1023–1039
Gruffydd ap Llywelyn ap Seisyll	1039–1063
Bleddyn ap Cynfyn	1063–1075
Trahaern ap Caradog	1075–1081
Gruffydd ap Cynan ab Iago	1081–1137
Owain Gwynedd	1137–1170
Dafydd ab Owain Gwynedd	1170–1194
Llywelyn Fawr, the Great	1194–1240
Dafydd ap Llywelyn	1240–1246
Llywelyn ap Gruffydd ap Llywelyn	1246–1282

English Princes, since A.D. 1301

Edward, b. 1284 (Edwd. II), cr. Pr. of Wales	1301
Edward the Black Prince, s. of Edward III	1343
Richard (Richard II), s. of the Black Prince	1377
Henry of Monmouth (Henry V)	1399
Edward of Westminster, son of Henry VI	1454
Edward of Westminster (Edward V)	1472
Edward, son of Richard III (d. 1484)	1483
Arthur Tudor, son of Henry VII	1489
Henry Tudor (Hen. VIII), s. of Henry VII	1503
Henry Stuart, son of James I (d. 1612)	1610
Charles Stuart (Charles I), s. of James I	1616
Charles (Charles II), son of Charles I	1630
James Francis Edward, "The Old Pretender" (d. 1766)	1688
George Augustus (Geo. II), s. of George I	1714
Frederick Lewis, s. of George II (d. 1751)	1727
George William Frederick (George III)	1751
George Augustus Frederick (George IV)	1762
Albert Edward (Edward VII)	1841
George (George V)	1901
Edward (Edward VIII)	1910
Charles Philip Arthur George	1958

THE FAMILY OF QUEEN VICTORIA

QUEEN VICTORIA *was born* May 24, 1819; *succeeded* to the Throne June 20, 1837; *married* Feb. 10, 1840 Albert, PRINCE CONSORT (*born* Aug. 26, 1819, *died* Dec. 14, 1861); *died* Jan. 22, 1901. Her Majesty had issue:—

1. H.R.H. Princess Victoria (*Princess Royal*) (1840–1901), married, 1858, Frederick, German Emperor; had issue:—

(1) H.I.M. William II (1859–1941), *German Emperor* 1888–1918, married Princess Augusta Victoria of Schleswig-Holstein-Sonderburg-Augustenburg (1858–1921), and secondly, Princess Hermine of Reuss (1887–1947). Had issue:—

(a) Prince William (1882–1951), (*Crown Prince* 1888–1918), married Duchess Cecilia of Mecklenburg-Schwerin (died 1954). (The Crown Prince's children:—Prince Wilhelm (1906–1940); Prince Louis Ferdinand, born 1907, married (1938) Grand Duchess Kira (died 1967), daughter of Grand Duke Cyril of Russia (and has issue four sons and two daughters); Prince Hubertus (1909–1950); Prince Frederick George (1911–1966); Princess Alexandrine Irene, born 1915; Princess Cecilia (1917–1975).

(b) Prince Eitel Frederick (1883–1942), married Duchess Sophie of Oldenburg (marriage dissolved 1926).

(c) Prince Adalbert (1884–1948), married Duchess Adelaide of Saxe-Meiningen. (Prince Adalbert's children:—Princess Victoria Marina, born 1917; Prince William Victor, born 1919.)

(d) Prince Augustus William (1887–1949), married Princess Alexandra of Schleswig-Glucksburg (marriage dissolved 1920). (Prince Augustus's son is Prince Alexander, born 1912.)

(e) Prince Oscar (1888–1958), married Countess von Ruppin. (Prince Oscar's children:—Prince Oscar (1915–1939); Prince Burchard, born 1917; Princess Herzeleide, born 1918; Prince William, born 1922.)

(f) Prince Joachim (1890–1920), married Princess Marie of Anhalt.

(g) Princess Victoria (1892–1980), married (1913)

the Duke of Brunswick. (Princess Victoria's children:—Prince Ernest, born 1914, married Princess Ortrud von Glucksburg, 1951; Prince George, born 1915; Princess Frederica (1917–1981), married Paul I, King of the Hellenes (*see below*); Prince Christian Oskar, born 1919; Prince Welf Heinrich, born 1923, married Princess Alexandra of Ysemburg, 1960).

(2) Princess Charlotte (1860–1919), married (1878) the Duke of Saxe-Meiningen. (Princess Charlotte's daughter, Princess Feodora (1879–1945), married (1898) the Prince Henry XXX. of Reuss.

(3) Prince Henry (1862–1929), married (1888) Princess Irene of Hesse (issue, Prince Waldemar (1889–1945); Prince Sigismund (1896–1978)).

(4) Princess Victoria (1866–1929), married firstly (1890) Prince Adolphus of Schaumburg-Lippe, secondly (1927) Alexander Zubkov.

(5) Prince Waldemar (1868–1879).

(6) Princess Sophia (1870–1932), married (1889) Constantine, *King of the Hellenes*, having issue:—

(a) George II. (1890–1947), *King of the Hellenes* 1922–24 and 1935–47, married Princess Elisabeth of Romania (marriage dissolved 1935).

(b) Alexander (1893–1920), *King of the Hellenes* 1917–1920, married (1919) Aspasia Manos; had issue Princess Alexandra (born 1921), who married, March 20, 1944, King Petar II. of Yugoslavia.

(c) Princess Helena (1896–1982), married (1921) King Carol of Romania, (marriage dissolved 1928), having issue, King Michael, G.C.V.O., born 1921, married (1948) Princess Anne of Bourbon Parma, and has issue, Princess Marguerite, born 1949, Princess Helene, born 1950, and Princess Irina, born 1953.

(d) Paul (1901–1964), *King of the Hellenes* 1947–1964, married 1938, Princess Frederica of Brunswick (*see above*); had issue Constantine (*Constantine XIII.*), born 1940, married 1964, H.R.H. Princess

Anne-Marie of Denmark, and has issue; Sophia, born 1938, married (1962) Don Juan Carlos, Prince of Spain (Juan Carlos I), and has issue; and Irene, born 1942.

(e) Princess Eirene (1904–1974), married (1939) the Duke of Aosta; had issue.

(f) Princess Catherine, born 1913, married (1947) Major R. C. A. Brandram and has issue.

(7) Princess Margarete (1872–1954), married Prince Frederick Charles of Hesse (issue Prince Frederick William (1893–1916); Prince Maximilian (1894–1914); Prince Philipp (1896–1980), married (1925) Princess Mafalda, daughter of King Victor Emmanuel III. of Italy (and has issue, Prince Maurice, born 1926, and Prince Henry, born 1927); Prince Wolfgang, born 1896; Prince Richard, born 1901.

2. **H.M. KING EDWARD VII** (*see* p. 216).

3. **H.R.H. Princess Alice** (1843–1878), married Prince Louis (afterwards reigning Grand Duke) of Hesse. Issue:—

(i) Victoria Alberta (1863–1950), married Admiral of the Fleet the Marquess of Milford Haven, having issue:—

(a) Alice (*H.R.H. Princess Andrew of Greece*) (1885–1969), married Prince Andrew of Greece; having issue (*see* p. 216).

(b) Lady Louise Mountbatten (*Queen of Sweden*) (1889–1965), married Nov. 3, 1923, H.R.H. The Crown Prince of Sweden, later King Gustaf VI. Adolf (died 1973).

(c) George, Marquess of Milford Haven, G.C.V.O., (1892–1938), Capt. R.N., married (1916) Countess Nadejda (died 1963), daughter of Grand Duke Michael of Russia; had issue:—Lady Elizabeth, born 1917; David Michael, Marquess of Milford Haven, O.B.E., D.S.O., Lieutenant, R.N. (ret.) (1919–1970), having issue, George Ivar Louis, *Marquess of Milford Haven, b.* 1963.

(d) Louis, Admiral of the Fleet Earl Mountbatten of Burma, K.G., P.C., G.C.B., O.M., G.C.S.I., G.C.I.E., G.C.V.O. (1900–1979), married 1922, Edwina Cynthia Annette (died 1960), daughter of Lord Mount Temple; having issue two daughters, Patricia (Countess Mountbatten of Burma), born 1924 and the Lady Pamela Hicks, born 1929.

(ii) Elizabeth Fedorovna (1864–1918), (*Grand Duchess Sergius of Russia*).

(iii) Irene (1866–1953), (*Princess Henry of Prussia*), married Prince Henry of Prussia (*see* p. 214).

(iv) Ernest Ludwig, Grand Duke of Hesse (1868–1937), having married (1905) Princess Eleonore of Solms-Hohensolmslich, with issue (a) George, Grand Duke of Hesse, born 1906, married Princess Cecilie of Greece and Denmark (*see* p. 216); *accidentally killed* (with mother, wife and two sons) Nov. 16, 1937; (b) Ludwig, Grand Duke of Hesse (1908–1968), married (Nov. 17, 1937) Margaret, daughter of 1st Lord Geddes.

(v) Frederick William (1870–1873).

(vi) Alix (*Tsaritsa of Russia*) (1872–1918), married (1894) Nicholas II. (*Tsar of All the Russias*), assassinated July 16, 1918, with the Tsar and their issue (Grand Duchess Olga; Grand Duchess Tatiana; Grand Duchess Marie; Grand Duchess Anastasia, and the Tsarevitch).

(vii) Mary (1874–1878).

4. **Admiral of the Fleet H.R.H. Prince Alfred**, *Duke of Edinburgh* (1844–1900), married 1874, Marie Alexandrovna (died 1920), only daughter of Alexander II, Emperor of Russia; succeeded as *Duke of Saxe-Coburg and Gotha* Aug. 22, 1893; had issue:—

(i) Alfred (*Prince of Saxe-Coburg*) (1874–1899).

(2) Marie (*Queen of Romania*) (1875–1938), married (1893), King Ferdinand of Romania; having issue:—

(a) King Carol II. of Romania (1893–1953), married (1921) Princess Helena of Greece (*see* p. 214).

(b) Elizabeth (*Queen of the Hellenes*) (1894–1956), married (1921) King George II of the Hellenes.

(c) Marie (1900–1961), married (1922) King Alexander of Yugoslavia, having issue:—Petar, King of Yugoslavia (1923–1970), married (1944) Princess Alexandra of Greece, having issue, Prince Alexander, born 1945; Prince Tomislav, born 1928, married (1957) Princess Margarita of Baden (*see* p. 216) and has issue, Prince Nicholas, born 1958; Prince Andrej, born 1929, married 1956, Princess Christina of Hesse).

(d) Prince Nicolas, born 1903.

(e) Princess Ileana, born 1909; married (1), Archduke Anton of Austria (having issue:—Stephen, born 1932); and, (2), Dr. Stefan Issarescu.

(f) Prince Mircea (1913–1916).

(3) Victoria (1876–1936), married (1894) Grand Duke of Hesse and (1905) the Grand Duke Cyril of Russia; having issue:—

(a) Marie (1907–1951), married (1925) Prince Friedrich Carl of Leiningen.

(b) Kira Cyrillovna (1909–1967), married (1938) Prince Ludwig of Germany.

(c) Vladimir Cyrillovitch, born 1917, married (1948) Princess Leonida Bagration-Moukhransky, and has issue, a daughter.

(4) Alexandra (1878–1942), married (1896) Prince of Hohenlohe Langenburg; had issue:—

(a) Gottfried (1897–1960).

(b) Maria (*Princess Friedrich of Holstein-Glucksburg*) (1899–1967).

(c) Princess Alexandra (1901–1963).

(d) Princess Irma, born 1902.

(5) Princess Beatrice (1884–1966), married (1909) Infante Alfonso Maria of Orleans (died 1975), and had issue.

5. **H.R.H. Princess Helena Augusta Victoria** (1846–1923), married 1866, General H.R.H. *Prince Christian of Schleswig-Holstein* (died 1917). Issue:—

(i) H.H. Prince Christian Victor (1867–1900).

(ii) H.H. Prince Albert (1869–1931).

(iii) H.H. Princess Helena Victoria (1870–1948).

(iv) H.H. Princess Marie Louise (1872–1956).

(v) H.H. Prince Harold (May 12–20, 1876).

6. **H.R.H. Princess Louise** (1848–1939), married 1871, the Marquess of Lorne, afterwards the 9th Duke of Argyll; without issue.

7. **Field Marshal H.R.H. Prince Arthur**, *Duke of Connaught* (1850–1942), married 1879, H.R.H. Princess Louisa of Prussia (died 1917). Issue:—

(i) H.R.H. Princess Margaret (1882–1920), married 1905, H.R.H. the Crown Prince of Sweden, later KING GUSTAV VI. ADOLF (died 1973) having issue:—

(a) Duke of Westerbotten (1906–1947), married (1932) Princess Sybil of Saxe-Coburg-Gotha (died 1972), having issue one son, now King Carl XVI Gustaf of Sweden, and 4 daughters.

(b) Duke of Upland (Count Sigvard Bernadotte), born 1907.

(c) Princess Ingrid (*Queen Mother of Denmark*), born 1910, married (1935) King Frederick IX. of Denmark (died 1972) and has issue 3 daughters.

(d) Duke of Halland, born 1912.

(e) Duke of Dalecarlia, born 1916.

(ii) Major-Gen. H.R.H. Prince Arthur (1883–1938), married 1913, H.H. the Duchess of Fife; had issue (see below).

(iii) H.R.H. Princess Patricia (*Lady Patricia Ramsay*) (1886–1974), married 1919, Adm. Hon. Sir Alexander Ramsay (died 1972), having issue Alexander Arthur Alfonso David, born 1919.

8. **H.R.H. Prince Leopold**, *Duke of Albany* (1853–1884), married Princess Helena of Waldeck (died 1922). Issue:—

(i) H.R.H. Princess Alice (*Countess of Athlone*)

(1883–1981), married 1904, Maj.-Gen. the Earl of Athlone (died 1957), having issue—
(a) Lady May Helen Emma, born 1906, married (1931) Sir Henry Abel-Smith, K.C.M.G., K.C.V.O., D.S.O., and has issue a son and 2 daughters.
(b) *Viscount Trematon* (1907–1928).
(ii) Charles Edward (1884–1954), *Duke of Saxe-Coburg-Gotha* (1900–1918), married (1905) Princess Victoria of Schleswig-Holstein; surviving issue 2 sons and 2 daughters.

9. **H.R.H. Princess Beatrice** (1857–1944), married

1885, H.R.H. Prince Henry of Battenberg (1858–1896); having issue:— (i) Alexander, *Marquess of Caris-brooke* (1886–1960), married Lady Irene Denison (died 1956); having issue a daughter, Lady Iris Mountbatten (1920–1982).
(ii) Victoria Eugénie (1887–1969), married 1906, His Majesty Alfonso XIII. (*King of Spain* 1886–1931; born 1886, died 1941), having issue.
(iii) Major Lord Leopold Mountbatten (1889–1922).
(iv) Maurice (1891–1914), died of wounds received in action.

THE FAMILY OF KING EDWARD VII

KING EDWARD VII, eldest son of Queen Victoria, *born* Nov. 9, 1841; *married* March 10, 1863, Her Royal Highness Princess Alexandra, eldest daughter of King Christian IX. of Denmark; *succeeded* to the Throne Jan. 22, 1901; *died* May 6, 1910. Issue:—

1. H.R.H. PRINCE ALBERT VICTOR, *Duke of Clarence and Avondale and Earl of Athlone* (1864–1892).

2. H.M. KING GEORGE V (*see* below). Assumed by Royal Proclamation (June 17, 1917) for his House and Family as well as for all descendants in the male line of Queen Victoria who are subjects of these Realms, the name of WINDSOR; (*see* p. 217).

3. H.R.H. LOUISE, *Princess Royal* (1867–1931), married July 27, 1889, 1st *Duke of Fife* (died 1912). Issue:—
(i) H.H. Princess Alexandra, Duchess of Fife (*H.R.H. Princess Arthur of Connaught*) (1891–1959), married 1913, H.R.H. Prince Arthur. Issue:—
Alastair Arthur, Duke of Connaught (1914–1943).
(ii) H.H. Princess Maud (1893–1945), married 1923, 11th Earl of Southesk. Issue:—

The Duke of Fife, born 1929; married (1956) Hon. Caroline Dewar (marriage dissolved, 1966) and has issue.

4. H.R.H. PRINCESS VICTORIA (1868–1935).

5. H.R.H. PRINCESS MAUD (1869–1938), married 1896, Haakon VII., King of Norway (died 1957). Issue:—
H.M. Olav V., K.G., K.T., G.C.B., G.C.V.O., KING OF NORWAY, born 1903, *married* 1929, H.R.H. Princess Marthe of Sweden (died 1954). Issue:—
(a) H.R.H. Princess Ragnhild, born 1930.
(b) H.R.H. Princess Astrid, born 1932.
(c) H.R.H. Harald, Crown Prince of Norway, G.C.V.O., born 1937.

6. H.R.H. PRINCE ALEXANDER JOHN CHARLES ALBERT (April 6–7, 1871).

THE FAMILY OF PRINCE ANDREW OF GREECE

Prince Andrew of Greece (1882–1944), *married* Princess Alice of Battenberg (*H.R.H. Princess Andrew of Greece*), who *died* 1969 (*see* p. 215); had issue:—
(1) Princess Margarita (1905–1981), *married* Prince Gottfried of Hohenlohe-Langenburg (*see* p. 215); issue, Prince Kraft, *born* 1935, Princess Beatrix, *born* 1936, Prince George, *born* 1938; Prince Ruprecht and Prince Albrecht, *born* 1944.
(2) Princess Theodora (1906–1969), *married* Prince Berthold of Baden (*died* 1963); issue, Princess Margarita, *born* 1932 (married, 1957, Prince Tomislav of Yugoslavia (see p. 215)), Prince Max, *born* 1933, Prince Louis, *born* 1937.
(3) Princess Cecilie, *born* 1911, *married* George, Grand Duke of Hesse, accidentally killed with husband and two sons, 1937 (*see* p. 215).
(4) Princess Sophie, born 1914, *married* (i) Prince Christopher of Hesse (died, 1944), having issue, Princess Christina, *born* 1933, Princess Dorothea, *born* 1934, Prince Charles, *born* 1937, Prince Rainer, *born* 1939, Princess Clarissa, *born* 1944); *married* (ii) Prince George of Hanover, and has further issue.
(5) Prince Philip (*H.R.H. the Prince Philip, Duke of Edinburgh*), *born* June 10, 1921 (*see* p. 218).

THE FAMILY OF KING GEORGE V

KING GEORGE V., second son of King Edward VII., *born* June 3, 1865; *married* July 6, 1893, Her Serene Highness Princess Victoria Mary Augusta Louise Olga Pauline Claudine Agnes (Queen Mary), *succeeded* to the throne May 6, 1910; *died* Jan. 20, 1936. Queen Mary died March 24, 1953. Issue:—

H.R.H. THE DUKE OF WINDSOR (EDWARD Albert Christian George Andrew Patrick David), *born* June 23, 1894, *succeeded* to the Throne as KING EDWARD VIII., Jan. 20, 1936; *abdicated* Dec. 11, 1936; *married* June 3, 1937, Mrs. Wallis Warfield (The Duchess of Windsor), *died* May 28, 1972.

H.M. KING GEORGE VI. (Albert Frederick Arthur George) *born* at York Cottage, Sandringham, Dec. 14, 1895; *married* April 26, 1923, to Lady Elizabeth Angela Marguerite (HER MAJESTY QUEEN ELIZABETH THE QUEEN MOTHER), daughter of the 14th Earl of Strathmore and Kinghorne, *succeeded* to the throne Dec. 11, 1936; *died* Feb. 6, 1952, having had issue (*see* pp. 218 and 219).

H.R.H. THE PRINCESS ROYAL (Victoria Alexandra Alice MARY), *born* April 25, 1897, *married* Feb. 28, 1922, the 6th Earl of Harewood (*born* Sept. 9, 1882; *died* May 24, 1947), *died* at Harewood House, Yorks., March 28, 1965, leaving issue:—
(1) George Henry Hubert Lascelles, *7th Earl of Harewood*, born Feb. 7, 1923; *married*, firstly, Sept. 29, 1949, Maria Donata (Marion), daughter of the late Erwin Stein (marriage dissolved 1967), and has issue, (i) David Henry George, Viscount Lascelles, *born* Oct. 21, 1950; (ii) James Edward, *born* Oct. 5, 1953,

married, April 4, 1973, Fredericka Duhrrson; (iii) Robert Jeremy Hugh, *born* Feb. 14, 1955; secondly, July 31, 1967, Mrs. Patricia Elizabeth Tuckwell, and has issue, Mark Hubert, *born* July 5, 1964.
(2) Gerald David Lascelles, *born* Aug. 21, 1924, *married* July 15, 1952, Miss Angela Dowding (marriage dissolved, 1978), and has issue, Henry Ulick, *born* May 19, 1953; secondly, Nov. 17, 1978, Mrs. Elizabeth Evelyn Colvin.

H.R.H. THE DUKE OF GLOUCESTER (Henry William Frederick Albert), Duke of Gloucester, Earl of Ulster and Baron Culloden, *born* March 31, 1900, *married* Nov. 6, 1935, Lady Alice Montagu-Douglas-Scott, daughter of the 7th Duke of Buccleuch (H.R.H. Princess Alice, Duchess of Gloucester, C.I., G.C.B., G.C.V.O., G.B.E., Grand Cordon of Al Kamal, Colonel-in-Chief of the Royal Hussars (Prince of Wales's Own), the King's Own Scottish Borderers, the Royal Corps of Transport, Deputy Colonel-in-Chief, Royal Anglian Regt., Air Chief Commandant W.R.A.F., *born* Dec. 25, 1901); *died* June 10, 1974, leaving issue:
(1) H.R.H. Prince William Henry Andrew Frederick, *born* Dec. 18, 1941; *accidentally killed* Aug. 28, 1972
(2) H.R.H. Prince Richard Alexander Walter George, *Duke of Gloucester*, G.C.V.O., Colonel-in-Chief, Gloucestershire Regiment, Grand Prior of the Order of St. John of Jerusalem, *born* Aug. 26, 1944, *married* July 8, 1972, Brigitte von Deurs and has issue, (i) Alexander Patrick George Richard, Earl of Ulster, *born* Oct. 24, 1974, (ii) Davina Elizabeth Alice Benedikte (Lady Davina Windsor), *born* Nov. 19, 1977 and (iii) Rose Victoria Brigitte Louise (Lady Rose Windsor), *born* March 1, 1980. *Residences*—Kensington Palace, W.8.; Barnwell Manor, Peterborough.

H.R.H. THE DUKE OF KENT (George Edward Alexander Edmund), Duke of Kent, Earl of St. Andrews and Baron Downpatrick, *born* Dec. 20, 1902, *married* Nov. 29, 1934, H.R.H. Princess Marina of Greece and Denmark (*born* Nov. 30, O.S., 1906; *died* Aug. 27, 1968). *Killed on Active Service*, Aug. 25, 1942 leaving issue:—
(1) H.R.H. Prince EDWARD George Nicholas Paul Patrick, *Duke of Kent*, G.C.M.G., G.C.V.O., *born* Oct. 9, 1935. Lt.-Col. The Royal Scots Dragoon Guards, Personal A.D.C. to the Queen, Colonel, Scots Guards, Colonel-in-Chief, Royal Regiment of Fusiliers, *married* June 8, 1961, Katharine Lucy Mary, G.C.V.O., Controller Commandant, Women's Royal Army Corps, Hon. Major-General, Colonel-in-Chief Army Catering Corps, daughter of Sir William Worsley, Bt., and has issue, (i) George Philip Nicholas, Earl of St. Andrews, *born* June 26, 1962; (ii) Helen Marina Lucy (Lady Helen Windsor), *born* April 28, 1964; (iii) Nicholas Charles Edward Jonathan (Lord Nicholas Windsor), *born* July 25, 1970. *Residences*—York House, St. James's Palace, S.W.1.; Anmer Hall, Norfolk.
(2) H.R.H. Princess ALEXANDRA Helen Elizabeth Olga Christabel, G.C.V.O., *born* Dec. 25, 1936, Colonel-in-Chief, 17th/21st Lancers, The King's Own Border Regiment, Deputy Colonel-in-Chief, The Light Infantry, Hon. Colonel North Irish Horse, Air Chief Commandant, Princess Mary's Royal Air Force Nursing Service, *married* April 24, 1963, Hon. Angus Ogilvy, son of the 12th Earl of Airlie, *born* Sept. 14, 1928, and has issue, (i) James Robert Bruce, *born* Feb. 29, 1964 and (ii) Marina Victoria Alexandra, *born* July 31, 1966. *Residence*—Thatched House Lodge, Richmond, Surrey. *Office*—22 Friary Court, St. James's Palace, S.W.1.
(3) H.R.H. Prince MICHAEL George Charles Franklin, *born* July 4, 1942, Major, Royal Hussars, *married* June 30, 1978, Baroness Marie-Christine von Reibnitz, and has issue, (i) Frederick Michael George David Louis (Lord Frederick Windsor), *born* April 6, 1979 and (ii) Gabriella Marina Alexandra Ophelia (Lady Ella Windsor), born April 23, 1981. *Residences*—Kensington Palace, W.8.; Nether Lypiatt Manor, Stroud, Glos.

H.R.H. PRINCE JOHN, *born* July 12, 1905; *died* Jan. 18, 1919.

THE HOUSE OF WINDSOR

Her Most Excellent Majesty ELIZABETH THE SECOND (Elizabeth Alexandra Mary of Windsor) by the Grace of God, of the United Kingdom of Great Britain and Northern Ireland and of Her other Realms and Territories Queen, Head of the Commonwealth, Defender of the Faith, Sovereign of the British Orders of Knighthood and Sovereign Head of the Order of St. John, Lord High Admiral of the United Kingdom, Colonel-in-Chief of The Life Guards, The Blues and Royals (Royal Horse Guards and 1st Dragoons), The Royal Scots Dragoon Guards (Carabiniers and Greys), 16th/5th The Queen's Royal Lancers, Royal Tank Regiment, Corps of Royal Engineers, Grenadier Guards, Coldstream Guards, Scots Guards, Irish Guards, Welsh Guards, The Royal Welch Fusiliers, The Queen's Lancashire Regiment, The Argyll and Sutherland Highlanders (Princess Louise's), The Royal Green Jackets, Royal Army Ordnance Corps, Corps of Royal Military Police, The Queen's Own Mercian Yeomanry, The Duke of Lancaster's Own Yeomanry, Canadian Forces Military Engineers Branch, The King's Own Calgary Regiment, Royal 22e Regiment, Governor-General's Foot Guards, The Canadian Grenadier Guards, Le Régiment de la Chaudière, 2nd Bn. Royal New Brunswick Regt. (North Shore), The 48th Highlanders of Canada, The Argyll and Sutherland Highlanders of Canada (Princess Louise's), The Calgary Highlanders, Royal Australian Engineers, Royal Australian Infantry Corps, Royal Australian Army Ordnance Corps, Royal Australian Army Nursing Corps, The Corps of Royal New Zealand Engineers, Royal New Zealand Infantry Regiment, Royal New Zealand Army Ordnance Corps, Royal Malta Artillery, Malawi Rifles, Captain-General of Royal Regiment of Artillery, The Honourable Artillery Company, Combined Cadet Force, Royal Regiment of Canadian Artillery, Royal Regiment of Australian Artillery, Royal Regiment of New Zealand Artillery, Royal New Zealand Armoured Corps, Air-Commodore-in-Chief, R. Aux.A.F., R.A.F. Regiment, Royal Observer Corps, Royal Canadian Air Force Auxiliary, Australian Citizen Air Force, Commandant-in-Chief, Royal Air Force College, Cranwell, Hon. Air Commodore, R.A.F. Marham, Hon. Commissioner, Royal Canadian Mounted Police, Master of the Merchant Navy and Fishing Fleets, Head of the Civil Defence Corps.

Elder daughter of His late Majesty King George VI and of Her Majesty Queen Elizabeth the Queen Mother; *born* at 17 Bruton Street, London, W.1, April 21, 1926, *succeeded* to the throne February 6, 1952, *crowned* June 2, 1953; having *married*, November 20, 1947, in Westminster Abbey, Philip, Duke of Edinburgh, Earl of Merioneth and Baron Greenwich (H.R.H. The Prince Philip, Duke of Edinburgh), K.G., P.C., K.T., O.M., G.B.E., Admiral of the Fleet, Field Marshal, Marshal of the Royal Air Force, Admiral of the Fleet, Royal Australian Navy, Field Marshal, Australian Military Forces, Marshal of the Royal Australian Air Force, Admiral of the Fleet, Royal New Zealand Navy, Field Marshal New Zealand Army, Marshal of the Royal New Zealand Air

Force, Captain General, Royal Marines, Colonel-in-Chief, The Queen's Royal Irish Hussars, The Duke of Edinburgh's Royal Regiment (Berkshire and Wiltshire), The Queen's Own Highlanders (Seaforth and Camerons), Corps of Royal Electrical and Mechanical Engineers, Intelligence Corps, Army Cadet Force, The Royal Canadian Regiment, The Royal Hamilton Light Infantry (Wentworth Regt.), The Cameron Highlanders of Ottawa, The Queen's Own Cameron Highlanders of Canada, The Seaforth Highlanders of Canada, The Royal Canadian Army Cadets, The Royal Australian Electrical and Mechanical Engineers, The Australian Cadet Corps, Corps of Royal New Zealand Electrical and Mechanical Engineers, Colonel of Grenadier Guards, Hon. Colonel, Edinburgh and Heriot-Watt Universities Officers' Training Corps, The Trinidad and Tobago Regiment, Admiral, Royal Canadian Sea Cadets, Air Commodore-in-Chief, Royal New Zealand Air Force, Air Training Corps, Royal Canadian Air Cadets, Colonel-in-Chief, Air Reserve Group of Air Command (Canada), Hon. Air Commodore, R.A.F. Kinloss, Master of the Corporation of Trinity House, Ranger of Windsor Park. *See* p. 216.

Residences—Buckingham Palace, S.W.1.; Windsor Castle, Berks.; Balmoral Castle, Aberdeenshire; Sandringham, Norfolk.

CHILDREN OF HER MAJESTY

H.R.H. THE PRINCE OF WALES (CHARLES Philip Arthur George), K.G., K.T., G.C.B, A.D.C., Prince of Wales and Earl of Chester, Duke of Cornwall and Duke of Rothesay, Earl of Carrick and Baron Renfrew, Lord of the Isles and Great Steward of Scotland, Personal A.D.C. to the Queen, Great Master of the Order of the Bath, Commander Royal Navy, Wing Commander Royal Air Force, Colonel-in-Chief 5th Royal Inniskilling Dragoon Guards, The Cheshire Regiment, The Royal Regiment of Wales (24th/41st Foot), The Gordon Highlanders, The Parachute Regiment, 2nd King Edward VII's Own Gurkha Rifles (The Sirmoor Rifles), Lord Strathcona's Horse (Royal Canadians), Royal Regiment of Canada, Royal Winnipeg Rifles, Royal Australian Armoured Corps, The Royal Pacific Islands Regiment, Air Reserve Group of Air Command (Canada), Air Commodore-in-Chief Royal New Zealand Air Force, Colonel Welsh Guards, Hon. Air Commodore, R.A.F. Brawdy, *born* November 14, 1948, *married* July 29, 1981, Lady Diana Frances Spencer (H.R.H. The Princess of Wales, *born* July 1, 1961), Colonel-in-Chief The Royal Hampshire Regiment, Hon. Air Commodore, R.A.F. Wittering, youngest daughter of the 8th Earl Spencer and the Hon. Mrs. Shand Kydd; and has issue, (i) William Arthur Philip Louis (H.R.H. Prince William of Wales), *born* June 21, 1982, and (ii) Henry Charles Albert David (H.R.H. Prince Henry of Wales), *born* Sept. 15, 1984.

Residences—Highgrove, Doughton, Tetbury, Glos.; Kensington Palace, W.8. *Office*—Buckingham Palace, S.W.1.

H.R.H. PRINCESS ANNE ELIZABETH ALICE LOUISE, G.C.V.O. Chief Commandant Women's Royal Naval Service, Colonel-in-Chief 14th/20th King's Hussars, Royal Corps of Signals, The Royal Scots (The Royal Regiment), The Worcestershire and Sherwood Foresters Regiment, 8th Canadian Hussars (Princess Louise's), Canadian Forces Communications and Electronics Branch, Grey and Simcoe Foresters, The Regina Rifle Regiment, Royal Australian Corps of Signals, Royal New Zealand Corps of Signals, Royal New Zealand Nursing Corps, Hon. Air Commodore, R.A.F. Lyneham, Commandant-in-Chief, Ambulance and Nursing Cadets, Commandant-in-Chief, Women's Transport Service (FANY), *born* August 15, 1950, *married* Nov. 14, 1973, Capt. Mark Anthony Peter Phillips, C.V.O. (*born* Sept. 22, 1948), Personal A.D.C. to the Queen, and has issue, (i) Peter Mark Andrew, *born* Nov. 15, 1977, and (ii) Zara Anne Elizabeth, *born* May 15, 1981.

Residence—Gatcombe Park, Minchinhampton, Stroud, Glos. *Office*—Buckingham Palace, S.W.1.

H.R.H. PRINCE ANDREW ALBERT CHRISTIAN EDWARD, C.V.O., *born* Feb. 19, 1960. Lieutenant, Royal Navy; Personal A.D.C. to the Queen.

H.R.H. PRINCE EDWARD ANTONY RICHARD LOUIS, *born* March 10, 1964. Second Lieutenant Royal Marines.

MOTHER OF HER MAJESTY

H.M. QUEEN ELIZABETH THE QUEEN MOTHER (Elizabeth Angela Marguerite) (daughter of the 14th Earl of Strathmore and Kinghorne), Lady of the Garter, Lady of the Thistle, Order of the Crown of India, Grand Master of the Royal Victorian Order, Dame Grand Cross of the Order of the British Empire, Royal Victorian Chain, Doctor of Civil Law, Doctor of Literature, Colonel-in-Chief 1st the Queen's Dragoon Guards, The Queen's Own Hussars, 9th/12th Royal Lancers (Prince of Wales's) The King's Regiment, The Royal Anglian Regiment, The Light Infantry, The Black Watch (Royal Highland Regiment), Royal Army Medical Corps, The Black Watch (Royal Highland Regiment) of Canada, The Toronto Scottish Regiment, Canadian Forces Medical Services, Royal Australian Army Medical Corps, Royal New Zealand Army Medical Corps, Hon. Colonel The Royal Yeomanry, The London Scottish, University of London Officers' Training Corps, Commandant-in-Chief R.A.F. Central Flying School, W.R.N.S., W.R.A.C., W.R.A.F., Air Chief Commandant, Women's Royal Australian Air Force, Patron St. Andrew's Ambulance Association, Commandant-in-Chief Nursing Corps and Divisions. *Born* August 4, 1900, *married* April 26, 1923, Prince Albert Frederick Arthur George of Windsor, Duke of York (*see* King GEORGE VI).

Residences.—Clarence House, St. James's Palace, S.W.1.; Royal Lodge, Windsor Great Park, Berks.; Castle of Mey, Caithness, Scotland.

SISTER OF HER MAJESTY

H.R.H. PRINCESS MARGARET ROSE (The Princess Margaret, Countess of Snowdon), C.I., G.C.V.O., Colonel-in-Chief, 15th/19th The King's Royal Hussars, The Royal Highland Fusiliers (Princess Margaret's Own Glasgow and Ayrshire Regiment), Queen Alexandra's Royal Army Nursing Corps, The Highland Fusiliers of Canada, The Princess Louise Fusiliers, Women's Royal Australian Army Corps, The Bermuda Regiment, Deputy Colonel-in-Chief, The Royal Anglian Regiment, Hon. Air Commodore, R.A.F. Coningsby, Commandant-in-Chief, St. John Ambulance Brigade Cadets, Grand President, St. John Ambulance Association and Brigade,

Dame Grand Cross of the Order of St. John of Jerusalem, President of the Girl Guides Association; *born* Aug. 21, 1930; *married* May 6, 1960 Anthony Charles Robert Armstrong-Jones, G.C.V.O. (*born* March 7, 1930, son of the late Ronald Armstrong-Jones, Q.C. and the Countess of Rosse, *created* Earl of Snowdon, 1961, Constable of Caernarvon Castle, *marriage dissolved*, 1978); and has issue, (i) David Albert Charles, Viscount Linley, *born* Nov. 3, 1961, and (ii) Sarah Frances Elizabeth (Lady Sarah Armstrong-Jones), *born* May 1, 1964.

Residence.—Kensington Palace, W.8.

Order of Succession to the Throne

1. H.R.H. Prince of Wales; 2. H.R.H. Prince William of Wales; 3. H.R.H. Prince Henry of Wales; 4. H.R.H. Prince Andrew; 5. H.R.H. Prince Edward; 6. H.R.H. Princess Anne, Mrs Mark Phillips; 7. Master Peter Phillips; 8. Miss Zara Phillips; 9. H.R.H. Princess Margaret, Countess of Snowdon; 10. Viscount Linley; 11. Lady Sarah Armstrong-Jones; 12. H.R.H. Duke of Gloucester; 13. Earl of Ulster; 14. Lady Davina Windsor; 15. Lady Rose Windsor; 16. H.R.H. Duke of Kent; 17. Earl of St. Andrews; 18. Lord Nicholas Windsor; 19. Lady Helen Windsor; 20. Lord Frederick Windsor; 21. Lady Gabriella Windsor; 22. H.R.H. Princess Alexandra, Hon. Mrs Angus Ogilvy; 23. Mr James Ogilvy; 24. Miss Marina Ogilvy.

Precedence in England

The Sovereign
The Prince Philip, Duke of Edinburgh.
The Prince of Wales, The Prince Andrew, The Prince Edward.
Princes of the Blood Royal.
Archbishop of Canterbury.
Lord High Chancellor.
Archbishop of York.
The Prime Minister.
Lord President of the Council.
Speaker of the House of Commons.
Lord Privy Seal.
High Commissioners of Commonwealth Countries and Ambassadors of Foreign States.
Dukes, according to their Patents of Creation:
(1) Of England; (2) of Scotland; (3) of Great Britain; (4) of Ireland; (5) those created since the Union.
Ministers and Envoys.
Eldest sons of Dukes of Blood Royal.
Marquesses, in same order as Dukes.
Dukes' eldest Sons.
Earls, in same order as Dukes.
Younger sons of Dukes of Blood Royal.
Marquesses' eldest Sons.
Dukes' younger Sons.
Viscounts, in same order as Dukes.
Earls' eldest Sons.
Marquesses' younger Sons.
Bishops of London, Durham and Winchester.
All other English Bishops, according to their seniority of Consecration.
Secretaries of State, if of the degree of a Baron.
Barons, in same order as Dukes.
Treasurer of H.M.'s Household.
Comptroller of H.M.'s Household.
Vice-Chamberlain of H.M.'s Household.
Secretaries of State under the degree of Baron.
Viscounts' eldest Sons.
Earls' younger Sons.
Barons' eldest Sons.

Knights of the Garter if Commoners.
Privy Councillors if of no higher rank.
Chancellor of the Exchequer.
Chancellor of the Duchy of Lancaster.
Lord Chief Justice of England.
Master of the Rolls.
President of the Family Division.
Vice-Chancellor.
The Lords Justices of Appeal.
Judges of the High Court.
Vice-Chancellor of County Palatine of Lancaster.
Viscounts' younger Sons.
Barons' younger Sons.
Sons of Life Peers.
Baronets of entire Kingdom, according to date of Patents.
Knights of the Thistle if Commoners.
Knights Grand Cross of the Bath.
Members of the Order of Merit.
Knights Grand Commanders of the Star of India.
Knights Grand Cross of St. Michael and St. George.
Knights Grand Commanders of the Indian Empire.
Knights Grand Cross of the Royal Victorian Order.
Knights Grand Cross of Order of the British Empire.
Companions of Honour.
Knights Commanders of the above Orders.
Knights Bachelor.
Official Referees of The Supreme Court.
Circuit judges and judges of the Mayor's and City of London Court.
Companions and Commanders *e.g.* C.B.; C.S.I.; C.M.G.; C.I.E.; C.V.O.; C.B.E.; D.S.O.; M.V.O. (4th); O.B.E.; I.S.O.
Eldest Sons of younger Sons of Peers.
Baronets' eldest Sons.
Eldest Sons of Knights in the same order as their Fathers.

M.V.O. (5th); M.B.E.
Younger Sons of the younger Sons of Peers.
Baronets' younger Sons.
Younger Sons of Knights in the same order as their Fathers.
Naval, Military, Air, and other Esquires by Office.

WOMEN

Women take the same rank as their husbands or as their brothers; but the daughter of a Peer marrying a Commoner retains her title as Lady or Honourable. Daughters of Peers rank next immediately after the wives of their elder brothers, and before their younger brothers' wives. Daughters of Peers marrying Peers of lower degree take the same order of precedency as that of their husbands; thus the daughter of a Duke marrying a Baron becomes of the rank of Baroness only while her sisters married to commoners retain their rank and take precedence of the Baroness. Merely official rank on the husband's part does not give any similar precedence to the wife.

Peeresses in their own right take the same Precedence as Peers of the same rank, i.e. from their date of creation.

LOCAL PRECEDENCE

ENGLAND AND WALES.—No written code of county or city order of precedence has been promulgated, but in Counties the Lord Lieutenant stands first, and secondly (normally) the Sheriff, and therefore in Cities and Boroughs the Lord Lieutenant has social precedence over the Mayor; but at City or Borough functions the Lord Mayor or Mayor will preside. At Oxford and Cambridge the High Sheriff takes precedence of the Vice-Chancellor.
SCOTLAND.—*See* Index.

THE QUEEN'S HOUSEHOLD

Lord Chamberlain, The Earl of Airlie, P.C., G.C.V.O.
Lord Steward, The Duke of Northumberland, K.G., P.C., G.C.V.O., T.D., F.R.S.
Master of the Horse, The Earl of Westmorland, K.C.V.O.
Treasurer of the Household, J. Cope, M.P.
Comptroller of the Household, Carol Mather, M.C., M.P.
Vice-Chamberlain, The Hon. Robert Boscawen, M.C., M.P.

Gold Stick, Maj.-Gen. Lord Michael Fitzalan Howard, G.C.V.O., C.B., C.B.E., M.C.; General Sir Desmond Fitzpatrick, G.C.B., D.S.O., M.B.E., M.C.
Vice-Admiral of the United Kingdom, Admiral Sir William O'Brien, K.C.B., D.S.C.
Rear-Admiral of the United Kingdom, Admiral Sir Derek Empson, G.B.E., K.C.B.
First and Principal Naval Aide-de-Camp, Admiral Sir William Staveley, G.C.B.
Flag Aide de Camp, Admiral Sir Peter Stanford, K.C.B., L.V.O.
Aides-de-Camp General, General Sir Thomas Morony, K.C.B., O.B.E.; General Sir Roland Guy, K.C.B., C.B.E., D.S.O.; General Sir Nigel Bagnall, K.C.B., C.V.O., M.C.; General Sir Edward Burgess, K.C.B., O.B.E.
Air Aides-de-Camp, Air Chief Marshal Sir Keith Williamson, G.C.B., A.F.C.; Air Chief Marshal Sir Thomas Kennedy, K.C.B., A.F.C.

Mistress of the Robes, The Duchess of Grafton, G.C.V.O.
Ladies of the Bedchamber, The Marchioness of Abergavenny, D.C.V.O.; The Countess of Airlie, C.V.O.
Extra Lady of the Bedchamber, The Countess of Cromer, C.V.O.
Women of the Bedchamber, Hon. Mary Morrison, D.C.V.O.; Lady Susan Hussey, D.C.V.O.; Lady Abel Smith, D.C.V.O.; Mrs. John Dugdale, D.C.V.O.
Extra Women of the Bedchamber, Mrs. John Woodroffe, C.V.O.; Lady Rose Baring, D.C.V.O.; Mrs. Michael Wall, D.C.V.O.
Extra Equerries, Vice-Admiral Sir Conolly Abel-Smith, G.C.V.O., C.B.; Vice-Adm. Sir Peter Ashmore, K.C.B., K.C.V.O., D.S.C.; Rear-Adm. the Earl Cairns, G.C.V.O., C.B.; Lt.-Col. The Lord Charteris of Amisfield, P.C., G.C.B., G.C.V.O., O.B.E., Q.S.O.; Vice-Adm. Sir Peter Dawnay, K.C.V.O., C.B., D.S.C.; Sir Edward Ford, K.C.B., K.C.V.O.; Rear-Adm. P. Greening; Brig. Sir Geoffrey Hardy-Roberts, K.C.V.O., C.B., C.B.E.; Sir William Heseltine, K.C.V.O., C.B.; Rear-Admiral Sir Hugh Janion, K.C.V.O.; Lt.-Col. Sir John Johnston, K.C.V.O., M.C.; Major Sir Rennie Maudslay, G.C.V.O., K.C.B., M.B.E.; Air Commodore Sir Dennis Mitchell, K.B.E., C.V.O., D.F.C., A.F.C.; The Rt. Hon Sir Philip Moore, G.C.B., G.C.V.O., C.M.G.; Rear-Adm. Sir Patrick Morgan, K.C.V.O., C.B., D.S.C.; Lt.-Col. Ririd Myddleton, M.V.O.; Lt.-Col. Sir Eric Penn, G.C.V.O., O.B.E., M.C.; Cdr. Sir Philip Row, K.C.V.O., O.B.E., R.N.; Air Vice-Marshal John Severne, L.V.O., O.B.E., A.F.C.; Group Capt. Peter Townsend, C.V.O., D.S.O., D.F.C.; Rear-Admiral Sir Richard John Trowbridge, K.C.V.O.; Lt.-Col. G. West; Air Commodore Sir Archie Little Winskill, K.C.V.O., C.B.E., D.F.C.

THE PRIVATE SECRETARY'S OFFICE
Buckingham Palace, S.W.1.

Private Secretary to The Queen, The Rt. Hon. Sir Philip Moore, G.C.B., G.C.V.O., C.M.G.
Deputy Private Secretary, Sir William Heseltine, K.C.V.O., C.B.
Assistant Private Secretary, R. Fellowes, L.V.O.
Defence Services Secretary, Air Vice-Marshal Richard Peirse, C.B.
Press Secretary, M. S. McA. Shea, L.V.O.
Assistant Press Secretaries, J. Haslam; V. Chapman, L.V.O. (*temp.*).
Chief Clerk, Miss A. Bowlby, M.V.O., M.B.E.
Secretary to the Private Secretary, Miss E. Pearce, M.V.O.
Clerks, Miss J. M. Damrel; Miss J. A. Adams, M.V.O.; Mrs. M. J. Atwell, M.V.O.; Mrs. J. Bean, M.V.O.; Mrs. W. I. Eldridge; Mrs. C. N. Good; Mrs. J. Rose; Mrs. C. Calkin; Miss K. E. May-Smith; Mrs. A. M. Neal, L.V.O. (*Press*); Miss F. M. Simpson, L.V.O. (*Press*); Miss S. P. Brennan, M.V.O. (*Press*); Miss K. McGrigor (*Press*).
Lady in Waiting's Office, Mrs. S. G. M. Gordon.

The Queen's Archives
Round Tower, Windsor Castle.

Keeper of The Queen's Archives, The Rt. Hon. Sir Philip Moore, G.C.B., G.C.V.O., C.M.G.
Assistant Keeper, O. Everett, L.V.O.
Registrar, Miss J. Langton, L.V.O.
Assistant Registrars, Miss E. Cuthbert, M.V.O.; Miss F. Dimond, M.V.O.; Mrs. G. de Bellaigue.

DEPARTMENT OF THE KEEPER OF THE PRIVY PURSE AND TREASURER TO THE QUEEN
Buckingham Palace, S.W.1.

Keeper of the Privy Purse and Treasurer to The Queen, P. T. Miles.

Privy Purse Office

Deputy Keeper of the Privy Purse, Major S. G. B. Blewitt, L.V.O.
Chief Accountant, G. H. Franklin, L.V.O.
Chief Clerk, D. Waters, L.V.O.
Accountant, Mrs. E. Smith, M.V.O.
Clerks, Miss C. Hall, Miss S. Ram.
Land Agent, Sandringham, J. Loyd, C.V.O.
Resident Factor, Balmoral, M. Leslie.

Treasurer's Office

Deputy Treasurer to The Queen, J. Parsons.
Chief Accountant and Paymaster, F. R. Mintram, L.V.O.
Assistant Chief Accountant and Paymaster, D. Walker, M.V.O.
Accountant, Mrs. J. Maitland, M.V.O.
Establishment Officer, P. Wright, C.V.O.
Clerks, Miss C. Auton, M.V.O.; Miss G. Wickham; Mrs. D. C. Mowbray; Miss C. Mackenzie; Miss C. McCarthy.
Print Unit, Miss I. Hoaen, M.V.O.; T. D. Byrne.

Royal Almonry

Lord High Almoner, The Rt. Rev. the Lord Bishop of Rochester.
Hereditary Grand Almoner, The Marquess of Exeter.
Sub-Almoner, Rev. Canon A. D. Caesar, M.A., MUS.B., F.R.C.O.
Secretary, P. Wright, C.V.O.
Assistant Secretary, D. Waters, L.V.O.

THE LORD CHAMBERLAIN'S OFFICE
St. James's Palace, S.W.1.

Comptroller, Lt.-Col. Sir John Johnston, K.C.V.O., M.C.
Assistant Comptroller, Lt.-Col. G. West.
Secretary, J. E. P. Titman, C.V.O.
Assistant Secretary, P. D. Hartley, M.V.O.
Registrar, M. E. Bishop, M.V.O.
State Invitations Assistant, Major J. C. Leech.

Clerks, D. Rankin-Hunt; Miss S. Hay; Miss A. Thomas; Mrs. S. Taylor; Miss K. Lynne; Mrs. M. Lewis; Miss J. Hockley; Miss S. Bowring.

Permanent Lords in Waiting, The Lord Cobbold, K.G., G.C.V.O.; Lt.-Col. The Lord Charteris of Amisfield, P.C., G.C.B., G.C.V.O., O.B.E., Q.S.O.; The Lord Maclean, P.C., K.T., G.C.V.O., K.B.E.

Lords in Waiting, The Lord Somerleyton; The Viscount Boyne; The Viscount Long; The Lord Skelmersdale; The Earl of Caithness; The Lord Brabazon of Tara; The Baroness Cox (*Baroness in Waiting*).

Gentlemen Ushers, Carron Greig, C.V.O.; Col. Gerard Leigh, C.V.O., C.B.E.; Lt.-Col. Sir Julian Paget, Bt., C.V.O.; Air Chief Marshal Sir Neville Stack, K.C.B., C.V.O., C.B.E., A.F.C.; Group-Capt. John Slessor; Major Nigel Chamberlayne-Macdonald, L.V.O., O.B.E.; Air Chief Marshal Sir Roy Austen-Smith, K.B.E., C.B., D.F.C.; Vice-Admiral Sir David Loram, K.C.B., M.V.O.; Capt. Michael Barrow, D.S.O., R.N.

Extra Gentlemen Ushers, Capt. Andrew Yates, L.V.O., R.N.; Major Thomas Harvey, C.V.O., D.S.O.; Air Vice-Marshal Sir Ranald Reid, K.C.B., D.S.O., M.C.; Esmond Butler, C.V.O.; Maj.-Gen. Sir Cyril Colquhoun, K.C.V.O., C.B., O.B.E.; Lt.-Col. Sir John Hugo, K.C.V.O., O.B.E.; Vice-Admiral Sir Ronald Brockman, K.C.B., C.S.I., C.I.E., C.V.O., C.B.E.; Air Marshal Sir Maurice Heath, K.B.E., C.B., C.V.O.; Maj.-Gen. Sir Peter Gillett, K.C.V.O., C.B., O.B.E.; Sir James Scholtens, K.C.V.O.; Sir Patrick O'Dea, K.C.V.O.; Brig.-Gen. Stewart Cooper, C.V.O., O.B.E., C.D.; Admiral Sir David Williams, G.C.B.; Capt. Michael Tufnell, C.V.O., D.S.C., R.N.; H. Davis, C.V.O.; Maj.-Gen. Roland Reid, C.V.O., M.C., C.D.; Lt.-Cmdr. John Holdsworth, C.V.O., O.B.E., R.N.

Gentleman Usher to the Sword of State, Air Chief Marshal Sir John Barraclough, K.C.B., C.B.E., D.F.C., A.F.C.

Gentleman Usher of the Black Rod, Air Chief Marshal Sir John Gingell, G.B.E., K.C.B.

Serjeants at Arms, P. A. Wright, C.V.O.; G. A. Harris, L.V.O., M.B.E.; J. E. P. Titman, C.V.O.

Marshal of the Diplomatic Corps, Lt.-Gen. Sir John Richards, K.C.B.

Vice-Marshal, The Hon. Eustace Gibbs.

Constable & Governor of Windsor Castle, Marshal of the Royal Air Force Sir John Grandy, G.C.B., K.B.E., D.S.O.

Keeper of the Jewel House, Tower of London, Maj.-Gen. Patrick MacLellan, C.B., M.B.E.

Surveyor of The Queen's Pictures, Sir Oliver Millar, K.C.V.O., F.B.A., F.S.A.

Assistant, Miss C. Crichton-Stuart.

Librarian, O. Everett, L.V.O.

Curator of the Print Room, The Hon. Mrs. Roberts, M.V.O.

Adviser for The Queen's Works of Art, Sir Francis Watson, K.C.V.O., F.S.A.

Surveyor of The Queen's Works of Art, Geoffrey de Bellaigue, C.V.O., F.S.A.

Assistant, Mrs D. Harland.

Personal Secretary, Miss S. McNeil.

Master of The Queen's Music, Malcolm Williamson, C.B.E.

Poet Laureate, E. Hughes.

Bargemaster, E. Hunt.

Keeper of the Swans, F. J. Turk, M.V.O.

Superintendent of the State Apartments, St. James's Palace, T. Taylor, M.V.O., M.B.E.

ASCOT OFFICE
St. James's Palace, S.W.1.

Her Majesty's Representative at Ascot, Col. P. Bengough, O.B.E.

Secretary, Miss L. Thompson-Royd.

ECCLESIASTICAL HOUSEHOLD
The College of Chaplains.

Clerk of the Closet, The Bishop of Bath and Wells.

Deputy Clerk of the Closet, Rev. Canon A. D. Caesar, M.A., MUS.B., F.R.C.O.

Chaplains to The Queen, Ven. E. J. G. Ward, M.V.O., M.A.; Rev. J. R. W. Stott, M.A.; Canon P. T. Ashton, M.V.O., M.A.; Rev. A. H. H. Harbottle, M.V.O., M.A.; Canon E. M. Pilkington, M.A.; Ven. T. Barfett, M.A.; Prof. Canon G. R. Dunstan, M.A., D.D., F.S.A.; Canon S. H. Hoffman, M.A.; Rev. Canon D. N. Griffiths, M.A.; Canon D. R. Vicary, M.A., B.SC.; Canon A. Glendining, L.V.O.; Ven. C. W. Borrett, M.A.; Canon J. G. Grimwade, M.A.; Canon J. S. Robertson, M.A.; Canon D. Landreth, T.D., M.A.; Canon J. V. Bean, M.A.; Ven. B. A. O'Ferrall, C.B., M.A.; Canon C. M. Ruston, M.A.; Canon P. A. Welsby, M.A., Ph.D.; Canon P. W. Miller; Canon G. Carnell, M.A.; Rev. K. Huxley, M.A.; Ven. R. Simpson, L.V.O., M.A.; Ven. P. Ashford; Canon G. A. Elcoat; Canon D. C. Gray, T.D., M.Phil., A.K.C.; Canon S. Wilkinson, A.K.C.; Canon J. Treadgold, B.A.; Ven. D. Scott, M.A.; Canon A. Russell, D.Phil.; Canon S. Barrington-Ward, M.A.; Canon E. James, M.A., A.K.C.; Canon J. Hester, M.A.; Rev. S. Pedley, M.A.; Rev. D. Tonge; Rev. Canon C. Craston.

Extra Chaplains, Canon J. S. D. Mansel, K.C.V.O., M.A., F.S.A.; Preb. S. A. Williams, C.V.O.; M.A.

Chapels Royal

Dean of the Chapels Royal, The Bishop of London.

Sub-Dean of Chapels Royal, Rev. Canon A. D. Caesar, M.A., MUS.B., F.R.C.O.

Priests in Ordinary, Rev. W. Booth, M.A.; Rev. A. Ford, M.A.; Rev. G. Watkins.

Organist, Choirmaster and Composer, R. J. Popplewell, F.R.C.O., F.R.C.M.

Domestic Chaplain—Buckingham Palace, Rev. Canon A. D. Caesar, M.A., MUS.B., F.R.C.O.

Domestic Chaplain—Windsor Castle, The Dean of Windsor.

Domestic Chaplain—Sandringham, Rev. J. G. M. W. Murphy, M.A.

Chaplain—Royal Chapel, Windsor Great Park, Rev. Canon J. Treadgold.

Chaplain—Hampton Court Palace, Rev. Canon M. Moore, M.A.

Chaplain—Tower of London, Rev. J. F. M. Llewellyn, L.V.O., M.A.

Organist and Choirmaster—Hampton Court Palace, Gordon Reynolds, L.V.O., A.R.C.M.

MEDICAL HOUSEHOLD

Head of the Medical Household and Physician, J. C. Batten, M.D., F.R.C.P.

Physicians, A. M. Dawson, M.D., F.R.C.P.; C. Elliot, M.R.C.G.P.

Serjeant Surgeon, W. Slack, M.Ch., F.R.C.S.

Surgeon Oculist, P. Holmes Sellors, M.A., B.M., B.Ch., F.R.C.S.

Surgeon Gynaecologist, G. D. Pinker, C.V.O., F.R.C.S.(Edin.), F.R.C.O.G.

Surgeon Dentist, N. A. Sturridge, L.D.S., B.D.S., D.D.S.

Physician to the Household, R. Thompson, D.M., F.R.C.P.

Surgeon to the Household, B. Jackson, M.S., F.R.C.S.

Surgeon Oculist to the Household, T. J. ffytche, F.R.C.S., L.R.C.P.

Apothecary to The Queen and to the Household, N. R. Southward, L.V.O., M.A., M.B., B.Chir., M.R.C.P.

Apothecary to the Household at Windsor, J. P. Clayton, L.V.O., M.A., M.B., B.Chir., M.R.C.S., L.R.C.P.

Apothecary to the Household at Sandringham, H. K. Ford, L.V.O., M.B., F.R.C.G.P.

Coroner of The Queen's Household, Lt.-Col. G. McEwan, M.B., Ch.B.

CENTRAL CHANCERY
OF THE ORDERS OF KNIGHTHOOD
St. James's Palace, S.W.1.

Secretary, Maj.-Gen. D. H. G. Rice, C.V.O., C.B.E.
Assistant Secretary, G. A. Harris, C.V.O., M.B.E.
Insignia Clerk, M. G. P. Kelly, M.V.O.
Clerks, J. McGurk, M.V.O.; Mrs. E. Searle; Miss S. Koller; Miss R. A. Wells; Miss T. Perfect; Miss H. Weir.

The Honorable Corps of Gentlemen at Arms
St. James's Palace, S.W.1.

Captain, The Lord Denham, P.C.; *Lieutenant*, Col. R. J. V. Crichton, M.C.; *Standard Bearer*, Major The Marquess of Donegall; *Clerk of the Cheque & Adjutant*, Major D. Jamieson, V.C.; *Harbinger*, Lt. Col. J. Eagles.

Gentlemen of the Corps

Brigadier, A. N. Breitmeyer.
Colonels, P. Pardoe; A. G. Way, M.C.; T. Hall, O.B.E.; P. Gengough, O.B.E.; Hon. N. Crossley, T.D.; T. Wilson.
Lieutenant-Colonels, N. H. R. Speke, M.C.; D. A. St. G. Laurie, O.B.E., M.C.; P. Hodgson; R. Steele, M.B.E.; W. S. P. Lithgow; Sir James Scott, Bt.; R. Mayfield, D.S.O.
Majors, Sir Richard Carne Rasch, Bt.; J. D. Dillon, D.S.C., R.M.; The Lord Suffield, M.C.; T. St. Aubyn; Sir Torquhil Matheson of Matheson, Bt.; F. J. H. Matheson; J. A. J. Nunn; Sir Philip Duncombe, Bt.; I. B. Ramsden, M.B.E.; M. J. Drummond-Brady; A. Arkwright; G. M. B. Colenso-Jones.
Captain, The Lord Monteagle of Brandon.

The Queen's Bodyguard of the Yeoman of the Guard
St. James's Palace, S.W.1.

Captain, The Earl of Swinton; *Lieutenant*, Col. Sir Hugh Brassey, K.C.V.O., O.B.E., M.C.; *Clerk of the Cheque and Adjutant*, Col. A. B. Pemberton, M.B.E.; *Ensign*, Major B. M. H. Shand, M.C.; *Exons.*, Capt. Sir Charles McGrigor, Bt.; Col. G. W. Tufnell.

MASTER OF THE HOUSEHOLD'S DEPARTMENT
Board of Green Cloth
Buckingham Palace, S.W.1.

Master of the Household, Vice-Admiral Sir Peter Ashmore, K.C.B., K.C.V.O., D.S.C.
Deputy Master of the Household, Lt.-Col. B. A. Stewart-Wilson, L.V.O.
Assistants to the Master of the Household, M. D. Tims, C.V.O.; M. Parker.
Chief Clerk, A. Hancock.
Deputy to Assistant, M. Jephson.
Senior Clerks, A. Bell; S. Stacy.
Clerks, Miss S. Derry, M.V.O.; Miss D. Graham; Mrs. A. Wise; Mrs. T. King; Miss A. Perkins; R. Smith.
Superintendent, Windsor Castle, Major Barrie Eastwood, M.B.E.
Assistant to Superintendent, Capt. R. McClosky.
Palace Steward, C. S. Dickman, R.V.M..
Chief Housekeeper, Miss A. de Trey-White.

ROYAL MEWS DEPARTMENT
Buckingham Palace, S.W.1.

Crown Equerry, Lt.-Col. Sir John Miller, K.C.V.O., D.S.O., M.C.
Equerries, Lt.-Col. B. A. Stewart-Wilson, L.V.O.; Major Hugh Lindsay; Capt. S. Holborow (*temp.*).

Veterinary Surgeon, Peter Scott Dunn, L.V.O., M.R.C.V.S.
Supt. Royal Mews, Buckingham Palace, Lt.-Col. William Marsh.
Comptroller of Stores, Major L. Marsham.
Chief Clerk, P. Almond.
Deputy Chief Clerk, J. Spencer.
Office Keeper, P. M. Goodman, M.V.O.

HER MAJESTY'S HOUSEHOLD
IN SCOTLAND

Hereditary Lord High Constable, The Earl of Erroll.
Hereditary Master of the Household, The Duke of Argyll.
Lord Lyon King of Arms, Malcolm R. Innes of Edingight, C.V.O., W.S.
Hereditary Bearer of the Royal Banner of Scotland, The Earl of Dundee, P.C.
Hereditary Bearer of the Scottish National Flag, The Earl of Lauderdale.
Hereditary Keepers:—
  Holyrood, The Duke of Hamilton and Brandon.
  Falkland, N. J. Crichton-Stuart.
  Stirling, The Earl of Mar and Kellie.
  Dunstaffnage, The Duke of Argyll.
Keeper of Dumbarton Castle, Brig. A. S. Pearson, C.B., D.S.O., O.B.E., M.C., T.D.
Governor of Edinburgh Castle, Lieut.-Gen. Sir Norman Arthur, K.C.B.
Dean of the Order of the Thistle, The Very Rev. Prof. J. McIntyre, C.V.O., M.A., B.D., D.Litt., D.D.
Dean of the Chapel Royal, Very Rev. Prof. R. A. S. Barbour, M.C., M.A., D.D.
Chaplains in Ordinary, Very Rev. R. A. S. Barbour, M.C., M.A., D.D.; Rev. W. J. Morris, D.D., LL.D., Ph.D.; Rev. H. W. McP. Cant, M.A., B.D.; Rev. K. MacVicar, M.B.E., D.F.C., T.D., M.A.; Very Rev. Prof. J. McIntyre, C.V.O., M.A., D.D., D.Litt.; Rev. A. J. C. Macfarlane, M.A.; Rev. J. McLeod, M.A.; Rev. G. I. Macmillan, M.A., B.D.; Very Rev. W. B. Johnston, M.A., B.D., D.D.; Rev. C. Forrester-Paton, M.A., B.D.
Extra Chaplains, Very Rev. J. A. Fraser, M.B.E., T.D., D.D.; Very Rev. the Lord MacLeod of Fuinary, M.C., D.D.; Very Rev. Prof. J. S. Stewart, D.D.; Rev. Prof. E. P. Dickie, M.C., D.D.; Very Rev. R. L. Small, C.B.E., D.D.; Very Rev. W. R. Sanderson, D.D.; Rev. W. H. Rogan, D.D.; Very Rev. R. W. V. Selby Wright, C.V.O., T.D., M.A., D.D., F.R.S.E., F.S.A.(scot.); Rev. T. J. T. Nicol, M.V.O., M.B.E., M.C., T.D.; Very Rev. G. T. H. Reid, M.C., M.A., D.D.; Very Rev. H. Douglas, K.C.V.O., C.B.E., M.A., D.D.
Domestic Chaplain, Balmoral, Rev. J. A. K. Angus, T.D., M.A.
Historiographer, Prof. G. Donaldson, M.A., Ph.D., F.B.A., F.R.S.E.
Botanist (vacant).
Painter and Limner, D. A. Donaldson, R.S.A., R.P.
Sculptor (vacant).
Astronomer, Prof. M. S. Longair, B.SC., Ph.D., M.A.
Physicians in Scotland, R. F. Robertson, C.B.E., M.D., P.R.C.P. (Ed.), F.R.C.P.; P. Brunt, M.D., F.R.C.P.
Surgeons in Scotland, T. J. McNair, M.D., F.R.C.S.; J. Engeset, ch.M., F.R.C.S.
Extra Surgeons in Scotland, Prof. Sir Charles Illingworth, C.B.E., M.D., F.R.C.S.Ed.; Prof. Sir Donald Douglas, M.B.E., ch.M., M.S., D.SC., F.R.C.S.
Apothecary to the Household at Balmoral, P. Crawford, M.B., ch.B., D.obst., R.C.O.G.
Apothecary to the Household at the Palace of Holyroodhouse, D. G. Illingworth, L.V.O., M.D., F.R.C.P., F.R.C.G.P.
Heralds & Pursuivants of Arms, (see page 374).

THE QUEEN'S BODYGUARD FOR SCOTLAND

The Royal Company of Archers.
Archers' Hall, Edinburgh.

Captain General and Gold Stick for Scotland, Col. The Earl of Stair, K.C.V.O., M.B.E.

Captains, Major The Lord Home of the Hirsel, K.T.; The Duke of Buccleuch and Queensberry, K.T., V.R.D.; Lt.-Col. Sir John Gilmour, Bt., D.S.O., T.D.; Col. The Lord Clydesmuir, K.T., C.B., M.B.E., T.D.

Lieutenants, Major The Lord Maclean, P.C., K.T., G.C.V.O., K.B.E.; Major Sir Hew Hamilton-Dalrymple, Bt., K.C.V.O.; Major The Earl of Wemyss and March, K.T.; The Earl of Airlie, G.C.V.O.

Ensigns, Lt.-Gen. Sir William Turner, K.B.E., C.B., D.S.O.; The Earl of Dalhousie, K.T., G.C.V.O., G.B.E., M.C. Capt. I. M. Tennant; Maj.-Gen. The Earl Cathcart, C.B., D.S.O., M.C.

Brigadiers, Capt. N. E. F. Dalrymple-Hamilton, C.V.O., M.B.E., D.S.C., R.N.; The Marquess of Lothian, K.C.V.O.; Commodore Sir John Clerk of Penicuik, Bt., C.B.E., V.R.D., R.N.R.; The Earl of Elgin and Kincardine, K.T.; Col. G. R. Simpson, D.S.O., L.V.O., T.D.; Major D. H. Butter, M.C.; The Earl of Minto, M.B.E.; Maj.-Gen. Sir John Swinton, K.C.V.O., O.B.E.; General Sir Michael Gow, G.C.B.; The Hon. Lord Elliott, M.C.; Maj. The Hon. L. H. C. Maclean; The Rt. Hon. George Younger, T.D., M.P.; Capt. G. Burnet, L.V.O.

Adjutant, Brig.-Maj. The Hon. L. H. C. Maclean.

Surgeon, Dr. M. D. Finlay.

Chaplain, Very Rev. R. W. V. Selby Wright, C.V.O., D.D., T.D., F.R.S.E.

President of the Council and Silver Stick for Scotland, Col. the Lord Clydesmuir, K.T., C.B., M.B.E., T.D.

Vice-President, Major Sir Hew Hamilton-Dalrymple, Bt., K.C.V.O.

Secretary, Col. H. F. O. Bewsher, O.B.E..

Treasurer, R. A. G. Douglas-Miller.

HOUSEHOLD OF THE PRINCE PHILIP, DUKE OF EDINBURGH

Private Secretary and Treasurer, B. H. McGrath.

Assistant Private Secretary, Brig. C. Robertson.

Equerry, Sqn. Ldr. T. J. Finneron.

Extra Equerries, J. B. V. Orr, C.V.O.; Sir Richard H. Davies, K.C.V.O., C.B.E.

Temporary Equerries, Major The Hon. A. Wigram, Grenadier Guards; Capt. I. Gardner, R.M.

Chief Clerk and Accountant, V. G. Jewell.

HOUSEHOLD OF QUEEN ELIZABETH THE QUEEN MOTHER

Lord Chamberlain, Major the Earl of Dalhousie, K.T., G.C.V.O., G.B.E., M.C.

Comptroller and Extra Equerry, Capt. Sir Alastair S. Aird, K.C.V.O.

Private Secretary and Equerry, Lt.-Col. Sir Martin Gilliat, G.C.V.O., M.B.E.

Treasurer and Equerry, Major Sir Ralph Anstruther, Bt., K.C.V.O., M.C.

Equerry, Major Raymond Seymour, L.V.O.

Press Secretary and Extra Equerry, Major Arthur J. S. Griffin, C.V.O.

Extra Equerry, The Lord Sinclair, L.V.O.

Equerry (Temp.), Capt. J. Lowther-Pinkerton.

Apothecary to the Household, Sir Ralph Southward, K.C.V.O., M.B., Ch.B., F.R.C.P.

Surgeon-Apothecary to the Household (Royal Lodge, Windsor), J. P. Clayton, L.V.O., M.A., M.B., B.chir., M.R.C.S., L.R.C.P.

Mistress of the Robes, The Dowager Duchess of Abercorn, G.C.V.O.

Ladies of the Bedchamber, The Dowager Viscountess Hambleden, D.C.V.O.; The Lady Grimthorpe, C.V.O.

Women of the Bedchamber, Ruth, Lady Fermoy, D.C.V.O., O.B.E.; Mrs Patrick Campbell-Preston, C.V.O.; Lady Elizabeth Basset, C.V.O.; Lady Angela Oswald.

Extra Women of the Bedchamber, Lady Victoria Wemyss, C.V.O.; The Hon. Mrs. Geoffrey Bowlby, C.V.O.; Lady Jean Rankin, D.C.V.O.

Clerk Comptroller, M. Blanch, L.V.O.

Chief Accountant, J. P. Kyle, M.V.O.

Clerks, Mrs. R. Murphy, M.V.O.; Miss F. Fletcher, M.V.O.

HOUSEHOLD OF THE PRINCE AND PRINCESS OF WALES

Private Secretary and Treasurer to The Prince and Princess of Wales (vacant).

Acting Private Secretary, D. Roycroft.

Acting Treasurer, J. Higgs.

Comptroller, Lt.-Col. P. Creasy.

Equerries to The Prince of Wales, Maj. J. M. W. Stenhouse, Gordon Highlanders; Capt. P. Owen-Edmunds (*temp.*).

Equerry to The Princess of Wales, Lt.-Cdr. P. Eberle, R.N.

Extra Equerry, Sqn.-Ldr. Sir David Checketts, K.C.V.O.; The Hon. Edward Adeane, C.V.O.

Temporary Equerry, Capt. S. Stephenson, Welsh Guards.

Lady in Waiting, Miss Anne Beckwith-Smith.

Extra Ladies in Waiting, The Hon. Mrs. Vivian Baring; Mrs. George West; Viscountess Campden.

HOUSEHOLD OF THE PRINCESS ANNE, MRS. MARK PHILLIPS

Private Secretary, Lt.-Col. Peter Gibbs.

Ladies in Waiting, Mrs. Andrew Feilden, L.V.O.; Miss Victoria Legge-Bourke; Mrs. Malcolm Innes; The Hon. Mrs. Legge-Bourke.

Extra Ladies in Waiting, Mrs. Richard Carew Pole, L.V.O.; The Countess of Lichfield.

Personal Secretary, Mrs. David Hodgson, M.V.O.

HOUSEHOLD OF THE PRINCESS MARGARET, COUNTESS OF SNOWDON

Private Secretary and Comptroller, The Lord Napier and Ettrick, C.V.O.

Personal Secretary, Miss M. Murray Brown, C.V.O.

Extra Ladies in Waiting, The Lady Elizabeth Cavendish, L.V.O.; Mrs. Alastair Aird, L.V.O.; Mrs. Robin Benson, L.V.O.; The Lady Juliet Townsend, L.V.O.; Mrs. Jane Stevens; The Hon. Mrs. Wills, L.V.O.; The Lady Glenconner; The Hon. Mrs. Whitehead; The Countess Alexander of Tunis; Mrs. Angus Blair.

THE DUKE AND DUCHESS OF GLOUCESTER'S HOUSEHOLD

Comptroller, Private Secretary and Equerry, Lt.-Col. Sir Simon Bland, K.C.V.O.

Ladies in Waiting, Mrs. Michael Wigley, L.V.O.; Mrs. Euan McCorquodale; Mrs. Howard Page.

Extra Lady in Waiting, Miss Jennifer Thomson.

PRINCESS ALICE, DUCHESS OF GLOUCESTER'S HOUSEHOLD

Comptroller, Private Secretary and Equerry, Lt.-Col. Sir Simon Bland, K.C.V.O.
Ladies in Waiting, Dame Jean Maxwell-Scott, D.C.V.O.; Mrs. Michael Harvey.
Extra Ladies in Waiting, Miss Dorothy Meynell, C.V.O.; Mrs. Cedric Holland, C.V.O.; Miss Diana Harrison; The Hon. Jane Walsh; Miss Jane Egerton Warburton, L.V.O.

THE DUKE AND DUCHESS OF KENT'S HOUSEHOLD

Treasurer, Sir Philip Hay, K.C.V.O., T.D.
Private Secretary, Lieut.-Cdr. Sir Richard Buckley, K.C.V.O., R.N.
Ladies in Waiting, Mrs. Alan Henderson, L.V.O.; Mrs. David Napier, L.V.O.; Miss Sarah Partridge.
Extra Lady in Waiting, Mrs. Peter Wilmot-Sitwell.

HOUSEHOLD OF PRINCESS ALEXANDRA

Lady in Waiting, The Lady Mary Fitzalan-Howard, C.V.O.
Private Secretary and Extra Lady in Waiting, Miss Mona Mitchell, C.V.O.
Extra Equerry, Maj. P. C. Clarke, C.V.O.

HOUSEHOLD OF PRINCE MICHAEL OF KENT

Private Secretary, Col. Michael Farmer.
Lady in Waiting, The Hon. Mrs. Leatham.
Extra Lady in Waiting, Miss Anne Frost.

HONORARY PHYSICIANS TO THE QUEEN (CIVIL)
(Appointed for three years from Feb. 1, 1984)

G. Crompton, *Chief Medical Officer, Welsh Office*; G. D. Duncan, *Regional Medical Officer, East Anglian Regional Health Authority*; I. Smith McDonald, *Deputy Chief Medical Officer, Scottish Office*; Miss P. G. Walsh Mason, *Senior Principal Medical Officer, Department of Health and Social Security*; P. C. Moore, *District Medical Officer, Shropshire*; T. K. Sweeney, *Senior Principal Medical Officer, Department of Health and Social Security.*

THE QUEEN'S BIRTHDAY, 1986

The date for the observance of the Queen's Birthday in 1986 both at home and abroad will be Saturday, June 14.

ROYAL SALUTES

On the Anniversaries of the Birth, Accession and Coronation of the Sovereign and on the Anniversaries of the birth of H.M. the Queen Mother and H.R.H. the Duke of Edinburgh a salute of 62 guns is fired on the wharf at the Tower of London.

On extraordinary and triumphal occasions, such as on the occasion of the Sovereign opening, proroguing or dissolving Parliament in Person, or when passing through London in procession, except when otherwise ordered, 41 guns only are fired.

On the occasion of the birth of a Royal infant a salute of 41 guns is fired from the two Saluting Stations in London, *i.e.* Hyde Park and the Tower of London.

Constable of the Royal Palace and Fortress of London, Field Marshal Sir Roland Gibb, G.C.B., C.B.E., D.S.O., M.C.

Lieutenant of the Tower of London, Lt.-Gen. Sir Hugh Cunningham, K.B.E.
Resident Governor and Keeper of the Jewel House, Maj.-Gen. A. P. W. MacLellan, M.B.E.
Master Gunner of St. James's Park, Lt.-Gen. Sir Thomas Morony, K.C.B., O.B.E.
Master Gunner within the Tower, Col. R. A. Burford, T.D.

THE ROYAL ARMS

QUARTERLY.—1st and 4th *gules,* three lions passant guardant in pale *or* (*England*); 2nd *or,* a lion rampant within a double tressure flory counterflory *gules* (*Scotland*); 3rd *azure,* a harp *or,* stringed *argent* (*Ireland*); the whole encircled with the Garter.
SUPPORTERS.—*Dexter:* a lion rampant guardant *or,* imperially crowned. *Sinister:* a unicorn *argent,* armed crined and unguled *or,* gorged with a coronet composed of crosses patées and fleurs de lis, a chain affixed passing between the forelegs and reflexed over the back.
BADGES.—The red and white rose united (*England*), a thistle (*Scotland*); a harp *or,* the strings *argent,* with a shamrock leaf *vert* (*Ireland*); upon a mount *vert,* a dragon passant wings elevated *gules* (*Wales*).

THE UNION JACK

The national flag of the United Kingdom is the Union Flag, generally known as the Union Jack, the name deriving from the use of the Union Flag on the jack-staff of naval vessels. It is a combination of the cross of the patron saint of England, St. George (*cross gules in a field argent*), the cross of the patron saint of Scotland, St. Andrew (*saltire argent in a field azure*) and a cross similar to that of St. Patrick, patron saint of Ireland (*saltire gules in a field argent*). The Union Flag was first introduced in 1606 after the union of England and Scotland, the cross of St. Patrick being added in 1801.

ANNUITIES TO THE ROYAL FAMILY

The annuity payable to Her Majesty is known as the Civil List, and is payable out of the Consolidated Fund under the authority of a Civil List Act following the recommendation of a Parliamentary Select Committee. The amount of the Civil List was fixed in the Civil List Act 1952 at £475,000, was increased from January 1, 1972, under the Civil List Act 1972 to £980,000, and has been variously increased since.

The allocation for the calendar year 1985 was as follows:—

The Queen	£3,976,200
Queen Elizabeth The Queen Mother	345,300
The Duke of Edinburgh	192,600
Prince Andrew	20,000
Prince Edward	20,000
The Princess Anne	120,000
The Princess Margaret	116,800
Princess Alice, Duchess of Gloucester	47,300
*Duke of Gloucester	94,000
*Duke of Kent	127,000
*Princess Alexandra	120,900
	5,180,100
*Refunded by The Queen	341,900
Total	4,838,200

These figures combine the sums payable directly from the Consolidated Fund with the supplements provided by the Royal Trustees from the grant made to them in the vote for economic and financial administration in the Estimates.

THE FLYING OF FLAGS

Days for hoisting the Union Flag on Government Buildings (from 8 A.M. to sunset).

February 6 (1952).—Her Majesty's Accession.

February 19 (1960).—Birthday of The Prince Andrew.

March 1.—St. David's Day (in Wales only).

March 10 (1964).—Birthday of The Prince Edward.

March 10.—Commonwealth Day 1986.

April 21 (1926).—Birthday of Her Majesty the Queen.

April 23.—St. George's Day (in England only). Where a building has two or more flagstaffs the Cross of St. George may be flown in addition to the Union Jack but not in a superior position.

June 2 (1953).—Coronation Day.

June 10 (1921).—Birthday of The Duke of Edinburgh.

June 14.—Queen's Official Birthday, 1986.

July 1 (1961).—Birthday of The Princess of Wales.

Aug. 4 (1900).—Birthday of Her Majesty Queen Elizabeth the Queen Mother.

Aug. 15 (1950).—Birthday of The Princess Anne.

Aug. 21 (1930).—Birthday of The Princess Margaret.

Nov. 9.—Remembrance Sunday, 1986.

Nov. 14 (1948).—Birthday of The Prince of Wales.

Nov. 20 (1947).—Her Majesty's Wedding Day.

Nov. 30.—St. Andrew's Day (in Scotland only).

And on the occasion of the opening and closing of Parliament by the Queen, flags should be flown on Government buildings in the Greater London area, whether or not Her Majesty performs the ceremony in person.

The only additions to the above list will be those notified to the Department of the Environment by Her Majesty's command and communicated by the Ministry to the other Departments. The list applies to all Government Buildings in London and elsewhere in the United Kingdom. In cases where it has been the practice to fly the Union Jack daily, *e.g.* on some Custom Houses, that practice may continue.

Flags will be flown at half-mast on the following occasions:...

(*a*) From the announcement of the death up to the funeral of the Sovereign, except on Proclamation Day, when they are hoisted right up from 11 A.M. to sunset.

(*b*) The funerals of members of the Royal Family, subject to special commands from Her Majesty in each case.

(*c*) The funerals of Foreign Rulers, subject to special commands from Her Majesty in each case.

(*d*) The funerals of Prime Ministers and ex-Prime Ministers of the United Kingdom.

(*e*) Other occasions by special command of Her Majesty.

On occasions when days for flying flags coincide with days for flying flags at half mast the following rules will be observed. Flags will be flown: (*a*) although a member of the Royal Family, or a near relative of the Royal Family, may be lying dead, unless special commands be received from Her Majesty to the contrary, and (*b*) although it may be the day of the funeral of a Foreign Ruler. If the body of a very distinguished subject is lying at a Government Office the flag may fly at half mast on that office until the body has left (provided it is a day on which the flag would fly) and then the flag is to be hoisted right up. On all other Government Buildings the flag will fly as usual.

The *Royal Standard* is only to be hoisted when the Queen is actually present in the building, and never when Her Majesty is passing in procession.

RED-LETTER DAYS

Scarlet Robes are worn by the Judges of the Queen's Bench Division on *Red-Letter Days.*

RED-LETTER DAYS AND STATE OCCASIONS, 1986.

Jan. 25. Conversion of St. Paul.

Feb. 2. Purification.

  ,, 6. Queen's Accession.

  ,, 12. Ash Wednesday.

Mar. 1. St. David.

  ,, 25. Annunciation.

Apr. 21. Queen's Birthday.

  ,, 25. St. Mark.

May 1. St. Philip and St. James.

  ,, 14. St. Matthias.

May 8. Ascension Day.

June 2. Coronation Day.

  ,, 10. Birthday of The Duke of Edinburgh.

  ,, 11. St. Barnabas.

  ,, 14. Queen's Official Birthday (1986).

  ,, 24. St. John the Baptist.

  ,, 29. St. Peter.

July 3. St. Thomas.

July 25. St. James.

Aug. 4. Birthday of Queen Elizabeth the Queen Mother.

Oct. 18. St. Luke.

  ,, 28. St. Simon and St. Jude.

Nov. 1. All Saints.

  ,, 8. Lord Mayor's Day.

  ,, 14. Birthday of The Prince of Wales.

  ,, 30. St. Andrew.

THE MILITARY KNIGHTS OF WINDSOR

Founded in 1348 after the Wars in France to assist English Knights, who, having been prisoners in the hands of the French, had become impoverished by the payments of heavy ransoms. They received a pension and quarters in Windsor Castle. Edward III founded the Order of the Garter later in the same year, incorporating the Knights of Windsor and the College of St. George into its foundation and raising the number of Knights to 26 to correspond with the number of the Knights of the Garter. Known later as the Alms Knights or Poor Knights of Windsor, their establishment was reduced under the will of King Henry VIII to 13 and Statutes were drawn up by Queen Elizabeth I.

In 1833 King William IV changed their designation to The Military Knights and granted them their present uniform which consists of a scarlet tail-coat with white cross sword-belt, crimson sash and cocked hat with plume. The badges are the Shield of St. George and the Star of the Order of the Garter. The Knights receive a small stipend in addition to their Army pensions and quarters in Windsor Castle. They take part in all ceremonies of the Noble Order of the Garter and attend Sunday morning service in St. George's Chapel as representatives of the Knights of the Garter.

Applications for appointment should be made to The Military Secretary, Ministry of Defence, Army Dept.

Governor, Maj.-Gen. Sir Peter Gillett, K.C.V.O., C.B., O.B.E.

Military Knights, Lt.-Colonel R. W. Dobbin, O.B.E.; Major H. Smith, M.B.E., R.V.M.; Lt.-Colonel A. R. Clark, M.C.; Lt.-Colonel C. A. Harvey; Major A. E. Wollaston, M.V.O.; Brigadier A. L. Atkinson, O.B.E.; Brigadier J. F. Linders, O.B.E., M.C.; Brigadier A. C. Tyler, C.B.E., M.C., D.L.; Major W. L. Thompson, M.V.O., M.B.E., D.C.M.; Major L. W. Dickerson; Major J. C. Cowley, D.C.M.; Brigadier C. J. Codner, C.B.E., M.C.

THE PEERAGE

The rules which govern the creation and succession of Peerages are extremely complicated. There are, technically, five separate Peerages, the Peerage of England, of Scotland, of Ireland, of Great Britain, and of the United Kingdom. The Peerage of Great Britain dates from 1707 when an Act of Union combined the two Kingdoms of England and Scotland and separate Peerages were discontinued; and the Peerage of the United Kingdom from 1801 when Great Britain and Ireland were combined under an Act of Union. Some Scottish Peers have received additional Peerages of Great Britain or of the United Kingdom since 1707, and some Irish Peers additional Peerages of the United Kingdom since 1801. The Peerage of Ireland was not entirely discontinued from 1801 but holders of Irish Peerages, whether pre-dating or created subsequent to the Union of 1801, are not entitled to sit in the House of Lords if they have no additional English, Scottish, Great Britain or United Kingdom Peerage. (However, they are eligible for election to the House of Commons and to vote in Parliamentary elections, which other Peers are not.) An Irish Peer holding a Peerage of a lower grade which enables him to sit in the House of Lords is introduced there by the title which enables him to sit, though for all other purposes he is known by his higher title. In the Peerage of Scotland there is no rank of Baron; the equivalent rank is Lord of Parliament, abbreviated to 'Lord'. All Peers of England, Scotland, Great Britain or the United Kingdom who are of full age (21 years) and of British nationality are entitled to sit in the House of Lords. Certain ancient Peerages pass on death to the nearest heir, male or female, and several are now held by women (*see also* p. 247). Since the Peerages Act, 1963, Peeresses in their own Right have been entitled to sit in the House of Lords, subject to the qualifications applying to Peers.

The Peerages Act, 1963, enables Peers or Peeresses to disclaim their Peerages for life: living Peers, within 12 months after the passing of the Act (July 31, 1963); a person subsequently succeeding to a Peerage, within 12 months (one month if an M.P.) after the date of succession, or of attaining his or her majority, if later. The disclaimer is irrevocable but does not affect the descent of the Peerage after the disclaimant's death, and the children of a disclaimed Peer may, if they wish, retain their precedence and any courtesy titles and styles borne as children of a Peer. Non-hereditary or Life Peerages, in the degree of Baron or Baroness, have been conferred by the Crown since 1876 on eminent judges, the Lords of Appeal or Law Lords, to enable them to carry out the judicial functions of the House of Lords, and since 1958 on men and women of distinction in public life, giving them seats in the House of Lords. Life Peers and Peeresses are addressed identically as an hereditary Peer or Peeress, and their children have the same courtesy style as the children of an hereditary Peer or Peeress.

No fees for Dignities have been payable since 1937. The House of Lords surrendered the ancient right of peers to be tried for treason or felons by their peers in 1948.

PEERAGES EXTINCT SINCE THE LAST ISSUE

EARLDOMS.—Avon (*cr.* 1961); Birkenhead (*cr.* 1922). VISCOUNTCIES.—Hall (*cr.* 1946). BARONIES.—Michelham (*cr.* 1905); St. Just (*cr.* 1935); Sherborne (*cr.* 1784).

DISCLAIMER OF PEERAGES

Earl of Durham; Earl of Home; Earl of Sandwich; Viscount Hailsham; Viscount Stansgate; Lord Altrincham; Lord Archibald; Lord Beaverbrook; Lord Fraser of Allander; Lord Merthyr; Lord Monkswell; Lord Reith; Lord Sanderson of Ayot; Lord Silkin; Lord Southampton.

PEERS WHO ARE MINORS

EARLS (2): Albemarle (*b.* 1965); Hardwicke (*b.* 1971). BARONS (3): Fermoy (*b.* 1967); Inverforth (*b.* 1966); VISCOUNTS (2): Goschen (*b.* 1965); Dillon (*b.* 1973). Wrottesley (*b.* 1968).

COMPOSITION OF THE HOUSE OF LORDS (At Aug. 3, 1985)

Archbishops and Bishops	26	
Peers by Succession	762	(18 Women)
Hereditary Peers of first creation (including the Prince of Wales)	29	
Life Peers under the Appellate Jurisdiction Act 1876	20	
Life Peers under the Life Peerages Act 1958	345	(47 Women)
TOTAL	1182	
Of whom:		
Peers without Writs of Summons	96	
Peers on Leave of Absence from the House	144	

Contractions and Symbols.—S. or I. appended to the date of creation denotes a *Scottish* or *Irish* title, the further addition of a * implies that the Peer in question holds also an *Imperial* title, which is specified (after the name) by its more definite description as *Engl., Brit.,* or *U.K.* When both titles are alike, as in the case of Argyll, this star is appended to the conjoined date below, and it then denotes that such date is that of the imperial creation. The mark ° signifies that there is no "of" in the Marquessate or Earldom so designated; *b.* signifies born; *s.,* succeeded; *m.,* married; *w.,* widower or widow; *M.,* minor; † Information on *Eldest Son or Heir* not ascertained at time of going to press.

ROYAL DUKES

Style, His Royal Highness the Duke of ——.
Addressed as, Sir, or more formally, May it please your Royal Highness.

1947 *Edinburgh,* The Prince Philip, Duke of Edinburgh, K.G., P.C., K.T., O.M., G.B.E., *b.* 1921, *m.* (*see* pp. 218 and 219).

1337 *Cornwall,* Charles, Prince of Wales, Duke of Cornwall (*Scottish Duke, Rothesay,* 1398). K.G., P.C., K.T., G.C.B., *b.* 1948, (*see* p. 218).

1928 *Gloucester* (2nd), Richard, Duke of Gloucester, G.C.V.O., *b.* 1944, *s.* 1974, *m.* (*see* p. 217.)

1934 *Kent* (2nd), Edward Duke of Kent, G.C.M.G., G.C.V.O., *b.* 1935, *s.* 1942, *m.* (*see* p. 217).

ARCHBISHOPS

Style, The Most Rev. His Grace the Lord Archbishop of——.
Addressed as, My Lord Archbishop; or, Your Grace.

Trans.

1980   *Canterbury* (102nd), Robert Alexander Kennedy Runcie. P.C., M.C., D.D., *b.* 1921, *m. Consecrated Bishop of St. Albans,* 1970.

1983   *York* (95th), John Stapylton Habgood, P.C., PH.D. *b.* 1927, *m. Consecrated Bishop of Durham,* 1973.

DUKES

Style, His Grace the Duke of——. *Addressed as,* My Lord Duke; or, Your Grace. The eldest sons of Dukes and Marquesses take, by courtesy, their father's second title. The other sons and the daughters are styled Lord Edward, Lady Caroline. etc.

Created.	*Title, Order of Succession, Name, etc.*	*Eldest Son or Heir.*
1868 I.*	*Abercorn* (5th), James Hamilton (6th *Brit. Marq.,* 1790, and 14th *Scott. Earl,* 1606 both *Abercorn), b.* 1934, *s.* 1979, *m.*	Marquess of Hamilton, *b.* 1969.
1701 s. ⎱ 1892* ⎰	*Argyll,* Ian Campbell (12th *Scottish* and 5th *U.K. Duke, Argyll), b.* 1937, *s.* 1973, *m.*	Marquess of Lorne, *b.* 1968.
1703 s.	*Atholl* (10th), George Iain Murray, *b.* 1931, *s.* 1957.	Godfrey P. *M.,* D.S.O., *b.* 1901.
1682	*Beaufort* (11th), David Robert Somerset, *b.* 1928, *s.* 1984, *m.*	Marquess of Worcester, *b.* 1952.
1694	*Bedford* (13th), John Robert Russell, *b.* 1917, *s.* 1953, *m.*	Marquess of Tavistock, *b.* 1940.
1663 s.*	*Buccleuch* (9th) & (11th) *Queensberry* (1684), Walter Francis John Montagu Douglas Scott, K.T., V.R.D. (8th *Engl. Earl, Doncaster,* 1662), *b.* 1923, *s.* 1973, *m.*	Earl of Dalkeith, *b.* 1954.
1694	*Devonshire* (11th), Andrew Robert Buxton Cavendish, P.C., M.C., *b.* 1920, *s.* 1950, *m.*	Marquess of Hartington, *b.* 1944.
1900	*Fife* (3rd), James George Alexander Bannerman Carnegie, *b.* 1929, *s.* 1959. *(see p. 216).*	Earl of Macduff, *b.* 1961.
1675	*Grafton* (11th), Hugh Denis Charles FitzRoy, K.G., *b.* 1919, *s.* 1970, *m.*	Earl of Euston, *b.* 1947.
1643 s.*	*Hamilton* (15th), Angus Alan Douglas Douglas-Hamilton (*Premier Peer of Scotland*; 12th *Brit. Duke, Brandon,* 1711), *b.* 1938, *s.* 1973, *m.*	Marquess of Douglas and Clydesdale, *b.* 1978.
1766 I.*	*Leinster* (8th), Gerald FitzGerald (*Premier Duke, Marquess and Earl of Ireland*; 8th *Brit. Visct., Leinster,* 1747) *b.* 1914, *s.* 1976, *m.*	Marquess of Kildare, *b.* 1948.
1719	*Manchester* (12th), Angus Charles Drogo Montagu, *b.* 1938, *m.*	Alexander C. D. D. *M., b.* 1962.
1702	*Marlborough* (11th), John George Vanderbilt Henry Spencer-Churchill, *b.* 1926, *s.* 1972, *m.*	Marquess of Blandford, *b.* 1955.
1707 s.*	*Montrose* (7th), James Angus Graham (5th *Brit. Earl, Graham,* 1722), *b.* 1907, *s.* 1954, *m.*	Marquess of Graham, *b.* 1935.
1756	*Newcastle* (*under Lyme*) (9th), Henry Edward Hugh Pelham-Clinton-Hope, O.B.E., *b.* 1907, *s.* 1941, *m.*	Edward C. *Pelham-Clinton, b.* 1920
1483	*Norfolk* (17th), Miles Francis Stapleton Fitzalan-Howard, K.G., C.B., C.B.E., M.C. (*Premier Duke and Earl*; 12th *Eng. Baron Beaumont,* 1309; 4th *U.K. Baron Howard of Glossop,* 1869), *b.* 1915, *s.* 1975, *m.* (*Earl Marshal*).	Earl of Arundel and Surrey, *b.* 1956.
1766	*Northumberland* (10th), Hugh Algernon Percy, K.G., P.C., G.C.V.O., T.D., F.R.S., *b.* 1914, *s.* 1940, *m.* (*Lord Steward*).	Earl Percy, *b.* 1953.
1716	*Portland* (9th), Victor Frederick William Cavendish-Bentinck, C.M.G. (5th *U.K. Baron, Bolsover,* 1880) *b.* 1897, *s.* 1980, *m.*	(None to Dukedom), to Earldom of Portland, Henry N. *B., b.* 1919.
1675	*Richmond* (9th) & *Gordon* (4th, 1876), Frederick Charles Gordon-Lennox (9th *Scott. Duke, Lennox,* 1675), *b.* 1904, *s.* 1935, *m.*	Earl of March and Kinrara, *b.* 1929.
1707 s.*	*Roxburghe* (10th), Guy David Innes-Ker (5th *U.K. Earl, Innes,* 1837), *b.* 1954, *s.* 1974, *m.* (*Premier Baronet of Scotland*).	Marquess of Bowmont, *b.* 1981.
1703	*Rutland* (10th), Charles John Robert Manners, C.B.E., *b.* 1919, *s.* 1940, *m.*	Marquess of Granby, *b.* 1959.
1684	*St. Albans* (13th), Charles Frederick Aubrey de Vere Beauclerk, O.B.E., *b.* 1915, *s.* 1964, *m.*	Earl of Burford, *b.* 1939.
1547	*Somerset* (19th), John Michael Edward Seymour, *b.* 1952, *s.* 1984, *m.*	Lord Seymour, *b.* 1982.
1833	*Sutherland* (6th), John Sutherland Egerton, T.D. (5th *U.K. Earl Ellesmere,* 1846), *b.* 1915, *s.* 1963, *m.*	Cyril R. *E., b.* 1905.
1814	*Wellington* (8th), Arthur Valerian Wellesley, M.V.O., O.B.E., M.C. (9th *Irish Earl, Mornington,* 1760), *b.* 1915, *s.* 1972, *m.*	Marquess of Douro, *b.* 1945.
1874	*Westminster* (6th), Gerald Cavendish Grosvenor, *b.* 1951, *s.* 1979, *m.*	(None).

MARQUESSES

Style, The Most Hon. the Marquess of——. *Addressed as,* My Lord Marquess. In titles marked ° the "of" is *not* used. For the style of Marquesses' sons and daughters, *see* under "DUKES," above.

1916   *Aberdeen and Temair* (6th), Alastair Ninian John Gordon (12th *Scott. Earl, Aberdeen,* 1682), *b.* 1920, *s.* 1984, *m.*   Earl of Haddo, *b.* 1955.

Created.	Title, Order of Succession, Name, etc.	Eldest Son or Heir.
1876	*Abergavenny* (5th), John Henry Guy Nevill, K.G., O.B.E., b. 1914, s. 1954, m.	Guy R. G. N., b. 1945.
1821	*Ailesbury* (8th), Michael Sidney Cedric Brudenell-Bruce, b. 1926, s. 1974, m.	Earl of Cardigan, b. 1952.
1831	*Ailsa* (7th), Archibald David Kennedy, O.B.E., (19th *Scott. Earl, Cassillis*, 1509), b. 1925, s. 1957, m.	Earl of Cassillis, b. 1956.
1815	*Anglesey* (7th), George Charles Henry Victor Paget, b. 1922, s. 1947, m.	Earl of Uxbridge, b. 1950.
1789	*Bath* (6th), Henry Frederick Thynne, b. 1905, s. 1946, m.	Viscount Weymouth, b. 1932.
1826	*Bristol* (7th), Frederick William John Augustus Hervey, b. 1954, m.	†
1796	*Bute* (6th), John Crichton-Stuart (11th *Scott. Earl, Dumfries*, 1633), b. 1933, s. 1956, m.	Earl of Dumfries, b. 1958.
1812	°*Camden* (6th), David George Edward Henry Pratt, b. 1930, s. 1983.	Earl of Brecknock, b. 1965.
1815	*Cholmondeley* (6th), George Hugh Cholmondeley, G.C.V.O., (10th *Irish Viscount, Cholmondeley*, 1661), b. 1919, s. 1968, m. (*Lord Great Chamberlain*).	Earl of Rocksavage, b. 1960.
1816 I*	°*Conyngham* (7th), Frederick William Henry Francis Conyngham (7th *U.K. Baron, Minster, U.K.* 1821), b. 1924, s. 1974, m.	Earl of Mount Charles, b. 1951.
1791 I.*	*Donegall* (7th), Dermot Richard Claud Chichester (7th *Brit. Baron, Fisherwick*, 1790, 6th *Brit. Baron, Templemore*, 1831), b. 1916, s. to Marquessate, 1975: to Templemore Barony, 1953, m.	Earl of Belfast, b. 1952.
1789 I.*	*Downshire* (7th), Arthur Wills Percy Wellington Blundell Trumbull Sandys Hill (7th *Brit. Earl, Hillsborough*, 1772), b. 1894, s. 1918, w.	A. Robin I. H., b. 1929.
1888	*Dufferin & Ava* (5th), Sheridan Frederick Terence Hamilton-Temple-Blackwood (11th *Irish Baron, Dufferin & Clandeboye*, 1800), b. 1938, s. 1945, m.	(None to Marquessate), to Irish Barony, Sir Francis G. *Blackwood*, Bt., b. 1916.
1801 I.*	*Ely* (8th) Charles John Tottenham (8th *U.K. Baron, Loftus*, 1801), b. 1913, s. 1969, m.	Viscount Loftus, b. 1943.
1801	*Exeter* (7th), William Martin Alleyne Cecil, b. 1909, s. 1981, m.	Lord Burghley, b. 1935.
1800 I.*	*Headfort* (6th), Thomas Geoffrey Charles Michael Taylour (4th *U.K. Baron, Kenlis*, 1831), b. 1932, s. 1960, m.	Earl of Bective, b. 1959.
1793	*Hertford* (8th), Hugh Edward Conway Seymour (9th *Irish Baron, Conway*, 1712), b. 1930, s. 1940, m.	Earl of Yarmouth, b. 1958.
1599 s.*	*Huntly* (12th), Douglas Charles Lindsay Gordon (*Premier Marquess of Scotland*) (4th *U.K. Baron, Meldrum*, 1815), b. 1908, s. 1937, m.	Earl of Aboyne, b. 1944.
1784	*Lansdowne* (8th), George John Charles Mercer Nairne Petty-Fitzmaurice, P.C. (8th *Irish Earl. Kerry*, 1723), b. 1912, s. 1944, m.	Earl of Shelburne, b. 1941.
1902	*Linlithgow* (3rd), Charles William Frederick Hope, M.C., T.D. (9th *Scott. Earl, Hopetoun* 1703), b. 1912, s. 1952, m.	Earl of Hopetoun, b. 1946.
1816 I.*	*Londonderry* (9th), Alexander Charles Robert Vane-Tempest-Stewart (6th *U.K. Earl, Vane*, 1823), b. 1937, s. 1955, m.	Viscount Castlereagh, b. 1972.
1701 s.*	*Lothian* (12th), Peter Francis Walter Kerr, K.C.V.O. (6th *U.K. Baron, Kerr*, 1821), b. 1922, s. 1940, m.	Earl of Ancram, M.P., b. 1945.
1917	*Milford Haven* (4th), George Ivar Louis Mountbatten, b. 1961, s. 1970.	Lord Ivar A. M. M., b. 1963.
1838	*Normanby* (4th), Oswald Constantine John Phipps, K.G., C.B.E. (8th *Irish Baron, Mulgrave*, 1767), b. 1912, s. 1932, m.	Earl of Mulgrave, b. 1954.
1812	*Northampton* (7th), Spencer Douglas David Compton, b. 1946, s. 1978, m.	Earl Compton, b. 1973.
1825 I.*	*Ormonde* (7th), James Hubert Theobald Charles Butler, M.B.E. (7th *U.K. Baron, Ormonde*, 1821), b. 1899, s. 1971, w.	(None to Marquessate), to Earldoms of Ormonde and Ossory, Viscount Mountgarret, b. 1936.
1682 s.	*Queensberry* (12th), David Harrington Angus Douglas, b. 1929, s. 1954, m.	Viscount Drumlanrig, b. 1967.
1926	*Reading* (4th), Simon Charles Henry Rufus Isaacs, b. 1942, s. 1980, m.	Lord Anthony M. R. I., b. 1943.
1789	*Salisbury* (6th), Robert Edward Peter Gascoyne-Cecil, b. 1916, s. 1972, m.	Viscount Cranborne, M.P., b. 1946.
1800 I.*	*Sligo* (10th), Denis Edward Browne (10th *U.K. Baron, Monteagle*, 1806), b. 1908, s. 1952, m.	Earl of Altamont, b. 1939.
1787	°*Townshend* (7th), George John Patrick Dominic Townshend, b. 1916, s. 1921, m.	Viscount Raynham, b. 1945.
1694 s.*	*Tweeddale* (13th), Edward Douglas John Hay (4th *U.K. Baron, Tweeddale*, 1881), b. 1947, s. 1979.	Lord Charles D. M. H., b. 1947.
1789 I.*	*Waterford* (8th), John Hubert de la Poer Beresford (8th *Brit. Baron, Tyrone*, 1786), b. 1933, s. 1934, m.	Earl of Tyrone, b. 1958.
1551	*Winchester* (18th), Nigel George Paulet (*Premier Marquess of England*), b. 1941, s. 1968, m.	Earl of Wiltshire, b. 1969.
1892	*Zetland* (3rd), Lawrence Aldred Mervyn Dundas (5th *U.K. Earl of Zetland*, 1838, 6th *Brit. Baron Dundas*, 1794), b. 1908, s. 1961, m.	Earl of Ronaldshay, b. 1937.

EARLS

Style (see also note, p. 247). The Right Hon. the Earl of ——. *Addressed as,* My Lord.
The eldest sons of Earls take, by courtesy, their father's second title, the younger sons
being styled the Hon. *e.g.* the Hon. John ——, but the daughters Lady Elizabeth ——,
etc. Where marked ° the "of" is not used

Created.	Title, Order of Succession, Name, etc.	Eldest Son or Heir.
1639 s.	*Airlie* (13th), David George Coke Patrick Ogilvy, P.C., G.C.V.O., *b.* 1926, *s.* 1968, *m.*	Lord Ogilvy, *b.* 1958.
1696	*Albemarle* (10th), Rufus Arnold Alexis Keppel, *b.* 1965, *s.* 1979, *M.*	Hon. Walter A. C. K., D.S.C., *b.* 1914.
1952	°*Alexander of Tunis* (2nd), Shane William Desmond Alexander, *b.* 1935, *s.* 1969, *m.*	Hon. Brian J. A., *b.* 1939.
1826	°*Amherst* (5th), Jeffery John Archer Amherst, M.C., *b.* 1896, *s.* 1927. *Annandale and Hartfell* (Full details to appear in next edition).	(None.)
1789 I.	°*Annesley* (10th), Patrick Annesley, *b.* 1924, *s.* 1979, *m.*	Hon. Philip H.A., *b.* 1927.
1785 I.	*Antrim* (9th), Alexander Randal Mark McDonnell, *b.* 1935, *s.* 1977, *m.* (*Viscount Dunluce.*)	Hon. Randal A. St. J. M., *b.* 1967.
1762 I.*	*Arran* (9th), Arthur Desmond Colquhoun Gore (5th *U.K. Baron Sudley,* 1884), *b.* 1938, *s.* 1983, *m.*	Paul A. G., C.M.G., C.V.O., *b.* 1921.
1955	°*Attlee* (2nd), Martin Richard Attlee, *b.* 1927, *s.* 1967, *m.*	Viscount Prestwood, *b.* 1956.
1714	*Aylesford* (11th), Charles Ian Finch-Knightley, *b.* 1918, *s.* 1958, *m.*	Lord Guernsey, *b.* 1947.
1937	°*Baldwin of Bewdley* (4th), Edward Alfred Alexander Baldwin, *b.* 1938, *s.* 1976, *m.*	Viscount Corvedale, *b.* 1973.
1922	*Balfour* (4th), Gerald Arthur James Balfour, *b.* 1925, *s.* 1968, *m.*	Eustace A. G. B., *b.* 1921.
1772	°*Bathurst* (8th), Henry Allen John Bathurst, *b.* 1927, *s.* 1943, *m.*	Lord Apsley, *b.* 1961.
1919	°*Beatty* (3rd), David Beatty, *b.* 1946, *s.* 1972, *m.*	Viscount Borodale, *b.* 1973.
1797 I.	*Belmore* (8th), John Armar Lowry-Corry, *b.* 1951, *s.* 1960, *m.*	Frederick H. L.-C., *b.* 1926.
1739 I.* } 1937 }	*Bessborough* (2nd), Frederick Edward Neuflize Ponsonby (10th *Irish Earl Bessborough*), *b.* 1913, *s.* 1956, *m.*	Arthur M. L. P., *b.* 1912 (to Irish Earldom only).
1815	*Bradford* (7th), Richard Thomas Orlando Bridgeman, *b.* 1947, *s.* 1981, *m.*	Viscount Newport, *b.* 1980.
1677 s.	*Breadalbane and Holland* (10th), John Romer Boreland Campbell, *b.* 1919, *s.* 1959.	(None.)
1469 s.*	*Buchan* (17th), Malcolm Harry Erskine, (8th *U.K. Baron Erskine* 1806), *b.* 1930, *s.* 1984, *m.*	Lord Cardross, *b.* 1960.
1746	*Buckinghamshire* (10th), (George) Miles Hobart-Hampden, *b.* 1944, *s.* 1983, *m.*	Sir Robert Hobart, Bt., *b.* 1915.
1800	°*Cadogan* (7th), William Gerald Charles Cadogan, M.C., *b.* 1914, *s.* 1933, *m.*	Viscount Chelsea, *b.* 1937.
1878	°*Cairns* (5th), David Charles Cairns, G.C.V.O., C.B., *b.* 1909, *s.* 1946, *m.*	Viscount Garmoyle, *b.* 1939.
1455 s.	*Caithness* (20th), Malcolm Ian Sinclair, *b.* 1948, *s.* 1965, *m.*	Lord Berriedale, *b.* 1981.
1800 I.	*Caledon* (7th), Nicholas James Alexander, *b.* 1955, *s.* 1980, *m.*	Earl Alexander of Tunis (*see* above).
1661	*Carlisle* (12th), Charles James Ruthven Howard, M.C. (*Scott. Baron, Ruthven of Freeland,* 1651), *b.* 1923, *s.* 1963, *m.*	Viscount Morpeth, *b.* 1949.
1793	*Carnarvon* (6th), Henry George Alfred Marius Victor Francis Herbert, *b.* 1898, *s.* 1923.	Lord Porchester, K.C.V.O., K.B.E., *b.* 1924.
1748 I.*	*Carrick* (9th), Brian Stuart Theobald Somerset Caher Butler (3rd *U.K. Baron, Butler,* 1912), *b.* 1931, *s.* 1957.	Viscount Ikerrin, *b.* 1953.
1800 I.	°*Castle Stewart* (8th), Arthur Patrick Avondale Stuart, *b.* 1928, *s.* 1961, *m.*	Viscount Stuart, *b.* 1953.
1814	°*Cathcart* (6th), Alan Cathcart, C.B., D.S.O., M.C. (15th *Scott. Baron, Cathcart,* 1447), *b.* 1919, *s.* 1927, *m.*	Lord Greenock, *b.* 1952.
1647 I.	*Cavan* (12th), Michael Edward Oliver Lambart, T.D., *b.* 1911, *s.* 1950, *m.*	Roger C. L., *b.* 1944.
1827	°*Cawdor* (6th), Hugh John Vaughan Campbell, *b.* 1932, *s.* 1970, *m.*	Viscount Emlyn, *b.* 1962.
1801	*Chichester* (9th), John Nicholas Pelham, *b.* 1944, *s.* 1944, *m.*	Richard A. H. P., *b.* 1952.
1803 I.*	*Clancarty* (8th), William Francis Brinsley Le Poer Trench (7th *U.K. Visct. Clancarty,* 1823), *b.* 1911, *s.* 1975, *m.*	Nicholas P. R. Le P. T., *b.* 1952.
1776 I.*	*Clanwilliam* (6th), John Charles Edmund Carson Meade (4th *U.K. Baron Clanwilliam,* 1828), *b.* 1914, *s.* 1953, *m.*	John H. M., *b.* 1919.
1776	*Clarendon* (7th), George Frederick Laurence Hyde Villiers, *b.* 1933, *s.* 1955, *m.*	Lord Hyde, *b.* 1976.
1620 I.*	*Cork & Orrery* (1660), Patrick Reginald Boyle (13th *Irish Earl* and 9th *Brit. Baron, Boyle of Marston,* 1711), *b.* 1910, *s.* 1967, *m.*	Hon. John W. B., D.S.C., *b.* 1916.
1850	*Cottenham* (8th), Kenelm Charles Everard Digby Pepys, *b.* 1948, *s.* 1968, *m.*	Viscount Crowhurst, *b.* 1983.
1762 I.*	*Courtown* (9th), James Patrick Montagu Burgoyne Winthrop Stopford (8th *Brit. Baron, Saltersford,* 1796), *b.* 1954, *s.* 1975, *m.*	Hon. Jeremy N. S., M.V.O., *b.* 1958.
1697	*Coventry* (11th), George William Coventry, *b.* 1934, *s.* 1940, *m.*	Viscount Deerhurst, *b.* 1957.
1857	°*Cowley* (7th), Garret Graham Wellesley, *b.* 1934, *s.* 1975, *m.*	Viscount Dangan, *b.* 1965.
1892	*Cranbrook* (5th), Gathorne Gathorne-Hardy, *b.* 1933, *s.* 1978, *m.*	Lord Medway, *b.* 1968.
1801	*Craven* (8th), Simon George Craven, *b.* 1961, *s.* 1983.	Rupert J. E. C., *b.* 1926.
1398 s.*	*Crawford* (29th) *and Balcarres* (12th), Robert Alexander Lindsay, P.C., (*Premier Earl on Union Roll and* 5th *U.K. Baron, Wigan,* 1826), *b.* 1927, *s.* 1975, *m.*	Lord Balniel, *b.* 1958.

Created.	Title, Order of Succession, Name, etc.	Eldest Son or Heir.
1861	*Cromartie* (4th), Roderick Grant Francis, Mackenzie, M.C., T.D., *b.* 1904, *s.* 1962, *m.*	Viscount Tarbat, *b.* 1948.
1901	*Cromer* (3rd), George Rowland Stanley Baring, K.G., G.C.M.G., M.B.E., P.C., *b.* 1918, *s.* 1953, *m.*	Viscount Errington, *b.* 1946.
1633 s.*	*Dalhousie* (16th), Simon Ramsay, K.T., G.C.V.O., G.B.E., M.C. (4th *U.K. Baron, Ramsay*, 1875), *b.* 1914, *s.* 1950, *m.*	Lord Ramsay, *b.* 1948.
1725 i.*	*Darnley* (11th), Adam Ivo Stuart Bligh (20th *English Baron, Clifton of Leighton Bromswold*, 1608), *b.* 1941, *s.* 1980, *m.*	Lord Clifton, *b.* 1968.
1711	*Dartmouth* (9th), Gerald Humphry Legge, *b.* 1924, *s.* 1962, *m.*	Viscount Lewisham, *b.* 1949.
1761	°*De La Warr* (10th), William Herbrand Sackville, *b.* 1921, *s.* 1976, *m.*	Lord Buckhurst, *b.* 1948.
1622	*Denbigh* (11th) *and Desmond* (10th), William Rudolph Michael Feilding (10th *Irish Earl, Desmond*, 1622), *b.* 1943, *s.* 1966, *m.*	Viscount Feilding, *b.* 1970.
1485	*Derby* (18th), Edward John Stanley, M.C., *b.* 1918, *s.* 1948, *m.*	Hon. Edward R. W. S., *b.* 1962.
1553	*Devon* (17th), Charles Christopher Courtenay, *b.* 1916, *s.* 1935, *m.*	Lord Courtenay, *b.* 1942.
1800 i.*	*Donoughmore* (8th), Richard Michael John Hely-Hutchinson (8th *U.K. Visct., Hutchinson*, 1821), *b.* 1927, *s.* 1981, *m.*	Viscount Suirdale, *b.* 1952.
1661 i.*	*Drogheda* (11th), Charles Garrett Ponsonby Moore, K.G., K.B.E. (2nd *U.K. Baron. Moore*, 1954), *b.* 1910, *s.* 1957, *m.*	Viscount Moore, *b.* 1937.
1837	*Ducie* (6th), Basil Howard Moreton, *b.* 1917, *s.* 1952, *m.*	Lord Moreton, *b.* 1951.
1860	*Dudley* (4th), William Humble David Ward, *b.* 1920, *s.* 1969, *m.*	Viscount Ednam, *b.* 1947.
1660 s.*	*Dundee* (12th), Alexander Henry Scrymgeour, (2nd *U.K. Baron, Glassary*, 1954), *b.* 1949, *s.* 1983, *m.*	Lord Scrymgeour, *b.* 1982.
1669 s.	*Dundonald* (14th), Ian Douglas Leonard Cochrane, *b.* 1918, *s.* 1958, *m.*	Lord Cochrane, *b.* 1961.
1686 s.*	*Dunmore* (11th), Kenneth Randolph Murray, *b.* 1913, *s.* 1981, *m.*	Viscount Fincastle, *b.* 1946.
1822 i.	*Dunraven and Mount-Earl* (7th), Thady Windham Thomas Wyndham-Quin, *b.* 1939, *s.* 1965, *m.*	(None).
1837	*Effingham* (6th), Mowbray Henry Gordon Howard (16th *E. Baron, Howard of Effingham*, 1554), *b.* 1905, *s.* 1946, *m.*	Lt.-Cmdr. David P. M. A. *H.*, *b.* 1939.
1507 s. } 1859* }	*Eglinton* (18th) *&* (9th) *Winton* (1600), Archibald George Montgomerie (6th *U.K. Earl Winton*, 1859), *s.* 1939, *s.* 1966, *m.*	Lord Montgomerie, *b.* 1966.
1733 i.*	*Egmont* (11th), Frederick George Moore Perceval (9th *Brit. Baron, Lovel & Holland*, 1762), *b.* 1914, *s.* 1932, *m.*	Viscount Perceval, *b.* 1934.
1821	*Eldon* (5th), John Joseph Nicholas Scott, *b.* 1937, *s.* 1976, *m.*	Viscount Encombe, *b.* 1962.
1633 s.*	*Elgin* (11th), *& Kincardine* (15th) (1647), Andrew Douglas Alexander Thomas Bruce, (4th *U.K. Baron, Elgin*, 1849), K.T., *b.* 1924, *s.* 1968, *m.*	Lord Bruce, *b.* 1961.
1789 i.*	*Enniskillen* (6th), David Lowry Cole, M.B.E., (4th *U.K. Baron, Grinstead*, 1815) *b.* 1918, *s.* 1963, *m.*	Viscount Cole, *b.* 1942.
1789 i.*	*Erne* (6th). Henry George Victor John Crichton (3rd *U.K. Baron, Fermanagh*, 1876), *b.* 1937, *s.* 1940, *m.*	Viscount Crichton, *b.* 1971.
1452 s.	*Erroll* (24th), Merlin Sereld Victor Gilbert Hay (*Hereditary Lord High Constable and Knight Marischal of Scotland*), *b.* 1948, *s.* 1978, *m.*	Lord Hay, *b.* 1984.
1661	*Essex* (10th), Robert Edward de Vere Capell, *b.* 1920, *s.* 1981, *m.*	Visct. Malden, *b.* 1944.
1711	°*Ferrers* (13th), Robert Washington Shirley, P.C., *b.* 1929, *s.* 1954, *m.*	Viscount Tamworth, *b.* 1952.
1789	°*Fortescue* (7th), Richard Archibald Fortescue, *b.* 1922, *s.* 1977, *m.*	Viscount Ebrington, *b.* 1951.
1841	*Gainsborough* (5th), Anthony Gerard Edward Noel, *b.* 1923, *s.* 1927, *m.*	Viscount Campden, *b.* 1950.
1623 s.*	*Galloway* (13th), Randolph Keith Reginald Stewart (6th *Brit. Baron, Stewart of Garlies*, 1796), *b.* 1928, *s.* 1978, *m.*	Alexander D. *S.*, M.B.E., T.D., *b.* 1914.
1703 s.*	*Glasgow* (10th), Patrick Robin Archibald Boyle (4th *U.K. Baron, Fairlie*, 1897), *b.* 1939, *s.* 1984, *m.*	Viscount of Kelburn, *b.* 1978.
1806 i.*	*Gosford* (7th), Charles David Nicholas Alexander John Sparrow Acheson (5th *U.K. Baron, Worlingham*, 1835), *b.* 1942, *s.* 1966.	Hon. Patrick B. V. M. *A.*, *b.* 1915.
1945	*Gowrie* (2nd), Alexander Patric Greysteil Hore-Ruthven, P.C. (3rd *U.K. Baron, Ruthven of Gowrie*, 1919), *b.* 1939, *s.* 1955, *m.*	Viscount Ruthven of Canberra, *b.* 1964.
1684 i.*	*Granard* (9th), Arthur Patrick Hastings Forbes, A.F.C. (4th *U.K. Baron, Granard*, 1806), *b.* 1915, *s.* 1948, *m.*	Peter A. E. H. *F.*, *b.* 1957.
1833	°*Granville* (5th), Granville James Leveson-Gower, M.C., *b.* 1918, *s.* 1953, *m.*	Lord Leveson, *b.* 1959.
1806	°*Grey* (6th), Richard Fleming George Charles Grey, *b.* 1939, *s.* 1963, *m.*	Philip K. *G.*, *b.* 1940.
1752	*Guilford* (9th), Edward Francis North, *b.* 1933, *s.* 1949, *m.*	Lord North, *b.* 1971.
1619 s.	*Haddington* (12th), George Baillie-Hamilton, K.T., M.C., T.D., *b.*1894, *s.* 1917, *m.*	Lord Binning, *b.* 1941.
1919	°*Haig* (2nd), George Alexander Eugene Douglas Haig, O.B.E., *b.* 1918. *s.* 1928, *m.*	Viscount Dawick, *b.* 1961.
1944	*Halifax* (3rd), Charles Edward Peter Neil Wood (5th *U.K. Viscount, Halifax*, 1866), *b.* 1944, *s.* 1980, *m.*	Lord Irwin, *b.* 1977.
1898	*Halsbury* (3rd), John Anthony Hardinge Giffard, F.R.S., *b.* 1908, *s.* 1943, *w.*	Adam E. *G.*, *b.* 1934.
1754	*Hardwicke* (10th), Joseph Philip Sebastian Yorke, *b.* 1971, *s.* 1974, *M.*	Richard C. J. *Y.*, *b.* 1916.
1812	*Harewood* (7th), George Henry Hubert Lascelles, *b.* 1923, *s.* 1947, *m.* (*See also* p. 217).	Viscount Lascelles, *b.* 1950.

Created.	Title, Order of Succession, Name, etc.	Eldest Son or Heir.
1742	*Harrington* (11th), William Henry Leicester Stanhope (8th *Brit. Viscount, Stanhope of Mahon,* 1717), *b.* 1922, *s.* 1929, *m.*	Viscount Petersham, *b.* 1945.
1809	*Harrowby* (6th), Dudley Ryder, *b.* 1892, *s.* 1956, *w.*	Viscount Sandon, *b.* 1922.
1821	°*Howe* (7th), Frederick Richard Penn Curzon, *b.* 1951, *s.* 1984, *m.*	James Q. P. C., *b.* 1923.
1529	*Huntingdon* (15th), Francis John Clarence Westenra Plantagenet Hastings, *b.* 1901, *s.* 1939, *m.*	Lt. Col. R. H. W. S. *H.,* D.S.O., O.B.E., M.C., *b.* 1917.
1885	*Iddesleigh* (4th), Stafford Henry Northcote, *b.* 1932, *s.* 1970, *m.*	Viscount St. Cyres, *b.* 1957.
1756	*Ilchester* (9th), Maurice Vivian de Touffreville Fox-Strangways, *b.* 1920, *s.* 1970, *m.*	Hon. Raymond G. *F.-S., b.* 1921.
1929	*Inchcape* (3rd), Kenneth James William Mackay, *b.* 1917, *s.* 1939, *m.*	Viscount Glenapp, *b.* 1943.
1919	*Iveagh* (3rd), Arthur Francis Benjamin Guinness, *b.* 1937, *s.* 1967.	Viscount Elveden, *b.* 1969.
1925	°*Jellicoe* (2nd), George Patrick John Rushworth Jellicoe, P.C., D.S.O., M.C., *b.* 1918, *s.* 1935, *m.*	Viscount Brocas, *b.* 1950.
1697	*Jersey* (9th), George Francis Child-Villiers (12th *Irish Visct., Grandison,* 1620), *b.* 1910, *s.* 1923, *m.*	Viscount Villiers, *b.* 1948.
1822 I.	*Kilmorey* (6th), Richard Francis Needham, M.P., *b.* 1942, *s.* 1977, *m.*	Viscount Newry and Morne, *b.* 1966.
1866	*Kimberley* (4th), John Wodehouse, *b.* 1924, *s.* 1941, *m.*	Lord Wodehouse, *b.* 1951.
1768 I.	*Kingston* (11th), Barclay Robert Edwin King-Tenison, *b.* 1943, *s.* 1948.	Viscount Kingsborough, *b.* 1969.
1633 s.*	*Kinnoull* (15th), Arthur William George Patrick Hay (9th *Brit. Baron, Hay of Pedwardine,* 1711), *b.* 1935, *s.* 1938, *m.*	Viscount Dupplin, *b.* 1962.
1677 s.*	*Kintore* (12th), (James) Ian Keith (2nd *U.K. Visct., Stonehaven,* 1938), *b.* 1908, *s.* to Viscountcy, 1941, to Earldom, 1974, *m.*	Lord Inverurie, *b.* 1939.
1914	°*Kitchener of Khartoum* (3rd), Henry Herbert Kitchener, T.D., *b.* 1919, *s.* 1937.	(None.)
1756 I.	*Lanesborough* (9th), Denis Anthony Brian Butler, T.D., *b.* 1918, *s.* 1950.	Cdr. T. B. J. D. *B.,* *b.* 1913.
1624 s.	*Lauderdale* (17th), Patrick Francis Maitland, *b.* 1911, *s.* 1968, *m.*	Viscount Maitland, *b.* 1937.
1837	*Leicester* (6th), Anthony Louis Lovel Coke, *b.* 1909, *s.* 1976, *m.*	Viscount Coke, *b.* 1936.
1641 s.	*Leven* (14th) & (13th) *Melville* (1690), Alexander Robert Leslie-Melville, *b.* 1924, *s.* 1947, *m.*	Lord Balgonie, *b.* 1954.
1831	*Lichfield* (5th), Thomas Patrick John Anson, *b.* 1939, *s.* 1960, *m.*	Viscount Anson, *b.* 1978.
1803 I.*	*Limerick* (6th), Patrick Edmund Pery, K.B.E. (6th *U.K. Baron, Foxford,* 1815), *b.* 1930, *s.* 1967, *m.*	Viscount Glentworth, *b.* 1963.
1633 s.	*Lindsay* (14th), William Tucker Lindesay-Bethune, *b.* 1901, *s.* 1943, *m.*	Viscount Garnock, *b.* 1926.
1626	*Lindsey* (14th) *and Abingdon* (9th) (1682), Richard Henry Rupert Bertie, *b.* 1931, *s.* 1963, *m.*	Lord Norreys, *b.* 1958.
1776 I.	*Lisburne* (8th), John David Malet Vaughan, *b.* 1918, *s.* 1965, *m.*	Viscount Vaughan, *b.* 1945.
1822 I.*	*Listowel* (5th), William Francis Hare, P.C., G.C.M.G. (3rd *U.K. Baron, Hare,* 1869), *b.* 1906, *s.* 1931, *m.*	Viscount Ennismore, *b.* 1964.
1905	*Liverpool* (5th), Edward Peter Bertram Savile Foljambe, *b.* 1944, *s.* 1969, *m.*	Viscount Hawkesbury, *b.* 1972.
1945	°*Lloyd George of Dwyfor* (3rd), Owen Lloyd George, *b.* 1924, *s.* 1968, *m.*	Viscount Gwynedd, *b.* 1951.
1785 I.*	*Longford* (7th), Francis Aungier Pakenham, K.G., P.C. (6th *U.K. Baron, Silchester,* 1821; 1st *U.K. Baron, Pakenham,* 1945), *b.* 1905, *s.* 1961, *m.*	Thomas F. D. *P.,* *b.* 1933.
1807	*Lonsdale* (7th), James Hugh William Lowther, *b.* 1922, *s.* 1953, *m.*	Viscount Lowther, *b.* 1949.
1838	*Lovelace* (5th), Peter Axel William Locke King (12th *British Baron, King,* 1725), *b.* 1951, *s.* 1964.	(None.)
1795 I.*	*Lucan* (7th), Richard John Bingham (3rd *U.K. Baron, Bingham,* 1934), *b.* 1934, *s.* 1964, *m.*	Lord Bingham, *b.* 1967.
1880	*Lytton* (5th), John Peter Michael Scawen Lytton (18th *English Baron, Wentworth,* 1529), *b.* 1950, *s.* 1985, *m.*	Viscount Knebworth, *b.* 1954.
1721	*Macclesfield* (8th), George Roger Alexander Thomas Parker, *b.* 1914, *s.* 1975, *m.*	Viscount Parker, *b.* 1943.
1800	*Malmesbury* (6th), William James Harris, T.D., *b.* 1907, *s.* 1950, *m.*	Viscount FitzHarris, *b.* 1946.
1776 & 1792	*Mansfield and Mansfield* (8th), William David Mungo James Murray (14th *Scott. Visct., Stormont,* 1621), *b.* 1930, *s.* 1971, *m.*	Viscount Stormont, *b.* 1956.
1565 s.	*Mar* (13th) & (15th) *Kellie* (1616), John Francis Hervey Erskine, *b.* 1921, *s.* 1955, *m.*	Lord Erskine, *b.* 1949.
1785 I.	*Mayo* (10th), Terence Patrick Bourke, *b.* 1929, *s.* 1962, *m.*	Lord Naas, *b.* 1953.
1627 I.*	*Meath* (14th), Anthony Windham Normand Brabazon (5th *U.K. Baron, Chaworth,* 1831), *b.* 1910, *s.* 1949, *m.*	Lord Ardee, *b.* 1941.
1766 I.	*Mexborough* (8th), John Christopher George Savile, *b.* 1931, *s.* 1980, *m.*	Viscount Pollington, *b.* 1959.
1813	*Minto* (6th), Gilbert Edward George Lariston Garnet Elliot-Murray-Kynynmound, M.B.E., *b.* 1928, *s.* 1975, *w.*	Viscount Melgund, *b.* 1953.
1562 s.*	*Moray* (20th) Douglas John Moray Stuart (12th *Brit. Baron, Stuart of Castle Stuart,* 1796), *b.* 1928, *s.* 1974, *m.*	Lord Doune, *b.* 1966.
1815	*Morley* (6th), John St. Aubyn Parker, *b.* 1923, *s.* 1962, *m.*	Visct. Boringdon, *b.* 1956.
1458 s.	*Morton* (22nd), John Charles Sholto Douglas, *b.* 1927, *s.* 1976, *m.*	Lord Aberdour, *b.* 1952.
1789	*Mount Edgcumbe* (8th), Robert Charles Edgcumbe, *b.* 1939, *s.* 1982, *m.*	Piers V. *E.,* *b.* 1946.
1831	*Munster* (7th), Anthony Charles FitzClarence, *b.* 1926, *s.* 1983, *m.*	(None.)

Created.	Title, Order of Succession, Name, etc.	Eldest Son or Heir.

1805 °*Nelson* (9th), Peter John Horatio Nelson, *b.* 1941, *s.* 1981, *m.* — Viscount Merton, *b.* 1971.

1660 s. *Newburgh* (11th), Prince Giulio Cesare Taddeo Cosimo Rospigliosi, *b.* 1907, *s.* 1977, *m.* — Viscount Kynnaird, *b.* 1942.

1827 i. *Norbury* (6th), Noel Terence Graham-Toler, *b.* 1939, *s.* 1955, *m.* — Viscount Glandine, *b.* 1967.

1806 i.* *Normanton* (6th), Shaun James Christian Welbore Ellis Agar (9th *Brit. Baron, Mendip*, 1791) (4th *U.K. Baron, Somerton*, 1873), *b.* 1945, *s.* 1967, *m.* — Viscount Somerton, *b.* 1982.

1647 s. *Northesk* (13th), Robert Andrew Carnegie, *b.* 1926, *s.* 1975, *m.* — Lord Rosehill, *b.* 1954.

1801 *Onslow* (7th), Michael William Coplestone Dillon Onslow, *b.* 1938, *s.* 1971, *m.* — Viscount Cranley, *b.* 1967.

1696 *Orkney* (8th), Cecil O'Bryen Fitz-Maurice, *b.* 1919, *s.* 1951, *m.* — O. Peter St. J. *F-M.*, *b.* 1938

1925 *Oxford & Asquith* (2nd), Julian Edward George Asquith, K.C.M.G., *b.* 1916, *s.* 1928, *m.* — Viscount Asquith, *b.* 1952.

1929 °*Peel* (3rd), William James Robert Peel (4th *U.K. Viscount Peel*, 1895), *b.* 1947, *s.* 1969, *m.* — Viscount Clanfield, *b.* 1976.

1551 *Pembroke* (17th) & (14th) *Montgomery* (1605), Henry George Charles Alexander Herbert, *b.* 1939, *s.* 1969. — Lord Herbert, *b.* 1978.

1605 s. *Perth* (17th), John David Drummond, P.C., *b.* 1907, *s.* 1951, *m.* — Viscount Strathallan, *b.* 1935.

1905 *Plymouth* (3rd), Other Robert Ivor Windsor-Clive (15th *English Baron, Windsor*, 1529), *b.* 1923, *s.* 1943, *m.* — Viscount Windsor, *b.* 1951.

1785 i. *Portarlington* (7th), George Lionel Yuill Seymour Dawson-Damer, *b.* 1938, *s.* 1959, *m.* — Viscount Carlow, *b.* 1965.

1743 *Portsmouth* (10th), Quentin Gerard Carew Wallop, *b.* 1954, *s.* 1984, *m.* — Viscount Lymington, *b.* 1981.

1804 *Powis* (6th), Christian Victor Charles Herbert (7th *Irish Baron, Clive*, 1762), *b.* 1904, *s.* 1974. — George W. *H.*, *b.* 1925.

1765 *Radnor* (8th), Jacob Pleydell-Bouverie, *b.* 1927, *s.* 1968. — Viscount Folkestone, *b.* 1955.

1831 i.* *Ranfurly* (6th), Thomas Daniel Knox, K.C.M.G. (7th *U.K. Baron, Ranfurly*, 1826), *b.* 1913, *s.* 1933, *m.* — Gerald F. N. *K.*, *b.* 1929.

1771 i. *Roden* (9th), Robert William Jocelyn, *b.* 1909, *s.* 1956, *m.* — Viscount Jocelyn, *b.* 1938.

1801 *Romney* (7th), Michael Henry Marsham, *b.* 1910, *s.* 1975, *m.* — Julian C. *M.*, *b.* 1948.

1703 s.* *Rosebery* (7th), Neil Archibald Primrose (3rd *U.K. Earl, Midlothian*, 1911), *b.* 1929, *s.* 1974, *m.* — Lord Dalmeny, *b.* 1967.

1806 i. *Rosse* (7th), William Brendan Parsons, *b.* 1936, *s.* 1979, *m.* — Lord Oxmantown, *b.* 1969.

1801 *Rosslyn* (7th), Peter St. Clair-Erskine, *b.* 1958, *s.* 1977, *m.* — Hon. David S. *St. C.-E.*, *b.* 1917.

1457 s. *Rothes* (21st), Ian Lionel Malcolm Leslie, *b.* 1932, *s.* 1975, *m.* — Lord Leslie, *b.* 1958.

1861 °*Russell* (4th), John Conrad Russell, *b.* 1921, *s.* 1970. — Hon. Conrad S. R. *R.*, *b.* 1937.

1915 °*St. Aldwyn* (2nd), Michael John Hicks-Beach, P.C., G.B.E., T.D., *b.* 1912, *s.* 1916, *m.* — Viscount Quenington, *b.* 1950.

1815 *St. Germans* (9th), Nicholas Richard Michael Eliot, *b.* 1914, *s.* 1960, *m.* — Lord Eliot, *b.* 1941.

1690 *Scarbrough* (12th), Richard Aldred Lumley (13th *Irish Visct., Lumley*, 1628), *b.* 1932, *s.* 1969, *m.* — Viscount Lumley, *b.* 1973.

1701 s. *Seafield* (13th), Ian Derek Francis Ogilvie-Grant, *b.* 1939, *s.* 1969, *m.* — Visct. Reidhaven, *b.* 1963.

1882 *Selborne* (4th), John Roundell Palmer, *b.* 1940, *s.* 1971, *m.* — Viscount Wolmer, *b.* 1971.

1646 s. *Selkirk* (10th) (George) Nigel Douglas-Hamilton, P.C., K.T., G.C.M.G., G.B.E., A.F.C., Q.C., *b.* 1906, *s.* 1940, *m.* — The Master of Selkirk, *b.* 1939.

1672 *Shaftesbury* (10th), Anthony Ashley-Cooper, *b.* 1938, *s.* 1961, *m.* — Lord Ashley, *b.* 1977.

1756 i.* *Shannon* (9th), Richard Bentinck Boyle (8th *Brit. Bn., Carleton* 1786), *b.* 1924, *s.* 1963. — Viscount Boyle, *b.* 1960.

1442 *Shrewsbury* (22nd) & *Waterford* (I. 1446), Charles Henry John Benedict Crofton Chetwynd Chetwynd-Talbot (*Premier Earl of England and Ireland; Earl Talbot*, 1784), *b.* 1952, *s.* 1980, *m.* — Viscount Ingestre, *b.* 1978.

1961 *Snowdon* (1st), Antony Charles Robert Armstrong-Jones, G.C.V.O., *b.* 1930, *m.* (*See also* p. 219). — Viscount Linley, *b.* 1961 (*see also* p. 219).

1880 °*Sondes* (5th), Henry George Herbert Milles-Lade, *b.* 1940, *s.* 1970. — (None.)

1633 s.* *Southesk* (11th), Charles Alexander Carnegie, K.C.V.O. (3rd *U.K. Baron, Balinhard*, 1869), *b.* 1893, *s.* 1941, *m.* — The Duke of Fife, *b.* 1929 (*see* pp. 216 and 227).

1765 °*Spencer* (8th), Edward John Spencer, M.V.O., *b.* 1924, *s.* 1975, *m.* — Viscount Althorp, *b.* 1964.

1703 s.* *Stair* (13th), John Aymer Dalrymple, K.C.V.O., M.B.E (6th *U.K. Baron, Oxenfoord*, 1841), *b.* 1906, *s.* 1961, *m.* — Viscount Dalrymple, *b.* 1961.

1984 *Stockton* (1st), (Maurice) Harold Macmillan, P.C., O.M., F.R.S., *b.* 1894. — Viscount Macmillan of Ovenden, *b.* 1943.

1821 *Stradbroke* (6th), Robert Keith Rous, *b.* 1937, *s.* 1983, *m.* — Hon. Robert K. *R.*, *b.* 1961.

1847 *Strafford* (8th), Thomas Edmund Byng, *b.* 1936, *s.* 1984, *m.* — Viscount Enfield, *b.* 1964.

1937 *Strathmore* (4th), Fergus Michael Claude Bowes-Lyon (17th *Scottish Earl, Strathmore & Kinghorne* 1606), *b.* 1928, *s.* 1972, *m.* — Lord Glamis, *b.* 1957.

1603 *Suffolk* (21st) & (14th) *Berkshire* (1626), Michael John James George Robert Howard, *b.* 1935, *s.* 1941, *m.* — Viscount Andover, *b.* 1974.

1955 *Swinton* (2nd), David Yarburgh Cunliffe-Lister, *b.* 1937, *s.* 1972, *m.* — Hon. Nicholas J. *C.-L.*, *b.* 1939.

1714 *Tankerville* (10th), Peter Grey Bennet, *b.* 1956, *s.* 1980. — Rev. the Hon. George A. G. *B.*, *b.* 1925.

Created.	Title, Order of Succession, Name, etc.	Eldest Son or Heir.
1822	°*Temple of Stowe* (7th), Ronald Stephen Brydges Temple-Gore-Langton, *b.* 1910, *s.* 1966.	W. Grenville A. *T.-G.-L.,* *b.* 1924.
1815	*Verulam* (7th), John Duncan Grimston (11th *Irish Visct., Grimston,* 1719; 16th *Scott. Baron, Forrester of Corstorphine,* 1633), *b.* 1951, *s.* 1973, *m.*	Viscount Grimston, *b.* 1978.
1729	°*Waldegrave* (12th), Geoffrey Noel Waldegrave, K.G., G.C.V.O., T.D., *b.* 1905, *s.* 1936, *m.*	Viscount Chewton, *b.* 1940.
1759	*Warwick* & °*Brooke* (1746), David Robin Francis Guy Greville (8th *Earl Brooke* and 8th *Earl of Warwick), b.* 1934, *s.* 1984.	Lord Brooke, *b.* 1957.
1633 s.*	*Wemyss* (12th) & (8th) *March* (1697), Francis David Charteris, K.T. (5th *U.K. Baron, Wemyss,* 1821), *b.* 1912, *s.* 1937, *m.*	Lord Neidpath, *b.* 1948.
1621 I.	*Westmeath* (13th), William Anthony Nugent, *b.* 1928, *s.* 1971, *m.*	Hon. Sean C. W. *N., b.* 1965.
1624	*Westmorland* (15th), David Anthony Thomas Fane, K.C.V.O., *b.* 1924, *s.* 1948, *m.* (*Master of the Horse*).	Lord Burghersh, *b.* 1951.
1876	*Wharncliffe* (4th), Alan James Montagu-Stuart-Wortley-Mackenzie, *b.* 1935, *s.* 1953, *m.*	Alan R. *Montagu-Stuart-Wortley, b.* 1927.
1801	*Wilton* (7th), Seymour William Arthur John Egerton, *b.* 1921, *s.* 1927, *m.*	Lord Ebury, *b.* 1934 (*see p.* 239).
1628	*Winchilsea* (16th) & (11th) *Nottingham* (1681), Christopher Denys Stormont Finch-Hatton, *b.* 1936, *s.* 1950, *m.*	Viscount Maidstone, *b.* 1967.
1766 I.	°*Winterton* (7th), Robert Chad Turnour, *b.* 1915, *s.* 1962, *m.*	N. Cecil *T.,* D.F.M., C.D., *b.* 1919.
1956	*Woolton* (3rd), Simon Frederick Marquis, *b.* 1958, *s.* 1969.	(None.)
1837	*Yarborough* (7th), John Edward Pelham, *b.* 1920, *s.* 1966, *m.*	Lord Worsley, *b.* 1963.
1922	*Ypres* (3rd), John Richard Charles Lambart French, *b.* 1921, *s.* 1948, *m.*	(None.)

VISCOUNTS

Style (see also note, p. 247), The Right Hon. the Viscount ——. *Addressed as,* My Lord. The eldest sons of Viscounts and Barons have no distinctive title; they, as well as their brothers and sisters, are styled the Hon. Robert, Hon. Mary, &c.

Created.	Title, Order of Succession, Name, etc.	Eldest Son or Heir.
1945	*Addison* (3rd), Michael Addison, *b.* 1914, *s.* 1976, *m.*	Hon. William M. W. *A., b.* 1945.
1946	*Alanbrooke* (3rd), Alan Victor Harold Brooke, *b.* 1932, *s.* 1972.	(None.)
1919	*Allenby* (3rd), Lt.-Col. Michael Jaffray Hynman Allenby, *b.* 1931, *s.* 1984, *m.*	Hon. Henry J. H. *A., b.* 1968.
1911	*Allendale* (3rd), Wentworth Hubert Charles Beaumont, *b.* 1922, *s.* 1956, *m.*	Hon. Wentworth P. I. *B., b.* 1948.
1642 s.	*Arbuthnott* (16th *Viscount of Arbuthnott*), John Campbell Arbuthnott, D.S.C., *b.* 1924, *s.* 1966, *m.*	Master of Arbuthnott, *b.* 1950.
1751 I.	*Ashbrook* (10th), Desmond Llowarch Edward Flower, K.C.V.O., M.B.E., *b.* 1905, *s.* 1936, *m.*	Hon. Michael L. W. *F., b.* 1935.
1917	*Astor* (4th), William Waldorf Astor, *b.* 1951, *s.* 1966, *m.*	Hon. William W. *A., b.* 1979.
1781 I.	*Bangor* (7th), Edward Henry Harold Ward, *b.* 1905, *s.* 1950, *m.*	Hon. William M. D. *W., b.* 1948.
1720 I.*	*Barrington* (11th), Patrick William Daines Barrington (5th *U.K. Baron Shute,* 1880), *b.* 1908, *s.* 1960.	(None.)
1925	*Bearsted* (3rd), Marcus Richard Samuel, T.D., *b.* 1909, *s.* 1948, *w.*	Hon. Peter M. S., M.C., T.D., *b.* 1911.
1963	*Blakenham* (2nd), Michael John Hare, *b.* 1938, *s.* 1982, *m.*	Hon. Caspar J. *H., b.* 1972.
1935	*Bledisloe* (3rd), Christopher Hiley Ludlow Bathurst, Q.C., *b.* 1934, *s.* 1979, *m.*	Hon. Rupert E. L. *B., b.* 1964.
1712	*Bolingbroke* & *St. John* (7th), Kenneth Oliver Musgrave St. John, *b.* 1927, *s.* 1974, *m.*	Hon. Henry F. *St. J., b.* 1957.
1960	*Boyd of Merton* (2nd), Simon Donald Rupert Neville Lennox-Boyd, *b.* 1939, *s.* 1983, *m.*	Hon. Benjamin A. *L.-B., b.* 1964.
1717 I.*	*Boyne* (10th), Gustavus Michael George Hamilton-Russell (4th *U.K. Baron, Brancepeth,* 1866), *b.* 1931, *s.* 1942, *m.*	Hon. Gustavus M. S. *H.-R., b.* 1965.
1929	*Brentford* (4th), Crispin William Joynson-Hicks, *b.* 1933, *s.* 1983, *m.*	Hon. Paul W. *J.-H., b.* 1971.
1929	*Bridgeman* (3rd), Robin John Orlando Bridgeman, *b.* 1930, *s.* 1982, *m.*	Hon. William O. C. *B., b.* 1968.
1868	*Bridport* (4th), Alexander Nelson Hood (7th *Duke of Brontë in Sicily,* 1799, *and* 6th *Irish Baron, Bridport* 1794), *b.* 1948, *s.* 1969, *m.*	Hon. Peregrine A. N. *H., b.* 1974.
1952	*Brookeborough* (2nd), John Warden Brooke, P.C. (N.I.), *b.* 1922, *s.* 1973, *m.*	Hon. Alan H. *B., b.* 1952.
1933	*Buckmaster* (3rd), Martin Stanley Buckmaster, O.B.E., *b.* 1921, *s.* 1974.	Hon. Colin J. *B., b.* 1923.
1939	*Caldecote* (2nd), Robert Andrew Inskip, D.S.C., *b.* 1917, *s.* 1947, *m.*	Hon. Piers J. H. *I., b.* 1947.
1941	*Camrose* (2nd), (John) Seymour Berry, T.D., *b.* 1909, *s.* 1954.	Lord Hartwell, M.B.E., T.D., *b.* 1911 (*see p.* 249).
1952	*Chandos* (3rd), Thomas Orlando Lyttelton, *b.* 1953, *s.* 1980.	Hon. Matthew P. A. *L., b.* 1956.

Created.	Title, Order of Succession, Name, etc.	Eldest Son or Heir.
1665 I.	*Charlemont* (13th), Charles Wilberforce Caulfeild (17th *Irish Baron, Caulfeild of Charlemont*, 1620), *b.* 1899, *s.* 1979, *m.*	John D. C., *b.* 1934.
1921	*Chelmsford* (3rd), Frederic Jan Thesiger, *b.* 1931, *s.* 1970, *m.*	Hon. Frederic C. P. *T.*, *b.* 1962.
1717 I.	*Chetwynd* (10th), Adam Richard John Casson Chetwynd, *b.* 1935, *s.* 1965, *m.*	Hon. Adam D. C., *b.* 1969.
1911	*Chilston* (4th), Alastair George Akers-Douglas, *b.* 1946, *s.* 1982, *m.*	Hon. Oliver I. *A.-D.*, *b.* 1973.
1902	*Churchill* (3rd), Victor George Spencer (5th *U.K. Baron Churchill*, 1815), *b.* 1934, *s.* 1973.	None to Viscountcy; to Barony, R. Harry R. S., *b.* 1926.
1718	*Cobham* (11th), John William Leonard Lyttelton (8th *Irish Baron, Westcote*, 1776), *b.* 1943, *s.* 1977, *m.*	Hon. Christopher C. *L.*, *b.* 1947.
1902	*Colville of Culross* (4th), John Mark Alexander Colville, Q.C. (13th *Scott. Baron, Colville of Culross*, 1604), *b.* 1933, *s.* 1945, *m.*	Master of Colville, *b.* 1959.
1826	*Combermere* (5th), Michael Wellington Stapleton-Cotton, *b.* 1929, *s.* 1969, *m.*	Hon. Thomas R. W. *S.-C.*, *b.* 1969.
1917	*Cowdray* (3rd), Weetman John Churchill Pearson, T.D. (3rd *U.K. Baron, Cowdray*, 1910), *b.* 1910, *s.* 1933, *m.*	Hon. Michael O. W. *P.*, *b.* 1944.
1927	*Craigavon* (3rd), Janric Fraser Craig, *b.* 1944, *s.* 1974.	(None).
1886	*Cross* (3rd), Assheton Henry Cross, *b.* 1920, *s.* 1932, *m.*	(None).
1943	*Daventry* (2nd), Robert Oliver FitzRoy, *b.* 1893, *s.* 1962, *w.*	Francis H. M. *FitzRoy-Newdegate*, *b.* 1921.
1937	*Davidson* (2nd), John Andrew Davidson, *b.* 1928, *s.* 1970, *m.*	Hon. Malcolm W. M. *D.*, *b.* 1934.
1956	*De L'Isle* (1st), William Philip Sidney, V.C., K.G., P.C., G.C.M.G., G.C.V.O., (6th *Baron De L'Isle and Dudley*, 1835), *b.* 1909, *m.*	Maj. Hon. Philip J. A. *S.*, M.B.E., *b.* 1945.
1776 I.	*De Vesci* (7th), Thomas Eustace Vesey (8th *Irish Baron, Knapton*, 1750), *b.* 1955, *s.* 1983.	Nicholas I. *V.*, *b.* 1954.
1917	*Devonport* (3rd), Terence Kearley, *b.* 1944, *s.* 1973.	Chester D. H. *K.*, *b.* 1932.
1964	*Dilhorne* (2nd), John Mervyn Manningham-Buller, *b.* 1932, *s.* 1980, *m.*	Hon. James E. *M.-B.*, *b.* 1956.
1622 I.	*Dillon* (22nd), Henry Benedict Dillon, *b.* 1973, *s.* 1982, *M.*	Hon. Richard A. L. *D.*, *b.* 1948.
1785 I.	*Doneraile* (10th), Richard Allen St. Leger, *b.* 1946, *s.* 1983, *m.*	Hon. Nathaniel W. R. St. J. *St. L.*, *b.* 1971.
1680 I.*	*Downe* (11th), John Christian George Dawnay (4th *U.K. Baron, Dawnay*, 1897), *b.* 1935, *s.* 1965, *m.*	Hon. Richard H. *D.*, *b.* 1967.
1959	*Dunrossil* (2nd), John William Morrison, C.M.G., *b.* 1926, *s.* 1961, *m.*	Hon. Andrew W. R. *M.*, *b.* 1953.
1964	*Eccles* (1st), David McAdam Eccles, C.H., P.C., K.C.V.O., *b.* 1904, *m.*	Hon. John D. *E.*, *b.* 1931.
1897	*Esher* (4th), Lionel Gordon Baliol Brett, C.B.E., *b.* 1913, *s.* 1963, *m.*	Hon. Christopher L. B. *B.*, *b.* 1936.
1816	*Exmouth* (10th), Paul Edward Pellew, *b.* 1940, *s.* 1970, *m.*	Hon. Edward F. *P.*, *b.* 1978.
1620 S.	*Falkland* (15th), Lucius Edward William Plantagenet Cary (*Premier Scottish Viscount on the Roll*), *b.* 1935, *s.* 1984, *m.*	Master of Falkland, *b.* 1963
1720	*Falmouth* (9th), George Hugh Boscawen (26th *Eng. Baron, Le Despencer*, 1264), *b.* 1919, *s.* 1962, *m.*	Hon. Evelyn A. H. *B.*, *b.* 1955.
1918	*Furness* (2nd), William Anthony Furness, *b.* 1929, *s.* 1940.	(None.)
1720 I.*	*Gage* (7th), George John St. Clere Gage, (6th *Brit. Baron, Gage*, 1790), *b.* 1932, *s.* 1982, *m.*	Hon. Henry N *G.*, *b.* 1934.
1727 I.	*Galway* (12th), George Rupert Monckton-Arundell, *b.* 1922, *s.* 1980, *m.*	Hon. John P. *M.-A.*, *b.* 1952.
1478 I.*	*Gormanston* (17th), Jenico Nicholas Dudley Preston (*Premier Viscount of Ireland*; 5th *U.K. Baron, Gormanston*, 1868), *b.* 1939, *s.* 1940, *w.*	Hon. Jenico F. T. *P.*, *b.* 1974.
1816 I.	*Gort* (8th), Colin Leopold Prendergast Vereker, *b.* 1916, *s.* 1975, *m.*	Hon. Foley R.S.P. *V.*, *b.* 1951.
1900	*Goschen* (4th), Giles John Harry Goschen, *b.* 1965, *s.* 1977, *M.*	(None.)
1849	*Gough* (5th), Shane Hugh Maryon Gough, *b.* 1941, *s.* 1951.	(None.)
1937	*Greenwood* (2nd), David Henry Hamar Greenwood, *b.* 1914, *s.* 1948.	Hon. Michael G. H. *G.*, *b.* 1923.
1891	*Hambleden* (4th), William Herbert Smith, *b.* 1930, *s.* 1948, *m.*	Hon. William H. B. *S.*, *b.* 1955.
1884	*Hampden* (6th), Anthony David Brand, *b.* 1937, *s.* 1975, *m.*	Hon. Francis A. *B.*, *b.* 1970.
1936	*Hanworth* (2nd), David Bertram Pollock, *b.* 1916, *s.* 1936, *m.*	Hon. David S. G. *P.*, *b.* 1946.
1791 I.	*Harberton* (10th), Thomas de Vautetort Pomeroy, *b.* 1910, *s.* 1980, *m.*	Hon. Robert W. *P.*, *b.* 1916.
1846	*Hardinge* (6th), Charles Henry Nicholas Hardinge, *b.* 1956, *s.* 1984.	Hon. Andrew H. *H.*, *b.* 1960.
1791 I.	*Hawarden* (8th), Robert Leslie Eustace Maude, *b.* 1926, *s.* 1958, *m.*	Hon. Robert C. W. L. *M.*, *b.* 1961.
1960	*Head* (2nd), Richard Antony Head, *b.* 1937, *s.* 1983, *m.*	Hon. Henry J. *H.*, *b.* 1980.
1550	*Hereford* (18th), Robert Milo Leicester Devereux (*Premier Viscount of England*), *b.* 1932, *s.* 1952.	Hon. Charles R. de B. *D.*, *b.* 1975.
1842	*Hill* (8th), Antony Rowland Clegg-Hill, *b.* 1931, *s.* 1974, *m.*	Peter D. R. C. *C.-H.*, *b.* 1945.
1796	*Hood* (7th), Alexander Lambert Hood (*Irish Baron, Hood*, 1782), *b.* 1914, *s.* 1981, *m.*	Hon. Henry L. A. *H.*, *b.* 1958.
1956	*Ingleby* (2nd), Martin Raymond Peake, *b.* 1926, *s.* 1966, *m.*	(None.)

Created.	Title, Order of Succession, Name, etc.	Eldest Son or Heir.
1945	*Kemsley* (2nd), (Geoffrey) Lionel Berry, *b.* 1909, *s.* 1968, *m.*	Richard G. *B.*, *b.* 1951.
1911	*Knollys* (3rd), David Francis Dudley Knollys, *b.* 1931, *s.* 1966, *m.*	Hon. Patrick N. M. *K.*, *b.* 1962.
1895	*Knutsford* (5th), Julian Thurston Holland-Hibbert, C.B.E., *b.* 1920, *s.* 1976.	Michael *H.-H.*, *b.* 1926.
1945	*Lambert* (2nd), George Lambert, T.D., *b.* 1909, *s.* 1958, *m.*	Hon. Michael J. *L.*, *b.* 1912.
1954	*Leathers* (2nd), Frederick Alan Leathers, *b.* 1908, *s.* 1965, *m.*	Hon. Christopher G. *L.*, *b.* 1941.
1922	*Leverhulme* (3rd), Philip William Bryce Lever, T.D., *b.* 1915, *s.* 1949, *w.*	(None.)
1781 I.	*Lifford* (8th), Alan William Wingfield Hewitt, *b.* 1900, *s.* 1954, *m.*	Hon. Edward J. W. *H.*, *b.* 1949.
1921	*Long* (4th), Richard Gerard Long, *b.* 1929, *s.* 1967, *m.*	Hon. James R. *L.*, *b.* 1960.
1957	*Mackintosh of Halifax* (3rd), (John) Clive Mackintosh, *b.* 1958, *s.* 1980, *m.*	Son, *b.* 1985.
1955	*Malvern* (3rd), Ashley Kevin Godfrey Huggins, *b.* 1949, *s.* 1978.	Hon. M. James *H.*, *b.* 1928.
1945	*Marchwood* (3rd), David George Staveley Penny, *b.* 1936, *s.* 1979, *m.*	Hon. Peter G. W. *P.*, *b.* 1965.
1942	*Margesson* (2nd), Francis Vere Hampden Margesson, *b.* 1922, *s.* 1965, *m.*	Hon. Richard F. D. *M.*, *b.* 1960.
1660 I.*	*Massereene* (13th) & (6th) *Ferrard* (1797), John Clotworthy Talbot Foster Whyte-Melville Skeffington (6th *U.K. Baron, Oriel,* 1821), *b.* 1914, *s.* 1956, *m.*	Hon. John D. C. W.-M. F. *S.*, *b.* 1940.
1802	*Melville* (9th), Robert David Ross Dundas, *b.* 1937, *s.* 1971, *m.*	Hon. Robert H. K. *D.*, *b.* 1984.
1916	*Mersey* (4th), Richard Maurice Clive Bigham, *b.* 1934, *s.* 1979, *m.*	Hon. Edward J. H. *B.*, *b.* 1966.
1717 I.	*Midleton* (11th), Trevor Lowther Brodrick (*Brit. Baron, Brodrick, Peper Harow,* 1796), *b.* 1903, *s.* 1979, *m.*	Alan H. *B.*, *b.* 1949.
1962	*Mills* (2nd), Roger Clinton Mills, *b.* 1919, *s.* 1968, *m.*	Hon. Christopher P. R. *M.*, *b.* 1956.
1716 I.	*Molesworth* (11th), Richard Gosset Molesworth, *b.* 1907, *s.* 1961, *w.*	Hon. Robert B. K. *M.*, *b.* 1959.
1801 I.*	*Monck* (7th), Charles Stanley Monck (4th *U.K. Baron, Monck,* 1866), *b.* 1953, *s.* 1982.	Hon. George S. *M.*, *b.* 1957.
1957	*Monckton of Brenchley* (2nd), Gilbert Walter Riversdale Monckton, C.B., O.B.E., M.C., *b.* 1915, *s.* 1965, *m.*	Hon Christopher W. *M.*, *b.* 1952.
1935	*Monsell* (2nd), Henry Bolton Graham Eyres-Monsell, *b.* 1905, *s.* 1969.	(None.)
1946	*Montgomery of Alamein* (2nd), David Bernard Montgomery, C.B.E, *b.* 1928, *s.* 1976, *m.*	Hon. Henry D. *M.*, *b.* 1954.
1550 I.*	*Mountgarret* (17th), Richard Henry Piers Butler (4th *U.K. Baron, Mountgarret,* 1911), *b.* 1936, *s.* 1966, *m.*	Hon. Piers J. R. *B.*, *b.* 1961.
1964	*Muirshiel* (1st), John Scott Maclay, P.C., K.T., C.H., C.M.G., *b.* 1905, *w.*	(None.)
1952	*Norwich* (2nd), John Julius Cooper, *b.* 1929, *s.* 1954, *m.*	Hon. Jason C. D. B. *C.*, *b.* 1959.
1651 S.	*Oxfuird* (12th), John Donald Alexander Arthur Makgill, *claim established* 1977, *b.* 1899, *m.*	George H. *M.*, *b.* 1934.
1873	*Portman,* (9th), Edward Henry Berkeley Portman, *b.* 1934, *s.* 1967, *m.*	Hon. Christopher E. B. *P.*, *b.* 1958.
1743 I.*	*Powerscourt* (10th), Mervyn Niall Wingfield (4th *U.K. Baron, Powerscourt,* 1885), *b.* 1935, *s.* 1973, *m.*	Hon. Mervyn A. *W.*, *b.* 1963.
1900	*Ridley* (4th), Matthew White Ridley, T.D., *b.* 1925, *s.* 1964, *m.*	Hon. Matthew W. *R.*, *b.* 1958.
1960	*Rochdale* (1st), John Durival Kemp, O.B.E., T.D. (2nd *U.K. Baron, Rochdale,* 1913), *b.* 1906, *m.*	Hon. St. John D. *K.*, *b.* 1938.
1919	*Rothermere* (3rd), Vere Harold Esmond Harmsworth, *b.* 1925, *s.* 1978, *m.*	Hon. Harold J. E. V. *H.*, *b.* 1967.
1937	*Runciman of Doxford* (2nd), Walter Leslie Runciman, O.B.E., A.F.C. (3rd *U.K. Baron, Runciman,* 1933), *b.* 1900, *s.* 1949, *m.*	Hon. Walter G. *R.*, F.B.A., *b.* 1934.
1918	*St. Davids* (2nd), Jestyn Reginald Austen Plantagenet Philipps (19th *English Baron, Strange of Knokin* 1299, 7th *English Baron, Hungerford,* 1426 *and De Moleyns,* 1445), *b.* 1917, *s.* 1938, *m.*	Hon. Colwyn J. J. *P.*, *b.* 1939.
1801	*St. Vincent* (7th), Ronald George James Jervis, *b.* 1905, *s.* 1940, *m.*	Hon. Edward R. J. *J.*, *b.* 1951.
1937	*Samuel* (3rd), David Herbert Samuel, PH.D., *b.* 1922, *s.* 1978, *m.*	Hon. Dan J. *S.*, *b.* 1925.
1911	*Scarsdale* (3rd), Francis John Nathaniel Curzon (7th *Brit. Baron, Scarsdale,* 1761), *b.* 1924, *s.* 1977, *m.*	Hon. Peter G. N. *C.*, *b.* 1949.
1905	*Selby* (4th), Michael Guy John Gully, *b.* 1942, *s.* 1959, *m.*	Hon. Edward T. W. *G.*, *b.* 1967.
1805	*Sidmouth* (7th), John Tonge Anthony Pellew Addington, *b.* 1914, *s.* 1976, *m.*	Hon. Christopher J. *A.*, *b.* 1941.
1940	*Simon* (2nd), John Gilbert Simon, C.M.G., *b.* 1902, *s.* 1954, *m.*	Hon. Jan D. *S.*, *b.* 1940.
1960	*Slim* (2nd), John Douglas Slim, O.B.E., *b.* 1927, *s.* 1970, *m.*	Hon. Mark W. R. *S.*, *b.* 1960.
1954	*Soulbury* (2nd), James Herwald Ramsbotham, *b.* 1915, *s.* 1971, *w.*	Hon. Sir Peter E. *R.*, G.C.M.G., G.C.V.O., *b.* 1919.
1776 I.	*Southwell* (7th), Pyers Anthony Joseph Southwell, *b.* 1930, *s.* 1960, *m.*	Hon. Richard A. P. *S.*, *b.* 1956.

Created.	Title, Order of Succession, Name, etc.	Eldest Son or Heir.
1959	*Stuart of Findhorn* (2nd), David Randolph Moray Stuart, *b.* 1924, *s.* 1971, *m.*	Hon. James D. *S.*, *b.* 1948.
1957	*Tenby* (3rd), William Lloyd George, *b.* 1927, *s.* 1983, *m.*	Hon. Timothy H. G. *L. G.*, *b.* 1962.
1952	*Thurso* (2nd), Robin Macdonald Sinclair, *b.* 1922, *s.* 1970, *m.*	Hon. John A. *S.*, *b.* 1953.
1983	*Tonypandy* (1st), (Thomas) George Thomas, P.C., *b.* 1909.	(None).
1721	*Torrington* (11th), Timothy Howard St. George Byng, *b.* 1943, *s.* 1961, *m.*	John L. *B.*, M.C., *b.* 1919.
1936	*Trenchard* (2nd), Thomas Trenchard, M.C., *b.* 1923, *s.* 1956, *m.*	Hon. Hugh *T.*, *b.* 1951.
1921	*Ullswater* (2nd), Nicholas James Christopher Lowther, *b.* 1942, *s.* 1949, *m.*	Hon. Benjamin J. *L.*, *b.* 1975.
1621 I.	*Valentia* (15th), Richard John Dighton Annesley, *b.* 1929, *s.* 1983, *m.*	Hon. Francis W. D. *A.*, *b.* 1959.
1960	*Ward of Witley* (1st), George Reginald Ward, P.C., *b.* 1907, *w.*	(None).
1964	*Watkinson* (1st), Harold Arthur Watkinson, P.C., C.H., *b.* 1910, *m.*	(None.)
1952	*Waverley* (2nd), David Alastair Pearson Anderson, *b.* 1911, *s.* 1958, *m.*	Hon. John D. F. *A.*, *b.* 1949.
1938	*Weir* (3rd), William Kenneth James Weir, *b.* 1933, *s.* 1975, *m.*	Hon. James W. H. *W.*, *b.* 1965.
1983	*Whitelaw* (1st), William Stephen Ian Whitelaw, P.C., C.H., M.C., *b.* 1918, *m.*	(None).
1918	*Wimborne* (3rd), Ivor Fox-Strangways Guest (4th *U.K. Baron, Wimborne*, 1880), *b.* 1939, *s.* 1967, *m.*	Hon. Ivor M.V.*G.*, *b.* 1968.
1923	*Younger of Leckie* (3rd), Edward George Younger, O.B.E., T.D., *b.* 1906, *s.* 1946, *w.*	Rt. Hon. George K. H. *Y.*, T.D., M.P., *b.* 1931.

BISHOPS

Style, The Right Rev. the Lord Bishop of ——. *Addressed as,* My Lord.

Apptd.		
1981	‡*London* (130th), Graham Douglas Leonard, P.C., D.D., *b.* 1921, *cons.* 1964, *trans.* 1973 and 1981, *m.*	
1984	‡*Durham* (92nd), Prof. David Edward Jenkins, M.A., *b.* 1925, *cons.* 1984, *m.*	
1985	*Winchester* (95th), Colin Clement Walter James, M.A., *b.* 1926, *cons.* 1973, *trans.* 1985, *m.*	
1975	‡*Bath and Wells* (74th), John Monier Bickersteth, M.A., *b.* 1921, *cons.* 1970, *trans.* 1975, *m.*	
1978	‡*Birmingham* (6th), Hugh William Montefiore, D.D., *b.* 1920, *cons.* 1970, *m.*	
1982	*Blackburn* (6th), David Stewart Cross, M.A., *b.* 1928, *cons.* 1976, *trans.* 1982, *m.*	
1984	*Bradford* (7th), Robert Kerr Williamson, *b.* 1932, *cons.* 1984, *m.*	
1985	‡*Bristol* (54th), Barry Rogerson, B.A., *b.* 1936, *cons.* 1979, *trans.* 1985, *m.*	
1972	‡*Carlisle* (64th), Henry David Halsey, B.A., *b.* 1919, *cons.* 1968, *trans.* 1972, *m.*	
	‡*Chelmsford* (vacant).	
1982	*Chester* (39th), Michael Alfred Baughen, *b.* 1930, *cons.* 1982, *m.*	
1974	‡*Chichester* (99th), Eric Waldram Kemp, D.D., *b.* 1915, *m.*	
	‡*Coventry* (vacant).	
1969	‡*Derby* (4th), Cyril William Johnston Bowles, M.A., *b.* 1916, *cons.* 1969, *m.*	
1977	‡*Ely* (66th), Peter Knight Walker, D.D., *b.* 1919, *cons.* 1972, *trans.* 1977, *m.*	
1985	‡*Exeter* (69th), Geoffrey Hewlett Thompson, M.A., *b.* 1929, *cons.* 1974, *trans.* 1985, *m.*	
1975	‡*Gloucester* (37th), John Yates, M.A., *b.* 1925, *cons.* 1972, *trans.* 1975, *m.*	
1983	*Guildford* (7th), Michael Edgar Adie, M.A. *b.* 1929, *cons.* 1983, *m.*	
1973	‡*Hereford* (103rd), John Richard Gordon Eastaugh, *b.* 1920, *cons.* 1973, *m.*	
1978	*Leicester* (4th), Cecil Richard Rutt, C.B.E., M.A., *b.* 1925, *cons.* 1966, *m.*	
1984	*Lichfield* (97th), Keith Norman Sutton, M.A., *b.* 1934, *cons.* 1978, *m.*	
1974	‡*Lincoln* (69th), Simon Wilton Phipps, M.C., M.A., *b.* 1921, *cons.* 1968, *trans.* 1974, *m.*	
1975	‡*Liverpool* (6th), David Stuart Sheppard, M.A., *b.* 1929, *cons.* 1969, *m.*	
1979	*Manchester* (9th), Stanley Eric Francis Booth-Clibborn, M.A., *b.* 1924, *m.*	
1981	*Newcastle* (10th), Andrew Alexander Kenny Graham, *b.* 1929, *cons.* 1977.	
1985	‡*Norwich* (70th), Peter John Nott, M.A., *b.* 1933, *cons.* 1977, *trans.* 1985, *m.*	
1978	‡*Oxford* (40th), Patrick Campbell Rodger, M.A., *b.* 1920, *cons.* 1970, *trans.* 1978, *m.*	
1984	*Peterborough* (36th), William John Westwood, M.A., *b.* 1925, *cons.* 1975, *m.*	
1985	*Portsmouth* (7th), Timothy John Bavin, M.A., *b.* 1935, *cons.* 1974.	
1977	‡*Ripon* (11th), David Nigel de Lorentz Young, M.A., *b.* 1931, *cons.* 1977, *m.*	
1961	*Rochester* (104th), Richard David Say, D.D., *b.* 1914, *cons.* 1961, *m.*	
1980	*St. Albans* (8th), John Bernard Taylor, M.A., *b.* 1929, *cons.* 1980, *m.*	
1978	‡*St. Edmundsbury & Ipswich* (7th), John Waine, B.A., *b.* 1930, *cons.* 1975, *m.*	
1982	*Salisbury* (76th), John Austin Baker, M.A., *b.* 1928, *cons.* 1982, *m.*	
1980	*Sheffield* (5th), David Ramsay Lunn, M.A., *b.* 1930, *cons.* 1980.	
1983	*Sodor & Man* (78th), Arthur Henry Attwell, B.D., M.Th., M.A., *b.* 1920, *cons.* 1983.	
1980	‡*Southwark* (7th), Ronald Oliver Bowlby, M.A., *b.* 1926, *cons.* 1972, *trans.* 1980, *m.*	
1985	*Southwell* (8th), Michael Humphrey Dickens Whinney, M.A., *b.* 1930, *cons.* 1982, *trans.* 1985, *m.*	
1981	*Truro* (12th), Peter Mumford, M.A., *b.* 1922, *cons.* 1974, *trans.* 1981, *m.*	
	‡*Wakefield* (vacant).	
1982	*Worcester* (111th), Philip Harold Ernest Goodrich, M.A., *b.* 1929, *cons.* 1973, *trans.* 1982, *m.*	

‡ Holds seat in House of Lords.

BARONS

Style (see *also* note, p. 247), The Right Hon. the Lord ——.
Addressed as, My Lord.

Created.	Title, Order of Succession, Name, etc.	Eldest Son or Heir.
1911	*Aberconway* (3rd), Charles Melville McLaren, *b.* 1913, *s.* 1953, *m.*	Hon. Henry C. *McL., b.* 1948.
1873	*Aberdare* (4th), Morys George Lyndhurst Bruce, P.C., K.B.E., *b.* 1919, *s.* 1957, *m.*	Hon. Alastair J. L. *B., b.* 1947.
1835	*Abinger* (8th), James Richard Scarlett, *b.* 1914, *s.* 1943, *m.*	Hon. James H. *S., b.* 1959.
1869	*Acton* (3rd), John Emerich Henry Lyon-Dalberg-Acton, C.M.G., M.B.E., T.D., *b.* 1907, *s.* 1924, *m.*	Hon. Richard G. *L.-D.-A., b.* 1941.
1887	*Addington* (6th), Dominic Bryce Hubbard, *b.* 1963, *s.* 1982, *M.*	Hon. Michael W. L. *H., b.* 1965.
1955	*Adrian* (2nd), Richard Hume Adrian, F.R.S., *b.* 1927, *s.* 1977, *m.*	(None.)
1921	*Ailwyn* (4th), Carol Arthur Fellowes, T.D., *b.* 1896, *s.* 1976, *m.*	(None.)
1907	*Airedale* (4th), Oliver James Vandeleur Kitson, *b.* 1915, *s.* 1958.	(None.)
1896	*Aldenham* (5th), and (3rd) *Hunsdon of Hunsdon* (1923), Antony Durant Gibbs, *b.* 1922, *s.* 1969, *m.*	Hon. Vicary T. *G., b.* 1948.
1962	*Aldington* (1st), Toby Austin Richard William Low, P.C., K.C.M.G., C.B.E., D.S.O., T.D., *b.* 1914, *m.*	Hon Charles H. S. *L., b.* 1948.
1902	*Allerton* (3rd), George William Lawies Jackson, *b.* 1903, *s.* 1925, *m.*	(None.)
1929	*Alvingham* (2nd), Maj.-Gen. Robert Guy Eardley Yerburgh, C.B.E., *b.* 1926, *s.* 1955, *m.*	Capt. Hon. Robert R. G. *Y., b.* 1956.
1892	*Amherst of Hackney* (4th), William Hugh Amherst Cecil, *b.* 1940, *s.* 1980, *m.*	Hon. Hugh W. A. *C., b.* 1968.
1881	*Ampthill* (4th), Geoffrey Denis Erskine Russell, *b.* 1921, *s.* 1973, *m.*	Hon. David W. E. *R., b.* 1947.
1947	*Amwell* (2nd), Frederick Norman Montague, *b.* 1912, *s.* 1966, *m.*	Hon. Keith N. *M., b.* 1943.
1863	*Annaly* (5th), Luke Robert White, *b.* 1927, *s.* 1970, *m.*	Hon. Luke R. *W., b.* 1954.
1903	*Armstrong* (3rd), William Henry Cecil John Robin Watson-Armstrong, *b.* 1919, *s.* 1972, *m.*	(None.)
1885	*Ashbourne* (4th), Edward Barry Greynville Gibson, *b.* 1933, *s.* 1983, *m.*	Hon. Edward C. D'O. *G., b.* 1967.
1835	*Ashburton* (6th), Alexander Francis St. Vincent Baring, K.G., K.C.V.O., *b.* 1898, *s.* 1938, *w.*	Hon. Sir John F. H. *B.,* C.V.O., *b.* 1928.
1892	*Ashcombe* (4th), Henry Edward Cubitt, *b.* 1924, *s.* 1962, *m.*	M. Robin *C., b.* 1936.
1911	*Ashton of Hyde* (3rd), Thomas John Ashton, T.D., *b.* 1926, *s.* 1983, *m.*	Hon. Thomas H. *A., b.* 1958.
1800 I.	*Ashtown* (6th), Christopher Oliver Trench, *b.* 1931, *s.* 1979, *m.*	Sir Nigel C. C. *T.,* K.C.M.G., *b.* 1916.
1956	*Astor of Hever* (3rd), John Jacob Astor, *b.* 1946, *s.* 1984, *m.*	Hon. Philip D. P. *A., b.* 1959.
1789 I. 1793*	} *Auckland* (9th), Ian George Eden (9th *Brit. Baron, Auckland*), *b.* 1926, *s.* 1957, *m.*	Hon. Robert I. B. *E., b.* 1962.
1313	*Audley* (25th), Richard Michael Thomas Souter, *b.* 1914, *s.* 1973, *m.*	Three co-heiresses.
1900	*Avebury* (4th), Eric Reginald Lubbock, *b.* 1928, *s.* 1971.	Hon. Lyulph A. J. *L., b.* 1954.
1718 I.	*Aylmer* (13th), Michael Anthony Aylmer, *b.* 1923, *s.* 1982, *m.*	Hon. A. Julian *A., b.* 1951.
1929	*Baden-Powell* (3rd), Robert Crause Baden-Powell, *b.* 1936, *s.* 1962, *m.*	Hon. David M. *B.-P., b.* 1940.
1780	*Bagot* (9th), Heneage Charles Bagot, *b.* 1914, *s.* 1979, *m.*	Hon. Charles H. S. *B., b.* 1944.
1953	*Baillieu* (3rd), James William Latham Baillieu, *b.* 1950, *s.* 1973, *m.*	Hon. Robert L. *B., b.* 1979.
1607 S.	*Balfour of Burleigh* (8th), Robert Bruce, *b.* 1927, *s.* 1967, *m.*	Hon. Victoria B., *b.* 1973.
1945	*Balfour of Inchrye* (1st), Harold Harington Balfour, P.C., M.C., *b.* 1897, *m.*	Hon. Ian *B., b.* 1924.
1924	*Banbury of Southam* (3rd), Charles William Banbury, *b.* 1953, *s.* 1981, *m.*	(None.)
1698	*Barnard* (11th), Harry John Neville Vane, T.D., *b.* 1923, *s.* 1964, *m.*	Hon. Henry F. C. *V., b.* 1959.
1887	*Basing* (5th), Neil Lutley Sclater-Booth, *b.* 1939, *s.* 1983, *m.*	Hon. Stuart W. *S.-B., b.* 1969.
1647 S.	*Belhaven & Stenton* (13th), Robert Anthony Carmichael Hamilton, *b.* 1927, *s.* 1961, *m.*	Master of Belhaven, *b.* 1953.
1848 I.	*Bellew* (7th), James Bryan Bellew, *b.* 1920, *s.* 1981, *m.*	Hon. Bryan E. *B., b.* 1943.
1856	*Belper* (4th), (Alexander) Ronald George Strutt, *b.* 1912, *s.* 1956.	Hon. Richard H. *S., b.* 1941.
1938	*Belstead* (2nd), John Julian Ganzoni, P. C., *b.* 1932, *s.* 1958.	(None.)
1922	*Bethell* (4th), Nicholas William Bethell, *b.* 1938, *s.* 1967.	Hon. James N. *B., b.* 1967.
1938	*Bicester* (3rd), Angus Edward Vivian Smith, *b.* 1932, *s.* 1968.	Hugh C. V. *S., b.* 1934.
1903	*Biddulph* (4th), Robert Michael Christian Biddulph, *b.* 1931, *s.* 1972, *m.*	Hon. Anthony N. C. M.*B., b.* 1959.
1938	*Birdwood* (3rd), Mark William Ogilvie Birdwood, *b.* 1938, *s.* 1962, *m.*	(None.)
1958	*Birkett* (2nd), Michael Birkett, *b.* 1929, *s.* 1962, *m.*	Hon. Thomas *B., b.* 1982.
1935	*Blackford* (4th), William Keith Mason, *b.* 1962, *s.* 1977.	(None.)
1907	*Blyth* (4th), Anthony Audley Rupert Blyth, *b.* 1931, *s.* 1977, *m.*	Hon. Riley A. J. *B., b.* 1955.
1797	*Bolton* (7th), Richard William Algar Orde-Powlett, *b.* 1929, *s.* 1963, *m.*	Hon. Harry A. N. *O.-P., b.* 1954.
1922	*Borwick* (4th), James Hugh Myles Borwick, M.C., *b.* 1917, *s.* 1961, *m.*	Hon. George S. *B., b.* 1922.
1761	*Boston* (10th), Timothy George Frank Boteler Irby, *b.* 1939, *s.* 1978, *m.*	Hon. George W. E. B. *I., b.* 1971.
1942	*Brabazon of Tara* (3rd), Ivon Anthony Moore-Brabazon, *b.* 1946, *s.* 1974, *m.*	Hon. Benjamin R. *M.-B., b.* 1983.
1880	*Brabourne* (7th), John Ulick Knatchbull, *b.* 1924, *s.* 1943, *m.*	Lord Romsey, *b.* 1947, *see* p. 247.

Created.	Title, Order of Succession, Name, etc.	Eldest Son or Heir.
1925	*Bradbury* (2nd), John Bradbury, *b.* 1914, *s.* 1950, *m.*	Hon. John *B.*, *b.* 1940.
1962	*Brain* (2nd), Christopher Langdon Brain, *b.* 1926, *s.* 1966, *m.*	Hon. Michael C. *B.*, D.M., *b.* 1928.
1981	*Brandon of Oakbrook*, Henry Vivian Brandon, P.C., M.C., *b.* 1920, *m.* (*Lord of Appeal*).	(Law Life Peerage.)
1938	*Brassey of Apethorpe* (3rd), David Henry Brassey, *b.* 1932, *s.* 1967, *m.*	Hon. Edward *B.*, *b.* 1964.
1788	*Braybrooke* (9th), Henry Seymour Neville, *b.* 1897, *s.* 1943, *m.*	Hon. Robin H. C. *N.*, *b.* 1932.
1529	*Braye* (7th), Thomas Adrian Verney-Cave, *b.* 1902, *m.*	Hon. Penelope M., *b.* 1941.
1980	*Bridge of Harwich*, Nigel Cyprian Bridge, P.C., *b.* 1917, *m.* (*Lord of Appeal*).	(Law Life Peerage.)
1957	*Bridges* (2nd), Thomas Edward Bridges, K.C.M.G., *b.* 1927, *s.* 1969, *m.*	Hon. Mark T. *B.*, *b.* 1954.
1982	*Brightman*, John (Anson) Brightman, P.C., *b.* 1911, *m.* (*Lord of Appeal*).	(Law Life Peerage.)
1945	*Broadbridge* (3rd), Peter Hewett Broadbridge, *b.* 1938, *s.* 1972, *m.*	Hon. Hugh T. *B.*, *b.* 1903.
1933	*Brocket* (3rd), Charles Ronald George Nall-Cain, *b.* 1952, *s.* 1967, *m.*	Hon. Alexander C. C. *N.-C.*, *b.* 1984.
1860	*Brougham and Vaux* (5th), Michael John Brougham, *b.* 1938, *s.* 1967.	Hon. Charles W. *B.*, *b.* 1971.
1945	*Broughshane* (2nd), Patrick Owen Alexander Davison, *b.* 1903, *s.* 1953, *m.*	Hon. Alexander *D.*, *b.* 1936.
1776	*Brownlow* (7th), Edward John Peregrine Cust, *b.* 1936, *s.* 1978, *m.*	Hon. Peregrine E. Q. *C.*, *b.* 1974.
1942	*Bruntisfield* (1st), Victor Alexander George Anthony Warrender, M.C., *b.* 1899, *m.*	Col. Hon. John R. *W.*, O.B.E., M.C., T.D., *b.* 1921.
1950	*Burden* (2nd), Philip William Burden, *b.* 1916, *s.* 1970, *m.*	Hon. Andrew P. *B.*, *b.* 1959.
1529	*Burgh* (7th), Alexander Peter Willoughby Leith, *b.* 1935, *s.* 1959, *m.*	Hon. Alexander G. D. *L.*, *b.* 1958.
1903	*Burnham* (5th), William Edward Harry Lawson, *b.* 1920, *s.* 1963, *m.*	Hon. Hugh J. F. *L.*, *b.* 1931.
1897	*Burton* (3rd), Michael Evan Victor Baillie, *b.* 1924, *s.* 1962, *m.*	Hon. Evan M. R. *B.*, *b.* 1949.
1643	*Byron* (12th), Richard Geoffrey Gordon Byron, D.S.O., *b.* 1899, *s.* 1983, *m.*	Hon. Robert J. *B.*, *b.* 1950.
1937	*Cadman* (3rd), John Anthony Cadman, *b.* 1938, *s.* 1966, *m.*	Hon. Nicholas A. J. *C.*, *b.* 1977.
1796	*Calthorpe* (10th), Peter Waldo Somerset Gough-Calthorpe, *b.* 1927, *s.* 1945, *m.*	(None.)
1945	*Calverley* (3rd), Charles Rodney Muff, *b.* 1946, *s.* 1971, *m.*	Hon. Jonathan E. *M.*, *b.* 1975.
1383	*Camoys* (7th), (Ralph) Thomas (Campion George Sherman) Stonor, *b.* 1940, *s.* 1976, *m.*	Hon. William *S.*, *b.* 1974.
1715 I.	*Carbery* (11th), Peter Ralfe Harrington Evans-Freke, *b.* 1920, *s.* 1970, *m.*	Hon. Michael P. *E.-F.*, *b.* 1942.
1834 I. ⎱ 1838* ⎰	*Carew* (6th), William Francis Conolly-Carew, C.B.E. (6th *U.K. Baron*, *Carew*, 1838), *b.* 1905, *s.* 1927, *m.*	Hon. Patrick T. *C.-C.*, *b.* 1938.
1916	*Carnock* (4th), David Henry Arthur Nicolson, *b.* 1920, *s.* 1982.	Nigel *N.*, M.B.E., *b.* 1917.
1796 I. ⎱ 1797* ⎰	*Carrington* (6th), Peter Alexander Rupert Carington, K.G., P.C., C.H., K.C.M.G., M.C. (6th *Brit. Baron*, *Carrington*, 1797), *b.* 1919, *s.* 1938, *m.*	Hon. Rupert F. J. *C.*, *b.* 1948.
1812 I.	*Castlemaine* (8th), Roland Thomas John Handcock, *b.* 1943, *s.* 1973, *m.*	Terence R. *H.*, *b.* 1902.
1936	*Catto* (2nd), Stephen Gordon Catto, *b.* 1923, *s.* 1959, *m.*	Hon. Innes G. *C.*, *b.* 1950.
1918	*Cawley* (3rd), Frederick Lee Cawley, *b.* 1913, *s.* 1954, *m.*	Hon. John F. *C.*, *b.* 1946.
1937	*Chatfield* (2nd), Ernle David Lewis Chatfield, *b.* 1917, *s.* 1967, *m.*	(None.)
1858	*Chesham* (5th), John Charles Compton Cavendish, P.C., *b.* 1916, *s.* 1952, *m.*	Hon. Nicholas C. *C.*, *b.* 1941.
1945	*Chetwode* (2nd), Philip Chetwode, *b.* 1937, *s.* 1950.	Hon. Roger *C.*, *b.* 1968.
1945	*Chorley* (2nd), Roger Richard Edward Chorley, *b.* 1930, *s.* 1978, *m.*	Hon. Nicholas R. D. *C.*, *b.* 1966.
1858	*Churston* (4th), Richard Francis Roger Yarde-Buller, V.R.D., *b.* 1910, *s.* 1930, *m.*	Hon. John F. *Y.-B.*, *b.* 1934.
1946	*Citrine* (2nd), Norman Arthur Citrine, *b.* 1914, *s.* 1983, *m.*	Hon. Ronald E. *C.*, *b.* 1919.
1800 I.	*Clanmorris* (7th), John Michael Ward Bingham, *b.* 1908, *s.* 1960, *m.*	Hon. Simon J. W. *B.*, *b.* 1937.
1672	*Clifford of Chudleigh* (13th) (Lewis) Hugh Clifford, O.B.E., *b.* 1916, *s.* 1964, *m.*	Hon. Thomas H. *C.*, *b.* 1948.
1299	*Clinton* (22nd), Gerard Neville Mark Fane Trefusis, *b.* 1934, *title called out of abeyance* 1965, *m.*	Hon. Charles P. R. F. *T.*, *b.* 1962.
1955	*Clitheroe* (2nd), Ralph John Assheton, *b.* 1929, *s.* 1984, *m.*	Hon. Ralph C. *A.*, *b.* 1962.
1919	*Clwyd* (2nd), (John) Trevor Roberts, *b.* 1900, *s.* 1955, *m.*	Hon. J. Anthony *R.*, *b.* 1935.
1948	*Clydesmuir* (2nd), Ronald John Bilsland Colville, K.T., C.B., M.B.E., T.D., *b.* 1917, *s.* 1954, *m.*	Hon. David R. *C.*, *b.* 1949.
1960	*Cobbold* (1st), Cameron Fromanteel Cobbold, K.G., P.C., G.C.V.O., *b.* 1904, *m.*	Hon. David A. F. *Lytton-Cobbold*, *b.* 1937.
1919	*Cochrane of Cults* (3rd), Thomas Charles Anthony Cochrane, *b.* 1922, *s.* 1968.	Hon. R. H. Vere *C.*, *b.* 1926.
1954	*Coleraine* (2nd), (James) Martin (Bonar) Law, *b.* 1931, *s.* 1980, *m.*	Hon. James P. B. *L.*, *b.* 1975.
1873	*Coleridge* (5th), William Duke Coleridge, *b.* 1937, *s.* 1984.	Hon. James D. *C.*, *b.* 1967.
1946	*Colgrain* (3rd), David Colin Campbell, *b.* 1920, *s.* 1973, *m.*	Hon. Alastair C. L. *C.*, *b.* 1951.
1917	*Colwyn* (3rd), (Ian) Anthony Hamilton-Smith, *b.* 1942, *s.* 1966, *m.*	Hon. Craig P. *H.-S.*, *b.* 1968.
1956	*Colyton* (1st), Henry Lennox D'Aubigné Hopkinson, P.C., C.M.G., *b.* 1902, *m.*	Hon. Nicholas H. E. *H.*, *b.* 1932.
1841	*Congleton* (8th), Christopher Patrick Parnell, *b.* 1930, *s.* 1967, *m.*	Hon. John P. C. *P.*, *b.* 1959.

Created.	Title, Order of Succession, Name, etc.	Eldest Son or Heir.
1927	*Cornwallis* (3rd), Fiennes Neil Wykeham Cornwallis, o.b.e., b. 1921, s. 1982, m.	Hon. Fiennes W. J. C., b. 1946.
1874	*Cottesloe* (4th), John Walgrave Halford Fremantle, g.b.e., t.d., b. 1900, s. 1956, m.	Hon. John T. F., b. 1927.
1929	*Craigmyle* (3rd), Thomas Donald Mackay Shaw, b. 1923, s. 1944, m.	Hon. Thomas C. S., b. 1960.
1899	*Cranworth* (3rd), Philip Bertram Gurdon, b. 1940, s. 1964, m.	Hon. Sacha W. R. G., b. 1970.
1959	*Crathorne* (2nd), Charles James Dugdale, b. 1939, s. 1977, m.	Hon. Thomas A. J. D., b. 1977.
1892	*Crawshaw* (4th), William Michael Clifton Brooks, b. 1933, s. 1946.	Hon. David G. B., b. 1934.
1940	*Croft* (2nd), Michael Henry Glendower Page Croft, b. 1916, s. 1947, w.	Hon. Bernard W. H. P. C., b. 1949.
1797 I.	*Crofton* (6th), Charles Edward Piers Crofton, b. 1949, s. 1974, m.	Hon. Guy P. G. C., b. 1951.
1375	*Cromwell* (7th), Godfrey John Bewicke-Copley, b. 1960, s. 1982.	Hon. Thomas D. B.-C., b. 1964.
1947	*Crook* (1st), Reginald Douglas Crook, b. 1901, m.	Hon. Douglas E. C., b. 1926.
1971	*Cross of Chelsea*, (Arthur) Geoffrey (Neale) Cross, p.c., b. 1904, m. *(Lord of Appeal, retired).*	(Law Life Peerage.)
1920	*Cullen of Ashbourne* (2nd), Charles Borlase Marsham Cokayne, m.b.e., b. 1912, s. 1932, m.	Hon. Edmund W. M. C., b. 1916.
1914	*Cunliffe* (3rd), Roger Cunliffe, b. 1932, s. 1963, m.	Hon. Henry C., b. 1962.
1927	*Daresbury* (2nd), Edward Greenall, b. 1902, s. 1938, w.	Hon. Edward G. G., b. 1928.
1924	*Darling* (2nd), Robert Charles Henry Darling, b. 1919, s. 1936, m.	Hon. Robert J. H. D., b. 1944.
1946	*Darwen* (2nd), Cedric Percival Davies, b. 1915, s. 1950, m.	Hon. Roger M. D., b. 1938.
1923	*Daryngton* (2nd), Jocelyn Arthur Pike Pease, b. 1908, s. 1949.	(None.)
1932	*Davies* (3rd), David Davies, b. 1940, s. 1944, m.	Hon. David D. D., b. 1975.
1812 I.	*Decies* (6th), Arthur George Marcus Douglas de la Poer Beresford, b. 1915, s. 1944, m.	Hon. Marcus H. T. de la P.B., b. 1948.
1299	*de Clifford* (27th), John Edward Southwell Russell, b. 1928, s. 1982, m.	Hon. William S. R., b. 1930.
1851	*De Freyne* (7th), Francis Arthur John French, b. 1927, s. 1935, m.	Hon. Fulke C. A. J. F., b. 1957.
1821	*Delamere* (5th), Hugh George Cholmondeley, b. 1934, s. 1979, m.	Hon. Thomas P. G. C., b. 1968.
1838	*de Mauley* (6th), Gerald John Ponsonby, b. 1921, s. 1962, m.	Col. Hon. Thomas M. P., t.d., b. 1930.
1937	*Denham* (2nd), Bertram Stanley Mitford Bowyer, p.c., b. 1927, s. 1948, m.	Hon. Richard G. B., b. 1959.
1834	*Denman* (5th), Charles Spencer Denman, c.b.e., m.c., t.d., b. 1916, s. 1971, m.	Hon. Richard T. S. D., b. 1946.
1957	*Denning*, Alfred Thompson Denning, p.c., b. 1899, m. *(Master of the Rolls, retired).*	(Law Life Peerage.)
1885	*Deramore* (6th), Richard Arthur de Yarburgh-Bateson, b. 1911, s. 1964, m.	(None.)
1887	*De Ramsey* (3rd), Ailwyn Edward Fellowes, k.b.e., t.d., b. 1910, s. 1925, m.	Hon. John A. F., b. 1942.
1264	*de Ros* (28th), Peter Trevor Maxwell, b. 1958, s. 1983 *(Premier Barony of England).*	Hon. Diana E. M., b. 1957.
1881	*Derwent* (4th), Patrick Robin Gilbert Vanden-Bempde-Johnstone, c.b.e., b. 1901, s. 1949, m.	Hon. Robin E. L. V.-B.-J., m.v.o., b. 1930.
1831	*De Saumarez* (6th), James Victor Broke Saumarez, b. 1924, s. 1969, m.	Hon. Eric D. S., b. 1956.
1910	*de Villiers* (3rd), Arthur Percy de Villiers, b. 1911, s. 1934.	Hon. Alexander C. de V., b. 1940.
1961	*Devlin*, Patrick Arthur Devlin, p.c., f.b.a., b. 1905, m. *(Lord of Appeal, retired).*	(Law Life Peerage.)
1930	*Dickinson* (2nd), Richard Clavering Hyett Dickinson, b. 1926, s. 1943, m.	Hon. Martin H. D., b. 1961.
1620 I. ⎱ 1765* ⎰	*Digby* (12th), Edward Henry Kenelm Digby, (6th *Brit. Baron, Digby),* b. 1924, s. 1964, m.	Hon. Henry N. K. D., b. 1954.
1968	*Diplock*, (William John) Kenneth Diplock, p.c., b. 1907, m. *(Lord of Appeal).*	(Law Life Peerage.)
1615	*Dormer* (16th), Joseph Spencer Philip Dormer, b. 1914, s. 1975.	Geoffrey H. D., b. 1920.
1943	*Dowding* (2nd), Derek Hugh Tremenheere Dowding, b. 1919, s. 1970, m.	Hon. Piers H. T. D., b. 1948.
1963	*Drumalbyn* (1st), Niall Malcolm Stewart Macpherson, p.c., k.b.e., b. 1908, m.	(None.)
1929	*Dulverton* (2nd), (Frederick) Anthony Hamilton Wills, c.b.e., t.d., b. 1915, s. 1956, m.	Hon. G. Michael H. W., b. 1944.
1800 I.	*Dunalley* (6th), Henry Desmond Graham Prittie, b. 1912, s. 1948, m.	Hon. Henry F. C. P., b. 1948.
1324 I.	*Dunboyne* (28th), Patrick Theobald Tower Butler, b. 1917, s. 1945, m.	Hon. John F. B., b. 1951.
1802	*Dunleath* (4th), Charles Edward Henry John Mulholland, t.d., b. 1933, s. 1956, m.	Sir Michael H. M., Bt., b. 1915.
1439 I.	*Dunsany* (19th), Randal Arthur Henry Plunkett (20th I., Baron, Killean, 1449), b. 1906, s. 1957, m.	Hon. Edward J. C. P., b. 1939.
1780	*Dynevor* (9th), Richard Charles Uryan Rhys, b. 1935, s. 1962.	Hon. Hugo G. U. R., b. 1966.
1928	*Ebbisham* (2nd), Rowland Roberts Blades, t.d., b. 1912, s. 1953, m.	(None.)
1857	*Ebury* (6th), Francis Egerton Grosvenor, b. 1934, s. 1957, m.	Hon. Julian F. M. G., b. 1959.
1974	*Edmund-Davies*, (Herbert) Edmund Edmund-Davies, p.c., b. 1906, m. *(Lord of Appeal, retired).*	(Law Life Peerage.)

Created.	Title, Order of Succession, Name, etc.	Eldest Son or Heir.
1643	*Elibank* (14th), Alan d'Ardis Erskine-Murray, *b.* 1923, *s.* 1973, *m.*	Master of Elibank, *b.* 1964.
1802	*Ellenborough* (8th), Richard Edward Cecil Law, *b.* 1926, *s.* 1945, *m.*	Capt. Hon. Rupert E. H. L., *b.* 1955.
1509 s.*	*Elphinstone* (18th), James Alexander Elphinstone (4th *U.K. Baron Elphinstone,* 1885), *b.* 1953, *s.* 1975, *m.*	Master of Elphinstone, *b.* 1980.
1934	*Elton* (2nd), Rodney Elton, T.D., *b.* 1930, *s.* 1973, *m.*	Hon. Edward P. *E.*, *b.* 1966.
1964	*Erroll of Hale* (1st), Frederick James Erroll, P.C., T.D., *b.* 1914, *m.*	(None.)
1964	*Erskine of Rerrick* (2nd), Iain Maxwell Erskine, *b.* 1926, *s.* 1980, *m.*	(None).
1627 s.	*Fairfax of Cameron* (14th), Nicholas John Albert Fairfax, *b.* 1956, *s.* 1964, *m.*	Hon. Edward N. T. *F.*, *b.* 1984.
1961	*Fairhaven* (3rd), Ailwyn Henry George Broughton, *b.* 1936, *s.* 1973, *m.*	Hon. James H. A. *B.*, *b.* 1963.
1916	*Faringdon* (3rd), Charles Michael Henderson, *b.* 1937, *s.* 1977, *m.*	Hon. James H. *H.*, *b.* 1961.
1756 I.	*Farnham* (12th), Barry Owen Somerset Maxwell, *b.* 1931, *s.* 1957, *m.*	Hon. Simon K. *M.*, *b.* 1933.
1856 I.	*Fermoy* (6th), Patrick Maurice Burke Roche, *b.* 1967, *s.* 1984, *M.*	Hon. E. Hugh B. *R.*, *b.* 1972.
1826	*Feversham* (6th), Charles Anthony Peter Duncombe, *b.* 1945, *s.* 1963, *m.*	Hon. Jasper O. S. *D.*, *b.* 1968.
1798 I.	*ffrench* (7th), Peter Martin Joseph Charles John ffrench, *b.* 1926, *s.* 1955 *m.*	Hon Robuck J. P. C. M. *ff.*, *b.* 1956.
1909	*Fisher* (3rd), John Vavasseur Fisher, D.S.C., *b.* 1921, *s.* 1955, *m.*	Hon. Patrick V. *F.*, *b.* 1953.
1295	*Fitzwalter* (21st), Fitzwalter Brook Plumptre, *b.* 1914 *called out of abeyance,* 1953, *m.*	Hon. Julian B. *P.*, *b.* 1952.
1776	*Foley* (8th), Adrian Gerald Foley, *b.* 1923, *s.* 1927, *m.*	Hon. Thomas H. *F.*, *b.* 1961.
1445 s.	*Forbes* (22nd), Nigel Ivan Forbes, K.B.E. (*Premier Baron of Scotland*), *b.* 1918, *s.* 1953, *m.*	Master of Forbes, *b.* 1946.
1821	*Forester* (8th), (George Cecil) Brooke Weld-Forester, *b.* 1938, *s.* 1977, *m.*	Hon Charles R. G. *W.-F.*, *b.* 1975.
1922	*Forres* (4th), Alastair Stephen Grant Williamson, *b.* 1946, *s.* 1978, *m.*	Hon George A. M. *W.*, *b.* 1972.
1917	*Forteviot* (3rd), Henry Evelyn Alexander Dewar, M.B.E., *b.* 1906, *s.* 1947, *m.*	Hon. John J. E. *D.*, *b.* 1938.
1975	*Fraser of Tullybelton,* Walter Ian Reid Fraser, P.C., *b.* 1911, *m.* (*Lord of Appeal*).	(Law Life Peerage.)
1951	*Freyberg* (2nd), Paul Richard Freyberg, O.B.E., M.C., *b.* 1923, *s.* 1963, *m.*	Hon. Valerian B. *F.*, *b.* 1970.
1917	*Gainford* (3rd), Joseph Edward Pease, *b.* 1921, *s.* 1971, *m.*	Hon. George *P.*, *b.* 1926.
1818 I.	*Garvagh* (5th), (Alexander Leopold Ivor) George Canning, *b.* 1920, *s.* 1956, *m.*	Hon. Spencer G. S. de R. *C.*, *b.* 1953.
1942	*Geddes* (3rd), Euan Michael Ross Geddes, *b.* 1937, *s.* 1975, *m.*	Hon. James G. N. *G.*, *b.* 1969.
1876	*Gerard* (4th), Robert William Frederick Alwyn Gerard, *b.* 1918, *s.* 1953.	Anthony R. H. *G.*, *b.* 1949.
1824	*Gifford* (6th), Anthony Maurice Gifford, Q.C., *b.* 1940, *s.* 1961, *m.*	Hon. Thomas A. *G.*, *b.* 1967.
1917	*Gisborough* (3rd), Thomas Richard John Long Chaloner, *b.* 1927, *s.* 1951, *m.*	Hon. Thomas P. L. *C.*, *b.* 1961.
1960	*Gladwyn* (1st), (Hubert Miles) Gladwyn Jebb, G.C.M.G., G.C.V.O., C.B., *b.* 1900, *m.*	Hon. Miles A. G. *J.*, *b.* 1930.
1899	*Glanusk* (4th), David Russell Bailey, *b.* 1917, *s.* 1948, *m.*	Hon. Christopher R. *B.*, *b.* 1942.
1918	*Glenarthur* (4th), Simon Mark Arthur, *b.* 1944, *s.* 1976, *m.*	Hon. Edward A. *A.*, *b.* 1973.
1911	*Glenconner* (3rd), Colin Christopher Paget Tennant, *b.* 1926, *s.* 1983, *m.*	Hon. Charles E. P. *T.*, *b.* 1957.
1964	*Glendevon* (1st), John Adrian Hope, P.C., *b.* 1912, *m.*	Hon. Julian J. S. *H.*, *b.* 1950.
1922	*Glendyne* (3rd), Robert Nivison, *b.* 1926, *s.* 1967, *m.*	Hon. John *N.*, *b.* 1960.
1939	*Glentoran* (2nd), Daniel Stewart Thomas Bingham Dixon, P.C., (N.I.), K.B.E., *b.* 1912, *s.* 1950, *w.*	Hon. Thomas R. V. *D.*, M.B.E., *b.* 1935.
1909	*Gorell* (4th), Timothy John Radcliffe Barnes, *b.* 1927, *s.* 1963, *m.*	Hon. Ronald A. H. *B.*, *b.* 1931.
1953	*Grantchester* (2nd), Kenneth Bent Suenson-Taylor, Q.C., *b.* 1921, *s.* 1976, *m.*	Hon. Christopher J. *S.-T.*, *b.* 1951.
1782	*Grantley* (7th), John Richard Brinsley Norton, M.C., *b.* 1923, *s.* 1954, *m.*	Hon. Richard W. B. *N.*, *b.* 1956.
1794 I.	*Graves* (8th), Peter George Wellesley Graves, *b.* 1911, *s.* 1963, *m.*	Evelyn P. *G.*, *b.* 1926.
1445 s.	*Gray* (22nd), Angus Diarmid Ian Campbell-Gray, *b.* 1931, *s.* 1946, *m.*	Master of Gray, *b.* 1964.
1950	*Greenhill* (2nd), Stanley Ernest Greenhill, M.D., *b.* 1917, *s.* 1967, *m.*	Hon. Malcolm *G.*, *b.* 1924.
1927	*Greenway* (4th), Ambrose Charles Drexel Greenway, *b.* 1941, *s.* 1975.	Hon. Mervyn S. K. *G.*, *b.* 1942.
1902	*Grenfell* (3rd), Julian Pascoe Francis St. Leger Grenfell, *b.* 1935, *s.* 1976, *m.*	Francis P. J. *G.*, *b.* 1938.
1944	*Gretton* (3rd), John Henrik Gretton, *b.* 1941, *s.* 1982, *m.*	Hon. John L. *G.*, *b.* 1975.
1869	*Greville* (4th), Ronald Charles Fulke Greville, *b.* 1912, *s.* 1952.	(None.)
1955	*Gridley* (2nd), Arnold Hudson Gridley, *b.* 1906, *s.* 1965, *m.*	Hon. Richard D. A. *G.*, *b.* 1956.
1985	*Griffiths,* (William) Hugh Griffiths, P.C., M.C., *b.* 1923, *m.* (*Lord of Appeal*).	(Law Life Peerage.)
1964	*Grimston of Westbury* (2nd), Robert Walter Sigismund Grimston, *b.* 1925, *s.* 1979, *m.*	Hon. Robert J. S. *G.*, *b.* 1951.
1886	*Grimthorpe* (4th), Christopher John Beckett, O.B.E., *b.* 1915, *s.* 1963, *m.*	Hon. Edward J. *B.*, *b.* 1954.
1945	*Hacking* (3rd), Douglas David Hacking, *b.* 1938, *s.* 1971, *m.*	Hon. Douglas F. *H.*, *b.* 1968.
1950	*Haden-Guest* (3rd), Richard Haden Haden-Guest, *b.* 1904, *s.* 1974, *m.*	Hon. Peter H. *H.-G.*, *b.* 1913.

Created.	Title, Order of Succession, Name, etc.	Eldest Son or Heir.
1886	*Hamilton of Dalzell* (3rd), John d'Henin Hamilton, K.C.V.O., M.C., b. 1911, s. 1952, m.	Hon. James L. H., b. 1938.
1874	*Hampton* (6th), Richard Humphrey Russell Pakington, b. 1925, s. 1974, m.	Hon. John H. A. P., b. 1964.
1939	*Hankey* (2nd), Robert Maurice Alers Hankey, K.C.M.G., K.C.V.O., b. 1905, s. 1963, m.	Hon. Donald R. A. H., b. 1938.
1958	*Harding of Petherton* (1st), John Harding, G.C.B., C.B.E., D.S.O., M.C., Field Marshal, b. 1896, w.	Hon. John C. H., b. 1928.
1910	*Hardinge of Penshurst* (3rd), George Edward Charles Hardinge, b. 1921, s. 1960, m.	Hon. Julian A. H., b. 1945.
1876	*Harlech* (6th), Francis David Ormsby-Gore, b. 1954, s. 1985.	†
1939	*Harmsworth* (2nd), Cecil Desmond Bernard Harmsworth, b. 1903, s. 1948, m.	Hon. Eric B. N. H., b. 1905.
1815	*Harris* (6th), George Robert John Harris, b. 1920, s. 1984.	Arthur T. H.-T., b. 1904.
1954	*Harvey of Tasburgh* (2nd), Peter Charles Oliver Harvey, b. 1921, s. 1968, m.	Hon. John W. H., b. 1923.
1295	*Hastings* (22nd), Edward Delaval Henry Astley, b. 1912, s. 1956, m.	Hon. Delaval T. H. A., b. 1960.
1835	*Hatherton* (7th), Thomas Charles Tasman Littleton, T.D., b. 1907, s. 1973, m.	Edward C. L., b. 1950.
1776	*Hawke* (10th), (Julian Stanhope) Theodore Hawke, b. 1904, m.	Hon. Edward G. H., b. 1950.
1927	*Hayter* (3rd), George Charles Hayter Chubb, K.C.V.O., C.B.E., b. 1911, s. 1967, m.	Hon. George W. M. C., b. 1943.
1945	*Hazlerigg* (2nd), Arthur Grey Hazlerigg, M.C., b. 1910, s. 1949, w.	Hon. Arthur G. H., b. 1951.
1797 I.	*Headley* (7th), Charles Rowland Allanson-Winn, b. 1902, s. 1969, m.	Hon. John R. A.-W., b. 1934.
1943	*Hemingford* (3rd), Dennis Nicholas Herbert, b. 1934, s. 1982, m.	Hon. Christopher D. C. H., b. 1973.
1906	*Hemphill* (5th), Peter Patrick Fitzroy Martyn Martyn-Hemphill, b. 1928, s. 1957, m.	Hon. Charles A. M. M.-H., b. 1954.
1799 I.*	*Henley* (8th), Oliver Michael Robert Eden (6th *U.K. Baron, Northington*, 1885), b. 1953, s. 1977, m.	Hon. Andrew F. E., b. 1955.
1800 I.*	*Henniker* (8th), John Patrick Edward Chandos Henniker-Major, K.C.M.G., C.V.O., M.C. (4th *U.K. Baron, Hartismere*, 1866), b. 1916, s. 1980, m.	Hon. Mark I. P. C. H.-M., b. 1947.
1886	*Herschell* (3rd), Rognvald Richard Farrer Herschell, b. 1923, s. 1929, m.	(None.)
1935	*Hesketh* (3rd), Thomas Alexander Fermor-Hesketh, b. 1950, s. 1955, m.	Hon. Robert F.-H., b.1951.
1828	*Heytesbury* (6th), Francis William Holmes à Court, b. 1931, s. 1971, m.	Hon. James W. H. à C., b. 1967.
1886	*Hindlip* (5th), Henry Richard Allsopp, b. 1912, s. 1966, m.	Hon. Charles H. A., b. 1940.
1950	*Hives* (2nd), John Warwick Hives, b. 1913, s. 1965, m.	Matthew P. H., b. 1971.
1912	*Hollenden* (3rd), Gordon Hope Hope-Morley, b. 1914, s. 1977, m.	Hon. Ian H.-M., b. 1946.
1897	*Holm Patrick* (3rd), James Hans Hamilton, b. 1928, s. 1942, m.	Hon. Hans. J. D. H., b. 1955.
1933	*Horder* (2nd), Thomas Mervyn Horder, b. 1911, s. 1955.	(None.)
1797 I.	*Hotham* (8th), Henry Durand Hotham, b. 1940, s. 1967, m.	Hon. William B. H., b. 1972.
1881	*Hothfield* (4th), Thomas Sackville Tufton, b. 1916, s. 1961.	George W. A. T., T.D., b. 1904.
1597	*Howard de Walden* (9th), John Osmael Scott-Ellis (5th *U.K. Baron, Seaford*, 1826), b. 1912, s. 1946, m.	Co-heiresses. To U.K. Barony, Colin H. F. Ellis, b. 1946.
1930	*Howard of Penrith* (2nd), Francis Philip Howard, b. 1905, s. 1939, m.	Hon. Philip E. H., b. 1945.
1960	*Howick of Glendale* (2nd), Charles Evelyn Baring, b. 1937, s. 1973, m.	Hon. David E. C. B., b. 1975.
1796 I.	*Huntingfield* (6th), Gerard Charles Arcedeckne Vanneck, b. 1915, s. 1969, m.	Hon. Joshua C. V., b. 1954.
1866	*Hylton* (5th), Raymond Hervey Jolliffe, b. 1932, s. 1967, m.	Hon. William H. M. J., b. 1967.
1933	*Iliffe* (2nd), Edward Langton Iliffe, b. 1908, s. 1960, m.	Robert P. R. I., b. 1944.
1543 I.	*Inchiquin* (18th), Conor Myles John O'Brien, b. 1943, s. 1982.	Murrough R. O'B., b. 1910.
1962	*Inchyra* (1st), Frederick Robert Hoyer Millar, G.C.M.G., C.V.O., b. 1900, m.	Hon. Robert C. R. H. M., b. 1935.
1964	*Inglewood* (1st), William Morgan Fletcher-Vane, T.D., b. 1909, w.	Hon. W. Richard F.-V., b. 1951.
1919	*Inverforth* (4th), Andrew Peter Weir, b. 1966, s. 1982, M.	Hon. John V. W., b. 1935.
1941	*Ironside* (2nd), Edmund Oslac Ironside, b. 1924, s. 1959, m.	Hon. Charles E. G. I., b. 1956.
1952	*Jeffreys* (2nd), Mark George Christopher Jeffreys, b. 1932, s. 1960, m.	Hon. Christopher H. M. J., b. 1957.
1924	*Jessel* (2nd), Edward Herbert Jessel, C.B.E., b. 1904, s. 1950, m.	(None.)
1906	*Joicey* (4th), Michael Edward Joicey, b. 1925, s. 1966, m.	Hon. James M. J., b. 1953.
1976	*Keith of Kinkel*, Henry Shanks Keith, b. 1922, m. (*Lord of Appeal*).	(Law Life Peerage.)
1937	*Kenilworth* (4th), John Randle Siddeley, b. 1954, s. 1981, m.	(None.)
1935	*Kennet* (2nd), Wayland Hilton Young, b. 1923, s. 1960, m.	Hon. William A. T. Y., b. 1957.
1776 I. 1886* }	*Kensington* (8th), Hugh Ivor Edwardes (*U.K. Baron, Kensington*), b. 1933, s. 1981, m.	Hon. William O. A. E., b. 1964.
1951	*Kenswood* (2nd), John Michael Howard Whitfield, b. 1930, s. 1963, m.	Hon. Michael C. W., b. 1955.
1788	*Kenyon* (5th), Lloyd Tyrell-Kenyon, C.B.E., b. 1917, s. 1927, m.	Hon. Lloyd T.-K., b. 1947.

Created.	Title, Order of Succession, Name, etc.	Eldest Son or Heir.
1947	*Kershaw* (4th), Edward John Kershaw, *b.* 1936, *s.* 1962, *m.*	Hon. John C. E. *K.*, *b.* 1971.
1943	*Keyes* (2nd), Roger George Bowlby Keyes, *b.* 1919, *s.* 1945, *m.*	Hon. Charles W. P. *K.*, *b.* 1951.
1909	*Kilbracken* (3rd), John Raymond Godley, D.S.C., *b.* 1920, *s.* 1950, *m.*	Hon. Christopher J. *G.*, *b.* 1945.
1971	*Kilbrandon*, Charles James Dalrymple Shaw, P.C., *b.* 1906, *m.* (*Lord of Appeal, retired*).	(Law Life Peerage.)
1900	*Killanin* (3rd), Michael Morris, M.B.E., T.D., *b.* 1914, *s.* 1927, *m.*	Hon. G. Redmond F. *M.*, *b.* 1947.
1943	*Killearn* (2nd), Graham Curtis Lampson, *b.* 1919, *s.* 1964, *m.*	Hon. Victor M. G. A. *L.*, *b.* 1941.
1789 I.	*Kilmaine* (7th), John David Henry Browne, *b.* 1948, *s.* 1978, *m.*	Hon. John F. S. *B.*, *b.* 1983.
1831	*Kilmarnock* (7th), Alastair Ivor Gilbert Boyd, *b.* 1927, *s.* 1975, *m.*	Hon. Robin J. *B.*, *b.* 1941.
1941	*Kindersley* (3rd), Robert Hugh Molesworth Kindersley, *b.* 1929, *s.* 1976, *m.*	Hon. Rupert J. M. *K.*, *b.* 1955.
1223 I.	*Kingsale* (35th), John de Courcy (*Premier Baron of Ireland*), *b.* 1941, *s.* 1969.	Nevinson R. *de C.*, *b.* 1920.
1682 s. ⎱ 1860* ⎰	*Kinnaird* (13th), Graham Charles Kinnaird (5th *U.K. Baron, Kinnaird*), *b.* 1912, *s.* 1972, *m.*	(None.)
1902	*Kinross* (5th), Christopher Patrick Balfour, *b.* 1949, *m.*	Hon. Alan I. *B.*, *b.* 1978.
1951	*Kirkwood* (3rd), David Harvie Kirkwood, PH.D., *b.* 1931, *s.* 1970, *m.*	Hon. James S. *K.*, *b.* 1937.
1979	*Lane*, Geoffrey Dawson Lane, P.C., A.F.C., *b.* 1918, *m.* (*Lord Chief Justice of England*).	(Law Life Peerage.)
1800 I.	*Langford* (9th), Geoffrey Alexander Rowley-Conwy, O.B.E., *b.* 1912, *s.* 1953, *m.*	Hon. Owen G. *R.-C.*, *b.* 1958.
1942	*Latham* (2nd), Dominic Charles Latham, *b.* 1954, *s.* 1970.	Anthony M. *L.*, *b.* 1954.
1431	*Latymer* (7th), Thomas Burdett Money-Coutts, *b.* 1901, *s.* 1949, *w.*	Hon. Hugo N. *M.-C.*, *b.* 1926.
1869	*Lawrence* (5th), David John Downer Lawrence, *b.* 1937, *s.* 1968.	(None.)
1947	*Layton* (2nd), Michael John Layton, *b.* 1912, *s.* 1966, *m.*	Hon. Geoffrey M. *L.*, *b.* 1947.
1859	*Leconfield* (7th), John Max Henry Scawen Wyndham (2nd *U.K. Baron, Egremont*, 1963), *b.* 1948, *s.* 1972, *m.*	Hon. George R. V. *W.*, *b.* 1983.
1839	*Leigh* (5th), John Piers Leigh, *b.* 1935, *s.* 1979, *m.*	Hon. Christopher D. P. *L.*, *b.* 1960.
1962	*Leighton of St. Mellons* (2nd), (John) Leighton Seager, *b.* 1922, *s.* 1963, *m.*	Hon. Robert W. H. L. *S.*, *b.* 1955.
1797	*Lilford* (7th), George Vernon Powys, *b.* 1931, *s.* 1949, *m.*	Hon. Mark V. *P.*, *b.*, 1975.
1945	*Lindsay of Birker* (2nd), Michael Francis Morris Lindsay, *b.* 1909, *s.* 1952, *m.*	Hon. James F. *L.*, *b.* 1945.
1758 I.	*Lisle* (7th), John Nicholas Horace Lysaght, *b.* 1903, *s.* 1919, *m.*	Patrick J. *L.*, *b.* 1931.
1925	*Lloyd* (2nd), Alexander David Frederick Lloyd, M.B.E., *b.* 1912, *s.* 1941, *m.*	(None.)
1895	*Loch* (4th), Spencer Douglas Loch, M.C., *b.* 1920, *s.* 1982, *m.*	(None.)
1850	*Londesborough* (9th), Richard John Denison, *b.* 1959, *s.* 1968.	(None.)
1541 I.	*Louth* (16th), Otway Michael James Oliver Plunkett, *b.* 1929, *s.* 1950, *m.*	Hon. Jonathan O. *P.*, *b.* 1952.
1458 s. ⎱ 1837* ⎰	*Lovat* (15th), Simon Christopher Joseph Fraser. D.S.O., M.C., T.D. (4th *U.K. Baron, Lovat*), *b.* 1911, *s.* 1933, *m.*	Master of Lovat, *b.* 1939.
1946	*Lucas of Chilworth* (2nd), Michael William George Lucas, *b.* 1926, *s.* 1967, *m.*	Hon. Simon W. *L.*, *b.* 1957.
1929	*Luke* (2nd), Ian St. John Lawson-Johnston, K.C.V.O., T.D., *b.* 1905, *s.* 1943, *m.*	Hon. Arthur C. St. J. *L.-J.*, *b.* 1933.
1839	*Lurgan* (5th), John Desmond Cavendish Brownlow, O.B.E., *b.* 1911, *s.* 1984.	(None.)
1914	*Lyell* (3rd), Charles Lyell, *b.* 1939, *s.* 1943.	(None.)
1859	*Lyveden* (6th), Ronald Cecil Vernon, *b.* 1915, *s.* 1973, *m.*	Hon. Jack L. *V.*, *b.* 1938.
1959	*MacAndrew* (2nd), Colin Nevil Glen MacAndrew, *b.* 1919, *s.* 1979, *m.*	Hon. Christopher A. C. *MacA.*, *b.* 1945.
1776 I.	*Macdonald* (8th), Godfrey James Macdonald, *b.* 1947, *s.* 1970, *m.*	Hon. Godfrey E. H. T. *M.*, *b.* 1982.
1949	*Macdonald of Gwaenysgor* (2nd), Gordon Ramsay Macdonald, *b.* 1915, *s.* 1966, *m.*	Hon. Kenneth L. *M.*, *b.* 1921.
1937	*McGowan* (3rd), Harry Duncan Cory McGowan, *b.* 1938, *s.* 1966, *m.*	Hon. Harry J. C. *Mc. G.*, *b.* 1971.
1922	*Maclay* (3rd), Joseph Paton Maclay, *b.* 1942, *s.* 1969, *m.*	Hon. Joseph P. *M.*, *b.* 1977.
1955	*McNair* (2nd), (Clement) John McNair, *b.* 1915, *s.* 1975, *m.*	Hon. Duncan J. *McN.*, *b.* 1947.
1951	*Macpherson of Drumochter* (2nd), James Gordon Macpherson, *b.* 1924, *s.* 1965, *m.*	Hon. James A. *M.*, *b.* 1979.
1937	*Mancroft* (2nd), Stormont Mancroft Samuel Mancroft, K.B.E., T.D., *b.* 1914, *s.* 1942, *m.*	Hon. Benjamin L. S. *M.*, *b.* 1957.
1807	*Manners* (5th), John Robert Cecil Manners, *b.* 1923, *s.* 1972, *m.*	Hon. John H. R. *M.*, *b.* 1956.
1922	*Manton* (3rd), Joseph Rupert Eric Robert Watson, *b.* 1924, *s.* 1968, *m.*	Lieut. Hon. Miles R. M. *W.*, *b.* 1958.
1908	*Marchamley* (3rd), John William Tattersall Whiteley, *b.* 1922, *s.* 1949, *m.*	Hon. William F. *W.*, *b.* 1968.

Created.	Title, Order of Succession, Name, etc.	Eldest Son or Heir.
1964	*Margadale* (1st), John Granville Morrison, T.D., b. 1906, w.	Hon. James I. M., T.D., b. 1930.
1961	*Marks of Broughton* (2nd), Michael Marks, b. 1920, s. 1964, m.	Hon. Simon R. M., b. 1950.
1930	*Marley* (2nd), Godfrey Pelham Leigh Aman, b. 1913, s. 1952, m.	(None.)
1964	*Martonmere* (1st), (John) Roland Robinson, P.C., G.B.E., K.C.M.G., b. 1907, m.	John S. R., b. 1963.
1776 I.	*Massy* (9th), Hugh Hamon John Somerset Massy, b. 1921, s. 1958, m.	Hon. David H. S. M., b. 1947.
1935	*May* (3rd), Michael St. John May, b. 1931, s. 1950, m.	Hon. Jasper B. St. J. M., b. 1965.
1928	*Melchett* (4th), Peter Robert Henry Mond, b. 1948, s. 1973.	(None.)
1925	*Merrivale* (3rd), Jack Henry Edmond Duke, b. 1917, s. 1951, m.	Hon. Derek J. P. D., b. 1948.
1919	*Meston* (3rd), James Meston, b. 1950, s. 1984, m.	Hon. Thomas J. D. M., b. 1977.
1838	*Methuen* (6th), Anthony John Methuen, b. 1925, s. 1975.	Hon. Robert A. H. M., b. 1931.
1711	*Middleton* (12th), (Digby) Michael Godfrey John Willoughby, M.C., b. 1921, s. 1970, m.	Hon. Michael C. J. W., b. 1948.
1939	*Milford* (2nd), Wogan Philipps, b. 1902, s. 1962, m.	Hon. Hugo J. L. P., b. 1929.
1933	*Milne* (2nd), George Douglass Milne, T.D., b. 1909, s. 1948, m.	Hon. George A. M., b. 1941.
1951	*Milner of Leeds* (2nd), Arthur James Michael Milner, b. 1923, s. 1967, m.	Hon. Richard J. M., b. 1959.
1947	*Milverton* (2nd), Rev. Fraser Arthur Richard Richards, b. 1930, s. 1978, m.	Hon. Michael H. R., b. 1936.
1873	*Moncreiff* (5th), Harry Robert Wellwood Moncreiff, b. 1915, s. 1942, m.	Hon. Rhoderick H. W. M., b. 1954.
1884	*Monk Bretton* (3rd), John Charles Dodson, b. 1924, s. 1933, m.	Hon. Christopher M. D., b. 1958.
1728	*Monson* (11th), John Monson, b. 1932, s. 1958, m.	Hon. Nicholas J. M., b. 1955.
1885	*Montagu of Beaulieu* (3rd), Edward John Barrington Douglas-Scott-Montagu, b. 1926, s. 1929, m.	Hon. Ralph D.-S.-M., b. 1961
1839	*Monteagle of Brandon* (6th), Gerald Spring Rice, b. 1926, s. 1946, m.	Hon. Charles J. S. R., b. 1953.
1943	*Moran* (2nd), (Richard) John (McMoran) Wilson, K.C.M.G., b. 1924, s. 1977, m.	Hon. James McM. W., b. 1952.
1918	*Morris* (3rd), Michael David Morris, b. 1937, s. 1975, m.	Hon. Thomas A. S. M., b. 1982.
1950	*Morris of Kenwood* (2nd), Philip Geoffrey Morris, b. 1928, s. 1954, m.	Hon. Jonathan D. M., b. 1968.
1945	*Morrison* (2nd), Dennis Morrison, b. 1914, s. 1953.	(None.)
1831	*Mostyn* (5th), Roger Edward Lloyd Lloyd-Mostyn, M.C., b. 1920, s. 1965, m.	Hon. Llewellyn R. L. L.-M., b. 1948.
1933	*Mottistone* (4th), David Peter Seely, C.B.E., b. 1920, s. 1966, m.	Hon. Peter J. P. S., b. 1949.
1945	*Mountevans* (3rd), Edward Patrick Broke Evans, b. 1943, s. 1974, m.	Hon. Jeffrey de C. R. E., b. 1948.
1283	*Mowbray* (26th), *Segrave* (27th) (1283), & *Stourton* (23rd) (1448), Charles Edward Stourton, C.B.E., b. 1923, s. 1965, m.	Hon. Edward W. S. S., b. 1953.
1932	*Moyne* (2nd), Bryan Walter Guinness, b. 1905, s. 1944, m.	Hon. Jonathan B. G., b. 1930.
1929	*Moynihan* (3rd), Antony Patrick Andrew Cairnes Berkeley Moynihan, b. 1936, s. 1965.	Hon. Colin B. M., M.P., b. 1955.
1781 I.	*Muskerry* (8th), Hastings Fitzmaurice Tilson Deane, b. 1907, s. 1966, m.	Hon. Robert F. D., b. 1948.
1627 s.*	*Napier and Ettrick* (14th), Francis Nigel Napier, M.V.O. (5th *U.K.* Baron, Ettrick, 1872), b. 1930, s. 1954, m.	Master of Napier, b. 1962.
1868	*Napier of Magdala* (5th), (Robert) John Napier, O.B.E., b. 1904, s. 1948, m.	Hon. Robert A. N., b. 1940.
1940	*Nathan* (2nd), Roger Carol Michael Nathan, b. 1922, s. 1963, m.	Hon. Rupert H. B. N., b. 1957.
1960	*Nelson of Stafford* (2nd), Henry George Nelson, b. 1917, s. 1962, m.	Hon. Henry R. G. N., b. 1943.
1959	*Netherthorpe* (3rd), James Frederick Turner, b. 1964, s. 1982.	Hon. Patrick A. T., b. 1971.
1946	*Newall* (2nd), Francis Storer Eaton Newall, b. 1930, s. 1963, m.	Hon. Richard H. E. N., b. 1961.
1776 I.	*Newborough* (7th), Robert Charles Michael Vaughan Wynn, D.S.C., b. 1917, s. 1965, m.	Hon. Robert V. W., b. 1949.
1892	*Newton* (4th), Peter Richard Legh, b. 1915, s. 1960, m.	Hon. Richard T. L., b. 1950.
1930	*Noel-Buxton* (3rd), Martin Connal Noel-Buxton, b. 1940, s. 1980.	Hon. Charles C. N.-B., b. 1975.
1957	*Norrie* (2nd), (George) Willoughby Moke Norrie, b. 1936, s. 1977, m.	Hon. Mark W. J. N., b. 1972.
1884	*Northbourne* (5th), Christopher George Walter James, b. 1926, s. 1982, m.	Hon. Charles W. H. J., b. 1960.
1866	*Northbrook* (5th), Francis John Baring, b. 1915, s. 1947, m.	Hon. Francis T. B., b. 1954.
1878	*Norton* (7th), John Arden Adderley, O.B.E., b. 1915, s. 1961, m.	Hon. James N. A. A., b. 1947.
1906	*Nunburnholme* (4th), Ben Charles Wilson, b. 1928, s. 1974, m.	Hon. Charles T. W., b. 1935.
1950	*Ogmore* (2nd), Gwilym Rees Rees-Williams, b. 1931, s. 1976, m.	Hon. Morgan R.-W., b. 1937.
1870	*O'Hagan* (4th), Charles Towneley Strachey, b. 1945, s. 1961, m.	Hon. Richard T. S., b. 1950.
1868	*O'Neill* (4th), Raymond Arthur Clanaboy O'Neill, T.D., b. 1933, s. 1944, m.	Hon. Shane S. C. O'N., b. 1965.
1836 I.*	*Oranmore and Browne* (4th), Dominick Geoffrey Edward Browne (2nd *U.K.* Baron Mereworth, 1926), b. 1901, s. 1927, m.	Hon. Dominick G. T. B., b. 1929.

Created.	*Title, Order of Succession, Name, etc.*	*Eldest Son or Heir.*
1933	*Palmer* (3rd), Raymond Cecil Palmer, O.B.E., b. 1916, s. 1950, m.	Hon. Gordon W. N. P., O.B.E., T.D., b. 1918.
1914	*Parmoor* (4th), (Frederick Alfred) Milo Cripps, b. 1929, s. 1977.	M. Anthony L. C., C.B.E., D.S.O., T.D., Q.C., b. 1913.
1962	*Pearce*, Edward Holroyd Pearce, P.C., b. 1901, m. (*Lord of Appeal, retired*).	(Law Life Peerage.)
1937	*Pender* (3rd), John Willoughby Denison-Pender, b. 1933, s. 1965, m.	Hon. Henry J. R. D.-P., b. 1968.
1866	*Penrhyn* (6th), Malcolm Frank Douglas-Pennant, D.S.O., M.B.E., b. 1908, s. 1967, m.	Hon. Nigel D.-P., b. 1909.
1603	*Petre* (17th), Joseph William Lionel Petre, b. 1914, s. 1915, m.	Hon. John P. L. P., b. 1942.
1918	*Phillimore* (3rd), Robert Godfrey Phillimore, b. 1939, s. 1947.	Hon. Claud S. P., b. 1911.
1945	*Piercy* (3rd), James William Piercy, b. 1946, s. 1981.	Hon. Mark E. P. P., b. 1953.
1827	*Plunket* (8th), Robin Rathmore Plunket, b. 1925, s. 1975, m.	Hon. Shaun A. F. S. P., b. 1931.
1831	*Poltimore* (7th), Mark Coplestone Bampfylde, b. 1957, s. 1978, m.	Son, b. 1985.
1690 s.	*Polwarth* (10th), Henry Alexander Hepburne-Scott, T.D., b. 1916, s. 1944, m.	Master of Polwarth, b. 1947.
1930	*Ponsonby of Shulbrede* (3rd), Thomas Arthur Ponsonby, b. 1930, s. 1976, m.	Hon. Frederick M. T. P., b. 1958.
1958	*Poole* (1st), Oliver Brian Sanderson Poole, P.C., C.B.E., T.D., b. 1911, m.	Hon. David C. P., b. 1945.
1852	*Raglan* (5th), FitzRoy John Somerset, b. 1927, s. 1964, m.	Hon. Geoffrey S., b. 1932.
1932	*Rankeillour* (4th), Peter St. Thomas More Henry Hope, b. 1935, s. 1967.	Michael R. H., b. 1940.
1953	*Rathcavan* (2nd), Phelim Robert Hugh O'Neill, P.C. (N.I.), b. 1909, s. 1982, m.	Hon. Hugh D. T. O'N., b. 1939.
1916	*Rathcreedan* (2nd), Charles Patrick Norton, T.D., b. 1905, s. 1930, m.	Hon. Christopher J. N., b. 1949.
1868 I.	*Rathdonnell* (5th), Thomas Benjamin McClintock Bunbury, b. 1938, s. 1959, m.	Hon. William L. McC. B., b. 1966.
1911	*Ravensdale* (3rd), Nicholas Mosley, M.C., b. 1923, s. 1966, m.	Hon. Shaun N. M., b. 1949.
1821	*Ravensworth* (8th), Arthur Waller Liddell, b. 1924, s. 1950, m.	Hon. Thomas A. H. L., b. 1954.
1821	*Rayleigh* (5th), John Arthur Strutt, b. 1908, s. 1947, w.	John G. S., b. 1960.
1937	*Rea* (3rd), John Nicolas, Rea, M.D., b. 1928, s. 1981, m.	Hon. Matthew J. R., b. 1956.
1628 s.	*Reay* (14th), Hugh William Mackay, b. 1937, s. 1963, m.	Master of Reay, b. 1965.
1902	*Redesdale* (5th), Clement Napier Bertram Mitford, b. 1932, s. 1963, m.	Hon. Rupert B. M., b. 1967.
1928	*Remnant* (3rd), James Wogan Remnant, C.V.O., b. 1930, s. 1967, m.	Hon. Philip J. R., b. 1954.
1806 I.	*Rendlesham* (8th), Charles Anthony Hugh Thellusson, b. 1915, s. 1943, m.	Hon. Charles W. B. T., b. 1954.
1933	*Rennell* (3rd), (John Adrian) Tremayne Rodd, b. 1935, s. 1978, m.	Hon. James R. D. T. R., b. 1978.
1964	*Renwick* (2nd), Harry Andrew Renwick, b. 1935, s. 1973, m.	Hon. Robert J. R., b. 1966.
1885	*Revelstoke* (4th), Rupert Baring, b. 1911, s. 1934.	Hon. John B., b. 1934.
1905	*Ritchie of Dundee* (5th), (Harold) Malcolm Ritchie, b. 1919, s. 1978, m.	Hon. Charles R. R. R., b. 1958.
1935	*Riverdale* (2nd), Robert Arthur Balfour, b. 1901, s. 1957, m.	Hon. Mark R. B., b. 1927.
1961	*Robertson of Oakridge* (2nd), William Ronald Robertson, b. 1930, s. 1974, m.	Hon. William B. E. R., b. 1975.
1938	*Roborough* (2nd), Massey Henry Edgcumbe Lopes, b. 1903, s. 1938, m.	Hon. Henry M. L., b. 1940.
1931	*Rochester* (2nd), Foster Charles Lowry Lamb, b. 1916, s. 1955, m.	Hon. David C. L., b. 1944.
1934	*Rockley* (3rd), James Hugh Cecil, b. 1934, s. 1976, m.	Hon. Anthony R. C., b. 1961.
1782	*Rodney* (9th), John Francis Rodney, b. 1920, s. 1973, m.	Hon. George B. R., b. 1953.
1651 s.*	*Rollo* (13th), Eric John Stapylton Rollo (4th *U.K. Baron, Dunning*, 1869), b. 1915, s. 1947, m.	Master of Rollo, b. 1943.
1959	*Rootes* (2nd), William Geoffrey Rootes, b. 1917, s. 1964, m.	Hon. Nicholas G. R., b. 1951.
1980	*Roskill*, Eustace Wentworth Roskill, P.C., b. 1911, m. (*Lord of Appeal*).	(Law Life Peerage.)
1796 I. 1838*	} *Rossmore* (7th), William Warner Westenra (6th *U.K. Baron, Rossmore*), b. 1931, s. 1958.	(None.)
1939	*Rotherwick* (2nd), (Herbert) Robin Cayzer, b. 1912, s. 1958, w.	Hon. H. Robin C., b. 1954.
1885	*Rothschild* (3rd), Nathanial Mayer Victor Rothschild, G.B.E., G.M., F.R.S., b. 1910, s. 1937, m.	Hon. N. C. Jacob R., b. 1936.
1911	*Rowallan* (3rd), Arthur Cameron Corbett, b. 1919, s. 1977.	Hon. John P. C. C., b. 1947.
1947	*Rugby* (2nd), Alan Loader Maffey, b. 1913, s. 1969, m.	Hon. Robert C. M., b. 1951.
1975	*Russell of Killowen*, Charles Ritchie Russell, P.C., b. 1908, m. (*Lord of Appeal, retired*).	(Law Life Peerage.)
1919	*Russell of Liverpool* (3rd), Simon Gordon Jared Russell, b. 1952, s. 1981, m.	Hon. Adam M. H. R., b. 1957.
1876	*Sackville* (6th), Lionel Bertrand Sackville-West, b. 1913, s. 1965, m.	Hugh R. I. S.-W., M.C., b. 1919.
1964	*St. Helens* (2nd), Richard Francis Hughes-Young, b. 1945, s. 1980, m.	(None.)
1559	*St. John of Bletso* (21st), Anthony Tudor St. John, b. 1957, s. 1978.	Edmund O. St. J., b. 1927.
1852	*St. Leonards* (4th), John Gerard Sugden, b. 1950, s. 1972.	Edward C. S., b. 1902.
1887	*St. Levan* (4th), John Francis Arthur St. Aubyn, D.S.C., b. 1919, s. 1978, m.	Hon. O. Piers St. A., M.C., b. 1920.
1885	*St. Oswald* (5th), Derek Edward Anthony Winn, b. 1919, s. 1984, m.	Hon. Charles R. A. W., b. 1959.
1972	*Salmon*, Cyril Barnet Salmon, P.C., b. 1903, m. (*Lord of Appeal, retired*).	(Law Life Peerage.)
1945	*Sandford* (2nd), Rev. John Cyril Edmondson, D.S.C., b. 1920, s. 1959, m.	Hon. James J. M. E., b. 1949.

Created.	Title, Order of Succession, Name, etc.	Eldest Son or Heir.
1871	*Sandhurst* (5th), (John Edward) Terence Mansfield, D.F.C., b. 1920, s. 1964, m.	Hon. Guy R. J. M., b. 1949.
1802	*Sandys* (7th), Richard Michael Oliver Hill, b. 1931, s. 1961, m.	Marcus T. H., b. 1931.
1888	*Savile* (3rd), George Halifax Lumley-Savile, b. 1919, s. 1931.	Hon. Henry L. T. L.-S., b. 1923.
1447	*Saye and Sele* (21st), Nathaniel Thomas Allen Fiennes, b. 1920, s. 1968, m.	Hon. Richard I. F., b. 1959.
1977	*Scarman*, Leslie George Scarman, P.C., O.B.E., b. 1911, m. (*Lord of Appeal*).	(Law Life Peerage.)
1932	*Selsdon* (3rd), Malcolm McEacharn Mitchell-Thomson, b. 1937, s. 1963, m.	Hon. Callum M. M. M.-T., b. 1969.
1916	*Shaughnessy* (3rd), William Graham Shaughnessy, b. 1922, s. 1938, m.	Hon. Michael J. S., b. 1946.
1783 I. 1839*	*Sheffield* (8th), Thomas Henry Oliver Stanley (8th *U.K. Baron, Stanley of Alderley* and 7th *U.K. Baron Eddisbury*, 1848), b. 1927, s. 1971, m.	Hon. Richard O. S., b. 1956.
1946	*Shepherd* (2nd), Malcolm Newton Shepherd, P.C., b. 1918, s. 1954, m.	Hon. Graeme G. S., b. 1949.
1964	*Sherfield* (1st), Roger Mellor Makins, G.C.B., G.C.M.G., b. 1904, w.	Hon. Christopher J. M., b. 1942.
1902	*Shuttleworth* (5th), Charles Geoffrey Nicholas Kay-Shuttleworth, b. 1948, s. 1975, m.	Hon. Thomas E. K.-S., b. 1976.
1963	*Silsoe* (2nd), David Malcolm Trustram Eve, Q.C., b. 1930, s. 1976, m.	Hon. Simon R. T. E., b. 1966.
1947	*Simon of Wythenshawe* (2nd), Roger Simon, b. 1913, s. 1960, m.	Hon. Matthew S., b. 1955.
1449 S.	*Sinclair* (17th), Charles Murray Kennedy St. Clair, M.V.O., b. 1914, s. 1957, m.	Master of Sinclair, b. 1968.
1957	*Sinclair of Cleeve* (2nd), John Robert Kilgour Sinclair, O.B.E., b. 1919, s. 1979, m.	Hon. John L. R. S., b. 1953.
1919	*Sinha* (3rd), Sudhindro Prosanno Sinha, b. 1920, s. 1967, m.	Hon. Sushanto S., b. 1953.
1828	*Skelmersdale* (7th), Roger Bootle-Wilbraham, b. 1945, s. 1973, m.	Hon. Andrew B.-W., b. 1977.
1916	*Somerleyton* (3rd), Savile William Francis Crossley, b. 1928, s. 1959, m.	Hon. Hugh F. S. C., b. 1971.
1784	*Somers* (8th), John Patrick Somers Cocks, b. 1907, s. 1953, m.	Philip S. S. C., b. 1948.
1917	*Southborough* (4th), Francis Michael Hopwood, b. 1922, s. 1982, m.	(None.)
1959	*Spens* (3rd), Patrick Michael Rex Spens, b. 1942, s. 1984, m.	Hon. Patrick N. G. S., b. 1968.
1640	*Stafford* (14th), Basil Francis Nicholas Fitzherbert, b. 1926, s. 1941, m.	Hon. Francis M. W. F., b. 1954.
1938	*Stamp* (3rd), Trevor Charles Stamp, M.D., b. 1907, s. 1941, m.	Hon. Trevor C. B. S., M.D., b. 1935.
1318	*Strabolgi* (11th), David Montague de Burgh Kenworthy, b. 1914, s. 1953, m.	Rev. the Hon. Jonathan M. A. K., b. 1916.
1954	*Strang* (2nd), Colin Strang, b. 1922, s. 1978, w.	(None.)
1955	*Strathalmond* (3rd), William Roberton Fraser, b. 1947, s. 1976, m.	Hon. William G. F., b. 1976.
1936	*Strathcarron* (2nd), David William Anthony Blyth Macpherson, b. 1924, s. 1937, m.	Hon. Ian D. P. M., b. 1949.
1955	‡*Strathclyde* (1st), Thomas Dunlop Galbraith, P.C., b. 1891, w.	Thomas G. D. du R. de B. G., b. 1960.
1900	*Strathcona and Mount Royal* (4th), Donald Euan Palmer Howard, b. 1923, s. 1959, m.	Hon. Donald A. S. H., b. 1961.
1836	*Stratheden & Campbell* (1841) (5th), Gavin Campbell, b. 1901, s. 1981, m.	Hon. Donald C., b. 1934.
1884	*Strathspey* (5th), Donald Patrick Trevor Grant, b. 1912, s. 1948, m.	Hon. James P. G., b. 1943.
1838	*Sudeley* (7th), Merlin Charles Sainthill Hanbury-Tracy, b. 1939, s. 1941, m.	Claud E. F. Hanbury-Tracy-Domvile, T.D., b. 1904.
1786	*Suffield* (11th), Anthony Philip Harbord-Hamond, M.C., b. 1922, s. 1951, m.	Hon. Charles A. A. H.-H., b. 1953.
1893	*Swansea* (4th), John Hussey Hamilton Vivian, b. 1925, s. 1934, m.	Hon. Richard A. H. V., b. 1957.
1907	*Swaythling* (3rd), Stuart Albert Samuel Montagu, O.B.E., b. 1898, s. 1927, m.	Hon. David C. S. M., b. 1928.
1919	*Swinfen* (3rd), Roger Mynors Swinfen Eady, b. 1938, s. 1977, m.	Hon. Charles R. P. S. E., b. 1971.
1935	*Sysonby* (3rd), John Frederick Ponsonby, b. 1945, s. 1956.	(None.)
1831 I	*Talbot of Malahide* (9th), Joseph Hubert George Talbot, b. 1899, s. 1975.	Reginald J. R. Arundell, b. 1931.
1946	*Tedder* (2nd), John Michael Tedder, SC.D., PH.D., D.SC., b. 1926, s. 1967, m.	Hon. Robin J. T., b. 1955.
1982	*Templeman*, Sydney (William) Templeman, P.C., M.B.E., b. 1920, m. (*Lord of Appeal*).	(Law Life Peerage).
1884	*Tennyson* (4th), Harold Christopher Tennyson, b. 1919, s. 1951.	Hon. Mark A. T., D.S.C., b. 1920.
1918	*Terrington* (4th), (James Allen) David Woodhouse, b. 1915, s. 1961, m.	Hon. C. Montague W., D.S.O., O.B.E., b. 1917.
1940	*Teviot* (2nd), Charles John Kerr, b. 1934, s. 1968, m.	Hon. Charles R. K., b. 1971.
1616	*Teynham* (20th), John Christopher Ingham Roper-Curzon, b. 1928, s. 1972, m.	Hon. David J. H. I. R.-C., b. 1965.
1964	*Thomson of Fleet* (2nd), Kenneth Roy Thomson, b. 1923, s. 1976, m.	Hon. David K. R. T., b. 1957.

‡ At time of going to press, it was confirmed that Baron Strathclyde had died.

Created.	Title, Order of Succession, Name, etc.	Eldest Son or Heir.
1792	*Thurlow* (8th), Francis Edward Hovell-Thurlow-Cumming-Bruce, K.C.M.G., *b.* 1912, *s.* 1971, *m.*	Hon. Roualeyn R. *H.-T.-C.-B.*, *b.* 1952.
1876	*Tollemache* (5th), Timothy John Edward Tollemache, *b.* 1939, *s.* 1975, *m.*	Hon. Edward J. H. *T.*, *b.* 1976.
1564 s.	*Torphichen* (15th), James Andrew Douglas Sandilands, *b.* 1946, *s.* 1975, *m.*	Douglas R. A. *S.*, *b.* 1926.
1947	*Trefgarne* (2nd), David Garro Trefgarne, *b.* 1941, *s.* 1960, *m.*	Hon. George G. *T.*, *b.* 1970.
1921	*Trevethin* (4th), *and Oaksey* (2nd), John Geoffrey Tristram Lawrence (2nd *U.K. Baron, Oaksey*, 1947), *b.* 1929, *s.* 1971, *m.*	Hon. Patrick J. T. *L.*, *b.* 1960.
1880	*Trevor* (4th), Charles Edwin Hill-Trevor, *b.* 1928, *s.* 1950, *m.*	Hon. Marke C. *H.-T.*, *b.* 1970.
1461 I.	*Trimlestown* (19th), Charles Aloysius Barnewall, *b.* 1899, *s.* 1937, *m.*	Hon. Anthony E. *B.*, *b.* 1928.
1940	*Tryon* (3rd), Anthony George Merrik Tryon, *b.* 1940, *s.* 1976, *m.*	Hon. Charles G. B. *T.*, *b.* 1976.
1935	*Tweedsmuir* (2nd), John Norman Stuart Buchan, C.B.E., C.D., *b.* 1911, *s.* 1940, *m.*	Hon. William *B.*, *b.* 1916.
1523	*Vaux of Harrowden* (10th), John Hugh Philip Gilbey, *b.* 1915, *s.* 1977, *m.*	Hon. Anthony W. *G.*, *b.* 1940.
1800 I.	*Ventry* (7th), Arthur Frederick Daubeney Olav Eveleigh-de-Moleyns, *b.* 1898, *s.* 1936.	Andrew W. *Daubeny-De M.*, *b.* 1943.
1762	*Vernon* (10th), John Lawrance Vernon, *b.* 1923, *s.* 1963, *m.*	Robert V. *Harcourt*, *b.* 1918.
1922	*Vestey* (3rd), Samuel George Armstrong Vestey, *b.* 1941, *s.* 1954, *m.*	Hon. William G. *V.*, *b.* 1983.
1841	*Vivian* (5th), Anthony Crespigny Claude Vivian, *b.* 1906, *s.* 1940, *w.*	Hon. Nicholas *V.*, *b.* 1935.
1934	*Wakehurst* (3rd), (John) Christopher Loder, *b.* 1925, *s.* 1970, *m.*	Hon. Timothy W. *L.*, *b.* 1958.
1723	*Walpole* (9th), Robert Henry Montgomerie Walpole, T.D., *b.* 1913, *s.* 1931, *m.*	Hon. Robert H. *W.*, *b.* 1938.
1780	*Walsingham* (9th), John de Grey, M.C., *b.* 1925, *s.* 1965, *m.*	Hon. Robert *de G.*, *b.* 1969.
1936	*Wardington* (2nd), Christopher Henry Beaumont Pease, *b.* 1924, *s.* 1950, *m.*	Hon. William S. *P.*, *b.* 1925.
1792 I.	*Waterpark* (7th), Frederick Caryll Philip Cavendish, *b.* 1926, *s.* 1948, *m.*	Hon. Roderick A. *C.*, *b.* 1959.
1942	*Wedgwood* (4th), Piers Anthony Weymouth Wedgwood, *b.* 1954, *s.* 1970.	John *W.*, M.D., *b.* 1919.
1861	*Westbury* (5th), David Alan Bethell, M.C., *b.* 1922, *s.* 1961, *m.*	Hon. Richard N. *B.*, M.B.E., *b.* 1950.
1944	*Westwood* (2nd), William Westwood, *b.* 1907, *s.* 1953, *m.*	Hon. William G. *W.*, *b.* 1944.
1935	*Wigram* (2nd), (George) Neville (Clive) Wigram, M.C., *b.* 1915, *s.* 1960, *m.*	Maj. Hon. Andrew F. C. *W.*, *b.* 1949.
1964	*Wilberforce*, Richard Orme Wilberforce, P.C., C.M.G., O.B.E., *b.* 1907, *m.* (*Lord of Appeal, retired*).	(Law Life Peerage.)
1491	*Willoughby de Broke* (20th), John Henry Peyto Verney, M.C., A.F.C., *b.* 1896, *s.* 1923, *m.*	Hon. Leopold D. *V.*, *b.* 1938.
1946	*Wilson* (2nd), Patrick Maitland Wilson, *b.* 1915, *s.* 1964, *m.*	(None.)
1937	*Windlesham* (3rd), David James George Hennessy, P.C., C.V.O., *b.* 1932, *s.* 1962, *m.*	Hon. James *H.*, *b.* 1968.
1951	*Wise* (2nd), John Clayton Wise, *b.* 1923, *s.* 1968, *m.*	Hon. Christopher J. C. *W.*, Ph.D., *b.* 1949.
1869	*Wolverton* (5th), Nigel Reginald Victor Glyn, *b.* 1904, *s.* 1932.	John P. R. *G.*, C.B.E., *b.* 1913.
1928	*Wraxall* (2nd), George Richard Lawley Gibbs, *b.* 1928, *s.* 1931.	Hon. Eustace H. B. *G.*, C.M.G., *b.* 1929.
1915	*Wrenbury* (3rd), John Burton Buckley, *b.* 1927, *s.* 1940, *m.*	Hon. William E. *B.*, *b.* 1966.
1838	*Wrottesley* (6th), Clifton Hugh Lancelot de Verdon Wrottesley, *b.* 1968, *s.* 1977, *M.*	Hon. Mark *W.*, *b.* 1951.
1919	*Wyfold* (3rd), Hermon Robert Fleming Hermon-Hodge, *b.* 1915, *s.* 1942.	(None.)
1829	*Wynford* (8th), Robert Samuel Best, M.B.E., *b.* 1917, *s.* 1943, *m.*	Hon. John P. *B.*, *b.* 1950.
1308	*Zouche* (18th), James Assheton Frankland, *b.* 1943, *s.* 1965, *m.*	Hon. William T. A. *F.*, *b.* 1984.

PEERESSES IN THEIR OWN RIGHT

Peerages are occasionally granted immediately to ladies of distinction or the widows of distinguished men; but frequently the instances falling under this heading are the result of regular inheritance in lines which are open to females in default of males. A Peeress in her Own Right retains her title after marriage, and if her husband's rank is the superior she is designated by the two titles jointly, the inferior one last: her hereditary claim still holds good in spite of any marriage whether higher or lower. No rank held by a woman can confer any title or even precedence upon her husband but the rank of a Peeress in her Own Right is inherited by her eldest son (or perhaps daughter), to whomsoever she may have been married.

COUNTESSES IN THEIR OWN RIGHT

Style, The Countess of —— *Addressed as,* My Lady.

Created.	Title, Name, etc.	Eldest Son or Heir.
1643 s.	*Dysart,* Rosamund Agnes Greaves, *b.* 1914, *s.* 1975.	Lady Katherine *Grant, b.* 1918.
1633 s.	*Loudoun,* Barbara Huddleston Abney-Hastings, *b.* 1919, *s.* 1960, *m.*	Lord Mauchline, *b.* 1942.
c. 1115 s.	*Mar,* Margaret of Mar (*Premier Earldom of Scotland*), *b.* 1940, *s.* 1975, *m.*	The Mistress of Mar, *b.* 1963.
1947	*Mountbatten of Burma,* Patricia Edwina Victoria Knatchbull, *b.* 1924, *s.* 1979, *m.*	Lord Romsey, *b.* 1947.
1235 s.	*Sutherland,* Elizabeth Millicent Sutherland, *b.* 1921, *s.* 1963, *m.*	Lord Strathnaver, *b.* 1947.

BARONESSES IN THEIR OWN RIGHT

Style, The Baroness —— *Addressed as,* My Lady.

Created.	Title, Name, etc.	Eldest Son or Heir.
1421	*Berkeley,* Mary Lalle Foley-Berkeley, *b.* 1905, *title called out of abeyance,* 1967.	Hon. Cynthia E. *Gueterbock, b.* 1909.
1455	*Berners,* Vera Ruby Williams, *b.* 1901, *s.* 1950, *m.*	Two co-heiresses.
1321	*Dacre,* Rachel Leila Douglas-Home, *b.* 1929, *title called out of abeyance,* 1970, *m.*	Hon. James T. A. *D.-H., b.* 1952.
1332	*Darcy de Knayth,* Davina Marcia Ingrams, *b.* 1938, *s.* 1943, *w.*	Hon. Caspar D. *I., b.* 1962.
1439	*Dudley,* Barbara Amy Felicity Wallace, *b.* 1907, *s.* 1972, *w.*	Hon. Jim. A. H. *W., b.* 1930.
1490 s.	*Herries,* Anne Elizabeth Fitzalan-Howard, *b.* 1938, *s.* 1975.	Lady Mary *F.-H.,* c.v.o., *b.* 1940.
1602 s.	*Kinloss,* Beatrice Mary Grenville Freeman-Grenville, *b.* 1922, *s.* 1944, *m.*	Master of Kinloss, *b.* 1953.
1663	*Lucas of Crudwell* (*Scottish Baroness, Dingwall* 1609), Anne Rosemary Palmer, *b.* 1919, *s.* 1958, *m.*	Hon. Ralph M. *P., b.* 1951.
1681 s.	*Nairne,* Katherine Evelyn Constance Bigham (*Katherine, Viscountess Mersey*), *b.* 1912, *s.* 1944, *m.*	Visct. Mersey, *b.* 1934 (see p. 235).
1945	*Portal of Hungerford,* Rosemary Ann Portal, *b.* 1923, *s.* 1971.	Hon. Mavis E. A. *P., b.* 1926.
1445 s.	*Saltoun,* Flora Marjory Fraser, *b.* 1930, *s.* 1979, *m.*	Hon. Katharine I. M. I. *F., b.* 1957.
1489 s.	*Sempill,* Ann Moira Sempill, *b.* 1920, *s.* 1965, *m.*	Master of Sempill, *b.* 1949.
1313	*Willoughby de Eresby,* Nancy Jane Marie Heathcote-Drummond-Willoughby, *b.* 1934, *s.* 1983.	Two co-heiresses.

THE PREFIX RIGHT HONOURABLE

"Right Honourable."—By long established custom, or courtesy, members of her Majesty's Most Honourable Privy Council are entitled to be designated "The Right Honourable," but, in practice, this prefix is sometimes absorbed in other designations; for example, a Prince of the Blood admitted a Privy Counsellor remains "His Royal Highness"; a Duke remains "His Grace"; a Marquess is still styled "Most Honourable". The style of all other Peers whether Privy Counsellors or not, is "Right Honourable", although it is more usual to describe them with the prefix "The", omitting the more elaborate styles. A Privy Counsellor who is not a Peer should be addressed as The Right (or Rt.) Hon.——. A Peer below the rank of Marquess who is a Privy Counsellor should be addressed as The Right (or Rt.) Hon. the Lord (or Earl or Viscount)——, P.C., or, less elaborately, The Lord (or Earl or Viscount)——P.C.

LIFE PEERS
Created under Life Peerages Act, 1958

(For Law Life Peerages *see* pp. 237–46)

BARONS

1974 *Alexander of Potterhill*, William Picken Alexander, PH.D., *b.* 1905, *m.*
1976 *Allen of Abbeydale*, Philip Allen, G.C.B., *b.* 1912, *m.*
1961 *Alport*, Cuthbert James McCall Alport, P.C., T.D., *b.* 1912, *w.*
1965 *Annan*, Noel Gilroy Annan, O.B.E., *b.* 1916, *m.*
1970 *Ardwick*, John Cowburn Beavan, *b.* 1910, *m.*
1973 *Ashby*, Eric Ashby, D.SC., F.R.S., *b.* 1904, *m.*
1967 *Aylestone*, Herbert William Bowden, P.C., C.H., C.B.E., *b.* 1905, *m.*
1977 *Baker*, John Fleetwood Baker, O.B.E., SC.D., F.R.S., *b.* 1901, *w.*
1982 *Bancroft*, Ian Powell Bancroft, G.C.B., *b.* 1922, *m.*
1974 *Banks*, Desmond Anderson Harvie Banks, C.B.E., *b.* 1918, *m.*
1974 *Barber*, Anthony Perrinott Lysberg Barber, P.C., T.D., *b.* 1920, *w.*
1983 *Barnett*, Joel Barnett, P.C., *b.* 1923, *m.*
1982 *Bauer*, Prof. Peter Thomas Bauer, *b.* 1915.
1967 *Beaumont of Whitley*, Timothy Wentworth Beaumont, *b.* 1928, *m.*
1979 *Bellwin*, Irwin Norman Bellow, *b.* 1923, *m.*
1981 *Beloff*, Max Beloff, *b.* 1913, *m.*
1981 *Benson*, Henry Alexander Benson, G.B.E., *b.* 1909, *m.*
1969 *Bernstein*, Sidney Lewis Bernstein, *b.* 1899, *m.*
1964 *Beswick*, Frank Beswick, P.C., *b.* 1912, *m.*
1971 *Blake*, Robert Norman William Blake, F.B.A., *b.* 1916, *m.*
1983 *Blanch*, Rt. Rev. Stuart Yarworth Blanch, P.C., *b.* 1918, *m.*
1978 *Blease*, William John Blease, *b.* 1914, *m.*
1964 *Blyton*, William Reid Blyton, *b.* 1899, *m.*
1980 *Boardman*, Thomas Gray Boardman, M.C., T.D., *b.* 1919, *m.*
1958 *Boothby*, Robert John Graham Boothby, K.B.E., *b.* 1900, *m.*
1976 *Boston of Faversham*, Terence George Boston, Q.C., *b.* 1930, *m.*
1983 *Bottomley*, Arthur George Bottomley, P.C., O.B.E., *b.* 1907, *m.*
1963 *Bowden*, Bertram Vivian Bowden, PH.D., *b.* 1910.
1972 *Boyd-Carpenter*, John Archibald Boyd-Carpenter, P.C., *b.* 1908, *m.*
1976 *Briggs*, Asa Briggs, *b.* 1921, *m.*
1974 *Briginshaw*, Richard William Briginshaw, *m.*
1976 *Brimelow*, Thomas Brimelow, G.C.M.G., O.B.E., *b.* 1915, *m.*
1964 *Brockway*, (Archibald) Fenner Brockway, *b.* 1888, *m.*
1975 *Brookes*, Raymond Percival Brookes, *b.* 1909, *m.*
1979 *Brooks of Tremorfa*, John Edward Brooks, *b.* 1927, *m.*
1983 *Broxbourne*, Derek Colclough Walker-Smith, P.C., T.D., Q.C., *b.* 1910, *m.*
1974 *Bruce of Donington*, Donald William Trevor Bruce, *b.* 1912, *m.*
1983 *Bruce-Gardyne*, John, (Jock), Bruce-Gardyne, *b.* 1930, *m.*
1976 *Bullock*, Alan Louis Charles Bullock, F.B.A., *b.* 1914, *m.*
1985 *Butterworth*, John Blackstock Butterworth, C.B.E., *b.* 1918, *m.*
1978 *Buxton of Alsa*, Aubrey Leland Oakes Buxton, M.C., *b.* 1918, *w.*
1965 *Caccia*, Harold Anthony Caccia, G.C.M.G., G.C.V.O., *b.* 1905, *m.*
1984 *Cameron of Lochbroom*, Kenneth John Cameron, P.C., Q.C., *b.* 1931, *m.*
1981 *Campbell of Alloway*, Alan Robertson Campbell, Q.C., *b.* 1917, *m.*
1974 *Campbell of Croy*, Gordon Thomas Calthrop Campbell, P.C., M.C., *b.* 1921, *m.*
1966 *Campbell of Eskan*, John Middleton Campbell, *b.* 1912, *w.*
1964 *Caradon*, Hugh Mackintosh Foot, P.C., G.C.M.G., K.C.V.O., O.B.E., *b.* 1907, *m.*
1983 *Carmichael of Kelvingrove*, Neil George Carmichael, *b.* 1921, *m.*
1975 *Carr of Hadley*, (Leonard) Robert Carr, P.C., *b.* 1916, *m.*
1977 *Carver*, (Richard) Michael (Power) Carver, G.C.B., C.B.E., D.S.O., M.C., *Field Marshal, b.* 1915, *m.*
1982 *Cayzer*, (William) Nicholas Cayzer, *b.* 1910, *m.*
1964 *Chalfont*, (Alun) Arthur Gwynne Jones, P.C., O.B.E., M.C., *b.* 1919, *m.*
1985 *Chapple*, Frank Joseph Chapple, *b.* 1921, *m.*
1978 *Charteris of Amisfield*, Martin Michael Charles Charteris, P.C., G.C.B., G.C.V.O., O.B.E., *b.* 1913, *m.*
1963 *Chelmer*, Eric Cyril Boyd Edwards, M.C., T.D., *b.* 1914, *m.*
1974 *Chelwood*, Tufton Victor Hamilton Beamish, M.C., *b.* 1917, *m.*
1977 *Chitnis*, Pratap Chidamber Chitnis, *b.* 1936, *m.*
1979 *Cledwyn of Penrhos*, Cledwyn Hughes, P.C., C.H., *b.* 1916, *m.*
1978 *Cockfield*, (Francis) Arthur Cockfield, P.C., *b.* 1916, *m.*
1980 *Coggan*, Rt. Rev. (Frederick) Donald Coggan, P.C., D.D., Royal Victorian Chain, *b.* 1909, *m.*
1964 *Collison*, Harold Francis Collison, C.B.E., *b.* 1909, *m.*
1981 *Constantine of Stanmore*, Theodore Constantine, C.B.E., *b.* 1910, *m.*
1966 *Cooper of Stockton Heath*, John Cooper, *b.* 1908, *m.*
1959 *Craigton*, Jack Nixon Browne, P.C., C.B.E., *b.* 1904, *m.*
1985 *Crawshaw of Aintree*, Lt.-Col. Richard Crawshaw, O.B.E., T.D., *b.* 1917, *m.*
1978 *Croham*, Douglas Albert Vivian Allen, G.C.B., *b.* 1917, *m.*
1973 *Crowther-Hunt*, Norman Crowther Crowther-Hunt, PH.D., *b.* 1920, *m.*
1974 *Cudlipp*, Hugh Cudlipp, O.B.E., *b.* 1913, *m.*
1979 *Dacre of Glanton*, Hugh Redwald Trevor-Roper, *b.* 1914, *m.*

1974 *Darling of Hillsborough*, George Darling, P.C., b. 1905, m.
1970 *Davies of Leek*, Harold Davies, P.C., b. 1904, w.
1974 *Davies of Penrhys*, Gwilym Elfed Davies, b. 1913, m.
1983 *Dean of Beswick*, Joseph Jabez Dean, b. 1923.
1976 *Delfont*, Bernard Delfont, b. 1909, m.
1970 *Diamond*, John Diamond, P.C., b. 1907, m.
1967 *Donaldson of Kingsbridge*, John George Stuart Donaldson, O.B.E., b. 1907, m.
1985 *Donoughue*, Bernard Donoughue, b. 1934, m.
1974 *Duncan-Sandys*, Duncan Edwin Duncan-Sandys, P.C., C.H., b. 1908, m.
1983 *Eden of Winton*, John Benedict Eden, P.C., b. 1925, m.
1985 *Elliott of Morpeth*, Robert William Elliott, b. 1920, m.
1972 *Elworthy*, (Samuel) Charles Elworthy, K.G., G.C.B., C.B.E., D.S.O., M.V.O., D.F.C., A.F.C., *Marshal of the Royal Air Force*, b. 1911, m.
1974 *Elwyn-Jones*, Frederick Elwyn-Jones, P.C., C.H., b. 1909, m.
1981 *Elystan-Morgan*, Dafydd Elystan Elystan-Morgan, b. 1932, m.
1980 *Emslie*, George Carlyle Emslie, P.C., M.B.E., b. 1919, m. (*Lord Justice-General of Scotland*).
1983 *Ennals*, David Hedley Ennals, P.C., b. 1922, m.
1978 *Evans of Claughton*, (David Thomas) Gruffydd Evans, b. 1928, m.
1983 *Ezra*, Derek Ezra, M.B.E., b. 1919, m.
1983 *Fanshawe of Richmond*, Anthony Henry Fanshawe Royle, K.C.M.G., b., 1927, m.
1958 *Ferrier*, Victor Ferrier Noel-Paton, E.D., b. 1900, m.
1983 *Fitt*, Gerard Fitt, b. 1926, m.
1970 *Fletcher*, Eric George Molyneux Fletcher, P.C., LL.D., b. 1903, m.
1979 *Flowers*, Brian Hilton Flowers, F.R.S., b. 1924, m.
1967 *Foot*, John Mackintosh Foot, b. 1909, m.
1982 *Forte*, Charles Forte, b. 1908, m.
1962 *Franks*, Oliver Shewell Franks, P.C., O.M., G.C.M.G., K.C.B., C.B.E., F.B.A., b. 1905, m.
1974 *Fraser of Kilmorack*, (Richard) Michael Fraser, C.B.E., b. 1915, m.
1966 *Fulton*, John Scott Fulton, b. 1902, m.
1982 *Gallacher*, John Gallacher, b. 1920, m.
1979 *Galpern*, Myer Galpern, b. 1903.
1963 *Gardiner*, Gerald Austin Gardiner, P.C., C.H., b. 1900, m.
1975 *Gibson*, (Richard) Patrick (Tallentyre) Gibson, b. 1916, m.
1979 *Gibson-Watt*, (James) David Gibson-Watt, P.C., M.C., b. 1918, m.
1977 *Glenamara*, Edward Watson Short, P.C., C.H., b. 1912, m.
1965 *Goodman*, Arnold Abraham Goodman, C.H., b. 1913.
1982 *Gormley*, Joseph Gormley, O.B.E., b. 1917, m.
1976 *Grade*, Lew Grade, b. 1906, m.
1983 *Graham of Edmonton*, (Thomas) Edward Graham, b.1925, m.
1967 *Granville of Eye*, Edgar Louis Granville, b. 1899, m.
1983 *Gray of Contin*, James, (Hamish), Hector Northey Gray, P.C., b. 1927, m.
1974 *Greene of Harrow Weald*, Sidney Francis Greene, C.B.E., b. 1910, m.
1974 *Greenhill of Harrow*, Denis Arthur Greenhill, G.C.M.G., O.B.E., b. 1913, m.
1975 *Gregson*, John Gregson, b. 1924.
1968 *Grey of Naunton*, Ralph Francis Alnwick Grey, G.C.M.G., G.C.V.O., O.B.E., b. 1910, m.
1983 *Grimond*, Joseph Grimond, P.C., T.D., b. 1913, m.
1970 *Hailsham of St. Marylebone*, Quintin McGarel Hogg, P.C., C.H., b. 1907, w. (*Lord High Chancellor*).
1983 *Hanson*, James Edward Hanson, b. 1922, m.
1974 *Harmar-Nicholls*, Harmar Harmar-Nicholls, b. 1912, m.
1974 *Harris of Greenwich*, John Henry Harris, b. 1930, m.
1979 *Harris of High Cross*, Ralph Harris, b. 1924, m.
1968 *Hartwell*, (William) Michael Berry, M.B.E., T.D., b. 1911, w.
1971 *Harvey of Prestbury*, Arthur Vere Harvey, C.B.E., b. 1906, m.
1974 *Harvington*, Robert Grant Grant-Ferris, P.C., b. 1907, m.
1978 *Hatch of Lusby*, John Charles Hatch, b. 1917.
1983 *Henderson of Brompton*, Peter Gordon Henderson, K.C.B., b. 1922, m.
1967 *Heycock*, Llewellyn Heycock, C.B.E., b. 1905, m.
1963 *Hill of Luton*, Charles Hill, P.C., M.D., b. 1904, m.
1979 *Hill-Norton*, Peter John Hill-Norton, G.C.B., *Admiral of the Fleet*, b. 1915, m.
1967 *Hirshfield*, Desmond Barel Hirshfield, b. 1913, m.
1979 *Holderness*, Richard Frederick Wood, P.C., b. 1920, m.
1974 *Home of the Hirsel*, Alexander Frederick Douglas-Home, P.C., K.T., b. 1903, m.
1979 *Hooson*, (Hugh) Emlyn Hooson, Q.C., b. 1925, m.
1974 *Houghton of Sowerby*, (Arthur Leslie Noel) Douglas Houghton, P.C., C.H., b. 1898, m.
1978 *Howie of Troon*, William Howie, b. 1924, m.
1961 *Hughes*, William Hughes, P.C., C.B.E., b. 1911, m.
1966 *Hunt*, (Henry Cecil) John Hunt, K.G., C.B.E., D.S.O., b. 1910, m.
1973 *Hunt of Fawley*, John Henderson Hunt, C.B.E., D.M., b. 1905, m.
1980 *Hunt of Tanworth*, John Joseph Benedict Hunt, G.C.B., b. 1919, m.
1978 *Hunter of Newington*, Robert Brockie Hunter, M.B.E., F.R.C.P., b. 1915, m.
1978 *Hutchinson of Lullington*, Jeremy Nicolas Hutchinson, Q.C., b. 1915, m.
1982 *Ingrow*, John Aked Taylor, O.B.E., T.D., b. 1917, m.
1979 *Irving of Dartford*, Sydney Irving, P.C., b. 1918, m.
1975 *Jacobson*, Sydney Jacobson, M.C., b. 1908, m.
1968 *Jacques*, John Henry Jacques, b. 1905, m.
1959 *James of Rusholme*, Eric John Francis James, b. 1909, m.
1981 *Jenkins of Putney*, Hugh Gater Jenkins, b. 1908, m.

1981 *John-Mackie*, John John-Mackie, *b.* 1909, *m.*
1983 *Kaberry of Adel*, Donald Kaberry, T.D., *b.* 1907, *m.*
1981 *Kadoorie*, Lawrence Kadoorie, C.B.E., *b.* 1899, *m.*
1976 *Kagan*, Joseph Kagan, *b.* 1915, *m.*
1965 *Kahn*, Richard Ferdinand Kahn, C.B.E., F.B.A., *b.* 1905.
1974 *Kaldor*, Nicholas Kaldor, F.B.A., *b.* 1908, *m.*
1970 *Kearton*, (Christopher) Frank Kearton, O.B.E., F.R.S., *b.* 1911, *m.*
1980 *Keith of Castleacre*, Kenneth Alexander Keith, *b.* 1916, *m.*
1985 *Kimball*, Marcus Richard Kimball, *b.* 1928, *m.*
1983 *King of Wartnaby*, John Leonard King, *m.*
1965 *Kings Norton*, Harold Roxbee Cox, PH.D., *b.* 1902, *m.*
1975 *Kirkhill*, John Farquharson Smith, *b.* 1930, *m.*
1974 *Kissin*, Harry Kissin, *b.* 1912, *m.*
1964 *Leatherland*, Charles Edward Leatherland, O.B.E., *b.* 1898, *m.*
1979 *Lever of Manchester*, Harold Lever, P.C., *b.* 1914, *m.*
1982 *Lewin*, Terence Thornton Lewin, K.G., G.C.B., M.V.O., D.S.C., *Admiral of the Fleet*, *b.* 1920, *m.*
1965 *Lloyd of Hampstead*, Dennis Lloyd, Q.C., LL.D., *b.* 1915, *m.*
1973 *Lloyd of Kilgerran*, Rhys Gerran Lloyd, C.B.E., Q.C., *b.* 1907, *m.*
1974 *Lovell-Davis*, Peter Lovell Lovell-Davis, *b.* 1924, *m.*
1979 *Lowry*, Robert Lynd Erskine Lowry, P.C., *b.* 1919, *m.* (*Lord Chief Justice of Northern Ireland*).
1980 *McAlpine of Moffat*, (Robert) Edwin McAlpine, *b.* 1907, *m.*
1983 *McAlpine of West Green*, (Robert) Alistair McAlpine, *b.* 1942, *m.*
1975 *McCarthy*, William Edward John McCarthy, *b.* 1925, *m.*
1976 *McCluskey*, John Herbert McCluskey, Q.C., *b.* 1929, *m.*
1966 *McFadzean*, William Hunter McFadzean, K.T., *b.* 1903, *m.*
1980 *McFadzean of Kelvinside*, Francis Scott McFadzean, *b.* 1915, *m.*
1978 *McGregor of Durris*, Oliver Ross McGregor, *b.* 1921, *m.*
1982 *McIntosh of Haringey*, Andrew Robert McIntosh, *b.* 1933, *m.*
1979 *Mackay of Clashfern*, James Peter Hymers Mackay, P.C., Q.C., *b.* 1927, *m.*
1974 *Mackie of Benshie*, George Yull Mackie, C.B.E., D.S.O., D.F.C., *b.* 1919, *m.*
1971 *Maclean*, Charles Hector Fitzroy Maclean, P.C., K.T., G.C.V.O., K.B.E., Royal Victorian Chain, *b.* 1916, *m.*
1982 *MacLehose of Beoch*, (Crawford) Murray MacLehose, K.T., G.B.E., K.C.M.G., K.C.V.O., *b.* 1917, *m.*
1967 *MacLeod of Fuinary*, Very Rev. George Fielden MacLeod, M.C., D.D., *b.* 1895, *m.*
1967 *Mais*, Alan Raymond Mais, G.B.E., T.D., E.R.D., *b.* 1911, *m.*
1981 *Marsh*, Richard William Marsh, P.C., *b.* 1928, *m.*
1985 *Marshall of Goring*, Walter Charles Marshall, C.B.E., F.R.S., *b.* 1932, *m.*
1980 *Marshall of Leeds*, Frank Shaw Marshall, *b.* 1915, *m.*
1980 *Matthews*, Victor Collin Matthews, *b.* 1919, *m.*
1983 *Maude of Stratford-upon-Avon*, Angus Edmund Upton Maude, P.C., T.D, *b.* 1912, *m.*
1971 *Maybray-King*, Horace Maybray Maybray-King, P.C., PH.D., *b.* 1901, *m.*
1981 *Mayhew*, Christopher Paget Mayhew, *b.* 1915, *m.*
1985 *Mellish*, Robert Joseph Mellish, P.C., *b.* 1913, *m.*
1979 *Miles*, Bernard James Miles, C.B.E., *b.* 1907, *m.*
1978 *Mishcon*, Victor Mishcon, *b.* 1915, *m.*
1981 *Molloy*, William John Molloy, *b.* 1918, *m.*
1961 *Molson*, (Arthur) Hugh (Elsdale) Molson, P.C., *b.* 1903, *m.*
1967 *Morris of Grasmere*, Charles Richard Morris, K.C.M.G., *b.* 1898, *m.*
1985 *Morton of Shuna*, Hugh Drennan Baird Morton, Q.C., *b.* 1930, *m.*
1971 *Moyola*, James Dawson Chichester-Clark, P.C. (N.I.), *b.* 1923, *m.*
1983 *Mulley*, Frederick William Mulley, P.C., *b.* 1918, *m.*
1985 *Murray of Epping Forest*, Lionel Murray, P.C., O.B.E., *b.* 1922, *m.*
1964 *Murray of Newhaven*, Keith Anderson Hope Murray, K.C.B., PH.D., *b.* 1903.
1979 *Murton of Lindisfarne*, (Henry) Oscar Murton, P.C., O.B.E., T.D., *b.* 1914, *m.*
1975 *Northfield*, (William) Donald Chapman, *b.* 1923.
1966 *Nugent of Guildford*, (George) Richard (Hodges) Nugent, P.C., *b.* 1907, *m.*
1973 *O'Brien of Lothbury*, Leslie Kenneth O'Brien, P.C., G.B.E., *b.* 1908, *m.*
1970 *Olivier*, Laurence Kerr Olivier, O.M., *b.* 1907, *m.*
1970 *O'Neill of the Maine*, Terence Marne O'Neill, P.C. (N.I.), *b.* 1914, *m.*
1976 *Oram*, Albert Edward Oram, *b.* 1913, *m.*
1971 *Orr-Ewing*, (Charles) Ian Orr-Ewing, O.B.E., *b.* 1912, *m.*
1974 *Paget of Northampton*, Reginald Thomas Paget, Q.C., *b.* 1908, *m.*
1975 *Parry*, Gordon Samuel David Parry, *b.* 1925, *m.*
1976 *Peart*, (Thomas) Frederick Peart, P.C., *b.* 1914, *m.*
1967 *Penney*, William George Penney, O.M., K.B.E., PH.D., D.SC., F.R.S., *b.* 1909, *m.*
1982 *Pennock*, Raymond (William) Pennock, *b.* 1920, *m.*
1979 *Perry of Walton*, Walter Laing Macdonald Perry, O.B.E., M.D., D.SC., F.R.S.E., F.R.C.P., *b.* 1921, *m.*
1983 *Peyton of Yeovil*, John Wynne William Peyton, P.C., *b.* 1919, *m.*
1975 *Pitt of Hampstead*, David Thomas Pitt, *b.* 1913, *m.*
1978 *Plant*, Cyril Thomas Howe Plant, C.B.E., *b.* 1910, *m.*
1959 *Plowden*, Edwin Noel Plowden, K.C.B., K.B.E., *b.* 1907, *m.*
1981 *Plummer of St. Marylebone*, (Arthur) Desmond (Herne) Plummer, T.D., *b.* 1914, *m.*
1973 *Porritt*, Arthur Espie Porritt, G.C.M.G., G.C.V.O., C.B.E., *b.* 1900, *m.*
1975 *Pritchard*, Derek Wilbraham Pritchard, *b.* 1910, *m.*
1982 *Prys-Davies*, Gwilym Prys Prys-Davies, *b.* 1923, *m.*
1982 *Quinton*, Anthony Meredith Quinton, *b.* 1925, *m.*
1974 *Ramsey of Canterbury*, Rt. Rev. Arthur Michael Ramsey, P.C., D.D., Royal Victorian Chain, *b.* 1904, *m.*
1978 *Rawlinson of Ewell*, Peter Anthony Grayson Rawlinson, P.C., Q.C., *b.* 1919, *m.*

1976 *Rayne,* Max Rayne, *b.* 1918, *m.*
1983 *Rayner,* Derek George Rayner, *b.* 1926.
1970 *Reigate,* John Kenyon Vaughan-Morgan, P.C., *b.* 1905, *m.*
1978 *Reilly,* Paul Reilly, *b.* 1912, *m.*
1979 *Renton,* David Lockhart-Mure Renton, P.C., K.B.E., T.D., Q.C., *b.* 1908, *m.*
1964 *Rhodes,* Hervey Rhodes, K.G., P.C., D.F.C., *b.* 1895, *w.*
1979 *Richardson,* John Samuel Richardson, M.V.O., M.D., F.R.C.P., *b.* 1910, *m.*
1983 *Richardson of Duntisbourne,* Gordon William Humphreys Richardson, K.G., P.C., M.B.E., T.D, *b.* 1915, *m.*
1961 *Robens of Woldingham,* Alfred Robens, P.C., *b.* 1910, *m.*
1969 *Roberthall,* Robert Lowe Roberthall, K.C.M.G., C.B., *b.* 1901, *m.*
1977 *Roll of Ipsden,* Eric Roll, K.C.M.G., C.B., *b.* 1907, *m.*
1979 *Ross of Marnock,* William Ross, P.C., M.B.E., *b.* 1911, *m.*
1975 *Ryder of Eaton Hastings,* Sydney Thomas Franklin (Don) Ryder, *b.* 1916, *m.*
1962 *Sainsbury,* Alan John Sainsbury, *b.* 1902, *m.*
1977 *Saint Brides,* John Morrice Cairns James, P.C., G.C.M.G., C.V.O., M.B.E., *b.* 1916, *m.*
1972 *Samuel of Wych Cross,* Harold Samuel, *b.* 1912, *m.*
1985 *Sanderson of Bowden,* Charles Russell Sanderson, *b.* 1933, *m.*
1979 *Scanlon,* Hugh Parr Scanlon, *b.* 1913, *m.*
1976 *Schon,* Frank Schon, *b.* 1912, *m.*
1972 *Seebohm,* Frederic Seebohm, T.D., *b.* 1909, *m.*
1978 *Sefton of Garston,* William Henry Sefton, *b.* 1915, *m.*
1958 *Shackleton,* Edward Arthur Alexander Shackleton, K.G., P.C., O.B.E., *b.* 1911, *m.*
1959 *Shawcross,* Hartley William Shawcross, P.C., G.B.E., Q.C., *b.* 1902, *w.*
1970 *Shinwell,* Emanuel Shinwell, P.C., C.H., *b.* 1884, *w.*
1980 *Sieff of Brimpton,* Marcus Joseph Sieff, O.B.E., *b.* 1913, *m.*
1985 *Silkin of Dulwich,* Samuel Charles Silkin, P.C., Q.C, *b.* 1918, *m.*
1971 *Simon of Glaisdale,* Jocelyn Edward Salis Simon, P.C., *b.* 1911, *m.* (*Lord of Appeal, retired*).
1978 *Smith,* Rodney Smith, K.B.E., F.R.C.S., *b.* 1914, *m.*
1978 *Soames,* (Arthur) Christopher (John) Soames, P.C., C.H., G.C.M.G., G.C.V.O., C.B.E., *b.* 1920, *m.*
1965 *Soper,* Rev. Donald Oliver Soper, PH.D., *b.* 1903, *m.*
1983 *Stallard,* Albert William Stallard, *b.* 1921, *m.*
1979 *Stewart of Fulham,* Robert Michael Maitland Stewart, P.C., C.H., *b.* 1906, *w.*
1981 *Stodart of Leaston,* James Anthony Stodart, P.C., *b.* 1916, *m.*
1983 *Stoddart of Swindon,* David Leonard Stoddart, *b.* 1926, *m.*
1969 *Stokes,* Donald Gresham Stokes, T.D., *b.* 1914, *m.*
1976 *Stone,* Joseph Ellis Stone, *b.* 1903, *m.*
1979 *Strauss,* George Russell Strauss, P.C., *b.* 1901, *m.*
1981 *Swann,* Michael Meredith Swann, PH.D., F.R.S., *b.* 1920, *m.*
1971 *Tanlaw,* Simon Brooke Mackay, *b.* 1934, *m.*
1958 *Taylor,* Stephen James Lake Taylor, M.D., *b.* 1910, *m.*
1978 *Taylor of Blackburn,* Thomas Taylor, C.B.E., *b.* 1929, *m.*
1968 *Taylor of Gryfe,* Thomas Johnston Taylor, *b.* 1912, *m.*
1982 *Taylor of Hadfield,* Francis Taylor, *b.* 1905, *m.*
1966 *Taylor of Mansfield,* Harry Bernard Taylor, C.B.E., *b.* 1895, *w.*
1981 *Thomas of Swynnerton,* Hugh Swynnerton Thomas, *b.* 1931, *m.*
1977 *Thomson of Monifieth,* George Morgan Thomson, P.C., K.T., *b.* 1921, *m.*
1967 *Thorneycroft,* (George Edward) Peter Thorneycroft, P.C., C.H., *b.* 1909, *m.*
1962 *Todd,* Alexander Robertus Todd, O.M., D.SC., D.Phil., F.R.S., *b.* 1907, *m.*
1981 *Tordoff,* Geoffrey Johnson Tordoff, *b.* 1928, *m.*
1974 *Tranmire,* Robert Hugh Turton, P.C., K.B.E., M.C., *b.* 1903, *m.*
1974 *Trend,* Burke St. John Trend, P.C., G.C.B., C.V.O., *b.* 1914, *m.*
1979 *Underhill,* (Henry) Reginall Underhill, C.B.E., *b.* 1914, *m.*
1985 *Vinson,* Nigel Vinson, L.V.O., *b.* 1931, *m.*
1964 *Wade,* Donald William Wade, *b.* 1904, *m.*
1974 *Wallace of Campsie,* George Wallace, *b.* 1915, *m.*
1974 *Wallace of Coslany,* George Douglas Wallace, *b.* 1906, *m.*
1961 *Walston,* Henry David Leonard George Walston, C.V.O., *b.* 1912, *m.*
1972 *Watkins,* Tudor Elwyn Watkins, *b.* 1903, *m.*
1977 *Wedderburn of Charlton,* Kenneth William Wedderburn, *b.* 1927, *m.*
1976 *Weidenfeld,* (Arthur) George Weidenfeld, *b.* 1919.
1980 *Weinstock,* Arnold Weinstock, *b.* 1924, *m.*
1965 *Wells-Pestell,* Reginald Alfred Wells-Pestell, *b.* 1910, *m.*
1978 *Whaddon,* John Derek Page, *b.* 1927, *m.*
1970 *Wheatley,* John Wheatley, P.C., *b.* 1908, *m.*
1974 *Wigoder,* Basil Thomas Wigoder, Q.C., *b.* 1921, *m.*
1985 *Williams of Elvel,* Charles Cuthbert Powell Williams, C.B.E., *b.* 1933, *m.*
1963 *Willis,* Edward Henry Willis, *b.* 1918, *m.*
1969 *Wilson of Langside,* Henry Stephen Wilson, P.C., Q.C., *b.* 1916, *m.*
1983 *Wilson of Rievaulx,* (James) Harold Wilson, K.G., P.C., O.B.E., F.R.S., *b.* 1916, *m.*
1975 *Winstanley,* Michael Platt Winstanley, *b.* 1918, *m.*
1965 *Winterbottom,* Ian Winterbottom, *b.* 1913, *m.*
1985 *Wolfson,* Leonard Gordon Wolfson, *b.* 1927, *m.*
1967 *Woolley,* Harold Woolley, C.B.E., *b.* 1905, *w.*
1978 *Young of Dartington,* Michael Young, PH.D., *b.* 1915, *m.*
1984 *Young of Graffham,* David Ivor Young, P.C., *b.* 1932, *m.*
1971 *Zuckerman,* Solly Zuckerman, O.M., K.C.B., F.R.S., M.D., D.SC., *b.* 1904, *m.*

BARONESSES

1979	*Airey of Abingdon*, Diana Josceline Barbara Neave Airey, *b.* 1919, *w.*
1970	*Bacon*, Alice Martha Bacon, P.C., C.B.E., *b.* 1911.
1967	*Birk*, Alma Birk, *b.* 1921, *m.*
1964	*Brooke of Ystradfellte*, Barbara Muriel Brooke, D.B.E., *b.* 1908, *w.*
1962	*Burton of Coventry*, Elaine Frances Burton, *b.* 1904.
1982	*Carnegy of Lour*, Elizabeth Patricia Carnegy of Lour, *b.* 1925.
1982	*Cox*, Caroline Anne Cox, *b.* 1937, *m.*
1978	*David*, Nora Ratcliff David, *b.* 1913, *m.*
1974	*Delacourt-Smith of Alteryn*, Margaret Rosalind Delacourt-Smith, *b.* 1916, *m.*
1978	*Denington*, Evelyn Joyce Denington, D.B.E., *b.* 1907, *m.*
1972	*Elles*, Diana Louie Elles, *b.* 1921, *m.*
1958	*Elliot of Harwood*, Katharine Elliot, D.B.E., *b.* 1903, *w.*
1981	*Ewart-Biggs*, (Felicity) Jane Ewart-Biggs, *b.* 1929, *w.*
1975	*Faithfull*, Lucy Faithfull, O.B.E., *b.* 1910.
1974	*Falkender*, Marcia Matilda Falkender, C.B.E., *b.* 1932.
1974	*Fisher of Rednal*, Doris Mary Gertrude Fisher, *b.* 1919, *w.*
1963	*Gaitskell*, Anna Dora Gaitskell, *w.*
1981	*Gardner of Parkes*, (Rachel) Trixie (Anne) Gardner, *b.* 1927, *m.*
1985	*Hooper*, Gloria Hooper, *b.* 1939.
1965	*Hylton-Foster*, Audrey Pellew Hylton-Foster, *b.* 1908, *w.*
1979	*Jeger*, Lena May Jeger, *b.* 1915, *w.*
1981	*Lane-Fox*, Felicity Lane-Fox, O.B.E., *b.* 1918.
1970	*Lee of Asheridge*, Janet Bevan, P.C., *b.* 1904, *w.*
1967	*Llewelyn-Davies of Hastoe*, Annie Patricia Llewelyn-Davies, P.C., *b.* 1915, *w.*
1978	*Lockwood*, Betty Lockwood, *b.* 1924, *m.*
1979	*McFarlane of Llandaff*, Jean Kennedy McFarlane, *b.* 1926.
1971	*Macleod of Borve*, Evelyn Hester Macleod, *b.* 1915, *w.*
1970	*Masham of Ilton*, Susan Lilian Primrose Cunliffe-Lister, *b.* 1935, *m.* (*Countess of Swinton*).
1982	*Nicol*, Olive Mary Wendy Nicol, *b.* 1923, *m.*
1963	*Northchurch*, Frances Joan Davidson, D.B.E. (*Dowager Viscountess Davidson*), *b.* 1894, *w.*
1964	*Phillips*, Norah Phillips, *b.* 1910, *w.*
1974	*Pike*, (Irene) Mervyn (Parnicott) Pike, D.B.E., *b.* 1918.
1981	*Platt of Writtle*, Beryl Catherine Platt, C.B.E., *b.* 1923, *m.*
1974	*Robson of Kiddington*, Inga-Stina Robson, *b.* 1919, *w.*
1979	*Ryder of Warsaw*, (Sue Ryder), C.M.G., O.B.E., *b.* 1924, *m.*
1971	*Seear*, (Beatrice) Nancy Seear, P.C., *b.* 1913.
1967	*Serota*, Beatrice Serota, *b.* 1919, *m.*
1966	*Sharp*, Evelyn Adelaide Sharp, G.B.E., *b.* 1903.
1973	*Sharples*, Pamela Sharples, *b.* 1923, *m.*
1974	*Stedman*, Phyllis Stedman, O.B.E., *b.* 1916, *m.*
1980	*Trumpington*, Jean Alys Barker, *m.*
1985	*Turner of Camden*, Muriel Winifred Turner.
1974	*Vickers*, Joan Helen Vickers, D.B.E., *b.* 1907.
1985	*Warnock*, Helen Mary Warnock, D.B.E., *b.* 1924, *m.*
1970	*White*, Eirene Lloyd White, *b.* 1909, *w.*
1958	*Wootton of Abinger*, Barbara Frances Wright, C.H., *b.* 1897, *w.*
1971	*Young*, Janet Mary Young, *b.* 1926, *m.*

THE ORDER OF ST. JOHN

The Most Venerable Order of the Hospital of St. John of Jerusalem
St. John's Gate, Clerkenwell, EC1M 4DA

Grand Prior, H.R.H. The Duke of Gloucester, G.C.V.O.

Lord Prior, Sir Maurice Dorman, G.C.M.G., G.C.V.O.   *Chancellor*, The Earl St. Aldwyn, P.C., G.B.E., T.D.
Vice-Chancellor, The Earl Cathcart, C.B., D.S.O., M.C.

Surnames of Peers and Peeresses differing from their Titles

Abney Hastings—
Loudoun
Acheson—*Gosford*
Adderley—*Norton*
Addington—*Sidmouth*
Agar—*Normanton*
Akers Douglas—*Chilston*
Alexander—*Alexander of Potterhill**
Alexander—*Alexander of Tunis*
Alexander—*Caledon*
Allen—*Allen of Abbeydale**
Allen—*Croham**
Allanson Winn—*Headley*
Allsopp—*Hindlip*
Aman—*Marley*
Anderson—*Waverley*
Annesley—*Valentia*
Anson—*Lichfield*
Armstrong Jones—
Snowdon
Arthur—*Glenarthur*
Ashley Cooper—
Shaftesbury
Ashton—*Ashton of Hyde*
Asquith—*Oxford & A.*
Assheton—*Clitheroe*
Astley—*Hastings*
Astor—*Astor of Hever*
Bailey—*Glanusk*
Baillie—*Burton*
Baille Hamilton—
Haddington
Baldwin—*Baldwin of Bewdley*
Balfour—*Kinross*
Balfour—*Riverdale*
Balfour—*Balfour of Inchrye*
Bampfylde—*Poltimore*
Banbury—*Banbury of Southam*
Baring—*Ashburton*
Baring—*Cromer*
Baring—*Howick of Glendale*
Baring—*Northbrook*
Baring—*Revelstoke*
Barker—*Trumpington**
Barnes—*Gorell*
Barnewall—*Trimlestown*
Bathurst—*Bledisloe*
Beamish—*Chelwood**
Beauclerk—*St. Albans*
Beaumont—*Allendale*
Beaumont—*Beaumont of Whitley**
Beavan—*Ardwick**
Beckett—*Grimthorpe*
Bellow—*Bellwin**
Bennet—*Tankerville*
Beresford—*Decies*
Beresford—*Waterford*
Berry—*Camrose*
Berry—*Hartwell**
Berry—*Kemsley*
Bertie—*Lindsey*
Best—*Wynford*
Bethell—*Westbury*
Bevan—*Lee of Asheridge**

Bewicke Copley—
Cromwell
Bigham—*Mersey*
Bigham—*Nairne*
Bingham—*Clanmorris*
Bingham—*Lucan*
Blades—*Ebbisham*
Bligh—*Darnley*
Bootle Wilbraham—
Skelmersdale
Boscawen—*Falmouth*
Boston—*Boston of Faversham**
Bourke—*Mayo*
Bowden—*Aylestone**
Bowes Lyon—*Strathmore*
Bowyer—*Denham*
Boyd—*Kilmarnock*
Boyle—*Cork and Orrery*
Boyle—*Glasgow*
Boyle—*Shannon*
Brabazon—*Meath*
Brand—*Hampden*
Brassey—*Brassey of Apethorpe*
Brett—*Esher*
Bridgeman—*Bradford*
Brodrick—*Midleton*
Brooke—*Alanbrooke*
Brooke—*Brooke of Ystradfellte**
Brooke—*Brookeborough*
Brooks—*Brooks of Tremorfa**
Brooks—*Crawshaw*
Brougham—*Brougham and Vaux*
Broughton—*Fairhaven*
Browne—*Craigton**
Browne—*Kilmaine*
Browne—*Oranmore and Browne*
Browne—*Sligo*
Brownlow—*Lurgan*
Bruce—*Aberdare*
Bruce—*Balfour of Burleigh*
Bruce—*Bruce of Donington**
Bruce—*Elgin and Kincardine*
Brudenell Bruce—
Ailesbury
Buchan—*Tweedsmuir*
Buckley—*Wrenbury*
Burton—*Burton of Coventry**
Butler—*Carrick*
Butler—*Dunboyne*
Butler—*Lanseborough*
Butler—*Mountgarret*
Butler—*Ormonde*
Buxton—*Buxton of Alsa**
Buxton—*Noel-Buxton*
Byng—*Strafford*
Byng—*Torrington*
Cameron—*Cameron of Lochbroom**
Campbell—*Argyll*
Campbell—*Breadalbane and Holland*
Campbell—*Campbell of Alloway**

Campbell—*Campbell of Croy**
Campbell—*Campbell of Eskan**
Campbell—*Cawdor*
Campbell—*Colgrain*
Campbell—*Stratheden and Campbell*
Campbell Gray—*Gray*
Canning—*Garvagh*
Capell—*Essex*
Carington—*Carrington*
Carmichael—*Carmichael of Kelvingrove**
Carnegie—*Fife*
Carnegie—*Northesk*
Carnegie—*Southesk*
Carr—*Carr of Hadley**
Cary—*Falkland*
Caulfeild—*Charlemont*
Cavendish—*Chesham*
Cavendish—*Devonshire*
Cavendish—*Waterpark*
Cavendish Bentinck—
Portland
Cayzer—*Rotherwick*
Cecil—*Amherst of Hackney*
Cecil—*Exeter*
Cecil—*Rockley*
Chaloner—*Gisborough*
Chapman—*Northfield**
Charteris—*Charteris of Amisfield**
Charteris—*Wemyss and March*
Cheshire—*Ryder of Warsaw**
Chetwynd Talbot—
Shrewsbury
Chichester—*Donegall*
Chichester Clark—
Moyola*
Child Villiers—*Jersey*
Cholmondeley—*Delamere*
Chubb—*Hayter*
Clegg Hill—*Hill*
Clifford—*Clifford of Chudleigh*
Clifton of Mar—*Mar*
Cochrane—*Cochrane of Cults*
Cochrane—*Dundonald*
Cocks—*Somers*
Cokayne—*Cullen of Ashbourne*
Coke—*Leicester*
Cole—*Enniskillen*
Colville—*Clydesmuir*
Colville—*Colville of Culross*
Compton—*Northampton*
Conolly Carew—*Carew*
Constantine—
Constantine of Stanmore*
Cooper—*Norwich*
Cooper—*Cooper of Stockton Heath**
Corbett—*Rowallan*
Courtenay—*Devon*
Cox—*Kings Norton**
Craig—*Craigavon*

Crawshaw—*Crawshaw of Aintree**
Crichton—*Erne*
Crichton Stuart—*Bute*
Cripps—*Parmoor*
Cross—*Cross of Chelsea*
Crossley—*Somerleyton*
Cubitt—*Ashcombe*
Cunliffe Lister—*Masham of Ilton**
Cunliffe Lister—*Swinton*
Curzon—*Howe*
Curzon—*Scarsdale*
Cust—*Brownlow*
Dalrymple—*Stair*
Darling—*Darling of Hillsborough**
Davidson—*Northchurch**
Davies—*Darwen*
Davies—*Davies of Leek**
Davies—*Davies of Penrhys**
Davison—*Broughshane*
Dawnay—*Downe*
Dawson Damer—
Portarlington
De Courcy—*Kingsale*
De Grey—*Walsingham*
Delacourt Smith—
Delacourt Smith of Alteryn*
De Yarburgh Bateson—
Deramore
Dean—*Dean of Beswick**
Deane—*Muskerry*
Denison—*Londesborough*
Denison Pender—*Pender*
Devereux—*Hereford*
Dewar—*Forteviot*
Dixon—*Glentoran*
Dodson—*Monk Bretton*
Donaldson—*Donaldson of Kingsbridge**
Douglas—*Morton*
Douglas—*Queensberry*
Douglas Hamilton—
Hamilton
Douglas Hamilton—
Selkirk
Douglas Home—*Dacre*
Douglas-Home—*Home of the Hirsel**
Douglas Pennant—
Penrhyn
Douglas Scott Montagu—
Montagu of Beaulieu
Drummond—*Perth*
Dugdale—*Crathorne*
Duke—*Merrivale*
Duncombe—*Feversham*
Dundas—*Melville*
Dundas—*Zetland*
Dutton—*Sherborne*
Eady—*Swinfen*
Eden—*Auckland*
Eden—*Avon*
Eden—*Henley*
Eden—*Eden of Winton**
Edgcumbe—*Mount Edgcumbe*
Edmondson—*Sandford*
Edwardes—*Kensington*
Edwards—*Chelmer**

* Life Peer created under Life Peerages Act, 1958

Egerton—Sutherland
Egerton—Wilton
Eliot—St. Germans
Elliot—Elliot of
  Harwood*
Elliot-Murray-
  Kynymound—Minto
Elliott—Elliott of
  Morpeth*
Erroll—Errol of Hale
Erskine—Buchan
Erskine—Erskine of
  Rerrick
Erskine—Mar & Kellie
Erskine Murray—
  Elibank
Evans—Evans of
  Claughton*
Evans—Mountevans
Evans Freke—Carbery
Eve—Silsoe
Eveleigh de Moleyns—
  Ventry
Eyres Monsell—Monsell
Fairfax—Fairfax of
  Cameron
Fane—Westmorland
Feilding—Denbigh
Fellowes—Ailwyn
Fellowes—De Ramsey
Fermor Hesketh—
  Hesketh
Fiennes—Saye & Sele
Finch Hatton—
  Winchilsea
Finch Knightley—
  Aylesford
Fisher—Fisher of
  Rednal*
Fitzalan Howard—
  Herries
Fitzalan Howard—
  Norfolk
FitzClarence—Munster
FitzGerald—Leinster
Fitzherbert—Stafford
FitzRoy—Daventry
FitzRoy—Grafton
Fletcher Vane—
  Inglewood
Flower—Ashbrooke
Foley Berkeley—Berkeley
Foljambe—Liverpool
Foot—Caradon*
Forbes—Granard
Fox Strangways—
  Ilchester
Frankland—Zouche
Fraser—Fraser of
  Kilmorack*
Fraser—Fraser of
  Tullybelton
Fraser—Lovat
Fraser—Saltoun
Fraser—Strathalmond
Freeman Grenville—
  Kinloss
Freeman Mitford—
  Redesdale
Fremantle—Cottesloe
French—De Freyne
French—Ypres
Galbraith—Strathclyde
Ganzoni—Belstead
Gardner—Gardner of
  Parkes*

Gascoyne Cecil—
  Salisbury
Gathorne Hardy—
  Cranbrook
Gibbs—Alderham
Gibbs—Wraxall
Gibson—Ashbourne
Giffard—Halsbury
Gilbey—Vaux of
  Harrowden
Glyn—Wolverton
Godley—Kilbracken
Gordon—Aberdeen
Gordon—Huntly
Gordon Lennox—
  Richmond
Gore—Arran
Gough Calthorpe—
  Calthorpe
Graham—Graham of
  Edmonton*
Graham—Montrose
Graham Toler—Norbury
Grant—Strathspey
Grant Ferris—
  Harvington*
Granville—Granville of
  Eye*
Gray—Gray of Contin*
Greaves—Dysart
Greenall—Daresbury
Greene—Greene of
  Harrow Weald*
Greenhill—Greenhill of
  Harrow*
Grenfell—St. Just
Greville—Warwick
Grey—Grey of Naunton*
Grimston—Grimston of
  Westbury
Grimston—Verulam
Grosvenor—Ebury
Grosvenor—Westminster
Guest—Wimborne
Guinness—Iveagh
Guinness—Moyne
Gully—Selby
Gurdon—Cranworth
Gwynne Jones—
  Chalfont*
Hamilton—Abercorn
Hamilton—Belhaven and
  Stenton
Hamilton—Hamilton of
  Dalzell
Hamilton—Holm Patrick
Hamilton Russel—
  Boyne
Hamilton Temple
  Blackwood—Dufferin
Hanbury Tracy—
  Sudeley
Handcock—Castlemaine
Harbord Hamond—
  Suffield
Harding—Harding of
  Petherton
Hardinge—Hardinge of
  Penshurst
Hare—Blakenham
Hare—Listowel
Harmsworth—
  Rothermere
Harris—Harris of
  Greenwich*

Harris—Harris of High
  Cross*
Harris—Malmesbury
Harvey—Harvey of
  Prestbury*
Harvey—Harvey of
  Tasburgh
Hastings—Huntingdon
Hatch—Hatch of Lusby*
Hay—Erroll
Hay—Kinnoull
Hay—Tweeddale
Heathcote-Drummond-
  Willoughby—
  Willoughby de Eresby
Hely Hutchinson—
  Donoughmore
Henderson—Henderson of
  Brompton*
Henderson—Faringdon
Hennessy—Windlesham
Henniker Major—
  Henniker
Hepburne Scott—
  Polwarth
Herbert—Carnarvon
Herbert—Hemingford
Herbert—Pembroke
Herbert—Powis
Hermon Hodge—Wyfold
Hicks Beach—St. Aldwyn
Hervey—Bristol
Hewitt—Lifford
Hill—Downshire
Hill—Hill of Luton*
Hill—Sandys
Hill Trevor—Trevor
Hobart Hampden—
  Buckinghamshire
Hogg—Hailsham of St.
  Marylebone*
Holland Hibbert—
  Knutsford
Holms à Court—
  Heytesbury
Hood—Bridport
Hope—Glendevon
Hope—Linlithgow
Hope—Rankeillour
Hope Morley—Hollenden
Hopkinson—Colyton
Hopwood—Southborough
Hore Ruthven—Gowrie
Houghton—Houghton of
  Sowerby*
Hovell Thurlow Cumming
  Bruce—Thurlow
Howard—Carlisle
Howard—Effingham
Howard—Howard of
  Penrith
Howard—Strathcona
Howard—Suffolk and
  Berkshire
Howie—Howie of Troon*
Hoyer Millar—Inchyra
Hubbard—Addington
Huggins—Malvern
Hughes—Cledwyn of
  Penrhos*
Hughes Young—St.
  Helens
Hunt—Hunt of Fawley*
Hunt—Hunt of
  Tanworth*

Hunter—Hunter of
  Newington*
Hutchinson—Hutchinson
  of Lullington*
Ingrams—Darcy de
  Knayth
Innes Ker—Roxburghe
Inskip—Caldecote
Irby—Boston
Irving—Irving of
  Dartford*
Isaacs—Reading
Jackson—Allerton
James—James of
  Rusholme*
James—Saint Brides*
James—Northbourne
Jebb—Gladwyn
Jervis—St. Vincent
Jocelyn—Roden
Jolliffe—Hylton
Joynson Hicks—
  Brentford
Kaberry—Kaberry of
  Adel*
Kay Shuttleworth—
  Shuttleworth
Kearley—Devonport
Keith—Keith of
  Castleacre*
Keith—Keith of Kinkel
Keith—Kintore
Kemp—Rochdale
Kennedy—Ailsa
Kenworthy—Strabolgi
Keppel—Albemarle
Kerr—Lothian
Kerr—Teviot
King—Lovelace
King—Maybray King*
King—King of Wartnaby*
King Tenison—Kingston
Kitchener—Kitchener of
  Khartoum
Kitson—Airedale
Knatchbull—Brabourne
Knatchbull—
  Mountbatten of Burma
Knox—Ranfurly
Lamb—Rochester
Lambart—Cavan
Lampson—Killearn
Larnach Nevill—
  Abergavenny
Lascelles—Harewood
Law—Coleraine
Law—Ellenborough
Lawrence—Trevethin
  and Oaksey
Lawson—Burnham
Lawson Johnston—
  Luke
Lee—Lee of Asheridge*
Le Poer Trench—
  Clancarty
Legge—Dartmouth
Legh—Newton
Leith—Burgh
Lennox Boyd—Boyd of
  Merton
Leslie—Rothes
Leslie Melville—Leven
Lever—Lever of
  Manchester*
Lever—Leverhulme

* Life Peer created under Life Peerages Act, 1958

Leveson Gower—*Granville*
Liddell—*Ravensworth*
Lindesay Bethune—*Lindsay*
Lindsay—*Crawford*
Lindsay—*Lindsay of Birker*
Littleton—*Hatherton*
Llewelyn-Davies—*Llewelyn-Davies of Hastoe**
Lloyd—*Lloyd of Hampstead**
Lloyd—*Lloyd of Kilgerran**
Lloyd George—*Lloyd George of Dwyfor*
Lloyd George—*Tenby*
Lloyd Mostyn—*Mostyn*
Loder—*Wakehurst*
Lopes—*Roborough*
Low—*Aldington*
Lowry Corry—*Belmore*
Lowther—*Lonsdale*
Lowther—*Ullswater*
Lubbock—*Avebury*
Lucas—*Lucas of Chilworth*
Lumley—*Scarbrough*
Lumley Savile—*Savile*
Lyon Dalberg Acton—*Acton*
Lysaght—*Lisle*
Lyttelton—*Chandos*
Lyttelton—*Cobham (Viscountcy)*
McAlpine—*McAlpine of Moffat**
McAlpine—*McAlpine of West Green**
McClintock Bunbury—*Rathdonnell*
Macdonald—*Macdonald of Gwaenysgor*
McDonnell—*Antrim*
McFadzean—*McFadzean of Kelvinside**
McFarlane—*McFarlane of Llandaff**
McGregor—*McGregor of Durris*
McIntosh—*McIntosh of Haringey**
Mackay—*Inchcape*
Mackay—*Mackay of Clashfern**
Mackay—*Reay*
Mackay—*Tanlaw**
Mackie—*John-Mackie**
Mackie—*Mackie of Benshie**
Mackintosh—*Mackintosh of Halifax*
McLaren—*Aberconway*
MacLehose—*MacLehose of Beoch**
Macleod—*Macleod of Borve**
MacLeod—*Macleod of Fuinary**
Maclay—*Muirshiel*
Macmillan—*Stockton*
Macpherson—*Drumalbyn*

Macpherson—*Macpherson of Drumochter*
Macpherson—*Strathcarron*
Maffey—*Rugby*
Maitland—*Lauderdale*
Makgill—*Oxfuird*
Makins—*Sherfield*
Manners—*Rutland*
Manningham Buller—*Dilhorne*
Mansfield—*Sandhurst*
Marks—*Marks of Broughton*
Marquis—*Woolton*
Marshall—*Marshall of Goring**
Marshall—*Marshall of Leeds**
Marsham—*Romney*
Martyn Hemphill—*Hemphill*
Mason—*Blackford*
Maude—*Hawarden*
Maude—*Maude of Stratford-upon-Avon**
Maxwell—*De Ros*
Maxwell—*Farnham*
Meade—*Clanwilliam*
Milles Lade—*Sondes*
Milner—*Milner of Leeds*
Mitchell Thomson—*Selsdon*
Monckton—*Galway*
Monckton—*Monckton of Brenchley*
Monckton—*Ruthven of Freeland*
Mond—*Melchett*
Money-Coutts—*Latymer*
Montagu—*Manchester*
Montagu—*Swaythling*
Montagu Douglas Scott—*Buccleuch*
Montagu Stuart Wortley Mackenzie—*Wharncliffe*
Montague—*Amwell*
Montgomerie—*Eglinton*
Montgomery—*Montgomery of Alamein*
Moore—*Drogheda*
Moore Brabazon—*Brabazon of Tara*
Moreton—*Ducie*
Morris—*Killanin*
Morris—*Morris of Grasmere**
Morris—*Morris of Kenwood*
Morrison—*Dunrossil*
Morrison—*Margadale*
Morton—*Morton of Shuna**
Mosley—*Ravensdale*
Mountbatten—*Edinburgh*
Mountbatten—*Milford Haven*
Mountbatten—*Mountbatten of Burma*
Muff—*Calverley*
Mulholland—*Dunleath*
Murray—*Atholl*
Murray—*Dunmore*

Murray—*Mansfield and Mansfield*
Murray—*Murray of Epping Forest**
Murray—*Murray of Newhaven**
Murton—*Murton of Lindisfarne**
Nall Cain—*Brocket*
Napier—*Napier and Ettrick*
Napier—*Napier of Magdala*
Neave—*Airey of Abingdon**
Needham—*Kilmorey*
Nelson—*Nelson of Stafford*
Neville—*Braybrooke*
Nicolson—*Carnock*
Nivison—*Glendyne*
Noel—*Gainsborough*
Noel Paton—*Ferrier**
North—*Guilford*
Northcote—*Iddesleigh*
Norton—*Grantley*
Norton—*Rathcreedan*
Nugent—*Nugent of Guildford**
Nugent—*Westmeath*
O'Brien—*Inchiquin*
O'Brien—*O'Brien of Lothbury**
Ogilvie Grant—*Seafield*
Ogilvy—*Airlie*
O'Neill—*O'Neill of the Maine**
O'Neill—*Rathcavan*
Orde Powlett—*Bolton*
Ormsby Gore—*Harlech*
Page—*Whaddon**
Paget—*Anglesey*
Paget—*Paget of Northampton**
Pakenham—*Lonford*
Pakington—*Hampton*
Palmer—*Lucas of Crudwell*
Palmer—*Selborne*
Parker—*Macclesfield*
Parker—*Morley*
Parnell—*Congleton*
Parsons—*Rosse*
Paulet—*Winchester*
Peake—*Ingleby*
Pearson—*Cowdray*
Pease—*Daryngton*
Pease—*Gainford*
Pease—*Wardington*
Pelham—*Chichester*
Pelham—*Yarborough*
Pelham Clinton Hope—*Newcastle*
Pellew—*Exmouth*
Penny—*Marchwood*
Pepys—*Cottenham*
Perceval—*Egmont*
Percy—*Northumberland*
Perry—*Perry of Walton**
Pery—*Limerick*
Petty Fitzmaurice—*Lansdowne*
Peyton—*Peyton of Yeovil**
Philipps—*Milford*
Philipps—*St. Davids*

Phipps—*Normanby*
Pitt—*Pitt of Hampstead**
Platt—*Platt of Writtle**
Pleydell Bouverie—*Radnor*
Plummer—*Plummer of St. Marylebone**
Plumptre—*Fitzwalter*
Pluckett—*Dunsany*
Plunkett—*Fingall*
Plunkett—*Louth*
Pollock—*Hanworth*
Pomeroy—*Harberton*
Ponsonby—*Bessborough*
Ponsonby—*De Mauley*
Ponsonby—*P. of Shulbrede*
Ponsonby—*Sysonby*
Portal—*Portal of Hungerford*
Powys—*Lilford*
Pratt—*Camden*
Preston—*Gormanston*
Primrose—*Rosebery*
Prittie—*Dunalley*
Ramsay—*Dalhousie*
Ramsey—*Ramsey of Canterbury**
Ramsbotham—*Soulbury*
Rawlinson—*Rawlinson of Ewell**
Rees Williams—*Ogmore*
Rhys—*Dynevor*
Richards—*Milverton*
Richardson—*Richardson of Duntisbourne**
Ritchie—*Ritchie of Dundee*
Robens—*Robens of Woldingham*
Roberts—*Clwyd*
Robertson—*Robertson of Oakridge*
Robinson—*Martonmere*
Robson—*Robson of Kiddington**
Roche—*Fermoy*
Rodd—*Rennell*
Roll—*Roll of Ipsden**
Roper Curzon—*Teynham*
Rospigliosi—*Newburgh*
Ross—*Ross of Marnock**
Rous—*Stradbroke*
Rowley Conwy—*Langford*
Royle—*Fanshawe of Richmond**
Runciman—*Runciman of Doxford*
Russell—*Ampthill*
Russell—*Bedford*
Russell—*De Clifford*
Russell—*Russell of Killowen*
Russell—*R. of Liverpool*
Ryder—*Harrowby*
Ryder—*Ryder of Eaton Hastings**
Sackville—*De La Warr*
Sackville West—*Sackville*
St. Aubyn—*St. Levan*
St. Clair—*Sinclair*
St. Clair Erskine—*Rosslyn*
St. John—*St. J. of Blesto*

* Life Peer created under Life Peerages Act, 1958

St. John—*Bolingbroke and St. John*
St. Leger—*Doneraile*
Samuel—*Bearsted*
Samuel—*Samuel of Wych Cross**
Sanderson—*Sanderson of Bowden**
Sandilands—*Torphichen*
Saumarez—*De Saumarez*
Savile—*Mexborough*
Scarlett—*Abinger*
Sclater Booth—*Basing*
Scott—*Eldon*
Scott Ellis—*Howard de Walden*
Scrymgeour Wedderburn—*Dundee*
Seager—*Leighton of St. Mellons*
Seely—*Mottistone*
Sefton—*Sefton of Garston**
Seymour—*Hertford*
Seymour—*Somerset*
Shaw—*Craigmyle*
Shaw—*Kilbrandon*
Shirley—*Ferrers*
Short—*Glenamara**
Siddeley—*Kenilworth*
Sidney—*De L'Isle*
Sieff—*Sieff of Brimpton**
Silkin—*Silkin of Dulwich**
Simon—*Simon of Glaisdale**
Simon—*Simon of Wythenshawe*
Sinclair—*Caithness*
Sinclair—*Sinclair of Cleeve*
Sinclair—*Thurso*
Skeffington—*Massereene*
Smith—*Bicester*
Smith—*Birkenhead*
Smith—*Colwyn*
Smith—*Hambleden*
Smith—*Kirkhill**
Somerset—*Beaufort*
Somerset—*Raglan*
Souter—*Audley*

Spencer—*Churchill*
Spencer Churchill—*Marlborough*
Spring Rice—*Monteagle of Brandon*
Stanhope—*Harrington*
Stanley—*Derby*
Stanley—*Sheffield*
Stapleton Cotton—*Combermere*
Stern—*Michelham*
Stewart—*Galloway*
Stewart—*Stewart of Fulham**
Stodart—*Stodart of Leaston**
Stoddart—*Stoddart of Swindon**
Stonor—*Camoys*
Stopford—*Courtown*
Stourton—*Mowbray*
Strachey—*O'Hagan*
Strutt—*Belper*
Strutt—*Rayleigh*
Stuart—*Castle Stewart*
Stuart—*Moray*
Stuart—*Stuart of Findhorn*
Suenson Taylor—*Grantchester*
Sugden—*St. Leonards*
Talbot—*T. of Malahide*
Taylor—*Taylor of Blackburn**
Taylor—*Taylor of Gryfe**
Taylor—*Taylor of Hadfield**
Taylor—*Taylor of Mansfield**
Taylour—*Headfort*
Temple Gore Langton—*Temple of Stowe*
Tennant—*Glenconner*
Thellusson—*Rendlesham*
Thesiger—*Chelmsford*
Thomas—*Thomas of Swynnerton**
Thomas—*Tonypandy*
Thomson—*Thomson of Fleet*

Thomson—*Thomson of Monifieth**
Thynne—*Bath*
Tottenham—*Ely*
Trefusis—*Clinton*
Trench—*Ashtown*
Trevor Roper—*Dacre of Glanton**
Tufton—*Hothfield*
Turner—*Netherthorpe*
Turner—*Turner of Camden**
Turnour—*Winterton*
Turton—*Tranmire**
Tyrell Kenyon—*Kenyon*
Vanden Bempde Johnstone—*Derwent*
Vane—*Barnard*
Vane Tempest Stewart—*Londonderry*
Vanneck—*Huntingfield*
Vaughan—*Lisburne*
Vaughan Morgan—*Reigate**
Vavasseur Fisher—*Fisher*
Vereker—*Gort*
Verney—*Willoughby de Broke*
Verney Cave—*Braye*
Vernon—*Lyveden*
Vesey—*De Vesci*
Villiers—*Clarendon*
Vintcent—*Wharton*
Vivian—*Swansea*
Walker-Smith—*Broxbourne**
Wallace—*Dudley (Barony)*
Wallace—*Wallace of Campsie**
Wallace—*Wallace of Coslany**
Wallop—*Portsmouth*
Ward—*Bangor*
Ward—*Dudley (Earldom)*
Ward—*Ward of Witley*
Warrender—*Bruntisfield*
Watson—*Manton*
Watson Armstrong—*Armstrong*

Wedderburn—*Wedderburn of Charlton**
Weir—*Inverforth*
Weld Forester—*Forester*
Wellesley—*Cowley*
Wellesley—*Wellington*
West—*Granville-West**
Westenra—*Rossmore*
White—*Annaly*
Whiteley—*Marchamley*
Whitfield—*Kenswood*
Willey—*Barnby*
Williams—*Berners*
Williams—*Williams of Elvel**
Williamson—*Forres*
Willoughby—*Middleton*
Wills—*Dulverton*
Wilson—*Moran*
Wilson—*Nunburnholme*
Wilson—*Wilson of Langside**
Wilson—*Wilson of Rievaulx**
Windsor—*Cornwall*
Windsor—*Gloucester*
Windsor—*Kent*
Windsor Clive—*Plymouth*
Wingfield—*Powerscourt*
Winn—*St. Oswald*
Winn—*Headley*
Wodehouse—*Kimberley*
Wood—*Halifax*
Wood—*Holderness**
Woodhouse—*Terrington*
Wright—*Wootton of Abinger**
Wyndham—*Leconfield*
Wyndham Quin—*Dunraven*
Wynn—*Newborough*
Yarde Buller—*Churston*
Yerburgh—*Alvingham*
Yorke—*Hardwicke*
Young—*Kennet*
Young—*Young of Dartington**
Young—*Young of Graffham**
Younger—*Y. of Leckie*

* Life Peer created under Life Peerages Act, 1958

COURTESY TITLES

Holders of Courtesy Titles are addressed in the same manner as holders of substantive titles.

From this list it will be seen that, for example, the "Marquess of Blandford" is heir to the Dukedom of Marlborough, and "Viscount Althorp" to the Earldom of Spencer. Titles of second heirs are also given, and the Courtesy Title of the father of a second heir is indicated by *; e.g., Earl of Burlington, eldest son of *Marquess of Hartington.

Marquesses

Blandford—*Marlborough*
Bowmont—*Roxburghe*
Douglas and Clydesdale—
  Hamilton
*Douro—*Wellington**
*Graham—*Montrose**
Granby—*Rutland*
Hamilton—*Abercorn*
*Hartington—*Devonshire**
*Kildare—*Leinster**
Lorne—*Argyll*
*Tavistock—*Bedford**
Worcester—*Beaufort*

Earls

*Aboyne—*Huntly**
Altamont—*Sligo*
Ancram—*Lothian*
Arundel and Surrey—
  Norfolk
Bective—*Headfort*
Belfast—*Donegall*
*Brecknock—*Camden**
*Burford—*St. Albans**
Burlington—**Hartington*
Cardigan—*Ailesbury*
Cassillis—*Ailsa*
Compton—*Northampton*
Dalkeith—*Buccleuch*
*Euston—*Grafton**
Haddo—*Aberdeen and*
  Temair
*Hopetoun—*Linlithgow**
Jermyn—*Bristol*
Macduff—*Fife*
*March and Kinrara—
  *Richmond**
*Mount Charles—
  *Conyngham**
Mornington—**Douro*
Mulgrave—*Normanby*
Offaly—**Kildare*
Percy—*Northumberland*
Rocksavage —
  Cholmondeley
*Ronaldshay—*Zetland**
St. Andrews—*Kent*
*Shelburne—*Lansdowne**
Tyrone—*Waterford*
Ulster—*Gloucester*
Uxbridge—*Anglesey*
Wiltshire—*Winchester*
Yarmouth—*Hertford*

Viscounts

Aithrie—**Hopetoun*
Althorp—*Spencer*

Andover—*Suffolk and*
  Berkshire
Anson—*Lichfield*
Asquith—*Oxford &*
  Asquith
Bayham—**Brecknock*
Boringdon—*Morley*
Borodale—*Beatty*
Boyle—*Shannon*
Brocas—*Jellicoe*
Calne and Calstone—
  *Shelburne
Campden—*Gainsborough*
Carlow—*Portarlington*
Castlereagh—
  Londonderry
Chelsea—*Cadogan*
Chewton—*Waldegrave*
Clanfield—*Peel*
Coke—*Leicester*
Cole—*Enniskillen*
Corvedale—*Baldwin of*
  Bewdley
Cranborne—*Salisbury*
Cranley—*Onslow*
Crichton—*Erne*
Crowhurst—*Cottenham*
Dalrymple—*Stair*
Dawick—*Haig*
Deerhurst—*Coventry*
Drumlanrig—
  Queensberry
Dupplin—*Kinnoull*
Ebrington—*Fortescue*
Ednam—*Dudley*
Elveden—*Iveagh*
Emlyn—*Cawdor*
Encombe—*Eldon*
Ennismore—*Listowel*
Enfield—*Strafford*
Errington—*Cromer*
Feilding—*Denbigh*
FitzClarence—*Munster*
FitzHarris—*Malmesbury*
Folkestone—*Radnor*
Garmoyle—*Cairns*
Garnock—*Lindsay*
Glandine—*Norbury*
Glenapp—*Inchcape*
Glentworth—*Limerick*
Grimston—*Verulam*
Gwynedd—*Lloyd George*
  of Dwyfor
Hawkesbury—*Liverpool*
Ikerrin—*Carrick*
Ingestre—*Shrewsbury*
Ipswich—**Euston*
Jocelyn—*Roden*
Kelburn—*Glasgow*
Kingsborough—*Kingston*

Knebworth—*Lytton*
Kynnaird—*Newburgh*
Lascelles—*Harewood*
Lewisham—*Dartmouth*
Linley—*Snowdon*
Loftus—*Ely*
Lowther—*Lonsdale*
Lumley—*Scarbrough*
Lymington—*Portsmouth*
Macmillan of Ovenden—
  Stockton
Maidstone — *Winchilsea*
  and Nottingham
Maitland—*Lauderdale*
Melgund—*Minto*
Merton—*Nelson*
Moore—*Drogheda*
Morpeth—*Carlisle*
Newport—*Bradford*
Newry and Mourne—
  Kilmorey
Parker—*Macclesfield*
Perceval—*Egmont*
Petersham—*Harrington*
Pollington—*Mexborough*
Prestwood—*Attlee*
Quenington—*St. Aldwyn*
Raynham—*Townshend*
Reidhaven—*Seafield*
Ruthven of Canberra and
  Dirleton—*Gowrie*
St. Cyres—*Iddesleigh*
Sandon—*Harrowby*
Slane—**Mount Charles*
Stormont—*Mansfield*
Strathallan—*Perth*
Stuart—*Castle Stewart*
Sudley—*Arran*
Suirdale—*Donoughmore*
Tamworth—*Ferrers*
Tarbat—*Cromartie*
Tiverton—*Halsbury*
Vaughan—*Lisburne*
Villiers—*Jersey*
Weymouth—*Bath*
Windsor—*Plymouth*
Wolmer—*Selborne*

Barons (Lord—)

Aberdour—*Morton*
Apsley—*Bathurst*
Ardee—*Meath*
Ashley—*Shaftesbury*
Balgonie—*Leven &*
  Melville
Berriedale—*Caithness*
Bingham—*Lucan*
Binning—*Haddington*
Brooke—*Warwick*

Bruce—*Elgin*
Buckhurst—*De La Warr*
Burghersh—
  Westmorland
Cardross—*Buchan*
Clifton—*Darnley*
Cochrane—*Dundonald*
Courtenay—*Devon*
Dalmeny—*Rosebery*
Delvin—*Westmeath*
Doune—*Moray*
Dundas—**Ronaldshay*
Eliot—*St. Germans*
Erskine—*Mar & Kellie*
Fintrie—**Graham*
Glamis—*Strathmore*
Greenock—*Cathcart*
Guernsey—*Aylesford*
Hay—*Erroll*
Herbert—*Pembroke*
Howland—**Tavistock*
Hyde—*Clarendon*
Inverurie—*Kintore*
Irwin—*Halifax*
Leslie—*Rothes*
Leveson—*Granville*
Mauchline—*Loudoun*
Medway—*Cranbrook*
Montgomerie—*Eglinton*
  and Winton
Moreton—*Ducie*
Naas—*Mayo*
Neidpath—*Wemyss &*
  March
Norreys—*Lindsey &*
  Abingdon
North—*Guilford*
Ogilvy—*Airlie*
Oxmantown—*Rosse*
Porchester—*Carnarvon*
Ramsay—*Dalhousie*
Romsey—*Mountbatten of*
  Burma
Rosehill—*Northesk*
Scrymgeour—*Dundee*
Settrington—**March*
  and Kinrara
Seymour—*Somerset*
Silchester—*Longford*
Strathavon and
  Glenlivet—**Aboyne*
Strathnaver—*Sutherland*
Vere of Hanworth—
  *Burford
Wodehouse—*Kimberley*
Worsley—*Yarborough*

THE PRIVY COUNCIL

Apart from Cabinet Ministers, who must be Privy Counsellors and are sworn in on first assuming office, membership of the Council (retained for life) is accorded by the Sovereign on the recommendation of the Prime Minister to eminent people in independent monarchical countries of the Commonwealth. Cabinet Ministers principally form the active Privy Council.

ORDERS OF CHIVALRY

The Most Noble Order of the Garter (1348)—K.G.

Ribbon, Garter Blue. *Motto*, Honi soit qui mal y pense (*Shame on him who thinks evil of it*).
The number of Knights Companions is limited to 24.

SOVEREIGN OF THE ORDER—THE QUEEN

Lady of the Garter—H.M. QUEEN ELIZABETH THE QUEEN MOTHER, 1936.
Extra Ladies of the Garter—H.M. JULIANA, QUEEN OF THE NETHERLANDS, 1958
H.M. THE QUEEN OF DENMARK, 1979

Royal Knights
H.R.H. the Duke of Edinburgh, 1947.
H.R.H. the Prince of Wales, 1958.

Extra Knights
H.M. the King of Norway, 1959.
H.M. the King of the Belgians, 1963.
H.I.M. the Emperor of Japan, 1971.
H.R.H. the Grand Duke of Luxemburg, 1972.
H.M. the King of Sweden, 1983

Knights Companions
The Duke of Northumberland, 1959.
The Viscount De L'Isle, 1968.

The Lord Ashburton, 1969.
The Lord Cobbold, 1970.
Sir Cennydd Traherne, 1970.
The Earl Waldegrave, 1971.
The Earl of Longford, 1971.
The Lord Rhodes, 1972.
The Earl of Drogheda, 1972.
The Lord Shackleton, 1974.
The Marquess of Abergavenny, 1974.
The Lord Wilson of Rievaulx, 1976.
The Duke of Grafton, 1976.
The Earl of Cromer, 1977.
The Lord Elworthy, 1977.
The Lord Hunt, 1979.
Sir Paul Hasluck, 1979.
Sir Richard Hull, 1980

The Duke of Norfolk, 1983
The Lord Lewin, 1983
The Lord Richardson of Duntisbourne, 1983
The Marquess of Normanby, 1985
The Lord Carrington, 1985
Prelate, The Bishop of Winchester.
Chancellor, The Marquess of Abergavenny, K.G., O.B.E.
Register, The Dean of Windsor.
Garter King of Arms, Lt.-Col. Sir Colin Cole, K.C.V.O., T.D.
Gentleman Usher of the Black Rod, Air Chief Marshal Sir John Gingell, G.B.E., K.C.B.
Secretary, Sir Walter Verco, K.C.V.O.

The Most Ancient and Most Noble Order of the Thistle—K.T.

Ribbon, Green. *Motto*, Nemo me impune lacessit (*No one provokes me with impunity*).
The number of Knights is limited to 16.

SOVEREIGN OF THE ORDER—THE QUEEN

Lady of the Thistle—H.M. QUEEN ELIZABETH THE QUEEN MOTHER, 1937

Royal Knights
H.R.H. the Duke of Edinburgh, 1952.
H.R.H. the Prince of Wales (*Duke of Rothesay*), 1977.

Extra Knight
H.M. the King of Norway, 1962.

Knights
The Earl of Haddington, 1951.
The Lord Home of the Hirsel, 1962.

The Earl of Wemyss and March, 1966.
The Lord Maclean, 1969.
The Earl of Dalhousie, 1971.
The Lord Clydesmuir, 1972.
The Viscount Muirshiel, 1973.
Sir Donald Cameron of Lochiel, 1973.
The Earl of Selkirk, 1976.
The Lord McFadzean, 1976.
The Hon. Lord Cameron, 1978.
The Duke of Buccleuch and Queensberry, 1978.
The Earl of Elgin and Kincardine, 1981.

The Lord Thomson of Monifieth, 1981.
The Lord MacLehose of Beoch, 1983.
Chancellor, The Lord Home of the Hirsel.
Dean, The Very Rev. Prof. J. McIntyre, M.A., B.D., D.Litt., D.D.
Secretary and Lord Lyon King of Arms, Malcolm R. Innes of Edingight, C.V.O., W.S.
Usher of the Green Rod, Rear-Admiral D.A. Dunbar-Nasmith, C.B., D.S.C.

The Most Honourable Order of the Bath (1725)

Ribbon, Crimson. *Motto*, Tria juncta in uno (*Three joined in one*). (Remodelled 1815, and enlarged many times since. The Order is divided into civil and military divisions.)

G.C.B. Mil. G.C.B. Civ. K.C.B. Mil. K.C.B. Civ. C.B. Mil.

THE SOVEREIGN; *Great Master and First or Principal Knight Grand Cross*, H.R.H. The Prince of Wales, K.G., K.T., G.C.B.; *Dean of the Order*, The Dean of Westminster; *Bath King of Arms*, Air Chief Marshal Sir David Evans, G.C.B., C.B.E.; *Registrar and Secretary*, Air Marshal Sir Denis Crowley-Milling, K.C.B., C.B.E., D.S.O., D.F.C.; *Genealogist*, Dr. C. Swan, M.V.O., PH.D.; *Gentleman Usher of the Scarlet Rod*, Rear-Admiral D. E. Macey, C.B.; *Deputy Secretary*, Maj.-Gen. D. H. G. Rice, C.V.O., C.B.E.; *Chancery*, Central Chancery of the Orders of Knighthood, St. James's Palace, S.W.1.—G.C.B., Knight (or Dame) Grand Cross; K.C.B., Knight Commander; D.C.B., Dame Commander; C.B., Companion. Women became eligible for the Order from Jan. 1, 1971.

The Order of Merit (1902)—O.M.
Ribbon, Blue and Crimson.

O.M.Mil.

This Order is designed as a special distinction for eminent men and women—without conferring a knighthood upon them. The Order is limited in numbers to 24, with the addition of foreign honorary members. Membership is of two kinds, Military and Civil, the badge of the former having crossed swords, and the latter oak leaves. Membership is denoted by the suffix o.M., which follows the first class of the Order of the Bath and precedes the letters designating membership of the inferior classes of the Bath and all classes of the lesser Orders of Knighthood.

O.M.Civ.

THE SOVEREIGN
H.R.H. THE DUKE OF EDINBURGH (1968)

Henry Spencer Moore, 1963.
Dorothy Hodgkin, 1965.
The Lord Zuckerman, 1968.
The Lord Penney, 1969.
Dame Veronica Wedgwood, 1969.
Sir Isaiah Berlin, 1971.
Sir George Edwards, 1971.

Sir Alan Hodgkin, 1973.
The Earl of Stockton, 1976.
Sir Ronald Syme, 1976.
The Lord Todd, 1977.
The Lord Franks, 1977.
Sir Frederick Ashton, 1977.
The Lord Olivier, 1981.

Sir Peter Medawar, 1981.
Gp. Capt. L. Cheshire, V.C., 1981.
Sir Andrew Huxley, 1983.
Sir Sidney Nolan, 1983.
Sir Michael Tippett, 1983.
Rev. Prof. Owen Chadwick, K.B.E., 1983.

Secretary and Registrar, Sir Edward Ford, K.C.B., K.C.V.O.
Chancery, Central Chancery of the Orders of Knighthood, St. James's Palace, S.W.1.

The Most Exalted Order of the Star of India (1861)

Ribbon, Light Blue, with White Edges. *Motto*, Heaven's Light our Guide.
THE SOVEREIGN; *Registrar*, Maj.-Gen. D. H. G. Rice, C.V.O., C.B.E.; G.C.S.I. Knight Grand
Commander; K.C.S.I., Knight Commander; C.S.I., Companion. No conferments since 1947.

G.C.S.I.

The Most Distinguished Order of St. Michael and St. George (1818)

Ribbon, Saxon Blue, with Scarlet centre. *Motto*, Auspicium melioris ævi (Token of a better age)
THE SOVEREIGN; *Grand Master*, H.R.H. The Duke of Kent, G.C.M.G., G.C.V.O.; *Prelate*, The Rt.
Rev. R. Woods, K.C.V.O.; *Chancellor*, The Lord Carrington, P.C., C.H., K.C.M.G., M.C.; *Secretary*, Sir
Antony Acland, K.C.M.G., K.C.V.O.; *Registrar*, Sir Charles Johnston, G.C.M.G.; *King of Arms*, The Lord
Saint Brides, P.C., G.C.M.G., C.V.O., M.B.E.; *Gentleman Usher of the Blue Rod*, Sir John Moreton,
K.C.M.G., K.C.V.O., M.C.; *Dean*, The Dean of St. Paul's; *Deputy Secretary*, Maj.-Gen. D. H. G. Rice, C.V.O.,
C.B.E. *Chancery*, Central Chancery of the Orders of Knighthood, St. James's Palace, S.W.1.—
G.C.M.G., Knight (or Dame) Grand Cross; K.C.M.G., Knight Commander; D.C.M.G., Dame
Commander; C.M.G., Companion.

The Most Eminent Order of the Indian Empire (1868)

Ribbon, Imperial Purple. *Motto*, Imperatricis auspiciis (*Under the auspices of the Empress*).
THE SOVEREIGN; *Registrar*, Maj.-Gen. D. H. G. Rice, C.V.O., C.B.E.; G.C.I.E., Knight Grand
Commander; K.C.I.E., Knight Commander; C.I.E., Companion. No conferments since 1947.

G.C.I.E.

The Royal Victorian Order (1896)

Ribbon, Blue, with Red and White Edges. *Motto*, Victoria.
THE SOVEREIGN; *Grand Master*, H.M. Queen Elizabeth the Queen Mother; *Chancellor*,
The Lord Chamberlain; *Secretary*, The Keeper of the Privy Purse; *Registrar*, The Secretary
of the Central Chancery of the Orders of Knighthood; *Chaplain*, The Rev. J. H. Williams.
Hon. Genealogist, Sir Walter Verco, K.C.V.O., G.C.V.O., Knight or Dame Grand Cross;
K.C.V.O., Knight Commander; D.C.V.O., Dame Commander; C.V.O., Commander; L.V.O.,
Lieutenant; M.V.O., Member.

The Royal Victorian Chain (1902)

Founded by King Edward VII, in 1902. It confers no precedence on its holders.
H.M. THE QUEEN
H.M. QUEEN ELIZABETH THE QUEEN MOTHER (1937).

H.M. Juliana, Queen of the Nether-
lands (1950).
H.M. the King of Norway (1955).
H.M. the King of Thailand (1960).
H.I.H. the Crown Prince of Ethiopia
(1965).
H.M. the King of Jordan (1966).

H.M. King Zahir Shah of Afghani-
stan (1971).
Rt. Hon. Roland Michener (1973).
H.M. the Queen of Denmark (1974).
The Right Rev. the Lord Ramsey of
Canterbury (1974).
H.M. the King of Nepal (1975).
H.M. the King of Sweden (1975).

The Right Rev. the Lord Coggan
(1980).
Ratu Sir George Cakobau (1982).
H.M. Queen Beatrix of the Nether-
lands (1982).
The Lord Maclean (1984).
General Antonio Eanes (1985).

The Most Excellent Order of the British Empire (1917)

Ribbon, Rose pink edged with pearl grey with vertical pearl stripe in centre (Military Division); without vertical pearl stripe (Civil Division). *Motto*, For God and the Empire.

G.B.E.   K.B.E.

THE SOVEREIGN: *Grand Master*, H.R.H. the Prince Philip, Duke of Edinburgh, K.G., P.C., K.T., O.M., G.B.E.; *Prelate*, The Bishop of London; *King of Arms*, Admiral Sir Anthony Morton, G.B.E., K.C.B.; *Registrar*, Maj.-Gen. D. H. G. Rice, C.V.O., C.B.E.; *Secretary*, Sir Robert Armstrong, G.C.B., C.V.O.; *Dean*, The Dean of St. Paul's; *Gentleman Usher of the Purple Rod*, Sir Robin Gillett, G.B.E.; *Chancery*, Central Chancery of the Orders of Knighthood, St. James's Palace, S.W.1. G.B.E., Knight or Dame Grand Cross; K.B.E. Knight Commander; D.B.E., Dame Commander; C.B.E., Commander; O.B.E., Officer; M.B.E., Member. The Order was divided into *Military* and *Civil* divisions in Dec. 1918.

Order of the Companions of Honour (June 4, 1917)—C.H.

Ribbon, Carmine, with Gold Edges.

This Order consists of one Class only and carries with it no title. It ranks after the 1st Class of the Order of the British Empire, *i.e.*, Knights and Dames Grand Cross (Mil. and Civ. Div.). The number of awards is limited to 65 (excluding honorary members) and the Order is open to both sexes. *Secretary and Registrar*, The Secretary of the Central Chancery of the Orders of Knighthood.

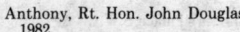

Anthony, Rt. Hon. John Douglas, 1982.
Ashley, Rt. Hon. Jack, 1975.
Ashton, Sir Frederick, 1970.
Aylestone, The Lord, 1975.
Carrington, The Lord, 1983.
Casson, Sir Hugh, 1985.
Cecil, Lord David Gascoyne, 1949.
Cledwyn of Penrhos, The Lord, 1977.
de Valois, Dame Ninette, 1982.
Duncan-Sandys, The Lord, 1973.
Eccles, The Viscount, 1984.
Elwyn-Jones, The Lord, 1976.
Fraser, Rt. Hon. Malcolm, 1977.
Freud, Lucian, 1983.
Gardiner, The Lord, 1975.
Gielgud, Sir John, 1977.
Glenamara, The Lord, 1976.
Goodman, The Lord, 1972.
Gorton, Rt. Hon. Sir John Grey, 1971.
Greene, Graham, 1966.

Hailsham of St. Marylebone, The Lord, 1974.
von Hayek, *Prof.* Friedrich, 1984.
Healey, Rt. Hon. Denis, 1979.
Houghton of Sowerby, The Lord, 1967.
Jones, James Larkin, 1978.
Larkin, Philip Arthur, 1985.
McMahon, Rt. Hon. Sir William, 1972.
Marshall, Rt. Hon. Sir John Ross, 1973.
Medawar, Sir Peter, 1972.
Moore, Henry Spencer, 1955.
Muirshiel, The Viscount, 1962.
Muldoon, Rt. Hon. Sir Robert, 1977.
Pasmore, Victor, 1981.
Perutz, *Prof.* Max Ferdinand, 1975.
Piper, John Egerton Christmas, 1972.
Popper, *Prof.* Sir Karl, 1982.
Porter, *Prof.* Rodney Robert, 1985.
Powell, Sir Philip, 1984.

Rahman, Tunku Abdul, 1960.
Runciman, *Hon.* Sir Steven, 1984.
Sanger, Frederick, 1981.
Shinwell, The Lord, 1965.
Sitwell, Sir Sacheverell, Bt., 1984.
Smith, Arnold Cantwell, 1975.
Soames, The Lord, 1980.
Somare, Rt. Hon. Michael Thomas, 1978.
Stewart of Fulham, The Lord, 1969.
Talboys, Rt. Hon. Brian Edward, 1981.
Thorneycroft, The Lord, 1980
Tippett, Sir Michael, 1979.
Trudeau, Rt. Hon. Pierre Elliot, 1984.
Watkinson, The Viscount, 1962.
Whitelaw, The Viscount, 1974.
Wootton of Abinger, The Baroness, 1977.
Honorary Members, M. René Massigli, 1954; Lee Kuan Yew, 1970; Dr. Joseph Luns, 1971.

The Royal Victoria and Albert (for Ladies)—V.A.

Instituted in 1862, and enlarged in 1864, 1865, and 1880. Badge, a medallion of Queen Victoria and the Prince Consort, surmounted by a crown, which was attached to a bow of white moiré ribbon. The honour did not confer any rank or title upon the recipient. The last holder of the honour, H.R.H. the Princess Alice, Countess of Athlone, died in 1981.

The Imperial Order of the Crown of India (for Ladies)—C.I.

Instituted Dec. 31, 1877. Badge, the royal cipher in jewels within an oval, surmounted by an Heraldic Crown and attached to a bow of light blue watered ribbon, edged white. The honour does not confer any rank or title upon the recipient. No conferments have been made since 1947.

H.M. THE QUEEN, 1947.
H.M. Queen Elizabeth the Queen Mother, 1931.

H.R.H. the Princess Margaret, Countess of Snowdon, 1947.
H.R.H. the Princess Alice, Duchess of Gloucester, 1937.

H.H. Maharani of Travancore, 1929.
Eugenie Marie, Countess Wavell, 1943.

The Imperial Service Order (1902)—I.S.O.

Ribbon, Crimson, with Blue Centre.

Appointment of Companion of this Order shall be open to those members of the Civil Services whose eligibility shall be determined by the grade held by such persons. The Order consists of The SOVEREIGN and Companions (not exclusively male) to a number not exceeding 1,700 of whom 1,100 may belong to the Home Civil Services and 600 to Overseas Civil Services. *Secretary*, Sir Robert Armstrong, G.C.B., C.V.O. *Registrar*, Maj.-Gen. D. H. G. Rice, C.V.O., C.B.E., St. James's Palace, S.W.1.

BARONETS, KNIGHTS GRAND CROSS, KNIGHTS GRAND COMMANDERS, KNIGHTS COMMANDERS AND KNIGHTS BACHELOR

Badge of Baronets
of England, Great Britain, U.K.,
(and Ireland marked I.).

Badge of Baronets
of Scotland or Nova Scotia
(marked S. or N.S.).

NOTES CONCERNING BARONETS

Clause II. of the Royal Warrant of February 8, 1910, ordains as follows:—"That no person whose name is not entered upon the Official Roll shall be received as a Baronet, or shall be addressed or mentioned by that title in any Civil or Military Commission, Letters Patent or other official document." When an obelisk (†) precedes a name it indicates that, *at the time of going to press*, the Baronet concerned has not been registered on the Official Roll of the Baronetage. The date of creation of the Baronetcy is given in parenthesis ( ).

Baronets are addressed as "Sir" (with Christian name) and in writing as "Sir Robert A—, Bt." Baronet's wives are addressed (formally) as "Your Ladyship" or "Lady A—," without any Christian name unless a daughter of a Duke, Marquess or Earl, in which case "The Lady Mary A—"; if daughter of a Viscount or Baron "The Hon. Lady A—."

NOTES CONCERNING KNIGHTS GRAND CROSS, ETC.

Knights Grand Cross, Knights Grand Commanders and Knights Commanders are addressed in the same manner as Baronets (*q.v.*), but in writing the appropriate initials (G.C.B., K.C.B., &c.) are appended to surname after "Bt." if they are also baronets or in place of "Bt." if they are not. Knights Bachelor are addressed as "Sir —— (first or Christian name)" and in writing as "Sir —— B —." The wife of a Knight Grand Cross, Knight Grand Commander, Knight Commander or Knight Bachelor is addressed as stated for the wife of a Baronet.

NOTES CONCERNING KNIGHTS BACHELOR

The Knights Bachelor do not constitute a Royal Order, but comprise the surviving representation of the ancient State Orders of Knighthood. The Register of Knights Bachelor, instituted by James I in the 17th century, lapsed, and in 1908 a voluntary Association was formed under the title of "The Society of Knights" (now "The Imperial Society of Knights Bachelor" by Royal command) with the primary objects of continuing the various registers dating from 1257 and obtaining the uniform registration of every created Knight Bachelor. In 1926 a design for a badge to be worn by Knights Bachelor was approved and adopted, a miniature reproduction being shown above; in 1974 a neck badge and miniature were added. The Officers of the Society are:—*Knight Principal,* Sir Colin Cole, K.C.V.O., T.D.; *Deputy Knight Principal,* Sir Gilbert Inglefield, G.B.E., T.D.; *Prelate,* Rt. Rev. and Rt. Hon. G. D. Leonard, D.D.; *Hon. Registrar,* Sir Arthur Driver; *Hon. Treasurer,* Sir John Howard; *Clerk to the Council,* R. M. Esden; Office, 21 Old Buildings, Lincoln's Inn, WC2A 3UJ.

BARONETAGE AND KNIGHTAGE
(Revised to Aug. 31, 1985)
Peers are not included in this list

A full entry in italic type indicates that the recipient of a Knighthood died during the year in which the honour was conferred. The name is included for purposes of record.

Aarvold, *His Hon.* Sir Carl Douglas, Kt., O.B.E., T.D.

Abal, Sir Tei, Kt., C.B.E.

Abbott, Sir Albert Francis, Kt., C.B.E.

Abdy, Sir Valentine Robert Duff, Bt. (1850).

Abel, Sir Seselo (Cecil) Charles Geoffrey, Kt., O.B.E.

Abeles, Sir (Emil Herbert) Peter, Kt.

Abell, Sir Anthony Foster, K.C.M.G.

Abell, Sir George Edmond Brackenbury, K.C.I.E., O.B.E.

Abercromby, Sir Ian George, Bt. (s. 1636).

Abraham, Sir Edward Penley, Kt., C.B.E., F.R.S.

Ackner, *Rt. Hon.* Sir Desmond James Conrad, Kt.

Ackroyd, Sir John Robert Whyte, Bt. (1956).

Acland, Sir Antony Arthur, K.C.M.G., K.C.V.O.

Acland, *Maj.* Sir Christopher Guy Dyke, Bt. (1890).

Acland, *Maj.-Gen.* Sir John Hugh Bevil, K.C.B., C.B.E.

Acland, Sir Richard Thomas Dyke, Bt. (1644).

Acton, Sir Harold Mario Mitchell, Kt., C.B.E.

Acutt, Sir Keith Courtney, K.B.E.

Adair, *Maj.-Gen.* Sir Allan Henry Shafto, Bt., G.C.V.O., C.B., D.S.O., M.C. (1838).

Adam, *Hon.* Sir Alistair Duncan Grant, Kt.

Adam, Sir Christopher Eric Forbes, Bt. (1917).

Adams, Sir Philip George Doyne, K.C.M.G.

Adams-Schneider, *Rt. Hon.* Sir Lancelot Raymond, K.C.M.G.

Adamson, Sir (William Owen) Campbell, Kt.

Adcock, Sir Robert Henry, Kt., C.B.E.

Addison, Sir William Wilkinson, Kt.

Ademola, *Rt. Hon.* Sir Adetokunbo Adegboyega, K.B.E.

Adrien, *Hon.* Sir Maurice Latour-, Kt.

Agnew, Sir Crispin Hamlyn, Bt. (s. 1629).

Agnew, Sir Geoffrey William Gerald, Kt.

Agnew, Sir (John) Anthony Stuart, Bt. (1895).

Agnew, *Cdr.* Sir Peter Garnett, Bt. (1957).

Agnew, Sir Robert David Garrick, Kt., C.B.E.

Agnew, Sir (William) Godfrey, K.C.V.O., C.B.

Ah-Chuen, Sir Moi Lin Jean Etienne, Kt.

Aiken, *Air Chief Marshal* Sir John Alexander Carlisle, K.C.B.

Ainley, Sir (Alfred) John, Kt., M.C.

Ainsworth, Sir (Thomas) David, Bt. (1916).

Aird, *Capt.* Sir Alastair Sturgis, K.C.V.O.

Aird, Sir (George) John, Bt. (1901).

Airey, Sir Lawrence, K.C.B.

Aisher, Sir Owen Arthur, Kt.

Aitchison, Sir Charles Walter de Lancey, Bt. (1938).

Aitken, Sir Robert Stevenson, Kt., M.D., D.Phil.

Akehurst, *Lt.-Gen.* Sir John Bryan, K.C.B., C.B.E.

Akers-Jones, Sir David, K.B.E., C.M.G.

Albert, Sir Alexis François, Kt., C.M.G., V.R.D.

Albery, Sir Donald Arthur Rolleston, Kt.

Albu, Sir George, Bt. (1912).

Aldington, Sir Geoffrey William, K.B.E., C.M.G.

Alexander, Sir Alexander Sandor, Kt.

Alexander, Sir Charles Gundry, Bt. (1945).

Alexander, Sir Claud Hagart-, Bt. (1886).

Alexander, *Hon.* Sir Darnley Arthur Raymond, Kt., C.B.E.

Alexander, Sir Desmond William Lionel Cable, Bt. (1809).

Alexander, Sir Douglas Hamilton, Bt. (1921).

Alexander, Sir (John) Lindsay, Kt.

Alexander, *Prof.* Sir Kenneth John Wilson, Kt.

Alexander, Sir Norman Stanley, Kt., C.B.E.

Allan, Sir Anthony James Allan Havelock-, Bt. (1858).

Allan, Sir Colin Hamilton, K.C.M.G., O.B.E.

Allard, Sir Gordon Laidlaw, Kt.

Allcroft, Sir Philip Magnus-, Bt., C.B.E. (1917).

Allen, *Prof.* Sir Geoffrey, Kt., Ph.D., F.R.S.

Allen, Sir Peter Christopher, Kt.

Allen, Sir Richard Hugh Sedley, K.C.M.G.

Allen, Sir (William) Denis, G.C.M.G., C.B.

Allen, Sir William Guilford, Kt.

Allen, Sir (William) Kenneth Gwynne, Kt.

Alleyne, *Rev.* John Olpherts Campbell, Bt., (1769).

Allinson, Sir (Walter) Leonard, K.C.V.O., C.M.G.

Alment, Sir (Edward) Anthony John, Kt.

Anderson, *Prof.* Sir (James) Norman (Dalrymple), Kt., O.B.E., Q.C., F.B.A.

Anderson, *General* Sir John D'Arcy, G.B.E., K.C.B., D.S.O.

Anderson, *Maj.-Gen.* Sir John Evelyn, K.B.E.

Anderson, Sir John Muir, Kt., C.M.G.

Anderson, Sir Kenneth, K.B.E., C.B.

Anderson, *Hon.* Sir Kenneth McColl, K.B.E.

Anderson, *Hon.* Sir Kevin Victor, Kt.

Anderson, *Vice-Adm.* Sir Neil Dudley, K.B.E., C.B.

Anderson, *Prof.* Sir (William) Ferguson, Kt., O.B.E.

Andrewes, Sir Christopher Howard, Kt., M.D., F.R.S.

Andrews, *Rt. Hon.* Sir John Lawson Ormrod, K.B.E.

Annamunthodo, *Prof.* Sir Harry, Kt., F.R.C.S.

Ansell, *Col.* Sir Michael Picton Kt., C.B.E., D.S.O.

Anson, *Vice-Adm.* Sir Edward Rosebery, K.C.B.

Anson, *Rear-Admiral* Sir Peter, Bt., C.B. (1831).

Anstey, *Brig.* Sir John, Kt., C.B.E., T.D.

Anstruther, Sir Ralph Hugo, Bt. K.C.V.O., M.C. (s. 1694).

Anthony, Sir (Michael) Mobolaji Bank-, K.B.E.

Antico, Sir Tristan Venus, Kt.

Antrobus, Sir Philip Coutts, Bt. (1815).

Arbuthnot, Sir John Sinclair-Wemyss, Bt., M.B.E., T.D. (1964).

Arbuthnot, Sir Keith Robert Charles, Bt. (1823).

Archdale, *Comdr.* Sir Edward Folmer, Bt., D.S.C., R.N. (1928).

Archer, *General* Sir (Arthur) John, K.C.B., O.B.E.

Archer, Sir Clyde Vernon Harcourt, Kt.

Arculus, Sir Ronald, K.C.M.G., K.C.V.O.

Armitage, *Air Marshal* Sir Michael John, K.C.B., C.B.E.

Armitage, Sir Robert Perceval, K.C.M.G., M.B.E.

Armstrong, Sir Andrew St. Clare, Bt. (1841).

Armstrong, Sir Robert Temple, G.C.B., C.V.O.

Armstrong, Sir Thomas Henry Wait, Kt., D.MUS.

Armytage, Sir John Martin, Bt. (1738).

Arnold, *Rt. Hon.* Sir John Lewis, Kt.

Arnott, Sir Alexander John Maxwell, Bt. (1896).

Arnott, *Prof.* Sir (William) Melville, Kt., T.D., M.D.

Arrindell, Sir Clement Athelston, G.C.M.G.

Arrowsmith, Sir Edwin Porter, K.C.M.G.

Arthur, Sir Stephen John, Bt. (1841).

Arthur, *Lt.-Gen.* Sir (John) Norman Stewart, K.C.B.

Arundell, *Brig.* Sir Robert Duncan Harris, K.C.M.G., O.B.E.

Arup, Sir Ove Nyquist, Kt., C.B.E.

Ashburnham, Sir Denny Reginald, Bt. (1661).

Ashe, Sir Derick Rosslyn, K.C.M.G.

Ashenheim, Sir Neville Noel, Kt., C.B.E.

Ashmore, *Admiral of the Fleet* Sir Edward Beckwith, G.C.B., D.S.C.

Ashmore, *Vice-Adm.* Sir Peter William Beckwith, K.C.B., K.C.V.O., D.S.C.

Ashton, Sir Frederick William Mallandaine, Kt., O.M., C.H., C.B.E.

Ashworth, Sir Herbert, Kt.

Aske, *Rev.* Sir Conan, Bt. (1922).

Astbury, Sir George, Kt.

Astley, Sir Francis Jacob Dugdale, Bt. (1821).

Aston, Sir Harold George, Kt., C.B.E.

Aston, *Hon.* Sir William John, K.C.M.G.

Astor, *Hon.* Sir John Jacob, Kt., M.B.E.

Astwood, *Hon.* Sir James Rufus, Kt.

Astwood, *Lt.-Col.* Sir Jeffrey Carlton, Kt., C.B.E., E.D.

Atcherley, Sir Harold Winter, Kt.

Atiyah, Sir Michael Francis, Kt., Ph.D., F.R.S.

Atkins, *Rt. Hon.* Sir Humphrey Edward Gregory, K.C.M.G., M.P.

Atkins, Sir William Sydney Albert, Kt., C.B.E.

Atkinson, *Air Marshal* Sir David William, K.B.E., Q.H.P.

Atkinson, Sir Frederick John, K.C.B.

Atkinson, Sir John Alexander, K.C.B., D.F.C.

Atkinson, Sir (John) Kenneth, Kt.

Atkinson, *Maj.-Gen.* Sir Leonard Henry, K.B.E.

Atkinson, Sir Robert, Kt., D.S.C.

Attenborough, Sir David Frederick, Kt., C.B.E., F.R.S.

Attenborough, Sir Richard Samuel, Kt., C.B.E.

Atwell, Sir John William, Kt., C.B.E., F.R.S.E.

Atwill, Sir (Milton) John (Napier), Kt.

Audley, Sir George Bernard, Kt.

Austin, Sir William Ronald, Bt. (1894).

Austin, *Vice-Admiral* Sir Peter Murray, K.C.B.

Auswild, Sir James Frederick John, Kt., C.B.E.

Ayer, *Prof.* Sir Alfred Jules, Kt., F.B.A.

Aykroyd, Sir Cecil William, Bt. (1929).

Aykroyd, Sir William Miles, Bt., M.C. (1920).

Aylmer, Sir Fenton Gerald, Bt. (I 1622).

Backhouse, Sir Jonathan Roger, Bt. (1901).

Bacon, Sir Nicholas Hickman Ponsonby, Bt. *Premier Baronet of England* (1611 and 1627).

Bacon, Sir Ranulph Robert Maunsell, Kt.

Bacon, Sir Sidney Charles, Kt., C.B.

Baddeley, Sir John Wolsey Beresford, Bt. (1922).

Baddiley, *Prof.* Sir James, Kt., Ph.D., D.SC., F.R.S., F.R.S.E.

Badenoch, Sir John, Kt., D.M., F.R.C.P.

Badger, Sir Geoffrey Malcolm, Kt.

Bagge, Sir John Alfred Picton, Bt. (1867).

Bagnall, *Gen.* Sir Nigel Thomas, G.C.B., C.V.O., M.C.

Bailey, Sir Brian Harry, Kt., O.B.E.

Bailey, Sir Derrick Thomas Louis, Bt., D.F.C. (1919).

Bailey, *Prof.* Sir Harold Walter, Kt., D.Phil., F.B.A.

Bailey, Sir Richard John, Kt., C.B.E.

Baillie, Sir Gawaine George Hope, Bt. (1823).

Baines, *Prof.* Sir George Grenfell-, Kt., O.B.E.

Baird, Sir David Charles, Bt. (1809).

Baird, *Prof.* Sir Dugald, Kt., M.D.

Baird, *Lt.-Gen.* Sir James Parlane, K.B.E., M.D.

Baird, Sir James Richard Gardiner, Bt., M.C. (s. 1695).

Baird, *Vice-Adm.* Sir Thomas Henry Eustace, K.C.B.

Bairsto, *Air Marshal* Sir Peter Edward, K.B.E., C.B.

Baker, Sir (Allan) Ivor, Kt., C.B.E.

Baker, Sir Humphrey Dodington Benedict Sherston-, Bt. (1796).

Baker, Sir (Stanislaus) Joseph, Kt., C.B.

Balcombe, *Rt. Hon.* Sir (Alfred) John, Kt.

Balderstone, Sir James Schofield, Kt.

Baldwin, Sir Peter Robert, K.C.B.

Balfour, *General* Sir (Robert George) Victor FitzGeorge-, K.C.B., C.B.E., D.S.O., M.C.

Ball, *Air Marshal* Sir Alfred Henry Wynne, K.C.B., D.S.O., D.F.C.

Ball, Sir Charles Irwin, Bt. (1911).

Ball, *Prof.* Sir Robert James, Kt., Ph.D.

Balmer, Sir Joseph Reginald, Kt.

Banks, Sir Maurice Alfred Lister, Kt.

Banner, Sir George Knowles Harmood-, Bt. (1924).

Bannerman, *Lt.-Col.* Sir Donald Arthur Gordon, Bt. (s. 1682).

Bannister, Sir Roger Gilbert, Kt., C.B.E., D.M., F.R.C.P.

Barber, Sir Derek Coates, Kt.

Barber, *Hon.* Sir (Edward Hamilton) Esler, Kt.

Barber, Sir William Francis, Bt., T.D. (1960).

Barclay, Sir Colville Herbert Sanford, Bt. (s. 1668).

Barclay, Sir Roderick Edward, G.C.V.O., K.C.M.G.

Barford, Sir Leonard, Kt.

Baring, Sir Charles Christian, Bt. (1911).

Baring, *Hon.* Sir John Francis Harcourt, Kt., C.V.O.

Baring, Sir Mark, K.C.V.O.

Barker, Sir Alwyn Bowman, Kt., C.M.G.

Barker, Sir Harry Heaton, Kt., K.B.E.

Barker, Sir William, K.C.M.G., O.B.E.

Barlow, Sir Christopher Hilaro, Bt. (1803).

Barlow, Sir (George) William, Kt.

Barlow, Sir John Denman, Bt. (1907).

Barlow, Sir Thomas Erasmus, Bt., D.S.C. (1902).

Barnard, Sir (Arthur) Thomas, Kt., C.B., O.B.E.

Barnard, *Capt.* Sir George Edward, Kt.

Barnes, Sir Denis Charles, K.C.B.

Barnes, Sir (Ernest) John (Ward), K.C.M.G., M.B.E.

Barnes, Sir James George, Kt., M.B.E.

Barnes, Sir Kenneth, K.C.B.

Barnes, Sir William Lethbridge Gorell-, K.C.M.G., C.B.

Barnett, *Air Chief Marshal* Sir Denis Hensley Fulton, G.C.B., C.B.E., D.F.C.

Barnett, Sir Oliver Charles, Kt., C.B.E., Q.C.

Barnewall, Sir Reginald Robert, Bt. (I 1623).

Barraclough, *Air Chief Marshal* Sir John, K.C.B., C.B.E., D.F.C., A.F.C.

Barraclough, Sir Kenneth James Priestley, Kt., C.B.E., T.D.

Barran, Sir David Haven, Kt.

Barran, Sir John Napoleon Ruthven, Bt. (1895).

Barratt, Sir Lawrence Arthur, Kt.

Barrett, *Lt.-Gen.* Sir David William Scott-, K.B.E., M.C.

Barrett, *Lt.-Col.* Sir Dennis Charles Titchener, Kt., T.D.

Barrie, Sir Walter, Kt.

Barrington, Sir Alexander (Fitzwilliam Croker), Bt. (1831).

Barrington, Sir Kenneth Charles Peto, Kt.

Barritt, Sir David Thurlow, Kt.

Barron, Sir Donald James, Kt.

Barrow, *Capt.* Sir Richard John Uniacke, Bt. (1835).

Barry, Sir (Lawrence) Edward (Anthony Tress), Bt. (1899).

Barry, Sir (Philip) Stuart Milner-, K.C.V.O., C.B., O.B.E.

Bartlett, Sir Henry David Hardington, Bt., M.B.E. (1913).

Barton, Sir Charles Newton, Kt., O.B.E., E.D.

Barton, *Prof.* Sir Derek Harold Richard, Kt., F.R.S., F.R.S.E.

Barttelot, *Lt.-Col.* Sir Brian Walter de Stopham, Bt., O.B.E. (1875).

Barwick, *Rt. Hon.* Sir Garfield Edward John, G.C.M.G.

Basten, Sir Henry Bolton, Kt., C.M.G.

Batchelor, Sir Ivor Ralph Campbell, Kt., C.B.E.

Bate, Sir David Lindsay, K.B.E.

Bate, Sir (Walter) Edwin, Kt., O.B.E.

Bateman, Sir Cecil Joseph, K.B.E.

Bateman, Sir Charles Harold, K.C.M.G., M.C.

Bateman, Sir Geoffrey Hirst, Kt., F.R.C.S.

Bateman, Sir Ralph Melton, K.B.E.

Bates, *Prof.* Sir David Robert, Kt., D.S.C., F.R.S.

Bates, *Maj.-Gen.* Sir (Edward) John (Hunter), K.B.E., C.B., M.C.

Bates, Sir Geoffrey Voltelin, Bt., M.C. (1880).

Bates, Sir John David, Kt., C.B.E., V.R.D.

Bates, Sir (John) Dawson, Bt., M.C. (1937).

Bates, Sir (Julian) Darrell, Kt., C.M.G., C.V.O.

Batho, Sir Maurice Benjamin, Bt. (1928).

Bathurst, Sir Frederick Peter Methuen Hervey-, Bt. (1818).

Bathurst, Sir Maurice Edward, Kt., C.M.G., C.B.E., Q.C.

Batsford, Sir Brian Caldwell Cook, Kt.

Batty, Sir William Bradshaw, Kt., T.D.

Baxendell, Sir Peter Brian, Kt., C.B.E.

Baxter, *Prof.* Sir (John) Philip, K.B.E., C.M.G.

Bayliss, *Prof.* Sir Noel Stanley, Kt., C.B.E.

Bayliss, Sir Richard Ian Samuel, K.C.V.O., M.D., F.R.C.P.

Bayly, *Vice-Adm.* Sir Patrick Uniacke, K.B.E., C.B., D.S.C.

Baynes, Sir John Christopher Malcolm, Bt. (1801).

Bazley, Sir Thomas Stafford, Bt. (1869).

Beach, *General* Sir (William Gerald) Hugh, G.B.E., K.C.B., M.C.

Beale, Sir William Francis, Kt., O.B.E.

Beament, Sir James William Longman, Kt., SC.D., F.R.S.

Beattie, *Hon.* Sir Alexander Craig, Kt.

Beattie, *Hon.* Sir David Stuart, G.C.M.G., G.C.V.O.

Beauchamp, Sir Christopher Radstock Proctor-, Bt. (1745).

Beaumont, Sir George (Howland Francis), Bt. (1661).

Beaumont, Sir Richard Ashton, K.C.M.G., O.B.E.

Beavis, *Air Chief Marshal* Sir Michael Gordon, K.C.B., C.B.E., A.F.C.

Becher, Sir William Fane Wrixon, Bt., M.C. (1831).

Beck, Sir Edgar Charles, Kt., C.B.E.

Beckett, *Capt.* Sir (Martyn) Gervase, Bt., M.C. (1921).

Beckett, Sir Terence Norman, Kt., C.B.E.

Bedbrook, Sir George Montario, Kt., O.B.E.

Bedingfeld, *Capt.* Sir Edmund George Felix Paston-, Bt. (1661).

Beecham, John Stratford Roland, Bt. (1914).

Beeck, Sir Marcus Truby, Kt.

Beeley, Sir Harold, K.C.M.G., C.B.E.

Beetham, *Marshal of the Royal Air Force* Sir Michael James, G.C.B., C.B.E., D.F.C., A.F.C.

Beevor, Sir Thomas Agnew, Bt. (1784).

Begg, *Admiral of the Fleet* Sir Varyl Cargill, G.C.B., D.S.O., D.S.C.

Beit, Sir Alfred Lane, Bt. (1924).

Beith, Sir John Greville Stanley, K.C.M.G.

Beldam, *Hon.* Sir (Alexander) Roy (Asplan), Kt., Q.C.

Bell, Sir Charles William, Kt., C.B.E.

Bell, Sir Gawain Westray, K.C.M.G., C.B.E.

Bell, Sir (George) Raymond, K.C.M.G., C.B.

Bell, Sir John Lowthian, Bt. (1885).

Bell, Sir (William) Ewart, K.C.B.

Bell, Sir William Hollin Dayrell Morrison-, Bt. (1905).

Bellew, *Hon.* Sir George Rothe, K.C.B., K.C.V.O., F.S.A.

Bellew, Sir Henry Charles Gratton-, Bt. (1838).

Bellinger, Sir Robert Ian, G.B.E.

Bellingham, Sir Noel Peter Roger, Bt. (1796).

Bowman-Shaw, Sir (George) Neville, Kt.

Bowmar, Sir Charles Erskine, Kt.

Boxer, *Air Vice-Marshal* Sir Alan Hunter Cachemaille, K.C.V.O., C.B., D.S.O., D.F.C.

Boyce, Sir Robert Charles Leslie, Bt. (1952).

Boyd, Sir Alexander Walter, Bt. (1916).

Boyd, Sir John McFarlane, Kt., C.B.E.

Boyd, *Prof.* Sir Robert Lewis Fullarton, Kt., C.B.E., D.SC., F.R.S.

Boyes, Sir Brian Gerald Barratt-, K.B.E.

Boyle, *Marshal of the Royal Air Force* Sir Dermot Alexander, G.C.B., K.C.V.O., K.B.E., A.F.C.

Boyle, Sir Lawrence, Kt., PH.D.

Boyle, Sir Stephen Gurney, Bt. (1904).

Boyne, Sir Henry Brian, Kt., C.B.E.

Boynton, Sir John Keyworth, Kt., M.C.

Brabham, Sir John Arthur, Kt., O.B.E.

Bradbury, *Surgeon Vice-Adm.* Sir Eric Blackburn, K.B.E., C.B.

Bradford, Sir Edward Alexander Slade, Bt. (1902).

Bradlaw, *Prof.* Sir Robert Vivian, Kt., C.B.E.

Bradman, Sir Donald George, Kt.

Bradshaw, *Lt.-Gen.* Sir Richard Phillip, K.B.E.

Brain, Sir (Henry) Norman, K.B.E., C.M.G.

Braine, *Rt. Hon.* Sir Bernard Richard, Kt., M.P..

Braithwaite, Sir (Joseph) Franklin Madders, Kt.

Bramall, *Field Marshal* Sir Edwin Noel Westby, G.C.B., O.B.E., M.C.

Bramall, Sir (Ernest) Ashley, Kt.

Bramley, *Prof.* Sir Paul Anthony, Kt.

Branch, Sir William Allan Patrick, Kt.

Brancker, Sir (John Eustace) Theodore, Kt., Q.C.

Branigan, Sir Patrick Francis, Kt., Q.C.

Brassey, *Col.* Sir Hugh Trefusis, K.C.V.O., O.B.E., M.C.

Bray, Sir Theodor Charles, Kt., C.B.E.

Braynen, Sir Alvin Rudolph, Kt.

Brearley, Sir Norman, Kt., C.B.E., D.S.O., M.C., A.F.C.

Bremridge, Sir John Henry, K.B.E.

Brennan, *Hon.* Sir (Francis) Gerard, K.B.E.

Brett, Sir Lionel, Kt.

Brickwood, Sir Basil Greame, Bt. (1927).

Bridges, *Hon.* Sir Phillip Rodney, Kt., C.M.G.

Briggs, *Hon.* Sir Geoffrey Gould, Kt.

Brinckman, Sir Theodore George Roderick, Bt. (1831).

Brinton, *Maj.* Sir (Esme) Tatton (Cecil), Kt.

Brisco, Sir Donald Gilfrid, Bt. (1782).

Briscoe, Sir John Leigh Charlton, Bt., D.F.C. (1910).

Brise, Sir John Archibald Ruggles-, Bt., C.B., O.B.E., T.D. (1935).

Bristow, *Hon.* Sir Peter Henry Rowley, Kt.

Britton, Sir Edward Louis, Kt., C.B.E.

Broackes, Sir Nigel, Kt.

Broadbent, Sir Ewen, K.C.B., C.M.G.

Broadbent, Sir William Francis, Bt. (1893).

Broadhurst, *Air Chief Marshal* Sir Harry, G.C.B., K.B.E., D.S.O., D.F.C., A.F.C.

Brockhoff, Sir Jack Stuart, Kt.

Brocklebank, Sir Aubrey Thomas, Bt. (1885).

Brockman, *Vice-Adm.* Sir Ronald Vernon, K.C.B., C.V.O., C.S.I., C.I.E., C.B.E.

Brockman, *Hon.* Sir Thomas Charles Drake-, Kt., D.F.C.

Brodie, Sir Benjamin David Ross, Bt. (1834).

Brogan, *Lt.-Gen.* Sir Mervyn Francis, K.B.E., C.B.

Bromhead, Sir John Desmond Gonville, Bt. (1806).

Bromley, Sir Rupert Charles, Bt. (1757).

Bromley, Sir Thomas Eardley, K.C.M.G.

Brook, Sir Robin, Kt., C.M.G., O.B.E.

Brooke, Sir Francis George Windham, Bt. (1903).

Brooke, Sir Alistair Weston, Bt. (1919).

Brooke, Sir (Norman) Richard (Rowley), Kt., C.B.E.

Brooke, Sir Richard Neville, Bt. (1662).

Brookes, Sir Wilfred Deakin, Kt., C.B.E., D.S.O.

Brooksbank, Sir (Edward) Nicholas, Bt. (1919).

Broom, *Air Marshal* Sir Ivor Gordon, K.C.B., C.B.E., D.S.O., D.F.C., A.F.C.

Broughton, *Air Marshal* Sir Charles, K.B.E., C.B.

Broughton, Sir Evelyn Delves, Bt. (1661).

Broun, Sir Lionel John Law, Bt. (s. 1686).

Brown, Sir Allen Stanley, Kt., C.B.E.

Brown, Sir (Arthur James) Stephen, K.B.E.

Brown, *Lt.-Col.* Sir Charles Frederick Richmond, Bt. (1863).

Brown, Sir (Charles) James Officer, Kt., M.D.

Brown, Sir (Cyril) Maxwell Palmer, K.C.B., C.M.G.

Brown, Sir David, Kt.

Brown, *Vice-Adm.* Sir David Worthington, K.C.B.

Brown, Sir Derrick Holden-, Kt.

Brown, Sir Douglas Denison, Kt.

Brown, Sir Edward Joseph, Kt., M.B.E.

Brown, *Prof.* Sir (Ernest) Henry Phelps, Kt., M.B.E., F.B.A.

Brown, Sir (Frederick Herbert) Stanley, Kt., C.B.E.

Brown, *Prof.* Sir (George) Malcolm, Kt., F.R.S

Brown, Sir John Douglas Keith, Kt.

Brown, Sir John Gilbert Newton, Kt., C.B.E.

Brown, Sir Mervyn, K.C.M.G., O.B.E..

Brown, *Hon.* Sir Ralph Kilner, Kt., O.B.E., T.D.

Brown, Sir Raymond Frederick, Kt., O.B.E.

Brown, Sir Robert Crichton-, K.C.M.G., C.B.E., T.D.

Brown, *Hon.* Sir Simon Denis, Kt.

Brown, *Rt. Hon.* Sir Stephen, Kt.

Brown, Sir Thomas, Kt.

Brown, *Air Commodore* Sir Vernon Sydney, Kt., C.B., Q.B.E.

Brown, Sir William Brian Piggott-, Bt. (1903).

Browne, Sir (Edward) Humphrey, Kt., C.B.E.

Browne, *Rt. Hon.* Sir Patrick Reginald Evelyn, Kt., O.B.E., T.D.

Browne, Sir Thomas Anthony Gore, Kt.

Brownrigg, Sir Nicholas (Gawen), Bt. (1816).

Bruce, Sir Arthur Atkinson, K.B.E., M.C.

Bruce, Sir (Francis) Michael Ian, Bt. (s. 1628).

Bruce, Sir Hervey James Hugh, Bt. (1804).

Bruce, *Rt. Hon.* Sir (James) Roualeyn Hovell-Thurlow-Cumming-, Kt.

Brunner, Sir John Henry Kilian, Bt. (1895).

Brunton, Sir (Edward Francis) Lauder, Bt. (1908).

Brunton, Sir Gordon Charles, Kt.

Bryan, Sir Andrew Meikle, Kt.

Bryan, Sir Arthur, Kt.

Bryan, Sir Paul Elmore Oliver, Kt., D.S.O., M.C., M.P.

Bryce, *Hon.* Sir (William) Gordon, Kt., C.B.E.

Bryden, Sir William James, Kt., C.B.E., Q.C.

Bryson, *Vice-Adm.* Sir Lindsay Sutherland, K.C.B.

Buchan, Sir John, Kt., C.M.G.

Buchanan, Sir Charles Alexander James Leith-, Bt. (1775).

Buchanan, Sir Andrew George, Bt. (1878).

Buchanan, *Prof.* Sir Colin Douglas, Kt., C.B.E.

Buchanan, *Vice-Adm.* Sir Peter William, K.B.E.

Buck, Sir (Philip) Antony (Fyson), Kt., Q.C., M.P.

Buckley, *Rt. Hon.* Sir Denys Burton, Kt., M.B.E.

Buckley, Sir John William, Kt.

Buckley, *Rear-Adm.* Sir Kenneth Robertson, K.B.E.

Buckley, *Lt.-Comdr.* Sir (Peter) Richard, K.C.V.O.

Bulkeley, Sir Richard Harry David Williams-, Bt., T.D. (1661).

Bull, Sir George, Bt. (1922).

Bull, Sir Graham MacGregor, Kt., M.D., F.R.C.P.

Bull, Sir Walter Edward Avenon, K.C.V.O.

Bullard, Sir Julian Leonard, K.C.M.G.

Bullus, Sir Eric Edward, Kt.

Bulmer, Sir William Peter, Kt.

Bultin, Sir Bato, Kt., M.B.E.

Bunbury, Sir Michael William, Bt. (1681).

Bunbury, Sir (Richard David) Michael Richardson-, Bt. (I 1787).

Bunch, Sir Austin Wyeth, Kt., C.B.E.

Bunting, Sir (Edward) John, K.B.E.

Burbidge, Sir Herbert Dudley, Bt. (1916).

Burbury, *Hon.* Sir Stanley Charles, K.C.M.G., K.C.V.O., K.B.E.

Burden, Sir Frederick Frank Arthur, Kt.

Burder, Sir John Henry, Kt.

Burdett, Sir Savile Aylmer, Bt. (1665).

Burgen, Sir Arnold Stanley Vincent, Kt., F.R.S.

Burgess, *General* Sir Edward Arthur, K.C.B., O.B.E.

Burgess, Sir John Lawie, Kt., O.B.E., T.D.

Burgh, Sir John Charles, K.C.M.G., C.B.

Burke, Sir Aubrey Francis, Kt., O.B.E.

Burke, *Prof.* Sir Joseph Terence, K.B.E.

Burke, Sir Thomas Stanley, Bt. (I 1797).

Burley, Sir Victor George, Kt., C.B.E.

Burman, Sir (John) Charles, Kt.

Burman, Sir Stephen France, Kt., C.B.E.

Burnet, Sir James William Alexander (Sir Alastair Burnet), Kt.

Burnett, *Air Chief Marshal* Sir Brian Kenyon, G.C.B., D.F.C., A.F.C.

Burnett, Sir David Humphery, Bt., M.B.E., T.D. (1913).

Burney, Sir Anthony George Bernard, Kt., O.B.E.

Burney, Sir Cecil Denniston, Bt. (1921).

Burns, Sir Charles Ritchie, K.B.E., M.D.

Burns, Sir John Crawford, Kt.

Burns, Sir Malcolm McRae, K.B.E.

Burns, Sir Terence, Kt.

Burns, *Maj.-Gen.* Sir (Walter Arthur) George, K.C.V.O., C.B., D.S.O., O.B.E., M.C.

Burrell, *Vice-Adm.* Sir Henry Mackay, K.B.E., C.B.

Burrell, Sir John Raymond, Bt. (1774).

Burrenchobay, Sir Dayendranath, K.B.E., C.M.G., C.V.O.

Burrows, Sir Bernard Alexander Brocas, G.C.M.G.

Burrows, Sir (Robert) John (Formby), Kt.

Burston, Sir Samuel Gerald Wood, Kt., O.B.E.

Burt, *Hon.* Sir Francis Theodore Page, K.C.M.G.

Burton, Sir Carlisle Archibald, Kt., O.B.E.

Burton, Sir George Vernon Kennedy, Kt., C.B.E.

Burton, *Air Marshal* Sir Harry, K.C.B., C.B.E., D.S.O.

Burton-Chadwick, Sir Joshua Kenneth, Bt. (1935).

Busby, Sir Matthew, Kt., C.B.E.

Bush, *Hon.* Sir Brian Drex, Kt.

Bush, *Admiral* Sir John Fitzroy Duyland, G.C.B., D.S.C.

Busk, Sir Douglas Laird, K.C.M.G.

Butler, Sir Clifford Charles, Kt., Ph.D., F.R.S.

Butler, Sir Michael Dacres, G.C.M.G.

Butler, Sir (Reginald) Michael (Thomas), Bt. (1922).

Butler, *Hon.* Sir Richard Clive, Kt.

Butler, *Col.* Sir Thomas Pierce, Bt., C.V.O., D.S.O., O.B.E. (1628).

Butt, Sir (Alfred) Kenneth Dudley, Bt. (1929).

Butterfield, *Prof.* Sir (William) John (Hughes), Kt., O.B.E., D.M., F.R.C.P.

Butterworth, Sir (George) Neville, Kt.

Buxton, Sir Thomas Fowell Victor, Bt. (1840).

Buzzard, Sir Anthony Farquhar, Bt. (1929).

Byatt, Sir Hugh Campbell, K.C.V.O., C.M.G.

Byers, Sir Maurice Hearne, Kt., C.B.E., Q.C.

Byford, Sir Lawrence, Kt., C.B.E., Q.P.M.

Byrne, Sir Clarence Askew, Kt., O.B.E., D.S.C.

Cable, Sir James Eric, K.C.V.O., C.M.G.

Cadbury, Sir (George) Adrian (Hayhurst), Kt.

Cadell, *Vice-Adm.* Sir John Frederick, K.B.E.

Cadwallader, Sir John, Kt.

Caffyn, *Brig.* Sir Edward Roy, K.B.E., C.B., T.D.

Cahn, Sir Albert Jonas, Bt. (1934).

Cain, Sir Edward Thomas, Kt., C.B.E.

Caine, Sir Sydney, K.C.M.G.

Cairncross, Sir Alexander Kirkland, K.C.M.G.

Cairns, *Rt. Hon.* Sir David Arnold Scott, Kt.

Cakobau, *Ratu* Sir George, G.C.M.G., G.C.V.O., O.B.E., Royal Victorian Chain.

Caldicott, *Hon.* Sir John Moore, K.B.E., C.M.G.

Caldwell, *Surgeon Vice-Adm.* Sir (Eric) Dick, K.B.E., C.B.

Callaghan, Sir Allan Robert, Kt., C.M.G.

Callaghan, Sir Bede Bertrand, Kt., C.B.E.

Callard, Sir Eric John, Kt.

Callaway, *Prof.* Sir Frank Adams, Kt., C.M.G., O.B.E.

Calley, Sir Henry Algernon, Kt., D.S.O., D.F.C.

Callinan, Sir Bernard James, Kt., C.B.E., D.S.O., M.C.

Calthorpe, Sir Euan Hamilton Anstruther-Gough-, Bt. (1929).

Cameron, *Lt.-Gen.* Sir Alexander Maurice, K.B.E., C.B., M.C.

Cameron of Lochiel, Sir Donald Hamish, Kt., C.V.O., T.D.

Cameron, Sir (Eustace) John, Kt., C.B.E.

Cameron, Sir James Clark, Kt., C.B.E., T.D.

Cameron, *Hon.* Sir John, Kt., D.S.C., Q.C. (Lord Cameron).

Cameron, Sir John Watson, Kt., O.B.E.

Camilleri, *His Hon.* Sir Luigi Antonio, Kt, LL.D.

Campbell, Sir Alan Hugh, G.C.M.G.

Campbell, Sir Clifford Clarence, G.C.M.G., G.C.V.O.

Campbell, Sir Colin Moffat, Bt., M.C. (s. 1668).

Campbell, *Col.* Sir Guy Theophilus Halswell, Bt., O.B.E., M.C. (1815).

Campbell, *Maj.-Gen.* Sir Hamish Manus, K.B.E., C.B.

Campbell, Sir Ilay Mark, Bt. (1808).

Campbell, Sir Matthew, K.B.E., C.B., F.R.S.E.

Campbell, Sir Niall Alexander Hamilton, Bt. (1831).

Campbell, Sir Ralph Abercromby, Kt.

Campbell, Sir Robin Auchinbreck, Bt. (S. 1628).

Campbell, Sir Thomas Cockburn-, Bt. (1821).

Campbell, *Hon.* Sir Walter Benjamin, Kt.

Campion, Sir Harry, Kt., C.B., C.B.E.

Cantley, *Hon.* Sir Joseph Donaldson, Kt., O.B.E.

Carberry, Sir John Edward Doston, Kt.

Carden, *Lt.-Col.* Sir Henry Christopher, Bt., O.B.E. (1887).

Carden, Sir John Craven, Bt. (I 1787).

Carew, Sir Rivers Verain, Bt. (1661).

Carey, Sir Peter Willoughby, G.C.B.

Carlill, *Vice-Adm.* Sir Stephen Hope, K.B.E., C.B., D.S.O.

Carlisle, Sir John Michael, Kt.

Carmichael, Sir David Peter William Gibson-Craig-, Bt. (s. 1702 and 1831).

Carmichael, Sir John, K.B.E.

Carnac, *Rev. Canon* Sir (Thomas) Nicholas Rivett-, Bt. (1836).

Carnegie, *Lt.-Gen.* Sir Robin Macdonald, K.C.B., O.B.E.

Carnegie, Sir Roderick Howard, Kt.

Carnwath, Sir Andrew Hunter, K.C.V.O.

Caröe, Sir (Einar) Athelstan (Gordon), Kt., C.B.E.

Carr, Sir James Henry Brownlow, Kt.

Carr, *Air Marshal* Sir John Darcy Baker-, K.B.E., C.B., A.F.C.

Carreras, *Lt.-Col.* Sir James, K.C.V.O., M.B.E.

Carrick, *Hon.* Sir John Leslie, K.C.M.G.

Carter, Sir Charles Frederick, Kt., F.B.A.

Carter, Sir Derrick Hunton, Kt., T.D.

Carter, *Hon.* Sir Douglas Julian, K.C.M.G.

Carter, Sir John, Kt., Q.C.

Carter, Sir William Oscar, Kt.

Cartland, Sir George Barrington, Kt., C.M.G.

Cartledge, Sir Bryan George, K.C.M.G.

Cary, Sir Roger Hugh, Bt. (1955).

Cash, Sir Gerald Christopher, G.C.M.G., K.C.V.O., O.B.E.

Cass, Sir John Patrick, Kt., O.B.E.

Cassel, Sir Harold Felix, Bt., T.D., Q.C. (1920).

Cassels, *Field Marshal* Sir (Archibald) James Halkett, G.C.B., K.B.E., D.S.O.

Cassels, *Admiral* Sir Simon Alastair Cassillis, K.C.B., C.B.E.

Cassidi, *Admiral* Sir (Arthur) Desmond, G.C.B.

Casson, Sir Hugh Maxwell, C.H., K.C.V.O., P.P.R.A., F.R.I.B.A.

Cater, Sir Jack, K.B.E.

Cater, Sir John Robert, Kt.

Catherwood, Sir (Henry) Frederick (Ross), Kt.

Catling, Sir Richard Charles, Kt., C.M.G., O.B.E.

Cato, *Hon.* Sir Arnott Samuel, K.C.M.G.

Caughey, Sir Thomas Harcourt Clarke, K.B.E.

Caulfield, *Hon.* Sir Bernard, Kt.

Cave, Sir Charles Edward Coleridge, Bt. (1896).

Cave, Sir (Charles) Philip Haddon-, K.B.E., C.M.G.

Cave, Sir Richard Guy, Kt., M.C.

Cave, Sir Richard Phillip, K.C.V.O., C.B.

Cave, Sir Robert Cave-Browne-, Bt. (1641).

Cawley, Sir Charles Mills, Kt., C.B.E., Ph.D.

Cayley, Sir Digby William David, Bt. (1661).

Cayzer, Sir James Arthur, Bt. (1904).

Cecil, *Rear-Adm.* Sir (Oswald) Nigel Amherst, K.B.E., C.B.

Chacksfield, *Air Vice-Marshal* Sir Bernard Albert, K.B.E., C.B.

Chadwick, Sir Albert Edward, Kt., C.M.G., M.S.M.

Chadwick, Sir John Edward, K.C.M.G.

Chadwick, *Rev. Prof.* (William) Owen, O.M., K.B.E., F.B.A.

Chalk, *Hon.* Sir Gordon William Wesley, K.B.E.

Chamberlain, *Hon.* Sir Reginald Roderic St. Clair, Kt.

Chan, *Rt. Hon.* Sir Julius, K.B.E.

Chance, Sir Roger James Ferguson, Bt., M.C. (1900).

Chancellor, Sir Christopher John, Kt., C.M.G.

Chandler, Sir Geoffrey, Kt., C.B.E.

Chaney, *Hon.* Sir Frederick Charles, K.B.E., A.F.C.

Chapman, Sir George Alan, Kt.

Chapman, Sir Robert Macgowan, Bt., C.B.E., T.D. (1958).

Chapman, *Hon.* Sir Stephen, Kt.

Chapple, *Lt.-Gen.* Sir John Lyon, K.C.B., C.B.E.

Charles, Sir Joseph Quentin, Kt.

Charnley, Sir (William) John, Kt., C.B.

Chau, *Hon.* Sir Sik-Nin, Kt., C.B.E.

Chaytor, Sir George Reginald, Bt. (1831).

Cheadle, Sir Eric Wallers, Kt., C.B.E.

Cheeketts, *Sqn. Ldr.* Sir David John, K.C.V.O.

Cheetham, Sir Nicolas John Alexander, K.C.M.G.

Chegwidden, Sir Thomas Sidney, Kt., C.B., C.V.O.

Chester, Sir (Daniel) Norman, Kt., C.B.E.

Chesterman, Sir (Dudley) Ross, Kt., Ph.D.

Chesterton, Sir Oliver Sidney, Kt., M.C.

Chetwynd, Sir Arthur Ralph Talbot, Bt. (1795).

Cheyne, Sir Joseph Lister Watson, Bt., O.B.E. (1908).

Chichester, Sir (Edward) John, Bt. (1641).

Child, Sir (Coles John) Jeremy, Bt. (1919).

Chilton, *Air Marshal* Sir (Charles) Edward, K.B.E., C.B.

Chilton, *Brig.* Sir Frederick Oliver, Kt., C.B.E., D.S.O.

Chilver, Sir (Amos) Henry, Kt., D.SC., F.R.S.

Chitty, Sir Thomas Willes, Bt. (1924).

Cholmeley, Sir Montague John, Bt. (1806).

Christie, Sir George William Langham, Kt.

Christie, *Hon.* Sir Vernon Howard Colville, Kt.

Christie, Sir William, Kt., M.B.E.

Christison, *Gen.* Sir (Alexander Frank) Philip, Bt., G.B.E., C.B., D.S.O., M.C. (1871).

Christofas, Sir Kenneth Cavendish, K.C.M.G., M.B.E.

Christopherson, Sir Derman Guy, Kt., O.B.E., D.Phil., F.R.S.

Chung, Sir Sze-yuen, Kt., C.B.E.

Clapham, Sir Michael John Sinclair, K.B.E.

Claringbull, Sir (Gordon) Frank, Kt., Ph.D.

Clark, Sir George Anthony, Bt. (1917).

Clark, Sir (Gordon Colvin) Lindesay, K.B.E., C.M.G., M.C.

Clark, Sir John Allen, Kt.

Clark, Sir John Douglas, Bt. (1886).

Clark, Sir John Stewart-, Bt. (1918).

Clark, Sir Robert Anthony, Kt., D.S.C.

Clark, Sir Robin Chichester-, Kt.

Clark, Sir William Gibson, Kt., M.P.

Clarke, Sir (Charles Mansfield) Tobias, Bt. (1831).

Clarke, *Prof.* Sir Cyril Astley, K.B.E., M.D., SC.D., F.R.S., F.R.C.P.

Clarke, Sir Ellis Emmanuel Innocent, G.C.M.G.

Clarke, Sir (Henry) Ashley, G.C.M.G., G.C.V.O.

Clarke, Sir Henry Osmond Osmond-, K.C.V.O., C.B.E.

Clarke, Sir Jonathan Dennis, Kt.

Clarke, Sir Rupert William John, Bt., M.B.E. (1882).

Clay, Sir Richard Henry, Bt. (1841).

Clayden, *Rt. Hon.* Sir (Henry) John Kt.

Clayson, Sir Eric Maurice, Kt.

Clayton, Sir David Robert, Bt., (1732).

Clayton, *Air Marshal* Sir Gareth Thomas Butler, K.C.B., D.F.C.

Clayton, Sir Robert James, Kt., C.B.E.

Clayton, *Prof.* Sir Stanley George, Kt., M.D.

Cleary, Sir Joseph Jackson, Kt.

Clegg, Sir Alexander Bradshaw, Kt.

Clegg, Sir Cuthbert Barwick, Kt.

Clegg, Sir Walter, Kt., M.P.

Clements, Sir John Selby, Kt., C.B.E.

Cleminson, Sir James Arnold Stacey, Kt., M.C.

Clerk, Sir John Dutton, Bt., C.B.E., V.R.D. (s. 1679)

Clerke, Sir John Edward Longueville, Bt. (1660).

Clifford, Sir (Geoffrey) Miles, K.B.E., C.M.G., E.D.

Clifford, Sir Roger Joseph, Bt. (1887).

Clothier, Sir Cecil Montacute, K.C.B., Q.C.

Clowes, *Col.* Sir Henry Nelson, K.C.V.O., D.S.O., O.B.E.

Clucas, Sir Kenneth Henry, K.C.B.

Clutterbuck, *Vice-Adm.* Sir David Granville, K.B.E., C.B.

Coates, Sir Ernest William, Kt., C.M.G.

Coates, Sir Frederick Gregory Lindsay, Bt. (1921).

Coats, Sir Alastair Francis Stuart, Bt. (1905).

Coats, Sir William David, Kt.

Cobban, Sir James Macdonald, Kt., C.B.E., T.D.

Cochrane, Sir (Henry) Marc (Sursock), Bt. (1903).

Cockburn, Sir John Elliot, Bt. (s. 1671).

Cockburn, Sir Robert, K.B.E., C.B., Ph.D.

Cockcroft, Sir Wilfred Halliday, Kt., D.Phil.

Cockerell, Sir Christopher Sydney, Kt., C.B.E., F.R.S.

Cockram, Sir John, Kt.

Cocks, Sir (Thomas George) Barnett, K.C.B., O.B.E.

Codrington, Sir Simon Francis Bethell, Bt. (1876).

Codrington, Sir William Alexander, Bt. (1721).

Coghill, Sir Egerton James Nevill Tobias, Bt. (1778).

Cohen, Sir Bernard Nathaniel Waley-, Bt. (1961).

Cohen, Sir Edward, Kt.

Cohen, Sir Rex Arthur Louis, K.B.E.

Coldstream, Sir George Phillips, K.C.B., K.C.V.O., Q.C.

Coldstream, *Prof.* Sir William Menzies, Kt., C.B.E.

Cole, Sir (Alexander) Colin, K.C.V.O., T.D.

Cole, Sir David Lee, K.C.M.G., M.C.

Cole, Sir (Robert) William, Kt.

Coles, Sir Kenneth Frank, Kt.

Coles, Sir Norman Cameron, Kt.

Colfox, Sir (William) John, Bt. (1939).

Collett, Sir Ian Seymour, Bt. (1934).

Collett, Sir (Thomas) Kingsley, Kt., C.B.E.

Collier, *Air Vice-Marshal* Sir (Alfred) Conrad, K.C.B., C.B.E.

Colingwood, *Lt.-Gen.* Sir (Richard) George, K.B.E., C.B., D.S.O.

Collins, Sir Arthur James Robert, K.C.V.O

Collins, Sir Geoffrey Abdy, Kt.

Collins, *Vice-Adm.* Sir John Augustine, K.B.E., C.B.

Colman, Sir Michael Jeremiah, Bt. (1907).

Colquhoun, *Maj.-Gen.* Sir Cyril Harry, K.C.V.O., C.B., O.B.E.

Colquhoun of Luss, Sir Ivar Iain, Bt. (1786).

Colt, Sir Edward William Dutton Bt. (1694).

Colthurst, Sir Richard La Touche, Bt. (1744).

Colville, Sir John Rupert, Kt., C.B., C.V.O.

Combs, Sir Willis Ide, K.C.V.O., C.M.G.

Compston, *Vice-Adm.* Sir Peter Maxwell, K.C.B.

Compton, Sir Edmund Gerald, G.C.B., K.B.E.

Compton Miller, Sir John (Francis), Kt., M.B.E., T.D.

Comyn, *Hon.* Sir James, Kt.

Conant, Sir John Ernest Michael, Bt. (1954).

Conran, Sir Terence Orby, Kt.

Constable, Sir Robert Frederick Strickland-, Bt. (1641).

Constantine, *Air Chief Marshal* Sir Hugh Alex, K.B.E., C.B., D.S.O.

Cook, Sir Christopher Wymondham Rayner Herbert, Bt. (1886).

Cook, Sir (Philip) Halford, Kt., O.B.E.

Cook, Sir William Richard Joseph, K.C.B., F.R.S.

Cooke, Sir Charles Fletcher-, Kt., Q.C.

Cooke, *Lt.-Col.* Sir David William Perceval, Bt. (1661).

Cooke, Sir John Fletcher-, Kt., C.M.G.

Cooke, Sir Robert Gordon, Kt.

Cooke, *Rt. Hon.* Sir Robin Brunskill, Kt.

Cooley, Sir Alan Sydenham, Kt., C.B.E.

Coop, Sir Maurice Fletcher, Kt.

Cooper, Sir William Daniel Charles, Bt. (1863).

Cooper, Sir Francis Ashmole, Bt., Ph.D. (1905).

Cooper, *Rt. Hon.* Sir Frank, G.C.B., C.M.G.

Cooper, *General* Sir George Leslie Conroy, G.C.B., M.C.

Cooper, Sir Gilbert Alexander, Kt., C.B.E., E.D.

Cooper, Sir Patrick Graham Astley, Bt. (1821).

Cooper, Sir William Henry, Kt., C.B.E.

Cooper, *Prof.* Sir (William) Mansfield, Kt.

Coote, Sir Christopher John, Bt., *Premier Baronet of Ireland* (I 1621).

Copas, *Most Rev.* Virgil, K.B.E., D.D.

Corbet, Sir John Vincent, Bt., M.B.E. (1808).

Corfield, *Rt. Hon.* Sir Frederick Vernon, Kt., Q.C.

Corfield, Sir Kenneth George, Kt.

Cork, Sir Kenneth Russell, G.B.E.

Corley, Sir Kenneth Sholl Ferrand, Kt.

Cormack, Sir Magnus Cameron, K.B.E.

Cornford, Sir (Edward) Clifford, K.C.B.

Cornforth, Sir John Warcup, Kt., C.B.E., D.Phil., F.R.S.

Cornwall, *General* Sir James Handyside Marshall-, K.C.B., C.B.E., D.S.O., M.C.

Corry, Sir James Perowne Ivo Myles, Bt. (1885).

Cortazzi, Sir (Henry Arthur) Hugh, G.C.M.G.

Cory, Sir Clinton James Donald, Bt. (1919).

Coslett, *Air Marshal* Sir (Thomas) Norman, K.C.B., O.B.E.

Costain, Sir Albert Percy, Kt.

Costar, Sir Norman Edgar, K.C.M.G.

Cotter, *Lt.-Col.* Sir Delaval James Alfred, Bt., D.S.O. (I. 1763).

Cotterell, Sir John Henry Geers, Bt. (1805).

Cotton, Sir John Richard, K.C.M.G., O.B.E.

Cotton, *Hon.* Sir Robert Carrington, K.C.M.G.

Cottrell, Sir Alan Howard, Kt., Ph.D., F.R.S.

Cotts, Sir (Robert) Crichton Mitchell, Bt. (1921).

Coulson, Sir John Eltringham, K.C.M.G.

Couper, Sir (Robert) Nicholas (Oliver), Bt. (1841).

Court, *Hon.* Sir Charles Walter Michael, K.C.M.G., O.B.E.

Coutts, Sir Walter Fleming, G.C.M.G., M.B.E.

Couzens, Sir Kenneth Edward, K.C.B.

Covacevich, Sir (Anthony) Thomas, Kt., D.F.C.

Cowen, *Rt. Hon. Prof.* Sir Zelman, G.C.M.G., G.C.V.O., Q.C.

Cowley, *Lt.-Gen.* Sir John Guise, K.B.E., C.B.

Cowper, Sir Norman Lethbridge, Kt., C.B.E.

Cowperthwaite, Sir John James, K.B.E., C.M.G.

Cox, Sir Anthony Wakefield, Kt., C.B.E., F.R.I.B.A.

Cox, *Prof.* Sir David Roxbee, Kt., F.R.S.

Cox, Sir (Ernest) Gordon, K.B.E., T.D., D.S.C., F.R.S.

Cox, Sir Geoffrey Sandford, Kt., C.B.E.

Cox, Sir (George) Trenchard, Kt., C.B.E., F.S.A.

Cox, *Vice-Adm.* Sir John Michael Holland, K.C.B.

Cox, Sir John William, Kt., C.B.E.

Cox, Sir Mencea Ethereal, Kt.,

Cradock, Sir Percy, G.C.M.G.

Craig, Sir (Albert) James (Macqueen), G.C.M.G.

Craig, *Air Chief Marshal* Sir David Brownrigg, G.C.B., O.B.E.

Cramer, *Hon.* Sir John Oscar, Kt.

Crane, Sir Harry Walter Victor, Kt., O.B.E.

Crane, Sir James William Donald, Kt., C.B.E.

Craufurd, Sir Robert James, Bt. (1781).

Craven, *Air Marshal* Sir Robert Edward, K.B.E., C.B., D.F.C.

Crawford, *Hon.* Sir George Hunter, Kt.

Crawford, Sir (Robert) Stewart, G.C.M.G., C.V.O

Crawford, *Prof.* Sir Theodore, Kt.

Crawford, *Vice-Adm.* Sir William Godfrey, K.B.E., C.B., D.S.C.

Crawshaw, *Hon.* Sir (Edward) Daniel (Weston), Kt.

Crawshay, *Col.* Sir William Robert, Kt., D.S.O., E.R.D., T.D.

Creagh, *Maj.-Gen.* Sir (Kilner) Rupert Brazier-, K.B.E., C.B., D.S.O.

Creasey, *General* Sir Timothy May, K.C.B., O.B.E.

Creswell, Sir Michel Justin, K.C.M.G.

Crichton, Sir Andrew James Maitland-Makgill-, Kt.

Cripps, Sir John Stafford, Kt., C.B.E.

Crisp, Sir (John) Peter, Bt. (1913).

Critchett, Sir Ian (George Lorraine), Bt. (1908).

Croft, Sir Owen Glendower, Bt. (1671).

Croft, Sir John Archibald Radcliffe, Bt. (1818).

Crofton, Sir (Hugh) Patrick Simon, Bt. (1801).

Crofton, *Prof.* Sir John Wenman, Kt.

Crofton, Sir Malby Sturges, Bt. (1838).

Croker, Sir Walter Russell, K.B.E.

Crookenden, *Lt.-Gen.* Sir Napier, K.C.B., D.S.O., O.B.E.

Croom, Sir John Halliday, Kt., T.D.

Cross, Sir Cecil Lancelot Stewart, Kt., C.B.E.

Cross, *Air Chief Marshal* Sir Kenneth Brian Boyd, K.C.B., C.B.E., D.S.O., D.F.C.

Crossland, Sir Leonard, Kt.

Crossley, Sir Christopher John, Bt. (1909).

Crossman, Sir Douglas Peter, Kt., T.D.

Crosthwaite, Sir (Ponsonby) Moore, K.C.M.G.

Crowe, Sir Colin Tradescant, G.C.M.G.

Crowley, Sir Brian Hurtle, Kt., M.M.

Crutchley, *Admiral* Sir Victor Alexander Charles, V.C., K.C.B., D.S.C.

Cruthers, Sir James Winter, Kt.

Cubbon, Sir Brian Crossland, G.C.B.

Cubitt, Sir Hugh Guy, Kt., C.B.E.

Cuckney, Sir John Graham, Kt.

Cumber, Sir John Alfred, Kt., C.M.G., M.B.E., T.D.

Cumming, Sir William Gordon Gordon-, Bt. (1804).

Cunard, Sir Guy Alick, Bt. (1859).

Cuninghame, Sir John Christopher Foggo Montgomery-, Bt. (N.S. 1672).

Cuninghame, Sir William Henry Fairlie-, Bt., (s. 1630).

Cunliffe, Sir David Ellis, Bt.

Cunningham, Sir Charles Craik, G.C.B., K.B.E., C.V.O.

Cunningham, *Lt.-Gen.* Sir Hugh Patrick, K.B.E.

Cunynghame, Sir Andrew David Francis, Bt. (s. 1702).

Cunynghame, Sir James Ogilvy Blair-, Kt., O.B.E.

Curle, Sir John Noel Ormiston, K.C.V.O., C.M.G.

Curlewis, *His Hon.* Sir Adrian Herbert, Kt., C.V.O., C.B.E.

Curran, Sir Samuel Crowe, Kt., D.SC., Ph.D., F.R.S., F.R.S.E.

Currie, *Prof.* Sir Alastair Robert, Kt., F.R.C.P., F.R.C.P.E., F.R.S.E.

Currie, Sir George Alexander, Kt.

Currie, Sir Neil Smith, Kt., C.B.E.

Currie, Sir William George Cubitt, Bt. (1847).

Curtis, Sir (Edward) Leo, Kt.

Curtis, Sir William Peter, Bt. (1802).

Curtiss, *Air Marshal* Sir John Bagot, K.C.B., K.B.E.

Cuthbert, *Vice-Adm.* Sir John Wilson, K.B.E., C.B.

Cuthbertson, Sir David Paton, Kt., C.B.E., M.D., D.SC.

Cuthbertson, Sir Harold Alexander, Kt.

Cutler, Sir (Arthur) Roden, V.C., K.C.M.G., K.C.V.O., C.B.E.

Cutler, Sir Charles Benjamin, K.B.E., E.D.

Cutler, Sir Horace Walter, Kt., O.B.E.

Dacie, *Prof.* Sir John Vivian, Kt., M.D., F.R.S.

Dainton, *Prof.* Sir Frederick Sydney, Kt., Ph.D., D.SC., F.R.S.

Daldry, Sir Leonard Charles, K.B.E.

Dale, Sir William Leonard, K.C.M.G.

Dalrymple, *Maj.* Sir Hew Fleetwood Hamilton-, Bt., K.C.V.O. (s. 1697).

Dalton, Sir Alan Nugent Goring, Kt., C.B.E.

Dalton, *Maj.-Gen.* Sir Charles James George, Kt., C.B., C.B.E.

Dalton, *Vice-Adm.* Sir Norman Eric, K.C.B., O.B.E.

Daly, *Lt.-Gen.* Sir Thomas Joseph, K.B.E., C.B., D.S.O.

Dalyell, Sir Tam, Bt., M.P. (N.S. 1685).

Daniel, Sir Goronwy Hopkin, K.C.V.O., C.B., D.Phil.

Daniell, Sir Peter Averell, Kt., T.D.

Danks, Sir Alan John, K.B.E.

Darby, Sir Peter Howard, Kt., C.B.E., Q.F.S.M.

Darell, Sir Jeffrey Lionel, Bt., M.C. (1795).

Dargie, Sir William Alexander, Kt., C.B.E.

Darling, Sir Clifford, Kt.

Darling, Sir James Ralph, Kt., C.M.G., O.B.E.

Darling, *General* Sir Kenneth Thomas, G.B.E., K.C.B., D.S.O.

Darlington, *Rear-Adm.* Sir Charles Roy, K.B.E.

Darvall, Sir (Charles) Roger, Kt., C.B.E.

Dashwood, Sir Francis John Vernon Hereward, Bt., *Premier Baronet of Great Britain* (1707).

Dashwood, Sir Richard James, Bt. (1684).

Davenport, *Lt.-Col.* Sir Walter Henry Bromley-, Kt., T.D.

Davidson, *Hon.* Sir Charles William, K.B.E.

Davie, *Rev.* Sir Arthur Patrick Ferguson-, Bt. (1847).

Davie, Sir Paul Christopher, Kt.

Davies, *Air Marshal* Sir Alan Cyril, K.C.B., C.B.E.

Davies, *Hon.* Sir (Alfred William) Michael, Kt.

Davies, Sir Alun Talfan, Kt., Q.C.

Davies, Sir (David) Arthur, K.B.E.

Davies, Sir David Henry, Kt.

Davies, *Hon.* Sir (David Herbert) Mervyn, Kt., M.C., T.D.

Davies, Sir David Joseph, Kt.

Davies, *Vice-Adm.* Sir Lancelot Richard Bell, K.B.E.

Davies, Sir Oswald, Kt., C.B.E.

Davies, Sir Richard Harries, K.C.V.O., C.B.E.

Davies, Sir Victor Caddy, Kt., O.B.E.

Davis, Sir Charles Sigmund, Kt., C.B.

Davis, Sir Colin Rex, Kt., C.B.E.

Davis, *Hon.* Sir (Dermot) Renn, Kt., O.B.E.

Davis, Sir (Ernest) Howard, Kt., C.M.G., O.B.E.

Davis, Sir John Gilbert, Bt. (1946).

Davis, *Air Chief Marshal* Sir John Gilbert, G.C.B., O.B.E.

Davis, Sir John Henry Harris, Kt.

Davis, Sir Maurice Herbert, Kt., O.B.E.

Davis, Sir Rupert Charles Hart-, Kt.

Davis, *Hon.* Sir Thomas Robert Alexander Harries, K.B.E.

Davis, *Admiral* Sir William Wellclose, G.C.B., D.S.O.

Davison, *Rt. Hon.* Sir Ronald Keith, G.B.E., C.M.G.

Dawbarn, Sir Simon Yelverton, K.C.V.O., C.M.G.

Dawnay, *Vice-Adm.* Sir Peter, K.C.V.O., C.B., D.S.C.

Dawson, *Hon.* Sir Daryl Michael, K.B.E., C.B.

Dawson, Sir Hugh Michael Trevor, Bt. (1920).

Dawson, *Air Chief Marshal* Sir Walter Lloyd, K.C.B., C.B.E., D.S.O.

Dawtry, Sir Alan (Graham), Kt., C.B.E., T.D.

Day, Sir Derek Malcolm, K.C.M.G.

Day, Sir Robin, Kt.

Deakin, Sir (Frederick) William (Dampier), Kt., D.S.O.

Dean, Sir (Arthur) Paul, Kt., M.P.

Dean, Sir John Norman, Kt.

Dean, Sir Patrick Henry, G.C.M.G.

Deane, *Hon.* Sir William Patrick, K.B.E.

Dearing, Sir Ronald Ernest, Kt., C.B.

Debenham, Sir Gilbert Ridley, Bt. (1931).

De Bunsen, Sir Bernard, Kt., C.M.G.

Deer, Sir (Arthur) Frederick, Kt., C.M.G.

de Gale, Sir Leo Victor, G.C.M.G., C.B.E.

de Hoghton, Sir (Richard) Bernard (Cuthbert), Bt. (1611).

De la Bère, Sir Cameron, Bt. (1953).

Delacombe, *Maj.-Gen.* Sir Rohan, K.C.M.G., K.C.V.O., K.B.E., C.B., D.S.O.

de la Mare, Sir Arthur James, K.C.M.G., K.C.V.O.

de la Rue, Sir Eric Vincent, Bt. (1898).

De Lestang, Sir Marie Charles Emmanuel Clement Nageon, Kt.

de Lotbinière, *Lt.-Col.* Sir Edmund Joly, Kt.

Delve, Sir Frederick William, Kt., C.B.E.

de Montmorency, Sir Arnold Geoffroy, Bt. (I 1631).

Denby, Sir Richard Kenneth, Kt.

Denholm, *Col.* Sir William Lang, Kt., T.D.

Denman, Sir (George) Roy, K.C.B., C.M.G.

Denning, *Lt.-Gen.* Sir Reginald Francis Stewart, K.C.V.O., K.B.E., C.B.

Denny, Sir Alistair Maurice Archibald, Bt. (1913).

Denny, Sir Anthony Coningham de Waltham, Bt. (I 1782).

Derham, *Prof.* Sir David Plumley, K.B.E., C.M.G.

Derham, Sir Peter John, Kt.

de Trafford, Sir Dermot Humphrey, Bt. (1841).

Deverell, Sir Colville Montgomery, G.B.E., K.C.M.G., C.V.O.

Devesi, Sir Baddeley, G.C.M.G., G.C.V.O.

Devitt, Sir Thomas Gordon, Bt. (1916).

Dewes, Sir Herbert John Salisbury, Kt., C.B.E.

Dewey, Sir Anthony Hugh, Bt. (1917).

Dewhurst, *Prof.* Sir (Christopher) John, Kt.

D'Eyncourt, Sir (John) Jeremy (Eustace) Tennyson-, Bt. (1930).

de Zulueta, Sir Philip Francis, Kt.

Dhenin, *Air Marshal* Sir Geoffrey Howard, K.B.E., A.F.C., G.M., M.D.

Dhrangadhra, H.H. the Maharaja Raj Saheb of, K.C.I.E.

Dibela, *Hon.* Sir Kingsford, G.C.M.G.

Dickens, Sir Louis Walter, Kt., D.F.C., A.F.C.

Dickinson, Sir Harold Herbert, Kt.

Dickinson, Sir Samuel Benson, Kt.

Dickson, *Marshal of the Royal Air Force* Sir William Forster, G.C.B., K.B.E., D.S.O., A.F.C.

Dilbertson, Sir Geoffrey, C.B.E.

Dilke, Sir John Fisher Wentworth, Bt. (1862).

Dill, Sir Nicholas Bayard, Kt., C.B.E.

Dillon, *Rt. Hon.* Sir (George) Brian (Hugh), Kt.

Dillon, Sir John Vincent, Kt., C.M.G.

Dillon, Sir Max, Kt.

Diver, *Hon.* Sir Leslie Charles, Kt.

Dixon, *Air Vice-Marshal* Sir (Francis Wilfred) Peter, K.B.E.

Dixon, Sir John George, Bt. (1919).

Dobson, Sir Denis William, K.C.B., O.B.E., Q.C.

Dobson, *General* Sir Patrick John Howard-, G.C.B.

Dobson, Sir Richard Portway, Kt.

Dodds, Sir Ralph Jordan, Bt. (1964).

Dodson, Sir Derek Sherborne Lindsell, K.C.M.G., M.C.

Dodsworth, Sir John Christopher Smith-, Bt. (1784).

Doig, Sir James Nimmo Crawford, Kt.

Doll, *Prof.* Sir (William) Richard (Shaboe), Kt., O.B.E., F.R.S., D.M., M.D., D.SC.

Donald, *Air Marshal* Sir John George, K.B.E.

Donaldson, Sir Dawson, K.C.M.G.

Donaldson, *Rt. Hon.* Sir John Francis, Kt.

Donne, *Hon.* Sir Gaven John, K.B.E.

Donne, Sir John Christopher, Kt.

Donner, Sir Patrick William, Kt.

Dookun, Sir Dewoonarain, Kt.

Dorman, *Lt.-Col.* Sir Charles Geoffrey, Bt., M.C. (1923).

Dorman, Sir Maurice Henry, G.C.M.G., G.C.V.O.

Dos Santos, Sir Errol Lionel, Kt., C.B.E.

Dougherty, *Maj.-Gen.* Sir Ivan Noel, Kt., C.B.E., D.S.O., E.D.

Douglas, *Prof.* Sir Donald Macleod, Kt., M.B.E.

Douglas, Sir (Edward) Sholto, Kt.

Douglas, *Very Rev.* Sir Hugh Osborne, K.C.V.O., C.B.E.

Douglas, Sir Robert McCallum, Kt., O.B.E.

Douglas, Sir Sholto Courtenay Mackenzie, Bt., M.C. (1831).

Douglas, *Rt. Hon.* Sir William Randolph, K.C.M.G.

Dove, Sir Clifford Alfred, Kt., C.B.E., E.R.D.

Dover, *Prof.* Sir Kenneth James, Kt., D.Litt., F.B.A., F.R.S.E.

Down, Sir Alastair Frederick, Kt., O.B.E., M.C., T.D.

Downey, Sir Gordon Stanley, K.C.B.

Downs, Sir Diarmuid, Kt., C.B.E.

Downward, Sir William Atkinson, Kt.

Dowse, *Maj.-Gen.* Sir Maurice Brian, K.C.V.O., C.B., C.B.E.

Dowson, Sir Philip Manning, Kt., C.B.E., A.R.A.

Doyle, Sir John Francis Reginald William Hastings, Bt. (1828).

D'Oyly, Sir John Rochfort, Bt. (1663).

Drake, Sir (Arthur) Eric (Courtney), Kt., C.B.E.

Drake, *Hon.* Sir (Frederick) Maurice, Kt., D.F.C.

Drake, Sir James, Kt., C.B.E.

Drew, Sir Arthur Charles Walter, K.C.B.

Drew, Sir Ferdinand Caire, Kt., C.M.G.

Drew, *Lt.-Gen.* Sir (William) Robert (Macfarlane), K.C.B., C.B.E., F.R.C.P.

Dreyer, *Admiral* Sir Desmond Parry, G.C.B., C.B.E., D.S.C.

Dring, *Lt.-Col.* Sir Arthur John, K.B.E., C.I.E.

Driver, Sir Arthur John, Kt.

Driver, Sir Eric William, Kt.

Drummond, *Lieut.-Gen.* Sir (William) Alexander (Duncan), K.B.E., C.B.

Dryden, Sir John Stephen Gyles, Bt. (1733 and 1795).

du Cann, *Rt. Hon.* Sir Edward Dillon Lott, K.B.E., M.P.

Duckmanton, Sir Talbot Sydney, Kt., C.B.E.

Duckworth, *Maj.* Sir Richard Dyce, Bt. (1909).

du Cros, Sir Claude Philip Arthur Mallet, Bt. (1916).

Dudding, Sir John Scarborough, Kt.

Duff, *Rt. Hon.* Sir (Arthur) Antony, G.C.M.G., C.V.O., D.S.O., D.S.C.

Duffus, *Hon.* Sir William Algernon Holwell, Kt.

Dugdale, Sir William Stratford, Bt., M.C. (1936).

du Heaume, Sir Francis Herbert, Kt., C.I.E., O.B.E.

Duke, *Maj.-Gen.* Sir Gerald William, K.B.E., C.B., D.S.O.

Dunbar, Sir Archibald Ranulph, Bt. (s 1700).

Dunbar, Sir David Hope-, Bt. (s 1664).

Dunbar, Sir Drummond Cospatrick Ninian, Bt., M.C. (s 1698).

Dunbar, Sir Jean Ivor, Bt. (s 1694).

Dunbar of Hempriggs, Dame Maureen Daisy Helen, Bt. (s 1706).

Duncan, Sir James Blair, Kt.

Duncombe, Sir Philip Digby Pauncefort-, Bt. (1859).

Dunham, Sir Kingsley Charles, Kt., Ph.D., F.R.S., F.R.S.E.

Dunlop, Sir (Ernest) Edward, Kt., C.M.G., O.B.E.

Dunlop, Sir Thomas, Bt. (1916).

Dunlop, Sir William Norman Gough, Kt.

Dunn, *Air Marshal* Sir Eric Clive, K.B.E., C.B., B.E.M.

Dunn, *Lt.-Col.* Sir (Francis) Vivian, K.C.V.O., O.B.E.

Dunn, *Air Marshal* Sir Patrick Hunter, K.B.E., C.B., D.F.C.

Dunn, *Rt. Hon.* Sir Robin Horace Walford, Kt., M.C.

Dunnett, Sir (Ludovic) James, G.C.B., C.M.G.

Dunning, Sir Simon William Patrick, Bt. (1930).

Dunphie, *Maj.-Gen.* Sir Charles Anderson Lane, Kt., C.B., C.B.E., D.S.O.

Dunstan, *Lt.-Gen.* Sir Donald Beaumont, K.B.E., C.B.

Duntze, Sir John Alexander, Bt. (1774).

Dupree, Sir Peter, Bt. (1921).

Dupuch, Sir (Alfred) Etienne (Jerome), Kt., O.B.E.

Durand, *Rev.* Sir (Henry Mortimer) Dickon, Bt. (1892).

Durham, Sir Kenneth, Kt.

Durie, Sir Alexander Charles, Kt., C.B.E.

Durkin, *Air Marshal* Sir Herbert, K.B.E., C.B.

Durlacher, *Admiral* Sir Laurence George, K.C.B., O.B.E., D.S.C.

Durrant, Sir William Henry Estridge, Bt. (1784).

Duval, Sir (Charles) Gaetan, Kt.

Dyer, *Prof.* Sir (Henry) Peter (Francis) Swinnerton, Bt., F.R.S. (1678).

Dyke, Sir Derek William Hart, Bt. (1677).

Earle, *Air Chief Marshal* Sir Alfred, G.B.E., C.B.

Earle, Sir (Hardman) George (Algernon), Bt. (1869).

East, Sir (Lewis) Ronald, Kt., C.B.E.

Eastham, *Hon.* Sir (Thomas) Michael, Kt.

Eastick, *Brig.* Sir Thomas Charles, Kt., C.M.G., D.S.O., E.D.

Easton, *Admiral* Sir Ian, K.C.B., D.S.C.

Easton, *Air Commodore* Sir James Alfred, K.C.M.G., C.B., C.B.E.

Eastwood, Sir John Bealby, Kt.

Eberle, *Admiral* Sir James Henry Fuller, G.C.B.

Ebrahim, Sir (Mahomed) Currimbhoy, Bt. (1910).

Eburne, Sir Sidney Alfred William, Kt., M.C.

Eccles, Sir John Carew, Kt., D.Phil., F.R.S.

Echlin, Sir Norman David Fenton, Bt. (I 1721).

Eckersley, Sir Donald Payze, Kt., O.B.E.

Edden, *Vice-Adm.* Sir (William) Kaye, K.B.E., C.B.

Edge, Sir William, Bt. (1937).

Edmenson, Sir Walter Alexander, Kt., C.B.E.

Edmonstone, Sir Archibald Bruce Charles, Bt. (1774).

Edwardes, Sir Michael Owen, Kt.

Edwards, Sir Christopher John Churchill, Bt. (1866).

Edwards, Sir George Robert, Kt., O.M., C.B.E., F.R.S.

Edwards, Sir (John) Clive (Leighton), Bt. (1921).

Edwards, Sir Llewellyn Roy, Kt.

Edwards, Sir Martin Llewellyn, Kt.

Edwards, *Prof.* Sir Samuel Frederick, Kt., F.R.S.

Egerton, Sir John Alfred Roy, Kt.

Egerton, Sir (Philip) John (Caledon) Grey-, Bt. (1617).

Egerton, Sir Seymour John Louis, G.C.V.O.

Eggleston, *Hon.* Sir Richard Moulton, Kt.

Eldridge, *Lt.-Gen.* Sir (William) John, K.B.E., C.B., D.S.O., M.C.

Eley, Sir Geoffrey Cecil Ryves, Kt., C.B.E.

Elliot, Sir John Blumenfeld, Kt.

Eliott of Stobs, Sir Arthur Francis Augustus Boswell, Bt. (s 1666).

Elliott, Sir Hugh Francis Ivo, Bt., O.B.E. (1917).

Elliott, Sir Norman Randall, Kt., C.B.E.

Elliott, Sir Randal Forbes, K.B.E.

Elliott, Sir Ronald Stuart, Kt.

Ellis, Sir John Rogers, Kt., M.B.E., M.D., F.R.C.P.

Ellis, Sir Ronald, Kt.

Ellison, *Rt. Rev.* and *Rt. Hon.* Gerald Alexander, K.C.V.O.

Ellison, *Col.* Sir Ralph Harry Carr-, Kt., T.D.

Ellwood, *Air Marshal* Sir Aubrey Beauclerk, K.C.B., D.S.C.

Elphinstone, Sir John, Bt. (s 1701).

Elphinstone, Sir (Maurice) Douglas (Warburton), Bt., T.D. (1816).

Elstub, Sir St. John de Holt, Kt., C.B.E.

Elton, Sir Charles Abraham Grierson, Bt. (1717).

Elyan, Sir (Isadore) Victor, Kt.

Emery, Sir Peter Frank Hannibal, Kt., M.P.

Empson, *Admiral* Sir (Leslie) Derek, G.B.E., K.C.B.

Emson, *Air Marshal* Sir Reginald Herbert, K.B.E., C.B., A.F.C.

Engholm, Sir Basil Charles, K.C.B.

Engineer, Sir Noshirwan Phirozshah, Kt.

Engle, Sir George Lawrence Jose, K.C.B., Q.C.

English, Sir Cyril Rupert, Kt.

English, Sir David, Kt.

Entwistle, Sir (John Nuttall) Maxwell, Kt.

Ereaut, Sir (Herbert) Frank Cobbold, Kt.

Errington, *Col.* Sir Geoffrey Frederick, Bt. (1963).

Errington, Sir Lancelot, K.C.B.

Erskine, Sir (Thomas) David, Bt. (1821).

Esmonde, Sir John Henry Grattan, Bt. (t 1629).

Espie, Sir Frank Fletcher, Kt., O.B.E.

Esplen, Sir William Graham, Bt. (1921).

Eustace, Sir Joseph Lambert, G.C.M.G.

Evans, Sir Anthony Adney, Bt. (1920).

Evans, Sir Athol Donald, K.B.E.

Evans, *Hon.* Sir Anthony Howell Meurig, Kt., R.D., Q.C.

Evans, *Air Chief Marshal* Sir David George, G.C.B., C.B.E.

Evans, Sir David Lewis, Kt., O.B.E., D.Litt.

Evans, *Lt.-Gen.* Sir Geoffrey Charles, K.B.E., C.B., D.S.O.

Evans, Sir Geraint Llewellyn, Kt., C.B.E.

Evans, *Hon.* Sir Haydn Tudor, Kt.

Evans, Sir Hywel Wynn, K.C.B.

Evans, Sir Ian William Gwynne-, Bt. (1913).

Evans, Sir Richard Mark, K.C.M.G.

Evans, Sir (Robert) Charles, Kt.

Evans, Sir (William) Vincent (John), G.C.M.G., M.B.E., Q.C.

Eveleigh, *Rt. Hon.* Sir Edward Walter, Kt., E.R.D.

Everard, *Maj.-Gen.* Sir Christopher Earle Welby-, K.B.E., C.B.

Everard, Sir Robin Charles, Bt. (1911).

Everson, Sir Frederick Charles, K.C.M.G.

Every, Sir John Simon, Bt. (1641).

Evetts, *Lt.-Gen.* Sir John Fullerton, Kt., C.B., C.B.E., M.C.

Ewart, Sir (William) Ivan (Cecil), Bt., D.S.C. (1887).

Ewbank, *Hon.* Sir Anthony Bruce, Kt.

Ewin, Sir (David) Ernest Thomas Floyd, Kt., O.B.E., M.V.O.

Ewing, *Vice-Adm.* Sir (Robert) Alastair, K.B.E., C.B., D.S.C.

Ewing, Sir Ronald Archibald Orr-, Bt. (1886).

Eyre, Sir Reginald Edwin, Kt., M.P.

Faber, Sir Richard Stanley, K.C.V.O., C.M.G.

Fadahunsi, Sir Joseph Odeleye, K.C.M.G.

Fagge, Sir John William Frederick, Bt. (1660).

Fairbairn, *Hon.* Sir David Eric, K.B.E., D.F.C.

Fairbairn, Sir (James) Brooke, Bt. (1869).

Fairbairn, Sir Robert Duncan, Kt.

Fairfax, Sir Vincent Charles, Kt., C.M.G.

Fairfax, Sir Warwick Oswald, Kt.

Fairgrieve, Sir (Thomas) Russell, Kt., C.B.E., T.D.

Fairhall, *Hon.* Sir Allen, K.B.E.

Falconer, *Hon.* Sir Douglas William, Kt., M.B.E.

Falk, Sir Roger Salis, Kt., O.B.E.

Falkiner, *Lt.-Col.* Sir Terence Edmond Patrick, Bt. (t 1778).

Falkner, Sir (Donald) Keith, Kt.

Falle, Sir Samuel, K.C.M.G., K.C.V.O., D.S.C.

Falshaw, Sir Donald, Kt.

Falvey, *Hon.* Sir John Neil, K.B.E., Q.C.

Faridkot, *Col.* H.H. the Raja of, K.C.S.I.

Farmer, Sir (Lovedin) George Thomas, Kt.

Farndale, *General* Sir Martin Baker, K.C.B.

Farquhar, *Lt.-Col.* Sir Peter (Walter), Bt., D.S.O. (1796).

Farquharson, *Hon.* Sir Donald Henry, Kt.

Farquharson, Sir James Robbie, K.B.E.

Farr, Sir John Arnold, Kt., M.P.

Farrar-Hockley, *General* Sir Anthony Heritage, G.B.E., K.C.B., D.S.O., M.C.

Farrer, Sir Charles Matthew, K.C.V.O.

Farrington, Sir Henry Francis Colden, Bt. (1818).

Faulkner, Sir Eric Odin, Kt., M.B.E.

Faulkner, Sir Percy, K.B.E., C.B.

Faulks, Sir Neville Major Ginner, Kt., M.B.E., T.D.

Fawcus, Sir (Robert) Peter, K.B.E., C.M.G.

Fawkes, Sir Randol Francis, Kt.

Fawcett, Sir James Edmund Sandford, Kt., D.S.C., Q.C.

Fayrer, Sir John Lang Macpherson, Bt., (1896).

Feilden, Sir Bernard Melchior, Kt., C.B.E.

Feilden, Sir Henry Wemyss, Bt., (1846).

Feldman, Sir Basil Samuel, Kt.

Fell, Sir Anthony, Kt.

Fellowes, Sir William Albemarle, K.C.V.O.

Fennessy, Sir Edward, Kt., C.B.E.

Ferens, Sir Thomas Robinson, Kt., C.B.E.

Ferguson, *Lt.-Col.* Sir Neil Edward Johnson-, Bt., T.D. (1906).

Fergusson of Kilkerran, Sir Charles, Bt. (s. 1703).

Fergusson, Sir James Herbert Hamilton Colyer-, Bt. (1866).

Feroze, Sir Rustam Moolan, Kt., F.R.C.S.

ffolkes, Sir Robert Francis Alexander, Bt. (1774)

Fieldhouse, Sir Harold, K.B.E., C.B.

Fieldhouse, *Admiral of the Fleet* Sir John David Elliott, G.C.B., G.B.E.

Fiennes, Sir John Saye Wingfield Twisleton-Wykeham-, K.C.B., Q.C.

Fiennes, Sir Maurice Alberic Twisleton-Wykeham-, Kt.

Fiennes, Sir Ranulph Twisleton-Wykeham-, Bt. (1916).

Figg, Sir Leonard Clifford William, K.C.M.G.

Figgess, Sir John George, K.B.E., C.M.G.

Figgures, Sir Frank Edward, K.C.B., C.M.G.

Figures, Sir Colin Frederick, K.C.M.G., O.B.E.

Fingland, Sir Stanley James Gunn, K.C.M.G.

Finlay, Sir Graeme Bell, Bt., E.R.D. (1964).

Finlay, *Prof.* Sir Moses, Kt., Ph.D., F.B.A.

Finley, Sir Peter Hamilton, Kt., O.B.E., D.F.C.

Finniston, Sir (Harold) Montague, Kt., Ph.D., F.R.S.

Finsberg, Sir Geoffrey, Kt., M.B.E., M.P.

Firth, *Prof.* Sir Raymond William, Kt., Ph.D., F.B.A.

Fisher, Sir George Read, Kt., C.M.G.

Fisher, *Hon.* Sir Henry Arthur Pears, Kt.

Fisher, Sir Nigel Thomas Loveridge, Kt., M.C.

Fison, Sir (Richard) Guy, Bt., D.S.C. (1905).

Fitch, *Vice-Adm.* Sir Richard George Alison, K.C.B.

Fitzgerald, *Rev.* (Sir) Edward Thomas, Kt. (1903).

FitzGerald, Sir George Peter Maurice, Bt., M.C., *The Knight of Kerry* (1880).

FitzGerald, Sir William James, Kt., M.C., Q.C.

FitzHerbert, Sir John Richard Frederick, Bt. (1784).

Fitzmaurice, *Lt.-Col.* Sir Desmond FitzJohn, Kt., C.I.E.

Fitzpatrick, *General* Sir (Geoffrey Richard) Desmond, G.C.B., D.S.O., M.B.E., M.C.

Fitzpatrick, *Air Marshal* Sir John Bernard, K.B.E., C.B.

Flanagan, Sir James Bernard, Kt., C.B.E.

Flavelle, Sir (Joseph) David Ellsworth, Bt. (1917).

Fleming, Sir Charles Alexander, K.B.E., F.R.S.

Fleming, *Instr. Rear-Adm.* Sir John, K.B.E., D.S.C.

Fleming, *Rt. Rev.* (William) Launcelot Scott, K.C.V.O., D.D.

Fletcher, *Hon.* Sir Alan Roy, Kt.

Fletcher, Sir James Muir Cameron, Kt.

Fletcher, Sir John Henry Lancelot Aubrey-, Bt. (1782).

Fletcher, Sir Leslie, Kt., D.S.C.

Fletcher, Sir Norman Seymour, Kt.

Fletcher, *Air Chief Marshal* Sir Peter Carteret, K.C.B., O.B.E., D.F.C., A.F.C.

Floyd, Sir Giles Henry Charles, Bt. (1816).

Foley, Sir (Thomas John) Noel, Kt., C.B.E.

Foot, Sir Geoffrey James, Kt.

Foots, Sir James William, Kt.

Forbes, *Hon.* Sir Alastair Granville, Kt.

Forbes, Sir Archibald Finlayson, G.B.E.

Forbes of Pitsligo, Sir Charles Edward Stuart-, Bt. (s 1626).

Forbes of Brux, *Hon.* Sir Ewan, Bt. (s 1630).

Forbes, *Hon.* Sir Hugh Harry Valentine, Kt.

Forbes, *Vice-Adm.* Sir John Morrison, K.C.B.

Forbes, *Maj.* Sir Hamish Stewart, Bt., M.B.E., M.C. (1823).

Ford, *Capt.* Sir Aubrey St. Clair-, Bt., D.S.O., R.N. (1793).

Ford, *Prof.* Sir Edward, Kt., O.B.E., M.D.

Ford, *Maj.* Sir Edward William Spencer, K.C.B., K.C.V.O.

Ford, *Air Marshal* Sir Geoffrey Harold, K.B.E., C.B.

Ford, *Prof.* Sir Hugh, Kt., F.R.S.

Ford, Sir John Archibald, K.C.M.G., M.C.

Ford, *Maj.-Gen.* Sir Peter St. Clair-, K.B.E., C.B., D.S.O.

Ford, Sir Richard Brinsley, Kt., C.B.E.

Ford, *General* Sir Robert Cyril, G.C.B., C.B.E.

Foreman, Sir Philip Frank, Kt., C.B.E.

Forman, Sir John Denis, Kt., O.B.E.

Forrest, Sir James Alexander, Kt.

Forrest, *Rear Adm.* Sir Ronald Stephen, K.C.V.O.

Forster, Sir Oliver Grantham, K.C.M.G., M.V.O.

Forwood, Sir Dudley Richard, Bt. (1895).

Foster, Sir John Gregory, Bt. (1930).

Foster, Sir Robert Sidney, G.C.M.G., K.C.V.O.

Foulis, Sir Ian Primrose Liston-, Bt. (s 1634).

Foulkes, Sir Nigel Gordon, Kt.

Fowden, Sir Leslie, Kt., F.R.S.

Fowke, Sir Frederick (Woollaston Rawdon), Bt. (1814).

Fowler, Sir (Edward) Michael Coulson, Kt.

Fox, Sir (Henry) Murray, G.B.E.

Fox, *Rt. Hon.* Sir Michael John, Kt.

Fox, Sir Theodore Fortescue, Kt., M.D., Ll.D.

Frame, Sir Alistair Gilchrist, Kt.

France, Sir Arnold William, G.C.B.

Francis, Sir Frank Chalton, K.C.B., F.S.A.

Frank, Sir Douglas George Horace, Kt., Q.C.

Frank, Sir (Frederick) Charles, Kt., O.B.E., F.R.S.

Frank, Sir Robert John, Bt. (1920).

Frankel, Sir Otto Herzberg, Kt., D.S.C., F.R.S.

Franklin, Sir Eric Alexander, Kt., C.B.E.

Franklin, Sir Michael David Milroy, K.C.B., C.M.G.

Franks, Sir Arthur Temple, K.C.M.G.

Fraser, Sir Angus McKay, K.C.B., T.D.

Fraser, Sir Basil Malcolm, Bt. (1921).

Fraser, Sir Bruce Donald, K.C.B.

Fraser, *General* Sir David William, G.C.B., O.B.E.

Fraser, Sir Douglas Were, Kt., I.S.O.

Fraser, *Air Marshal Rev.* Sir (Henry) Paterson, K.B.E., C.B., A.F.C.

Fraser, Sir Hugh, Bt. (1961).

Fraser, Sir Ian, Kt., D.S.O., O.B.E.

Fraser, Sir (James) Campbell, Kt.

Fraser, *Prof.* Sir James David, Bt. (1943).

Fraser, Sir William Kerr, K.C.B.

Frederick, Sir Charles Boscawen, Bt. (1723).

Freeland, Sir John Redvers, K.C.M.G.

Freeman, *His Eminence* James Darcy, K.B.E.

Freeman, Sir James Robin, Bt. (1945).

Freeman, Sir (Nathaniel) Bernard, Kt., C.B.E.

Freeman, Sir Ralph, Kt., C.V.O., C.B.E.

Freer, *Air Chief Marshal* Sir Robert William George, G.B.E., K.C.B.

Freeth, *Hon.* Sir Gordon, K.B.E.

French, *Hon.* Sir Christopher James Saunders, Kt.

Fretwell, Sir George Herbert, K.B.E., C.B.

Fretwell, *Maj.* Sir John Emsley, K.C.M.G.

Frew, Sir John Lewtas, Kt., O.B.E.

Froggatt, Sir Leslie Trevor, Kt.

Froggatt, Sir Peter, Kt.

Frossard, Sir Charles Keith, Kt.

Frost, *Hon.* Sir (Thomas) Sydney, Kt.

Fry, Sir Francis Wilfrid, Bt., O.B.E. (1894).

Fry, *Hon.* Sir William Gordon, Kt.

Fryberg, Sir Abraham, Kt., M.B.E.

Fuchs, Sir Vivian Ernest, Kt., Ph.D.

Fuller, *Hon.* Sir John Bryan Munro, Kt.

Fuller, Sir John William Fleetwood, Bt. (1910).

Fung, *Hon.* Sir Kenneth Ping-Fan, Kt., C.B.E.

Furness, Sir Stephen Roberts, Bt. (1913).

Gadsden, Sir Peter Drury Haggerston, G.B.E.

Gage, Sir Berkeley Everard Foley, K.C.M.G.

Gairy, *Rt. Hon.* Sir Eric Matthew, Kt.

Gaitskell, Sir Arthur, Kt., C.M.G.

Gallwey, Sir Philip Frankland Payne-, Bt. (1812).

Galsworthy, Sir Arthur Norman, K.C.M.G.

Galsworthy, Sir John Edgar, K.C.V.O., C.M.G.

Gamble, Sir David Hugh Norman, Bt. (1897).

Gandell, Sir Alan Thomas, Kt., C.B.E.

Ganilau, *Ratu* Sir Penaia Kanatabatu, G.C.M.G., K.C.V.O., K.B.E., D.S.O.

Gardner, Sir Douglas Bruce Bruce-, Bt. (1945).

Gardner, Sir Edward Lucas, Kt., Q.C., M.P.

Gardner-Thorpe, *Col.* Sir Ronald, G.B.E., T.D.

Garland, *Hon.* Sir Ransley Victor, Kt.

Garlick, Sir John, K.C.B.

Garner, Sir Anthony Stuart, Kt.

Garran, Sir (Isham) Peter, K.C.M.G.

Garrett, *Hon.* Sir Raymond William, Kt., A.F.C.

Garrioch, Sir (William) Henry, Kt.

Garthwaite, Sir William Francis Cuthbert, Bt., D.S.C. (1919).

Garvey, Sir Ronald Herbert, K.C.M.G., K.C.V.O., M.B.E.

Garvey, Sir Terence Willcocks, K.C.M.G.

Gascoigne, *Maj.-Gen.* Sir Julian Alvery, K.C.M.G., K.C.V.O., C.B., D.S.O.

Geddes, Sir (Anthony) Reay (Mackay), K.B.E.

Gentry, *Maj.-Gen.* Sir William George, K.B.E., C.B., D.S.O.

George, Sir Arthur Thomas, Kt.

Gethin, *Lt.-Col.* Sir Richard Patrick St. Lawrence, Bt. (I 1665).

Ghurburrun, Sir Rabindrah, Kt.

Gibbon, *General* Sir John Houghton, G.C.B., O.B.E.

Gibbons, Sir (John) David, K.B.E.

Gibbons, Sir William Edward Doran, Bt. (1752).

Gibbs, *Air Marshal* Sir Gerald Ernest, K.B.E., C.I.E., M.C.

Gibbs, *Rt. Hon.* Sir Harry Talbot, G.C.M.G., K.B.E.

Gibbs, *Rt. Hon.* Sir Humphrey Vicary, G.C.V.O., K.C.M.G., O.B.E.

Gibbs, *Field-Marshal* Sir Roland Christopher, G.C.B., C.B.E., D.S.O., M.C.

Gibson, Sir Alexander Drummond, Kt., C.B.E.

Gibson, Sir Christopher Herbert, Bt. (1931).

Gibson, *Rev.* Sir David, Bt. (1926).

Gibson, *Vice-Adm.* Sir Donald Cameron Ernest Forbes, K.C.B., D.S.C.

Gibson, Sir Donald Evelyn Edward, Kt., C.B.E.

Gibson, *Hon.* Sir Marcus George, Kt.

Gibson, *Rt. Hon.* Sir Maurice White, Kt.

Gibson, Sir Peter Leslie, Kt.

Gibson, *Hon.* Sir Ralph Brian, Kt.

Gibson, Sir Ronald George, Kt., C.B.E., F.R.C.S.

Giddings, *Air Marshal* Sir (Kenneth Charles) Michael, K.C.B., O.B.E., D.F.C., A.F.C.

Gielgud, Sir (Arthur) John, Kt., C.H.

Giffard, Sir (Charles) Sydney (Rycroft), K.C.M.G.

Gilbert, *Brig.* Sir Herbert Ellery, K.B.E., D.S.O.

Gilbert, *Air Marshal* Sir Joseph Alfred, K.C.B., C.B.E.

Gilbertson, Sir Geoffrey, Kt., C.B.E.

Gilbey, Sir (Walter) Derek, Bt. (1893).

Gilchrist, Sir Andrew Graham, K.C.M.G.

Gilchrist, Sir (James) Finlay (Elder), Kt., C.B.E.

Giles, Sir Alexander Falconer, K.B.E., C.M.G.

Gilkison, Sir Alan Fleming, Kt., C.B.E.

Gillard, *Hon.* Sir Oliver James, Kt.

Gillett, *Maj.-Gen.* Sir Peter Bernard, K.C.V.O., C.B., O.B.E.

Gillett, Sir Robin Danvers Penrose, Bt., G.B.E., R.D. (1959).

Gilliat, *Lt.-Col.* Sir Martin John, G.C.V.O., M.B.E.

Gilmour, *Rt. Hon.* Sir Ian Hedworth John Little, Bt., M.P. (1926).

Gilmour, Sir John Edward, Bt., D.S.O., T.D. (1897).

Gingell, *Air Chief Marshal* Sir John, G.B.E., K.C.B.

Gladstone, Sir (Erskine) William, Bt. (1846).

Glass, Sir Leslie Charles, K.C.M.G.

Glasspole, Sir Florizel Augustus, G.C.M.G, G.C.V.O.

Glen, Sir Alexander Richard, K.B.E., D.S.C.

Glenn, Sir (Joseph Robert) Archibald, Kt., O.B.E.

Glidewell, *Rt. Hon.* Sir Iain Derek Laing, Kt.

Glock, Sir William Frederick, Kt., C.B.E.

Glover, Sir Gerald Alfred, Kt.

Glover, *General* Sir James Malcolm, K.C.B., M.B.E.

Glubb, *Lt.-Gen.* Sir John Bagot, K.C.B., C.M.G., D.S.O., O.B.E., M.C.

Glyn, Sir Anthony Geoffrey Leo Simon, Bt. (1927).

Glyn, Sir Richard Lindsay, Bt., (1759 and 1800).

Goad, Sir (Edward) Colin (Viner), K.C.M.G.

Godber, Sir George Edward, G.C.B., D.M.

Goddard, *Air Marshal* Sir (Robert) Victor, K.C.B., C.B.E.

Goff, *Rt. Hon.* Sir Robert Lionel Archibald, Kt.

Goff, Sir Robert (William) Davis-, Bt. (1905).

Gold, Sir Arthur Abraham, Kt., C.B.E.

Gold, Sir Joseph, Kt.

Goldberg, *Prof.* Sir Abraham, Kt., M.D., D.SC., F.R.C.P.

Goldman, Sir Samuel, K.C.B.

Goldsmid, *Maj.-Gen.* Sir James Arthur d'Avigdor-, Bt., C.B., O.B.E., M.C. (1934).

Goldsmith, Sir James Michael, Kt.

Gombrich, *Prof.* Sir Ernst Hans Josef, Kt., C.B.E., Ph.D., F.B.A., F.S.A.

Gomes, Sir Stanley Eugene, Kt.

Gooch, Sir (Richard) John Sherlock, Bt. (1746).

Gooch, Sir Robert Douglas, Bt. (1866).

Goodall, Sir Reginald, Kt., C.B.E.

Goode, Sir William Allmond Codrington, G.C.M.G.

Goodenough, Sir Richard Edmund, Bt. (1943).

Goodhart, Sir Philip Carter, Kt., M.P.

Goodhart, Sir Robert Anthony Gordon, Bt. (1911).

Goodhew, Sir Victor Henry, Kt.

Goodison, Sir Alan Clowes, K.C.M.G.

Goodison, Sir Nicholas Proctor, Kt.

Goodson, *Lt.-Col.* Sir Alfred Lassam, Bt. (1922).

Goodwin, Sir Reginald Eustace, Kt., C.B.E.

Goodwin, *Lt.-Gen.* Sir Richard Elton, K.C.B., C.B.E., D.S.O.

Goody, *Most Rev.* Launcelot John, K.B.E.

Goold, Sir George Leonard, Bt. (1801).

Goold, Sir James Duncan, Kt.

Gordon, Sir Andrew Cosmo Lewis Duff-, Bt. (1813).

Gordon, Sir Charles Addison Somerville Snowden, K.C.B.

Gordon, Sir John Charles, Bt. (s 1706).

Gordon, Sir Keith Lyndell, Kt., C.M.G.

Gordon, Sir (Lionel) Eldred (Peter) Smith-, Bt. (1838).

Gordon, Sir Sidney Samuel, Kt., C.B.E.

Gore, Sir Richard Ralph St. George, Bt. (I 1622).

Goring, Sir William Burton Nigel, Bt. (1627).

Gorton, *Rt. Hon.* Sir John Grey, G.C.M.G., C.H.

Goschen, Sir Edward Christian, Bt., D.S.O. (1916).

Gosling, Sir (Frederick) Donald, Kt.

Gould, *Hon.* Sir Trevor Jack, Kt.

Goulding, *Hon.* Sir (Ernest) Irvine, Kt.

Goulding, Sir (William) Lingard Walter, Bt. (1904).

Gourlay, *General* Sir (Basil) Ian (Spencer), K.C.B., O.B.E., M.C., R.M.

Govan, Sir Lawrence Herbert, Kt.

Gow, *Gen.* Sir (James) Michael, G.C.B.

Gowans, *Hon.* Sir (Urban) Gregory, Kt.

Gowans, Sir James Learmonth, Kt., C.B.E., F.R.C.P., F.R.S.

Gower, Sir (Herbert) Raymond, Kt., M.P.

Gowing, *Prof.* Sir Lawrence Burnett, Kt., C.B.E.

Graaff, Sir de Villiers, Bt., M.B.E. (1911).

Grace, Sir John Te Herekiekie, K.B.E., M.V.O.

Graesser, *Col.* Sir Alastair Stewart Durward, Kt., D.S.O., O.B.E., M.C., T.D.

Graham, Sir Charles Spencer Richard, Bt. (1783).

Graham, Sir James Bellingham, Bt. (1662).

Graham, Sir John Alexander Noble, Bt., K.C.M.G. (1906).

Graham, Sir John Moodie, Bt. (1964).

Graham, Sir (John) Patrick, Kt.

Graham, Sir Norman William, Kt., C.B.

Graham, Sir Ralph Wolfe, Bt. (1629).

Grandy, *Marshal of the Royal Air Force* Sir John, G.C.B., K.B.E., D.S.O.

Grant, Sir Archibald, Bt. (s 1705).

Grant, Sir Clifford, Kt.

Grant, Sir (John) Anthony, Kt., M.P.

Grant, Sir Kenneth Lindsay, Kt., O.B.E.

Grant, Sir Patrick Alexander Benedict, Bt. (s 1688).

Grantham, *Admiral* Sir Guy, G.C.B., C.B.E., D.S.O.

Granville, Sir Keith, Kt., C.B.E.

Gray, Sir John Archibald Browne, Kt., SC.D., F.R.S.

Gray, *Vice-Adm.* Sir John Michael Dudgeon, K.B.E., C.B.

Gray, Sir William Hume, Bt. (1917).

Gray, Sir William Stevenson, Kt.

Grayson, Sir Ronald Henry Rudyard, Bt. (1922).

Greatbatch, Sir Bruce, Kt., K.C.V.O., C.M.G., M.B.E.

Green, Sir (Edward) Stephen (Lycett), Bt., C.B.E. (1886).

Green, Sir George Ernest, Kt.

Green, *Hon.* Sir Guy Stephen Montague, K.B.E.

Green, Sir Owen Whitley, Kt.

Green, Sir Peter James Frederick, Kt.

Greenaway, Sir Derek Burdick, Bt., C.B.E. (1933).

Greenborough, Sir John, K.B.E.

Greene, Sir Hugh Carleton, K.C.M.G., O.B.E.

Greene, Sir (John) Brian Massy-, Kt.

Greening, *Rear-Adm.* Sir Paul Woollven, K.C.V.O.

Greenwell, Sir Edward Bernard, Bt. (1906).

Greeves, *Maj.-Gen.* Sir Stuart, K.B.E., C.B., D.S.O., M.C.

Grenside, Sir John Peter, Kt., C.B.E.

Gretton, *Vice-Adm.* Sir Peter William, K.C.B., D.S.O., O.B.E., D.S.C.

Grey, Sir Anthony Dysart, Bt. (1814).

Grey, Sir Paul Francis, K.C.M.G.

Grierson, Sir Richard Douglas, Bt. (s 1685).

Grieve, Sir (Herbert) Ronald (Robinson), Kt.

Grieve, *Prof.* Sir Robert, Kt.

Griffin, *Admiral* Sir Anthony Templer Frederick Griffith, G.C.B.

Griffin, Sir (Charles) David, Kt., C.B.E.

Griffin, Sir John Bowes, Kt., Q.C.

Griffiths, Sir Eldon Wylie, Kt., M.P.

Griffiths, Sir (Ernest) Roy, Kt.

Griffiths, Sir Percival Joseph, K.B.E., C.I.E.

Griffiths, Sir John Norton-, Bt. (1922).

Griffiths, Sir Reginald Ernest, Kt., C.B.E.

Grimwade, Sir Andrew Sheppard, Kt., C.B.E.

Grindrod, *Most Rev.* John Basil Rowland, K.B.E.

Groom, Sir (Thomas) Reginald, Kt.

Groom, *Air Marshal* Sir Victor Emmanuel, K.C.V.O., K.B.E., C.B., D.F.C.

Grotrian, Sir Philip Christian Brent, Bt. (1934).

Grove, Sir Charles Gerald, Bt. (1874).

Grove, Sir Edmund Frank, K.C.V.O.

Groves, Sir Charles Barnard, Kt., C.B.E.

Grugeon, Sir John Drury, Kt.

Grundy, *Air Marshal* Sir Edouard Michael FitzFrederick, K.B.E., C.B.

Guinness, Sir Alec, Kt., C.B.E.

Guinness, Sir Howard Christian Sheldon, Kt., V.R.D.

Guinness, Sir Kenelm Ernest Lee, Bt. (1867).

Guise, Sir John, G.C.M.G., K.B.E.

Guise, Sir John Grant, Bt. (1783).

Gujadhur, Sir Radhamohun, Kt., C.M.G.

Gull, Sir Michael Swinnerton Cameron, Bt. (1872).

Gunn, *Prof.* Sir John Currie, Kt., C.B.E.

Gunn, Sir William Archer, K.B.E., C.M.G.

Gunning, Sir Robert Charles, Bt. (1778).

Gunston, Sir Richard Wellesley, Bt. (1938).

Gurden, Sir Harold Edward, Kt.

Gutch, Sir John, K.C.M.G., O.B.E.

Guthrie, Sir Malcolm Connop, Bt., (1936)

Guthrie, *Hon.* Sir Rutherford Campbell, Kt., C.M.G.

Guy, *General* Sir Roland Kelvin, K.C.B., C.B.E., D.S.O.

Habakkuk, Sir John Hrothgar, Kt., F.B.A.

Hackett, *General* Sir John Winthrop, G.C.B., C.B.E., D.S.O., M.C.

Haddow, Sir (Thomas) Douglas, K.C.B.

Hadley, Sir Leonard Albert, Kt.

Hadow, Sir Gordon, Kt., C.M.G., O.B.E.

Hadow, Sir (Reginald) Michael, K.C.M.G.

Hague, *Prof.* Sir Douglas Chalmers, Kt., C.B.E.

Haines, Sir Cyril Henry, K.B.E.

Hale, *Prof.* Sir John Rigby, Kt.

Haley, Sir William John, K.C.M.G.

Hall, Sir Arnold Alexander, Kt., F.R.S.

Hall, Sir Basil Brodribb, K.C.B., M.C., T.D.

Hall, *Air Marshal* Sir Donald Percy, K.C.B., C.B.E., A.F.C.

Hall, Sir Douglas Basil, Bt., K.C.M.G. (s 1687)

Hall, Sir (Frederick) John (Frank), Bt. (1923).

Hall, Sir John Bernard, Bt. (1919).

Hall, Sir Peter Reginald Frederick, Kt., C.B.E.

Hall, Sir Robert de Zouche, K.C.M.G.

Hall, *Brig.* Sir William Henry, K.B.E., D.S.O., E.D.

Hallett, *Vice-Adm.* Sir (Cecil) Charles Hughes-, K.C.B., C.B.E.

Halliday, Sir George Clifton, Kt.

Halliday, *Vice-Adm.* Sir Roy William, K.B.E., D.S.C.

Hallifax, *Vice-Adm.* Sir David John, K.C.B., K.B.E.

Hallinan, Sir (Adrian) Lincoln, Kt.

Halsey, *Rev.* Sir John Walter Brooke, Bt. (1920).

Halstead, Sir Ronald, Kt., C.B.E.

Hambling, Sir (Herbert) Hugh, Bt. (1924).

Hamburger, Sir Sidney Cyril, Kt., C.B.E.

Hamer, *Hon.* Sir Rupert James, K.C.M.G., E.D.

Hamill, Sir Patrick, Kt., Q.P.M.

Hamilton, Sir (Charles) Denis, Kt., D.S.O.

Hamilton, Sir Edward Sydney, Bt. (1776 and 1819).

Hamilton, Sir James Arnot, K.C.B., M.B.E.

Hamilton, *Admiral* Sir John Graham, G.B.E., C.B.

Hamilton, Sir Michael Aubrey, Kt.

Hamilton, Sir Patrick George, Bt. (1937).

Hamilton, Sir (Robert Charles) Richard Caradoc, Bt. (s 1646).

Hamilton, Sir Bruce Stirling-, Bt. (s 1673).

Hammett, *Hon.* Sir Clifford James, Kt.

Hammick, Sir Stephen George, Bt. (1834).

Hampshire, Sir Stuart Newton, Kt., F.B.A.

Hanbury, Sir John Capel, Kt., C.B.E.

Hancock, *Lt.-Col.* Sir Cyril Percy, K.C.I.E., O.B.E., M.C.

Hancock, Sir David John Stowell, K.C.B.

Hancock, *Air Marshal* Sir Valston Eldridge, K.B.E., C.B., D.F.C.

Hancock, *Prof.* Sir (William) Keith, K.B.E., F.B.A.

Hand, *Most Rev.* Geoffrey David, K.B.E.

Handley, Sir David John Davenport-, Kt., O.B.E.

Hanham, Sir Michael William, Bt., D.F.C. (1667).

Hanley, Sir Michael Bowen, K.C.B.

Hanmer, Sir John Wyndham Edward, Bt. (1774).

Hanson, Sir Anthony Leslie Oswald, Bt. (1887).

Hanson, Sir (Charles) John, Bt. (1918).

Harcourt-Smith, *Air Marshal* Sir David, K.C.B., D.F.C.

Harders, Sir Clarence Waldemar, Kt., O.B.E.

Hardie, Sir Charles Edgar Mathewes, Kt., C.B.E.

Harding, Sir George William, K.C.M.G., C.V.O.

Harding, Sir Harold John Boyer, Kt.

Harding, *Air Chief Marshal* Sir Peter Robin, K.C.B.

Harding, Sir Roy Pollard, Kt., C.B.E.

Hardinge, Sir Robert Arnold, Bt. (1801).

Hardingham, Sir Robert Ernest, Kt., C.M.G., O.B.E.

Hardman, Sir Fred, Kt., M.B.E.

Hardman, Sir Henry, K.C.B.

Hardy, Sir James Douglas, Kt., C.B.E.

Hardy, Sir James Gilbert, Kt., O.B.E.

Hardy, Sir Rupert John, Bt., (1876).

Hare, Sir Thomas, Bt. (1818).

Harford, Sir James Dundas, K.B.E., C.M.G.

Harford, Sir (John) Timothy, Bt. (1934).

Harington, *General* Sir Charles Henry Pepys, G.C.B., C.B.E., D.S.O., M.C.

Harington, Sir Nicholas John, Bt. (1611).

Harland, *Air Marshal* Sir Reginald Edward Wynyard, K.B.E., C.B.

Harley, Sir Thomas Winlack, Kt., M.B.E., M.C.

Harman, Sir Cecil William Francis Stafford-King-, Bt. (1914).

Harman, *General* Sir Jack Wentworth, G.C.B., O.B.E., M.C.

Harman, *Hon.* Sir Jeremiah LeRoy, Kt.

Harmer, Sir Frederic Evelyn, Kt., C.M.G.

Harmer, Sir (John) Dudley, Kt., O.B.E.

Harmsworth, Sir Hildebrand Harold, Bt. (1922).

Harper Gow, Sir Leonard Maxwell, Kt., M.B.E.

Harpham, Sir William, K.B.E., C.M.G.

Harris, *Prof.* Sir Alan James, Kt., C.B.E.

Harris, Sir Anthony Kyrle Travers, Bt. (1953).

Harris, *Prof.* Sir Charles Herbert Stuart-, Kt., C.B.E., M.D.

Harris, Sir Charles Joseph William, K.B.E.

Harris, *Lt.-Gen.* Sir Ian Cecil, K.B.E., C.B., D.S.O.

Harris, *Maj.-Gen.* Sir Jack Alexander Sutherland-, K.C.V.O., C.B.

Harris, Sir Jack Wolfred Ashford, Bt. (1932).

Harris, Sir Lewis Edward, Kt., O.B.E.

Harris, Sir Philip Charles, Kt.

Harris, Sir Ronald Montague Joseph, K.C.V.O., C.B.

Harris, Sir William Gordon, K.B.E., C.B.

Harris, Sir William Woolf, Kt., O.B.E.

Harrison, Sir Ernest Thomas, Kt., O.B.E..

Harrison, Sir Francis Alexander Lyle, Kt., M.B.E., Q.C.

Harrison, Sir Geoffrey Wedgwood, G.C.M.G., K.C.V.O.

Harrison, *Surgeon Vice-Adm.* Sir John Albert Bews, K.B.E.

Harrison, *Hon.* Sir (John) Richard, Kt., E.D.

Harrison, Sir Michael James Harwood, Bt. (1961).

Harrison, *Prof.* Sir Richard John, Kt., F.R.S.

Harrison, Sir (Robert) Colin, Bt. (1922).

Harrop, Sir Peter John, K.C.B.

Hart, Sir Byrne, Kt., C.B.E., M.C.

Hart, Sir Francis Edmund Turton-, K.B.E.

Hartley, *Air Marshal* Sir Christopher Harold, K.C.B., C.B.E., D.F.C., A.F.C.

Hartley, Sir Frank, Kt., C.B.E., ph.D.

Hartnett, Sir Laurence John, Kt., C.B.E.

Hartopp, Sir John Edmund Cradock-, Bt. (1796).

Hartwell, Sir Brodrick William Charles Elwin, Bt. (1805).

Harvey, Sir Charles Richard Musgrave, Bt. (1933).

Harvey-Jones, Sir John Henry, Kt., M.B.E.

Haskard, Sir Cosmo Dugal Patrick Thomas, K.C.M.G., M.B.E.

Haslam, *Hon.* Sir Alec Leslie, Kt.

Haslam, *Rear-Adm.* Sir David William, K.B.E., C.B.

Haslam, Sir Robert, Kt.

Hasluck, *Rt. Hon.* Sir Paul Meernaa Caedwalla, K.G., G.C.M.G., G.C.V.O.

Hassan, Sir Joshua Abraham, Kt., C.B.E., M.V.O., Q.C.

Hassett, *General* Sir Francis George, K.B.E., C.B., D.S.O., M.V.O.

Hastings, Sir Stephen Lewis Edmonstone, Kt., M.C.

Hatty, *Hon.* Sir Cyril James, Kt.

Haughton, Sir James, Kt., C.B.E., Q.P.M.

Havelock, Sir Wilfrid Bowen, Kt.

Havers, *Rt. Hon.* Sir (Robert) Michael (Oldfield), Kt., Q.C., M.P.

Hawker, Sir (Frank) Cyril, Kt.

Hawkings, Sir (Francis) Geoffrey, Kt.

Hawkins, Sir Arthur Ernest, Kt.

Hawkins, Sir Humphry Villiers Caesar, Bt. (1778).

Hawkins, Sir Paul Lancelot, Kt., T.D., M.P.

Hawkins, *Vice-Adm.* Sir Raymond Shayle, K.C.B.

Hawley, *Maj.* Sir David Henry, Bt. (1795).

Hawley, Sir Donald Frederick, K.C.M.G., M.B.E.

Haworth, Sir (Arthur) Geoffrey, Bt. (1911).

Haworth, *Hon.* Sir William Crawford, Kt.

Hawthorne, *Prof.* Sir William Rede, Kt., C.B.E., SC.D., F.R.S.

Hay, Sir (Alan) Philip, K.C.V.O., T.D.

Hay, Sir Arthur Thomas Erroll, Bt., I.S.O. (s 1663).

Hay, Sir David Osborne, Kt., C.B.E., D.S.O.

Hay, Sir Frederick Baden-Powell, Bt. (s 1703).

Hay, Sir James Brian Dalrymple-, Bt. (1798).

Hayday, Sir Frederick, Kt., C.B.E.

Haydon, Sir Walter Robert, K.C.M.G.

Hayes, Sir Brian David, K.C.B.

Hayes, Sir Claude James, K.C.M.G.

Hayes, *Vice-Adm.* Sir John Osier Chattock, K.C.B., O.B.E.

Hayman, Sir Peter Telford, K.C.M.G., C.V.O., M.B.E.

Hayter, Sir William Goodenough, K.C.M.G.

Hayward, Sir Alfred, K.B.E.

Hayward, Sir Anthony William Byrd, Kt.

Hayward, Sir Richard Arthur, Kt., C.B.E.

Head, Sir Francis David Somerville, Bt. (1838).

Healey, Sir Charles Arthur Chadwyck-, Bt., O.B.E., T.D. (1919).

Heap, Sir Desmond, Kt.

Heath, Sir Barrie, Kt., D.F.C.

Heath, Sir Mark Evelyn, K.C.V.O., C.M.G.

Heath, *Air Marshal* Sir Maurice Lionel, K.B.E., C.B., C.V.O.

Heathcoat Amory, Sir Ian, Bt. (1874).

Heathcote, Sir Michael Perryman, Bt. (1733).

Heaton, Sir Yvo Robert Henniker-, Bt. (1912).

Hein, Sir (Charles Henri) Raymond, Kt., Q.C.

Hele, Sir Ivor Thomas Henry, Kt., C.B.E.

Hellaby, Sir (Frederick Reed) Alan, Kt.

Hellings, *General* Sir Peter William Cradock, K.C.B., D.S.C., M.C., R.M.

Helpmann, Sir Robert Murray, Kt., C.B.E.

Henare, Sir James Clendon Tau, K.B.E., D.S.O.

Henderson, Sir Guy Wilmot McLintock, Kt., Q.C.

Henderson, Sir James Thyne, K.B.E., C.M.G.

Henderson, Sir (John) Nicholas, G.C.M.G.

Henderson, Sir Neville Vicars, Kt., C.B.E.

Henderson, *Admiral* Sir Nigel Stuart, G.B.E., K.C.B.

Henderson, Sir William MacGregor, Kt., D.SC., F.R.S.

Henley, Sir Douglas Owen, K.C.B.

Henley, *Rear-Adm.* Sir Joseph Charles Cameron, K.C.V.O., C.B.

Hennessy, Sir James Patrick Ivan, K.B.E., C.M.G.

Hennessy, Sir John Wyndham Pope-, Kt., C.B.E., F.B.A., F.S.A.

Henniker, *Brig.* Sir Mark Chandos Auberon, Bt., C.B.E., D.S.O., M.C. (1813).

Henry, Sir Denis Aynsley, Kt., O.B.E., Q.C.

Henry, Sir James Holmes, Bt., C.M.G., M.C., T.D., Q.C. (1923).

Henry, *Hon.* Sir Trevor Ernest, Kt.

Hepburn, Sir Ninian Buchan Archibald John Buchan-, Bt. (1815).

Herbecq, Sir John Edward, K.C.B.

Herbert, *Admiral* Sir Peter Geoffrey Marshall, K.C.B., O.B.E.

Hermon, Sir John Charles, Kt., O.B.E.

Heron, Sir Conrad Frederick, K.C.B., O.B.E.

Herries, Sir Michael Alexander Robert Young-, Kt., O.B.E., M.C.

Heseltine, Sir William Frederick Payne, K.C.V.O., C.B.

Hetherington, Sir Arthur Ford, Kt., D.S.C.

Hetherington, Sir Thomas Chalmers, K.C.B., C.B.E., T.D., Q.C.

Heward, *Air Chief Marshal* Sir Anthony Wilkinson, K.C.B., O.B.E., D.F.C., A.F.C.

Hewetson, Sir Christopher Raynor, Kt., T.D.

Hewetson, *General* Sir Reginald Hackett, G.C.B., C.B.E., D.S.O.

Hewett, Sir John George, Bt., M.C. (1813).

Hewitt, Sir (Cyrus) Lenox (Simson), Kt., O.B.E.

Hewitt, Sir Nicholas Charles Joseph, Bt. (1921).

Heygate, Sir George Lloyd, Bt. (1831).

Heyman, Sir Horace William, Kt.

Heywood, Sir Oliver Kerr, Bt. (1838).

Hezlet, *Vice-Adm.* Sir Arthur Richard, K.B.E., C.B., D.S.O., D.S.C.

Hibbert, Sir Reginald Alfred, G.C.M.G.

Hickey, Sir Justin, Kt.

Hickman, Sir (Richard) Glenn, Bt. (1903).

Hicks, *Col.* Sir Denys Theodore, Kt., O.B.E., T.D.

Hicks, Sir John Richard, Kt., F.B.A.

Higgins, Sir Christopher Thomas, Kt.

Higgs, Sir (John) Michael (Clifford), Kt.

Hildred, Sir William Percival, Kt., C.B., O.B.E.

Hildreth, *Maj.-Gen.* Sir (Harold) John (Crossley), K.B.E.

Hildyard, Sir David Henry Thoroton, K.C.M.G., D.F.C.

Hiley, *Hon.* Sir Thomas Alfred, K.B.E.

Hilgendorf, Sir Charles, Kt., C.M.G.

Hill, *Prof.* Sir Austin Bradford, Kt., C.B.E., Ph.D., D.SC., F.R.S.

Hill, Sir George Alfred Rowley, Bt. (t 1779).

Hill, Sir James Frederick, Bt. (1917).

Hill, Sir John McGregor, Kt., ph.D.

Hill, Sir John Maxwell, Kt., c.B.E., D.F.C.

Hill, Sir Robert Erskine-, Bt. (1945).

Hillary, Sir Edmund, K.B.E.

Hilton, Sir Derek Percy, Kt., M.B.E.

Himsworth, Sir Harold Percival, K.C.B., M.D., F.R.S.

Hine, *Air Chief Marshal* Sir Patrick Bardon, K.C.B.

Hines, Sir Colin Joseph, Kt., O.B.E.

Hinsley, *Prof.* Sir Francis Harry, Kt., O.B.E., F.B.A.

Hirsch, *Prof.* Sir Peter Bernhard, Kt., Ph.D., F.R.S.

Hirst, *Hon.* Sir David Cozens-Hardy, Kt.

Hoare, Sir Frederick Alfred, Bt. (1962).

Hoare, Sir Peter Richard David, Bt. (1786).

Hoare, Sir Timothy Edward Charles, Bt. (t 1784).

Hobart, *Lt.-Cdr.* Sir Robert Hampden, Bt., R.N. (1914).

Hobday, Sir Gordon Ivan, Kt.

Hobhouse, Sir Charles Chisholm, Bt., T.D. (1812).

Hobson, Sir Harold, Kt., c.B.E.

Hockaday, Sir Arthur Patrick, K.C.B., C.M.G.

Hodge, Sir John Rowland, Bt., M.B.E. (1921).

Hodge, Sir Julian Stephen Alfred, Kt.

Hodges, *Air Chief Marshal* Sir Lewis MacDonald, K.C.B., C.B.E., D.S.O., D.F.C.

Hodgkin, *Prof.* Sir Alan Lloyd, O.M., K.B.E., F.R.S., SC.D.

Hodgkinson, *Air Chief Marshal* Sir (William) Derek, K.C.B., C.B.E., D.F.C., A.F.C.

Hodgson, Sir Maurice Arthur Eric, Kt.

Hodgson, *Hon.* Sir (Walter) Derek (Thornley), Kt.

Hodson, Sir Michael Robin Adderley, Bt. (t 1789).

Hoffenberg, *Prof.* Sir Raymond, K.B.E.

Hoffman, *Hon.* Sir Leonard Hubert, Kt., Q.C.

Hogan, Sir Michael Joseph Patrick, Kt., C.M.G.

Hogg, Sir Christopher Anthony, Kt.

Hogg, *Vice-Adm.* Sir Ian Leslie Trower, K.C.B., D.S.C.

Hogg, Sir John Nicholson, Kt., T.D.

Hogg, *Maj.* Sir Arthur Ramsay, Bt., M.B.E. (1846).

Hogg, Sir William Lindsay Lindsay-, Bt. (1905).

Holcroft, Sir Peter George Culcheth, Bt. (1921).

Holden, Sir David Charles Beresford, K.B.E., C.B., E.R.D.

Holden, Sir Edward, Bt. (1893).

Holden, Sir John David, Bt. (1919).

Holder, Sir John Eric Duncan, Bt. (1898).

Holder, *Air Marshal* Sir Paul Davie, K.B.E., C.B., D.S.O., D.F.C., Ph.D.

Holderness, Sir Richard William, Bt. (1920).

Holdsworth, Sir (George) Trevor, Kt.

Holland, Sir Clifton Vaughan, Kt.

Holland, Sir Guy (Hope), Bt. (1917).

Holland, Sir Kenneth Lawrence, Kt., C.B.E., Q.F.S.M.

Holland, Sir Philip Welsby, Kt., M.P.

Hollings, *Hon.* Sir (Alfred) Kenneth, Kt., M.C.

Hollis, *Hon.* Sir Anthony Barnard, Kt.

Hollom, Sir Jasper Quintus, K.B.E.

Holloway, *Hon.* Sir Barry Blyth, K.B.E.

Holmes, *Prof.* Sir Frank Wakefield, Kt.

Holmes, Sir Maurice Andrew, Kt.

Holmes, Sir Stanley, Kt.

Holt, Sir James Richard, K.B.E.

Holt, Sir John Anthony Langford-, Kt.

Home, Sir David George, Bt. (s 1671).

Hone, *Maj.-Gen.* Sir (Herbert) Ralph, K.C.M.G., K.B.E., M.C., T.D., Q.C.

Honywood, Sir Filmer Courtenay William, Bt. (1660).

Hood, Sir Alexander William Fuller-Acland-, Bt. (1806).

Hood, Sir Harold Joseph, Bt., T.D. (1922).

Hood, *Col.* Sir Tom Fielden, K.B.E., C.B., T.D.

Hookway, Sir Harry Thurston, Kt.

Hoole, Sir Arthur Hugh, Kt.

Hooper, Sir Anthony Robin Maurice, Bt. (1962).

Hooper, Sir Leonard James, K.C.M.G., C.B.E.

Hooper, Sir Robin William John, K.C.M.G., D.S.O., D.F.C.

Hope, Sir Archibald Philip, Bt., O.B.E., D.F.C. (s 1628).

Hope, Sir (Charles) Peter, K.C.M.G., T.D.

Hope, Sir Robert Holms-Kerr, Bt. (1932)

Hopkin, Sir (William Aylsham) Bryan, Kt., c.B.E.

Hopkins, *Admiral* Sir Frank Henry Edward, K.C.B., D.S.O., D.S.C.

Hopkins, Sir James Sidney Rawdon Scott-, Kt.

Hopkinson, Sir (Henry) Thomas, Kt., c.B.E.

Hordern, Sir Michael Murray, Kt., C.B.E.

Hordern, Sir Peter Maudslay, Kt., M.P.

Horlick, *Vice-Adm.* Sir Edwin John, K.B.E.

Horlick, Sir John James Macdonald, Bt. (1914).

Hornby, Sir (Roger) Antony, Kt.

Horne, Sir Alan Gray Antony, Bt. (1929).

Horsfall, Sir John Musgrave, Bt., M.C., T.D. (1909).

Horsley, *Air Marshal* Sir (Beresford) Peter (Torrington), K.C.B., C.B.E., M.V.O., A.F.C.

Hort, Sir James Fenton, Bt. (1767).

Hoskyns, Sir Benedict Leigh, Bt. (1676).

Hoskyns, Sir John Austin Hungerford Leigh, Kt.

Houldsworth, Sir (Harold) Basil, Bt. (1956).

Houldsworth, Sir Reginald Douglas Henry, Bt., O.B.E., T.D. (1887).

Hounsfield, Sir Godfrey Newbold, Kt., C.B.E.

House, *Lt.-Gen.* Sir David George, G.C.B., K.C.V.O., C.B.E., M.C.

Houssemayne du Boulay, Sir Roger William, K.C.V.O., C.M.G.

How, Sir Friston Charles, Kt., c.B.

Howard, Sir Douglas Frederick, K.C.M.G., M.C.

Howard, Sir (Hamilton) Edward de Coucey, Bt., G.B.E. (1955).

Howard, Sir John Alfred Golding, Kt.

Howard, *Maj.-Gen.* Lord Michael Fitzalan-, G.C.V.O., C.B., C.B.E., M.C.

Howard, Sir Walter Stewart, Kt., M.B.E.

Howe, *Rt. Hon.* Sir (Richard Edward) Geoffrey, Kt., Q.C., M.P.

Howie, Sir James William, Kt., M.D.

Howlett, *Lt.-Gen.* Sir Geoffrey Hugh Whitby, K.B.E., M.C.

Hoyle, *Prof.* Sir Fred, Kt., F.R.S.

Hoyos, *Hon.* Sir Fabriciano Alexander, Kt.

Huckle, Sir (Henry) George, Kt., O.B.E.

Huddie, Sir David Patrick, Kt.

Hudleston, *Air Chief Marshal* Sir Edmund Cuthbert, G.C.B., C.B.E.

Hudson, Sir Havelock Henry Trevor, Kt.

Hudson, *Lt.-Gen.* Sir Peter, K.C.B., C.B.E.

Huggins, *Hon.* Sir Alan Armstrong, Kt.

Hugh-Jones, Sir Wynn Normington, Kt., M.V.O.

Hughes, Sir David Collingwood, Bt. (1773).

Hughes, *Prof.* Sir Edward Stuart Reginald, Kt., C.B.E.

Hughes, Sir Jack William, Kt.

Hughes, *Air Marshal* Sir (Sidney Weetman) Rochford, K.C.B., C.B.E., A.F.C.

Hughes, Sir Trevor Poulton, K.C.B.

Hughes, Sir Trevor Denby Lloyd-, Kt.

Hugo, *Lt.-Col.* Sir John Mandeville, K.C.V.O., O.B.E.

Hull, *Field Marshal* Sir Richard Amyatt, K.G., G.C.B., D.S.O.

Hulme, *Hon.* Sir Alan Shallcross, K.B.E.

Hulse, Sir (Hamilton) Westrow, Bt. (1739).

Hulton, Sir Edward George Warris, Kt.

Hulton, Sir Geoffrey Alan, Bt. (1905).

Hume, Sir Alan Blyth, Kt., c.B.

Humphreys, Sir Olliver William, Kt., C.B.E.

Humphreys, Sir (Raymond Evelyn) Myles, Kt.

Hunn, Sir Jack Kent, Kt., C.M.G.

Hunt, Sir David Wathen Stather, K.C.M.G., O.B.E.

Hunt, *Admiral* Sir Nicholas John Streynsham, K.C.B., L.V.O.

Hunt, *General* Sir Peter Mervyn, G.C.B., D.S.O., O.B.E.

Hunt, Sir Rex Masterman, Kt., C.M.G.

Hunt, Sir Robert Frederick, Kt., C.B.E.

Hunter, *Hon.* Sir Alexander Albert, K.B.E.

Hunter, Sir Ian Bruce Hope, Kt., M.B.E.

Hurley, Sir John Garling, Kt., C.B.E.

Hutchinson, Sir Joseph Burtt, Kt., C.M.G., SC.D., F.R.S.

Hutchinson, *Hon.* Sir Ross, Kt., D.F.C.

Hutchison, *Lt.-Cdr.* Sir (George) Ian Clark, Kt., R.N.

Hutchison, *Hon.* Sir Michael, Kt., Q.C.

Hutchison, Sir Peter, Bt. (1939).

Hutchison, Sir Peter Craft, Bt. (1956).

Hutchison, Sir (William) Kenneth, Kt., C.B.E., F.R.S.

Hutson, Sir Francis Challenor, Kt., C.B.E.

Hutton, Sir Leonard, Kt.

Huxley, *Prof.* Sir Andrew Fielding, Kt., O.M., F.R.S.

Huxley, Sir Leonard George Holden, K.B.E., D.Phil., Ph.D.

Huxtable, *Lt.-Gen.* Sir Charles Richard, K.C.B., C.B.E.

Hyatali, *Hon.* Sir Isaac Emanuel, Kt.

Ibbs, Sir (John) Robin, Kt.

Illingworth, *Prof.* Sir Charles Frederick William, Kt., C.B.E.

Inch, Sir John Ritchie, Kt., C.V.O., C.B.E.

Ingilby, Sir Thomas Colvin William, Bt. (1866).

Inglefield, Sir Gilbert Samuel, G.B.E., T.D.

Inglefield, *Col.* Sir John Frederick Crompton-, Kt., T.D.

Inglis, Sir Brian Scott, Kt.

Inglis of Glencorse, Sir Roderick John, Bt. (s 1703).

Ingram, Sir James Herbert Charles, Bt. (1893).

Innes, Sir Charles Kenneth Gordon, Bt. (N.S. 1686).

Innes, Sir (Ronald Gordon) Berowald, Bt., O.B.E. (s 1628).

Inniss, *Hon.* Sir Clifford de Lisle, Kt.

Irish, Sir Ronald Arthur, Kt., O.B.E.

Irving, *Rear-Adm.* Sir Edmund George, K.B.E., C.B.

Irwin, Sir James Campbell, Kt., O.B.E., E.D.

Isham, Sir Ian Vere Gyles, Bt. (1627).

Issigonis, Sir Alec Arnold Constantine, Kt., C.B.E., F.R.S.

Jack, *Hon.* Sir Alieu Sulayman, Kt.

Jackling, Sir Roger William, G.C.M.G.

Jackman, *Air Marshal* Sir (Harold) Douglas, K.B.E., C.B.

Jackson, Sir William Thomas, Bt. (1869)

Jackson, Sir Geoffrey Holt Seymour, K.C.M.G.

Jackson, Sir (John) Edward, K.C.M.G.

Jackson, *Hon.* Sir Lawrence Walter, K.C.M.G.

Jackson, Sir Michael Roland, Bt. (1902).

Jackson, Sir Nicholas Fane St. George, Bt. (1913).

Jackson, *Air Vice-Marshal* Sir Ralph Coburn, K.B.E., C.B.

Jackson, Sir Robert, Bt. (1815).

Jackson, *Comdr.* Sir Robert Gillman Allen, K.C.V.O., C.M.G., O.B.E.

Jackson, *General* Sir William Godfrey Fothergill, G.B.E., K.C.B., M.C.

Jacob, *Lt.-Gen.* Sir (Edward) Ian (Claud), G.B.E., C.B.

Jacob, Sir Isaac Hai, Kt., Q.C.

Jacobs, *Hon.* Sir Kenneth Sydney, K.B.E.

Jacobs, Sir Wilfred Ebenezer, G.C.M.G., K.C.V.O., O.B.E., Q.C.

Jacomb, Sir Martin Wakefield, Kt.

Jaffray, Sir William Otho, Bt. (1892).

Jagatsingh, *Hon.* Sir Kher, Kt.

Jakeway, Sir (Francis) Derek, K.C.M.G., O.B.E.

Jakobovits, Rabbi Immanuel, Kt.

James, Sir Cynlais Morgan, K.C.M.G.

James, Sir Gerard Bowes Kingston, Bt. (1823).

Janion, *Rear-Adm.* Sir Hugh Penderel, K.C.V.O.

Janvrin, *Vice-Adm.* Sir (Hugh) Richard Benest, K.C.B., D.S.C.

Jardine, *Maj.* Sir (Andrew) Rupert (John) Buchanan-, Bt., M.C. (1885).

Jardine, Sir Andrew Colin Douglas, Bt. (1916).

Jardine of Applegirth, *Col.* Sir William Edward, Bt., O.B.E., T.D. (s 1672).

Jarratt, Sir Alexander Anthony, Kt., C.B.

Jarrett, Sir Clifford George, K.B.E., C.B.

Jawara, *Hon.* Sir Dawda Kairaba, Kt.

Jeewoolall, Sir Ramesh, Kt.

Jeffcoate, Sir (Thomas) Norman (Arthur), Kt., M.D., F.R.C.S.

Jefferson, Sir George Rowland, Kt., C.B.E.

Jefferson, Sir Mervyn Stewart Dunnington-, Bt. (1958).

Jeffreys, Sir Harold, Kt., D.SC., F.R.S.

Jehangir, Sir Hirji, Bt. (1908).

Jejeebhoy, Sir Rustom, Bt. (1857).

Jellicoe, Sir Geoffrey Alan, Kt., C.B.E., F.R.I.B.A.

Jenkins, Sir Evan Meredith, G.C.I.E., K.C.S.I.

Jenkins, Sir Owain Trevor, Kt.

Jenkinson, Sir Anthony Banks, Bt. (1661).

Jenks, Sir Richard Atherley, Bt. (1932).

Jennings, Sir Albert Victor, Kt.

Jennings, Sir Raymond Winter, Kt., Q.C.

Jennings, *Prof.* Sir Robert Yewdall, Kt., Q.C.

Jenour, Sir (Arthur) Maynard (Chesterfield), Kt., T.D.

Jephcott, *Hon.* Sir Bruce Reginald, Kt., C.B.E.

Jephcott, Sir (John) Anthony, Bt. (1962).

Jessel, Sir Charles John, Bt. (1883).

Joel, *Hon.* Sir Asher Alexander, K.B.E.

John, Sir Rupert Godfrey, Kt.

Johnson, *Rt. Hon.* Sir David Powell Croom-, Kt., D.S.C., V.R.D.

Johnson, Sir Henry Cecil, K.B.E.

Johnson, Sir Peter Colpoys Paley, Bt. (1755).

Johnson, Sir Ronald Ernest Charles, Kt., C.B.

Johnson, Sir Victor Philipse Hill, Bt. (1818).

Johnson Smith, Sir Geoffrey, Kt., M.P.

Johnston, Sir Alexander, G.C.B., K.B.E.

Johnston, Sir Charles Collier, Kt., T.D.

Johnston, Sir Charles Hepburn, G.C.M.G.

Johnston, Sir (David) Russell, Kt., M.P.

Johnston, Sir John Baines, G.C.M.G., K.C.V.O.

Johnston, *Lt.-Gen.* Sir Maurice Robert, K.C.B., O.B.E.

Johnston, Sir Thomas Alexander, Bt. (s 1626).

Johnstone, Sir Frederic Allan George, Bt. (s 1700).

Jolliffe, Sir Anthony Stuart, G.B.E.

Jones, Sir Brynmor, Kt., Ph.D., SC.D.

Jones, *General* Sir Charles Phibbs, G.C.B., C.B.E., M.C.

Jones, Sir Christopher Lawrence-, Bt. (1831).

Jones, *Air Marshal* Sir Edward Gordon, K.C.B., C.B.E., D.S.O., D.F.C.

Jones, *Rt. Hon.* Sir Edward Warburton, Kt.

Jones, Sir (Edward) Martin Furnival, Kt., C.B.E.

Jones, Sir Eric Malcolm, K.C.M.G., C.B., C.B.E.

Jones, Sir Ewart Ray Herbert, Kt., D.SC., Ph.D., F.R.S.

Jones, Sir Francis Avery, Kt., C.B.E., F.R.C.P.

Jones, *Air Marshal* Sir George, K.B.E., C.B., D.F.C.

Jones, Sir Glyn Smallwood, G.C.M.G., M.B.E.

Jones, Sir Harry Ernest, Kt., C.B.E.

Jones, Sir (Harry) Vincent Lloyd-, Kt.

Jones, Sir Henry Frank Harding, G.B.E.

Jones, Sir James Duncan, K.C.B.

Jones, *Air Marshal* Sir (John) Humphrey Edwardes, K.C.B., C.B.E., D.F.C., A.F.C.

Jones, Sir (John) Kenneth (Trevor), Kt., C.B.E., Q.C.

Jones, Sir John Lewis, K.C.B., C.M.G.

Jones, Sir John Prichard-, Bt. (1910).

Jones, Sir Keith Stephen, Kt.

Jones, *Hon.* Sir Kenneth George Illtyd, Kt.

Jones, Sir (Owen) Trevor, Kt.

Jones, Sir Samuel Owen, Kt.

Jones, Sir Simon Warley Frederick Benton, Bt. (1919).

Jones, Sir (William) Elwyn (Edwards), Kt.

Jones, Sir (William) Emrys, Kt.

Jones, *Hon.* Sir William Lloyd Mars-, Kt., M.B.E.

Jordan, *Air Marshal* Sir Richard Bowen, K.C.B., D.F.C.

Joseph, *Maj.* Sir (Herbert) Leslie, Kt.

Joseph, *Rt. Hon.* Sir Keith Sinjohn, Bt., M.P. (1943).

Jungius, *Vice-Adm.,* Sir James George, K.B.E.

Junor, Sir John Donald Brown, Kt.

Jupp, *Hon.* Sir Kenneth Graham, Kt., M.C.

Kalo, Sir Kwamala, Kt., M.B.E.

Kan Yuet-Keung, Sir, G.B.E.

Karimjee, Sir Tayabali Hassanali Alibhoy, Kt.

Katsina, The Emir of, K.B.E., C.M.G.

Katz, Sir Bernard, Kt., F.R.S.

Kavali, Sir Thomas, Kt., C.B.E.

Kay, *Prof.* Sir Andrew Watt, Kt.

Kaye, Sir Emmanuel, Kt., C.B.E.

Kaye, Sir John Phillip Lister Lister-, Bt. (1812).

Kaye, Sir David Alexander Gordon, Bt. (1923).

Keane, Sir Richard Michael, Bt. (1801).

Keatinge, Sir Edgar Mayne, Kt., C.B.E.

Keeble, Sir (Herbert Ben) Curtis, G.C.M.G.

Kellett, Sir Brian Smith, Kt.

Kellett, Sir Stanley Charles, Bt. (1801).

Kelliher, Sir Henry Joseph, Kt.

Kelly, *Rt. Hon.* Sir (John William) Basil, Kt.

Kelly, Sir William Theodore, Kt., O.B.E.

Kemp, Sir Leslie Charles, K.B.E.

Kemsley, *Col.* Sir Alfred Newcombe, K.B.E., C.M.G., E.D.

Kendrew, *Maj.-Gen.* Sir Douglas Anthony, K.C.M.G., C.B., C.B.E., D.S.O.

Kendrew, Sir John Cowdery, Kt., C.B.E., SC.D., F.R.S.

Kenilorea, *Rt. Hon.* Sir Peter, K.B.E.

Kennard, *Lt.-Col.* Sir George Arnold Ford, Bt. (1891).

Kennaway, Sir John Lawrence, Bt. (1791).

Kennedy, Sir Albert Henry, Kt.

Kennedy, Sir Clyde David Allen, Kt.

Kennedy, Sir George Ronald Derrick, Bt., O.B.E. (1836).

Kennedy, *Hon.* Sir Paul Joseph Morrow, Kt., Q.C.

Kennedy, *Air Chief Marshal* Sir Thomas Lawrie, G.C.B., A.F.C.

Kennedy-Good, Sir John, K.B.E.

Kennon, *Vice-Adm.* Sir James Edward Campbell, K.C.B., C.B.E.

Kenny, *Lt.-Gen.* Sir Brian Leslie Graham, K.C.B., C.B.E.

Kenny, Sir Patrick John, Kt.

Kent, Sir Harold Simcox, G.C.B., Q.C.

Kent, Sir Percy Edward (Sir Peter Kent), Kt., D.SC., Ph.D., F.R.S.

Kenyon, Sir George Henry, Kt.

Kerr, *Rt. Hon.* Sir John Robert, G.C.M.G., G.C.V.O.

Kerr, *Rt. Hon.* Sir Michael Robert Emanuel, Kt.

Kerr, *Hon.* Sir Alastair Blair-, Kt.

Kerruish, Sir (Henry) Charles, Kt., O.B.E.

Kerry, Sir Michael James, K.C.B., Q.C.

Kershaw, Sir (John) Anthony, Kt., M.C., M.P.

Keswick, Sir William Johnston, Kt.

Keville, Sir (William) Errington, Kt., C.B.E.

Kidd, Sir Robert Hill, K.B.E., C.B.

Kidu, *Hon.* Sir Buri (William), Kt.

Kikau, *Ratu* Sir Jone Latianara, K.B.E.

Kiki, *Hon.* Sir (Albert) Maori, K.B.E.

Killen, *Hon.* Denis James, K.C.M.G.

Killick, Sir John Edward, K.C.M.G.

Kilpatrick, Sir William John, K.B.E.

Kimber, Sir Charles Dixon, Bt. (1904).

Kinahan, Sir Robert George Caldwell, Kt., E.R.D.

King, Sir Albert, Kt., O.B.E.

King, *General* Sir Frank Douglas, G.C.B., M.B.E.

King, Sir James Granville Le Neve, Bt., T.D. (1888).

King, Sir Richard Brian Meredith, K.C.B., M.C.

King, Sir Sydney Percy, Kt., O.B.E.

King, Sir Wayne Alexander, Bt. (1815).

Kingman, *Prof.* Sir John Frank Charles, Kt., F.R.S.

Kingsland, Sir Richard, Kt., C.B.E., D.F.C.

Kingsley, Sir Patrick Graham Toler, K.C.V.O.

Kininmonth, Sir William Hardie, Kt., P.P.R.S.A., F.R.I.B.A.

Kinloch, Sir David, Bt. (s 1686).

Kinloch, Sir John, Bt. (1873).

Kirby, *Hon.* Sir Richard Clarence, Kt.

Kirkley, Sir (Howard) Leslie, Kt., C.B.E.

Kirkpatrick, Sir Ivone Elliott, Bt. (s 1685).

Kirwan, Sir (Archibald) Laurence Patrick, K.C.M.G., T.D.

Kitson, *General* Sir Frank Edward, G.B.E., K.C.B., M.C.

Kitson, Sir Timothy Peter Geoffrey, Kt.

Kitto, *Rt. Hon.* Sir Frank Walters, K.B.E.

Kleinwort, Sir Kenneth Drake, Bt. (1909).

Knight, Sir Allan Walton, Kt., C.M.G.

Knight, Sir Arthur William, Kt.

Knight, Sir Harold Murray, K.B.E., D.S.C.

Knight, *Air Marshal* Sir Michael William Patrick, K.C.B., A.F.C.

Knights, Sir Philip Douglas, Kt., C.B.E., Q.P.M.

Knill, Sir John Kenelm Stuart, Bt. (1893).

Knipe, Sir Leslie Francis, Kt., M.B.E.

Knott, Sir John Laurence, Kt., C.B.E.

Knowles, Sir Charles Francis, Bt. (1765).

Knowles, Sir Leonard Joseph, Kt., C.B.E.

Knox, *Hon.* Sir William Edward, Kt.

Kornberg, *Prof.* Sir Hans Leo, D.SC., SC.D., Ph.D., F.R.S.

Krusin, Sir Stanley Marks, Kt., C.B.

Kyle, *Air Chief Marshal* Sir Wallace Hart, G.C.B., K.C.V.O., C.B.E., D.S.O., D.F.C.

Labouchere, Sir George Peter, G.B.E., K.C.M.G.

Lacon, Sir Edmund Vere, Bt. (1818).

Lacy, Sir Hugh Maurice Pierce, Bt. (1921).

Lagesen, *Air Marshal* Sir Philip Jacobus, K.C.B., D.F.C., A.F.C.

Laidlaw, Sir Christophor Charles Fraser, Kt.

Laing, Sir Hector, Kt.

Laing, Sir (John) Maurice, Kt.

Laing, Sir (William) Kirby, Kt.

Laithwaite, Sir (John) Gilbert, G.C.M.G., K.C.B., K.C.I.E., C.S.I.

Lake, Sir (Atwell) Graham, Bt. (1711).

Laker, Sir Frederick Alfred, Kt.

Lakin, Sir Michael, Bt. (1909).

Laking, Sir George Robert, K.C.M.G.

Lamb, Sir Albert (Larry), Kt.

Lamb, Sir Albert Thomas, K.B.E., C.M.G., D.F.C.

Lamb, Sir Lionel Henry, K.C.M.G., O.B.E.

Lambart, Sir Oliver Francis, Bt. (1911).

Lambert, Sir Anthony Edward, K.C.M.G.

Lambert, Sir Edward Thomas, K.B.E., C.V.O.

Lambert, Sir Greville Foley, Bt. (1711).

Lambert, Sir John Henry, K.C.V.O., C.M.G.

Lancaster, *Vice-Adm.* Sir John Strike, K.B.E., C.B.

Lancaster, Sir Osbert, Kt., C.B.E.

Lane, Sir David William Stennis Stuart, Kt.

Lane, Sir Peter Stewart, Kt.

Lang, *Lt.-Gen.* Sir Derek Boileau, K.C.B., D.S.O., M.C.

Langham, Sir James Michael, Bt. (1660).

Langley, *Maj.-Gen.* Sir Henry Desmond Allen, K.C.V.O., M.B.E.

Langman, Sir John Lyell, Bt. (1906).

Langrishe, Sir Hercules Ralph Hume, Bt. (I 1777).

Lapsley, *Air Marshal* Sir John Hugh, K.B.E., C.B., D.F.C., A.F.C.

Lapun, *Hon.* Sir Paul, Kt.

Larcom, Sir (Charles) Christopher Royde, Bt. (1868).

Larmour, Sir Edward Noel, K.C.M.G.

Lartigue, Sir Louis Cools-, Kt., O.B.E.

Lasdun, Sir Denys Louis, Kt., C.B.E., F.R.I.B.A.

Laskey, Sir Denis Seward, K.C.M.G., C.V.O.

Latey, *Hon.* Sir John Brinsmead, Kt., M.B.E.

Latham, Sir Joseph, Kt., C.B.E.

Latham, Sir Richard Thomas Paul, Bt. (1919).

Latimer, Sir (Courtenay) Robert, Kt., C.B.E.

Latimer, Sir Graham Stanley, K.B.E.

Laucke, *Hon.* Sir Condor Louis, K.C.M.G.

Lauder, Sir Piers Robert Dick-, Bt. (s 1690).

Laurantus, Sir Nicholas, Kt., M.B.E.

Laurence, Sir Peter Harold, K.C.M.G., M.C.

Laurie, Sir Robert Bayley Emilius, Bt. (1834).

Lavan, *Hon.* Sir John Martin, Kt.

Law, *Hon.* Sir Eric John Ewan, Kt.

Law, *Admiral* Sir Horace Rochfort, G.C.B., O.B.E., D.S.C.

Lawes, Sir (John) Michael Bennet, Bt. (1882).

Lawler, Sir Peter James, Kt., O.B.E.

Lawrence, Sir David Roland Walter, Bt. (1906).

Lawrence, Sir Guy Kempton, Kt., D.S.O., O.B.E., D.F.C.

Lawrence, Sir John Waldemar, Bt., O.B.E. (1858).

Lawrence, Sir William, Bt. (1867).

Lawson, Sir Christopher Donald, Kt.

Lawson, *Col.* Sir John Charles Arthur Digby, Bt., D.S.O., M.C. (1900).

Lawson, *Hon.* Sir Neil, Kt.

Lawson, *Gen.* Sir Richard George, K.C.B., D.S.O., O.B.E.

Lawson, Sir William Howard, Bt. (1841).

Lawton, *Prof.* Sir Frank Ewart, Kt.

Lawton, *Rt. Hon.* Sir Frederick Horace, Kt.

Layfield, Sir Frank Henry Burland Willoughby, Kt., Q.C.

Lazarus, Sir Peter Esmond, K.C.B.

Lea, *Lt.-Gen.* Sir George Harris, K.C.B., D.S.O., M.B.E.

Lea, *Vice-Adm.,* Sir John Stuart Crosbie, K.B.E.

Lea, Sir Thomas Claude Harris, Bt. (1892).

Leach, *Prof.* Sir Edmund Ronald, Kt., Ph.D., F.B.A.

Leach, *Admiral of the Fleet* Sir Henry Conyers, G.C.B.

Leach, Sir Ronald George, G.B.E.

Leahy, Sir John Henry Gladstone, K.C.M.G.

Lean, Sir David, Kt., C.B.E.

Leask, *Lt.-Gen.* Sir Henry Lowther Ewart Clark, K.C.B., D.S.O., O.B.E.

Leather, Sir Edwin Hartley Cameron, K.C.M.G., K.C.V.O.

Leaver, Sir Christopher, G.B.E.

Le Bailly, *Vice-Adm.* Sir Louis Edward Stewart Holland, K.B.E., C.B.

Le Cheminant, *Air Chief Marshal* Sir Peter de Lacey, G.B.E., K.C.B., D.F.C.

Lechmere, Sir Berwick Hungerford, Bt. (1818).

Ledger, Sir Frank, (Joseph Francis), Kt.

Ledwidge, Sir (William) Bernard (John), K.C.M.G.

Lee, Sir Arthur James, K.B.E., M.C.

Lee, *Air Chief Marshal* Sir David John Pryer, G.B.E., C.B.

Lee, Sir (George) Wilton, Kt.

Lee, *Col.* Tun Sir Henry Hau Shik, K.B.E.

Lee, Sir (Henry) Desmond (Pritchard), Kt.

Lee, *Brig.* Sir Leonard Henry, Kt., C.B.E.

Lee, *Col.* Sir William Allison, Kt., O.B.E., T.D.

Leeds, Sir Christopher Anthony, Bt. (1812).

Lees, *Air Marshal* Sir Ronald Beresford, K.C.B., C.B.E., D.F.C.

Lees, Sir Thomas Edward, Bt. (1897).

Lees, Sir Thomas Harcourt Ivor, Bt. (1804).

Lees, Sir (William) Antony Clare, Bt. (1937).

Leese, Sir John Henry Vernon, Bt. (1908).

le Fleming, Sir William Kelland, Bt. (1705).

Legard, Sir Charles Thomas, Bt. (1660).

Leggatt, *Hon.* Sir Andrew Peter, Kt., Q.C.

Leggett, Sir Clarence Arthur Campbell, Kt., M.B.E.

Leggo, Sir Jack Frederick, Kt., D.F.C.

Leigh, Sir John, Bt. (1918).

Leigh, Sir Neville Egerton, K.C.V.O.

Leighton, Sir Michael John Bryan, Bt. (1693).

Leitch, Sir George, K.C.B., O.B.E.

Leith, Sir Andrew George Forbes-, Bt. (1923).

Le Marchant, Sir Denis, Bt. (1841).

Le Marchant, Sir Spencer, Kt.

Le Masurier, Sir Robert Hugh, Kt., D.S.C.

Lemon, Sir (Richard) Dawnay, Kt., C.B.E.

Leng, *General* Sir Peter John Hall, K.C.B., M.B.E., M.C.

Lennard, *Rev.* Sir Hugh Dacre Barrett-, Bt. (1801).

Lennox, *Rear Adm.* Sir Alexander Henry Charles, K.C.V.O., D.S.O.

Lennox, *Lt.-Gen.* Sir George Charles Gordon, K.B.E., C.B., C.V.O., D.S.O.

Leon, Sir John Ronald, Bt. (1911).

Leonard, *Hon.* Sir (Hamilton) John, Kt., Q.C.

Leonard, Sir Reginald Byron, Kt., C.M.G., O.B.E.

Leonard, Sir Walter McEllister, Kt., D.F.C.

Le Quesne, Sir (Charles) Martin, K.C.M.G.

Le Quesne, Sir (John) Godfray, Kt., Q.C.

Leslie, Sir John Norman Ide, Bt. (1876).

†Leslie, Sir (Percy) Theodore, Bt. (s 1625).

Lethbridge, Sir Thomas Periam Hector Noel, Bt. (1804).

Leuchars, Sir William Douglas, K.B.E.

Leuchars, Sir William Douglas, K.B.E.

Lever, Sir (Tresham) Christopher Arthur Lindsay, Bt. (1911).

Levey, Sir Michael Vincent, Kt., M.V.O.

Levine, Sir Montague Bernard, Kt.

Levinge, Sir Richard George Robin, Bt. (I 1704).

Levy, Sir (Enoch) Bruce, Kt., O.B.E.

Levy, Sir Ewart Maurice, Bt. (1913).

Lewando, Sir Jan Alfred, Kt., C.B.E.

Lewis, Sir Allen Montgomery, G.C.M.G., Q.C.

Lewis, *Admiral* Sir Andrew Mackenzie, K.C.B.

Lewis, Sir Ian Malcolm, Kt.

Lewis, *Prof.* Sir Jack, Kt., F.R.S.

Lewis, Sir Kenneth, Kt., M.P.

Lewis, Sir William Arthur, Kt.

Lewthwaite, Sir William Anthony, Bt. (1927).

Ley, Sir Francis Douglas, Bt., M.B.E., T.D. (1905).

Leyland, Sir Vivyan Edward Naylor-, Bt. (1895).

Lickley, Sir Robert Lang, Kt., C.B.E.

Lidbury, Sir John Towersey, Kt.

Lidderdale, Sir David William Shuckburgh, K.C.B.

Liddle, Sir Donald Ross, Kt.

Liggins, Sir Edmund Naylor, Kt., T.D.

Lighthill, Sir (Michael) James, Kt., F.R.S.

Lighton, Sir Christopher Robert, Bt., M.B.E. (I 1791).

Lim, Sir Han-Hoe, Kt., C.B.E.

Lincoln, Sir Anthony Handley, K.C.M.G., C.V.O.

Lincoln, *Hon.* Sir Anthony Leslie Julian, Kt.

Lindley, Sir Arnold Lewis George, Kt.

Lindop, Sir Norman, Kt.

Lindsay, Sir James Harvey Kincaid Stewart, Kt.

Lindsay, Sir Ronald Alexander, Bt., (1962).

Lindsay, Sir William, Kt., C.B.E.

Lindsay-Fynn, Sir Basil Mortimer, Kt.

Linstead, Sir Hugh Nicholas, Kt., O.B.E.

Lintott, Sir Henry John Bevis, K.C.M.G.

Lithgow, Sir William James, Bt. (1925).

Little, *Hon.* Sir Douglas Macfarlan, Kt.

Little, *Most Rev.* Thomas Francis, K.B.E.

Littler, Sir (James) Geoffrey, K.C.B.

Livermore, Sir Harry, Kt.

Llewellyn, Sir David Treharne, Kt.

Llewellyn, Sir (Frederick) John, K.C.M.G.

Llewellyn, Sir Henry Morton, Bt., C.B.E. (1922).

Llewellyn, *Col.* Sir (Robert) Godfrey, Bt., C.B., C.B.E., M.C., T.D. (1959).

Llewelyn, Sir John Michael Dillwyn-Venables-, Bt. (1890).

Lloyd, *Rt. Hon.* Sir Anthony John Leslie, Kt.

Lloyd, *Maj.* Sir (Ernest) Guy (Richard), Bt., D.S.O. (1960).

Lloyd, Sir (John) Peter (Daniel), Kt.

Loane, *Most Rev.* Marcus Lawrence, K.B.E.

Lobo, Sir Rogerio Hyndman, Kt., C.B.E.

Lock, *Comdr.* Sir (John) Duncan, Kt.

Lockhart, Sir Muir Edward Sinclair-, Bt. (s 1636).

Lockhart-Mummery, Sir Hugh Evelyn, K.C.V.O., M.D., F.R.C.S.

Lockspeiser, Sir Ben, K.C.B., F.R.S.

Lockwood, Sir Joseph Flawith, Kt.

Loder, Sir Giles Rolls, Bt. (1887).

Lodge, Sir Thomas, Kt.

Loehnis, Sir Clive, K.C.M.G.

Loewen, *General* Sir Charles Falkland, G.C.B., K.B.E., D.S.O.

Logan, Sir Donald Arthur, K.C.M.G.

Logan, Sir Douglas William, Kt., D.Phil.

Logan, Sir Raymond Douglas, Kt.

Lokoloko, Sir Tore, G.C.M.G., G.C.V.O., O.B.E.

Lomax, Sir John Garnett, K.B.E., C.M.G., M.C.

Long, Sir Ronald, Kt.

Longden, Sir Gilbert James Morley, M.B.E.

Longland, Sir David Walter, Kt., C.M.G.

Longland, Sir John Laurence, Kt.

Longley, Sir Norman, Kt., C.B.E.

Looker, Sir Cecil Thomas, Kt.

Loram, *Vice-Adm.* Sir David Anning, K.C.B., M.V.O.

Lorimer, Sir (Thomas) Desmond, Kt.

Lousada, Sir Anthony Baruh, Kt.

Lovell, Sir (Alfred Charles) Bernard, Kt., O.B.E., F.R.S.

Lovelock, Sir Douglas Arthur, K.C.B.

Loveridge, Sir John Henry, Kt., C.B.E.

Low, Sir Alan Roberts, Kt.

Low, Sir James Richard Morrison-, Bt. (1908).

Lowe, *Air Chief Marshal* Sir Douglas Charles, G.C.B., D.F.C., A.F.C.

Lowe, *Air Vice-Marshal* Sir Edgar Noel, K.B.E., C.B.

Lowe, Sir Francis Reginald Gordon, Bt. (1918).

Lowry, Sir John Patrick, Kt., C.B.E.

Lowson, Sir Ian Patrick, Bt. (1951).

Lowther, *Maj.* Sir Charles Douglas, Bt. (1824).

Loyd, Sir Francis Alfred, K.C.M.G., O.B.E.

Lubbock, Sir Alan, Kt., F.S.A.

Lucas, Sir Cyril Edward, Kt., C.M.G., F.R.S.

Lucas, Sir Thomas Edward, Bt. (1887).

Luckhoo, *Hon.* Sir Joseph Alexander, Kt.

Luckhoo, Sir Lionel Alfred, K.C.M.G., C.B.E., Q.C.

Lucy, Sir Edmund John William Hugh Cameron-Ramsay-Fairfax-, Bt. (1836).

Luddington, Sir Donald Collin Cumyn, K.B.E., C.M.G., C.V.O.

Luke, *Hon.* Sir Emile Fashole, K.B.E.

Luke, Sir Stephen Elliot Vyvyan, K.C.M.G.

Lumby, Sir Henry, Kt., C.B.E.

Lumsden, Sir David James, Kt.

Lus, *Hon.* Sir Pita, Kt., O.B.E.

Lush, *Hon.* Sir George Hermann, Kt.

Lushington, Sir Henry Edmund Castleman, Bt. (1791).

Lusty, Sir Robert Frith, Kt.

Luyt, Sir Richard Edmonds, G.C.M.G., K.C.V.O., D.C.M.

Lygo, *Admiral* Sir Raymond Derek, K.C.B.

Lyle, Sir Gavin Archibald, Bt. (1929).

Lyons, Sir Edward Houghton, Kt.

Lyons, Sir (Isidore) Jack, Kt., C.B.E.

Lyons, Sir James Reginald, Kt.

Lyons, *His Hon.* Sir Rudolph, Kt., Q.C.

McAdam, Sir Ian William James, Kt., O.B.E.

Macadam, Sir Peter, Kt.

McAllister, Sir Reginald Basil, Kt., C.M.G., C.V.O.

McAlpine, *Hon.* Sir John Kenneth, K.C.M.G.

McAlpine, Sir Robin, Kt., C.B.E.

Macara, Sir (Charles) Douglas, Bt. (1911).

McArthur, *Col.* Sir Malcolm Hugh, Kt., O.B.E.

Macartney, Sir John Barrington, Bt. (1 1799).

Macaulay, Sir Hamilton, Kt., C.B.E.

McAvoy, Sir (Francis) Joseph, Kt., C.B.E.

McCaffrey, Sir Thomas Daniel, Kt.

McCall, Sir (Charles) Patrick Home, Kt., M.B.E., T.D.

McCarthy, *Rt. Hon.* Sir Thaddeus Pearcey, K.B.E.

McCauley, *Air Marshal* Sir John Patrick Joseph, K.B.E., C.B.

McCaw, *Hon.* Sir Kenneth Malcolm, Kt., Q.C.

McClintock, Sir Eric Paul, Kt.

McConnell, *Cdr.* Sir Robert Melville Terence, Bt., V.R.D. (1900).

McCowan, *Hon.* Sir Anthony James Denys, Kt., Q.C.

McCowan, Sir Hew Cargill, Bt. (1934).

McCrea, *Prof.* Sir William Hunter, Kt., F.R.S.

McCullough, *Hon.* Sir (Iain) Charles (Robert), Kt.

McCusker, Sir James Alexander, Kt.

MacDermot, Sir Dermot Francis, K.C.M.G., C.B.E.

McDermott, Sir (Lawrence) Emmet, K.B.E.

MacDonald, *General* Sir Arthur Leslie, K.B.E., C.B.

McDonald, *Air Chief Marshal* Sir Arthur William Baynes, K.C.B., A.F.C.

McDonald, Sir Duncan, Kt., C.B.E.

Macdonald, Sir Herbert George deLorme, K.B.E.

Macdonald of Sleat, Sir Ian Godfrey Bosville, Bt. (s 1625).

McDonald, Sir James, K.B.E.

Macdonald, *Vice-Adm.* Sir Roderick Douglas, K.B.E.

McDonald, *Hon.* Sir William John Farquhar, Kt.

MacDougall, Sir (George) Donald (Alastair), Kt., C.B.E., F.B.A.

McDowell, Sir Henry McLorinan, K.B.E.

McEvoy, *Air Chief Marshal* Sir Theodore Newman, K.C.B., C.B.E.

McEwen, Sir John Roderick Hugh, Bt. (1953).

McEwin, *Hon.* Sir (Alexander) Lyell, K.B.E.

McFarland, Sir Basil (Alexander Talbot), Bt., C.B.E. (1914).

McFarlane, Sir Ian, Kt.

Macfarlane, Sir George Gray, Kt., C.B.

Macfarlane, Sir James Wright, Kt.

Macfarlane, Sir Norman Somerville, Kt.

MacFarquhar, Sir Alexander, K.B.E., C.I.E.

McGeoch, *Vice-Adm.* Sir Ian Lachlan Mackay, K.C.B., D.S.O., D.S.C.

Macgregor, Sir Edwin Robert, Bt. (1828).

MacGregor of MacGregor, Sir Gregor, Bt. (1795).

McGregor, Sir Ian Alexander, Kt., C.B.E., F.R.S.

McGrigor, *Capt.* Sir Charles Edward, Bt. (1831).

McInerney, *Hon.* Sir Murray Vincent, Kt.

McIntosh, *Vice-Adm.* Sir Ian Stewart, K.B.E., C.B., D.S.O., D.S.C.

Macintosh, Sir Robert Reynolds, Kt., M.D.

McIntosh, Sir Ronald Robert Duncan, K.C.B.

McKaig, *Admiral* Sir (John) Rae, K.C.B., C.B.E.

McKay, *Hon.* Sir Donald Norman, K.C.M.G.

Mackay, Sir (George Patrick) Gordon, Kt., C.B.E.

Mackay, Sir James Mackerron, K.B.E., C.B.

McKay, Sir James Wilson, Kt.

McKay, Sir John Andrew, Kt., C.B.E.

Mackay, Sir William Calder, Kt., O.B.E., M.C.

McKee, *Air Marshal* Sir Andrew, K.C.B., C.B.E., D.S.O., D.F.C., A.F.C.

McKee, *Maj.* Sir (William) Cecil, Kt., E.R.D.

MacKenna, Sir Bernard Joseph Maxwell, Kt.

McKenzie, Sir Alexander, K.B.E.

Mackenzie, Sir Alexander Alwyne Henry Charles Brinton Muir-, Bt. (1805).

Mackenzie, Sir (Alexander George Anthony) Allan, Bt. (1890).

Mackenzie, *Vice-Adm.* Sir Hugh Stirling, K.C.B., D.S.O., D.S.C.

Mackenzie, Sir Robert Evelyn, Bt. (s 1673).

Mackenzie, *Capt.* Sir Roderick (Edward François McQuhae), Bt. (s 1703).

Mackeson, Sir Rupert Henry, Bt. (1954).

Mackie, Sir Maitland, Kt., C.B.E.

MacKinlay, Sir Bruce, Kt., C.B.E.

MacKintosh, Sir Angus Mackay, K.C.V.O., C.M.G.

McKissock, Sir Wylie, Kt., O.B.E., F.R.C.S.

Macklin, Sir Bruce Roy, Kt., O.B.E.

Mackworth, *Cdr.* Sir David Arthur Geoffrey, Bt. (1776).

Maclaren, Sir Hamish Duncan, K.B.E., C.B., D.F.C.

Maclean, Sir Fitzroy Hew, Bt., C.B.E. (1957).

McLean, Sir Francis Charles, Kt., C.B.E.

MacLean, *Vice-Adm.* Sir Hector Charles Donald, K.B.E., C.B., D.S.C.

McLean, *Lt.-Gen.* Sir Kenneth Graeme, K.C.B., K.B.E.

Maclean, Sir Donald Og Grant, Kt.

Maclean, Sir Robert Alexander, K.B.E.

MacLellan, Sir (George) Robin (Perronet), Kt., C.B.E.

Maclennan, Sir Ian Morrison Ross, K.C.M.G.

McLennan, Sir Ian Munro, K.C.M.G., K.B.E.

McLeod, Sir Charles Henry, Bt. (1925).

McLeod, Sir Ian George, Kt.

McLintock, Sir William Traven, Bt. (1934).

Maclure, Sir John Robert Spencer, Bt. (1898).

McMahon, Sir Brian Patrick, Bt. (1817).

McMahon, *Rt. Hon.* Sir William, G.C.M.G., C.H.

McMichael, Sir John, Kt., M.D., F.R.S., F.R.C.P.

MacMillan, Sir Kenneth, Kt.

MacMillan, *General* Sir Gordon Holmes Alexander, K.C.B., K.C.V.O., C.B.E., D.S.O., M.C.

Macmillan, Sir Alexander McGregor Graham, Kt.

Macmillan, Sir (James) Wilson, K.B.E.

Macnab, *Brig.* Sir Geoffrey Alex Colin, K.C.M.G., C.B.

Macnaghten, Sir Patrick Alexander, Bt. (1836).

McNamara, *Air Chief Marshal* Sir Neville Patrick, K.B.E.

McNee, Sir David Blackstock, Kt., Q.P.M.

McNeice, Sir (Thomas) Percy (Fergus), Kt., C.M.G., O.B.E.

McNeill, *Hon.* Sir David Bruce, Kt.

McNicoll, *Vice-Adm.* Sir Alan Wedel Ramsay, K.B.E., C.B., G.M.

McPetrie, Sir James Carnegie, K.C.M.G., O.B.E.

MacPherson, Sir Keith Duncan, Kt.

Macpherson, *Hon.* Sir William Alan, Kt., T.D., Q.C.

Macready, Sir Nevil John Wilfrid, Bt. (1923).

Macrory, Sir Patrick Arthur, Kt.

McShine, *Hon.* Sir Arthur Hugh, Kt.

Mactaggart, Sir Ian Auld, Bt. (1938).

McTiernan, *Rt. Hon.* Sir Edward Aloysius, K.B.E.

Madden, *Admiral* Sir Charles Edward, Bt., G.C.B. (1919).

Maddock, Sir Ieuan, Kt., C.B., O.B.E., F.R.S.

Maddocks, Sir Kenneth Phipson, K.C.M.G., K.C.V.O.

Maddox, Sir (John) Kempson, Kt., V.R.D., M.D.

Madigan, Sir Russel Tullie, Kt., O.B.E.

Magarey, Sir James Rupert, Kt.

Magill, Sir Ivan Whiteside, K.C.V.O.

Maguire, *Air Marshal* Sir Harold John, K.C.B., D.S.O., O.B.E.

Mahon, Sir George Edward John, Bt. (1819).

Main, Sir Peter Tester, Kt., E.R.D.

Maini, Sir Amar Nath, Kt., C.B.E.

Mais, *Hon.* Sir (Robert) Hugh, Kt.

Maitland, Sir Donald James Dundas, G.C.M.G., O.B.E.

Maitland, Sir Richard John, Bt. (1818).

Makins, Sir Paul Vivian, Bt. (1903).

Malcolm, Sir David Peter Michael, Bt. (s. 1665).

Malet, *Col.* Sir Edward William St. Lo, Bt., O.B.E. (1791).

Mallabar, Sir John Frederick, Kt.

Mallet, Sir (William) Ivo, G.B.E., K.C.M.G.

Mallinson, Sir (William) Paul, Bt. (1935).

Malone, *Hon.* Sir Denis Eustace Gilbert, Kt.

Mamo, Sir Anthony Joseph, Kt., O.B.E.

Mander, Sir Charles Marcus, Bt. (1911).

Mann, *Hon.* Sir Michael, Kt., Q.C.

Mann, Sir Rupert Edward, Bt. (1905).

Mansel, *Rev. Canon* James Seymour Denis, K.C.V.O.

Mansel, Sir Philip, Bt. (1622).

Mansergh, *Vice-Adm.* Sir (Cecil) Aubrey (Lawson), K.B.E., C.B., D.S.C.

Mansfield, *Vice-Adm.* Sir (Edward) Gerard (Napier), K.B.E., C.V.O.

Mansfield, Sir Philip (Robert Aked), K.C.M.G.

Mant, Sir Cecil George, Kt., C.B.E.

Mara, *Rt. Hon. Ratu* Sir Kamisese Kapaiwai Tuimacilai, G.C.M.G., K.B.E.

Marchant, Sir Herbert Stanley, K.C.M.G., O.B.E.

Margetson, *Maj.* Sir Philip Reginald, K.C.V.O., M.C.

Marjoribanks, Sir James Alexander Milne, K.C.M.G.

Mark, Sir Robert, G.B.E.

Markham, Sir Charles John, Bt. (1911).

Marking, Sir Henry Ernest, K.C.V.O., C.B.E., M.C.

Marks, Sir John Hedley Douglas, Kt., C.B.E.

Marling, Sir Charles William Somerset, Bt., (1882).

Marr, Sir Leslie Lynn, Bt. (1919).

Marre, Sir Alan Samuel, K.C.B.

Marriner, Sir Neville, Kt., C.B.E.

Marriott, Sir Ralph George Cavendish Smith-, Bt. (1774).

Marsack, Sir Charles Croft, K.B.E.

Marsden, Sir Nigel John Denton, Bt., (1924).

Marshall, Sir Arthur Gregory George, Kt., O.B.E.

Marshall, Sir Denis Alfred, Kt.

Marshall, Sir Hugo Frank, K.B.E, C.M.G.

Marshall, *Rt. Hon.* Sir John Ross, G.B.E., C.H.

Marshall, *Prof.* Sir (Oshley) Roy, Kt., C.B.E.

Marshall, Sir Peter Harold Reginald, K.C.M.G.

Marshall, Sir Robert Braithwaite, K.C.B., M.B.E.

Martell, *Vice-Adm.* Sir Hugh Colenso, K.B.E., C.B.

Marten, *Rt. Hon.* Sir Neil, Kt.

Martin, *Air Marshal* Sir Harold Brownlow, K.C.B., D.S.O., D.F.C., A.F.C.

Martin, *Vice-Adm.* Sir John Edward Ludgate, K.C.B., D.S.C.

Martin, *Prof.* Sir (John) Leslie, Kt., Ph.D.

Martin, Sir John Miller, K.C.M.G., C.B., C.V.O.

Martin, Sir Sidney Launcelot, Kt.

Marwick, Sir Brian Allan, K.B.E., C.M.G.

Marychurch, Sir Peter Harvey, K.C.M.G.

Masefield, Sir Peter Gordon, Kt.

Mason, *Hon.* Sir Anthony Frank, K.B.E.

Mason, Sir (Basil) John, Kt., C.B., D.SC., F.R.S.

Mason, *Vice-Adm.* Sir Frank Trowbridge, K.C.B.

Mason, Sir Frederick Cecil, K.C.V.O., C.M.G.

Mason, Sir John Charles Moir, K.C.M.G.

Mason, *Prof.* Sir Ronald, K.C.B., F.R.S.

Mather, *Prof.* Sir Kenneth, C.B.E., D.SC., F.R.S.

Mather, Sir William Loris, Kt., O.B.E., M.C., T.D.

Mathers, Sir Robert William, Kt.

Matheson, Sir (James Adam) Louis, K.B.E., C.M.G.

Matheson of Matheson, Sir Torquhil Alexander, Bt. (1882).

Mathias, Sir Richard Hughes, Bt. (1917).

Matthews, Sir Bryan Harold Cabot, Kt., C.B.E., SC.D., F.R.S.

Matthews, Sir Peter Alec, Kt.

Matthews, Sir Peter Jack, Kt., C.V.O., O.B.E., Q.P.M.

Matthews, Sir Russell, Kt., O.B.E.

Matthews, Sir Stanley, Kt., C.B.E.

Maudslay, *Major* Sir (James) Rennie, G.C.V.O., K.C.B., M.B.E.

Mavor, *Air Marshal* Sir Leslie Deane, K.C.B., A.F.C.

Maxwell, Sir Aymer, Bt. (s 1681).

Maxwell, Sir Nigel Mellor Heron-, Bt. (s 1683).

Maxwell, Sir Robert Hugh, K.B.E.

May, *Rt. Hon.* Sir John Douglas, Kt.

May, Sir Kenneth Spencer, Kt., C.B.E.

Mayall, Sir (Alexander) Lees, K.C.V.O., C.M.G.

Maycock, Sir William d'Auvergne, Kt., C.B.E., M.V.O., M.D., F.R.C.P.

Mayhew, Sir Patrick Barnabas Burke, Kt., Q.C., M.P.

Mayhew-Sanders, Sir John Reynolds, Kt.

Maynard, *Air Chief Marshal* Sir Nigel Martin, K.C.B., C.B.E., D.F.C., A.F.C.

Meade, Sir (Richard) Geoffrey (Austin), K.B.E., C.M.G., C.V.O.

Meaney, Sir Patrick Michael, Kt.

Medawar, Sir Peter Brian, Kt., O.M., C.H., C.B.E., D.SC., F.R.S.

Medlycott, Sir (James) Christopher, Bt. (1808).

Meere, Sir Francis Anthony, Kt., C.B.E.

Megarry, *Rt. Hon.* Sir Robert Edgar, Kt., F.B.A.

Megaw, *Rt. Hon.* Sir John, Kt., C.B.E., T.D.

Meinertzhagen, Sir Peter, Kt., C.M.G.

Mellor, Sir John Serocold Paget, Bt. (1924).

Melville, Sir Eugene, K.C.M.G.

Melville, Sir Harry Work, K.C.B., PH.D., D.SC., F.R.S.

Melville, Sir Leslie Galfreid, K.B.E.

Melville, Sir Ronald Henry, K.C.B.

Mensforth, Sir Eric, Kt., C.B.E.

Menter, Sir James Woodham, Kt., PH.D., SC.D., F.R.S.

Menteth, Sir James Wallace Stuart-, Bt. (1838).

Menuhin, Sir Yehudi, K.B.E.

Menzies, Sir Peter Thomson, Kt.

Merrison, Sir Alexander Walter, Kt., F.R.S.

Merton, *Air Chief Marshal* Sir Walter Hugh, G.B.E., K.C.B., K.C.B.

Meyer, Sir Anthony John Charles, Bt., M.P. (1910).

Meyjes, Sir Richard Anthony, Kt.

Meyrick, *Lt.-Col.* Sir George David Elliott Tapps-Gervis-, Bt., M.C. (1791).

Meyrick, Sir David John Charlton, Bt. (1880).

Michelmore, Sir Walter Harold Strachan, Kt., M.B.E.

Micklethwait, Sir Robert Gore, Kt., Q.C.

Middlemore, Sir William Hawkslow, Bt. (1919).

Middleton, Sir George Humphrey, K.C.M.G.

Middleton, Sir George Proctor, K.C.V.O.

Middleton, Sir Peter Edward, K.C.B.

Middleton, Sir Stephen Hugh, Bt. (1662).

Miers, Sir (Henry) David Alastair Capel, K.B.E., C.M.G.

Milbank, Sir Anthony Frederick, Bt. (1882).

Milburn, Sir Anthony Rupert, Bt. (1905).

Miles, Sir (Arnold) Ashley, Kt., C.B.E., M.D., F.R.S.

Miles, Sir William Napier Maurice, Bt. (1859).

Millais, Sir Ralph Regnault, Bt. (1885).

Millar, Sir Oliver Nicholas, K.C.V.O., F.B.A.

Millar, Sir Ronald Graeme, Kt.

Millard, Sir Guy Elwin, K.C.M.G., C.V.O.

Miller, Sir Douglas Sinclair, K.C.V.O., C.B.E.

Miller, Sir (Ian) Douglas, Kt.

Miller, Sir John Holmes, Bt. (1705).

Miller, *Lt.-Col.* Sir John Mansel, K.C.V.O., D.S.O., M.C.

Miller, Sir (Joseph) Holmes, Kt., O.B.E.

Miller, Sir (Oswald) Bernard, Kt.

Miller, Sir Richard Hope, Kt.

Miller, Sir Stephen James Hamilton, K.C.V.O., M.D., F.R.C.S.

Miller of Glenlee, Sir (Frederick William) Macdonald, Bt. (1788).

Milling, *Air Marshal* Sir Denis Crowley-, K.C.B., C.B.E., D.S.O., D.F.C.

Millis, Sir Leonard William Francis, Kt., C.B.E.

Mills, *Vice-Adm.* Sir Charles Piercy, K.C.B., C.B.E., D.S.C.

Mills, Sir Frank, K.C.V.O., C.M.G.

Mills, Sir John Lewis Ernest Watts, Kt., C.B.E.

Mills, Sir Peter Frederick Leighton, Bt. (1921).

Mills, Sir Peter McLay, Kt., M.P.

Milman, Sir Dermot Lionel Kennedy, Bt. (1800).

Milmo, *Hon.* Sir Helenus Patrick Joseph, Kt.

Milner, Sir (George Edward) Mordaunt, Bt. (1717).

Milnes Coates, Sir Anthony Robert, Bt. (1911).

Minhinnick, Sir Gordon Edward George, K.B.E.

Minogue, *Hon.* Sir John Patrick, Kt., Q.C.

Miskin, *Hon.* Sir James William, Kt., Q.C.

Mitchell, *Air Cdre.* Sir (Arthur) Dennis, K.B.E., C.V.O., D.F.C., A.F.C.

Mitchell, Sir Derek Jack, K.C.B., C.V.O.

Mitchell, Sir Hamilton, K.B.E.

Mitchell, Sir (Seton) Steuart Crichton, K.B.E., C.B.

Moberly, Sir John Campbell, K.B.E., C.M.G.

Mocatta, Sir Alan Abraham, Kt., O.B.E.

Moffat, *Lt.-Gen.* Sir William Cameron, K.B.E.

Mogg, *General* Sir (Herbert) John, G.C.B., C.B.E., D.S.O.

Moir, Sir Ernest Ian Royds, Bt. (1916).

Moller, *Hon.* Sir Lester Francis, Kt.

†Molony, Sir Thomas Desmond, Bt. (1925).

Monro, Sir Hector Seymour Peter, Kt., M.P.

Monson, Sir (William Bonnar) Leslie, K.C.M.G., C.B.

Montgomery, Sir (Basil Henry) David, Bt. (1801).

Montgomery, Sir (William) Fergus, Kt., M.P.

Mookerjee, Sir Birendra Nath, Kt.

Moon, Sir (Edward), Bt., M.C. (1887).

Moon, Sir Edward Penderel, Kt., O.B.E.

Moon, Sir Peter James Scott, K.C.V.O., C.M.G.

Moon, Sir Peter Wilfred Giles Graham-, Bt. (1855).

Moore, Sir Edward Stanton, Bt., O.B.E. (1923).

Moore, Sir Francis Thomas, Kt.

Moore, Sir Henry Roderick, Kt., C.B.E.

Moore, *Hon.* Sir John Cochrane, Kt.

Moore, *Maj.-Gen.* Sir (John) Jeremy, K.C.B., O.B.E., M.C.

Moore, Sir John Michael, K.C.V.O., C.B., D.S.C.

Moore, *Prof.* Sir Norman Winfrid, Bt. (1919).

Moore, *Rt. Hon.* Sir Philip Brian Cecil, G.C.B., G.C.V.O., C.M.G.

Moore, Sir William Roger Clotworthy, Bt., T.D. (1932).

Moores, Sir John, Kt., C.B.E.

Mootham, Sir Orby Howell, Kt.

Mordaunt, Sir Richard Nigel Charles, Bt. (1611).

Mordecai, Sir John Stanley, Kt., C.M.G.

More, Sir Jasper, Kt.

Moreton, Sir John Oscar, K.C.M.G., K.C.V.O., M.C.

Morgan, Sir Clifford Naunton, Kt.

Morgan, *Maj.-Gen.* Sir David John Hughes-, Bt., C.B., C.B.E. (1925).

Morgan, Sir Ernest Dunstan, K.B.E.

Morgan, *Rear-Adm.* Sir Patrick John, K.C.V.O., C.B., D.S.C.

Morgan-Giles, *Rear-Adm.* Sir Morgan Charles, Kt., D.S.O., O.B.E., G.M.

Morley, Sir Godfrey William Rowland, Kt., O.B.E., T.D.

Morony, *Gen.* Sir Thomas Lovett, K.C.B., O.B.E.

Morpeth, Sir Douglas Spottiswoode, Kt., T.D.

Morris, *Air Marshal* Sir Arnold Alec, K.B.E., C.B.

Morris, *Air Marshal* Sir Douglas Griffith, K.C.B., C.B.E., D.S.O., D.F.C.

Morris, Sir Robert Byng, Bt. (1806).

Morrow, Sir Ian Thomas, Kt.

Morse, Sir Christopher Jeremy, K.C.M.G.

Morton, *Admiral* Sir Anthony Storrs, G.B.E., K.C.B.

Morton, Sir Brian, Kt.

Morton, Sir Ralph John, Kt., C.M.G., O.B.E., M.C.

Moseley, Sir George Walker, K.C.B.

Moser, *Prof.* Sir Claus Adolf, K.C.B., C.B.E., F.B.A.

Moses, Sir Charles Joseph Alfred, Kt., C.B.E.

Moss, Sir John Herbert Theodore Edwards-, Bt. (1868).

Mostyn, Sir Jeremy John Anthony, Bt. (1670).

Mostyn, *Lt.-Gen.* Sir Joseph David Frederick, K.C.B., C.B.E.

Mott, Sir John Harmer, Bt. (1930).

Mott, Sir Nevill Francis, Kt., F.R.S.

Mount, Sir James William Spencer, Kt., C.B.E., B.E.M.

Mount, Sir William Malcolm, Bt. (1921).

Mountain, Sir Denis Mortimer, Bt. (1922).

Mowbray, Sir John, Kt.

Mowbray, Sir John Robert, Bt. (1880).

Moynihan, Sir Noel Henry, Kt.

Muir, Sir David John, Kt., C.M.G.

Muir, Sir John Harling, Bt. (1892).

Muir, Sir Laurence Macdonald, Kt.

Muir Wood, Sir Alan Marshall, Kt., F.R.S.

Muirhead, Sir David Francis, K.C.M.G., C.V.O.

Muldoon, *Rt. Hon.* Sir Robert David, G.C.M.G., C.H.

Mulholland, Sir Michael Henry, Bt. (1945).

Mumford, Sir Albert Henry, K.B.E.

Munn, Sir James, Kt., O.B.E.

Munro, Sir Ian Talbot, Bt. (s 1634).

Munro, *Hon.* Sir Robert Lindsay, Kt., C.B.E.

Munro, Sir Sydney Douglas Gun-, G.C.M.G., M.B.E.

Munro, Sir Alasdair Thomas Ian Bt. (1825).

Murdoch, *Air Marshal* Sir Alister Murray, K.B.E., C.B.

Murless, Sir (Charles Francis) Noel, Kt.

Murley, Sir Reginald Sydney, K.B.E., T.D., F.R.C.S.

Murphy, Sir Leslie Frederick, Kt.

Murray, *Rear-Adm.* Sir Brian Stewart, K.C.M.G.

Murray, Sir Donald Frederick, K.C.V.O., C.M.G.

Murray, *General* Sir Horatius, G.C.B., K.B.E., D.S.O.

Murray, Sir James, K.C.M.G.

Murray, Sir Nigel Andrew Digby, Bt. (s 1628).

Murray, Sir Patrick Ian Keith, Bt. (s 1673).

Murray, Sir Rowland William Patrick, Bt. (s 1630).

Murrie, Sir William Stuart, G.C.B., K.B.E.

Mursell, Sir Peter, Kt., M.B.E.

Musgrave, Sir Christopher Patrick Charles, Bt. (1611).

Musgrave, Sir (Frank) Cyril, K.C.B.

Musgrave, Sir Richard James, Bt. (1 1782).

Musker, Sir John, Kt.

Musson, *General* Sir Geoffrey Randolph Dixon, G.C.B., C.B.E., D.S.O.

Mustill, *Rt. Hon.* Sir Michael John, Kt.

Myers, Sir Kenneth Ben, Kt., M.B.E.

Myers, Sir Philip Alan, Kt., O.B.E., Q.P.M.

Myers, *Prof.* Sir Rupert Horace, K.B.E.

Mynors, Sir Humphrey Charles Baskerville, Bt. (1964).

Mynors, *Prof.* Sir Roger Aubrey Baskerville, Kt., F.B.A.

Nabarro, Sir John David Nunes, Kt., M.D., F.R.C.P.

Nairn, Sir Michael, Bt. (1904).

Nairn, Sir Robert Arnold Spencer-, Bt. (1933).

Nairne, *Rt. Hon.* Sir Patrick Dalmahoy, G.C.B., M.C.

Nalder, *Hon.* Sir Crawford David, Kt.

Nall, Sir Michael Joseph, Bt., R.N. (1954).

Napier, Sir Joseph William Lennox, Bt., O.B.E. (1867).

Napier, Sir Oliver John, Kt.

Napier, Sir William Archibald, Bt. (s 1627).

Napley, Sir David, Kt.

Narain, Sir Sathi, K.B.E.

Neal, Sir Eric James, Kt.

Neal, Sir Leonard Francis, Kt., C.B.E.

Neale, Sir Alan Derrett, K.C.B., M.B.E.

Neave, Sir Arundell Thomas Clifton, Bt. (1795).

Nedd, *Hon.* Sir Robert Archibald, Kt.

Neill, *Rt. Hon.* Sir Brian Thomas, Kt.

Neill, Sir Francis Patrick, Kt., Q.C.

Neill, *Rt. Hon.* Sir Ivan K., Kt.

Nelson, *Maj.-Gen.* Sir (Eustace) John (Blois), K.C.V.O., C.B., D.S.O., O.B.E., M.C.

Nelson, *Air Marshal* Sir (Sidney) Richard (Carlyle), K.C.B., O.B.E., M.D.

Nelson, *Maj.* Sir William Vernon Hope, Bt., O.B.E. (1912).

Nepean, *Lt.-Col.* Sir Evan Yorke, Bt. (1802).

Ness, *Air Marshal* Sir Charles Ernest, K.C.B., C.B.E.

Nevill, *Air Vice-Marshal* Sir Arthur de Terrotte, K.B.E., C.B.

Neville, Sir Richard Lionel John Baines, Bt. (1927).

Neville, *Maj.-Gen.* Sir Robert Arthur Ross, K.C.M.G., C.B.E., M.C.

Newbold, Sir Charles Demorée, K.B.E., C.M.G., Q.C.

Newman, Sir Geoffrey Robert, Bt. (1836).

Newman, Sir Gerard Robert Henry Sigismund, Bt. (1912).

Newman, Sir Jack, Kt., C.B.E.

Newman, Sir Kenneth Leslie, Kt.

Newns, Sir (Alfred) Foley (Francis Polden), K.C.M.G., C.V.O.

Newton, Sir (Harry) Michael (Rex), Bt. (1900).

Newton, Sir Hubert, Kt.

Newton, Sir Kenneth Garnar, Bt., O.B.E., T.D. (1924).

Newton, Sir (Leslie) Gordon, Kt.

Ngata, Sir Henare Kohere, K.B.E.

Niall, Sir Horace Lionel Richard, Kt., C.B.E.

Nicholas, Sir Herbert Richard, Kt., O.B.E.

Nicholas, Sir John William, K.C.V.O., C.M.G.

Nicholls, *Hon.* Sir Donald James, Kt., Q.C.

Nicholls, Sir Douglas Ralph, K.C.V.O., O.B.E.

Nicholls, *Air Marshal* Sir John Moreton, K.C.B., C.B.E., D.F.C., A.F.C.

Nichols, Sir Edward Henry, Kt., T.D.

Nicholson, *Hon.* Sir David Eric, Kt.

Nicholson, Sir Godfrey, Bt. (1958).

Nicholson, Sir John Charles, Bt. (1859).

Nicholson, Sir John Norris, Bt., K.B.E., C.I.E. (1912).

Nicholson, Sir Robin Buchanan, Kt., PH.D., F.R.S.

Nickerson, Sir Joseph, Kt.

Nicolson, Sir David Lancaster, Kt.

Nield, Sir Basil Edward, Kt., C.B.E., Q.C.

Nield, Sir William Alan, G.C.M.G., K.C.B.

Nightingale, Sir Charles Manners Gamaliel, Bt. (1628).

Nightingale, Sir John Cyprian, Kt., C.B.E., B.E.M., Q.P.M.

Nimmo, *Hon.* Sir John Angus, Kt., C.B.E.

Niven, Sir (Cecil) Rex, Kt., C.M.G., M.C.

Nixon, Sir Edwin Ronald, Kt., C.B.E.

Nixon, *Rev.* Sir Kenneth Michael John Basil, Bt. (1906).

Noad, Sir Kenneth Beeson, Kt., M.D.

Noble, Sir Andrew Napier, Bt., K.C.M.G. (1923).

Noble, Sir Marc Brunel, Bt. (1902).

Noble, Sir Peter Scott, Kt.

Noble, Sir (Thomas Alexander) Fraser, Kt., M.B.E.

Nock, Sir Norman Lindfield, Kt.

Noel, Sir Claude, Kt., C.M.G.

Nolan, *Hon.* Sir Michael Patrick, Kt., Q.C.

Nolan, Sir Sidney Robert, Kt., O.M., C.B.E.

Nordmeyer, *Hon.* Sir Arnold Henry, K.C.M.G.

Norman, Sir Arthur Gordon, K.B.E., D.F.C.

Norman, *Rt. Rev.* Edward Kinsella, K.B.E., D.S.O., M.C.

Norman, *Vice-Adm.* Sir (Horace) Geoffrey, K.C.V.O., C.B., C.B.E.

Norman, Sir Mark Annesley, Bt. (1915).

Norman, Sir Robert Wentworth, Kt.

Norris, Sir Alfred Henry, K.B.E.

Norris, *Vice-Adm.* Sir Charles Fred Wivell, K.B.E., C.B., D.S.O.

Norris, *Air Chief Marshal* Sir Christopher Neil Foxley-, G.C.B., D.S.O., O.B.E.

Norris, Sir Eric George, K.C.M.G.

Norris, *Hon.* Sir John Gerald, Kt., E.D.

North, Sir Thomas Lindsay, Kt.

North, Sir (William) Jonathan (Frederick), Bt. (1920).

Northam, Sir William Herbert, Kt., C.B.E.

Norton, Sir Clifford John, K.C.M.G., C.V.O.

Norwood, Sir Walter Neville, Kt.

Nossal, Sir Gustav Joseph Victor, Kt., C.B.E.

Nott, *Rt. Hon.* Sir John William Frederic, K.C.B.

Nourse, *Rt. Hon.* Sir Martin Charles, Kt.

Nugent, Sir John Edwin Lavallin, Bt. (1 1795).

Nugent, *Maj.* Sir Peter Walter James, Bt. (1831).

Nugent, Sir Robin George Colborne, Bt. (1806).

Nuttall, Sir Nicholas Keith Lillington, Bt. (1922).

Nutting, *Rt. Hon.* Sir (Harold) Anthony, Bt. (1903).

Oakeley, Sir (Edward) Atholl, Bt. (1790).

Oakes, Sir Christopher, Bt. (1939).

Oakeshott, Sir Walter Fraser, Kt., F.B.A., F.S.A.

Oakshott, *Hon.* Sir Anthony Hendrie, Bt. (1959).

Oates, Sir Thomas, Kt., C.M.G., O.B.E.

Oatley, Sir Charles William, Kt., O.B.E., F.R.S.

Obolensky, *Prof.* Sir Dimitri, Kt.

O'Brien, Sir Frederick William Fitzgerald, Kt.

O'Brien, Sir Timothy John, Bt. (1849).

O'Brien, Sir Richard, Kt., D.S.O., M.C.

O'Brien, *Admiral* Sir William Donough, K.C.B., D.S.C.

O'Connell, Sir Morgan Donal Conail, Bt. (1869).

O'Connor, *Lt.-Gen.* Sir Denis Stuart Scott, K.B.E., C.B.

O'Connor, *Rt. Hon.* Sir Patrick McCarthy, Kt.

O'Dea, Sir Patrick Jerad, K.C.V.O.

Ogilvie, Sir Alec Drummond, Kt.

Ogilvy, Sir David John Wilfrid, Bt. (s 1626).

O'Halloran, Sir Charles Ernest, Kt.

Ohlson, Sir Brian Eric Christopher, Bt. (1920).

Okeover, *Capt.* Sir Peter Ralph Leopold Walker-, Bt. (1886).

Oldman, *Col.* Sir Hugh Richard Deare, K.B.E., M.C.

Olewale, *Hon.* Sir Niwia Ebia, Kt.

Oliphant, Sir Mark (Marcus Laurence Elwin), K.B.E., F.R.S.

Oliver, Sir (Frederick) Ernest, Kt., C.B.E., T.D.

Oliver, *Rt. Hon.* Sir Peter Raymond, Kt.

O'Loghlen, Sir Colman Michael, Bt. (1838).

Olver, Sir Stephen John Linley, K.B.E., C.M.G.

O'Neil, *Hon.* Sir Desmond Henry, Kt.

O'Neill, *Hon.* Sir Con Douglas Walter, G.C.M.G.

Onslow, Sir John Roger Wilmot, Bt. (1797).

Oppenheim, Sir Alexander, Kt., O.B.E., D.SC., F.R.S.E.

Oppenheim, Sir Duncan Morris, Kt.

Oppenheimer, Sir Michael Bernard Grenville, Bt. (1921).

Oppenheimer, Sir Philip Jack, Kt.

Opperman, *Hon.* Sir Hubert Ferdinand, Kt., O.B.E.

Orde, Sir John Alexander Campbell-, Bt. (1790).

O'Regan, *Hon.* Sir John Barry, Kt.

Organe, *Prof.* Sir Geoffrey Stephen William, Kt., M.D.

Ormond, Sir John Davies Wilder, Kt., B.E.M.

Ormrod, *Rt. Hon.* Sir Roger Fray Greenwood, Kt.

Orr, *Rt. Hon.* Sir Alan Stewart, Kt., O.B.E.

Orr, Sir David Alexander, Kt., M.C.

Orr, Sir John Henry, Kt., O.B.E., Q.P.M.

Osborn, Sir Richard Henry Danvers, Bt. (1662).

Osborn, Sir John Holbrook, Kt, M.P.

Osborne, Sir Basil, Kt., C.B.E.

Osborne, Sir Peter George, Bt. (1 1629).

Osifelo, Sir Frederick Aubarua, Kt., M.B.E.

Osman, Sir (Abdool) Raman Mahomed, G.C.M.G., C.B.E.

Osmond, Sir Douglas, Kt., C.B.E.

Osmond, Sir (Stanley) Paul, Kt., C.B.

Otton, Sir Geoffrey John, K.C.B.

Otton, *Hon.* Sir Philip Howard, Kt., Q.C.

Oulton, Sir Antony Derek Maxwell, K.C.B., Q.C.

Outerbridge, *Col. Hon.* Sir Leonard Cecil, Kt., C.B.E., D.S.O.

Outram, Sir Alan James, Bt. (1858).

Overall, Sir John Wallace, Kt., C.B.E., M.C.

Overton, Sir Hugh Thomas Arnold, K.C.M.G.

Owen, Sir Hugo Dudley Cunliffe-, Bt. (1920).

Owen, Sir Hugh Bernard Pilkington, Bt. (1813).

Owen, Sir Ronald Hugh, Kt.

Owo, The Olowo of, Kt.

Packard, *Lieut.-Gen.* Sir (Charles) Douglas, K.B.E., C.B., D.S.O.

Padmore, Sir Thomas, G.C.B.

Pagan, *Brig.* Sir John Ernest, Kt., C.M.G., M.B.E., E.D.

Page, Sir Alexander Warren, Kt., M.B.E.

Page, Sir (Arthur) John, Kt., M.P.

Page, Sir Frederick William, Kt., C.B.E.

Page, Sir John Joseph Joffre, Kt., O.B.E.

Paget, Sir John Starr, Bt. (1886).

Paget, Sir Julian Tolver, Bt., C.V.O. (1871).

Pain, *Lt.-Gen.* Sir (Horace) Rollo (Squarey), K.C.B., M.C.

Pain, *Hon.* Sir Peter Richard, Kt.

Palliser, *Rt. Hon.* Sir (Arthur) Michael, G.C.M.G.

Palmer, Sir (Charles) Mark, Bt. (1886).

Palmer, Sir Geoffrey Christopher John, Bt. (1660).

Palmer, Sir John Chance, Kt.

Palmer, Sir John Edward Somerset, Bt. (1791).

Palmer, *Maj.-Gen.* Sir (Joseph) Michael, K.C.V.O.

Palmer, *Brig.* Sir Otho Leslie Prior-, Kt., D.S.O.

Panckridge, *Surgeon Vice-Adm.* Sir (William) Robert (Silvester), K.B.E., C.B.

Pao, Sir Yue-Kong, Kt., C.B.E.

Pape, *Hon.* Sir George Augustus, Kt.

Pararajasingam, Sir Sangarapillai, Kt.

Parbo, Sir Arvi Hillar, Kt.

Parham, *Admiral* Sir Frederick Robertson, G.B.E., K.C.B., D.S.O.

Parish, Sir David Elmer Woodbine, Kt., C.B.E.

Park, *Hon.* Sir Hugh Eames, Kt.

Parker, Sir (Arthur) Douglas Dodds-, Kt.

Parker, Sir Douglas William Leigh, Kt., O.B.E.

Parker, Sir John Edward, Kt.

Parker, Sir Karl Theodore, Kt., C.B.E., Ph.D., F.B.A.

Parker, Sir Peter, Kt., M.V.O.

Parker, Sir Richard (William) Hyde, Bt. (1681).

Parker, *Rt. Hon.* Sir Roger Jocelyn, Kt.

Parker, *Vice-Adm.* Sir (Wilfred) John, K.B.E., C.B., D.S.C.

Parker, Sir (William) Alan, Bt. (1844).

Parkes, Sir Alan Sterling, Kt., C.B.E., Ph.D., D.SC., SC.D., F.R.S.

Parkes, Sir Basil Arthur, Kt., O.B.E.

Parkes, Sir Edward Walter, Kt.

Parkinson, Sir Nicholas Fancourt, Kt.

Parry, Sir Ernest Jones-, Kt.

Parry, Sir (Frank) Hugh (Nigel), Kt., C.B.E.

Parry-Evans, *Air Marshal* Sir David, K.C.B., C.B.E.

Parsons, Sir Anthony Derrick, G.C.M.G., M.V.O., M.C.

Parsons, Sir (John) Michael, Kt.

Parsons, Sir Richard Edmund (Clement Fownes), K.C.M.G.

Part, Sir Antony Alexander, Kt., G.C.B., M.B.E.

Pascoe, *Lt. Gen.* Sir Robert Alan, K.C.B., M.B.E.

Pasley, Sir John Malcolm Sabine, Bt. (1794).

Patch, *Air Chief Marshal* Sir Hubert Leonard, K.C.B., C.B.E.

Paterson, Sir Dennis Craig, Kt.

Paterson, Sir George Mutlow, Kt., O.B.E., Q.C.

Paterson, Sir John Valentine Jardine, Kt.

Paton, *Prof.* Sir George Whitecross, Kt.

Paton, Sir Leonard Cecil, Kt., C.B.E., M.C.

Paton, *Capt.* Sir Stuart Henry, K.C.V.O., C.B.E., R.N. *(ret.).*

Paton, Sir (Thomas) Angus (Lyall), Kt., C.M.G., F.R.S.

Paton, *Prof.* Sir William Drummond Macdonald, Kt., C.B.E., D.M., F.R.S., F.R.C.P.

Pattinson, *Hon.* Sir Baden, K.B.E.

Paul, Sir John Warburton, G.C.M.G., O.B.E., M.C.

Payne, Sir Norman John, Kt., C.B.E.

Peacock, Sir Geoffrey Arden, Kt., C.V.O.

Pearce, Sir Austin William, Kt., C.B.E., Ph.D.

Pearce, Sir Eric Herbert, Kt., O.B.E.

Peard, *Rear-Adm.* Sir Kenyon Harry Terrell, K.B.E.

Pearman, *Hon.* Sir James Eugene, Kt., C.B.E.

Pears, Sir Peter Neville Luard, Kt., C.B.E.

Pearson, Sir Francis Fenwick, Bt., M.B.E. (1964).

Pearson, Sir (James) Denning, Kt.

Pearson, *General* Sir Thomas Cecil Hook, K.C.B., C.B.E., D.S.O.

Peart, *Prof.* Sir William Stanley, Kt., M.D., F.R.S.

Pease, Sir (Alfred) Vincent, Bt. (1882).

Pease, Sir Richard Thorn, Bt. (1920).

Peat, Sir Henry, K.C.V.O., D.F.C.

Peck, Sir Edward Heywood, G.C.M.G.

Peck, Sir John Howard, K.C.M.G.

Pedder, *Vice-Adm.* Sir Arthur Reid, K.B.E., C.B.

Pedder, *Air Marshal* Sir Ian Maurice, K.C.B., O.B.E., D.F.C.

Pedler, Sir Frederick Johnson, Kt.

Peek, Sir Francis Henry Grenville, Bt. (1874).

Peek, *Vice-Adm.* Sir Richard Innes, K.B.E., C.B., D.S.O.

Peel, Sir John Harold, K.C.V.O.

Peel, Sir (William) John, Kt.

Peierls, Sir Rudolf Ernst, Kt., C.B.E., D.SC., D.Phil., F.R.S.

Peile, *Vice-Adm.* Sir Lancelot Arthur Babington, K.B.E., C.B., D.S.O., M.V.O.

Peirse, Sir Henry Grant de la Poer Beresford-, Bt. (1814).

Pelly, Sir John Alwyne, Bt. (1840).

Pemberton, Sir Francis Wingate William, Kt., C.B.E.

Pendred, *Air Marshal* Sir Lawrence Fleming, K.B.E., C.B., D.F.C.

Penn, *Lt.-Col.* Sir Eric Charles William Mackenzie, G.C.V.O., O.B.E., M.C.

Penruddock, Sir Clement Frederick, Kt., C.B.E.

Percival, Sir Anthony Edward, Kt., C.B.

Percival, *Rt. Hon.* Sir (Walter) Ian, Kt., Q.C., M.P.

Pereira, Sir (Herbert) Charles, Kt., D.SC., F.R.S.

Perkins, *Surgeon Vice-Adm.* Sir Derek Duncombe Steele-, K.C.B., K.C.V.O.

Perkins, Sir (Walter) Robert Dempster, Kt.

Perrin, Sir Michael Willcox, Kt., C.B.E.

Perring, Sir Ralph Edgar, Bt. (1963).

Perris, Sir David (Arthur), Kt., M.B.E.

Perry, Sir (David) Norman, Kt., M.B.E.

Pestell, Sir John Richard, K.C.V.O.

Peterkin, Sir Neville, Kt.

Petersen, Sir Jeffrey Charles, K.C.M.G.

Peterson, Sir Arthur William, K.C.B., M.V.O.

Petit, Sir Dinshaw Manockjee, Bt. (1890).

Peto, Sir Henry George Morton, Bt. (1855).

Peto, Sir Michael Henry Basil, Bt. (1927).

Petrie, Sir (Charles) Richard (Borthwick), Bt., T.D. (1918).

Pettigrew, Sir Russell Hilton, Kt.

Pettingel, Sir William Walter, Kt., C.B.E.

Pettit, Sir Daniel Eric Arthur, Kt.

Philips, *Prof.* Sir Cyril Henry, Kt.

Philipson, Sir Robert James, (Sir Robin Philipson), Kt., R.A.

Phillips, *Prof.* Sir David Chilton, Kt., Ph.D., F.R.S.

Phillips, Sir Fred Albert, Kt., C.V.O.

Phillips, Sir Henry Ellis Isidore, Kt., C.M.G., M.B.E.

Phillips, Sir Horace, K.C.M.G.

Phillips, Sir John Grant, K.B.E.

Phillips, Sir Robin Francis, Bt. (1912).

Phipps, *Vice-Adm.* Sir Peter, K.B.E., D.S.C., V.R.D.

Pickard, Sir Cyril Stanley, K.C.M.G.

Pickering, Sir Edward Davies, Kt.

Pickthorn, Sir Charles William Richards, Bt. (1959).

Piers, Sir Charles Robert Fitzmaurice, Bt. (I 1661).

Pigot, *Maj.-Gen.* Sir Robert Anthony, Bt., C.B., O.B.E. (1764).

Pigott, Sir Berkeley Henry Sebastian, Bt. (1808).

Pike, Sir Philip Ernest Housden, Kt., Q.C.

Pike, Sir Theodore Ouseley, K.C.M.G.

Pike, *Lt.-Gen.* Sir William Gregory Huddleston, K.C.B., C.B.E., D.S.O.

Pilcher, Sir (Charlie) Dennis, Kt., C.B.E.

Pilcher, Sir John Arthur, G.C.M.G.

Pilditch, Sir Richard Edward, Bt. (1929).

Pile, Sir Frederick Devereux, Bt. M.C. (1900).

Pile, Sir William Dennis, G.C.B., M.B.E.

Pilkington, Sir Lionel Alexander Bethune, (Sir Alastair), Kt., F.R.S.

Pilkington, Sir Thomas Henry Milborne-Swinnerton-, Bt. (s 1635).

Pillar, *Admiral* Sir William Thomas, G.B.E., K.C.B.

Pim, *Capt.* Sir Richard Pike, K.B.E., V.R.D., R.N.V.R.

Pindling, *Rt. Hon.* Sir Lynden Oscar, K.C.M.G.

Pinsent, Sir Christopher Roy, Bt. (1938).

Piper, Sir David Towry, Kt., C.B.E.

Pippard, *Prof.* Sir (Alfred) Brian, Kt., F.R.S.

Pirbhai, Sir Eboo, Kt., O.B.E.

Pirie, *Gp. Capt.* Sir Gordon Hamish, Kt., C.B.E.

Pitblado, Sir David Bruce, K.C.B., C.V.O.

Pitman, Sir Hubert Percival Lancaster, Kt., O.B.E.

Pitman, Sir (Isaac) James, K.B.E.

Pitoi, Sir Sere, Kt., C.B.E.

Pitt, Sir Harry Raymond, Kt., Ph.D., F.R.S.

Pitts, Sir Cyril Alfred, Kt.

Pixley, Sir Neville Drake, Kt., M.B.E., V.R.D.

Pizey, *Admiral* Sir (Charles Thomas) Mark, G.B.E., C.B., D.S.O.

Plaister, Sir Sydney, Kt., C.B.E.

Platt, Sir Harry, Bt., M.D. (1958).

Platt, *Prof.* Hon. Sir Peter, Bt. (1959).

Playfair, Sir Edward Wilder, K.C.B.

Pleass, Sir Clement John, K.C.M.G., K.C.V.O., K.B.E.

Pliatzky, Sir Leo, K.C.B.

Plimmer, Sir Clifford Ulric, K.B.E.

Plimsoll, Sir James, Kt., C.B.E.

Plowman, Sir (John) Anthony, Kt.

Plowman, *Hon.* Sir John Robin, Kt., C.B.E.

Plumb, Sir (Charles) Henry, Kt.

Plumb, *Prof.* Sir John Harold, Kt.

Pochin, Sir Edward Eric, Kt., C.B.E., M.D., F.R.C.P.

Poett, *General* Sir (Joseph Howard) Nigel, K.C.B., D.S.O.

Pole, *Col.* Sir John Gawen Carew, Bt., D.S.O., T.D. (1628).

Pole, Sir Peter Van Notten, Bt. (1791).

Pollard, Sir (Charles) Herbert, Kt., C.B.E.

Pollen, Sir John Michael Hungerford, Bt. (1795).

Pollock, Sir George, Kt., Q.C.

Pollock, Sir George Frederick, Bt. (1866).

Pollock, Sir Giles Hampden Montagu-, Bt. (1872).

Pollock, *Admiral of the Fleet* Sir Michael Patrick, G.C.B., M.V.O., D.S.C.

Pollock, Sir William Horace Montagu-, K.C.M.G.

Pond, *Prof.* Sir Desmond Arthur, Kt., M.D., F.R.C.P.

Ponsonby, Sir Ashley Charles Gibbs, Bt., M.C. (1956).

Pontin, Sir Frederick William, Kt.

Poore, Sir Herbert Edward, Bt. (1795).

Pope, *Vice-Adm.* Sir (John) Ernle, K.C.B.

Pope, Sir Joseph Albert, Kt., D.SC., Ph.D.

Popper, *Prof.* Sir Karl Raimund, Kt., C.H., Ph.D., F.R.S.

Popplewell, *Hon.* Sir Oliver Bury, Kt., Q.C.

Portal, Sir Jonathan Francis, Bt. (1901).

Porter, Sir Andrew Marshall Horsbrugh-, Bt., D.S.O. (1902).

Porter, *Prof.* Sir George, Kt., F.R.S., PH.D., SC.D.

Porter, Sir Leslie, Kt.

Porter, *Air Marshal* Sir (Melvin) Kenneth (Drowley), K.C.B., C.B.E.

Porter, *Hon.* Sir Murray Victor, Kt.

Porter, *Rt. Hon.* Sir Robert Wilson, Kt., Q.C.

Posnett, Sir Richard Neil, K.B.E., C.M.G.

Potter, Sir (Joseph) Raymond (Lynden), Kt.

Potter, *Maj.-Gen.* Sir (Wilfrid) John, K.B.E., C.B.

Potter, Sir (William) Ian, Kt.

Pound, Sir John David, Bt. (1905).

Pountain, Sir Eric John, Kt.

Powell, Sir (Arnold Joseph) Philip, Kt., C.H., O.B.E., R.A., F.R.I.B.A.

Powell, Sir Nicholas Folliott Douglas, Bt. (1897).

Powell, Sir Richard Royle, G.C.B., K.B.E., C.M.G.

Power, Sir Alastair John Cecil, Bt. (1924).

Powles, Sir Guy Richardson, K.B.E., C.M.G., E.D.

Powlett, *Vice-Adm.* Sir Peveril Barton Reibey Wallop William-, K.C.B., K.C.M.G., C.B.E., D.S.O.

Poynton, Sir (Arthur) Hilton, G.C.M.G.

Prain, Sir Ronald Lindsay, Kt., O.B.E.

Prendergast, Sir John Vincent, K.B.E., C.M.G., G.M.

Prentice, *Hon.* Sir William Thomas, Kt., M.B.E.

Prescott, Sir Mark, Bt. (1938).

Preston, Sir Kenneth Huson, Kt.

Preston, Sir Peter Sansome, K.C.B.

Preston, Sir Ronald Douglas Hildebrand, Bt. (1815).

Pretyman, Sir Walter Frederick, K.B.E.

Prevost, *Capt.* Sir George James Augustine, Bt. (1805).

Price, Sir Charles Keith Napier Rugge-, Bt. (1804).

Price, Sir David Ernest Campbell, Kt., M.P.

Price, Sir Francis Caradoc Rose, Bt. (1815).

Price, Sir Frank Leslie, Kt.

Price, Sir (James) Robert, K.B.E.

Price, Sir Leslie Victor, Kt., O.B.E.

Price, Sir Norman Charles, K.C.B.

Price, Sir Robert John Green-, Bt. (1874).

Prichard, Sir Montague Illtyd, Kt., C.B.E., M.C.

Prickett, *Air Chief Marshal* Sir Thomas Other, K.C.B., D.S.O., D.F.C.

Prideaux, Sir Humphrey Povah Treverbian, Kt., O.B.E.

Prideaux, Sir John Francis, Kt., O.B.E.

Primrose, Sir Alasdair Neil, Bt. (1903).

Pringle, *Air Marshal* Sir Charles Norman Seton, K.B.E.

Pringle, *Lt.-Gen.* Sir Steuart (Robert), Bt., K.C.B., R.M. (s 1683).

Pritchard, Sir Asa Hubert, Kt.

Pritchard, Sir John Michael, Kt., C.B.E.

Pritchard, Sir Neil, K.C.M.G.

Pritchett, Sir Victor Sawdon, Kt., C.B.E.

Proby, Sir Peter, Bt. (1952).

Proctor, Sir (George) Philip, K.B.E.

Proctor, Sir Roderick Consett, Kt., M.B.E.

Proud, Sir John Seymour, Kt.

Pryke, Sir David Dudley, Bt. (1926).

Pugh, Sir Idwal Vaughan, K.C.B.

Pugsley, *Prof.* Sir Alfred Grenvile, Kt., O.B.E., D.SC., F.R.S.

Pullinger, Sir (Francis) Alan, Kt., C.B.E.

Pumphrey, Sir (John) Laurence, K.C.M.G.

Purchas, *Rt. Hon.* Sir Francis Brooks, Kt.

Pyke, Sir Louis Frederick, Kt., E.D.

Quayle, Sir (John) Anthony, Kt., C.B.E.

Quilter, Sir Anthony Raymond Leopold Cuthbert, Bt. (1897).

Quinlan, Sir Michael Edward, K.C.B.

Quirk, *Prof.* Sir (Charles) Randolph, C.B.E., F.B.A.

Rabukawaqa, Sir Josua Rasilau, K.B.E., M.V.O.

Raby, Sir Victor Harry, K.B.E., C.B., M.C.

Radcliffe, Sir Sebastian Everard, Bt. (1813).

Radclyffe, Sir Charles Edward Mott-, Kt.

Radford, Sir Ronald Walter, K.C.B., M.B.E.

Radzinowicz, *Prof.* Sir Leon, Kt., Ll.D.

Rae, *Hon.* Sir Wallace Alexander Ramsay, Kt.

Raeburn, Sir Michael Edward Norman, Bt. (1923).

Raeburn, *Maj.-Gen.* Sir (William) Digby (Manifold), K.C.V.O., C.B., D.S.O., M.B.E.

Raikes, Sir (Henry) Victor (Alpin MacKinnon), K.B.E.

Raikes, *Vice-Adm.* Sir Iwan Geoffrey, K.C.B., C.B.E., D.S.C.

Ralli, Sir Godfrey Victor, Bt., T.D. (1912).

Ramgoolam, *Rt. Hon.* Sir Seewoosagur, G.C.M.G.

Rampton, Sir Jack Leslie, K.C.B.

Ramsay, Sir Alexander William Burnett, Bt. (1806).

Ramsay, *Cdre.* Sir James Maxwell, K.C.M.G., K.C.V.O., C.B.E., D.S.C.

Ramsay, Sir Neis Alexander, Bt. (s 1666).

Ramsay, Sir Thomas Meek, Kt., C.M.G.

Ramsbotham, *Hon.* Sir Peter Edward, G.C.M.G., G.C.V.O.

Ramsden, Sir Geoffrey Charles Frescheville, Kt., C.I.E.

Ramsden, Sir (Geoffrey) William Pennington-, Bt. (1689).

Ramsey, Sir Alfred Ernest, Kt.

Randle, *Prof.* Sir Philip John, Kt.

Ranger, Sir Douglas, Kt., F.R.C.S.

Rank, Sir Benjamin Keith, Kt., C.M.G.

Rankin, Sir Hugh (Charles Rhys), Bt. (1898).

Rankine, Sir John Dalzell, K.C.M.G., K.C.V.O.

Raper, *Vice-Adm.* Sir (Robert) George, K.C.B.

Rasch, *Maj.* Sir Richard Guy Carne, Bt. (1903).

Rashleigh, Sir Richard Harry, Bt. (1831).

Rault, Sir Louis Joseph Maurice, Kt.

Rawlins, *Surgeon Vice-Adm.* Sir John Stuart Pepys, K.B.E.

Rawlinson, Sir Anthony Henry John, Bt. (1891).

Rawlinson, Sir Anthony Keith, K.C.B.

Raymond, Sir Stanley Edward, Kt.

Read, *Air Marshal* Sir Charles Frederick, K.B.E., C.B., D.F.C., A.F.C.

Read, *General* Sir (John) Antony (Jervis), G.C.B., C.B.E., D.S.O., M.C.

Read, Sir John Emms, Kt.

Read, *Lt.-Gen.* Sir John Hugh Sherlock, K.C.B., O.B.E.

Reade, Sir Clyde Nixon, Bt. (1661).

Readhead, Sir James Templeman, Bt. (1922).

Reay, *Lt.-Gen.* Sir (Hubert) Alan John, K.B.E.

Redfearn, Sir Herbert, Kt.

Redgrave, *Maj.-Gen.* Sir Roy Michael Frederick, K.B.E., M.C.

Redman, *Lt.-Gen.* Sir Harold, K.C.B., C.B.E.

Redmayne, Sir Nicholas, Bt. (1964).

Redmond, Sir James, Kt.

Redshaw, Sir Leonard, Kt.

Redwood, Sir Peter Boverton, Bt. (1911).

Reece, Sir Gerald, K.C.M.G., C.B.E.

Reed, *Hon.* Sir Nigel Vernon, Kt., C.B.E.

Rees, Sir (Charles William) Stanley, Kt., T.D.

Rees-Mogg, Sir William, Kt.

Reeve, *Hon.* Sir (Charles) Trevor, Kt.

Reeves, *Most Rev.* Paul Alfred, Kt.

Reffell, *Vice-Adm.* Sir Derek Roy, K.C.B.

Refshauge, *Maj.-Gen.* Sir William Dudley, Kt., C.B.E.

Reid, Sir Alexander James, Bt. (1897).

Reid, *Hon.* Sir George Oswald, Kt., Q.C.

Reid, *Air Vice-Marshal* Sir (George) Ranald Macfarlane, K.C.B., D.S.O., M.C.

Reid, Sir Hugh, Bt. (1922).

Reid, Sir John James Andrew, K.C.M.G., C.B., T.D.

Reid, Sir John Thyne, Kt., C.M.G.

Reid, Sir Norman Robert, Kt.

Reid, Sir Robert Basil, Kt., C.B.E.

Reid, Sir William, Kt., C.B.E.

Reilly, Sir (D'Arcy) Patrick, G.C.M.G., O.B.E.

Reiss, Sir John Anthony Ewart, Kt., B.E.M.

Renals, Sir Stanley, Bt. (1895).

Rendell, Sir William, Kt.

Rennie, Sir Alfred Baillie, Kt.

Rennie, Sir John Shaw, G.C.M.G., O.B.E.

Renshaw, Sir (Charles) Maurice Bine, Bt. (1903).

Renwick, Sir Richard Eustace, Bt. (1921).

Reporter, Sir Shapoor Ardeshirji, K.B.E.

Revans, Sir John, Kt., C.B.E.

Rex, *Hon.* Sir Robert Richmond, K.B.E., C.M.G.

Reynolds, Sir David James, Bt. (1923).

Reynolds, Sir Peter William John, Kt., C.B.E.

Rhodes, Sir John Christopher Douglas, Bt. (1919).

Rhodes, Sir Peregrine Alexander, K.C.M.G.

Richards, *Hon.* Sir Edward Trenton, Kt., C.B.E.

Richards, Sir (Francis) Brooks, K.C.M.G., D.S.C.

Richards, Sir Gordon, Kt.

Richards, Sir James Maude, Kt., C.B.E.

Richards, *Lt.-Gen.* Sir John Charles Chisholm, K.C.B., R.M.

Richards, Sir Rex Edward, Kt., D.SC., F.R.S.

Richardson, *General* Sir Charles Leslie, G.C.B., C.B.E., D.S.O.

Richardson, Sir Egerton Rudolf, Kt., C.M.G.

Richardson, Sir (Horace) Frank, Kt.

Richardson, Sir (John) Eric, Kt., C.B.E.

Richardson, Sir Anthony Lewis, Bt. (1924).

Richardson, *Lt.-Gen.* Sir Robert Francis, K.C.B., C.V.O., C.B.E.

Richardson, Sir Simon Alaisdair Stewart-, Bt. (s 1630).

Richardson, Sir William Robert, Kt.

Riches, Sir Derek Martin Hurry, K.C.M.G.

Riches, Sir Eric William, Kt., M.C.

Riches, *General* Sir Ian Hurry, K.C.B., D.S.O.

Richmond, Sir Alan James, Kt.

Richmond, *Rt. Hon.* Sir Clifford Parris, K.B.E.

Richmond, Sir John Christopher Blake, K.C.M.G.

Richmond, Sir John Frederick, Bt. (1929).

Richmond, *Vice-Adm.* Sir Maxwell, K.B.E., C.B., D.S.O.

Rickett, Sir Denis Hubert Fletcher, K.C.M.G., C.B.

Ricketts, Sir Robert Cornwallis Gerald St. Leger, Bt. (1828).

Ricks, Sir John Plowman, Kt.

Riddell, Sir John Charles Buchanan, Bt. (s 1628).

Ridley, Sir Sidney, Kt.

Ridsdale, Sir Julian Errington, Kt., C.B.E., M.P.

Rigby, *Lt.-Col.* Sir (Hugh) John (Macbeth), Bt. (1929).

Rigby, *Hon.* Sir Ivo Charles Clayton, Kt.

Riley, Sir Ralph, Kt., F.R.S.

Ring, Sir Lindsay Roberts, G.B.E.

Ringadoo, *Hon.* Sir Veerasamy, Kt.

Ripley, Sir Hugh, Bt. (1880).

Risk, Sir Thomas Neilson, Kt.

Risson, *Maj.-Gen.* Sir Robert Joseph Henry, Kt., C.B., C.B.E., D.S.O., E.D.

Ritchie, Sir James Edward Thomson, Bt., T.D. (1918).

Rix, Sir John, Kt., M.B.E.

Roberts, Sir Bryan Clieve, K.C.M.G., Q.C.

Roberts, Sir David Arthur, K.B.E., C.M.G., C.V.O.

Roberts, *Hon.* Sir Denys Tudor Emil, K.B.E., Q.C.

Roberts, Sir (Edward Fergus) Sidney, Kt., C.B.E.

Roberts, Sir Frank Kenyon, G.C.M.G., G.C.V.O.

Roberts, Sir Geoffrey Newland, Kt., C.B.E., A.F.C.

Roberts, *Brig.* Sir Geoffrey Paul Hardy-, K.C.V.O., C.B., C.B.E.

Roberts, Sir Gilbert Howland Rookehurst, Bt. (1809).

Roberts, Sir Gordon James, Kt., C.B.E.

Roberts, *General* Sir Ouvry Lindfield, G.C.B., K.B.E., D.S.O.

Roberts, Sir Samuel, Bt. (1919).

Roberts, Sir Stephen James Leake, Kt.

Roberts, Sir William James Denby, Bt. (1909).

Robertson, *Prof.* Sir Alexander, Kt., C.B.E.

Robertson, Sir James Anderson, Kt., C.B.E.

Robertson, *Prof.* Sir Rutherford Ness, Kt., C.M.G.

Robinson, Sir Albert Edward Phineas, Kt.

Robinson, Sir David, Kt.

Robinson, Sir Dove-Myer, Kt.

Robinson, *Prof.* Sir (Edward) Austin (Gossage), Kt., C.M.G., O.B.E., F.B.A.

Robinson, Sir George Gilmour, Kt.

Robinson, Sir John Beverley, Bt. (1854).

Robinson, Sir John James Michael Laud, Bt. (1660).

Robinson, *Rt. Hon.* Sir Kenneth, Kt.

Robinson, Sir Niall Bryan Lynch-, Bt., D.S.C. (1920).

Robinson, Sir Wilfred Henry Frederick, Bt. (1908).

Robson, *Prof.* Sir James Gordon, Kt., C.B.E.

Robson, Sir Thomas Buston, Kt., M.B.E.

Robson, *Vice-Adm.* Sir (William) Geoffrey (Arthur), K.B.E., C.B., D.S.O., D.S.C.

Roche, Sir David O'Grady, Bt. (1838).

Rodger, Sir William Glendinning, Kt., O.B.E.

Rodgers, Sir John Charles, Bt. (1964).

Rodrigues, Sir Alberto Maria, Kt., C.B.E., E.D.

Roe, *Air Chief Marshal* Sir Rex David, G.C.B., A.F.C.

Rogers, *Air Chief Marshal* Sir John Robson, K.C.B., C.B.E.

Rogers, Sir Philip, G.C.B., C.M.G.

Rogers, Sir Philip James, Kt., C.B.E.

Roll, *Rev.* Sir James William Cecil, Bt. (1921).

Rooke, Sir Denis Eric, Kt., C.B.E.

Roper, *Hon.* Sir Clinton Marcus, Kt.

Ropner, Sir John Bruce Woollacott, Bt. (1952).

Ropner, Sir Robert Douglas, Bt. (1904).

Roscoe, Sir Robert Bell, K.B.E.

Rose, Sir Alec Richard, Kt.

Rose, *Hon.* Sir Christopher Dudley Roger, Kt., Q.C.

Rose, Sir Clive Martin, G.C.M.G.

Rose, Sir David Lancaster, Bt. (1874)

Rose, Sir Julian Day, Bt. (1872 and 1909).

Rosier, *Air Chief Marshal* Sir Frederick Ernest, G.C.B., C.B.E., D.S.O.

Roskill, Sir Ashton Wentworth, Kt., Q.C.

Ross, Sir Alexander, Kt.

Ross, Sir Archibald David Manisty, K.C.M.G.

Ross, *Hon.* Sir (Dudley) Bruce, Kt.

Ross, Sir (James) Keith, Bt., R.D., F.R.C.S. (1960).

Ross, Sir Lewis Nathan, Kt., C.M.G.

Rosser, Sir Melvyn Wynne, Kt.

Rossi, Sir Hugh Alexis Louis, Kt., M.P.

Rossiter, *Hon.* Sir John Frederick, K.B.E.

Rostron, Sir Frank, Kt., M.B.E.

Roth, *Prof.* Sir Martin, Kt., M.D., F.R.C.P.

Rothenstein, Sir John Knewstub Maurice, Kt., C.B.E., Ph.D.

Rothnie, Sir Alan Keir, K.C.V.O., C.M.G.

Rous, Sir Stanley Ford, Kt., C.B.E.

Rous, Sir Anthony Gerald Roderick, K.C.M.G., O.B.E.

Row, *Hon.* Sir John Alfred, Kt.

Row, *Cdr.*, Sir Philip John, K.C.V.O., O.B.E., R.N.

Rowe, Sir Henry Peter, K.C.B., Q.C.

Rowell, Sir John Joseph, Kt., C.B.E.

Rowland, *Air Marshal* Sir James Anthony, K.B.E., D.F.C., A.F.C.

Rowlands, *Air Marshal* Sir John Samuel, K.B.E., G.C.

Rowlandson, Sir (Stanley) Graham, Kt., M.B.E.

Rowley, Sir Charles Robert, Bt. (1836).

Rowley, Sir Joshua Francis, Bt. (1786).

Rowling, *Rt. Hon.* Sir Wallace Edward, K.C.M.G.

Rowntree, Sir Norman Andrew Forster, Kt.

Roxburgh, *Vice-Adm.* Sir John Charles Young, K.C.B., C.B.E., D.S.O., D.S.C.

Royden, Sir Christopher John, Bt. (1905).

Rucker, Sir Arthur Nevil, K.C.M.G., C.B., C.B.E.

Rugg, Sir (Edward) Percy, Kt.

Rumbold, Sir (Horace) Algernon (Fraser), K.C.M.G., C.I.E.

Rumbold, Sir Henry John Sebastian, Bt. (1779).

Rumbold, Sir Jack Seddon, Kt.

Runciman, *Hon.* Sir Steven ; (James Cochran Stevenson), Kt., C.H.

Rundall, Sir Francis Brian Anthony, G.C.M.G., O.B.E.

Rusby, *Vice-Adm.* Sir Cameron, K.C.B., M.V.O.

Russell, Sir Archibald Edward, Kt., C.B.E., F.R.S.

Russell, Sir Charles Ian, Bt. (1916).

Russell, Sir Evelyn Charles Sackville, Kt.

Russell, Sir George Michael, Bt. (1812).

Russell, Sir (Robert) Mark, K.C.M.G.

Russell, *Hon.* Sir (Thomas) Patrick, Kt.

Russo, Sir Peter George, Kt., C.B.E.

Ryan, Sir Derek Gerald, Bt. (1919).

Rycroft, Sir Richard Newton, Bt. (1784).

Ryland, Sir (Albert) William (Cecil), Kt., C.B.

Rymill, Sir Arthur Campbell, Kt.

Ryrie, Sir William Sinclair, K.C.B.

Sainsbury, Hon. Sir John Davan, Kt.

Sainsbury, Sir Robert James, Kt.

Saint, Sir (Sidney) John, Kt., C.M.G., O.B.E.

St. Aubyn, Sir John Molesworth-, Bt., C.B.E. (1689).

St. George, Sir Denis Howard, Bt. (1 1766).

St. Johnston, *Col.* Sir (Thomas) Eric, Kt., C.B.E.

Sakzewski, Sir Albert, Kt.

Salomon, Sir Walter Hans, Kt.

Salt, Sir Anthony Houlton, Bt. (1869).

Salt, Sir (Thomas) Michael John, Bt. (1899).

Samuel, Sir Jon Michael Glen, Bt. (1898).

Samuels, Sir Alexander, Kt., C.B.E.

Samuelson, Sir (Bernard) Michael (Francis), Bt. (1884).

Sanders, Sir Harold George, Kt., Ph.D.

Sanders, Sir Robert Tait, K.B.E., C.M.G.

Sanderson, Sir (Frank Philip) Bryan, Bt. (1920).

Sandford, Sir Folliott Herbert, K.B.E., C.M.G.

Sandilands, Sir Francis Edwin Prescott, Kt., C.B.E.

Sarell, Sir Roderick Francis Gisbert, K.C.M.G., K.C.V.O.

Sargant, Sir (Henry) Edmund, Kt.

Saunders, *Air Chief Marshal* Sir Hugh William Lumsden, G.C.B., K.B.E., M.C., D.F.C., M.M.

Saunders, *Hon.* Sir John Anthony Holt, Kt., C.B.E., D.S.O., M.C.

Saunders, Sir Owen Alfred, Kt., D.SC., F.R.S.

Saunders, Sir Peter, Kt.

Sauzier, Sir (André) Guy, Kt., C.B.E., E.D.

Savage, Sir Ernest Walter, Kt.

Saville, *Hon.* Sir Mark Oliver, Kt., Q.C.

Savory, Sir Reginald Charles Frank, Kt., C.B.E.

Sayer, *Vice-Adm.* Sir Guy Bourchier, K.B.E., C.B., D.S.C.

Sayers, *Prof.* Sir Edward George, Kt., C.M.G., M.D.

Scarlett, Sir Peter William Shelley Yorke, K.C.M.G., K.C.V.O.

Scholtens, Sir James Henry, K.C.V.O.

Schubert, Sir Sydney, Kt.

Schultz, Sir (Joseph) Leopold, Kt., O.B.E.

Schuster, Sir (Felix) James Moncrieff, Bt., O.B.E. (1906).

Scoon, Sir Paul, G.C.M.G., O.B.E.

Scoones, *Maj.-Gen.* Sir Reginald Laurence, K.B.E., C.B., D.S.O.

Scopes, Sir Leonard Arthur, K.C.V.O., C.M.G., O.B.E.

Scott, Sir Bernard Francis William, Kt., C.B.E., T.D.

Scott, Sir (Charles) Hilary, Kt.

Scott, Sir (Charles) Peter, K.B.E., C.M.G.

Scott, Sir David Aubrey, G.C.M.G.

Scott, Sir David John Montagu Douglas, K.C.M.G., O.B.E.

Scott, Sir Anthony Percy, Bt. (1913).

Scott, Sir Eric, Kt., O.B.E.

Scott, Sir George Edward, Kt., C.B.E.

Scott, Sir Ian Dixon, K.C.M.G., K.C.V.O., C.I.E.

Scott, Sir James Walter, Bt. (1962).

Scott, Sir Michael, K.C.V.O., C.M.G.

Scott, Sir Michael Fergus Maxwell, Bt. (*E* 1642).

Scott, Sir Oliver Christopher Anderson, Bt. (1909).

Scott, Sir Peter Markham, Kt., C.B.E., D.S.C.

Scott, *Hon.* Sir Richard Rashleigh Folliott, Kt., Q.C.

Scott, Sir Terence Charles Stuart Morrison-, Kt., D.S.C., D.SC.

Scott, Sir Walter, Bt. (1907).

Scott, *Rear-Adm.* Sir (William) David (Stewart), K.B.E., C.B.

Scowen, Sir Eric Frank, Kt., M.D., D.SC., LL.D., F.R.C.P., F.R.C.S.

Scragg, *Air Vice-Marshal* Sir Colin, K.B.E., C.B., A.F.C.

Scrivenor, Sir Thomas Vaisey, Kt., C.M.G.

Seale, Sir John Henry, Bt. (1838).

Seaman, Sir Keith Douglas, K.C.V.O., O.B.E.

Sebright, Sir Peter Giles Vivian, Bt. (1626).

Secombe, Sir Harry Donald, Kt., C.B.E.

Seconde, Sir Reginald Louis, K.C.M.G., C.V.O.

Seely, Sir Nigel Edward, Bt. (1896).

Seeyave, Sir Rene Sow Choung, Kt., C.B.E

Selby, Sir Kenneth, Kt.

Seligman, Sir Peter Wendel, Kt., C.B.E.

Sellors, Sir Thomas Holmes, Kt., D.M.

Sells, Sir David Perronet, Kt.

Senior, Sir Edward Walters, Kt., C.M.G.

Sergeant, Sir Patrick, Kt.

Series, Sir (Joseph Michel) Emile, Kt., C.B.E.

Serpell, Sir David Radford, K.C.B., C.M.G., O.B.E.

Seton, Sir (Christopher) Bruce, Bt. (s 1663).

Seton, Sir Robert James, Bt. (s 1683).

Sewell, Sir (John) Allan, Kt., I.S.O.

Seymour, *Cdr.* Sir Michael Culme-, Bt., R.N. (1809).

Shakerley, Sir Geoffrey Adam, Bt. (1838).

Shakespeare, Sir William Geoffrey, Bt. (1942).

Shankland, Sir Thomas Murray, Kt., C.M.G.

Shann, Sir Keith Charles Owen, Kt., C.B.E.

Shapland, Sir William Arthur, Kt.

Sharp, Sir Edward Harold Wilfred, Bt. (1922).

Sharp, Sir Eric, Kt., C.B.E.

Sharp, Sir George, Kt., O.B.E.

Sharp, Sir Kenneth Johnston, Kt., T.D.

Sharp, Sir Milton Reginald, Bt. (1920).

Sharp, Sir Richard Lyall, K.C.V.O., C.B.

Sharp, Sir (William Harold) Angus, K.B.E., Q.P.M.

Sharpe, Sir Frank Victor, Kt., C.M.G., O.B.E., E.D.

Sharpe, *Hon.* Sir John Henry, Kt., C.B.E.

Sharpe, Sir Reginald Taaffe, Kt., Q.C.

Shattock, Sir Gordon, Kt.

Shaw, Sir (Charles) Barry, Kt., C.B., Q.C.

Shaw, Sir John Michael Robert Best-, Bt. (1665).

Shaw, Sir Michael Norman, Kt., M.P.

Shaw, Sir Robert, Bt. (1821).

Shaw, Sir Roy, Kt.

Shaw, Sir Run Run, Kt., C.B.E.

Sheen, *Hon.* Sir Barry Cross, Kt.

Sheffield, Sir Reginald Adrian Berkeley, Bt. (1755).

Shehadie, Sir Nicholas Michael, Kt., O.B.E.

Shelbourne, Sir Philip, Kt.

Sheldon, *Hon.* Sir (John) Gervase (Kensington), Kt.

Shelley, Sir John Richard, Bt. (1611).

Shepheard, Sir Peter Faulkner, Kt., C.B.E.

Shepheard, Sir Victor George, K.C.B.

Shepherd, Sir Peter Malcolm, Kt., C.B.E.

Sherlock, Sir Philip Manderson, K.B.E.

Sherman, Sir Alfred, Kt.

Sherman, Sir Louis, Kt., O.B.E.

Shields, Sir Neil Stanley, Kt., M.C.

Shiffner, Sir Henry David, Bt. (1818).

Shillington, Sir (Robert Edward) Graham, Kt., C.B.E.

Sholl, *Hon.* Sir Reginald Richard, Kt.

Shone, Sir Robert Minshull, Kt., C.B.E.

Short, *Brig.* Sir Noel Edward Vivian, Kt., M.B.E., M.C.

Shuckburgh, Sir (Charles Arthur) Evelyn, G.C.M.G., K.C.B.

Shuckburgh, Sir Charles Gerald Stewkley, Bt. (1660).

Sich, Sir Rupert Leigh, Kt., C.B.

Siddall, Sir Norman, Kt., C.B.E.

Sidey, *Air Marshal* Sir Ernest Shaw, K.B.E., C.B., M.D.

Sie, Sir Banja Tejan-, G.C.M.G.

Simeon, Sir John Edmund Barrington, Bt. (1815).

Simogun, Sir Petar, Kt., M.B.E., B.E.M.

Simonet, Sir Louis Marcel Pierre, Kt., C.B.E.

Simpson, *Hon.* Sir Alfred Henry, Kt.

Simpson, *General* Sir Frank Ernest Wallace, G.B.E., K.C.B., D.S.O.

Simpson, Sir William James, Kt.

Sinclair, Sir Clive Marles, Kt.

Sinclair, Sir George Evelyn, Kt., C.M.G., O.B.E.

Sinclair, Sir Ian McTaggart, K.C.M.G., Q.C.

Sinclair, Sir John Rollo Norman Blair, Bt. (s 1704).

Sinclair, *Prof.* Sir Keith, Kt., C.B.E.

Sinclair, *Air Vice-Marshal* Sir Laurence Frank, K.C.B., G.C., C.B.E., D.S.O.

Sinclair, Sir Ronald Ormiston, K.B.E.

Singh, *Hon.* Sir Vijay Raghubir, Kt.

Singhania, Sir Padampat, Kt.

Singhateh, *Alhaji'i* Sir Farimang, G.C.M.G.

Singleton, Sir Edward Henry Sibbald, Kt.

Sinnamon, Sir Hercules, Kt., O.B.E.

Sisson, Sir Roy, Kt.

Sitwell, Sir Sacheverell, Bt., C.H. (1808).

Skelhorn, Sir Norman John, K.B.E., Q.C.

Skellerup, Sir Valdemar Reid, Kt., C.B.E.

Skinner, *Hon.* Sir Henry Albert, Kt.

Skinner, Sir Thomas Edward, K.B.E.

Skinner, Sir (Thomas) Keith (Hewitt), Bt. (1912).

Skipwith, Sir Patrick Alexander d'Estoteville, Bt. (1622).

Skyrme, Sir (William) Thomas (Charles), K.C.V.O., C.B., C.B.E., T.D.

Slade, Sir Benjamin Julian Alfred, Bt. (1831).

Slade, *Rt. Hon.* Sir Christopher John, Kt.

Slaney, *Prof.* Sir Geoffrey, K.B.E.

Slattery, *Rear-Adm.* Sir Matthew Sausse, K.B.E., C.B.

Sleight, Sir John Frederick, Bt. (1920).

Slimmings, Sir William Kenneth MacLeod, Kt., C.B.E.

Slynn, *Hon.* Sir Gordon, Kt.

Smallpeice, Sir Basil, K.C.V.O.

Smallwood, *Air Chief Marshal* Sir Denis Graham, G.B.E., K.C.B., D.S.O., D.F.C.

Smart, *Prof.* Sir George Algernon, Kt., M.D., F.R.C.P.

Smart, Sir Jack, Kt., C.B.E.

Smedley, Sir Harold, K.C.M.G., M.B.E.

Smeeton, *Vice-Adm.* Sir Richard Michael, K.C.B., M.B.E.

Smiley, Sir Hugh Houston, Bt. (1903).

Smirk, Sir (Frederick) Horace, K.B.E., M.D.

Smith, Sir Alan, Kt., C.B.E., D.F.C.

Smith, Sir Alexander Mair, Kt., Ph.D.

Smith, Sir (Alexander) Rowland, Kt.

Smith, Sir Arthur Henry, Kt.

Smith, *Maj.-Gen.* Sir Cecil Miller, K.B.E., C.B., M.C.

Smith, Sir Christopher Sydney Winwood, Bt. (1809).

Smith, Sir Dudley (Gordon), Kt., M.P.

Smith, *Maj.-Gen.* Sir Edmund Hakewill, K.C.V.O., C.B., C.B.E., M.C.

Smith, *Vice-Adm.* Sir (Edward Michael) Conolly Abel, G.C.V.O., C.B.

Smith, *Maj.-Gen.* Sir (Francis) Brian Wyldbore-, Kt., C.B., D.S.O., O.B.E.

Smith, Sir (Frank) Ewart, Kt.

Smith, *Vice-Adm.* Sir Geoffrey Thistleton-, K.B.E., C.B., G.M.

Smith, Sir Charles Bracewell-, Bt. (1947).

Smith, *Col.* Sir Henry Abel, K.C.M.G., K.C.V.O., D.S.O.

Smith, Sir Henry Thompson, K.B.E., C.B.

Smith, Sir Howard Frank Trayton, G.C.M.G.

Smith, *Hon.* Sir James Alfred, Kt., C.B.E., T.D.

Smith, Sir (James) Eric., Kt., C.B.E., Sc.D., F.R.S.

Smith, Sir John Hamilton-Spencer-, Bt. (1804).

Smith, Sir John Kenneth Newson-, Bt. (1944).

Smith, Sir Laurence Barton Grafftey-, K.C.M.G., K.B.E.

Smith, Sir Leonard Herbert, Kt., C.B.E.

Smith, Sir Leslie Edward George, Kt.

Smith, *Hon.* Sir Murray Stuart-, Kt.

Smith, Sir Raymond Horace, K.B.E.

Smith, Sir Reginald Beaumont, Kt.

Smith, Sir Richard Rathbone Vassar-, Bt., T.D. (1917).

Smith, Sir (Richard) Robert Law-, Kt., C.B.E., A.F.C.

Smith, Sir Robert Hill, Bt., (1945).

Smith, *Air Marshal* Sir Roy David Austen-, K.B.E., C.B., D.F.C.

Smith, *Prof.* Sir Thomas Broun, Kt., Q.C.

Smith, Sir (Thomas) Gilbert, Bt. (1897).

Smith, *Admiral* Sir Victor Alfred Trumper, K.B.E., C.B., D.S.C.

Smith, Sir William Reardon Reardon-, Bt. (1920).

Smith, Sir (William) Reginald Verdon, Kt.

Smith, Sir (William) Richard Prince-, Bt. (1911).

Smithers, *Prof.* Sir David Waldron, Kt., M.D.

Smithers, Sir Peter Henry Berry Otway, Kt., V.R.D., D.Phil.

Smithers, *Hon.* Sir Reginald Allfree, Kt.

Smyth, Sir Thomas Weyland Bowyer-, Bt., (1661).

Smyth, Sir Timothy John, Bt. (1955).

Snedden, *Rt. Hon.* Sir Billy Mackie, K.C.M.G., Q.C.

Snelling, Sir Arthur Wendell, K.C.M.G., K.C.V.O.

Snelson, Sir Edward Alec Abbott, K.B.E.

Soame, Sir Charles John Buckworth-Herne-, Bt. (1697).

Sobell, Sir Michael, Kt.

Sobers, Sir Garfield St. Auburn, Kt.

Solomon, Sir David Arnold, Kt., M.B.E.

Solomons, *Hon.* Sir (Louis) Adrian, Kt.

Solti, Sir Georg, K.B.E.

Somerset, Sir Henry Beaufort, Kt., C.B.E.

Somerville, *Brig.* Sir John Nicholas, Kt., C.B.E.

Somerville, Sir Robert, K.C.V.O.

Sopwith, Sir Charles Ronald, Kt.

Sopwith, Sir Thomas Octave Murdoch, Kt., C.B.E.

Sorsbie, Sir Malin, Kt., C.B.E.

Soutar, *Air Marshal* Sir Charles John Williamson, K.B.E.

South, Sir Arthur, Kt.

Southby, Sir (Archibald) Richard (Charles), Bt., O.B.E., (1937).

Southern, Sir Richard William, Kt., F.B.A.

Southern, Sir Robert, Kt., C.B.E.

Southey, Sir Robert John, Kt., C.M.G.

Southward, Sir Ralph, K.C.V.O., F.R.C.P.

Southwood, *Prof.* Sir (Thomas) Richard (Edmund), Kt., F.R.S.

Southworth, Sir Frederick, Kt., Q.C.

Souyave, *Hon.* Sir (Louis) Georges, Kt.

Sowrey, *Air Marshal* Sir Frederick Beresford, K.C.B., C.B.E., A.F.C.

Soysa, Sir Warusahennedige Abraham Bastian, Kt., C.B.E.

Sparkes, Sir Robert Lyndley, Kt.

Sparrow, Sir John, Kt.

Spearman, Sir Alexander Young Richard Mainwaring, Bt. (1840).

Speed, Sir Robert William Arney, Kt., C.B., Q.C.

Speelman, *Jonkheer* Sir Cornelis Jacob, Bt. (1686).

Speight, *Hon.* Sir Graham Davies, Kt.

Speir, Sir Rupert Malise, Kt.

Spencer, Sir Kelvin Tallent, Kt., C.B.E., M.C.

Spender, *Prof.* Sir Stephen Harold, Kt., C.B.E.

Spicer, Sir Peter James, Bt. (1906).

Spooner, Sir James Douglas, Kt.

Spotswood, *Marshal of the Royal Air Force* Sir Denis Frank, G.C.B., C.B.E., D.S.O., D.F.C.

Springer, Sir Hugh Worrell, G.C.M.G., C.B.E.

Spry, *Brig.* Sir Charles Chambers Fowell, Kt., C.B.E., D.S.O.

Spry, *Hon.* Sir John Farley, Kt.

Spurling, *Hon.* Sir (Arthur) Dudley, Kt., C.B.E.

Stabb, *Hon.* Sir William Walter, Kt., Q.C.

Stack, *Air Chief Marshal* Sir (Thomas) Neville, K.C.B., C.V.O., C.B.E., A.F.C.

Staine, *Hon.* Sir Albert Llewellyn, Kt., C.B.E.

Stainton, Sir Anthony Nathaniel, K.C.B., Q.C.

Stainton, Sir (John) Ross, Kt., C.B.E.

Stallard, Sir Peter Hyla Gawne, K.C.M.G., C.V.O., M.B.E.

Stallworthy, Sir John Arthur, Kt., F.R.C.S.

Stamer, Sir (Lovelace) Anthony, Bt. (1809).

Stanbridge, *Air Vice-Marshal* Sir Brian Gerald Tivy, K.C.V.O., C.B.E., A.F.C.

Stanford, *Admiral* Sir Peter Maxwell, K.C.B., L.V.O.

Stanier, *Brig.* Sir Alexander Beville Gibbons, Bt., D.S.O., M.C. (1917).

Stanier, *General* Sir John Wilfred, G.C.B., M.B.E.

Staples, Sir John Richard, Bt. (I. 1628).

Stapleton, Sir (Henry) Alfred, Bt. (1679).

Stark, Sir Andrew Alexander Steel, K.C.M.G., C.V.O.

Starke, *Hon.* Sir John Erskine, Kt.

Starkey, Sir John Philip, Bt. (1935).

Starrit, Sir James, K.C.V.O.

Statham, Sir Norman, K.C.M.G., C.V.O.

Staughton, *Hon.* Sir Christopher Stephen Thomas Jonathan Thayer, Kt.

Staveley, Sir John Malfroy, K.B.E., M.C.

Staveley, *Admiral* Sir William Doveton Minet, G.C.B.

Stebbings, Sir John Chalmer, Kt.

Stedman, Sir George Foster, K.B.E., C.B., M.C.

Steedman, *Air Chief Marshal* Sir Alasdair (Alexander McKay Sinclair), G.C.B., C.B.E., D.F.C.

Steel, Sir David Edward Charles, Kt., D.S.O., M.C., T.D.

Steel, *Maj.* Sir (Fiennes) William Strang, Bt. (1938).

Steel, Sir James, Kt., C.B.E.

Steel, Sir (Joseph) Lincoln (Spedding), Kt.

Steele, Sir Kenneth Charles, Kt., D.F.C.

Steele, Sir (Philip John) Rupert, Kt.

Steere, Sir Ernest Henry Lee-, K.B.E.

Stenhouse, Sir Nicol, Kt.

Stening, *Col.* Sir George Grafton Lees, Kt., E.D.

Stephen, Sir James Alexander, Bt. (1891).

Stephen, *Rt. Hon.* Sir Ninian Martin, G.C.M.G., G.C.V.O., K.B.E.

Stephens, Sir David, K.C.B., C.V.O.

Stephenson, Sir Henry Upton, Bt. (1936).

Stephenson, *Rt. Hon.* Sir John Frederick Eustace, Kt.

Stephenson, Sir William Samuel, Kt., M.C., D.F.C.

Sterling, Sir Jeffrey Maurice, Kt., C.B.E.

Sternberg, Sir Sigmund, Kt.

Stevens, *Air Marshal* Sir Alick Charles, K.B.E., C.B.

Stevens, *Vice-Adm.* Sir John Felgate, K.B.E., C.B.

Stevens, Sir Laurence Houghton, Kt., C.B.E.

Stevenson, *Rt. Hon.* Sir (Aubrey) Melford (Steed), Kt.

Stevenson, *Vice-Adm.* Sir (Hugh) David, K.B.E.

Stevenson, Sir Simpson, Kt.

Steward, Sir William Arthur, Kt.

Stewart, Sir Alan, Kt.

Stewart, Sir Alan d'Arcy, Bt. (I 1623).

Stewart, Sir David Brodribb, Bt., T.D. (1960).

Stewart, Sir David James Henderson-, Bt. (1957).

Stewart, Sir Edward Jackson, Kt.

Stewart, *Prof.* Sir Frederick Henry, Kt., PH.D., F.R.S., F.R.S.E.

Stewart, Sir Hector Hamilton, K.B.E.

Stewart, Sir Herbert Ray, Kt., C.I.E.

Stewart, Sir Houston Mark Shaw-, Bt., M.C., T.D. (s. 1667).

Stewart, Sir Hugh Charlie Godfray, Bt. (1803).

Stewart, Sir Iain Maxwell, Kt.

Stewart, Sir James Douglas, Kt.

Stewart, Sir James Watson, Bt. (1920).

Stewart, Sir Michael Norman Francis, K.C.M.G., O.B.E.

Stewart, Sir Robertson Huntly, Kt., C.B.E.

Stewart, Sir Ronald Compton, Bt. (1937).

Steyn, *Hon.* Sir Johan Van Zyl, Kt., Q.C.

Stinson, Sir Charles Alexander, K.B.E.

Stirling, Sir Alexander John Dickson, K.B.E., C.M.G.

Stirling, Sir Charles Norman, K.C.M.G., K.C.V.O.

Stoby, Sir Kenneth Sievewright, Kt.

Stockdale, Sir Edmund Villiers Minshull, Bt. (1960).

Stocker, *Hon.* Sir John Dexter, Kt., M.C., T.D.

Stockwell, *General* Sir Hugh Charles, G.C.B., K.B.E., D.S.O.

Stoker, *Prof.* Sir Michael George Parke, Kt., C.B.E., F.R.C.P., F.R.S., F.R.S.E.

Stone, *Prof.* Sir (John) Richard (Nicholas), Kt., C.B.E.

Stonhouse, Sir Philip Allan, Bt. (1628).

Storey, *Hon.* Sir Richard, Bt. (1960).

Stormonth Darling, Sir James Carlisle, Kt., C.B.E., M.C., T.D.

Stott, Sir Adrian George Ellingham, Bt. (1920).

Stourton, Sir Ivo Herbert Evelyn Joseph, Kt., C.M.G., O.B.E.

Stow, Sir Christopher Philipson-, Bt., D.F.C. (1907).

Stow, Sir John Montague, G.C.M.G., K.C.V.O.

Stowe, Sir Kenneth Ronald, K.C.B., C.V.O.

Stracey, Sir John Simon, Bt. (1818).

Strachey, Sir Charles, Bt. (1801).

Straker, Sir Michael Ian Bowstead, Kt., C.B.E.

Strasser, Sir Paul, Kt.

Stratton, Sir Richard James, K.C.M.G.

Stratton, *Lt.-Gen.* Sir William Henry, K.C.B., C.V.O., C.B.E., D.S.O.

Strawson, *Prof.* Sir Peter Frederick, Kt., F.B.A.

Street, *Hon.* Sir Laurence Whistler, K.C.M.G.

Strong, Sir Charles Love, K.C.V.O.

Strong, Sir Roy Colin, Kt., PH.D., F.S.A.

Stronge, Sir James Anselan Maxwell, Bt. (1803).

Strutt, Sir Nigel Edward, Kt., T.D.

Stuart, Sir Kenneth Lamonte, Kt.

†Stuart, Sir Phillip Luttrell, Bt. (1660).

Stuart-Smith, *Hon.* Sir Murray, Kt.

Stubblefield, Sir (Cyril) James, Kt., D.SC., F.R.S.

Stubbs, Sir James Wilfrid, K.C.V.O., T.D.

Stucley, *Lt.* Sir Hugh George Coplestone Bampfylde, Bt. (1859).

Studd, Sir Edward Fairfax, Bt. (1929).

Studd, Sir Peter Malden, G.B.E., K.C.V.O.

Studholme, Sir Henry Gray, Bt., C.V.O. (1956).

Style, *Lt. Cdr.* Sir Godfrey William, Kt., C.B.E., D.S.C., R.N.

Style, Sir William Montague, Bt. (1627).

Suffield, Sir (Henry John) Lester, Kt.

Sugden, Sir Arthur, Kt.

Sullivan, Sir Desmond John, Kt.

Sullivan, Sir Richard Arthur, Bt. (1804).

Summerfield, *Hon.* Sir John Crampton, Kt., C.B.E.

Summerhayes, Sir Christopher Henry, K.B.E., C.M.G.

Summers, Sir Felix Roland Brattan, Bt. (1952).

Summerson, Sir John Newenham, Kt., C.B.E., F.B.A., F.S.A.

Sunderland, *Prof.* Sir Sydney, Kt., C.M.G.

Surridge, Sir (Ernest) Rex (Edward), Kt., C.M.G.

Sutherland, Sir (Frederick) Neil, Kt., C.B.E.

Sutherland, Sir Iain Johnstone Macbeth, K.C.M.G.

Sutherland, Sir John Brewer, Bt. (1921).

Sutherland, Sir Maurice, Kt.

Suttie, Sir (George) Philip Grant-, Bt. (s 1702).

Sutton, Sir Frederick Walter, Kt., O.B.E.

Sutton, Sir Richard Lexington, Bt. (1772).

Sutton, Sir Stafford William Powell Foster-, K.B.E., C.M.G., Q.C.

Swaffield, Sir James Chesebrough, Kt., C.B.E., R.D.

Swallow, Sir William, Kt.

Swann, Sir Anthony Charles Christopher, Bt., C.M.G., O.B.E., (1906).

Swanwick, Sir Graham Russell, Kt., M.B.E.

Swartz, *Hon.* Sir Reginald William Colin, K.B.E., E.D.

Swayne, Sir Ronald Oliver Carless, Kt., M.C.

Swinson, Sir John Henry Alan, Kt., O.B.E.

Swinton, *Maj.-Gen.* Sir John, K.C.V.O., O.B.E.

Swire, Sir Adrian Christopher, Kt.

Swiss, Sir Rodney Geoffrey, Kt., O.B.E.

Swynnerton, Sir Roger John Massy, Kt., C.M.G., O.B.E., M.C.

Sykes, Sir Francis Godfrey, Bt. (1781).

Sykes, Sir John Charles Anthony le Gallais, Bt. (1921).

Sykes, Sir Tatton Christopher Mark, Bt. (1783).

Syme, Sir Colin Yorke, Kt.

Syme, Sir Ronald, Kt., O.M., F.B.A.

Symington, *Prof.* Sir Thomas, Kt., M.D., F.R.S.E.

Synge, Sir Robert Carson, Bt. (1801).

Tait, *Admiral* Sir (Allan) Gordon, K.C.B., D.S.C.

Tait, Sir James Sharp, Kt., D.Sc., LlD., Ph.D.

Tait, Sir Peter, K.B.E.

Tait, *Air Vice-Marshal* Sir Victor Hubert, K.B.E., C.B.

Talbot, *Vice-Adm.* Sir (Arthur Allison) FitzRoy, K.B.E., C.B., D.S.O.

Talbot, *Hon.* Sir Hilary Gwynne, Kt.

Tallack, Sir Hugh Mackay, Kt.

Tancred, Sir Henry Lawson-, Bt. (1662).

Tang, Sir Shiu-kin, Kt., C.B.E.

Tange, Sir Arthur Harold, Kt., C.B.E.

Tansley, Sir Eric Crawford, Kt., C.M.G.

Tapp, *Maj.-Gen.* Sir Nigel Prior Hanson, K.B.E., C.B., D.S.O.

Tapsell, Sir Peter Hannay Bailey, Kt., M.P.

Tate, *Lt.-Col.* Sir Henry, Bt. (1898).

Taukala, Sir David Dawea, Kt., M.B.E.

Taylor, *Lt.-Gen.* Sir Allan Macnab, K.B.E., M.C.

Taylor, Sir Alvin Burton, Kt.

Taylor, Sir (Arthur) Godfrey, Kt.

Taylor, Sir Charles Stuart, Kt., T.D.

Taylor, Sir George, Kt., D.Sc., F.R.S., F.R.S.E.

Taylor, Sir Henry Milton, Kt.

Taylor, Sir James, Kt., M.B.E., D.Sc.

Taylor, Sir John Lang, K.C.M.G.

Taylor, Sir Nicholas Richard Stuart, Bt. (1917).

Taylor, *Hon.* Sir Peter Murray, Kt.

Tebbit, Sir Donald Claude, G.C.M.G.

Te Heuheu, Sir Hepi Hoani, K.B.E.

Telford, Sir Robert, Kt., C.B.E.

Temple, Sir John Meredith, Kt.

Temple, Sir Rawden John Afamado, Kt. C.B.E., Q.C.

Temple, *Maj.* Sir Richard Anthony Purbeck, Bt., M.C. (1876).

Tennant, Sir Mark Dalcour, K.C.M.G., C.B.

Tennant, Sir Peter Frank Dalrymple, Kt., C.M.G., O.B.E.

Teo, Sir Fiatau Penitala, G.C.M.G., G.C.V.O., I.S.O., M.B.E.

Terry, Sir Andrew Henry Bouhier Imbert-, Bt. (1917).

Terry, Sir George Walter Roberts, Kt., C.B.E., Q.P.M.

Terry, Sir John Elliott, Kt.

Terry, *Air Chief Marshal* Sir Peter David George, G.C.B., A.F.C.

Tetley, Sir Herbert, K.B.E., C.B.

Tett, Sir Hugh Charles, Kt.

Thalben-Ball, Sir George Thomas, Kt., C.B.E.

Thiess, Sir Leslie Charles, Kt., C.B.E.

Thomas, Sir Frederick William, Kt.

Thomas, Sir (Godfrey) Michael (David) Bt. (1694).

Thomas, Sir John Maldwyn, Kt.

Thomas, Sir Patrick Muirhead, Kt., D.S.O., T.D.

Thomas, Sir Robert Evan, Kt.

Thomas, *Hon.* Sir Swinton Barclay, Kt., Q.C.

Thomas, Sir William James Cooper, Bt., T.D. (1919).

Thomas, Sir (William) Michael (Marsh), Bt. (1918).

Thompson, Sir Edward Hugh Dudley, Kt., M.B.E., T.D.

Thompson, Sir Edward Walter, Kt.

Thompson, Sir (Humphrey) Simon Meysey-, Bt. (1874).

Thompson, *Hon.* Sir John, Kt.

Thompson, Sir Paul Anthony, Bt. (1963).

Thompson, Sir Christopher Peile, Bt. (1890).

Thompson, Sir Peter Anthony, Kt.

Thompson, Sir Ralph Patrick, Kt.

Thompson, Sir Richard Hilton Marler, Bt. (1963).

Thompson, Sir Robert Grainger Ker, K.B.E., C.M.G., D.S.O., M.C.

Thompson, Sir (Thomas) Lionel Tennyson, Bt. (1806).

Thomson, Sir Adam, Kt., C.B.E.

Thomson, Sir Evan Rees Whitaker, Kt.

Thomson, Sir (Frederick Douglas) David, Bt. (1929).

Thomson, Sir Ivo Wilfrid Home, Bt. (1925).

Thomson, Sir John, K.B.E., T.D.

Thomson, Sir John Adam, G.C.M.G.

Thomson, Sir John (Ian) Sutherland, K.B.E., C.M.G.

Thorley, Sir Gerald Bowers, Kt., T.D.

Thorn, Sir John Samuel, Kt., O.B.E.

Thorne, *Maj.-Gen.* Sir David Calthrop, K.B.E.

Thorne, Sir Peter Francis, K.C.V.O., C.B.E.

Thornton, *Lt.-Gen.* Sir Leonard Whitmore, K.C.B., C.B.E.

Thornton, Sir Peter Eustace, K.C.B.

Thorold, Sir Anthony Henry, Bt., O.B.E., D.S.C. (1642).

Thouron, Sir John Rupert Hunt, K.B.E.

Throckmorton, Sir Robert George Maxwell, Bt. (1642).

Thwin, Sir U, Kt.

Tibbits, *Capt.* Sir David Stanley, Kt., D.S.C., R.N.(ret).

Tickell, Sir Crispin Charles Cervantes, K.C.V.O.

Tikaram, Sir Moti, K.B.E.

Tilney, Sir John Dudley Robert Tarleton, Kt., T.D.

Tippet, *Vice-Adm.* Sir Anthony Sanders, K.C.B.

Tippett, Sir Michael Kemp, Kt., O.M., C.H., C.B.E.

Titterton, *Prof.* Sir Ernest William, Kt., C.M.G.

Tizard, Sir John Peter Mills, Kt.

Tod, *Air Marshal* Sir John Hunter Hunter-, K.B.E., C.B.

Todd, Sir Bryan James, Kt.

Todd, Sir Geoffrey Sydney, K.C.V.O., O.B.E.

Todd, Sir Herbert John, Kt., C.I.E.

Tollemache, *Maj.-Gen.* Sir Humphry Thomas, Bt., C.B., C.B.E., R.M. (1793).

Tololo, Sir Alkan, K.B.E.

Tombs, Sir Francis Leonard, Kt.

Tomkins, Sir Alfred George, Kt., C.B.E.

Tomkins, Sir Edward Emile, G.C.M.G., C.V.O.

Tomlinson, Sir (Frank) Stanley, K.C.M.G.

Tooley, Sir John, Kt.

Tooth, Sir Hugh Vere Huntly Duff Munro-Lucas-, Bt. (1920).

Tooth, *Hon.* Sir (Seymour) Douglas, Kt.

Toothill, Sir John Norman, Kt., C.B.E.

ToRobert, Sir Henry Thomas, K.B.E.

Tory, Sir Geofroy William, K.C.M.G.

Touche, Sir Anthony George, Bt. (1920).

Touche, Sir Rodney Gordon, Bt. (1962).

Tovey, Sir Brian John Maynard, K.C.M.G.

Townley, Sir John Barton, Kt.

Townsend, *Rear-Adm.* Sir Leslie William, K.C.V.O., C.B.E.

Townsing, Sir Kenneth Joseph, Kt., C.M.G.

Trafford, Sir (Joseph) Anthony Porteous, Kt.

Traherne, Sir Cennydd George, K.G., T.D.

Traill, Sir Alan Towers, G.B.E.

Trant, *General* Sir Richard Brooking, K.C.B.

Travancore, *Maj.-Gen.* H.H. the Maharajah of, G.C.S.I., G.C.I.E.

Travers, Sir Thomas à'Beckett, Kt.

Treacher, *Admiral* Sir John Devereux, K.C.B.

Trehane, Sir (Walter) Richard, Kt.

Trelawny, Sir John Barry Salusbury-, Bt. (1628).

Trench, Sir David Clive Crosbie, G.C.M.G., M.C.

Trench, Sir Nigel Clive Cosby, K.C.M.G.

Trench, Sir Peter Edward, Kt., C.B.E., T.D.

Trescowthick, Sir Donald Henry, K.B.E.

Trethowan, Sir (James) Ian (Raley), Kt.

Trethowan, *Prof.* Sir William Henry, Kt. C.B.E., F.R.C.P.

Trevaskis, Sir (Gerald) Kennedy (Nicholas), K.C.M.G., O.B.E.

Trevelyan, Sir George Lowthian, Bt. (1874).

Trevelyan, Sir Norman Irving, Bt. (1662).

Trewby, *Vice-Adm.* Sir (George Francis) Allan, K.C.B.

Trinder, Sir (Arnold) Charles, G.B.E.

Tritton, Sir Anthony John Ernest, Bt. (1905).

Trollope, Sir Anthony Owen Clavering, Bt. (1642).

Trotter, Sir Ronald Ramsay, Kt

Troubridge, Sir Peter, Bt. (1799).

Troughton, Sir Charles Hugh Willis, Kt., C.B.E., M.C., T.D.

Troup, *Vice-Adm.* Sir (John) Anthony (Rose), K.C.B., D.S.C.

Trowbridge, *Rear-Adm.* Sir Richard John, K.C.V.O.

Truscott, Sir Denis Henry, G.B.E., T.D.

Truscott, Sir George James Irving, Bt. (1909).

Trusted, Sir Harry Herbert, Kt., Q.C.

Tuck, Sir Bruce Adolph Reginald, Bt. (1910).

Tucker, Sir Henry James, K.B.E.

Tuckwell, Sir Edward George, K.C.V.O., F.R.C.S.

Tudor Price, *Hon.* Sir David William, Kt.

Tuite, Sir Christopher Hugh, Bt., Ph.D. (1622).

Tuivaga, Sir Timoci Uluiburotu, Kt.

Tuke, Sir Anthony Favill, Kt.

Tupper, Sir Charles Hibbert, Bt. (1888).

Turbott, Sir Ian Graham, Kt., C.M.G., C.V.O.

Turing, Sir John Leslie, Bt., M.C. (s 1638).

Turnbull, Sir Francis Fearon, K.B.E., C.B., C.I.E.

Turnbull, Sir Richard Gordon, G.C.M.G.

Turner, *Rt. Hon.* Sir Alexander Kingcome, K.B.E.

Turner, *Admiral* Sir (Arthur) Francis, K.C.B., D.S.C.

Turner, *Lt.-Gen.* Sir William Francis Robert, K.B.E., C.B., D.S.O.

Tuttle, *Air Marshal* Sir Geoffrey William, K.B.E., C.B., D.F.C.

Tuzo, *General* Sir Harry Craufurd, G.C.B., O.B.E., M.C.

Twiss, *Admiral* Sir Frank Roddam, K.C.B., K.C.V.O., D.S.C.

Tyler, *Maj.-Gen.* Sir Leslie Norman, K.B.E., C.B.

Tymms, Sir Frederick, K.C.I.E., M.C.

Tyree, Sir (Alfred) William, Kt., O.B.E.

Tyrrell, Sir Murray Louis, K.C.V.O., C.B.E.

Tyrwhitt, Sir Reginald Thomas Newman, Bt. (1919).

Udoma, *Hon.* Sir (Egbert) Udo, Kt.

Unsworth, Hon. Sir Edgar Ignatius Godfrey, Kt., C.M.G.

Unwin, Sir Keith, K.B.E., C.M.G.

Urquhart, Sir Andrew, K.C.M.G., M.B.E.

Urwick, Sir Alan Bedford, K.C.V.O., C.M.G.

Usher, Sir Peter Lionel, Bt. (1899).

Vallat, Sir Francis Aimé, G.B.E., K.C.M.G., Q.C.

Vanderfelt, Sir Robin Victor, K.B.E.

van der Post, Sir Laurens Jan, Kt., K.B.E.

Vane, Sir John Robert, Kt., D.Phil., D.SC., F.R.S.

Vangeke, *Most Rev.* Louis, K.B.E.

Vanneck, *Air Commodore* Hon. Sir Peter Beckford Rutgers, G.B.E., C.B., A.F.C.

van Straubenzee, Sir William Radcliffe, Kt., M.B.E., M.P.

Vaughan, Sir (George) Edgar, K.B.E.

Vaughan, Sir Gerard Folliott, Kt., M.P., F.R.C.P.

Vavasour, *Cdr.* Sir Geoffrey William, Bt., D.S.C., R.N. (1828).

Veale, Sir Alan John Ralph, Kt.

Verco, Sir Walter John George, K.C.V.O.

Verney, Sir John, Bt., M.C., T.D. (1946).

Verney, Sir Ralph Bruce, Bt., K.B.E. (1818).

Vernon, Sir James, Kt., C.B.E.

Vernon, Sir Nigel John Douglas, Bt. (1914).

Vesey, Sir (Nathaniel) Henry (Peniston), Kt., C.B.E.

Vestey, Sir (John) Derek, Bt. (1921).

Vial, Sir Kenneth Harold, Kt., C.B.E.

Vick, Sir (Francis) Arthur, Kt., O.B.E., Ph.D.

Vickers, *Lt.-Gen.* Sir Richard Maurice Hilton, K.C.B., M.V.O., O.B.E.

Vickery, Sir Philip Crawford, Kt., C.I.E., O.B.E.

Victoria, Sir (Joseph Aloysius) Donatus, Kt., C.B.E.

Villiers, Sir Charles Hyde, Kt., M.C.

Villiers, *Vice-Adm.* Sir (John) Michael, K.C.B., O.B.E.

Vincent, *Lt.-Gen.* Sir Richard Frederick, K.C.B., D.S.O.

Vincent, Sir William Percy Maxwell, Bt. (1936).

Vinelott, *Hon.* Sir John Evelyn, Kt.

Vines, Sir William Joshua, Kt., C.M.G.

Virtue, *Hon.* Sir John Evenden, Kt.

Vyse, *Lt.-Gen.* Sir Edward Dacre Howard-, K.B.E., C.B., M.C.

Vyvyan, Sir John Stanley, Bt. (1645).

Waddell, Sir Alexander Nicol Anton, K.C.M.G., D.S.C.

Waddell, Sir James Henderson, Kt., C.B.

Wade, *Col.* Sir George Albert, M.C.

Wade, *Prof.* Sir Henry William Rawson, Kt., Q.C., F.B.A.

Wade, *Air Chief Marshal* Sir Ruthven Lowry, K.C.B., D.F.C.

Wade, Sir (William) Oulton, Kt.

Wade-Gery, Sir Robert Lucian, K.C.M.G., K.C.V.O.

Waechter, Sir (Harry Leonard) d'Arcy, Bt. (1911).

Wagner, Sir Anthony Richard, K.C.B., K.C.V.O.

Waite, *Hon.* Sir John Douglas, Kt.

Wake, Sir Hereward, Bt., M.C., (1621).

Wakefield, Sir (Edward) Humphry (Tyrell), Bt. (1962).

Wakefield, Sir Peter George Arthur, K.B.E., C.M.G.

Wakeford, *Air Marshal* Sir Richard Gordon, K.C.B., M.V.O., O.B.E., A.F.C.

Wakeley, Sir John Cecil Nicholson, Bt., F.R.C.S. (1952).

Wakeman, Sir (Offley) David, Bt. (1828).

Walker, *Rev.* Alan Edgar, Kt., O.B.E.

Walker, Sir Allan Grierson, Kt., Q.C.

Walker, Sir Baldwin Patrick, Bt. (1856).

Walker, Sir (Charles) Michael, G.C.M.G.

Walker, *Vice-Adm.* Sir (Charles) Peter (Graham), K.B.E., C.B., D.S.C.

Walker, Sir Michael Leolin Forestier-, Bt. (1835).

Walker, Sir Edward Ronald, Kt., C.B.E.

Walker, *Air Chief Marshal* Sir (George) Augustus, G.C.B., C.B.E., D.S.O., D.F.C., A.F.C.

Walker, Sir Gervas George, Kt.

Walker, *Maj.* Sir Hugh Ronald, Bt. (1906).

Walker, Sir James Graham, Kt., M.B.E.

Walker, Sir James Heron, Bt. (1868).

Walker, *General* Sir Walter Colyear, K.C.B., C.B.E., D.S.O.

Walker, Sir William Giles Newsom, Kt., T.D.

Wall, Sir Patrick Henry Bligh, M.C., V.R.D., M.P.

Wallace, Sir Gordon, Kt.

Wallace, Sir Ian James, Kt., C.B.E.

Waller, *Rt. Hon.* Sir George Stanley, Kt., O.B.E.

Waller, Sir (John) Keith, Kt., C.B.E.

Waller, Sir John Stainer, Bt. (1815).

Waller, Sir Robert William, Bt. (1 1780).

Walley, Sir John, K.B.E., C.B.

Walmsley, *Air Marshal* Sir Hugh Sydney Porter, K.C.B., K.C.I.E., C.B.E., M.C., D.F.C.

Walsh, Sir Alan, Kt., D.SC., F.R.S.

Walsh, Sir David Philip, K.B.E., C.B

Walsh, Prof. Sir John Patrick, K.B.E.

Walsham, *Rear-Adm.* Sir John Scarlett Warren, Bt., C.B., O.B.E. (1831).

Walter, Sir Harold Edward, Kt.

Walters, *Prof.* Sir Alan Arthur, Kt.

Walters, Sir Frederick Donald, Kt.

Walters, Sir Peter Ingram, Kt.

Walters, Sir Roger Talbot, K.B.E., F.R.I.B.A.

Walton, *Prof.* Sir John Nicholas, Kt., T.D., F.R.C.P.

Walton, Sir John Robert, Kt.

Walton, *Hon.* Sir Raymond Henry, Kt.

Wan, Sir Wamp, Kt., M.B.E.

Wanstall, *Hon.* Sir Charles Gray, Kt.

Ward, Sir Arthur Hugh, K.B.E.

Ward, *General* Sir Dudley, G.C.B., K.B.E., D.S.O.

Ward, Sir Aubrey Ernest, Kt.

Ward, Sir John Guthrie, G.C.M.G.

Ward, Sir Joseph James Laffey, Bt. (1911).

Ward, *Maj.-Gen.* Sir Philip John Newling, K.C.V.O., C.B.E.

Ward, *General* Sir Richard Erskine, G.B.E., K.C.B., D.S.O., M.C.

Ward, Sir Terence George, Kt., C.B.E.

Wardale, Sir Geoffrey Charles, K.C.B.

Wardlaw, Sir Henry (John), Bt. (s 1631).

Wardle, Sir Thomas Edward Jewell, Kt.

Ware, Sir Henry Gabriel, K.C.B.

Waring, Sir (Alfred) Holburt, Bt. (1935).

Wark, Sir Ian William, Kt., C.M.G., C.B.E., Ph.D., D.SC.

Warmington, *Lt.-Cdr.* Sir Marshall George Clitheroe, Bt., R.N. (1908).

Warner, Sir (Edward Courtenay) Henry, Bt. (1910).

Warner, Sir Edward Redston, K.C.M.G., O.B.E.

Warner, Sir Frederick Archibald, G.C.V.O., K.C.M.G.

Warner, Sir Frederick Edward, Kt., F.R.S.

Warner, *Hon.* Sir Jean-Pierre Frank Eugene, Kt.

Warren, Sir Alfred Henry, Kt., C.B.E.

Warren, Sir (Harold) Brian (Seymour), Kt.

Warren, Sir Brian Charles Pennefather, Bt. (1784).

Warren, Sir Frederick Miles, K.B.E.

Wass, Sir Douglas William Gretton, G.C.B.

Waterhouse, Sir Ellis Kirkham, Kt., C.B.E.

Waterhouse, *Hon.* Sir Ronald Gough, Kt.

Waterlow, Sir Christopher Rupert, Bt. (1873).

Waterlow, Sir (James) Gerard, Bt. (1930).

Wates, Sir Ronald Wallace, Kt.

Watkins, *Rt. Hon.* Sir Tasker, Kt., V.C.

Watson, Sir Bruce Dunstan, Kt.

Watson, *Capt.* Sir Derrick William Inglefield Inglefield-, Bt., T.D. (1895).

Watson, Sir Francis John Bagott, K.C.V.O., F.B.A., F.S.A.

Watson, Sir (James) Andrew, Bt. (1866).

Watson, Sir Michael Milne-, Bt., C.B.E. (1937).

Watson, Sir (Noel) Duncan, K.C.M.G.

Watson, *Vice-Admiral* Sir Philip Alexander, K.B.E., M.V.O.

Watson, *Vice-Adm.* Sir (Robert) Dymock, K.C.B., C.B.E.

Watt, Sir Alan Stewart, Kt., C.B E.

Watt, Sir George Steven Harvie-, Bt., T.D., Q.C. (1945).

Watt, *Surgeon Vice-Adm.* Sir James, K.C.B., F.R.C.S.

Wauchope, Sir Patrick George Don-, Bt. (s 1667).

Way, Sir Richard George Kitchener, K.C.B., C.B.E.

Wayne, *Prof.* Sir Edward Johnson, Kt., M.D., Ph.D.

Weaver, Sir Tobias Rushton, Kt., C.B.

Webb, *Lt.-Gen.* Sir Richard James Holden, K.B.E., C.B.

Webb, Sir Thomas Langley, Kt.

Webster, *Hon.* Sir Peter Edlin, Kt.

Webster, Sir Richard James, Kt., D.S.O.

Wedderburn, Sir Andrew John Alexander Ogilvy-, Bt. (1803).

Wedderspoon, Sir Thomas Adam, Kt.

Wedgwood, Sir John Hamilton, Bt., T.D. (1942).

Weeks, Sir Hugh Thomas, Kt., C.M.G.

Weipers, *Prof.* Sir William Lee, Kt.

Weir, Sir Michael Scott, K.C.M.G.

Weir, Sir Roderick Bignell, Kt.

Weiss, Sir Eric, Kt.

Welby, Sir (Richard) Bruno Gregory, Bt. (1801).

Welch, Sir John Reader, Bt. (1957).

Weld, *Col.* Sir Joseph William, Kt., O.B.E., T.D.

Weldon, Sir Anthony William, Bt. (t. 1723).

Welensky, *Rt. Hon.* Sir Roy, (Roland), K.C.M.G.

Wellings, Sir Jack Alfred, Kt., C.B.E.

Wells, Sir Charles Maltby, Bt., T.D. (1944).

Wells, Sir John Julius, Kt., M.P.

Westall, *General* Sir John Chaddesley, K.C.B., C.B.E., R.M.

Westerman, Sir (Wilfred) Alan, Kt., C.B.E.

Wheatley, Sir (George) Andrew, Kt., C.B.E.

Wheeler, Sir Ernest Richard, K.C.V.O., M.B.E.

Wheeler, Sir Frederick Henry, Kt., C.B.E.

Wheeler, *Air Chief Marshal* Sir (Henry) Neil (George), G.C.B., C.B.E., D.S.O., D.F.C., A.F.C.

Wheeler, Sir John Hieron, Bt. (1920).

Wheeler, *Hon.* Sir Kenneth Henry, Kt.

Wheldon, Sir Huw Pyrs, Kt., O.B.E., M.C.

Wheler, *Capt.* Sir Trevor Wood, Bt. (1660).

Whishaw, Sir Charles Percival Law, Kt.

Whitaker, *Maj.* Sir James Herbert Ingham, Bt. (1936).

White, *Hon.* Sir Alfred John, Kt.

White, Sir Christopher Robert Meadows, Bt. (1937).

White, Sir Dick Goldsmith, K.C.M.G., K.B.E.

White, Sir Frederick William George, K.B.E., Ph.D., F.R.S.

White, Sir George Stanley James, Bt. (1904).

White, Sir Harold Leslie, Kt., C.B.E.

White, *Wing-Cdr.* Sir Henry Arthur Dalrymple-, Bt., D.F.C. (1926).

White, *Hon.* Sir John Charles, Kt., M.B.E.

White, Sir John Woolmer, Bt. (1922).

White, Sir Lynton Stuart, Kt., M.B.E.- T.D.

White, *Admiral* Sir Peter, G.B.E.

White, Sir Thomas Astley Woollaston, Bt. (1802).

White, Sir (Vincent) Gordon (Lindsay), K.B.E.

Whitehead, Sir Rowland John Rathbone, Bt. (1889).

Whiteley, Sir Hugo Baldwin Huntington-, Bt. (1918).

Whiteley, *General* Sir Peter John Frederick, G.C.B., O.B.E., R.M.

Whitford, *Hon.* Sir John Norman Keates, Kt.

Whitley, *Air Marshal* Sir John René, K.B.E., C.B., D.S.O., A.F.C.

Whitmore, Sir Clive Anthony, K.C.B., C.V.O.

Whitmore, Sir John Henry Douglas, Bt. (1954).

Whitteridge, Sir Gordon Coligny, K.C.M.G., O.B.E.

Whittle, *Air Commodore* Sir Frank, K.B.E., C.B., F.R.S.

Whyte, Sir William Erskine Hamilton, K.C.M.G.

Wicks, *Hon.* Sir James, Kt.

Wicks, Sir James Albert, Kt.

Wigan, Sir Alan Lewis, Bt. (1898).

Wiggin, Sir John Henry, Bt., M.C. (1892).

Wigglesworth, Sir Vincent Brian, Kt., C.B.E., M.D., F.R.S.

Wigram, *Rev. Canon* Sir Clifford Woolmore, Bt. (1805).

Wilbraham, Sir Richard Baker, Bt. (1776).

Wilcox, Sir Malcolm George, Kt., C.B.E.

Wilford, Sir (Kenneth) Michael, G.C.M.G.

Wilkins, Sir Graham John, Kt.

Wilkins, *Lt.-Gen.* Sir Michael Compton Lockwood, K.C.B., O.B.E.

Wilkinson, Sir (David) Graham (Brook) Bt. (1941).

Wilkinson, *Prof.* Sir Denys Haigh, Kt., F.R.S.

Wilkinson, *Prof.* Sir Geoffrey, Kt., F.R.S.

Wilkinson, *Rt. Hon.* Sir Nicolas Christopher Henry Browne-, Kt.

Wilkinson, Sir Harold, Kt., C.M.G.

Wilkinson, Sir Peter Allix, K.C.M.G., D.S.O., O.B.E.

Wilkinson, Sir (Robert Francis) Martin, Kt.

Willatt, Sir (Robert) Hugh, Kt.

Willcocks, Sir David Valentine, Kt., C.B.E., M.C.

Williams, Sir Alwyn, Kt., PH.D., F.R.S.

Williams, Sir Anthony James, K.C.M.G.

Williams, Sir Brandon Meredith Rhys-, Bt., M.P. (1918).

Williams, *Prof.* Sir Bruce Rodda, K.B.E.

Williams, *Admiral* Sir David, G.C.B.

Williams, Sir David Innes, Kt.

Williams, Sir Donald Mark, Bt. (1866).

Williams, Sir Edgar Trevor, Kt., C.B., C.B.E., D.S.O.

Williams, *Hon.* Sir Edward Stratten, K.C.M.G., K.B.E.

Williams, Sir Francis John Watkin, Bt., Q.C. (1798).

Williams, Sir Gwilym Tecwyn, Kt., C.B.E.

Williams, Sir Henry Morton Leech, Kt., M.B.E.

Williams, Sir Henry Sydney, Kt., O.B.E.

Williams, Sir (John) Leslie, Kt., C.B.E.

Williams, *Capt.* Sir John Protheroe, Kt., C.M.G., O.B.E.

Williams, Sir John Robert, K.C.M.G.

Williams, Sir Leonard, K.B.E., C.B.

Williams, Sir Osmond, Bt., M.C. (1909).

Williams, Sir Peter Watkin, Kt.

Williams, *Prof.* Sir Robert Evan Owen, Kt., M.D., F.R.C.P.

Williams, Sir (Robert) Philip Nathaniel, Bt. (1915).

Williams, Sir Robin Philip, Bt. (1953).

Williams, Sir Rolf Dudley-, Bt. (1964).

Williams, Sir (William) Maxwell (Harries), Kt.

Williams, Sir (William) Thomas, Kt., Q.C.

Williamson, *Marshal of the Royal Air Force* Sir Keith Alec, G.C.B., A.F.C.

Williamson, Sir (Nicholas Frederick) Hedworth, Bt. (1642).

Willink, Sir Charles William, Bt. (1957).

Willis, *Hon.* Sir Eric Archibald, K.B.E., C.M.G.

Willis, *Vice-Adm.* Sir (Guido) James, K.B.E.

Willis, Sir John Ramsay, Kt.

Willison, *Lt.-Gen.* Sir David John, K.C.B., O.B.E., M.C.

Willison, Sir John Alexander, Kt., O.B.E.

Willoughby, *Maj.-Gen.* Sir John Edward Francis, K.B.E., C.B.

Wills, Sir David Seton, Bt. (1904).

Wills, Sir (Hugh) David Hamilton, Kt., C.B.E., T.D.

Wills, Sir John Spencer, Kt.

Wills, Sir John Vernon, Bt., T.D. (1923).

Wilmot, Sir Henry Robert, Bt. (1759).

Wilmot, *Cdr.* Sir John Assheton Eardley-, Bt., M.V.O., D.S.C., R.N. (1821).

Wilson, Sir Alan Herries, Kt., F.R.S.

Wilson, *Lt.-Gen.* Sir (Alexander) James, K.B.E., M.C.

Wilson, Sir Angus Frank Johnstone, Kt., C.B.E.

Wilson, Sir Austin George, Kt., O.B.E.

Wilson, Sir Charles Haynes, Kt.

Wilson, Sir David, Bt. (1920).

Wilson, Sir David Mackenzie, Kt.

Wilson, Sir Geoffrey Masterman, K.C.B., C.M.G.

Wilson, Sir Graham Selby, Kt., M.D., F.R.S.

Wilson, Sir James William Douglas, Bt. (1906).

Wilson, Sir John Foster, Kt., C.B.E.

Wilson, Sir John Gardiner, Kt., C.B.E.

Wilson, Sir John Martindale, K.C.B.

Wilson, Sir Keith Cameron, Kt.

Wilson, Sir (Mathew) Martin, Bt. (1874).

Wilson, Sir Reginald Holmes, Kt.

Wilson, *Rt. Rev.* Roger Plumpton, K.C.V.O., D.D.

Wilson, Sir Roland, K.B.E.

Wilson, *Hon.* Sir Ronald Darling, K.B.E., C.M.G.

Wilton, Sir (Arthur) John, K.C.M.G., K.C.V.O., M.C.

Wiltshire, Sir Frederick Munro, Kt., C.B.E.

Windeyer, Sir Brian Wellingham, Kt.

Windeyer, *Rt. Hon.* Sir (William John) Victor, K.B.E., C.B., D.S.O., E.D.

Wingate, *Capt.* Sir Miles Buckley, K.C.V.O.

Winneke, *Hon.* Sir Henry Arthur, K.C.M.G., K.C.V.O., O.B.E.

Winnifrith, Sir (Alfred) John (Digby), K.C.B.

Winnington, Sir Francis Salwey William, Bt. (1755).

Winskill, *Air Commodore* Sir Archibald Little, K.C.V.O., C.B.E., D.F.C.

Winterbottom, Sir Walter, Kt., C.B.E.

Winterton, *Maj.-Gen.* Sir (Thomas) John (Willoughby), K.C.B., K.C.M.G., C.B.E.

Wiseman, Sir John William, Bt. (1628).

Wolfson, Sir David, Kt.

Wolfson, Sir Isaac, Bt., F.R.S. (1962).

Wollen, Sir (Ernest) Russell (Storey), K.B.E.

Wolseley, Sir Charles Garnet Richard Mark, Bt. (1628).

Wolseley, Sir Garnet, Bt. (1 1745).

Wolstenholme, Sir Gordon Ethelbert Ward, Kt., O.B.E.

Wombwell, Sir George Philip Frederick, Bt. (1778).

Womersley, Sir Peter John Walter, Bt. (1945).

Wontner, Sir Hugh Walter Kingwell, G.B.E., C.V.O.

Wood, Sir Anthony John Page, Bt. (1837).

Wood, Sir Arthur Michael, Kt., C.B.E.

Wood, Sir David Basil Hill-, Bt. (1921).

Wood, Sir Frederick Ambrose Stuart, Kt.

Wood, Sir Henry Peart, Kt., C.B.E.

Wood, Sir Ian Jeffreys, Kt., M.B.E.

Wood, *Prof.* Sir John Crossley, Kt., C.B.E.

Wood, *Hon.* Sir John Kember, Kt., M.C.

Wood, Sir Kenneth Millns, Kt.

Wood, Sir Russell Dillon, K.C.V.O., V.R.D.

Wood, Sir William Alan, K.C.V.O., C.B.

Woodfield, Sir Philip John, K.C.B., C.B.E.

Woodhouse, *Rt. Hon.* Sir (Arthur) Owen, K.B.E., D.S.C.

Woodroffe, *Most Rev.* George Cuthbert Manning, K.B.E.

Woodroofe, Sir Ernest George, Kt., PH.D.

Woodruff, *Prof.* Sir Michael Francis Addison, Kt., D.S.C., F.R.S., F.R.C.S.

Woods, Sir Colin Philip Joseph, K.C.V.O., C.B.E.

Woods, *Most Rev.* Frank, K.B.E., D.D.

Woods, *Rt. Rev.* Robert Wilmer, K.C.V.O.

Woodward, *Hon.* Sir (Albert) Edward, Kt., O.B.E.

Woodward, *Vice-Adm.* Sir John Forster, K.C.B.

Woolf, *Hon.* Sir Harry Kenneth, Kt.

Woolf, Sir John, Kt.

Woollaston, Sir (Mountford) Tosswill, Kt.

Woolley, Sir Richard van der Riet, Kt., O.B.E., F.R.S.

Wordie, Sir John Stewart, Kt., C.B.E., V.R.D.

Worsley, *Lt.-Gen.* Sir John Francis, K.B.E., C.B., M.C.

Worsley, *General* Sir Richard Edward, G.C.B., O.B.E.

Worsley, Sir (William) Marcus (John), Bt. (1838).

Worthington, *Air Vice Marshal* Sir Geoffrey Luis, K.B.E., C.B.

Wraight, Sir John Richard, K.B.E., C.M.G.

Wrangham, Sir Geoffrey Walter, Kt.

Wraxall, Sir Charles Frederick Lascelles, Bt. (1813).

Wrey, Sir (Castel Richard) Bourchier, Bt. (1628).

Wright, Sir Allan Frederick, K.B.E.

Wright, Sir Denis Arthur Hepworth, G.C.M.G.

Wright, Sir Edward Maitland, Kt., D.Phil.,Ll.D., D.S.C., F.R.S.E.

Wright, Sir (John) Oliver, G.C.M.G., G.C.V.O., D.S.C.

Wright, Sir Patrick Richard Henry, K.C.M.G.

Wright, Sir Paul Hervé Giraud, K.C.M.G., O.B.E.

Wright, *Hon.* Sir Reginald Charles, Kt.

Wright, Sir Richard Michael Cory-, Bt. (1903).

Wright, Sir Rowland Sydney, Kt., C.B.E.

Wrightson, Sir Charles Mark Garmondsway, Bt. (1900).

Wyatt, Sir Woodrow Lyle, Kt.

Wykeham, *Air Marshal* Sir Peter Guy, K.C.B., D.S.O., O.B.E., D.F.C., A.F.C.

Wylie, Sir Campbell, Kt., E.D., Q.C.

Wyndham, Sir Harold Stanley, Kt., C.B.E.

Wynn, *Col.* Sir (Owen) Watkin Williams-, Bt., C.B.E. (1688).

Wynter, Sir Luther Reginald, Kt., C.B.E.

Yapp, Sir Stanley Graham, Kt.

Yarrow, Sir Eric Grant, Bt., M.B.E. (1916).

Yeend, Sir Geoffrey John, Kt., C.B.E.

Yellowlees, Sir Henry, K.C.B.

Yocklunn, Sir John (Soong Chung), K.C.V.O.

Yonge, Sir (Charles) Maurice, Kt., C.B.E., D.SC., F.R.S., F.R.S.E.

Yorston, Sir (Robert) Keith, Kt., C.B.E.

Youde, Sir Edward, G.C.M.G., M.B.E.

Youens, Sir Peter William, Kt., C.M.G., O.B.E.

Young, Sir Brian Walter Mark, Kt.

Young, *Lt.-Gen.* Sir David Tod, K.B.E., C.B., D.F.C.

Young, *Prof.* Sir Frank George, Kt., D.SC., Ph.D., F.R.S.

Young, Sir George Samuel Knatchbull, Bt., M.P. (1813).

Young, *Most Rev.* Guilford, K.B.E.

Young, *Hon.* Sir Harold William, K.C.M.G.

Young, *Hon.* Sir John McIntosh, K.C.M.G.

Young, Sir John Kenyon Roe, Bt. (1821).

Young, Sir Leslie Clarence, Kt., C.B.E.

Young, Sir Norman Smith, Kt.

Young, Sir Richard Dilworth, Kt.

Young, Sir Robert Christopher Mackworth-, G.C.V.O.

Young, Sir Roger William, Kt.

Young, Sir Stephen Stewart Templeton, Bt. (1945).

Young, Sir William Neil, Bt. (1769).

Younger, *Maj.-Gen.* Sir John William, Bt., C.B.E. (1911).

Younger, Sir William McEwan, Bt., D.S.O. (1964).

Zeidler, Sir David Ronald, Kt. C.B.E.

Zoleveke, Sir Gideon Pitabose, K.B.E.

Zurenuo, *Rt. Rev.* Zurewe Kamong, Kt., O.B.E.

Dames Grand Cross and Dames Commanders of the Order of the Bath, the Order of St. Michael and St. George, the Royal Victorian Order and the Order of the British Empire

NOTE.—Dames Grand Cross (G.C.B., G.C.M.G., G.C.V.O. or G.B.E.) and Dames Commanders (D.C.B., D.C.M.G., D.C.V.O. or D.B.E.) are addressed in a manner similar to that of Knights Grand Cross or Knights Commanders, *e.g.* "Miss Florence Smith" after receiving the honour would be addressed as "Dame Florence", and in writing as "Dame Florence Smith, G. (or D.) C.B., G. (or D.) C.M.G., G. (or D.) C.V.O., OR G. (or D.) B.E." Where such award is made to a lady already in enjoyment of a higher title the appropriate letters are appended to her name, *e.g.* "The Countess of —— G.C.V.O." Peeresses in their own right, and Life Peeresses, are not included in this list. Dames Grand Cross rank after wives of Baronets and before wives of Knights Grand Cross. Dames Commanders rank after the wives of Knights Grand Cross and before the wives of Knights Commanders.

DAMES GRAND CROSS AND DAMES COMMANDERS

H.M. Queen Elizabeth The Queen Mother, K.G., K.T., C.I., G.M.V.O.

H.R.H. The Princess Margaret, Countess of Snowdon, C.I., G.C.V.O.

H.R.H. The Princess Alice, Duchess of Gloucester, G.C.B., C.I., G.C.V.O., G.B.E.

H.R.H. The Princess Alexandra of Kent, G.C.V.O.

H.R.H. The Princess Anne, G.C.V.O.

H.R.H. The Duchess of Kent, G.C.V.O.

Abercorn, Mary, Duchess of, G.C.V.O.

Ackroyd, Dame (Dorothy) Elizabeth, D.B.E.

Albemarle, The Countess of, D.B.E.

Alexander of Tunis, Margaret Diana, Countess, G.B.E.

Anderson, Dame Judith, D.B.E.

Anderson, *Brig.* Hon. Dame Mary Mackenzie (Mrs. Pihl), D.B.E.

Anglesey, (Elizabeth) Shirley Vaughan, Marchioness of, D.B.E.

Ashcroft, Dame Peggy (Mrs. Hutchinson), D.B.E.

Austin, Dame (Mary) Valerie Hall, D.B.E.

Aves, Dame Geraldine Maitland, D.B.E.

Baker, Dame Janet Abbott, D.B.E.

Baring, Lady Rose Gwendolen Louisa, D.C.V.O.

Barnes, Dame (Alice) Josephine (Mary Taylor), (Dame Josephine Warren), D.B.E., F.R.C.P., F.R.C.S.

Barnett, Dame (Mary) Henrietta, D.B.E.

Bate, Dame Zara Kate, D.B.E.

Beaurepaire, Dame Beryl Edith, D.B.E.

Berry, Dame Alice Miriam, D.B.E.

Bishop, Dame (Margaret) Joyce, D.B.E.

Blackwood, Dame Margaret, D.B.E.

Blaxland, Dame Helen Frances, D.B.E.

Bolte, Edith Lilian, Lady, D.B.E.

Booth, *Hon.* Dame Margaret Myfanwy Wood, D.B.E.

Bottomley, Dame Bessie Ellen, D.B.E.

Bowles, Dame Ann Parker, D.C.V.O., C.B.E.

Brazill, Dame Josephine (Sister Mary Philippa), D.B.E.

Brecknock, Marjorie Countess of, D.B.E.

Breen, Dame Marie Freda, D.B.E.

Bridges, Dame Mary Patricia, D.B.E.

Brown, Dame Beryl Paston, D.B.E.

Browne, Lady Moyra Blanche Madeleine, D.B.E.

Bryans, Dame Anne Margaret, D.B.E.

Bryce, Dame Isabel Graham, D.B.E.

Buckley, Hon. Dame Ruth Burton, D.B.E.

Burnside, Dame Edith, D.B.E.

Buttfield, Dame Nancy Eileen, D.B.E.

Bynoe, Dame Hilda Louisa, D.B.E.

Campbell, Dame Kate Isabel, D.B.E., M.D.

Cartwright, Dame Mary Lucy, D.B.E., SC.D., D.Phil., F.R.S.

Cayford, Dame Florence Evelyn, D.B.E.

Cleland, Dame Rachel, D.B.E.

Clode, Dame (Emma) Frances (Heather), D.B.E.

Cockayne, Dame Elizabeth, D.B.E.

Coker, Dame Elizabeth, D.B.E.

Coles, Dame Mabel Irene, D.B.E.

Colvin, *Brig.* Dame Mary Katherine Rosamond, D.B.E., T.D.

Cooper, Dame Whina, D.B.E.

Coulshed, Dame (Mary) Frances, D.B.E., T.D.

Cozens, *Brig.* Dame (Florence) Barbara, D.B.E., R.R.C.

Cramer, Dame Mary Theresa, D.B.E.

Crowe, Dame Sylvia, D.B.E.

Daws, Dame Joyce Margaretta, D.B.E.

De La Warr, Sylvia, Countess, D.B.E.

Dell, Dame Miriam Patricia, D.B.E.

de Valois, Dame Ninette, C.H., D.B.E.

Devonshire, Mary Alice, Duchess of, G.C.V.O., C.B.E.

Dickson, Dame Violet Penelope, D.B.E.

Donaldson, Dame (Dorothy) Mary, G.B.E.

Doughty, Dame Adelaide Baillieu, D.B.E.

Doyle, *Air Commandant* Dame Jean Lena Annette Conan (Lady Bromet), D.B.E.

Drake, *Brig.* Dame Jean Elizabeth Rivett Rivett-, D.B.E.

Drummond, Dame (Edith) Margaret, D.B.E.

Dugdale, Dame Kathryn Edith Helen, D.C.V.O.

du Maurier, Dame Daphne (Lady Browning), D.B.E.

Durack, Dame Mary (Mrs. H. C. Miller), D.B.E.

Elgin & Kincardine, Katherine, Countess of, D.B.E.

Evans, Lady Olwen Elizabeth Carey, D.B.E.

Fell, Dame Honor Bridget, D.B.E., F.R.S.

Fermoy, Ruth Sylvia, Lady, D.C.V.O., O.B.E.

Fitton, Dame Doris Alice (Mrs. Mason), D.B.E.

Fonteyn, Dame Margot, D.B.E.

Friend, Dame Phyllis Muriel, D.B.E.

Frink, Dame Elisabeth, D.B.E., R.A.

Frost, Dame Phyllis Irene, D.B.E.

Gallagher, Dame Monica Josephine, D.B.E.

Gardiner, Dame Helen Louisa, D.B.E., M.V.O.

Gardner, Dame Frances, D.B.E.

Gardner, Dame Helen Louise, D.B.E.

Gibbs, Dame Molly Peel, D.B.E.

Giles, *Air Commandant* Dame Pauline, D.B.E., R.R.C.

Godwin, Dame (Beatrice) Anne, D.B.E.

Golding, Dame (Cecilie) Monica, D.B.E.

Gordon, Dame Minita Elmira, G.C.M.G.

Grafton, The Duchess of, G.C.V.O.

Green, Dame Mary Georgina, D.B.E.

Guilfoyle, Dame Margaret Georgina Constance. D.B.E.

Hall, Dame Catherine Mary, D.B.E.

Hambleden, Patricia, Viscountess, D.C.V.O.

Hammond, Dame Joan Hood, D.B.E.

Harris, Dame (Muriel) Diana Reader-, D.B.E.

Hart, *Rt. Hon.* Dame Judith Constance Mary, D.B.E., M.P.

Heilbron, *Hon.* Dame Rose, D.B.E.

Henrison, Dame Anne Elizabeth Rosina, D.B.E.

Herbison, Dame Jean Marjory, D.B.E., C.M.G.

Hill, Dame Elizabeth Mary, D.B.E.

Hill, *Air Commodore* Dame Felicity Barbara, D.B.E.

Hiller, Dame Wendy (Mrs. Gow), D.B.E.

Holland-Martin, Rosamund Mary, Lady, D.B.E.

Hunter, Dame Pamela, D.B.E.

Hussey, Lady Susan Katharine, D.C.V.O.

Isaacs, Dame Albertha Madeline, D.B.E.

James, Dame Naomi Christine, D.B.E.

Jenkins, Dame (Mary) Jennifer, D.B.E.

Kelleher, Dame Joan, D.B.E.

Kettlewell, *Commandant* Dame Marion Mildred, D.B.E.

Kidd, Dame Margaret Henderson (Mrs. Macdonald), D.B.E., Q.C.

Kilroy, Dame Alix Hester Marie (Lady Meynell), D.B.E.

Kirk, Dame (Lucy) Ruth, D.B.E.

Knight, Dame Joan Christabel Jill, D.B.E., M.P.

Kramer, *Prof.* Dame Leonie Judith, D.B.E.

Lancaster, Dame Jean, D.B.E.

Lane, Dame Elizabeth Kathleen, D.B.E.

Lister, Dame Unity Viola, D.B.E.

Litchfield, Dame Ruby Beatrice, D.B.E.

Lloyd, Dame Hilda Nora, D.B.E.

Lowrey, *Air Commandant* Dame Alice, D.B.E., R.R.C.

Lynn, Dame Vera (Mrs. Lewis), D.B.E.

Mackinnon, Dame (Una) Patricia, D.B.E.

Macknight, Dame Ella Annie Noble, D.B.E., M.D.

Macmillan of Ovenden, Katharine, Viscountess, D.B.E.

Mann, Dame Ida Caroline, D.B.E., D.SC., F.R.C.S.

Markova, Dame Alicia, D.B.E.

Maxwell-Scott, Dame Jean Mary Monica, D.C.V.O.

Menzies, Dame Pattie Maie, G.B.E.

Miles, Dame Margaret, D.B.E.

Miller, Dame Mabel Flora Hobart, D.B.E.

Mitchell, *Hon.* Dame Roma Flinders, D.B.E.

Morant, Dame Mary Maud (Sister Mary Regis), D.B.E.

Morrison, *Hon.* Dame Mary Anne, D.C.V.O.

Munro, Dame Alison, D.B.E.

Murdoch, Dame Elisabeth Joy, D.B.E.

Murray, Dame (Alice) Rosemary, D.B.E., D.Phil.

Neagle, Dame Anna (Mrs. Wilcox), D.B.E.

Niccol, Dame Kathleen Agnes, D.B.E.

Norris, Dame Ada May, D.B.E., C.M.G.

Ollerenshaw, Dame Kathleen Mary, D.B.E., D.Phil.

Origo, *Marchesa* Iris, D.B.E.

Parker, Dame Marjorie Alice Collett, D.B.E.

Paterson, Dame Betty Fraser Ross, D.B.E.

Pepys, Lady (Mary) Rachel, D.C.V.O.

Pickerill, Dame Cecily Mary Wise, D.B.E.

Plowden, The Lady, D.B.E.

Prentice, Dame Winifred Eva, D.B.E.

Purves, Dame Daphne Helen, D.B.E.

Pyke, The Lady, D.B.E.

Railton, *Brig.* Dame Mary, D.B.E.

Railton, Dame Ruth (Mrs. Cecil Harmsworth King), D.B.E.

Rankin, Dame Annabelle Jane Mary, D.B.E.

Rankin, Lady Jean Margaret Florence, D.C.V.O.

Raven, Dame Kathleen Annie (Mrs. J. T. Ingram), D.B.E.

Reader, Dame Audrey Tattie Hinchcliff, D.B.E.

Rees, Dame Dorothy Mary, D.B.E.

Riddelsdell, Dame Mildred, D.C.B., C.B.E.

Ridley, Dame (Mildred) Betty, D.B.E.

Roberts, Dame Jean, D.B.E.

Roberts, Dame Joan Howard, D.B.E.

Roberts, Dame Shelagh Marjorie, D.B.E.

Robertson, *Commandant* Dame Nancy Margaret, D.B.E.

Roe, Dame Raigh Edith, D.B.E.

Rosebery, Eva, Countess of, D.B.E.

Saunders, Dame Cicely Mary Strode, D.B.E., F.R.C.P.

Scott, Dame Catherine Campbell, D.B.E.

Scott, Dame Margaret, (Dame Catherine Margaret Mary Denton), D.B.E.

Seccombe, Dame Joan Anna Dalziel, D.B.E.

Shepherd, Dame Margaret Alice, D.B.E.

Sherlock, *Prof.* Dame Sheila Patricia Violet, D.B.E., M.D., F.R.C.P.

Sloss, Hon. Dame (Ann) Elizabeth (Oldfield) Butler-, D.B.E.

Smieton, Dame Mary Guillan, D.B.E.

Smith, Lady Abel, D.C.V.O.

Smith, Dame Enid Mary Russell Russell-, D.B.E.

Smith, Dame Margot, D.B.E.

Snagge, Dame Nancy Marion, D.B.E.

Soames, The Lady, D.B.E.

Springman, Dame Ann Marcella, D.B.E.

Stark, Dame Freya (Mrs. Perowne), D.B.E.

Stephens, *Air Commandant* Dame Anne, D.B.E.

Stevenson, Dame Hilda Mabel, D.B.E.

Stewart, Dame Muriel Acadia, D.B.E.

Sutherland, Dame Joan (Mrs. Bonynge), D.B.E.

Tangney, Dame Dorothy Margaret, D.B.E.

Taylor, Dame Jean Elizabeth, D.C.V.O.

Te Atairangikaahu, Arikinui, D.B.E.

Te Kanawa, Dame Kiri Janette (Mrs. Park), D.B.E.

Tilney, Guinevere, Lady, D.B.E.

Tizard, Dame Catherine Anne, D.B.E.

Turner, Dame Eva, D.B.E.

Turner, *Brig.* Dame Margot, D.B.E., R.R.C.

Tylecote, Dame Mabel, D.B.E.

Tyrwhitt, *Brig.* Dame Mary Joan Caroline, D.B.E., T.D.

Uatioa, Dame Mere, D.B.E.

Uvarov, Dame Olga, D.B.E.

Van Praagh, Dame Peggy, D.B.E.

Varley, Dame Joan Fleetwood, D.B.E.

Vaughan, Dame Janet Maria, (Mrs. Gourlay), D.B.E., F.R.S.

Wakehurst, Margaret, Lady, D.B.E.

Walker, Dame Susan Armour, D.B.E.

Wall, (Alice) Anne, (Mrs. Michael Wall), D.C.V.O.

Warburton, Dame Anne Marion, D.C.V.O., C.M.G.

Wedega, Dame Alice, D.B.E.

Wedgwood, Dame (Cicely) Veronica, O.M., D.B.E.

Welsh, Dame (Ruth) Mary (Eldridge), D.B.E., T.D.

Weston, Dame Margaret Kate, D.B.E.

Whateley, Dame Leslie Violet, D.B.E., T.D.

Williamson, Dame (Elsie) Marjorie, D.B.E., Ph.D.

Winner, Dame Albertine Louise, D.B.E., M.D.

Woollcombe, Dame Jocelyn May, D.B.E.

Wormald, Dame Ethel May, D.B.E.

Yarwood, Dame Elizabeth Ann, D.B.E.

Yonge, Dame (Ida) Felicity (Ann), D.B.E.

THE VICTORIA CROSS, V.C.

For Conspicuous Bravery

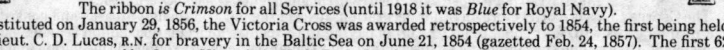

The ribbon *is Crimson* for all Services (until 1918 it was *Blue* for Royal Navy).

Instituted on January 29, 1856, the Victoria Cross was awarded retrospectively to 1854, the first being held by Lieut. C. D. Lucas, R.N. for bravery in the Baltic Sea on June 21, 1854 (gazetted Feb. 24, 1857). The first 62 Crosses were presented by Queen Victoria in Hyde Park, London, on June 26, 1857.

The V.C. is worn before all other decorations, on the left breast, and consists of a cross-pattée of bronze, 1½ inches in diameter, with the Royal Crown surmounted by a lion in the centre, and beneath there is the inscription "For Valour." Holders of the V.C. receive a tax-free annuity of £100, irrespective of need or other conditions. In 1911, the right to receive the Cross was extended to Indian soldiers, and in 1920 a Royal Warrant extended the right to Matrons, Sisters and Nurses, and the Staff of the Nursing Services and other services pertaining to Hospitals and Nursing, and to Civilians of either sex regularly or temporarily under the orders, direction or supervision of the Naval, Military, or Air Forces of the Crown.

Surviving Recipients of the Victoria Cross

Agansing Rai, *Havildar* (Gurkha Rifles), *World War* 1944

Ali Haidar, *Jemadar* (Frontier Force Rifles), *World War* 1945

Anderson, *Lt.-Col.* C. G. W., M.C. (Australian M.F.), *World War*......................1942

Annand, *Capt.* R. W. (Durham L.I.), *World War* 1940

Bhanbhagta Gurung, *Capt.* (2nd Gurkha Rifles), *World War*.........................1945

Bhandari Ram, *Capt.* (Baluch R.), *World War* ..1944

Burton, *Corpl.* R. H. (Duke of Wellington's R.), *World War* 1944

Campbell, *Brigadier* L. M., D.S.O., O.B.E., T.D. (A. & S. Highrs.), *World War*...........1943

Carne, *Col.* J. P., D.S.O. (Glos. R.), *Korea* 1951

Chapman, *Sergt.* E. T., B.E.M. (Monmouthshire R.), *World War* 1945

Cheshire, *Group Capt.* G. L., D.S.O., D.F.C. (R.A.F.), *World War* 1944

Cruickshank, *Fl. Lt.* J. A. (R.A.F.V.R.), *World War* 1944

Crutchley, *Admiral* Sir Victor Alexander, K.C.B., D.S.C. (R.N.), *Gt. War* 1918

Currie, *Maj.* D. V., C.B.E. (S. Alberta R., Canada), *World War* 1944

Cutler, Sir A. R., K.C.M.G., K.C.V.O., C.B.E. (Australia), *World War* 1941

Dean, *Col.* D. J., O.B.E. (R. W. Kent R.), *Gt. War* 1918

De L'Isle, *Maj.* The Viscount, K.G., P.C., G.C.M.G., G.C.V.O. (*Hon.* W. P. Sidney) (Gren. Gds.), *World War* 1944

Eardley, *Sergt.* G. H., M.M. (K.S.L.I.), *World War* 1944

Elliott, *Lt.* the Rev. K. (N.Z.M.F.), *World War* ..1942

Ervine-Andrews, *Lt.-Col.* H. M. (E. Lancs. R.), *World War* 1940

Foote, *Maj.-Gen.* H. R. B., C.B., D.S.O. (R. Tank R.), *World War* 1942

Foote, Rev. J. W. (Canada), *World War* 1942

Fraser, *Cdr.* I. E., D.S.C. (R.N.R.), *World War* ..1945

Ganju Lama, *Jemadar*, M.M. (Gurkha Rifles), *World War* 1944

Gardner, *Capt.* P. J., M.C. (R.T.R.), *World War* ..1941

Ghale, *Subedar* Gaje (Gurkha Rifles), *World War*...1943

Gian Singh, *Jemadar* (Punjab R.), *World War* ..1945

Gordon, *W.O. II* J. H. (Australia), *World War* 1941

Gould, *Lt.* T. W. (R.N.), *World War* 1942

Hinton, *Sergt.* J. D. (N.Z.M.F.), *World War* 1941

Jackson, *W.O.* N. C. (R.A.F.V.R.), *World War*...1944

Jamieson, *Maj.* D. A. (R. Norfolk R.), *World War* 1944

Joynt, *Lt.-Col.* W. D. (Aust. I. F.), *Gt. War* 1918

Kenna, *Pte.* E. (Australian M.F.), *World War* ..1945

Kenneally, *C.-Q.-M.-S.* J. P. (Irish Gds.), *World War* 1943

Lachiman Gurung, *Rifleman* (Gurkha Rifles), *World War* 1945

Laurent, *Lt.* H. J. (N.Z. Rif. Bgde.), *Gt. War* 1918

Learoyd, *Wing-Cmdr.* R. A. B. (R.A.F.), *World War* 1940

Magennis, *L/S* J. J. (R.N.), *World War* 1945

Mahony, *Lt.-Col.* J. K., C.D. (Westminster R., Canada), *World War* 1944

Merritt, *Lt.-Col.* C. C. I., C.D. (S. Saskatchewan R.), *World War* 1942

Moon, *Lt.* Rupert V. (Aust. Inf.), *Gt. War* 1917

Norton, *Capt.* G. R., M.M. (S.A.M.F.), *World War* 1944

Parkash Singh, *Maj.* (Punjab R.), *World War* ..1943

Payne, *W.O.* K. (Australian Army), *Vietnam* ...1969

Place, *Rear-Adm.* B. C. G., C.B., D.S.C. (R.N.), *World War* 1943

Porteous, *Brig.* P. A. (R.A.), *World War* 1942

Rambahadur Limbu, *Lt.* (Gurkha Rifles), *Sarawak* 1965

Rattey, *Sergt.* R. R. (Australia), *World War* 1945

Reid, *Fl.-Lt.* W. (R.A.F.V.R.), *World War* 1943

Rutherford, *Capt.* C. S., M.C., M.M. (Quebec R.), *Gt. War* 1918

Ryder, *Capt.* R. E. D. (R.N.), *World War* 1942

THE GEORGE CROSS, G.C. (1940)

FOR GALLANTRY

The ribbon is *dark blue* threaded through a bar adorned with laurel leaves.

INSTITUTED *September, 24th,* 1940 (with amendments, *November 3rd,* 1942).

The George Cross is worn before all other decorations (except the V.C.) on the left breast § and consists of a plain silver cross with four equal limbs, the cross having in the centre a circular medallion bearing a design showing St. George and the Dragon. The inscription "For Gallantry" appears round the medallion and in the angle of each limb of the cross is the Royal cypher "G VI" forming a circle concentric with the medallion. The reverse is plain and bears the name of the recipient and the date of the award. The cross is suspended by a ring from a bar adorned with laurel leaves on dark blue ribbon 1½ inches wide.

The cross is intended primarily for civilians and awards to the fighting services are confined to actions for which purely military honours are not normally granted. It is awarded only for acts of the greatest heroism or of the most conspicuous courage in circumstances of extreme danger. From April 1, 1965, holders of the Cross have received a tax-free annuity of £100.

§ When worn by a woman it may be worn on the left shoulder from a ribbon of the same width and colour fashioned into a bow.

Empire Gallantry Medal.—The Royal Warrant which ordained that the grant of the Empire Gallantry Medal should cease authorized holders of that medal to return it to the Central Chancery of the Orders of Knighthood and to receive in exchange the George Cross. A similar provision applied to posthumous awards of the Empire Gallantry Medal made after the outbreak of war in 1939.

In October 1971 all surviving holders of the Albert Medal and the Edward Medal exchanged those decorations for the George Cross.

THE DISTINGUISHED SERVICE ORDER (1886)—D.S.O.

Ribbon, Red, with Blue Edges.

Bestowed in recognition of especial services in action of commissioned officers in the Navy, Army and Royal Air Force and (1942) Mercantile Marine. The members are Companions only and rank immediately before the 4th Class of the Royal Victorian Order. A Bar may be awarded for any additional act of service.

PRINCIPAL DECORATIONS AND MEDALS (in order of Precedence)

Victoria Cross.—1856.—V.C.

George Cross.—1940.—G.C.

British Orders of Knighthood, Etc. (For D.S.O. *see* p. 300).

Royal Red Cross.—1883—R.R.C. (Class I).—For ladies.

Distinguished Service Cross.—1914.—D.S.C.—In substitution for the Conspicuous Service Cross, 1901; is for officers of R.N. below the rank of Captain, and Warrant Officers.

Military Cross.—Dec. 1914.—M.C.—Awarded to Captains, Lieutenants, and Warrant Officers (Cl I. and II.) in the Army and Indian and Colonial Forces.

Distinguished Flying Cross.—1918.—D.F.C.—For Bestowal upon Officers and Warrant Officers in the Royal Air Force (and Fleet Air Arm from April 9, 1941) for acts of gallantry when flying in active operations against the enemy.

Air Force Cross.—1918.—A.F.C.—Instituted as preceding but for acts of courage or devotion to duty when flying, although not in active operations against the enemy (extended to Fleet Air Arm since April 9, 1941).

Royal Red Cross (Class II—A.R.R.C.).

Order of British India.

Kaisar-i-Hind Medal.

Order of St. John.

Albert Medal.—1866.—A.M.—"For Gallantry in Saving Life at Sea" or "on Land." (Holders receive £100 tax-free annuity).

Union of South Africa Queen's Medal for Bravery, in Gold.

Medal for Distinguished Conduct in the Field.—1854.—D.C.M.—Awarded to warrant officers, non-commissioned officers and men of the Army and R.A.F.

Conspicuous Gallantry Medal.—1874.—C.G.M.—Is bestowed upon warrant officers and men of the R.N. and since 1942 of Mercantile Marine and R.A.F.

The George Medal.—G.M.—Established by King George VI in 1940 is a recognition of acts of gallantry.

The Edward Medal.—1907.—In recognition of heroic acts by miners or quarrymen, or of others who have endangered their lives in rescuing those so employed. (Holders receive £100 tax-free annuity.)

Royal West African Frontier Force Distinguished Conduct Medal.

King's African Rifles Distinguished Conduct Medal.

Union of South Africa Queen's Medal for Bravery in Silver.

Distinguished Service Medal.—1914.—D.S.M.—For chief petty officers, petty officers, men, and boys of all branches of the Royal Navy, and since 1942 of Mercantile Marine, to non-commissioned officers and men of the Royal Marines, and to all other persons holding corresponding positions in Her Majesty's Service afloat.

Military Medal.—1916.—M.M.—For warrant and non-commissioned officers and men and serving women.

Distinguished Flying Medal.—1918.—D.F.M.—and the Air Force Medal.—A.F.M.—For warrant and non-commissioned officers and men for equivalent services as for D.F.C. and A.F.C. (extended to Fleet Air Arm, April 9, 1941).

Constabulary Medal (Ireland).

Medal for Saving Life at Sea.

Colonial Police Medal for Gallantry (C.P.M.)

Queen's Gallantry Medal.—1974.

British Empire Medal.—B.E.M.—(formerly the Medal of the Order of the British Empire, for Meritorious Service; also includes the Medal of the Order awarded before Dec. 29, 1922).

Queen's Police (Q.P.M.) and Fire Services Medals for Distinguished Service, (Q.F.S.M.).

Queen's Medal for Chiefs.

War Medals and Stars (in order of date).

Polar Medals (in order of date).

Royal Victorian Medal (Gold, Silver and Bronze).

Imperial Service Medal.

Police Medals for Valuable Service.

Badge of Honour.

Jubilee, Coronation and Durbar Medals.

King George V, King George VI and Queen Elizabeth II Long and Faithful Service Medals.

Medal for Meritorious Service.

Long Service and Good Conduct Medal.

Naval Long Service and Good Conduct Medal.

Royal Marine Meritorious Service Medal.

Royal Air Force Meritorious Service Medal.

Royal Air Force Long Service and Good Conduct Medal.

Royal West African Frontier Force Long Service and Good Conduct Medal.

King's African Rifles Long Service and Good Conduct Medal.

Police and Fire Brigade Long Service and Good Conduct Medal.

Colonial Police and Fire Brigades Long Service Medal.

Colonial Prison Service Medal.

Army Emergency Reserve Decoration.—E.R.D.

Volunteer Officer's Decoration.—V.D.

Volunteer Long Service Medal.

Volunteer Officer's Decoration (for India and the Colonies).

Volunteer Long Service Medal (for India and the Colonies).

Colonial Auxiliary Forces Long Service Medal.

Medal for Good Shooting (Naval).

Militia Long Service Medal.

Imperial Yeomanry Long Service Medal.

Territorial Decoration.—1908.—T.D.

Efficiency Decoration.—E.D.

Territorial Efficiency Medal.

Efficiency Medal.

Special Reserve Long Service and Good Conduct Medal.

Decoration for Officers, Royal Navy Reserve.—1910.—R.D.

Decoration for Officers, R.N.V.R.—V.R.D.

Royal Naval Reserve Long Service and Good Conduct Medal.

R.N.V.R. Long Service and Good Conduct Medal.

Royal Naval Auxiliary Sick Berth Reserve Long Service and Good Conduct Medal.

Royal Fleet Reserve Long Service and Good Conduct Medal.

Royal Naval Wireless Auxiliary Reserve Long Service and Good Conduct Medal.

Air Efficiency Award.—1942.—A.E.

The Queen's Medal.—(For Champion Shots in the Army, T.A. and R.A.F.).

Cadet Forces Medal.—1950.

Coast Life Saving Corps Long Service Medal.—1911.

Special Constabulary Long Service Medal.

Royal Observer Corps Medal.

Civil Defence Long Service Medal.

Service Medal of the Order of St. John.

Badge of the Order of the League of Mercy.

Voluntary Medical Service Medal.—1932.

Women's Royal Voluntary Service Medal.

Colonial Special Constabulary Medal.

Foreign Orders, Decorations and Medals (in order of date).

THE UNITED KINGDOM CONSTITUTION

The United Kingdom constitution is not contained in any single document but has evolved in the course of time, formed partly by statute, partly by common law and partly by convention. A constitutional monarchy, the United Kingdom is governed by Ministers of the Crown in the name of the Sovereign, who is head both of the state and the government.

The organs of government are the *legislature* (Parliament), the *executive* and the *judiciary*. The executive consists of Her Majesty's Government (Cabinet and other Ministers), government departments (*see* pp. 369–449), local authorities (*see* Index), and public corporations operating nationalised industries or social or cultural services (*see* pp. 369–449). The judiciary, *i.e.* judges, pronounce on the law, both written and unwritten, interpret statutes and are responsible for the enforcement of the law; the judiciary is independent of both the legislature and the executive (*see* Law Courts and Offices).

THE MONARCHY

The Sovereign personifies the state and is, in law, an integral part of the legislature, head of the executive, head of the judiciary, the Commander-in-Chief of all armed forces of the Crown and the 'Supreme Governor' of the Church of England. The seat of the monarchy is in the United Kingdom. In the Channel Islands and the Isle of Man, which are Crown dependencies, the Sovereign is represented by a Lieutenant-Governor: in the member states of the Commonwealth of which the Sovereign is head of state, her representative is a Governor-General (*see also* p. 693): in United Kingdom dependencies the Sovereign is usually represented by a Governor, who is responsible to the British Government.

Although the powers of the monarchy are now very limited, restricted mainly to the advisory and ceremonial, there are important acts of government which require the participation of the Sovereign. These include summoning, proroguing and dissolving Parliament, giving Royal Assent to Bills passed by Parliament, appointing important office-holders, *e.g.* government ministers, judges, bishops, and governors, conferring peerages, knighthoods and other honours, and granting pardon to a person wrongly convicted of a crime. An important function is appointing a Prime Minister, by convention the leader of the political party which enjoys, or can secure, a majority of votes in the House of Commons. In international affairs the Sovereign as head of State has the power to declare war and make peace, to recognise foreign states and governments, to conclude treaties and to annex or cede territory. However, as the Sovereign entrusts executive power to Ministers of the Crown and acts on the advice of her Ministers, which she cannot ignore, in practice royal prerogative powers are exercised by Ministers, who are responsible to Parliament.

Ministerial responsibility does not diminish the Sovereign's importance to the smooth working of government. She holds meetings of the Privy Council, gives audiences to her Ministers and other officials at home and overseas, receives accounts of Cabinet decisions, reads dispatches and signs state papers; she must be informed and consulted on every aspect of national life; and she must show complete impartiality.

In the event of the Sovereign's absence abroad, it is necessary to appoint *Counsellors of State* under Letters Patent to carry out the chief functions of the Monarch, including the holding of Privy Councils and giving Royal Assent to Acts passed by Parliament. The normal procedure is to appoint as Counsellors three or four members of the Royal Family among those remaining in the United Kingdom. In the event of the Sovereign on accession being under the age of eighteen years, or at any time unavailable or incapacitated by infirmity of mind or body for the performance of the royal functions, provision is made for a Regency.

THE PRIVY COUNCIL

The Sovereign in Council, or Privy Council, was the chief source of executive power until the system of Cabinet government developed. Now its main function is to advise the Sovereign to approve Orders in Council and to advise on the issue of royal proclamations. The Council's own statutory responsibilities (independent of the powers of the Sovereign in Council) include powers of supervision over the registering bodies for the medical and allied professions. A full Council is summoned only on the death of the Sovereign or when the Sovereign announces his or her intention to marry (for full list of Counsellors, *see* pp. 258–259).

There are a number of advisory Privy Council committees, whose meetings the Sovereign does not attend. Some are prerogative committees, such as those dealing with legislative matters submitted by the legislatures of the Channel Islands and the Isle of Man or with applications for charters of incorporation; and some are provided for by statute, *e.g.* those for the universities of Oxford and Cambridge and the Scottish universities.

The Judicial Committee of the Privy Council is the final court of appeal from courts of the United Kingdom dependencies, courts of independent Commonwealth countries which have retained the right of appeal, courts of the Channel Islands and the Isle of Man, some professional and disciplinary committees and church sources. The Committee is composed of all Privy Counsellors who hold, or have held, high judicial office, although usually only three or five hear each case.

Administrative work is carried out by the Privy Council Office under the direction of the Lord President of the Council, a Cabinet Minister.

PARLIAMENT

Parliament is the supreme law-making authority and can legislate for the United Kingdom as a whole or for any parts of it separately (the Channel Islands and the Isle of Man are Crown dependencies and not part of the United Kingdom). The main functions of Parliament are to pass laws, to provide (by voting taxation) the means of carrying on the work of government and to scrutinise government policy and administration, particularly proposals for expenditure. By custom, Parliament is also consulted before the ratification of international treaties and agreements.

Parliament emerged during the late thirteenth and early fourteenth centuries. The nucleus of early Parliaments were the officers of the King's household and the King's judges, joined by such ecclesiastical and lay magnates as the King might summon, and occasionally by the knights of the shires, burgesses and proctors of the lower clergy. By the end of Edward III's reign a "House of Commons" was beginning to appear: the first known Speaker was elected in 1377.

Parliamentary procedure is based on custom and precedent, partly formulated in the Standing Orders of both Houses (*see* p. 308), and each House has the right to control its own internal proceedings and to commit for contempt. The system of debate in the two Houses is similar; when a subject has been moved and seconded, the Speaker proposes the question as the subject of a debate. Members speak from wherever they have been sitting. Questions are decided by a vote on a simple majority. Draft legislation is introduced, in either House, as a public Bill. Public Bills can be introduced by a Government Minister or a private Member, but in practice the majority of Bills which become law are introduced by the Government. To become law, a Bill must be passed by each House (for parliamentary stages, *see* Bill, p. 306) and then sent to the Sovereign for the Royal Assent, after receipt of which it becomes an Act of Parliament.

Proceedings of both Houses are public, except on extremely rare occasions. The minutes (called Votes and Proceedings in the Commons, and Minutes of Proceedings in the Lords) and the speeches (The Official Report of Parliamentary Debates, *Hansard*) are published daily. Proceedings are also recorded for sound transmission on radio and television; a Parliamentary Sound Archive has been established. In January 1985, the House of Lords started a 6-month experiment of allowing television cameras into its debates.

By the Parliament Act of 1911, the maximum duration of a Parliament is five years, if not previously dissolved, the term being reckoned from the date given on the writs for the new Parliament. The maximum life has been prolonged by legislation in such rare circumstances as the two world wars (Jan. 31, 1911–Nov. 25, 1918: Nov. 26, 1935–June 15, 1945). Dissolution and writs for a general election are ordered by the Queen on the advice of the Prime Minister. The life of a Parliament is divided into *sessions*, usually of one year in length, beginning and ending most often in October or November.

THE HOUSE OF LORDS

The House of Lords consists of the Lords Spiritual and Temporal. The Lords Spiritual are the Archbishops of Canterbury and York, the Bishops of London, Durham and Winchester, and the 21 senior diocesan Bishops of the Church of England. The Lords Temporal consist of all hereditary Peers and Peeresses of England, Scotland, Great Britain and the United Kingdom who have not disclaimed their Peerages, Life Peers and Peeresses, and those Lords of Appeal in Ordinary created Life Peers (Law Lords). Disclaimants of an hereditary Peerage lose their right to sit

in the House of Lords but gain the right to vote at Parliamentary elections and to offer themselves for election to the House of Commons. (*See also* p. 226). Peers who do not wish to attend sittings of the House of Lords may apply for leave of absence for the duration of a Parliament.

Until the beginning of this century the House of Lords had considerable power, being able to vote any Bill submitted to it by the House of Commons, but those powers were greatly reduced by the Parliament Act of 1911 and subsequently by the Parliament Act of 1949 (*see* **Parliament Acts 1911 and 1949**, p. 307).

Combined with its legislative role, the House of Lords has judicial powers as the ultimate Court of Appeal for Courts in Great Britain and Northern Ireland, except for criminal cases in Scotland. These powers are exercised by the Lord Chancellor and the Law Lords.

Members of the House of Lords are unpaid. However, they are entitled to reimbursement of travelling expenses on parliamentary business within the U.K. and certain other expenses incurred for the purpose of attendence at sittings of the House, within a maximum for each day of £43·00 for overnight subsistence, £18·00 for day subsistence and incidental travel, and £18·00 for secretarial costs, postage and certain additional expenses.

The House is presided over by the Lord Chancellor, who is *ex officio* Speaker of the House. A panel of deputy Speakers is appointed by Royal Commission. The first deputy Speaker is the Lord Chairman of Committees, appointed at the beginning of each session, a salaried officer of the House who takes the chair in Committee of the whole House and in some Select Committees. He is assisted by a panel of Deputy Chairmen, headed by the salaried Principal Deputy Chairman of Committees, who is also Chairman of the European Communities Committee of the House. The permanent officers include the Clerk of the Parliament and other Clerks who, with other officers of the House, are collectively known as the Parliament Office; the Gentleman-Usher of the Black Rod, who is also Serjeant at Arms in attendence upon the Lord Chancellor and is responsible for security and for accommodation and services in the House of Lords; and the Yeoman Usher who is Deputy Serjeant at Arms and assists Black Rod in his duties.

OFFICERS OF THE HOUSE OF LORDS

Speaker, The Rt. Hon. Quintin McGarel Hogg, C.H., Lord Hailsham of St. Marylebone.
   Private Secretary, M. H. Collon.
Chairman of Committees, The Rt. Hon. Lord Aberdare, K.B.E. £29,320
Principal Deputy Chairman of Committees, The Rt. Hon. Baroness Llewelyn-Davies of Hastoe £26,340

Clerk of the Parliaments, J. C. Sainty £45,500
*Clerk Assistant and Principal Clerk, Public
   Bills,* J. E. Grey, C.B. £36,500
Reading Clerk and Clerk of the Journals,
   M. A. J. Wheeler-Booth £30,865
Counsel to Chairman of Committees, D. Rippengal, C.B., Q.C. £36,500
Second Counsel, K. Newman, C.B. £30,865
Assistant Counsel, G. A. Preston ... £22,329–£26,898
Principal Clerks, J. A. Vallance White (*Judicial Office and Fourth Clerk at the Table*);
   J. M. Davies (*Private Bills and Overseas
   Offices*); P. D. G. Hayter (*Committees*) £30,865
Chief Clerks, C. A. J. Mitchell; M. G. Pownall;
   B. P. Keith .... £22,329–£26,898
Senior Clerks, D. R. Beamish (*Seconded as
   Secretary to the Leader of the House and
   Chief Whip*); R. H. Walters, D.Phil.; D. F.
   Slater; Miss F. M. MacLeod ..... £14,873–£19,728
Clerk of the Records, H. S. Cobb, F.S.A.
   .... £22,329–£26,898
Deputy Clerk of the Records, D. J. Johnson,
   F.S.A. .... £18,416–£22,662

Assistant Clerks of the Records, J. C. Morgan
   (*Sound Archives*); S. K. Ellison .. £13,431–£19,728
Accountant, E. W. Field .... £14,873–£24,291
Assistant Accountant, C. Preece ... £12,345–£15,166
Judicial Taxing Clerk, C. G. Osborne
   .... £12,345–£15,166
Librarian, R. H. V. C. Morgan ..... £22,329–£26,898
Deputy Librarian, D. L. Jones...... £18,416–£22,662
Library Clerks, P. G. Davis, PH.D.; Miss E. M.
   McInnes....................... £13,431–£19,728
Examiners of Petitions for Private Bills,
   H. M. Barclay; J. M. Davies.
Gentleman-Usher of the Black Rod and Serjeant-at-Arms, Air Chief Marshal Sir John
   Gingell, G.B.E., K.C.B. £29,095
*Yeoman Usher of the Black Rod and Deputy
   Serjeant-at-Arms,* Brigadier D. M. Stileman, O.B.E. .... £14,062–£18,627
Staff Superintendent, Maj. F. P. Horsfall, M.B.E.
Shorthand Writer, Mrs. E. M. C. Holland   fees
Editor, Official Report (Hansard), Mrs.
   M. E. E. C. Villiers £23,251
Asst. do. W. Frensham.................... £19,151

THE HOUSE OF COMMONS

The Members of the House of Commons are elected by universal adult suffrage. For electoral purposes, the United Kingdom is divided into constituencies, each of which returns one Member to the House of Commons, the Member being the candidate who obtains the largest number of votes cast in the constituency. To ensure equitable representation the four Boundary Commissions keep constituency boundaries under review and recommend any redistribution of seats which may seem necessary due to population movements, etc. The number of seats was raised to 640 in 1945, then reduced to 625 in 1948, and subsequently rose to 630 in 1955, 635 in 1970 and 650 in 1983. Of the present 650 seats there are 523 for England, 38 for Wales, 72 for Scotland and 17 for Northern Ireland. Elections are by secret ballot, each elector casting one vote: voting is not compulsory. When a seat becomes vacant between General Elections, a by-election is held.

British subjects and citizens of the Irish Republic can stand for election as Members of Parliament (M.P.s) provided they are 21 or over and not subject to disqualification. Those disqualified from sitting in the House include undischarged bankrupts, people sentenced to more than one year's imprisonment, clergy of the Church of England, Church of Scotland, Church of Ireland and Roman Catholic Church, peers, and holders of certain offices listed in the House of Commons Disqualification Act 1975 (*e.g.* members of the judiciary, Civil Service, regular armed forces, police forces, some local government officers and some members of public corporations and government commissions). A candidate does not require any party backing but his or her nomination for election must be supported by the signatures of ten people registered in the constituency. A candidate must also deposit with the returning officer £150, which is forfeit if the candidate does not receive more than 12·5 per cent of the votes cast. (The Representation of the People Bill, 1984–85, which was due to become law as the Almanack went to press, raises the deposit to £500 and lowers the forfeiture limit to 5 per cent of votes cast.) All election expenses, except the candidate's personal expenses, are subject to a statutory limit of £2,700, plus 2·3 pence for each elector in a borough constituency or 3·1 pence for each elector in a county constituency. (*See* pp. 312–319 for an alphabetical list of M.P.s, pp. 320–345 for the results of the last General Election and subsequent by-elections).

The week's business of the House is outlined each Thursday by the Leader of the House, after consultation between the Chief Government Whip and the Chief Opposition Whip. About the half of the time will be taken up by the Government's legislative programme, and the rest by other business, e.g. question time. As a rule Bills likely to raise political controversy are introduced in the Commons before going on to the Lords, and the Commons claims exclusive control in respect of national taxation and expenditure, and in respect of local rates and charges upon them. Bills such as the Finance Bill, which imposes taxation, and the Consolidated Fund Bills, which authorise expenditure, must begin in the Commons. A Bill of which the financial provisions are subsidiary may begin in the Lords; and the Commons may waive their rights in regard to Lords' amendments affecting finance.

The Commons has a public register of M.P.s financial, and certain other, interests. Members must also disclose any relevant financial interest or benefit in a matter before the House when taking part in a debate, in any other proceedings of the House or in consultations with other Members, with Ministers or civil servants.

Since 1911 Members of the House of Commons have received payments and travelling facilities; they are entitled to claim income tax relief on expenses incurred in the course of their Parliamentary duties. Salary rates since 1911 as follows:

	p.a.			p.a.
1911	£400	1978 June		£6,897
1937	600	1978 June		9,450
1946	1,000	1980 June		11,750
1957	1,750	1981 June		13,950
1964	3,250	1982 June		14,510
1972 Jan	4,500	1983 June		15,308
1975 June	5,750	1984 Jan		16,106
1976 June	6,062	1985 Jan		16,904
1977 July	6,270			

In October 1969 Members were granted an allowance for secretarial and research expenses.

	p.a.			p.a.
1969 Oct	£500	1979 June		£4,600
1972 Jan	1,000	1980 Feb		6,750
1974 Aug	1,750	1980 Aug		8,000
1975 June	3,200	1981 June		8,480
1976 June	3,512	1982 June		8,820
1977 June	3,687	1983 June		12,000
1978 June	4,200	1984 June		12,546

Also, since January 1972, Members can claim reimbursement for the additional cost of staying overnight away from their main residence while on Parliamentary business.

	p.a.			p.a.
1972	£750	1979 July		£3,866
1974 Aug	1,050	1980 Aug		4,903
1975 July	1,814	1981 Aug		5,206
1976 July	2,038	1982 Aug		5,674
1977 July	2,534	1983 Aug		6,163
1978 July	3,046	1984 Aug		6,696

From March 1980 provision was made enabling each Member in receipt of Secretarial and Research Allowance to contribute sums to an approved pension scheme for the provision of a pension, or other benefits, for or in respect of persons whose salary is met by him.

To 31 March 1981	£786 p.a.
1982	838
1983	875
1984	1,136
1985	1,254

The cost of travel allowances for 1984/85 was stated in June 1985 to be £3,920,685 (car mileage claims £2,630,000, rail travel £458,540 and air travel £399,888, spouse/children travel £275,008, extended travel within U.K. £49,374, and secretarial travel £106,975).

The Ministerial Salaries and Members' Pensions Act 1965 established a contributory pension fund providing pensions for former Members of Parliament and for dependents of deceased former Members. The Fund was reconstituted and the scheme restructured to bring it into line with pension schemes in the public sector by the Parliamentary and Other Pensions Acts 1972: further Acts modifying the arrangements for Members, Ministers and certain officeholders are the Parliamentary and Other Pensions and Salaries Act 1976; the Parliamentary Pensions Act 1978; the House of Commons Members' Fund and Parliamentary Pensions Act 1981 and the Parliamentary Pensions. etc., Act 1984. The arrangements now provide a pension of one-fiftieth of salary for each year of pensionable service with a maximum of 2/3rds of salary at age 65. Pension is normally payable at age 65, for men and women, or on later retirement. Pensions may be paid earlier e.g. on ill-health retirement. The widow of a former Member receives a pension of one-half her late husband's pension. Pensions are index-linked. Members contribute 9 per cent of salary to the pension fund: there is an Exchequer contribution, currently just over three times the amount contributed by Members, but under review.

The House of Commons Members' Fund provides for annual or lump sum grants to ex-Members, their widows and children whose incomes are below certain limits. Alternatively, payments of £1,282 per annum to ex-Members with at least ten years service and who left the House of Commons before October 1964 and £641 per annum to their widows are made as of right. Members contribute £24 per annum and the Exchequer £115,000 per annum to the Fund. The income of the Fund in 1983–84 was £210,094 and estimated expenditure on grants and payments was £162,159. The net assets of the Fund as at September 30, 1984 amounted to £954,738.

The House of Commons is presided over by the Speaker, who has considerable powers to maintain order in the House. His deputy, the Chairman of Ways and Means, and two Deputy Chairmen, all of whom may preside over sittings of the House of Commons, are elected by the House; they, like the Speaker, neither speak nor vote other than in their official capacity. The staff of the House are employed by a Commission chaired by the Speaker. The Clerk of the House of Commons, the Serjeant at Arms and the other Heads of Departments (see below) are permanent officers of the House, not M.P.s. The Clerk of the House is the principal adviser to the Speaker on the privileges and procedures of the House and his department's responsibilities relate to the conduct of the business of the House and its Committees. The Serjeant at Arms, who attends upon the Speaker on ceremonial occasions, is responsible for security and for accommodation and services in the Commons part of the building.

OFFICERS AND OFFICIALS OF THE HOUSE OF COMMONS

Speaker, The Rt. Hon. Bernard Weatherill, M.P. for Croydon North East £40,340
Chairman of Ways and Means, The Rt. Hon. Harold Walker, M.P. for Doncaster Central £30,410
First Deputy Chairman of Ways and Means, The Rt. Hon. Ernest Armstrong, M.P. for Durham North West £27,920
Second Deputy Chairman of Ways and Means, Sir Paul Dean, M.P. for Woodspring £27,920

Offices of the Speaker and Chairman of Ways and Means

Speaker's Secretary, W. A. Beaumont, O.B.E., A.E.
  £22,329–£26,898
Speaker's Counsel, H. Knorpel, C.B.; G. E. Gammie, C.B. £30,865
Chaplain to the Speaker, The Rev. Canon T. Beeson.
Staff Inspector, H. W. Bunkell ..... £14,873–£19,728

Department of the Clerk of the House

Clerk of the House of Commons, K. A. Bradshaw, C.B. £45,500
Clerk Asst., C. J. Boulton, C.B. £36,500
Clerk of Committees, D. A. M. Pring, C.B., M.C. £36,500
Principal Clerks—
  Public Bills, J. H. Willcox £30,865
  Select Committees, R. S. Lankester £30,865
  Table Office, D. W. Limon £30,865
  Private Bills, H. M. Barclay £30,865
  Journals, M. T. Ryle £30,865
  Overseas Office, J. F. Sweetman, T.D. £30,865
  Standing Committees, A. A. Barrett £28,274
  Second Clerk, Select Committees, C. B. Winnifrith £28,274
  Financial Committees, W. R. McKay £28,274
Deputy Principal Clerks, J. R. Rose; A. J. Hastings; R. J. Willoughby; S. A. L. Panton; R. B. Sands; G. Cubie; M. R. Jack, PH.D.; D. G. Millar; Mrs. J. Sharpe; Ms. A. Milner-Barry; R. W. G. Wilson; W. A. Proctor; F. A. Cranmer; C. R. M. Ward, PH.D.; Ms. H. E. Irwin; D. W. N. Doig
  £22,329–£26,898
Senior Clerks, R. J. Rogers; A. Sandall; M. Litt; M. H. Cooper, PH.D.; D. L. Natzler; D. J. Cairncross; E. P. Silk; Mrs. S. A. de Ste. Croix; A. R. Kennon; D. W. Robson; L. C. Laurence Smyth; A. R. Gren; D. F. Harrison; S. J. Priestley; C. P. R. Bennett; A. H. Doherty; P. A. Evans; R. I. S. Phillips; P. D. Brittain (*acting*) J. Hallowell (*acting*); .... £13,649–£17,906
Examiners of Private Bills, H. M. Barclay; J. M. Davies.
Taxing Officer, H. M. Barclay.

Department of the Serjeant at Arms

Serjeant at Arms, Major G. V. S. Le Fanu ... £30,865
Deputy Serjeant at Arms, Major P. N. W. Jennings .... £22,329–£26,898
Assistant Serjeant at Arms, M. J. A. Cummins .... £19,169–£22,988
Deputy Assistant Serjeant at Arms, P. A. J. Wright .... £15,821–£19,728

Department of the Library

Librarian, D. Menhennet, D.Phil £30,865
Deputy Librarian, D. J. T. Englefield
  £22,329–£26,898

Library and Information Service

Assistant Librarians, H. J. Palmer; G. F. Lock .... £22,329–£25,265
Deputy Assistant Librarians, J. B. Poole, Ph.D.; Miss J. B. Tanfield; S. Z. Young; Mrs. H. R. Coates; Miss P. J. Baines; K. G. Cuninghame; Mrs. J. M. Wainwright; Mrs. C. B. Andrews .... £18,416–£22,662
Senior Library Clerks, Miss E. K. Andrews, D.PHIL.; Mrs. B. L. Miller; Mrs. J. M. Lourie; Mrs. F. Poole; Mrs. J. M. Fiddick; C. C. Pond, PH.D.; C. R. Barclay; Mrs. C. M. Gillie; Miss C. E. Nield; R. C. Clements; R. J. Ware, D.Phil; Ms. D. Gore, PH.D; R. J. Twigger; B. K. Winetrobe; T. N. Edmonds; R. J. Cracknell; Mrs. G. L. Allen (*temp.*)
  £11,682–£19,728

Vote Office

Deliverer of the Vote, G. R. Russell . £17,653–£24,291
Deputy Deliverer of the Vote, H. C. Foster
  £12,345–£16,274

Administration Department

Head of Administration Department, A. C. J. Poole £30,865
Accountant, J. L. G. Dobson ..... £22,329–£26,898
Deputy Accountant, A. J. Lewis.... £18,365–£24,291
Senior Assistant Accountant, G. P. Brown (*temp.*) .... £17,653–£20,799
Assistant Accountants, G. P. Brown; F. W. Brewer; A. R. Marskell; M. J. Barram; A. C. Langford, M.B.E. (*temp.*); Miss M. M. McColl (*temp.*) .... £12,345–£17,546

Head of Establishments Office (vacant)
                                    £22,329–£26,246
Deputy Head of Establishments Office, J. A.
    Robb .... £18,365–£24,291
Assistant Head of Establishments Office, D. J.
    Mouat .... £12,345–£16,926
Computer Development Officer, R. S. Morgan
                                    £20,434–£26,246

Department of the Official Report

Editor, K. S. Morgan .... £25,488–£26,898
Deputy Editor, L. R. Johns £20,894
Principal Assistant Editors, R. V. Hadlow; J.
    Gourley £19,599

Senior Assistant Editors, F. G. Brotherston;
    C. R. G. Watson £19,599
Assistant Editor, P. Walker .... £17,653–£18,946
Deputy Assistant Editors, E. Holland; I.
    Church £18,046

Refreshment Department

General Manager, W. J. J. Smillie £24,129
Deputy General Manager, E. J. Nash
                                    £14,873–£19,728
Catering Accountant, D. R. W. Wood
                                    £14,873–£19,728

PARLIAMENTARY INFORMATION
The following is a short glossary of aspects of work of Parliament:
(*Unless otherwise stated, references are to* House of Commons *procedures*.)

Adjournment Debate.—Usually a half-hour debate introduced by a backbencher at the end of business for the day. The subjects raised are often local or personal issues.

Bill.—Proposed legislation is termed a *Bill*. The stages of a Public Bill in the House of Commons are as follows:

First Reading: There is no debate at this stage, which nowadays merely constitutes an order to have the Bill printed.

Second Reading: The debate on the principle of the Bill.

Committee Stage: The detailed examination of a Bill, clause by clause. In most cases this takes place in a *Standing Committee*, or the whole House may act as a Committee. Rarely, a Bill may be examined by a *Select Committee* (*see* below).

Report Stage: Detailed review of a Bill as amended in Committee.

Third Reading: Final debate on a Bill.

Public Bills go through the same stages in the House of Lords, except that in almost all cases the Committee Stage is taken in the Committee of the Whole House.

Some Public Bills may start in the House of Lords, in which case the Lords stages are taken first.

Both Houses have to agree the same text of a Bill, so that the *Amendments* made by the second House are then considered in the originating House and if not agreed, sent back or themselves amended, until agreement is reached.

Chiltern Hundreds.—A legal fiction, a nominal office of profit under the Crown, the acceptance of which requires a Member to vacate his seat. The Manor of Northstead is similar. These are the only means by which an M.P. may resign.

Closure & Guillotine.—To prevent deliberate waste of time of either house, a motion may be made that the question be now put. In the House of Commons, if the Speaker decides that the rights of a minority are not being prejudiced and 100 members support the motion, it is put to the vote immediately, and, if carried, the original motion is put to the House, without further debate. The *Guillotine* represents a more rigorous and systematic application of the Closure. Under this system, a Bill proceeds in accordance with a rigid timetable and discussion is limited to the time allotted to each group of clauses. The Closure is possible in the House of Lords, but is hardly ever used. There is, however, no procedure for a guillotine. The completion of business in the Lords is traditionally ensured by mutual agreement from all sides of the House.

Consolidated Fund Bill.—A Bill to authorize issue of sums to maintain Government service. The Bill is dealt with without debate, but afterwards members may raise topics of public or local importance.

Delegated Legislation.—This consists, principally, of Statutory Instruments within the meaning of the Statutory Instruments Act 1946. These fall into three broad categories:—(i) "Affirmative Instruments", which are subject to approval by resolutions of both Houses before they can come into or remain in force; (ii) "Negative Instruments", which are subject to annulment by resolution of either House; and (iii) "General Instruments", which include those not required to be laid before Parliament and those which are required to be so laid but are not subject to approval or annulment. There are in addition Special Procedure Orders, which are another form of delegated legislation, subject to procedures which allow time for petitions to be lodged against them.

Dissolution.—Parliament comes to an end either by Dissolution by the Sovereign or the expiration of the term of five years for which the House of Commons was elected. Dissolution is normally effected by a Royal Proclamation.

Early Day Motion.—A motion put on the Order Paper by an M.P. without in general the real prospect of its being debated. Such motions are expressions of backbench opinion.

Emergency Debate.—In the Commons a method of obtaining prompt discussion of a matter of urgency is by moving the adjournment under Standing Order No. 10 for the purpose of discussing a specific and important matter that should have urgent consideration. A member may ask leave to make this motion by giving written notice to the Speaker, usually before 12 noon, and if the Speaker considers the matter of sufficient importance and it obtains the support of 40 members, it is discussed usually at 7 p.m. on the following day.

Father of the House.—The Member whose continuous service in the House of Commons, is the longest. The present Father of the House is the Rt. Hon. James Callaghan, elected first in 1945.

General Synod Measure.—A measure passed by the national assembly of the Church of England under the Church of England Assembly (Powers) Act 1919. These measures are considered by the Ecclesiastical Committee, who make a report, and are then considered by both Houses, and if approved, sent for the Royal Assent.

Hansard.—The official report of debates in both Houses (and in Standing Committees) published by H.M.S.O., normally on the day after the sitting concerned.

Hours of Meeting.—The House of Commons meets on Monday, Tuesday, Wednesday and Thursday at 2.30 p.m., and on Friday at 9.30 a.m. The House of Lords normally meets during the Session at 2.30 p.m. on Monday, Tuesday and Wednesday and at 3 p.m. on Thursday. In the latter part of the Session, the House sometimes sits on Fridays at 11 a.m.

Hybridity.—A Public Bill which is considered to affect specific private or local interests, as distinct from *all* such interests of a single category, is called a Hybrid Bill and is subject to a special form of scrutiny.

Leader of the Opposition.—In 1937 the office of Leader of the Opposition was recognized and a salary of £2,000 per annum was assigned to the post, thus following a practice which had prevailed in the Dominion of Canada since 1906. In Jan. 1985 the salary was £40,310. The present Leader of the Opposition is the Rt. Hon. Neil Kinnock.

The Lord Chancellor.—The Lord High Chancellor of Great Britain is (*ex officio*) the Speaker of the House of Lords. Unlike the Speaker of the House of Commons, he is a member of the Government, and takes part in debates and votes in divisions. He has none of the powers to maintain order that the Speaker in the Commons has, these powers being exercised in the Lords by the House as a whole. The Lord Chancellor sits in the Lords on one of the *Woolsacks*, couches covered with red cloth and stuffed with wool. If he wishes to address the House in any way except formally as Speaker, he leaves the Woolsack and steps towards his place as a peer.

Naming.—When a member has been named, *i.e.* contrary to the practice of the House called by surname and not addressed as the "Hon. Member for ... (his constituency)", the Leader of the House moves that he "be suspended from the service of the House" for (in the case of a first offence) a period of a week. The period of suspension is increased, should the member offend again.

Opposition Day.—A day on which the topic for debate is chosen by the Opposition. There are 20 such days in a normal session. On 17 days, subjects are chosen by the Leader of the Opposition; on the remaining three days by the leader of the next largest opposition party.

Parliament Acts 1911 and 1949.—Under these Acts certain Bills may become law without the consent of the Lords.

Since at least the 18th century the Commons have had the privilege of having bills concerned with supply (*i.e.* taxation and money matters) passed without amendment by the Lords; though until 1911 the Lords retained the right to reject such bills outright.

By the Parliament Act 1911 a Bill which has been endorsed by the Speaker of the House of Commons as a Money Bill and has been passed by the Commons and sent up to the Lords at least one month before the end of a session can become law without the consent of the Lords if it is not passed by them without amendment within a month.

Under the Parliament Act 1911 and 1949, if the Lords reject any other Public Bill (except those dealing with certain subjects such as the prolongation of Parliament) which has been passed by the Commons in two successive sessions then that Bill shall (unless the Commons direct to the contrary) become law without the consent of the Lords.

The effect of the Parliament Acts is therefore that the Lords have power to delay a Public Bill for thirteen months from its first Second Reading in the House of Commons.

Prime Minister's Questions.—The Prime Minister answers questions from 3.15 to 3.30 pm on Tuesdays and Thursdays. Nowadays the "open question" predominates. Members ask the Prime Minister what are his or her official engagements for the day or whether an official visit will be made to such and such a place. A supplementary question on virtually any topic can then be put.

Private Bill.—A Bill promoted by a body or an individual to give powers additional to, or in conflict with, the general law, and to which a separate procedure applies.

Private Members' Bill.—A Public Bill promoted by a Member who is not a member of H.M. Government.

Private Notice Question.—A question adjudged of urgent importance on submission to Mr. Speaker, answered at the end of oral questions—usually at 3.30 p.m.

Privilege.—The following are covered by the privilege of Parliament: (i) freedom from interference in going to, attending at, and going from, Parliament; (ii) freedom of speech; (iii) the printing and publishing of anything relating to the proceedings of the two Houses is subject to privilege; (iv) each House is the guardian of its dignity and may punish any insult to the House as a whole.

Prorogation.—The bringing to an end, by the Sovereign on the advice of the Government, of a Session of Parliament. All Public Bills which have not completed their stages lapse on Prorogation.

Queen's Speech.—The Speech delivered by H.M. The Queen at the State Opening of Parliament, in which the Government's programme for the year is set forth. The Speech is, of course, drafted for and approved by the Cabinet.

Question Time.—Oral questions are answered in the Commons from 2.30 to 3.30 pm every day except Friday. They are also taken at the start of the Lords sittings, with a daily limit of four oral questions.

Royal Assent.—The Royal Assent is signified by Letters Patent to such Bills and Measures as have passed both Houses of Parliament (or Bills which have been passed under the Parliament Acts 1911 and 1949). The Sovereign has not given Royal Assent in person since 1854. On occasion, for instance in the Prorogation of Parliament, Royal Assent may be pronounced to the two Houses by Lords Commissioners; but more usually Royal Assent is notified to each House sitting separately in accordance with the Royal Assent Act 1967. The Norman formulae for Royal Assent are then endorsed on the Acts by the Clerk of the Parliaments.

The power to withold assent (colloquially known as the Royal Veto) resides with the Sovereign, but has not been exercised in the United Kingdom since 1707, in the reign of Queen Anne.

Select Committees consisting usually of 10–15 members of all parties are a means used by both Houses in order to investigate certain matters.

Most Select Committees in the House of Commons are now tied to Departments—each Committee investigates subjects within a Government Department's remit. At the time of going to press these were: Agriculture, Defence, Education Science and Arts, Employment, Energy, Environment, Foreign Affairs, Home Affairs, Scottish Affairs, Social Services, Trade and Industry, Transport, Treasury and Civil Service, Welsh Affairs.

There are other House of Commons Select Committees dealing with Public Accounts (*i.e.* the spending by H.M. Government of money voted by Parliament), European Legislation and Statutory Instruments, and also domestic committees dealing, for example, with Privilege and Services. Public Select Committees usually take evidence in public: their evidence and reports are published by H.M. Stationery Office.

The principal Select Committee in the House of Lords is that on the European Communities, which has, at present, seven sub-committees dealing with all areas of community policy. The House of Lords also has a Select Committee on Science and Technology, which appoints sub-committees to deal with specific subjects. In addition, *ad hoc* Select Committees have been set up from time to time to investigate specific subjects, *e.g.* Unemployment, Overseas Trade. There are also some Joint Committees of the two Houses, *e.g.* the Joint Committee on Statutory Instruments.

The Speaker.—The Speaker of the House of Commons is the spokesman and president of the Chamber. He is elected by the House at the beginning of each Parliament or when the previous Speaker retires or dies. He neither speaks in debates nor votes in divisions except when the voting is equal. His position in the precedence of the Kingdom is high, only the Prime Minister and the Lord President of the Council (when not peers) among Commoners going before him. He takes precedence of all Lords, except the two Archbishops and the Lord Chancellor, and Speakers are almost invariably raised to the Peerage on vacating their office.

Standing Orders.—Rules which have from time to time been agreed by each House of Parliament to regulate the conduct of its business. These orders are not irrevocable, may be revised, amended or repealed, and are from time to time suspended or dispensed with.

State Opening.—This marks the start of each new Parliament or new session of Parliament. Parliament is normally opened, in the presence of both Houses, by the Queen in person, who makes the Speech from the Throne which outlines the Government's policies for the coming session (*see* Queen's Speech). In the absence of the Queen, Parliament is opened by Royal Commission, and the Queen's Speech is read by one of the Lords Commissioner specially appointed by Letters Patent for the occasion.

Strangers.—Anyone who is not a Member or Officer of the House is a *stranger*. Visitors are generally admitted to debates of both Houses but may be excluded if the House so decides. In practice this happens only in time of war.

Ten Minute Rule.—A colloquial term for Standing Order No. 15, under which backbenchers have an opportunity on Tuesdays and Wednesdays to introduce a bill and speak in its favour for about ten minutes. Time is also available for a short opposing speech.

Vacant Seats.—When a vacancy occurs in the House of Commons during a session of Parliament the Writ for the by-election is moved, by a Whip of the party to whom the member whose seat has been vacated belonged. If the House is in recess, the Speaker can issue a warrant for a writ, should two members certify to him that a seat is vacant.

Whips.—In order to secure the attendance of Members of a particular party in Parliament on all occasions, and particularly on the occasion of an important division, Whips (originally known as "Whippers-in") are appointed for the purpose. The written appeal or circular letter issued by them is also known as a "whip", its urgency being denoted by the number of times it is underlined. Neglect to respond to a three-lined whip, headed "Most important", is tantamount in the Commons to secession (at any rate temporarily) from the party. Whips are officially recognized by Parliament and are provided with office accommodation in both Houses. In the House of Commons, Government and some Opposition Whips receive salaries from public funds.

PUBLIC INFORMATION SERVICE.—Enquiries from the general public and organizations of all kinds about the work, composition and history of the House of Commons are answered by the Public Information Office, House of Commons, S.W.1 (01-219 4272). This office also edits the House of Commons Weekly Information Bulletin (published by H.M. Stationery Office). The Journal and Information Office, House of Lords, S.W.1 (01-219 3107) answers queries relating to the procedure and practice of the Lords.

HER MAJESTY'S GOVERNMENT

Her Majesty's Government is the body of Ministers responsible for the administration of national affairs, determining policy and introducing into Parliament any legislation necessary to give effect to government policy. The majority of Ministers are members of the House of Commons but members of the House of Lords may also hold Ministerial responsibility, and certain offices, *e.g.* Lord Chancellor, are always held by members of the House of Lords. The Prime Minister is, by recent convention, always a member of the House of Commons.

THE PRIME MINISTER

The office of Prime Minister, which had been in existence for nearly 200 years, was officially recognised in 1905 and its holder was granted a place in the Table of Precedence. The Prime Minister, by tradition also First Lord of the Treasury and Minister for the Civil Service, is appointed by the Sovereign and is usually the leader of the party which enjoys, or can secure, a majority in the House of Commons. Other Ministers are appointed by the Sovereign on the recommendation of the Prime Minister, who also allocates functions amongst Ministers and has the

power to obtain their resignation or dismissal individually.

The Prime Minister informs the Sovereign of state and political matters, advises on the dissolution of Parliament, and makes recommendations for important Crown appointments, the award of honours, etc.

As the chairman of Cabinet meetings and leader of a political party, the Prime Minister is responsible for translating party policy into government activity: and as leader of the Government the Prime Minister is responsible to Parliament and to the electorate for the policies and their implementation.

The Prime Minister also represents the nation in international affairs, *e.g.* summit conferences.

THE CABINET

The Cabinet developed during the 18th century as an inner committee of the Privy Council, which was the chief source of executive power until that time. It is composed of about 20 Ministers chosen by the Prime Minister, usually the heads of government departments (known as Secretaries of State or Ministers unless they have a special title, *e.g.* Chancellor of the Exchequer) and the holders of various traditional offices. Ministers of State can be given a seat in the Cabinet.

The Cabinet's functions are the final determination of policy, control of government and co-ordination of government departments. The exercise of its functions is dependent upon enjoying majority support in the House of Commons. Cabinet meetings are held in private, taking place once or twice a week during parliamentary sittings and less often during a recess. Proceedings are confidential, the members being bound by their oath as Privy Counsellors not to disclose information about the proceedings.

The convention of collective responsibility means that the Cabinet acts unanimously even when Cabinet Ministers do not all agree on a subject. The policies of departmental Ministers must be consistent with the policies of the Government as a whole, and once the Government's policy has been decided, each Minister is expected to support it or resign.

The convention of Ministerial responsibility holds a Minister, as the political head of his or her department, accountable to Parliament for the department's work. Departmental Ministers usually decide all matters within their responsibility, although on matters of political importance they normally consult their colleagues collectively. A decision by a departmental Minister is binding on the Government as a whole.

HER MAJESTY'S MINISTRY
(*See* also "Occurrences during Printing")
THE CABINET

Prime Minister, First Lord of the Treasury and Minister for the Civil Service, THE RT. HON. MARGARET HILDA THATCHER, M.P., F.R.S, *born* Oct. 13, 1925.

Secretary of State for the Home Department, The Rt. Hon. Leon Brittan, Q.C., M.P., *born* Sept. 25, 1939.

Lord High Chancellor, The Rt. Hon. Lord Hailsham of St. Marylebone, C.H., *born* Oct. 9, 1907.

Secretary of State for Foreign and Commonwealth Affairs, The Rt. Hon. Sir Richard Edward Geoffrey Howe, Q.C., M.P., *born* Dec. 20, 1926.

Chancellor of the Exchequer, The Rt. Hon. Nigel Lawson, M.P., *born* March 11, 1932.

Secretary of State for Trade and Industry and President of the Board of Trade, The Rt. Hon. Norman Beresford Tebbit, M.P., *born* March 29, 1931.

Secretary of State for Defence, The Rt. Hon. Michael Ray Dibdin Heseltine, M.P., *born* March 21, 1933.

Lord Privy Seal and Leader of the House of Commons, The Rt. Hon. (William) John Biffen, M.P., *born* Nov. 3, 1930.

Secretary of State for Employment, The Rt. Hon. Thomas Jeremy King, M.P., *born* June 13, 1933.

Lord President of the Council and Leader of the House of Lords, The Viscount Whitelaw, P.C., C.H., M.C., *born* June 28, 1918.

Minister of Agriculture, Fisheries and Food, The Rt. Hon. Thomas Michael Jopling, M.P., *born* Dec. 10, 1930.

Secretary of State for the Environment, The Rt. Hon. Charles Patrick Fleeming Jenkin, M.P., *born* Sept. 7, 1926.

Secretary of State for Scotland, The Rt. Hon. George Kenneth Hotson Younger, T.D., M.P., *born* Sept. 22, 1931.

Secretary of State for Wales, The Rt. Hon. Roger Nicholas Edwards, M.P., *born* Feb. 25, 1934.

Secretary of State for Northern Ireland, The Rt. Hon. Douglas Richard Hurd, C.B.E., M.P., *born* March 8, 1930.

Secretary of State for Social Services, The Rt. Hon. Peter Norman Fowler, M.P., *born* Feb. 2, 1938.

Secretary of State for Energy, The Rt. Hon. Peter Edward Walker, M.B.E., M.P., *born* March 25, 1932.

Secretary of State for Education and Science, The Rt. Hon. Sir Keith Sinjohn Joseph, Bt., M.P., *born* Jan. 17, 1918.

Chief Secretary to the Treasury, The Rt. Hon. Peter Wynford Innes Rees, Q.C., M.P., *born* Dec. 9, 1926.

Secretary of State for Transport, The Rt. Hon. Nicholas Ridley, M.P., *born* Feb 17, 1929.

Chancellor of the Duchy of Lancaster, The Earl of Gowrie, P.C., *born* Nov. 26, 1939 (*Minister for the Arts*).

Minister Without Portfolio, The Lord Young of Graffham, P.C., *born* Feb. 27, 1932.

LAW OFFICERS

Attorney-General, The Rt. Hon. Sir Robert Michael Oldfield Havers, Q.C., M.P., *born* 1923.

Lord Advocate, The Lord Cameron of Lochbroom, P.C., Q.C.

Solicitor-General, Sir Patrick Barnabas Burke Mayhew, Q.C., M.P., *born* 1929.

Solicitor-General for Scotland, Peter Lovat Fraser, Q.C., M.P., *born* 1945.

MINISTERS NOT IN THE CABINET

Parliamentary Secretary to the Treasury, The Rt. Hon. John Wakeham, M.P., *born* 1932.

Economic Secretary to the Treasury, Ian Stewart, M.P., *born* 1935.

Financial Secretary to the Treasury, John Edward Michael Moore, M.P., *born* 1937.

Paymaster General, John Selwyn Gummer, M.P., *born* 1939.

Ministers of State:

Agriculture, Fisheries and Food, John Roddick Russell MacGregor, M.P., O.B.E., *born* 1937; The Lord Belstead, P.C., *born* 1932.

Defence, John Paul Stanley, M.P., *born* 1942 (*Armed Forces*); The Rt. Hon. Adam Courtauld Butler, M.P., *born* 1931 (*Procurement*).

Employment, Hon. Peter Hugh Morrison, M.P., *born* 1944.

Environment, The Lord Elton, T.D., *born* 1930.

Energy, The Rt. Hon. Alick Laidlaw Buchanan-Smith, M.P., *born* 1932.

Foreign and Commonwealth Office, The Baroness Young, P.C., *born* 1926; Malcolm Leslie Rifkind, M.P., *born* 1946; Richard Napier Luce, M.P., *born* 1936; The Rt. Hon. Timothy Hugh Francis Raison, M.P., *born* 1929 (*Minister for Overseas Development*).

Health, The Rt. Hon. Kenneth Harry Clarke, Q.C., M.P., *born* 1940.

Home Office, Giles Shaw, M.P., *born* 1931; The Lord Glenarthur, *born* 1944; David Waddington, Q.C., M.P., *born* 1929.

Housing and Construction, Ian Gow, M.P., T.D., *born* 1937.
Industry, Norman Stewart Hughson Lamont, M.P., *born* 1942.
Information Technology, Geoffrey Edwin Pattie, M.P., *born* 1936.
Local Government, Rt. Hon. Kenneth Wilfred Baker, M.P., *born* 1934.
Northern Ireland Office, Dr. Rhodes Boyson, M.P., *born* 1925.
Scottish Office, The Lord Gray of Contin, P.C., *born* 1927.
Social Security, Anthony Harold Newton, O.B.E., M.P., *born* 1937.
Trade, The Rt. Hon. Paul Channon, M.P., *born* 1935.
Transport, Mrs. Lynda Chalker, M.P., *born* 1942.
Treasury, Barney Hayhoe, M.P., *born* 1925.
Welsh Office, John Stradling Thomas, *born* 1925.

PARLIAMENTARY UNDER SECRETARIES, ETC.

Agriculture, Fisheries and Food, Mrs. P. Fenner, M.P.
Defence, The Lord Trefgarne; J. Lee, M.P.
Education and Science, R. Dunn, M.P.; Hon. P. Brooke, M.P.
Employment, P. Bottomley, M.P.; Hon. A. Clark, M.P.
Energy, A. Goodlad, M.P.; D. Hunt, M.P.; P. G. Malone, M.P.
Environment, Sir George Young, Bt., M.P.; N. Mac-Farlane, M.P.; Hon. W. Waldegrave, M.P.
Foreign and Commonwealth Affairs, T. Renton, M.P.
Health and Social Security, R. Whitney, O.B.E., M.P.; J. Patten, M.P.; The Baroness Trumpington.
Home Office, D. Mellor, M.P.
Northern Ireland Office, N. P. Scott, M.B.E., M.P.; C. Patten, M.P; The Lord Lyell.
Scottish Office, M. Ancram, M.P.; J. A. Stewart, M.P.; J. MacKay, M.P.
Trade and Industry, A. Fletcher, M.P.; J. Butcher, M.P.; D. Trippier, M.P.; The Lord Lucas of Chilworth.
Transport, D. Mitchell, M.P.; M. Spicer, M.P.
Treasury, Lords Commissioners, The Hon. D. Thompson, M.P.; The Hon. I. Lang, M.P.; The Hon. T. Garel-Jones, M.P.; The Hon. A. Hamilton, M.P.
Welsh Office, I. W. P. Roberts, M.P.

GOVERNMENT WHIPS

The Government Whips in the House of Lords are: The Captain of the Honourable Corps of the Gentlemen at Arms (Lord Denham), the Captain of the Queen's Bodyguard of the Yeoman of the Guard (Earl of Swinton), the political Lords in Waiting (Viscount Long, Lord Skelmersdale, The Lord Brabazon of Tara, Earl of Caithness).

The Government Whips in the House of Commons are: *Chief Whip*, the Parliamentary Secretary to the Treasury (Rt. Hon. J. Wakeham): *Deputy Chief Whip*, the Treasurer, H.M. Household (J. Cope); the Comptroller, H.M. Household (C. Mather): the Vice-Chamberlain, H.M. Household (R. Boscawen); Lords Commissioners (D. Thompson, I. Lang, T. Garel-Jones, Hon. A. Hamilton, J. Major): *Assistant Whips*, Hon. T. Sainsbury, M. Neubert, T. Durant, P. Lloyd, Hon. M. Lennox-Boyd.

GOVERNMENT BY PARTY

Before the reign of William and Mary the principal Officers of State were chosen by and were responsible to the Sovereign alone and not to Parliament or the nation at large. Such officers acted sometimes in concert with one another, but more often independently, and the fall of one did not, of necessity, involve that of others, although all were liable to be dismissed at any moment.

In 1693 the Earl of Sunderland recommended to William III the advisability of selecting a Ministry from the political party which enjoyed a majority in the House of Commons and the first united Ministry was drawn in 1696 from the Whigs, to which party the King owed his throne, the principal members being Russell (the Admiral), Somers (the Advocate), Lord Wharton and Charles Montague (afterwards Chancellor of the Exchequer). This group became known as the *Junto* and was regarded with suspicion as a novelty in the political life of the nation, being a small section meeting in secret apart from the main body of Ministers. It may be regarded as the forerunner of the *Cabinet* and in course of time it led to the establishment of the principle of joint responsibility of Ministers, so that internal disagreement caused a change of personnel or resignation of the whole body of Ministers.

The accession of George I, who was unfamiliar with the English language, led to a disinclination on the part of the Sovereign to preside at meetings of his Ministers and caused the appearance of a *Prime Minister*, a position first acquired by Robert Walpole in 1721 and retained without interruption for 20 years and 326 days.

In 1828 the old party of the Whigs became known as *Liberals*, a name originally given to it by its opponents to imply laxity of principles, but gradually accepted by the party to indicate its claim to be pioneers and champions of political reform and progressive legislation. In 1861 a Liberal Registration Association was founded and Liberal Associations became widespread. As the outcome of a conference at Birmingham in 1877 a National Liberal Federation was formed, with headquarters in London. The Liberal Party was in power for long periods during the second half of the nineteenth century in spite of the set-back during the Home Rule crisis of 1886, which resulted in the secession of the Liberal Unionists, and for several years during the first quarter of the twentieth century, but after a further split into National and Independent Liberals it numbered only 59 in all after the General Election of 1929, with a further fall to 12 (excluding National Liberals) after the 1945 Election.

Soon after the change from Whig to Liberal the Tory Party became known as *Conservative*, a name traditionally believed to have been invented by John Wilson Croker in 1830 and to have been generally adopted about the time of the passing of the Reform Act of 1832 to indicate that the preservation of national institutions was the leading principle of the party. After the Home Rule crisis of 1886 the dissentient Liberals entered into a compact with the Conservatives, under which the latter undertook not to contest their seats, but a separate *Liberal Unionist* organization was maintained until 1912, when it was united with the Conservatives.

The Labour Party.—Labour candidates for Parliament made their first appearance at the General Election of 1892, when there were 27 standing as "Labour" or "Liberal-Labour."

In 1900 the *Labour Representation Committee* was set up in order to establish a distinct Labour Group in Parliament, with its own whips, its own policy, and a readiness to co-operate with any party which might be engaged in promoting legislation in the direct interest of labour. In 1906 the L.R.C. became known as *The Labour Party*.

Social Democratic Party.—The Council for Social Democracy was announced by four former Labour Cabinet Ministers—Roy Jenkins, David Owen, William Rodgers and Mrs. Shirley Williams—on Jan. 25, 1981. Subsequently a number of sitting Labour Members of Parliament, together with one Conservative, crossed the floor of the Commons to join the new group, and on March 26, 1981 the Social Democratic Party was launched in London, followed by eight regional launches. Later in the year the S.D.P. and the Liberal Party formed an electoral *Alliance*, though each party decides its own policy and maintains its own party organisation.

The government of the day is formed by the party which wins the largest number of seats in the House of Commons at a General Election, or which has the support of a majority of members in the House of Commons. By tradition, the leader of the majority party is asked by the Sovereign to form a government, while the largest minority party becomes the official Opposition with its own leader and own "Shadow Cabinet". Leaders of the Government and Opposition sit on the front benches of the Commons with their supporters (the back-benchers) sitting behind them.

When a party is in Opposition and its leadership becomes vacant, it makes its free choice among the various personalities available; but if the party is in office, the Sovereign's choice may anticipate, and in a certain sense forestall, the decision of the party.

POLITICAL PARTIES

CONSERVATIVE AND UNIONIST PARTY, Central Office, 32 Smith Square, SW1P 3HH.—*Party Chairman*, J. S. Gummer, M.P.; *Vice Chairmen*, T. Arnold, M.P.; H. Miller, M.P.; J. Spicer, M.P.; Miss E. Nicholson; Sir Geoffrey Finsberg, M.B.E., M.P.; Lord Marshall of Leeds; *Hon. Treasurer*, Lord McAlpine of West Green; *Dir. of Organisation*, Sir Anthony Garner.

SCOTTISH CONSERVATIVE PARTY, Central Office, 3 Chester Street, Edinburgh EH3 7RF.—*Chairman*, Sir James Goold; *Deputy Chairman*, Dr. A. Smith, C.B.E.; *Dir.*, W. Henderson.

LABOUR PARTY, 150 Walworth Road, SE17 1JT.— *Chairman*, A. Hadden; *Vice-Chairman*, N. Hough; *Treasurer*, S. McLuskie; *Gen. Sec.*, L. Whitty; *Parliamentary Party Leader*, Rt. Hon. N. Kinnock, M.P.; *Deputy Leader*, Rt. Hon. R. Hattersley, M.P.; *Leader of the Labour Peers*, Lord Cledwyn of Penrhos.

SHADOW CABINET, 1984–85.—Rt. Hon. N. Kinnock, M.P. (*Leader of the Opposition*); Rt. Hon. R. Hattersley, M.P. (*Treasury and Economic Affairs*); Rt. Hon. D. Healey, M.P. (*Foreign and Commonwealth Affairs*); Rt. Hon. G. Kaufman, M.P. (*Home Affairs*); Rt. Hon. P. Shore, M.P. (*Leader of the House*); Rt. Hon. J. Smith, M.P. (*Trade and Industry*); Dr. J. Cunningham, M.P. (*Environment*); J. Prescott, M.P. (*Employment*); Hon. Gwyneth Dunwoody, M.P. (*Transport*); D. Davies, M.P. (*Defence*); Rt. Hon. P. Archer, M.P. (*Northern Ireland*); B. Jones, M.P. (*Wales*); D. Dewar, M.P. (*Scotland*); R. Cook, M.P. (*Campaign Co-ordinator*); M. Meacher, M.P. (*Health and Social Security*); G. Radice, M.P. (*Education*); Rt. Hon. S. Orme, M.P. (*Energy*).

Labour Whips in the House of Lords are: *Chief Whip*, Lord Ponsonby of Shulbrede; *Deputy Chief Whip*, Baroness David; Lord John-Mackie, Lord Graham of Edmonton, Lord Stoddart of Swindon, Lord Dean of Beswick, Baroness Nicol. Labour Whips in the House of Commons are: *Chief Whip*, Rt. Hon M. F. L. Cocks (standing down, autumn 1985); *Deputy Chief Whip*, N. Hogg, M.P.; R. Corbett, L. Cunliffe, D. Dixon, J. Hamilton, F. Haynes, J. Home-Robertson, A. McKay, J. McWilliam, A. Mitchell, Dr. R. Thomas.

LIBERAL PARTY, Headquarters, 1 Whitehall Place, SW1A 2HE.—*Chairman*, P. Tyler; *Vice Chairmen*, A. Ellis, O.B.E.; P. Harris; *Hon. Treasurers*, Sir Hugh Jones, L.V.O., A. Jacobs; *Sec. Gen.*, J. Spiller, M.B.E.; *Parliamentary Party Leader*, Rt. Hon. D. Steel, M.P.; *Leader of the Liberal Peers*, Lady Seear, P.C.

The Liberal Whip in the House of Lords is Lord Tordoff. Liberal Whips in the House of Commons are: *Chief Whip*, D. Alton; *Deputy Chief Whip*, M. Meadowcroft.

SCOTTISH LIBERAL PARTY, 4 Clifton Terrace, Edinburgh EH12 5DR.—*Leader*, R. Johnston, M.P.; *President*, Lord Mackie of Benshie; *Chairman*, R. Finnie; *Political Director*, R. Waddell; *Party Sec.*, Mrs. R. Grant.

WELSH LIBERAL PARTY, Dumfries Chambers, 91 St. Mary's Street, Cardiff CF1 1DW.—*Chairman*, N. Phillips; *Vice Chairman*, G. Griffiths; *Hon. Treasurers*, P. Davies, Dr. G. Morrison; *Sec.*, Mrs. L. Scharer.

PLAID CYMRU, 51 Cathedral Road, Cardiff CF1 9HD.—*Chairman*, S. Morgan; *Deputy Chairman*, Janet Davies; *Hon. Treasurer*, J. Dixon; *Sec.*, D. Williams; *Party President*, D. E. Thomas, M.P.; *Vice-President*, D. Iwan.

SCOTTISH NATIONAL PARTY, 6 North Charlotte Street, Edinburgh, EH2 4JH.—*Chairman*, G. Wilson, M.P.; *Senior Vice-Chairman*, Mrs. M. Ewing; *Hon. Treasurer*, A. Morgan; *National Sec.*, N. R. McCallum; *Parliamentary Party Leader*, Rt. Hon. D. Stewart, M.P.

SOCIAL DEMOCRATIC PARTY, 4 Cowley Street, SW1P 3NB.—*President*, Rt. Hon. Mrs. S. Williams; *Vice-President*, Rt. Hon. W. Rodgers; *National Sec.*, R. Newby; *Parliamentary Party Leader*, Rt. Hon. Dr. D. Owen, M.P.; *Deputy Leader*, Rt. Hon. R. Jenkins, M.P.

The S.D.P. Whip in the House of Lords is Lord Kilmarnock. The S.D.P. Whip in the House of Commons is J. Cartwright, M.P.

NORTHERN IRELAND

SOCIAL DEMOCRATIC AND LABOUR PARTY, 38 University Street, Belfast BT7 1FZ.—*Chairman*, A. Maginness; *Deputy Chairmen*, M. Boyd, F. McIlvanna; *Hon. Treasurer*, P. Brannigan; *Gen. Sec.*, E. Hanna; *Parliamentary Party Leader*, J. Hume, M.P.; *Deputy Leader*, S. Mallon.

ULSTER DEMOCRATIC UNIONIST PARTY, 296 Albertbridge Road, Belfast BT5 4GW.—*Chairman*, J. McClure; *Deputy Chairman*, S. Gibson; *Hon. Treasurer*, D. Herron; *Sec.*, A. Kane; *Parliamentary Party Leader*, Dr. I. Paisley, M.P.; *Deputy Leader*, P. Robinson, M.P.

ULSTER UNIONIST PARTY, Council Headquarters, 3 Glangall Street, Belfast BT12 5AE.—*Chairman*, Mrs. H. Bradford; *Deputy Chairman*, J. Allen; *Hon. Treasurer*, J. Cunningham; *Sec.*, F. Millar; *Parliamentary Party Leader*, Rt. Hon. J. H. Molyneaux, M.P.

ALPHABETICAL LIST OF MEMBERS OF THE HOUSE OF COMMONS

For abbreviations, *see* page 320.

Maj.

SMALL MAJORITIES

The following M.P.s were returned in June 1983 with majorities of fewer than 500 votes.

THE PRINCIPAL PARTIES IN PARLIAMENT (1931–1983)

General Election	Conservative	Liberal	Labour
1931	471	72 (a)	65 (b)
1935	387	54 (c)	166 (d)
1945	189	25 (e)	396 (f)
1950	298 (g)	9	315 (h)
1951	320 (i)	6	296 (h)
1955	344 (i)	6	277 (j)
1959	365 (i)	6	258 (k)
1964	303 (i)	9	317
1966	253 (i)	12	363 (l)
1970	330 (m)	6	287 (n)
1974 (February) .	296	14	301 (o)
1974 (October) ..	276	13	319 (p)
1979	339	11	268 (q)
1983	397	23 (r)	209 (s)

NOTES.—(a) Liberal National 35 (Simon); Liberal 33 (Samuel); 4 (Lloyd George). (b) National Labour 13 (MacDonald); Labour 52 (Henderson). (c) Liberal National 33; Liberal 21. (d) National Labour 8; Labour 154; I.L.P. 4. (e) Liberal National 13; Liberal

12. (f) Labour 393; I.L.P. 3. (g) Incl. Nat. Liberal. (h) Irish Nationalists (2) and Speaker make total of 625. (i) Including associates. (j) Sinn Fein (2) and Speaker make total of 630. (k) Independent (1) makes total of 630. (l) Republican Labour (1) makes total of 630. (m) Including Ulster Unionists. (n) Scottish Nationalists (1); Independent (5) and Speaker make total of 630. (o) United Ulster Unionist Council (11), Scottish Nationalists (7), Plaid Cymru (2); Social Democratic and Labour Party (1); Social Democrat (1); Independent Labour (1); and Speaker make total of 635. (p) Scottish Nationalists (11); United Ulster Unionist (10); Plaid Cymru (3); Social Democratic and Labour Party (1); Independent (1) and Speaker make a total of 635. (q) Ulster Unionist (5); Democratic Unionist (3); Plaid Cymru (2); Scottish Nationalists (2); Social Democratic and Labour (1); United Ulster Unionist (1); Independent (2) and Speaker make a total of 635. (r) Liberal 17; S.D.P. 6. (s) Official Unionist (11); Democratic Unionist (3); Scottish Nationalists (2); Plaid Cymru (2); Ulster Popular Unionist (1); Social Democratic and Labour Party (1) and Provisional Sinn Fein (1) make a total of 650.

THE HOUSE OF COMMONS BY CONSTITUENCIES, JUNE 1983

The figures following the name of the Constituency denote the total number of *Electors* in the Parliamentary Division at the General Election of June 9, 1983.

ABBREVIATIONS — *C.* = Conservative; *D.U.P.* = Democratic Unionist Party; *Ind.* = Independent; *L./All. S.D.P./ All.* = Liberal and Social Democratic Alliance; *Lab.* = Labour; *O.U.P.* = Official Unionist Party; *P.C.* = Plaid Cymru; *S.D.L.P.* = Social Democratic and Labour Party; *S.F.* = Sinn Fein; *S.N.P.* = Scottish National Party; *U.P.U.P.* = Ulster Popular Unionist Party.

A.B. = Assassin's Bullet; *A.C.I.E.* = Against Cuts In Education; *A.C.M.* = Anti-Common Market; *A.Corr.* = Anti-Corruption; *All.* = Alliance (N.I.); *A.V.* = Anti-Vivisection; *B.B.H.* = Belgrano, Blood, Hunger; *B.E.L.L.S.* = Ban Every Licensing Law Society; *B.N.P.* = British National Party; *C.A.C.M.* = Conservative Against Common Market; *C.B.W.U.* = Campaign for Black and White Unity; *C.D.* = Christian Democrat; *C.F.C.P.* = Conservative For Capital Punishment; *C.M.P.* = Common Market Party; *Com.* = Community; *Comm.* = Communist; *Corn Nat.* = Cornish Nationalist; *C.U.I.* = Council for United Ireland; *Eco.* = Ecology; *Eth. Min.* = Ethnic Minority; *F.A.M.P.* = Freddie's Alternative Medicine Party; *F.D.P.* = Fancy Dress Party; *F.P.* = Feudal Party; *F.W.D.* = Freedom from World Domination; *I.F.P.* = Islington and Finsbury Party; *Ind. Pow.* = Independent Powellite; *I.N.P.* = Irish National Party; *I.W.R.P.* = Isle of White Resident's Party; *J.A.H.C.* = Jesus And His Cross; *J.D.F.* = Justice for Divorced Fathers; *L.A.O.* = Law And Order; *L.I.L.* = Local Independent Labour; *L.M.* = Loony Monster; *Loony Soc.* = Loony Society; *L.T.U.* = Labour and Trade Union; *M.D.P.* = Modern Democratic Party; *M.K.* = Mebyon Kernow; *M.P.P.* = Multiracial Political Party; *N.A.* = Noise Abatement; *Nat. Lab.* = National Labour Party; *N.F.* = National Front; *O.N.C.* = One Nation Conservative; *P.A.L.* = Party of Associates with Licensees; *P.F.A.* = Prosperity For All; *P.R.* = Proportional Representation; *R.A.P.* = Radical and Anti-Parliamentarian; *R.C.C.P.* = Restoration of Capital and Corporal Punishment; *Rev. Comm.* = Revolutionary Communist; *R.H.C.P.* = Reintroduction of Hanging and Corporal Punishment; *S.A.C.A.* = Servicemen's and Citizen's Association; *S.B.I.L.P.* = Southport Back In Lancashire Party; *S.D.B.P.* = Stop Deportation of Black People; *S.E.E.* = Spare the Earth Ecology; *S.P.G.B.* = Socialist Party of Great Britain; *T.E.F.* = Traditional English Food; *T.V.C.A.B.L.* = Tactically Vote Conservative Annihilate Bennites Livingstoneites; *U.P.* = Unemployed Party; *W.C.P.P.P.* = Workers' Charter with Pensioners' Political Power; *W.F.L.O.E.* = Women For Life On Earth; *W.P.* = Workers' Party; *W.P.W.S.* = Workers' Party for a Workers' State; *W.Reg.* = Wessex Regionalist; *Wrld Gv.* = World Government; *W.R.P.* = Workers' Revolutionary Party.

An asterisk * denotes membership of the last House. In the seats where there has been either a minor change or no change at all to the boundary, the 1979 majorities are shown below the 1983 result.

ENGLAND

Aldershot (Hants)
E. 77,593

*J. M. G. Critchley, C.		31,288
N. Westbrook, L/All.		19,070
A. Crawford, Lab.		6,070
C. maj.		12,218

Aldridge-Brownhills
(W. Midlands)
E. 60,803

*R. C. S. Shepherd C.		24,148
R. T. Burford, Lab.		11,864
P. Gunn, S.D.P./All.		11,599
C. maj.		12,284

Altrincham and Sale
(Gtr. Manchester)
E. 65,984

*W. F. Montgomery C.		25,321
B. Clancy, L/All.		14,410
A. Erwin, Lab.		7,684
Mrs. C. Marsh, Eco.		629
L. J. Wolstenholme, Ind.		152
C. Maj.		10,911

Amber Valley (Derbys)
E. 66,720

P. A. C. L. Oppenheim, C.		21,502
D. M. Bookbinder, Lab.		18,184
B. Johnson, L/All.		10,989
P. Griffiths, Ind.		856
C. maj.		3,318

Arundel (W. Sussex)
E. 74,849

*R. M. Marshall, C.		31,096
J. Walsh, L/All.		15,391
G. C. Rees, Lab.		4,302
J. Wadman, C.F.C.P.		1,399
C. maj.		15,705

Ashfield (Notts)
E. 68,791

*D. F. Haynes, Lab.		21,859
R. Seligman, C.		15,772
Mrs. F. Stein, L/All.		13,812
Lab. maj.		6,087

Ashford (Kent)
E. 65,442

*H. K. Speed, R.D., C.		27,230
Mrs. J. Hawkes, S.D.P./All.		13,319
P. Lewis, Lab.		6,167
Dr. C. A. Porter, Eco.		569
J. W. King, Nat. Lab.		456
R. E. Lockwood, B.N.P.		195
C. maj.		13,911
(May '79, C. maj. 13,638)		

Ashton-under-Lyne
(Gtr. Manchester)
E. 58,963

*Rt. Hon. R. E. Sheldon, Lab.		20,987
R. Spring, C.		13,290
J. Adler, S.D.P./All.		7,521
D. Hallsworth, Rev. Comm.		407
Lab. maj.		7,697
(May '79, Lab. maj. 8,379)		

Aylesbury (Bucks)
E. 72,792

*Rt. Hon. T. H. F. Raison, C.		30,230
M. Soole, S.D.P./All.		15,310
M. P. Moran, Lab.		6,364
T. Chapman, Ind.		166
C. maj.		14,920

Banbury (Oxon)
E. 65,324

A. B. Baldry, C.		26,225
K. Fitchett, S.D.P./All.		13,200
J. B. Hodgson, Lab.		9,343
D. N. Brough, Loony Soc.		383
C. maj.		13,025

Barking (Gtr. London)
E. 52,362

*Ms. J. Richardson, Lab.		14,415
H. Summerson, C.		10,389
J. Gibb, L/All.		8,770
I. Newport, N.F.		646
Lab. maj.		4,026

Barnsley (S. Yorks)
CENTRAL E. 55,115

*Rt. Hon. R. Mason, Lab.		21,847
H. Oldfield, C.		7,674
Rev. G. Reid, L./All.		7,011
Lab. maj.		14,173

EAST E. 53,611

T. Patchett, Lab.		23,905
P. Tomlinson, L./All.		6,413
G. England, C.		5,749
Lab. maj.		17,492

WEST AND PENISTONE E. 60,648

*A. McKay, Lab.		22,560
T. Hartley, C.		12,218
J. Evans, S.D.P./All.		9,624
Lab. maj.		10,342

Barrow and Furness (Cumbria)
E. 67,896

C. S. Franks, C.		22,284
*Rt. Hon. A. E. Booth, Lab.		17,707
D. Cottier, S.D.P./All.		11,079
C. maj.		4,577

Basildon (Essex)
E. 69,604

D. A. A. Amess, *C.*	17,516
J. G. H. Fullbrook, *Lab.*	16,137
Miss S. Slipman, *S.D.P./*	
All.	11,634
C. maj.	1,379

Basingstoke (Hants)
E. 71,975

A. R. F. Hunter, *C.*	28,381
*G. E. Hudson Davies,	
S.D.P./All.	15,931
J. McAllister, *Lab.*	10,646
I. Wilson, *B.N.P.*	344
C. maj.	12,450

Bassetlaw (Notts)
E. 65,721

*J. W. Ashton, *Lab.*	22,231
M. Cleasby, *C.*	18,400
B. Withnall, *S.D.P./All.*	8,124
Lab. maj.	3,831

Bath (Avon)
E. 64,325

*C. F. Patten, *C.*	22,544
J. M. Dean, *S.D.P./All.*	17,240
A. J. Pott, *Lab.*	7,259
D. Grimes, *Eco.*	441
R. S. Wardle, *Prog. L.*	319
G. S. Young, *Wrld. Gv.*	67
C. maj.	5,304
(May '79, C. maj. 9,112)	

Batley and Spen (W. Yorks)
E. 73,798

Mrs. E. J. Peacock, *C.*	21,433
*K. J. Woolmer, *Lab.*	20,563
D. S. Woollery, *S.D.P./All.*	11,678
C. Lord, *Eco.*	493
C. maj.	870

Battersea (Gtr. London)
E. 65,938

*A. Dubs, *Lab.*	19,248
R. Allason, *C.*	15,972
M. Harris, *S.D.P./All.*	7,675
M. J. Salt, *N.F.*	539
Mrs. S. Wilmington, *Eco.*	377
T. Jackson, *C.B.W.U.*	86
Mrs. K. Purie-Harwell,	
Com.	22
Lab. maj.	3,276

Beaconsfield (Bucks)
E. 66,168

*T. J. Smith, *C.*	30,552
D. Ive, *L./All.*	12,252
J. S. Smith, *Lab.*	5,107
C. maj.	18,300

Beckenham (Gtr. London)
E. 58,719

*Sir P. C. Goodhart, *C.*	23,606
Mrs. C. Forrest, *L./All.*	10,936
J. P. Dowd, *Lab.*	6,386
G. W. Younger, *B.N.P.*	203
C. maj.	12,670
(May '79, C. maj. 13,751)	

Bedfordshire

MID. *E.* 75,558

*N. W. Lyell, q.c., *C.*	33,042
Mrs. M. Howes, *L./All.*	15,661
J. Tizard, *Lab.*	9,420
C. maj.	17,381

NORTH *E.* 71,491

*T. H. H. Skeet, *C.*	27,969
B. K. Gibbons, *L./All.*	14,120
Miss P. Healy, *Lab.*	11,323
N. J. Hughes, *Ind.*	344
C. maj.	13,849

SOUTH WEST *E.* 76,298

*W. D. Madel, *C.*	31,767
R. Byfield, *S.D.P./All.*	16,036
W. Cochrane, *Lab.*	9,899
C. maj.	15,731

Berwick-upon-Tweed (Nthmb)
E. 53,585

*A. J. Beith, *L./All.*	21,958
J. Brazier, *C.*	13,743
Mrs. V. Baird, *Lab.*	5,975
L./All. maj.	8,215

Bethnal Green and Stepney
(Gtr. London)
E. 55,333

*Rt. Hon. P. D. Shore, *Lab.*	15,740
S. Charters, *L./All.*	9,382
D. Argyropulo, *C.*	4,323
V. J. Clark, *N.F.*	800
J. Rees, *Com.*	243
B. Chadhuri, *Ind.*	214
P. Mahoney, *R.A.P.*	136
Lab. maj.	6,358

Beverley (Humberside)
E. 75,813

*Sir P. H. B. Wall, m.c.,	
v.r.d., *C.*	31,233
M. Pitts, *L./All.*	17,364
E. M. Morley, *Lab.*	6,921
C. maj.	13,869

Bexhill and Battle
(E. Sussex)
E. 61,785

C. F. Wardle, *C.*	30,329
P. Smith, *L./All.*	10,583
I. Pearson, *Lab.*	3,587
Miss. A. Rix, *Eco.*	538
C. maj.	19,746

Bexleyheath
(Gtr. London)
E. 59,263

*C. D. Townsend, *C.*	23,411
B. Standen, *L./All.*	13,153
A. Erlam, *Lab.*	7,560
C. maj.	10,258

Billericay (Essex)
E. 74,779

*K. H. Proctor, *C.*	29,635
E. Bonner, *L./All.*	15,020
S. Sewell, *Lab.*	10,528
C. maj.	14,615

Birkenhead (Merseyside)
E. 67,293

*F. Field, *Lab.*	23,249
T. Peet, *C.*	13,535
G. Lindsay, *L./All.*	9,782
Miss H. Clarke, *Eco.*	337
Lab. maj.	9,714

Birmingham (W. Midlands)

EDGBASTON *E.* 55,063

*Mrs. J. C. J. Knight, m.b.e.,	
C.	19,585
J. Binns, *S.D.P./All.*	8,167
P. A. Bilson, *Lab.*	7,647
J. Hurdley, *Eco.*	516
S. T. Hardwick, *Ind. C.*	293
Ms. P. A. Davies, *Comm.*	169
Miss. D. C. Howlett,	
J.A.H.C.	97
C. maj.	11,418

ERDINGTON *E.* 56,019

R. Corbett, *Lab.*	14,930
D. Moylan, *C.*	14,699
C. Barber, *S.D.P./All.*	7,915
Lab. maj.	231

HALL GREEN *E.* 61,023

*R. E. Eyre, *C.*	21,142
M. H. Willis, *Lab.*	11,769
J. Hemming, *L./All.*	10,175
C. maj.	9,373

HODGE HILL *E.* 61,234

*T. A. G. Davis, *Lab.*	19,692
P. Roe, *C.*	14,600
G. A. Gospill, *L./All.*	6,557
N. Tomkinson, *N.F.*	529
Lab. maj.	5,092

LADYWOOD *E.* 60,441

Ms. C. Short, *Lab.*	19,278
Mrs. P. Le Hunte, *C.*	10,248
K. Hardeman, *L./All.*	7,758
B. Bakhtaura, *S.D.B.P.*	355
R. W. Atkinson, *W.R.P.*	198
Lab. maj.	9,030

NORTHFIELD *E.* 74,326

R. D. King, *C.*	22,596
*J. Spellar, *Lab.*	19,836
D. Webb, *L./All.*	10,045
P. Sheppard, *Comm.*	420
C. maj.	2,760

PERRY BARR *E.* 74,371

*J. W. Rooker, *Lab.*	27,061
M. D. Portillo, *C.*	19,659
C. E. G. Williams, *L./All.*	4,773
Lab. maj.	7,402

SELLY OAK *E.* 71,671

*A. M. Beaumont-Dark, *C.*	23,008
J. Turner, *Lab.*	17,612
K. Wheldall, *S.D.P./All.*	10,613
C. maj.	5,396

SMALL HEATH *E.* 59,376

*Rt. Hon. D. H. Howell,	
Lab.	22,874
P. Nischal, *C.*	7,622
A. Bostock, *S.D.P./All.*	5,722
Lab. maj.	15,252

SPARKBROOK *E.* 53,612
Rt. Hon. R. S. G. Hattersley, Lab. 19,757
P. Douglas-Osborn, *C.* 9,209
O. S. Parmar, *S.D.P./All.* ... 3,416
Ms. F. Eden, *Rev. Comm.* . 305
C. S. A. Chinn, *Ind.* 281
   Lab. maj. 10,548

YARDLEY *E.* 57,707
*A. D. G. Bevan, *C.* 17,986
R. D. Godsiff, *Lab.* 15,121
D. Bennett, *S.D.P./All.* 8,109
R. Jones, *N.F.* 415
   C. maj. 2,865

Bishop Auckland (Durham)
E. 71,142
*D. Foster, *Lab.* 22,750
B. Legg, *C.* 18,444
A. Collinge, *L./All.* 10,070
   Lab. maj. 4,306

Blaby (Leics)
E. 71,930
*Rt. Hon. N. Lawson, *C.* ... 32,689
R. Lustig, *L./All.* 15,573
C. Wrigley, *Lab.* 6,838
P. Gegan, *N.F.* 568
   C. maj. 17,116
   (May '79, C. maj. 20,640)

Blackburn (Lancs)
E. 76,078
*J. W. Straw, *Lab.* 25,400
G. Mather, *C.* 22,345
E. Fairbrother, *S.D.P./All.* . 8,174
D. A. Riley, *N.F.* 864
   Lab. maj. 3,055

Blackpool (Lancs)
NORTH *E.* 57,576
N. A. Miscampbell, Q.C., C. 20,592
C. Heyworth, *L./All.* 10,440
M. J. Hindley, *Lab.* 8,730
A. S. Hanson, *N.F.* 514
   C. maj. 10,152
   (May '79, C. maj. 10,229)

SOUTH *E.* 56,201
*Sir P. A. R. Blaker, *C.* ... 19,852
F. J. Jackson, *Lab.* 9,714
A. Cox, *S.D.P./All.* 9,417
W. Smith, *N.F.* 263
   C. maj. 10,138
   (May '79, C. maj. 8,848)

Blaydon (Tyne & Wear)
E. 65,481
*J. D. McWilliam, *Lab.* ... 21,285
A. Williams, *C.* 14,063
M. Carr, *S.D.P./All.* 12,607
   Lab. maj. 7,222

Blyth Valley (Nthmb)
E. 57,639
*J. Ryman, *Lab.* 16,583
Ms. R. Brownlow, *S.D.P./All.* 13,340
A. Hargreaves, *C.* 11,657
S. Robinson, *Ind.* 406
   Lab. maj. 3,243

Bolsover (Derbys)
E. 64,769
*D. E. Skinner, *Lab.* 26,514
S. Roberts, *C.* 12,666
S. Reddish, *S.D.P./All.* ... 7,886
   Lab. maj. 13,848

Bolton (Gtr. Manchester)
NORTH EAST *E.* 58,918
P. G. Thurnham, *C.* 19,632
*Mrs. W. A. Taylor, *Lab.* .. 17,189
J. Alcock, *S.D.P./All.* 8,311
D. P. Ball, *B.N.P.* 186
T. L. Keen, *Ind.* 104
   C. maj. 2,443

SOUTH EAST *E.* 67,527
*D. W. Young, *Lab.* 23,984
J. Walsh, *C.* 15,231
Mrs. M. Rothwell, *L./All.* .. 10,157
T. L. Keen, *P.R.* 296
   Lab. maj. 8,753

WEST *E.* 67,354
Hon. T. G. Sackville, *C.* .. 23,731
D. Green, *Lab.* 16,579
R. Baker, *S.D.P./All.* 12,321
   C. maj. 7,152

Boothferry (Humberside)
E. 72,370
Sir P. E. O. Bryan, D.S.O., M.C., C. 30,536
A. Ellis, *L./All.* 13,116
T. Geraghty, *Lab.* 9,271
   C. maj. 17,420

Bootle (Merseyside)
E. 75,354
*A. Roberts, *Lab.* 27,282
R. Watson, *C.* 12,143
J. Wall, *S.D.P./All.* 12,068
   Lab. maj. 15,139

Bosworth (Leics)
E. 73,097
*Rt. Hon. A. C. Butler, *C.* . 31,663
M. Fox, *S.D.P./All.* 14,369
D. J. M. Janner, *Lab.* 11,120
   C. maj. 17,294

Bournemouth (Dorset)
EAST *E.* 70,711
*D. A. Atkinson, *C.* 25,176
Dr. J. Millward, *L./All.* ... 13,760
M. J. Shutler, *Lab.* 4,026
Mrs. M. Hogarth, *Ind. C.* . 3,644
T. Dykes, *Eco.* 273
J. Stooks, *L.M.* 225
   C. maj. 11,416

WEST *E.* 72,297
J. V. Butterfill, *C.* 28,466
M. James, *L./All.* 15,135
K. Horrocks, *Lab.* 6,243
J. H. Morse, *B.N.P.* 180
   C. maj. 13,331

Bow and Poplar (Gtr. London)
E. 57,768
*I. Mikardo, *Lab.* 15,878
E. Flounders, *L./All.* 10,017
S. Eyres, *C.* 5,129
Miss S. Bartlett, *N.F.* 596
A. J. Snooks, *Lab. Ind.* ... 266
K. R. Scotcher, *W.R.P.* ... 117
   Lab. maj. 5,861

Bradford (W. Yorks)
NORTH *E.* 66,439
G. J. Lawler, *C.* 16,094
C. P. Wall, *Lab.* 14,492
P. Birkby, *S.D.P./All.* 11,962
*B. T. Ford, *Ind. Lab.* 4,018
A. Howarth, *Loony Soc.* .. 194
M. Easter, *B.N.P.* 193
   C. maj. 1,602

SOUTH *E.* 69,588
*T. W. Torney, *Lab.* 18,542
G. T. Hall, *C.* 18,432
D. A. Pearl, *S.D.P./All.* ... 12,143
R. Adsett, *Eco.* 308
   Lab. maj. 110

WEST *E.* 71,296
M. F. Madden, *Lab.* 19,499
S. Day, *C.* 16,162
*E. Lyons, *S.D.P./All.* 13,301
Ms. B. Slaughter, *W.R.P.* . 139
   Lab. maj. 3,337

Braintree (Essex)
E. 73,548
A. H. Newton, O.B.E., C. . 29,462
I. Bing, *S.D.P./All.* 16,021
Mrs. J. M. Dyson, *Lab.* ... 10,551
   C. maj. 13,441
   (May '79, C. maj. 12,518)

Brent (Gtr. London)
EAST *E.* 61,489
*Rt. Hon. R. Freeson, *Lab.* . 18,363
R. Lacey, *C.* 13,529
M. Rosen, *S.D.P./All.* 6,598
J. O'Leary, *I.N.P.* 289
G. Downing, *W.R.P.* 222
K. Radclyffe, *Ind.* 88
   Lab. maj. 4,834

NORTH *E.* 62,679
*Dr. R. R. Boyson, *C.* 24,842
Mrs. S. Jackson, *Lab.* 10,191
T. Mann, *S.D.P./All.* 9,082
   C. maj. 14,651

SOUTH *E.* 62,783
*L. A. Pavitt, *Lab.* 21,259
C. Smedley, *C.* 10,740
R. Billins, *L./All.* 7,557
R. Sawh, *Eth. Min.* 356
   Lab. maj. 10,519

Brentford and Isleworth (Gtr. London)
E. 69,170
*B. J. Hayhoe, *C.* 24,515
P. Rowlands, *Lab.* 15,128
M. Wilks, *S.D.P./All.* 11,438
P. Andrews, *N.F.* 427
R. Simmerson, *C.A.C.M.* . 179
   C. maj. 9,387
   (May '79, C. maj. 4,994)

Brentwood and Ongar (Essex)
E. 65,976

*R. A. McCrindle, C.		29,484
N. Amor, L./All.		15,282
J. W. Orpe, Lab.		5,739
C. maj.		14,202

Bridgwater (Somerset)
E. 64,224

*Rt. Hon. T. J. King, C.		25,107
Mrs. R. Farley, S.D.P./All.		14,410
A. J. May, Lab.		8,524
C. maj.		10,697

Bridlington (Humberside)
E. 76,718

*J. E. Townend, C.		31,284
Mrs. E. Martin, S.D.P./All.		14,675
M. Craven, Lab.		7,370
S. Tooke, Eco.		803
C. maj.		16,609

Brigg and Cleethorpes
(Humberside)
E. 77,471

*M. R. Brown, C.		28,893
G. Wigginton, L./All.		16,704
J. D. Hough, Lab.		11,404
C. maj.		12,189

Brighton (E. Sussex)
KEMPTOWN E. 60,877

*A. Bowden, M.B.E., C.		22,265
R. Fitch, Lab.		12,887
D. T. Burke, S.D.P./All.		8,098
E. Budden, N.F.		290
		9,378

PAVILION E. 59,761

*Rt. Hon. H. J. Amery, C.		21,323
M. Neves, S.D.P./All.		10,191
H. Spillman, Lab.		9,879
C. maj.		11,132

Bristol (Avon)
EAST E. 66,296

J. Sayeed, C.		19,844
*Rt. Hon. A. N. W. Benn, Lab.		18,055
P. Tyrer, L./All.		10,404
E. Andrews, N.F.		343
G. Dorey, Eco.		311
C. maj.		1,789

NORTH WEST E. 72,996

M. C. Stern, C.		24,617
Dr. Sarah Palmer, Lab.		18,290
Mrs. H. Long, S.D.P./All.		13,228
C. maj.		6,327

SOUTH E. 72,067

*Rt. Hon. M. F. L. Cocks, Lab.		21,824
A. Gammell, C.		17,405
D. Stanbury, S.D.P./All.		9,674
G. Collard, Eco.		352
A. Chester, Comm.		224
Mrs. L. Byrne, W.R.P.		113
Lab. maj.		4,419

West E. 73,190

*Hon. W. A. Waldegrave, C.		25,400
G. Ferguson, L./All.		15,222
Mrs. P. Tatlow, Lab.		10,094
J. Scott, Eco.		872
S. Boyle, Ind.		142
C. maj.		10,178

Bromsgrove (H & W)
E. 66,146

*H. D. Miller, C.		27,911
A. J. Milligan, S.D.P./All.		10,736
G. Titley, Lab.		10,280
J. Churchman, Eco.		716
C. maj.		17,175

Broxbourne (Herts)
E. 67,387

Mrs. M. A. Roe, C.		29,328
B. Pollock, L./All.		11,862
M. J. Stears, Lab.		8,159
J. R. Smith, B.N.P.		502
C. maj.		17,466

Broxtowe (Notts)
E. 69,760

*J. T. Lester, C.		28,522
K. Melton, L./All.		13,444
M. Warner, Lab.		11,368
C. maj.		15,078

Buckingham
E. 62,758

G. G. H. Walden, C.M.G., C.		27,552
R. Ryder, L./All.		13,584
M. Groucutt, Lab.		7,272
C. maj.		13,968

Burnley (Lancs)
E. 66,542

P. L. Pike, Lab.		20,178
I. Bruce, C.		19,408
M. Steed, L./All.		11,195
Lab. maj.		770

Burton (Staffs)
E. 71,849

*I. J. Lawrence, Q.C., C.		27,874
R. E. G. Slater, Lab.		16,227
Mrs. J. Garner, L./All.		10,420
C. maj.		11,647
(May '79, C. maj. 9,801)		

Bury (Gtr. Manchester)
NORTH E. 66,065

A. J. H. Burt, C.		23,923
*F. R. White, Lab.		21,131
Mrs. E. Wilson, L./All.		7,550
C. maj.		2,792

SOUTH E. 64,827

D. A. G. Sumberg, C.		21,718
D. Boden, Lab.		17,998
K. Evans, S.D.P./All.		9,628
C. maj.		3,720

Bury St. Edmunds (Suffolk)
E. 72,875

*E. W. Griffiths, C.		31,081
Sir R. Harland, S.D.P./All.		14,959
W. Moszczynski, Lab.		6,666
C. maj.		16,122

Calder Valley (W. Yorks)
E. 71,309

*D. Thompson, C.		24,439
D. Shutt, L./All.		16,440
Ms. A. Holmes, Lab.		15,108
C. maj.		7,999

Cambridge
E. 67,018

*R. V. R. Rhodes James, C.		20,931
M. Oakeshott, S.D.P./All.		14,963
Ms. J. Jones, Lab.		14,240
J. Dougrez-Lewis, Loony Soc.		286
C. maj.		5,968

Cambridgeshire
NORTH EAST E. 69,894

*C. R. Freud, L./All.		26,936
N. Duval, C.		21,741
R. J. Harris, Lab.		4,625
L./All. maj.		5,195

SOUTH EAST E. 66,885

*Rt. Hon. F. L. Pym, M.C., C.		28,555
C. Slee, S.D.P./All.		14,791
Ms. M. Jackson, Lab.		6,261
C. maj.		13,764

SOUTH WEST E. 76,228

*Sir J. A. Grant, C.		32,521
D. Nicholls, L./All.		18,654
J. Gluza, Lab.		6,703
C. maj.		13,867

Cannock and Burntwood (Staffs)
E. 66,188

J. G. D. Howarth, C.		20,976
*G. E. Roberts, Lab.		18,931
J. W. Withnall, S.D.P./All.		11,336
C. maj.		2,045

Canterbury (Kent)
E. 73,464

*D. L. Crouch, C.		29,029
J. Purchese, L./All.		13,287
Ms. J. Gould, Lab.		7,906
D. Conder, Eco.		962
J. White, Ind.		226
C. maj.		15,742

Carlisle (Cumbria)
E. 54,515

*R. H. Lewis, Lab.		15,618
R. Sowler, C.		15,547
R. Hunt, S.D.P./All		10,471
Lab. maj.		71
(May '79, Lab. maj. 4,556)		

Carshalton and Wallington
(Gtr. London)
E. 68,682

*F. N. Forman, C.		25,396
J. Ensor, S.D.P./All.		14,641
Mrs. J. Baker, Lab.		8,655
R. Steel, Eco.		784
C. maj.		10,755
(May '79, C. maj. 10,371)		

Castle Point (Essex)
E. 64,023

*Sir B. R. Braine, C.	......	26,730
Ms. A. Bastow, *S.D.P./All.*		11,313
Ms. L. Cunningham, *Lab.*		7,621
C. maj.	....	15,417

Cheadle
(Gtr. Manchester)
E. 66,474

*T. Normanton, T.D., C.	....	28,452
P. Clark, *L./All.*		19,072
K. Parker, *Lab.*	....	3,553
C. maj.	....	9,380

Chelmsford (Essex)
E. 78,849

Rt. Hon. N. A. F. St. John-		
*Stevas, C.		29,824
S. Mole, *L./All.*	....	29,446
C. Playford, *Lab.*	......	3,208
P. D. P. Waite, *Ind.*	......	127
C. maj.	....	378

Chelsea (Gtr. London)
E. 53,864

*N. P. Scott, M.B.E., C.	.....	19,122
J. Fryer, *L./All.*	....	7,101
N. Palmer, *Lab.*	....	3,876
Ms. A. Fielding, *Ind.*	.....	139
C. maj.	....	12,021
(May '79, C. maj. 15,690)		

Cheltenham (Glos.)
E. 76,068

*C. G. Irving, C.	....	29,187
R. Holme, *L./All.*	....	23,669
Mrs. J. M. James, *Lab.*	...	4,390
D. Swindley, *Eco.*	......	479
C. maj.	....	5,518

Chertsey and Walton (Surrey)
E. 70,210

*G. E. Pattie, C.	....	29,679
R. de St. Croix, *S.D.P./All.*		13,980
D. Green, *Lab.*	....	6,902
F. Barrett, *F.A.M.P.*	.....	318
C. maj.	....	15,699
(May '79, C. maj. 12,024)		

Chesham and Amersham
(Bucks)
E. 69,980

Rt. Hon. Sir I. H. J. L.		
*Gilmour, BT., C.	......	32,435
R. Bradnock, *L./All.*	.....	16,556
C. Duncan, *Lab.*	....	4,150
C. maj.	....	15,879

Chesterfield (Derbys)
E. 68,486

Rt. Hon. E. G. Varley,		
*Lab.	....	23,881
N. Bourne, *C.*	....	16,118
M. Payne, *L./All.*	....	9,705
Lab. maj.	....	7,763
(*see* by-election on p. 345)		

Chichester (W. Sussex)
E. 77,259

*R. A. Nelson, C.	......	35,482
H. Gibson, *S.D.P./All.*	...	15,365
R. H. Rhodes, *Lab.*	....	3,995
J. Sherlock, *Eco.*	......	838
C. maj.	....	20,117
(May '79, C. maj. 23,776)		

Chingford (Gtr. London)
E. 56,228

*Rt. Hon. N. B. Tebbit, C.	..	22,541
R. Hoskins, *L./All.*	....	10,127
W. D. Shepherd, *Lab.*	....	7,239
J. Morgan, *Eco.*	....	479
B. Cheetham, *N.F.*	....	380
J. Neighbour, *Ind.*	....	104
S. Barklem, *Ind.*	....	34
C. maj.	....	12,414
(May '79, C. maj. 12,383)		

Chipping Barnet (Gtr. London)
E. 58,423

*S. B. Chapman, C.	......	23,164
C. Perkin, *L./All.*	....	10,771
N. J. M. Smith, *Lab.*	......	6,599
E. Parry, *Eco.*	....	552
J. Hopkins, *Ind.*	....	195
C. maj.	....	12,393
(May '79, C. maj. 14,007)		

Chislehurst (Gtr. London)
E. 54,567

*R. E. Sims, C.	....	22,108
P. Lingard, *L./All.*	....	10,047
A. H. McDonald, *Lab.*	....	7,320
A. Waite, *B.N.P.*	....	201
C. maj.	....	12,061
(Maj. '79, C. maj. 9,765)		

Chorley (Lancs)
E. 72,841

*D. R. Dover, C.	....	27,861
I. Taylor, *Lab.*	....	17,586
P. O'Neill, *S.D.P./All.*	...	11,691
A. S. Holgate, *Eco.*	....	451
Mrs. E. Rokas, *Ind.*	......	114
C. maj.	....	10,275

Christchurch (Dorset)
E. 65,489

*R. J. Adley, C.	....	31,722
S. Alexander, *S.D.P./All.*		11,984
J. R. Mitchell, *Lab.*	......	3,590
C. maj.	....	19,738

Cirencester and Tewkesbury
(Glos)
E. 80,067

*Rt. Hon. N. Ridley, C.	....	34,282
P. Beckerlegge, *L./All.*	...	20,455
T. J. R. Penny, *Lab.*	......	5,243
C. maj.	....	13,827

City of Chester
E. 64,508

*Hon. P. H. Morrison, C.	..	22,645
D. E. Robertson, *Lab.*	...	13,546
A. Stunell, *L./All.*	....	11,874
C. maj.	....	9,099

**The City of London and
Westminster South**
E. 67,773

*Hon. P. L. Brooke, C.	.....	20,754
A. Walker-Smith, *L./All*	.	7,367
S. Jones, *Lab.*	....	6,013
R. Shorter, *Eco.*	....	419
A. Reeve, *N.F.*	....	248
A. Spence, *Comm.*	....	161
W. Litvin, *Ind.*	....	147
C. maj.	....	13,387

Colchester (Essex)

NORTH E. 77,292

*Sir P. A. F. Buck, Q.C., C.	.	29,921
R. Montgomerie, *L./All.*	.	14,873
R. C. Allen, *Lab.*	....	10,397
D. Wilkinson, *Ind. C.*	....	784
R. Davies, *Ind.*	....	510
C. maj.	....	15,048

SOUTH, AND MALDON E. 79,582

*Rt. Hon. J. Wakeham, C.	.	31,296
J. Stevens, *S.D.P./All.*	...	19,131
H. J. Barnard, *Lab.*	......	7,932
C. maj.	....	12,165

Colne Valley (W. Yorks)
E. 69,634

*R. S. Wainwright, *L./All.*	21,139
J. Holt, *C.*	....	17,993
A. Williams, *Lab.*	....	13,668
T. L. Keen, *Ind.*	....	260
L./All. maj.	....	3,146

Congleton (Cheshire)
E. 63,897

Mrs. J. A. Winterton, C.	..	23,895
C. Smedley, *L./All.*	....	15,436
E. Gill, *Lab.*	....	9,783
C. maj.	....	8,459

Copeland (Cumbria)
E. 54,216

Dr. J. A. Cunningham,		
*Lab.	....	18,756
Mrs. V. Wilson, *C.*	....	16,919
J. Beasley, *S.D.P./All.*	...	6,722
Lab. maj.	....	1,837
(May '79, Lab. maj. 5,455)		

Corby (Northants)
E. 63,067

W. R. Powell, *C.*	....	20,827
*W. D. Homewood, *Lab.*	...	17,659
T. G. Whittington, *L./*		
All.	....	9,905
Miss R. Stanning, *Eco.*	...	505
C. maj.	....	3,168

Cornwall

NORTH E. 66,813

*G. A. Neale, C.	....	28,146
D. Chambers, *L./All.*	.....	23,087
J. Hayday, *Lab.*	....	2,096
J. C. A. Whetter, *Corn.*		
Nat.	....	364
C. maj.	....	5,059

SOUTH EAST   E. 65,166
*R. A. Hicks, *C.* 28,326
D. Blunt,*L./All.* 19,972
A. J. Bebb, *Lab.* 2,507
J. Chadwick, *Eco.* 337
Mrs. J. Dent, *Ind.* 94
C. maj. 8,354

Coventry (W. Midlands)
NORTH EAST   E. 67,037
*G. M. Park, *Lab.* 22,190
D. Weeks, *C.* 13,415
D. Simmons, *S.D.P./All.* ... 10,251
R. Prince, *W.R.P.* 342
J. Meacham, *Comm.* 193
Lab. maj. 8,775

NORTH WEST   E. 52,072
*G. Robinson, *Lab.* 17,239
A. Coombs, *C.* 14,201
W. Talbot, *L./All.* 7,479
Lab. maj. 3,038

SOUTH EAST   E. 52,538
D. J. Nellist, *Lab.* 15,307
J. Arnold, *C.* 12,625
G. Kilby, *L./All.* 9,323
Lab. maj. 2,682

SOUTH WEST   E. 65,077
*J. P. Butcher, *C.* 22,223
D. Edwards, *Lab.* 15,776
Mrs. M. Lyle, *S.D.P./All.* .. 11,174
Mrs. W. Williamson, *Nat.*
  Party 214
C. maj. 6,447

Crawley (W. Sussex)
  E. 70,713
Hon. A. N. W. Soames, *C.* . 25,963
L. Jahn, *Lab.* 14,149
T. Forester, *S.D.P./All.* ... 13,900
C. maj. 11,814

Crewe and Nantwich (Cheshire)
  E. 71,787
*Hon. Mrs. G. P. Dunwoody,
  Lab. 22,031
P. Rock, *C.* 21,741
J. Pollard, *S.D.P./All.* 9,820
Lab. maj. 290

Crosby (Merseyside)
  E. 83,274
*G. M. Thornton, *C.* 30,604
*Mrs. S. V. Williams, *S.D.P./
  All.* 27,203
R. Waring, *Lab.* 6,611
P. Hussey, *Eco.* 415
C. maj. 3,401

Croydon (Gtr. London)
CENTRAL   E. 56,531
*J. E. M. Moore, *C.* 20,866
A. S. McKinley, *Lab.* 9,045
T. Burgess, *S.D.P./All.* ... 8,864
C. maj. 11,821

NORTH EAST   E. 62,923
*Rt. Hon. B. B. Weatherill,
  C. 22,292
J. Goldie, *S.D.P./All.* 10,665
Ms. K. Riley, *Lab.* 9,503
C. maj. 11,627

NORTH WEST   E. 58,333
*H. J. Malins, *C.* 16,674
*W. H. Pitt, *L./All.* 12,582
I. Smedley, *Lab.* 9,561
N. Griffin, *N.F.* 336
R. Rowe, *Eco.* 286
C. maj. 4,092

SOUTH   E. 64,482
*Sir W. G. Clark, *C.* 29,842
J. Forrest, *L./All.* 12,402
R. C. E. Brooks, *Lab.* 3,568
C. maj. 17,440
(May '79, C. maj. 20,868)

Dagenham (Gtr. London)
  E. 62,960
B. C. Gould, *Lab.* 15,665
R. Neill, *C.* 12,668
Mrs. J. Horne, *S.D.P./All.* 10,769
J. A. Pearce, *N.F.* 645
D. Walshe, *Comm.* 141
Lab. maj. 2,997

Darlington (Durham)
  E. 65,233
M. C. Fallon, *C.* 22,434
*O. O'Brien, *Lab.* 18,996
R. Dutton, *S.D.P./All.* ... 8,737
A. Clark, *C.D.* 108
C. maj. 3,438
(May '79, Lab. maj. 1,052)

Dartford (Kent)
  E. 71,622
*R. J. Dunn, *C.* 28,199
D. Townsend, *Lab.* 14,636
J. Mills, *L./All.* 11,204
A. H. Crockford, *F.D.P.* .. 374
G. E. Nye, *N.F.* 282
C. maj. 13,563

Daventry (Northants)
  E. 64,314
*Rt. Hon. R. E. Prentice, *C.* . 26,357
D. Collins, *S.D.P./All.* 13,221
D. Middleton, *Lab.* 9,840
C. maj. 13,136

Davyhulme (Gtr. Manchester)
  E. 64,363
*W. S. Churchill, *C.* 22,055
D. Wrigley, *L./All.* 13,041
S. Rogers, *Lab.* 12,887
C. maj. 9,014

Denton and Reddish
  (Gtr. Manchester)
  E. 68,661
*A. F. Bennett, *Lab.* 22,123
J. Snadden, *C.* 16,998
J. Begg, *S.D.P./All.* 10,869
Lab. maj. 5,125

Derby
NORTH   E. 70,374
G. Knight, *C.* 22,303
*P. Whitehead, *Lab.* 18,797
S. Connolly, *L./All.* 9,924
C. maj. 3,506

SOUTH   E. 68,578
Mrs. M. M. Beckett, *Lab.* . 18,169
G. Hales, *C.* 17,748
I. Smith, *S.D.P./All.* 9,976
E. Wall, *Eco.* 297
Lab. maj. 421

Derbyshire
NORTH EAST   E. 68,273
*R. J. Ellis, *Lab.* 21,094
I. Bridge, *C.* 19,088
S. Hardy, *S.D.P./All.* 11,494
Lab. maj. 2,006

SOUTH   E. 75,391
Mrs. E. Currie, *C.* 25,909
P. Kent, *Lab.* 17,296
R. MacFarquhar, *S.D.P./
  All.* 15,959
C. maj. 8,613

WEST   E. 68,668
*M. F. Parris, *C.* 29,695
V. Bingham, *L./All.* 14,370
J. S. March, *Lab.* 9,060
C. maj. 15,325

Devizes (Wilts)
  E. 83,211
*Hon. C. A. Morrison, *C.* .. 33,644
Mrs. E. Palmer, *S.D.P./All.* 18,020
D. Hulme, *Lab.* 10,468
Mrs. G. Ewen, *W. Reg.* ... 234
C. maj. 15,624
(May '79, C. maj. 16,088)

Dewsbury (W. Yorks)
  E. 83,211
J. Whitfield, *C.* 20,297
D. Ripley, *Lab.* 18,211
*D. Ginsburg, *S.D.P./All.* . 13,065
C. maj. 2,086

Doncaster (S. Yorks)
CENTRAL   E. 71,039
*Rt. Hon. H. Walker, *Lab.* . 21,154
J. Somers, *C.* 18,646
T. Stables, *S.D.P./All.* 10,524
Lab. maj. 2,508

NORTH   E. 72,184
*M. C. Welsh, *Lab.* 26,626
B. M. L. Stephen, *C.* 13,915
D. Orford, *S.D.P./All.* 9,916
Lab. maj. 12,711

Don Valley (S. Yorks)
  E. 73,112
M. Redmond, *Lab.* 23,036
Mrs. B. Utting, *C.* 16,570
D. Lange, *L./All.* 11,482
Lab. maj. 6,466

Dorset
NORTH   E. 67,524
*N. B. Baker, *C.* 30,058
Dr. G. Tapper, *L./All.* 18,678
Ms. J. Fox, *Lab.* 2,710
D. C. T. Fox, *W. Reg.* 294
C. maj. 11,380

SOUTH *E.* 68,998

Viscount Cranborne, C. ..	28,631
S. Head, *S.D.P./All.*	13,533
D. Hewitt, *Lab.*	7,831
Mrs. B. Smith, *Ind.*	151
C. maj.	15,098

WEST *E.* 60,997

J. W. Spicer, C.	27,030
T. Jones, *L./All.*	13,078
D. Cash, *Lab.*	5,168
C. maj.	13,952

Dover (Kent)
E. 67,922

Rt. Hon. P. W. I. Rees, Q.C., *C.*	25,454
S. Love, *Lab.*	16,234
G. Nice, *S.D.P./All.*	10,601
M. Potter, *Eco.*	404
C. maj.	9,220

Dudley (W. Midlands)
EAST *E.* 74,765

Rt. Hon. Dr. J. W. Gilbert, *Lab.*	24,441
Mrs. S. Gillies, *C.*	18,625
C. Simon, *S.D.P./All.* ...	10,272
Lab. maj.	5,816

WEST *E.* 77,795

J. G. Blackburn, C.	27,250
W. Price, *Lab.*	18,527
G. Lewis, *L./All.*	13,251
C. maj.	8,723

Dulwich (Gtr. London)
E. 56,596

G. F. Bowden, C.	15,424
Ms. C. Huey, *Lab.*	13,565
D. Taverne, *S.D.P./All.* ..	8,376
R. Barker, *N.F.*	338
R. Baker, *Eco.*	237
R. W. Vero, *Loony Soc.* ...	99
C. maj.	1,859

Durham
CITY OF *E.* 66,925

W. M. Hughes, Lab.	18,163
D. Stoker, *S.D.P./All.* ...	16,190
M. Lavis, *C.*	15,438
Lab. maj.	1,973

NORTH *E.* 71,256

G. H. Radice, Lab.	26,404
D. Howarth, *L./All.*	12,967
S. Popat, *C.*	12,418
Lab. maj.	13,437

NORTH WEST *E.* 60,747

Rt. Hon. E. Armstrong, *Lab.*	19,135
J. T. Middleton, *C.*	12,779
C. Foote Wood, *L./All.* ...	11,008
Lab. maj.	6,356

Ealing (Gtr. London)
ACTON *E.* 62,078

Sir G. S. K. Young, BT., *C.* .	22,051
G. J. Daniel, *Lab.*	11,959
P. Mitchell, *S.D.P./All.* ..	10,593
S. Pulley, *Comm.*	192
C. maj.	10,092

NORTH *E.* 68,538

H. Greenway, C.	23,128
H. J. Benn, *Lab.*	16,837
A. Miller, *L./All.*	11,021
J. Shore, *B.N.P.*	306
C. maj.	6,291

SOUTHALL *E.* 71,441

S. J. Bidwell, Lab.	26,664
N. Linacre, *C.*	15,548
M. Nadeen, *L./All.*	8,059
E. Pendrous, *N.F.*	555
S. Paul, *Ind.*	150
Lab. maj.	11,116
(May '79, Lab. maj. 11,278)	

Easington (Durham)
E. 65,732

J. D. Dormand, Lab.	25,912
F. Patterson, *L./All.*	11,120
C. J. Coulson-Thomas, *C.* .	7,342
Lab. maj.	14,792

East Berkshire
E. 81,512

A. J. MacKay, C.	33,967
K. O'Sullivan, *S.D.P./All.* .	17,868
Ms. E. Rogers, *Lab.*	7,953
C. maj.	16,099

Eastbourne (E. Sussex)
E. 72,980

I. R. E. Gow, T.D., *C.*	31,501
P. Driver, *L./All.*	18,015
C. Clark, *Lab.*	3,790
C. maj.	13,486

Eastleigh (Hants)
E. 82,447

Sir D. E. C. Price, C.	32,393
M. Kyrle, *L./All.*	19,385
P. Hallman, *Lab.*	11,736
C. maj.	13,008

East Lindsey (Lincs)
E. 69,715

P. H. B. Tapsell, C.	27,151
J. Sellick, *L./All.*	19,634
G. R. Lowis, *Lab.*	4,299
C. maj.	7,517

Eccles (Gtr. Manchester)
E. 67,230

L. Carter-Jones, Lab.	21,644
D. Philp, *C.*	15,639
K. A. Hemsley, *L./All.*	9,392
B. Cottam, *Comm.*	485
Lab. maj.	6,005

Eddisbury (Cheshire)
E. 71,056

A. R. Goodlad, C.	28,407
R. Fletcher, *L./All.*	13,561
D. G. Hanson, *Lab.*	11,169
C. maj.	14,846

Edmonton (Gtr. London)
E. 64,809

I. D. Twinn, C.	18,968
T. E. Graham, Lab.	17,775
L. Brass, *L./All.*	7,523
D. J. Bruce, *B.N.P.*	372
C. maj.	1,193

Ellesmere Port and Neston
(Cheshire)
E. 69,992

M. Woodcock, *C.*	24,371
A. Davies, *Lab.*	17,284
L. George, *S.D.P./All.*	11,413
C. maj.	7,087

Elmet (W. Yorks)
E. 67,008

S. L. Batiste, C.	23,909
R. Wilson, *Lab.*	16,053
Mrs. G. Paterson, *S.D.P./* *All.*	10,589
C. maj.	7,856

Eltham (Gtr. London)
E. 55,062

P. J. Bottomley, C.	19,530
C. P. Moore, *Lab.*	11,938
E. Randall, *L./All.*	9,030
P. Banks, *B.N.P.*	276
C. maj.	7,592

Enfield (Gtr. London)
NORTH *E.* 67,980

T. J. C. Eggar, C.	25,456
B. G. Grayson, *Lab.*	13,740
J. Daly, *S.D.P./All.*	9,452
Miss T. Persighetti, *Eco.* .	320
J. Billingham, *B.N.P.*	268
C. maj.	11,716

SOUTHGATE *E.* 65,438

Hon. Sir A. G. Berry, C. ..	26,451
D. Morgan, *L./All.*	10,632
Ms. M. Honeyball, *Lab.* ...	8,132
M. Braithwaite, *B.N.P.* ..	318
C. maj.	15,819
(*see* by-election on p. 345)	

Epping Forest (Essex)
E. 66,578

Sir J. A. Biggs-Davison, C.	27,373
M. Pettman, *S.D.P./All.* ...	11,995
Ms. H. J. Bryan, *Lab.*	8,289
R. Boenke, *Eco.*	452
S. Smith, *B.N.P.*	330
C. maj.	15,378
(May '79, C. maj. 15,453)	

Epsom and Ewell (Surrey)
E. 70,630

Hon. A. G. Hamilton, C. ..	30,737
M. Anderson, *L./All.*	13,542
W. R. Carpenter, *Lab.* ...	6,587
C. maj.	17,195

Erewash (Derbys)
E. 73,335

P. L. Rost, C.	25,167
W. Moore, *Lab.*	13,848
J. Corbett, *S.D.P./All.*	12,331
W. G. Camm, *Ind. Lab.*	4,158
C. maj.	11,319

Erith and Crayford
(Gtr. London)
E. 56,066

D. A. Evennett, C.	15,289
A. J. Wellbeloved, S.D.P./ *All.*	14,369
M. G. Smart, *Lab.*	11,260
O. Hawke, *B.N.P.*	272
C. maj.	920

Esher (Surrey)
E. 61,745

*D. C. M. Mather, M.C., C.	.	28,577
C. Wheatley, L./All.	.	12,665
Ms. D. D. Plaskow, Lab.	.	3,250
W. Wellie, Loony Soc.	.	664
C. maj.		15,912

Exeter (Devon)
E. 73,441

*J. G. Hannam, C.	.	26,660
S. Mennell, S.D.P./All.	.	16,780
R. Evans, Lab.	.	13,088
P. Frings, Eco.	.	779
C. maj.		9,880
(May '79, C. maj. 8,027)		

Falmouth and Camborne
(Cornwall)
E. 65,624

*W. D. Mudd, C.	.	24,614
D. Fieldsend, S.D.P./All.	.	13,589
A. Bunt, Lab.	.	10,446
R. Jenkin, M.K.	.	582
C. maj.		11,025

Fareham (Hants)
E. 71,901

*P. R. C. Lloyd, C.	.	32,762
S. Yolland, L./All.	.	16,446
D. Sommerville, Lab.	.	3,808
C. maj.		16,316

Faversham (Kent)
E. 76,467

*R. D. Moate, C.	.	29,849
M. Goyder, S.D.P./All.	.	15,252
C. M. Bromley, Lab.	.	11,130
C. maj.		14,597

Feltham and Heston
(Gtr. London)
E. 78,366

*R. P. Ground, Q.C., C.	.	23,724
R. W. Kerr, Lab.	.	21,576
A. Alagappa, L./All.	.	8,706
S. Glass, N.F.	.	696
C. maj.		2,148
(May '79, Lab. maj. 4,105)		

Finchley (Gtr. London)
E. 55,638

*Rt. Hon. Mrs. M. H. Thatcher, C.	.	19,616
L. G. Spigel, Lab.	.	10,302
Dr. Margaret Joachim, L./All.	.	7,763
Ms. S. Wilkinson, W.F.L.O.E.	.	279
D. Sutch, Loony Soc.	.	235
A. J. Noonan, B.E.L.L.S.	.	75
Miss H. M. Anscomb, Ind.	.	42
A. P. Whitehead, L.A.O.	.	37
D. A. Webb, Anti-Censor	.	28
B. C. Wareham, P.A.L.	.	27
B. C. Wedmore, B.B.H.	.	13
C. maj.		9,314
(May '79, C. maj. 7,878)		

Folkestone and Hythe (Kent)
E. 67,802

M. Howard, C.	.	27,261
J. MacDonald, L./All.	.	15,591
L. Lawrie, Lab.	.	4,700
P. A. Todd, Ind.	.	318
C. maj.		11,670
(May '79. C. maj. 16,020)		

Fulham (Gtr. London)
E. 51,833

*M. Stevens, C.	.	18,204
A. Powell, Lab.	.	13,415
D. Rendel, L./All.	.	7,194
Ms. J. Grimes, Eco.	.	277
R. Pearce, N.F.	.	229
J. Keats, Ind. L.	.	102
C. maj.		4,789
(May '79, C. maj. 1,499)		

Fylde (Lancs)
E. 62,238

*Sir E. L. Gardner, Q.C., C.	.	27,879
Mrs. E. A. Smith, L./All.	.	10,777
D. J. King, Lab.	.	4,821
H. Fowler, Ind.	.	863
C. maj.		17,012

Gainsborough and Horncastle
(Lincs)
E. 67,115

E. J. E. Leigh, C.	.	25,625
A. Phillips, L./All.	.	20,558
C. James, Lab.	.	3,886
G. Dixon, Eco.	.	279
C. maj.		5,067

Gateshead East (Tyne & Wear)
E. 68,364

*B. Conlan, Lab.	.	22,981
F. Rogers, C.	.	12,659
P. Nunn, S.D.P./All.	.	11,920
Lab. maj.		10,322

Gedling (Notts)
E. 66,656

*Sir P. W. Holland, C.	.	27,207
A. Berkeley, S.D.P./All.	.	12,543
J. Peck, Lab.	.	10,330
J. Szatter, Ind.	.	186
C. maj.		14,664

Gillingham (Kent)
E. 69,256

J. R. Couchman, C.	.	26,381
C. Lewcock, L./All.	.	15,538
A. S. West, Lab.	.	9,084
C. maj.		10,843
(May '79, C. maj. 10,499)		

Glanford and Scunthorpe
(Humberside)
E. 71,962

R. S. Hickmet, C.	.	20,356
J. Ellis, Lab.	.	19,719
C. Nottingham, S.D.P./All.	.	12,819
C. maj.		637

Gloucester
E. 74,268

*Rt. Hon. Mrs. S. Oppenheim, C.	.	27,235
C. W. V. Hinds, Lab.	.	14,698
M. Golder, S.D.P./All.	.	13,499
J. Waters, Eco.	.	479
R. Rhodes, B.N.P.	.	260
C. maj.		12,537

Gosport (Hants)
E. 64,877

*P. J. Viggers, C.	.	28,179
P. Chegwyn, L./All.	.	13,728
B. B. Bond, Lab.	.	4,319
R. A. McMillan, Ind.	.	241
C. maj.		14,451

Grantham (Lincs)
E. 75,047

*Hon. D. M. Hogg, C.	.	31,692
S. Titley, L./All.	.	12,781
T. E. Savage, Lab.	.	10,677
C. maj.		18,911

Gravesham (Kent)
E. 71,150

*T. D. Brinton, C.	.	25,968
J. F. Ovenden, Lab.	.	17,505
M. Horton, S.D.P./All.	.	10,826
P. Johnson, N.F.	.	420
M. Sewell, Eco.	.	103
C. maj.		8,463

Great Grimsby (Humberside)
E. 68,388

*A. V. Mitchell, Lab.	.	18,330
C. Hancock, C.	.	17,599
P. Genney, S.D.P./All.	.	14,552
Lab. maj.		731
(May '79, Lab. maj. 6,241)		

Great Yarmouth
(Norfolk)
E. 62,809

M. R. H. Carttiss, C.	.	22,423
O. Lloyd, Lab.	.	11,223
E. Minett, L./All.	.	10,803
C. maj.		11,200

Greenwich (Gtr. London)
E. 51,586

*N. G. Barnett, Lab.	.	13,361
A. Rolfe, C.	.	12,150
T. Ford, S.D.P./All.	.	8,783
I. Dell, B.N.P.	.	259
R. Mallone, Fellowship	.	242
Ms. F. Hook, Comm.	.	149
Lab. maj.		1,211

Guildford (Surrey)
E. 75,134

*Rt. Hon. D. A. R. Howell, C.	.	30,016
Mrs. M. Sharp, L./All.	.	18,192
K. Chesterton, Lab.	.	5,853
A. Farrell, P.A.L.	.	425
C. maj.		11,824

Hackney (Gtr. London)

NORTH AND STOKE NEWINGTON
E. 66,754

*E. A. C. Roberts, *Lab.*	18,989
E. Hartley-Booth, *C.*	10,444
D. Ash, *L./All.*	5,746
D. Fitzpatrick, *Eco.*	492
M. Goldman, *Comm.*	426
J. Field, *N.F.*	396
Lab. maj.	8,545

SOUTH AND SHOREDITCH E. 71,304

B. C. J. Sedgemore, *Lab.*	16,621
P. Croft, *C.*	8,930
*R. W. Brown, *S.D.P./All.*	7,025
J. Roberts, *Ind.L.*	3,724
S. Quilty, *L.I.L.*	704
R. Ashton, *N.F.*	593
Mrs. V. Tyndall, *B.N.P.*	374
D. Green, *Comm.*	246
R. Goldstein, *W.R.P.*	141
Lab. maj.	7,691

Halesowen and Stourbridge
(W. Midlands)
E. 76,403

*J. H. R. Stokes, *C.*	28,250
T. Clitheroe, *S.D.P./All.*	14,934
C. Ellison, *Lab.*	14,611
D. Rudd, *Eco.*	582
C. maj.	13,316

Halifax (W. Yorks)
E. 72,747

R. Galley, *C.*	22,321
*Dr. Shirley Summerskill, *Lab.*	20,452
F. Cockroft, *S.D.P./All.*	11,868
C. maj.	1,869

Halton (Cheshire)
E. 72,743

*Rt. Hon. G. J. Oakes, *Lab.*	24,752
P. Pedley, *C.*	17,923
R. Tilling, *S.D.P./All.*	10,649
Lab. maj.	6,829

Hammersmith (Gtr. London)
E. 46,718

*C. S. Soley, *Lab.*	13,645
N. Mansfield, *C.*	11,691
M. Starks, *S.D.P./All.*	4,925
S. Knott, *Ind. L.*	1,912
Mrs. L. Bennett, *N.F.*	250
Ms. D. Sutherland, *Eco.*	325
Ms. C. Dixon, *W.R.P.*	81
P. Dick, *Ind.*	73
Lab. maj.	1,954
(May '79, Lab. maj. 3,506)	

Hampshire

EAST E. 79,303

*M. J. Mates, *C.*	36,968
Ms. R. Bryan, *L./All.*	18,641
S. J. Cowan, *Lab.*	3,247
C. maj.	18,327

NORTH WEST E. 65,780

*D. B. Mitchell, *C.*	28,044
I. Willis, *L./All.*	15,922
M. J. Davis, *Lab.*	4,957
C. maj.	12,122

Hampstead and Highgate
(Gtr. London)
E. 66,554

*G. Finsberg, M.B.E., *C.*	18,366
J. McDonnell, *Lab.*	14,996
Mrs. A. Sofer, *S.D.P./All.*	11,030
J. Stevenson, *Poet*	156
C. maj.	3,370

Harborough (Leics)
E. 72,177

*J. A. Farr, *C.*	32,957
T. Swift, *L./All.*	14,472
M. Upham, *Lab.*	6,285
B. Fewster, *Eco.*	802
J. Taylor, *B.N.P.*	280
C. maj.	18,485
(May '79, C. maj. 21,978)	

Harlow (Essex)
E. 69,715

J. J. J. Hayes, *C.*	21,924
*A. S. Newens, *Lab.*	18,250
J. Bastick, *L./All.*	12,891
J. Ward, *Ind.*	256
C. maj.	3,674
(May '79, Lab. maj. 1,392)	

Harrogate (N. Yorks)
E. 72,815

*R. G. Banks, *C.*	30,269
J. Burney, *S.D.P./All.*	14,381
J. Dixon, *Lab.*	5,128
D. Kelly, *R.H.C.P.*	316
P. Vessey, *N.F.*	163
C. maj.	15,888

Harrow (Gtr. London)

EAST E. 79,926

*H. J. Dykes, *C.*	28,834
R. Hains, *L./All.*	16,166
D. Brough, *Lab.*	12,941
C. maj.	12,668

WEST E. 73,151

*A. J. Page, *C.*	28,056
S. Bayliss, *S.D.P./All.*	17,035
K. A. Toms, *Lab.*	7,811
C. maj.	11,021

Hartlepool (Cleveland)
E. 69,346

*E. L. Leadbitter, *Lab.*	22,048
F. Rodgers, *C.*	18,958
N. Bertram, *S.D.P./All.*	7,422
Lab. maj.	3,090
(May '79, Lab. maj. 8,162)	

Harwich (Essex)
E. 72,179

*Sir J. E. Ridsdale, C.B.E., *C.*	27,422
R. Goodenough, *L./All.*	14,920
R. Knight, *Lab.*	8,302
C. maj.	12,502

Hastings and Rye (E. Sussex)
E. 69,747

*K. R. Warren, *C.*	25,626
D. Amies, *L./All.*	14,646
N. Knowles, *Lab.*	7,304
G. McNally, *Ind.*	503
C. maj.	10,980

Havant (Hants)
E. 73,096

*I. S. Lloyd, *C.*	29,148
Mrs. E. Cleaver, *S.D.P./All.*	17,192
R. J. Norris. *Lab.*	6,335
C. maj.	11,956

Hayes and Harlington
(Gtr. London)
E. 57,620

T. P. Dicks, *C.*	16,451
P. Fagan, *Lab.*	12,217
*N. D. Sandelson, *S.D.P./All.*	11,842
F. Hill, *Freedom*	324
C. maj.	4,234
(May '79, Lab. maj. 3,302)	

Hazel Grove (Gtr. Manchester)
E. 63,630

*T. R. Arnold, *C.*	22,627
A. Vos, *L./All.*	20,605
J. Comyn-Platt, *Lab.*	5,895
C. maj.	2,022

Hemsworth (W. Yorks)
E. 54,323

*A. Woodall, *Lab.*	22,081
J. Woofindin, *L./All.*	7,891
D. Williamson, *C.*	7,291
Lab. maj.	14,190

Hendon (Gtr. London)

NORTH E. 54,505

*J. M. Gorst, *C.*	18,499
K. Craig, *S.D.P./All.*	9,474
A. M. Williams, *Lab.*	8,786
B. Franklin, *Nat.*	194
R. Clayton, *Ind. Dem.*	116
C. maj.	9,025
(May '79, C. maj. 6,392)	

SOUTH E. 53,929

*Rt. Hon. P. J. M. Thomas, Q.C., *C.*	17,115
M. Palmer, *L./All.*	10,682
Mrs. D. N. Neall, *Lab.*	7,415
C. maj.	6,433
(May '79, C. maj. 8,750)	

Henley (Oxon)
E. 62,120

*Rt. Hon. M. R. D. Heseltine, *C.*	27,039
I. Brook, *L./All.*	13,258
I. Roxburgh, *Lab.*	4,282
Ms. R. Johnson, *W.F.L.O.E.*	517
T. Rogers, *O.N.C.*	213
C. maj.	13,781

Hereford
E. 64,051

*C. R. Shepherd, *C.*	23,334
C. Green, *L./All.*	21,057
J. Evans, *Lab.*	3,690
Ms. V. Murray, *Eco.*	463
C. maj.	2,277
(May '79, C. maj. 4,970)	

Hertford and Stortford
E. 68,615

*P. B. Wells, C.		29,039
R. Wotherspoon, S.D.P./		
All.		16,110
J. Carr, Lab.		6,203
G. Wiles, B.N.P.		304
P. Cullen, P.F.A.		221
C. maj.		12,929

Hertfordshire

NORTH E. 75,439

*B. H. I. H. Stewart, C.		29,302
G. Binney, L./All.		19,359
J. Reilly, Lab.		11,104
C. maj.		9,943

SOUTH WEST E. 74,371

*R. L. Page, C.		30,217
I. Blair, L./All.		18,023
E. Playfair, Lab.		7,818
M. Lupton, Ind.		307
C. maj.		12,194

WEST E. 76,597

R. B. Jones, C.		28,436
N. Hollinghurst, S.D.P./		
All.		18,860
P. Boateng, Lab.		13,583
C. maj.		9,576

Hertsmere (Herts)
E. 72,997

*Rt. Hon. C. E. Parkinson,		
C.		28,628
Mrs. Z. Gifford, L./All.		13,758
I. D. D. Reed, Lab.		10,315
R. Parkinson, Ind. Comm.		1,116
C. maj.		14,870

Hexham (Nthmb)
E. 54,341

*Rt. Hon. A. G. F. Rippon,		
Q.C., C.		21,374
E. Robson, L./All.		13,066
S. J. Byers, Lab.		7,056
C. maj.		8,308

Heywood and Middleton
(Gtr. Manchester)
E. 59,870

*J. Callaghan, Lab.		18,111
Mrs. C. Hodgson, C.		14,137
A. Rumbelow, S.D.P./All.		9,262
K. Henderson, B.N.P.		316
Lab. maj.		3,974

High Peak (Derbys)
E. 67,358

C. J. Hawkins, C.		24,534
D. Marquand, S.D.P./All.		14,594
D. J. Wilcox, Lab.		13,755
C. maj.		9,940

Holborn and St. Pancras
(Gtr. London)
E. 71,604

*F. G. Dobson, Lab.		20,486
A. Kerpel, C.		13,227
W. Jones, L./All.		9,242
R. Price, W.R.P.		155
Lab. maj.		7,259

Holland with Boston (Lincs)
E. 63,562

*R. B. Body, C.		24,962
Mrs. C. Le Brun, L./All.		13,226
J. A. Moore, Lab.		6,970
C. maj.		11,736

Honiton (Devon)
E. 72,232

*Sir P. F. H. Emery, C.		32,602
A. Sampson, S.D.P./All.		17,833
R. A. C. Sharpe, Lab.		3,377
C. maj.		14,769

Hornchurch (Gtr. London)
E. 61,741

*R. C. Squire, C.		21,393
A. R. Williams, Lab.		12,209
J. Martin, S.D.P./All.		11,251
Mrs. A. Joyce, N.F.		402
M. Crowson, Eco.		219
C. maj.		9,184
(May '79, C. maj. 769)		

Hornsey and Wood Green
(Gtr. London)
E. 73,870

*Sir H. A. L. Rossi, C.		22,323
Mrs. V. Veness, Lab.		18,424
M. Burrell, S.D.P./All.		10,995
P. Lang, Eco.		854
C. maj.		3,899

Horsham (W. Sussex)
E. 80,407

*P. M. Hordern, C.		37,897
G. Archibald, S.D.P./All.		16,112
G. R. Ward, Lab.		4,999
P. Spurrier, Eco.		925
C. maj.		21,785

Houghton and Washington
(Tyne & Wear)
E. 75,686

R. Boyes, Lab.		26,168
R. Kenyon, S.D.P./All.		12,347
R. Vane, C.		12,104
Lab. maj.		13,821

Hove (E. Sussex)
E. 71,918

*Hon. T. A. D. Sainsbury, C.		28,628
Mrs. T. Beamish, L./All.		11,409
C. Wright, Lab.		6,550
T. Layton, S.E.E.		524
K. Lillie, M.D.P.		189
C. maj.		17,219
(May '79, C. maj. 19,449)		

Huddersfield (W. Yorks)
E. 68,174

*B. J. Sheerman, Lab.		20,051
J. Tweddle, C.		16,096
Mrs. K. J. L. Hasler, L./All.		12,027
H. Hirst, Ind.		271
Lab. maj.		3,955

Hull (Humberside)
E. 70,037

EAST E. 70,037

*J. L. Prescott, Lab.		23,615
D. Bunting-Leng, C.		13,541
Mrs. C. Gurevitch, L./All.		10,172
Lab. maj.		10,074

NORTH E. 74,543

*J. K. McNamara, Lab.		21,365
C. Hayward, C.		15,337
T. A. Smith, S.D.P./All.		13,381
R. Tenney, Nat.		222
Lab. maj.		6,028

WEST E. 57,702

S. J. Randall, Lab.		15,361
M. Humphreys, C.		11,707
W. Unwin, S.D.P./All.		9,575
Lab. maj.		3,654

Huntingdon (Cambs)
E. 76,668

*J. Major, C.		34,254
Mrs. S. Gatiss, L./All.		13,906
M. Slater, Lab.		6,317
T. Eiloart, Eco.		444
C. maj.		20,348

Hyndburn (Lancs)
E. 59,341

J. K. Hargreaves, C.		19,405
*A. Davidson, Lab.		19,384
J. Bridgen, S.D.P./All.		6,716
F. Smith, Eco.		226
P. Gateson, Ind.		169
C. maj.		21

Ilford (Gtr. London)

NORTH E. 60,248

*V. W. H. Bendall, C.		22,042
M. J. Gapes, Lab.		10,841
I. Roxburgh, S.D.P./All.		10,052
C. maj.		11,201

SOUTH E. 58,208

*N. G. Thorne, O.B.E., T.D., C.		18,672
J. H. Hogben, Lab.		14,106
R. Scott, L./All.		7,999
R. A. Martin, B.N.P.		316
C. maj.		4,566

Ipswich (Suffolk)
E. 67,292

*K. T. Weetch, Lab.		22,191
Dr. Elizabeth Cottrell, C.		21,114
Mrs. P. Miernik, L./All.		7,220
A. Pearson, B.N.P.		235
Lab. maj.		1,077

Isle of Wight
E. 94,226

*S. S. Ross, L./All.		38,407
Mrs. V. Bottomley, C.		34,904
Mrs. C. Wilson, Lab.		1,828
B. McDermott, I.W.R.P.		208
L./All. maj.		3,503
(May '79, L. maj. 352)		

Islington (Gtr. London)

NORTH E. 59,984

J. B. Corbyn, Lab.		14,951
D. Coleman, C.		9,344
*J. Grant, S.D.P./All.		8,268
*M. O'Halloran, Ind. Lab.		4,091
L. Bearsford-Walker,		
B.N.P.		176
R. Lincoln, C.U.I.		134
Lab. maj.		5,607

SOUTH AND FINSBURY *E.* 59,795
C. R. Smith, Lab.		13,460
*G. Cunningham, *S.D.P./*		
All.		13,097
A. Johnston, *C.*		9,894
J. Donegan, *N.F.*		341
J. Murphy, *I.F.P.*		102
D. Stentiford, *B.N.P.*		94
C. Slapper, *S.P.G.B.*		85
Lab. maj.		363

Jarrow (Tyne & Wear)
E. 63,770
D. Dixon, Lab.		25,151
Miss S. Copland, *C.*		11,274
J. A. Lennox, *L./All.*		9,094
Lab. maj.		13,877

Keighley (W. Yorks)
E. 63,678
G. P. A. Waller, C.		21,370
R. Cryer, Lab.		18,596
J. Wells, *L./All.*		9,951
M. Penney, *Eco.*		302
C. maj.		2,774

Kensington (Gtr. London)
E. 49,584
Sir B. M. Rhys Williams,		
BT., *C.*		14,274
B. T. Bousquet, *Lab.*		9,173
W. Goodhart, *S.D.P./All.*		6,873
J. Porritt, *Eco.*		649
T. Knight, *Ind.*		86
C. maj.		5,101
(May '79, C. maj. 5,463)		

Kettering (Northants)
E. 62,819
R. N. Freeman, C.		23,223
Mrs. C. Goodhart, *S.D.P./*		
All.		14,637
A. Gordon, *Lab.*		10,119
C. maj.		8,586

Kingston upon Thames
(Gtr. London)
E. 56,794
N. S. H. Lamont, C.		22,094
R. Hayes, *L./All.*		13,222
P. J. Smith, *Lab.*		4,977
Miss A. Presant-Collins,		
Eco.		290
P. Dodd, *Loony Soc.*		259
C. maj.		8,872
(May '79, C. maj. 13,544)		

Kingswood (Avon)
E. 72,159
R. A. Hayward, C.		22,573
T. Walker, *Lab.*		20,776
M. Gilbert, *S.D.P./All.*		12,591
C. maj.		1,797

Knowsley (Merseyside)
NORTH *E.* 55,606
R. Kilroy-Silk, Lab.		24,949
A. Birch, *C.*		7,758
B. McColgan, *S.D.P./All.*		5,715
J. Simons, *W.R.P.*		246
Lab. maj.		17,191

SOUTH *E.* 68,114
S. F. Hughes, *Lab.*		25,727
Miss E. Lamont, *C.*		13,958
I. Smith, *L./All.*		8,173
Lab. maj.		11,769

Lancaster (Lancs)
E. 56,040
Mrs. M. E. Kellett-Bow-		
man, C.		21,050
C. Harkins, *Lab.*		10,414
W. Booth, *L./All.*		10,214
S. R. Leach, *Ind.*		179
C. maj.		10,636

Langbaurgh (Cleveland)
E. 77,387
J. R. Holt, *C.*		24,239
Mrs. G. Johnson, *Lab.*		18,215
R. Ashby, *L./All.*		15,615
C. maj.		6,024

Leeds (W. Yorks)
CENTRAL *E.* 63,299
D. J. Fatchett, Lab.		18,706
P. Wrigley, *L./All.*		10,484
M. Ashley-Brown, *C.*		9,192
G. Cummins, *B.N.P.*		331
J. M. Rogers, *Comm.*		314
Lab. maj.		8,222

EAST *E.* 63,611
Rt. Hon. D. W. Healey, C.H.,		
M.B.E., *Lab.*		18,450
A. Bell, *C.*		12,355
Mrs. M. Clay, *L./All.*		10,884
A. H. Brons, *N.F.*		475
Lab. maj.		6,095

NORTH EAST *E.* 65,226
Rt. Hon. Sir K. S. Joseph,		
BT., *C.*		21,940
P. Crystal, *S.D.P./All.*		12,945
R. Sedler, *Lab.*		10,951
E. Tibbitts, *A. Corr.*		128
P. Holton, *A.C.I.E.*		123
C. maj.		8,995

NORTH WEST *E.* 68,004
Dr. K. Hampson, C.		22,579
N. Jones, *S.D.P./All.*		14,042
J. Battle, *Lab.*		10,757
A. Laurence, *Eco.*		673
C. G. Haygreen, *Ind. C.*		437
C. maj.		8,537

WEST *E.* 67,538
M. J. Meadowcroft, *L./All.*		17,908
J. Dean, Lab.		15,860
Miss J. Keeble, *C.*		12,515
A. Braithwaite, *B.N.P.*		334
L./All. maj.		2,048

Leicester
EAST *E.* 67,071
P. N. E. Bruinvels, *C.*		19,117
Ms P. Hewitt, *Lab.*		18,184
T. Bradley, S.D.P./All.		10,362
R. V. Ganatra, *Ind.*		970
R. L. Sutton, *B.N.P.*		459
C. maj.		933
(May '79, Lab. maj. 2,856)		

SOUTH *E.* 73,573
D. H. Spencer, Q.C., *C.*		21,424
J. Marshall, Lab.		21,417
R. Renold, *L./All.*		9,410
C. Davis, *Eco.*		495
C. Pickard, *B.N.P.*		280
D. P. Roberts, *W.P.W.S.*		161
C. maj.		7
(May '79, Lab. maj. 1,998)		

WEST *E.* 67,691
Hon. G. E. Janner, Lab.		20,837
R. Meacham, *C.*		19,125
S. Fernando, *S.D.P./All.*		5,935
R. Hill, *B.N.P.*		469
B. J. Prangle, *W.R.P.*		176
Lab. maj.		1,712
(May '79, Lab. maj. 8,838)		

Leigh (Gtr. Manchester)
E. 68,063
L. F. Cunliffe, Lab.		25,477
P. Johnston, *C.*		13,163
D. Eccles, *S.D.P./All.*		10,468
Lab. maj.		12,314

Leominster (H & W)
E. 66,286
P. Temple-Morris, C.		29,276
R. Pincham, *L./All.*		19,490
D. Wilcox, *Lab.*		1,932
Miss F. M. Norman, *Eco.*		668
C. maj.		9,786

Lewes (E. Sussex)
E. 67,366
J. R. Rathbone, C.		29,261
D. Bellotti, *L./All.*		15,357
Ms S. Sander, *Lab.*		4,244
R. Mutter, *Eco.*		1,221
C. maj.		13,904

Lewisham (Gtr. London)
DEPTFORD *E.* 58,663
Rt. Hon. J. E. Silkin, Lab.		17,360
R. Wheatley, *C.*		11,328
Miss D. Abbott, *S.D.P./All.*		6,734
P. Wilson, *B.N.P.*		317
S. B. Housego, *A.B.*		173
Lab. maj.		6,032

EAST *E.* 61,216
Hon. C. B. Moynihan, *C.*		17,168
R. Moyle, Lab.		15,259
Ms. P. Toynbee, *S.D.P./All.*		9,351
R. C. Edmonds, *B.N.P.*		288
A. Hassard, *Eco.*		270
G. Roberts, *Comm.*		135
P. Gibson, *W.R.P.*		71
C. maj.		1,909

WEST *E.* 63,043
J. C. Maples, C.		19,521
C. Price, Lab.		17,015
H. Mooney, *L./All.*		7,470
R. F. Hoy, *B.N.P.*		336
C. maj.		2,506

Leyton (Gtr. London)
E. 57,770
H. M. Cohen, *Lab.*		16,504
W. Neilson-Hansen, *C.*		11,988
B. Magee, S.D.P./All.		9,448
Lab. maj.		4,516
(May '79, Lab. maj. 5,734)		

Lincoln
E. 72,887

*K. M. Carlisle, C.	....	25,244
M. Withers, Lab.	.....	14,958
F. Stockdale, S.D.P./All.	.	13,631
G. Blades, Ind.	....	523
C. maj.	....	10,286

Littleborough and Saddleworth
(Gtr. Manchester)
E. 64,018

*G. K. Dickens, C.	....	20,510
R. Knowles, L./All.	.....	14,860
S. Moore, Lab.	....	12,106
R. Barry, R.C.C.P.	....	398
C. maj.	....	5,650

Liverpool

BROADGREEN E. 63,826

T. Fields, Lab.	....	18,802
D. Dougherty, C.	....	15,002
R. Pine, Ind. L.	....	7,021
*Lt. Col. R. Crawshaw, O.B.E., T.D., S.D.P./All.	.	5,169
Lab. maj.	....	3,800

GARSTON E. 64,326

E. Loyden, Lab.	....	21,450
J. Ross, C.	....	17,448
Miss R. Cooper, L./All.	...	7,153
Lab. maj.	....	4,002

MOSSLEY HILL E. 62,789

*D. P. Alton, L./All.	......	18,845
B. Keefe, C.	....	14,650
A. C. Snowden, Lab.	.....	12,352
M. Erikson-Rohrer, N.F.	.	212
L./All. maj.	....	4,195

RIVERSIDE E. 61,638

*R. Parry, Lab.	....	24,978
T. Morrison, C.	....	7,600
P. Zentner, S.D.P./All.	...	5,381
J. Blevin, Comm.	....	261
D. Latchford, W.R.P.	....	234
Lab. maj.	....	17,378

WALTON E. 73,532

*E. S. Heffer, Lab.	....	26,980
A. Maddox, C.	....	12,865
D. Croft, L./All.	....	10,970
D. J. M. McKechnie, B.N.P.	....	343
Lab. maj.	....	14,115

WEST DERBY E. 63,088

R. N. Wareing, Lab.	......	23,905
W. Trelawney, C.	....	12,062
*E. Ogden, S.D.P./All.	....	7,871
Lab. maj.	....	11,843

Loughborough (Leics)
E. 70,668

*S. J. Dorrell, C.	....	29,056
M. Jones, Lab.	....	12,876
J. Frears, S.D.P./All.	...	12,189
D. Whitebread, Eco.	....	591
J. A. Peacock, B.N.P.	....	228
C. maj.	....	16,180

Ludlow (Salop)
E. 63,256

*E. P. Cockeram, C.	....	26,278
D. Lane, S.D.P./All.	.....	14,975
P. M. Davis, Lab.	....	5,949
C. maj.	....	11,303

Luton (Beds)

NORTH E. 69,805

*J. R. Carlisle, C.	....	26,115
K. Hopkins, Lab.	.....	14,134
D. Stephen, S.D.P./All.	..	13,769
C. maj.	....	11,981

SOUTH E. 71,015

*G. F. J. Bright, C.	....	22,531
I. M. Clemitson, Lab.	.....	17,910
D. Franks, L./All.	....	13,395
C. maj.	....	4,621

Macclesfield (Cheshire)
E. 73,082

*N. R. Winterton, C.	......	32,538
Mrs. R. Coleman, L./All.	..	11,859
P. B. Kelly, Lab.	....	9,923
M. Reeman, Ind.	....	488
C. maj.	....	20,679

Maidstone (Kent)
E. 70,357

*J. J. Wells, C.	....	26,420
J. Burnett, L./All.	......	19,194
G. T. Carey, Lab.	....	6,280
C. maj.	....	7,226

Makerfield (Gtr. Manchester)
E. 69,176

*M. T. F. McGuire, Lab.	...	25,114
E. Hay, C.	....	14,238
R. Grayson, L./All.	......	11,633
Lab. maj.	....	10,876

Manchester

BLACKLEY E. 60,106

*K. Eastham, Lab.	....	20,132
P. Ridgway, C.	....	13,676
J. Cookson, L./All.	......	8,081
Lab. maj.	....	6,456

CENTRAL E. 69,188

*R. K. Litherland, Lab.	...	27,353
D. Eager, C.	....	8,868
A. Ahmed, S.D.P./All.	....	4,956
A. Coles, N.F.	....	729
Lab. maj.	....	18,485

GORTON E. 64,645

*Rt. Hon. G. B. Kaufman, Lab.	....	22,460
J. Kershaw, C.	....	12,495
K. Whitmore, L./All.	.....	8,348
M. Cowle, Comm.	....	333
L. C. Andrews, B.N.P.	...	231
Lab. maj.	....	9,965

WITHINGTON E. 64,606

*F. J. Silvester, C.	....	18,329
Mrs. F. W. Done, Lab.	....	15,956
B. Lever, S.D.P./All.	.....	12,231
M. G. Gibson, F.P.	....	184
C. maj.	....	2,373

Wythenshawe E. 60,995

*Rt. Hon. A. Morris, Lab.	..	23,172
Mrs. J. Jacobs, C.	....	12,488
D. Sandiford, L./All.	....	6,766
Lab. maj.	....	10,684
(May '79, Lab. maj. 12,113)		

Mansfield (Notts)
E. 65,277

*Rt. Hon. J. D. Concannon, Lab.	....	18,670
R. Wrenn, C.	....	16,454
S. Taylor, S.D.P./All.	.....	11,036
Lab. maj.	....	2,216

Medway (Kent)
E. 63,387

*Mrs. P. E. Fenner, C.	.....	22,507
R. E. Bean, Lab.	....	13,851
F. Winckless, S.D.P./All.	.	9,658
C. maj.	....	8,656

Meriden (W. Midlands)
E. 74,161

*I. C. Mills, C.	....	28,474
*E. J. Sever, Lab.	....	13,456
Mrs. P. M. Dunbar, S.D.P./All.	....	10,674
C. L. Collins, N.F.	....	460
C. maj.	....	15,018

Middlesbrough (Cleveland)
E. 62,950

S. Bell, Lab.	....	21,220
Mrs. L. Campey, C.	......	11,551
D. Sanders, L./All.	......	8,871
M. Simpson, W.R.P.	.....	207
Lab. maj.	....	9,669

Mid Kent
E. 66,510

A. Rowe, C.	....	25,400
Mrs. A. Wainman, L./All.	12,857
V. Hull, Lab.	....	8,928
D. Delderfield, New Brit.	.	324
C. maj.	....	12,543

Mid Sussex
E. 77,005

*R. T. Renton, C.	....	35,310
J. Campbell, L./All.	......	18,566
Mrs. P. A. Hawkes, Lab.	..	3,470
J. Bray, Ind.	....	196
C. maj.	....	16,744

Milton Keynes (Bucks)
E. 79,229

*W. R. Benyon, C.	....	28,181
Mrs. J. Nightingale, S.D.P./All.	....	16,659
J. Thakoordin, Lab.	.....	13,045
A. Francis, Eco.	....	494
R. G. W. Rickord, B.N.P.	.	290
C. maj.	....	11,522

Mitcham and Morden
(Gtr. London)
E. 63,535

*Mrs. A. C. R. Rumbold,		
C.B.E., C.	....	19,827
D. Nicholas, *Lab.*	....	13,376
B. Douglas-Mann, *S.D.P./*		
All.	....	12,720
J. Perryman, *N.F.*	....	539
C. maj.	....	6,451
(May '79, Lab. maj. 618)		

Mole Valley (Surrey)
E. 65,067

*K. W. Baker, C.	....	29,691
Ms. S. Thomas, *L./All.*	....	14,973
Ms. F. Lines, *Lab.*	......	4,147
C. maj.	....	14,718

Morecambe and Lunesdale
(Lancs)
E. 53,238

*Hon. M. A. Lennox-Boyd,		
C.	....	21,968
T. Clare, *S.D.P./All.*	....	9,774
A. C. Bryning, *Lab.*	......	6,882
Mrs. I. Woods, *Ind.*	......	208
C. maj.	....	12,194

Morley and Leeds South
(W. Yorks)
E. 60,864

*Rt. Hon. M. Rees, Lab.	...	18,995
W. Hyde, *C.*	....	13,141
P. Burley, *S.D.P./All.*	....	9,216
Lab. maj.	....	5,854

Newark (Notts)
E. 64,008

*R. T. Alexander, C.	......	26,334
J. McGuigan, *Lab.*	......	12,051
S. Thompstone, *S.D.P./All.*		10,076
Mrs. P. Hewis, *Eco.*	......	463
C. maj.	....	14,283

Newbury (Berks)
E. 71,343

*R. M. C. McNair-Wilson, C.		31,836
A. Richards, *L./All.*	......	18,798
R. C. Knight, *Lab.*	....	3,027
C. maj.	....	13,038

Newcastle-under-Lyme (Staffs)
E. 65,400

*J. Golding, Lab.	....	21,210
L. Lawrence, *C.*	....	18,406
A. Thomas, *L./All.*	......	10,916
Lab. maj.	....	2,804

Newcastle upon Tyne

CENTRAL   E. 62,687

P. R. G. Merchant, *C.*	....	18,161
N. Todd, *Lab.*	....	15,933
*J. Horam, S.D.P./All.	....	9,923
D. N. Jacques, *Eco.*	......	478
C. maj.	....	2,228

EAST   E. 59,587

N. H. Brown, *Lab.*	......	19,247
A. Barnes, *C.*	....	11,755
*M. Thomas, S.D.P./All.	....	11,293
Lab. maj.	....	7,492

NORTH   E. 69,432

*R. C. Brown, Lab.	....	18,985
P. Straw, *C.*	....	16,429
J. Shipley, *L./All.*	......	15,136
Lab. maj.	....	2,556

New Forest (Hants)
E. 70,033

*P. M. E. D. McNair-Wilson,		
C.	....	34,157
R. Harrison, *L./All.*	......	13,232
D. T. James, *Lab.*	....	4,075
C. maj.	....	20,925

Newham (Gtr. London)

NORTH EAST   E. 62,463

*R. Leighton, Lab.	......	19,282
Mrs. H. Gardener, *C.*	.....	10,773
Mrs. A. Winfield, *L./All.*	..	7,943
F. Adams, *N.F.*	....	794
Lab. maj.	....	8,509
(May '79, Lab. maj. 10,040)		

NORTH WEST   E. 49,814

T. Banks, *Lab.*	....	13,042
K. D. Irons, *C.*	....	6,124
A. Kellaway, *S.D.P./All.*	..	5,204
*A. Lewis, *Ind. Lab.*	......	3,074
M. Hipperson, *N.F.*	......	525
Lab. maj.	....	6,918
(May '79, Lab. maj. 10,455)		

SOUTH   E. 50,362

*N. J. Spearing, Lab.	.....	13,561
A. Reilly, *S.D.P./All.*	.....	6,250
N. Thompson, *C.*	......	6,212
I. H. M. Anderson, *N.F.*	..	993
Lab. maj.	....	7,311
(May '79, Lab. maj. 12,773)		

Norfolk

MID   E. 68,953

R. A. Ryder, O.B.E., *C.*	....	29,032
D. Cargill, *S.D.P./All.*	....	13,517
L. J. Potter, *Lab.*	....	8,950
M. McNee, *Ind. Pow.*	....	405
C. maj.	....	15,515

NORTH   E. 65,101

*R. F. Howell, C.	......	26,230
J. Elworthy, *S.D.P./All.*	..	13,007
E. A. Barber, *Lab.*	......	9,317
C. maj.	....	13,223

NORTH WEST   E. 69,181

H. C. Bellingham, *C.*	.....	23,358
*C. Brocklebank-Fowler,		
S.D.P./All.	......	20,211
M. Tilbury, *Lab.*	....	10,139
C. maj.	....	3,147

SOUTH   E. 73,523

*J. R. R. MacGregor, O.B.E.,		
C.	....	30,747
R. Carden, *L./All.*	......	18,612
H. A. Holzer, *Lab.*	......	7,408
C. maj.	....	12,135

SOUTH WEST   E. 70,398

*Sir P. L. Hawkins, T.D., C.		28,632
B. Baxter, *L./All.*	....	13,722
A. L. Rosenberg, *Lab.*	....	9,072
C. maj.	....	14,910

Normanton (W. Yorks)
E. 61,249

W. O'Brien, *Lab.*	....	18,782
A. Paul, *C.*	....	14,599
P. Pantelli, *S.D.P./All.*	...	9,741
Lab. maj.	....	4,183

Northampton

NORTH   E. 68,370

*A. R. Marlow, C.	......	23,129
D. Offenbach, *Lab.*	......	13,269
A. Rounthwaite, *L./All.*	..	12,829
C. maj.	....	9,860

SOUTH   E. 68,910

*M. W. L. Morris, C.	....	26,824
K. Kyle, *S.D.P./All.*	......	11,698
M. Coleman, *Lab.*	....	11,533
C. maj.	....	15,126

Northavon (Avon)
E. 73,553

*J. A. Cope, C.	....	30,790
Dr. G. Conrad, *L./All.*	...	17,807
Mrs. N. P. J. Norris, *Lab.*	..	8,243
K. Radmall, *Eco.*	....	499
C. maj.	....	12,983

North Devon
E. 63,638

*A. Speller, C.	......	28,066
R. Blackmore, *L./All.*	....	19,339
P. E. James, *Lab.*	....	2,893
R. Joanes, *Eco.*	....	669
C. maj.	....	8,727

North Shropshire
E. 73,333

*Rt. Hon. W. J. Biffen, C.	..	28,496
D. Evans, *L./All.*	....	16,829
Miss H. Jones, *Lab.*	......	7,860
J. L. Phillimore, *Ref.*	.....	135
C. maj.	....	11,667

North Warwickshire
E. 68,625

Hon. F. A. A. Maude, C.	..	22,452
J. E. Tomlinson, *Lab.*	....	19,867
H. Kerry, *S.D.P./All.*	.....	11,207
C. maj.	....	2,585

North West Leicestershire
E. 68,510

D. G. Ashby, *C.*	....	24,760
Mrs. I. Read, *Lab.*	......	18,098
G. Cort, *L./All.*	....	12,043
Mrs. D. Freer, *Eco.*	......	637
C. maj.	....	6,662

North Wiltshire
E. 76,150

*R. F. Needham, C.	....	30,924
C. S. M. Graham, *L./All.*	..	23,692
S. R. Allsop, *Lab.*	....	2,888
E. Barnham, *Eco.*	....	678
H. Baile de la Perrière,		
J.D.F.	....	113
C. maj.	....	7,232
(May '79, C. maj. 4,697)		

Norwich (Norfolk)

NORTH *E.* 62,781

H. P. Thompson, C.		21,355
Rt. Hon. D. Ennals, Lab.		15,476
G. Jones, L./All.		10,796
Ms. F. Cairns, W.R.P.		194
C. maj.		5,879

SOUTH *E.* 64,100

J. A. Powley, C.		18,998
J. Garrett, Lab.		17,286
J. Hardie, S.D.P./All.		11,968
A. Carter, Eco.		468
P. Williams, N.F.		145
J. Ward, Ind.		91
C. maj.		1,712

Norwood (Gtr. London)
E. 55,663

J. D. Fraser, Lab.		16,280
J. P. Parfitt, C.		13,397
M. Noble, S.D.P./All.		6,371
Miss C. M. Williams, N.F.		343
J. Sanderson, Ind.		123
Lab. maj.		2,883

Nottingham

EAST *E.* 63,638

M. Knowles, C.		17,641
M. Sloman, Lab.		16,177
M. Bird, S.D.P./All.		8,385
D. S. Merrick, Ind. C.		1,421
C. maj.		1,464

NORTH *E.* 71,807

R. G. J. Ottaway, C.		18,730
W. Whitlock, Lab.		18,368
L. Williams, S.D.P./All.		9,200
J. Peck, Comm.		1,184
C. maj.		362

SOUTH *E.* 65,059

M. M. Brandon-Bravo, C.		22,238
K. S. Coates, Lab.		16,523
R. Poynter, L./All.		9,697
C. maj.		5,715

Nuneaton (Warwicks)
E. 66,072

L. D. Stevens, C.		20,666
J. Haynes, Lab.		15,605
Ms. R. Levitt, S.D.P./All.		14,264
G. E. Davis, Ind. Lab.		504
C. maj.		5,061

Old Bexley and Sidcup
(Gtr. London)
E. 50,255

Rt. Hon. E. R. G. Heath,		
M.B.E., C.		22,422
P. Vickers, L./All.		9,704
C. A. Kiff, Lab.		5,116
C. maj.		12,718

(May '79, C. maj. 13,456)

Oldham (Gtr. Manchester)

CENTRAL AND ROYTON
E. 67,177

J. A. Lamond, Lab.		18,611
J. Farquahar, C.		15,299
M. Jackson, S.D.P./All.		11,022
Lab. maj.		3,312

West *E.* 57,445

M. H. Meacher, Lab.		17,690
D. Dickinson, C.		14,510
R. A. M. Smith, L./All.		7,745
J. Street, W.C.P.P.P.		180
Lab. maj.		3,180

Orpington (Gtr. London)
E. 58,759

I. R. Stanbrook, C.		25,569
J. W. Cook, L./All.		15,418
D. M. Bean, Lab.		3,439
L. T. Taylor, B.N.P.		215
C. maj.		10,151

Oxford

EAST *E.* 63,613

S. J. Norris, C.		18,808
A. D. Smith, Lab.		17,541
Mrs. M. Godden, L./All.		10,690
C. maj.		1,267

WEST AND ABINGDON *E.* 67,413

J. H. C. Patten, C.		23,778
D. E. T. Luard, S.D.P./All.		16,627
J. Jacottet, Lab.		8,440
Ms. S. Starmer, Eco.		544
R. Jones, Loony Soc.		267
C. N. Smith, U.P.		95
P. Doubleday, Ind.		86
Ms. R. Pinder, Ind.		26
C. maj.		7,151

Peckham (Gtr. London)
E. 59,128

Ms. H. Harman, Lab.		16,616
T. Eckersley, C.		7,792
A. Sawdon, S.D.P./All.		7,006
Mrs. M. Bailey, N.F.		800
Lab. maj.		8,824

Pendle (Lancs)
E. 64,483

J. R. L. Lee, C.		22,739
G. Rogers, Lab.		16,604
G. Lishman, L./All.		12,056
C. maj.		6,135

Penrith and The Border
(Cumbria)
E. 68,164

Rt. Hon. W. S. I. Whitelaw,		
C.H., M.C., C.		29,304
M. Young, L./All.		13,883
A. L. Williams, Lab.		6,612
C. maj.		15,421

(see p. 344 for by-election result)

Peterborough (Cambs.)
E. 78,957

Dr. B. S. Mawhinney, C.		27,270
B. Fish, Lab.		16,831
The Lady Walston, S.D.P./All.		13,142
N. Callaghan, Eco.		511
D. Hyland, W.R.P.		155
P. Gallagher, Ind. Lab.		0
C. maj.		10,439

Plymouth (Devon)

DEVONPORT *E.* 61,813

Rt. Hon. Dr. D. A. L. Owen,		
S.D.P./All.		20,843
Miss. A. Widdecombe, C.		15,907
J. Priestley, Lab.		9,845
J. E. Sullivan, Ind. C.		292
R. Bearsford-Walker,		
B.N.P.		72
Mrs. F. Hill, C.D.		21
S.D.P./All. maj.		4,936

DRAKE *E.* 52,383

Miss J. E. Fookes, C.		19,718
W. Fitzgerald, S.D.P./All.		11,133
Ms. S. A. Cresswell, Lab.		7,921
C. W. Bradbury, B.N.P.		163
C. maj.		8,585

SUTTON *E.* 59,890

Hon. A. K. M. Clark, C.		25,203
A. Puttick, L./All.		13,516
Ms. F. Holland, Lab.		6,538
S. Shaw, Eco.		470
C. maj.		11,687

Pontefract and Castleford
(W. Yorks)
E. 64,878

G. Lofthouse, Lab.		24,990
B. Howell, C.		11,299
D. Dale, L./All.		7,452
Lab. maj.		13,691

Poole (Dorset)
E. 70,731

J. D. Ward, C.B.E., C.		30,358
B. Clements, L./All.		15,929
M. V. Castle, Lab.		5,595
A. Foster, S.A.C.A.		177
C. maj.		14,429

Portsmouth (Hants)

NORTH *E.* 77,923

P. H. S. Griffiths, C.		31,413
S. Luxon, S.D.P./All.		13,414
N. Beard, Lab.		12,013
C. maj.		17,999

SOUTH *E.* 74,357

R. B. Pink, C.B.E., V.R.D., C.		25,101
M. Hancock, S.D.P./All.		12,766
Mrs. S. T. Thomas, Lab.		11,324
A. J. Evens, Ind. L.		554
G. A. Knight, N.F.		279
D. W. Fry, T.E.F.		172
C. maj.		12,335

(see by-election on p. 345)

Preston (Lancs)
E. 64,969

S. G. Thorne, Lab.		21,810
T. Huntley, C.		14,832
M. Connolly, S.D.P./All.		10,039
Lab. maj.		6,978

Pudsey (W. Yorks)
E. 70,583

J. G. D. Shaw, C.		24,455
J. Cummins, L./All.		19,141
Ms. S. M. Price, Lab.		9,542
R. Smith, Ind.		387
C. maj.		5,314

Putney (Gtr. London)
E. 68,853

*D. J. Mellor, C.		21,863
P. Hain, *Lab.*		16,844
C. Welchman, *L./All.*		7,668
M. Connolly, *N.F.*		290
Mrs. R. Baillie-Grohman, *Eco.*		190
L. Chalk, *Soc.*		88
W. Williams, *Ind.*		41
C. maj.		5,019
(May '79, C. maj. 2,634)		

Ravensbourne (Gtr. London)
E. 58,811

*J. L. Hunt, C.		27,143
Mrs. C. M. Boston, *S.D.P./All.*		11,631
J. R. Holbrook, *Lab.*		4,037
A. T. Shotton, *B.N.P.*		242
C. maj.		15,512

Reading (Berks)

EAST   *E.* 67,511

*Dr. G. F. Vaughan, C.		24,516
C. Huhne, *S.D.P./All.*		13,008
K. Boyle, *Lab.*		9,218
G. Darnton, *Eco.*		519
P. Baker, *B.N.P.*		147
B. Shone, *C.M.P.*		113
C. maj.		11,508

WEST   *E.* 66,080

*R. A. B. Durant, C.		24,948
R. J. Day, *L./All.*		13,549
R. Evans, *Lab.*		9,220
E. Lilley, *Ind.*		161
C. maj.		11,399

Redcar (Cleveland)
E. 63,447

*J. Tinn, Lab.		18,348
P. Bassett, *C.*		15,244
G. Nightingale, *S.D.P./All.*		11,614
Lab. maj.		3,104
(May '79, Lab. maj. 8,053)		

Reigate (Surrey)
E. 70,320

*G. A. Gardiner, C.		29,932
Mrs. E. Pamplin, *S.D.P./All.*		13,625
B. A. Symons, *Lab.*		6,114
D. Newell, *Eco.*		1,029
C. maj.		16,307

Ribble Valley (Lancs)
E. 59,982

*D. C. Waddington, Q.C., C.		29,223
M. Carr, *S.D.P./All.*		10,632
E. A. Saville, *Lab.*		6,214
C. maj.		18,591

Richmond and Barnes
(Gtr. London)
E. 55,845

J. J. Hanley, C.		20,695
A. J. Watson, *L./All.*		20,621
K. Vaz, *Lab.*		3,156
C. maj.		74

Richmond (N. Yorks)
E. 75,196

*Rt. Hon. L. Brittan, Q.C., C.		32,373
D. Raw, *L./All.*		14,307
Mrs. B. L. M. Hawkins, *Lab.*		4,997
C. maj.		18,066

Rochdale (Gtr. Manchester)
E. 66,976

*C. Smith, M.B.E., L./All.		21,858
Ms. V. Broon, *Lab.*		14,271
A. Fearn, *C.*		10,616
P. Barker, *N.F.*		463
P. Courtney, *U.P.*		204
L./All. maj.		7,587
(May '79, L. maj. 5,294)		

Rochford (Essex)
E. 69,392

Dr. M. Clark, C.		29,495
R. Boyd, *L./All.*		16,393
M. Witzer, *Lab.*		5,105
C. maj.		13,102

Romford (Gtr. London)
E. 55,758

*M. J. Neubert, C.		20,771
J. Bates, *L./All.*		10,197
J. Hoepelman, *Lab.*		7,494
Mrs. M. P. Caine, *N.F.*		432
C. maj.		10,574
(May '79, C. maj. 8,812)		

Romsey and Waterside (Hants)
E. 70,782

*M. K. B. Colvin, C.		30,361
A. Bloss, *S.D.P./All.*		16,671
M. Knight, *Lab.*		6,604
C. maj.		13,690

Rossendale and Darwen (Lancs)
E. 74,401

*D. A. Trippier, C.		27,214
C. Robinson, *Lab.*		18,393
M. Taylor, *L./All.*		12,246
C. maj.		8,821

Rotherham (S. Yorks)
E. 61,165

*J. S. Crowther, Lab.		22,236
C. Middleton, *C.*		10,527
P. Bowler, *L./All.*		8,192
Lab. maj.		11,709
(May '79, Lab. maj. 13,435)		

Rother Valley (S. Yorks)
E. 65,127

K. J. Barron, Lab.		21,781
J. Derrick, *C.*		13,156
J. Boddy, *S.D.P./All.*		11,903
Lab. maj.		8,625

Rugby and Kenilworth
(Warwicks)
E. 74,501

*J. F. Pawsey, C.		29,622
D. Owen-Jones, *L./All.*		15,381
P. Blundell, *Lab.*		13,180
C. maj.		14,241

Ruislip-Northwood
(Gtr. London)
E. 56,378

*J. A. D. Wilkinson, C.		24,498
R. Stephenson, *L./All.*		11,516
M. O'Brien, *Lab.*		5,105
C. maj.		12,982
(May '79, C. maj. 17,207)		

Rushcliffe (Notts)
E. 70,333

*K. H. Clarke, Q.C., C.		33,253
J. Hamilton, *L./All.*		13,033
V. R. Coaker, *Lab.*		7,290
Mrs. M. Pooks, *Eco.*		518
C. maj.		20,220
(May '79, C. maj. 22,484)		

Rutland and Melton (Leics)
E. 75,180

*M. A. Latham, C.		33,262
D. J. Farrer, *L./All.*		14,909
J. Whitby, *Lab.*		6,414
Ms. H. A. Goddard, *Eco.*		532
C. maj.		18,353

Ryedale (N. Yorks)
E. 78,388

*J. D. Spence, C.		33,312
Mrs. E. Shields, *L./All.*		17,170
P. Bloom, *Lab.*		5,816
C. maj.		16,142

Saffron Walden (Essex)
E. 69,385

*A. G. B. Haselhurst, C.		30,869
J. Torode, *S.D.P./All.*		15,620
R. P. Trory, *Lab.*		6,078
W. D. Smedley, *A.C.M.*		797
C. maj.		15,249
(May '79, C. maj. 15,363)		

St. Albans (Herts)
E. 72,849

P. B. Lilley, C.		29,676
A. S. B. Walkington, *L./All.*		21,115
Mrs. R. Austin, *Lab.*		6,213
C. maj.		8,561

St. Helens (Merseyside)

NORTH   *E.* 71,059

*J. Evans, Lab.		25,334
A. Rhodes, *C.*		16,075
N. Derbyshire, *L./All.*		11,525
Lab. maj.		9,259

SOUTH   *E.* 69,172

G. E. Bermingham, Lab.		22,906
R. Bull, *C.*		13,244
P. Briers, *S.D.P./All.*		10,939
M. Davies, *Ind.*		1,780
Lab. maj.		9,662

St. Ives (Cornwall)
E. 64,012

D. A. Harris, C.		24,297
H. Carter, *S.D.P./All.*		16,438
Ms. M. Crowley, *Lab.*		5,310
P. Prior, *M.K.*		569
H. Hoptrough, *Eco.*		439
N. Horner, *Ind.*		219
C. maj.		7,859

Salford East
(Gtr. Manchester)
E. 63,946

*Rt. Hon. S. Orme, Lab.	...	21,373
S. Cole, C.	....	11,832
A. Williams, S.D.P./All.		6,190
S. Carter, W.R.P.	....	417
Lab. maj.	....	9,541

Salisbury (Wilts)
E. 74,189

S. R. Key, C.	....	28,876
J. Lakeman, L./All.	......	21,702
Mrs. C. K. Lamberth, Lab.		3,139
Miss M. Kemp, W. Reg.	...	182
T. Abbott, Ind.	....	86
C. maj.	....	7,174

Scarborough (N. Yorks)
E. 72,362

*Sir M. N. Shaw, C.	....	27,977
Mrs. R. Jordan, S.D.P./All.		14,048
J. Battersby, Lab.	....	9,545
C. maj.	....	13,929

Sedgefield (Durham)
E. 61,702

A. C. L. Blair, Lab.	......	21,401
T. Horton, C.	....	13,120
D. Shand, S.D.P./All.	....	10,183
M. Logan-Salton, Ind.	....	298
Lab. maj.	....	8,281

Selby (N. Yorks)
E. 65,365

*Rt. Hon. M. J. H. Alison, C.	....	26,712
W. Whitaker, L./All.	.....	10,747
Mrs. S. Haines, Lab.	.....	9,687
C. maj.	....	15,965

Sevenoaks (Kent)
E. 71,327

*G. M. Wolfson, C.	....	30,722
S. Jakobi, L./All.	....	15,016
R. Gooding, Lab.	....	6,439
G. L. Burnett, N.F.	......	416
C. maj.	....	15,706

Sheffield (S. Yorks)

ATTERCLIFFE E. 64,204

*A. E. P. Duffy, Lab.	.....	23,067
G. Millward, C.	....	11,455
Ms. I. Addison, S.D.P./All.		10,241
Lab. maj.	....	11,612

BRIGHTSIDE E. 67,260

*Miss V. J. Maynard, Lab.	.	25,531
F. Butler, L./All.	....	10,322
D. Grayson, C.	....	7,888
P. A. Spinks, N.F.	....	286
Lab. maj.	....	15,209

CENTRAL E. 66,769

R. G. Caborn, Lab.	....	24,759
Miss P. Major, S.D.P./All.		7,969
Miss P. Rawlings, C.	.....	7,908
Miss V. Gill, Comm.	......	296
C. Barrett, Rev. Comm.	...	222
Lab. maj.	....	16,790

HALLAM E. 78,878

*Sir J. H. Osborn, C.	......	26,851
M. Johnson, L./All.	.....	15,077
Ms. J. McCrindle, Lab.	...	10,463
P. Booler, Ind. C.	....	656
C. maj.	....	11,774

HEELEY E. 74,659

W. Michie, Lab.	....	24,111
S. Cordle, C.	....	15,743
J. M. Day, S.D.P./All.	....	12,813
Lab. maj.	....	8,368

HILLSBOROUGH E. 74,422

*M. H. Flannery, Lab.	....	20,901
D. Chadwick, L./All.	.....	19,355
Mrs. C. Smith, C.	....	15,881
Lab. maj.	....	1,546

Sherwood (Notts)
E. 69,091

A. S. Stewart, C.	....	21,595
W. Bach, Lab.	....	20,937
Mrs. M. E. Cooper, S.D.P./ All.	....	10,172
C. maj.	....	658

Shipley (W. Yorks)
E. 67,584

*J. M. Fox, M.B.E., C.	....	25,866
W. Wallace, L./All.	......	14,421
M. A. Leathley, Lab.	.....	11,218
S. Shepherd, Eco.	....	521
C. maj.	....	11,445

Shoreham (W Sussex)
E. 69,720

*R. N. Luce, C.	....	31,679
J. Ingram, L./All.	....	15,913
Mrs. S. J. Hurcombe, Lab.		3,794
C. maj.	....	15,766

Shrewsbury and Atcham (Salop)
E. 66,554

D. L. Conway, C.	....	24,397
A. Bowen, L./All.	....	15,773
A. Mosley, Lab.	....	9,080
C. maj.	....	8,624
(May '79, C. maj. 10,184)		

Skipton and Ripon
(N. Yorks)
E. 69,421

*J. G. B. Watson, C.	....	31,509
Mrs. K. C. Brooks, L./All.		16,463
Ms. M. A. Billing, Lab.	...	4,044
C. maj.	....	15,046

Slough (Berks)
E. 71,907

J. A. Watts, C.	....	22,064
*Miss J. Lestor, Lab.	......	18,958
N. Bosanquet, S.D.P./All.		9,519
G. John, N.F.	....	528
I. Flindall, Eco.	....	325
C. maj.	....	3,106

Solihull (W. Midlands)
E. 73,677

J. M. Taylor, C.	....	31,947
I. Gillett, L./All.	....	14,553
I. Jamieson, Lab.	....	6,075
C. maj.	....	17,394

Somerton and Frome
(Somerset)
E. 64,695

*Hon. R. T. Boscawen, C.	..	26,988
N. Hinton, S.D.P./All.	...	17,761
J. B. Osborn, Lab.	....	4,867
C. maj.	....	9,227

Southampton (Hants)

ITCHEN E. 72,233

C. R. Chope, C.	....	21,937
*R. Mitchell, S.D.P./All.	..	16,647
J. Denham, Lab.	....	14,324
C. maj.	....	5,290

TEST E. 74,668

*S. J. A. Hill, C.	....	24,657
A. P. V. Whitehead, Lab.	.	15,311
A. Vinson, S.D.P./All.	...	14,592
C. maj.	....	9,346

Southend (Essex)

EAST E. 57,690

*E. M. Taylor, C.	....	21,743
C. George, S.D.P./All.	....	11,052
C. O. O'Brien, Lab.	......	6,188
C. maj.	....	10,691
(May '79, C. maj. 10,774)		

WEST E. 67,486

*Rt. Hon. H. P. G. Channon, C.	....	26,360
G. Grant, L./All.	....	18,327
Mrs. J. Nisbet, Lab.	......	3,675
C. maj.	....	8,033
(May '79, C. maj. 16,864)		

South Hams (Devon)
E. 74,276

*A. D. Steen, C.	....	31,855
A. Rogers, L./All.	....	19,454
G. J. Morris, Lab.	....	3,824
Ms. W. Morgan, Eco.	.....	518
C. maj.	....	12,401

Southport (Merseyside)
E. 70,089

*Sir W. I. Percival, Q.C., C.	.	25,612
I. B. Brodie-Brown, L./All.		20,573
F. P. Brady, Lab.	....	4,233
K. L. Wood, S.B.I.L.P.	...	374
C. maj.	....	5,039
(May '79, C. maj. 6,527)		

South Ribble (Lancs)
E. 72,401

*R. J. Atkins, C.	....	27,625
F. Duffy, Lab.	....	14,966
R. Walker, L./All.	....	13,690
C. maj.	....	12,659

South Shields (Tyne & Wear)
E. 61,924

*D. G. Clark, Lab.	....	19,055
P. Groves, C.	....	12,653
P. Angus, S.D.P./All.	....	9,288
Lab. maj.	....	6,402

Southwark and Bermondsey
(Gtr. London)
E. 55,839

*S. H. W. Hughes, *L./All.*	..	17,185
*J. Tilley, *Lab.*	....	12,021
R. Hughes, *C.*	....	4,481
J. S. Sneath, *N.F.*	......	474
K. T. Mason, *New Brit.*	...	154
A. Farehk, *Rev. Comm.*	...	54
S. C. McKenzie, *Nat.*	.....	50
T. L. Keen, *Ind.*	....	50
L./All. maj.	....	5,164

Spelthorne (Surrey)
E. 72,236

*Rt. Hon. Sir H. E. G. Atkins,		
C.	....	26,863
A. Layton, *S.D.P./All.*	...	13,357
M. C. Rowlands, *Lab.*	......	7,926
R. Adams, *Ind. C.*	....	2,816
E. Butterfield, *A.C.M.*	......	325
C. maj.	....	13,506
(May '79, C. maj. 16,153)		

Stafford
E. 70,570

*Rt. Hon. Sir H. C. P. J.		
Fraser, *M.B.E.*, *C.*	......	27,639
D. Dunn, *S.D.P./All.*	......	13,362
M. J. D. Poulter, *Lab.*	....	12,789
J. Caruso, *Gizza Job*	....	212
C. maj.	....	14,277
(see by-election on p. 345)		

Staffordshire

MID   E. 67,425

*B. J. Heddle, *C.*	....	27,210
T. Jones, *L./All.*	....	13,330
P. Lane, *Lab.*	....	11,720
C. maj.	....	13,880

MOORLANDS   E. 72,466

*D. L. Knox, *C.*	....	30,079
B. Campbell, *Lab.*	....	13,513
P. Gubbins, *S.D.P./All.*	...	12,370
C. maj.	....	16,566

SOUTH   E. 73,038

*P. T. Cormack, *C.*	....	32,764
J. Chambers, *L./All.*	......	13,004
M. J. Cartwright, *Lab.*	....	9,568
C. maj.	....	19,760
(May '79, C. maj. 17,433)		

SOUTH EAST   E. 63,324

D. L. Lightbown, *C.*	......	24,556
Mrs. C. M. Crawley, *Lab.*	..	13,658
M. Lynch, *S.D.P./All.*	......	10,220
C. maj.	....	10,898

Stalybridge and Hyde
(Gtr. Manchester)
E. 67,916

*T. Pendry, *Lab.*	....	21,798
B. Silvester, *C.*	....	17,436
J. Hughes, *L./All.*	....	8,339
B. Nylan, *N.F.*	....	294
Lab. maj.	....	4,362
(May '79, Lab. maj. 6,580)		

Stamford and Spalding (Lincs)
E. 65,955

*Sir K. Lewis, *C.*	....	27,728
P. Lee, *S.D.P./All.*	....	15,972
Ms. A. Mullender, *Lab.*	...	5,354
C. maj.	....	11,756

Stevenage (Herts)
E. 67,706

T. J. R. Wood, *C.*	....	20,787
B. R. M. Stoneham, *S.D.P./*		
All.	....	19,032
Mrs. S. Reeves, *Lab.*	.....	12,673
D. R. Bowmaker, *B.N.P.*	...	236
C. maj.	....	1,755

Stockport (Gtr. Manchester)
E. 58,908

A. R. Favell, *C.*	....	18,517
P. R. Ward, *Lab.*	....	12,731
*T. McNally, *S.D.P./All.*	...	12,129
M. Shipley, *Eco.*	....	369
K. Walker, *Nat.*	....	194
C. maj.	....	5,786

Stockton (Cleveland)

NORTH   E. 70,277

F. Cook, *Lab.*	....	18,339
H. Davies, *C.*	....	16,469
*Rt. Hon. W. Rodgers,		
S.D.P./All.	....	14,630
Lab. maj.	....	1,870

SOUTH   E. 73,790

*I. W. Wrigglesworth,		
S.D.P./All.	....	19,550
T. Finnegan, *C.*	....	19,448
F. Griffiths, *Lab.*	....	13,998
D. Fern, *Ind.*	....	205
S.D.P./All. maj.	....	102

Stoke-on-Trent (Staffs)

CENTRAL   E. 66,934

*M. Fisher, *Lab.*	....	21,194
K. Mans, *C.*	....	12,944
Ms. V. Freeman, *S.D.P./*		
All.	....	9,458
C. S. Cook, *Loony Soc.*	....	504
Lab. maj.	....	8,250

NORTH   E. 75,251

*J. S. Forrester, *Lab.*	......	24,721
R. Ibbs, *C.*	....	16,518
T. Beswick, *S.D.P./All.*	....	12,186
Lab. maj.	....	8,203

SOUTH   E. 70,600

*Rt. Hon. J. Ashley, *C.H.*,		
Lab.	....	23,611
P. Maxwell, *C.*	....	16,506
W. Walley, *L./All.*	....	9,050
Lab. maj.	....	7,105

Stratford-on-Avon (Warwicks)
E. 76,649

A. T. Howarth, *C.B.E.*, *C.*	..	34,041
W. J. B. Taylor, *L./All.*	...	16,124
*F. O. Hooley, *Lab.*	....	5,731
C. maj.	....	17,917

Streatham (Gtr. London)
E. 60,032

*W. J. M. Shelton, *C.*	......	18,264
Mrs. M. Long, *Lab.*	......	12,362
P. Billenness, *L./All.*	.....	8,321
K. Handy, *N.F.*	....	321
C. maj.	....	5,902

Stretford (Gtr. Manchester)
E. 57,448

A. J. Lloyd, *Lab.*	....	18,028
W. Sweeney, *C.*	....	13,686
D. Wilks, *S.D.P./All.*	.....	8,141
S. A. Ud-Din, *Ind. Lab.*	...	336
Lab. maj.	....	4,342

Stroud (Glos)
E. 77,528

*Sir J. A. Kershaw, *M.C.*,		
C.	....	30,896
G. Fallon, *L./All.*	....	19,182
D. R. Parsons, *Lab.*	......	10,141
C. maj.	....	11,714

Suffolk

CENTRAL   E. 75,641

M. Lord, *C.*	....	30,096
N. Baldwin, *L./All.*	......	15,365
Mrs. M. Sierakowski, *Lab.*	10,828
C. maj.	....	14,731

COASTAL   E. 71,521

*J. S. Gummer, *C.*	....	31,240
D. Houseley, *S.D.P./All.*	..	15,618
D. Ballantyne, *Lab.*	......	6,780
C. maj.	....	15,622

SOUTH   E. 76,209

T. S. K. Yeo, *C.*	....	29,469
R. Kemp, *L./All.*	....	18,200
S. Billcliffe, *Lab.*	....	10,516
C. maj.	....	11,269

Sunderland
(Tyne & Wear)

NORTH   E. 78,520

R. A. Clay, *Lab.*	....	24,179
C. Lewis, *C.*	....	16,983
D. McCourt, *L./All.*	......	11,090
Lab. maj.	....	7,196

SOUTH   E. 75,124

*G. A. T. Bagier, *Lab.*	.....	22,869
A. Mitchell, *C.*	....	17,321
J. Anderson, *S.D.P./All.*	..	9,865
Lab. maj.	....	5,548

Surbiton (Gtr. London)
E. 46,949

R. P. Tracey, *C.*	....	18,245
C. Nowakowski, *S.D.P./*		
All.	....	9,496
N. D. Waskett, *Lab.*	......	5,173
J. Maclellan, *Eco.*	....	551
C. maj.	....	8,749
(May '79, C. maj. 10,802)		

Surrey

EAST   E. 58,485

*Rt. Hon. Sir R. E. G. Howe,		
Q.C., *C.*	....	27,272
Mrs. S. Liddell, *L./All.*	...	11,836
H. Pincott, *Lab.*	....	4,249
C. maj.	....	15,436
(May '79, C. maj. 19,400)		

NORTH WEST *E.* 78,377
*W. M. J. Grylls, C. 35,297
J. Weedon, *L./All.* 14,279
J. Burrow, *Lab.* 5,452
C. maj. 21,018
(May '79, C. maj. 25,456)

SOUTH WEST *E.* 69,875
*Rt. Hon. M. V. Macmillan,
C. 31,067
G. Scott, *L./All.* 16,716
S. E. D. Williams, *Lab.* ... 4,239
C. maj. 14,351
(*see* by-election on p 345)

Sutton and Cheam
(Gtr. London)
E. 63,099

*D. N. Macfarlane, C. 26,782
C. Caswill, *L./All.* 16,518
G. S. Dixon, *Lab.* 3,568
C. maj. 10,264
(May '79, C. maj. 15,706)

Sutton Coldfield (W. Midlands)
E. 67,695

*Rt. Hon. P. N. Fowler, C. .. 31,753
A. Jones, *L./All.* 12,769
C. C. Gibbons, *Lab.* 4,066
C. maj. 18,984
(May '79, C. maj. 26,107)

Swindon (Wilts)
E. 76,833

S. C. Coombs, *C.* 22,310
*D. Stoddart, Lab. 20,915
D. J. Scott, *S.D.P./All.* ... 13,743
C. maj. 1,395
(May '79, Lab. maj. 5,899)

Tatton (Cheshire)
E. 68,747

M. N. Hamilton, *C.* 27,877
D. Levy, *S.D.P./All.* 13,917
D. W. Davies, *Lab.* 9,295
C. maj. 13,960

Taunton (Somerset)
E. 70,359

*Rt. Hon. E. D. L. du Cann,
C. 28,112
M. Cocks, *S.D.P./All.* 15,545
J. Gray, *Lab.* 9,498
C. maj. 12,567
(May '79, C. maj. 12,724)

Teignbridge (Devon)
E. 67,515

P. C. M. Nicholls, *C.* 28,265
J. Alderson, *L./All.* 20,047
M. Loughlin, *Lab.* 3,749
A. Hope, *Loony Soc.* 241
C. maj. 8,218

Thanet (Kent)

NORTH *E.* 66,678
R. J. Gale, *C.* 26,801
W. MacMillan, *S.D.P./All.* 12,256
Ms. C. Booth, *Lab.* 6,482
B. Dobing, *B.N.P.* 324
C. maj. 14,545

SOUTH *E.* 61,989
*J. W. P. Aitken, C. 24,512
I. Josephs, *L./All.* 10,461
M. Clark, *Lab.* 8,429
C. maj. 14,051

Thurrock (Essex)
E. 66,300

*Dr. Oonagh McDonald,
Lab. 17,600
Miss J. Tallon, *C.* 15,878
D. Benson, *S.D.P./All.* ... 9,761
M. J. Bibby, *Ind.* 1,220
R. W. Sinclair, *B.N.P.* 252
J. Paul, *Comm.* 199
Lab. maj. 1,722

Tiverton (Devon)
E. 63,828

*R. J. Maxwell-Hyslop, C. . 27,101
D. Morrish, *L./All.* 19,215
D. A. Gorbutt, *Lab.* 3,154
C. maj. 7,886

Tonbridge and Malling (Kent)
E. 72,549

*J. P. Stanley, C. 30,417
F. Freeman, *S.D.P./All.* .. 16,897
D. J. Bishop, *Lab.* 6,896
C. maj. 13,520
(May '79, C. maj. 16,252)

Tooting (Gtr. London)
E. 68,083

*T. M. Cox, Lab. 19,640
R. Harris, *C.* 16,981
Mrs. J. Neuberger, *S.D.P./*
All. 8,317
P. Berbridge, *N.F.* 355
Ms. E. Shaw, *Eco.* 255
R. E. Lewis, *Comm.* 181
H. Patel, *Eth. Min.* 146
C. Redgrave, *W.R.P.* 72
Lab. maj. 2,659

Torbay (Devon)
E. 67,337

*Sir F. M. Bennett, C. 25,721
M. Mitchell, *L./All.* 19,166
P. W. Rackley, *Lab.* 3,521
Mrs. A. M. L. Murray,
Ratepayer 500
C. maj. 6,555

Torridge and West Devon
E. 70,648

*Sir P. M. Mills, C. 31,156
V. Howell, *L./All.* 18,805
W. A. Tupman, *Lab.* 3,531
M. J. Beale, *Ind.* 116
Miss H. E. Rous, *W. Reg.* .. 113
C. maj. 12,351

Tottenham (Gtr. London)
E. 67,944

*N. Atkinson, Lab. 22,423
P. Murphy, *C.* 13,027
A. L'Estrange, *L./All.* 6,990
W. G. Hurry, *Ind. C.* 652
Lab. maj. 9,396

Truro (Cornwall)
E. 68,514

*D. C. Penhaligon, L./All. . 31,279
P. Buddell, *C.* 20,799
Ms. J. M. Beecroft, *Lab.* .. 2,479
L./All. maj. 10,480

Tunbridge Wells (Kent)
E. 73,700

*Sir P. B. B. Mayhew, Q.C.,
C. 31,199
P. Blaine, *L./All.* 16,073
S. J. Casely, *Lab.* 6,042
D. Smith, *N.F.* 236
C. maj. 15,126
(May '79, C. maj. 20,536)

Twickenham (Gtr. London)
E. 64,116

*T. F. H. Jessel, C. 25,110
J. Waller, *L./All.* 20,318
Ms. P. A. Nicholas, *Lab.* .. 3,732
J. Clarke, *Eco.* 424
T. Denville-Faulkner, *N.F.* 234
R. W. Kenyon, *Ind.* 40
C. maj. 4,792

Tyne Bridge
(Tyne & Wear)
E. 60,808

*H. L. Cowans, Lab. 21,127
R. Crawley, *C.* 9,434
A. Dawson, *L./All.* 6,852
Lab. maj. 11,693

Tynemouth
(Tyne & Wear)
E. 74,549

*N. G. Trotter, C. 27,029
P. J. Cosgrove, *Lab.* 17,420
D. Mayhew, *L./All.* 11,153
C. maj. 9,609

Upminster (Gtr. London)
E. 66,445

*Sir N. C. Bonsor, BT., C. .. 25,153
D. Osman, *S.D.P./All.* 12,339
A. Hughes, *Lab.* 9,829
G. Nobes-Pride, *N.F.* 566
C. maj. 12,814
(May '79, C. maj. 9,065)

Uxbridge (Gtr. London)
E. 61,615

*J. M. Shersby, C. 23,875
P. Russell, *S.D.P./All.* 11,038
P. J. Magee, *Lab.* 9,611
C. maj. 12,837
(May '79, C. maj. 7,995)

Vauxhall (Gtr. London)
E. 64,867

*S. K. Holland, Lab. 18,234
K. Manning, *C.* 10,454
R. Liddle, *S.D.P./All.* 9,515
J. Wright, *N.F.* 508
P. J. Lingard, *Loony Soc.* .. 266
D. Cook, *Comm.* 199
G. B. Shorter, *W.P.* 38
Lab. maj. 7,780

Wakefield (W. Yorks)
E. 68,416

*Rt. Hon. W. Harrison, Lab.	19,166
N. Hazell, C.	18,806
Dr. D. Carlton, S.D.P./All.	9,166
Mrs. V. Parker, B.N.P.	295
Lab. maj.	360

Wallasey (Merseyside)
E. 68,462

*Mrs. L. Chalker, C.	22,854
J. A. Robertson, Lab.	16,146
J. Richardson, S.D.P./All.	10,717
C. maj.	6,708
(May '79, C. maj. 5,381)	

Wallsend (Tyne & Wear)
E. 76,268

*W. E. Garrett, Lab.	26,615
Miss M. Leigh, C.	14,101
Mrs. J. Phylactou, S.D.P./All.	13,522
Lab. maj.	12,514

Walsall (W. Midlands)
NORTH E. 68,868

*D. J. Winnick, Lab.	20,782
N. Stephens, C.	17,958
A. Bentley, L./All.	10,141
Lab. maj.	2,824

SOUTH E. 67,257

*B. T. George, Lab.	21,735
D. Nicholson, C.	21,033
B. Silver, S.D.P./All.	6,586
J. Parker, B.N.P.	632
Lab. maj.	702

Walthamstow (Gtr. London)
E. 48,324

*E. P. Deakins, Lab.	13,241
A. Amos, C.	11,936
P. Leighton, S.D.P./All.	7,192
P. Mitchell, N.F.	444
S. Lambert, Eco.	424
Lab. maj.	1,305
(May '79, Lab. maj. 4,403)	

Wansbeck (Nthmb)
E. 63,398

J. Thompson, Lab.	21,732
J. A. Thompson, L./All.	13,901
C. Michell, C.	10,563
Lab. maj.	7,831

Wansdyke (Avon)
E. 71,094

*J. H. Aspinwall, C.	28,434
R. Denton-White, L./All.	15,368
L. Williams, Lab.	12,168
A. Stout, W. Reg.	213
C. maj.	13,066

Wanstead and Woodford (Gtr. London)
E. 57,705

*Rt. Hon. C. P. F. Jenkin, C.	23,765
K. Crawford, L./All.	9,411
Mrs. L. S. Hilton, Lab.	5,334
Mrs. C. Warth, Eco.	476
H. Marshall, N.F.	456
C. maj.	14,354
(May '79, C. maj. 17,750)	

Wantage (Oxon)
E. 63,950

R. V. Jackson, C.	25,992
Mrs. W. Tumin, S.D.P./All.	15,867
A. J. D. Popper, Lab.	7,115
A. P. Barrett Mockler, W. Reg.	183
C. maj.	10,125

Warley (W. Midlands)
EAST E. 57,439

*A. M. W. Faulds, Lab.	18,036
M. Whitby, C.	14,645
B. Hamer, S.D.P./All.	6,697
H. Singh Randhawa, Comm.	217
Lab. maj.	3,391

WEST E. 57,165

*Rt. Hon. P. K. Archer, Q.C., Lab.	18,272
Miss A. McIntyre, C.	13,004
A. G. Baines, L./All.	7,485
Lab. maj.	5,268

Warrington (Cheshire)
NORTH E. 69,850

*E. D. H. Hoyle, Lab.	20,873
S. Sexton, C.	15,596
D. Harrison, S.D.P./All.	13,951
I. Sloan, B.N.P.	267
Lab. maj.	5,277

SOUTH E. 72,803

*Rt. Hon. M. Carlisle, Q.C., C.	22,740
Dr. D. Colin-Thome, Lab.	16,275
I. Marks, L./All.	14,827
N. Chantrell, Eco.	403
C. maj.	6,465

Warwick and Leamington
E. 70,858

*Sir D. G. Smith, C.	26,512
R. Behrens, S.D.P./All.	13,480
R. Chessum, Lab.	11,463
N. Charlton, Eco.	685
C. maj.	13,032

Watford (Herts)
E. 71,992

*W. A. T. T. Garel-Jones, C.	26,273
P. Burton, S.D.P./All.	14,267
I. Wilson, Lab.	14,247
C. maj.	12,006

Waveney (Suffolk)
E. 77,960

*Rt. Hon. J. M. L. Prior, C.	30,371
J. A. Lark, Lab.	16,073
Ms. G. Artis, S.D.P./All.	12,234
C. maj.	14,298

Wealden (E. Sussex)
E. 69,244

*Sir G. J. Johnson Smith, C.	31,926
D. Pace, S.D.P./All.	14,741
Mrs. P. Knight, Lab.	3,060
C. maj.	17,185

Wellingborough (Northants)
E. 67,598

*P. D. Fry, C.	25,715
J. Mann, Lab.	13,659
L. Stringer, L./All.	12,994
Miss D. M. P. Garnett, Ind.	228
C. maj.	12,056

Wells (Somerset)
E. 62,159

D. P. Heathcoat-Amory, C.	25,385
A. Butt-Philip, L./All.	18,810
A. M. Leigh, Lab.	3,747
G. Livings, Ind.	273
C. maj.	6,575

Welwyn Hatfield (Herts)
E. 72,644

*C. P. Y. Murphy, C.	27,498
Dr. L. Granshaw, S.D.P./All.	15,252
J. France, Lab.	14,898
C. maj.	12,246

Wentworth (S. Yorks)
E. 62,057

*P. Hardy, Lab.	25,538
R. Norton, C.	9,603
M. Tildsley, S.D.P./All.	8,082
Lab. maj.	15,935

West Bromwich (W. Midlands)
EAST E. 59,391

*P. C. Snape, Lab.	15,894
C. Cole, C.	15,596
M. Smith, L./All.	10,200
Lab. maj.	298

WEST E. 58,341

*Miss B. Boothroyd, Lab.	18,896
D. Harman, C.	12,257
A. Collingbourne, S.D.P./All.	6,094
Lab. maj.	6,639
(May '79, Lab. maj. 9,468)	

Westbury (Wilts)
E. 80,244

*D. Walters, M.B.E., C.	31,133
D. Hughes, L./All.	22,627
H. W. Thomas, Lab.	6,058
P. Ekins, Eco.	609
J. C. Banks, W. Reg.	131
C. maj.	8,506

West Gloucestershire
E. 74,266

*P. Marland, C.	27,092
J. Watkinson, S.D.P./All.	17,440
M. J. Hodkinson, Lab.	14,572
C. maj.	9,652
(May '79, C. maj. 4,174)	

West Lancashire

K. H. Hind, *C.*		25,458
Ms. J. Farrington, *Lab.*		18,600
A. Sackville, *S.D.P./All.*		10,983
C. maj.		6,858

Westminster North
(Gtr. London)
E. 68,988

*J. D. Wheeler, *C.*		19,134
A. Latham, *Lab.*		17,424
G. Halliwell, *S.D.P./All.*		6,956
T. Cooper, *Eco.*		527
T. L. Keen, *T.V.C.A.B.L.*		148
B. Fisher, *Ind.*		73
C. maj.		1,710

Westmorland and Lonsdale
(Cumbria)
E. 67,161

*Rt. Hon. T. M. Jopling, *C.*		29,775
K. Hulls, *L./All.*		13,188
C. Stott, *Lab.*		4,798
R. Gibson, *Eco.*		805
C. maj.		16,587

Weston-Super-Mare (Avon)
E. 71,439

*A. W. Wiggin, T.D., *C.*		27,948
J. Marks, *S.D.P./All.*		18,457
R. L. Berry, *Lab.*		5,781
C. maj.		9,491

Wigan (Gtr. Manchester)
E. 72,390

*R. Stott, C.B.E., *Lab.*		29,859
J. Piggott, *L./All.*		12,554
H. Cadman, *C.*		12,320
Lab. maj.		17,305

Wimbledon (Gtr. London)
E. 64,132

*Rt. Hon. Sir R. M. O. Havers, Q.C., *C.*		24,169
D. Twigg, *L./All.*		12,623
R. B. Tansey, *Lab.*		8,806
A. Jones, *Eco.*		717
E. Weakner, *P.A.L.*		114
C. maj.		11,546
(May '79, C. maj. 13,315)		

Winchester (Hants)
E. 72,792

*J. E. D. D. Browne, *C.*		31,908
J. MacDonald, *S.D.P./All.*		18,861
W. H. Allchin, *Lab.*		4,512
S. Winkworth, *W. Reg.*		155
C. maj.		13,047

Windsor and Maidenhead
(Berks)
E. 78,619

*Dr. A. Glyn, E.R.D., *C.*		32,191
P. Winner, *L./All.*		13,988
Mrs. V. I. Price, *Lab.*		6,383
W. O. Board, *Ind. C.*		1,842
G. F. C. Gillmore, *N.F.*		511
P. B. Illesley, *Ind.*		300
C. R. Bex, *W. Reg.*		68
C. maj.		18,203

Wirral (Merseyside)
E. 60,864

*G. B. Porter, *C.*		24,766
P. Hollingworth, *S.D.P./All.*		10,928
K. J. S. Rimmer, *Lab.*		10,411
C. maj.		13,838

West *E.* 61,646

*D. J. F. Hunt, M.B.E., *C.*		25,276
S. Mulholland, *L./All.*		10,125
J. McCabe, *Lab.*		9,855
C. maj.		15,151

Witney (Oxon)
E. 69,362

*Rt. Hon. D. R. Hurd, C.B.E., *C.*		28,695
P. J. Baston, *L./All.*		15,983
Mrs. C. B. Douse, *Lab.*		7,145
C. maj.		12,712

Woking (Surrey)
E. 78,327

*C. G. D. Onslow, *C.*		32,748
P. Goldenberg, *L./All.*		16,511
Mrs. D. B. Broer, *Lab.*		6,566
D. Comens, *P.A.L.*		368
C. maj.		16,237
(May '79, C. maj. 18,392)		

Wokingham (Berks)
E. 71,725

*Sir W. R. van Straubenzee, M.B.E., *C.*		32,925
J. Leston, *L./All.*		17,227
M. Orton, *Lab.*		4,362
C. maj.		15,698

Wolverhampton (W. Midlands)

North East *E.* 63,716

*Mrs. R. Short, *Lab.*		17,941
A. Burnside, *C.*		17,727
R. Yarnell, *L./All.*		8,524
C. Baugh, *N.F.*		585
Lab. maj.		214

South East *E.* 56,428

*R. Edwards, *Lab.*		17,440
P. McLoughlin, *C.*		12,428
J. Wernick, *L./All.*		9,112
Lab. maj.		5,012

South West *E.* 68,847

*N. W. Budgen, *C.*		25,214
R. M. Jones, *Lab.*		13,694
E. Harwood, *S.D.P./All.*		10,724
J. Deary, *A.C.M.*		201
C. maj.		11,520

Woodspring (Avon)
E. 71,280

*A. P. Dean, *C.*		31,932
R. Morgan, *L./All.*		16,800
D. H. White, *Lab.*		6,536
D. M. Robyns, *W. Reg.*		177
C. maj.		15,132

Woolwich (Gtr. London)
E. 56,297

J. C. Cartwright, S.D.P./All.		15,492
Mrs. A. Wise, *Lab.*		12,767
Mrs. P. Drummond-Brown, *C.*		9,616
T. C. Fitz-Gerald, *B.N.P.*		384
S.D.P./All. maj.		2,725
(May '79, Lab. maj. 10,460)		

Worcester
E. 66,531

*Rt. Hon. P. E. Walker, M.B.E., *C.*		24,381
C. Phipps, *S.D.P./All.*		13,510
J. Rudd, *Lab.*		11,208
K. A. Axon, *B.N.P.*		208
C. maj.		10,871

Worcestershire

Mid *E.* 74,254

E. Forth, *C.*		28,159
R. E. Maher, *Lab.*		13,954
Mrs. M. Fairhead, *S.D.P./All.*		12,866
D. W. Fletcher, *N.P.*		386
C. maj.		14,205

South *E.* 73,278

*W. M. H. Spicer, *C.*		30,095
D. Phillips, *L./All.*		18,706
P. Sandland-Nielson, *Lab.*		4,183
G. Woodford, *Eco.*		866
G. R. G. Pass, *Ind.*		113
C. maj.		11,389
(May '79, C. maj. 20,380)		

Workington (Cumbria)
E. 56,119

*D. N. Campbell-Savours, *Lab.*		23,239
M. Smith, *C.*		16,111
N. Blackshaw, *L./All.*		5,311
Lab. maj.		7,128
(May '79, Lab. maj. 5,756)		

Worsley (Gtr. Manchester)
E. 71,987

T. Lewis, *Lab.*		21,675
S. Windle, *C.*		17,536
*J. F. Roper, *S.D.P./All.*		14,545
Lab. maj.		4,139

Worthing (W. Sussex)
E. 75,772

*Rt. Hon. T. L. Higgins, *C.*		32,807
A. Clare, *L./All.*		17,554
A. Minto, *Lab.*		3,158
M. Wingfield, *N.F.*		292
D. Monks, *B.N.P.*		103
C. maj.		15,253
(May '79, C. maj. 20,380)		

The Wrekin (Salop)
E. 77,226

*P. W. Hawksley, *C.*		22,710
B. Grocott, *Lab.*		21,379
M. Biltcliffe, *S.D.P./All.*		14,208
C. maj.		1,331

Wycombe (Bucks)
E. 70,065

*R. W. Whitney, o.b.e., C.		27,221
A. Page, S.D.P./All.		14,024
C. Bastin, Lab.		8,636
M. Amin, M.P.P.		327
C. maj.		13,197

Wyre (Lancs)
E. 65,934

*Sir W. Clegg, C.		26,559
I. Murdoch, S.D.P./All.		11,748
W. Goldsmith, Lab.		8,743
C. maj.		14,811

Wyre Forest (H & W)
E. 68,298

*J. E. Bulmer, C.		24,809
A. Batchelor, L./All.		16,632
R. B. Williams, Lab.		9,850
C. maj.		8,177

Yeovil (Somerset)
E. 66,102

J. J. D. Ashdown, L./All.		26,608
D. Martin, C.		23,202
P. J. Brushett, Lab.		2,928
L./All. maj.		3,406

York (N. Yorks)
E. 78,311

C. R. Gregory, C.		24,309
*A. W. Lyon, Lab.		20,662
J. V. Cable, S.D.P./All.		13,523
A. J. Lister, Ind.		204
T. G. Brattan, B.N.P.		148
C. maj.		3,647
(May '79, Lab. maj. 1,250)		

WALES

Aberavon (W. Glam.)
E. 53,443

*Rt. Hon. J. Morris, Q.C., Lab.		23,745
Mrs. S. Cutts, L./All.		8,206
G. Bailey, C.		6,605
G. Phillips, P.C.		1,859
Lab. maj.		15,539

Alyn and Deeside (Clwyd)
E. 56,618

*S. B. Jones, Lab.		17,806
S. Burns, C.		16,438
E. C. H. Owen, S.D.P./All.		9,535
A. Shore, P.C.		413
Lab. maj.		1,368

Blaenau Gwent
E. 55,948

*Rt. Hon. M. M. Foot, Lab.		30,113
G. Atkinson, L./All.		6,408
T. Morgan, C.		4,816
S. Morgan, P.C.		1,624
Lab. maj.		23,705

Brecon and Radnor (Powys)
E. 47,277

*T. E. Hooson, C.		18,255
D. Morris, Lab.		9,471
R. Livsey, L./All.		9,226
Ms. S. Meredudd, P.C.		640
R. Booth, Ind.		278
C. maj.		8,784
(see by-election on p. 345)		

Bridgend (Mid Glam)
E. 53,918

P. C. Hubbard-Miles, C.		15,950
J. A. Fellows, Lab.		14,623
R. Smart, S.D.P./All.		9,630
K. Bush, P.C.		1,312
C. maj.		1,327

Caernarfon (Gwynedd)
E. 44,147

*D. W. Wigley, P.C.		18,308
D. Jones, C.		7,319
Mrs. B. H. Williams, Lab.		6,736
O. G. Griffiths, L./All.		2,356
P.C. maj.		10,989
(May '79, P.C. maj. 8,724)		

Caerphilly (Mid Glam)
E. 63,479

R. Davies, Lab.		21,570
A. Lambert, L./All.		10,017
C. Welby, C.		9,295
L. Whittle, P.C.		6,414
Lab. maj.		11,553

Cardiff (S. Glam)

CENTRAL E. 53,815

*I. Grist, C.		16,090
M. German, L./All.		12,638
R. T. Davies, Lab.		9,387
P. Morgan, P.C.		704
C. maj.		3,452

NORTH E. 53,377

G. H. Jones, C.		19,433
A. W. Jeremy, S.D.P./All.		12,585
Ms. J. Hutt, Lab.		8,256
Dr. D. Huws, P.C.		974
C. maj.		6,848

SOUTH AND PENARTH E. 59,520

*Rt. Hon. L. J. Callaghan, Lab.		17,448
D. Tredinnick, C.		15,172
W. Roddick, L./All.		8,816
Ms. S. Edwards, P.C.		673
B. T. Lewis, F.W.D.		165
Lab. maj.		2,276

WEST E. 58,538

S. Terlezki, C.		15,472
D. Seligman, Lab.		13,698
*J. Thomas, S.D.P./All.		10,388
M. Parri, P.C.		848
G. Jones, Eco.		352
C. maj.		1,774

Carmarthen (Dyfed)
E. 63,468

*Dr. R. G. Thomas, Lab.		16,459
N. M. Thomas, C.		15,305
G. Evans, P.C.		14,099
Mrs. J. Colin, S.D.P./All.		5,737
B. Kingzett, Eco.		374
C. Grice, B.N.P.		154
Lab. maj.		1,154

Ceredigion and Pembroke North (Dyfed)
E. 60,523

*G. W. Howells, L./All.		19,677
T. Raw-Rees, C.		14,038
G. E. Hughes, Lab.		6,840
C. Dafis, P.C.		6,072
Miss M. Smith, Eco.		431
L./All. maj.		5,639

Clwyd

NORTH WEST E. 62,503

*Sir A. J. C. Meyer, BT., C.		23,283
J. Lewis, L./All.		13,294
I. Campbell, Lab.		7,433
Mrs. M. Rhys, P.C.		1,669
		9,989

SOUTH WEST E. 55,792

R. L. Harvey, C.		14,575
*R. T. Ellis, S.D.P./All.		13,024
D. B. Carter, Lab.		11,829
T. Schiavone, P.C.		3,684
		1,551

Conwy (Gwynedd)
E. 51,567

*I. W. P. Roberts, C.		16,413
Rev. J. R. Roberts, L./All.		12,145
I. Walters, Lab.		6,731
D. Iwan, P.C.		4,105
C. maj.		4,268

Cynon Valley (Mid Glam)
E. 50,284

*I. L. Evans, Lab.		20,668
F. Aubel, S.D.P./All.		7,594
J. Arbuthnot, C.		5,240
Mrs. P. Jarman, P.C.		3,421
Lab. maj.		13,074
(see by-election on p. 345)		

Delyn (Clwyd)
E. 62,483

K. W. Raffan, C.		20,242
J. Colbert, Lab.		14,298
J. H. Parry, L./All.		12,545
H. Huws, P.C.		1,558
C. maj.		5,944

Gower (W. Glam.)
E. 56,693

*G. L. Wardell, Lab.		16,972
Dr. A. R. T. Kenyon, C.		15,767
G. Jones, S.D.P./All.		10,450
N. Williams, P.C.		1,444
Lab. maj.		1,205

Islwyn (Gwent)
E. 50,259

*N. G. Kinnock, Lab.		23,183
D. Johnson, S.D.P./All.		8,803
M. Bevan, C.		5,511
A. Richards, P.C.		1,574
Lab. maj.		14,380

Llanelli (Dyfed)
E. 63,826

*Rt. Hon. D. J. D. Davies, Lab.		23,207
N. Kennedy, C.		9,601
K. Rees, L./All.		9,076
H. T. Edwards, P.C.		5,880
R. E. Hitchon, Comm.		371
Lab. maj.		13,606

Meirionnydd Nant Conwy
(Gwynedd)
E. 30,459

*D. E. Thomas, P.C.	......	9,709
D. Lloyd, *C.*	......	7,066
D. Roberts, *S.D.P./All.*	...	4,254
G. Williams, *Lab.*	....	3,735
P.C. maj.	....	2,643

Merthyr Tydfil and Rhymney
(Mid Glam)
E. 59,486

*E. Rowlands, Lab.	....	29,053
P. Owen, *L./All.*	......	6,323
R. Blauston, *C.*	......	5,449
G. Howells, *P.C.*	......	2,058
T. Gould, *W.R.P.*	....	256
Lab. maj.	....	22,730

Monmouth (Gwent)
E. 56,112

*J. Stradling-Thomas, C.	..	21,746
C. Lindley, *S.D.P./All.*	...	12,403
C. Short, *Lab.*	....	9,593
G. Williams, *P.C.*	....	493
C. maj.	....	9,343

Montgomery (Powys)
E. 37,474

A. C. Carlile, *L./All.*	.....	12,863
*D. Williams, C.	......	12,195
J. Wilson, *Lab.*	....	2,550
C. Clowes, *P.C.*	....	1,585
D. W. Rowlands, *Ind.*	....	487
L./All. maj.	....	668
(May '79, C. maj. 1,593)		

Neath (W. Glam)
E. 55,272

*D. R. Coleman, C.B.E., *Lab.*	....	22,670
K. Davies, *S.D.P./All.*	...	9,066
R. Buckley, *C.*	....	7,350
D. I. Owen, *P.C.*	....	3,046
J. Donovan, *Comp. Dem.*	.	150
Lab. maj.	....	13,604

Newport (Gwent)

EAST *E.* 52,503

*R. J. Hughes, Lab.	....	15,931
R. Thomason, *C.*	....	13,301
Ms. F. David, *S.D.P./All.*	..	10,293
D. Thomas, *P.C.*	....	697
Lab. maj.	....	2,630

WEST *E.* 54,125

M. N. F. Robinson, *C.*	....	15,948
B. Davies, *Lab.*	....	15,367
Dr. W. Jones, *L./All.*	....	10,163
D. Watkins, *P.C.*	....	477
C. maj.	....	581

Ogmore (Mid Glam)
E. 51,378

*R. Powell, Lab.	....	23,390
J. Parsons, *L./All.*	....	6,026
R. O'Sullivan, *C.*	....	5,806
E. J. Merriman, *P.C.*	......	3,124
Dr. N. Thomas, *Eco.*	......	1,161
Lab. maj.	....	17,364

Pembroke (Dyfed)
E. 67,885

*Rt. Hon. R. N. Edwards, C.	....	24,860
A. P. Griffiths, *Lab.*	......	15,504
Rev. J. Pullin, *S.D.P./All.*		10,983
O. Osmond, *P.C.*	....	1,073
D. Hoffmann, *Eco.*	....	478
G. S. Phillips, *Ind.*	....	136
C. maj.	....	9,356

Pontypridd (Mid Glam)
E. 60,883

*B. T. John, Lab.	....	20,188
R. Langridge, *S.D.P./All.*		11,444
R. Evans, *C.*	....	10,139
Mrs. J. Davies, *P.C.*	......	2,065
A. K. Jones, *Eco.*	....	449
Lab. maj.	....	8,744

Rhondda (Mid Glam)
E. 62,587

A. R. Rogers, *Lab.*	......	29,448
A. Lloyd, *S.D.P./All.*	.....	8,078
G. Davies, *P.C.*	....	4,845
P. Meyer, *C.*	....	3,973
A. True, *Comm.*	....	1,350
Lab. maj.	....	21,370
(May '79, Lab. maj. 31,481)		

Swansea (W. Glam)

EAST *E.* 57,285

*D. Anderson, Lab.	......	22,297
M. Shrewsbury, *L./All.*	...	8,762
N. O'Shaughnessy, *C.*	....	8,080
C. Reid, *P.C.*	....	1,531
W. R. Jones, *Comm.*	......	294
Lab. maj.	....	13,535

WEST *E.* 58,237

*Rt. Hon. A. J. Williams, Lab.	....	18,042
Dr. J. Lewis, *C.*	....	15,692
P. Berry, *S.D.P./All.*	.....	8,036
Mrs. M. Pennar, *P.C.*	.....	795
G. E. Oubridge, *Eco.*	.....	265
Lab. maj.	....	2,350

Torfaen (Gwent)
E. 58,739

*L. Abse, Lab.	....	20,678
G. Blackburn, *L./All.*	....	12,393
P. Martin, *C.*	....	9,751
Mrs. P. Cox, *P.C.*	....	896
Lab. maj.	....	8,285
(May '79, Lab. maj. 17,368)		

Vale of Glamorgan (S. Glam)
E. 62,885

*Sir H. R. Gower, C.	......	22,421
M. E. Sharp, *Lab.*	....	12,028
A. Evans, *S.D.P./All.*	.....	11,154
J. Dixon, *P.C.*	....	1,068
C. maj.	....	10,393

Wrexham (Clwyd)
E. 60,707

J. Marek, *Lab.*	....	16,120
Mrs. K. Wood, *C.*	....	15,696
M. Thomas, *L./All.*	......	13,974
J. Thomas, *P.C.*	....	1,239
Lab. maj.	....	424

Ynys Môn/Anglesey
(Gwynedd)
E. 50,359

*K. L. Best, T.D., *C.*	....	15,017
I. W. Jones, *P.C.*	....	13,333
T. Williams, *Lab.*	....	6,791
D. Thomas, *S.D.P./All.*	...	4,947
C. maj.	....	1,684
(May '79, C. maj. 2,817)		

SCOTLAND

Aberdeen (Grampian)

NORTH *E.* 63,049

*R. Hughes, Lab.	....	19,262
C. S. Deans, *S.D.P./All.*	..	10,118
Mrs. G. Scanlan, *C.*	......	7,426
J. McGugan, *S.N.P.*	......	3,790
Ms. M. Harty, *Eco.*	....	367
Lab. maj.	....	9,144

SOUTH *E.* 57,540

P. G. Malone, *C.*	......	15,393
R. Middleton, *Lab.*	......	11,812
I. G. Philip, *S.D.P./All.*	...	10,372
S. Coull, *S.N.P.*	....	1,974
C. maj.	....	3,581

Angus East (Tayside)
E. 59,359

*P. L. Fraser, Q.C., *C.*	......	19,218
A. Welsh, *S.N.P.*	......	15,691
Miss P. Hammond, *S.D.P./ All.*	....	4,978
C. McConnell, *Lab.*	......	3,497
Mrs. P. Ross, *Eco.*	....	239
C. maj.	....	3,527

Argyll and Bute (S'clyde)
E. 47,497

*J. J. MacKay, C.	......	13,380
Mrs. J. R. Michie, *L./All.*	.	9,536
I. Smith, *S.N.P.*	....	8,514
C. McCafferty, *Lab.*	......	3,204
C. maj.	....	3,844

Ayr (S'clyde)
E. 65,010

*Rt. Hon. G. K. H. Younger, T.D., C.	....	21,325
K. MacDonald, *Lab.*	......	13,338
C. Brodie, *L./All.*	....	12,740
I. Goldie, *S.N.P.*	....	2,431
C. maj.	....	7,987

Banff and Buchan (Grampian)
E. 60,403

*A. McQuarrie, C.	......	16,072
D. Henderson, *S.N.P.*	....	15,135
E. Needham, *S.D.P./All.*	..	6,084
I. F. R. Lloyd, *Lab.*	......	3,150
C. maj.	....	937

Caithness and Sutherland
(H'land)
E. 30,871

*R. A. R. Maclennan, S.D.P./All.	....	12,119
A. Scouller, *C.*	....	5,276
D. Carrigan, *Lab.*	....	3,325
J. Ingram, *S.N.P.*	....	2,568
S.D.P./All. maj.	....	6,843
(May '79, Lab. maj. 2,539)		

Carrick, Cumnock and Doon Valley (S'clyde)
E. 55,925

*G. Foulkes, Lab.		21,394
J. McInnes, C.		10,024
R. Logan, S.D.P./All.		7,421
R. Wyllie, S.N.P.		2,694
Lab. maj.		11,370

Clackmannan (Central)
E. 47,642

*M. J. O'Neill, Lab.		16,478
Mrs. J. Jones, S.N.P.		6,839
C. Hendry, C.		6,490
Mrs. H. Campbell, S.D.P./All.		6,205
Lab. maj.		9,639

Clydebank and Milngavie (S'clyde)
E. 50,831

*H. McCartney, Lab.		17,288
J. Gourlay, S.D.P./All.		9,573
R. Graham, C.		7,852
A. Aitken, S.N.P.		3,566
J. Bollan, Comm.		308
Lab. maj.		7,715
((May '79, Lab. maj. 12,003))		

Clydesdale (S'clyde)
E. 60,240

*Rt. Hon. Dame Judith Hart, D.B.E., Lab.		17,873
P. Bainbridge, C.		13,007
Miss M. Craig, S.D.P./All.		9,908
T. McAlpine, S.N.P.		5,271
Lab. maj.		4,866

Cumbernauld and Kilsyth (S'clyde)
E. 44,190

*N. Hogg, Lab.		16,629
D. Herbison, S.D.P./All.		6,701
G. Murray, S.N.P.		5,875
Mrs. A. Thompson, C.		4,590
Lab. maj.		9,928

Cunninghame (S'clyde)

NORTH E. 53,126

*J. A. Corrie, C.		15,557
J. N. Carson, Lab.		13,920
R. Leishman, S.D.P./All.		7,268
C. Cameron, S.N.P.		3,460
C. maj.		1,637

SOUTH E. 48,552

*D. Lambie, Lab.		19,344
P. Gallie, C.		7,576
J. Boss, L./All.		6,370
Mrs. K. Ullrich, S.N.P.		2,451
Lab. maj.		11,768

Dumbarton (S'clyde)
E. 57,373

*I. Campbell, Lab.		15,810
I. Lawson, C.		13,695
R. Sawyer, S.D.P./All.		9,813
I. Bayne, S.N.P.		3,768
Lab. maj.		2,115
(May '79, Lab. maj. 6,457)		

Dumfries (D & G)
E. 57,594

*Sir H. S. P. Monro, C.		18,730
J. McCall, S.D.P./All.		10,036
T. McAughtrie, Lab.		8,764
E. Gibson, S.N.P.		4,527
C. maj.		8,694

Dundee (Tayside)

EAST E. 62,752

*R. G. Wilson, S.N.P.		20,276
C. Bowman, Lab.		15,260
Mrs. B. Vaughan, C.		7,172
S. Rottger, L./All.		3,546
S.N.P. maj.		5,016
(May '79, S.N.P. maj. 2,519)		

WEST E. 62,703

*E. Ross, Lab.		20,288
D. Senior, C.		10,138
Mrs. E. Dick, S.D.P./All.		7,976
J. Lynch, S.N.P.		7,973
P. Marks, Eco.		302
Lab. maj.		10,150
(May '79, Lab. maj. 10,457)		

Dunfermline (Fife)

EAST E. 49,881

J. G. Brown, Lab.		18,515
D. Harcus, L./All.		7,214
C. Shenton, C.		6,764
G. Hunter, S.N.P.		2,573
A. Maxwell, Comm.		864
Lab. maj.		11,301

WEST E. 49,075

*R. G. Douglas, Lab.		12,998
Dr. P. Davison, C.		10,524
F. Moyes, S.D.P./All.		9,434
J. Fairlie, S.N.P.		2,798
S. Dobson, Eco.		321
Lab. maj.		2,474

East Kilbride (S'clyde)
E. 61,420

*Dr. M. S. Miller, Lab.		17,535
D. Sullivan, S.D.P./All.		13,199
R. Dalkeith, (Earl of Dalkeith) C.		11,483
D. Urquhart, S.N.P.		4,795
W. Doolan, Comm.		256
Lab. maj.		4,336

East Lothian
E. 62,351

*J. D. Home Robertson, Lab.		20,934
M. Fry, C.		14,693
M. Kibby, L./All.		9,950
R. Knox, S.N.P.		2,083
Lab. maj.		6,241

Eastwood (S'clyde)
E. 59,378

*J. A. Stewart, C.		21,072
J. Pickett, S.D.P./All.		12,477
J. McGuire, Lab.		9,083
Ms. J. Herriot, S.N.P.		2,618
C. maj.		8,595

Edinburgh (Lothian)

CENTRAL E. 57,064

*A. M. Fletcher, C.		14,095
R. Kelley, Lab.		11,529
Dr. Marion Macleod, S.D.P./All.		9,498
R. Halliday, S.N.P.		1,810
D. Carson, Comm.		119
C. maj.		2,566

EAST E. 51,156

*G. S. Strang, Lab.		16,169
P. Martin, C.		10,303
R. Mcleod, L./All.		7,570
P. Scott, S.N.P.		1,976
Lab. maj.		5,866

LEITH E. 60,562

*R. D. M. Brown, Lab.		16,177
D. Graham, S.D.P./All.		11,204
B. Cooklin, C.		10,706
J. Young, S.N.P.		2,646
Lab. maj.		4,973

PENTLANDS E. 59,295

*M. L. Rifkind, C.		17,051
K. Smith, S.D.P./All.		12,742
E. Milligan, Lab.		10,390
N. MacCormick, S.N.P.		2,642
A. Nicol-Smith, Eco.		687
C. maj.		4,309

SOUTH E. 62,517

*M. A. F. J. Ancram (Earl of Ancram), C.		16,485
J. Godfrey, S.D.P./All.		12,830
R. A. McCreadie, Lab.		12,824
N. MacCallum, S.N.P.		2,256
Mrs. L. Hendry, Eco.		450
C. maj.		3,655

WEST E. 61,050

*Lord James Douglas-Hamilton, C.		17,646
D. King, L./All.		17,148
A. Wood, Lab.		9,313
J. Nicoll, S.N.P.		2,126
C. maj.		498

Falkirk (Central)

EAST E. 52,045

*H. Ewing, Lab.		17,956
D. Masterton, C.		7,895
A. Wedderburn, S.D.P./All.		6,967
J. MacGregor, S.N.P.		4,490
Miss F. McGregor, Comm.		334
Lab. maj.		10,061

WEST E. 49,402

*D. A. Canavan, Lab.		16,668
I. Mitchell, C.		7,690
M. Harris, L./All.		7,477
B. Cochrane, S.N.P.		4,739
Lab. maj.		8,978

Fife

CENTRAL E. 54,389

*W. W. Hamilton, Lab.		17,008
Mrs. T. Little, L./All.		9,214
D. Mason, C.		8,863
J. Taggart, S.N.P.		4,039
D. Allison, Eco.		297
Lab. maj.		7,794

NORTH EAST *E.* 50,476
*J. S. B. Henderson, C.	....	17,129
M. Campbell, *L./All.*	.....	14,944
Dr. J. K. M. Hulbert, *S.N.P.*	....	2,442
D. Caldwell, *Lab.*	....	2,429
T. G. Flinn, *Eco.*	....	242
C. maj.	....	2,185

Galloway and Upper Nithsdale
(D & G)
E. 51,831
*I. B. Lang, C.	....	17,579
G. Thompson, *S.N.P.*	...	12,118
G. Douglas, *L./All.*	....	5,129
M. B. Miller, *Lab.*	....	4,464
C. maj.	....	5,461

Glasgow (S'clyde)

CATHCART *E.* 51,055
*J. A. Maxton, Lab.	....	16,037
D. May, *C.*	....	11,807
K. Bloomer, *S.D.P./All.*	..	8,710
W. Steven, *S.N.P.*	....	2,151
Lab. maj.	....	4,230

CENTRAL *E.* 51,217
*R. McTaggart, Lab.	......	17,066
W. Harvey, *C.*	....	6,104
Mrs. I. Nelson, *L./All.*	.....	5,366
P. Mallan, *S.N.P.*	....	3,300
J. McGoldrick, *Comm.*	....	347
Lab. maj.	....	10,962

GARSCADDEN *E.* 50,589
*D. C. Dewar, Lab.	....	19,635
W. Lyden, *S.D.P./All.*	.....	6,161
K. Macleod, *C.*	....	5,368
N. MacLeod, *S.N.P.*	....	3,566
S. A. Barr, *Comm.*	....	218
Lab. maj.	....	13,474
(May '79, Lab. maj.		15,198

GOVAN *E.* 51,754
*Rt. Hon. B. Millan, Lab.	..	20,370
I. McDonald, *S.D.P./All.*	.	7,313
A. Mackenzie, *C.*	....	7,180
P. Kindlen, *S.N.P.*	....	2,207
Lab. maj.	....	13,057

HILLHEAD *E.* 57,016
*Rt. Hon. R. H. Jenkins, S.D.P./All.	......	14,856
*N. Carmichael, Lab.	.....	13,692
M. Tosh, *C.*	....	9,638
G. Leslie, *S.N.P.*	....	2,203
J. Davidson, *Ind. C.*	......	249
A. Whitelaw, *Eco.*	....	239
J. Robins, *A.V.*	....	139
S.D.P./All. maj.	....	1,164

MARYHILL *E.* 51,847
*J. M. Craigen, Lab.	......	18,724
Ms. E. Attwooll, *L./All.*	..	7,521
J. Gibbs, *C.*	....	5,014
I. Morrison, *S.N.P.*	......	2,408
P. Smith, *Comm.*	....	274
Lab. maj.	....	11,203

POLLOK *E.* 53,217
*J. White, Lab.	....	18,973
J. Carlaw, *C.*	....	7,441
G. McKell, *L./All.*	....	6,308
F. Hannigan, *S.N.P.*	.....	3,585
Lab. maj.	....	11,532

PROVAN *E.* 47,706
*H. D. Brown, Lab.	....	20,040
A. Heron, *S.D.P./All.*	....	4,655
Miss S. Gordon, *C.*	......	3,374
Mrs. P. Kennedy, *S.N.P.*	.	2,737
J. Jackson, *Comm.*	....	294
Lab. maj.	....	15,385
(May '79, Lab. maj. 18,844)		

RUTHERGLEN *E.* 59,209
*Rt. Hon. J. G. Mackenzie, Lab.	....	21,510
R. Brown, *L./All.*	....	12,384
Mrs. H. Hodgins, *C.*	.....	8,017
K. Fee, *S.N.P.*	....	2,438
C. Corrigan, *W.R.P.*	.....	148
Lab. maj.	....	9,126

SHETTLESTON *E.* 51,955
*D. Marshall, Lab.	....	19,203
I. Henderson, *C.*	....	6,787
S. Strachen, *L./All.*	......	6,568
D. Hood, *S.N.P.*	....	2,801
K. Hill, *B.N.P.*	....	103
Lab. maj.	....	12,416

SPRINGBURN *E.* 53,373
*M. J. Martin, Lab.	....	22,481
J. Kelly, *L./All.*	....	4,882
D. Tweedie, *C.*	....	4,565
J. McLaughlin, *S.N.P.*	..	2,804
Lab. maj.	....	17,599

Gordon (Grampian)
E. 65,537
M. G. Bruce, *L./All.*	......	20,134
J. Cran, *C.*	....	19,284
G. Grant, *Lab.*	....	3,899
K. Guild, *S.N.P.*	....	2,636
L./All. maj.	....	850

Greenock and Port Glasgow
(S'clyde)
E. 59,437
N. A. Godman, *Lab.*	.....	20,650
A. Blair, *L./All.*	....	16,025
C. Chrichton, *C.*	....	4,314
A. Clayton, *S.N.P.*	....	2,989
G. McKinlay, *W.R.P.*	....	114
Lab. maj.	....	4,625
(May '79, Lab. maj. 11,282)		

Hamilton (S'clyde)
E. 61,430
*G. I. M. Robertson, Lab.	..	24,384
S. Donaldson, *L./All.*	.....	9,365
Mrs. M. Scott, *C.*	....	8,940
Mrs. M. Whitehead, *S.N.P.*	3,816
Lab. maj.	....	15,019

Inverness, Nairn and Lochaber
(H'land)
E. 63,645
*D. R. Johnston, L./All.	...	20,671
D. G. Maclean, *C.*	....	13,373
D. McMillan, *Lab.*	....	6,448
H. Vernal, *S.N.P.*	....	4,395
L./All. maj.	....	7,298

Kilmarnock and Loudoun
(S'clyde)
E. 61,394
*W. McKelvey, Lab.	....	20,250
R. Leckie, *C.*	....	11,450
A. Ross, *S.D.P./All.*	......	10,545
C. Calman, *S.N.P.*	....	4,165
Lab. maj.	....	8,800
(May '79, Lab. maj. 11,467)		

Kincardine and Deeside
(Grampian)
E. 59,552
*Rt. Hon. A. L. Buchanan-Smith, C.	....	20,293
S. Waugh, *L./All.*	....	12,497
Mrs. M. Morell, *Lab.*	.....	6,472
A. Tuttle, *S.N.P.*	....	3,297
C. maj.	....	7,796

Kirkcaldy (Fife)
E. 53,078
*H. P. H. Gourlay, Lab.	...	15,380
I. Walker, *C.*	....	10,049
M. Black, *S.D.P./All.*	....	9,274
D. Wood, *S.N.P.*	....	3,452
Lab. maj.	....	5,331

Linlithgow (Lothian)
E. 58,111
*T. Dalyell, Lab.	....	19,694
C. Jones, *C.*	....	8,333
D. Ramsey, *S.N.P.*	....	8,026
P. Cockcroft, *S.D.P./All.*	.	7,432
Dr. Morag Parnell, *Comm.*	199
Lab. maj.	....	11,361

Livingston (Lothian)
E. 53,284
*R. F. Cook, Lab.	....	14,255
A. Henderson, *L./All.*	....	9,304
J. Campbell, *C.*	....	9,129
K. MacAskill, *S.N.P.*	.....	5,090
Lab. maj.	....	4,951

Midlothian
E. 60,496
*A. Eadie, B.E.M., Lab.	....	19,401
A. Dewar, *S.D.P./All.*	....	13,245
D. Menzies, *C.*	....	9,922
Mrs. M. Hird, *S.N.P.*	.....	2,826
Lab. maj.	....	6,156

Monklands (S'clyde)

EAST *E.* 49,030
*Rt. Hon. J. Smith, Lab.	...	18,358
J. Love, *C.*	....	8,559
A. Rennie, *L./All.*	....	5,721
T. Johnston, *S.N.P.*	......	3,185
Lab. maj.	....	9,799

WEST *E.* 50,345
*T. Clarke, C.B.E., Lab.	....	20,642
L. Cameron, *C.*	....	8,378
R. Ackland, *S.D.P./All.*	..	6,605
A. Lyon, *S.N.P.*	....	2,473
Lab. maj.	....	12,264

Moray (Grampian)
E. 60,804
*A. Pollock, C.	....	16,944
H. Watt, *S.N.P.*	....	15,231
M. Burnett, *L./All.*	......	7,901
J. Kiddie, *Lab.*	....	3,139
C. maj.	....	1,713

Motherwell (S'clyde)

NORTH *E.* 56,512

*J. Hamilton, C.B.E., Lab.	..	24,483
R. Hargrave, C.		6,589
G. Whitelaw, L./All.		5,970
R. Lyle, S.N.P.		5,333
Lab. maj.		17,894

SOUTH *E.* 52,183

*Dr. J. W. Bray, Lab.		19,939
P. Walker, C.		7,590
B. Ashley, S.D.P./All.		6,754
J. Wright, S.N.P.		3,743
Lab. maj.		12,349
(May '79, Lab. maj. 10,937)		

North Tayside
E. 51,972

*W. C. Walker, C.		19,269
A. Morgan, S.N.P.		9,170
D. Skene, L./All.		7,255
N. Wylie, Lab.		2,057
C. maj.		10,099

Orkney and Shetland (Islands)
E. 30,087

J. R. Wallace, L./All.		9,374
*D. Myles, C.		5,224
Mrs. W. Ewing, S.N.P.		3,147
Ms. R. Goodlad, Lab.		2,665
L./All. maj.		4,150
(May '79, L. maj. 6,810)		

Paisley (S'clyde)

NORTH *E.* 50,464

*A. Adams, Lab.		15,782
Miss A. McCartin, S.D.P./All.		8,195
B. Townsend, C.		7,425
H. Morrell, S.N.P.		2,783
Dr. Nicolette Carlaw, Eco.		439
Lab. maj.		7,587

SOUTH *E.* 52,031

*N. F. Buchan, Lab.		15,633
Mrs. E. Buchanan, L./All.		9,104
J. Knox, C.		7,819
J. Mitchell, S.N.P.		4,918
D. Mellor, Eco.		271
Lab. maj.		6,529

Perth and Kinross (Tayside)
E. 61,478

*N. H. Fairbairn, Q.C., C.	..	17,888
G. D. Crawford, S.N.P.		11,155
B. Coutts, L./All.		10,997
A. J. Stuart, Lab.		4,414
C. maj.		6,733

Renfrew West and Inverclyde
(S'clyde)
E. 53,510

Mrs. A. A. McCurley, C.	..	13,669
*Dr. J. D. Mabon, S.D.P./All.		12,347
G. Doherty, Lab.		12,139
W. Taylor, S.N.P.		3,653
C. maj.		1,322

Ross, Cromarty and Skye
(H'land)
E. 48,401

C. P. Kennedy, S.D.P./All.		13,528
*Rt. Hon. H. Gray, C.		11,824
M. Elder, Lab.		4,901
Miss K. Matheson, S.N.P.		4,863
S.D.P./All. maj.		1,704

Roxburgh and Berwickshire
(Borders)
E. 41,702

A. J. Kirkwood, L./All.	....	15,920
*I. Sproat, C.		12,524
D. Briggs, Lab.		2,326
R. Shirley, S.N.P.		852
L./All. maj.		3,396

Stirling (Central)
E. 56,302

M. B. Forsyth, C.		17,039
M. Connarty, Lab.		11,906
R. Finnie, L./All.		10,174
W. Houston, S.N.P.		3,488
C. maj.		5,133

Strathkelvin and Bearsden
(S'clyde)
E. 60,500

M. W. Hirst, C.		17,501
R. Waddell, L./All.		13,801
A. P. Ingram, Lab.		12,308
Mrs. M. Bain, S.N.P.		4,408
C. maj.		3,700

Tweeddale, Ettrick and Lauderdale
(Borders)
E. 37,075

*Rt. Hon. D. M. S. Steel, L./All.		16,868
A. Ballentine, C.		8,329
M. Saren, Lab.		2,200
A. Macartney, S.N.P.		1,455
L./All. maj.		8,539

Western Isles (Islands)
E. 22,822

*Rt. Hon. D. J. Stewart, S.N.P.		8,272
B. D. H. Wilson, Lab.		4,560
M. Morrison, C.		1,460
N. McLeod, L./All.		876
S.N.P. maj.		3,712
(May '79, S.N.P. maj. 3,063)		

NORTHERN IRELAND

Antrim

EAST *E.* 58,863

R. Beggs, O.U.P.		14,293
J. Allister, D.U.P.		13,926
S. Neeson, All.		7,620
M. O'Cleary, S.D.L.P.		1,047
W. Cunning, Ind.		741
A. Kelly, W.P.		581
O.U.P. maj.		367

NORTH *E.* 63,254

*Rev. I. R. K. Paisley, D.U.P.		23,922
Rev. R. Coulter, O.U.P.	..	10,749
S. Farren, S.D.L.P.		6,193
P. McMahon, S.F.		2,860
M. H. Samuel, Eco.		451
D.U.P. maj.		13,173

SOUTH *E.* 59,321

C. Forsythe, O.U.P.		17,727
R. Thompson, D.U.P.	....	10,935
G. Mawhinney, All.		4,612
A. Maginness, S.D.L.P.		3,377
S. Laverty, S.F.		1,629
K. Smyth, W.P.		549
O.U.P. maj.		6,792

Belfast

EAST *E.* 55,581

*P. D. Robinson, D.U.P.	....	17,631
D. J. M. Burchill, O.U.P.		9,642
O. Napier, All.		9,373
D. Donaldson, S.F.		682
Mrs. M. Tang, L.T.U.		584
P. Prendiville, S.D.L.P.		519
F. Cullen, W.P.		421
H. Boyd, N.A.		59
D.U.P. maj.		7,989

NORTH *E.* 61,128

A. C. Walker, O.U.P.	....	15,339
G. Searight, D.U.P.		8,260
B. Feeney, S.D.L.P.		5,944
J. Austin, S.F.		5,451
P. Maguire, All.		3,879
S. Lynch, W.P.		2,412
W. Gault, Ind. D.U.P.	....	1,134
O.U.P. maj.		7,079

SOUTH *E.* 53,694

*Rev. W. M. Smyth, O.U.P.		18,669
D. Cook, All.		8,945
R. S. McRae, D.U.P.		4,565
Dr. A. McDonnell, S.D.L.P.		3,216
S. McKnight, S.F.		1,107
G. Carr, W.P.		856
O.U.P. maj.		9,724

WEST *E.* 59,750

G. Adams, S.F.		16,379
Dr. J. Hendron, S.D.L.P.	..	10,934
*G. Fitt, Ind.		10,326
T. Passmore, O.U.P.		2,435
G. A. Haffey, D.U.P.		2,399
Ms. M. McMahon, W.P.	..	1,893
S.F. maj.		5,445

Down

NORTH *E.* 61,574

*J. A. Kilfedder, U.P.U.P.	..	22,861
J. Cushnahan, All.		9,015
R. McCartney, O.U.P.		8,261
C. O'Baoill, S.D.L.P.		645
U.P.U.P. maj.		13,846

SOUTH *E.* 66,968

*Rt. Hon. J. E. Powell, M.B.E., O.U.P.		20,693
E. McGrady, S.D.L.P.	....	20,145
P. Fitzsimmons, S.F.		4,074
C. Harvey, D.U.P.		3,743
P. M. D. Forde, All.		1,823
Ms. M. Magee, W.P.		851
O.U.P. maj.		548

East Londonderry
E. 67,365

*W. Ross, O.U.P.		19,469
J. McClure, D.U.P.		12,207
A. Doherty, S.D.L.P.		9,397
J. Davey, S.F.		7,073
Mrs. M. McGrath, All.	...	2,401
F. Donnelly, W.P.		819
O.U.P. maj.		7,262

Fermanagh and South Tyrone
E. 67,880

K. Maginnis, O.U.P.	28,630
O. Carron, S.F.	20,954
Mrs. R. Flanaghan, *S.D.L.P.*	9,923
D. Kettyles, *W.P.*	649
O.U.P. maj.	7,676

Foyle
E. 67,432

J. Hume, *S.D.L.P.*	24,071
G. Campbell, *D.U.P.*	15,923
M. McGuiness, *S.F.*	10,607
G. O'Grady, *All.*	1,108
E. Melaugh, *W.P.*	582
S.D.L.P. maj.	8,148

Lagan Valley
E. 60,099

Rt. Hon. J. H. Molyneaux, O.U.P.	24,017

Rev. W. Beattie, *D.U.P.* 6,801
S. Close, *All.* 4,593
C. Boomer, *S.D.L.P.* 2,603
R. McAuley, *S.F.* 1,751
G. Loughlin, *W.P.* 809
O.U.P. maj. 17,216

Newry and Armagh
E. 62,387

J. F. Nicholson, *O.U.P.*	18,988
S. Mallon, *S.D.L.P.*	17,434
J. McAllister, *S.F.*	9,928
T. Moore, *W.P.*	1,070
O.U.P. maj.	1,554

Strangford
E. 60,232

Rt. Hon. J. D. Taylor, O.U.P.	19,086
S. Gibson, *D.U.P.*	11,716
A. Morrow, *All.*	6,171
J. Curry, *S.D.L.P.*	1,713

R. Heath, *Ind. L.* 430
O.U.P. maj. 7,370

Ulster, Mid-
E. 63,899

Rev. R. T. W. McCrea, D.U.P.	16,174
D. G. Morrison, *S.F.*	16,096
P. D. Haughey, *S.D.L.P.*	12,044
W. J. Thompson, *O.U.P.*	7,066
Dr. J. A. Lagan, *All.*	1,735
T. A. Owens, *W.P.*	766
D.U.P. maj.	78

Upper Bann
E. 60,795

J. H. McCusker, O.U.P.	24,888
J. McDonald, *S.D.L.P.*	7,807
J. Wells, *D.U.P.*	4,547
B. Curran, *S.F.*	4,110
T. French, *W.P.*	2,392
O.U.P. maj.	17,081

BY-ELECTIONS (Since 1983 General Election)

Penrith and The Border
(July 28, 1983)

D. Maclean, *C.*	17,530
M. Young, *L./All.*	16,978
L. Williams, *Lab.*	2,834
D. Sutch, *Ind.*	412
E. Morgan, *Ind.*	150
H. Anscomb, *Ind.*	72
J. Connell, *Ind.*	69
P. Smith, *Ind.*	35
C. maj.	552

Chesterfield
(March 1, 1984)

Rt. Hon. T. Benn, *Lab.*	24,633
M. Payne, *Lib./All.*	18,369
N. Bourne, *C.*	8,028
B. Maynard, *Ind.*	1,355
D. Sutch, *Ind.*	178
D. Bentley, *Ind.*	116
J. Davey, *Ind.*	83
T. A. Layton, *Ind.*	46
Helen Anscomb, *Ind.*	34
J. Bardwaj, *Ind.*	33
D. Butler, *Ind.*	24
P. Nicholls-Jones, *Ind.*	22
S. Shaw, *Ind.*	20
C. Hill, *Ind.*	17
G. R. Piccaro, *Ind.*	15
D. Cahill, *Ind.*	12
J. Connell, *Ind.*	7
Lab. maj.	6,264

Cynon Valley
(May 3, 1984)

Ann Clwyd, *Lab.*	19,389
F. Aubel, *S.D.P./All.*	6,554
C. Jones, *P.C.*	3,619
J. Arbuthnot, *C.*	2,441
Mary Winter, *Comm.*	642
N. Recontre, *Ind.*	215
P. Nicholls-Jones, *Ind.*	122
Lab. maj.	12,835

Stafford
(May 3, 1984)

W. Cash, *C.*	18,713
D. Dunn, *S.D.P./All.*	14,733
M. Poulter, *Lab.*	12,677
C. Teasdale, *Ind.*	210
C. maj.	3,980

Surrey South West
(May 3, 1984)

Virginia Bottomley, *C.*	21,545
G. Scott, *L./All.*	18,946
Barbara Roche, *Lab.*	2,949
V. Litvin, *Ind.*	117
Helen Anscomb, *Ind.*	82
P. Smith, *Ind.*	29
C. maj.	2,599

Portsmouth South
(June 14, 1984)

M. T. Hancock, *S.D.P./All.*	15,358
P. R. J. Rock, *C.*	14,017
Sally Thomas, *Lab.*	10,846
G. A. Knight, *N.F.*	226
T. A. F. Mitchell, *Ecology*	190
A. J. Evans, *Ind.*	113
T. A. Layton, *Ind.*	50
A. N. Andrews, *Ind.*	42
P. R. Smith, *Ind.*	41
S.D.P./All. maj.	1,341

Enfield Southgate
(December 13, 1984)

M. D. X. Portillo, *C.*	16,684
T. Slack, *L./All.*	11,973
W. F. Hamid, *Lab.*	4,000
A. Polydorou, *Turkish Troops out of Cyprus*	687
J. W. Kershaw, *Nationalist*	80
R. E. Shenton, *English Nationalist*	78
I. I. Burgess, *Abolish Greater London, Restore Middx.*	50
G. Weiss, *Captain Rainbow Universal*	48
H. M. Anscomb, *Death off Roads, Freight on Rail*	45
C. maj.	4,711

Brecon and Radnor
(July 4, 1985)

R. A. L. Livesey, *L./All.*	13,753
R. Willey, *Lab.*	13,194
C. Butler, *C.*	10,631
Mrs J. Davies, *P.C.*	435
D. E. Sutch, *Monster Raving Loony*	202
R. Everest, *One Nation C.*	154
A. Genillard, *Cure MS.*	3
L./All. maj.	559

EUROPEAN PARLIAMENT (U.K. MEMBERS AND ELECTIONS)

UNITED KINGDOM MEMBERS OF THE EUROPEAN PARLIAMENT

An asterisk* denotes membership of the previous parliament.

*Gordon J. Adam (*Lab.*), Northumbria; *Richard A. Balfe (*Lab.*), London, South Inner; *Robert C. Battersby (*C.*), Humberside; Christopher J. P. Beazley (*C.*), Cornwall and Plymouth; *Peter G. Beazley (*C.*), Bedfordshire, S.; *The Lord Bethell (*C.*), London, N.W.; *Miss Beata A. Brookes (*C.*), Wales, N.; *Mrs. Janey Buchan (*Lab.*), Glasgow; Bryan M. D. Cassidy (*C.*), Dorset E. and Hampshire W.; *Rt. Hon. Mrs. Barbara A. Castle (*Lab.*), Greater Manchester, W.; *Sir Frederick Catherwood (*C.*), Cambridge and Bedfordshire N.; *Kenneth D. Collins (*Lab.*), Strathclyde, E.; *Richard J. Cottrell (*C.*), Bristol; Mrs. Christine M. Crawley (*Lab.*), Birmingham, E.; G. Robert Cryer (*Lab.*), Sheffield; *David M. Curry (*C.*), Essex, N.E.; Mrs. Margaret M. Daly (*C.*), Somerset and Dorset W.; *John de Courcy Ling (*C.*), Midlands, Central; *Basil R. V. Z. de Ferranti (*C.*), Hampshire, Central; *The Marquess of Douro (*C.*), Surrey, W.

*The Baroness Elles (*C.*), Thames Valley; James E. M. Elles (*C.*), Oxford and Buckinghamshire; Michael N. Elliott (*Lab.*), London, W.; *Mrs. Winifred M. Ewing (*S.N.P.*), Highlands and Islands; Mrs. I. Sheila Faith (*C.*), Cumbria and Lancashire, N.; Alec Falconer (*Lab.*), Scotland Mid and Fife; J. Glyn Ford (*Lab.*), Greater Manchester, W.; *Winston J. Griffiths (*Lab.*), Wales, S.; Michael J. Hindley (*Lab.*), Lancashire, E.; Geoffrey W. Hoon (*Lab.*), Derbyshire; *Paul F. Howell (*C.*), Norfolk; Leslie J. Huckfield (*Lab.*), Merseyside, E.; Stephen S. Hughes (*Lab.*), Durham; *John Hume (*S.D.L.P.*), N. Ireland; *Alasdair H. Hutton (*C.*), Scotland, S.; Mrs. Caroline F. Jackson (*C.*), Wiltshire; *Christopher M. Jackson (*C.*), Kent, E.; Michael L. Kilby (*C.*), Nottingham.

*Alfred Lomas (*Lab.*), London, N.E.; Michael McGowan (*Lab.*), Leeds; Hugh McMahon (*Lab.*), Strathclyde, W.; Edward H. C. Macmillan Scott (*C.*), York; *John L. Marshall (*C.*), London, N.; David W. Martin (*Lab.*), Lothians; *Thomas Megahy (*Lab.*), Yorkshire, S.W.; C. James O. Moorhouse (*C.*), London S. and Surrey E.; D. Richard Morris (*Lab.*), Wales, Mid and W.; A. Stanley Newens (*Lab.*), London, Central; Edward Newman (*Lab.*), Greater Manchester, Central; *William F. Newton Dunn (*C.*), Lincolnshire; *Tom Normanton (*C.*), Cheshire, E.; *The Lord O'Hagan (*C.*), Devon; *Rev. Ian R. K. Paisley (*D.U.P.*), N. Ireland; *George B. Patterson (*C.*), Kent, W.; *Andrew Pearce (*C.*), Cheshire, W.; Terence J. Pitt (*Lab.*), Midlands, W.; *Sir Henry Plumb (*C.*), The Cotswolds; *Derek Prag (*C.*), Hertfordshire; *Peter N. Price (*C.*), London, S.E.; *Christopher J. Prout (*C.*), Shropshire and Stafford; *James L. C. Provan (*C.*), Scotland, N.E.; *Miss Joyce G. Quin (*Lab.*), Tyne and Wear; *Dame Shelagh M. Roberts (*C.*), London, S.W.

*Sir James Scott-Hopkins (*C.*), Hereford and Worcester; *Barry H. Seal (*Lab.*), Yorkshire, W.; *R. Madron Seligman (*C.*), Sussex, W.; *Dr. Alexander Sherlock (*C.*), Essex, S.W.; *Richard J. Simmonds (*C.*), Wight and Hampshire, E.; *Anthony. M. H. Simpson (*C.*), Northamptonshire; Llewellyn Smith (*Lab.*), Wales, S.E.; George W. Stevenson (*Lab.*), Staffordshire, E.; Kenneth Stewart (*Lab.*), Merseyside, W.; *Sir John Stewart-Clark (*C.*), Sussex, E.; *Rt. Hon. John Taylor (*O.U.P.*), N. Ireland; John E. Tomlinson (*Lab.*), Birmingham, W.; Mrs. Carol Tongue (*Lab.*), London, E.; *Frederick A. Tuckman (*C.*), Leicester; *Amédée E. Turner (*C.*), Suffolk; *Hon. Sir Peter B. R. Vanneck (*C.*), Cleveland and Yorkshire N.;*Michael J. Welsh (*C.*), Lancashire, Central; Norman West (*Lab.*), Yorkshire, South.

UNITED KINGDOM ELECTIONS TO EUROPEAN PARLIAMENT

(June 14, 1984)

An asterisk * denotes membership of the previous Parliament. For abbreviations, *see* p. 320

Bedfordshire, South
E. 524,974

*P. G. Beazley, *C.*	72,088
W. Cochrane, *Lab.*	57,106
P. A. Dixon, *L./All.*	36,444
C. maj.	*14,982*

Birmingham, East
E. 548,899

Mrs. C. M. Crawley, *Lab.*	76,377
*Miss N. E. Forster, *C.*	54,994
D. A. Bennett *S.D.P./All.*	21,927
Miss D. Howell, *Ind.*	1,440
Lab. maj.	*21,383*

Birmingham, West
E. 518,707

J. E. Tomlinson, *Lab.*	61,946
C. Hart, *C.*	55,702
J. C. Binns, *S.D.P./All.*	19,422
Lab. maj.	*6,244*

Bristol
E. 569,765

*R. J. Cottrell, *C.*	94,652
R. L. Berry, *Lab.*	77,008
P. J. Farley, *S.D.P./All.*	33,698
C. maj.	*17,644*

Cambridge and Bedfordshire North
E. 523,899

*Sir Frederick Catherwood, *C.*	86,117
H. G. Bottomley, *Lab.*	38,901
A. N. Duff, *L./All.*	36,341
C. maj.	*47,216*

Cheshire, East
E. 498,568

*T. Normanton, *C.*	71,182
A. Stephenson, *Lab.*	52,806
J. P. Corbett, *S.D.P./All.*	31,374
C. maj.	*18,376*

Cheshire, West
E. 539,761

*A. Pearce, *C.*	74,579
D. G. Hanson, *Lab.*	64,887
E. C. H. Owen, *S.D.P./All.*	30,470
C. maj.	*9,692*

Cleveland and Yorkshire North
E. 566,083

*Hon. Sir P. Vanneck,, *C.*	73,217
P. F. Tinnion, *Lab.*	70,592
C. Beever, *S.D.P./All.*	35,916
C. maj.	*2,625*

Cornwall and Plymouth
E. 506,004

C. J. P. Beazley, *C.*	81,627
J. C. Marks, *S.D.P./All.*	63,876
J. D. Cosgrove, *Lab.*	35,952
A. I. Parkin, *Ind.*	5,645
R. J. Trevallion, *Ind.*	2,981
J. Whetter, *Ind.*	1,892
C. maj.	*17,751*

The Cotswolds
E. 527,081

*Sir H. Plumb, *C.*	94,740
Miss M. E. Burton, *L./All.*	45,798
Miss J. A. Royall, *Lab.*	36,738
C. maj.	*48,942*

Cumbria and Lancashire North
E. 547,433

Mrs. I. S. Faith, *C.*	86,127
J. R. Atkinson, *Lab.*	62,332
Mrs. K. C. Brooks, *L./All.*	39,622
C. maj.	*23,795*

Derbyshire
E. 553,020

G. W. Hoon, *Lab.*	79,466
*T. N. B. Spencer, *C.*	72,613
Miss J. M. Elles, *S.D.P./All.*	30,824
Lab. maj.	*6,853*

Devon
E. 560,807

*Lord O'Hagan, C.	....	110,129
P. G. Driver, L./All.	.....	53,519
D. A. Gorbutt, Lab.	.....	30,017
P. S. Christie, Eco.	....	6,919
Lady Rous, W. Reg.	....	659
C. maj.	....	56,610

Dorset East and Hampshire West
E. 565,709

B. M. D. Cassidy, C.	.....	109,072
J. M. Goss, L./All.	.....	49,181
D. T. James, Lab.	....	31,223
C. maj.	....	59,891

Durham
E. 530,104

S. S. Hughes, Lab.	.....	106,073
Hon. W. R. Fletcher-Vane, C.	....	44,846
C. Foote Wood, L./All.	...	32,307
Lab. maj.	....	61,227

Essex, N.E.
E. 574,022

*D. M. Curry, C.	....	97,138
B. L. Stapleton, Lab.	....	42,836
A. E. Ross, S.D.P./All.	..	34,769
C. maj.	....	54,302

Essex, S.W.
E. 557,704

*Dr. A. Sherlock, C.	....	72,190
C. O'Brien, Lab.	....	56,169
A. F. C. Morris, L./All.	...	29,385
C. maj.	....	16,021

Glasgow
E. 518,178

*Mrs. J. Buchan, Lab.	....	91,015
Miss S. Chadd, C.	.....	25,282
C. Mason, L./All.	.....	20,867
N. MacLeod, S.N.P.	.....	16,456
Lab. maj.	....	65,733

Greater Manchester, Central
E. 507,941

E. Newman, Lab.	....	76,830
T. R. M. Sewell, C.	.....	48,753
G. E. A. O. Weddell, L./All.	....	24,192
K. J. Martin, Ind.	....	1,430
Lab. maj.	....	28,077

Greater Manchester, East
E. 510,586

J. G. Ford, Lab.	....	65,101
T. K. Thornber, C.	....	56,450
Mrs. B. Gaskin, S.D.P./All.	....	27,801
M. J. Shipley, Eco.	....	3,158
Lab. maj.	....	8,651

Greater Manchester, West
E. 528,896

*Rt. Hon. Mrs. B. A. Castle, Lab.	....	93,740
*W. J. Hopper, C.	....	56,042
J. R. Boddy, S.D.P./All.	...	17,894
Lab. maj.	....	37,698

Hampshire, Central
E. 524,649

*B. R. V. Z. de Ferranti, C.	..	84,086
F. B. Jacobs, S.D.P./All.	...	39,265
M. V. Castle, Lab.	....	39,228
C. maj.	....	44,821

Hereford and Worcester
E. 560,654

*Sir J. Scott-Hopkins, C.	....	84,077
P. E. S. Nielson, Lab.	.....	44,143
I. D. Phillips, L./All.	.....	37,854
Mrs. F. M. Norman, Eco.	...	8,179
C. maj.	....	39,934

Hertfordshire
E. 505,206

*D. Prag, C.	....	87,603
A. McWalter, Lab.	.....	41,671
Mrs. F. M. Beckett, S.D.P./All.	....	40,877
C. maj.	....	45,932

Highlands and Islands
E. 307,265

*Mrs. W. M. Ewing, S.N.P.	...	49,410
D. R. Johnston, L./All.	...	33,133
D. Webster, C.	....	18,847
Rev. J. McArthur, Lab.	.....	16,644
S.N.P. maj.	....	16,277

Humberside
E. 503,080

*R. C. Battersby, C.	....	61,952
P. D. Crampton, Lab.	.....	53,937
S. W. Unwin, S.D.P./All.	...	27,318
C. maj.	....	8,015

Kent, East
E. 554,808

*C. M. Jackson, C.	....	92,340
D. A. Enright, Lab.	.....	43,473
A. Kinch, S.D.P./All.	.....	34,601
S. Dawe, Eco.	....	5,405
C. maj.	....	48,867

Kent, West
E. 565,693

*G. B. Patterson, C.	....	85,414
A. Woodhams, Lab.	......	50,784
P. H. Billenness, L. All.	.....	33,306
Mrs. C. A. Bunyan, Eco.	...	4,991
C. maj.	....	34,630

Lancashire, Central
E. 524,132

*M. J. Welsh, C.	....	82,370
Miss H. M. Jones, Lab.	.....	56,175
*M. Gallagher, S.D.P./All.	..	24,936
C. maj.	....	26,195

Lancashire, East
E. 534,542

M. J. Hindley, Lab.	.....	75,711
*E. T. Kellett-Bowman, C.	..	67,806
A. G. Lishman, L./All.	.....	26,320
Lab. maj.	....	7,905

Leeds
E. 527,653

M. McGowan, Lab.	......	70,535
J. G. Holt, C.	....	60,178
S. J. Cooksey, L./All.	.....	36,097
Lab. maj.	....	10,357

Leicester
E. 564,350

*F. A. Tuckman, C.	....	72,508
P. A. Soulsby, Lab.	.....	69,616
D. N. Simmonds, S.D.P./All.	....	29,656
A. G. Barrett, Ind.	....	3,249
C. maj.	....	2,892

Lincolnshire
E. 551,904

*W. F. Newton Dunn, C.	...	92,606
C. W. Sewell, Lab.	.....	47,161
G. Purves, L./All.	.....	37,244
C. maj.	....	45,445

London, Central
E. 543,825

A. S. Newens, Lab.	....	77,842
*A. D. Fergusson, C.	....	64,545
E. Wistrich, S.D.P./All.	...	30,269
J. E. Porritt, Eco.	....	5,945
R. J. Maynard, Ind.	....	1,569
Lab. maj.	....	13,297

London, East
E. 537,831

Miss C. Tongue, Lab.	....	73,870
*A. R. Tyrrell, C.	....	61,711
Mrs. J. Horne, S.D.P./All.	..	26,379
Lab. maj.	....	12,159

London, North
E. 564,359

*J. L. Marshall, C.	....	74,846
E. Large, Lab.	....	69,993
J. Skinner, L./All.	....	31,344
P. S. J. Lang, Eco.	....	4,682
C. maj.	....	4,853

London, N.E.
E. 513,781

*A. Lomas, Lab.	....	79,907
M. Batchelor, C.	....	27,242
J. P. Heppell, L./All.	....	17,344
Mrs. J. Lambert, Eco.	.....	4,797
Lab. maj.	....	52,665

London, N.W.
E. 518,365

*The Lord Bethell, C.	....	69,803
Ms. P. Healy, Lab.	....	62,381
A. Ketteringham, L./All.	...	29,609
C. maj.	....	7,422

London, S.E.
E. 561,984

*P. N. Price, C.	....	81,508
S. J. Cowan, Lab.	....	61,493
J. H. Fryer, L./All.	....	38,614
W. E. Turner, Ind.	....	989
C. maj.	....	20,015

London, S.W.
E. 499,273

*Dame Shelagh M. Roberts, C.	....	70,490
Miss A. J. Pollack, Lab.	...	63,623
D. J. Twigg, L/All.	....	32,268
Mrs. S. G. Willington, Eco.	..	3,066
C. maj.	....	6,867

London South and Surrey East
E.505,393

*C.J.O. Moorhouse, C.	82,122
A.S. MacKinlay, Lab.	37,465
J.G. Parry, L./All.	34,522
C.maj.	*44,657*

London, South Inner
E.530,672

*R.A. Balfe, C.	77,661
Mrs. D. Miller, C.	46,180
J. Daly, S.D.P./All.	25,391
Mrs. J. Owens, Eco.	3,281
Lab.maj.	*31,481*

London, West
E.516,661

M.N. Elliot, Lab.	79,554
*B.H. Hord, C.	74,325
C. Layton, S.D.P./All.	36,687
Mrs. D. M. Sutherland, Eco.	4,361
Lab.maj.	*5,229*

Lothians
E.516,068

D.W. Martin, Lab.	74,989
I.J. Henderson, C.	49,065
Dr. J.D. Mabon, S.D.P./All.	36,636
Dr. D. Stevenson, S.N.P.	22,331
Miss L. Hendry, Eco.	2,560
Lab.maj.	*25,924*

Merseyside, East
E.537,285

L.J. Huckfield, Lab.	87,086
T.G.D.R.B. Galbraith, C.	38,047
T. Bishop, S.D.P./All.	17,259
Lab.maj.	*49,039*

Merseyside, West
E.551,532

K. Stewart, Lab.	65,915
*Miss G.D. Hooper, C.	52,718
P.R. Clark, L./All.	37,303
Lab.maj.	*13,197*

Midlands, Central
E.533,798

*J. de Courcy Ling, C.	67,884
D.J. Blackman, Lab.	55,155
P. Langmead, S.D.P./All.	27,912
A. Enstone, Ind.	1,494
C.maj.	*12,729*

Midlands, West
E.533,796

T.J. Pitt, Lab.	74,091
A.T. Burnside, C.	54,406
C. Carter, L./All.	17,709
Lab.maj.	*19,685*

Norfolk
E.543,214

*P.F. Howell, C.	95,459
A.E.B. Heading, Lab.	58,602
L. Williams, S.D.P./All.	37,703
C.maj.	*36,857*

Northamptonshire
E.547,188

*A.M.H. Simpson, C.	88,668
J. Dickie, Lab.	48,809
Mrs. C. M. Goodhart, S.D.P./All.	37,421
Mrs. A. Bryant, Ind.	3,330
C.maj.	*39,859*

Northumbria
E.512,979

*G.J. Adam, Lab.	78,417
C.M.M. Crichton, C.	62,717
G. Scott, L./All.	42,946
Lab.maj.	*15,700*

Nottingham
E.554,473

M.L. Kilby, C.	82,500
K. Coates, Lab.	66,374
K.M. Melton, L./All.	33,169
C.maj.	*16,126*

Oxford and Buckinghamshire
E.542,343

J.E.M. Elles, C.	94,136
R.J. Liddle, S.D.P./All.	45,055
J.G. Power, Lab.	39,164
C.maj.	*49,081*

Scotland, Mid. and Fife
E.528,529

A. Falconer, Lab.	80,038
*J.R. Purvis, C.	52,872
Mrs. J.T. Jones, S.N.P.	30,511
A. A. I. Wedderburn, S.D.P./All.	24,220
Lab.maj.	*27,166*

Scotland, North-East
E.548,711

*J.L.C. Provan, C.	53,809
F. Doran, Lab.	44,638
D. Hood, S.N.P.	33,448
I.G. Philip, S.D.P./All.	25,490
C.maj.	*9,171*

Scotland, South
E.484,760

*A.H. Hutton, C.	60,843
R. Stewart, Lab.	57,706
Mrs. E. M. Buchanan, L./All.	23,598
I.R. Goldie, S.N.P.	22,242
C.maj.	*3,137*

Sheffield
E.558,984

G.R. Cryer, Lab.	93,530
D.R. Grayson, C.	47,247
Miss M. Holmstedt, L./All.	23,935
Lab.maj.	*46,283*

Shropshire and Stafford
E.562,823

*C.J. Prout, C.	82,291
D.J.A. Hallam, Lab.	57,359
R.M. Burman, L./All.	37,209
C.maj.	*24,932*

Somerset and Dorset West
E.540,393

Mrs. M. Daly, C.	98,928
R.G. Moore, L./All.	58,677
Mrs. J. Linden, Lab.	36,836
C.maj.	*40,251*

Staffordshire, East
E.563,376

G.W. Stevenson, Lab.	76,753
*R.J. Moreland, C.	68,886
R. Fox, S.D.P./All.	26,093
Lab.maj.	*7,867*

Strathclyde, East
E.498,458

*K.D. Collins, Lab.	90,792
G. Leslie, S.N.P.	27,330
P.R. Leckie, C.	24,857
Ms. P. de Seume, L./All.	11,883
Lab.maj.	*63,462*

Strathclyde, West
E.499,162

H. McMahon, Lab.	70,234
Miss J. Lait, C.	47,196
Mrs. J. Herriot, S.N.P.	28,866
D.J. Herbison, S.D.P./All.	25,955
Lab.maj.	*23,038*

Suffolk
E.516,050

*A.E. Turner, C.	88,243
W. Moszczynski, Lab.	41,145
C. Leakey, L./All.	34,084
C.maj.	*47,098*

Surrey, West
E.504,923

*The Marquess of Douro, C.	96,675
E. Mortimer, S.D.P./All.	44,087
N.K.A.S. Vaz, Lab.	22,531
C.maj.	*52,588*

Sussex, East
E.537,397

*Sir J. Stewart-Clark, Bt., C.	102,287
J. Busby, S.D.P./All.	36,666
H. Spillman, Lab.	32,213
Mrs. E. Evelyn, Eco.	5,401
C.maj.	*65,621*

Sussex, West
E.531,934

*R.M. Seligman, C.	104,257
Dr. J.M.M. Walsh, L./All.	46,755
G.C. Rees, Lab.	22,857
D. Aherne, Eco.	3,842
C.maj.	*57,502*

Thames Valley
E.519,564

*The Baroness Elles, C.	74,928
R.B. Bastin, Lab.	36,123
R.W. Bradnock, L./All.	32,704
C.maj.	*38,805*

Tyne and Wear
E.543,955

*Miss J.G. Quin, Lab.	89,024
R.R. Cook, C.	39,610
B.P. Carroll, S.D.P./All.	19,081
Lab.maj.	*49,414*

Wales, Mid and West
E.533,644

D.R. Morris, Lab.	89,362
D. Lewis, C.	52,910
D. Lloyd, L./All.	35,168
Dr. P. Williams, P.C.	32,880
Miss M.A. Smith, Eco.	4,266
Lab.maj.	*36,452*

Wales, North
E.516,153

*Miss B. A. Brooks, C.	69,139
R. T. Ellis, S.D.P./All.	56,861
C. I. Campbell, Lab.	54,768
D. Iwan, P.C.	38,117
C. maj.	*12,278*

Wales, South
E.509,434

*W. J. Griffiths, Lab.	99,936
Miss J. R. Pattman, C.	55,678
Mrs. J. Davis, L./All.	26,588
Dr D. Huws, P.C.	13,201
Lab. maj.	*44,258*

Wales, S.E.
E.565,739

L. Smith, Lab.	131,916
R. Whyatt, C.	36,359
C. D. Lindley, S.D.P./All.	28,330
S. Morgan, P.C.	18,833
Lab. maj.	*95,557*

Wight and Hampshire, East
E.544,189

*R. J. Simmonds, C.	96,666
Mrs. S. Ludford, L./All.	53,738
J. A. Phillips, Lab.	36,445
C. maj.	*42,928*

Wiltshire
E.531,501

Mrs. C. F. Jackson, C.	86,873
J. B. Ainslie, L./All.	60,404
P. Whiteside, Lab.	35,457
C. maj.	*26,469*

York
E.517,592

E. H. C. McMillan-Scott, C.	80,636
Mrs. S. Haines, Lab.	44,234
M. G. Howard, S.D.P./All.	33,356
C. maj.	*36,402*

Yorkshire, South
E.516,431

N. West, Lab.	98,020
Mrs. R. P. N. Pockley, C.	30,271
D. Eden, S.D.P./All.	19,306
Lab. maj.	*67,749*

Yorkshire, S.W.
E.518,423

*T. Megahy, Lab.	88,464
A. J. A. Lodge, C.	44,291
J. F. Crossley, L./All.	26,964
Lab. maj.	*44,173*

Yorkshire, West
E.560,190

*B. H. Seal, Lab.	86,259
I. C. Bruce, C.	65,405
E. Lyons, S.D.P./All.	28,709
Lab. maj.	*20,854*

Northern Ireland
E.1,077,605

First Preference

*Rev. I. R. K. Paisley, D.U.P.	230,251
*J. Hume, S.D.L.P.	151,399
*Rt. Hon. J. D. Taylor, O.U.P.	147,169
D. Morrison, S.F.	91,476
D. Cook, All.	34,046
J. Kilfedder, U.P.U.P.	20,092
S. Lynch, W.P.	8,712
C. McGuigan, Eco.	2,172

Rev. I. R. K. Paisley, J. Hume, and *Rt. Hon. J. D. Taylor* were elected by the single transferable voting system.

VOTES CAST AT U.K. GENERAL ELECTIONS, 1974–83

General Election, February 1974*

Conservative	11,868,906
Labour	11,639,243
Liberal	6,063,470
Scottish Nationalist	632,032
Plaid Cymru	171,634
Communist	32,741
Others	207,884

General Election, October, 1974*

Labour	11,456,597
Conservative	10,464,675
Liberal	5,346,800
Scottish Nationalist	839,628
Plaid Cymru	166,321
Others	195,065

General Election, 1979*

Conservative	13,697,753
Labour	11,506,741
Liberal	4,305,324
Scottish Nationalist	504,259
National Front	191,706
Plaid Cymru	132,544
Others	188,063

General Election, 1983*

Conservative	13,012,602
Labour	8,457,124
Liberal/S.D.P. Alliance	7,780,587
Scottish Nationalist	331,975
Plaid Cymru	125,309
Others	198,383

*Excluding Northern Ireland

MAJORITIES IN THE HOUSE OF COMMONS SINCE 1945

Year	Party	Majority	Year	Party	Majority
1945	Labour	146	1966	Labour	99
1950	Labour	8	1970	Conservative	31
1951	Conservative	16	1974 (Feb.)	No Majority	
1955	Conservative	59	1974 (Oct.)	Labour	5
1959	Conservative	100	1979	Conservative	43
1964	Labour	5	1983	Conservative	144

PARLIAMENTARY SUMMARY, LORDS AND COMMONS, 1984–85

Re-assembling earlier than the Commons following the summer recess, the Lords met on Oct. 16 when Viscount Whitelaw made a statement about the Brighton bombing. On Oct. 18, Lord Shinwell attended the House on his 100th birthday for a celebration in the Royal Gallery and later in the Chamber, where high tributes were paid to him. On Oct. 22, the Commons re-assembled and party spokesmen joined in further condemnation of the Brighton bombing. The Home Secretary (Mr. Brittan) declared: "We will not be bombed into bolt holes by terrorists" and spoke of new arrangements centrally for countering I.R.A. terrorists' threats. Parliament was prorogued on Oct. 31 following a debate in the Lords on the Warnock inquiry into human fertilisation and embryology. In the Commons, the last of the major debates of the session was on the unemployment situation, but Labour's attack was beaten-off by 264 to 189 votes.

THE QUEEN'S SPEECH

The Queen opened the new session of Parliament on Nov. 6 and in her speech which outlined the Government's legislative proposals said: "I look forward with great pleasure to receiving the President of Malawi and the President of Mexico on State visits during the next 12 months, to paying a State visit to Portugal in March, and to visiting the Caribbean in the autumn on the occasion of the Commonwealth Heads of Government Meeting in the Bahamas.

My Government consider as their highest priority the maintenance of national security and the preservation of peace. They will, accordingly, continue to play an active part in the Atlantic Alliance. They will promote Western defence interests outside the N.A.T.O. area. They will make vigorous efforts to combat international terrorism.

With the allies of the United Kingdom, my Government will contribute to arms control and disarmament negotiations and will work for the resumption of negotiations where these have been broken off. They will work continually for a greater atmosphere of trust between East and West.

Following the agreement at Fontainebleau on the fairer sharing of the Community's budget burden and on the overall control of Community spending, my Government look forward to the further development of the European Community.

They will continue to press for improvements in the Common Agricultural Policy and for completion of the common market in goods and services.

They will work for the early conclusion of the negotiations to enable Spain and Portugal to join the Community, and to conclude a new agreement to succeed the Lomé Convention.

My Government will continue fully to discharge their obligations to the people of the Falkland Islands, while seeking more normal relations between this country and Argentina.

They will consider the views expressed by the people of Hong Kong on the draft agreement with China, and report to Parliament.

They reaffirm their commitment to the people of Gibraltar and hope to see the early implementation of the Lisbon statement.

My Government will continue to work for a settlement in Namibia, a solution to the Arab/Israel dispute and the restoration of the independence and non-aligned status of Afghanistan.

My Government will continue fully to support the Commonwealth, to play a constructive role in the United Nations, to maintain a substantial aid programme, and to encourage investment in developing countries.

My Government will continue to work closely with other nations and international institutions to strengthen and spread economic recovery; and to co-operate on issues connected with the settlement of international debts.

My Government will continue to pursue policies founded on sound money and lower public borrowing and aimed at securing a further reduction in inflation.

While noting that the numbers of people in work are steadily rising, my Government remains deeply concerned about unemployment and will continue policies designed to achieve better opportunities for employment and to help the unemployed obtain the training or work experience needed to fill them.

Firm control of public spending will be maintained. My Government will work for a more flexible and competitive economy through lower taxation, further reform of the tax system, increased efficiency in the public sector and encouragement of initiative and enterprise which will sustain rising standards.

In order to promote efficiency and growth, my Government will continue their policies of exposing State-owned businesses to competition and, where appropriate, returning them to the private sector.

A Bill will be introduced to increase competition in the provision of local bus services in Great Britain and to transfer to the private sector the operations of the National Bus Company.

A Bill will be introduced to increase competition in retail banking by completing the transition of the Trustee Savings Banks to private sector status.

Bills will be introduced to reform insolvency law in England and Wales, and in Scotland, and to remove the statutory levy on cinema admissions and establish an environment for the film and cinema industries free from regulation.

A Bill will be introduced to abolish the Greater London Council and the metropolitan county councils.

Legislation will be introduced to extend the franchise to certain British citizens resident abroad, to change absent voting arrangements in order to enable those on holiday to vote, and to increase the parliamentary election deposit but reduce the threshold for forfeiture.

A Bill will be introduced to establish a national prosecution service independent of the police in England and Wales and to enable the Attorney General to refer Crown Court sentences for the opinion of the Court of Appeal.

A further Bill will establish a new and comprehensive statutory framework governing the interception of communications.

Measures will be introduced for the administration of justice in England and Wales and making further reforms in the law following reports of the Law Commission.

There will be a measure dealing with the international aspects of child abduction and the custody of children.

A Bill will be introduced to improve the occupational pension rights of people who leave schemes before pensionable age and to ensure that members are able to obtain information about their schemes.

Legislation will be introduced for the better protection of food and the environment.

A Bill will be introduced to give parents of children educated at public expense the right to exempt them from corporal punishment. My Government will continue to develop policies to raise educational standards.

My Government will encourage the constitutional parties in Northern Ireland to consider how powers can be restored to local administration on a basis acceptable to all sides of the community, and will seek to maintain good relations with the Government of the Republic of Ireland.

The security forces will continue to receive my Government's full support. Legislation will be introduced to prevent impersonation at elections in Northern Ireland.

Bills will be introduced to establish trustee bodies to manage certain Scottish institutions, and to reform Scots law, including provisions on matrimonial property and financial provision on divorce, following reports by the Scottish Law Commission."

Debate on The Queen's Speech

The Lords discussed the Speech for four days and the Commons for six days. Mr. Kinnock, Labour leader, declared it would do nothing to lower unemployment or stimulate investment and trade. Mrs. Thatcher retorted that the Opposition by their words denounced unemployment, but by their deeds they created it; the Government would continue with policies designed to achieve higher employment. The Liberal leader, Mr. Steel, criticized the Speech for not addressing itself to the two major problems of the chronic level of unemployment and the increasingly divided nature of British society. On Nov. 12, a Labour motion attacking the Government for failing to propose measures to rebuild the nation's industrial base and create new opportunities for employment was defeated by 353 to 196 votes. On the last day of debate (Nov. 13), a Labour amendment attacking policies which they claimed had already severely damaged the economy and which would continue to hold back the prospects of recovery, was defeated by 364 to 205 votes. A Liberal–S.D.P. amendment also attacking the programme for offering no policies to reduce unemployment was rejected by 364 to 200 votes. Then the programme embodied in the Speech was approved by 352 to 202 votes.

ECONOMIC STATEMENT

On Nov. 12, the Chancellor of the Exchequer (Mr. Lawson) made his autumn statement in the Commons when he promised net tax cuts of about £1½ billion in the 1985 Budget. In his statement, the Chancellor said he was laying before the House the Government's outline public expenditure plans for 1985–86, proposals for National Insurance contributions next year, and the forecast of economic prospects for 1985 required by the 1975 Industry Act. Mr. Lawson continued: "The Government remains committed to reducing taxation, and to keeping firm control over Government spending.

"Following this year's public expenditure review, the public expenditure planning total for next year, 1985–86, has been set at £132 billion. This is within the provisional figure for 1985–86 published in the Public Expenditure White Paper in February.

"The Government has thus succeeded for the third year running in holding the planning total to the level announced in previous White Papers.

"After allowing for inflation, public expenditure next year is planned to be broadly the same as was planned for this year and below the likely out-turn for this year, which has been inflated by the cost of maintaining electricity supplies during the coal strike.

"With the economy continuing to expand, public expenditure as a percentage of national output should fall next year to its lowest level for six years.

"The revised plans contain a reserve for contingencies of £3 billion. This is £½ billion less than the provisional reserve for 1985–86 allowed for in the February White Paper, when departmental spending plans for 1985–86 were less well defined, but £½ billion more than this year's reserve.

"The allocation of this £½ billion to specific expenditure programmes, coupled with an increase in forecast receipts from the privatisation programme, has enabled most, though not all, programmes to show an increase in spending over the White Paper figures.

"To contain these increases to dimensions compatible with the overall £132 billion planning total has required some hard decisions, however.

"Thus there will be increased spending on the National Health Service, but individual health authorities will be expected to become more efficient and to absorb any pay and price increases within the money made available to them.

"In addition, the Secretary of State for Social Services has already announced important measures to cut costs by limitations on N.H.S. prescribing, and there will have to be increases in charges.

"Again, spending on social security will increase, but to contain the scale of the increase my right honourable friend will be announcing a number of new measures including substantial savings in supplementary benefit provision for board and lodgings claimants.

"The five per cent abatement of invalidity pension which has applied since 1980 will, however, be restored from next November.

"Yet again, there will be increased provision for education, partly offset by a reduction in spending on student grants.

"By contrast, because fewer young people than expected have needed to take up places on the Youth Training Scheme, the Secretary of State for Employment is able to apply some of the consequential savings to expand other employment and training measures, including the Enterprise Allowance Scheme, within a reduced overall total.

"Other programmes to have reduced provision include domestic assistance to agriculture and housing."

Mr. Lawson continued: "Fuller details of these and other changes are contained in the autumn statement itself, but the Treasury will be making its own contribution to the need for savings.

"The £1 coin has 50 times the life of the note, yet costs less than twice as much to produce. Accordingly, I have instructed the Bank of England to cease issuing £1 notes after the end of this year, although the note will continue to be legal tender for at least a year. This will save £3 million on public expenditure in the first year alone. The ½p, which has not been issued since March 29 this year, will cease to be legal tender after Dec. 31. On Thursday of this week, the Bank of England will be issuing a new version of the £20 note which should be more difficult to forge."

Mr. Lawson continued: "This year's review of expenditure plans has, as usual, also covered the Government's public spending plans for the two later years, 1986–87 and 1987–88.

"The details will show that total pub ic spending is planned to remain broadly constant in real terms right up to 1987–88, which implies a continuing steady reduction as a proportion of G.D.P.

Mr. Lawson said the Government had conducted the usual autumn review of National Insurance contributions in the light of advice from the Government Actuary on the prospective income and expenditure of the National Insurance Fund.

"As last year, we have decided to reduce the taxpayer's contribution to the fund—the so-called Treasury Supplement—by 2 per cent., bringing it down to 9 per cent., but this will not require any corresponding increase in contribution rates.

"Thus the full Class 1 rate will remain unchanged at 9 per cent., for employees and 10·45 per cent. for employers.

"In addition, employers will be relieved of the

burden of contributions on payments under the statutory sick pay scheme, which in due course will be extended to cover the first 28 weeks of sickness.

"As usual, the earnings limits will need to be increased broadly in line with inflation and from next April the lower earnings limit will rise to £35·50 a week and the upper earnings limit to £265 a week.

"Next year, employers will enjoy the full benefit of the abolition of the National Insurance surcharge, which took effect only last month.

"Taking this into account, the total burden on employers in 1985–86 is expected to be significantly less in real terms than in the current year, 1984–85, despite a rising labour force.

"Since the Budget, the economy has had to endure a number of testing developments, both at home and abroad, of a sort which not so long ago would have driven it off course, this time, they have not done so.

"Monetary growth has been in line with the targets I set at the time of the Budget, and inflation has remained low: perhaps 4½ per cent. in the last quarter of this year.

"Total national output, which reached its highest level ever last year, looks set to rise by a further 2¼ per cent. this year. Had it not been for the coal strike, growth this year would probably have been 3½ per cent.

"Investment has been rising particularly strongly; indeed, over the economy as a whole, I expect it to reach a new all-time high this year.

"Employment has been rising at a brisk pace since early 1983, but not yet strongly enough to check the rise in the numbers of those registering as unemployed.

"The outlook for jobs, will, however, have been helped by the recent fall in interest rates which largely reverses the increase during the summer. Provided we stick firmly to present policies, the prospect is of further interest rate cuts ahead.

"This year's P.S.B.R. is likely to turn out higher than the £7¼ billion I envisaged at the time of the Budget, chiefly as a result of the coal strike.

"If the strike were to end at Christmas, it would add some £1¼ billion to borrowing this financial year; and the public expenditure planning total would be exceeded by about the same amount.

"On that basis, I estimate that the P.S.B.R. for 1984–85 would be some £8½ billion, subject to the usual margin of uncertainty at this time of the year. A P.S.B.R. of this size would still be comfortably the smallest proportion of G.D.P. for well over a decade.

"For next year, with continued firm monetary and fiscal policies, inflation is expected to edge down slightly to 4½ per cent. by the fourth quarter.

"Output and employment will continue to rise, with total output expected to be up by a further 3½ per cent. in 1985, of which about 1 per cent. represents the assumed recovery from the coal strike.

"Within this total, the forecast suggests that 1985 will be another good year for exports and industrial investment. Indeed, investment by non-North Sea businesses is expected to rise in real terms by seven per cent. next year, following an 11 per cent. rise this year.

"The forecast makes the conventional assumptions that Income Tax and excise duties are both indexed in line with prices and that the P.S.B.R. is held next year to the £7 billion, or two per cent. of G.D.P., indicated in the medium term financial strategy published at the time of the last Budget.

"It also takes into account the changes made in this year's Finance Act which will take full effect next year and reduce taxation in 1985–86 by some £1¾ billion.

"Beyond that, the margin of uncertainty at this stage is very considerable and the House will understand that the prospects for 1985–86 will need to be reviewed again, in the light of more up-to-date information, before I make my Budget judgment next year.

"On this basis, it does look as if there will be scope for some further net reductions in taxes in next year's Budget.

"The best figure I can put on it at present time is about £1½ billion.

"The autumn statement shows that for the third year running—that is, for every single year since the Government introduced cash planning for public expenditure—spending plans have been held at or below previous White Paper totals.

"It shows too that we are now in the fourth year of steady growth, with a further year of investment and export-led growth in prospect, and with no sign whatever of a resurgence of inflation, and the numbers in work are rising strongly for only the third time since the 'sixties," the Chancellor concluded.

Debate on the Economic Statement

Mr. Roy Hattersley, Shadow Chancellor, accused the Government of intentionally deflating the economy and of budgeting for a permanent pool of three million unemployed as an essential ingredient of Tory policy. Dr. David Owen, S.D.P. leader, said what the Chancellor was doing with public expenditure would do nothing other than add considerably to unemployment. There was a debate on the Chancellor's autumn statement on Dec. 6 when a Labour motion accusing the Government of calculating on a high level of unemployment and condemning the expenditure cuts was defeated by 346 to 199 votes. The Government's motion to approve the programme was carried by 343 to 198 votes.

Sitting suspended

The Speaker suspended the sitting of the Commons on Nov. 21 amid uproar over an announcement that the families of striking miners, and other strikers, would receive less than other people when social security benefits were increased from Nov. 26. Some 30 Labour M.P.s vacated their seats and assembled in front of the Mace with angry gesticulations. Mr. Fowler, Social Services Secretary, was prevented from making an emergency statement which Opposition M.P.s had demanded some hours previously. When the M.P.s refused to move after a ten-minute suspension, the Speaker adjourned the House. The next day, the Speaker and the Prime Minister condemned those Labour M.P.s who caused the suspension; the Speaker warned M.P.s that such conduct undermined the authority of Parliament and Mrs. Thatcher described the demonstration as "a very ugly incident". Later in the day, eight Tories voted against the Government with 40 others abstaining after Sir Geoffrey Howe (Foreign Secretary) announced all-round economies at the Foreign Office which caused back-bench concern that the overseas aid budget would be affected. Among the abstainers were Mr. Heath, former Prime Minister, and Mr. Pym, former Foreign Secretary, and all the officers of the Tory back-bench foreign affairs committee. A Liberal motion opposing any cuts in expenditure on overseas aid, the British Council and the External Service of the B.B.C. was defeated by 311 to 184 votes, a large number of Labour M.P.s being absent.

On Nov. 26, Mr. Fowler, Social Services Secretary, refuted Labour accusations that he had cut £1 from the benefits paid to the families of strikers in order to defeat the N.U.M. Mr. Michael Meacher, Shadow Social Services Secretary, moved a motion charging the Government with having postponed announcing the deduction until the last possible moment in order to stifle debate. After a three-hour emergency debate on the benefit changes the Government won a division by 279 to 185 votes.

The Opposition initiated a debate on Nov. 27 alleging failure of Government policies to safeguard the natural environment and the national heritage of Britain, but their motion calling for greater action was defeated by 276 to 190 votes. The same day, the Opposition launched another attack, this time deploring the deepening crisis in the shipbuilding industry and the massive redundancies already announced and in prospect. Their motion demanding urgent action to maintain the industry was defeated by 267 to 188 votes and a Government amendment endorsing the decision to return British Shipbuilders warship building interests to the private sector was carried by 259 to 185 votes. In the Lords, peers voted to admit television cameras to the Chamber for a six-month experiment.

A two-day debate on the second reading of the Local Government Bill to abolish the Greater London Council and the six metropolitan county councils opened on Dec. 3 in the Commons. Mr. Jenkin, Environment Secretary, said abolition was a clear manifesto pledge on which the Conservatives fought and won the last General Election, but Dr. Cunningham, Labour Shadow Environment Secretary, denounced the measure and described it as a Bill for centralisation with over 40 new powers for ministers. There were critics of the Bill from all parties and prominent among Tories were Mr. David Howell, former Transport Minister, and Mr. Heath. However, the second reading was obtained by 354 to 219 votes, with about a dozen Tory M.P.s abstaining. A Labour amendment to reject a second reading was defeated by identical voting figures.

Students grants

Proposed changes in the system of student grants announced by Sir Keith Joseph, Education Secretary, on Dec. 4, provoked angry response from Conservative M.P.s. They attacked his plans to abolish minimum grants, raise parental contributions and to charge wealthier parents tuition fees. On the following day, Sir Keith announced a partial withdrawal of these proposals and said he would drop the plan for parental contributions to tuition fees. But he was unable now to provide all the £38 million planned to add to the science budget.

On Dec. 10, the Government secured a second reading for the Representation of the People Bill, which extended the franchise to qualified persons living abroad, raised the amount of the General Election deposit, and enabled holiday-makers to vote by post or proxy.

Lord Cledwyn of Penrhos, Opposition leader in the Lords, moved a motion on Dec. 12 which recognized the human misery and waste caused by current unemployment of labour and resources and deplored the lack of urgency shown by the Government in tackling the problem. Lord Young of Graffham, Minister without Portfolio, recognized unemployment as the central issue of our time on which they all shared profound concern. The motion was defeated by 134 to 105 votes.

The Local Government Bill

In the Commons on Dec. 12, on the committee stage of the Local Government Bill, Mr. Jack Straw, a Labour spokesman on Environment, moved an amendment calling for an impartial investigation by a royal commission, a tribunal, or the Audit Commission, but it was defeated by 233 to 182 votes. Later a Tory back-bench move to set up a new elected strategic body for London after G.L.C. abolition was defeated by a majority of only 23, nineteen Conservatives voting for the proposal and a large number abstaining. During further committee stage discussion on Dec. 13, an Alliance move to waive the six metropolitan county councils from abolition was outvoted by 268 to 14. Mr. Simon Hughes, the Liberal spokesman, chastised Labour for failing to vote the previous night in support of an Alliance amendment to save the G.L.C. but not the metropolitan counties, an argument which produced sharp party backbiting. Ultimately the clause to abolish the G.L.C. and the metropolitan county councils effective from April 1, 1986, was approved by 277 to 156 votes.

Local authority assets

Mr. Jenkin, Environment Secretary, came under all-round attack on Dec. 18 when he announced new restraints on local authorities in the use of assets raised largely through the sale of council houses. Former Cabinet ministers, Mr. Pym and Mr. Geoffrey Rippon, joined the Opposition in assailing the proposals and the Speaker granted a request for an emergency debate. This took place next day and the Speaker had frequently to call for order as Mr. Jenkin defended his proposals as necessary to avoid the risk of a large overspend in local government next year. At the end of the day when the House divided on the formal motion to adjourn, on which the debate was initiated, the Government won the vote by 325 to 225 with only three Tories voting against the Government and some 30 others abstaining. On Feb. 27, an Opposition motion attacking the Government's decision further to restrict the use local authorities could make of receipts realised through the sale of assets was defeated by 314 to 206 votes. Mr. Gow, Housing Minister, announced that certain low-cost home ownership schemes operated by local authorities were to be exempt from Government curbs on the use of receipts from council house sales. On Mar. 13, a few Conservatives voiced criticism along with the main stream of the Opposition of Government plans to stop councils spending £1 billion receipts from the sale of council houses on new work; Labour's attempt to overturn the proposals was defeated by 313 to 192 votes.

M.L.R. reintroduced

The Chancellor of the Exchequer (Mr. Lawson) defended his decision to reintroduce a minimum lending rate when he told the Commons on Jan. 14 of the Government's resolve to do nothing to weaken the fight against inflation and that higher interest rates would have to continue as long as was necessary to achieve that. Mr. Lawson made his statement against the background of the decline in the value of sterling and most Tory M.P.s supported his action although Opposition members charged him with panic measures. Mr. Hattersley, Shadow Chancellor, said the statement indicated the Government's economic policy was a shambles. On Jan. 15, Mrs. Thatcher staunchly defended the Chancellor during question time after Mr. Kinnock declared he should be sacked to help the pound. Mr. Hattersley moved a Labour motion on the reduction of unemployment through public investment and condemning the Government for its failure. Mr. Lawson hit back by saying the best hope for the jobless was the economic recovery now based on a durable foundation with a low tax economy the best way to create jobs. Mr. Heath again made an onslaught on the Government's economic policies, but Mr. Tom King, Employment Secretary, riposted that the Government had halted the haemorrhage of loss of jobs. Labour's motion was defeated by 383 to 182 votes.

The Miners' Strike

Throughout the session the on-going national coalminers' strike became the subject for regular questions to the Prime Minister and other involved ministers at question time with ministerial statements but merely a few full-scale debates. However, on Jan. 17, Labour M.P.s demanded a debate with such vocal force that the Speaker suspended the sitting for 20 minutes. Labour back-benchers continued to demand a debate in Government time and when the Speaker tried to proceed to the next business, 16 of them rose from their seats. Mr. Weatherill complained that the M.P.s were behaving in a very unruly way and against all their traditions that members should not seek to challenge the authority of the chair. When the M.P.s refused to resume their seats, the Speaker suspended the sitting. On Feb. 4, M.P.s discussed a Labour motion on the coalmining dispute amid noisy, angry vociferous scenes, though Labour's bid to condemn the Government's attitude to negotiations was defeated by 378 to 200 votes.

Mr. Brittan, Home Secretary, told the Commons on Jan. 22 that difficult decisions would have to be made about the security arrangements for future party conferences and similar major political events when commenting on the conclusions of an inquiry into the Brighton bombing. He said a new counter-terrorist working group was to be set up with representatives from the police, the security services and the Army. Mr. Kaufman, Shadow Home Secretary, described the inquiry report as inadequate and complacent. Both sides of the Commons questioned Government moves to make a £119 million supplementary payment to the Common Market but the amount was later sanctioned by 349 to 189 votes, with 10 Tories voting against and others abstaining.

Televising of the Lords

The Earl of Stockton, the former Conservative Prime Minister, was the star of the first televised debate in the Lords on Jan. 23, although his speech was delayed briefly by a demonstration in the Strangers' Gallery in support of the miners. Lord Beswick opened the debate for the Opposition and called for economic and social policies which would unite the nation and create employment.

On Jan. 24, a proposal to allow the Attorney General to seek the Court of Appeal's opinion on sentences imposed in Crown Courts was tossed aside in the Lords by 140 to 98 votes.

Corporal punishment

Sir Keith Joseph, Education Secretary, moved on Jan. 28 the second reading of the Education (Corporal Punishment) Bill to secure compliance with the judgment of the European Court on Human Rights, but he was chided by M.P.s from all round the Commons. The Bill gave parents the right to decide whether or not their children at State schools should be eligible for the cane. Labour moved to refuse the measure a second reading but this was defeated by 298 to 168 votes and the Bill was read a second time by 290 to 171 votes. However, on July 4, the Lords, dealing with the self-same Bill, voted by 108 to 104 for the total abolition of corporal punishment in all schools, both State and independent.

Labour censure motion

In the Commons on Jan. 31, Mr. Kinnock moved a censure motion on the Government for its gross mismanagement of the economy and claimed their secretive dithering over sterling had made Britain the punchbag of the world's currency speculators.

The Prime Minister nonetheless rejected exchange controls and other measures to discourage speculation against the pound and stated that the Government had had the guts necessary to take the measures to maintain their strategy. The Opposition motion was defeated by 395 to 222 votes, and a Tory amendment congratulating the Government on its firm action in maintaining sound financial conditions and medium-term strategy was carried by 392 to 221 votes.

There was more trouble among Government supporters on Feb. 7 when Mr. Gow, Environment Minister, defended the decision to make water authorities impose higher charges than they actually wanted. The imposition of higher charges was attacked from both sides.

On Feb. 12, the Transport Bill, which introduced competition on bus routes and denationalized the National Bus Company, was championed for a second reading by Mr. Ridley, Transport Minister, but he ran into opposition from Mr. Peter Fry (Con. Wellingborough), a member of the All-Party Select Committee on Transport, who moved an amendment declining to give the Bill a second reading until there had been an opportunity to study the Select Committee's report on the industry. When Mr. Fry offered to withdraw his amendment because of a concession on this point, Labour and Alliance M.P.s forced a division which the Government won by 83 votes; three Tories voted against the Bill and a dozen others abstained.

The sinking of the "Belgrano"

There were hectic moments in the Commons on Feb. 12 when Mr. Kinnock declined to accept the Prime Minister's statement that she had played no part in the decision to prosecute Mr. Clive Ponting over the leaking of documents on the sinking of the *Belgrano*. With Conservatives shouting at Mr. Kinnock to withdraw, Mrs. Thatcher declared she had said explicitly and before the whole House that she was not involved in the decision to prosecute Mr. Ponting. Mr. Kinnock demanded to know Mrs. Thatcher's precise role in the decision to prosecute but the Prime Minister said the decision was the duty of the Attorney-General and the Director of Public Prosecutions. There were irate cries of "scandalous" and "withdraw" when Mr. Kinnock said he frankly did not believe Mrs. Thatcher was not involved in the decision to prosecute. The Prime Minister was angry herself now and called on Mr. Kinnock to accept what she had said. Sir Michael Havers, the Attorney-General, questioned about how the decision to prosecute had been taken, said Mrs. Thatcher was not consulted. On Feb. 13, the Speaker rejected attempts by Tories to change a ruling made in the previous day's exchanges and said he stood by his decision that Mr. Kinnock's statement, that he did not believe Mrs. Thatcher, did not amount to calling her a liar. Inevitably this provoked more heated inter-party exchanges, which overspilled into Feb. 14 when Mrs. Thatcher stoutly rejected Opposition accusations that ministers had misled Parliament over the sinking of the Argentine warship. Mr. Kinnock said he accepted Mrs. Thatcher's assurances that she was not involved in the decision by the law officers to prosecute Mr. Ponting but the supercharged atmosphere was unabated for another 15 minutes of exchanges. On Feb. 18, there was a full debate on the sinking of the *Belgrano* opened by Mr. Heseltine, Defence Secretary, who rejected the account given by Mr. Ponting of the reasons for his decision to leak official documents on the action. Mr. Denzil Davies, Labour Defence spokesman, accused Mr. Heseltine of trying to carry out a character assassination of the former civil servant acquitted at the Central Criminal Court of contravening the Official Secrets Act. He moved the Opposition amendment which accused the Government of seeking to conceal information and to purvey distorted and misleading information to the Commons and its Foreign Affairs Committee and of having betrayed its responsibility to Parliament. It was heavily defeated by 350 to 202 votes. The Government motion recognizing the sinking was a necessary and legitimate action in the Falklands campaign was carried by 351 votes to nil.

Speaker's Chair damaged

Mr. Enoch Powell's private member's Bill to prohibit research on human embryos was given a second reading by 238 to 66 votes in the Commons on Feb. 15 after Mr. Kenneth Clarke, Health Minister, had indicated the Government proposed to introduce its own legislation on the issues raised by the Warnock Report on human fertilisation within the lifetime of this Parliament. There were some extraordinary scenes on May 3 when the Bill was scheduled to make progress through its remaining stages. Opponents of Mr. Powell's Unborn Children (Protection) Bill talked at length on a preceding measure of modest aims which left little time for much progress. After a long discussion on one amendment, Mr. Powell moved the closure which the Deputy Speaker (Mr. Walker) accepted and then there was uproar. M.P.s opposed to the Bill rushed to the Speaker's Chair, and Mr. Dafydd Wigley (Plaid Cymru, Caernarfon) thumped the Chair with his fist and a ledge from it fell to the floor. A group of Labour M.P.s had collected before the Chair and were resting on it when it was damaged. Ultimately, after agreeing to the closure motion which provoked the rumpus, M.P.s defeated by 157 to 82 votes a move by the Bill's opponents to limit the power of courts to convict in cases where experimentation on embryos was deliberately intended.

Marathon speech

There was a debate on the Government's expenditure plans for 1985–86 in the Commons on Mar. 4, but a Labour amendment deploring the proposals was defeated by 357 to 182 votes.

On Mar. 5, a group of M.P.s opposed to adding fluoride to the water supply kept the Commons sitting all night discussing the Water (Fluoridation) Bill and the debate continued right through to Mar. 6 for 21 hours in all when the measure received a third reading. Mr. Ivan Lawrence (Con. Burton) made a speech lasting 4 hours 23 minutes, claimed as the longest continuous speech in the Commons this century. A move to make fluoridation subject to annual review was defeated. The Bill affirmed the right of water authorities to add fluoride to supplies if health authorities asked them to do so. In the Lords, on April 18, an amendment to give local councils the power to veto the addition of fluoride to water supplies was defeated.

Mr. King, Employment Secretary, told M.P.s on Mar. 11 it was a cruel deception to imply there was a magic wand which would cure unemployment when Labour attacked the Government in a debate on its policies towards unemployment and industry, in which the Opposition was defeated by 301 to 197 votes. A motion endorsing Government policies was approved by 299 to 196 votes.

The Home Secretary successfully moved on Mar. 12 the second reading of the Interception of Communications Bill which for the first time provided a statutory framework for interception of phone calls or letters. He also announced the Government was to bring forward further legislation to safeguard people who were the victims of improper use of surveillance or bugging devices.

The National Health Service (general medical and pharmaceutical services) amendment regulations were considered on Mar. 18. Mr. Fowler, Social Services Secretary, assured M.P.s he had no plans to extend his blacklist of drugs as he averted a Conservative revolt against his proposals to limit the drugs which might be prescribed on the N.H.S. However, Mr. Meacher, Labour's Front Bench spokesman, called the amended regulations a squalid little cost-cutting measure. Only six Tories voted against the regulations in the event with the Government having a 127-vote majority.

THE BUDGET

The Chancellor of the Exchequer (Mr. Lawson) presented his second Budget on Mar. 19 and in his statement said: "Once again we can look back on a year of steady growth and low inflation. During 1984 as a whole, inflation remained at around five per cent., output grew by a further 2½ per cent., with investment up by 6½ per cent. and non-oil exports by 9 per cent., to reach the all-time record levels in each case.

"Manufacturing industry recovered particularly strongly, with output up by 3½ per cent.—the biggest rise in any single year since 1973—exports up by 10 per cent. and investment by 13 per cent. The current account of the balance of payments has remained in surplus for the fifth successive year.

"By international standards, too, the economy has performed well.

"Our growth was above, and our inflation below, the European Community average.

"Moreover, this progress has been achieved in the teeth of the coal strike, for which, in the short term, the nation has had to pay a heavy price.

"In the current financial year the coal strike has reduced the level of national output by over 1¼ per cent. and worsened the Balance of Payments by some £4 billion.

"It has increased public expenditure by £2½ billion and public sector borrowing by £2¾ billion. It has cost us confidence abroad and jobs at home.

"But the cost, both economic and constitutional, of submitting to this strike would have been infinitely greater than the costs that have been incurred in successfully resisting it.

"It is a remarkable tribute to the underlying strength of the British economy that it has been able to withstand so long and damaging a strike in such good shape.

"Looking ahead, we are now about to embark on what will be the fifth successive year of steady growth, with output in 1985 as a whole set to rise by a further 3½ per cent.

"Inflation may edge up for a time, perhaps to six per cent. by the middle of the year, but should then fall back to five per cent. by the end of the year and lower still in 1986.

"While there can be no disputing the strength and durability of the economic upswing, there is equally no disputing the fact that it is marred by an unacceptably high level of unemployment.

"And this, despite the fact that the latest figures suggest that employment has risen by half-a-million over the past two years, with a further increase likely over the year ahead.

"If at home the past year has been overshadowed by the coal strike, internationally it has been dominated by the relentless surge of the dollar, which rose by a further 30 per cent. against all the major European currencies.

FINANCIAL STRATEGY

On the medium-term financial strategy, Mr. Lawson said: "We have already shown that we are not afraid to take action, however unpalatable, to keep the medium-term financial strategy on course in an unpredictable and uncertain world.

"That strategy was first launched five years ago next week. Our commitment to it remains as firm today as it was then.

"It was designed to bring down the rate of inflation and to ensure a reasonable growth of demand in money terms; and it has succeeded on both counts.

"We are determined to maintain steady downward pressure on inflation.

"The Government's economic strategy has two key components: a monetary policy designed to bring down inflation, and a supply side policy designed to improve the competitive performance of the economy.

"There can be no doubt about the Government's commitment to maintain monetary conditions that will continue to bring down inflation. Short-term interest rates will be held at the level needed to achieve this.

"While monetary policy is at the heart of the medium-term financial strategy, it needs to be buttressed by an appropriate fiscal policy.

"The out-turn for the public sector borrowing requirement for 1983–84 was £9¾ billion, or 3¼ per cent. of G.D.P. In my Budget last year I planned to reduce it substantially in 1984–85 to £7¼ billion, or 2¼ per cent. of G.D.P.

"In the event, this year's P.S.B.R. looks like turning out at £10½ billion, or 3¼ per cent. of G.D.P.—the same as last year.

"All but £½ billion of this substantial overrun is directly attributable to the cost of the coal strike.

"I believe it was right to meet the large but once-for-all cost of keeping the economy going throughout the coal strike by borrowing, thus in effect spreading the cost over a number of years, but it is now necessary to return to the path I outlined last year.

"That means that the P.S.B.R. for the coming year, 1985–86, will be set at £7 billion, equivalent to two per cent. of G.D.P. As this year, some £3 billion will be financed through national savings.

"For the coming year, a substantial reduction in the P.S.B.R. must take precedence over objectives for reducing the burden of tax.

"Given the need to ensure that the Budget deficit is of a size that can and will be soundly financed, lower taxes can only be achieved by maintaining the firmest control of public expenditure.

"It now looks as if this year's public expenditure planning total will be exceeded by nearly £3½ billion of which over two-thirds is attributable to the coal strike.

"But quite apart from the coal strike, the upward pressures on public spending remain intense, not least from increased take-up of social security benefits and further local authority overspending.

"In addition, we have had to accommodate the effects of higher interest rates and a lower exchange rate.

"I have therefore reassessed the adequacy of the reserves for 1985–86, 1986–87 and 1987–88 provided in the January White Paper.

"To provide a more realistic basis on which to plan and control the level of public spending, I have judged it prudent to add £2 billion to the reserve and thus to the White Paper planning totals for each of the three years.

"At the same time, I have further increased the estimate for debt interest in each year.

"These increases in the size of the reserve will raise the planning totals for the next three years by about 1½ per cent.

"On the other side of the public accounts, tax receipts too are now expected to be higher over the next three years, partly for related reasons. But not by as much.

"The scope I have for tax cuts this year is therefore only half the amount I indicated might be available in my statement to the House in November.

"In other words, the net effect after indexation of the measures I shall announce will be to contribute some £¾ billion to the £7 billion borrowing requirement I have set for 1985–86.

"In determining the nature of those measures within the overall framework of the medium-term financial strategy, my overriding objective has been to improve the prospect for jobs.

"In setting financial policy for the year ahead I have had one object in mind: the continuing reduction of inflation.

"Equally, in deciding my individual Budget proposals within that overall framework. I have sought throughout to make those changes that will do most to promote enterprise and employment.

EMPLOYMENT AND TRAINING

My Budget today represents a further step along the road we have been taking since 1979. It will help us to ensure that more new jobs are created and that they will be jobs that last.

"I begin with some measures directly related to employment and training. One of the most long-standing problems in this country is our failure to prepare our school-leavers adequately for work.

"Since it was first launched in 1983, the Youth Training Scheme has proved to be a very successful bridge between school and work. It has also helped to make young people's pay expectations more realistic.

"The Government has therefore decided to promote a substantial expansion of the Youth Training Scheme. Provided employers contribute a major share of the cost, the Government is prepared to provide further funds to launch this new initiative, over and above the existing £800 million a year of public expenditure on the Y.T.S.

"The expanded scheme would offer places lasting two years for the 16-year-old and one year for the 17-year-old school-leavers, leading to a recognized qualification.

"The existing Y.T.S. provides foundation training and preparation for work. The expanded scheme will also involve occupational training for both the employed and the unemployed, geared to the needs of business and industry.

"In the long run, we expect employers to meet the full cost as those in other countries do.

"I am therefore prepared to set aside a fixed sum in public funds to launch this new initiative and get it moving in the right direction.

"Provided the outcome is satisfactory, I have undertaken to increase the Department of Employment's programme by £125 million in 1986–87 and £300 million in 1987–88.

"This expenditure will be partly offset by savings in social security payments and the ending of the Young Workers Scheme, which will close for applications at the end of March 1986.

"I am also providing the M.S.C. with an additional £20 million in 1986–87 to finance a programme of appropriate inservice teacher training courses.

Mr. Lawson said it had become increasingly evident that the output of graduates in high technology disciplines was not keeping pace with the expanding needs of industry.

"The Education Secretary would therefore be announcing a special programme, costing about £40 million over the next three years, to provide additional places in engineering and technology at selected higher education institutions.

"Under the community programme, local authorities and voluntary bodies provided temporary work for the long-term unemployed on projects of community benefit.

"This scheme, which at present provided 130,000 places, had proved its worth, with a significant proportion of those who left it going on to other jobs."

Mr. Lawson announced that he had agreed to make funds available to provide an additional 100,000 community programme places by June 1986.

"These places will be for 18 to 24-year-olds who have been unemployed for six months or more, and other adults who have been unemployed for over a year."

To accommodate this, the Employment Department's programme would be further increased by £140 million in 1985–86 and £460 million in 1986–87.

"The net addition to public expenditure as a result of all the proposals I have announced will be £75 million in 1985–86, £300 million in 1986–87, and £400 million in 1987–88."

More needed to be done to remove legislative impediments to the effective working of the labour market, the Chancellor went on.

"Accordingly, the Secretary of State for Employment will be extending to all employers the provisions on unfair dismissal which currently apply to small firms. The qualifying period for unfair dismissals will thus become two years for all new employees."

The Employment Secretary would also be issuing a consultative document about the future of the wages councils later this week.

TAX REFORM

"I am satisfied that the right way to proceed with major tax reform is to issue a Green Paper first, as a basis for full and informed discussion, followed by legislation when the results of that discussion have been fully digested.

"I therefore propose to issue a Green Paper later this year on the reform of personal income tax.

"The computerisation of P.A.Y.E. makes this the right time to review the system of personal taxation. Most of the work will be complete by the end of 1987 and the full range of facilities will be available by 1989."

The Chancellor went on: "It is the Government's firm policy to reduce the burden of income tax.

"The present structure of personal income tax is far from satisfactory. Too many young people start paying tax at too low a level, and too many families find themselves in the poverty and unemployment traps.

"There is a strong case for changing to a new system of personal allowances more suited to today's economic and social needs.

"Under this, everyone, man or woman, married or single, would have the same standard allowance. But if either a wife or a husband were unable to make full use of their allowance, the unused portion could be transferred, if they so wished, to their partner.

"This reform would produce a more logical and straightforward system. Far more people could be taken out of the poverty and unemployment traps, and indeed taken out of tax altogether, for a given sum of overall tax relief than is possible under the present system.

"Husbands and wives would each be taxed separately on their own income irrespective of the income of the other. The aggregation for tax purposes of a wife's earned income and investment income with her husband's would end, thus removing what has become an increasing source of resentment among women.

"After an appropriate period for consultation, it would be possible to legislate in 1987 and have a system on these lines in place by the end of the decade.

"The present indexation provision unfairly discriminates against those who acquired their assets prior to 1982. For them the allowance is based not on the 1982 value of the asset but on its original cost.

"I propose to remedy this injustice. The indexation allowance will henceforth be based on March 1982 values.

"Combined with the statutory indexation of the exempt amount, which will rise in 1985–86 to £5,900, these changes will remove some 15,000 taxpayers from liability altogether.

"Increasingly the tax will be levied on real and not inflationary gains.

"With these reforms, I believe the tax is now on a broadly acceptable and sustainable basis."

The combined cost of this reform was £155 million in a full year, but none of it fell in 1985–86.

Turning to stamp duties, Mr. Lawson said he had decided the time had come to simplify and modernize "these ancient duties."

"I propose to sweep away 15 separate duties, including the contract note duty and the one per cent. duty on gifts.

"Altogether, the changes I am proposing should reduce by over 40 per cent. the number of documents which require to be stamped.

"I have decided to abolish Development Land Tax altogether, with immediate effect.

"At the same time I propose to cancel all deferred charges under the tax.

"The net cost will be some £20 million in 1985–86 and £50 million in a full year."

Development gains would continue to be subject to Income Tax, Corporation Tax and Capital Gains Tax, in the same way as any income or capital gains.

BUSINESS TAXATION

Turning to business taxation, the Chancellor said: "From next year, a business will be able to exclude from its general pool of capital expenditure any assets which it believes will have only a short life: so that if the asset is subsequently scrapped after, say, four years, it will be fully written off for tax over that period.

"The benefit to business could rise to about £300 million in the early 1990s.

"The number of employee share schemes has increased from 30 when we first took office in 1979 to some 850 today.

"To maintain and build on this progress I propose to reduce the retention period for profit sharing schemes from seven years to five.

"I propose to take action to deal with tax avoidance by partnerships, following the consultative document issued last year.

"In my last Budget I removed a competitive disadvantage to British manufacturers by levying V.A.T. on imports. I have decided to modify the new regime in two respects.

"I propose to relieve from V.A.T. certain goods which are imported into this country solely for repair, or for processing which does not change their identity, and are then re-exported to their owners overseas.

"Second, goods which are temporarily exported from the U.K. and then reimported after repair or processing abroad, will beat V.A.T. only on the value of the repair or processing. These reliefs will take effect on June 1 and have a once-for-all cost in 1985–86 of £30 million.

"I propose to introduce secondary legislation to remove the constraint imposed by the Banking Act which prevents companies from financing themselves by a series of issues of short-term securities. This should provide a useful alternative to bank borrowing.

"I have no major new proposals this year on the taxation of North Sea oil.

"My only proposal for change is to remove immediate Petroleum Revenue Tax Relief for onshore exploration and appraisal expenditure.

"I propose to implement many of the proposals contained in last year's consultative document on Capital Gains Tax retirement relief, notably to reduce the age for full relief to 60 and to extend relief to those who are obliged by ill-health to retire before that age.

"This relief is particularly important to proprietors of small businesses concerned at the Capital Gains Tax they might have to pay when they come to sell their business on retirement.

"Although the Business Expansion Scheme has been in existence only two years, it has already made an impressive contribution to the promotion and growth of new businesses.

"Last year almost 20,000 people took advantage of the tax reliefs offered by the Business Expansion Scheme to invest some £100 million in more than 500 companies. Over half of this went to provide equity capital for new businesses.

"I propose to include within the scheme companies formed to carry out research and development.

"I propose to exclude from the scheme certain ventures which primarily involve property development. Building and construction will, of course, continue to be a qualifying trade.

"Last year I undertook to review the scope of V.A.T. relief for bad debts, a matter of considerable concern to small businesses.

"In the light of legislation now proceeding on the reform of the insolvency law, I propose to widen the scope of the existing relief.

"The new rules will take effect as soon as the provisions of the Insolvency Bill are implemented and will cost some £25 million in a full year.

"I propose to increase the V.A.T. threshold to £19,500 from midnight tonight."

Mr. Lawson said that over the past five years the ranks of the self-employed had risen by well over half-a-million, or some 30 per cent. At present none of the National Insurance contribution paid by the self-employed can be set against tax at all.

"I propose to remedy this grievance. As from April 6, tax relief will be allowed for half the graduated Class 4 National Insurance contribution paid by the self-employed.

"In addition, I have agreed with the Secretary of State for Social Services that, as from the beginning of October, the flat rate Class 2 National Insurance contribution payable by the self-employed will be reduced from £4·75 to £3·50 a week.

"The benefit of these reliefs to the self-employed will be £55 million in 1985–86 and £155 million in a full year."

PERSONAL TAXATION

Turning to the taxation of personal income and spending, Mr. Lawson said:

"I propose to increase the revenue from the Excise Duties by rather more than is required simply to keep pace with inflation—a less painful task now that inflation is relatively low.

"I propose to increase the duty on cigarettes and hand-rolling tobacco by the equivalent, including V.A.T. of sixpence on a packet of 20 cigarettes.

"I do not, however, propose any increase in the duties on cigars and pipe tobacco.

"I propose increases which, including V.A.T., will put between a penny and twopence a pint on most beer (depending on its strength); a penny a pint on cider; sixpence on a bottle of table wine and about 10p a bottle on sparkling or fortified wine.

"In recognition of the current difficulties of the Scotch whisky industry, however, I propose to increase the duty on spirits by only 10p a bottle.

"I propose to increase the duty on petrol and derv by amounts which, including V.A.T., will raise the price at the pumps by approximately four pence and three pence halfpenny a gallon respectively. As last year, I do not propose any change in the duty on heavy fuel oil.

"I propose however, to raise more revenue from the Vehicle Excise Duty. For cars and light vans the duty will go up by £10 to £100.

"On the advice of the Secretary of State for Transport, the pattern of duty on lorries will be changed to correspond more closely to the amount of wear and tear they cause to the roads.

"While there will be substantial increases in duty for some of the heaviest rigid lorries, for most lorries the rates will remain unchanged.

"These changes in the excise duties will, all told, raise an extra £820 million in 1985–86, some £235 million more than is required to keep pace with inflation.

"The overall impact effect on the R.P.I. of these changes will be one half of one per cent. Apart from one change I do not intend to make any further extensions of the V.A.T. base during the lifetime of this Parliament.

"The one extension I propose to make concerns newspapers and magazines. At present, while all other advertising is taxed, newspaper and magazine advertising is not.

"There is no justification for this anomaly.

"Accordingly, I propose that from May, newspaper and magazine advertising should be subject to V.A.T. This will raise £30 million in 1985–86 and £50 million in a full year.

"I also propose to change the V.A.T. treatment of credit cards and similar payment cards—a part of the financial sector which has enjoyed exceptional growth over the past few years.

"I propose that from May 1 transactions between the companies providing the cards and the outlets which accept them should be classified as exempt. This means that the companies will not be able to recover V.A.T. in respect of such transactions.

"This will raise £15 million in 1985–86 and £20 million a full year.

"I have decided to extend the existing V.A.T. relief for medical or scientific equipment bought with donated funds for use in hospitals and the like to cover computer equipment for certain medical uses.

"Following extensive consultations. I propose to include in this year's Finance Bill legislation to implement most of the recommendations of the first two volumes of the Keith Report on the enforcement powers of the Revenue departments, including measures to deal with the problem of the late payment of V.A.T.

"This is expected to bring in extra revenue of about £50 million in 1985–86; by 1988–89 there will have been a cumulative once-for-all revenue gain of about £600 million. Proposals on the Inland Revenue aspects of the Keith Report will follow in next years Finance Bill.

"The V.A.T. changes I have proposed will bring in £90 million in 1985–86, rising eventually to £215 million in a full year."

Turning to capital transfer tax the Chancellor said:

"Since 1979 the burden of this tax has been very significantly reduced, and I propose to maintain that position this year by raising the threshold and rate bands set last year in line with statutory indexation.

"In addition, I propose to widen the scope of the existing exemption for amenity land surrounding a house of outstanding heritage quality. This will be welcomed by all those concerned with the preservation of our national heritage.

"Turning to income tax, on April 6 the banks will move over to the composite rate system for the payment of tax on bank interest. I need to legislate to put the corresponding composite rate payments by building societies on a similar footing starting next year.

"This will not produce any additional revenue. As an administrative saving, I also propose to legislate this year to bring new loans above the mortgage interest relief ceiling into the Miras system by April 1987. The ceiling itself will remain at £30,000 for 1985–86.

"I need to set the 1986–87 car benefit scales for those whose employers provide them with the use of a car. As last year, I propose to increase both the car and fuel scales by 10 per cent. with effect from April 1986.

"To give further help to charities, I propose to increase from £5,000 to £10,000 the limit to which relief at the higher rates of tax is allowed for covenants."

Of his main income tax proposals Mr. Lawson said: "I propose to make no change this year in the rates of income tax. I believe it is right to concentrate most of the limited resources at my disposal on raising the starting point for tax.

"The statutory indexation formula means I should increase all the principal income tax allowances and bands by 4·6 per cent., the increase in the R.P.I. over the year to last December, rounded up.

"For the higher rate threshold and bands I propose this year to do just that. The first higher rate of 40 per cent. will be reached at a taxable income of £16,200 and the top rate of 60 per cent. will apply to taxable income above £40,200.

"For the basic thresholds I can do more. Statutory indexation would imply an increase in the single person's allowance of precisely twice as much—£100. I propose to increase it £200—from £2,005 to £2,205.

"Statutory indexation would imply an increase in the married man's allowance of £150. Again, I propose to raise it by precisely twice as much—£300—from £3,155 to £3,455.

"I propose to increase the age allowances this year by the same cash amount as the corresponding basic allowances. Thus the single age allowance will rise by £200 from £2,490 to £2,690 and the married age allowance will go up by £300 from £3,955 to £4,255.

"These increases mean that most single people will enjoy an income tax cut of at least £1·15 a week and most married couples an income tax cut of at least £1·73 a week.

"Some 800,000 people on low incomes—100,000 of them widows—who would have paid tax if thresholds had not been increased will pay no tax at all.

"That is almost twice as many as would have been taken out of tax had the allowances merely been indexed.

"The income tax changes I have announced will take effect under P.A.Y.E. on the first pay day after May 17. The cost is considerable: £1·6 billion in 1985–86, of which roughly half represents the cost of indexation.

"The increase in the basic allowances of almost 10 per cent. or some five per cent. in real terms, means that for 1985–86 they will be more than 20 per cent. higher in real terms than they were in 1978–79, Labour's last year."

NATIONAL INSURANCE

"Turning to National Insurance contributions, Mr. Lawson said he had already set out the broad lines of the Government's strategy to improve the prospects for jobs.

"I have concluded that an effective response to this problem must include direct action in two related areas—to cut the costs of employing the young and unskilled, and to sharpen their own incentive to work at wages which employers can afford to pay."

He therefore proposed, in collaboration with the Social Services Secretary, a radical reform of the structure of National Insurance contributions.

Essential features of the contributory principle would be preserved and changes would affect both employers' and employees' contributions.

"Given the limited resources at my disposal, I cannot afford this year to make a further substantial reduction in the overall burden of employment costs, following the abolition of the National Insurance Surcharge in last year's Budget.

"I therefore propose to abolish the upper earnings limit for the employer's National Insurance contribution, which for 1985–86 has been set at £265 a week.

"Under the new, and arguably fairer, scheme I am now proposing, the employer's liability will be the same flat 10·45 per cent. of earnings as at present applies below the upper earnings limit.

"The £800 million raised by this change in a full year enables me to make a substantial reduction in the cost of employing people at the lower end of the earnings scale.

"There, instead of the uniform 10·45 per cent., I propose to introduce a system of graduated rates.

"As now, there will be no National Insurance payable for those earning below the lower earnings limit, which for 1985–86 has been set at £35·50 a week, broadly in line with the single person's pension.

"But for employees earning between this and £55 a week, the employer will in future have to pay only five per cent. instead of 10·45 per cent.: for employees earning between £55 a week and £90 a week the new rate for employers will be seven per cent.: and for those earning between £90 and £130 a week the employer will pay nine per cent.

"The full employers' rate of 10·45 per cent. will apply only for those earning over £130 a week.

"These changes represent substantial reductions in the cost of employing the lower paid.

"I propose to introduce a similar system of graduated National Insurance contribution rates for the employees themselves at the lower end of the earnings scale.

"At present, those earning more than the lower earnings limit pay a flat rate of nine per cent. on total earnings up to the upper earnings limit, and nothing on any amount they may earn above that limit.

"This system makes National Insurance contributions a particularly heavy burden for the low paid.

"I propose that, in future, those earning between £33·50 and £55 a week pay at the rate of five per cent., and those earning between £55 and £90 a week seven per cent. "Only those who earn above £90 a week will be liable to the full nine per cent. on their earnings.

"But I do not propose to abolish the upper earnings limit for employees' contributions. In addition, as I have already indicated, I propose a corresponding reduction in the contributions paid by the self-employed. The flat rate Class 2 contributions will be reduced from £4·75 to £3·50 a week.

"I should make it clear that these changes are not intended to affect benefit rights, and new rules will be introduced to protect those rights. Nor will the changes affect arrangements for the contracted-out rebate.

"The overall cost of these changes will be £450 million in a full year, made up of £80 million less in employers' contributions, £270 million less in employees' contributions, and £100 million less in contributions from the self-employed. In 1985–86, the total cost will be £160 million.

"The effect on job prospects will, over time, be substantial. The radical restructuring I have announced will encourage employers to take on the young and unskilled, and give them, in turn, an incentive to seek work at wages that employers can afford.

"These are changes of a major order. They amount to a direct and powerful attack on disincentives to employment.

"They tackle the problem of unemployment where it is most acute. They complete my Budget for jobs," the Chancellor concluded.

The debate on the Budget

Mr. Kinnock charged Mr. Lawson with delivering a stalemate Budget when what the country needed was expansion, opportunity, and most of all jobs. The Chancellor, he said, had again turned his back on millions of fellow citizens who were unemployed and millions who were poor and he would not be forgiven. Mr. Richard Wainwright, for the Liberals, said the Budget was the most austere for four years and said the raising of tax thresholds was an extraordinary way of scattering largesse so that a few crumbs reached the poor. Debate on the Chancellor's proposals occupied four days and on Mar. 25 at the conclusion of the usual "inquest" the Government secured approval of the general contents by 355 to 202 votes.

The Lords debated the Budget proposals and their consequences on unemployment on April 3 when Lord Murray of Epping Forest, former general secretary of the T.U.C. made his maiden speech. When the second reading of the Local Government Bill was discussed in the Lords on April 15, over fifty peers announced their intention to participate and it turned out to be a long, long day for the Upper House although in the result the Government won its motion.

Government defeated

The Earl of Stockton joined other Tory peers who combined with Opposition and cross-bench members to defeat the Government. By 101 to 90 votes, a majority of 11 against the Government, they inserted an amendment during the third reading of the Insolvency Bill to reduce from 12 to six months the period before insolvency in which "Crown preference" was given to V.A.T. payments over other debtor claims in bankruptcy cases.

On April 22, Labour launched a debate on the Welfare State and Mr. Meacher, Shadow Social Services Secretary, called on the Government to withdraw its plans to abolish the State Earnings-Related Pension Scheme. Labour's motion accusing the Government of dismantling the Welfare State was rejected by 276 to 167 votes.

Proceedings disrupted

Labour M.P.s were responsible for a row in the Commons on April 23 about where Dr. Owen, S.D.P. leader, should stand to make a speech which called for a strengthening of Government legislation on the trade unions. The problem began when Left-wing M.P.s occupied all the places where the S.D.P. M.P.s sit before Dr. Owen and his colleagues could do so.

Dr. Owen then attempted to speak from the Opposition despatch box until finally the Deputy Speaker (Mr. Walker) suspended the proceedings for 16 minutes because of the disruption by Labour members. After talks outside the Chamber, Dr. Owen began his speech, nearly an hour late, from the bench where other S.D.P. M.P.s normally sit.

A Government amendment welcoming the success of its step-by-step approach to the reform of industrial relations law was carried by 224 to 167 votes. In the Lords, Lord Home of the Hirsel, former Conservative Prime Minister, challenged the new Russian leadership to prove its desire for better relations with the West by honouring treaty commitments. Lord Cledwyn of Penrhos, Opposition leader, welcomed Mr. Gorbachev's apparently more realistic approach while Lord Shinwell said there were irreconcilable differences between the two world super-powers; the answer was to have a constructive deterrent. The Commons staged a foreign affairs' debate on April 25.

On April 29, the Lords voted down Opposition plans to set up an inquiry into the future of services now run by the G.L.C. and the metropolitan county councils, when during the committee stage of the Local Government Bill they rejected by 196 to 137 votes a Labour amendment designed for this purpose.

The House of Lords unusually received a constitutional ticking-off from the Speaker of the Commons on April 30. Mr. Weatherill ruled that the Upper Chamber had committed a major infringement of the rights of M.P.s by voting for the imposition of a levy on TV films and blank and recorded video tapes. He declared that the Lords' action in amending the Films Bill had violated the sole right of the Commons to levy general taxes and called on the Government to have the provision deleted. This action was moved by Mr. Lamont, Minister of State, Industry, and was approved by the Commons without a division.

Further Government defeats

On May 7, the Government sustained two defeats in the Lords on its Local Government Bill. First the House voted to insert a requirement that before fixing a date for the abolition of the authorities the Environment Secretary must present a report to Parliament, this being carried by 152 to 135 votes, a majority of 17 against the Government. Secondly, the House voted to set up city-wide highway authorities for the G.L.C. and the six counties after the Bill became law, voting being 117 to 103, a majority against the Government of 14. On May 9, there was another Lords' defeat for the same Bill when by 170 to 166 votes the House accepted a paving amendment to open the way for establishing that Greater London and the six counties should each have its own corporate waste disposal authority. A fourth Government defeat came on May 13 when the Lords voted by 142 to 133 to reduce ministerial powers to review the I.L.E.A. administration. On July 2, Lord Elton, Environment Minister, disclosed that Greater London was to have a joint planning committee when peers gave a third reading to the Local Government Bill. On July 8, the Commons began consideration of the Lords' amendments, to the Bill. Mr. Jenkin, Environment Secretary, told M.P.s the Government would oppose only two of the major changes made by the Upper House—those setting up highway and waste disposal authorities for London. These two changes were duly reversed in the division lobbies, but the Commons did accept 76 of the 98 amendments made by the Lords. When the Commons' treatment of their amendments was conveyed to the Lords on July 15, peers agreed to the final changes to the Bill and also accepted the Commons' decision on highways and waste disposal authorities by 217 to 153 and 213 to 154 respectively.

National security

The Prime Minister on May 9 made a statement on the report of the Security Commission on their inquiry into the case of Michael Bettaney, the former security service officer sentenced to 23 years imprisonment for Official Secrets Act offences. The Commission, she said, had made a number of recommendations for changes in positive vetting procedures in the security services and also recommended that the revised and improved arrangements which applied at present only to the more senior grades should be extended to all staff. Mr. Kinnock said Mrs. Thatcher's statement did not meet the real seriousness of the problems illustrated by the Bettaney case and he accused the Prime Minister of complacency. Dr. Owen, S.D.P. leader, said an all-party Parliamentary Select Committee of both Houses should be able to scrutinize the security and intelligence services.

On May 13, the Home Secretary announced a judicial inquiry and other action aimed at improving safety at all sports grounds in Britain. In a surprise move on May 17, the Commons gave a private member's Bill to outlaw kerb-crawling and sponsored by Miss Janet Fookes (Con. Plymouth Drake) an unopposed third reading after its opponents, two Tory M.P.s, had previously apparently blocked the passage of the measure.

Sunday trading laws

The Home Secretary was at the receiving end of criticism from some of his own back-benchers as well as Opposition opponents on May 20 when he spoke in support of the Government's decision to reform the law on Sunday opening of shops; the Commons was debating the Auld Report which recommended the abolition of the Sunday trading laws. While Government M.P.s were subject to a three-line whip on this issue, Labour M.P.s were allowed a free vote. The Government won backing to scrap these laws by 304 to 184 votes; 26 Tories voted against the Government and a similar number abstained while three Labour M.P.s voted with the Government.

Reform of Social Security

On June 3, Mr. Fowler, Social Services Secretary, made a statement on publication of the Government Green Paper, "Reform of Social Security," a consultative document on major changes to the system. Mr. Meacher, the Opposition spokesman, described it as "this black day for the people of Britain," and denounced the proposals as the reintroduction of Victorian values with invidious distinctions between the deserving and undeserving poor. On June 18, there was a six-hour debate on the Green Paper proposals when a Labour amendment condemning the reforms suggested was defeated by 335 to 178. A Government motion welcoming the Green Paper was carried by 335 to 196 votes. Liberals and S.D.P. abstained on the Labour amendment and voted against the Government's motion.

The 1985 Defence Estimates consumed two days of debate on June 12 and 13 at the end of which they were approved by 353 to 168 votes. Previously Labour's attack on the defence plans in which they claimed the policy of buying Trident at an ever-increasing cost would lead to further damaging cuts in Britain's real defence and the conventional contribution to N.A.T.O., was defeated by 367 to 157 votes. On June 17, the White Paper on airports policy was discussed by M.P.s who voted to approve the proposals. A Labour amendment opposing the White Paper because they claimed it would encourage

further airport developments in the south-east to the disadvantage of many local communities was rejected.

The subject of Government-imposed price increases was raised on June 19 when Labour accused the Conservatives of deliberately putting-up public sector charges, causing higher prices in the private sector by raising V.A.T. and producing record interest rates through mismanagement of the economy. The Opposition's critical motion was voted down by 272 to 166. A Government amendment of support for its sound financial policies was carried by 271 to 165 votes. Nineteen Tory M.P.s voted against the Government on June 25 and another 10 abstained in protest at the European Communities Bill to increase Britain's payments to the E.E.C. The Bill nonetheless received a second reading by 352 to 184 votes.

The Government's Sporting Events Bill banning alcohol at soccer matches and other sports fixtures was presented in the Commons on June 26 and was given a formal first reading. M.P.s began consideration of all stages of the measure on July 3 and rushed them through by early morning on July 4. On July 17, the Bill passed all its stages unamended in the Lords.

On July 15, an Alliance motion, which was supported by Labour, called on the Government to provide extra money from the contingency reserve to avoid damaging and unacceptable reductions in health care while welcoming recent pay rises to doctors and nurses as legitimate and deserved; the motion was defeated by 233 to 154 votes.

Top salaries

The storm clouds began to gather in the Commons on July 19 over the previous day's announcement of the recommendations of the Top Salaries Review Body with increases rising to 48 per cent. Leading the Opposition attack was Mr. Roy Hattersley, Deputy leader, whose emergency question was dealt with by Mr. Peter Rees, Chief Secretary, Treasury, and whose critical reaction was also reflected among Conservative back-benchers. On July 23, the elements broke loose when a test case of Parliament's judgment on these awards was provided with a Government motion to approve the Order to increase the Lord Chancellor's salary from £66,250 to £77,000 was debated. There was plenty of incisive across-party mauling of the implementation decision and the row continued until the early hours of next morning, July 24, when at 2 a.m. the vote was taken. There was a revolt by 48 Tory M.P.s who voted against the Government and about another 50 Tories abstained resulting in the Order being approved with a slim Government majority of 17, the figures being 249 to 232. With the Government's overall majority of 138, it was the Tories' lowest majority in this Parliament. Tory M.P.s claimed that as many as 38 Labour M.P.s failed to support their party in the division. Later in the day of July 24, a Labour amendment seeking to delay the summer recess until the Prime Minister had participated in a debate on the pay awards was defeated by 311 to 172 votes. During angry exchanges previous to the debate on the Order, Mrs. Thatcher at Question Time, strongly defended the decision of implementation and accused Mr. Hattersley of "cant and humbug" and told Dr. Owen, S.D.P. leader, he deserved to be treated with "utter contempt". On July 29, the Lords considered a motion also to increase the salary of the Lord Chancellor as recommended and this was another opportunity for the critics to deploy their arguments with the result that although the salary rise was unaffected a Labour amendment expressing regret at the Government's insensitive pay decision for top people was carried by 140 to 135 votes, majority of five against the Government and a shock defeat for the Tories. However, the defeat was produced mainly because of the joining of forces by Labour, Liberal– S.D.P. Alliance and the cross-benches. Only five Conservative peers voted against the Government but there was a significant absence from the lobbies of Tory supporters.

Earlier on July 23, there was a debate in the Commons on changes to the immigration rules to comply with the terms of the European Court on Human Rights' rules and a motion to approve these was carried by 307 to 192 votes. There was an announcement too by Mr. Heseltine, Defence Secretary, of the takeover by commercial management of the running of the Royal Dockyards at Devonport and Rosyth and Mr. Denzil Davies, Shadow Defence

Secretary, promised that Labour would take both yards back into public ownership. The Lords voted against a proposal that the TV experiment of their proceedings should end as planned after a six-month period, and then endorsed a motion for it to continue until a final decision was taken early in 1986.

There was considerable Tory support for Mr. Jenkin, Environment Secretary, on July 25 when he announced that the present system of targets and penalties to control local authority expenditure would not apply next year. Dr. John Cunningham, Labour's spokesman, however, regarded the statement as "a massive increase in more authoritarian control" of local authority expenditure and budgets.

On July 26, the Commons departed for the summer recess while the Lords continued until July 31 when they too adjourned.

PUBLIC ACTS OF PARLIAMENT 1984–85

This list of Public Acts commences with 3 Public Acts which received the Royal Assent before September 1984 and which were mentioned briefly in the last summary. Those Public Acts which follow received the Royal Assent after August 1984. The date stated after each Act is the date on which it came into operation.

Road Traffic Regulation Act 1984 (s. 90 and Sched. 8 para. 3 day or days to be appointed, remainder on September 26, 1984) consolidates the 1967 Act and certain related enactments with amendments to give effect to recommendations of the Law Commission and the Scottish Law Commission.

Housing Defects Act 1984 (s. 28 on July 31, 1985; remainder on December 1, 1984) makes provision in connexion with defective dwellings disposed of by public sector authorities and provides for certain provisions in agreements between building societies to be disregarded for the purposes of the Restrictive Trade Practices Act 1956. For example, the Act enables the Secretary of State to designate a class of buildings where it appears to him that buildings in that class are defective due to their design or construction then, broadly speaking, the individual owner of such a building who bought without knowledge of the defects will be eligible for assistance providing several other conditions are fulfilled.

Parliamentary Pensions etc. Act 1984 (July 31, 1984) makes further provision with respect to the contributory pensions schemes for MPs and for the holders of certain Ministerial and other offices; makes further provision for the alleviation of hardship; and provides for payments to be made, in certain circumstances, to persons who cease to hold Ministerial and other offices or to be MEPs.

Roads (Scotland) Act 1984 (part on January 1, 1985 the remainder on a day or days to be appointed) makes provisions as regards roads in Scotland. The Act codifies the law relating to roads in Scotland. Its main effect is to end the situation under which there were different provisions relating to the former burgh areas from those relating to the landward areas.

Building Act 1984 (part on December 1, 1984 the rest on a day or days to be appointed) consolidates certain enactments concerning buildings and buildings and related matters.

Foster Children (Scotland) Act 1984 (January 1, 1985) consolidates certain enactments relating to foster children as they have effect in Scotland.

Co-operative Development Agency and Industrial Development Act 1984 (part on October 31, 1984, part on November 29, 1984, the remainder on a day to be appointed) amends the Co-operative Development Agency Act 1978 and gives the Secretary of State power to dissolve the Agency; amends and replaces provisions in the Industrial Development Act 1982 relating to designate assisted areas and regional development grants.

Rent (Scotland) Act 1984 (January 31, 1985) consolidates in relation to Scotland certain enactments relating to rents and tenants' rights and connected matters.

Ordnance Factories and Military Service Act 1984 (October 31, 1984) makes provision for the transfer to a company or companies of certain property, rights and liabilities to which Her Majesty or a Minister of the Crown is entitled or subject and which are attributable to the operations of the Royal Ordnance Factories and for the extinction of certain liabilities of those factories; makes provision for the transfer of property, etc. to or from those and certain other companies; makes provision about the powers of special constables; and for other similar or connected purposes.

Police and Criminal Evidence Act 1984 (part on January 1, 1985, part on March 1, 1985, remainder on a day or days to be appointed) makes provision in relation to the powers and duties of the police persons in police detention, criminal evidence, police discipline and complaints against the police—makes arrangements for obtaining the views of the community on policing and for a rank of deputy chief constable; and amends the law relating to the Police Federations and Police Forces and Police Cadets in Scotland. For example, the Act contains convoluted provisions prescribing limits for which persons may be detained without charge whereby the initial period of 24 hours may be extended; and gives the police increased powers to set up road blocks.

Consolidated Fund (No. 2) Act 1984 (December 20, 1984) applies certain sums out of the Consolidated Fund to the service of the years ending March 31, 1985 and 1986.

Friendly Societies Act 1984 (December 20, 1984) validates certain contracts of insurance entered into by registered friendly societies before June 1, 1984 and modifies, with both retrospective and prospective effect, provisions relating to the financial limits in the 1974 Act s. 64 and the Taxes Act 1970 s. 332.

Consolidated Fund Act 1985 (January 24, 1985) applies a sum out of the Consolidated Fund to the service of the year ending March 31, 1985.

Elections (Northern Ireland) Act 1985 (part on January 24, 1985 the remainder on a day or days to be appointed) makes further provision for preventing personation at elections in Northern Ireland.

Brunei and Maldives Act 1985 (March 11, 1985) makes provision in connexion with the admission of Brunei and Maldives to membership of the Commonwealth.

Milk (Cessation of Production) Act 1985 (s. 6 on a day to be appointed the remainder on May 11, 1985) provides for the payment of compensation for the discontinuance or reduction of milk production to those who are or have been registered in the direct sales register or a wholesale register maintained under the Dairy Produce Quotas Regulations 1984; and for connected purposes.

New Towns and Urban Development Corporations Act 1985 (May 11, 1985) facilitates the completion and subsequent winding-up of the new towns programme in England and Wales. It also makes minor changes to the legislation governing new towns.

Companies Act 1985 (s. 243(3) and (4) on a day to be appointed, the remainder on July 1, 1985) consolidates the greater part of the Companies Acts.

Business Names Act 1985 (July 1, 1985) consolidates certain enactments relating to the names under which persons may carry on business in Great Britain.

Company Securities (Insider Dealing) Act 1985 (July 1, 1985) consolidates the enactments relating to insider dealing in company securities.

Companies Consolidation (Consequential Provisions) Act 1985 (July 1, 1985) deals with the transitional matters, savings, repeals and amendments consequential upon the 1985 consolidation of company statute law.

London Regional Transport (Amendment) Act 1985 (March 11, 1985) specifies the amount (c. £258m) which the GLC is to pay to London Regional Transport under s. 49 of the 1984 Act.

Consolidated Fund (No. 2) Act 1985 (March 27, 1985) applies certain sums out of the Consolidated Fund to the service of the years ending March 31, 1984 and 1985.

Mineral Workings Act 1985 (part on March 27, 1985, part on April 1, 1985 the remainder on May 27, 1985) repeals certain provisions of the 1951 and 1971 Acts, transfers the assets of the Ironstone Restoration Fund to the British Steel Corporation, makes further provision about agricultural ironstone land and forestry on ironstone land and confers powers in connexion with the reclamation, improvement or bringing into use of certain land and for connected purposes.

Cinemas Act 1985 (June 27, 1985) consolidates the Cinematograph Acts 1909 to 1982 and certain related enactments with an amendment to give effect to a recommendation of the Law Commission.

Shipbuilding Act 1985 (March 27, 1985) extends the period in relation to which schemes under the Shipbuilding (Redundancy Payments) Act 1978 have effect and extinguishes all outstanding liabilities in respect of the loan made to Upper Clyde Shipbuilders Ltd. by the Shipbuilding Industry Board.

Hong Kong Act 1985 (April 4, 1985) makes provision for and in connexion with the ending of British sovereignty and jurisdiction over Hong Kong.

National Heritage (Scotland) Act 1985 (various dates) transfers responsibility for the Royal Scottish Museum and the National Museum of Antiquities of Scotland to a new Board of Trustees of the National Museums of Scotland; establishes a Board of Trustees of the Royal Botanic Garden, Edinburgh; makes provision as to the status functions and powers of the new Boards; makes further provision in relation to the National Galleries of Scotland and the National Library of Scotland; and for various other purposes connected with the Scottish heritage.

Reserve Forces (Safeguard of Employment) Act 1985 (August 9, 1985) consolidates certain enactments as to the reinstatement in civil employment of members of the reserve and auxiliary forces who have been called into whole-time service in the armed forces of the Crown, and for the protection of the employment of those liable to be called into such service.

Betting Gaming and Lotteries (Amendment) Act 1985 (part on July 9, 1985, the remainder on a day to be appointed) removes restrictions under the 1963 to 1984 Acts as to the occasions on which betting may take place on racecourses and other tracks and as to the events in connexion with which betting may take place on dog racecourses and makes further provision with respect to the operation of totalizators on such racecourses.

Town and Country Planning (Compensation) Act 1985 (May 9, 1985) restricts the circumstances in which compensation is payable under the 1971 Act ss. 165 and 169 and the Scottish 1972 Act ss. 154 and 158.

Charities Act 1985 (day or days to be appointed) makes further provision with respect to charities in England and Wales, dealing with the submission of and publicity for charities' accounts; alteration of objects by old charities; power for certain charity trustees to transfer property to another charity and power for very small charities to spend capital.

Films Act 1985 (part on May 23, 1985 the remainder on July 23, 1985) repeals the Acts 1960 to 1980 which regulated the exhibition and distribution of commercial films and makes provision as to the termination of the levy on cinema receipts. It also makes provision in connexion with the dissolution of the National Film Finance Corporation and introduces fresh provision for financial assistance for purposes connected with British films.

Dangerous Vessels Act 1985 (July 23, 1985) empowers harbour masters to give directions to prohibit vessels from entering the areas of jurisdiction of their respective harbour authorities or to require the removal of vessels from those areas where those vessels present a grave and imminent danger to the safety of any person or property, or risk of obstruction to navigation; enables the Secretary of State to give further directions countermanding the harbour masters' directions.

Prosecution of Offences Act 1985 (various dates some to be appointed) establishes an independent

Crown Prosecution Service for England and Wales; makes provision as to costs in criminal cases and makes various procedural changes including enabling the Secretary of State to set time limits in relation to the preliminary stages of criminal proceedings. The Act does not affect the right of private prosecution.

Rent (Amendment) Act 1985 (May 23, 1985) inter alia makes further provision as to the circumstances in which possession of a dwellinghouse is recoverable under Case 11 in the Rent Act 1977 Sched. 15 and Case 11 in the Rent (Scotland) Act 1984 Sched. 2 (The Act reverses the Court of Appeal decision in *Pocock* v. *Steel* which held that an owner occupier could only make use of Case 11 if his occupation immediately preceded the grant of the tenancy in question).

Industrial Development Act 1985 (s. 3 on April 1, 1986 the remainder on August 13, 1985) makes provision with respect to the English Industrial Estates Corporation and extends the borrowing powers of the Welsh Development Agency.

Intoxicating Substances (Supply) Act 1985 (August 13, 1985) prohibits the supply to persons under the age of 18 of certain substances which may cause intoxication if inhaled.

Coal Industry Act 1985 (June 13, 1985) provides for grants by the Secretary of State to the NCB in respect of group deficits and makes further provision with respect to certain grants and payments by the Secretary of State under the 1977 Act.

Motor-Cycle Crash-Helmets (Restriction of Liability) Act 1985 (August 13, 1985) exempts persons other than the actual offender from criminal liability in respect of the offence of driving or riding on a motor cycle in contravention of the regulations requiring the wearing of crash-helmets.

Enduring Powers of Attorney Act 1985 (day to be appointed) enables powers of attorney to be created which will survive any subsequent mental incapacity of the donor.

Ports (Finance) Act 1985 (day or days to be appointed) provides for grants to be made to the National Dock Labour Board; increases the limit on the amount of financial assistance to the PLA and the Mersey Docks and Harbour Company; and makes further provision in connection with borrowing and audits of certain harbour authorities and repeals Harbours Act 1964 s. 9 (control of harbour development).

Wildlife and Countryside (Amendment) Act 1985 (August 26, 1985) amends provisions of the 1981 Act relating to areas of scientific interest and maps of National Parks showing certain areas of moor and heath, the Badgers Act 1973 relating to the taking, injuring or killing of badgers and the Forestry Act 1967 relating to the Forestry Commission.

Hill Farming Act 1985 (August 26, 1985) extends the provision in the 1946 Act regulating or prohibiting the burning of heather and grass so as to include bracken, gorse and vaccinium.

Rating (Revaluation Rebates) (Scotland) Act 1985 (August 26, 1985) provides for rebates in respect of rates on certain properties in Scotland whose rateable values were increased at the 1985 revaluation to more than three times their previous level.

Road Traffic (Production of Documents) Act 1985 (September 16, 1985) amends certain provisions relating to the production of documents under the Road Traffic Act 1972 and the Transport Act 1982.

Gaming (Bingo) Act 1985 (day or days to be appointed) amends the Gaming Act 1968 in respect of games which are played on bingo club premises and in which the players may be in different bingo club premises.

Agricultural Training Board Act 1985 (September 16, 1985) makes provision with respect to the functions of the Agricultural Training Board.

Family Law (Scotland) Act 1985 (day or days to be appointed) makes fresh provision in the law of Scotland regarding aliment, financial and other consequences of decrees of divorce and of declarator of nullity of marriage; and property rights and legal capacity of married persons.

Prohibition of Female Circumcision Act 1985 (September 16, 1985) prohibits female circumcision except where it is necessary for the physical or mental health of the person on whom it is performed or is performed on a person who is in any stage of labour or has just given birth and is performed for purposes connected with that labour or birth.

Controlled Drugs (Penalties) Act 1985 (September 16, 1985) increases the penalties (e.g. to life imprisonment for class A drugs) for certain offences relating to controlled drugs.

Licensing (Amendment) Act 1985 (July 16, 1985) amends the Licensing Act 1964 in relation to orders for extended hours at premises providing entertainment and in relation to special hours certificates.

Copyright (Computer Software) Amendment Act 1985 (September 16, 1985) amends the Copyright Act 1956 in its application to computer programs and computer storage. The effect is that the 1956 Act applies in the same way to a computer program as it does to a literary work.

Hospital Complaints Procedure Act 1985 (day to be appointed) obliges health authorities in England and Wales and Health Boards in Scotland to establish a complaints procedure for hospital patients and to draw such a procedure to the attention of patients.

Local Government (Access to Information) Act 1985 (April 1, 1986) provides for greater public access to local authority meetings, reports and documents subject to special confidentiality provisions. It also imposes upon local authorities duties to publish certain information.

Sexual Offences Act 1985 (September 16, 1985) makes provision for penalizing in certain circumstances the soliciting of women for sexual purposes by men and increases the penalties under the 1956 Act for certain offences against women. The particular offences covered relate to kerb crawling and the persistent soliciting of a woman for prostitution.

Charter Trustees Act 1985 (July 16, 1985) provides for the continuation of the charter trustees of any city or town and for the presentation of their powers and of the privileges and rights of the inhabitants of their area upon that area becoming comprised in a borough.

Insurance (Fees) Act 1985 (July 16, 1985) provides for the payment of certain fees by insurance companies and the Council of Lloyd's.

Further Education Act 1985 (various dates some to be appointed) empowers local authorities to supply goods and services through further education establishments and to make loans to certain other persons to enable them to do so; and repeals Sex Discrimination Act 1975 s. 28(b) (exception for a course designed for teachers of physical training).

Food and Environment Protection Act 1985 (various dates some to be appointed) authorizes the making in an emergency of orders specifying activities which are to be prohibited as a precaution against the consumption of food rendered unsuitable for human consumption in consequence of an escape of substances; replaces the Dumping At Sea Act 1974 which fresh provision for controlling the deposit of substances and articles in the sea; makes provision for the control of the deposit of substances and articles under the sea-bed; and regulates pesticides and substances, preparations and organisms prepared or used for the control of pests or for protection against pests.

Surrogacy Arrangements Act 1985 (July 16, 1985) regulates certain activities in connexion with arrangements with a view to women carrying children as surrogate mothers. It is designed to prevent the commercial exploitation of surrogacy by making advertising and payment, etc. offences.

Representation of the People Act 1985 (various dates some to be appointed) amends the law relating to parliamentary elections in the U.K. and local government elections in Great Britain, provides for combining polls taken on the same date at such elections and elections to the European Communities' Assembly, extends the franchise at elections to that Assembly, amends the law relating to the effect of the demise of the Crown on the summoning and duration of a new Parliament and repeals the 1918 Act s. 21(3) (time appointed for meeting of Parliament after the proclamation summoning it).

Local Government Act 1985 (July 16, 1985) abolishes, with effect from April 1, 1986, the GLC and the metropolitan county councils; transfers their functions to the local authorities in their areas and, in some cases, to other bodies; and provides for other matters consequential on, or connected with, the abolition of those councils.

Town and Country Planning (Amendment) Act 1985 (September 22, 1985) extends the 1971 Act s. 62 and the 1972 (Scotland) Act s. 60 (which concern the replacement of trees) to trees in woodlands.

Finance Act 1985 (July 25, 1985) grants certain duties, alters others and amends the law relating to the National Debt and the Public Revenue and makes further provision in connexion with Finance. Inter alia the Act exempts gilt edged securities from capital gains tax but subjects them to anti-avoidance of income tax legislation, increases the exemption from excess liability for covenanted payments to charity (to £10,000 p.a.), and simplifies and modernizes stamp duties.

Appropriation Act 1985 (July 25, 1985) applies a sum out of the Consolidated Fund to the service of the year ending March 31, 1986, appropriates the supplies granted in the present Session of Parliament, and repeals certain Consolidated Fund and Appropriation Acts.

Sporting Events (Control of Alcohol etc.) Act 1985 (July 25, 1985) in the aftermath of the Brussels disaster, this Act seeks to control alcohol on coaches and trains carrying passengers to or from designated sporting events, and to control alcohol, containers etc. at sports grounds. It also makes provision for the regulation of the sale and supply of alcohol and the closing of bars at designated sports grounds by a uniformed constable.

Wildlife and Countryside (Service of Notices) Act 1985 (July 25, 1985) applies Town and Country Planning Act 1971 s. 283 and Town and Country Planning (Scotland) Act 1972 s. 269 to notices and other documents required or authorized to be served or given under the Wildlife and Countryside Act 1981.

Social Security Act 1985
Interception of Communications Act 1985
Trustee Savings Banks Act 1985
Child Abduction and Custody Act 1985

PARLIAMENTARY ASSOCIATIONS

COMMONWEALTH PARLIAMENTARY ASSOCIATION (1911)

The Commonwealth Parliamentary Association consists of 127 branches in the national, state, provincial or territorial parliaments in the countries of the Commonwealth. Commonwealth Parliamentary conferences and general assemblies are held every year in different countries of the Commonwealth.

President (1984–85), Hon. H. Swan, M.L.A., Speaker of the Legislative Assembly of Saskatchewan (*Canada*).

Vice President (1984–85), Rt. Hon. Sir Geoffrey Howe, Q.C., M.P., Secretary of State for Foreign and Commonwealth Affairs (*United Kingdom*).

Secretary-General, Sir Robin Vanderfelt, K.B.E., Palace of Westminster, S.W.1.

Secretary, United Kingdom Branch, P. Cobb, Westminster Hall, Houses of Parliament, S.W.1.

THE INTER-PARLIAMENTARY UNION (1889)

To facilitate personal contact between Members of all Parliaments in the promotion of representative institutions, peace and international co-operation. *Secretary General,* Pio Carlo Terenzio, Place du Petit-Saconnex, B.P. 99, 1211 Geneva 19, Switzerland.

BRITISH GROUP

Palace of Westminster, SW1

Hon. President, The Lord Chancellor; Mr. Speaker.
President, The Rt. Hon. Margaret Thatcher, M.P.
Secretary, Capt. P. J. Shaw, R.N.

THE QUEEN'S AWARDS FOR EXPORT AND TECHNOLOGY

The Queen's Award for Export Achievement and The Queen's Award for Technological Achievement were instituted by Royal Warrant in 1976, the two separate Awards taking the place of The Queen's Award to Industry which had been instituted in 1965. This was the major change made as a result of a number of recommendations by a committee chaired by the Duke of Edinburgh that reviewed all aspects of the Award scheme in 1975 after its second 5-year period of operation; all the recommendations were accepted by the Government. The reports of the 3 committees that have considered the scheme, in 1965, 1970, and 1975—under the chairmanship of the Duke of Edinburgh, Lord McFadzean and the Duke of Edinburgh respectively—are available on loan from The Queen's Awards Office.

The Awards are designed to recognize and encourage outstanding achievements in exporting goods or services from the United Kingdom and in advancing process or product technology. They differ from a personal Royal honour in that they are given to a unit as a whole—management and employees working as a team.

They may be applied for by any organization within the United Kingdom, the Channel Islands or the Isle of Man producing goods or services which meet the criteria for the Awards. Eligibility is not influenced in any way by the particular activities of the unit applying, its location, or size. Units or agencies of central and local government with industrial functions, as well as research associations, educational institutions and bodies of a similar character, are also eligible, provided that they can show they have contributed to industrial efficiency.

The criteria on which recommendations for the Awards are based are:

1. Export Achievement

A substantial and sustained increase in export earnings to a level which is outstanding for the products or services concerned and for the size of the applicant unit's operations. Account will be taken of any special market factors described in the application. Applicants for the Award will be expected to explain the basis of the achievement (e.g. improved marketing organization or new initiative to cater for export markets) and this will be taken into consideration. Export earnings considered will include receipts by the applicant unit in this country from the export of goods produced in this country, and the provision of services to non-residents. Account will be taken of the overseas expenses incurred other than marketing expenses. Income from profits (after overseas tax) remitted to this country from the applicant unit's direct investments in its overseas branches, subsidiaries or associates in the same general line of business will be taken into account, but not receipts from profits on other overseas investments or by interest on overseas loans or credits.

2. Technological Achievement

A significant advance, leading to increased efficiency, in the application of technology to a production or development process in British industry or the production for sale of goods which incorporate new and advanced technological qualities.

Each award is formally conferred by a Grant of Appointment and is symbolized by a representation of its emblem cast in stainless steel and encapsulated in a transparent acrylic block. Presentations are usually made on behalf of The Queen by Her Majesty's Lord Lieutenants at the principal place of business or production of the unit. A reception is given annually by The Queen at Buckingham Palace for representatives of the winners of the Awards.

Awards are held for five years and holders are entitled to fly the appropriate Award flag and to display the emblem on the packaging of goods produced in this country, on the goods themselves, on the unit's stationery, in advertising and on certain articles used by employees: units may also display the emblem of any previous current Awards during the 5 years.

Awards are announced on April 21—the actual birthday of Her Majesty the Queen—and published formally in a special supplement to the London Gazette. All enquires about the scheme and requests for application forms—completed forms must be returned by October 31—should be made to: The Secretary, The Queen's Awards Off.ce, Dean Bradley House, 52 Horseferry Road, London SW1P 2AG. Telephone: 01-222 2277.

Export Achievement Awards

In 1985, the Queen's Award was conferred on the following concerns for export achievement:

A & M Hearing Aids Ltd., Crawley, West Sussex; Aerial Access Equipment Ltd., Longbenton, Tyne and Wear; Amek Systems & Controls Ltd., Salford; Anglo Blackwells Ltd., Widnes, Cheshire; Armstrong Competition Motorcycles Ltd., Bolton, Lancashire; Associated Retail Development International Ltd., London W.1; Autotype International Ltd., Wantage, Oxfordshire; Barnett International Ltd., Wolverhampton, West Midlands; Beacon Publications PLC, Northampton; The Heavy Media Separation Division of Birds Commercial Metals Ltd., Stratford-upon-Avon, Warwickshire; Henry Boot International Ltd., Dronfield, Sheffield; Bridge of Weir Leather Co. Ltd., Bridge of Weir, Renfrewshire; Brightside Mechanical & Electrical Services Group Ltd., Birmingham; The Scottish Division of the Aircraft Group of British Aerospace PLC, Prestwick, Ayrshire; Brown Brothers & Co. Ltd., Edinburgh; James Burrough PLC, London S.E.11; Carrington Hull Associates Ltd., London E.C.1; Coopervision Optics Ltd., Southampton; Coutinho Caro UK Ltd., London E.C.4; D B Factors Ltd., Sheffield, South Yorkshire; Data Recording Heads Ltd., Staines, Middlesex; Donvand Ltd., London E.C.1; Dunkirk Metals Ltd., Dunkirk, Nottingham; Edendeck Ltd., Burnley, Lancashire; Ferranti Electronics Ltd., Oldham, Lancashire; First Intertia Switch Ltd., Hartley Wintney, Hampshire; Flogates Ltd., Sheffield, South Yorkshire; Floorlife-Andek Ltd., Hove, East Sussex; Foster Wheeler Petroleum Development Ltd., London W.C.2; Franklin Hodge Industries Ltd., Hereford; Garrett Airsearch Ltd., Skelmersdale, Lancashire; H R & H Marketing Research International Ltd., London W.1; Harrods Ltd., London S.W.1; Hazleton Securities Ltd., Richmond, Surrey; Houbigant Ltd., Horley, Surrey; The House of Darts, Bristol; Hydraroll Limited, Gaerwen, Gwynedd; The Plant Protection Division of Imperial Chemical Industries PLC, Fernhurst, Surrey; Jaguar Cars Ltd., Coventry, West Midlands; Justerini and Brooks Ltd., London S.W.1; The Walter Kidde Co. Ltd., Northolt, Middlesex; Kigass Engineering Ltd., Leamington Spa, Warwickshire; Kirkpatrick Linron (Ballyclare) Ltd., Ballyclare, Co. Antrim, Northern Ireland; Linear Ltd., Newton Aycliffe, County Durham; Link Systems Ltd., High Wycombe, Buckinghamshire; Linton &

Hirst Ltd., Swindon, Wiltshire; Longdin & Browning (Surveys) Ltd., Swansea, West Glamorgan; The Lygon Arms Ltd, Broadway, Worcestershire; The Frimley Unit of Marconi Command and Control Systems Ltd., Camberley, Surrey; James Martin Associates Ltd., London S.W.19; Mayer Newman & Co. Ltd., Erith, Kent; Mitchell Cotts Chemicals Ltd., Mirfield, West Yorkshire; Morgan-Bryant Marketing Ltd., London W.3; Mostyn Chemicals Ltd., Stockport, Cheshire; Naim Audio Ltd., Salisbury, Wiltshire; Netlon Ltd., Blackburn, Lancashire; Oilfield Inspection Services Ltd., Great Yarmouth, Norfolk; Oxford Magnet Technology Ltd., Eynsham, Oxford; Pipeline Induction Heat Ltd., High Wycombe, Buckinghamshire; Redpath Dorman Long Ltd., Bedford; Regent Belt Co. Ltd., Walgrave, Northamptonshire; John Reid & Sons (Strucsteel) Ltd., Christchurch, Dorset; Renishaw Electrical Ltd., Wotton-under-Edge, Gloucestershire; Saga Holidays PLC, Folkestone, Kent; Scanro Ltd., Newcastle-upon-Tyne, Tyne and Wear; Schmidt Manufacturing & Equipment (UK) Ltd., Ely, Cambridgeshire; Sheppard Robson, London N.W.1; The Aircraft Division of Short Brothers PLC, Belfast, Northern Ireland; Silver Spring Mineral Water Co. Ltd., Folkestone, Kent; Singer Link-Miles Ltd., Lancing, West Sussex; Soundcraft Electronics Ltd., Borehamwood, Hertfordshire; Spectramass Ltd., Congleton, Cheshire; Spheric Engineering Ltd., Crawley, West Sussex; The Medal Division of Spink & Son Ltd., London S.W.1; T M Services Ltd., London W.1; Tame Valley Alloys Ltd., Tamworth, Staffordshire; Charles Tanqueray & Co. Ltd., London E.C.1; Tape Automation Ltd., Harlow, Essex; Thermaflex Ltd., Glenrothes, Fife; Thorn EMI Screen Entertainment Ltd., London W.C.2; John R. Timme & Son Ltd., Bradford West Yorkshire; Tiphook Container Rental Co. Ltd., Bromley, Kent; Titan Converting Equipment Ltd., Bishops Stortford, Hertfordshire; Trusthouse Forte PLC, London W.1; Tusting and Burnett (1938) Ltd., Odell, Bedfordshire; Tweedvale Woollens Ltd., London W.1; United Pig Breeders PLC, Huntingdon, Cambridgeshire; Vista Optics Ltd., Loughborough, Leicestershire; Windsong Record Exports Ltd., Croydon, Surrey; Yardley & Co. Ltd., London W.1.

Awards for Technological Achievement 1985

In 1985, the following concerns received the Queen's Award for technological achievement:

BP Petroleum Development (North West Europe) Ltd., London E.C.2 (*Magnus deep water oil and gas project*); The Research Department of The Boots Company PLC, Nottingham (*"Ibuprofen" drug for treatment of rheumatic diseases*); The Civil Division of the Aircraft Group of British Aerospace PLC, Hatfield, Hertfordshire (*BAe 146 passenger aircraft*); The Optical Materials and Low Loss Fibre Section of the British Telecom Research Laboratories of British Telecommunications PLC, Ipswich, Suffolk (*Single mode optical fibres*); Celltech Ltd., Slough, Berkshire (*Monoclonal antibodies*); City Technology Ltd., London E.C.1 (*Toxic gas sensors*); Cossor Electronics Ltd., Harlow, Essex (*Monopulse secondary surveillance radar system*); Crosfield Electronics Ltd., Hemel Hempstead, Hertfordshire (*Electronic magazine publishing and communications system*); Datron Instruments Ltd., Norwich, Norfolk (*Programmable multifunction calibrator*); Domino Printing Sciences Ltd., Barr Hill, Cambridgeshire (*High speed industrial ink jet printing systems*); Dunlop Slazenger International Ltd., Wakefield, West Yorkshire (*Carbon fibre tennis rackets*); Filtronic Components Ltd., Shipley, West Yorkshire (*Suspended substrate stripline microwave filters and multiplexers*); The Airborne Display Division of GEC Avionics Ltd., Rochester, Kent (*Aircraft head-up display systems*); GEC Transmission & Distribution Projects Ltd., Stafford (*"Transidrive"—electrical power converter*); Glaxo Group Research Ltd., Greenford, Middlesex (*Ranitidine "Zantac" treatment for peptic ulcers*); Hurley Moate Engineering Company Ltd., Oldham, Lancashire (*"In Register" splicer machine for printing and paper industries*); The Mainframe Systems Division of ICL PLC, Manchester (*Content-addressable file store information search processor*); Interface Developments Ltd., Hawkhurst, Kent (*Flexible diamond cloth*); Lucas Cookson Syalon Ltd., Solihull, West Midlands (*Engineering ceramics*); The Mining Research and Development Establishment of the National Coal Board, Burton-on-Trent, Staffordshire (*Filtration dust collector*); Oxford Magnet Technology Ltd., Oxford (*Magnet systems for magnetic resonance scanners and In Vivo spectroscopy*); Picker International Ltd., Wembley, Middlesex (*Magnetic resonance imaging systems*); Quantel Ltd., Kenley, Surrey (*Digital "Paint Box" electronic graphic system*); Rank Film Laboratories Ltd., Denham, Buckinghamshire (*4,000 metre motion picture film printing system*); The Pharmaceutical Division of Reckitt & Colman Products Ltd., Kingston-upon-Hull (*Buprenorphine (Temgesic R)—pain killer*); Rendel Palmer & Tritton, London S.E.1 (*Design of the Thames Flood Barrier*); Rotabolt Ltd., Dudley, West Midlands (*Fastening device*); Sira Ltd., Chislehurst, Kent (*"SPATE 8000" stress analyser*); The Wellcome Research Laboratories of the Wellcome Foundation Ltd., Beckenham, Kent (*Acyclovir "Zovirax" antiviral drug for the treatment of herpes*).

BRITISH OIL STATISTICS (million tonnes)

	1979	1980	1981	1982	1983
Oil production†					
Land	0·1	0·2	0·2	0·3	0·3
Offshore	77·8	80·2	89·2	103·1	114·6
Refinery output	90·6	79·2	72·0	70·7	70·9
Deliveries of petroleum products for inland consumption	84·6	71·2	66·3	67·2	64·5
Exports (including re-exports):					
Crude petroleum	38·8	38·5	51·4	60·4	68·4
Refined petroleum products and process oils	14·4	16·1	13·1	14·5	15·9
Imports:					
Crude petroleum	57·9	44·8	33·1	28·3	22·8
Refined petroleum products and process oils	16·0	14·1	14·1	17·2	17·4

† Crude oil plus condensates and petroleum gases derived at onshore treatment plants.

CIVIL SERVICE STAFF

Analysis by ministerial responsibility at 1 April in each year

† Full-time equivalents (thousands)

	1978	1979	1980	1981	1982	1983	1984
Total civil and defence departments	735·7	732·3	704·9	689·6	666·4	648·9	624·0
of which Non-industrials	*567·3*	*565·8*	*547·5*	*539·9*	*528·0*	*518·5*	*504·3*
Industrials	*168·4*	*166·5*	*157·4*	*149·7*	*138·4*	*130·4*	*119·7*
Total civil departments	485·3	484·6	465·1	460·0	449·4	440·0	424·8
Agriculture, Fisheries and Food	14·6	14·5	14·3	13·6	13·1	12·7	12·1
Chancellor of the Exchequer's	128·9	128·2	119·0	114·9	121·0	117·4	112·4
Departments:							
Customs and Excise	28·8	28·8	27·2	26·8	26·2	25·4	25·1
Inland Revenue	85·2	84·6	78·3	75·6	74·0	73·1	69·8
Department for National Savings	10·9	10·8	10·4	10·0	9·1	8·3	8·0
Treasury and others	4·0	4·0	3·1	2·5	11·7	10·6	9·5
Education and Science	3·7	3·7	3·7	3·6	3·5	3·5	2·4
Employment	53·7	53·6	50·7	53·8	58·7	57·9	56·4
Energy	1·3	1·3	1·3	1·2	1·1	1·1	1·1
Environment	57·3	56·0	51·7	47·0	42·1	39·4	36·6
Foreign and Commonwealth	12·1	12·1	11·6	11·4	11·1	11·1	10·0
Home	33·2	33·5	34·1	35·4	34·6	35·1	36·4
Industry	9·5	9·5	9·1	8·8	8·3	7·7	–
Scotland	13·5	13·7	13·6	13·6	13·4	13·1	12·8
Social Services	99·5	100·9	98·9	100·1	98·0	96·4	92·6
Trade	9·7	9·6	9·4	9·3	8·9	8·9	–
Trade and Industry	–	–	–	–	–	–	14·7
Transport	14·5	13·9	13·5	13·7	13·0	13·0	14·2
Wales	2·5	2·6	2·5	2·3	2·3	2·2	2·2
Other civil departments	31·3	31·4	31·7	31·3	20·2	20·5	20·9
Total Ministry of Defence	250·4	247·7	239·8	229·6	216·9	208·9	199·2

† Part-time employees are counted as half units.

POLICE FORCES (Authorised establishment and strength)

Number

	1977	1978	1979	1980	1981	1982	1983
England and Wales							
Regular police							
Authorised establishment	116,980	117,668	118,322	118,930	120,008	120,125	120,447
Strength:							
Men	98,935	99,134	102,360	105,563	107,379	108,517	108,519
Women...................	7,789	8,477	9,394	10,355	10,702	10,935	10,995
Seconded:							
Men	1,400	1,386	1,477	1,430	1,424	1,419	1,407
Women...................	77	78	78	75	70	80	82
Additional constables:							
Men	97	85	114	96	90	89	84
Women...................	–	1	2	1	1	1	2
Scotland							
Regular police							
Authorised establishment:							
Men	13,144	13,162	13,148	13,187	13,195	13,205	13,261
Women...................							
Strength:							
Men	11,069	11,477	12,280	12,419	12,379	12,433	12,435
Women...................	763	746	786	771	749	719	713
Central service:							
Men	52	51	56	60	54	55	65
Women...................	3	4	4	5	2	2	2
Seconded:							
Men	78	72	72	69	78	73	68
Women...................	8	5	3	2	5	4	3
Additional regular police:							
Authorised establishment ..	174	179	126	72	67	62	60
Strength	174	176	148	71	66	62	60
Northern Ireland							
Royal Ulster Constabulary							
Strength:							
Men	5,140	5,495	5,938	6,224	6,622	7,017	7,328
Women...................	552	615	676	711	712	701	675

GOVERNMENT AND PUBLIC OFFICES

All salaries throughout the section were supplied by individual Offices and are subject to variation. At the time of going to press, it was not possible to confirm the information required.

In January 1984, the Home Civil Service introduced a unified pay and grading structure for senior personnel. The new grades with the previous equivalent are shown below:

Unified Grade	Previous Title
1	Permanent Secretary.
1A	Second Permanent Secretary.
2	Deputy Secretary.
3	Under Secretary.
4	Chief Scientific Officer B, Professional and Technology Directing A and equivalent levels.
5	Assistant Secretary, Deputy Chief Scientific Officer, Professional and Technology Directing B and equivalent levels.
6	Senior Principal, Senior Principal Scientific Officer, Professional and Technology Superintending Grade and equivalent levels.

ADVISORY, CONCILIATION AND ARBITRATION SERVICE
11–12 St. James's Square, SW1Y 4LA
[01–214 6000]

The Advisory, Conciliation and Arbitration Service (ACAS) is an independent organisation set up under the Employment Protection Act, 1975, under the management of a Council appointed by the Secretary of State for Employment. The functions of the Service are to provide facilities for conciliation, mediation and arbitration as a means of avoiding and resolving industrial disputes; and to provide advisory services to industry on industrial relations matters.
Chairman, Sir Pat Lowry, C.B.E.
Chief Conciliation Officer, D. G. Boyd.
Director of Resources and General Policy Branch, E. Norcross.

MINISTRY OF AGRICULTURE, FISHERIES AND FOOD
Whitehall Place, SW1A 2HH†
[01–233 3000]

The Ministry of Agriculture, Fisheries and Food is responsible for administering government policy for agriculture, horticulture and fishing in England and for many food matters in the United Kingdom. Some of the Ministry's responsibilities for animal health extend to Great Britain. In association with the Intervention Board for Agricultural Produce and the other Agricultural Departments in the United Kingdom it is responsible for the administration of the EEC common agricultural and fisheries policy and for various national support schemes. It also administers schemes for the control and eradication of animal and plant diseases and for assistance to capital investment in farm and horticultural businesses and land drainage; it exercises responsibilities relating to applied research and development. The Agricultural Development and Advisory Service (ADAS) is part of the Ministry. The Ministry sponsors the food and drink manufacturing industries and distribution trades. It is concerned with the supply and quality of food, food compositional standards, hygiene, labelling and advertising of food

†Unless otherwise stated, this is the main address of Divisions of the Ministry.

and has certain responsibilities for ensuring public health standards in the manufacture, preparation and distribution of basic foods.

Salary List

Minister	£32,208
Minister of State (Commons)	£22,378
Minister of State (Lords)	£29,320
Parliamentary Secretary	£16,648
Permanent Secretary (Grade 1)	£52,750
Deputy Secretary (Grade 2)	£38,325 to £39,250
Under Secretary (Grade 3)	£30,975 to £31,750
Assistant Secretary (Grade 5)	£20,964 to £25,533
Senior Principal (Grade 6)	£17,000 to £22,926
Principal	£13,508 to £18,363
Assistant Solicitor (Grade 5)	£20,964 to £25,533
Chief Scientific Officer (Grade 4)	£27,551 to £28,301
Deputy Chief Scientific Officer (Grade 5)	£20,964 to £25,533
Senior Principal Scientific Officer (Grade 6)	£17,000 to £22,926
Chief Statistician (Grade 5)	£20,964 to £25,533

Minister, THE RT. HON. MICHAEL JOPLING, M.P.
  Private Secretary (Principal), C. I. Llewelyn.
  Parliamentary Private Secretary, P. Marland, M.P.
  Special Adviser, T. Boswell.
Ministers of State, JOHN MACGREGOR, M.P., O.B.E.; THE LORD BELSTEAD, P.C.
  Private Secretaries, (to Mr. MacGregor), Mrs. S. Stagg; *(to Lord Belstead),* T. D. Rossington.
Parliamentary Private Secretary (to Mr. MacGregor), M. Lord, M.P.
Parliamentary Secretary, Mrs. P. Fenner, M.P.
  Private Secretary, M. C. Bourke.
Parliamentary Clerk Miss B. J. Richards.
Permanent Secretary, Sir Michael Franklin, K.C.B., C.M.G.
  Private Secretary, Mrs. C. M. Adams.

ESTABLISHMENT DEPARTMENT
Director of Establishments (G3), G. Stapleton.

Manpower Division
Victory House, 30–34 Kingsway, WC2B 6TU
[01–405 4310]
Head of Division (G5), Mrs. A. M. Blackburn.

Establishments (General) Division
Victory House, 30–34 Kingsway, WC2B 6TU
[01–405 4310]
Head of Division (G5), A. V. Vickery.

Staff Training Branch*
Principal, J. M. Lynes.

Welfare Branch
Victory House, 30–34 Kingsway, WC2B 6TU
[01–405 4310]
Chief Welfare Officer (Senior Executive Officer), R. R. J. Huckins.

Personnel Division
Victory House, 30–34 Kingsway, WC2B 6TU
[01–405 4310]
Head of Division (G5), C. J. A. Barnes.

FINANCE DEPARTMENT
Principal Finance Officer (G3), G. W. Wilson.

Finance Division I*
Head of Division (G5), G. A. Hollis.

*At Great Westminster House, Horseferry Road, SW1P 2AE [01–216 6311].

Finance Division II*
Head of Division (G5), J. A. Brown.

Financial Management Team
Head of Division (G5), D. J. Coates.

Audit Division*
Director of Audit (G5), S. T. K. Hester.
Assistant Director of Audit (G6), F. W. Martin.

LEGAL DEPARTMENT
55 Whitehall, SW1A 2EY
[01–217 3000]

Legal Adviser and Solicitor (G2), G. J. Jenkins.
Principal Assistant Solicitors (G3), A. E. Munir; J. McElheran.

Legal Division A1
Assistant Solicitor (G5), J. O. Stansfield.

Legal Division A2
Assistant Solicitor (G5), A. Yavash.

Legal Division A3
Assistant Solicitor (G5), J. H. Jordan.

Legal Division B1
Assistant Solicitor (G5), J. F. McCleary.

Legal Division B2
Assistant Solicitor (G5), G. R. J. Robertson.

Legal Division B3
Assistant Solicitor (G5), Miss E. A. Stephens.

Legal Division B4
Assistant Solicitor (G5), B. T. Atwood.

MANAGEMENT SERVICES

Under Secretary (G3), J. E. Dixon.

Computer Services Division
Government Buildings, Epsom Road,
Guildford, Surrey GU1 2LD
[0483 68121]
Head of Division (G5), D. F. Reed.

Office Services Division
Head of Division (G6), J. E. Nunn, D.F.C.

Management Services Division
Victory House, 30–34 Kingsway, WC2B 6TU
[01-405 4310]
Head of Division (G5), G. B. Hopley.

Information Division
Chief Information Officer-A (G5), J. A. Colmer.
Chief Press Officer, G. Shepherd.
Principal Librarian, T. C. J. Norton.

**Information Technology and Procedures
Division**
Victory House, 30–34 Kingsway, WC2B 6TU
[01-405 4310]
Head of Division (G5), W. J. Willis.

CHIEF SCIENTIST'S GROUP

Chief Scientist (Fisheries and Food) (G3), R. N. Crossett, D.Phil.*
Chief Scientist (Agriculture and Horticulture) (G3), G. H. O. Burgess, Ph.D.*

RESEARCH AND DEVELOPMENT
REQUIREMENTS DIVISION*

Head of Division (G5), G. K. Bruce.

*At Great Westminster House, Horseferry Road, SW1P 2AE [01–216 6311].

FOOD SCIENCE DIVISION
65 Romney Street, S.W.1
[01–212 7676]

Deputy Chief Scientific Officer (G5), M. E. Knowles, Ph.D.

AGRICULTURAL COMMODITIES

Deputy Secretary (G2), D. H. Andrews, C.B., C.B.E.

EUROPEAN AND EXTERNAL RELATIONS

Under Secretary (G3), D. A. Hadley.

European Community Division I
Head of Division (G5), vacant.

European Community Division II
Head of Division (G5), R. E. Melville.

External Relations
Head of Division (G5), P. A. Cocking.

CEREALS AND SUGAR

Under Secretary (G3), G. E. Myers, C.M.G.

Cereals Division
Head of Division (G5), R. C. Lowson.

Sugar, Oils and Fats Division
Head of Division (G5), P. P. Nash.

MEAT

Under Secretary (G3), Mrs. J. M. Archer.

Pigs, Eggs and Poultry Division
Head of Division (G5), M. Ring.

Beef Division
Head of Division (G5), D. P. Hunter.

Sheep and Livestock Subsidies Division
Head of Division (G5), Mrs. A. M. Pickering.

MILK

Under Secretary (G3), B. H. B. Dickinson.

Milk and Milk Products Division I
Head of Division (G5), S. Wentworth.

Milk and Milk Products Division II
Head of Division (G5), I. C. Redfern.

Milk and Milk Products Division III
Head of Division (G5), A. R. Cruickshank.

FISHERIES AND FOOD

Deputy Secretary (G2), W. E. Mason, C.B.

FISHERIES DEPARTMENT*

Fisheries Secretary (G3), D. H. Griffiths.

Fisheries Division I
Head of Division (G5), G. R. Waters.

Fisheries Division II
Head of Division (G5), J. C. Edwards.

Fisheries Division III
Head of Division (G5), M. T. Haddon.

Sea Fisheries Inspectorate
Chief Inspector (G6), P. J. Derham, O.B.E.

*At Great Westminster House, Horseferry Road, SW1P 2AE [01–216 6311].

Fisheries Research
*Director of Fisheries Research and Development for
Great Britain (G4)*, A. Preston.
Deputy Directors of Fisheries Research (G5), H. W.
Hill; D. J. Garrod, PH.D.

Fisheries Laboratory
Pakefield Road, Lowestoft, Suffolk NR33 0HT
[0502 62244]

Fisheries Laboratory
Remembrance Avenue, Burnham-on-Crouch,
Essex CM0 8HA
[0621 782658]

Fisheries Experiment Station
Benarth Road, Conwy, Gwynedd LL32 8UB
[049 263 3883]
Inspector of Salmon and Freshwater Fisheries, B.
Stott.*

Fish Diseases Laboratory
The Nothe, Weymouth, Dorset DT4 8UB
[03057 72137]
Officer-in-charge (Principal Scientific Officer), B. J.
Hill, PH.D.

Torry Research Station
P.O. Box 31, 135 Abbey Road,
Aberdeen AB9 8DG
[0224 877071]
Director (G5), J. J. Connell, PH.D.

FOOD, DRINK AND MARKETING POLICY
Under Secretary (G3), R. J. Packer.

Food Policy and Exports Promotion Division
Head of Division (G5), B. E. Camp.

Alcoholic Drinks Division
Head of Division (G5), C. R. Bodrell.

Tropical Foods*
Head of Division (G5), R. S. Thomas.

Marketing Policy and Potatoes Division
Head of Division (G5), G. P. McLachlan.

EMERGENCIES, FOOD QUALITY AND PEST
CONTROLS*
Under Secretary (G3), Mrs. E. A. J. Attridge.

Standards Division*
Head of Division (G5), C. A. Cockbill.

Emergencies Division
Head of Division (G5), A. Jeffrey Smith.

Pesticides and Infestation Control*
Head of Division (G5), G. M. Trevelyan.

LAND AND RESOURCES
Deputy Secretary (G2), E. J. G. Smith, C.B.

LAND
Under Secretary (G3), J. A. Anderson.

Land Improvement Division*
Head of Division (G5), M. Madden.

Land Use and Tenure Division*
Head of Division (G5), P. W. Murphy.

Land Drainage Division*
Head of Division (G5), R. C. McIvor.

* At Great Westminster House, Horseferry Road,
SW1P 2AE [01–216 6311].

ANIMAL HEALTH
Under Secretary (G2), J. W. Hepburn.

Animal Health Division I
Government Buildings, Hook Rise South,
Tolworth, Surbiton, Surrey KT6 7NF
[01–337 6611]
Head of Division (G5), W. R. Small.

Animal Health Division II
Government Buildings, Hook Rise South,
Tolworth, Surbiton, Surrey KT6 7NF
[01–337 6611]
Head of Division (G5), A. R. Burne.

Animal Health Division III
Tolworth Tower, Surbiton, Surrey KT6 7DX
[01–399 5191]
Head of Division (G5), K. W. Wilkes.

Meat Hygiene Division
Tolworth Tower, Surbiton, Surrey KT6 7DX
[01–399 5191]
Head of Division (G5), P. M. Boyling.

AGRICULTURAL RESOURCES POLICY,
HORTICULTURE, PLANT HEALTH AND
SEEDS
Under Secretary (G3), C. R. Cann.

Horticulture Division*
Senior Economic Adviser & Head of Division (G5),
R. E. Mordue.

Agricultural Resources Policy Division
Eagle House, 90/96 Cannon Street, EC4N 6HT
[01–623 4266]
Head of Division (G5), H. R. Neilson.

Plant Variety, Rights Office and Seeds
White House Lane, Huntingdon Road,
Cambridge CB3 0LF
[0223 277151]
Head of Division (G5), F. H. Goodwin.

Plant Health Divison*
Head of Division (G6), Miss E. M. Price.

ECONOMICS AND STATISTICS
Director of Economics and Statistics (G3), C. W.
Capstick, C.M.G.

Economics (Farm Business) Division
Senior Economic Adviser (G5), Mrs. S. M. Dickinson.

Economics (International) Division
Senior Economic Adviser (G5), R. W. Irving.

Economics (Resource Use) Division
55 Whitehall, SW1A 2EY
[01–233 3000]
Senior Economic Adviser (G5), A. P. Power, PH.D.

Statistics (Agricultural Commodities) Division
Chief Statistician (G5), P. Roberts.

Statistics (Census and Prices) Division
Chief Statistician (G5), D. E. Bradbury.

Economics and Statistics (Food)
Senior Economic Adviser (G5), J. M. Slater, PH.D.

REGIONAL ORGANIZATION
Deputy Secretary (G2), E. J. G. Smith, C.B.

*At Great Westminster House, Horseferry Road,
SW1P 2AE [01–216 6311].

Eastern Region
Block C, Government Buildings,
Brooklands Avenue, Cambridge CB2 2DR
[0223 358911]
Chief Regional Officer (G5), T. W. Nicol.

Northern Region
Block 2, Government Buildings, Lawnswood,
Leeds S16 5PY
[0532 674411]
Chief Regional Officer (G5), A. F. Baines.

South Eastern Region
Block A, Government Offices,
Coley Park, Reading RG1 6DT
[0734 581222]
Chief Regional Officer (G5), J. A. Bamford.

South Western Region
Block 3, Government Bldgs., Burghill Road,
Westbury-on-Trym, Bristol BS10 6NJ
[0272 500000]
Chief Regional Officer (G5), B. F. Shorney.

Midlands and Western Region
Woodthorne, Wolverhampton WV6 8TQ
[0902 754190]
Chief Regional Officer (G5), R. J. D. Carden.

**AGRICULTURAL DEVELOPMENT AND
ADVISORY SERVICE (A.D.A.S.)**

Director General and Chief Scientific Advisor (G2),
Prof. R. L. Bell, ph.d.

AGRICULTURE*

Chief Agricultural Officer (G3), J. J. North.
Senior Agricultural Officers (G4), G. A. Mansfield; P. Ingram.
Senior Horticultural Officer (G4), D. J. Fuller.
Superintending Horticultural Marketing Inspector (G6), J. P. Blakey.

AGRICULTURAL SCIENCE

Head of Service (G3), P. J. Bunyan, d.sc., ph.d.*
Senior Agricultural Scientists (G4), D. C. Drummond* *(Research and Development)*; R. C. Little, ph.d.* *(Advice and Promotion)*.

Pest Infestation Control Laboratory
London Road, Slough, Berks. SL3 7HJ
[75 34626]
Director of Slough, Tolworth and Worplesdon Laboratories (G5), P. I. Stanley, ph.d.

**Plant Pathology Laboratory and Plant Health
and Seeds Inspectorate**
Hatching Green, Harpenden, Herts. AL5 2BD
[0582 75241/46]
Director of Harpenden Laboratory (G5), H. J. Gould.
Chief Plant Health and Seeds Inspector (G6), W. J. Stubbs.

Great Westminster House, Horseferry Road,
SW1P 2AE
[01—216 8311]
Staff Officer, Science Service (G6), K. G. Gostick.

LAND AND WATER SERVICE*

Director (G3), D. B. S. Fitch.
Assistant Director (G5), B. D. Trafford.

*At Great Westminster House, Horseferry Road,
SW1P 2AE [01-216 6311].

VETERINARY
Government Buildings, Hook Rise South,
Tolworth, Surbiton, Surrey KT6 7NF
[01—337 6611]
Chief Veterinary Officer (G3), W. H. G. Rees.
Director of Veterinary Field Services (G3), J. G. Loxam.

Central Veterinary Laboratory, New Haw,
Weybridge, Surrey KT15 3NB
[91 41111]
Director of Veterinary Laboratories (G3), A. J. Stevens.

Lasswade Veterinary Laboratory, Eskgrove,
Lasswade, Midlothian EH18 1HU
[031—663 6525]

Cattle Breeding Centre, Shinfield, Reading,
Berks. RG2 9BZ
[0734 883157]

ADAS ADMINISTRATION

Director (G3), G. P. Jupe.
Senior A.D.A.S. Officer (Wales) (G5), T. M. K. Evans.

Agricultural Development and Advice Division
Head of Division (G5), A. H. Abbott.*

**AGRICULTURAL AND FOOD RESEARCH
COUNCIL**
160 Great Portland Street, W1N 6DT
[01-580 6655]

The former Agricultural Research Council was incorporated by Royal Charter in 1931. The Science and Technology Act, 1965, transferred responsibility for the Research Council to the Secretary of State for Education and Science and a new Charter received Royal approval in 1967. In 1983, the Council formally adopted the title Agricultural and Food Research Council in recognition of the increasing importance of food research and the expanding contribution the Council expects to make to it. It is principally financed from the Parliamentary vote of the Department of Education and Science and the Ministry of Agriculture, Fisheries and Food, but also receives some funds from industry and other outside bodies. The Council, an autonomous body, is charged with the organisation and development of agricultural and food research in Great Britain. To this end it supports a number of scientific research establishments; by direct funding of its own institutes located throughout Great Britain; by the allocation of grants to other institutes in England and Wales which, though under the Council's auspices, are directly responsible to their own governing bodies; and by the allocation of various other grants.

The term Agricultural and Food Research Service applies to all Institutes and Units in England, Wales and Scotland which, though funded in various different ways are responsible to the Council. It also applies to the Scottish Agricultural Research Institutes which, though funded by the Department of Agriculture and Fisheries for Scotland, look to the Council for advice on their research programmes.

Chairman, The Earl of Selborne; *(Members)*, Prof. R. L. Bell, ph.d.; Prof. D. Boulter, d.Phil.; Dr. G. H. O. Burgess, f.r.s.e.; J. E. Cross; R. N. Crossett, d.Phil.; Prof. B. Crossland, c.b.e., f.r.s.; Prof. B. K. Follett, f.r.s.; Prof. I. M. Glynn, f.r.s.; A. C. Green; L. P. Hamilton; Prof. J. L. Harper, f.r.s.; C. Mackey; M. Mackie; J. A. Parry, c.b.e.; B. C. Read, c.b.e.; Prof. D. C. Smith, f.r.s.; E. J. G. Smith, c.b.; Prof. E. J. L. Soulsby, ph.d.; Prof. R. Whittenbury, ph.d.

* At Great Westminster House, Horseferry Road, SW1P 2AE [01—216 6311].

Assessors, W. H. G. Rees; Prof. W. D. P. Stewart, F.R.S.; Dr. C. Wright.
Deputy Chairman and Secretary, Prof. J. L. Jinks, C.B.E., F.R.S.
Second Secretary, J. A. F. Rook, D.SC., F.R.S.E.
Under-Secretary, G. M. P. Myers.
Heads of Divisions, R. Prideaux; Prof. G. Cheeseman; J. Dickens; R. J. Harris; B. G. Jamieson, PH.D.; Dr. J. V. Lake.
Policy Group, W. S. Wise.
Principal Information Officer, M. F. Goodwin.
For the Research Institutes under the control of the Council, *see* Index.

EXECUTIVE COUNCIL OF THE COMMONWEALTH AGRICULTURAL BUREAUX
Farnham House, Farnham Royal, Slough, Berks. SL2 3BN
[Farnham Common : 2281]

The Commonwealth Agricultural Bureaux, founded in 1929, consist of four Institutes and ten Bureaux, under the control of an Executive Council, comprising representatives of the Commonwealth countries which contribute to its funds. Each Institute and Bureau is concerned with its own particular branch of agricultural science and acts as a clearing house for the dissemination of information of value to research workers throughout the world. They deal respectively with entomology, mycology, helminthology and nematology, biological control, agricultural economics, animal breeding and genetics, animal health, nutrition, dairy science and technology, forestry, horticulture and plantation crops, pastures and field crops, plant breeding and genetics, and soils and fertilizers. The information is published in journals which have a monthly circulation of 32,000 in 150 countries. The abstract journals are produced by computer-assisted processes, and the whole data base has been consolidated and is available in machine-readable form. Review articles, books, maps, monographs and annotated bibliographies on particular subjects are also issued.
Chairman, Dr. M. Moore (*Australia*).
Vice-Chairman, S. Mutondo (*Zambia*).
Director General, D. Mentz.

Institutes

Commonwealth Institute of Entomology, 56 Queen's Gate, S.W.7. *Director,* J. M. Harley.
Commonwealth Mycological Institute, Ferry Lane, Kew, Richmond, Surrey. *Director,* D. L. Hawksworth, PH.D.
Commonwealth Institute of Biological Control, Gordon Street, Curepe, Trinidad. *Director,* F. D. Bennett, PH.D.
Commonwealth Institute of Parasitology, 395A Hatfield Road, St. Albans, Herts. *Director,* R. L. J. Muller, PH.D.

Bureaux

Agricultural Economics, Dartington House, Little Clarendon Street, Oxford.—*Director,* Miss M. A. Bellamy.
Animal Breeding and Genetics, Animal Breeding Research Organization, The King's Buildings, West Mains Road, Edinburgh, Scotland.—*Director,* J. D. Turton.
Animal Health, Central Veterinary Laboratory, New Haw, Weybridge, Surrey.—*Director,* R. M. Mack.
Dairy Science and Technology, Lane End House, Shinfield, Reading.—*Director,* E. J. Mann.
Forestry, Commonwealth Forestry Institute, South Parks Road, Oxford.—*Director,* W. Finlayson.

Horticulture and Plantation Crops, East Malling Research Station, Maidstone, Kent.—*Director,* D. O'D. Bourke.
Nutrition, Rowett Research Institute, Bucksburn, Aberdeen, Scotland.—*Director,* D. J. Fleming.
Pastures and Field Crops, Hurley, Maidenhead, Berks.—*Director,* P. J. Boyle.
Plant Breeding and Genetics, Department of Applied Biology, Pembroke Street, Cambridge.—*Director,* Miss O. Holbek.
Soils, Rothamsted Experimental Station, Harpenden, Herts.—*Director,* B. Butters.

COLLEGE OF ARMS OR HERALDS COLLEGE
Queen Victoria Street, E.C.4
[01–248 2762]

The College of Arms is open daily from 10–4 (Mondays to Fridays) when an Officer of Arms is in attendance to deal with enquiries by the public, though such enquiries may also be directed to any of the Officers of Arms, either personally or by letter.

There are 13 officers of the College, 3 Kings of Arms, 6 Heralds and 4 Pursuivants, who specialize in genealogical and heraldic work for their respective clients. The College possesses the finest records on these subjects in the world. It is the official repository of the Arms and pedigrees of English, Northern Irish, and Commonwealth families and their descendants, and its records include official copies of the records of Ulster King of Arms, the originals of which remain in Dublin.

Arms have been and still are granted by Letters Patent from the Kings of Arms under Authority delegated to them by the Sovereign, such authority having been expressly conferred on them since at least the fifteenth century. A right to Arms can only be established by the registration in the official records of the College of Arms of a pedigree showing direct male line descent from an ancestor already appearing therein as being entitled to Arms, or by making application through the College of Arms for a Grant of Arms.
Earl Marshal, His Grace the Duke of Norfolk, K.G., C.B., C.B.E., M.C.

Kings of Arms

Garter, Sir Colin Cole, K.C.V.O., T.D., F.S.A.
Clarenceux, Sir Anthony Richard Wagner, K.C.B., K.C.V.O., D.Litt., F.S.A.
Norroy and Ulster, John Phillip Brooke Brooke-Little, C.V.O., F.S.A.

Heralds

York (and Registrar), Conrad Marshall John Fisher Swan, L.V.O., PH.D., F.S.A.
Chester, David Hubert Boothby Chesshyre, F.S.A.
Windsor, Theobald David Mathew.
Richmond, Michael Maclagan, F.S.A.
Lancaster, Peter Llewellyn Gwynn-Jones.
Somerset, Thomas Woodcock.

Earl Marshal's Secretary, Sir Walter John George Verco, K.C.V.O., Surrey Herald Extraordinary.

Pursuivants

Rouge Dragon, Patric Laurence Dickinson.
Portcullis, Peter Brotherton Spurrier.
Bluemantle, Terence David McCarthy.
Rouge Croix, Henry Edgar Paston-Bedingfeld.

COURT OF THE LORD LYON
H.M. New Register House, Edinburgh EH1 3YT
[031–556 7255]

The Scottish Court of Chivalry, including the genealogical jurisdiction of the *Ri-Sennachie* of Scotland's Celtic Kings, adjudicates rights to arms and administration of *The Scottish Public Register of All Arms and Bearings* (under 1672 cap. 47) and *Public Register of All Genealogies*. The Lord Lyon presides and judicially establishes rights to existing arms or succession to Chiefship, or for cadets with scientific "differences" showing position in clan or family. Pedigrees are also established by decrees of Lyon Court, and by Letters Patent. As *Royal Commissioner in Armory*, he grants Patents of Arms (which constitute the grantee and heirs noble in the Noblesse of Scotland) to "virtuous and well-deserving" Scotsmen, and petitioners (personal or corporate) in Her Majesty's overseas realms of Scottish connection, and issues birthbrieves. In Scots Law, Arms are protected by Statute; their usurpation is punishable, and the Registration Fees of Honour on patents and matriculations are payable to H.M. Exchequer.

Lord Lyon King of Arms, Malcolm Rognvald Innes of Edingeth, c.v.o., w.s., f.s.a. *Scot.*

Heralds

Islay, John I. D. Pottinger, l.v.o.
Marchmont, Major David Maitland Maitland-Titterton, t.d., f.s.a. *Scot.*
Albany, John A. Spens, r.d., w.s.
Rothesay Extraordinary, Lt.-Col. Harold Andrew Balvaird Lawson, c.v.o.

Pursuivants

Unicorn, Sir Crispin Agnew of Lochnaw, Bt.
Dingwall, Charles J. Burnett.

Lyon Clerk and Keeper of Records, John I. D. Pottinger, l.v.o.
Procurator-Fiscal, Ivor R. Guild, w.s.
Herald Painter, Mrs. J. Phillips.
Macer, Thomas C. Gray.

ART GALLERIES, ETC.

OFFICE OF ARTS AND LIBRARIES
(*see* entry on page 425)

ARTS COUNCIL OF GREAT BRITAIN
105 Piccadilly, W1V 0AU
[01-629 9495]

The Arts Council is Great Britain's principal channel for public financial support of the arts. It funds the major arts organizations in England, the Regional Arts Associations and the Scottish and Welsh Arts Councils. It also provides a service of advice, information and help to artists, arts organizations and the general public. In addition, the Council runs the Hayward and Serpentine Galleries, the Wigmore Hall and the Poetry Library in London, organizes art exhibitions and co-ordinates tours of drama, opera, dance and contemporary music.

It is an independent body established by Royal Charter in 1946. Its aims are: (a) to develop and improve the knowledge, understanding and practice of the arts; (b) to increase the accessibility of the arts to the public throughout Great Britain; (c) to advise and co-operate with government departments, local authorities and other bodies on any matters concerned whether directly or indirectly with these aims. The arts with which the Council is mainly concerned are dance and mime, drama, literature, music and opera, and the visual arts, including photography and arts films.

The Council receives a grant-in-aid from the Government, and for the year 1985–86 the amount is £105,000,000.
Chairman, Sir William Rees-Mogg.
Secretary-General, L. Rittner.

ROYAL FINE ART COMMISSION
2 Carlton Gardens, SW1Y 5AA
[01–930 3935]

Appointed in May, 1924, "to enquire into such questions of public amenity or of artistic importance as may be referred to them from time to time by any of our Departments of State, and to report thereon to such Department; and, furthermore, to give advice on similar questions when so requested by public or quasi-public bodies, where it appears to the said Commission that their assistance would be advantageous." In August, 1933, a Royal Warrant extended the Terms of Reference of the Commission—"so that it shall also be open to the said Commission, if they so desire, to call the attention of any of Our Departments of State, or of the appropriate public or quasi-public bodies, to any project or development which in the opinion of the said Commission may appear to affect amenities of a national or public character"; in May, 1946, a Royal Warrant further extended the Terms of Reference of the Commission as follows:—

We Do give and grant unto you, or any three or more of you, full power to call before you such persons as you shall judge likely to afford you any information upon the subject of this Our Commission; and also to call for, have access to and examine all such books, documents, registers and records as may afford you the fullest information on the subject, and to inquire of and concerning the premises by all other lawful ways and means whatsoever: We Do authorize and empower you, or any three or more of you, to visit and personally inspect such places as you may deem it expedient so to inspect for the more effectual carrying out of the purposes aforesaid:

Chairman, Rt. Hon. N. St. John-Stevas, m.p., ph.d.
Commissioners, The Countess of Airlie, c.v.o.; Miss Elizabeth Chesterton, o.b.e.; Sir Anthony Cox, c.b.e.; Sir Philip Dowson, c.b.e.; Sir Ralph Freeman, c.v.o., c.b.e.; Mark Girouard, ph.d.; A. J. Gordon, c.b.e.; The Duke of Grafton, k.g., f.s.a.; R. MacCormac; P. Nuttgens, c.b.e., ph.d.; Sir David Piper, c.b.e.; Sir Philip Powell, c.h., o.b.e., r.a.; Miss W. Taylor; W. Whitfield, c.b.e.
Secretary, S. Cantacuzino.

ROYAL FINE ART COMMISSION FOR SCOTLAND
9 Atholl Crescent,
Edinburgh EH3 8HA
[031–229 1109]

Commissioners, Prof. A. J. Youngson, d.litt. (*Chairman*); Miss Louise G. Annand, m.b.e.; J. P. Boys, a.r.s.a., f.r.i.b.a.; B. Klein, c.b.e.; W. K. Mackay; Prof. I. Metzstein, a.r.s.a.; Prof. F. N. Morcos-Asaad, ph.d.; A. Morrocco, ll.d., r.s.a.; J. D. Richards, c.b.e., a.r.s.a.; R. R. Steedman, r.s.a.; Mrs. F. M. E. Walker, o.b.e., p.r.s.a., f.r.i.b.a.
Secretary, C. Prosser.

NATIONAL GALLERY
Trafalgar Square, WC2N 5DN
[01–839 3321]

Hours of opening.—Weekdays 10 to 6, Sundays 2 to 6. Closed on Good Friday, Christmas Eve, Christmas Day, Boxing Day, New Year's Day and May Day Bank Holiday.

The National Gallery was founded in 1824, following a Parliamentary grant of £60,000 for the purchase and exhibition of the Angerstein collection of pictures. The present site was first occupied in 1838 and enlarged and improved at various times throughout the years. A substantial extension to the north of the building with a public entrance in Orange Street was opened in 1975. Expenses for 1985–86 are estimated at £6,639,000.

Trustees

Hon. J. Rothschild (*Chairman*); S. Young; Miss B. Riley, C.B.E.; Hon. Sir John Baring, C.V.O.; The Marquess of Dufferin and Ava; Sir Rex Richards, F.R.S., D.Phil.; M. Sacher; Mrs. C. Hubbard; M. Cowdy.

Officers

Director, Sir Michael Levey, M.V.O., F.B.A. £32,350
Keeper and Deputy Director, A. J. W. Braham
£20,964 to £23,900
Keeper, Education and Exhibitions, A. J. W. Smith
£20,964 to £23,900
Deputy Keepers, C. P. H. Brown; M. J. Wilson
£17,051 to £21,297
Assistant Keepers, Dr. D. R. Gordon; M. J. C. Helston .... £10,317 to £18,363
Scientific Adviser, R. H. G. Thomson, C.B.E.
£20,964 to £23,900
Chief Restorer, M. H. Wyld ...... £20,964 to £23,900
Finance and Establishments, D. C. E. Gunn
£10,980 to £13,801

NATIONAL PORTRAIT GALLERY
St. Martin's Place, WC2H 0HE
[01–930 1552]

Open Monday to Friday 10 to 5. Saturday 10 to 6. Sunday 2 to 6.

The first grant was made in 1856 to form a gallery of the portraits of the most eminent persons in British history, the collections being successively housed in Great George Street, Westminster, in South Kensington, and in Bethnal Green. The present building was opened in 1896, £80,000 being contributed to its cost by Mr. W. H. Alexander; an extension erected at the expense of Lord Duveen was opened in 1933.

Chairman, The Lord Kenyon, C.B.E., F.S.A.
Trustees, The Lord President of the Council (*ex officio*); The President of the Royal Academy of Arts (*ex officio*); Prof. Sir Lawrence Gowing, C.B.E.; The Duke of Grafton, K.G., F.S.A.; J. P. Ehrman, F.B.A., F.S.A.; Sir Oliver Millar, K.C.V.O., F.B.A., F.S.A.; Prof. J. Roberts; Prof. B. R. Morris; The Rev. Prof. W. O. Chadwick, K.B.E., D.D., F.B.A.; Mrs. Susan Crosland; Prof. M. Gowing, C.B.E., F.B.A.; Sir Huw Wheldon, O.B.E., M.C.; The Marquess of Anglesey, F.S.A.; The Lord Rockley; H. Keswick.
Director, J. T. Hayes, Ph.D., F.S.A £25,533
Keeper and Deputy Director, M. Rogers, D.Phil.
£20,964 to £23,900

TATE GALLERY
Millbank, SW1P 4RG
[01–821 1313]

Hours of opening.—Weekdays 10 to 5.50. Sundays 2 to 5.50. Closed on New Year's Day, Good Friday, May Day Holiday, Christmas Eve, Christmas Day and Boxing Day.

The Tate Gallery comprises three national collec-

tions: (a) British painting of all periods; (b) modern foreign painting; (c) modern sculpture. Works are displayed at the Gallery as two collections: The British Collection, in which Hogarth, Blake, Turner, Constable and the Pre-Raphaelites are particularly well represented and the Modern Collection, which includes major works by virtually all leading artists and a fine collection of contemporary prints. There is an almost continuous programme of major loan exhibitions, and free lectures, films and guided tours are offered nearly every day throughout the year. The Gallery was opened in 1897, the cost of erection (£80,000) being defrayed by Sir Henry Tate, who also contributed the nucleus of the present collection. The Turner Wing, built at the expense of Sir Joseph Duveen was opened in 1920. Lord Duveen defrayed the cost of galleries to contain the collection of modern foreign painting, completed in 1926, and a new sculpture hall, completed in 1937. The latest and largest extension to the Tate Gallery was opened by Her Majesty Queen Elizabeth II on May 24, 1979. This extension, costing £3,200,000, has increased the public areas of the Gallery 50 per cent and also includes purpose-built accommodation for the Conservation Department and the Photographic Department, and extra accommodation for the reserve collection. The Clore Gallery for the Turner Collection is being built adjoining the Tate Gallery and is due to open in 1986. Nearly £6,000,000 is being donated from the Clore Foundation. Expenses for 1985–86 are estimated at £5,645,000.

Director, A. Bowness, C.B.E. £30,865
Trustees, R. Rogers (*Chairman*); P. Palumbo; The Countess of Airlie, C.V.O.; A. Caro, C.B.E.; G. de Botton; J. Golding; P. Heron, C.B.E.; Sir Rex Richards, D.SC., F.R.S.; M. Weinberg; Mrs. C. Hubbard.
Keeper of the British Collection, M. R. F. Butlin
£22,329 to £25,260
Keeper of the Modern Collection, R. E. Alley
£22,329 to £25,260
Keeper of Museum Services, M. G. Compton
£22,329 to £25,260
Keeper of Conservation, The Viscount Dunluce
£22,329 to £25,260
Deputy Keepers, R. E. Morphet; L. A. Parris; Miss R. Rattenbury; R. Perry .... £18,416 to £19,728
Administration Officer, R. Aylward
£14,873 to £19,728

WALLACE COLLECTION
Hertford House, Manchester Square, W1M 6BN
[01–935 0687]

Admission free. Open on weekdays 10 a.m. to 5 p.m.: Sundays 2 p.m. to 5 p.m. Closed on Good Friday, December 24–26, January 1 and May Day.

The Wallace Collection was bequeathed to the nation by the widow of Sir Richard Wallace, Bt., K.C.B., M.P., on her death in 1897, and Hertford House was subsequently acquired by the Government. The collection includes pictures, drawings and miniatures, French furniture, sculpture, bronzes, porcelain, armour and miscellaneous *objets d'art*. The total net expenses were estimated at £877,000 in 1985–86.

Director, J. A. S. Ingamells.
Assistants to Director, P. Hughes; Miss R. J. Savill.
Establishment and Finance Officer, A. W. Houldershaw.

NATIONAL GALLERIES OF SCOTLAND
The Mound, Edinburgh EH2 2EL
[031–556 8921]

Director, T. Clifford £25,533
Trustees, R. W. Begg, C.B.E., (*Chairman*); The Marquess of Bute; Prof. H. A. D. Miles; J. Notman; Prof. M. Kemp; J. Knox.

Restorer, J. P. Dick .... £17,051 to £21,297
Curator of Education and Information, vacant
£12,066 to £18,363
Secretary, J. Gordon .... £10,980 to £13,801
Comprising:

National Gallery of Scotland
The Mound, Edinburgh
[031–556 8921]

Open: Monday to Saturday 10 to 5; Sunday 2 to 5;
Closed 25, 26, 27, 31 December; 1, 2, 3 January.
Keeper, H. Macandrew .... £17,051 to £21,297
Assistant Keepers, M. Clarke (£10,317 to £13,801);
Miss L. M. Errington, ph.d. (£17,066 to £18,363).
Keeper of Prints and Drawings, K. K. Andrews
£17,051 to £21,297

Scottish National Portrait Gallery
1 Queen Street, Edinburgh
[031–556 8921]

Hours—as for National Gallery of Scotland.
Keeper, D. Thomson, ph.d. ...... £17,051 to £21,297
Assistant Keepers, Miss R. K. Marshall, ph.d.; J. E.
Holloway .... £17,066 to £18,363

Scottish National Gallery of Modern Art
Belford Road, Edinburgh EH4 3DR
[031 556 8921]

Hours—as for National Gallery of Scotland.
Keeper, W. D. Hall .... £20,964 to £23,900
Assistant Keeper, K. S. Hartley .. £17,066 to £18,363

(For other British Art Galleries, *see* Index.)

ASSOCIATED BRITISH PORTS
150 Holborn, EC1N 2LR
[01-430 1177]

Constituted under the Transport Act, 1981. A.B.P.
owns and operates 19 active ports and traffic through
them in 1984 totalled 81,941,000 tonnes. Net registered tonnage of shipping entering and leaving the
ports in 1984 totalled 123,150,000 tons and passengers
in transit totalled 2,540,000. Net loss, before tax,
1984, £6,423,000.
Chairman, J. K. Stuart £58,749
Deputy Chairman, Sir Charles Ball.
Deputy Chairman and Joint Managing Director, D.
Stringer, o.b.e.
Joint Managing Director, J. Williams.

UNITED KINGDOM ATOMIC ENERGY
AUTHORITY
11 Charles II Street, SW1Y 4QP
[01–930 5454]

Established by the Atomic Energy Authority Act,
1954, the Authority is responsible for providing
research and development support for the U.K.
nuclear power programme. It also undertakes work
on other civil applications of nuclear energy and on
various projects outside the nuclear field on repayment. The UKAEA has eight laboratories and a
London headquarters employing some 14,000 people.
The total annual operating expenditure is some
£400m.
Chairman, A. Allen, c.b.e. £54,340
Deputy Chairman and Chief Executive, (vacant).
Members (*Full-time*), Dr. T. N. Marsham, c.b.e.; Dr.
L. E. J. Roberts, c.b.e., f.r.s. £41,500

(*Part-time*) Sir Peter Hirsch, f.r.s.; Sir John Mc-
Farlane Boyd, c.b.e.; Prof. N. L. Franklin, c.b.e.,
f.r.s.; J. Bullock; R. E. J. Roberts; C. Allday, c.b.e.;
Sir Alan Cottrell, f.r.s.; M. J. B. Parker (*each
£4,675*); F. E. Bonner, c.b.e.; I. T. Manley, c.b. (*each
unpaid*).
Secretary, R. L. R. Nicholson.

THE BANK OF ENGLAND
Threadneedle Street, EC2R 8AH

The Bank of England was incorporated in 1694
under Royal Charter. It is the banker of the
Government on whose behalf it manages the Note
Issue and the National Debt. As central reserve bank
of the country, the Bank keeps the accounts of British
banks, who maintain with it a proportion of their
cash resources, and of most overseas central banks.
Governor, R. Leigh-Pemberton.
Deputy Governor, C. W. McMahon.
Directors, Dr. D. V. Atterton, c.b.e.; Hon. Sir John
Baring, c.v.o.; G. Blunden; Sir Adrian Cadbury;
F. B. Corby; G. A. Drain, c.b.e.; R. D. Galpin; E. A.
J. George; Prof. B. Griffiths; Sir Robert Haslam;
Sir Hector Laing; A. D. Loehnis; A. Lord, c.b.; The
Lord Nelson of Stafford; D. G. Scholey, c.b.e.; D. A.
Walker.
Associate Director, Banking Supervision, W. P. Cooke.
Adviser to the Governor, Economics, J. S. Flemming.
Assistant Directors, M. J. Balfour; A. L. Coleby; D.
A. Dawkins; B. Quinn; C. J. Farrow.
Chief Adviser, D. G. Holland, c.m.g.
Chief of Banking Department (*Chief Cashier*), D. H.
F. Somerset.
Chief Registrar, J. G. Drake.
General Manager, Printing Works, G. L. Wheatley.
Secretary, P. E. Towndrow.
Head of Information Division, P. H. Kent.
The Auditor, L. G. Lloyd.

(For "Banking" section *see* Index.)

BOUNDARY COMMISSIONS

The Commissions are constituted under the House
of Commons (Redistribution of Seats) Act 1949 as
amended by the House of Commons (Redistribution
of Seats) Act 1958. The Speaker of the House of
Commons is ex-officio chairman of all four Commissions in the United Kingdom. Each of the four
Commissions is required by law to keep the parliamentary constituencies in their part of the United
Kingdom under review. Each of the three Commissions in Great Britain is required by law to keep the
European Assembly constituencies in their part of
Great Britain under review.

England
St. Catherines House, 10 Kingsway, WC2B 6JP
[01–242 0262]

Deputy Chairman, The Hon. Mr. Justice Walton.
Joint Secretaries, G. P. Barnes and A. N. Pickersgill.

Wales
St. Catherines House, 10 Kingsway, WC2B 6JP
[01–242 0262]

Deputy Chairman, The Hon. Mr. Justice Kenneth
Jones.
Joint Secretaries, G. P. Barnes and A. N. Pickersgill.

Scotland
St. Andrew's House, Edinburgh EH1 3DE
[031–556 8501]

Deputy Chairman, The Hon. Lord Ross.
Secretary, A. Simmen.

Northern Ireland
c/o Northern Ireland Office,
Whitehall, SW1A 2AZ
[01–273 5480]

Deputy Chairman, The Hon. Mr. Justice Hutton.
Secretary, G. D. Fergusson.

BRITISH AEROSPACE p.l.c.
Headquarters: Brooklands Road, Weybridge,
Surrey, KT13 OSJ
[0932 53444]

100 Pall Mall, SW1Y 5HR
[01–930 1020]

British Aerospace was formed in 1977 by the merging of the British Aircraft Corporation, Scottish Aviation, and the aircraft and dynamics divisions of Hawker Siddeley as a then nationalised industry. The company was denationalised in 1981 with H.M. Government retaining a 48% shareholding. The U.K. arm of Sperry Gyroscope was later acquired. The fully privatised status was achieved in the spring of 1985 when H.M. Government's shareholding was sold in conjunction with a substantial rights issue.

British Aerospace is primarily engaged in the design, development, production and sale of military and civil aircraft, guided weapons and space systems, in electronics and related technologies and in the provision of support services.

Employing over 75,000 people in the U.K. and overseas British Aerospace is one of the largest U.K. exporters of manufactured goods with customers worldwide and collaborative agreements in 19 countries. British Aerospace has subsidiary companies in the U.S.A. and Australia.

Chairman, Sir Austin Pearce, C.B.E., Ph.D.
Managing Director and Chief Executive, Sir Raymond Lygo, K.C.B.
Deputy Managing Directors, I. R. Yates, C.B.E. (*Aircraft*); H. Metcalfe, O.B.E. (*Dynamics*).
Finance Director, B. E. Friend.
Secretary and Legal Adviser, B. Cookson.
Corporate Executive Public Affairs, D. Mc Clen.

BRITISH AIRPORTS AUTHORITY
Head Office: Gatwick Airport, W. Sussex RH6 0HZ
[0293 517755]

Set up under the *Airports Authority Acts*, 1965 and 1975, the Authority owns and manages seven major airports—Heathrow, Gatwick, Stansted, Glasgow, Prestwick, Edinburgh and Aberdeen. The Authority's total assets are £1,179,200,000.
Chairman, Sir Norman Payne, C.B.E. £56,600
Managing Director, J. Mulkern.

BRITISH AIRWAYS p.l.c.
Speedbird House, Heathrow Airport (London),
Middlesex TW6 2JA [01–759 5511]

Pursuant to the Civil Aviation Act, 1980 and the Orders made thereunder, the undertaking of British Airways Board became vested in British Airways p.l.c. as from April 1, 1984. British Airways has four main subsidiary companies: British Airways Helicopters, British Airways Engine Overhaul, British Airtours and British Airways Tour Operations Ltd.

British Airways has 196 aircraft in service (165 fixed wing and 31 helicopters), and at the operating level, the provisional and unaudited results for the year to March 31, 1985, showed a surplus before interest and other charges of £315 million. The audited result in the previous year was a profit of £313 million.
Chairman, The Lord King of Wartnaby, C.B.E.
Chief Executive, C. M. Marshall.

BRITISH BROADCASTING CORPORATION
Broadcasting House, W1A 1AA
[01–580 4468]

The BBC was incorporated under Royal Charter as successor to the British Broadcasting Company, Ltd., whose licence expired Dec. 31, 1926. Its present Charter came into force Aug. 1, 1981, for 15 years. The Chairman, Vice-Chairman and other Governors are appointed by the Queen in Council. The BBC is financed by revenue from receiving licences for the Home services and by a Grant in Aid from Parliament for the External services. The total number of receiving licences in the U.K. at March 31, 1985 was 18,715,937, of which 2,896,263 were for monochrome receivers and 15,819,674 for colour receivers. Annual television fees are: monochrome £18; colour £58.

Board of Governors

Chairman, S. Young. £28,408
Vice-Chairman, Sir William Rees-Mogg. £7,235
Governors, The Lady Faulkner of Downpatrick (*N. Ireland*) (£7,235); W. Peat, C.B.E. (*Scotland*) (£7,235); A. Roberts (*Wales*) (£7,235); Miss D. M. S. D. Park, C.M.G., O.B.E.; Sir John Johnston, G.C.M.G., K.C.V.O.; Miss J. Barrow, O.B.E.; Sir John Boyd, C.B.E.; M. McAlpine; The Lady Parkes; The Earl of Harewood .... (*each*) £3,620

Board of Management

Director-General, A. D. G. Milne.
Deputy Director-General, M. Checkland.
Managing Directors, A. S. Kark (*External Services*); R. T. L. Francis (*Radio*); W. F. Cotton, O.B.E. (*Television*).
Assistant Director-General, A. Protheroe, M.B.E., T.D.
Directors, G. Buck (*Finance*); T. B. McCrirrick (*Engineering*); J. F. Wilkinson (*Public Affairs*); B. G. Wenham (*Programmes, Television*); C. Martin (*Personnel*).

Other Senior Staff

Deputy Managing Director, Radio, C. J. McLelland.
Deputy Managing Director, External Services, C. Bell.
Deputy Director of Engineering, G. Cook.
Deputy Director of Personnel, R. Chase.
General Manager, Publications, J. G. Holmes.
Legal Adviser, A. Jennings.
Chief Assistant to Director-General, Margaret Douglas.
Secretary, D. Holmes.
Managing Director, B.B.C. Enterprises, B. Parkin.
Controller BBC-1, M. Grade.
Controller BBC-2, G. McDonald.
Controller Radio 1, J. Beerling.
Controller Radio 2, B. Marriot.
Controller Radio 3, I. McIntyre.
Controller Radio 4, D. Hatch.
Controller Information Services, M. Bunce.
Deputy Secretary, Patricia Hodgson.

Controllers of Regional Offices

English Regions, M. Alder, Broadcasting Centre, Pebble Mill Road, Birmingham.
Scotland, P. E. B. Chalmers, Broadcasting House, Queen Margaret Drive, Glasgow.
Wales, S. G. Jones, Broadcasting House, Llantrisant Road, Llandaff, Cardiff.
Northern Ireland, J. S. Hawthorne, C.B.E., Broadcasting House, 25–27 Ormeau Avenue, Belfast.

THE BRITISH COUNCIL
10 Spring Gardens, SW1A 2BN
[01–930 8466]

The British Council was established in 1934 and incorporated by Royal Charter in 1940. Its principal aims and functions are: to promote a wider knowledge of Britain and the English language abroad, to develop closer cultural relations between Britain and other countries and to administer educational aid programmes. The Council receives grants from the Foreign and Commonwealth Office and the Overseas Development Administration (estimated for 1985/86 at £83,900,000); acts as the agent of the Overseas Development Administration in specific aid programmes (totalling £64,800,000); as the agent of the Foreign and Commonwealth Office in specific student support programmes (£8,300,000); and gains, from sources other than the British taxpayer, earnings from English language teaching, paid educational services, and acting for international organizations, including U.N. agencies (£43,800,000).

Chairman, Sir David Orr, M.C.
Director-General, Sir John Burgh, K.C.M.G., C.B.

BRITISH RAILWAYS BOARD
Euston Square, P.O. Box 100, NW1 2DZ
[01–262 3232]

The British Railways Board came into being on Jan. 1, 1963 under the terms of the Transport Act, 1962. The Board became responsible for the provision of railway services in Great Britain and for associated shipping, hotel, catering and other services formerly carried on by the British Transport Commission.

Chairman, Sir Robert Reid, C.B.E. £66,800
Deputy Chairman, Sir Richard Cave, M.C. (part-time).
Vice-Chairmen, D. Fowler, C.B.E.; G. Myers, C.B.E.
Members, S. D. Jenkins*; Prudence Leith*; H. R. Macleod*; J. J. O'Brien; A. Sheppard.*
  * Part-time members, paid *pro rata*.
Secretary, J. Batley.

BRITISH SHIPBUILDERS
Headquarters: Benton House, 136 Sandyford Road, Newcastle upon Tyne, NE2 1QE
[0632 326772]

Established under the Aircraft and Shipbuilding Industries Act of 1977, British Shipbuilders is a national corporation responsible for all publicly-owned shipyards, etc. in England and Scotland.
Chairman and Chief Executive, J. G. Day.
Corporation Secretary, P. C. M. Thompson.

BRITISH STANDARDS INSTITUTION
British Standards House, 2 Park Street, W.1
[Enquiry Section: B.S.I., Linford Wood, Milton Keynes, MK14 6LE. Tel. 0908 320066]

The British Standards Institution is the recognized authority in the U.K. for the preparation and publication of national standards for industrial and consumer products. The Institution originated in 1901, when the Institutions of Civil, Mechanical and Electrical Engineers, together with the Iron and Steel Institute and the Institution of Naval Architects, formed a joint Engineering Standards Committee—which subsequently became the British Engineering Standards Association. A Royal Charter was granted in 1929 and with the extension of the scope of the organization to include the building, chemical and textile industries its title was later changed to "British Standards Institution".

The Institution, in consultation with the interests concerned, now prepares standards relating to nearly every sector of the nation's industry and trade. There are over 9,500 British Standards covering specifications of quality, construction dimensions,

performance or safety; methods of test and analysis; glossaries of terms; and codes of practice. Over 600 new and revised British Standards are published each year.

British Standards are issued for voluntary adoption though in a number of cases compliance with a British Standard is required by legislation. The Institution operates certification schemes under which industrial and consumer products are certified as complying with the relevant British Standard and manufacturers satisfying the requirements of such schemes may use the Institution's certification trade marks known as the "Kitemark" and the "Safety Mark". Other testing and certification services, together with information services, are available to industry, including help in meeting technical requirements in export markets.

The Institution is financed by voluntary subscriptions, an annual Government grant, the sale of its publications and fees for testing and certification. There are more than 17,000 subscribing members of B.S.I.

Director General, D. G. Spickernell, C.B.

BRITISH STEEL CORPORATION
9 Albert Embankment, SE1 7SN
[01–735 7654]

The British Steel Corporation was established under the Iron and Steel Act 1967 which vested in the Corporation the shares of the fourteen major steel companies. The Corporation's main duty is to supply such iron and steel products as it thinks fit in sufficient quantities and at such prices as will meet reasonable demand.

Chairman, Sir Robert Haslam.
Deputy Chairman and Chief Executive, R. Scholey, C.B.E.
Members (full-time), Dr. D. Grieves; M. E. Llowarch; G. H. Sambrook; J. G. Stewart.
Members (part-time), Sir John Boyd, C.B.E.; The Lord Gregson; S. J. Gross, C.M.G.; R. Halstead, C.B.E.; I. K. MacGregor; A. E. Wheatley.
Secretary, I. M. P. Evans.

BRITISH TECHNOLOGY GROUP
101 Newington Causeway, SE1 6BU
[01–403 6666]

British Technology Group (BTG) is the name under which the National Research Development Corporation and the National Enterprise Board have been co-operating since 1981. BTG's primary function is to promote the development and commercialization of technology derived from U.K. public sector sources, i.e. universities, polytechnics, research councils, government research establishments and other public bodies. BTG takes responsibility for protecting and licensing inventions from these sources, provides funds for development, seeks licensees and negotiates licence agreements with industry. The general aim is to ensure that maximum advantage is taken of the commercial potential of successful U.K. research and development.

Chairman, C. Barker.

BRITISH TELECOM
(*see* Index for entry)

BRITISH TOURIST AUTHORITY
Thames Tower, Black's Road, W6 9EL
[01–846 9000]

Under the Development of Tourism Act, 1969, four co-equal statutory Tourist Boards were established: the British Tourist Authority, the English Tourist Board, the Scottish Tourist Board and the Wales Tourist Board. Each is financed mainly by direct grant-in-aid from Government and is an independent statutory body. The British Tourist Authority has specific responsibility for promoting tourism to Great Britain from overseas. It also has a general responsibility for tourism within Great Britain as a whole.

Chairman, D. R. Y. Bluck, O.B.E. (*part-time*).
Director General, L. J. Lickorish, C.B.E.

English Tourist Board

Thames Tower, Black's Road, W6 9EL

Scottish Tourist Board

23, Ravelston Terrace, Edinburgh

Wales Tourist Board

3 Castle Street, Cardiff

BRITISH WATERWAYS BOARD

Melbury House, Melbury Terrace, NW1 6JX
[01–262 6711]

Chairman, Sir Leslie Young, C.B.E. (*part-time*).
Vice-Chairman, Dr. A. Robertson, C.B.E.
Members (all part-time), P. R. Lisle, O.B.E.; J. Weston; Rear Admiral D. A. Dunbar-Nasmith; M. Everard; H. G. C. Aldous.
Chief Executive, D. G. McCance.
Secretary and Deputy Chief Executive, T. T. Luckcuck.

BRITOIL p.l.c.

150 St. Vincent Street, Glasgow G2 5LJ
[041–204 2525]

Chairman, Sir Philip Shelbourne.
Chief Executive, D. Walker.
Joint Managing Directors, I. Clark; M. Ford.
Executive Directors, J. Evans; M. Kelly; R. Speirs; Sir Archie Lamb, K.B.E.

CABINET OFFICE

The Cabinet Office comprises the Secretariat, who support Ministers collectively in the conduct of Cabinet business; the Management and Personnel Office (M.P.O.) which is responsible for the management and organization of the Civil Service and recruitment into it, training, efficiency, personnel management and senior appointments; the Central Statistical Office; and the Historical Section. Other functions are from time to time laid on the Office, some ephemerally and some permanently. Non-departmental Ministers may be attached to the Office.

The functions of the Cabinet Office (M.P.O.) are in support of the Prime Minister in her capacity as Minister for the Civil Service, with responsibility for day-to-day supervision delegated to the Chancellor of the Duchy of Lancaster.

The Prime Minister.
Principal Private Secretary to the Prime Minister, F. E. R. Butler.
Private Secretaries to the Prime Minister, C. Powell (*Overseas Affairs*); A. Turnbull (*Economic Affairs*); T. J. Flesher (*Parliamentary Affairs*); M. E. Addison (*Home Affairs and Diary*).
Personal Assistant to the Prime Minister, Mrs. C. M. Ryder.
Secretary for Appointments, J. R. Catford.
Political Secretary, S. Sherbourne.
Foreign Affairs Adviser, Sir Percy Cradock, G.C.M.G.
Adviser on Efficiency, Sir Robin Ibbs.
Policy Unit, J. Redwood; Hon. C. Monckton; N. C. Owen; D. Willets; P. T. Warry; J. B. Wybrew; O. Letwin; D. Hobson.
Chief Press Secretary, B. Ingham.
Deputy Chief Press Secretary, Miss J. Caines.
Assistant Private Secretaries to Prime Minister, Miss J. Drever; Mrs J. Cole.
Parliamentary Private Secretary, The Rt. Hon. M. Alison, M.P.
Secretary to the Cabinet and Head of Home Civil Service, Sir Robert Armstrong, G.C.B., C.V.O.   £63,125

SECRETARIAT

70 Whitehall, SW1A 2AS
[01–233 3000]

Second Permanent Secretary (*G1A*), The Rt. Hon. Sir Antony Duff, G.C.M.G., C.V.O., D.S.O., D.S.C.   £48,500
Deputy Secretaries (*G2*), Sir Colin Figures, K.C.M.G., O.B.E.; Sir Robin Nicholson; C.L.G. Mallaby, C.M.G.; J. B. Unwin; D. F. Williamson, C.B.
                              £38,325 to £39,250
Under Secretaries (*G3*), C. J. S. Brearley; A. J. Wiggins, D. E. J. Jago; G. Stapleton; M. R. Morland. . . . .   £30,975 to £31,750
Assistant Secretaries (*G5*), Brig. J. A. J. Budd; H. Burke; D. R. C. Christopher; J. B. Donnelly; J. R. Fonblanque; Brig. C. L. G. G. Henshaw; J. James; M. H. Jay; J. M. Mackintosh, C.M.G.; D. K. A. Reynolds; M. W. Townley; R. Watson
                              £20,964 to £25,533
Senior Principal (*G6*), J. L. Wright, O.B.E.
                              £17,000 to £22,926

MANAGEMENT AND PERSONNEL OFFICE

Great George Street, SW1P 3AL
[01–233 3000]

Second Permanent Secretary (*G1A*), Miss A. E. Mueller, C.B. £48,500
Director, Top Management Programme (*Deputy Secretary*) (*G2*), J. F. Mayne . . . . . . £38,325 to £39,250
Security Adviser, Air Vice Marshal B. G. Lock, C.B., C.B.E., A.F.C.

Senior and Public Appointment, Conduct, Machinery of Government

Director, Public Appointments Unit (*Under Secretary*) (*G3*), C. V. Peterson, C.V.O. . . . . . . £30,975 to £31,750
Assistant Secretaries (*G5*), Ms. E. C. Turton; G. T. Morgan; G. J. Court . . . . £20,964 to £25,533

Security Division

Assistant Secretary, S. R. Davie.

Management and Efficiency

Under Secretary (*G3*), I. B. Beesley
                              £30,975 to £31,750
Assistant Secretaries (*G5*), K. Chivers; Miss K. Jenkins . . . . £20,964 to £25,533
Senior Principal (*G6*), E. Brown . . £17,000 to £22,926

Personnel Management

Under Secretary (*G3*), J. A. Chilcot
                              £30,975 to £31,750
Assistant Secretaries (*G5*), D. P. Laughrin; P. D. Ewins; C. D. Stevens . . . . £20,964 to £25,533

Central Unit on Purchasing

Director, M. J. O. Willacy.
Deputy Director (*G5*), R. B. Brown
                              £20,964 to £25,533

Joint Management Unit

Grade 3, Mrs. V. Strachan . . . . £30,975 to £31,750

Training and Civil Service College

Sunningdale Park, Ascot, Berks SL5 0QE
[0990 23444]
London: 11 Belgrave Road, SW1V 1RB
[01-834 6644]

Principal (*G3*), N. E. A. Moore . . . £30,975 to £31,750
Head of Training Division (*Assistant Secretary*) (*G5*), P. R. Coster . . . . £20,964 to £25,533
College Secretary (*Assistant Secretary*) (*G5*), vacant
                              £20,964 to £25,533
Directors (*Assistant Secretaries*) (*G5*), P. Hearson; E. J. Henstridge; R. J. Eason; G. Gammon; Dr. P. Lund . . . . £20,964 to £25,533

Civil Service Commission
Alencon Link, Basingstoke, Hants. RG21 1JB
[0256 29222]

First Commissioner (Deputy Secretary) (G2), D. J. Trevelyan, C.B. . . . . £38,325 to £39,250
Commissioners (Under Secretaries) (G3), E. J. Morgan (*Director, Civil Service Selection Board*), N. B. J. Gurney . . . . £30,975 to £31,750
Commissioners (part-time), N. Johnson; Dr. J. S. MacFarlane.
Assistant Secretary (G5), A. W. Duncan
£20,964 to £25,533
Senior Principals (G6), J. D. Diston; P. J. Wiggett; A. Halford; R. Payne . . . . £17,000 to £22,926

Civil Service Selection Board
Kirkland House, 22 Whitehall, SW1A 2ED

Director (Under Secretary) (G3), E. J. Morgan
£30,975 to £31,750
Deputy Director (G5), G. H. Wollen
£20,964 to £25,533
Chief Psychologist (Senior Principal Psychologist), D. J. McLeod.

Medical Advisory Service
Tilbury House, Petty France, SW1H 9EU
[01-213 3000]

Medical Adviser, Dr. A. M. Semmence.
Principal Medical Officers, Dr. P. J. Constable; Dr. M. L. E. Espir.

CENTRAL STATISTICAL OFFICE
Great George Street, SW1P 3AQ
[01-233 3000]

Director and Head of the Government Statistical Service, J. Hibbert £48,500
Private Secretary, Mrs. C. D. Bates.
Under Secretaries (G3), D. W. Flaxen; M. J. M. Erritt; J. D. Wells . . . . £30,975 to £31,750
Assistant Secretaries (G5), P. Altobell; Miss S. P. Carter; A. A. Croxford; T. J. Griffin; P. B. Kenny; K. Mansell; D. Ramprakash; R. G. Ward; Dr. J. H. Ludley.

HISTORICAL SECTION
Hepburn House, Marsham Street, SW1P 4HW
[01-211 6605]

Departmental Records Adviser (Senior Principal) (G6), Mrs. H. E. Forbes.

ESTABLISHMENT OFFICER'S GROUP

Principal Establishment and Finance Officer, Under Secretary (G3), J. W. Stevens . . £30,975 to £31,750
Deputy Establishment Officer (G5), A. Phillips
£20,964 to £25,533

Finance

Senior Finance Officer (Senior Principal) (G6), C. J. Parry . . . . £17,000 to £22,926

Information Services

Chief Press Officer (Senior Principal) (G6), J. Stubbs
£17,000 to £22,926

Internal Audit

Principal, A. Holman.

CABLE AUTHORITY
Gillingham House, 38–44 Gillingham Street, SW1V 1HU
[01-821 6161]

The Cable Authority is the statutory body established by the Cable and Broadcasting Act, 1984 to grant franchises for the operation of new cable systems and to licence and regulate the provision of cable programme services.
Chairman, R. Burton.
Deputy Chairman, Prof. J. Ring, C.B.E.
Members, Mrs. A. Ballard; P. Johnson; Mrs. E. MacDonald-Brown; P. Paine, C.B.E., D.F.C.
Director-General, J. Davey.
Director of Finance and Operations, K. Miles.
Director of Services, K. Morrison.

CHARITY COMMISSION
Ryder Street, St. James's, SW1Y 6AH
[01-214 6000]
Northern Office:
Graeme House, Derby Square, Liverpool L2 7SB
[051-227 3191]
Central Register of Charities,
St. Alban's House, Haymarket, SW1Y 4QX
[01-214 6000]

The Charity Commission was constituted under Act of Parliament in 1853 and reconstituted under the Charities Act, 1960, with the general function of promoting the effective use of charitable monies and a duty to keep a register of charities in England and Wales. The Official Custodian for Charities holds investments for charities and remits the income, free of income tax, to trustees.

Chief Commissioner, D. A. Peach £32,350
Commissioners, C. A. H. Parsons; F. W. Trinder.
Deputy Commissioners, R. W. Groves; J. Farquharson; M. A. Rao; J. F. Claricoat; Mrs. J. F. R. Quint; G. S. Goodchild . . . . £20,964 to £25,533
Assist. Commissioners, Mrs. F. E. Middleton; H. K. Udvadia; Mrs. H. M. Phillips; Miss D. F. Taylor; S. K. Sen; J. A. Dutton; K. M. Dibble; P. P. White; N. M. Mackenzie; D. C. Raikes; R. W. Tomlinson
£15,688 to £21,297
Secretary and Asst. Commissioner, D. Forrest
£20,964 to £25,533
Principals, R. E. Hatton (*Asst. Commissioner*); D. McNaught (*Asst. Commissioner*); Miss S. M. St. C. Smith (*Asst. Commissioner*); J. H. Vining
£13,508 to £18,363
Official Custodian for Charities, S. H. Way
£17,000 to £22,926
Deputy Official Custodian, R. J. Crick
£13,508 to £18,363
Establishment Officer, J. M. Samuels
£13,508 to £18,363

CHURCH COMMISSIONERS
1 Millbank, SW1P 3JZ
[01-222 7010]

The Church Commissioners were established on April 1, 1948, by the amalgamation of *Queen Anne's Bounty* (established 1704) and the *Ecclesiastical Commissioners* (established 1836).

The Commissioners' main task is to improve the stipends and housing of the Church of England clergy and to provide them and their widows with adequate pensions and assistance with housing in retirement. They also carry out administrative duties in connection with pastoral reorganization and redundant churches, and have been designated by the General Synod as the Central Stipends Authority of the Church of England.

The Commissioners' income for the year ended Dec. 31, 1984, was derived from the following sources:—

	£'s million
Stock exchange investments	35·4
Land and property	40·9
Mortgages, loans, etc.	7·3
Trust income, and diocesan/parish contributions for stipends	42·8
	£126·4

This income was applied as follows:—

Clergy stipends	74·9
Clergy and widows' pensions	28·0
Clergy houses	9·1
Episcopal administration and payments to Chapters	4·3
Church buildings	2·5
Administrative expenses of the Commissioners and related bodies	7·3
	£126·1

Constitution

The 2 Archbishops, the 41 diocesan Bishops, 5 deans or provosts, 10 other clergy and 10 laymen appointed by the General Synod; 4 laymen nominated by the Queen; 4 persons nominated by the Archbishop of Canterbury; The Lord Chancellor; The Lord President of the Council; the First Lord of the Treasury; The Chancellor of the Exchequer; The Secretary of State for the Home Dept; The Speaker of the House of Commons; The Lord Chief Justice; The Master of the Rolls; The Attorney-General; The Solicitor-General; The Lord Mayor and two Aldermen of the City of London; The Lord Mayor of York and one representative from each of the Universities of Oxford and Cambridge.

Church Estates Commissioners

First, Sir Douglas Lovelock, K.C.B.
Second, Sir William van Straubenzee, M.B.E., M.P.
Third, Mrs. B. E. Haworth.

Officers

Secretary, J. E. Shelley.
Private Secretary, A. D. Guthrie-Jones.
Deputy Secretary, P. Locke.
Assistant Secretaries, D. I. Archer (*Chief Accountant*); J. R. Beard (*Estates*); C. P. Canton (*Establishment Officer*); J. M. Davies (*Redundant Churches*); D. J. Day (*Pastoral*); M. D. Elengorn (*Stipends*); J. W. Ferguson (*Computer*); D. N. Goodwin (*Houses*); W. J. Pennel (*Bishoprics*); vacant (*Investments*).
Deputy Accountant and Trust Officer, G. C. Baines.
Deputy Estates Secretary, P. H. P. Shaw, L.V.O.
Deputy Establishment Officer, Mrs. B. A. Bartlett.
Computer Manager, J. W. Ferguson.
Press & Information Officer, J. C. Reddington.
Principals, A. W. Atkins; W. R. Herbert; M. J. Symon; R. M. Hutchings; E. G. Peacock; Miss A. M. Mackie.

Legal Department

Official Solicitor, E. W. Wills.
Deputy Solicitor, A. J. L. Campbell.
Assistant Solicitor, J. P. Guy.
Senior Legal Assistants, Miss J. M. Bland; J. D. Carter; Rev. B. G. Hall; Miss S. M. S. Jones; R. D. C. Murray; Mrs. S. E. Prosser; Miss I. E. Slaughter.

Main Agents

Messrs. Cluttons, 5 Great College Street, Westminster, S.W.1; Messrs. Smiths Gore, The King's Lodgings, Minster Precincts, Peterborough; Messrs. Chestertons, 40 Connaught Street, W.2. and 26 Clifton Road, W.9.

CIVIL AVIATION AUTHORITY
C.A.A. House, 45–59 Kingsway, WC2B 6TE
[01–379 7311]

Chairman, J. Dent, C.B.E. (*part-time*) £38,000
Managing Director, J. L. Curle.
Secretary, Miss G. M. E. White.

COMMONWEALTH DEVELOPMENT CORPORATION
33 Hill Street, W1A 3AR
[01–629 8484]

The Corporation's area of operations covers Commonwealth countries which have achieved independence since 1948, the remaining territories dependent upon Britain and, with Ministerial approval, any other developing country. The Corporation is authorized to borrow up to £750,000,000.
Chairman (part-time), The Lord Kindersley.
Deputy Chairman (part-time), Sir Colin Campbell, Bt., M.C.
Members (part-time), H.R.H. The Prince of Wales; J. M. Clay; C. F. Sedcole; Mrs. A. Wright; V. Robertson, O.B.E.; D. Warburton.
General Manager, J. D. Eccles, C.B.E.

COMMONWEALTH OFFICE
See **Foreign and Commonwealth Office**

COMMONWEALTH SECRETARIAT
(*see* p. 694)

COUNTRYSIDE COMMISSION
John Dower House, Crescent Place,
Cheltenham, Glos. GL50 3RA
[0242 521381]

The Countryside Commission is an independent agency set up in 1968 to promote the conservation and enhancement of landscape beauty in England and Wales, to encourage the provision and improvement of facilities in the countryside for enjoyment, including the need to secure access for open air recreation. Since April 1982 the Commission has been funded by annual grant from the Department of the Environment. Its executive powers and responsibilities are defined under the Countryside Act, 1949, the Local Government Act, 1974 and the Wildlife & Countryside Act, 1981. Members of the Commission are appointed by the Secretary of State for the Environment and the Secretary of State for Wales acting jointly.
Chairman, Sir Derek Barber £14,957
Deputy Chairman, (vacant).
Director, A. A. C. Phillips.................. £29,500
Assistant Directors, R. Clarke (*Policy*); M. J. Kirby (*Regions*) .... £20,964 to £25,533
National Heritage Adviser, Mrs. M. D. Laverack
£17,000 to £22,926
Secretary, M. J. Burchell .... £13,508 to £18,363
Head of Conservation Branch, M. E. Taylor
£13,508 to £18,363

Head of Recreation & Access Branch, J. W. B. Worth
.... £13,508 to £18,363
Head of Communications Branch, M. H. Glen
.... £13,508 to £18,363
Regional Officers, C. G. Coggins (*Newcastle*); B. Walbank (*Cambridge*); Dr. S. A. Bucknall (*Leeds*); R. J. Lloyd (*Bristol*); R. T. Thomas (*Manchester*); D. E. Coleman (*London*); F. S. Walmsley (*Birmingham*) .... £13,508 to £18,363

Office for Wales
8 Broad Street, Newtown, Powys
[0686 26799]

Chairman, R. E. M. Rees £8,428
Principal Officer, A. M. H. Fitton £13,508 to £18,363

COUNTRYSIDE COMMISSION FOR SCOTLAND
Battleby, Redgorton, Perth
[0738 27921]

Established under the Countryside (Scotland) Act, 1967, with functions for the provision, development and improvement of facilities for the enjoyment of the Scottish countryside, and for the conservation and enhancement of the natural beauty and amenity thereof.

Chairman, D. W. Nickson, C.B.E.* (*part-time*).
Commissioners, J. M. S. Arnott; Mrs. F. Ballantyne; Dr. D. J. Bennet; I. R. Thomson; A. W. Driver; Prof. C. H. Gimingham; G. R. Marwick; D. Ross; R. R. Steedman; G. G. Stewart.
Director, M. Taylor.
Deputy Director, T. Huxley.
Secretary, W. B. Prior.
Asst. Directors, J. M. Fladmark (*Research and Development*); J. R. Turner (*Planning*).
*J. R. Carr from Jan. 1, 1986.

COVENT GARDEN MARKET AUTHORITY
Covent House, New Covent Garden Market,
SW8 5NX
[01–720 2211]

The Covent Garden Market Authority is constituted under the Covent Garden Market Acts, 1961 to 1977, the members being appointed by the Minister of Agriculture, Fisheries and Food. The Authority owns a 60-acre site comprising a fruit and vegetable market, a flower market and an administration building. The Authority is empowered to borrow capital up to £45,000,000.

Chairman, P. Firmston-Williams, O.B.E. (*part-time*)
.... £18,718
Members (*part-time*), Sir Adrian Cadbury; P. J. Hunt; E. I. Kingston; R. Pierson; J. A. Harvey ... £3,620
General Manager, C. M. G. Allen, C.B.E.
Secretary, Dr. P. M. Liggins.

CRIMINAL INJURIES COMPENSATION BOARD
Whittington House, 19 Alfred Place, WC1E 7EJ
[01–631 4467 and 01–636 2812]

The Board was constituted in 1964 to administer the Government scheme for *ex gratia* payments of compensation to victims of crimes of violence.
Chairman, M. Ogden, Q.C.
Members, I. J. Black, Q.C.; D. Calcutt, Q.C.; H. Carlisle, Q.C.; B. W. Chedlow, Q.C.; Miss B. Cooper, Q.C.; J D. Crowley, Q.C.; Sir Alun Davies, Q.C.; Sir Richard Denby; C. Fawcett, Q.C.; Sir Arthur Hoole; J. Law, Q.C.; Sir Denis Marshall; M. Morland, Q.C.; The

Lord Morton of Shuna, Q.C.; A. S. Myerson, Q.C.; C. W. F. Newman, Q.C.; Sir John Palmer; I. M. S. Park, C.B.E.; Miss S. Ritchie, Q.C.; L. Stuart Shields, Q.C.; R. I. Sutherland, Q.C.; D. M. Thomas, O.B.E., Q.C.; D. B. Weir, Q.C.; C. H. Whitby, Q.C.
Secretary and Solicitor, D. M. North.
Deputy Secretary, D. J. White.
Chief Executive, T. F. Corbett.

CROWN AGENTS FOR OVERSEA GOVERNMENTS AND ADMINISTRATIONS
4 Millbank, S.W.1
[01–222 7730]

The Crown Agents act as financial, commercial and professional agents for almost 100 governments and over 300 public authorities and international bodies. Their services are available to any government and to any organization in the public sector. They are a public service and do not act for individuals or for commercial concerns in the private sector.

The Crown Agents also act for the United Nations and as authorised agents for projects financed by the International Bank for Reconstruction and Development (The World Bank), the International Development Association and the Asian Development Bank.

Chairman, P. A. Graham, O.B.E.

CROWN ESTATE COMMISSIONERS
13/15 Carlton House Terrace, SW1Y 5AH
[01–214 6000]
78 Pall Mall, SW1Y 5ES

THE CROWN ESTATE (formerly The Crown Lands).—The Land Revenues of the Crown in *England and Wales* have been collected on the public account since 1760, when George III surrendered them and received a fixed annual payment or *Civil List*. At the time of the surrender the gross revenues amounted to about £89,000 and the net return to about £11,000.

In the year ended March 31, 1985, the total Receipts by the Commissioners were £44,205,000. The Expenditure was £22,231,000. The sum of £23,000,000 was paid to the Exchequer in 1984–85 as *Surplus Revenue*, being a net sum from which no deductions have been made for administration.

The Land Revenues in *Ireland* have been carried to the Consolidated Fund since 1820; from April 1, 1923, as regards Southern Ireland, they have been collected and administered by the Irish Free State (Republic of Ireland).

The Land Revenues in *Scotland* were transferred to the Commissioners in 1833.

First Commissioner and Chairman (*part-time*), The Earl of Mansfield and Mansfield.
Second Commissioner (*and Secretary*), Dr. K. Dexter, C.B. £36,500
Commissioners (*part-time*), R. B. Caws, C.B.E.; P. Sober; O. H. Colburn; G. D. Lillingston; Capt. I. M. Tennant; J. N. C. James.
Deputy Commissioners, D. J. Chapman; R. G. L. Osborne .... £20,964 to £25,333
Crown Estate Surveyor, C. F. Hynes
.... £17,000 to £22,926
Deputy Crown Estate Surveyor, K. W. Dytor
.... £14,392 to £17,322
Crown Estate Receiver for Scotland, M. J. Gravestock (10 Charlotte Square, Edinburgh)
.... £13,508 to £18,363
Principals, J. Stumbke; D. B. Cooke; F. G. Parrish
.... £13,508 to £18,363
Organization and Establishments Officer and Clerk to the Board, A. Barker .... £13,508 to £18,363

Accountant and Receiver-General, R. G. Bell
£13,508 to £18,363
Legal Adviser and Assistant Solicitor, M. L. Davies
£20,964 to £25,533
Senior Legal Assistants, M. R. Brocklehurst; I. R. Colquhoun; M. A. J. Cordingley; J. B. Postgate; H. Turnsek; A. M. Spratt .... £15,688 to £21,297
Solicitor, Scotland, D. F. Stewart.

Windsor Estate

Surveyor and Deputy Ranger, A. R. Wiseman, M.V.O.
£26,909

BOARD OF CUSTOMS AND EXCISE
King's Beam House, Mark Lane, EC3R 7HE
[01-626 1515]

Commissioners of Customs were first appointed in 1671 and housed by the King in London, the present "Long Room" in the Custom House, Lower Thames Street, E.C.3, replaced that built by Charles II and was rebuilt after destruction by fire in 1718 and 1814. The Excise Department was formerly under the Inland Revenue Department and was amalgamated with the Customs Department on April 1, 1909.

H.M. Customs and Excise is responsible for collecting and administering customs and excise duties and value added tax and advises the Chancellor of the Exchequer on any matters connected with them. The Department is also responsible for preventing and detecting the evasion of revenue laws and for enforcing a range of prohibitions and restrictions on the importation of certain classes of goods. In addition, the Department undertakes certain agency work on behalf of other departments, including the compilation of U.K. overseas trade statistics from customs import and export documents.

The Board

Chairman, Sir Angus Fraser, K.C.B., T.D. £52,750
Private Secretaries, Ms. A. French; Ms. C. W. Appleton.
Deputy Chairmen, B. H. Knox; L. D. Hawken, C.B.
£38,325 to £39,250
Commissioners, N. E. Godfrey; L. J. Harris; D. J. Howard; P. Jefferson Smith; A. W. Russell; R. Weston.............................. £29,500

Headquarters Office

Assistant Secretaries, I. D. Savins; P. R. H. Allen; J. Vaughan; R. I. Bolt; N. J. Collings; R. S. Bielby; P. Nash; P.Kent; P. St. Quinton; D. A. Walton; P. Hammond; R. A. Mechem; P. J. Webb; D. F. O. Battle; B. E. M. Prophet; K. Berry; D. J. Fellingham; R. N. Lewis; R. H. C. Stiff; P. Wilmott; V. Matthews; B. J. Cockerell; E. N. Taylor; J. W. Tracey; P. S. Jenkins; W. D. Whitmore; W. F. McGuigan; G. F. Taylor; D. F. W. Fryett; R. D. Goddard; P. Hogg .... £20,964 to £25,533
Head of Press and Information Division, G. G. Hammond .... £13,508 to £18,363

V.A.T. Central Unit

Controller, R. A. Huband .... £20,964 to £25,533
Deputy Controller, M. J. Wardle .. £17,000 to £22,926

Solicitor's Office

Solicitor, A. J. Jeddere-Fisher ... £38,325 to £39,250
Principal Assistant Solicitors, R. G. C. King; P. V. H. Smith .... £30,975 to £31,750
Assistant Solicitors, P. Breuer; P. J. C. Ellis; M. Michael; D. E. J. Nissen; Miss E. S. Thomas; R. D. S. Wylie; G. F. Butt; D. W. Levett-Yeats; M. A. Cooper; G. W. M. McFarlane; D. E. T. S. Keefe; I. W. Gardner; M. C. K. Gasper .. £20,964 to £25,533

Accountant and Comptroller-General's Office

Accountant and Comptroller-General, C. A. Bray
£20,964 to £25,533

Deputy Accountant-Generals, M. H. Smith; A. Aitchison; J. E. Ebery .... £17,000 to £22,926

Statistical Office

Controller, C. C. Finlinson .... £20,964 to £25,533

Investigation Division

Chief Investigation Officer, R. L. H. Lawrence
£20,964 to £25,533

Collectors of Customs and Excise
England and Wales

Birmingham: H. L. Hellier.
Dover: A. Collie.
East Anglia: W. K. Herbert.
East Midlands: C. J. Packman.
Leeds: N. T. Hodson.
Liverpool: P. J. Little.
London Airports: R. Craggs.
London City and South: W. Crawford.
London Port: A. C. Morrow.
London North and West: A. G. Smith.
Manchester: D. Smith.
Northampton: G. D. Town.
Northern England: D. R. Inglis.
Reading: J. H. Tee.
Southampton: S. J. C. Jones.
South Wales and the Borders: A. Ferguson.
South West England: R. E. Grimstead.

Scotland

Aberdeen: G. W. Sharpe.
Edinburgh: A. C. Sawyer.
Glasgow & Clyde: I. McLeod.

Northern Ireland

Belfast: B. E. Barclay.
Salaries:
All £20,964 to £25,533.

MINISTRY OF DEFENCE
See **Armed Forces Section**

DESIGN COUNCIL
28 Haymarket, S.W.1

The Design Council's aim is to improve the design of British products by: advising companies on up-to-date practice in engineering and industrial design; selecting well designed British goods for The Design Centre and for the annual Design Council Awards; publishing information to help manufacturers, designers, and others professionally involved in design; and promoting improvements in design education at all levels. The Design Centres in London and Glasgow mount exhibitions showing new developments in design and include shops selling selected British products. There is a smaller Design Centre in Cardiff and offices in Belfast, Wolverhampton and Manchester. Publications include the monthly *Design* and *Engineering* magazines, the termly *Designing* magazine for schools, as well as books and other periodicals. There is a comprehensive design bookshop in the London Design Centre. The Design Council is funded partly by a Government grant-in-aid and partly by earned revenues.

Chairman, Sir William Barlow.
Director, K. Grant.

DEVELOPMENT COMMISSION
11 Cowley Street, SW1P 3NA
[01-222 9134]

The Development Commission, England's rural development agency, is a statutory body funded by Government grant-in-aid which undertakes economic and social problems in rural areas and advises the Government on related rural matters in England.

It concentrates its resources in priority areas—Rural Development Areas—but some assistance, particularly through its main agency, the Council for Small Industries in Rural Areas, is available both within and outside the RDAs.

Chairman, The Lord Vinson, L.V.O.

Other Commissioners, Mrs. P. Batty Shaw, C.B.E.; Prof. M. D. I. Chisholm; D. J. C. Davenport; The Lord Gisborough; M. Schreiber; C. V. Wilkinson; A. Leavett.

Chief Executive, J. V. Williams.

THE DUCHY OF CORNWALL
10 Buckingham Gate, SW1E 6LA
[01–834 7346]

The Duchy of Cornwall was instituted by Edward III in 1337 for the support of his eldest son, Edward, the Black Prince, and since 1503 the eldest surviving son of the Sovereign has, as heir apparent, succeeded to the Dukedom by inheritance. As the oldest of the English Duchies, it has enjoyed a long association with the Crown. Before elevation to a dukedom, it was an earldom from 1227, when Richard, King of the Romans and younger brother of Henry III, was created Earl of Cornwall.

The Prince's Council

H.R.H. The Prince of Wales, K.G., K.T., G.C.B; The Lord Franks, O.M., P.C., G.C.M.G., K.C.B., C.B.E., F.B.A. (*Lord Warden of the Stannaries*); Hon. Sir John Baring, C.V.O. (*Receiver General*); P. T. Miles; R. A. Morritt, Q.C. (*Attorney-General to the Prince of Wales*); J. W. Y. Higgs (*Secretary and Keeper of the Records*); Sir Nicholas Henderson, G.C.M.G.; J. E. Pugsley; F. J. Williams.

Other Officers of the Duchy of Cornwall

Auditors, J. H. Bowman; P. L. Ainger; H. Hughes.
Solicitor, M. H. Boyd-Carpenter.
Assistant Secretary, K. J. S. Knott.
Sheriff (1985–86), Maj.-Gen. E. M. Hall, C.B., M.B.E.

THE DUCHY OF LANCASTER
Lancaster Place, Strand, WC2E 7ED
[01–836 8277]

The estates and jurisdiction known as the Duchy and County Palatine of Lancaster have been attached to the Crown since 1399, when John of Gaunt's son came to the throne as Henry IV. As the Lancaster inheritance it goes back to 1265. Edward III erected Lancashire into a County Palatine in 1351.

Chancellor of the Duchy of Lancaster, THE EARL OF GOWRIE, P.C. (*Minister for the Arts*).
Private Secretary, P. Thomas.
Attorney-General and Attorney and Serjeant within the County Palatine of Lancaster, J. L. Knox, Q.C.
Receiver-General, P. T. Miles.
Vice-Chancellor, His Hon. A. J. Blackett-Ord.
Clerk of the Council and Keeper of Records, M. K. Ridley.
Solicitor, W. O. Farrer.
Asst. Solicitor, I. J. Dicker.
Chief Clerk, P. C. Clarke, C.V.O.

ECONOMIC AND SOCIAL RESEARCH COUNCIL
160 Great Portland Street, W1N 6DT
[01–637 1499]

The E.S.R.C. was set up by Royal Charter in 1965 for the promotion of social science research. The Council carries out its role by awarding research grants, by initiating research and research contracts, by funding designated research centres, and by awarding postgraduate studentships and bursaries.

In addition, the Council provides advice and disseminates knowledge on the social sciences. A list of publications is available from the E.S.R.C. Information Office.

Chairman, Prof. Sir Douglas Hague, C.B.E.
Secretary, Mrs. S. Reeve.

DEPARTMENT OF EDUCATION AND SCIENCE
Elizabeth House, York Road, SE1 7PH
[01–934 9000]

The Government Department of Education was, until the establishment of a separate office, a Committee of the Privy Council appointed in 1839 to supervise the distribution of certain grants which had been made by Parliament since 1834. The Act of 1899 established the Board of Education, with a President and Parliamentary Secretary, and created a Consultative Committee. The Education Act of 1944 established the Ministry of Education. In April 1964 the office of the Minister of Science was combined with the Ministry to form the Department of Education and Science. The cost of administration for the financial year 1985–86 was estimated at £50,186,000.

Salary List

Secretary of State	£42,980
Parliamentary Under Secretaries	£28,120
Permanent Secretary (Grade 1)	£52,750
Deputy Secretaries (Grade 2)	£38,325 to £39,250
Under Secretaries (Grade 3)	£30,975 to £31,750
Chief Inspectors (Grade 4)	£26,909
Assistant Secretaries	
Chief Information Officer (A)	
Senior Economic Adviser	
Chief Statisticians	
Professional and Technical	*(Grade 5)* £20,964 to £25,533
Directing Grade B	
Staff Inspectors	
Divisional Inspectors	
Chief Architect	
Senior Principals	
Professional and Technological	*(Grade 6)* £17,000 to £22,926
Superintendents	
Senior Principal Scientific Officers	
H.M. Inspectors (Grade 6)	£17,000 to £22,926
Principals	
Economic Advisers	
Principal Catering Officer	£13,508 to £18,363
Statisticians	
Principal Research Officers	
Principal Scientific Officers	£11,343 to £14,931

Secretary of State for Education and Science, THE RT. HON. SIR KEITH JOSEPH, BT., M.P.
Private Sec., R. L. Smith.
Parliamentary Private Secretary, G. Walden, M.P.
Parliamentary Under Secretaries of State, R. Dunn, M.P.; Hon. P. Brooke, M.P.
Permanent Secretary, Sir David Hancock, K.C.B.
Deputy Secretaries, R. H. Bird, C.B.; W. O. Ulrich; P. H. Halsey, M.V.O.
Under Secretaries, J. H. Thompson (*Director of Establishments*); A. E. D. Chamier; C. A. Clark; N. W. Stuart (*Accountant General*); J. I. Langtry; D. G. Libby; B. M. Norbury; N. Summers; D. W. Tanner; N. B. W. Thompson; W. B. Wakefield (*Director of Statistics*); C. R. Walker.

Architects, Building and Schools II Branch

Assistant Secretaries, J. S. Beastall; A. S. Gann; G. J. Mungeam; B. C. Peatey.

Principals, Miss A. F. Brown; W. M. Caldow; Miss M. d' Armenia; S. F. Denning; R. D. Hull; P. S. Lewis; P. J. Middleton; P. J. Parramore; J. K. Sawtell; G. R. E. Stewart; M. J. P. Vann; J. N. Walmsley.
Chief Architect, J. D. Kay.
Superintending Architects, R. Clynes; D. H. Griffin; M. S. Hacker; G. E. Hughes; R. L. Thompson.
Superintending Engineer (Mechanical and Electrical), (vacant).
Superintending Quantity Surveyor, B. G. Whitehouse.
Principal Architects, R. W. U. Alcock; A. J. Branton; Miss C. G. Edwards; Miss R. Hall; Miss E. J. Lloyd-Jones; P. Marriott; D. S. Nightingale; G. J. Parker; T. W. Prosser; O. M. Stepan; D. F. Wicks; J. J. Wilson.
Principal Quantity Surveyors, G. C. Battersby; T. W. A. Carden; W. P. Horsnell; J. L. S. Sinclair.
Architects, Grade I, A. J. Benson-Wilson; E. C. Bissell; J. R. C. Brooke; P. Lenssen; Miss K. M. S. Livingston; Miss B. M. T. Sanders; A. C. Thompson.
Quantity Surveyor, Grade I, A. A. Jones.
Engineer (Mechanical and Electrical), Grade I, M. J. Patel.

Establishments and Organization Branch

Assistant Secretaries, E. B. Granshaw; Miss D. C. Fordham.
Senior Principals, G. J. Aylett; A. J. Holloway; R. E. Judd.
Principals, B. Bekhradnia; J. A. C. Cooke; K. W. Cawdron; G. H. N. Evans; Mrs. S. G. Evans; P. L. Jones.

Library

Librarian, D. N. Allum.

Finance Branch

Assistant Secretaries, R. D. Horne; Miss J. A. Gilbey (*Deputy Accountant General*).
Senior Principal, W. Gamble.
Principals, E. A. Alcock; P. J. Edwards; W. A. Irvine; D. J. Jones; A. J. Stewart; C. E. Treen; A. J. Wye.

Further and Higher Education Branch 1

Assistant Secretaries, D. M. Forrester; C. H. Saville; M. J. G. Smith.
Senior Principal, E. J. Herbert.
Principals, M. A. Aldridge; Miss N. M. Hill; D. R. Pollard; Mrs. S. L. Scales; R. L. Smith; D. K. Timms; A. R. Williams.

Further and Higher Education Branch 2

Assistant Secretaries, J. C. Hedger; R. P. Ritzema; A. G. B. Woollard.
Principals, P. F. Curran; K. L. R. English; J. S. Harris; M. McBride; W. H. Miller; A. J. Shaw; R. E. Troedson; S. R. Williams.

Further and Higher Education Branch 3

Assistant Secretaries, G. Etheridge; D. W. R. Lewis; D. V. Stafford.
Principals, Miss N. Bartman; A. Callaghan; P. W. Fulford-Jones; Mrs. K. H. Jameson; J. Nicholls.

Legal Branch

Assistant Legal Adviser, D. H. Ingham.
Senior Legal Assistant, Miss M. E. Trefgarne; M. A. Widdrington; D. J. Aries.

Pensions Branch

Mowden Hall, Staindrop Road,
Darlington, Co. Durham DL3 9BG
[Darlington: 460155]

Assistant Secretary, F. M. Scott.
Principals, A. F. Cowan; D. G. Halladay; P. Ramsden; K. M. Miles.

Teachers 2, External Relations and General Branch

Assistant Secretaries, Mrs. C. M. Chattaway; R. W. Chattaway; Mrs. H. K. Douglas.
Senior Economic Adviser, B. D. Cullen.
Principals, A. D. Adamson; Mrs. M. J. Lawrence; Mrs. C. K. Saville; C. J. Dowe; Miss J. P. Partington.
Chief Information Officer, N. S. Gaffin.
Principal Scientific Officer, R. B. Ladley.
Economic Adviser, K. J. Sear.
Staff Inspector, (vacant).

Schools Branch I

Assistant Secretaries, M. M. Capey; E. R. Morgan; J. W. Whitaker.
Principals, Miss A. M. J. Benham; Mrs. G. W. Dishart; D. H. Griffiths; Miss P. I. Laidlaw; M. Williams; A. N. Brown; Miss J. F. Cramphorn; J. S. Street; A. Wilshaw.

Schools Branch III

Assistant Secretaries, B. L. Baish; A. J. C. Edwards; N. J. Sanders.
Staff Inspector, A. Clegg.
Principals, H. H. Barrick; S. W. Cosser; Miss B. M. Ellington; B. D. Glickman; R. J. Green; Mrs. P. Masters.

Science Branch

Assistant Secretaries, R. P. Norton; Mrs. H. M. Williams.
Principals, K. C. Humphrey; L. B. Webb; A. B. McClean; K. D. J. Root.

Statistics Branch

Assistant Secretary, L. R. F. Wiggins.
Chief Statisticians, P. L. Turnbull; J. W. Gardner.
Senior Principal, A. J. Harley.
Principals, A. Allison; K. Baxter; J. K. Bushnell; K. Coombs; A. M. Cooper; P. D. Gott.
Statisticians, R. E. Dew; R. K. Jain; Mrs. S. Keith; T. C. Knight; Mrs. I. M. MacDonald-Davies; Mrs. I. R. Magill; Mrs. A. E. Mellor.
Principal Research Officer, D. J. Hodges.

Teachers 1 Branch (Salaries and Qualification)

Assistant Secretaries, Mrs. I. Wilde; D. A. Wilkinson.
Senior Principal, (vacant).
Principals, S. T. Crowne; R. S. Daruwalla; E. W. Grogan; T. B. Jeffery; M. J. F. Rabarts; J. Wilde.

H.M. Inspectorate (England)

Senior Chief Inspector, E. J. Bolton.
Chief Inspectors, B. C. Arthur; J. A. Everson; A. R. Marshall; T. P. Melia; E. Norris; Mrs. P. Perry; A. J. Rose.

Divisional Inspectors, B. A. Chaplin; J. T. G. Chugg; E. C. Cordell; Miss V. J. Evans; W. G. Hamflett; B. W. Howes; D. T. E. Marjoram.

Staff Inspectors, T. W. F. Allan; R. Arnold; A. Ashbrook; T. H. Bennetts; R. J. Brake; J. K. Brierley; P. Brown; T. Carroll; A. G. Clegg; A. T. Cox; Miss S. Crisp; D. A. Denegri; B. Denton; Mrs. G. M. Dolden; D. Flanagan; G. R. Frater; A. Gibson; G. Goldstein; V. Green; B. W. V. Hawes; R. A. S. Hennessey; G. A. Hicks; M. W. Himsworth; D. Hollingsworth; L. Jackson; D. G. S. Lambert; J. G. Lavender; M. Le Guillou; T. L. Lilley; A. G. Loosemore; P. F. Marlow; C. P. Marshall; J. H. Mayhew; R. F. Mildon; Miss A. C. Millett; R. W. Mycock; D. W. McAllister; Mrs. R. W. Peacocke; G. T. Peaker; C. W. Rowland; I. P. Salisbury; P. Samuel; E. Scott; C. H. Selby; B. D. Short; J. G. Slater; Mrs. M. M. Smart; M. E. Sprinks; K. W. Thomas; M. J. Tomlinson; D. R. Trainor; A. F. Turberfield; Mrs. S. P. Twite; J. R. Ungoed-Thomas; D. G.Vallis; W. H. Wainwright; D. E. Walker; R. C. Williams; M. Wylie; T. Wylie; R. E. Young.

HM Inspectors, Mrs. C. A. Agambar; W. Agnew; Miss J. A. Aldwinckle; Mrs. G. M. V. Alexander; D. J. Allen; T. I. Ambrose; K. J. Anglesey; P. T. Armitstead; Miss J. L. Atkin; D. Baillie; W. G. Bakehouse; Mrs. C. A. Baker; C. Banks; A. M. Barnes; J. H. Barnes; G. Barratt; R. E. Barrett; Mrs. E. P. Baxell; P. E. B. Belshaw; J. F. Bennett; S. G. L. Bignell; D. B. F. Billimore; Miss V. Blackburn; A. J. Boddington; Mrs. C. M. Bond; Miss J. M. Bonner; P. R. Booth; R. G. Booth; A. C. Boucher; Mrs. E. J. Boucher; D. M. W. Boulton; Miss E. Bourne; C. Bowring-Carr; Mrs. M. T. Boyd-Clarke; G. R. H. Boys; D. J. Bradbury; P. L. Bradbury; M. H. Bradley; T. E. Brand; Mrs. H. S. Bridge; E. F. H. Brittain; J. Broadbent; R. H. Brock; F. Brook; Miss C. M. Brooks; A. W. Brown; Mrs. M. A. Buckingham; D. G. Buckland; M. J. Buckley; T. A. Burdett; K. R. Burford; J. M. Burgess; Mrs. G. M. Burke; J. W. Butler; P. Cadenhead; Miss M. E. Caistor; R. A. Callender; M. J. Campbell; P. Candlish; N. Carr; Mrs. J. Carswell; M. J. Caton; Mrs. E. Cave; R. B. Chalmers; Miss J. A. Cheong; B. J. Chopping; Miss D. H. Chorley; D. Clare; P. R. Clarke; G. Clay; D. G. Close; D. A. Coe; J. E. M. Cohn; B. Colbeck; M. J. Collier; M. J. Convey; Mrs. M. A. Cooke; D. A. Cormican; P. Cradock; G. Cranmer; Mrs. G. K. Crawford; J. Creedy; L. S. Crickmore; Mrs. M. E. Crisp; Miss K. Cross; R. S. Crowcroft; R. Daniels; Mrs. J. Darroch; C. M. Davies; T. Dickinson; T. Dillon; A. Dobson; Lady Donoughue; J. A. S. Dossett; Mrs. M. E. Eade; P. D. Edwards; Mrs. C. Elliott; D. L. Elliott; J. A. Elliott; M. A. Emery; Mrs. V. E. Emmett; Mrs. J. E. Ensing; K. J. Evans; Mrs. G. Everson; J. H. Fairhurst; Mrs. C. Farrell; V. A. Farthing; Mrs. B. E. Fawcett; Mrs. B. R. D. Fisher; B. P. Fitzgerald; J. Fitzpatrick; D. H. M. Foster; R. S. Fowler; R. C. Fox; D. Fraser; P. S. Friend; C. C. Frost; R. C. Frost; J. P. Fulton; P. Gannon; P. H. W. Garwood; I. Gera; Mrs. J. E. A. Gifford; G. A. Gill; M. D. Gill; C. R. Gillings; M. S. Girling; C. Goodhead; Mrs. K. N. Gosling; C. Goulding; J. G. Goulding; Miss S. Gracey; D. I. Grant; J. D. Green; B. Gregson-Allcott; N. Grenyer; R. H. Griffiths; R. M. Griffiths; Mrs. P. E. Guest-Jones; E. E. J. Haidon; D. S. Hale; D. J. Halligan; N. J. Hallmark; J. A. Hamer; J. N. Hardwick; R. A. Hargreaves; B. R. Harris; C. R. Hart; D. J. Hart; Miss K. M. Hart; R. Hartley; A. Harvey; K. N. Hastings; F. W. Hawkins; G. H. Haworth; B. P. Hayes; G. M. Hearnshaw; Miss L. M. Hencher; M. L. Hening; J. F. Herbert; Mrs. J.

S. Herbert; J. A. Hertrich; P. M. Hesketh; T. Higginbottom; P. Highfield; J. F. H. Hilbourne; J. A. Hill; W. J. Hill; Mrs. G. A. Hindhaugh; J. R. Holmes; C. Hooper; D. J. House; M. J. Howarth; B. A. F. Hubbard; V. C. Hughes; J. B. Hurn; J. B. Huskins; J. N. Hutchinson; A. J. Hymans; E. S. Ingledew; P. F. J. Irvine; A. R. Ivatts; M. J. Ive; T. M. Jardine; B. D. Jelly; K. Jennings; D. W. John; Miss S. H. Johns; P. W. R. Johnson; D. A. Jones; Mrs. M. E. Jones; W. D. Kaye; Mrs. A. C. Keelan-Towner; M. Kerrigan; M. A. Khan; B. L. King; D. P. King; K. King; J. B. Knox; D. G. Labon; A. J. Lacey; G. N. E. Lageard; B. M. Lane; J. W. Langley; J. W. F. Learmonth; E. H. Leaton; J. P. Leigh; Miss B. J. Lewis; D. F. Lewis; L. D. Johnson; Mrs. J. M. Lingard; E. R. B. Little; A. W. Littlewood; Miss B. M. Lockwood; A. B. Lomax; R. Long; R. S. Long; Mrs. E. M. Lowe; T. L. Lusty; J. A. Mabey; Mrs. H. M. Macdonald; Mrs. P. R. Maclay; M. E. Madden; D. J. Marjoram; Miss R. J. Marlor; G. D. Marrow; J. G. Marshall; E. S. Martin; Mrs. M. M. Martin; T. W. Martin; W. P. Massam; Miss E. M. Matthews; J. E. Mattick; M. R. E. Mealing; Miss B. E. Megson; Mrs. R. Melling; G. Merlane; B. E. Merton; H. Millington; J. K. Millington; D. Mills; Miss H. A. Moffat; A. R. H. Monk; P. Muschamp; H. Myers; C. McCall; J. McGinn; Mrs. J. C. McGinty; J. McGuire; D. C. McIntosh; M. McLaughlin; Mrs. J. McLean; I. A. McNally; C. Needham; Miss D. A. Nelson; R. Nicholls; A. J. Nisbett; P. M. Nixon; M. Norman; J. P. O'Connor; Mrs. G. I. Oldham; P. J. H. Oliver; P. I. Orr; A. Owen; W. E. Owen; Ms. J. H. Paraskeva-Hunt; Miss P. Park; K. Parker; D. J. Parks; J. M. Parsons; I. M. Paterson; P. J. Pearson; Mrs. D. M. Penn; Miss I. Perlmutter; Miss J. M. Phillips; K. Pinder; B. J. Pitchers; M. W. A. Pitts; M. R. Potter; C. Potts; C. P. Power; H. A. Price; Mrs. M. P. Pryce; M. E. Pullee; Mrs. P. E. Pulver; J. Reynolds; C. M. Richards; J. C. Richardson; A. S. Robertson; G. Robson; I. A. Rodger; S. J. A. Rogers; R. Roundhill; A. C. Rowe; C. Rowe; D. H. Rutt; M. V. Salter; Mrs. J. Sartain; Mrs. K. J. Saunders; B. Sayer; J. C. Schenk; P. L. Seaborne; E. L. Sewell; D. T. V. Sharman; D. I. Shelton; J. R. Shirtcliff; Mrs. V. M. Sida; P. J. Silvester; Mrs. D. E. Simmonds; P. Singh; G. Sleightholme; B. J. Smith; P. J. C. Smith; P. R. Smith; R. T. Smith; D. E. Soulsby; Mrs. B. Staniland; J. Stanyer; J. W. Steel; J. M. Steels; B. Stevenson; Mrs. M. T. Stiles; R. W. Stockdale; M. M. Stone; C. F. Stoneman; Mrs. J. E. Storrie; Miss M. E. Stride; R. Summersby; D. P. Swain; A. Sykes; D. W. Sylvester; D. W. Taylor; J. A. Taylor; Miss P. M. M. Taylor; R. S. Taylor; A. F. Thomas; D. L. Thorburn; R. M. Thorpe; J. Tierney; M. J. Todd; B. D. Tomkins; J. E. Trickey; A. D. J. Turner; Mrs. J. W. Turner; B. C. L. Walker; A. Walmsley; Miss P. Walters; M. Wardlow; Mrs. A. P. Warren; R. K. Warren; N. G. Warwick; D. H. Watts; M. R. Webb; R. R. Weir; D. J. Wells; D. L. West; P. E. Weston; R. Whitburn; C. G. White; Miss F. White; J. White; F. Whiteman; D. G. Whittaker; Mrs. O. Whittingham; C. C. B. Wightwick; J. B. Willcock; D. G. Williams; H. G. Williams; J. R. Williams; K. G. Williams; Mrs. S. A. Williams; D. P. T. Woodgate; J. D. Woodhouse; Mrs. S. A. Woodroffe; J. A. Woodrow; J. I. Wragg; Miss B. M. Wright; F. P. Young; A. J. Youngs.

Attached to HM Inspectorate, C. Booth (*Staff Inspector attached*); Mrs. C. Hague; G. A. N. Smith.

H.M. Inspectorate Support Services

Principal, P. J. Thorpe.
Senior Executive Officer, P. A. Clarke.

H.M. Inspectorate (Wales)

(*See* Welsh Office)

ELECTRICITY AUTHORITIES

THE ELECTRICITY COUNCIL
30 Millbank, SW1P 4RD
[01–834 2333]

Chairman, T. P. Jones, C.B. £61,000
Deputy Chairman, A. Plumpton, C.B.E.
£45,000 to £50,000
Members, R. W. Orson, C.B.E.; R. A. Farrance
£35,000 to £45,000
Members from the Central Electricity Generating Board, The Lord Marshall of Goring, C.B.E., F.R.S.; F. E. Bonner, C.B.E.; G. A. W. Blackman, C.B.E.
Secretary, R. Savinson.

CENTRAL ELECTRICITY GENERATING BOARD
Sudbury House, 15 Newgate Street, EC1A 7AU
[01–634 5111]

Chairman, The Lord Marshall of Goring, C.B.E., F.R.S. £61,000
Deputy Chairman, F. E. Bonner, C.B.E.
£50,000 to £55,000
Members, D. A. Davis, G. A. W. Blackman, C.B.E.; J. W. Baker .... £35,000 to £45,000
Part-time Members, R. M. Dantzic; Sir Eric Sharp, C.B.E.; R. V. Giordano (*each*) £4,270
Secretary, G. H. Hadley.

ELECTRICITY BOARDS
The 12 Area Electricity Boards

(The Chairmen of Area Boards receive a salary of £30,000 to £40,000.)
London, Templar House, 81–87 High Holborn, WC1V 6NU. *Chairman*, D. G. Jefferies. *Sec.*, D. G. Rees.
South Eastern, Grand Avenue, Hove, East Sussex BN3 2LS. *Chairman*, G. A. Squair. *Sec.*, S. M. Wide.
Southern, Southern Electricity House, Littlewick Green, Maidenhead, Berks. *Chairman*, D. A. Ross. *Sec.*, R. C. Collier.
South Western, Electricity House, Colston Avenue, Bristol BS1 4TS. *Chairman*, K. F. Whittle. *Sec. and Solicitor*, S. G. Marshall.
Eastern, P.O. Box 40, Wherstead, Ipswich, Suffolk 1P9 2AQ. *Chairman*, J. C. Smith. *Sec.*, W. L. M. French.
East Midlands, P.O. Box 4, North P.D.O., 398 Coppice Road, Arnold, Nottingham NG5 7HX. *Chairman*, J. F. Harris. *Sec.*, T. F. C. Walker.
Midlands, P. O. Box 8 Mucklow Hill, Halesowen, West Midlands B62 8BP. *Chairman*, J. J. Wilson. *Sec.*, R. K. Young.
South Wales, St. Mellons, Cardiff CF3 9XW. *Chairman*, J. Wynford Evans. *Sec.*, A. Worth.
Merseyside and North Wales, Sealand Road, Chester. *Chairman*, B. H. Weston, *Sec.*, C. W. Leonard.
Yorkshire, Wetherby Road, Scarcroft, Leeds LS14 3HS. *Chairman*, J. Porteous. Sec. and Solicitor, R. Dickinson.
North Eastern, Carliol House, Newcastle upon Tyne NE99 1SE. *Chairman*, T. Rutherford, C.B.E., *Sec.*, J. W. Dalgleish.
North Western, Cheetwood Road, Manchester M8 8BA. *Chairman*, B. R. Hastings. *Sec.*, B. Benson.

NORTH OF SCOTLAND HYDRO-ELECTRIC BOARD
16 Rothesay Terrace, Edinburgh EH3 7SE
[031–225 1361]

Chairman, M. Joughin, C.B.E. (*part-time*) £19,300
Deputy Chairman and Chief Executive, K. R. Vernon, C.B.E.

Members (*part-time*), A. T. H. Tulloch; Mrs. C. A. M. Davis (*Chairman of Consultative Council*).; M. G. N. Walker; D. J. Miller; C. S. Macphie; D. F. Myles; G. Barrie (£3,250 to £4,500).
Secretary, J. E. M. Watts.

SOUTH OF SCOTLAND ELECTRICITY BOARD
Spean Street, Glasgow G44 4BE
[041–637 7177]

Chairman, D. J. Miller £45,000
Deputy Chairman, I. M. H. Preston £37,500
Part-time Members, A. Barr; D. McLean; N. C. Kuensberg; Prof. D. I. MacKay; Mrs. J. A. Thomson (£3,500); M. Joughin, C.B.E. (*unpaid*); G. B. Whyte (*unpaid*).
Secretary, D. A. S. MacLaren.

DEPARTMENT OF EMPLOYMENT
Caxton House, Tothill Street, SW1H 9NF
[01–213 3000]

The Department of Employment is responsible for Government policies on the working of the labour market and the needs and conditions of people at work. These policies include the encouragement of employment and of effective training for it, the provision of special measures to deal with unemployment, and the promotion of good industrial relations and a healthy and safe working environment. The Department publishes a wide range of statistics and other information bearing on these matters, including the movement of prices and earnings.

Many of the executive functions carried out in the Department's area of policy interest are exercised by separate national agencies reporting to the Secretary of State for Employment.

Secretary of State for Employment, THE RT. HON. THOMAS KING, M.P. £31,271
  Private Secretary, D. J. Normington.
  Assistant Private Secretaries, I. A. Mackinnon; C. M. Snell.
  Parliamentary Private Secretary, Dr. B. Mawhinney, M.P.
Minister of State, HON. P. MORRISON, M.P. ... £21,881
Under Secretaries of State, P. Bottomley, M.P.; Hon. A. Clark, M.P. £16,411
Permanent Secretary, Sir Michael Quinlan, K.C.B.
£52,750
Deputy Secretaries, R. J. Dawe, O.B.E.; D. B. Smith, C.B. .... £38,325 to £39,250
Solicitor, G. E. McClelland ...... £38,325 to £39,250

Industrial Relations

Grade 3, R. S. Allison; E. G. Whybrew
£30,975 to £31,750
Grade 5, D. G. Talintyre; N. Covington; N. H. Reed; A. G. Johnson .... £20,964 to £25,533
Chief Wages Inspector, J. A. Dyble £20,964 to £25,533
Secretary of Wages Councils, S. Cottingham
£13,508 to £18,363

Manpower Policy

Grade 3 (*Division 1*), P. Mackay .. £30,975 to £31,750
Grade 3 (*Division 2*), M. E. G. Fogden
£30,975 to £31,750
Grade 4 (*Unemployment Benefit Service*), J. W. Cooper £26,909
Grade 5, J. M. Dewsbury; R. A. David; D. W. Brown; I. A. W. Fair; J. B. Shaw; M. J. Brimmer
£20,964 to £25,533

Overseas Division

Grade 3, W. R. B. Robinson ...... £30,975 to £31,750
Grade 5, J. S. Lambert; Miss M. E. Green
£20,964 to £25,533

Economic and Social Division

Grade 3, G. L. Reid .... £30,975 to £31,750
Grade 5, C. F. Tucker; M. W. Smart; P. Brannen;
Mrs. Z. Hornstein; D. Stanton . £20,964 to £25,533

Personnel and Management Services Division

Director of Personnel, A. W. Brown £29,500
Head of Business Services, B. P. White £26,909
Grade 5, (*Group Personnel Unit*), S. Tolson
£20,964 to £25,533
Director of Computing, S. Elliott   £20,964 to £25,533

Information Division

Head of Information, A. E. Moorey
£20,964 to £25,533
Deputy Head of Information, S. Reardon
£17,000 to £22,926

Finance Division

Accountant-General, F. J. Bayliss £29,500
Grade 5, G. Kahan; R. H. Chambers
£20,964 to £25,533

Solicitor's Office

Solicitor, G. E. McClelland .... £38,325 to £39,250

Statistics Division

Director of Statistics, P. D. Dworkin £29,500
Grade 5, B. J. Buckingham; Mrs. A. V. Wheatcroft;
D. J. Sellwood; D. E. Allnutt ... £20,964 to £25,533

Health and Safety Commission

Chairman, Dr. J. Cullen £45,500
Members of the Commission, D. Mason; Dr. M. C.
Shannon; Dr. C. M. Thomas; R. F. Eberlie; P.
Jacques; R. W. Buckton; Dr. A. H. Raper; W.
Greendale.
Secretary, Miss C. Johnson ...... £17,000 to £22,926

Health and Safety Executive

Director General, J. D. Rimington £39,250
Deputy Director General, J. D. G. Hammer .. £36,500
Secretary, Miss S. C. Newton .... £17,000 to £22,926
Solicitor, A. D. Osborne £26,909

Resources and Planning Division

Director, A. B. Martin £29,500

Hazardous Substances Division

Director, C. D. Burgess £29,500

Safety Policy and Information Services Division

Director, D. J. Hodgkins £29,500

Medical Division

Director of Medical Services, Dr. J. T. Carter £32,350

Technology and Air Pollution Division

Director, A. C. Barrell £29,500
H.M. Chief Industrial Air Pollution Inspector, R. J.
Perriman £26,909

Factory and Agricultural Inspectorates Division

H.M. Chief Inspector of Factories, D. C. T. Eves
£29,500
H.M. Chief Agricultural Inspector, C. Boswell
£20,964 to £25,533

H.M. Mines and Quarries Inspectorate

H.M. Chief Inspector of Mines and Quarries, A.
Harley £35,144

H.M. Nuclear Installations Inspectorate

H.M. Chief Inspector of Nuclear Installations, R. D.
Anthony £29,500

Research and Laboratory Services Division

Director, (vacant).

DEPARTMENT OF ENERGY

Thames House South,
Millbank, SW1P 4QJ (unless otherwise stated)
[01–211 3000]

The Department of Energy is responsible within
the Government for the development of policies in
relation to all forms of energy. It also discharges
governmental functions connected with the publicly-
owned coal, gas and electricity industries. It is
responsible for the Atomic Energy Authority; is the
sponsoring Department for the nuclear power industry and is responsible for the development of oil and
gas resources on the British sector of the Continental
Shelf. It is the sponsoring Department for the oil
industry and is responsible for international aspects
of energy problems, including relations and co-
operation with oil producing countries. The Department is the co-ordinating body for energy efficiency
policy and for encouraging the development of new
sources of energy.

Salary List

Secretary of State £42,980
Minister of State £33,500
*Parliamentary Under-Secre-
tary of State* £28,120
*Permanent Under-Secretary of
State* £52,750
Deputy Secretary .... £38,325 to £39,250
Director of P.E.D. £41,853
Head of Information £25,533
Under Secretary .... £30,975 to £31,750
*Reservoir Evaluation Specialist
I* £37,903
Assistant Secretary £25,533
*Reservoir Evaluation Specialist
II* £35,647
Senior Principal £22,926
*Chief Electrical Engineering
Inspector* £25,533
Deputy Chief Scientific Officer . £25,533
*Senior Principal Scientific
Officer* £22,926
Chief Statistician £25,533
Senior Economic Adviser £25,533
*Director (Gas and Oil Measure-
ment Branch)* £25,533
Petroleum Specialist II £31,153
A.D./Accounts £23,600
Director of Engineering £25,533
*Assistant Director of Engin-
eering* £22,926

Secretary of State for Energy, THE RT. HON. PETER
WALKER, M.B.E., M.P.
Principal Private Secretary, G. S. Dart.
Parliamentary Private Secretary, S. Dorrell, M.P.
Assistant Private Secretaries, P. R. Evans; E. G.
Huke; K. R. Loader.
Minister of State for Energy, THE RT. HON. ALICK
BUCHANAN-SMITH, M.P.
Private Secretary, Miss S. A. Killen.
Parliamentary Private Secretary, J. Watson, M.P.
Assistant Private Secretary, Miss J. A. Bennington.
Parliamentary Under-Secretaries of State, A. Goodlad,
M.P.; D. Hunt, M.P.; P. G. Malone, M.P.
Permanent Under Secretary of State, P. Gregson, C.B.
Private Secretary, E. F. Quilty.
Deputy Secretaries, J. R. S. Guinness; I. T. Manley.
Chief Scientific Adviser, Sir Sam Edwards.
Parliamentary Clerk, G. L. Davey.

Establishment and Finance Division

*Principal Establishment and Finance Officer (Under
Secretary)*, R. T. J. Wilson.

Assistant Secretaries, R. Beasley; G. W. Thynne; C. C. Wilcock; L. F. Barclay; M. H. Atkinson; Dr. W. S. Burroughs.

Electricity Division

Under Secretary, M. S. Buckley.
Assistant Secretaries, P. G. P. D. Fullerton; Dr. F. R. Heathcote.
Chief Electrical Engineering Inspector, (vacant).

Coal Division

Under Secretary, (vacant).
Assistant Secretaries, Ms. A. Beaton; Mrs. S. D. Brown.

Atomic Energy Division

Under Secretary, D. I. Morphet.
Assistant Secretaries, G. H. Stevens; J. R. Bretherton; N. A. C. Hirst.

Energy Technology Division

Chief Scientist (Under Secretary), Dr. D. Pooley.
Deputy Chief Scientific Officers, D. C. Gore; Dr. R. G. S. Skipper.
Assistant Secretary, Dr. D. H. Metz.
Senior Principal Scientific Officers, H. F. Ferguson; G. S. Dearnley; Dr. G. Preston; E. G. Bevan; W. Macpherson; Dr. D. Fairmaner.

Energy Policy

Under Secretary, B. Emmett.
Assistant Secretaries, Miss P. A. Boys; E. Pash; J. Whaley; P. H. Agrell.

Energy Efficiency Office

Director General, W. I. MacIntyre.
Directors, R. C. Courtney; Dr. E. G. Finer; G. D. Meredith; J. R. Wakely.

Economics and Statistics Division

Under Secretary, E. H. M. Price.
Chief Statistician, J. J. M. Harris.
Senior Economic Advisers, A. J. Meyrick; S. A. Price; Dr. K. J. Wigley.

Oil Division

Under Secretary, A. J. Wiggins.
Assistant Secretaries, Dr. C. J. Myerscough; S. W. Fremantle; A. J. Dorken; P. T. Harding; W. C. F. Butler.

Gas Division

Under Secretary, D. R. Davis.
Assistant Secretaries, Dr. J. G. Wright; C. P. Carter; Dr. W. D. Evans; M. F. Reidy.

Gas and Oil Measurement Branch
Government Buildings, Saffron Road, Wigston, Leicester
[0533 785354]

Director, J. Plant.

Petroleum Engineering Division

Director of P.E.D., P. J. Walmsley, M.B.E..
Reservoir Evaluation Specialist I, K. R. J. Trott.
Reservoir Evaluation Specialists II, J. R. V. Brooks; D. W. Mann.
Petroleum Specialists II, R. Giles; D. R. Clementson; J. R. Petrie.
Senior Principal, P. D. Atkinson.
Senior Principal Scientific Officer, J. N. Mansfield.
Assistant Director Engineer, G. N. Marriott.

Offshore Supplies Office
Headquarters Office:
Alhambra House, 45 Waterloo Street,
Glasgow G2 6AS
[041–221 8777]

Director General, J. E. d'Ancona.
Director Industry, W. E. Allison.
Director Policy and Administration, A. E. Maule.
Director Research and Development, Dr. J. E. P. Miles.
Director China Unit, Dr. K. P. Forrest.
Senior Principal Business Development, H. Holden.
Senior Principal Scientific Officers, C. J. Hughes; D. W. Partridge.
Assistant Director Engineers, H. M. Whiteside; P. R. Taylor.

Information Division

Head of Information, Miss R. C. A. Christopherson.

DEPARTMENT OF THE ENVIRONMENT
2 Marsham Street, SW1P 3EB
[01–212 3434]

The Department of the Environment is responsible for planning and land use; local government; housing, construction; inner city areas; new towns; environmental protection; conservation areas and countryside affairs; royal parks and palaces; historic buildings and ancient monuments; sport and recreation. The Property Services Agency is responsible for all construction activities, supplies and transport at home and abroad for all Government departments including the Ministry of Defence and some repayment clients including British Telecom.

Salary List

Secretary of State	£31,271		
Minister of State (Local Govt. & Environmental Services)	£28,000		
Minister of State (Housing & Construction)	£21,881		
Parliamentary Under Secretary of State	£16,411		
Permanent Secretary (Grade 1)	£52,750		
Second Permanent Secretary (1A)	£48,500		
Chief Executive (1A)	£48,500		
Deputy Secretary (2)	£38,325	to	£39,250
Director General (2)	£38,325	to	£39,250
Solicitor and Legal Adviser (2)	£38,325	to	£39,250
Chief Economic Adviser (2)	£38,325	to	£39,250
Director, B.R.S., U.I.P.P.L. (3)	£32,350		
Under Secretary (3)	£30,975	to	£31,750
Director, Information (4)	£26,909		
Director, Regional Office (3)	£30,975	to	£31,750
Director Works, P.S.A. London (3)	£30,975	to	£31,750
Chief Planning Inspector (3)	£30,975	to	£31,750
Principal Establishment Officer (3)	£30,975	to	£31,750
Principal Finance Officer (Under Sec.) (3)	£30,975	to	£31,750
Principal Assistant Solicitor (3)	£30,975	to	£31,750
Chief Scientific Officer (B) (4)	£26,909		
Director Contracts (P.S.A.) (4)	£26,909		
Deputy Director Research (B.R.E.) (4)	£26,909		
Deputy Chief Planner (4)	£26,909		
Director, P.S.A. Regions (4)	£26,909		
Deputy Chief Scientific Officer (5)	£20,964	to	£25,533
Assistant Director/Director "B" (5)	£20,964	to	£25,533
Assistant Chief Planner (5)	£20,964	to	£25,533
Assistant Secretary (5)	£20,964	to	£25,533
Controller, Regional Office (5)	£20,964	to	£25,533

Chief Statistician (5) .... £20,964 to £25,533
Senior Economic Adviser (5) .. £20,964 to £25,533
Controller of Accounts (5)..... £20,964 to £25,533

Secretary of State for the Environment, THE RT. HON. PATRICK JENKIN, M.P.
  Private Secretary, R. U. Young.
Special Advisers, Sir Robert Cooke; A. Tyrie.
  Parliamentary Private Secretary, R. Needham, M.P.

Minister for Local Government, THE RT. HON. KENNETH WILFRED BAKER, M.P.
  Private Secretary, M. J. Bailey.
Special Adviser, P. Davis.
Minister of State, THE LORD ELTON, T.D.
  Private Secretary, S. Watts.

Minister for Housing and Construction, IAN GOW, M.P.
  Private Secretary, N. A. J. Kinghan.
Parliamentary Under-Secretaries of State:—
  N. MacFarlane, M.P.; Sir George Young, BT., M.P.; Hon. W. Waldegrave, M.P.
  Private Secretaries, P. Dykins (*to Mr. MacFarlane*); N. G. P. Mitchell (*to Sir George Young*); Ms. B. G. Jones (*to Mr. Waldegrave*).
  Parliamentary Clerk, L. Peacock.
Permanent Secretary, T. M. Heiser, C.B.
  Private Secretary, Miss B. Campbell.
Lord in Waiting, The Lord Skelmersdale.
  Private Secretary, D. J. Prior.
Second Permanent Secretary, Sir Peter Harrop, K.C.B.
  Private Secretary, W. Hills.
Chief Executive, Second Permanent Secretary, Property Services Agency, A. G. Manzie, C.B..

Information

Director, D. A. McDonald.

Merseyside Task Force

Under Secretary (G3), D. C. Renshaw.
Grade 5, R. W. Bunce; D. J. Morrison.

PROPERTY SERVICES AGENCY

Chief Executive, A. G. Manzie, C.B..
Private Secretary, P. Handley.

DEPUTY CHIEF EXECUTIVE 1

Deputy Secretary (G2), G. H. Chipperfield, C.B.

Home Regional Services

Director (G3), A. J. Aveling.
Grade 5, M. Clayton; H. R. Webber; J. W. Deane.

Property Services Agency Regions (Home)

Director (G3):
  London, G. Hopkinson.
Directors (G4):
  Eastern, A. S. Kennedy.
  Midland, K. H. A. Allen.
  North East, G. Flanagan.
  North West, H. Rogers.
  South East, P. J. M. Butter.
  South West, J. M. Rex.
  Southern, R. A. Munday.
  Central Office for Wales, J. H. Clemits.

Scottish Services

Director (G3), A. G. Gosling.
Grade 5, D. R. Smith; P. M. Livesey; J. S. Wilson.

DEPUTY CHIEF EXECUTIVE 2

Grade 2, H. P. Johnston, C.B.

Defence Services I

Director (G3), R. A. Gomme.
Grade 5, G. J. Skinner; C. D. Boylan; H. L. Froome-Lewis; J. Jacobs; R. T. Turner.

Defence Services II

Director (G3), P. S. Draper.
Grade 5, J. S. Stevens; P. Kitchen; A. Levy; S. G. D. Duguid; M. R. Sutton; D. K. Warren.

Civil Accommodation

Director (G3), R. G. S. Johnston.
Chief Estate Surveyor (G4), R. P. Hore.
Grade 5, R. J. Dorrington; B. E. Fensome; A. K. W. Morgan; M. G. Stuart; J. A. Owen.

Defence Estates Services Division

Grade 5, M. D. Clarke.

DIRECTOR GENERAL OF DESIGN SERVICES

Grade 2, J. B. Jefferson, C.B.E.

Building and Quantity Surveying Services

Director (G4), E. J. Bowman.
Grade 5, K. A. Miles.

Civil Engineering Services

Director (G4), R. F. Hughes.
Grade 5, G. H. Sowden; I. T. Millar.

Mechanical and Electrical Engineering Services

Director (G3), A. W. Loten, C.B..
Grade 5, D. S. Ashworth.

Directorate of Architectural Services

Director (G4), J. P. Lynch.
Grade 5, C. A. P. Crooke.

Establishments, Property Services Agency

Principal Establishment Officer (G3), A. R. Atherton.
Grade 5, G. N. Bendon; R. A. Stead; R. C. Cracknell.

Information Technology

Director (G4), Mrs. E. M. Causley Cooper.
Grade 5, L. W. Culver; D. Evans.

Finance, Property Services Agency

Principal Finance Officer (G3), M. V. Hawtin.
Director of Contracts (G4), C. Pink.
Grade 5, A. E. Coules; J. E. Quinlin; J. W. C. Wilton.
Comptroller of Accounts (G5), J. A. Pearson.

THE CROWN SUPPLIERS

Controller (G3), J. A. Dole.
Assistant Controllers (G5), E. L. Pinfold; A. H. Pollington; P. L. Leonard.
Financial Controller (G5), J. Cousins.

PLANNING, INNER CITIES, NEW TOWNS, LONDON, REGIONAL DEVELOPMENT

Deputy Secretary (G2), J. Delafons, C.B.

Inner Cities

Under Secretary (G3), K. E. C. Sorensen.
Grade 5, N. Sanders; J. S. Parker; M. B. Gahagan; W. B. Solesbury.

Regional Policy and Development and New Towns

Under Secretary (G3), D. C. L. Wroe.
Grade 5, P. J. Plowman; A. J. C. Simcock.

Greater London

Under Secretary (G3), P. C. McQuail.
Grade 5, R. Williams; J. G. Grevatt; A. Buchanan.

Planning Land Use Policy

Under Secretary (G3), N. W. Summerton.
Grade 5, D. N. Donaldson; G. I. Fuller; I. H. Nicol; R. C. Mabey.

Land and Property

Chief Estate Officer (G4), C. K. Howes.
Grade 6, J. C. White.

Planning Services

Director (G4), Dr. M. R. Richardson.
Grade 5, R. A. Bird; P. F. Everall.
Grade 6, P. Morgan; D. C. Stroud; W. G. B. Phillips.

HOUSING AND CONSTRUCTION

Deputy Secretary (G2), W. I. McIndoe.
Under Secretaries (G3), B. D. Ponsford; R. J. A. Sharp;
R. G. Brown; D. T. Routh.
Chief Architect (G4), Miss P. R. Tindale.
Grade 5, P. F. Emms; A. H. Corner; J. J. Rendell; J.
A. Penfold; R. J. Gibson; J. M. Hope; I. G. Urquhart;
J. P. Henry; D. T. I. G. Davies; I. C. MacPherson;
A. E. Holmans; B. C. Isherwood; J. Vaughan; G. L.
Laufer; P. J. J. Britton; S. T. McQuillan; Mrs. J.
M. Williams.
Grade 6, Mrs. J. Littlewood.

WATER DIRECTORATE

Under Secretary (G3), J. A. L. Gunn.
Grade 5, P. T. McIntosh; Mrs. L. A. C. Simcock; M.
G. Healey; H. Wenban-Smith.

FINANCE AND LOCAL GOVERNMENT

Deputy Secretary, Principal Finance Officer (G2), K.
F. J. Ennals, C.B.

Local Government Finance Policy

Under Secretary (G3), C. J. S. Brearley.
Grade 5, P. J. Fletcher; J. Hobson; J. Kidgell; M. J.
C. Faulkner; D. L. H. Roberts; L. B. Hicks.

Housing, Water and Central Finance

Under Secretary (G3), F. A. Osborn.
Grade 5, D. R. Bradley; D. A. C. Heigham; A. G.
Watson.
Director Accountant (Grade 5), B. Redfern.
Grade 6, A. J. Pike.

Local Government

Under Secretary (G3), D. C. Pickup.
Grade 5, M. J. Wanstall; C. J. Griffin; D. J. Phillips.
Grade 6, P. G. Iredale.

Local Government Reorganisation

Under Secretary (G3), J. P. G. Rowcliffe.
Grade 5, Mrs. D. S. Phillips; D. P. Walley; R. J.
Brown; Mrs. L. A. Thomas.

Local Government Finance Studies

Under Secretary (G3), P. F. Owen.
Grade 5, R. A. J. Mayer; P. D. Ward; R. M. F. Bright;
J. W. Smith.

ENVIRONMENTAL PROTECTION, RURAL AFFAIRS AND SPORT

Deputy Secretary (G2), Dr. M. W. Holdgate, C.B.

Central Directorate on Environmental Protection

Under Secretary (G3), D. Gruffydd Jones.
Grade 4, Dr. D. A. Everest.
Grade 5, Miss F. McConnell; Dr. N. J. King; P. S.
MacCormack; P. G. Burgess.
Grade 6, Dr. P. J. Corcoran; Dr. D. L. Simms.

Directorate of Waste Disposal

Under Secretary (G3), P. Critchley.
Grade 5, Dr. F. S. Feates; R. G. D. Osmond; J. F.
Ballard.

Directorate of Rural Affairs

Under Secretary (G3), T. R. Hornsby.
Grade 5, A. Flexman; F. C. Argent.
Grade 6, J. C. Peters.

Sports and Recreation

Under Secretary (G3), D. T. Routh.
Grade 5, D. V. Teasdale.

ANCIENT MONUMENTS AND HISTORIC BUILDINGS DIRECTORATE

Director (Under Secretary) (G3), T. R. Hornsby.
Grade 5, B. Strong; R. Jones.
Grade 6, R. A. Stephenson, M.V.O.

DEPARTMENTS OF THE ENVIRONMENT AND TRANSPORT REGIONAL OFFICES

West Midlands (Birmingham)

*Chairman, Regional Board and Regional Director
(G3)*, H. F. Ellis-Rees.
Regional Controllers (G5), S. Jones; D. L. Saunders;
N. H. Perry.

Yorkshire and Humberside (Leeds)

*Chairman, Regional Board and Regional Director
(G3)*, R. J. Green.
Regional Controllers (G5), J. B. Wilson; K. Beaumont.

North West (Manchester)

*Chairman, Regional Board and Regional Director
(G3)*, F. Kendall.
Regional Controllers (G5), D. R. Ritchie; D. J.
Morrison; J. W. Glester.

Northern (Newcastle upon Tyne)

*Chairman, Regional Board and Regional Director
(G3)*, A. G. Balls.
Regional Controllers (G5), J. A. M. Hastings; R. G.
Bell.

South West (Bristol)

*Chairman, Regional Board and Regional Director
(G3)*, G. M. Wedd.
Regional Controller (G5), J. Ashbridge.

East Midlands (Nottingham)

*Chairman, Regional Board and Regional Director
(G4)*, P. M. Hewitt, O.B.E.
Regional Controller (G5), N. H. Perry.

South East

*Chairman, Regional Board and Regional Director
(G3)*, J. Peeler.
Regional Controllers (G5), N. Thompson; M. W. McD.
Cairns; J. A. Colley.

Eastern

*Chairman, East Anglia Regional Board and Regional
Director (G3)*, D. G. Crane.
Regional Controllers (G5), J. J. Parsons; A. F.
Richardson.

STATISTICS (ENVIRONMENT)

Under Secretary (G3), D. C. L. Wroe.
Grade 5, R. F. Sellwood; F. D. Sando; W. H. Stott; J.
E. Kidgell; P. S. MacCormack; D. L. H. Roberts.

CHIEF ECONOMIC ADVISER (ENVIRONMENT)

Deputy Secretary (G2), H. J. D. Cole.
Grade 5, B. C. Isherwood; A. A. E. Holmans; D. A. C.
Heigham; H. B. Wenban-Smith; P. S. MacCormack.

CHIEF SCIENTIST (ENVIRONMENT)

Deputy Secretary (G2), Dr. M. W. Holdgate, C.B.

Environment Science Policy Unit

Director (G4), Dr. D. Everest.
Grade 5, C. L. Robson.

Building Research Establishment

Director (G3), Dr. R. G. H. Watson.
Deputy Director (G4), R. E. Jeanes.
Grade 5, T. J. Griffiths; Dr. S. J. Leach; Dr. J. B. Menzies; K. N. Palmer; J. M. Baker.

LEGAL

Solicitor and Legal Adviser (G2), M. J. Ware.
Principal Assistant Solicitor (G3), Mrs. A. S. Granham.

DEPARTMENTS OF THE ENVIRONMENT AND TRANSPORT—COMMON SERVICES
2 Marsham Street, SW1P 3EB
(01–212 3434)

ORGANIZATION AND ESTABLISHMENTS

Director General of Organisation and Establishments (G2), D. J. Burr.

Establishments Organisation Division

Grade 5, J. F. Stoker.

Senior Staff Management

Under Secretary (G3), F. W. Girling.
Grade 5, B. Taylor; H. D. Hallett.
Chief Librarian (G6) P. Kirwan.
Grade 6, F. H. Elders; F. R. Gill.

Personnel Management and Training

Under Secretary (G3), E. B. C. Osmotherly.
Grade 5, C. R. Grimsey; P. Stringfellow; G. D. Edmonds; Mrs. M. McDonald; C. R. Hook.
Grade 6, A. Cowan; D. Farrow; B. L. W. Dexter; G. R. Wells; G. Bray; M. S. Barratt; J. England, O.B.E.
Chief Welfare Officer (Principal), R. J. Wood.

Administrative Resources

Under Secretary (G3), Miss D. A. Nichols.
Grade 4, J. G. Handby.
Grade 5, A. Z. Levy; Ms. E. A. Hopkins; C. P. Evans; R. G. Jones.
Grade 6, R. H. Cheeseman; R. W. MacGregor.

PLANNING INSPECTORATE

Chief Planning Inspector (G3), Miss E. B. Haran.
Deputy Chief Planning Inspectors (G4), J. D. Adshead; R. J. Amblin.
Assistant Chief Planning Inspectors (G5), M. M. Cross; A. S. Barnes; F. E. Booth; S. Crow; N. E. Heijne; T. M. Millington; P. J. Roberts; J. Mossop.
Head of Administration (G5), R. D. Compton.

ROYAL COMMISSION ON ENVIRONMENTAL POLLUTION
Church House, Great Smith Street, SW1P 3BL
[01–212 8620]

Set up on Feb. 20, 1970, "to advise on matters, both national and international, concerning the pollution of the environment; on the adequacy of research in this field; and the future possibilities of danger to the environment."

Chairman, Prof. Sir Richard Southwood, F.R.S.
Members, A. Archer; Prof. C. Blake; Prof. B. E. Clayton; Prof. G. R. Conway; The Earl of Cranbrook; J. W. Edmonds; Prof. G. E. Fogg, C.B.E., F.R.S.; The Lord Nathan; Prof. D. E. Newland; J. P. R. Pope; Dr. C. W. Suckling, F.R.S.; Prof. M. P. Vessey; Prof. H. Charnock, F.R.S.; L. C. G. Gilling, O.B.E..
Secretary, T. E. Radice.

EQUAL OPPORTUNITIES COMMISSION
Overseas House, Quay Street, Manchester M3 3HN
[061–833 9244]

Press Office: 1 Bedford Street. W.C.2
[01–379 6323]

Regional Offices: 249 West George Street,
Glasgow [041–226 4591]

Caerwys House, Windsor Place, Cardiff
[0222–43552]

Chairman, The Baroness Platt of Writtle ... £30,080
Deputy Chairman, Mrs. J. Finlay £16,832
Members, Prof. Angela Bowey; Mrs. R. Brown; J. Dunlop; D. Guereca; B. Marks; Mrs. T. Marsland; Ann Robinson; Miss D. Rookledge; Lady Turner; Mrs. P. Turner.
Chief Executive, A. E. Hart.

EXCHEQUER AND AUDIT DEPARTMENT
See National Audit Office

EXPORT CREDITS GUARANTEE DEPARTMENT
P.O. Box 272, Aldermanbury House,
Aldermanbury, EC2P 2EL
[01–382 7000]

The Export Credits Guarantee Department is responsible to the Secretary of State for Trade. The Export Guarantees and Overseas Investment Act 1978 enables E.C.G.D. to encourage U.K. exports by making available export credit insurance to British firms engaged in selling overseas and to guarantee repayment to banks in Britain providing finance for export credit. Guarantees under Section 1 of the Act are given after consultation with an Advisory Council of bankers and businessmen.

The Act also empowers E.C.G.D. to insure British private investment overseas against political risks, such as war, expropriation and restrictions on remittances.

Secretary, J. Gill C.B. £35,278
Deputy to the Secretary, (vacant).
Under Secretaries, R. T. Kemp; D. C. Smith; D. H. Twyford; F. J. Chapman £28,583
Assistant Secretaries, K. G. Lockwood; C. M. Bossom; G. Bromley; C. E. Breach; J. G. M. Cochrane; R. Wild; J. W. Coggins; R. A. Ranson; J. K. Sedman; W. J. C. Pinnell; A. J. Bray; C. Foxall; B. J. Davison; Miss S. E. Harding; J. R. Weiss .... £19,243 to £23,159
Senior Principals, A. P. Fowell; G. C. Bird; D. C. Cooper; K. Dixey; F. Wilmot; M. J. Long
      £15,605 to £20,794
Principals, J. S. Anderson; P. Armstrong; D. D. Baird; R. Bennett; T. R. Black; G. Blackburn; D. Q. Bryars; P. J. Callaghan; J. D. Cameron; A. P. C. Carcas; A. L. Childs; D. Collins; D. R. Coombe; A. B. Coyne; M. J. Crane; Mrs. R. Q. Davies; R. A. Dew; C. L. W. Durning; R. I. Fear; R. X. Fear; G. C. Fisher; J. M. Foster; R. R. Fryatt; P. C. Gaudoin; R. Gotts; D. A. Green; R. T. Griffiths; R. Hardy; G. H. Hill; R. Holloway; T. M. Jaffray; P. F. Jennings; G. G. Jones; R. Jones; N. A. Lambert; R. F. Lethbridge; G. J. A. Link; V. P. Lunn-Rockliffe; J. S. McKibbin; Mrs. M. Maddox; Miss R. M. Martin; D. W. Miller; D. Miner; J. Moon; A. J. E. Muckersie; P. L. Neal; D. W. Overy; M. D. Pentecost; R. J. Pomeroy; S. C. Pond; Mrs. V. A. Randall; I. L. S. L. Robertson; S. Rosenthal; M. Russell; R. Scott; B. M. Sidwell, T.D.; K. Smith; J. Snowden; C. T. Spillane; R. M. Sutton; C. M. Thorogood; D. A. H. Tickner; D. L. Townley; J. A. Tyler; P. M. Walker; E. J. Walsby; A. R. Watt; R. A. Watt; Miss J.West; D. L. Wyatt; G. A. Young ..... £12,399 to £16,656

Principal Information Officer, M. J. Ricketts
£12,399 to £16,656
Principal Scientific Officer, A. P. G. Hare
£11,343 to £14,931

Regional Offices

Belfast: Windsor House, 9–15 Bedford Street, Belfast (0232 231743); *Birmingham:* Colmore Centre, 115 Colmore Row, Birmingham (021–233 1771); *Bristol:* 1 Redcliffe Street, Bristol (0272–299971); *Cambridge:* 72–80 Hills Road, Cambridge (0223–68801); *City of London:* Clements House, 14–18 Gresham Street, E.C.2 (01–726 4050); *Croydon:* Sunley House, Bedford Park, Croydon (01–680 5030); *Glasgow:* Fleming House, 134 Renfrew Street, Glasgow (041–332 8707); *Leeds:* West Riding House, 67 Albion Street, Leeds (0532–450631); *Manchester:* Townbury House, Blackfriars Street, Salford (061–834 8181).

Export Guarantees Advisory Council

Chairman, W. J. Benson.
Deputy Chairman, R. J. Dent.
Other Members, J. N. Scott; M. M. Baker; W. A. J. Dacombe; M. D. McWilliam; W. G. Barrett; R. H. George; W. Hogbin; E. L. Brooks.

OFFICE OF FAIR TRADING
Field House, Bream's Buildings, EC4A 1PR
[01–242 2858]

The Office of Fair Trading is a government department responsible for the administration of the Fair Trading Act, 1973, the Consumer Credit Act, 1974, the Restrictive Trade Practices Act, 1976, the Estate Agents Act, 1979, and the Competition Act, 1980. Under the supervision of the Director General of Fair Trading the office keeps under review commercial activities in the United Kingdom and aims to protect the consumer against unfair practices and is divided between five main areas: consumer affairs, consumer credit, monopolies and mergers, restrictive trade practices and anti-competitive practices.

Director General, Sir Gordon Borrie £45,000
Deputy Director General, Miss E. M. Llewellyn-Smith £36,500

Consumer Affairs Division

Director, C. T. Newton £28,583
Assistant Directors, D. G. Hyde; M. D. C. Johnson; S. G. Linstead . . . . £20,964 to £25,533

Competition Policy Division

Director, Dr. M. Howe £29,500
Assistant Directors, Mrs. E. C. Jones; D. W. Lightfoot; J. C. Octon; D. R. Ford . . . . £20,964 to £25,533

Legal Division

Director, B. J. O'Toole £28,583

Chief Information Officer, J. E. Perry
£17,000 to £22,926
Senior Economic Adviser, A. G. Atkinson
£20,964 to £25,533
Establishment and Finance Officer, J. F. H. Craven
£13,508 to £18,363

FOREIGN AND COMMONWEALTH OFFICE
Downing Street, SW1A 2AL
[01-233 3000]

On the recommendations of the Committee on Representational Services Overseas appointed by the Prime Minister under the Chairmanship of Lord Plowden in 1962, H.M. Diplomatic Service was created on Jan. 1, 1965, by the amalgamation of the Foreign Service, the Commonwealth Service, and the Trade Commission Service, and is now responsible for the manning of the overseas posts of these three former services. On Aug. 1, 1966, the Colonial Office was merged into the Commonwealth Relations Office to form the Commonwealth Office. The Foreign Office and Commonwealth Office combined on Oct. 1, 1968.

In November 1970 overseas development became the ultimate responsibility of the Secretary of State for Foreign and Commonwealth Affairs, although it remained in the day-to-day charge of the Minister for Overseas Development (now the Overseas Development Administration), except for the period from March 1974 to June 1975 when the Ministry of Overseas Development reverted to its independent status.

Secretary of State, THE RT. HON. SIR GEOFFREY HOWE, Q.C., M.P. £42,980
  Private Secretary, L. V. Appleyard.
  Assistant Private Secretaries, C. R. Budd; P. F. Ricketts; J. Houston.
  Social Secretary, Miss R. J. Hazell.
Ministers of State for Foreign and Commonwealth Affairs, THE BARONESS YOUNG, P.C. (£25,350); MALCOLM RIFKIND, M.P.; RICHARD LUCE, M.P. (*each* £30,410).
Minister of State for Foreign and Commonwealth Affairs (Minister for Overseas Development), RT. HON. TIMOTHY RAISON, M.P. £30,410
Parliamentary Under Secretary of State, T. Renton, M.P. £25,460
Permanent Under Secretary of State and Head of the Diplomatic Service, Sir Antony Acland, K.C.M.G., K.C.V.O. £51,250
  Private Secretary, S. L. Cowper-Coles.
Deputy Under Secretaries, J. S. Whitehead, C.M.G., C.V.O. (*Chief Clerk*); Sir William Harding, C.M.G., C.V.O.; E. A. J. Fergusson; R. Q. Braithwaite, C.M.G.; A. D. S. Goodall, C.M.G.; Sir Crispin Tickell, K.C.V.O.; D. M. D. Thomas, C.M.G. (*and Political Director*) £36,500
Assistant Under Secretaries, I. S. Winchester, C.M.G. (*Director of Communications*); N. J. Barrington, C.M.G., C.V.O.; S. L. Egerton, C.M.G.; M. R. H. Jenkins, C.M.G.; C. H. Imray, C.M.G. (*Chief Inspector and Deputy Chief Clerk*); J. R. Johnson, C.M.G.; K. G. MacInnes, C.M.G. (*Principal Finance Officer*); R. J. O'Neill, C.M.G.; R. W. Renwick, C.M.G.; D. C. Thomas, C.M.G.; Hon. H. Maud, C.M.G.; P. J. Weston; D. C. Wilson £29,500
Inspectors, (vacant) (*Head of Home Inspectorate*); A. J. Pover; J. R. Leeland; P. A. McLean; R. Westbrook . . . . £22,329 to £26,898
Legal Adviser, Sir John Freeland, K.C.M.G.
Second Legal Adviser, H. G. Darwin, C.M.G.
Deputy Legal Advisers, A. D. Watts, C.M.G.; P. R. N. Fifoot, C.M.G.
Legal Counsellors, D. H. Anderson; F. Burrows, C.M.G.; D. M. Edwards; Mrs. E. M. Denza, C.M.G.; A. I. Aust; J. D. P. Bickford; M. R. Eaton
£23,209 to £26,898
Senior Economic Advisers, Miss P. I. J. Harvey; J. M. C. Rollo . . . . £22,329 to £26,898
International Labour Adviser, A. E. Smith
£22,329 to £26,898
Overseas Police Adviser, R. P. Bryan, O.B.E.
£22,329 to £26,898

Signals Department (Government Communications Headquarters)
Priors Road, Cheltenham, Gloucestershire
[0242–21491]

Director, Sir Peter Marychurch, K.C.M.G. £32,500
Principal Establishment Officer, J. Adye £26,750

Heads of Departments

(£22,329 to £26,898. Assistant Heads of Dept., £21,217 or £14,873 to £19,728; except where stated)

Aid Policy Dept., B. Ireton; *Asst.*, M. Elliott.

Arms Control and Disarmament Dept., Hon. M. Pakenham; *Asst.*, S. I. Soutar.

Central African Dept., Miss T. A. H. Solesby; *Asst.*, D. I. Lewty.

Claims Dept., D. M. Kerr, O.B.E.

Commonwealth Co-ordination Dept., D. Le Breton, C.B.E.; *Asst.*, J. Illman.

Communications Administration Dept., B. B. Bushell; *Assts.*, V. A. Lister, M.B.E.; D. Hughes.

Communication Engineering Dept., R. Castle-Smith, M.B.E. *Deputy Head of Dept.*, P. J. Rothery.

Communications Operations Dept., B. P. Austin; *Assts.*, G. Feast; E. G. B. Jarman.

Communications Planning Staff, C. K. Davies.

Communications Technical Services Dept., P. Mason; *Assts.*, C. Higham; N. L. Allen; E. V. Toreson.

Consular Dept., J. Harrison, L.V.O.; *Assts.*, N. Jarrold; T. Abbott.

Cultural Relations Dept., J. E. C. Macrae; *Assts.*, W. T. Hull, M.B.E.; L. W. Boyes.

Defence Dept., R. J. Alston; *Assts.*, C. D. Crabbie; D. M. Bell.

East African Dept., W. N. Wenban-Smith; *Asst.*, P. Gregory-Hood.

Eastern European Dept., J. A. Birch; *Asst.*, D. C. A. Madden.

Economic Relations Dept., M. L. Tait, M.V.O.; *Asst.*, G. Stegmann.

Economic Advisers, S. H. Broadbent; *Deputy Head*, J. M. C. Rollo.

Energy Science and Space Dept., D. E. S. Blatherwick, O.B.E.; *Asst.*, S. J. L. Wright.

European Community Dept. (External), J. Shepherd; *Asst.*, G. Evans.

European Community Dept. (Internal), P. S. Fairweather; *Asst.*, J. S. Wall, M.V.O.

Falkland Islands Dept., A. E. Palmer, C.V.O.; *Deputy Head*, D. Lamont.

Far Eastern Dept., M. Elliott; *Asst.*, I. C. Orr.

Finance Dept., M. A. Marshall; *Deputy Head of Dept.*, G. F. Griffiths (£22,329 to £26,898); *Assts.*, R. E. Escritt; A. H. Ellis.

Govt. Hospitality Fund, Brig. A. Cowan, M.B.E. (Secretary) £22,329 to £26,898.

Hong Kong Dept., A. C. Galsworthy, C.M.G..

Information Dept., P. Hinchcliffe, C.V.O.; *Assts.* P. J. W. Le Breton; A. Free-Gore.

Information Technology Dept., A. C. Thorpe; *Asst.*, J. Duffy.

Library and Records Dept., Miss E. C. Blayney; H. Hannam.

Maritime, Aviation and Environment Dept., J. W. D. Gray; *Asst.*, D. Broad.

Mexico and Caribbean Dept., D. Joy, C.B.E.; *Asst.*, Miss M. L. Croll.

Middle East Dept., S. P. Day; *Asst.*, R. A. M. Hendrie.

Migration and Visa Dept., A. J. Cambridge; *Asst.*, D. O. Amy, O.B.E.

Nationality and Treaty Dept., D. W. Partridge; *Asst.*, Miss Y. J. E. Veale, O.B.E.

Near East and North Africa Dept., C. W. Long; *Asst.*, P. M. Nixon, O.B.E.

News Dept., C. J. R. Meyer; *Deputy Head*, I. A. Roberts.

North America Dept., P. Fowler; *Asst.*, Miss S. Darling Rogerson.

Nuclear Energy Dept., I. R. Kenyon; *Asst.*, T. N. Young.

Office Services and Transport Unit, D. M. Harrison, O.B.E. (£19,257)

Overseas Estate Dept., R. J. Carrick, C.M.G., M.V.O.; *Deputy Head*, J. Owen, M.B.E.

Permanent Under Secretary's Dept., P. G. Wallis; *Deputy Head*, G. J. B. Williams.

Personnel Operations Dept., A. M. Wood; *Deputy Head*, S. W. J. Fuller; *Assts.*, J. B. Horrocks, M.B.E.; E. Clay; N. M. McCarthy; R. Beveridge.

Personnel Policy Dept., K. E. H. Morris; *Asst.*, B. Dinwiddy.

Personnel Services Dept., J. T. Masefield; *Assts.*, B. E. Bowley; M. Sullivan.

Planning Staff, Miss L. P. Neville-Jones.

Protocol Dept., Hon. E. Gibbs, C.M.G. (*H.M. Vice-Marshal of the Diplomatic Corps*) £26,898; S. W. F. Martin, M.V.O. (*First Assistant Marshal of the Diplomatic Corps*). *Assts.*, J. S. Jasper, O.B.E.; D. K. Sprague.

Republic of Ireland Dept., G. Clark.

Research Dept., P. E. Hall (*Director*).

Security Dept., Mrs. V. E. Sutherland; *Asst.*, P. Sullivan.

South America Dept., P. McLean; *Asst.*, D. Coates.

South Asian Dept., T. C. Wood; *Asst.*, B. E. Cleghorn.

South-East Asian Dept., J. D. Hartland-Swann; *Asst.*, D. J. Carter.

Southern African Dept., A. Reeve; *Asst.*, N. J. Thorpe.

Southern-European Dept., R. A. Neilson, M.V.O.; *Asst.*, H. N. H. Synott.

South Pacific Dept., J. S. Chick; *Asst.*, D. Pragnell, M.V.O., O.B.E..

Soviet Dept., N. H. R. A. Broomfield; *Asst.*, J. M. Macgregor.

Trade Relations and Exports Dept., N. Smith; *Assts.*, A. A. Joy; J. MacDonald.

Training Dept., Mrs. J. J. Campbell.

Director of Language Centre, J. Moore.

United Nations Dept., P. Lever; *Assts.*, R. B. Janvrin; T. N. Byrne.

West African Dept., M. Daly; *Asst.*, P. J. Priestley.

West Indian and Atlantic Dept., C. Sanderson; *Asst.*, Dr. C. Brown.

Western European Dept., M. Llewelyn-Smith; *Asst.*, C. Munro.

CORPS OF QUEEN'S MESSENGERS

Superintendent of the Queen's Messenger Service, Lt.-Col. E. M. T. Crump.

Queen's Diplomatic Service Messengers, R. J. Angel; Col. B. C. F. Arkle, M.B.E., T.D.; Maj. I. G. M. Bamber; Cdr. R. D. D. Bamford; Sqn.-Ldr. L. C. Bazalgette; Maj. G. M. Benson; Lt.-Cdr. B. R. Bezance; Capt. D. F. A. Bloom, G.M.; Lt.-Col. J. B. Clee; Major F. C. W. Courtenay-Thompson; Col. J. M. Deans; Maj. P. T. Dunn; Maj. A. M. Farmer; Lt.-Col. J. W. A. Fleming; J. W. Hannah, M.B.E.; Lt.-Col. K. Hitchcock; J. O. Hollis; Cdr. R. G. E. Howe; Lt.-Col. P. S. Kerr-Smiley; Lt.-Col. J. M. C. Kimmins; Maj. D. B. Metcalfe; G. F. Miller; Maj. J. K. Nairne; Wg.-Cdr. R. A. Nash; Maj. L. M. Phillips; Lt.-Col. H. M. L. Smith; Col. W. H. F. Stevens, O.B.E., A.D.C.; Col. D. W. F. Taylor; Sqn.-Ldr. J. A. Watson; Lt.-Cdr. R. N. J. Wright.

FOREIGN COMPENSATION COMMISSION

Alexandra House, Kingsway, WC2B 6TT

[01–438 7045]

The Commission was set up by the Foreign Compensation Act 1950, primarily to distribute under Orders in Council funds received from other governments in accordance with agreements to pay compensation for expropriated British property and other losses sustained by British nationals. Amending Acts followed: the Foreign Compensation Act 1962 dealt with Egyptian compensation and the Foreign Compensation Act 1969 with claims for losses in the Baltic States and ceded territories of the USSR. The Commission has since 1950 completed the determination of claims and distribution of funds in respect of

Egypt (1962), Yugoslavia, Czechoslovakia, Bulgaria, Poland, Hungary, Romania (1961), and moneys received from the Board of Trade under the USSR Order in Council 1969, dealing with the Baltic States and ceded territories. The Commission has also completed the determination of claims in respect of Egypt (1971) and Romania (1976) and made a final payment from each fund. The Commission has the further duty of registering claims for British-owned property in contemplation of agreements with other countries, and it has done so in seven instances since 1950, the most recent being under the German Democratic Republic (Registration) Order, 1975, and the People's Republic of China (Registration) Order, 1980. The latter Order came into operation on January 5, 1981, and enabled certain claims of United Kingdom nationals relating to property in, and debts or pensions owing from persons in, the territory controlled by the People's Republic of China to be registered and reported on by the Commission.

An agreement was made on January 29, 1982, between the United Kingdom and Czechoslovakia on the settlement of certain outstanding claims and financial issues. The Czechoslovakia Order in Council 1982 came into operation on September 1, 1982, and provides for payments to the Commission by H.M. Government of compensation received under this agreement, and for the determination of claims to such compensation and its distribution by the Commission. Adjudication of these claims continues.

Chairman, A. W. E. Wheeler, C.B.E.
Commissioner, J. A. S. Hall, D.F.C., Q.C.
Secretary and Chief Examiner, D. H. Wright.

FORESTRY COMMISSION
231 Corstorphine Road, Edinburgh EH12 7AT
[031–334 0303]

The Forestry Commissioners are charged with the general duty of promoting in Great Britain the interests of forestry, the development of afforestation, the production and supply of timber and, in discharging their functions, endeavouring to achieve a reasonable balance between the needs of forestry and conservation. The Commission manages some 890,000 hectares of productive forest and has a continuing policy of developing its forests for recreation by the general public. It is also the Forestry Authority for Great Britain with responsibility for a range of regulatory functions, including the administration of grant-aid schemes for planting by private owners, the licensing of tree felling and the control of tree pests and diseases.

Chairman, Sir David Montgomery (*part-time*)
.... £17,210
Director-General and Deputy Chairman, G. D. Holmes, C.B. £36,500
Head of Private Forestry and Development, (vacant) £29,500
Head of Administration and Finance, D. T. J. Rutherford £29,500
Head of Operations, G. J. Francis £29,500
Senior Officer, Wales (Victoria House, Aberystwyth), D. Y. M. Robertson £24,317

REGISTRY OF FRIENDLY SOCIETIES (CENTRAL OFFICE) AND OFFICE OF THE INDUSTRIAL ASSURANCE COMMISSIONER
15–17 Great Marlborough Street, W1V 2AX
[01–437 9992]

The Department acts as a public registry for mutual organizations registered under, mainly, the Building Societies Act 1962, Friendly Societies Act 1974 and the Industrial and Provident Societies Act 1965. This function includes certifying that the rules are within

the law, receiving and checking annual returns and putting both rules and annual returns on the public record files which are open to search by the public.

The Department's main responsibility, however, is the prudential supervision of those mutual organizations which hold investors' money, particularly the building societies and larger friendly societies, to protect the money placed with those societies by investors. The Department acts as the main channel of communication between the Government and building societies and friendly societies, and is responsible for offering advice to Ministers on policy issues affecting those societies.

The Chief Registrar has certain powers to arbitrate in disputes between members and registered societies.

Chief Registrar and Industrial Assurance Commissioner, J. M. Bridgeman £38,325
Asst. Registrar and Deputy Head of Department, A. Wilson £26,909
Assistant Registrars, R. L. Devlins; P. D. Davis
.... £20,964 to £25,533
Grade 6, S. Whitehead .... £17,000 to £22,926
Establishment and Finance Officer and Head of Establishments & Records Branch, G. S. Royston
.... £17,000 to £22,926
Senior Legal Assistants, C. B. E. White; A. Lawton; R. C. Perkins .... £15,688 to £21,297
Registrations Branch (Head), R. E. Merrick
.... £13,508 to £18,363
Monitoring (F&P) Branch (Head), T. R. Richards
.... £13,508 to £18,363
Monitoring (BS)Branch (Head), F. da Rocha
.... £13,508 to £18,363
Inspections Branch (Head), C. Bell
.... £13,508 to £18,363
Policy and Parliamentary Principal, Ms. M. L. Hindmarch .... £13,508 to £18,363
Computer Project Manager, F. Gold
.... £13,508 to £18,363
Financial Appraisal Group (Statistician), A. G Tebbutt .... £13,508 to £18,363

Registry of Friendly Societies, Scotland
58 Frederick Street, Edinburgh, EH2 1AB
[031–226 3224]

Assistant Registrar, J. L. J. Craig, W.S.

GAMING BOARD FOR GREAT BRITAIN
Berkshire House, 168–173 High Holborn,
WC1V 7AA
[01–240 0821]

Established on October 25, 1968, to maintain a broad oversight of developments in gaming in Great Britain, to check prospective gaming licensees management and staff, and to advise the Home Secretary on making regulations which may be needed for the further control of gaming.

Chairman, Sir Anthony Rawlinson, K.C.B. (*part-time*) £18,048
Members, Mrs. E. B. Y. Hunter-Jones; P. B. Kavanagh, C.B.E., Q.P.M.; N. A. Ward-Jones, V.R.D. (*part-time*) £7,235
Secretary, M. H. Hogan.

BRITISH GAS CORPORATION
152 Grosvenor Road, SW1V 3JL
[01–821 1444]

British Gas was established in 1973. It explores for, purchases and transmits gas, and through its 12 Regions supplies gas to over 16 million customers throughout Great Britain.

Chairman, Sir Denis Rooke, C.B.E., F.R.S. £58,100
Chief Executive, R. Evans.
Secretary, G. C. Hogg.

GAS REGIONS

Scottish, Granton House, 4 Marine Drive, Edinburgh EH5 1YB. *Chairman*, R. W. Hill.

Northern, Norgas House, P.O. Box 1GB, Killingworth, Newcastle-upon-Tyne NE99 1GB. *Chairman*, K. Summersgill.

North Western, Welman House, Altrincham, Cheshire WA15 8AE. *Chairman*, R. H. Greenfield.

North Eastern, New York Road, Leeds LS2 7PE. *Chairman*, N. Blacker.

East Midlands, P.O. Box 145, De Montfort Street, Leicester LE1 9DB. *Chairman*, E. A. Haynes.

West Midlands, Wharf Lane, Solihull, West Midlands B91 2JP. *Chairman*, H. V. Keating.

Wales, Helmont House, Churchill Way, Cardiff CF1 4NB. *Chairman*, D. H. Fisher.

Eastern, Star House, Potters Bar, Herts. EN6 2PD. *Chairman*, D. H. Griffiths, O.B.E.

North Thames, North Thames House, London Road, Staines, Middx. TW18 4AE. *Chairman*, J. Gadd.

South Eastern, Segas House, Katherine Street, Croydon CR9 1JU. *Chairman*, A. A. Dove.

Southern, 80 St. Mary's Road, Southampton SO9 5AT. *Chairman*, D. A. Young.

South Western, Riverside, Temple Street, Keynsham, Bristol BS18 1EQ. *Chairman*, A. I. D. Frith.

THE GOVERNMENT ACTUARY
22 Kingsway, WC2B 6LE
[01–242 6828]

Government Actuary, E. A. Johnston, C.B. £39,250
Directing Actuaries, C. D. Daykin; D. H. Loades; G. G. Newton £30,800
Chief Actuaries, D. G. Ballantine; C. L. Cannon; J. L. Field; R. T. Foster; M. A. Pickford; A. G. Young £27,275
Senior Actuaries, B. J. Coode; C. A. Harris*; T. W. Hewitson; P. H. Hinton*; P. M. Hodgett; F. A. Honeysett; A. I. Johnston; Mrs. I. W. Lane; C. F. Morrison; A. P. Pavelin; D. F. Renn*; Miss P. M. Webster .... £18,411 to £24,291
*£22,329 to £26,898

GOVERNMENT HOSPITALITY FUND
2 Carlton Gardens, SW1Y 5AA
[01–214 6000]

Instituted in 1908 for the purpose of organizing official hospitality on a regular basis, with a view to the promotion of international goodwill.
Minister in Charge, R. Luce, M.P.
Secretary, Brig. A. Cowan, M.B.E.

DEPARTMENT OF HEALTH AND SOCIAL SECURITY
Alexander Fleming House, Elephant and Castle, SE1 6BY
[01–407 5522]

The Department of Health and Social Security was created on November 1, 1968, from the Ministry of Health and Ministry of Social Security. The Department performs the functions of the two former Ministries.

The Department is responsible for the administration of the National Health Service in England and for the personal social services run by local authorities in England for children, the elderly, infirm, handicapped and other persons in need. It has functions relating to food hygiene and welfare foods. The Department is also concerned with the medical and surgical treatment of war pensioners in England, the Channel Isles, Isle of Man or living in the Irish Republic, and is responsible for the ambulance and first aid services in emergency, under the Civil

Defence Act, 1948. The Department represents the United Kingdom on the World Health Organization of the United Nations. Responsibility for the administration of the Health Services in Wales was transferred to the Welsh Office on April 1, 1969. The Department is responsible for the social security services in England, Scotland and Wales. These services comprise schemes for war pensions, national insurance, child benefit, industrial injuries, attendance allowances, mobility allowances and supplementary benefits.

Secretary of State for Social Services, THE RT. HON. (PETER) NORMAN FOWLER, M.P............ £38,910
Private Secretary, S. A. Godber . £20,013 to £24,317
Assistant Private Secretaries, S. H. F. Hickey; Miss E. Mothersill.
Parliamentary Private Secretary, C. Wardle, M.P.
Special Adviser to the Secretary of State, N. True.
Minister of State for Social Security, ANTONY HAROLD NEWTON, O.B.E., M.P. £30,410
Minister of State (Health), THE RT. HON. KENNETH HARRY CLARKE, Q.C., M.P. £30,410
Parliamentary Under Secretaries of State, R. Whitney, O.B.E., M.P.; J. Patten, M.P. (*Health and Personal Social Services*) £25,460; The Baroness Trumpington (*Health and Social Security*) £21,450
Permanent Secretary, Sir Kenneth Stowe, K.C.B., C.V.O. £52,750
Private Secretary, M. Kerin.
Second Permanent Secretary, Sir Geoffrey Otton, K.C.B.
Private Secretary, S. Bird.
Deputy Secretaries, B. R. Rayner; G. G. Hulme; C. W. France; G. A. Hart; J. S. Heppell; N. E. Clarke; M. Fairey .... £38,325 to £39,250
Chairman of N.H.S. Management Board, V. Paige.
Private Secretary, T. Kingham.
Chief Medical Officer, Dr. E. D. Acheson £42,000
Chief Works Officer, J. Bolton £30,500
Librarian, J. Wormald .... £13,508 to £18,363
Chief Scientist, Prof. Sir Desmond Pond, M.D., F.R.C.P. £36,500
Assistant Chief Scientist, Prof. R. J. Cole, PH.D. £27,791

Solicitor's Office

Solicitor, J. St. L. Brockman £36,500
Principal Assistant Solicitors, P. K. J. Thompson; R. J. Butcher £29,500

Establishment and Personnel Division I

Director of Establishment and Personnel (Departmental) Under Secretary, B. Bridges £30,975 to £31,750
Assistant Secretaries, J. F. Shaw; J. N. Wray; G. R. West .... £20,964 to £25,533

Establishment and Personnel Division II

Director of Establishment and Personnel (Headquarters) Under Secretary, M. C. Malone-Lee £30,975 to £31,750
Assistant Secretaries, P. V. Foster; Ms. K. Caines £20,964 to £25,533

Regional Directorate

Under Secretary, B. W. Taylor ... £30,975 to £31,750
Assistant Secretaries, Miss A. E. Perkins; R. J. Tilney; J. Moyes .... £20,964 to £25,533

Statistics and Research Division

Director of Statistics and Research, A. R. Smith £29,500
Chief Statisticians, B. Mahon; Ms. P. A. Stewart; J. A. Rowntree; M. V. Wilde; D. Wallace; R. J. Scott; C. P. Hogan .... £21,014 to £25,513

International Relations (Health)

Under Secretary, (vacant) .... £30,975 to £31,750
Assistant Secretary, G. C. M. Lupton
£20,013 to £24,317

Information Division

Director of Information, Mrs. J. Hewlett-Davies
£29,500
Deputy Director, P. Wilson ...... £20,013 to £24,317

Economic Adviser's Office

Chief Economic Adviser, C. H. Smee £29,500
Senior Economic Advisers, N. J. Glass; J. W. Hurst;
M. A. Parsonage .... £20,013 to £24,317

Social Security Division A

Under Secretary, D. Storer ...... £30,975 to £31,750
Assistant Secretaries, M. E. H. Platt; P. L. Adeane;
Mrs. A. De Peyer .... £20,964 to £25,533

Social Security Division B

Under Secretary, C. M. Regan .... £30,975 to £31,750
Assistant Secretaries, T. Whiteley; J. W. White
£20,964 to £25,533

Social Security Division C

Under Secretary, J. H. Ward ..... £30,975 to £31,750
Assistant Secretaries, J. R. Simpson; J. E. Knight;
I. D. Alexander............... £20,964 to £25,533

Social Security Supplementary Benefits Division

Under Secretary, B. Walmsley ... £30,975 to £31,750
Assistant Secretaries, J. Tross; D. Brerton; Mrs.
E. A. Woods................. £20,964 to £25,533

Finance Divisions

Under Secretary (*Health*), Mrs. G. T. Banks
£30,975 to £31,750
Assistant Secretaries, J. H. James; I. Jewesbury;
M. G. Lillywhite .... £20,013 to £24,317
Under Secretary (*Health*), R. A. Birch
£30,975 to £31,750
Assistant Secretaries, R. A. Cubitt; R. Smith; A. T.
Skinner; P. Fletcher......... £20,013 to £24,317
Under Secretary (*Social Security*), T. S. Heppell
£30,975 to £31,750
Assistant Secretaries, G. R. L. Osborne; R. A.
Wallace; M. Whippman .... £20,013 to £24,317

Medical Divisions (Health)

Deputy Chief Medical Officers, E. L. Harris, C.B.;
M. E. Abrams; E. L. Harris, C.B.; R. M. Oliver
£36,500
Senior Principal Medical Officers, Barbara Macgib-
bon; N. P. Halliday; Pamela Mason; D. C. Ower,
T.D.; J. S. Metters; G. C. Rivett; Diana M. Walford;
G. Jones................................ £29,500
Principal Medical Officers, A. W. G. English; J.
Heckford; J. L. Hunt; R. D. Mann; G. K. Matthew,
M.B.E.; R. G. Penn; R. Wawman; R. H. Smith;
J. H. Steadman; R. Wilkins; Alison Smithies; G.
Pincherle............................... £26,594
Medical Staff Officers, L. B. Hunt; Dr. T. K. Sweeney.

Medical Division (Social Security)

Chief Medical Adviser, Dr. P. R. Greenfield . £29,500
Principal Medical Officers, B. Purdy; W. R. O.
Eggington; D. F. Rice; T. J. G. Phillips.... £26,594

N.H.S. PERSONNEL DIVISIONS
Division FPS

Under Secretary, J. G. Pilling ... £30,975 to £31,750
Assistant Secretaries, Mrs. S. Reeve; R. W. D.
Venning; Mrs. C. Palmer; Mrs. P. Petrie
£20,013 to £24,317

Division HAP

Under Secretary, P. J. Wormald .. £30,975 to £31,750
Assistant Secretaries, N. Illingworth; B. A. R. Smith;
R. M. Drury; Mrs. M. A. Robinson
£20,013 to £24,317

Division MME

Assistant Secretary, W. Robertson
£20,013 to £24,317

Superannuation Branch

Deputy Secretary, N. E. Clarke ... £38,325 to £39,250
Assistant Secretary, J. M. Bankier
£20,013 to £24,317

Supply Division

Controller of Supply, F. R. Higson £29,500
Assistant Secretary, J. Harley .... £20,013 to £24,317
Director of Scientific and Technical Branch, R. T.
Rogers £27,791
Superintendents, R. W. B. Allen; Miss M. N. Duncan;
Dr. D. C. Potter; Dr. N. A. Slark; A. D. C. Shipley
£16,229 to £21,834

Community Services Division

Under Secretary, J. S. Scott-Whyte
£30,975 to £31,750
Assistant Secretaries, Mrs. V. M. Demmery; Mrs.
E. Shaw; R. Orton ...... £20,013 to £24,317
Senior Principal, C. E. Stone.

Mental Health Division

Under Secretary, E. B. McGinnis . £30,975 to £31,750
Assistant Secretaries, B. A. Harrison; Mrs. P. M.
Williamson; Mrs. M. A. J. Pearson
£20,013 to £24,317

Regional Liaison Division

Under Secretary, C. Graham ..... £30,975 to £31,750
Assistant Secretaries, A. J. Davies; D. J. Morris; Mrs.
M. A. Robinson .... £20,013 to £24,317

Central Management Services

Under Secretary, M. E. G. Fogden
£30,975 to £31,750
Assistant Secretaries, J. W. E. Clutterbuck; T. A.
Howell; M. J. Pinches; J. Y. Marshall; J. M. Wray
£20,013 to £24,317

Prevention, Primary, Maternity and Child Health Division

Under Secretary, Mrs. J. M. Firth
£30,975 to £31,750
Assistant Secretaries, C. H. Wilson; R. P. S. Hughes;
A. I. Ratcliffe .... 20,013 to £24,317

Social Services Inspectorate

Chief Inspector (*Deputy Secretary*), W. B. Utting
£38,325 to £39,250
Deputy Chief Inspectors, M. Phillips; J. H. Barnes
£26,909
Principal Social Work Service Officers (*HQ*), Miss
P. M. Baker; J. H. Barnes; D. E. Gregory; D. G.
Gilroy; Miss M. I. Denham; J. Hodder; Mrs. I.
Midforth; Miss P. P. Thayer ... £19,069 to £23,898
Principal Social Work Officers (*Regions*), Miss C. M.
Clark; H. J. Devey; Miss M. I. Ellis; A. B. Hannan;
J. F. Corcoran; W. A. Hollingberry; Miss C. F.
Jayne; Miss M. S. Markham; Mrs. E. I. Tate.

Medicines Division

Under Secretary, N. M. Hale ..... £30,975 to £31,750
Assistant Secretary, D. O. Hagger
£20,013 to £24,317

Health Service Division

Under Secretary, J. P. Cashman .. £30,975 to £31,750
Assistant Secretaries, A. B. Barton; J. B. Sharp;
M. A. Harris; P. M. C. Winterton
£20,013 to £24,317

Catering and Dietetics Branch

Chief Officer on Catering and Dietetics, A. R. Horton
£16,343 to £20,794
Deputy Chief Officer, Miss E. J. Young (*acting*)
£13,508 to £18,363

Domestic Services Management Branch

Chief Officer, Miss M. Mawson ... £17,000 to £22,926
Deputy Chief Officer, Miss I. D. Oliver
£13,508 to £18,363

Works Group

Chief Works Officer (Director-General of Works), J.
Bolton £36,500

Directorate of Works Development

Director or Works Development and Chief Architect,
R. H. Goodman £29,500
Assistant Chief Architects, M. A. Meager; P. L. Ward
£20,013 to £24,317
Superintending Architects, B. Hitchcox; G. Mayers;
A. J. Noakes; J. Ward .... £15,605 to £20,794
Assistant Chief Engineer, (vacant)
£20,013 to £24,317
Superintending Engineers, J. M. Singh; G. Fisher
£15,605 to £20,794

Directorate of Works Operations

Director of Works Operations and Chief Engineer,
(vacant) £29,500
Assistant Chief Architect, C. Davies
£20,013 to £24,317
Superintending Architects, J. D. Twells; M. F. Kemp
£15,605 to £20,794
Assistant Chief Engineers, S. Ratcliffe; I. E. G.
Mahon .... £20,013 to £24,317
Superintending Engineers, R. S. Body; T. Wagstaff;
R. J. Tuthill; B. C. Oliver...... £15,605 to £20,794
Superintending Surveyor, B. K. Gilbert
£15,605 to £20,794

Directorate of Works Construction and Cost Intelligence

Director of Works Construction and Chief Surveyor,
K. W. Hudson £29,500
Assistant Chief Architect, M. J. Bench
£20,013 to £24,317
Superintending Architect, D. J. Burnett
£15,605 to £20,794
Superintending Engineer, (vacant)
£15,605 to £20,794
Assistant Chief Surveyor, D. A. Butler
£20,013 to £24,317
Superintending Surveyors, N. J. M. Barton; D. W.
Luscombe .... £15,605 to £20,794

Administrative Support and Land Branch

Assistant Secretary, J. Garlick ... £20,013 to £24,317

Dental Division

Chief Dental Officer, M. C. Downer £29,500
Deputy Chief Dental Officer, D. R. Whittington
£26,594
Senior Dental Officers, W. G. Everett; Dr. Burnapp;
W. N. McL. Niven; J. Rodgers, D.F.M.; C. Howard
£24,317

Nursing Division

Chief Nursing Officer, Mrs. A. A. B. Poole ... £29,500
Deputy Chief Nursing Officer, Miss S. P. C. Wright-
Warren £26,112

Principal Nursing Officers, M. A. Clark; Dr. S.
LeLean; Mrs. D. A. Patey; Mrs. E. B. Rivett; J.
Tait; Miss J. Wheeler £22,975

Operational Strategy Directorate

Director, Dr. J. W. C. Spackman.
Assistant Secretary, G. H. Bardwell; (one vacancy).

Pharmaceutical Division

Chief Pharmaceutical Officer, Dr. B. A. Wills
£29,500
Deputy Chief Pharmaceutical Officer, Dr. C. A.
Johnson...................... £20,013 to £24,317
Superintending Pharmaceutical Officers, R. Baker;
Dr. J. Purves; A. G. Stewart; B. H. Hartley
£17,000 to £22,926
Principal Pharmaceutical Officers, K. J. Ayling; D. I.
R. Begg; J. P. Betts; A. C. Cartwright; Miss R.
Coulson; Miss P. O. Creed; B. A. Curran; J.
Davenport; Mrs. L. Davidson; Mrs. M. A. Dow;
A. T. Gray; D. Haythorn Thwaite; Miss D. Hepburn;
W. J. Hewlett; Dr. A. Islam; J. R. V. Merrills;
A. J. Middleton; Miss M. J. E. Millar; Miss S. A.
Norton; Miss M. L. Rabouhans; A. R. Rogers; J. R.
Sharp; Miss R. J. Smith; R. L. Smith; R. B. Trigg;
J. L. Turner; J. A. Wandless ... £15,150 to £18,232

North Fylde Central Office

Controller, J. M. Bankier .... £20,013 to £24,317

Newcastle upon Tyne Central Office

Controller, D. V. Chislett £29,500
Assistant Secretaries, E. H. W. Luxton; J. Wailes; J.
W. W. Nairn .... £20,013 to £24,317

Scotland

Argyle House, 2 Lady Lawson Street, Edinburgh
Controller, F. S. Clark .... £20,013 to £24,317

Regional Organization [England and Wales]

North Eastern, Government Buildings, Lawnswood,
Leeds and Arden House, Regent Centre, Regent
Farm Road, Gosforth, Newcastle upon Tyne.
Regional Controller, R. Walton.
London North, Olympic House, Olympic Way, Wem-
bley, Middx. *Regional Controller*, J. F. Jones.
London South, Sutherland House, 29–37 Brighton
Road, Sutton, Surrey and Grosvenor House, Basing
View, Basingstoke, Hants. *Regional Controller*,
Mrs. S. P. Maunsell.
Wales and South Western, Gabalfa, Cardiff and
Flowers Hill, Bristol. *Regional Controller*, G.
Griffiths.
West Midlands, Five Ways Tower, Frederick Road,
Edgbaston, Birmingham. *Regional Controller*, J. T.
Green.
North Western, St. Martin's House, Stanley Precinct,
Bootle, Merseyside. *Regional Controller*, J. B.
Griffin.

INDUSTRIAL INJURIES ADVISORY COUNCIL

Friars House, 157–168 Blackfriars Road,
SE1 8EU
[01–703 6380]

The Industrial Injuries Advisory Council is a
statutory body under the Social Security Act, 1975,
which considers and advises the Secretary of State
for Social Services on Regulations and other questions relating to industrial injuries benefit or its
administration.
Chairman, Prof. J. M. Harrington.
Members, J. R. Boddy, M.B.E.; D. W. Boydell; B. L.
Cawley; Prof. D. M. Conning; Dr. R. J. Donaldson,
O.B.E.; Dr. P. C. Elmes; P. R. A. Jacques; J. Ll.
McQuitty, O.B.E., Q.C.; T. W. Mawer; Dr. M. L.

Newhouse; Dr. A. J. Newman Taylor; S. J. Stanbrook; D. W. Vallis; Mrs. S. M. Anderson; G. Lloyd, C.B.E.

Secretary, B. O'Gorman.

NATIONAL INSURANCE JOINT AUTHORITY
151 Great Titchfield Street, W1P 8AD
[01–636 1696]

Members, The Secretary of State for Social Services; the Head of the Department of Health and Social Services for Northern Ireland.

Deputies for the Secretary of State for Social Services, Sir Kenneth Stowe, K.C.B., C.V.O., D. G. Storer; for the Head of the Department of Health and Social Services for Northern Ireland, N. Dugdale; R. F. Mills.

Joint Financial Advisers, E. A. Johnston; T. S. Heppell; F. A. Elliott.

Secretary, J. D. Leach.

SOCIAL SECURITY—OFFICE OF THE CHIEF ADJUDICATION OFFICER
Cumberland House,
15/17 Cumberland Place, Southampton SO9 2DD
[0703–34541]

Chief Adjudication Officer, T. A. Parsons, C.B.

SOCIAL SECURITY ADVISORY COMMITTEE
New Court, Carey Street, W.C.2.
[01–831 6111]

The Social Security Advisory Committee (SSAC) was established by the Social Security Act 1980 to advise the Secretary of State for Social Services and the Department of Health and Social Services for Northern Ireland on all Social Security matters except those relating to benefits for industrial injuries and diseases and occupational pensions. The Social Security Housing Benefit Act 1982 added housing benefit to the Committee's responsibilities.

Chairman, P. M. Barclay, C.B.E.

Members, Mrs. J. Browning, O.B.E.; Mrs. J. Cheetham; Dr. R. J. Donaldson, O.B.E.; Rev. G. H. Good, O.B.E.; H. Hodge; P. Jacques; Mrs. J. L. Lysaght, C.B.E.; T. S. McLeod; Dr. D. Ray; Dr. A. V. Stokes, O.B.E.; Prof. Olive Stevenson; H. G. Simpson, C.B.E.; R. G. Wendt.

Secretary, Miss G. Moore.

NATIONAL HEALTH SERVICE REGIONAL HEALTH AUTHORITIES

England is divided between 14 Regional Health Authorities, each with at least one university medical school within its boundaries. Each Region contains a number of district health authorities (which are the operational NHS authorities, responsible for assessing needs in their areas, for planning, organizing and administering district health services to meet them). The district health authorities are generally coterminous with the local authorities which provide complementary personal social services. Four of the postgraduate teaching hospitals are now managed by district health authorities and eight are now managed by special health authorities. The Chairmen, and members of Regional Health Authorities and special health authorities, and the Chairmen of district health authorities are appointed by the Secretary of State for Social Services.

Regions

Northern, Benfield Road, Walker Gate, Newcastle upon Tyne. *Chairman*, Prof. B. E. Tomlinson, C.B.E., M.D. *Regional Administrator*, D. Hague.

Yorkshire, Park Parade, Harrogate. *Chairman*, B. Askew. *Regional Administrator*, W. A. H. Holroyd.

Trent, Fulwood House, Old Fulwood Road, Sheffield. *Chairman*, Sir John Carlisle. *Regional Administrator*, B. Edwards.

East Anglia, Union Lane, Chesterton, Cambridge. *Chairman*, Sir Arthur South. *Regional Administrator*, J. H. Stewart.

North East Thames, 40 Eastbourne Terrace, W2. *Chairman*, D. Berniman. *Regional Administrator*, M. J. Fairey.

North West Thames, 40 Eastbourne Terrace, W2. *Chairman*, Dame Betty Paterson; D.B.E. *Regional Administrator*, D. J. Kenny.

South East Thames, Thrift House, Collington Avenue, Bexhill-on-Sea, E. Sussex. *Chairman*, Sir Peter Baldwin. *Regional Administrator*, P. H. J. Le Fleming.

South West Thames, 40 Eastbourne Terrace, W2. *Chairman*, A. V. Driver. *Regional Administrator*, A. J. Kember.

Wessex, Highcroft, Romsey Road, Winchester, Hants. *Chairman*, B. Thwaites, PH.D. *Regional Administrator*, J. Hoare.

Oxford, Old Road, Headington, Oxford. *Chairman*, Sir Gordon Roberts, C.B.E. *Regional Administrator*, P. M. Cooke.

South Western, King Square House, 26–27 King Square, Bristol. *Chairman*, W. V. S. Seccombe. *Regional Administrator*, R. Nicholls.

West Midlands, Arthur Thompson House, 146–150 Hagley Road, Birmingham. *Chairman*, J. Ackers. *Regional Administrator*, K. F. Bales.

Mersey, Wilberforce House, The Strand, Liverpool. *Chairman*, R. D. Wilson. *Regional Administrator*, D. Nichol.

North Western, Gateway House, Piccadilly South, Manchester. *Chairman*, Sir John Page. *Regional Administrator*, Dr. J. L. Roberts.

SCOTTISH HOME AND HEALTH DEPARTMENT
and
NATIONAL HEALTH SERVICE, SCOTLAND
See **Scottish Office**

HIGHLANDS AND ISLANDS DEVELOPMENT BOARD
Bridge House, 27 Bank Street,
Inverness IV1 1QR
[0463 234171]

The Board, a grant-aided body, responsible to the Secretary of State for Scotland, has two broad objectives. These are (1) to assist the people of the Highlands and Islands to improve their economic and social conditions; (2) to enable the Highlands and Islands to play a more effective part in the economic and social development of the nation. To this end the Board will concert, promote, assist or undertake measures for economic and social development.

Chairman, R. Cowan.

Secretary, J. A. MacAskill.

HISTORIC BUILDINGS AND MONUMENTS COMMISSION FOR ENGLAND
Fortress House,
23 Savile Row, W1X 2HE
[01–734 6010]

Under the National Heritage Act, 1983, the duties of the Commission are: (i) to secure the preservation of ancient monuments and historic buildings situated in England; (ii) to promote the preservation and enhancement of the character and appearance of conservation areas situated in England; (iii) to promote the public's enjoyment of, and advance their knowledge of, ancient monuments and historic buildings situated in England and their preservation. The Commission has two statutory advisory committees (*see* below).

Chairman, The Lord Montagu of Beaulieu.
Deputy Chairman, H.R.H. the Duke of Gloucester, G.C.V.O.
Commissioners, J. Beecham; J. Benson; P. M. Burnham; H. M. Colvin; Prof. R. Cramp; Sir Arthur Drew, K.C.B.; A. H. Emery; D. W. Insall; Mrs. J. Jenkins; Prof. A. C. Renfrew; The Earl of Shelburne.
Chief Executive, P. W. Rumble.

Historic Buildings Advisory Committee
25 Savile Row, W.1.
[01–734 6010]

Chairman, Mrs. J. Jenkins.
Secretary, Mrs. E. J. Sharman.

Ancient Monuments Advisory Committee
23 Savile Row, W.1.
[01–734 6010]

Chairman, Sir Arthur Drew, K.C.B.
Secretary, A. F. W. Swift.

HISTORIC BUILDINGS COUNCIL (WALES)
Brunel House, 2 Fitzalan Road,
Cardiff CF2 1UY
[0222–465511]

Chairman, The Marquess of Anglesey, F.S.A.
Members, W. Lindsay Evans; Prof. J. Eynon, F.R.I.B.A., F.S.A.; The Earl Lloyd George of Dwyfor; T. Lloyd; Prof. Glanmor Williams, C.B.E., D.Litt., F.S.A.; R. Haslam.
Secretary, R. J. Bolus.

HISTORIC BUILDINGS COUNCIL (SCOTLAND)
25 Drumsheugh Gardens, Edinburgh EH3 7RN
[031–226 3611–4]

Chairman, The Marquess of Bute.
Members, I. Begg; Mrs. K. Dalyell; Prof. J. Dunbar-Nasmith, C.B.E.; M. Ellington; I. Hutchison, O.B.E.; The Hon. Lord Jauncey, Q.C.; Dr. M. Lindsay, C.B.E., T.D.; C. McWilliam; K. Newis, C.B., C.V.O.; K. Nugent; H. F. Smith, M.B.E.
Secretary, D. J. Christie.

HISTORICAL MANUSCRIPTS COMMISSION
See page 431

ROYAL COMMISSION ON HISTORICAL MONUMENTS [ENGLAND]
Fortress House, 23 Savile Row, W1X 1AB
[01–734 6010]

The Royal Commission on Historical Monuments (England) was appointed in 1908 to survey and publish accounts of historically significant buildings, earthworks and stone constructions up to the year 1714. A new Royal Warrant in 1963 allowed the Commissioners to extend this date limit at their discretion; for practical purposes 1850 is normally taken as the limit. The Commission has published up to the present inventories covering in whole or in part eleven counties and five cities and has also published numerous other works including national and local surveys of types of monument. It is

primarily a recording body though the Commissioners recommend that certain structures should be preserved. A part of the Commission is the National Monuments Record, the public archive of information, documents and photographs of archaeological sites and historic buildings.

Chairman, The Earl Ferrers, P.C.
Commissioners, Prof. R. J. C. Atkinson, C.B.E., F.S.A.; Prof. M. W. Beresford; R. A. Buchanan, PH.D.; Prof. J. D. Evans, PH.D., F.S.A.; P. Kidson, PH.D., F.S.A.; Prof. G. I. Meirion-Jones, PH.D., F.S.A.; Prof. C. Renfrew, PH.D., F.B.A., F.S.A.; Prof. A. L. F. Rivet, F.B.A., F.S.A.; J. Thirsk, PH.D., F.B.A.; Sir Harry Hookway; Prof. J. K. Downes, PH.D., F.S.A.; Prof. A. C. Thomas, PH.D., F.S.A.; Prof. M. Biddle, F.S.A.; Prof. P. E. Lasko, C.B.E., F.B.A., F.S.A.
Secretary, P. J. Fowler, PH.D., F.S.A.

ROYAL COMMISSION ON ANCIENT AND HISTORICAL MONUMENTS IN WALES
Edleston House, Queens Road,
Aberystwyth SY23 2HP
[Aberystwyth: 4381]

The Commission was appointed in 1908 to make an inventory of the Ancient and Historical Monuments in Wales and Monmouthshire. The Commission now includes the National Monuments Record for Wales.
Chairman, Prof. R. J. C. Atkinson, C.B.E., F.S.A.
Commissioners, M. R. Apted, PH.D., F.S.A.; G. C. Boon, F.S.A.; R. W. Brunskill, PH.D.; Prof. D. Ellis Evans, D.Phil., F.B.A.; J. G. Jenkins, D.SC., F.S.A.; Prof. E. M. Jope, F.B.A., F.S.A.; J. B. Smith; Prof. Dewi-Prys Thomas; Prof. Glanmor Williams, Litt.D., F.S.A.; Prof. J. G. Williams.
Secretary, P. Smith, F.S.A.

ROYAL COMMISSION ON ANCIENT AND HISTORICAL MONUMENTS OF SCOTLAND
54 Melville Street, Edinburgh EH3 7HF
[031–225 5994]

The Commission was appointed in 1908 to make an inventory of the Ancient and Historical Monuments of Scotland and to specify those that seem most worthy of preservation. It also has a responsibility to record monuments threatened with destruction, including a statutory duty to record historic buildings for which Listed Building Consent for demolition has been granted. The National Monuments Record of Scotland, a branch of the Commission, contains an extensive collection of pictorial and documentary material relating to Scottish ancient monuments and historic buildings and is open daily for public reference. It also supplies archaeological information to the Ordnance Survey for mapping purposes.
Chairman, The Earl of Crawford and Balcarres, P.C.
Commissioners, Prof. A. A. M. Duncan; Prof. J. D. Dunbar-Nasmith, C.B.E., F.R.I.B.A.; Prof. Rosemary Cramp, F.S.A.; H. M. Colvin, C.B.E., F.B.A.; Prof. L. Alcock, F.S.A., F.R.S.E.; Prof. G. Jobey, D.S.O., F.S.A; Prof. J. Butt; Mrs. P. E. Durham.
Secretary, J. G. Dunbar, F.S.A.

ANCIENT MONUMENTS BOARD (WALES)
Brunel House, 2 Fitzalan Road, Cardiff CF2 1UY
[0222–465511]

Chairman, Prof. G. Williams, C.B.E., D.Litt., F.S.A.
Members, Prof. R. J. C. Atkinson, C.B.E., F.S.A.; G. C. Boon, F.S.A.; R. B. Heaton; The Lord Kenyon, C.B.E., F.S.A.; Prof. R. R. Davies, D.Phil.; D. Moore, F.S.A.
Secretary, A. Huws.

ANCIENT MONUMENTS BOARD (SCOTLAND)
3–11, Melville Street, Edinburgh EH3 7QD
[031 226 2570]

Chairman, M. Magnusson, F.R.S.E., F.S.A.Scot.
Members, J. G. Dunbar, F.S.A., F.S.A.Scot.; Prof. G. Jobey, D.S.O., F.S.A., F.S.A.Scot.; Dr. G. G. Simpson, F.S.A., F.S.A.Scot; Dr. A. Fenton, F.S.A., F.S.A.Scot.; Mrs. M. M. Paterson, F.S.A.Scot.; H. F. Smith, M.B.E.; The Rt. Hon. Lady Grimond; Prof. L. Alcock, F.S.A., F.R.S.E., F.S.A.Scot.; J. Simpson, F.S.A.Scot.; Sir Jamie Stormonth Darling, C.B.E., M.C., T.D., W.S.; Prof. J. J. Wilkes, Ph.D., F.S.A.; Prof. E. C. Fernie, F.S.A., F.S.A.Scot.
Secretary, I. J. MacKenzie, F.S.A.Scot.

HOME-GROWN CEREALS AUTHORITY
Hamlyn House, Highgate Hill, N19 5PR

Constituted under the Cereals Marketing Act, 1965, the Authority consists of 9 members representing U.K. cereal growers, 9 representing dealers in, or processors of, grain and 3 independent members. The purpose of the Authority is to improve the marketing of U.K. grain, production of which was about 26·5 million tonnes in 1984. One of the major functions of the Authority is to provide a market information service. It also supports research related to improving the marketing of cereals and has initiated other developments with the same aim. The Authority also acts as the agent of the Intervention Board for Agricultural Produce in respect of intervention buying, storage and disposal of cereals and oilseed rape within the U.K. under the Common Agricultural Policy and for certain other aspects of the E.E.C. arrangements for cereals in the U.K.
Chairman, A. Laing, C.B.E.
General Manager, C. J. Ames.

HOME OFFICE
50 Queen Anne's Gate, SW1H 9AT
[01–213 3000]

The Home Office deals with those internal affairs in England and Wales which have not been assigned to other Departments. The Home Secretary is particularly concerned with the administration of justice; criminal law; the treatment of offenders including probation and the prison service; the police; immigration and nationality; passport department; community relations; certain public safety matters; fire and civil defence services and also with broad questions of national broadcasting policy. He personally is the link between The Queen and the public and exercises certain powers on Her behalf including that of the Royal Pardon.

Other subjects dealt with include electoral arrangements; addresses and petitions to The Queen; ceremonial and formal business connected with honours; requests for extradition of criminals; scrutiny of local authority byelaws; grant of licences for scientific experiments on animals; cremations, burials and exhumations; firearms; dangerous drugs and poisons, general policy on laws relating to shops, liquor licensing, gaming and lotteries, charitable collections and marriage; theatre and cinema licensing; coordination of government action in relation to the voluntary social services; and sex discrimination policy.

Salary List
Secretary of State	£38,910
Ministers of State	£30,410
Permanent Under Secretary of State (Grade 1)	
	£52,750

Deputy Under Secretary of State (G2)
£38,325 to £39,250
Assistant Under Secretary of State (G3)
£30,975 to £31,750
Assistant Secretary (G5) .... £20,964 to £25,533
Senior Principal (G6) .... £17,000 to £22,926
Principal and Deputy Director ... £13,508 to £18,363
Principal Psychologist .... £13,508 to £18,363
Principal Scientific Officer ...... £12,357 to £16,462
Principal Professional and Technology Officers
£14,392 to £17,322

Secretary of State for the Home Department, The Rt. Hon. Leon Brittan, Q.C., M.P.
  Principal Private Secretary (G5), S. W. Boys Smith.
  Private Secretaries, Ms. C. J. Heald; W. R. Fittall.
  Parliamentary Private Secretaries, G. Bright, M.P.; P. Nicholls, M.P.; T. Smith, M.P.
  Parliamentary Clerk, J. Acton.
Ministers of State, Giles Shaw, M.P.; The Lord Glenarthur; David Waddington, Q.C., M.P.
Parliamentary Under-Secretary of State, D. Mellor, M.P.
Permanent Under Secretary of State (G1), Sir Brian Cubbon, G.C.B.
  Private Secretary, H. S. Webber.
Deputy Under Secretaries of State (G2), D. E. R. Faulkner, C.B.; W. N. Hyde; J. Nursaw, C.B. (*Legal Adviser*); M. J. A. Partridge, C.B.; M. J. Moriarty (*Principal Establishment Officer*); C. J. Train (*Director-General of the Prison Service*).
Chief Medical Officer (at Department of Health and Social Security), E. D. Acheson, D.M., F.R.C.P.

Broadcasting Department
Assistant Under-Secretary of State (G3), Q. J. Thomas.
Assistant Secretary (G5), C. L. Scoble.
Principals, F. H. Eggleston; W. R. Fittall; R. Eagle; D. C. Houghton; N. C. Sanderson; Miss J. Stewart.

Community Programmes and Equal Opportunities Department
Assistant Under-Secretary of State (G3), A. P. Wilson.
Assistant Secretary (G5), J. L. Goddard.
Principals, M. J. Gillespie; Mrs. C. Lehman; Dr. G. L. Thomas; M. Whittaker.

Voluntary Services Unit.
Assistant Secretary (G5), Mrs. P. A. Lee.
Senior Principal (G6), P. E. Bolton.
Principal, F. N. Jasper.

Criminal Department
Assistant Under-Secretary of State (G3), W. J. Bohan.
Assistant Secretaries (G5), W. A. Jeffrey; G. P. Pratt; G. K. Sandiford; N. R. Varney; R. R. G. Watts.
Principals, M. P. Bolt; Mrs. M. E. Bowden; M. K. Brenchley; A. Cogbill; R. G. W. Cook; Miss L. F. Gill; Miss R. E. Henn; R. W. B. Hurley; B. Johnson; Miss B. Latimer; Mrs. R. M. Mitev; Miss G. Moody; S. S. Mundy; J. S. Nottingham; Mrs. S. Street; Miss P. M. Strong; G. Sutton; Mrs. D. M. White; M. Youngs.
Chief Probation Inspector (G5), R. S. Taylor.
Assistant Chief Probation Inspectors (G6), R. A. Betteridge; D. F. Duchemin; Miss M. D. Samuels; C. T. Swann.

Research and Planning Unit
Head of Unit (G5), Mrs. M. Tuck.
Grade 6, J. F. Macleod; R. Tarling.
Principals, J. M. Hough; A. D. Maclean; T. F. Marshall; Mrs. P. Mayhew; Ms. P. M. Morgan; Miss J. W. Mott; Ms. M. J. Shaw; Dr. D. E. Smith; Ms. J. Vennard; G. R. Walmsley.

Establishment Department

Assistant Under-Secretary of State (G3), Miss M. A. Clayton (*Personnel*).
Assistant Secretaries (G5), M. H. Davies; J. A. Ingham; W. J. Stephens; F. J. A. Warne.
Senior Principals (G6), S. W. Bennett; F. R. Hayhurst; J. Smedley; P. G. Spurgeon.
Principals, Miss M. V. A. Allibone; D. J. Blackwood; R. C. Case; C. I. Dickinson; J. C. Dilling; Miss A. Edwards; B. J. Flaherty; Mrs. E. I. France; D. H. Gannon; D. Grant; P. H. Gibson; Mrs. M. G. Hollocks; D. G. Jones; B. J. Jordan; W. R. Mann; R. Ritchie; K. E. R. Rogers; D. G. Ross; M. P. Scandrett; J. C. Smith; R. E. Stockdale.

Home Office Unit at Civil Service Selection Board
Kirkland House, 22 Whitehall, SW1A 2ED
[01–273 3529]

Assistant Secretary, R. J. Miles.
Principal Psychologist, R. T. Feltham.

Finance and Manpower Department

Assistant Under-Secretary of State (Principal Finance Officer) (G3), J. F. Halliday.
Assistant Secretaries (G5), J. V. Dance; C. H. Taylor; Mrs. V. V. R. Harris; J. E. Hayzelden.
Senior Principals (G6), J. W. Cane; R. M. Hoare; J. P. Nicholson.
Principals, G. Allison; I. J. Babbage; J. Bowles; M. J. Brown; J. I. Chisholm; I. M. Clark; D. R. Dewick; P. F. Hewett; M. P. B. Kennedy; J. W. Maloney; M. R. Matthews; Mrs. P. W. Nice; A. Norbury; G. C. Robertson; Mrs. M. R. Ryan; A. V. H. Stainer.

Fire and Emergency Planning Department

Assistant Under-Secretary of State (G3), R. M. Morris.
Assistant Secretaries (G5), P. Canovan; Miss G. M. B. Owen; J. A. Howard; Mrs. J. Thompson.
Grade 6, B. S. Luetchford.
Principals, E. Alley; W. F. Bryant; T. K. Cobley; K. H. Cooper; T. P. R. Crompton; C. Farrington; Mrs. D. M. Grice; J. Holloway; Miss S. R. Muir; I. Rich; P. A. Stanton; G. Underwood; J. Wake; A. Walmsley; T. J. Wilson.

Fire Service Inspectorate

Chief Inspector, Sir Peter Darby, C.B.E., Q.F.S.M.
Inspectors (Grade I), H. R. C. Boyce, Q.F.S.M.; A. R. Brannon, O.B.E.; C. G. Burgon; R. D. H. Doyle, C.B.E.; T. D. Jones, O.B.E.; N. F. Roundell, Q.F.S.M.; A. A. Winning, C.B.E.
Inspectors (Grade II), S. D. Christian; J. Dukelow; C. Green; T. Greenwood; A. F. Kilford; S. Platt; W. C. Perry; H. V. Reed; G. L. Tinley.
Senior Engineering Inspector, R. M. Simpson

Fire Service College
Moreton-in-Marsh, Gloucestershire
[Moreton-in-Marsh: 50831]

Commandant, G. Clarke, C.B.E.
Deputy Commandant, D. Holland, M.B.E..
Secretary (Principal), J. A. Gibbs.

Civil Defence College
The Hawkhills, Easingwold, Yorks.
[Easingwold: 21406]

Principal, J. B. Bettridge, C.B.E.
Vice-Principal, G. E. Harrison.

Home Office H.Q. U.K. Warning and Monitoring Organization
James Wolfe Road, Cowley, Oxford
[Oxford 776005]

Director (G6), R. F. Cooke.
Deputy Director, W. P. Lawrie.

General Department

Assistant Under-Secretary of State (G3), M. E. Head.
Assistant Secretaries (G5), S. S. Bampton; N. M. Johnson; N. Nagler; Mrs. J. E. Reisz.
Principals, B. M. Caffarey; Mrs. F. Clarkson; R. G. Ferguson; Miss G. M. Griffiths; D. J. Hardwick; A. N. Pickersgill; Miss G. M. Romney; R. B. Snow; C. P. S. Stevens; K. D. Sutton; R. J. Weatherill; Miss M. S. Wooldridge.
Chief Inspector of Drugs (G6), H. B. Spear.

Cruelty to Animals Inspectorate

Chief Inspector, M. A. Richards.
Superintending Inspector, C. B. Hart.

Immigration and Nationality Department
Lunar House, Wellesley Road, Croydon, Surrey,
CR9 2BY
[01–686 0333]

Assistant Under-Secretary of State (G3), G. H. Phillips.
Assistant Secretaries (G5), P. R. Burleigh; Mrs. B. H. Fair; R. J. Fries; J. K. Moore; A. R. Rawsthorne.
Senior Principals (G6), R. A. McDowell; D. M. McQueen.
Principals, M. Boyle; M. Copley; J. G. Daly; P. Durbin; J. P. Emery; T. M. Harris; R. Haugh; Mrs. J. M. Kidd; J. F. C. Love; D. J. M. McDonough; R. C. Masefield; G. H. Sonnenberg; R. S. Weeks.

Immigration Service

Chief Inspector (G4), P. Tompkins.
Deputy Chief Inspectors (G6), C. B. Manchip; A. A. Holton; D. G. Stephens.
Assistant Chief Inspectors, G. Boiling, M.B.E.; K. Butterworth; I. J. Caffrey; J. M. de Llanos; J. M. Durose; J. D. Smith; G. H. C. Thomas; G. A. Treadwell.

Passport Department
Clive House, Petty France, SW1H 9HD
[01–213 3000]

Head of Unit (G5), A. Holmes, C.B.E.
Deputy Head of Unit (G6), F. H. Keens.
Principals, Miss M. A. N. Ashton; N. K. Finlayson; T. Lonsdale; J. F. Nicholson; Miss H. E. Wells.

Legal Adviser's Branch

Legal Adviser (G2), J. Nursaw, C.B.
Principal Assistant Legal Advisers (G3), A. H. Hammond; J. Pakenham-Walsh.
Assistant Legal Advisers, D. Bentley; R. J. Clayton; Miss P. Edwards; Mrs. S. A. Evans; A. W. D. Wilson.
Senior Legal Assistants, A. M. C. Inglese; J. O'Meara; C. M. L. Osborne; D. Seymour.

Police Department

Assistant Under-Secretaries of State (G3), G. L. Angel; D. H. J. Hilary; G. J. Wasserman.
Assistant Secretaries (G5), N. C. Abbott; D. J. Belfall; B. O. Bubbear; Miss J. M. Goose; A. Harding; R. A. Harrington; E. Soden.
Senior Principals (G6), K. H. Heal; Dr. R. A. Hinder; M. H. Rumble.
Principals, R. J. Baxter; C. E. Birt; J. D. Cleary; Miss K. J. Collins; G. E. Dunkley; B. R. Gange; P. R. A. Fulton; P. Harris; R. E. Hawkes; R. J. D. Hazell; N. F. M. Home; Miss S. G. Kippax; K. Mackenzie; T. C. Morris; Mrs. L. Pallett; J. Sibson; A. G. Thomson; G. A. Treadwell; M. L. Winspear; R. C. Yeates.

Police National Computer Unit
Horseferry House,
Dean Ryle Street, S.W.1
[01–211 3000]

Assistant Secretary (G5), A. G. Bailey.
Senior Principals (G6), G. M. Cole; D. W. Punshon; D. A. Quarmby.

Principals, E. L. Brannan; G. Coulthard; Mrs. A. Cowley; R. F. Cumings; D. C. Moulton; R. Reason; R. T. Robinson; B. G. Stocking; R. H. Watt; T. W. Wrighton.

Directorate of Telecommunications
Horseferry House,
Dean Ryle Street, S.W.1
[01–211 3000]

Director of Telecommunications (G5), P. L. T. Owen, O.B.E.

Deputy Directors (G6), G. E. Guy; D. A. Hendon; R. M. Hughes; H. Woodmansey.

Principals, D. J. Moss; D. Mullarky.

Senior Communications Officer, D. W. Hart.

Chief Telecommunications Engineers, I. Aitken; R. C. Eaton; A. Hulme; A. N. Kent; J. E. Lebutt; G. J. Mewett; J. L. Mumford; M. A. Parker; M. J. Phillips; D. C. J. Theobald; P. M. Tomlinson.

H.M. Inspectorate of Constabulary

H.M. Chief Inspector of Constabulary, Sir Lawrence Byford, C.B.E., Q.P.M.

H.M. Inspectors, R. S. Barratt, C.B.E., Q.P.M.; J. H. Brownlow, C.B.E., Q.P.M.; Sir Philip Myers, O.B.E., Q.P.M.; B. Weigh, C.B.E., Q.P.M.; J. Woodcock, C.B.E., Q.P.M.

Scientific Research and Development Branch
Horseferry House,
Dean Ryle Street, S.W.1
[01–211 3000]

Director (G5), A. N. Rapsey.

Deputy Directors (G6), T. R. Mann; Dr. D. M. S. Peace; Dr. G. Turnbull; Dr. P. A. Young.

Principal Scientific Officers, Dr. B. J. Blain; Dr. G. A. Carr-Hill; Dr. A. Ganson; Dr. S. Hadjipavlou; Dr. J. A. Harwood; T. Kent; D. J. Meakin; J. A. Miles; K. Millard; D. D. O'Brien; C. D. Payne; Dr. F. H. Preston; J. E. Simes; Dr. J. R. Stealey; R. C. Stephen; F. Venables; Dr. R. W. Walker; A. M. Western; Dr. I. P. Williamson.

Principal Professional and Technology Officer, R. Oliver.

Police Staff College
Bramshill House, Basingstoke, Hampshire
[Hartley Wintney 2931]

Commandant, B. N. Pain, C.B.E., Q.P.M.

Deputy Commandant and Director of Courses, J. Radley, Q.P.M.

Dean of Academic Studies, I. A. Watt.

Principal, A. F. G. Hitchman.

Headquarters Forensic Science Service
Horseferry House
Dean Ryle Street, S.W.1.
[01–211 3000]

Controller (G4), Miss M. Pereira, C.B.E.

Assistant to Controller (G6), Dr. T. J. Rothwell.

Principal, (vacant).

Principal Scientific Officer, Dr. M. P. Stephenson.

Prison Service
Cleland House, Page Street, SW1P 4LN
[01–211 3000]

Director-General of the Prison Service (G2), C. J. Train.

Deputy Director-General of the Prison Service (G3), G. H. Lakes, M.C.

Prisons Board

Assistant Under Secretaries of State (Directors) (G3), E. Caines (*Personnel and Finance*); A. J. Langdon (*Operational Policy*); T. C. Platt (*Regimes and Services*); Dr. J. Kilgour (*Medical Services*).

Regional Directors (G5), A. W. Driscoll (*South-East*);

C. P. Honey (*Northern*); J. R. Sandy (*Midland*); I. Dunbar (*South West*).

Non-Executive Members, Miss D. N. Barrett; P. Custis.

Assistant Secretaries (G5), M. J. Addison; A. J. Butler; B. A. Emes; P. C. Edwards; P. J. C. Mawer; A. H. Turney; R. M. Whalley; L. P. Wright.

Deputy Director of Prison Medical Services (G4), Dr. P. J. Hynes.

Principal Medical Officers (G4), Dr. P. Arrowsmith; Dr. D. A. F. Doherty; Dr. R. J. Wool.

Senior Principals (G6), D. R. Birleson; J. A. Pemberton; D. F. Scagell; A. C. Stott; L. A. Scudder.

Governors I, D. Brown; G. D. Dadds; J. Gadd.

Principals, Mrs. P. R. Atkins; N. Benger; D. J. Blackman; B. G. Chaplin; P. Cook; D. A. L. Cooke; Mrs. C. Crawford; H. M. C. Crudge; P. Done; E. A. Grant; J. Gundersen; D. J. Hollis; R. Hulley; J. C. Imber; M. J. D. Jones; E. J. Kings; J. LeVay; B. Lockett; Miss D. Loudon; A. D. McFarlane; W. F. McCay; Ms. E. B. Moody; M. J. Murphy; Mrs. S. Murray; T. R. Peters; P. G. V. Pike; J. Plumridge; D. E. Powell; J. A. K. de Quidt; M. J. A. Prowse; Ms. P. Ransford; P. M. Scott; S. Spence; G. N. Stadlen; Mrs. H. Wigoder; R. A. Wright.

Governors II, J. F. Bailey; A. J. Barclay; J. J. Childs; R. Clarke; Miss J. M. Fowler; H. D. Jones; P. J. Kitteridge; D. G. Longley; A. K. Rawson; D. Twiner.

Prison Service Chaplaincy (G6), (vacant).

Director of Psychological Services, P. H. Shapland.

Chief Education Officer, (vacant).

Chief Physical Education Officer, M. Denton.

Governors III, J. W. Dring; Miss A. W. Hair; C. F. Lambert; I. Lockwood; D. M. Morrison; T. M. O'Sullivan; T. N. Pitt-Brook; M. F. W. Watson-Jackson.

Chief Architect's Branch and Directorate of Works
Abell House, John Islip Street, SW1P 4LH
[01–211 3000]

Chief Architect and Director of Works (G4), H. J. M. McMaster.

Superintending Architects (G6), M. A. Brooks; J. H. Cooper; G. E. F. Slatter; R. W. T. Haines; T. R. Jones; P. A. G. Walker.

Principal Professional and Technology Officers, O. P. Astaniotis; D. G. Baines; H. G. S. Banks; M. J. Bridgford; G. F. Burgess; B. D. Charlson; G. W. Chrisp; C. R. Cope; H. J. Davies; C. F. Drewitt; A. W. Gillman; D. W. Harris; M. C. Hayes; G. E. Hickey; J. V. R. Hillyer; F. Home; M. J. Ireson; J. F. Keeler; R. T. Lewis; S. L. Mahraj; A. W. Orchard; R. J. Perham; C. A. G. Poole; R. S. Putland; J. F. Sheldon; B. A. Stickley; M. Sweeny; E. C. Webber.

Principal, D. Mannings.

Prison Service Industries and Farms
Lunar House, Wellesley Road, Croydon,
Surrey CR9 2BY
[01–686 0333]

Director (G5), C. J. Walters.

Group Managers (G6), M. Codd; N. Fennemore; A. M. Gold; J. H. Smith; C. J. Welsh.

Principals, J. H. Henderson; J. F. Rogers; C. Tredger.

Principal Professional & Technology Officers, D. Field; R. Fisher; G. A. Hallam; T. Senior; M. Sweeney.

Supply and Transport Branch
Crown House, 53 Elizabeth Street,
Corby, Northants.
[Corby 202101]

Director (G6), J. D. Lodder.

Principals, R. C. Brett; M. Fitzgerald; J. Harvey; A. S. Thompson.

Prison Service Regional Offices

Birmingham:
Regional Director (G5), J. R. Sandy.
Deputy Regional Director, F. B. O'Friel.
Assistant Regional Directors, E. C. Bennett (*Administration*); J. Blakey (*Young Offenders*); I. A. E. Boon (*Operations*).

Bristol:
Regional Director (G5), I. Dunbar.
Deputy Regional Director, A. H. Rayfield.
Assistant Regional Directors, T. C. Newell (*Adult Offenders*); D. V. Horsley (*Administration*); G. W. A. Ellington (*Young Offenders*).

Manchester:
Regional Director (G5), W. Driscoll.
Deputy Regional Director, J. Jones.
Assistant Regional Directors, L. Edgar (*Administration*); C. B. Scott (*Adult Males*); M. Langdon (*Females*); G. Walker (*Young Offenders*).

Tolworth:
Regional Director (G5), C. P. Honey.
Deputy Regional Director, J. F. Perriss.
Assistant Regional Directors, J. Walsh (*Administration*); J. Dugdale (*Operations*); E. R. Campbell (*Young Offenders*).

PRISONS
Governors

Acklington, Northumberland, A. Stapleton.
Albany, I.O.W., P. D. R. Meech.
Ashwell, Leics., R. Curtis.
Askham Grange, Yorks., J. Hunter.
Bedford, J. L. Uzzell.
Birmingham, R. J. Kendrick.
Blundeston, Suffolk, G. H. Cropper.
Bristol, J. Williams.
Brixton, S.W.2., Miss J. Kinsley.
Camp Hill, I.O.W., S. Brumby.
Canterbury, Maj. R. A. Stratford-Tuke.
Cardiff, G. W. Axe.
Channings Wood, Devon, W. J. Keast.
Chelmsford, J. R. Penson.
Coldingley, Surrey, Mrs. M. M. Donnelly.
Cookham Wood, J. D. Yates.
Dartmoor, D. Thompson.
Dorchester, P. R. Pope.
Drake Hall, Stafford, R. Mitchell.
Durham, A. H. Papps.
Exeter, D. Alderson.
Featherstone, Wolverhampton, (vacant).
Ford, Sussex, P. L. Pye.
Frankland, Durham, R. Mole.
Gartree, Leics., R. R. Tilt.
Gloucester, N. W. A. Wall.
Grendon and Spring Hill, Bucks., M. F. G. Selby.
Haverigg, Cumbria, B. McLuckie.
Highpoint, Newmarket, D. V. Hickson.
Holloway, N.7., C. Allen.
Hull, B. V. Smith.
Kingston, Portsmouth, Miss M. R. Allen.
Kirkham, Lancs., K. L. Taylor.
Lancaster, B. A. Wilson.
Leeds, W. A. Martin.
Leicester, J. R. Wilkinson.
Lewes, D. A. Brown.
Leyhill, Glos., W. E. McEvoy.
Lincoln, P. L. Harrap.
Liverpool, J. Richardson.
Long Lartin, Worcs., M. D. Jenkins.
Maidstone, (vacant).
Manchester, J. D. U. Lewis.
Northeye, Sussex, D. C. Ozanne.

Norwich, R. E. Withers.
Nottingham, J. R. Marriott.
Oxford, M. A. Lewis.
Parkhurst, I.O.W., J. Rumball.
Pentonville, B. A. Marchant.
Preston, A. N. Joseph.
Ranby, T. Davies.
Reading, B. C. Hayday.
Rudgate, N. Berry.
Shepton Mallet, R. D. Dixon.
Shrewsbury, L. M. Wiltshire.
Stafford, C. Heald.
Standford Hill, J. M. Reid.
Stocken, E. P. Polkinghorne.
Styal, Cheshire, J. H. M. Anderson.
Sudbury, L. Stones.
Swansea, S. R. Robinson.
The Verne, Dorset, D. L. Long.
Wakefield, J. E. Simmons.
Wakefield Service College, R. S. Duncan.
Wandsworth, S.W.18., D. A. Marsden.
Wayland, C. A. Brown.
Winchester, M. V. Roberts.
Wormwood Scrubs, W.12., D. Brooke.
Wymott, Preston, E. S. Nash.

YOUTH CUSTODY CENTRES
Governors

Aylesbury, T. C. H. Newth.
Bullwood Hall, Essex, Miss U. M. B. McCollam.
Castington, M. R. J. Gander.
Deerbolt, P. A. Whitehouse.
Dover, D. Aram.
East Sutton Park, Kent, B. H. Coatsworth.
Erlestoke, Wilts., A. F. Mills.
Everthorpe, Humberside, T. M. Turner.
Feltham, A. F. H. Arnold.
Gaynes Hall, Cambs, M. J. Jehan.
Glen Parva, Leics., E. V. H. Williams.
Guys Marsh, Dorset, Maj. R. B. Coombs.
Hatfield, Yorks., R. Elvy.
Hewell Grange, Worcs., Miss M. A. Carden.
Hindley, Lancs, G. Shore.
Hollesley Bay Colony, Suffolk, J. C. G. Williams.
Huntercombe and Finnamore Wood, Oxon., F. Crowe.
Lowdham Grange, Notts., W. J. Cooper.
Northallerton, F. Weigh.
Onley, Warwicks., J. Whitty.
Portland, Dorset, T. W. Abbott.
Rochester, J. S. Shulman.
Stoke Heath, Salop, A. Cruikshank.
Swinfen Hall, Staffs., J. Semple.
Thorn Cross, D. Hall.
Usk, Gwent, J. Capel.
Wellingborough, E. Martin.
Wetherby, Yorks., F. E. C. Jones.

REMAND CENTRES
Governors

Ashford, Middx., S. C. A. Pryor.
Brockhill, Worcs., (vacant).
Latchmere House, Surrey, J. L. Smith.
Low Newton, Co. Durham, (vacant).
Pucklechurch, Bristol, Miss S. F. McCormick.
Risley, Cheshire, N. F. Low.
Thorp Arch, Wetherby, D. Whitehead.

DETENTION CENTRES
Governors

Aldington, Kent, G. Gregory-Smith.
Blantyre House, Kent, R. Croxford.
Buckley Hall, Lancs., E. F. Callaghan.
Campsfield House, Oxford, K. B. Owen.
Eastwood Park, Glos., D. W. Chapman.
Foston Hall, Derby, Maj. L. J. Henwood.
Gringley, B. Tyreman.
Haslar, Hants., B. Sutton.

Kirklevington, Cleveland, D. G. McNaughton.
Medomsley, C. Harder.
New Hall, Yorks., B. E. N. Lyte.
North Sea Camp, Lincs., J. W. Hanson.
Send, Surrey, J. R. Dovell.
Werrington House, Staffs., M. K. Pascoe.
Whatton, Notts., J. M. Sharples.

Inspectorate of Prisons

H.M. Chief Inspector of Prisons, Sir James Hennessy, K.B.E., C.M.G.
H.M. Deputy Chief Inspector of Prisons (G5), A. J. Pearson.
Inspectors, D. Campbell; H. D. Hillier; O. Shaw; J. Tuck; B. J. Wells; B. Wilson, B.E.M.
Principal, A. F. C. Crook.

Public Relations Branch

Director of Information Services, B. L. Mower.
Chief Information Officer, (vacant).
Principal Information Officers, Ms. E. Drummond; R. Windsor.

Statistical Department
Tolworth Tower, Tolworth, Surrey
[01–399 5191]

Assistant Under-Secretary of State (G3), Miss R. J. Maurice.
Chief Statisticians (G5), C. G. Lewis; P. W. Ward; T. J. Kavanagh.

Women's Royal Voluntary Service
17 Old Park Lane, W1Y 4AJ
[01–499 6040]

National Chairman, Mrs. B. Shenfield.

HORSERACE TOTALISATOR BOARD
74 Upper Richmond Road, S.W.15
[01–874 6411]

Established by the Betting, Gaming and Lotteries Act, 1963, as successor in title to the Racecourse Betting Control Board established by the Racecourse Betting Act, 1928.

Its function is to operate totalisators on approved racecourses in Great Britain, and it also provides off-course cash and credit offices. Under the Horserace Totalisator and Betting Levy Board Act, 1972, it is further empowered to offer bets at starting price (or other bets at fixed odds) on any sporting event.
Chairman, Sir Woodrow Wyatt £38,000
Members, The Lord Chapple; Mrs. P. Hastings; The Duke of Devonshire, P.C., M.C.; Hon. D. Montagu; P. S. Winfield; J. F. Sanderson.

HOUSING CORPORATION
149 Tottenham Court Road, W1P 0BN
[01–387 9466]

A Government agency established in 1964 which registers, supervises and funds non-profit making housing associations throughout the United Kingdom. Under the 1974 Housing Act the Corporation was given a new and central role in promoting the housing association movement and funding an expanded programme of housing schemes by associations mainly for fair rent. The Act also gave the Corporation the responsibility for the registering of the housing associations before they could be eligible for public funds and supervising and controlling their activities to ensure accountability for the public money in their care. The Corporation has now registered over 2,500 associations under the 1974 Act.

Since 1974 the Corporation has supported housing associations in the rehabilitation of older houses and in new building, much of it to help people with special needs, including the elderly, the handicapped, and the single homeless. Following the 1980 Housing Act the Corporation is encouraging and backing new initiatives by housing associations to extend the range of housing available through schemes for shared equity, leasehold for the elderly and improvement for sale. All housing associations may now sell to their tenants and tenants of non-charitable housing associations have the right to buy their homes. *Chairman*, Sir Hugh Cubitt, C.B.E.

INDEPENDENT BROADCASTING AUTHORITY
70 Brompton Road, S.W.3
[01–584 7011]

The Independent Television Authority was created by Act of Parliament in July, 1954 to provide an additional television broadcasting service to that provided by the British Broadcasting Corporation. In July, 1972, under the Sound Broadcasting Act, 1972, it was renamed the Independent Broadcasting Authority and its functions were extended to cover the provision of Independent Local Radio. The Television Act, 1964, and the Sound Broadcasting Act, 1972 were consolidated into the Independent Broadcasting Authority Act, 1973. The Broadcasting Act, 1980, provided for the setting up of the Channel Four Television Company as a subsidiary of the IBA; it started broadcasting in England, Scotland and Northern Ireland on Nov. 2, 1982. A separate Welsh Fourth Channel Authority was also established by this Act and started broadcasting on Nov. 2, 1982. The Broadcasting Act, 1981 has consolidated a number of Acts relating to the IBA. As part of its review of the ITV system, the Authority, in December 1980, offered a contract to broadcast a new national breakfast-time television service (which started in Feb. 1983) to TV-*am*. In addition, changes were made to some ITV companies.

The Authority consists of a Chairman and eleven members appointed by the Home Secretary (of whom three make Scotland, Wales and Northern Ireland their respective responsibilities) and a permanent staff under the Director General. The four main functions of the Authority are to appoint the ILR and ITV programme companies; to own and operate the transmitters; to supervise the programmes provided by the contractors and the Channel Four Television Company and their scheduling; and to control the advertising. The programme companies pay the Authority a rental to enable it to carry out its duties. Fifteen ITV programme companies provide programmes in 14 regions (two companies operate in London, one at the weekends, the other during the week). By June, 1985, 47 Independent Local Radio contractors were broadcasting in 42 areas of the U.K. (in London, there are two companies, one providing a news and information service, and the second general entertainment and information). Both Independent Television and ILR are financed mainly by the sale of advertising time.
Chairman, The Lord Thomson of Monifieth, P.C., K.T.
Deputy Chairman, Sir John Riddell.
Members, Mrs. P. Ridley; M. H. Caine; R. A. Grantham; Mrs. J. D. M. Jowitt; Mrs. J. McIvor (*Northern Ireland*); J. R. Purvis (*Scotland*); G. R. Peregrine (*Wales*); Mrs. Y. Conolly; G. Russell; Prof. A. Cullen, O.B.E., F.R.S.
Director General, J. Whitney.
Director of Administration, Mrs. S. Littler.
Director of Television, D. Glencross.
Director of Radio, J. B. Thompson, C.B.E.
Director of Engineering, T. Robson, O.B.E.
Director of Finance, P. Rogers.
Controller of Advertising, H. Theobalds.
Controller of Information Service, Miss B. Hosking, O.B.E.

Secretary, B. Rook.
Regional and National Officers, F. W. L. G. Bath *(South-West England, Channel Islands);* M. J. Fay *(Yorkshire);* E. Lewis *(Wales and West of England);* A. D. Fleck *(Northern Ireland);* Miss S. Thane *(East of England);* D. Lee *(North-West England);* B. Marjoribanks *(Scotland);* R. J. F. Lorimer *(North-East England and the Borders);* N. J. Reedy *(East and West Midlands);* J. B. Scott *(South and South-East England).*

CENTRAL OFFICE OF INFORMATION
Hercules Road, SE1 7DU
[01–928 2345]

The Central Office of Information is a common service department which produces information and publicity material, and supplies publicity services, for other Government departments on a repayment basis. In the United Kingdom it conducts Government display press, television and poster advertising, produces and distributes booklets, leaflets, films, television material, exhibitions, photographs and other visual material; and distributes departmental press notices. For the overseas departments it supplies British Information posts overseas with press, radio and television material, booklets, magazines, reference services, films, exhibitions, photographs, display and reading room material; arranges tours in the United Kingdom for official visitors from overseas. Administrative responsibility for the Central Office of Information rests with H.M. Treasury Ministers, while the ministers whose departments it serves are responsible for the policy expressed in its work.

SALARY LIST

Director General	£32,350
Deputy Director General	£27,791
Principal Establishment Officer	£25,533 *(maximum)*
Principal Finance Officer	£25,533 *(maximum)*
Group Director	£25,533 *(maximum)*
Head of Information Officer Management Unit	£25,533 *(maximum)*
Director	£22,926 *(maximum)*
Regional Director (Leeds, London, Birmingham and Manchester)	£22,926 *(maximum)*
Regional Director (Newcastle, Cambridge and Bristol)	£18,363 *(maximum)*

Director-General, N. Taylor.
  Private Secretary, Mrs. M. M. Habershon.
  Head of Information Officer Management Unit, A. J. Brooks.
Deputy Director-General, Miss S. Jefferies.

Establishment and Organization Division
Principal Establishment Officer, E. Bridger.

Finance and Accounts Division
Principal Finance Officer, A. H. Robinson.

OVERSEAS PUBLICITY GROUP
Group Director, A. E. Bevens.

Overseas Press Services
Director, R. N. Hooper.

Overseas Publications & Foreign Languages
Director, S. C. Lyle Smythe.

Overseas Visitors & Information Studies
Director, D. A. Smith.

VISUAL MEDIA AND RADIO GROUP
Group Director, (vacant).

Films & Television
Director, R. J. Hall.

Radio and Photographic Services
Director, J. A. Leys.

Exhibitions
Director, D. A. Loxley.

HOME PUBLICITY GROUP
Group Director, J. Bolitho.

Advertising
Director, K. C. Belben.

Home Publications & Printing
Director, D. A. Low.

Research
Director, R. J. H. Jones.

CLIENT SERVICES GROUP
Group Director, P. T. Brazier.

Media Co-ordination & Customer Relations
Director, J. W. Coe.

Regional Offices
North Eastern
Wellbar House, Gallowgate,
Newcastle upon Tyne
Regional Director, J. F. Dougray.

Yorkshire and Humberside
City House, New Station Street, Leeds
Regional Director, A. S. Poole.

Eastern
Three Crowns House, 72–80 Hills Road, Cambridge
Regional Director, P. J. Woodford.

London and South Eastern
Hercules Road, SE1 7DU
Regional Director, J. K. Holroyd, L.V.O.

South Western
The Pithay, Bristol, 1
Regional Director, P. D. Yorke.

Midlands
Five Ways Tower, Frederick Road, Edgbaston,
Birmingham 15
Regional Director, R. F. Long.

North Western
Sunley Building, Piccadilly Plaza, Manchester
Regional Director, O. J. B. Prince-White.

BOARD OF INLAND REVENUE
Somerset House, WC2R 1LB
[01–438 6622]

The Board of Inland Revenue was constituted under the Inland Revenue Board Act, 1849, by the consolidation of the Board of Excise and the Board of Stamps and Taxes. In 1909 the administration of excise duties was transferred to the Board of Customs. The Board of Inland Revenue administers and collects direct taxes—mainly income tax, corporation tax, capital gains tax, capital transfer tax, stamp duty, development land tax and petroleum revenue tax—and advises the Chancellor of the Exchequer on policy questions involving them. The Head Office is in London and there are Inspectors of Taxes offices and Collection offices throughout the United Kingdom. The Department's Valuation Office is responsible for valuing property for tax purposes, for compensation and for compulsory purchase and (in England and Wales) for local rating purposes. In 1984/85 Inland Revenue collected over £50,500,000,000 tax.

SALARY LIST

Unified Grade 1 .... £52,750
  2 .... £39,250 (maximum)
  3 .... £31,750 (maximum)
  4 .... £26,909
  5 .... £25,533 (maximum)
  6 .... £22,926 (maximum)
Departmental Variations:
Deputy Chief Valuer (England and Wales)
        £29,500 (maximum)
Chief Valuer (Scotland) £26,604
Assistant Chief Valuer (England and Wales) £25,975
Solicitor (Scotland) £25,300
Senior Legal Assistant (Scotland)
        £21,297 (maximum)
Chief Examiner (CTO) .... £18,509 (maximum)

The Board

Chairman (Grade 1), Sir Lawrence Airey, K.C.B.
  Private Secretary, Miss J. L. Pattison.
Deputy Chairmen (Grade 2), A. J. G. Isaac, C.B.; A. M. W. Battishill.
Directors General (Grade 2), D. B. Rogers, C.B.; B. Pollard.
Commissioners: Chief Valuer (Grade 2), A. B. Fallows; (Grade 3), J. D. Taylor-Thompson.

Policy Divisions

Grade 3, R. A. Blythe; C. W. Corlett; B. T. Houghton; L. J. H. Beighton; J. D. Taylor-Thompson, C.B.; D. Y. Pitts.
Grade 5, B. A. Mace; T. A. Symons; J. D. Farmer; P. W. Fawcett; J. B. Shepherd; N. C. Munro; D. G. Draper; O. T. Morgan; M. J. G. Elliott; J. P. B. Bryce; M. Prescott; G. H. Bush; R. G. Lusk; R. I. McConnachie; M. F. Cayley; I. R. Spence; E. McGivern; Mrs. C. B. Hubbard; Miss M. A. Hill; C. Stewart.
Controller of Development Land Tax Office (Grade 6), R. F. Moore.

Central Division

Grade 3, T. J. Painter.
Grade 5, P. Lewis; R. R. Martin.
Senior Economic Adviser (Grade 5), R. Weeden.

Technical Division

Directors (Grade 3), J. E. Lawrance; J. H. Roberts.
Assistant Directors (Grade 4), M. D. Whitear; K. A. Skinner; R. E. German; R. W. Parker; J. Moule; M. D. E. Newstead; E. K. Pearson; E. Pattison; G. F. Hamilton; W. Northend; J. M. L. Davenport; J. C. Campbell; D. W. Hugo; I. N. Hunter; B. Sadler; J. F. Hall.
Assistant Director (Grade 5), A. J. O'Brien.
Principal Inspectors of Taxes (Grade 5), M. L. Gordon; M. Templeman; J. Potter; R. J. Smith; R. E. Creed; J. White; C. H. Coleman; P. C. Fielder; I. R. Drummond; J. Bishton; P. Farmer; B. Carter; K. H. Colmer; P. Harrison; J. S. Marshall; E. J. Gribbon; D. A. Johnson; R. G. Jasper.
Controller of Oil Taxation Office (Grade 4), R. M. Elliss.

Management Divisions

Director of Personnel (Grade 3), P. B. G. Jones.
Assistant Directors (Grade 4), G. Findley (Grade 5); R. A. Hutton, B. O'Connor; F. W. Newcombe; J. T. Tudor.

Controller of Office Services (Grade 6), B. R. Spooner.
Director of Manpower and Training (Grade 3), J. M. Crawley.
Assistant Directors (Grade 4), G. J. Lyall (Grade 5); R. K. Freeman; J. Marshall; D. K. Matthews.
Head of Operational Research (Grade 6), A. A. Holt.
Director of Data Processing (Grade 3), S. C. T. Matheson.
Assistant Directors (Grade 5), R. A. Hamilton; J. C. Cockcroft; D. Selwood.
Director of Operations (Grade 3), C. Cherry.
Assistant Directors (Grade 4), D. S. Aldridge (Grade 5); J. E. Yard; R. H. Allen; D. H. Stanton; P. J. Hodgson; J. C. Jones; J. Gant.
Head of Communications Group (Grade 4), D. W. Muir.
Press Secretary, Ms. S. E. Tyrrell.
Controller, Enforcement Office (Grade 5), R. F. Bruford.

Finance Division

Principal Finance Officer (Grade 3), J. M. Crawley.
Assistant Secretaries (Grade 5), A. G. Nield; J. A. Pinder.
Controller, Central Accounting Office (Grade 6), J. Gray.
Chief Internal Auditor (Grade 6), T. D. C. Meadows.

Statistics Division

Director (Grade 3), J. W. S. Walton.
Chief Statisticians (Grade 5), J. B. Dearman; W. Gonzalez; F. A. Fitzpatrick; J. Calder.
Management (Grade 6), E. F. Smith.

Office of the Controller of Stamps
Bush House, South-West Wing, Strand, WC2B 4QN and Barrington Road, Worthing, Sussex

Controller (Grade 6), D. E. Pipe.

Capital Taxes Office
Minford House, Rockley Road, W14 0DF

Controller (Grade 4), G. A. Spencer.
Deputy Controllers (Grade 5), B. D. Kent; R. J. Draper.
Asst. Controllers (Grade 6), G. Allcock; A. S. Johnson; M. Swann; A. L. Barton; I. P. Gunn; D. J. Ferley; C. A. Oldridge; H. V. Capon; R. T. Kablean; J. Blagden; T. J. Plumb.

Solicitor of Inland Revenue
Somerset House, WC2R 1LB

Solicitor (Grade 2), R. S. Boyd.
Principal Assistant Solicitors (Grade 3), P. D. Hall; J. F. Easton; R. K. Miller.
Assistant Solicitors (Grade 5), A. L. L. Alexander; C. J. C. Baron; R. T. Brand; K. O. Butterfield; B. R. D. Clarke; B. E. Cleave; M. C. Furey, C.B.E.; J. F. W. Hinson; E. O. Jackson, C.B.E.; J. D. H. Johnston; N. R. Phillips; J. G. H. Bates; P. L. Ridd.

Superannuation Funds Office
Lynwood Road, Thames Ditton, Surrey KT7 0DP

Controller (Grade 5), H. B. Thompson.
Assistant Controllers (Grade 6), J. Horrell; I. A. Young.

Inspector of Foreign Dividends Office
Lynwood Road, Thames Ditton, Surrey KT7 0DP

Inspector of Foreign Dividends (Grade 6), D. J. Critchley.

Office of the Chief Valuer
New Court, Carey Street, WC2A 2JE

Chief Valuer (Grade 2), A. B. Fallows.
Deputy Chief Valuers, P. G. Heard; R. R. B. Shutler.
Assistant Chief Valuers, P. J. Borrett; R. D. E. Gilbard; S. H. Keith; A. J. Langford; R. J. Sellick.

Superintending Valuers (Grade 5), P. R. Garrett; D. B. Hardy; M. J. Loveridge; D. I. Mabey; A. S. Murton; A. B. Prior; R. J. Schumacher; C. J. Thompson.

INLAND REVENUE (SCOTLAND)
80 Lauriston Place, Edinburgh EH3 9SL

Controller (Grade 4), W. S. Linkie.
Group Controllers (Grade 5), J. Brown; H. S. MacRae; O. J. Clarke; M. J. Hodgson.

Controller (Stamps)
16 Picardy Place, Edinburgh EH1 3NF
Controller, Mrs. M. M. Wynne.

Capital Taxes Office
16 Picardy Place, Edinburgh EH1 3NF

Registrar (Grade 5), J. B. M. McKean.
Deputy Registrar (Grade 6), P. G. Bruce, M.B.E.
Chief Examiners, Miss M. M. M. Armstrong; F. F. King; G. Mackie; T. E. Naysmith; Mrs. J. A. Templeton; J. R. Telford; W. Young.

Solicitor's Office
80 Lauriston Place, Edinburgh EH3 9SL

Solicitor, T. H. Scott.
Senior Legal Assistants, I. K. Laing; Miss E. M. M. McLean; D. S. Wishart.

Office of the Chief Valuer, Scotland
15 Drumsheugh Gardens, Edinburgh EH3 7UN

Chief Valuer, J. Fergus.
Assistant Chief Valuers (Grade 5), J. A. Sutherland; M. A. Newbury.

INTERVENTION BOARD FOR AGRICULTURAL PRODUCE
Fountain House, 2 Queen's Walk, Reading RG1 7QW
[Reading: 583626]

The Board was formed as a Government Department on November 22, 1972, and is responsible under the Agricultural Ministers for the implementation within the United Kingdom of the guarantee functions of the Common Agricultural Policy of the European Economic Community. Policy matters are the responsibility of the Agricultural Ministers of the United Kingdom.

SALARY LIST

Grade 3	£31,750 (*maximum*)
Grade 4	£26,909
Grade 5	£20,964 to £25,533
Grade 6	£17,000 to £20,926
Principals	£13,508 to £18,363
Commodity Specialists	£14,538 to £19,567

Chairman, D. C. G. Jessel.
Chief Executive (Grade 3), A. K. H. Atkinson, C.B.
Finance Officer and Director of Management Services (Grade 4), P. G. Horscroft.

Establishments Branch
Principal, J. Bird.

Finance Division
Grade 5, J. N. Diserens.
Principals, H. MacKinnon; E. R. Asprey; R. Bryant.

Audit Branch
Principal, R. Howes.

Computer Services
Grade 6, E. M. Abbott.
Principal, D. F. Horler.

Internal Market Division
Grade 5, D. M. L. Macgregor.
Grade 6, G. R. Holloway.
Principals, P. J. Offer; M. E. Statham; J. A. Sutton.
Commodity Specialists, J. R. Edmunds; B. C. Cook.

External Market Division
Grade 5, R. J. Attwell.
Principals, G. N. Dixon; N. P. J. Rowe; G. Donkin.

United Kingdom Seeds Executive
Prof. J. D. Ivins (*Chairman*); Prof. J. P. Cooper, C.B.E.; J. S. Denton, O.B.E.; F. H. Goodwin; P. R. Hayward, O.B.E.; G. G. Lyall; D. J. Palmer; W. P. Watt.

H.M. LAND REGISTRY
Lincoln's Inn Fields, WC2A 3PH
[01-405 3488]

The registration of title to land was first introduced in England and Wales by the Land Registry Act, 1862. Many changes have been made to the original system by subsequent legislation and H.M. Land Registry operates today under the Land Registration Acts, 1925 to 1971. The object of registering title to land is for dealings with it to be made more simple and economical. This is achieved by maintaining a register of land owners whose title is guaranteed by the State and by providing simple forms for the transfer, mortgage and other dealings with real property. Under the Land Registration Act, 1966, the voluntary first registration of land in non-compulsory areas was severely curtailed in order to facilitate an accelerated programme for the extension of the compulsory system to cover all the built-up areas of the country as soon as possible. The intention is that registration of title shall ultimately be universal throughout England and Wales. Nevertheless, before the 1966 Act a great deal of land became registered voluntarily and it is still possible in non-compulsory areas to register building estates, upon certain conditions, and other classes of property in specified circumstances. H.M. Land Registry is administered under the Lord Chancellor by the Chief Land Registrar and the work is decentralized to a number of regional offices. The Chief Land Registrar is also responsible for the Land Charges Department and the Agricultural Credits Department.

Headquarters Office

Chief Land Registrar, E. J. Pryer	£36,500
Chief Executive, C. Hotham	£29,500
Senior Land Registrar, C. J. West	£20,964 to £25,533
Land Registrar, Mrs. J. G. Totty	£19,243 to £23,159
Assistant Land Registrars, M. L. Wood; M. Croker; M. G. Garwood	£15,688 to £21,297
Assistant Secretaries, J. J. Manthorpe (*Controller Registration*); R. J. Fenn (*Controller of Management Services*)	£20,964 to £25,533
Senior Principal, P. J. Smith	£17,000 to £22,926
Principals, P. J. Brenchley; J. E. Deas; J. Hodder; I. Leach; P. Morris; V. J. C. Shorney; J. W. Wallis	£13,508 to 18,363

Establishment and Accounts

Principal Establishment Officer, E. F. Martin	£20,964 to £25,533
Assistant Establishment Officers, B. Gaskell; E. G. Beardsall	£13,508 to £18,363
Principal Finance Officer, B. R. Elliott	£13,508 to £18,363
Head of Office Services, R. A. Davis	£13,508 to £18,363

Birkenhead District Land Registry
76 Hamilton Street, Birkenhead,
Merseyside L41 5JW
[051–647 5661]

District Land Registrar, J. L. Inskipp
£20,964 to £25,533
Assistant Land Registrars, G. A. Hughes; I. E. Hardman; M. Taylor; S. R. Coveney
£15,688 to £21,297
Area Manager, J. Eccles......... £17,000 to £22,926

Croydon District Land Registry
Sunley House, Bedford Park, Croydon CR9 3LE
[01–686 8833]

District Land Registrar, M. H. Baines
£20,964 to £25,533
Assistant Land Registrars, A. E. Farwell; C. H. Johnson; Miss W. V. Drake.... £15,688 to £21,297
Area Manager, J. O. Sheldon ... £17,000 to £22,926

Durham District Land Registry
Southfield House, Southfield Way,
Durham DH1 5TR
[0385–66151]

District Land Registrar, P. H. Curnow
£20,964 to £25,533
Assistant Land Registrars, Miss C. A. Lever; H. M. Taylor; R. E. P. Underwood; C. W. Martin; G. J. Wadsworth .... £15,688 to £21,297
Area Manager, D. F. Price....... £17,000 to £22,926

Gloucester District Land Registry
Twyver House, Bruton Way,
Gloucester GL1 1DQ
[0452–28666]

District Land Registrar, Miss A. M. Phillips
£20,964 to £25,533
Assistant Land Registrars, M. E. Burn; D. M. J. Moss; P. M. Ratcliffe; S. G. Taverner . £15,688 to £21,297
Area Manager, M. H. Spooner ... £17,000 to £22,926

Harrow District Land Registry
Lyon House, Lyon Road, Harrow,
Middlesex HA1 2EU
[01–427 8811]

District Land Registrar, H. S. Early
£20,964 to £25,533
Assistant Land Registrars, Miss J. E. Bagshaw; T. H. O. Lewis; C. J. T. Brierley; J. H. Gill; C. Tate
£15,688 to £21,297
Area Manager, D. I. Whyte...... £17,000 to £22,926

Land Charges and Agricultural Credits Department
Burrington Way, Plymouth PL6 3LP
[0752–779831]

Superintendent of Land Charges, J. C. O'Brien
£13,508 to £18,363

Lytham District Land Registry
Birkenhead House, Lytham St. Annes,
Lancs. FY8 5AB
[0253–736999]

District Land Registrar, J. G. Cooper
£20,964 to £25,533
Assistant Land Registrars, J. F. Bamber; J. G. Dickinson; J. B. Duckworth; R. H. Hargreaves
£15,688 to £21,297
Area Manager, E. J. Stringer .... £17,000 to £22,926

Nottingham District Land Registry
Chalfont Drive, Nottingham NG8 3RN
[0602–291111]

District Land Registrar, P. J. Timothy
£20,964 to £25,533

Assistant Land Registrars, D. M. Adams; P. A. Brown; K. G. Harvey; M. C. Jefferies; P. D. Smith; Mrs. P. M. Reeson .... £15,688 to £21,297
Area Manager, P. F. Taylor...... £17,000 to £22,926

Peterborough District Land Registry
Aragon Court, Northminster Road,
Peterborough PE1 1XN
[0733 46048]

District Land Registrar, M. Avens £20,964 to £25,533
Assistant Land Registrars, T. J. Reacher; J. T. Scott; S. T. Abdulhusein .... £15,688 to £21,297
Area Manager, G. N. French..... £17,000 to £22,926

Plymouth District Land Registry
Plumer House, Tailyour Road,
Crownhill, Plymouth PL6 5HY
[0752–701234]

District Land Registrar, P. A. Meehan
£20,964 to £25,533
Assistant Land Registrars, W. J. Perry; E. G. Thomas; S. P. Kelway; L. M. Pope; A. J. Pain
£15,688 to £21,297
Area Manager, B. Hall .... £17,000 to £22,926

Stevenage District Land Registry
Brickdale House, Danestrete, Stevenage,
Herts. SG1 1XG
[0438–314488]

District Land Registrar, D. M. T. Mullett
£20,964 to £25,533
Assistant Land Registrars, F. G. D. Emler; I. M. Jeffrey; O. D. Christopherson .. £15,688 to £21,297
Area Manager, A. Gould .... £17,000 to £22,926

Swansea District Land Registry
37, The Kingsway, Swansea, Glam. SA1 5LF
[0792–476677]

District Land Registrar, A. P. Roberts
£20,964 to £25,533
Assistant Land Registrars, C. D. Hinds; N. M. Jones; T. M. Lewis .... £15,688 to £21,297
Area Manager, B. E. G. Martin .. £17,000 to £22,926

Tunbridge Wells District Land Registry
Curtis House, Hawkenbury, Tunbridge Wells,
Kent TN2 5AQ
[0892–26141]

District Land Registrar, A. Gould £20,964 to £25,533
Assistant Land Registrars, J. S. R. Bevington; P. L. Cook; G. R. Tooke .... £15,688 to £21,297
Area Manager, B. E. Kitching ... £17,000 to £22,926

Weymouth District Land Registry
1 Cumberland Drive, Weymouth,
Dorset DT4 9TT
[03057–76161]

District Land Registrar, K. L. Charles
£20,964 to £25,533
Assistant Land Registrars, W. W. Budden; J. B. Rhodes; M. A. Roche .... £15,688 to £21,297
Area Manager, R. R. C. Green ... £17,000 to £22,926

Computer Services Division
Plumer House, Tailyour Road,
Crownhill, Plymouth PL6 5HY
[0752–701234]

Head of Computer Services Division, A. A. Restorick
£17,000 to £22,926
Principals, N. G. Worcester; R. J. Smith; R. T. Davis
£13,508 to £18,363

LAW COMMISSION

England and Wales

Conquest House, 37–38 John Street,
Theobalds Road, WC1N 2BQ
[01–242 0861]

Set upon June 16, 1965, under the Law Commissions Act, 1965, to make proposals to the Government for the examination of the law and for its revision where it is unsuited for modern requirements, obscure, or otherwise unsatisfactory. It recommends to the Lord Chancellor programmes for the examination of different branches of the law and suggests whether the examination should be carried out by the Commission itself or by some other body. The Commission is also responsible for the preparation of Consolidation and Statute Law (Repeals) Bills.

Chairman, The Hon. Mr. Justice Ralph Gibson.
Members, T. M. Aldridge; B. J. Davenport, Q.C.; Prof. J. T. Farrand; Mrs. B. M. Hoggett.
Secretary, J. G. H. Gasson.

Scottish Law Commission

140 Causewayside, Edinburgh

Chairman, The Hon. Lord Maxwell.
Commissioners, Dr. E. M. Clive; C. G. B. Nicholson, Q.C. (*full-time*); R. D. D. Bertram, W.S.; J. Murray, Q.C. (*part-time*).

LAW OFFICERS' DEPARTMENT

Attorney-General's Chambers,
Royal Courts of Justice, WC2A 2LL

The Law Officers of the Crown for England and Wales (the Attorney-General and the Solicitor-General) represent the Crown in courts of justice, advise Government departments and represent them in court. The Attorney-General has also certain administrative functions, including supervision of the Director of Public Prosecutions.

Attorney General, THE RT. HON. SIR (ROBERT) MICHAEL (OLDFIELD) HAVERS, Q.C., M.P. . . £34,308†
Parliamentary Private Secretary, N. W. Lyell, Q.C., M.P.
Solicitor General, SIR PATRICK (BARNABAS BURKE) MAYHEW, Q.C., M.P. £27,878†
Parliamentary Private Secretary, M. Howard, Q.C., M.P.
Legal Secretary, H. Steel, C.M.G., O.B.E. £36,500
Asst. Legal Sec., M. L. Saunders. £30,800
† From Jan. 1, 1986.

LIBRARIES

OFFICE OF ARTS AND LIBRARIES
(*see* entry on page 425)

THE BRITISH LIBRARY

2 Sheraton Street, W1V 4BH
[01–636 1544]

The British Library was established on July 1, 1973, under the British Library Act, 1972, to provide, on a national scale, comprehensive reference, lending, bibliographic and other services based on its vast collections of books, manuscripts, maps, music, periodicals and other material. It was created by bringing together under a management board a number of national library organizations

The Library is organized into three divisions: Reference, Lending and Bibliographic Services, and two departments: the National Sound Archive and the Research and Development Department. It has a Central Administration.

The Reference Division comprises the Departments of Printed Books, Manuscripts, Oriental Manuscripts and Printed Books; the India Office Library and Records (since 1982), the Newspaper Library at Colindale, the Library Association Library, the Science Reference Library and, since 1983, the Preservation Service. The Division contains about 11,770,000 volumes of printed books and periodicals, about 85,000 volumes of Western Manuscripts and 41,000 volumes of Oriental Manuscripts, and outstanding collections of newspapers, official papers, papyri, charters, seals, maps, music and postage stamps. Admission to the Great Russell Street reading rooms and those of the Department of Oriental Manuscripts and Printed Books, the India Office Library and Records and the Newspaper Library is by reader's pass only. The Science Reference Library is the principal public reference library in the U.K. for contemporary literature of science and technology; no reader's pass is needed. In 1983, the Library established a Preservation Service within the Division. It is concerned with preservation policies and practices in the U.K., runs conservation studios and binderies, reprographic and photographic services for the Library, provides consultancy services and supports research and training in preservation. The National Preservation Office is wholly funded by the British Library and provides an information and advisory service to U.K. libraries.

The Lending Division in Yorkshire operates a rapid postal loan or photocopy service for organizations and currently receives 2,871,000 requests a year from British and foreign libraries. Individuals should apply through their local libraries. The stock contains 4,500,000 volumes of books and periodicals, 3,500,000 documents in microfilm and large quantities of semi-published materials such as reports, translations and theses.

The Bibliographic Services Division creates records both for forthcoming publications, from advance information received under the cataloguing-in-publication programme, and for books and other items received by legal deposit at the Copyright Receipt Office. The Division publishes the records in a range of printed bibliographies, including the British National Bibliography, and in machine-readable form as UKMARC, available on-line through the BLAISE-LINE information retrieval scheme, or on magnetic tape, through various record supply services. These records can be further processed by the BLAISE-LOCAS service which offers centralized file building and catalogue production facilities. In addition, the Division offers the specialist biomedical and toxicological information service, BLAISE-LINK.

The National Sound Archive (founded as the British Institute of Recorded Sound in 1947) became a department of the British Library in April 1983. Its collections include more than 500,000 discs and over 35,000 hours of tape recordings. Public access to the collections is through a free listening service in London and at the reading room of the Lending Division in Boston Spa.

The Research and Development Department promotes and supports research and development related to library and information operations in all subject fields and is directed to the benefit of the national library and information system as a whole.

Board Members

Chairman, Sir Frederick Dainton, F.R.S.
Chief Executive, K. R. Cooper.
Directors General, A. Wilson; P. R. Lewis; M. B. Line.
Part-time Members, Sir Robert Clayton, C.B.E.; W. G. Graham, M.C.; Sir Denis Hamilton, D.S.O.; Prof. B. Morris; D. Owen; Miss D. Park; Prof. I. G. Stewart; Prof. P. A. Larkin; Sir Robin Mackworth-Young, K.C.V.O.

Central Administration
2 Sheraton Street, W1V 4BH
[01-636 1544]

Secretary to the Board and Director of Central Administration, L. Bell.
Head of Press and Public Relations, Mrs. M. Treen.

Reference Division
Director General, A. Wilson.

Department of Printed Books
Gt. Russell St., London, W.C.1
[01-636 1544]

Keepers, R. J. Fulford; I. P. Gibb.

Library Association Library
7 Ridgmount St., W.C.1.
[01-636 1544]

Librarian, A. N. Macgregor.

Newspaper Library
Colindale Ave., N.W.9
[01-200 5515]

Head of Newspaper Library, (vacant).

Department of Manuscripts
Gt. Russell St., W.C.1
[01-636 1544]

Director and Keeper, Dr. D. P. Waley.

Department of Oriental Manuscripts and Printed Books
14 Store St., WC1E 7DG
[01-636 1544]

Keeper, B. C. Bloomfield.

India Office Library and Records
Orbit House, 197 Blackfriars Rd., SE1 8NG
[01-928 9531]

Director, B. C. Bloomfield.

Science Reference Library
25 Southampton Buildings, Chancery Lane, W.C.2
and
9 Kean St., W.C.2

Director, M. W. Hill.

National Preservation Office
Great Russell Street, W.C.1.
[01-636 1544]

National Preservation Officer, Miss L. J. Carr.

Lending Division
Boston Spa, Wetherby, West Yorks.
[0937 843434]

Director General, M. B. Line.
Executive Director, K. P. Barr.

Bibliographic Services Division
2 Sheraton St., W.1
[01-636 1544]

Director General, P. R. Lewis.
Director of Automated Services, M. D. Martin.

National Sound Archive
29 Exhibition Road, S.W.7
[01-589 6603]

Director, Dr. C. Roads.

Research and Development Department
2 Sheraton St., W.1
[01-636 1544]

Director, B. J. Perry.

NATIONAL LIBRARY OF SCOTLAND
George IV Bridge, Edinburgh EH1 1EW
[031-226 4531]

Open free. Reading Room, weekdays, 9.30 a.m. to 8.30 p.m. Saturdays 9.30 to 1. Map Room, weekdays, 9.30 to 5 p.m.; Saturdays, 9.30 to 1. Exhibition, weekdays, 9.30 a.m. to 5 p.m. Saturdays, 9.30 to 1; Sundays 2 to 5 (closed on Sundays Oct. to April).

The Library, which had been founded as the Advocates' Library in 1682, became the National Library of Scotland by Act of Parliament in 1925. It continues to share the rights conferred by successive Copyright Acts since 1710. Its collections of printed books and MSS., augmented by purchase and gift, are very large and it has an unrivalled Scottish collection. The present building was opened by H.M. the Queen in 1956.

The Reading Room is for reference and research which cannot conveniently be pursued elsewhere. Admission is by ticket issued to an approved applicant.

Chairman of the Trustees, M. F. Strachan, C.B.E. F.R.S.E.
Librarian and Secretary to the Trustees, Prof. E. F. D. Roberts, PH.D., F.R.S.E. £25,533
Secretary of the Library and Deputy Librarian, B. G. Hutton .... £20,964 to £23,900
Curators Grade C, M. C. Graham; J. E. McIntyre; A. M. Marchbank, PH.D.; Elspeth D. Yeo
£12,066 to £18,363
Keepers of Printed Books, W. H. Brown, E.R.D.; R. Donaldson, PH.D.; I. D. McGowan; Ann Matheson, PH.D. .... £17,051 to £21,297
Curators Grade C, M. A. Begg; A. M. Cain, PH.D.; T. A. F. Cherry; R. Duce; Alison E. Harvey Wood; B. P. Hillyard, D.Phil.; S. Holland; Ruth I. Hope; Alexia F. Howe; W. A. Kelly; J. M. Morris; J. Margaret Wilkes .... £12,066 to £18,363
Keepers of Manuscripts, P. M. Cadell; T. I. Rae, PH.D.
£17,051 to £21,297
Curators Grade C, I. G. Brown, PH.D., F.S.A.; I. C. Cunningham; I. F. Maciver; S. M. Simpson
£12,066 to £18,363
Director of Scottish Library Network (SCOLCAP), B. Gallivan .... £17,051 to £21,297
Curators Grade C, B. Royan; R. F. Guy
£12,066 to £18,363

THE NATIONAL LIBRARY OF WALES
Llyfrgell Genedlaethol Cymru
Aberystwyth, Dyfed SY23 3BU

Readers' room open on weekdays, 9.30 a.m. to 6 p.m. (Saturdays, 5 p.m.); closed on Sundays and Bank Holidays. Admission by Reader's Ticket.

Founded by Royal Charter, 1907, and maintained by annual grant from the Treasury. One of the six libraries entitled to most privileges under Copyright Act. Contains about 3,000,000 printed books, 40,000 manuscripts, 4,000,000 deeds and documents, and numerous maps, prints and drawings. Specializes in manuscripts and books relating to Wales and the Celtic peoples. Repository for pre-1858 Welsh probate records. Approved by the Master of the Rolls as a repository for manorial records and tithe documents, and by the Lord Chancellor for certain legal records. Bureau of the Regional Libraries Scheme for Wales.

Librarian, B. F. Roberts, PH.D.
Secretary, D. B. Lloyd.
Heads of Departments, D. Huws (*Manuscripts and Records*); P. A. L. Jones (*Printed Books*); D. H. Owen (*Pictures and Maps*).

COMMISSION FOR LOCAL ADMINISTRATION IN ENGLAND
21 Queen Anne's Gate, SW1H 9BU
[01–222 5622]

Local Commissioners are responsible for investigating complaints from members of the public in England who claim to have suffered injustice because of maladministration by a local authority, a water authority or a police authority. Certain types of action are excluded from investigation, particularly personnel matters and commercial transactions unless they relate to the purchase or sale of land. Complaints must normally be made through a member of the authority against which the complaint is made although a complaint can be put to a Local Commissioner direct if a member fails or refuses to refer it. A free booklet "Your Local Ombudsman" is available from the Commission's office.

Chairman of the Commission and Local Commissioner, D. C. M. Yardley, D.Phil. £45,500
Vice Chairman and Local Commissioner, F. G. Laws
. . . . £37,500
Local Commissioner, F. P. Cook £36,950
Member, The Parliamentary Commissioner for Administration
Secretary, M. R. Hyde £27,903

LONDON REGIONAL TRANSPORT
55 Broadway, SW1H 0BD
[01–222 5600]

Subject to the financial objectives and principles approved by the Secretary of State for Transport, London Regional Transport has a general duty to provide or secure the provision of public transport services for Greater London.

Chairman, Dr. K. Bright £47,500
Members, Dr. T. M. Ridley; J. Telford Beasley; B. G. Dale £41,000

LORD ADVOCATE'S DEPARTMENT
Fielden House, 10 Great College Street,
SW1P 3SL
[01–212 7676]

The Law Officers for Scotland are the Lord Advocate and the Solicitor-General for Scotland. The Lord Advocate's Department is responsible for drafting Scottish legislation, for providing legal advice to other departments on Scottish questions and for assistance to the Law Officers for Scotland in certain of their legal duties.

Lord Advocate, The Lord Cameron of Lochbroom, P.C., Q.C. £34,890
Solicitor-General for Scotland, P. L. Fraser, Q.C., M.P. £23,538
Legal Secretary and First Parliamentary Draftsman, N. J. Adamson, C.B., Q.C. £42,000
Senior Asst. Legal Secs. and Parlty. Draftsmen, G. M. Clark; D. J. S. Duncan; J. C. McCluskie . . . £34,000
Asst. Legal Secs. and Deputy Parlty. Draftsmen, J. D. Harkness; G. Kowalski; P. J. Layden, T.D.; C. A. M. Wilson . . . . £21,844 to £25,533
Junior Legal Sec. and Asst. Parlty. Draftsman, D. C. Macrae . . . . £15,688 to £21,297

LORD CHANCELLOR'S DEPARTMENT
House of Lords, SW1A 0PW
[01–219 3000]

The Lord Chancellor is responsible for promoting general reforms in the civil law, for the procedure of the civil courts and for the administration of the Supreme Court (Court of Appeal, High Court and Crown Court) and county courts in England and Wales, and for legal aid schemes. He is responsible for advising the Crown on the appointment of judges

and certain other officers and is himself responsible for the appointment of Masters and Registrars of the High Court and District and County Court Registrars and magistrates. He is responsible for ensuring that letters patent and other formal documents are passed in the proper form under the Great Seal of the Realm, of which he is the custodian. The work in connection with this is carried out under his direction in the Office of the Clerk of the Crown in Chancery.

Lord Chancellor, THE RT. HON. THE LORD HAILSHAM OF ST. MARYLEBONE, C.H. £71,500
Private Secretary to the Lord Chancellor, R. C. Stoate
. . . . £15,688 to £21,297
Permanent Secretary, Sir Derek Oulton, K.C.B., Q.C.
. . . . £52,750
Private Secretary to the Permanent Secretary, G. Pulford . . . . £8,896 to £11,265

Crown Office

Clerk of the Crown in Chancery, Sir Derek Oulton, K.C.B., Q.C.
Deputy Clerk of the Crown in Chancery, P. D. Robinson, C.B. £39,250
Clerk of the Chamber, Miss J. L. Waine
. . . . £10,980–£13,801

Legal Administration Division
Neville House, Page Street, S.W.1
[01–211 8104]

Deputy Secretary, P. D. Robinson, C.B. £39,250
Under Secretary, R. E. K. Holmes £31,750
Assistant Solicitors, P. M. Harris; R. H. H. White
. . . . £20,964 to £25,533
Assistant Secretaries, C. W. Everett; D. E. Staff
. . . . £20,964 to £25,533

Appointments Division
House of Lords, S.W.1.
[01–219 3000]

Deputy Secretary, T. S. Legg, C.B. £39,250
Assistant Solicitor, Mrs. N. A. Oppenheimer
. . . . £20,964–£25,533

Secretary of Commissions
4th Flr, Thames House North, Millbank, S.W.1.
[01–211 0067]

Secretary of Commissions (Under Secretary), B. Cooke £31,750
Joint Deputy Secretaries of Commissions, R. V. Grobler; W. B. Scott.

Legislation Division
House of Lords, S.W.1.
[01–219 3000]

Under Secretary, C. R. Seaton £31,750
Assistant Solicitors, P. M. Harris; M. H. Collon
. . . . £20,964–£25,533

Establishment and Finance Division
Neville House, Page Street, S.W.1
[01–211 8623]

Principal Establishment and Finance Officer, D. J. Wiblin £31,750
Assistant Secretaries, Miss J. E. Court; A. D. Fagin; D. S. Mortimer; I. R. Tapster; Miss J. Court
. . . . £20,964–£25,533
Senior Principal, C. F. Tye . . . . £17,000–£22,926
Principal Information Officer, G. E. Moggridge
. . . . £13,508–£18,363

Courts Funds Office
Royal Courts of Justice, WC2A 2LL

Accountant General, Sir Derek Oulton, K.C.B.
Deputy Accountant General, P. D. Lewis, T.D.
. . . . £20,964 to £25,533
Head of Courts Fund Office, I. J. MacBean
. . . . £13,508 to £18,363

Ecclesiastical Patronage
10 Downing Street, S.W.1
[01–233 3000]

Secretary for Ecclesiastical Patronage, J. R. Catford.
Assistant Secretary for Ecclesiastical Patronage, (vacant) . . . . £13,508–£18,363

See also Law Courts and Offices

LORD GREAT CHAMBERLAIN'S OFFICE
House of Lords, SW1A 0PW
[01–219 3100]

The Lord Great Chamberlain is a Great Officer of State, the office being hereditary since the grant of Henry I to the family of De Vere, Earls of Oxford.
Lord Great Chamberlain, The Marquess of Cholmondeley, G.C.V.O., M.C.
Secretary to the Lord Great Chamberlain, Air Chief Marshal Sir John Gingell, G.B.E., K.C.B.
Clerk to the Lord Great Chamberlain, Miss C. A. Sansbury.

LORD PRIVY SEAL
Privy Council Office,
Whitehall, SW1A 2AT

Lord Privy Seal, and Leader of the House of Commons, THE RT. HON. JOHN BIFFEN, M.P.
Private Secretary, D. R. Morris.
Assistant Private Secretary, Miss A. J. Smith.

OFFICE OF MANPOWER ECONOMICS
22 Kingsway, WC2B 6JY
[01–405 5944]

The Office of Manpower Economics was set up in 1971. It is an independent non-statutory organization which is responsible for servicing independent review bodies which advise on the pay of various public service groups (*see* entries under "Review Bodies"), the Pharmacists Review Panel, the Police Negotiating Board and the Civil Service Arbitration Tribunal. The Office is also responsible for servicing *ad hoc* bodies of inquiry and for undertaking research into pay and associated matters as requested by Government.
Director, R. W. Williams
Assistant Secretaries, G. E. Johnson; D. A. Roberts; D. R. Bower.
Chief Statistician, H. J. M. Jones.

MANPOWER SERVICES COMMISSION
Head Office: Moorfoot, Sheffield S1 4PQ
[0742 753275]

Chairman, B. H. Nicholson £45,500
Members, F. A. Baker, C.B.E.; Miss S. I. Elkin, O.B.E.; K. Graham, O.B.E.; Dr. M. R. Green; W. H. Keys; J. A. Lawton, C.B.E.; W. Longden; H. Orr-Ewing; N. J. Payne, C.B.E.
Director, G. Holland £32,500

Employment Division

Chief Executive, B. D. Emmett £26,250
General Employment Service, M. Weston £21,654
Planning, J. S. Child £20,500
Disabled Person's Services, B. Swindell £23,159
SEPACS and Sheltered Employment, D. J. Sullivan £20,550
Special Employment Measures, J. B. Surr . . . £22,302
PER Director, D. Rees £22,700
Executive Directors:
  T. R. R. O'Connor (*Wales and the South*); M. Weston (*Scotland and the North*).

Training Division

Chief Executive, R. J. Dawe, O.B.E. £28,265
Director of Occupational Training, Miss J. H. Bacon £26,250
Director of Youth Training, K. N. Atkinson . £25,000
Open Tech Unit, J. D. Tinsley £23,159
Occupational Policy, J. Wiltshire £23,159
Adult Training, J. A. Robertson £20,728
Sectors Training, P. D. Carr £23,421
YTS Programmes, Mrs. V. J. Bayliss £23,387
YTS Strategy, Evaluation and Research, M. G. Mellish.
Quality Branch, Dr. G. Tolley.
Training, Economics and Statistics Branch, Mrs. J. Marquand.
Statistics, N. H. W. Davis.
Regional and Area Operations, J. Wild £23,387

Skillcentre Training Agency

Chief Executive, R. C. Stephenson £24,077
Skill Centre Operations, S. Loveman £21,426
Product Development, J. Mannell £20,794
Promotional Services, J. Turner.
Financial and Accounting Services, T. Kent.

Personnel and Central Services Division

Director, D. B. Price.
Personnel, A. T. Wisbey.
Computer Branch, I. E. Turl.
Marketing Information Branch, N. Stone.
Psychological Services, Dr. M. C. Killcross.
Staff Training, J. Corbett.

Planning and Resources Division

Director, I. A. Johnston.
Accounts, J. S. Cousins.
Finance Policy, D. J. Howells.
Manpower and Efficiency, G. Kendall.
Central Planning, J. F. Smith.

MEDICAL RESEARCH COUNCIL
20 Park Crescent, W1N 4AL
[01–636 5422]

Chairman, The Earl Jellicoe, P.C., D.S.O., M.C.
Deputy Chairman and Secretary, Sir James Gowans, C.B.E., F.R.S.
Members, E. D. Acheson, D.M., F.R.C.P.; B. H. Bailey, O.B.E.; Belinda Banham, C.B.E.; Prof. I. D. Bouchier, M.D., F.R.C.P.; J. T. Carter; Prof. A. Cowey, D.Phil.; D. L. Crouch, M.P.; Prof. M. A. Epstein, M.D., D.SC., F.R.S.; Prof. R. E. Kendell, M.D., F.R.C.P.; Prof. June Lloyd, M.D., F.R.C.P.; Prof. P. J. Morris, PH.D.; Prof. J. M. Newsom-Davis, M.D., F.R.C.P.; Prof. D. K. Peters, F.R.C.P.; D. A. Rees, D.SC., F.R.S.; J. J. A. Reid, C.B., T.D., M.D., D.SC., F.R.C.P.; Sir Michael Stoker, C.B.E., F.R.S.; Prof. L. Wolpert, PH.D., F.R.S.
Administrative Secretary, D. Noble.

Neurobiology and Mental Health Board

Chairman, Prof. J. M. Newsom-Davis, M.D., F.R.C.P.

Cell Biology and Disorders Board

Chairman, Prof. L. Wolpert, PH.D., F.R.S.

Physiological Systems and Disorders Board

Chairman, Prof. June Lloyd, M.D., F.R.C.P.

Tropical Medicine Research Board

Chairman, Sir Christopher Booth, M.D., F.R.C.P.

HEADQUARTERS OFFICE

Medical Division

Principal Medical Officers, Katherine Levy; Barbara Rashbass; J. Alwen, PH.D.

Administrative Division

Administrative Secretary, D. Noble.
Assistant Secretaries, Norma Morris; N. H. Winterton; J. E. A. Hay.

Secretariat and Universities Division

Assistant Secretary, B. C. Dodd.

Headquarters Establishments and O & M Section and Computing Services

Head of Section, D. C. Brunton.

National Institute for Medical Research
Mill Hill, N.W.7
[01-959 3666]

Director, D. A. Rees, D.SC., F.R.S.

Clinical Research Centre
Watford Road, Harrow, Middlesex
[01-864 5311]

Director, Sir Christopher Booth, M.D., F.R.C.P.

Research Units

Anatomical Neuropharmacology Unit, Dept. of Pharmacology, University of Oxford, South Park Road, Oxford OX1 3QT. *Director*, Prof. A. D. Smith.
Applied Psychology Unit, 15 Chaucer Road, Cambridge. *Director*, A. D. Baddeley, PH.D.
Biochemical Parasitology Unit, Molteno Institute, Downing Street, Cambridge. *Director*, B. A. Newton, PH.D.
Biostatistics Unit, University Medical School, Hills Road, Cambridge. *Director*, I. Sutherland, D.PHIL.
Blood Group Unit, University College, London, Wolfson House, 4 Stephenson Way, N.W.1. *Director*, Patricia Tippett, PH.D.
Blood Pressure Unit, Western Infirmary, Glasgow. *Director*, A. F. Lever, F.R.C.P.
Brain Metabolism Unit, University Dept. of Pharmacology, 1 George Square, Edinburgh. *Director*, G. Fink, M.D.
Cell Biophysics Unit, Dept. of Biophysics, King's College, 26–29 Drury Lane, W.C.2. *Hon. Director*, Prof. B. B. Boycott, F.R.S.
Cell Mutation Unit, University of Sussex, Falmer, Brighton. *Director*, Prof. B. A. Bridges, PH.D.
Cellular Immunology Unit, Sir William Dunn School of Pathology, Oxford. *Director*, Dr. A. F. Williams.
Child Psychiatry Unit, Institute of Psychiatry, De Crespigny Park, Denmark Hill, SE5 8AF. *Director*, Prof. M. Rutter.
Clinical and Population Cytogenetics Unit, Western General Hospital, Crewe Road, Edinburgh. *Director*, Prof. H. J. Evans, PH.D., F.R.S.E.
Clinical Oncology and Radiotheraupeutics Unit, Medical School, Hills Road, Cambridge. *Hon. Director*, Prof. N. M. Bleehen, F.R.C.P.
Clinical Pharmacology Unit, University Department of Clinical Pharmacology, Radcliffe Infirmary, Oxford. *Hon. Director*, Prof. D. G. Grahame-Smith, PH.D., F.R.C.P.
Cognitive Development Unit, 17–19 Gordon Street, W.C.1. *Director*, J. Morton, PH.D.
Cyclotron Unit, Hammersmith Hospital, Ducane Road, W.12. *Director*, D. D. Vonberg, C.B.E.
Dental Research Unit, London Hospital Medical College, Turner Street, E1 2AD. *Director*, Prof. N. W. Johnson.
Unit on the Development and Integration of Behaviour, Subdept. of Animal Behaviour, Madingley, Cambridge. *Hon. Director*, Prof. R. A. Hinde, SC.D., F.R.S
Development Neurobiology Unit, 33 St. John's Mews, W.C.1. *Director*, R. Balazs, M.D., D.Phil.
Dunn Nutrition Unit, Milton Road, Cambridge. *Director*, R. G. Whitehead, PH.D.

Environmental Epidemiology Unit, Southampton General Hospital. *Director*, Prof. D. J. P. Barker, M.D., Ph.D., F.R.C.P.
Epidemiology and Medical Care Unit, Northwick Park Hospital, Harrow, Middx. *Director*, T. W. Meade.
Epidemiology Unit (South Wales), 4 Richmond Road, Cardiff. *Director*, P. C. Elwood, M.D.
Unit for Epidemiological Studies in Psychiatry, University of Psychiatry, Royal Edinburgh Hospital, Morningside Park, Edinburgh. *Director*, N. B. Kreitman, M.D.
Experimental Embryology and Teratology Unit, M.R.C. Laboratories, Woodmansterne Road, Carshalton, Surrey. *Director*, D. G. Whittingham.
Human Biochemical Genetics Unit, Galton Laboratory University College London, Wolfson House, 4 Stephenson Way, N.W.1. *Hon. Director*, D. A. Hopkinson, M.D.
Immunochemistry Unit, University Department of Biochemistry, South Parks Road, Oxford. *Hon. Director*, Prof. R. R. Porter, Ph.D., F.R.S.
Institute of Hearing Research, The Medical School, University of Nottingham. *Director*, M. P. Haggard, Ph.D.
M.R.C. Laboratories, Carshalton, Woodmansterne Road, Carshalton, Surrey. *Admin. Officer*, B. H. Goodfellow.
M.R.C. Laboratories, The Gambia, Fajara, The Gambia, W. Africa. *Director*, B. M. Greenwood, M.D.
M.R.C. Laboratories, Jamaica, University of the West Indies, Mona, Kingston, Jamaica. *Director*, G. R. Serjeant, M.D.
Leukaemia Unit, Royal Postgraduate Medical School, Ducane Road, W.12. *Hon. Director*, Prof. D. A. G. Galton, M.D., F.R.C.P.
Mammalian Development Unit, University College London, Wolfson House, 4 Stephenson Way, N.W.1. *Director*, Anne McLaren, D.Phil., F.R.S.
Mammalian Genome Unit, Dept. of Zoology, University of Edinburgh, West Mains Road, Edinburgh. *Director*, E. M. Southern, Ph.D.
Mechanisms in Tumour Immunity Unit, University Medical School, Hills Road, Cambridge. *Director*, Prof. P. J. Lachmann, SC.D., F.R.C.P.
Medical Sociology Unit, 5–6, Lilybank Gardens, Glasgow. *Director*, Sally Macintyre, M.SC., Ph.D.
Mineral Metabolism Unit, The General Infirmary, Great George Street, Leeds. *Acting Director*, M. Peacock, F.R.C.P.
Laboratory of Molecular Biology, University Postgraduate Medical School, Hills Road, Cambridge. *Director*, S. Brenner, D.Phil., F.R.S.
Molecular Haematology Unit, John Radcliffe Hospital, Headington, Oxford. *Director*, Prof. D. J. Weatherell, M.D., F.R.C.P., F.R.S.
Unit of Neural Mechanisms of Behaviour, 3 Malet Place, W.C.1. *Director*, I. Steele Russell, Ph.D.
Neurochemical Pharmacology Unit, University Dept. of Pharmacology, Hills Road, Cambridge. *Director*, (vacant).
Neuroendocrinology Unit, Newcastle General Hospital, Westgate Road, Newcastle upon Tyne. *Director*, J. A. Edwardson, Ph.D.
Neurological Prostheses Unit, Institute of Psychiatry, De Crespigny Park, Denmark Hill, S.E.5. *Hon. Director*, Prof. G. S. Brindley, M.D., F.R.C.P., F.R.S.
Neuro-Ontology Unit, Institute of Neurology, National Hospital, Queen Square, W.C.1. *Director*, J. D. Hood, Ph.D., D.SC.
Neuropathogenesis Unit, West Mains Road, Edinburgh. *Director*, A. G. Dickinson, Ph.D.
Perceptual and Cognitive Performance Unit, Experimental Psychology Laboratory, University of Sussex, Falmer, Brighton. *Director*, Prof. W. P. Colquhoun, Ph.D.

Radiobiology Unit, Harwell, Didcot, Oxon. *Director*, Prof. G. E. Adams, ph.d., d.sc.

Reproductive Biology Unit, 37 Chalmers St., Edinburgh. *Director*, D. W. Lincoln, ph.d., d.sc.

Social and Applied Psychology Unit, Dept. of Psychology, University of Sheffield. *Director*, P. B. Warr, ph.d.

Social Psychiatry Unit, Institute of Psychiatry, De Crespigny Park, Denmark Hill, S.E.5. *Director*, Prof. J. K. Wing, m.d., Ph.d.

Toxicology Unit, M.R.C. Laboratories, Woodmansterne Road, Carshalton, Surrey. *Director*, T. A. Connors, d.sc.

Trauma Unit, Oxford Road, Manchester. *Director*, Prof. H. B. Stoner, m.d.

Tuberculosis and Chest Diseases Unit, Brompton Hospital, Fulham Road, S.W.3. *Director*, Prof. W. Fox, c.m.g., m.d., f.r.c.p.

Tuberculosis and Related Infections Unit, Royal Postgraduate Medical School, Du Cane Road, W12 0HS. *Director*, Dr. J. Ivanyi.

Virology Unit, Institute of Virology, Church Street, Glasgow. *Hon. Director*, Prof. J. H. Subak-Sharpe, ph.d., f.r.s.e.

THE ROYAL MINT
Llantrisant, nr. Pontyclun,
Mid-Glamorgan CF7 8YT
[0443–222111]

Master Worker and Warden, The Chancellor of the Exchequer (*ex officio*).
Deputy Master and Comptroller, Dr. D. J. Gerhard.

MONOPOLIES AND MERGERS COMMISSION
48 Carey Street, WC2A 2JT
[01–831 6111]

The Commission was established under the Monopolies and Restrictive Practices (Inquiry and Control) Act, 1948 as the Monopolies and Restrictive Practices Commission and was reconstituted on subsequent occasions. It became the Monopolies and Mergers Commission when the Fair Trading Act, 1973, came into operation on November 1, 1973. The Commission has the duty of investigating and reporting on questions referred to it in accordance with the Act with respect to (*a*) the existence or possible existence of monopolies not registrable under the Restrictive Trade Practices Act, 1976, which consolidated earlier legislation, and relating to the supply of goods or services in the United Kingdom or part of the United Kingdom or to the supply of goods for export; (*b*) the transfer of a newspaper or newspaper's assets; (*c*) the creation or possible creation of a merger qualifying for investigation within the meaning of the Act.

In monopoly references (except those "limited to the facts") and in merger references it is the duty of the Commission to report on the effect of the facts which they find on the public interest and to consider and, if they think fit, to recommend the action to be taken to remedy or prevent adverse effects. In addition the Fair Trading Act, 1973, provides for references to the Commission on the general effect on the public interest of specified monopoly or other uncompetitive practices and of restrictive labour practices.

The Competition Act, 1980, provides for the reference to the Commission of particular anti-competitive practices and of questions of efficiency, costs, service provided and possible abuse of monopolies in the public sector.

The Telecommunications Act 1984 provides for references by the Director General of Telecommunications: (a) where the Director General is not able to

reach an acceptable agreement on the modification of a licence under the Act; and (b) in the case of possible monopoly situations in commercial activities connected with telecommunications and of anti-competitive practices in connection with the production, supply or acquisition of telecommunications apparatus or the supply or securing of telecommunication services.

Chairman, Sir Godfray Le Quesne, q.c. £51,120
Deputy Chairmen, (*part-time*), H. H. Hunt (£18,268); Sir Alan Neale, k.c.b., m.b.e. (£18,268); D. G. Richards (£21,008).
Members, J. G. Ackers; C. C. Baillieu; M. B. Bunting; K. S. Carmichael, c.b.e.; Sir Robert Clayton, c.b.e.; P. H. Dean; Prof. K. D. George; H. L. G. Gibson, o.b.e.; Prof. R. M. Goode, o.b.e.; D. G. Goyder; G. D. Gwilt; L. Kelly; M. S. Lipworth; Prof. S. C. Littlechild; Miss P. K. R. Mann; S. McDowall, c.b.e.; L. A. Mills; B. C. Owens; Prof. R. Rees; J. S. Sadler, c.b.e.; N. L. Salmon; R. G. Smethurst; Sir Ronald Swayne, m.c.; D. P. Thomson; C. A. Unwin, m.b.e.; S. Wainwright, c.b.e. . . . . *each* £6,180
Secretary, N. E. D. Burton.

MUSEUMS

MUSEUMS AND GALLERIES COMMISSION
2 Carlton Gardens, SW1Y 5AA
[01–930 0995]

The Commission was established in 1931 as the Standing Commission on Museums and Galleries. From its inception its remit has covered the whole of Great Britain. In 1981, the Government decided to strengthen the Commission, changing its name with a revised formal mandate:— (i) to advise generally on the most effective development of museums and galleries and to advise, and take action as appropriate, on any specific matters which may be referred to them from time to time; (ii) to promote co-operation between musuems and galleries and particularly between the national and provincial institutions; (iii) to stimulate the generosity and direct the efforts of those who aspire to become public benefactors. The Commission is funded through the Office of Arts and Libraries. Its present executive functions include the control of the services of the National Security Adviser, the allocation of grants to the 7 Area Museum Councils (AMCs) in England and the monitoring of the 9 U.K. AMCs generally, and co-ordination of the funding and monitoring the work of the Museum Documentation Association. The Commission also directly administers a capital grant scheme for non-national museums and, in 1984, a significant new scheme of conservation grants. In addition, the Commission exercises an important role in advising the Government on indemnities and the acceptance of works of art in lieu of Capital Transfer Tax.

Chairman, Prof. B. Morris, d.phil.
Members, The Marchioness of Anglesey, d.b.e.; T. Clifford; Hon. J. Davies; Prof. Sir John Hale, f.b.a.; T. W. I. Hodgkinson, c.b.e.; T. A. Hume, c.b.e., f.s.a.; J. Last; H. F. J. Leggatt; Admiral of the Fleet the Lord Lewin, k.g., g.c.b., m.v.o., d.s.c.; Prof. G. D. Sims, o.b.e.; Prof. H. A. D. Miles; The Lord Windlesham, c.v.o., p.c.; (one vacancy).
Secretary, P. Longman.

THE BRITISH MUSEUM
Great Russell Street, WC1B 3DG
[01–636 1555]

Antiquities Departments: Egyptian, Greek and Roman, Medieval and Later, Oriental, Prehistoric and Romano-British; Western Asiatic; also, Coins and Medals, Prints and Drawings, Ethnography.

Main entrance, Great Russell Street, W.C.1; *North entrance*, Montague Place, W.C.1. Open weekdays (including Bank Holidays) 10 to 5 and Sundays 2.30 to 6. Closed on Good Friday, Christmas Eve, Christmas Day, Boxing Day, New Year's Day and the first Monday in May. The ethnographical collections are displayed in The Museum of Mankind at 6 Burlington Gardens, W.1. Opening times as above.

The British Musuem may be said to date from 1753, when Parliament granted funds to purchase the collections of Sir Hans Sloane and the Harleian manuscripts, and for their proper housing and maintenance. The building (Montagu House) was opened in 1759. The present buildings were erected between 1823 and the present day, and the original collection has increased to its present dimensions by gifts and purchases. The administrative expenses were estimated at £13,053,000 in 1985–86, and were met by a vote under "Museums, Galleries and the Arts", Class X of the Civil Estimates. The constitution of the British Museum was revised under the terms of the British Museum Act, 1963.

Under the provisions of the British Library Act 1972 and the British Library Act (Appointed Day) Order 1973, the Library Departments of the British Museum were transferred on July 1, 1973, from the responsibility of the Trustees of the British Museum to that of the British Library Board and became part of the British Library.

Board of Trustees

Appointed by the Sovereign: H.R.H. The Duke of Gloucester, G.C.V.O. *Appointed by the Prime Minister:* The Lord Trend, P.C., G.C.B., C.V.O., (*Chairman*); Sir Arthur Drew, K.C.B.; Graham C. Greene; Prof. E. T. Hall, D.Phil., F.S.A., F.B.A.; C. E. A. Hambro; Sir Denis Hamilton, D.S.O.; Prof. Sir Harry Hinsley, O.B.E., F.B.A.; Sir Denys Lasdun, C.B.E., F.R.I.B.A.; J. L. Thorn; The Lord Windlesham, P.C., C.V.O.; The Lord Charteris of Amisfield, P.C., G.C.B., G.C.V.O., O.B.E.; Mrs. M. Moore; Prof. G. H. Treitel, D.C.L., F.B.A., Q.C.; Sir Ian Trethowan; The Lord Weinstock.

Nominated by the Royal Society, Royal Academy, British Academy and Society of Antiquaries of London: The Lord Adrian, M.D., F.R.S. (*Royal Society*); Dame Elisabeth Frink, D.B.E., R.A. (*Royal Academy*); The Lord Blake, F.B.A. (*British Academy*); Prof. W. Watson, C.B.E., F.S.A., F.B.A. (*Society of Antiquaries*)

Appointed by the Trustees of the British Museum: Sir David Attenborough, C.B.E.; Sir Martyn Beckett, BT., M.C., R.I.B.A.; Prof. Rosemary Cramp, F.S.A.; Prof. P. Lasko, C.B.E., F.S.A., F.B.A.; Sir Francis Sandilands, C.B.E.

Officers

Director, Sir David Wilson £36,500
Deputy Director, Jean M. Rankine £23,776 to £25,533
Secretary, G. B. Morris .... £17,051 to £21,297
Administrative Assistant, Marjorie L. Caygill
.... £12,066 to £18,363
Head of Public Services (Deputy Keeper), G. A. L. House .... £17,051 to £21,297
Head of Design (Deputy Keeper), Margaret Hall, O.B.E.
.... £17,051 to £21,297
Assistant Keeper, Education Office, J. F. Reeve
.... £12,066 to £18,363
Head of Press and Public Relations, E. Balfour
.... £10,980 to £13,801
Press and Public Relations Officer, A. Hamilton
.... £8,896 to £11,265
Head of Administration (Senior Principal), B. A. Wilson .... £17,000 to £22,926
Museum Superintendent (Principal), P. E. Youngs..................... £13,508 to £18,363

Keeper of Prints and Drawings, J. K. Rowlands
.... £20,964 to £23,900
Deputy Keeper, A. V. Griffiths ... £17,051 to £21,297
Assistant Keepers, Frances A. Carey; N. J. L. Turner; Lindsay Stainton; M. B. Royalton-Kisch
.... £12,066 to £18,363
Keeper of Coins and Medals, J. P. C. Kent
.... £20,964 to £23,900
Deputy Keepers, M. J. Price; N. M. Lowick
.... £17,051 to £21,297
Assistant Keepers, M. G. Powell-Jones; Marion M. Archibald; A. M. Burnett; B. J. Cook .. £12,066 to
.... £18,363
Keeper of Egyptian Antiquities, T. G. H. James
.... £20,964 to £23,900
Deputy Keeper, W. V. Davies .... £17,051 to £21,297
Assistant Keepers, M. L. Bierbrier; A. J. Spencer
.... £12,066 to £18,363
Keeper (Acting) of Western Asiatic Antiquities, T. C. Mitchell..................... £20,964 to £23,900
Assistant Keepers, J. E. Curtis; C. B. F. Walker; I. L. Finkel .... £12,066 to £18,363
Keeper of Greek and Roman Antiquities, B. F. Cook
.... £20,964 to £23,900
Deputy Keeper, K. S. Painter .... £17,051 to £21,297
Assistant Keepers, Susan E. C. Walker; Veronica Tatton-Brown; D. J. R. Williams ...... £12,066 to
.... £18,363
Keeper of Medieval and Later Antiquities, N. M. Stratford .... £20,964 to £23,900
Deputy Keepers, G. H. Tait; J. Cherry; Leslie E. Webster .... £17,051 to £21,297
Assistant Keepers, D. Kidd; D. Buckton; M. D. Collins; T. H. Wilson .... £12,066 to £18,363
Keeper of Prehistoric and Romano-British Antiquities, I. H. Longworth .... £20,964 to £23,900
Deputy Keeper, G. de G. Sieveking; I. M. Stead
.... £17,051 to £21,297
Assistant Keepers, I. A. Kinnes; T. W. Potter; Marilyn R. Bruce-Mitford .... £12,066 to £18,363
Keeper of Oriental Antiquities, L. R. H. Smith
.... £20,964 to £23,900
Deputy Keepers, Jessica M. Rawson; J. M. Rogers
.... £17,051 to £21,297
Assistant Keepers, W. Zwalf; Anne S. L. Farrer; J. R. Knox .... £12,066 to £18,363
Keeper of Ethnography, M. D. McLeod
.... £20,964 to £23,900
Deputy Keeper, B. Durrans ...... £17,051 to £21,297
Assistant Keepers, Elizabeth M. Carmichael; Shelagh G. Weir; Dorota Starzecka; J. C. H. King; J. B. Mack; N. F. Barley .... £12,066 to £18,363
Keeper of Scientific Research and Conservation, M. Tite......................... £20,964 to £23,900
Principal Scientific Officers, P. T. Craddock; M. J. Hughes; I. C. Freestone.
Keeper of Conservation, W. A. Oddy
.... £17,051 to £21,297
Principal Scientific Officer, V. D. Daniels.
Principal Conservator, Hannah P. Lane .. £12,066 to
.... £18,363

THE BRITISH MUSEUM (NATURAL HISTORY)
Cromwell Road, SW7 5BD
[01–589 6323]

Open free Monday to Saturday (except New Year's Day, Good Friday, May Day, Christmas Eve, Christmas Day and Boxing Day) 10 to 6, and on Sundays from 2.30 to 6.

The Natural History Museum originates from the natural history departments of the British Museum, Bloomsbury. During the 19th century the natural history collections grew so extensively that it became necessary to find new quarters for them and in 1881 they were moved to South Kensington. The British Museum Act, 1963, made the Natural History Museum completely independent with its own body of Trustees. The Zoological Museum, Tring, bequeathed by the second Lord Rothschild, has formed part of the Museum since 1938. On April 1, 1985, the Geological Museum, formerly part of the British Geological Survey, merged with the Natural History Museum (opening times are as given above). Research workers are admitted to the libraries and study collections by Student's Ticket, applications for which should be made in writing to the Director. There are lectures for visitors at 3 p.m. on week-days and lectures are also available at other times for special parties by arrangement with the Department of Public Services.

The administrative expenses were estimated at £9,751,000 in 1984–85.

Board of Trustees

Chairman, Prof. Sir Richard Harrison, F.R.S.
Appointed by the Prime Minister: The Earl of Cranbrook; Prof. Sir Frederick Stewart, F.R.S.; The Lord Swann, F.R.S.; The Lord Adrian, F.R.S.; Dr. W. F. Bodmer, F.R.S.; Prof. D. Spencer Smith.
Nominated by the Royal Society: Prof. Sir Andrew Huxley, O.M., P.R.S.
Appointed by the Trustees of the British Museum (Natural History): Prof. H. B. Whittington, F.R.S.; Sir James Hamilton, K.C.B., M.B.E.

Director (G3), R. H. Hedley, D.SC. £32,350
Deputy Director (G5), A. C. Bishop, PH.D.
.... £20,964 to £25,533
Secretary (G5), R. Saunders ...... £20,964 to £25,533
Assistant to the Director, R. F. Eastwood, PH.D.
.... £12,357 to £16,462

Department of Zoology

Keeper (G6), J. F. Peake .... £17,000 to £22,926
Deputy Keepers (G6), C. R. Curds, D.SC.; R. J. Lincoln, PH.D. .... £17,000 to £22,926
Senior Principal Scientific Officer (G6), P. H. Greenwood, D.SC. .... £17,000 to £22,926
Principal Scientific Officers, E. N. Arnold, PH.D.; K. E. Banister, PH.D.; I. R. Bishop, O.B.E.; G. A. Boxhall, PH.D.; Miss A. M. Clark; Miss P. L. Cook; P. F. S. Cornelius, PH.D.; A. A. Fincham, PH.D.; J. D. George, PH.D.; D. I. Gibson, PH.D.; J. E. Hill; R. W. Ingle, PH.D.; Mrs. J. Jewell, PH.D.; H. M. Platt, PH.D.; D. Rollinson, PH.D.; R. W. Sims; V. R. Southgate, PH.D.; J. D. Taylor, PH.D.; A. C. Wheeler; P. J. P. Whitehead, PH.D. .... £12,357 to £16,462

Ornithology Section
Park Street, Tring, Herts.
[Tring: 4181]

Principal Scientific Officers, P. J. K. Burton, PH.D.; C. J. O. Harrison, PH.D. .... £12,357 to £16,462

Department of Entomology

Keeper (G6), L. A. Mound, D.SC. ... £17,000 to £22,926
Deputy Keepers (G6), D. R. Ragge, PH.D.; R. I. Vane-Wright .... £17,000 to £22,926
Senior Principal Scientific Officers (G6), R. W. Crosskey, D.SC.; V. F. Eastop, D.SC. .... £17,000 to £22,926
Principal Scientific Officers, R. L. Blackman, PH.D.; B. Bolton; I. D. Gauld, PH.D.; P. M. Hammond; D. Hollis; W. J. Knight, PH.D.; A. C. Pont; R. D. Pope; K. S. O. Sattler, PH.D.; A. J. Shelley, PH.D.; K. G. V. Smith; R. T. Thompson; W. G. Tremewan; Miss C. M. F. von Hayek; A. Watson; P. E. S. Whalley, D.SC. .... £12,357 to £16,462

Department of Botany

Keeper (G5), J. F. M. Cannon ... £20,964 to £25,533
Deputy Keeper (G6), P. W. James . £17,000 to £22,926

Principal Scientific Officers, A. O. Chater; A. Eddy; C. J. Humphries, PH.D.; L. M. Irvine; A. C. Jermy; D. M. John, PH.D.; R. J. Pankhurst; J. M. Pettitt, PH.D.; J. H. Price; N. K. B. Robson, PH.D.£12,357 to £16,462

Department of Palaeontology

Keeper (G5), H. W. Ball, PH.D. .... £20,964 to £25,533
Deputy Keepers (G6), L. R. M. Cocks, D.SC.; M. K. Howarth, PH.D. .... £17,000 to £22,926
Senior Principal Scientific Officers (G6), C. Patterson, PH.D.; C. G. Adams, O.B.E., PH.D.£17,000 to £22,926
Principal Scientific Officers, P. J. Andrews, PH.D.; C. H. C. Brunton, PH.D.; A. J. Charig, PH.D.; P. L. Forey, PH.D.; R. A. Fortey, D.SC.; A. W. Gentry, D.Phil.; R. P. S. Jefferies, PH.D.; N. J. Morris, D.Phil.; C. P. Nuttall; H. G. Owen, PH.D.; J. B. Richardson, PH.D.; B. R. Rosen, PH.D.; C. B. Stringer, PH.D.; A. J. Sutcliffe, PH.D.; D. Tills, PH.D.£12,357 to £16,462

Department of Mineralogy

Keeper (G5), A. C. Bishop, PH.D. .. £20,964 to £25,533
Deputy Keeper (G6), D. R. C. Kempe, D.Phil.
.... £17,000 to £22,926
Senior Principal Scientific Officers (G6), P. Henderson, D.Phil.; R. Hutchison, PH.D. .... £17,000 to £22,926
Principal Scientific Officers, A. M. Clark, PH.D.; P. G. Embrey; A. L. Graham, PH.D.; R. R. Harding, PH.D.; R. F. Symes, PH.D.; A. R. Woolley, PH.D.£12,357 to £16,462

Department of Administrative Services

Head and Establishment Officer (G6), R. Saunders
.... £20,964 to £25,533
Administration Officer, J. A. Street ...... £13,508 to £18,363
Finance and Organization, E. G. Hartman
.... £13,508 to £18,363

Department of Central Services

Head (G6), G. B. Corbet, PH.D. ..... £17,000 to £22,926
Biometrics and Computing Services, R. F. Eastwood, PH.D. .... £12,357 to £16,462
Publications Officer, R. S. Cross .. £13,508 to £18,363

Department of Library Services

Head (G6), A. P. Harvey .... £17,000 to £22,926
Deputy Head, R. E. R. Banks ...... £12,357 to £16,462
Principal Scientific Officer, Miss P. Gilbert
.... £12,357 to £16,462

Department of Public Services

Head (G6), R. S. Miles, D.SC. .... £17,000 to £22,926
Deputy Head, G. C. S. Clarke, PH.D.
.... £12,357 to £16,462
Operations Manager, M. J. Grant £13,508 to £18,363

Geological Museum
Exhibition Road, South Kensington, SW7 2DE
[01-589 3444]

The Museum's three public galleries have major displays of gems and basic earth science, including 'Treasures of the Earth', 'The Story of the Earth', 'The Building of Britain', British regional geology and the economic geology of the world.
Curator (Grade 6), F. W. Dunning, O.B.E. . £17,000 to £22,926

MUSEUM OF LONDON
London Wall, EC2Y 5HN
[01-600 3699]

The Museum of London was opened in December 1976 in its new building at the corner of London Wall and Aldersgate Street in the City. It is based on the amalgamation of the former Guildhall Museum and London Museum. The Museum is controlled by a

Board of Governors, appointed (6 each) by the Government, the Corporation of London and the Greater London Council. The exhibition illustrates the history of London from prehistoric times to the present day.
Chairman of Board of Governors, R. M. Robbins, C.B.E., F.S.A.
Director, M. G. Hebditch, F.S.A.

THE SCIENCE MUSEUM
South Kensington, SW7 2DD
[01–589 3456]

Open on weekdays 10 to 6; Sundays 2.30 to 6. Closed on Good Friday, Christmas Eve, Christmas Day, Boxing Day, New Year's Day and May Day Bank Holiday.
For Science Museum Library, *see* below.
The Science Museum, which is the National Museum of Science and Industry, was instituted in 1853 under the Science and Art Department as a part of the South Kensington Museum, and opened in 1857; to it were added in 1883 the collections of the Patent Museum. In 1909 the administration of the Science Collection was separated from that of the Art Collections, which were transferred to the Victoria and Albert Museum. The collections in the Science Museum illustrate the development of science and engineering and related industries.
The administrative expenses of the Museum, Library, the National Railway Museum and the National Museum of Photography, Film and Television were estimated at £8,492,000 for 1984–85.
Director and Secretary, Dame Margaret Weston, D.B.E. £31,750
Museum Administrator, K. J. Rhodes, M.B.E.
£17,000 to £22,926

Department of Physical Sciences
Keeper I, Dr. D. B. Thomas . . . . . . £20,964 to £23,900
Keeper II, Dr. R. F. Bud . . . . £17,051 to £21,297
Assistant Keepers, Dr. D. Vaughan; Dr. A. Q. Morton; Dr. A. K. Newmark; Dr. J. Darius . . . . . £12,066 to £18,363

Wellcome Museum of the History of Medicine
Keeper I, Dr. B. Bracegirdle . . . . . £20,964 to £23,900
Assistant Keeper, Dr. G. M. Skinner
£12,066 to £18,363

Department of Engineering
Keeper I, Dr. E. J. S. Becklake. . . . £20,964 to £23,900
Assistant Keepers, Dr. B. P. Bowers; W. K. E. Geddes; J. C. Robinson; A. E. Butcher; P. D. Stephens; J. Smart; Dr. A. McConnell . . . . . . £12,066 to £18,363

Department of Transport
Keeper I, G. W. B. Lacey . . . . £20,964 to £23,900
Assistant Keepers, Dr. T. Wright; J. A. Bagley; A. Hall-Patch; P. R. Mann . . . . £12,066 to £18,363

Department of Museum Services
Keeper I, Dr. D. A. Robinson . . . . . £20,964 to £23,900
Keeper II, M. R. Preston. . . . . £17,051 to £21,297
Assistant Keepers, I. M. Ball; Dr. A. W. Wilson; G. R. Mummery . . . . £12,066 to £18,363

Library
SCIENCE MUSEUM LIBRARY, South Kensington, SW7 5NH.—A national library of science, specializing in the history of science and technology, 480,000 volumes, 21,000 periodicals and transactions of learned societies, about 6,400 current. Bibliographies supplied.—Open on weekdays 10 to 5.30. Closed on Sundays and Bank Holiday weekends. Photocopying and microfilm service.

Keeper I, L. R. Day . . . . £20,964 to £23,900
Assistant Keepers, D. J. Bryden; Dr. L. D. Will
£12,066 to £18,363

National Railway Museum
Leeman Road, York
[0904–21261]

Keeper I, Dr. J. A. Coiley . . . . £20,964 to £23,900
Assistant Keeper, P. W. B. Semmens
£12,066 to £18,363

National Museum of Photography, Film and Television
Princes View, Bradford
[0274 727488]

Keeper II, C. Ford . . . . £17,051 to £21,297
Assistant Keeper, Miss M. Benton
£12,066 to £18,363

THE VICTORIA AND ALBERT MUSEUM
South Kensington, SW7 2RL
[01–589 6371]

Hours 10 to 5.50 (weekdays and Bank Holidays); Sundays, 2.30 to 5.50. Closed every Friday, Christmas Eve, Christmas Day, Boxing Day, New Year's Day and May Day. The National Art Library is open on weekdays (except Fridays) from 10 to 5 (closed 1 to 2 Saturdays) and the Print Room from 10 to 4.30 (except Fridays). A museum of all branches of fine and applied art, it descends direct from the Museum of Manufactures (later called Museum of Ornamental Art), opened in Marlborough House in 1852. The Museum was moved in 1857 to become part of the collective South Kensington Museum. It was renamed the Victoria and Albert Museum in 1899. The branch museum at Bethnal Green was opened in 1872 and the building is the most important surviving example of the type of glass and iron construction used by Paxton for the Great Exhibition of 1851. The Victoria and Albert Museum also administers the Wellington Museum (Apsley House), Ham House, Richmond, Osterley Park, Middlesex, and the Theatre Museum.
Director and Secretary, Sir Roy Strong, PH.D., F.S.A.
Deputy Director, Dr. M. D. Darby.

Department of Ceramics
Keeper, J. V. Mallet. . . . . £20,964 to £23,900
Deputy Keeper, D. M. Archer.
Assistant Keepers, Miss A. G. Somers-Cocks; Dr. O. Watson.

Department of Conservation
Keeper, Dr. J. Ashley-Smith . . . . . £20,964 to £23,900
Deputy Keeper, Mrs. G. F. Miles.

Department of Education
Keeper, G. Opie . . . . £17,051 to £21,297
Assistant Keeper, R. D. Parkinson.

Far Eastern Department
Keeper, J. V. Earle . . . . £20,964 to £23,900
Assistant Keepers, A. C. Clunas; Miss R. Kerr.

Department of Furniture and Interior Design
Keeper, J. H. Morley . . . . £20,964 to £23,900
Deputy Keeper, S. S. Jervis.
Assistant Keeper, J. J. S. L. Hardy.

Indian Department
Keeper, R. W. Skelton . . . . £20,964 to £23,900
Assistant Keepers, Dr. D. Swallow; J. S. Guy.

Library

Keeper, Mrs. E. A. L. Esteve-Coll . £20,964 to £23,900
Deputy Keepers, Dr. D. Haldane; C. Hogben.
Assistant Keeper, Dr. R. Watson.

Metalwork Department

Keeper, R. Lightbown . . . . £20,964 to £23,900
Assistant Keepers, Mrs. P. Glanville; Miss M. Campbell; E. R. Edgecumbe.

Museum Services Department

Keeper, Dr. M. D. Darby . . . . £20,964 to £23,900
Deputy Keeper, D. R. Coachworth.

Prints, Drawings, Photographs and Paintings Department

Keeper, Dr. C. M. Kauffmann . . . . £20,964 to £23,900
Deputy Keepers, Miss S. B. Lambert; J. D. W. Murdoch.
Assistant Keepers, L. S. Lambourne; M. Haworth-Booth; M. Snodin.

Department of Sculpture

Keeper, A. F. Radcliffe . . . . £20,964 to £23,900
Assistant Keepers, M. Baker; P. E. D. Williamson.

Department of Textiles and Dress

Keeper, Miss S. Levey . . . . £20,964 to £23,900
Deputy Keeper, Miss N. K. A. Rothstein.
Assistant Keepers, Mrs. M. Ginsburg; Mrs. V. D. Mendes; Miss W. Hefford.

Theatre Museum

Keeper, A. Schouvaloff . . . . £17,051 to £21,297
Assistant Keeper, Dr. J. Fowler.

Administration

Chief Administrative Officer, J. Close
£17,000 to £22,926

Bethnal Green Museum of Childhood
Cambridge Heath Road, Bethnal Green, E2 9PA
[01–980 3204]

Hours 10 to 6 on Mondays to Thursdays and Saturdays (including Bank Holidays); Sundays 2.30 to 6. Closed every Friday, May Day, Christmas Eve, Christmas Day, Boxing Day and New Year's Day. A branch of the Victoria and Albert Museum, opened in 1872. Toys, dolls, dolls' houses, model theatres, optical toys, games and children's costume. Also Spitalfields silk and wedding dresses.
Keeper, A. P. Burton . . . . £17,051 to £21,297

THE COMMONWEALTH INSTITUTE
Kensington High Street, W.8
[01–603 4535]

The Commonwealth Institute is a centre for information about the Commonwealth. It is funded by the British Government with contributions from other Commonwealth Governments. The Institute is controlled by a Board of Governors which includes the High Commissioners of all Commonwealth countries represented in London. The Institute has permanent exhibitions on all Commonwealth nations, an arts centre, library and education department.

Gallery opening hours: Monday to Saturday 10 a.m. to 5.30 p.m.; Sundays 2 p.m. to 5 p.m. Admission is free. Closed Good Friday, May Day, Christmas Eve, Christmas Day, Boxing Day and New Year's Day.
Director, J. F. Porter.
Deputy Director, R. R. Bourne.
Chief Education Officer, (vacant)
£13,508 to £18,363

Chief Exhibition Officer, A. E. Cobbold
£13,508 to £18,363
Art Director, R. Atkins . . . . £13,508 to £18,363
Chief Administration Officer, M. J. Dunleavy
£13,508 to £18,363
Librarian, M. J. Foster . . . . £10,980 to £13,801
Senior Education Officer, Miss M. Butcher
£10,980 to £13,801
Senior Exhibition Officer, R. Varney
£10,980 to £13,801

IMPERIAL WAR MUSEUM
Lambeth Road, SE1 6HZ
[01–735 8922]

Open daily (except Good Friday, Christmas Eve, Christmas Day, Boxing Day, New Year's Day and May Bank Holiday) 10 a.m.–5.50 p.m. (Sundays 2 p.m.–5.50 p.m.) Reference Depts. open Monday–Friday (except on public holidays), 10 a.m.–5.00 p.m.

The Museum, which was founded in 1917 and established by Act of Parliament in 1920, illustrates and records all aspects of the two world wars and other military operations involving Britain and the Commonwealth since 1914. It was opened in its present home, formerly Bethlem Hospital or Bedlam, in 1936. Its extensive collections include aircraft, armoured fighting vehicles, artillery, uniforms, models, orders and decorations, badges and insignia, works of art, posters, photographs, films, books, documents and sound recordings. The Museum also administers H.M.S. *Belfast* in the Pool of London, Duxford Airfield near Cambridge and The Cabinet War Rooms in Westminster.

The Museum provides regular programmes of films and talks for visiting parties from schools, colleges and the armed services. Expenses for 1985–86 are estimated at £4,445,000.

Director, A. C. N. Borg, Ph.D., F.S.A.
£20,964 to £25,533
Deputy Director and Head of the Research and Information Office, R. W. K. Crawford
£20,964 to £23,900
Secretary, J. J. Chadwick . . . . . . £17,051 to £21,297
Special Assistant to the Director, Mrs. J. C. Andrew
£12,066 to £18,363
Establishment and Finance Officer (Principal), J. F. Golding . . . . £13,505 to £18,363
Senior Keeper and Keeper of Audio-Visual Records, G. T. C. Coultass . . . . £20,964 to £23,900
Keeper of Duxford Airfield, E. O. Inman
£20,964 to £23,900
Keeper of H.M.S. Belfast, Capt. A. W. Wheeler, R.N.
£20,964 to £23,900
Keeper of the Department of Museum Services, C. Dowling, D.Phil. . . . . £17,051 to £21,297
Keeper of the Department of Documents, R. W. A. Suddaby . . . . £17,051 to £21,297
Keeper of the Department of Exhibits and Firearms, D. J. Penn . . . . £17,051 to £21,297
Keeper of the Department of Printed Books, G. M. Bayliss, Ph.D. . . . . £17,051 to £21,297
Keeper of the Department of Art, Miss A. H. Weight
£12,066 to £18,363
Keeper of the Department of Film, Miss A. E. Fleming
£12,066 to £18,363
Keeper of the Department of Information Retrieval, R. B. N. Smither . . . . £12,066 to £18,363
Keeper of the Department of Photographs, Miss K. J. Carmichael . . . . £12,066 to £18,363
Keeper of the Department of Sound Records, Mrs. M. A. Brooks . . . . £12,066 to £18,363
Curator of the Cabinet War Rooms, E. J. Wenzel
£8,452 to £11,265

NATIONAL MARITIME MUSEUM
Greenwich, SE10 9NF
[01–858 4422]

Open weekdays 10 till 6 (Mon.–Fri. in winter, 10–5, Sats. 10–5.30); Sundays 2 to 5.30 (2 to 5 in winter). Closed Good Friday, Christmas Eve, Christmas Day, Boxing Day, New Year's Day and May Day.

Reading Room open on weekdays 10 to 5; tickets of admission on written application to the Director.

The National Maritime Museum was established by Act of Parliament in 1934, for the illustration of the maritime history, archæology, art and science of Great Britain. The museum is in two groups of buildings, in Greenwich Park, the Main Buildings, centred round the Queen's House (built by Inigo Jones, 1616–35) and the Old Royal Observatory, including Wren's Flamsteed House, to the south. The collections include paintings; actual craft and ship-models; ships' lines; prints and drawings; maps, atlases and charts; navigational and astronomical instruments; uniforms and relics; books and MSS. The amount for salaries and expenses, including a Grant-in-Aid, was estimated at £4,304,000 for 1984–85.

Director and Accounting Officer, Dr. N. Cossons, O.B.E.
£26,236
Deputy Director (Curator A), P. G. W. Annis
£20,964 to £23,900
Assistant Deputy Director (Conservator A), Miss G. M. Lewis..................... £20,964 to £23,900
Secretary (Principal), Col. W. B. Mansell, M.C., R.M. (ret.).......................... £13,508 to £18,363

Information Project Group
Curator B, Dr. R. J. B. Knight ... £17,051 to £21,297
Curators C, Dr. J. L.Cutbill; S. M. Riley
£12,066 to £18,363
Curator D, B. K. W. Booth ...... £10,317 to £13,801

Department of Museum Services
Curator B, C. St. J. H. Daniel .... £17,051 to £21,297
Curator C, L. J. Willis (*Design Services*)
£12,066 to £18,363
Curators D, P. Sugg (*Film Officer*); G. P. Stewart (*D.O.E. Liaison Officer*) .... £10,317 to £13,801

Department of Astronomy and Navigation
Curator A, Prof. S. R. C. Malin ... £20,964 to £23,900
Curator B, A. N. Stimson M.V.O. (*Navigation*)
£17,051 to £21,297
Curators C, C. W. Terrell (*Hydrography*); B. Hutchinson (*Horology*) .... £12,066 to £18,363
Curator D, Ms. C. Stott (*Astronomy*)
£10,317 to £13,801

Department of Pictures
Curator A, R. L. Ormond .... £20,964 to £23,900
Curator B, Dr. D. M. B. Cordingly £17,051 to £21,297
Curator D, D. S. Stonham (*Historic Photographs*)
£10,317 to £13,801

Department of Conservation
Conservator A, Miss G. M. Lewis . £20,964 to £23,900
Chief Antiques Conservator (Conservator C), P. C. Van Geersdaele .... £17,051 to £21,297
Conservators C, Miss K. Leane; Mrs. C. E. Hampton
£17,051 to £21,297
Conservators D, Mrs. E. Boyd; C. J. Wheatley; Miss E. G. Hamilton-Eddy.......... £10,317 to £13,801

Department of Printed Books and Manuscripts
Curator A, D. V. Proctor .... £20,964 to £23,900
Curators C, Mrs. M. Patrick (*Librarian*); A. W. H. Pearsall; Dr. M. W. B. Sanderson; Mrs. A. M. Shirley; Mrs. S. G. Vaz........ £17,051 to £21,297

Department of Ships
Curator A, Dr. A. P. McGowan ... £20,964 to £23,900
Curators C, Miss R. Prentice (*Weapons and Antiquities*); F. M. Walker (*Naval Architecture & Shipbuilding*); A. J. Viner .... £17,051 to £21,297
Curator D, D. J. Lyon .... £10,317 to £13,801

Archaeological Research Centre
Curator A, Dr. J. F. Coates .... £20,964 to £23,900
Curator D, Miss S. V. E. Heal .... £10,317 to £13,801

Department of Administration
Principal, Col. W. B. Mansell, M.C., R.M. (*ret.*)
£13,508 to £18,363
Senior Executive Officers, E. A. Skinner, M.B.E. (*Finance Officer*); Miss D. E. Williams (*Establishments Officer*) .... £10,980 to £13,801
Security Officer, J. Stacey........ £9,211 to £10,355

NATIONAL ARMY MUSEUM
Royal Hospital Road, SW3 4HT
[01–730 0717]

Established by Royal Charter (1960). History of five centuries of the British Army: includes the story of the Indian Army up to Independence in 1947. Open, Mon.–Sat., 10–5.30; Sun. 2–5.30. Indian Army room and the regimental collections of 5 Irish infantry regiments disbanded in 1922 at R.M.A. Sandhurst, Camberley, Surrey may be viewed by appointment only, Mon. to Fri.

Director, W. Reid, F.S.A.
Personal Assistant to the Director, Miss E. Christie.
Deputy Director and Keeper of Records, B. Mollo, T.D.
Assistant Director and Keeper of Uniform, Mrs. D. B. Willcox.

ROYAL AIR FORCE MUSEUM
Hendon, NW9 5LL
[01–205 2266]

The museum covers all aspects of the history of the Royal Air Force and its predecessors, and the history of aviation generally. The museum building is sited on ten acres of the historic former airfield at Hendon. Its aircraft hall, which occupies two hangars dating from the First World War, displays some 40 aircraft from the museum's total collection of over 100 machines. Admission is free.

Adjacent to the R.A.F. Museum is the Battle of Britain Museum, which contains a unique collection of British, German and Italian aircraft. Admission: £1·00; children and O.A..P.s 50p.

Also located on the same site is the new Bomber Command Museum which contains an impressive collection of historic bomber aircraft. Admission: £1; children and O.A.P.s 50p. Open Mons.–Sats., 10 a.m.–6 p.m. (Sundays, 2 p.m.–6 p.m.). Closed 24, 25, 26 Dec., 1 Jan., Good Fri. and May Day.

Director, J. Tanner, C.B.E., D.Litt., F.S.A.
Keepers, R. F. Barker; D. C. R. Elliott; P. Murton; R. Simpson; Wg. Cmdr. W. Wood, O.B.E.

GEOLOGICAL MUSEUM
See British Museum (Natural History)

(For other Museums in England—*see* Index)

THE NATIONAL MUSEUM OF WALES
(Amgueddfa Genedlaethol Cymru)
Cardiff CF1 3NP
[0222 397951]

Open Tues.–Sat., 10 a.m. to 5 p.m. Sundays 2.30 to 5 p.m. Closed on Mondays, Christmas Eve, Christmas Day, Boxing Day, New Year's Day, May Day and Good Friday. Admission free.

President, W. A. Twiston-Davies.
Vice-President, Hon. J. Davies.
Director, D. A. Bassett, ᴘʜ.ᴅ.
Secretary, D. W. Dykes, ᴘʜ.ᴅ., ꜰ.ꜱ.ᴀ.
Keepers, (*Geology*) M. G. Bassett, ᴘʜ.ᴅ.; (*Botany*) B. A. Thomas, ᴘʜ.ᴅ.; (*Zoology*) P. M. Morgan; (*Archaeology*) G. C. Boon, ꜰ.ꜱ.ᴀ.; (*Art*) P. Cannon-Brookes, ᴘʜ.ᴅ.

Welsh Folk Museum
(Amgueddfa Werin Cymru)
St. Fagans, Nr. Cardiff

The museum is situated 4 miles west of Cardiff. Open weekdays 10–5, Sundays 2.30–5. Admission charged. Closed on Christmas Eve, Christmas Day, Boxing Day, New Year's Day, Good Friday and May Day.
Curator, T. M. Owen, ꜰ.ꜱ.ᴀ.
Keepers, V. H. Phillips; E. Scourfield.

Legionary Museum of Caerleon
Caerleon, Gwent.

Contains material found on the site of the Roman fortress of Isca and its suburbs. [Nᴏᴛᴇ. The Museum is closed for redevelopment until 1987.]

Turner House Art Gallery
Penarth, Nr. Cardiff

Open Tues.–Sat. 11 a.m.–12.45 p.m. and 2 p.m. to 5 p.m. Sundays, 2 p.m. to 5 p.m. Closed Mondays, except Bank Holidays, and on Christmas Eve, Christmas Day, Boxing Day, New Year's Day, Good Friday, and May Day. Admission free.

Oriel Eryri
Llanberis, Gwynedd

An environmental centre interpreting the rich natural history of Snowdonia. Open mid-June till mid-Sept.; weekdays 10–5; Sundays 2.30–5. Admission free.

Welsh Slate Museum
Llanberis, Gwynedd

Open 9.30 a.m.–5.30 p.m. Easter to 30 April; 9.30 a.m. to 6.30 p.m. May to Sept. Admission 80p; children and pensioners 40p.

Segontium Roman Fort Museum
Beddgelert Road, Caernarfon, Gwynedd

Open weekdays at 9.30, Sundays at 2. Closes at 6 from May to September, at 5.30 in March, April and October, at 4 from November to February. Closed Christmas Eve, Christmas Day, Boxing Day, New Year's Day, Good Friday and May Day. Admission free. On the site of the fort, in the guardianship of the Welsh Office. Contains mostly material excavated there.

Museum of the Woollen Industry
Dre-fach Felindre, Dyfed

It occupies part of a working mill, the Cambrian Mills. Open 10 a.m. to 5 p.m. Monday–Saturday from April 1 to September 30. Closed May Day. Admission free.

Welsh Industrial and Maritime Museum
Bute Street, Cardiff

Open Tues.–Sat. 10–5; Sundays 2.30–5. Closed Mondays, Christmas Eve, Christmas Day, Boxing Day, New Year's Day, Good Friday and May Day. Admission free.
Curator, J. G. Jenkins, ᴘʜ.ᴅ., ꜰ.ꜱ.ᴀ.

Yr Hen Gapel
Tre'r-ddôl, nr. Aberystwyth, Dyfed

The museum portrays 19th century religious life in Wales. Open 10–5 Monday–Saturday from April–September. Closed May Day. Admission free.

ROYAL SCOTTISH MUSEUM
Chambers Street, Edinburgh EH1 1JF
[031–225 7534]

Open, Mon.–Sat., 10 a.m. to 5 p.m.; and Sun., 2 to 5 p.m.
Director, R. G. W. Anderson, ᴅ.ᴘʜil. £25,455
Keeper, Department of Art and Archaeology, Miss D. Idiens .... £20,013 to £22,762
Keeper, Department of Geology, (vacant)
£20,013 to £22,762
Keeper, Department of Natural History, M. Shaw, ᴅ.ᴘʜil. .... £20,013 to £22,762
Keeper, Department of Technology, J. D. Storer
£20,013 to £22,762
Deputy Keepers, Sheila Brock, ᴘʜ.ᴅ.; H. G. Macpherson, ᴘʜ.ᴅ.; I. H. J. Lyster; S. Wood
£16,278 to £20,283

NATIONAL MUSEUM OF ANTIQUITIES OF SCOTLAND
Queen Street, Edinburgh EH2 1JD
[031–557 3550]

Founded in 1781 by the Society of Antiquaries of Scotland, and transferred to the Nation in 1858. Open free. Weekdays, 10 a.m. to 5 p.m.; Sundays 2–5 p.m.
Director, Dr. A. Fenton £24,516
Deputy Keeper, Dr. D. V. Clarke.
Assistant Keepers, G. Sprott; Miss M. Bryden; Dr. D. Caldwell; H. G. Cheape.

Scottish Agricultural Museum
Royal Highland Showground, Ingliston, Midlothian

Open weekdays 10 a.m.–4 p.m. May to September; at other times by arrangement. Admission free.

NATIONAL AUDIT OFFICE
Audit House, Victoria Embankment, EC4Y 0DS†
[01–353 8901]

The National Audit Office, created by the National Audit Act 1983, replaced the Exchequer and Audit Department on January 1, 1984. The Comptroller and Auditor General, who is head of the National Audit Office, is an Officer of the House of Commons and is appointed by Letters Patent under the Great Seal on an address from the House of Commons made by the Prime Minister after agreement with the Chairman of the Committee of Public Accounts. He can be removed from Office only by the Queen on an address from both Houses of Parliament. His full title is "Comptroller General of the Receipt and Issue of Her Majesty's Exchequer and Auditor General of Public Accounts". As Comptroller General, he authorizes the issue of public funds to Government Departments and other public sector bodies. As Auditor General, his statutory duties are to certify the accounts of all Government Departments and a wide range of other public sector bodies; to examine revenue and store accounts; and to report the results of his examinations to Parliament. He also has wide statutory powers to carry out and report to Parliament on, examinations of economy, efficiency and effectiveness in the use of resources by those bodies he audits or to which he has rights of access. In addition to his statutory audits, the Comptroller and Auditor General is also the auditor by agreement of the accounts of many bodies, generally in receipt of public funds, and of certain international organizations.
Comptroller and Auditor General, Sir Gordon Downey, ᴋ.ᴄ.ʙ. £45,500

Deputy Comptroller and Auditor General, H. D. Myland £36,500
Assistant Auditor Generals, J. A. Collens; D. A. Dewar; M. J. Goodson; R. A. Birch £29,500
Director of Establishments and Accounts, B. D. Baker.
Directors of Audit, P. M. Jefford; G. W. Garside; M. R. J. Paul; P. J. Beck; J. A. Davies; I. R. W. Hargest; R. W. Locke; T. Dobson; P. O'Keefe; A. G. Brown; E. S. Young; T. J. Lovett; A. C. Pyatt; G. H. B. Spear; G. J. S. Frith; D. A. Reeve; R. N. Le Marechal; A. I. A. Oyarzabal; C. L. Press; W. D. Turner; C. K. Beauchamp; J. A. Higgins
£24,450 to £32,675
Deputy Directors of Audit, A. W. Bird; W. E. Harle; E. J. Weeks; C. J. Day; D. C. Page; G. T. Morgan; J. E. Smith; K. E. Turner; B. Hogg; R. J. McCourt; A. R. Murray; W. L. Ewing; G. J. McKeown; L. H. Hughes; A. M. Pearce; M. C. Pfleger; R. M. Bennett; M. V. Pettet; R. E. Spurgeon; A. G. Roberts; R. A. Skeen; A. Cunningham; D. S. Dodge; G. G. Jones; K. MacLean .... £21,025 to £28,125

† As from Dec. 1985, address will be Buckingham Palace Road, SW1W 9SP (01–798 7000).

NATIONAL BUS COMPANY
172 Buckingham Palace Road, SW1W 9TN
[01–730 3453]

The National Bus Company is a statutory body under the provisions of the Transport Act, 1968. It controls 49 operating companies covering almost every part of England and Wales outside London and the municipal and Passenger Transport Executive undertakings. The N.B.C. bus and coach fleets total about 14,000 vehicles and it employs a staff of about 50,000.
Chairman, R. Brook, C.B.E. £50,000
Members (full time), I. Dalton (*Vice Chairman*); (*part-time*): R. H. Grierson; G. Heywood, M.B.E.; C. Hollick; I. S. Irwin, C.B.E.; R. T. Kanter; Miss K. Mortimer; J. D. Orme; G. J. Parker.

NATIONAL COAL BOARD
Hobart House, Grosvenor Place, S.W.1.
[01–235 2020]

The National Coal Board was constituted in 1946. It took over the mines on January 1, 1947.
Chairman, I. MacGregor.
Deputy Chairman, J. R. Cowan, C.B.E.
Members, H. M. Spanton, O.B.E.; (two vacancies).
Members (part-time), Sir Melvyn Rosser; R. T. S. Macpherson, C.B.E.; P. C. Michael, C.B.E.; D. L. Donne; D. K. Newbigging, O.B.E.; C. Barker.
Secretary, D. G. Brandrick, C.B.E.

NATIONAL CONSUMER COUNCIL
18 Queen Anne's Gate, S.W.1
[01–222 9501]

Chairman, M. J. Montague, C.B.E. £11,420
Director, J. Mitchell.

NATIONAL DEBT OFFICE, *see* NATIONAL INVESTMENT AND LOANS OFFICE

NATIONAL DOCK LABOUR BOARD
22–26 Albert Embankment, SE1 7TE
[01–735 7271–9]

The National Dock Labour Board administers the scheme for giving permanent employment to dock workers under the Dock Workers (Regulation of Employment) (Amendment) Scheme 1967. The Board was reconstituted as a body corporate on August 1, 1977 under the Dock Work Regulation Act 1976 which made further provision for regulating the allocation and performance of the work of cargo-handling in and about the ports of Great Britain.
Chairman, R. H. Thompson.
General Manager, K. T. Percy.

NATIONAL ECONOMIC DEVELOPMENT OFFICE
Millbank Tower, Millbank, SW1P 4QX
[01–211 6998]

Council

Government Members, The Chancellor of the Exchequer (*Chairman*); the Secretaries of State for Employment, Education and Science, Energy, and Trade and Industry; Minister without Portfolio.
Management Members, Sir Terence Beckett, C.B.E.; Sir Donald Barron; Sir James Cleminson, M.C.; Dr. J. S. McFarlane; D. Nickson, C.B.E.; A. E. Stote.
Trade Union Members, D. Basnett; R. Bickerstaffe; T. Duffy; C. Jenkins; R. Todd; N. Willis. *Independent Members*, B. Nicholson; Sir Robert Haslam; R. Leigh-Pemberton; The Lord Marshall of Goring, C.B.E., F.R.S.; Mrs. R. E. Waterhouse, C.B.E.
Director-General, J. Cassels, C.B.
Secretary, P. V. Dixon.
Industrial Director, B. Quilter.
Economic Director, M. Posner.

NATIONAL ENTERPRISE BOARD
See **British Technology Group**

NATIONAL FREIGHT CONSORTIUM p.l.c.
The Merton Centre,
45 St. Peters Street, Bedford.
[0234 67444]

The National Freight Consortium p.l.c. purchased the whole of the issued share capital of the National Freight Company Limited from the Secretary of State for Transport in February 1982. 82½ per cent of the issued share capital of the Consortium is held by the employees, pensioners and their families, whilst the remaining 17½ per cent is held by a consortium of bankers.
Chairman, Sir Peter Thompson.
Deputy Chairmen, J. K. Watson (*Finance*); D. H. White.
Chief Executive, J. D. Mather.
Executive Directors, J. L. Copland; P. A. Mayo (*Legal Services*); G. F. Pygall; E. A. Wall.
Non-Executive Directors, H. L. Batty; F. S. Law, C.B.E.; V. G. Paige, C.B.E.; J. W. Robb; R. H. Watson.
Secretary, A. J. Staley, M.B.E.

NATIONAL GALLERIES
See **Art Galleries**

NATIONAL INVESTMENT AND LOANS OFFICE
Royex House, Aldermanbury Square, EC2V 7LR
[01–606 7321]

The National Investment and Loans Office was set up on April 1, 1980 by merging the staffs of the National Debt Office and the Public Works Loan Board. The Department provides staff and services for the National Debt Commissioners and the Public Works Loan Commissioners.
Director, P. A. Goodwin.
Establishment Officer, A. G. Ladd.

National Debt Office
Comptroller General, P. A. Goodwin.

Public Works Loan Board

Chairman, J. E. A. R. Guinness.
Deputy Chairman, W. Bowdell, c.b.e.
Other Commissioners, Miss F. M. Cook; R. W. E. Law;
Miss V. J. Di Palma; G. Ross Russell; W. H. P.
Davison; P. Brackfield; S. G. Dunster; D. H. Adams;
R. A. Chapman; J. Broadfoot.
Secretary, P. A. Goodwin.
Assistant Secretary, I. H. Peattie.

NATIONAL RADIOLOGICAL PROTECTION BOARD
Chilton, Didcot, Oxon. OX11 0RQ
[0235–831600]

The National Radiological Protection Board is an
independent statutory body created by the Radiological Protection Act 1970. The Government's purpose
was to establish a national point of authoritative
reference in radiological protection.
Chairman, Sir Richard Southwood, f.r.s.
Director, H. J. Dunster, c.b.

NATIONAL RESEARCH DEVELOPMENT CORPORATION
See **British Technology Group**

DEPARTMENT FOR NATIONAL SAVINGS
Charles House, 375 Kensington High Street,
W14 8SD
[01–603 2000]

The Department for National Savings was established as a Government Department when the former
Post Office Savings Department became separated
from the Post Office on October 1, 1969. The
Department is responsible for the administration of
a range of schemes for personal savers. These include
Savings Certificates, both fixed interest and index-
linked, Yearly Plan, Income Bonds, Deposit Bonds,
Investment Accounts, Ordinary Accounts and Pre-
mium Bonds. The National Savings Stock Register
sells Government stock through post offices.
Director of Savings, S. W. Gilbert, c.b. £36,500
Deputy Director, J. A. Patterson £29,500
Establishment Officer, R. T. Rowland
  £20,964 to £25,533
Finance Officer, D. E. L. Whittall £20,964 to £25,533
Controllers, J. Stamp; P. N. S. Hickman Robertson
  (*Marketing & Information*); R. S. Watts; G. R.
  Wilson .... £20,964 to £25,533
Senior Principals, W. E. H. Westlake; C. Ward; E. B.
  Senior; D. W. Kellaway; I. T. Standen; R. H. Lee;
  J. K. Hill .... £17,000 to £22,926
Principals, J. G. Booth; I. B. Arkinstall; F. Bardsley;
  H. Johnson; N. Booth; D. H. Monaghan; K. M. J.
  Harbridge; A. S. McGill; D. S. Speedie; I. Forsyth;
  D. Newton; W. J. Herd; C. B. Taylor; J. W. Davison;
  T. Threlfall; A. Brown; R. H. Stansfield; W. J.
  Ferrier; A. G. Muir; F. McGourhty; T. J. F.
  McMahon; D. K. Paterson; H. Webster; J.
  Wheatley; C. McVey; J. B. Dunphy; P. Finnie; A.
  B. Wood; A. T. Stevenson ..... £13,508 to £18,363
Statistician, M. J. Barker .... £13,508 to £18,363
Principal Information Officers, P. G. Hutchings; Mrs.
  S. M. Cullum .... £13,508 to £18,363
Principal Research Officer, T. J. Bedeman
  £13,508 to £18,363

NATIONAL TRUST
36 Queen Anne's Gate, SW1H 9AS
[01–222 9251]

The National Trust was founded in 1895 by Miss
Octavia Hill, Sir Robert Hunter and Canon Rawnsley,
their object being to preserve as much as possible the
history and beauty of their country for its people. It
became an organization incorporated by Act of
Parliament (1907) to ensure the preservation of lands
and buildings of historic interest or natural beauty
for public access and benefit. It is independent of the
State and relies on the voluntary support of private
individuals for working funds. As a charity, however,
it is allowed certain tax exemptions.
The Trust protects more than 600,000 acres, much
of it superb hill country in the Lake District,
Snowdonia, the Peak District and other National
Parks. The Trust also owns and opens to the public
some 270 country houses, other buildings and gardens and preserves villages, nature reserves,
archæological sites and many farms.
In 1965 the Trust launched Enterprise Neptune, a
campaign to acquire as much as possible of the most
beautiful stretches of coastline which were under
threat from development. The Trust now protects
more than 450 miles of coastline.
The Trust has now some 1,200,000 members paying
an annual subscription and more than 150,000 new
members are joining each year. Rents, admission
fees, legacies and gifts are other important sources of
support and income.
The policy of the Trust is determined by the
governing body, the Council. Half of its members are
appointed by national institutions, such as the
British Museum, the National Gallery, the Ramblers'
Association and the Royal Horticultural Society; the
other half are elected by Trust members at the annual
general meeting. The Council appoints the Executive
Committee, which in turn has established Regional
Committees responsible for the management of the
Trust's properties.

NATIONAL TRUST FOR SCOTLAND
5 Charlotte Square, Edinburgh 2

The National Trust for Scotland was founded in
1931, and its objects are similar to those of the
National Trust. Like that organization, it is incorporated by Act of Parliament, is dependent for finance
upon legacies, donations and the subscriptions of its
members, is recognized as a charity for tax exemption
purposes, and enjoys certain privileges under various
Finance Acts regarding capital transfer tax and
capital gains tax.
The Trust administers 97 properties covering over
100,000 acres. Great houses in its care include:—The
House of The Binns, West Lothian; Brodick Castle,
Isle of Arran; Crathes Castle, Kincardineshire;
Culzean Castle, Ayrshire; Falkland Palace, Fife; Hill
of Tarvit and Kellie Castle, Fife; Drum Castle, Castle
Fraser, Leith Hall, Craigievar Castle and Haddo
House, Aberdeenshire; and Brodie Castle, Moray-
shire. In Edinburgh are two contrasting houses—
the Georgian House in the New Town and Gladstone's
Land in the Old Town; and in Helensburgh is Charles
Rennie Mackintosh's The Hill House.
In the Trust's care are also several noteworthy
gardens. Some are associated with the great houses,
others are:—Inverewe, in Wester Ross; the re-
created 17th century garden of Pitmedden in Aber-
deenshire; Threave in Kirkcudbrightshire, where a
School of Gardening is run; Branklyn Garden, Perth;
Inveresk Lodge Garden, near Edinburgh, and Green-
bank, Clarkston, Glasgow.
Among the mountainous country owned by the
Trust is the Pass of Glen Coe and the mountain group
"The Five Sisters of Kintail" and the estate of
Torridon in Wester Ross, and Ben Lomond.
Islands in the Trust's care include the St. Kilda
group, Fair Isle, Iona and Canna. At Bannockburn,
Killiecrankie, Glenfinnan and Culloden, the Trust
owns sites associated with Scottish history.

Among smaller properties are houses associated with famous Scots:— the birthplaces of Barrie in Kirriemuir, Carlyle in Ecclefechan, and Hugh Miller in Cromarty; and Burns' Bachelors' Club, Tarbolton and Souter Johnnie's House, Kirkoswald in Ayrshire.

At Culross, in other Fife coastal villages, and at Dunkeld, Perthshire, the restoration of architecturally attractive groups of houses led to the creation of the Little Houses Improvement Scheme, under which properties are bought, restored and re-sold. Since its inception over 160 houses reflecting the vernacular architecture of Scotland have been restored throughout the country. The operation was one of the four pilot projects in the U.K. selected for special allocation during European Architectural Heritage Year, 1975 and in 1976 was awarded the European Prize for the Preservation of Ancient Monuments, given by the F.V.S. Foundation of Hamburg. In addition to its other activities, the Little Houses Improvement Scheme operates a property marketing service.

NATURAL ENVIRONMENT RESEARCH COUNCIL
Polaris House, North Star Avenue, Swindon, Wilts. SN2 1EU
[0793 40101]

The Natural Environment Research Council was established by Royal Charter on June 1, 1965, under the Science and Technology Act, 1965, to encourage, plan and conduct research in the physical and biological sciences which relate to man's natural environment and its resources.

The Council carries out research and training through its own institutes and grant-aided institutes, and by grants, fellowships and post-graduate awards to universities and other institutions of higher education.
Chairman, H. Fish.
Secretary, J. C. Bowman, Ph.D.

RESEARCH INSTITUTES

British Geological Survey
Nicker Hill, Keyworth, Nottingham NG12 5GG
[06077 6111]
Director, Sir Malcolm Brown, D.SC., Ph.D., F.R.S., F.R.S.E.

Institute of Oceanographic Sciences
Wormley Laboratory, Godalming, Surrey GU8 5UB
[042879 4141]
Director, A. S. Laughton, Ph.D., F.R.S.
Bidston Observatory, Birkenhead L43 7RA
[051–052 8639]

Institute for Marine Environmental Research
Prospect Place, The Hoe, Plymouth PL1 3DH
[0752 21371]
Director, B. L. Bayne, Ph.D.

Institute of Marine Biochemistry
St. Fittick's Road, Aberdeen AB1 3RA
[0224 875695]
Acting Director, Prof. J. R. Sargent.

Sea Mammal Research Unit
c/o British Antarctic Survey, Madingley Road, Cambridge CB3 0ET
[0223 311354]
Director, R. M. Laws, C.B.E., Ph.D., F.R.S.

Institute of Hydrology
Maclean Building, Crowmarsh Gifford, Wallingford, Oxon. OX10 8BB
[0491 38800]
Director, J. S. G. McCulloch, Ph.D.

Institute of Terrestrial Ecology
Merlewood Research Station, Grange-over-Sands, Cumbria LA11 6JU
[04484 2264/6]
Director, J. N. R. Jeffers.
Research Stations: Cambridge; Monks Wood; Furzebrook; Edinburgh; Banchory; Bangor; Culture Centre of Algae and Protozoa, Cambridge.

Institute of Virology
Mansfield Road, Oxford OX1 3SR
[0865–512361]
Director, Dr. D. H. L. Bishop.

Unit of Comparative Plant Ecology
Department of Botany, University of Sheffield, Western Bank, Sheffield S10 2TN
[0742 78555]
Head of Unit, Prof. I. H. Rorison, D.Phil.

British Antarctic Survey
Madingley Road, Cambridge CB3 0ET
[0223 61188]
Director, R. M. Laws, C.B.E., Ph.D., F.R.S.

GRANT-AIDED INSTITUTES

Marine Biological Association of the U.K.
The Laboratory, Citadel Hill, Plymouth PL1 2PB
[0752 21761]
Director, Prof. E. J. Denton, C.B.E., F.R.S.

Scottish Marine Biological Association
Dunstaffnage Marine Research Laboratory
P.O. Box No. 3, Oban, Argyll PA34 4AD
[0631 62244]
Director, Prof. R. I. Currie, C.B.E.

Freshwater Biological Association
The Ferry House, Far Sawrey, Ambleside, Cumbria LA22 0LP
[09662 24689]
Director, R. T. Clarke, Ph.D.

SPECIAL SERVICES

N.E.R.C. Scientific Services
Polaris House, North Star Avenue, Swindon, Wilts. SN2 1EU
[0793 40101]
Director, B. F. Rule.

NATURE CONSERVANCY COUNCIL
Northminster House, Peterborough PE1 1UA
[0733 40345]

Establishes, maintains and manages National Nature Reserves, advises generally on nature conservation, gives advice to the Government on nature conservation policies and on how other policies may affect nature conservation, and supports, commissions and undertakes relevant research.
Chairman, W. H. N. Wilkinson.
Director General, R. C. Steele.
Chief Scientist, Dr. D. A. Ratcliffe.
Country Headquarters:
England: Northminster House, Peterborough PE1 1UA.
  Director, Dr. F. B. O'Connor.
Scotland: 12 Hope Terrace, Edinburgh EH9 2AS.
  [031–447 4784]
  Director, Dr. J. Francis.
Wales: Plas Penrhos, Penrhos Road, Bangor, Gwynedd LL57 2LQ.
  [0248–355141]
  Director, Dr. T. Pritchard.

NORTHERN IRELAND OFFICE
Whitehall, SW1A 2AZ
[01–273 3000]
Stormont House, Belfast
[0232 63255]
Stormont Castle, Belfast
[0232 63011]
Dundonald House,
Upper Newtownards Road, Belfast
[0232 63255]

The Northern Ireland Office is the office of the Secretary of State for Northern Ireland, who is the Cabinet Minister responsible for Northern Ireland. Through the Northern Ireland Office he has direct responsibility for constitutional developments, law and order and security and electoral matters. Under the Northern Ireland Act 1974, the Northern Ireland departments are also subject to the direction and control of the Secretary of State during direct rule.

Secretary of State for Northern Ireland, THE RT. HON.
DOUGLAS HURD, C.B.E., M.P. £42,980
  Private Secretary, J. A. Daniell.
  Assistant Private Secretaries, R. P. Cleasby*; N. D. Ward.
  Parliamentary Clerk, Miss S. Marshall.
  Special Adviser, E. S. C. Bickham.
  Parliamentary Private Secretary, K. Carlisle, M.P.
Minister of State, DR. RHODES BOYSON, M.P. .. £33,590
  Private Secretary, W. R. Gamble.
  Parliamentary Private Secretary, J. Pawsey, M.P.
Parliamentary Under Secretaries of State, The Lord Lyell (£24,229); N. Scott, M.B.E., M.P.; C. Patten, M.P.
£28,120
  Private Secretaries, Mrs. L. M. Rogers; A. J. Whysall; Miss A. Porter.
Permanent Under Secretary of State, R. J. Andrew, C.B. £52,750
  Private Secretary, J. A. Stephens.
Second Permanent Under Secretary of State, Head of the NICS, K. P. Bloomfield, C.B.* £48,500
  Private Secretary, Ms. E. Sung.*
Deputy Secretaries (G2), A. W. Stephens, C.M.G.; A. J. E. Brennan, C.B. .... £38,325 to £39,250
Under Secretaries (G3), P. W. J. Buxton*; D. Chesterton; D. Gilliland, C.B.E.*; A. J. Merifield*; S. G. Norris (*Principal Establishment and Finance Officer*); B. D. Palmer* .... £30,975 to £31,750
Assistant Secretaries (G5), P. N. Bell; P. M. Coston*; P. Coulson*; N. R. Cowling; Miss D. F. E. Elliott; J. B. Forsythe*; S. C. Jackson*; W. J. Kerr, O.B.E.*; L. J. McClelland*; S. McKillop*; D. G. McNeill*; C. Radcliffe*; R. S. Reeve*.
Chief Information Officer (G5), A. Wood.
Deputy Chief Scientific Officer (G5), R. A. Hall, O.B.E.*

* Located in Northern Ireland.

OFFICE OF ARTS AND LIBRARIES
Great George Street, SW1P 3AL
[01–233 3073]

The Office of Arts and Libraries became a separate, free-standing department in July 1983, having been formerly part of the Department of Education and Science. It has general responsibilities for arts policy and its broad objectives are to assist the provision and development of the performing and visual arts, to maintain and enhance the collections of national museums and art galleries, to help preserve the national heritage and to sustain and develop national collections of literary and archive material. It directly funds some 20 bodies including the Arts Council, the nine national museums and galleries and the British Library. The Office of Arts and Libraries also has policy responsibilities towards the public library and local museum services. The Government Art Collection, which is responsible for the acquisition, maintenance and display of works of art in major government buildings in this country and abroad, forms part of the Office of Arts and Libraries.

Chancellor of the Duchy of Lancaster and Minister for the Arts, The Earl of Gowrie, P.C.
  Private Secretary, C. P. Thomas.
  Parliamentary Private Secretary, T. Rathbone, M.P.
Head of the Office of Arts and Libraries (Deputy Secretary), R. W. L. Wilding, C.B.

Arts and Heritage
Assistant Secretary, R. H. Stone.
Principals, P. J. Fallon; Miss M. J. Lamont; D. H. A. Lodge.

Finance, Establishments and Museums
Assistant Secretary, M. D. Phipps.
Principals, D. Barwick; J. F. Cammack; Miss C. R. Morrison.

Libraries and Information Services
Assistant Secretary, C. C. Leamy.
Principal, P. J. Walsh.
Library Advisers, P. J. Beauchamp; D. F. Fuegi; Miss C. R. Luytens.

Government Art Collection
Curator, Dr. W. Baron.

OFFICE OF THE PRESIDENT OF SOCIAL SECURITY APPEAL TRIBUNALS AND MEDICAL APPEAL TRIBUNALS
Almack House, 26–28 King Street, SW1Y 6RB

An independent statutory authority set up under the Health and Social Services and Social Security Adjudications Act 1983 to exercise judicial and administrative control over social security appeal tribunals and medical appeal tribunals throughout England, Wales and Scotland.
President, His Honour Judge John Byrt, Q.C.
Secretary, O. C. L. Thorpe.

ORDNANCE SURVEY
Romsey Road, Maybush, Southampton SO9 4DH
[Southampton 775555]

Director-General, P. McMaster.
Directors (each £25,533):
  Surveys and Production, A. S. Macdonald.
  Marketing, Planning and Development, J. Leonard.
  Overseas Surveys, B. E. Furmston.
  Finance, D. P. E. Mason.
Heads of Functions:
  Production, D. Toft.
  Topographic Surveys, P. Wesley.
  Geodesy, Photogrammetry and Computations, A. P. Atkinson.
  Marketing, K. Nolan.
  Research and Development, M. Sowton.
  Manager of Finance, J. G. Curtis.
  Establishments, W. Rayer.
  Overseas Surveys, I. T. Logan.

OVERSEAS DEVELOPMENT ADMINISTRATION
Eland House, Stag Place, SW1E 5DH
[01–213 3000]
Abercrombie House, Eaglesham Road, East Kilbride,
Glasgow G75 8EA
[03552 41199]

The Overseas Development Administration deals with British development assistance to overseas countries. This includes both capital aid on concessional terms and technical assistance (mainly in the form of specialist staff abroad and training facilities in the United Kingdom), whether provided directly to developing countries or through the various multilateral aid organizations, including the United Nations and its specialized agencies.

Minister for Overseas Development, THE RT. HON. TIMOTHY RAISON, M.P.
Private Secretary, M. J. Dinham.
Permanent Secretary, Sir Crispin Tickell £52,750
Private Secretary, J. G. Lingham.
Deputy Secretary, R. A. Browning £38,325 to £39,250
Under Secretaries, R. M. Ainscow; N. B. Hudson; J. L. F. Buist; J. M. M. Vereker; A. T. Wilson; H. J. Arbuthnot; Dr. J. M. Healey... £30,975 to £31,750

Economic Service

Head of the Economic Service (Under Secretary), Dr. J. M. Healey .... £30,975 to £31,750
Senior Economic Advisers, J. B. Wilmshurst; J. C. H. Morris; J. T. Roberts; G. P. Sandersley
.... £20,964 to £25,533
Economic Advisers, A. G. Coverdale; D. B. Crapper; A. D. Davis; K. E. Gubbins; Dr. G. Haley; E. Hawthorn; P. J. A. Landymore; P. L. Owen; J. D. Patel; J. N. Stevens; C. J. B. White; Mrs. J. M. White .... £13,508 to £18,363
Chief Statistician, R. M. Allen .. £20,964 to £25,533
Statisticians, C. J. Allison; J. R. B. King; M. W. Kirsop; M. C. Walmsley ...... £13,508 to £18,363

Information Department

Head of Information Dept., J. C. Machin.
Principal Information Officer, J. E. Murphy
.... £13,508 to £18,363

Heads of Development Divisions

Caribbean (Bridgetown), M. G. Bawden; *East Africa (Nairobi).* R. M. Graham-Harrison; *Pacific (Suva)*, A. J. Bennett; *South-East Asia (Bangkok)*, V. J. McLean; *Southern Africa (Lilongwe)*, J. V. Kerby .... £20,964 to £25,533
U.K. Permanent Delegation to U.N.E.S.C.O. (Paris)
Permanent Delegate, J. Gordon .. £20,964 to £25,533
Assistant Secretaries, M. G. Bawden; G. A. Beattie; M. L. Cahill; W. T. A. Cox; R. F. R. Deare; J. A. L. Faint; P. D. M. Freeman; K. G. W. Frost; W. Hobman; B. R. Ireton; C. R. O. Jones; M. C. McCulloch; P. S. McLean, O.B.E.; R. G. M. Manning; Dr. D. G. Osborne; R. G. Pettitt; M. A. Power; J. E. Rednall; D. F. Smith; D. L. Stanton; Ms. S. Unsworth; Mrs. P. M. Wilkinson; K. A. F. Woolverton; R. W. Wootton .... £20,964 to £25,533
Senior Principals, F. Crampsey; L. E. Fitzpatrick; A. F. Watkins; D. S. Fish; Mrs. S. Jay; G. A. Williams; D. Sands Smith; J. C. Machin .. £17,000 to £22,926
Principals, J. D. Aitken; S. I. Alexander; J. A. Anning; G. A. Armstrong; D. W. Baker; E. T. Barnes; D. J. Batt; D. G. Bell; W. T. Birrell; H. Britton; W. A. Brownlie; P. J. Burton; D. G. Camps; R. O. Carter; P. H. Charters; Miss D. W. Cherry; D. J. Church; T. F. G. Connor; B. Cook; G. Crabtree; D. R. Curran; M. J. Dinham; J. R. Drummond; C. T. Gerard; J. R. Gilbert; K. D. Grimshaw; C. W. Hall; Miss J. V. Hanna; P. Harris; Ms. P. J. Hilton; M. I. Holland; N. Hoult; W. Jardine; B. T. Jordan; Mrs. B. M. Kelly; Mrs. J. Laurance; D. Lawless; G. G. Leader; C. A. Metcalf; J. C. Millett; B. A. Mitchell; G. A. Mustard; S. C. Pennock; P. T. Perris; B. G. Peskett; S. Ray; R. S. Ridgwell; G. F. Roberts; M. K. Robson; C. R. Roth; J. M. Scoular; R. J. Smith; M. J. Sexton; Q. M. Stegmann; I. F. Stickels; I. D. Stuart; A. J. Sutherland; C. M. Taylor; E. C. N. Taylor; N. Thomas; A. Thorpe; D. Trotter; D. P. Turner; Miss M. H. Vowles; R. J. Walsgrove; C. W. Warren; S. A. Wheeler; R. S. White; D. M. Whitecross; M. A. Wickstead; P. M. Wilson; R. J. Wilson, J. M. Winter .... £13,508 to £18,363

Advisory and Specialist Staff

Principal Education Adviser, Dr. R. O. Iredale
.... £20,964 to £25,533
Education Advisers, M. D. Francis; P. G. Scopes; Dr. B. L. Steele .... £17,000 to £22,926
Principal Engineering Adviser, T. D. Pike
.... £20,964 to £25,533
Engineering Advisers, J. N. Bulman; J. R. Hyde; D. Gillett; B. G. Little .... £17,000 to £22,926
Assistant Engineering Advisers, C. I. Ellis; R. J. Cadwallader; C. S. Reid ...... £13,508 to £18,363
Energy Adviser, Dr. J. L. D. Harrison.
Electrical and Mechanical Engineering Adviser, R. P. Jones.
Architectural Adviser, J. B. Shelley
.... £17,000 to £22,926
Architectural & Planning Adviser, H. W. Housego-Woolgar.
Manpower and Employment Adviser, Prof. J. Fyfe
.... £17,000 to £22,926
Chief Medical Adviser, (vacant).
Principal Medical Adviser, Dr. A. M. Baker.
Medical Advisers, Dr. P. Key; Dr. N. A. Ward
.... £17,000 to £22,926
Principal Nursing and Health Services Adviser, Mrs. B. M. Bubb .... £20,964 to £25,533
Nursing and Health Services Adviser, Miss M. Pollock .... £17,000 to £22,926
Chief Natural Resources Adviser, A. T. Wilson
.... £29,500
Deputy Chief National Resources Adviser, A. W. Peers .... £20,964 to £25,533
Deputy Chief Natural Resources Adviser, Dr. J. C. Davies (Research) .... £20,964 to £25,533
Agricultural Advisers, J. R. Goldsack; R. W. Smith (Research); P. Tuley; A. R. Stobbs
.... £17,000 to £22,926
Assistant Agricultural Adviser, J. R. F. Hansell
.... £13,508 to £18,363
Animal Health Advisers, G. G. Freeland; (one vacancy) .... £17,000 to £22,926
Fisheries Advisers, J. Stoneman; Dr. J. Tarbit
.... £17,000 to £22,926
Forestry Advisers, R. H. Kemp; W. J. Howard
.... £17,000 to £19,317
Financial Management Advisers, D. W. Heffer; D. J. Sanderson .... £17,000 to £22,926
Senior Procurement Adviser, K. S. Breyer
.... £13,500 to £18,363
Overseas Police Adviser, (vacant)   ⎫ *See also Foreign*
Deputy Overseas Police Adviser, ⎬ *and Common-*
R. G. W. Lamb   ⎭ *wealth Office.*
Senior Social Development Adviser, Dr. D. A. P. Butcher .... £17,000 to £19,317
Social Development Adviser, Dr. S. J. Conlin
.... £13,508 to £18,363

Land Resources Development Centre
Tolworth Tower, Surbiton, Surrey KT6 7DY
[01-399 5281]

Director, A. J. Smyth .... £20,964 to £25,533

Tropical Development Research Institute
56-62 Gray's Inn Road, WC1X 8LU
[01-242 5412]
College House, Wrights Lane, W.8

Director, Dr. E. M. Thain £24,077

OFFICE OF THE PARLIAMENTARY COMMISSIONER AND HEALTH SERVICE COMMISSIONER
Church House, Great Smith Street, SW1P 3BW
[01-212 7676]

The Parliamentary Commissioner for Administration is responsible for investigating complaints referred to him by Members of the House of Commons from members of the public who claim to have sustained injustice in consequence of maladministration in connection with administrative action taken by or on behalf of Government Departments. Certain types of action by Departments are excluded from investigation. Actions taken by other public bodies (such as local authorities, the police, the Post Office and nationalised industries) are outside the Commissioner's scope.

The Health Service Commissioners for England, for Scotland and for Wales are responsible for investigating complaints against National Health Service authorities that are not dealt with by those authorities to the satisfaction of the complainant. Complaints can be referred direct by the member of the public who claims to have sustained injustice or hardship in consequence of the failure in a service provided by a relevant body, failure of that body to provide a service or in consequence of any other action by that body. Certain types of action are excluded, in particular, action taken solely in consequence of the exercise of clinical judgment. The three offices are presently held by the Parliamentary Commissioner.

Parliamentary Commissioner and Health Service Commissioner, A. R. Barrowclough, Q.C. . . £45,500
Secretaries, D. G. Allen, C.M.G.; G. V. Marsh . £29,500
Directors, V. J. Dean; K. H. Green; Mrs. J. M. Fowler; M. D. Randall; J. C. Bateman; J. H. Carruthers
£20,493 to £24,409
Principals, P. J. Belsham; C. H. Hemmings; J. F. Hanna (*Establishment Officer*); G. M. Keil; D. S. Martin; C. McCabe; M. Padgham; R. A. Smith; A. Watson; R. Church; P. Godden-Kent; Ms. S. I. Jolly; Mrs. C. Bentley; N. H. Hodgkiss
£13,649 to £17,906

PARLIAMENTARY COUNSEL
36 Whitehall, SW1A 2AY
[01–273 3000]

First Counsel, Sir George Engle, K.C.B., Q.C. . . £45,500
Second Counsel, C. H. de Waal, C.B. £39,250
Counsel, P. Graham, C.B.; J. D. M. Rennie; J. C. Jenkins; J. S. Mason; Miss S. P. Burns; D. W. Saunders; E. G. Caldwell; E. G. Bowman
up to £36,500

PAROLE BOARD
Abell House, John Islip Street, SW1P 4LH
[01–211 3000]

The Board was constituted under section 59 of the Criminal Justice Act, 1967.

The function of the Board is to advise the Secretary of State for the Home Department with respect to: (1) Release on licence under section 60 (i) or 61 and recall under section 62 of the Criminal Justice Act, 1967 of persons whose cases have been referred to the Board by the Secretary of State; (2) The conditions of such licences, and the variation and cancellation of such conditions; and (3) any other matter so referred which is connected with release on licence or recall of persons to whom section 60 or 61 of the Act applies.

Chairman, The Lord Windlesham, P.C., C.V.O.
Vice-Chairman, The Rt. Hon. Lord Justice Lloyd.
Secretary, J. Glaze.

PATENT OFFICE
(and Industrial Property and Copyright Department)
Department of Trade and Industry,
State House, 66–71 High Holborn,
WC1R 4TP
[01–831 2525]
Sale Branch : Orpington, Kent

The duties of the Department consist in the administration of the Patent Acts, the Registered Designs Act and the Trade Marks Act and in dealing with questions relating to the Copyright Acts. The Department also provides information service about patent specifications. In 1984 the Office granted 18,867 patents and registered 6,697 designs and 16,083 trade marks.

Comptroller-General, I. J. G. Davis, C.B. £33,715
Assistant Comptrollers, T. W. Sage; V. Tarnofsky
£29,156
Superintending Examiners, D. C. L. Blake; N. G. Tarnofsky; J. P. Britton; M. F. Vivian; A. Sugden; J. Sharrock; G. K. Lindsey; E. F. Blake . . . £26,898
Principal Examiners, R. E. Bridges; C. G. Harrison; R. M. Bennett; C. S. Richenberg; M. Fox; P. E. Taylor; C. I. C. Byrne; M. G. Currell; S. A. Goodchild; J. Winter; A. J. Needs; H. R. Bailey; P. L. Eggington; Miss C. M. Edwards; A. C. N. Woodcock; D. R. Barratt; P. A. Gill; N. L. Sands; B. C. Faulkner; S. J. Rutland; W. J. Lyon; K. E. Panchen; C. D. Kopkin; D. H. Rowland; E. J. Lawrence; B. J. Phillips; D. B. Johnson; C. G. M. Hoptroff; S. Southworth; B. G. Harden; J. Hillman; M. W. Hills; L. Lewis; P. S. Michaelis; N. J. Miles; K. C. Thomas; R. S. Vidler; Miss Y. J. Pegler
£23,933 to £25,888
Assistant Registrar, Trade Marks, J. M. Myall
£22,329 to £26,898
Senior Principals, A. B. Clarke; R. V. Egan; A. Holt
£18,365 to £24,291
Senior Examiner, Information Retrieval Services, W. Preacher . . . . £15,821 to £22,662

Manchester Office
Room 921A, Sunley Buildings,
Piccadilly Plaza, M1 4BA
[01–236 2171]

PAYMASTER GENERAL
70 Whitehall, SW1A 2AS
[01–233 7051]
Sutherland House, Russell Way, Crawley, West Sussex RH10 1UH

The Paymaster General's Office was formed by the consolidation in 1835 of various separate pay departments then existing, some of which dated back at least to the Restoration of 1660. Its function is that of paying agent for Government Departments, other than the Revenue Departments. Most of its payments are made through banks, to whose accounts the necessary transfers are made at the Bank of England. The payment of approximately one million public service pensions is an important feature of its work.

Paymaster General, JOHN SELWYN GUMMER, M.P.
Assistant Paymaster General, L. A. Andrews
£20,964 to £25,533
Senior Principals, D. R. L. Breed; A. J. McClatchey
£17,000 to £22,926
Principals, D. R. Alexander; O. J. Breeden; E. D. Hatswell; K. Sullens; G. Thomas; M. D. West
£13,508 to £18,363

POLICE COMPLAINTS AUTHORITY
10 Great George Street, SW1P 3AB
[01–213 5392]

The Police Complaints Authority was established under the Police and Criminal Evidence Act 1984 to introduce a further independent element into the procedure for dealing with complaints by members of the public against police officers in England and Wales. The Authority has powers to supervise the investigation of certain categories of serious complaints and certain statutory functions in relation to the disciplinary aspects of complaints.

Chairman, Sir Cecil Clothier, K.C.B., Q.C.
Deputy Chairman (Discipline), Rear-Admiral J. A. Bell.
Deputy Chairman (Investigations), Rt. Hon. R. Moyle.
Members, V. Clements; Mrs E. Crawley; M. C. Hazlewood; J. Lyttle; B. V. Moore; Brig. J. Pownall: Capt. N. Taylor; Mrs. R. Vickers; Mrs. R. Wolff.

POLITICAL HONOURS SCRUTINY COMMITTEE
Cabinet Office, Great George Street, SW1P 3AL
[01–233 3000]

Chairman, The Lord Shackleton, K.G., P.C., O.B.E.
Members, The Lord Carr of Hadley, P.C.; The Lord Franks, P.C., O.M., G.C.M.G., K.C.B., C.B.E., F.B.A.
Secretary, Mrs. M. Hedley-Miller, C.B.

OFFICE OF POPULATION CENSUSES AND SURVEYS
St. Catherine's House, 10, Kingsway, WC2B 6JP
[01–242 0262]

The Office of Population Censuses and Surveys was created by a merger in May 1970 of the General Register Office and the Government Social Survey Department. The Registrar General controls the local registration service in England and Wales in the exercise of its registration and marriage duties. Copies of the original registrations of births, still-births, marriages and deaths are kept in London. A register of adopted children is held at Titchfield. Central indexes are compiled quarterly and certified copies of entries may be obtained on payment of certain fees. Since 1841 the Registrar General has been responsible for taking the census of population. He also prepares and publishes a wide range of statistics and appropriate commentary relating to population, fertility, births, still-births, marriages, deaths and cause of death, infectious diseases, sickness and injuries. The Registrar General also maintains, at Southport, a central register of persons on doctors' lists, for the purposes of the National Health Service.

Hours of public access, Mon.–Fri., 8.30 a.m.–4.30 p.m.
Director and Registrar General, A. R. Thatcher, C.B.
£36,500
Deputy Director, F. W. Whitehead £29,500
Senior Principal Medical Officer, M. R. Alderson
£29,500
Deputy Registrar General, J. V. Ribbins
£20,964 to £25,533
Assistant Secretaries, Miss R. D. B. Pease (*Establishment Officer*); P. H. Kenney; M. L. Pennington
£20,964 to £25,533
Chief Statisticians, J. Craig (*Population*); Miss J. H. Thompson (*Population*) . . . . £20,964 to £25,533
Senior Statisticians (*Medical*), J. S. Ashley; A. G. McCormick; A. J. Swerdlow £25,535
Chief Social Survey Officer "A", R. Barnes
£20,964 to £25,533
Senior Principals, G. P. Barnes; I. K. G. Arnold; J. P. Hisley; W. Jenkins; D. L. Pearce
£17,000 to £22,926
Chief Social Survey Officers "B", Mrs. K. H. Dunnell; Mrs. M. L. Durant; R. K. Thomas; I. B. Knight
£17,000 to £22,926
Statistician (*Medical*), M. F. G. Murphy £23,515
Statisticians, R. I. Armitage; F. L. Ashwood; R. J. Beacham; M. S. Britton; Miss A. C. Brown; L. Bulusu; Miss S. B. Claydon; T. L. F. Devis; J. M. Dixie; A. J. Fox; P. O. Goldblatt; Mrs. M. E. Lane; M. E. McDowall; J. B. Werner . £13,508 to £18,363

Principals, B. S. T. Alcock; Mrs. P. E. Astbury; N. E. Auckland; R. A. P. Bailey; E. Barton; T. B. Bryson; A. M. Clark; J. Denton; I. M. Golds; P. Howell; A. F. Jones; Miss E. M. McCrossan; R. McLeod; B. W. Meakings; Mrs. J. S. Morris; R. M. Nicholls; Miss D. M. Pace; J. A. Rampton; T. A. Russell; K. J. Stalker; Mrs. D. M. Stobart; A. W. Tester
£13,508 to £18,363
Principal Social Survey Officers, Miss J. Atkinson; Mrs. M. R. Bone; M. J. Bradley; R. J. Butcher; Mrs. J. R. Gregory; P. J. Heady; A. J. Marsh; Mrs. J. Martin; Mrs. I. Rauta; R. U. Redpath; K. K. Sillitoe; Miss J. E. Todd; P. R. Wilson
£13,508 to £18,363
Principal Information Officer, (vacant).
Principal Research Officer, C. J. Denham
£13,508 to £18,363

PORT OF LONDON AUTHORITY
Head Office, Leslie Ford House,
Tilbury Docks,
Tilbury, Essex RM18 7EH
[03752 3444]

Under the Port of London Authority (Constitution) Revision Order 1975, the membership of the Board consists of a minimum of nine and a maximum of 17 members. In addition to the Chairman a minimum of seven and a maximum of 10 non-executive members are appointed by the Minister of Transport.
A minimum of one executive member and a maximum of six executive members may be appointed by the Chairman and other non-executive members.
Chairman, Sir Brian Kellett.
Deputy Chairman and Chief Executive, J. N. Black.
Director of Tilbury, J. S. McNab.
Director of Administration, J. C. Jenkinson, M.V.O.
Director of Finance, T. R. MacMaster.
Secretary, G. E. Ennals.

THE POST OFFICE
33 Grosvenor Place, SW1X 1PX
[01–235 8000]

Crown services for the carriage of Government despatches were set up about 1516. The conveyance of public correspondence began in 1635 and the mail service was made a Parliamentary responsibility with the setting up of a Post Office in 1657. Telegraphs came under the Post Office control in 1870 and the Post Office Telephone Service began in 1880. The National Girobank service of the Post Office began in 1968. The Post Office ceased to be a Government Department on October 1, 1969, following the Post Office Act 1969. The office of Postmaster General was abolished and responsibility for the running of the postal, telecommunications, and giro and remittance services was transferred to the new public authority called the Post Office. The 1981 British Telecommunications Act separated the functions of the Post Office. The Post Office is now solely responsible for postal services and National Girobank. The Act reaffirmed the Post Office basic letter monopoly but added some specific exclusions. The Chairman and members of the Post Office Board are appointed by the Secretary of State but responsibility for the running of the Post Office as a whole rests with the Board in its corporate capacity.

Post Office Board
Chairman, Sir Ronald Dearing, C.B.
Acting Managing Director, National Giorobank, A. K. Hanton.

Members, R. A. Clinton (*Counter Services*); W. Cockburn (*Royal Mail Operations*); K. M. Young, C.B.E. (*Personnel and Industrial Relations*); A. D. Garrett (*Royal Mail Marketing*); P. E. Sellers (*Finance*).

Part-time Members, C. E. Beauchamp, C.B.E.; D. O. Gladwin, C.B.E.; E. Cole; Sir Clifford Cornford, K.C.B.; P. E. Moody, C.B.E.; S. Wainwright.

PRIVY COUNCIL OFFICE
Whitehall, SW1A 2AT

Lord President of the Council (and Leader of the House of Lords), THE VISCOUNT WHITELAW, C.H., M.C.

Private Secretary, Miss J. MacNaughton.

Clerk of the Council, G. I. de Deney	£32,433
Deputy Clerk of the Council, C. E. S. Horsford, C.V.O.	£26,898
Senior Clerk, R. P. Bulling	£15,481

PUBLIC HEALTH LABORATORY SERVICE
Headquarters Office:
61 Colindale Avenue, NW9 5EQ
[01–200 1295]

Members of the Board, C. E. G. Smith, C.B., M.D. (*Chairman*); A. D. Bostock; Prof. A. R. Buchan, M.D.; A. E. Eames; A. P. Haines; E. L. Harris, C.B.; P. Higham; Prof. R. Hurley, M.D.; Prof. F. W. O'Grady, C.B.E., T.D., M.D.; A. J. Rowland; M. Sackwood; C. C. Stevens, O.B.E.; Prof. A. J. Zuckerman, D.SC., M.D.; and three others to be appointed.

Director, J. W. G. Smith, M.D.
Deputy Directors, J. R. Davies, M.D.; P. D. Meers, M.D.
Secretary to the Board, R. B. Paget.

Central Public Health Laboratory
Colindale Avenue, N.W.9

Director, Prof. A. A. Glynn, M.D.
Division of Enteric Pathogens, B. Rowe, T.D.
Division of Hospital Infection, E. M. Cooke, M.D.
Division of Microbiological Reagents and Quality Control, A. G. Taylor, PH.D. (*acting*).
Food Hygiene Laboratory, R. J. Gilbert, PH.D.
Hepatitis Epidemiology Unit (Division of Epidemiology), S. Polakoff, M.D.
Mycological Reference Laboratory, Prof. D. W. R. Mackenzie, PH.D.
National Collection of Type Cultures, L. R. Hill, D.SC.
Virus Reference Laboratory, M. S. Pereira, M.D.

Centre for Applied Microbiology and Research
Porton Down, Salisbury

Director, P. M. Sutton.
Bacterial Metabolism Research Laboratory, M. J. Hill, PH.D.
Experimental Pathology Laboratory, A. Baskerville, D.V.SC., PH.D.
Microbial Technology Laboratory, Prof. A. Atkinson, PH.D.
Molecular Genetics Laboratory, P. J. Greenaway, PH.D.
Special Pathogens Reference Laboratory, E. T. W. Bowen, O.B.E., PH.D.
Therapeutic Products Laboratory, H. E. Wade, PH.D.
Vaccine Research and Production Laboratory, Prof. J. Melling, PH.D.

Other Special Laboratories and Units

Anaerobe Reference Unit, Public Health Laboratory, Luton: A. T. Willis, M.D.

Communicable Disease Surveillance Centre (Division of Epidemiology), 61 Colindale Avenue, N.W.9: N. S. Galbraith.
Gonococcus Reference Unit, Public Health Laboratory, Bristol: A. E. Jephcott, M.D.
Influenza Research Unit, Public Health Laboratory, Guildford: J. R. Davies, M.D.
Leptospira Reference Unit, Public Health Laboratory, Hereford: S. A. Waitkins, PH.D.
Malaria Reference Laboratory, London School of Hygiene and Tropical Medicine, W.C.1: Prof. D. J. Bradley, D.M.; Prof. W. Peters, M.D., D.SC.
Mycobacterium Reference Unit, Public Health Laboratory, Cardiff: P. A. Jenkins, PH.D.

Regional Laboratories

Birmingham, J. G. P. Hutchison, M.D.; *Bristol,* A. E. Jephcott, M.D.; *Cambridge,* C. E. D. Taylor, M.D.; *Cardiff,* C. H. L. Howells, M.D.; *Leeds,* R. N. Peel; *Liverpool,* G. C. Turner, M.D.; *Manchester,* D. M. Jones, M.D.; *Newcastle,* A. E. Wright, T.D., M.D.; *Oxford,* J. B. Selkon, T.D.; *Portsmouth,* O. A. Okubadejo, M.D.; *Sheffield,* B. W. Barton.

Area Laboratories

Ashford, C. Dulake; *Bath,* D. G. White; *Brighton,* B. T. Thom; *Carlisle,* M. A. Knowles; *Carmarthen,* H. D. S. Morgan; *Chelmsford,* R. E. Tettmar, D.PATH.; *Chester,* J. H. Pennington, M.D.; *Coventry,* P. R. Mortimer, M.D.; *Dorchester,* P. Gill; *Epsom,* E. I. Tanner; *Exeter,* R. J. C. Hart; *Gloucester,* K. A. V. Cartwright; *Guildford,* R. Y. Cartwright; *Hereford,* I. R. Ferguson; *Hull,* S. L. Mawer; *Ipswich,* P. H. Jones; *Leicester,* C. J. Mitchell; *Lincoln,* J. G. Wallace; LONDON: *Central Middlesex Hospital,* D. A. McSwiggan (*Honorary*); *Dulwich,* A. H. C. Uttley, PH.D.; *Tooting,* D. G. Fleck, M.D.; *Whipps Cross,* B. Chattopadhyay, M.D.; *Luton,* A. T. Willis, M.D.; *Middlesbrough,* E. McKay-Ferguson, M.D.; *Norwich,* W. Shepherd, M.D.; *Nottingham,* M. J. Lewis, M.D.; *Peterborough,* R. S. Jobanputra, M.D.; *Plymouth,* P. J. Wilkinson; *Poole,* W. L. Hooper; *Preston,* D. N. Hutchinson; *Reading,* J. V. Dadswell; *Rhyl,* F. B. Jackson; *Salisbury,* S. Patrick; *Shrewsbury,* C. A. Morris, M.D.; *Southampton,* A. D. Pearson; *Stoke-on-Trent,* J. Gray; *Swansea,* D. H. M. Joynson; *Taunton,* J. V. S. Pether; *Truro,* W. A. Telfer Brunton; *Watford,* M. T. Moulsdale; *Wolverhampton,* R. G. Thompson.

REGISTRAR OF PUBLIC LENDING RIGHT
4th Floor, Bayheath House,
Prince Regent Street,
Stockton-on-Tees,
Cleveland, TS18 1DF
[0642 604699]

Under the Public Lending Right system payment is made from public funds to authors whose books are lent out from public libraries. The Public Lending Right Act (1979) established the legal right to be administered by a Registrar, appointed by the Minister for the Arts. Payment is made once a year (in February) and the amount each author receives is proportionate to the number of times (established from a sample) that books were lent out during the previous year.

From the applications he receives the Registrar of PLR compiles, to hold on his computer, the register of authors and books. Only living authors resident in the United Kingdom or West Germany are eligible to apply. The term "author" covers writers, illustrators, translators, and some editors/compilers.

A representative sample of loans is recorded consisting of all issues from 20 public libraries. This is then multiplied in proportion to total library lending to produce for each book an estimate of its total annual loans throughout the country. Annually the computer compares the register with the estimated loans to discover how many loans are credited to each registered book for the calculation of PLR payments. The computer uses code numbers—in most cases the ISBN printed in the book.

Parliament allocates a sum each year for PLR (£2 million in 1984/85; £2.75 million in 1985/86). This Fund pays the administrative costs of PLR and reimburses local authorities for recording loans in the sample libraries. The remaining money is then divided to work out how much can be paid for each estimated loan of a registered book; this was 0.92 pence in 1984/85, and will change annually.

There is a top limit of £5,000 for the books of any one registered author: the money for loans above this level is used to augment the remaining PLR payments.

In February 1985, the sum of £1,657,000 was made available for distribution to 7,622 registered authors and assignees as the second annual payment of PLR. *Registrar,* J. W. Sumsion.

PUBLIC RECORD OFFICE
See **Record Offices**

PUBLIC TRUSTEE OFFICE
Stewart House, Kingsway, WC2B 6JX
[01–405 4300]

The Public Trustee is a Trust corporation created to undertake the business of executorship and trusteeship; he can act as executor or administrator of the estate of a deceased person, or as a trustee of a will or settlement (either by original appointment or by transfer at a later stage) alone or jointly with others in the same manner and under the same legal obligations as a private individual or commercial trust corporation, but with a guarantee that all breaches of trust will be made good out of the Consolidated Fund. He cannot accept a trust which is foreign, exclusively charitable or for the benefit of creditors, nor an insolvent estate. He can accept the trusteeship of and manage pension funds, disaster funds and the funds of private individuals or institutions. He also administers common investment funds for moneys in Court. Fees are charged for his services, the Office being self supporting but non profit making.
Public Trustee, J. A. Boland £30,800
Assistant Public Trustee, R. C. Annis
£22,264 to £26,833
Chief Administrative Officer, J. P. Hamilton
£22,264 to £26,833
Chief Investment Manager, H. Stevenson
£18,300 to £24,226
Finance Officer, F. A. Boocock ... £18,300 to £24,226
Chief Property Adviser, A. C. Nightingale
£15,692 to £18,622
Acceptance Officer, R. A. Cunningham
£14,808 to £19,663

PUBLIC WORKS LOAN BOARD
See **National Investment and Loans Board**

COMMISSION FOR RACIAL EQUALITY
Elliot House, 10–12 Allington Street, SW1E 5EH
[01–828 7022]

Established on June 13, 1977, under the Race Relations Act 1976, to work towards elimination of discrimination and promote equality of opportunity and good relations between different racial groups generally. (Replaces Community Relations Commission and Race Relations Board).

Chairman, P. Newsam.
Deputy Chairman, C. Robinson, O.B.E.
Members, Mrs. S. Flather; A. W. Gayton; Dr. F. Hashmi, O.B.E.; G. E. B. Tyler; L. Crawford; Mrs. L. Khan; Prof. B. Parekh; G. S. Sarang; K. Gill; Ethel M. Houston, O.B.E.; E. Gilmour Jones; W. Morris; K. R. Whitesides.

RECORD OFFICES, ETC.

THE PUBLIC RECORD OFFICE
Chancery Lane, WC2A 1LR
[01-405 0741]
Ruskin Avenue, Kew,
Richmond, Surrey TW9 4DU
[01-876 3444]

The Office, originally established in 1838 under the Master of the Rolls, was placed by the Public Records Act 1958 under the direction of the Lord Chancellor. He appoints a Keeper of Public Records, whose duties are to co-ordinate and supervise the selection of records of government departments and the English Law Courts for permanent preservation, to safeguard the records under his charge, and to make them available to the public.

The Office holds records of central government dating from *Domesday Book* (1086) to 1984. Under the 1967 Public Records Act they are normally open to inspection when 30 years old, and are then available, without charge, in the reading rooms, Monday to Friday, 9.30 to 5.

During 1986 the traditional Museum display in Chancery Lane is replaced by a *Domesday Book* 900th anniversary exhibition, April to September, Monday to Saturday, 10 to 6.
Keeper of Public Records, G. H. Martin, D.PHIL., F.S.A.
£30,865
Deputy Keeper, Dr. P. M. Barnes . £21,729 to £26,298
Records Administration Officer, M. Roper
£21,729 to £26,298
Officer-in-Charge, Chancery Lane, Dr. R. F. Hunnisett
£22,329 to £25,265
Establishment Officer, J. G. Wickham
£14,273 to £19,128
Principal Assistant Keepers, C. D. Chalmers; Mrs. J. M. Cox; Dr. N. G. Cox; N. E. Evans; Dr. A. A. H. Knightbridge; Mrs. A. N. Nicol; J. L. Walford
£17,816 to £22,662
Assistant Keepers, Mrs. M. K. Banton; Miss G. L. Beech; Miss A. S. Bevan; Dr. T. M. Chalmers; Miss M. M. Condon; Dr. D. Crook; Dr. H. Forde; Dr. M. R. Foster; Dr. E. M. Hallam Smith; Ms. S. M. F. Healy; Dr. E. J. Higgs; Mrs. H. E. Jones; Dr. M. J. Jubb; Mrs. A. E. Morton; T. R. Padfield; Dr. J. B. Post; Dr. N. A. M. Rodger; Dr. D. L. Thomas
scale rising to max. of £19,728
Principal, Repository and Reprographic Services, P. F. McCaffrey .... £14,273 to £19,128
Principal Inspecting Officer, D. Ashton
£14,273 to £19,128
Inspecting Officers, D. Barlow; A. W. H. Medlicott; J. S. Harley; J. A. Keene; C. B. Townshend; K. J. Smith; F. McCall; Miss H. R. Shelton .. £11,823 to £14,566
Head of Information Technology Unit, Mrs. M. Wilkinson .... £11,823 to £14,566
Deputy Establishment Officer, C. J. Edwards . £11,823 to £14,566

ADVISORY COUNCIL ON PUBLIC RECORDS
Public Record Office, Chancery Lane, WC2A 1LR
[01-405 0741]

Chairman, The Master of the Rolls.
Members, The Lord Bancroft, G.C.B.; Dr. R. D'O.

Butler, C.M.G.; W. Clarke, C.B.E.; Prof. D. N. Dilks; Prof. G. R. Elton, F.B.A.; Prof. P. D. A. Harvey; Prof. M. E. Howard, C.B.E., M.C., F.B.A.; Dr. M. Hughes, M.P.; Prof. Sir Hans Kornberg, F.R.S.; Rt. Hon. Sir Robert Megarry, F.B.A.; Dr. J. Morgan; Sir Paul Osmond, C.B.; W. R. Serjeant; R. S. Wainwright, M.P.; M. A. Latham, M.P.; Prof. E. A. Wrigley.

Assessors, D. J. Wiblin; Dr. G. H. Martin.
Secretary, Dr. M. J. Jubb.

HOUSE OF LORDS RECORD OFFICE
House of Lords, SW1A 0PW
[01-219 3074]

Since 1497, the records of Parliament have been kept within the Palace of Westminster. They are in the custody of the Clerk of the Parliaments, who in 1946 established a record department to supervise their preservation and their production to students. The Search Room of this office is open to the public throughout the year, Mondays to Fridays inclusive from 9.30 a.m. to 5 p.m. The records preserved number some 3,000,000 documents, and include Acts of Parliament from 1497, Journals of the House of Lords from 1510. Minutes and Committee proceedings from 1610, and Papers laid before Parliament from 1531. Amongst the records are the Petition of Right, the Death Warrant of Charles I, the Declaration of Breda and the Bill of Rights. The House of Lords Record Office also has charge of the Journals of the House of Commons (from 1547), and other surviving records of the Commons (from 1572), which include plans and annexed documents relating to Private Bill legislation from 1818. Among other documents are the records of the Lord Great Chamberlain, the political papers of certain members of the two Houses (including the papers of Lloyd George, Bonar Law and other statesmen previously preserved in the Beaverbrook Library), and documents relating to Parliament acquired on behalf of the nation. All the manuscripts and other records are preserved in the Victoria Tower of the Houses of Parliament. A permanent exhibition was established in the Royal Gallery in 1979.

Clerk of the Records, H. S. Cobb, F.S.A.
              £22,329 to £26,898
Deputy Clerk of the Records, D. J. Johnson, F.S.A.
              £18,416 to £22,662
Assistant Clerks of the Records, J. C. Morgan (*Sound Archives*); S. K. Ellison .... £13,431 to £19,728

ROYAL COMMISSION ON HISTORICAL MANUSCRIPTS
Quality House, Quality Court, Chancery Lane,
WC2A 1HP
[01-242 1198]

The Commission was set up by Royal Warrant in 1869 to enquire and report on collections of papers of value for the study of history in private hands. In 1959 a new warrant enlarged these terms of reference to include all historical records, wherever situated, outside the Public Records and gave it added responsibilities, as a central co-ordinating body, to promote, assist and advise on their proper preservation and storage. The Commission has published over 200 volumes of reports. It holds a further 28,000 unpublished reports in the National Register of Archives, available for consultation in its search room. It also administers the Manorial and Tithe Documents Rules on behalf of the Master of the Rolls.

Chairman, The Lord Blake, F.B.A.
Commissioners, Prof. J. C. Beckett; Sir Robert Somerville, K.C.V.O., F.S.A.; The Lord Kenyon, C.B.E., F.S.A.; The Lord Fletcher, P.C., F.S.A.; ; The Duke of Northumberland, K.G., P.C., G.C.V.O., F.R.S.; J. P. W.

Ehrman, F.B.A., F.S.A.; The Earl of Wemyss and March, K.T.; Prof. S. F. C. Milsom, F.B.A.; Sir John Habakkuk, F.B.A.; G. E. Aylmer, F.B.A.; P. T. Cormack, F.S.A., M.P.; H. M. Colvin, C.B.E., F.B.A., F.S.A.; Prof. G. W. S. Barrow, F.B.A.; Valerie L. Pearl, F.S.A.; The Marquess of Anglesey; Prof. Owen Chadwick, O.M., K.B.E., F.B.A.
Secretary, B. S. Smith, F.S.A.

SCOTTISH RECORD OFFICE
H.M. General Register House, Edinburgh EH1 3YY
[031-556 6585]

The history of the national archives of Scotland can be traced back to the 13th century. The present headquarters of the Scottish Record Office, the General Register House, was founded in 1774 and built to designs by Robert Adam, later modified by Robert Reid. Here are preserved the administrative records of pre-Union Scotland, the registers of central and local courts of law, the public registers of property rights and legal documents, and many collections of local and church records and private archives. Certain groups of records, mainly the modern records of government departments in Scotland, the Scottish railway records, and the plans collection, are preserved in the branch repository at the West Register House in Charlotte Square—the former St. George's Church which was designed by Robert Reid. The Search Rooms in both buildings open daily from 9 to 4.45 (Mondays to Fridays). A permanent exhibition at the West Register House and changing exhibitions at the General Register House are open to the public on weekdays from 10 to 4. The National Register of Archives (Scotland), which is a branch of the Scottish Record Office, is based in the West Register House.
Keeper of the Records of Scotland, Dr. A. L. Murray.

DEPARTMENT OF THE REGISTERS OF SCOTLAND
Meadowbank House, 153 London Road,
Edinburgh EH8 7AU
[031-661 6111]

The Registers of Scotland consist of:—
(1) General Register of Sasines and Land Register of Scotland; (2) Register of Deeds in the Books of Council and Session; (3) Register of Protests; (4) Register of English and Irish Judgments; (5) Register of Service of Heirs; (6) Register of the Great Seal; (7) Register of the Quarter Seal; (8) Register of the Prince's Seal; (9) Register of Crown Grants; (10) Register of Sheriffs' Commissions; (11) Register of the Cachet Seal; (12) Register of Inhibitions and Adjudications; (13) Register of Entails; (14) Register of Hornings.
The General Register of Sasines and the Land Register of Scotland form the chief security in Scotland of the rights of land and other heritable (or real) property.
Keeper of the Registers of Scotland, W. Russell
              £26,909
Deputy Keeper, J. Robertson ..... £20,964 to £25,533
Senior Assistant Keepers, R. C. Brown; A. A. Snowdon; G. C. Warrender .... £17,000 to £22,926
Assistant Keepers, J. Cogle; B. J. Corr; A. M. Falconer; R. C. Fulton; J. Knox; Mrs. A. McDonald; J. MacDonald; L. J. Morrison; D. L. Nicoll; A. W. Ramage; A. G. Rennie; I. M. Tainsh
              £13,508 to £18,363

CORPORATION OF LONDON RECORDS OFFICE
Guildhall, EC2P 2EJ
[01-606 3030]

Contains the municipal archives of the City of London which are regarded as the most complete

collection of ancient municipal records in existence. Includes charters of William the Conqueror, Henry II, and later Kings and Queens to 1957; ancient custumals: Liber Horn, Dunthorne, Custumarum, Ordinacionum, Memorandorum and Albus, Liber de Antiquis Legibus, and collections of Statutes; continuous series of judicial rolls and books from 1252 and Council minutes from 1275; records of the Old Bailey and Guildhall Sessions from 1603, and financial records from the 16th century, together with the records of London Bridge from the 12th century and numerous subsidiary series and miscellanea of historical interest. A Guide was published in 1951. Readers' Room open Monday to Friday, 9.30 a.m. to 4.45 p.m.
Keeper of the City Records, The Town Clerk.
Deputy Keeper, J. R. Sewell.
Assistant Keeper, Mrs. J. M. Bankes.

REVIEW BODIES

ARMED FORCES PAY

The Review Body on Armed Forces Pay was appointed in September 1971 to advise the Prime Minister on the pay and allowances of members of Naval, Military and Air Forces of the Crown and of any women's service administered by the Defence Council.

The members of the Review Body are: Sir Peter Matthews (*Chairman*); M. Bett; D. P. M. Hudson; Mrs. J. Hughes; L. A. Mills; Admiral Sir Anthony Morton, G.B.E., K.C.B.; J. R. Sargent.

DOCTORS' AND DENTISTS' REMUNERATION

The Review Body on Doctors' and Dentists' Remuneration was appointed in July 1971 to advise the Prime Minister on the remuneration of doctors and dentists taking any part in the National Health Service.

The members of the Review Body are: Sir Robert Clark, D.S.C. (*Chairman*); Dr. Anne Hogg; J. L. Kirkpatrick, C.B.E.; Prof. P. G. Moore, T.D.; D. G. Richards; Prof. G. F. Thomason, C.B.E.; Sir Graham Wilkins; J. K. Warburton, C.B.E.

TOP SALARIES

The Review Body on Top Salaries was appointed in May, 1971 to advise the Prime Minister on the remuneration of the higher judiciary and other judicial appointments; senior civil servants; and senior officers of the armed forces. Until August 1980 the remit also included the Chairmen and members of the Boards of nationalized industries. The Review Body has also been asked on a number of occasions to advise on the remuneration of Members of Parliament and of Ministers and on the level of the Peers' expenses allowances.

The members of the Review Body are: The Lord Plowden, K.C.B., K.B.E. (*Chairman*); Sir Harold Atcherley; The Lord Chorley; Sir Robin Ibbs; Sir Peter Matthews; A. Morritt, Q.C.; Sir David Orr; Sir Thomas Skyrme, K.C.V.O., C.B., C.B.E., T.D.

NURSING STAFF, MIDWIVES, HEALTH VISITORS AND PROFESSIONS ALLIED TO MEDICINE

The Review Body for nursing staff, midwives, health visitors and professions allied to medicine was set up in July 1983 to advise the Prime Minister on the remuneration of nursing staff, midwives and health visitors employed in the National Health Service; and physiotherapists, radiographers, remedial gymnasts, occupational therapists, orthoptists, chiropodists, dietitians and related grades employed in the National Health Service.

The members of the Review Body are: Sir John Greenborough, K.B.E. (*Chairman*); Miss B. Cooper, Q.C.; Mrs. S. Harold; Sir John Herbecq, K.C.B.; Dr. G. Hills; Mrs. J. Hughes; I. H. Phillipps; Prof. G. F. Thomason, C.B.E.

NOTE.—The secretariat for the above bodies is provided by the Office of Manpower Economics (*see separate entry*).

ROYAL BOTANIC GARDENS, KEW
Richmond, Surrey TW9 3AB
[01-940 1171]
Also at: Wakehurst Place, Ardingly, near Haywards
Heath,
West Sussex RH17 6TN
[0444 892701]

The Royal Botanic Gardens (RBG), Kew were founded in 1759 by H.R.H. Princess Augusta. In 1841, they became a public institution; in 1847, the Museums of Economic Botany were opened, and in 1852, the Herbarium and Library were established. The Jodrell Laboratory opened in 1876. In 1965, the garden at Wakehurst Place was acquired; it is owned by the National Trust and managed by RBG Kew. From 1903 to 1984, RBG Kew was part of the Ministry of Agriculture, Fisheries and Food. Under the National Heritage Act 1983, a Board of Trustees was set up to administer the Gardens which, on 1 April, 1984, then became an independent body supported by a grant-in-aid.

The functions of RBG Kew are to carry out research into plant sciences, to disseminate knowledge about plants and to provide the public with the opportunity to gain knowledge and enjoyment from the Gardens' collections. The expertise of the RBG Kew is in plant taxonomy, distribution, genetics, anatomy, biochemistry, propagation, conservation and utilisation. There are extensive national reference collections of living and preserved plants and a comprehensive library and archive. The main emphasis is on tropical and subtropical plants.

Open daily, except Christmas Day and New Year's Day, from 10 a.m. The closing hour varies from 4 p.m. in mid-winter to 7 p.m. on week-days, and 8 p.m. at week-ends and Bank Holidays, in mid-summer. Admission, 15p. Museums open 10 a.m.; Glasshouses, 11 a.m. to 4.50 p.m. (weekdays); to 5.50 p.m. (Sundays). No dogs except guide-dogs for the blind.

BOARD OF TRUSTEES

Chairman, Hon. J. D. Eccles.
Members, Sir Leslie Fowden, F.R.S.; Prof. W. G. Chaloner, F.R.S.; Prof. E. C. D. Cocking, F.R.S.; J. P. Cousins; Sir Philip M. Dowson, C.B.E.; Prof. G. E. Fogg, C.B.E., F.R.S.; Prof. V. H. Heywood, PH.D., D.SC.; Sir Charles Pereira, D.SC., F.R.S.; Prof. Elizabeth B. Robson, PH.D.; Cdr. L. M. Saunders Watson, R.N. (*ret*); Sir Huw Wheldon, O.B.E., M.C.
Director, Prof. E. A. Bell.

ROYAL COMMISSION FOR THE EXHIBITION OF 1851
1 Lowther Gardens, Exhibition Road, SW7 2AA
[01–589 3665]

Incorporated by Supplemental Charter as a permanent Commission after winding up the affairs of the Great Exhibition of 1851. It has for its object the promotion of scientific and artistic education by means of funds derived from its Kensington Estate, purchased with the surplus left over from the Great Exhibition.

President, H.R.H. The Duke of Edinburgh, K.G., P.C., K.T., O.M., G.B.E.
Chairman, Board of Management, Sir Richard Way, K.C.B., C.B.E.
Secretary to Commissioners, C. A. H. James.

SCIENCE AND ENGINEERING RESEARCH COUNCIL
Polaris House, North Star Avenue,
Swindon, Wilts. SN2 1ET
[0793–26222]

Chairman, Prof. E. W. J. Mitchell.
Members, Prof. Sir Michael Atiyah; Prof. B. L. Clarkson; Prof. A. H. Cook; Prof. D. E. N. Davies; Prof. B. E. F. Fender; G. R. Hall; Prof. C. Hilsum; Dr. M. W. Holdgate; R. B. Horton; Prof. M. A. Jeeves; Prof. R. O. C. Norman; Prof. D. H. Perkins; Dr. C. H. Reece; O. Roith; D. T. Shore; Prof. J. J. Turner; Prof. R. Wilson; (one vacancy).

SCOTTISH OFFICE
Dover House, Whitehall, SW1A 2AU
[01–233 3000]

Secretary of State for Scotland, THE RT. HON. GEORGE KENNETH HOTSON YOUNGER, T.D., M.P. .. £40,930
Private Secretary, R. S. B. Gordon
£20,964 to £25,533
Assistant Private Secretaries, A. Rinning; K. M. Robbie.
Minister of State for Agriculture and Fisheries, The Lord Gray of Contin, P.C. £26,670
Parliamentary Under Secretaries of State, J. Allan Stewart, M.P. (*Industry and Education*); J. MacKay, M.P. (*Health and Social Work*); M. Ancram, M.P. (*Home Affairs and the Environment*) £26,780
Permanent Under Secretary of State, Sir William Fraser, G.C.B. £52,750
Private Secretary, R. N. Irvine.
Parliamentary Clerk, J. F. Rowell.
Liaison Staff:
Assistant Secretaries, I. C. Freeman; R. H. Scott
£20,964 to £25,533
Principals, I. A. Sneddon; G. A. D. Philip
£13,508 to £18,363

New St. Andrew's House,
Edinburgh EH1 3SX
[031–556 8400]

MANAGEMENT GROUP SUPPORT STAFF
Principal, D. Macniven .... £13,508 to £18,363

CENTRAL SERVICES
Deputy Secretary (Central Services), I. D. Penman
£38,325 to £39,250

Establishment Division
Under Secretary, A. H. Bishop (*Principal Establishment Officer*) .... £30,975 to £31,750
Assistant Secretaries, Miss M. Maclean; J. Hamill
£20,964 to £25,533
Senior Principals, J. N. Davison; A. B. Fairweather, T.D.; W. A. Smith .... £17,000 to £22,926
Principals, W. E. Bennet; J. Blaikie; D. J. Chalmers; D. A. Christie; W. Davidson; M. Finnigan; J. R. M. Flucker; H. J. Graham; I. C. Henderson; D. Macniven; Mrs. J. Niven; B. V. Surridge; Miss M. A. Wood .... £13,508 to £18,363

Directorate of Computers and Telecommunications
Broomhouse Drive, Edinburgh
[031–443 4040]
Computer Services
Manager (Assistant Secretary), J. Duffy
£20,944 to £25,533

Deputy Manager (Senior Principal), C. B. Knox
£17,000 to £22,926
Principals, A. M. Brown; J. A. Brown; I. W. Goodwin
£13,508 to £18,363

Telecommunications
St. Andrew's House, Edinburgh
(031–556 8501)

Director, A. F. Harrison .... £17,000 to £22,926

Finance Division
Finance Group
Under Secretary, K. J. MacKenzie (*Principal Finance Officer*) .... £30,975 to £31,750
Assistant Secretaries, J. W. Elvidge; I. G. F. Gray; T. E. McGreevy; G. Murray; H. Robertson, M.B.E.
£20,964 to £25,533
Senior Principals, I. Nicholson; W. T. Tait; A. Walker .... £17,000 to £22,926
Principals, J. S. Aldridge; A. G. Beattie; S. W. E. Davidson; L. P. S. Dunbar; T. W. Forsyth; I. W. Gordon; D. A. Howe; W. A. Lamberton; I. A. McLeod; D. R. Mayer; W. Moyes; D. F. Middleton; D. Muir; I. M. Nicol; J. Porter; I. M. Smith; I. T. Wallace; R. K. West; R. G. B. Wilkie
£13,508 to £18,363

Local Government Finance Group
Assistant Secretaries, N. G. Campbell; B. V. Philp
£20,964 to £25,533
Principals, P. S. Collings; C. C. Forsyth; J. A. Rennie; T. Winwick .... £13,508 to £18,363

Solicitor's Office
(*For the Scottish Departments and certain U.K. services including H.M. Treasury, in Scotland.*)
Solicitor, A. A. McMillan £36,500
Deputy Solicitor, R. Brodie £29,500
Divisional Solicitors, J. B. Allan; K. F. Barclay; N. W. Boe; *R. Eadie; G. Jackson; J. L. Jamieson; *Mrs. L. A. Lilliker; J. A. Stewart; T. G. Walters
£20,964 to £25,533
*Seconded to Scottish Law Commission

Scottish Information Office
(*For the Scottish Departments and certain U.K. services*)
Director, C. F. Corbett .... £20,964 to £25,533
Deputy Director, D. C. M. Beveridge
£17,000 to £22,926

Statistics
Chief Statistician, A. M. Burnside
£20,964 to £25,533

Inquiry Reporters
16 Waterloo Place, Edinburgh
[031–556 9191]
Chief Reporter, A. G. Bell £29,500
Deputy Chief Reporter, W. D. Campbell
£20,964 to £25,533

DEPARTMENT OF AGRICULTURE AND FISHERIES FOR SCOTLAND
Chesser House, 500 Gorgie Road, Edinburgh
EH11 3AW
[031–443 4020]
Dover House, Whitehall, London, SW1A 2AU
[01–233 3000]

Secretary, L. P. Hamilton £36,500
Under Secretary, D. G. Mackay £29,500
Fisheries Secretary, B. Gordon £29,500
Assistant Secretaries, T. A. Cameron; A. D. F. Findlay; J. W. L. Lonie; G. G. Lyall; L. V. McEwan; A. B. Scott; G. M. D. Thomson; E. J. Weeple; I. M. Whitelaw .... £20,964 to £25,533

Principals, D. J. Baird; C. Barbour; D. I. Dalgetty; D. R. Dickson; J. G. Donnelly; J. H. F. Finnie; A. Johnston; F. J. Lawrie; A. Lindsey; A. Lister; B. E. McAdam; J. McGhee; C. K. McIntosh; D. Reid; W. B. Ritchie; D. A. Robertson; D. M. Rowand; N. A. Stewart; D. Stott; R. J. Walker
£13,508 to £18,363
Chief Agricultural Officer (Under Secretary), C. Mackay .... £30,975 to £31,750
Deputy Chief Agricultural Officer, J. F. Hutcheson
£20,964 to £25,533
Assistant Chief Agricultural Officers, W. K. Boyd; R. Macdonald; W. A. Macgregor; G. M. B. Redpath; J. I. Woodrow .... £17,000 to £22,926
Chief Agricultural Economist, J. M. Dunn, D.Phil.
£17,000 to £22,926
Chief Fatstock Officer, A. Bain ... £13,508 to £18,363
Chief Food and Dairy Officer, M. E. M. Anderson
£14,538 to £19,567
Chief Surveyor, N. Taylor .... £17,000 to £22,926
Scientific Adviser, A. M. Raven, PH.D.
£20,964 to £25,533
Senior Principal Scientific Officers, T. W. Hegarty, PH.D.; D. Thornton .... £17,000 to £22,926

Royal Botanic Garden
Inverleith Row, Edinburgh EH3 5LR
[031–552 7171]

Regius Keeper, Prof. D. M. Henderson, C.B.E., F.R.S.E.
£20,964 to £25,533
Assistant Keeper, J. Cullen, PH.D.   £17,000 to £22,926

Agricultural Scientific Services
East Craigs, Edinburgh EH12 8NJ
[031–339 2355]

Director, D. C. Graham, PH.D., F.R.S.E.
£20,964 to £25,533
Deputy Director, R. D. Seaton ... £17,000 to £22,926
Senior Principal Scientific Officers, J. R. Cutler; M. J. Richardson .... £17,000 to £22,926

Fisheries Research Services
Marine Laboratory, P.O. Box 101,
Victoria Road, Torry, Aberdeen AB9 8DB
[0224 876544]

Director, Prof. A. D. McIntyre, D.SC., F.R.S.E. . £26,909
Deputy Director, A. D. Hawkins, PH.D.
£20,964 to £25,533
Senior Principal Scientific Officers, R. Jones; D. N. MacLennan; A. L. S. Munro, PH.D.; C. S. Wardle, PH.D. .... £17,000 to £22,926

Freshwater Fisheries Laboratory,
Faskally, Pitlochry, Perthshire PH16 5LB
[0796 2060]

Senior Principal Scientific Officers, R. G. J. Shelton, PH.D.; J. E. Thorpe, PH.D. ...... £17,000 to £22,926

Sea Fisheries Inspectorate

Chief Inspector of Sea Fisheries, J. W. S. Kinnaird
£17,000 to £22,926
Inspector of Salmon and Freshwater Fisheries, R. B. Williamson .... £12,867 to £16,462
Marine Superintendent, Captain D. R. Corse
£22,332 to £22,692

Crofters Commission
4/6 Castle Wynd, Inverness IV2 3EQ
[0463 237231]

Chairman (part-time), J. F. M. Macleod £18,500
Members (part-time), A. I. Macarthur; N. A. MacAskill (£12,025); A. Fraser, PH.D.; B. T. Hunter; D. A. Morrison; P. Morrison; I. G. Munro £6,013
Secretary, I. A. Macpherson ..... £17,000 to £22,926

Red Deer Commission
Knowsley, 82 Fairfield Road, Inverness IV3 5LH
[0463 231751]

Chairman, I. K. Mackenzie £9,715
Secretary, N. H. McCulloch ...... £10,980 to £13,801

SCOTTISH DEVELOPMENT DEPARTMENT
New St. Andrew's House, Edinburgh EH1 3SZ
[031–556 8400]
Dover House, Whitehall, London, SW1A 2AU
[01–233 3000]

Secretary, T. R. H. Godden, C.B. £36,500
Under Secretaries, H. H. Mills; J. Walker
£30,975 to £31,750
Director, Historic Buildings and Monuments, T. M. Band.
Assistant Secretaries, Ms. L. Clare; M. J. P. Cunliffe; D. J. Essery; J. S. B. Martin; I. Maxwell; K. W. Moore; F. H. Orr; G. Robson; N. W. Smith; R. E. Smith; Mrs. G. M. Stewart; Miss M. B. Tait
£20,964 to £25,533
Principals, M. T. Affolter; J. R. Brown; D. J. Christie; W. M. Giles; R. Gordon; J. L. Helm; J. C. Henderson; I. P. Hetherington; A. R. Irons; J. W. H. Irvine; J. C. Judson; G. M. Lee; B. J. Lincoln; Miss I. M. Low; C. M. A. Lugton; G. A. McHugh; I. J. MacKenzie; P. M. McLaren; K. Macrae; Mrs. M. J. Martyn; A. J. Matheson; J. Meldrum; D. N. G. Reid; P. J. Robinson; D. M. Rowand; P. M. Russell; J. M. Thornton; R. Walker; J. O. Wastle; M. R. Wilson .... £13,508 to £18,363

Professional Staff

Chief Engineer, S. C. Agnew £29,500
Deputy Chief Engineer, R. McGillivray
20,964 to £25,533
Assistant Chief Engineers, W. Ferguson; N. G. Semple; J. O. Thorburn ...... £17,000 to £22,926
Director of Building and Chief Architect, J. E. Gibbons, PH.D............................ £29,500
Deputy Director of Building and Deputy Chief Architect, M. R. Miller .... £20,964 to £25,533
Deputy Director of Building and Chief Quantity Surveyor, D. C. Russell .... £20,964 to £25,533
Assistant Director and Deputy Chief Quantity Surveyor, A. Duncan .... £17,000 to £22,926
Assistant Director and Chief Mechanical and Electrical Engineer, R. A. E. Quartermaine
£17,000 to £22,926
Assistant Directors, A. R. H. Bott; H. R. McGallum; R. W. Naismith; R. I. Watson .. £17,000 to £22,926
Chief Planner, W. D. C. Lyddon, C.B., D.Litt. . £29,500
Deputy Chief Planner, A. Mackenzie
£20,964 to £25,533
Assistant Chief Planners, D. R. Dare; A. W. Denham; S. G. Fulton; P. D. McGovern, PH.D.
£17,000 to £22,926
Chief Research Officer, C. C. MacDonald
£20,964 to £25,533
Senior Principal Research Officers, C. P. A. Levein, PH.D.; C. L. Wood .... £17,000 to £22,926
Chief Road Engineer, J. A. M. MacKenzie ... £28,583
Deputy Chief Engineer (Roads), G. S. Marshall
£20,964 to £25,533
Deputy Chief Engineer (Bridges), W. R. Varley
£20,964 to £25,533
Assistant Chief Engineers, J. Patience; R. D. Udall; (one vacancy) .... £17,000 to £22,926
H.M. Chief Industrial Pollution Inspector, I. W. W. Wright....................... £20,964 to £25,533
Chief Estates Officer, R. I. K. White
£17,000 to £22,926
Principal Inspector of Ancient Monuments for Scotland, I. MacIvor .... £16,757 to £19,314
Principal Inspector of Historic Buildings, D. M. Walker...................... £16,757 to £19,314

INDUSTRY DEPARTMENT FOR SCOTLAND
New St. Andrew's House, Edinburgh
[031–556 8400]
and
Dover House, Whitehall, S.W.1
[01–233 3000]

Secretary and Chief Economic Adviser to the Secretary of State for Scotland, R. G. L. McCrone, C.B., Ph.D. £36,500
Under Secretaries, J. F. Laing; W. W. Scott
£30,975 to £31,750
Assistant Secretaries, D. Connelly; R. S. Crofts; W. J. Fearnley; Miss E. A. Mackay; A. M. Russell
£20,964 to £25,533
Senior Economic Advisers, J. A. Peat; W. M. McNie .... £20,964 to £25,533
Principals, A. C. King; A. W. Fraser; M. A. Grant; D. M. Henderson; W. A. McKenzie; Mrs. R. N. Menlowe; Ms. J. E. Morgan; B. Naylor; D. N. G. Reid; Mrs. A. Robson; P. M. Russell; D. R. Semple
£13,508 to £18,363

Industrial Expansion
Alhambra House, 45 Waterloo Street, Glasgow
[041–248 2855]

Under Secretary, G. R. Wilson ... £30,975 to £31,750
Industrial Adviser, D. E. Guy.
Assistant Secretaries, S. F. Hampson; P. McKinlay
£20,964 to £25,533
Senior Principals, J. E. Milne, O.B.E.; G. M. Stark
£17,000 to £22,926
Principals, W. C. Alison; D. A. Brew; C. H. Coulthard; D. J. Fowles; E. D. F. McGaughrin; A. J. Stewart
£13,508 to £18,363

Locate in Scotland
120 Bothwell Street, Glasgow
[041–248 2700]

Director, I. S. Robertson £26,909
Senior Principal, J. Laydon ..... £17,000 to £22,926
Principal, (vacant).
Assistant Secretary, D. Harrison (*U.S.A.*)

SCOTTISH EDUCATION DEPARTMENT
New St. Andrew's House, St. James Centre,
Edinburgh
[031–556 8400]
and
Dover House, Whitehall, London, S.W.1
[01–233 3000]

Secretary, J. A. Scott, L.V.O. £36,500
Under Secretaries, R. R. Hillhouse; I. M. Wilson, C.B. .... £30,975 to £31,750
Assistant Secretaries, D. A. Campbell; D. J. Crawley; J. R. Cuthbert, Ph.D. (*Chief Statistician*); E. C. Davison; E. W. Frizzell; J. Linn; E. C. Reavley; D. Wishart .... £20,964 to £25,533
Senior Principal, G. E. Brewerton £17,000 to £22,926
Principals, I. R. Anderson; Mrs. E. E. R. Barnwell; T. Blacklock; R. G. H. Brown; D. G. Campbell; M. A. Duffy; T. B. Haig, O.B.E.; J. C. Halley; F. H. Hunter; M. J. Hunter; A. R. Irons; Miss J. M. Lawson; J. McCallum; J. C. McLean; N. MacLeod; Miss M. M. Marshall; I. A. Perrett; N. Pittman; I. M. Watt; W. Weir .... £13,508 to £18,363

H.M. Inspectors of Schools

Senior Chief Inspector, J. A. Ferguson £29,500
Deputy Senior Chief Inspectors, W. R. Ritchie; H. F. Smith £26,909
Chief Inspectors, W. F. L. Bigwood; L. Clark; A. H. Ferguson; T. N. Gallacher; J. Howgego; R. S. Johnston; S. E. McClelland, Ph.D.; D. W. Mack; A. M. Rankin; J. H. Thomson .... £20,964 to £25,533

Inspectors, J. N. Alison; M. T. J. Axford; P. Banks; W. T. Beveridge; Mrs. W. Binnie; J. Boyes; Miss C. L. Boyle; M. J. Brown; Mrs. M. M. Browning; J. W. Burdin; D. C. Burgess; Miss G. C. Campbell; T. N. Carr; D. G. Carter; C. Cleall; A. W. Constable; M. Q. Cramb; A. H. B. Davidson; G. B. Debling; G. A. Dell; R. F. Dick; J. C. Dignan; G. H. C. Donaldson; J. T. Donaldson; D. W. Duncan; Miss K. M. Fairweather; A. W. Finlayson; B. Fryer; A. R. Gallon; K. G. Gavin; A. B. Giovanazzi; G. P. D. Gordon; G. D. Gray, Ph.D.; T. O. Greig; R. A. Hawke; J. Hay, Ph.D.; K. A. Hope; L. A. Hunter; M. Jack; J. Jackson, Ph.D.; E. S. Kelly; D. E. Kelso; J. Kiely; D. G. Kirkpatrick; I. Lawson; R. E. Lygo; M. McAllan; J. McAlpine; I. M. MacAskill; L. McCallum; D. McCalman; H. K. McCorkindale; J. J. McDonald; Mrs. M. A. Macfarlane; A. S. McGlynn; Ms. I. S. McGregor; H. M. MacLaren; C. R. MacLean; M. Macleod; D. R. McNicoll; A. J. Macpherson; A. Maltby; H. L. Martin; A. C. T. Mascarenhas; G. Mathison; W. M. Mein; Mrs. J. M. Millar; A. Milne; S. Milne, Ph.D.; J. Mitchell; Miss E. R. Mowat; R. H. Nelson; B. Nickerson, Ph.D.; A. M. Noble, Ph.D.; D. A. Osler; I. P. Pascoe; J. Picken; Miss A. H. M. Prain; R. B. Prescott; A. M. Rankin; T. A. Rankin; J. C. Rankine; S. A. Ritchie; W. M. Roach, Ph.D.; I. D. S. Robertson; J. N. Robertson; A. L. Robson; M. Roebuck; J. Rorrison; D. M. Russell; A. L. Small; E. P. Spencer; H. Stalker; A. M. Steele; Mrs. J. A. Stewart; W. P. Stewart; J. W. Thomson; R. M. S. Tuck; G. Wallis; R. S. Weir; Miss G. A. White; R. G. Wilson; J. G. L. Wright; D. B. Young; R. W. J. Young, Ph.D.
£15,688 to £22,933

Social Work Services Group
43 Jeffrey Street, Edinburgh EH1 1DN
[031–556 9233]

The Social Work Services Group, which is attached to the Scottish Education Department, administers the provisions of the Social Work (Scotland) Act, 1968.

Under-Secretary, D. A. Leitch .... £30,975 to £31,750
Assistant Secretaries, D. A. Bennet; R. E. S. Robinson; D. Stevenson .... £20,964 to £25,533
Senior Principal, G. W. Tucker .. £17,000 to £22,926
Principals, D. J. Baird; Miss A. E. Hamilton; D. G. Kerr; J. C. McLean; I. F. Munro; W. F. Robertson; D. Stewart .... £13,508 to £18,363
Chief Social Work Adviser, D. Colvin £26,909
Deputy Chief Social Work Advisers, D. S. Roulston; D. K. Naik .... £20,964 to £25,533
Senior Advisers, A. C. Adams; Miss D. M. Boardman; Ms. M. L. Hunt; W. J. McCollam; F. A. O'Leary; A. R. Sabine; J. I. Smith .... £19,069 to £23,898

SCOTTISH HOME AND HEALTH DEPARTMENT
St. Andrew's House,
Edinburgh EH1 3DE
[031–556 8501]
Dover House, Whitehall, London, SW1A 2AU
[01–233 3000]

Secretary, W. K. Reid, C.B. £36,500
Under Secretaries, W. Baird; Miss P. A. Cox; J. E. Fraser; H. Morison .... £30,975 to £31,750
Assistant Secretaries, G. P. H. Aitken, T.D.; G. A. Anderson; J. W. Barron; C. M. Baxter; R. J. W. Clark; Mrs. E. C. G. Craghill; J. G. Davies; K. W. McKay; A. M. Macpherson; G. N. Munro; N. E. Sharp; J. W. Sinclair .... £20,964 to £25,533
Principals, D. C. Anderson; P. A. Brady; D. H. Brown; J. T. Brown; R. A. Catto; J. A. Clare; D. J. Davidson; D. H. F. Dee; M. Ewart; P. J. Fleming; J. D. Gallagher; C. A. Heggie; C. D. Henderson; W. A. Howat; N. D. Ingram; D. K. C. Jeffrey; J. F.

Kerr; R. C. Lawson; S. M. Liddle; M. J. Lowndes; R. S. T. MacEwen; K. B. T. MacKenzie; D. C. Macnab; A. J. Matheson; C. Moir; Mrs. N. S. Munro; R. Patton; G. A. Paul; D. A. Robertson; A. J. Rushworth; A. Simmen; T. Spence; A. Stephenson; P. D. Stephenson; I. C. Stewart; R. S. Stewart; R. Tait; G. P. Walker; A. W. Wallace; A. G. Young £13,508 to £18,363

Medical Services

Chief Medical Officer, I. S. Macdonald £36,500
Deputy Chief Medical Officer, G. A. Scott £29,500
Principal Medical Officers, M. Ashley-Miller; Margaret Hennigan; A. D. McIntyre; A. T. B. Moir; R. A. Ratcliff; B. C. S. Slater, o.b.e.; A. B. Young £26,594
Senior Medical Officers, R. E. G. Aitken; J. T. Boyd; P. W. Brooks; R. G. Covell; D. C. Drummond; J. B. P. Ferguson; C. F. Fleming; G. I. Forbes; W. Forbes; J. M. Forrester; G. Gilray; L. F. Howitt; H. McBain; R. M. Melville, o.b.e.; J. A. Morton; J. S. Patterson; O. A. Thores £25,533
Senior Regional Medical Officers, I. G. Conn; A. C. McBlane; D. E. Walker £26,594
Regional Medical Officers, P. I. Brown; Elspeth C. Carrick; J. A. Fergusson; T. E. S. Fergusson; W. M. Gilmour; Elizabeth M. Melville; J. B. Morris; H. D. R. Munro; W. M. Reid; P. I. T. Walker £16,597 to £23,515
Chief Scientist, Prof. A. P. M. Forrest.
Chief Dental Officer, N. K. Colquhoun £26,594
Deputy Chief Dental Officer, J. Gall £25,533
Regional Dental Officers, T. G. L. Bell; F. D. Murray; G. A. Reid ....£16,597 to £23,515
Chief Nursing Officer, Miss M. G. Auld £28,899
Chief Pharmacist, G. Calder ..... £15,605 to £20,794

Miscellaneous Appointments

H.M. Chief Inspector of Constabulary, A. Morrison, c.v.o., q.p.m. £39,488
H.M. Chief Inspector of Prisons (part-time), D. A. P. Barry, c.b.e. £15,320
Commandant, Scottish Police College, Maj.-Gen. D. C. Alexander, c.b. £29,499
H.M. Chief Inspector of Fire Services, R. J. Knowlton, c.b.e., q.f.s.m. ....£25,881 to £28,915
Commandant, Scottish Fire Service Training School, A. Jones, o.b.e., q.f.s.m. ......£15,201 to £15,900
Secretary, Scottish Health Service Planning Council, (vacant).

Prisons Group
St. Margaret's House, 151 London Road,
Edinburgh EH8 7TQ
[031–661 6181]

Director of Scottish Prison Service, A. M. Thomson £27,791
Assistant Secretary, Deputy Director (Administration), T. J. Kelly ....£20,964 to £25,533
Assistant Controller, Deputy Director (Operations), D. M. MacIver £26,803
Assistant Secretary, Deputy Director (Personnel and Supplies), R. D. Jackson ....£20,964 to £25,533
Senior Principal, Deputy Director (Regime Services), T. Collinson ....£17,000 to £22,926

Prison Governors

Aberdeen, M. J. Milne .... £14,456 to £17,581
Barlinnie, A. Gallacher £23,735
Barlinnie Special Unit, W. Davidson £14,456 to £17,581
Castle Huntly Young Offenders Institution, J. S. Bertram......................£14,456 to £17,581
Cornton Vale, J. Meiklejohn ...... 17,804 to £21,297
Dumfries Prison, G. R. Bond ..... £14,456 to £17,581

Dungavel, Strathaven, R. R. Glen £14,456 to £17,581
Edinburgh, J. M. Brownlee £23,735
Friarton Detention Centre, R. Park £12,181 to £14,128
Glenochil Young Offenders Institution and Detention Centre, W. McVey £23,735
Greenock, A. R. Walker .... £14,456 to £17,581
Inverness, F. Sankey............ £14,456 to £17,581
Longriggend Remand Institution, A. M. Webster £14,456 to £17,581
Low Moss, J. Milne............. £14,456 to £17,581
Noranside Young Offenders Institution, L. W. G. Hewitson....................£14,456 to £17,581
Penninghame, D. F. Houston .... £12,181 to £14,128
Perth, W. G. Walker .... £17,804 to £21,297
Peterhead, A. J. Smith £23,735
Polmont Young Offenders Institution, G. B. Duncan £17,804 to £21,297
Shotts, G. W. Jackson .... £14,456 to £17,581
Scottish Prison Service College, A. Thomson £14,456 to £17,581

Mental Welfare Commission for Scotland
22 Melville Street, Edinburgh EH3 7NS
[031–225 7034]

Chairman, P. C. Millar, o.b.e.
Commissioners, Prof. Annie T. Altschul, c.b.e.; P. H. Brodie; Prof. T. D. Campbell; R. G. Davis; Mrs. J. B. M. Ellis, o.b.e.; Ms. A. M. Green; Mrs. A. I. Huggins; D. A. Macdonald, o.b.e.; Mrs. H. S. Mein; Dr. H. S. Ross; H. F. Smith, m.b.e.; J. G. Sutherland.
Medical Commissioners, H. C. Fowlie; W. Boyd.
Secretary, J. S. Graham.

Counsel to the Secretary of State for Scotland under the Private Legislation Procedure (Scotland) Act, 1936 (50 Frederick Street, Edinburgh)
Senior Counsel, G. S. Douglas, q.c.
Junior Counsel, P. K. Vandore, q.c.

NATIONAL HEALTH SERVICE, SCOTLAND
Health Boards

Argyll and Clyde, Gilmour House, Paisley. *Chairman*, J. D. Ryan. *Secretary*, A. K. Skirving.
Ayrshire and Arran, P.O. Box 13, Hunters Avenue, Ayr. *Chairman*, W. S. Fyfe. *Secretary*, M. S. Abbott.
Borders, Huntlyburn, Melrose, Roxburghshire. *Chairman*, J. Gibb. *Secretary*, D. A. Peters.
Dumfries and Galloway, Nithbank, Dumfries. *Chairman*, J. A. M. McIntyre. *Secretary*, R. B. K. MacGregor.
Fife, Glenrothes House, North Street, Glenrothes. *Chairman*, J. C. Balfour. *Secretary*, I. G. Dorward.
Forth Valley, 33 Spittal Street, Stirling. *Chairman*, L. S. M. Hynd. *Secretary*, J. M. Eckford.
Grampian, 1–7 Albyn Place, Aberdeen. *Chairman*, C. W. Ellis. *Secretary*, Dr. H. R. M. Wilson.
Greater Glasgow, 225 Bath Street, Glasgow. *Chairman*, D. F. Mcquaker. *Secretary*, R. D. R. Gardner, c.b.e.
Highland, Reay House, 17 Old Edinburgh Road, Inverness. *Chairman*, J. McWilliam. *Secretary*, R. R. W. Stewart.
Lanarkshire, 14 Beckford Street, Hamilton, Lanarkshire. *Chairman*, Mrs. B. M. Gunn, o.b.e. *Secretary*, F. Clark.
Lothian, 11 Drumsheugh Gardens, Edinburgh. *Chairman*, A. Findlay. *Secretary*, R. Mitchell.
Orkney, Balfour Hospital, New Scapa Road, Kirkwall, Orkney. *Chairman*, J. D. M. Robertson. *Secretary*, J. A. Muir.
Shetland, 28 Burgh Road, Lerwick. *Chairman*, Mrs. F. Graines. *Secretary*, D. C. March.

Tayside, P.O. Box 75, Vernonholme, Riverside Drive, Dundee. *Chairman*, D. B. Grant. *Secretary*, G. G. Savage, O.B.E.
Western Isles, 37 South Beach Street, Stornoway, Isle of Lewis. *Chairman*, Mrs. M. A. Macmillan. *Secretary*, J. Glover.

Common Services Agency
Trinity Park House, South Trinity Road, Edinburgh
Secretary, J. R. Y. Mutch. *Treasurer*, J. W. Morrison.

GENERAL REGISTER OFFICE (Scotland)
New Register House, Edinburgh EH1 3YT
[031–556 3952]

Registrar General, Dr. C. M. Glennie £24,077
Deputy Registrar General, J. N. Randall
£19,243 to £23,159
Statisticians, D. Salmond; D. A. Orr
£12,399 to £16,656
Principals, G. F. Baird; I. G. Bowie; I. G. Dewar
£12,399 to £16,656

SEA FISH INDUSTRY AUTHORITY
Sea Fisheries House, 10 Young Street,
Edinburgh EH2 4JQ
[031–225 2515]

Chairman, J. P. Rettie, T.D.
Chief Executive, J. C. H. Richman.
Deputy Chief Executive, P. D. Chaplin.
Finance Director, A. Downie.
Technical Director, A. G. Hopper.
Marketing Director, R. M. Kennedy.
Secretary, R. A. Davie.

SOCIAL SCIENCE RESEARCH COUNCIL
See Economic and Social Research Council

OFFICE OF THE SOCIAL SECURITY COMMISSIONERS
6 Grosvenor Gardens, SW1W 0DH
[01–730 9236]
23 Melville Street, Edinburgh EH3 7PW
[031–225 2201]
16 Park Grove, Cardiff CF1 3BN
[0222 387898]

The Commissioners are the final Statutory Authority to decide claims under the Social Security Acts, and the Child Benefit Acts.
Chief Commissioner, L. J. Bromley, Q.C.
Secretary, Miss H. Baker.

HER MAJESTY'S STATIONERY OFFICE
St. Crispins, Duke Street, Norwich NR3 1PD
[0603–622211]

Her Majesty's Stationery Office was established in 1786 and is the British Government's central organization for the supply of printing, binding, office supplies and office machinery of all kinds, for the Public Service at home and abroad; H.M.S.O. is also the Government's publisher and has bookshops for the sale of Government publications in London, Edinburgh, Manchester, Bristol, Birmingham and Belfast. H.M.S.O. obtains most of its supplies from commercial sources by competitive tender, except that about one quarter of its printing requirements is done in its own printing works.
Since April 1, 1980, H.M.S.O. has been a trading fund established under the Government Trading Funds Act, 1973.
Controller and Chief Executive, W. J. Sharp, C.B.
£36,500
Director General of Printing and Publishing, K. A. Allen £27,791

Director General of Corporate Services, A. A. Smith
£26,909
Head of Internal Audit and Manpower Branch, C. G. Wood .... £13,508 to £18,363
Adviser on Typography, J. Miles.

Publications Division
Director, C. J. Penn .... £20,964 to £25,533
General Manager Publications Centre, S. M. Rae .... £17,000 to £22,926
Deputy Directors, A. M. Cole; B. J. Jackson; A. A. Smith; J. Saville; B. Wilson ... £13,508 to £18,363

Supply Division
Director, D. W. Ray .... £20,964 to £25,533
Deputy Directors, P. Barnard; Miss V. Bailey; A. A. Gummett; C. E. Harrold; F. R. Payne; C. T. B. L. Robinson .... £13,508 to £18,363

Finance and Planning Division
Director, A. J. Davies .... £20,964 to £25,533
Head of Systems Co-ordination, C. N. Southgate
£13,508 to £18,363
Deputy Directors, V. G. Bell; J. J. Dain; R. T. Wykes
£13,508 to £18,363

Personnel Services Division
Director, D. J. Balls .... £20,964 to £25,533
Deputy Directors, R. C. Barnard; R. A. Dunn
£13,508 to £18,363

Industrial Personnel Division
Director, D. J. Wintle .... £17,000 to £22,926
Deputy Directors, M. B. Moore; G. A. James
£13,508 to £18,363

Computer Services Division
Director, J. V. Moore .... £17,000 to £22,926
Deputy Directors, B. L. Cleland; M. J. M. Salt; D. C. Kerry .... £13,508 to £18,363

Production Division
Director, E. B. McKendrick ...... £20,964 to £25,533
Director of Parliamentary and Classified Printing, D. G. Forbes .... £17,000 to £22,926
Director of Reprographics, R. S. Moore
£13,508 to £18,363
Printing Press Managers, G. H. R. Parfitt; A. Mackie; E. Hendry .... £13,508 to £18,363
Head of Works Management Accounting, R. W. Chapman .... £13,508 to £18,363

Technical Services
Head of Technical Services (Origination), T. J. Soutar
£13,508 to £18,363
Head of Technical Services (Printing), H. S. Todd
£13,508 to £18,363
Head of Engineering Services, Safety Adviser & Energy Manager, R. Miller .... £13,739 to £16,497

Print Procurement Division
Director, M. D. Lynn .... £20,964 to £25,533
Deputy Directors, K. J. Lowe; P. J. Macdonald; J. McDonald .... £13,508 to £18,363
Deputy Director Management Accounting, P. J. Macdonald .... £12,399 to £16,656

Scotland
Bankhead Avenue, Edinburgh EH11 4AB
Bookshop: 13A Castle Street, Edinburgh EH2 3AR
Director, G. A. H. Turner .... £13,508 to £18,363

Northern Ireland
Chichester Street, Belfast BT1 4PS
Retail and Trade Bookshop: Chichester Street, Belfast BT1 4JY
Director, Miss V. J. Wilson ...... £10,980 to £13,801

London

Britannia House, 7 Trinity Street, SE1 1DA

Publications Centre: 51 Nine Elms Lane, SW8 5BR.
Bookshops: Retail—49 High Holborn, W.C.1.
Wholesale and Post Orders—P. O. Box 276, SW8 5DT.

Manchester

Broadway, Chadderton, Oldham, Lancs. OL9 9QH

Bookshop: 9–21 Princess Street, Manchester M60 8AS.

Bristol

Ashton Vale Road, Bristol BS3 2HN

Bookshop: Southey House, Wine Street, Bristol BS1 2BQ.

Birmingham

Bookshop: 258 Broad Street, Birmingham B1 2HE.

STATUTE LAW COMMITTEE
House of Lords, SW1A 0PW

Chairman, The Lord Chancellor.
Vice-Chairman, Mr. Justice Ralph Gibson.
Members, The Attorney-General; the Lord Advocate; N. J. Adamson, C.B., Q.C.; P. K. Archer, Q.C., M.P.; J. B. Bailey, C.B.; K. A. Bradshaw, C.B.; The Lord Brightman, P.C.; Sir Antony Buck, Q.C., M.P.; Sir Brian Cubbon, K.C.B.; Sir George Engle, K.C.B.; The Lord Fraser of Tullybelton; Sir William Fraser, K.C.B.; H. W. Gamon, C.B.E.; Sir Michael Kerry, K.C.B.; The Lord Lowry, P.C.; The Hon. Lord Maxwell; J. Morris, Q.C., M.P.; Sir George Moseley, K.C.B.; Miss A. Mueller, C.B.; Sir Derek Oulton, K.C.B.; D. Rippengal, C.B., Q.C.; J. C. Sainty; W. J. Sharp, C.B.; T. R. F. Skemp, C.B.
Secretary, C. A. J. Mitchell.

Statutory Publications Office
Queen Anne's Chambers,
28 Broadway, SW1H 9JS
[01–273 3000]

Editor, C. R. Crockett.

OFFICE OF TELECOMMUNICATIONS
Atlantic House, 50 Holborn Viaduct, EC1N 2HQ
[01–353 4020]

OFTEL is a non-Ministerial Government Department headed by a Director-General, which has been given responsibility for supervising telecommunications activities in the U.K.

Its principal functions are to ensure that holders of telecommunications licences comply with their licence conditions; to maintain and promote effective competition in telecommunications; to promote, in respect of prices, quality and variety the interests of consumers, purchasers and other users of telecommunication services and apparatus.

The Director-General has a duty to promote competition in the provision of telecommunication services and in the supply and production of telecommunication apparatus. He has powers to deal with anti-competitive practices and monopoly situations.

The Director-General also has a duty to consider all complaints and representations about telecommunication apparatus and services.
Director-General, Prof. B. Carsberg.
Deputy Director-General, W. R. B. Wigglesworth.
Director of P.T.O. Licensing, A. W. G. Catto.
Director of Apparatus Approval, J. P. Compton.
Head of Consumer Affairs, Mrs. J. Percy-Davis.
Head of Information, D. C. Redding.

NATIONAL THEATRE BOARD
South Bank, SE1 9PX
[01–928 2033]

Chairman, The Lord Rayne.
Members, R. Baird; R. Brew, C.B.E.; T. Burrill; The Lord Chorley; R. Clutton; J. Hannam, M.P.; H. Hinds; Sonia Melchett; R. M. Mills; The Lord Mishcon; Sir Derek Mitchell, K.C.B., C.V.O.; J. Mortimer, Q.C.; P. Pitt; The Lady Plowden, D.B.E.; Lois Sieff; J. Whitney.
Secretary, D. Gosling.

DEPARTMENT OF TRADE AND INDUSTRY
1 Victoria Street, SW1H 0ET
[01–215 7877]

The Department is responsible for:
(a) International trade policy, including the promotion of U.K. trade interests in the European Community, G.A.T.T., O.E.C.D., U.N.C.T.A.D. and other international organizations.
(b) Under the direction of the British Overseas Trade Board, the promotion of U.K. exports and assistance to exporters.
(c) Policy in relation to industry, including the general promotion of the interests of industry and assistance to industry; specific interest in all manufacturing and service industries apart from those covered by other Departments; regional policy and regional industrial assistance (some of this applying only to England); policy towards small firms; and policy in relation to the public bodies British Shipbuilders, the British Steel Corporation, the Post Office, British Telecom and the British Technology Group.
(d) Competition policy and consumer protection, including relations with the Office of Fair Trading and the Monopolies and Mergers Commission, and the National Weights and Measures Laboratory.
(e) Policy on science and technology and research and development matters, standards and designs, support for innovation, and the administration of the National Physical Laboratory, National Engineering Laboratory, Warren Spring Laboratory and the Laboratory of the Government Chemist.
(f) The administration of company legislation and the Companies Registration Office; the Insolvency Service; the regulation of the insurance industry; the regulation of radio frequencies; and the Patent Office.
(g) The Business Statistics Office.

Salary List

Secretary of State	£31,271
Ministers of State	£21,881
Parliamentary Under Secretaries of State	£16,411
Permanent Secretary (Grade 1)	£52,750
Deputy Secretary (Grade 2)	£38,325 to £39,250
The Solicitor (Grade 2)	£38,325 to £39,250
Under Secretary (Grade 3)	£30,975 to £31,750
Grade 4	£26,909
Grade 5	£20,964 to £25,533
Grade 6	£17,000 to £22,926
Principal	£13,508 to £18,363
Controller, Export Licensing Branch	£13,508 to £18,363
Inspector General of the Insolvency Service	£29,500
Deputy Inspectors General	£25,975
Inspector of Companies	£25,975

Research Establishments

Director, National Physical Laboratory	£32,350
Director, National Engineering Laboratory	£29,500
Government Chemist	£29,500
Director, Warren Spring Laboratory	£29,500

Secretary of State for Trade and Industry and President of the Board of Trade, THE RT. HON. NORMAN TEBBIT, M.P.
  Principal Private Secretary, J. F. Mogg.
  Parliamentary Private Secretary, I. Mills, M.P.
Minister for Trade, THE RT. HON. PAUL CHANNON, M.P.
  Private Secretary, M. Cocks.
  Parliamentary Private Secretary, D. Atkinson, M.P.
Minister of State for Information Technology, GEOFFREY EDWIN PATTIE, M.P.
  Private Secretary, T. P. Abraham.
Minister of State for Industry, NORMAN LAMONT, M.P.
  Private Secretary, E. N. R. Hosker.
Parliamentary Under Secretary of State for Corporate and Consumer Affairs, Alexander Fletcher, M.P.
  Private Secretary, D. P. Griffiths.
Parliamentary Under Secretary of State for Industry, John Butcher, M.P.
  Private Secretary, D. M. Halldearn.
Parliamentary Under Secretary of State for Industry, David Trippier, M.P.
  Private Secretary, P. D. Madden.
Parliamentary Under Secretary of State, The Lord Lucas of Chilworth.
  Private Secretary, Mrs. L. C. Cassidy.
Joint Permanent Secretary, Sir Brian Hayes, K.C.B.
  Private Secretary, J. L. Startup.
Deputy Secretaries, D. M. Dell; A. J. P. Macdonald; O. Roith (*Chief Scientist and Engineer*); R. Mountfield; B. W. Oakley, C.B.E. (*Alvey Directorate*); J. Caines, C.B.; C. W. Roberts; R. Williams; H. H. Liesner, C.B. (*Chief Economic Adviser*); J. B. K. Rickford (*The Solicitor*); R. C. M. Cooper, C.B. (*Principal Establishment and Finance Officer*).
Parliamentary Clerk, T. A. Hardbattle.
Policy Planning Unit (G5), Dr. T. E. H. Walker.

International Trade Policy Division
[01–215 7877]

Under Secretary, A. J. Lane.
Heads of Branch (G5), A. J. Pryor; P. Gent; T. Sharp.

Overseas Trade Divisions
[01–215 7877]

Division 1 (*Projects and Export Policy*)
Under Secretary, C. B. Benjamin.
Heads of Branch (G5), M. M. Baker; J. P. S. Crawford; J. H. Chapman.

Division 2
(*N. America, N.E. and S.E. Asia and Australasia*)
Under Secretary, A. C. Hutton.
Heads of Branch (G5), D. J. Hall; W. J. Hall; J. M. Healey.

Division 3
Under Secretary, A. J. Hunter.

Administration and Finance
Head of Branch (G5), R. M. Rumbelow.

Export to Europe Branch
Head of Branch (G5), L. F. Standen.

Export Data Branch
Director (G5), M. J. Morrison.
(1 Victoria Street, SW1H 0ET. Tel. 01–215 7877.)

Fairs and Promotion Branch
Director (G5), P. Robinson.

Soviet Union and Eastern Europe
Director (G5), K. W. N. George.

Division 4 (*Middle East, Africa and Latin America*)
Under Secretary, A. Titchener.
Heads of Branch (G5), H. R. Owen; M. Petter; B. J. Everett.

European Commercial and Industrial Policy Division
[01–215 7877]

Under Secretary, N. P. Brecknell.
Heads of Branch (G5), A. Berry; O. H. Kemmis.

British Overseas Trade Board
1 Victoria Street, SW1H 0ET
[01–215 7877]

Chairman, The Earl Jellicoe, P.C., D.S.O., M.C.
Vice-Chairman, H.R.H. The Duke of Kent, G.C.M.G., G.C.V.O.
Members, P. E. G. Bates; Sir Gordon Booth, K.C.M.G., C.V.O.; Sir Neville Bowman-Shaw; R. Q. Braithwaite, C.M.G.; Gisela Burg; T. T. Candlish; T. Duffy; A. K. Edwards, M.B.E.; J. Gill, C.B.; Sir Robert Haslam; The Earl of Limerick, K.B.E.; R. G. S. Messervy; J. W. Parsons; M. R. Rendle; C. W. Roberts; C. F. Sedcole; The Lord Selsdon; Dr. N. B. Smith, C.B.; N. C. Thompson; G. S. Tucker, C.B.E.; R. J. Withers, C.B.E.
Chief Executive, C. W. Roberts.
Secretary (G5), R. M. Rumbelow.
Chief Information Officer (G6), P. W. Probert.

Patent Office and Industrial Property and Copyright Department
25 Southampton Buildings, WC2A 1AY
[01–405 8721]

Comptroller General of Patents, Designs and Trade Marks, I. J. G. Davis.
Assistant Comptrollers, R. Bowen; V. Tarnofsky.
Assistant Registrar of Trade Marks, J. M. Myall.

Insurance Division
Sanctuary Bldgs., 16–20 Gt. Smith Street, SW1P 3DB
[01–215 7877]

Under Secretary, T. Muir.
Heads of Branch (G5), V. F. Lane; M. Z. Wasilewski; P. S. Salvidge; M. D. Oldham.

Financial Services Division
Sanctuary Bldgs., 16–20 Gt. Smith Street, SW1P 3DB
[01–215 7877]

Under Secretary, B. J. G. Hilton.
Heads of Branch (G5), A. C. G. Lowry; R. H. S. Wells.

Companies Division
Sanctuary Bldgs., 16–20 Great Smith Street, SW1P 3DB
[01–215 7877]

Under Secretary, A. A. Duguid.
Heads of Branch (G5), D. Steel; Mrs. M. A. Wilks.
2–14 Bunhill Row, E.C.1
[01–606 4071]

Companies Investigation Branch, Inspector of Companies, R. B. Howard.

Companies Registration Office
Companies House, Crown Way, Maindy, Cardiff CF4 3UZ
[0222 388588]

Registrar of Companies for England and Wales (G5), D. B. Nottage.
London Search Room, 55–71 City Road, EC1Y 1BB
[01–253 9393]

102 George Street, Edinburgh EH2 3DJ
[031–225 5774]
Registrar for Scotland, E. T. K. Lougheed.

Department of Commerce
64 Chichester Street, Belfast
[0232 34488]
Registrar for Northern Ireland, H. Lytk.

The Insolvency Service
2–14 Bunhill Row, EC1Y 8LL
[01–606 4071]

Inspector General of the Insolvency Service, M. Clark.
Deputy Inspectors General, P. D. Pink; J. B. Clemetson; A. K. Sales.

Consumer Affairs Division
Millbank Tower, Millbank, SW1P 4QU
[01–211 3000]

Under Secretary, S. N. Burbridge.
Heads of Branch (G5), D. L. Gatland; R. P. Hope; F. W. Willis.
Trading Standards Adviser, D. Jones.

Air Division
Ashdown House, 123 Victoria Street, SW1E 6RB
[01–212 7676]

Under Secretary, M. J. Michell.
Heads of Branch (G5), M. K. O'Shea; J. M. Bowder.
Grade 6, J. R. Collingbourne; A. W. R. Allcock.

Space, Post Office and Films Division
29 Bressenden Place, SW1E 5DT
[01–213 3000]

Under Secretary, J. C. Leeming.
Heads of Branch (G5), A. C. Nicholas; M. J. C. Butcher.

Research and Technology Policy Division
Ashdown House, 123 Victoria Street, SW1E 6RB
[01–212 7676]

Under Secretary, A. Williams.
Heads of Branch (G5), A. W. Keddie; D. J. Wiseman; Dr. A. J. Wallard; T. Garrett, C.B.E.

National Physical Laboratory
Teddington, Middlesex TW11 0LW
[01–977 3222]

Director (G3), Dr. P. Dean, C.B.

Laboratory of the Government Chemist
Cornwall House, Stamford Street, SE1 9NQ
[01–928 7900]

Government Chemist, Dr. R. F. Coleman

National Engineering Laboratory
East Kilbride, Glasgow G75 0QU
[03552 20222]

Director (G3), Dr. D. A. Bell.

Warren Spring Laboratory
Gunnels Wood Road, Stevenage, Herts SG1 2BX
[0438 3388]

Director, P. J. Cooper.

National Weights and Measures Laboratory
26 Chapter Street, SW1P 4NS
[01–211 3000]

Director (G5), Dr. P. B. Clapham.

General Policy Division
1 Victoria Street, SW1H 0ET
[01–215 7877]

Under Secretary, E. Wright.
Heads of Branch (G5), A. Whiting; G. M. Field; M. J. Vile; N. R. Thornton.

Quality and Education Division
Ashdown House, 123 Victoria Street, SW1E 6RB
[01–212 7676]

Under Secretary, M. C. McCarthy.
Heads of Branch (G5), Dr. E. B. Bates; P. Goodman; M. R. Cohen.

Inward Investment, Tourism and Service Industries Division
Kingsgate House, 66–74 Victoria Street, SW1E 6SJ
[01–212 7676]

Under Secretary, J. F. J. Jardine.
Heads of Branch (G5), F. E. Wildman; D. Harrison-Harvey; J. Woodrow.

Regional Policy Division
Kingsgate House, 66/74 Victoria Street, SW1E 6SJ
[01–212 7676]

Under Secretary, J. E. Cammell.
Heads of Branch (G5), E. W. Pearcey; J. G. Walmsley; B. Winkett.

Small Firms Division
Ashdown House, 123 Victoria Street, SW1E 6RB
[01–212 7676]

Under Secretary, J. F. J. Jardine.
Head of Branch (G5), Dr. P. J. Graham.

Industrial Development Unit
Kingsgate House, 66–74 Victoria Street, SW1E 6SJ
[01–212 7676]

Director (G2), D. M. Dell.
Deputy Directors, E. Middleton; R. Ford; D. Kell; R. A. M. Ramsay; E. J. Fairweather.
Secretariat and General Policy:
Head of Branch (G5), D. R. Coates.

Radio Regulatory Division
Waterloo Bridge House, Waterloo Road, SE1 8UA
[01–275 3000]

Under Secretary, A. J. Nieduseynski.
Heads of Branch (G5), A. Marshall; M. V. Coolican.
Director (G5), Dr. J. Durkin.

Alvey Directorate
Millbank Tower, Millbank, SW1P 4QU
[01–211 3000]

Minerals and Metals Division
Ashdown House, 123 Victoria Street, SW1E 6RB
[01–212 7676]

Under Secretary, B. Murray.
Heads of Branch (G5), N. M. K. Worman; M. A. R. Lunn; R. L. Long; N. M. K. Worman.

Chemicals, Textiles, Paper, Timber and Other Miscellaneous Industries Division
Ashdown House, 123 Victoria Street, SW1E 6RB
[01–212 7676]

Under Secretary, P. M. S. Corley.
Heads of Branch (G5), M. S. Bremner; B. E. Armstrong; J. K. Chapman; P. J. Gregory.

Shipbuilding Policy Division
Ashdown House, 123 Victoria Street, SW1E 6RB
[01–212 7676]

Under Secretary, S. W. Treadgold.
Heads of Branch (G5), D. M. Hoddinott; D. R. C. Durie.

Mechanical and Electrical Engineering Division
Ashdown House, 123 Victoria Street, SW1E 6RB
[01–212 7676]

Under Secretary, F. R. Mingay.
Heads of Branch (G5), J. C. S. Priston; Mrs. P. A. Denham; R. McVickers; Dr. R. C. Dobbie.

Vehicles Division
Ashdown House, 123 Victoria Street, SW1E 6RB
[01–212 7676]

Under Secretary, M. J. A. Cochlin.
Heads of Branch (G5), R. A. Brown; R. J. Meadway; A. J. Mantle.

Information Technology Division
29 Bressenden Place, SW1E 5DT
[01–213 3000]

Under Secretary, W. B. Willott.
Heads of Branch (G5), B. W. Smith; R. Foster; D. M. March; W. M. S. Owsianka.

Electronics Applications Division
29 Bressenden Place, SW1E 5DT
[01–213 3000]

Under Secretary, J. H. Major.
Heads of Branch (G5), J. G. Noyes; M. E. Farry; H. J. Ivey; A. Conway.

Telecommunications Division
Ashdown House, 123 Victoria Street, SW1E 6RB
[01–212 7676]

Under Secretary, R. J. Priddle.
Heads of Branch (G5), J. E. Avery; L. G. Faulkner; J. F. R. Martin.

DEPARTMENT OF TRADE AND INDUSTRY SERVICES ORGANIZATION
Sanctuary Buildings, 16/20 Great Smith Street, SW1P 3DB
[01–215 7877]

Deputy Secretaries, H. H. Liesner, c.b. (*Chief Economic Adviser*); J. B. K. Rickford (*The Solicitor*); R. C. M. Cooper, c.b. (*Principal Establishment and Finance Officer*).

Personnel Management Division
Sanctuary Buildings
16–20 Great Smith Street, SW1P 3DB
[01–215 7877]

Under Secretary, N. F. Ledsome.
Heads of Branch (G5), Miss M. T. Neville-Rolfe; D. W. F. Johnson; J. F. Bailes; Dr. R. Wood.

Management Services and Manpower Division
Sanctuary Buildings,
16–20 Great Smith Street, SW1P 3DB
[01–215 7877]

Under Secretary, P. E. Dougherty.
Heads of Branch (G5), R. Nicholls; K. J. Doyle; R. W. Simpson; R. A. C. Hewes.
Senior Principal Scientific Officer (G6), N. Bernard.

Finance and Resource Management Division
Kingsgate House, 66/74 Victoria Street, SW1E 6SJ
[01–212 7676]

Under Secretary, A. C. Russell.
Heads of Branch (G5), E. H. Whitaker; H. V. B. Brown; A. C. Elkington; P. R. S. Hartnack.

Accounts Branch
24–26 Newport Road, Cardiff
[0222 492611]

Director of Accounts, A. C. Elkington.

Internal Audit
Ebury Bridge House, Ebury Bridge Road, SW1W 8QD
[01–730 9678]

Head of Internal Audit, K. Holt

Solicitor's Department
10–18 Victoria Street, S.W.1
[01–215 7877]

The Solicitor, J. B. K. Rickford.
Under Secretaries, R. J. Ayling; J. R. Mallinson; J. R. Woolman.
Assistant Solicitors (G5), P. H. Bovey; Mrs. N. M. P. Chappell; Mrs. T. J. Dunstan; R. D. Fayers; R. Higgins; K. A. M. Johnson; C. S. Kerse; R. M.

Malbey; Miss J. Richardson; J. W. Roberts; C. B. Robson; Mrs. F. A. Scarborough; J. M. Stanley; A. M. Susman; E. A. Thompson.

Information Division
1 Victoria Street, SW1H 0ET

Head of Information (G5), Miss C. Bowe.
Deputy Head of Information (G6), A. Williams.
Chief Press Officers, Miss G. P. Samuel; P. Burke; G. A. Nissen.

Economics Divisions
1 Victoria Street, SW1H 0ET
[01–215 7877]

Chief Economic Adviser (G2), H. H. Liesner, c.b.

Division 1
Ashdown House, 123 Victoria Street, SW1E 6RB
[01–212 7676]

Under Secretary, J. R. Shepherd.
Heads of Branch (G5), R. D. Rees; B. M. Nonehebel; J. M. Barber.

Division 2
1 Victoria Street, SW1H 0ET
[01–215 7877]

Under Secretary, N. K. Gardner.
Heads of Branch (G5), R. Van Slooten; P. J. Goate; M. S. Bradbury.

Statistics Divisions
1 Victoria Street, SW1H 0ET
[01–215 7877]

Division 1
Millbank Tower, Millbank, SW1P 4QU
[01–211 3000]

Under Secretary, N. Harvey.
Heads of Branch (G5), R. C. Woods; R. L. Butchart; J. Walker.

Division 2
1 Victoria Street, SW1H 0ET
[01–215 7877]

Under Secretary, J. Hibbert.
Heads of Branch (G5), W. E. Boyd; P. H. Richardson; G. Jenkinson.

Business Statistics Office
Cardiff Road, Newport, Gwent
[0633 56111]

Director, R. Ash.
Heads of Branch (G5), C. C. Maskall; Dr. B. Mitchell; R. M. Norton; S. R. Curtis; D. R. Lewis.
Grade 6, W. D. Knight.

Industrial Development Unit-Accountancy Services Division
Millbank Tower, Millbank, SW1P 4QU
[01–211 3000]

Under Secretary, J. A. Knox.
Directors (G5), G. T. Pearson; H. J. Charman.

REGIONAL ORGANIZATION

North Eastern Regional Office
Stanegate House, 2 Groat Market, Newcastle upon Tyne NE1 1YN
[0632 324722]

Regional Director (*Under Secretary*), W. R. Atkinson, c.b.
Regional Industrial Adviser, A. Chitty.

North Western Regional Office
Sunley Bldg., Piccadilly Plaza, Manchester M1 4BA
[061–236 2171]

Regional Director (G3), Dr. J. C. J. Thynne.
Regional Industrial Adviser, G. D. Yates.

Yorkshire and Humberside Regional Office
Priestley House, Park Row, Leeds LS1 5LF
[0532 443171]

Regional Director (Under Secretary), J. W. Preston.

West Midlands Regional Office
Ladywood House, Stephenson Street, Birmingham
B2 4DT
[021–632 4111]

Regional Director (G5), H. M. Lanyon.

East Midlands Regional Office
Severns House, 20 Middle Pavement, Nottingham
NG1 7DW
[0602 56181]

Regional Director (G5), K. J. Green.

South Western Regional Office
The Pithay, Bristol BS1 2PB
[0272 291071]

Regional Director (G5), D. B. Lodge.

South West Industrial Development Office
Phoenix House, Notte Street, Plymouth PL1 2HF
[0752 21891]

Deputy Director, M. G. Brown.

South Eastern Regional Office (Industry)
Ebury Bridge House, Ebury Bridge Road,
SW1W 8QD
[01–730 9678]

Regional Director (G5), G. J. Bradshaw.

South Eastern Regional Office (Exports)
Ebury Bridge House, Ebury Bridge Road,
SW1W 8QD
[01–730 9678]

Director (G6), Dr. H. A. P. Fisher.

DEPARTMENT OF TRANSPORT
2 Marsham Street, SW1P 3EB
[01–212 3434]

The Department of Transport has overall responsibility for land, sea and air transport. This entails general sponsorship of the transport industries, with particular responsibility for the nationalized airline, rail and bus industries; domestic and international civil aviation policy; shipping policy and the ports industry; navigational lights; pilotage; H.M. Coastguard; oversight of road transport, including vehicle registration and licensing, driver licensing and road safety; responsibility for construction and maintenance of motorways and trunk roads; and general oversight of the transport planning of local authorities, including payments of grant from central Government.

SALARY LIST

Secretary of State	£31,271
Minister of State	£21,881
Parliamentary Secretary	£16,411
Permanent Secretary (Grade 1)	£52,750
Deputy Secretary (G2)	£38,325 to £39,250
Director TRRL (G3)	£30,975 to £31,750
Chief Highway Engineer (G3)	£30,975 to £31,750
Under Secretary (G3)	£30,975 to £31,750
Director of Regional Offices (G3)	£30,975 to £31,750
Director, (Transport) (G4)	£26,909
Chief Inspecting Officer, Railways (G4)	£26,909
Deputy Chief Highway Engineer (G4)	£26,909
Deputy Chief Scientific Officer (G5)	£20,964 to £25,533
Assistant Chief Planner (G5)	£20,964 to £25,533
Chairman of Traffic Commissioners	£25,533
Assistant Secretary (G5)	£20,964 to £25,533

Controller, Regional Office (G5)	£20,964 to £25,533
Senior Economic Adviser (G5)	£20,964 to £25,533
Chief Statistician (G5)	£20,964 to £25,533

Secretary of State for Transport, THE RT. HON. NICHOLAS RIDLEY, M.P.
Private Secretary, R. A. Allan.
Parliamentary Private Secretary, Mrs. A. Rumbold, C.B.E., M.P.
Minister of State, MRS. LYNDA CHALKER, M.P.
Private Secretary, C. H. Bowden.
Parliamentary Private Secretary, R. Squire, M.P.
Parliamentary Under Secretaries, D. Mitchell, M.P.; M. Spicer, M.P.
Private Secretary, R. C. Bennett.
Private Secretary, Mrs. S. J. Rooke.
Parliamentary Clerk, M. Carty.
Permanent Under Secretary of State (G1), Sir Peter Lazarus, K.C.B.
Private Secretary, A. J. H. Picton.

Information
Head of Information (G5), G. M. Devereau.

DEPUTY SECRETARY *(G2):* J. Palmer.

Railways
Under Secretary (G3), J. R. Coates.
Grade 5, G. D. Miles; B. D. Goodfellow; P. Wood.
Chief Inspecting Officer (G4), Maj. C. F. Rose *(ret.).*

Passenger Transport
Under Secretary (G3), A. P. Brown.
Grade 5, P. E. Pickering; H. C. T. Fawcett; Mrs. G. M. Ashmore.

Public Transport London and Metropolitan
Under Secretary (G3), A. J. Goldman.
Grade 5, F. Gale; Miss C. M. Egerton.

Freight and Local Transport
Under Secretary (G3), W. P. Jackson.
Grade 5, M. S. Albu.
Grade 6, J. Winder; R. A. O'Sullivan.

Traffic Area Offices
Chairmen of Traffic Commissioners and Licensing Authorities

Eastern (Nottingham and Cambridge), K. Peter.
Metropolitan (Acton), (vacant).
North Eastern (Newcastle upon Tyne and Leeds), F. Whalley.
North Western (Manchester), R. D. Hutchings.
Scottish (Edinburgh), H. McNamara.
South Eastern (Eastbourne), R. S. Thornton.
Western (Bristol), Maj.-Gen. V. H. J. Carpenter, C.B., M.B.E.
South Wales (Cardiff), R. R. Jackson.

DEPUTY SECRETARY *(G2):* W. M. Knighton, C.B.

Shipping Policy
Under Secretary (G3), G. R. Sunderland.
Grade 5, J. D. Henes; M. L. Fielder.

Marine and Ports
Under Secretary (G3), J. W. S. Dempster.
Grade 5, J. A. Battersby; J. R. Fells.
Chief Coastguard (G5), Lt.-Cdr. J. T. Fetherstone-Dilke, R.N. *(ret.).*

Marine Pollution Control Unit
Director (G4), Rear-Adm. M. L. Stacey, C.B.
Surveyor General, Dr. J. Cowley, C.B.E.
Grade 5, Capt. J. H. Shone; D. J. Fowler; D. C. Gilbert; G. Thompson.

Road and Vehicle Safety

Under Secretary (G3), T. W. Hall.
Grade 5, D. J. Lyness; D. M. Smith; R. J. Oliver; E. Dunn.

Vehicle Engineering Development Unit

Chief Mechanical Engineer (G4), D. V. Jones.

Driver and Vehicle Licensing

Director (G4), G. R. Wattley.
Grade 5, M. A. Robinson; R. Bird; R. J. Verge.

Driver Licensing, Vehicle Taxation and Insurance

Grade 5, D. S. Evans.

DEPUTY SECRETARY (G2): J. E. Hannigan, c.b.

Highways Policy and Programme

Under Secretary(G3), H. J. Blanks.
Grade 5, D. A. R. Peel; M. R. Egerton; P. E. Butler; R. T. Stirland.

Highways, Contracts, Administration and Maintenance

Under Secretary (G3), A. A. Pelling.
Grade 5, W. Walker; P. R. Smith; J. W. Fellows; B. J. Bennett.

Highways Engineering

Chief Highway Engineer (G3), K. Sriskandan.
Grade 4, T. A. Rochester.
Grade 5, G. P. Mallett; R. S. Wilson; S. Chatterjee; J. Denning; S. Rose.

Traffic and Greater London Roads

Under Secretary (G3), Mrs. J. M. Bridgeman.
Grade 5, A. M. White; N. T. Rees; W. E. Gallagher.

PRINCIPAL FINANCE OFFICER AND DEPUTY SECRETARY (G2): D. Holmes, c.b.

Civil Aviation Policy

Under Secretary (G3), R. E. Clarke.
Grade 5, A. T. Baker; J. A. Rhodes; D. J. Rowlands; I. C. Douek; B. D'Oliveira, o.b.e.

International Aviation

Under Secretary (G3), H. M. G. Stevens.
Grade 5, A. Fortnam; E. J. Lindley; D. C. Moss.

Accidents Investigation Branch

Chief Inspector of Accidents (G4), G. C. Wilkinson, a.f.c.
Grade 5, D. A. Cooper.

International Transport

Under Secretary (G3), A. G. Lyall.
Grade 5, C. M. Woodman; Miss J. J. Lambert.

Finance

Under Secretary (G3), I. Yass.
Grade 5, P. R. Smethurst; B. J. Billington; J. D. Noulton; R. Griffins; L. S. Moyle.
Accountancy Adviser (G5), G. M. Dennett.

Transport Policy Review Unit

Grade 5, J. W. B. Robins.

ECONOMICS AND STATISTICS (TRANSPORT)

Chief Economic Adviser (G3), H. J. D. Cole.
Grade 5, G. A. C. Searle; M. B. Egerton; C. T. B. Smith; A. J. Nichols.

Statistics (Transport)

Under Secretary (G3), E. J. Thompson.
Grade 5, H. M. Dale; Miss B. J. Wood; H. Collings; G. R. Emes.

Science and Research

Chief Scientific Adviser, Deputy Secretary (G2), Dr. M. W. Holdgate, c.b.

DEPUTY SECRETARY, RESEARCH AND DEVELOPMENT (G2): H. J. D. Cole.

Transport and Road Research Laboratory

Director (G3), G. Margason.
Deputy Director (G4), D. F. Cornelius.
Grade 5, N. W. Lister; Dr. L. J. Griffin; Dr. A. J. M. Hitchcock; F. V. Webster; R. S. Hinsley; D. I. Robertson.

Science and Research Policy and Programmes

Grade 5, P. G. O'Neill.

CHIEF SCIENTIFIC ADVISER (G2): Dr. M. W. Holdgate, c.b.

DEPARTMENTS OF THE ENVIRONMENT AND TRANSPORT REGIONAL OFFICES AND COMMON SERVICES

See under **Department of the Environment**

THE TREASURY
Parliament Street, SW1P 3AG
[01–233 3000]

The Office of the Lord High Treasurer has been continuously in commission for well over 200 years: the Lord High Commissioners of H.M. Treasury consist of the First Lord of the Treasury (who is also the Prime Minister), the Chancellor of the Exchequer and five Junior Lords. This Board of Commissioners is assisted at present by the Chief Secretary, a Parliamentary Secretary who is the Chief Whip, a Financial Secretary, an Economic Secretary, a Minister of State and by the Permanent Secretary. The Prime Minister and First Lord is not primarily concerned in the day to day aspects of Treasury business. The Parliamentary Secretary and the Junior Lords are Government whips in the House of Commons. The management of the Treasury devolves upon the Chancellor of the Exchequer and, under him, the Chief Secretary, the Financial Secretary, The Economic Secretary and the Minister of State. The Chief Secretary is responsible for the control of public expenditure, general business of the public services and industry groups, overseas aid and export credit; efficiency in the public sector (including general policy on civil service numbers and financial management in government); and procurement policy. The Financial Secretary discharges the traditional responsibility of the Treasury for the largely formal procedure for the voting of funds by Parliament. He also has responsibility for other Parliamentary financial business, Inland Revenue duties and taxes and privatisation policy. The Economic Secretary has responsibility for monetary policy; Treasury responsibility for the financial system, U.K. membership of E.C. Budget Council, the Royal Mint, Department for National Savings, Registry of Friendly Societies and the National Loans Office. The Minister of State deals with Customs & Excise matters, public sector pay and pensions, H.M. Stationery Office, Central Office of Information and Government Actuaries Department. He also answers questions in the House of Commons on Civil Service matters. All Treasury Ministers are concerned in tax matters.

Prime Minister and First Lord of the Treasury, THE RT. HON. MARGARET HILDA THATCHER, M.P., F.R.S. £31,271
Lord Commissioners of the Treasury, The Hon. D. Thompson, M.P.; The Hon. I. Lang, M.P.; The Hon. T. Garel-Jones, M.P.; The Hon. A. Hamilton, M.P. £13,601

Chancellor of the Exchequer, THE RT. HON. NIGEL LAWSON, M.P. £31,271
Principal Private Secretary, Mrs. J. R. Lomax.
Private Secretary, Miss M. O'Mara.
Chief Secretary to the Treasury, THE RT. HON. PETER REES, Q.C., M.P. £31,271
Private Secretary, R. J. Broadbent.
Assistant Private Secretary, P. Peglar.
Parliamentary Secretary to the Treasury and Government Chief Whip, THE RT. HON. JOHN WAKEHAM, M.P. £25,881
Private Secretary, M. Maclean.
Financial Secretary, JOHN MOORE, M.P. £21,881
Private Secretary, Miss V. Life.
Economic Secretary, IAN STEWART, M.P.
Private Secretary, A. M. Ellis.
Minister of State, THE RT. HON. BARNEY HAYHOE, M.P. £21,881
Private Secretary, M. W. Norgrove.
Treasurer of H.M. Household and Deputy Chief Whip, J. Cope, M.P. £21,881
(NOTE.—All salaries shown above do not include Parliamentary salary.)
Assistant Whips, Hon. T. Sainsbury, M.P.; M. Neubert, M.P.; T. Durant, M.P.; P. Lloyd, M.P.; Hon. M. Lennox-Boyd, M.P.
Permanent Secretary (G1), Sir Peter Middleton, K.C.B.
Private Secretary, (vacant).
Second Permanent Secretaries (G1A), Sir Geoffrey Littler, K.C.B. (*Overseas Finance*); A. M. Bailey, C.B. (*Public Services*) £48,500
Head of Government Economics Service and Chief Economic Adviser to the Treasury, Sir Terence Burns.
Deputy Secretaries (G2), F. Cassell (*Public Finance*); R. G. Lavelle (*Overseas Finance*); J. Anson, C.B. (*Public Services*); J. Anson, C.B. (*General Expenditure*); E. P. Kemp (*Pay and Allowances*); N. J. Monck (*Industry*) .... £38,325 to £39,250
Deputy Chief Economic Adviser to the Treasury, I. C. R. Byatt £36,500

Public Services Sector

Industry, Agriculture and Employment Group:
Under Secretary (G3), T. U. Burgner
£30,975 to £31,750
Assistant Secretaries (G5), Ms. E. Conn; R. B. Butt; P. A. Shaw .... £20,964 to £25,533
Public Enterprises:
Under Secretary (G3), D. J. Moore £30,975 to £31,750
Assistant Secretaries (G5), S. A. Robson; G. E. Grimstone; J. G. Colman ...... £20,964 to £25,533
Social Services and Territorial:
Under Secretary (G3), G. W. Watson
£30,975 to £31,750
Assistant Secretaries (G5), Ms. D. Seammen; P. M. Rayner; W. J. E. Norton ...... £20,964 to £25,533
Local Government:
Under Secretary (G3), J. R. Jameson
£30,975 to £31,750
Assistant Secretaries (G5), C. C. Allan; D. R. Instone
£20,964 to £25,533
Home Transport and Education:
Under Secretary (G3), B. T. Gilmore
£30,975 to £31,750
Assistant Secretaries (G5), F. K. Jones; T. Burr
£20,964 to £25,533

Expenditure Support:
Under Secretary (G3), (vacant) ... £30,975 to £31,750
Assistant Secretary (G5), R. B. Willis
£20,964 to £25,533
Chief Statistician, J. Draper ..... £20,964 to £25,533
Chief Scientific Officer, T. P. Turner
£20,964 to £25,533
Senior Economic Adviser, M. J. Spackman
£20,964 to £25,533

Accounts and Purchasing:
Under Secretary (G3), C. H. A. Judd
£30,975 to £31,750
Senior Principal (G6), R. J. Allwood
£17,000 to £22,926
Central Computer and Telecommunications Agency:
Under Secretary (G3), P. Freeman £30,975 to £31,750
Assistant Secretaries (G5), W. A. Beard; C. D. Butler; W. Houldsworth; R. A. Ballard; R. M. Paynter; M. O'Connor; R. E. Dibble .... £20,964 to £25,533
Directing Grade Engineer B, C. R. D. Tatham
£20,964 to £25,533
General Expenditure Policy:
Under Secretary (G3), M. C. Scholar
£30,975 to £31,750
Assistant Secretaries (G5), P. R. C. Gray; M. L. Williams; C. C. Allan ...... £20,964 to £25,533
Senior Principal (G6), E. I. Cooper
£17,000 to £22,926
Defence Policy and Material:
Under Secretary (G3), P. J. Kitcatt
£30,975 to £31,750
Assistant Secretaries (G5), D. R. Norgrove; N. M. Hansford .... £20,964 to £25,533
Civil Service Catering Organization:
Executive Director, D. S. B. Simpson
£30,975 to £31,750

Overseas Finance Sector

Overseas Finance:
Finance Economic Unit:
Under Secretary (G3), P. N. Sedgwick
£30,975 to £31,750
Aid and Export Finance:
Under Secretary (G3), P. Mountfield
£30,975 to £31,750
Assistant Secretaries (G5), J. S. Beastall, Mrs. A. F. Case .... £20,964 to £25,533
European Community:
Under Secretary (G3), G. E. Fitchew
£30,975 to £31,750
Assistant Secretaries (G5), J. E. Mortimer; G. W. Hopkinson .... £20,964 to £25,533
External Finance:
Under Secretary (G3), R. G. Lavelle
£30,975 to £31,750
Assistant Secretary (G5), C. W. Kelly
£20,964 to £25,533

Chief Economic Adviser's Sector

Forecast and Analysis:
Under Secretary (G3), H. P. Evans £30,975 to £31,750
Senior Economic Advisers, S. J. Davies; C. J. Mowl
£20,964 to £25,533
Senior Principal (G6), R. James .. £17,000 to £22,926
Medium Term and Policy Analysis:
Under Secretary (G3), J. C. Odling-Smee
£30,975 to £31,750
Senior Economic Advisers, C. Mellis; C. J. Riley
£20,964 to £25,533

Public Enterprises Analytic Unit and Economics of Taxation and Social Security Division

Under Secretary (G3), I. C. Byatt . £30,975 to £31,750
Assistant Secretary (G3), G. A. C. D. Houston
£20,964 to £25,533

Senior Economic Advisers, R. B. Stannard; G. P. Smith . . . . £20,964 to £25,533
Fiscal Policy:
Under Secretary (G3), G. W. Monger
£30,975 to £31,750
Assistant Secretaries (G5), R. I. G. Allen; H. M. Griffiths . . . . £20,964 to £25,533
Home Finance:
Under Secretary (G3), T. P. Lankester
£30,975 to £31,750
Assistant Secretary (G5), M. A. Hall
£20,964 to £25,533
Senior Principals (G6), L. Watts; T. F. Mathews
£17,000 to £22,926

Pay and Allowances Command

Pay:
Under Secretary (G3), (vacant)
£30,975 to £31,750
Assistant Secretaries (G5), P. G. F. Davis; D. M. Williams; J. F. Gilhooly . . . . £20,964 to £25,533
Industrial Relations:
Assistant Secretary (G5), R. B. Butt
£20,964 to £25,533

Superannuation:
Assistant Secretary (G5), D. M. Williams
£20,964 to £25,533

Central Area

Establishment and Organization:
Under Secretary (G3), Miss J. Kelley
£30,975 to £31,750
Assistant Secretary (G5), B. M. Fox
£20,964 to £25,533

Senior Economic Adviser, J. Dixon
£20,964 to £25,533
Senior Principals (G6), E. J. Needle; R. N. Edwards
£17,000 to £22,926
Central Unit:
Under Secretary (G3), A. M. W. Battishill
£30,975 to £31,750
Economic Briefing (Assistant Secretary) (G5), M. T. Folger.
Information:
Assistant Secretary (G5), R. P. Culpin
£20,964 to £25,533
Deputy Head of Division and Press Secretary to the Chief Secretary, J. J. Monaghan £17,000 to £22,926

Treasury Representatives in U.S.A.

Economic Minister and U.K. Representative IMF/IBRD, N. L. Wicks, C.B.E.

Rating of Government Property Department
Jameson House, 69 Notting Hill Gate, W.11

Treasury Valuer, P. J. Dahlhoff.
Deputy Treasury Valuer, J. F. Olney.

THE TREASURY SOLICITOR
Department of H.M. Procurator-General and Treasury Solicitor
Queen Anne's Chambers, 28 Broadway, SW1H 9JS
[01–273 3000]

Procurator-General and Treasury Solicitor, J. B. Bailey, C.B. £40,500
Deputy Treasury Solicitor, G. A. Hosker £32,500

Advisory Division

Under Secretary (Legal), (vacant) £30,975 to £31,750
Assistant Solicitors, R. P. Ellis; J. E. Collins; Miss J. L. Wheldon . . . . £20,964 to £25,533
Senior Legal Assistants, M. R. M. Davis; A. J. Perrett; M. Lewis; P. D. Coopman; H. R. Morrison; D. Brummell; P. C. Jenkins; J. R. J. Braggins; M. J. Hemming . . . . £15,688 to £21,297

Litigation Divisions

Under Secretaries, (Legal), T. J. G. Pratt; R. D. Munrow; D. A. Watson . . . . £30,975 to £31,750
Assistant Solicitors, M. J. C. Haines; D. A. Hogg; A. Leithead; C. G. Leonard; R. Lines; M. E. Mead; Miss V. M. Peto; A. D. Preston; R. N. Ricks; J. H. Wilkinson . . . . £20,964 to £25,533
Senior Legal Assistants, A. P. M. Aylett; Mrs. D. Babar; A. Belchambers; Miss P. J Carroll; Mrs. G. Dagtoglou; J. N. Desai; Miss V. F. Dewhurst; H. Grange; P. D. F. Grant; N. J. Harington; Mrs. S. Hay; I. Hood; J. D. Howes; R. A. D. Jackson; J. E. Jones; Mrs. A. D. B. McFee; B. E. McHenry; Mrs. A. M. Morris; C. J. P. Muttukumaru; D. A. Pearson; R. J. Phillips; A. J. Sandal; R. E. Seely; G. Stimson; M. B. Sturdy; P. F. O. Whitehurst; S. C. Willey
£15,688 to £21,297
Principals, D. Palmer; D. A. Stalker; J. M. Hawkins; F. G. O'Connell . . . . £13,508 to £18,363

Queen's Proctor Division

Queen's Proctor, J. B. Bailey, C.B.
Assistant Queen's Proctor, G. F. Sills
£20,964 to £25,533

Conveyancing Division

Under Secretary (Legal), I. T. Lewis
£30,975 to £31,750
Assistant Solicitors, D. E. T. Bevan; R. W. M. Cooper; A. P. Millar; P. L. Noble; A. M. Scarfe; D. A. J. Simpson; J. Wyer . . . . £20,964 to £25,533
Senior Legal Assistants, M. H. M. Anderson; M. Benmayor; J. J. Briars; P. W. M. Cooke; R. L. Coward; M. Drayton; I. R. S. Falconer; Miss R. C. Farmer; T. Forrester; D. J. C. Garnett; Miss G. Gilder; D. M. Gleed; M. W. Harrison; J. B. Howe; Mrs. M. Jordan; L. Levy; A. R. Lilleystone; Miss J. M. Matthews; D. P. Moloney; P. F. Nockles; A. L. Norris; C. L. Oastler; G. E. Papes; I. P. Parker; R. M. Pierce; M. F. Rawlins; S. W. Rock; M. R. Rosenfeld; Miss P. E. Slatter; R. J. B. Stenhouse; T. J. Sylvester-Jones; B. D. Thurley; S. A. Tobin; Miss C. E. M. Troddyn; D. M. Webster; W. F. Williams; H. W. C. Wilson . . . . . £15,688 to £21,297
Principals, R. D. Harris; F. F. H. Hayter
£13,508 to £18,363

Statutory Publications Office

Assistant Solicitor, J. M. Gibson.
Senior Legal Assistant, C. E. J. Carey.

Establishment, Finance and General Services Division

Establishment and Legal Personnel Officer (Assistant Secretary), G. Roberts . . . . £20,964 to £25,533
Senior Legal Assistant, P. C. Jenkins
£15,688 to £21,297
Chief Accountant, B. C. Shephard £13,508 to £18,363
Head of Costs Branch, A. M. Niven
£13,508 to £18,363

Bona Vacantia Division

Assistant Solicitor, J. C. Leck . . . . £20,964 to £25,533
Senior Legal Assistant, Miss S. L. Sargant
£15,688 to £21,297
Principal, D. B. Green . . . . £13,508 to £18,363

Department of Energy Branch
Thames House South, Millbank, SW1P 4QJ
[01–211 6046]

Legal Adviser (Under Secretary (Legal)), G. B. Claydon . . . . £30,975 to £31,750
Assistant Solicitors, D. R. M. Long; R. M. C. Venables; D. H. Ingham; B. J. Ecclestone . £20,964 to £25,533
Senior Legal Assistants, M. A. Blythe; F. Croft; D. A. E. Michaels; D. F. W. Pickup
£15,688 to £21,297

Department of Education and Science Branch
Elizabeth House, York Road, SE1 7PH
[01-934 9958]

Legal Adviser (*Under Secretary*), J. E. Coleman.
Assistant Solicitor, A. G. Jones... £20,964 to £25,533
Senior Legal Assistants, Miss M. Trefgarne; D. J. Aries; M. A. Widdrington..... £15,688 to £21,297

Department of Transport Branch
2 Marsham Street, SW1P 3EB
[01-212 3434]

Under Secretary, G. H. Beetham.
Assistant Solicitors, R. G. Bellis; C. W. M. Ingram; B. W. James; D. F. Pascho; L. Oates.
Senior Legal Assistants, F. D. W. Clarke; Mrs. P. A. Dayer; J. H. Francis; B. J. Hammersley; A. K. Johnston; D. W. Jordan; Miss M. Lind-Smith; J. S. Reynolds.

COUNCIL ON TRIBUNALS
GKN House, 22 Kingsway, W.C.2

The Council on Tribunals are an independent body established in 1958 by the *Tribunals and Inquiries Act* of that year, to act as an advisory body in the field of administrative tribunals and statutory inquiries. They now operate under the Tribunals and Inquiries Act, 1971. Under the Act they keep under review the constitution and working of the various tribunals which have been placed under their general supervision, and consider and report on administrative procedures relating to statutory inquiries.

The Council must be consulted both about procedural regulations for the tribunals under their supervision and about many procedural rules for statutory inquiries. They are also frequently consulted on proposals for legislation affecting tribunals and inquiries and on proposals where the need for an appeals procedure may arise.

The numerous tribunals which have been placed under the Council's supervision are concerned with a wide variety of matters ranging from agriculture and road traffic to immigration, taxation, pensions, and the allocation of school places. They include social security and National Health Service Tribunals, the Lands Tribunal, Industrial Tribunals, Mental Health Review Tribunals, Local Valuation Courts and the Civil Aviation Authority. The Council's jurisdiction is from time to time extended to additional tribunals, inquiries and hearings.

The Scottish Committee of the Council generally considers Scottish tribunals and matters relating only to Scotland.

Members of the Council are appointed by the Lord Chancellor and the Lord Advocate. The Scottish Committee is composed partly of members of the Council designated by the Lord Advocate and partly others appointed by him. The Parliamentary Commissioner for Administration is *ex officio* a member of both the Council and the Scottish Committee.

The Council submit an annual report on their work and that of the Scottish Committee to the Lord Chancellor and the Lord Advocate, which must be laid before Parliament.

Chairman, The Lord Gibson-Watt, P.C., M.C.
Members, A. R. Barrowclough, Q.C.; Prof. L. N. Brown; D. Bruce; D. C. Calcutt, Q.C.; Mrs. M. P. Case; Sir Kenneth Clucas, K.C.B.; A. C. Heywood; D. W. Jones-Williams, O.B.E., M.C., T.D.; Miss E. R. Littlejohn, O.B.E.; R. N. M. MacLean, Q.C. (*also Chairman of Scottish Committee*); N. Robertson; Mrs. S. H. Spence; Prof. A. Webb; The Lord Wigoder, Q.C.
Secretary, M. W. Sayers.

Scottish Committee
20 Walker Street, Edinburgh EH3 7HR
[031-225 3236]

Chairman, R. N. M. MacLean, Q.C.
Members, A. R. Barrowclough, Q.C. (*Parliamentary Commissioner for Administration*); Mrs. E. Anderson; D. Bruce; P. M. Gemmill; G. S. Peterkin; N. Robertson; R. B. Weatherstone.
Secretary, Mrs. E. M. Chalmers.

SPECIAL COMMISSIONERS OF INCOME TAX
Turnstile House, 98 High Holborn, WC1V 6LQ
[01-438 7413]

The Special Commissioners are an independent body appointed by the Lord Chancellor to hear appeals concerning income tax, surtax, corporation tax, capital gains tax, capital transfer tax, development land tax and petroleum revenue tax.
Presiding Special Commissioner, R. H. Widdows
£33,000
Special Commissioners, A. K. Tavare; Miss E. Wix; B. M. F. O'Brien; T. H. K. Everett........ £29,865
Clerk to Special Commissioners, M. H. Gledhill
£14,873 to £19,728

CORPORATION OF TRINITY HOUSE
Trinity House, Tower Hill, EC3N 4DH
[01-480 6601]

Trinity House, the first General Lighthouse and Pilotage Authority in the Kingdom, was a body of importance when Henry VIII granted the institution its first charter in 1514. The Corporation is the General Lighthouse Authority for England and Wales, the Channel Islands and Gibraltar, with certain statutory jurisdiction over aids to navigation maintained by local harbour authorities. It is also responsible for dealing with wrecks dangerous to navigation, except those occurring within port limits or wrecks of H.M. ships. The Trinity House Lighthouse Service is maintained out of the General Lighthouse Fund which is provided from light dues levied on ships using the ports of the United Kingdom and Eire. The Corporation is also the principal pilotage authority in the United Kingdom and is responsible for London and 39 other districts. Certain charitable trusts are administered by the Corporation for the relief of aged or distressed mariners and their dependants. The affairs of the Corporation are managed by a Board of ten active Elder Brethren and the Secretary, assisted by administrative, engineering and marine staff. The active Elder Brethren also act as nautical assessors in marine causes in the Admiralty Division of the High Court of Justice.

Elder Brethren

Master, H.R.H. the Duke of Edinburgh, K.G. *Deputy Master*, Sir Miles Buckley Wingate, K.C.V.O. *Elder Brethren*, Capt. D. J. Cloke; Capt. I. R. C. Saunders; H.R.H. the Prince of Wales, K.G.; Capt. G. P. McCraith; Capt. R. J. Galpin, R.D., R.N.R. (*ret.*); Capt. Sir George Barnard; Capt. R. N. Mayo, C.B.E.; Capt. Sir David Tibbits, D.S.C., R.N.; Capt. D. A. G. Dickens; Capt. J. E. Bury; Capt. J. A. N. Bezant, D.S.C., R.D., R.N.R. (*ret.*); The Lord Wilson of Rievaulx, K.G., O.B.E., F.R.S.; Rt. Hon. E. R. G. Heath, M.B.E., M.P.; The Visct. Runciman of Doxford, O.B.E., A.F.C.; Capt. P. F. Mason, C.B.E.; Capt. T. Woodfield, O.B.E.; Sir Arthur Drake, C.B.E.; The Lord Simon of Glaisdale, P.C.; Admiral of the Fleet the Lord Lewin, K.G., G.C.B., M.V.O., D.S.C.; Capt. D. T. Smith, R.N.; Commander Sir Robin Gillett, G.B.E., R.D., R.N.R.; Capt. P. M. Edge; The Lord Shackleton, K.G., O.B.E., P.C.; Sir John Cuckney; Capt. D. J. Orr; The Lord Carrington, K.G., C.H., K.C.M.G., M.C., P.C.

Officers

Secretary, J. R. Backhouse.
Deputy Secretary, A. W. Snook.
Director of Engineering, R. J. Shergold.
Operations Manager, M. J. Faulkner.
Administration Manager, J. B. Fuller.
Personnel Manager, A. J. Smith.
Surveyor of Shipping, J. K. Rankin.
Principal, Pilotage Department, H. E. Oliver.
Principal, Corporate Department, J. A. Liddle.
Public Relations Officer, P. W. Ridgway.

CLYDE PORT AUTHORITY
16 Robertson Street, Glasgow G2 8DS

Chairman, R. W. S. Easton, C.B.E.
Managing Director, J. Mather.
Secretary, G. P. Johnston.

COMMISSIONERS OF NORTHERN LIGHTHOUSES
84 George Street, Edinburgh.
[031-226 7051]

The Commissioners of Northern Lighthouses are the General Lighthouse Authority for Scotland and the Isle of Man. The present Board owes its origin to an Act of Parliament passed in 1786 which authorized the erection of 4 lighthouses; 19 Commissioners were appointed to carry out the Act. At the present time the Commissioners operate under the Merchant Shipping Act, 1894 and are 19 in number.
The Commissioners control 47 Major manned Lighthouses, 42 Major unmanned Lighthouses, 101 Minor Lights and many Lighted and Unlighted Buoys. They have a fleet of 3 Motor Vessels.

Commissioners

The Lord Advocate, the Solicitor General, the Lords Provost of Edinburgh, Glasgow and Aberdeen; the Provost of Inverness; the Chairman of Argyll & Bute District Council; the Sheriffs-Principal of North Strathclyde; Tayside, Central & Fife; Grampian, Highlands & Islands: South Strathclyde, Dumfries & Galloway; Lothians & Borders; and Glasgow & Strathkelvin; W. D. H. Gregson, C.B.E.; T. Macgill; Capt. J. A. MacLeod; Capt. A. F. Dickson, O.B.E.; Rev. Capt. A. W. G. Kissack; A. J. Struthers.

Officers

General Manager, Cdr. J. M. Mackay, M.B.E.
Secretary, J. R. Welsh.
Engineer-in-Chief, J. H. K. Williamson.

UNIVERSITY GRANTS COMMITTEE
14 Park Crescent, W1N 4DH
[01-636 7799]

The Committee was appointed by the Chancellor of the Exchequer in July, 1919, and its present terms of reference are as follows:
"To enquire into the financial needs of university education in the U.K.; to advise the Government as to the application of any grants made by Parliament towards meeting them; to collect, examine, and make available information relating to university education throughout the United Kingdom; and to assist, in consultation with the universities and other bodies concerned, the preparation and execution of such plans for the development of the universities as may from time to time be required in order to ensure that they are fully adequate to national needs."
Chairman, Sir Peter Swinnerton-Dyer, F.R.S. £39,500
Other Members, Sir Peter Baxendell, C.B.E.; Prof. P. M. Bromley; Prof. J. Cannon, C.B.E.; D. Clarke; Sir Robert Clayton, C.B.E.; Dr. S. Cotson; Prof. C. T. Dollery; Prof. A. J. Forty; Prof. B. G. Gowenlock,

F.R.S.E.; Prof. M. B. Harris; Prof. Mary Hesse; Prof. G. R. Higginson; R. S. Johnson, C.B.E.; Prof. D. S. Jones, M.B.E., F.R.S.; Prof. P. R. G. Layard; Prof. J. G. Morris; Prof. R. Needham; W. D. C. Semple; Prof. J. Sizer; Mrs. T. Thomas, O.B.E..
Secretary, N. T. Hardyman, C.B. £29,500
Assist. Secretaries, E. C. Appleyard; M. B. Baker; H. W. B. Davies .... £20,013 to £24,317
Principals, Miss M. J. Darby; G. E. Huggins; M. C. Hutchison (*Statistician*); Mrs. R. McDonagh; Miss A. Lawson; A. H. Prosser; M. H. Sharpe.

VALUE ADDED TAX TRIBUNALS

A person dissatisfied with a decision of the Commissioners of Customs and Excise relating to certain aspects of value added tax may appeal to a tribunal. VAT Tribunals are entirely independent of the Commissioners and are under the supervision of the Council on Tribunals. They are intended to determine disputes concerning VAT speedily and with a minimum of formality and to assist in the uniform application of the tax throughout the United Kingdom. VAT Tribunals are established in London, Manchester and Edinburgh. Tribunals also sit in Belfast, Birmingham, Bristol, Cardiff, Exeter, Leeds and Newcastle as necessary.

15/17 Great Marlborough Street, W1V 1AF
[01-437 6337]

President, The Lord Grantchester, Q.C.
Registrar, J. M. Busby.

Tribunal Centres

London: 15/17 Great Marlborough Street, W1V 1AF
[01-437 6543].
Chairman, N. P. M. Elles.
Edinburgh (*including Belfast and Newcastle*): 44 Palmerston Place, Edinburgh.
Vice-President, Scotland, R. A. Bennett, Q.C.
Manchester: Warwickgate House, Warwick Road, Old Trafford, Manchester [061-872-6471]
Chairman, P. A. Ferns, T.D.

COMMONWEALTH WAR GRAVES COMMISSION
2 Marlow Road, Maidenhead, Berkshire SL6 7DX
[Maidenhead: 34221]

The Commonwealth War Graves Commission (formerly Imperial War Graves Commission) was founded by Royal Charter in 1917. It is responsible for the commemoration of 1,695,000 members of the forces of the Commonwealth who fell in the two world wars. More than one million graves are maintained in 23,361 burial grounds throughout the world. Over three-quarters of a million men and women who have no known grave or who were cremated are commemorated by name on memorials built by the Commission.
The funds of the Commission are derived from the six Governments participating in its work—the United Kingdom, Canada, Australia, New Zealand, South Africa and India.

President, H.R.H. The Duke of Kent, G.C.M.G., G.C.V.O.
Chairman, The Secretary of State for Defence.
Vice-Chairman, Air Chief Marshal Sir John Barraclough, K.C.B., C.B.E., D.F.C., A.F.C., F.R.S.A.
Members, The Minister for Housing and Construction; The High Commissioners for Canada, the Commonwealth of Australia, New Zealand, and India; the Ambassador for the Republic of South Africa; Sir Edward Gardner, Q.C., M.P.; The Lord Wallace of Coslany; Sir Edward Goschen, Bt., D.S.O.; Admiral Sir David Williams, G.C.B.; General

Sir Robert Ford, G.C.B., C.B.E.; Sir David Muirhead, K.C.M.G., C.V.O; Sir Donald Maitland, G.C.M.G., O.B.E.; The Baroness McFarlane of Llandaff.
Director-General, Sir Arthur Hockaday, K.C.B., C.M.G.
Deputy Director-General, P. R. Matthew.
Assistant Directors-General, W. J. Symons, O.B.E. (*Operations*); J. Saynor (*Administration*).
Legal Adviser and Solicitor, G. C. Reddie.
Director of External Relations, P. H. M. Swan.
Director of Works, N. B. Osborn.
Director of Horticulture, J. B. Paton, O.B.E.
Director of Informations Services, S. G. Campbell, M.C.
Establishment Officer, H. Westland.
Chief Finance Officer, M. S. Johnson.
Organization and Audit Officer, D. R. Parker.
Hon. Consulting Engineer, P. A. Scott.
Hon. Botanical Adviser, Prof. E. A. Bell, Ph.D.
Hon. Artistic Adviser, Prof. Sir Peter Shepheard, C.B.E.

Imperial War Graves Endowment Fund

Trustees, Sir John Hogg, T.D.; E. M. P. Welman; Air Chief Marshal Sir John Barraclough, K.C.B., C.B.E., D.F.C., A.F.C., F.R.S.A.
Hon. Secretary to the Trustees, M. S. Johnson.

WELSH OFFICE
Gwydyr House, Whitehall, SW1A 2ER
[01–233 3000]

Cathays Park, Cardiff CF1 3NQ
[0222 825111]

Ty Glas Road, Llanishen,
Cardiff CF4 5PL
[0222 753271]

Plas Crug, Aberystwyth,
Dyfed SY23 1NG
[0970 3162]

Brunel House, Fitzalan Road,
Cardiff CF2 1UY
[0222 465511]

(All staff are based at Cathays Park unless otherwise indicated. Staff marked * are located in London, those marked ° in Llanishen, those marked † in Aberystwyth and those marked ‡ in Brunel House.)
Secretary of State, THE RT. HON. (ROGER) NICHOLAS EDWARDS, M.P.* £31,271
  Private Secretary, R. C. Williams.*
  Assistant Private Secretaries, J. Carter*; P. D. L. Skellon.*
  Parliamentary Private Secretary, M. Robinson, M.P.*
Minister of State, JOHN STRADLING THOMAS, M.P.*
  £21,881
  Private Secretary, R. C. O'Sullivan.*
Parliamentary Under-Secretary of State, I. W. P. Roberts, M.P.* £16,411
  Private Secretary, S. Morris.*
  Parliamentary Clerk, Mrs. S. Rees.*
Head of Department, R. A. Lloyd Jones, C.B. . £45,500
  Private Secretary, G. M. Quarrell.
Deputy Head of Department, I. H. Lightman, C.B.
  £36,500

Permanent Secretary's Division
Head of Division, Mrs. M. Evans*
  £20,964 to £25,533
Principal, D. M. Rolph .... £13,508 to £18,363

Establishment Group
Principal Establishment Officer, J. W. Lloyd . £29,500
Heads of Divisions, E. A. J. Carr‡ (£29,400); W. L. Chapman; Miss E. N. M. Davies £20,964 to £25,533
Senior Economic Adviser, O. T. Hooker
  £20,964 to £25,533

Chief Statistician, D. Adams Jones
  £20,964 to £25,533
Superintending Architect, J. D. Hogg‡
  £17,000 to £22,926
Principal Inspector of Ancient Monuments and Historic Buildings, R. Avent ...... £16,757 to £19,314
Principals, R. J. Bolus‡; P. Davenport; D. R. Davies; Miss E. M. Jones; W. A. Vinall . £13,508 to £18,363
Economic Adviser, (vacant).
Principal Research Officers, I. I. Thomas; E. Darwin; Mrs. M. A. J. Gronow .... £13,508 to £18,363
Statisticians, G. J. Cockell; Miss W. K. Fader; K. Francombe; J. A. Grimes; E. Swires Hennessey; J. D. James; R. Jones; J. D. Kinder; Mrs. B. J. M. Wilson .... £13,508 to £18,363
Inspectors of Ancient Monuments and Historic Buildings, J. K. Knight; A. D. McLees; Dr. S. E. Rees
  £9,952 to £17,465

Finance Group
Principal Finance Officer, M. G. Jeremiah . . . £29,500
Heads of Divisions, L. L. Ginn, T.D.; C. L. Jones; L. Pritchard .... £20,964 to £25,533
Principals, M. G. Horlock; P. G. C. Lunn; G. Morgan; D. A. Pritchard; C. E. Taylor; B. O. Valentine
  £13,508 to £18,363
Chief Internal Auditor, B. R. Davies
  £13,508 to £18,363

Health Professional Group
Chief Medical Officer, G. Crompton £29,500
Deputy Chief Medical Officers, A. M. George; Deidre J. Hine £26,594
Senior Medical Officers, G. J. Moses; D. J. W. Anderson; D. M. Gambier; D. Ferguson Lewis
  £25,533
Chief Dental Officer, (vacant).
Medical Officers, R. Buntwal; Mary Cotter; J. W. Crossley; D. E. Davies; S. H. Killey; Jennifer Lloyd; H. G. Penrhys Jones; D. H. Richards; N. E. Thomas .... £16,597 to £23,515
Dental Officers, A. Cobb; J. D. O. Parkholm; T. A. Williams .... £16,597 to £23,515
Scientific Adviser, Dr. J. A. V. Pritchard
  £17,000 to £22,926
Pharmaceutical Adviser, D. L. Thomas
  £17,000 to £22,926

Housing, Health and Social Services Policy Group
Head of Group, J. I. Davies, M.B.E. £29,500
Heads of Divisions, P. R. Gregory; J. A. Morgan; A. E. Peat .... £20,964 to £25,533
Chief Social Work Service Officer, Miss Z. E. Williams .... £20,964 to £25,533
Chief Architect, H. O. M. Coleman £17,000 to £22,926
Principal Social Work Service Officers, D. G. Evans; B. F. Norman .... £19,069 to £23,898
Grade 6, G. T. Evans .... £17,000 to £22,926
Principals, Mrs. J. D. Annand; A. C. Elmer; P. S. Gray; M. H. Harper; R. Hughes; D. H. Jones; S. H. Martin; D. B. Quinlin; D. T. Richards; Ms. J. H. Roberts; Mrs. H. F. O. Thomas . £13,508 to £18,363
Social Work Service Officers, G. H. Davies; J. K. Fletcher; J. F. Mooney; Miss A. M. Perrott; C. D. Vyvyan; A. G. Williams; R. C. Woodward
  £13,508 to £18,777
Principal Professional and Technology Officers, R. Broad; T. A. Campden; C. Eyres; G. N. Harding; H. D. Harry; I. Smith; E. T. Williams
  £14,392 to £17,322

National Health Service Directorate
Director of the NHS in Wales, J. W. Owen . . . £45,000
Heads of Divisions, L. M. Lloyd, M.B.E.; J. C. Price; N. E. Thomas .... £20,964 to £25,533

Principals, W. M. Cooper; R. J. Davies; W. G. Davies;
N. S. Jones, I.S.O.; Miss J. E. Paulett; D. Simpson
£13,508 to £18,363
Principal Research Officer, A. S. Dredge
£13,508 to £18,363
Ambulance Adviser, P. J. Hunt .. £13,508 to £20,644
Principal Professional and Technology Officers, M.
W. Grist; J. W. Wallington .... £14,392 to £17,322
Catering and Domestic Services Adviser, C. H.
Bearpark .... £10,980 to £13,801

Nursing Division

Chief Nursing Officer, Mrs. Y. Moores £26,112
Deputy Chief Nursing Officer, Mrs. G. M. Stephens
£22,975
Nursing Officers, Dr. M. F. Alexander; Mrs. P. A.
Bryant; Miss M. Hope; Mrs. B. Melvin; M. F.
Tonkin; Mrs. D. J. Vass .... £17,551 to £20,642

Legal Division

Legal Adviser, A. J. Beale £29,500
Assistant Solicitors, D. G. Lambert; P. J. Murrin
£21,844 to £25,533
Senior Legal Assistants, A. B. Cole; J. D. H. Evans;
A. K. Gillard; C. P. Jones; C. G. Longville; A. J.
Park; Mrs. A. T. Parkes; Mrs. T. C. Shellens; J. H.
Turnbull; H. Warman; A. J. Watkins .. £15,688 to
£21,297

Information Division

Chief Information Officer, H. G. Roberts
£20,964 to £25,533
Principal Information Officer, E. M. Bowen, M.V.O.
£13,508 to £18,363

Economic and Regional Policy Group

Head of Group, J. A. Annand £29,500
Heads of Divisions, H. R. Bollington; G. C. G. Craig;
D. I. Westlake .... £20,964 to £25,533
Principals, R. Abel; L. Conway; Ms. J. M. Gordon; B.
J. Mitchell; F. G. Watson; B. Wilcox
£13,508 to £18,363

Industry Department

Director, O. Rees £29,500
Finance Director, (vacant).
Heads of Divisions, J. F. Craig; C. W. Harris
£20,964 to £25,533
Senior Principal Scientific Officer, Dr. J. N. M.
Firth.................................... £22,926
Principals, P. Bishop; C. J. Burdett; R. O. Evans; M.
Jewell; D. Pugh (at Colwyn Bay); W. P. Roderick;
C. J. Tudor .... £13,508 to £18,363
Principal Professional and Technology Officer, F. J.
Davies .... £14,392 to £17,322
Principal Scientific Officers, P. Bragg; G. A. Madden
£12,357 to £16,462

Water and Environmental Protection Division

Head of Division, L. E. Taylor .... £20,964 to £25,533
Superintending Engineer, A. S. R. Mutch
£17,000 to £22,926
Grade 6, B. S. Millwood .... £17,000 to £22,926
Principals, J. A. Evans; L. A. Pavelin; A. Whitaker
£13,508 to £18,363
Principal Scientific Officer, R. A. Page
£12,357 to £16,462

Education Department

Head of Department, R. H. Jones, C.V.O. £29,500
Heads of Divisions, H. Evans; R. D. Potter, C.B.E.
(£20,964 to £25,533); D. M. Timlin
£17,000 to £22,926
Principals, D. F. J. Beames; D. A. Bullen; R. J. Callen;
J. B. Davies; M. L. Evans; J. W. Jones; Miss C. M.
Owen .... £13,508 to £18,363

H. M. Inspectorate

Chief Inspector, I. R. Lloyd £26,909
Staff Inspectors, S. J. Adams; R. L. James; R. E. Jones;
P. Thomas; R. Thomas; P. C. Webb; M. J. F. Wynn
£20,964 to £25,533
H. M. Inspectors, C. Abbott; Mrs. G. Briwnant Jones;
H. W. Davies; R. G. Davies; D. G. Evans; J. R. N.
Evans; K. M. Evans; N. B. Evans; Mrs. L.
Gainsbury; A. G. George; J. Griffiths; A. Hamilton
Jones; A. Higgins; Mrs. R. James; W. R. Jenkins;
M. John; G. D. Jones; O. E. Jones; Mrs A. Keane;
J. M. Laugharane; M. J. Law; I. M. Lewis; J. R.
Lewis; R. A. Lowe; A. Morgan; I. G. Morgan; J.
Nicholas; Miss P. A. Nicholas; Miss E. Ogwen; T.
E. Parry; T. G. Prosser; W. H. Raybould; D. G. H.
Rees; G. O. Roberts; Miss D. Selleck; Mrs. Y. Scott;
M. W. Stone; R. Raylor; G. Thomas; Glyndwr
Thomas; Mrs. I. Thomas; Miss L. Thomas; P. B.
Walker; G. Warren; B. Wigley; W. E. L. Williams;
D. P. Williams................ £17,000 to £22,926

Transport, Highways and Planning Group

Head of Group, R. W. Jarman° £29,500
Director of Engineering, G. Mercer° £26,909
Heads of Divisions, G. G. Elliott°; A. H. H. Jones°; J.
C. Lewis .... £20,964 to £25,533
£16,288 to £21,753
Chief Planner, C. J. Curry .... £20,964 to £25,533
Principal Housing and Planning Inspector, Miss B.
Ellis .... £21,595 to £24,230
Superintending Engineers, J. G. Evans°; J. E. Morgan,
O.B.E.°; R. Lober .... £17,000 to £22,926
Superintending Estates Officer, G. K. Hoad
£17,000 to £22,926
Senior Housing and Planning Inspectors, T. W.
Barnes; R. Pierce; J. L. S. Whalley; J. D. Grainger;
Brig. A. D. R. Saunders; D. Sheers; G. Sloan
£16,288 to £21,753
Principals, G. Davies°; R. W. Jenkins°; A. V. Price°;
J. Shortridge°; R. C. Simpson°; K. L. Smith°; S. H.
Spackman .... £13,508 to £18,363
Principal Planning Officers, D. B. Courtier; G.
Fairhurst; J. O. Pryce; B. G. Taylor
£14,392 to £17,322
Principal Research Officers, G. R. Jones; I. E. Thompson .... £13,508 to £18,363
Landscape Adviser, C. W. W. Smart°
£14,392 to £17,322
Principal, Professional and Technology Officers, P. I.
Adams°; P. Dunstan°; B. H. Hawker°; D. G. Minas°;
B. J. W. Martin°; S. D. Padfield°; W. H. Prosser°; J.
R. Rees°; D. P. Soane°; E. G. Whitcutt°
£14,392 to £17,322

Agriculture Department

Head of Department, R. Hall Williams £29,500
Heads of Divisions, M. E. Bevan; G. Owen, O.B.E.; D.
J. Palmer† .... £20,964 to £25,533
Principals, P. Finnigan†; W. K. Griffiths; R. E.
Hughes†; T. W. Hunter; R. F. Patterson; Mrs. C. J.
Peat; J. M. Thomas .... £13,508 to £18,363
Divisional Executive Officers, J. C. Alexander (*Carmarthen*); D. W. Evans (*Ruthin*); R. G. Gairey
(*Cardiff*); D. R. Thomas (*Caernarfon*); R. J. E.
Wilcox (*Llandrindod Wells*) ... £13,508 to £18,363

LAND AUTHORITY FOR WALES
The Custom House, Custom House Street,
Cardiff CF1 5AP
[0222 499077]

The Authority is responsible for acquiring and
disposing of land needed for private development in
Wales.
Chairman, D. H. Pryce Thomas, C.B.E. (*part-time*)
£18,265
Chief Executive, B. Ryan.

LAW COURTS AND OFFICES

LAW SITTINGS (1986)—*Hilary*, Jan. 11 to March 26; *Easter*, April 8 to May 23; *Trinity*, June 3 to July 31; *Michaelmas*, Oct. 1 to Dec. 21.

THE JUDICIAL COMMITTEE OF THE PRIVY COUNCIL

The Judicial Committee of the Privy Council is the final court of appeal from courts of the United Kingdom dependencies, courts of independent Commonwealth countries which have retained the right of appeal, courts of the Channel Islands and the Isle of Man, some professional and disciplinary committees and church sources. The Committee is composed of all Privy Counsellors who hold, or have held, high judicial office, although usually only three or five hear each case.

The Judicial Committee includes the Lord Chancellor, the Lords of Appeal in Ordinary (*see* below) and such other members of the Privy Council as shall from time to time hold or have held "high judicial office," and certain judges from the Commonwealth.

Office—Downing Street, S.W.1.
Registrar of the Privy Council, D. H. O. Owen.
Chief Clerk, D. Rushton.

THE JUDICATURE OF ENGLAND AND WALES

The legal system of England and Wales is separate from those of Scotland and Northern Ireland and differs from them in law, judicial procedure and court structure, although there is a common distinction between civil law (disputes between individuals) and criminal law (acts harmful to the community).

The supreme judicial authority for England and Wales is the House of Lords, which is the ultimate Court of Appeal from all courts in Great Britain and Northern Ireland (except criminal courts in Scotland). As a Court of Appeal it consists of the Lord Chancellor and the Lords of Appeal in Ordinary (Law Lords). The Supreme Court of Judicature comprises the Court of Appeal, the Crown Court and the High Court of Justice. The High Court of Justice is the superior civil court and is divided into three Divisions. The Chancery Division is concerned mainly with equity, bankruptcy and contentious probate business; the Queen's Bench Division deals with commercial and maritime law, with civil cases not assigned to other courts, and hears appeals from lower courts; and the Family Division, which deals with matters relating to family law. Sittings are held at the Royal Courts of Justice in London or at 24 Crown Court centres outside the capital. High Court judges sit alone to hear cases at first instance. Appeals from lower courts are heard by two or three judges, or by single judges of the appropriate Division.

The decision to prosecute in cases tried on indictment and in summary cases of a serious nature rests in England and Wales with the police. Some offences, however, can be prosecuted only with the consent of the Attorney-General or by, or with the consent of the Director of Public Prosecutions on behalf of the Attorney-General. A number of other offences must also be reported by the police to the Director of Public Prosecutions, although the Director does not always prosecute all such cases and may leave prosecution to the police. (An independent prosecution service is to be established, however, and is expected to come into operation in 1986.)

Minor criminal offences (summary offences) are dealt with in magistrates' courts, which usually consist of three unpaid lay magistrates (justices of the peace) sitting without a jury, who are advised on points of law and procedure by a legally-qualified clerk to the justices: in busier courts a full-time, salaried and legally-qualified stipendiary magistrate presides alone. Cases involving people under 17 are heard in juvenile courts, specially constituted magistrates' courts which sit apart from other courts. Preliminary proceedings in a serious case to decide whether there is evidence to justify committal for trial in the Crown Court are also held in the magistrates' courts. Appeals from magistrates' courts against sentence or conviction are made to the Crown Court. Appeals upon a point of law are made to the High Court, and may go on to the House of Lords.

The Crown Court sits in about 90 centres, divided into six circuits, and is presided over by High Court judges, full-time circuit judges, and part-time recorders, sitting with a jury in all trials which are contested. It deals with trials of the more serious criminal offences, the sentencing of offenders committed for sentence by magistrates' courts (when the magistrates' consider their own power of sentence inadequate), and appeals from lower courts. Magistrates usually sit with a circuit judge or recorder to deal with appeals and committals for sentence. Appeals from the Crown Court, either against sentence or conviction, are made to the Court of Appeal (Criminal Division), presided over by the Lord Chief Justice. A further appeal from the Court of Appeal to the House of Lords can be brought if a point of law of general public importance is considered to be involved.

Most minor civil cases are dealt with by the county courts, of which there are about 300. For cases involving small claims there are special arbitration facilities and simplified procedures: cases involving claims which exceed set limits may be tried in the county courts with the consent of the parties, or in certain circumstances on transfer from the High Court. Undefended divorce cases and, outside London, bankruptcy proceedings can be heard in designated county courts. Magistrates' courts can deal with certain classes of civil case, mostly those relating to the family, and committees of magistrates licence public houses, clubs and betting shops. Appeals in matrimonial, adoption and guardianship proceedings heard in the magistrates' courts go to the Family Division of the High Court: affiliation appeals and appeals from decisions of the licensing committees of magistrates to the Crown Court. Appeals from the High Court and county courts are heard in the Court of Appeal (Civil Division), presided over by the Master of the Rolls, and may go on to the House of Lords, the final court of appeal in civil cases.

Coroners' courts investigate violent and unnatural deaths or sudden deaths where the cause is unknown. Cases may be brought before a local coroner (a senior lawyer or doctor) by doctors, the police, various public authorities or members of the public. Where a death is sudden and the cause is unknown the coroner may order a post-mortem examination to determine the cause of death rather than holding an inquest in court.

THE HOUSE OF LORDS (as final Court of Appeal)

The Lord High Chancellor—
The Rt. Hon. the Lord Hailsham of St. Marylebone, C.H. (*born* 1907, *apptd.* 1979), £71,500.

Lords of Appeal in Ordinary (each £63,750)

	Apptd.
Rt. Hon. Lord Diplock, *born* 1907	1968
Rt. Hon. Lord Fraser of Tullybelton, *born* 1911	1975
Rt. Hon. Lord Keith of Kinkel, *born* 1922	1977
Rt. Hon. Lord Scarman, O.B.E., *born* 1911	1977
Rt. Hon. Lord Roskill, *born* 1911	1980
Rt. Hon. Lord Bridge of Harwich, *born* 1917	1980
Rt. Hon. Lord Brandon of Oakbrook, M.C., *born* 1920	1981
Rt. Hon. Lord Brightman, *born* 1911	1982
Rt. Hon. Lord Templeman, M.B.E., *born* 1920	1982
Rt. Hon. Lord Griffiths, *born* 1923	1985

Registrar: The Clerk of the Parliaments, J. Sainty.

SUPREME COURT OF JUDICATURE
COURT OF APPEAL

Ex officio Judges.—The Lord High Chancellor, the Lord Chief Justice of England, the Master of the Rolls, the President of the Family Division, and the Vice-Chancellor.

The Master of the Rolls (£63,750)
The Rt. Hon. Sir John Donaldson (*born* 1920, *apptd.* 1982).

Secretary, Miss V. Seymour; *Clerk,* K. H. L. Smeeton.
Lords Justices of Appeal (each £60,750)—

	Apptd.
Rt. Hon. Sir Frederick Horace Lawton, *born* 1911	1972
Rt. Hon. Sir Desmond James Conrad Ackner, *born* 1920	1980
Rt. Hon. Sir Peter Raymond Oliver, *born* 1921	1980
Rt. Hon. Sir Tasker Watkins, V.C., *born* 1918	1980
Rt. Hon. Sir Patrick McCarthy O'Connor, *born* 1914	1980
Rt. Hon. Sir Michael Fox, *born* 1921	1981
Rt. Hon. Sir Michael Robert Emanuel Kerr, *born* 1921	1981
Rt. Hon. Sir John Douglas May, *born* 1923	1982
Rt. Hon. Sir Christopher John Slade, *born* 1927	1982
Rt. Hon. Sir Francis Brooks Purchas, *born* 1919	1982
Rt. Hon. Sir Robert Lionel Archibald Goff, *born* 1926	1982
Rt. Hon. Sir George Brian Hugh Dillon, *born* 1923	1982
Rt. Hon. Sir Stephen Brown, *born* 1929	1983
Rt. Hon. Sir Roger Jocelyn Parker, *born* 1923	1983
Rt. Hon. Sir David Powell Croom-Johnson, D.S.C., *born* 1914	1984
Rt. Hon. Sir Anthony John Leslie Lloyd, *born* 1929	1984
Rt. Hon. Sir Brian Thomas Neill, *born* 1923	1985
Rt. Hon. Sir Michael John Mustill, *born* 1931	1985
Rt. Hon. Sir Martin Charles Nourse, *born* 1932	1985
Rt. Hon. Sir Iain Derek Laing Glidewell, *born* 1924	1985
Rt. Hon. Sir Alfred John Balcombe, *born* 1925	1985

Court of Appeal (Criminal Division)

Judges, The Lord Chief Justice of England, The Master of the Rolls, Lord Justices of Appeal and the Judges of the Queen's Bench Division.

Courts-Martial Appeal Court

Judges, The Lord Chief Justice of England, The Master of the Rolls, Lords Justice of Appeal, and Judges of the Queen's Bench Division.

HIGH COURT OF JUSTICE
CHANCERY DIVISION
President, The Lord High Chancellor

The Vice-Chancellor (£60,750)
The Rt. Hon. Sir Nicolas Christopher Henry Browne-Wilkinson
(*born* 1930, *apptd.* 1985)

Secretary (vacant); *Clerk,* W. Northfield.
Judges (each £55,625)

	Apptd.
Hon. Sir John Norman Keates Whitford, *born* 1913	1970
Hon. Sir (Ernest) Irvine Goulding, *born* 1910	1971
Hon. Sir Raymond Henry Walton, *born* 1915	1973
Hon. Sir John Evelyn Vinelott, *born* 1923	1978
Hon. Sir Douglas William Falconer, M.B.E., *born* 1914	1981
Hon. Sir Jean-Pierre Frank Eugene Warner, *born* 1924	1981
Hon. Sir Peter Leslie Gibson, *born* 1934	1981
Hon. Sir David Herbert Mervyn Davies, M.C., T.D., *born* 1918	1982
Hon. Sir Jeremiah LeRoy Harman, *born* 1930	1982
Hon. Sir Donald James Nicholls, *born* 1933	1983
Hon. Sir Richard Rashleigh Folliott Scott, *born* 1934	1983
Hon. Sir Leonard Hubert Hoffman, *born* 1934	1985

High Court of Justice in Bankruptcy

Judges, The Rt. Hon. the Vice-Chancellor; The Hon. Mr. Justice Goulding; The Hon. Mr. Justice Walton; The Hon. Mr. Justice Vinelott; The Hon. Mr. Justice Nourse; The Hon. Mr. Justice Warner; The Hon. Mr. Justice Peter Gibson; The Hon. Mr. Justice Mervyn Davies; The Hon. Mr. Justice Harman; The Hon. Mr. Justice Nicholls; The Hon. Mr. Justice Scott.

Companies Court

Judges, The Hon. Mr. Justice Vinelott; The Hon. Mr. Justice Mervyn Davies; The Hon. Mr. Justice Harman.

Patent Court (Appellate Section)

Judges, The Hon. Mr. Justice Whitford; The Hon. Mr. Justice Falconer.

QUEEN'S BENCH DIVISION
The Lord Chief Justice of England (£69,500)
The Rt. Hon. The Lord Lane, A.F.C.
(*born* 1918, *apptd.* 1980)

Secretary, Mrs. J. Simpson; *Clerk,* G. Curtis.
Judges (each £55,625)—

	Apptd.
Hon. Sir Joseph Donaldson Cantley, O.B.E., *born* 1910	1965
Hon. Sir Bernard Caulfield, *born* 1914	1968
Hon. Sir William Lloyd Mars-Jones, M.B.E., *born* 1915	1969
Hon. Sir Peter Henry Rowley Bristow, *born* 1913	1970
Hon. Sir Hugh Harry Valentine Forbes, *born* 1917	1970
Hon. Sir Leslie Kenneth Edward Boreham, *born* 1918	1972
Hon. Sir (Alfred William) Michael Davies, *born* 1921	1973
Hon. Sir John Dexter Stocker, M.C., T.D., *born* 1918	1973
Hon. Sir Kenneth George Illtyd Jones, *born* 1921	1974
Hon. Sir Haydn Tudor Evans, *born* 1920	1974

Hon. Sir Peter Richard Pain, *born* 1913	1975
Hon. Sir Kenneth Graham Jupp, M.C., *born* 1917	1975
Hon. Sir Ralph Brian Gibson, *born* 1922	1977
Hon. Sir (Walter) Derek (Thornley) Hodgson, *born* 1917	1977
Hon. Sir James Peter Comyn, *born* 1921	1978
Hon. Sir (Frederick) Maurice Drake, D.F.C., *born* 1923	1978
Hon. Sir Barry Cross Sheen, *born* 1918	1978
Hon. Sir David Bruce McNeill, *born* 1922	1979
Hon. Sir Harry Kenneth Woolf, *born* 1933	1979
Hon. Sir Christopher James Saunders French, *born* 1925	1979
Hon. Sir Thomas Patrick Russell, *born* 1926 .	1980
Hon. Sir Peter Edlin Webster, *born* 1929	1980
Hon. Sir Thomas Henry Bingham, *born* 1933 .	1980
Hon. Sir Henry Albert Skinner, *born* 1926 ...	1980
Hon. Sir Peter Murray Taylor, *born* 1930	1981
Hon. Sir Murray Stuart-Smith, *born* 1927	1981
Hon. Sir Christopher Stephen Thomas Jonathan Thayer Staughton, *born* 1933	1981
Hon. Sir Donald Henry Farquharson, *born* 1928	1981
Hon. Sir Anthony James Denys McCowan, *born* 1928	1981
Hon. Sir (Iain) Charles (Robert) McCullough, *born* 1931	1981
Hon. Sir Hamilton John Leonard, *born* 1926 .	1981
Hon. Sir Alexander Roy Asplan Beldam, *born* 1925	1981
Hon. Sir David Cozens-Hardy Hirst, *born* 1925	1982
Hon. Sir John Stewart Hobhouse, *born* 1932 .	1982
Hon. Sir Michael Mann, *born* 1930	1982
Hon. Sir Andrew Peter Leggatt, *born* 1930 ...	1982
Hon. Sir Michael Patrick Nolan, *born* 1928 ..	1982
Hon. Sir Oliver Bury Popplewell, *born* 1927 ..	1983
Hon. Sir William Alan Macpherson, T.D., *born* 1926	1983
Hon. Sir Philip Howard Otton, *born* 1933	1983
Hon. Sir Paul Joseph Morrow Kennedy, *born* 1935	1983
Hon. Sir Michael Hutchison, *born* 1933	1983
Hon. Sir Simon Denis Brown, *born* 1937	1984
Hon. Sir David William Tudor Price, *born* 1931	1984
Hon. Sir Anthony Howell Meurig Evans, *born* 1934	1984
Hon. Sir Mark Oliver Saville, *born* 1936	1985
Hon. Sir Johan Van Zyl Steyn, *born* 1932	1985
Hon. Sir Christopher Dudley Roger Rose, *born* 1937	1985
Hon. Mr. Richard Howard Tucker, Q.C., *born* 1931	1985

FAMILY DIVISION
President (£61,500)

Rt. Hon. Sir John Lewis Arnold (*born* 1915, *apptd.* 1979).
Secretary, Mrs. E. Coles; *Clerk*, C. Beardsmore.
Judges (each £55,625)—

	Apptd.
Hon. Sir John Brinsmead Latey, M.B.E., *born* 1914	1965
Hon. Sir (Alfred) Kenneth Hollings, M.C., *born* 1918	1971
Hon. Sir (Charles) Trevor Reeve, *born* 1915 ..	1973
Hon. Dame Rose Heilbron, D.B.E., *born* 1914...	1974
Hon. Sir Brian Drex Bush, *born* 1925	1976
Hon. Sir John Kember Wood, M.C., *born* 1922 .	1977
Hon. Sir Ronald Gough Waterhouse, *born* 1926	1978
Hon. Sir (John) Gervase (Kensington) Sheldon, *born* 1913	1978
Hon. Sir (Thomas) Michael Eastham, *born* 1920	1978

Hon. Dame Margaret Myfanwy Wood Booth, D.B.E., *born* 1933	1979
Hon. Sir Anthony Leslie Julian Lincoln, *born* 1920	1979
Hon. Dame (Ann) Elizabeth (Oldfield) Butler-Sloss, D.B.E. *born* 1933	1979
Hon. Sir Anthony Bruce Ewbank, *born* 1925 .	1980
Hon. Sir John Douglas Waite, *born* 1932	1982
Hon. Sir Anthony Barnard Hollis, *born* 1927 .	1982
Hon. Sir Swinton Barclay Thomas, *born* 1931.	1985

RESTRICTIVE PRACTICES COURT

Judicial Members, The Hon. Mr. Justice Anthony Lincoln (*Principal*); The Hon. Mr. Justice McNeill; The Hon. Mr. Justice Warner; Lord Ross; Lord Justice Gibson.

Lay Members, N. C. Pearson, O.B.E., T.D.; N. L. Salmon; I. G. Stewart; B. M. Currie; L. Robertson.

LORD CHANCELLOR'S DEPARTMENT
See Government and Public Offices.

SUPREME COURT DEPARTMENTS AND OFFICES
Royal Courts of Justice, WC2A 2LL

Administrator, S. Orchard .... £20,964–£25,533

Central Office of the Supreme Court
Royal Courts of Justice, WC2A 2LL

Senior Master of the Supreme Court (Q.B.D.), and Queen's Remembrancer, J. R. Bickford-Smith, T.D. £36,500
Masters of the Supreme Court (Q.B.D.), S. J. Waldman; I. S. Warren; C. W. S. Lubbock; P. B. Creightmore; K. W. Topley; D. L. Prebble; A. A. Grant; G. H. Hodgson; R. L. Turner £29,925
Chief Clerk (Central Office), R. P. Knight £13,508–£18,363
Chief Clerk to the Q.B. Judges in Chambers, C. F. Jones .... £13,508–£18,363

Crown Office of the Supreme Court
Royal Courts of Justice, WC2A 2LL

Master of the Crown Office, and Queen's Coroner and Attorney, D. R. Thompson, C.B., Q.C.

Official Referees of the Supreme Court

His Honour Judge Sir William Stabb, Q.C.; His Honour Judge Hawser, Q.C.; His Honour Judge Newey, Q.C.; His Honour Judge Smout, Q.C.

Court of Appeal (Civil Division) Office
Royal Courts of Justice, WC2A 2LL

Registrar, J. D. R. Adams.

Criminal Appeal Office
Royal Courts of Justice, WC2A 2LL

Registrar, D. R. Thompson, C.B., Q.C. £36,500
Assistant Registrar, J. A. D. Heal ... £20,964–£25,533
Assistant Solicitor, R. A. Venne .... £20,964–£25,533
Chief Clerk, A. F. P. Ottway ..... £13,508–£18,363

Courts-Martial Appeals Office
Royal Courts of Justice, WC2A 2LL

Registrar, D. R. Thompson, C.B., Q.C. £36,500
Chief Clerk, A. F. P. Ottway.

Supreme Court Taxing Office

Chief Master, F. T. Horne £36,500
Masters of the Supreme Court, M. A. Clews; F. G. Berkeley; A. J. Wright; C. R. N. Martyn; M. N. Devonshire, T.D.; P. T. Hurst; C. A. Prince £29,925
Chief Clerk, D. Hutchings .... £13,508–£18,363

Examiners of the Court
(Empowered to take Examination of Witnesses in all Divisions of the High Court)
M. F. Meredith-Hardy; B. Rathbone; N. W. Briggs; R. Jacobs.

Chancery Chambers,
Royal Courts of Justice, WC2A 2LL

Masters of the Supreme Court, R. Chamberlain, T.D. *(Chief Master),* £36,500; M. B. Cholmondeley Clarke; J. M. Dyson; J. S. Gowers; G. A. Barratt £29,925
Chief Clerk, A. T. D. Higgs . . . . £13,508–£18,363
Conveyancing Counsel of the Supreme Court, J. Monckton; S. G. Maurice; M. J. Roth.

Bankruptcy Department
Thomas More Building, Royal Courts of Justice, Strand, WC2A 2LL

Chief Registrar, J. Bradburn £36,500
Principal Clerk, R. L. Jones.

Official Receivers' Department

Senior Official Receiver, J. B. Clemetson.
Official Receivers, D. A. Thorne; D. E. Dolman.
Assistant do. E. A. Ashcroft; A. G. L. Billing; D. E. I. Peet; W. Jenner; S. E. Rhodes; J. A. Booth; M. J. Pugh.

Companies Court
Thomas More Building, Royal Courts of Justice, WC2A 2LL

Registrar, J. Bradburn.
Chief Clerk, J. R. Baker . . . . £13,508–£18,363
Senior Official Receiver, Companies Department, J. B. Clemetson.

Restrictive Practices Court
Thomas More Building, Royal Courts of Justice, WC2A 2LL

Clerk of the Court, J. Bradburn.
Chief Clerk, J. R. Baker.

Principal Registry (Family Division)
Somerset House, WC2R 1LP

Senior Registrar, B. P. Tickle £36,500
Registrars, B. Garland; C. F. Turner; T. G. Guest; D. H. Colgate; D. E. Morris; J. E. Artro-Morris; R. B. Rowe; G. B. N. A. Angel; B. P. F. Kenworthy-Browne; G. A. Terian; Mrs. K. T. Moorhouse; D. T. A. Davies; Mrs. N. Pearce £29,925
Secretary, R. Conn . . . . £13,508–£18,363

District Probate Registrars

Birmingham and Stoke-on-Trent, A. M. Teasdale.
Brighton and Maidstone, G. R. Garrett.
Bristol, Exeter and Bodmin, P. L. Speyer.
Ipswich, Norwich and Peterborough, E. R. Alexander.
Leeds, Lincoln and Sheffield, C. S. Fisher.
Liverpool, Lancaster and Chester, J. D. Hemingway.
Llandaff, Bangor, Carmarthen and Gloucester, D. W. Jones.
Manchester and Nottingham, M. A. Moran.
Newcastle, Carlisle, York and Middlesbrough, A. Bertram.
Oxford and Leicester, Miss M. L. Farmborough.
Winchester, A. K. Biggs.

Admiralty Registry and Marshal's Office
Royal Courts of Justice, WC2A 2LL

Registrar, J. D. H. Rochford £29,925
Marshal and Chief Clerk, V. E. Ricks
£13,508–£18,363

Court of Protection
25 Store Street, W.C.1.

Master, Mrs. A. B. MacFarlane.
Chief Clerk, P. D. Lewis, T.D.

Protection Division
Head of Protection Division, E. J. Dober.

Management Division
48–49 Chancery Lane, W.C.2.
Head of Management Division, J. R. Ellis.

Official Solicitor's Department
Penderel House, 287 High Holborn, W.C.1.

Official Solicitor to the Supreme Court, H. D. S. Venables £31,750
Dep. Do., H. J. Baker . . . . £20,964–£25,533
Assistant Solicitor, W. H. McBryde
£20,964–£25,533
Chief Clerk, A. J. Simpson . . . . £13,508–£18,363

OFFICE OF THE LORD CHANCELLOR'S VISITORS
Neville House, Page Street, S.W.1

Legal Visitor, M. H. Fauvelle.
Medical Visitors, W. A. Heaton-Ward; E. Carr; F. E. Kenyon; R. J. Kerry; P. A. Morris.

OFFICE OF THE JUDGE ADVOCATE 0F THE FLEET
Queen Elizabeth Building, Temple, EC4Y 9BS

Judge Advocate of the Fleet, W. M. Howard, Q.C.

OFFICE OF THE JUDGE ADVOCATE GENERAL OF THE FORCES
(*Joint Service for the Army and the Royal Air Force*)
4th Floor, St. Dunstan's House, Fetter Lane, EC4A 1BT

Judge Advocate General, J. Stuart-Smith . . . £33,000
Vice Judge Advocate General, G. L. Chapman
£31,000
Assistant Judge Advocates General, C. G. Gould; G. E. Empson; G. R. Canner; E. G. Moelwyn-Hughes; A. P. Pitts; S. B. Spence . . . . £20,964–£25,533
Deputy Judge Advocates, A. Labor; D. M. Berkson; M. A. Hunter . . . . £15,688–£21,297

HIGH COURT AND CROWN COURT CENTRES

First-tier centres deal with both civil and criminal cases and are served by High Court and Circuit Judges. Second-tier centres deal with criminal cases only but are served by both High Court and Circuit Judges. Third-tier centres deal with criminal cases only and are served only by Circuit Judges.

Midland and Oxford Circuit

First-tier—Birmingham, Lincoln, Nottingham, Stafford, Warwick. *Second-tier*—Leicester, Northampton, Oxford, Shrewsbury, Worcester. *Third-tier*—Coventry, Derby, Dudley, Grimsby, Hereford, Peterborough, Stoke-on-Trent, Walsall, Wolverhampton.
Circuit Administrator, M. C. Blair, 2 Newton Street, Birmingham B4 7LU.
Courts Administrators, Birmingham Group, C. A. Green; *Nottingham Group,* P. H. Martin; *Stafford Group,* A. F. Parker.

North Eastern Circuit

First-tier—Leeds, Newcastle upon Tyne, Sheffield, Teesside. *Second-tier*—York. *Third-tier*—Beverley, Doncaster, Durham, Huddersfield, Kingston-upon-Hull, Wakefield.

Circuit Administrator, M. D. Huebner, National Westminster House, 4th Floor, 29 Bond Street, Leeds LS1 5BQ.

Courts Administrators, Leeds Group, C. A. White; *Newcastle upon Tyne Group*, F. I. Lance; *Sheffield Group*, J. Scott.

Northern Circuit

First-tier—Carlisle, Liverpool, Manchester, Preston. *Third-tier*—Barrow-in-Furness, Bolton, Burnley, Kendal, Lancaster.

Circuit Administrator, R. Potter, Aldine House, West Riverside, New Bailey Street, Salford M3 5EU.

Courts Administrators, Manchester Group, G. F. Addicott; *Liverpool Group*, B. H. Whittaker; *Preston Group*, G. Davies.

South Eastern Circuit

First-tier—Greater London, Chelmsford, Lewes, Norwich (The High Court in Greater London sits at the Royal Courts of Justice. The Crown Court in Greater London sits at the following locations: Acton, Central Criminal Court, Croydon, Kingston-upon-Thames, Knightsbridge, Newington Causeway, Snaresbrook, Southwark and Wood Green). *Second-tier*—Ipswich, Maidstone, Reading, St. Albans. *Third-tier*—Aylesbury, Bedford, Bury St. Edmunds, Cambridge, Canterbury, Chichester, Kings Lynn, Southend.

Circuit Administrator, J. L. Heritage, New Cavendish House, 18 Maltravers Street, W.C.2.

Deputy Circuit Administrator, M. McKenzie.

Courts Administrators, Chelmsford Group, K. H. A. Henderson; *Maidstone Group*, G. R. Nicholls; *Kingston Group*, P. M. Thomas; *London* (*Civil*), S. M. Orchard; *London* (*Crime*), J. Howe.

Wales and Chester Circuit

First-tier—Caernarvon, Cardiff, Chester, Mold, Swansea. *Second-tier*—Carmarthen, Newport, Welshpool. *Third-tier*—Dolgellau, Haverfordwest, Knutsford, Merthyr Tydfil, Warrington.

Circuit Administrator, S. W. L. James, Churchill House, Churchill Way, Cardiff.

Courts Administrators, Cardiff Group, G. Jones; *Chester Group*, A. H. Howard.

Western Circuit

First-tier—Bodmin, Bristol, Exeter, Winchester. *Second-tier*—Dorchester, Gloucester, Plymouth. *Third-tier*—Barnstaple, Bournemouth/Poole, Devizes, Newport (I.O.W.), Portsmouth, Salisbury, Southampton, Swindon, Taunton.

Circuit Administrator, I. E. Ashworth, Bridge House, Clifton, Bristol BS8 4BN.

Courts Administrators, Bristol Group, A. C. Burden; *Exeter Group*, J. F. Brindley; *Winchester Group*, J. K. W. Phipps.

CIRCUIT JUDGES
(each £36,500)

Midland and Oxford Circuit

W. A. L. Allardice; F. A. Allen; M. J. Astill; F. A. Blennerhassett, Q.C.; J. F. Blythe, T.D.; F. L. Clark, Q.C.; P. Clark; R. Cole; J. M. Coulson; I. T. R. Davidson, Q.C.; W. N. Davison; A. de Piro, Q.C.; T. M. Dillon, Q.C.; A. R. M. Ellis; J. F. Evans, Q.C.; B. A. Farrer, Q.C.; H. G. A. Gosling; M. K. Harrison-Hall; T. R. Heald; J. R. Hopkin; R. H. Hutchinson; J. E. M. Irvine; J. G. Jones; E. F. Jowitt, Q.C.; J. T. C. Lee; J. R. Macgregor; M. H. Mander, Q.C.; K. Matthewman, Q.C.; P. W. Medd, O.B.E., Q.C.; K. S. W. Mellor, Q.C.; N. Micklem; A. J. H. Morrison; M. D. Mott; P. C. Northcote; F. M. Potter; H. C. Rigby, D.F.C.; D. E. Roberts; J. Ross, Q.C.; C. S. Stuart-White; H. C.

Tayler, Q.C.; K. J. Taylor; R. J. Toyn; M. B. Ward; R. L. Ward, Q.C.; G. G. A. Whitehead, D.F.C.; D. J. R. Wilcox; H. Wilson; J. W. Wilson; B. Woods; C. H. Wootton; C. G. Young.

Northern Circuit

H. H. Andrew, Q.C.; J. R. Arthur, D.F.C.; A. W. Bell; R. M. Bingham, T.D., Q.C.; A. J. Blackett-Ord (*Vice Chancellor, County Palatine of Lancaster*); A. S. Booth, Q.C.; Joyanne W. Bracewell, Q.C.; D. D. Brown, Q.C.; I. B. Campbell; F. B. Carter, Q.C.; G. P. Crowe, Q.C.; J. W. Da Cunha; J. M. Davies, Q.C.; B. Duckworth; Ann Marian Ebsworth; A. A. Edmondson; J. FitzHugh, Q.C.; D. M. Forster; D. G. F. Franks; R. J. Hardy; Mary Holt; G. W. Humphries; W. H. W. Jalland; A. C. Jolly; H. A. Kershaw; H. L. Lachs; R. R. Leech; C. N. Lees; J. M. Lever, Q.C.; R. Lockett; J. H. Lord; I. H. Morris-Jones, Q.C.; F. J. Nance; M. O'Donoghue; F. D. Paterson; R. E. I. Pickering; A. M. Prestt, Q.C.; M. A. G. Sachs; N. W. M. Sellers, V.R.D.; H. S. Singer; J. A. Stannard; I. R. Taylor, Q.C.; E. S. Temple, M.B.E., Q.C. (*Recorder of Liverpool*); V. B. Webster; W. R. Wickham; R. Wood.

North Eastern Circuit

G. Baker, Q.C.; P. Baker, Q.C.; J. M. A. Barker; H. C. Beaumont, M.B.E.; H. G. Bennett, Q.C.; B. Bush; C. D. Chapman, Q.C.; Myrella Cohen, Q.C.; J. Coles, Q.C.; J. A. Cotton; C. R. Dean, Q.C.; D. S. Forrester-Paton, Q.C.; A. N. Fricker, Q.C.; M. Gibbon, Q.C.; S. S. Gill; M. Gosnay; H. G. Hall; P. H. Hallam; J. A. Henham; D. Herrod, Q.C.; H. Hewitt; V. R. Hurwitz; A. E. Hutchinson, Q.C.; J. R. Johnson; A. C. Lauriston, Q.C.; A. C. Macdonald; G. Milner; A. L. Myerson, Q.C.; D. A. Orde; Miss H. E. Paling, Q.C.; R. A. Percy; J. Pickles; J. H. E. Randolph; D. M. Savill, Q.C.; A. Simpson; L. B. Stephen; J. Stephenson; R. A. R. Stroyan, Q.C.; J. D. Walker; M. Walker; P. H. C. Walker; O. Wrighton.

South Eastern Circuit

J. S. R. Abdela, T.D., Q.C.; F. J. Aglionby; A. K. Allen, O.B.E.; M. J. Anwyl-Davies, Q.C.; M. V. Argyle, M.C., Q.C.; A. P. Babington; J. A. Baker; J. B. Baker, Q.C.; P. V. Baker; R. M. N. Band, M.C., Q.C.; R. A. Barr; P. T. S. Batterbury, T.D.; F. E. Beezley; G. J. Binns; M. Birks; J. C. C. Blofeld, Q.C.; P. M. Blomefield; J. Bolland; L. J. Bromley, Q.C.; A. E. Brooks; G. N. Butler, Q.C.; N. M. Butter, Q.C.; H. J. Byrt, Q.C.; C. V. Callman; Sir Harold Cassel, Bt., T.D., Q.C.; B. R. Clapham; A. W. Clark; D. J. Clarkson, Q.C.; J. L. Clay, T.D.; Patricia Coles, Q.C.; C. C. Colston, Q.C.; R. K. Cooke, O.B.E.; M. R. Coombe; Margaret D. Cosgrave; A. G. W. Coulthard; P. H. Counsell; A. E. Cox; P. V. Crocker; N. H. Curtis-Raleigh; J. Davies, Q.C.; W. L. M. Davies, Q.C.; J. J. Dean; W. N. Denison, Q.C.; K. M. Devlin; G. L. S. Dobry, C.B.E., Q.C.; The Lord Dunboyne; J. B. S. Edwards; Q. T. Edwards, Q.C.; J. H. Ellison, V.R.D.; J. K. Q. Evans; P. R. Fallon, M.C.; A. L. Figgis; I. Finestein, Q.C.; J. A. R. Finlay, Q.C.; J. R. B. Fox-Andrews, Q.C.; A. Garfitt; L. Gerber; F. E. H. G. Gibbens; P. W. Goldstone; M. B. Goodman; J. H. Gower, Q.C.; P. B. Greenwood; D. J. Griffiths; Jean Graham Hall; R. E. Hammerton; J. P. Harris, D.S.C., Q.C.; C. L. Hawser, Q.C.; J. D. W. Hayman; J. B. R. Hazan, Q.C.; A. H. Head; M. R. Hickman; C. R. Hilliard; D. E. Hill-Smith, V.R.D.; D. Holden; F. Honig; A. C. W. Hordern, Q.C.; J. Hunter; T. F. Hutton; H. J. Hyam; C. P. James; W. Kee; M. Kennedy, Q.C.; J. F. Kingham; L. G. Krikler; C. G. Lea, M.C.; N. Lermon, Q.C.; E. Lewis; A. C. L. Lewisohn; A. Lipfriend; D. T. Lloyd; G. D. Lovegrove, Q.C.; D. B. D. Lowe; Noreen M. Lowry; R. J. Lowry, Q.C.; R. D. Lymbery, Q.C.; D. L. McDonnell, O.B.E.; K. M. McHale; I. G. McLean; J. L. E. MacManus, T.D., Q.C.; M. B. Macmullen; M. J. P. Macnair; K. A. Machin; J. R. Main, Q.C.; A. Marder, Q.C.; O. S.

Martin, Q.C.; G. F. P. Mason, Q.C.; J. H. E. Mendl; Sir James Miskin, Q.C. (*Recorder of London*); E. F. Monier-Williams; S. A. Morton, T.D.; J. D. F. Moylan; J. I. Murchie; J. H. R. Newey, Q.C.; Suzanne F. Norwood; C. R. Oddie; A. Owen; J. A. D. Owen, Q.C.; D. A. Paiba; R. H. S. Palmer; M. C. Parker, Q.C.; B. H. Pearce, Q.C.; Miss V. A. Pearlman; F. H. L. Petre; A. L. Phelan; T. H. Pigot, Q.C.; H. C. Pownall, Q.C.; J. E. Pullinger; R. D. Ranking; J. W. Rant, Q.C.; E. V. P. Reece; G. R. Rice; E. B. B. Richards; G. H. Rooke, T.D., Q.C.; Deborah M. Rowland; K. W. Rubin; J. H. A. Scarlett; J. D. Sheerin; G. J. Shindler, Q.C.; M. Singh, Q.C.; J. K. E. Slack, T.D.; S. C. Sleeman; P. M. J. Slot; M. B. Smith; D. A. L. Smout, Q.C.; A. P. Solomon; R. O. C. Stable, Q.C.; D. J. Stinson; E. Stockdale; J. S. Streeter; J. H. A. Stucley, D.S.C.; J. B. Taylor, M.B.E., T.D.; D. A. Thomas, M.B.E.; A. H. Tibber; A. M. Troup; S. Tumim; J. T. Turner; M. T. Underhill, Q.C.; L. J. Verney, T.D.; A. O. R. Vick, Q.C.; R. W. Vick; G. M. Vos; B. J. Wakley, M.B.E.; A. F. Waley, V.R.D., Q.C.; M. E. Ward; J. R. Warde; D. B. Watling, Q.C.; V. B. Watts; D. S. West-Russell; F. J. White; D. H. Wild; J. E. Williams; Sir Thomas Williams, Q.C.; W. G. Wingate, Q.C.; G. N. Worthington; E. E. Wrintmore; E. E. Youds.

Wales and Chester Circuit

K. I. R. Crowther, Q.C.; R. D. G. David, Q.C.; T. M. Evans, Q.C.; W. N. Francis; M. Gibbon, Q.C.; B. F. Griffiths, Q.C.; D. W. Howells; G. Jones; T. E. I. Lewis-Bowen; D. T. Lloyd-Jones, V.R.D.; G. Morgan; P. T. Hopkin Morgan, Q.C.; D. Morgan Hughes; D. A. Phillips; C. N. Pitchford; D. W. Powell; H. W. J. ap Robert; H. E. P. Roberts, Q.C.; J. C. Rutter; D. B. Williams, T.D., Q.C.; H. Williams; R. G. Woolley.

Western Circuit

G. B. Best; N. R. Blaker, Q.C.; B. R. Braithwaite; A. C. Bulger; R. C. Chope; Sir Jonathan Clarke; P. H. F. Clarke; Hazel Counsell; J. A. Cox; M. Dyer; P. Fallon, Q.C.; B. J. F. Galpin; A. C. Goodall, M.C.; I. Starforth Hill, Q.C.; G. B. Hutton; J. H. Inskip, Q.C.; M. G. King; Sir Ian Lewis; D. McCarraher, V.R.D.; H. E. L. McCreery, Q.C.; Sheila M. D. McKinney; G. G. Macdonald; E. B. McLellan; E. G. Neville; K. C. L. Smithies; R. Stock, Q.C.; H. M. J. Tucker; D. H. W. Vowden, Q.C.; K. M. Willcock, Q.C.; J. H. Wroath.

RECORDERS

J. R. S. Adams; I. D. G. Alexander; J. D. Alliott, Q.C.; W. P. Andreae-Jones; B. J. Appleby, Q.C.; J. F. A. Archer, Q.C.; The Rt. Hon. P. K. Archer, Q.C., M.P.; A. J. Arlidge; R. Ashton; P. Ashworth, Q.C.; T. G. F. Atkinson; R. E. Auld, Q.C.; W. S. Ayler; P. Back, Q.C.; P. G. N. Badge; M. J. D. Baker; T. S. G. Baker, Q.C.; A. F. Balston; B. J. Barker; D. Barker, Q.C.; R. O. Barlow; D. M. W. Barnes; C. J. A. Barnett, Q.C.; W. E. Barnett, Q.C.; A. R. Barrowclough, Q.C.; S. J. Bates, Q.C.; R. J. A. Batt; P. M. Beard; C. H. Beaumont; C. O. M. Bedingfield, T.D., Q.C.; R. E. Bell, Q.C.; The Hon. M. J. Beloff; P. Bennett, Q.C.; D. R. Bentley; D. M. Berkson; Miss I. Bernstein; R. H. Bernstein, D.F.C., Q.C.; M. Bethel, Q.C.; J. C. Beveridge, Q.C.; I. J. Black, Q.C.; J. W. Black, Q.C.; M. S. Blackburn; C. Bloom; J. G. Boal; C. L. Boothman; L. A. F. Borrett; M. R. Bowley, Q.C.; P. C. Bowsher, Q.C.; I. R. Boyd; P. N. Brandt; D. J. Brennan; G. J. B. G. Brice, Q.C.; J. N. W. Bridges-Adams; P. J. Briggs; S. E. Brodie, Q.C.; J. L. Brodrick; H. Brooke, Q.C.; R. Brown; J. M. Bull, Q.C.; J. P. Burgess; J. P. Burke, Q.C.; J. K. Burke; R. D. M. Bursell; A. J. Butcher, Q.C.; A. N. L. Butterfield; D. C. Calcutt, Q.C.; Mrs. B. A. Calvert, Q.C.; Miss S. M. C. Cameron, Q.C.; The Lord Campbell of Alloway, Q.C.; B. E. Capstick, Q.C.; H. B. H. Carlisle, Q.C.; M. Carlisle, Q.C., M.P.; E. S. Cazaler, Q.C.; J. A. Chadwin, Q.C.; D. R. Chance; B. L. Charles; P. J. Charlesworth;

B. W. Chedlow, Q.C.; D. Clark; P. N. R. Clark; A. P. Clarke; D. C. Clarke, Q.C.; P. C. Clegg; R. N. B. Clegg, Q.C.; J. M. Collins, Q.C.; J. M. Collins; C. D. Compston; P. R. C. Coni, Q.C.; M. B. Connell, Q.C.; M. J. Cook; G. H. Coombe; Miss B. P. Cooper, Q.C.; Rt. Hon. Sir Frederick Corfield, Q.C.; Miss D. R. Cotton, Q.C.; J. S. Coward, Q.C.; D. M. Cowley, Q.C.; B. R. E. Cox, Q.C.; P. J. Cox, D.S.C., Q.C.; J. Crabtree; P. F. Crane; P. J. Crawford, Q.C.; W. H. R. Crawford, Q.C.; C. J. Crespi, Q.C.; M. A. L. Cripps, C.B.E., D.S.O., T.D., Q.C.; D. L. Croft, Q.C.; F. P. Crowder, Q.C.; J. D. Crowley, Q.C.; E. J. R. Crowther, O.B.E., Q.C.; W. R. M. Crowther; Miss E. A. M. Curnow; R. H. Curtis, Q.C.; G. H. L. M. Daniel; G. W. Davey; Sir Alun T. Davies, Q.C.; R. E. Davies, Q.C.; J. J. Deave; J. B. Deby, Q.C.; C. F. Dehn, Q.C.; W. E. Denny, C.B.E., Q.C.; S. C. Desch, Q.C.; A. E. J. Diamond, Q.C.; J. B. S. Diehl; Miss A. E. Downey; D. P. Draycott, Q.C.; J. M. Drinkwater, Q.C.; R. D. L. Du Cann, Q.C.; L. S. B. Duncan; W. H. Dunn, Q.C.; C. H. Durman.

C. M. Edwards; D. E. H. Edwards; G. O. Edwards; D. F. Elfer; G. Elias, Q.C.; The Lord Elystan-Morgan; G. A. Ensor; D. A. Evans, Q.C.; D. M. Evans, Q.C.; F. P. L. Evans; Miss M. A. P. Evans; E. C. Evans-Lombe, Q.C.; G. N. Eyre, Q.C.; W. D. Fairclough; P. D. Fanner; D. J. Farrer, Q.C.; M. H. Fauvelle; S. J. D. Fawcus; J. D. A. Fennell, O.B.E., Q.C.; T. G. Field-Fisher, T.D., Q.C.; J. J. Finney; Miss E. N. Fisher; W. R. Fitch; J. E. Fletcher; N. H. Freeman; W. M. Gage, Q.C.; M. Gale, Q.C.; P. N. Garland, Q.C.; M.S. Garner; L. N. H. George; R. J. H. Gibbs, Q.C.; A. T. Glass; W. J. Glover, Q.C.; Miss A. F. Goddard; H. K. Goddard, Q.C.; S. A. Goldstein; A. A. Gordon; J. P. Gorman, Q.C.; The Lord Grantchester, Q.C.; G. Gray, Q.C.; R. I. Gray, Q.C.; R. M. K. Gray, Q.C.; A. D. Green; B. S. Green, Q.C.; S. P. Grenfell; R. D. Grey, Q.C.; R. Grey, Q.C.; W. P. Grieve, Q.C.; I. O. Griffiths, Q.C.; J. C. Griffiths, Q.C.; L. Griffiths; M.G. Grills; Mrs. H. M. Grindrod, Q.C.; R. B. Groves; A. S. Haching, Q.C.; M. F. Haigh; J. Hall; D. T. Hallchurch, T.D.; P. J. Halnan; J. H. Hames, Q.C.; A. W. Hamilton, Q.C.; G. M. Hamilton, T.D., Q.C.; R. G. Hamilton; J. A. Hammond; J. Hampton; Miss R. S. A. Hare, Q.C.; B. Hargrove, O.B.E., Q.C.; R. D. Harman, Q.C.; F. D. Hart, Q.C.; C. A. Hart-Leverton, Q.C.; C. S. Harvey, M.B.E., T.D.; R. J. S. Harvey, Q.C.; T. S. A. Hawkesworth, Q.C.; R. G. Hawkins, Q.C.; R. W. P. Hay; M. Heald, Q.C.; G. E. Heggs; R. A. Henderson, Q.C.; R. H. Q. Henriques; D. R. M. Henry, Q.C.; J. C. Hicks, Q.C.; A. B. Hidden, Q.C.; B. J. Higgs, Q.C.; A. M. Hill, Q.C.; E. M. Hill, Q.C.; J. D. Hitchen; A. N. Hitching; T. D. T. Hodson; D. A. Hollis, V.R.D., Q.C.; A. T. Hoolahan, Q.C.; The Lord Hooson, Q.C.; R. Houlker, Q.C.; W. M. Howard, Q.C.; M. J. Hubbard; F. M. S. Hudson; Maj.-Gen. Sir David Hughes-Morgan, Bt, C.B.E.; J. Hugill, Q.C.; J. G. Hull, Q.C.; P. J. Hunt; R. Hunt; B. A. Hytner, Q.C.; N. E. J. Inglis-Jones, Q.C.; A. A. M. Irvine, Q.C.; N. F. Irvine, Q.C.; F. C. Irwin, Q.C.; D. M. Jack; M. R. Jackson; P. J. E. Jackson; C. E. F. James; N. F. B. Jarman; D. A. Jeffreys, Q.C.; J. Jeffs, Q.C.; C. W. L. Jervis; D. B. Johnson, Q.C.; M. H. Johnson; R. L. Johnson, Q.C.; E. S. Jones, Q.C.; G. R. Jones; T. G. Jones; W. H. Joss; I. Judge, Q.C.; M. D. L. Kalisher, Q.C.; J. W. Kay, Q.C.; D. St. J. Keane, Q.C.; D. N. Keating, Q.C.; R. W. M. Keeling; D. A. M. Kemp, Q.C.; I. A. Kennedy, Q.C.; A. M. Kenny; T. D. Kent-Jones; P. M. Kershaw, Q.C.; R. I. Kidwell, Q.C.; G. E. Kilfoil; R. C. Klevan, Q.C.

L. H. C. Lait; D. N. R. Latham; G. F. B. Laughland, Q.C.; T. Lawrence; L. D. Lawton, Q.C.; M. K. Lee, Q.C.; R. T. L. Lee; C. H. de V. Leigh; Sir Godfrey Le Quesne, Q.C.; S. Levine; M. E. Lewer, Q.C.; A. K. Lewis, Q.C.; M. ap G. Lewis, Q.C.; G. M. Lightfoot; C. D. Lindsay; R. J. D. Livesey, Q.C.; C. G. Llewellyn-Jones; J. Lloyd-Eley, Q.C.; F. R. Lockhart; R. H. Lownie; P. D. Loy; J. A. T. Loyd, Q.C.; N. W. Lyell, Q.C.; E. Lyons, Q.C.; J. R. V. McAulay, Q.C.; D. D. McEvoy, Q.C.; S. N. McKinnon, Q.C.; I. S. Mackintosh;

N. R. B. Macleod, Q.C.; Miss M. B. MacMurray, Q.C.; K. C. Macrae; J. G. McNaught; E. A. Machin, Q.C.; B. C. Maddocks; Miss A. Mallalieu; R. G. Marshall-Andrews; R. B. Martin, Q.C.; H. R. Mayor; N. A. Medawer, Q.C.; M. Meggerson; J. M. Meredith; A. L. Mildon, Q.C.; J. T. Milford; R. A. Miller; Mrs. B. J. L. Mills; J. B. M. Milmo, Q.C.; N. A. Miscampbell, Q.C., M.P.; S. G. Mitchell; H. J. Montlake; L. J. J. Morgan; W. G. O. Morgan, Q.C.; G. E. Moriarty, Q.C.; M. Morland, Q.C.; D. G. Morris; The Rt. Hon. J. Morris, Q.C., M.P.; J. B. Mortimer, Q.C.; T. H. Moseley; F. J. Muller, Q.C.; A. S. Myerson, Q.C.; N. J. Mylne; G. K. Naylor, T.D.; C. W. F. Newman, Q.C.; G. M. Newman, Q.C.; J. D. Newton; A. J. D. Nicholl; C. V. Nicholls, Q.C.; C. A. A. Nicholls, Q.C.; M. C. Nicholson; A. S. T. E. Nicol; Mrs. M. F. Norrie; D. P. O'Brien, Q.C.; E. M. Ogden, Q.C.; H. H. Ognall, Q.C.; B. R. Oliver; S. K. O'Malley; S. K. Overend; G. V. Owen, Q.C.; S. R. Page; A. W. Palmer, Q.C.; E. O. Parry; N.S. K. Pascoe; J. G. Paulusz; J. R. Peppitt, Q.C.; Sir Ian Percival, Q.C., M.P.; D. S. Perrett, Q.C.; N. A. Phillips, Q.C.; D. A. Pirie; M. T. Pill, Q.C.; C. J. Pitchers; Miss E. F. Platt, Q.C.; A. G. S. Pollock, Q.C.; D. A. Poole, Q.C.; F. H. Potts, Q.C.; M. J. Pratt, Q.C.; T. W. Preston, Q.C.; A. J. Price, Q.C.; J. A. Price, Q.C.; V. W. C. Price, Q.C.; E. J. Prosser, Q.C.; B. H. Pryor; A. G. Purnell, Q.C.; P. O. Purnell, Q.C.

A. Rankin, Q.C.; A. D. Rawley, Q.C.; L. F. Read, Q.C.; P. Rees; J. R. Reid, Q.C.; H. A. Richardson; K. A. Richardson; Miss S. A. Ritchie, Q.C.; G. Rivlin, Q.C.; P. B. Roberts; J. M. G. Roberts; D. E. H. Robson, Q.C.; J. O. Roch, Q.C.; D. A. H. Rodwell, Q.C.; J. M. T. Rogers, Q.C.; J. W. Rogers, Q.C.; P. H. Rolf; A. M. T. Rose, M.C.; R. G. Rougier, Q.C.; J. J. Rowe, Q.C.; R. R. Russell; T. R. G. F. Ryland; N. T. Salts, Q.C.; J. E. A. Samuels, Q.C.; K. M. T. Schiemann, Q.C.; A. F. B. Scrivener, Q.C.; R. J. Seabrook, Q.C.; C. Seagroatt, Q.C.; R. A. W. Sears, Q.C.; H. M. Self, Q.C.; Col. D. M. D. Selwood; J. A. O. Shand; M. D. Sherrard, Q.C.; L. Shield; L. S. Shields, Q.C.; J. M. Shorrock; R. M. G. Simpson, Q.C.; A. T. Smith, Q.C.; C. H. Smith; D·A. Smith, Q.C.; J. R. S. Smyth; R. E. Snape; R. J. Southan; Miss J. M. Southworth, Q.C.; G. C. H. Spafford; M. H. Spence, Q.C.; D. H. Spencer, Q.C., M.P.; J. A. C. Spokes, Q.C.; S. A. Stamler, Q.C.; Miss A. H. Steel, Q.C.; D. H. Stembridge; S. M. Stephens, Q.C.; J. S. H. Stewart, Q.C.; R. M. Stewart, Q.C.; D. M. A. Stokes; E. D. R. Stone, Q.C.; P. J. Stretton; M. Stuart-Moore; J. Stuart-Smith; F. R. C. Such; A. B. Suckling, Q.C.; D. M. Sumner; L. Swift, Q.C.; A. B. Taylor; E. Taylor; N. Taylor, Q.C.; K. J. Tetley; D. M. Thomas, Q.C.; D. O. Thomas, Q.C.; J. Thomas, Q.C.; Rt. Hon. P. J. M. Thomas, Q.C., M.P.; A. A. R. Thompson, Q.C.; R. N. Titheridge, Q.C.; M. A. Thorpe, Q.C.; J. K. Toulmin, Q.C.; J. B. S. Townend, Q.C.; R. H. Tucker, Q.C.; S. L. Tuckey, Q.C.; M. W. Turcan; M. J. Turner, Q.C.; C. J. M. Tyrer; A. R. Tyrrell, Q.C.; Mrs. A. P. Uziell-Hamilton; A. R. Vandermeer, Q.C.; D. C. Waddington, Q.C., M.P.; J. P. Wadsworth; D. St. J. R. Wagstaff; R. M. Wakerley, Q.C.; W. H. Waldron, Q.C.; J. J. Walker-Smith; B. Walsh, Q.C.; C. D. G. P. Waud; D. McL. Webster, Q.C.; P. A. Webster; M. Weisman; P. Weitzman, Q.C.; C. P. C. Whelon; C. H. Whitby, Q.C.; A. Whitfield, Q.C.; J. R. Whitley; D. G. Widdicombe; Miss N. Wilkins; G. H. G. Williams, Q.C.; G. W. Williams, Q.C.; J. G. Williams, Q.C.; J. L. Williams; S. W. Williamson, Q.C.; J. C. Willis; S. M. Willis; J. G. Wilmers, Q.C.; A. M. Wilson, Q.C.; C. Wilson Smith; D. A. Wood; D. R. Woolley, Q.C.; N. G. Wootton; J. M. Wright, Q.C.; E. G. Wrintmore; G. N. Barr Young; K. H. Zucker, Q.C.

STIPENDIARY MAGISTRATES

Greater Manchester, William Derrick Fairclough (1982); Cecil Thomas Latham, O.B.E. (1976).
Humberside, Neville Helme White (1985).

Leeds, Francis David Lindley Loy (1972); Ian Robertson Boyd (1982).
Merseyside, Norman Godfrey Wootton (1976).
Mid Glamorgan, David Powys Rowland (1961); Benjamin Rhys Oliver (1983).
South Glamorgan, Sir (Adrian) Lincoln Hallinan (1976).
South Yorkshire, Ian William Crompton (1983); James Edward Barry (1985).
West Midlands, Frederick Henry Hatchard (1981); James Robert Staples Smyth (1978); William Michael Probert (1983).

INNER LONDON MAGISTRATES

Chief Metropolitan Stipendiary Magistrate and Chairman of Committee of Magistrates for Inner London Area, David Armand Hopkin (*Bow Street*). £33,000

Committee of Magistrates for Inner London Area

3rd Floor, North-West Wing,
Bush House, Aldwych, WC2B 4PJ
Principal Chief Clerk and Clerk to the Committee,
I. Fowler £27,409
Chief Clerk (Training), J. W. Greenhill £24,033

Magistrates
(*each* £28,500)

Bow Street, William Edward Charles Robins; Ronald David Bartle; Barrington Black.

Camberwell Green, Maurice Juniper Guymer, O.B.E.; Ralph Hamilton Lownie; George Alfred Bathurst Norman; Sir Bryan Clieve Roberts, K.C.M.G., Q.C.; Charles Peter Morton Davidson; David Benjamin Meier.

Clerkenwell, John Denis Purcell; Mark Lemon Robert Romer; Christopher John Bourke.

Greenwich and Woolwich, Miss Pamela Marjorie Long; Stanley Graham Clixby; David Quentin Miller.

Highbury Corner, David Barr; David Melvyn Fingleton; Geoffrey Parkinson; Anthony Rodger Davies.

Horseferry Road, Eric Crowther, O.B.E.; James Hobson Jobling; Ronald Trevor Moss; Mrs. Norma Negus.

Marlborough Street, Kenneth John Heastey Nichols; Jeremy George Connor.

Marylebone, Peter Duncan Fanner; Geoffrey Lindsay James Noel; John Quentin Campbell; Keith Maitland-Davies.

Old Street, Patrick John Halnan; Terence Maher.

South Western, John Jeremy Fordham; Miss Dawn Angela Freedman; Anura Cooray.

Thames, Peter Gilmour Noto Badge; Brian John Canham.

Tower Bridge, Roger Benedict Sanders; Christopher David Voelcker; Mrs. Jacqueline Roberta Comyns.

Wells Street, Christopher Besley; Edward James Branson; Miss Audrey Mary Jennings; Michael Anthony Johnstone; Peter Fingret.

West London, David Fairbairn; Harold Cook.

Unattached Magistrates, David Kennett Brown; Roger David Connor.

DIRECTOR OF PUBLIC PROSECUTIONS
4/12 Queen Anne's Gate, SW1H 9AZ

Director, Sir Thomas Hetherington, K.C.B., C.B.E., T.D., Q.C.
Deputy Director, K. Dowling, C.B.
Principal Assistant Directors, J. Walker; D. G. Williams; J. Wood.

THE SCOTTISH JUDICATURE

Scotland has a legal system separate and differing greatly from the English legal system in enacted law, judicial procedure and the structure of courts.

There is in Scotland a system of public prosecution headed by the Lord Advocate which is independent of the police, who have no say in the decision to prosecute. The Lord Advocate, discharging his functions through the Crown Office in Edinburgh, is responsible for prosecutions in the High Court, sheriff courts and district courts. Prosecutions in the High Court are prepared by the Crown Office and conducted in court by one of the Law Officers or an advocate-depute. In the inferior courts the decision to prosecute is made and prosecution is preferred by procurators fiscal, who are lawyers and full-time civil servants, subject to the directions of the Crown Office. A permanent legally-qualified civil servant known as the Crown Agent is responsible for the running of the Crown Office and the organization of the Procurator Fiscal Service, of which he is the head.

Scotland is divided into six Sheriffdoms, each with a full-time Sheriff Principal. The Sheriffdoms are further divided into sheriff court districts, each of which has a legally-qualified, resident sheriff or sheriffs, who are the judges of the court.

In criminal cases sheriffs principal and sheriffs have the same powers: sitting with a jury of 15 members, they may try more serious cases on indictment, or, sitting alone, may try lesser cases under summary procedure. Minor summary offences are dealt with in district courts which are administered by the district and the islands local government authorities and presided over by lay justices of the peace, and, in Glasgow only, by stipendiary magistrates. Juvenile offenders (children under 16) may be brought before an informal children's hearing comprising three local lay people. The superior criminal court is the High Court of Justiciary which is both a trial and an appeal court. Cases on indictment are tried by a High Court Judge, sitting with a jury of 15, in Edinburgh and on circuit in other towns. Appeals from the lower courts against conviction or sentence are heard also by the High Court, which sits as an appeal court only in Edinburgh. There is no further appeal to the House of Lords in criminal cases.

In civil cases the jurisdiction of the sheriff court extends to most kinds of action. Appeal against decisions of the sheriff may be made to the Sheriff Principal and thence to the Court of Session, or direct to the Court of Session, which sits only in Edinburgh. The Court of Session is divided into the Inner and the Outer House. The Outer House is a court of first instance in which cases are heard by judges sitting singly, sometimes with a jury of 12. The Inner House, itself subdivided into two Divisions of equal status, is mainly an appeal court. Appeals may be made to the Inner House from the Outer House as well as from the sheriff court: an appeal may be made from the Inner House to the House of Lords.

The Judges of the Court of Session are the same as those of the High Court of Justiciary, the Lord President of the Court of Session also holding the office of Lord Justice General in the High Court.

The office of coroner does not exist in Scotland: the local procurator fiscal inquires privately into sudden and suspicious deaths and may report findings to the Crown Agent. In some cases a fatal accident inquiry may be held before the sheriff.

COURT OF SESSION (Established 1532) and HIGH COURT OF JUSTICIARY

The Lord President and Lord Justice General, The Rt. Hon. the Lord Emslie, M.B.E.

INNER HOUSE.—*First Division.*

The Lord President, The Rt. Hon. Lord Emslie, George Carlyle Emslie, M.B.E. £63,750
Hon. Lord Cameron, Sir John Cameron, K.T., D.S.C.
Hon. Lord Grieve, William Robertson Grieve, V.R.D.
Hon. Lord Brand, David William Robert Brand.

Second Division

Lord Justice Clerk, The Hon. Lord Ross, Donald MacArthur Ross £60,750
Hon. Lord Hunter, John Oswald Mair Hunter, V.R.D.
Hon. Lord Robertson, Ian Macdonald Robertson, T.D.
Hon. Lord Dunpark, Alastair McPherson Johnston, T.D.

OUTER HOUSE

Hon. Lord Kincraig, Robert Smith Johnston
Hon. Lord Maxwell, Peter Maxwell (*seconded to Scottish Law Commission*)
Hon. Lord McDonald, Robert Howat McDonald, M.C.
Rt. Hon. Lord Wylie, Norman Russell Wylie, V.R.D.
Hon. Lord Stewart, Ewan George Francis Stewart, M.C.
Hon. Lord Allanbridge, William Ian Stewart
Hon. Lord Cowie, William Lorn Kerr Cowie
Hon. Lord Jauncey, Charles Eliot Jauncey
Rt. Hon. Lord Murray, Ronald King Murray
Hon. Lord Mayfield, Ian MacDonald, M.C.
Hon. Lord Davidson, Charles Kemp Davidson
Rt. Hon. Lord McCluskey, John Herbert McCluskey.
(SALARIES: All judges other than the Lord President and Lord Justice Clerk .... £55,625)

Court of Session and High Court of Justiciary
Parliament House, Parliament Square, Edinburgh

Principal Clerk of Session and Justiciary, A. M. Campbell .... £20,964–£25,533
Deputy Principal Clerk of Session and Extractor, H. S. Foley .... £13,508–£18,363
Deputy Principal Clerk (Administration) and of Justiciary, J. Robertson .... £13,508–£18,363
Keeper of the Rolls, V. A. Woods .. £13,508–£18,363
Depute Clerks of Session, Outer House, W. Gillon; M. Weir; M. Bonar; N. J. Dowie; I. Smith; J. A. R. Cowie; T. Higgins; E. A. Cumming; B. Watson; P. J. McGonigle; A. Brown; W. McCulloch; Q. Oliver; F. Shannly; P. Crow; T. B. Cruickshank
.... £10,980–£13,801
Depute Clerks of Justiciary, W. J. Burns; J. Cumming; T. Fyffe; A. Hogg .... £10,980–£13,801

Scottish Courts Administration
26–27 Royal Terrace, Edinburgh EH7 5AH

Director, W. A. P. Weatherston.

Crown Office
5/7 Regent Road, Edinburgh

Crown Agent, I. Dean £36,500
Deputy Crown Agent, J. D. Lowe £26,909

Companies Registration Office
102 George Street, Edinburgh EH2 3DJ

Registrar, E. T. K. Lougheed.

Sheriff Court of Chancery
16 North Bank Street, Edinburgh

Sheriff of Chancery, Sir Frederick O'Brien, Q.C.

H.M. Commissary Office
16 North Bank Street, Edinburgh

Commissary Clerk, D. B. White.

SCOTTISH LAND COURT
1 Grosvenor Crescent, Edinburgh

Chairman, The Hon. Lord Elliott, M.C.
Members, A. B. Campbell, O.B.E.; A. Gillespie, M.B.E.; D. D. McDiarmid.

SHERIFFS PRINCIPAL, SHERIFFS, SHERIFF CLERKS AND PROCURATORS FISCAL IN SCOTLAND

SHERIFFDOM AND SHERIFF PRINCIPAL	SHERIFFS	SHERIFF CLERKS	PROCURATORS FISCAL
Grampian, Highland and Islands.— S. E. Bell, Q.C.	*Aberdeen, Stonehaven,* A. M. G. Russell, Q.C.; A. L. Stewart; D. J. Risk; R. J. D. Scott.	J. Rodden .... I. P. Smith	A. S. Jessop. J. T. O'Donnell.
	Banff and Peterhead, N. Mc-Partlin.	W. H. Connon ...... P. J. O'Hara	P. W. Johnston. I. S. McNaughtan.
	Elgin..........................	I. Munro	A. Wither.
	Wick and Dornoch, E. Stewart (*also Tain*).	K. A. MacColl	D. R. Hingston. J. D. McNaughton. T. F. Aitchison.
	Inverness, Lochmaddy, Portree, Stornoway, Dingwall, Tain, W. J. Fulton; D. Booker-Milburn; J. O. A. Fraser.	R. M. Sinclair ...... W. Dunn	A. Haughney. C. S. Mackenzie. W. M. S. Carnegie. H. T. Westwater.
	Kirkwall, Lerwick, A. A. Mac-Donald.	J. Rodden	A. W. Wright. D. J. McLeay.
	Fort William, D. Noble (*also Oban and Campbeltown*)	R. M. Sinclair	J. I. M. MacGillivray.
Tayside, Central and Fife.— R. R. Taylor, Q.C., PH.D.	*Arbroath, Forfar,* S. O. Kermack	A. G. Pryde .... R. G. Davis	C. D. G. Hillary. A. L. Ingram.
	Dundee, E. F. Bowen; G. L. Cox	A. A. Steele	D. R. Smith.
	Perth, J. F. Wheatley	Miss J. Telfer	M. MacPhail.
	Falkirk, A. V. Sheehan; R. E. G. Younger (*also Stirling*)	E. G. Appelbe	G. E. Scott.
	Stirling, W. C. Henderson	K. MacKenzie......	K. Valentine.
	Alloa, W. M. Reid	R. D. Sinclair	Miss M. W. Robertson.
	Cupar, J. C. McInnes (*also Perth*)	Miss A. I. Thompson	R. A. S. Brown.
	Dunfermline, J. S. Forbes; W. M. Reid (*also Alloa*)	J. M. Hay	R. T. Hamilton.
	Kirkcaldy, W. J. Christie; C. R. Macarthur, Q.C.	J. M. Clark	Mrs. I. Guild.
Lothian and Borders.— Sir Frederick O'Brien, Q.C.	*Edinburgh,* N. E. D. Thomson; W. T. Hook; K. W. B. Middleton (*also Haddington*); R. D. Ireland, Q.C.; J. L. M. Mitchell; Miss I. A. Poole*; G. W. S. Presslie*; P. G. B. McNeill, PH.D.; Miss H. J. Aronson; R. G. Craik, Q.C.; G. I. W. Shiach.	D. B. White	J. D. Allan.
	Peebles, N. E. D. Thomson (*also Edinburgh*).	D. B. White	F. J. M. Brown.
	Linlithgow, I. D. MacPhail; M. Stone	G. W. Waddell	H. R. Annan.
	Haddington, K. W. B. Middleton (*also Edinburgh*).	D. V. Flynn	I. D. Douglas.
	Jedburgh, Duns, J. V. Paterson.	J. R. Jenkins	D. W. Batchelor. J. C. Whitelaw.
	Selkirk, J. V. Paterson	G. C. McKillop	D. J. F. Howdle.
North Strathclyde.— P. I. Caplan, Q.C.	*Oban and Campbeltown,* D. Noble (*also Fort William*).	J. Shaw .... J. S. Doig	D. H. McNeill. I. Henderson. J. I. M. MacGillivray.
	Dumbarton, J. P. Murphy; D. Kelbie; F. H. Hamilton*.	J. S. Doig	J. Cardle.
	Paisley, A. K. F. Hunter; H. R. MacLean; R. G. Smith.	J. Shaw	J. B. R. Mackinnon.
	Greenock, J. Irvine Smith; Sir Stephen Young (*also Dunoon and Rothesay*).	A. P. McPherson ...	A. T. W. Wilson. W. D. Stewart. Miss C. McNaughton.
	Kilmarnock, T. M. Croan; D. B. Smith; T. F. Russell.	W. B. Davidson	J. L. McLeod.

*Floating Sheriffs.

Sheriffdom and Sheriff Principal	Sheriffs	Sheriff Clerks	Procurators Fiscal
Glasgow and Strathkelvin.— J. A. Dick, M.C., Q.C.	*Glasgow,* N. D. MacLeod; A. C. Horsfall; J. J. Maguire; A. A. Bell, Q.C.; J. S. Mowat; B. Kearney; G. H. Gordon, Q.C.; A. C. McKay; A. Lothian; J. C. M. Jardine; Mrs. D. J. B. Robertson; B. A. Lockhart; I. G. Pirie; Miss A. L. A. Smith; W. G. Stevenson, Q.C.; G. J. Evans; E. H. Galt; F. J. Keane; A. C. Henry; A. M. Bell; J. K. Mitchell; A. G. Johnston; C. Smith*.	C. McLay	J. M. Tudhope.
South Strathclyde, Dumfries and Galloway.— M. G. Gillies, T.D., Q.C.	*Hamilton,* J. R. Fiddes, Q.C.; L. S. Lovat; A. C. MacPherson; W. F. Lunny; I. A. MacMillan, C.B.E.	B. J. Young	S. W. Lockhart, C.B.E.
	Lanark, R. G. McEwan, Q.C.	J. G. Barr	S. R. Houston.
	Ayr, D. M. K. Grant; N. Gow, Q.C.	T. D. McIntosh	N. G. O'Brien.
	Stranraer, Kirkcudbright, J. A. Farrell (*also Dumfries*).	L. McFarlane	F. Walkingshaw. R. F. Gibb.
	Dumfries, K. G. Barr; N. J. G. Ramsay.	W. Jones	J. T. MacDougall.
	Airdrie, J. H. Stewart; J. S. Boyle.	H. Findlay	W. G. Carmichael.

*Floating Sheriffs.

NORTHERN IRELAND JUDICATURE

In Northern Ireland the legal system and the structure of courts closely resemble those of England and Wales; there are, however, often differences in enacted law.

The Supreme Court of Judicature of Northern Ireland comprises the Court of Appeal, the Crown Court and the High Court of Justice, and the practice and procedure of these Courts is similar to those in England. The superior civil court is the High Court of Justice, from which an appeal may be made to the Court of Appeal; the House of Lords is the final civil appeal court.

The decision to prosecute in cases tried on indictment and in summary cases of a serious nature rests in Northern Ireland with the Director of Public Prosecutions, who is responsible to the Attorney General. Minor summary offences are prosecuted by the police.

Minor criminal offences are dealt with in magistrates' courts by a full-time, legally qualified resident magistrate and, where an offender is under 17, by juvenile courts consisting of the resident magistrate and two lay members specially qualified to deal with juveniles (at least one of whom must be a woman). Appeals from magistrates' courts are heard by the county court. The Crown Court, served by High Court and county court judges, deals with criminal trials on indictment. Cases are heard before a judge and, except those involving offences specified under emergency legislation, a jury. Appeals from the Crown Court against conviction or sentence are heard by the Northern Ireland Court of Appeal; the House of Lords is the final court of appeal.

Magistrates' courts in Northern Ireland can deal with certain classes of civil case but most minor civil cases are dealt with in county courts. Judgments of all civil courts are enforceable through a centralized procedure administered by the Enforcement of Judgments Office.

SUPREME COURT OF JUDICATURE

The Royal Courts of Justice, Belfast.

Lord Chief Justice of Northern Ireland, The Rt. Hon. The Lord Lowry.

Judges, The Rt. Hon. Lord Justice (Sir Maurice White) Gibson; The Rt. Hon. Lord Justice (Turlough) O'Donnell; The Rt. Hon. Lord Justice (Sir John William Basil) Kelly; The Hon. Mr. Justice (John Clarke) MacDermott; The Hon. Mr. Justice (Donald Bruce) Murray; The Hon. Mr. Justice (James Brian Edward) Hutton; The Hon. Mr. Justice (John Patrick Basil) Higgins; The Hon. Mr. Justice (Robert Douglas) Carswell.

Lord Chief Justice's Office

Principal Secretary to the Lord Chief Justice and Clerk of the Crown for Northern Ireland, J. A. L. McLean, Q.C.
Legal Secretary to the Lord Chief Justice, R. T. Millar.

Central Office

Master, V. A. Care, Q.C.

Office of Care and Protection

Master, R. L. G. Davison.

Chancery Office

Master, V. G. Bridges.

Bankruptcy and Companies Office

Master, J. M. Hunter, C.B.E.

Probate and Matrimonial Office

Master, D. W. G. Heatly.

High Court

Master, J. W. William.

Taxing Office

Master, A. E. Anderson, C.B.E.

Court Funds Office

Accountant, R. A. Guiler.

Recorders

Belfast, J. K. Pringle, Q.C.
Londonderry, J. J. Curran, Q.C.

County Court Judges

Judge Babington, D.S.C., Q.C.; Judge Chambers, Q.C.; Judge Donaldson, Q.C.; Judge Gibson, Q.C.; Judge

Hart, q.c.; Judge McKee, q.c.; Rt. Hon. Judge Sir Robert Porter, q.c.; Judge Rowland, q.c.; Judge Russell, q.c.; Judge Watt, q.c.

Crown Solicitor, H. A. Nelson.
Director of Public Prosecutions, Sir Barry Shaw, c.b., q.c.

ECCLESIASTICAL COURTS

Judge, John Arthur Dalziel Owen, q.c.
[Judge of the Provincial Courts of Canterbury and York under "The Ecclesiastical Jurisdiction Measure, 1963."].

Court of Arches

Registry, 16 Beaumont Street, Oxford.
Dean, The Rt. Worshipful J. A. D. Owen, q.c.

Court of Faculties

[Registry and Office for Marriage Licences (Special and Ordinary). Appointment of Notaries Public, &c., 1, The Sanctuary, Westminster, S.W.1. Office hours, 10 to 4; Saturdays, 10 to 12].
Master, The Rt. Worshipful J. A. D. Owen, q.c.

Vicar General's Office of the Province of Canterbury

16 Beaumont Street, Oxford

Vicar General and Chancellor, The Worshipful Miss S. M. Cameron, q.c.

Chancery Court of York

Auditor, The Rt. Worshipful J. A. D. Owen, q.c.
Registrar, G. P. Knowles.

Office of the Vicar General of the Province of York

Vicar General, The Worshipful T. A. C. Coningsby.
Registrar, G. P. Knowles.

INDUSTRIAL AND OTHER TRIBUNALS

The Industrial Tribunals

Central Office (England and Wales)
93 Ebury Bridge Road, S.W.1
President, His Honour Judge D. S. West-Russell £36,000

Central Office (Scotland)
St. Andrew House, 141 West Nile Street, Glasgow
President, R. C. Hay, w.s.................. £32,750

Immigration Appeal Tribunal
Thanet House, 231 Strand, WC2R 1DA

President, D. L. Neve.
Vice-Presidents, G. W. Farmer; Prof. D. C. Jackson.

Lands Tribunal
5 Chancery Lane, W.C.2

President, Sir Douglas Frank, q.c.
Members, J. H. Emlyn Jones, m.b.e.; V. G. Wellings, q.c.; W. H. Rees; C. R. Mallett; Wm. Hall, d.f.c.
Registrar, C. A. McMullan.

Lands Tribunal for Scotland
1 Grosvenor Crescent, Edinburgh

President, The Hon. Lord Elliott, m.c.
Members, W. Hall, d.f.c. (*full-time*); W. D. C. Andrews, c.b.e., w.s.; T. Finlayson (*part-time*).

Patents Court (Appellate Section)
Room 163, Chancery Chambers,
Royal Courts of Justice, WC2A 2LL

Judges, The Hon. Mr. Justice Whitford; The Hon. Mr. Justice Falconer.

Pensions Appeal Tribunals
St. Dunstan's House, Fetter Lane, EC4A 1BT

President, Sir Geoffrey Briggs.

Performing Right Tribunal
Room 1509, State House, 66–71 High Holborn, W.C.1

Chairman, A. M. Morison, q.c.
Secretary, E. J. Barnett.

Transport Tribunal
Golden Cross House,
Duncannon Street, WC2N 4JF

President, Judge Inskip, q.c.

Parliamentary and Local Government Election Petitions Office
Room 118, Royal Courts of Justice, WC2A 2LL

Prescribed Officer, J. R. Bickford Smith.

POLICE AUTHORITIES IN THE UNITED KINGDOM

Police Force	Headquarters	Actual Strength	Chief Constable (†Chief Officer)	Chairman of Police Authority/Committee
England				
Avon and Somerset	Bristol	2,994	R. Broome, O.B.E., Q.P.M.	T. E. Turvey, O.B.E.
Bedfordshire	Bedford	1,007	A. Dyer	F. S. Lester
Cambridgeshire	Huntingdon	1,133	I. H. Kane, Q.P.M.	Dr. D. C. Nicholls
Cheshire	Chester	1,793	D. J. Graham, Q.P.M.	J. H. Collins, O.B.E.
Cleveland	Middlesbrough	1,447	C. F. Payne, Q.P.M.	Mrs. I. Cole
Cumbria	Penrith	1,097	B. D. F. Price, Q.P.M.	Maj. T. R. Riley
Derbyshire	Ripley	1,765	A. O. Smith (acting)	H. Lowe
Devon and Cornwall	Exeter	2,730	D. Elliott, Q.P.M.	J. R. W. R. Carew-Pole
Dorset	Dorchester	1,150	B. H. Weight, Q.P.M.	Maj. Gen. H. M. G. Bond
Durham	Durham	1,290	E. J. Boothby, Q.P.M.	S. Cutler
Essex	Chelmsford	2,637	R. S. Bunyard, Q.P.M.	G. C. Waterer, M.B.E.
Gloucestershire	Cheltenham	1,164	L. A. G. Soper, Q.P.M.	C. P. Hay
Hampshire (& I.o.W.)	Winchester	3,054	J. Duke, Q.P.M.	Capt. M. P. R. Boyle
Hertfordshire	Welwyn Garden City	1,566	T. A. Morris, Q.P.M.	Dr. A. J. R. Anderson, C.B.E.
Humberside	Hull	1,972	D. Hall, C.B.E., Q.P.M.	G. Stroud
Kent	Maidstone	2,875	F. L. Jordan, Q.P.M.	J. A. Spence
Lancashire	Preston	3,019	R. B. Johnson, Q.P.M.	J. Entwistle
Leicestershire	Leicester	1,700	A. Goodson, O.B.E., Q.P.M.	R. R. Angrave
Lincolnshire	Lincoln	1,183§	S. W. Crump, Q.P.M.	M. D. Kennedy
Greater Manchester	Manchester 16	6,714	C. J. Anderton, C.B.E., Q.P.M.	Mrs. G. I. Cox
Merseyside	Liverpool 69	4,571	K. G. Oxford, C.B.E., Q.P.M.	Mrs. M. B. Simey
Norfolk	Norwich	1,275	G. Charlton, Q.P.M.	J. S. Peel, M.C.
Northamptonshire	Northampton	1,018	M. Buck, O.B.E., Q.P.M.	A. A. Morby
Northumbria	Newcastle upon Tyne	3,362	S. E. Bailey, C.B.E., Q.P.M.	J. E. Hornsby
Nottinghamshire	Nottingham	2,156	C. McLachlan, C.B.E., Q.P.M.	F. Taylor
Staffordshire	Stafford	2,084	C. H. Kelly, Q.P.M.	Miss I. H. Moseley
Suffolk	Ipswich	1,127	S. L. Whiteley, C.B.E., Q.P.M.	Capt. R. J. Sheepshanks
Surrey	Guildford	1,589	B. Hayes, Q.P.M.	J. F. Whitfield
Sussex	Lewes	2,830	R. Birch, Q.P.M.	F. W. E. Keen
Thames Valley	Oxford	3,317	C. Smith, C.V.O.	R. J. Clibbon
Warwickshire	Warwick	918	P. D. Joslin, Q.P.M.	Maj. S. W. T. Birch, T.D.
West Mercia	Worcester	1,923	A. A. Mullett, Q.P.M.	Mrs. J. Hadley
West Midlands	Birmingham 4	6,658	G. J. Dear, Q.P.M.	E. T. Shore
Wiltshire	Devizes	1,045	D. Smith, O.B.E., Q.P.M.	J. E. H. Church.
Yorkshire, North	Northallerton	1,341	P. J. Nobes	C. Thorpe
Yorkshire, South	Sheffield	2,854	P. Wright, O.B.E.	G. H. Moores
Yorkshire, West	Wakefield	4,992	C. Sampson, Q.P.M.	R. Darrington
Wales				
Dyfed-Powys	Carmarthen	921	R. B. Thomas, C.B.E., Q.P.M.	W. R. Nicholl
Gwent	Cwmbran	967	J. E. Over, Q.P.M.	B. J. Hearth
North Wales	Colwyn Bay	1,264	D. Owen, Q.P.M.	W. R. Webb
South Wales	Bridgend	3,078	D. A. East, Q.P.M.	P. Squire, O.B.E.
Scotland				
Central Scotland	Stirling	552	I. T. Oliver, Q.P.M.	W. Douglas
Dumfries and Galloway	Dumfries	317	J. M. Boyd, Q.P.M.	Rev. R. Hamill
Fife	Kirkcaldy	656	W. M. Moodie, Q.P.M.	W. G. Anderson
Grampian	Aberdeen	957	A. G. Lynn, Q.P.M.	J. A. S. McPherson, C.B.E.
Lothian and Borders	Edinburgh 4	2,361	W. G. M. Sutherland, Q.P.M.	A. H. Lester
Northern	Inverness	600	H. C. MacMillan	J. S. Munro
Strathclyde	Glasgow 2	6,757	A. Sloan, Q.P.M.	J. Irvine
Tayside	Dundee	957	J. W. Bowman, Q.P.M.	W. Johnston, O.B.E.
Northern Ireland				
Royal Ulster Constabulary	Belfast 5	8,161	Sir John Hermon, O.B.E.	Sir Myles Humphreys
Islands				
Isle of Man	Douglas	175	F. Weedon, Q.P.M.	E. M. Ward, B.E.M.
States of Jersey	St. Helier	206	†D. Parkinson	J. W. Ellis
Guernsey	St. Peter Port	131	†M. Le Moignan	M. W. Torode

§Authorized establishment

METROPOLITAN POLICE OFFICE
New Scotland Yard, Broadway, SW1H 0BG
[01–230 1212]

Commissioner, Sir Kenneth Newman, Q.P.M. £45,500
Deputy Commissioner, P. M. Imbert, Q.P.M. . . £38,775
Receiver, A. D. Gordon-Brown £36,500
Deputy Receiver, B. G. David £27,791

Territorial Operations Department

Assistant Commissioner, G. D. McLean, Q.P.M.
£35,250
Deputy Assistant Commissioners, C. F. Dinsdale; R.
Innes; D. J. O'Dowd £28,200
Commanders, Miss J. Hilton; R. C. Marsh; L. T.
Roach; A. W. Young £24,750
Senior Principal, W. T. Davis £17,000–22,926

Area Headquarters

Deputy Assistant Commissioners, R. A. Hunt, O.B.E.;
J. F. Newing; M. D. Richards; T. J. Siggs £28,200
Commanders, W. E. E. Boreham; A. W. F. Hemming-
way; T. A. Lloyd-Hughes; D. J. Mitchell, Q.P.M.
£24,750
*Metropolitan Police Special Constabulary, Chief Com-
mandant*, A. A. Hammond, O.B.E.

Specialist Operations Department

Assistant Commissioner, J. A. Dellow, C.B.E. . £35,250
Deputy Assistant Commissioners, J. H. Cracknell,
L.V.O.; C. V. Hewett, O.B.E., Q.P.M.; G. W. Jones;
B. R. C. Worth £28,200
Commanders, D. R. E. Bicknell, Q.P.M.; M. R. Camp-
bell; P. H. Corbett; S. R. A. Crawshaw; R. A.
Dowling; A. McNair; E. Mitchell; P. Phelan, Q.P.M.;
C. J. Rideout; W. Taylor; D. H. Williams, Q.P.M.
£24,750

Metropolitan Police Laboratory

Director, R. L. Williams £26,909
Deputy Directors, G. J. Lee; M. R. Loveland; P. D.
Martin; E. F. Pearson £17,000–22,926
Senior Principal Scientific Officer, B. B. Wheals
£17,000–22,926

Personnel and Training Department

Assistant Commissioner, H. N. Annesley £35,250
Deputy Assistant Commissioners, M. J. Evans; J.
Thornton, Q.P.M. £28,200
Commanders, J. M. M. Huins; B. H. Skitt, B.E.M.;
K. W. Masterson £24,750
Welfare Officer, K. F. T. Rivers, M.B.E
£13,508–18,363

Metropolitan Police Cadet Corps

Commander, K. W. Masterson £24,750

Medical and Dental Branch

Chief Medical Officer, E. C. A. Bott

Management Support Department

Assistant Commissioner, C. B. J. Sutton, Q.P.M.
£35,250

Complaints Investigation Bureau

Deputy Assistant Commissioner, (vacant).
Commander, K. J. Merton £24,750

Public Information Department

Director of Information, R. B. Wells £28,200
Deputy Director of Information, H. B. Colver
£17,000–22,926

Directorate of Management Services

Director, N. E. Hand £20,964–25,533
Deputy Director, J. E. Tubb £17,000–22,926

Force Inspectorate

Deputy Assistant Commissioner, J. A. Smith £28,200
Commander, M. A. Ferguson £24,750

Solicitor's Department

Solicitor, D. M. O'Shea £36,500
Deputy Solicitor, D. W. Warran £29,500
Assistant Solicitors, P. R. Essex; W. S. Frost; H. B.
Hargrave; R. L. Kiley; R. E. Marsh; R. J. Mays;
J. R. McCann; C. S. Porteous; R. N. D. Thorne;
J. M. Tuff £20,964–25,533
The following departments are responsible to the
Receiver through the Deputy Receiver.

"E" Department
Establishments and Secretariat

Establishment Officer, R. B. Jones . . . £20,964–25,533
Deputy Establishment Officers, J. A. Crutchlow;
M. W. Maidment; E. R. Bright £17,000–22,926

"F" Department
Finance

Director of Finance, R. V. Clark £20,964–25,533
Deputy Directors of Finance, J. L. Davies; A. M. J.
Williams; D. Wilson £17,000–22,926

Supplies and Services Department

Director, N. N. I. Batten £17,000–22,926

Catering Department

Director of Catering, Col. R. R. Owens, O.B.E.
£17,000–22,926

Property Services Department

Director of Property Services, M. L. Belchamber
£20,964–25,533
Deputy Directors, R. M. Boa; J. A. Chipchase; K. R.
Sewell £17,000–22,926

Chief Engineer's Department

Chief Engineer, Col. J. E. Owen £20,964–25,533
Deputy Chief Engineers, N. Boothman; D. Hale,
O.B.E.; J. M. Wardle; D. A. Woolgar
£17,000–22,926

Department of Computing Services

Director of Computing Services, R. G. Gregory
£20,964–25,533
Deputy Directors of Computing Services, D. K. Dun-
kin; T. Egan £17,000–22,926

CITY OF LONDON POLICE
26 Old Jewry, EC2R 8DJ

Commissioner, O. Kelly £38,775
Assistant Commissioner, W. Taylor £30,225
Commander, H. J. Moore £24,750
Chief Superintendents, A. Martin (*Administration*);
D. Perry ("*B*" *Divn.*); R. Fowlie ("*C*" *Divn.*); K.
Richiardi (*Traffic & Communications*); B. A. Tar-
bun (*C.I.D.*); G. Squires (*C.I.D/Fraud*)
£21,540–22,794

City of London Special Constabulary

Chief Commandant, F. A. D. Ralfe.
Staff Officer, P. Redman.

BRITISH TRANSPORT POLICE
15 Tavistock Place, WC1H 9SJ
[01–388 7541]

The Force provides a policing service to the British
Railways Board and its wholly-owned subsidiary
companies, London Regional Transport, and Sealink
British Ferries. Police posts are located throughout
England, Wales and Scotland.

Chief Constable, K. H. Ogram, Q.P.M.
Deputy Chief Constable, G. E. Coles.
Assistant Chief Constables, T. H. S. Buckle (*Administration*); W. I. McGregor (*Operations*); J. Nixon (*Personnel & Training*); W. F. Palmer (*London Transport Division*); A. M. Mackenzie (*Scottish Division*).

MINISTRY OF DEFENCE POLICE
Ministry of Defence, Empress State Building,
Lillie Road, SW6 1TR
[01–385 1244]

The Ministry of Defence Police are responsible chiefly for the policing of military establishments in Great Britain.
Chief Constable, J. R. T. Bailey, C.B.E., G.M.
Deputy Chief Constable, J. Aspinall.
Head of M.D.P. Secretariat, J. A. Horley.
Assistant Chief Constable (*Operations*), S. G. Edwards.

Area Headquarters
Central Area, Apsley House, Stockport, Cheshire.—*Assistant Chief Constable*, E. L. Morton.
Northern Area, Hilton Road, Rosyth, Fife.—*Assistant Chief Constable*, C. Bucke.
Southern Area, Aldershot, Hants.—*Assistant Chief Constable*, L. C. A. Knight, Q.P.M.
Western Area, Medmenham, Marlow, Bucks.—*Assistant Chief Constable*, I. S. McGregor.

STAFF ASSOCIATIONS

ASSOCIATION OF CHIEF POLICE OFFICERS OF ENGLAND, WALES AND NORTHERN IRELAND, Room 1133, New Scotland Yard, Broadway, SW1H 0BG. Represents the Chief Constables, Deputy Chief Constables and Assistant Chief Constables of England, Wales and N. Ireland, and officers of the rank of Commander and above in the Metropolitan and City of London Police. *Gen. Sec.*, B. Morrissey, O.B.E., Q.P.M.

THE POLICE SUPERINTENDENTS' ASSOCIATION OF ENGLAND AND WALES, 46A Reading Road, Pangbourne RG8 7JD. Represents officers of the rank of Superintendent and Chief Superintendent. *Sec.*, Chief Supt. J. Keyte, O.B.E.

THE POLICE FEDERATION OF ENGLAND AND WALES, 15–27 Langley Road, Surbiton, Surrey KT6 6LP. Represents officers up to and including the rank of Chief Inspector. *Gen. Sec.*, P. Tanner.

ASSOCIATION OF CHIEF POLICE OFFICERS (SCOTLAND), Police Headquarters, Fettes Avenue, Edinburgh EH4 1RB. Represents the Chief Constables, Deputy Chief Constables and Assistant Chief Constables of the Scottish police forces. *Hon. Sec.*, Chief Constable W. G. M. Sutherland, Q.P.M.

THE ASSOCIATION OF SCOTTISH POLICE SUPERINTENDENTS, Hon. Secretary's Office, Strathclyde Police, Force Headquarters, 173 Pitt Street, Glasgow G2 4JS. Represents officers of the rank of Superintendent and Chief Superintendent. *Hon. Sec.*, Chief Supt. D. L. Allan.

THE SCOTTISH POLICE FEDERATION, 5 Woodside Place, Glasgow G3 7PD. Represents officers up to and including the rank of Chief Inspector. *Gen. Sec.*, A. Gowl.

THE SUPERINTENDENTS ASSOCIATION OF NORTHERN IRELAND, Ormiston House, Hawthornden Road, Belfast BT4 3NH. Represents Superintendents and Chief Superintendents in the R.U.C. *Hon. Sec.*, W/ Chief Supt. A. Donald.

THE POLICE FEDERATION FOR NORTHERN IRELAND, Royal Ulster Constabulary, Garnerville, Garnerville Road, Belfast BT4 2NX. Represents officers up to and including the rank of Chief Inspector. *Gen. Sec.*, J. Elder.

CRIMINAL STATISTICS
ENGLAND AND WALES
Notifiable offences recorded by the police (thousands)

	Total	Violence against the person	Sexual offences	Burglary	Robbery	Theft and handling stolen goods	Fraud and forgery	Criminal damage	Other
1981	2,963·8	100·2	19·4	723·2	20·3	1,603·2	106·7	386·7	4·1
1982	3,262·4	108·7	19·7	810·6	22·8	1,755·9	123·1	417·8	3·8
1983	3,247·0	111·3	20·4	813·4	22·1	1,705·9	121·8	443·3	8·7†
1984	3,499·1	114·2	20·2	897·5	24·9	1,808·0	126·1	497·8	10·4†
1985 1st quarter	865·9	26·7	4·7	223·7	6·5	444·8	35·3	121·5	2·6†

†Includes from the beginning of 1983 offences of 'trafficking in controlled drugs'.

SCOTLAND
Crimes and offences recorded by the police (thousands)

	Total crimes and offences (annual)	†Total crimes and offences (monthly)	Non-sexual crimes of violence against the person	Crimes involving indecency	Crimes involving dishonesty	Fire-raising, malicious and reckless conduct	Other crimes	Miscellaneous offences	Offences relating to motor vehicles
1981	744·7	740·6	12·2	4·8	318·5	61·3	9·5	117·8	216·4
1982	762·5	766·1	12·3	5·0	343·2	66·4	12·0	115·8	211·5
1983	799·9	800·3	13·3	5·5	345·2	72·9	14·1	112·8	236·6
1984	809·5	811·4	13·9	5·7	360·6	79·3	17·1	115·2	219·6
1985 1st quarter	196·4		3·6	1·4	82·7	19·0	4·2	26·5	59·0

†Components may not add to totals due to separate rounding.

THE ARMED FORCES

MINISTRY OF DEFENCE
Main Building, Whitehall, SW1A 2HB
[01–218 9000]

Secretary of State for Defence, THE RT. HON. MICHAEL
HESELTINE, M.P. £42,980
Private Secretary, R. C. Mottram.
Assistant Private Secretaries, N. R. H. Evans; B. P.
Neale; S. H. Lowe; Miss W. Anderton.
Parliamentary Private Secretary, N. B. Baker, M.P.
Minister of State for the Armed Forces, THE RT. HON.
JOHN STANLEY, M.P. £33,500
Private Secretary, P. M. W. Francis.
Minister of State for Defence Procurement, THE RT.
HON. ADAM COURTAULD BUTLER, M.P. £33,500
Private Secretary, Dr. A. S. Kemp.
*Parliamentary Under Secretary of State for the Armed
Forces*, The Lord Trefgarne £22,520
*Parliamentary Under Secretary of State for Defence
Procurement*, J. Lee, M.P. £28,120
Chief of Defence Staff, Admiral Sir John Fieldhouse,
G.C.B., G.B.E., A.D.C.
Deputy Chief of The Defence Staff, Air Marshal Sir
Donald Hall, K.C.B., C.B.E., A.F.C.
*Assistant Chief of The Defence Staff (Policy and
Nuclear)*, Rear-Admiral J. C. K. Slater, L.V.O.
Assistant Chief of Defence Staff (Intelligence), Rear
Admiral T. Bevan.
Assistant Chief of The Defence Staff (Overseas), Air
Vice Marshal J. M. D. Sutton, C.B.
*Assistant Chief of The Defence Staff (Command,
Control, Communications and Information Sys-
tems)*, Major-General G. R. Oehlers.
Director-General of Intelligence, Vice-Admiral Sir
Roy Halliday, K.B.E., D.S.C. (retd.).
Chief of The Defence Staff (Intelligence), Lt.-Gen. D.
Boorman, C.B.
Defence Services Secretary, Air Vice-Marshal R. C. F.
Peirse, C.B.
Chief of The Naval Staff and First Sea Lord, Admiral
Sir William Staveley, G.C.B., A.D.C.
Vice Chief of The Naval Staff, Admiral Sir Peter
Stanford, K.C.B., L.V.O., A.D.C.
Commandant-General Royal Marines, Lt.-Gen. Sir
Michael Wilkins, K.C.B., O.B.E.
Chief of The General Staff, General Sir Nigel Bagnall
K.C.B., C.V.O., M.C., A.D.C. (Gen.).
Vice Chief of The General Staff, Gen. Sir James
Glover, K.C.B., M.B.E.
Chief of The Air Staff, Air Chief Marshal Sir David
Craig, G.C.B., O.B.E.
Vice Chief of The Defence Staff, Air Chief Marshal Sir
Patrick Hine, K.C.B.
Chief Scientific Adviser, Prof. R. O. C. Norman
£45,500
Assistant Chief Scientific Advisers, N. H. Hughes
(Projects); H. G. R. Robinson, O.B.E. (Research);
J. D. Culshaw (Studies); D. C. Fakley, O.B.E.
(Nuclear) £29,500
*Director, Defence Operational Analysis Establish-
ment*, J. D. Culshaw £29,500
Chief Scientist (Royal Navy), Dr. F. A. Johnson
£29,500
Chief Scientist (Army), L. R. Gray £29,500
Chief Scientist (Royal Air Force), D. E. Humphries
£29,500
Chief of Naval Personnel and Second Sea Lord,
Admiral Sir Simon Cassels, K.C.B., C.B.E.
Naval Secretary, Rear-Admiral R. C. Dimmock.
Chaplain of The Fleet, Ven. N. D. Jones, Q.H.C.
Chief of Fleet Support, Vice-Admiral Sir Anthony
Tippett, K.C.B.
Chief Executive Royal Dockyards, Rear-Admiral A. S.
George, C.B. £32,350
Principal Director of Planning and Policy, G. Allin.

Director of Establishments and Personnel, R. J. C.
Stone.
Director, Finance, A. G. Maxfield.

Military Secretary, Lt.-Gen. Sir David Mostyn, K.C.B.,
C.B.E.

Adjutant-General, Gen. Sir Roland Guy, K.C.B., C.B.E.,
D.S.O.

Quartermaster-General, Gen. Sir Richard Trant,
K.C.B.

Chaplain-General, Ven. W. F. Johnston, C.B., Q.H.C.

Air Member for Personnel, Air Chief Marshal Sir
Thomas Kennedy, K.C.B., A.F.C.

Chaplain-in-Chief, R.A.F., Ven. G. R. Renowden,
Q.H.C.

Air Member for Supply and Organisation, Air Marshal Sir Michael Knight, K.C.B., A.F.C.

Permanent Under Secretary of State, Sir Clive Whit-
more, K.C.B., C.V.O. £45,500
Second Permanent Under Secretary of State, J. N. H.
Blelloch, C.B. £39,500
Deputy Under-Secretaries of State, K. C. Macdonald,
(Resource and Programmes); J. G. Ashcroft, (Fi-
nance); R. M. Hastie-Smith (Civilian Manage-
ment); B. E. Robson (Personnel and Logistics)
£36,500
Assistant Under-Secretaries of State, M. Gainsbor-
ough, (Programmes); W. D. Reeves, (Systems); C.
T. McDonnell (Resources); N. Bevan, (General
Finance); R. L. Facer, (Personnel and Logistics);
W. F. Mumford, (R&D Establishment and Research
Admin.); M. D. Tidy (Ordnance); T. J. Brack,
(Naval Personnel); K. J. Pritchard, C.B. (Director-
General Supplies and Transport (Naval)) . . £29,500
Commandant, Royal College of Defence Studies, Gen.
Sir Michael Gow, K.C.B., O.B.E.

Procurement Executive

Chief of Defence Procurement, P. K. Levene . . £45,500
Private Secretary, Miss E. G. Cassidy.
Deputy Under-Secretary of State (Policy) (P.E.), K. C.
Macdonald, C.B. £36,500
*Assistant Under-Secretary of State (Equipment Col-
laboration)* J. L. Roberts £29,500
*Assistant Under-Secretary of State (Royal Ordnance
Factories Bill)*, B. M. Norbury £29,500
Director-General Quality Assurance, D. Brighton
£29,500
Director-General of Defence Contracts, B. R. Haigh
£29,500
Head of Defence Sales, C. Chandler.
Director-General of Marketing, T. F. W. B. Knapp.
Assistant Under-Secretary, C. H. Henn (Sales
Admin.) £29,500
*Controller Research and Development Establish-
ments, Research and Nuclear*, C. C. Fielding, C.B.
£39,250
*Assistant Under-Secretary of State Research and
Development Establishments, and Research Ad-
ministration*, W. F. Mumford £29,500
*Deputy Controller and Adviser (Research and Tech-
nology)*, Dr. G. G. Pope £36,500
*Deputy Controller Research and Development Estab-
lishments Resources and Personnel*, J. F. Barnes,
C.B. £36,500
*Director-General Research A and Chief Scientist
(Royal Navy)*, Dr. F. A. Johnson £29,500
*Director, Admiralty Marine Technology Establish-
ment*, Dr. D. J. L. Smith £29,500
Director, Admiralty Surface Research Establishment,
I. B. Bott £32,350

Director, Royal Signals and Radar Establishment, Dr. A. C. Baynham £32,350
Director-General Research B and Chief Scientist (Army), L. R. Gray...................... £29,500
Director, Atomic Weapons Research Establishment, P. G. E. F. Jones £39,055
Director, Chemical Defence Establishment, Dr. G. S. Pearson £29,500
Deputy Director Vehicles Department, J. Ellis £32,350
Director, Propellants, Explosives and Rocket Motor Establishment, Dr. B. H. Newman £29,500
Director, Royal Armament Research and Development Establishment, Dr. T. P. McLean £32,350
Director-General Research and Technology Chief Scientist (Royal Air Force), D. E. Humphries £29,500
Commandant, Aeroplane and Armament Experimental Establishment, Air Commodore G. C. Williams.
Director, Royal Aircraft Establishment, Dr. G. G. Pope £36,500
Assistant Controller (Nuclear), Dr. E. D. Dracott £29,740
Controller of the Navy, Vice-Admiral Sir Derek Reffell, K.C.B.
Assistant Under-Secretary of State (Material-Naval), C. H. O'D. Alexander £29,500
Principal Director of Navy and Nuclear Contracts, A. J. Figes.............................. £27,791
Deputy Controller Warships, P. W. Jarvis ... £34,250
Director-General Surface Ships, Rear Admiral H. L. O. Thompson.
Director-General Submarines, S. A. T. Warren £29,500
Chief Naval Weapons Systems Engineer, Dr. D. G. Kiely £29,500
Director-General Future Material Projects (Naval), P. E. Chamberlain £29,500
Deputy Controller Warship Equipment, Rear-Admiral G. G. W. Marsh.
Director-General Surface Weapons, H. Perkins £29,500
Director-General Underwater Weapons, Commodore C. L. Wood.
Chief Strategic Systems Executive, Rear Admiral J. S. Cooper, O.B.E.
Deputy Chief Strategic Systems Executive, Cdre. M. C. Powys Maurice.
Master-General of the Ordnance, Lt. General Sir Richard Vincent, K.C.B., D.S.O.
Vice Master-General of the Ordnance, Major-General M. T. Skinner.

Assistant Under-Secretary of State (Ordnance), M. D. Tidy £29,500
Principal Director of Contracts (Ordnance), R. G. Woodman £27,791
Director-General Guided Weapons and Electronics, Dr. P. G. Smith £29,500
Director-General of Fighting Vehicles and Engineer Equipment, Major-General S. R. A. Stopford, M.B.E.
Director-General of Weapons (Army), Major-General R. J. Crossley, C.B.E.
Controller, Aircraft, Air Chief Marshal Sir John Rogers, K.C.B., C.B.E.
Assistant Under-Secretary of State/Air (Procurement Executive), J. M. Moss £29,500
Principal Director of Contracts/Air, B. J. Slade £27,791
Deputy Controller Aircraft, D. M. Spiers..... £36,500
Director-General Engines (Procurement Executive), M. C. Neale £29,500
Director-General Aircraft 1, M. T. Peters £36,500
Director-General Aircraft 2, Air Vice-Marshal J. A. Porter, O.B.E.
Deputy Controller Aircraft Weapons and Electronics, P. R. Wallis £32,350
Director-General of Air Weapons Electronic Systems, Dr. T. Buckley £29,500
Director-General of Strategic Electronic Systems, Air Vice-Marshal F. M. Holroyd £29,500

Meteorological Office

London Road, Bracknell, Berks.
[Bracknell: 20242]

The Meteorological Office is the State Meteorological Service. It forms part of the Ministry of Defence, the Director General being ultimately responsible to the Secretary of State for Defence.

Except for the common services provided by other government departments as part of their normal functions, the cost of the Meteorological Office is borne by Defence Votes.

Of the expenditure chargeable to Defence Votes about £34,000,000 represents expenditure associated with staff and £35,100,000 on stores, communications and miscellaneous services. About £21,800,000 is recovered from outside bodies for special services rendered, sales of meteorological equipment, etc.
Director-General, Prof. J. T. Houghton, C.B.E., D.Phil., F.R.S............................... £36,500
Director of Research, P. Goldsmith £27,791
Director of Services, F. H. Bushby £29,500

THE ROYAL NAVY

THE QUEEN

Admirals of the Fleet

H.R.H. The Prince Philip, Duke of Edinburgh, K.G., P.C., K.T., O.M., G.B.E., *born* June 10, 1921 ..... Jan. 15, 1953
Sir Varyl Begg, G.C.B., D.S.O., D.S.C., *born* Oct. 1, 1908 .... Aug. 12, 1968
The Lord Hill-Norton, G.C.B., *born* Feb. 8, 1915 .... March 12, 1971
Sir Michael Pollock, G.C.B., M.V.O., D.S.C., *born* Oct. 19, 1916 .... March 1, 1974
Sir Edward Ashmore, G.C.B., D.S.C., *born* Dec. 11, 1919 .... Feb. 9, 1977
The Lord Lewin, K.G., G.C.B., M.V.O., D.S.C., *born* Nov. 19, 1920 .... July 6, 1979
Sir Henry Leach, G.C.B., *born* Nov. 18, 1923 .... Dec. 1, 1982
Sir John Fieldhouse, G.C.B., G.B.E., A.D.C., (*Chief of Defence Staff*), *born* Feb. 12, 1928 .... Nov. 1, 1985

Admirals

Staveley, Sir William, G.C.B., A.D.C., (*First Sea Lord and Chief of Naval Staff*).

Cassels, Sir Simon, K.C.B., C.B.E., (*Second Sea Lord and Chief of Naval Personnel and Admiral President Royal Naval College Greenwich*).

Stanford, Sir Peter, K.C.B., L.V.O., A.D.C., (*C-in-C Naval Home Command*).

Hunt, Sir Nicholas, K.C.B., L.V.O., (*C. in C. Fleet, Allied C.-in-C. Channel and C.-in-C. Eastern Atlantic Area*).

Vice-Admirals

Hallifax, Sir David, K.C.B., K.B.E., (*Deputy Supreme Allied Commander Atlantic*).

Tippet, Sir Anthony, K.C.B., (*Chief of Fleet Support*).

Reffell, Sir Derek, K.C.B., (*Controller of the Navy*).

Fitch, R. G. A.

Woodward, Sir John, K.C.B., (*Deputy Chief of Defence Staff, Commitments*).

Gerken, R. W. F., C.B.E., (*Flag Officer, Plymouth, Port Admiral Devonport, Commander Central Sub. Area, Eastern Atlantic and Commander Plymouth Sub Area Channel*).

Dalton, G. T. J. O., (*Deputy Supreme Allied Commander Atlantic*).

Symons, P. J., (*Chief of Staff to Commander, Allied Naval Forces, Southern Europe*).

Vallings, G. M. F., (*Flag Officer Scotland and Northern Ireland, Commander Northern Sub Area Eastern Atlantic, and Commander N O R E Sub Area Channel, and Port Admiral Rosyth*).

Webster, J. M., (*Chief of Staff to C.-in-C. Fleet*).

Rear-Admirals

Grove, J. S., C.B., O.B.E., (*Chief Strategic Systems Executive*).

Eckersly-Maslin, D. M., C.B., (*Assistant, Command, Control, Communications and Information Systems*).

Higgins, W. A., C.B., C.B.E., (*Director-General Naval Personnel Services and Chief Naval Supply and Secretariat Officer*).

Marsh, G. G. W., C.B., O.B.E., (*Deputy Controller Warship Equipment and Chief Naval Engineer Officer*).

Oswald, J. J. R., (*Flag Officer Third Flotilla and Commander Anti-Submarine Group Two*).

Vallis, M. A., (*Director-General Marine Engineering and Senior Naval Representative Bath*).

Thomas, W. R. S., O.B.E., (*Flag Officer, Second Flotilla*).

Middleton, L. E., D.S.O., (*Flag Officer Naval Air Command*).

Barker, J. P.

Simpson, M. F.

Black, J. J., D.S.O., M.B.E., (*Assistant Chief of Naval Staff*).

MacLean, E., (*Director-General Fleet Support Policy and Services*).

Thompson, H. L. O., (*Director-General Surface Ships*).

Bathurst, D. B., (*Director General Naval Manpower and Training*).

Burgess, J., M.V.O., (*Managing Director, H.M. Dockyard, Rosyth*).

Heaslip, R. G., (*Flag Officer Submarines and COMSUBEASTLANT*).

Hogg, R. I. T., (*Flag Officer First Flotilla*).

Livesay, M. H., (*Flag Officer Sea Training*).

Snow, K. A., (*Deputy Asst. Chief of Staff (Operations) on the staff of the Supreme Allied Commander, Europe*).

Bevan, T. M., (*Assistant Chief of the Defence Staff (Intelligence)*).

Kerr, J. B. (*Assistant Chief of Staff, Defence, Operational Requirements, Sea Systems*).

Hitchens, G. A. F., (*Chief Staff Officer (Engineering) to C.-in-C. Fleet*).

Richmond, A. J., (*Assistant Chief of the Defence Staff, (Logistics, Policy and Plans)*).

King, N. R. D., (*Commander British Navy Staff Washington, Naval Attache Washington, UK National Liason Representative to SACLANT*).

Holley, R. V. (*Director-General Aircraft (Naval)*).

Morris, R. O., (*Hydrographer of the Navy*).

Dimmock, R. C., (*Naval Secretary*).

Dingemans, R. G. V., D.S.O., (*Flag Officer Gibraltar, and Naval Base Commander and COMGIBMED*).

Slater, J. C. K., L.V.O., (*Assistant Chief of the Defence Staff (Policy and Nuclear)*).

Garnier, J., C.B.E., L.V.O., (*Flag Officer Royal Yachts*).

Wheatley, A., (*Flag Officer and Naval Base Commander Portsmouth and Head of Establishment of the Fleet Maintenance, and Repair Organisation*).

Marsden, P. N., (*Senior Naval Member of Directing Staff, Royal College of Defence Studies*).

Grenier, P. F., (*Chief of Staff to C.-in-C. Chief Naval Home Command*).

HER MAJESTY'S FLEET

Type/Class	No.	Operational or engaged in preparing for service or trials or training	No.	Undergoing restorative or major refit or conversion, on standby etc.
Submarines				
Polaris	3	Renown, Resolution, Revenge	1	Repulse
Fleet	12	Valiant, Warspite, Churchill, Conqueror, Sovereign, Swiftsure, Sceptre, Spartan, Splendid, Trafalgar, Turbulent, Tireless	2	Courageous, Superb
Oberon Class	8	Orpheus, Oberon, Olympus, Oracle, Ocelot, Osiris, Opossum, Opportune	5	Odin, Otter, Onslaught, Onyx, Otus
Porpoise Class	2	Sealion, Walrus		
ASW Carrier	3	Invincible, Illustrious, Ark Royal*		
ASW/Commando Carriers			1	Hermes†
Assault Ships	2	Fearless†, Intrepid		
Guided-Missile Destroyers				
County	2	Glamorgan, Fife		
Type 82			1	Bristol
Type 42	12	Birmingham, Cardiff, Newcastle, Glasgow, Exeter, Southampton, Nottingham, Liverpool, Manchester, Gloucester*, Edinburgh*, York		

Frigates

Type 22	6	Broadsword, Battleaxe, Brilliant, Brazen, Boxer, Beaver, Brave*	
Type 21	5	Active, Amazon, Arrow, Alacrity, Avenger	1 Ambuscade
Leander Class	18	Leander, Ajax, Galatea, Naiad, Arethusa, Cleopatra, Phoebe, Argonaut, Minerva, Danae, Penelope, Andromeda, Charybdis, Achilles, Diomede, Scylla, Hermione, Jupiter	5 Euryalus, Sirius, Ariadne, Apollo, Aurora
Rothesay Class	4	Rothesay, Plymouth, Yarmouth, Berwick	
Navigation Training Ship ...	1	Juno†	

Offshore Patrol

Island Class	6	Alderney, Guernsey, Jersey, Lindisfarne, Orkney, Shetland	1 Anglesey
Castle Class	2	Dumbarton Castle, Leeds Castle	

MCMVs

Minesweepers Ton Class	7	Alfriston, Bickington, Crichton, Hodgeston, Soberton, Stubbington, Walkerton	2 Cuxton, Upton
River Class	11	Waveney, Carron, Dovey, Helford*, Humber, Blackwater*, Itchen*, Helmsdale*, Orwell*, Ribble*, Spey*	
Minehunters Ton Class	13	Bildeston, Brereton, Brinton, Gavinton, Iveston, Keddleston, Kellington, Kirkliston, Maxton, Nurton, Sheraton, Wilton, Hubberston	2 Bossington, Bronington
Hunt Class	10	Brecon, Brocklesby, Cattistock, Cottesmore, Dulverton, Ledbury, Middleton, Chiddingfold, Hurworth*, Bicester*	

Patrol Craft

Bird Class	4	Cygnet, Kingfisher, Peterel†, Sandpiper†	
Loyal Class	2	Alert, Vigilant	
Coastal Training Craft	15	Attacker†, Fencer†, Hunter†, Chaser†, Striker†, Archer†*, Biter†*, Smiter†*, Pursuer†*, Trumpeter†*, Blazer†*, Dasher†*, Puncher†*, Charger†*, Ranger†*	
Coastal Patrol Craft	2	Monkton, Wolverton	
Peacock Class	5	Peacock, Plover, Starling, Swallow, Swift	
Falkland Islands Patrol Vessels	3	Protector, Guardian, Sentinel	

Support Ships

Submarine Tender			1 Wakeful
MCM Support Ship	1	Abdiel	
Seabed Operations Vessel....	1	Challenger	

Royal Yacht/Hospital Ship .. 1 Britannia

Training Ships

Fleet Tenders	4	Manly†, Mentor†, Messina, Millbrook

Ice Patrol Ship .... 1 Endurance

Survey Ships	8	Beagle, Bulldog, Fawn, Fox, Hecate, Herald, Hydra, Gleaner	1 Hecla

Notes:

(i) This table includes ships due for completion or disposal during the course of 1985/86 and the numbers of each type are not therefore an accurate indication of the ships available at any one time. It does not include those ships solely engaged in harbour training duties.

(ii) Ships marked * were under construction on 1 April 1985 and are planned to enter service during 1985/86.

(iii) Ships marked † are engaged partially on trials or training.

(iv) Ships approved during 1984/85 for disposal: Antrim, Lowestoft, Falmouth, Torquay, Lewiston, Pollington, Shavington, Wotton, Wasperton, Yarnton, Waterwitch, Woodlark, Echo, Enterprise, Egeria, Beachampton and the hovercraft BH7.

Royal Naval Auxiliary Service.—The Royal Naval Auxiliary Service (RNXS) is a uniformed civilian volunteer service, administered by the Ministry of Defence and trained by the Royal Navy to operate at ports and anchorages, for duty in emergencies and war. RNXS units are situated on the coasts of the United Kingdom and organised and run by the Area Flag Officers. The role of the RNXS is to assist with the defence of ports and anchorages by manning local headquarters and supporting the Naval Control of Shipping Organisation. The strength is 2,800.

ROYAL MARINES

The Corps of Royal Marines, about 7,100 strong, first formed in 1664, is part of the Naval Service. The Royal Marines provide Britain's sea soldiers and in particular 3 Commando Brigade Royal Marines, two thirds of which is trained and equippped for arctic warfare. Royal Marines also serve in H.M. Ships, provide landing craft crews, special boat sections and other detachments for naval and amphibious operations. They also provide the Naval Band Service.

The Royal Marines Reserve of about 1,200 volunteers consists of five main centres in London, Bristol, Liverpool, Newcastle and Glasgow.
Commandant-General, Royal Marines, Lieutenant General Sir Michael Wilkins, K.C.B., O.B.E.
Major-Generals, J. C. Hardy, C.B., L.V.O. *(H.Q. AF-NORTH)*; J. M. C. Garrod, O.B.E. *(Chief of Staff)*; J. H. A. Thompson, C.B., O.B.E. *(Training, Reserve and Special Forces)*; J. St. J. Grey *(Commando Forces)*.

QUEEN ALEXANDRA'S ROYAL NAVAL NURSING SERVICE (Q.A.R.N.N.S.)

The first nursing sisters were appointed to naval hospitals in 1884 and the service gained its current title under the patronage of Queen Alexandra in 1902. Nursing ratings were introduced in 1960 and from 1982 a number of men have taken the opportunity to join Q.A.R.N.N.S. as both officers and ratings. Still largely based at the Royal Naval Hospitals, Q.A.R.N.N.S. continue their responsibility for the health and fitness of naval personnel. The strength is about 600.
Patron, H.R.H. Princess Alexandra.
Matron-in-Chief and Director of Defence Nursing Services, Miss J. Robertson, R.R.C., Q.H.N.S., Q.A.R.N.N.S.

WOMEN'S ROYAL NAVAL SERVICE (W.R.N.S.)

Originally founded in 1917, the W.R.N.S. were temporarily disbanded between World Wars I and II. The contribution of the Service is now firmly established as a professional and integral part of the Royal Navy with personnel serving in the United Kingdom and abroad in a wide range of specialist roles. Although W.R.N.S. do not serve at sea, they provide an essential nucleus of about 3,000 trained personnel ashore in order to release men to H.M. Ships.
Chief Commandant, H.R.H. Princess Anne.
Director W.R.N.S., Commandant D. P. Swallow, Hon. A.D.C., W.R.N.S.

THE ARMY

THE QUEEN

Field-Marshals

H.R.H. The Prince Philip, Duke of Edinburgh, K.G., P.C., K.T., O.M., G.B.E., Field-Marshal, Australian Military Forces, Col.-in-Chief, Q.R.I.H., D.E.R.R., Q.O. Hldrs., Corps of Royal Electrical and Mechanical Engineers, A.C.F., Col. G.G., *born* June 10, 1921 .... Jan. 15, 1953
The Lord Harding of Petherton, G.C.B., C.B.E., D.S.O., M.C., *born* Feb. 10, 1896 .... July 21, 1953
Sir Richard A. Hull, K.G., G.C.B., D.S.O., *born* May 7, 1907 .... Feb. 8, 1965
Sir A. James H. Cassels, G.C.B., K.B.E., D.S.O., *born* Feb. 28, 1907 .... Feb. 29, 1968
The Lord Carver, G.C.B., C.B.E., D.S.O., M.C., *born* April 24, 1915 .... July 18, 1973
Sir Roland Gibbs, G.C.B., C.B.E., D.S.O., M.C., *born* June 22, 1921 .... July 13, 1979

Generals

Stanier, Sir John, G.C.B., M.B.E.

Gow, Sir Michael, G.C.B., Col. Comdt. Int. Corps *(Comdt. Royal College of Defence Studies)*.

Bagnall, Sir Nigel, K.C.B., C.V.O., M.C., A.D.C. *(Gen.)*, Col. Comdt. A.P.T.C., Col. Comdt. R.A.C., *(Chief of the General Staff)*.

Morony, Sir Thomas, K.C.B., O.B.E., A.D.C. *(Gen.)*, Col. Comdt. R.H.A., Col. Comdt. R.A. *(U.K. MILREP N.A.T.O.)*.

Lawson, Sir Richard, K.C.B., D.S.O., O.B.E. *(C.-in-C. Allied Forces Northern Europe)*.

Guy, Sir Roland, K.C.B., C.B.E., D.S.O., A.D.C. *(Gen.)*, Col. Comdt. 1 R.G.J., Col. Comdt. S.A.S.C. *(Adjutant General)*.

Burgess, Sir Edward, K.C.B., O.B.E., A.D.C. *(Gen.)*, Col. Comdt. R.A. *(DSACEUR)*.

Trant, Sir Richard, K.C.B., Col. Comdt. R.A.O.C., Col. Comdt. R.A.E.C. *(Quartermaster General)*.

Glover, Sir James, K.C.B., M.B.E., Col. Comdt. 3 R.G.J., Col. Comdt. R.M.P. *(C.-in-C. U.K. Land Forces)*.

Farndale, Sir Martin, K.C.B., Col. Comdt. R.A. and A.A.C. *(C.-in-C. B.A.O.R. and Commander Northern Army Group)*.

Lieutenant-Generals

Boswell, Sir Alexander, K.C.B., C.B.E., Col. Comdt. The Scottish Division.

Richardson, Sir Robert, K.C.B., C.V.O., C.B.E., Col. R.S.

Mostyn, Sir David, K.C.B., C.B.E., Col. Comdt. The Light Division, Col. Comdt. A.L.C. *(Military Secretary)*.

Howlett, Sir Geoffrey, K.B.E., M.C., Col. Comdt. P.A.R.A., Col. Comdt. A.C.C. *(G.O.C. South East District)*.

Akehurst, Sir John, K.C.B. C.B.E., Dep. Col. R. Anglian *(Comd. U.K. Fd. Army & Insp. Gen. T.A.)*.

Vincent, Sir Richard, K.C.B., D.S.O., Col. Comdt. R.A. and R.E.M.E. *(Master General of the Ordnance)*.

Huxtable, Sir Charles, K.C.B., C.B.E., Col. Comdt. The King's Division, Col. D.W.R. *(Comd. Training and Arms Directors)*.

Chapple, Sir John, K.C.B., C.B.E., *(Deputy Chief of the Defence Staff (Programme and Personnel))*.

Arthur Sir Norman, K.C.B., Col. Comdt. M.P.S.C., Col. Comdt. Scots D.G., *(G.O.C. Scotland & Governor of Edinburgh Castle)*.

Kenny, Sir Brian, K.C.B., C.B.E., Col. Comdt. R.A.V.C., Col. Q.R.I.H., *(Commander 1 (B.R.) Corps)*.

Pascoe, Sir Robert, K.C.B., M.B.E., *(G.O.C.D. Mil. Operations Northern Ireland)*.

Moffat, Sir Cameron, K.B.E., Q.H.S., *(Surgeon General)*.

Major-Generals

Langley, Sir Desmond, K.C.V.O., M.B.E.

Watts, J. P. B. C., C.B., C.B.E., M.C. (*C.D.S. & Chief of Operations Sultan of Oman's Armed Forces*).

Boorman, D., C.B., Col. 6 G.R. (*Chief of Defence Staff (Intelligence)*).

Matthews, M., C.B. (*Engineer-in-Chief (Army)*).

Reynolds, M. F., C.B. (*Assistant Director, Plans & Policy Division, International Military Staff N.A.T.O.*).

Lane, B. M., C.B., O.B.E., Col. L.I. (*G.O.C. South West District*).

Chiswell, P. I., C.B., C.B.E.

Reilly, J. C., D.S.O., Dep. Col. R.R.F. (*A.C.D.S. (Concepts) M.O.D.*).

Thorne, Sir David, K.B.E., Dep. Col. R. Anglian (*Comd. 1 Armd. Div.*).

Woodford, D. M., C.B.E., Col. R.R.F. (*Comdt. Joint Service Defence College*).

Gray, M. S., O.B.E. (*Chief of Staff H.Q. B.A.O.R.*).

Walker, A. K. F., Col. Comdt. R.T.R. (*Chief of Staff H.Q. U.K. Land Forces*).

Boam, T. A., C.B.E. (*C.B.F. Hong Kong & Major General Brigade of Gurkhas*).

Boyne, J., M.B.E. (*Director General of Electrical and Mechanical Engineering*).

Davis, B. W., C.B., C.B.E. (*Director General Logistic Planning (Army) M.O.D.*).

Keightley, R. C. (*Comdt. R.M.A.S.*).

MacMillan, J. R. A., C.B.E., Col. Gordons (*Assistant Chief of the General Staff*).

Palmer, C. P. R., C.B.E., Col. A. & S.H. (*Comdt. Staff College*).

Watkins, G. H., O.B.E. (*Director General Army Manning and Recruiting*).

Eyre, J. A. C. G., C.V.O., C.B.E. (*G.O.C. London District & Major General Comd. The Household Division*).

Rougier, C. J.

Steele, M. C. M., M.B.E. (*Chief Joint Liaison Organisation Bonn*).

Bartlett, J. L., C.B. (*Paymaster in Chief*).

Davies, D. M., O.B.E. (*G.O.C. North West District*).

Whalley, W. L., C.B.

Pryn, W. J., O.B.E., Q.H.S. (*Director of Army Surgery*).

Benbow, R. (*Signal Officer in Chief (Army)*).

Bowman, J. F. (*Director Army Legal Services*).

Goodman, J. D. W. (*Director Army Air Corps*).

Gordon Lennox, B. C., M.B.E. (*G.O.C. Berlin*).

New, L. A. W., C.B.E.

Oehlers, G. R. (*Assistant Chief of the Defence Staff (Communication & Information Systems)*).

Shortis, C. T., C.B.E., Col. Comdt. P.O.W. Div. (*Director of Infantry*).

Stibbon, J. J., O.B.E. (*Assistant Chief of the General Staff (Operational Requirements)*).

Waters, C. J., C.B.E. Col. Glosters (*Comd. 4 Armd. Div.*).

Webster, B. C., C.B.E. (*Director of Army Quartering*).

Welsh, P. M., O.B.E., M.C. (*President Regular Commissions Board*).

Braggins, D. H. (*Director General of Transport & Movements*).

Miller, D. E., C.B.E., M.C., Col. Ray's Own Border (*Chief of Staff LIVE OAK*).

Burch, K., C.B., C.B.E.

Pank, J. D. G. (*Director General of Personal Services (Army)*).

Spacie, K., O.B.E. (*Director Army Training*).

Ryan, D. E., LL.B. (*Director of Army Education*).

Thompson, C. N. (*Director Military Survey*).

Airy, C. J., C.B.E. (*Senior Army Member R.C.D.S.*).

Inge, P. A. (*G.O.C. North East District & Comd. 2 Inf. Div.*).

McGuinness, B. P. (*G.O.C. Western District*).

Paton, D. S., C.B.E., Q.H.P. (*Comd. Medicine B.A.O.R.*).

Livesey, B., Q.H.S. (*Comdt. Royal Army Medical College*).

Roberts, D. M., Q.H.P. (*Director Army Medicine*).

Yeoman, A. (*Comd. Communications B.A.O.R.*).

Cornock, C. G., M.B.E. (*Director Royal Artillery*).

Crossley, R. J., C.B.E. (*Director General Weapons (Army)*).

Billiere, P. E. de la C. de la, C.B.E., D.S.O., M.C. (*G.O.C. Wales*).

Cooper, S. C. (*Director Royal Armoured Corps*).

Ramsbotham, D. J., C.B.E. (*Comd. 3 Armd. Div.*).

Johnson, G. D., O.B.E., M.C., Col 10 G.R. (*Assistant Chief of the Defence Staff (N.A.T.O. & U.K.)*).

Ramsay, C. A., O.B.E. (*G.O.C. East District*).

Learmont, J. H., C.B.E. (*Commander Artillery 1 (B.R.) Corps*).

Jones, C. E. W., C.B.E. (*Director General Territorial Army and Organisation*).

Jeapes, A. S., O.B.E., M.C. (*Commander Land Forces Deputy Director Operations Northern Ireland*).

Stopford, S. R. A., M.B.E. (*Director General Fighting Vehicles & Engineer Equipment*).

Berragon, G. B. (*Director General Ordnance Services*).

Evans, J. A. M. (*Commandt. R.M.C.S.*).

CONSTITUTION OF THE BRITISH ARMY

The Regular Forces include the following Arms, Branches and Corps. Soldiers' Record Offices are shown at the end of each group; records of officers are maintained at the Ministry of Defence.

The Arms

Household Cavalry.—The Life Guards; The Blues and Royals (Royal Horse Guards and 1st Dragoons). *Records,* Horse Guards, London, S.W.1.

Royal Armoured Corps.—Cavalry Regiments: 1st The Queen's Dragoon Guards; The Royal Scots Dragoon Guards (Carabiniers and Greys); 4th/7th Royal Dragoon Guards; 5th Royal Inniskilling Dragoon Guards; The Queen's Own Hussars; The Queen's Royal Irish Hussars; 9th/12th Royal Lancers (Prince of Wales's); The Royal Hussars (Prince of Wales's Own), 13th/18th Royal Hussars (Queen Mary's Own); 14th/20th King's Hussars; 15th/19th The King's Royal Hussars; 16th/5th The Queen's Royal Lancers; 17th/21st Lancers; Royal Tank Regiment comprising four regular regiments. *Records,* Queen's Park, Chester.

Artillery.—Royal Regiment of Artillery. *Records,* Imphal Barracks, Fulford Road, York.

Engineers.—Corps of Royal Engineers. *Records,* Ditchling Road, Brighton.

Signals.—Royal Corps of Signals. *Records,* Balmore House, Caversham, Reading.

Infantry.—The Brigades/Regiments of Infantry of the Line are grouped in Divisions as follows:—

Guard's Division—Grenadier, Coldstream, Scots, Irish and Welsh Guards. Divisional HQ: HQ Household Division, Horse Guards, S.W.1. *Depot:* Pirbright Camp, Brookwood, Surrey. *Records:* The Foot Guards Regimental Manning and Record Office, Wellington Barracks, Birdcage Walk, London, S.W.1.

Scottish Division—The Royal Scots (The Royal Regiment); The Royal Highland Fusiliers (Princess Margaret's Own Glasgow and Ayrshire Regiment); The King's Own Scottish Borderers; The Black Watch (Royal Highland Regiment); Queen's Own Highlanders (Seaforth and Camerons); The Gordon Highlanders; The Argyll and Sutherland Highlanders (Princess Louise's). *Divisional HQ,* The Castle, Edinburgh. *Depôts,* Scottish Divisional Depôts, Glencorse, Milton Bridge, Midlothian and Albemarle Barracks, Ouston, Newcastle. *Records,* Imphal Barracks, Fulford, York.

Queen's Division—The Queen's Regiment, The Royal Regiment of Fusiliers, The Royal Anglian Regiment. *Divisional HQ*, Bassingbourn Barracks, Royston, Herts. *Depôt*, Bassingbourn Barracks, Royston, Herts. *Records*, Higher Barracks, Exeter, Devon.

King's Division—The King's Own Royal Border Regiment, The King's Regiment; The Prince of Wales's Own Regiment of Yorkshire; The Green Howards (Alexandra, Princess of Wales's Own Yorkshire Regiment); The Royal Irish Rangers (27th (Inniskilling) 83rd and 87th); The Queen's Lancashire Regiment; The Duke of Wellington's Regiment (West Riding). *Divisional HQ*, Imphal Barracks, York. *Depôts*, The King's Division Depôt (Yorkshire), Queen Elizabeth Barracks, Strensall, Yorks., and Albemarle Barracks, Ouston, Newcastle. The King's Division Depôt (Royal Irish Rangers), St. Patrick's Barracks, Ballymena, Northern Ireland. *Records*, Imphal Barracks, Fulford, York.

Prince of Wales's Division—The Devonshire and Dorset Regiment; The 22nd (Cheshire) Regiment; The Royal Welch Fusiliers, The Royal Regiment of Wales (24th/41st Foot); The Gloucestershire Regiment; The Worcestershire and Sherwood Foresters Regiment (29th/45th Foot); The Royal Hampshire Regiment; The Staffordshire Regiment (The Prince of Wales's); The Duke of Edinburgh's Royal Regiment (Berkshire and Wiltshire). *Divisional HQ*, Whittington Barracks, Lichfield, Staffs. *Depôts*, Mercian Depôt, The Prince of Wales's Division, Whittington Barracks, Lichfield, Staffs; Welsh Depôt, The Prince of Wales's Division, Cwrt-y-Gollen, Crickhowell, Powys. *Records*, Imphal Barracks, Fulford, York.

Light Division—The Light Infantry; The Royal Green Jackets. *Divisional HQ*, Peninsula Barracks, Winchester, Hants. *Depôts*, The Light Division Depôt (Shrewsbury), Sir John Moore Barracks, Copthorne, Shrewsbury, Salop. The Light Division Depôt (Winchester), Peninsula Barracks, Winchester, Hants. *Records*, Higher Barracks, Exeter.

Brigade of Gurkhas—2nd King Edward VII's Own Gurkha Rifles (The Sirmoor Rifles); 6th Queen Elizabeth's Own Gurkha Rifles; 7th Duke of Edinburgh's Own Gurkha Rifles; 10th Princess Mary's Own Gurkha Rifles, The Queen's Gurkha Engineers, Queen's Gurkha Signals, Gurkha Transport Regt. *Brigade HQ*, H.M.S. *Tamar*, Hong Kong, B.F.P.O. 1. *Depôt*, Training Depôt, Brigade of Gurkhas, Malaya Lines, Sek Kong, B.F.P.O. 1. *Records*, Record Office, Brigade of Gurkhas, Hong Kong, B.F.P.O. 1.

The Parachute Regiment (Three regular battalions)—*Depôt*, Browning Barracks, Aldershot, Hants. *Records*, Higher Barracks, Exeter.

Special Air Service Regiment—*Regimental HQ*, Duke of York's Headquarters, Sloane Square, S.W.3. *Depôt*, Stirling Lines, Hereford. *Records*, Higher Barracks, Exeter, Devon.

Army Air Corps—Regimental H.Q. and Depôt, Middle Wallop, Hants. *Records*, Higher Barracks, Exeter.

The Services

Royal Army Chaplain's Department—Regimental H.Q. and Depôt, Bagshot Park, Surrey.

Royal Corps of Transport, *Records*, Ore Place, Hastings.

Royal Army Medical Corps, Royal Army Dental Corps, Queen Alexandra's Royal Army Nursing Corps, and Women's Royal Army Corps. *Records*, Queen's Park, Chester.

Royal Army Ordnance Corps, Corps of Royal Electrical and Mechanical Engineers. *Records*, Glen Parva Barracks, Saffron Road, Wigston, Leicester.

Small Arms School Corps. *Records*, Higher Barracks, Exeter.

General Service Corps. *Records*, Imphal Barracks, Fulford Road, York.

Corps of Royal Military Police, Royal Army Pay Corps, Royal Army Veterinary Corps, Royal Pioneer Corps, Intelligence Corps, Army Catering Corps, Military Provost Staff Corps, Royal Army Educational Corps, Army Physical Training Corps, Army Legal Corps, Band of the Royal Military Academy, Sandhurst, Officers Training Corps. *Records*, Higher Barracks, Exeter, Devon.

The Territorial Army (T.A.) is designed to provide a highly trained and well equipped force which will complete the Regular Army order of battle in a time of national emergency. Its establishment is approximately 75,000 and it is planned that this will rise to 86,000 by 1990. A new element of the T.A., The Home Service Force, designed to produce a low cost guard force, is being expanded to some 5,000 posts by 1990.

The Ulster Defence Regiment (U.D.R.) was raised under authority of the *U.D.R. Act* 1969 and assists the Regular Army in Northern Ireland. H.Q., Magheralave Road, Lisburn, Co. Antrim. *Records*, Imphal Barracks, Fulford Road, York.

QUEEN ALEXANDRA'S ROYAL ARMY NURSING CORPS (Q.A.R.A.N.C.)

Founded in 1902 as Q.A.I.M.N.S., became Q.A.R.A.N.C. in 1959. Q.A.R.A.N.C. has trained nurses for the register and roll since 1950 and has four other employment categories. There was an introduction of a non-nursing officer element in 1959 for personnel work. The Q.A.R.A.N.C. provides service in military hospitals world-wide—United Kingdom (including N. Ireland), B.A.O.R., Hong Kong, Dharan, Cyprus, Falkland Islands and Belize.

Colonel-in-Chief, H.R.H. Princess Margaret.
Directorate of Defence Nursing Services, Miss J. Robertson, R.R.C., Q.H.N.S., Q.A.R.N.N.S.

WOMEN'S ROYAL ARMY CORPS (W.R.A.C.)

The W.R.A.C. was formed on February 1, 1949 as a Corps of the Regular Army. The Corps predecessors were Q.M.A.A.C. in World War I, and A.T.S. in World War II. The present role of the W.R.A.C. is to be organised and trained, as an integral part of the Army, to carry out those tasks for which its members are best suited and qualified, so that it will contribute to the maximum efficiency of the Army as a whole. The Corps is approximately 8,500 (Regular and T.A.) and is employed by 36 sponsors in 60 employments in 500 units world-wide in the British Army.

Commandant-in-Chief, H.M. Queen Elizabeth The Queen Mother.
Controller Commandant, H.R.H. The Duchess of Kent.
Deputy Controller Commandant, Brigadier E. J. Nolan, C.B.
Director, Women's Royal Army Corps, Brigadier H. G. Meechie, M.A.

THE ROYAL AIR FORCE

THE QUEEN

Marshals of the Royal Air Force

H.R.H. the Prince Philip, Duke of Edinburgh, K.G., P.C., K.T., O.M., G.B.E. (*Air Commodore-in-Chief, Air Training Corps, Marshal of the R.A.A.F.*) *born* June 10, 1921 .... Jan. 15, 1953
Sir William F. Dickson, G.C.B., K.B.E., D.S.O., A.F.C., *born* Sept. 24, 1898 .... June 1, 1954
Sir Dermot A. Boyle, G.C.B., K.C.V.O., K.B.E., A.F.C., *born* Oct. 2, 1904 .... Jan 1, 1958
The Lord Elworthy, K.G., G.C.B., C.B.E., D.S.O., M.V.O., D.F.C., A.F.C., *born* March 23, 1911 .... April 1, 1967
Sir John Grandy, G.C.B., K.B.E., D.S.O., *born* Feb. 8, 1913 (*Governor and Constable of Windsor Castle*) .... April 1, 1971
Sir Denis Spotswood, G.C.B., C.B.E., D.S.O., D.F.C., *born* Sept. 26, 1916 .... March 31, 1974
Sir Michael Beetham, G.C.B., C.B.E., D.F.C., A.F.C., A.D.C., *born* May 17, 1923 .... Oct. 15, 1982
Sir Keith Williamson, G.C.B., A.F.C., *born* Feb. 25, 1928 .... Oct. 15, 1985

Air Chief Marshals

Kennedy, Sir Thomas, G.C.B., A.F.C., A.D.C. (*Air Member for Personnel*).
Craig, Sir David, G.C.B., O.B.E. (*Chief of the Air Staff*).
Rogers, Sir John, K.C.B., C.B.E. (*Controller Aircraft*).
Beavis, Sir Michael, K.C.B., C.B.E., A.F.C. (*Deputy C.-in-C., Allied Forces Central Europe*).
Harding, Sir Peter, K.C.B., (*A.O.C. in C. S.T.C. U.K. Air Forces*).
Hine, Sir Patrick, K.C.B., (*Vice Chief of the Defence Staff*).

Air Marshals

Knight, Sir Michael, K.C.B., A.F.C. (*Air Member for Supply and Organisation*).
Hall, Sir Donald, K.C.B., C.B.E., A.F.C. (*Deputy Chief of the Defence Staff*).
Armitage, Sir Michael, K.C.B., C.B.E. (*Deputy Chief of the Defence Staff (Intelligence)*).
Fitzpatrick, Sir John, K.B.E., C.B. (*A.O.C. No. 18 Group*).
Harcourt-Smith, Sir David, K.C.B., D.F.C. (*A.O.C.-in-C., R.A.F. Support Command*).
Gilbert, Sir Joseph, K.C.B., C.B.E. (*Deputy C.-in-C Strike Command*).
Dunn, Sir Eric, K.B.E., C.B., B.E.M. (*Chief Engineer (R.A.F.)*).
Donald, Sir John, K.B.E., Q.H.S. (*Deputy Surgeon General (Operations) and Director General R.A.F. Medical Services*).
Parry-Evans, Sir David, K.C.B., C.B.E., (*C.-in-C. R.A.F. Germany and Cmdr. 2 A.T.A.F.*).

Air Vice-Marshals

Sutton, J. M. D., C.B. (*Assistant Chief of the Defence Staff (Overseas)*).

Skingsley, A. G., C.B. (*Assistant Chief of the Air Staff (Policy)*).
Hayr, K. W., C.B., C.B.E., A.F.C. (*Commander British Forces Cyprus and Administrator Sovereign Base Areas*).
Bennett, E. P., C.B. (*Commander, Sultan of Oman's Air Force*).
Peirse, R. C. F., C.B. (*Defence Services Secretary*).
Duxbury, J. B., C.B.E. (*Air Secretary*).
Jones, L. A., C.B., A.F.C. (*Assistant Chief of the Defence Staff (Programmes)*).
White, G. A., C.B., A.F.C. (*Commandant, R.A.F. College, Bracknell*).
Adams, M. K., A.F.C. (*Assistant Chief of the Defence Staff (Operational Requirements)*).
Sanderson, K. F. (*Air Officer Administration, Strike Command*).
Spottiswood, J. D., C.V.O., A.F.C. (*Director-General of Training (R.A.F.)*).
Stuart-Paul, R. I., M.B.E. (*Air Officer Training R.A.F. Support Command*).
Tetley, J. F. H., C.V.O. (*Air Officer Scotland and N. Ireland*).
Newton, B. H., O.B.E. (*Senior Directing Staff (Air), Royal College of Defence Studies*).
Simmons, M. G., A.F.C. (*Air Officer Commanding, No. 1 Group*).
Hann, D. N. (*Chief of Staff, No. 18 Group*).
Richardson, D. W. (*Air Officer Engineering Strike Command*).
White, T. P. (*Air Officer Maintenance, R.A.F. Support Command*).
Holroyd, F. M., C.B. (*Director-General Strategic Electronic Systems*).
Perrin, N. A. (*President Ordnance Board*).
Porter, J. B., O.B.E. (*Director-General Aircraft 2*).
Lees, R. L., C.B., M.B.E. (*Air Officer Administration, R.A.F. Support Command*).

King, P. F., O.B.E., Q.H.S. (*Dean of Air Force Medicine*).
Jones, J. M., Q.H.D.S. (*Director of Dental Services (R.A.F.) and Director of Defence Dental Services*).
Forman, G. N. (*Director of Legal Services (R.A.F.)*).
Jackson, B. J. (*Assistant Chief of Staff (Policy) Supreme H.Q. Allied Powers Europe*).
Huxley, B. (*Deputy Controller, National Air Traffic Services*).
Hurrell, F. C., O.B.E., Q.H.P. (*Principal Medical Officer, Strike Command*).
Black, G. P., O.B.E., A.F.C. (*Deputy Chief of Staff (Operations), Allied Air Forces Central Europe*).
Dick, R. (*Head of British Defence Staff and Defence Attaché, Washington*).
Bryant, D. T., C.B.E. (*Deputy Commander, R.A.F. Germany*).
Beill, A. (*Director General of Supply (R.A.F.)*).
Alcock, R. J. M. (*Director General of Communications Information Systems and Organisation (R.A.F.)*).
Macey, E. H., O.B.E. (*Air Officer Commanding and Commandant R.A.F. College, Cranwell*).
Allison, D. (*Director of Management & Support of Intelligence*).
Livingston, G., Q.H.S. (*Principal Medical Officer, R.A.F. Support Command*).
Stear, M. J. D., C.B.E. (*Air Officer Commanding, No. 11 Group*).
Campbell, K. A. (*Director General of Personal Services (R.A.F.)*).
Walker, J. R., C.B.E., A.F.C. (*Senior Air Staff Officer, Strike Command*).
Kemball, R. J., C.B.E. (*Commander British Forces, Falkland Islands*).
Leech, D. B., C.B.E. (*Commandant General R.A.F. Regiment and Director General of Security (R.A.F.)*).

PRINCESS MARY'S ROYAL AIR FORCE NURSING SERVICE (P.M.R.A.F.N.S.)

The Princess Mary's Royal Air Force Nursing Service is open to suitable male and female candidates who wish to train for or already hold the Enrolled Nurse Certificate (G). Registered General Nurses are eligible to apply for an initial 4 years' short service commission.
Matron-in-Chief, Princess Mary's R.A.F. Nursing Service, Air Commodore I. J. Harris, C.B., R.R.C.

WOMEN'S ROYAL AIR FORCE (W.R.A.F.)

Formed on 1 April 1918, the Women's Royal Air Force was disbanded on 1 April 1920 and reformed on 1 February 1949 from the Women's Auxiliary Air Force, the World War II Service, which had been formed on 28 June 1939, and from the R.A.F. Companies of the Auxiliary Territorial Service.

W.R.A.F. officers and airwomen, respectively, serve in most of the R.A.F. ground branches and trades and also as Air Loadmaster aircrew. W.R.A.F. personnel are employed at R.A.F. stations and higher formations at home and abroad, and they compete, on equal terms, with their R.A.F. counterparts for appointments, promotion and places on training courses.

Commandant-in-Chief, H.M. Queen Elizabeth the Queen Mother.
Air Chief Commandant, H.R.H. Princess Alice, Duchess of Gloucester.
Director, Air Commodore H. F. Renton, C.B., A.D.C.

CONSTITUTION OF THE ROYAL AIR FORCE

The Royal Air Force consists of 3 Commands: Strike Command and Support Command in the United Kingdom, and R.A.F. Germany. Strike Command is responsible for providing the air defence of the United Kingdom and reinforcement forces for N.A.T.O.; its roles include strike/attack, air defence, control and reporting, maritime surveillance, air reconnaissance, air-to-air refuelling, offensive support, air transport, aero-medical facilities, and search and rescue. Support Command is responsible for air and ground training, communications, engineering support, logistics, hospitals and for providing a range of administrative support. R.A.F. Germany provides tactical air support in N.A.T.O.'s Central Region; its roles include strike/attack, interdiction, counter air operations, air defence, close air support of land forces, tactical reconnaissance and helicopter support.

To carry out its tasks, the Royal Air Force is equipped with Victor, Tornado, Buccaneer, Phantom, Lightning, Harrier, Jaguar, Canberra, Hunter, Nimrod, Shackleton, VC10, Tristar, Hercules, Hawk, Jet Provost, Chipmunk and Bulldog aircraft; Puma, Wessex, Sea King and Chinook helicopters; miscellaneous communications aircraft, etc.; and Bloodhound and Rapier missiles.

ROYAL OBSERVER CORPS
Bentley Priory, Stanmore, Middlesex

Established 1925, the Royal Observer Corps is a uniformed voluntary civilian organization originally set up to identify and track the movement of aircraft in war. In 1955 the Corps assumed the modern role of detecting nuclear bursts and monitoring radioactive fall-out in support of the United Kingdom Warning and Monitoring Organization. The Corps is affiliated to the Royal Air Force and is administered by Strike Command.

Air Commodore-in-Chief, H.M. THE QUEEN.
Commandant, Air Commodore J. Broughton, R.A.F.

THE UNION JACK SERVICES CLUBS

Patron-in-Chief: Her Majesty the Queen.
Patron: Major-Gen. Sir Julian Gascoigne, K.C.M.G., K.C.V.O., C.B., D.S.O.
President: Major-Gen. Sir Robert Pigot, Bt., C.B., O.B.E., R.M.
Comptroller: Brig. J. N. Ghika, C.B.E.
Club Secretary: L. F. Moulton.

THE UNION JACK CLUB
Sandell Street, S.E.1
[Tel.: 01–928 6401]

The Union Jack Club provides residential accommodation for service and ex-service men and women and their families. All serving men and women below commissioned rank are members. Ex-service membership is by election. Honorary membership is extended to the Forces of other nations visiting the United Kingdom, to members of the Police, Fire, Ambulance and Prison Services, to members of the Merchant Navy, Royal Observer Corps, Coast Guards, Civil Service, Royal British Legion, and Corps of Commissionaires, and those sponsored by various other organizations approved by the Governing Council.

RELATIVE RANK—SEA, LAND AND AIR

ROYAL NAVY	ARMY	ROYAL AIR FORCE
1. Admiral of the Fleet.	1. Field-Marshal.	1. Marshal of the R.A.F.
2. Admiral.	2. General.	2. Air Chief Marshal.
3. Vice-Admiral.	3. Lieutenant-General.	3. Air Marshal.
4. Rear-Admiral.	4. Major-General.	4. Air Vice-Marshal.
5. Commodore (1st & 2nd Class).	5. Brigadier.	5. Air Commodore.
6. Captain.	6. Colonel.	6. Group Captain.
7. Commander.	7. Lieutenant-Colonel.	7. Wing Commander.
8. Lieutenant-Commander.	8. Major.	8. Squadron Leader.
9. Lieutenant.	9. Captain.	9. Flight-Lieutenant.
10. Sub-Lieutenant.	10. Lieutenant.	10. Flying Officer.
11. Acting Sub-Lieutenant.	11. Second Lieutenant.	11. Pilot Officer.

SERVICE SALARIES AND PENSIONS

The following rates of pay have been introduced as part of the 1985 pay award for service personnel. The Government accepted the recommendations of the Armed Forces Pay Review Body, which advises on pay levels for all ranks up to and including Brigadier. The award was paid in full from 1 April 1985. The Government, however, decided to stage in two parts the recommendations of the Top Salaries Review Body, which advises on ranks above Brigadier. The first stage took effect from 1 July 1985 with the full amount (shown below) being introduced from 1 March 1986. Salaries for the Women's Services reflect equal pay for equal work and conditions, but because the X-Factor addition for women is lower than for men (7½% compared to 10%) women's rates approximate to 98% of the rates for men. Since 1970 the determining factor of the Review Bodies' recommendations has been the relation of forces' salaries to civilian earnings by a carefully detailed process of job evaluation.

ROYAL NAVY AND ROYAL MARINES
Normal Rates

Rank	Daily £	Annual £
Midshipman	14·41	5,260
After 1 year	17·90	6,533
Sub-Lieutenant and Acting Lieutenant RM	20·52	7,490
After 2 years	26·52	9,680
After 3 years	28·62	10,446
Lieutenant	33·47	12,217
After 1 year	34·37	12,545
After 2 years	35·27	12,874
After 3 years	36·17	13,202
After 4 years	37·07	13,531
After 5 years	37·97	13,859
After 6 years	38·87	14,188
Lieutenant Commander/Captain RM	42·31	15,443
After 1 year	43·36	15,826
After 2 years	44·41	16,210
After 3 years	45·46	16,593
After 4 years	46·51	16,976
After 5 years	47·56	17,359
After 6 years	48·61	17,743
After 7 years	49·66	18,126
After 8 years	50·71	18,509
Commander/Major R.M.	57·70	21,060
After 2 years or 19 years service	59·22	21,615
After 4 years or 21 years service	60·74	22,170
After 6 years or 23 years service	62·26	22,725
After 8 years or 25 years service	63·78	23,280
Captain/Lieutenant-Colonel RM	66·92	24,426
After 2 years	68·68	25,068
After 4 years	70·44	25,711
With 6 years seniority/Colonel RM	80·55	29,401
Rear-Admiral/Major-General R.M.	93·15*	34,000*
Vice-Admiral/Lieutenant-General RM	115·07*	42,000*
Admiral/General RM	164·38*	60,000*
Admiral of the Fleet	205·48*	75,000*

* as at 1 March 1986

ARMY
Normal Rates

Rank	Daily £	Annual £
Second Lieutenant	20·52	7,490
Lieutenant		
On appointment	26·52	9,680
After 1 year in the rank	27·22	9,935
After 2 years in the rank	27·92	10,191
After 3 years in the rank	28·62	10,446
After 4 years in the rank	29·32	10,702
Captain		
On appointment	33·47	12,217
After 1 year in the rank	34·37	12,545
After 2 years in the rank	35·27	12,874
After 3 years in the rank	36·17	13,202
After 4 years in the rank	37·07	13,531
After 5 years in the rank	37·97	13,859
After 6 years in the rank	38·87	14,188
Major		
On appointment	42·31	15,443
After 1 year in the rank	43·36	15,826
After 2 years in the rank	44·41	16,210
After 3 years in the rank	45·46	16,593
After 4 years in the rank	46·51	16,976
After 5 years in the rank	47·56	17,359
After 6 years in the rank	48·61	17,743
After 7 years in the rank	49·66	18,126
After 8 years in the rank	50·71	18,509
Special List Lieutenant Colonel.	57·40	20,951
Lieutenant-Colonel		
On appointment with less than 19 years' service	57·70	21,060
After 2 years in rank or with 19 years service	59·22	21,615
After 4 years in rank or with 21 years service	60·74	22,170
After 6 years or with 23 years service	62·26	22,725
After 8 years in rank or with 25 years service	63·78	23,280
Colonel		
On appointment	66·92	24,426
After 2 years in rank	68·68	25,068
After 4 years in rank	70·44	25,711
After 6 years in rank	72·20	26,353
After 8 years in rank	73·96	26,995
Brigadier	80·55	29,401
Major-General	93·15*	34,000*
Lieutenant-General	115·07*	42,000*
General	164·38*	60,000*
Field Marshal	205·48*	75,000*

* as at 1 March 1986

ROYAL AIR FORCE
Normal rates

Rank	Daily	Annual	Rank	Daily	Annual
	£	£		£	£
Acting Pilot Officer.............	17·90	6,533	After 5 years.................	47·56	17,359
After 6 months in the rank			After 6 years.................	48·61	17,743
(aircrew officers only)......	18·31	6,683	After 7 years.................	49·66	18,126
Pilot Officer	20·52	7,490	After 8 years.................	50·71	18,509
Flying Officer	26·52	9,680	Wing Commander		
After 1 year or 3 years	27·22	9,935	On appointment with less than		
After 2 years or 4 years	27·92	10,191	19 years	57·70	21,060
After 3 years or 5 years	28·62	10,446	After 2 years or 19 years	59·22	21,615
After 4 years or 6 years	29·32	10,702	After 4 years or 21 years	60·74	22,170
Flight Lieutenant.............	33·47	12,217	After 6 years or 23 years	62·26	22,725
After 1 year or 7 years	34·37	12,545	After 8 years or 25 years	63·78	23,280
After 2 years or 8 years	35·27	12,874	Group Captain	66·92	24,426
After 3 years or 9 years	36·17	13,202	After 2 years	68·68	25,068
After 4 years or 10 years	37·07	13,531	After 4 years	70·44	25,711
After 5 years or 11 years	37·97	13,859	After 6 years	72·20	26,353
After 6 years or 12 years	38·87	14,188	After 8 years	73·96	26,995
Squadron Leader.............	42·31	15,443	Air Commodore	80·55	29,401
After 1 year.................	43·36	15,826	Air Vice-Marshal	93·15*	34,000*
After 2 years.................	44·41	16,210	Air Marshal	115·07*	42,000*
After 3 years.................	45·46	16,593	Air Chief Marshal.............	164·38*	60,000*
After 4 years.................	46·51	16,976	Marshal of the Royal Air Force .	205·48*	75,000*

c.s. = commissioned service.

* as at 1 March 1986

ROYAL NAVY AND ROYAL MARINES SPECIAL DUTIES LIST OFFICERS
Army Male Officers commissioned from the ranks, and Royal Air Force Branch Officers

Years of commissioned service	Years of Non-commissioned service from age 18					
	Under 12 years		12 years and under 15 years		15 years and over	
	Daily	Annual	Daily	Annual	Daily	Annual
	£	£	£	£	£	£
On appointment...................	36·47	13,312	38·27	13,969	40·07	14,626
After 1 year.....................	37·37	13,640	39·17	14,297	40·75	14,874
After 2 years....................	38·27	13,969	40·07	14,626	41·43	15,122
After 3 years....................	39·17	14,297	40·75	14,874	42·11	15,370
After 4 years....................	40·07	14,626	41·43	15,122	42·79	15,618
After 5 years....................	40·75	14,874	42·11	15,370	43·47	15,867
After 6 years....................	41·43	15,122	42·79	15,618	44·15	16,115
After 8 years....................	42·11	15,370	43·47	15,867	44·83	16,363
After 10 years...................	42·79	15,618	44·15	16,115	44·83	16,363
After 12 years...................	43·47	15,867	44·83	16,363	44·83	16,363
After 14 years...................	44·15	16,115	44·83	16,363	44·83	16,363
After 16 years...................	44·83	16,363	44·83	16,363	44·83	16,363

ROYAL NAVY
Artificers, Medical and Communications Technicians—Daily Rates

Rating	Less than 6 years Scale A	6 years but less than 9 years Scale B	9 years or more Scale C
	£	£	£
FCPO Artificer/Technician	37·84	38·14	38·59
CCPO Artificer/Technician	36·33	36·63	37·08
CPO Artificer....... } 1st Class Technician . } Scale I	34·92	35·22	35·67
CPO Artificer....... } 1st Class Technician . } Scale II...................	33·58	33·88	34·33
PO Artificer.. } 2nd Class Technician .... }	29·67	29·97	30·42
Probationary or Acting PO Artificer .... } 3rd Class Technician .... }	28·30	28·60	29·05
4th Class Technician (Leading)	24·70	25·00	25·45
Leading Artificer .... } Acting/4th Class Technician .... }	23·21	23·51	23·96
Acting Leading Artificer............................	20·99	21·29	21·74
5th Class Technician (Able)	19·91	20·21	20·66

ROYAL NAVY AND ROYAL MARINES—OTHER BRANCHES

New rates of pay for those committed to serve for:

Rating	Scale	Less than 6 years Scale A	6 years but less than 9 years Scale B	9 years or more Scale C
		£	£	£
Fleet Chief Petty Officer/Warrant Officer Class I	I	35·00	35·30	35·75
Chief Petty Officer	I	30·91	31·21	31·66
Chief Petty Officer	II	30·35	30·65	31·10
Petty Officer/Sergeant	I	27·54	27·84	28·29
Petty Officer/Sergeant	II	27·04	27·34	27·79
Leading Rating/Corporal	I	24·70	25·00	25·45
Leading Rating/Corporal	II	23·21	23·51	23·96
Able Rating/Marine 1st Class	I	19·91	20·21	20·66
Able Rating/Marine 1st Class	II	18·69	18·99	19·44
Able Rating/Marine 1st Class	III	16·72	17·02	17·47
Ordinary Rating/Marine 2nd Class	I	14·59	14·89	15·34
Ordinary Rating/Marine 2nd Class	II	13·40	13·70	14·15

ARMY

Daily rates of pay for those committed to serve for:

Rank	Less than 6 years Scale A			6 years but less than 9 years Scale B			9 years or more Scale C		
	Band 1	Band 2	Band 3	Band 1	Band 2	Band 3	Band 1	Band 2	Band 3
	£	£	£	£	£	£	£	£	£
Private Class IV ...	13·40	—	—	13·70	—	—	14·15	—	—
Class III ...	14·50	16·72	—	14·80	17·02	—	15·25	17·47	—
Class II ...	15·91	18·13	—	16·21	18·43	—	16·66	18·88	—
Class I ...	17·08	19·30	21·69	17·38	19·60	21·99	17·83	20·05	22·44
Lance Corporal									
Class III ...	17·08	19·30	—	17·38	19·60	—	17·83	20·05	—
Class II ...	18·30	20·52	—	18·60	20·82	—	19·05	21·27	—
Class I ...	19·60	21·82	24·21	19·90	22·12	24·51	20·35	22·57	24·96
Corporal Class II ...	20·99	23·21	—	21·29	23·51	—	21·74	23·96	—
Class I ...	22·48	24·70	27·09	22·78	25·00	27·39	23·23	25·45	27·84

	Band 4	Band 5	Band 6	Band 7	Band 4	Band 5	Band 6	Band 7	Band 4	Band 5	Band 6	Band 7
	£	£	£	£	£	£	£	£	£	£	£	£
Sergeant	24·60	27·04	29·67	—	24·90	27·34	29·97	—	25·35	27·79	30·42	—
Staff Sergeant	26·16	28·60	31·23	34·07	26·46	28·90	31·53	34·37	26·91	29·35	31·98	34·82
Warrant Officer Class I	27·96	30·40	33·03	35·87	28·26	30·70	33·33	36·17	28·71	31·15	33·78	36·62
Warrant Officer Class I	29·93	32·37	35·00	37·84	30·23	32·67	35·30	38·14	30·68	33·12	35·75	38·59

ROYAL AIR FORCE
Airmen (Aircrew)

Rank	Less than 6 years Scale A			6 years but less than 9 years Scale B			9 years or more Scale C		
	Band 5	Band 6	Band 7	Band 5	Band 6	Band 7	Band 5	Band 6	Band 7
	£	£	£	£	£	£	£	£	£
Pilots, Navigators, Air Electronics Operators and Air Engineers (A)									
Sergeant	—	29·67	—	—	29·97	—	—	30·42	—
Flight Sergeant	—	—	34·95	—	—	35·25	—	—	35·70
Master Aircrew	—	—	37·84	—	—	38·14	—	—	38·59
Air Signallers and Air Loadmasters									
Sergeant	27·04	—	—	27·34	—	—	27·79	—	—
Flight Sergeant	—	32·11	—	—	32·41	—	—	32·86	—
Master Aircrew	—	35·00	—	—	35·30	—	—	35·75	—

ROYAL AIR FORCE

Airmen (Ground Trades, Apprentices and P.M.R.A.F.N.S.)

New rates of pay for those committed to serve for:

Rank/Category	less than 6 years Scale A			less than 9 years but not less than 6 years—Scale B			9 years or more Scale C		
	Band 1	Band 2	Band 3	Band 1	Band 2	Band 3	Band 1	Band 2	Band 3
	£	£	£	£	£	£	£	£	£
Aircraftmen over 17½ on entry	13·40	13·40	13·40	13·70	13·70	13·70	14·15	14·15	14·15
Leading Aircraftmen	14·50	16·72	19·11	14·80	17·02	19·41	15·25	17·47	19·86
Senior Aircraftmen	17·08	19·30	21·19	17·38	19·60	21·99	17·83	20·05	22·44
Junior Technician	19·60	21·82	24·21	19·90	22·12	24·51	20·35	22·57	24·96
Corporal	22·21	24·43	27·09	22·51	24·73	27·39	22·96	25·18	27·84

	Band 4	Band 5	Band 6	Band 7	Band 4	Band 5	Band 6	Band 7	Band 4	Band 5	Band 6	Band 7
	£	£	£	£	£	£	£	£	£	£	£	£
Sergeant	24·60	27·04	29·67	—	24·90	27·34	29·97	—	25·35	27·79	30·42	—
Chief Technician	25·82	28·26	30·89	33·73	26·12	28·56	31·19	34·03	26·57	29·01	31·64	34·48
Flight Sergeant	27·04	29·48	32·11	34·95	27·34	29·78	32·41	35·25	27·79	30·23	32·86	35·70
Warrant Officer	29·93	32·37	35·00	37·84	30·23	32·67	35·30	38·14	30·68	33·12	35·75	38·59

Officers of W.R.N.S.

Rank	Daily	Annual
	£	£
Probationary 3rd Officer	20·05	7,318
Third Officer on confirmation	22·01	8,033
After 2 years	25·92	9,461
After 3 years	26·60	9,709
After 4 years	27·28	9,957
After 5 years	27·97	10,209
After 6 years	28·65	10,457
Second Officer	31·71	11,939
After 1 year	33·59	12,260
After 2 years	34·47	12,582
After 3 years	35·35	12,903
After 4 years	36·23	13,224
After 5 years	37·11	13,545
After 6 years	37·99	13,866
First Officer	41·35	15,093
After 1 year	42·37	15,465
After 2 years	43·40	15,841
After 3 years	44·43	16,217
After 4 years	45·45	16,589
After 5 years	46·48	16,965
After 6 years	47·51	17,341
After 7 years	48·53	17,713
After 8 years	49·56	18,089
Chief Officer	56·39	20,582
After 2 years or with 19 years' service	57·89	21,123
After 4 years or with 21 years' service	59·36	21,666
After 6 years or with 23 years' service	60·88	22,221
After 8 years or with 25 years' service	62·40	22,776
Superintendent	66·00	24,090
After 2 years	67·76	24,732
After 4 years	69·52	25,375
After 6 years	71·28	26,017
After 8 years	73·04	26,660
Director, W.R.N.S.	80·09	29,233

Officers of W.R.A.C., and Q.A.R.A.N.C.

Rank	Daily	Annual
	£	£
Second-Lieutenant	20·05	7,318
Lieutenant—On appointment	25·92	9,461
After 1 year	26·60	9,709
After 2 years	27·28	9,957
After 3 years	27·97	10,209
After 4 years	28·65	10,457
Captain—On appointment	32·71	11,939
After 1 year	33·59	12,260
After 2 years	34·47	12,582
After 3 years	35·35	12,903
After 4 years	36·23	13,224
After 5 years	37·11	13,545
After 6 years	37·99	13,866
Major—On appointment	41·35	15,093
After 1 year	42·37	15,465
After 2 years	43·40	15,841
After 3 years	44·43	16,217
After 4 years	45·45	16,589
After 5 years	46·48	16,965
After 6 years	47·51	17,341
After 7 years	48·53	17,713
After 8 years	49·56	18,089
Lieutenant-Colonel—On appointment with less than 19 years' service	56·39	20,582
With 19 years service or after 2 years in rank	57·87	21,123
With 21 years service or after 4 years in rank	59·36	21,666
With 23 years service or after 6 years in rank	60·88	22,221
With 25 years service or after 8 years in rank	62·40	22,776
Colonel—On appointment	66·00	24,090
After 2 years	67·76	24,732
After 4 years	69·52	25,375
After 6 years	71·28	26,017
After 8 years	73·04	26,660
Brigadier	80·09	29,233

Officers of W.R.A.F.

Rank	Daily	Annual
	£	£
Acting Pilot Officer	17·49	6,384
Pilot Officer	20·05	7,318
Flying Officer	25·92	9,461
After 1 year or 3 years c.s.	26·60	9,709
After 2 years or 4 years c.s.	27·28	9,957
After 3 years or 5 years c.s.	27·97	10,209
After 4 years or 6 years c.s.	28·65	10,457
Flight Lieutenant	32·71	11,939
After 1 year or 7 years c.s.	33·59	12,260
After 2 years or 8 years c.s.	34·47	12,581
After 3 years or 9 years c.s.	35·35	12,902
After 4 years or 10 years c.s.	36·23	13,223
After 5 years or 11 years c.s.	37·11	13,545
After 6 years or 12 years c.s.	37·99	13,866
Squadron Leader	41·35	15,092
After 1 year	42·37	15,465
After 2 years	43·40	15,841
After 3 years	44·43	16,216
After 4 years	45·45	16,589
After 5 years	46·48	16,965
After 6 years	47·51	17,341
After 7 years	48·53	17,713
After 8 years	49·56	18,089
Wing Commander		
On appointment with less than 19 years c.s.	56·39	20,582
After 2 years or 19 years c.s.	57·87	21,122
After 4 years or 21 years c.s.	59·36	21,666
After 6 years or 23 years c.s.	60·88	22,221
After 8 years or 25 years c.s.	62·40	22,776
Group Captain	66·00	24,090
After 2 years	67·76	24,732
After 4 years	69·52	25,374
After 6 years	71·28	26,017
After 8 years	73·04	26,659
Air Commodore	80·09	29,232

c.s. = commissioned service

W.R.N.S. Ratings and Naval Nurses

Rating	Scale	New rates of pay		
		Band 1	Band 2	Band 3
		£	£	£
Ordinary Rating	under 17½	9·90	—	
	at 17½	13·10	13·10	
Able Rating	III	14·16	16·23	18·67
	II	16·09	18·26	20·60
	I	17·28	19·45	21·79
Leading Rating	II	20·51	22·68	25·02
	I	21·96	24·13	26·47
		Band 4	Band 5	Band 6	Band 7
		£	£	£	£
Petty Officer	II	23·78	26·16	28·73	31·51
	I	24·30	26·68	29·25	32·03
Chief Petty Officer	II	25·75	28·13	30·70	33·48
	I	26·37	28·75	31·32	34·10
Fleet Chief Petty Officer	I	29·25	31·63	34·20	36·98

W.R.A.C. and Q.A.R.A.N.C.
New rates of pay for those who have served for:

Rank		Less than 6 years			6 years but less than 9 years			9 years or more		
	Band	1	2	3	1	2	3	1	2	3
		£	£	£	£	£	£	£	£	£
Private Class IV Age 17–17½.		9·60	—	—	—	—	—	—	—	—
Class IV		13·09	—	—	13·39	—	—	13·84	—	—
Class III		14·16	16·33	—	14·46	16·63	—	14·91	17·08	—
Class II		15·54	17·71	—	15·84	18·01	—	16·29	18·46	—
Class I		16·68	18·85	21·19	16·98	19·15	21·49	17·43	19·60	21·94
Lance Corporal Class III		16·68	18·85	—	16·98	19·15	—	17·43	19·60	—
Class II		17·88	20·05	—	18·18	20·35	—	18·63	20·80	—
Class I		19·15	21·32	23·66	19·45	21·62	23·96	19·90	22·07	24·41
Corporal Class II		20·51	22·68	—	20·81	22·98	—	21·26	23·43	—
Class I		21·96	24·13	26·47	22·26	24·43	26·77	22·71	24·88	27·22
	Band	4	5	6	7	4	5	6	7	4	5	6	7
		£	£	£	£	£	£	£	£	£	£	£	£
Sergeant		24·04	26·42	28·99	—	24·34	26·72	29·29	—	24·79	27·17	29·74	—
Staff Sergeant		25·56	27·94	30·51	33·29	25·86	28·24	30·81	33·59	26·31	28·69	31·26	34·04
Warrant Officer Class II		27·32	29·70	32·27	35·05	27·62	30·00	32·57	35·35	28·07	30·45	33·02	35·80
Class I		29·25	31·63	34·20	36·98	29·55	31·93	34·50	37·28	30·00	32·38	34·95	37·73

W.R.A.F. AIRWOMEN (Ground Trades) and P.M.R.A.F.N.S.
Daily rates of pay for those who have served for:

Rank	Less than 6 years			Less than 9 years but not less than 6 years			9 years or more		
	Band 1	Band 2	Band 3	Band 1	Band 2	Band 3	Band 1	Band 2	Band 3
	£	£	£	£	£	£	£	£	£
Aircraftwoman under age 17½	9·90	—	—	—	—	—	—	—	—
Aircraftwoman at age 17½	13·09	13·09	13·09	—	—	—	—	—	—
Leading Aircraftwoman	14·16	16·33	18·67	14·46	16·63	18·97	14·91	17·08	19·42
Senior Aircraftwoman	16·68	18·85	21·19	16·98	19·15	21·49	17·43	19·60	21·94
Junior Technician	19·15	21·32	23·66	19·45	21·62	23·96	19·90	22·07	24·41
Corporal	21·70	23·87	26·47	22·00	24·17	26·77	22·45	24·62	27·22

Rank	Band 4	Band 5	Band 6	Band 7	Band 4	Band 5	Band 6	Band 7	Band 4	Band 5	Band 6	Band 7
	£	£	£	£	£	£	£	£	£	£	£	£
Sergeant	24·04	26·42	28·99	—	24·34	26·72	29·29	—	24·79	27·17	29·74	—
Chief Technician	25·23	27·61	30·18	32·96	25·53	27·91	30·48	33·26	25·98	28·36	30·93	33·71
Flight Sergeant	26·42	28·80	31·31	34·15	26·72	29·10	31·67	34·45	27·17	29·55	32·12	34·90
Warrant Officer	29·25	31·63	34·20	36·98	29·55	31·93	34·50	37·28	30·00	32·38	34·95	37·73

CHARGES FOR MARRIED AND SINGLE QUARTERS

Married Quarters

Type of quarter	Annual* charge			
	Grade 1	Grade 2	Grade 3	Grade 4
	£	£	£	£
Officers				
I	2,442	2,212	1,745	1,223
II	2,190	1,982	1,566	1,095
III	1,916	1,734	1,369	960
IV	1,690	1,529	1,208	843
V	1,478	1,340	1,058	741
Other Ranks				
D/WO	1,157	1,048	829	580
C	1,029	934	737	515
B	905	821	646	453
A	631	573	453	318

Single Quarters

Rank	Annual* charge			
	Grade 1	Grade 2	Grade 3	Grade 4
	£	£	£	£
Major and above	989	898	708	496
Captain and below	829	752	595	416
Warrant Officer and Senior N.C.O.	584	529	420	292
Corporal and below	307	281	219	153
Young serviceman receiving less than the minimum adult (ie Private IV) rate	226	208	164	113

*Annual charges are derived from daily rates in whole pence and rounded to the nearest £.

Female officers of Q.A.R.N.N.S.

Rank	Daily	Annual
	£	£
Nursing Officer On appointment	25·92	9,461
After 1 year	26·60	9,709
After 2 years	27·28	9,957
After 3 years	27·97	10,209
After 4 years	28·65	10,457
Senior Nursing Officer On appointment	32·71	11,939
After 1 year	33·59	12,260
After 2 years	34·47	12,582
After 3 years	35·35	12,903
After 4 years	36·23	13,224
After 5 years	37·11	13,545
After 6 years	37·99	13,866
Superintending Nursing Officer On appointment	41·35	15,093
After 1 year	42·37	15,465
After 2 years	43·40	15,841
After 3 years	44·43	16,217
After 4 years	45·45	16,589
After 5 years	46·48	16,965
After 6 years	47·57	17,341
After 7 years	48·53	17,713
After 8 years	49·56	18,089
Chief Nursing Officer On appointment with less than 19 years service	56·39	20,582
With 19 years service or after 2 years in the rank	57·87	21,123
With 21 years in service or after 4 years in the rank	59·36	21,666
With 23 years service or after 6 years in the rank	60·88	22,221
With 25 years service or after 8 years in the rank	62·40	22,776
Principal Nursing Officer On appointment	66·00	24,090
After 2 years	67·76	24,732
After 4 years	69·52	25,375
After 6 years	71·28	26,017
After 8 years	73·04	26,659
Matron-in-Chief	80·09	29,233

SERVICE RETIREMENT BENEFITS, ETC.

NOTE—Those who leave the Forces having served at least five years, but not long enough to qualify for the appropriate immediate pension, now qualify for a preserved pension and terminal grant both of which are payable at age 60. The tax-free resettlement grants shown below are payable on release to those who qualify for a preserved pension and who have completed 9 years service from age 21 (officers) or 12 years from age 18 (other ranks).

RETIREMENT BENEFITS (MEN) Officers*—All Services

No. of years reckonable service over age 21	Capt. (incl. Q.M.) and below	Major (incl. Q.M.)	Lt.-Col. (Q.M.)	Lt.-Col.	Col. and Deputy Chaplain General	Brigadier	Major-General, etc.	Lieutenant-General, etc.	General, etc.
	£p.a.	£p.a.	£p.a.	£p.a.	£p.a.	£p.a.	£p.a.	£p.a.	£p.a.
16	4,044	4,838	5,481	6,160					
17	4,231	5,068	5,711	6,445					
18	4,418	5,298	5,941	6,730	7,805				
19	4,605	5,528	6,171	7,015	8,136				
20	4,792	5,758	6,401	7,300	8,466				
21	4,978	5,988	6,631	7,585	8,797				
22	5,165	6,218	6,861	7,870	9,127	10,339			
23	5,352	6,448	7,091	8,155	9,458	10,666			
24	5,539	6,678	7,321	8,440	9,788	10,992	Not available at time of going to press		
25	5,726	6,907	7,550	8,726	10,119	11,319			
26	5,913	7,137	7,780	9,011	10,449	11,646			
27	6,100	7,367	8,010	9,296	10,780	11,972			
28	6,287	7,597	8,240	9,581	11,110	12,299			
29	6,474	7,827	8,470	9,866	11,441	12,626			
30	6,660	8,057	8,700	10,151	11,771	12,952			
31	6,847	8,287	8,930	10,436	12,102	13,279			
32	7,034	8,517	9,160	10,721	12,432	13,606			
33	7,221	8,747	9,390	11,006	12,763	13,932			
34	7,408	8,972	9,620	11,291	13,093	14,259			

* Including those male officers holding equivalent ranks in the Q.A.R.N.N.S.

Ratings, Soldiers and Airmen*

Number of years reckonable service	Below Corporal	Corporal	Sergeant	Staff Sergeant	Warrant Officer Class II	Warrant Officer Class I
	£p.a.	£p.a.	£p.a.	£p.a.	£p.a.	£p.a.
22	2,399	3,044	3,357	3,811	3,918	4,299
23	2,483	3,150	3,474	3,944	4,057	4,454
24	2,567	3,257	3,591	4,077	4,196	4,610
25	2,650	3,363	3,708	4,210	4,335	4,765
26	2,734	3,469	3,826	4,343	4,475	4,921
27	2,818	3,575	3,943	4,476	4,614	5,076
28	2,902	3,682	4,060	4,609	4,753	5,231
29	2,986	3,788	4,177	4,742	4,892	5,387
30	3,069	3,894	4,294	4,875	5,031	5,542
31	3,153	4,000	4,411	5,008	5,170	5,698
32	3,237	4,107	4,528	5,141	5,309	5,853
33	3,321	4,213	4,645	5,274	5,448	6,008
34	3,405	4,319	4,763	5,407	5,588	6,164
35	3,488	4,425	4,880	5,540	5,727	6,319
36	3,572	4,532	4,997	5,673	5,866	6,475
37	3,656	4,638	5,114	5,806	6,005	6,630

* Including male nurses serving in the Q.A.R.N.N.S. holding equivalent rank.

RETIREMENT BENEFITS (WOMEN)

Q.A.R.N.N.S., W.R.N.S., Q.A.R.A.N.C., W.R.A.C., P.M.R.A.F.N.S., W.R.A.F. (The annual rates for W.R.A.C. are given: these apply to equivalent ranks in all Services, including the Nursing Services).

OFFICERS (16–34 years' service).—Captain, £3,953–£7,241; Major, £4,729–£8,775; Lt.-Col., £6,021–£11,037; Colonel, £7,707–£12,929; Brigadier £10,287–£14,188.

SERVICEWOMEN (22–37 years' service).—Below Corporal, £2,345–£3,574; Corporal, £2,976–£4,534; Sergeant, £3,281–£4,999; Staff Sergeant, £3,725–£5,675; Warrant Officer II, £3,830–£5,870; Warrant Officer I, £4,202–£6,481.

NOTES

Terminal grants are in each case three times the rate of retired pay or pension. There are special rates of retired pay for Chaplains, Flight Lieutenants (Specialist Aircrew), and certain other ranks not shown above. Deductions may be made in cases of voluntary retirement.

The normal rates of gratuity for officers with short service commissions are £1,375 (men) and £1,344 (women) for each year completed. Resettlement grants are: officers £4,729 (men) and £4,623 (women); non-commissioned ranks £3,169 (men), £3,098 (women).

THE CHURCH OF ENGLAND

THE GENERAL SYNOD OF THE CHURCH OF ENGLAND

The General Synod was constituted in 1970, under the Synodical Government Measure 1969, in succession to the former Church Assembly. There are in total some 560 members of the General Synod, divided into three distinct houses—the House of Bishops, the House of Clergy and the House of Laity. It is presided over jointly by the Archbishops of Canterbury and York and normally meets three times each year—in February, July and November.

The function of the General Synod is to consider and make provision for all matters concerning the Church of England, and to consider the express opinion on any other matters of religious or public interest. The Synod appoints a number of Committees, Boards and Councils which deal with, or advise the Synod on, a wide range of matters affecting the Church and its Ministry.

Under the Church of England Assembly (Powers) Act 1919 the General Synod has the power—delegated by Parliament—to frame Statute Law on any matter concerning the Church of England, which are known as Measures. A Measure, once approved by General Synod, must be laid before both Houses of Parliament who may accept or reject it but may not amend it. If the Measure is accepted it is then submitted for Royal Assent and when this has been given the Measure has the full force of Law just as an Act of Parliament.

The Synod also has the power to make Canons and other ecclesiastical regulations provided that they do not conflict with statutory law. Canons have to be submitted to the Crown before they can come into effect.

OFFICES.—Church House, Dean's Yard, SW1P 3NZ— *Presidents*, The Archbishop of Canterbury; The Archbishop of York; *Sec.-Gen.*, W. D. Pattinson. THE HOUSE OF BISHOPS.—*Chairman*, The Archbishop of Canterbury; *Vice-Chairman*, The Archbishop of York. THE HOUSE OF CLERGY.—*Chairman*, The Archdeacon of Leicester; *Vice-Chairman*, Canon P. H. Boulton. THE HOUSE OF LAITY, *Chairman*, O. W. H. Clark, C.B.E.; *Vice-Chairman*, Prof. J. D. McClean.

Stipends (from April 1985)

Archbishop of Canterbury	£26,085
Archbishop of York	£22,770
Bishop of London	£21,175
Bishop of Durham	£18,615
Bishop of Winchester	£15,415
Diocesan Bishop	£13,845
Dean or Provost	£11,270
Canons Residentiary	£9,100

Province of Canterbury

CANTERBURY

102nd Archbishop and Primate of All England, Most Rev. and Rt. Hon. Robert Alexander Kennedy Runcie, M.C., D.D. (Lambeth Palace, S.E.1), *cons.* 1970, *trs.* 1980. [Signs Robert Cantuar] 1980

Bishops Suffragan

Dover, Rt. Rev. Richard Henry McPhail Third, M.A. (Upway, St. Martin's Hill, Canterbury) (*cons.* 1976) 1980
Maidstone, Rt. Rev. Robert Maynard Hardy, M.K. (Bishop's House, Egerton, Ashford, Kent) 1980
Assistant Bishops, Rt. Rev. John Taylor Hughes, C.B.E. (*cons.* 1956), 1977; Rt. Rev. Harold Isherwood, M.V.O., O.B.E. (*cons.* 1974), 1979; Rt. Rev. The Lord Coggan, P.C., D.D. (*cons.* 1956), 1980.

Dean

Very Rev. Victor Alexander de Waal, M.A. 1976

Canons Residentiary

A. M. Allchin, M.A., B.Litt., D.D. 1973	Archd. Simpson 1981
	P. Brett, M.A. 1983
J. H. R. De Sausmarez 1981	

Organist, Allan Wicks, M.A., F.R.C.O. 1961

Archdeacons

Canterbury, Ven. J. A. Simpson, M.A. 1981
Maidstone, Ven. A. M. Percival-Smith, M.A. 1979
Clergy, 241.
Vicar-General of Province and Diocese, Miss S. Cameron, Q.C.
Commissary General, J. H. R. Newey, Q.C., M.A., LL.B. 1971
Joint Registrars of the Province, F. E. Robson, 16 Beaumont Street, Oxford; B. J. T. Hanson, Church House, Dean's Yard, S.W.1.
Registrar of the Diocese of Canterbury, A. O. E. Davies, 9 The Precincts, Canterbury.

LONDON

130th Bishop, Rt. Rev. and Rt. Hon. Graham Douglas Leonard, D.D., S.T.D., *cons.* 1964, *trs.* 1973 and 1981 (8 Barton Street, SW1P 3RX) [Signs Graham Londin:] 1981

Bishops Suffragan

Kensington, Rt. Rev. Mark Santer, M.A. (19 Campden Hill Square, W.8) 1981
Willesden, Rt. Rev. Tom Butler, PH.D. (173 Willesden Lane, Brondesbury, N.W.6) 1985
Edmonton, Rt. Rev. Brian John Masters, M.A. (13 North Audley Street, W.1.) 1984
Stepney, Rt. Rev. James Lawton Thompson, M.A. (23 Tredegar Square, E.3) 1978
Fulham, Rt. Rev. C. John Klyberg (4 Cambridge Place, W.8.) 1985

Dean of St. Paul's

Very Rev. Alan Brunskill Webster, M.A., B.D., The Deanery, 9 Amen Court, E.C.4 1977

Canons Residentiary

Archd. Harvey 1978	K. G. Routledge, M.A.1982
K. J. Woollcombe, M.A., S.T.D. 1981	P. Ball, M.A. 1984

Organist, C. H. Dearnley, M.A., B.MUS., F.R.C.O. .. 1968
Receiver of St. Paul's, Commander C. Shears, O.B.E., R.N. (*ret.*)

Archdeacons

London, Ven. F. W. Harvey, M.A. 1978
Middlesex, Ven. T. J. Raphael, B.A. 1983
Northolt, Ven. E. Shirras 1985
Hampstead, Ven. R. Coogan 1984
Hackney, Ven. R. E. D. Sharpley, M.A. 1981
Beneficed Clergy, 403; *Curates, &c.*, 185
Chancellor and Commissary of the Dean and Chapter, G. H. Newsom, Q.C., M.A. 1971
Registrar, D. W. Faull, 22 Greencoat Place, S.W.1 1969

WESTMINSTER

The Collegiate Church of St. Peter—(A Royal Peculiar)
Dean, (vacant).

Canons Residentiary

Bishop E. G. Knapp- Fisher 1975	S. Charles, B.comm., B.D. 1978
T. R. Beeson, M.A., A.K.C. 1976	A. E. Harvey, M.A. ..1982

Archdeacon, Rt. Rev. E. G. Knapp-Fisher, M.A. .1975
Chapter Clerk, Registrar and Receiver General,
W. R. J. Pullen, C.V.O., Ll.B. 1959
Organist, S. Preston, M.A., B.Mus. 1980
Legal Secretary, C. L. Hodgetts, Ll.B. 1973

WINCHESTER

95th Bishop, Rt. Rev. Colin Clement Walter
James, M.A. (Wolvesey, Winchester SO23 9ND)
[Signs Colin Winton:] 1985

Bishops Suffragan

Southampton, Rt. Rev. Edward David Cart-
wright, M.A. (Jollers, Winchester SO21 2NS) .1984
Basingstoke, Rt. Rev. Michael Richard John
Manktelow, M.A. (1 The Close, Winchester
SO23 9LS) 1977

Dean

Very Rev. Michael Staffurth Stancliffe, M.A. ..1969

Dean of Jersey, Very Rev. Basil Arthur O'Ferrall,
C.B., M.A., R.N. 1985
Dean of Guernsey, Very Rev. John William
Foster, R.N. 1978

Canons Residentiary

A. G. Wedderspoon, M.A., B.D. 1970	E. G. Job, M.A. ....1979 P. A. Britton, M.A. ..1980
Bp. of Basingstoke ..1977	

Organist, Martin Neary, M.A., F.R.C.O. 1972

Archdeacons

Winchester, Ven. A. G. Clarkson, M.A. 1984
Basingstoke, Ven. T. G. Nash, M.A. 1982
Beneficed Clergy, 220; *Curates, &c.*, 55
Chancellor, John Spokes, Q.C. 1985
Registrar and Legal Secretary, P. M. White, B.A. 1981

BATH AND WELLS

74th Bishop, Rt. Rev. John Monier Bickersteth,
M.A. (cons. 1970). (The Palace, Wells BA5 2PD)
[Signs John Bath & Wells]..................1975

Bishop Suffragan

Taunton, (vacant).

Dean

Very Rev. Patrick Reynolds Mitchell, M.A., F.S.A. 1973

Canons Residentiary of Wells

D. R. Vicary, M.A. ...1975	C. E. Thomas 1983
S. R. Cutt, M.A. 1979	

Organist, A. Crossland 1970

Archdeacons

Bath, Ven. J. E. Burgess, B.D. 1975
Taunton, Ven. L. E. Olyott, B.A. 1977
Wells, Ven. C. E. Thomas, B.A.................1983
Beneficed Clergy, 225; *Other Clergy*, 35.
Chancellor, G. H. Newsom, Q.C. 1970
Registrar, Sec. & Chapt. Clerk, N. M. Cavender,
Wells.

BIRMINGHAM

6th Bishop, Rt. Rev. Hugh William Montefiore,
D.D. (cons. 1970) (Bishop's Croft, Harborne,
Birmingham B17 0BG) [Signs Hugh
Birmingham] 1978

Bishop Suffragan

Aston, Rt. Rev. Colin Ogilvie Buchanan, M.A. (60
Handsworth Wood Road, Birmingham) 1982

Provost

Very Rev. Basil Stanley Moss, M.A. 1972

Canons Residentiary

D. McLean, M.A. 1972	Archd. Cooper 1982
L. M. Davies, B.A. ...1981	

Archdeacons

Aston, Ven. J. L. Cooper, B.D. 1982
Birmingham, Ven. J. Duncan, M.A. 1974
Beneficed Clergy, 159; *Curates, &c.*, 73
Organist, H. Best, B.Mus., A.R.C.O..............1978
Chancellor, His Honour Judge Aglionby, M.A. ..1970
Registrar and Legal Secretary, M. Shaw (85
Cornwall Street, Birmingham).

BRISTOL

54th Bishop, Rt. Rev. Barry Rogerson (Bishop's
House, Clifton Hill, Bristol BS8 1BW) [Signs
John Bristol] 1985

Bishop Suffragan

Malmesbury, Rt. Rev. Peter James Firth, M.A. ..1983

Dean

Very Rev. Alfred Hounsell Dammers, M.A.......1973

Canons Residentiary

D. E. R. Isitt, M.A. ...1977	J. Rogan, M.A. 1983
J. M. Free, B.D. 1982	

Organist, M. Archer, M.A., F.R.C.O., A.R.C.M. 1983

Archdeacons

Bristol, Ven. A. J. Balmforth, M.A..............1979
Swindon, Ven. K. Clark, M.A. 1982
Beneficed Clergy, 123; *Curates, &c.*, 30
Chancellor, D. C. Calcutt, Ll.B., Mus.B..........1971
Registrar and Sec., T. R. Urquhart 1972

CHELMSFORD

Bishop, (vacant) (Bishopscourt, Margaretting
Ingatestone CM4 0HD).

Bishops Suffragan

Colchester, Rt. Rev. Roderic Norman Coote, D.D.
(Bishop's House, 32 Inglis Road, Colchester)
(cons. 1951) 1966
Barking, Rt. Rev. James William Roxburgh, M.A.
(670 High Road, Buckhurst Hill) 1983
Bradwell, Rt. Rev. Charles Derek Bond, A.K.C.
(188 New London Road, Chelmsford) 1976
Provost, Very Rev. J. H. Moses, Ph.D., B.A. 1982
Organist, G. Elliott, Mus.B., F.R.C.O. 1981

Archdeacons

Southend, Ven. J. S. Bailey, M.A..............1982
West Ham, Ven. P. S. Dawes, B.A..............1980
Colchester, Ven. E. C. F. Stroud, B.A............1983
Beneficed Clergy, 384; *Curates, &c.*, 99
Chancellor, Miss S. M. Cameron, M.A. 1970
Diocesan Registrar, D. W. Faull, 22 Greencoat
Place, S.W.1 1963

CHICHESTER

99th *Bishop*, Rt. Rev. Eric Waldram Kemp, D.D.
(The Palace, Chichester PO19 1PY) [Signs Eric
Cicestr:] 1974

Bishops Suffragan

Lewes, Rt. Rev. Peter John Ball, M.A. (Litlington
Rectory, nr. Polegate) 1977
Horsham, Rt. Rev. Ivor Colin Docker, M.A.
(Bishop's Lodge, Worth, nr. Crawley).......1975
Assistant Bishops, Rt. Rev. William Warren
Hunt, M.A. (cons. 1955) 1980; Rt. Rev. Mark
Green (cons. 1972) 1982

Dean

Very Rev. Robert Tinsley Holtby, M.A., B.D......1977

Canons Residentiary

R. T. Greenacre, | J. F. Hester, M.A. ...1985
M.A., ...1975 |
Organist, A. J. Thurlow, B.A., F.R.C.O...........1980

Archdeacons

Chichester, Ven. K. Hobbs, M.A. 1981
Horsham, Ven. W. C. L. Filby, ...1983
Lewes and Hastings, Ven. M. L. Godden, M.A...1975
  Beneficed Clergy, 320; *Curates, &c.*, 69
Chancellor, Q. T. Edwards, Q.C..................1978
*Legal Secretary to the Bishop, and Diocesan
Registrar*, C. L. Hodgetts, Ll.B.

COVENTRY

Bishop, (vacant) (The Bishop's House, 23 Davenport Road, Coventry CV5 6PW).

Bishop Suffragan

Warwick, Rt. Rev. Keith Appleby Arnold, M.A...1980
Provost, Very Rev. Colin Semper, M.A. 1982
Organist, P. Wright, M.A., F.R.C.O. 1984

Canons Residentiary

P. A. Berry, M.A.....1973 | S. S. Smalley, M.A.,
                        | B.D., Ph.D 1977

Archdeacons

Warwick, Ven. P. S. G. Bridges................1983
Coventry, Ven. A. W. Morgan, B.A. 1983
  Beneficed Clergy, 104; *Curates, &c.*, 49
Chancellor, W. M. Gage, M.A. 1980
Registrar, D. J. Dumbleton, Ll.B., Coventry 1978

DERBY

4th *Bishop*, Rt. Rev. Cyril William Johnston
Bowles, M.A. (The Bishop's House, 6 King
Street, Duffield, Derby DE6 4EU) [Signs Cyril
Derby] 1969

Bishop Suffragan

Repton, Rt. Rev. Francis Henry Arthur Rich-
mond, M.A. (Repton House, Lea, Matlock) 1985
Assistant Bishop, Rt. Rev. Cecil Allan Warren,
M.A. (cons 1965) 1983
Provost, Very Rev. Benjamin Hugh Lewers, M.A.1981

Canons Residentiary

Archd. Dell ....1981 | I. Gatford..........1984

Archdeacons

Chesterfield, Ven. G. R. Phizacklerley, M.A. 1978
Derby, Ven. R. S. Dell, M.A. 1973
Organist, P. Gould, F.R.C.O. 1982
  Beneficed Clergy, 190; *Curates, &c.*, 23
Chancellor, J. W. M. Bullimore, Ll.B............1981
Registrar, J. R. S. Grimwood-Taylor, M.A., Derby.

ELY

66th *Bishop*, Rt. Rev. Peter Knight Walker, D.D.
(cons. 1972, trans. 1977) (The Bishop's House,
Ely CB7 4DW) [Signs Peter Elien:] 1977

Bishop Suffragan

Huntingdon, Rt. Rev. William Gordon Roe, M.A.,
D.Phil. (Powchers Hall, The College, Ely) 1980

Dean

Very Rev. William James Patterson, M.A. 1984

Canons Residentiary

D. J. Green ....1980 | M. S. MacDonald,
Bp. of Huntingdon . . 1980 | M.A. 1982
Organist, A. W. Wills, MUS. DOC., F.R.C.O........1959

Archdeacons

Ely, Ven. D. Walser, M.A. 1981
Wisbech, Ven. D. Fleming 1984
Huntingdon, Ven. R. K. Sledge, M.A. 1978
  Incumbents, 155; *Curates, &c.*, 10
Chancellor, Rev. Canon K. G. Routledge, M.A., LL.B.
Registrar, W. H. Godfrey 1978
Joint Registrar, P. F. B. Beesley, LL.B. 1 The
Sanctuary, S.W.1.

EXETER

69th *Bishop*, Rt. Rev. Geoffrey Hewlett Thompson (cons. 1974) (The Palace, Exeter) [Signs
Hewlett Exon:] 1985

Bishops Suffragan

Crediton, Rt. Rev. Peter Coleman, M.A. (10 The
Close, Exeter) 1984
Plymouth, Rt. Rev. K. A. Newing, M.A...........1982
Assistant Bishops, Rt. Rev. John Armstrong,
C.B., O.B.E. (cons. 1963); Rt. Rev. Charles Robert
Claxton, D.D. (cons. 1946); Rt. Rev. Ronald
Cedric Osbourne Goodchild, M.A. (cons. 1964);
Rt. Rev. Philip John Pasterfield, M.A. (cons.
1974).

Dean

Very Rev. Richard Montague Stephens Eyre,
M.A. 1981

Canons Residentiary

Archd. Richards ...1981 | A. C. Mawson, M.A. .1979
J. A. Thurmer, M.A. .1973 |
Organist, L. Nethsingha, M.A., F.R.C.O. 1972
Chapter Clerk, J. F. Eden, M.A. 1966

Archdeacons

Barnstaple, Ven. R. G. Herniman, B.A. 1970
Totnes, Ven. R. S. Hawkins, M.A., B.Phil. 1981
Plymouth, Ven. R. G. Ellis, M.A. 1982
Exeter, Ven. J. Richards, M.A. 1981
  Beneficed Clergy, 275; *Curates, &c.*, 38
Chancellor, D. C. Calcutt, Q.C., M.A., Ll.B., MUS.B .1971
Registrar, J. F. G. Michelmore, T.D., M.A., 18
Cathedral Yard, Exeter 1963
Diocesan Secretary, Sqn. Ldr. W. McDonald,
D.F.C., Diocesan House, Palace Gate, Exeter ..1976

GIBRALTAR IN EUROPE

Bishop, Rt. Rev. John Richard Satterthwaite (5A
Gregory Place, W8 4NG).

Bishop Suffragan

In Europe, Rt. Rev. Ambrose Walter Marcus Weekes,
C.B.

Auxiliary Bishops, Rt. Rev. E. M. H. Capper, O.B.E.;
Rt. Rev. D. de Pina Cabral; Rt. Rev. H. Isherwood,
M.V.O., O.B.E.

Vicar-General, Rev. P. O. Deacon.
Bishop's Commissaries, Canon J. A. Taylor; Canon H. Wybrew; Preb. D. W. C. Mossman, O.B.E.; Canon J. D. Beckwith.
Dean, Cathedral Church of the Holy Trinity, Gibraltar, (vacant).
Chancellor, Pro-Cathedral of St. Paul, Valletta, Malta, (vacant).
Chancellor, Pro-Cathedral of the Holy Trinity, Brussels, Belgium, Ven. J. Lewis.

Archdeacons

Aegean, Ven. G. B. Evans.
N.W. Europe, Ven. J. Lewis.
N. France, (vacant).
Gibraltar, Ven. R. B. Ney, O.B.E.
Italy, Ven. G. L. C. Westwell.
Riviera, Ven. J. Livingstone.
Scandinavia, Ven. B. Horlock, O.B.E.
Switzerland, Ven. A. R. Nind.

GLOUCESTER

37th Bishop, Rt. Rev. John Yates, M.A. (*cons.* 1972) (Bishopscourt, Gloucester GL1 2BQ) [Signs John Gloucestr:] 1975

Bishop Suffragan

Tewkesbury, (vacant).

Dean

Very Rev. K. N. Jennings, M.A. 1982

Canons Residentiary

| Archd. Evans ...... 1969 | A. L. Dunstan, M.A. .1978 |
| D. C. St. V. Welander, B.D. .... 1975 | R. D. M. Grey, A.K.C. .... 1982 |
Organist, J. D. Sanders, M.A., MUS.B., F.R.C.O., A.R.C.M. 1967

Archdeacons

Gloucester, Ven. C. J. H. Wagstaff, B.A.
Cheltenham, Ven. T. E. Evans, M.A. 1975
    Beneficed Clergy, 184; *Curates, &c.*, 23
Chancellor & Vicar-Gen., Rev. E. Garth Moore, M.A. 1957
Diocesan Registry, 34 Brunswick Road, Gloucester.
Joint Registrars, J. R. Stayt, M.A.; C. G. Peak, M.A.
Diocesan Sec., R. Anderton.

GUILDFORD

7th Bishop, Rt. Rev. Michael Edgar Adie, M.A. (Willow Grange, Woking Road, Guildford GU4 7QS) [Signs Michael Guildford] 1983

Bishop Suffragan

Dorking, Rt. Rev. David Peter Wilcox, M.A. 1985
Assistant Bishop, Rt. Rev. Gilbert Hindley Baker, (*cons.* 1966) 1983
Dean, Very Rev. Antony Cyprian Bridge 1968

Canons Residentiary

F. S. Telfer, M.A. .... 1973 | P. G. Croft, M.A. ... 1983
Organist, A. T. S. Millington, M.A., F.R.C.O. 1983

Archdeacons

Surrey, Ven. P. E. Barber, M.A. 1980
Dorking, Ven. P. G. Hogben 1982
    Beneficed Clergy, 147; *Curates, &c.*, 55
Chancellor, M. B. Goodman, M.A.
Legal Sec., P. F. B. Beesley, Ll.B.
Registrar of Diocese, P. F. B. Beesley, Ll.B.
Registrar of the Archdeaconries, P. F. B. Beesley, Ll.B.

HEREFORD

103rd Bishop, Rt. Rev. John Richard Gordon Eastaugh, B.A. (The Palace, Hereford HR4 9BN) [Signs John Hereford] 1973

Bishop Suffragan

Ludlow, Rt. Rev. Stanley Mark Wood (*cons.* 1971) 1982

Dean

Very Rev. Peter Haynes 1982

Canons Residentiary

Archd. Woodhouse . 1982 | P. Iles 1983
J. Tiller .... 1984 |
Organist, Roy Massey, B.MUS., F.R.C.O. 1974

Archdeacons

Hereford, Ven. A. H. Woodhouse 1982
Ludlow, Ven. I. Griggs 1984
    Beneficed Clergy, 98; *Curates, &c.*, 43
Chancellor, J. M. Henty 1977
Joint Registrars, V. T. Jordan, 5 St. Peter Street, Hereford; P. Beesley, 1 The Sanctuary, Westminster, S.W.1.

LEICESTER

4th Bishop, Rt. Rev. Cecil Richard Rutt, C.B.E., M.A. (*cons.* 1966) (Bishop's Lodge, Leicester LE2 3BD) [Signs Richard Leicester] 1978
Assistant Bishop, Rt. Rev. John Ernest Llewellyn Mort, C.B.E., M.A. (*cons.* 1952) 1972
Provost, Very Rev. Alan Christopher Warren, M.A. 1978

Canons Residentiary

D. W. Gundry, B.D., | Bp. Mort 1970
M.Th. .... 1963 |
Organist, Peter White, M.A., MUS.B., F.R.C.O. 1968

Archdeacons

Leicester, Ven. R. D. Silk, B.A. 1980
Loughborough, Ven. H. Lockley, PH.D. 1963
    Beneficed Clergy, 160; *Curates, &c.*, 29
Chancellor, N. H. Freeman 1979
Registrar, K. J. Moore, 10 Friar Lane, Leicester.

LICHFIELD

97th Bishop, Rt. Rev. Keith Norman Sutton, M.A. (*cons.* 1978) (Bishop's House, The Close, Lichfield WS13 7LG) [Signs Keith Lichfield] 1984

Bishops Suffragan

Shrewsbury, Rt. Rev. Leslie Lloyd Rees (68 London Road, Shrewsbury) 1980
Stafford, Rt. Rev. John Stevens Waller, M.A. (Park Lodge, 3 Beech Court, Stone, Staffs.) ... 1979
Wolverhampton, (vacant).

Dean

Very Rev. John Harley Lang, M.A. 1980

Canons Residentiary

Archd. Ninis 1974	G. M. Smallwood,
A. N. Barnard, M.A. .1977	M.A. 1978
	W. J. Turner, B.A. . 1983
Organist, J. Rees-Williams, M.A., F.R.C.O. 1978

Archdeacons

Lichfield, Ven. R. B. Ninis, M.A. 1974
Salop, Ven. R. M. C. Jeffery, B.D. 1980
Stoke on Trent, Ven. J. D. Delight, B.A. 1982
    Beneficed Clergy, 352; *Curates, &c.*, 76
Chancellor, Rev. Canon K. G. Routledge, M.A., LL.B.
Diocesan Registrar and Bishop's Sec., M. B. S. Exham.

LINCOLN

69*th Bishop*, Rt. Rev. Simon Wilton Phipps, M.C., M.A. (*cons.* 1968, *trans.* 1974), (Bishop's House, Eastgate, Lincoln LN2 1QQ) [Signs Simon Lincoln:] 1974

Bishops Suffragan

Grimsby, Rt. Rev. David Tustin, M.A. (43 Abbey Park Road, Grimsby) 1979
Grantham, Rt. Rev. Dennis Gascoyne Hawker, M.A. (Fairacre, Barrowby High Road, Grantham) 1972
Assistant Bishops, Rt. Rev, Anthony Otter, M.A. (*cons.* 1949)(1965); Rt. Rev. Gerald Fitzmaurice Colin, M.A. (*cons.* 1966) 1979

Dean

Very Rev. the Hon. Oliver William Twisleton-Wykeham-Fiennes, M.A. 1968

Canons Residentiary

D. C. Rutter, M.A. ... 1965	J. S. Nurser, M.A.,
B. R. Davis, M.A. 1977	Ph.D. 1977
	Archd. Lawrence,
	M.A. 1985

Organist, Philip Marshall, MUS.DOC., F.R.C.O. 1966

Archdeacons

Stow, Ven. D. Scott, M.A. 1975
Lincoln, Ven. R. J. Milner, M.A. 1983
Lindsey, Ven. J. H. C. Lawrence, M.A. 1985
Beneficed Clergy, 280; *Curates, &c.*, 50
Chancellor, His Honour Judge M. B. Goodman, M.A. 1971
Registrar, D. M. Wellman, M.A., 5–6 Bank Street, Lincoln.

NORWICH

Bishop, 70*th Bishop* (and 111*th of East Anglia*), Rt. Rev. Peter John Nott, M.A. (The Bishop's House, Norwich, NR3 1SB)
[Signs Peter Norvic] 1985

Bishops Suffragan

Lynn, (vacant).
Thetford, Rt. Rev. Timothy Dudley-Smith, M.A. .1981

Dean

Very Rev. John Paul Burbridge, M.A. 1983

Canons Residentiary

J. F. Poulton, B.A. ..1979	C. Beswick 1984
D. H. Bishop 1980	

Organist, M. B. Nicholas, M.A., F.R.C.O. 1971

Archdeacons

Norfolk, Ven. P. Dawson, M.A. 1977
Norwich, Ven. A. M. Handley, M.A. 1981
Lynn, Ven. G. F. Grobecker, M.B.E., M.A. 1980
Beneficed Clergy, 225; *Curates, &c.*, 15
Chancellor, His Hon. J. H. Ellison, V.R.D., M.A. . .1955
Joint Registrars and Secs., B. O. L. Prior, M.B.E., T.D.; J. A. Linton, M.A.

OXFORD

40*th Bishop*, Rt. Rev. Patrick Campbell Rodger (*cons.* 1970, *trs.* 1978), (Diocesan Church House, North Hinksey, Oxford OX2 0NB) [Signs Patrick Oxon] 1978

Bishops Suffragan

Buckingham, Rt. Rev. Simon Hedley Burrows, M.A. (Sheridan, Grimms Hill, Great Missenden) 1974
Dorchester, Rt. Rev. Conrad John Eustace Meyer, M.A. (151 Wroslyn Road, Freeland, Oxon.) 1979

Reading

Rt. Rev. Ronald Gregory Graham Foley, B.A. (Greenbanks, Old Bath Road, Sonning, Reading) 1982
Assistant Bishops, Rt. Rev. Sydney Cyril Bulley, M.A., D.D., 1979; Rt. Rev. A. K. Cragg, M.A., D.D., 1982; Rt. Rev. Eric Wild, M.A., 1982; Rt. Rev. L. J. Ashton, C.B. 1984

Dean of Christ Church

Very Rev. Eric William Heaton, M.A. 1979

Canons Residentiary

W. R. F. Browning,	Archd. Weston 1982
M.A., B.D. (*Canon of*	O. M. T. O'Donovan,
the Cathedral	D.Phil. 1982
Church) 1965	R. D. Williams, M.A.
M. F. Wiles, D.D. 1970	D.Phil. 1985
J. C. Fenton, M.A., B.D.	
................1978	

Organist, S. Darlington, M.A., F.R.C.O.

Archdeacons

Oxford, Ven. F. V. Weston, M.A. 1982
Berks., Ven. J. E. Brown, B.D. 1978
Bucks., Ven. J. F. E. Bone, M.A. 1978
Chancellor, P. T. S. Boydell 1958
Registrar and Legal Sec., F. E. Robson 1969

WINDSOR

(*The Queen's Free Chapel of St. George within Her Castle of Windsor—A Royal Peculiar*)
Dean, Rt. Rev. Michael Ashley Mann..........1976

Canons Residentiary

D. J. Burgess, M.A. ..1978	J. A. White 1982
J. D. Treadgold 1981	D. M. Stainsby 1985

Organist, C. J. Robinson, M.A., B.MUS., F.R.C.O. 1975
Chapter Clerk, Maj.-Gen. R. L. C. Dixon, C.B., M.C. 1981

PETERBOROUGH

36*th Bishop*, Rt. Rev. William John Westwood, M.A. (The Palace, Peterborough PE1 1YA) [Signs William Petriburg] 1984
Assistant Bishop, Rt. Rev. William Alfred Franklin, O.B.E. 1978

Dean

Very Rev. Randolph George Wise, M.A. 1981

Canons Residentiary

Archd. Fernyhough 1977	T. R. Christie, M.A. .1980
	J. Higham, M.A. 1983

Master of the Music, C. S. Gower, M.A., F.R.C.O. ...1977

Archdeacons

Northampton, Ven. B. R. Marsh, B.A. 1964
Oakham, Ven. B. Fernyhough, B.A. 1977
Beneficed Clergy, 250; *Curates, &c*, 30
Chancellor, Rev. Canon K. C. Routledge, M.A., LL.B.
Registrar, R. Hemingray, 37 Priestgate, Peterborough.

PORTSMOUTH

7*th Bishop*, Rt. Rev. Timothy John Bavin, M.A. (Bishopswood, Fareham, Hants.) [Signs Timothy Portsmouth] 1985
Provost, Very Rev. David Staffurth Stancliffe, M.A. 1982
Organist, A. Froggatt, MUS.B., A.R.C.O.

Canons Residentiary

N. H. Crowder, M.A. .1975	R. Eckersley 1984
S. G. Platten 1982	P. J. Cotton 1984

Archdeacons

Portsmouth, Ven. R. V. Scruby, M.A. 1977
I. of Wight, Ven. F. C. Carpenter, M.A. 1977
  Beneficed Clergy, 94; *Curates, &c.*, 64
Chancellor, His Honour Judge Aglionby, M.A. . . 1978
Registrar, T. S. Blower, M.A. 1976

ROCHESTER

104th Bishop, Rt. Rev. Richard David Say, D.D.
  (Bishopscourt, Rochester ME1 1TS) [Signs
  David Roffen:] 1961

Bishop Suffragan

Tonbridge, Rt. Rev. David Henry Bartleet, M.A.
  (Bishop's Lodge, St. Botolph's Road,
  Sevenoaks) 1982

Dean

Very Rev. John Robert Arnold, M.A. 1978

Canons Residentiary

P. A. Welsby, M.A.,	E. R. Turner, M.A. . . 1981
PH.D. 1966	Archd. Turnbull . . . 1984
H. E. G. Stapleton,	
M.A. 1980	

Organist, B. Ferguson, M.A., F.R.C.O. 1977

Archdeacons

Bromley, Ven. E. R. Francis 1979
Rochester, Ven. A. M. A. Turnbull, M.A. 1984
Tonbridge, Ven. R. J. Mason 1977
  Beneficed Clergy, 200; *Curates, &c.*, 50
Chancellor, His Honour Judge M. B. Goodman,
  M.A. 1971
Registrar, O. R. Woodfield, Rochester 1955
Sec. D. W. Faull, 22 Greencoat Place, S.W.1. 1963

ST. ALBANS

8th Bishop, Rt. Rev. John Bernard Taylor, M.A.
  (Abbey Gate House, St. Albans AL3 4HD)
  [Signs John St. Albans] 1980

Bishops Suffragan

Bedford, Rt. Rev. David John Farmbrough, M.A. 1981
Hertford, Rt. Rev. Kenneth Harold Pillar, M.A. . 1982

Dean

Very Rev. Peter Clement Moore, M.A., D.Phil. . . . 1973
Organist, C. Walsh 1985

Archdeacons

St. Albans, Ven. E. M. Norfolk 1982
Bedford, Ven. C. J. Mayfield 1979
  Beneficed Clergy, 249; *Curates, &c.*, 83
Chancellor, G. H. Newsom, Q.C., M.A. 1958
Registrar and Legal Sec., D. N. Cheetham,
  Holywell Lodge, 41 Holywell Hill, St. Albans . 1978

ST. EDMUNDSBURY AND IPSWICH

7th Bishop, Rt. Rev. John Waine, B.A. (Bishop's
  House, Ipswich IP1 3ST), *cons.* 1975 [Signs
  John St. Edm. & Ipswich] 1978

Bishop Suffragan

Dunwich, Rt. Rev. Eric Nash Devenport, B.A. . . . 1980
Provost, Very Rev. Raymond Furnell 1981

Canons Residentiary

D. A. Payne, M.A. . . . 1973 | G. J. Tarris, M.A. . . . 1982

Archdeacons

Ipswich, Ven. G. D. J. Walsh, M.A. 1976
Suffolk, Ven. T. A. Gibson, M.A. 1984
Sudbury, Ven. D. J. Smith 1984
Organist, P. Treptre, M.A., F.R.C.O. 1985
Beneficed Clergy, 139; *Clergy of incumbent status*, 38;
  Curates, 17
Chancellor, His Honour Judge Blofeld, Q.C., M.A. 1974
Registrar, J. D. Mitson, M.A., LL.B. 22–28 Museum
  Street, Ipswich.

SALISBURY

76th Bishop, Rt. Rev. John Austin Baker, M.A.,
  M. Litt. (South Canonry, The Close, Salisbury
  SP1 2ER) [Signs John Sarum] 1982

Bishops Suffragan

Sherborne, Rt. Rev. John Dudley Galtrey Kirk-
  ham, M.A. (Little Bailie, Sturminster Marshall,
  Wimborne) 1976
Ramsbury, Rt. Rev. John Robert Geoffrey
  Neale, A.K.C. (Bishop's House, Urchfont, Dev-
  izes, Wilts.) 1974

Dean

Very Rev. Sydney Hall Evans, C.B.E., M.A., D.D. . . 1977

Canons Residentiary

I. G. D. Dunlop, M.A.,	R. G. Askew, M.A. . . . 1983
F.S.A. 1972	D. J. C. Davies, M.A. . 1985

Organist, R. G. Seal, M.A., F.R.C.O. 1968

Archdeacons

Sherborne, Ven. J. K. Oliver, M.A. 1985
Sarum, Ven. N. S. McCulloch, M.A. 1979
Wilts, Ven. B. J. Smith 1980
Dorset, Ven. G. E. Walton 1982
  Beneficed Clergy, 255; *Curates, &c.*, 38
Chancellor of the Diocese, His Hon. J. H. Ellison,
  V.R.D., M.A. 1955
Registrar and Legal Secretary, F. M. Broadbent,
  M.A., 42 Castle Street, Salisbury.

SOUTHWARK

7th Bishop, Rt. Rev. Ronald Oliver Bowlby, M.A.
  (Bishop's House, 38 Tooting Bec Gardens,
  SW16 1QZ) (*cons.* 1973, *trans.* 1980) [Signs
  Ronald Southwark] 1980
Assistant Bishops, Rt. Rev. Edward George
  Knapp-Fisher, M.A. (*cons.* 1960), 1975; Rt. Rev.
  Edmund Michael Hubert Capper, O.B.E. (*cons.*
  1967), 1981; Rt. Rev. Archibald Ronald Mc-
  Donald Gordon (*cons.* 1975) 1984

Bishops Suffragan

Croydon, Rt. Rev. Wilfred Denniston Wood 1985
Kingston on Thames, Rt. Rev. Peter Stephen
  Maurice Selby, M.A. 1984
Woolwich, Rt. Rev. Albert Peter Hall, M.A. 1984
Provost, Very Rev. David Lawrence Edwards,
  M.A. 1983

Canons Residentiary

P. H. Penwarden,	G. A. Parrott . . . 1977
M.A. 1971	R. Garrard 1979
I.G. Smith-Cameron,	J. S. Cox, M.A. . . . 1983
B.A. 1972	

Organist, H. Bramma 1976

Archdeacons

Southwark, (vacant).
Lewisham, Ven. C. J. Lacey 1985
Kingston, Ven. B. V. Jacob, M.A. 1977
Wandsworth, Ven. P. B. Coombs, M.A. 1975
Chancellor, Rev. E. Garth Moore, M.A. 1948
Registrar, D. W. Faull, 30 Causton Street, S.W.1. 1963

TRURO

12th Bishop, Rt. Rev. Peter Mumford, M.A. (Lis Escop, Truro TR3 6QQ) [Signs Peter Truron:] 1981

Bishop Suffragan

St. Germans, Rt. Rev. Richard Llewellin (32 Falmouth Road, Truro) 1985
Assistant Bishop, Rt. Rev. R. F. Cartwright, M.A..1982

Dean

Very Rev. David John Shearlock, B.A. 1982

Canons Residentiary

P. L. Maddock, B.A. .1976	W. J. P. Boyd, Ph.D. .1985
Archd. Wood 1981	

Organist, J. Winter............................1971

Archdeacons

Cornwall, Ven. A. Wood......................1981
Bodmin, Ven. G. Temple 1981
Beneficed Clergy, 164; *Curates, &c.*, 20
Chancellor, P. T. S. Boydell, Q.C. 1957
Registrar and Secretary, R. W. Money, 2 Princes Street, Truro.

WORCESTER

111th Bishop, Rt. Rev. Philip Harold Ernest Goodrich, M.A. (The Bishop's House, Hartlebury Castle, Kidderminster) [Signs Philip Worcester] 1982
Assistant Bishops, Rt. Rev. David Howard Nicholas Allenby, M.A. (cons. 1962) (1968); Rt. Rev. Oliver Stratford Tomkins, D.D. (cons. 1959), 1975; Rt. Rev. John Arthur Arrowsmith Maund (cons. 1950); Rt. Rev. Stanley Chapman Pickard (cons. 1958).

Bishop Suffragan

Dudley, Rt. Rev. Anthony Charles Dumper, M.A. (The Bishop's House, Brooklands, Halesowen Road, Cradley Heath) 1977

Dean

Very Rev. Thomas George Adames Baker, M.A. .1975

Canons Residentiary

J. R. Fenwick, M.A. .1978	Archd. Bentley 1984
N. Robinson 1983	

Organist, D. Hunt, MUS.D., F.R.C.O. 1975

Archdeacons

Dudley, Ven. R. Bennett 1985
Worcester, Ven. F. Bentley 1984
Beneficed Clergy, 120; *Curates, &c.*, 50
Chancellor, P. T. S. Boydell, Q.C. 1959
Registrar, Rev. J. A. Dale, Diocesan Registry, Little Comberton Rectory, Pershore.

Province of York

YORK

95th Archbishop and Primate of England Most Rev. and Rt. Hon. John Stapylton Habgood, P.C., D.D., cons. 1973 (Bishopthorpe, York YO2 1QE) [Signs John Ebor:] 1983
Assistant Bishops, Rt. Rev. George Eyles Irwin Cockin, B.A. (cons. 1959) (1969); Rt. Rev. Richard Knyvet Wimbush, M.A. (cons. 1963) (1977); Rt. Rev. George Edward Holderness (cons. 1955) 1980

Bishops Suffragan

Selby, Rt. Rev. Clifford Condor Barker, T.D., M.A. (8 Bankside Close, Upper Poppleton, York) ...1983
Hull, Rt. Rev. Donald George Snelgrove, T.D., M.A. (Hullen House, Woodfield Lane, Hessle, Hull) 1981
Whitby, Rt. Rev. Gordon Bates (60 West Green, Stokesley, Middlesbrough) 1983

Dean

Very Rev. John Eliot Southgate 1984

Canons Residentiary

M. E. Bowering 1981	R. Mayland 1982
R. A. Hockley, M.A. .1976	J. Toy, M.A., Ph.D. ..1983

Organist, P. J. Moore, B.MUS., A.R.C.M., F.R.C.O.

Archdeacons

York, Ven. L. C. Stanbridge, M.A..............1972
East Riding, Ven. M. E. Vickers, M.A. 1981
Cleveland, Ven. R. J. Woodley 1984
Beneficed Clergy, 255; *Curates, &c.*, 39
Official Principal and Auditor of the Chancery Court, J. A. D. Owen, Q.C.
Chancellor of the Diocese, T. A. C. Coningsby, M.A...1977
Vicar-General of the Province and Official Principal of the Consistory Court, T. A. C. Coningsby, M.A.
Registrar and Secretary, G. P. Knowles, M.A., LL.B. 1968

DURHAM

92nd Bishop, Rt. Rev. David Edward Jenkins, M.A. (Auckland Castle, Bishop Auckland DL14 7NR) [Signs David Dunelm] 1984

Bishop Suffragan

Jarrow, Rt. Rev. Michael Thomas Ball, M.A., C.G.A. (Melkridge House, Gilesgate, Durham DH1 1JB)..................................1980

Dean

Very Rev. Peter Richard Baelz, M.A., B.D........1980

Canons Residentiary

D. R. Jones, M.A.....1964	R. L. Coppin, M.A....1974
Archd. Perry 1970	Archd. Hodgson 1983
S. W. Sykes, M.A. 1974	T. Hart, M.A. 1983

Organist, R. Lloyd, MUS.B., F.R.C.O. 1974

Archdeacons

Durham, Ven. M. C. Perry, M.A.................1970
Auckland, Ven. J. D. Hodgson, B.A.............1983
Clergy, 306
Chancellor, Rev. E. Garth Moore, M.A. 1954
Registrar and Legal Secretary, W. K. Wills, LL.B. .1975

BLACKBURN

6th Bishop, Rt. Rev. David Stewart Cross, M.A. (Bishop's House, Ribchester Road, Blackburn BB1 9EF) [Signs Stewart Blackburn] 1982

Bishops Suffragan

Lancaster, Rt. Rev. Ian Harland, M.A. (Wheatfield, Dallas Road, Lancaster LA1 1TN) 1985
Burnley, Rt. Rev. Richard Charles Challinor Watson, M.A. (Palace House, Burnley) 1970
Provost, Very Rev. Lawrence Jackson, A.K.C. ...1973

Canons Residentiary

G. A. Williams, M.A. .1965	B. M. Beaumont,
J. M. Taylor 1975	M.A. 1977

Archdeacons

Lancaster, Ven. K. H. Gibbons, B.SC.............1981
Blackburn, Ven. C. W. D. Carroll, M.A..........1973
Organist, D. A. Cooper, M.A., F.R.C.O.............1983
    Beneficed Clergy, 230; Curates, &c., 50
Chancellor, Quentin T. Edwards, Q.C..........1977
Registrar, Leslie Ranson, LL.B. 1954

BRADFORD

7th Bishop, Rt. Rev. Robert Kerr Williamson
    (Bishopscroft, Ashwell Road, Heaton, Brad-
    ford) [Signs Robert Bradford BD9 4AU]......1984
Provost, Very Rev. Brandon Donald Jackson,
    Ll.B. 1977

Canons Residentiary

K. H. Cook, A.K.C. ...1977 | C. Hayward........1983
Organist, G. Weaver, M.A., A.R.C.O. 1982

Archdeacons

Bradford, Ven. D. H. Shreeve, M.A. 1984
Craven, Ven. D. A. Rogers, M.A. 1977
    Beneficed Clergy, 123; Curates, &c., 23
Chancellor, D. M. Savill, Q.C.................1976
Registrar and Secretary, J. G. H. Mackrell, 18
    Devonshire Street, Keighley 1977

CARLISLE

64th Bishop, Rt. Rev. Henry David Halsey, B.A.
    (Rose Castle, Dalston, Carlisle CA5 7BZ), (cons.
    1968) [Signs David Carliol] 1972

Bishop Suffragan

Penrith, Rt. Rev. George Lanyon Hacker, M.A.
    (The Rectory, Gt. Salkeld, Penrith).........1979

Dean

Very Rev. John Howard Churchill, M.A. 1973

Canons Residentiary

R. A. Chapman, M.A.1978 | R. J. W. Bevan 1982
Organist, R. A. Seivewright, M.A., A.R.C.O. 1960

Archdeacons

Carlisle, Ven. C. P. Stannard 1984
West Cumberland, Ven. T. R. B. Hodgson, B.D. ..1979
Westmorland and Furness, Ven. P. Vaughan,
    M.A...1983
    Beneficed Clergy, 190
Chancellor, His Hon. D. J. Stinson, M.A. 1971
Registrar and Sec., I. S. Sutcliffe, M.A., LL.B.,
    Carlisle 1964

CHESTER

39th Bishop, Rt. Rev. Michael Alfred Baughen,
    B.D. (Bishop's House, Chester CH1 2JD) [Signs
    Michael Cestr:] 1982

Bishops Suffragan

Stockport, Rt. Rev. Frank Pilkington Sargeant,
    B.A. (32 Park Gate Drive, Cheadle Hulme,
    Cheshire SK8 7DS) 1983
Birkenhead, Rt. Rev. Ronald Brown, B.A. (Traf-
    ford House, Queen's Park, Chester) 1974

Dean

Very Rev. Thomas Wood Ingram Cleasby, M.A. .1978

Canons Residentiary

K. M. Maltby, M.A., | L. R. Barker, M.A. ...1984
    B.D. ....1974 |
W. H. Vanstone, M.A., |
    S.T.M. ....1978 |
Organist, R. A. Fisher, M.A., F.R.C.O. 1967

Archdeacons

Chester, Ven. H. L. Williams, B.A. 1975
Macclesfield, Ven. R. Simpson, L.V.O., M.A......1978
Chancellor, H. H. Lomas, M.A..................1977
Registrar and Legal Secretary, A. K. McAllester,
    Friars, 20 White Friars, Chester.

LIVERPOOL

6th Bishop, Rt. Rev. David Stuart Sheppard, M.A.
    (cons. 1969) (Bishop's Lodge, Woolton Park,
    Liverpool) [Signs David Liverpool] 1975

Bishop Suffragan

Warrington, Rt. Rev. Michael Henshall, B.A.
    (Martinsfield, Elm Avenue, Great Crosby,
    Liverpool) 1975
Asst. Bishops, Rt. Rev. William Scott Baker, M.A.
    (cons. 1943), 1968; Rt. Rev. John William
    Hawkins Flagg (cons. 1969) 1978

Dean

Very Rev. R. D. C. Walters, B.SC 1983

Canons Residentiary

M. M. Wolfe ....1982 | K. J. Riley 1983
D. J. Hutton ....1983 | N. A. Frayling 1983
Organist, Ian Tracey........................1980

Archdeacons

Liverpool, Ven. G. H. G. Spiers 1979
Warrington, Ven. C. D. S. Woodhouse...........1981
    Beneficed Clergy, 234; Curates, &c., 66
Chancellor, R. G. Hamilton, M.A.
Registrar and Cathedral Chapter Clerk, R. H.
    Arden, 1 Hanover Street, Liverpool 1.

MANCHESTER

9th Bishop, Rt. Rev. Stanley Eric Francis Booth-
    Clibborn, M.A. (Bishopscourt, Bury New Road,
    Manchester M7 0LE) [Signs Stanley
    Manchester]................................1979

Bishops Suffragan

Bolton, Rt. Rev. David George Galliford, M.A. (4
    Standfield Drive, Lostock, Bolton) 1984
Hulme, Rt. Rev. Colin Scott, M.A. (1 Raynham
    Avenue, Didsbury, Manchester 20) 1984
Middleton, Rt. Rev. Donald Alexander Tytler,
    M.A., (The Hollies, Manchester Road,
    Rochdale) 1982
Assistant Bishops, Rt. Rev. Edward Ralph Wick-
    ham, B.D. (cons. 1959), 1982; Rt. Rev. Kenneth
    Venner Ramsey, M.A., B.D. (cons. 1953) 1975

Dean

Very Rev. Robert Waddington, B.A. (The
    Deanery, 44 Shrewsbury Road, Prestwich M25
    8GQ) 1984

Canons Residentiary

G. O. Morgan, B.SC. .1971 | J. Nicholls, A.K.C. ...1983
Archd. R. B. Harris .1980 | J. R. Atherton, M.A.,
    | PH.D. 1984
Organist, G. Stewart.

Archdeacons

Manchester, Ven. R. B. Harris, M.A. 1980
Bolton, Ven. W. Brison 1985
Rochdale, Ven. D. Bonser, M.A.................1982
    Beneficed Clergy, 300; Curates, &c., 110
Chancellor, G. C. H. Spafford, M.A., LL.B. 1976
Registrar and Bishop's Secretary, J. Maloney, 90
    Deansgate, Manchester 1972

NEWCASTLE

10th *Bishop*, Rt. Rev. Andrew Alexander Kenny Graham (*cons.* 1977) (Bishop's House, 29 Moor Road South, Gosforth, Newcastle upon Tyne NE3 1PA) [Signs A. Newcastle] 1981
Assistant Bishop, Rt. Rev. Kenneth Edward Gill (*cons.* 1972) 1980
Provost, Very Rev. Christopher Garnett Howsin Spafford, M.A. 1976

Canons Residentiary

D. A. Carrette, M.A. ..1978 | R. Langley..........1985
W. J. Thomas, M.A. .1983 |
Organist, Russell A. Missin, F.R.C.O. 1967

Archdeacons

Northumberland, Ven. W. J. Thomas, M.A. 1983
Lindisfarne, Ven. D. J. Smith 1981
Beneficed Clergy, 116; *other Clergy of incumbent status*, 38; *Curates, &c.*, 33
Chancellor, His Hon. A. J. Blackett-Ord, M.A. 1971
Registrar and Sec., R. R. V. Nicholson, 46 Grainger Street, Newcastle upon Tyne.

RIPON

11th *Bishop*, Rt. Rev. David Nigel de Lorentz Young, M.A. (Bishop Mount, Ripon HG4 5DP.) [Signs David Ripon] 1977

Bishop Suffragan

Knaresborough, Rt. Rev. John Dennis, M.A. (16 Shaftesbury Avenue, Leeds) 1979

Dean

Very Rev. Christopher Russell Campling, M.A. ...1984

Canons Residentiary

R. B. McFadden, | P. J. Marshall, M.A. ..1985
M.A. ....1979 |
D. G. Ford ....1980 |
Organist, Ronald Perrin, F.R.C.O. 1966

Archdeacons

Leeds, Ven. A. J. Comber, M.SC. 1982
Richmond, Ven. N. G. L. R. McDermid, M.A. 1983
Beneficed Clergy, 132; *Curates, &c.*, 40
Chancellor, J. B. Mortimer, Q.C., M.A. 1971
Registrar and Legal Secretary, J. R. Balmforth, M.A., Phoenix House, South Parade, Leeds.

SHEFFIELD

5th *Bishop*, Rt. Rev. David Ramsay Lunn, M.A. (Bishopscroft, Snaithing Lane, Sheffield S10 3LG) [Signs David Sheffield] 1980

Bishop Suffragan

Doncaster, Rt. Rev. William Michael Dermot Persson (5 Park Lane, Sheffield 10) 1982
Provost, Very Rev. Wilfred Frank Curtis, A.K.C. 1974

Archdeacons

Sheffield, Ven. M. J. M. Paton, M.A. 1978
Doncaster, Ven. D. Carnelley 1985

Organist, G. Matthews, B.MUS., F.R.C.O. 1967
Beneficed Clergy, 163; *Curates, &c.*, 46
Chancellor, G. B. Graham, Q.C. 1971
Registrar and Legal Sec. P. T. Ward, 30 Bank Street, Sheffield.

SODOR AND MAN

78th *Bishop*, Rt. Rev. Arthur Henry Attwell, B.D., M.Th., M.A. (Bishop's House, Quarterbridge Road, Douglas, Isle of Man) [Signs Arthur Sodor and Man] 1983
Archdeacon, D. A. Willoughby, B.A.

Canons Residentiary

B. H. Kelly, M.A. | J. D. Gelling, M.A.
D. Baggaley, M.A. | B. H. Partinston
Beneficed Clergy, 20; *Curates, &c.*, 21
Vicar-General and Registrar, P. W. S. Farrant, 24 Athol Street, Douglas.
Assistant Secretary, J. Wilson.

SOUTHWELL

8th *Bishop*, Rt. Rev. Michael Humphrey Dickens Whinney, M.A. (Bishop's Manor, Southwell) [Signs Michael Southwell] 1985

Bishop Suffragan

Sherwood, Rt. Rev. Harold Richard Darby, B.A. (Applegarth, Halam, Southwell) 1975
Provost, Very Rev. John Murray Irvine, M.A. ...1978

Canons Residentiary

D. P. Keene, M.A. ...1981 | I. G. Collins 1985
Organist, K. Beard, M.A., MUS.B., F.R.C.O. 1959

Archdeacons

Newark, Ven. D. Leaning 1979
Nottingham, Ven. G. C. Handford 1984
Beneficed Clergy, 172; *Curates, &c.*, 42
Chancellor, J. Shand, M.A., LL.B. 1981
Registrar, P. H. Mellors, M.A., Ll.B. 1970

WAKEFIELD

Bishop, (vacant).

Bishop Suffragan

Pontefract, Rt. Rev. Thomas Richard Hare, M.A. (306 Barnsley Road, Wakefield) 1971
Asst. Bishops, Rt. Rev. Patrick Burnet Harris, M.A. (cons. 1973) 1981; Rt. Rev. Ralph Emmerson, B.D. (cons. 1972) 1979; Rt. Rev. Anselm Genders, M.A. (cons. 1977) 1982
Provost, Very Rev. John Edward Allen. 1982

Archdeacons

Pontefract, Ven. K. Unwin, M.A. 1981
Halifax, Ven. A. D. Chesters, M.A. 1985
Organist, J. L. Bielby, M.A., MUS.B., F.R.C.O. 1971
Beneficed Clergy, 176; *Curates, &c.*, 27
Chancellor, G. B. Graham, Q.C., Ll.B. 1959
Registrar and Sec., E. Chapman, B.A., Burton Street, Wakefield.........................1979

THE CHURCH IN WALES

BANGOR

79th *Bishop*, Rt. Rev. John Cledan Mears, M.A., *b.* 1922, *cons.* 1982.

LLANDAFF

Bishop, (vacant).

MONMOUTH

6th *Bishop and* 8th *Archbishop of Wales*, Most Rev. Derrick Greenslade Childs, B.A., *b.* 1918, *cons.* 1972, *elected* Archbishop of Wales, 1983.

ST. ASAPH

74th *Bishop*, Rt. Rev. Alwyn Rice Jones, M.A., *b.*, 1934.....................................1982

ST. DAVID'S

124th *Bishop*, Rt. Rev. George Noakes, B.A., *b.*
1924 1982

SWANSEA AND BRECON

6th *Bishop*, Rt. Rev. Benjamin Noel Young
Vaughan, M.A., *b.* 1917 1976

(Stipend of diocesan bishop of the Church of Wales is £14,000 p.a. from Jan. 1, 1986)

OVERSEAS

Sees	Apptd.

CANADA
Primate
The Most Rev. Edward Walter Scott 1971

Province of Canada
The Most Rev. Archbishop
Fredericton, Harold Lee Nutter, *b.* 1923
(*cons.*1971), *Archbishop and Metropolitan* 1980

The Rt. Rev. Bishops
Central Newfoundland, M. Genge 1975
Eastern Newfoundland and Labrador M. Mate .1980
Montreal, R. Hollis 1975
Nova Scotia, A. G. Peters .1982
Quebec, A. Goodings 1977
Western Newfoundland, S. S. Payne, *b.* 1932 1978

Province of Rupert's Land
The Most Rev. Archbishop
Qu'Appelle, Michael Geoffrey Peers, *b.* 1934 (*cons.*
1977), *Archbishop and Metropolitan* 1982

The Rt. Rev. Bishops
Arctic, J. R. Sperry, *b.* 1924 1974
Athabasca, G. F. Woolsey .1983
Brandon, J. F. S. Conlin 1975
Calgary, J. B. Curtis 1983
Edmonton, E. K. Clarke (*cons.* 1976) 1980
Keewatin, H. J. P. Allan, *b.* 1928 1974
Qu' Appelle (see above)
Rupert's Land, W. H. Jones (*cons.* 1970) 1983
Saskatchewan, T. O. Morgan 1985
Saskatoon, R. A. Wood 1981

Province of Ontario
The Most Rev. Archbishop
Toronto, Lewis Samuel Garnsworthy, *b.* 1922
(*cons.* 1968), *Archbishop and Metropolitan* . . .1980

The Rt. Rev. Bishops
Algoma, L. E. Peterson 1983
Huron, D. D. Jones (*cons.* 1982) 1984
Moosonee, C. Lawrence 1980
Niagara, J. C. Bothwell (*cons.* 1971) 1973
Ontario, A. A. Read (*cons.* 1972) 1981
Ottawa, E. K. Lackey 1981
Toronto (see above)

Province of British Columbia
The Most. Rev. Archbishop
New Westminster, Douglas Walter Hambidge, *b.*
1927 (*cons.* 1969), *Archbishop and
Metropolitan* 1981

The Rt. Rev. Bishops
British Columbia R. F. Shepherd 1984
Caledonia, J. E. Hannen 1981
Cariboo, J. S. P. Snowden .1974
Kootenay, R. E. F. Berry 1971
New Westminster (see above)
Yukon, R. C. Ferris 1981

Sees	Apptd.

AUSTRALIA
Primate of Australia
The Most Rev. John Basil Rowland Grindrod,
K.B.E., Archbishop of Brisbane.

Province of New South Wales
Archbishop and Metropolitan
Sydney, D. W. B. Robinson, *b.* 1922 (*cons.* 1973) . .1982
Asst. Bps., J. R. Reid, *b.* 1928 (1972); K. H. Short,
b. 1927 (1975); E. D. Cameron, *b.* 1926 (1975); R.
H. Goodhew, *b.* 1931 (1982).
Armidale, P. Chiswell, *b.* 1934 1976
Bathurst, H. A. J. Witt (*cons.* 1965) 1981
Canberra and Goulburn, O. D. Dowling (*cons.*
1981) 1983
Grafton B. A. Schultz (*cons.* 1985)
Newcastle, A. C. Holland *b.* 1927 (*cons.* 1970) 1978
Riverina, B. R. Hunter, *b.* 1927 (*cons.* 1971) 1971

Province of Victoria
Archbishop and Metropolitan
Melbourne, The Most Rev. David John Penman,
b. 1936 (*cons.* 1982) 1984
Bps. Coadj., J. A. Grant, *b.* 1931 (1970); D. H. W.
Shand; *b.* 1921 (1973); J. C. Stewart *b.* 1940
(1984); R. L. Butterss *b.* 1931 (1985); P. J.
Hollingworth *b.* 1935 (1985); J. W. Wilson *b.*
1937 (1985).

The Rt. Rev. Bishops
Ballarat, J. Hazlewood, *b.* 1924 1975
 Assistant Bp, G. H. Warden, *b.* 1931 1981
Bendigo, O. S. Heyward, *b.* 1926 1975
Gippsland, N. J. Chynoweth, *b.* 1922 (*cons.* 1974) 1980
Wangaratta, R. G. Beal, *b.* 1929 1985

Province of Queensland
Archbishop and Metropolitan
Brisbane, The Most Rev. J. B. R. Grindrod, K.B.E.,
b. 1919 1980
Bp. for Southern Region, R. Wicks, O.B.E., *b.* 1921
. . . . 1973
Bp. for Western Region, Rt. Rev. A. Charles *b.*
1926 1983

The Rt. Rev. Bishops
Carpentaria, A. Hall-Matthews, *b.* 1940 1984
N. Queensland, H. J. Lewis, *b.* 1926 1971
Northern Territory, C. Wood, *b.* 1936 1983
Rockhampton, G. A. Hearn, *b.* 1935 1981

Province of Western Australia
Archbishop and Metropolitan
Perth, The Most Rev. Peter Frederick Carnley,
(*cons.* 1981) 1981
Asst. Bps., M. B. Challen (1978); B. R. Kyme . .1982

The Rt. Rev. Bishops
Bunbury, H. J. U. Jamieson 1984
N. W. Australia, G. B. Muston 1982

Sees	Apptd.

Province of South Australia

Archbishop and Metropolitan

Adelaide, The Most Rev. Keith Rayner, *b.* 1929
  (*cons.* 1969) 1975

The Rt. Rev. Bishops

The Murray, R. G. Porter, *b.* 1924 (*cons.* 1967)... 1970
Willochra, S. B. Rosier, *b.* 1928 (*cons.* 1967) 1970

Extra-Provincial Diocese

Tasmania, P. K. Newell, *b.* 1930 (*cons.* 1982) 1982

PROVINCE OF PAPUA NEW GUINEA

Archbishop

Popondota, The Most Rev. G. S. Ambo (*cons.*
  1960) 1984

The Rt. Rev. Bishops

Aipo Rongo, J. C. Ashton 1976
Asst. Bp., B. Kerina 1981
Dogura, R. Sanana 1976
New Guinea Is., B. S. Meredith 1967
Port Moresby, I. R. Gadebo 1983

PROVINCE OF NEW ZEALAND

Primate and Archbishop

Auckland, (vacant).
  Asst. Bps., G. E. A. Wilson, *b.* 1926 (1980); E.
  G. Buckle, *b.* 1926 (1981)

The Rt. Rev. Bishops

Aotearoa, W. Vercoe, *b.* 1928 1981
Christchurch, M. J. Goodall, *b.* 1928 1984
Dunedin, P. W. Mann, *b.* 1924 1976
Nelson, P. E. Sutton, *b.* 1923 1965
Polynesia, J. L. Bryce, *b.* 1935 1975
Waiapu, P. G. Atkins, *b.* 1936 1983
Waikato, B. N. Davis, *b.* 1934 1980
Wellington, E. K. Norman, K.B.E., *b.* 1916 1973
  Asst. Bp., W. J. W. Rosevear, *b.* 1918 1981

PROVINCE OF MELANESIA

Archbishop

Central Melanesia, The Most Rev. Norman
Kitchener Palmer, C.M.G., M.B.E., *b.* 1928 1975

The Rt. Rev. Bishops

Malaita, W. A. Pwaisiho 1981
Temotu, A. S. Waiaru 1981
Vanuatu, H. Tevi (*cons.* 1979) 1980
Ysabel, E. Pogo 1981

PROVINCE OF SOUTH AFRICA

Archbishop and Metropolitan

Cape Town, The Most Rev. Philip Welsford
Richmond Russell, *b.* 1919 (*cons.* 1966) 1981
  Bps. Suff., P. M. Matolengwe, *b.* 1937 (1976);
  C. H. Albertyn *b.* 1928 (1983).

The Rt. Rev. Bishops

Bloemfontein, T. S. Stanage, *b.* 1932 1982
George, D. G. Damant *b.* 1933 1985
Grahamstown, K. C. Oram, *b.* 1919 1974
Johannesburg, D. M. B. Tutu *b.* 1931 1985
  Bps. Suff., M. S. Ndwandwe, *b.* 1928 (1978);
  J. S. Nkoane, *b.* 1929 (1982).
Kimberley & Kuruman, G. A. Swartz, *b.* 1928 ... 1983
Lebombo, D. S. Sengulane, *b.* 1946 1976
Lesotho, P. S. Mokuku, *b.* 1935 1978
  Bp. Suff., D. P. Nestor, *b.* 1938 1980
Namibia, J. H. Kauluma, *b.* 1933 1981

Sees	Apptd.

Natal, M. Nuttall, *b.* 1934 1982
  Bp. Suff., A. Mkhize, *b.* 1929 1980
Niassa, (vacant).
Port Elizabeth, B. R. Evans, *b.* 1929 1974
Pretoria, R. A. Kraft, *b.* 1936 1982
  Bp. Suff., J. H. G. Ruston, *b.* 1929 1983
St. Helena, E. A. C. Cannan, *b.* 1920 1974
St. John's, J. Z. Dlamini, *b.* 1935 1985
Swaziland, B. L. N. Mkhabela, *b.* 1926 1975
Zululand, L. B. Zulu, *b.* 1937 1975

PROVINCE OF THE WEST INDIES

Archbishop of West Indies

Windward Islands, The Most Rev. George Cuthbert Manning Woodroffe, K.B.E., *Archbishop
and Metropolitan, b.* 1918 (*cons.* 1969) 1980

The Rt. Rev. Bishops

Antigua, O. U. Lindsay, *b.* 1928 (*cons.* 1970) 1970
Barbados, D. W. Gomez, *b.* 1937 (*cons.* 1972) .. 1972
Belize, K. A. McMillan (*cons.* 1980) 1980
Guyana, R. O. George, *b.* 1924 (*cons.* 1976) 1980
Jamaica, N. W. de Souza (*cons.* 1973) 1979
  Bps. Suff. (*Mandeville*), W. A. Murray (1976);
  (*Montego Bay*), A. C. Reid (1980)
Nassau and the Bahamas, M. H. Eldon, C.M.G.
  (*cons.* 1971) 1972
Trinidad, C. O. Abdulah (*cons.* 1970) 1970
Windward Islands, (see above).

As the Province of Nigeria came into being on
Feb. 24, 1979, the rest of the Province of West Africa
continues to function as the (On-going) Province of
West Africa:

PROVINCE OF WEST AFRICA

Archbishop

Liberia, The Most Rev. George Daniel Browne,
D.D.
  Bp. Suff., Rt. Rev. Edward W. Neufville.

The Rt. Rev. Bishops

Accra, F. W. B. Thompson; *Bo*, M. Keili; *Cape
Coast*, J. Ackon; *Freetown*, P. E. S. Thompson;
Kumasi, E. K. Yeboah; *Gambia and Guinea*, J.
R. Elisee; *Liberia*, (see above); *Koforidua*, R.
Okine; *Sekondi*, T. Annobil; *Sunyani/Tamale*,
J. Dadson.

PROVINCE OF NIGERIA

Archbishop

Ibadan, The Most Rev. Timothy Omotayo Olu-
fosoye (*cons.* 1965) *elected Archbp. of Nigeria* .1979

The Rt. Rev. Bishops

Lagos, J. A. Adetuloge 1985
The Niger, J. A. Onyemelukwe................. 1975
Niger Delta, S. O. Elenwa 1981
Ondo, S. O. Aderin 1981
Kaduna, T. E. Ogbonyomi 1975
Owerri, B. C. Nwankiti....................... 1968
Benin, J. K. George 1985
Ekiti, J. A. Adetiloye 1970
Enugu, G. N. Otubelu 1969
Aba, H. A. I. Afonya 1957
Kwara, H. Haruna........................... 1974
Ilesa, G. I. O. Olajide 1981
Egba-Egbado, T. I. Akintayo 1977
Ijebu, E. O. I. Ogundana 1984
Asaba, R. N. C. Nwosu 1977
Kano, B. B. Ayam 1980
Jos, T. E. I. Adesola 1985
Warri, J. O. Dafiewhare 1980
Akure, E. B. Gbonigi 1983
Owo, A. O. Awosan 1983

Sees	Apptd.
Akoko, J. L. Akeredolu	1983
Akigwe/Orlu, S. C. N. Ebo	1985

PROVINCE OF CENTRAL AFRICA

Archbishop

Botswana, The Most Rev. W. P. K. Makhulu, *b.* 1935 (*cons.* 1979) 1980

The Rt. Rev. Bishops

Central Zambia, C. W. Hlanya, *b.* 1933 (*cons.* 1984)	1984
Lake Malawi, P. N. Nyanja, *b.* 1940 (*cons.* 1978)	1978
Lundi, J. Siyachitema, *b.* 1932 (*cons.* 1981)	1981
Lusaka, S. S. Mumba, *b.* 1939 (*cons.* 1981)	1981
Manicaland, E. Masuko (*cons.* 1981)	1981
Mashonaland, R. P. Hatendi, *b.* 1927 (*cons.* 1979)	1981
Matabeleland, R. W. S. Mercer, *b.* 1935 (*cons.* 1977)	1977
Northern Zambia, J. Mabula, *b.* 1922 (*cons.* 1971)	1971
Southern Malawi, D. D. Ainani, *b.* 1921 (*cons.* 1979)	1981

PROVINCE OF KENYA

Archbishop

Nairobi, The Most Rev. Manasses Kuria 1979

The Rt. Rev. Bishops

Eldoret	
Maseno North, J. Mundia	1970
Maseno South, H. Okullu	1974
Asst. Bp., D. J. Omolo	1981
Mombasa, P. Mwang'ombe	1964
Bp. Coadjutor, C. Nzano, (*cons.* 1975)	1978
Mount Kenya East, D. Gitari	1975
Mount Kenya South, (vacant).	
Nakuru, L. Kamau	1979

PROVINCE OF TANZANIA

Archbishop

Zanzibar and Tanga, The Most Rev. J. Ramadhani 1984

The Rt. Rev. Bishops

Central Tanganyika, Y. Madinda, *b.* 1926 (*cons.* 1964)	1971
Dar es Salaam, C. Mlangwa	1984
Kagera, Christoper Ruhuza	1985
Mara, Gershom Nyaronga	1985
Masasi, C. R. Norgate	1984
Morogoro, G. Chitemo	1965
Ruvuma, M. Ngahyoma	1971
South West Tanganyika, C. Mwaigoga	1983
Victoria Nyanza, J. Rusibamayila	1976
Western Tanganyika, G. E. Mpango	1983
Mount Kilimanjaro, A. Mohamed	1982

PROVINCE OF UGANDA

Archbishop

Kampala, The Most Rev. Dr. Y. Okoth (*cons.* 1972)	1984
Asst. Bp., A. L. Gonahasa	1985

The Rt. Rev. Bishops

Ankole, A. Betungura	1970
Bukedi, N. E. Okille	1984
Bunyoro, Y. Rwakaikara	1981
Busoga, C. Bamwoze	1972
Karamoja, H. Davies	1981
Kigezi, F. Kivengere	1972
Asst. Bp., W. Rukirande	1975
Lango, M. Otim	1976
Asst. Bp., W. Okodi	1979
Madi and West Nile, R. Ringtho (*cons.* 1976)	1977

Sees	Apptd.
Mbale, A. M. Wesonga	1981
Mityana, Y. Mukasa	1977
Mukono, L. Mpalanyi-Nkoyoyo	1985
Namirembe, M. Kauma	1985
North Kigezi, Y. Ruhindi	1981
Northern Uganda, B. Ogwal	1974
Asst. Bp., G. Oboma	1979
Ruwenzori, E. Kamanyire	1981
Soroti, G. Ilukor	1976
South Ruwenzori, Zebedee Masereka	1984
West Ankole, Y. Bamunoba	1977
West Buganda, C. Senyonjo	1974

PROVINCE OF BURUNDI, RWANDA AND ZAIRE

Archbishop

Butare, The Most Rev. J. Ndandali (*cons.* 1975) 1982

The Rt. Rev. Bishops

Boga Zaire, P. Njojo	1980
Bukavu, B. Dirokpa	1982
Asst. Bp., K. Mbona	1980
Bujumbura, S. Sindamuka	1975
Buye, S. Ndayisenga	1979
Kigali, A. Sebununguri.	
Kisangani, S. T. Mugera	1980
Shyira, A. Nshamihigo.	

PROVINCE OF THE INDIAN OCEAN

Archbishop

Seychelles, F. Chang-Him 1984

The Rt. Rev. Bishops

Antananarivo, R. Rabenirina	1984
Antsiranana, K. Benzies	1982
Mauritius, R. Donat	1984
Toamasina, F. Razakariasy	1984

ANGLICAN COUNCIL OF SOUTH AMERICA

The Rt. Rev. Bishops

Argentina and E. S. America, R. S. Cutts	1975
Chile, C. F. Bazley (*cons.* 1969)	1977
Asst. Bps., I. Morrison (1977); B. Skinner	1978
Northern Argentina, D. Leake (*cons.* 1969)	1980
Asst. Bp., M. Mariño	1975
Paraguay, O. Ortiz (*cons.* 1982)	1985
Peru and Bolivia, D. Evans	1978

UNDER THE ARCHBISHOP OF CANTERBURY

The Rt. Rev. Bishops

Bermuda, C. C. Luxmoore.	
Pusan, W. Choi	1974
Kuching, (vacant).	
Lusitanian Church in Portugal, F. Soares	1981
Sabah, Chhoa Heng Sze	1971
Seoul, S. S. Kim.	
Singapore, M. Tay	1982
Spanish Reformed Episcopal Church, A. Sanchez	1982
Taejon, M. Pae	1974
West Malaysia, J. G. Savarimuthu	1973

THE EPISCOPAL CHURCH IN JERUSALEM AND THE MIDDLE EAST

President-Bishop, Rt. Rev. H. B. Dehqani-Tafti	1976
Asst. Bp., A. K. Cragg	1970
Jerusalem, S. Kafity	1984

Sees	Apptd.
Iran, H. B. Dehqani-Tafti	1961
Egypt, G. Abdel Malik	1984
Cyprus and the Gulf, H. Moore	1983

PROVINCE OF BRAZIL

Primate

(Acting) Rt. Rev. E. K. Sherrill, *b.* 1925 *(cons. 1959)* ... 1983

The Rt. Rev. Bishops

Brasilia, A. G. Sória, *b.* 1922 *(cons. 1977)* ... 1985
Central Brazil, S. A. Ruiz, *b.* 1932 *(cons. 1985)* ... 1985
Northern Brazil, C. E. Rodrigues, *b.* 1935 *(cons. 1985)* ... 1986
South Central Brazil, S. Takatsu, *b.* 1927 *(cons. 1977)* ... 1977
Southern Brazil, C. V. S. Gastal, *b.* 1937 *(cons. 1984)* ... 1985
Southwestern Brazil, O. V. Luiz, *b.* 1938 *(cons. 1976)* ... 1976

PROVINCE OF BURMA

Archbishop

Rangoon, The Most Rev. Gregory Hla Gyaw, *(cons. 1973)* ... 1979

Sees	Apptd.
The Rt. Rev. Bishops	
Akyab, B. Theaung Hawi, *(cons. 1973)*	1980
Mandalay, T. Mya Wah, *(cons. 1984)*	1984
Pa'an, G. Kyaw Mya, *(cons. 1979)*	1979

THE HOLY CATHOLIC CHURCH IN JAPAN

(Nippon Sei Ko Kai)

Primate

Hokkaido, The Rt. Rev. John Masanao Watanabe, *b.* 1916 *(cons. 1969)* ... 1983

The Rt. Rev. Bishops

Chubu, A. J. Uematsu, *b.* 1916 *(cons. 1976)* ... 1976
Kita Kanto, J. T. Yashiro, *b.* 1931 *(cons. 1985)* ... 1985
Kobe, P. K. Yashiro, *b.* 1924 *(cons. 1984)* ... 1984
Kyoto, St. George J. Yagi, *b.* 1928 *(cons. 1979)* ... 1979
Kyushu, J. N. Iida, *b.* 1929 *(cons. 1982)* ... 1982
Okinawa, P. S. Nakamura, *b.* 1927 *(cons. 1972)* ... 1972
Osaka, C. I. Kikawada, *b.* 1925 *(cons. 1975)* ... 1975
Tohoku, C. Y. Tazaki, *b.* 1923 *(cons. 1979)* ... 1979
Tokyo, J. J. Yamada, *b.* 1917 *(cons. 1982)* ... 1982
Yokohama, R. S. Kajiwara, *b.* 1932 *(cons. 1984)* ... 1984

THE CHURCH OF SCOTLAND

Church Office, 121 George Street, Edinburgh EH2 4YN

THE CHURCH OF SCOTLAND is Presbyterian in constitution, and is governed by Kirk Sessions, Presbyteries, Synods, and the General Assembly, which consists of both representative ministers and elders, in equal numbers from each of the Presbyteries. It is presided over by a Moderator (chosen annually by the Assembly), to whom Her Majesty the Queen has granted precedence in Scotland, during his term of office, next after the Lord Chancellor of Great Britain. The Sovereign, if not present in person, is represented by a Lord High Commissioner, who is appointed each year by the Crown. The country, for Church purposes, is divided into 12 Synods and 46 Presbyteries, and there are about 2,000 ministers and licentiates engaged in ministerial and other work. The figures at Dec. 31, 1984, were:—

Congregations, 1,765; total membership 887,165. There are 135 ministers and other personnel working with partner Churches and in expatriate charges in 26 countries.

LORD HIGH COMMISSIONER (1985), The Lord Maclean, P.C., K.T., G.C.V.O., K.B.E.

MODERATOR OF THE ASSEMBLY (1985), Right Rev. D. M. B. A. Smith, M.A.
Principal Clerk, Rev. J. L. Weatherhead, M.A.
Deputy Clerk, Rev. A. G. McGillivray, M.A., B.D.
Procurator, G. Penrose, Q.C.
Law Agent and Solicitor of the Church, R. A. Paterson, M.A. Ll.B.
Parliamentary Solicitor, Colin McCulloch (London).
General Treasurer, W. G. P. Colledge, C.A.

THE PRESBYTERIAN CHURCH IN IRELAND.—The largest of the Presbyterian churches in Ireland consists of 22 presbyteries, 426 ministers, 566 congregations, with 132,802 communicants, 124,048 families and 6,624 Sunday-school teachers. During the 12 months ended Dec. 31, 1984, there was contributed by congregational effort £3,187,869 plus IR£237,284 for religious, charitable, and missionary purposes. The total income for the period raised by congregations for all purposes was £15,024,181 plus IR£1,093,703.—
General Sec., Very Rev. T. J. Simpson, M.A., D.D., Church House, Belfast, BT1 6DW.

UNITED REFORMED CHURCH

The United Reformed Church was formed by the union of the Congregational Church in England and Wales and the Presbyterian Church of England on October 5, 1972. The Re-formed Association of Churches of Christ were joined to the URC on September 26, 1981. It is divided into 12 Provinces, each with a Provincial Moderator, and 70 Districts. There are 136,000 members and 1,000 serving ministers of whom 100 are auxiliary and 500 give voluntary service. It shares an international mission through the Council for World Mission and is a member of the

British and World Council of Churches. Its ministers are trained at five recognized colleges.
General Sec., Rev. B. G. Thorogood, M.A., 86 Tavistock Place, WC1H 9RT

The majority of those members of the Congregational Church who did not join the United Reformed Church comprise the Congregational Federation. *Sec.*, J. B. Wilcox, The Congregational Centre, 4 Castle Gate, Nottingham.

THE EPISCOPAL CHURCH IN SCOTLAND

Sees. The Rt. Rev. Bishops.	Cons. Clgy.	Stipd.
Aberdeen and Orkney, Frederick Charles Darwent	1978..12	£8,635
Argyll and the Isles, George Kennedy Buchanan Henderson, M.A., *b.* 1921	1977..11	£10,238
Brechin, Lawrence Edward Luscombe, *b.* 1925	1975..16	£6,549
Edinburgh, Alastair Iain Macdonald Haggart, M.A., *b.* 1915.	1975..65	£8,064

Sees. The Rt. Rev. Bishops.	Cons. Clgy.	Stipd.
Glasgow and Galloway, Derek Alec Rawcliffe, O.B.E., *b.* 1919	1981..41	£8,349
Moray, Ross and Caithness, George Minshull Sessford, M.A., *b.* 1928	1970..17	£6,800
St. Andrews, Dunkeld and Dunblane, Michael Geoffrey Hare-Duke, M.A., *b.* 1925	1969..26	£6,770

Registrar of the Episcopal Synod, I. R. Guild, W.S., 16 Charlotte Square, Edinburgh EH2 4YS
Churches, Mission Stations, &c., 339. Clergy, 221; Communicants, 38,420.

THE CHURCH OF IRELAND

Sees	Archbishops	Apptd.	Clgy.
Armagh*	Most Rev. John Ward Armstrong, D.D., *b.* 1915 (*cons.* 1968)	1980	52
Dublin	Most Rev. Donald Arthur Caird, D.D., *b.* 1925 (*cons.* 1970)	1985	63
	Bishops		
Meath & Kildare	(vacant)		23
Cashel & Ossory	Rt. Rev. Noel Vincent Willoughby, M.A., *b.* 1926	1980	35
Clogher	Rt. Rev. Gordon McMullan, Ph.D., B.Sc., *b.* 1934	1980	29
Connor	Rt. Rev. William John McCappin, B.D., *b.* 1919	1981	98
Cork, Cloyne & Ross	Rt. Rev. Samuel Greenfield Poyntz, Ph.D., B.D., *b.* 1926	1978	24
Derry & Raphoe	Rt. Rev. James Mehaffey, B.D., Ph.D., *b.* 1931	1980	49
Down & Dromore	Rt. Rev. Robert Henry Alexander Eames, Ll.B., Ph.D., *b.* 1937 (*cons.* 1975)	1980	96
Kilmore, Elphin & Ardagh	Rt. Rev. William Gilbert Wilson, B.D., Ph.D., *b.* 1918	1981	21
Limerick & Killaloe	Rt. Rev. Walton Newcombe Francis Empey, B.D., *b.* 1934	1981	15
Tuam	Rt. Rev. John Coote Duggan, B.D., *b.* 1918	1969	9

**Primate.*

St. Patrick's National Cathedral, Dublin. *Dean and Ordinary,* Very Rev. V. G. B. Griffin, Ph.D., B.A.

Chief Officer and Secretary to the Representative Church Body, H. R. Roberts, Church of Ireland House, Church Avenue, Rathmines, Dublin 6.

THE METHODIST CHURCH

The Methodist Church is governed primarily by the Conference, secondarily by the District Synods (held in the autumn and the spring), consisting of all the ministers and of selected laymen in each district, over which a chairman, who is a minister, is appointed by the Conference; and thirdly by the circuit meeting of the ministers and lay officers of each circuit. The authority of both Synods and Circuit Meetings is subordinate to the Conference, which has the supreme legislative and judicial power in Methodism.

President of the Conference (July 1985–86), Rev. C. Hughes Smith, M.A.
Vice-President of the Conference (July 1985–86), L. Murray, J.P.
Secretary of the Conference, Rev. B. E. Beck, D.D., 1 Central Buildings, Westminster, S.W.1.
President Designate (1986–87), Rev. N. L. Gilson, D.F.C., M.A.
Vice-President Designate (1986–87), Mrs. A. M. Knighton.

Statistics.—In 1984 in association with the Conference in Great Britain there were 3,457 Ministers, 13,984 Local Preachers, 458,592 Members in 7,659 churches. Statistics are published triennially.

The World Methodist Council, founded 1881, reorganized 1951, associates Methodism throughout the world in 90 countries.

The Methodist Church was founded in 1739 by the two brothers Wesley and rapidly spread throughout the British Isles and to America before 1770. The Methodist Church in Great Britain was united in 1932 by the fusion of the Wesleyan Methodist Church which was the original section, the Primitive Methodist Church, which arose through the evangelists Hugh Bourne and William Clowes in 1810, and the United Methodist Church, itself a fusion in 1907 of the Methodist New Connexion which dated from 1797, the Bible Christian Methodist Church, which dated from 1815 and the United Methodist Free Churches which originated in controversies in 1828 and 1849. The United Methodist Church of America was formed by a union of United Methodist denominations with the United Evangelical Brethren.

Methodist Church in Ireland

The Methodist Church in Ireland has 195 Ministers, 280 Lay Preachers, 20,949 Adult and 13,894 Junior Members.

President, (1985–86), Rev. H. Skillen.

Secretary, Rev. C. G. Eyre, B.A., 3 Upper Malone Road, Belfast, BT9 6TD.

The United Church of Canada

85 St. Clair Ave. E., Toronto, Ontario M4T 1M8

The United Church of Canada is the result of the union (1925) of Methodist, Presbyterian and Congregational Churches in Canada. Subsequently several other communions have become part of the Church.

Moderator, Rt. Rev. Robert F. Smith, TH.D.

Secretary, Rev. P. A. Cline.

Independent Methodists

Independent Methodists.—This body is Congregational in its organization, with an unpaid Ministry. Its first Conference was held in 1805. In 1985 there

were in Great Britain 135 Ministers, 4,246 Members, 114 Churches and 3,986 Sunday scholars. *Gen. Sec.,* Rev. J. M. Day, The Old Police House, Croxton, Stafford ST21 6PE.

Wesleyan Reform Union

This Union is Methodist in doctrine, Congregational in government, with, if any church desires it, a paid ministry. It is the remnant of the original Reformers expelled from Wesleyan Methodism in 1849. The adherents are mainly in the Midland and Northern counties. In 1985 there were in Great Britain 20 Ministers, 133 Lay Preachers, 3,331 Members, 133 Churches and 2,412 Sunday School scholars.—*President,* H. Sykes, Wombwell, Barnsley. *General Secretary and Connexional Editor,* Rev. D. A. Morris, Wesleyan Reform Church House, 123 Queen Street, Sheffield 1.

THE PRESBYTERIAN CHURCH OF WALES

The PRESBYTERIAN OR CALVINISTIC METHODIST CHURCH OF WALES is the only Church of purely Welsh origin, and embraces a very large section of the Welsh-speaking population. Its form of government is Presbyterian, and it is a constituent of the World Alliance of Reformed Churches.

In 1985 the body numbered—chapels and other buildings, 1,200; ministers in pastoral charge, 168; elders, 4,917; communicants, 75,092; Sunday scholars, 25,343.

The *Association in the East* which includes nine of the English Presbyteries was formed in 1947.

Moderator of General Assembly (1985–86), Rev. T. Noel Roberts, Ruthin.

Moderators of Associations (1985–86) *South Wales,* R. G. A. Richards, Swansea; *North Wales,* Rev. T. J. Griffith, Llandrillo-yn-Rhos, Clwyd; *East Wales,* Rev. G. Evans, Wenvoe, Cardiff CF5 6AD.

General Secretary, Rev. D. H. Owen, 53 Richmond Road, Cardiff CF2 3UP

The Baptists have over 35,000,000 members in all countries. In Britain they are for the most part grouped in Associations of churches, and the majority of these belong to the Baptist Union, which was formed in 1812. Current statistics show that there are 2,070 churches and 166,688 members. There also exist separate Baptist Unions of Scotland (159 churches and 16,471 members); Wales (599 churches and 33,146 members); Ireland (91 churches and 7,949 members). *President of the Baptist Union of Great Britain and Ireland,* (1985–86), Rev. N. P. Wright. *Secretary,* Rev. B. Green, M.A., B.D. *Office,* 4 Southampton Row, WC1B 4AB

THE JEWS

It is estimated that about 410,000 Jews are resident in the British Isles, some 280,000 being domiciled in Greater London.

The *Board of Deputies of British Jews,* established in 1760, is the representative body of British Jewry and is recognized by H.M. Government. The basis of representation is mainly synagogal, but secular organizations are also represented. It is a deliberative body and its objects are to watch over the interests of British Jewry, to protect Jews against any disability which they may suffer by reason of their creed and to take such action as may be conducive to their welfare.

President, Dr. Lionel Kopelowitz, J.P.

Secretary General, Hayim Pinner.

Office, Woburn House, Upper Woburn Place, W.C.1.

CHIEF RABBI—Sir Immanuel Jakobovits, KT., PH.D.

Executive Officer, S. Cohen. *Office,* Adler House, Tavistock Square, W.C.1.

The *Beth Din* (Court of Judgment) is a rabbinic body consisting of *Dayanim* (Assessors) and the Chief Rabbi, who is President of the Court. The Court arbitrates when requested in cases between Jew and Jew and Jew and non-Jew and gives decisions on religious questions. The decisions are based on Jewish Law and practice and do not conflict with the law of the land. The *Beth Din* also deals with matters concerning dietary law and marriages and divorces, according to Jewish Law.

Dayanim, Rabbi C. Ehrentreu; Rabbi Dr. I. Lerner; Rabbi C. D. Kaplin; Rabbi I. D. Berger.

Clerk to the Court, Rabbi B. Berkovits, Adler House, Tavistock Square, W.C.1.

OTHER RELIGIOUS DENOMINATIONS

The General Assembly of Unitarian and Free Christian Churches has about 95 ministers, 250 chapels and other places of worship in Great Britain and Ireland. *Gen. Sec.,* Dr. R. W. Smith, Essex Hall, Essex Street, WC2R 3HY

The Salvation Army, first known as the Christian Mission, was founded by William Booth in the East End of London in 1865. In 1878 it took its present name and adopted a quasi-military method of government. Since then it has become established in over

80 countries of the world. The head of the denomination, known as the General, is elected by a High Council, consisting of all active Commissioners and Territorial Commanders who have held the rank of Colonel for at least two years. In 1983 there were in Great Britain, 1,044 Corps (Churches), 125 Social Services Centres and 1,812 Officers engaged in evangelistic and social work. The latest statistics for the world (1983) are 15,135 Corps, 4,449 Social Services Centres (including institutions and schools) and 24,808 Officers. *General,* Jarl Wahlström. *Interna-*

tional Headquarters:— 101 Queen Victoria Street, E.C.4.

The Religious Society of Friends (Quakers), founded in the 17th century, has no separated ministry. There are in Great Britain 447 places of worship and 18,045 members (world membership 210,398). *Central Offices (Great Britain),* Friends House, Euston Road, NW1 2BJ; *(Ireland),* 6 Eustace Street, Dublin.

The First Church of Christ, Scientist, in Boston Massachusetts, U.S.A. (District Manager, Committees on Publication for Great Britain and Ireland, 108 Palace Gardens Terrace, W.8), has about 240 branch churches and societies in Great Britain and Ireland.

The Moravian Church, 5 Muswell Hill, N.10, has in the U.K. 40 congregations with 4,000 members.

The Free Church of England (otherwise called The Reformed Episcopal Church) has 33 churches in England. *Gen. Sec.,* Rt. Rev. A. Ward, 28 Sedgebrook, Swindon, Wilts.

The Seventh Day Adventists (*Hdqrs.,* Stanborough Park, Watford, Herts. WD2 6JP), have more than 200 organized churches and companies and more than 15,950 members in the British Isles. *Executive Sec.,* E. W. Howell.

The Spiritualists in Britain have 900 churches and societies.

THE ROMAN CATHOLIC CHURCH

HIS HOLINESS POPE JOHN PAUL II (Karol Wojtyla), *born* in Wadowice, Poland, May 18, 1920; *ordained priest* November 1, 1946; appointed *Archbishop of Krakow* January 13, 1964, created *Cardinal* at a Consistory on June 26, 1967. Formally assumed Pontificate October 16, 1978.

THE SACRED COLLEGE OF CARDINALS, when complete, consisted of six Cardinal Bishops, fifty Cardinal Priests and fourteen Cardinal Deacons. This number was fixed by Pope Sixtus V in 1586. Pope John XXIII created 52 new Cardinals. Pope Paul VI created 27 new Cardinals on Feb. 22, 1965, 27 on June 26, 1967, 33 on Apr. 28 1969, 30 on March 5, 1973, 20 on May 24, 1976, 4 on June 27, 1977; Pope John Paul II created 15 new Cardinals on June 30, 1979, 18 on Feb. 2, 1983, 28 on May 25, 1985. In July 1985 there were 153 Cardinals. The Cardinals are advisers and assistants of the Sovereign Pontiff and form the supreme council or Senate of the Church. On the death of the Pope they elect his successor. The assembly of the Cardinals at the Vatican for the election of a new Pope is known as the Conclave in which, in complete seclusion, the Cardinals elect by secret ballot; a two-thirds majority is necessary before the vote can be accepted as final. When a Cardinal receives the necessary votes the Dean of the Sacred College formally asks him if he will accept election and the name by which he wishes to be known. On his acceptance of the office the Conclave is dissolved and the First Cardinal Deacon announces the election to the assembled crowd in St. Peter's Square. On the first Sunday or Holyday following the election the new Pope assumes the pontificate at High Mass in St. Peter's Square. A new pontificate is dated from the assumption of the pontificate.

FORMS OF ADDRESS: *Cardinal,* "His Eminence Cardinal . . ." (if an Archbishop, "His Eminence the Cardinal Archbishop of . . ."); *Archbishop,* "The Most Rev. Archbishop of . . ."; *Bishop,* "The Rt. Rev. Bishop of . . ."

THE CURIA

The Curia or governing body of the Roman Catholic Church is made up of various administrative departments headed by the Secretariat of State and the Sacred Council for the Public Affairs of the Church. Below these are congregations, secretariats and tribunals assisted by commissions and offices. All are headed by Cardinals who have as their British equivalent the Ministers or Secretaries of State heading the various government departments.

The Vatican State has as with any nation its own diplomatic service although its representatives are officially acknowledged in different ways throughout the countries of the World. Where the representation is only to the local churches and not to the government of that country then the man appointed is an Apostolic Delegate as was the case in Britain until recently. However where the representative is recognized as having diplomatic status by a particular government then he is known as either a nuncio, pro nuncio or inter nuncio. Nuncios are Papal Ambassadors who are given precedence over all other ambassadors by their appointed country and are the doyens of the diplomatic corps. In countries where precedence is not recognized, as in Britain, the papal representative is known as a pro nuncio.

Apostolic Pro Nuncio to Great Britain, awaiting appointment, 54 Parkside, Wimbledon, SW19.

British Ambassador Extraordinary and Plenipotentiary to the Holy See, His Excellency Sir Mark Evelyn Heath, K.C.V.O., C.M.G., Via Condotti 91, 00187 Rome, Italy.

THE BISHOPS' CONFERENCES

The Roman Catholic church **in England and Wales** is governed by:

1. **The Bishops' Conference** which consists of the local ordinaries (the Diocesan Bishops) of any rite; coadjutor bishops and auxiliaries; and titular bishops with special tasks. They are headed by the President, Cardinal Basil Hume and Vice President, Archbishop Worlock, Archbishop of Liverpool.

2. **The Bishops' Standing Committee** made up of the Metropolitans (Archbishops) and department heads. It has general responsibility for continuity and policy between the Plenary Sessions of the Conference and for the preparation of the agenda and implementation of Conference decisions. This committee is serviced by the General Secretariat.

There are six departments each with an episcopal chairman which look after the life of the church within England and Wales. The departments and their heads are as follows:

(a) Department for Christian Life and Worship: Archbishop Bowen (*Southwark*).
(b) Department for Mission and Unity: Bishop Clark (*East Anglia*).
(c) Department for Christian Doctrine and Formation: Bishop Konstant (*Central London*).
(d) Department for Social Responsibility: Bishop Harris (*Middlesbrough*).
(e) Department for Christian Citizenship: Bishop McCartie (*Auxiliary in Birmingham*).
(f) Department for International Affairs: Bishop O'Brien (*Hertfordshire*).

As well as the above the Conference has agencies and consultative bodies affiliated to it and all are serviced by the General Secretariat headed by a General Secretary namely:

England & Wales: *President*, H. E. Cardinal George Basil Hume, Archbishop of Westminster, Archbishop's House, Westminster, London, SW1P 1QJ

Scotland: *President*, H. E. Cardinal Gordon Joseph Gray, Archbishop of St. Andrews and Edinburgh, Archbishop's House, 42 Grenhill Gardens, Edinburgh, EH10 4BJ

Ireland (there is one hierarchy covering both North and South): *President*, H. E. Cardinal Tomás Ó Fiaich, Archbishop of Armagh, "Ara Coeli", Armagh, Ireland.

ENGLAND AND WALES

Apostolic Pro-Nuncio to the United Kingdom of Great Britain and Northern Ireland, The Most Rev. Bruno Heim.

The Most Revd. Archbishops		Cons.	Clgy.
Westminster, H.E. Cardinal Basil Hume			
(1976)		1976	926
Auxil., Basil C. Butler		1966	
Auxil., Victor Guazzelli		1970	
Auxil., Philip Harvey		1977	
Auxil., David Konstant		1977	
Auxil., Gerald Mahon		1970	
Auxil., James J. O'Brien		1977	
Birmingham, Maurice Couve de Murville			
(1982)		1982	526
Auxil., Joseph Cleary		1965	
Auxil., Patrick L. McCartie		1977	
Cardiff, John A. Ward (1983)		1981	186
Auxil., Daniel Mullins		1970	
Liverpool, Derek Worlock (1976)		1965	563
Auxil., Anthony Hitchen		1979	
Auxil., Kevin O'Connor		1979	
Auxil., John Rawsthorne		1982	
Southwark, Michael Bowen (1977)		1970	573
Auxil., Charles Henderson		1972	
Auxil., Howard Tripp		1980	
Auxil., John Jukes		1980	

The Rt. Revd. Bishops		
Arundel and Brighton, Cormac Murphy-O'Connor	1977	331
Brentwood, Thomas McMahon (1980)	1980	214
Clifton, Mervyn Alexander (1975)	1972	246
East Anglia, Alan Clark (1976)	1969	125
Hallam, Gerald Moverley (1980)	1968	106
Hexham and Newcastle, Hugh Lindsay (1975)	1970	340
Auxil., Owen Swindelhurst	1977	
Lancaster, Brian C. Foley	1962	265
Coadjutor, John Brewer (1971)	1983	
Auxil., Thomas Pearson	1949	
Leeds, William Gordon Wheeler (1966)	1964	299
Menevia (Wales), James Hannigan	1983	141
Middlesbrough, Augustine Harris (1978)	1966	208
Auxil., Thomas O'Brien	1982	
Northampton, Francis Thomas	1982	182
Nottingham, James McGuinness (1975)	1972	250
Plymouth, Cyril Restieaux	1955	187
Portsmouth, Anthony Emery (1976)	1968	355
Salford, Patrick Kelly	1984	490
Auxil., Geoffrey Burke	1967	
Shrewsbury, Joseph Gray (1980)	1969	255

SCOTLAND

The Most Revd. Archbishops		
St. Andrews & Edinburgh, H.E. Cardinal Gordon Gray	1951	250
Auxil., James Monaghan	1970	

Glasgow, Thomas Winning (1974)	1972	374
Auxil., John Mone		
Auxil., Charles Renfrew	1977	

The Rt. Revd. Bishops		
Aberdeen, Mario Conti	1977	57
Argyll & Isles, Colin MacPherson	1969	39
Dunkeld, Vincent Logan	1981	75
Galloway, Maurice Taylor	1981	82
Motherwell, Joseph Devine		203
Paisley, Stephen McGill (1969)	1960	94

NORTHERN IRELAND†

Nuncio to Ireland, Most Rev. Gaetano Alibrandi (Archbishop of Bindi)

The Most Revd. Archbishop

Armagh, H.E. Cardinal Thomas O'Fiaich	1977	278
Auxil., James Lennon	1980	

The Rt. Revd. Bishops		
Clogher, Joseph Duffy	1979	140
Derry, Edward Daly	1974	155
Down & Connor, Cahal Daly (1982)	1967	
Dromore, Francis Brooks	1976	74
Kilmore, Francis McKiernan	1972	133

RESIDENTIAL ARCHBISHOPRICS THROUGHOUT THE WORLD

NOTE: This list is set out with the name of the relevant country first; then the name of the diocese; and finally the Archbishop's name. It does not include England and Wales or Scotland which are above.

Albania

Durrës, vacant.
Shkodrë, vacant. (Apostolic Administrator: Monsignor Ernesto Coba.)

Algeria

Alger, H.E. Cardinal Leon-Etienne Duval.

Angola

Huambo, Manuel Franklin da Costa.
Luanda, Eduardo André Muaca.
Lubango, H.E. Cardinal Alexandre do Nascimento.

Argentina

Bahia Blanca, Jorge Mayer.
Buenos Aires, H.E. Cardinal Juan Carlos Aramburu.
Cordoba, H.E. Cardinal Raúl Francisco Primatesta.
Corrientes, Fortunato A. Rossi.
La Plata, Antonio José Plaza.
Mendoza, Candido Genaro Rubido.
Paraná, Adolfo Servando Tortolo.
Resistencia, Juan J. Iriarte.
Rosario, vacant.
Salta, Moises J. Blanchoud.
San Juan de Cuyo, Italo Severino Di Stefano.
Santa Fe, Edgardo Gabriel Storni.
Tucumán, Horatio A. Bozzoli.

Australia

Adelaide, James William Gleeson.
Brisbane, Francis Roberts Rush.
Canberra, Francis P. Carroll.
Hobart, Guilford Clyde Young.
Melbourne, Thomas Francis Little.

---

† There is one hierarchy for the whole of Ireland. Several of the Dioceses listed above have territory partly in the Republic of Ireland and partly in Northern Ireland.

Perth, William J. Foley.
Sydney, Edward B. Clancy.

Austria

Salzburg, Karl Berg.
Wien, H.E. Cardinal Franz Konig.

Bangladesh

Dhaka, Michael Rozario.

Belgium

Malines-Bruxelles, H.E. Cardinal Godfried Danneels.

Benin

Cotonou, Christophe Adimou.

Bolivia

Cochabamba, Gennaro Prata.
La Paz, Jorge Manrique Hurtado.
Santa Cruz de la Sierra, Luis Rodriguez Pardo.
Sucre, Rene Fernandez Apaza.

Brazil

Aparacida, Geraldo Maria de Morais Penido.
Aracaju, Luciano José Cabral Duarte.
Belem do Pará, Alberto Guadêncio Ramos.
Belo Horizonte, João Rezende Costa.
Botucatú, Vincent Marchetti Zioni.
Brasilia, Jose Freire Falcao.
Campinas, Gilberto Pereira Lopes.
Campo Grande, Antonio Barbosa.
Cascavel, Armando Cirio.
Cuiaba, Bonifacio Piccinini.
Curitiba, Pedro Antonio Fedalto.
Diamantina, Geraldo Majelo Reis.
Florianópolis, Afonso Niehues.
Fortaleza, H.E. Cardinal Aloisio Lorscheider.
Goiania, Fernando Gomes Dos Santos.
Juiz de Fora, Juvenal Roriz.
Londrina, Geraldo Majela Agnelo.
Maceió, vacant.
Manaus, vacant.
Mariana, Oscar de Oliveira.
Maringá, Jaime Luis Coelho.
Natal, Nivaldo Monte.
Niteroi, José Gonçalves da Costa.
Olinda & Recife, Helder Reçsoa Câmara.
Paraiba, José M. Pires.
Porto Alegre, Claudio Colling.
Porto Velho, José Martins da Silva.
Pouso Alegre, José D'Angelo Neto.
Ribeirão Preto, Romeu Alberti.
São Luis do Maranhão, Paulo Eduardo Andrade Ponte.
São Paulo, H.E. Cardinal Paulo Evaristo Arns.
São Salvador da Bahia, H.E. Cardinal Avelar Brandão Vilela.
São Sebastião do Rio de Janeiro, H.E. Cardinal Eugenio de Araújo Sales.
Teresina, Miguel F. Camara Filho.
Uberaba, Benedito de Ulhôa Vieira.
Vitória, Silvestre L. Scandian.

Burma

Mandalay, Alphonse U. Than Aung.
Rangoon, Gabriel Thohey.

Burundi

Gitega, Joachim Ruhuna.

Cameroon

Bamenda, Paul Verdzekov.
Douala, Simon Tonyé.
Garoua, Christian W. Tumi.
Yaoundé, Jean Zoa.

Canada

Edmonton, Joseph N. MacNeil.
Grouard-McLennon, Henri Légaré.
Halifax, James Martin Hayes.
Keewatin-Le Pas, Paul Dumouchel.
Kingston, Francis John Spence.
Moncton, Donat Chiasson.
Montréal, Paul Grégoire.
Ottawa, Joseph Aurèle Plourde.
Québec, H.E. Cardinal Louis-Albert Vachon.
Regina, Charles Halpin.
Rimouski, Gilles Ouellet.
St Boniface, Antoine Hacault.
St Johns, Newfoundland, Alphonsus L. Penney.
Sherbrooke, Jean Marie Fortier.
Toronto, H.E. Cardinal Gerald Emmett Carter.
Vancouver, James Francis Carney.
Winnipeg, Latin Rite–Adam Exnen; Ukrainian Rite–Maxim Hermaniuk.

Central Africa

Bangui, Joachim N'Dayen.

Chad

N'Djamena, Charles Vandame.

Chile

Antofagasta, Carlos Oviedo Cavada.
Conception, José Manuel Santos Ascarza.
La Serena, Bernardino Pinera Carvallo.
Puerto Montt, Eladio Vicuña Aránguiz.
Santiago de Chile, H.E. Cardinal Juan F. Fresno Larrain.

China

Anking, Huai-Ning, vacant.
Canton, Dominic Tang Yee-Ming.
Changsha, vacant.
Chunking, vacant.
Foochow, Min-Hou, vacant.
Hangchow, vacant.
Hangkow, vacant.
Kaifeng, vacant.
Kunming, vacant.
Kweyang, vacant.
Lanchow, vacant.
Mukden, vacant.
Nanchang, vacant.
Nanking, vacant.
Nanning, vacant.
Peking, vacant.
Sian, vacant.
Suiyüan, Francis Wong Hsueh-Ming.
Taiyuan, Dominic Luke Capozi (expelled 11 April 1946, now living in Nazareth, Israel).
Tsinan, vacant. (Apostolic Administrator: John P'ing Ta-Kuam).

Colombia

Barranquilla, Germán Villa Gaviria.
Bogota, Mario Revollo Bravo.
Bucaramanga, Hector Rueda Hernández.
Cali, Alberto Uribe Urdeneta.
Cartegena, Carlos Jose Ruiseco.
Ibagué, José Joaquin Flórez Hernández.
Manizales, José de Jesús Pimiento Rodriguez.
Medellin, H.E. Cardinal Alfonso López Trujillo.
Nueva Pamplona, vacant.
Popayán, Samuel Silverio Buitrago.
Tunja, Augusto Trujillo Arango.

Congo

Brazzaville, Barthélémy Batantu.

Costa Rica

San José de Costa Rica, Román Arrieta Villalobos.

Cuba

San Cristóbal de la Habana, Jaime Lucas Ortega y Alamino.
Santiago de Cuba, Pedro Meurice Estiu.

Czechoslovakia

Olomouc, vacant.
Praha, H.E. Cardinal František Tomášek.
Trnava, vacant. (Apostolic Administrator: Monsignor Julius Gábriš).

Dominican Republic

Santo Domingo, Nicolás de Jesús López Rodriguez.

Ecuador

Cuenca, Alberto Luna Tobar.
Guayaquil, Bernardino Echeveria Ruiz.
Quito, H.E. Cardinal Pablo, Muñoz Vega.

El Salvador

San Salvador, Arturo Rivero Damas.

Equatorial Guinea

Malabo, Rafael Nze Abuy.

Ethiopia

Addis Ababa, H.E. Cardinal Paul Tzadua.

Federal Republic of Germany

Bamberg, Elmar Maria Kredel.
Freiburg Im Breisgau, Oskar Saier.
Koln, H.E. Cardinal Joseph Höffner.
Munich & Freising, H.E. Cardinal Friedrich Wetter.
Paderborn, Johannes Joachim Degenhardt.

France

Aix, Bernard Panafieu.
Albi, Robert Coffy.
Auch, vacant.
Avignon, Raymond Bouchex.
Besançon, Lucien Daloz.
Bordeaux, Marius Maziers.
Bourges, Pierre Plateau.
Cambrai, Jacques Delaporte.
Chambéry, André Bontems.
Lyon, H.E. Cardinal Albert Decourtray.
Marseilles, vacant.
Paris, Jean-Marie Lustiger.
Reims, Jacques Ménager.
Rennes, H.E. Cardinal Paul Gouyon.
Rouen, Joseph Duval.
Sens, Eugene Ernoult.
Tolouse, André Collini.
Tours, Jean Honoré.

French Polynesia

Papeete, Michel Coppenrath.

Gabon

Libreville, André Fernand Anguilé.

Ghana

Cape Coast, John Kodwo Amissah.
Tamale, Peter Poreiku Dery.

Greece

Athenai, Nicola Foscolos.
Corfu, Antonio Varthalitis.
Naxos, Jean Perris.
Rodi, vacant (Apostolic administrator Michel Pierre Franzidis).

Guatemala

Guatemala, Prospero Penandos del Barrio.

Guinea

Conakry, Robert Sarah.

Haiti

Port au Prince, François-Wolff Ligondé.

Haute Volta

Ouagadougou, H.E. Cardinal Paul Zoungrana.

Honduras

Tegucigalpa, Hector Enrique Santos Hernández.

Hungary

Eger, László Kádár.
Esztergom, H.E. Cardinal László Lekai.
Kalocsa, József Ijjas.

India

Agra, Cecil de Sa.
Bangalore, Packiam Arokiaswamy.
Bhopal, Eugene D'Souza.
Bombay, Simon Ignatius Pimenta.
Calcutta, H.E. Cardinal Lawrence Trevor Picachy.
Changanacherry, Anthony Padiyara.
Cuttack-Bhubaneswar, Henry Sebastian D'Souza.
Delhi, Angelo Innocent Fernandes.
Ernakulam, vacant.
Goa and Damao, Raul Nicolau Gonsalves.
Hyderabad, Saminini Arulappa.
Madras and Mylapore, Rayappa Arulappa.
Madurai, Justin Diraviam.
Nagpur, Leobard D'Souza.
Pondicherry and Cuddalore, Venmani S. Selvanather.
Ranchi, Pius Kerketta.
Shillong-Gauhati, Hubert D'Rosario.
Trivandrum, [Syrian Melekite Rite], Benedict Varghese Mar Gregorios Thangalathil.
Verapoly, Joseph Kelanthara.

Indonesia

Ende, Donatus Djagom.
Jakarte, Leo Soekoto.
Medan, Alfred Gonti Pius Datubara.
Merauke, Jacobus Duivenvoorde.
Pontianak, Hieronymus Herculanus Bumbun.
Semarang, Julius R. Darmaatmadja.
Ujong Pandang, vacant.

Iran

Ahwaz, Hanna Zora.
Tehran, Youhannan Semaan Issayi.
Urmyā, Thomas Meram.

Iraq

Arbil, Stephane Babeka.
Baghdad, Paul Dahdah.
Basra, Yousif Thomas.
Kerkuk, André Sana.
Mossul, Georges Garmo.

Ireland

Armagh, H.E. Cardinal Tomás Ó Fiaich.
Cashel, Thomas Morris.
Dublin, Kevin McNamara.
Tuam, Joseph Cunnane.

Israel

Akka [Greek Melekite Catholic Rite], Maximos Salloum.

Italy

Acerenza, Francis Cuccarese.
Amalfi, Ferdinand Palatucci.
Ancona, Carlo Maccari.
Bari, Mariano Magrassi.

Benevento, Carlo Minchiatti.
Bologna, H.E. Cardinal Giacomo Biffi.
Brindisi, Settimio Todisco.
Cagliari, Giovanni Canestri.
Camerino, Bruno Frattegiani.
Campobasso-Boiano, Pietro Santoro.
Capua, Luigi Diligenza.
Catonia, Domenico Picchinenna.
Catanzaro, Antonio Cantisani.
Chieti, Antonio Valentini.
Conza, Antonio Nuzzi.
Cosenza, Dino Trabalzini.
Fermo, Cleto Bellucci.
Ferrara, Luigi Maverna.
Florence, H.E. Cardinal Silvano Piovanelli.
Foggia, Salvatore De Giorgi.
Gaeta, Luigi Carli.
Genoa, H.E. Cardinal Guiseppe Siri.
Gorizia and Gradisca, Antonio Vitale Bommarco.
Lanciano, Enzio d'Antonio.
L'Aquila, Mario Peressin.
Lecce, Michele Mincuzzi.
Lucca, Guiliano Agresti.
Manfredonia, Valentino Vailati.
Matera, Michele Giordano.
Messina, Ignas Cannavó.
Milano, H.E. Cardinal Carlo Maria Martini.
Modina, Santo B. Quadri.
Monreale, Salvatore Cassisa.
Napoli, H.E. Cardinal Corrado Ursi.
Oristano, Francesco Spanedda.
Otranto, Vincenzo Franco.
Palermo, H.E. Cardinal Salvatore Pappalardo.
Perugia, Cesare Pagani.
Pescara-Penne, Antonio Jannucci.
Pisa, Benbenuto Matteucci.
Potenza, Guiseppe Vairo.
Ravenna, Ersilio Tonini.
Reggio Calabria, vacant.
Rossano, Serafino Sprovieri.
Salerno, Guerino Grimaldi.
Santa Severina, Giuseppi Agostino.
Sassari, Salvatore Isgró.
Siena, Ismaele Mario Castellano.
Siracusa, Calogero Lauricella.
Sorrento, Antonio Zama.
Spoleto, Ottorino Pietro Alberti.
Taranto, Guglielmo Motolese.
Torino, H.E. Cardinal Anastasio Alberto Ballestrero.
Trani and Barletta, Giuseppe Carata.
Trento, Alessandro Maria Gottardi.
Udine, Alfredo Battisti.
Urbino, Donato U. Bianchi.
Vercelli, Albino Mensa.

Ivory Coast
Abidjan, Bernard Yago.

Jamaica
Kingston in Jamaica, Samuel Emmanuel Carter.

Japan
Nagasaki, H.E. Cardinal Joseph Asajiro Satowaki.
Osaka, Paul Hisao Yasuda.
Tōkyō, Peter Seiichi Shirayanagi.

Jordan
Petra and Filadelfia [Greek Melekite Catholic Rite],
Saba Youakim.

Kenya
Nairobi, H.E. Cardinal Maurice Otunga.

Korea
Kwang Ju, Victorinus Kong-Hi Youn.
Seoul, H.E. Cardinal Stephen Sou Hwan Kim.
Tae Gu, John B. Bong-Kil Sye.

Lebanon
Baalbek, Eliopoli [Greek Melekite Catholic Rite],
Elias Zoghbi.
Beirut [Greek Melekite Catholic Rite], Habib Bacha.
Cipro, Elie Farah.
Saïdā [Greek Melekite Catholic Rite], Ignace Raad.
Tripoli del Libano [Maronite Rite], Antoine Joubeir;
[Greek Melekite Catholic Rite], Elias Nijmé.
Tyr [Greek Melekite Catholic Rite], Georges Haddad;
[Maronite Rite], Joseph Khoury.
Zahleh and Furzol [Greek Melekite Catholic Rite],
Andre Haddad.

Lesotho
Maseru, Alfonso Ligouri Morapeli.

Liberia
Monrovia, Michael Kpakala Francis.

Lithuania
Kaunas, vacant.
Vilna, vacant (Apostolic administrator, Monsignor
Edward Kisiel).

Madagascar
Diego Suarez, Albert Joseph Tsiahoana.
Fianarantsoa, Gilbert Ramanantoanina.
Tananarive, H.E. Cardinal Victor Razafimahatratra.

Malawi
Bamako, Luc Auguste Sangaré.

Malaysia
Kuching, Peter Chung Hoan Ting.

Malta
Malta, Joseph Mercieca.

Martinique
Fort de France, Maurice Marie-Sainte.

Mexico
Acapulco, Rafael Bello Ruiz.
Antequera, Bartolomé Carrasco Briseno.
Chihuahua, Adalberto Almeida Merino.
Hermosillo, Carlos Quintero Arce.
Jalapa, Sergio Obeso Rivero.
Mexico, H.E. Cardinal Ernesto Corripio Ahumada.
Monterray, Adolfo Suarez Rivera.
Morelia, Estanislao Alcarez Figueroa.
Puebla de los Angeles, Rosendo Huesca Pacheco.
Yucatán, Manuel Castro Ruiz.

Monaco
Monaco, vacant.

Morocco
Rabat, Hubert Michon.
Tanger, Antonio J. Peteiro Freire.

Mozambique
Maputo, Alexandre José Maria dos Santos.
Nampula, Manuel Vieira Pinto.

Netherlands
Utrecht, H.E. Cardinal Adrianus J. Simonis.

New Guinea
Port Moresby, Peter Kurongku.

New Zealand
Wellington, Thomas Stafford Williams.

Nicaragua
Managua, H.E. Cardinal Miguel Obando Bravo.

Nigeria

Kaduna, Peter Yariyok Jatau.
Lagos, Anthony Okogie.
Onitsha, H.E. Cardinal Francis Arinze.

Oceania

Agaña, Felixberto Flores.
Honiara, Adrian Thomas Smith.
Nouméa, Michel-Marie-Bernard Calvet.
Samoa Apia and Tokelau, H.E. Cardinal Pio Taofin-u'u.
Suva, Petero Mataca.

Pakistan

Karachi, H.E. Cardinal Joseph Cordeiro.

Panamá

Panamá, Marcos Gregorio McGrath.

Papua New Guinea

Madang, Leo Arkfield.
Mount Hagen, George Bernarding.
Rabaul, Albert Bundervoet.

Paraguay

Asuncion, Ismael Blas Rolon Silvero.

Peru

Arequipa, Fernando Vargas Ruiz de Somocurcio.
Ayacucho o Huamanga, Federico Richter Fernandez-Prada.
Cuzco, Alcides Mendoza Castro.
Huancayo, vacant.
Lima, H.E. Cardinal Juan Landózuri Ricketts.
Piura, Oscar Rolando Cantuarias Pastor.
Trujillo, Manuel Prado Pérez-Rosas.

Philippines

Caceras, Leonardo Legazpi.
Cagayan de Oro, Patrick H. Cronin.
Capiz, Antonio Frondosa.
Cebu, Nome di Gesù, H.E. Cardinal Ricardo Vidal.
Cotabato, Philip Frances Smith.
Davao, Antonio Mabutas y Lloren.
Jaro, Artemio G. Casas.
Lingayan-Dagupan, Federico G. Limon.
Lipa, Mariano Gaviola Garcés.
Manila, H.E. Cardinal Jaime L. Sin.
Nueva Segovia, José T. Sanchez.
Ozamis, Jesus Desado.
Palo, Cipriano Urgel.
San Fernando, Oscar Cruz.
Tuguegarao, Teodulfo S. Domingo.
Zamboanga, Francisco Raval Cruces.

Poland

Gniezno, H.E. Cardinal Józef Glemp. (See also Warszawa).
Kraków, H.E. Cardinal Franciszek Macharski.
Lwów, H.E. Cardinal Myroslav Lubachisky.
Poznan, Jerzy Stroba.
Warszawa, H.E. Cardinal Józef Glemp.
Wroclaw, H.E. Cardinal Henryk Roman Gulbinowicz.

Portugal

Braga, Eurico Dias Nogueira.
Evora, Maurilio Jorge Quintal de Gouveia.

Puerto Rico

San Juan de Puerto Rico, H.E. Cardinal Luis Aporte Martinez.

Romania

Bucarest, vacant.

Rwanda

Kigali, Vincent Nsengiyumva.

Senegal

Dakar, H.E. Cardinal Hyacinthe Thiandoum.

Sierra Leone

Freetown & Bo, Joseph Ganda.

Singapore

Singapore, Gregory Yong Sooi Nghean.

South Africa

Bloemfontein, Peter John Butelezi.
Cape Town, Stephen Naidoo.
Durban, Denis Eugene Hurley.
Pretoria, George Francis Daniel.

Spain

Barcelona, H.E. Cardinal Narciso Jubany Arnau.
Burgos, Theodoro C. Fernandez.
Granada, José Méndez Asensio.
Madrid, H.E. Cardinal Angel Suquia Goicoechea.
Oviedo, Gabino Diaz Merchán.
Pamplona, José Mariá Cirardo Lachiondo.
Santiago de Compostella, Antonio Rouco Varela.
Sevilla, Carlos Amigo Vallejo.
Tarragona, Ramon Torrella Cascante.
Toledo, H.E. Cardinal Marcelo González Martin.
Valencia, Miguel Roca Cabanellas.
Valladolid, José Delicado Baeza.
Zaragoza, Eliaz Yanez Alvarez.

Sri Lanka

Colombo, Nicholas Marcus Fernando.

Sudan

Khartoum, Gabriel Zubeir Wako.

Syria

Alep, Beroea, Halab [Greek Melekite Catholic Rite], Néophytes Edelby.
Baniyas, Nicholas Hajj.
Bosra, Bostra, Boulos Nassif Borkhoche.
Damascus [Greek Melekite Catholic Rite], vacant.
Hassaké-Nisibi, Georges Habib Hafouri.
Homs, Emesa [Syrian Catholic Rite], Jean Dahi.
Laodicea di Siria [Greek Melekite Catholic Rite], Michel Yatim.

Taiwan

Taipeh, Matthew Kia Yen-Wen.

Tanzania

Dar Es Salaam, H.E. Cardinal Laurean Rugambwa.
Tabora, Mark Mihayo.

Thailand

Bangkok, Michael Michai Kitbunchu.
Tharé and Nonseng, Lawrence Khai Saen-Phon-On.

Togo

Lomé, Robert Casimir Dosseh-Anyron.

Trinidad

Port of Spain, Gordon Anthony Pantin.

Turkey

Diarbekir, Paul Karatas.
Istanbul, Constantinople, Jean Tcholakian.
Izmir, Giuseppe G. Bernardini.

Uganda

Kampala, H.E. Cardinal Emmanuel Nsubuga.

Uruguay

Montevideo, Carlos Porteli.

U.S.A.

Anchorage, Francis Thomas Hurley.

Atlanta, Thomas A. Donnellan.
Baltimore, William D. Borders.
Boston, H.E. Cardinal Bernard F. Law.
Chicago, H.E. Cardinal Joseph L. Bernardin.
Cincinnati, Daniel E. Pilarczyk.
Denver, James Vincent Casey.
Detroit, Edmund C. Szoka.
Dubuque, Daniel W. Kucera.
Hartford, John F. Whealon.
Indianapolis, Edward T. O'Meara.
Kansas City in Kansas, Ignatius J. Strecker.
Los Angeles, H.E. Cardinal Timothy Manning.
Louisville, Thomas C. Kelly.
Miami, Edward A. McCarthy.
Milwaukee, Rembert G. Weakland.
Mobile, Oscar H. Lipscomb.
Newark, Peter L. Gerety.
New Orleans, Philip M. Hannan.
New York, H.E. Cardinal John J. O'Connor.
Oklahoma City, Charles A. Salatka.
Omaha, Daniel E. Sheehan.
Philadelphia, H.E. Cardinal John Joseph Krol.
Pittsburgh, Stephen J. Kocisko.
Portland in Oregon, Cornelius M. Power.
St Louis (Missouri), John L. May.
St Paul & Minneapolis, John Robert Roach.
San Antonio, Patrick F. Flores.
San Francisco, John R. Quinn.
Sante Fe, Robert F. Sanchez.
Seattle, Raymond G. Hunthausen.
Washington, James A. Hickey.

U.S.S.R.

Mohilev, there is an **unnamed** Apostolic Administrator in the following Russian Dioceses: Mohilev, Moscow, Leningrad, Kharkov, Kazan, Samara and Sinibirsk.

Venezuela

Barquisimeto, Julio Manuel Chirivella Varela.
Caracas, H.E. Cardinal José Ali Lebrún Moratinos.
Ciudad Bolivar, Crisanto Mata Cova.
Maracaibo, Domingo Roa Pérez.
Meridia, Miguel Antonio Salas Salas.
Valencia, Luis Eduardo Henriquez Jiménez.

Vietnam

Hanoi, H.E. Cardinal Joseph-Marie Trinh ván Căn.
Huê, Philippe Nguyen-Kim-Diên.
Thanh-Phô Hôchiminh, Paul Nguyên Van Binh.

West Indies

Castries, Kelvin Edward Felix.

Yugoslavia

Bar, Petar Perkolić.
Beograd, Alojz Turk.
Ljubljana, Alojzij Suštar.
Rijeka-Senj, Josip Paulišić.
Split-Makarska, Frane Franić.
Vrhbosna, Marco Jozinović.
Zadar, Marijan Oblak.
Zagreb, Franjo Kuharić.

Zaire

Bukavu, Mulindwa Mutabesha.
Kananga, Bakole wa Ilunga.
Kinshasa, H.E. Cardinal Joseph Malula.
Kisangani, Fataki.
Lubumbashi, Kabanga Songasonga.
Mbandaka-Bikoro, Etsou-Nzabi-Bamungwabi.

Zambia

Kasama, Elias Mutale.
Lusaka, Adrian Mungandu.

Zimbabwe

Harare, Patrick Chakaipa.

ARCHBISHOPS OF TITULAR SEES

Acrida, Mario Schierano.
Amasya, James Patrick Carroll.
Amida, Flavien Zacharie Melkie.
Beroe, Victor Sartre.
Cesarea in Palaestina [Greek Melekite Catholic Rite]: Hilarion Capucci.
Claudiopolis in Honoriade, Alfredo Bruniera.
Corinthus, Gennaro Verolino.
Dara, Nicholas T. Elko.
Doclea, H.E. Cardinal Jozef Tomko.
Edessa in Osrhoëne [Greek Melekite Catholic Rite]: Pierre Rai; [Syrian Catholic Rite]: Gregoire Ephrem Jarjour.
Emerita Augusta, Justo Mullor Garcia.
Egina, Raffaele Forni.
Ephesus, John Henry Boccella.
Gabala, Gérard de Milleville.
Gangra, Antonio Ferreira de Macedo.
Giustiniana prima, Edouard Gagnon.
Gortina, Victor F. Foley.
Gradum, José López Ortiz.
Hadrianopolis in Haemimonto, Lino Zanini.
Heraclea in Europa, Mario Cagna.
Justiniana prima, H.E. Cardinal Edouard Gagnon.
Kaškar, Emmanuel-Karim Delly.
Laodicea in Syria, Martin John O'Connor.
Macra, John Dooley.
Marcianopolis, Teofilo Camomot Bastida.
Mesembria, Loris Francesco Capovilla.
Myra, Basile Khoury.
Nazareth, Giuseppe Carata.
Nicaea Parva, Paolino Limongi.
Nicosia, Aurelio Signora.
Nubia, Paul Antaki.
Pelusium [Greek Melekite Catholic Rite]: Pierre Medawar.
Salamis, Joseph Kuo.
Scytopolis, Joseph Raya.
Selymbria, Emile Socquet.
Soteropolis, Ettore Cunial.
Tarsus [Maronite Rite]: Nasrallah Sfeir; [Greek Melekite Catholic Rite]: Loutfi Laham.
Tiburnia, Donato Squicciarini.
Velebusdo, Jose M. Estepa Llaurens.
Viminacium, Franco Brambilla.

ORTHODOX CHURCH

Greek Orthodox Church (Archdiocese of Thyateira and Great Britain), Most Rev. Archbishop Methodios Fouyas, Ph.D., D.D., 5 Craven Hill, W.2.

Serbian Orthodox Church (Patriarchate of Serbia) Right Rev. Bishop Lavrentije, 89 Lancaster Road, W.11.

Polish Orthodox Church Abroad, Right Rev. Bishop Matthew, 53 Shakespeare Road, NW7 4BA

Russian Orthodox Church (Patriarchate of Moscow), Most Rev. Metropolitan Anthony of Sourozh, Russian Cathedral, Ennismore Gardens, S.W.7.

Russian Orthodox Church Outside Russia. His Grace Bishop Constantine, Dormition Cathedral, Emperor's Gate, S.W.7. Mission Administrator Hegumen Seraphim, 14 St. Dunstan's Road, N.W.6.

The Ukrainians, Latvians, Byelorussians and Romanians also have congregations in this country.

LONDON CATHEDRALS, CHURCHES, ETC.

Church of England

St. Paul's Cathedral, City of London, EC4M 8AD (1675–1710), cost £747,660. The cross on the dome is 365 ft. above the ground level, the inner cupola 218 ft. above the floor. "Great Paul," in S.W. tower weighs 17 tons. Organ by Father Smith (enlarged by Willis and rebuilt by Mander) in case carved by Grinling Gibbons (who also carved the choir stalls). The choir and high altar were restored in 1958 after war damage and the North Transept in 1962. The American War Memorial Chapel was consecrated in November, 1958. The Chapel of the Most Excellent Order of the British Empire in the Crypt of the Cathedral was dedicated on May 20, 1960. Nave and transepts free; Fees to the following parts (on weekdays only, 10 a.m. (Sat. 11 a.m.) to 3.15 p.m. and—during Summer Time only—to 4.15 p.m.); Crypt, Treasury and historical display, 75p; whispering gallery, stone gallery, 80p (children reduced price). Service on Sundays at 8, 10.30, 11.30 and 3.15. Weekdays at 7.30, 8, 4 (winter), 5 (summer).

Westminster Abbey, S.W.1. (built A.D. 1050–1745).—Open on weekdays 9 a.m. to 6 p.m., (8 p.m., Wednesdays). Admission to the Royal Chapels, Poets' Corner, Quire and Statesmen's Aisle £1.40 (student card holders 70p; O.A.P.s and children 40p). Last admission Monday–Friday 4 p.m., Saturday 5 p.m. Wednesdays 6 p.m.–8 p.m. free. Nave open on Sundays between services. Services: Sundays, Holy Communion 8 a.m., Matins 10.30, Holy Communion 11.40 (sung every second and fourth Sundays in month), Evensong 3 p.m., Congregational Service 6.30 p.m., generally preceded by an organ recital. Monday–Friday, Matins 7.30 a.m., Holy Communion 8 a.m., Holy Communion 12.30 p.m. (Wednesdays, Lunchhour Service), Evensong 5 p.m. Saturdays, Holy Communion 8 a.m., Matins 9 a.m., Evensong 3 p.m. Chapel of Henry VII, Chapter House and Cloisters; King Edward the Confessor's shrine, A.D. 1269, tombs of kings and queens (Henry III, Edward I, Edward III, Henry V, Mary Queen of Scots, Queen Elizabeth I), and many other monuments and objects of interest, including the grave of "The Unknown Warrior" and Poets' Corner. The Coronation Chair encloses the "Stone of Scone", which was removed from Scotland by Edward I in 1296.

Southwark Cathedral, south side of the Thames, near London Bridge, S.E.1.—Mainly 13th century, but the nave is largely rebuilt. Open 7.30 a.m. to 6 p.m., free. Sunday services, Eucharist 11 a.m., Evensong, 3 p.m. Weekdays: Matins 12.30 p.m., Holy Communion 12.45 p.m., Evensong (sung on Tuesdays and Fridays) 5.30 p.m., Saturdays, Holy Communion, 12 noon.

The tomb of John Gower (1330–1408) is between the Bunyan and Chaucer memorial windows, in the N. aisle; Shakespeare effigy backed by view of Southwark and Globe Theatre in S. aisle; the altar screen (erected 1520) has been restored; the tomb of Bishop Andrews (died 1626) is near screen. The Early English Lady Chapel (behind the choir), restored 1930, was the scene of the Consistory Courts of the reign of Mary (Gardiner and Bonner); and is still used as a Consistory Court. John Harvard, after whom Harvard University is named, was baptized here in 1607.

Temple Church, The Temple, E.C.4.—The nave formed one of five remaining round churches in England, the others being at Cambridge, Northampton, Little Maplestead (Essex), and Ludlow Castle. Rebuilding of the church was completed in 1958. Sunday morning services, open to the public, 11.15 a.m., except in August and September. *Master of the Temple*, Rev. Canon J. Robinson, M.Th., B.D. *Reader*, Rev. Preb. W. D. Kennedy-Bell, M.A.

Church of Scotland

Crown Court Church, Russell Street, Covent Garden, W.C.2.—Sundays, 11.15 (Holy Communion, first Sunday of Month) and 6.30. Mid week Service, Thursdays, 1.30.

St. Columba's, Pont Street, SW1X 0BD. Sundays, 11 and 6.30. *Minister*, Very Rev. J. F. McLuskey, M.C., D.D.

United Reformed

City Temple, Holborn Viaduct, E.C.1.—Sundays, 11 and 6.30 and Thursdays, 1.15. *Assistant Minister*, Rev. C. Flashman.

Independent Evangelical

Westminster Chapel, Buckingham Gate, SW1E 6BS—Sundays, 11 and 6.30. *Minister*, Rev. Dr. R. T. Kendall.

Methodist

Wesley's Chapel, City Road, EC1Y 1AU—Sunday service 11 a.m. *Minister*, Rev. Dr. R. C. Gibbins.

Central Hall, Westminster, SW1H 9NU—Sunday Services, 11 a.m. and 6.30 p.m. *Minister*, Rev. Dr. R. J. Tudor.

West London Mission, Hinde Street Methodist Church, W.1.—Sundays at 10, 11 and 6.30. *Superintendent*, Rev. J. A. Newton, M.A., Ph.D., D.Litt.

Baptist

Bloomsbury Central Baptist Church, Junction of Shaftesbury Avenue and New Oxford Street, W.C.2.—Sundays 11 and 6.30. *Minister*, Rev. H. Howard Williams, Ph.D.

Religious Society of Friends

Friends' House, Euston Road, N.W.1.

Roman Catholic

Westminster Cathedral, Ashley Place, Westminster, SW1P 1QW (close to Victoria Station), built 1895–1903 from the designs of J. F. Bentley (the campanile is 283 feet high.—*Sundays:* Masses, 7, 8, 9, 10.30 (sung), 12 noon, 5.30 p.m. and 7 p.m.; Solemn Vespers and Benediction, 3.30. *Weekdays.* (Mon.-Fri.) Masses, 7, 8, 8.30, 9, 10.30, 12.30, 1.05 5.30 (sung). Lauds, 7.40 a.m.; Vespers, 5 p.m.; (Saturday) Masses, 7, 8, 8.30, 9, 10.30 (sung), 12.30, 6 p.m.; Lauds, 7.40 a.m.; Vespers, 5.30 p.m. *Holy days of obligation.* Low Masses, 7, 8, 8.30, 9, 10.30, 12.30, 1.05, 5.30 (sung), 7 p.m. Cathedral open 6.45 a.m. to 8 p.m.

The Oratory, Brompton, S.W.7.—*Sundays:* Masses, 7, 8, 9, 10, 11; (High Mass); 12.30, 4.30, 7; Vespers and Benediction, 3.30. *Weekdays:* Masses, 7, 8, 10; 12.30, 6 p.m. (no 12.30 on Sats.). Service Thurs. 8 p.m. *Holy days:* Masses 7, 8, 10, 12.15, 1.15, 4.30, and 8 p.m.; 6 p.m. (High Mass). On the eve, Vespers and Benediction, 5.30 p.m.

ARCHBISHOPS OF CANTERBURY SINCE 1414

1414 Henry Chichele	1633 William Laud	1828 William Howley
1443 John Stafford	1660 William Juxon	1848 John Bird Sumner
1452 John Kemp	1663 Gilbert Sheldon	1862 Charles Thomas Longley
1454 Thomas Bourchier	1678 William Sancroft	1868 Archibald Campbell Tait
1486 John Morton	1691 John Tillotson	1883 Edward White Benson
1501 Henry Dean	1695 Thomas Tenison	1896 Frederick Temple
1503 William Warham	1716 William Wake	1903 Randall Thomas Davidson
1533 Thomas Cranmer	1737 John Potter	1928 Cosmo Gordon Lang
1556 Reginald Pole	1747 Thomas Herring	1942 William Temple
1559 Matthew Parker	1757 Matthew Hutton	1945 Geoffrey Francis Fisher
1576 Edmund Grindal	1758 Thomas Secker	1961 Arthur Michael Ramsey
1583 John Whitgift	1768 Hon. Frederick Cornwallis	1974 Frederick Donald Coggan
1604 Richard Bancroft	1783 John Moore	1980 Robert Runcie
1611 George Abbot	1805 Charles Manners Sutton	

ARCHBISHOPS OF YORK SINCE 1606

1606 Tobias Matthew	1724 Launcelot Blackburn	1891 William Connor Magee
1628 George Montague	1743 Thomas Herring	1891 William Dalrymple Maclagan
1629 Samuel Harsnett	1747 Matthew Hutton	1909 Cosmo Gordon Lang
1632 Richard Neile	1757 John Gilbert	1929 William Temple
1641 John Williams	1761 Robert Hay Drummond	1942 Cyril Forster Garbett
1660 Accepted Frewen	1777 William Markham	1956 Arthur Michael Ramsey
1664 Richard Sterne	1808 Edward Venables Vernon	1961 Frederick Donald Coggan
1683 John Dolben	Harcourt	1975 Stuart Yarworth Blanch
1688 Thomas Lamplugh	1848 Thomas Musgrave	1983 John Stapylton Habgood
1691 John Sharp	1860 Charles Thomas Longley	
1714 William Dawes	1862 William Thomson	

POPES FROM 1800

Sovereign Pontiff	Family Name	Elected	Sovereign Pontiff	Family Name	Elected
Pius VII	Chiaramonti	1800	Pius XII	Pacelli	1939
Leo XII	della Genga	1823	John XXIII	Roncalli	1958
Pius VIII	Castiglioni	1829	Paul VI	Montini	1963
Gregory XVI	Cappellari	1831	John Paul I	Luciani	1978
Pius IX	Mastai-Ferretti	1846	John Paul II	Wojtyla	1978
Leo XIII	Pecci	1878			
Pius X	Sarto	1903			
Benedict XV	della Chiesa	1914			
Pius XI	Ratti	1922			

Adrian IV (Nicholas Breakspear, the only English-man elected Pope) was born at Langley, near St. Albans; elected Pope, on the death of Anastasius IV, 1154; died 1159.

PATRON SAINTS

St. George, Patron Saint of England.—St. George is believed to have been born in Cappadocia, of Christian parents, in the latter part of the 3rd century and to have served with distinction as a soldier under the Emperor Doicletian, including a visit to England on a military mission. When the persecution of Christians was ordered, St. George sought a personal interview to remonstrate with the Emperor and after a profession of faith resigned his military commission. Arrest and torture followed and he was martyred at Nicomedia on April 23, 303, a day ordered to be kept in remembrance as a national festival by the Council of Oxford in 1222, although it was not until the reign of Edward III that he was made patron saint of England. His connection with a dragon seems to date from the close of the 6th century and to be due to the transfer of his remains from Nicomedia to Lydda, close to the scene of the legendary exploit of Perseus in rescuing Andromeda and slaying the sea monster, credit for which became attached to the Christian martyr.

St. David, Patron Saint of Wales.—St. David is believed to have been born near the beginning and to have died towards the end of the 6th century. St. David was an eloquent preacher, who founded the monastery at Menevia, now St. David's. He became the patron of Wales, but there is no record of any

papal Canonization before 1181. His annual festival is observed on March 1.

St. Andrew, Patron Saint of Scotland.—St. Andrew, one of the Christian Apostles and brother of Simon Peter, was born at Bethsaida on the Lake of Galilee and lived at Capernaum. He preached the Gospel in Asia Minor and in Scythia along the shores of the Black Sea and became the patron saint of Russia. It is believed that he suffered crucifixion at Patras in Achaea, on a *crux decussata* (now known as St. Andrew's Cross) and that his relics were removed from Patras to Constantinople and thence to St. Andrews, probably in the 8th century, since which time he has been the patron saint of Scotland. The festival of St. Andrew is held on November 30, a church festival indicated in the calendar by red letters.

St. Patrick, Patron Saint of Ireland.—St. Patrick was born in England about 389 and was carried off to Ireland as a slave about sixteen years later, escaping to Gaul at the age of 22. He was ordained deacon at Auxerre and having been consecrated Bishop in 432 was despatched to Wicklow to reorganize the Christian communities in Ireland. He founded the see of Armagh and introduced Latin into Ireland as the language of the Church. He died in 461 and his festival is celebrated on March 17.

EDUCATION DIRECTORY

UNIVERSITIES

The universities have power to award their own degrees. They grant 70 per cent. of all first degrees awarded in Britain and 95 per cent. of all higher degrees. They provide most of the basic and much of the applied research undertaken in Britain, and are responsible for the initial training of virtually all research workers. The universities make the chief contribution to wholly new knowledge through fundamental research.

THE UNIVERSITY OF OXFORD

FULL TERMS, 1986

Hilary, Jan. 19 to Mar. 15; *Trinity*, April 27 to June 21; *Michaelmas*, Oct. 12 to Dec. 6

Number of Undergraduates in Residence 1984–85: Men, 5,814; Women, 3,640

UNIVERSITY OFFICES, etc.   Elect.

Chancellor, Rt. Hon. the Earl of Stockton, O.M., F.R.S., *Balliol*	1960
High Steward, The Lord Wilberforce, P.C., C.M.G., O.B.E., M.A., *All Souls*	1967
Vice-Chancellor, Sir Patrick Neill, Q.C., M.A., Warden of *All Souls*	1985
Proctors, Mrs. R. L. Deech, M.A., *St. Anne's*; L. G. Black, D.phil., *Oriel*	1985
Assessor, A. J. Ryan, M.A., *New College*	1985
Public Orator, G. W. Bond, M.A., *Pembroke*	1980
Bodley's Librarian, (vacant)	
Keeper of Archives, T. H. Aston, M.A., *Corpus Christi*	1969
Director of the Ashmolean Museum, C. J. White, M.A., *Worcester*	1985
Registrar of the University, A. J. Dorey, M.A., D.Phil., *Linacre*	1979
Surveyor to the University, (vacant)	
Secretary of Faculties, A. P. Weale, M.A. *Worcester*	1984
Secretary of the Chest and Chief Accountant, (vacant)	
Deputy Registrar (Admin.), D. W. Roberts, M.A., *Pembroke*	

Oxford Colleges and Halls
(With dates of foundation)

All Souls (1438), Sir Patrick Neill, Q.C., B.C.L., M.A., *Warden* (1977).
Balliol (1263), A. J. P. Kenny, PH.D., M.A., D.Phil., D.Litt., F.B.A., F.R.S.E., *Master* (1978).
Brasenose (1509) Prof. J. K. B. M. Nicholas, M.A., *Principal* (1978).
Christ Church (1546), Very Rev. E. W. Heaton, M.A., *Dean*, (1979).
Corpus Christi (1517), Sir Kenneth Dover, M.A., D.Litt., F.R.S.E., F.B.A., *President* (1976).
Exeter (1314), The Lord Crowther-Hunt, PH.D., M.A., *Rector* (1982).
Green (1979), Sir John Walton, M.A., D.SC., *Warden* (1983).
Hertford (1874), G. J. Warnock, M.A., *Principal* (1971).
Jesus (1571), Dr. P. M. North, M.A., D.C.L. *Principal* (1984).
Keble (1868), C. J. E. Ball, M.A., *Warden* (1979).
Lady Margaret Hall (1878), D. M. Stewart, M.A., *Principal* (1979).
Linacre (1962), J. B. Bamborough, M.A., *Principal* (1962).

Lincoln (1427), Rev. V. H. H. Green, D.D., *Rector* (1983).
Magdalen (1458), K. B. Griffin, M.A., D.Phil., *President* (1979).
Merton (1264), J. M. Roberts, D.Phil., *Warden* (1985).
New College (1379), H. McGregor, Q.C., M.A., *Warden* (1985).
Nuffield (1937), M. G. Brock, C.B.E, M.A., *Warden* (1978).
Oriel (1326), Rt. Hon. Sir Zelman Cowen, A.K., G.C.M.G., G.C.V.O., Q.C., M.A., D.C.L., *Provost* (1982).
Pembroke (1624), Sir Roger Bannister, C.B.E., M.A., D.M., F.R.C.P., *Master* (1985).
Queen's (1340), The Lord Blake, M.A., D.Litt., F.B.A., *Provost* (1968).
St. Anne's (1952) (Originally Society of Oxford Home-Students (1879)), Dr. C. Palley, PH.D., *Principal* (1984).
St. Antony's (1950), A. R. M. Carr, M.A., D.Litt., *Warden* (1968).
St. Catherine's (1962), Rt. Hon. Sir Patrick Nairne, G.C.B., M.C., M.A., *Master* (1981).
St. Cross (1965), G. H. Stafford, C.B.E., M.A., PH.D., F.R.S., *Master* (1980).
St. Edmund Hall (c. 1278), J. C. B. Gosling, M.A., *Principal* (1983).
St. John's (1555), Sir John Kendrew, C.B.E., SC.D., PH.D., M.A., D.SC., D.Phil., F.R.S., *President* (1981).
St. Peter's (1929), Prof. G. E. Aylmer, M.A., D.Phil., F.B.A., *Master* (1978).
Trinity (1554), The Lord Quinton, M.A., F.B.A., *President* (1978).
University (1249), The Lord Goodman, C.H., LL.M., M.A., *Master* (1976).
Wadham (1612), Sir Claus Moser, K.C.B., C.B.E., F.B.A., *Warden* (1984).
Wolfson (1966), Sir Raymond Hoffenberg, M.D., PH.D., P.R.S.P., *President* (1985).
Worcester (1714), The Lord Briggs, M.A., F.B.A., *Provost* (1976).
Campion Hall (1896), Rev. P. Hackett, M.A., *Master* (1984).
St. Benet's Hall (1897), Rev. P. D. Holdsworth, O.S.B., M.A., S.T.L., *Master* (1980).
Mansfield (1886), D. A. Sykes, M.A., D.Phil., *Principal* (1977).
Regent's Park (1810), Rev. B. R. White, M.A., D.Phil., *Principal* (1972).
Greyfriars (1910), Very Rev. T. M. Mann, M.A., *Warden* (1981).

COLLEGES FOR WOMEN ONLY

St. Hilda's (1893), Mrs. G. M. Moore, M.A., *Principal* (1980).
St. Hugh's (1886), Miss M. R. Trickett, M.A., *Principal* (1973).
Somerville (1879), Miss D. M. S. D. Park, C.M.G., O.B.E., M.A., *Principal* (1980).

THE UNIVERSITY OF CAMBRIDGE

FULL TERMS, 1986

Lent, Jan. 14 to Mar. 14; *Easter*, Apr. 22 to June 6; *Michaelmas*, Oct. 7 to Dec. 5

Number of Undergraduates in Residence 1984–85: Men, 6,135; Women, 3,346

UNIVERSITY OFFICES, &C.   Elect.

Chancellor, H.R.H. The Duke of Edinburgh, K.G., K.T., O.M., G.B.E.	1977

† *Vice-Chancellor*, Prof. the Lord Adrian, M.A., M.D., F.R.S., *Master of Pembroke College* 1985
High Steward, The Lord Devlin, P.C., M.A., F.B.A., *Chr.* 1966
Deputy High Steward, The Lord Richardson of Duntisbourne, P.C., M.B.E., T.D. 1983
Commissary, The Lord Salmon, P.C., M.A., *Pemb.* 1979
Proctors, J. A. Trevithick, M.A., *King's*; P. H. W. Hawkins, *Sid* 1985
Orator, J. Diggle, M.A., PH.D., *Queen's.* 1982
Registrary, S. G. Fleet, M.A., PH.D., *Down* 1983
Deputy Registrary, R. F. Holmes, M.A., *Darw....* 1972
Librarian, F. W. Ratcliffe, M.A., PH.D., *Corp.* 1980
Treasurer, M. P. Halstead, PH.D., *Cai.* 1985
Secretary General of the Faculties, K. J. R. Edwards, M.A., *St. John's* 1984
Director of the Fitzwilliam Museum, Prof. A. M. Jaffé, Litt.D., *King's* 1973

Cambridge Colleges
(With dates of foundation)

Christ's (1505), Prof. Sir Hans Kornberg, SC.D., F.R.S., *Master* (1983).
Churchill (1960), Prof. Sir Hermann Bondi, K.C.B., M.A., F.R.S., *Master* (1982).
Clare (1326), Prof. R. C. O. Matthews, C.B.E., M.A., F.B.A., *Master* (1975).
Clare Hall (1966), Sir Michael Stoker, C.B.E., M.A., M.D., F.R.S., *President* (1980).
Corpus Christi (1352), M. W. McCrum, M.A., *Master* (1980).
Darwin (1964), Sir Arnold Burgen, M.D., F.R.S., *Master* (1982).
Downing (1800), Prof. Sir John Butterfield, O.B.E., M.A., D.M., M.D., *Master* (1978).
Emmanuel (1584), Prof. D. S. Brewer, Litt.D., *Master* (1977).
Fitzwilliam (1966), Prof. J. C. Holt, M.A., D.Phil., F.B.A., *Master* (1981).
Girton (1869), Lady Warnock, M.A., *Mistress* (1984).
Gonville & Caius (1348), Prof. Sir Henry Wade, M.A., LL.D., D.C.L., F.B.A., Q.C., *Master* (1976).
Jesus (1496), Sir Alan Cottrell, M.A., PH.D., SC.D., F.R.S., *Master* (1974).
King's (1441), B. A. O. Williams, M.A., F.B.A., *Provost* (1979).
Pembroke (1347), Prof. Lord Adrian, M.A., M.D., F.R.S., *Master* (1981).
Peterhouse (1284), Lord Dacre of Glanton, M.A., F.B.A., *Master* (1980).
Queens' (1448), Prof. E. R. Oxburgh, M.A., F.R.S., *President* (1982).
Robinson (1977), Prof. Sir Jack Lewis, M.A., PH.D., D.SC., M.A., SC.D., F.R.S., *Warden* (1977).
St. Catharine's (1473), *Master* Prof. B. E. Supple, PH.D (1984).
St. Edmund's House (1896), R. M. Laws, C.B.E., PH.D, *Master* (1986).
St. John's (1511), Prof. Sir Francis Hinsley, O.B.E., M.A., *Master* (1979).
Selwyn (1882), Prof. A. H. Cook, SC.D., F.R.S., *Master* (1983).
Sidney Sussex (1596), Prof. D. H. Northcote, PH.D., SC.D., F.R.S., *Master* (1976).
Trinity (1546), Sir Andrew Huxley, P.R.S., *Master* (1984).
Trinity Hall (1350), J. Lyons, M.A., PH.D., *Master* (1984).
Wolfson (1965), Prof. D. G. T. Williams, M.A., LL.B., *President* (1980).

---

† Correspondence for the *Vice-Chancellor* and other administrative officers should be sent to the *University Offices*, The Old Schools, Cambridge.

COLLEGE FOR MEN ONLY

Magdalene (1542), D. Calcutt, Q.C., *Master* (1985).

COLLEGES FOR WOMEN ONLY

New Hall (1954), Mrs. V. L. Pearl, M.A., D.Phil., *President* (1981).
Newnham (1871), Miss S. J. Browne, M.A., C.B., *Principal* (1983).

APPROVED SOCIETIES

Homerton (1824) (for B.Ed. Students), A. G. Bamford, M.A., *Principal* (1985).
Hughes Hall (*formerly Cambridge T.C.*) (1885), (for post-graduate students), B. M. Herbertson, M.A., M.D., *President* (1984).
Lucy Cavendish Collegiate Society (1965) (for women research students and mature undergraduates), Dame Anne Warburton, *President* (1985).

THE UNIVERSITY OF ASTON IN BIRMINGHAM (1966)
Aston Triangle, Birmingham B4 7ET

Full-time Students (1984–85), 3,861.
Chancellor, Sir Adrian Cadbury, M.A.
Vice-Chancellor Prof. F. W. Crawford, M.SC., PH.D., D.Eng., D.SC.
Secretary, (vacant).

UNIVERSITY OF BATH (1966)
Claverton Down, Bath BA2 7AY

Full-time Students (1984–85), 3,681.
Chancellor, Lord Kearton, O.B.E., F.R.S.
Vice-Chancellor, J. R. Quayle, M.A., PH.D., F.R.S.
Registrar and Secretary, R. M. Mawditt, M.SC., F.R.S.A.

THE UNIVERSITY OF BIRMINGHAM (1900)
P.O. Box 363, Birmingham B15 2TT

Full-time Students (1985), 8,497.
Chancellor, Sir Alex Jarratt, C.B.
Vice-Chancellor and Principal, Prof. E. A. Marsland, PH.D., F.R.C. Path.
Secretary, H. Harris, B.SC. (ECON.), LL.B.
Registrar, Mrs. A. M. Hutton, M.A.

UNIVERSITY OF BRADFORD (1966)
Bradford BD7 1DP

Full-time Students (1984–85), 4,248.
Chancellor, J. Harvey-Jones, M.B.E.,
Vice-Chancellor and Principal, Prof. J. C. West, C.B.E., PH.D., D.SC.
Registrar and Secretary, I. M. Sanderson, M.B.E., B.SC.

THE UNIVERSITY OF BRISTOL (1909)
Bristol BS8 1TH

Full-time Students (1984–85), 7,045.
Chancellor, Prof. Dorothy Hodgkin, O.M., M.A., PH.D, F.R.S. (1971).
Vice-Chancellor, Sir John Kingman, M.A., F.R.S.
Registrar and Secretary, E. C. Wright, M.A. (1978).

BRUNEL UNIVERSITY (1966)
Uxbridge, Middlesex UB8 3PH

Full-time Students (1984–85), 3,316.
Chancellor, The Earl of Halsbury, F.R.S.
Vice-Chancellor, Prof. R. E. D. Bishop, C.B.E., PH.D., F.R.S.
Secretary General and Registrar, D. Neave, L.L.M..

UNIVERSITY OF BUCKINGHAM (1983)
(Founded 1976 as University College at Buckingham)
Buckingham MK18 1EG

Full-time Students (1985), 581
Independent of state finance.
Chancellor, The Lord Hailsham of St. Marylebone, P.C., C.H., F.R.S.
Vice-Chancellor, Dr. A. M. Barrett, PH.D.
Registrar, S. P. J. Ellis, M.A.
Bursar and Sec., P. Quick, M.A.

THE CITY UNIVERSITY (1966)
Northampton Square, EC1V 0HB

Full-time Students (1984–85), 2,939.
Chancellor, The Lord Mayor of London.
Vice-Chancellor, R. N. Franklin, M.A., D.Phil., D.SC.
Academic Registrar, A. H. Seville, M.A., PH.D.
Secretary, M. M. O'Hara.

THE UNIVERSITY OF DURHAM
(Founded 1832; re-organized 1908, 1937 and 1963)
Old Shire Hall, Durham DH1 3HP

Full-time Students (1984–85), 4,636.

Chancellor, Dame Margot Fonteyn de Arias.
Vice-Chancellor and Warden, Prof. F. G. T. Holliday, C.B.E., F.R.S.E.
Registrar and Secretary, I. E. Graham, M.A.

Colleges

University, E. C. Salthouse, PH.D., *Master*
Hatfield, J. P. Barber, M.A., P.H.D., *Master*.
Grey, E. Halladay, M.A., *Master*.
Van Mildert, A. T. von S. Bradshaw, M.A., *Master*.
Collingwood, J. A. Tuck, M.A., PH.D., *Master*.
St. Chad's, Rev. R. C. Trounson, M.A., *Principal*.
St. John's, Miss D. R. Etchells, M.A., *Principal*.
St. Mary's, Miss J. M. Kenworthy, M.A., *Principal*.
St. Aidan's, Miss I. Hindmarsh, M.A., *Principal*.
Trevelyan, Miss D. Lavin, M.A., *Principal*.
St. Hild and St. Bede, J. V. Armitage, PH.D., *Principal*.
St. Cuthbert's Society, Prof. J. L. Brooks, M.A., *Principal (acting)*.
The Graduate Society, G. Kohnstam, PH.D., *Principal*.
Ushaw, Very Rev. Canon P. F. J. Walton, *President*.

THE UNIVERSITY OF EAST ANGLIA (1963)
Norwich NR4 7TJ

Full-time Students (1984–85), 4,140.
Chancellor, Rev. Prof. W. O. Chadwick, O.M., K.B.E., D.D., F.B.A.
Vice-Chancellor, Prof. M. W. Thompson, D.SC.
Registrar and Secretary, M. G. E. Paulson-Ellis, M.A.

THE UNIVERSITY OF ESSEX (1964)
Wivenhoe Park, Colchester CO4 3SQ

Full-time Students (1984–85), 2,881.
Chancellor, Rt. Hon. Sir Patrick Nairne G.C.B., M.C., M.A., LL.D.
Vice-Chancellor, A. E. Sloman, C.B.E., M.A., D.Phil.
Registrar and Sec., E. Newcomb, B.A.

THE UNIVERSITY OF EXETER (1955)
Northcote House, Exeter EX4 4QJ

Full-time Students (1983–84), 4,856.
Chancellor, Sir Rex Richards, D.SC., F.R.S., F.R.S.C. (1982).
Vice-Chancellor, D. Harrison, M.A., PH.D., SC.D., F.R.S.C.
Academic Registrar and Secretary, M. J. Hislop.

THE UNIVERSITY OF HULL (1954)
Cottingham Road, Hull HU6 7RX

Full-time Students (1984–85), 4,666.
Chancellor, The Lord Wilberforce, P.C., C.M.G., O.B.E. (1978).
Vice-Chancellor, Prof. W. Taylor, C.B.E., PH.D. (1985).
Registrar, F. T. Mattison, M.A., LL.B.

THE UNIVERSITY OF KEELE (1962)
Keele, Staffordshire ST5 5BG

Full-time Students (1984–85), 2,769.
Chancellor, H.R.H. The Princess Margaret, Countess of Snowdon, C.I., G.C.V.O. (until Feb., 1986).
Vice-Chancellor, Prof. B. E. F. Fender, C.M.G., PH.D.
Registrar, D. Cohen, M.A., PH.D., F.R.S.C.

UNIVERSITY OF KENT AT CANTERBURY (1965)
Canterbury, Kent CT2 7NZ

Full-time Students (1984–85), 4,136.
Chancellor, The Lord Grimond, P.C., T.D.
Vice-Chancellor, D. J. E. Ingram, M.A., D.Phil.
Registrar and Finance Officer, A. D. Linfoot, M.A.

THE UNIVERSITY OF LANCASTER (1964)
Bailrigg, Lancaster LA1 4YW

Full-time Students (1984–85), 4,345.
Chancellor, H.R.H. The Princess Alexandra, G.C.V.O.
Vice-Chancellor, Prof. H. J. Hanham, PH.D.
Registrar, M. D. Forster, M.A.
Secretary, G. M. Cockburn, M.A.

THE UNIVERSITY OF LEEDS (1904)
Leeds LS2 9JT

Full-time Students (1984–85), 10,381.
Chancellor, H.R.H. The Duchess of Kent, G.C.V.O. (1966).
Vice-Chancellor, Sir Edward Parkes, M.A.,PH.D., SC.D.
Registrar, J. J. Walsh, M.A. (1979).
Bursar, R. Head (1976).

THE UNIVERSITY OF LEICESTER (1957)
Leicester LE1 7RH

Full-time Students (1984–85), 4,643.
Chancellor, (vacant).
Vice-Chancellor, M. Shock, M.A.
Registrar, J. W. Walmsley (1983).

THE UNIVERSITY OF LIVERPOOL (1903)
P.O. Box 147, Liverpool L69 3BX

Full-time Students (1984–85), 7,425.
Chancellor, The Viscount Leverhulme, T.D.
Vice-Chancellor, Prof. J. F. Norbury, PH.D. (*acting*).
Registrar, R. A. Hind, M.A.
Secs., D. R. Holmes, M.A. (*Academic*); S. Guy (*Admin.*).

THE UNIVERSITY OF LONDON (1836)
Senate House, WC1E 7HU

Internal Students (1984–85), 40,280, External Students, 16,948.
Visitor, H.M. The Queen in Council.
Chancellor, H.R.H. The Princess Anne, G.C.V.O.
Vice-Chancellor, The Lord Flowers, F.R.S.
Chairman of the Court, The Lord Scarman, P.C., O.B.E. M.A.
Chairman of Convocation, Prof. J. P. Quilliam, M.B., D.SC.
Principal, P. Holwell.

Principal Officers

Clerk of the Court, P. Holwell.
Clerk of the Senate, P. Taylor.
Academic Registrar, Mrs. G. Roberts.
Secretary to University Entrance and School Examinations Council, A. R. Stephenson, M.A.
Director of Central Library Services, V. T. H. Parry, M.A.

Schools of the University

Birkbeck College, Malet Street, WC1E 7HX, Prof. W. G. Overend, PH.D., D.SC., *Master*.
Imperial College of Science and Technology, South Kensington, SW7 2AZ, Dr. E. A. Ash, C.B.E., PH.D., F.R.S., *Rector*.
Institute of Education, 20 Bedford Way, WC1H 0AL, Prof. D. Lawton, PH.D., *Dir.*
King's College (includes former Chelsea College and Queen Elizabeth College), Strand, WC2R 2LS, Prof. S. R. Sutherland, M.A., *Principal*.
London School of Economics and Political Science, Houghton Street, WC2A 2AE, Prof. I. Patel, *Director*.
Queen Mary College, Mile End Road, E1 4NS, Sir James Menter, M.A., PH.D., SC.D., F.R.S., *Principal*.
Royal Holloway and Bedford New College, Egham Hill, Egham, Surrey TW20 0EX, Prof. Dorothy E. C. Wedderburn, *Principal*.
Royal Veterinary College, Royal College Street, NW1 0TU, A. O. Betts, M.A., PH.D., *Principal and Dean*.
School of Oriental and African Studies, Malet Street, WC1E 7HP, Prof. C. D. Cowan, M.A., PH.D., *Dir.*
School of Pharmacy, 29–39 Brunswick Square, WC1N 1AX, F. Fish, PH.D., *Dean*.
University College, Gower Street, WC1E 6BT, Sir James Lighthill, F.R.S., *Provost*.
Westfield College, Kidderpore Avenue, Hampstead, NW3 7ST, Prof. J. E. Varey, PH.D., D.Litt., *Principal*.
Wye College, Wye, Ashford, Kent TN25 5AH, I. A. M. Lucas, C.B.E., M.SC., *Principal*.
*Heythrop College, 11–13 Cavendish Square, W1M 0AN, Rev. B. Callaghan, S.J., M.A., *Principal*.

Senate Institutes

British Institute in Paris, 9–11 Rue de Constantine, 75007, Paris, Prof. C. L. Campos, L-ès-L., PH.D., *Dir.* London office: 15 Woburn Square, WC1H 0NS.
Courtauld Institute of Art, 20 Portman Square, W1H 0BE, Prof. C. M. Kauffman, PH.D., *Dir.*
Institute of Advanced Legal Studies, Charles Clore House, 17 Russell Square, WC1B 5DR, Prof. A. L. Diamond, LL.M., *Dir.*
Institute of Archæology, 31–34 Gordon Square, WC1H 0PY, Prof. J. D. Evans, PH.D., Litt.D., F.B.A., F.S.A., *Dir.*
Institute of Classical Studies, 31–34 Gordon Square, WC1H 0PY, Prof. J. P. Barron, M.A., *Dir.*
Institute of Commonwealth Studies, 27–28 Russell Square, WC1B 5DS, Prof. Shula E. Marks, PH.D., *Dir.*
Institute of Germanic Studies, 29 Russell Square, WC1B 5DP, Prof. R. A. Wisbey, M.A., *Hon. Dir.*
Institute of Historical Research, Senate House, Malet Street, WC1E 7HU, Prof. F. M. L. Thompson, D.Phil., F.B.A., *Dir.*
Institute of Latin American Studies, 31 Tavistock Square, WC1H 9HA, Prof. J. Lynch, PH.D., *Dir.*
Institute of United States Studies, 31 Tavistock Square, WC1H 9EZ, Prof. P. J. Parish, *Dir.*
School of Slavonic and E. European Studies, University of London, Senate House, WC1E 7HU, M. A. Branch, PH.D., *Dir.*

---

*Not in receipt of U.G.C. grants.

Warburg Institute, Woburn Square, WC1H 0AB, Prof. J. B. Trapp, M.A., F.B.A., *Dir.*

Institutions having Recognized Teachers

Goldsmiths' College, Lewisham Way, New Cross, SE14 6NW, A. Rutherford, M.A., *Warden*.
Jews' College, 44a Albert Road, NW4 25J, Rabbi Dr. J. Sacks, *Principal.*
London Graduate School of Business Studies, Sussex Place, NW1 4SA, Prof. P. G. Moore, PH.D., *Principal.*
Royal Academy of Music, Marylebone Road, NW1 5HT, Sir David Lumsden, D.Phil., MUS.B., F.R.C.M., *Principal.*
Royal College of Music, Prince Consort Road, SW7 2BS, Sir David Willcocks, C.B.E., *Director.*
Trinity College of Music, Mandeville Place, W1M 6AQ, M. Davies, C.B.E., M.A., *Principal.*

UNDERGRADUATE MEDICAL COLLEGES AND SCHOOLS OF THE UNIVERSITY OF LONDON

CHARING CROSS AND WESTMINSTER MEDICAL SCHOOL, The Reynolds Building, St. Dunstan's Road, W6 8RP; Horseferry Road, Westminster, SW1P 2AR.—*Dean*, Prof. T. W. Glenister, C.B.E., T.D., D.SC.; *Secretary*, G. K. Buckley.
KING'S COLLEGE SCHOOL OF MEDICINE AND DENTISTRY, Denmark Hill, SE5 8RX.
THE LONDON HOSPITAL MEDICAL COLLEGE, Turner Street, E1 2AD.—*Dean*, Prof. M. A. Floyer, M.A., M.D., F.R.C.P.; *Secretary*, D. L. Edwards.
THE MIDDLESEX HOSPITAL MEDICAL SCHOOL, Mortimer Street, W1P 7PN.—*Dean*, Prof. W. W. Slack, M.A., F.R.C.S.; *Secretary*, Dr. D. Sanders.
ROYAL FREE HOSPITAL SCHOOL OF MEDICINE, Rowland Hill Street, NW3 2PF.—*Dean*, B. B. MacGillivray, F.R.C.P.; *Secretary*, B. A. Blatch.
ST. BARTHOLOMEW'S HOSPITAL MEDICAL COLLEGE, West Smithfield, EC1A 7BE.—*Dean*, Dr. I. Kelsey Fry, D.M., F.R.C.P.; *Secretary*, D. J. Brown, M.B.E., M.A.
ST. GEORGE'S HOSPITAL MEDICAL SCHOOL, Cranmer Terrace, Tooting, SW17 0RE.—*Dean*, Dr. R. J. West, M.D., F.R.C.P., D.Ch.; *Secretary*, R. B. Hill, M.A., M.SC.
ST. MARY'S HOSPITAL MEDICAL SCHOOL, Norfolk Place, Paddington, W2 1PG.—*Dean*, Prof. P. Richards, M.A., PH.D., M.D., F.R.C.P.; *Secretary*, K. Lockyer.
UNITED MEDICAL AND DENTAL SCHOOLS OF GUY'S AND ST. THOMAS'S HOSPITALS, Guy's Campus: London Bridge, SE1 9RT; St. Thomas's Campus: Lambeth Palace Road, SE1 7EH.—*Deans*, B. Creamer, M.D., F.R.C.P., Prof. T. J. H. Clark, M.D., F.R.C.P.; *Dean of Dental Studies*, Prof. A. H. R. Rowe; *Secretary*, D. G. Bompas, C.M.G., M.A.
UNIVERSITY COLLEGE, LONDON, SCHOOL OF MEDICINE, Gower Street WC1E 6BT.

POSTGRADUATE MEDICAL SCHOOLS OF THE UNIVERSITY OF LONDON

LONDON SCHOOL OF HYGIENE AND TROPICAL MEDICINE, Keppel Street WC1E 7HT. Dr. C. E. Gordon Smith, C.B., M.D., F.R.C.P., *Dean*.
ROYAL POSTGRADUATE MEDICAL SCHOOL, Du Cane Road W12 0SH. Dr. D. N. S. Kerr, F.R.C.P., *Dean*.

BRITISH POSTGRADUATE MEDICAL FEDERATION (University of London), 33 Millman Street, WC1N 3EJ. Sir David Innes Williams M.D., M.Chir., F.R.C.S., *Director*.
Comprises:—
INSTITUTE OF BASIC MEDICAL SCIENCES, 35–45 Lincoln's Inn Fields, WC2A 3PN. Prof. G. P. Lewis, *Academic Dean*.

INSTITUTE OF CANCER RESEARCH, Royal Cancer Hospital, 17a Onslow Gardens SW7 3AL. Prof. R. A. Weiss, *Director.*

CARDIOTHORACIC INSTITUTE, Fulham Road, SW3 6HP. Prof. Margaret Turner-Warwick, F.R.C.P., *Dean.*

INSTITUTE OF CHILD HEALTH, 30 Guilford Street, W.C.1. Prof. P. J. Graham, F.R.C.P., *Dean.*

INSTITUTE OF DENTAL SURGERY, Eastman Dental Hospital, Gray's Inn Road, WC1X 8LD. Prof. G. B. Winter, D.Ch., F.D.S., *Dean.*

INSTITUTE OF DERMATOLOGY, St. John's Hospital for Diseases of the Skin, Lisle Street, W.C.2. Prof. E. Wilson Jones, F.R.C.P., F.R.C.Path, *Dean.*

INSTITUTE OF LARYNGOLOGY AND OTOLOGY, Royal National Throat, Nose and Ear Hospital, 330–332 Gray's Inn Road, WC1X 8EE. P. McKelvie, F.R.C.S., *Dean.*

INSTITUTE OF NEUROLOGY, National Hospital, Queen Square, WC1N 3BG. Prof. J. Marshall, D.SC., M.D., F.R.C.P., *Dean.*

INSTITUTE OF OBSTETRICS AND GYNÆCOLOGY, Queen Charlotte's Maternity Hospital, Goldhawk Road, W6 0XG. Prof. M. G. Elder, *Dean.*

INSTITUTE OF OPHTHALMOLOGY, Judd Street, WC1H 9QS. R. K. Blach, M.D., F.R.C.S., *Dean.*

INSTITUTE OF ORTHOPÆDICS, Royal National Orthopædic Hospital, Brockley Hill, Stanmore, Middx. HA7 4LP. E. L. Trickey, F.R.C.S., *Dean.*

INSTITUTE OF PSYCHIATRY, De Crespigny Park, Denmark Hill, SE5 8AF. Dr. R. M. Murray, M.D., M.R.C.psych., *Dean.*

INSTITUTE OF UROLOGY, 172 Shaftsbury Avenue, WC2H 8JE. F. D. Thompson, F.R.C.P., *Dean.*

LOUGHBOROUGH UNIVERSITY OF TECHNOLOGY (1966)
Loughborough LE11 3TU

Full-time Students (1984–85), 5,150.
Chancellor, Sir Arnold Hall, M.A., F.R.S.
Vice-Chancellor, Prof. J. G. Phillips, PH.D.
Registrar, H. Brooks, B.SC. (Econ.).

THE UNIVERSITY OF MANCHESTER
Oxford Road, Manchester M13 9PL

(Founded 1851; re-organized 1880 and 1903).

Full-time Students (1984–85), 15,499.
Chancellor, The Duke of Devonshire, P.C., M.C. (1965).
Vice-Chancellor, Prof. M. H. Richmond, PH.D., SC.D., F.R.S. (1981).
Registrar, K. E. Kitchen, M.A. (1979).

UNIVERSITY OF MANCHESTER INSTITUTE OF SCIENCE AND TECHNOLOGY (1824)
P.O. Box 88, Manchester M60 1QD

Full-time Students (1984–85), 3,948.
President, Sir John Mason, F.R.S.
Principal, Prof. H. C. A. Hankins, PH.D.
Secretary and Registrar, D. H. McWilliam, B.A.

THE UNIVERSITY OF NEWCASTLE UPON TYNE
(Founded 1852; re-organized 1908, 1937 and 1963)
Newcastle upon Tyne NE1 7RU

Full-time Students (1984–85), 7,532.
Chancellor, The Duke of Northumberland, K.G., P.C., G.C.V.O., T.D., F.R.S. (1963).
Vice-Chancellor, Prof. L. W. Martin, M.A., Ph.D.
Registrar, D. E. T. Nicholson, M.A.

THE UNIVERSITY OF NOTTINGHAM (1948)
University Park, Nottingham NG7 2RD

Full-time Students (1984–85), 6,839.
Chancellor, Sir Gordon Hobday, PH.D., F.R.S.C.
Vice-Chancellor, B. C. L. Weedon, C.B.E., PH.D., D.SC., F.R.S., F.R.S.C.
Registrar, G. E. Chandler, B.A.

THE UNIVERSITY OF READING (1926)
Whiteknights, P.O. Box 217, Reading RG6 2AH

Full-time Students (1984–85), 5,599.
Chancellor, The Lord Sherfield, G.C.B., G.C.M.G. (1970).
Vice-Chancellor, E. S. Page, M.A., PH.D. (1979).
Registrar, T. Bottomley, B.A. (1982).
Bursar, R. H. C. Ascott, M.A.

UNIVERSITY OF SALFORD (1967)
Salford M5 4WT

Full-time Students (1984–85), 3,528.
Chancellor, H.R.H. The Prince Philip, Duke of Edinburgh, K.G., P.C., K.T., O.M., G.B.E., F.R.S.
Vice-Chancellor, J. M. Ashworth, PH.D., M.A.
Registrar, S. R. Bosworth, B.A.

THE UNIVERSITY OF SHEFFIELD (1905)
Sheffield S10 2TN

Full-time Students (1984–85), 7,478.
Chancellor, Sir Frederick Dainton, PH.D., SC.D., M.A., F.R.S. (1979).
Vice-Chancellor, Prof. G. D. Sims, O.B.E., M.SC., PH.D. (1974).
Registrar and Secretary, J. S. Padley, PH.D. (1982).

THE UNIVERSITY OF SOUTHAMPTON (1952)
Highfield, Southampton SO9 5NH

Full-time Students (1984–85), 6,377.
Chancellor, The Earl Jellicoe, P.C., D.S.O., M.C.
Vice-Chancellor, Dr. G. R. Higginson, PH.D.
Secretary and Registrar, D. A. Schofield, M.A. (1978).
Academic Registrar, Miss A. E. Clarke, B.A. (1978).

UNIVERSITY OF SURREY (1966)
Guildford, Surrey GU2 5XH

Full-time Students (1984–85), 3,170.
Chancellor, H.R.H. The Duke of Kent, G.C.M.G., G.C.V.O.
Vice-Chancellor, A. Kelly, PH.D., SC.D., F.R.S.
Academic Registrar, G. Haigh, PH.D.
Secretary, L. J. Kail.

THE UNIVERSITY OF SUSSEX (1961)
Falmer, Brighton BN1 9RH

Full-time Students (1984–85), 4,298.
Chancellor, The Earl of March and Kinrara.
Vice-Chancellor, Prof. Sir Denys Wilkinson, M.A., Ph.D., F.R.S.
Registrar and Secretary, G. Lockwood, D.phil.

THE UNIVERSITY OF WARWICK (1965)
Coventry CV4 7AL

Full-time Students (1984–85), 5,432.
Chancellor, The Lord Scarman, P.C., O.B.E., M.A.
Vice-Chancellor, C. L. Brundin, Ph.D.
Registrar, M. L. Shattock, M.A.

THE UNIVERSITY OF YORK (1963)
Heslington, York YO1 5DD

Full-time Students (1984–85), 3,383.
Chancellor, The Lord Swann, Ph.D., F.R.S.
Vice-Chancellor, Prof. S. B. Saul, Ph.D.
Registrar, Anne B. Riddell.

ROYAL COLLEGE OF ART, 1837
Kensington Gore SW7 2EU

Under Royal Charter (1967) the Royal College of Art grants the degrees of Doctor, Doctor of Philosophy, Master of Arts and Master of Design (RCA).
Students (1985), 616 (all postgraduate).
Provost, Sir Hugh Casson, C.H., K.C.V.O., P.P.R.A., M.A.
Registrar, B. M. Cooper, B.A..

CRANFIELD INSTITUTE OF TECHNOLOGY 1969
Cranfield, Bedford MK43 0AL

Under Royal Charter (1969) the Cranfield Institute of Technology grants degrees in applied science, engineering, technology and management.
Full-time Students (1984–85), 1,858.
Chancellor, The Lord Kings Norton, Ph.D., D.I.C.
Vice-Chancellor, Sir Henry Chilver, Ph.d., F.R.S.
General Secretary, P. A. Digger.

THE OPEN UNIVERSITY (1969)
Walton Hall, Milton Keynes MK7 6AA

Students (1984), 120,000.
Tuition by correspondence linked with special radio and television programmes, summer schools and a locally-based tutorial and counselling service. Under Royal Charter the University awards degrees of B.A., B.Phil., M.A., M.Sc., M.Phil., Ph.D., D.Sc. and D.Litt. There are six faculties—arts, School of Education, mathematics, science, social sciences and technology and a wide range of continuing education courses.
Chancellor, The Lord Briggs, M.A.
Vice-Chancellor, J. H. Horlock, Ph.D., Sc.D., F.R.S.
Secretary, D. J. Clinch.

THE UNIVERSITY OF WALES (1893)
Cathays Park, Cardiff

Chancellor, H.R.H. The Prince of Wales, K.G., K.T., G.C.B., A.D.C. (1976).
Pro-Chancellor, The Lord Cledwyn of Penrhos, P.C., C.H. (1985).
Vice-Chancellor, Dr. G. Owen, D.Sc.
Registrar, M. A. R. Kemp, Ph.D.

Colleges

University College of Wales, Aberystwyth.—*Princ.*, G. Owen, D.Sc. (1979).
University College of North Wales, Bangor.—*Princ.*, Prof. E. Sunderland, M.A., Ph.D. (1984).
University of Wales Institute of Science and Technology, Cardiff.—*Princ.*, A. F. Trotman-Dickenson, M.A., Ph.D., D.Sc. (1968).
Cardiff (University College).—*Princ.*, C. W. L. Bevan, C.B.E., D.Sc., F.R.S.C. (1966).
Lampeter (St. David's College).—*Princ.*, Prof. B. R. Morris, M.A., D.Phil. (1980).
Swansea (University College).—*Princ.*, Prof. B. L. Clarkson, B.Sc., Ph.D., (1982).
University of Wales College of Medicine, Cardiff.—*Provost*, Prof. H. L. Duthie, M.D., Ch.M., F.R.C.S. (1979).

SCOTLAND

UNIVERSITY OF ABERDEEN (1495)
Regent Walk, Aberdeen AB9 1FX

Undergraduates (1984–85), 5,472.
Chancellor, Lord Polwarth, T.D., F.R.S.E., F.R.S.A.
Principal, Prof. G. P. McNicol, M.D., Ph.D., F.R.C.P. (1981).
Secretary, W. M. Bradley.
Rector (1984–87), H. Watt.

UNIVERSITY OF EDINBURGH (1583)
Old College, South Bridge, Edinburgh EH8 9YL

Full-time Students (1984–85), 9,802.
Chancellor, H.R.H. The Prince Philip, Duke of Edinburgh, K.G., K.T., O.M., G.B.E., P.C., F.R.S. (1952).
Vice-Chancellor and Principal, J. H. Burnett, M.A., D.Phil., F.R.S.E. (1979).
Secretary, A. M. Currie, O.B.E. (1978).
Rector, A. MacPherson, (1985–88).

UNIVERSITY OF DUNDEE (1967)
Dundee DD1 4HN

Full-time Students (1984–85), 3,588.
Chancellor, The Earl of Dalhousie, K.T., G.C.V.O., G.B.E., M.C. (1977).
Principal and Vice-Chancellor, Prof. A. M. Neville, M.C., T.D., M.Sc., Ph.D., F.R.S.E. (1978).
Secretary, R. Seaton, M.A., LL.B. (1973).
Rector, R. Gordon Wilson, M.P. (1983–86).

UNIVERSITY OF GLASGOW (1451)
Glasgow G12 8QQ

Full-time Students (1984–85), 10,085.
Chancellor, Sir Alec Cairncross, K.C.M.G., F.B.A.
Vice-Chancellor, Sir Alwyn Williams, Ph.D., F.R.S., F.R.S.E. (1976).
Registrar, F. Gillanders, M.A.
Secretary to the University Court, R. Ewen, O.B.E., T.D.
Rector, M Kelly, Ph.D. (1984–87).

HERIOT-WATT UNIVERSITY (1966)
Chambers Street, Edinburgh EH1 1HX

Full-time Students (1984–85), 3,155.
Chancellor, The Lord Thomson of Monifieth, P.C., K.T. (1977).
Principal and *Vice-Chancellor*, T. L. Johnston, M.A., Ph.D., F.R.S.E. (1981).
Registrar, D. Sturgeon, B.L.
Secretary, D. I. Cameron, B.L. (1966).

UNIVERSITY OF ST. ANDREWS (1411)
College Gate, St. Andrews KY16 9AJ

Full-time Students (1984–85), 6,380.
Chancellor, Sir Kenneth Dover, M.A., D.Litt., F.R.S.E., F.B.A. (1981).
Principal and Vice-Chancellor, J. S. Watson, M.A., F.R.S.E. (1966).
Registrar and Secretary, M. J. B. Lowe, Ph.D. (1981).
Rector, Katharine Whitehorn (1982–85).

UNIVERSITY OF STIRLING (1967)
Stirling FK9 4LA

Full-time Students (1984–85), 2,700.
Chancellor, Sir Monty Finniston, Ph.D., F.R.S. (1978).
Principal and Vice-Chancellor, Sir Kenneth Alexander, B.Sc., F.R.S.E. (1980).
Secretary, R. G. Bomont, B.Sc. (Econ.) (1973).

UNIVERSITY OF STRATHCLYDE (1964)
16 Richmond Street, Glasgow G1 1XQ

Full-time Students (1984–85), 7,401.
Chancellor, The Lord Todd, O.M., M.A., D.SC., D.Phil., F.R.S., F.R.S.C., P.P.R.S. (1965).
Principal and Vice-Chancellor, G. J. Hills, Ph.D., D.SC., F.R.S.E., F.R.S.C. (1980).
Registrar, D. W. J. Morrell, M.A., LL.B. (1973).

NORTHERN IRELAND

THE QUEEN'S UNIVERSITY OF BELFAST (1908)

Full-time Students (1984–85), 6,936.
Chancellor, Sir Rowland Wright, C.B.E., D.SC., F.R.S.A.
President and Vice-Chancellor, Sir Peter Froggatt, K.B., M.A., M.D., Ph.D. (1976).
Registrar, F. Smyth, LL.B.
Administrative Secretary, D. H. Wilson.

UNIVERSITY OF ULSTER (1984)
Coleraine, Co. Londonderry BT52 1SA
(Amalgamation of New University of Ulster and Ulster Polytechnic)

Full-time Students (1984–85), 7,475.
Chancellor, The Lord Grey of Naunton, G.C.M.G., G.C.V.O., O.B.E. (1980).

Vice-Chancellor, D. S. Birley, M.A.
Academic Registrar, P. J. Conway.
Secretary, J. A. Hunter, M.A.

REPUBLIC OF IRELAND

UNIVERSITY OF DUBLIN TRINITY COLLEGE (1592)
Dublin 2

Full-time Students (1984–85), 6,166.
Chancellor, F. J. C. O'Reilly, LL.D.
Provost, W. A. Watts, M.A., SC.D. (1981).
Registrar, E. Sagarra, M.A., D.Phil. (1981).
Secretary, G. H. H. Giltrap, M.A.

NATIONAL UNIVERSITY OF IRELAND, DUBLIN (1908)
49 Merrion Square, Dublin 2

Full-time Students (1984–85), 18,434.
Chancellor, Dr. T. K. Whitaker.
Vice-Chancellor, Dr. C. ó h Eocha, Ph.D.
Registrar, Dr. M. Gilheany, B.A., B.Comm., M.ECON.SC.

Constituent Colleges
Presidents
Univ. Coll., Dublin, T. Murphy, M.D., D.SC.
Univ. Coll., Cork, T. ó Ciardha, M.A., Ph.D.
Univ. Coll. Galway, C.ó h Eocha, Ph.D.

THE ASSOCIATION OF COMMONWEALTH UNIVERSITIES
36 Gordon Square, WC1H 0PF

The Association holds quinquennial Congresses of the Universities of the Commonwealth and other meetings in the intervening years; publishes the *Commonwealth Universities Yearbook*, handbooks listing scholarships and fellowships, etc.; acts as a general information centre on universities in U.K. and other Commonwealth countries; provides an advisory service for the filling of university teaching staff appointments overseas; administers travelling fellowships for university administrators as well as Commonwealth Foundation and Edward Boyle bursaries for medical students; and runs the Third World Academic Exchange Programme. It also supplies the secretariat for the Commonwealth Scholarship Commission in the United Kingdom and for the Marshall Aid Commemoration Commission.
Secretary General, A. Christodoulou, C.B.E., M.A.

COUNCIL FOR NATIONAL ACADEMIC AWARDS
344–354 Gray's Inn Road, WC1X 8BP

Established in 1964 with powers to award degrees and other academic distinctions, comparable in standard with awards granted and conferred by universities to students in polytechnics and other institutions of higher education in the United Kingdom which do not have the power to award their own degrees. The Council awards degrees and honours degrees of B.A., B.Ed., B.SC., B.Eng. and M.Eng. and higher and research degrees and doctorates. On Sept. 1, 1974, the Council assumed responsibility for the work formerly undertaken by the National Council for Diplomas in Art and Design, and in September, 1976, for the Diploma on Management Studies.
President, H.R.H. The Prince of Wales, K.G., K.T., G.C.B.
Chairman, Sir Alastair Pilkington, F.R.S.
Chief Officer, E. Kerr, B.SC., Ph.D.

POLYTECHNICS

The 30 polytechnics constitute a substantial part of the higher education system in England and Wales. Overall they provide an educational environment for some 260,000 students each year, about half of them following full-time or sandwich courses. Within the public sector their total entry includes over 75% of all first-year enrolments to degree courses and others recognised as being of the same standard. In many cases, their student enrolments at this level match those of most universities. In addition the polytechnics play a major part in the national provision of other advanced courses which do not lead to a degree or degree-equivalent qualifications. The polytechnics' function is to provide virtually the full range of courses, albeit with a pronounced vocational flavour. Together engineering, science and technology currently account for little more than one-third of the enrolments. A further third is involved in administrative, business and social studies and some 13% occur in education. The remaining 22% are spread over other professional and vocational subjects (e.g. architecture, librarianship and catering); music, drama and visual arts; languages (3%) and other arts (3%). Full-time and sandwich course students for the year 1984–85 are shown in parentheses.

CITY OF BIRMINGHAM POLYTECHNIC, Perry Barr, Birmingham B42 2SU (4,687).—*Dir.*, P. C. Knight.
BRIGHTON POLYTECHNIC, Moulsecoomb, Brighton BN2 4AT (4,027).—*Dir.*, G. R. Hall, C.B.E.
BRISTOL POLYTECHNIC, Coldharbour Lane, Frenchay, Bristol BS16 1QY (5,675).—*Dir.*, Dr. W. Birch.
COVENTRY (LANCHESTER) POLYTECHNIC, Priory Street, Coventry CV1 5FB (6,691).—*Dir.*, G. Holroyde.
HATFIELD POLYTECHNIC, P.O. Box 109, College Lane, Hatfield, Herts AL10 9AB (3,900).—*Dir.*, J. Illston, Ph.D., D.SC.
HUDDERSFIELD POLYTECHNIC, Queensgate, Huddersfield HD1 3DH (4,443).—*Rector*, K. J. Durrands.
KINGSTON POLYTECHNIC, Penrhyn Road, Kingston upon Thames KT1 2EE (5,269).—*Dir.*, R. C. Smith, Ph.D.

LANCASHIRE POLYTECHNIC, Preston PR1 2TQ (4,500).—*Dir.*, E. E. Robinson.

LEEDS POLYTECHNIC, Calverley Street, Leeds LS1 3HE (5,500).—*Dir.*, P. J. Nuttgens, C.B.E., ph.D.

LEICESTER POLYTECHNIC, P.O. Box 143, Leicester LE1 9BH (4,494).—*Dir.*, Dr. D. Bethel, C.B.E.

LIVERPOOL POLYTECHNIC, Rodney House, 70 Mount Pleasant, Liverpool L3 5UX (7,025).—*Rector*, J. C. McKenzie.

LONDON:

CITY OF LONDON POLYTECHNIC, 117–119 Houndsditch, EC3A 7BU (2,657).—*Prov.*, J. M. Edwards, Q.C.

MIDDLESEX POLYTECHNIC, 114 Chase Side N14 5PN (7,000).—*Dir.*, R. M. W. Rickett, C.B.E., ph.D.

NORTH-EAST LONDON POLYTECHNIC, Romford Road, E15 4LZ (5,065).—*Dir.*, G. T. Fowler, M.A.

POLYTECHNIC OF CENTRAL LONDON, 309 Regent Street, W1R 8AL (4,120).—*Rector*, Prof. T. E. Burlin, D.SC., ph.D.

POLYTECHNIC OF NORTH LONDON, Holloway Road N7 8DB (5,000).—*Dir.*, (vacant).

POLYTECHNIC OF THE SOUTH BANK, Borough Road, SE1 0AA (4,796).—*Dir.*, J. Beishon, D.Phil.

THAMES POLYTECHNIC, Wellington Street, Woolwich, SE18 6PF (3,978).—*Dir.*, N. Singer, ph.D.

MANCHESTER POLYTECHNIC, All Saints, Manchester M15 6BH (9,444).—*Dir.*, K. Green, M.A.

NEWCASTLE UPON TYNE POLYTECHNIC, Ellison Place, Newcastle upon Tyne NE1 8ST (4,644).—*Dir.*, Prof. L. Barden.

NORTH STAFFORDSHIRE POLYTECHNIC, Beaconside, Stafford ST18 0AD (4,637).—*Dir.*, J. F. Dickenson, ph.D.

OXFORD POLYTECHNIC, Headington, Oxford OX3 0BP (4,320).—*Dir.*, B. L. Tonge, ph.D.

PLYMOUTH POLYTECHNIC, Drake Circus, Plymouth PL4 8AA (4,834).—*Dir.*, R. F. M. Robbins, ph.D.

PORTSMOUTH POLYTECHNIC, Museum Road, Portsmouth PO1 2QQ (6,463).—*Pres.*, H. D. Law, ph.D.

SHEFFIELD CITY POLYTECHNIC, Pond Street, Sheffield S1 1WB (7,750).—*Principal*, J. M. Stoddart.

SUNDERLAND POLYTECHNIC, Langham Tower, Ryhope Road, Sunderland SR2 7EE (4,334).—*Rector*, E. P. Hart, ph.D.

TEESSIDE POLYTECHNIC, Borough Road, Middlesbrough, Cleveland TS1 3BA (3,394).—*Dir.*, M. D. Longfield, ph.D.

TRENT POLYTECHNIC, Burton Street, Nottingham NG1 4BU (7,563).—*Dir.*, Prof. J. O'Neill.

WOLVERHAMPTON POLYTECHNIC, Wulfruna Street, Wolverhampton WV1 1SB (4,579).—*Dir.*, M. J. Harrison, M.A.

POLYTECHNIC OF WALES, Pontypridd, Mid Glamorgan CF37 1DL (4,300).—*Dir.*, J. D. Davies, O.B.E., M.SC., ph.D., D.SC.

COLLEGES

It is not possible to name here all the colleges offering courses of higher or further education. The list that follows is confined to colleges providing at least one full-time course leading to a *first degree* granted by a university or by the Council for National Academic Awards (C.N.A.A.). It does not include colleges forming part of a polytechnic or of a university.

After the name of each college the abbreviated title of the appropriate degree or degrees is given, but the very many *other* qualifications for which the colleges also provide courses are not listed.

ABERDEEN COLLEGE OF EDUCATION (*B.Ed.*), Hilton Place, Aberdeen AB9 1FA.—*Principal*, D. Adams.

BATH COLLEGE OF HIGHER EDUCATION (*B.A., B.Sc., B.Ed.*), Newton Park, Bath BA2 9BN.—*Director*, B. L. Gomes da Costa.

BEDFORD COLLEGE OF HIGHER EDUCATION (*B.A., B.Ed.*), 37 Lansdowne Road, Bedford MK40 2BZ.—*Director*, Dr. P. Mansell.

BISHOP GROSSETESTE COLLEGE (*B.Ed.*), Lincoln, Lincolnshire LN1 3DY.—*Principal*, L. G. Marsh.

BOLTON INSTITUTE OF HIGHER EDUCATION (*B.A., B.Sc., B.Ed., B.Eng.*), Deane Road, Bolton BL3 5AB.—*Principal*, Dr. R. Oxtoby.

BRADFORD AND ILKLEY COMMUNITY COLLEGE (*B.A., B.Ed.*), Great Horton Road, Bradford BD7 1AY.—*Principal*, Dr. P. J. Gallagher.

BRETTON HALL COLLEGE OF HIGHER EDUCATION (*B.A., B.Ed.*), West Bretton, Wakefield, West Yorkshire WF4 4LG.—*Principal*, Dr. J. L. Taylor.

BUCKINGHAMSHIRE COLLEGE OF HIGHER EDUCATION (*B.A., B.Sc.*), Queen Alexandra Road, High Wycombe, Bucks. HP11 2JZ.—*Director*, D. J. Everett.

BULMERSHE COLLEGE OF HIGHER EDUCATION (*B.A., B.Ed.*), Woodlands Avenue, Earley, Reading RG6 1HY.—*Principal*, H. Silver, ph.D.

CAMBERWELL SCHOOL OF ART AND CRAFTS (*B.A.*), Peckham Road, London SE5 8UF—*Principal*, I. E. T. Jenkin. O.B.E.

CAMBORNE SCHOOL OF MINES (*B.Eng.*), Pool, Redruth, Cornwall TR15 3SE.—*Principal*, Dr. P. Hackett.

CAMBRIDGESHIRE COLLEGE OF ARTS AND TECHNOLOGY (*B.A., B.Sc.*), East Road, Cambridge CB1 1PT—*Principal*, R. L. Helmore, C.B.E.

CANTERBURY COLLEGE OF ART (*B.A.*), New Dover Road, Canterbury CT1 3AN.—*Principal*, G. G. Bellamy.

CENTRAL SCHOOL OF ART AND DESIGN (*B.A.*), Southampton Row, London WC1 4AP.—*Principal*, T. H. Pannell.

CENTRAL SCHOOL OF SPEECH AND DRAMA (*B.Ed., B.Sc.*), Embassy Theatre, Eton Avenue, London NW3 3HY.—*Principal*, G. Kitson.

CHARLOTTE MASON COLLEGE (*B.Ed.*), Ambleside, Cumbria LA22 9BB.—*Principal*, J. Thorley, M.A., ph.D.

CHELSEA SCHOOL OF ART (*B.A.*), Manresa Road, London SW3 6LS—*Principal*, J. Barnicoat.

CHESTER COLLEGE (*B.A., B.Ed.*), Cheyney Road, Chester CH1 4BJ.—*Principal*, Dr. M. V. J. Seaborne.

CHRIST CHURCH COLLEGE OF HIGHER EDUCATION (*B.A., B.Sc., B.Ed.*), North Holmes Road, Canterbury, Kent CT1 1QU—*Principal*, M. H. A. Berry, T.D.

COLCHESTER INSTITUTE (*B.A.*), Sheepen Road, Colchester CO3 3LL.—*Director*, J. M. Threlfall.

CRAIGIE COLLEGE OF EDUCATION (*B.Ed.*), Ayr KA8 0SR.—*Principal*, R. C. McNaught.

CREWE AND ALSAGER COLLEGE OF HIGHER EDUCATION (*B.A., B.Ed.*), Crewe Road, Crewe CW1 1DU.—*Director*, Miss B. P. R. Ward, C.B.E.

DARTINGTON COLLEGE OF ARTS (*B.A.*), Totnes, Devon TQ9 6EJ.—*Principal*, C. Roosevelt.

DE LA SALLE COLLEGE (*B.A., B.Sc., B.Ed.*), Hopwood Hall, Middleton, Manchester M24 3XH.—*Principal*, Rev. Br. Wilfrid, M.A.

DERBYSHIRE COLLEGE OF HIGHER EDUCATION (*B.Comb.Studs., B.A., B.Sc., B.Ed.*), Kedleston Road, Derby DE3 1GB.—*Director*, J. May, T.D., ph.D.

DORSET INSTITUTE OF HIGHER EDUCATION (*B.A., B.Sc.*), Wallisdown Road, Wallisdown, Poole BH12 5BB—*Director*, B. R. MacManus.

DUNCAN OF JORDANSTONE COLLEGE OF ART (*B.A., B.Sc., B. Arch.*), Perth Road, Dundee DD1 4HT.—*Principal*, M. Lacome.

DUNDEE COLLEGE OF EDUCATION (*B.Ed.*), Gardyne Road, Dundee DD5 1NY.—*Principal*, W. A. Illsley, ph.D.

DUNDEE COLLEGE OF TECHNOLOGY (*B.A., B.Sc., B.Eng.*), Bell Street, Dundee DD1 1HG.—*Principal*, H. G. Cuming, C.B.E., ph.D.

DUNFERMLINE COLLEGE OF PHYSICAL EDUCATION (*B.Ed.*, *B.A.*), Cramond Road North, Edinburgh EH4 6JD.—*Principal*, Miss J. A. Carroll.

EALING COLLEGE OF HIGHER EDUCATION (*B.A.*), St. Mary's Road, Ealing, London W5 5RF—*Director*, N. Merritt.

EDGE HILL COLLEGE OF HIGHER EDUCATION (*B.A.*, *B.Ed.*, *B.Sc.*), St. Helens Road, Ormskirk, Lancs. L39 4QP.—*Director*, H. Webster.

EDINBURGH COLLEGE OF ART (*B.A.*, *B.Sc.*, *B.Arch.*), Lauriston Place, Edinburgh EH3 9DF.—*Principal*, J. L. Paterson.

ESSEX INSTITUTE OF HIGHER EDUCATION (*B.A.*, *B.Sc.*, *B.Ed.*), Victoria Road South, Chelmsford, Essex CM1 1LL.—*Director*, M. Salmon.

EXETER COLLEGE OF ART AND DESIGN (*B.A.*), Earl Richards Road North, Exeter EX26AS.—*Principal*, D. Jeremiah, PH.D.

FALMOUTH SCHOOL OF ART (*B.A.*), Wood Lane, Falmouth, Cornwall TR11 4RA—*Principal*, T. Cross.

GLASGOW COLLEGE OF BUILDING AND PRINTING (*B.Sc.*), 60 North Hanover Street, Glasgow G1 2BP.—*Principal*, D. McEwan.

GLASGOW COLLEGE OF TECHNOLOGY (*B.A.*, *B.Sc.*), Cowcaddens Road, Glasgow G4 0BA.—*Director*, Dr. N. G. Meadows.

GLASGOW SCHOOL OF ART (*B.A.*, *B.Arch.*), 167 Renfrew Street, Glasgow G3 6RQ.—*Director*, Prof. A. E. Jones.

GLOUCESTERSHIRE COLLEGE OF ARTS AND TECHNOLOGY (*B.A.*, *B.Sc.*), Oxstalls Lane, Gloucester GL2 9HW.—*Principal*, D. Williams.

GWENT COLLEGE OF HIGHER EDUCATION (*B.A.*, *B.Sc.*, *B.Ed.*, *B.Eng.*), Clarence Place, Newport, Gwent NP9 0UW.—*Principal*, M. I. Harris.

HARROW COLLEGE OF HIGHER EDUCATION (*B.A.*), Watford Road, Northwick Park, Harrow, Middlesex HA1 3TP.—*Principal*, Dr. H. R. Harris.

HERTFORDSHIRE COLLEGE OF ART AND DESIGN (*B.A.*), 7 Hatfield Road, St. Albans, Herts. AL1 3RS.

HERTFORDSHIRE COLLEGE OF HIGHER EDUCATION (*B.Ed.*), Wall Hall, Aldenham, Watford WD28AT—*Principal*, D. Haslam, PH.D.

HUMBERSIDE COLLEGE OF HIGHER EDUCATION (*B.A.*, *B.Ed.*, *B.Sc.*), Cottingham Road, Hull HU6 7RT.—*Director*, J. Earls, PH.D.

JEWS' COLLEGE (*B.A.*), Albert Road, Hendon, NW4 2SJ.—*Principal*, Rabbi Dr. J. Sacks.

JORDANHILL COLLEGE OF EDUCATION (*B.Ed.*), Southbrae Drive, Jordanhill, Glasgow G13 1PP.—*Principal*, Dr. T. R. Bone.

KIDDERMINSTER COLLEGE OF FURTHER EDUCATION (*B.A.*), Hoo Road, Kidderminster, Worcs DY10 1LX.—*Principal Designate*, Dr. T. Seddon.

KING ALFRED'S COLLEGE OF HIGHER EDUCATION (*B.A.*, *B.Ed.*), Sparkford Road, Winchester SO22 4NR.—*Principal*, J. A. Cranmer.

LABAN CENTRE FOR MOVEMENT AND DANCE, GOLDSMITHS' COLLEGE (*B.A.*), New Cross, London SE14 6NW.—*Director*, Marion North, PH.D.

LA SAINTE UNION COLLEGE OF HIGHER EDUCATION (*B.A.*, *B.Th.*, *B.Ed.*), The Avenue, Southampton SO9 5HB.—*Principal*, Sister Maria Bernard.

COLLEGE OF LIBRARIANSHIP WALES (*B.Lib.*), Llanbadarn Fawr, Aberystwyth SY23 3AS.—*Acting Principal*, D. Mason.

LIVERPOOL INSTITUTE OF HIGHER EDUCATION (*B.A.*, *B.Ed.*), *Rector*, Dr. J. Burke, P.O. Box 6, Stand Park Road, Liverpool L16 9JD; Christ's and Notre Dame College—*Principal*, Mgr. B. Doyle; S. Katharine's College—*Head of College*, Rev. E. V. Binks.

LONDON BIBLE COLLEGE (*B.A.*), Green Lane, Northwood, Middlesex HA6 2UW.—*Principal*, Dr. M. C. Griffiths.

LONDON COLLEGE OF PRINTING (*B.A.*), Elephant and

Castle, London SE1 6SB.—*Principal*, R. Hedley Lewis.

LOUGHBOROUGH COLLEGE OF ART AND DESIGN (*B.A.*), Radmoor, Loughborough, Leics.—*Principal*, R. H. Hampson.

LUTON COLLEGE OF HIGHER EDUCATION (*B.Sc.*), Park Square, Luton.—*Director*, Dr. R. W. Steed.

MAIDSTONE COLLEGE OF ART (*B.A.*), Oakwood Park, Oakwood Road, Maidstone, Kent.—*Principal*, K. Gribble.

MORAY HOUSE COLLEGE OF EDUCATION (*B.Ed.*), Holyrood Road, Edinburgh EH8 8AQ.—*Principal*, G. Kirk.

NAPIER COLLEGE OF COMMERCE AND TECHNOLOGY (*B.A.*, *B.Sc.*, *B.Eng.*), Colinton Road, Edinburgh EH10 5DT and Sighthill Court, Edinburgh.—*Principal*, Dr. W. A. Turmeau.

NENE COLLEGE (*B.A.*, *B.Sc.*, *B.Ed.*), Moulton Park, Northampton NN2 7AL.—*Director*, Dr. E. Ogilvie.

NEWMAN COLLEGE (*B.Ed.*), Genners Lane, Bartley Green, Birmingham B32 3NT.—*Principal*, Joan Cuming, PH.D.

NONINGTON COLLEGE (*B.A.*), Nonington, Dover, Kent CT15 4HH.—*Principal*, S. Beaumont.

NORMAL COLLEGE (*B.A.*, *B.Ed.*), Bangor, North Wales.—*Principal*, R. Williams.

NORTH CHESHIRE COLLEGE (*B.A.*), Fearnhead, Warrington WA2 0DB.—*Director*, W. E. Buckley.

NORTH EAST SURREY COLLEGE OF TECHNOLOGY (*B.Sc.*), Reigate Road, Ewell, Epsom, Surrey KT17 3DS.

NORTH E. WALES INSTITUTE OF HIGHER EDUCATION (*B.A.*, *B.Ed.*), Cefn Road, Wrexham, Clwyd LL13 9HL.—*Principal*, Prof. G. O. Phillips, PH.D.

NORTH RIDING COLLEGE (*B.Ed.*), Filey Road, Scarborough, North Yorkshire YO11 3AZ.—*Principal*, F. W. Wright.

NORWICH SCHOOL OF ART (*B.A.*), St. George Street, Norwich, Norfolk NR3 1BB.—*Principal*, W. G. English.

OAK HILL COLLEGE (*B.A.*), Chase Side, Southgate, N14 4PS.—*Principal*, Rev. Canon D. H. Wheaton.

PAISLEY COLLEGE OF TECHNOLOGY (*B.A.*, *B.Sc.*, *B.Eng.*), High Street, Paisley PA1 2BE.—*Principal*, T. M. Howie.

QUEEN MARGARET COLLEGE (*B.A.*, *B.Sc.*), 36 Clerwood Terrace, Edinburgh EH12 8TS.—*Principal*, D. F. Leach.

THE QUEEN'S COLLEGE, GLASGOW (*B.A.*, *B.Sc.*), 1 Park Drive, Glasgow G3 6LP.—*Principal*, Dr. G. A. Richardson.

RAVENSBOURNE COLLEGE OF ART AND DESIGN (*B.A.*), Walden Road, Chislehurst, Kent BR7 5SN.—*Principal*, N. J. Frewing.

RIPON AND YORK ST. JOHN COLLEGE OF HIGHER EDUCATION (*B.A.*, *B.Sc.*, *B.Ed.*), Lord Mayor's Walk, York YO3 7EX.—*Principal*, Dr. G. P. McGregor.

ROBERT GORDON'S INSTITUTE OF TECHNOLOGY (*B.A.*, *B.Sc.*, *B.Eng.*), Schoolhill, Aberdeen AB9 1FR.—*Principal*, Dr. D. A. Kennedy.

ROEHAMPTON INSTITUTE OF HIGHER EDUCATION (*B.A.*, *B.Sc.*, *B.Ed.*), Roehampton Lane, London SW15 5PJ.—*Rector*, K. W. Keohane, C.B.E., PH.D.

ROLLE COLLEGE (*B.A.*, *B.Ed.*), Exmouth, Devon EX8 2AT.—*Principal*, M. Preston, PH.D.

ROSE BRUFORD COLLEGE OF SPEECH AND DRAMA (*B.A.*), Lamorbey Park, Sidcup, Kent DA15 9DF.—*Principal*, J. N. Benedetti.

ROYAL ACADEMY OF MUSIC (*B.Mus.*), Marylebone Road, London NW1 5HT.—*Principal*, Dr. D. Lumsden.

ROYAL COLLEGE OF MUSIC (*B.Mus.*), Prince Consort Road, South Kensington, London SW7 2BS.—*Director*, M. G. Matthews, F.R.C.M.

ROYAL NAVAL ENGINEERING COLLEGE (*B.Eng.*), Manadon, Plymouth PL5 3AQ.—*Dean*, Capt. A. O. Holding.

ROYAL SCOTTISH ACADEMY OF MUSIC AND DRAMA (*B.A.*), St. George's Place, Glasgow G.2.

S. MARTIN'S COLLEGE OF HIGHER EDUCATION (*B.A., B.Ed.*), Bowerham, Lancaster LA1 3JD.—*Principal*, R. Clayton.

ST. ANDREW'S COLLEGE OF EDUCATION (*B.Ed.*), Bearsden, Glasgow G61 4QA.—*Principal*, Sr. Margaret Sheridan.

ST. JOHN'S SEMINARY (*B.Th.*), Wonersh, Guildford GU5 0QX.—*Rector*, Rev. Mgr. H. C. Budd.

ST. JOSEPH'S COLLEGE OF EDUCATION (*B.Ed.*), Trench House, Stewartstown Road, Belfast.—*Principal*, Very Rev. Canon M. Dallat.

COLLEGE OF ST. MARK AND ST. JOHN (*B.A., B.Ed.*), Derriford Road, Plymouth PL6 8BH.—*Principal*, J. E. Anderson.

ST. MARTIN'S SCHOOL OF ART (*B.A.*), 107–109 Charing Cross Road, London WC2H 0DU.—*Principal*, I. Simpson.

ST. MARY'S COLLEGE (*B.A., B.Sc., B.Ed.*), Strawberry Hill, Twickenham, Middlesex TW1 4SX.—*Principal*, Rev. D. A. Beirne.

ST. MARY'S COLLEGE OF EDUCATION (*B.Ed.*), 191 Falls Road, Belfast BT12 6FE.—*Principal*, Very Rev. Canon M. Dallat.

COLLEGE OF ST. PAUL AND ST. MARY (*B.A., B.Sc., B.Ed.*), The Park, Cheltenham, Glos. GL50 2RH.—*Principal*, G. D. Barnes.

SALISBURY AND WELLS THEOLOGICAL COLLEGE (*B.Th.*), Salisbury SP1 2EE.—*Principal*, Rev. Canon R. J. A. Askew.

SCOTTISH COLLEGE OF TEXTILES (*B.A., B.Sc.*), Netherdale, Galashiels, Selkirkshire TD1 3HF.—*Principal*, J. C. Furniss.

SOUTHAMPTON INSTITUTE OF HIGHER EDUCATION (*B.A., B.Sc.*), East Park Terrace, Southampton SO9 4WW.—*Principal*, J. W. Longden.

SOUTH GLAMORGAN INSTITUTE OF HIGHER EDUCATION (*B.A., B.Sc., B.Ed.*), Western Avenue, Llandaff, Cardiff CF5 2YB.—*Principal*, Dr. E. J. Brent.

SPURGEON'S COLLEGE (*B.A.*), South Norwood Hill, London SE25 6DJ.—*Principal*, Rev. R. Brown, PH.D.

STOCKPORT COLLEGE OF TECHNOLOGY (*B.Sc., B.Eng.*), Wellington Road South, Stockport SK1 3UQ.

STOURBRIDGE COLLEGE OF TECHNOLOGY AND ART (*B.A.*), Hagley Road, Stourbridge, West Midlands.—*Principal*, T. H. Jenkins.

STRANMILLIS COLLEGE (*B.Ed.*), Stranmillis Road, Belfast BT9 5DY.—*Principal*, R. J. Rodgers, PH.D.

THEOLOGICAL COLLEGE (*B.Th.*), Chichester PO19 3ES.—*Principal*, Rev. Canon J. W. Hind.

TRINITY AND ALL SAINTS' COLLEGE (*B.A., B.Sc., B.Ed.*), Brownberrie Lane, Horsforth, Leeds LS18 5HD.—*Principal*, Dr. H. M. Hallaway.

TRINITY COLLEGE (*B.A.*), Stoke Hill, Bristol BS9 1JP.—*Principal*, Rev. G. Carey, PH.D.

TRINITY COLLEGE (*B.A., B.Ed.*), Carmarthen, Dyfed, SA31 3EP.—*Principal*, D. C. Jones-Davies.

TRINITY COLLEGE OF MUSIC (*B.Mus.*), 11–13 Mandeville Place, London W1M 6AQ.—*Principal*, M. Davies, C.B.E.

WATFORD COLLEGE (*B.Sc.*), Hempstead Road, Watford, WD1 3EZ.—*Principal*, T. J. Howard, PH.D.

WELSH COLLEGE OF MUSIC AND DRAMA (*B.A., B.Ed.*), Castle Grounds, Cathays Park, Cardiff.—*Principal*, P. Fletcher.

WEST GLAMORGAN INSTITUTE OF HIGHER EDUCATION (*B.A., B.Ed.*), Townhill Road, Cockett, Swansea SA2 0UT.—*Principal*, G. Stockdale, PH.D.

WESTHILL COLLEGE (*B.Ed.*), Hamilton Building, Weoley Park Road, Selly Oak, Birmingham B29 6LL.—*Principal*, Rev. G. Bamford, C.B.E.

WEST LONDON INSTITUTE OF HIGHER EDUCATION (*B.A., B.Sc., B.Ed.*), Lancaster House, Borough Road, Isleworth, Middlesex TW7 5DU.—*Principal*, J. E. Kane, M.Ed., PH.D.

WEST MIDLANDS COLLEGE OF HIGHER EDUCATION (*B.A., B.Ed.*), Gorway, Walsall.—*Principal*, T. J. Cox.

WESTMINSTER COLLEGE (*B.A., B.Ed.*), North Hinksey, Oxford OX2 9AT.—*Principal*, Rev. Dr. K. B. Wilson.

WEST SURREY COLLEGE OF ART AND DESIGN (*B.A.*), Falkner Road, The Hart, Farnham, Surrey GU9 7DS.—*Principal*, R. J. Morris.

WEST SUSSEX INSTITUTE OF HIGHER EDUCATION (*B.A., B.Ed.*), The Dome, Upper Bognor Road, Bognor Regis, West Sussex PO21 1HR.—*Director*, J. F. Wyatt.

WIMBLEDON SCHOOL OF ART (*B.A.*), Merton Hall Road, Wimbledon, London SW19 3QA.—*Principal*, M. Murphy.

WINCHESTER SCHOOL OF ART (*B.A.*), Park Avenue, Winchester, Hampshire SO23 8DL.—*Principal*, D. C. Sherlock, F.R.S.A..

WORCESTER COLLEGE OF HIGHER EDUCATION (*B.A., B.Sc., B.Ed.*), Henwick Grove, Worcester WR2 6AJ.—*Principal*, D. R. Shadbolt, D.PHIL.

GRANTS FOR STUDENTS

Post-School

Students in England and Wales who plan to take a full-time or sandwich course of further study after leaving school may be eligible for a grant from their local education authority (L.E.A.). Enquiries should be made to the authority in the area in which the student normally lives. There is a list on pages 514–515. Application forms are available from schools and L.E.A.s. Completed forms should be sent to the appropriate L.E.A. as early as possible. For courses beginning in the autumn, applications should, however, not be made earlier than the preceding January.

Types of grant. Grants are of two kinds: mandatory and discretionary. *Mandatory grants* (370,500 in 1982–83) are those which L.E.A.s *must* pay to students who are attending what are called "designated courses" and who can satisfy certain other conditions; such a grant is normally to enable the student to attend only one designated course and there is no general entitlement to an award for any particular number of years. *Discretionary grants* (45,400 full value awards in 1982–83) are those for which each L.E.A. has discretion to decide its own policy.

Designated courses include those which are *full-time or sandwich* and lead to a university or C.N.A.A. (*see* p. 510) degree; the diploma of higher education; the higher national diploma of the Business & Technician Education Council; and initial teacher-training courses including courses for the postgraduate certificate in education and the art teachers' certificate or diploma. Also included may be *part-time* initial teacher-training courses designated for this purpose.

Eligibility. To be eligible for a grant, students admitted to a designated course must, *inter alia*:—

(a) have been ordinarily resident in the United Kingdom for the three years immediately preceding the academic year in which the course begins. (If the student was absent because his or her family was temporarily employed abroad, the L.E.A. should be consulted for advice.)

(b) have not previously attended one or more courses of advanced further education of more than two years' duration. Attendance for up to one term on such a course is disregarded;

(c) apply for the grant before the end of the first term of the course.

Condition (b) above does not apply to students wishing to take a course leading to a postgraduate certificate in education or the art teachers' certificate or diploma.

Value. A means-tested maintenance grant, usually paid once a term through the university or college office, covers periods of attendance during term and the Christmas and Easter vacations but not the summer vacation. It is subject to deduction on account of the student's own income and his/her parents' or spouse's income. (70 per cent of all dependent students in 1982–83 getting full value awards had parents who were assessed as having to pay a contribution towards the maintenance element of the grant.) Tuition fees in full are usually paid direct to the university or college by the L.E.A.

Cost. Local authority expenditure on student maintenance in 1982–83 was £557·3 million.

In Scotland corresponding awards are made by the Scottish Education Department and in Northern Ireland by Education and Library Boards.

Postgraduate awards

A number of schemes of postgraduate bursaries or studentships for U.K. residents are administered by the Department of Education and Science and the five research councils (agricultural and food, economic and social science, medical, natural environment, science and engineering). 14,800 awards were made in 1982–83.

LOCAL EDUCATION AUTHORITIES

English and Welsh Counties

AVON, P.O. Box 57, Avon House North, St. James Barton, Bristol BS99 7EB.—*Director*, P. Coleman.

BEDFORDSHIRE, County Hall, Bedford MK42 9AP.— *Chief Education Officer*, D. P. J. Browning.

BERKSHIRE, Shire Hall, Shinfield Park, Reading RG2 9XD.—*Director*, P. E. Edwards.

BUCKINGHAMSHIRE, County Hall, Aylesbury HP20 1UA.—*Chief Education Officer*, C. Garrett.

CAMBRIDGESHIRE, Shire Hall, Castle Hill, Cambridge CB3 0AP.—*Chief Education Officer*, G. H. Morris.

CHESHIRE, County Hall, Chester CH1 1SF.—*Director*, N. Fitton.

CLEVELAND, Woodlands Road, Middlesbrough.— *County Education Officer*, A. H. R. Calderwood.

CLWYD, Shire Hall, Mold CH7 6NB.—*Director*, H. K. Evans.

CORNWALL, County Hall, Truro TR1 3AY.—*Secretary for Education*, N. W. Barr.

CUMBRIA, 5 Portland Square, Carlisle CA1 1PU.— *Director*, P. C. Boulter.

DERBYSHIRE, County Offices, Matlock DE4 3AG.— *Director*, J. G. Evans.

DEVON, County Hall, Exeter EX2 4QG.—*Chief Education Officer*, J. G. Owen, C.B.E.

DORSET, County Hall, Dorchester DT1 1XJ.—*Director*, P. L. Gedling.

DURHAM, County Hall, Durham DH1 5UJ.—*Director*, D. J. W. Sowell.

DYFED, Pibwrlwyd, Carmarthen.—*Director*, W. J. Phillips.

ESSEX, Threadneedle House, Market Road, Chelmsford CM1 1LD.—*County Education Officer*, J. O. Morris.

GLOUCESTERSHIRE, Shire Hall, Gloucester GL1 2TP.— *Chief Education Officer*, K. D. Anderson.

GWENT, County Hall, Cwmbran NP44 2XH.—*Director*, E. H. Loudon.

GWYNEDD, County Offices, Shirehall Street, Caernarfon LL55 1SH.—*Director*, G. E. Humphreys.

HAMPSHIRE, The Castle, Winchester SO23 8UG.— *County Education Officer*, R. D. Clark.

HEREFORD AND WORCESTER, 25 Castle Street, Worcester WR1 3AG.—*County Education Officer*, J. W. Turnbull.

HERTFORDSHIRE, County Hall, Hertford SG13 8DF.— *County Education Officer*, D. Fisher.

HUMBERSIDE, County Hall, Beverley HU17 9BA.— *Director*, J. Bower.

ISLE OF WIGHT, County Hall, Newport PO30 1UD.— *County Education Officer*, R. O. Burton.

KENT, Springfield, Maidstone.—*County Education Officer*, B. Oatley.

LANCASHIRE, P.O. Box 61, County Hall, Preston PR1 8RJ.—*Chief Education Officer*, A. J. Collier.

LEICESTERSHIRE, County Hall, Glenfield, Leicester LE3 8RF.—*Director*, K. H. Wood-Allum.

LINCOLNSHIRE, County Offices, Lincoln LN1 1YQ.— *Director*, F. G. Rickard.

MID GLAMORGAN, County Hall, Cathays Park, Cardiff CF1 3NE.—*Director*, K. S. Hopkins.

NORFOLK, County Hall, Norwich NR1 2DH.—*County Education Officer*, M. H. Edwards.

NORTHAMPTONSHIRE, Northampton House, Northampton.—*County Education Officer*, M. J. Henley.

NORTHUMBERLAND, County Hall, Morpeth NE61 2EF.—*Director*, C. C. Tipple.

NOTTINGHAMSHIRE, County Hall, West Bridgford, Nottingham NG2 7QP.—*Director*, A. J. Fox.

OXFORDSHIRE, Macclesfield House, New Road, Oxford OX1 1NA.—*Chief Education Officer*, T. R. P. Brighouse.

POWYS, The Lindens, Spa Road, Llandrindod Wells.— *Director*, R. W. Bevan.

SHROPSHIRE, Shirehall, Abbey Foregate, Shrewsbury SY2 6ND.—*County Education Officer*, J. Boyers.

SOMERSET, County Hall, Taunton TA1 4DY.—*Director*, B. Taylor.

SOUTH GLAMORGAN, County Offices, Kingsway, Cardiff.—*Director*, L. J. Cule.

STAFFORDSHIRE, County Education Offices, Tipping Street, Stafford.—*Chief Education Officer*, Dr. P. J. Hunter.

SUFFOLK, St. Andrew House, County Hall, Ipswich IP4 1LJ.—*County Education Officer*, D. G. Graham.

SURREY, County Hall, Kingston upon Thames.— *County Education Officer*, M. C. Pinchin.

SUSSEX (East), County Hall, Lewes.—*County Education Officer*, J. A. Carter.

SUSSEX (West), County Hall, Chichester PO19 1RQ.— *Director*, R. D. C. Bunker.

WARWICKSHIRE, P.O. Box 24, 22 Northgate Street, Warwick CV34 4SR.—*County Education Officer*, M. L. Ridger.

WEST GLAMORGAN, County Hall, Swansea SA1 3SN.—*Director*, J. Beale.

WILTSHIRE, County Hall, Trowbridge BA14 8JN.— *Chief Education Officer*, I. M. Slocombe.

YORKSHIRE (North), County Hall, Northallerton DL7 8AE.—*County Education Officer*, F. F. Evans.

London

INNER LONDON EDUCATION AUTHORITY.—*Controller of Education*, W. H. Stubbs.

Education Officers

BARKING, Town Hall, Dagenham IG11 7LU.—A. W. Bush.

BARNET, Town Hall, Friern Barnet N11 3DL.—J. Dawkins.

BEXLEY, Town Hall, Crayford DA1 4EN.—*Director*, P. Geen.

BRENT, Chesterfield House, Park Lane, Wembley HA9 7RW.—*Director*, A. Parsons.

BROMLEY, Town Hall, Bromley, Kent BR1 1SB.—G. Grainge.

CROYDON, Taberner House, Park Lane CR9 3JS.— *Director*, D. Naismith.

EALING, Hadley House, Uxbridge Road W5 2EY.—R. J. Hartles, C.B.E.

ENFIELD, Civic Centre, Silver Street, Enfield EN1 3XA.—*Director,* G. Hutchinson.

HARINGEY, 48–62 Station Road N22 4TY.—A. Lenney.

HARROW, Civic Centre, Station Road, Harrow HA1 2UW.—*Director,* J. F. Mann.

HAVERING, Mercury House, Mercury Gardens, Romford, Essex RM1 3DR.—*Director,* B. H. Laister.

HILLINGDON, Civic Centre, High Street, Uxbridge, Middx UB8 1UW.—*Director,* J. Lyn-Jones.

HOUNSLOW, Civic Centre, Lampton Road, TW3 4DN.—*Director,* J. Cooper.

KINGSTON UPON THAMES, Guildhall, KT1 1EU.—*Director,* R. J. McCloy.

MERTON, Crown House, London Road, Morden, Surrey SM4 5DX.—*Director,* R. Davies.

NEWHAM, 29 Broadway, Stratford E.15.—(vacant).

REDBRIDGE, Lynton House, 255–259 High Road, Ilford, Essex IG1 1NN.—K. G. M. Ratcliffe.

RICHMOND UPON THAMES, Regal House, London Road, Twickenham, Middx. TW1 3AA.—*Director,* I. Waters.

SUTTON, The Grove, Carshalton, Surrey SM5 3AL.—*Director,* C. Melville.

WALTHAM FOREST, Municipal Offices, High Road, Leyton E10 5QJ.—I. Smith.

Metropolitan District Councils

BARNSLEY, Berneslai Close, Barnsley S70 2TA.—*Education Officer,* T. Brooks.

BIRMINGHAM, Margaret Street, Birmingham B3 3BU.—*Chief Education Officer,* J. M. Crawford.

BOLTON, Paderborn House, Civic Centre, Bolton BL1 1JW.—*Director,* B. Hughes.

BRADFORD, Provincial House, Bradford.—*Director,* W. R. Knight.

BURY, Athenaeum House, Market Street, Bury.—*Director,* M. Gray.

CALDERDALE.—Northgate House, Northgate, Halifax HX1 1UN.—*Chief Education Officer,* A. Pickvance.

COVENTRY, Council House, Earl Street, CV1 5RR.—*Education Officer,* R. Aitken.

DONCASTER, Princegate DN1 3BN.—*Director,* M. J. Pass.

DUDLEY, 2 St. James's Road, Dudley.—*Chief Education Officer,* R. K. Westerby.

GATESHEAD, Prince Consort Road South NE8 4LP.—*Education Officer,* W. H. Cubitt.

KIRKLEES, Oldgate House, 2 Oldgate, Huddersfield HD1 6QW.—*Education Officer,* P. G. Davies.

KNOWSLEY, Huyton Hey Road, Huyton, Merseyside L36 5YH.—*Education Officer,* P. M. Neafsey.

LEEDS, Merrion House, Merrion Centre LS2 8JY.—*Director,* S. Johnson, C.B.E.

LIVERPOOL, 14 Sir Thomas Street L1 6BJ.—*Education Officer,* K. A. Antcliffe.

MANCHESTER, Cumberland House, Crown Square M60 3BB.—*Chief Education Officer,* G. Hainsworth.

NEWCASTLE UPON TYNE, Civic Centre, Barrass Bridge NE99 2BN.—*Director,* B. M. O'Reilly.

NORTH TYNESIDE, The Chase, North Shields NE29 0HW.—*Education Officer,* J. F. Partington.

OLDHAM, Old Town Hall, Chadderton.—*Education Officer,* T. J. Farrington.

ROCHDALE, Municipal Offices, Smith Street, Rochdale.—*Chief Education Officer,* A. N. Naylor.

ROTHERHAM, Norfolk House, Walker Place.—*Education Officer,* K. Snowden.

ST. HELENS, Century House, Hardshaw Street.—*Education Officer,* N. D. Nelson.

SALFORD, Chapel Street M3 5LT.—*Education Officer,* B. Grady.

SANDWELL, P.O. Box 41, Highfields, High Street, West Bromwich B70 3RG.—*Education Officer,* G. A. Brinsdon.

SEFTON, Town Hall, Oriel Road, Bootle, Merseyside L20 7AE.—*Education Officer,* J. A. Marsden.

SHEFFIELD, P.O. Box 67, Leopold Street.—*Education Officer,* W. S. Walton.

SOLIHULL, P.O. Box 20, The Council House B91 3QU.—*Education Officer,* C. Humphrey.

SOUTH TYNESIDE, Town Hall, Jarrow.—*Director,* K. Stringer.

STOCKPORT, Stopford House, Town Hall, Piccadilly SK1 3XE.—*Education Officer,* J. E. Hendy.

SUNDERLAND, P.O. Box 101, Town Hall and Civic Centre SR2 7DN.—*Education Officer,* J. Hall.

TAMESIDE, Council Offices, Wellington Road, Ashton-under-Lyne OL6 6DL.—*Education Officer,* M. J. Mason.

TRAFFORD, P.O. Box 19, Town Hall, Sale M33 1YR.—*Education Officer,* D. J. Hatfield.

WAKEFIELD, 8 Bond Street.—*Education Officer,* W. H. Wright.

WALSALL, Civic Centre, Darwall Street, Walsall WS1 1DQ.—*Director,* R. D. Nixon.

WIGAN, Gateway House, Standishgate, WN1 1XL.—*Director of Education,* J. K. Hampson.

WIRRAL, Municipal Offices, Cleveland Street, Birkenhead L41 6NH.—*Director,* M. Nichol.

WOLVERHAMPTON, Civic Centre, St. Peters Square WV1 1RG.—*Director,* P. N. Harris.

Channel Islands, etc.

JERSEY, P.O. Box 142, Highlands, St. Saviour.—*Director,* J. S. Rodhouse.

GUERNSEY, P.O. Box 32, La Couperderie, St. Peter Port.—*Director,* M. D. Hutchings.

ISLE OF MAN, Government Offices, Bucks Road, Douglas.—*Director,* J. A. Davies.

ISLES OF SCILLY, Town Hall, St. Mary's TR21 0LW.—*Secretary for Education,* I. Glover.

Scottish Regional and Islands Councils

BORDERS, Regional Headquarters, Newtown St. Boswells TD6 0SA.—*Director,* J. McLean.

CENTRAL, Viewforth, Stirling FK8 2ET.—*Director,* I. Collie.

DUMFRIES AND GALLOWAY, 30 Edinburgh Road, Dumfries.—*Director,* J. K. Purves.

FIFE, Fife House, North Street, Glenrothes KY7 5LT.—*Director,* M. More.

GRAMPIAN, Woodhill House, Ashville Road West, Aberdeen AB9 2LU.—*Director,* J. A. D. Michie.

HIGHLAND, Regional Buildings, Glenurquhart Road, Inverness IV3 5NX.—*Director,* Dr. C. E. Stewart.

LOTHIAN, 40 Torphichen Street, Edinburgh EH3 8JJ.—*Director,* W. D. C. Semple.

ORKNEY, Council Offices, Kirkwall KW15 1NY.—*Director,* A. Bain.

SHETLAND, 1 Harbour Street, Lerwick.—*Director,* R. A. Barnes.

STRATHCLYDE, Strathclyde House, 20 India Street, Glasgow G2 4PF.—*Director,* E. Miller.

TAYSIDE, Tayside House, 28 Crichton Street, Dundee DD1 3RA.—*Director,* D. G. Robertson.

WESTERN ISLES, Council Offices, Sandwick Road, Stornoway, Isle of Lewis PA87 2BW.—*Director,* N. R. Galbraith.

Northern Ireland
Education and Library Boards

BELFAST, Board Headquarters, 40 Academy Street, Belfast 1.—*Chief Officer,* T. G. J. Moag.

NORTH-EASTERN, County Hall, 182 Galgorm Road, Ballymena, Co. Antrim BT42 1HN.—*Chief Officer,* R. A. Hamilton.

SOUTH-EASTERN, 18 Windsor Avenue, Belfast BT9 6EF.—*Chief Officer,* T. Nolan.

SOUTHERN, 3 Charlemont Place, The Mall, Armagh BT61 9AX.—*Chief Officer,* J. G. Kelly.

WESTERN, 1 Hospital Road, Omagh, Co. Tyrone BT79 0AW.—*Chief Officer,* M. H. F. Murphy.

ADULT EDUCATION

'Adult Education' covers a broad spectrum of educational activities ranging from non-vocational courses of general interest, through the acquiring of special vocational skills needed in industry or commerce, to study for a degree at the Open University. It has been defined as "the provision of non-formal and informal education for adult people: that is, courses excluding the normal range of provision in colleges and universities for young people immediately following the statutory school leaving age, but including the full range of recurrent educational opportunities designed for people of more mature years, and related to any or all aspects of adult life".

Providers. Courses are provided by many bodies: local education authorities (regional authorities in Scotland, education and library boards in Northern Ireland), residential colleges, the Open University, the extra-mural departments of other universities (and Birkbeck College of the University of London), the BBC, ITV and local radio stations, and various voluntary bodies. The local education authorities operate through 'area' adult education centres, institutes or colleges and the adult studies departments of colleges of further education. The Open University, in partnership with the BBC, provides distance teaching leading to ordinary or honours first degrees, and also offers post-experience and higher degree courses. Nearly 40 other universities have extra-mural or adult education or continuing education departments which serve their local areas or regions. The BBC has a Continuing Education Advisory Council and the Independent Broadcasting Authority an Educational Advisory Council which has an Adult Education Section. Of the voluntary bodies the biggest and best-known is the Workers' Educational Association (*see below*).

Courses. Although lengths vary, most courses are part-time. Long-term residential colleges (*see below*) provide full-time courses lasting one or two years. Adult education courses are of two main kinds – those involving face-to-face teaching with teacher and student in the same room and the distance teaching provided through TV and radio, and/or correspondence courses.

Numbers. There are no comprehensive statistics covering all aspects of adult education but it is known that enrolments in November 1983 at L.E.A. adult education and youth centres in England were about 1·6 million, an increase of 6 per cent over the previous year. About 116,000 students were enrolled at the Open University in 1984, including 66,500 undergraduates and 48,500 students on continuing education courses. In 1983–84, some 314,000 students attended courses of liberal adult education provided by university extra-mural departments and the W.E.A. in England and Wales. This was 8,000 more than in 1982–83.

NATIONAL INSTITUTE OF ADULT CONTINUING EDUCATION (England and Wales), 19b De Montfort Street, Leicester LE1 7GE. (*Dir.*, A. K. Stock). The institute provides a means of consultation and cooperation between all the forces in adult education. It provides information and advice to organizations and individuals on all aspects of adult continuing education; it conducts enquiries into problems of adult education; organizes conferences and other meetings; and issues publications. Recently, it has set up a special Unit for the Development of Adult Continuing Education with additional D.E.S. finance and also administers the local development of the D.E.S.'s Education for Adult Unemployed project. The government-funded Adult Literacy and Basic Skills Unit operates as an agency of the National Institute.

SCOTTISH INSTITUTE OF ADULT EDUCATION, 30 Rutland Square, Edinburgh EH1 2BW. (*Dir.*, Dr. Elizabeth Gerver). The institute is an advisory and consultative body which arranges conferences and training courses, undertakes research, acts as an information centre about current activities, and produces publications.

UNIVERSITIES COUNCIL FOR ADULT AND CONTINUING EDUCATION, consisting of one representative from each university, was established in 1947 for the interchange of ideas and the formulation of common policies on extra-mural education – *Hon. Secretary*, W. Forster, M.A., Dept. of Adult Education, The University, Leicester.

WORKERS EDUCATIONAL ASSOCIATION, Temple House, 9 Upper Berkeley Street, London W1H 8BY. (*Gen. Secretary*, R. Lochrie). Founded in 1903, the WEA consists of about 900 branches and nearly 1,500 affiliated educational and workers' organisations. Non-sectarian and non-party-political, it aims to stimulate and to satisfy the demands of workers for education, and to further the advancement of education generally. The W.E.A. is organised in 21 districts. Each district in England and Wales is recognized by the Department of Education and Science as a 'responsible body' for the provision of educational facilities in respect of which it receives grants under Departmental regulations. LEAs also make grants towards administrative expenses.

RESIDENTIAL COLLEGES FOR ADULT EDUCATION

Long term:
The eight long-term colleges listed below offer one- and two-year courses for adults and are grant-aided by the Department of Education and Science. Students are eligible for grants under an Adult Education State Bursaries Scheme.

COLEG HARLECH, Harlech, Gwynedd LL46 2PU. (For men and women).—*Warden*, J. W. England.
CO-OPERATIVE COLLEGE, Stanford Hall, Loughborough, Leics. LE12 5QR (For men and women).—*Principal*, Dr. R. Houlton.
FIRCROFT COLLEGE, 1018 Bristol Road, Selly Oak, Birmingham B29 6LH. (For men and women).—*Principal*, B. J. Wicker.
HILLCROFT COLLEGE, Surbiton, Surrey KT6 6DF. (For women).—*Principal*, Ms. P. Lambert.
NEWBATTLE ABBEY, Dalkeith, Edinburgh EH22 3LL. (For men and women).—*Principal*, A. D. Reid.
NORTHERN COLLEGE, Wentworth Castle, Stainborough, Barnsley, South Yorks. S75 3ET. (For men and women).—*Principal*, R. H. Fryer.
PLATER COLLEGE, Pullens Lane, Oxford OX3 0DT. (For men and women).—*Principal*, D. G. Chiles.
RUSKIN COLLEGE, Oxford OX1 2HE. (For men and women).—*Principal*, J. D. Hughes.

Short term:
The short-term colleges and centres listed below offer residential courses, lasting from a day or two to two or three weeks, in a wide range of subjects. LEAs directly sponsor many of the colleges while others are sponsored by universities or voluntary organizations. A booklet listing such *Residential Short Courses* is published by the National Institute of Adult Education (see above).

ALSTON HALL COLLEGE, Longridge, Nr. Preston; ASHRIDGE MANAGEMENT COLLEGE, Berkhamsted, Herts.; AVONCROFT COLLEGE, Stoke Heath, Bromsgrove, Worcs.; BEAMISH HALL RESIDENTIAL COLLEGE FOR ADULT EDUCATION, Stanley, County Durham; BELSTEAD HOUSE, Nr. Ipswich, Suffolk; BRAZIERS ADULT COLLEGE, Ipsden, Oxford; BURTON MANOR, Burton, South Wirral, Cheshire; BURWELL HOUSE RESIDENTIAL CENTRE, Burwell, Cambridge; DEBDEN HOUSE, Debden Green, Loughton, Essex; DENMAN COLLEGE, Marcham, Nr. Abingdon, Oxon.; DEVON CENTRE FOR FURTHER EDUCATION, Dartington College of Arts, Totnes; DILLINGTON COLLEGE FOR ADULT EDUCATION, Ilminster, Somerset; DYFFRYN HOUSE, St. Nicholas, Nr. Cardiff; EARNLEY CONCOURSE, Nr. Chichester, Sussex; EASTHAMPTEAD PARK EDUCATIONAL CENTRE, Wokingham, Berkshire; GRAFHAM WATER RESIDENTIAL CENTRE, West Perry, Huntingdon; GRANTLEY HALL, Ripon, North Yorkshire; HAWKWOOD COLLEGE, Stroud, Glos.; HENLEY—THE MANAGEMENT COLLEGE, Greenlands, Henley-on-Thames, Oxon.; HIGHAM HALL, Bassenthwaite Lake, Cockermouth, Cumbria; THE HILL, Pen-y-Pound, Abergavenny, Gwent; HOLLY ROYDE COLLEGE, West Didsbury, Manchester; HORNCASTLE RESIDENTIAL COLLEGE, Horncastle, Lincs.; KINGSGATE HOUSE, Convent Road, Broadstairs, Kent; KNUSTON HALL, Irchester, Wellingborough, Northants.; LANCASHIRE COLLEGE FOR ADULT EDUCATION, Southport Road, Chorley; LOSEHILL HALL, Castleton, Derbyshire; MADINGLEY HALL, Madingley, Cambridge; MARYLAND COLLEGE, Woburn, Milton Keynes; THE OLD RECTORY, Fittleworth, Pulborough, Sussex; PENDRELL HALL, Codsall Wood, Wolverhampton; REWLEY HOUSE, 3–7 Wellington Square, Oxford; ROFFEY PARK MANAGEMENT COLLEGE, Forest Road, Horsham, Sussex; RURAL MUSIC SCHOOLS ASSOCIATION, Little Benslow Hills, Ibberson Way, Hitchin, Herts.; SPODE CONFERENCE CENTRE, Hawkesyard Priory, Rugeley, Staffs.; THEOBALDS PARK COLLEGE, Waltham Cross, Herts.; URCHFONT MANOR, Nr. Devizes, Wilts.; WANSFELL COLLEGE, Theydon Bois, Epping, Essex; WEDGWOOD MEMORIAL COLLEGE, Barlaston, Stoke-on-Trent, Staffs.; WENSUM LODGE, King Street, Norwich, Norfolk; WEST DEAN COLLEGE, West Dean, Chichester, Sussex; WESTHAM HOUSE COLLEGE, Barford, Warwick.

PROFESSIONAL EDUCATION
(excluding *postgraduate* study)

NOTE.—References to university courses in the sections following are not claimed to be comprehensive and cover only *full-time* courses leading to *first degrees*. A full list appears in the *Compendium of University Entrance Requirements* produced annually by the universities. The considerable facilities available for postgraduate study or research are not treated here.

POSTGRADUATE STUDY AND RESEARCH. All universities provide facilities for postgraduate study and research. They co-operatively issue each year the *British Universities' Guide to Graduate Study* which lists all "taught courses" but does not cover research. In general, universities can provide facilities for research in at least some aspects of all the subjects in which first degrees are offered.

Courses at postgraduate level leading to master's-level degrees of the Council for National Academic Awards (C.N.A.A.) are offered by polytechnics and other colleges. They are listed in the C.N.A.A.'s annual *Directory of Postgraduate and Post-Experience Courses*. It is also possible to undertake research at polytechnics leading to an M. Phil. or Ph.D. granted by the C.N.A.A.

ACCOUNTANCY

(*See also* Business, Management and Administration).

First Degrees in *Accounting* or *Accountancy* are granted by the Universities of Belfast, Birmingham, Dundee, East Anglia, Exeter, Glasgow, Hull, Kent, Liverpool, Stirling, Strathclyde, Ulster and Wales (Aberystwyth and Cardiff University Colleges and Institute of Science and Technology). At several other universities one of these subjects can be combined with, e.g., Financial Administration, Finance or Economics.

Courses leading to first degrees in *Accounting, Accountancy* or *Accounting and Finance* granted by the Council for National Academic Awards are provided by City of Birmingham Polytechnic, Brighton Polytechnic, Bristol Polytechnic, City of London Polytechnic, Dundee College of Technology, Ealing College of Higher Education, Glasgow College of Technology, Huddersfield Polytechnic, Kingston Polytechnic, Lancashire Polytechnic, Leeds Polytechnic, Liverpool Polytechnic, Manchester Polytechnic, Middlesex Polytechnic, Napier College, Newcastle upon Tyne Polytechnic, North East London Polytechnic (*Finance with Accounting*), Polytechnic of North London, Portsmouth Polytechnic, Sheffield City Polytechnic (*Accounting and Financial Control*), Trent Polytechnic and Polytechnic of Wales.

Professional Bodies.—The main bodies granting membership on examination after a period of practical work are:

INSTITUTE OF CHARTERED ACCOUNTANTS IN ENGLAND AND WALES, P.O. Box 433, Moorgate Place, EC2P 2BJ.—*Sec.*, E. J. D. Warne, C.B.E.

INSTITUTE OF CHARTERED ACCOUNTANTS OF SCOTLAND, 27 Queen Street, Edinburgh EH2 1LA and 218 St. Vincent Street, Glasgow.—*Sec.*, E. Tait, M.B.E.

ASSOCIATION OF CERTIFIED ACCOUNTANTS, 29 Lincolns Inn Fields, WC2A 3EE.—*Sec.*, R. A. Dudman.

CHARTERED INSTITUTE OF PUBLIC FINANCE AND ACCOUNTANCY, 3 Robert Street, WC2N 6BH.—*Sec.*, N. P. Hepworth.

INSTITUTE OF COST AND MANAGEMENT ACCOUNTANTS, 63 Portland Place, W1N 4AB.

ACTUARIAL SCIENCE

First Degrees in *Actuarial Science* are granted by the City University and the Universities of Kent and London (London School of Economics and Political Science); and in *Actuarial Mathematics and Statistics* by Heriot-Watt University.

Two professional organizations grant qualifications after examination:

INSTITUTE OF ACTUARIES, Staple Inn Hall, High Holborn, WC1V 7QJ.—*Sec. General*, C. D. A. Mackie.

FACULTY OF ACTUARIES IN SCOTLAND, *Hall and Library*, 23 St. Andrew Square, Edinburgh EH2 1AQ.—*Sec.*, W. Wallace Mair.

AERONAUTICS
and Aeronautical Engineering

First Degrees in *Aeronautical Engineering* are granted by the Universities of Bath, Belfast, Bristol, Cambridge, the City University, the Universities of Glasgow, London (Imperial College of Science and Technology; Queen Mary College (also *Avionics—Aeronautical/Electrical*), Loughborough (*Aeronautical Engineering and Design*), Manchester, Salford and (*Aeronautics and Astronautics* and *Aerospace Systems Engineering*) Southampton; and in *Air Transport Engineering* by the City University.

Courses leading to first degrees in *Aeronautical Engineering* granted by the Council for National Academic Awards are provided by Hatfield Polytechnic and Kingston Polytechnic.

CHELSEA COLLEGE OF AERONAUTICAL AND AUTOMOBILE ENGINEERING, Shoreham Airport, West Sussex BN4 5FJ.

AGRICULTURE

First Degrees in *Agriculture* or *Agricultural Science(s)* are granted by the Universities of Aberdeen, Belfast, Edinburgh, Glasgow, Leeds, London (Wye College), Newcastle upon Tyne, Nottingham, Reading and Wales (University Colleges of Aberystwyth and Bangor); in *Agricultural Technology and Management* by Cranfield Institute of Technology; and in *Horticulture* by Bath, London (Wye College), Nottingham, Reading and Strathclyde.

Courses leading to first degrees in *Agriculture* granted by the Council for National Academic Awards are provided by Plymouth Polytechnic/Seale Hayne College and Wolverhampton Polytechnic/Harper Adams Agricultural College.

Other schools of agriculture are:

ABERDEEN, North of Scotland College of Agriculture, 581 King Street, AB9 1UD.—*Principal*, Prof. G. A. Lodge, Ph.D.

CIRENCESTER, Royal Agricultural College, GL7 6JS.—*Principal*, H. V. Hughes.

EDINBURGH SCHOOL OF AGRICULTURE, The, West Mains Road, Edinburgh EH9 3JG.—*Principal*, Prof. P. N. Wilson, Ph.D.

SHUTTLEWORTH AGRICULTURAL COLLEGE, Old Warden Park, Biggleswade, Bedfordshire SG18 9DX.—*Principal*, J. E. Scott.

WEST OF SCOTLAND AGRICULTURAL COLLEGE, Auchincruive, Ayr KA6 5HW.—*Principal*, Prof. J. M. M. Cunningham, C.B.E., Ph.D., F.R.S.E.

There are in addition over twenty country Agricultural Institutes giving a one-year course.

ARCHÆOLOGY

First Degrees in *Archæology* or *Archæological Sciences/Studies* are granted by the Universities of Belfast, Bradford, Durham, Edinburgh, Exeter, Glasgow, Lancaster, Leicester, Liverpool, London (Institute of Archæology, King's and University Colleges; School of Oriental and African Studies), Newcastle upon Tyne, Nottingham, Reading, Southampton, Wales (University College of Cardiff) and York. At several other universities archæology can be combined with another subject, e.g. ancient history, classics or anthropology.

ARCHITECTURE

The Education and Professional Development Committee of THE ROYAL INSTITUTE OF BRITISH ARCHITECTS, 66 Portland Place, W1N 4AD, *Pres.*, L. A. L. Rolland; *Sec.*, P. K. Harrison, C.B.E., sets standards and guides the whole system of architectural education throughout the United Kingdom. Courses at the following Schools are recognized by the R.I.B.A. They are visited regularly by the R.I.B.A. Visiting Board to ensure that they meet the minimum standards for exemption from the R.I.B.A.'s own examinations.

UNIVERSITY SCHOOLS

(Subject to exceptions noted below, courses are full-time for five years, leading to a first degree and final diploma; number of students and name of Head of School or Department of Architecture are included.)

BATH: University School of Architecture and Building Engineering, Claverton Down BA2 7AY (240).—Prof. E. Happold (6-yr. sandwich course in architecture in conjunction with 4-year sandwich course in building engineering).

BELFAST: Queen's University BT7 1NN (161).—Prof. W. J. Kidd.

CAMBRIDGE: Department of Architecture (190).—Prof. C. St. J. Wilson.

CARDIFF: The Welsh School of Architecture, University of Wales Institute of Science and Technology CF1 3XE (253).— Prof. J. Eynon.

DUNDEE: Dept. of Architecture, University of Dundee DD1 4HT: Duncan of Jordanstone College of Art, Perth Road (215).—Prof. J. Paul.

EDINBURGH: University of Edinburgh, Dept. of Architecture (184).—Prof. I. Metzstein.

—Heriot-Watt University (joint course with Edinburgh College of Art), Lauriston Place EH3 9DF (250).—Prof. J. D. Dunbar-Nasmith, C.B.E.

GLASGOW: Mackintosh School of Architecture, Glasgow University and Glasgow School of Art, 177 Renfrew Street G3 6RQ (303).—Prof. A. MacMillan. University of Strathclyde, Dept. of Architecture and Building Science, 131 Rottenrow G4 0NG (180).—P. A. Reed.

LIVERPOOL: The Liverpool School of Architecture, Leverhulme Building, Abercromby Square, P.O. Box 147, L69 3BX. (186).—Prof. J. N. Tarn.

LONDON: Bartlett School of Architecture and Planning, University College London (190).—Prof. J. Musgrove.

MANCHESTER: University of Manchester School of Architecture M13 9PL (200).—A. Roderick Males.

NEWCASTLE UPON TYNE: University School of Architecture NE1 7RU (140).—Prof B. Farmer.

NOTTINGHAM: University Dept. of Architecture NG7 2RD (140).—Prof. C. Riley.

SHEFFIELD: University Dept. of Architecture (200).—Prof. K. H. Murta.

OTHER SCHOOLS

(Subject to the exceptions noted below, courses are full-time for five years, leading to a first degree and final diploma. Number of students and name of Head of School are shown.)

ABERDEEN: Scott Sutherland School of Architecture, Robert Gordon's Institute of Technology (180).—R. Webster.

BIRMINGHAM: School of Architecture, City of Birmingham Polytechnic, B42 2SU (250).—A. D. Collier.

BRIGHTON: School of Architecture and Interior Design, Brighton Polytechnic, Lewes Road, Brighton BN2 4AT (225).—R. Macleod.

CANTERBURY: School of Architecture, Canterbury College of Art, New Dover Road, CT1 3AN (164).—M. Crux.

HUDDERSFIELD: Polytechnic School of Architecture, Queensgate.—Dr. A. Forward. (Part 1 only).

HULL: School of Architecture, Humberside College of Higher Education, Strand Close, HU2 9BT (185).—C. Padamsee.

KINGSTON UPON THAMES: Polytechnic School of Architecture, Knights Park, KT1 2QJ (210).—D. Berry.

LEEDS: School of Architecture and Landscape, Leeds Polytechnic, Brunswick Terrace, LS2 8BU (353).—W. T. Bradshaw.

LEICESTER: Polytechnic School of Architecture, P.O. Box 143, LE1 9BH (230).—Prof. T. Matoff.

LIVERPOOL: Polytechnic (B.A. (Hons.) Architectural Studies).—K. E. Martin.

LONDON: Architectural Association School of Architecture, 34–36 Bedford Square, W.C.1 (400).—A. Boyarsky.

Department of Architecture, Polytechnic of the South Bank, S.W.8 (121).—H. Haenlein.

School of Architecture, Faculty of Environment. Polytechnic of Central London, 35 Marylebone Road, NW1 5LS (255).—A. Cunningham.

Dept. of Environmental Design, Polytechnic of North London, Holloway, N7 8DB (450).—W. Briscoe.

School of Architecture, North East London Polytechnic, Holbrook Road, E15 3EA.—N. Silver.

Thames Polytechnic, School of Architecture and Landscape, Oakfield Lane, Dartford, Kent DA1 2SZ (476).—Dr. J. Paul.

MANCHESTER: Polytechnic School of Architecture, Dept. of Architecture and Landscape, Loxford Tower, Lower Chatham Street, M15 6HA (319).—R. P. Burton.

OXFORD: Dept. of Architecture, Oxford Polytechnic, Gypsy Lane, OX3 0BP (400).

PLYMOUTH: Polytechnic School of Architecture, Hoe Centre, Notte Street, PL1 2AR (204).—Prof. A. Gale.

PORTSMOUTH: Polytechnic School of Architecture, King Henry I Street, PO1 2DY (175).—Prof. G. H. Broadbent.

ART AND DESIGN

First Degrees in *Art, Fine Art* or *History of Art* are granted by the Universities of Aberdeen, Cambridge, East Anglia, Edinburgh, Essex, Glasgow, Lancaster (*Visual Arts*),Leeds, Leicester, London (Courtauld Institute of Art; Birkbeck, University and Westfield Colleges; School of Oriental and African Studies), Loughborough (*Design and Technology*), Manchester, Manchester Institute of Science and Technology (*Textile Design and Design Management*), Newcastle upon Tyne, Nottingham, Oxford, Reading, St. Andrews, Stirling, Sussex, Wales (University College, Aberystwyth—*Visual Art*; Cardiff University College—*Textiles and Design*) and Warwick. At several other universities art or history of art are combined with another subject. The degrees in *Art* granted by the Royal College of Art are higher degrees.

Courses leading to first degrees in *Art and Design* (*Fine Art, Graphic Design, Textiles/Fashion or Three-Dimensional Design*) granted by the Council for National Academic Awards are provided by more than 40 colleges/schools of art and polytechnics some of which also offer C.N.A.A. degree courses in other subjects in the field of Art and Design, including *Furniture Design, Graphic Design, Industrial Design and Interior Design.*

LONDON.—Royal Academy Schools of Painting and Sculpture, Burlington Gardens, W1V 0DS (80).—*Keeper*, Edward Middleditch; *Secretary*, Laura Scott; *Curator*, I. Tregarthen-Jenkin.

LONDON.—The Slade School of Fine Art, University College, WC1E 6BT, provides undergraduate and graduate courses in Fine Art.—*Slade Professor*, Patrick George; *Sec.*, M. Watson.

OXFORD, The Ruskin School of Drawing and Fine Art, at 74 High Street, Oxford OX1 4BG (60 undergraduates).—*Ruskin Master of Drawing*, David Tindle. Course in Drawing, Painting, Printmaking, Sculpture and History of Art. The University awards a Bachelor of Fine Art degree.

ASTRONOMY

First Degrees in *Astronomy* are granted by the Universities of Glasgow, London (Queen Mary and University Colleges); and in *Astrophysics* by the Universities of Edinburgh, London (Queen Mary

College) and Wales (University College, Cardiff). Various combinations of Astronomy, Mathematics, Physics and Astrophysics are also available.

Astronomy may be taken as part of a C.N.A.A. degree course at certain polytechnics.

BANKING

First Degrees with specialization in *Banking and Finance* are granted by the Universities of Birmingham (*Money, Banking and Finance*), Loughborough, Ulster and Wales (Institute of Science and Technology; also *Banking, Insurance and Finance* at Bangor University College), and the City University (*Banking and International Finance*).

Professional organizations granting qualifications after examination:—

THE INSTITUTE OF BANKERS, 10 Lombard Street, EC3V 9AS.—*Sec. General*, E. Glover.

THE INSTITUTE OF BANKERS IN SCOTLAND, 20 Rutland Square, Edinburgh EH1 2DE.—*Sec.*, B. McKenna.

BIOLOGY, CHEMISTRY, PHYSICS

First Degrees in these subjects are granted by many universities. Courses leading to first degrees, granted by the Council of National Academic Awards, are provided by many polytechnics. Professional qualifications are awarded by:—

THE INSTITUTE OF BIOLOGY, 20 Queensberry Place, SW7 2DZ.—*Gen. Sec.*, P. N. O'Donoghue.

THE INSTITUTE OF PHYSICS, 47 Belgrave Square, SW1X 8QX.—*Sec.*, Dr. Louis Cohen.

THE ROYAL SOCIETY OF CHEMISTRY, Burlington House, Piccadilly W1V 0BN.—*President*, Prof. R. O. C. Norman, D.S.C., F.R.S.C., F.R.S., *Sec. Gen.*, Dr. R. D. Guthrie, F.R.S.C.

BREWING

First Degrees in Brewing are granted by Heriot-Watt University.

BUILDING

(*See also* Architecture, Estate Management and Surveying)

First Degrees in *Building, Building Engineering* or *Building Technology* are granted by the following Universities: Aston in Birmingham (*Building Technology and Management*), Bath, Heriot-Watt (also *Building Economics and Quantity Surveying*), Liverpool (*Building Construction Engineering, Building Services Engineering*), London (University College), Manchester (Manchester Institute of Science and Technology—also *Building Services Engineering* and *Construction Management*), Reading (*Building Construction & Management, Quantity Surveying* and *Building Surveying*), Salford (*Building Surveying*, also *Quantity Surveying and Construction Economics*) and Ulster (also *Building Services Engineering* and *Quantity Surveying*).

Courses leading to first degrees in *Building* granted by the Council for National Academic Awards are provided by Brighton Polytechnic, Bristol Polytechnic, Polytechnic of Central London, Coventry (Lanchester) Polytechnic, Glasgow College of Technology with Glasgow College of Building and Printing, Leeds Polytechnic, Liverpool Polytechnic, Sheffield City Polytechnic (*Construction*), the Polytechnic of the South Bank, Trent Polytechnic, and Polytechnic of Wales; in *Building Surveying* by Leicester Polytechnic, Liverpool Polytechnic, Polytechnic of the South Bank, Thames Polytechnic; and in *Building Services Engineering* by Newcastle upon

Tyne Polytechnic, Wolverhampton Polytechnic and the Polytechnic of the South Bank (*Environmental Engineering*).

Examinations are also conducted by:—

THE CHARTERED INSTITUTE OF BUILDING, Englemere, King's Ride, Ascot, Berks. SL5 8BJ.

THE INSTITUTE OF CLERKS OF WORKS OF GREAT BRITAIN, 41 The Mall, Ealing, W5 3TJ.—*Sec.*, A. P. Macnamara.

THE INSTITUTION OF MUNICIPAL ENGINEERS, 25 Eccleston Square, S.W.1 (Chartered Engineers', Building Control Officers' Ordinary and Higher Certificates).

BUSINESS, MANAGEMENT AND ADMINISTRATION

First Degrees in *Business Studies* are granted by the Universities of Bath (*Business Administration*), Belfast (*Business Administration*), Bradford, City, East Anglia (*Business Information Systems*), Edinburgh, Heriot-Watt (*Business Organization*), Liverpool, Loughborough (*Business Administration with a Modern Language*), Salford (*Business and Administration, Business Operation and Control*), Sheffield, Stirling, Ulster (also *European Business Studies and International Business Communication* (provisional)), Wales (University College, Aberystwyth: *Economics and Business*) (University College, Swansea: also *European Business Studies*), Wales (Institute of Science and Technology) (*Business Administration*; also *Business Economics*); in *Administration* by the Universities of Aston in Birmingham (*Managerial and Administrative Studies*), Birmingham (*Public Policy Making and Administration*), Essex (*Policy-making and Administration*) and Salford (*Business and Administration*); in *Management Sciences/Studies* by the City University (and *Systems Management*), Loughborough University of Technology, and the Universities of Bradford, Cambridge, Hull, Kent at Canterbury (also *Public Administration and Management*, and *European Management Science*), Lancaster, Leeds (*Textile Management*), London (London School of Economics), Loughborough, Manchester (Institute of Science and Technology ; also *Textile Economics and Management*), St. Andrews, Stirling, Wales (Cardiff University College), Swansea University College: also *American Management Studies* and *European Management Science*), and Warwick; in *Marketing* by the Universities of Lancaster and Strathclyde; and in *Commerce* by the University of Birmingham. A variety of other combinations in these fields are available at some of these universities and these subjects also form part of degree courses in other universities.

Courses leading to first degrees in *Business Studies* or *Business Administration* granted by the Council for National Academic Awards are provided by City of Birmingham Polytechnic, Brighton Polytechnic, Bristol Polytechnic, Polytechnic of Central London, City of London Polytechnic, Coventry (Lanchester) Polytechnic, Dorset Institute of Higher Education, Dundee College of Technology (also *Commerce*), Ealing College of Higher Education, Glasgow College of Technology (also *Commerce*), Hatfield Polytechnic, Huddersfield Polytechnic, Humberside College of Higher Education, Kingston Polytechnic, Lancashire Polytechnic, Leeds Polytechnic, Leicester Polytechnic, Liverpool Polytechnic, Manchester Polytechnic, Middlesex Polytechnic, Napier College of Commerce and Technology (also *Commerce*), Newcastle upon Tyne Polytechnic, North East London Polytechnic (also *Manufacturing Studies*), Polytechnic of N. London, N. Staffordshire Polytechnic, Oxford Polytechnic, Paisley College of Technology

(*Business Economics*), Plymouth Polytechnic, Portsmouth Polytechnic, Robert Gordon's Institute of Technology, Sheffield City Polytechnic (also *Industrial Studies*), Polytechnic of the South Bank, Sunderland Polytechnic, Teesside Polytechnic, Thames Polytechnic, Trent Polytechnic (also *Industrial Studies*), Polytechnic of Wales, West Glamorgan Institute of Higher Education and Wolverhampton Polytechnic.

Courses leading to first degrees in *European Business Studies/Administration* granted by the Council for National Academic Awards are provided by Buckinghamshire College of Higher Education, Humberside College of Higher Education, Middlesex Polytechnic and Trent Polytechnic.

The Thames Polytechnic provides courses for C.N.A.A. first degrees in *International Marketing*; and Manchester Polytechnic in *Retail Marketing*. Huddersfield Polytechnic provides courses for C.N.A.A. degrees in *Marketing (Engineering)* and *Textile Marketing*; and Humberside College of Higher Education courses for C.N.A.A. degrees in *Secretarial Studies and Office Systems Management*.

Leicester, Manchester, Sheffield City, Teesside and Trent Polytechnics, the Polytechnic of Wales, Glasgow College of Technology, Robert Gordon's Institute of Technology provide courses for C.N.A.A. first degrees in *Public Administration*; and Leeds Polytechnic in *Administration Studies*.

Glasgow College of Technology provides courses for C.N.A.A. first degrees in *Risk Management*.

Professional bodies conducting training and/or examinations in Administration and Management include:

ROYAL INSTITUTE OF PUBLIC ADMINISTRATION, 3 Birdcage Walk, SW1H 9JH.—*Dir. Gen.*, W. Plowden.

THE INSTITUTE OF HEALTH SERVICE MANAGEMENT, 75 Portland Place, W1N 4AN.—*Sec.*, L. B. Akid.

THE INSTITUTE OF PERSONNEL MANAGEMENT, IPM House, Camp Road, Wimbledon SW19 4UW.

INSTITUTION OF INDUSTRIAL MANAGERS, Industrial Management House, Cardiff Road, Luton, Beds. LU1 1RQ.

INSTITUTE OF HOUSING, 12 Upper Belgrave Street, S.W.1.

INSTITUTE OF ADMINISTRATIVE MANAGEMENT, 40 Chatsworth Parade, Petts Wood, Orpington, Kent BR5 1RW.—*Sec.*, M. J. Ainsworth.

HENLEY—THE MANAGEMENT COLLEGE, Greenlands, Henley-on-Thames, Oxon RG9 3AU.—*Princ.*, Prof. T. Kempner (1972).

LONDON BUSINESS SCHOOL, Sussex Place, Regent's Park, NW1 4SA.—*Princ.*, Prof. P. G. Moore.

MANCHESTER BUSINESS SCHOOL, Booth Street West, Manchester M15 6PB.—*Dir.*, Dr. R. G. J. Telfer.

SCOTTISH BUSINESS SCHOOL, 79 St. George's Place, Glasgow G2 1EU.

INSTITUTE OF MARKETING, Moor Hall, Cookham, Maidenhead, Berks. SL6 9QH.—*Dir.-Gen.*, P. B. Blood.

Courses of advanced training in most branches of commerce, including preparation for examinations of the recognized professional organizations as well as for the National Certificates in Business Studies are available at the Polytechnics listed by cities on p. 510–511.

Throughout the country commercial education at a lower level is provided at *Evening Institutes*, particulars of which may be obtained from the Local Education Authority.

There are also numbers of well-established private schools awarding certificates which are widely accepted.

Institutions awarding Professional Qualifications in Commerce:—

A. GENERAL

THE ROYAL SOCIETY OF ARTS EXAMINATIONS BOARD, 8 John Adam Street, Adelphi, WC2N 6EZ.

THE LONDON CHAMBER OF COMMERCE AND INDUSTRY, Commercial Education Scheme, Marlowe House, Station Road, Sidcup, Kent.

THE EAST MIDLAND FURTHER EDUCATIONAL COUNCIL, Robins Wood House, Robins Wood Road, Aspley, Nottingham NG8 3NH.

THE NORTHERN COUNCIL FOR FURTHER EDUCATION, 5 Grosvenor Villas, Grosvenor Road, Newcastle upon Tyne NE2 2RU.

THE WEST MIDLANDS ADVISORY COUNCIL FOR FURTHER EDUCATION (incorporating Union of Educational Institutions), Norfolk House, Smallbrook Queensway, Birmingham B5 4NB.

NORTH WESTERN REGIONAL ADVISORY COUNCIL FOR FURTHER EDUCATION (incorporating the Union of Lancashire and Cheshire Institutes), Town Hall, Walkden Road, Worsley, Manchester M28 4QE.

THE YORKSHIRE AND HUMBERSIDE ASSOCIATION FOR FURTHER AND HIGHER EDUCATION, Bowling Green Terrace, Leeds LS11 9SX.

WELSH JOINT EDUCATION COMMITTEE, 245 Western Avenue, Cardiff CF5 2YX.

B. SPECIALIZED

THE INSTITUTE OF CHARTERED SECRETARIES AND ADMINISTRATORS, 16 Park Crescent, W1N 4AH.

THE FACULTY OF SECRETARIES AND ADMINISTRATORS LTD., P.O. Box 7, Godalming, Surrey GU7 1PR.

THE INSTITUTE OF EXPORT, World Trade Centre, E1 9AA.

THE INSTITUTE OF CHARTERED SHIPBROKERS, 24 St. Mary Axe, EC3A 8DE.—*Sec.*, J. H. Parker.

INSTITUTE OF MARKETING, Moor Hall, Cookham, Maidenhead, Berks. SL6 9QH.—*Sec.*, W. E. Hinder.

THE CHARTERED INSTITUTE OF TRANSPORT, 80 Portland Place, W1N 4DP.—*Dir. Gen. and Sec.*, J. C. F. Cameron.

THE CAM FOUNDATION, Abford House, 15 Wilton Road SW1V 1NJ.

INSTITUTE OF PRACTITIONERS IN ADVERTIZING, 44 Belgrave Square SW1X 8QS.—*Dir.*, C. Channon.

INSTITUTE OF PURCHASING AND SUPPLY, Easton House, Easton on the Hill, Stamford, Lincs. PE9 3NZ.—*Dir. Gen.*, J. G. S. Groundwater.

INSTITUTE OF PERSONNEL MANAGEMENT, IPM House, Camp Road, Wimbledon, S.W.19.

BUSINESS AND TECHNICIAN EDUCATION COUNCIL Central House, Upper Woburn Place, WC1H 0HH

The Business & Technician Education Council (BTEC) is responsible for planning, administering and reviewing a wide range of courses, below degree level, in areas such as business, finance, distribution, public sector administration, computing, engineering, construction, science, agriculture, catering and design in England, Wales and Northern Ireland.

Chairman, H. N. Raine.
Chief Executive, J. E. Sellars.

COMPUTER SCIENCE

First Degrees in *Computer/Computing Science(s)/ Computing, Computational Science* are granted by Brunel (also *Applied Computer Systems*), City (also *Business Computing Systems*), Heriot-Watt and Loughborough (also *Data Processing* and *Information Technology & Human Factors*) Universities and by the Universities of Aberdeen, Aston in Birmingham, Belfast (also *Information Technology*), Birmingham

(*Software Engineering*), Bradford (also *Computing & Information Systems Science*), Bristol, Cambridge, Dundee, East Anglia, Edinburgh, Essex (also *Computer & Microprocessor Systems*), Exeter, Glasgow, Hull, Keele, Kent (also *Computer Systems Engineering*), Lancaster, Leeds (also *Data Processing*), Liverpool, London (Imperial (also *Software Engineering*), King's (also *Computer Systems with Microelectronics*), Queen Mary (also *Computer Systems with Microelectronics*), Royal Holloway and Bedford New, and University Colleges; London School of Economics and Political Science), Manchester (also *Computing & Information Systems*), Manchester Institute of Science and Technology, Newcastle upon Tyne, Reading, St. Andrews (also *Information Processing*), Salford (*Electronic Computer Systems*), Sheffield, Southampton, Stirling, Strathclyde (also *Computer Science and Microprocessor Systems*), Sussex, Ulster (also *Computing Science for Business* and *Computing Science (Data Processing)*), Wales (University College, Aberystwyth; University College, Cardiff: also *Computer Systems*; University College, Swansea), Warwick and York (also *Computer Systems & Software Engineering*).

Courses leading to first degrees in *Computer Science/Studies* or *Computing* granted by the Council for National Academic Awards are provided by Brighton Polytechnic also (*Microelectronics & Information Processing*), Bristol Polytechnic (*Systems Analysis*), Coventry (Lanchester) Polytechnic, Glasgow College of Technology (*Computer Information Systems*), Hatfield Polytechnic, Huddersfield Polytechnic (*Computing in Business*), Kingston Polytechnic (also *Information Systems Design*), Leeds Polytechnic (*Computing and Operational Research*), Leicester Polytechnic (also *Information Technology*), Napier College of Commerce and Technology (*Computing and Data Processing*), North East London Polytechnic, North Staffordshire Polytechnic (also *Information Systems* and *Information Technology*), Paisley College of Technology, Plymouth Polytechnic (*Computing and Informatics*), Portsmouth Polytechnic, Sheffield City Polytechnic, Polytechnic of the South Bank, Teesside Polytechnic, Thames Polytechnic, Wolverhampton Polytechnic and Polytechnic of Wales; and in *Data Processing* by Sunderland Polytechnic.

These subjects also form part of other degree courses, often as *Mathematics/Statistics and Computer Science*, at many universities and colleges.

DANCE

(*See also* Physical Education)

First degrees in *Dance in Society* are granted by the University of Surrey.

Courses leading to first degrees in *Dance Theatre* granted by the Council for National Academic Awards are provided by the Laban Centre for Movement and Dance in association with Goldsmiths' College. Dance also forms part of C.N.A.A. degree courses, often called *Performing Arts* or *Creative Arts*, at several polytechnics and colleges. For first degree courses in *Human Movement Studies* see under 'Recreation, Sport and Human Movement Studies'.

THE ROYAL ACADEMY OF DANCING (incorporated by Royal Charter), 48 Vicarage Crescent, SW11 3LT.—*Directors*, Julia Farron, D. Scrimgeour, Priscilla Yates, D. Wall.

THE ROYAL BALLET SCHOOL, 155 Talgarth Road, W14 9DE, and White Lodge, Richmond Park.—*Director*, Merle Park, C.B.E.

IMPERIAL SOCIETY OF TEACHERS OF DANCING (1904), Euston Hall, Birkenhead Street, WC1H 8BE.—*Dir.*, K. Abraham.

DEFENCE

First Degrees in *Peace Studies* are granted by the universities of Bradford and Ulster.

Royal Naval Colleges
ROYAL NAVAL COLLEGE
Greenwich, SE10 9NN

Admiral President, Admiral Sir Richard Fitch, K.C.B.
Head of Dept. of History and International Affairs, Prof. P. Nailor.
Dean of the College and Director, Dept. of Nuclear Science and Technology, Prof. J. R. A. Lakey, Ph.D.

INSTITUTE OF NAVAL MEDICINE
Alverstoke, Hants PO12 2DL

Surgeon Commodore (Naval Medicine and Training) and Dean of Naval Medicine, Surgeon Cdre J. W. Richardson, O.B.E., Q.H.S., F.R.C.S.

BRITANNIA ROYAL NAVAL COLLEGE
Dartmouth, Devon TQ6 0HJ

Captain, Capt. G. M. Tullis.
Commander, Cdr. C. J. Esplin-Jones, O.B.E.
Dir. of Studies, C. H. Christie, M.A.

ROYAL NAVAL ENGINEERING COLLEGE
Manadon, Plymouth PL5 3AQ.

The college provides a broad based engineering education leading to B.Eng. and M.Sc. degrees together with specialist training in naval engineering at chartered engineer standards. Students are selected uniformed officers of the Royal Navy, Commonwealth and foreign navies, and civilians.
Captain, Capt. R. A. Isaac.
Dean, Capt. G. C. George.
Executive Officer, Cdr. C. W. Crichton.
Dir. of Naval Engineering, Cdr. M. L. D. Kendrick.
Dir. of Postgraduate Studies, Cdr. D. J. Cooke.
Dir. of Undergraduate Studies, Cdr. K. S. Hart.

Military Colleges
STAFF COLLEGE, CAMBERLEY
Surrey GU15 4NP

Officers who graduate at the college have the letters *psc.* after their names in Service Lists.
Commandant, Maj.-Gen. C. P. R. Palmer, C.B.E.
Deputy Commandant, Brig. J. A. M. Evans.

ROYAL MILITARY ACADEMY SANDHURST
Camberley, Surrey GU15 4PQ

The Royal Military Academy, Woolwich, founded in 1741, and the Royal Military College, Sandhurst, founded in 1799, were amalgamated in 1947 under the above title.
Mons Officer Cadet School, Aldershot, opened in 1942 for the training of short service officers, also became part of RMA Sandhurst in 1972.
Commandant, Maj.-Gen. R. C. Keightley.

ROYAL MILITARY COLLEGE OF SCIENCE
Shrivenham, nr. Swindon, Wilts SN6 8LA

The College was founded at Woolwich in 1864 and transferred to Shrivenham in 1946. It has now been integrated into Cranfield Institute of Technology but is still located at Shrivenham. Officer students from U.K., Commonwealth and foreign armies and some civilian students are prepared for degrees awarded by Cranfield Institute.

Commandant, Maj.-Gen. J. A. M. Evans.
Dean, Prof. F. R. Hartley, D.Phil.
Academic Registrar, vacant.

ARMOUR SCHOOL
R.A.C. CENTRE
Bovington Camp, nr. Wareham, Dorset BH20 6LZ

Commanding Officer and Chief Instructor, Col. A. T. Lindsay.

WELBECK COLLEGE
Worksop, Notts. S80 3LN

Principal, Col. G. H. Silvey.
Bursar, Col. R. Mathews.

INSTITUTE OF ARMY EDUCATION
Court Road, Eltham, SE9 5NR

Director, Maj.-Gen. D. E. Ryan.

Royal Air Force Colleges
ROYAL AIR FORCE STAFF COLLEGE
Bracknell, Berks.

Opened at Andover on 3 April 1922, the College is now the centre for Command and Staff Training in the Royal Air Force. The principal course held each year aims to prepare selected senior officers, from the UK Armed Forces and many countries overseas, for high-grade command and staff appointments and for promotion to the highest ranks in their Services.
Air Officer Commanding and Commandant, Air Vice-Marshal A. G. Skingsley, C.B.

ROYAL AIR FORCE COLLEGE
Cranwell, Lincs NG34 8HB

Founded in 1920, the College provides initial officer training for Royal Air Force, Women's Royal Air Force and Princess Mary's Royal Air Force Nursing Service officers, and initial specialist training for officers of the Engineer and Supply Branches. Advanced specialist training is provided for officers of the General Duties, Engineer and Supply Branches. Flying training for pilots of the General Duties Branch is provided by the Flying Training School, Cranwell. The headquarters of the University Air Squadrons is at the College.

Air Officer Commanding and Commandant, Air Vice-Marshal E. H. Macey, O.B.E.

ROYAL AIR FORCE SCHOOL OF EDUCATION AND TRAINING SUPPORT
R.A.F. Newton, Nottingham NG13 8HL

Commanding Officer, Gp. Capt. J. F. Jarvis, O.B.E.

DENTISTRY

First Degrees in Dentistry are granted by the University of Belfast, Birmingham, Bristol, Dundee, Edinburgh, Glasgow, Leeds, Liverpool, London (United Medical and Dental Schools of Guy's and St. Thomas's Hospitals, King's College School of Medicine and Dentistry, London Hospital Medical College, University College), Manchester, Newcastle upon Tyne, Sheffield, Wales (University College, Cardiff, and Welsh National School of Medicine).
To be entitled to be registered in the Dentists Register a person must hold the degree or diploma in dental surgery of a University in the United Kingdom or Republic of Ireland or the diploma of any of the Licensing Authorities (The Royal College of Sur-

geons of England, of Edinburgh and in Ireland, and the Royal College of Physicians and Surgeons of Glasgow).

DIETETICS
(See also Food and Nutrition Science)

Courses in *Dietetics* leading to first degrees granted by the University of Wales are provided by South Glamorgan Institute of Higher Education. Courses leading to first degrees in *Dietetics* granted by the Council for National Academic Awards are provided by Leeds Polytechnic, Queen Margaret College, Paisley College of Technology with Queen's College and Robert Gordon's Institute of Technology (*Nutrition and Dietetics*).

The professional association is The British Dietetic Association, Daimler House, Paradise Street, Birmingham B1 2BJ. Full membership is open to dietitians holding a recognized qualification, who may also become State Registered Dietitians through the Council for Professions Supplementary to Medicine (*q.v.*).

DRAMA

First Degrees in *Drama* are granted by the Universities of Birmingham (*Drama and Theatre Arts*), Bristol, East Anglia, Exeter, Glasgow (*Dramatic Studies*—in conjunction with Royal Scottish Academy of Music and Drama), Hull, Kent (*Drama and Theatre Studies*), London (Royal Holloway and Bedford New College: *Drama and Theatre Studies*), Loughborough, Manchester and Wales (University Colleges of Aberystwyth and Bangor); and in *Theatre Studies & Dramatic Arts* by the University of Warwick. Drama also forms part of degree courses in other universities. Courses in Drama leading to first degrees granted by the University of Lancaster are provided at Liverpool Polytechnic and by the University of Leeds at Bretton Hall College of Higher Education.

Courses leading to first degrees granted by the Council for National Academic Awards are provided by Crewe and Alsager College of Higher Education (*Drama Studies*), Dartington College of Arts (*Theatre*), King Alfred's College of Higher Education (*Drama (Theatre and TV Studies)*) and Rose Bruford College of Speech and Drama (*Theatre Arts*).

The national validating body for courses providing training in drama is the National Council for Drama Training. It currently has courses at the following: Arts Educational Schools; Birmingham School of Speech Training & Dramatic Art; Bristol Old Vic Theatre School; Central School of Speech and Drama; Drama Centre, London; Guildford School of Acting; Guildhall School of Music and Drama (see p. 530); London Academy of Music and Dramatic Art; Rose Bruford College of Speech and Drama; Royal Academy of Dramatic Art (*see below*); Royal Scottish Academy of Music and Drama; Webber Douglas Academy of Dramatic Art; Welsh College of Music and Drama.

ROYAL ACADEMY OF DRAMATIC ART (founded by Sir Herbert Beerbohm Tree, 1904), 62–64 Gower Street, WC1E 6ED.—*Principal*, O. Neville, PH.D.; *Administrator-Registrar*, R. O'Donoghue.

BRITISH THEATRE ASSOCIATION (formerly BRITISH DRAMA LEAGUE), 9 Fitzroy Square W1P 6AE.—*Dir.*, Jane Hackworth-Young.

ECONOMICS

Almost all universities grant first degrees in economics. Courses leading to first degrees in Economics granted by the Council for National Academic Awards are provided by some 20 Polytechnics and Colleges.

ENGINEERING
(See separate subjects below)

The Council of Engineering Institutions ceased operations in Sept. 1983 and its major functions are now carried on by The Engineering Council, 10 Maltravers Street, WC2R 3ER.—*Sec.*, J. Carlill. The fifteen principal qualifying bodies are:—

ROYAL AERONAUTICAL SOCIETY, 4 Hamilton Place, W1V 0BQ.—*Sec.*, B. P. Laight.

INSTITUTE OF ENERGY, 18 Devonshire Street, W.1.

INSTITUTION OF CHEMICAL ENGINEERS, 165/171 Railway Terrace, Rugby, Warwickshire CV21 3HQ; London Office, 12 Gayfere Street, SW1P 3HP.—*Gen. Sec.*, Dr. T. J. Evans.

INSTITUTION OF CIVIL ENGINEERS, 1–7 Great George Street SW1P 3AA.—*Sec.*, J. C. McKenzie.

INSTITUTION OF ELECTRICAL ENGINEERS, Savoy Place, WC2R 0BL.

INSTITUTION OF ELECTRONIC AND RADIO ENGINEERS, 99 Gower Street, WC1E 6AZ.—*Sec.*, D. D. Duffett.

INSTITUTION OF GAS ENGINEERS, 17 Grosvenor Crescent, S.W.1.

INSTITUTE OF MARINE ENGINEERS, 76 Mark Lane, EC3R 7JN.—*Sec.*, J. Stuart Robinson.

INSTITUTION OF MECHANICAL ENGINEERS, 1 Birdcage Walk, SW1H 9JJ.

INSTITUTION OF METALS, 1 Carlton House Terrace SW1Y 5DB.

INSTITUTION OF MINING ENGINEERS, Danum House, 6A South Parade, Doncaster DN1 2DY.

INSTITUTION OF MINING AND METALLURGY, 44 Portland Place, W1N 4BR.

INSTITUTION OF PRODUCTION ENGINEERS, Rochester House, 66 Little Ealing Lane, W5 4XX.—*Sec.*, R. J. Miskin.

INSTITUTION OF STRUCTURAL ENGINEERS, 11 Upper Belgrave Street, SW1X 8BH.

ROYAL INSTITUTION OF NAVAL ARCHITECTS, 10 Upper Belgrave Street, S.W.1.

ENGINEERING, GENERAL AND ENGINEERING SCIENCE

First Degrees in *General Engineering* or *Engineering Science* are granted by the Universities of Aberdeen, Aston in Birmingham, Cambridge, Durham, Edinburgh, Exeter, Lancaster, Leicester, Liverpool, London (Queen Mary College), Loughborough, Oxford, Reading, Surrey, Ulster and Warwick. Courses leading to first degrees in *Engineering* granted by the Council for National Academic Awards are provided by polytechnics and colleges.

Aeronautical Engineering

See main heading:
AERONAUTICS AND AERONAUTICAL ENGINEERING

Agricultural Engineering

First Degrees in *Agricultural Engineering* and *Agricultural Mechanization* are granted by the University of Newcastle upon Tyne. Courses in *Agricultural Engineering* and *Agricultural Technology & Management* leading to degrees granted by Cranfield Institute of Technology are provided at Silsoe College.

Chemical Engineering

First Degrees are granted by the Universities of Aston in Birmingham (*Chemical Process Engineering*), Bath, Belfast, Birmingham, Bradford, Cambridge, Edinburgh, Exeter, Heriot-Watt, Leeds, London (Imperial College of Science and Technology; University College), Loughborough, Manchester

(Manchester Institute of Science and Technology), Newcastle upon Tyne, Nottingham, Salford, Sheffield (*Chemical Process Engineering*), Strathclyde, Surrey, Wales (University College, Swansea).

Courses leading to first degrees granted by the Council for National Academic Awards are provided by North East London Polytechnic, Polytechnic of the South Bank, Teesside Polytechnic and Polytechnic of Wales.

Civil, Electrical & Mechanical Engineering

First Degrees in *Civil, Electrical* (or *Electrical and Electronic*) *and Mechanical Engineering* are granted by Aberdeen, Aston in Birmingham, Bath, Belfast, Birmingham, Bradford, Bristol, Brunel (*E. & M.*), Cambridge, City, Dundee, Durham, Edinburgh, Exeter, Glasgow, Heriot-Watt, Lancaster, Leeds, Leicester, Liverpool, London (Imperial College of Science and Technology, King's College, Queen Mary College, University College), Loughborough, Manchester, *also* Manchester Institute of Science and Technology, Newcastle upon Tyne, Nottingham, Oxford, Reading (*E. & M.*), Salford, Sheffield, Southampton, Strathclyde, Surrey, Sussex, Ulster (*C. & Manufacturing E.*), Wales (University Colleges at Cardiff and Swansea; Institute of Science and Technology, Cardiff; University College, Bangor E.), and Warwick.

Some 40 polytechnics or colleges provide courses (in one or more of civil, electrical/electronic and mechanical engineering) leading to first degrees granted by the Council for National Academic Awards.

Electronic Engineering & Electronics

First Degrees in *Electronic Engineering* or *Electronics* or *Electrical and Electronic Engineering* or *Electrical Engineering (including Electronics)* are granted by the following universities: Aberdeen, Aston, Bath, Belfast, Birmingham, Bradford, Bristol, Brunel, Cambridge, City, Dundee, Durham, East Anglia (*Electronic Systems Engineering*), Edinburgh, Essex, Exeter, Glasgow, Heriot-Watt, Hull, Keele, Kent at Canterbury, Lancaster, Leeds, Leicester, Liverpool, London (Imperial College of Science and Technology, King's, Queen Mary and University Colleges), Loughborough, Manchester (*also* Manchester Institute of Science and Technology), Newcastle upon Tyne, Nottingham, Oxford, Reading, Salford, Sheffield, Southampton, Strathclyde, Surrey, Sussex, Ulster, Wales (University Colleges of Bangor (also *Ocean Electronics*), Cardiff and Swansea, Institute of Science and Technology), Warwick (also *Engineering Electronics*), York.

Courses leading to first degrees in *Electronic Engineering* or in *Electrical and Electronic Engineering*, granted by the Council for National Academic Awards are provided by nearly 30 polytechnics or colleges.

Marine Engineering and Naval Architecture

First Degrees in *Marine Engineering* and *Naval Architecture and Shipbuilding* are granted by the University of Newcastle upon Tyne; in *Naval Architecture and Ocean Engineering* by the Universities of Glasgow and London (University College); in *Naval Architecture* by the University of Strathclyde; in *Ship Science* by the University of Southampton, in *Maritime Studies* by the University of Wales (Institute of Science and Technology) and in *Civil and Maritime Engineering* by the University of Liverpool.

Courses leading to first degrees in *Mechanical Engineering (Marine)* granted by the Council for National Academic Awards are provided by Liverpool Polytechnic.

Nuclear Engineering

First Degrees are granted by the Universities of London (Queen Mary College—also *Nuclear Reactor Science and Technology*), and Manchester.

Offshore Engineering

First Degrees are granted by Heriot-Watt University.

Production Engineering

First Degrees in *Production Engineering, Manufacturing Engineering* or *Industrial Engineering* are granted by the following Universities: Aston in Birmingham, Bath, Brunel, Cambridge, City, Hull (*Engineering Design and Manufacture*), Loughborough, Manchester and Manchester Institute of Science and Technology, Nottingham, Oxford, Strathclyde, Ulster and Wales (Institute of Science and Technology).

Courses leading to first degrees in *Production Engineering* granted by the Council for National Academic Awards are provided by Coventry (Lanchester) Polytechnic, Kingston Polytechnic, Leeds Polytechnic, Trent Polytechnic; in *Industrial Engineering* by Hatfield Polytechnic, Paisley College of Technology; in *Manufacturing Engineering* by Liverpool Polytechnic; in *Manufacturing Studies* by North East London Polytechnic; in *Manufacturing Systems Engineering* by Sheffield City Polytechnic; and in *Plant Engineering* by Trent Polytechnic.

Structural Engineering

First Degrees in *Civil and Structural Engineering* are granted by the Universities of Aberdeen, Bath, Bradford, Heriot-Watt (*Structural Engineering*), Liverpool, London (University College: *Civil, Structural and Environmental Engineering*), Sheffield, Sussex, and Wales (University College, Cardiff).

ESTATE MANAGEMENT AND SURVEYING
(*See also* Building)

First Degrees are granted by the Universities of Aberdeen (*Land Economy*), Cambridge (*Land Economy*), Heriot-Watt (*Estate Management*), Reading (*Land Management*) and Ulster (*Estate Management*).

First Degrees in *Surveying Science* are granted by the University of Newcastle upon Tyne, in *Building Economics and Quantity Surveying* by Heriot-Watt University, in *Quantity Surveying* by Ulster University, in *Property Valuation and Management* by the City University, in *Quantity Surveying and Building Surveying* by the University of Reading, and in *Quantity Surveying and Construction Economics* and *Building Surveying* by the University of Salford.

Courses leading to first degrees granted by the Council for National Academic Awards are provided by the following: in *Estate Management* by the City of Birmingham Polytechnic, Kingston Polytechnic, Oxford Polytechnic, Polytechnic of the South Bank and Thames Polytechnic; in *General Practice Surveying* by Newcastle upon Tyne Polytechnic; in *Housing* by Bristol Polytechnic; in *Housing Studies* by Sheffield City Polytechnic; in *Land Administration* by North East London Polytechnic; in *Land Economics* by Paisley College of Technology; in *Land Management* by Leicester Polytechnic; in *Minerals Estate Management* by Sheffield City Polytechnic; in *Quantity Surveying* by City of Birmingham Polytechnic, Bristol Polytechnic, Polytechnic of Central London,

Dundee College of Technology, Glasgow College of Technology with Glasgow College of Building and Printing, Kingston Polytechnic, Leeds Polytechnic, Liverpool Polytechnic, Newcastle upon Tyne Polytechnic, Portsmouth Polytechnic, Robert Gordon's Institute of Technology, Polytechnic of the South Bank, Thames Polytechnic, Trent Polytechnic and Polytechnic of Wales; in *Surveying and Mapping Sciences* by North East London Polytechnic; in *Urban Estate Management* by Polytechnic of Central London, Liverpool Polytechnic and the Polytechnic of Wales; in *Urban Estate Surveying* by Trent Polytechnic; in *Urban Land Administration* by Portsmouth Polytechnic; in *Urban Land Economics* by Sheffield City Polytechnic; and in *Valuation and Estate Management* by Bristol Polytechnic.

Qualifying professional bodies include:

THE INCORPORATED SOCIETY OF VALUERS AND AUCTIONEERS, 3 Cadogan Gate, SW1X 0AS.—*Sec.*, M. Astbury.

RATING AND VALUATION ASSOCIATION, 115 Ebury Street, SW1W 9QT.—*Sec.*, B. L. Hill.

THE INCORPORATED ASSOCIATION OF ARCHITECTS AND SURVEYORS, Jubilee House, Billing Brook Road, Weston Favell, Northampton NN3 4NW.—*Hon. Sec.*, W. J. Clark.

THE ROYAL INSTITUTION OF CHARTERED SURVEYORS (incorporating The Institute of Quantity Surveyors), 12 Great George Street, Parliament Square, SW1P 3AD.—*Sec. Gen.*, M. Pattison.

THE FACULTY OF ARCHITECTS AND SURVEYORS, with which is incorporated the Institute of Registered Architects, 15 St. Mary Street, Chippenham, Wilts.—*Sec.*, A. D. G. Webb.

FISHERY SCIENCE

First Degrees in *Wildlife and Fisheries Management* are granted by the University of Edinburgh.

Courses leading to first degrees in *Fishery Science/ Studies* granted by the Council for National Academic Awards are provided by Humberside College of Higher Education, and Plymouth Polytechnic.

FOOD AND NUTRITION SCIENCE
(See also Dietetics, Home Economics and Hotelkeeping)

First Degrees in *Food Science* are granted by the Universities of Belfast, Leeds, London (King's College), Nottingham, Reading (also *Food Science, Food Economics & Marketing* and *Food Technology*), Strathclyde, Surrey (*Nutrition & Food Science*) and Ulster (*Food Processing Technology*) (Provisional); and in *Nutrition* by the Universities of London (King's College), Nottingham and Surrey.

Courses leading to first degrees in *Food Science* granted by the Council for National Academic Awards are provided by the Polytechnic of the South Bank; in *Catering* by Oxford Polytechnic; in *Catering Administration* by Dorset Institute of Higher Education; in *Catering and Accommodation Studies* by Napier College of Commerce and Technology; in *Catering and Applied Nutrition* by Huddersfield Polytechnic; in *Catering Systems* by Sheffield City Polytechnic; in *Food and Accommodation Studies* by Leeds Polytechnic; in *Food Marketing Sciences* by Sheffield City Polytechnic; in *Food, Textiles & Consumer Studies* by the Polytechnic of the South Bank; in *Industrial Food Technology* by Humberside College of Higher Education; in *Nutrition and Dietetics* by Robert Gordon's Institute of Technology.

Scientific and professional bodies include: NUTRITION SOCIETY, Chandos House, 2 Queen Anne Street, W1M 9LE; FOOD SCIENCE & TECHNOLOGY INSTITUTE, 20 Queensberry Place, SW7 2DR.—*Exec. Sec.*, Ms. H. G. Wild.

FORESTRY AND TIMBER STUDIES

First Degrees in Forestry are granted by the Universities of Aberdeen, Edinburgh (*Agriculture, Forestry & Rural Economy*) (Provisional), and (also *Wood Science* and *Agroforestry*) Wales (University College, Bangor).

Courses leading to first degrees in *Timber Technology* granted by the Council for National Academic Awards are provided by Buckinghamshire College of Higher Education.

Professional Organizations

THE COMMONWEALTH FORESTRY ASSOCIATION, c/o CFI, South Parks Road, Oxford OX1 3RB.—*Sec.*, W. Hockey.

THE ROYAL FORESTRY SOCIETY OF ENGLAND, WALES AND NORTHERN IRELAND, 102 High Street, Tring, Herts. HP23 4HU.—*Dir.*, E. H. M. Harris.

THE ROYAL SCOTTISH FORESTRY SOCIETY, 10–11 Atholl Crescent, Edinburgh EH3 3HE.—*Sec.*, W. B. C. Walker.

THE INSTITUTE OF CHARTERED FORESTERS, 22 Walker Street, Edinburgh EH3 7HR.—*Sec.*, Mrs. M. W. Dick.

FUEL AND ENERGY STUDIES
(See also Nuclear Engineering)

First Degrees in *Fuel and Combustion Science* and in *Fuel and Energy Engineering* are granted by the University of Leeds; in *Petroleum Engineering* by London (Imperial College of Science and Technology); in *Mining and Petroleum Engineering* by the University of Strathclyde; in *Natural Gas Engineering* by the University of Salford; in *Fuel Technology* by the University of Sheffield; and in *Fuel and Energy and Management Studies* by the University of Leeds. These subjects may also form part of other degree courses.

Courses leading to first degrees in *Energy Engineering* granted by the Council for National Academic Awards are provided by Napier College of Commerce and Technology, and in *Power Engineering* by Derbyshire College of Higher Education.

Courses leading to certificates and qualification by professional bodies are available at many Technical Colleges.

The principal professional bodies are:—

THE INSTITUTION OF GAS ENGINEERS, 17 Grosvenor Crescent, S.W.1.

THE INSTITUTE OF ENERGY, 18 Devonshire Street, W.1.

THE INSTITUTE OF PETROLEUM, 61 New Cavendish Street W1M 8AR.—*Gen. Sec.*, D. C. Payne..

GEOLOGY

First Degrees in *Geology* or *Geological Sciences* or *Applied Geology* are granted by the Universities of Aberdeen (also *Petroleum Geology*), Aston in Birmingham, Belfast, Birmingham, Bristol, Cambridge, Durham, East Anglia (*Environmental Sciences*), Edinburgh, Exeter, Glasgow, Hull, Keele, Leeds, Leicester, Liverpool, London, Birkbeck College, Goldsmith's College, Imperial College of Science and Technology (also *Mining Geology*), Queen Mary College, Royal Holloway & Bedford New College, University College), Manchester, Newcastle upon Tyne (also *Engineering Geology*), Nottingham, Oxford, Reading, St. Andrews, Sheffield, Southampton, Strathclyde, Wales (University Colleges at Aberystwyth, Cardiff and Swansea).

Degree courses in *Geophysics* and *Geophysical Sciences* are also provided by universities.

Courses leading to first degrees in *Geology* granted by the Council for National Academic Awards are provided by City of London Polytechnic, Derbyshire College of Higher Education (*Earth and Life Studies*), Kingston Polytechnic and Portsmouth Polytechnic; in *Geology and Environment* by Oxford Polytechnic; and in *Engineering Geology and Geotechnics* by Portsmouth Polytechnic.

HOME ECONOMICS AND CATERING
(See also Dietetics, Food, Hotelkeeping and Institutional Management).

First Degrees are granted by the Universities of Ulster (*Home Economics* and *Catering Administration*), Wales (Cardiff University College: *Home Economics*), Strathclyde (*Hotel and Catering Management*) and Surrey (*Hotel and Catering Management*). Courses leading to first degrees in *Home Economics* granted by the University of Bath are provided at Bath College of Higher Education.

Courses leading to first degrees granted by the Council for National Academic Awards are provided by Bradford and Ilkley Community College (*Home and Community Studies*), Dorset Institute of Higher Education (*Catering Administration*), Huddersfield Polytechnic (*Catering and Applied Nutrition; Hotel and Catering Administration*); Leeds Polytechnic (*Home Economics*); Liverpool Polytechnic (*Home Economics*), Manchester Polytechnic (*Home Economics* and *Hotel and Catering Studies*); Middlesex Polytechnic (*Hotel and Catering Administration*); Napier College of Commerce and Technology (*Catering and Accommodation Studies*); Newcastle upon Tyne Polytechnic (*Home Economics*); Oxford Polytechnic (*Catering*); Portsmouth Polytechnic/Highbury College of Technology (*Hotel and Catering Management*); Queen Margaret College (*Home Economics*); Queen's College (*Home Economics*); Robert Gordon's Institute of Technology (*Home Economics; Hotel, Catering and Institutional Administration*); and Sheffield City Polytechnic (*Catering Systems*).

HOTELKEEPING
(See also Institutional Management)

First Degrees are granted by the Universities of Strathclyde (*Hotel and Catering Management*), Surrey (*Hotel Management* and *Hotel and Catering Management*) and Ulster (*Hotel and Tourism Management*).

Courses leading to first degrees in *Hotel and Catering Administration/Studies/Management* granted by the Council for National Academic Awards are provided by Huddersfield, Manchester and Middlesex Polytechnics and by Portsmouth Polytechnic/Highbury College of Technology; and in *Hotel, Catering and Institutional Management* by Robert Gordon's Institute of Technology.

INDUSTRIAL RELATIONS

First Degrees in Industrial Relations are granted by the Universities of Birmingham, Kent at Canterbury, London (London School of Economics and Political Science), Strathclyde and Wales (Cardiff University College). Industrial relations also forms part of degree courses at other universities.

INSTITUTIONAL MANAGEMENT
(See also Hotelkeeping)

First Degrees in Institutional Management are granted by the University of Wales (Cardiff University College).

Courses leading to first degrees in *Institutional Management* granted by the Council for National

Academic Awards are provided by the Polytechnic of North London; and in *Hotel, Catering and Institutional Management* by Robert Gordon's Institute of Technology.

Qualifying professional body in the three subjects above is:

HOTEL, CATERING AND INSTITUTIONAL MANAGEMENT ASSOCIATION, 191 Trinity Road, SW17 7HN.—*Dir.*, Elizabeth Gadsby.

INSURANCE

First Degrees in *Banking, Insurance and Finance* are granted by the University of Wales (University College, Bangor) and in *Industrial Economics with Insurance* by the University of Nottingham.

Courses leading to first degrees in *Risk Management* granted by the Council for National Academic Awards are provided by the Glasgow College of Technology.

Organizations conducting examinations and awarding diplomas:—

THE CHARTERED INSURANCE INSTITUTE, 20 Aldermanbury, EC2V 7HY.—*Sec. Gen.*, P. V. Saxton.

THE ASSOCIATION OF AVERAGE ADJUSTERS, Irongate House, Dukes Place, EC3A 7LP.

THE CHARTERED INSTITUTE OF LOSS ADJUSTERS, Manfield House, 376 Strand, W.C.2.

JOURNALISM

Courses for trainee newspaper journalists are available at 11 centres. One-year full-time courses are available for selected students. Particulars of all these courses are available from the Director of the National Council for Training of Journalists, Carlton House, Hemnall Street, Epping, Essex.

Short courses for experienced journalists are also arranged by the National Council. For periodical journalists courses are offered at a London college through N.C.T.J. enrolment including a one-year full-time course.

LANGUAGES

First Degrees in English and in a very wide range of Foreign Languages (including Oriental and African languages) are granted by universities. Degrees in *Linguistics* are awarded by the Universities of East Anglia, Essex (also *Language Studies Psycholinguistics*), Hull, Lancaster, Leeds (*Linguistics and Phonetics*), London (School of Oriental and African Studies and University College), Newcastle upon Tyne, Reading (also *Linguistics and Language Pathology*), Sussex and Wales (University College, Bangor); in *Applied Languages* (Provisional) by the University of Ulster; in *Language and Linguistics (African, Asian and European Languages*) by the University of York; and in *Languages (Interpreting and Translating*) by Heriot-Watt University. These subjects also form part of degree courses at many other universities.

Courses leading to first degrees in various *Foreign Languages* granted by the Council for National Academic Awards are provided by some 15 Polytechnics and Colleges.

LAW

First Degrees in Law are granted by the Universities of Aberdeen, Belfast, Birmingham, Bristol, Brunel, Cambridge, Dundee, Durham, East Anglia, Edinburgh, Essex, Exeter, Glasgow, Hull, Kent at Canterbury (also *Industrial Relations (Law)*), Lancaster, Leeds, Leicester, Liverpool, London (King's College; London School of Economics and Political

Science; Queen Mary College; School of Oriental and African Studies; University College), Manchester, Newcastle upon Tyne, Nottingham, Oxford, Reading, Sheffield, Southampton, Stirling (*Business Law*), Strathclyde (also *Business Law*), Sussex, Wales (University Colleges at Aberystwyth and Cardiff, Institute of Science and Technology) and Warwick.

Courses leading to first degrees in Law granted by the Council for National Academic Awards are provided by City of Birmingham Polytechnic, Bristol Polytechnic, Polytechnic of Central London, Chelmer Institute of Higher Education, City of London Polytechnic (also *Business Law*), Coventry (Lanchester) Polytechnic (*Business Law*), Ealing College of Higher Education, Huddersfield Polytechnic (*Business Law*), Kingston Polytechnic, Lancashire Polytechnic, Leeds Polytechnic, Leicester Polytechnic, Liverpool Polytechnic, Manchester Polytechnic, Middlesex Polytechnic, Newcastle upon Tyne Polytechnic, North East London Polytechnic, Polytechnic of North London, North Staffordshire Polytechnic, Polytechnic of the South Bank, Trent Polytechnic and Wolverhampton Polytechnic; and Polytechnic of Wales.

Qualifications for Barrister are obtainable only at one of the Inns of Court or Faculty of Advocates; for Solicitor, from the Law Society or its equivalent in Scotland or Ireland.

THE INNS OF COURT
THE SENATE OF THE INNS OF COURT AND THE BAR
11 South Square, Gray's Inn, WC1R 5EL

The governing body of the Barristers' branch of the legal profession, established in 1974 assuming the functions of the former Senate of the Four Inns of Court and the former General Council of the Bar.
Vice Chancellor, The Rt. Hon. Lord Justice Browne-Wilkinson.
Chairman, R. Alexander, Q.C.
Treasurer, J. Roch, Q.C.
Secretary, M. Murray.

THE INNER TEMPLE, EC4Y 7HL

Treasurer (1985), His Honour Sir William Stabb.
Sub-Treasurer, Capt. P. T. Sheehan, C.B.E.
Deputy Sub-Treasurer, Miss J. Morris.
Master of the Library, D. G. Widdicombe, Q.C.

THE MIDDLE TEMPLE EC4Y 9AT

Treasurer (1985), J. Mills, O.B.E., Q.C.
Under-Treasurer, Rear Adm. J. R. Hill.
Deputy Under-Treasurer, P. F. Gee.
Deputy Treasurer, The Rt. Hon. Sir John Donaldson.

LINCOLN'S INN, WC2A 3TL

Treasurer (1985), The Hon. Mr. Justice Warner.
Master of the Library, M. M. Wheeler.
Under-Treasurer, Capt. P. M. Carver.
Deputy do., E. M. T. Segar.

GRAY'S INN, W.C.1

Treasurer (1985), The Hon. Dame Rose Heilbron, D.B.E.
Master of Library, L. Caplan, Q.C.
Under-Treasurer, Rear Adm. C. M. Bevan, C.B.
Deputy do., P. A. A. Simmonds.

COUNCIL OF LEGAL EDUCATION
Gray's Inn Place, WC1R 5DX

Established by the four Inns of Court to superintend the Education and Examination of Students for the Bar of England and Wales.
Chairman, The Hon. Mr. Justice Bingham.

Vice-Chairman and Chairman, Board of Studies, The Hon. Mr. Justice Hobhouse.
Vice-Chairman and Chairman of the Finance Committee, His Hon. Judge E. F. Monier-Williams.
Inns of Court School of Law, Dean of Faculty, Mrs. M. A. Phillips.
Sub-Dean, E. Tenenbaum.

FACULTY OF ADVOCATES
Advocates' Library, Edinburgh EH1 1RF

Application for admission as an Advocate of the Scottish Bar is made by Petition to the Court of Session. The candidate is remitted for examination to the Faculty of Advocates. Enquiries should be addressed to The Clerk of Faculty.
Dean of Faculty, W. D. Prosser, Q.C.
Vice-Dean, J. A. Cameron, Q.C.
Treasurer, A. C. M. Johnston, Q.C.
Clerk of Faculty, N. M. P. Morrison.
Keeper of the Library, J. T. Cameron, Q.C.
Law Agent, P. C. Millar.

NORTHERN IRELAND

Admission to the Bar of Northern Ireland is controlled by the Honorable Society of the Inn of Court of Northern Ireland (established Jan. 11, 1926), Royal Courts of Justice, Belfast BT1 3JF.
Treasurer (1985), W. P. McCollum, Q.C.
Under-Treasurer and Librarian, J. A. L. McLean, Q.C.

THE LAW SOCIETY
113 Chancery Lane, WC2A 1LP

The Society controls the education and examination of articled clerks, and the admission of solicitors in England and Wales. It also regulates professional standards and conduct. Number of members, over 40,000.
President of the Society (1985–86), C. A. B. Leslie.
Vice-President (1985–86), J. M. Wickerson.
Secretary-General, J. L. Bowron.
Secretaries, D. Edwards (*Deputy Sec. Gen., and Legal Aid*); J. M. D. Hoyle (*Education and Training*); W. Merricks (*Professional Purposes*); G. Lee (*Professional and Public Relations*); A. J. Merrett (*Finance and Administration*); A. J. Lockley (*Contentious Business*); M. C. Leaf (*Non-Contentious Business*); H. Adamson (*Law Reform and International Relations*); Mrs. A. N. Brice (*Council Business*).

THE COLLEGE OF LAW, Braboeuf Manor, St. Catherine's, Guildford, Surrey GU3 1HA (and at 33–35 Lancaster Gate, W2 3LU, 2 Breams Buildings, Chancery Lane, EC4A 1DP, and Christleton Hall, Chester CH3 7AB), provides courses for The Law Society examinations.

LAW SOCIETY OF SCOTLAND
Law Society's Hall, 26 Drumsheugh Gardens, Edinburgh EH3 7YR

The Society comprises all practising solicitors in Scotland. It controls the examination of legal trainees and the admission of solicitors in Scotland and acts as registrar of solicitors under the Solicitors (Scotland) Act, 1980.

The Law Society of Scotland administers the Legal Aid and Advice Scheme set up under the Legal Aid and Advice (Scotland) Acts, 1967 and 1972.
President of the Society (1985–86), N. M. Stewart.
Secretary, K. W. Pritchard.
Secretary (*Legal Education*), Mrs. C. Slater.

LIBRARIANSHIP AND INFORMATION SCIENCE

First Degrees are granted by the University of Belfast (*Library and Information Studies*), Loughborough University of Technology (*Library Studies*), and the University of Wales (Aberystwyth) (*Librarianship* with another subject) (jointly with the College of Librarianship, Wales), and by the University of Strathclyde (*Librarianship* with another subject).

Courses leading to first degrees in *Librarianship/Library Studies* or *Librarianship/Library Studies with Information Studies/Science* granted by the Council for National Academic Awards are provided by City of Birmingham Polytechnic, Brighton Polytechnic, Ealing College of Higher Education, Leeds Polytechnic, Liverpool Polytechnic, Manchester Polytechnic, Newcastle upon Tyne Polytechnic, Polytechnic of North London and Robert Gordon's Institute of Technology; and in *Information Science* by Leeds Polytechnic.

The Library Association, 7 Ridgmount Street, WC1E 7AE, maintains the professional register of Chartered Librarians (Fellows and Associates). *Chief Exec.*, G. Cunningham.

MATERIALS STUDIES (including Metallurgy)

First Degrees in *Materials Science, Materials Technology, or Materials Science and Technology* are granted by the following universities: Bath, Birmingham (also *Metallurgy/Materials Engineering*), Brunel, Cambridge (*Metallurgy and Materials Science*), Leeds, Liverpool, London (Imperial College of Science and Technology: *Metallurgy and Materials*, Queen Mary College), Loughborough (*Materials Engineering*), Manchester and Manchester Institute of Science and Technology, Newcastle upon Tyne, Nottingham (*Metallurgy and Materials Science*), Oxford (*Metallurgy and Science of Materials*), Sheffield, Strathclyde (*Science of Engineering Materials*), Surrey and Wales (University College, Swansea, and (*Metallurgy and Materials Science*) Cardiff). First Degrees in *Polymer Technology/Polymer Science* are granted by London (Queen Mary College) and Sheffield. First Degrees in *Ceramics Science and Engineering/Technology* are granted by the Universities of Leeds and Sheffield; and in *Science and Technology of Glasses* by the University of Sheffield. First Degrees in *Metallurgy* and/or *Metallurgical Engineering* are granted by the following universities: Birmingham (*Metallurgy/Materials Engineering*), Brunel, Cambridge (*Metallurgy and Materials Science*), Leeds, Liverpool, London (Imperial College of Science and Technology: *Metallurgy and Materials*), Manchester and Manchester Institute of Science and Technology, Newcastle upon Tyne, Nottingham (*Metallurgy and Materials Science*), Oxford (*Metallurgy and Science of Materials*), Salford (*Engineering Metallurgy*), Sheffield, Strathclyde, Surrey, Wales (University Colleges at Cardiff (*Metallurgy and Materials Science*) and Swansea).

Courses leading to first degrees in *Materials Science/Technology* or *Metallurgy* or *Metallurgy and Materials* granted by the Council for National Academic Awards are provided by the City of London Polytechnic, Coventry (Lanchester) Polytechnic, Sheffield City Polytechnic (*Metallurgy and Microstructural Engineering*), Sunderland Polytechnic, Thames Polytechnic. Courses leading to first degrees in *Polymer Science and Technology* granted by the Council for National Academic Awards are provided by Manchester Polytechnic and the Polytechnic of North London; in *Mineral Processing Technology* by Camborne School of Mines; and in *Timber Technology* by Buckinghamshire College of Higher Education.

The Institution of Metals, 1 Carlton House Terrace SW1Y 5DB, is a qualifying body.

MATHEMATICS

First Degrees in *Mathematics* and/or *Applied Mathematics* are granted by all universities.

Courses leading to first degrees in *Mathematics* granted by the Council for National Academic Awards are provided by about a dozen Polytechnics and Colleges.

MEDICINE

First Degrees in *Medicine and Surgery* are granted by the Universities of Aberdeen, Belfast, Birmingham, Bristol, Cambridge, Dundee, Edinburgh, Glasgow, Leeds, Leicester, Liverpool, London (medical schools/colleges:— Charing Cross and Westminster M.S., King's College S.M.D., London H.M.C., Middlesex H.M.S., Royal Free H.M.S., St. Bart's. H.M.C., St. George's H.M.S., St. Mary's H.M.S., United M.D.S. (Guy's and St. Thomas's), University College), Manchester, Newcastle upon Tyne, Nottingham, Oxford, Sheffield, Southampton, Wales (University College, Cardiff, and Welsh National School of Medicine).

Licensing Corporations granting Diplomas

The Royal College of Physicians of London and the Royal College of Surgeons of England, Examining Board in England, Lincoln's Inn Fields, WC2A 3PN.

The Society of Apothecaries, Black Friars Lane, EC4V 6EJ.—*Registrar*, D. H. C. Barrie.

Royal College of Obstetricians and Gynæcologists, 27 Sussex Place, Regent's Park, NW1 4RG.—*Sec.*, A. G. S. Taylour.

The Royal College of Physicians of Edinburgh, 9 Queen Street, Edinburgh EH2 1JQ.—*Sec.*, Dr. T. M. Chalmers

The Royal College of Surgeons of Edinburgh, Nicolson Street, Edinburgh EH8 9DW.—*Sec.*, P. Edmond, C.B.E., Q.H.S.

The Royal College of Physicians and Surgeons of Glasgow, 234–242 St. Vincent Street, Glasgow G2 5RJ.—*Sec.*, A. Beattie, F.R.C.P.

The Scottish Triple Qualification Board, Nicolson Street, Edinburgh EH8 9DW and 242 St. Vincent Street, Glasgow.

Professions Supplementary to Medicine

The standard of professional education in chiropody, dietetics, medical laboratory sciences, occupational therapy, orthoptics, physiotherapy, radiography and remedial gymnastics is the responsibility of eight professional boards, which also publish an annual register of qualified practitioners. The work of the Boards is co-ordinated and supervised by The Council for Professions Supplementary to Medicine (Park House, 184 Kennington Park Road, SE11 4BU). F. Whitehill, *Registrar*.

CHIROPODY

Professional qualifications are granted by the Society of Chiropodists, 53 Welbeck Street, W1M 7HE, to students who have passed the qualifying examination after attending a course of full-time training for three years at one of the ten recognized schools in England and Wales, two in Scotland and one in Northern Ireland. Qualifications granted by the Society are approved by the Chiropodists Board for the purpose of State Registration, which is a condition of employment within the National Health Service. *Sec.*, G. C. Jenkins.

DIETETICS

(*See* main heading, p. 523)

MEDICAL LABORATORY SCIENCE

First Degrees in *Medical Laboratory Science* are granted by Bradford University and the University of Ulster.

Courses leading to first degrees in Medical Laboratory Science granted by the Council for National Academic Awards are provided by several polytechnics.

Qualifications from higher or further education establishments and training in medical laboratories are required for progress to the professional examinations and qualifications of the Institute of Medical Laboratory Sciences, 12 Queen Anne Street, W1M 0AU.

OCCUPATIONAL HYGIENE

Courses leading to first degrees in *Occupational Hygiene* granted by the Council for National Academic Awards are provided by the Polytechnic of the South Bank.

OCCUPATIONAL THERAPY

First Degrees in *Occupational Therapy* are (provisional) granted by the University of Ulster. Professional qualifications are awarded after examination by the College of Occupational Therapists, 20 Rede Place, Bayswater, W2 4TU, which recognizes 16 training schools in England, Wales, Scotland, N. Ireland and Eire.

ORTHOPTICS

Orthoptists undertake the diagnosis and treatment of all types of squint and other anomalies of binocular vision, working in close collaboration with ophthalmologists. The training and maintenance of professional standards are the responsibility of the Orthoptists Board of the Council for the Professions Supplementary to Medicine. The examining and qualifying body is the British Orthoptic Society. Training consists of a three-year course at one of 9 approved Orthoptic Schools in England and Wales and 1 in Scotland.

The Professional Association is the British Orthoptic Society, Tavistock House North, Tavistock Square, WC1H 9HX.

(*See also* under Ophthalmic Optics.)

PHYSIOTHERAPY

First Degrees are granted by the University of Ulster.

Courses leading to first degrees in *Physiotherapy* granted by the Council for National Academic Awards are provided by North East London Polytechnic and the Queen's College.

Full-time three- or four-year degree or diploma courses available at 32 recognised Schools in the U.K. Examinations leading to Membership of The Chartered Society of Physiotherapy and to State Registration. Information from The Chartered Society of Physiotherapy, 14 Bedford Row, London WC1R 4ED.

RADIOGRAPHY AND RADIOTHERAPY

Examinations leading to qualification are conducted by The College of Radiographers, 14 Upper Wimpole Street, W1M 8BN.

There are recognized training centres in radiography and radiotherapy at many cities and towns in England and Wales, Scotland and Northern Ireland.

In London courses are available at the London Teaching Hospitals listed on p. 507–508; and at Hammersmith, St. Thomas' and Royal Northern Hospitals, at Bromley and Greenwich.

METEOROLOGY

First Degrees in *Meteorology* are granted by the University of Reading. The subject is also included in degree courses at some other universities.

MINING AND MINING ENGINEERING

First Degrees in *Mining* or *Mining Engineering* are granted by the following universities: Leeds (also *Mineral Engineering*), London (Imperial College of Science and Technology (also *Mineral Technology*)), Newcastle upon Tyne, Nottingham, Strathclyde (*Mining and Petroleum Engineering*), Wales (University College, Cardiff: also *Mineral Processing*).

Courses leading to first degrees granted by the Council for National Academic Awards are provided by Camborne School of Mines (*Mining Engineering* and *Mineral Processing Engineering*) and North Staffordshire Polytechnic (*Mining Engineering*).

Miscellaneous Authorities

THE INSTITUTION OF MINING ENGINEERS, Danum House, 6A South Parade, Doncaster DN1 2DY.

THE ENGINEERING COUNCIL, Canberra House, Maltravers Street, W.C.2.

MUSIC

First Degrees in *Music* are granted by the Universities of Aberdeen (also *History of Music*), Bath (course at Bath College of Higher Education), Belfast, Birmingham, Bristol, Cambridge, City, Durham, East Anglia, Edinburgh, Exeter, Glasgow (also *Music Education* and *Music Performance* in conjunction with Royal Scottish Academy of Music and Drama), Hull, Lancaster, Leeds (also at Bretton Hall College), Leicester (*Musicianship*), Liverpool, London (King's College, Royal Holloway and Bedford New College; *also* Goldsmiths' College, Royal Academy of Music, Royal College of Music, and Trinity College of Music), Manchester, Newcastle upon Tyne, Nottingham, Oxford, Reading, Sheffield, Southampton, Stirling (*Music/History of Music*), Surrey (*Academic & Practical Applications of Music*; *Music & Sound Recording* (*Tonmeister*)), Sussex, Ulster, Wales (University Colleges at Aberystwyth, Bangor and Cardiff; also at Welsh College of Music and Drama), and York.

Courses leading to first degrees in Music granted by the Council for National Academic Awards are provided by City of Birmingham Polytechnic, Colchester Institute, Dartington College of Arts, Huddersfield Polytechnic and Kingston Polytechnic (*Music Education*).

ASSOCIATED BOARD OF THE ROYAL SCHOOLS OF MUSIC
14 Bedford Square, WC1B 3JG

Conducts the local examinations in music and speech for the four Royal Schools of Music—the Royal Academy of Music and the Royal College of Music in London, the Royal Northern College of Music, Manchester and the Royal Scottish Academy of Music and Drama, Glasgow.

Chief Exec. and Dir. of Examinations, R. Smith.

ROYAL ACADEMY OF MUSIC (1822)
Marylebone Road, NW1 5HT

Full training facilities are provided for students seeking a professional career in all branches of music. Courses lead to Professional Certificate, G.R.S.M. (Hons) or B.Mus. (London) after three years' full time study. Dip.R.A.M. (Performers) may be obtained after four years. The L.R.A.M. Diploma is open to both internal and external candidates.

Principal, Sir David Lumsden, M.A., D.Phil., MUS.B.
Administrator, J. Bliss.
Warden, P. James, PH.D., B.MUS.

ROYAL COLLEGE OF MUSIC (1883)
Prince Consort Road, South Kensington, S.W.7

M.MUS., B.MUS., G.R.S.M., Dip.R.C.M. and A.R.C.M. awarded by examination.
No. of Students, 600.
Director, M. G. Matthews, F.R.C.M., A.R.C.O.
Vice-Director, I. Horsbrugh.
Registrar, J. Thorogood.
Bursar, A. P. Millar.

GUILDHALL SCHOOL OF MUSIC AND DRAMA (1880)
Silk Street, Barbican, EC2Y 8DT

Full-time and part-time courses in Music, Speech, Drama and Stage Management. Awards Diplomas of Graduate (G.G.S.M.), Associate (A.G.S.M.) and Licentiate (L.G.S.M.). The Diploma of Graduate (G.G.S.M.) carries graduate honours status.
Principal, J. Hosier, C.B.E., F.R.C.M.
Director of Drama, T. Church.
Director of Music, L. East.
Director of Administration, G. Derbyshire.

TRINITY COLLEGE OF MUSIC (1872)
11–13 Mandeville Place, W1M 6AQ

Complete training in music for teachers and performers. Courses lead to the university degree of B.MUS., the Graduate Diploma which carries Graduate Honours status, the Teacher's Diploma in Music and the Performer's Diploma in Music.
Principal, M. Davies, C.B.E., F.R.C.M.
Vice-Principal, D. Pettit.
Dir. of Examinations, D. Gulliver.

LONDON COLLEGE OF MUSIC
47 Great Marlborough Street, W1V 2AS

Comprehensive full-time musical training for performers and teachers. Graduate Course recognized by the Dept. of Education and Science and Burnham Committee.
Director, J. McCabe, MUS.B., F.R.C.M.
Secretary, K. R. Beard.

ROYAL COLLEGE OF ORGANISTS (1864)
Kensington Gore, SW7 2QS

For the promotion of the highest standard in organ playing and choir-training. Awards Diplomas of Associateship (A.R.C.O.) and Fellowship (F.R.C.O.); and Choir-Training (CHM).
Clerk, K. B. Lyndon.

BIRMINGHAM SCHOOL OF MUSIC
Paradise Circus, Birmingham B3 3HG

Head, L. Carus, F.R.C.M.

THE CURWEN INSTITUTE
17 Primrose Avenue, Chadwell Heath, Romford, Essex RM6 4QB

International examining body maintained by The John Curwen Society (1975).

ROYAL SCHOOL OF CHURCH MUSIC
Addington Palace, Croydon CR9 5AD
Founded (1927) for the advancement of good music in the Church.

Director, Dr. L. Dakers, C.B.E., D.MUS., F.R.C.O., F.R.A.M.
Secretary, V. E. Waterhouse.

ROYAL NORTHERN COLLEGE OF MUSIC
124 Oxford Road, Manchester M13 9RD

Principal, J. Manduell, C.B.E., F.R.A.M., F.R.N.C.M., F.R.C.M., F.R.S.A.M.D.

ROYAL MILITARY SCHOOL OF MUSIC
Kneller Hall, Twickenham TW2 7DU

Commandant, Col. C. A. Ewing, O.B.E.
Director of Music and Chief Instructor, Lt.-Col. D. R. Beat, L.V.O.

ROYAL MARINES SCHOOL OF MUSIC
Deal, Kent CT14 7EH

Commandant, Lt.-Col. E. G. R. Sale, R.M.
Principal Director of Music, Lt.-Col. G. A. C. Hoskins, M.V.O., A.R.A.M., R.M. (Eight Bands in Commission in 1985).

ROYAL SCOTTISH ACADEMY OF MUSIC AND DRAMA
St. George's Place, Glasgow G2 1BS

Curriculum provides for all branches of study necessary for entry into the professions of music and drama. Special Degree Courses for those who wish to teach music and drama in schools.
Principal, P. Ledger, C.B.E., MUS.B., L.R.A.M.

NAUTICAL STUDIES
(*See also* Marine Engineering, Fishery Science)

The University of Wales grants first degrees in *Maritime Commerce* and *Maritime Geography* (courses at Institute of Science and Technology).

Courses leading to first degrees in *Nautical Studies* granted by the Council for National Academic Awards are provided by Liverpool Polytechnic (*Maritime Studies*), Plymouth Polytechnic and Sunderland Polytechnic.

Merchant Navy Training Schools
For Officers

MERCHANT NAVY COLLEGE, Greenhithe, Kent DA9 9NY.—*Principal*, G. Emmons, M.SC., PH.D.
THE COLLEGE OF MARITIME STUDIES, Warsash, Southampton SO3 6ZL. *Director*, Capt. C. N. Phelan.

For Seamen

INDEFATIGABLE AND NAUTICAL SEA TRAINING SCHOOL FOR BOYS (Independent; in receipt of government grant (Residential)), Plas Llanfair, Llanfairpwll, Anglesey (150); *Captain Headmaster*, Capt. R. T. Youngman; *Sec.*, L. R. Ridyard, Room 22, Oriel Chambers, 14 Water Street, Liverpool, 2.
NATIONAL SEA TRAINING COLLEGE, Denton, Gravesend, Kent. *Princ.*, Capt. P. H. Adlam.

NURSING

Courses in which academic study leading to a degree at a University may be combined with nursing training/practical nursing in hospitals are provided by the following universities: Brunel (*Mental Nursing*), City, Edinburgh, Glasgow, Hull, Liverpool, London (Goldsmiths', King's and Queen Mary Colleges), Manchester, Southampton, Surrey, Ulster and Wales (Welsh National School of Medicine).

Courses leading to first degrees in *Nursing* granted by the Council for National Academic Awards are provided by Bristol Polytechnic, Dundee College of Technology, Glasgow College of Technology, Leeds Polytechnic, Queen Margaret College, Sheffield City Polytechnic and Polytechnic of the South Bank.

Three-year courses for State Registration in general, sick children's mental and mental deficiency nursing. Two-year course for State enrolment. Training schools in many parts of Great Britain.

THE ROYAL COLLEGE OF NURSING
OF THE UNITED KINGDOM
20 Cavendish Square, W1M 0AB

The Royal College of Nursing, within its Institute of Advanced Nursing Education, provides education at post-basic level in hospital, occupational health and community health fields. Advanced courses are held in preparation for senior posts in administration and teaching; and other short and special courses. *Director of Education,* Miss M. D. Green.

NATIONAL BOARDS FOR NURSING, MIDWIFERY AND HEALTH VISITING
FOR ENGLAND
170 Tottenham Court Road, W1P 0HA
Chief Exec. Officer, Dr. E. Bendall.

FOR SCOTLAND
22 Queen Street, Edinburgh EH2 1JX
Chief Exec. Officer., Miss M. W. Thomson.

FOR WALES
Pearl Assurance House, Floor 13,
Greyfriars Road,Cardiff CF1 3AG
Chief Exec., W. Preece.

FOR NORTHERN IRELAND
79 Chichester Street, Belfast BT1 4JE
Chief Exec., J. J. Walsh.

OPHTHALMIC OPTICS

First Degrees in *Ophthalmic Optics* are granted by the following Universities: Aston in Birmingham, Bradford, City, Manchester (Manchester Institute of Science and Technology), and Wales (Institute of Science and Technology).

Courses leading to first degrees in *Ophthalmic Optics* granted by the Council for National Academic Awards are provided by the Glasgow College of Technology.

Examining bodies granting qualifications as an ophthalmic optometrist or dispensing optician:—

THE BRITISH COLLEGE OF OPHTHALMIC OPTICIANS (OPTOMETRISTS), 10 Knaresborough Place, SW5 0TG.

THE ASSOCIATION OF DISPENSING OPTICIANS, 22 Nottingham Place, W1M 4AT (training institution; qualification as dispensing optician).

FACULTY OF DISPENSING OPTICIANS, Apothecaries' Hall, Blackfriars Lane, EC4V 6EL.

OSTEOPATHY

LONDON COLLEGE OF OSTEOPATHIC MEDICINE (Incorporating London College of Osteopathy), 8–10 Boston Place, N.W.1.

PHARMACY

First Degrees in *Pharmacy* are granted by the Universities of Aston in Birmingham, Bath, Belfast, Bradford, Heriot-Watt, London (King's College and the School of Pharmacy), Manchester, Nottingham, Strathclyde, Wales (Institute of Science and Technology).

Courses leading to first degrees in Pharmacy granted by the Council for National Academic Awards are provided by Brighton Polytechnic, Leicester Polytechnic, Liverpool Polytechnic, Portsmouth Polytechnic, Robert Gordon's Institute of Technology, and Sunderland Polytechnic.

Information may be obtained from The Registrar, The Pharmaceutical Society of Great Britain, 1 Lambeth High Street, SE1 7JN.

PHOTOGRAPHY, FILM AND TV STUDIES

First Degrees in *Film and Media Studies* are granted by the University of Stirling. At some other universities *Film* may be studied as part of a first degree course.

Courses leading to first degrees granted by the Council for National Academic Awards are provided by Derbyshire College of Higher Education (*Photographic Studies*), Harrow College of Higher Education/Middlesex Polytechnic (*Applied Photography, Film and TV*), London College of Printing (*Photography, Film and TV*), Napier College of Commerce and Technology (*Photographic Studies*), Polytechnic of Central London (*Film and Photographic Arts* and *Photographic Sciences*), Trent Polytechnic (*Photography*), West Surrey College of Art and Design (*Photography, Film and Video, Animation*).

BRITISH INSTITUTE OF PROFESSIONAL PHOTOGRAPHY, Amwell End, Ware, Herts. SG12 9HN.—*Secretary,* P. A. Large.

PRINTING

First Degrees in *Typography and Graphic Communication* are awarded by the University of Reading.

Courses leading to first degrees in *Printing and Packaging Technology* granted by the Council for National Academic Awards are provided by Watford College of Technology.

Courses in technical and general, design and administrative aspects of printing are available at technical colleges throughout the United Kingdom. Details can be obtained from the Institute of Printing and the British Printing Industries Federation (*see below*).

In addition to the examining and organizing bodies listed below, examinations are held by various independent regional examining boards in further education.

INSTITUTE OF PRINTING (1961), 8 Lonsdale Gardens, Tunbridge Wells, Kent TN1 1NU.

JOINT COMMITTEE (AND SCOTTISH JOINT COMMITTEE) FOR NATIONAL CERTIFICATES IN PRINTING.

BRITISH PRINTING INDUSTRIES FEDERATION, 11 Bedford Row, WC1R 4DX.

RECREATION, SPORT, AND HUMAN MOVEMENT STUDIES

(*See also* Dance)

First Degrees are granted by the University of Birmingham (*Physical Education*), Loughborough University of Technology (*Physical Education and Sports Science*; also *Physical Education, Sports Science and Recreation Management*) and Ulster (*Sports Studies*).

Courses in *Sports Science/Studies* leading to first degrees granted by the Council for National Academic Awards are provided by Bedford College of Higher Education, Brighton Polytechnic, Crewe and Alsager College of Higher Education, Jordanhill College of Education (*Sport in the Community*), Liverpool Polytechnic, Newcastle upon Tyne Polytechnic with Sunderland Polytechnic, North Staffordshire Polytechnic (*Sport and Recreation Studies*), Sheffield City Polytechnic, Trent Polytechnic (*Sport—Administration and Science*) and West Sussex Institute of Higher Education; and in *Recreation* by Dunfermline College of Physical Education, and College of St. Mark and St. John (*Recreation and Community*).

First degrees in *Human Movement Studies* are granted by the University of Wales (courses at South Glamorgan Institute of Higher Education) and by the Council for National Academic Awards (courses at Leeds Polytechnic: also *Leisure Studies*).

Physical Education and *Sports Science/Studies* also form part of a degree course at many other colleges/polytechnics.

ROBOTICS

(*See also* Computer Science)

First Degrees in *Electronic Control and Robot Engineering* are granted by the University of Hull.

SOCIAL WORK

First Degrees in *Social Studies* or in *Social Sciences* are granted by most universities. Courses leading to first degrees in *Social Science* or *Social Sciences/ Applied Social Science or Sociology* granted by the Council for National Academic Awards are provided by some 30 polytechnics and colleges.

CENTRAL COUNCIL FOR EDUCATION AND TRAINING IN SOCIAL WORK, Derbyshire House, St. Chad's Street, London WC1H 8AD.—*Dir.*, Miss P. H. F. Young, C.B.E. The Council is an independent body financed by the Government. It has statutory authority throughout the U.K. to promote education and training for social work and for certain other kinds of work in the personal social services. It recognizes or approves courses, schemes or programmes. The C.C.E.T.S.W.'s award, the Certificate of Qualification in Social Work, is the professional qualification for social workers and courses that lead to it are available at universities, polytechnics, colleges and institutes.

BRITISH ASSOCIATION OF SOCIAL WORKERS, 16 Kent Street, Birmingham B5 6RD. *Gen. Sec.*, D. Jones.

THE INSTITUTE OF HOUSING, 12 Upper Belgrave Street, SW1X 8BA.—*Dir.*, P. J. McGurk.

SPEECH SCIENCE

(*See also* Languages)

First Degrees in *Speech* are awarded by the University of Newcastle upon Tyne, in *Speech Science* by the University of Sheffield, in *Speech Sciences* by the University of London (University College), in *Speech Pathology and Therapy* by the University of Manchester (and at Manchester Polytechnic), in *Speech Pathology and Therapeutics* (with courses at Jordanhill College of Education) by the University of Glasgow; and in *Speech Therapy* by the University of Ulster and (with courses at South Glamorgan Institute of Higher Education) by the University of Wales.

Courses leading to first degrees in *Speech Therapy* granted by the Council for National Academic Awards are provided by Central School of Speech and Drama, City of Birmingham Polytechnic (*Speech and Language Pathology and Therapeutics*), Leeds Polytechnic, Leicester Polytechnic (*Speech Pathology and Therapy*) and Queen Margaret College (*Speech Pathology and Therapy*).

The Directory of qualified Speech Therapists is published by the College of Speech Therapists, Harold Poster House, 6 Lechmere Road, NW2 5BU. Courses leading to B.Sc.(Hons.) degree and Licentiateship of The College of Speech Therapists are available at:

THE CENTRAL SCHOOL OF SPEECH AND DRAMA (Department of Speech Therapy), Embassy Theatre, Swiss Cottage, NW3 3HY.

CITY OF BIRMINGHAM POLYTECHNIC SCHOOL OF SPEECH THERAPY, Perry Bar, Birmingham.

LEEDS POLYTECHNIC, School of Health and Applied Sciences, Speech Therapy Section, Calverley Street, Leeds LS1 3HE.

QUEEN MARGARET COLLEGE, Department of Speech Therapy, Clerwood Terrace, Edinburgh EH12 8TS.

CARDIFF SCHOOL OF SPEECH THERAPY, South Glamorgan Institute of Higher Education, Western Avenue, Cardiff CF5 2YB.

LEICESTER POLYTECHNIC, School of Speech Pathology, Scraptoft, Leicester LE7 9SU.

NATIONAL HOSPITALS COLLEGE OF SPEECH-SCIENCES, 59 Portland Place, W1N 3AJ.

SURVEYING

(*See* Estate Management and Surveying)

TEACHING

There are now three main ways to gain the qualification needed to become a teacher:

(a) The first is to follow a three- or four-year course leading to a B.Ed. degree. B.Ed. courses are provided by some 70 colleges of education/institutes of higher education/polytechnics. The degrees are awarded either by universities or by the Council for National Academic Awards (C.N.A.A.).

(b) The second, for those who are already graduates with a degree other than a B.Ed., is to follow a one-year course leading to a postgraduate certificate in education.

(c) The third is to take a course at one of the few institutions, mainly universities, that offer concurrent courses (normally four years) leading to a degree (other than B.Ed.) *and* a teaching qualification.

TECHNICAL EDUCATION

First Degrees in one or more technologies are awarded by almost all universities; and many polytechnics and colleges of technology provide courses leading to first degrees granted by the Council for National Academic Awards. Details are given under individual subject headings.

(*See also*: Aeronautics; Building; Computer Science; Engineering; Fuel and Energy Studies; Mining; Ophthalmic Optics; Printing, and Textiles.)

CITY AND GUILDS OF LONDON INSTITUTE
76 Portland Place, W1N 4AA

An independent educational organization founded in 1878 and incorporated by Royal Charter. The Institute offers examinations on its published regulations and syllabuses, and awards certificates of prevocational and vocational training in a wide range of technical subjects. Its syllabuses are taught in secondary schools, colleges of further education, and other educational and training establishments in the United Kingdom and overseas. The Institute provides the administrative services for the National Examinations Board for Supervisory Studies, and, with the Business and Technician Education Council, has established the Joint Board for Pre-Vocational Education.

President, H.R.H. the Duke of Edinburgh, K.G., K.T.
Chairman, H. M. Neal.
Director-General, H. Knutton, C.B.
Secretary, B. B. Phillips.
Dean of the City and Guilds College, Prof. H. Sawistowski.

TECHNICIAN EDUCATION COUNCIL
(*See* "Business and Technician Education Council" on page 521).

Regional Advisory Councils

Set up in 1947 (i) to bring education and industry together to find out the needs of young workers and advise on the provision required, and (ii) to secure reasonable economy of provision. They also have certain responsibilities in connection with the procedure for the approval by the Department of Education and Science of advanced courses, and issue handbooks, etc., giving, for the guidance of students and teachers, information about the facilities available within a region or district for various types of training (e.g. electrical engineering, textiles, building and chemistry). There are ten Regional Advisory Councils in England and Wales:—

1 (LONDON AND SOUTH EASTERN).—Regional Advisory Council for Technological Education, Tavistock House South, Tavistock Square, WC1H 9LR.
2 (SOUTHERN).—Regional Council for Further Education, 26 Bath Road, Reading RG1 6NT.
3 (SOUTH WEST).—Regional Council for Further Education, Wessex Lodge, 11–13 Billetfield, Taunton TA1 3NN.
4 (WEST MIDLANDS).—Advisory Council for Further Education, Norfolk House, Smallbrook Queensway, Birmingham B5 4NB.
5 (EAST MIDLANDS).—East Midlands Further Education Council, Robins Wood House, Robins Wood Road, Aspley, Nottingham NG8 3NH.
6 (EAST ANGLIAN).—Regional Advisory Council for Further Education, 2 Looms Lane, Bury St. Edmunds, Suffolk IP33 1HE.
7 (YORKSHIRE AND HUMBERSIDE).—Association for Further and Higher Education, Bowling Green Terrace, Leeds LS11 9SX.
8 (NORTH-WESTERN).—North Western Regional Advisory Council for Further Education (incorporating the Union of Lancashire and Cheshire Institutes), Town Hall, Walkden Road, Worsley, Manchester M28 4QE.
9 (NORTHERN).—Northern Council for Further Education, 5 Grosvenor Villas, Grosvenor Road, Newcastle upon Tyne NE2 2RU.
10 (WALES).—Welsh Joint Education Committee, 245 Western Avenue, Cardiff CF5 2YX.

Industry Training Boards

AGRICULTURAL, Bourne House, 32–34 Beckenham Road, Beckenham, Kent BR3 4PB.—*Dir.*, R. C. Swan.
CLOTHING AND ALLIED PRODUCTS, Tower House, Merrion Way, Leeds LS2 8NY.—*Director*, J. W. Dearden.
CONSTRUCTION, Radnor House, 272 London Road, Norbury, SW16 4EL.—*Sec.*, J. A. Reynolds, O.B.E.
ENGINEERING, P.O. Box 176, 54 Clarendon Road, Watford, Herts. WD1 1LB.—*Sec.*, E. P. Jones.
HOTEL AND CATERING INDUSTRY TRAINING BOARD, P.O. Box 18, Ramsey House, Central Square, Wembley, Middx. HA9 7AP.—*Sec.*, B. Smart.
LOCAL GOVERNMENT TRAINING BOARD, 4th Floor, Arndale Centre, Luton, Beds. LU1 2TS.—*Dir.*, M. Clarke.
MAN-MADE FIBRES INDUSTRY TRAINING ADVISORY BOARD, Gable House, 40 High Street, Rickmansworth, Herts. WD3 1ES.—*Gen. Manager*, D. W. Ashby.
OFFSHORE PETROLEUM, Forties Road, Montrose, Angus DD10 9ET.—*Sec.*, P. J. Bing, O.B.E.
PLASTICS PROCESSING, Brent House, 950 Great West Road, Brentford, Middx. TW8 9ES.—*Gen. Manager*, D. Titterton.
ROAD TRANSPORT, Capitol House, Empire Way, Wembley, Middx.—*Dir. Gen.*, T. E. Tindall.

Industrial Training Foundation
91 Waterloo Road, S.W.1.

The Industrial Training Foundation provides a consultancy service to British and overseas governments, industry and commerce, on technical education and training. It is a non profit-making institution registered under the Charities Act and charges fees only to cover its costs. Its objectives are to promote the development of vocational and industrial education and training in its broadest sense.

ITF has acted for, or in association with, all relevant Government departments, and international and institutional bodies. It was formed in 1964 with British Government support and the experience gained in Britain was later put to use in developing training services for overseas countries.

ITF advises Governments and industry on the necessary steps for the institution, development and implementation of training programmes ranging from courses to cover a specific problem to fully integrated comprehensive projects.

TEXTILES

First Degrees in *Textiles* are awarded by the Universities of Leeds and Manchester (Manchester Institute of Science and Technology).

Courses leading to first degrees in *Textile Marketing* granted by the Council for National Academic Awards are provided by Huddersfield Polytechnic; in *Textile and Knitwear Technology* by Leicester Polytechnic; in *Textiles with Clothing Studies* by Scottish College of Textiles; in *Clothing Studies* by Manchester Polytechnic; in *Food, Textiles and Consumer Studies* by Polytechnic of the South Bank; and in various aspects of *Textiles/Fashion* by some 20 Polytechnics and Colleges.

THE TEXTILE INSTITUTE, 10 Blackfriars Street, Manchester M3 5DR.—*Gen. Sec.*, R. G. Denyer.

THEOLOGY

First Degrees in *Theology* or *Divinity* are granted by the Universities of Aberdeen, Belfast, Birmingham, Bristol (*Theology and Religious Studies*), Cambridge (*Theological and Religious Studies*), Durham, Edinburgh, Exeter, Glasgow, Hull, Kent at Canterbury, Leeds (*Theology and Religious Studies*), London (Heythrop and King's Colleges), Manchester, Nottingham, Oxford, St. Andrews, Southampton (at La Sainte Union College of Higher Education), and Wales (Aberystwyth, Bangor, Cardiff, and, also *Theology and Religious Studies*, St. David's University Colleges); in *Biblical Studies* by the Universities of London (King's College), Manchester, Newcastle upon Tyne, Sheffield and Wales (Bangor University College); and in *Religious Studies* by the Universities of Aberdeen, Bristol (*Theology and Religious Studies*), Cambridge (*Theological and Religious Studies*), Edinburgh, Lancaster, Leeds (*Theology and Religious Studies*), London (King's College), Manchester (*Comparative Religion*) (provisional), Newcastle upon Tyne, Stirling, and Wales (University College, Cardiff and, also *Theology and Religious Studies*, St. David's University College).

Courses leading to first degrees in *Theology* or *Theological Studies* granted by the Council for National Academic Awards are provided by London Bible College, Spurgeon's College, Trinity College, Bristol and Westminster College, Oxford; in *Theological and Pastoral Studies* by Oak Hill College; and in *Jewish Studies* by Jews' College.

Theological Colleges
Church of England and Church in Wales

BANGOR (University Anglican Chaplaincy) (Church Hostel) (28).—*Warden*, Rev. Canon B. C. Morgan.
BIRMINGHAM (Queen's Coll., Somerset Road, Edgbaston, B15 2QH) (70).—*Princ.*, Rev. G. S. Wakefield (Ecumenical College).
BRISTOL (Trinity College, BS9 1JP) (130).—*Princ.*, Rev. G. Carey, PH.D.

CAMBRIDGE (Ridley Hall, CB3 9HG) (56).—*Princ.*, Rev. H. F. de Waal.

CAMBRIDGE (Westcott House, Jesus Lane, CB5 8BP) (50).—*Princ.*, Rev. Dr. R. W. N. Hoare.

CHICHESTER (Westgate, PO19 3ES) (60).—*Princ.*, Rev. Canon J. W. Hind.

CUDDESDON (Ripon College, Oxon OX9 9EX) (70).—*Princ.*, Rev. Canon D. P. Wilcox.

DURHAM.—*See* University of Durham—St. Chad's; St. John's.

LAMPETER (St. David's College)—*See* University of Wales.

LINCOLN (Theological College, LN1 3BP) (70).—*Warden*, Rev. Canon F. H. A. Richmond.

LLANDAFF (St. Michael's, Cardiff CF5 2YJ) (32).—*Warden*, Rev. Canon J. G. Hughes, PH.D.

LONDON (King's College, W.C.2.).—*See* University of London.

MIRFIELD (College of the Resurrection, WF14 0BW) (43).—*Princ.*, Rev. D. Lloyd, C.R.

NOTTINGHAM (St. John's College, Bramcote, NG9 3DS) (125).—*Princ.*, Rev. Dr. A. Thiselton.

OAK HILL (Southgate, N14 4PS) (75).—*Princ.*, Rev. Canon D. H. Wheaton.

OXFORD (St. Stephen's House, OX4 1JX) (58).—*Princ.*, Rev. D. Thomas.

OXFORD (Wycliffe Hall) (90).—*Princ.*, Rev. G. N. Shaw.

SALISBURY AND WELLS (19 The Close, Salisbury SP1 2EE) (82).—*Princ.*, Rev. Canon R. J. A. Askew.

Church of Scotland

ABERDEEN (Christ's Coll., AB1 1YD) (143).—*Master*, Rev. H. R. Sefton, PH.D.

EDINBURGH (New Coll., Faculty of Divinity, Univ. of Edinburgh, EH1 2LU) (237).—*Princ.*, Rev. Prof. A. C. Cheyne.

GLASGOW (Trinity Coll.) (150).—*Princ.*, Rev. Prof. R. Davidson, B.D.

ST. ANDREWS (College of St. Mary, University of St. Andrews) (170).—*Princ.*, Very Rev. W. McKane.

Scottish Episcopal Church

EDINBURGH (Rosebery Crescent, EH12 5JT) (26).—*Princ.*, Rev. Canon J. M. Armson.

Presbyterian

BELFAST (Union Theological Coll., BT7 1JT) (79).—*Princ.*, Rev. Prof. E. A. Russell.

Presbyterian Church of Wales

ABERYSTWYTH (United Theological Coll.) (38).—*Princ.*, Rev. Prof. E. ap Nefydd Roberts.

Methodist

BELFAST (Edgehill Theological Coll.) (22).—*Princ.*, Rev. Dr. Dennis Cooke.

BRISTOL (Wesley Coll., Westbury-on-Trym, BS10 7QD.) (55).—*Princ.*, Rev. Dr. W. D. Stacey.

CAMBRIDGE (Wesley House) (20).—*Princ.*, Rev. Dr. I. H. Jones.

Congregational and United Reformed

ABERYSTWYTH (Memorial College) (14).—*Princ.*, Rev. Dr. D. E. Davies.

BANGOR (Bala-Bangor Independent Coll., LL57 2EH) (16).—*Princ.*, R. T. Jones, D.PHIL., D.D.

CAMBRIDGE (Westminster Coll., Madingley Road, CB3 0AA) (30).—*Princ.*, Rev. M. H. Cressey.

EDINBURGH (Scottish Congregational College, 9 Rosebery Crescent, EH12 5YN) (27).—*Princ.*, Rev. H. Smith.

MANCHESTER (Northern College, College Road, M16 8BP) (35).—*Princ.*, Rev. Dr. R. J. McKelvey.

OXFORD (Mansfield College) (160).—*Princ.*, D. A. Sykes, D.PHIL.

Roman Catholic
(Colleges for the Diocesan Clergy)

ALLEN HALL, 28 Beaufort Street, Chelsea, SW3 5AA. (55).—*Rector*, Rt. Rev. Mgr. J. Coghlan.

GLASGOW (St. Peter's Coll., 33 Briar Road, Glasgow) (37).—*Rector*, Very Rev. M. Ward, PH.L.

OSCOTT COLL., Sutton Coldfield, West Midlands B73 5AA (98).—*Rector*, Rt. Rev. Mgr. M. J. Kirkham.

OSTERLEY, Middlesex (Campion House, 112 Thornbury Road, TW7 4NN) (60).—*Superior*, Rev. D. Blackledge, S.J.

UPHOLLAND, Skelmersdale, Lancs. WN8 0PZ (now St. Joseph's College School and the Upholland Northern Institute for Adult Christian Education) (114).—*Pres.*, Rt. Rev. Bishop J. Rawsthorne.

USHAW (Durham DH7 9RH) (175).—*Pres.*, Rt. Rev. Mgr. P. Walton.

WONERSH, Guildford GU5 0QX (St. John's) (70).—*Rector*, Father P. Smith.

Baptist

BANGOR (North Wales Baptist Coll., LL57 2EH) (3).—*Princ.*, Rev. J. R. Rowlands.

BRISTOL (Baptist Coll., Woodland Road, BS8 1UN) (40).—*Pres.*, Rev. Dr. W. M. S. West.

CARDIFF (S. Wales Baptist Coll., CF2 3UR.) (16).—*Princ.*, Rev. N. Clark.

GLASGOW (The Scottish Baptist College, 12 Aytoun Road, G41 5RT) (16).—*Princ.*, Rev. G. W. Martin, PH.D.

LONDON (Spurgeon's Coll., South Norwood Hill, SE25 6DJ) (62).—*Princ.*, Rev. R. Brown, PH.D.

MANCHESTER (Northern Baptist College, Brighton Grove, Rusholme, M14 5JP) (affiliated to Manchester Univ.)—*Princ.*, to be appointed.

OXFORD (Regent's Park College, OX1 2LB) (80).—*Princ.*, Rev. B. R. White, D.Phil.

Unitarian

MANCHESTER (Unitarian College, Brighton Grove, Rusholme, M14 5JP.) (4).—*Princ.*, Rev. A. J. Long.

Interdenominational—Unitarian

OXFORD (Manchester Coll.) (70).—*Princ.*, Rev. A. J. Cross.

Jewish

JEWS' COLLEGE, Albert Road, Hendon, NW4 2SJ. (40).—*Princ.*, Rabbi Dr. J. Sacks.

LEO BAECK COLLEGE, The Manor House, 80 East End Road, N3 2SY (21).—*Princ.* Rabbi Dr. J. Magonet.

TOWN AND COUNTRY PLANNING

First Degrees are granted by Heriot-Watt University (*Town Planning*), and by the Universities of Belfast (*Environmental Planning*), Dundee (*Town and Regional Planning* in association with Duncan of Jordanstone College of Art), Glasgow (*Planning*), London (University College: *Environmental Studies and Planning*), Manchester (*Town and Country Planning*), Newcastle upon Tyne (*Town and Country Planning, Landscape Design*), Nottingham (*Architecture and Environmental Design*), Sheffield (*Urban Studies*), Stirling (*Urban Studies and Social Policy*), and Wales (Institute of Science and Technology: *Town Planning Studies*).

Courses leading to first degrees in *Town Planning* granted by the Council for National Academic Awards are provided by City of Birmingham Polytechnic, Leeds Polytechnic and Polytechnic of the South Bank; in *Town and Country Planning* by Bristol Polytechnic; in *Planning Studies* by Oxford Polytechnic; in *Environmental Planning* by Chelmer Institute of Higher Education; in *Urban Planning*

Studies by the Polytechnic of Central London; and in *Urban and Regional Planning* by Coventry (Lanchester) Polytechnic.

The ROYAL TOWN PLANNING INSTITUTE, 26 Portland Place, W.1, recognizes a number of Degree and Diploma courses in town planning.

TRANSPORT

First Degrees are granted by the Universities of Aston (*Transport Operation and Planning*), Loughborough (*Transport Management and Planning*), Wales (*Institute of Science and Technology: International Transport*) and Ulster (*Transport Technology*). The City University awards a first degree in *Air Transport Engineering*.

Courses leading to first degrees granted by the Council for National Academic Awards are provided by Huddersfield Polytechnic (*Transport and Distribution*) and Napier College of Commerce and Technology (*Transportation Engineering*).

The CHARTERED INSTITUTE OF TRANSPORT, 80 Portland Place, London W.1, conducts qualifying examinations in transport management leading to chartered professional status.

VETERINARY STUDIES

First Degrees in *Veterinary Science/Medicine and Surgery* are granted by the Universities of Bristol, Cambridge, Edinburgh, Glasgow, Liverpool and London (Royal Veterinary College).

HEADMASTERS' CONFERENCE SCHOOLS

THE HEADMASTERS' CONFERENCE.—*Chairman* (1986), C. H. D. Everett (Tonbridge); *Gen. Sec.*, T. P. Snape, Chancery House, 107 St Paul's Road, N.1.;*Deputy Sec.*, F. G. R. Fisher. The annual meetings are, as a rule, held at the end of September.

In considering applications for election to membership the Committee will have regard to the scheme or other instrument under which the school is administered (taking particularly into consideration the degree of independence enjoyed by the Headmaster and the Governing Body); the number of pupils over thirteen years of age in the school; the number of pupils in proportion to the size of the school who are in the sixth form, *i.e.* engaged on studies at the Advanced Level of the General Certificate of Education.

Name of School	F'ded.	No. of Boys	Annual Fees D = Day Boys	Headmaster (With date of Appointment)
England and Wales				
Abingdon, Oxfordshire	1256	702	£3,648 .... D£1,824	M. St. J. Parker (1975)
Aldenham, Elstree, Herts.	1597	340†	£5,085 .... D£3,075	M. Higginbottom (1983)
Alleyn's School, Dulwich, S.E.22	1619	861†	.... D£2,250	D. A. Fenner (1976)
Allhallows, Rousdon, Dorset	1515	270†	£5,040 .... D£2,376	P. S. Larkman (1983)
Ampleforth College (*R.C.*), York	1802	700	£4,950	Rev. D. L. Milroy, O.S.B. (1980)
Ardingly Coll., Haywards Heath, Sussex*	1858	475†	£5,040 .... D£3,825	J. W. Flecker (1980)
Arnold School, Blackpool	1896	725†	£3,462 .... D£1,734	R. D. W. Rhodes (1979)
Ashville College, Harrogate	1877	410†	£3,576 .... D£1,875	D. E. Norfolk (1977)
Bancroft's, Woodford Green, Essex	1727	688†	.... D£2,335	Dr. P. C. D. Southern (1985)
Barnard Castle, Co. Durham	1883	500†	£3,420 .... D£1,806	F. S. McNamara (1980)
Bedales, Petersfield, Hants.	1893	350†	£5,490 .... D£3,735	E. A. M. MacAlpine (1981)
Bedford School	1552	703	£4,386 .... D£2,514	C. I. M. Jones (1975)
Bedford Modern School	1566	912	£3,342 .... D£1,773	P. J. Squire (1977)
Berkhamsted, Herts.	1541	448	£4,245 .... D£2,289	C. J. Driver (1983)
Birkenhead, Merseyside	1860	700	.... D£1,605	J. A. Gwilliam (1963)
Bishop's Stortford College, Herts.	1868	350†	£4,785 .... D£3,405	S. G. G. Benson (1984)
Bloxham School, Banbury, Oxon.*	1860	350†	£5,100 .... D£3,420	M. W. Vallance (1982)
Blundell's, Tiverton	1604	450†	£5,160 .... D£3,150	A. J. D. Rees (1980)
Bolton	1524	870	.... D£1,626	A. W. Wright (1983)
Bootham, York.	1823	245†	£4,410 .... D£2,640	J. H. Gray (1972)
Box Hill School, Mickleham, Dorking	1959	260†	£4,775 .... D£2,775	R. McComish (1959)
Bradfield College, Berks.	1850	507†	£5,340 .... D£3,738	P. B. Smith (1985)
Bradford Grammar, Yorks.	1662	1000†	.... D£1,494	D. A. G. Smith (1974)
Brentwood School, Essex	1557	835†	£3,996 .... D£2,244	J. A. E. Evans (1981)
Brighton College, Sussex	1845	458†	£4,365 .... D£2,835	W. S. Blackshaw (1971)
Bristol Cathedral School	1542	440†	.... D£1,770	C. S. Martin (1979)
Bristol Grammar School	1532	957†	.... D£1,782	J. R. Avery (1975)
Bromsgrove, Worcs.	1553	415†	£4,443 .... D£2,910	Rev. J. N. F. Earle (1971)
Bryanston School, Blandford	1928	600†	£5,790 .... D£3,861	T. D. Wheare (1983)
Bury Grammar, Lancs.	1634	650	.... D£1,335	J. Robson (1969)
Canford, Wimborne, Dorset	1923	520†	£5,520 .... D£3,865	M. Marriott (1976)
Caterham, Surrey	1811	440†	£4,164 .... D£2,286	S. R. Smith (1974)
Charterhouse, Godalming	1611	700†	£5,670 .... D£4,680	P. J. Attenborough (1982)
Cheadle Hulme	1855	850†	£3,990 .... D£1,860	D. C. Firth (1977)
Cheltenham College	1841	560†	£5,430 .... D£3,615	R. M. Morgan (1978)
Chigwell, Essex	1629	300	£4,320 .... D£2,706	B. J. Wilson (1971)
Christ College, Brecon	1541	293	£3,585 .... D£2,688	S. W. Hockey (1982)

† Pupils.   * A Woodard Corporation School.

Name of School	F'ded.	No. of Boys	Annual Fees D = Day Boys	Headmaster (With date of Appointment)
Christ's Hospital, Horsham	1553	720	Various	J. Hansford (1985)
Churcher's College, Petersfield, Hants. .	1722	440†	£4,131 .... D£1,995	J. F. Fishley (1985)
City of London, E.C.4	1442	775	.... D£2,535	J. M. Hammond (1984)
City of London Freemen's School, Ashtead Park, Surrey	1854	350	£3,882 .... D£2,466	M. J. Kemp (1964)
Clifton College, Bristol................	1862	650	£5,550 .... D£3,783	S. M. Andrews (1975)
Colfe's School, Lee, S.E.12	1652	630†	.... D£1,974	V. S. Anthony (1976)
Colston's, Bristol.....................	1710	310†	£4,020 .... D£2,535	G. W. Searle (1975)
Coventry School (Bablake and King Henry VIII, *amal.* 1977)	—	1647	.... D£1,497	R. Cooke (*Director*) (1977)
Cranleigh, Surrey	1863	565†	£6,045 .... D£4,215	A. Hart (1984)
Culford School, Bury St. Edmunds	1881	450†	£4,068 .... D£2,442	D. Robson (1971)
Dame Allan's Sch., Newcastle on Tyne..	1705	440	.... D£1,680	F. Wilkinson (1970)
Dauntsey's, Devizes	1543	520†	£4,425 .... D£2,505	C. R. Evans (1985)
Dean Close, Cheltenham	1884	416†	£5,430 .... D£3,480	C. J. Bacon (1979)
Denstone College, Uttoxeter, Staffs.* ...	1873	392†	£4,550 .... D£3,330	T. G. Beynon (1978)
Douai (*R.C.*), Woolhampton	1903	317	£4,176 .... D£2,781	Rev. P. W. Sollom, O.S.B. (1975)
Dover College, Kent	1871	360†	£5,142 .... D£3,372	J. K. Ind (1981)
Downside (*R.C.*), Stratton-on-the-Fosse, Somerset	1607	471	£4,580 .... D£3,066	Rev. P. Jebb (1980)
Dulwich College, S.E.21	1619	1370	£5,205 .... D£2,595	D. A. Emms (*Master*) (1975)
Durham	1414	350	£4,836 .... D£3,225	M. A. Lang (1982)
Eastbourne College, Sussex............	1867	552†	£4,967 .... D£3,655	C. J. Saunders (1981)
Ellesmere College, Shropshire*	1884	372†	£4,800 .... D£3,360	F. E. Maidment (1982)
Eltham College, S.E.9	1842	514†	£4,749 .... D£1,980	C. D. Waller, PH.D. (1983)
Emanuel School, S.W.11................	1594	620	.... D£2,325	P. F. Thomson (1984)
Epsom College, Surrey	1855	630†	£5,100 .... D£3,525	J. B. Cook, PH.D. (1982)
Eton College, Windsor	1440	1250	£5,310	W. E. K. Anderson (1980)
Exeter, Devon	1633	600	£3,435 .... D£1,845	G. T. Goodall (1979)
Felsted, Dunmow, Essex	1564	470†	£5,340 .... D£4,275	E. J. H. Gould (1983)
Forest School, Snaresbrook, E.17.......	1834	680†	£3,759 .... D£2,583	J. C. Gough (*Warden*) (1983)
Framlingham College, Suffolk	1864	500†	£4,254 .... D£2,736	L. I. Rimmer (1971)
Giggleswick, Settle, Yorks............	1512	315†	£5,130 .... D£3,420	I. D. Watson (1978)
Gresham's, Holt, Norfolk	1555	422†	£4,920 .... D£3,255	H. R. Wright (1985)
Haberdashers' Aske's, Elstree, Herts....	1690	1100	.... D£2,400	B. H. McGowan (1973)
Haileybury, Herts.	1862	631†	£5,205 .... D£3,125	D. M. Summerscale (*Master*) (1976)
Hampton, Middlesex	1557	840	.... D£1,965	H. G. Alexander (1970)
Harrow, Middlesex	1571	750	£5,850 .... D£4,388	I. D. S. Beer (1981)
Hereford, Cathedral School	1384	566†	£3,348 .... D£1,863	B. B. Sutton (1975)
Highgate, N.6	1565	620	£4,842 .... D£2,643	R. C. Giles (1974)
Hulme Grammar School, Oldham	1611	685	.... D£1,431	D. R. Ward (1980)
Hurstpierpoint College, Sussex*	1849	408	£4,950 .... D£3,900	R. N. P. Griffiths (1964)
Hymers College, Hull	1889	630†	.... D£1,248	B. G. Bass (1983)
Ipswich, Suffolk	1390	600†	£3,948 .... D£2,283	Dr. J. M. Blatchly, F.S.A. (1972)
The John Lyon School, Harrow	1876	470	.... D£1,980	D. Dixon (1983)
Kelly College, Tavistock	1877	300†	£5,238 .... D£3,492	C. H. Hirst (1985)
Kent College, Canterbury	1885	579†	£4,083 .... D£2,211	R. J. Wicks (1980)
Kimbolton, Cambs.	1600	500†	£4,125 .... D£2,160	D. W. Donaldson (1973)
King Edward VI School, Southampton ..	1553	850	.... D£1,923	C. Dobson (1971)
King Edward VII School, Lytham	1908	540	.... D£1,479	D. Heap (1982)
King Edward's, Bath, Avon	1552	620†	.... D£1,614	J. P. Wroughton (1982)
King Edward's, Birmingham	1552	700	.... D£1,854	M. J. W. Rogers (*Master*) (1982)
King Edward's, Witley, Surrey	1553	512†	£4,140 .... D£2,625	R. W. Wilkinson (1985)
King's College, Taunton*	1880	471†	£4,965 .... D£3,600	J. M. Batten (1969)
King's College Sch., Wimbledon, S.W.19	1829	630	.... D£2,460	R. M. Reeve (1980)
King's School, Bruton	1519	290†	£5,010 .... D£3,510	A. H. Beadles (1985)
King's School, Canterbury	600	695†	£5,535 .... D£3,765	—
King's School, Chester	1541	440	.... D£1,890	A. R. D. Wickson (1981)
King's School, Ely	970	430†	£4,836 .... D£3,084	H. Ward (1970)
King's School, Macclesfield	1502	900	.... D£1,905	A. H. Cooper (1966)
King's School, Rochester	604	445†	£4,041 .... D£2,325	R. A. Ford (1975)
King's School, Worcester	1541	690†	£3,825 .... D£2,175	Dr. J. M. Moore (1983)
Kingston Grammar, Surrey	1561	570†	.... D£2,205	S. J. Miller (1977)
Kingswood School, Bath	1748	480†	£4,845 .... D£3,045	L. J. Campbell (1970)
Lancing College, Sussex*.............	1848	540	£5,370 .... D£3,645	J. S. Woodhouse (1981)
Latymer Upper, Hammersmith, W.6	1624	960	.... D£2,295	M. L. R. Isaac (1971)
Leeds Gr. School, Leeds 6.............	1552	1082	.... D£1,660	A. C. F. Verity (1976)
Leighton Park Sch., Reading	1890	330†	£4,689 .... D£3,285	J. Hunter (1981)
The Leys School, Cambridge...........	1875	400†	£5,025 .... D£3,705	B. T. Bellis (1975)

† Pupils.   * A Woodard Corporation School.

Name of School	F'ded	No. of Boys	Annual Fees D = Day Boys	Headmaster (With date of Appointment)
Liverpool College, Liverpool 18	1840	368†	£3,414 .... D£1,821	R. V. Haygarth (1979)
Llandovery College	1848	230†	£3,870 .... D£2,400	R. Brinley Jones, ph.d. (1976)
Lord Wandsworth Coll., Long Sutton, Hants.	1912	400	£4,344 .... D£3,396	G. A. G. Dodd (1982)
Loughborough Grammar	1495	820	£3,993 .... D£1,839	D. N. Ireland (1984)
Magdalen College School, Oxford	1480	497	£3,693 .... D£1,794	W. B. Cook (*Master*) (1972)
Malvern College, Worcester	1865	605	£5,100 .... D£3,675	R. de C. Chapman (1983)
Manchester Grammar School	1515	1440	.... D£1,900	J. G. Parker (*High Master*) (1985)
Marlborough College, Wilts.	1843	900†	£5,250	R. W. Ellis, c.b.e. (*Master*) (1972)
Merchant Taylors', Crosby	1620	630	.... D£1,800	D. R. Johnston-Jones (1979)
Merchant Taylors', Northwood	1561	700	£4,425 .... D£2,925	D. J. Skipper (1982)
Mill Hill, N.W.7	1807	535†	£5,070 .... D£3,360	A. C. Graham (1979)
Monkton Combe, Bath	1868	340†	£4,968 .... D£3,591	R. A. C. Meredith (1978)
Monmouth	1614	530	£3,867 .... D£2,094	R. D. Lane (1982)
Mount St. Mary's College, Spinkhill, Derbyshire (*R.C.*)	1842	292†	£4,047 .... D£2,679	Rev. J. F. Grumitt, s.j. (1976)
Newcastle-under-Lyme School	1874	1200†	.... D£1,575	J. W. Donaldson (*Principal*) (1974)
Norwich School	1250	600	£4,278 .... D£1,878	C. D. Brown (1984)
Nottingham High School	1513	800	.... D£1,680	D. T. Witcombe, ph.d. (1970)
Oakham, Rutland, Leics.	1584	720†	£4,872 .... D£2,613	G. Smallbone (1985)
The Oratory (*R.C.*), Woodcote, Reading.	1859	360	£4,335 .... D£3,024	A. Snow (1972)
Oundle, Peterborough, Northants.	1556	740	£5,535	D. B. McMurray (1984)
Pangbourne College, Berks.	1917	330	£4,920 .... D£3,630	P. D. C. Points (1969)
Perse Sch., Cambridge	1615	465	£3,879 .... D£1,839	A. E. Melville (1969)
Plymouth College	1877	640†	£3,765 .... D£1,935	A. M. Joyce (1983)
Pocklington School, York.	1514	634†	£3,462 .... D£1,680	A. D. Pickering (1981)
Portsmouth Gr. Sch.	1732	700†	.... D£1,665	A. C. V. Evans (1983)
Prior Park Coll. (*R.C.*), Bath	1830	275†	£4,132 .... D£2,340	P. F. J. Tobin (1981)
Queen Elizabeth's Gr., Blackburn	1567	1020†	.... D£1,590	P. F. Johnston (1978)
Queen Elizabeth Gr. Sch., Wakefield	1591	700	£3,117 .... D£1,872	R. P. Mardling (1985)
Queen Elizabeth's Hospital, Bristol	1590	460	£3,249 .... D£1,755	Dr. R. Gliddon (1985)
Queen's College, Taunton, Som.	1843	430†	£5,145 .... D£2,850	A. P. Hodgson (1979)
Radley Coll., Abingdon	1847	590	£5,280	D. R. W. Silk (*Warden*) (1968)
Ratcliffe Coll. (*R.C.*), Leicester	1844	310†	£4,200 .... D£2,750	Rev. L. G. Hurdidge (1984)
Reed's, Cobham, Surrey	1813	345	£4,275 .... D£3,135	D. E. Prince (1983)
Reigate Grammar	1675	820†	.... D£2,025	J. G. Hamlin (1982)
Rendcomb Coll., Cirencester, Glos.	1920	265†	£4,515	R. M. A. Medill (1971)
Repton School, Derby	1557	545†	£5,250 .... D£3,900	D. J. Jewell (1979)
Rossall, Fleetwood, Lancs.	1844	480†	£5,397 .... D£3,777	J. Sharp, d.Phil. (1972)
Royal Grammar School, Guildford	1552	720	.... D£2,250	J. Daniel (1977)
Royal Grammar Sch., Newcastle-upon-Tyne	1545	950	.... D£1,650	A. S. Cox (1972)
Royal Grammar School, Worcester	1291	750	£3,735 .... D£1,935	T. E. Savage (1978)
Rugby, Warwickshire	1567	774†	£5,535 .... D£2,910	O. R. S. Bull (1985)
Rydal, Colwyn Bay, Clwyd	1885	320†	£4,185 .... D£2,985	P. F. Watkinson (1968)
Ryde School, Isle of Wight	1921	295†	£3,480 .... D£1,740	P. D. V. Wilkes (1984)
St. Albans, Herts.	1570	670	.... D£2,010	S. C. Wilkinson (1984)
St. Anselm's Coll., Birkenhead.	1933	650	.... D£1,404	Rev. Br. M. G. Miller (1981)
St. Bees, Cumbria	1583	380†	£4,890 .... D£3,300	M. T. Thyne (1980)
St. Benedict's, Ealing, W.5 (*R.C.*).	1902	600†	.... D£1,932	Dom. A. Gee (1978)
St. Dunstan's, Catford, S.E.6.	1888	662	.... D£2,100	B. D. Dance (1973)
St. Edmund's, Canterbury.	1749	290†	£4,530 .... D£3,165	J. V. Tyson (1978)
St. Edmund's Coll. (*R.C.*), Ware, Herts.	1568	360†	£4,410 .... D£2,646	D. J. J. McEwen (1984)
St. Edward' Coll., Liverpool	1853	665	.... D£1,560	B. D. Sassi (1984)
St. Edward's, Oxford	1863	559†	£5,280 .... D£3,960	J. C. Phillips (*Warden*) (1978)
St. George's Coll., Weybridge (*R.C.*)	1869	650†	£4,158 .... D£2,805	Rev. P. C. Hunting (1977)
St. John's, Leatherhead	1851	440	£4,500 .... D£3,450	D. E. Brown (1985)
St. Lawrence Coll., Ramsgate	1879	330†	£5,055 .... D£3,360	J. H. Binfield (1983)
St. Mary's College, Gt. Crosby	1919	620†	.... D£1,536	Rev. Br. N. D. O'Halloran (1972)
St. Paul's, Lonsdale Rd., Barnes, S.W.13	1509	750	£4,686 .... D£2,925	Rev. Canon P. Pilkington (*High Master*) (1985)
St. Peter's, York	627	440†	£4,452 .... D£2,544	R. N. Pittman (1985)
Sedbergh, Cumbria	1525	470	£5,145 .... D£3,600	R. G. Baxter (1982)
Sevenoaks School, Kent.	1418	900†	£5,049 .... D£3,042	R. P. Barker (1981)
Sherborne, Dorset	1550	660	£5,115 .... D£3,840	R. D. Macnaghten (1974)
Shrewsbury School	1552	650	£5,460 .... D£3,900	S. J. B. Langdale (1981)
Silcoates, Wakefield	1820	499†	£3,654 .... D£2,115	J. C. Baggaley (1978)

† Pupils.

Name of School	F'ded.	No. of Boys	Annual Fees D = Day Boys		Headmaster (With date of Appointment)
Solihull, Warwicks	1560	800†	£3,432	D£1,935	A. Lee (1983)
Stamford, Lincs.	1532	800	£3,468	D£1,740	G. J. Timm (1978)
Stockport Grammar Sch., Cheshire	1487	974†		D£1,782	D. R. J. Bird (1985)
Stonyhurst Coll. (*R.C.*), nr. Whalley, Lancs.	1794	480	£4,860		Dr. R. G. G. Mercer (1985)
Stowe, Bucks.	1923	628	£5,760	D£3,975	C. G. Turner (1979)
Sutton Valence, Kent	1576	375†	£4,875	D£3,120	M. R. Haywood (1980)
Taunton, Somerset	1847	650†	£4,229	D£3,384	N. S. Roberts (1970)
Tettenhall College, Staffs.	1863	400†	£3,990	D£2,457	W. J. Dale (1968)
Tonbridge, Kent	1553	650	£5,370	D£3,720	C. H. D. Everett (1975)
Trent Coll., Long Eaton, Derbyshire	1868	575†	£4,770	D£2,652	A. J. Maltby (1968)
Trinity School, Croydon	1596	640		D£2,088	R. J. Wilson (1972)
Truro, Cornwall	1879	856†	£2,994	D£1,764	D. W. Burrell (1959)
University Coll. School, Frognal, N.W.3	1830	520		D£2,475	G. D. Slaughter (1983)
Uppingham, Leics.	1584	626†	£5,250		N. R. Bomford (1982)
Warwick	914	812	£3,714	D£1,728	J. A. Strover (1977)
Wellingborough, Northants	1595	395†	£4,131	D£2,526	G. Garrett (1973)
Wellington Coll., Crowthorne, Berks.	1856	800†	£4,950	D£3,570	D. H. Newsome, Ph.D. (1980)
Wellington Sch., Somerset	1841	750†	£3,660	D£1,950	J. Kendall-Carpenter (1973)
Wells Cathedral School, Somerset	1180	497†	£3,726	D£2,094	A. K. Quilter (1964)
West Buckland School, Barnstaple, Devon	1858	377†	£3,870	D£2,085	M. Downward (1979)
Westminster, Dean's Yard, S.W.1	1560	600†	£5,025	D£3,075	J. M. Rae, Ph.D. (1970)
Whitgift, Croydon	1596	850		D£2,220	D. A. Raeburn (1970)
William Hulme's G. S.	1887	774		D£1,899	P. A. Filleul (1974)
Winchester College	1382	630	£5,760	D£4,320	J. P. Sabben-Clare (1985)
Wolverhampton Grammar School	1512	600†		D£2,025	P. H. Hutton (1978)
Woodbridge School, Suffolk	1662	500†	£3,945	D£2,235	D. Younger (1985)
Woodhouse Grove School, Bradford	1812	520†	£3,675	D£2,130	D. A. Miller (1972)
Worcester Coll. for the Blind	1866	85	£9,000	D£6,000	Rev. B. R. Manthorp (1980)
Worksop Coll., Notts.*	1895	360†	£4,800	D£3,300	R. J. Roberts (1975)
Worth School, Crawley, Sussex (*R.C.*)	1959	330	£4,725		Rev. R. S. Ortiger (1983)
Wrekin Coll., Wellington, Shropshire	1880	315†	£5,085	D£3,480	J. H. Arkell (1983)
Wycliffe Coll., Stonehouse, Glos.	1882	350†	£5,106	D£3,285	R. C. Poulton (1980)

Scotland

Name of School	F'ded.	No. of Boys	Annual Fees D = Day Boys		Headmaster (With date of Appointment)
Daniel Stewart's and Melville Coll., Edinburgh (*amalgamated*, 1973)	1832	775	£3,675	D£1,860	R. M. Morgan (1977)
Dollar Academy, Perthshire	1818	897†	£3,594	D£1,536	L. Harrison (*Rector*) (1984)
Dundee High School, Tayside	1239	1135†		D£1,596	R. Nimmo (*Rector*) (1977)
The Edinburgh Academy	1824	640†	£4,574	D£2,280	L. E. Ellis (*Rector*) (1977)
Fettes College, Edinburgh	1870	415†	£4,860	D£3,270	A. J. C. Cochrane (1979)
George Heriot's, Edinburgh	1659	1350†		D£1,515	K. P. Pearson (1983)
George Watson's Coll., Edinburgh	1741	1049†	£3,675	D£1,860	F. E. Gerstenberg (1985)
Glasgow Academy	1845	545		D£1,665	C. W. Turner (*Rector*) (1983)
Glenalmond College, Perthshire	1841	400	£5,100		J. N. W. Musson (*Warden*) (1972)
Gordonstoun, Elgin, Morayshire	1934	460†	£5,478	D£3,510	M. B. Mavor (1979)
Hutcheson's Gr. School, Glasgow	1641	1100†		D£1,200	P.Brian (*Rector*) (1984)
Kelvinside Academy, Glasgow	1878	500		D£1,790	J. H. Duff (*Rector*) (1980)
Loretto Sch., Musselburgh, Midlothian	1827	300†	£4,500	D£2,700	Rev. N. W. Drummond (1984)
Merchiston Castle, Edinburgh	1833	335	£4,800	D£3,120	D. M. Spawforth (1981)
Morrison's Academy, Perthshire	1860	800†	£3,600	D£1,380	H. A. Ashmall (*Rector*) (1979)
Robert Gordon's Coll., Aberdeen	1729	850	£1,671	D£1,425	G. A. Allan (1978)
Strathallan, Forgandenny, Perthshire	1913	450†	£4,860		C. D. Pighills (1975)

Northern Ireland

Name of School	F'ded.	No. of Boys	Annual Fees D = Day Boys		Headmaster (With date of Appointment)
Bangor Gr. School, Co. Down	1856	890		D£615	T. W. Patton (1979)
Belfast Methodist College	1868	1602†	£2,611	D£913	J. Kincade, Ph.D. (1974)
Belfast Royal Academy	1785	1230†		D£800	W. M. Sillery (1980)
Campbell Coll., Belfast	1894	470	£3,684	D£1,599	B. W. J. G. Wilson (1977)
Coleraine Academical Institution	1856	1110	£2,270	D£780	R. S. Forsythe (1984)
Portora Royal School, Enniskillen	1618	425†	£3,448	D£955	R. L. Bennett (1983)
Royal Belfast Academical Instn.	1810	950		D£1,024	T. J. Garrett (1978)

Channel Islands, Isle of Man, etc.

Name of School	F'ded.	No. of Boys	Annual Fees D = Day Boys		Headmaster (With date of Appointment)
Elizabeth Coll., Guernsey	1563	534	£2,560	D£840	R. A. Wheadon (1972)
Victoria Coll., Jersey	1852	590†	£3,801	D£1,267	M. H. Devenport (1967)
King William's Coll., Isle of Man	1668	300†	£4,635	D£3,075	P. K. Bregazzi, Ph.D. (1979)

† Pupils.   * A Woodard Corporation School.

Name of School	F'ded.	No. of Boys	Annual Fees D = Day Boys	Headmaster (*With date of Appointment*)
		OVERSEAS		
Africa				
Diocesan Coll., Rondebosch, S. Africa ...	1849	605	R6,670 ... DR3,600	J. S. B. Peake (1983)
Falcon College, Esigodini, Zimbabwe ...	1954	432	$Z3,300	P. N. Todd (1985)
Peterhouse, Maranderer, Zimbabwe	1955	480	$Z3,753 .... D$Z495	Rev. Dr. A. J. Megahey (*Rector*) (1984)
St George's Coll., Harare, Zimbabwe	1896	850	$Z2,500 .. D$Z1,000	J. C. Berry (*Rector*) (1984)
Australia				
A.C.T.:				
Canberra G.S.	1929	865	$6,420 .... D$2,805	P. J. McKeown (1959)
N.S.W.:				
Armidale Sch., Armidale	1894	524	$6,870 .... D$3,144	G. C. S. Andrews (1982)
Barker Coll., Hornsby	1890	1130†	$6,000 .... D$3,000	T. J. McCaskill (1963)
Church of England G.S. N. Sydney	1889	950	$10,890 .... D$3,600	R. A. I. Grant (1983)
Cranbrook Sch., Sydney	1918	780	$7,665 .... D$3,840	Dr. B. N. Carter (1985)
The King's School, Parramatta	1831	910	$7,410 .... D$4,110	J. A. Wickham (1984)
Knox G.S., Wahroonga	1924	1250	$7,350 .... D$3,450	Dr. I. Paterson (1969)
Newington Coll., Stanmore	1863	1050	$8,010 .... D$3,960	A. J. Rae (1972)
St. Patrick's College, Goulburn	1874	580	$2,745 ..... D$870	Br. F. D. Marzorini (*President*) (1975)
The Scots College, Sydney	1893	1005	$7,635 .... D$3,915	G. A. W. Renney (1980)
Sydney Grammar School	1857	1130	.... D$4,215	A. M. Mackerras (1969)
Queensland:				
Anglican Church G.S. Brisbane	1912	1256	$5,180 .... D$2,320	W. Hayward (1974)
Southport School	1901	782	$5,100 .... D$2,400	J. H. Day (1972)
South Australia:				
Prince Alfred Coll., Adelaide	1869	770	$7,800 .... D$3,540	G. B. Bean (1970)
St. Peter's Coll., Adelaide	1847	761	$7,263 .... D$3,180	Dr. A. J. Shinkfield (1978)
Scotch Coll., Adelaide.................	1919	......		W. M. Miles (1975)
Tasmania:				
Hutchins School, Hobart	1846	600	$4,800 .... D$2,400	Dr. D. B. Clarke (1971)
Victoria:				
Ballarat and Clarendon Coll., Ballarat ..	1864	800†	$6,780 .... D$3,030	R. M. Horner (1964)
Brighton Grammar School, Brighton ...	1882	1046	.... D$3,816	R. L. Rofe (1967)
Camberwell G. S., Balwyn	1886	930	.... D$3,380	A. Dyer (1966)
Carey Baptist School, Kew	1923	995†	.... D$4,125	G. L. Cramer (1964)
Caulfield Grammar Sch., East Kilda ...	1881	1430	$7,110 .... D$3,660	Rev. A. S. Holmes (1977)
Church of England G.S., Melbourne ...	1856	786	$7,560 .... D$3,960	N. A. H. Creese (1970)
Eltham College	1974	660†	.... D$3,000	Dr. B. J. Webber (1984)
Geelong Coll., Geelong, Corio	1861	572†	$8,490 .... D$3,990	S. P. Gebhardt (1976)
Haileybury Coll., Keysborough	1892	1750	.... D$3,900	A. M. H. Aikman (1974)
Peninsular Church of England, Mt. Eliza	1961	779	$6,624 .... D$3,924	H. A. Macdonald (1971)
Scotch Coll., Hawthorn, Melbourne ...	1851	1340	$8,000 .... D$4,000	Dr. F. G. Donaldson (1983)
Wesley Coll., Melbourne	1866	1450†	.... D$3,660	D. H. Prest (1972)
West Australia:				
Christ Church Grammar School, Claremont	1910	779	$6,675 .... D$3,135	A. J. de V. Hill (1982)
Guildford Grammar Sch.	1896	763	$6,420 .... D$3,060	J. M. Moody (1979)
Hale School, Wembley Downs	1858	650	$6,000 .... D$3,000	Dr. K. G. Tregonning, M.B.E. (1967)
Scotch Coll., Swanbourne	1897	745	$6,510 .... D$3,105	W. R. Dickinson (1972)
Canada				
Appleby Coll., Ontario	1911	280	$11,600 . D$7,700	A. S. Troubetzkoy (1981)
Ashbury Coll., Ottawa	1891	300†	$11,500 ... D$6,300	A. M. Macoun (1981)
Brentwood Coll., School, Vancouver ...	1961	360†	$11,220 ... D$5,705	W. T. Ross (1985)
Hillfield Strathallan Coll.,Ont.	1901	914†	.... D$5,200	M. B. Wansbrough (1969)
Pickering Coll., Ont.	1842	150	$12,000 . D$6,000	S. H. Clark (1978)
St. Andrew's Coll., Ont.	1899	450	$12,130 ... D$6,600	R. P. Bedard (1981)
Shawnigan Lake School, B.C.	1916	......		D. J. Farrant (1978)
Toronto French School, Ont.	1962	330†	$11,250 ... D$5,850	W. H. Giles (1962)
Trinity Coll. Sch., Port Hope, Ont.	1865	375	$11,750 ... D$6,700	R. C. N. Wright (1983)
Upper Canada Coll., Toronto	1829	620	$11,550 ... D$6,300	R. H. Sadleir (1975)

† Pupils.

Name of School	F'ded.	No. of Boys	Annual Fees D=Day Boys	Headmaster (With date of Appointment)
Europe				
Aiglon Coll., Switzerland	1949	260†	SFr.27,300 .... DSFr.18,780	P. Parsons (1976)
British School of Brussels	1970	1050†	.... D£3,935	J. Jackson, PH.D. (1983)
British School in the Netherlands	.....	500†	.... Dfl12,420	B. D. Davidson (1979)
Campion School, Athens	1970	915†	Drachmae1,282,538 D Drachmae380,000	A. F. Eggleston, O.B.E. (1982)
The English School, Cyprus	1900	780†	.... D£C1,021	D. H. Humphreys, O.B.E. (1968)
St. Columba's Coll., Dublin	1843	300†	IR£4,080DIR£2,130	D. S. Gibbs, O.B.E. (Warden) (1974)
St. George's English School, Rome	1958	810†	......DL9,000,000	H. J. Deelman (1980)
Far East				
Island School, Hong Kong	1967	1158†	.... D$17,000	C. H. R. Niven (1983)
India				
Lawrence School, Lovedale,	1858	470†	Rs.8,850	L. A. Vyas (1972)
Lawrence School, Sanawar	1847	550†	Rs.7,500	S. R. Das (1974)
St. Paul's School, Darjeeling	1823	......		H. Dang (Rector) (1977)
Yadavindra Public School, Patiala	1947	470†	Rs.6,600 . DRs.2,400	H. N. Kashyap (1969)
New Zealand				
Christchurch Boys' High Sch., Canterbury	1881	1096	$2,250 ..... D$30	I. D. Leggat (1976)
Christ's Coll., Christchurch, Canterbury	1850	627	$4,800 .... D$2,400	Dr. M. J. Rosser (1985)
The Collegiate School, Wanganui	1854	535	$6,330 .... D$3,195	I. D. McKinnon (1980)
King's Coll., Auckland	1896	700†	$5,655 .... D$3,183	I. P. Campbell (1971)
Rathkeale Coll., Masterton	1963	487†	$5,994 .... D$2,490	J. S. Taylor (1979)
St. Andrew's Coll., Christchurch	1916	650	$5,385 .... D$2,685	A. J. Rentoul, PH.D. (1982)
Timaru Boys' High Sch., Canterbury	1880	730	$2,310 ..... D$60	I. W. Sawers (1982)
Waitaki Boys' High School	1883	700	$3,000 ...... D$30	G. Tait (1985)
South America				
Markham Coll., Lima, Peru	1946	600	........D$U.S.1,100	R. C. Pinchbeck, O.B.E. (1966)
St. George's Coll., Argentina	1898	230†	$U.S.5,000 .... D$U.S.3,750	C. T. Gill Leech (1980)
West Indies				
Harrison Coll., Barbados	1729	805†	Nil.......... DNil	C. W. Thorpe (1983)
Munro Coll., Jamaica	1856	694	$J300 ..... D$J218	V. Forbes (1983)

NOTE.—The Headmasters of the following schools are additional members, by invitation, of the H.M.C.: Cavendish School, Devizes School, Henbury School, Highlands School, High Wycombe Royal G.S., Richmond School, Sexey's School, Strand College, Thirsk School, Tiffin School, Watford G.S. and Westcliff H.S.

SOCIETY OF HEADMASTERS OF INDEPENDENT SCHOOLS

Secretary, A. E. R. Dodds, Green Garth, Horsell Rise, Woking, Surrey.

Name of School	F'ded.	No. of Boys	Annual Fees D=Day Boys	Headmaster (With date of Appointment)
Abbotsholme, Uttoxeter, Staffs.	1889	250†	£5,070 .... D£3,380	D. J. Farrant (1984)
Ackworth, Pontefract	1779	417†	£4,005 .... D£2,322	G. R. McKee (1971)
Austin Friars, Carlisle (R.C.)	1951	290	£3,300 .... D£1,800	Rev. T. Lyons, O.S.A. (1981)
Bearwood Coll., Wokingham, Berks.	1827	346	£4,800 .... D£2,700	The Hon. Martin Penney (1980)
Bedstone College, Shropshire	1948	204†	£4,185 .... D£2,460	G. S. Wilson (1971)
Belmont Abbey, Hereford (R.C.)	1926	274	£3,705 .... D£2,025	Rev. S. McGurk (1983)
Bembridge, Isle of Wight	1919	190†	£3,210 .... D£2,040	R. L. Whitby, L.V.O. (1974)
Bentham Grammar, N. Yorks	1726	310†	£3,450 .... D£1,725	R. S. Repper (1983)
Bethany School, Goudhurst, Kent	1866	290	£4,056 .... D£2,700	C. A. H. Lanzer (1970)
Carmel Coll., Wallingford, Oxon.	1948	268†	£6,060 .... D£3,366	P. D. Skelker (1984)
Chetham's School of Music, Manchester	1653	270†	£7,356 .... D£5,697	J. Vallins, O.B.E. (1974)
Claysmore, Iwerne Minster, Blandford	1896	350†	£4,630 .... D£3,310	M. P. Hawkins (1979)
Cokethorpe School, Nr. Witney, Oxon.	1957	140†	£4,650 .... D£3,210	D. F. Goldsmith (1979)
Cotton College, Oakamoor, Staffs. (R.C.)	1763	180†	£3,330 .... D£1,920	R. J. Hutchings (1983)
Cranbrook, Kent	1518	740†	£2,418 .... DNil	M. C. Pavey (1981)
Fort Augustus School, Inverness-shire (R.C.)	1878	92	£3,804 .... D£2,283	Rev. M. Benedict Seed, O.S.B. (1985)

† Pupils.

Name of School	F'ded.	No. of Boys	Annual Fees D = Day Boys	Headmaster (With date of Appointment)
Frensham Heights, Farnham, Surrey ...	1925	265†	£5,415 .... D£3,255	A. L. Pattinson (1973)
Fulneck Boys' School, W. Yorkshire....	1753	360†	£3,075 .... D£1,626	I. D. Cleland (1980)
Grenville College, Bideford, Devon*....	1954	350	£4,299 .... D£2,190	D. C. Powell-Price, T.D., PH.D. (1975)
Keil School, Dumbarton	1915	180†	£3,879 .... D£2,250	C. H. Tongue (1984)
Kingham Hill School, Oxon.	1886	250	£3,600 .... D£2,400	D. Shepherd (1981)
King's School, Gloucester	1541	360†	£3,879 .... D£2,304	Rev. A. C. Charters (1983)
Kirkham Grammar, nr. Preston, Lancs..	1549	485†	£2,985 .... D£1,545	M. J. Summerlee (1972)
Lord Mayor Treloar College, Holybourne, Hants.	1908	272†	£12,198 .... D£9,150	A. Macpherson (1974)
Milton Abbey Sch., nr. Blandford, Dorset	1954	285	£4,980	S. R. D. Hall (1974)
Oswestry, Shropshire	1407	330†	£3,672 .... D£2,226	I. G. Templeton (1985)
Pierrepont School, Farnham, Surrey ...	1947	260†	£4,575 .... D£2,766	J. Payne (1983)
Purcell School (Music), Harrow, Middx.	1962	160†	£4,890 .... D£2,490	K. J. Bain (1983)
Rannoch School, Perthshire	1959	235†	£4,230 .... D£2,520	M. Barratt (1982)
Reading Blue Coat School, Berks.	1646	480	£3,690 .... D£2,190	A. C. E. Sanders (1974)
Rishworth School, Ripponden, W. Yorks.	1724	400†	£3,705 .... D£2,010	Rev. J. Williams (1968)
Royal Hospital School, Holbrook, Suffolk	1712	700	£2,580	M. Kirk (1983)
Royal Russell School, Croydon, Surrey .	1853	420†	£3,825 .... D£2,391	R. D. Balaam (1981)
Royal Wolverhampton Sch., Staffs.	1850	350†	£3,648 .... D£2,136	R. Hawkins (1977)
Ruthin School, Clwyd	1574	160	£4,326 .... D£2,817	F. R. Ullman (1986)
St. David's Coll., Llandudno	1965	235	£4,200 .... D£2,700	J. A. Mayor (1965)
Scarborough College, Yorks............	1898	460†	£4,050 .... D£2,160	D. S. Hempsall (1985)
Seaford College, Petworth, Sussex	1884	430	£3,900	Rev. C. E. Johnson (1944)
Shebbear College, Beaworthy, Devon ...	1841	300	£3,729 .... D£1,893	R. J. Buley (1983)
Shiplake College, Henley, Oxon.	1959	320	£4,305 .... D£2,700	P. H. Lapping (1979)
Sidcot School, Winscombe, Somerset ...	1808	270†	£4,365 .... D£2,295	T. C. Leimdorfer (1977)
Stanbridge Earls School, Romsey	1952	170†	£5,370 .... D£3,580	H. Moxon (1984)

† Pupils.   * A Woodard Corporation School.

NOTE.—The Headmasters of Bedales School, City of London Freemen's School, Colston's School, Churcher's College, Lord Wandsworth College, Pangbourne College, Rendcomb College, Ryde School, St. Edmund's College, St. George's College, Weybridge, Silcoates School, Tettenhall College, Wells Cathedral School, West Buckland School and Woodbridge School are also Members of the Society. Details of these schools are included in the list of Headmasters' Conference Schools.

GIRLS' SCHOOLS ASSOCIATION MEMBERS

THE GIRLS' SCHOOLS ASSOCIATION, 29 Gordon Square, W.C.1.—*Sec.*, Miss S. M. Chapman.

Name of School	F'ded.	No. of Girls	Annual Fees D = Day Girls	Headmistress (a) Headmaster (With date of Appointment)
The Abbey School, Reading...........	1887	750	.... D£1,614	S. M. Hardcastle (1960)
Abbot's Hill, Hemel Hempstead	1912	148	£4,200 .... D£2,895	Mrs. J. Kingsley (1979)
Adcote School, Shrewsbury	1907	135	£3,930 .... D£2,400	Mrs. S. B. Cecchet (1979)
The Alice Ottley School, Worcester ...	1883	520	£3,765 .... D£1,893	C. Sibbit (1986)
All Hallows School, Ditchingham, Bungay, Suffolk	1864	170	£3,498 .... D£2,151	A. C. Harris (1984)
Ancaster House, Bexhill-on-Sea	1906	150	£3,960 .... D£2,415	Mrs. S. V. Chapman (1985)
The Atherley School, Southampton (CSC)	1926	330	.... D£1,635	A. Ward (1973)
Badminton School, Bristol	1858	275	£4,485 .... D£3,345	(a) C. J. T. Gould (1981)
*Bath High School	1875	526	.... D£1,515	M. A. Winfield (1985)
Battle Abbey School, E. Sussex	1912	120	£3,525 .... D£2,025	(a) D. J. A. Teall (1982)
Bedford High School.................	1882	800	£3,726 .... D£1,854	Mrs. M. E. A. Kaye (1976)
Bedgebury School, Goudhurst, Kent ...	1860	380	£4,540 .... D£2,694	(a) J. H. Delany (1978)
*Belvedere School, Liverpool	1880	513	.... D£1,515	S. Downs (1972)
Benenden School, Cranbrook, Kent	1923	400	£5,070	Mrs. du Charme (1985)
Beresford House, Eastbourne	1902	150	£3,945 .... D£2,064	A. M. Barnett (1965)
Berkhamsted School for Girls.........	1888	432	£3,603 .... D£1,812	V. E. M. Shepherd (1980)
*Birkenhead High	1901	933	.... D£1,515	F. Kellett (1971)
*Blackheath High	1880	518	.... D£1,605	Mrs. H. E. W. Williams (1978)
Bolton School, Lancs	1877	812	.... D£1,626	Mrs. M. A. Spurr (1979)
Bradford Grammar School for Girls ...	1875	611	.... D£1,548	R. M. Gleave (1976)
*Brighton and Hove High, Brighton ...	1876	735	£3,225 .... D£1,515	Mrs. J. B. E. Wells (1978)
*Bromley High School	1883	622	.... D£1,605	J. A. Plowman (1984)
Bruton School for Girls, Somerset	1900	574	£3,240 .... D£1,800	J. M. Thomson (1980)

Name of School	F'ded.	No. of Girls	Annual Fees D = Day Girls		Headmistress (a) Headmaster (With date of Appointment)
Burgess Hill, Sussex	1906	285	£3,924	D£2,121	Mrs. B. H. Webb (1979)
Bury Grammar School	1884	740	....	D£1,335	J. E. Batty (1979)
Casterton School, Kirkby Lonsdale, Cumbria	1823	381	£3,792	D£2,289	(a) G. Vinestock (1984)
*Central Newcastle High School	1895	776	....	D£1,515	Mrs. A. M. Chapman (1985)
Channing School, Highgate, N.6	1885	280	....	D£2,160	Mrs. A. T. D. Macaire (1978)
Charters Towers, Bexhill-on-Sea	1929	180	£3,783	D£1,935	D. L. Howe (1972)
Cheltenham Ladies' College	1853	850	£4,488	D£2,961	J. Sadler (1979) (Principal)
City of London, Barbican, E.C.2......	1894	557	....	D£1,980	L. E. Mackie (1972)
Clarendon School, Bedford	1898	230	£4,200	D£2,280	J. L. Howell (1978)
Clifton High School for Girls, Bristol ..	1877	492	£3,285	D£1,575	Mrs. J. D. Walters (1985)
Cobham Hall, Gravesend, Kent	1962	297	£4,785	D£3,195	S. Cameron (1985)
Colston's Girls' School, Bristol......	1891	640	....	D£1,497	A. C. Parkin (1981)
Combe Bank, Sevenoaks, Kent.......	1868	242	....	D£1,863	Mrs. A. J. K. Austin (1982)
Commonweal Lodge, Purley, Surrey ..	1916	138	....	D£1,863	J. M. Brown (1982)
The Convent of the Assumption, Richmond, Yorks.	1852	165	£3,900	D£2,085	Sr. M. Connor (1978)
The Convent of the Sacred Heart, Woldingham, Surrey	1842	400	£3,855	D£2,370	Sr. M. Hinde
Cranborne Chase, Tisbury, Wilts.	1946	135	£4,650	D£1,983	Mrs. M. Simmons (1983)
Cranford House, Wallingford	1931	106	....	D£1,770	T. A. Spencer (1980)
Croft House, Shillingstone, Dorset	1941	185	£4,185	D£2,790	Mrs. S. Rawlinson (1985)
Croham Hurst, S. Croydon, Surrey	1899	360	....	D£1,680	D. J. Seward (1970)
*Croydon High School	1874	1051	....	D£1,605	A. M. Mark (1980)
Dame Alice Harpur School, Bedford ..	1882	790	....	D£1,548	S. M. Morse (1970)
Dame Allan's Girls', Newcastle-on-Tyne	1705	440	....	D£1,680	J. Graham (1970)
Derby High School	1892	240	....	D£2,073	(a) G. H. Goddard (1983)
Dodderhill School, Droitwich	1973	125	....	D£1,890	(a) I. U. Andersson (1984)
Downe House, Cold Ash, Newbury	1907	410	£4,695	D£3,045	S. E. Farr (1978)
Durham High School	1884	386	....	D£1,521	(a) I. J. Walkley (1979)
Edgbaston Church of England Coll. ...	1886	316	....	D£1,494	V. R. Belton (1967)
Edgbaston High School	1876	545	....	D£1,494	V. R. Belton (1967)
Edgehill Coll., Bideford, Devon	1884	352	£3,795	D£1,920	D. W. Ballantyne (1980)
Ellerslie, Great Malvern	1922	260	£4,620	D£3,075	P. M. Binyon (1974)
Elmslie School, Blackpool	1918	450	....	D£1,440	E. M. Smithies (1978)
Eothen, Caterham, Surrey (CSC)	1892	210	....	D£1,830	D. C. Raine (1973)
Farlington, Horsham, W. Sussex	1896	242	£3,900	D£2,400	Mrs. O. M. Peto (1977)
Farnborough Hill Convent, Hants.	1889	496	....	D£1,953	Sr. S. Cousins (1983)
Farringtons, Chislehurst............	1911	300	£3,570	D£2,010	Mrs. F. V. Hatton (1972)
Felixstowe College, Suffolk	1929	340	£4,185	D£2,550	E. D. Guinness (1979)
Fernhill Manor, New Milton, Hants. ..	1890	137	£3,450	D£2,205	(a) Rev. A. Folks (1985)
Francis Holland, Clarence Gate, N.W.1.	1878	350	....	D£2,100	A. E. Holt (1974)
Francis Holland, Graham Terr., S.W.1.	1881	170	....	D£2,100	Mrs. J. A. Anderson (1982)
Godolphin, Salisbury	1726	290	£4,653	D£2,793	E. A. S. Hannay (1980)
Godolphin and Latymer Sch., W.6	1905	690	....	D£2,055	M. Rudland (1986)
Greenacre, Banstead, Surrey	1933	265	£3,855	D£2,025	M. E. Haggerty (1977)
The Grove, Hindhead, Surrey	1877	185	£3,792	D£2,202	(a) C. Brooks (1984)
Guildford High School (CSC)	1888	403	....	D£1,920	J. E. Dutton (1977)
Haberdashers' Aske's, Elstree	1873	840	....	D£1,530	Mrs. S. Wiltshire (1974)
Haberdashers' Monmouth School for Girls........................	1891	501	£3,087	D£1,656	Mrs. P. M. Phillips (1981)
Harrogate College	1893	430	£3,810	D£2,535	Mrs. J. C. Lawrance (1974)
Headington School, Oxford	1915	530	£3,855	D£1,977	E. M. Tucker (1982)
Heathfield School, Ascot	1900	185	£5,025		Mrs. S. E. Watkins (1982)
Heathfield School, Pinner	1900	300	....	D£1,785	Mrs. W. E. Ribchester (1974)
Hethersett Old Hall, Norwich	1928	154	£3,165	D£1,695	Mrs. V. M. Redington (1983)
Holy Child School, Edgbaston	1933	242	£2,790	D£1,530	Sr. W. Gradon (1983)
Howell's School, Denbigh	1859	300	£4,800	D£3,000	(a) Dr. J. T. Armstrong (1983)
*Howell's School, Llandaff	1860	567	£3,465	D£1,605	J. P. Turner (1978)
Hull High School (CSC)	1890	250	£2,340	D£1,680	C. M. B. Radcliffe (1976)
Hulme Grammar School, Oldham	1895	440	....	D£1,520	Mrs. A. Groom (1985)
Hunmanby Hall, nr. Filey	1928	320	£3,875	D£2,395	J. E. Jefferson (1979)
Huyton College, Liverpool	1894	268	£4,080	D£1,884	W. E. Edwards (1984)
*Ipswich High School	1878	590	....	D£1,515	P. M. Hayworth (1971)
James Allen's Girls', Dulwich, S.E.22 ..	1741	625	....	D£1,860	Mrs. B. Davies (1984)
School of Jesus and Mary, Ipswich	1860	160	....	D£1,425	Mrs. E. A. C. McKay (1982)
Kent College, Tunbridge Wells	1885	329	£4,023	D£2,400	(a) Rev. J. C. A. Barrett (1983)
King Edward VI H.S., Birmingham ...	1883	530	....	D£1,677	E. W. Evans (1977)
King's High School, Warwick	1879	537	....	D£1,584	M. Leahy (1970)
Kingsley School, Leamington........	1884	326	£3,030	D£1,620	E. C. Fairhurst (1977)

Name of School	F'ded.	No. of Girls	Annual Fees D = Day Girls	Headmistress (a) Headmaster (With date of Appointment)
La Sagesse Convent High, Newcastle-upon-Tyne	1906	330	.... D£1,665	Sr. Pauline (1967)
La Sagesse Convent, Romsey	1896	150	£2,385 .... D£1,065	Sr. Thomas (1977)
Lady Eleanor Holles, Hampton, Middx.	1711	586	.... D£1,905	E. M. Candy (1981)
Lavant House, Chichester	1952	150	£3,800 .... D£2,265	D. M. Ellis (1982)
Lawnside, Great Malvern	1818	140	£4,095	D. M.M. Stewart (1971)
Leeds Girls' High	1876	765	.... D£1,590	P. A. Randall (1977)
Loughborough High School	1850	527	£2,970 .... D£1,635	J. E. L. Harvatt (1978)
Luckley-Oakfield School, Wokingham	1895	265	£3,225 .... D£2,015	(a) R. C. Blake (1984)
Malvern Girls' College	1893	520	£4,320 .... D£2,880	Mrs. E. Stamers-Smith (1984)
Manchester High School for Girls	1874	733	.... D£1,593	M. M. Moon (1983)
Manor House School, Little Bookham, Surrey	1920	170	£4,110 .... D£2,025	Mrs. J. Findlay (1985)
Maynard School, Exeter	1877	440	.... D£1,707	F. Murdin (1980)
Merchant Taylors' School, Crosby	1888	506	.... D£1,800	Mrs. M. E. Davies (1963)
Micklefield School, Seaford, Sussex	1910	230	£4,200 .... D£2,340	Mrs. M. M. Payton (1969)
Moira House, Eastbourne	1875	260	£4,290 .... D£2,400	(a) A. R. Underwood (1975)
More House School, Pont Street, S.W.1	1953	245	.... D£2,600	Mrs. P. M. Mathias (1974)
Moreton Hall, Oswestry	1913	310	£4,410 .... D£2,940	(a) E. J. Cussell (1976)
Mount School, York	1831	296	£4,104 .... D£2,536	D. J. Ellis (1977)
New Hall, Chelmsford	1642	536	£4,455 .... D£2,688	Sr. M. Francis (1963)
Newcastle-upon-Tyne Church H.S.	1885	384	.... D£1,638	P. E. Davies (1974)
North Foreland Lodge, Sherfield-on-Loddon, Hants.	1909	164	£4,500	D. L. Matthews (1983)
North London Collegiate School, Edgware	1850	700	.... D£1,860	M. M. N. McLauchlan (1965)
Northampton High School	1878	500	.... D£1,623	S. Lightburne (1964)
Northwood College, Middx.	1878	320	£3,153 .... D£1,743	M. D. Hillyer-Cole (1966)
*Norwich High School	1875	722	.... D£1,515	Mrs. V. C. Bidwell (1985)
*Nottingham High School for Girls	1875	964	.... D£1,515	Mrs. C. Bowering (1984)
*Notting Hill and Ealing High	1873	736	.... D£1,605	Mrs. C. J. Fitz (1983)
Oakdene, Beaconsfield	1911	400	£3,300 .... D£2,055	C. S. Artley, Ph.D. (1983)
Old Palace School, Croydon	1887	600	.... D£1,380	K. L. Hilton (1974)
*Oxford High School	1875	598	.... D£1,515	Mrs. J. Townsend (1981)
Park School, Yeovil	1851	154	£4,005 .... D£1,875	(a) D. M. Upton (1977)
Parsons Mead, Ashstead, Surrey	1897	300	£4,173 .... D£2,280	M. M. Dees (1979)
Penrhos Coll., Colwyn Bay	1880	306	£4,020 .... D£2,580	(a) N. C. Peacock (1974)
Perse School for Girls, Cambridge	1881	540	.... D£1,812	M. R. Bateman (1980)
Pipers Corner School, High Wycombe	1930	245	£3,780 .... D£2,055	Dr.M. M. Wilson (1986)
Polam Hall, Darlington	1848	318	£4,215 .... D£2,091	M. C. Bright (1985)
Portland House, Leicester	1906	249	.... D£1,695	Mrs. D. Buchan (1982)
*Portsmouth High School	1882	609	.... D£1,515	Mrs. J. M. Dawtrey (1984)
Princess Helena Coll., Hitchin, Herts.	1820	181	£4,260 .... D£2,835	(a) D. Clarke, Ph.D. (1971)
Prior's Field, Godalming	1902	200	....	Mrs. M. W. Dawson
*Putney High School, S.W.15	1893	753	.... D£1,605	Mrs. N. Silver (1979)
Queen Anne's, Caversham	1698	365	£4,383 .... D£2,700	A. M. Scott (1977)
†Queen Ethelburga's, Harrogate	1912	160	£4,050 .... D£2,460	Mrs. M. C. James (1984)
†Queen Margaret's, Escrick Park, York	1901	215	£3,895 .... D£2,430	(a) C. S. McGarrigle (1983)
Queen Mary, Lytham	1930	685	.... D£1,479	M. C. Ritchie (1981)
Queen's College, Harley Street, W.1	1848	375	£3,225 .... D£2,025	Mrs. P. J. Fleming (1983)
Queen's Gate School, Queen's Gate, S.W.7	1891	177	.... D£2,325	Mrs. C. M. Newnham (1971)
Queen's School, Chester	1878	421	.... D£1,467	M. Farra (1973)
Queenswood, Hatfield, Herts.	1894	360	£4,743	Mrs. A. M. B. Butler (1981)
Redland High School, Bristol	1882	450	.... D£1,518	E. A. Hobbs (1986)
The Red Maids', Bristol	1634	470	£3,021 .... D£1,521	E. Castle (1982)
Rickmansworth Masonic School	1788	500	£3,950 .... D£2,370	(a) D. L. Curtis (1980)
Roedean School, Brighton	1885	450	£4,629	Mrs. A. R. Longley (1984)
Rosemead, Littlehampton	1919	222	£3,975 .... D£2,163	Mrs. S. Dickerson (1981)
Royal Naval School, Haslemere, Surrey	1840	300	£4,296 .... D£2,859	D. M. Otter (1970)
Royal School for Daughters of Officers of the Army, Bath	1864	400	£3,960 .... D£2,370	Mrs. S. Greig (1982)
Runton Hill, Runton, Cromer	1911	180	£3,975 .... D£2,673	Mrs. M. Sheelin Cuthbert (1976)
Rye St. Anthony, Oxford	1930	300	£3,150 .... D£1,635	P. M. Sumpter (1976)
Sacred Heart, Tunbridge Wells	1915	250	£3,951 .... D£2,298	(a) J. A. Fallon, Ph.D. (1979)
St. Albans High School	1889	457	.... D£1,665	E. M. Diggory (1983)
St. Andrew's, Bedford	1897	180	.... D£1,335	K. M. Smith (1981)
St. Anne's, Windermere	1863	310	£3,900 .... D£2,430	(a) M. B. McC. Brown (1984)
St. Antony's-Leweston, Sherborne, Dorset	1891	407	£4,140 .... D£2,805	Mrs. P. Cartwright (1983)
St. Audries, West Quantoxhead, nr. Taunton	1906	223	£3,603 .... D£2,013	(a) A. J. Tough (1975)

Name of School	F'ded	No. of Girls	Annual Fees D = Day Girls	Headmistress (a) Headmaster (With date of Appointment)
St. Brandon's, Clevedon, Avon	1831	275	£4,155 .... D£2,250	(a) J. S. Davey (1978)
St. Catherine's, Bramley, Guildford	1885	410	£3,795 .... D£2,325	(a) J. R. Palmer (1982)
†School of St. Clare, Penzance	1889	110	£3,900 .... D£2,214	M. M. Coney (1969)
St. David's, Ashford, Middx.	1716	195	£3,246 .... D£1,884	Mrs. J. G. Ireland (1985)
St. Dunstan's Abbey, Plymouth	1850	250	£2,850 .... D£1,590	H. L. Abley (1970)
St. Elphin's Church of England School, Matlock	1844	260	£4,089 .... D£2,265	(a) A. P. C. Pollard (1979)
St. Felix, Southwold, Suffolk	1897	370	£4,335 .... D£3,051	Mrs. A. Mustoe (1978)
St. Francis' College, Letchworth, Herts.	1933	255	£3,510 .... D£1,785	D. B. Ganderton (1984)
S. Gabriel's, Newbury	1929	130	.... D£1,983	Mrs. P. Gott (1980)
St. George's, Ascot	1923	235	£4,425 .... D£2,970	Mrs. J. M. Goodland (1982)
S. Helen & S. Katharine, Abingdon	1903	508	£2,797 .... D£1,455	Y. Paterson (1973)
St. Helen's, Northwood, Middx.	1899	539	£3,405 .... D£1,815	J. D. Leader (1966)
S. Hilary's, Alderley Edge	1880	245	.... D£1,575	(a) N. H. Norman (1976)
S. Hilary's, Sevenoaks	1942	200	.... D£1,560	Mrs. P. Miles (1977)
St. James's and the Abbey, West Malvern (*amalgamated* 1979)	1896	170	£4,455 .... D£2,270	J. M. Nixon (1978)
St. Joseph's, Lincoln	1905	160	£3,030 .... D£1,530	Mrs. A. Scott (1983)
St. Joseph's Convent, Reading	1909	435	.... D£1,716	M. Ball (1985)
St. Leonards-Mayfield School, East Sussex (*amalgamated* 1954)	—	528	£3,690 .... D£2,460	Sr. J. Sinclair (1980)
St. Margaret's, Bushey, Herts	1749	353	£3,900 .... D£2,400	S. Law (1985)
†St. Margaret's, Exeter	1904	350	£2,736 .... D£1,635	Mrs. J. M. Giddings (1984)
Saint Martin's, Solihull	1941	230	.... D£1,725	Mrs. H. P. Roxborough (1984)
St. Mary's Convent, Ascot	1885	320	£4,500 .... D£2,700	Sr. M. Orchard (1982)
St. Mary's Convent, Shaftesbury	1945	320	£3,720 .... D£2,130	Sr. C. Livesey (1985)
St. Mary's Hall, Brighton	1836	370	£4,275 .... D£2,430	M. F. C. Harvey (1981)
St. Mary's, Calne, Wilts.	1872	314	£4,380 .... D£2,595	D. H. Burns (1985)
St. Mary's, Cambridge	1898	500	£2,875 .... D£1,605	Sr. M. C. Kenworthy-Brown (1977)
St. Mary's, Colchester	1908	270	.... D£1,545	Mrs. G. M. G. Mouser (1981)
St. Mary's, Gerrards Cross	1872	245	.... D£1,825	Mrs. J. D. G. Smith (1984)
St. Mary's, Wantage, Oxon.	1873	300	£4,425	Mrs. P. H. Johns (1980)
St. Michael's, Limpsfield, Oxted	1850	200	£3,795 .... D£2,205	(a) B. F. Long, ph.d. (1983)
†St. Michael's, Petworth, Sussex	1844	206	£4,650 .... D£3,150	Mrs. M. Steeves (1981)
St. Paul's Girls', Brook Green, W.6	1904	600	.... D£2,751	Mrs. H. Brigstocke (*High Mistress*) (1974)
St. Stephen's Coll., Broadstairs	1867	148	£4,365 .... D£2,700	B. Seymour (1974)
St. Swithun's, Winchester	1884	411	£4,596 .... D£2,916	N. O. Davies (1973)
*Sheffield High School	1878	637	.... D£1,515	D. M. Skilbeck (1983)
Sherborne School, Dorset	1899	455	£3,455 .... D£2,970	J. M. Taylor (1985)
*Shrewsbury High School	1885	558	.... D£1,515	E. M. Gill (1982)
Sir William Perkins's, Chertsey	1725	445	.... D£1,620	Mrs. A. F. Darlow (1982)
*South Hampstead High School	1876	664	.... D£1,605	Mrs. D. A. Burgess (1975)
Stamford High School, Lincs.	1876	738	£2,904 .... D£1,614	G. K. Bland (1978)
Stonar, Atworth, Melksham, Wilts.	1921	265	£4,251 .... D£2,205	Mrs. S. Hopkinson (1985)
Stover School, Newton Abbot	1932	190	£3,594 .... D£1,965	C. A. Smith (1969)
Stratford House School, Bromley	1912	250	.... D£1,845	Mrs. A. Williamson (1974)
*Streatham Hill and Clapham High	1887	457	.... D£1,605	G. M. Ellis (1979)
Sunderland High School (*CSC*)	1884	225	.... D£1,620	Mrs. M. Thrush (1980)
Surbiton High School (*CSC*)	1884	400	.... D£1,785	Mrs. R. A. Thynne (1979)
*Sutton High School, Surrey	1884	809	.... D£1,605	A. E. Cavendish (1980)
*Sydenham High School, S.E.26	1887	634	.... D£1,605	M. I. J. Hamilton (1966)
Talbot Heath, Bournemouth	1886	485	£3,162 .... D£1,650	C. E. Austin-Smith (1976)
Teesside High, Cleveland	1970	409	.... D£1,638	J. Sawyer (1982)
Tormead School, Guildford	1905	360	£3,546 .... D£1,665	Mrs. J. V. Crouch-Smith (1977)
Truro High School	1880	412	£3,450 .... D£1,740	Mrs. J. F. Marshall (1984)
Tudor Hall School, Banbury	1850	242	£4,440 .... D£2,889	N. Godfrey (1984)
Upper Chine, Shanklin, I.O.W.	1799	300	£2,925 .... D£2,055	B. A. Philpott (1981)
Ursuline Convent, Westgate-on-Sea	1904	345	£4,059 .... D£2,058	Sr. M. Murphy (1976)
Ursuline High School, Ilford	1903	400	.... D£1,590	P. Dixon (1984)
Wadhurst College, Sussex	1930	230	£4,305 .... D£2,550	D. Swatman (1971)
Wakefield High School	1878	710	.... D£1,686	Y. J. Hand (1974)
Walthamstow Hall, Sevenoaks, Kent	1838	400	£3,933 .... D£2,130	Mrs. J. S. Lang (1984)
Wentworth Milton Mt., Bournemouth	1962	312	£3,300 .... D£2,025	M. Vokins (1982)
Westfield, Newcastle-upon-Tyne	1962	230	.... D£1,536	Mrs. M. Hill (1979)
West Heath, Sevenoaks, Kent	1867	145	£4,425 .... D£3,195	R. M. Rudge (1965)
Westholme, Blackburn	1923	590	.... D£1,425	J. Bond, ph.d. (1968)
Westonbirt, Tetbury, Glos.	1928	250	£4,794 .... D£3,135	(a) H. A. Nickols (1981)
*Wimbledon High School	1880	678	.... D£1,605	Mrs. R. A. Smith (1982)
Withington School, Manchester	1890	460	.... D£1,512	M. Hulme (1961)

(a) Headmaster

Name of School	F'ded.	No. of Girls	Annual Fees D = Day Girls	Headmistress (a) Headmaster (With date of Appointment)
Wroxhall Abbey School, Warwick.....	1872	165	£4,395 .... D£2,979	Mrs. I. D. M. Iles (1980)
Wycombe Abbey, Bucks.	1896	480	£5,025	P. M. Lancaster (1974)
York College (CSC).................	1908	206	.... D£1,830	Mrs. J. L. Clare (1982)
Scotland				
Laurel Bank, Glasgow	1903	280	.... D£1,800	L. G. Egginton (1984)
Mary Erskine School, Edinburgh	1694	650	£3,675 .... D£1,860	(a) R. M. Morgan (1978)
Park School, Glasgow	1880	322	.... D£1,665	J. Rutherford (1974)
St. Denis and Cranley, Edinburgh.....	1858	250	£3,690 .... D£1,770	Mrs. J. M. Munro (1984)
St. George's, Edinburgh..............	1888	580	£3,885 .... D£1,875	Mrs. J. L. Clanchy (1976)
St. Leonards, St. Andrews, Fife	1877	400	£4,920 .... D£2,175	M. Hamilton (1970)
St. Margaret's, Aberdeen.............	1846	224	£3,171 .... D£1,401	M. D. Bosomworth (1970)
St. Margaret's, Edinburgh	1890	800	£3,725 .... D£1,725	Mrs. M. J. Cameron (1984)
Channel Islands				
The Ladies' College, Guernsey	1872	350	.... D £780	J. Honey (1976)

* Girls' Public Day School Trust, 26 Queen Anne's Gate, S.W.1

† Woodard Corporation School.

CSC Church Schools Company, 1a Doughty Street, W.C.1

G.B.A. and G.B.G.S.A.

The Governing Bodies Association (G.B.A.) and the Governing Bodies of Girls' Schools Association (G.B.G.S.A.) together comprise 531 independent secondary schools all of which are educational charities. Both Associations are constituent members of the Independent Schools Joint Council. The Headmasters or Headmistresses of almost all these schools are members of either the Headmasters Conference (H.M.C.), the Girls Schools Association (G.S.A.) or the Society of Headmasters of Independent Schools (S.H.M.I.S.). The total number of pupils in G.B.A. and G.B.G.S.A. schools is approximately 274,000. Sec., Lt. Col. C. J. M. Hamilton, O.B.E., The Flat, The Lambdens, Beenham, Reading, Berks.

EVENTS OF THE YEAR (*SEPT. 1, 1984–AUG. 31, 1985*)

THE ROYAL HOUSE

(1984) Sept. 3. The Duke of Kent attended the 40th anniversary celebrations of the liberation of Brussels in Belgium. **4.** The Duke of Kent opened the Football Association's National School at Lilleshall. **14.** Princess Margaret visited Glasgow. **15.** The Princess of Wales gave birth to a boy weighing 6 lb. 14 oz. at St. Mary's Hospital, Paddington; on Sept. 16 it was announced that the new Prince was to be named Henry Charles Albert David and to be known as Harry. **18.** Princess Anne opened New College, Swindon. **19.** Princess Anne opened a shopping centre in Bracknell. **23.** The Prince of Wales attended a service of remembrance at Oosterbeek War Cemetery to mark the 40th anniversary of the Battle of Arnhem. **24.** The Queen and the Duke of Edinburgh left Heathrow Airport for tour of Canada; the Duke returned to London on Oct. 5 and the Queen on Oct. 16 after her private stay in the U.S.A. Princess Anne visited Gainsborough, Lincs. **28.** The Queen Mother presided at the opening of the 30th conference of the Commonwealth Parliamentary Association in Douglas, Isle of Man.

Oct. 1. Princess Anne visited the Isle of Man. **5.** The Duke of Edinburgh left Heathrow Airport to undertake engagements in Cyprus, Egypt, Saudi Arabia and Japan. **10.** Princess Anne visited Shropshire; on Oct. 16 she visited Cornwall. **19.** Princess Alexandra and the Hon. Angus Ogilvy left Heathrow Airport to visit Cannes, France, on the occasion of the celebrations to mark the 150th anniversary of the founding of the town. **22.** Princess Anne, President of the Save the Children Fund, left Heathrow Airport to visit Bangladesh and India. The Prince of Wales visited Hartlepool. **23.** President Mitterrand of France arrived in London on a four-day State visit. Princess Margaret left Heathrow Airport to visit Bermuda and Dallas. **24.** The Queen Mother left Heathrow Airport for Italy to visit Venice. **28.** The Prince of Wales left R.A.F. Lyneham to undertake engagements in Italy. **29.** The Queen Mother was present at a service in Westminster Abbey to mark the centenary of the foundation of Toynbee Hall. **31.** The Queen and the Duke of Edinburgh visited Maidstone, Rochester and Gillingham.

Nov. 2. The Duke of Edinburgh visited Cardiff. **6.** The Queen, accompanied by the Prince and Princess of Wales, opened the new session of Parliament. The Queen Mother visited Newcastle upon Tyne. **7.** The Queen attended a service of thanksgiving at St. Paul's Cathedral to mark the centenary of the N.S.P.C.C. **8.** The Queen Mother planted a cross in the Royal British Legion Field of

Remembrance at St. Margaret's Church, Westminster. **10.** The Queen and the Duke of Edinburgh, the Queen Mother, and the Prince and Princess of Wales, Princess Anne, and Princess Alexandra were present at the Royal British Legion Festival of Remembrance at the Royal Albert Hall. **11.** The Queen and the Duke of Edinburgh and the Prince of Wales laid wreaths at the Cenotaph on Remembrance Day. **13.** The Prince of Wales, Patron of the Operation Raleigh youth venture project, attended the sailing of the flagship *Sir Walter Raleigh* at Hull. **14.** The President of Finland visited the Queen and the Duke of Edinburgh at Buckingham Palace. The Queen with the Duke of Edinburgh dined with the Commonwealth High Commissioners at Marlborough House. **15.** The Queen and the Duke of Edinburgh visited the College of Arms to mark its quincentenary. The Princess of Wales named the new P. & O. cruise liner *Royal Princess* at Southampton. **27.** Princess Margaret visited British Aerospace at Stevenage and opened new spacecraft assembly hall. **28.** Princess Anne visited Bradford; on the following day she visited Liverpool. **30.** Princess Anne left Heathrow Airport to visit the United Arab Emirates where she was subsequently joined by Capt. Mark Phillips.

Dec. 4. The Princess of Wales visited the Royal School for the Blind at Leatherhead, Surrey. Princess Margaret visited Derbyshire. **5.** The Queen Mother visited the Royal Smithfield Show at Earls Court. **6.** The Queen and the Duke of Edinburgh gave a reception on board *Britannia* in the Pool of London. **11.** The Queen visited the Household Cavalry Regiment at Hyde Park Barracks. **12.** The Prince of Wales visited Liverpool; on Dec. 18 he visited Stirling and Glasgow. **21.** Prince Henry of Wales was christened in St. George's Chapel, Windsor. **25.** The Queen made her traditional broadcast to the Commonwealth. **31.** The New Year's Honours List was published and included four life peerages.

(1985) Jan. 6. Princess Margaret underwent a minor lung operation at the Brompton Hospital; she returned to Kensington Palace on Jan. 13. **16.** The Prince and Princess of Wales visited Horton Hospital, Epsom. **17.** The Queen Mother was present at the Royal Albert Hall to pay tribute to the eleven Regiments celebrating their 300th anniversary. **29.** The Prince and Princess of Wales visited Bridgend and Mid and South Glamorgan.

Feb. 5. The Princess of Wales visited Dr. Barnardo's Headquarters at Barkingside, Ilford, Essex. **8.** The Prince of Wales visited Macclesfield. **13.** The Queen visited "The Golden Age of Anglo-Saxon Art" exhibition at the British Museum. **14.** The Duke of Edinburgh unveiled a memorial to the Earl and Countess Mountbatten of Burma in Westminster Abbey, other members of the royal family also attending. **18.** Princess Anne, President, Save the Children Fund, left Heathrow Airport to resume her earlier visit to India. **19.** The Prince of Wales visited Derby. **26.** The Duke of Edinburgh attended the City and Guilds College centenary banquet at Guildhall. **27.** The President of the Irish Republic visited the Queen at Buckingham Palace. The Queen Mother visited the Headquarters of the Intelligence Corps at Ashford, Kent. **28.** The Queen and the Duke of Edinburgh visited *The Times* to mark its bicentenary.

Mar. 1. The Duke of Edinburgh, President, World Wildlife Fund International, left Heathrow Airport for visits to Switzerland, Algeria, Niger, Mali, Senegal, The Gambia and Mauritania, and later Madeira. The Prince of Wales became a blood donor for the first time at a transfusion centre in London. **4.** The Queen attended a reception at 12 Downing Street given by the Vice-Chamberlains of the Royal Household of her reign. **5.** The Queen opened a new wing of the Royal Hospital and Home for Incurables at Putney. **6.** The Queen attended a service in St. Paul's Cathedral to mark the golden jubilee of King George's Jubilee Trust. **7.** The Prince and Princess of Wales visited Nottinghamshire. **10.** The Queen Mother opened the Museum of Eton Life at Eton College. **11.** The Queen attended the Commonwealth Day observance service in Westminster Abbey. **14.** President Mubarak of Egypt visited the Queen at Buckingham Palace. **15.** The Queen visited Derbyshire. **18.** The Queen Mother, accompanied by the Prince and Princess of Wales and Princess Anne and Capt. Mark Phillips, was present at the royal film performance of *A Passage to India* in London. **19.** President Nyerere of Tanzania visited the Queen at Buckingham Palace. **20.** The Prime Minister of St. Lucia had an audience of the Queen. **22.** The Queen visited the new Hampshire Fire Brigade Headquarters at Eastleigh. The Prince of Wales visited a North Sea oil rig in the Forties Field. **25.** The Queen left Heathrow Airport for a four-day State visit to Portugal where she was joined by the Duke of Edinburgh. **30.** Princess Anne attended the Grand National at Aintree.

April 3. The Prince and Princess of Wales opened the Wolfson Galleries. **4.** The Queen and the Duke of Edinburgh attended the Maundy Service at Ripon Cathedral at which the Queen distributed the Royal Maundy. **11.** The Princess of Wales visited New Scotland Yard. **16.** President Banda of Malawi arrived in Windsor on a four-day State visit to Britain. **18.** Princess Margaret arrived in

Hungary on a four-day visit. **19.** The Queen Mother visited Stratford-upon-Avon. The Prince and Princess of Wales left Heathrow Airport for their 17-day visit to Italy. **22.** The Prime Minister of Papua New Guinea lunched with the the Queen and the Duke of Edinburgh at Windsor Castle. **26.** Princess Margaret visited Humberside.

May 1. The Prime Minister of Canada lunched with the Queen at Buckingham Palace. **2.** Princess Margaret visited Glasgow. **3.** Princess Anne opened the Regent Arcade, Cheltenham. **8.** The Queen and the Duke of Edinburgh accompanied by Prince Edward attended a service in Westminster Abbey to commemorate the 40th anniversary of the end of the Second World War, other members of the royal family also attending. Princess Anne visited Northern Ireland. The Duchess of Kent left for a three-day visit to the Channel Islands. **9.** The Queen unveiled a statue of Field Marshal Earl Alexander of Tunis at Wellington Barracks. **10.** Princess Margaret visited Gwent. **14.** The President of the Cameroon lunched with the Queen at Buckingham Palace. **17.** The Queen visited Colchester. **20.** The Queen and other members of the royal family visited the Chelsea Flower Show. **21.** The Prince and Princess of Wales visited Tyne and Wear. **24.** The Queen visited the Lake District. **27.** Princess Alice, Duchess of Gloucester, was present at a banquet to mark the 400th anniversary of the granting of the Charter to Corby, Northamptonshire. **30.** The Princess of Wales visited the Isle of Wight.

June 2. The Prince of Wales accepted the freedom of the borough of Dinefwr, Dyfed, and also accepted the freedom on behalf of the Royal Regiment of Wales. **3.** The Duke of Edinburgh left Blackpool Airport for Canada. Princess Anne visited Suffolk. **5.** The Queen accompanied by the Queen Mother, Princess Anne, and Princess Alexandra visited Epsom Races. **6.** The Queen gave a lunch party for the Chinese Prime Minister at Buckingham Palace. The Queen Mother embarked in *Britannia* at Portsmouth to visit the West Country and the Isles of Scilly. Princess Anne took the salute at the Founder's Day parade at the Royal Hospital, Chelsea, and later opened the bone marrow transplant unit at Westminster Children's Hospital. **11.** The President of Mexico arrived in London on a State visit. **13.** Princess Anne visited Cambridge. **14.** The Queen unveiled the South Atlantic campaign memorial in St. Paul's Cathedral. **15.** The Queen's Birthday Honours List was published and included two life peers among 671 people honoured. The Queen was present at her Birthday Parade on Horse Guards Parade. **18, 19, 20 and 21.** The Queen with the Duke of Edinburgh was present at

Ascot Races. **21.** The Queen and the Duke of Edinburgh gave a dinner party followed by a dance at Windsor Castle to celebrate the 21st birthdays of Prince Edward, Lady Sarah Armstrong-Jones, Lady Helen Windsor, and James Ogilvy. **23.** Prince Andrew left Heathrow Airport to visit Canada. **24.** Princess Margaret was present at a candle-lighting ceremony in the forecourt of Buckingham Palace to mark the 75th anniversary of girl guiding. **26.** Princess Anne visited Devon. **28.** The Queen visited Lord's Cricket Ground and met members of the Australian and England cricket teams. Princess Margaret visited Glasgow. The Duke and Duchess of Gloucester left Heathrow Airport to visit Tenerife to inaugurate the British Isaac Newton Telescope in the new international observatory on La Palma.

July 2. The Queen and the Duke of Edinburgh visited Perth and Kinross. The Prince and Princess of Wales began a three-day visit to the Western Isles. **3.** The Duke of Edinburgh opened Murrayfield Hospital in Edinburgh. **11.** The Duke of Edinburgh visited the Greater Manchester area. The Prince of Wales opened the new terminal building at Luton airport. **12.** The Queen Mother left Heathrow Airport for a visit to Canada. Princess Margaret visited Aberdeen. **13.** The Prince and Princess of Wales attended the opening of the "Live Aid" concert at Wembley Stadium. **16.** The Prince and Princess of Wales visited Middlesbrough. **19.** The Princess of Wales visited the Army Staff College, Camberley, Surrey. **24.** The Queen and the Duke of Edinburgh attended a service of thanksgiving in Westminster Abbey to mark the quatercentenary of the City of Westminster. **25.** The Queen, accompanied by the Duke of Edinburgh, in the garden of Buckingham Palace, presented a new standard to the Queen's Body Guard of the Yeomen of the Guard on the occasion of its quincentenary. **26.** The Queen and the Duke of Edinburgh visited Cardiff and Bristol to mark the 150th anniversary of the Great Western Railway. **28.** The Princess of Wales opened the international Stoke Mandeville paraplegic games. **30.** The Prince of Wales visited an open-air celebration to mark the 350th anniversary of the inauguration of the Royal Mail at Bagshot Park, Surrey.

Aug. 1. The Queen and the Duke of Edinburgh visited Great Yarmouth and Lowestoft. **15.** The Queen, accompanied by the Duke of Edinburgh, visited Inverness and opened new harbour board development and the new Raigmore Hospital. **27.** The Prince and Princess of Wales visited hospitals in Greater Manchester to see survivors of the Manchester Airport disaster. **28.** The Queen Mother visited Thurso. **29.** Princess Margaret undertook engagements in Dundee.

BRITISH POLITICS

(1984) Sept. 9. The four-day annual conference of the Social Democratic Party opened at Buxton, Derbyshire. **10.** The Prime Minister announced Cabinet changes with Mr. Douglas Hurd as Ulster Secretary in succession to Mr. James Prior and Mr. David Young, chairman of the Manpower Services Commission, who was to become a life peer, as Minister without Portfolio with special responsibility for the growth of enterprise and the creation of jobs; the Earl of Gowrie became Chancellor of the Duchy of Lancaster in place of Lord Cockfield; it was also announced that Lord Cockfield and Mr. Stanley Clinton Davis, former Labour M.P., were being nominated as the two British members of the European Commission. **13.** The Labour Party issued its new policy statement on the economy entitled "A Future that Works." **14.** The Police Federation accepted a 5·4 per cent. pay rise for those below the rank of superintendent. **17.** The Liberal Party assembly opened at Bournemouth; on Sept. 20 delegates voted for the immediate withdrawal of all Cruise missiles from Britain. **19.** The Prime Minister defended the decision to sink the Argentinian cruiser, *General Belgrano*, during the Falklands conflict. **20.** Mr. Kenneth Livingstone and three Labour colleagues won four G.L.C. by-elections caused by their resignations; Conservatives boycotted the elections.

Oct. 1. The Labour Party conference opened at Blackpool and voted to give uncritical support to the N.U.M. in passing a resolution which condemned "organised violence" by the police against miners' pickets and their families; delegates also rejected all moves to involve the membership as a whole in decisions on re-selection of M.P.s; on the following day, Mr. Kinnock, the Labour leader, condemned all picket-line violence whether by police or striking miners; on Oct. 3 conference delegates confirmed by a four to one majority support for unilateral nuclear disarmament. **6.** The Prime Minister set up an Enterprise Unit in the Cabinet Office to promote the creation of jobs. **9.** The Conservative Party conference opened in Brighton, with the miners' strike predominant and the Home Secretary telling delegates of new measures to help local authorities, chief constables, and the courts in combating picket-line violence and intimidation; on the following day, Mr. Kenneth Clarke, Minister for Health, announced the introduction of life sentences for drug pushers; on Oct. 11, Employment Secretary (Mr. King) told conference that the number of adult training places was to be doubled and Trade and Industry Secretary (Mr. Tebbit) said the privatisation programme would continue; on the following day the conference continued despite the I.R.A. bomb attack (*see* **"Crimes, Trials, Etc."**) and the

THE QUEEN IN PORTUGAL

The Queen with university students during her visit to Portugal in March. President Eanes (*left*) looks on.

The Prince and Princess of Wales in Venice during their visit to Italy in the spring.

THE 40TH ANNIVERSARY OF VE-DAY

The Queen and the Duke of Edinburgh and other members of the royal family at the service in Westminster Abbey to commemorate the 40th anniversary of the end of the Second World War.

THE BRADFORD FIRE DISASTER

Football fans watch as fire sweeps the entire length of Bradford City's main stand in May.

THE BRUSSELS FOOTBALL TRAGEDY

The scene at the Heysel Stadium before the European Cup Final in May.

THE MANCHESTER JET FIRE

The burned-out shell of the British Airtours Boeing 737 which burst into flames during its take-off for Corfu at Manchester Airport in August.

THE HANDSWORTH RIOTS

The aftermath of rioting in the Handsworth district of Birmingham in September.

FAMINE IN ETHIOPIA

Famine victims waiting for aid in one of the relief camps in Ethiopia.

LIVE AID

The "Live Aid" concert at Wembley Stadium in July.

INDIA'S LEADERSHIP

Mrs. Indira Gandhi (*inset*), Prime Minister of India, was assassinated in Oct. 1984 and was succeeded by her son, Mr. Rajiv Gandhi. Mr. Gandhi is seen putting the torch to his mother's funeral pyre.

SOUTH AFRICA

Unrest and violence flared in South Africa's black townships and a state of emergency was declared in July.

OBITUARIES

Sir Michael Redgrave (*top left*), Sir Robert Mayer (*top right*), Lord George-Brown (*bottom left*) and Dickie Henderson.

Boris Becker, the 17-year-old West German, holding the trophy after winning the men's singles at the Wimbledon Lawn Tennis Championships. He became the first unseeded champion and the youngest-ever winner.

IRELAND'S HERO

Barry McGuigan, the new world featherweight boxing champion, during a victory parade through Belfast.

England players celebrate at the Oval after winning the Test series against Australia by three matches to one.

BRITISH TRIUMPHS

Steve Cram (*left*), the British athlete, who broke three world records in 19 days in the summer. Sandy Lyle kisses the trophy after becoming the first Briton to win the Open Golf Championship since 1969.

Prime Minister told delegates that terrorism would not prevail. **16.** The Prime Minister and Mr. Kinnock, the Labour leader, stood side by side at the Bar of the House of Lords to listen to Viscount Whitelaw, deputy Prime Minister, make a statement on the bombing of the Grand Hotel in Brighton. **18.** Lord Shinwell attended the House of Lords on his 100th birthday for celebrations in the Royal Gallery and later in the Chamber replied to all-party tributes. **22.** In a statement to the Commons on the Brighton bombing, the Home Secretary revealed he had set in hand new arrangements centrally for countering the Irish terrorist threat, with a Whitehall committee channelling information from the Special Branch and other security agencies and co-ordinating counter-measures. **24.** President Mitterrand of France addressed peers and M.P.s in the Royal Gallery of the House of Lords. **25.** In the Shadow Cabinet elections, Mr. Wedgwood Benn failed to regain a place and Mr. Eric Heffer also lost his seat. The Prime Minister condemned the planting of explosives in the grounds of the French Embassy in London by one of President Mitterrand's bodyguards to test the efficiency of British security. **29.** Twenty-seven Tory M.P.s rebelled in the Commons and voted against legislation to make racial discrimination by police a disciplinary offence.

Nov. 6. The Queen opened the new session of Parliament. The Royal Navy admitted that a log of the nuclear submarine, *Conqueror*, which sank the Argentine cruiser *General Belgrano* in 1981, had been mislaid; on the following day Mr. Heseltine, the Defence Secretary, told the Commons that the log was a "routine" document of technical information. **12.** The Chancellor of the Exchequer made his autumn financial statement (*see* **"Parliamentary Summary"**) in the Commons and also announced that no more £1 notes would be issued by the Bank of England after Dec. 31 and they would be replaced by the £1 coin. Mr. Dennis Skinner, Labour M.P. for Bolsover, was ordered out of the Commons by the Speaker after referring to Dr. David Owen, the S.D.P. leader, as a "pompous sod." **13.** President Koivisto of Finland arrived in London for talks. The Earl of Stockton delivered his maiden speech at the age of 90 in the House of Lords. The six-day debate on the Queen's Speech concluded in the Commons where a Labour amendment critical of Government policies was defeated by 364 to 205 votes and an S.D.P.-Liberal amendment critical of policies to reduce unemployment was also defeated by 364 to 200 votes; the programme set out in the Speech was approved by 352 to 202 votes. **15.** Mr. Edward du Cann, chairman of the Conservative back-bench 1922 Committee, was defeated in an election for the position by Mr.

Cranley Onslow. **19.** Mrs. Thatcher and Dr. Fitzgerald, the Irish Prime Minister, held talks at Chequers, the venue having been switched from Dublin on security grounds. **21.** The Speaker suspended the sitting of the Commons during uproar over a Government announcement that families of striking miners and other strikers would receive less than other people when social security benefits were increased; 30 Labour M.P.s gathered in front of the Mace shouting abusively at Ministers; the Speaker adjourned the House after a 10-minute break when the Labour M.P.s refused to move. Mr. Kinnock, the Labour Party leader, and Mr. Denis Healey, Shadow Foreign Secretary, arrived in Moscow for talks with the Soviet leadership. **22.** Eight Tory M.P.s voted against the Government and 40 others abstained after the Foreign Secretary announced economies at the Foreign Office which provoked backbench concern that the overseas aid budget would be affected; the Foreign Secretary also served notice to terminate at the end of 1985, U.K. membership of U.N.E.S.C.O. unless changes were made in its spending programme. **26.** Pensions and all other social security benefits were increased lifting the cost of State welfare to a record of nearly £40 billion. An emergency Commons debate on a Labour motion relating to changes in benefits affecting strikers ended in the Government winning the division by 279 to 185 votes. Mr. Lamont, Minister of State for Industry, announced a £100 million aid programme for areas affected by closures and redundancies in the steel, ship-building, and textile industries. **27.** The House of Lords gave final approval to plans to televise proceedings in the Chamber for a six-month experimental period. **28.** Government announced that aid to the regions would be reduced by £300 million in a plan to cut automatic assistance to firms.

Dec. 4. The Bill to abolish the G.L.C. and the six metropolitan councils was given a second reading in the Commons by 354 to 219 votes with a dozen Tory M.P.s abstaining; a Labour amendment declining to give the Bill a second reading was defeated by identical voting figures. **5.** Sir Keith Joseph, Education Secretary, announced a partial withdrawal of his proposals to cut student grants and increase the parental contribution following threats of a large-scale revolt by Tory M.P.s; parental contributions to tuition fees were to be dropped. The Commons approved the Government's intention to sign the agreement on the future of Hong Kong. **6.** In the Commons, a Labour motion condemning the expenditure cuts in the autumn financial statement was defeated by 346 to 199 votes; the Government motion approving the programme being carried by 343 to 198 votes. **11.** Mr. Jenkin, Environment Secretary, announced that 13 high-spending councils—12

Labour and one Conservative—must reduce their rates next year and that five other councils would have a limit set on the amount by which they could raise rates. New methods of Government purchasing were announced to produce savings of £400 million a year in the way departments bought goods and services. 12. The Commons Foreign Affairs Select Committee published its report on the Falkland Islands. 13. In the Enfield Southgate by-election, the Conservatives retained the seat with a majority reduced from 15,819 at the General Election to 4,711; the Liberal/Alliance was second and the Labour candidate, who lost his deposit, was third. 15. Mr. Mikhail Gorbachev of the Soviet Union arrived in Britain for a week-long visit during which he had a three-hour meeting at Chequers with Mrs. Thatcher. 17. The Earl of Gowrie, Minister for the Arts, announced an overall increase of 5·8 per cent. in Government support for the arts, museums and libraries. 18. Mr. Jenkin, Environment Secretary, announced new restraints on local authorities in the use of assets raised mainly through the sale of council houses; on Dec. 19 an emergency motion initiated by the Opposition on the £1 billion curbs was defeated by 325 to 225 votes; three Tories voted against the Government and some 30 others abstained. The Lords approved the Order extending the term of office of members of the G.L.C. and the metropolitan county councils to be abolished under the Local Government Bill. 20. Mr. Ridley, Transport Secretary, told the Commons that the Civil Aviation Bill, which had been blocked in committee by Tory and Labour M.P.s would not be proceeded with until after a decision on the development of Stansted Airport. It was announced that a South Atlantic campaign memorial bearing the names of the men who lost their lives in the Falklands Conflict, was to be erected in the crypt of St. Paul's Cathedral.

(1985) Jan. 1. The 1954 Cabinet papers were released under the 30-year rule. 4. A message from Mrs. Thatcher to President Chernenko in reply to the Russian leader's note in Dec. was delivered at the Foreign Ministry in Moscow; it referred to the development of bilateral relations and other international issues. 10. The Prime Minister told the Commons the Government had no plans to reintroduce chemical weapons but said the situation had to be kept under constant review because of the "massive Soviet capability" in such weapons. 15. In the Commons, a Labour motion condemning the Government's refusal to implement policies to reduce unemployment was defeated by 383 to 182 votes. Mr. Tebbit, Trade and Industry Secretary, told M.P.s the Government was to sell its remaining shareholding in British Aerospace. The Prime Minister announced the Government would arrange a suitable com-

memoration to mark this year's 40th anniversary of VE-Day; this reversed an earlier decision to rule out any official Government-sponsored celebration. 16. The Rate Support Grant proposals were approved in the Commons by 343 to 211 votes, with a handful of Tories voting against the Government. 17. Labour M.P.s pressing for a debate on the miners' dispute forced the Speaker to adjourn the sitting of the Commons for twenty minutes when 16 of them refused to sit down; the Speaker said the M.P.s were behaving in "a very unruly way"; at a meeting of the Parliamentary Labour Party later, Mr. Kinnock accused the M.P.s of "utter self indulgence and utter self-indiscipline." 21. The second reading of the Hong Kong Bill was unopposed in the Commons. 22. A White Paper on the Government's expenditure plans to 1987–88 was published. The Home Secretary announced that a special team of chief constables was being set up to prepare security plans for political party conferences this year. 23. The proceedings of the House of Lords were televised for the first time; striking miners briefly disrupted proceedings as the Earl of Stockton rose to speak. 24. The Government was defeated by 140 to 98 in the Lords when an amendment was carried to remove a clause from the Prosecution of Offences Bill which would give the Attorney-General new power to refer a lenient sentence for review by the Court of Appeal. Increased payments from public funds to finance the work of Opposition parties in Parliament were approved in the Commons with the Labour Party receiving £440,000, the Liberals £88,000, the S.D.P. £62,000, and other parties sharing £40,000. 25. The Sexual Offences Bill, a private member's measure designed to protect women from "kerb-crawlers" was given an unopposed second reading in the Commons. 28. Seven Tory M.P.s voted against the Government in the Commons and a dozen others abstained in protest against a Bill to allow parents to exempt their children from corporal punishment at school; however, the Bill received a second reading by 290 to 171 votes. 30. Mr. Larry Whitty was elected general secretary of the Labour Party. 31. An Opposition censure motion on the Government's economic policy was defeated in the Commons by 395 to 222 votes. On a formal motion to adjourn the House, on which Ministers were instructed to abstain so as not to prejudge the issue, a debate on the development of Stanstead as London's third airport ended with the adjournment being carried by 247 votes to nil, 70 Tory rebels voting with Labour, after criticisms from the anti-Stanstead M.P.s.

Feb. 4. In the Commons, a Labour motion condemning the Government's attitude to negotiations in the coal strike was defeated by 378 to 200 votes. 7. Nineteen Tory M.P.s voted against the Government and four others abstained in the Commons in a protest at proposals to force water authorities to impose higher charges than they wanted; the Government won the division by 295 to 191 votes. **8.** Sir Geoffrey Howe, Foreign Secretary, announced that Britain and Libya were to reopen contacts following the release of the four Britons held hostage in Libya. **12, 13, 14.** The Prime Minister and Mr. Kinnock, Labour leader, were engaged in a continuing war of words over the *General Belgrano* secrets case and exchanged letters after Mr. Kinnock refused to accept Mrs. Thatcher's repeated assurance in the Commons that she had not been involved in the decision to prosecute Mr. Clive Ponting (*see* "Crimes, Trials, etc."). **14.** M.P.s approved a compromise increase in the deposit for Parliamentary elections from £150 to £500 and agreed that five per cent. of votes necessary to save it should replace the present 12½ per cent. **15.** By 238 to 66 votes, the Commons approved the second reading of Mr. Enoch Powell's private Member's Bill to prohibit research on human embryos. **18.** After a debate in the Commons on the sinking of the *General Belgrano*, a Labour motion accusing the Government of seeking to conceal information and of having betrayed its responsibility to Parliament was defeated by 350 to 202 votes. **19.** Mrs. Thatcher left Heathrow Airport for a three-day visit to the U.S.A. where she addressed both Houses of Congress on Feb. 20. **21.** Mr. Dennis Skinner, Labour M.P. for Bolsover, was ordered out of the Commons after accusing Mr. Biffen, Leader of the House, of being a liar. **28.** The Prime Minister ordered an urgent official inquiry into allegations in a television documentary that MI5 had been improperly tapping the telephones of union leaders and anti-nuclear campaigners; on Mar. 6, Mrs. Thatcher announced that as a result of the inquiry, the Government and Administrations back to 1970 had been cleared of authorising improper telephone-tapping.

Mar. 4. A Commons' debate on the Government's expenditure plans resulted in a Labour amendment deploring the policies being defeated by 357 to 182 votes. **6.** Mr. Ivan Lawrence, Tory M.P. for Burton-on-Trent, spoke for four hours 23 minutes in the Commons, the longest continuous speech there this century. **13.** Eighteen Tories voted against the Government with 30 others abstaining in protest at an Order imposing restrictions on councils' freedom to spend money from the sale of homes on further building; the Labour motion to block the restrictions was defeated by 313 to 192 votes. It was announced in the Commons that the Government was to abolish the British National Oil Corporation. **19.** The Chancellor of the Exchequer (Mr. Lawson) presented his Budget in Parliament (*see* **"Parliamentary Summary" for details**). **25.** The Commons four-day debate on the Budget was concluded and the Budget itself was approved in general by 355 to 202 votes. **27.** Mr. Brittan, Home Secretary, announced in the Commons that television licence fees were to rise from Mar. 28 from £46 to £58 for colour sets and from £15 to £18 for black and white. **28.** Mr. King, Employment Secretary, published a White Paper on long-term employment strategy. **29.** The Government published its Surrogacy Arrangements Bill to outlaw commercial surrogacy agencies.

April 2. The Conservative Party suspended £30,000 in grants to the Federation of Conservative Students because of alleged serious vandalism during the students' conference at Loughborough University. **3.** The names of 12 new working peers were announced by the Prime Minister—six Conservatives, five Labour, and one S.D.P. **12.** Mr. Brittan, Home Secretary, announced there was to be a review of instructions to immigration officers. **14.** Mrs. Thatcher arrived back in London at the end of her 11-day tour of Asian countries and Saudi Arabia. **15.** The Government's Bill to ban commercial surrogate motherhood agencies and the advertising of surrogacy agencies was given a second reading in the Commons. **18.** The Foreign Office ordered two Russians—a diplomat and a manager of the airline Aeroflot—to leave Britain within seven days for spying; on April 22 the Soviet Union expelled three British diplomats in reprisal and it was disclosed in London that five, not two, Russian officials, had been ordered out of Britain earlier. **22.** In the Commons, a Labour motion accusing the Government of dismantling the welfare state was defeated by 276 to 167 votes.

May 1. A statement on the Defence Estimates, 1985, was published. **2.** Elections in 47 English and Welsh county councils resulted in a big swing to the Liberal-S.D.P. Alliance parties. **3.** The Speaker's chair was damaged in the Commons amid heated scenes involving M.P.s opposed to Mr. Enoch Powell's Bill to outlaw all scientific research on human embryos. **7.** The Government had two defeats in the Lords on the Bill to abolish the G.L.C. and the six metropolitan counties; the Government suffered another defeat on May 9. **9.** The Prime Minister announced changes in the procedures of the security services after informing the Commons that MI5 had made serious errors of judgment about Michael Bettaney, the counter-espionage officer who passed secrets to the Russians. **16.** The Home Secretary announced new police and court powers to combat violence at demonstrations, picket lines, and football matches. **17.** M.P.s gave a third reading in the Commons to a private member's Bill, which imposed fines of up to £2,000 on drivers who solicited women in their cars. **20.** A Government motion on the report of the Auld Committee of Inquiry on proposals to amend the Shops Act and its decision to reform the law on Sunday opening of shops was carried by 304 to 184 votes. **23.** The Prime Minister told the Commons that sterner penalties for drug traffickers and a law change to allow proceeds of trafficking to be confiscated were to be introduced; the Commons all-party Home Affairs Committee published an interim report on the drug menace facing Britain. **30.** It was announced the Government was giving £250,000 to the disaster fund set up by the Italian Government following the tragedy at the European Cup Final in Brussels.

June 3. Mr. Fowler, Social Services Secretary, published a Green Paper, "Reform of Social Security," which included the phasing out of the State Earnings Related Pension Scheme. Mrs. Thatcher and Zhao Ziyang, Chinese Prime Minister, signed an agreement at 10 Downing Street on economics and the peaceful use of nuclear power. **6.** The Prime Minister announced the Government had agreed to implement the pay increases recommended by review bodies for nurses, doctors, and dentists, and the Armed forces in settlements of nine per cent. for nurses in two stages, 6·4 per cent. for doctors and dentists, and 7·3 per cent. for the Forces. **11.** The British Labour group in the European Parliament voted to replace Mrs. Barbara Castle as their leader with Mr. Alfred Lomas. **17.** Mr. Tebbit, Trade and Industry Secretary, told the Commons he had cleared the British Leyland plan to proceed with a £1,800 million investment programme to ensure survival of Austin Rover and given approval in principle for a new collaboration agreement with Honda of Japan. **18.** Mr. Fowler, Social Services Secretary, announced that pensions, unemployment pay and most other social security benefits would rise by seven per cent. in Nov. but child benefits would rise by less than the rate of inflation and alterations in housing benefit rates would mean about two million householders would have smaller rates rebates. A Government motion approving the Green Paper proposals on the reform of social security was carried by 335 to 196 votes. **25.** Nineteen Tory M.P.s voted against the Government and a further 10 abstained in protest at the Bill to increase Britain's payments to the Common Market.

July 3. A Bill to ban the sale of alcohol at football grounds from the start of the new season was rushed through the Commons. Mrs. Thatcher and U.S. Vice-President, Mr. George Bush, launched a joint effort for stronger international action against terrorism after talks at Downing Street. **4.** The Liberal–S.D.P. Alliance won Brecon and Rad-

nor from the Conservatives in a by-election by 559 votes with Labour second. The Lords voted 108 to 104 in favour of the total abolition of corporal punishment in both State and independent schools. **8.** Britain lifted import restrictions against Argentina. **15.** The Government's Bill to abolish the G.L.C. and the six metropolitan county councils completed its passage when the Lords approved Commons amendments; it received the royal assent on the following day. **16.** A Government White Paper setting out measures by which it was proposed to ease the burden on businesses was published. **17.** Mr. King, Employment Secretary, announced the Government was to remove the rights of Wages Councils to set minimum pay for workers under 21 and reduce their powers to fix adult rates. **18.** The Prime Minister announced pay increases ranging from 5·1 per cent. to 48 per cent. for "top people," the rises averaging 17·6 per cent. for senior service officers, 16·3 per cent. for judges, and 12·2 per cent. for senior civil servants. **22.** Peers voted in favour of continuing the experimental televising of their proceedings. **23.** Mr. Heseltine, Defence Secretary, announced the Government was to proceed with its plan to give the management of the naval dockyards at Rosyth and Devonport to commercial contractors. A motion in the Commons to approve the raising of the Lord Chancellor's salary resulted in a large-scale revolt by Tory M.P.s, the Government order being carried by a majority of only 17. **24.** The Commons Foreign Affairs Committee published its report on its inquiry into the sinking of the Argentine cruiser *General Belgrano.* **25.** Mr. Jenkin, Environment Secretary, announced the present system of targets and penalties to control local authority expenditure would not apply next year and the aggregate Exchequer grant to local authorities would be £11·8 billion, the same as the current year's settlement. **29.** The Government was defeated in the Lords when an Opposition amendment to a motion to accept the recommendation to raise the Lord Chancellor's salary was carried by 140 to 135 votes, a majority against the Government of five; the amendment expressed regret at the Government's "insensitive" pay decision.

Aug. 6. A joint Labour–T.U.C. document— "A new partnership—a new Britain"—was launched.

IRELAND

(See also "Crimes, Trials, etc.")

(1984) Sept. 14. Power supplies in the Republic were back to normal following widespread cuts on Sept. 13 in a dispute over new shift rosters for workers at generating plants. **18.** Ten loyalist hunger strikers at Magilligan Prison, Co. Londonderry, who were demanding separation from Republican inmates, agreed to take minimum sustenance while negotiations continued with the Northern Ireland Office. **29.** An Irish Navy patrol boat seized a huge haul of weapons and ammunition being smuggled from the U.S.A. to the I.R.A. when it forced an Irish trawler, the *Marita Ann*, to stop off the south-west coast of Ireland.

Nov. 1. The report of an independent inquiry on Northern Ireland, headed by Lord Kilbrandon, was published.

(1985) Jan. 22. The Duchess of Kent arrived in Ulster for a two-day visit.

Feb. 19. The Dublin Parliament rushed through legislation enabling the Eire Government to seize I.R.A. funds held at a bank in the Republic. **20.** A government bill to legalise over-the-counter sales of contraceptives in the Republic passed through the Dail by a majority of three votes.

Mar. 15. It was announced that the Irish Government had stepped in to rescue the Insurance Corporation of Ireland from collapse.

April 16. The annual report of the Chief Constable of the Royal Ulster Constabulary disclosed that terrorism fell in Northern Ireland last year to its lowest level since 1970. **30.** Dr. Garret FitzGerald, the Irish Republic's Prime Minister, made a surprise visit to Londonderry.

May 8. Princess Anne began a visit to Northern Ireland. **16.** District council elections in Northern Ireland resulted in Sinn Fein winning 59 seats.

July 14. Two days of violent clashes in Northern Ireland while security forces organized an operation to prevent Orangemen parading through a Catholic area of Portadown, Co. Armagh, left 53 policemen and some 19 civilians injured with 48 arrests.

Aug. 14. The Irish Government ordered a year's pay freeze from Jan. 1986 for public service workers in the Republic.

ACCIDENTS AND DISASTERS

(1984) Sept. 1. Up to 1,000 people were believed to have died in the worst tropical storm in the Philippines for years. **8.** Two more deaths brought the total to 24 from the outbreak of food poisoning at the Stanley Royd psychiatric hospital in Wakefield, W. Yorks.

Oct. 2. One person was drowned and five others were missing after a pleasure launch hired for a birthday party collided with a barge on the River Elbe in Hamburg. **11.**

Three people died and 18 were injured in a rush-hour rail crash involving a crowded commuter train and a freight train at Wembley Central station. **15.** Official sources in Dacca stated that floods in Bangladesh had killed more than 700 people. **19.** According to reports in Moscow, an Aeroflot airliner had crashed into a fuel tanker in Omsk killing all 150 people on board.

Nov. 19. A total of 473 people died and another 1,300 were missing in a Mexico City suburb after a gas plant explosion. **23.** Hundreds of passengers were evacuated from Tube trains after fire broke out at Oxford Street underground station.

Dec. 3. A leakage of poisonous gas from an American-owned pesticide factory at Bhopal in India caused some 2,500 deaths and thousands suffered injury. **4.** Two people died and more than 70 were injured when a passenger express ploughed into the rear of a train hauling tankers of fuel oil at Salford, Greater Manchester; leaking fuel exploded into a fireball destroying the first two coaches of the passenger train. **11.** Nine people died in a pile-up of 22 vehicles in fog on the M25 between Godstone, Surrey, and Sevenoaks, Kent. **20.** A goods train was derailed in a tunnel under the moors on the Lancashire-Yorkshire border and fuel tankers exploded. **26.** It was reported that at least 17 people, eight from one family, had died in Britain in fires at their homes over Christmas.

(1985) Jan. 9. Twenty-four old people died when a fire swept through a home in a village near Beauvais in northern France. **10.** Eight people were killed and seven injured when a gas explosion wrecked a block of flats at Putney Hill, west London; six firemen were also injured during rescue operations. **11.** Three American soldiers died when a missile burst into flames as it was being unpacked at a U.S. camp, north of Stuttgart. **17.** It was reported from Ethiopia that over 400 people had been killed when a train plunged into a ravine.

Feb. 10. Nine people died on the M6 motorway in Staffordshire when swirling snow suddenly reduced visibility, causing a pile-up of lorries and cars. **11.** In W. Germany, nineteen people died, 17 of them R.A.F. bandsmen, when their bus collided with a petrol tanker north of Munich; on Feb. 14 the number of dead bandsmen rose to 19. **19.** An Iberia Airlines Boeing 727 crashed near Bilbao in Spain killing all 148 passangers and crew. **25.** Twenty-two French miners were killed in an explosion at a pit in the Lorraine basin.

Mar. 27. More than 40 schoolchildren died when a bus burst a tyre and fell into a dam near Johannesburg. **30.** Four people were killed when the hovercraft *Princess Margaret* crashed against a breakwater in gale-force winds in Dover harbour.

April 27. Eighty people died and many were injured when a fire gutted a mental hospital in Buenos Aires.

May 6. Four boys in a Buckinghamshire school party were drowned when they were swept into the sea at Land's End. **9.** Twelve people were killed including five children, when the roof of an indoor swimming pool collapsed near Zurich. **11.** Fifty-three soccer spectators died and over 200 were injured when fire swept through the main stand at Bradford City's football ground during the match with Lincoln City; the death toll subsequently rose to 55. **17.** More than sixty coal miners were killed in a gas explosion in Hokkaido, Japan. **25.** Thousands of people died when a cyclone and tidal waves struck the coast of Bangladesh. **26.** Thirty-four people were killed when two oil tankers exploded at the Spanish port of San Roque. **29.** Seven Britons, including five children, died in a school holiday coach crash in the South of France.

June 23. An Air India jumbo jet disintegrated as it plunged into the sea about 120 miles off Ireland and all 327 people on board were killed, the plane having taken off from Montreal for London and Bombay.

July 8. Eight people were killed when the Le Havre–Paris express train hit a lorry on an unmanned level crossing in Normandy. **19.** Water and mud from a burst dam swept down the Fiemme valley in northern Italy killing many people and destroying hotels and homes; on July 31, the number of bodies recovered reached 232 with another 38 missing, presumed dead.

Aug. 3. Thirty-five people were killed when two trains collided in the Lot region of central France. **12.** A Japanese Boeing 747 with 509 pasengers and 15 crew crashed and burst into flames on a remote wooded mountainside 70 miles north-west of Tokyo; it was the worst disaster in aviation history involving a single plane; on Aug. 13 rescue teams discovered four people still alive—the only survivors. **15.** The nine members of the crew of the *Virgin Atlantic Challenger* were rescued when the catamaran powerboat was holed while attempting the fastest sea crossing of the Atlantic; the crew were picked-up from their life-rafts 130 miles west of Land's End. **22.** Fifty-four people died and 83 escaped when a British Airtours Boeing 737 burst into flames as the pilot aborted its take-off for Corfu at Manchester Airport; two firemen were also hurt; on Aug. 28, the death toll rose to 55 when an injured man died in hospital. **31.**

Forty-three people were killed when an express train jumped the rails south of Paris and was struck by a train travelling in the opposite direction.

CRIMES, TRIALS, ETC.

(1984) Sept. 4. A terrorist car-bomb explosion in the crowded centre of Newry, Co. Down, injured 71 people. **10.** John Eadie, a rapist, who terrorised Southend for eight years and who admitted raping six women and girls and committing indecent assault on two other women, was jailed for life at Chelmsford Crown Court. **11.** Dr. Brian Richards was sentenced.to four years in prison in California for soliciting the murder of Mr. Peter Stephan, his colleague in a Harley Street clinic, his bail being continued while he pursued an appeal. **14.** Arthur Hutchinson, the wedding-night killer of a bride's father, mother, and brother and the rapist of her sister, was given three life sentences at Durham Crown Court for the murder of the three members of the Laitner family in Oct. 1983 and eight years for rape with five years for aggravated burglary; the judge recommended that he served a minimum of 18 years.

Oct. 4. A sea-going vessel, several small boats, and two lorries were seized in a police and Customs raid on a gang trying to unload a large quantity of cannabis on the River Crouch, Essex. **9.** Steven Korser-Acquah, aged 22, and Derrick Rossi, aged 29, both from Tottenham, convicted of attempting to murder a policeman when fleeing from a £35,000 bank robbery in Bristol city centre in April 1983 and of attempting to wound another policeman with intent to resist arrest, were each jailed for life at the Central Criminal Court; they were cleared of attempted murder or wounding of a third police officer. **10.** Two men were sentenced to life imprisonment (one of them recommended to serve 20 years) in Glasgow High Court for murdering a family of six in Glasgow's so-called "ice-cream war" and four other men were jailed for their parts in the violence. **12.** Sir Anthony Berry, M.P. for Enfield Southgate, was one of four people who were killed in an I.R.A. terrorist bomb attack on the Grand Hotel, Brighton, headquarters of the party leaders at the annual Conservative conference; among the injured in the attempt to assassinate the Prime Minister and members of the Cabinet and Government were Mr. Norman Tebbit, Trade and Industry Secretary, and his wife, Mr. John Wakeham, Government Chief Whip, whose wife was one of the dead, and Sir Walter Clegg, M.P. for Wyre and his wife; on Nov. 13 the death toll rose to five when Mrs. Muriel McLean, wife of the Scottish Conservatives' president, died. **19.** The jury hearing the case at Southwark Crown Court against

Dr. Keith Hampson, a Conservative M.P., failed to reach a verdict on a charge of indecently assaulting a police constable and they were discharged; on Oct. 25 the prosecution said it was dropping the retrial and the judge directed a verdict of not guilty be recorded. **28.** Six kilograms of pure heroin worth up to £4 million on the addicts' market were seized by Scotland Yard's Drugs Squad in London. **30.** A Libyan believed to be a senior officer in Col. Gaddafi's secret service, had been deported, it was confirmed by the Home Office.

Nov. 2. Three robbers who tortured a London newsagent and his wife were jailed for 18, 15 and 13 years respectively at the Central Criminal Court for what the judge called "unspeakable offences which make the blood run cold." Velma Barfield, who killed her mother, her boyfriend, and two others with arsenic, was executed by lethal injection in North Carolina, the first woman to be executed in the U.S.A. for 22 years. **14.** John Gibson, an Ulster Volunteer Force terrorist, who turned "supergrass", was given concurrent jail sentences totalling 1,762 years at Belfast Crown Court for 143 crimes including the murders of four Roman Catholics. **26.** Roy Garner, of Southgate, a businessman stated to have masterminded a £2,200,000 gold tax fraud, was jailed for four years, fined £150,000, and ordered to pay £90,000 costs at the Central Criminal Court. **30.** Two striking miners, aged 20 and 21, were charged with murdering Mr. David Wilkie who died when his taxi was hit by concrete as it passed under a bridge while he was driving a miner to work in south Wales; a third striking miner was later charged with the murder. A letter bomb addressed to the Prime Minister at Downing Street was intercepted by a Post Office sorter in Nine Elms, south London.

Dec. 2. Michael McAvoy, aged 32, and Brian Robinson, aged 41, both from south London, were found guilty of Britain's biggest robbery of £27 million in gold bullion and other valuables from a Brink's Mat warehouse near Heathrow; on the following day they were jailed for 25 years each. **3.** George Best, the former footballer, was freed on bail by a High Court judge pending his appeal against a 12-week prison sentence for a drink-driving charge, assaulting a policeman, and failing to answer bail; on Dec. 17 his appeal was dismissed. **4.** Vincent Evans, who terrorised the town of Newport for three months, was jailed for life at Cardiff Crown Court after admitting rape, and one charge of attempted rape, indecent assault and common assault. **7.** Stacy Keach, an American actor, was jailed for nine months at Reading Crown Court after he admitted smuggling £4,500 worth of cocaine into Britain. **11.** Three I.R.A. gunrunners were each jailed for 10 years in Dublin; they had been captured on board the trawler *Marita Ann* in Sept. (*see* "Ireland"). **14.** Mr. Arthur Scargill, N.U.M. President, was fined £250 with £750 costs in court at Rotherham for obstruction while picketing. A British soldier, Pte. Ian Richard Thain, aged 19, was found guilty at Belfast Crown Court of murder during the course of his duty; he was jailed for life for murdering Thomas Reilly, road manager of a pop group, in August 1984. **17.** Colin Evans, of Reading, killer of four-year-old Marie Payne, was jailed for at least 30 years after pleading guilty to the murder at the Central Criminal Court. **18.** Belfast Crown Court acquitted 35 people implicated in alleged terrorist crimes on the evidence of an informer. **20.** Eight people involved in a Mafia-backed V.A.T. plot which defrauded the Customs and Excise of £3·9 million were jailed at the Central Criminal Court to terms ranging from six years to six months. **23.** Fifteen people were killed when a terrorist bomb exploded aboard a train travelling from Naples to Milan. **24.** Dominic McGlinchey, Ireland's most wanted terrorist during nearly seven years on the run, was jailed for life at Belfast Crown Court for the murder of Mrs. Hester McMullan in 1977.

(1985) Jan. 7. Nine striking miners were jailed at Derby Crown Court for setting fire to N.C.B. buses used to take working miners across picket lines; one received three years for arson and the others and a farm-worker two-and-a-half years. **11.** A striking miner was sentenced to five years' jail and another to three years' youth custody after being convicted at Chelmsford Crown Court of attacking a policeman on picket duty. **14.** Allan Pearey, aged 35, of Kidbrooke, was jailed for life at the Central Criminal Court after admitting six rapes and four indecent assaults between April 1983 and July 1984. **17.** Two unarmed soldiers and a retired major were murdered after a Land-Rover carrying a £17,000 Army pay roll was ambushed in the Pentland Hills south of Edinburgh. It was announced that Richard Haynes, who stole art treasures from stately homes, had been jailed for 15 years. **22.** Raymond Williams, a senior civil servant at the Ministry of Defence in Bath, was convicted at Bristol Crown Court of selling Ministry documents to a newspaper and was jailed for six months. **24.** Four striking miners who carried out a £75,000 arson attack on coaches used to convey working miners through picket lines were each jailed for two years at Stoke-upon-Trent Crown Court; a fifth miner was given two years' youth custody. **28.** Three life sentences were passed on Peter Murray, aged 36, of Cheadle Heath, at Manchester Crown Court for his part in the murder of two teenagers at a Peak District beauty spot near Buxton, Derbyshire, in 1983; three other members of Murray's gang were each given three life sentences also.

Feb. 1. A leading West German industrialist died in Munich after being shot in the head by Red Army Faction terrorists. **4.** Two Kashmiri students were found guilty at Birmingham Crown Court of murdering an Indian diplomat kidnapped and shot dead in the Midlands a year ago; on Feb. 7 they were jailed for life and three other men received prison sentences ranging from 20 years to two years. **7.** Two senior secret policemen charged with the murder of the pro-Solidarity priest Father Jerzy Popieluszko were each given maximum 25-year jail sentences in Poland. **11.** Clive Ponting, a senior civil servant at the Ministry of Defence, who admitted leaking documents on the sinking of the Argentinian cruiser *General Belgrano*, was cleared by a jury at the Central Criminal Court of breaching the Official Secrets Act. **12.** Alexander Barak, an Israeli businessman and the kidnap gang leader, was jailed for 14 years at the Central Criminal Court after he and three other men admitted kidnapping and drugging Mr. Umaru Dikko, former Nigerian transport minister. **14.** Ian Botham, the England cricketer, was fined £100 at Scunthorpe after admitting possessing cannabis. **18.** Graham Backhouse, a Cotswold farmer, who tried to kill his wife in a car bombing for £100,000 insurance money and later shot dead a neighbour as a scapegoat for the explosion, was jailed for life at Bristol Cown Court after a jury found him guilty of murder and attempted murder. **20.** Three Libyan students were given jail sentences ranging from 12 to 5 years at Manchester Crown Court after being found guilty of plotting and causing explosions in Manchester in March 1984. **21.** Northern Ireland's fifth informer trial collapsed when a judge at Belfast Crown Court rejected the evidence of a Loyalist "supergrass". **22.** Kevin Kearsley, who terrorised women in the bed-sit area of East Oxford for six months in 1984, was jailed for 16 years at Northampton Crown Court for rape, indecent assault and burglary. **23.** A bomb exploded in the Paris branch of Marks and Spencer, killing one person and injuring 15 others. **26.** Malcolm Fairley, the hooded rapist known as "The Fox", who terrorised villagers in five counties, was sentenced to six life terms and a total of 82 years' jail at St. Albans Crown Court; he admitted three rapes, two indecent assaults, three aggravated burglaries and five burglaries. **28.** Nine members of the Royal Ulster Constabulary were killed when the I.R.A. launched a mortar attack on the police station in Newry, Co. Down; about ten R.U.C. personnel and civilians were seriously injured.

Mar. 7. Two Provisional I.R.A. terrorists, Paul Kavanagh and Thomas Quigley, members of a unit which carried out a month-long bombing campaign in London in 1981, were jailed at the Central Criminal Court for a minimum of 35 years on their five life sentences for murder; Natalino Vella, who pleaded guilty to acting as quartermaster to the unit, was jailed for 15 years. **8.** Peter Hogg, former airline pilot, was jailed at the Central Criminal Court for killing his wife, whose body was dumped in Wast Water in the Lake District in 1976; acquitted of murder, Hogg was convicted of manslaughter and received three years with another 12 months consecutively for obstructing a coroner and committing perjury in divorce proceedings begun after his wife's death. **11.** Four leaders of a gang who forced prostitutes throughout the country to work for them were jailed for from seven years to 2½ years at the Central Criminal Court. **12.** A Libyan student, who took part in a weekend series of bombings in London a year ago, was jailed for 15 years at the Central Criminal Court. **21.** A football hooligan who kicked a rival supporter in the face was jailed for five years at Swindon Crown Court. **22.** James Baigrie, a murderer on the run from jail, shot himself in a van in Earl's Court, London, where he had been beseiged by police who exploded two tear-gas canisters under the vehicle. **28.** Three men were sentenced to death in Dublin for the machine-gun killing of a policeman during an I.R.A. post office robbery in the Irish Republic last year; a fourth man was found guilty of common murder which is not subject to the death sentence. Maurice Beckford, who battered his four-year-old stepdaughter to death after starving and torturing her for ten months, was jailed for 10 years for manslaughter at the Central Criminal Court; his common law wife, Beverly Lorrington, was sentenced to 18 months for wilful neglect and cruelty to her daughter.

April 2. Stephen Korsa-Acquah and Derek Rossi, already serving life sentences for shooting a policeman in the face, were each given two more life sentences at the Central Criminal Court and prison terms totalling 425 years for a series of hold-ups and use of guns. Two of West Germany's most notorious Left-wing terrorists, Brigitte Mohnhaupt and Christian Klar, were given multiple life sentences in Stuttgart for a series of murders of prominent West Germans in 1977. **3.** Five Kent miners who fire-bombed the yard of a haulier were jailed for three years at Chelmsford Crown Court. **12.** A terrorist bomb in a restaurant outside Madrid killed 18 people and injured over 80. **25.** A striking Yorkshire miner who set fire to the home of a strike-breaker was jailed for three years at Wakefield Crown Court.

May 10. One of three miners accused of killing taxi-driver David Wilkie as he took a working miner to his pit during the coal strike, was cleared of murder on the direction of the judge at Cardiff Crown Court; on May 16, the other two miners, Dean Hancock and Russell Shankland, both aged 21, of Rhymney, Mid-Glamorgan, were jailed for life after being found guilty of Mr. Wilkie's murder. **17.** Cpl. Andrew Walker, of the Royal Scots, was jailed at Edinburgh High Court for a minimum of 30 years for machine-gunning three other soldiers to death in a payroll robbery in January on the Pentland Hills south of Edinburgh. **20.** Four young members of the Royal Ulster Constabulary, including a woman police constable, were killed when their armour-plated car was blown to pieces by an I.R.A. bomb hidden in a lorry trailer only yards from the Irish border near Newry. **21.** Twenty-five soccer hooligans, supporters of Cambridge United, were sentenced to terms ranging from five years' jail to five months' youth custody at the Central Criminal Court.

June 7. John Knight, of Wheathampstead, Herts, and Terence Perkins, of Enfield, were convicted at the Central Criminal Court of being part of the armed gang who carried out the £6 million Security Express raid in London two years ago; on June 10 they were jailed for 22 years. **10.** In a Rhode Island court, Claus Von Bulow was acquitted of twice trying to murder his heiress wife with injections of insulin. **14.** Walter Fraser, of Muswell Hill, London, one of the leaders of a worldwide drug-smuggling ring, was jailed for 24 years at the Central Criminal Court after being found guilty of conspiring to handle and supply cocaine. At Belfast Crown Court, six Loyalist terrorists from the Ulster Volunteer Force were jailed for life for their parts in five sectarian murders. **19.** Three people, two of them children, were killed when a bomb exploded at Frankfurt Airport. **23.** Forty minutes after a Canadian Pacific Boeing 747 carrying 390 people landed from Vancouver at Narita airport in Japan a bomb exploded in a container loaded with cases from the plane. An I.R.A. bomb planted in the Rubens Hotel in Buckingham Palace Road, London, was defused after a tip-off to police. **24.** Anti-terrorist branch detectives questioned suspects after uncovering a plot by the I.R.A. to plant bombs in hotels at 12 seaside resorts and ferry terminals at the height of the holiday season; on June 25, Sir Kenneth Newman, Metropolitan Police Commissioner, was placed in overall command of the search operation for the bombs and 15 of 21 people arrested during the past few days were being held for questioning concerning the seaside bombing campaign, last Oct.'s Brighton bombing, and other terrorist attacks; on June 29. Patrick Joseph Magee, from Belfast, was charged with murdering five people in an explosion at the Grand Hotel, Brighton; six people were also charged with him in connec-

tion with terrorist related offences. **26.** Michael Burke, of Cork City, a former Irish soldier, was jailed for 12 years at Dublin's Special Criminal Court for his part in the kidnap of Mr. Don Tidey, head of a stores group. **28.** Christopher Ogleton, a 17 year-old from East Dulwich, who inflicted serious injuries with a butcher's knife on a police constable when robbing a sweet shop, was sentenced to nine years youth custody at the Central Criminal Court.

July 1. Several people were injured when a bomb exploded at Rome's Leonardo da Vinci airport. A terrorist explosion killed a woman and injured 28 people at British Airways sales office in Madrid. **2.** Anti-terrorist detectives gave the all-clear to the 12 seaside towns in Britain which had been faced with the threat of an I.R.A. bomb campaign. **5.** Five men involved in an attempt to smuggle 4½ tons of cannabis resin worth £10·8 million into Britain were jailed at Chelmsford Crown Court for terms of 5 to 10 years. **10.** Four men were jailed at Birmingham Crown Court for their part in an international conspiracy to smuggle military components to South Africa. **12.** Mr. Noel Fellowes, a former policeman who served four years of a seven-year jail term for killing a coin dealer in 1970, was declared innocent in the Court of Appeal which quashed his conviction for manslaughter and set aside the sentence. **22.** Three members of a Jewish underground group were sentenced to life imprisonment in Jerusalem after being found guilty of killing Palestinians in the Israeli-occupied West Bank. Robert Drew, aged 35, of Ropley, Hants, who shot a policeman, kidnapped two others and held a solicitor and his family hostage was jailed for 18 years at Lewes Crown Court. **25.** Andrew Neil, the 20-year-old father who murdered his baby daughter Tyra Henry, whose body was covered in human bite marks and who had massive brain injuries, was jailed for life at the Central Criminal Court. **31.** Susan Stock, and her boyfriend, Malcolm Poole, who lived in Birkenhead, were sentenced to life imprisonment at Liverpool Crown Court for the murder of four-year-old Christopher Stock, who was stated to have been bitten and battered in his last six weeks of life. Two men whose bull terrier bitches were matched against each other in an illegal dog fight ending in the death of one of the animals were given custodial sentences of two months at Cheshunt.

Aug. 9. Peter Brophy, of Hammersmith, on trial with his wife at the Central Criminal Court accused of assaulting their six-month-old child, who was blinded in his right eye and suffered damage to the other, leapt to his death from a multi-storey car park shortly before he was due to reappear at his trial; later, charges against his wife were dropped.

14. Three anglers were each fined £20 at Alnwick court for digging for bait in a nature reserve on the Northumberland coast. **24.** A five-year-old boy was shot dead during a police raid on a flat in Birmingham; the raid was one of three in the Birmingham area which followed an armed robbery at a South Wales restaurant. **28.** An East German couple living in London were remanded in custody on charges under the Official Secrets Act and other charges relating to false passports.

ECCLESIASTICAL

(1984) Sept. 9. The Pope arrived in Quebec for a 12-day visit to Canada.

Oct. 4. Statistics published by the General Synod of the Church of England showed that the number of clergymen was less than half of what it was 100 years ago. **15.** The Pope ruled that the old Latin Mass ceremony might again be legally used in churches provided Roman Catholics asked their bishops to reinstate it.

Nov. 14. The General Synod of the Church of England voted in favour of a resolution calling for legislation to achieve the ordination of women as priests.

(1985) Jan. 26. The Pope began a two-week Latin American tour.

Feb. 13. The Church of England General Synod accepted the Bishops' recommendation that decisions on church marriages for divorcees be left to the parish priest, who should consult with his bishop; the Synod also debated "the nature of Christian belief" in which discussion revolved around the public views of the Bishop of Durham (Rt. Rev. David Jenkins) on the Virgin Birth and the Resurrection.

April 24. Herr Honecker, the East German President, had an audience with the Pope in Rome. **29.** It was announced that the Church of England's first black bishop to serve in Britain was to be the Ven. Wilfred Wood, who was to be consecrated Bishop of Croydon.

May 12. The Pope started a four-day visit to the Netherlands followed by a two-day visit to Luxemburg.

July 2. The Church of England General Synod approved by a majority vote in all three of its houses to allow women to be ordained as deacons. **3.** The Methodist Conference accepted overwhelmingly a report which rejected Freemasonry and decided that Masonic lodges would no longer be allowed to hold meetings on the Church's premises. **4.** It was reported that after 30 years in prison, Ignatius Gong Pinmei, the former R.C. Bishop of Shanghai, had been released. **14.** It was announced that Miss Vivienne Faull, a dea-

coness, had been appointed the first woman college chaplain at Cambridge University.

Aug. 8. The Pope began a seven nation African tour.

EDUCATION

(1984) Oct. 31. British companies pledged about £15 million to set up a new university, the Institute of Information Technology, at Milton Keynes.

Nov. 15. Local authority education leaders published a plan for reforming the teaching profession.

Dec. 18. The Government allocated £620 million for 1985–86 for polytechnics and colleges of higher education.

(1985) Jan. 4. Sir Keith Joseph, Education Secretary, outlined proposals to improve the standard of teaching in schools and colleges. **10.** A new qualification for 17-year-olds known as the Certification of Pre-Vocational Education was published. **29.** Oxford University dons voted overwhelmingly not to grant an honorary doctorate to Mrs. Thatcher.

Mar. 14. The report of the inquiry into the education of children from ethnic minority groups under Lord Swann's chairmanship was published. **15.** A standard criteria agreed by the examination boards, the Secondary Examinations Council, and the Education Secretary for the new G.C.S.E. test on a national basis was published. **26.** A White Paper was published, outlining changes in education designed to give parents more influence, improve teaching and discipline, and reform the examination system.

May 18. Dr. Robert Morris, an American psychologist, was appointed Britain's first professor of the paranormal by Edinburgh University. **21.** A Green Paper, "The Development of Higher Education into the 1990s," was published by the Dept. of Education and Science. **23.** In a major report, the Government's school inspectors warned that school buildings in England were reaching a crisis point of neglect and bad repair.

ENVIRONMENT AND LOCAL AFFAIRS

(1984) Sept. 6. The Commons Environment Committee reported that Britain's power stations were responsible for a "plague of acid rain" across Europe. **17.** The first of the companies granted pilot cable television licences for new areas went into action in Swindon.

Nov. 21. The report of the Government committee of inquiry into shopping laws was published and recommended the end of all legal restrictions on shop opening hours and Sunday trading. **28.** The Government published a consultative document on the future of dog licensing.

Dec. 13. The Post Office announced there would be a freeze on basic postal charges at least until Sept. 1985. The Environment Secretary (Mr. Jenkin) announced that the London Zoo, which was facing bankruptcy, would receive grants totalling £8,750,000 over the next three years.

(1985) Jan. 16. The Docklands Development Corporation announced a £1 billion scheme to build a new city five miles from the centre of London. **21.** A D.H.S.S. report dealing with cot deaths was published. **22.** The Medical Research Council announced a system to license the work carried out in test-tube baby clinics and to check all laboratories carrying out experiments on human embryos. **24.** Mr. Jenkin, Environment Secretary, announced that proposals to store radio-active waste at Billingham, Cleveland, had been dropped.

Feb. 20. Mr. Clarke, Health Minister, announced that AIDS was not to be made a notifiable disease but that health authorities would be given powers to detain victims in exceptional circumstances. **26.** The Environment Secretary announced the setting-up of five city action teams with the aim of promoting more effectively the different Government programmes in the inner city partnership areas.

Mar. 7. After a record 340 days, the Sizewell B nuclear power station public inquiry ended at Snape Maltings, Suffolk. **8.** It was announced that a £9.5 million gallery of modern art was to be established in restored dockland buildings in Liverpool. **10.** The G.L.C. voted to set a legal rate of 33.92p. **11.** It was announced that prescription charges for N.H.S. medicines were to rise by 40p to £2 an item from April 1 with increases also being made in the cost of dental treatment and charges for private treatment in N.H.S. pay beds. **15.** The Public Health Service Laboratory announced a £4 million programme to test all two million blood donors for the disease AIDS.

April 12. Haringey Borough Council became the first of the rate-capped Labour authorities to announce a legal rate and a legal budget. **18.** Mr. Jenkin, Environment Secretary, announced that five city action teams had been formed to deal with dereliction and unemployment in inner cities. **24.** Labour-controlled Manchester City Council voted to abolish the ceremony, pomp, and

pageantry of the office of Lord Mayor while retaining the title in name only. **25.** The Nature Conservancy Council announced three new national nature reserves in Scotland at Dunnet Links and Blar nam Faoileag, Caithness, and Cragbank Wood in the Borders.

May 13. An outbreak of Legionnaire's Disease in Staffordshire claimed two more lives to bring the death total to 36 with a further 68 patients still being treated for symptoms. The Department of Health ordered a review into the sale of human kidneys for transplant operations. **21.** Councillor Mohammed Ajeeb became Britain's first Asian Lord Mayor when he took office in Bradford.

June 27. It was disclosed that one of the best-preserved Bronze Age buildings found in Britain had been discovered by a team of archaeologists at Flag Fen on the outskirts of Peterborough.

July 3. Lambeth council voted by a majority of one to set a legal rate. **23.** The Post Office announced a 1p cut in basic second-class letter prices from Nov. **25.** The report was published of the National Federation of Housing Association's inquiry into British housing, chaired by the Duke of Edinburgh. **26.** The Transport Secretary (Mr. Ridley) announced in the Commons his decision that the by-pass round Okehampton in Devon would be built to the south of the town through Dartmoor National Park.

FINANCE

(1984) Sept. 8. Mexico said it had reached agreement with creditor banks for stretching out repayment of most of its foreign debt over 14 years at lower interest rates. **18.** Chile devalued the peso by 19 per cent.

Oct. 1. The Bank of England acquired Johnson Matthey Bankers after a special accountants' investigation had revealed an estimated £150 million worth of loan losses. **16.** Norway cut charges for North Sea oil by $1–$1.50 a barrel; on the following day the British Government approved a cut of $1.35 a barrel. **17.** Sharp falls in share prices and sterling were recorded in London; on the following day the pound fell to a new low of $1.1860 and Nigeria cut its crude oil by $2 to $28 a barrel; on Oct. 19 stocks and shares rallied strongly in London but the pound closed at its lowest ever all round level. **25.** Lloyds Bank announced it was opening selected branches on Saturdays. **29.** Members of O.P.E.C. meeting in Geneva agreed to an 8½ per cent. production cut in efforts to avoid a price war.

Dec. 2. It was announced that the £3·9 billion issue of British Telecom shares was four times oversubscribed with applications worth £16·5 billion being made for the 86 per cent. of the stock on offer to British investors with 2,060,000 members of the public making applications; 7,500 applicants seeking to buy batches of more than 100,000 shares had been squeezed out completely. **18.** It was announced that the Trustee Savings Bank was to be sold to the private sector. **20.** Saleninvest, one of the world's largest shipping companies, filed for bankruptcy in Stockholm.

(1985) Jan. 1. The Israeli State Controller blamed the collapse of the country's stock exchange on illegal share manipulation by major banks. **4.** P. & O. sold its five-ship English Channel car ferry fleet for £12,500,000 to European Ferries. **11.** The clearing banks raised base lending rates one per cent. to 10½ per cent. **14.** The Government took emergency action to stop the fall in the value of the pound by the first use of minimum lending rate since it was suspended in 1981; a 1½ point rise in bank base rates to 12 per cent. followed. **18.** It was announced that home loan rates were to rise by between one per cent. and 1¼ per cent. in February. **21.** The Israeli budget was presented for the first time in American dollars instead of shekels. **28.** Bank base rates were increased to 14 per cent.

Feb. 11. The pound fell below $1.10 for the first time in London as the dollar reached new heights against most major currencies; on Feb. 12 the pound closed at a new low of $1.0870; on Feb. 13 it closed at $1.0860, on Feb. 25 at $1.0560 on Feb. 26 at $1.0535 after earlier falling to $1.0360; on Feb. 27 large sales of dollars by European central banks sent the U.S. currency into free fall with the pound jumping more than five cents before closing in London at $1.09. **28.** ICI reported a profit of £1,034 million for 1984.

Mar. 6. The Midland Bank reported a drop from £225 million to £135 million in its 1984 pre-tax profits after losing £222 million in America through its Californian subsidiary, Crocker National. **18.** The closure of 70 savings banks in Ohio, U.S.A. was extended for a further 48 hours to enable the state legislature to devise a plan to strengthen the institutions after the crisis in the past week following a multi-million-dollar run on deposits; on Mar. 15 the Governor had ordered all savings banks with funds covered by state insurance to close their doors for three days. **19.** The Chancellor of the Exchequer presented his Budget in the Commons (*see* **"Parliamentary Summary"**). **20.** Bank base rates were cut by half a point to 13½ per cent.; there was a further cut to 13 per cent. on Mar. 28. **22.** The building societies announced increases in the mortgage rates of one per cent. to 14 per cent. from April.

April 3. Barclays and Midland banks reduced their base lending rates by ¼ of a percentage point to 13¾ and a further half per cent. on April 12. **18.** Bank interest charges in the Irish Republic were cut by 1¼ per cent. **19.** Inflation rose to 6·1 per cent. in the year to mid-March. Nat West and Lloyds cut their base lending rates by ½ per cent.

May 8. British Airways announced a record operating surplus for 1984–85 of £315 million. **16.** Bolivia devalued its currency by 40 per cent. **17.** The yearly inflation rate rose to 6·9 per cent. in May. The U.S. Federal Reserve Board cut its discount rate from 8 per cent. to 7·5 per cent., the lowest for seven years. **25.** It was confirmed that the Lear Fan executive jet aircraft project in Northern Ireland had collapsed with the loss of £57 million of public money.

June 1. Poland devalued its currency by 13·2 per cent. **7.** A £200 million rescue operation was launched by the Hong Kong Government to halt a major banking crisis developing in the colony. **14.** The annual rate of inflation rose to seven per cent. **20.** The Chancellor of the Exchequer (Mr. Lawson) proposed major changes in banking law following the collapse of Johnson Matthey.

July 10. World-wide demand for sterling forced up the pound to $1·40, its best level since May 1984. **12.** The Nationwide and Woolwich building societies confirmed their intention of merging. British Airways and 11 other air companies agreed to pay £35 million to Laker Airways' creditors to halt legal action in the U.S.A.; Sir Freddie Laker was offered nearly £6 million on condition he dropped all claims against the firms. British Petroleum and Esso cut 6p a gallon from their four-star petrol with Shell following suit. **15.** The clearing banks in London reduced base rates by a half per cent. to 12 per cent. Western creditor nations gave Poland until 1996 to repay instalments on its foreign debt. **17.** Mr. Lawson Chancellor of the Exchequer told the Commons the City of London Police had been called in to investigate the affairs of Johnson Matthey Bank. **20.** The Italian Government announced the lira was to be devalued by six per cent. within the European Monetary System and the other currencies in the system would be revalued by two per cent. **23.** British Gas reported a £200 million drop in annual profits. **25.** An immediate cut in mortgage rate was announced for new borrowers by the Halifax and the Abbey National building societies, the basic rate dropping from 14 per cent. to 13¼ per cent. **26.** The Post Office made record pre-tax annual profits of £163,800,000. **29.** The National Coal

Board's annual report and accounts disclosed that more than £2·6 billion was provided by the Government to see the industry through the pit strike.

Aug. 1. In its annual report, the Electricity Council revealed that extra costs resulting from the coal strike were just over £2,200 million otherwise the industry would have produced an operating profit of £702 million. British Airports Authority reported a record annual profit of £72 million. **13.** The bonus to be paid for the three-year term of Mr. Ian MacGregor as chairman of British Steel before he became chairman of the National Coal Board was fixed by the Government at £875,000. The world's largest operator of shipping tankers, the Sanko Steamship Company of Japan, collapsed financially. **15.** Building societies announced a reduction in mortgage interest rates by 1¼ per cent. from the start of Sept. **25.** Israel decided to change its currency with the new money to be called the new shekel with its value equal to 1,000 old shekels.

LABOUR AND TRADE UNIONS

(1984) Sept. 3. The T.U.C. conference opened in Brighton and voted to give total support to the N.U.M. in its dispute with the N.C.B., but leaders of the steel and electricity supply workers said their members could not and would not accede to the demand not to cross miners' picket lines; on the following day, Mr. Kinnock, the Labour Party leader, told conference that the miners' case "must be put without violence". **4.** Mr. Norman Willis was elected to succeed Mr. Len Murray as T.U.C. General Secretary. An arbitration committee recommended a 5·1 per cent. pay rise for teachers in England and Wales who had claimed a substantial increase on the employers' offer of 4·5 per cent. Unions representing Britain's ambulancemen accepted a 4·5 per cent. pay rise back-dated to April. **14.** Coal strike settlement talks collapsed after a week-long series of meetings between the N.C.B. and N.U.M. **18.** Transport union port delegates voted to call-off the dock strike after 22 days during which resistance by many dockers had prevented the full national stoppage planned by union leaders. **21.** The steel unions rejected the N.U.M.'s appeal to stop production. **28.** Leaders of nine electricity supply unions decided in London they were unable to reach a joint decision on support for the miners; the pit deputies' union, N.A.C.O.D.S., announced an 82·5 per cent. vote for all-out strike action.

Oct. 3. The 14-week Cammell Laird sit-in at Birkenhead ended as the remaining men surrendered to police and a bailiff at the shipyard; they were taken to Walton jail to join others who were arrested on Oct. 1 to

serve a 28-day sentence for contempt in defying a High Court order. N.A.C.O.D.S. presented a set of proposals to A.C.A.S. aimed at ending the coal strike. **4.** Unemployment in Sept. rose to 3,283,640. **15.** Talks aimed at ending the pit strike collapsed after four days of negotiations between the N.C.B. and N.U.M. at A.C.A.S.; on the following day, leaders of N.A.C.O.D.S. decided to call their members out on strike from Oct. 24. **18.** British Rail's corporate plan forecast a reduction in staff of 13,000 by 1990. **19.** Electricians in power stations voted to reject the T.U.C.'s policy of "total support" for the N.U.M.'s strike. **20.** The N.C.B. announced it had appointed Mr. Michael Eaton as a new co-ordinator to take charge of communications and publicity during the miners' strike. **23.** Union negotiators agreed a 7·2 per cent. pay deal with local authority employers for 40,000 firemen. **24.** The threatened strike by members of N.A.C.O.D.S. was called off when the union executive unanimously voted to accept peace terms offered by the N.C.B. The T.U.C. general council voted to rejoin the National Economic Development Council. **31.** Talks between the N.C.B. and the N.U.M. collapsed after 10 hours at A.C.A.S.; on Nov. 2 and Nov. 3 the N.C.B. offered pre-Christmas pay incentives to induce striking miners to return to work.

Nov. 5. It was stated that the London Ambulance Service's closed shop had been abolished because fewer than 85 per cent. of union members voting in a secret ballot supported it. **9.** It was reported that 2,200 miners had returned to work during the week. Jaguar car workers voted to accept a revised 22 per cent. pay offer and call off their nine-day old strike. **13.** The Electrical, Electronic, Telecommunications and Plumbing Union decided to accept Government money for postal ballots. **15.** Union negotiators for Ford's car workers accepted a seven per cent. pay offer. **19.** A record 2,282 striking miners returned to work; it was also stated that in the previous week 5,016 miners had returned. **20.** Miners' leaders in north Wales declared officially they could no longer back the strike, saying their members had "voted with their feet" and returned to work. **21.** N.U.M. leaders had talks in York about the miners' strike with church leaders. The Austin Rover pay strike was called off after workers at Longbridge, Birmingham, the last plant on strike, voted overwhelmingly to return. **30.** The N.C.B. said 15,505 members of the N.U.M, including white collar staff, had returned to work during Nov. with N.U.M. members now working at 146 of the 174 pits.

Dec. 3. An emergency delegate conference of the N.U.M. decided to continue its defiance of the courts and called on the T.U.C. general council to "mobilise industrial action" in support; on Dec. 6, the T.U.C. reaffirmed its support for the striking miners but drew back from offering any assistance which might place it in contempt of court. **17.** Computer staff at the D.H.S.S. offices in Newcastle-upon-Tyne and Washington, Tyne and Wear, who had been on strike for seven months over new shift-working patterns and had disrupted payment of pensions and child benefit, voted to return to work in the New Year. **20.** Delegates representing the Nottinghamshire miners voted overwhelmingly to place their coalfield outside the control of the N.U.M. and its disciplinary rules. **28.** A strike by 270 sewing machinists which stopped Ford car production for over a month ended when the strikers accepted a peace formula to take their demand for re-grading to independent arbitration.

(1985) Jan. 10. The N.U.M. executive decided that all its members should be involved in future strike negotiations. **14.** A pay settlement of just over 5 per cent. was agreed between the Engineering Employers' Federation and union leaders. **17.** A one-day strike called by the N.U.R. and A.S.L.E.F. in the Midlands in protest against alleged victimisation of men blacking coal trains caused disruption to British Rail services. **21.** Local government white collar workers were awarded pay increases of between 4.6 per cent. and 5.6 per cent. by A.C.A.S. **24.** Dockers at Southampton accepted wage cuts and lower manning levels to end a three-month dispute which threatened to close the port's container terminals. **28.** Teachers' union leaders rejected a four per cent. pay rise and an offer of immediate arbitration from their local authority employers during talks in London. **29.** Members of the A.U.E.W. voted to accept Government funds to pay for ballots. **31.** Unemployment rose by 121,552 in Jan. to a new record of 3,340,958.

Feb. 1. The N.C.B. decided to withdraw from any further informal discussions to try to find a basis for peace talks in the pit strike because the N.U.M. would not accept a commitment to close uneconomic pits. **8.** N.C.B. stated that 3,754 miners had returned to work in the last week. The *Daily Mail* resumed publication in London after a three-day stoppage involving the clerical chapel of S.O.G.A.T. **19.** The Prime Minister met T.U.C. leaders at Downing Street to discuss the miners' strike and then Mr. Walker, Energy Secretary, consulted with Mr. MacGregor, N.C.B. Chairman, before inviting the T.U.C. monitoring group to his Department; on Feb. 20, N.U.M. leaders unanimously rejected new peace proposals negotiated between the N.C.B. the T.U.C., and the Energy Secretary; on Feb. 21, miners' delegates voted unanimously to continue the strike; on Feb. 22, the N.C.B. stated 2,278 miners had returned to

work for the first time during the week; on Feb. 25, there was a record one-day return to work of 3,807 miners, the Nottinghamshire area of N.U.M. scrapped the national ban on overtime, and union leaders in South Wales, Durham, and Northumberland decided to discuss calls for a general return; on Feb. 27, the N.C.B. stated the gross total of working miners had reached 93,500, or more than 50 per cent. of the workforce; on Mar. 1, the N.C.B. reported the week's total of strikers returning to work was 9,456; on Mar. 3, delegates of the N.U.M. voted 98 to 91 to return to work on Mar. 5 without a settlement with the N.C.B.; the Prime Minister and the N.C.B. said they would not consider a general amnesty for those miners dismissed during the dispute and that there was no question of re-employing pickets convicted of crimes of violence and of serious damage to N.C.B. property; on Mar. 5, the N.C.B. stated that 85 per cent. of its workforce had reported for work; Scottish miners voted on Mar. 6 to return and in Yorkshire all but two of the area's pits were working; on Mar. 26, the result of a ballot among N.U.M. members on a proposed 50p-a-week levy to support the men dismissed during the strike was: 50,429 (46 per cent.) in favour, 58,721 (54 per cent.) against. **26.** Industrial action over teachers' pay began and the N.U.T. staged the first of its strikes.

Mar. 1. Members of SOGAT '82 employed on national newspapers voted to accept a five per cent. pay offer backdated to Jan. 1. **5.** Farm workers were awarded a pay rise of 8.5 per cent. overall. **26.** Production of *The Sun* newspaper was resumed after settlement of a dispute which had stopped its publication since Mar. 19. **28.** The N.U.M. executive decided to recommend that the 17-month overtime ban be called-off.

April 1. Disruption of postal services began when 800 staff at London's Mount Pleasant sorting office ignored a High Court injunction and walked out in protest at the introduction of new technology; on the following day the postmen called off their action and returned to duty in compliance with a legal order obtained by management; on April 5 the Union of Telecommunication Workers' national executive accepted management's package proposals on technology, productivity, and manning. **2.** The National Union of Railwaymen and A.S.L.E.F. accepted a 4·85 per cent. pay offer. N.U.M. delegates voted 122 to 74 to call-off their 17-month overtime ban. **10.** Members of the Civil and Public Services Association voted narrowly not to strike in support of their pay claim. **18.** Miners' leaders decided to accept two missed annual pay offers of 5·2 per cent. each. **20.** Post Office workers began clearing a backlog of 20 million letters held-up by unofficial strike action by the Union of Communication Workers which had begun in Northampton a week ago over payments for delivery of local election polling cards; staff returned to normal working on April 21. **22.** Nissan, the Japanese motor vehicle manufacturer, made an agreement to give the A.U.E.W. sole bargaining rights at its new assembly plant in Washington, Tyne and Wear. Decisions to increase the number of teachers' strikes and other disruptive action were taken by the two biggest teachers' unions. **25.** The national executive of the T.G.W.U. voted to hold a new election to choose its next general secretary following allegations of ballot-rigging in the previous poll which elected Mr. Ron Todd. Ford sewing machinists learned their jobs were to be up-graded on the recommendation of an independent arbitration panel. **28.** A 5·6 per cent. pay deal in the water industry was accepted in a ballot of the General, Municipal, Boilermakers and Allied Trades Union.

May 1. An independent inquiry found clear evidence of ballot rigging in last year's election for the general secretaryship of the T.G.W.U. **15.** Plans were announced to reduce the number of workers at British Rail's manufacturing and repair workshops by 4,800 before March 1987. **16.** Pit deputies voted to impose an immediate national overtime ban because they claimed the N.C.B. had reneged on an agreement during the miners' strike that no pit would be closed without going through a revised colliery review procedure. **17.** The N.U.R.'s national executive committee voted unanimously to call out its members working on the London Underground despite a High Court injunction ordering the union not to strike until a ballot of affected members had been held; on May 20, the union ended its strike after only 12 hours when thousands of its members ignored the stop-work call. **24.** The Coal Board stated it was to cut 2,500 jobs in the Doncaster area by March 1986.

June 6. Plans were announced by the N.C.B. for a £450 million pit employing more than 1,800 men at full production in 11 years at a site west of Coventry. **8.** British Rail announced it was to abolish its closed shop deal with the unions. **15.** Mr. Ron Todd was again elected general secretary of the T.G.W.U. in a fresh ballot. **25.** The N.U.R. decided to hold ballots of members before calling strikes.

July 1. Mr. Scargill, N.U.M. president, told the union's annual conference in Sheffield that the decision to return to work without an agreement at the end of the year-long strike was a fundamental mistake; conference overwhelmingly endorsed the union's tactics including its refusal to call a national ballot; more than £2,500,000 of the N.U.M.'s assets

sent to Ireland before the strike was returned to Britain at the request of the union. **3.** The N.U.M. conference confirmed the dismissal of Mr. Roy Lynk, leader of Nottinghamshire miners, as a national official of the union. Postal workers balloted to support a package of productivity changes including acceptance of new technology and more part-time staff. **4.** Mr. Scargill became president for life of the N.U.M. when conference delegates voted by the necessary two-thirds majority for rule changes. **6.** Leaders of Nottinghamshire's miners voted overwhelmingly to breakaway from the N.U.M. and to form their own union. **12.** The employers' negotiating team made an improved pay offer to give all teachers a rise of just over 7·5 per cent. by the end of their pay year next April with over 11 per cent. for those at the bottom of the scale.

Aug. 2. A new union of miners independent of the N.U.M. was formed in the Nottinghamshire and South Derbyshire areas and the Durham miners' association. **5.** Sir Keith Joseph, Education Secretary, offered teachers £1,250 million spread over four years in addition to any pay deal negotiated in an effort to break the deadlock on pay. **7.** British Steel Corporation confirmed the closure of the Gartcosh rolling mill, near Ravenscraig, Scotland. **13.** British Rail threatened to dismiss 270 guards who had been on stike in South Wales and Scotland over one-man trains which with local stoppages and work-to-rule sanctions had disrupted passenger and freight services for five weeks. **14.** Mr. Raymond Chadburn was dismissed as president of the breakaway Nottinghamshire Union of Mineworkers for his failure to support the area's policy during and after the pit strike. **19.** A wildcat strike by some Southern region rail guards affected thousands of London commuters; staff walked-out in protest over the dismissal of 233 strikers in Glasgow and South Wales; on Aug. 20 talks between British Rail and N.U.R. on driver-only trains and reinstatement of dismissed guards collapsed; on Aug. 28 the result of the ballot of guards was announced with 4,815 (52·5 per cent.) voting against strike action over the introduction of driver-only trains and 4,360 (47·5 per cent.) for. **29.** The T.U.C. general council instructed the Amalgamated Union of Engineering Workers not to apply for any more Government money for secret ballots. **30.** Mr. Robert Maxwell, publisher of Mirror Group Newspapers, said he had decided it was no longer possible to print any of its newspapers at its London Headquarters and announced he was to sell the *Sporting Life*, which was at the centre of a lengthy dispute with the National Graphical Association; publication of the *Mirror* and other M.G.N. titles had been stopped for the past 10 days.

LEGAL

(1984) Sept. 21. Sequestrators of assets of the south Wales miners union were given authority in the High Court to pay contempt of court fines from union funds in a Sheffield bank. 26. A High Court judge in Manchester gave a group of workers until midnight on Sept. 30 to end their sit-in at Cammell Laird's Birkenhead shipyard or face a month in jail for contempt; on Oct. 10 an appeal by the Official Solicitor against the sentences was dismissed by three Appeal Court judges. 28. In two separate decisions, a High Court judge granted miners in Yorkshire and Derbyshire injunctions declaring strikes in those areas unlawful and restraining union officers there from claiming the strike to be official; the judge ordered elections to be held for branch officials in Yorkshire and banned the N.U.M.'s new disciplinary committee from acting against any Derbyshire or Yorkshire miner. The Employment Appeals Tribunal ruled that a trade unionist who was deeply dissatisfied with his union's performance had the legal right to resign from it even if a closed-shop agreement was in operation.

Oct. 4. Contempt of court proceedings brought by two Yorkshire miners against the N.U.M. and its president, Mr. Scargill, were adjourned by a High Court judge to give Mr. Scargill and the N.U.M. time to reflect on their position; on Oct. 10, the judge imposed fines of £200,000 on the N.U.M. and £1,000 on its president for contempt of court. 9. The Queen's Bench Divisional Court in London upheld the legal validity of the Lion Intoximeter 3000 breath test machine. 22. The South African Government forfeited £400,000 bail when four of its nationals failed to appear at Coventry magistrates' court to answer arms smuggling charges. 25. Sequestration of all the assets of the N.U.M was ordered by the High Court after the union's failure to pay a £200,000 contempt of court fine. The Law Lords by a majority of one rejected an appeal by the *Guardian* newspaper against the court order which forced it to reveal the name of the Foreign Office "mole", Sarah Tisdall. 26. Capt. Kent Kirk, a Danish trawler-owner, fined £30,000 last year for fishing within the British 12-mile limit, had his conviction quashed on appeal at the Central Criminal Court and the money returned to him.

Nov. 1. The High Court ruled that a motorist who refused to provide a breath specimen for analysis in a police station could be convicted under drink-driving laws even if he claimed he was wrongly arrested and was not driving. 5. Assets of the N.U.M. totalling £2,785,000 were temporarily frozen in an Irish bank account on the orders of a Dublin High Court judge. 12. Three Bromley schoolgirls made legal history when the local

council agreed to pay them £351 each in compensation for sexual discrimination in the classroom. 14. A High Court judge ruled that Labour-controlled Hackney Borough Council acted unlawfully when it banned a Liberal councillor from sub-committee meetings and documents. 22. Five Law Lords unanimously dismissed the trade unions' case for the lifting of the ban on their operating at G.C.H.Q. 26. The High Court imposed a fine of £200,000 on the Transport and General Workers' Union for contempt of court in defying court orders to call off the Austin Rover strike. 30. In the High Court, a Derbyshire solicitor, Mr. Herbert Brewer, was appointed receiver of the entire assets of the N.U.M.; on Dec. 1, three Appeal Court judges unanimously rejected the N.U.M.'s appeal against the appointment of a receiver; on Dec. 7, Mr. Michael Arnold, a City of London chartered accountant, took over as receiver.

Dec. 11. The High Court ordered the unpaid £200,000 contempt of court fine imposed on the T.G.W.U. should be collected by the Queen's Remembrancer. 19. The N.U.M. lost a High Court action to stop the union's Nottinghamshire area council from voting on proposed rule changes which would give the area union greater autonomy. 20. Mrs. Victoria Gillick won her Appeal Court action against girls under 16 being given contraceptives without their parents' consent.

(1985) Jan. 22. A test case brought by a striking miner to overturn the D.H.S.S. decision to stop £16 a week from supplementary benefit to strikers' families was refused a hearing by two High Court judges who said the claim should be made through the D.H.S.S.'s appeals process. 30. Nearly £5 million of the assets sent abroad by the N.U.M. was recovered by the receiver appointed by the High Court and part of the money was used to pay the £200,000 fine imposed on the union for contempt of court.

Feb. 11. A group of South Wales working miners were granted an injunction by a High Court judge to stop their local union from organising mass intimidatory picketing to the five pits where they worked.

Mar. 29. An industrial tribunal in Bristol ordered the T.G.W.U. to pay compensation to the three dismissed tugboat men; they had refused to rejoin the union when the national docks strike ended. A High Court judge found the actions taken to exclude the Professional Association of Teachers from Burnham Committee sub-committees "wholly unreasonable" and decided that the National Union of Teachers was "frustrating the intention of Parliament" by refusing to accept Association representatives on the sub-committees.

June 13. The High Court in London ruled that the police could legitimately stop motorists at random and prosecute them under the drink-driving laws. **24.** The National Graphical Association was fined £15,000 for contempt in the High Court for giving clandestine approval to the continued blacking of the Wolverhampton Express & Star group of newspapers in defiance of a court order. **28.** A High Court judge upheld the Football Association's ban on English soccer clubs playing in Europe following the Brussels tragedy.

July 10. The High Court rejected an application by the former general secretary and former president, Nottinghamshire area, N.U.M., which would have returned control of the area to the N.U.M. until its constitution could be revised by ballot. **23.** British Rail obtained a High Court order requiring the National Union of Railwaymen to lift an instruction to guards to refuse to work with 25 new rail buses. Mr. Patrick Hope-Johnstone, a Scottish landowner, was given the right by a decision of the House of Lords Committee of Privileges to use the title of the Earl of Annandale and Hartfell.

Aug. 1. Magistrates at Reading juvenile court made legal history by declaring that a baby born a "junkie" was ill-treated before birth because her drug-addict mother took drugs while pregnant. **30.** A judge in the Edinburgh Court of Session ruled that whooping cough vaccine could not be proved to have been the cause of severe brain damage which ruined the life of a four-month-old baby boy, now aged nine years.

SPORT

(1984) Oct. 21. Steve Jones, an R.A.F. corporal from south Wales, recorded a world best marathon in Chicago with a time of 2 hr. 8 m. 6 s.

Nov. 12. The West Indies became the first team in Test history to win nine consecutive matches when they beat Australia in Perth.

Dec. 8. With victory over Scotland at Murrayfield, Australia's touring rugby side gained its first grand slam in the British Isles. Stirling Albion beat Selkirk, an amateur side from the Borders, by 20 goals to nil in the first round of the Scottish Cup, the highest score in British football since 1887.

(1985) Jan. 2. The West Indies cricket team's run of 27 unbeaten Test matches ended in Sydney when Australia won the final Test of the series. **11.** The Football Association ordered a replay behind closed doors of the F.A. Cup-tie between Burton Albion, beaten 6–1 on Jan. 5, when their goal-keeper was knocked unconscious by a missile thrown from the crowd, and Leicester. **15.** Double centuries were scored by Graeme Fowler and Mike Gatting in the first innings of the fourth Test against India at Madras, the first time this feat had been achieved by two Englishmen in the same innings. **18.** Celtic football club were ordered to play their next home match against a European team behind closed doors and fined £17,000 by U.E.F.A. after attacks by their supporters on players from Rapid Vienna.

Feb. 12. The British Amateur Athletics Board announced it was to introduce an open register for athletes willing to have random drug tests and that only those who signed would be eligible for major competitions. **16.** Demonstrators forced Zola Budd to drop out of the English women's cross-country championships at Birkenhead by running on to the course.

Mar. 13. Hundreds of Millwall supporters ran riot at Luton's football ground and in the town itself after an F.A. Cup quarter final match during which the referee took the teams off the pitch for 25 minutes when Millwall fans spilled on to the field; 31 policemen and 16 other people were injured and thousands of pounds of damage was done to the ground and a soccer special train. **18.** The Football Association decided against closing Chelsea's ground following rioting a fortnight before. **29.** It was announced that the friendly football match between England and Scotland was to be moved from Wembley to Hampden Park.

April 1. At a meeting at 10 Downing Street chaired by Mrs Thatcher, measures were agreed to try to eliminate hooliganism at football matches. **6.** Henrietta Shaw became the first woman to cox Cambridge in the boat race. **9.** The Football Association fined Millwall £7,500 because of its supporters' violence in the March cup-tie with Luton. **21.** The London Marathon attracted a world record figure of 17,500 entrants. **23.** Princess Anne made her flat-racing debut at Epsom in an invitation event for charity and finished fourth.

May 9. Mr. John Smith, chairman of Liverpool Football Club, was appointed the new part-time chairman of the Sports Council. **11.** About 150 people, including nearly 70 police officers, were hurt during violent clashes at the Birmingham City versus Leeds football match in Birmingham and there were 125 arrests; on May 12, a 15-year-old boy died from injuries received after a wall collapsed. **13.** The Home Secretary announced that all third and fourth division clubs in the Football League would have to apply for safety certificates following the tragedy at Bradford. **18.** Kevin Moran of Manchester United became the first player in the history of the F.A. Cup Final to be sent off. **29.** Thirty-eight people died, many of them trampled to death, when a wall and a safety fence collapsed during rioting before the European Cup Final between Liverpool and Juventus in the Heysel Stadium, Brussels; 454 were injured; on May 31, the F.A. ordered the withdrawal of all English clubs from European competitions for the coming season; the Belgian Government banned all British football clubs from playing in Belgium; on June 2, U.E.F.A. announced that English football clubs had been banned from competing in Europe for an indefinite period; on June 6, F.I.F.A. banned English professional soccer clubs from playing anywhere outside England; on June 8, British Rail announced it was to stop running football specials for soccer fans and to end cheap excursion fares to fans travelling on scheduled services; on June 12, the Prime Minister met the F.A. and Football League at Downing Street to discuss soccer hooliganism; on June 20, Liverpool were banned by U.E.F.A. from all European club competitions for three seasons.

July 3. Football League clubs officially rejected the Prime Minister's plan for a national membership card scheme for supporters. **7.** Boris Becker, the 17-year-old West German, defeated Kevin Curren in the Wimbledon men's final to become the first unseeded champion and the youngest winner as well as the first German to take the title. **11.** F.I.F.A. lifted the world-wide ban on English football clubs who were now to be allowed to play matches outside Europe. **12.** The British Olympic Association decided unanimously that Birmingham should seek the nomination of the International Olympic Committee to stage the 1992 Olympic Games. **13.** An interim injunction in the High Court, Wellington, New Zealand, stopped the departure for South Africa of the All Blacks rugby union team; on July 14 the New Zealand R.F.U. announced it would not appeal against the decision. **24.** Mr. Justice Popplewell published his interim report on crowd safety at sports grounds. **29.** An F.A. disciplinary commission fined Birmingham City £5,000 following the riot with Leeds supporters at Birmingham in May.

Aug. 4. Steve Cram, the British athlete, broke the world 2,000 metres record in Budapest, his third world record in 19 days; he had previously broken the 1,500 metres and one mile records. **8.** Liverpool F.C. lost its appeal to U.E.F.A. against a three-year ban on taking part in all competition in Europe. **15.** David Robertson, the Scottish international golfer, who was disqualified from the Open Championship for incorrectly marking his ball on the greens, was fined £5,000 and suspended for 20 years by the P.G.A. European Tour.

TRANSPORT

(1984) Sept. 29. The last link of a new trans-Siberian railway was completed after ten years' work.

Oct. 4. British Rail announced it was to keep open the Settle-Carlisle Pennine route for at least the next five years. **5.** British Airways and British Caledonian agreed an exchange of routes to resolve the controversy between them over Government plans to review airline competition policy.

Nov. 15. The British and French Governments decided to form a new working party to consider schemes to be financed by private enterprise for construction of a Channel tunnel. **16.** British Rail announced that train fares were to rise by about 6½ per cent.

Dec. 10. The report of the inquiry into the future of Stansted and Heathrow airports was published. It was announced that the ban on smoking on the London Underground was to be extended to cover stations following a serious fire at Oxford Circus in Nov.

(1985) Jan. 10. Sir Clive Sinclair launched his electric C5 three-wheeler machine.

Mar. 21. The British and French Governments gave approval for a tunnel or bridge between the two countries.

April 12. London to Moscow Concorde flight.

May 23. Mr. Jenkin, Environment Secretary, gave outline planning permission for a Stolport—short take-off and landing airport—to be built in east London.

June 5. The Government White Paper on airports policy was published, dealing with the development, structure, ownership, and regulation of the regional and London airports, and with the announcement that Stansted was to be developed as London's third major airport.

July 1. British Rail's plan to reopen the Snow Hill tunnel under the City with direct electric trains between Southern and London Midland regions was given Government approval.

Aug. 27. The Civil Aviation Authority ordered immediate checks on airliners powered by engines similar to the one involved in the Manchester Airport disaster.

COMMONWEALTH

(1984) Sept. 4. Mr. Brian Mulroney's Progressive Conservative Party won a landslide victory in the Canadian general election. In Zimbabwe, Bishop Abel Muzorewa was released after 10 months' detention. **21.** Brunei was admitted to the United Nations.

Oct. 10. In Malta, a one-day general strike was widely observed in protest against Government's lock-out of teachers. **18.** Hong Kong's legislative council approved the Sino-British draft agreement on the Colony's future. **26.** A Royal Commission in Australia into drug-running and organised crime presented its report to the Federal and Victoria Governments. **31.** Mrs. Indira Gandhi, Prime Minister of India, was shot dead by two Sikh members of her bodyguard in New Delhi, and was succeeded by her son, Mr. Rajiv Gandhi; violence flared in cities across India following the assassination, with many deaths.

Nov. 20. A number of police and civilians died when Tamil separatists bombed a major police station in Sri Lanka's northern province of Jaffna. **25.** Canadian Government announced plans to reduce immigration to preserve jobs for Canadians. **27.** Two gunmen assassinated Mr. Percy Norris, the British Deputy High Commissioner in Bombay, who was ambushed and shot as he was being driven to his office, an extremist Islamic organisation claiming responsibility. The Foreign Secretary (Sir Geoffrey Howe) and the Spanish Foreign Minister reached agreement in Brussels for the future of Gibraltar which provided for the re-establishment of direct communications between the Rock and Spain on matters such as free movement of goods and traffic and airspace. **28.** In New Zealand, Sir Robert Muldoon was replaced as leader of the Opposition by his deputy.

Dec. 1. The Labour Government was returned to office in Australia's general election with a reduced majority. **2 to 10.** Increasing violence was reported from Sri Lanka stemming from Tamil separatist activities. **3.** The first general election since 1976 took place in Grenada with the New National Party led by Mr. Herbert Blaize winning 14 of the 15 seats. **14.** The first general election in Belize since independence resulted in victory for the United Democratic Party led by Mr. Manuel Esquivel. **20.** Mrs. Thatcher visited Hong Kong. **22.** Mr. Dom Mintoff resigned as Prime Minister of Malta. **24.** Polling in the Indian general election began; on Dec. 28 it was announced that Mr. Rajiv Gandhi's Congress(I) party had won 401 seats in a landslide victory.

(1985) Jan. 12. President Nyerere of Tanzania said he would not stand for re-election when his term expired at the end of the year.

Feb. 4. The border between Gibraltar and Spain was fully reopened at midnight. **12.** Mr.

Robert Oates, Canada's Defence Minister, resigned after it was disclosed that he had visited a strip club while in West Germany.

Mar. 2. Twenty people at least were killed in Eastern India when police fired on mobs and rival party workers who clashed during state elections. **12.** Mr. Bernard St. John took over as Prime Minister of Barbados following the death of Mr. Tom Adams. **21.** In a referendum in Bangladesh, Lt. Gen. Ershad received a vote of confidence and approval for his continuation in office as President. **28.** President Devan Nair of Singapore resigned after admitting he was an alcoholic.

April 5. Mrs. Thatcher arrived in Kuala Lumpur, Malaysia, at the start of her 11-day South-East Asia tour to seven countries. **8.** The Indian Government sued the Union Carbide Corporation in New York over the chemical leak which caused the Bhopal tragedy. **26.** Hundreds of people were reported killed in an outbreak of religious violence in Nigeria. **28.** The Maltese Government and the Vatican reached agreement on a settlement of the dispute which had effectively closed all Roman Catholic schools in Malta.

May 3. Nigeria opened its borders to allow Africans from neighbouring countries to begin leaving before the May 10 deadline banning illegal aliens. **10.** A wave of bombings in India killed 35 people as violence escalated; on May 12 the death toll reached 87 and police arrested over 1,000 people. **12.** Prince Andrew opened the new airport at Mount Pleasant on the Falkland Islands. **14.** Tamil guerrillas killed at least 86 Sri Lankan civilians when they opened fire on the streets of Anuradhapura; on May 15, the death toll reached 146.

June 21. The separatist Premier of Quebec Province, Mr. Rene Levesque, announced his resignation. **27.** Mr. Ian Smith, former Prime Minister of Rhodesia, retained his seat in the general election in Zimbabwe for white seats.

July 7. It was stated in Zimbabwe that Mr Mugabe's ruling Zanu–PF party had won 63 of the 79 contested common-roll seats in the general election. **8.** The Canadian Government banned its parliamentarians from accepting expenses-paid trips to South Africa. **21.** It was reported that 32 people were killed in clashes between communal groups and police in Gujarat, western India, bringing the death toll in the State through riots since last Nov. to more than 250. **24.** Mr. Gandhi, India's Prime Minister, and the leader of the Sikh party, Akali Dal, signed an agreement to end the political dispute in Punjab State; on July 26, the Akali Dal party called-off its three-year protest campaign and endorsed the agreement with Mr. Gandhi. **27.** The Ugandan Army's 10th Brigade seized the capital,

Kampala, in a *coup* which overthrew President Obote, who fled to neighbouring Kenya; on July 29, Maj.-Gen. Tito Okello, commander of the Army, was sworn-in as the country's new leader; on July 30 a military council was set up.

Aug. 6. Australia, New Zealand and six South Pacific island States signed the Treaty of Rarotonga declaring a nuclear-free zone covering most of the Pacific Ocean south of the equator. Mr. Desmond Hoyte, former Prime Minister, was sworn in as President of Guyana after the death on Aug. 5 of President Forbes Burnham. **15.** Vice-President Ali Hassan Mwinyi, President of Zanzibar, was chosen by Tanzania's ruling party to succeed President Julius Nyerere. Mr. Gandhi, Indian Prime Minister, signed an accord with militant leaders from Assam. **16.** An announcement in Canberra stated that Australia and Britain had reached agreement on severing their remaining constitutional links. The Indian Government banned the export of human skeletons. **17.** Ethnic violence erupted in Sri Lanka as talks between the Government and leaders of the Tamil separatists collapsed. **20.** In India, the Sikh leader, Sant Harchand Singh Longowal, was assassinated by four Sikh extremist gunmen hours after four other Sikhs shot and killed a leader of the ruling Congress(I) party. New Zealand's Minister of Finance announced taxation changes which included a 25 per cent. income tax cut. **27.** In a bloodless *coup* in Nigeria, a group of dissident Army officers seized power; on Aug. 31, the new Government released Mr. Graham Coveyduck, a British businessman held for a year without trial.

MIDDLE EAST

(1984) Sept. 13. In Israel, Mr. Shimon Peres, leader of the Labour Party, formed a government of national unity with the Likud front and a number of smaller parties; the government received a vote of confidence in the Knesset by 98 votes to 18 with one abstention; on Sept. 17 the shekel was devalued by 9 per cent. **20.** Several people were killed in a suicide car bomb explosion in Lebanon which wrecked the new U.S. Embassy building in East Beirut. **25.** Jordan and Egypt agreed to resume diplomatic relations.

Oct. 17. Mr. Peres, Israel's Prime Minister, set out terms for an Israeli withdrawal from Lebanon as the government in Beirut authorised direct negotiations between Lebanese and Israeli military officers. **23.** The Israeli Government accepted proposals to freeze wages, prices and taxes. **28.** The Foreign Secretary (Sir Geoffrey Howe) arrived in Israel for talks after an unscheduled visit to President Gemayel of Lebanon.

Nov. 23. The Palestine National Council meeting opened in Amman. **26.** President Mitterrand of France arrived in Damascus for a two-day official visit to Syria.

(1985) Jan. 3. It was disclosed in Jerusalem that thousands of Jews had been flown secretly to Israel from the famine-stricken areas of Ethiopia. **14.** The Israeli Cabinet approved a unilateral step-by-step withdrawal of troops from Lebanon; the withdrawal began on Jan. 20. **16.** Israel's four religious parties were defeated in an attempt to grant Israeli Orthodox rabbis the exclusive authority to determine who is a Jew. **20.** Four days of talks between the leaders of the Greek and Turkish communities in Cyprus ended in failure at the U.N. in New York.

Feb. 10. Israeli planes bombed a Palestinian guerrilla base in the Bekaa Valley after attacks on Israeli forces in south Lebanon; two car bomb explosions in Tripoli and Beirut killed 10 people. **11.** King Hussein of Jordan and Yasser Arafat, the P.L.O. leader agreed on joint political action to achieve Middle East peace.

Mar. 3. The Israeli Cabinet decided to start immediately the second stage of the withdrawal of its forces from Lebanon. **4.** Fifteen people were killed and 55 injured by a bomb which exploded in a Shi'ite village mosque in Israeli-occupied southern Lebanon. **8.** A huge car bomb killed 62 people in Moslem West Beirut and injured 200 more. **10.** Twelve Israeli soldiers were killed and 14 injured when a suicide attacker drove a truck packed with explosives into a convoy of troops being withdrawn from Lebanon. **13.** Christian militiamen broke away from the political wing of President Gemayel of Lebanon's Phalange party and sent their men onto the streets of East Beirut to seize control of many key points; on Mar. 16 Syrian troops and tanks moved into new positions in north Lebanon to support the Gemayel Government. **15.** Britain's Ambassador in Lebanon advised Britons to leave the country unless they had compelling reasons to stay after the kidnapping of a second Briton in 24 hours; on Mar. 18 the British Embassy closed its offices in West Beirut. **21.** Israeli troops occupied nine south Lebanon villages and killed at least 21 suspected terrorists. **22.** Gunmen kidnapped a French diplomat and two other French embassy employees in Moslem West Beirut in increasing violence against the dwindling foreign community in Lebanon; on Mar. 25 a third Briton was kidnapped.

April 17. At least 20 were killed in Beirut's heaviest inter-Moslem battle in more than a year. **21.** Israel's Cabinet decided that the final withdrawal of its troops from Lebanon would take place by the beginning of June.

22. An Israeli missile-carrying boat sank a terrorist ship off Tel Aviv. **28.** Druze and Moslem militias intensified their assault on Christian villages in south Lebanon capturing the main Beirut to Sidon coast road and driving thousands of families from their homes.

May 20. The three Israeli soldiers held prisoner by Palestinians since the invasion of Lebanon in 1982 were released in Geneva as part of an exchange for 1,500 Palestinian prisoners held by Israel. **22.** More than 50 people, including 15 children in a school bus, were killed by a car bomb in Beirut's Christian district. **26.** Hundreds of Palestinian families were reported to have fled from the fighting in the Beirut refugee camps under siege by Shi'ite Amal militiamen and Beirut hospital sources said 245 people had been killed and 1,000 wounded; on June 18, an agreement to end the siege was signed in Damascus.

June 7. Twenty-four Finnish soldiers serving with the United Nations force in Lebanon were captured by the Israeli-backed South Lebanese Army; the Finns were released, after Israeli intervention, on June 15. **10.** The Israeli Government presented its own plan for Middle East peace talks. **11.** Six Shi'ite Moslem gunmen hijacked a Jordanian jet at Beirut and demanded to be flown to Tunis; after two unsuccessful attempts to land at Tunis, they returned to Beirut where they blew-up the aircraft just after its passengers and crew had been released. **14.** A sky-jacked Trans World airliner with 145 passengers, mostly Americans, arrived back in Beirut from Algiers after a series of threats by three Shi'ite Moslem terrorists to kill hostages; the Boeing 727 with a crew of nine was seized during a flight from Athens to Rome and ordered to fly to Beirut where 19 American women and children were freed; later in Algiers a further 22 passengers including 17 American women and a child were released; the sky-jackers demanded the release of all Shi'ite Moslem prisoners in Israel; back in Beirut, the terrorists killed an American marine; on June 15, 109 people had been set free but with the plane at Algiers airport, 43 Americans were still being held hostage; on June 16, the plane was ordered to Beirut for a third time; on June 17, Mr. Nabih Berri, the Lebanese Shi'ite leader, said he had had the American hostages removed to a secret location in Moslem West Beirut; U.S. naval and marine forces moved into the eastern Mediterranean; on June 18, three more hostages were freed, including Demis Roussos, the Greek pop singer; on June 30, the 16-day ordeal of the hostages ended when they were freed in Beirut and driven in a Red Cross convoy to Damascus before flying to a U.S. air base near Frankfurt, West Germany, to be reunited with their families.

July 3. Israel released 300 Lebanese prisoners from Atlit detention camp in northern Israel. **16.** In Israel, a meeting between the Prime Minister, the labour leader, and employers' representatives resulted in a new contract with the private sector which averted a threatened general strike

Aug. 17. Fifty-four people were killed when a car bomb exploded outside a crowded supermarket on Christian East Beirut's waterfront with 120 others wounded, mostly women and children; on Aug 19, two car bombs exploded in Moslem militia-controlled neighbourhoods of West Beirut killing at least 31 people and wounding 90; on Aug. 20, factional warfare resulted in another 70 deaths with 250 wounded in Tripoli and Beirut and its suburbs; on Aug. 21, Christian and Moslem militiamen shelled rival neighbourhoods, killing 15 people.

U.S.A.

(1984) Sept. 24. President Reagan offered Russia to exchange long-range military plans and visits to each other's nuclear test sites. **28.** The President held talks at the White House with Mr. Andrei Gromyko, the Soviet Foreign Minister.

Oct. 4. The space shuttle *Challenger* lifted-off from Cape Canaveral with a record crew of seven, including two women, one of whom (Dr. Kathryn Sullivan) subsequently became the first American woman to walk in space.

Nov. 6. The presidential elections resulted in a landslide win for President Reagan who won 49 of the 50 States and 525 of the 538 electoral college votes, the remaining 13 going to Mr. Walter Mondale, the Democratic candidate; in the popular vote, Reagan polled 59 per cent. and Mondale 41 per cent. It was confirmed that the State Department in Washington had warned Russia against sending high-performance jet fighters to Nicaragua; on Nov. 9 the U.S.A. denied that it was embarking on an invasion of Nicaragua and Administration officials said the Russians had assured America there were no jet fighters aboard a Russian cargo ship in a Nicaraguan port. **8.** The space shuttle, *Discovery*, took off from Cape Canaveral; during its mission, two rogue satellites were salvaged. **19.** President Reagan ordered the closing of the anti-trust investigation into Laker Airways' bankruptcy.

Dec. 5. The President presented his Cabinet with a plan to cut $34 billion from domestic programmes in the Budget; on the following day he proposed a one year five per cent. pay cut for the Government's federal civilian employees. **13.** Britain's request for the extradition of an I.R.A. gunman (John Doherty) convicted of the murder of a British Army captain was refused by a federal judge in New York on the grounds that the killing was a "political" act. **19.** America confirmed it would withdraw from U.N.E.S.C.O. at the end of the month. The U.S.A. accused Soviet troops of conducting genocide against the Afghan people.

(1985) Jan. 3. The President announced an additional $411 million worth of emergency aid for African famine victims. **13.** The U.S. Navy announced plans to install 758 nuclear Tomahawk cruise missiles in 106 of its nuclear-powered hunter-killer submarines. **20.** President Reagan was sworn in for a second term at the White House. **24.** The space shuttle *Discovery* was launched from Cape Canaveral on a secret military mission. **30.** The U.S.A. reported a record trade deficit of $123.3 billion last year.

Feb. 5. The White House cancelled a naval exercise in the Pacific with Australia and New Zealand as a protest against the New Zealand Government's refusal of port facilities for a U.S. destroyer with a potential nuclear capability; on Feb. 7, President Reagan and Mr. Bob Hawke, Australian Prime Minister discussed the question of Anzus co-operation in Washington. **20.** Mrs. Thatcher addressed a joint session of Congress and later had talks with President Reagan.

Mar. 5. The Chief Minister of the British Caribbean colony of Turks and Caicos and another Minister were arrested on drug-related charges in Miami. Mr. Weinberger, U.S. Defence Secretary, suspended payments to the General Dynamic Corporation, the country's largest defence contractor, during a Pentagon inquiry into charges that the company billed the Government for improper expenses. **15.** Mr. Raymond Donovan, U.S. Secretary of Labour, resigned after being ordered by a judge to stand trial on fraud and larceny charges arising from when he was an executive with a construction company. **19.** The Senate voted to approve funds for 21 more MX nuclear missiles; the House of Representatives gave its approval on Mar. 26.

April 12. The space shuttle, *Discovery*, was launched from Cape Canavarel with Senator Jack Garn on board as the first civilian observer to travel in space; it returned on April 19. **26.** America announced the expulsion of a Soviet assistant military attache in retaliation for Moscow's refusal to accept the blame for the recent shooting of a U.S. Army major by a Russian sentry in East Germany.

May 1. An order banning all U.S. trade with Nicaragua and prohibiting Nicaraguan ships and aircraft from entering America was

signed by President Reagan. **2.** The Senate voted to freeze defence spending at its present level plus an allowance for inflation for the next three years; on May 23, the House of Representatives approved a defence budget of £775 billion for 1986, about the present level. **3.** Washington expelled four Polish diplomats in retaliation for Poland's expulsion of two American officials accused of taking part in a May Day protest by Solidarity supporters. **7.** The city of New York honoured its 250,000 Vietnam veterans. **27.** President Reagan opened a nationwide campaign to sell his new tax reform plan.

June 6. The Senate approved $38 million of humanitarian aid to the Nicaraguan "Contra" rebels over the next two years; on June 12, the House of Representatives approved similar aid of $27 million over the next nine months. **20.** The lifting by the House of Representatives of a 16-year ban on the production of chemical wapons was welcomed by the White House. **25.** Britain and the U.S.A. signed in Washington a treaty closing the loophole under which I.R.A. terrorists in America could avoid extradition to face trial by pleading their offences were "political". **27.** The House of Representatives gave the President authority to send troops into combat in Central America under certain conditions without first seeking Congressional approval.

July 1. President Reagan ordered measures to isolate Beirut Airport. **2.** The President welcomed home 30 of the U.S. hostages held in Beirut. A Nov. summit meeting between President Reagan and Mr. Gorbachev, the Soviet leader, was confirmed. **12.** The Senate voted 80 to 12 for anti-apartheid sanctions against South Africa, following a similar vote by the House of Representatives. **13.** President Reagan underwent an operation for the removal of a growth in his intestines; on July 15, doctors announced the tumour removed was malignant but they believed all of the cancer had been removed; on July 20, the President left hospital and returned to the White House. **23.** President Reagan interrupted his convalescence to welcome the President of China to the White House.

Aug. 1. The White House stated that President Reagan had had a patch of skin removed from his nose for testing to see if an infection was malignant; the President subsequently disclosed it was diagnosed as a mild form of skin cancer. The House of Representatives voted 380 to 48 for a Bill imposing economic sanctions on South Africa. **5.** President Reagan offered to join Russia in stopping all underground nuclear tests after the U.S.A. had concluded its current series of explosions. **14.** Mr. Bush, the U.S. Vice-President led a service of commemoration in

San Francisco to mark the end of the 1939–45 War and the 40th anniversary of the defeat of Japan. **20.** The U.S.A. announced it was to begin testing weapons targeted to destroy space satellites. **21.** The State Department accused the Soviet Union of spraying a chemical which might cause cancer on cars and other possessions of Americans in Moscow to enable secret police to keep track of them and their contacts.

COMMON MARKET

(1984) Sept. 17. Common Market grants to Britain totalling nearly £78 million were announced for road, rail, telecommunications and tourist developments.

Oct. 1. An agreement over the future control of Common Market expenditure was reached by E.E.C. finance ministers in Luxemburg, which effectively left budgetary control in their hands. **18.** The European Commission announced the release of £587 million as settlement of Britain's claim for a 1983 E.E.C. budget rebate. **22.** Foreign ministers of the E.E.C. agreed on a mini-package for Spain and Portugal's entry to the Common Market, but left open the issues of fishing and wine. **25.** The E.E.C. made an immediate grant of £1,800,000 to cover two months' famine relief work in Ethiopia.

Nov. 12. Britain was successful in its long campaign to control Common Market farm spending and limit the amount the E.E.C. could spend overall in any one year; E.E.C. finance ministers agreed on a detailed text which gave national treasuries the right to specify each year what the Community could spend. **23.** The Common Market reached agreement in Brussels on a new five-year trade and aid pact with Third World countries.

Dec. 4. At the E.E.C. summit meeting in Dublin, heads of government solved all technical problems for Spanish and Portuguese entry but Greece insisted on maintaining a right of vote over the applications; the summit leaders agreed on a new budgetary discipline for future years and pledged £275 million worth of food aid next year to feed famine victims in Africa.

(1985) Jan. 24. Another £226 million in grants to Britain were announced by the regional development fund of the Common Market.

Feb. 1. Greenland's withdrawal from the Common Market took effect.

Mar. 29. Foreign ministers of the E.E.C. agreed basic terms in Brussels under which

Spain and Portugal could join the Common Market.

April 24. Common Market budget ministers agreed to add £1·2 billion to the £16 billion budget they had agreed last year for 1985; an extra £1·8 billion had been requested by the Commission.

May 8. More than 30 Left-wing Euro-M.P.s walked out when President Reagan addressed the European Parliament.

June 12. Spain and Portugal signed the treaty of accession to the Common Market. The West German Government used its veto powers for the first time at an E.E.C. Farm Ministers' meeting in Luxembourg to block a planned 1·8 per cent. cut in Common Market cereal prices. **13.** Euro-M.P.s in Strasbourg approved a revised £16 billion E.E.C. budget for this year. **15.** The E.E.C. Commission in Brussels announced that Britain's contributions would be reduced by £800 million next year as a result of the automatic system of rebates. **28.** A campaign to defeat international terrorism was launched in Milan by the heads of the ten Common Market governments at the start of the E.E.C. summit meeting; on the following day, on a majority vote, it was decided to hold a conference on changes to the Treaty of Rome.

July 22. Common Market foreign ministers meeting in Brussels condemned the declaration of a state of emergency in South Africa.

AFRICA

(See also "Commonwealth")

(1984) Sept. 3. Fourteen people were killed when thousands of blacks rampaged in townships south of Johannesburg; on the following day the death toll rose to 26. **13.** Six Indian opposition leaders, freed from detention by order of a Natal supreme court judge on Sept. 7, took refuge in the offices of the British Consulate in Durban when fresh detention orders were issued; on Oct. 6 three of the men left the Consulate and were promptly arrested; the three remaining fugitives left the Consulate on Dec. 12, two of them being arrested. **14.** Mr. P. W. Botha formally took office as President of South Africa. **18.** Several black miners were killed in a clash with police near Johannesburg as President Botha opened the new tri-racial Parliament of South Africa. **24.** South Africa said it would not return to Britain four South Africans charged with attempting to smuggle weapons components in reprisal for refusal by the U.K. to order the removal of the six fugitives from the British Consulate in Durban. **25.** French and Libyan troops began withdrawing from Chad following an evacuation agreement reached the previous week in Tripoli. **26.** The South African Government freed five prominent anti-apartheid leaders from detention without trial. **28.** The Southern African bishops' conference in Johannesburg called for a commission of inquiry into the cause of recent unrest in the black townships.

Oct. 3. It was reported that South African troops would monitor an unconditional cease-fire in Mozambique between the Frelimo Government and the resistance movement. **23.** Seven thousand South African troops and police were deployed in a cordon and search operation of the black townships of Sebokeng, Sharpeville and Boipatong. **28.** The World Food Programme reported that a food crisis was developing in Chad which was the worst outside Ethiopia.

Nov. 2. An Ethiopian government minister said the food airlift to Ethiopia must continue for at least a year to keep millions from starvation. **6.** At least sixteen people died and many were injured during widespread unrest in South Africa's black townships. **12.** Morocco walked out of the African summit in Addis Ababa and withdrew from the Organisation of African Unity because of the decision to seat the Polisario guerrilla group at the conference. Western diplomats reported that the Ethiopian Government had suffered a serious reverse in Eritrea when rebels had wiped out a battalion of some 400 troops. **21.** It was revealed that a mass movement of people from drought-stricken regions of North Ethiopia to more fertile areas had been started by the military regime. **30.** Details were released of a five-year military co-operation agreement between Libya and Malta.

Dec. 29. Three Britons were among a group of 22 foreign hostages abducted by Unita guerrillas during an attack on a diamond mining town in north-east Angola; all the hostages were subsequently released on March 16, 1985.

(1985) Jan. 25. President Botha of South Africa announced proposals to increase the political, social and economic influence of the country's black population.

Feb. 5. Four Britons held as political hostages in Libya for nearly nine months were released in Tripoli and returned to the U.K. on Feb. 7 with Mr. Terry Waite, the Archbishop of Canterbury's special envoy who had negotiated to secure their freedom.

Mar. 21. South African riot police fired on a crowd of several thousand blacks, killing 19, as they marched to a funeral at Uitenhage.

April 6. Sudan's Army seized power in a bloodless *coup* and deposed President Numeiry. **8.** Somalia said it was restoring diplomatic relations with Libya. **15.** The South African Government accepted immediately the recommendations of a Parliamentary select committee that laws forbidding sex and marriage across the colour line should be abolished. **17.** The last of the South African troops in southern Angola withdrew to the border with Namibia; on April 18, it was announced South Africa would permit political parties in Namibia to form a transitional government while retaining its present powers over the territory.

June 11. The report of the judicial inquiry into the circumstances in which 19 blacks were shot dead in a funeral procession near Uitenhage in March was published and laid blame on South African police. **14.** Fifteen people were killed when South African troops attacked suburban homes in Gaborone, the Botswana capital. **17.** A transitional Government of national unity was installed in Namibia, but with South Africa retaining control over foreign affairs, defence, and internal security. **28.** The South African Council of Churches adopted a resolution supporting a campaign of civil disobedience.

July 5. It was stated that loyal Guinean troops had foiled an attempted *coup* by a former prime minister. **20.** President Botha declared a state of emergency in South Africa in 36 areas giving magistrates and police wide powers to deal with the wave of unrest and violence in the black townships; extended powers were also granted to the security forces; on July 21, police detained at least 113 people; the death toll in Durban's black townships rose to 42 on Aug. 9 as Zulu mobs continued to rampage through Indian areas and over 2,000 Indians and their families fled their homes and businesses; on Aug 11, three blacks including a policeman were burned to death in separate incidents and another three people were killed as the death toll rose to 65; on Aug. 15, President Botha in a speech eagerly awaited around the world made it clear he was standing firm on his previously-stated policies of gradual reform of apartheid and that the Government would not give in to outside demands.

Aug. 21. It was announced that Tunisia was to expel 253 Libyan nationals for "spying" after Libya had decided the previous week to expel 96,000 Tunisians. **28.** Four people were shot dead in one of Cape Town's black townships when a banned march to demand the release of the jailed black political leader, Nelson Mandela, was stopped by police and troops; there were also clashes between students and police; on Aug. 29, police engaged in pitched battles with youths in black townships around Cape Town and six people were killed; on Aug. 30, violence flared again in Cape Town's non-white suburbs bringing the toll of three days and nights of rioting to 28 dead and over 150 injured.

OTHER COUNTRIES

(1984) Sept. 4. Under Russian pressure, Herr Erich Honecker, the *East German* leader, cancelled his first visit to West Germany. **6.** Marshal Nikolai Ogarkov was unexpectedly replaced as Chief of the *Soviet* General Staff. **12.** President Mitterrand of *France* presented the draft budget for 1985 which provided for a five per cent. reduction in personal income tax. **18.** Western diplomats in Islamabad reported that 200 to 300 *Afghan* resistance fighters were killed in a Russian sweep of the Panjshir Valley, north of Kabul. **26.** In *Peking*, the chief Chinese negotiator, and Sir Richard Evans, British Ambassador, initialled the agreement to return Hong Kong to China in 1997.

Oct. 2. Three *Russian* cosmonauts returned to earth after a record-breaking eight months in space. **5.** *Argentina* ceded to *Chile* a dozen small islands off Tierra del Fuego; on Oct. 18 the two countries signed a peace pact over the future of the Beagle Channel. **10.** *Russia* signed a 20-year friendship treaty with *North Yemen*. The *French* Cabinet announced wives and children of foreign workers would no longer be admitted to France unless heads of families could furnish proof they could support them. **14.** *Russia* announced it had started fitting strategic bombers and submarines with cruise missiles. **15.** President Ceausescu of *Romania* arrived in Bonn for a three-day State visit to *West Germany*. **16.** According to Western diplomats in Kabul, the number of Russian troops in *Afghanistan* had risen by 30,000 in the last few days. *West Germany's* agricultural ministry published a report which stated more than 50 per cent. of the country's forest area had been visibly damaged by acid rain and air pollution. *El Salvador's* opposing factions agreed to set up a peace commission to try to end the five-year civil war. **17.** The *French* Government announced new measures to combat poverty with a new levy on private wealth. **18.** *Iran* launched a reportedly major offensive in the war with *Iraq*. **20.** A *Spanish* trawler sank off the Cornish coast after an *Irish* gunboat fired against it when it allegedly ignored instructions to heave-to; all 16 crew members were rescued. A document was published by Teng Hsiao-Ping, *China's* leader introducing economic reforms which abolished price controls, rejected Maoist theories of egalitarianism, and called for more enterprise. **23.** President Chernenko blamed bad management, waste and laziness as the causes of the *Soviet*

Union's poor agricultural performance. **25.** Power from the world's largest hydro-electric dam began to flow after inauguration by the Presidents of *Brazil* and *Paraguay* of the Itaipu dam on the Parana River.

Nov. 1. *Argentina* failed to secure E.E.C. support for a U.N. motion calling for negotiations on sovereignty of the Falklands. **2.** It was confirmed by the Kremlin that Stalin's daughter, Svetlana, who defected to the West in 1967, had returned to *Moscow*. **5.** Senor Daniel Ortega, leader of *Nicaragua's* Left-wing junta, declared himself the winner of the country's presidential election. Mr. Rifkind, Foreign Office Minister, made the first visit to *Poland* by a British Government Minister since martial law was declared in 1981. **11.** Two young deserters from the Soviet army in Afghanistan, who had been living in London since being granted political asylum in June, returned to *Russia*. **15.** President Mitterrand of France and Col. Gaddafi of Libya held a surprise meeting in *Crete* on troop withdrawals from Chad. Six Russian helicopters and several aircraft were shot down in *Afghanistan* last week according to Western diplomatic reports reaching Islamabad of guerrilla operations. **26.** President Chernenko had talks in *Moscow* with Mr. Kinnock, the Labour leader. **27.** *Russia* announced the largest increase since the 1960s in its official defence budget for 1985.

Dec. 1. Melanesian rebels unilaterally proclaimed the territory of *New Caledonia* independent of France. Cardinal Glemp, *Polish* primate, ordered a curb on political activity by Polish priests. **8.** The Common Market and 66 of the world's poorer countries signed a new trade and aid agreement in the Togo capital of Lomé. **11.** A *Belgian* terrorist group claimed responsibility for six bomb attacks on N.A.T.O. oil pipelines in Belgium which caused serious damage. **13.** The *Swiss* Parliament completed its approval of a Government proposal to apply to join the *U.N.* **18.** The U.N. General Assembly agreed to spend £62 million on a conference centre in Addis Ababa, *Ethiopia*. **19.** The *Chinese* leader, Teng Hsiao-ping, greeted Mrs. Thatcher in the Great Hall of the People in Peking where she and the Chinese Premier signed the handover document transferring Hong Kong to China; Mrs. Thatcher announced the Queen was to visit China, probably in the second half of 1986.

(1985) Jan. 2. A Russian missile strayed over *Norway* and *Finland* on Dec. 28, the Defence Ministry in Oslo stated, and was believed to have come down in Finnish Lapland; on Jan. 4, Russia apologised to both countries after admitting the missile might have flown over their territory. **8.** After talks between Mr. Shultz, U.S. Secretary of State, and Mr. Gromyko, Soviet Foreign Minister, in *Geneva*, it was announced that both countries had agreed to enter into full negotiations on nuclear and space weapons. **9.** Mr. Kinnock, the British Labour Party leader, arrived in *Nicaragua* to attend the inauguration of President Daniel Ortega; on Jan. 13, Mr. Kinnock and Fidel Castro, the Cuban leader, had talks in Managua. **15.** Sr. Tancredo Neves won a landslide election victory to become *Brazil's* first civilian president since 1964. **18.** President Mitterrand of France arrived in *New Caledonia* to discuss the independence of the French Pacific territory. **24.** A political controversy began in *Austria* after the Defence Minister personally received Walter Reder, a convicted war criminal, upon his return to Austria following his release from prison in Italy. **28.** A Royal Navy frigate was among six N.A.T.O. vessels which came under fire in *Lisbon's* harbour in an abortive terrorist attack.

Feb. 8. Sir Geoffrey Howe, Foreign Secretary began a visit to *Romania* and subsequently visited *Bulgaria*. **19.** Two-day talks on Middle East issues between delegations from the U.S.A. and Russia opened in *Vienna*.

Mar. 10. It was reported that hundreds of people had been killed in *Iraqi* missile, artillery and air attacks on *Iranian* towns and cities. President Karamanlis of *Greece* resigned after the Socialist party withdrew support for his re-election. Right-wing parties won big gains in local polls throughout *France*. **11.** Mr. Mikhail Gorbachev became head of the *Soviet* Communist party, being named as general secretary within hours of the announcement of the death of Mr. Konstantin Chernenko; on Mar. 13, world leaders attended the funeral of President Chernenko in Moscow. **12.** The arms control negotiations between the Russians and Americans began in *Geneva*. **15.** The *Belgian* Government announced that 16 U.S. cruise missiles would be deployed in Belgium on schedule before the end of the month. **17.** Thousands of casualties were reported in the battle for the Hawizah marshes area in south-east Iraq and both *Iran* and *Iraq* attacked ships in the Gulf; on Mar. 18, President Mubarak of Egypt and King Hussein of Jordan flew to Baghdad for talks on the situation in the Gulf. **24.** A member of the U.S. military liaison mission in *East Germany* was shot dead by a Russian sentry. **31.** *El Salvador* held a general election in which the Christian Democratic Party of President Duarte claimed victory.

April 3. The *French* Government announced that next year's general election for the French National Assembly was to be held under a single-ballot system of proportional representation at department level. **8.** Sir Geoffrey Howe arrived in East Berlin on the first visit by a British Foreign Secretary to *East Germany*. **10.** *Pakistan* named its first all-civilian Cabinet in eight years. **26.** In *Warsaw*, Mr. Gorbachev, the Russian leader, signed a 20-year extension of the Warsaw Pact with his East European allies. **29.** President Ortega of *Nicaragua* and Mr. Gorbachev, the Soviet leader, had talks in Moscow.

May 3. The two-day seven-nation economic summit of Western countries opened in *Bonn*. **5.** In *West Germany*, President Reagan visited the former Belsen concentration camp and Bitburg war cemetery; the President subsequently visited Spain and Portugal and addressed the European Parliament in Strasbourg. **8.** *Europe* celebrated 40 years of peace with services and ceremonies to mark the anniversary of VE-Day. **14.** According to Western diplomatic despatches reaching Islamabad, over 1,000 civilians had been killed by Soviet troops in north-eastern *Afghanistan*. **23.** President Eanes of Portugal announced in Peking he had reached agreement with China to begin talks on the return to mainland control of *Macao*.

June 2. The *Greek* general election resulted in the re-election of Mr. Andreas Papandreou and his Pan-Hellenic Socialist Movement. **11.** In *Berlin*, the biggest East-West spy exchange for 40 years took place with the U.S.A. handing over four people convicted of espionage for 23 people held in Polish and East German prisons as Western agents. **21.** Experts agreed that the body exhumed in *Brazil* two weeks ago was that of Josef Mengele, the Nazi war criminal.

July 10. *China* and *Russia* signed an £11 billion five-year trade agreement. **22.** *Britain* and *Spain* signed an extradition treaty. **29.** Mr. Gorbachev, the Soviet leader, announced a five-month ban on all *Soviet* nuclear testing from August. **31.** Diplomatic sources in Islamabad reported that Mujihadeen resistance fighters had launched a major offensive against Afghan and Soviet forces in south-east *Afghanistan*.

Aug. 23. It was announced that Hans Tiedge, the head of *West Germany's* counterespionage department, had defected to East Germany.

MISCELLANEOUS

(1984) Sept. 5. Scotland Yard announced guidelines to its police officers concerning membership of Freemasonry.

Oct. 16. The British Medical Association announced it was to launch a public health campaign against cigarette smoking. **27.** It was reported from California that surgeons had transplanted a baboon's heart into a dying baby; the baby died on Nov. 16.

Dec. 6. Roger de Grey was elected President of the Royal Academy in succession to Sir Hugh Casson. **19.** Ted Hughes was appointed the new Poet Laureate.

(1985) Jan. 3. The Australian Royal Commission into the conduct of the atomic weapons test programme of the 1950s opened in London. **4.** Mrs. Kim Cotton, believed to be the first commercial surrogate mother in Britain, gave birth to a girl; on Jan. 8, the baby was made a ward of court; on Jan. 14, a High Court judge explained why he allowed the baby subsequently to go to America with her sperm-donor father and his wife. **29.** It was announced that Britain would join the U.S. project for a manned space station to be launched in 1992 and later this year would set up a British National Space Centre.

Feb. 14. The General Medical Council decided that doctors must no longer treat or advise girls under-16 who asked for the contraceptive pill without their parents' knowledge, except in an emergency.

Mar. 5. The report of the Government-instigated inquiry into the workings of the B.B.C. was published.

April 18. The Getty Museum of California paid a record £7,500,000 for Mantegna's painting, "Adoration of the Magi." **25.** It was announced that Sqd.-Ldr. Nigel Wood, an R.A.F. test pilot, was to be Britain's first man in space and would be a member of the crew of the American space shuttle in June 1986.

June 13. Mr. John Paul Getty, jun., established an endowment fund for the National Gallery worth £20 million initially.

July 13. The 16-hour Live Aid concert at Wembley and Philadelphia attracted a world television audience estimated at 1,500 million and raised £50 million world-wide for Africa's starving populations. **17.** The B.B.C. announced plans for a radical restructuring of the organization. **30.** Following intervention by the Home Secretary, the B.B.C. Governors decided not to transmit in its present form the television documentary, "At the Edge of the Union," a production about political extremism in Northern Ireland; on Aug. 7, the B.B.C. announced the film would be shown in due course but a 24-hour strike by broadcasting journalists blacked out nearly all television and radio news bulletins and some live programmes on both B.B.C. and I.T.V.; the B.B.C.'s External Services went off the air for the first time.

Aug. 9. The Austrian Justice Minister announced that a number of people were under arrest and others were being investigated in connection with the doctoring of wine by the use of diethylene glycol.

OBITUARY, SEPT. 16, 1984–AUG. 31, 1985

Addams, Dawn, film actress, aged 54—*May* 7.
Aitken, Sir Max, BT., D.S.O., D.F.C., newspaper publisher, aged 75—*April* 30.
Bailey, Sir Donald, O.B.E., designer of wartime bridge, aged 83—*May* 5.
Balogh, Baron, former economic adviser to Labour Governments, aged 79—*Jan.* 20.
Beeching, Baron, PH.D., aged 71—*March* 23.
Berry, *Hon.* Sir Anthony, Conservative M.P. for Enfield, Southgate, aged 59—*Oct.* 12, 1984 (*see* page 570).
Bloom, Ursula, writer, aged 91—*Oct.* 29, 1984.
Böll, Heinrich, West German novelist, aged 67—*July* 16.
Boulting, John, film producer and director, aged 71—*June* 17.
Brambell, Wilfrid, actor, aged 72—*Jan.* 18.
Brown, Baron, P.C., M.B.E., industrialist and former Labour Minister, aged 76—*March* 17.
Bryant, Sir Arthur, C.H., C.B.E., historian, aged 85—*Jan.* 22.
Burnham, Forbes, President of Guyana, aged 62—*Aug.* 6.
Caldwell, Taylor, novelist, aged 84—*Aug.* 30.
Cameron of Balhousie, *Marshal of the Royal Air Force,* Baron, K.T., G.C.B., C.B.E., D.S.O., D.F.C., former Chief of Defence Staff, aged 64—*Jan.* 29.
Cameron, James, C.B.E., journalist and broadcaster, aged 73—*Jan.* 26.
Chagall, Marc, artist, aged 97—*March* 28.

Chernenko, Konstantin, Soviet leader, aged 73—*March* 10.
Clitheroe, 1st Baron, P.C., K.C.V.O., former Chairman of Conservative Party, aged 83—*Sept.* 18, 1984.
Compton, Leslie, former footballer and cricketer, aged 72—*Dec.* 1984.
Dirac, *Prof.* Paul, O.M., physicist, aged 82—*Oct.* 1984.
Dixon, Reginald, organist, aged 80—*May* 9.
Dyall, Valentine, actor, aged 77—*June* 24.
Fender, Percy, cricketer, aged 92—*June* 15.
Fraser, Sir Robert, O.B.E., first Director-General of Independent Television Authority, aged 80—*Jan.* 20.
Gandhi, Mrs. Indira, Prime Minister of India (*assassinated*), aged 66—*Oct.* 31, 1984.
George-Brown, Baron, P.C., former Foreign Secretary and deputy leader of Labour Party, aged 70—*June* 2.
Gordon, Noele, actress, aged 61—*April* 14.
Harlech, 5th Baron, P.C., K.C.M.G., former British Ambassador in Washington (*accidentally killed*), aged 66—*Jan.* 26.
Hendry, Ian, actor, aged 53—*Dec.* 1984.
Hooson, Tom, Conservative M.P. for Brecon and Radnor, aged 52—*May* 8.
Horrocks, *Lt.-Gen.* Sir Brian, K.C.B., K.B.E., D.S.O., M.C., distinguished wartime commander, aged 89—*Jan.* 4.
Howard of Henderskelfe, Baron, former chairman of the B.B.C., aged 64—*Nov.* 27, 1984.

Hoxha, Enver, Albanian leader, aged 76—*April* 11.

Lawford, Peter, film actor, aged 61—*Dec.* 24, 1984.

Littler, Sir Emile, theatrical impresario, aged 81—*Jan.* 23.

Lodge, Henry Cabot, leading U.S. diplomat, aged 82—*Feb.* 27.

Lyons, Sir William, founder of Jaguar Cars, aged 83—*Feb.* 8.

Mayer, Sir Robert, C.H., K.C.V.O., founder of Children's Concerts, aged 105—*Jan.* 9.

Moncreiffe of that Ilk, Sir Iain, BT., C.V.O., Q.C., aged 65—*Feb.* 27.

Monro, Matt, the singer, aged 54—*Feb.* 7.

Naipaul, Shiva, author, aged 40—*Aug.* 13.

Negus, Arthur, O.B.E., antiques expert, aged 82—*April* 5.

Nemon, Oscar, sculptor, aged 79—*April* 13.

O'Brien, Edmond, actor, aged 69—*May* 8.

Ormandy, Eugene, conductor, aged 85—*March* 12.

Peckinpah, Samuel, film director, aged 59—*Dec.* 28, 1984.

Pidgeon, Walter, film actor, aged 86—*Sept.* 25, 1984.

Plomley, Roy, O.B.E., writer and broadcaster, aged 71—*May* 28.

Raymond, Rene (James Hadley Chase), author, aged 78—*Feb.* 6.

Redgrave, Sir Michael, C.B.E., distinguished actor, aged 77—*March* 21.

Robins, Denise, romantic novelist, aged 88—*May* 1.

Robinson, Stanford, O.B.E., conductor, aged 80—*Oct.* 25, 1984.

Rossiter, Leonard, actor, aged 57—*Oct.* 5, 1984.

Ryle, Sir Martin, pioneer of radio astronomy, aged 66—*Oct.* 14, 1984.

St. Oswald, 4th Baron, M.C., former junior Conservative Minister, aged 68—*Dec.* 19, 1984.

Simpson, *Prof.* Keith, C.B.E., renowned pathologist, aged 78—*July* 21.

Smallwood, Norah, O.B.E., publisher, aged 74—*Oct.* 11, 1984.

Trevelyan, Baron, K.G., G.C.M.G., C.I.E., O.B.E., distinguished diplomat and administrator, aged 79—*Feb.* 8.

Truffaut, Francois, film director, aged 52—*Oct.* 21, 1984.

Williams, Dorian, O.B.E., show jumping commentator, aged 71—*July* 21.

Wolfenden, Baron, C.B.E., distinguished services to social reform and education, aged 78—*Jan.* 18.

Wolstenholme, Guy, golfer, aged 53—*Oct.* 9, 1984.

CENTENARIES

One Hundred Years Ago (1886).—A selection follows of "Remarkable Occurrences" (as "Events of the Year" was then called) as printed in the 1887 and 1888 editions of *Whitaker's Almanack* covering the year 1886:

JANUARY.

1. The annexation of Upper Burmah to the British Empire formally proclaimed.

4. A company formed at Amsterdam for draining the Zuyder Zee.

10. Col. Gordon carried a Dacoit entrenched position near Sagaing, at point of bayonet.

14. At a meeting of the Submarine Continental Railway Co. it was resolved to proceed with a bill for maintenance and continuance of the tunnel under the Straits of Dover.

17. The Emperor of Russia performed the ceremony of blessing the waters of the Neva.

18. Burmese defeated with heavy loss: six guns taken.

20. The tunnel under the Mersey, from Liverpool to Birkenhead, opened by the Prince of Wales.

—. The Queen opened Parliament in person.

21. Bank rate lowered from 4 to 3 per cent.

FEBRUARY.

1. Mutiny in the Mersey on board the Roman Catholic reformatory ship *Clarence.*

4. The French Chamber resolve to comply with a petition to sell the Crown jewels to provide a superannuation fund for aged workmen.

5. While excavating at the Acropolis, 3 colossal statues of women, completely coloured, belonging to the period before Phidias, were discovered.

8. Serious rioting in London; the mob doing much damage to houses and property on their way from Trafalgar Square to Hyde Park, and afterwards to Oxford Street.

11. Rioting in Leicester; the mob attacking the hosiery factories.

13. Russians made formal entry into Penjdeh.

16. Prize fight in the Forest of St. Germain between two English pugalists.

17. The members of Mr. Gladstone's third administration kissed hands on their appointment.

18. Bank rate reduced from 3 to 2 per cent.

23. The Queen decorated officers and men of the Soudan campaign.

25. Equestrian entertainment by Hengler, attended by the Queen; first time since the death of the Prince Consort.

MARCH.

10. Terrible railway collision at Monte Carlo and Mentone Railway: several carriages fell into the sea; many persons killed and wounded.

13. From this day soldiers of all arms and all regiments allowed to wear their beards.

17. The Duchess of Connaught gave birth to a daughter at Buckingham Palace.

18. Riotous demonstration at Manchester.

23. The P. and O. steamer *Carthage* made the passage of Suez Canal at night by means of the electric light.

29. Mr. Chamberlain and Mr. Trevelyan resigned their places in the Ministry, and were succeeded by Mr. Stansfeld and Lord Dalhousie.

APRIL.

7. The Abbé Liszt visited the Queen at Windsor, and played some musical selections.

17. Opening of new deep-water docks at Tilbury; constructed at a cost of £3,000,000.

22. Crystal Palace Gas Company fined for supplying impure gas.

23. Suspension of the Cardiff Savings Bank, with over 5,000 depositors on its books.

MAY.

6. Derby theatre burnt: one of the actors suffocated.

—. Bank rate raised from 2 to 3 per cent.

7. Duel between M. Rochefort and M. Portalis; four shots exchanged without effect.

16. Suakin evacuated by the British troops.

17. Birth (posthumous) of the King of Spain.

24. A florist at Stratford obtained £500 damages against the Great Eastern Railway Co. for damage done by smoke from locomotives.

28. Fresh discovery of gold in Western Australia announced.

JUNE.

3. Rule against soldiers smoking in the street done away with; may smoke after 5 p.m. between Oct. 1st and March 31st, and after 6 p.m. between April 1st and Sept. 30th.

4. Serious riots, resulting in loss of life, commence in Belfast.

9. Eruption of Mount Tarawera, New Zealand, and destruction of Wairoa and the famous Pink Terraces near Lake Rotomahana.

10. Bank rate reduced from 3 to 2½ per cent.

13. King of Bavaria drowned himself in the Starnberg lake; Dr. Gudden also drowned in attempting to save the King.

14. Vancouver, British Columbia, destroyed by fire.

21. The foundation-stone of the new Tower Bridge across the Thames laid by the Prince of Wales.

22. A bill for the expulsion of the Royal Princes from France passed by 137 votes to 122: to take effect from the 24th.

JULY.

1. Commencement of the elections for a new Parliament.

2. The Queen reviewed nearly 15,000 troops at Aldershot.

17. Shocking accident at Woolwich: a man's body embedded in a block of steel.

24. Sale of the Blenheim pictures: the Rubens's obtained high prices; the day's sale amounting to £34,834.

25. Rioting in Amsterdam: 23 persons killed and about 90 wounded.

31. Renewed riots in Belfast: the mob fired on by the police.

—. 200 marines landed at Tiree to assist in serving notices on the crofters.

AUGUST.

3. The Marquess of Salisbury and other ministers attend at Windsor and accept the seals of office.

5. The new Parliament meets for the election of Speaker.

8. The Emperors of Germany and Austria met at Gastein.

14. Several persons killed and many wounded owing to riots in Belfast.

19. Parliament opened by Royal Commission.

26. Bank rate raised from 2½ to 3½ per cent.

31. Earthquake in the southern States of America, and destruction of Charleston.

SEPTEMBER.

1. The Severn Tunnel opened for passenger traffic.

7. Prince Alexander of Bulgaria quitted Sofia on abdicating the throne.

13. Royal National Eisteddfod inaugurated at Carnarvon.

—. The *Volta*, propelled by electricity, crossed the Channel from Dover to Calais.

19. Rioting again broke out in Belfast, when two people were killed.

OCTOBER.

2. Twenty-one lives lost by an explosion in the Silkstone Colliery, Altofts, near Wakefield.

21. Bank rate raised from 3½ to 4 per cent.

NOVEMBER.

9. The *London Gazette* announced the establishment of a new naval and military order, to be styled the "Distinguished Service Order".

19. Fire at Hampton Court Palace, causing serious damage, and endangering the many valuable works of art contained in the palace.

DECEMBER.

3. Resignation of the French Ministry.

—. *Punch* summoned for libel: charge dismissed as "monstrous".

10. New French Cabinet announced.

—. Two lifeboats capsized near Southport, with loss of 27 lives.

16. Bank rate raised from 4 to 5 per cent.

23. Lord Randolph Churchill resigned the Chancellorship of the Exchequer.

29. Delegates from Bulgaria received at the Foreign Office.

THE CENTENARIES OF 1986

Died 1886	
Jan. 16	Amilcare Ponchielli, Italian composer.
May 15	Emily Dickinson, American poet.
May 23	Leopold von Ranke, German historian.
July 31	Franz Liszt, Hungarian pianist and composer.
Nov. 8	Fred Archer, champion jockey.
Nov. 18	Chester A. Arthur, U.S. President 1881–85.
Born 1886	
July 23	Sir Arthur Whitten Brown, aviator and companion of Alcock on first transatlantic flight.
Oct 16	David Ben-Gurion, first Prime Minister of Israel.
Died 1786	
Aug. 17	Frederick the Great, King of Prussia 1740–86.
Born 1786	
Feb. 24	Wilhelm Grimm, German philologist and folklorist.
Aug. 17	Davy Crockett, American frontiersman and Congressman.
Nov. 18	Carl von Weber, German composer.
Died 1686	
Nov. 11	Louis, Prince of Condé, French soldier.
Born 1686	
May 14	Gabriel D. Fahrenheit, German physicist and inventor of the mercury thermometer.
Died 1586	
Oct. 17	Sir Philip Sidney, Elizabethan poet and soldier.
Events 1886	
Jan. 29	Patenting of first successful petrol-driven car, built by Karl Benz.
March 10	First Cruft's Dog Show in London.
Sept. 4	Surrender of Geronimo, leader of the last great American Indian rebellion.
Oct. 28	Statue of Liberty unveiled.
Events 1586	
July 28	First potatoes arrive in Britain (at Plymouth) from Colombia.
Sept. 22	Battle of Zutphen.

THE CENTENARIES OF 1987

Died 1887	
July 14	Alfred Krupp, German arms manufacturer.
Nov. 2	Jenny Lind, Swedish operatic soprano.

Born 1887
Jan. 28	Artur Rubinstein, concert pianist.
May 15	Edwin Muir, author.
Aug. 3	Rupert Brooke, poet.
Sept. 26	Sir Barnes Wallis, aircraft designer.
Oct. 31	Chiang Kai Shek, Chinese general and head of the Nationalist Government.
Nov. 1	L. S. Lowry, artist.
Nov. 17	Viscount Montgomery of Alamein.

Died 1787
Nov. 15	Christoph Gluck, German operatic composer.

Born 1787
March 16	George S. Ohm, German physicist.
March 17	Edmund Kean, actor.

Died 1687
Nov.	Nell Gwynn, mistress of Charles II.

Died 1587
Feb. 8	Mary, Queen of Scots.
April 18	John Foxe, martyrologist.

Born 1387
Sept. 16	Henry V.

Died 1087
Sept. 9	William I (the Conqueror).

DISTANCES FROM LONDON (Heathrow) BY AIR

A list of the distances in statute miles from London to various places abroad. They have been supplied by IAL, Southall, Middx.

To	Miles	To	Miles	To	Miles
Ajaccio	790	Dublin	279	New York (J. F. Kennedy)	3,440
Algiers	1,035	Düsseldorf	310	Nice	645
Alicante	911	Entebbe	4,033	Oporto	806
Amsterdam	230	Faro	1,063	Oslo (Fornebu)	723
Ankara	1,770	Frankfurt	406	Palermo	1,128
Athens	1,500	Geneva	468	Palma/Majorca	836
Auckland	11,404	Gibraltar	1,084	Paris	215; (Orly 227)
Baghdad	2,551	Gothenburg (Landvetter)	664	Perth/Australia	9,008
Bahrain	3,163	Hamburg	463	Prague	649
Bangkok	5,928	Helsinki (Vantaa)	1,147	Rangoon	5,581
Barbados	4,193	Hong Kong	5,990	Reykjavik	1,167
Barcelona	712	Honolulu	7,220	Rhodes	1,743
Basle	447	Istanbul	1,560	Rome (Fiumicino)	895
Beirut	2,161	Johannesburg	5,634	Salzburg	652
Bergen	648	Karachi	3,935	Shannon	369
Berlin (Templehof)	592	Khartoum	3,071	Singapore	6,756
Bermuda	3,428	Kingston/Jamaica	4,668	Sofia	1,266
Bombay	4,478	Kuala Lumpur	6,557	Stockholm (Arlanda)	908
Bordeaux	458	Kuwait	2,903	Sydney (Australia)	10,568
Brisbane	10,273	Larnaca/Cyprus	2,036	Tangier	1,120
Brussels	217	Leningrad	1,314	Teheran	2,741
Budapest	923	Lisbon	972	Tel Aviv	2,229
Cagliari	959	Madrid	773	Tokyo (Narita)	5,956
Cairo	2,194	Malaga	1,041	Toronto	3,545
Calcutta	4,958	Malta	1,305	Trinidad (Port of Spain)	4,405
Chicago (O'Hare)	3,941	Marseilles	614	Tripoli	1,468
Cologne	331	Mauritius	6,075	Turin (Caselle)	570
Colombo	5,411	Milan	609	Valencia	826
Copenhagen	608	Montego Bay	4,687	Venice (Tessera)	715
Corfu	1,273	Montreal (Mirabel)	3,241	Vienna (Schwechat)	790
Dar-es-Salaam	4,662	Moscow (Sheremetievo)	1,557	Warsaw	912
Darwin	8,613	Munich	588	Zagreb	848
Delhi	4,180	Nairobi	4,248	Zürich	490
Detroit	3,754	Naples	1,011		
Doha	3,253	Nassau	4,332		

Value of United Kingdom exports (fob) (£ million)
Analysis by sections and divisions

	1980	1981	1982	1983
Total UK exports	47,357·1	50,998·1	55,557·8	60,533·7
Food and live animals chiefly for food	2,050·8	2,338·5	2,508·3	2,748·6
Live animals chiefly for food	139·9	175·6	179·1	187·4
Meat and meat preparations	327·2	328.9	347·5	496·2
Dairy products and birds' eggs	298.4	307.2	325.6	305.9
Fish, crustaceans and molluscs, and preparations thereof	145·6	150·2	162·3	203·6
Cereals and cereal preparations	455·7	697·8	773·9	736·7
Vegetables and fruit	152·5	152·2	154·0	163·2
Sugar, sugar preparations and honey	112·2	116·4	121·1	144·9
Coffee, tea, cocoa, spices, and manufactures thereof	261·1	245·2	252·2	291·3
Feeding stuff for animals (not including un-milled cereals)	63·6	60·9	69·0	78·7
Miscellaneous edible products and preparations	94·6	104·0	123·8	140·7
Beverages and tobacco	1,205·9	1,311·7	1,451·5	1,486.2
Beverages	897·9	951·6	1,060·1	1,051·2
Tobacco and tobacco manufactures	308·0	360·1	391·4	435·0
Crude materials, inedible, except fuels	1,378·5	1,247·6	1,293·7	1,527·3
Hides, skins and furskins, raw	189·9	173·9	180·5	200·2
Oil seeds and oleaginous fruit	2·9	4·5	7·9	37·8
Crude rubber (including synthetic and re-claimed)	75·6	108·1	122·8	141·7
Cork and wood	16·0	27·2	28·6	24·1
Pulp and waste paper	22·8	13·9	11·6	15·8
Textile fibres (other than wool tops) and their wastes (not manufactured into yarn or fabric)	312·9	298·3	314·2	374·7
Crude fertilisers and crude minerals (excluding coal, petroleum and precious stones)	235·3	227·0	224·2	223·9
Metalliferous ores and metal scrap	474·4	347·8	346·6	444·2
Crude animal and vegetable materials	48·6	46·9	57·3	64·9
Mineral fuels, lubricants and related materials	6,428·8	9,616·5	11,237·1	13,126·5
Petroleum, petroleum products and related materials	6,133·2	9,107·5	10,685·7	12,525·0
Coal, coke, gas and electric current	295·6	508·9	551·4	601·6
Animal and vegetable oils, fats and waxes	71·0	65·1	46·5	59·1
Chemicals and related products*	5,286·2	5,550·1	6,119·3	6,929·3
Organic chemicals	1,297·6	1,496·3	1,592·3	1,927·3
Inorganic chemicals	619·9	586·5	694·9	699·8
Dyeing, tanning and colouring materials	432·5	433·6	464·1	568·7
Medicinal and pharmaceutical products	744·8	851·9	978·0	1,074·2
Essential oils and perfume materials; toilet, polishing and cleansing materials	464·7	483·3	525·1	574·3
Fertilisers, manufactured	52·3	62·3	48·8	69·7
Explosives and pyrotechnic products	36·6	39·4	36·8	40·1
Artificial resins and plastic materials, and cellu-lose esters and ethers	874·4	810·7	875·3	980·1
Chemical materials and products, not elsewhere specified	763·4	786·2	904·1	995·0

Value of United Kingdom exports (fob) (£ million)—*Continued*
Analysis by sections and divisions

	1980	1981	1982	1983
Total UK exports	47,357·1	50,998·1	55,557·8	60,533·7
Manufactured goods classified chiefly by material*	8,754·0	7,719·3	7,940·5	8,862·2
Leather, leather manufactures, nes, and dressed furskins	212·2	207·2	202·1	232·9
Rubber manufactures, nes	447·1	464·6	417·9	451·8
Cork and wood manufactures (excluding furniture)	84·4	86.4	83·2	85·2
Paper, paperboard, and articles of paper pulp, of paper or of paperboard	475·0	461·5	503·1	543·1
Textile yarn, fabrics, made-up articles, nes, and related products	1,363·0	1,202·7	1,192·0	1,284·6
Non-metallic mineral manufactures, nes	2,110·2	1,538·2	1,609·9	1,995·0
Iron and steel	983·4	1,239·4	1,291·8	1,330·9
Non-ferrous metals	1,770·6	1,244·1	1,244·7	1,614·5
Manufactures of metal, nes	1,308·0	1,275·2	1,395·6	1,324·0
Machinery and transport equipment*	16,267·3	16,784·1	18,100·9	18,313·7
Power generating machinery and equipment	2,230·8	2,642·2	2,809·1	2,472·5
Machinery specialised for particular industries	2,573·6	2,557·9	2,601·3	2,336·3
Metalworking machinery	486·4	510·8	522·4	416·2
General industrial machinery and equipment, nes, and machine parts, nes	2,316·8	2,305·7	2,411·8	2,333·2
Office machines and automatic data processing equipment	1,345·5	1,291·8	1,599·5	2,049·2
Telecommunications, sound recording and reproducing apparatus and equipment	712·5	820·5	897·2	991·7
Electrical machinery, apparatus and appliances, nes, and electrical parts thereof (including non-electrical counterparts, nes, of electrical household type equipment)	1,798·6	1,758·7	2,117·0	2,289·5
Road vehicles (including air cushion vehicles)	3,158·0	3,170·5	3,109·0	3,084·1
Other transport equipment	1,645·1	1,726·2	2,033·5	2,341·1
Miscellaneous manufactured articles*	4,503·7	4,844·6	5,151·8	5,814·1
Sanitary, plumbing, heating and lighting fixtures and fittings, nes	109·0	113·0	107·0	108·3
Furniture and parts thereof	239·2	222·1	240·9	257·8
Travel goods, handbags and similar containers	19·5	20·1	19·1	19·3
Articles of apparel and clothing accessories	807·5	846·6	840·0	865·4
Footwear	130·4	121·2	114·9	123·4
Professional, scientific and controlling instruments and apparatus, nes	948·3	1,107·5	1,255·4	1,472·4
Photographic apparatus, equipment and supplies and optical goods, nes, watches and clocks	519·5	504·6	551·9	573·6
Miscellaneous manufactured articles, nes	1,730·4	1,909·4	2,022·7	2,393·8
Manufactured goods (total*)	34,811·2	34,898·0	37,312·6	39,919·1
Commodities and transactions not classified elsewhere	1,411·0	1,520·7	1,708·2	1,666·9

Value of United Kingdom imports (cif) (£ million)
Analysis by sections and divisions

	1980	1981	1982	1983
Total UK imports	49,772·9	51,168·6	56,978·2	65,993·1
Food and live animals chiefly for food	5,477·8	5,785·2	6,414·1	6,891·3
Live animals chiefly for food	102·1	109·5	133·1	170·3
Meat and meat preparations	1,225·5	1,260·0	1,370·9	1,313·5
Dairy products and birds' eggs	493·7	592·2	567·9	629·2
Fish, crustaceans and molluscs, and preparations thereof	348·8	403·5	404·2	505·6
Cereals and cereal preparations	603·2	565·9	549·9	595·3
Vegetables and fruit	1,238·9	1,389·4	1,608·3	1,718·9
Sugar, sugar preparations and honey	391·7	393·8	429·5	424·4
Coffee, tea, cocoa, spices and manufactures thereof	676·6	579·5	722·4	800·0
Feeding stuff for animals (not including unmilled cereals)	248·9	328·7	446·6	523·6
Miscellaneous edible products and preparations	148·4	162·8	181·1	210·4
Beverages and tobacco	674·8	752·1	836·7	962·1
Beverages	439·8	482·7	517·5	617·3
Tobacco and tobacco manufactures	235·0	269·5	319·2	344·7
Crude materials, inedible, except fuels	3,788·5	3,736·8	3,612·9	4,364·5
Hides, skins and furskins, raw	227·6	192·5	189·5	184·9
Oil seeds and oleaginous fruit	264·8	305·3	259·6	216·9
Crude rubber (including synthetic and reclaimed)	182·8	171·5	182·9	197·4
Cork and wood	683·1	603·7	673·8	938·0
Pulp and waste paper	398·7	438·5	412·0	428·0
Textile fibres (other than wool tops) and their wastes (not manufactured into yarn or fabric)	376·1	376·0	410·8	475·6
Crude fertilisers and crude minerals (excluding coal, petroleum and precious stones)	302·8	255·9	263·5	285·7
Metalliferous ores and metal scrap	1,168·6	1,185·0	977·5	1,358·1
Crude animal and vegetable materials	183·9	208·4	243·3	279·9
Mineral fuels, lubricants and related materials	6,875·4	7,166·4	7,408·6	7,067·1
Petroleum, petroleum products and related materials	6,072·7	6,235·6	6,276·9	5,738·0
Coal, coke, gas and electric current	802·7	930·8	1,131·6	1,329·0
Animal and vegetable oils, fats and waxes	260·9	263·3	317·0	358·8
Chemicals and related products*	3,146·9	3,596·6	4,179·1	5,119·5
Organic chemicals	897·4	1,062·4	1,171·9	1,456·3
Inorganic chemicals	432·9	454·4	539·3	561·3
Dyeing, tanning and colouring materials	145·7	170·7	198·0	235·1
Medicinal and pharmaceutical products	222·6	298·3	374·6	470·1
Essential oils and perfume materials; toilet, polishing and cleansing materials	174·7	203·6	242·2	305·3
Fertilisers, manufactured	89·9	104·9	127·1	172·5
Explosives and pyrotechnic products	7·5	7·7	10·9	14·1
Artificial resins and plastic materials, and cellulose esters and ethers	763·2	862·9	1,017·7	1,323·4
Chemical materials and products, not elsewhere specified	413·1	431·7	497·4	581·3

Value of United Kingdom imports (cif) (£ million)—*Continued*
Analysis by sections and divisions

	1980	1981	1982	1983
Total UK imports	49,772·9	51,168·6	56,978·2	65,993·1
Manufactured goods classified chiefly by material*	10,333·8	8,936·3	9,852·5	11,840·1
Leather, leather manufactures, nes, and dressed furskins	137·1	140·7	154·6	184·0
Rubber manufactures, nes	263·5	281·0	326·2	419·6
Cork and wood manufactures (excluding furniture)	368·9	443·0	436·3	578·8
Paper, paperboard, and articles of paper pulp, of paper or of paperboard	1,286·7	1,536·9	1,675·1	1,906·3
Textile yarn, fabrics, made-up articles, nes, and related products	1,543·7	1,761·6	1,927·6	2,320·1
Non-metallic mineral manufactures, nes	1,938·0	1,443·4	1,520·3	2,085·5
Iron and steel	1,448·0	1,089·5	1,367·3	1,260·7
Non-ferrous metals	2,487·4	1,425·3	1,495·7	1,976·3
Manufactures of metal, nes	860·5	815·1	949·5	1,108·9
Machinery and transport equipment*	12,565·6	13,399·2	16,464·2	20,230·7
Power generating machinery and equipment	961·1	1,272·8	1,482·7	1,569·2
Machinery specialised for particular industries	1,205·2	1,183·3	1,485·9	1,731·8
Metalworking machinery	408·4	346·4	380·6	342·4
General industrial machinery and equipment, nes, and machine parts, nes	1,414·7	1,394·9	1,634·4	1,845·6
Office machines and automatic data processing equipment	1,393·4	1,631·7	2,121·9	3,019·9
Telecommunications and sound recording and reproducing apparatus and equipment	823·6	1,291·4	1,586·2	1,916·4
Electrical machinery, apparatus and appliances, nes, and electrical parts thereof (including non-electrical counterparts, nes, of electrical household type equipment)	1,518·5	1,759·6	2,179·1	2,807·3
Road vehicles (including air cushion vehicles)	3,351·6	3,408·1	4,489·6	5,753·7
Other transport equipment	1,488·9	1,111·1	1,103·8	1,244·4
Miscellaneous manufactured articles*	5,130·7	6,061·1	6,618·4	7,714·7
Sanitary, plumbing, heating and lighting fixtures and fittings, nes	78·1	81·8	103·5	126·7
Furniture and parts thereof	283·2	349·2	400·1	490·5
Travel goods, handbags and similar containers	94·9	117·7	108·6	131·1
Articles of apparel and clothing accessories	1,230·7	1,438·4	1,500·0	1,601·5
Footwear	354·0	415·6	468·3	542·0
Professional, scientific and controlling instruments and apparatus, nes	743·5	865·6	1,052·1	1,303·7
Photographic apparatus, equipment and supplies and optical goods, nes, watches and clocks	655·0	749·0	761·0	862·3
Miscellaneous manufactured articles, nes	1,691·3	2,043·8	2,224·9	2,657·0
Manufactured goods (total*)	31,177·0	31,993·2	37,114·2	44,905·0
Commodities and transactions not classified elsewhere	1,518·5	1,471·6	1,274·8	1,444·3

INSOLVENCY

Bankruptcies, etc. (England and Wales)

	1976	1977	1978	1979	1980	1981	1982	1983
Number of bankruptcies, etc.								
Debtors adjudicated bankrupt	6,681	4,078	3,526	3,158	3,634	4,730	5,303	6,555
Compositions and schemes of arrangement	—	2	—	1	7	3	2	4
Administration orders of deceased debtors' estates	19	15	14	11	11	11	14	17
Liabilities (£ thousand)								
Debtors adjudicated bankrupt	76,692	104,674	205,809	65,805	68,580	169,608	210,615	226,277
Compositions and schemes of arrangement	—	11	—	18	116	46	39	81
Administration orders of deceased debtors' estates	1,517	774	427	532	421	573	380	709
Assets (£ thousand)								
Debtors adjudicated bankrupt	22,300	15,834	20,093	21,768	39,327	39,433	34,464	54,117
Compositions and schemes of arrangement	—	3	—	8	75	63	43	47
Administration orders of deceased debtors' estates	212	319	145	124	155	166	135	225

Sequestrations (bankruptcies) in Scotland

	1976	1977	1978	1979	1980	1981	1982	1983
Number of sequestrations	80	76	80	66	111	117	144	174
Liabilities (£ thousand)	3,171	3,213	4,338	2,470	4,843	12,266	9,757	18,434
Assets (£ thousand)	1,305	1,025	648	994	2,060	4,228	3,975	5,601

Company Liquidations

	1976	1977	1978	1979	1980	1981	1982	1983
England and Wales								
Compulsory liquidations	2,511	2,425	2,265	2,064	2,935	2,771	3,745	4,807
Voluntary liquidations:								
Creditors'	3,428	3,406	2,821	2,473	3,955	5,825	8,322	8,599
Members'	4,173	3,650	3,615	4,030	3,970	3,638	3,908	3,808
Total liquidations notified (all types)	10,112	9,481	8,701	8,567	10,860	12,234	15,975	17,214
Scotland								
Compulsory liquidations	84	67	78	56	135	158	177	263
Voluntary liquidations:								
Creditors'	145	204	196	182	244	280	326	258
Members'	299	222	230	214	242	248	253	243
Total liquidations notified (all types)	528	493	504	452	621	686	756	764
Northern Ireland								
Compulsory liquidations	7	1	8	7	8	16	10	15
Voluntary liquidations:								
Creditors'	42	31	45	27	66	83	111	96
Members'	38	42	36	37	39	39	41	52
Total liquidations notified (all types)	87	74	89	71	113	138	162	163

HOME FINANCE

Central government financial transactions

£ million

	Consolidated Fund			National Loans Fund				Central government borrowing requirement
					Other transactions			
	Revenue	Expenditure	Consolidated fund deficit	Receipts	Payments	Deficit	Other funds and accounts	
1982	84,896	−89,237	−4,341	11,023	−14,008	−7,326	−529	−7,855
1983	86,610	−96,257	−9,647	11,511	−16,201	−14,337	−156	−14,493
1984	95,194	−103,385	−8,191	12,799	−14,844	−10,236	45	−10,191
Financial years								
1982–83	83,270	−90,470	−7,200	10,824	−15,288	−11,664	−1,069	−12,733
1983–84	88,364	−97,450	−9,086	11,833	−15,245	−12,498	214	−12,284
1984–85	98,247	−105,608	−7,361	12,916	−15,418	9,863	−220	−10,083
1985 1st quarter ..	30,594	−29,248	1,346	3,727	−4,641	432	−384	−48
1984 March	8,287	−11,554	−3,267	2,988	−1,011	−1,290	−550	−1,840
April	6,321	−8,128	−1,807	702	−696	−1,801	−86	−1,887
May	7,216	−8,795	−1,579	1,477	−1,652	−1,754	130	−1,624
June	6,362	−7,606	−1,244	522	−681	−1,403	−33	−1,436
July	8,130	−9,193	−1,063	1,609	−1,209	−663	241	−422
August	7,069	−8,226	−1,157	947	−1,027	−1,237	270	−967
September ..	7,286	−7,743	−457	967	−1,344	−834	−56	−890
October	9,512	−8,635	877	923	−1,329	471	−1,224	−753
November ..	7,309	−9,561	−2,252	1,477	−2,266	−3,041	619	−2,422
December ..	8,448	−8,473	−25	565	−573	−33	303	270
1985 January ...	12,373	−8,972	3,401	193	−2,032	1,562	510	2,072
February ...	8,741	−7,837	904	363	−1,443	−176	361	185
March	9,480	−12,439	−2,959	3,171	−1,166	−954	−1,255	−2,209
April	7,442	−9,003	−1,561	949	−1,021	−1,633	714	−919
May	7,504	−9,012	−1,508	1,564	−1,624	−1,568	208	−1,360

Public sector borrowing requirement

£ million

	Total		Contributions by			Financed by				
						Non-bank private sector		Monetary sector	Overseas sector	
									External finance	
	Unadjusted	Seasonally adjusted†	Central government*	Local authorities	Public corporations	Notes and coin	Other	Borrowing in sterling from banks	Foreign currency borrowing from banks	Direct external finance
1982	4,954		7,855	−2,108	−793	462	5,906	−2,273	−52	1,407
1983	11,605		14,493	−2,422	−466	674	11,509	−2,039	115	1,450
1984	10,250		10,191	−447	506	294	8,095	892	293	1,392
Financial years										
1982–83	8,865		12,733	−2,629	−1,239	1,418	9,227	−3,331	−64	1,902
1983–84	9,731		12,284	−2,198	−355	222	8,973	−921	79	1,690
1984–85	10,166		10,083	−916	999	756	15,422	−4,491	423	−553
1983 1st quarter	1,801	4,321	2,269	−13	−455	544	2,563	−1,922	—	375
2nd quarter	3,167	1,861	5,460	−1,468	−825	−349	3,356	−88	−20	887
3rd quarter	3,702	2,916	3,519	83	100	225	2,798	−123	−50	433
4th quarter	2,935	2,835	3,245	−1,024	714	254	2,792	94	185	−245
1984 1st quarter	−73	2,119	60	211	−344	92	27	−826	−36	615
2nd quarter	4,601	3,257	4,947	58	−404	236	5,084	−1,054	43	338
3rd quarter	2,805	2,765	2,279	492	34	25	966	1,200	103	425
4th quarter	2,918	2,045	2,905	−1,208	1,220	−59	2,018	1,572	183	−6
1985 1st quarter	−157	2,099	−48	−258	149	554	7,354	−6,209	94	−1,310

†Financial year constrained.   *An increase in debt is shown positive.

BALANCE OF PAYMENTS OF THE UNITED KINGDOM (£ million)

	1978	1979	1980	1981	1982	1983
Current account						
Visible trade						
Exports (fob)	35,063	40,687	47,422	50,977	55,565	60,625
Imports (fob)	36,605	44,136	45,909	47,325	53,181	61,341
Visible balance	−1,542	−3,449	+1,513	+3,652	+2,384	−716
Invisibles						
Credits	19,134	23,861	25,934	29,644	31,307	34,975
Debits	16,430	20,937	23,818	26,075	28,485	31,343
Invisible balance	+2,704	+2,924	+2,116	+3,569	+2,822	+3,632
of which:						
Services balance	*+3,858*	*+4,155*	*+4,356*	*+4,458*	*+3,706*	*+3,902*
Interest, profits and dividends balance	*+623*	*+1,034*	*−161*	*+1,056*	*+1,165*	*+1,948*
Transfers balance	*−1,777*	*−2,265*	*−2,079*	*−1,945*	*−2,049*	*−2,218*
CURRENT BALANCE	+1,162	−525	+3,629	+7,221	+5,206	+2,916
Capital transfers	−	−	−	−	−	−
Investment and other capital transactions						
Overseas investment in United Kingdom						
Direct	+1,261	+1,740	+2,541	+998	+1,085	+2,457
Investment by oil companies	+666	+1,215	+1,714	+1,882	+1,770	+1,263
Portfolio	−85	+1,253	+851	+508	+450	+1,640
of which: British government stocks	*−3*	*+929*	*+571*	*+201*	*+495*	*+709*
Miscellaneous investment	+35	+75	+100	+70	+120	+85
Total overseas investment in United Kingdom	+1,877	+4,283	+5,206	+3,458	+3,425	+5,445
United Kingdom private investment overseas						
Direct	−2,710	−3,035	−3,317	−5,152	−2,530	−2,609
Oil and miscellaneous investment	−821	−2,858	−1,566	−1,418	−1,984	−1,841
Portfolio	−1,073	−909	−3,150	−4,090	−6,210	−6,110
Total	−4,604	−6,802	−8,033	−10,660	−10,724	−10,560
Official long-term capital	−336	−401	−91	−336	−337	−389
Import credit	+292	+64	−254	+130	−220	−33
Export credit	−922	−856	−902	−969	−1,165	−1,484
Foreign currency borrowing or lending abroad	−434	+1,622	+2,054	+1,462	+4,271	+1,167
Exchange reserves in sterling:						
British government stocks	−113	+247	+945	+267	−52	+194
Banking and money market liabilities, etc.	—	+509	+317	−118	+438	+714
Other external banking and money market liabilities in sterling	+293	+2,580	+2,558	+2,607	+4,134	+3,225
External sterling lending by United Kingdom banks	−504	+205	−2,500	−2,954	−3,299	−1,386
Other external borrowing or lending						
United Kingdom public sector	+22	−7	−166	−18	−105	−87
United Kingdom private sector	+84	+456	−341	−323	+194	+10
Other transactions	+81	−66	−243	+101	+253	−464
Total investment and other capital transactions	−4,264	+1,834	−1,450	−7,353	−3,187	−3,648
Allocation of SDRs	—	+195	+180	+158	—	—
Official financing						
Net transactions with overseas monetary authorities	−1,016	−596	−140	−145	−163	−36
Foreign currency borrowing (net)	−187	−250	−941	−1,587	+26	+249
Official reserves (drawings on +/additions to −)	+2,329	−1,059	−291	+2,419	+1,421	+603
Total official financing	+1,126	−1,905	−1,372	+687	+1,284	+816
Balancing item	+1,976	+401	−987	−713	−3,303	−84

PERSONAL INCOME AND EXPENDITURE (£ million)

	1978	1979	1980	1981	1982	1983
Income before tax						
Income from employment:						
Wages and salaries	84,236	98,466	116,305	124,803	133,527	143,348
Pay in cash and kind of HM Forces	1,645	2,020	2,436	2,689	2,905	3,121
Total	85,881	100,486	118,741	127,492	136,432	146,469
Employers' contributions:						
National insurance, etc.	6,084	6,947	8,330	8,940	9,525	10,632
Other	7,123	8,301	9,862	11,722	12,226	12,971
Total income from employment	99,088	115,734	136,933	148,154	158,183	170,072
Income from self-employment:						
After deducting stock appreciation	13,667	15,689	16,835	18,676	21,240	22,674
Stock appreciation	439	753	750	561	287	449
Total	14,106	16,442	17,585	19,237	21,527	23,123
Rent, dividends and net interest:						
Receipts by life assurance and superannuation schemes	4,766	6,406	7,790	8,758	10,116	11,313
Imputed rent of owner-occupied dwellings	5,367	6,525	7,827	9,103	10,106	10,895
Other receipts, net	2,695	4,261	5,194	4,161	4,184	3,034
Total	12,828	17,192	20,811	20,022	24,406	25,242
Current transfers to charities from companies	45	51	52	62	66	74
National insurance benefits and other current grants from general government	17,872	20,960	25,468	31,137	36,375	39,528
Imputed charge for capital consumption of private non-profit making bodies	199	226	269	300	311	321
Total personal income	144,138	170,605	201,118	220,912	240,868	258,360
Deductions from income						
UK taxes on income	19,459	21,570	25,554	28,802	31,436	32,822
National insurance, etc. contributions	10,107	11,531	13,944	15,923	18,141	20,643
Transfers abroad (net)	74	207	256	259	205	211
Personal disposable income	114,498	137,297	161,364	175,928	191,086	204,684
Expenditure						
Consumers' expenditure	99,486	117,912	136,789	152,125	166,477	182,427
Balance saving	15,012	19,385	24,575	23,803	24,609	22,257
Total	114,498	137,297	161,364	175,928	191,086	204,684
Memorandum items						
Saving ratio (per cent)	*13.1*	*14.1*	*15.2*	*13.5*	*12.9*	*10.9*
Real personal disposable income:						
At 1980 prices	151,197	159,821	161,364	158,106	158,554	161,578
1980 = 100	93.7	99.0	100.0	98.0	98.3	100.1

CONSUMERS' EXPENDITURE

£ million

	Total consumers' expenditure	Durable goods				Other goods								Services	
		Total	Cars, motor cycles and other vehicles	Furniture and floor coverings	Other durable goods	Food (household expenditure)	Beer	Other alcoholic drink	Tobacco	Clothing other than footwear	Footwear	Energy products	Other goods	Rent, rates and water charges	Other services
At current prices															
1980	136,789	13,320	6,307	3,429	3,584	22,873	5,320	4,634	4,822	8,103	1,760	10,957	14,369	16,044	34,587
1981	152,125	13,885	6,511	3,513	3,861	24,170	5,970	5,183	5,515	8,406	1,853	13,367	15,538	19,465	38,773
1982	166,538	15,165	7,064	3,698	4,403	25,590	6,453	5,554	5,882	8,854	2,067	14,954	16,809	22,399	42,811
1983	182,420	18,310	9,142	4,150	5,018	27,148	7,140	6,232	6,208	9,804	2,310	16,212	18,292	23,576	47,188
1984	194,581	18,846	9,076	4,398	5,372	28,151	7,734	6,683	6,621	10,637	2,536	16,929	19,864	25,166	51,414
Unadjusted															
1982 1st quarter	38,806	3,792	1,904	893	995	6,106	1,400	1,022	1,396	1,843	424	3,992	3,751	5,313	9,767
2nd quarter	40,268	3,388	1,679	827	882	6,519	1,707	1,181	1,460	1,994	491	3,322	3,953	5,600	10,653
3rd quarter	42,549	4,204	2,242	893	1,069	6,335	1,704	1,278	1,496	2,088	523	3,254	4,072	5,704	11,891
4th quarter	44,915	3,781	1,239	1,085	1,457	6,630	1,642	2,073	1,530	2,929	629	4,386	5,033	5,782	10,500
1983 1st quarter	42,787	4,722	2,544	1,005	1,173	6,346	1,566	1,128	1,475	1,984	453	4,523	4,083	5,794	10,713
2nd quarter	44,082	4,154	2,138	971	1,045	6,652	1,788	1,314	1,558	2,235	568	3,779	4,349	5,851	11,834
3rd quarter	46,912	5,176	3,025	983	1,168	6,898	1,971	1,439	1,569	2,329	590	3,421	4,416	5,916	13,187
4th quarter	48,639	4,258	1,435	1,191	1,632	7,252	1,815	2,351	1,606	3,256	699	4,489	5,444	6,015	11,454
1984 1st quarter	45,820	4,834	2,537	1,071	1,226	6,761	1,700	1,243	1,568	2,105	485	4,905	4,345	6,098	11,776
2nd quarter	47,617	4,531	2,432	996	1,103	7,113	1,971	1,435	1,640	2,420	616	3,837	4,761	6,309	12,984
3rd quarter	49,299	4,983	2,676	1,063	1,244	7,013	2,052	1,565	1,690	2,535	661	3,421	4,806	6,347	14,141
4th quarter	51,845	4,498	1,431	1,268	1,799	7,264	2,011	2,440	1,723	3,577	774	4,681	5,962	6,417	12,513
1985 1st quarter	49,100	5,052	2,559	1,151	1,342	6,950	1,860	1,278	1,683	2,371	560	5,286	4,874	6,527	12,659
Revalued at 1980 prices															
1980	136,789	13,320	6,307	3,429	3,584	22,873	5,320	4,634	4,822	8,103	1,760	10,957	14,369	16,044	34,587
1981	136,429	13,486	6,366	3,354	3,766	22,676	5,000	4,612	4,470	8,189	1,696	10,992	14,420	16,279	34,609
1982	137,581	14,193	6,510	3,424	4,259	22,587	4,838	4,545	4,128	8,329	1,810	11,038	14,624	16,530	34,959
1983	143,011	16,459	7,909	3,724	4,826	22,858	4,914	4,816	4,082	8,892	1,948	11,129	14,968	16,764	36,181
1984	145,241	16,290	7,294	3,754	5,242	22,468	4,943	5,041	3,944	9,392	2,051	11,238	15,528	16,978	37,368
Unadjusted															
1982 1st quarter	32,941	3,552	1,747	839	966	5,431	1,089	871	1,027	1,768	377	3,120	3,346	4,108	8,252
2nd quarter	33,273	3,171	1,555	764	852	5,683	1,286	970	1,027	1,890	432	2,488	3,468	4,128	8,730
3rd quarter	34,917	3,917	2,051	828	1,038	5,635	1,267	1,030	1,034	1,959	456	2,377	3,528	4,139	9,575
4th quarter	36,450	3,553	1,157	993	1,403	5,838	1,196	1,674	1,040	2,712	545	3,053	4,282	4,155	8,402
1983 1st quarter	34,086	4,327	2,280	916	1,131	5,458	1,108	897	998	1,832	388	3,116	3,411	4,172	8,379
2nd quarter	34,616	3,724	1,854	870	1,000	5,650	1,235	1,016	1,022	2,042	479	2,615	3,572	4,184	9,077
3rd quarter	36,561	4,564	2,558	883	1,123	5,772	1,351	1,099	1,024	2,108	496	2,374	3,585	4,199	9,989
4th quarter	37,748	3,844	1,217	1,055	1,572	5,978	1,220	1,804	1,038	2,910	585	3,024	4,400	4,209	8,736
1984 1st quarter	34,795	4,249	2,106	932	1,211	5,465	1,126	940	1,004	1,893	402	3,253	3,452	4,224	8,787
2nd quarter	35,474	3,851	1,934	853	1,064	5,642	1,268	1,086	964	2,141	503	2,568	3,742	4,237	9,472
3rd quarter	36,547	4,248	2,136	898	1,214	5,592	1,303	1,180	984	2,247	528	2,373	3,744	4,252	10,096
4th quarter	38,425	3,942	1,118	1,071	1,753	5,769	1,246	1,835	992	3,111	618	3,044	4,590	4,265	9,013
1985 1st quarter	35,329	4,261	1,977	969	1,315	5,300	1,140	938	957	2,057	438	3,343	3,640	4,278	8,977
Seasonally adjusted															
1981 1st quarter	33,980	3,271	1,450	830	991	5,601	1,210	1,126	1,060	2,067	446	2,740	3,638	4,108	8,713
2nd quarter	34,118	3,358	1,516	828	1,014	5,714	1,231	1,128	1,021	2,056	443	2,739	3,637	4,128	8,665
3rd quarter	34,489	3,647	1,678	867	1,102	5,593	1,193	1,118	1,018	2,085	455	2,784	3,673	4,139	8,784
4th quarter	34,994	3,917	1,866	899	1,152	5,679	1,204	1,175	1,029	2,121	466	2,775	3,676	4,155	8,797
1982 1st quarter	35,139	4,001	1,935	906	1,160	5,645	1,224	1,167	1,025	2,148	462	2,748	3,707	4,172	8,840
2nd quarter	35,539	3,966	1,841	940	1,185	5,669	1,185	1,183	1,022	2,223	491	2,864	3,735	4,184	9,017
3rd quarter	36,106	4,263	2,150	925	1,188	5,729	1,274	1,198	1,008	2,246	495	2,779	3,733	4,199	9,182
4th quarter	36,227	4,229	1,983	933	1,293	5,815	1,231	1,268	1,027	2,275	500	2,738	3,793	4,209	9,142
1984 1st quarter	35,960	3,973	1,799	923	1,251	5,662	1,242	1,228	1,028	2,234	482	2,877	3,766	4,224	9,257
2nd quarter	36,430	4,106	1,910	923	1,273	5,661	1,219	1,258	966	2,336	516	2,814	3,921	4,237	9,396
3rd quarter	36,193	4,003	1,772	942	1,289	5,597	1,224	1,280	969	2,394	526	2,778	3,899	4,252	9,320
4th quarter	36,645	4,208	1,813	966	1,429	5,597	1,258	1,275	981	2,428	527	2,769	3,942	4,265	9,395
1985 1st quarter	36,450	4,000	1,698	958	1,344	5,495	1,258	1,219	980	2,410	520	2,938	3,956	4,278	9,396

UNEMPLOYMENT (Thousands)

	United Kingdom		Great Britain				Northern Ireland			
	Total	Percent-age rate	Total	Percent-age rate	Males	Females	Total	Percent-age rate	Males	Females
1980	1,664·9	6·8	1,590·5	6·7	1,129·1	461·3	74·5	12·8	51·5	22·9
1981 Monthly	2,520·4	10·4	2,422·4	10·2	1,773·3	649·1	98·0	16·8	70·0	27·9
1982 averages	2,916·9	12·1	2,808·5	11·9	2,055·9	752·6	108·3	18·7	77·3	31·0
1983	3,104·7	12·9	2,987·6	12·7	2,133·5	854·0	117·1	20·2	85·1	32·0
1984	3,159·8	13·1	3,038·4	12·9	2,109·6	928·8	121·4	20·9	87·7	33·7
1981 October 8	2,771·6	11·4	2,667·7	11·3	1,932·0	735·7	103·9	17·9	73·4	30·5
November 12	2,769·5	11·4	2,667·7	11·3	1,941·7	726·0	101·8	17·5	72·5	29·4
December 10	2,764·1	11·4	2,663·0	11·2	1,952·9	710·0	101·2	17·4	72·3	28·9
1982 January 14	2,896·3	12·0	2,790·5	11·8	2,047·2	743·3	105·8	18·3	75·5	30·2
February 11	2,870·2	11·9	2,765·5	11·7	2,031·6	734·0	104·7	18·1	74·9	29·8
March 11	2,820·8	11·7	2,717·6	11·5	1,999·4	718·1	103·2	17·8	74·1	29·2
April 15	2,818·5	11·7	2,714·3	11·5	2,000·3	714·0	104·2	18·0	74·7	29·5
May 13	2,800·5	11·6	2,694·3	11·4	1,988·1	707·2	105·1	18·2	75·3	29·8
June 10	2,769·6	11·5	2,663·8	11·3	1,967·1	696·7	105·8	18·3	75·8	30·0
July 8	2,852·5	11·8	2,744·4	11·6	2,011·6	732·8	108·2	18·7	76·7	31·4
August 12	2,898·8	12·0	2,789·7	11·8	2,036·6	753·1	109·0	18·8	77·2	31·9
September 9	3,066·2	12·7	2,950·3	12·5	2,127·3	823·0	115·8	20·0	81·3	34·5
October 14	3,049·0	12·6	2,935·3	12·4	2,127·4	807·9	113·7	19·7	80·1	33·7
November 11	3,063·0	12·7	2,950·8	12·5	2,147·6	803·2	112·2	19·4	80·8	31·4
December 9	3,097·0	12·8	2,984·7	12·7	2,186·4	798·3	112·3	19·4	81·6	30·7
1983 January 13	3,225·2	13·4	3,109·0	13·3	2,270·6	838·4	116·2	20·1	84·2	32·0
February 10	3,199·4	13·3	3,084·7	13·2	2,252·7	832·0	114·7	19·8	83·9	30·8
March 10	3,172·4	13·2	3,058·7	13·0	2,236·0	822·7	113·7	19·6	83·4	30·2
April 14	3,169·9	13·2	3,053·5	13·0	2,221·1	832·5	116·4	20·1	85·3	31·1
May 12	3,049·4	12·7	2,934·4	12·5	2,115·0	819·4	115·0	19·9	84·4	30·6
June 9	2,983·9	12·4	2,870·5	12·2	2,061·8	808·7	113·4	19·6	82·9	30·5
July 14	3,020·6	12·6	2,903·5	12·4	2,059·4	844·1	117·1	20·2	84·6	32·6
August 11	3,009·9	12·5	2,892·9	12·3	2,040·6	852·4	117·0	20·2	84·5	32·5
September 8	3,167·4	13·2	3,043·7	13·0	2,116·3	927·4	123·7	21·4	88·3	35·4
October 13	3,094·0	12·9	2,974·2	12·7	2,075·9	898·3	119·8	20·7	86·5	33·4
November 10	3,084·4	12·8	2,964·7	12·6	2,072·4	892·2	119·7	20·7	86·6	33·2
December 8	3,079·4	12·8	2,960·9	12·6	2,080·7	880·3	118·4	20·5	86·2	32·2
1984 January 12	3,199·7	13·2	3,077·4	13·0	2,156·6	920·9	122·2	21·0	88·8	33·5
February 9	3,186·4	13·2	3,063·8	13·0	2,147·4	916·5	122·5	21·1	89·5	33·0
March 8	3,142·8	13·0	3,021·9	12·8	2,116·6	905·3	120·9	20·8	88·4	32·4
April 5	3,107·7	12·8	2,987·6	12·7	2,092·5	895·2	120·1	20·7	87·6	32·5
May 10	3,084·5	12·5	2,963·9	12·6	2,073·4	890·5	120·6	20·8	87·7	32·8
June 14	3,029·7	12·5	2,910·8	12·3	2,033·5	877·3	118·9	20·5	86·1	32·8
July 12	3,100·5	12·8	2,978·9	12·6	2,063·2	915·7	121·6	20·9	87·0	34·7
August 9	3,115·9	12·9	2,995·2	12·7	2,064·6	930·5	120·7	20·8	86·5	34·2
September 13	3,283·6	13·6	3,156·6	13·4	2,155·6	1,000·9	127·1	21·9	90·0	37·1
October 11	3,225·1	13·3	3,103·2	13·1	2,130·8	972·4	122·0	21·0	87·2	34·8
November 8	3,222·6	13·3	3,101·6	13·1	2,135·7	965·9	121·0	20·8	87·0	34·0
December 6	3,219·4	13·3	3,100·0	13·1	2,145·8	954·2	119·4	20·5	86·7	32·7
1985 January 10	3,341·0	13·8	3,217·9	13·6	2,226·8	991·0	123·1	21·2	89·2	33·9
February 14	3,323·7	13·7	3,200·7	13·6	2,220·1	980·6	123·0	21·2	89·8	33·2
March 14	3,267·6	13·5	3,145·9	13·3	2,180·3	965·6	121·7	20·9	88·9	32·8
April 11	3,272·6	13·5	3,150·3	13·3	2,181·8	968·5	122·3	21·0	88·9	33·3
May 9	3,240·9	13·4	3,120·0	13·2	2,155·8	964·2	120·9	20·8	87·9	33·0
June 13	3,178·6	13·1	3,057·2	13·0	2,109·2	948·0	121·4	20·9	87·6	33·8

Employees in employment: all industries

At June   Industries analysed according to the Standard Industrial Classification 1980   Thousands

	1976	1977	1978	1979	1980	1981	1982	1983	1984
Total employees in employment..	22,543	22,619	22,777	23,158	22,972	21,871	21,418	21,081	21,152
Males	13,392	13,363	13,389	13,479	13,306	12,547	12,160	11,855	11,839
Females	9,152	9,256	9,388	9,679	9,666	9,324	9,258	9,226	9,313
of which: Total production and con-struction industries	9,254	9,260	9,215	9,234	8,918	8,069	7,634	7,267	7,131
Agriculture, forestry and fishing....	393	388	382	368	361	352	354	349	340
Coal, oil and natural gas extraction and processing	350	353	358	356	357	344	329	313	290
Electricity, gas, other energy and water supply	370	365	358	366	370	365	354	342	340
Manufacturing industries..........	7,281	7,328	7,290	7,258	6,940	6,221	5,898	5,609	5,517
Construction	1,252	1,215	1,208	1,253	1,252	1,138	1,053	1,003	983
Wholesale distribution and repairs ..	1,039	1,058	1,087	1,128	1,163	1,127	1,112	1,097	1,174
Retail distribution	2,061	2,087	2,101	2,174	2,175	2,090	2,031	2,018	2,137
Hotels and catering...............	864	877	898	950	979	950	965	935	1,013
Transport	1,025	1,030	1,048	1,051	1,047	985	935	896	875
Postal services and communications.	431	419	415	422	437	438	434	427	426
Banking, finance, insurance........	1,494	1,518	1,571	1,663	1,714	1,740	1,748	1,755	1,881
Public administration	1,990	1,989	1,999	2,001	1,972	1,905	1,869	1,883	1,865
Education	1,618	1,602	1,608	1,647	1,630	1,604	1,591	1,590	1,586
Medical and other health services, veterinary services..............	1,174	1,184	1,207	1,229	1,254	1,289	1,313	1,315	1,337
Other services	1,193	1,204	1,245	1,291	1,323	1,325	1,323	1,297	1,377

Distribution of working population

Thousands

	Unadjusted								Seasonally adjusted	
	Working popu-lation	Unemployed excluding students	Employed labour force	Employees in employment			Self-employed persons (with or without em-ployees)	HM Forces	Working population	Employees in employ-ment
				Total	Males	Females				
At June										
1976	26,093	1,265	24,828	22,543	13,392	9,152	1,949	336	26,131	22,524
1977	26,209	1,359	24,850	22,619	13,363	9,256	1,904	327	26,241	22,606
1978	26,342	1,343	24,999	22,777	13,389	9,388	1,904	318	26,372	22,762
1979	26,610	1,235	25,375	23,158	13,479	9,679	1,903	314	26,646	23,139
1980	26,819	1,513	25,306	22,972	13,306	9,666	2,011	323	26,869	22,950
1981	26,718	2,395	24,323	21,870	12,547	9,323	2,118	334	26,784	21,845
1982										
Mar.	26,724	2,821	23,903	21,382	12,186	9,197	2,193	328	26,842	21,519
June	26,730	2,770	23,960	21,418	12,160	9,258	2,218	324	26,803	21,390
Sept.	26,942	3,066	23,876	21,310	12,119	9,191	2,243	323	26,790	21,224
Dec.	26,842	3,097	23,745	21,156	11,967	9,189	2,268	321	26,803	21,126
1983										
Mar.	26,703	3,172	23,531	20,917	11,837	9,079	2,293	321	26,816	21,052
June	26,705	2,984	23,721	21,081	11,855	9,226	2,318	322	26,786	21,054
Sept.	27,003	3,167	23,836	21,168	11,910	9,258	2,343	325	26,845	21,081
Dec.	26,960	3,079	23,881	21,188	11,845	9,344	2,368	325	26,922	21,162
1984										
Mar.	26,904	3,143	23,761	21,009	11,814	9,195	2,426	326	27,001	21,135
June	27,002	3,030	23,972	21,152	11,839	9,313	2,494	326	27,098	21,125
Sept.	27,375	3,284	24,092	21,238	11,892	9,346	2,526	328	27,220	21,159
Dec.	27,402	3,219	24,183	21,299	11,840	9,459	2,557	327	27,365	21,270

FUEL AND POWER

ELECTRICITY

Electricity Industry Finance 1983–85

	£ million	
	1983–84	1984–85
Turnover		
Electricity Supply	9,026·3	9,354·8
Contracting	147·2	152·9
Appliance Marketing	388·5	433·8
TOTAL	9,562·0	9,941·5
Operating Costs		
Electricity Supply	8,130·5	10,651·4(a)
Contracting	142·6	147·7
Appliance Marketing	371·2	405·2
TOTAL	8,644·3	11,204·3
Operating profit/loss before monetary working capital adjustment		
Electricity Supply	895·8	−1,296·6
Contracting	4·6	5·2
Appliance Marketing	17·3	28·6
TOTAL	917·7	−1,262·8
Monetary working capital adjustment	3·3	14·3
Profit/loss on ordinary activities before interest	914·4	−1,277·1
Interest payable	450·3	431·0(b)
Profit/loss before extraordinary charge	464·1	−1,708·1
Extraordinary charge	—	15·0
Profit/loss for the year transferred to reserves	464·1	−1,723·1
Exceptional costs Costs included above attributable to the miners' strike:		
(a) Electricity supply operating costs		1,979·0
(b) Interest		41·0
TOTAL		2,020·0
Excluding the electricity supply exceptional costs, the operating profit before MWCA would have been		716·2

COAL PRODUCTION†

Year (*March*)	NCB Mines	Open Cast	Other	Total
1983	104·7	14·7	1·5	120·9
1984	90·0	13·8	1·5	105·3
1985	27·6	13·6	1·5	42·7

† million tonnes.

	£ million	
Income	1984†	1985†
From Sales (Net)		
Coal	4,153	1,811
Coke	137	64
Gas, Benzole, Tar, etc.	37	13
Processed Fuel	112	44
Miscellaneous Products, Services and Rents	221	86
	4,660	2,018
Other Receipts	367	232
NET INCOME	5,027	2,250

	£ million	
Expenditure	1984†	1985†
Wages, Salaries, Pensions, etc.	2,457	1,292
Past Employee Costs	445	331
Contract work	328	334
Materials, Repairs, Power	1,250	800
Depreciation and other expenses	957	1,195
TOTAL EXPENDITURE	5,437	3,952
PROFIT (LOSS)	(410)	(1,702)
Less Interest Payable, etc.	465	525
Surplus (Deficit) for year	(875)	(2,225)
Government deficit grant	875	2,225
SURPLUS (DEFICIT) CARRIED TO RESERVES	—	—

†April to March.

GAS SUPPLY

	1983–84	1984–85
	(Million Therms)	
GAS SOLD AND USED		
Domestic	9,128	9,278
Industrial	5,753	5,966
Commercial	2,400	2,500
Total gas sold	17,281	17,744
Used for own purposes	133	138
TOTAL GAS SOLD AND USED	17,414	17,882

British Gas Corporation Finance

	1983–84	1984–85
	£ million	
TURNOVER		
Gas (excluding own use)	5,821	6,291
Oil	29	5
Installation and contracting	229	236
Appliances	219	237
Other	124	144
TOTAL	6,422	6,913
COSTS Prime materials		
Natural gas and feedstocks	2,291	2,885
Gas levy	527	504
TOTAL PRIME MATERIALS	2,818	3,389
OPERATING COSTS		
Salaries, wages and associated costs	1,147	1,179
Replacement expenditure	287	303
Other trading costs	925	972
Conversion costs and displaced plant written off	—	—
Tangible fixed assets— historical depreciation	118	140
supplementary depreciation	250	221
Monetary working capital and cost of sales adjustments	28	58
TOTAL OPERATING COSTS	2,755	2,873
Operating profit	849	651
Net interest receivable	99	85
Taxation	(168)	(199)
Extraordinary charge	(3)	—
Interest payable on capital liabilities	(13)	(13)
PROFIT RETAINED	764	524
OPERATING PROFIT—HISTORICAL COST BASIS	1,127	930

AGRICULTURE

Agricultural land: area and harvest

	Area at the June Census (thousand hectares)				Estimated quantity harvested (thousand tonnes)			
	1981	1982	1983	1984	1981	1982	1983	1984
Cereals								
Wheat	1,491	1,663	1,695	1,933	8,710	10,320	10,800	14,980
Barley	2,327	2,222	2,143	1,978	10,230	10,960	9,980	11,030
Oats	144	129	108	106	620	575	465	545
Mixed corn for threshing	11	10	8	8	44	39	35	36
Rye for threshing	6	6	7	6	25	25	24	28
Potatoes								
Early crop	24	25	24	198	375	430	320	395
Main crop	167	167	171		5,840	6,445	5,565	7,005
Fodder crops								
Beans for stockfeeding	45	40	34	32	123	122	105	125
Turnips and swedes	79	71	66	64	4,795	4,575	3,655	3,960
Fodder beet and mangolds	5	5	5	8	320	370	295	570
Maize for threshing or stockfeeding	18	16	15	16	635	635	550	580
Kale, cabbage, savoys, kohl rabi and rape for stockfeeding	49	43	40	39	2,195	1,985	1,660	1,805
Peas harvested dry for stockfeeding				42			85	170
Other crops for stockfeeding	26	31	25	22				
Horticultural crops								
Orchards and small fruit	62	61	58	56				
Vegetables grown in the open:								
Brussels sprouts	13	13	11	11	203	216		
Cabbage (all kinds), cauliflower and broccoli	26	27	25	25	897	829		
Carrots	17	14	13	14	711	576		
Parsnips		3	2	3	54	52		
Turnips and swedes	3	3			110	82		
Beetroot	2	2	2	2	99	102		
Onions	8	9	8	8	258	259		
Leeks					37	39		
Beans (broad, runner and french)	11	12	11	10	83	105		
Peas, green for market	55	56	47	46	25	24		
Peas, green for processing					256	242		
Peas, for harvesting dry	28	27	18	14	87	88		
Celery	1	1	1	1	50	50		
Lettuce	4	4	4	4	131	146		
Rhubarb					39	37		
Other vegetables	10	9	10	10				
Flowers, nursery stock, bulbs grown in open:								
Hardy nursery stock	7	7	7	7				
Bulb flowers and bulbs	5	5	4	4				
Other flowers	1	1	1	1				
Area under glass	2	2	2	2				
Other crops								
Sugar beet	210	204	199	199	7,395	10,005	7,495	9,015
Rape grown for oilseed	125	174	222	269	325	581	565	925
Hops	6	6	6	5	9	10	9	80
Other crops not for stockfeeding	7	7	6	6				
Bare fallow	76	55	97	42				
Total tillage	5,071	5,127	5,124	5,196				
Lucerne								
All grasses under five years old	1,911	1,859	1,846	1,794				
Total arable	6,982	6,986	6,970	6,990				
All grasses five years old and over	5,103	5,097	5,107	5,105				
Total crops and grass	12,085	12,083	12,078	12,095				
Rough grazing								
Sole rights	5,021	4,984	4,927	4,889				
Common (estimated)	1,214	1,214	1,212	1,214				
Woodland on agricultural holdings	277	285	292	299				
All other land on agricultural holdings	211	217	227	218				
Total agricultural area	18,808	18,783	18,735	18,716				
Total area of the United Kingdom	24,089	24,088	24,088	24,088				

AGRICULTURE

Cattle, Sheep, Pigs and Poultry on Agricultural Holdings (Thousands)

Cattle and Calves	Total cattle and calves	Cows and heifers in milk		Cows in calf but not in milk		Heifers in calf with first calf		Bulls for service	All other cattle and calves		
		Dairy	Beef	Dairy	Beef	Dairy	Beef		2 years old and over	1 year old and under 2	Under 1 year old
1979 June	13,589	2,975	1,303	317	240	684	180	90	1,033	3,123	3,644
December	13,363	2,662	739	690	797	442	169	86	1,044	3,114	3,621
1980 June	13,426	2,938	1,241	290	238	677	161	86	1,005	3,153	3,636
December	13,062	2,608	701	669	750	449	171	82	972	3,086	3,575
1981 June	13,138	2,907	1,191	284	228	700	162	84	963	3,041	3,576
December	12,959	2,615	678	678	732	441	178	82	948	3,034	3,573
1982 June	13,244	2,984	1,161	266	227	688	163	84	937	3,057	3,676
December	13,173	2,684	673	673	708	437	177	82	970	3,095	3,674
1983 June	13,290	3,058	1,132	274	225	688	159	83	904	3,059	3,707
December	13,157	2,736	700	693	642	416	169	81	939	3,134	3,648
1984 June	13,213	2,977	1,124	303	227	658	170	80	905	3,069	3,716
December†	12,985	2,637	674	674	675	397	170	78	921	3,088	3,671

Sheep and Lambs	Total sheep and lambs	Sheep 1 year old and over				Lambs under 1 year old
		Ewes for breeding	Two tooth ewes (shearlings)	Rams for service	Others	
1979 June	29,946	11,709	2,870	342	974	14,051
December	21,609	13,640		375	889	6,705
1980 June	31,446	12,178	2,745	353	927	15,243
December	21,604	14,038		378	714	6,473
1981 June	32,097	12,528	2,743	358	841	15,628
December	22,200	14,430		386	709	3,683
1982 June	33,067	12,909	2,871	366	877	16,044
December	22,944	14,926		397	838	6,783
1983 June	34,069	13,310	2,933	383	831	16,612
December	23,317	15,249		414	795	6,859
1984 June	34,802	13,648	2,892	393	788	17,080
December†	23,946	15,465		426	750	7,306

Pigs	Total pigs	Sows and gilts for breeding				Boars for service	Barren sows for fattening	All other pigs				
		Sows in pig	Gilts in pig	Other sows kept for breeding	50 kg gilts (110 lb) and over expected to be used for breeding			110 kg (240 lb) and over	80 kg (175 lb) and under 110 kg (240 lb)	50 kg (110 lb) and under 80 kg (175 lb)	20 kg (45 lb) and under 50 kg (110 lb)	Under 20 kg (45 lb)
1979 June	7,864	528	109	215	82	43	14	112	695	1,770	2,258	2,040
December	7,813	521	91	208	91	42	13	107	661	1,766	2,288	2,026
1980 June	7,815	517	109	204	84	42	12	102	657	1,772	2,240	2,074
December	7,770	514	101	203	89	42	14	109	634	1,773	2,244	2,047
1981 June	7,828	522	112	203	87	43	11	90	638	1,776	2,227	2,119
December	7,910	532	108	197	90	43	12	93	627	1,837	2,281	2,090
1982 June	8,023	543	122	200	89	45	12	117	630	1,824	2,281	2,163
December	8,210	558	114	204	92	46	15	105	661	1,892	2,308	2,216
1983 June	8,174	542	110	204	82	45	15	100	605	1,868	2,362	2,241
December	7,782	510	96	184	75	43	16	87	610	1,826	2,244	2,091
1984 June	7,689	518	105	178	77	42	12	91	599	1,787	2,198	2,082
December†	7,793	526	107	181	84	43	14	101	600	1,831	2,200	2,106

Poultry	Total poultry	Fowls for producing eggs for eating			Fowls for breeding (including cocks and cockerels)	Broilers and other table fowls	Total fowls	Other poultry		
		Birds that have been in the laying flock for:		Growing pullets (from day old to point of lay)				Ducks	Geese	Turkeys
		less than 12 months	12 months or more							
1979 June	135,345	35,890	12,230	15,504	6,657	57,153	127,433	1,552		6,359
December	124,542	33,502	13,140	13,642	6,651	49,045	115,979	1,269	109	7,186
1980 June	135,105	34,415	11,596	14,457	6,678	59,917	127,063	1,390	133	6,519
December	119,297	32,296	12,074	11,959	5,642	47,975	109,947	1,226	123	8,001
1981 June	132,286	31,737	12,736	14,219	6,117	57,830	122,639	1,333	148	8,167
December	123,596	31,368	11,760	12,663	6,039	53,032	114,862	1,316	120	7,298
1982 June	135,363	32,711	12,081	14,766	6,457	60,075	126,091	1,443	157	7,672
December	113,866	32,408	11,726	12,726	5,586	49,788	112,234	1,402	122	
1983 June	128,260	32,917	11,546	12,079	6,012	58,887	118,496	1,410	138	8,198
December	125,667	30,371	11,719	12,645	5,555	52,834	113,124	1,468	123	10,937
1984 June	129,436	30,083	11,843	13,163	6,396	59,341	120,826	1,365	145	7,084
December†	—	30,258	10,615	12,122	6,041	53,258	112,295	—	—	—

† Provisional

ROADS

On April 1, 1984, the total mileage of public roads in Great Britain, excluding green lanes, was 215,453 of which 163,935 were in England, 31,385 in Scotland and 20,133 in Wales.

Highway Authorities

The powers and responsibilities of highway authorities in England and Wales are set out in the Highways Acts 1980. They are concerned mainly with the construction, improvement and maintenance of highways. The Secretary of State for Transport and the Secretary of State for Wales are the highway authorities for the trunk roads in England and in Wales respectively. (Trunk roads constitute the national system of routes for through traffic and include most motorways.)

Under the Local Government Act 1972, since April 1, 1974, the county councils are the highway authorities for all highways in England (outside Greater London) and Wales, other than trunk roads. However, the district councils have a right to maintain unclassified urban roads, footpaths and bridleways and may under agency arrangements carry out other highway functions on behalf of the county councils. In Greater London the most important non-trunk roads are metropolitan roads, for which the Greater London Council is highway authority. The Common Council of the City of London and the London borough councils are highway authorities for all other non-trunk roads in their areas.

For Scotland there is separate legislation under which the Secretary of State for Scotland is the highway authority for trunk roads. The highway authorities for non-trunk public roads are the Regional and Islands Councils. There are general powers available in the Local Government (Scotland) Act 1973, which would enable them if they wished to delegate functions to the District Councils.

Transport Supplementary Grant was introduced on 1 April 1975, to replace a variety of grants towards expenditure. It was a block grant which was paid to the G.L.C. and county councils in respect of their current and capital expenditure. From April 1982, T.S.G. in Wales became payable on capital expenditure only, grant in respect of current expenditure having been subsumed into the Rate Support Grant. In England, T.S.G. was payable on current and capital expenditure and is restricted to highways and the regulation of traffic. For 1985–86 the rate of grant is 50 per cent. of Council's estimate of expenditure. From April 1985, in Wales, T.S.G. will be payable in respect of new schemes only if over £5m. For the financial year 1985–86 local authorities in England received £160,000,000 in transport supplementary grants.

Motorways

The network in England and Wales is based on five main routes—London–Yorkshire (M1), London–South Wales (M4), Birmingham–Bristol–Exeter (M5), Birmingham–Carlisle (M6) and Lancashire–Yorkshire (M62). Other important motorways in use include: Medway Towns (M2); London–Basingstoke (M3); London–Cambridge (M11); Rotherham–Goole (M18); London–Folkestone (M20); London orbital route (M25); London–Oxford (M40); North Cheshire (M56); and South Humberside (M180). Motorways in use in Scotland include: Edinburgh–Glasgow–Greenock (M8); Edinburgh–Stirling (M9); Maryville–Mollisburn (M73); Millbank–Maryville (M74); Stirling–Haggs (M80); Friarton Bridge, Perth (M85); Inverkeithing–Perth (M90) and (M80)–Kincardine Bridge (M876).

On April 1, 1984, 1,729 miles of trunk and principal motorway were open to traffic in Great Britain (England 1,508, Scotland 147 and Wales 74). 74 miles were under construction, all of them in England.

Motor Vehicles

The number of vehicles in Great Britain with current licences in 1984 totalled 20,765,000; private and light goods vehicles 17,792,000; motor cycles, scooters and mopeds 1,225,000; public transport vehicles 116,000; heavy goods vehicles 1,565,000; agricultural tractors 375,000; others 730,000. There were 648,000 vehicles exempt from licensing.

Driving Tests

The number of driving tests conducted in Great Britain in the year 1984 was 1,784,112, of which 50·93 per cent resulted in failure.

Expenditure

Expenditure on roads in England during 1983–84 was £2,038m compared with £2,031m in 1982–83. The expenditure during 1983–84 may be broken down as follows: New Construction and Improvement £971m (Trunk roads £518m; Principal and other roads, £435m); Maintenance (including road safety), £1,067m (Trunk roads, £191m, Principal and other roads, £876m); Cleansing, Gritting and Snow-Clearing, and other expenditure. Road Lighting costs of £141m are included. In addition the cost of vehicle parking was £92m (gross).

Expenditure on new construction and in improvement of trunk roads and motorways in England during 1983–84 was £518m. In Scotland and Wales, the figures were £86·7m and £135·8m respectively. Expenditure on new construction and improvement of principal and other roads in 1983–84 was £453m in England, £112·3m in Scotland and £57·8m in Wales.

Road Casualties

In 1984 in Great Britain there were 60 vehicles for every kilometre of road or one vehicle for every 17 metres. Fifteen road users were killed and 873 injured on an average day. Of those killed 39% were car users, 33% pedestrians, 17% users of two-wheeled motor vehicles; 19% of all those killed were children.

Year	Killed	Injured	Year	Killed	Injured
1965	7,952	389,985	1975	6,366	318,584
1966	7,985	384,472	1976	6,570	333,103
1967	7,319	362,659	1977	6,614	341,447
1968	6,810	342,398	1978	6,831	342,964
1969	7,365	345,529	1979	6,362	328,000
1970	7,499	355,869	1980	6,010	323,000
1971	7,699	344,328	1981	5,846	318,994
1972	7,763	351,964	1982	5,934	328,362
1973	7,406	346,374	1983	5,445	303,139
1974	6,833	318,035	1984	5,599	318,715

Deaths more than 30 days after the accident are excluded.

BRITISH RAILWAYS 1984–85

The British Railways Board was set up, along with our other separate nationalized transport undertakings, by the terms of the Transport Act, 1962. This Act dissolved the British Transport Commission and shared its assets between the new bodies which assumed their responsibilities on January 1, 1963. Under the Act the finances of the railways were reconstructed and previous restrictions were modified to give them greater commercial freedom than they had enjoyed in the past.

The Transport Act of 1968 reduced the railways' commencing debt and enabled the Secretary of State for the Environment to make grants for the maintenance of unremunerative passenger services.

The Railways Act of 1974 further reduced the Board's capital debt but increased its borrowing powers. It also introduced a new system of financial support in accordance with E.E.C. regulations; the Secretary of State is authorized to impose general obligations on the Board in respect of passenger services and is empowered to compensate the Board for meeting these obligations. The Secretary of State's power to make grants for unremunerative passenger services was withdrawn. The Transport Act of 1981 empowered the Secretary of State to direct the board to dispose of assets. This power has not been exercised, but the Board's former shipping, harbour and hotel businesses have been sold to the private sector.

The railway business is broken down into five distinct business sectors each with its own Director. The sectors focus on three passenger businesses of Intercity; London & S.E.; and Provincial Services; together with the Railfreight and parcel businesses. In addition for the purposes of management and operation the railways are divided into Regions. They cover the following areas:

1. London Midland Region—bounded by a line joining Carlisle, Oldham, Nottingham, Bedford, London, Banbury, Kidderminster, Aberystwyth.
2. Western Region—west of a line joining Yeovil, Westbury, Reading, London and the southern border of the L.M. Region.
3. Southern Region—south of a line joining Dorchester, Salisbury, London and the Thames.
4. Eastern Region—east of a line joining London, Peterborough, Sheffield, Bradford and Carlisle.
5. Scottish Region—north of a line joining Carlisle and Berwick.

Staff.—On Mar. 31, 1985, British Rail employed a total staff of 147,219 compared with 155,423 on Dec. 31, 1983.

Financial Results, 1984–85.—The Profit and Loss Account for 1984–85 showed a deficit of £408·3m compared with a surplus of £7·8m for 1983, while the railway working surplus (before taking interest charges or revenue from other activities into account) was £235·4m, compared with a surplus of £62·2m for the previous year.

Railways	£ million 1984–5	
Gross receipts:		
Passenger (including Grants)..	2,679·3	
Freight (inc. parcels and mails)	557·1	
Miscellaneous	6·3	
TOTAL..............		3,242·7
Working expenses:		
Train services	1,560·7	
Terminal	333·2	
Miscellaneous traffic expenses .	121·7	
Track and signalling..........	789·5	
General expenses.............	590·7	
Provision for replacement of assets	125·0	
TOTAL..................		3,520·8
Railway net loss...............		278·1
Net income from Operational Property (Letting), Advertising and Catering....		42·7
OPERATING LOSS		235·4

OPERATING STATISTICS

At Mar. 31, 1985, British Rail had 24,698 miles of standard gauge lines and sidings in use, representing 10,441 miles of route of which 2,360 miles were electrified. Standard rail on main line has a weight of 110 lbs. per yard. British Rail had 2,711 locomotives (diesel and diesel electric, 2,467 and electric, 244); 2,617 diesel multiple-unit vehicles, 7,078 electric multiple-unit vehicles and 3,869 locomotive-hauled passenger carriages with a capacity of 939,860 seats or berths in 1984. Loaded train miles run in passenger service totalled 238·9m. 857·2m passenger journeys were made during the year, including 383·5m made by holders of season tickets. The average distance of each passenger journey on ordinary fare was 34·8 miles; and on season ticket, 16 miles. Passenger stations in use in 1985 numbered 2,376 and freight stations 148.

Freight.—There were 45,189 freight-vehicles and 2,130 other vehicles in the non-passenger-carrying stock. Loaded train miles run in freight service totalled 29·8m.

Casualties in Train Accidents
(includes British Railways, London Transport and other railways).

	1982	1983
Fatal accidents....	5	0
Passengers killed ..	0	2
Passengers seriously injured ...	3	9
Railwaymen killed	8	1
Railwaymen seriously injured ...	12	8
Other persons killed	3	7
Other persons seriously injured ...	3	4
Passengers carried per passenger killed	—	—
Passenger miles run per passenger killed	—	—

Railway Accidents in which 20 Persons and over were Killed in the United Kingdom since 1948

Year	Date	Name of Accident	Railway	Number Killed	Cause
1948	Apl. 17	Winsford	L.M. Region	24	Collision.
1952	Oct. 8	Harrow	L.M. Region	112	Collision.
1957	Dec. 4	Lewisham	S. Region	90	Collision in fog.
1967	Nov. 5	Hither Green	S. Region	49	Track failure.
1975	Feb. 28	Moorgate	L.T.E.	43	Terminal overrun.

AERODROMES AND AIRPORTS

Aerodromes in Great Britain, Northern Ireland, the Isle of Man and the Channel Islands which are either State owned, operated by the Civil Aviation Authority or licensed for use by civil aircraft. A number of unlicensed airfields not included in this list are also available for private use by permission of the owner or controlling authority. Aerodromes designated as Customs airports are printed in bold type. Customs facilities are available at certain other aerodromes by special arrangement.

S = Owned and operated by the State.
CAA = Operated by the Civil Aviation Authority.
BAA = Operated by the British Airports Authority.
M = Owned or operated by Municipal Authority.

J = Military airfield available for civil use by prior permission.
H = Licensed helicopter station.

ENGLAND AND WALES

Aberporth, Dyfed. S
Abingdon, Oxon. J
Andrewsfield, Essex.
Barrow (Walney Island), Cumbria.
Bembridge, I.O.W.
Benson, Oxon. J
Biggin Hill, Kent.
Birmingham, W. Midlands. M
Blackbushe, Hants.
Blackpool, Lancs. M
Bodmin, Cornwall.
Bourn, Cambridge.
Bournemouth, (Hurn), Dorset. M
Bridlington, Humberside.
Bristol, Avon. M
Brize Norton, Oxford. J
Caernarfon, Gwynedd.
Cambridge.
Cardiff, S. Glamorgan. M
Carlisle, Cumbria. M
Chichester (Goodwood), Sussex.
Chivenor, Devon. J
Church Fenton, N. Yorks. J
Clacton, Essex.
Compton Abbas, Dorset.
Cosford, Wolverhampton. J
Coventry, W. Midlands. M
Cranfield, Beds.
Cranwell, Lincs. J
Culdrose, Cornwall. J
Denham, Bucks.
Dishforth, N. Yorks. J
Doncaster, S. Yorks.
Dunkeswell, Devon.
Duxford, Cambs. M
Earls Colne, Halstead.
East Midlands, Derby. M
Elstree, Herts.
Elvington, Yorks. J
Exeter, Devon.
Fairoaks, Surrey.
Farnborough, Hants. S
Fenland, Lincs.
Finningley, S. Yorks. J
Gloucester/Cheltenham (Staverton), Glos. M
Great Yarmouth (North Denes), Norfolk.
Halfpenny Green, Staffs.
Hamble, Hants.
Hatfield, Herts.
Haverfordwest, Dyfed. M
Hawarden, Clywd.
Holyhead Heliport, Gwynedd. H
Hucknall, Notts.
Humberside. M
Ipswich, Suffolk.
Isle of Wight (Sandown).
Kemble, Glos. J
Land's End (St. Just), Cornwall.
Lashenden, Headcorn, Kent.

Leavesden, Herts.
Leeds and Bradford, Yorks. M
Leeming, N. Yorks. J
Lee-on-Solent, Hants. J
Leicester, Leics.
Linton-on-Ouse, Yorks. J
Liverpool, Merseyside. M
London (Gatwick). BAA
London (Heathrow). BAA
London (Stansted). BAA
London (Westland Heliport). H
Luton, Beds. M
Lydd, Kent.
Lyneham, Wilts. J
Manchester International. M
Manchester (Barton).
Manston, Kent. J
Nether Thorpe, S. Yorks.
Newcastle, Tyne and Wear. M
Newton, Notts. J
Northampton (Sywell), Northants.
Northolt, Mddx. J
Norwich, Norfolk. M
Nottingham, Notts.
Oxford (Kidlington), Oxfordshire.
Panshanger, Herts.
Penzance, Cornwall. H
Peterborough (Conington).
Peterborough (Sibson), Cambs.
Plymouth (Roborough), Devon.
Portland Naval, Dorset. JH
Redhill, Surrey.
Rochester, Kent.
St. Mawgan, Cornwall. J
Sandtoft, Humberside.
Scilly Isles (St. Mary's).
Seething, Norfolk.
Shawbury, Shropshire. J
Sherburn-in-Elmet, N. Yorks.
Shipdham, Norfolk.
Shobdon, Herefordshire.
Shoreham, W. Sussex. M
Silverstone, Northants.
Skegness (Ingoldmells), Lincs.
Sleap, Shropshire.
Southampton, Hants.
Southend, Essex. M
Stapleford, Essex.
Sturgate, Lincs.
Swansea, W. Glam. M
Teesside, Cleveland. M
Thruxton, Hants.
Tresco, Isles of Scilly. H
Valley, Gwynedd. J
Waddington, Lincs. J
Warton, Lancs.
Wattisham, Suffolk. J
Wellesbourne Mountford, Warwick.
Weston, Avon. H
White Waltham, Berks.
Wickenby, Lincs.
Woodford, Gtr. Manchester.

Woodvale, Merseyside. J
Wycombe Air Park (Booker), Bucks.
Yeovil, Somerset.
Yeovilton, Somerset. J

SCOTLAND

Aberdeen (Dyce). BAA
Barra, Hebrides.
Benbecula, Hebrides. CAA
Dounreay (Thurso). S
Dundee, Angus. M
Eday. M
Edinburgh. BAA
Fair Isle.
Fetlar, Shetlands.
Fife/Glenrothes.
Flotta, Orkneys.
Glasgow. BAA
Hoy Longhope, Orkneys. M
Inverness (Dalcross). CAA
Islay (Port Ellen). CAA
Isle of Skye. M
Kinloss. J
Kirkwall. CAA
Lerwick (Tingwall). M
Leuchars. J
Lossiemouth. J
Machrihanish, Kintyre, J
North Ronaldsay, Orkneys. M
Papa Westray, Orkneys. M
Perth (Scone).
Prestwick. BAA
Rothesay, Bute. H
Sanday, Orkneys. M
Scatsta.
Stornoway, Hebrides. CAA
Stronsay, Orkneys. M
Sumburgh, Shetlands. CAA
Tiree. CAA
Unst, Shetland. M
West Freugh, Wigtown. S
Westray, Orkneys. M
Whalsay, Shetlands.
Wick. CAA

NORTHERN IRELAND

Belfast (Aldergrove). S
Belfast (Harbour).
Enniskillen (St. Angelo). M
Londonderry (Eglinton). M
Newtownards.

ISLE OF MAN

Ronaldsway.

CHANNEL ISLANDS

Alderney. S
Guernsey. S
Jersey. S

MERCHANT SHIPPING

PRINCIPAL MERCHANT FLEETS OF THE WORLD. Source: *Lloyd's Register of Shipping*

Flag	1973 No.	1973 Tons Gross	1978 No.	1978 Tons Gross	1983 No.	1983 Tons Gross	1984 No.	1984 Tons Gross
Liberia	2,289	49,904,744	2,523	80,191,329	2,062	67,664,201	1,934	62,024,700
Japan	9,469	36,785,094	9,321	39,182,079	10,593	40,751,915	10,425	40,358,479
Greece	2,536	19,295,143	3,666	33,956,693	3,169	37,477,642	2,904	35,058,593
Panama	1,692	9,568,954	3,640	20,748,679	5,316	34,655,508	5,499	37,244,233
*U.S.S.R.	7,123	17,396,900	7,991	22,261,927	7,753	24,549,350	7,095	24,492,469
*U.S.A.	4,063	14,912,432	4,746	16,187,636	6,437	19,358,496	6,441	19,291,868
Norway	2,758	23,621,096	2,646	26,128,428	2,340	19,299,966	2,271	19,372,916
United Kingdom	3,628	30,159,543	3,359	30,896,696	2,570	19,551,405	2,468	15,875,062
†China, People's Republic of	296	2,946,303	1,517	6,788,493	1,693	9,868,075	1,905	13,258,776
Italy	1,726	8,847,205	1,694	11,491,873	1,609	10,015,211	1,590	9,157,867
France	1,376	8,288,773	1,317	12,197,354	1,173	7,504,690	1,174	8,945,046
Spain	2,420	4,833,048	2,753	8,056,080	2,589	7,009,106	2,529	7,004,852
Singapore	387	2,004,269	954	7,489,205	855	6,896,961	825	6,512,344
Germany, Fed. Republic of	2,234	7,914,679	1,999	9,736,667	1,769	6,386,002	1,813	6,242,467
Korea (South)	617	1,103,925	1,148	2,975,389	1,733	6,226,646	1,799	6,771,402
India	430	2,886,595	591	5,769,224	677	5,807,906	710	6,414,741
Brazil	469	2,103,319	565	3,701,731	698	5,296,798	706	5,721,821
Saudi Arabia	43	58,530	154	1,246,112	435	5,515,697	422	3,968,272
Denmark	1,362	4,106,525	1,397	5,530,408	1,312	4,383,906	1,301	4,585,991
Netherlands	1,989	5,029,443	1,238	5,351,492	1,294	4,383,526	1,337	5,784,336
Hong Kong	98	1,322,529	130	874,850	294	3,686,127	340	3,267,281
Poland	631	2,072,531	796	3,490,887	812	3,450,241	783	3,520,352
Cyprus	589	2,935,775	793	2,599,529	593	3,432,683	737	6,727,887
Sweden	831	5,669,340	696	6,508,255	674	3,384,677	679	3,441,076
Canada	1,235	2,432,802	1,289	2,964,499	1,300	2,964,472	1,310	3,449,496
Philippines	404	947,210	577	1,264,995	884	2,546,638	946	3,124,711
Kuwait	162	676,879	251	2,240,030	235	2,548,112	250	2,551,074
Yugoslavia	382	1,667,183	468	2,365,630	479	2,524,374	480	2,681,879
Turkey	353	756,907	460	1,358,779	687	2,399,846	776	2,666,820
Argentina	351	1,452,552	432	2,200,679	532	2,398,764	530	2,406,714
Romania	96	474,497	229	1,429,041	339	2,358,127	393	2,168,471
Finland	390	1,543,426	341	2,358,623	322	2,273,503	332	2,172,850
Belgium	236	1,161,609	288	1,684,692	322	2,022,481	338	1,856,967
Australia	373	1,160,205	426	1,531,739	578	1,949,699	622	2,105,549
Indonesia	573	668,964	1,093	1,272,387	1,391	1,794,642	1,484	1,073,871
Iran	93	192,386	208	1,194,675	270	1,561,417	306	1,489,120
Iraq	46	228,274	115	1,305,907	161	1,475,048	153	1,664,312
Mexico	248	453,024	336	727,201	619	1,475,104	624	1,492,245
Malaysia	117	226,350	182	552,456	376	1,420,834	429	1,421,714
German Dem. Rep.	432	1,219,037	452	1,539,994	416	1,365,662	409	1,366,149
Algeria	56	102,832	121	1,352,986	143	1,357,681	147	1,571,007
Portugal	438	1,271,815	342	1,282,663	357	1,293,277	357	1,282,962
Bulgaria	159	756,749	189	1,082,477	197	—	197	—
Bahamas	—	—	—	—	—	—	163	3,191,971
Malta	—	—	—	—	—	—	195	1,366,149
Venezuela	—	—	—	—	—	—	250	1,003,381

* Including ships of the United States Reserve Fleet. † Including 3,968,418 gross tonnage for Taiwan.

TONNAGE CLASSED WITH LLOYD'S REGISTER.

At 30th June, 1984, 24·85 per cent (104,047,773 tons) of the tonnage owned in the world was classed by Lloyd's Register.

MERCHANT SHIPPING

MOTORSHIPS COMPLETED IN THE WORLD DURING 1984
Source: *Lloyd's Register of Shipping*

Country of Build	Total		For Registration in	Total	
	No.	Gross Tonnage		No.	Gross Tonnage
Japan	902	9,711,381	Panama	308	3,900,662
Korea (South)	87	1,472,887	Japan	422	2,660,111
*†China, People's Republic of	61	1,150,842	Liberia	80	1,751,622
Germany, Federal Republic of	109	516,590	‡China, People's Republic of	69	1,340,601
Denmark	46	474,181	U.S.S.R.	325	997,105
United Kingdom	46	444,743	Greece	45	846,381
U.S.S.R.	210	395,584	Hong Kong	27	488,483
German Democratic Republic	58	366,841	Germany, Federal Republic of	97	486,761
*Romania	18	365,211	U.S.A.	44	464,903
Spain	92	354,955	United Kingdom	39	459,369
Finland	30	340,358	India	46	441,805
France	36	326,552	Norway	41	430,747
Sweden	13	303,620	Romania	12	350,613
Poland	52	302,013	Philippines	16	303,353
Italy	30	273,701	Denmark	39	295,946
Brazil	23	271,450	Brazil	38	280,120
Yugoslavia	21	270,797	Italy	21	255,358
Netherlands	68	153,977	Sweden	11	252,564
Bulgaria	9	153,292	Singapore	34	246,247
Belgium	11	152,255	Netherlands	56	219,975
Norway	39	111,519	Korea (South)	24	195,064
U.S.A.	73	83,738	France	19	157,993
Turkey	33	67,613	Belgium	11	152,255
Argentina	7	67,115	Egypt	15	116,199
India	9	36,827	Iran	34	111,796
Greece	7	36,347	Poland	7	106,188
Singapore	43	30,393			
Canada	5	26,083			
Other Countries	72	73,186	Other Countries	330	1,021,840
WORLD TOTAL	2,210	18,334,061		2,210	18,334,061

Included in the table above are 6 steamships, 2 of 49,071 in France, 3 of 306,065 in Japan and 1 of 80,912 in Sweden.
Tonnage completed to Lloyd's Register Class.—Of the world tonnage completed during 1984, 22·8 per cent (4,171,446 gross tonnage) was to Lloyd's Register Class.
* Information incomplete.   † Including 821,879 gross tonnage from Taiwan.   ‡ Including 776,239 gross tonnage for Taiwan.

DEFENCE MANPOWER STRENGTHS

Thousands

At 1 April U.K. SERVICE PERSONNEL	1978	1979	1980	1981	1982	1983	1984
All services: total	320·7	315·0	320·6	333·8	327·6	320·6	325·9
Male	306·1	299·7	304·4	316·8	311·9	305·2	309·7
Female	14·6	15·3	16·2	16·9	15·7	15·4	16·2
Royal Navy: total	67·8	65·1	64·4	66·4	65·1	64·0	63·7
Male	63·8	61·2	60·5	62·3	61·1	60·1	59·8
Female	4·0	3·8	3·8	4·1	4·0	3·9	3·9
Royal Marines: total	7·5	7·4	7·6	7·9	7·9	7·8	7·6
Male	7·5	7·4	7·6	7·9	7·9	7·8	7·6
Army: total	160·8	156·2	159·0	166·0	163·2	159·1	161·5
Male	155·1	150·4	152·8	159·4	157·2	152·9	155·0
Female	5·7	5·8	6·3	6·6	6·0	6·1	6·6
Royal Air Force: total	84·6	86·3	89·6	93·5	91·5	89·8	93·1
Male	79·7	80·7	83·5	87·2	85·7	84·5	87·3
Female	4·9	5·6	6·1	6·3	5·8	5·4	5·7
Personnel Locally Entered overseas: total	8·4	8·4	8·2	9·7	10·1	10·1	9·6
Regular Reserves: total	179·5	188·5	192·6	196·5	196·4	193·4	198·0
Royal Navy	26·3	28·4	27·0	26·8	24·7	23·9	23·5
Royal Marines	2·4	2·4	2·2	2·2	2·2	2·2	2·2
Army	118·5	127·0	133·1	137·5	140·2	138·3	143·2
Army General Reserve	–	–	–	–	–	–	–
Royal Air Force	32·3	30·8	30·3	30·1	29·3	28·9	29·0
Volunteer Reserves and Auxilliary Forces: total	75·3	73·5	77·0	83·9	86·3	87·3	85·7
Royal Navy	5·4	5·4	5·0	5·4	5·4	5·4	5·2
Royal Marines	1·0	0·9	0·8	0·9	1·1	1·1	1·0
Territorial Army	60·6	59·4	63·3	69·5	72·1	72·8	71·4
Ulster Defence Regiment	7·9	7·6	7·4	7·5	7·1	7·1	6·8
Home Service Force	–	–	–	–	–	0·3	0·3
Royal Air Force	0·4	0·3	0·5	0·6	0·6	0·6	1·0
Cadet Forces: total	142·2	140·0	141·5	144·1	144·6	142·0	141·2
Royal Navy	25·0	23·9	22·7	24·5	24·6	22·4	23·1
Army	73·4	72·6	74·6	75·1	74·1	74·5	73·8
Royal Air Force	43·8	43·5	44·1	44·4	45·9	45·1	44·3

Recruitment of U.K. Service personnel to each Service

Number

	1976/77	1977/78	1978/79	1979/80	1980/81	1981/82	1982/83	1983/84
All Services: total	40,244	38,237	43,366	50,652	50,488	22,607	21,647	36,991
Male	36,390	34,188	38,774	46,206	46,693	21,188	19,342	33,760
Female	3,854	4,049	4,592	4,446	3,795	1,419	2,305	3,231
Royal Navy: total	8,195	7,167	6,791	8,526	9,088	3,805	3,584	4,785
Male	7,238	6,269	5,978	7,701	8,130	3,353	3,078	4,223
Female	957	898	813	825	958	452	506	562
Royal Marines: total	929	903	1,282	1,676	1,674	699	447	447
Male	929	903	1,282	1,676	1,674	699	447	447
Army: total	24,088	22,550	25,254	29,189	28,871	14,204	13,071	22,348
Male	22,344	20,868	23,528	27,164	27,241	13,603	11,679	20,811
Female	1,744	1,682	1,726	2,025	1,630	601	1,392	1,537
Royal Air Force: total	7,032	7,617	10,039	11,261	10,855	3,899	4,545	9,411
Male	5,879	6,148	7,986	9,665	9,648	3,533	4,138	8,279
Female	1,153	1,469	2,053	1,596	1,207	366	407	1,132

HOUSING

Permanent dwellings completed

	United Kingdom				England and Wales			
	Total	For local housing authorities	For private owners	Other	Total	For local housing authorities	For private owners	Other
1963	307,714	123,903	177,787	6,024	270,655	97,015	168,242	5,398
1964	383,192	154,754	221,264	7,174	336,505	119,468	210,432	6,605
1965	391,234	164,957	217,162	9,115	347,181	133,024	206,246	7,911
1966	396,009	176,871	208,647	10,491	349,480	142,430	197,502	9,548
1967	415,455	199,749	204,208	11,498	362,898	159,347	192,940	10,611
1968	425,835	187,984	226,068	11,783	371,726	148,049	213,273	10,404
1969	378,324	180,958	185,916	11,450	324,165	139,850	173,377	10,938
1970	362,226	176,926	174,342	10,958	307,266	134,874	162,084	10,308
1971	364,475	154,894	196,313	13,268	309,776	117,215	179,998	12,563
1972	330,936	120,431	200,755	9,750	287,294	93,635	184,622	9,037
1973	304,637	102,604	191,080	10,953	264,047	79,289	174,413	10,345
1974	279,582	121,017	145,177	13,388	241,173	99,423	129,626	12,124
1975	321,936	150,526	154,528	16,882	278,694	122,857	140,381	15,456
1976	324,769	151,824	155,229	17,716	278,660	124,152	138,477	16,031
1977	314,093	143,250	143,905	26,938	276,011	121,246	128,688	26,077
1978	288,603	112,340	152,166	24,097	254,001	96,752	134,578	22,671
1979	251,805	88,485	144,055	19,265	220,722	77,192	125,306	18,224
1980	240,364	88,229	130,571	21,564	213,273	78,261	114,761	20,251
1981	204,126	68,143	116,381	19,602	177,354	58,219	101,803	17,332
1982	176,629	39,828	123,781	13,020	154,123	33,298	109,577	11,248
1983	197,531	38,902	142,979	15,650	171,591	31,409	126,370	13,812

	Scotland				Northern Ireland			
	Total	For local housing authorities	For private owners	Other	Total	For local housing authorities	For private owners	Other
1963	28,217	21,164	6,622	431	8,842	5,724	2,923	195
1964	37,171	29,156	7,662	353	9,516	6,130	3,170	216
1965	35,116	26,584	7,553	979	8,937	5,349	3,363	225
1966	36,029	27,515	7,870	644	10,500	6,926	3,275	299
1967	41,458	33,222	7,498	738	11,099	7,180	3,770	149
1968	41,989	32,011	8,720	1,258	12,120	7,924	4,075	121
1969	42,628	33,932	8,326	370	11,531	7,176	4,213	142
1970	43,126	34,360	8,220	546	11,884	7,692	4,038	104
1971	40,783	28,577	11,614	592	13,916	9,102	4,701	113
1972	31,992	19,593	11,835	564	11,650	7,203	4,298	149
1973	30,033	17,349	12,215	469	10,557	5,966	4,452	139
1974	28,336	16,182	11,239	915	10,073	5,412	4,312	349
1975	34,323	22,784	10,371	1,168	8,919	4,885	3,776	258
1976	36,527	21,154	13,704	1,669	9,582	6,518	3,048	16
1977	27,320	14,328	12,132	860	10,762	7,676	3,085	1
1978	25,759	9,907	14,443	1,409	8,843	5,681	3,145	17
1979	23,782	7,857	15,175	750	7,301	3,436	3,574	291
1980	20,611	7,455	12,242	914	6,480	2,513	3,568	399
1981	20,015	7,065	11,021	1,929	6,757	2,859	3,557	341
1982	16,432	3,716	11,532	1,184	6,074	2,814	2,672	588
1983	17,765	3,449	13,039	1,277	8,175	4,044	3,570	561

BIRTHS AND MARRIAGES (Thousands)

| | Live births | | | | | Marriages | | | | |
| | United Kingdom | England and Wales | | Scotland | Northern Ireland | United Kingdom | England and Wales | | Scotland | Northern Ireland |
		Total	Wales				Total	Wales		
1979	734·6	638·0	36·2	68·4	28·2	416·9	368·9	20·2	37·9	10·2
1980	753·7	656·2	37·4	68·9	28·6	418·4	370·0	21·1	38·5	9·9
1981	730·8	634·5	35·8	69·1	27·3	397·8	352·0	19·8	36·2	9·6
1982	719·2	625·9	35·7	66·2	27·0	387·0	342·2	19·0	34·9	9·9
1983	721·5	629·1	35·5	65·1	27·3	389·3	344·3	19·9	35·0	10·0
1984	729·6	636·8	35·9	65·1	27·7	395·8	349·0	19·2	36·3	10·4
1982 1st quarter	176·7	153·4	8·6	16·6	6·7	62·2†	54·9	3·1	5·8	1·5†
2nd quarter	180·2	157·0	9·0	16·3	6·9	108·8†	96·5	5·3	9·6	2·7†
3rd quarter	185·9	162·1	9·3	16·7	7·0	138·0†	121·9	6·7	12·1	4·1†
4th quarter	176·5	153·4	8·8	16·7	6·4	78·0†	68·9	3·9	7·5	1·7†
1983 1st quarter	175·3	152·4	8·7	16·1	6·8	61·9†	54·7	4·0	5·6	1·6†
2nd quarter	184·6	161·3	9·0	16·3	7·0	108·9†	96·7	5·2	9·5	2·7†
3rd quarter	187·4	163·4	9·1	16·9	7·1	140·5†	124·2	6·8	12·3	4·0†
4th quarter	174·1	151·9	8·6	15·8	6·3	78·0†	68·8	4·0	7·6	1·7†
1984 1st quarter	176·1	153·5	8·6	15·7	6·9	61·2†	54·4	3·1	5·4	1·5†
2nd quarter	180·7	157·7	8·8	15·9	7·0	115·0†	102·1	5·5	10·1	2·9†
3rd quarter	191·0	167·1	9·4	16·9	7·0	146·2†	129·0	7·1	12·9	4·2†
4th quarter	181·8	158·4	9·0	16·7	6·7	73·4†	63·7	3·5	7·9	1·7†
1985 1st quarter	189·0†	166·0		16·0†	6·9†				5·1†	

† Estimated.

DEATHS REGISTERED* (Thousands)

| | Total | | | | | Infants under one year | | | | |
| | United Kingdom | England and Wales | | Scotland | Northern Ireland | United Kingdom | England and Wales | | Scotland | Northern Ireland |
		Total	Wales				Total	Wales		
1980	661·5	581·4	35·1	63·3	16·8	9·11	7·90	0·43	0·83	0·38
1981	658·0	577·9	35·0	63·8	16·3	8·16	7·02	0·45	0·78	0·36
1982	662·8†	581·9	35·2	65·0	15·9†	7·90†	6·78	0·38	0·75	0·37†
1983	659·1†	579·6	35·2	63·5	16·0†	7·36†	6·38	0·38	0·65	0·33†
1984	644·9†	566·9	33·7		15·7†	7·00†	6·04	0·31		0·29†
1981 1st quarter	182·4	160·6	9·8	17·3	4·6	2·30	1·96	0·15	0·24	0·09
2nd quarter	156·8	137·6	8·4	15·2	3·9	1·96	1·70	0·10	0·17	0·09
3rd quarter	146·7	128·8	7·8	14·3	3·5	1·78	1·55	0·09	0·16	0·07
4th quarter	172·1	150·9	9·0	17·0	4·2	2·12	1·82	0·12	0·20	0·09
1982 1st quarter	190·5†	166·5	9·9	19·4	4·7†	2·24†	1·95	0·09	0·18	0·11†
2nd quarter	160·1†	141·1	8·6	15·2	3·9†	1·83†	1·55	0·08	0·19	0·09†
3rd quarter	144·5†	126·9	7·9	14·2	3·4†	1·73†	1·47	0·09	0·19	0·07†
4th quarter	167·6†	147·4	8·8	16·3	3·9†	2·08†	1·80	0·11	0·20	0·08†
1983 1st quarter	190·5†	167·6	10·5	18·1	4·8†	2·10†	1·86	0·11	0·17	0·08†
2nd quarter	157·5†	138·3	8·4	15·3	3·9†	1·79†	1·54	0·08	0·15	0·10†
3rd quarter	147·8†	130·0	8·0	14·2	3·5†	1·64†	1·41	0·10	0·16	0·08†
4th quarter	163·3†	143·6	8·3	15·8	3·8†	1·82†	1·57	0·09	0·17	0·07†
1984 1st quarter	179·8†	158·1	9·4	17·2	4·4†	2·09†	1·82	0·10	0·18	0·08†
2nd quarter	161·6†	142·0	8·4	15·6	4·1†	1·69†	1·44	0·07	0·16	0·09†
3rd quarter	140·4†	123·2	7·2	13·8	3·3†	1·47†	1·26	0·07	0·16	0·06†
4th quarter	163·1†	143·5	8·6	15·7†	3·8†	1·75†	1·52	0·07	0·17	0·06†
1985 1st quarter				17·5†					0·17†	

* Excluding stillbirths. † Provisional.

Deaths Analysed by Cause (England and Wales)

	1979	1980	1981	1982	1983
Total deaths	593,019	581,385	577,890	581,861	579,608
Deaths from natural causes	571,866	561,089	558,102	562,251	560,599
Infections and parasitic diseases	2,273	2,239	2,102	2,116	2,043
Cholera	—	—	—	—	1
Typhoid fever	2	1	2	3	1
Shigellosis and amoebiasis	8	5	8	4	7
Enteritis and other diarrhoeal diseases	176	141	149	134	119
Tuberculosis of respiratory system	490	474	432	454	375
Other tuberculosis, including late effects	446	429	332	296	324
Diphtheria	—	—	—	1	—
Whooping cough	7	6	5	14	5
Streptococcal sore throat and scarlatina	7	3	4	3	2
Meningococcal infection	97	71	85	70	70
Acute poliomyelitis	—	—	—	—	—
Smallpox	—	1	—	—	—
Measles	17	26	15	13	16
Louse-borne typhus and other rickettsioses	1	—	—	—	1
Malaria	6	8	2	10	7
Syphilis	76	59	55	46	47
Neoplasms	129,638	130,556	131,691	132,448	134,270
Malignant neoplasm of stomach	11,305	10,900	10,652	10,211	10,502
Malignant neoplasm of trachea, bronchus and lung	34,760	35,168	34,727	34,832	35,572
Malignant neoplasm of breast	12,174	12,245	12,597	12,492	12,759
Malignant neoplasm of uterus	3,598	3,576	3,537	3,512	3,464
Leukaemia	3,298	3,340	3,349	3,462	3,481
Benign neoplasms and neoplasms of unspecified nature	1,065	1,011	1,240	1,532	956
Endocrine, nutritional, metabolic diseases and immunity disorders	6,462	6,440	6,195	5,963	6,153
Diabetes mellitus	4,809	4,781	4,626	4,534	4,516
Nutritional deficiencies	91	105	124	91	107
Diseases of blood and blood-forming organs	1,729	1,672	1,588	1,588	1,512
Anaemias	1,252	1,163	1,134	1,035	949
Mental disorders	3,211	3,308	3,441	3,757	4,142
Diseases of nervous system and sense organs	6,934	6,483	6,975	7,558	7,624
Meningitis	285	277	266	286	281
Diseases of the circulatory system	298,436	290,395	286,258	284,246	282,815
Acute rheumatic fever	3	4	2	4	1
Chronic rheumatic heart disease	3,396	3,248	3,120	2,904	2,884
Hypertensive disease	6,506	5,588	5,413	5,160	4,725
Ischaemic heart disease	155,647	154,371	155,196	154,605	156,550
Diseases of pulmonary circulation and other forms of heart disease	36,419	34,645	32,751	32,259	30,529
Cerebrovascular disease	74,378	71,443	69,651	69,028	67,785
Diseases of the respiratory system	85,925	83,405	83,507	88,111	86,633
Influenza	838	514	626	716	796
Pneumonia	54,376	53,704	54,057	56,529	55,513
Bronchitis, emphysema	21,627	19,255	17,530	17,297	15,410
Asthma	1,477	1,480	1,603	1,577	1,645
Diseases of the digestive system	16,255	16,140	16,447	16,456	15,838
Ulcer of stomach and duodenum	4,361	4,418	4,457	4,608	4,259
Appendicitis	222	179	164	155	136
Hernia of abdominal cavity and other intestinal obstruction	2,114	1,999	1,959	1,908	1,861
Chronic liver disease and cirrhosis	2,186	2,218	2,212	2,152	2,184
Diseases of the genito-urinary system	7,913	7,735	7,970	8,132	7,830
Nephritis, nephrotic syndrome and nephrosis	4,380	4,482	4,766	4,950	4,742
Hyperplasia of prostate	818	722	749	694	621
Complications of pregnancy, child birth and puerperium	74	70	57	42	54
Abortion	9	13	10	6	8
Diseases of the skin and subcutaneous tissue	439	473	516	493	505
Diseases of musculo-skeletal system & connective tissue	3,047	3,104	3,112	3,224	3,241
Congenital anomalies	3,498	3,404	3,039	3,037	2,944
Certain conditions originating in the perinatal period	3,424	3,148	2,659	2,464	2,422
Birth trauma, hypoxia, birth asphyxia and other respiratory conditions	1,921	1,731	1,445	1,336	1,268
Signs, symptoms and other ill-defined conditions	2,608	2,507	2,545	2,616	2,573
Deaths by violence	21,153	20,296	19,788	19,610	19,009
All accidents	14,846	14,032	. .	13,297	12,823
Motor vehicle accidents	5,855	5,831	. .	5,310	5,146
Suicide and self-inflicted injury	4,195	4,321	4,419	4,279	4,279
All other external causes	2,112	1,943	. .	2,034	1,907

THE UNITED KINGDOM

Area.—The land area of the United Kingdom* (England, Wales, Scotland and N. Ireland) is 93,051 sq. miles. The area of inland water in the United Kingdom is 1,196 sq. miles. Total 94,247 sq. miles.

Sq. miles	England	Wales	Scotland	N. Ireland
Land	50,081	7,969	29,795	5,206
Inland Water	281	50	619	246
Total	50,362	8,019	30,414	5,452

* Excludes the Isle of Man (227 sq. miles) and the Channel Islands (75 sq. miles)

POPULATION : CENSUS RESULTS, 1801–1981   Thousands

	United Kingdom			England and Wales			Scotland			Northern Ireland†		
	Total	Male	Female	Total	Male	Female	Total	Male	Female	Total	Male	Female
1801	11,944	5,692	6,252	8,893	4,255	4,638	1,608	739	869	1,443	698	745
1811	13,368	6,368	7,000	10,165	4,874	5,291	1,806	826	980	1,397	668	729
1821	15,472	7,498	7,974	12,000	5,850	6,150	2,092	983	1,109	1,380	665	715
1831	17,835	8,647	9,188	13,897	6,771	7,126	2,364	1,114	1,250	1,574	762	812
1841	20,183	9,819	10,364	15,914	7,778	8,137	2,620	1,242	1,378	1,649	800	849
1851	22,259	10,855	11,404	17,928	8,781	9,146	2,889	1,376	1,513	1,443	698	745
1861	24,525	11,894	12,631	20,066	9,776	10,290	3,062	1,450	1,612	1,396	668	728
1871	27,431	13,309	14,122	22,712	11,059	11,653	3,360	1,603	1,757	1,359	647	712
1881	31,015	15,060	15,955	25,974	12,640	13,335	3,736	1,799	1,936	1,305	621	684
1891	34,264	16,593	17,671	29,003	14,060	14,942	4,026	1,943	2,083	1,236	590	646
1901	38,237	18,492	19,745	32,528	15,729	16,799	4,472	2,174	2,298	1,237	590	647
1911	42,082	20,357	21,725	36,070	17,446	18,625	4,761	2,309	2,452	1,251	603	648
1921	44,027	21,033	22,994	37,887	18,075	19,811	4,882	2,348	2,535	*1,258*	*610*	*648*
1931	46,038	22,060	23,978	39,952	19,133	20,819	4,843	2,326	2,517	*1,243*	*601*	*642*
1951	50,225	24,118	26,107	43,758	21,016	22,742	5,096	2,434	2,662	1,371	668	703
1961	52,709	25,481	27,228	46,105	22,304	23,801	5,179	2,483	2,697	1,425	694	731
1971	55,515	26,952	28,562	48,750	23,683	25,067	5,229	2,515	2,714	1,536	755	781
1981	55,776	27,064	28,701	49,154	23,873	25,281	5,130	2,466	2,664	1,491	725	756

NOTES.—1. Before 1801 there existed no official return of the population of either England or Scotland. Estimates of the population of England at various periods, calculated from the number of baptisms, burials and marriages, are: in 1570, 4,160,221; 1600, 4,811,718; 1630, 5,600,517; 1670, 5,773,646; 1700, 6,045,008; 1750, 6,517,035. Because of the War there was no Census in 1941.

2. The last official Census of Population in respect of England and Wales, Scotland, Northern Ireland, the Isle of Man and Guernsey, was taken on the night of April 5, 1981.

3. † All figures refer to the area which is now Northern Ireland. Figures for N. Ireland in 1921 and 1931 are estimates based on the Censuses held in 1926 and 1937.

ISLANDS.—*The figures given above do not include islands of the British seas.* Populations of these islands at census years since 1900 were:—

	ISLE OF MAN			JERSEY			GUERNSEY		
	Total	Male	Female	Total	Male	Female	Total	Male	Female
1901	54,752	25,496	29,256	52,576	23,940	28,636	43,042	21,140	21,902
1911	52,016	23,937	28,079	51,898	24,014	27,884	45,001	22,215	22,786
1921	60,284	27,329	32,955	49,701	22,438	27,263	40,529	19,303	21,226
1931	49,308	22,443	26,865	50,462	23,424	27,038	42,743	20,675	22,068
1951	55,123	25,749	29,464	57,296	27,282	30,014	45,747	22,094	23,380
1961	48,151	22,060	26,091	57,200	27,200	30,000	47,178	22,890	24,288
1971	56,289	26,461	29,828	72,532	35,423	37,109	52,708	25,382	27,326
1981	64,679	30,901	33,778	77,000	37,000	40,000	56,000	27,000	29,000

INCREASE OF THE PEOPLE, ETC.

In Great Britain 6·3 per cent of the usually resident population was born outside the United Kingdom, and in England and Wales this figure was 6·6 per cent. Some 4·5 per cent of the population of England and Wales lived in households whose head was born in the New Commonwealth or Pakistan. Britain's total population is expected, on 1981 estimates, to be 56·4 million in 1986, 58 million in 2001 and 58·8 million in 2016. Annual births have fallen since the mid-1960s and the average size of family in 1982 was 1·75, below the level of 2·1 required for replacement of the population. The number of live births in 1983 was 694,000 (2,000 more than in 1982), of which over 14 per cent were illegitimate.

Although the total population has remained relatively stable in the last decade there have been changes in the age and sex structure. The proportion of people under 16 is about 22 per cent; 16–64 years, 63 per cent; 65 and over, 15 per cent. Some 18 per cent were over normal retirement age (60 for women, 65 for men). There are about 6 per cent more male than female births every year, but the higher mortality of men at all ages, means that at about 50 years of age the number of women begins to exceed the number of men.

LOCAL GOVERNMENT IN ENGLAND AND WALES

The Local Government Act, 1972 provided for the reorganisation of local government in England (outside Greater London whose local government was reorganised in 1965) and Wales. On April 1, 1974 the former county, county borough, and county district councils were abolished. Two tiers of new local authorities, county and district councils, covering metropolitan and non-metropolitan counties and districts, replaced them.

Structures and Areas in England

Six *metropolitan counties* cover the main conurbations outside Greater London: Tyne and Wear, West Midlands, Merseyside, Greater Manchester, West Yorkshire and South Yorkshire. Each metropolitan county extends to the edge of the general continuously built-up area of the conurbation. The six metropolitan counties are divided into 36 *metropolitan districts*, most of which have a population of over 200,000 and include a former county borough.

There are 39 *non-metropolitan counties*; each of these is divided into *non-metropolitan districts*, of which there are 296. These districts have populations broadly between 60,000 and 100,000. About one third of the non-metropolitan districts, however, have populations above this range because of the need to avoid dividing large towns. Some districts, mainly in sparsely populated areas, have populations below 60,000.

Permanent Local Government Boundary Commissions for England and Wales have been set up to keep the areas and electoral arrangements of the new local authorities under review.

Constitution and Elections

The county and district councils consist of directly elected councillors. The broad range of sizes of councils are: county councils 60–100 members; metropolitan district councils 50–80 members; non-metropolitan district councils 30–60 members. The councillors elect annually one of their number as chairman.

The general pattern in England is that councillors serve 4 years and there are no elections of district and parish councillors in county elections year. All new authorities were elected *en bloc* in 1973 (as "shadow" authorities until they took on their functions on April 1, 1974). All county councils were elected together in 1977 and every four years thereafter (i.e. 1981, 1985, etc.). In metropolitan districts one-third of the councillors for each ward are elected each year except in the year of county elections. Non-metropolitan districts can choose whether to have elections by thirds or whole council elections. In the former case, one-third of the council, as nearly as may be, is elected in each year of metropolitan district elections. If they choose whole council elections these are held in the mid-year of the county cycle (i.e. 1979, 1983, etc.). Local elections are normally held on the first Thursday in May.

Elections to local authorities in *Greater London* have been brought into line with the rest of England so that the normal term of office for councillors on the G.L.C. and the London Borough Councils is now four years instead of three. Greater London Council elections have taken place in the same year as county council elections since 1977.

In anticipation of their impending abolition (see below), the elections to the G.L.C. and the six metropolitan county councils which were due to be held in May 1985 were cancelled.

Generally speaking, all British subjects or citizens of the Republic of Ireland of 18 years or over, resident on the qualifying date in the area for which the election is being held are entitled to vote at local government elections. A register of electors is prepared and published annually by local electoral registration officers.

A returning officer has the overall responsibility for an election. Voting takes place at polling stations, arranged by the local authority and under the supervision of a presiding officer specially appointed for the purpose. Candidates, who are subject to various statutory qualifications and disqualifications designed to secure that they are suitable persons to hold office, must be nominated by electors for the electoral area concerned.

Internal Organisation and Local Government Services in England

The council are the final decision-making body within any authority. They are free to a great extent to make their own internal organisational arrangements. Normally questions of major policy are settled by the full council, while the administration of the various services is the responsibility of committees of members. Day to day decisions are delegated to the council's officers, who act within the policies laid down by the members.

Many councils have set up corporate management teams of the Chief Executive and chief officers, who consider the operations of their authority as a whole, rather than dealing with each service separately, as was often the case in the past.

Local authorities are empowered or required by various Acts of Parliament to carry out functions in their areas. The legislation concerned comprises public general Acts and "local" Acts which local authorities have promoted as private bills. Functions are divided everywhere between two tiers of authorities, though their allocation within the metropolitan areas is somewhat different from outside, the metropolitan district councils exercising more functions than the non-metropolitan district councils.

Responsibility for the main local government functions is allocated as follows (though responsible authorities may involve other authorities in the provision of certain of their services through agency arrangements):

County councils: Strategic planning (e.g. structure plans; major projects); traffic, transport and highways; police; fire service; consumer protection (other than hygiene); refuse disposal; smallholdings.

Non-metropolitan county and metropolitan district councils: Education; social services; libraries.

District Councils: Local planning; housing; highways (maintenance of certain urban roads and off-street car parks); building regulations; environmental health; refuse collection; cemeteries and crematoria.

Concurrent (county and district councils): Recreation (e.g. parks, playing fields, swimming pools); museums; encouragement of the arts.

The sewerage and sewage disposal functions of local authorities have been transferred to 9 new water authorities in England and the Welsh Water Authority. Water authorities, however, are expected to make agreements whereby the new district councils discharge sewerage functions on an agency basis. Apart from these functions, the water authorities are responsible for water supply and conservation; river pollution control and river management; fisheries; land drainage; and use of water space for recreation and amenity purposes.

The personal health functions of local authorities were transferred in 1977 to area health authorities, whose areas were the same as non-metropolitan and Welsh counties and metropolitan districts. From April 1982 this two-tier structure was replaced by about 199 District Health Authorities. They work in close collaboration with local education, social services and environment health authorities.

London.—The Greater London Area embraces the old counties of London and Middlesex (except Potters Bar, Staines and Sunbury-on-Thames) and parts of the neighbouring counties of Essex, Herts., Kent and Surrey and the whole of the county boroughs of Croydon, East Ham and West Ham.

The Greater London Council is responsible for traffic, major roads and overall planning. All other matters are the concern of the 32 London borough councils; the City of London, besides retaining its previous functions, has the powers of a London borough.

Local Government Reorganisation

Under the Local Government Act 1985, which comes into effect on April 1, 1986, the Greater London Council and the six metropolitan county councils are to be abolished and most of their functions made the responsibility of the existing borough and district councils. In addition, new joint authorities, composed of borough and district councillors, will run the fire service in London and the fire, police and public transport services in the metropolitan counties. Education in Inner London will become the responsibility of a new directly elected Inner London Education Authority. Residuary bodies will deal with other business of the Councils after abolition. The chairmen of the bodies are:

Greater London, Sir Godfrey Taylor.
Greater Manchester, J. P. B. Hadfield.
Merseyside, L. F. Pocock.
South Yorkshire, B. Cotton.
Tyne and Wear, A. S. Robertson.
West Midlands, Dr. M. D. Skillicorn.
West Yorkshire, T. McDonald.

Parishes

The rural parishes in England were not, in general, affected by local government reorganisation except that the powers of parish councils were extended and a few of them were divided by the boundaries of new counties and districts. 300 former small borough and urban district councils became parish councils with the same powers as other parish councils.

Parishes with 200 or more electors must generally have parish councils, and about three-quarters of the parishes have councils. A parish council comprises at least 5 members, the number being fixed by the district council. All parishes have parish meetings, comprising the electors of the parish.

Parish council functions include: allotments; arts and crafts; community halls, recreational facilities (e.g. open spaces, swimming pools), cemeteries and crematoria; and many minor functions. They must also be given an opportunity to comment on planning applications. They may, like county and district councils, spend up to a 2p rate for the general benefit of the parish. They precept on the district councils for their rate funds. In general, parish councils are elected every four years, in the year in which the local district councillor is elected.

Civic dignities

District councils may petition for a royal charter granting borough status to the district. In boroughs the chairman of the council is the mayor. The status "city" and the right to call the mayor "Lord Mayor" may also be granted by letters patent. Parish councils may call themselves "town councils", in which case their chairman is the "town mayor".

Charter trustees are established for those former boroughs which are too large to have parish councils and are situated in districts without city or borough status. The charter trustees are the district councillors representing the former borough and they elect a mayor, continue civic tradition, and look after the charters, insignia and civic plate of the former borough.

Local Commissioners for England and Wales

There exist Local Commissioners for England and Wales whose duty it is to investigate complaints of maladministration in many aspects of local government.

Wales

Since 1974 Wales, including the former Monmouthshire, has been divided into eight counties; Gwynedd; Clwyd; Powys; Dyfed; West, Mid and South Glamorgan; and Gwent. There are 37 districts in Wales, many of those in the less populated parts reflecting the areas of former Welsh counties.

The arrangements for Welsh counties and districts are generally similar to those for English nonmetropolitan counties and districts. There are some differences in functions: Welsh district councils have refuse disposal as well as refuse collection functions and they may provide on-street as well as off-street car parks with the consent of the county council. A few districts have also been designated as library authorities.

In Wales parishes have been replaced by communities. Unlike England, where many areas are not in any parish, communities have been established for the whole of Wales; approximately 1,000 communities in all. Community meetings may be convened as and when desired. Community councils exist in about 750 communities and further councils may be established at the request of a community meeting. Community councils have broadly the same range of powers as English parish councils. Community councillors are elected *en bloc* on the same basis as parish councillors in England, i.e. at the same time as a district council election and for a term of four years.

Local Government Finance

Local government is financed from various sources. (1) *Rates.*—Levied by district councils and in London by the City Corporation and the London boroughs. Sums required by the Greater London Council, by county councils and parish or community councils are included in the rates levied by London boroughs and district councils. From April 1, 1986 when the G.L.C. and Metropolitan County Councils are abolished under the Local Government Act 1985, new joint boards for police, fire and transport services and a new I.L.E.A. will be able to precept on district councils, while new residuary bodies, set up to inherit the property and legal rights and liabilities not assigned to specific successor bodies, will be able to make levies on those authorities. Rates are levied by a poundage tax on the rateable value of property in the area of the rating authority. Under the General Rate Act, 1967, rating authorities are required to charge a lower rate in the pound on dwellings than on property generally in their area. A differential of 18½p for both England and Wales has been prescribed since 1982–83. Rental values are annual rental values, on certain statutory assumptions, determined as at the date of the current valuation lists. The current valuation lists, prepared by valuation officers of the

Board of Inland Revenue, came into force on April 1, 1973. New property is added to the list and significant changes to existing property necessitate amendments to the rateable value. The lists remain in force until the next general revaluation. Certain types of property are exempt from rates, e.g. agricultural land and buildings, and places of public religious worship. Some charities and other non-profit-making organizations can receive full or partial exemption. Under the General Rate Act, 1967, as amended by the Local Government Act, 1974 and the Local Government Planning and Land Act 1980, local authorities can resolve to rate specified classes of empty property by an amount up to 100 per cent of the full rates, subject to a maximum of 50 per cent on non-domestic properties from 1 April 1981. From April 19, 1984 local authorities' powers to levy rates on empty industrial properties have been suspended and from April 1, 1985 this has been extended to empty warehouses. The Social Security and Housing Benefits Act 1982 (administered by the D.H.S.S.) makes provision for rate rebates for domestic ratepayers, eligibility depending on income, rates payable and number of people in the household. The Rating (Disabled Persons) Act 1978 provides rate relief in respect of certain facilities needed by disabled persons.

(2) *Government Grants.*—In addition to specific Government grants in aid of revenue expenditure on particular services, from April 1, 1981 grants known as rate support grants are payable to local authorities under the provisions of Part VI of the Local Government, Planning and Land Act, 1980. These grants, which replace the block grants previously paid under the Local Government Act, 1974, consist of two elements: block grant and domestic rate relief grant. The block grant, which is a single grant payment, replaces the needs and resources element under the previous system, and is payable to non-metropolitan counties and districts, metropolitan districts, London boroughs, the City of London, and the Isles of Scilly. The block grant is intended to enable all authorities to provide comparable standards of service at the same poundage cost to local ratepayers. The domestic rate relief grant, like the previous domestic element, is payable to all rating authorities to reimburse them for the cost of giving the domestic rate relief prescribed for the year.

In order to arrive at the total amount of the rate support grants to local authorities in England for any year (the new grant system provides for Wales to be administered separately), the aggregate of Exchequer grants to local authorities in respect of their relevant expenditure for the year is determined in advance (housing subsidies and specific grants towards expenditure on rate rebates and mandatory awards to students and trainee teachers are outside this aggregate amount) and from this is deducted the estimated amount of specific grants for the year in aid of revenue expenditure and the supplementary grants for transport purposes and in connection with national parks; the resulting balance is the amount of rate support grant. The Local Government Finance Act 1982 gives the Secretary of State power to abate the block grant of local authorities which exceed expenditure guidance which he has issued.

Forecasts of local authority relevant expenditure for 1985–86 in England adopted by the Government for rate support grant purposes were as follows. The amounts given are at 1985–86 cash prices.

Service	£M
Education	9,963
School Meals and Milk	296
Libraries, Museums and Art Galleries	347
Personal Social Sevices and Port Health	2,332
Police	2,493
Fire	549
Other Home Office Services	356
Local Transport	1,544
Local Environmental Services	2,420·5
Land Drainage and Flood Protection	90
Consumer Protection	52·5
Employment	73·5
Non-Housing Revenue Account Housing	110·5
Housing Benefits	93
Allocated Current Expenditure	£20,720
Unallocated Current Expenditure	594
Total Current Expenditure	£21,314
Revenue Contributions to Capital Outlay	599
Loan Charges (including leasing)	2,377
Rate Fund Contributions to Housing Revenue Account	316
Interest Receipts	−445
Total Relevant Expenditure	£24,161

The aggregate amount of Exchequer grants for 1985–86 was determined at £11,764 million. Of this, the specific grants and the Transport and National Parks Supplementary grants were estimated at £2,579 million, giving a total for rate support grants of £9,188 million, of which £8,489 million was in respect of the block grant and £699 million the domestic rate relief grant.

Rates and Rateable Values.—The total rateable value for England on April 1, 1984 was £7,444 million (figure for 1985 not yet available) and an estimate of the amount to be raised in rates, gross of rebates, in 1985–86 is £13,286 million.

Average Rates.—The estimated average rates levied in England in 1985–86 were: Inner London Boroughs, *domestic* rate 188·60p, *non-domestic* rate 187·02p; Outer London, 169·17p and 192·50p; Metropolitan Districts, 206·78p and 228·83p. The average rates levied in England were estimated at 173·43p (domestic) and 193·18p (non-domestic). In Wales the estimated average rates levied were, *domestic* rate 177·78p, *non-domestic* rate 196·12p.

SCOTLAND

Since 1975 Scotland has been divided into 9 regions, and 3 islands areas covering respectively Orkney, Shetland and the Western Isles. Within the regions there is a second independent tier of 53 districts. Regional and district councils have separate responsibility for specific functions. Islands councils are most-purpose authorities and are each responsible in their areas for the functions (except police, fire and valuation) which are carried out by regions and districts.

Regional Functions.—The regional authorities are responsible for strategic planning, for the provision of infrastructure such as roads, water and sewerage, for flood prevention, coast protection, and for certain public transport services. They also carry out among others the education, social work and consumer protection functions and have responsibility for police, fire, civil defence and electoral registration.

District Functions.—The district authorities deal with more local matters such as local planning;

development control; building control; housing; leisure and recreation; tourism; libraries; environmental health including cleansing, refuse collection and disposal, food hygiene, inspection of shops, offices and factories, clean air, markets and slaughterhouses, burial and cremation; licensing, including liquor, cinemas and theatres, betting, gaming and dogs, taxis, charitable collections.

Community Councils.—Provision is also made in the Act for setting up community councils under schemes prepared by each district and islands authority. Such councils are not local authorities but have a statutory base. They have no statutory functions but are expected to take such action in the community as appears to their members to be desirable and practicable.

Local Government Electors.—In April 1985 there were 3,957,276 electors in Scotland. Elections are next due to take place in 1986 for region and island councils and in 1988 for district councils.

Rates and Rateable Values.—In 1981–82, the latest year for which final figures were available, a total of £1,271,870,000 was received from the general rates of local government in Scotland and £50,562,000 from domestic water rates. The rateable value on which rates were leviable was £1,296,122,000 on the general rates and £469,173,000 on the domestic water rates. The average general rate levied was 108·5p and the domestic water rate levied was 6·6p.

Provisional figures for 1984–85 show total receipts from general rates of £1,535,780,000 and £59,154,698 from domestic water rates. The rateable value leviable for 1984–85 was £1,325,066,000 (general) and £599,421,041 (domestic water rate). The average rate per £ levied for 1984–85 was 126·4p (general) and 9·9p (domestic water rate).

NORTHERN IRELAND

For the purpose of local government Northern Ireland has a system of 26 single-tier district councils. There are 566 members of the councils, elected for periods of four years at a time on the principle of proportional representation.

The district councils all have the same three main roles. These are:

(a) an executive role in which the councils are responsible for a wide range of local services including the provision of recreational, social, community, and cultural facilities; environmental health; consumer protection; the enforcement of building regulations; the promotion of tourist development schemes; gas supply; street cleansing; refuse collection and disposal; litter prevention; and miscellaneous licensing and registration provisions, including dog control;

(b) a representative role in which they nominate representatives to sit as members of the various statutory bodies responsible for the administration of regional services such as education and libraries, health and personal social services, drainage, fire and electricity; and

(c) a consultative role in which they act as the media through which the views of local people are expressed on the operation in their area of other regional services notably planning, roads, and conservation (including water supply and sewerage services) provided by those departments of central government which have an obligation, either statutorily or otherwise, to consult the district councils about proposals affecting their areas.

WATER AUTHORITIES

The Water Act 1973, which provided for the reorganization of the water services in England and Wales, resulted in the creation of ten autonomous multipurpose water authorities (nine regional authorities in England and the Welsh Water Authority).

The water authorities are responsible for water supply, water conservation, sewerage and sewage disposal, prevention of river pollution, fisheries, land drainage and the recreational use of their waters. Between them the authorities employ about 52,000 people, have an annual revenue expenditure of some £1,950 million and an investment budget of about £825 million a year.

Under the Water Act 1983 the Water Authorities Association was set up by the regional water authorities. The Association enables the water authorities to discuss amongst themselves and with the Government and other bodies matters of common concern, co-ordinates any necessary joint action by the water authorities, and provides press and public relations services.

THE WATER AUTHORITIES ASSOCIATION, 1 Queen Anne's Gate, S.W.1.—*Sec.*, A. Semple.

Regional Water Authorities

THAMES WATER AUTHORITY, Nugent House, Vastern Road, Reading RG1 8DB.—*Managing Director*, K. West.

SOUTHERN WATER AUTHORITY, Guildborne House, Worthing, Sussex.—*Chief Executive*, B. R. Thorpe.

SEVERN TRENT WATER AUTHORITY, Abelson House, 2297 Coventry Road, Sheldon, Birmingham.—*Chief Executive*, D. A. D. Reeve, C.B.E..

WESSEX WATER AUTHORITY, Wessex House, Passage Street, Bristol.—*Chief Executive*, K. F. Roberts, C.B.E.

ANGLIAN WATER AUTHORITY, Ambury House, Huntingdon.—*Chief Executive*, P. H. Bray.

SOUTH WEST WATER AUTHORITY, Peninsula House, Rydon Lane, Exeter EX2 7HR.—*Chief Executive*, A. G. C. Williams.

NORTHUMBRIAN WATER AUTHORITY, Northumbria House, Regent Centre, Gosforth, Newcastle-upon-Tyne.—*Chief Executive*, W. F. Ridley.

NORTH WEST WATER AUTHORITY, Dawson House, Great Sankey, Warrington.—*Chief Executive*, J. B. Oldfield.

YORKSHIRE WATER AUTHORITY, West Riding House, 67 Albion Street, Leeds.

WELSH WATER AUTHORITY, Cambrian Way, Brecon, Powys.—*Chief Executive*, B. Doyle.

Party Representation in Local Government

Abbreviations: *A.* = Liberal/S.D.P. Alliance; *C.* = Conservative; *Com.* = Communist; *D.Lab.* = Democratic Labour; *Ind.* = Independent; *Lab.* = Labour; *L.* = Liberal; *M.K.* = Mebyon Kernow; *N.P.* = Non-Political/Non-Party; *P.C.* = Plaid Cymru; *R.A.* = Ratepayers'/Residents' Associations; *S.D.P.* = Social Democratic Party; *S.N.P.* = Scottish National Party.

ENGLAND

Non-Metropolitan Counties (as at end May 1985)

Avon .... *Lab.* 37, *C.* 31, *A.* 8.
Bedford ..... *C.* 29, *Lab.* 29, *A.* 14 (1 Vac.).
Berkshire .. *C.* 42, *Lab.* 17, *L.* 15, *R.A.* 1, *S.D.P.* 1.
Bucks. ...... *C.* 49, *Lab.* 12, *A.* 9, *Ind.* 1
Cambridge.. *C.* 29, *Lab.* 21, *L.* 19, *S.D.P.* 7, *Ind.* 1.
Cheshire .. *Lab.* 32, *C.* 27, *A.* 11, *Ind.* 1.
Cleveland .. *Lab.* 51, *C.* 20, *A.* 6.
Cornwall .... *L.* 28, *Ind.* 27, *C.* 16, *Lab.* 5, *A.* 2, *M.K.* 1.
Cumbria.... *Lab.* 39, *C.* 36, *Ind.* 3, *L.* 3, *A.* 2.
Derbyshire .. *Lab.* 54, *C.* 24, *A.* 4, *Ind.* 1, *Ind.* *C.* 1.
Devon .... *C.* 37, *A.* 36, *Lab.* 10, *Ind.* 2
Dorset ...... *C.* 42, *A.* 26, *Lab.* 4, *Ind.* 2, *Ind.* *C* 2, *R.A.* 1.
Durham .... *Lab.* 50, *A.* 7, *C.* 5, *Ind.* 5, *Others* 5.
Essex .... *C.* 45, *Lab.* 29, *A.* 23, *R.A.* 1.
Gloucester... *L.* 20, *C.* 18, *Lab.* 14, *Ind.* *C.* 5, *S.D.P.* 3, *Ind.* 2, *Others* 1.
Hampshire ..*C.* 50, *A.* 30, *Lab.* 19, *Ind.* 2, (1 Vac.).
Hereford and
  Worcester ..*C.* 39, *Lab.* 18, *L.* 13, *Ind.* 4, *S.D.P.* 2.
Herts........ *C.* 36, *Lab.* 27, *A.* 14.
Humberside .*Lab.* 36, *C.* 35, *A.* 4.

Kent .... *C.* 57, *Lab.* 23, *L.* 16, *S.D.P.* 2, (1 Vac.).
Lancashire ..*Lab.* 48, *C.* 42, *L.* 8, (1 Vac.).
Leicester .... *C.* 42, *Lab.* 32, *A.* 11.
Lincolnshire .*C.* 40, *A.* 20, *Lab.* 14, *Ind.* 2, *R.A.* 1.
Norfolk .....*C.* 44, *Lab.* 25, *A.* 15.
Northants. .. *C.* 34, *Lab.* 29, *L.* 4, *Ind.* 1.
Northumb. .. *Lab.* 30, *A.* 20, *C.* 13, *Ind.* 2, (1 Vac.).
Notts........ *Lab.* 47, *C.* 38, *A.* 2, (1 Vac.).
Oxfordshire . *C.* 31, *Lab.* 20, *A.* 18, *Ind.* 1.
Shropshire .. *Lab.* 25, *C.* 24, *A.* 10, *Ind.* 7.
Somerset .. *A.* 26, *C.* 24, *Lab.* 7.
Staffordshire *Lab.* 48, *C.* 30, *L.* 4
Suffolk ...... *C.* 50, *Lab.* 23, *Ind.* 4, *A.* 3.
Surrey ...... *C.* 52, *A.* 12, *Lab.* 7, *Ind.* 3, *R.A.* 2.
Sussex, East .*C.* 35, *L.* 20, *Lab.* 12, *S.D.P.* 1.
Sussex, West .*C.* 46, *A.* 17, *Lab.* 8.
Warwicks.... *C.* 26, *Lab.* 24, *L.* 6, *S.D.P.* 4, *Ind.* 1, *R.A.* 1.
Wight, I.o. .. *L.* 27, *C.* 11, *Ind.* 2, *A.* 1, *N.P.* 1, *S.D.P.* 1.
Wiltshire .... *C.* 30, *A.* 25, *Lab.* 17, *Ind.* 2, *R.A.* 1.
Yorks., N. ...*C.* 43, *A.* 26, *Lab.* 20, *Ind.* 7.

Metropolitan Counties (as at end May 1985)

Greater Manchester .*Lab.* 76, *C.* 18, *L.* 10, *S.D.P.* 1, (1 Vac.).
Merseyside .... *Lab.* 52, *C.* 26, *L.* 17, (4 Vac.).
South Yorkshire .... *Lab.* 83, *C.* 12, *A.* 4, *R.A.* 1.
Tyne and Wear ..... *Lab.* 72, *C.* 23, *L.* 7, *Ind.* *L.* 1, *R.A.* 1.

West Midlands ...... *Lab.* 73, *C.* 24, *L.* 5, *Ind.* 1. (1 Vac.).
West Yorkshire ..... *Lab.* 63, *C.* 14, *L.* 11.

Metropolitan District Councils (as at end May 1985)

GREATER MANCHESTER

Bolton .... *Lab.* 36, *C.* 20, *L.* 4.
Bury .... *C.* 26, *Lab.* 22.
Manchester........ *Lab.* 79, *C.* 14, *L.* 6.
Oldham .... *Lab.* 40, *C.* 16, *A.* 4.
Rochdale .... *Lab.* 28, *C.* 17, *L.* 12, *A.* 2 (1 Vac.).
Salford .... *Lab.* 53, *C.* 6, *L.* 1.
Stockport .... *C.* 28, *Lab.* 15, *L.* 15, *R.A.* 3, *Ind.* *Lab.* 2.
Tameside .... *Lab.* 45, *C.* 9, *L.* 3.
Trafford .... *C.* 36, *Lab.* 19, *L.* 8.
Wigan .... *Lab.* 61, *L.* 8, *C.* 3.

MERSEYSIDE

Knowsley .... *Lab.* 55, *C.* 9, *L.* 2.
Liverpool.......... *Lab.* 56, *L.* 30, *C.* 13.
St. Helens .... *Lab.* 39, *C.* 12, *L.* 2, *S.D.P.* 1.
Sefton............. *C.* 36, *Lab.* 22, *A.* 10, *Ind.* 1.
Wirral .... *C.* 34, *Lab.* 24, *A.* 8.

SOUTH YORKSHIRE

Barnsley .... *Lab.* 60, *C.* 3, *L.* 1, *Ind.* 1, *R.A.* 1.
Doncaster .... *Lab.* 51, *C.* 11, *L.* 1.
Rotherham .... *Lab.* 61, *C.* 3, *A.* 1, *Ind.* 1.
Sheffield .... *Lab.* 63, *C.* 15, *L.* 8, *A.* 1.

TYNE AND WEAR

Gateshead .... *Lab.* 57, *C.* 7, *L.* 1, *R.A.* 1.
Newcastle upon
  Tyne .... *Lab.* 45, *C.* 22, *L.* 10, *S.D.P.* 1.
North Tyneside ..... *Lab.* 33, *C.* 20, *A.* 6, *Ind.* *Lab.* 1.
South Tyneside ..... *Lab.* 47, *C.* 3, *L.* 1, *Others* 9.
Sunderland .... *Lab.* 52, *C.* 13, *L.* 6, *S.D.P.* 1, *Ind.* *Lab.* 2, (1 Vac.).

WEST MIDLANDS

Birmingham .... *Lab.* 61, *C.* 52, *L.* 3, *S.D.P.* 1.
Coventry .... *Lab.* 34, *C.* 20.
Dudley .... *Lab.* 35, *C.* 35, *Ind.* 2.
Sandwell .... *Lab.* 53, *C.* 13, *L.* 5, (1 Vac.).
Solihull .... *C.* 33, *Lab.* 13, *R.A.* 4, *L.* 1.
Walsall............. *Lab.* 25, *C.* 19, *L.* 9, *Ind.* 7.
Wolverhampton..... *Lab.* 35, *C.* 23, *A.* 2.

WEST YORKSHIRE

Bradford .... *Con.* 43, *Lab.* 41, *L.* 6.
Calderdale .... *Lab.* 23, *C.* 16, *L.* 14, *A.*1.
Kirklees............ *Lab.* 36, *C.* 18, *L.* 14, *S.D.P.* 3, (1 Vac.).
Leeds .... *Lab.* 53, *C.* 34, *L.* 10, *S.D.P.* 1, *Ind.* 1.
Wakefield .... *Lab.* 54, *A.* 4, *C.* 4, *Ind.* 1.

Non-Metropolitan District Councils (as at end May 1985)
(* one-third of councillors of Councils so denoted retire each year, except in those years when County Council elections are held)

*Adur . . . . *C.* 19, *L.* 18, *R.A.* 2.
Allerdale . . . . *Lab.* 27 *Ind.* 18, *C.* 10.
Alnwick . . . . *L.* 8, *C.* 6, *Ind.* 3, *Ind. Lab.* 2, *Lab.* 1, *Others* 9.
*Amber Valley . . *Lab.* 22, *C.* 10, *A.* 7, *Ind.* 3, *N.P.* 1.
Arun . . . . *C.* 51, *A.* 4, *Lab.* 1.
Ashfield . . . . *Lab.* 27, *L.* 3, *C.* 1, *S.D.P.* 1, (1 Vac.).
Ashford . . . . *C.* 27, *A.* 7, *Ind.* 6, *Lab.* 6, *Ind. L.* 1, *R.A.* 1, *Other* 1
Aylesbury Vale . . *C.* 34, *Ind.* 12, *A.* 6, *Lab.* 4, (2 Vac.).
Babergh . . . . *C.* 18, *Ind.* 7, *Lab.* 3, *A.* 2, *Others* 12.
*Barrow-in-
Furness . . . . . . *Lab.* 26, *C.* 11, *Ind.* 1.
*Basildon . . . . *Lab.* 24, *C.* 15, *L.* 3.
*Basingstoke &
Deane . . . . *C.* 29, *Lab.* 19, *Ind.* 7, *L.* 2, *S.D.P.* 2.
*Bassetlaw . . . . . . *Lab.* 26, *C.* 20, *Ind.* 3, *Ind. C.* 1.
*Bath . . . . *C.* 30, *Lab.* 11, *A.* 7.
Berwick upon
Tweed . . . . *C.* 8, *L.* 7, *Ind.* 5, *Lab.* 3, *Others* 5.
Beverley . . . . *C.* 35, *L.* 11, *Lab.* 5, *Ind.* 1, (1 Vac.).
Blaby . . . . *C.* 19, *A.* 5, *Ind.* 4, *R.A.* 1, *Others* 10.
*Blackburn . . . . . *Lab.* 30, *C.* 22, *L.* 5, *R.A.* 3.
Blackpool . . . . . . *C.* 32, *Lab.* 9, *L.* 3.
Blyth Valley . . . . *Lab.* 32, *A.* 11, *C.* 3, *L.* 1.
Bolsover . . . . *Lab.* 34, *Ind.* 2, (1 Vac.).
Boothferry . . . . . . *C.* 20, *Ind.* 8, *Lab.* 6, *S.D.P.* 1.
Boston . . . . *C.* 17, *Ind.* 9, *Lab.* 4, *L.* 4.
Bournemouth . . . *C.* 37, *A.* 6, *Lab.* 5, *Ind.* 3, *Ind. C.* 3, *L.* 1, *Others* 2
Bracknell . . . . *C.* 40.
Braintree . . . . *C.* 25, *Lab.* 16, *Ind.* 11, *L.* 5, *R.A.* 2, (1 Vac.).
Breckland . . . . . . *C.* 25, *N.P.* 15, *Lab.* 8, *Ind.* 4, *A.* 1.
*Brentwood . . . . . *C.* 28, *L.* 9, *Lab.* 2.
Bridgnorth . . . . . *Ind.* 19, *C.* 9, *L.* 3, *Lab.* 2.
Brighton . . . . *C.* 22, *Lab.* 22, *A.* 4.
*Bristol . . . . *Lab.* 33, *C.* 29, *L.* 6.
*Broadland . . . . . *C.* 39, *Ind.* 6, *A.* 4.
Bromsgrove . . . . . *C.* 29, *Lab.* 8, *R.A.* 3, *L.* 1.
*Broxbourne . . . . *C.* 32, *Lab.* 5, *A.* 3, (2 Vac.).
Broxtowe . . . . *C.* 37, *Lab.* 10, *Ind.* 1, (1 Vac.).
*Burnley . . . . *Lab.* 39, *C.* 12, *A.* 2, *L.* 1.
*Cambridge . . . . . *Lab.* 22, *C.* 10, *L.* 9, *SDP.* 1.
*Cannock Chase . *Lab.* 19, *L.* 16, *C.* 5, *Ind.* 1, *Ind. L.* 1.
Canterbury . . . . . *C.* 37, *Lab.* 7, *A.* 3, *Ind.* 2.
Caradon . . . . *Ind.* 31, *C.* 4, *A.* 3, *R.A.* 2, *Lab.* 1.
Carlisle . . . . *Lab.* 26, *C.* 22, *L.* 2, *Ind.* 1.
Carrick . . . . *C.* 22, *Ind.* 11, *L.* 11, *Lab.* 1.
Castle Morpeth . . *A.* 6, *C.* 6, *L.* 5, *Ind.* 3, *Lab.* 2, *R.A.* 2, *Others*, 10.
Castle Point . . . . *C.* 37, *Lab.* 2.
Charnwood . . . . . *C.* 38, *Lab.* 12, *Ind. C.* 1, (1 Vac.).
Chelmsford . . . . . *A.* 31, *C.* 26, *Ind.* 3.
*Cheltenham . . . . *L.* 14, *C.* 12, *R.A.* 4, *Lab.* 2, *Ind.* 1.
*Cherwell . . . . . . *C.* 35, *Lab.* 11, *A.* 5, *Ind.* 1.
*Chester . . . . *C.* 33, *Lab.* 16, *L.* 10, *Ind.* 1.
Chesterfield . . . . . *Lab.* 35, *C.* 10, *A.* 1, (1 Vac.).
Chester-le-Street *Lab.* 23, *Ind.* 5, *L.* 4, *C.* 1.
Chichester . . . . . . *C.* 28, *A.* 13, *Ind.* 4, *N.P.* 3, *R.A.* 2.
Chiltern . . . . *C.* 42, *A.* 2, *Lab.* 2, *Ind.* 1, *L.* 1, *R.A.* 1, (1 Vac.).
*Chorley . . . . *C.* 23, *Lab.* 22, *Ind.* 1, *S.D.P.* 1.
Christchurch . . . . *C.* 13, *Ind.* 9, *Lab.* 3.
Cleethorpes . . . . . *C.* 16, *Lab.* 8, *L.* 8, *Ind.* 7, *A.* 1, *Ind. Lab.* 1.
*Colchester . . . . . *C.* 35, *Lab.* 11, *A.* 10, *R.A.* 3, *Ind.* 1.
*Congleton . . . . . *C.* 27, *L.* 14, *Lab.* 4.
Copeland . . . . . . *Lab.* 29, *C.* 16, *Ind.* 4, *A.* 1, *R.A.* 1.
Corby . . . . *Lab.* 23, *C.* 3, (1 Vac.).
Cotswold . . . . . . *N.P.* 22, *C.* 9, *Ind.* 8, *A.* 2, *L.* 2, *Lab.* 1, (1 Vac.).
*Craven . . . . *C.* 18, *L.* 8, *Ind.* 5, *Lab.* 2, *S.D.P.* 1.

*Crawley . . . . *Lab.* 19, *C.* 13.
*Crewe and
Nantwich . . . . . *C.* 27, *Lab.* 25, *L* 3, *S.D.P.* 2.
Dacorum . . . . *C.* 37, *Lab.* 17, *A.* 3, *Ind.* 1.
Darlington . . . . . . *Lab.* 27, *C.* 20, *Ind.* 3, *A.* 1, *L.* 1.
Dartford . . . . *C.* 26, *Lab.* 16, *R.A.* 2, *Ind. Lab.* 1.
*Daventry . . . . . . *C.* 20, *Lab.* 8, *Ind.* 5, *A.* 2.
*Derby . . . . *Lab.* 24, *C.* 18, *L.* 2.
Derwentside . . . . *Lab.* 34, *Ind.* 12, *C.* 5, *A.* 2, (2 Vac.).
Dover . . . . *C.* 39, *Lab.* 17.
Durham . . . . *Lab.* 27, *Ind.* 8, *A.* 5, *L.* 4, *C.* 2, *N.P.* 2, *Ind. Lab.* 1.
Easington . . . . . . *Lab.* 34, *L.* 7, *Ind.* 6, *A.* 2, *Ind. Lab.* 2.
*Eastbourne . . . . *C.* 14, *A.* 8, *L.* 7, *Lab.* 1.
East Cambs. . . . . . *Ind. C.* 4, *C.* 3, *Ind.* 3, *A.* 2, *Ind. L.* 2, *L.* 1, *Lab.* 1, *Others* 20, (1 Vac.).
*East Devon . . . . *C.* 43, *A.* 13, *Ind. C.* 3, *Lab.* 1.
East Hampshire . *C.* 29, *A.* 7, *Ind.* 6.
East Herts. . . . . . . *C.* 31, *Ind.* 7, *R.A.* 6, *A.* 3, *Lab.* 2, *Ind. C.* 1.
*Eastleigh . . . . . . *C.* 20, *L.* 14, *Lab.* 10.
East Lindsey . . . . *C.* 7, *Ind.* 5, *A.* 4, *L.* 3, *Lab.* 3, *Others* 38.
East Northants. . . *C.* 30, *Lab.* 6.
East Staffs. . . . . . . *C.* 21, *Lab.* 22, *Ind. C.* 2, *L.* 1.
East Yorkshire . . . *C.* 30, *Ind.* 7, *Lab.* 2, *L.* 1, *Others* 3.
Eden . . . . *N.P.* 37.
*Ellesmere Port &
Neston . . . . *Lab.* 27, *C.* 13, (1 Vac.).
*Elmbridge . . . . . *C.* 32, *R.A.* 18, *A.* 5, *Lab.* 5.
*Epping Forest . . *C.* 36, *Lab.* 12, *R.A.* 6, *Ind.* 2, *A.* 2, *Ind. C.* 1.
Epsom & Ewell . . *R.A.* 33, *A.* 3, *Lab.* 3.
Erewash . . . . *C.* 27, *Lab.* 20, *Ind. C.* 2, *Ind. Lab.* 1, (2 Vac.).
Exeter . . . . *C.* 16, *Lab.* 14, *L.* 5, *Ind.* 1.
*Fareham . . . . *C.* 25, *A.* 12, *R.A.* 4, *Lab.* 1.
Fenland . . . . *C.* 21, *Ind.* 7, *Lab.* 6, *L.* 5, *A.* 1.
Forest Heath . . . . *C.* 13, *N.P.* 6, *Ind.* 4, *Lab.* 2.
Forest of Dean . . *Lab.* 21, *Ind.* 20, *A.* 4, *C.* 4.
Fylde . . . . *C.* 22, *R.A.* 10, *N.P.* 8, *Ind.* 2, *Ind. C.* 2, *A.* 1, *L.* 1, *Lab.* 1, (2 Vac.).
Gedling . . . . *C.* 38, *Lab.* 8, *A.* 5, *Ind.* 2, *Ind. C.* 1, (1 Vac.).
*Gillingham . . . . *C.* 23, *A.* 11, *Lab.* 7, *Ind. L.* 1.
Glanford . . . . *C.* 24, *Ind.* 12, *Lab.* 2, *A.* 1, *SDP.* 1, (1 Vac.).
*Gloucester . . . . . *C.* 16, *Lab.* 11, *L.* 6.
*Gosport . . . . *C.* 24, *L.* 3, *Lab.* 3.
Gravesham . . . . . *C.* 23, *Lab.* 20, *S.D.P.* 1.
*Great Grimsby . *Lab.* 19, *C.* 18, *A.* 7, *Ind.* 1.
Great Yarmouth . *C.* 26, *Lab.* 18, *L.* 4.
Guildford . . . . *C.* 31, *Lab.* 6, *A.* 5, *L.* 2, *Ind.* 1.
*Halton . . . . *Lab.* 34, *C.* 8, *S.D.P.* 2, *Ind.* 1, *L.* 1, *N.P.* 1
Hambleton . . . . . . *N.P.* 20, *C.* 12, *Ind.* 10, *A.* 3, *Lab.* 2.
Harborough . . . . . *C.* 24, *Ind.* 8, *A.* 2, *Lab.* 2, (1 Vac.).
*Harlow . . . . *Lab.* 33, *L.* 5, *C.* 4.
Harrogate . . . . . . *C.* 36, *Ind.* 8, *L.* 8, *Lab.* 2, *Others* 5, (1 Vac.).
*Hart . . . . *C.* 12, *L.* 12, *Ind.* 8, *S.D.P.* 2, *Ind. C.* 1.
*Hartlepool . . . . . *Lab.* 33, *C.* 11, *N.P.* 2, *L.* 1.
*Hastings . . . . *C.* 13, *L.* 10, *Lab.* 8, *Ind.* 1.
*Havant . . . . *C.* 25, *Lab.* 9, *A.* 5, *Ind.* 2, *N.P.* 1.
*Hereford . . . . *L.* 14, *C.* 7, *Lab.* 4, *Ind.* 2.
*Hertsmere . . . . . *C.* 23, *Lab.* 12, *A.* 4.
High Peak . . . . . . *C.* 20, *Lab.* 14, *A.* 5, *Ind.* 4, *R.A.* 1.
Hinckley and
Bosworth . . . . . *C.* 26, *Lab.* 4, *L.* 3, (1 Vac.).
Holderness . . . . . . *Ind.* 28, *C.* 3.
Horsham . . . . *C.* 36, *Ind.* 3, *A.* 2, *R.A.* 1.

*Stratford-on-
  Avon. ....*C*. 37, *Ind*. 10, *A*. 6, *Lab*. 2.
*Stroud ....*C*. 28, *Ind*. 10, *A*. 9, *Lab*. 9.
Suffolk Coastal .. *C*. 44, *Ind*. 5, *N.P*. 4, *Lab*. 2.
Surrey Heath ... *C*. 36.
*Swale ....*C*. 28, *Lab*. 10, *A*. 9, *Ind*. 1, *Ind*. C.
  1.
*Tamworth .....*C*. 16, *Lab*. 11.
*Tandridge ... *C*. 35, *A*. 3, *Lab*. 3, *Ind*. 1.
Taunton Deane .. *C*. 31, *Lab*. 10, *Ind*. 6, *S.D.P*. 1, (1
  Vac.).
Teesdale ....*Ind*. 28, *Lab*. 3.
Teignbridge .. *C*. 20, *N.P*. 20, *Ind*. 8, *A*. 5, *Lab*. 4,
  (1 Vac.).
Tendring ....*C*. 30, *Lab*. 9, *R.A*. 8, *A*. 7, *Ind*. 4,
  S.D.P. 2.
Test Valley .....*C*. 28, *A*. 6, *N.P*. 6, *Ind*. 2, *Lab*. 1, (1
  Vac.).
Tewkesbury .... *C*. 13, *Ind*. 8, *N.P*. 4, *A*. 1, *L*. 1,
  Others 18.
*Thamesdown ... *Lab*. 32, *C*. 14, *A*. 2, *Ind*. 1.
Thanet ....*Ind*. C. 16, *Ind*. 13, *C*. 8, *Lab*, 7, *A*. 5,
  N.P. 3, (2 Vac.).
*Three Rivers ... *C*. 23, *A*. 14, *Lab*. 10.
*Thurrock ....*Lab*. 27, *C*. 10, *Ind*. *Lab*. 2.
*Tonbridge &
  Malling ....*C*. 35, *A*. 11, *Lab*. 5, *Ind*. 1.
*Torbay ....*C*. 28, *A*. 4, *R.A*. 2, *Ind*. 1, *L*. 1.
Torridge .......*N.P*. 29, *C*. 3, *L*. 3, *Lab*. 1.
*Tunbridge Wells *C*. 41, *A*. 5, *Ind*. 1, *Lab*. 1.
Tynedale ....*Ind*. 17, *C*. 12, *L*. 11, *Lab*. 7.
Uttlesford ......*C*. 26, *A*. 7, *Ind*. 1, *Others* 8.
Vale of White   *C*. 39, *S.D.P*. 6, *Ind*. 2, *L*. 2, *Lab*. 1,
  Horse ....   (1 Vac.).
Vale Royal ......*C*. 29, *Lab*. 23, *Ind*. 5, *L*. 1, *R.A*. 1,
  S.D.P. 1.
Wansbeck ......*Lab*. 39, *L*. 7.
Wansdyke ......*C*. 33, *Lab*. 11, *Ind*. 3.
Warrington .....*Lab*. 36, *C*. 21, *A*. 2, *Ind*. *Lab*. 1.

Warwick ....*C*. 31, *Lab*. 7, *A*. 4, *R.A*. 3.
*Watford ....*Lab*. 22, *C*. 14.
Waveney ....*C*. 26, *Lab*. 19, *L*. 2, *Ind*. 1.
Waverley ......*C*. 42, *A*. 7, *Ind*. 5, *Lab*. 2, *Ind*. C. 1.
Wealden ......*C*. 45, *R.A*. 6, *A*. 4, *Ind*. 2, (1 Vac.).
Wear Valley ...*Lab*. 27, *Ind*. 4, *N.P*. 4, *C*. 3, *L*. 2.
Wellingborough ..*C*. 18, *Lab*. 12, *Ind*. 3, *L*. 1.
*Welwyn
  Hatfield ......*Lab*. 24, *C*. 19.
West Derbyshire *C*. 26, *A*. 5, *N.P*. 3, *Lab*. 2, *Ind*. 1,
  Ind. C. 1, *L*. 1.
*West Devon ....*NP*. 15, *C*. 9, *Ind*. 5, *A*. 1.
*West Dorset....*C*. 15, *N.P*. 8, *Ind*. 4, *L*. 4, *A*. 1, *Ind*.
  C. 1, *Lab*. 1, *Others* 20, (1 Vac.).
*W. Lancashire .*C*. 30, *Lab*. 19, *A*. 3, *Ind*. 3.
*West Lindsey ..*A*. 15, *Ind*. 11, *C*. 8, *Lab*. 3.
*W. Oxon. ......*C*. 25, *Ind*. 12, *A*. 8, *Lab*. 4.
West Somerset ..*N.P*. 24, *C*. 4, *Ind*. 3, *A*. 1.
West Wilts. .....*C*. 33, *Lab*. 4, *A*. 3, *Ind*. 3.
*Weymouth and
  Portland ....*C*. 15, *Lab*. 12, *Ind*. 3, *R.A*. 3, *L*. 2.
Wimborne ......*C*. 27, *A*. 3, *Ind*. 3, *L*. 1, *R.A*. 1, (1
  Vac.).
*Winchester ....*C*. 37, *A*. 8, *Ind*. 5, *Lab*. 5.
Windsor and
  Maidenhead ..*C*. 47, *L*. 7, *R.A*. 4.
*Woking........*C*. 20, *A*. 8, *Lab*. 7.
*Wokingham ....*C*. 45, *L*. 7, *Lab*. 1, (1 Vac.).
*Woodspring ....*C*. 46, *Ind*. 5, *Lab*. 4, *A*. 2, *S.D.P*. 1,
  (1 Vac.).
*Worcester .....*C*. 18, *Lab*. 18.
Worthing ......*C*. 24, *A*. 7, *L*. 5.
Wrekin ....*Lab*. 32, *C*. 7, *Ind*. 6, *A*. 1.
Wychavon ......*C*. 18, *Ind*. 8, *L*. 5, *Lab*. 3, *Others* 15.
Wycombe ......*C*. 50, *Lab*. 9, *L*. 1.
Wyre ....*C*. 46, *Lab*. 8, *L*. 2.
*Wyre Forest .. *C*. 17, *L*. 15, *Lab*. 7, *Ind*. 3.
*York ....*Lab*. 19, *C*. 18, *L*. 8.

Greater London Boroughs (as at end May 1985)

Barking and   *Lab*. 36, *C*. 3, *L*. 3, *R.A*. 3, *Ind*.
  Dagenham........   2, (1 Vac.).
Barnet ....*C*. 47, *Lab*. 13.
Bexley ....*C*. 38, *Lab*. 14, *A*. 9, (1 Vac.).
Brent ....*Lab*. 32, *C*. 31, *L*. 3.
Bromley ....*C*. 50, *A*. 5, *Lab*. 5.
Camden ....*Lab*. 33, *C*. 26.
Croydon ....*C*. 62, *Lab*. 5, *R.A*. 3.
Ealing ....*C*. 34, *Lab*. 30, *A*. 3, *Ind*. 2, *Ind*.
  C. 1.
Enfield ....*C*. 47, *Lab*. 19.
Greenwich ....*Lab*. 43, *C*. 17, *A*. 3.
Hackney ....*Lab*. 50, *L*. 7, *C*. 3.
Hammersmith
  and Fulham ......*C*. 23, *Lab*. 21, *Ind*. *Lab*. 3, *L*. 3.
Haringey ....*Lab*. 36, *C*. 22, *Ind*. 1.
Harrow ....*C*. 40, *L*. 13, *Lab*. 6, *R.A*. 4.
Havering ....*C*. 37, *Lab*. 12, *R.A*. *Ind*. 9, *A*. 5.
Hillingdon ....*C*. 57, *Lab*. 10, *A*. 2.

Hounslow ....*Lab*. 33, *C*. 27.
Islington ....*Lab*. 49, *S.D.P*. 3.
Kensington and
  Chelsea ....*C*. 39, *Lab*. 14, *Ind*. 1.
Kingston-on-Thames *C*. 38, *L*. 9, *Lab*. 3.
Lambeth ....*Lab*. 34, *C*. 26, *A*. 4.
Lewisham ....*Lab*. 39, *C*. 27, (1 Vac.).
Merton ....*C*. 43, *Lab*. 13, *R.A*. 1.
Newham ....*Lab*. 55, *S.D.P*. 3, *L*. 2.
Redbridge ....*C*. 49, *Lab*. 12, *A*. 2.
Richmond-on-
  Thames ....*A*. 28, *C*. 24.
Southwark ....*Lab*. 50, *C*. 8, *A*. 3, *Ind*. *Lab*. 3.
Sutton ....*C*. 41, *A*. 8, *Lab*. 7.
Tower Hamlets ......*Lab*. 30, *L*. 19, *Ind*. 1.
Waltham Forest .....*C*. 25, *Lab*. 25, *L*. 7.
Wandsworth ....*C*. 33, *Lab*. 25, *L*. 2, (1 Vac.).
Westminster ....*C*. 42, *Lab*. 15, *Ind*. 1, *Ind*. C. 1,
  Ind. *Lab*. 1.

WALES
County Councils (as at end May 1985)

Clwyd ......*Lab*. 27, *Ind*. 23, *C*. 14, *L*. 2.
Dyfed ....*Ind*. 33, *Lab*. 31, *L*. 8, *P.C*. 5, *Ind*. *Lab*.
  1, *R.A*. 1, *S.D.P*. 1.
Gwent ......*Lab*. 67, *C*. 9, *L*. 1, *P.C*. 1.
Gwynedd ....*N.P*. 42, *A*. 7, *P.C*. 7, *Lab*. 6, *C*. 3, (1
  Vac.).

Mid Glam. ...*Lab*. 69, *P.C*. 7, *Ind*. 3, *A*. 1, *C*. 1, *Com* 1,
  L. 1, *R.A*. 1, *Others* 1.
Powys.......*Ind*. 42, *Lab*. 8, *A*. 2, *L*. 1.
S. Glam. .....*Lab*. 34, *C*. 18, *A*. 9, *P.C*. 1.
W. Glam. ....*Lab*. 54, *C*. 7, *A*. 5, *Ind*. 3, *N.P*. 1,

District Councils (as at end May 1985)

Aberconwy .....*N.P.* 19, *C.* 9, *A.* 5, *Ind.* 3, *L.* 3, *Lab.* 2.

Afan ....*Lab.* 25, *R.A.* 6.

Alyn & Deeside..*Lab.* 23, *C.* 13, *A.* 4, *Ind.* 4, *R.A.* 1.

Arfon ....*Ind.* 15, *P.C.* 11, *Lab.* 10, *L.* 4.

Blaenau Gwent..*Lab.* 39, *R.A.* 4, *Ind.* 2, *P.C.* 2, *C.* 1, *Ind. Lab.* 1, *L.* 1.

Brecknock ......*Ind.* 32, *Lab.* 16, *L.* 1, *P.C.* 1, (1 Vac.).

Cardiff ....*C.* 34, *Lab.* 26, *A.* 4, *Ind.* 1.

Carmarthen.....*Ind.* 24, *Lab.* 6, *L.* 3, *R.A.* 2, *P.C.* 1

Ceredigion......*Ind.* 30, *L.* 4, *A.* 3, *Lab.* 3, *P.C.* 2, *S.D.P.* 1.

Colwyn.........*N.P.* 12, *L.* 12, *C.* 6, *R.A.* 2, *Ind. C.* 1, *Lab.* 1.

Cynon Valley ...*Lab.* 28, *P.C.* 6, *Com.* 1, *Ind.* 1, *Others* 2.

Delyn ....*Lab.* 17, *Ind.* 14, *L.* 3, *C.* 2, *P.C.* 2, *N.P.* 1, (1 Vac.).

Dinefwr ....*Lab.* 14, *Ind.* 10, *P.C.* 4, *Ind. Lab.* 2, *N.P.* 2.

Dwyfor ........*P.C.* 3, *Others* 26.

Glyndwr........*Ind.* 31, *Lab.* 2.

Islwyn.........*Lab.* 24, *P.C.* 8, *Ind.* 1, *A.* 1 (1 Vac.).

Llanelli ....*Lab.* 30, *A.* 2, *Other* 1.

Lliw Valley .....*Lab.* 25, *Ind.* 3, *Ind. Lab.* 2, *C.* 1, *P.C.* 1.

Meirionnydd ....*N.P.* 30, *P.C.* 5, *Lab.* 3, *Ind.* 1.

Merthyr Tydfil ..*Lab.* 30, *R.A.* 2, *Ind.* 1.

Monmouth......*C.* 26, *Lab.* 7, *Ind.* 4, *A.* 2.

Montgomery ....*Ind.* 5, *P.C.* 2, *C.* 1, *L.* 1, *Lab.* 1, *Others* 39.

Neath ....*Lab.* 30, *P.C.* 2, *Ind.* 1, *A.* 1.

Newport........*Lab.* 35, *C.* 11, *A.* 1.

Ogwr...........*Lab.* 28, *C.* 18, *Ind.* 6, *P.C.* 2, *L.* 1, *R.A.* 1, (1 Vac.).

Preseli.........*Ind.* 42, *Lab.* 2.

Radnor ....*Ind.* 33.

Rhondda........*Lab.* 26, *R.A.* 4, *P.C.* 2, *Ind.* 1.

Rhuddlan.......*N.P.* 12, *Ind.* 9, *C.* 4, *Lab.* 4, *A.* 2, *R.A.* 1.

Rhymney Valley .*Lab.* 35, *P.C.* 8, *Ind.* 2, *R.A.* 2, *A.* 1.

S. Pembroke. ....*Ind.* 25, *Lab.* 4.

Swansea ....*Lab.* 31, *C.* 16, *Ind.* 2, *L.* 1, *R.A.* 1.

Taff-Ely ....*Lab.* 31, *Ind.* 6, *P.C.* 5, *L.* 3, *R.A.* 2, *C.* 1.

Torfaen........*Lab.* 32, *Ind.* 8, *Com.* 1, *C.* 1, *RA.* 1.

Vale of

Glamorgan.....*C.* 32, *Lab.* 10, *Ind.* 2, *P.C.* 2.

Wrexham Maelor *Lab.* 23, *C.* 9, *Ind.* 5, *L.* 3, *P.C.* 1, *Others* 3.

Ynys Môn ......*N.P.* 40, *Lab.* 3, *Ind.* 1, *L.* 1.

SCOTLAND
Scottish Regional Councils (as at end May 1985)

Borders .....*Ind.* 12, *N.P.* 1, *C.* 8, *A.* 2.

Central .....*Lab.* 22, *S.N.P.* 5, *C.* 4, *Ind.* 2, *A.* 1.

Dumfries & *Ind.* 11, *N.P.* 11, *C.* 4, *Lab.* 4, *S.N.P.* 3, Galloway .. *A.* 2.

Fife ....*Lab.* 27, *C.* 9, *A.* 5, *Ind.* 2, *Com.* 1, *SNP.* 1.

Grampian ...*C.* 26, *Lab.* 15, *A.* 7, *S.N.P.* 3, *Ind.* 2, (1 Vac.).

Highland ....*Ind.* 16, *Lab.* 5, *C.* 2, *L.* 2, *S.N.P.* 2, *Others* 25.

Lothian .....*Lab.* 23, *C.* 21, *A.* 3, *Ind.* 1, *S.N.P.* 1.

Orkney .....*N.P.* 24.

Shetland ....*Ind.* 22, *Lab.* 3.

Strathclyde..*Lab.* 80, *C.* 14, *A.* 4, *Ind.* 2, *S.N.P.* 2, *N.P.* 1.

Tayside .....*C.* 27, *Lab.* 13, *S.N.P.* 4, *Ind.* 2.

Western Isles *N.P.* 30.

Scottish District Councils (as at end May 1985)

Aberdeen ....*Lab.* 26, *A.* 17, *C.* 7.

Angus ..........*S.N.P.* 11, *C.* 8, *Ind.* 2.

Annandale

& Eskdale .....*Ind.* 9, *A.* 4, *N.P.* 3.

Argyll & Bute ...*Ind.* 13, *N.P.* 9, *C.* 3, *S.N.P.* 1.

Badenoch and

Strathspey ....*N.P.* 11.

Banff & Buchan .*Ind.* 6, *N.P.* 6, *S.N.P.* 5, *C.* 1.

Bearsden and

Milngavie ....*C.* 6, *A.* 2, *Ind.* 1, *Lab.* 1.

Berwickshire ...*C.* 8, *Ind.* 3, *A.* 1.

Caithness ......*Ind.* 15, *L.* 1.

Clackmannan ...*Lab.* 9, *S.N.P.* 2, *C.* 1.

Clydebank .....*Lab.* 11, *C.* 1.

Clydesdale .....*Ind.* 6, *Lab.* 6, *S.N.P.* 3, *Ind. Lab.* 1.

Cumbernauld

& Kilsyth .....*Lab.* 8, *S.N.P.* 4.

Cumnock &

Doon Valley ...*Lab.* 10.

Cunninghame ...*Lab.* 23, *C.* 5, *N.P.* 2.

Dumbarton ....*Lab.* 11, *C.* 2, *A.* 1, *Ind.* 1, *N.P.* 1.

Dundee ....*Lab.* 25, *C.* 14, *A.* 2, *S.N.P.* 24, *Ind.* *C.* 1.

Dunfermline ....*Lab.* 24, *A.* 6, *C.* 2, *Com.* 1, *SNP.* 1.

East Kilbride ....*Lab.* 14, *C.* 2..

East Lothian ....*Lab.* 11, *C.* 6.

Eastwood ....*C.* 10, *R.A.* 2.

Edinburgh ......*Lab.* 34, *C.* 22, *A.* 4, *SNP.* 2.

Ettrick and

Lauderdale ...*Ind.* 8, *Lab.* 2, *C.* 1, *Others* 5.

Falkirk ....*Lab.* 25, *SNP.* 7, *C.* 2, *Ind.* 2.

Glasgow ....*Lab.* 59, *C.* 5, *A.* 2.

Gordon ....*Ind.* 7, *C.* 3, *L.* 1, *A.* 1.

Hamilton ....*Lab.* 17, *L.* 2, *C.* 1.

Inverclyde ......*Lab.* 11, *L.* 9.

Inverness.......*Ind.* 18, *Lab.* 8, *L.* 2.

Kilmarnock and

Loudoun......*Lab.* 14, *C.* 3, *S.N.P.* 1.

Kincardine and

Deeside ......*Ind.* 7, *C.* 3, *L.* 1, *S.N.P.* 1.

Kirkcaldy ......*Lab.* 30, *A.* 3, *C.* 3, *Ind.* 2, *R.A.* 1, *S.N.P.* 1.

Kyle & Carrick ..*C.* 11, *Lab.* 11, *Ind. Lab.* 1, *Others* 2.

Lochaber ....*Ind.* 5, *Lab.* 5, *N.P.* 3, *Ind. Lab.* 2.

Midlothian .....*Lab.* 14, *L.* 1.

Monklands......*Lab.* 18, *C.* 2.

Moray .........*N.P.* 10, *Ind.* 5, *S.N.P.* 2, *Lab.* 1.

Motherwell .....*Lab.* 23, *C.* 2, *SNP.* 2, *Com.* 1, *Others* 1, (1 Vac.).

Nairn ....*Ind.* 9, *Lab.* 1.

Nithsdale ....*C.* 7, *Ind.* 7, *S.N.P.* 7, *Lab.* 6, *Ind. Lab.* 1.

N.-E. Fife ....*A.* 11, *C.* 5, *Ind.* 2.

Perth & Kinross .*C.* 13, *Lab.* 6, *A.* 5, *Ind.* 3.

Renfrew ....*Lab.* 35, *C.* 5, *S.N.P.* 3, *A.* 2.

Ross &

Cromarty .....*N.P.* 20, *C.* 1, *Lab.* 1.

Roxburgh ......*Ind.* 6, *C.* 5, *A.* 3, *N.P.* 2.

Skye & Lochalsh .*Ind.* 10, *S.D.P.* 1.

Stewartry ......*N.P.* 7, *Ind.* 3, *Others* 2

Stirling ....*Lab.* 11, *C.* 8, *Ind.* 1.

Strathkelvin ....*Lab.* 11, *C.* 4.

Sutherland .....*N.P.* 14.

Tweeddale ......*Ind.* 10.

West Lothian ...*Lab.* 19, *Ind.* 3, *S.N.P.* 2.

Wigtown .......*N.P.* 13, *S.N.P.* 1.

The Kingdom of England

Position and Extent.—The Kingdom of England lies between 55° 46′ and 49° 57′ 30″ N. latitude (from a few miles north of the mouth of the Tweed to the Lizard), and between 1° 46′ E. and 5° 43′ W. (from Lowestoft to Land's End). England is bounded on the north by the Cheviot Hills; on the south by the English Channel; on the east by the Straits of Dover (Pas de Calais) and the North Sea; and on the West by the Atlantic Ocean, Wales and the Irish Sea.

It has a total area of 50,362 sq. miles (land 50,081; inland water 281). The population (1981 Census) was 46,362,836 (males 22,520,723; females 23,842,113). The average density of the population in 1981 was 915 per square mile.

Relief.—There is a marked division between the upland and lowland areas of England. In the extreme north the Cheviot Hills (highest point, *The Cheviot*, 2,674 ft.) form a natural boundary with the Kingdom of Scotland. Running south from the Cheviots, though divided from them by the Tyne Gap, is the Pennine range (highest point, *Cross Fell*, 2,930 ft.), the main orological feature of the country. The Pennines culminate in the Peak District of Derbyshire (*Kinder Scout*, 2,088 ft.). West of the Pennines are the Cumbrian Mountains, which include *Scafell Pike* (3,210 ft.), the highest peak in England, and to the east are the Yorkshire Moors, their highest point being *Urra Moor* (1,490 ft.).

In the west, the foothills of the Welsh mountains extend into the bordering English counties of Shropshire (the *Wrekin*, 1,334 ft.; *Long Mynd*, 1,694 ft.) and Hereford and Worcester (the Malvern Hills—*Worcestershire Beacon*, 1,394 ft.). Extensive areas of high land and moorland are also to be found in the southwestern peninsular formed by Somerset, Devon and Cornwall: principally Exmoor (*Dunkery Beacon*, 1,704 ft.), Dartmoor (*High Willhays*, 2,038 ft.) and Bodmin Moor (*Brown Willy*, 1,377 ft.). Ranges of low, undulating hills run across the south of the country, including the Cotswolds in the Midlands and southwest, the Chilterns to the north of Greater London, and the North (Kent) and South (Sussex) Downs of the south-east coastal areas.

The lowlands of England lie in the Vale of York, East Anglia and the area around the Wash, the lowest lying being the Cambridgeshire Fens in the valleys of the Great Ouse and the River Nene, which are below sea-level in places; since the 17th century extensive drainage has brought much of the Fens under cultivation. The North Sea coast between the Thames and the Humber, low-lying and formed of sand and shingle for the most part, is subject to erosion and defences against further incursion have been built along many stretches.

Hydrography.—The *Severn* is the longest river in Great Britain, rising in the north-eastern slopes of Plinlimmon (Wales) and entering England in Shropshire with a total length of 220 miles from its source to its outflow into the Bristol Channel, where it receives on the east the Bristol Avon, and on the west the Wye, its other tributaries being the Vrynwy, Tern, Stour, Teme and Upper (or Warwickshire) Avon. The Severn is tidal below Gloucester, and a high bore or tidal wave sometimes reverses the flow as high as Tewkesbury (13½ miles above Gloucester). The scenery of the greater part of the river is very picturesque and beautiful, and the Severn is a noted salmon river, some of its tributaries being famous for trout. Navigation is assisted by the Gloucester and Berkeley Ship Canal (16¾ miles), which admits vessels of 350 tons to Gloucester. The *Severn Tunnel*, begun in 1873 and completed in 1886 (at a cost of £2,000,000) after many difficulties from flooding, is 4 miles 628 yards in length (of which 2¼ miles are under the river). The Severn road bridge between Haysgate, Gwent, and Almondsbury, Glos., with a centre span of 3,240 ft. was opened in 1966.

The longest river wholly in England is the *Thames*, with a total length of 215 miles from its source in the Cotswold hills to the Nore, and is navigable by ocean-going ships to London Bridge. The Thames is tidal to Teddington (69 miles from its mouth) and forms county boundaries almost throughout its course; on its banks are situated London, Windsor Castle, the home of the Sovereign, Eton College, the first of the public schools, and Oxford, the oldest university in the kingdom.

Of the remaining English rivers those flowing into the North Sea are the Tyne, Wear, Tees, Ouse and Trent from the Pennine Range, the Great Ouse (160 miles) from Northamptonshire, and the Orwell and Stour from the hills of East Anglia. Flowing into the English Channel are the Sussex Ouse from the Weald, the Itchen from the Hampshire Hills, and the Axe, Teign, Dart, Tamar and Exe from the Devonian Hills; and flowing into the Irish Sea are the Mersey, Ribble and Eden from the western slopes of the Pennines and the Derwent from the Cumbrian Mountains. The *English Lakes*, noteworthy for their picturesque scenery and poetic associations, lie in Cumbria, the largest being Windermere (10 miles long), Ullswater and Derwentwater.

Islands.—The *Isle of Wight* is separated from Hampshire by the Solent; total area 147 sq. miles, population about 120,400. The climate is mild and healthy, making the island a popular holiday resort. Capital, Newport, at the head of the estuary of the Medina, Cowes (at the mouth) being the chief port; other centres are Ryde, Sandown, Shanklin, Ventnor, Freshwater, Yarmouth, Totland Bay, Seaview and Bembridge.

Lundy (= Island) 11 miles N.W. off Hartland Point, Devon, is about 2 miles long and about ½ mile broad (average), with a total area of about 1,116 acres, and a population of about 20; it became the property of the National Trust in 1969 and is now principally a bird sanctuary.

(*See also* The Isles of Scilly, p. 692.)

Climate.—England has a generally mild and temperate climate. Because of the prevailing south-westerly winds, the weather day to day is variable, being affected mainly by depressions moving eastwards across the Atlantic Ocean. This maritime influence means that the west of the country tends to experience wetter but also milder weather than the east. Rainfall also increases with altitude, the mountainous areas of the north and west having more rain than the lowlands of the south and east. Rain is fairly well-distributed throughout the year in all areas but, on average, the driest months are March to June, and the wettest September to January.

The mean annual temperature reduced to sea-level varies from 11°C in the south-west to 9°C near Berwick-on-Tweed. In winter, temperatures tend to be higher in the south and west than in the east, while the warmest in summer are the south and inland areas. Latitude for latitude the mean annual temperature is lower in the east; the decrease of mean temperature with height is about 0·6°C per 100 metres.

EARLY INHABITANTS

Prehistoric Man.—Archaeological evidence suggests that England has been inhabited since at least the Palaeolithic period, though the extent of the various Palaeolithic cultures was dependent upon the degree of glaciation. The succeeding Neolithic and Bronze Age cultures have left abundant remains throughout the country, the best-known of these being the henges and stone circles of Stonehenge (10 miles north of Salisbury, Wilts.) and Avebury (Wilts.), both of which are believed to have been of religious significance. In the latter part of the Bronze Age the *Goidels*, a people of Celtic race, and in the Iron Age other Celtic races of *Brythons* and *Belgae*, invaded the country and brought with them Celtic civilization and dialects, place names in England bearing witness to the spread of the invasion over the whole kingdom.

The Roman Conquest.—The Roman conquest of Gaul (57–50 B.C.) brought Britain into close contact with Roman civilization, but although Julius Cæsar raided the south of Britain in 55 B.C., and 54 B.C., conquest was not undertaken until nearly 100 years later. In A.D. 42 the Emperor Claudius dispatched Aulus Plautius, with a well-equipped force of 40,000, and himself followed with reinforcements in the same year. Success was delayed by the resistance of *Caratacus* (Caractacus), the British leader from A.D. 48–51, who was finally captured and sent to Rome, and by a great revolt in A.D. 61 led by *Boudicca* (Boadicea), Queen of the Iceni; but the south of Britain was secured by A.D. 70, and Wales and the area north to the Tyne by about A.D. 80.

In A.D. 122, the Emperor Hadrian visited Britain and built a continuous rampart, since known as *Hadrian's Wall*, from Wallsend to Bowness (Tyne to Solway). The work was entrusted by the Emperor Hadrian to Aulus Platorius Nepos, legate of Britain from 122 to 126, and it formed the northern frontier of the Roman Empire in the west for three and a half centuries.

The Romans administered Britain as a Province under a Governor, with a well-defined system of local government, each Roman municipality ruling itself and surrounding territory, while London was the centre of the road system and the seat of the financial officials of the Province of Britain. Colchester, Lincoln, York, Gloucester and St. Albans stand on the sites of five Roman municipalities, and Wroxeter, Caerleon, Chester, Lincoln and York were at various times the sites of legionary fortresses. Well-preserved Roman towns have been uncovered at (or near) *Silchester* (Calleva Atrebatum), 10 miles south of Reading, *Wroxeter* (Viroconium), near Shrewsbury, and *St. Albans* (Verulamium) in Hertfordshire.

Four main groups of roads radiated from London, and a fifth (the Fosse) ran obliquely from Lincoln through Leicester, Cirencester and Bath to Exeter. Of the four groups radiating from London one ran S.E. to Canterbury and the coast of Kent, a second to Silchester and thence to parts of Western Britain and South Wales, a third (later known as *Watling Street*) ran through Verulamium to Chester, with various branches, and the fourth reached Colchester, Lincoln, York and the eastern counties.

In the 4th century Britain was subject to raids along the east coast by Saxon pirates, which led to the establishment of a system of coast defence from the Wash to Southampton Water, with forts at Brancaster, Burgh Castle (Yarmouth), Walton (Felixstowe), Bradwell, Reculver, Richborough, Dover, Lympne, Pevensey and Porchester (Portsmouth). The Irish (Scoti) and Picts in the north were also becoming more aggressive; from about A.D. 350 incursions became more frequent and more formid-able. As the Roman Empire came under attack increasingly towards the end of the 4th century many troops were removed from Britain for service in other parts of the Empire. The island was cut off from Rome by the Teutonic conquest of Gaul early in the 5th century, and with the withdrawal of the last Roman garrison in A.D. 442, the Romano-British were left to themselves.

According to legend, the British King *Vortigern* called in the Saxons to defend him against the Picts, the Saxon chieftains being *Hengist* and *Horsa*, who landed at Ebbsfleet, Kent, and established themselves in the Isle of Thanet; but the events during the 150 years between the final break with Rome and the re-establishment of Christianity are unclear. However, it would appear that in the course of this period the raids turned into large-scale settlement by invaders traditionally known as Angles (England north of the Wash and East Anglia), Saxons (Essex and southern England) and Jutes (Kent and the Weald), which pushed the Romano-British into the mountainous areas of the north and west, Celtic culture outside Wales and Cornwall surviving only in topographical names. Various kingdoms were established at this time which attempted to claim overlordship of the whole country, hegemony finally being achieved by *Wessex* (capital, Winchester) in the 9th century. This century also saw the beginning of raids by the Vikings (Danes), which were resisted by *Alfred the Great* (871–899), the greatest of the Wessex kings, who fixed a limit to the advance of Danish settlement by the Treaty of Wedmore (878), giving them the area north and east of Watling Street, on condition they adopt Christianity.

In the 10th century the Kings of Wessex recovered the whole of England from the Danes, but subsequent rulers were unable to resist a second wave of invaders. England paid tribute (*Danegeld*) for many years, and was invaded in 1013 by the Danes and ruled by Danish Kings from 1016 until 1042, when Edward the Confessor was recalled from exile in Normandy. In 1066 Harold Godwineson (brother-in-law of Edward and son of Earl Godwin of Wessex) was chosen King of England, but after defeating (at Stamford Bridge, Yorkshire, Sept. 25) an invading army under Harald Hadraada, King of Norway (aided by Harold Godwineson's younger brother, the outlawed Earl Tostig of Northumbria), he was himself defeated at the *Battle of Hastings* on Oct. 14, 1066, and the Norman Conquest secured the throne of England for Duke William of Normandy, a cousin of Edward the Confessor.

Christianity reached the Roman province of Britain from Gaul in the 3rd century (or possibly earlier), *Alban*, traditionally Britain's first martyr, being put to death as a Christian during the persecution of Diocletian (June 22, 303), at his native town Verulamium; and the Bishops of Londinium, Eboracum (York), and Lindum (Lincoln) attended the Council of Arles in 314. However, the Anglo-Saxon invasions submerged the Christian religion in England until the 6th century when conversion was undertaken in the north from 563 by Celtic missionaries from Ireland led by St. Columba, and in the south by a mission sent from Rome in 597 which was led by St. Augustine, who became the first archbishop of Canterbury. England appears to have been converted again by the end of the 7th century and followed, after the Council of Whitby in 663, the practices of the Roman Church, which brought the country into the mainstream of European thought and culture.

AREA AND POPULATION OF ENGLISH COUNTIES

County	Administrative Headquarters	Area (*hectares*)	Population	Rateable Value	Actual Rateable Value per head§
				£	£
Avon	Avon House, The Haymarket, Bristol	134,614	935,900	12,509,805	135·17
Bedfordshire......	*Bedford	123,460	516,900	88,600,000	161·10
Berkshire	†Reading	125,890	707,744	131,198,000	185·37
Buckinghamshire .	*Aylesbury	188,284	608,700	106,622,000	175·16
Cambridgeshire ...	†Cambridge	340,892	611,100	88,805,577	145·32
Cheshire	*Chester	232,846	933,200	142,000,000	151·00
Cleveland	Municipal Buildings, Middlesbrough	58,308	564,700	81,354,197	144·00
Cornwall	*Truro	354,792‡	437,100	48,858,539	111·78
Cumbria..........	The Courts, Carlisle	681,012	483,000	50,406,000	104·36
Derbyshire	County Offices, Matlock	263,094	911,100	109,163,012	120·00
Devon............	*Exeter	671,088	980,400	116,837,416	120·74
Dorset	*Dorchester	265,375	617,800	89,839,788	145·41
Durham	*Durham	243,592	606,800	59,684,538	98·36
Essex	*Chelmsford	367,192	1,496,700	244,629,518	164·00
Gloucestershire ..	†Gloucester	264,266	508,000	67,000,000	131·88
Hampshire	The Castle, Winchester	377,698	1,499,400	217,967,000	145·36
Hereford and Worcester	*Worcester	392,650	648,600	89,257,109	138·81
Hertfordshire.....	*Hertford	163,415	979,800	174,598,400	178·20
Humberside	*Beverley, N. Humberside	351,212	854,000	100,193,200	117·00
Kent	*Maidstone	373,060	1,494,200	196,478,867	131·49
Lancashire	*Preston	306,346	1,384,400	146,976,000	106·17
Leicestershire ..	*Leicester	255,293	863,700	119,040,050	137·03
Lincolnshire......	County Offices, Lincoln	591,485	557,609	66,261,309	143·50
Greater London	*S.E.1.	157,946	6,756,000	2,025,538,254	301·50
Greater Manchester.....	*Piccadilly Gardens, Manchester	128,674	2,586,400	338,494,829	130·50
Merseyside	Metropolitan House, Old Hall St., Liverpool	65,202	1,500,800	189,002,000	131·90
Norfolk	*Norwich	536,776	714,500	96,134,852	133·65
Northamptonshire	*Northampton	236,737	547,200	78,074,835	142·68
Northumberland ..	*Morpeth	503,165	302,000	33,964,879	112·47
Nottinghamshire..	*Nottingham	216,365	1,000,100	127,819,000	128·00
Oxfordshire	*Oxford	260,782	558,300	85,048,507	154·00
Shropshire	†Shrewsbury	349,014	390,000	46,709,225	119·76
Somerset	*Taunton	345,094	440,600	53,053,914	120·41
Staffordshire	County Buildings, Stafford	271,615	1,018,000	130,700,000	128·40
Suffolk	*Ipswich	379,663	618,800	81, 647,147	131·94
Surrey	*Kingston-upon-Thames	167,924	1,014,400	180,663,563	178·10
Sussex, East	Pelham House, St. Andrew's Lane, Lewes	179,512	673,800	103,516,193	153·63
Sussex, West......	*Chichester	198,935	687,600	103,400,000	141·00
Tyne and Wear ...	Sandyford House, Archbold Terr., Newcastle	54,006	1,145,300	130,793,968	114·20
Warwickshire	†Warwick	198,053	477,700	70,171,887	146·89
West Midlands	*Lancaster Circus, Birmingham	89,943	2,657,000	416,575,000	182·30
Wight, Isle of	*Newport, I.O.W.	38,066	121,000	14,337,847	118·49
Wiltshire.........	*Trowbridge	348,070	539,900	64,945,781	147·00
Yorkshire, North .	*Northallerton	830,865	684,700	78,739,037	114·99
Yorkshire, South..	*Barnsley	156,049	1,310,500	140,727,168	107·38
Yorkshire, West...	*Wakefield	203,912	2,063,300	220,444,000	106·00

* County Hall. † Shire Hall. ‡ Excluding Isles of Scilly. § Actual Rateable Value per head at April 1, 198

ENGLISH COUNTIES AND SHIRES

LORD LIEUTENANTS AND HIGH SHERIFFS

County or Shire	Lord Lieutenant	*High Sheriff, 1985–86
Avon	Sir John Wills, Bt., T.D.	R. E. J. Bernays
Bedfordshire	Lt. Col. H. C. Hanbury, L.V.O., M.C.	The Hon. Pearl Lawson Johnstone, O.B.E.
Berkshire	Col. The Hon. G. W. N. Palmer, O.B.E., T.D.	R. O. Steel
Buckinghamshire	Cdr. The Hon. J. Tapling Fremantle, R.N.(Rtd)	V. G. A. Hoare Nairne
Cambridgeshire	M. G. M. Bevan	J. S. Martin, C.B.E.
Cheshire	The Rt. Hon. The Viscount Leverhulme, T.D.	R. D. Wilson
Cleveland	The Rt. Hon. The Lord Gisborough	J. M. Wright
Cornwall	The Rt. Hon. The Viscount Falmouth	Maj. Gen. E. M. Hall, C.B., M.B.E.
Cumbria	Sir Charles Graham, Bt.	Maj. A. J. R. Harrison
Derbyshire	Col. P. Hilton, M.C.	I. F. Ley
Devon	Lt. Col. The Rt. Hon. The Earl of Morley	M. F. Heathcote Amory
Dorset	The Rt. Hon. The Lord Digby	C. J. R. Pope, T.D.
Durham	The Rt. Hon. The Lord Barnard, T.D.	D. J. Grant, C.B.E.
Essex	Adm. Sir Andrew Lewis, K.C.B.	D. W. R. Evans
Gloucestershire	Col. M. St. J. V. Gibbs, C.B., D.S.O., T.D.	Maj. M. T. N. H. Wills
Hampshire	Lt. Col. Sir James Scott, Bt.	J. A. Leavett-Shenley
Hereford and Worcester	Capt. T. R. Dunne	Capt. C. P. Hazlehurst (Rtd)
Hertfordshire	Maj.-Gen. Sir George Burns, K.C.V.O., C.B., D.S.O., O.B.E., M.C.	G. N. P. C. De Boinville, M.C., T.D.
Humberside	R. A. Bethell	J. H. Goodhart
Kent	R. Leigh-Pemberton	Maj. Sir Marc Noble, Bt.
Lancashire	S. Towneley	E. C. Parker
Leicestershire	Col. R. A. St. G. Martin, O.B.E.	Hon. D. G. Brooks
Lincolnshire	H. N. Nevile	M. J. Worth
Greater London	Commission of Deputy Lieutenants pending new appointment	P. C. Macnamara
Greater Manchester	Sir William Downward	Col. T. Sherman, O.B.E., V.R.D.
Merseyside	Wing Cmdr. K. M. Stoddart, A.E.	D. F. Moore
Norfolk	T. Colman	Brig. Sir Jeffrey Darell, Bt, M.C.
Northamptonshire	J. L. Lowther, C.B.E.	C. H. Cripps
Northumberland	The Rt. Hon. The Viscount Ridley, T.D.	T. W. Sale
Nottinghamshire	Sir Gordon Hobday	N. J. F. Hardy
Oxfordshire	Sir Ashley Ponsonby, Bt., M.C.	A. Tyser
Shropshire	J. R. S. Dugdale	C. S. Motley
Somerset	Lt. Col. G. W. F. Luttrell, M.C.	J. S. B. White
Staffordshire	Sir Arthur Bryan	A. P. Bamford
Suffolk	Sir Joshua Rowley, Bt.	Capt. C. B. H. Wake-Walker, R.N.
Surrey	The Rt. Hon. The Lord Hamilton of Dalzell, K.C.V.O., M.C.	J. F. Whitfield
Sussex, East	The Most Hon. The Marquess of Abergavenny, K.G., O.B.E.	M. R. Toynbee
Sussex, West	Her Grace Lavinia, Duchess of Norfolk, C.B.E.	Maj. Gen. Sir Philip Ward, K.C.V.O., C.B.E.
Tyne and Wear	Sir Ralph Carr-Ellison, T.D.	A. I. Welch, O.B.E.
Warwickshire	C. M. T. Smith-Ryland	J. L. M. Graham
West Midlands	The Rt. Hon. The Earl of Aylesford	R. L. Harris
Wight, Isle of	Sir John Nicholson, Bt., K.B.E.	V. G. Walker
Wiltshire	Col. Sir Hugh Brassey, K.C.V.O., O.B.E., M.C.	Lt. Col. J. G. Jeans
Yorkshire, North	The Most Hon. The Marquess of Normanby, K.G., C.B.E.	M. T. Barstow
Yorkshire, South	J. H. Neill, C.B.E., T.D.	J. R. Archdale
Yorkshire, West	The Rt. Hon. The Lord Ingrow, O.B.E., T.D.	J. Lyles

* High Sheriffs are nominated by the Queen on November 12 and come into office after Hilary Term.

ENGLISH COUNTIES AND SHIRES

CHIEF EXECUTIVES, TREASURERS AND CHAIRMEN OF COUNTY COUNCILS

County or Shire	Chief Executive	County Treasurer	Chairman of C.C.
Avon	N. J. L. Pearce	D. G. Morgan	W. Greaves
Bedfordshire	J. W. Elven	V. F. Phillips	A. C. Chapman
Berkshire	R. W. Gash	M. C. Beasley	I. E. Morgan
Buckinghamshire	E. M. E. White	H. Springthorpe	W. A. Rooke
Cambridgeshire	J. K. Barratt	J. E. Barton	K. P. Leonard
Cheshire	R. G. Wendt	J. E. H. Whiteoak	R. Carey, B.E.M.
Cleveland	A. J. Hodgkinson†	B. Stevenson	W. Ferrier
Cornwall	G. K. Burgess	C. E. J. Cainey	F. J. Williams
Cumbria	T. J. R. Whitfield	J. R. Ford	S. H. Murray
Derbyshire	E. Cobb*	E. Cobb	Mrs. J. Platts
Devon	D. D. Macklin	B. J. Weston	D. G. Potter
Dorset	K. A. Abel, C.B.E.	D. M. Gasson	Air Cmmdre. K. J. McIntyre, C.B., C.B.E.
Durham	P. Dawson	K. W. Smith	J. E. Paterson
Essex	R. W. Adcock	E. A. Twelvetree	R. M. Williams
Gloucestershire	J. V. Miller	T. N. Hobson	E. J. Radley
Hampshire	A. R. Hodgson	J. E. Scotford	C. M. Jones
Hereford and Worcester	G. A. Price	J. Rocke	J. T. Arnett
Hertfordshire	M. J. Le Fleming	K. S. Cliff	F. J. Cogan
Humberside	P. R. Wellings*	J. A. Parkes	H. Dalton
Kent	W. U. Jackson, C.B.E.	W. B. Taylor	Mrs. R. M. P. Nesham
Lancashire	B. Hill	W. O. Jolliffe	Mrs. M. P. Case
Leicestershire	S. Jones	R. Hale	Dr. P. Hill
Lincolnshire	R. J. D. Procter	D. G. Barrett	P. Newton
Greater London	M. F. Stonefrost, C.B.E.	J. E. G. Crockford	A. L. Banks, M.P.
Greater Manchester	G. A. Harrison	J. M. Marriott	G. Colin
Merseyside	R. F. O'Brien	D. F. Smith	Mrs. E. Lawrenson
Norfolk	B. J. Capon	C. A. Boar	J. Mack
Northamptonshire	A. J. Greenwell	J. Smith	G. Pollard
Northumberland	C. B. Rodger	R. Wolstenholme	J. E. Teasdale
Nottinghamshire	A. Sandford	G. S. Luff	Mrs. M. E. Gray
Oxfordshire	A. T. Brown, C.B.E.	J. T. Vokins	H. G. H. Clifton
Shropshire	W. N. P. Jones	M. N. Davis	J. Turner
Somerset	J. E. Whittaker	B. M. Tanner	W. M. Drower, M.B.E.
Staffordshire	B. A. Price	B. Smith	F. A. Cholerton, C.B.E.
Suffolk	C. W. Smith	P. B. Atkinson	Miss M. M. P. MacRae
Surrey	F. A. Stone	D. J. Thomas	J. Macfarlane
Sussex, East	R. M. Beechey	M. R. Hancock	J. F. Chatfield, C.B.E.
Sussex, West	J. R. Hooley	B. E. Fieldhouse	P. G. Shepherd
Tyne and Wear	J. J. Gardner	P. J. Smith	Mrs. E. J. Shearan
Warwickshire	J. W. Hayes	J. P. Hunt	J. C. Brindley
West Midlands	J. D. Hender	K. E. Rose	Mrs. G. M. Pemberton
Wight, Isle of	J. S. Horsnell	D. A. Tuck	H. D. Howe
Wiltshire	I. A. Browning	A. F. Gould	J. B. Ainslie, O.B.E.
Yorkshire, North	H. J. Evans	K. R. Hounsome	L. Backhouse
Yorkshire, South	J. C. Harris	R. C. Johnston	T. W. McLean
Yorkshire, West	W. Miles	G. S. Pollard	D. Daniel

† Secretary.   * Director.

MUNICIPAL DIRECTORY OF ENGLAND

A list of METROPOLITAN BOROUGH AND CITY COUNCILS. Those accorded CITY status are in SMALL CAPITALS.

Metropolitan Boroughs	Popula-tion	Rateable Value 1985 £	Chief Executive	Mayor †Lord Mayor *Chairman 1985–86
GREATER MANCHESTER				
Bolton	261,800	28,908,868	K. P. Bounds	W. Hardman
Bury	174,800	19,741,816	J. A. McDonald	A. Colleran
MANCHESTER	448,000	78,714,660	R. M. W. Taylor	*K. Strath
Oldham	220,900	23,591,244	C. Smith	A. B. McConnell
Rochdale	205,500	21,603,681	J. Towey	L. Worsley
SALFORD	245,000	32,510,810	R. C. Rees	F. Brockbank
Stockport	288,000	39,485,204	A. L. Wilson	B. J. Warwick
Tameside	216,300	22,279,353	G. Mayall	T. Marsden
Trafford	218,700	39,515,368	R. M. C. Shields	R. Mee
Wigan	309,200	32,110,000	P. Johnson	G. Lockett
MERSEYSIDE				
Knowsley	168,500	21,697,355	R. Penn	Mrs. F. Kneale
LIVERPOOL	497,300	70,347,610	A. J. Stocks, C.B.E.	*H. Dalton
St. Helens	192,000	23,664,649	B. S. Lace	G. J. Shuttleworth
Sefton	294,300	37,156,344	A. G. Corless	B. M. Rimmer
Wirral	338,500	42,925,649	C. D. Darley	G. C. Lindsay
SOUTH YORKSHIRE				
Barnsley	225,890	19,718,817	A. Bleasby	D. E. Lloyd
Doncaster	289,800	30,057,144	C. B. Jeynes	L. N. Hall, B.E.M.
Rotherham	250,000	23,727,799	D. I. Shackleton	T. R. Sharman
SHEFFIELD	545,800	67,446,005	I. L. Podmore	†Mrs. D. Walton
TYNE AND WEAR				
Gateshead	212,900	21,779,000	L. Elton	W. E. Ainsworth
NEWCASTLE UPON TYNE	280,100	42,617,487	C. J. Davies	†R. C. Burgess
North Tyneside	195,000	21,768,133	E. B. Lincoln	T. H. Bryson
South Tyneside	159,000	15,792,145	S. Clark	Mrs. M. C. Pearson
Sunderland	293,919	28,865,980	G. P. Key	R. Baxter
WEST MIDLANDS				
BIRMINGHAM	1,003,000	166,520,934	T. Caulcott	†F. W. Carter
COVENTRY	314,100	44,812,014	R. Tarr	†W. McKernan
Dudley	300,900	45,222,250	J. F. Mulvehill	Dr. K. C. Rogers
Sandwell	308,700	50,193,408	G. A. Hadley	D. L. Crump
Solihull	199,900	30,561,023	J. Scampion	R. M. Scannell
Walsall	265,600	39,455,798	A. V. Astling	W. H. Westwood
Wolverhampton	255,400	43,114,171	M. T. Lyons‡	G. F. Howells
WEST YORKSHIRE				
BRADFORD	464,400	45,574,666	G. C. Moore	†M. Ajeeb
Calderdale	193,000	17,169,223	M. Ellison	T. Lawlor
Kirklees	377,300	33,512,819	D. A. Ansbro	C. C. Walker
LEEDS	716,100	92,500,000	J. Rawnsley‡	†S. Symmonds
WAKEFIELD	312,200	33,877,759	J. G. Stanbury	L. Harrison

‡ Chief Officer.

DISTRICT COUNCILS

A list of non-Metropolitan District Councils in England. Those accorded CITY status are in SMALL CAPITALS, those with Borough status are distinguished by having § prefixed.

District	Popula-tion	Rateable value 1985 £	Chief Executive (*Clerk)	Chairman 1985–86 (a) Mayor (b) Lord Mayor
Adur, West Sussex	58,570	8,603,146	F. M. G. Staden	A. J. A. Merrick
Allerdale, Cumbria	94,244	9,228,013	A. C. Crane	T. Tweddle
Alnwick, Northumberland	29,100	3,100,000	A. G. A. Groome	W. J. Mitchell
Amber Valley, Derbyshire	109,590	14,847,000	J. Ragsdale	E. Eldred
Arun, West Sussex	124,900	17,225,524	J. V. Midgley	A. R. Shingler
Ashfield, Nottinghamshire	105,800	10,608,078	S. Beedham	Mrs. A. A. Flynn
§Ashford, Kent	87,500	12,017,050	E. H. W. Mexter	(a) T. A. Richards
Aylesbury Vale, Bucks.	140,000	21,090,012	J. L. Guest	E. R. McLean
Babergh, Suffolk	75,600	9,598,303	D. C. Bishop	J. W. Baxter
§Barrow in Furness, Cumbria	73,900	6,565,036	D. G. B. Lyon	(a) Mrs. I. Lucas

District	Population	Rateable value 1985 £	Chief Executive (*Clerk)	Chairman 1985–86 (a) Mayor (b) Lord Mayor
Basildon, Essex	160,200	25,955,000	R. C. Mitchinson	Mrs. E. Gelder
§Basingstoke and Deane, Hants.	136,300	21,410,631	D. W. Pilkington, R.D.	(a) P. J. Horrigan
Bassetlaw, Notts.	103,700	16,833,959	R. D. Blair	D. G. Wells
BATH, Avon	85,000	11,095,000	(vacant)	(a) Mrs. J. F. Hole
§Berwick-upon-Tweed, Northumberland	26,400	3,113,479	J. Healy	(a) K. K. Dickenson
§Beverley, Humberside	107,400	12,433,952	W. J. H. Thomas	(a) Mrs. E. R. Standing
Blaby, Leics.	77,800	9,259,552	J. E. Meakin	E. C. Rodgers
§Blackburn, Lancs.	142,800	13,997,000	S. Jones	(a) E. Smith
§Blackpool, Lancs.	147,000	18,875,912	I. B. Prosser	(a) J. R. H. Battersby
§Blyth Valley, Northumberland	78,000	7,404,354	D. Crawford †	(a) D. Raffle
§Bolsover, Derbys.	70,900	6,182,007	C. A. Tucker	N. Jackson
§Boothferry, Humberside	61,000	5,665,000	J. W. Barber	K. Sherwood
§Boston, Lincs.	53,669	6,552,507	R. E. Coley	(a) A. A. Goodson
§Bournemouth, Dorset	145,100	24,849,348	K. Lomas	(a) R. F. Wotton
Bracknell, Berks.	89,100	15,094,143	A. J. Targett	T. G. Ainscough
Braintree, Essex	115,500	15,838,600	C. Daybell	A. F. Millam
Breckland, Norfolk	99,100	11,855,891	J. B. Heath	Canon F. J. Room
Brentwood, Essex	72,800	13,253,263	C. P. Sivell	A. Witts
Bridgnorth, Salop	51,000	6,016,298	G. C. Nutley	Mrs. R. E. J. Yeomans
§Brighton, East Sussex	149,000	25,300,000	R. G. Morgan	(a) R. J. Cristofoli
BRISTOL, Avon	399,300	60,632,532	P. M. McCarthy	(b) J. Bosdet
Broadland, Norfolk	99,900	10,649,899	B. R. Grayling	A. S. Watts
Bromsgrove, Hereford and Worcs.	88,200	11,683,722	G. F. Badham	Mrs. S. J. Bushby
§Broxbourne, Herts.	81,000	12,869,198	C. Campbell	Mrs. M. J. Dowsett
§Broxtowe, Notts.	104,200	12,000,591	A. E. Hodder	(a) G. Stanley
§Burnley, Lancs.	93,300	8,573,966	B. Whittle	(a) J. Wyld
CAMBRIDGE	101,300	22,150,843	G. G. Datson	(a) A. J. Johnson
Cannock Chase, Staffs.	85,800	11,182,086	B. E. Rastall	M. J. Holder
CANTERBURY, Kent	119,000	15,219,353	C. C. Gay	(a) Mrs. H. McCabe
Caradon, Cornwall	71,400	6,967,080	L. J. Gawley	K. Hodge
CARLISLE, Cumbria	101,200	11,063,000	R. Wilson	(a) K. Aitken
Carrick, Cornwall	76,104	9,524,195	A. R. Grint	C. D. Cocking
§Castle Morpeth, Northumberland	49,800	6,523,883	M. Cole	(a) Mrs. D. W. McBryde
Castle Point, Essex	86,100	11,647,543	A. R. Neighbour	D. J. Mitchell
§Charnwood, Leics.	141,290	20,035,688	D. L. Harris	(a) A. Dodd, B.E.M.
§Chelmsford, Essex	144,000	24,567,623	R. M. C. Hartley	(a) D. Ashford
§Cheltenham, Glos.	86,000	14,825,000	B. N. Wynn	(a) P. G. Penner
Cherwell, Oxon.	116,300	17,344,516	A. M. Brace	B. E. Prestidge
CHESTER, Cheshire	116,657	18,665,437	D. F. Burton	(a) J. D. Owens-Kay
§Chesterfield, Derbys.	97,200	12,063,882	D. R. Shaw	(a) T. E. Whyatt
Chester-le-Street, Durham	52,300	4,674,389	A. Golightly	J. Willis
Chichester, West Sussex	99,900	14,328,275	P. G. Lomas	N. Best
Chiltern, Bucks.	92,500	16,408,728	D. G. Sainsbury	J. A. A. Creswell
§Chorley, Lancs.	92,300	8,981,306	A. B. Webster	(a) A. M. Crook
§Christchurch, Dorset	40,800	6,752,130	C. H. Dewsnap	(a) Ms. N. K. Fox
§Cleethorpes, Humberside	68,700	8,768,937	R. W. Bull	(a) Mrs. N. M. Field
§Colchester, Essex	140,700	19,768,312	J. Allen	(a) J. R. H. Williams
§Congleton, Cheshire	82,600	10,798,283	A. Molyneux	(a) R. B. Parish
§Copeland, Cumbria	72,500	7,540,764	P. N. Denson	(a) E. Calvin
Corby, Northants.	51,500	8,956,198	D. Hall	G. Crawley
Cotswold, Glos.	70,300	9,443,292	D. Waring	H. N. E. Groves
Craven, North Yorks	47,653	5,072,146	A. Howell*	R. Nicholson
§Crawley, West Sussex	83,500	18,587,172	M. Sander	(a) G. Todd
§Crewe and Nantwich, Cheshire	98,217	12,833,431	R. Mather	(a) P. Kent
Dacorum, Herts.	135,000	23,744,165	R. H. Davis	J. Taunton
§Darlington, Durham	99,982	13,262,060	H. R. C. Owen	(a) J. A. Anderson
§Dartford, Kent	77,315	12,684,323	R. J. Duck	(a) K. Pearsall
Daventry, Northants.	58,800	9,084,390	R. Symons	E. H. Westaway
§DERBY	215,000	31,078,861	F. R. Tagg	(a) W. H. Matthews
Derwentside, Durham	87,300	7,547,694	T. M. Hodgson	S. C. Walker
Dover, Kent	103,500	11,794,080	J. P. Moir	P. E. Buss
DURHAM	88,900	9,217,546	R. J. B. Morris	(a) A. Crooks
Easington, Durham	98,000	7,703,539	D. C. Kelly	C. F. Short, M.B.E.
§Eastbourne, East Sussex	80,000	14,226,340	C. A. Bloor	L. Mason
East Cambridgeshire	55,200	5,956,809	T. T. G. Hardy	Mrs. M. R. Cook
East Devon	108,017	13,502,103	C. A. Moseley	Capt. C. G. E. Cottrell

† Chief Officer.

District	Population	Rateable value 1985 £	Chief Executive (*Clerk)	Chairman 1985–86 (a) Mayor (b) Lord Mayor
East Hampshire	95,000	12,750,501	H. S. Fry	Mrs. B. H. Edwards
East Hertfordshire	111,200	17,400,000	D. J. Anstey	F. Clay
§Eastleigh, Hants.	97,600	14,714,599	M. C. Brainsby	(a) N. Garnett
East Lindsey, Lincs.	106,700	12,883,304	A. W. Silcox-Crowe	H. Fainlight, M.B.E.
East Northamptonshire	62,866	6,964,517	D. B. Adnitt	Mrs. E. M. Dicks
East Staffordshire	95,300	13,133,589	F. W. Saunders	K. Clarke
§East Yorkshire, Humberside	76,200	7,381,340	J. H. Gibson	(a) P. Barker
Eden, Cumbria	43,984	4,569,040	J. D. Brown	E. Bain
§Ellesmere Port and Neston, Cheshire	81,200	16,827,576	S. Ewbank	H. Evans
§Elmbridge, Surrey	111,100	22,953,888	D. W. L. Jenkins	(a) W. M. D. Gibson
Epping Forest, Essex	117,000	19,443,937	A. V. Hackman	A. J. T. Bryant, B.E.M.
§Epsom and Ewell, Surrey	69,400	11,903,190	D. R. Grimes	(a) Mrs. E. M. F. Catmur
§Erewash, Derbys.	103,500	11,933,281	J. M. Parker	(a) P. Cresswell
Exeter, Devon	100,800	14,855,782	B. Frowd	(a) R. Slack
§Fareham, Hants.	90,875	13,157,675	O. D. Ellis	(a) Mrs. H. M. Joyce, O.B.E.
Fenland, Cambs.	68,600	8,181,484	E. S. Thompson	R. C. Lake
Forest Heath, Suffolk	56,100	6,461,689	J. F. Gale	The Lady Petre
Forest of Dean, Glos.	73,000	6,892,000	K. W. Harris	A. C. Cooper
§Fylde, Lancs.	69,200	9,182,500	B. J. Smith	(a) J. Payne
§Gedling, Notts.	104,075	11,579,890	W. Brown	(a) E. Frost
§Gillingham, Kent.	94,500	10,752,176	G. C. Jones	(a) Mrs. J. A. Ward-McNally
§Glanford, Humberside	67,300	8,960,947	D. D. H. Cameron	(a) F. A. Bunyan
Gloucester	94,400	13,152,927	H. R. T. Shackleton	(a) Miss E. N. Hedge
§Gosport, Hants.	77,100	9,790,126	W. D. Hooper	D. J. Lucas
Gravesham, Kent	95,329	12,357,935	R. D. Dewar	(a) F. Gibson
§Great Grimsby, Humberside	92,400	11,651,989	R. V. Hughes	F. A. Coleman
§Great Yarmouth, Norfolk	82,600	11,934,230	K. G. Ward	(a) J. M. Benson
§Guildford, Surrey	122,000	23,141,167	D. T. Watts	(a) J. Patrick
§Halton, Cheshire	122,800	17,684,315	R. Turton	(a) J. E. Hughes
Hambleton, North Yorks.	75,400	8,296,873	C. Spencer	Col. M. C. W. P. Consett
Harborough, Leics.	62,200	8,047,687	F. T. Berry	Mrs. A. M. Harris
Harlow, Essex	79,000	14,206,446	H. Platt	A. Jones
§Harrogate, North Yorks.	142,600	17,348,664	J. V. Lovell	(a) Mrs. B. A. Towler
Hart, Hants.	78,939	10,502,316	M. W. Tyler	Mrs. M. Stocks
§Hartlepool, Cleveland	93,400	11,092,740	N. D. Abram	(a) M. Boagey
§Hastings, East Sussex	77,800	9,991,673	R. A. Carrier	(a) D. W. Thornton
§Havant, Hants.	117,400	15,469,066	D. E. Ridley	(a) Mrs. T. J. Daines
Hereford	47,800	6,900,779	C. E. S. Willis	(a) S. J. Stroucken
§Hertsmere, Hertfordshire	88,500	16,743,121	S. J. Evans	I. C. Harding
High Peak, Derbys.	82,142	9,197,405	G. D. Jones	(a) Mrs. B. M. Langham
§Hinckley and Bosworth, Leics.	90,400	11,839,602	F. Shaw†	(a) S. Heath
§Holderness, Humberside	48,000	5,164,186	D. B. Law	(a) J. Overvoorde
Horsham, West Sussex	102,880	14,754,809	M. J. Pearson	A. H. Windrum
§Hove, East Sussex	89,000	15,365,889	G. H.Longden	(a) R. J. Allen
Huntingdon, Cambs.	133,400	16,366,661	L. Bly	M. F. Newman
§Hyndburn, Lancs.	78,210	6,707,888	N. D. Macgregor	(a) E. F. Hill
§Ipswich, Suffolk	120,000	19,126,529	J. R. Savage	(a) E. Grant
Kennet, Wilts.	66,100	6,877,263	S. L. A. Jaques	J. M. Read
Kerrier, Cornwall	84,900	8,523,906	S. G. Stevens	R. S. Godolphin
§Kettering, Northants.	71,700	8,410,216	R. M. Eagland	(a) J. Meads
§King's Lynn and W. Norfolk	123,500	16,670,546	J. McGhee	(a) T. C. R. Legge
Kingston upon Hull, Humberside	268,300	29,394,027	A. B. Wood	(b) J. M. Paton
Kingswood, Avon	86,800	8,648,550	A. Smith	G. Wells
Lancaster, Lancs.	126,800	14,667,642	W. Pearson	(a) J. H. Ball
§Langbaurgh, Cleveland	149,300	22,035,000	K. Abigail*	(a) A. S. Seed
Leicester	282,300	42,710,178	D. Mellor	(b) Mrs. J. M. Setchfield
Leominster, Hereford and Worcs.	37,600	3,750,977	G. A. Robson	B. R. Lowe, O.B.E.
Lewes, East Sussex	82,700	12,548,337	C. W. Mann	S. R. Bleach
§Lichfield, Staffs.	89,900	12,639,871	J. T. Thompson	H. D. Brooks
Lincoln	77,100	10,785,230°	C. J. Thomas	(a) Mrs. I. E. Campbell
§Luton, Beds.	165,000	32,038,977	A. Collins	(a) Mrs. A. L. Bush
§Macclesfield, Cheshire	148,500	23,162,004	B. W. Longden	(a) G. Sutton
§Maidstone, Kent	131,800	17,568,704	A. F. Hargraves	(a) Mrs. R. E. Graham
Maldon, Essex	50,500	7,586,798	E. Robinson	H. L. Frost

† Chief Officer.   ° 1984 figure.

District	Population	Rateable value 1985 £	Chief Executive (*Clerk)	Chairman 1985–86 (a) Mayor (b) Lord Mayor
Malvern Hills, Hereford and Worcs.	85,200	10,364,404	L. J. Martin	Mrs. B. E. Bomphrey
Mansfield, Notts.	100,000	10,208,341	C. Evans	D. E. Cruickshanks
§Medina, Isle of Wight	68,700	8,282,209	D. Carmichael	(a) R. J. Price
§Melton, Leics.	43,700	5,646,846	P. J. G. Herrick*	(a) D. F. Sanders
Mendip, Somerset	91,800	10,314,531	G. Jeffs	E. G. Wright, G.M.
Mid Bedfordshire	108,000	14,272,868	P. A. Freeman	W. H. Russell.
Mid Devon (Tiverton)	58,700	5,646,918	R. C. Greensmith	D. Coulthard
§Middlesbrough, Cleveland	148,600	17,935,998	J. R. Foster, O.B.E.	(a) J. Jones
Mid Suffolk	72,490	8,477,041	H. McFarlane	H. F. Griffiths, O.B.E.
Mid Sussex, West Sussex	114,235	17,164,599	B. J. Grimshaw	E. L. Cox
§Milton Keynes, Bucks.	145,800	25,190,492	M. J. Murray	(a) L. H. Cowley
Mole Valley, Surrey	77,300	12,649,292	A. A. Huggins	Mrs. T. A. E. Martin
Newark, Notts.	104,300	11,425,000	V. G. Crawley	S. A. Wilford
Newbury, Berks.	128,277	20,196,014	B. J. Thetford	Mrs. R. A. G. Sanders-Rose
§Newcastle under Lyme, Staffs.	119,100	13,730,172	A. G. Owen	(a) Mrs. M. Platt
§New Forest, Hants.	154,300	24,017,234	P. A. Bassett	Mrs. J. C. Safe
§Northampton	164,000	28,627,518	A. C. Parkhouse	(a) R. E. Linsdell
Northavon, Avon	122,000	16,975,698	F. Maude	A. G. Higgs
§North Bedfordshire	133,000	21,339,092	J. F. Hayward	(a) B. F. Dillingham
North Cornwall	66,100	7,447,884	I. Whiting	G. Facks-Martin
North Devon	79,000	8,378,526	M. J. Clare	G. E. Andrews
North Dorset	49,700	5,433,253	A. J. Bridgeman	Mrs. M. E. Cossins
North East Derbyshire	97,300	9,213,783	R. S. Billington	G. W. Marshall, B.E.M.
North Hertfordshire	108,900	19,205,969	J. S. Philp	M. K. Tatham
North Kesteven, Lincs.	79,380	8,290,636	Dr. G. J. Coady	Dr. M. E. Jones
North Norfolk	85,500	10,790,619	T. V. Nolan	Mrs. V. H. Bensley
North Shropshire	51,500	5,052,900	K. Flood	Mrs. P. M. Collins
§North Warwickshire	60,000	8,502,000	D. Monks	(a) D. Mott
North West Leicestershire	79,100	10,324,075	J. E. White	Mrs. A. M. Hall
North Wiltshire	107,700	10,840,553	H. Miles	M. E. Flintoff
NORWICH, Norfolk	123,700	23,351,407	A. R. H. Glover	(b) Mrs. B. E. E. Stevenson
NOTTINGHAM	277,100	42,851,015	M. H. F. Hammond	(b) D. F. Tongue
§Nuneaton and Bedworth, Warks.	114,700	14,007,853	I. J. Clarke	(a) A. H. Walker
§Oadby and Wigston, Leics.	53,100	7,037,364	J. B. Burton	(a) R. Hughes
§Oswestry, Shropshire	31,580	3,154,011	D. A. Towers	(a) D. G. Lloyd, M.B.E.
OXFORD	116,500	21,314,800	E. J. Patrick	(b) R. A. Dudman
§Pendle, Lancs.	85,566	6,423,995	C. A. Simmonds	(a) N. Walker
Penwith, Cornwall	53,900	5,969,000	J. C. Moore, M.B.E.	H. Storer
PETERBOROUGH, Cambs.	140,625	22,577,451	P. B. Sidebottom	R. E. Burke
PLYMOUTH, Devon	255,200	30,933,952	A. F. Watson	(b) J. L. Mills
§Poole, Dorset	125,150	20,869,448	I. K. D. Andrews	Mrs. D. M. Hackforth
PORTSMOUTH, Hants.	191,600	27,909,132	R. Trist	(b) F. Warner
§Preston, Lancs.	125,800	15,784,347	A. Owens	(a) Mrs. J. Ainscough
Purbeck, Dorset	40,414	5,724,531	A. J. James	D. B. Humphry
§Reading, Berks.	136,400	28,882,050	W. H. Tee	(a) B. Fowles
§Redditch, Hereford and Worcs.	73,820	11,503,796	Ms. A. C. Griffin	(a) W. G. L. Lock
§Reigate and Banstead, Surrey	116,700	19,424,348	C. T. Pollard	(a) Mrs. K. Waters
§Restormel, Cornwall	78,900	10,310,440	D. Brown	(a) F. J. Parkin
§Ribble Valley, Lancs.	51,500	5,400,702	M. Jackson	(a) Mrs. J. Lilburn
Richmondshire, North Yorks.	45,400	4,486,110	M. F. Tooze	C. W. C. Watson
ROCHESTER UPON MEDWAY, Kent	146,000	23,043,765	R. E. Painter	(a) D. P. Rossiter
Rochford, Essex	74,800	10,641,015	A. G. Cooke	J. A. Sheaf
§Rossendale, Lancs.	65,000	5,221,944	J. S. Hartley‡	(a) V. R. Clegg
Rother, East Sussex	78,000	11,384,494	D. F. Powell	F. Price
§Rugby, Warwicks.	86,700	12,764,667	J. S. R. Lawton	(a) B. Levy
§Runnymede, Surrey	73,700	12,132,627	E. W. Andrews	(a) A. W. Read
§Rushcliffe, Notts.	92,800	12,970,899	J. Saxton	(a) Mrs. C. W. Whiting
§Rushmoor, Hants.	80,600	12,469,229	D. Hartley	C. Balchin
Rutland, Leics.	33,800	3,868,000	A. S. Jowett	R. A. Pedder
Ryedale, North Yorks.	86,200	7,969,338	A. Pearson	M. J. Bradley
ST. ALBANS, Herts.	126,600	23,338,502	R. H. Braddon	(a) Rev. R. F. Donald
§St. Edmundsbury, Suffolk	87,820	12,419,870	G. R. N. Toft	(a) N. R. Whitwell
Salisbury, Wilts.	102,800	13,289,515	F. W. Colquhoun	A. J. Burden
§Scarborough, North Yorks.	102,100	11,314,521	J. M. Trebble	(a) S. H. Rowe

‡ Borough Director.

District	Population	Rateable value 1985 £	Chief Executive (*Clerk)	Chairman 1985–86 (a) Mayor (b) Lord Mayor
§Scunthorpe, Humberside	65,000	12,245,712	K. Lescure	(a) R. Mitchell
Sedgefield, Durham	91,200	9,538,940	A. J. Roberts	S. Brown
Sedgemoor, Somerset	90,000	11,033,445	M. V. P. Hart	Mrs. H. M. Ellis-Jones
Selby, North Yorks.	82,000	13,446,452	D. J. Jenkins	J. Tate
Sevenoaks, Kent	110,000	13,759,234	P. Hodgson	Mrs. M. J. Thompsett
Shepway, Kent	86,500	13,089,734	R. H. Summers	H. W. M. D. Service
§Shrewsbury and Atcham, Shropshire	89,300	12,459,145	D. M. Clark	(a) E. T. B. Butcher
§Slough, Berks.	96,715	24,115,498	C. F. Lakin	(a) W. F. Back
SOUTHAMPTON, Hants.	203,900	31,820,833	E. A. Urquhart	(a) G. M. Ranger
South Bedfordshire	109,000	20,592,935	T. D. Rix	R. Cook
South Bucks.	61,400	14,181,192	S. R. Jobson	Sir Duncan Lock
South Cambridgeshire	113,700	16,874,208	B. J. Hancock	S. T. L. Symonds
South Derbyshire	68,800	9,757,658	I. F. Baylis	P. D. Richardson
§Southend-on-Sea, Essex	157,700	27,668,961	F. R. Peacock	P. H. Herbert
South Hams, Devon	68,000	8,070,116	F. G. Palmer	C. J. Eales
South Herefordshire	47,587	5,189,752	D. T. Cole	Mrs. E. M. Saunders
South Holland, Lincs.	63,412	6,929,704	J. T. Brindley	T. Barker
South Kesteven, Lincs.	98,800	12,344,000	K. R. Cann	J. H. Foster
South Lakeland, Cumbria	96,400	11,211,605	A. F. Winstanley	J. Noble
South Norfolk	98,300	10,882,260	A. G. T. Kellett	A. W. Cook
South Northamptonshire	65,196	7,876,105	C. M. Major	Mrs. K. A. Riggall
South Oxfordshire	133,100	18,867,462	J. B. Chirnside	Mrs. P. Clarke
§South Ribble, Lancs.	98,000	10,167,701	R. N. L. Hamm	(a) J. R. Jenkinson
South Shropshire	34,200	3,448,742	G. Kellet, M.B.E.	T. J. Marston
South Somerset	135,200	15,646,501	D. J. Ashford	S. C. Harding
South Staffordshire	103,400	12,737,793	G. J. Hayward	D. W. Watson
South Wight, I.O.W.	50,200	6,055,638	D. W. Jaggar	(a) A. K. Snelling
§Spelthorne, Surrey	91,000	21,661,212	G. F. Hilbert	(a) H. Pugh
§Stafford	117,300	16,701,154	R. E. Humphreys	(a) A. G. Will
Staffordshire Moorlands	95,500	9,872,437	A. W. Law	A. F. J. Povey
§Stevenage, Herts.	75,700	14,200,000	S. W. Catchpole	(a) S. E. Greenfield
§Stockton-on-Tees, Cleveland	178,000	27,777,000	F. F. Theobalds	(a) S. Redican
STOKE-ON-TRENT, Staffs.	250,400	32,583,938	S. W. Titchener	(b) J. P. Birkin
Stratford-on-Avon, Warwicks.	101,200	16,202,815	T. J. W. Foy	Ms. P. L. Joslin
Stroud, Glos.	104,900	12,110,000	D. F. Collins	R. P. Nicholas
Suffolk Coastal	99,900	14,568,182	D. L. Blay	J. L. Geater
§Surrey Heath	78,400	13,395,224	M. Orlik	(a) P. J. Tompkins
§Swale, Kent	110,200	12,854,000	H. White, C.B.E., D.F.C., A.F.C.	(a) R. Moreton
§Tamworth, Staffs.	67,500	8,133,449	P. E. Thorpe	(a) S. Munn
Tandridge, Surrey	77,900	10,184,182	C. W. Rockall	(a) Mrs. L. M. Narcisi
§Taunton Deane, Somerset	88,900	11,015,595	P. F. Berman	(a) J. Hall
Teesdale, Durham	24,700	2,288,604	A. E. Pooley	J. H. Harding
Teignbridge, Devon	93,679	11,484,154	P. B. Young	P. C. Riggs
Tendring, Essex	118,597	16,060,624	D. Mitchell-Gears	A. P. Rayner
§Test Valley, Hants.	95,500	14,021,031	G. Blythe	(a) W. S. White
§Tewkesbury, Glos.	80,815	11,200,000	R. A. Wheeler	(a) P. J. Prior
§Thamesdown, Wilts.	157,000	22,248,000	D. M. Kent	(a) P. L. Jefferies
Thanet, Kent	121,400	15,242,000	I. G. Gill	B. R. White, B.E.M.
Three Rivers, Herts.	77,800	12,986,613	G. A. Deans	C. Stewart
§Thurrock, Essex	125,300	28,412,026	G. V. Semain	(a) A. A. Clarke
Tonbridge and Malling, Kent	99,800	13,595,436	S. W. Stanford	M. Ferry, T.D.
§Torbay, Devon	113,100	17,047,946	D. P. Hudson	(a) A. T. C. Sawyer
Torridge, Devon	48,800	4,091,431	L. S. Mogridge	W. H. Trace
§Tunbridge Wells, Kent	95,245	12,510,506	W. E. Battersby	(a) Mrs. O. M. Eames
Tynedale, Northumberland	54,800	6,183,758	A. Baty	D. M. Bell
Uttlesford, Essex	63,805	9,140,884	J. F. Vernon	P. M. MacPhail
Vale of White Horse, Oxon.	105,800	18,435,974	J. C. Neville Wood	V. G. Day
Vale Royal, Cheshire	112,100	15,418,259	W. R. T. Woods	Mrs. M. B. Birkenhead
Wansbeck, Northumberland	62,200	7,877,542	J. D. McHardy	J. Devon
Wansdyke, Avon	76,099	8,711,416	H. St. J. Smith†	Mrs. M. N. Pope
§Warrington, Cheshire	176,200	26,658,923	W. H. Lawton, T.D.	(a) P. Mounfield
Warwick	115,600	19,664,380	M. J. Ward	Mrs. A. L. Leddy
§Watford, Herts.	76,000	16,808,788	R. B. McMillan	(a) Mrs. I. Tunstall Dunn
Waveney, Suffolk	102,000	11,941,739	M. Berridge	P. D. Plummer
§Waverley, Surrey	112,800	17,447,009	G. W. Nuttall	K. N. F. Cruden
Wealden, East Sussex	123,800	14,653,798	D. R. Holness	H. Smith
Wear Valley, Durham	64,300	5,983,521	M. R. Sutcliff	J. Jones

† Secretary.

District	Population	Rateable value 1985 £	Chief Executive (*Clerk)	Chairman 1985–86 (a) Mayor (b) Lord Mayor
§Wellingborough, Northants....	65,000	8,735,012	W. B. Veal	(a) Maj. D. F. Hooton, T.D.
Welwyn Hatfield, Herts.	92,665	19,122,711	L. Asquith	J. McDonald
West Derbyshire	66,783	7,269,251	R. Bubb	F. W. Glossop
§West Devon...................	43,500	4,109,508	J. S. Ligo	N. F. Guy
West Dorset	81,400	9,285,000	M. B. Taylor	H. W. Haward
West Lancashire	106,385	13,052,825	J. C. Cowdall	K. I. Vincent
West Lindsey, Lincs.	76,100	8,080,325	A. W. Hancock	Mrs. J. M. Westgarth
West Oxfordshire	86,700	10,905,325	N. J. B. Robson	M. L. Chadwick
West Somerset	29,500	5,985,872	H. Close	S. E. Brown
West Wiltshire................	99,301	11,669,707	G. A. F. Garland	Mrs. M. E. Pearce
§Weymouth and Portland, Dorset	57,175	6,598,397	R. E. F. Norman	(a) P. E. G. Harvey
Wimborne, Dorset.............	74,000	10,660,000	W. G. Press	W. Wells.
Winchester, Hants............	92,500	13,742,776	D. H. Cowan	(a) Mrs. J. D. Freeman
§Windsor and Maidenhead, Berks......................	134,600	26,502,187	G. B. Blacker	(a) R. E. Shaw
§Woking, Surrey	85,200	15,771,424	P. Russell	(a) Mrs. P. E. Bohling
Wokingham, Berks.	129,700	19,416,301	N. E. Butler	Col. J. R. Cole
Woodspring, Avon	167,638	20,179,588	R. H. Moon	R. L. Harrison
Worcester	75,700	13,017,177	P. Stanton	(a) F. Poole
§Worthing, West Sussex	94,200	14,881,278	T. L. Elliott	(a) S. D. Moore
Wrekin, Shropshire	128,500	16,575,619	R. E. Paine	B. Norton
Wychavon, Hereford and Worcs.	97,350	14,408,380	P. G. Rust	Mrs. J. M. Jones
Wycombe, Bucks...............	157,500	29,589,114	W. C. Roberts	Mrs. A. S. Moore
§Wyre, Lancs..................	99,400	11,310,646	A. K. B. Boatswain	(a) F. C. Moreland
Wyre Forest, Hereford and Worcs.	91,169	13,297,265	A. S. Dick	J. W. Wardle
York, North Yorks.	99,910	11,809,621	J. Cairns	(b) Mrs. M. S. Bwye

THE PRINCIPAL ENGLISH CITIES

BIRMINGHAM

Birmingham (West Midlands), Britain's second city and the largest metropolitan district in the country, is the chief centre of the hardware trade and motor components industry. It is estimated that over 1,500 distinct trades are carried on in the city. The generally accepted derivation of "Birmingham" is the *ham* or dwelling-place of the *ing* or the family of *Beorma* presumed to have been a Saxon. Between the 11th and 16th centuries the de Berminghams were Lords of the Manor. Recent development includes the National Exhibition Centre (opened in 1976), the Aston Science Park for high technology industries, and a partnership between the City Council, Lloyd's Bank and Aston University to provide risk-capital for such industries. Birmingham is also a regional centre for the media.

The principal buildings are the Town Hall, built in 1832–1834; the Council House (1878); Victoria Law Courts(1891); the University (1909); the 13th century Church of St. Martin (rebuilt 1873); the Cathedral (formerly St. Philip's Church); the Roman Catholic Cathedral of St. Chad (Pugin) and the Methodist Central Hall.

Under local government reorganization in 1974, Birmingham was merged with Sutton Coldfield, to become a Metropolitan District in the West Midlands Metropolitan County.

BRADFORD

Bradford (West Yorkshire), 192 miles N.N.W. of London, is the administrative centre of the Metropolitan District of Bradford. The District covers an area of 91,444 acres and lies on the southern edge of the Yorkshire Dales National Park, including within its boundaries the village of Haworth, home of the Brontë sisters, and Ilkley Moor.

Originally a Saxon township, Bradford received a market charter in 1251 but developed only slowly until the industrialisation of the textile industry brought rapid growth during the 19th century. The prosperity of that period is reflected in much of the city's architecture, particularly the public buildings—City Hall (1873), Wool Exchange (1867), St George's Hall (Concert Hall, 1853), Cartwright Hall (Art Gallery, 1904) and Technical College (1882). Other chief buildings are the Cathedral (15th century) and Bolling Hall (14th century).

Textiles still play an important part in the city's economy but industry is now more broadly based, including engineering and micro-electronics. The city has a strong banking, insurance and building society sector, and a growing tourism industry.

BRISTOL

Bristol (Avon) is the largest non-metropolitan district in population in the country, and lies 119 miles W. of London. The present municipal area is 10,954 hectares.

Bristol's port systems at Avonmouth, Royal Portbury and Portishead are the largest municipally owned docks in the country, handling imports of fresh and processed foods, molasses, vehicles, animal feeding stuffs, chemicals, petroleum products, metals and forest products. Goods exported through the port include vehicles, metals and all types of manufactured goods. The Royal Portbury Dock is capable of handling six 70,000 d.w.t. vessels at any one time. It has the largest lock entrance in the U.K. and has direct access to the M.5 motorway.

The chief buildings include the 12th century Cathedral (with later additions), with Norman Chapter House and gateway, the 14th century Church of St. Mary Redcliffe, Wesley's Chapel, Broadmead, the Merchant Venturers' Almshouses, the Council House (1956), Guildhall, Exchange (erected from the designs of John Wood in 1743), Cabot Tower, the University and Clifton College, Red Lodge (Tudor), Georgian House and Blaise Folly and Mansion. The Roman Catholic Cathedral at Clifton was opened in 1973.

The *Clifton Suspension Bridge*, with a span of 702 feet over the Avon, was projected by Brunel in 1836 but was not completed until 1864. Brunel's *SS Great Britain*, the first ocean going propeller driven ship, is now being restored in the City Docks from where she was launched in 1843.

Bristol was a Royal Borough before the Norman Conquest. The earliest form of the name is *Bricgstow*. In 1373 it received from Edward III a charter granting it county status.

CAMBRIDGE

CAMBRIDGE, a settlement far older than its ancient University, lies on the Cam or Granta, 51 miles north of London and 65 miles south-west of Norwich. It has an area of 10,060 acres.

The city is a county town and regional headquarters. Its industries include electronics, flour milling, cement making and the manufacture of scientific instruments. Among its open spaces are Jesus Green, Sheep's Green, Coe Fen, Parker's Piece, Christ's Pieces, the University Botanic Garden, and the Backs, or lawns and gardens through which the Cam winds behind the principal line of college buildings. East of the Cam, King's Parade, upon which stand Great St. Mary's Church, Gibbs' Senate House and King's College Chapel with Wilkins' screen, joins Trumpington Street to form one of the most beautiful throughfares in Europe.

University and College buildings provide the outstanding features of Cambridge architecture but several churches (especially St. Benet's, the oldest building in the City, and St. Sepulchre's the Round Church) also are notable. The modern Guildhall (1939) stands on a site of which at least part has held municipal buildings since 1224.

CANTERBURY

CANTERBURY, the Metropolitan City of the Anglican Communion, has a history going back to prehistoric times. It was the Roman Durovernum and the Saxon Cant-wara-byrig (stronghold of the men of Kent). Here in 597 St. Augustine began the conversion of the English to Christianity, when Ethelbert, King of Kent, was baptized.

Of the Benedictine St. Augustine's Abbey, burial place of the Jutish Kings of Kent (whose capital Canterbury was) only extensive ruins remain. St. Martin's Church, on the eastern outskirts of the City, is stated by Bede to have been the place of worship of Queen Bertha, the Christian wife of King Ethelbert, before the advent of St. Augustine.

In 1170 the rivalry of Church and State culminated in the murder in Canterbury Cathedral, by Henry II's knights, of Archbishop Thomas Becket, whose shrine became a great centre of pilgrimage as described by Chaucer in his *Canterbury Tales*. After the Reformation pilgrimages ceased, but the prosperity of the City was strengthened by an influx of Huguenot refugees, who introduced weaving. The Elizabethan poet and playwright Christopher Marlowe was born and reared in Canterbury, and there are literary associations also with Defoe, Dickens, Joseph Conrad and Somerset Maugham.

The Cathedral, with architecture ranging from the eleventh to the fifteenth centuries, is world famous. Modern pilgrims are attracted particularly to the Martyrdom, The Black Prince's Tomb, the Warriors' Chapel and the many examples of mediæval stained glass.

The medieval City Walls are built on Roman foundations and the fourteenth century West Gate is one of the finest buildings of its kind in the country.

The 1,000 seat Marlowe Theatre is the base for the Canterbury International Festival of the Arts each autumn.

Before the institution of the Mayoralty in 1448 the City was governed by bailiffs and earlier still by prefects or provosts.

CARLISLE

CARLISLE is situated at the confluence of the River Eden and River Caldew, 309 miles north west of London and a few miles from the Scottish border. It has an area of 254,955 acres, and was granted a charter in 1158.

The city stands at the western end of Hadrian's Wall and dates from the original Roman settlement of *Luguvalium*. Granted to Scotland in the 10th century, Carlisle is not included in the Doomsday Book. William Rufus reclaimed the area in 1092 and the Castle and city walls were built to guard Carlisle and the western border; the Citadel is a Tudor addition to protect the south of the city. Until the Union of the Crowns in 1603, Carlisle changed hands several times and was frequently besieged. During the Civil War the city remained Royalist; in 1745 it supported the Young Pretender.

The Cathedral, originally a 12th century Augustinian priory, was enlarged in the 13th and 14th centuries after the diocese was created in 1133. To the south are the restored remains of the medieval priory and nearby the 18th century church of St. Cuthbert, the third to stand on a site dating from the 7th century.

Carlisle is the major commercial and agricultural centre for the area, and industries include the manufacture of metal goods, biscuits and textiles. However, the largest employer is the services sector, notably in retailing and transport. The city has an important communications position at the centre of a network of major roads, as an important stage on the main west coast rail services and with its own airport at Crosby.

CHESTER

CHESTER is situated on the River Dee, 189 miles north west of London. The city administers an area of 173 square miles and was granted Borough and City status in 1974.

Chester's recorded history dates from the 1st century when the Romans founded the fortress of *Deva*. The city's name is derived from the Latin *castra* (a camp or encampment). During the Middle Ages, Chester was the principal port of north west England but declined with the silting of the Dee estuary and competition from Liverpool. The city was also an important military centre, notably during Edward I's Welsh campaigns and the Elizabethan Irish campaigns. During Civil War, Chester supported the King and was besieged from 1643–6. Chester's first charter was granted *c* 1175 and the city was incorporated in 1506. The office of Sheriff is the earliest created in the country (*c* 1120's), and the Mayor also enjoys the title "Admiral of the Dee".

The city's architectural features include the city walls (an almost complete two mile circuit), the unique Rows (covered galleries above the street level shops), the Victorian Gothic Town Hall (1869), the

Castle (rebuilt 1788 and 1822) and numerous half-timbered buildings. The Cathedral was a Benedictine abbey until the Dissolution. Remaining monastic buildings include the chapter house, refectory and cloisters and there is a modern free-standing bell tower. The Norman church of St. John the Baptist was a Cathedral church in the early Middle Ages.

Chester's principal industry is tourism, and the city is also a shopping centre for North Wales and the North West. Other industries include light engineering and manufacture of car components.

COVENTRY

COVENTRY (West Midlands) is a city 92 miles N.W. of London, and an important industrial centre, producing cars, machine tools, agricultural machinery and telecommunications equipment.

The city owes its beginning to Leofric, Earl of Mercia and his wife Godiva who, in 1043, founded a Benedictine monastery. The guildhall of St. Mary dates from the 14th century, three of the city's churches date from the 14th and 15th centuries and 16th century almshouses may still be seen. Coventry's first cathedral was destroyed at the Reformation, its second in the 1940 blitz (its walls and spire remain) and the new cathedral designed by Sir Basil Spence, consecrated in 1962, now draws innumerable visitors.

Post-war public buildings include the Art Gallery and Museum, Lanchester Polytechnic, the Civic Theatre, Museum of British Road Transport, new swimming baths and sports centre.

DERBY

DERBY stands on the banks of the River Derwent, 127 miles N.N.W. of London, and covers an area of 30 square miles. The name Derby dates back to 880 when the Danes settled in the locality and changed the original Saxon name of "Northworthy" to "Deoraby".

Derby has a wide range of industries: its products include the aero engines of Rolls Royce Ltd., lawn mowers, pipework, specialised mechanical engineering equipment, textiles, chemicals, plastics and the Royal Crown Derby porcelain. The city is an established railway centre, the site of British Rail's Technical Centre with its research laboratories.

Buildings of interest include St Peter's Church, (14th century), the Cathedral (1525), St Mary's Roman Catholic Church (1839), the Industrial Museum, formerly the Old Silk Mill (1721), and the Old Abbey Building dating from the 14th century. Two recent developments are the Assembly Rooms in the Market Place and the Eagle Centre, a shopping precinct covering twelve acres, including a market and the new Derby Playhouse.

The first charter granting a Mayor and Aldermen was that of Charles I in 1637. Previous charters date back to 1154. It was granted City status in 1977.

DURHAM

The city of DURHAM is a district in the county of Durham and covers an area of 73 square miles. The city is the major tourist attraction in the county because of its prominent Norman Cathedral and Castle set high on a wooded peninsula overlooking the River Wear. The Cathedral was founded as a shrine for the body of St. Cuthbert in 995. The present building dates from 1093 and among its many treasures is the tomb of the Venerable Bede (673–735). Durham's Prince Bishops had unique powers up to 1836, being lay rulers as well as religious leaders. As a palatinate Durham could have its own army, nobility, coinage and courts. The Castle was the main seat of the Prince Bishops for nearly 800 years; it is now used as a College by the University.

The University, founded on the initiative of Bishop William Van Mildert, is England's third oldest. Its students live in 14 colleges spread across the city.

Among other buildings of interest is the Guildhall in the Market Place which dates originally from the 14th century. Much work has been carried out to conserve this area, forming part of the city's major contribution to the Council of Europe's Urban Renaissance Campaign. Annual events include Durham's Regatta in June (claimed to be the oldest rowing event in Britain) and the Miners' Gala in July.

In the past 20 years the economy of Durham has undergone a significant change with the replacement of mining as the dominant feature by "white collar" employment. The majority of this employment is in local government service industries and the University.

EXETER

EXETER lies on the River Exe 170 miles south west of London and 10 miles from the sea. It covers an area of 11,037 acres and was granted a Royal Charter by Henry II.

The Romans founded *Isca Dumnoniorum* in the 1st century A.D., and in the 3rd century a stone wall (most of which remains) was built, providing protection against Saxon, and then Danish invasions. After the Conquest, the city led resistance to William in the west, until reduced by siege. The Normans built the motte and bailey castle of Rougemont, the gatehouse and one tower of which remain, although the rest was pulled down in 1784. The first bridge across the Exe was built in the 13th century. The city's role as a port declined due to the silting of the river, but was somewhat restored by the construction in the 1560's of the first ship canal in England. Exeter was the Royalist headquarters in the West during the Civil War.

The diocese of Exeter was established by Edward the Confessor in 1050, although a church existed on the Cathedral site in the early 10th century. A new cathedral was built in the 12th century but the present building was begun c 1275 in the Gothic style, although incorporating the Norman towers, and completed about a century later with the West Front. The Guildhall dates from the 12th century and there are many other medieval buildings in the city, as well as architecture in the Georgian and Regency styles (Custom House, The Quay). Damage suffered by bombing in 1942 led to the redevelopment of the city centre.

Exeter's prosperity from medieval times was based on trade in wool and woollen cloth (commemorated by Tuckers Hall), which remained at its height until the late 18th century when export trade was hit by the French Wars. Subsequently Exeter has developed as an administrative and commercial centre, notably in the distributive trades and light manufacturing industries.

KINGSTON UPON HULL

HULL (officially "Kingston upon Hull") lies in the mostly rural County of Humberside, at the junction of the River Hull with the Humber, 22 miles from the North Sea and 205 miles N. of London. The municipal area is 17,535 acres.

Hull is one of the great seaports of the United Kingdom. It has docks covering a water area of 172 acres, equipped to handle cargoes by unit-load techniques, and is a departure point for car ferry services to the continent. There is a great variety of industry and service industries, as well as increasing tourism and conference business.

The city, restored after very heavy air raid damage during World War II, has good office and administrative buildings, its municipal centre being the Guildhall, its educational centre the University of Hull and its religious centre the Parish Church of the Holy Trinity. The old Town area is being renovated and includes a new marina and plans for a shopping complex. Just west of the city is the Humber Bridge, the world's longest single span suspension bridge, which was officially opened by H.M. the Queen in July 1981.

Kingston upon Hull was so named by Edward I. City status was accorded in 1897 and the office of Mayor raised to the dignity of Lord Mayor in 1914.

LEEDS

LEEDS (West Yorkshire), a Metropolitan District from April 1, 1974, is a junction for road, rail, canal and air services and an important commercial centre, situated in the lower Aire Valley, 195 miles by road N.N.W. of London. The metropolitan area is 138,915 acres.

The main manufacturing industries are mechanical engineering, printing, publishing and clothing. However, 65 per cent of employment is in sevices, notably professional and scientific, particularly education and medicine, distributive trades, finance and banking.

The principal buildings are the Civic Hall (1933), the Town Hall (1858), the Municipal Buildings and Art Gallery (1884) with the Henry Moore Gallery (1982), the Corn Exchange (1863) and the University. The Parish Church (St. Peter's) was rebuilt in 1841; the 17th century St. John's Church has a fine interior with a famous English renaissance screen; the last remaining 18th century church is Holy Trinity, Boar Lane (1727). Kirkstall Abbey (about 3 miles from the centre of the city), founded by Henry de Lacy in 1152, is one of the most complete examples of Cistercian houses now remaining. Temple Newsam, birthplace of Lord Darnley, was acquired by the Council in 1922. The present house was largely re-built by Sir Arthur Ingram in about 1620. Adel Church, about 5 miles from the centre of the city, is a fine Norman structure.

Leeds was first incorporated by Charles I in 1626. The earliest forms of the name are *Loidis* or *Ledes*, the origins of which are obscure.

LEICESTER

LEICESTER is situated geographically in the centre of England, 100 miles north of London. The City dates back to pre-Roman times and was one of the five Danish *Burhs*. In 1589 Queen Elizabeth I granted a Charter to the City and the ancient title was confirmed by Letters Patent in 1919. Under local government reorganization Leicester's area remained unchanged at 18,141 acres, and it retains its designation as a City.

The principal industries of the city are hosiery, and knitwear, footwear manufacturing and engineering. The growth of Leicester as a hosiery centre increased rapidly from the introduction there of the first stocking frame in 1670 and to-day it has some of the largest hosiery factories in the world, with much of the output being exported.

The principal buildings in the city are the Town Hall; the New Walk Centre; the University; Leicester Polytechnic and De Montfort Hall, one of the finest concert halls in the provinces seating over 2,750 persons. The ancient Churches of St. Martin (now Leicester Cathedral), St. Nicholas, St. Margaret, All Saints, St. Mary de Castro, and buildings such as the Guildhall, the 14th century Newarke Gate, the Castle and the Jewry Wall Roman site still exist. The Haymarket Theatre, an integral part of a large new shopping and car-parking complex, was opened in 1973.

LINCOLN

Situated 143 miles north of London and 40 miles inland on the River Witham, LINCOLN derives its name from a contraction of *Lindum Colonia*, the settlement founded in A.D. 48 by the Romans to command the crossing of Ermine Street and Fosse Way. Sections of the 3rd century Roman city wall can be seen, including an extant gateway (Newport Arch), and excavations have discovered traces of a sewerage system unique in Britain. The Romans also drained the surrounding fenland and created a canal system, laying the foundations of Lincoln's agricultural prosperity, and also of the city's importance in the medieval wool trade as a port and Staple town. As one of the Five Boroughs of the Danelaw, Lincoln was an important trading centre in the 9th and 10th centuries and medieval prosperity from the wool trade lasted until the 14th century, enabling local merchants to build parish churches (of which three survive), and attracting in the 12th century a Jewish community (Jew's House and Court, Aaron's House). However, the removal of the Staple to Boston in 1369 heralded a decline from which the city only recovered fully in the 19th century when improved fen drainage made Lincoln agriculturally important, and improved canal and rail links led to industrial development, mainly in the manufacture of machinery, components and engineering products.

The Castle was built shortly after the Conquest and is unusual in having two mounds; on one motte stands a Keep (Lucy's Tower) added in the 12th century. The Cathedral was begun c1073 when the first Norman bishop moved the see of Lindsey to Lincoln, but was mostly destroyed by fire and earthquake in the 12th century. Rebuilding was begun by St. Hugh and completed over a century later. The Wren library contains manuscripts including one of the four surviving originals of the Magna Carta. Other notable architectural features of the city are the 12th century High Bridge, the oldest in Britain still to carry buildings, and the Guildhall situated above the 15–16th century Stonebow gateway.

LIVERPOOL

LIVERPOOL (Merseyside) on the right bank of the river Mersey, 3 miles from the Irish Sea and 194 miles N.W. of London, is one of the greatest trading centres of the world and the principal port in the United Kingdom for the Atlantic trade. The municipal area of 27,819 acres includes 2,840 acres in the bed of the river Mersey.

There are 7 miles of docks on both sides of the river and the Gladstone and Royal Seaforth Docks can accommodate the largest vessels afloat. Gross tonnage of ships entering and leaving the port annually is 19,000,000 tonnes. The main imports are petroleum, grain, ores, edible oils, timber, containers and break bulk cargo. The Royal Seaforth Dock, opened in 1973, is the latest development. It comprises container, timber and grain terminals and is within the Liverpool Free Port, superimposed upon 600 acres of active dockland.

Liverpool was created a borough in 1207 and a city in 1880. From the early eighteenth century it expanded rapidly with the growth of the port. Surviving buildings from this date include the Bluecoat Chambers (1718, formerly the Bluecoat School), the Town Hall (1754, rebuilt to the original design, 1795), and buildings in Rodney Street, Canning Street and the suburbs. Notable from the nineteenth and twentieth centuries are the Anglican Cathedral, built from the designs of Sir Giles Gilbert Scott (the foundation stone was laid in 1904, and the building was only completed in 1980): the Catholic Metropolitan Cathedral (designed by Sir Frederick Gibberd, consecrated 1967) and St. George's Hall, (1838–1854), regarded as one of the finest modern examples of classical architecture. In 1852 an Act was obtained for establishing a public library, museum and art gallery; as a result Liverpool had one of the first public libraries in the country. The Brown, Picton & Hornby libraries now form the largest city central libraries in Europe. The Victoria Building of Liverpool University, The Royal Liver, Cunard and Mersey Docks & Harbour Company buildings at the Pier Head, the Municipal Buildings and the Philharmonic Hall are other examples of the City's fine buildings.

Constructed between 1925 and 1934, the first Mersey Tunnel was named "Queensway". The second Mersey Tunnel—"Kingsway"—was opened on 24 June 1971, and a similar tunnel adjacent to it was opened on 14th February 1974. In 1969 the Merseyside Passenger Transport Executive was formed to improve and co-ordinate local transport throughout Merseyide, and, in partnership with British Rail, developed the Merseyside Loop/Link system, opened in 1977 to link Southport, Ormskirk and Garston with the City Centre stations and lines to the Wirral.

In 1984 a 250 acre area of Liverpool's southern waterfront was cleared and landscaped to accommodate Britain's first International Garden Festival.

MANCHESTER

MANCHESTER (the *Mancunium* of the Romans, who occupied it in A.D. 78) is 189 miles N.W. of London and covers about 43 square miles.

Manchester is a commercial and industrial centre with a population engaged in engineering, chemical, clothing, food processing and textile industries. Banking and insurance are among the prime commercial activities. The city is connected with the sea by the Manchester Ship Canal, opened in 1894, 35½ miles long, and accommodating ships up to 15,000 tons. Manchester Airport handles more than 5 million passengers yearly.

The principal buildings are the Town Hall, erected in 1877 from the designs of Alfred Waterhouse, R.A., together with a large extension of 1938; the Royal Exchange (1869, enlarged 1921) the Central Library (1934); Heaton Hall; the 17th century Chetham Library; the Rylands Library (1899), which includes the Althorp collection; the University precinct; the 15th-century Cathedral (formerly the parish church) and the Free Trade Hall. Manchester is the home of the Hallé Orchestra, the Royal Northern College of Music, the Royal Exchange Theatre and seven public art galleries.

The town received its first charter of incorporation in 1838 and was created a city in 1853. The title of city was retained under local government reorganization.

NEWCASTLE UPON TYNE

NEWCASTLE UPON TYNE (Tyne and Wear) a Metropolitan District on the north bank of the River Tyne, is 8 miles from the North Sea, 272 miles N. of London and has an area of 27,640 acres. A Cathedral and University City, it is the administrative, commercial and cultural centre for north-east England and the principal port. It is an important manufacturing centre with a wide variety of industries.

The principal buildings include the Castle Keep (12th century), Black Gate (13th century), Blackfriars (13th century), West Walls (13th century), St. Nicholas's Cathedral (15th century, fine lantern tower), St. Andrew's Church (12th–14th century), St. John's (14th–15th century), All Saints (1786 by Stephenson), St. Mary's Roman Catholic Cathedral (1844), Trinity House (17th century), Sandhill (16th century houses), Guildhall (Georgian), Grey Street (1834–39), Central Station (1846–50), Laing Art Gallery (1904), University of Newcastle Physics Building (1962), Civic Centre (1963), Central Library (1969) and Eldon Square Development (1976). Open spaces include the Town Moor (927 acres) and Jesmond Dene. Eight bridges span the Tyne at Newcastle.

The City derives its name from the "new castle" (1080) erected as a defence against the Scots. In 1400 it was made a County, and in 1882 a City.

NORWICH

NORWICH (Norfolk) is an ancient City 110 miles N.E. of London. It grew from an early Anglo-Saxon settlement near the confluence of the Rivers Yare and Wensum, and now serves as provincial capital for the predominantly agricultural region of East Anglia. The name is thought to relate to the most northerly of a group of Anglo-Saxon villages or "wics". The present City has an area of 9,655 acres. The City's first known Charter was granted in 1158 by Henry II.

Norwich serves its surrounding area as a market town and commercial centre, banking and insurance being prominent among the City's businesses. From the 14th century until the Industrial Revolution, Norwich was the regional centre of the woollen industry, but now the biggest single industry is the manufacturing of shoes and other principal trades are engineering, printing, and the production of chemicals, clothing, confectionery and other foodstuffs. Norwich is accessible to seagoing vessels by means of the River Yare, entered at Great Yarmouth, 20 miles to the east.

Among many historic buildings are the Cathedral (completed in the twelfth century and surmounted by a fifteenth century spire 315 feet in height), the Keep of the Norman Castle (now a museum and art gallery), the fifteenth century flint-walled Guildhall, some thirty medieval parish churches, St. Andrew's and Blackfriars' Halls, the Tudor houses preserved in Elm Hill and the Georgian Assembly House. The University of East Anglia has been established in Norwich on a spacious site at Earlham on the City's western boundary and received its first students in 1963.

NOTTINGHAM

NOTTINGHAM (Nottinghamshire) stands on the River Trent, 124 miles N.N.W. of London in one of the most valuable coalfields of the country connected by canal with the Atlantic and the North Sea. The municipal area is 18,364 acres.

The principal industries are hosiery, lace, bleaching, dyeing and spinning, tanning, engineering and cycle works, brewing, the manufacture of tobacco, chemicals, furniture, typewriters and mechanical products.

The chief buildings are the 17th century Nottingham Castle (restored in 1878, and now the City Museum and Gallery of Art), Wollaton Hall (1580–88) owned by the City Council and now a Natural History Museum, St. Mary's, St. Peter's, and St. Nicholas's Churches, the Roman Catholic Cathedral (Pugin, 1842–4), the Council House (1929), the Guildhall and Court House (1888), Shire Hall, Albert Hall, the University, Trent Polytechnic, Newstead Abbey, home of Lord Byron, the Theatre Royal (1865), the Playhouse (1963) and the Royal Concert Hall (1982).

Snotingaham or *Notingeham*, "the village or home of the sons of Snot" (the Wise), is the Anglo-Saxon name for the Celtic *Tuigogobauc*, "Cave Homes". The City possesses a Charter of Henry II, and was created a City in 1897. Under local government reorganization, the style of city was reaccorded from April, 1974.

OXFORD

OXFORD is a University City, an important industrial centre, and a market town, with an area of 8,785 acres. Industry played a minor part in Oxford until the motor industry was established in 1912.

It is for its architecture that Oxford is of most interest to the visitor, its oldest specimens being the reputed Saxon tower of St. Michael's church, the remains of the Norman castle and city walls and the Norman church at Iffley. It is chiefly famous however, for its Gothic buildings, such as the Divinity Schools, the Old Library at Merton College, William of Wykeham's New College, Magdalen College and Christ Church and many other college buildings. Later centuries are represented by the Laudian quadrangle at St. John's College, the Renaissance Sheldonian Theatre by Wren, Trinity College Chapel, and All Saints Church; Hawksmoor's mock-Gothic at All Souls College, and the eighteenth century Queens' College. In addition to individual buildings, High Street and Radcliffe Square, just off it, both form architectural compositions of great beauty. Most of the Colleges have gardens, those of Magdalen, New College, St. John's (designed by "Capability" Brown) and Worcester being the largest.

PLYMOUTH

PLYMOUTH is situated on the borders of Devon and Cornwall at the confluence of the Rivers Tamar and Plym, 210 miles from London, with an area of 19,572 acres. The city has a long maritime history; it was the home port of Sir Francis Drake and the starting point for his circumnavigation of the world, as well as the last port of call for the Mayflower when the Pilgrim Fathers sailed for the New World in 1620. The Barbican harbour area has many Elizabethan buildings, and on Plymouth Hoe stands the first lighthouse to be built on the Eddystone Rocks, some miles offshore.

Following extensive war damage, the city centre comprising a large shopping centre, municipal offices, law courts and public buildings, has been re-built. The main employment is provided by H.M.Dockyard, though many new industrial firms have become established in the post-war period and the city is a growing tourism centre: in 1982 the Theatre Royal was opened. In conjunction with the Cornwall County Council, the Tamar Bridge was constructed linking the City by road with Cornwall.

PORTSMOUTH

PORTSMOUTH occupies Portsea Island, Hampshire, with boundaries extending to the mainland. It has an area of 15½ sq. miles and is 70 miles from London.

Portsmouth is a centre of industry and commerce, including many high technology and manufacturing industries. It is the U.K. headquarters of a major computer company and two insurance companies. H.M. Naval Base still has a substantial work force, although this has decreased in recent years. The commercial port and Continental Ferry Port is owned and run by the City Council, and carries passengers and vehicles to France and the Channel Islands.

A major port since the 16th century, Portsmouth is also a thriving seaside resort catering for thousands of visitors and day-trippers annually. Among many historic attractions are Lord Nelson's flagship, H.M.S. *Victory*; the Tudor warship *Mary Rose*; the D-Day Museum; Charles Dickens' birthplace at 393 Old Commercial Road; the Royal Naval and Royal Marine museums; Southsea Castle (built by Henry VIII), the Round Tower and Point Battery, which for hundreds of years have guarded the entrance to Portsmouth Harbour; and Fort Widley on Portsdown Hill.

ST. ALBANS

Twenty-five miles north west of London and situated on the River Ver, ST. ALBANS' origins stem from the major Roman town of *Verulamium*. Named after the first Christian martyr in Britain, who was executed here, St. Albans has developed around the Norman Abbey and Cathedral Church (consecrated 1115), the second longest in Britain, built partly of materials from the old Roman city. The museums house Iron Age and Roman artifacts and the Roman Theatre, unique in Britain, has a stage as opposed to an amphitheatre. Archæological excavations in the city centre continue also to reveal evidence of pre-Roman, Saxon and medieval occupation.

The town's significance grew to the extent that it was a signatory and venue for the drafting of the Magna Carta. It was also the scene of major riots during the Peasants' Revolt; the French King John was imprisoned there after the Battle of Poitiers, and heavy fighting took place during the Wars of the Roses; but it is as a Roman town that it is best recognized.

Previously controlled by the Abbot, the town achieved a Royal Charter in 1553 and City status in 1877. The street market, first established in 1553, is still an important feature of the city, as are many hotels and inns which survive from the days when St. Albans was an important coach stop. Tourist attractions include historic churches and houses, and a 15th century clock tower.

The advent of the railway saw the gradual expansion of the city, and the area now contains a wide range of firms, with special emphasis on micro-technology and electronics, particularly in the medical field. In addition, it is the home of the Royal National Rose Society, and of Rothamsted Park, the agricultural research centre.

In 1974 the City and District of St. Albans was formed, taking in the town of Harpenden and many villages, and it now covers an area of 63 square miles.

SHEFFIELD

SHEFFIELD (South Yorkshire), the centre of the special steel and cutlery trades, is situated 159 miles N.N.W. of London, at the junction of the Sheaf, Porter, Rivelin and Loxley with the River Don.

Sheffield has an area of 91,000 acres (nearly 150 square miles), including 4,619 acres of publicly owned parks and woodland. Though its cutlery, silverware and plate have long been famous, Sheffield has other and now more important industries—special and alloy steels, engineering and tool-making. Research in glass, metallurgy, radiotherapy and other fields is carried on.

The parish church of St. Peter and St. Paul, founded in the twelfth century, became the Cathedral Church of the Diocese of Sheffield in 1914. The Roman Catholic Cathedral Church of St. Marie (founded 1847) was created Cathedral for the new diocese of Hallam in 1980. Parts of the present building date from about 1435. The principal buildings are the Town Hall (1897, 1923 and 1977), the Cutlers' Hall (1832), the University (1905 and recent extensions, including 19-storey Arts Tower), City Hall (1932), Graves Art Gallery (1934), Castle Market Building

(1959), the retail market (1973), Mappin Art Gallery and the Crucible Theatre.

Sheffield was created a city in 1893 and on April 1, 1974 became a Metropolitan District Council incorporating Stocksbridge and most of the Wortley Rural area, and retained city status.

Master Cutler (1984–85) 361st *Master of the Company of Cutlers in Hallamshire*, I. Porter.

SOUTHAMPTON

SOUTHAMPTON is Britain's premier passenger and a fast-growing container port. In 1984 a Free Trade Zone was established in the port. The first Charter was granted by Henry II and Southampton was created a county of itself in 1447. In February, 1964, Her Majesty the Queen granted city status by Royal Charter. The city has an area of 12,071 acres excluding tidal waters.

There have been Roman and Saxon settlements on the site of the city, which has been an important port since the time of the Conquest due to its natural deep-water harbour. The oldest church is St. Michael's (1070) which has a black tournai marble font and an unusually tall tower, a landmark for navigators of Southampton Water. Other buildings and monuments within the city walls are the Tudor Merchants Hall, the Weigh-house, West Gate, King John's House, Long House, Holy Rood Church, St. Julien's Church and the Mayflower Memorial. Public open spaces total over 1,000 acres in extent and comprise 9 per cent. of the city's area. The Common covers an area of 328 acres in the central district of the city and is mostly natural parkland.

STOKE-ON-TRENT

STOKE-ON-TRENT (Staffordshire), familiarly known as The Potteries, stands on the River Trent 157 miles N. of London. The present municipal area is 22,916 acres (36 square miles) and the city is the main centre of employment for the population of North Staffordshire. It is the largest clayware producer in the world (china, earthenware, sanitary goods, refractories, bricks and tiles) and has a considerable coal mining output drawn from one of the richest coalfields in Western Europe. The city has steelworks, foundries, chemical works, engineering plants, rubber works, paper mills, and a very wide range of manufactures. The city is also the venue for the 1986 National Garden Festival.

Extensive reconstruction has been carried on in recent years. A unique feature of the city is that it has six "centres" and more shops and public halls than other areas of comparable size. The City was formed by the federation in 1910 of the separate municipal authorities of Tunstall, Burslem, Hanley, Stoke-upon-Trent, Fenton, and Longton, all of which are now combined in the present City of Stoke-on-Trent.

WINCHESTER

WINCHESTER, the ancient capital of England, is situated on the River Itchen 65 miles S.W. of London and 12 miles north of Southampton. Since local government reorganization in 1974, the style of City has been accorded to the whole of the new district of Winchester, which embraces an area of 162,921 acres of Mid-Hampshire.

Winchester is rich in architecture of all types but the cathedral takes first place. The longest Gothic cathedral in the world, it was built in 1079–1093 and exhibits examples of Norman, Early English and Perpendicular styles. Winchester College, founded in 1382, is one of the most famous public schools, the original building (of 1393) remaining unaltered. St. Cross Hospital, another great medieval foundation, lies 1 mile south of the city. Founded in 1136 by Bishop Henry de Blois, the Almshouses were re-established in 1445 by Cardinal Henry Beaufort. The Chapel and dwellings are of great architectural interest, and visitors may still receive the "Wayfarer's Dole" of bread and ale.

Recent excavations have done much to clarify the origins and development of Winchester. Part of the forum and several of the streets of the Roman town have been discovered; and excavations in the Cathedral Close have uncovered the entire site of the Anglo-Saxon cathedral (known as the Old Minster) and parts of the New Minster, built by Alfred's son Edward the Elder, and the burial place of the Alfredian dynasty. The original burial place of St. Swithun, before his remains were translated to a site in the present cathedral, was also uncovered.

Excavations in other parts of the City have thrown much light on Norman Winchester, notably on the site of the Royal Castle, adjacent to which the new Law Courts have been built, and in the grounds of the Bishop's Palace at Wolvesey, where the great house built by Bishops Giffard and Henry of Blois in the 12th century has been uncovered.

YORK

The City of YORK is a District in the County of North Yorkshire, and is an archiepiscopal seat. The City has an area of 7,295 acres.

The recorded history of York dates from A.D. 71, when the Roman Ninth Legion established a base under Petilius Cerealis which later became the fortress of Eboracum. In Anglo-Saxon times the city was the royal and ecclesiastical centre of Northumbria, and was captured by a Viking army in A.D. 866, after which it became the capital of the Viking kingdom of Jorvik. By the 14th century the city had become a great mercantile centre, chiefly owing to its control of the wool trade, and was used as the chief base against the Scots. Under the Tudors its fortunes declined, though Henry VIII made it the headquarters of the Council of the North. Recent excavations on many sites, including Coppergate, has greatly expanded knowledge of Roman, Viking and medieval urban life.

With its development as a railway centre in the 19th century the commercial life of York expanded and it is now a flourishing modern city. The principal industries are the manufacture of chocolate, railway coaches, scientific instruments, and sugar. The City is also an important tourist centre.

It is rich in examples of architecture of all periods. The earliest church (built, 627) was succeeded by several others until, in the 12th to the 15th centuries, the present Minster was built in a succession of styles. The finest features are the West front with its two towers, the spacious transepts and the stained glass. Other examples within the city are the medieval city walls and gateways, churches and guildhalls. Domestic architecture includes the Georgian mansions of The Mount, Micklegate and Bootham. Its museums are world-famous and include the Castle Museum, one of the best-known folk museums in Great Britain, the National Railway Museum, and the Jorvik Viking Centre.

THE NATIONAL PARKS

The ten National Parks described below in their order of designation have been established in England and Wales. These areas are not public property and although many public paths exist and some areas of open land are available for walking visitors are not free to wander over private land within the Park boundaries. They have been marked out for special care aimed at two prime purposes: to conserve and enhance their natural beauty, and to promote their enjoyment by the public.

Peak District National Park (542 sq. miles).— Mainly in Derbyshire but extending into Staffordshire, Cheshire, South Yorkshire, West Yorkshire and Greater Manchester. In the south and east are limestone uplands, and finely wooded dales, while northwards, moorlands, edged by gritstone crags, attract hill walkers and climbers. There are information centres at Bakewell, Edale (open all year) and Castleton (Easter–October and possibly winter weekends), and information points in Goyt Valley and at Hartington (summer weekends and Bank Holidays). An information caravan tours the Park and there is a residential study centre at Losehill Hall.

Lake District National Park (866 sq. miles).—In Cumbria. Spectacular mountain scenery with wooded lower slopes enhanced by lakes and tarns. The area includes England's highest mountains (Scafell Pike, Helvellyn and Skiddaw) and largest lakes. Walking and rock-climbing are the principal recreations, but there are fishing, swimming, sailing, boating and winter sports as well. There are information centres at Keswick, Kendal, Ambleside, Waterhead, Hawkshead, Seatoller and Bowness. Information vans are sited at Coniston, Glenridding and Pooley Bridge. At Brockhole on the shore of Windermere, is a National Park centre.

Snowdonia National Park (838 sq. miles).—In Gwynedd in North Wales. A mountainous region of lakes, forest, wooded valleys, reservoirs and power stations and traversed by high passes, offering some of the finest rock-climbing and mountain walking for both beginner and expert. There are information centres at Aberdyfi, Bala, Betws y Coed, Blaenau Ffestiniog, Conwy, Harlech, Dolgellau, Llanberis, Llanrwst and Plas Tan y Bwlch, at which there is also a residential study centre.

Dartmoor National Park (365 sq. miles).—In Devon, the highest area of high moorland in southern England, famous for its granite "tors" often weathered into strange shapes. Fine hanging oak woods adorn the river valleys which lead up into the Moor. The Park is rich in prehistoric relics and offers fine walking and riding. Information vans are sited at Newbridge, Tavistock, Bovey Tracey, Steps Bridge, Princeton and Postbridge.

Pembrokeshire Coast National Park (225 sq. miles).—A spectacular section of Britain's coastline, where rock cliffs alternate with bays and sandy coves. In the north is Mynydd Preseli, abounding in prehistoric relics. The Park includes the fine Milford Haven waterway reaches, Tenby, the cathedral of St. David's, and Carew and other Norman castles. There are information centres at Tenby, St. David's, Pembroke, Newport, Kilgetty, Haverfordwest and Broad Haven.

North York Moors National Park (553 sq. miles).—In North Yorkshire and Cleveland, the Park stretches from the Hambleton Hills in the west to the coastline above Scarborough. On the coast sheltered bays and sandy beaches alternate with headlands harbouring villages such as Staithes and Robin Hood's Bay. The heart of the Park offers tracts of open moorland, intersected by wooded valleys. Mount Grace Priory and the abbeys of Rievaulx and Byland are within the Park. There are information centres at Danby Lodge, Pickering, Sutton Bank, Ravenscar, Helmsley and Hutton-le-Hole, and a day study centre at Danby Lodge.

Yorkshire Dales National Park (680 sq. miles).— An area of upland moors, cut by deep valleys, mostly in North Yorkshire but extending into Cumbria. The Park includes some of the finest limestone scenery in Britain: Kilnsey Crag in Wharfedale, Gordale Scar, and Malham Cove in Malhamdale. In the Park also are Swaledale and Wensleydale, the three peaks of Ingleborough, Whernside and Pen-y-Ghent, and many relics of the past such as the Roman fort at Bainbridge and Bolton Abbey in Wharfedale. There are information centres at Clapham, Grassington, Hawes, Aysgarth Falls, Malham and Sedbergh, and a national park cave and fell centre at Whernside Manor.

Exmoor National Park (265 sq. miles).—Mainly in Somerset but extending into Devon, this is a moorland plateau with finely wooded combes encompassing the well-known coastline between Minehead and Combe Martin Bay in the north and the Brendon Hills in the east. There are information centres at Lynmouth, County Gate and Dulverton. An information van is sited at Combe Martin.

Northumberland National Park (398 sq. miles).—A region of hills and moorland, stretching from Hadrian's Roman Wall in the south to the Cheviot Hills on the Scottish Border. The area is rich in historic interest. There are information centres at Byrness, Ingram, Once Brewed, Rothbury, Housesteads, Hexham and Harbottle Hills. An information caravan is sited at Cawfields.

Brecon Beacons National Park (519 sq. miles).— The most recent National Park, established in 1957, is centred on "The Beacons" with its three peaks: Pen y Fan, Corn Du and Cribyn rising to nearly 3,000 feet. But it includes the Black Mountains to the east and the Black Mountain to the west, thus taking in parts of Gwent and Dyfed as well as southern Powys and a small area of Mid-Glamorgan. The Upper Usk Valley, Llangorse Lake, Brecon Cathedral, Carreg Cennen Castle and Llanthony Priory are all within the Park. There are information centres at Brecon, Craig-y-nos Country Park, Abergavenny, Llandovery, a study centre at Danywenallt and a day visitor centre near Libanus, Brecon.

AREAS OF OUTSTANDING NATURAL BEAUTY

These are designated solely for landscape conservation purposes. They are listed below, in alphabetical order, having been designated between December, 1956 and October, 1983.

Anglesey (83 sq. miles).—Except for breaks around the urban areas and in the vicinity of Wylfa, the designated area extends along the entire coastline.

The varied scenery is famed for its beauty, as also are the Menai Straits, separating the island from the mainland.

Arnside and Silverdale (29 sq. miles).—Lying along the upper half of Morecambe Bay, the area embraces the Kent estuary where it adjoins the Lake District National Park and includes extensive tidal flats in the Bay. The varied coastal landscape contains several limestone hills, woodland and bog areas locally known as "mosses". Known for its wildfowl breeding grounds, the whole area is of considerable ecological value.

Cannock Chase (26 sq. miles).—This is an area of high heathland in Staffordshire, relieved by varied scenery in which parklands adjoin farms, woodlands and pleasant villages. Deer continue to roam over the Chase.

Chichester Harbour (29 sq. miles).—Well known for its small boating and sailing facilities, the area extends from Hayling Island in the west to Apuldram in the east and contains the whole of Thorney Island.

Chilterns (309 sq. miles).—The well-known chalk downlands from Goring in South Oxfordshire north-eastwards through Buckinghamshire, Hertfordshire and Bedfordshire to Dunstable and Luton, including the outlying group of hills beyond Luton. Contains several National Trust properties and Whipsnade Zoo.

Cornwall (360 sq. miles).—Comprising a number of separate areas including Bodmin Moor and some of the finest and best-known coastal scenery in Britain. Most of the Land's End peninsula; the coast between St. Michael's Mount and St. Austell with Falmouth omitted; and the Fowey Estuary are all included: in north Cornwall most of the coast to Bedruthan Steps, north of Newquay, and between Perranporth and Godrevy Towans. In 1983 10 sq. miles of the Camel Estuary were added to the designated area.

Cotswolds (582 sq. miles).—Contains the great limestone escarpment overlooking the Vales of Gloucester and Evesham. The remainder is high undulating country and narrow wooded valleys traversed by shallow rapid streams. Noted for its beautiful villages.

Cranborne Chase and West Wiltshire Downs (370 sq. miles).—This area, covering parts of Wilt-shire, Dorset, Hampshire and Somerset, contains extensive tracts of chalkland, with steep-sided combes and scarps, and the wooded remnants of the ancient Chase. To the west the area is bounded by wooded greensand hills and the Vale of Wardour.

Dedham Vale (28 sq. miles).—This is the flat land of water meadows with hedges and woodland, border-ing Essex and Suffolk, where John Constable (1776-1837) painted during much of his life. Flatford Mill, Willy Lott's Cottage and the church of Stoke-by-Nayland still stand.

East Devon (103 sq. miles).—The area comprises the fine stretch of coastline between Orcombe Rocks, near Exmouth, and the Dorset area near Lyme Regis, with Sidmouth, Beer and Seaton omitted. Inland Gittisham Hill, East Hill and Woodbury and Ayle-beare Commons are all included.

North Devon (66 sq. miles).—Comprising three sections of fine coastline—the whole of the Hartland peninsula; from Bideford Bar to the western limits of Ilfracombe, and from east of Ilfracombe to the boundary of the Exmoor National Park. Clovelly, Braunton Burrows, Woolacombe and Combe Martin are all included.

South Devon (128 sq. miles).—It includes the magnificent coast between Bolt Head and Bolt Tail, a National Trust property; Salcombe, Slapton Sands and Dartmouth, and the four estuaries and valleys of the Yealm, Erme, Avon and Dart.

Dorset (400 sq. miles).—Takes in the whole of the coastline between Lyme Regis and Poole, with the Isle of Portland and Weymouth omitted, and stretches inland to include the Purbeck Hills and the downs, heaths and wooded valleys of the Hardy country.

Forest of Bowland (310 sq. miles).—A fine tract of high open moorland running westward from near Settle and Bolton by Bowland in the Pennines, to Caton and Scorton in Central Lancashire. A small outlying area east of the River Ribble includes Pendle Hill and Pendleton Moor.

Gower (73 sq. miles).—In the county of West Glamorgan, South Wales, the area is known for its beautiful coastline, its rocky limestone cliffs, sandy bays and coves and for its wooded ravines stretching inland.

East Hampshire (151 sq. miles).—This mainly chalkland area stretches from the outskirts of Winchester to the Hampshire/Sussex border at a distance of about 10 miles inland from the south coast.

South Hampshire Coast (30 sq. miles).—14 miles of coastline on the northern shores of the Solent, between Hurst Castle and Calshot Castle, south-east of Fawley, with the central part of the area extending inland up the Beaulieu River for about six miles, including a beautiful part of the New Forest. Along much of the coast woods of oak and Scots pine stretch down to the water's edge, while at the western end are some attractive salt marshes.

High Weald (560 sq. miles).—Based on the central sandstone hills of the Weald of South-East England, the area covers parts of East and West Sussex, Kent and Surrey. It is predominantly wooded, with copses of deciduous woodland as well as larger heathland areas like Ashdown Forest, the remnants of the old Wealden forests. Orchards and cultivated land are also characteristic, as are landscaped parks, historic buildings and villages, and hammer ponds, the relics of the ancient iron industry.

Kent Downs (326 sq. miles).—Running from the Surrey border near Westerham (its boundary adjoin-ing that of the Surrey Hills area), about 60 miles to the coast near Dover and Folkestone, with a coastal outlier at South Foreland and a narrow strip of the old sea cliff escarpment west of Hythe overlooking Romney Marsh. Pleasant pastoral scenery, pictur-esque villages, ancient churches and castles, with the Downs rising to 600 feet.

Lincolnshire Wolds (216 sq. miles).—The area extends in a south-east direction from Laceby and Caistor in the north to the region of Spilsby, about ten miles west of Skegness. Its charm is derived from the undulating terrain, sparse settlement pattern and the excellent views from the chalk escarpments. The wolds are extensively farmed and contain numerous small, attractive villages.

Lleyn (60 sq. miles).—An isolated peninsula in Gwynedd, North Wales, of unique character, still largely unspoilt by the hand of man.

Malvern Hills (40 sq. miles).—The area embodies the whole range of the Malvern Hills in the county of Hereford and Worcester, just touching Gloucester-shire. Such well-known features as the Worcester-shire Beacon, North Hill, the Herefordshire Beacon, and Midsummer Hill, a National Trust property, are within the area.

Mendip Hills (78 sq. miles).—Comprising over half of the Mendip Hills, the area stretches, west to east, from Bleadon Hill to the A.39 road north of Wells. Blagdon Lake and Chew Magna Lake are within the boundary which, in the south, takes in Cheddar Gorge. The plateau, rising to over 1,000 ft., commands fine views over the Bristol Channel and surrounding countryside. Noted for its caves, including Wookey Hole, the area is of great scientific and historic interest.

Norfolk Coast (174 sq. miles).—With coastal scenery ranging from salt marsh and mudflats, sand-dunes and shingle ridges to sea cliffs, this area includes six miles of the south-east coast of the Wash, an almost continuous coastal strip three to five miles in depth from Hunstanton to Bacton, with a further small strip between Sea Palling and Winterton-on-Sea. The area, which is rich in wild-life, also includes part of the Sandringham Estate.

Northumberland Coast (50 sq. miles).—Low cliffs and rocky headlands with active fishing villages comprise this area which stretches from just south of Berwick to Amble. It includes Holy Island, with the oldest monastic ruins in the country; the Farne Islands, and the great castles of Bamburgh, Dunstan-burgh and Warkworth.

Quantock Hills (38 sq. miles).—The main feature of this area in Somerset is the range of red sandstone hills rising to a height of 1,260 feet at Will's Neck above Crow Combe.

Isles of Scilly (6 sq. miles).—There are about 140 islands and skerries in the Scillies group of which only five are inhabited. Geologically, the formation is similar to Land's End and other granite areas in Cornwall. The coastline is dramatically rocky, inter-spersed with sheltered sandy beaches and areas of dune of bleached decomposed granite, glistening with mica and shells. There are coastal paths round the larger islands, and a number of sites of special scientific interest, identified by the Nature Conser-vancy Council.

Shropshire Hills (300 sq. miles).—This area in-cludes the fine landscape around Church Stretton, with Caer Caradoc, the Long Mynd, the Stiperstones, and the long ridge of Wenlock Edge from which it extends north-east to the Wrekin and the Ercall.

Solway Coast (41 sq. miles).—A stretch of beautiful coastline in Cumbria from above Maryport to the estuaries of the Rivers Eden and Esk (with Silloth omitted) backed by the Solway Plain and noted for its historic and scientific interests.

Suffolk Coast and Heaths (151 sq. miles).—Takes in 38 miles of coastline and parts of the Stour and Orwell estuaries, while the Deben, Alde and Blyth flow through it. With heath, woodland, marsh and beaches, the scenery is attractively varied and the area important to ornithologists.

Surrey Hills (160 sq. miles).—The Hog's Back and the ridge of the North Downs from Guildford to Titsey in the east are within this area, as are Leith Hill, Hindhead Common, the Devil's Punch Bowl; the well-known villages of Abinger, Shere, Hamble-don and Chiddingfold; Box Hill and Frensham Ponds.

Sussex Downs (379 sq. miles).—The area includes the chalk escarpment of the South Downs from Beachy Head to the West Sussex/Hampshire border, with such well-known features as Firle Beacon and Chanctonbury Ring, and stretches down to the coast between Eastbourne and Seaford. In the west the boundary adjoins the East Hampshire and Surrey Hills areas.

North Wessex Downs (671 sq. miles).—An upland area in Hampshire, Wiltshire, Oxfordshire and Berk-shire, bounded by the Marlborough and Lambourn Downs in the west and the Chiltern Hills in the east. To the south of the downs the area is intersected by the Kennet Valley, the Vale of Pewsey and Enbourne Vale, with Savernake Forest in the midst. The southern section comprises the North Hampshire Downs where they descend to the Test Valley which, together with Salisbury Plain, form the southern limit of what is so far the largest area designated.

Isle of Wight (73 sq. miles).—A number of separate areas comprising unspoiled stretches of coastline, the Yar Valley, the high downland behind Ventnor and the fine chalk downland ridge east of Newport to Culver Cliff and Foreland.

Wye Valley (125 sq. miles).—This area lies within the counties of Gwent, Gloucestershire and Hereford and Worcester. The lower Wye Valley landscape is characterised by its steeply-wooded slopes, cliffs and gorges where the river has cut through limestone outcrops. Further north the valley is broader and the river meanders through pleasant pastureland. Tintern Abbey and the well-known viewpoint from Symonds Yat are within this beautiful area. The flora include many rare species.

HISTORIC MONUMENTS

England

A select list of monuments under the control, since its creation in April 1984, of the Historic Buildings and Monuments Commission for England.

Charges for admission represent the figures obtain-ing in 1985.

Reduced admission prices for retirement pension-ers and children under 16. 10 per cent. discount for parties of 11 or more. Annual membership passes are available at £8 for adults and £4 for pensioners and children upon application to the Commission, 25 Savile Row, London W1X 2BT.

Standard hours of opening (marked *) are as follows:

	Weekdays	Sundays
Mar. 15–Oct. 15	9.30 a.m.–6.30 p.m.	2.00–6.30 p.m.
Oct. 16–Mar. 14	9.30 a.m.–4.00 p.m.	2.00–4.00 p.m.

Monuments not marked * open April–Sept. only.

Those marked † open on Sundays at 9.30 a.m. from April–Sept. inclusive.

All monuments are closed on Christmas Eve, Christmas Day, Boxing Day and New Year's Day. Some smaller sites may close for the lunch-hour, which is normally 1–2 p.m.

BEESTON CASTLE, Cheshire. 80p*. Thirteenth-century inner ward with gatehouse and towers, and considerable remains of large outer ward.

BERKHAMSTED CASTLE, Hertfordshire*. Extensive remains of a large 11th-century motte-and-bailey castle with later stone wall.

BOLSOVER CASTLE, Derbyshire. 60p†*. established in Norman times, it is now notable for its exception-ally interesting 17th-century buildings.

BOSCOBEL HOUSE, Salop. 60p*†. Timber-framed early 17th-century hunting lodge with later altera-tions. Charles II's "Royal Oak" is nearby.

BRINKBURN PRIORY, Northumberland. 50p†*. An Augustinian priory; the church (c. 1200, repaired in 1858) and parts of the claustral buildings survive.

BROUGHAM CASTLE, Cumbria. 50p†*. Extensive remains of the keep (c. 1170), and of other buildings of periods up to the 17th century.

BYLAND ABBEY, North Yorkshire. 50p*. Consider-able remains of church and conventual buildings date from the abbey's foundation in 1177 by the Cistercians.

CARISBROOKE CASTLE, Isle of Wight. Summer £1.50, Winter 60p†*. Extensive motte-and-bailey castle with shell keep.

CARLISLE CASTLE, Cumbria. Summer £1·00, Winter 50p†*. The Castle was begun by William Rufus. The keep houses the Regimental Museum of the Border Regiment.

CASTLE ACRE PRIORY, Norfolk. 50p†*. Extensive remains include the church with its elaborate west front, and the prior's lodgings.

CASTLE RISING, Norfolk. 60p†*. A fine 12th-century keep stands in a massive earthwork with its gatehouse and bridge.

CHESTERS ROMAN FORT, Northumberland. Summer 80p, Winter 40p†*.

CHYSAUSTER ANCIENT VILLAGE, Cornwall, 50p†*. Iron-Age village of courtyard houses.

CLEEVE ABBEY, Somerset. 60p†* Much of the claustral buildings survive including timber-roofed frater, but only foundations of the church.

CORBRIDGE ROMAN STATION, Northumberland. 80p*. Excavations have revealed the central area of the Roman town and military base of Corstopitum.

DEAL CASTLE, Kent. 60p†*. The largest and most complete of the castles erected by Henry VIII for coastal defence.

DOVER CASTLE, Kent. Keep—Summer £1·20, Winter 60p†*; Underground Works 50p*; Grounds—free. One of the largest and most important English castles.

DUNSTANBURGH CASTLE, Northumberland. 50p†*. The castle, standing on a cliff above the sea, has a 14th-century gatehouse-keep.

FARLEIGH CASTLE, Somerset. 50p†*. Late 14th-century castle of two courts. The chapel contains fine tomb of Sir Thomas Hungerford.

FARNHAM CASTLE, Surrey. 30p. Keep, April–Sept. Built by the Bishops of Winchester, the motte of the castle is enclosed by a large 12th-century shell keep.

FINCHALE PRIORY, Durham. 30p†. Benedictine house on banks of River Wear with considerable 13th-century remains.

FOUNTAINS ABBEY, North Yorkshire. (Closed for renovation)

FRAMLINGHAM CASTLE, Suffolk. 50p†*. Impressive castle with high curtain-walls of late 12th-century enclosing a poor-house of 1639.

FURNESS ABBEY, Cumbria. 60p*. Founded in 1127 by Stephen, afterwards King of England; extensive remains of church and conventual buildings.

GOODRICH CASTLE, Hereford and Worcester. 60p†*. Extensive remains of beautiful 14th-century castle incorporating interesting 12th-century keep.

GRIMES GRAVES, Norfolk. 60p†*. Extensive group of flint mines dating from the Stone Age. Several shafts can be inspected.

HAILES ABBEY, Gloucestershire. 60p†*. Ruins of a Cistercian monastery founded in 1246. Museum contains some fine architectural fragments.

HELMSLEY CASTLE, North Yorkshire. 50p†*. Twelfth-century keep and curtain wall with 16th-century domestic buildings against west wall.

HOUSESTEADS ROMAN FORT, Northumberland. Summer 80p, Winter 40p†*. Excavation has exposed this infantry fort on Hadrian's Wall with its extra-mural civilian settlement.

KENILWORTH CASTLE, Warwickshire. 80p*. One of the finest and most extensive castles in England, showing many styles of building from 1155 to 1649.

LANERCOST PRIORY, Cumbria. 50p. The nave of the priory church is still used and there are remains of other claustral buildings.

LINDISFARNE PRIORY, Northumberland. 50p†*. An Anglican monastery destroyed by the Danes, it was re-established by the Benedictine abbey of Durham.

LULLINGSTONE ROMAN VILLA, Kent. Summer £1·00, Winter 50p†*. A large villa occupied through much of the Roman period; fine mosaics and a unique Christian chapel.

MIDDLEHAM CASTLE, North Yorkshire. 60p*. The fine keep of 1170 stands in the centre of 13th-century inner ward.

MOUNT GRACE PRIORY, North Yorkshire. 60p*. Carthusian monastery, with remains of monks' separate houses.

NETLEY ABBEY, Hampshire. Free*. Extensive remains of 13th-century church, claustral buildings and abbot's house, incorporating much fine detail.

OLD SARUM, Wiltshire. 50p†*. Large 11th-century earthworks enclosing the excavated remains of the castle and the cathedral.

ORFORD CASTLE, Suffolk. 50p*†. Circular keep of c. 1170 and remains of coastal defence castle built by Henry II.

PENDENNIS CASTLE, Cornwall. 60p†*. Well-preserved castle erected by Henry VIII for coast defence and enlarged by Elizabeth I.

PEVENSEY CASTLE, East Sussex. 50p†*. Extensive remains of a Roman fort of the Saxon Shore enclosing an 11th-century castle.

PEVERIL CASTLE, Derbyshire. 60p*†. In a picturesque and nearly impregnable position, this 12th-century castle is defended on two sides by precipitous rocks.

PORTCHESTER CASTLE, Hampshire. 60p†*. A Roman fort of the Saxon Shore enclosing a fine Norman keep and priory church.

RECULVER CASTLE and ROMAN FORT, Kent. 30p. Remains of Saxon church with 12th-century towers standing in a Roman fort.

RICHBOROUGH CASTLE. Kent. 60p†*. The landing-site of the Claudian invasion, it became a supply-base and a Saxon Shore fort.

RICHMOND CASTLE, North Yorkshire. 60p†*. This very fine 12th-century keep, with 11th-century curtain-wall and gatehouse, commands Swaledale.

RIEVAULX ABBEY, North Yorkshire. Summer 80p, Winter 40p†*. Extensive remains include an early Cistercian nave (1140) and fine 13th-century choir and claustral buildings.

ROCHESTER CASTLE, Kent. 60p*†. Eleventh-century wall, partly overlying the Roman city wall, encloses splendid square keep of c. 1130.

ST. AUGUSTINE'S ABBEY, Canterbury, Kent. 50p†*. Founded by St. Augustine in 598; 7th- and 11th-century churches underlie the medieval abbey.

ST. MAWES CASTLE, Cornwall. 50p†*. Coast defence castle built by Henry VIII consisting of central tower and three bastions.

SCARBOROUGH CASTLE, North Yorkshire. 60p†*. Remains of 12th-century keep and curtain-walls dominating the town.

STONEHENGE, Wiltshire. £1·00†*. Sundays from 9.30 a.m. all year. World-famous prehistoric monument consisting of central stone circles surrounded by bank and ditch.

TILBURY FORT, Essex. 60p*. Built to guard the Thames against the Dutch, the fort is a fine example of 17th-century fortification.

TINTAGEL CASTLE, Cornwall. 80p†*. Twelfth-century castle on cliff-top site and remains of a Celtic monastery.

TYNEMOUTH PRIORY and CASTLE, Tyne and Wear. 60p†*. Anglian monastery destroyed by the Danes and re-established in 1090, with 14th-century defensive system.

WALMER CASTLE, Kent. Summer £1·00, Winter 50p†*. Closed Mon. (unless Bank Holiday) and when Lord Warden is in residence. One of Henry VIII's coast defence castles, it is the residence of the Lord Warden of the Cinque Ports.

WARKWORTH CASTLE, Northumberland. 60p†. Magnificent early 15th-century keep built by the Percys, with other remains from earlier periods.

WHITBY ABBEY, North Yorkshire. 50p†*. A Saxon foundation destroyed by the Danes with considerable remains of fine 13th-century church.

WROXETER ROMAN CITY, Shropshire 50p†*. The public baths and part of the forum remain of the Roman town of Viroconium.

Wales

A select list of monuments under the control of Cadw: Welsh Historic Monuments. Charges for admission represent the figures obtaining in 1985. Concessionary rates are available for children, etc. Hours of opening are as shown for English monuments.

BEAUMARIS CASTLE, Anglesey, Gwynedd. 90p†. The finest example of the concentrically planned castle in Britain, it is still almost intact.

CAERLEON ROMAN AMPHITHEATRE, Gwent. 50p†. Late 1st-century oval arena surrounded by bank for spectators with entrance passages.

CAERLEON ROMAN FORTRESS BATHS, Gwent. 50p†. Rare example of a legionary bath-house.

CAERNARFON CASTLE, Gwynedd. Summer £1.60, Winter £1.00†. The most important of the Edwardian castles, built together with the town wall between 1283 and 1330.

CAERPHILLY CASTLE, Glamorgan. 80p†. Concentrically planned castle (c. 1270) notable for its great scale and use of water defences.

CASTELL COCH, S. Glamorgan. 90p. Rebuilt 1875–90 on medieval foundations.

CHEPSTOW CASTLE, Gwent. 80p†. Fine rectangular keep in the middle of extensive fortifications.

CONWY CASTLE, Gwynedd. 90p†. Built by Edward I to guard the Conway ferry, it is a magnificent example of medieval architecture.

CRICCIETH CASTLE, Gwynedd. 60p†. A native Welsh castle of the early 13th century, much altered by Edward I.

DENBIGH CASTLE, Clwyd. 60p†. The remains of the castle, which dates from 1282–1322, include unusual triangular gatehouse.

HARLECH CASTLE, Gwynedd. 90p†. Well preserved Edwardian castle with a concentric plan sited on rocky outcrop above the former shore-line.

RAGLAN CASTLE, Gwent. 70p†. Extensive and imposing remains of 15th-century castle with moated hexagonal keep.

ST. DAVID'S, BISHOP'S PALACE, Dyfed. 60p†. Extensive remains of principal residence of Bishop of St. David's dating from 1280–1350.

TINTERN ABBEY, Gwent. 90p†. Very extensive remains of the fine 13th-century church and conventual buildings of this Cistercian monastery.

Scotland

A select list of monuments under the control of the Scottish Development Department.

Charges for admission represent the figures obtaining in 1985. Concessionary rates are available for children, etc.

Standard hours of opening (marked S.) are as follows:

	Weekdays	Sundays
April–Sept.	9.30–7.00 p.m.	2.00–7.00 p.m.
Oct.–March	9.30–4.00 p.m.	2.00–4.00 p.m.

Monuments open at any reasonable time are indicated by A.

ABERLEMNO, Tayside. Four Pictish stones. A. Closed in Winter. Admission free.

ANTONINE WALL, Central and Strathclyde Regions. A. Admission free.

ARNOL BLACKHOUSE, Western Isles. S. 40p. Traditional Hebridean dwelling.

BONAWE, Strathclyde. A. Closed in Winter. 50p. Mid-18th century iron-furnace.

BROUGH OF BIRSAY, Orkney. A. 50p. Remains of the Norse period.

BROWN AND WHITE CATERTHUNS, Tayside. A. Admission free. Iron Age hill forts.

CAERLAVEROCK CASTLE, Dumfries and Galloway. S. 50p.

CAIRNPAPPLE HILL, Lothian. S. 50p. Closed Mon. a.m. and Fri. A prehistoric ritual complex and Bronze Age cairn.

CALLANISH, Western Isles. A. Admission free. Standing Stones.

CAMSTER CAIRNS, Highland. A. Admission free.

CLAVA CAIRNS, Highland. A. Admission free.

DRYBURGH ABBEY, Borders. S. £1·00.

EARLS AND BISHOPS PALACES, Kirkwall, Orkney. S. 50p.

EDINBURGH CASTLE, including Scottish National War Memorial, Scottish United Services Museum and Historic Apartments. Admission to War Memorial, free; to all other areas, Adults £2·00, Senior Citizens and Children £1·00, Family Ticket £4·00. There is no reduction for parties. Members of H.M. Forces in uniform free. Open Oct.–March, weekdays 9.30–5.05, Sun. 12.30–4.20; April–Sept. weekdays 9.30–5.50, Sun. 11.00–5.50.

Alterations may also be made to opening hours during the Tattoo, State and Military events.

EDZELL CASTLE, Tayside. S. 50p.

ELGIN CATHEDRAL, Grampian. S. 50p.

FORT GEORGE, Highland. S. 50p.

GLASGOW CATHEDRAL, Strathclyde. S. Admission free.

GLENELG BROCHS, Highland. A. Admission free.

HERMITAGE CASTLE, Borders. S. 50p.

HUNTLY CASTLE, Grampian. S. 50p.

JARLSHOF, Shetland. S. 50p. Closed Tues. and Wed. p.m. Remains of villages from Bronze Age to Viking times.

JEDBURGH ABBEY, Borders. S. 50p. Closed Thurs. p.m.

KELSO ABBEY, Borders. S. Admission free.

LINLITHGOW PALACE, Lothian. S. £1·00.

LOANHEAD STONE CIRCLE, Grampian. A. Admission free.

MAES HOWE, Orkney. S. £1·00. Prehistoric tomb.

MEIGLE MUSEUM, Tayside. S. 50p. Closed Sun. Pictish stones.

MELROSE ABBEY, Borders. S. £1·00.

MOUSA BROCH, Shetland. A. Admission free.

NETHER LARGIE CAIRNS, Strathclyde. A. Admission free.

NEW ABBEY CORN MILL, Dumfries and Galloway. S. 50p. Closed Wed. and Thurs. a.m.

RING OF BROGAR, Orkney. A. Admission free.

RUTHWELL CROSS, Dumfries and Galloway. A. Admission free.

ST. ANDREWS' CASTLE AND CATHEDRAL, Fife. S. 50p. Cathedral, admission free.

SKARA BRAE, Orkney. S. £1·00. Prehistoric village.

SMAILHOLM TOWER, Borders. S. Closed in Winter. 50p.

STIRLING CASTLE, Central. Oct.–March, weekdays 9.30–5, Sun. 12.30–4.20; April–Sept., weekdays 9.30–6, Sun. 11–5.30. £1.20.

TANTALLON CASTLE, Lothian. S. £1·00.

THREAVE CASTLE, Dumfries and Galloway. S. Admission free. Ferry charge 50p.

HOUSES OPEN TO THE PUBLIC

Times of summer opening and admission fees shown are those which obtained in 1985, and are subject to modification. Space permits only a selection of some of the more noteworthy houses in the U.K. which are open to the public. A fuller description of some houses in or near London will be found on pages 665–675. (*Property of the National Trust.)

ALNWICK CASTLE, Northumberland. Seat of the Duke of Northumberland.—May 5–Oct. 4, Daily (except Sat.) 1–5. Admission, £1.50.

A LA RONDE, Exmouth.—April–Oct., Mon.–Sat., 10–6; Sun., 2–7. Admission, £1.20.

ALTHORP, Northampton.—All year, Daily, 2.30–5.30. Aug., 2.30–6, Bank Holidays, 11–6. Admission, £2.50, Weds., £3.50 (Connoisseurs' Day).

*ANGLESEY ABBEY, Cambs.—April 21–Oct. 13, Wed., Thurs., Fri., Sat., Sun. and Bank Holiday Mons. 2–6. Mar. 31–April 15, weekends only. Admission, £1.90.

ARUNDEL CASTLE, W. Sussex. Seat of the Duke of Norfolk.—April 1–Oct. 25, 1–5; June–Aug. and Bank Hols., 12–5. Closed Sats.

*AVEBURY MANOR, Marlborough.—April–Sept., Mon. to Sat., 11.30–6.30; Sun. 1.30–6.30. Oct.–March, Sat. and Sun., 1.30–5.

BADMINTON, Avon.—Closed in 1986.

BANTRY HOUSE, Co. Cork.—All year, Daily, 9–6. Admission, £2.

*BASILDON PARK, Berks.—April–Oct., 2–6 (Wed. to Sat.); Suns. and Bank Holiday Mons., 12–6. Admission, £1.60.

BEAULIEU, Hants.—Easter–Sept., Daily, 10–6. Oct.–Easter, Daily 10–5 (see also page 652).

*BELTON HOUSE, Grantham.—April–Oct., Weds.–Suns. and Bank Hol. Mons., 1–5.30. Admission, £2.

BELVOIR CASTLE, nr. Grantham. Seat of the Duke of Rutland.—March 19–Sept. 29, Tues., Wed., Thurs., Sat and Good Friday, 12–6; Bank Holidays, 11–7; Suns., 12–7. Oct., Suns., 2–6. Admission, £2.00.

BERKELEY CASTLE, Glos.—May–Aug., Daily, except Mon. (but including Bank Holidays), 11–5; Sun. 2–5; April and Sept., 2–5; Bank Holidays, 11–5; Oct., Suns., 2–4.30. Admission, £1.80.

BLAIR CASTLE, Tayside. Seat of the Duke of Atholl.—April, Suns. and Mons. April 21–Oct. 13, Daily, 10–5 (Suns. 2–5). Admission, £1.80.

BLENHEIM PALACE, Oxon. Seat of the Duke of Marlborough.—March 11–Oct. 31, Daily, 11–6.

BOUGHTON HOUSE, Northants. Seat of the Duke of Buccleuch & Queensberry.—April weekends; 2 weekends in May; July 28–Sept. 16, Daily (except Fri.); Sept. 18–Oct. 27, Wed., to Sun., 2–6. Admission, £3.

BOWHILL, Selkirk.—May–Sept., Mon., Wed., Thurs., Sat. and Sun. (July and Aug., Daily except Fri.) 12–5; Suns., 2–6. Admission, £1.50.

BROADLANDS, Hants.—April–Sept., Daily (closed Mon., except Aug., Sept. and Bank Holidays), 10–6. Admission, £2.40.

BROUGHTON CASTLE, Oxon.—mid May–mid Sept., Weds. and Suns. (also Thurs. in July and Aug.) and Bank Holidays, 2–5. Admission, £1.60.

*BUCKLAND ABBEY, Devon. Including Drake relics.—Good Fri.–Sept. (also Bank Holidays) 11–6; Suns. 2–6. Oct.–Easter, Wed. and weekends, 2–5. Admission, £1.30.

BURGHLEY HOUSE, Stamford.—April–6 Oct. (closed Sept. 7), Daily 11–5; Good Fri. and Suns., 2–5.

CARDIFF CASTLE.—May–Sept., Daily, 10–6; Nov.–Feb., Daily, 10–4; Mar., April, Oct., Daily, 10–5.

CARLTON TOWERS, N. Yorks.—Suns. only May to Sept., plus Bank Holidays, 1–5. Admission charged.

CASTLE ASHBY, Northants.—August (except day of Horse Trials), 2–6. Open all year to parties by prior arrangement.

*CASTLE COOLE, Enniskillen.—Closed for restoration work. Parklands remain open.

*CASTLE DROGO, Devonshire.—April–Oct., Daily, 11–6. Admission, £2·20.

CASTLE HOWARD, N. Yorks.—March 25–Oct., Daily, 11–5.

CAWDOR CASTLE, Inverness.—May–Sept., Daily, 10–5.30. Admission, £1.80.

*CHARTWELL, Kent. Home of Sir Winston Churchill.—March–Nov., Sat., Sun. and Wed., 11–4; Apr. 2–Oct. 31, Tues., Wed. and Thurs., 12–5; Sat., Sun. and Bank Hol. Mon., 11–5. Admission £2·30.

CHATSWORTH, Derbyshire. Seat of the Duke of Devonshire.—March 31–Oct. 27, Daily, 11.30–4.30.

CHICHELEY HALL, Newport Pagnell.—April 5–Sept. 29, Suns. and Bank Holidays, also Weds. in Aug., 2.30–6. Admission, £1.60.

*CLIVEDEN, Maidenhead.—Gardens, Daily, 11–6 (closed Jan. and Feb.); House, Apr.–Oct., Sats. and Suns., 2–6, (closed Bank Holidays and Good Friday). Admission, £2.

*COMPTON CASTLE, nr. Paignton.—April–Oct., Mons., Weds. and Thurs., 10–12.15, 2–5. Admission, £1.20.

*CROFT CASTLE, Herefordshire.—May–Sept., Weds.–Suns., 2–6 (also Bank Holidays). Apr. and Oct., weekends and Easter Bank Hol. Mon., 2–5. Admission £1.40.

DARWIN AND DOWN HOUSE, Downe, Orpington, Kent.—March–Jan. 31; 1–6; not Mons. (except Bank Hols.), Fris. or Dec. 24–26. Admission, £1·20; O.A.P.s, 60p; children, 30p.

DRUMLANRIG CASTLE, Dumfries.—Easter and April 5–8; May and June, Daily (except Fri.), 1.30–5 (Sun. 2–6); July and Aug., Daily (except Fri.), 11–5; Suns., 2–6. Admission, £2.00.

GLAMIS CASTLE, Angus.—May–Sept., Daily (except Sats.), also Easter, 1–5. Admission, £1.80.

*HARDWICK HALL, Derbyshire.—Apr.–Oct., Daily (not Mons. (except Bank Hols.) Tues. and Fris.), 1–5.30. Admission, £2·20.

HAREWOOD HOUSE, Leeds.—April–Oct., Daily, from 11 a.m.

HATFIELD HOUSE, Herts.—March 26–Oct. 13, Daily (except Mons.), 12–5; Suns., 2–5.30; Bank Holidays, 11–5. Admission, £2.45.

HEVER CASTLE, Kent.—April–Oct. 6, Daily (except Thurs.), 12–6. Admission, £2·75.

HOLKER HALL, Cumbria.—Easter Sun.–Oct. 27, Daily (except Sats.), 10.30–4.30. Admission, £1·50.

HOLKHAM HALL, Wells.—June–Sept., Sun., Mon., Thurs., 1.30–5; also Weds. in July and Aug. (and Spring and Summer Bank Hol. Mons.,) 11.30–5. Admission £1·30, Pensioners £1·00., Children 50p. Also Bygones Collection £1·00/75p/50p.

HOPETOUN HOUSE, nr. Edinburgh.—Easter and April 26–Sept. 16, Daily, 11–5.30. Admission £1·90.

HOUGHTON HALL, Norfolk.—Easter Sun.–Sept. 29, Thurs. and Bank Holidays, 12–5.30; Suns., 1.30–5.30. Admission, £1.50.

*HUGHENDEN MANOR, High Wycombe. Disraeli's home—April–Oct., Weds.–Sats., 2–6; Suns. and Bank Hol. Mons., 12–6. Mar. weekends, 2–6 or dusk. Admission, £1.60.

INVERARAY CASTLE, Argyll. Seat of the Duke of Argyll.—April 6–Oct. 13, Daily (except Fri.), 10–1, 2–6 (July and Aug., Daily, 10–6); Suns., 1–6. Admission, £1.80.

KELMSCOTT MANOR, nr. Lechlade.—April–Sept., 1st Wed. in each month, 11–1, 2–5. Admission, £2.

KNEBWORTH HOUSE, Herts.—April–May, Suns. and Bank Hols.; May 25–Sept. 15, Daily (except Mons.); also Bank Hol. Mons. 11.30–5.30.

*KNOLE, Kent.—April–Oct., Weds. to Sats., 11–5 (also Bank Holidays); Suns., 2–5. Admission, £2.

LEEDS CASTLE, Kent.—April–Oct., Daily (except non Bank Hol. Mons. in April, May and Oct.), 11–5. Nov.–March, weekends only, 12–4.

*LITTLE MORETON HALL, Cheshire.—April–Sept., Daily (except Tues.), Mar. and Oct., weekends, 2–6. Admission, £1.60. Weekends and Bank Hols. £1·80.

LONGLEAT HOUSE, Warminster.—All year, Daily, 10–6 (Oct.–Easter, 10–4).

LUTON HOO, Beds.—March 30–Oct. 13, Daily (except Tues. and Fris.), also Good Friday, 11–6; Suns., 2–6. Admission, £1.80.

MELBOURNE HALL, Derbyshire.—June 1–Oct. 1, Suns., 2–6. Admission, £2.

MICHELHAM PRIORY, E. Sussex.—April 5–Oct. 20, Daily, 11–5.30. Admission, £1.30.

*MONTACUTE HOUSE, Yeovil.—April–Nov. 10, Daily (except Tues.), 12.30–6. Admission, £2.

*MOUNT STEWART, Co. Down.—April–Sept., Daily (except Fris.), 2–6. Also Good Friday. Admission, £1.40.

OSBORNE HOUSE, I.O.W. State and Private Apartments.—April 2–Oct. 13, 11–5, (July and Aug., 10–5); not Suns. Admission, £2.

*PENRHYN CASTLE, Bangor.—April 5–Oct. 27, Daily (except Tues.), 12–5 (June–Sept., Bank Holidays 11–5). Admission, £1.90.

PENSHURST PLACE, Kent.—April–Oct. 6, Daily (except Mons.), 1–5.30. Admission, £2.40.

*PETWORTH HOUSE, W. Sussex.—April–Oct., Daily (except Mons., Tues. and Fris.), also Bank Holiday Mons., 2–6. Admission, £2.40.

PORTMEIRION, Gwynedd.—April–Oct., Daily, 9.30–5.30. Admission charge.

POWDERHAM CASTLE, Exeter.—For opening times contact the Administrator, (0626) 890 243.

*POWIS CASTLE, Powys.—April 6–Sept. 29, Weds. to Suns. (also Tues. in July and Aug.). 1–6. Bank Hol. Mons., 11.30–6. Admission, £1.90.

RABY CASTLE, Durham.—April 10–June 30 and Sept., Weds. and Suns.; July–Sept., Daily (except Sats.), 2–5. Also Bank Hols. Admission, £1.50.

RAGLEY HALL, Warwicks.—April–Sept., Daily (except Mons. and Fris.), also Bank Hols., 1.30–5.30. Admission, £2.

ROCKINGHAM CASTLE, Corby.—Easter Sun.–Sept., Suns., Thurs., Tues. in Aug and Bank Hols. (Mon. and Tues.), 2–6. Admission, £1.70.

*RUFFORD OLD HALL, Lancashire—April–Oct., Daily (except Fri., but incl. Good Fri.), 2–6. Admission, £1.30.

RUSSBOROUGH, Co. Wicklow.—Easter–Oct., Suns., Bank Hols.; also Weds. (June–Aug.), Sats. (July–Aug.), 2.30–5.30. Admission, £1.80.

SANDRINGHAM, Norfolk.—April 7–Sept. 26 (except Fris. and Sats., and closed July 22–Aug. 10), 11–4.45 (Suns., 12–4.45). Admission, £1.50.

SCONE PALACE, Perth.—Good Friday–mid Oct., Daily, 10–5.30; Suns., 2–5.30 (July and Aug., 11–5.30). Admission, £1.90.

SHEFFIELD PARK, East Sussex.—Apr. 2–Nov. 10, Tues. to Sat., 11–6, Sun., Bank Hols., 2–6. Admission, May, Oct. and Nov. £2·30. April, June, Sept. £1·80.

SHERBORNE CASTLE, Dorset.—Easter Sat.–Sept., Thurs., Sat., Sun. and Bank Hol. Mons., 2–6.

*SHUGBOROUGH, Staffs.—mid March–Oct., Tues. to Fris. and Bank Hol. Mons., 10.30–5.30; Sats. and Suns., 2–5.30. Admission, £2.00.

*SISSINGHURST, Kent.—April–Oct. 15, Tues.–Fri., 1–6.30; Sats., Suns. and Good Friday, 10–6.30. Closed Bank Holidays. Admission, £2.30 (Suns. £2.80).

SKIPTON CASTLE, N. Yorks.—Mons.–Sats., 10–6; Suns, 2–6. Admission charge.

*SMALLHYTHE PLACE, Tenterden. Dame Ellen Terry's home.—April–Oct., Daily (except Tues. and Fris.) 2–6. Admission, £1.

*SNOWSHILL MANOR, Broadway.—April and Oct., Sats., Suns. and Easter Mon., 11–1, 2–5; May–Sept., Weds. to Suns. (incl. Bank Holidays), 11–1, 2–6. Admission, £2.10.

STANFORD HALL, Leics.—Easter Sun.–Sept., Thurs., Sats. and Suns. (also Bank Hol. Mons. and following Tues.), 2.30–6. Admission, £1.60.

STONOR PARK, Oxon.—April–Sept., Weds., Thurs. and Suns. (also Sats. in Aug.), 2–5.30. Bank Hol. Mons., 11–5.30. Admission £1.70.

STONELEIGH ABBEY, Warwicks.—Easter Mon.–Sept. 30, Suns., Mons. and Thurs. 1–5.30. Admission, £2.20.

*STOURHEAD, Wilts.—May–Sept., Daily (except Fris.); Apr. and Oct.–Nov. 10, Daily (except Thurs., Fri.), 2–6. Admission, £1.70. Gardens, Daily, 8–7. Admission, £1.30.

STRATFIELD SAYE HOUSE, Reading.—Easter Sat., Sun. and Mon, April weekends, then May 1–Sept. 28, Daily (except Fris.), 11.30–5.

*SUDBURY HALL, Derbys.—April–Oct., Daily (except Mons. and Tues.), also Bank Hols. 1–5.30. Admission, £1.80.

SUDELEY CASTLE, Glos.—April–Oct., Daily, 12–5. Admission, £2.80.

SULGRAVE MANOR, Northants. Home of the Washington family.—Feb.–Dec., Daily (except Weds.), 10.30–1, 2–5.30 (closes 4 p.m. in winter). Admission, £1.00.

*TRERICE, Cornwall.—April–Oct., Daily, 11–6. Admission, £1.80.

*THE VYNE, Basingstoke.—April–Oct. 20, Daily (except Mons. and Fris.), 2–6; Bank Hol. Mons., 11–6. Admission, £1.60.

TYN-Y-RHOS HALL, Shropshire—May–Sept., Weds., Thurs., Sats., Suns. and Bank Hol. Mons., 2.30–6. Admission, 80p.

*WADDESDON MANOR, Bucks.—March 27–Oct. 27, Weds. (except after Bank Hol.) to Suns., 2–6. Also Bank Hols., 11–6. Admission, £2.00.

WARWICK CASTLE.—March–Oct., Daily, 10–5.30; Nov.–Feb., Daily, 10–4.30.

WILTON HOUSE, Wilts.—April 2–Oct. 13, Tues. to Sats. and Bank Hol. Mons., 11–6; Suns., 1–6. Admission, £2·20.

*WIMPOLE HALL, Cambs.—March 30–Nov. 3, Daily (except Fris.) and Bank Hol. Mons., 2–6. Admission, £1.90.

WINSLOW HALL, Bucks.—July to Sept. 15, Daily (except Mons.) also Bank Hols., 2.30–5.30. Sept. 15–30, weekends only. Admission, £1·25.

WOBURN ABBEY, Beds. Seat of the Duke of Bedford.—April 1–Oct. 27, 11–5.45, Suns., 11–6.15. Oct. 28–Mar. 31, weekends only, 11–4.45.

MUSEUMS AND ART GALLERIES OUTSIDE LONDON

(For National Art Galleries and Museums outside London see pages 375–6, 418 and 420–21.)

Avebury.—*Great Barn Folk Life Museum.* April–Oct., open daily 10–5.30; most weekends Nov.–Mar. 2–4. Admission charge.

Barnard Castle, Co. Durham.—*The Bowes Museum.* Important collections of British and European fine art, from medieval period to 19th century Fine porcelain and glass, tapestries and furniture. Music and costume galleries. English period rooms from Elizabeth I to Victoria; French decorative arts of 18th and 19th centuries; local antiquities. Temporary Exhibitions. Open weekdays, May–Sept., 10–5.30; March, April and October, 10–5; Nov.–Feb., 10–4. Sundays, 2–5 (Summer); 2–4 (Winter). Admission £1·20; children and O.A.P.s, 35p.

Bath.—*Roman Baths Museum.* Roman Baths complex including newly excavated Temple precinct. Admission (including Pump Room), £1·50; children 90p. *Museum of Costume,* Assembly Rooms. Fashion from 16th century to current year. (Winter) weekdays 9–5; Sundays 11–5. (Summer) weekdays 9–6; Sundays 10–6. Admission £1.25; children 75p. *American Museum in Britain,* Claverton Manor. American decorative arts from late-17th to mid-19th centuries. Open 28 Mar.–2 Nov., daily (except Mons.), 2–5; Bank Holiday Mons. and preceding Suns., 11–5. During winter only on application. Admission charge. *Victoria Art Gallery,* Bridge Street. Open Mon.–Fri. 10–6; Sat. 10–5. Closed Suns. and Bank Holidays. Admission free.

Beaulieu.—*National Motor Museum.* Displays of vehicles dating from 1895 to present day. Open daily 10–6 (winter, 10–5). Admission charge.

Belfast.—*Ulster Museum,* Botanic Gardens. Collections of Irish antiquities, natural and local history, fine and applied arts. Open Mon.–Fri. 10–5, Sat. 1–5, Sun. 2–5. *Ulster Folk Museum,* Holywood. Indoor and outdoor exhibits of all aspects of Ulster folklife. Open Oct.–April, weekdays 11–5, Sun. 2–5 (May–Sept. open to 6 p.m.). May–June (Wed. only) 10–9. Admission 50p, children and O.A.P.s, 20p. *Transport Museum,* Holywood and Witham Street. History of land, sea and air transport in Ireland and road, rail and sea vehicles. Holywood site—open as for Folk Museum. Witham Street site open weekdays 10–6. Admission 20p, children and O.A.P.s 10p. Special arrangements apply at both museums over Christmas and Easter.

Beverley, N. Humberside.—*Museum of Army Transport.* Exhibits include field workshop, amphibious assault landing, railway section and aircraft. Open daily 10–5. Admission: Adults £1., Children and O.A.P.s, 50p.

Birmingham.—*City Museum and Art Gallery.* British and European masters from 14th to 20th centuries (particularly the Pre-Raphaelite movement), sculpture, European gold, silver and jewellery, pottery and porcelain, furniture, textiles and costume, archaeology, local and natural history. Open, free, Weekdays and Sat., 10–5; Sundays, 2–5. Closed Christmas Day, Boxing Day, New Year's Day and Good Friday.

Museum of Science and Industry, Newhall Street. The history of science from the Industrial Revolution to the present; many working machines under steam, gas, etc. Open, free, Weekdays, 10–5; Saturdays, 10–5, Sundays, 2–5. Other Birmingham museums are: *Aston Hall, Blakesley Hall, Birmingham Nature Centre, Sarehole Mill,* and *Weoley Castle.*

Bradford.—*Cartwright Hall,* Lister Park. Contains European and British fine art from the 16th century onwards. *Bolling Hall,* off Wakefield Road, a furnished house dating from the 15th century. *Industrial Museum,* Moorside Mills, illustrates the local wool and worsted industries and transport. *Cliffe Castle,* Keighley. Natural and local history. *Manor House,* Ilkley, is an Elizabethan Manor House with exposed wall of Roman Fort. Open 10–5 (April–Sept., 10–6, except Industrial museum). Closed Good Friday, Christmas Day, Boxing Day and Mons. (except Bank Holidays). Admission free.

Brighton.—*The Royal Pavilion, Palace of George IV.* Chinoiserie interiors, much of the original furniture returned on loan from H.M. the Queen. Open daily 10–5 (10–6.30, June to September). Closed Christmas Day and Boxing Day. Admission £1·85 (reduced rates for children, O.A.P.s, parties, etc.).

Art Gallery and Museum, Church Street (adjacent Royal Pavilion). Old master paintings; Willett pottery and porcelain collection, 20th-century art and furniture, ethnography, archæology, costume gallery. Open, free, 10–5.45 Tuesdays to Saturdays; Sundays 2–5. Closed Christmas Day, Boxing Day, Good Friday, Mondays and Jan. 1st.

Preston Manor, Preston Park. (Thomas-Stanford: Macquoid bequests of English period furniture, furnishings, china and silver.) Closed Christmas Day, Boxing Day, Good Friday, Mondays and Jan. 1st. Open 10–5, Admission 80p (reduced rates for children, O.A.P.s, parties). Gardens open, free.

The Grange, Art Gallery and Museum, Rottingdean. Sussex Room, Kipling Room and collections of National Toy Museum. Open, free, 10–5 weekdays; Sundays, 2–5. Closed Christmas Day, Boxing Day, Wednesdays and Jan. 1st.

The Booth Museum of Natural History, Dyke Road. Open, free, 10–5, Sundays, 2–5. Closed Christmas Day, Boxing Day, Good Friday, Thursdays and Jan. 1st.

Bristol.—*City Museum and Art Gallery.* Collections of Egyptology, British archæology, natural and local history. Collection of Old Masters, 19th cent. and modern paintings, Chinese ceramics, glass, English silver, glass, porcelain and delftware, English and foreign embroideries. Open weekdays, 10–5. *Bristol Industrial Museum,* Prince's Wharf. Collections of manufacturing equipment and transport, including unique steam carriage and Bristol-built aero-engines. Open daily (except Thurs. and Fri.) 10–1, 2–5. *Maritime Heritage Centre* including *SS Great Britain*, open daily 10–6, 10–5 (winter). Closed Christmas Eve and Day. *St. Nicholas Church Museum*. Church plate and vestments, local medieval antiquities, Hogarth altarpiece. Brass-rubbing centre. Open Mon.–Sat. 10–5. Also *Red Lodge, Blaise Castle House Museum, Kingsweston Roman Villa* and *Georgian House*.

National Life-boat Museum, Princes Wharf, Wapping Road. Displays of life-boats, models and equipment. Open From April, daily 10.30–4.30. Admission 50p, children 30p, O.A.P.s 30p.

Cambridge.—*Fitzwilliam Museum*. Egyptian, Greek, Near Eastern and Roman antiquities, coins and medals, medieval manuscripts, paintings and drawings, prints, Oriental and Occidental pottery and porcelain, textiles, arms and armour, medieval and renaissance objects of art, and a library. Open free, Tues.–Sat., Lower Galleries 10–2, Upper Galleries 2–5; Sun. 2.15–5. Closed Dec. 24 to Jan. 1 and Good Friday. Closed Mons. incl. May Day Bank Holiday but not Easter and Bank Holiday Mons.

Canterbury.—*Royal Museum and Art Gallery, and Buffs Regimental Museum*. Collections include archaeology, porcelain, prints and pictures. Open free weekdays, 10–5. *Roman Pavement Museum*. Roman material from post-war excavations of Canterbury. *Westgate Tower Museum*. Arms and armour and display of city walls and gates. (Roman and Westgate Museums open 10–1, 2–5; Oct.–March, 2–4 only.) Admission 25p, children, 10p.

Carlisle.—*Tullie House Museum and Art Gallery*, Castle Street. Collections of archæology, natural and social history, fine and decorative arts in Jacobean house. Open weekdays 9–7 (Oct.–March, 9–5); Spring and Summer Bank Holidays, and Suns. June–Aug., 2.30–5. *Guildhall*, Greenmarket. Civic and Guild history and artefacts. Contact Tullie House Museum for opening information.

Chester.—*Grosvenor Museum*, Grosvenor Street. Collection of Roman antiquities from legionary fortress; natural history, art and folk-life. Open weekdays 10.30–5, Sun., 2–5. *King Charles Tower* on City Walls. Civil War displays. Open daily (summer), weekends (winter), times vary. Admission charge.

Colchester.—*Colchester and Essex Museum, The Castle* contains local archæological antiquities, especially those from Roman Colchester. The *Holly Trees Mansion* (1718) covers social life of the 18th and 19th centuries. *Natural History Museum*, All Saints Church. Natural history of Essex. *Museum of Social History*, Holy Trinity Church. Domestic life and crafts. Open, weekdays, 10–5, Sat, 10–4 (branches closed 1–2 p.m.). Castle only, Sundays 2.30–5 (April–Sept.); admission 55p; Children 20p, O.A.P.s free. Branches free all year.

Coventry.—*Herbert Art Gallery and Museum*, Jordan Well. Archæology, natural and local history, fine and decorative arts. Open weekdays 10–6, Sun., 2–5. Closed Good Friday and Christmas period. *Museum of British Road Transport*, St. Agnes Lane, Hales Street. April–Sept., 10–4 (Mon.–Fri.), 10–5.30 (weekends); Oct.–March, Fri., Sat. and Sun. only. Admission 90p; children and O.A.P.s 45p. *Lunt Roman Fort*, Baginton. June–Sept., 12–6 (closed Mons. and Thurs.).

Crich, Nr. Matlock, Derbyshire—*National Tramway Museum*. Open air working museum with collection of trams from Britain and abroad. Mile-long scenic line. Open, Sats., Suns. and Bank Holidays 10.30–5.30 (Easter–Oct.); also daily (except Fri.) 10.00–4.30 (May–Sept.)

Derby.—*Museum and Art Gallery*, Strand. Archaeology, military, social history, natural history. Collections of paintings by Joseph Wright of Derby; Derby porcelain, costume, model theatres. Open Tues.–Sat. 10–5. *Industrial Museum*, Silk Mill, Full Street, Rolls Royce collection of aero engines etc. Tues.–Fri. 10–5. (Saturdays 10–4.45). Closed on all Bank Holidays.

Dorchester.—*Dorset County Museum*. Geology, archæology, local and natural history and rural crafts of Dorset. Collection of Thomas Hardy's manuscripts, books, notebooks, drawings, etc. Open weekdays 10–5, closed Christmas Day, Boxing Day and Good Friday. Admission 60p, children and O.A.P.s 30p.

Durham.—*Light Infantry Museum and Arts Centre*. County Regiment's 200 year history displayed; arts and crafts exhibitions. Open weekdays (except Mons.) 10–5, Sun. and Bank Holiday Mons., 2–5. Closed Christmas Day and Boxing Day. Admission 30p, children and O.A.P.s 10p. *Oriental Museum*, The University. Collections ranging from Ancient Egypt to China and Japan. Open weekdays 9.30–1, 2.15–5. Weekends, closed Nov.–Feb.; Mar.–Oct. Sats. 9.30–12, 2.15–5, Suns. 2.15–5. *Cathedral Treasury*. Relics of St. Cuthbert, church plate, medieval seals, manuscripts and vestments. Open weekdays 10–4.30, Sun., 2–4.30. Admission 45p, children 10p.

Edinburgh.—*City Art Centre*, 2 Market Street. Late 19th and 20th century art, mostly Scottish, and temporary exhibitions. Open weekdays 10–5 (June–Sept., 10–6). Admission free. *Canongate Tolbooth*, 163 Canongate. Courthouse and prison for 300 years; temporary exhibitions. Open weekdays 10–5 (June–Sept., 10–6). Admission free. *Huntly House*, 142 Canongate. Local history, collections of Edinburgh silver, glass and Scottish pottery. Open weekdays 10–5 (June–Sept., 10–6). Admission free. Also: *Lady Stair's House*, Lawnmarket. Mon.–Sat., 10–5 (June–Sept., 10–6). *Lauriston Castle*, Cramond Road South, April–Oct., Daily (except Fri.), 11–1, 2–5; Nov.–March, weekends only.

Exeter.—*Royal Albert Memorial Museum and Art Gallery*, Queen Street. English art, ceramics and glass, Exeter silver, costume, natural and social history. Open Tues.–Sat. 10–5.15. *Maritime Museum*, The Quay. Collection of working boats. Open daily 10–5 (Jun.–Sept., 10–6). Admission charge. *Underground Passages*, Princesshay. Medieval aqueducts. Tues.–Sat., 2–4.40.

Fort William.—*West Highland Museum*, Cameron Square. Historical, natural history and folk exhibits, including those of the '45 Rising. Daily (except Sun.) 10–1 and 2–5; June and Sept. 9.30–5.30; July and Aug. 9.30–9.

Glasgow.—*Art Gallery and Museum*, Kelvingrove. Old Masters, 19th century French paintings; archæology and natural history, special collection of armour. *Museum of Transport*, 25 Albert Drive. Road and rail vehicles, ship models. *People's Palace*, Glasgow Green. History of city from 1175 to present. *The Burrell Collection*, Pollok Park. Textiles, furniture, ceramics, stained glass, silver and other art objects, paintings, especially 19th century French. *Pollok House*, Pollok Park. Spanish paintings, furniture, silver, ceramics. *Haggs Castle Museum*, St. Andrews Drive. Childrens museum. All open weekdays 10–5, Sun. 2–5. Admission free.

Guildford.—*Guildford Museum*, Castle Arch. Local museum for archæology and history of Surrey including collections of the Surrey Archæological Society. Open every day except Sunday, 11–5. Closed on Good Friday and Christmas.

Hull.—*Ferens Art Gallery.* Collection of European art, especially Dutch 17th century; British portraits of 18th–20th centuries; Humberside marine paintings; contemporary art and changing exhibitions. *Wilberforce House.* Jacobean merchant's house, birthplace of Wilberforce; collection of slavery relics, period furniture, costume and ceramics. *Transport and Archæology Museum.* Veteran cars, trams, coaches and velocipedes; archæological finds from Humberside, including Roman mosaics. *Town Docks Museum.* Whaling, fishing, trawling, ships and shipping. All open Mon.–Sat., 10–5; Sun., 1.30–4.30. *Posterngate Gallery.* Exhibitions and one-man shows. Tues.–Sat.

Huntingdon.—*Cromwell Museum.* Remaining portion of the 12th-century Hospital of St. John housing portraits of Cromwell, his family and Parliamentary notables, and Cromwelliana—documents, armour, coins, etc. Open, free, Sun. 2–4; Tues. to Fri., 11–1, 2–5, Sat., 11–1, 2–4. Closed Mon. and Bank Holidays other than Good Friday.

Ipswich.—*Ipswich Museum.* Collections of Suffolk geology, archæology and natural history and ethnology. Temporary exhibitions. *Christchurch* (Branch Museum) Tudor house contains furniture, Suffolk portraits, English porcelain, pottery and glass. Mon.–Sat. 10–5; Sun. 2.30–4.30. *Wolsey Art Gallery*, attached, houses Borough collections of paintings (local artists, Gainsborough, Constable, Munnings, etc.). Modern prints, sculpture. Open, weekdays 10–5. Closed on some Bank Holidays.

Leeds.—*City Art Gallery.* English watercolours. British and European painting, modern sculpture, incl. Henry Moore gallery. Open weekdays, 10–6, Suns., 2–5. Print Room and Art library contains study collection of drawings and prints. Wed., 10–9, Sat., 10–4, other weekdays 10–5.30, closed Sun.
Temple Newsam House. Tudor/Jacobean house, furnished in style of 17th and 18th cents., with silver, European porcelain and pottery, pictures, etc. Open daily (except Mons.), 10.30–6.15 or dusk; Weds. (May–Sept.), 10.30–8.30. Open all Bank Holidays (except Christmas). Admission 50p; children (with adults 20p), O.A.P.s 20p. *Lotherton Hall*, Gascoigne art and silver collection, oriental gallery, costume collection, 19th century furniture, ceramics, park and gardens. open daily (except Mons.), 10.30–6.15 or dusk; Thurs. (May–Sept.), 10.30–8.30. Open all Bank Holidays (except Christmas). Admission to Hall, 50p; children (with adults 20p), O.A.P.s 20p. *Abbey House Museum*, folk museum including three full-sized streets. Open Oct.–Mar., weekdays 10–5, Sun. 2–5, (to 6, April–Sept.). *Industrial Museum.* Open April–Sept., Tues.–Sat. 10–5, Sun. 2–5 (to 4, Oct.–March). Open Bank Holidays.

Leicester.—*Leicestershire Museum and Art Gallery*, New Walk (1849). Natural history, geology, Egyptology, 18th–20th century English paintings, ceramics, silver. *Newarke Houses*, The Newarke. Social history of Leicestershire from 1500 A.D.; musical instruments; local clocks. *Jewry Wall Museum*, St. Nicholas Circle. Archaeology (prehistoric–1500). Roman Jewry Wall and Baths, mosaics. Belgrave Hall, Church Road. A Queen Anne house with furniture and garden of note. Coaches and agricultural collection. *Museum of the Royal Leicestershire Regiment*, The Magazine, Oxford Street. *Museum of Technology*, Corporation Road. Knitting industry and Power galleries. Horse-drawn and motor vehicles, beam engines. *Wygston's House Museum of Costume*, Applegate. Costume from 1789–1924. All museums open weekdays (except Fri.) 10–5.30; Sun., 2–5.30. Closed Christmas Day, Boxing Day and Good Friday.

Lewes.—*Museum of Sussex Archæology*, Barbican House, near Castle. Prehistoric, Roman, Saxon and mediæval collections relating to Sussex; local pictures and prints. Open weekdays, 10–5.30, Sundays (April–Oct.), 11–5.30. Admission, 75p; Children, 40p.
Anne of Cleves House, Southover. Local history and folk museum. Open weekdays (mid. Feb.–mid. Nov.), 10–5.30. Suns. (April–Oct.), 2–5.30. Admission, 70p; Children 35p.

Lincoln.—*Usher Gallery.* Watches, miniatures, porcelain, silver, etc., Peter de Wint collection of oils and watercolours, Lincolnshire topographical drawings, *personalia* associated with Tennyson family. Coins and medals. Open weekdays, 10–5.30; Sun., 2.30–5. *City and County Museum*, The Greyfriars. Geology, natural history and archæology of Lincolnshire. Special collection of armour. Open weekdays, 10–5.30; Sun., 2.30–5. *Museum of Lincolnshire Life.* Collections illustrate life and work in Lincolnshire since 17th century. Open weekdays, 10–5.30; Sun., 2.30–6. Closed December and January. *National Cycle Museum*, Brayford Wharf North. Collection of vintage and veteran cycles. Open Easter to Oct. 10–5 daily; Oct. to Easter Fri., Sat., and Sun. 10–5.

Liverpool.—*Walker Art Gallery.* European painting from 14th century–present day, particularly strong in early Italian and Northern, Pre-Raphaelite and Academic 19th century paintings. Open, weekdays, 10–5; Suns., 2–5. Closed on Good Friday, Christmas Eve, Christmas Day, Boxing Day and New Year's Day. *Sudley Art Gallery* (Emma Holt Bequest), Mossley Hill Road. 18th and 19th-century paintings, mainly English, including Gainsborough, Millais and Turner. Open as for Walker Art Gallery.
Merseyside County Museums, William Brown Street. Established with the Mayer and Derby collections, including the Mayer-Fejervary Gothic ivories, the Bryan Fausett group of Anglo-Saxon antiquities, and the Lord Derby and Tristram ornithological collections. Displays include vivarium and aquarium, land transport, local and natural history, archæology, ethnology, timekeeping and space gallery; also a Planetarium. Open weekdays, 10–5; Sun., 2–5. Closed New Year's Day, Good Friday, Christmas Eve, Christmas Day and Boxing Day. Admission free (except to Planetarium). *Merseyside Maritime Museum*, Pier Head. Displays on local maritime history in restored waterfront buildings. Also craft demonstrations, working exhibits and floating vessels. Open Easter–Autumn, daily 10.30–5.30. Admission charge. *Prescot Museum of Clock and Watch Making*, 34 Church Street, Prescot. Clocks, watches, tools and workshop reconstructions. Open Tues.–Sat. and Bank Hol. Mon. 10–5; Sun. 2–5. Closed Mon., Christmas Eve, Christmas Day, Boxing Day, New Year's Day and Good Friday. Admission free.
Speke Hall. Half-timbered Tudor house administered by the County Museums for the National Trust. Open weekdays 10–5, Sun. 2–7 (2–5 Oct.–March). Admission charge. *Croxteth Hall and County Park.* Ancestral home of the Earls of Sefton. A working estate within the boundary of a major city. Hall, farm etc. open daily, Easter to Sept., 11–5. Admission charge. Park open all year; free.

Manchester.—*City Art Gallery*, Mosley Street. Old Masters, Turner, Pre-Raphaelites, Impressionists; sculpture, porcelain, silver. *Athenaeum Gallery*, Princess Street. Both Mon.–Sat., 10–6. Sun., 2–6. Admission free. *Whitworth Art Gallery*, Oxford Road. Watercolours, drawings, prints, textiles and wallpapers collections, and 20th century British art. Mon.–Sat., 10–5 (Thurs. 10–9); closed Suns. *North Western Museum of Science and Industry*, Grosvenor Street. Development of industry in region. *National Paper Museum*, history of papermaking. Both open Mon.–Sat. 10–5. Admission free. *Gallery of English Cos-*

tume, Platt Hall, Rusholme. Exhibits from 17th century to present. Also *Heaton Hall*, Prestwich, *Wythenshawe Hall*, Northenden and *Fletcher Moss Museum*, Didsbury. Opening times vary.

Newcastle-upon-Tyne.—*Laing Art Gallery*, Higham Place. Fine art from 17th century, pottery, glass, silver and metalwork. Open weekdays 10–5.30, Sun. 2.30–5.30. *Keep Museum*, St. Nicholas Street. History of site. Oct.–March, Mon.–Sat. 10–4.30 (April–Sept. open to 5.30 p.m.). Closed Christmas Day, Boxing Day, New Year's Day and Good Friday. *Trinity Maritime Centre* and *Trinity House*, Broad Chare. Centre open weekends 11–3. Trinity House Apr.–Oct., 2–4, Tues., Wed., Thurs. *Military Vehicle Museum*, Exhibition Park. Open daily 10–5. *Museum of Science and Engineering*, West Blandford Street. Mon.–Fri. 10–5.30, Sat. 10–4.30. *Newburn Hall Motor Museum*, Townfield Gdns. Tues.–Sat. 10–10 p.m. *Blackgate Bagpipe Museum*, St. Nicholas Street. Mon.–Sat. 10–5.30 (winter 4.30); Sun 11–5.30 (winter 4.30).

Newmarket.—*National Horse racing Museum.* Five galleries of displays relating to the development of horseracing and to the horses and people connected with the sport. Open 29 March–8 Dec., Tues.–Sat. 10–5, Sun. 2–5. Closed Mon. except Aug. and Bank Holidays. Admission £1·50, children, O.A.P.s 75p.

Norwich.—*Castle Museum.* Exhibits of art (including Norwich School), local archæology, social and natural history, pottery and glass. Open, Mon.–Sat., 10–5; Sun. 2–5. *Strangers' Hall*, Charing Cross. Late medieval mansion furnished as a museum of urban domestic life, 16th–19th centuries. Open, Mon.–Sat., 10–5. *Bridewell Museum of Local Industries*, Bridewell Alley. Transport, crafts and industries of Norfolk and North Suffolk. Open, Mon.–Sat., 10–5. *St. Peter Hungate Church Museum*, Princes Street. 15th century church used for display of church art and antiquities. Open, Mon.–Sat., 10–5.

Nottingham.—*Castle Museum and Art Gallery.* English and Dutch paintings and drawings 17th–20th centuries; special collections of Bonington and Paul Sandby. Ceramics, silver, glass, medieval Nottingham alabaster carvings, local historical and archaeological displays, classical, oriental and ethnographical antiquities; the regimental collection of the Sherwood Foresters. Open, Summer, 10–5.45; Winter, 10–4.45. Closed Christmas Day. Admission free, small charge on Sundays and Bank Holidays.

Industrial Museum, Wollaton Park. Industrial, lacemaking machinery, steam engines, transport. Open, April–Sept., Mon.–Sat. 10–6; Sunday, 2–6; Oct.–April, Thurs. and Sat., 10–4.30; Sunday, 1.30–4.30. Closed Christmas Day. Admission free, small charge on Sun. and Bank Holidays.

Canal Museum, Canal Street. Open Easter–Oct., Wed.–Sat., 10–5.45, (Sun. 1–5.45); Oct.–Easter, Wed.–Sat., 1–5.00; Sun. 1–5. Admission free.

Natural History Museum, Wollaton Hall. Open, Summer 10–7 (Sun. 2–5); Winter, 10 till dusk (Sun. 1.30–4.30). Closed Christmas Day. Admission free except Sun. and Bank Holidays.

Newstead Abbey, 11½ miles N. of Nottingham. Collections associated with poet Byron. Abbey open Good Friday to end of September, every day, 2–6, admission charge.

Castlegate Museum of Costumes and Textiles. Open daily 10–5. Closed Christmas Day. Admission free.

Brewhouse Yard Museum, Castle Boulevard. Everyday life from the 17th century to present. Open daily 10–12, 1–5, admission free. Closed Christmas Day.

Oakham, *Rutland County Museum*, Catmose Street.—Archæology, local history, craft tools and agricultural implements. Open Tues.–Sat., 10–1, 2–5; Sun. (April–Oct.) 2–5, and Bank Holiday Mons.

Oxford, *Ashmolean Museum.*—Collections of European and Oriental fine and applied arts; Classical, Near-Eastern archæology and Numismatics. Open Tues.–Sat., 10–4, Sundays, 2–4. Admission free.

Plymouth.—*City Museum and Art Gallery*, Drake Circus. Fine art, including Cottonian collection and Reynolds' portraits, Plymouth porcelain, archaeology, local and natural history. Mon.–Fri., 10–5.30; Sat., 10–5. Admission free.

Portsmouth.—*City Museum and Art Gallery*, Museum Road. Decorative and fine arts, local and social history. Daily 10.30–5.30. Admission charge. Also 6 branch museums including fortifications, military history, archæology, natural science, technology and D-Day Museum. *Royal Naval Museum*, H.M. Naval Base. Nelson collection, ship and naval artifacts, the Victorian Navy, W.W.2 at Sea, The South Atlantic campaign displays, *Mary Rose* and an exhibition of her treasures. Weekdays 10.30–5; Sundays 1–5. Admission charge.

Port Sunlight Village, Merseyside. *Lady Lever Art Gallery.* Paintings and watercolour drawings (mainly British School), antique, renaissance and British sculpture, English furniture, mainly 18th cent., Chinese pottery and porcelain, and important collection of old Wedgwood. Open weekdays 10–5, Sundays 2–5.

St. Albans.—*City Museum*, Hatfield Road. Natural history, geology, craft and trade tools. Open weekdays 10–5. Admission free. *Verulamium Museum*, St. Michael's. Roman and Belgic material including mosaics, one *in situ* in Hypercaust annexe. Open weekdays 10–4, Sun. 2–4 (to 5.30 p.m. in summer). Admission, 60p; children, students and O.A.P.s, 35p.

Sheffield.—*City Museum, Weston Park.* Includes the Bateman Collection of antiquities from Peak District Bronze Age barrows, cutlery and old Sheffield plate collections. Open, weekdays, Sept.–May, 10–5; June–Aug. 10–8; Sun. 11–5 (Closed Christmas Eve, Christmas Day and Boxing Day). *Mappin Art Gallery*, Weston Park. Paintings and sculpture of 18th–20th centuries (mainly British School) and contemporary works. Open weekdays 10–5 (Jun.–Aug. open to 8 p.m.), Sun. 2–5. *Abbeydale Industrial Hamlet*, Abbeydale Road South. A late 18th–early 19th century scythe and steel works with associated housing. Open, weekdays 10–5, Sun. 11–5. *Kelham Island Industrial Museum.* Open Wed.–Sat., 10–5; Sun. and Bank Holiday Mon., 11–5. *Shepherd Wheel*, Whiteley Wood. Water-powered cutlery grinding establishment. Open 10–12.30, 1.30–5 (opens at 11 on Sun.). Closed Mon. and Tues. *Bishops' House, Meersbrook Park*; museum of local history in timber-framed domestic building. Open, Wed.–Sat., 10–5; Sun. 11–5.

Stoke-on-Trent.—*City Museum and Art Gallery*, Bethesda Street, Hanley. Major ceramic collections. Open daily (except Sun.) 10.30–5 p.m. *Chatterley Whitfield Mining Museum*, Tunstall. Coal mine open daily (except Mon.) 9–5 (last tour 3.30). Admission, Adults £2·90, O.A.P.s £2·35, Children £1·80. *Gladstone Pottery Museum*, Longton. A working Victorian pottery. Open daily (except Mon. in winter) 10.30–5.30, Sun. 2–6. Admission, Adults £1, O.A.P.s 70p, Children 50p.

Pottery Factory Tours: Tours are available at the following: *Minton*, London Road; *Royal Doulton*, Nile Street; *Spode*, Church Street, all Stoke. *Beswick*, Gold Street; *Melba-Wain*, Heathcote Road; *Healacraft China*, Weston Coyney Road, all Longton, *Coalport and Crown Staffordshire*, Park Street, Fenton and *Wedgwood's* at Barlaston.

Stratford-upon-Avon.—*Shakespeare's Birthplace*, contains period furniture, rare books, MSS and objects of Shakespearean interest with new Shakespeare Centre nearby. *Anne Hathaway's Cottage*, Shottery, early home of Shakespeare's wife. *Mary Arden's House*, Wilmcote, Tudor farmhouse home of Shakespeare's mother. *New Place*, where Shakespeare died. *Hall's Croft*, half-timbered home of Shakespeare's daughter and her family. *Grammar School* attended by Shakespeare. *Royal Shakespeare Theatre* burnt down 1926, rebuilt 1932 with 1,500 seats.

Styal.—*Quarry Bank Mill*, Cheshire. History of the cotton industry, weaving demonstrations. Closed Mon. except June–Sept. Oct.–March, daily, 11–4. April–Sept., daily, 11–5. Admission £2·00; children £1·30; family ticket £5·30.

Winchester.—*City Museum.* Weekdays 10–5; Sundays 2–5 (closed Mons. in winter). *Cathedral Library.* MSS and other exhibits from 10th century onwards. Weekdays 10.30–12.30, 2.30–4.30. Admission charge. *Cathedral Treasury.* Exhibition of church silver and other pieces. Weekdays 11–5; Sundays 2.30–4.30. Admission charge.

Worcester.—*City Museum and Art Gallery.* Natural history of Worcestershire and temporary art exhibitions; also museum of the Worcestershire Regiment and the Worcester Yeomanry Cavalry. Open weekdays 9.30–6, Sat. 9.30–5. Closed Thurs. *The Commandery*, Sidbury. 15th century building housing Civil War displays. Weekdays 10.30–5; Sun. 2.30–6. *Tudor House Museum*, Friar Street. Local domestic and social history. Mon.–Sat., 10.30–5 (closed Thurs.). *Dyson Perrins Museum of Worcester Porcelain*, Severn Street. Mon. to Fri. 9.30–5, Sat. 10–5.

York.—*Castle Museum.* Folk museum of Yorkshire life of the past four centuries. Open weekdays, 9.30–5, Suns., 10–5 (closes 6.30 p.m., April–Sept.). Admission, £1.50; children and O.A.P.s 75p (special party rates Nov.–March).

Jorvik Viking Centre, Coppergate. Reconstruction of Viking York and display of artifacts. Open daily (incl. Suns.) 9–5.30 (7 p.m. Easter–Oct.). Admission £2, children £1.

Yorkshire Museum and Gardens, Museum Street, Roman Life gallery, archæology, decorative arts, geology, natural history. Open weekdays, 10–5; Sun., 1–5. Admission, 80p; children, O.A.P.s, etc., 40p. Gardens, Roman, Anglian and medieval ruins. Open weekdays, 8–dusk; Sun. 10–dusk. *The York Story*, Castlegate. Open weekdays 10–5; Sun. 1–5. Admission, 75p; children 40p.

Art Gallery, Exhibition Square. European paintings, 14th–20th century; watercolours and prints of Yorkshire; modern English stoneware pottery. Open weekdays, 10–5; Sun., 2.30–5. Admission free.

Treasurer's House (National Trust). Chapter House Street. Open, April–Oct., 10.30–6. Admission charge.

H.M. COASTGUARD

Founded in 1822 to guard our coasts against smuggling, H.M. Coastguard's role today is a very different one—that of complete dedication to the guarding and saving of all life at sea. Administered by the Department of Transport, it is responsible for co-ordinating all civil marine search and rescue operations around the 2,500 mile coastline of Great Britain and Northern Ireland, and 1,200 miles into the Atlantic, as well as co-operating with search and rescue organizations of neighbouring countries both in Western Europe and around the Atlantic seaboard. In addition the Service maintains a 24-hour watch on the Dover Strait, providing a Channel Navigation Information Service for all shipping in one of the busiest sea lanes in the world.

Since 1978 H.M. Coastguard has been organized into six Regions, each with a Regional Controller operating from a Maritime Rescue Co-ordination Centre. Each Region is subdivided into Districts under District Controllers, operating from Maritime Rescue Sub-Centres. In all there are 24 of these major centres. They are on 24-hour watch and are fitted with a comprehensive range of communications and rescue equipment. They are supported by some 350 smaller stations manned by Auxiliary Coastguards under the direction of Regulars, each of which keeps its parent centre fully informed of day to day casualty risk, particularly on the more remote danger spots around the coast.

Between January 1 and December 31, 1984, the 560 Regular and 9,000 Auxiliary Coastguards co-ordinated 4,879 incidents requiring search and rescue facilities, resulting in assistance being given to 8,516 persons. All distress telephone and radio calls are centralized on the 25 centres, which are particularly on the alert for people or vessels in distress, shipping hazards and oil slicks. Using their modern telecommunications equipment and the facilities provided by British Telecom's Coast Radio Stations, they can alert and co-ordinate the most appropriate rescue facilities: RNLI lifeboats, Royal Navy or RAF helicopters, fixed-wing aircraft, Naval vessels, ships in the vicinity, and Coastguard shore and cliff rescue teams.

For those who regularly sail in local waters, or make longer passages, the Coastguard Yacht and Boat Safety Scheme provides a valuable free service. Its aim is to give the Coastguard a record of the details of craft, their normal operating areas and their passage plans. Yacht and Boat Safety Scheme Cards are available from all Coastguard stations, harbourmasters' offices and most yacht clubs and marinas.

Members of the public who see an accident or a potentially dangerous incident on or around the coast should without hesitation dial '999' and ask for the Coastguard.

LONDON BOROUGHS

City or Borough (*Inner London Borough)	Municipal Offices	Population	Rateable Value April 1, 1985	Town Clerk (*Chief Executive)	Mayor or (a) Lord Mayor
			£		
City of Westminster*	City Hall, Victoria St., S.W.1.	184,100	325,471,735	R. G. Brooke	(a) R. Bramble
Barking and Dagenham	‡Dagenham, Essex.	149,100	26,977,197	D. C. J. Farr	G. H. Shaw
Barnet	†The Burroughs, Hendon, N.W.4.	295,000	61,958,500	E. M. Bennett	Mrs. B. Langstone
Bexley	‡Bexleyheath, Kent.	217,900	31,365,000	*T. Musgrave	R. J. Passey
Brent	†Forty Lane, Wembley.	251,238	52,164,954	*M. G. Bichard	R. Stone
Bromley	†Bromley, Kent.	299,500	51,727,000	*N. T. Palk	R. D. Foister
Camden*	†Euston Road, N.W.1.	175,500	117,571,095	F. Nickson	J. Fulbrook
Croydon	†Taberner House, Park Lane, Croydon.	320,600	70,582,039	F. S. H. Birch	G. Smith
Ealing	†Ealing, W.5.	288,700	57,364,605	B. T. Collins	V. Kopecky
Enfield	‡Enfield.	261,000	49,372,925	W. D. Day	J. D. Reed
Greenwich*	†Wellington St., Woolwich, S.E.18.	209,873	33,037,806	*A. Glover	J. Gillman
Hackney*	Mare St., E.8.	187,900	37,962,620	*Ms. P. Gordon	Ms. D. Shanks
Hammersmith and Fulham*	†King St., W.6.	148,447	36,412,696	*A. J. Allen	K. G. F. B. Howe, O.B.E.
Haringey	Wood Green, N.22.	202,650	36,834,895	*R. C. Limb	J. Gardner
Harrow	‡Station Rd., Harrow.	197,700	35,301,142	*D. Adams	P. H. Pitt
Havering	†Romford, Essex.	241,500	38,503,258	*R. W. J. Tridgell	E. Mundam
Hillingdon	‡Uxbridge.	228,220	59,369,260	*P. A. Johnson	G. A. L. Sullivan
Hounslow	‡Lampton Rd., Hounslow	200,829	50,676,814	*R. D. Jefferies	E. Pauling, M.B.E.
Islington*	†Upper St., N.1.	165,200	54,915,889	*E. W. Dear	Ms. M. Ogilvy-Webb
Kensington and Chelsea (Royal Borough)*	†Hornton St., W.8.	136,000	72,974,703	R. S. Webber	D. Campion
Kingston upon Thames (Royal Borough)	Guildhall, Kingston upon Thames.	133,600	29,189,931	G. N. Hollis (Co-ordinator)	F. J. Steptoe
Lambeth*	Brixton Hill, S.W.2.	244,000	60,398,822	A. J. George	L. Leon
Lewisham*	†Catford, S.E.6.	231,900	35,001,577	J. W. Harwood	Ms. M. Sandra
Merton	†Broadway, Wimbledon, S.W.19	165,400	31,642,196	*W. McKee	Mrs. D. Harris
Newham	†East Ham Road, E.6.	209,400	36,362,663	*J. Samuel	T. Nolan
Redbridge	High Road, Ilford	227,000	37,000,000	*G. U. Price	R. E. Smith
Richmond upon Thames	§Twickenham, Middx.	160,800	33,013,954	M. J. Honey	A. I. Simmonds
Southwark*	†Peckham Rd., S.E.5.	215,400	59,800,000	*J. B. Parker (acting)	P. Sullivan
Sutton	‡St. Nicholas Way, Sutton, Surrey.	170,100	30,023,520	*A. Taylor	R. F. Johnson
Tower Hamlets*	†Patriot Square, E.2.	144,000	48,254,727	*D. Regan	P. Beasley
Waltham Forest	†Walthamstow, E.17.	215,100	31,948,289	*L. G. Knox	A. J. Simmons
Wandsworth*	†Wandsworth, S.W.18.	258,100	44,003,555	*A. J. Newman	M. A. S. Heaster

†Town Hall.　　‡Civic Offices.　　§Municipal Offices.

GREATER LONDON COUNCIL
(*see* also p. 619–620)

The Greater London Council and 32 London Borough Councils were constituted under the London Government Act, 1963. They replaced, on April 1, 1965, the London County Council, the Middlesex County Council, the County Borough Councils of Croydon, East Ham and West Ham, 28 metropolitan borough, 39 non-county borough and 15 urban district councils. The boundaries and constitution of the Corporation of the City of London were not affected.

Under the Act, Greater London became for the first time a clearly defined local government area including, in addition to the former counties of London and the greater part of Middlesex, parts of Metropolitan Essex, Kent, Surrey and Hertfordshire.

The Greater London Council at present consists of 92 councillors. Councillors are elected for single-member electoral divisions which are coterminous with the parliamentary constituencies. Councillors hold office for four years. The Chairman, Vice-Chairman and Deputy Chairman are elected annually by the councillors. The political head of the administration is the Leader of the Council, elected by the majority party. The Council meets at three weekly intervals at 2.30 p.m. on Tuesdays except in holiday periods. Most committees and sub-committees meet at three- or six-weekly intervals.

GREATER LONDON COUNCIL

Chairman, A. Banks.
Vice-Chairman, H. Kay.
Deputy-Chairman, H. H. Sandford, O.B.E., D.F.M.
Leader of the Council, K. Livingstone.
Leader of the Opposition, A. Greengross.
Arbour, A. F. (*C.*)...........*Surbiton*
Avery, Dr. D. J. (*C.*) ....*The City of London and Westminster South*
Bailey, Dr. G. N. A. (*C.*) ....*Brentford and Isleworth*
Banks, A. L., M.P. (*Lab. & Co-op*)...................*Tooting*
Bays, A. W. (*C.*) ....*Upminster*
Beale, N. (*C.*)...............*Finchley*
Bell, W. A. O. J. (*C.*) ....*Chelsea*
Black, P. B. (*C.*) ....*Hendon South*
Boateng, P. (*Lab.*) ....*Walthamstow*
Bolton, S. C. (*C.*) ....*Wimbledon*
Bramall, Sir Ashley (*Lab.*)..*Tower Hamlets*
Branagan, J. (*Lab.*)........*Stepney and Poplar*
Brew, R. M., C.B.E. (*C.*) .....*Chingford*
Bundred, S. (*Lab.*) ....*Islington North*
Carr, J. A. (*Lab.*) ....*Hackney Central*
Cassidy, B. M. D. (*C.*) ......*Hendon North*
Clack, Mrs. J. E. (*C.*) ....*Harrow Central*
Copland, Mrs. S. (*C.*).......*Carshalton*
Cutler, Sir Horace, O.B.E.
(*C.*) ....*Harrow West*
Daniel, G. J. (*Lab.*) ....*Ealing North*
Davies, N. (*Lab.*) ....*Woolwich West*
Dawe, P. J. (*Lab.*) ....*Leyton*
Dobson, J. C. (*C.*) ....*Acton*
Edwards, A. F. G. (*Lab.*)....*Newham North West*
Fletcher, Ms. J. (*Lab.*) .....*Tottenham*
Gardner of Parkes, Baroness
(*C.*) ....*Southgate*
Garside, M. E. (*Lab.*).......*Woolwich East*
Gent, R. C. (*C.*) ....*Sidcup*
Gill, P. S. (*C.*) ....*Croydon South*
Gouge, E. S. (*Lab.*).........*Ilford South*
Greengross, A. D. (*C.*).......*Hampstead*
Gumbel, Mrs. M. (*C.*).......*Sutton and Cheam*
Hammond, L. (*Lab.*) ....*Dulwich*
Handy, E. (*Lab.*)............*Erith and Crayford*
Hardy, A. (*C.*) ....*Brent North*
Harrington, I. (*Lab.*).......*Brent South*
Hart, Dr. A. B. (*Lab.*) ......*Hornsey*
Herbert, A. L. (*Lab.*) ....*Lewisham West*
Hinds, H. W. (*Lab. & Co-op*) *Peckham*
Howard, N. (*Lab.*) ....*Brent East*
Hughes, R. G. (*C.*) ....*Croydon Central*
Jenkins, Ms. M. A. (*Lab..*) ..*Putney*
Jenkinson, T. A. (*Lab.*) ....*Newham South*
Judge, A. R. (*Lab.*) ....*Mitcham and Morden*
Kay, H. (*Lab.*).............*Dagenham*

Langton, V. R. M. (*C.*) .....*Bexleyheath*
Lemkin, J. A. (*C.*) ....*Uxbridge*
Little, K. W. (*Lab.*) ....*Edmonton*
Livingstone, K. R. (*Lab.*) ...*Paddington*
Lucas, N. (*Lab.*) ....*Battersea North*
McBrearty, A. (*Lab.*) ....*Enfield North*
McDonnell, J. (*Lab.*).......*Hayes and Harlington*
Mackay, A. C. (*Lab.*).......*Deptford*
Major, J. R. (*C.*) ....*Chipping Barnet*
Mitchell, R., O.B.E. (*C.*) .....*Wanstead and Woodford*
Moore, P. D. (*Lab.*) ....*Lambeth Central*
Morgan, Ms. J. M. (*Lab.*) ...*Hackney South and Shoreditch*
Morrell, Ms. F. M. (*Lab.*) ...*Islington South and Finsbury*
Mote, H. T. (*C.*)............*Harrow East*
Neill, R. J. M. (*C.*) ....*Romford*
Nicholson, G. E. (*Lab.*) .....*Bermondsey*
Pitt, P. S. (*Lab.*) ....*Feltham and Heston*
Randall, S. J. C. (*C.*) ......*Beckenham*
Ripley, S. W. L. (*C.*).........*Kingston upon Thames*
Roe, Mrs. M. A., M.P. (*C.*) ..*Ilford North*
Rolfe, A. J. (*C.*).............*Croydon North East*
Ross, G. (*Lab. & Co-op*)......*Hackney North and Stoke Newington*
Rossi, C. A. (*Lab.*) ....*Holborn and St. Pancras South*
Rossi, P. N. (*S.D.P.*) ....*Lewisham*
Sandford, H. H., O.B.E. (*C.*) .*St. Marylebone*
Sieve, Mrs. Y. (*Lab.*) ....*Southall*
Slade, A. C. (*Lib.*)..........*Richmond*
Smith, Prof. N. J. D. (*C.*)....*Norwood*
Sofer, A. (*S.D.P.*) ....*St. Pancras North*
Stead, B. J. (*Lab.*) ....*Fulham*
Stewart, S. J. (*C.*)..........*Croydon North-West*
Tatham, Mrs. J. (*C.*) ....*Orpington*
Taylor, C. J. H. (*C.*) ....*Ruislip-Northwood*
Tremlett, G., O.B.E. (*C.*).....*Twickenham*
Tuffrey, M. W. (*Lib.*).......*Vauxhall*
Turney, S. J. (*Lab.*) ....*Islington Central*
Vigars, R. L. (*C.*) ....*Kensington*
Ward, J. B. (*Lab.*) ....*Barking*
Ward, M. (*Lab.*) ....*Wood Green*
Wetzel, D. C. (*Lab.*).........*Hammersmith North*
Weyer, F. W. (*C.*)...........*Streatham*
Wheeler, M. J. (*C.*) ....*Ravensbourne*
Williams, A. R. (*Lab.*) ......*Hornchurch*
Wilson, J. (*Lab.*) ....*Newham North East*
Wise, Ms. V. (*Lab.*) ....*Battersea South*
Wood, D. F. M. (*Lab.*) ......*Greenwich*
Wykes, Mrs. J. K. (*C.*)......*Chislehurst*

Director-General and Clerk to the Council, M. F. Stonefrost, C.B.E.

G.L.C. SERVICES

(*see* also p. 619–620)

The services provided by the G.L.C. include planning, roads, traffic management and control, fire services, refuse disposal, housing, parks and licensing. For certain services it shares responsibility with the London Borough Councils and the City Corporation.

Education.—The local education authority for an area corresponding with the area of the twelve inner London boroughs and the City of London is the Inner London Education Authority, a special committee of the G.L.C. consisting of the members of the Council elected for the inner London boroughs together with a representative of each inner London Borough Council and of the Common Council. The Council charges to the rating authorities in the Inner London Education Area the expenditure of the I.L.E.A., the amount being determined by the Authority. This unique arrangement preserves the continuity of the service which has developed since 1870 as a unity without regard to local boundary divisions.

The total number of pupils on the rolls of the Authority's nursery, primary and secondary schools (including special schools for handicapped children) is 300,852. There are 1,084 schools, staffed by the equivalent of 20,772 full-time teachers. Vocational instruction, cultural studies and recreational activities for persons over compulsory school age are arranged at the various establishments for further education. The Authority maintains 26 colleges and makes grants to 5 polytechnics and 3 other institutions. Part-time classes are offered at 24 adult education and literary institutes, and 83 youth centres, including 2 drama centres. The 20 outer London Borough Councils are the education authorities for their Boroughs.

Housing.—The Council shares with the London Borough Councils responsibility for housing in London. In line with the development of its strategic housing role the Council has now transferred most of its housing management functions to the Borough Councils. For the future, the Council intends to concentrate on analysing London's overall housing needs, presenting a co-ordinated view of action required, with a much reduced range of executive activities, although it will continue to carry out new building programmes and improvement work on older properties. This work is set out in the Council's London Housing Appraisal and its annual Housing Investment Programme submission to the Department of the Environment

Planning and Transportation.—Planning responsibilities in London are shared between the G.L.C. and the London Borough Councils. The G.L.C. is the planning authority for London as a whole and its strategic policies are set out in the G.L.D.P.—the structure plan for Greater London. Within the framework of the G.L.D.P., London Borough Councils may prepare their own local plans which together with the G.L.D.P. then form the basis for controlling development.

Town planning control of development proposals is mainly the concern of the London Boroughs (or the London Docklands Development Corporation), but the G.L.C. has some responsibilities in this field. As planner and developer the Council is involved in many major schemes. The Council and its District Surveyors are responsible for making and administering building control regulations in the inner London boroughs, and the Council is also responsible for planning controls respecting buildings of historical or architectural interest, or in conservation areas.

The Council is responsible for the construction, improvement and maintenance of principal roads. As the traffic authority for all roads in Greater London it prepares or approves traffic management schemes and devises special projects for assisting cyclists and pedestrians, installs and controls traffic signals, bus only lanes, waiting and loading restrictions and speed limits and makes the orders which enforce them. It maintains the Thames tunnels, all but four of the Thames bridges (London, Tower, Blackfriars and Southwark, which are maintained by the Corporation of London), and maintains and operates the Woolwich free ferry.

The G.L.C.'s responsibility, through the London Transport Executive, for transport services in London was transferred in June 1984 to the London Regional Transport board, which is responsible to the Secretary of State for Transport.

Expanding towns.—The Council continues to have agreements with a number of towns for the provision of homes and jobs out of London, but negotiations are now well advanced for their termination where this can be done by agreement.

Parks and Open Spaces.—The Council maintains some 5,500 acres of parks and open spaces. The London Borough Councils and the City Corporation between them provide a further 28,500 acres. Up to 800 open-air entertainments are arranged in G.L.C. parks each summer and almost all games and sports are provided for. At Crystal Palace, in addition to the Council's 106 acre park is the Crystal Palace National Sports Centre, owned by the Council and managed by the Sports Council.

Other features of the G.L.C.'s administration include its responsibility for the Royal Festival Hall, Queen Elizabeth Hall and Purcell Room, and the Hayward Gallery, which is leased by the G.L.C. to the Arts Council; the maintenance of The Iveagh Bequest, Kenwood, many other buildings of historic interest and two museums, and the maintenance and operation of Thames piers. The Greater London Record Office and Library house official records and other manuscripts, books, maps, drawings and photographs relating to London and are open to the public for reference purposes. The Research and Intelligence unit is concerned with information and research on any matters concerning Greater London. The results of its work will be available to government departments, local authorities and the public.

Solid waste disposal.—The Council is responsible for the disposal of refuse throughout Greater London—some 3,250,000 tonnes currently being handled each year. It operates a number of transfer stations and one incinerator. Refuse is used for infilling at thirty-four land reclamation sites. The Boroughs continue to be responsible for refuse collection. Over 12,000 old vehicles and more than 300,000 tonnes of bulky household refuse (the latter deposited direct by members of the public but included in the total of 3,250,000 tonnes) are also dealt with as a means of improving the environment under the Refuse Disposal (Amenity) Act, 1978. The Council provide separate containers for glass, metal, textiles, etc. to facilitate re-cycling. The G.L.C. is also responsible, under the Control of Pollution Act, 1974, for the issue of waste disposal licences and for monitoring the movement of hazardous waste through the London area.

Land Drainage and Flood Prevention.—The G.L.C. and the Borough Councils exercise land drainage functions on certain watercourses within a 400 sq. mile area in and adjoining Greater London known as the London Excluded Area. The G.L.C. undertakes flood prevention works and maintains unobstructed flows in main metropolitan watercourses including the Ravensbourne, Beverley Brook, Wandle, Crane and Brent rivers. The Council also has flood prevention functions along some 120 miles of riverbank of the Thames and its tidal tributaries. A moveable barrier across the Thames at Silvertown was completed in 1982 and, with associated bank raising schemes, will provide flood protection against surge tides.

Licensing.—The Council is the licensing authority in Greater London for certain places of entertainment, greyhound race tracks and petroleum installations.

Fire Services.—The Council is the fire authority for its whole area.

The London Fire Brigade set up on April 1, 1965, under the London Government Act, 1963, consists of the Brigades of the former counties of London and Middlesex (excluding the districts of Staines, Sunbury and Potters Bar), the former county boroughs of East Ham, West Ham and Croydon and of parts of Essex, Herts., Kent and Surrey. *Headquarters*, 8 Albert Embankment, S.E.1.

The Brigade has 114 land stations. Wholetime authorized establishment, 7,067. There are 640 firefighting appliances and support vehicles and a new fire-boat was recently commissioned.

Chief Officer, R. A. Bullers, q.f.s.m.
Deputy Chief Officer, G. D. Clarkson.

Finance.—The Greater London Council's original gross budget for 1984–85 (including London Transport Executive) amounts to £3,570 million of which £3,063 million is revenue expenditure (including £1,066 million for the Inner London Education Authority and £741 million for L.T.E.) and £507 million is capital expenditure (£20 million for the Inner London Education Authority and £172 million for L.T.E.).

Revenue expenditure during the year will be met by precept on the London Borough Councils (£1,631 million); income from charges, rents, reimbursements for fees and salaries, sale of balances etc. (£651 million); London Transport fares etc. (£488 million); and by Exchequer grants for certain works and services (£293 million). The Inner London Education Authority determines the amount the Council must precept on the rating authorities in Inner London for education purposes.

Capital expenditure on housing and education and on loans is financed by external borrowing; capital expenditure on all other services is financed internally through a capital fund.

THE CORPORATION OF LONDON

The City of London is the historic centre at the heart of London known as "the square mile" around which the vast metropolis has grown over the centuries. The City's residential population is 5,300 (1981 Census). The civic government is carried on by the Corporation of London through the Court of Common Council, a body consisting of the Lord Mayor, 24 other Aldermen and 136 Common Councilmen. The legal title of the Corporation is "the Mayor and Commonalty and Citizens of the City of London."

The City is the financial and business centre of London and includes the head offices of the principal banks, insurance companies and mercantile houses, in addition to buildings ranging from the historic interest of the Roman Wall and the 15th century Guildhall, to the massive splendour of St. Paul's Cathedral and the architectural beauty of Wren's spires.

The City of London was described by Tacitus in A.D. 62 as "a busy emporium for trade and traders". Under the Romans it became an important administration centre and hub of the road system. Little is known of London in Saxon times when it formed part of the kingdom of the East Saxons. In 886 Alfred recovered London from the Danes and reconstituted it a burgh under his son-in-law. In 1066 the citizens submitted to William the Conqueror who in 1067 granted them a charter, which is still preserved, establishing them in the rights and privileges they had hitherto enjoyed. The mayoralty was established on the recognition of the corporate unity of the citizens by Prince John in 1191, the first Mayor being Henry Fitz Ailwyn who filled the office for 21 years and was succeeded by Fitz Alan (1212–14). A new charter was granted by King John in 1215, directing the Mayor to be chosen annually, which has ever since been done, though in early times the same individual often held the office more than once. A familiar instance is that of "Whittington, thrice Lord Mayor of London" (in reality four times, A.D. 1397, 1398, 1406, 1419); and many modern cases have occurred. The earliest instance of the phrase "Lord Mayor" in English is in 1414. It is used more generally in the latter part of the 15th century and becomes invariable from 1535 onwards. At Michaelmas the Liverymen in Common Hall choose two Aldermen who have served the office of Sheriff for

presentation to the Court of Aldermen, and one is chosen to be Lord Mayor for the ensuing mayoral year. The Lord Mayor is presented to the Lord Chief Justice at the Royal Courts of Justice on the second Saturday in November to make the final declaration of office, having been sworn in at Guildhall on the preceding day. The procession to the Royal Courts of Justice is popularly known as the *Lord Mayor's Show.*

Aldermen are mentioned in the 11th century and their office is of Saxon origin. They were elected annually between 1377 and 1394, when an Act of Parliament of Richard II directed them to be chosen for life. The *Common Council*, elected annually on the first Friday in December, was, at an early date, substituted for a popular assembly called the *Folkmote.* At first only two representatives were sent from each ward, but the number has since been greatly increased.

Sheriffs were Saxon officers: their predecessors were the *wic-reeves* and *portreeves* of London and Middlesex. At first they were officers of the Crown, and were named by the Barons of the Exchequer; but Henry I (in 1132) gave the citizens permission to choose their own Sheriffs, and the annual election of Sheriffs became fully operative under King John's charter of 1199. The citizens lost this privilege, as far as the election of Sheriff of Middlesex is concerned, by the Local Government Act, 1888; but the Liverymen continue, as heretofore, to choose two Sheriffs of the City of London, who are appointed on Midsummer Day, and take office at Michaelmas.

Officers.—The Recorder was first appointed in 1298. The office of Chamberlain is an ancient one, the first contemporary record of which is 1237. The Town Clerk (or Common Clerk) is mentioned in 1274 and the Common Serjeant in 1291.

Activities.—The work is assigned to a number of committees which present reports to the Court of Common Council. These Committees are:—City Lands and Bridge House Estates, Policy and Resources, Coal, Corn and Rates Finance, Planning and Communications, Central Markets, Billingsgate and Leadenhall Markets, Spitalfields Market, Police, Port and City of London Health and Social Services, Library (Library, Records, Art Gallery), Boards of Governors of Schools, Music (Guildhall School of

Music and Drama), Establishment, Housing, Gresham (City side), Epping Forest and Open Spaces, West Ham Park, Privileges, Barbican Residential and Barbican Centre (Barbican Arts and Conference Centre).

The Honourable the *Irish Society*, which manages the Corporation's Estates in Ulster, consists of a Governor and 5 other Aldermen, the Recorder, and 19 Common Councilmen, of whom one is elected Deputy Governor.

The *City's Estate*, in the possession of which the Corporation of London differs from other municipalities, is managed by the City Lands and Bridge House Estates Committee, the Chairmanship of which carries with it the title of "Chief Commoner."

The Right Honourable the Lord Mayor 1984–1985*

Sir Alan Towers Traill, G.B.E., *born* 1935; Alderman of *Langbourn*, 1975; *Sheriff of London*, 1982; *Lord Mayor*, 1984.

Secretary, Rear-Admiral A. J. Cooke, C.B.

Recorder, Sir James Miskin, Q.C., 1975; *Chamberlain*, Bernard Peter Harty, 1983; *Town Clerk*, Geoffrey William Rowley, 1982; *Common Serjeant*, Thomas Herbert Pigott, Q.C., 1984.

The Aldermen

Aldermen	Ward	Born	C.C.	Ald.	Shff.	Lord Mayor
Sir Edward de Coucey Howard, Bt., G.B.E.	Cornhill	1915	1951	1963	1966	1971
Cdr. Sir Robin Danvers Penrose Gillett, Bt., G.B.E., R.D., R.N.R.	Bassishaw	1925	1965	1969	1973	1976
Sir Peter Drury Haggerston Gadsden, G.B.E.	Farringdon Wt.	1929	1969	1971	1970	1979
Col. Sir Ronald Laurence Gardner-Thorpe, G.B.E., T.D.	Bishopsgate	1917	....	1972	1978	1980
Sir Christopher Leaver, G.B.E.	Dowgate	1937	1973	1974	1979	1981
Dame Mary Donaldson, G.B.E.	Coleman St.	1921	1966	1975	1981	1983
Sir Alan Towers Traill, G.B.E.	Langbourn	1935	1970	1975	1982	1984
All the above have passed the Civic Chair						
William Allan Davis	Cripplegate	1921	1971	1976	1982	....
David Kenneth Rowe-Ham	Bridge	1935	....	1976	1984	....
Col. Greville Douglas Spratt, T.D.	Castle Baynard	1927	....	1978	1984	....
Christopher Collett	Broad Street	1931	1973	1979	1985	....
Hugh Charles Philip Bidwell	Billingsgate	1934	....	1979	....	....
Alexander Michael Graham	Queenhithe	1938	1978	1979	....	....
Brian Garton Jenkins	Cordwainer	1935	....	1980	....	....
Francis McWilliams, T.D.	Aldersgate	1926	1978	1980	....	....
Paul Henry Newall, T.D.	Walbrook	1934	1980	1981	....	....
Christopher Rupert Walford	Farringdon Wn.	1935	....	1982	....	....
Roderic Neil Young	Bread Street	1933	1980	1982	....	....
Roger William Cork	Tower	1947	1978	1983	....	....
Brian Edward Toye	Lime Street	1938	....	1983	....	....
Richard Everard Nichols	Candlewick	1938	1983	1984	....	....
Peter Anthony Bull	Cheap	1937	1968	1984	....	....
Peter Keith Levene	Portsoken	1941	1983	1984	....	....
Leonard John Chalstrey	Vintry	1931	1981	1984	....	....
Clive Haydn Martin, O.B.E.	Aldgate	1935	....	1985	....	....

* The Lord Mayor for 1985–86 was elected on Michaelmas Day (*See* "Occurrences During Printing").

The Sheriffs 1985–1986

Christopher Collett (*see above*) and Jack Edward Neary (*see below*), elected July 8; *assumed office* September 27, 1985.

THE COMMON COUNCIL OF LONDON

Allday, P. F. (1972) . . . . *Bishopsgate*
Ballard, K. A., M.C. (1969) . . . . *Castle Baynard*
Balls, *Deputy* H. D. (1970) . . . . *Cripplegate*
Barker, J. A. (1981) . . . . *Cripplegate Wt.*
Beale, M. J. (1949) . . . . *Lime Street*
Begg, M. Henderson (1977) . . . . *Coleman Street*
Bigley, Miss A. F. (1982) . . . . *Cripplegate Wn.*
Bird, J. L. (1977) . . . . *Bridge*
Birkett, *Lt. Col.*, D., M.C. (1983) . . . . . *Aldersgate*
Block, S. A. A. (1983) . . . . *Cheap*
Bramwell, F. M. (1983) . . . . *Langbourn*
Brighton, R. L. (1984) . . . . *Portsoken*
Brooks, W. I. B. (1979) . . . . *Cripplegate Wn.*
Brown, B. J., C.B.E. (1973) . . . . *Aldersgate*
Brown, D. C. G. (1976) . . . . *Aldgate*
Brown, D. T. (1971) . . . . *Walbrook*

Cassidy, M. J. (1980) . . . . *Aldersgate*
Catt, B. F. (1982) . . . . *Farringdon Wn.*
Challis, G. H. (1978) . . . . *Langbourn*
Champness, *Deputy* P. H. (1966) . . . . . *Walbrook*
Chandler, E. G., C.B.E. (1982) . . . . *Cornhill*
Clements, *Deputy* G. E. I. (1960) . . . . *Farringdon Wt.*
Cohen, J. M. (1980) . . . . *Queenhithe*
Cohen, *Deputy* S E., C.B.E. (1951) . . . . *Farringdon Wt.*
Cole, *Lt.-Col.*, Sir Colin, K.C.V.O., T.D. (1964) . . . . *Castle Baynard*
Colover, D. (1975). . . . . *Bishopsgate*
Cope, Dr. J. (1963) . . . . *Farringdon Wt.*
Coven, *Deputy* Mrs. E. O. (1972) . . . . . *Dowgate*
Daltrey, D. H. J. (1973) . . . . *Billingsgate*
David, C. P. (1984) . . . . *Aldgate*
Deith, R. C. (1944) . . . . *Farringdon Wn.*

Delderfield, D. W. (1982) . . . . *Aldersgate*
Denny, A. M. (1971) . . . . *Billingsgate*
De Silva, (1980) . . . . *Farringdon Wt.*
Dewhirst, *Deputy* W. (1971) . . . . *Cripplegate*
Donnelly, T. A., M.B.E. (1982) . . . . *Bread Street*
Duckworth, *Deputy* H. C.B.E. (1960) . *Lime St.*
Durand, Mrs. B. J. (1975) . . . . *Farringdon Wt.*
Durnin, J. C. (1976) . . . . *Cordwainer*
Edwards, R. D. K. (1978) . . . . *Bassishaw*
Eskenzi, A. N. (1971) . . . . *Farringdon Wn.*
Evans, Mrs. J. (1975) . . . . *Farringdon Wt.*
Eve, R. A. (1980) . . . . *Cheap*
Ewin, *Deputy* Sir David Floyd-,
  M.V.O., C.B.E. (1963) . . . . *Castle Baynard*
Falk, F. A. (1984) . . . . *Farringdon Wt.*
Farrow, M. W. W. (1983) . . . . *Cripplegate*
Farthing, R. B. C. (1981) . . . . *Aldgate*
Fell, J. A. (1982) . . . . *Queenhithe*
Fisher, *Deputy* D. G. (1958) . . . . *Cornhill*
Fitzgerald, R. C. A. (1981) . . . . *Bread Street*
Frappell, C. E. (1973) . . . . *Bread St.*
Fraser, W. B. (1981) . . . . *Vintry*
Galloway, A. D. (1981) . . . . *Bread Street*
Gass, *Deputy* G. J. (1967) . . . . *Coleman St.*
Gold, R. (1965) . . . . *Castle Baynard*
Gordon, Miss C. F. (1978) . . . . *Cripplegate Wn.*
Gugan, K., ph.D. (1974) . . . . *Dowgate*
Harding, N. H. (1970) . . . . *Farringdon Wn.*
Harris, R. P. (1980) . . . . *Cripplegate.*
Harris, W. H. Wylie (1957) . . . . *Farringdon Wn.*
Hart, *Deputy* M. G. (1970) . . . . *Bridge*
Hatfield, A. F. R. (1968) . . . . *Bishopsgate*
Henderson, *Deputy* J. S. (1975) . . . . . *Langbourn*
Holland, *Deputy* J. (1972) . . . . *Aldgate*
Horlock, *Deputy* H. W. S. (1969) . . . . *Farringdon Wn.*
Howard, D. H. S. (1973) . . . . *Cornhill*
Humphrays, Mrs. R. (1976) . . . . *Cripplegate*
Ide, W. R. (1972) . . . . *Castle Baynard*
Jackson, L. St. J. T. (1978) . . . . *Bassishaw*
James, A. J. (1973) . . . . *Cordwainer*
James, J. F. (1977) . . . . *Farringdon Wt.*
Jenks, M. A. B. (1972) . . . . *Coleman St.*
Kemp, D. L. (1984) . . . . *Coleman St.*
Knowles, S. K. (1984) . . . . *Candlewick*
Langmead, A. D. G., T.D. (1982) . . . . . *Tower*
Laurie, P. D. Northall- (1975) . . . . *Walbrook*
Lawson, G. C. H. (1972) . . . . *Portsoken*
Lawrence, D. W. O. (1979) . . . . *Bridge*
Liss, *Deputy* H. (1965) . . . . *Aldersgate*
Luke, A. L. (1968) . . . . *Bishopsgate*
McAuley, *Deputy*, C. (1957) . . . . *Bread St.*
McNeil, I. D. (1977) . . . . *Lime Street*
Malins, J. H. (1981) . . . . *Farringdon Wt.*
Mills, A. P. (1969) . . . . *Bassishaw*

Mitchell, C. R. (1972) . . . . *Castle Baynard*
Mizen, *Deputy* D. H. (1979) . . . . *Broad Street*
Morgan, *Deputy* B. L., C.B.E. (1963) . . *Bishopsgate*
Murkin, *Deputy* C. H., O.B.E. (1969) . . *Vintry*
Nash, Mrs. J. C. (1983) . . . . *Aldersgate*
Neary, J. E. (1982) . . . . *Aldgate*
Newby, J. (1982) . . . . *Lime Street*
Oliver, J. M. Y. (1980) . . . . *Bishopsgate*
Olson, A. H. F. (1972) . . . . *Dowgate*
Oram, *Deputy* M. H., T.D. (1963) . . . . *Cordwainer*
Owen, Mrs. J. (1975) . . . . *Langbourn*
Owen-Ward, J. R. (1983) . . . . *Bridge*
Packard, Brig. J. J. (1973) . . . . *Cripplegate*
Peacock, R. W., C.B.E. (1956) . . . . *Vintry*
Pearson, T. A. S. (1979) . . . . *Queenhithe*
Pembroke, *Deputy* Mrs. A. M. F.
  (1978) . . . . *Cheap*
Ponsonby of Shulbrede, The Lady
  (1981) . . . . *Farringdon Wt.*
Prince, *Deputy* L. B., C.B.E. (1950) . . . *Bishopsgate*
Pulman, G. A. (1983) . . . . *Tower*
Ratner, R. A., T.D. (1981) . . . . *Broad Street*
Reed, E. J. (1978) . . . . *Tower*
Reed, *Deputy* J. L., M.B.E. (1967) . . . . . *Farringdon Wn.*
Rigby, P. P. (1972) . . . . *Farringdon Wn.*
Rodgers, S. C. (1969) . . . . *Farringdon Wt.*
Rogers, Miss E. H. L. (1982) . . . . *Cornhill*
Roney, *Deputy* E. P. T. (1974) . . . . *Bishopsgate*
Rowlandson, Sir Graham, M.B.E.
  (1961) . . . . *Coleman Street*
Samuel, *Deputy* Mrs. I. (1972) . . . . *Portsoken*
Saunders, *Deputy* R. (1975) . . . . *Candlewick*
Savory, M. B. (1980) . . . . *Broad Street*
Scriven, R. G. (1984) . . . . *Candlewick*
Shalit, D. M. (1973) . . . . *Farringdon Wn.*
Sharp, *Deputy* Mrs. I. M. (1974) . . . . . *Queenhithe*
Sheppard, S., O.B.E. (1957) . . . . *Billingsgate*
Shindler, *Deputy* A. B. (1966) . . . . *Billingsgate*
Silk, D. (1979) . . . . *Cripplegate*
Smith, P. A. Revell- (1959) . . . . *Vintry*
Spanner, J. H. T.D. (1984) . . . . *Broad St*
Spurrier, H. J. (1974) . . . . *Dowgate*
Stevenson, J. L. (1970) . . . . *Coleman Street*
Stitcher, G. M., C.B.E. (1966) . . . . *Farringdon Wt.*
Sunderland, O., T.D. (1968) . . . . *Billingsgate*
Turner, *Deputy* R. L. (1973) . . . . *Tower*
Welch, Sir John, Bt. (1975) . . . . *Walbrook*
Wilmot, R. T. D. (1973) . . . . *Cordwainer*
Wilson, *Deputy* A. B. (1960) . . . . *Aldersgate*
Wilson, E. S. (1979) . . . . *Aldersgate*
Wixley, *Deputy* G. R. A., C.B.E., T.D.
  (1964) . . . . *Bassishaw*
Woodward, C. D. (1972) . . . . *Cripplegate*

Deputies.—In the preceding list each Common Councilman so described serves as *Deputy* to the Alderman of his Ward.

FREEMEN'S GUILDS

London.—Guild of Freemen of the City of London, 4 Dowgate Hill, EC4M 7DE. *Clerk*, D. Reid.

Berwick upon Tweed.—Freemen's Guild of Berwick upon Tweed. *Sec.*, J. R. Reay, 9 Church Street.

Chester.—Freemen and Guilds of the City of Chester. The Guildhall, Chester.

Coventry.—City of Coventry Freemen's Guild. *Hon. Clerk.*, H. J. McCranor, 89 Brinklow Road, Binley, Coventry, CV3 2JB.

Grimsby.—Enrolled Freemen of Grimsby. *Clerk*, W. J. Savage, St. Mary's Chambers, Grimsby.

Lincoln.—Lincoln Freemen's Committee. *Clerk*, A. J. Gadd, 45 Skellingthorpe Road, Lincoln.

Newcastle upon Tyne.—Gild of Freemen of the City of Newcastle upon Tyne. *Hon. Sec.*, G. T. Henzell, 8 Leyburn Drive, High Heaton, Newcastle-upon-Tyne, NE7 7AP.

Oxford.—Oxford Freemen's Committee. *Sec.*, C. R. Butterfield, 126 High Street, Oxford, OX1 4DG

Shrewsbury.—Association of Shrewsbury Freemen, *Hon. Sec.* D. Morris, 7 Canonbury, Kingsland, Shrewsbury.

York.—Gild of Freemen of the City of York. *Hon. Clerk*, Mrs. J. Steel, 9 Spalding Avenue, Clifton, York.

THE CITY GUILDS (LIVERY COMPANIES)

The Livery Companies of the City of London derive their name from the assumption of a distinctive dress or livery by their members in the 14th century.

The order of precedence (according to 2nd Report of Municipal Corporations' Commissioners, 1837), omitting extinct companies, is given in parentheses after the name of each Company.

About 20,400 Liverymen of the Guilds are entitled to vote at elections in *Common Hall.*

MERCERS *(1). Hall,* Ironmonger Lane, EC2V 8HE. *Livery,* 220.—*Clerk,* G. M. M. Wakeford; *Master,* C. S. Clayton.

GROCERS *(2). Hall,* Princes Street, EC2R 8AQ. *Livery,* 320.—*Clerk,* C. P. G. Chavasse; *Master,* A. P. Sparks.

DRAPERS *(3). Hall,* Throgmorton Street, EC2N 2DQ. *Livery,* 230.—*Clerk,* R. C. G. Strick; *Master,* D. G. Stern.

FISHMONGERS *(4). Hall,* London Bridge, EC4R 9EL. *Livery,* 296.—*Clerk,* E. S. Earl; *Prime Warden,* Maj.-Gen. The Duke of Norfolk, K.G., C.B., C.B.E., M.C.

GOLDSMITHS *(5). Hall,* Foster Lane, EC2V 6BN. *Livery,* 260.—*Clerk,* C. P. de B. Jenkins, M.B.E., M.C.; *Prime Warden,* Prof. E. T. Hall.

SKINNERS *(6* and *7). Hall,* 8 Dowgate Hill, EC4R 2SP. *Livery,* 370.—*Clerk,* M. H. Glover; *Master,* M. C. Cowdrey, C.B.E.

MERCHANT TAYLORS *(6* and *7). Hall,* 30 Threadneedle Street, EC2R 8AY. *Livery* 328.—*Clerk,* A. T. Langdon-Down; *Master,* Rt. Hon. Lord Newall.

HABERDASHERS *(8). Hall,* Staining Lane, EC2V 7DD. *Livery,* 320.—*Clerk,* Capt. M. E. Barrow, D.S.O., R.N.; *Master,* M. W. D. Northcott

SALTERS *(9). Hall,* Fore Street, EC2Y 5DE. *Livery,* 158.—*Clerk,* J. M. Montgomery; *Master,* Maj. Lord Robertson of Oakridge.

IRONMONGERS *(10). Hall,* Barbican, EC2Y 8AA. *Livery,* 99.—*Clerk,* R. B. Brayne, M.B.E.; *Master,* Hon. Patrick Best.

VINTNERS *(11). Hall,* Upper Thames Street, EC4V 3BE. *Livery,* 319.—*Clerk,* Brig. G. Read, C.B.E. *Master,* A. L. Davies.

CLOTHWORKERS *(12). Hall,* Dunster Court, Mincing Lane, EC3R 7AH. *Livery,* 185.—*Clerk,* C. M. Mowll; *Master,* P. M. Luttman-Johnson.

The above are the Twelve "Great" London Companies in order of Civic precedence.

ACCOUNTANTS *(86). Livery,* 327.—*Clerk,* O. Sunderland, T.D., Shelley House, 3 Noble Street, EC2V 7DQ; *Master,* Sir Kenneth Cork, G.B.E.

ACTUARIES *(91). Livery,* 119.—*Clerk,* A. K. Tudor, 8 Madgeways Close, Great Amwell, Herts., SG12 9RU; *Master,* J. R. Haigh.

AIR PILOTS AND AIR NAVIGATORS, GUILD OF *(81). Livery,* 400.—*Grand Master,* H.R.H. the Prince Philip, Duke of Edinburgh, K.G.; *Clerk,* Cpl P. Wilson, 30 Eccleston Square, S.W.1; *Master,* T. W. Brooke-Smith.

APOTHECARIES, SOCIETY OF *(58). Hall,* Black Friars Lane, EC4V 6EJ. *Livery,* 1,100.—*Clerk,* Maj. J. C. O'Leary; *Master,* Prof. J. A. Dudgeon.

ARBITRATORS *(93). Livery,* 160.—*Clerk,* B. W. Vigrass, O.B.E., V.R.D., 75 Cannon Street, EC4N 5BH; *Master,* F. McWilliams.

ARMOURERS AND BRASIERS *(22). Hall,* 81 Coleman Street, EC2R 5BJ. *Livery,* 120.—*Clerk,* Lt. Col. R. R. F. Cowe; *Master,* Dr. R. M. S. Perrin.

BAKERS *(19). Hall,* Harp Lane, Lower Thames Street, E.C.3. *Livery,* 360.—*Clerk,* P. F. Wilson, D.F.C.; *Master,* H. M. Joseph.

BARBERS *(17). Hall,* Monkwell Square, E.C.2. *Livery,* 178.—*Clerk,* B. W. Hall, *Master,* P. Lambert.

BASKETMAKERS *(52). Livery,* 500.—*Clerk,* D. J. Farrier, 5 The Spinney, Warren Road, Purley, CR2 1AB; *Prime Warden,* E. Darlow.

BLACKSMITHS *(40). Livery,* 250.—*Clerk,* J. Green, 280 Balham High Road, SW17 7AL; *Prime Warden,* A. W. Pennington.

BOWYERS *(38). Livery,* 92.—*Clerk,* A. Black, 2 Serjeants' Inn, Fleet Street, EC4Y 1LL; *Master,* B. MacDermot.

BREWERS *(14). Hall,* Aldermanbury Square, EC2V 7HR. *Livery,* 113.—*Clerk,* Rr. Adm. M. L. Wemyss, C.B; *Master,* J. S. Fox.

BRODERERS *(48). Livery,* 100.—*Clerk,* S. G. B. Underwood, 11A Bridge Road, East Molesey, KT8 9EY; *Master,* J. F. Tearle.

BUILDERS MERCHANTS *(88). Livery,* 200.—*Clerk,* A. G. P. Lincoln, M.C., T.D. 128 Queen Victoria Street, E.C.4; *Master,* J. S. Faulder.

BUTCHERS *(24). Hall,* 87 Bartholomew Close, EC1A 7EB. *Livery,* 650.—*Clerk,* Cmdr. P. B. Cowan, R.N.; *Master,* D. L. Franks.

CARMEN *(77). Livery,* 433.—*Clerk,* Lt. Col. G. T. Pearce, M.B.E., St. Olave's Rectory, 8 Hart Street, EC3R 7NB; *Master,* O. Sunderland, T.D..

CARPENTERS *(26). Hall,* 1 Throgmorton Avenue, EC2N 2JJ. *Livery,* 150.—*Clerk,* Capt. K. G. Hamon, R.N.; *Master,* A. T. C. Binny.

CITY OF LONDON SOLICITORS *(79). Livery,* 413.—*Clerk,* E. C. Robbins, 13–14 Charterhouse Square, EC1M 6AX; *Master,* E. P. T. Roney.

CLOCKMAKERS *(61). Livery,* 281.—*Clerk,* Air Cdre. B. G. Frow, D.S.O, D.F.C., 2 Greycoat Place, SW1P 1SD; *Master,* Sir Charles Ball.

COACHMAKERS *(72). Livery,* 405.—*Clerk,* Maj. W. H. Wharfe, R.M., 149 Banstead Road, Ewell, Epsom. KT17 3HL; *Master,* R. D. C. Dallimore

COOKS *(35). Livery,* 75.—*Clerk,* H. J. Lavington, T.D. 49 Queen Victoria Street, E.C.4.

COOPERS *(36). Hall,* 13 Devonshire Square, EC2M 4TH. *Livery,* 255.—*Clerk,* J. A. Newton; *Master,* Rev. F. S. Skelton, D.S.O., D.F.C.

CORDWAINERS *(27). Livery* 136.—Clerk, Capt. C. T. Codrington, 30 Fleet Street, EC4Y 1AA; *Master,* M. O. Skinner.

CURRIERS *(29). Livery,* 85.—*Clerk,* I. R. McNeil, 43 Church Road, Hove, BN3 2BT; *Master,* F. Allen.

CUTLERS *(18). Hall,* 4 Warwick Lane, EC4M 7BR. *Livery,* 110.—*Clerk,* K. S. G. Hinde; *Master,* D. Randolph.

DISTILLERS *(69). Livery,* 210.—*Clerk,* B. Dehn, 1 Vintners Place, E.C.4; *Master,* T. N. Ritchie, T.D.

DYERS *(13). Hall,* 11–13 Dowgate Hill, EC4R 2ST. *Livery,* 134.—*Clerk,* J. R. Chambers; *Prime Warden,* R. T. S. MacPherson.

ENGINEERS *(94). Livery,* 300.—*Clerk,* M. W. Leonard, C.V.O., 2 Little Smith Street, SW1P 3DL; *Master,* Sir Denis Rooke, C.B.E.

FAN MAKERS *(76). Livery,* 217.—*Clerk,* R. Southcombe, Ludgate House, 107–111 Fleet Street, EC4A 2AB; *Master,* S. J. Shelton.

FARMERS *(80). Livery,* 294.—*Clerk,* I. G. Williamson. 7/8 King's Bench Walk, Temple, EC4Y 7DT; *Master,* C. T. Muddiman.

FARRIERS *(55). Livery,* 375.—*Clerk,* H. W. H. Ellis, 37 The Uplands, Loughton, Essex, IG10 1NQ; *Master,* H.R.H. The Princess Anne, Mrs. Mark Phillips, G.C.V.O.

FELTMAKERS *(63). Livery,* 350.—*Clerk,* E. J. P. Elliott, 53 Davies Street, Berkeley Square, W1Y 2BL; *Master,* D. Watling.

FLETCHERS *(39). Livery,* 110.—*Clerk,* J. R. Garnett, 118 Old Broad Street, EC2N 1AR; *Master,* D. J. Eldridge.

FOUNDERS *(33). Hall,* 13 St. Swithin's Lane, EC4N 8AL. *Livery,* 165.—*Clerk,* H. Wilson Wiley; *Master,* N. C. Crighton.

FRAMEWORK KNITTERS (64). *Livery*, 225.—*Clerk*, H. C. Weale, 51 Dulwich Wood Avenue, SE19 1HG; *Master*, H. R. Ellis.

FRUITERERS (45). *Livery*, 268.—*Clerk*, Mrs. Pauline Halliday, 19 Woburn Place, WC1H 0LU; *Master*, M. W. Mack.

FURNITURE MAKERS (83). *Livery*, 238.—*Clerk*, Wg.-Cdr. G. Acklam, M.B.E., 30 Harcourt Street, W1H 2AA; *Master*, D. B. Ercolani.

GARDENERS (66). *Livery*, 250.—*Clerk*, P. de V. Rudolph, Inigo Place, 31 Bedford Street, WC2E 9EH; *Master*, W. P. Maclagan.

GIRDLERS (23). *Hall*, Basinghall Avenue, E.C.2. *Livery*, 80.—*Clerk*, P. H. White.

GLASS-SELLERS (71). *Livery*, 180.—*Hon. Clerk*, P. J. Willoughby, 25 New Street Square, EC4A 3LN; *Master*, D. Williams-Thomas.

GLAZIERS (53). *Livery*, 300.—*Clerk*, R. B. Hodgetts, Glaziers Hall, 9 Montague Close, London Bridge, S.E.1; *Master*, Sir William Carter.

GLOVERS (62). *Livery*, 300.—*Clerk*, Capt. D. G. F. Palmer, O.B.E., Glovers, Tismans Common, Rudgwick, W. Sussex, RH12 3DU; *Master*, F. W. Caine

GOLD AND SILVER WYREDRAWERS (74). *Livery*, 350.—*Clerk*, D. Reid, P.O. Box 153, 40a Ludgate Hill, EC4M 7DE; *Master*, R. W. E. Payne.

GUNMAKERS (73). *Livery*, 200.—*Clerk*, F. B. Brandt, 12 Devonshire Square, E.C.2.

HORNERS (54). *Livery*, 430.—*Clerk*, Dr. E. M. Hunt, 11 Hobart Place, SW1W 0HL; *Master*, M. G. Spofforth.

INNHOLDERS (32). *Hall*, College Street, Dowgate Hill, E.C.4. *Livery*, 107.—*Clerk*, J.R. Edwardes Jones.

INSURERS (92). *Livery*, 271.—*Clerk*, V. D. Webb, The Hall, 20 Aldermanbury, EC2V 7HY; *Master*, F. R. D. Holland.

JOINERS (41). *Livery*, 117.—*Clerk*, D. A. Tate, Parkville House, Bridge Street, Pinner, HA5 3JD; *Master*, A. Stevens.

LAUNDERERS (89). *Livery*, 180.—*Clerk*, W. E. Kingsland, 34 Broadhurst, Ashtead, Surrey, KT21 1QD; *Master*, R. Le Poidevin.

LEATHERSELLERS (15). *Hall*, 15 St. Helens Place, EC3A 6DQ. *Livery*, 150.—*Clerk*, Capt. C. N. MacEacharn, C.B.E., R.N.; *Master*, A. W. Russell.

LORINERS (57). *Livery*, 352.—*Clerk*, J. R. Williams, 2/5 Benjamin Street, EC1M 5QL; *Master*, R. A. J. Bowman.

MARKETORS (90). *Livery*, 142.—*Clerk*, B. F. Catt, 29 Queen Street, EC4R 1BH; *Master*, C. Austin Nunn.

MASONS (30). *Livery*, 111.—*Clerk*, H. J. Maddocks, 9 New Square, WC2A 3QN; *Master*, E. H. Turner.

MASTER MARINERS, HONOURABLE COMPANY OF (78). H.Q.S. *Wellington*, Temple Stairs, WC2R 2PN. *Livery*, 300.—*Clerk*, D. H. W. Field; *Admiral*, H.R.H. the Duke of Edinburgh, K.G.; *Master*, Capt. C. F. Vine, R.N.R..

MUSICIANS (50). *Livery*, 260.—*Clerk*, W. R. I. Crewdson, 4 St. Paul's Churchyard, E.C.4; *Master*, J. S. P. Morley.

NEEDLEMAKERS (65). *Livery*, 230.—*Clerk*, M. G. Cook, 4 Staple Inn, WC1V 7QW; *Master*, J. A. Miller.

PAINTER STAINERS (28). *Hall*, 9 Little Trinity Lane, EC4V 2AD. *Livery*, 400.—*Clerk*, A. G. P. Lincoln, M.C., T.D.; *Master* E. A. Osorio.

PATTERNMAKERS (70). *Livery*, 250.—*Clerk*, A. J. Hucker, 6 Raymond Bldgs., Gray's Inn, WC1R 5BZ; *Master*, A. J. Hucker.

PAVIORS (56). *Livery*, 250.—*Clerk*, R. F. Coe, Cutlers' Hall, Warwick Lane, EC4M 7BR; *Master*, D. J. Hodges.

PEWTERERS. (16). *Hall*, Oat Lane, EC2V 7DE. *Livery*, 110.—*Clerk*, Maj. J. M. Halford, R.M.; *Master*, Sir Geoffrey Peacock, C.V.O.

PLAISTERERS (46). *Hall*, 1 London Wall, EC2Y 5JU. *Livery*, 193.—*Clerk*, H. Mott; *Master*, D. L. Robinson.

PLAYING CARD MAKERS (75). *Livery*, 149.—*Clerk*, M. J. Smyth, 1 Serjeants' Inn, Fleet Street, EC4Y 1JD; *Master*, P. A. Simkins.

PLUMBERS (31). *Livery*, 279.—*Clerk*, Col. E. M. P. Hardy, Ironmongers Hall, Barbican, EC2Y 8AA; *Master*, M. B. Caroe.

POULTERS (34). *Livery*, 164.—*Clerk*, I. G. Williamson, 7–8 King's Bench Walk, Temple, EC4Y 7DT; *Master*, H. Duckworth.

SADDLERS (25). *Hall*, Gutter Lane, Cheapside, EC2V 6BR. *Livery*, 90.—*Clerk*, Gp. Capt. K. M. Oliver, R.A.F. (retd.); *Master*, T. P. Salisbury.

SCIENTIFIC INSTRUMENT MAKERS (84). *Livery*, 213.—*Clerk*, Maj. Gen. E. Younson, O.B.E., 9 Montague Close, SE1 9DD; *Master*, G. G. Zahler O.B.E.

SCRIVENERS (44).—*Clerk*, H. J. W. Harman, Chancery House, 53/64 Chancery Lane, W.C.2; *Master*, J. P. B. Brook-Little.

SECRETARIES AND ADMINISTRATORS (87). *Livery*, 223.—*Hon. Clerk*, G. H. Challis, The Irish Chamber, Guildhall Yard, EC2V 5AE; *Master*, R. M. Clarke.

SHIPWRIGHTS (59). *Livery*, 500.—*Clerk*, C. H. Baylis, C.B., Ironmongers' Hall, Barbican, EC2Y 8AA; *Permanent Master*, H.R.H. the Duke of Edinburgh, K.G., K.T.; *Prime Warden*, R. C. L. Charvet.

SPECTACLEMAKERS (60). *Livery*, 303.—*Clerk*, C. J. Eldridge, Apothecaries' Hall, EC4V 6EL.

STATIONERS AND NEWSPAPER MAKERS (47). *Hall*, Stationers' Hall, Ave Maria Lane, Ludgate Hill, EC4M 7DD. *Livery*, 450.—*Clerk*, Capt. P. Hames, R.N.; *Master*, R. S. Tindle, O.B.E.

SURVEYORS (85). *Livery*, 310.—*Clerk*, W. J. Preston, 12 Great George Street, Parliament Square, SW1P 3AD; *Master*, R. W. P. Luff.

TALLOWCHANDLERS (21). *Hall*, 4 Dowgate Hill, EC4R 2SH. *Livery*, 174.—*Clerk*, Col. M. ff. Woodhead, O.B.E.; *Master*, Lt. Col. T. A. Donnelly, M.B.E.

TIN PLATE WORKERS (67). *Livery*, 209.—*Clerk*, A. Hill, 71 Lincolns Inn Fields, WC2A 3JF; *Master*, D. W. Llewellyn, O.B.E.

TOBACCO PIPE MAKERS AND TOBACCO BLENDERS (82). *Livery*, 185.—*Clerk*, I. J. Kimmins, Bouverie House, 154 Fleet Street, EC4A 2HX; *Master*, G. E. S. Widdowson.

TURNERS (51). *Livery*, 170.—*Clerk*, N. M. A. Evelegh, 1 Serjeants' Inn, EC4Y 1JD; *Master*, Sir David Pryke, Bt.

TYLERS AND BRICKLAYERS (37). *Livery*, 124.—*Clerk*, F. A. G. Rider, 6 Bedford Row, WC1R 4DQ; *Master*, J. B. F. Mathews.

UPHOLDERS (49). *Livery*, 200.—*Clerk*, R. C. H. Twyford, 1 Leathermarket, Weston Street SE1 3ER; *Master*, S. A. G. Rust.

WAX CHANDLERS (20). *Hall*, Gresham Street, EC2V 7AD. *Livery*, 100.—*Clerk*, T. Wood.

WEAVERS (42). *Livery*, 125.—*Clerk*, J. G. Ouvry, 1 The Sanctuary, SW1P 3JT; *Upper Bailiff*, O. A. E. J. Makower.

WHEELWRIGHTS (68). *Livery*, 268.—*Clerk*, M. R. Francis, Greenup, Milton Avenue, Gerrards Cross, Bucks., SL9 8QW; *Master*, R. H. Gould.

WOOLMEN (43). *Livery*, 145.—*Clerk*, R. J. R. Cousins, 3rd Floor, 192–198 Vauxhall Bridge Rd., SW1V 1HF; *Master*, P. Gilbert.

PARISH CLERKS (No livery) (Brethren, 100).—*Clerk*, R. H. Adams, T.D., F.S.A., 14 Dale Close, Oxford, OX1 1TU; *Master*, A. H. Green.

WATERMEN AND LIGHTERMEN (No livery. Craft Owning Freemen, 272).—*Hall*, 18 St. Mary-at-Hill, EC3R 8EE.—*Clerk*, W. B. G. Wilson; *Master*, D. J. Piper.

ENVIRONMENTAL CLEANERS.—*Hall*, Mark Lane, E.C.3.—*Clerk*, E. W. Hill, T.D.; *Master*, D. G. Wells.

NOTE.—In certain companies the election of Master or Prime Warden for the year does not take place till the autumn. In such cases the Master or Prime Warden for 1984–85 is given.

LONDON AND ITS ENVIRONS

(For National Art Galleries and Museums in London and for London Cathedrals, Churches, etc. see Index.)

Adelphi, Strand, W.C.2.—Adelphi Terrace and district commemorate the four Adam brothers, James, John, Robert and William, who laid out the district (formerly Durham House) at the close of the 18th century, though few 18th century buildings now remain. Four of the streets were formerly called after the brothers but are now Adam Street, John Adam Street, Robert Street and Durham House Street. In the neighbourhood of the Adelphi was York House, built by the Duke of Buckingham in 1625 (the Water Gate of which still stands in Embankment Gardens), the commemorative streets being *Charles* Street, *Villiers* Street, *Duke* Street, *Buckingham* Street.

Alexandra Palace and Park, Muswell Hill, N.10.—Set in a park of 200 acres, the second Palace was completed in 1875 at a cost of £400,000. Although it suffered severe damage from a fire in July 1980 plans for restoration include the provision of facilities for exhibitions, concerts, sport and leisure activities. Meanwhile, events continue in the ALEXANDRA PAVILION adjacent to the Palace. Trusteeship of the Palace devolved onto the G.L.C. in 1965, who passed it to Haringey Council on Jan. 1, 1980.

Baltic Exchange, St. Mary Axe, E.C.3.—The world market for the chartering of cargo ships. The present Exchange was built in 1903 and the new wing opened by H.M. The Queen on Nov. 21, 1956.

Bank of England, Threadneedle Street, E.C.2. (Not open to the public)—The Bank of England, founded in 1694, has always been closely connected with the Government. The present building, completed in 1940 to the designs of Sir Herbert Baker, incorporates features reminiscent of the earlier architects, Sampson (1734), Sir Robert Taylor (1765) and Sir John Soane (1788).

Banqueting House, Whitehall, S.W.1.—The only important building left of the great Palace of Whitehall. The previous banqueting house was burnt down in 1619, and replaced by the present structure designed by Inigo Jones. In 1635 it was enriched with Rubens' ceiling paintings. Charles I was executed on a scaffold set up just in front of the present entrance. Open, Tues.–Sat., 10–5; Sun., 2–5. Closed Mons. Admission (1984), 50p; children and O.A.P.s 25p.

Barbican Arts Centre, EC2Y 8DS.—Owned, funded and managed by the Corporation of London, the Barbican Centre was opened on 3 March 1982 by H.M. The Queen, and is the largest complex of its kind in Western Europe. It houses the 1,166 seat Barbican Theatre, now the London base of the Royal Shakespeare Company along with a smaller 200 seat studio theatre (The Pit), and the 2,026 seat Barbican Hall for concerts by the London Symphony Orchestra. There are also three cinemas, an art gallery, a sculpture court and a large lending library, in addition to facilities for trade exhibitions and conferences, as well as bars and restaurants.

Bridges.—The bridges over the Thames (from East to West) are the *Tower Bridge* (built by the Corporation of London and opened in 1894), with its bascules, operated now by new electrically-run machinery. The walkway was opened to the public in 1982 and a museum in 1983. *London Bridge* (opened after rebuilding in 1831 by Rennie; the new London Bridge was completed in 1973 and opened by H.M. The Queen on March 16, 1973); *Southwark Bridge* (opened in 1819, also by Rennie; rebuilt by the Corporation of London, 1922); *Blackfriars Bridge* (opened in 1769, rebuilt, 1869, and widened by the Corporation of London in 1909); *Waterloo Bridge*

(Rennie), opened in 1817, commanding a fine view of western London, rebuilt by L.C.C. and reopened 1944; *Hungerford Bridge*, 1863 (railway bridge with a footbridge); *Westminster Bridge* (built in 1750 and then presenting a view that inspired Wordsworth's sonnet; rebuilt and re-opened in 1862; width, 84 ft.) with Thomas Thornycroft's *Boadicea* at the north-eastern end; this bridge leads from Westminster Abbey and the Houses of Parliament to the County Hall and St. Thomas's Hospital; *Lambeth Bridge* (built 1862, rebuilt 1932) leading from Lambeth Palace to Millbank; *Vauxhall Bridge* (built in 1811–16, rebuilt in 1906), leading to Kennington Oval; *Chelsea Bridge*, leading from Chelsea Hospital to Battersea Park (reconstructed and widened; 1937) and *Albert Bridge* (1873); *Battersea Bridge* (opened in 1890); *Wandsworth Bridge* opened in 1873; rebuilt and re-opened in 1940); *Putney Bridge* (built 1729, rebuilt 1884, widened in 1933), where the Oxford and Cambridge Boat Race is started for Mortlake; *Hammersmith Bridge* (rebuilt 1887); *Barnes Bridge* (for pedestrians only, 1933); *Chiswick Bridge* (opened in 1933); *King Edward VII Bridge, Kew* (rebuilt in 1902, opened 1903), leading to the Royal Botanic Gardens, Kew; *Twickenham Lock Bridge; Twickenham Bridge* (opened 1933); *Richmond Bridge* (opened in 1777); *Kingston Bridge* (built 1828 and widened 1914) and *Hampton Court Bridge* (rebuilt, 1933).

Buckingham Palace, St. James's Park, S.W.1. (Not open to the public.)—Purchased by King George III in 1762 from the heir of the Duke of Buckingham, the Palace has been the London home of the Sovereign since Queen Victoria's accession in 1837. It was altered by Nash for King George IV, and refronted in stone (part of the Queen Victoria Memorial) by Sir Aston Webb in 1913.

The Queen's Gallery, containing a changing selection of the finest pictures and works of art from all parts of the royal collection, was opened to the public on July 25, 1962. Open: Tues.–Sat., and Bank Holidays 11–5 p.m.; Sundays. 2–5 p.m. Admission charges are payable, entering from Buckingham Palace Road.

The Royal Mews is open to visitors on Weds. and Thurs. throughout the year (except in Ascot Week), 2–4 p.m. Admission charges, the net proceeds of which are devoted to charities, are payable at the entrance.

Canada House, Trafalgar Square, S.W.1.—Designed by Sir Robert Smirke and built in 1824–7, it underwent major alterations to incorporate the former Royal College of Physicians building, also by Smirke, between 1964–67. Certain interior features of the original building, now housing the Canadian High Commission, are preserved including the spacious, richly furnished room now occupied by the High Commissioner.

Canonbury Tower, Canonbury, N.1.—The largest remaining part of a 16th-century house originally built by the Priors of St. Bartholomew, and since 1952 used as the headquarters of a non-professional theatre company. Contains the "Spencer" and "Compton" oak-panelled rooms. Other relics of Canonbury House can be seen nearby.

Carlyle's House, 24 Cheyne Row, Chelsea, S.W.3. The home of Thomas Carlyle for 47 years until his death in 1881, and containing many of his effects. Now the property of the National Trust. Open daily, except Mons., Tues. 11–5, from April 1–Oct. 31. Admission £1·20; children 60p.

Catholic Central Library, St. Francis Friary, 47 Francis Street, S.W.1.—Founded as a private library in 1914, it was taken over in 1959 by the Franciscan Friars of the Atonement. It is an up-to-date lending and research library of over 55,000 volumes, 150 periodicals, for the general reader, student and ecumenist. Books are sent by post when required. Hours of opening: Mon.-Fri. 10-5; Sat. 10-1.30.

Cemeteries.—In *Kensal Green Cemetery*, North Kensington, W.10 (70 acres), are tombs of W. M. Thackeray, Anthony Trollope, Sydney Smith, Shirley Brooks, Wilkie Collins, Tom Hood, W. Mulready, George Cruikshank, John Leech, Leigh Hunt, Brunel ("Great Eastern"), Ross (Arctic), Charles Kemble and Charles Mathews (actors). In *Highgate Cemetery*, N.6, are the tombs of George Eliot, Herbert Spencer, Michael Faraday, Karl Marx and G. J. Holyoake. In *Abney Park Cemetery*, Stoke Newington, N.16 are the tomb of General Booth, founder of the Salvation Army, and memorials to many Nonconformist Divines. In the *South Metropolitan Cemetery*, Norwood, S.E.27, are the tombs of C. H. Spurgeon, Lord Alverstone, Douglas Jerrold, John Belcher, R.A., Theodore Watts-Dunton, Dr. Moffat (missionary), Sir H. Bessemer, Sir H. Maxim, Sir J. Barnby, Sir A. Manns, Mrs. Beeton, Sir Henry Tate and J. Whitaker, F.S.A. (*Whitaker's Almanack*). In the churchyard of the former *Marylebone Chapel* are buried Allan Ramsay (poet), Hoyle (whist), Ferguson (astronomer), Charles Wesley (hymn writer) and his son Samuel Wesley (musician). The chapel itself was demolished in 1949. **Crematoria.**—*Ilford* (City of London); *Norwood*; *Hendon*; *Streatham Park*; *Finchley* (St. Marylebone) and *Golder's Green* (12 acres), near Hampstead Heath, with "Garden of Rest" and memorials to famous men and women.

Cenotaph, Whitehall, S.W.1.—(Literally "empty tomb"). Monument erected "To the Glorious Dead", as a memorial to all ranks of the Sea, Land and Air Forces who gave their lives in the service of the Empire during the First World War. Designed by Sir Edwin Lutyens. Erected as a temporary memorial in 1919 and replaced by a permanent structure in 1920. Unveiled by King George V on Armistice Day, 1920. An additional inscription was added after the 1939-45 War, to commemorate those who gave their lives in that conflict.

Charterhouse. Sutton's Hospital, Charterhouse Square, E.C.1. (*Master,* E. E. Harrison, M.A., F.S.A.; *Registrar and Clerk to the Governors,* J. C. Moss), a Carthusian monastery from 1371-1537, when it came into the possession of Sir Edward (later first Lord) North, who sold it in 1565 to the fourth Duke of Norfolk, who renamed it Howard House. After his execution in 1572, following the Ridolfi Plot, hatched at Charterhouse, it was eventually granted by Queen Elizabeth, in 1587, to Norfolk's second son, Thomas Howard, Earl of Suffolk, who in 1608 sold it to Thomas Sutton, who endowed it as a Hospital for aged men "of gentle birth" and a School for Boys (removed to Godalming in 1872). The buildings are partly 14th but mainly 15th and 16th century. The Duke's private palace was destroyed by enemy action in the second World War, but the Hall, Chapel and Great Chamber are intact or restored and now accommodate some 30 Brothers. Roger Williams, founder and governor of Rhode Island, was a scholar on the Foundation. Among other famous pupils were John Wesley, Lord Baden-Powell, the poets and writers Crashaw, Lovelace, Beddoes and Thackeray, who described the School as "Greyfriars" in "The Newcombes" and more recently Lord Beveridge, Lord Ismay and Lord Weeks. Visitors are shown round on Wednesdays at 2.45 p.m. from April to July inclusive (charge £1).

Chelsea Physic Garden, 66 Royal Hospital Road, SW3 4HS.—A garden of general botanical research,

maintaining a wide range of rare and unusual plants. Established in 1673 by the Society of Apothecaries, now administered by the Chelsea Physic Garden Ltd. Open to the public on a regular basis during summer months. All enquiries to the Curator at above address.

Chelsea, Royal Hospital (founded by Charles II, in 1682, and built by Wren; opened in 1692), Royal Hospital Road, Chelsea, S.W.3, for old and disabled soldiers. Great Hall, Chapel and Museum open daily 10 to 12 and 2 to 4 (Museum closed on Sunday afternoons from October to March). The extensive grounds include the former Ranelagh Gardens, and are the venue for the Chelsea Flower Show held each May by the Royal Horticultural Society. *Governor,* General Sir Robert Ford, G.C.B., C.B.E.; *Lieut-Governor and Secretary,* Major-Gen. A. L. Watson, C.B.

City Business Library (Corporation of London), 55 Basinghall Street, E.C.2. Open Mon.-Fri. 9.30-5.00.

College of Arms or Heralds' College, Queen Victoria Street, E.C.4—Her Majesty's Officers of Arms (Kings, Heralds and Pursuivants of Arms) were first incorporated by Richard III, and granted Derby House on the site of the present College building by Philip and Mary. The building now in use dates from 1671-88. The powers vested by the Crown in the Earl Marshal (The Duke of Norfolk) with regard to State ceremonial are largely exercised through the College, which is also the official repository of English pedigrees and all Arms granted to subjects of the Queen (except in Scotland). Enquiry may be made to the Officer on duty in the Public Office, Mon.-Fri. between 10 a.m. and 4 p.m.

Commonwealth Institute, Kensington High Street, W.8.—A permanent exhibition opened on Nov. 6, 1962, by Her Majesty the Queen, replacing the former Imperial Institute opened in 1893 in S. Kensington. An interesting feature of the building is its paraboloid copper-sheathed roof. The Institute contains, in 60,000 square feet arranged in 3 galleries, a visual representation of the history, geography and ways of life of the Commonwealth countries and dependencies; on the ground floor, exhibits of Australia, New Zealand, Bangladesh, Canada, India, Sri Lanka, the Pacific and Atlantic islands and Antartica; on the middle gallery, the African countries, Mauritius and Seychelles; and on the upper gallery, the Caribbean countries, Bermuda, Cyprus, Gibraltar and Malta, Brunei, Hong Kong, Malaysia, Singapore, Belize, Guyana, Papua New Guinea, Isle of Man and the Channel Islands. Art Galleries; Cinema; Theatre; Library services; Restaurant, Bookshop.

Open, weekdays, 10-5.30; Sundays, 2.00-5.00. Admission free. Closed Christmas Eve, Christmas Day, Boxing Day, New Year's Day, Good Friday and May Day.

County Hall, Westminster Bridge, S.E.1.—The Headquarters of the Greater London Council (*see* pp. 658-60) built on the Pedlar's Acre, Bishop's acre, Four Acres and Float Mead, Lambeth, from the designs of Ralph Knott, with a river façade of 750 ft. The main building was completed in 1933. The building of the North and South blocks on a site to the East of the main building started in the early 1930s. They were occupied in 1939 but not finally completed until 1963. The Council, when in session, meets in public in the council chamber every third Tuesday afternoons at 2.30 p.m.

Courtauld Institute Galleries, University of London, Woburn Square, WC1.—The galleries of the University of London contain the Lee collection and the Gambier-Parry collections (14th century to 18th century old masters); the important Courtauld collection of Impressionist and Post-Impressionist paintings; the Roger Fry collection and the Witt and Spooner collections (old master drawings and English water-colours). A major new bequest, the Princes Gate collection of old master paintings and drawings, was opened to the public in July 1981. Open weekdays, 10–5; Sundays, 2–5. Admission £1; children, OAPs, and students (except London University students), 50p.

Custom House, Lower Thames Street, E.C.3.—Built 1813–17, with a wide quay on Thames. The *Long Room* is about 190 ft. long.

Dickens House, 48, Doughty Street, W.C.1.—In this house Charles Dickens lived from 1837 to 1839, and here he completed *Pickwick Papers.* It is the headquarters of the Dickens Fellowship and contains many relics of the novelist. It is open to the public daily, 10 to 5 (Sundays and Bank Holidays excepted); admission £1; students 75p; children, 50p; families, £2.

Downing Street.—Number 10, Downing Street, S.W.1, is the official town residence of the Prime Minister, No. 11 of the Chancellor of the Exchequer and No. 12 is the office of the Government Whips. The street was named after Sir George Downing, Bt. soldier and diplomatist, who was M.P. for Morpeth from 1660 to 1684.

Chequers, a Tudor mansion in the Chilterns, about 3 miles from Princes Risborough, was presented together with a maintenance endowment by Lord and Lady Lee of Fareham in 1917 to serve, from Jan. 1, 1921, as a country residence for the Prime Minister of the day, the Chequers estate of 700 acres being added to the gift by Lord Lee in 1921. The mansion contains a famous collection of Cromwellian portraits and relics.

Dr. Johnson's House, Gough Square, Fleet Street, E.C.4.—A tall late 17th-century house in which Samuel (and his wife) lived between 1748 and 1759. His *Dictionary* was compiled here. The house is furnished with 18th century pieces and there is an excellent collection of Johnsoniana. Open daily (except Sundays and Bank Holidays) from 11 to 5.30 (Winter 5). Admission £1; students and O.A.P.s, 50p.

Dulwich, S.E.21.—Contains *Dulwich College* (founded by Edward Alleyn in 1619), the *Horniman Museum* (q.v.) and the *Dulwich Picture Gallery,* built by Sir John Soane to house the collection bequeathed by the artist Sir Francis Bourgeois. The gallery was damaged in the Second World War but rebuilt with the aid of a grant from the Pilgrim Trust and reopened in 1953. *Dulwich Village* retains many of the rural characteristics of the pre-suburban period.

Eltham, S.E.9.—Contains remains of 13th–15th century *Eltham Palace,* the birthplace of John of Eltham (1316), son of Edward II. The hall, built by Edward IV, has a hammer-beam roof of chestnut. In the churchyard of St. John the Baptist is the tomb of *Thomas Doggett,* the comedian and founder of the Thames Watermen's championship (Doggett's Coat and Badge).

Ely Place, Holborn Circus, E.C.1.—Previously the site of the London house of the Bishop of Ely, Ely Place is a private street (built in 1773) whose affairs are administered by Commissioners under a special Act of Parliament. The 14th-century chapel, now St. Etheldreda's (R.C.) Church, is open daily until dusk.

Eton College.—The most famous of English public schools, founded by Henry VI in 1440. Buildings date from 1442.

Fulham Palace, Bishop's Avenue, Fulham, S.W.6.—The courtyard is 16th century, remainder 18th and 19th century. Former residence of the Bishop of London. Grounds of about 9 acres.

Geffrye Museum, Kingsland Road, E.2.—Open on Tuesdays to Saturdays 10 to 5, Sundays 2 to 5. Closed on Christmas Day and on Mondays except Bank Holidays. Admission free.

The Museum is housed in a building erected originally as almshouses in 1713. It was eventually purchased by the London County Council and opened as a museum in 1914. The Exhibits are shown in a series of period rooms dating from 1600 to 1939, each containing furniture and domestic equipment of middle-class English home. An 18th century woodworker's shop, an openhearth kitchen and the original chapel are also shown, together with a selection of costume. Temporary exhibitions are held in the Exhibition Hall. There is a reference library of books on furniture, social history and art. Special arrangements for children visiting the Museum in school parties (which must be booked in advance) and in their leisure time. *Director,* J. Daniels.

George Inn, Southwark.—Near London Bridge Station. Given to National Trust in 1937. Last galleried inn in London, built in 1677. Open during licensed hours.

Greenwich, S.E.10.—*Greenwich Hospital* (since 1873, the Royal Naval College) was built by Charles II, largely from designs by John Webb, and by Queen Anne and William III, from designs by Wren, on the site of an ancient royal palace, and of the more recent *Palace of Placentia,* an enlarged edition of the palace, constructed by Humphrey, Duke of Gloucester (1391–1447), son of Henry IV. Henry VIII, Queen Mary I and Queen Elizabeth I were born in the Royal Palace (which reverted to the Crown in 1447) and King Edward VI died there. In the principal quadrangle is a marble statue of George II, by Rysbraeck. (For *National Maritime Museum,* see Index.) *Painted Hall* and *Chapel* open daily except Thursdays from 2.30 p.m. to 5 p.m. Visitors are also admitted to Sunday Service in the Chapel at 11 a.m., summer and winter, except during College vacations. *Greenwich Park* (196¼ acres) was enclosed by Humphrey, Duke of Gloucester, and laid out by Charles II, from the designs of Le Nôtre. *The Queen's House,* begun in 1616, was designed for Anne of Denmark by Inigo Jones (Closed for repairs from Oct. 1984). On a hill in Greenwich Park is the former Royal Observatory (founded 1675). Part of its buildings at Greenwich have been taken over by the Maritime Museum and named *Flamsteed House,* after John Flamsteed (1646–1719), first Astronomer Royal. Astronomical and navigational equipment is exhibited, and the time ball and zero meridian of longitude can also be seen. The Parish church of Greenwich (*St. Alfege*) was rebuilt by Hawksmoor (Wren's pupil) in 1728, and restored after severe damage during the Second World War. General Wolfe (Heights of Abraham) and Tallis ("the father of Church Music") are buried in the church. Henry VIII was christened in the former church. *Charlton House:* built in the early 17th century (1607–1612) for Adam Newton, tutor to Prince Henry, brother to Charles I. The house is largely in the Jacobean style of architecture. *Cutty Sark,* the last of the famous tea clippers, which has been preserved as a memorial to ships and men of a past era. The ship is fully restored and re-rigged, with a museum of sail on board. Open to visitors: weekdays, 11 to 5 (Summer, 6 p.m.); Sundays and Boxing Day, 2.30 to 5. The yacht *Gipsy Moth IV* in which Sir Francis Chichester sailed single-handed round the world, 1966–67, is preserved alongside the *Cutty Sark.*

Guildhall, Gresham Street, City, E.C.2.—Scene of civic government for the City for more than a thousand years. Built *c.* 1440; façade built 1788–9;

damaged in the Great Fire, 1666, and by incendiary bombs, 1940. The main hall and crypt (the most extensive medieval crypt in London) have been restored. Events in Guildhall include the annual election of Lord Mayor, election of Sheriffs, receptions in honour of Sovereigns and Heads of State, and the meetings of the Court of Common Council (*see* "Corporation of London"). Open free; weekdays, 10–5; Sundays (May to Sept.) 10–5. *Keeper of the Guildhall,* J. H. Lucioni.

The Library and Museum of the Clockmakers' Company are housed in new premises, and are open to the public, Mon. to Fri., 10–5. Admission free (entrance in Aldermanbury). The Library contains Plans of London, 1570; Deed of Sale with Shakespeare's signature; first, second and fourth folios of Shakespeare's plays etc. (*See also* City Business Library).

Ham House, Richmond.—A notable example of 17th-century domestic architecture, long the home of the Tollemache family (Earls of Dysart). The contents, described as "probably the finest and most varied collection of Charles II's reign to survive", were purchased for the Victoria and Albert Museum which now administers the house. Ham House may be seen on Tues.–Sun. inclusive and on Bank Holidays, 11–5 p.m. Closed Mon. (except Bank Holidays), Christmas Eve, Christmas Day, Boxing Day, Good Friday, New Year's Day and May Day. Admission £1·50; children, students and O.A.P.s, 75p.

Hampton Court.—Sixteenth-century Palace built by Cardinal Wolsey, with additions by Sir Christopher Wren for William and Mary, 15 miles from London. Fine view of river. Beautiful gardens with maze and prolific grape vine (planted in 1769). State Apartments and collection of pictures. Tennis Court, built by King Henry VIII in 1530. Collection of Mantegna paintings. The Palace is *closed* on Christmas Eve, Christmas Day, Boxing Day, New Year's Day. State Apartments: (1985) £2. Children under sixteen and O.A.P.s £1. Mantegna Gallery 10p; Maze 39p. 10 per cent group discount. Tennis Court, Banqueting House, Mantegna Gallery closed Oct.–Mar. Maze closed Nov.–Feb. Palace open Oct.–Mar. 9.30–5 p.m. (Sun. 2–5 p.m.); April–Sept. 9.30–6 p.m. (Sun. 11–6 p.m.).

Harrow.—Public school founded by John Lyon in 1571. The "Fourth Form Room" dates from 1608.

Honourable Artillery Company's Headquarters, City Road, E.C.1.—The H.A.C. (*Chief Exec.* Capt. G. C. Lloyd, C.B.E., R.N.) received its charter of incorporation from Henry VIII in 1537, and has occupied its present ground since 1641. The Armoury House dates from 1735. The present castellated barracks date from 1860. Four of its members who emigrated in the 17th century, founded in 1638 the Ancient and Honorable Artillery Company of Massachusetts. The H.A.C. is the senior regiment of the Territorial Army Volunteer Reserves, and maintains a Headquarters, four squadrons, a gun troop, and two companies of the Home Service Force.

Horniman Museum and Library, London Road, Forest Hill, S.E.23. Open daily (except Christmas Eve and Christmas Day), 10.30 to 6, Sundays 2 to 6. Only the Lecture Hall is open on Boxing Day afternoon. Admission free. The Museum was presented in 1901 to the London County Council by the founder, Mr. F. J. Horniman, M.P. It is now administered by the I.L.E.A. on behalf of the G.L.C. The Museum has three main departments, ethnography, musical instruments and natural history. In the ethnography department the large collections include exhibits illustrating man's progress in the arts and crafts from prehistoric times. The natural history department

includes an aquarium. Reference library (except Mondays). Schools Service. Free concerts and lectures (autumn and spring). Special exhibitions. *Director,* D. M. Boston, O.B.E.

Horse Guards, Whitehall, S.W.1.—Archway and offices built about 1753. The mounting of the guard (Life Guards, or the Blues and Royals) at 11 a.m. (10 a.m. on Sundays) and the dismounted inspection at 4 p.m. are picturesque ceremonies. Only those on the Lord Chamberlain's list may drive through the gates and archway into *Horse Guard's Parade* (230,000 sq. ft.), where the Colour is "trooped" on the Queen's Official Birthday.

The Houses of Parliament, Westminster, S.W.1.—An ordinance issued in the reign of Richard II stated that "Parliament shall be holden or kepid wheresoever it pleaseth the King" and at the present day the Sovereign summons Parliament to meet and prescribes the time and place of meeting. The royal palace of Westminster, originally built by Edward the Confessor (Westminster Hall (*q.v.*) being added by William Rufus), was the normal place of Parliament from about 1340. St. Stephen's Chapel (first mentioned in the reign of John) was used from about 1550 for the meetings of the House of Commons, which had previously been held in the Chapter House or Refectory of Westminster Abbey. The House of Lords met in an apartment of the royal palace.

The fire of 1834 destroyed the whole palace, except Westminster Hall, and the present Houses of Parliament were erected on the site from the designs of Sir Charles Barry and Augustus Welby Pugin between 1840 and 1867, at a cost of £2,198,000. The Chamber of the House of Commons was destroyed by enemy action in 1941 and the foundation stone of a new building, from the designs of Sir Giles Gilbert Scott, was laid by the Speaker on May 26, 1948. The new Chamber was used for the first time on Oct. 26, 1950.

The Victoria Tower of the House of Lords is about 330 ft. high, and when Parliament is sitting the Union Flag flies by day from its flagstaff. *The Clock Tower* of the House of Commons is about 320 ft. high and contains "Big Ben", the hour bell said to be named after Sir Benjamin Hall, First Commissioner of Works when the original bell was cast in 1856. This bell, which weighed 16 tons 11 cwt., was found to be cracked in 1857. The present bell (13½ tons) is a recasting of the original and was first brought into use in July, 1859. The dials of the clock are 23 ft. in diameter, the hands being 9 ft. and 14 ft. long (including balance piece). A light is displayed from the Clock Tower at night when Parliament is sitting.

The Houses of Parliament are not open to the general public. All arrangements for visits must be made direct with a Member of Parliament.

Admission to the Strangers' Gallery of the House of Lords as arranged by a Peer or by queue *via* the St. Stephen's Entrance. Admission to the Strangers' Gallery of the House of Commons, by Members' order (Members' orders should be sought well in advance), or by queue *via* St. Stephen's Entrance. Queues are sometimes shorter after 6 p.m., Mon.–Thurs. Overseas visitors may obtain cards of introduction from their Embassy or High Commission.

Inns of Court.—The *Inner* and *Middle Temple,* S. of Fleet Street, E.C.4, and N. of Victoria Embankment, to which the gardens extend, have occupied (since early 14th century) the site of the buildings of the Order of Knights Templars. *Inner Temple Hall* (rebuilt in 1955 after bomb damage) is open to the public Mon.–Fri. 10.30–11.30, 3–4 on application to Treasurer's Office during law sittings. *Temple Church,* restored in 1958 after severe damage by bombing, is open on weekdays 9.30–4 p.m. and the public are admitted to Sunday services. *Middle Temple Hall* (1562–70) is open to the public when not in use, Monday–Friday, 10–12 and 3–4.30 p.m.; Saturday when staff are available. Closed, Public Holidays. In Middle Temple Gardens (not open to the public) Shakespeare (Henry VI, Part I) places the incident which led to the "Wars of the Roses" (1455–85). *Lincoln's Inn*, from Chancery Lane to Lincoln's Inn Fields, W.C.2, occupies the site of the palace of a former Bishop of Chichester and of a Black Friars monastery. The records show the Society as being in existence in 1422. The Hall and Library Buildings are of 1845, although the Library is first mentioned in 1474, and the old Hall early 16th century, the Chapel was rebuilt *c.* 1619–23. Halls open to public by appointment, Chapel and Gardens, Mon.–Fri. 12–2.30. Chapel services, Sun. 11.30 a.m. during Law Terms. *Lincoln's Inn Fields* (7 Acres); the Square, laid out by Inigo Jones, contains many fine old houses with handsome interiors. *Gray's Inn*, Holborn/Gray's Inn Road, W.C.1. Early 14th century. Hall (1556–60); Chapel (largely rebuilt in 1698). Services 11.15 a.m. (during Law Dining Terms only.) Holy Communion 1st Sunday in every month except Aug.–Sept. Public welcome. Library (41,000 vols., mss. and printed books) may be viewed by appointment. Gardens open to the public from 12 noon to 2.30 p.m. (May–Sept.). The Inn, although badly damaged during the last war, has been completely restored to its former beauty with gracious red brick buildings overlooking grass covered squares and gardens. Strong Elizabethan associations. No other "Inns" are active, but what remains of *Staple Inn* is worth visiting as a relic of Elizabethan London; though heavy damage was done by a flying-bomb, it retains a picturesque gabled front on Holborn (opposite Gray's Inn Road). *Clement's Inn* (near St. Clement Danes' Church), *Clifford's Inn*, Fleet Street, and *Thavies Inn*, Holborn Circus, are all rebuilt. *Serjeant's Inn*, Fleet Street (damaged by bombing) and another (demolished 1910) of the same name in Chancery Lane, were composed of Serjeants-at-Law, the last of whom died in 1922.

Jewish Museum, Woburn House, Upper Woburn Place, W.C.1.—Opened in 1932, the Museum contains a comprehensive collection of objects and antiquities, illustrating Jewish life, history and religion. Open Tues.–Thurs. (and Fri. in summer) 10–4, Sun. (and Fri. in winter) 10–12.45. Closed Mon., Sat., Public and Jewish holidays. Group visits by arrangement with Secretary.

Keats House, Keats Grove, Hampstead, N.W.3.—In two houses here, now made into one, John Keats lived at various times between 1818 and 1820. Restored 1974–75. Open weekdays, 10–1 a.m., 2–6 p.m.; Sundays and Bank Holidays, 2 p.m.–5 p.m. Closed—Christmas Day, Boxing Day, New Year's Day, Good Friday, Easter Eve and May Day. The Keats Memorial Library contains over 7,000 volumes.

Kensington Palace, W.8.—The original house was bought by William III in 1689 and enlarged by Christoper Wren. The birthplace of Queen Victoria in 1819. The State Apartments are open to the public and contain pictures and furniture from the royal collections. A suite of rooms devoted to the memory of Queen Victoria is also shown. Admission: £1; children, O.A.P.s 50p.

The *Court Dress Collection* is also open, and includes three restored rooms, the Red Saloon, the Teck Saloon and the room where Queen Victoria is said to have been born. Admission: £2·00; children, O.A.P.s, £1·00p. *Both open*, weekdays 9–5; Suns. 1–5.

Kew, Surrey.—A favourite home of the early Hanoverian monarchs. Kew House, the residence of Frederick, Prince of Wales, and later of his son,

George III, was pulled down in 1803, but the earlier Dutch House, now known as Kew Palace, survives. It was built in 1631 and acquired by George III as an annexe to Kew House in 1781. The famous Kew Gardens (*see* Index) were originally laid out as a private garden for Kew House for George III's mother in 1759 and were much enlarged in the nineteenth century, notably by the inclusion of the grounds of the former Richmond Lodge.

Kneller Hall, Twickenham.—Royal Military School of Music. A band of up to 120 instrumentalists gives concerts in the grounds on Wednesdays throughout the summer, commencing at 8 p.m. Admission 50p (Grand concerts, £1). Season tickets and party bookings available.

Lambeth Palace, S.E.1.—The official residence of the Archbishop of Canterbury, on south bank of Thames; the oldest part is 13th century, the house itself is early 19th century. For leave to visit the historical portions, applications should be made by letter to the Archbishop's Chaplain.

Livery Companies' Halls.—The Principal Companies (*see* Index) have magnificent halls but admission to view them has generally to be arranged beforehand. Among the finest or more interesting may be mentioned the following: Goldsmiths' Hall, Foster Lane. The present hall was completed in 1835, and contains some magnificent rooms. Exhibitions of plate have been shown here periodically in recent years. Fishmongers' Hall, London Bridge (built 1831–3), now admirably restored after severe bomb damage, also contains fine rooms. Apothecaries' Hall, Black Friars Lane, was rebuilt in 1670, after the Great Fire, and has library, hall and kitchen which are good examples of this period, together with a pleasant courtyard. Vintners' Hall, Upper Thames Street, was also rebuilt after the Great Fire, and its hall has very fine late 17th century panelling. The Watermen and Lightermen's Company is not, strictly speaking, a Livery Company, but its hall, in St. Mary at Hill, is a good example of a smaller 18th century building, with pilastered façade. It was completed in 1780. Stationers' Hall, in Stationers' Hall Court, behind Ludgate Hill, another post-fire Hall, standing in its own court, has a particularly finely carved screen; its façade dates from 1800. Barbers' Hall, Monkwell Street, with a Hall attributed to Inigo Jones, was completely destroyed by bombing, but has now been rebuilt. The new hall was built some 30 ft. from the old site to enable one of the bastions and part of the wall of the Roman fort to remain exposed to view.

Lloyd's, Lime Street, E.C.3.—Housed in the Royal Exchange for 150 years and in Leadenhall Street from 1928–1957. The present building was opened by H.M. Queen Elizabeth the Queen Mother on Nov. 14, 1957. The underwriting space has an area of 44,250 sq. ft. and houses the Lutine Bell.

London Planetarium, Marylebone Road, N.W.1.—Open daily (except Dec. 25), star shows from 11–4.30. Admission charge.

London Transport Museum, Covent Garden, W.C.2.—Housed in the former Flower Market, the Museum contains a collection of buses, trams, trolley-buses, trains, working displays and London Transport paraphernalia. There is a research library and lecture theatre. Open every day, 10 a.m. to 6.00 p.m. (except Dec. 24, 25 and 26). Admission: £2·20; children, UB40s, students and O.A.P.s, £1.

Lord's Cricket Ground, St. John's Wood Road, N.W.8.—The headquarters (since 1814) of the Marylebone Cricket Club (founded 1787), the premier cricket club in England, the scene of some of the principal matches of the season and Middlesex

County headquarters. Real tennis court and squash courts in building behind members' pavilion.

The Cricket Memorial Gallery, a museum of cricket, open to the public on match days (except Sundays) until 5 p.m. Adults, 50p; children and O.A.P.s, 25p. In winter and on non-match days admission is by prior arrangement with the Curator.

Madame Tussaud's Exhibition, Marylebone Road, N.W.1.—Open daily (except Dec. 25), 10–5.30; Admission charge.

Mansion House, City, E.C.4.—(Built 1739–53, reconstructed 1930–31.) The official residence of the Lord Mayor; the Egyptian Hall and Ballroom are the chief attractions. Admission by order from the Lord Mayor's Secretary.

Marble Hill House, Twickenham.—Example of the English Palladian style, built 1724–9 for Henrietta Howard, Countess of Suffolk, mistress of George II. Reopened 1966, after restoration work on the elevations of the house, entrance hall, main staircase and first floor rooms. The Great Room and mahogany staircase are noteworthy. Open daily (except Fri.) 10 a.m.–5 p.m. (closes 4, Nov.–Jan.). Admission free. Now houses fine collection of early 18th century paintings and furniture including original overmantel and overdoors by Panini.

Markets.—The London markets (administered by the Corporation of the City of London) provide foodstuffs for 8,500,000 to 9,000,000 people. *Central Meat, Fish, Fruit, Vegetable, and Poultry Markets,* Smithfield (present buildings, 1866) the largest meat market in the world and site of St. Bartholomew's Fair from 9th to 19th century; *Leadenhall Market* (Meat and Poultry built 1881, part recently demolished); *Billingsgate* (Fish), Thames Street (built 1875, part recently demolished) a market site for over 1,000 years (moved to the Isle of Dogs in Jan. 1982); *Spitalfields,* E.1. (Vegetables, Fruit, etc.), enlarged 1928, and opened by the late Queen Mary; *London Fruit Exchange,* Brushfield Street (built by Corporation of London 1928–29) faces Spitalfields Market. Other markets are—*Covent Garden* (now moved to Nine Elms) established under a charter of Charles II, in 1661, and *Borough Market,* S.E.1, for vegetables, fruit, flowers, etc.

Marlborough House, Pall Mall, S.W.1.—Built by Wren for the first Duke of Marlborough and completed in 1711, the house finally reverted to the Crown in 1835. Prince Leopold lived there until 1831, and Queen Adelaide from 1837 until her death in 1849. In 1863 it became the London house of the Prince of Wales and was the London home of Queen Mary until her death in 1953. The Queen's Chapel, Marlborough Gate, begun in 1623 from the designs of Inigo Jones for the Infanta Maria of Spain, and completed for Queen Henrietta Maria, is open to the public for services on Sundays at 8.30 a.m. and 11.15 a.m. between Easter Day and end July (*see also* St. James's Palace for winter services in The Chapel Royal). In 1959 Marlborough House was given by the Queen as a centre for Commonwealth Government conferences and it was opened as such in March, 1962.

London Monument (commonly called "The Monument"), Monument Street, E.C.3.—Built from designs of Wren, 1671–77, to commemorate the *Great Fire of London,* which broke out in Pudding Lane, Sept. 2, 1666. The fluted Doric column is 120 ft. high (the moulded cylinder above the balcony supporting a flaming vase of gilt bronze is 42 ft. in addition), and is based on a square plinth 40 ft. high, with fine carvings on W. face (making a total height of 202 ft.). Splendid views of London from gallery at top of column (311 steps). Admission (until 20 minutes before closing time), Mon.–Fri., 9 a.m. to 2 p.m., 3

p.m.–6 p.m. (Oct.–March to 4 p.m.). Sat. 9 a.m.–2 p.m., 3 p.m.–4 p.m. (Oct.–Mar.); Sat. and Sun. 2 p.m.–6 p.m. (Apr.–Sept.) Entrance fee. Closed Christmas Day, Boxing Day and Good Friday.

Monuments.—*Albert Memorial,* South Kensington; *Royal Air Force,* Victoria Embankment, Beaconsfield, Parliament Square; *Beatty, Jellicoe* and *Cunningham,* Trafalgar Square; *Belgian Gratitude* (Reginald Blomfield), Victoria Embankment; *Boadicea* (or "Boudicca"), Queen of the Iceni, E. Anglia (Thomas Thornycroft), Westminster Bridge; *Brunel* (Marochetti), Victoria Embankment; *Burghers of Calais* (Rodin), Victoria Tower Gardens, Westminster; *Burns,* Embankment Gardens; *Carlyle* (Boehm), Cheyne Walk, Chelsea; *Cavalry,* Hyde Park; *Cavell,* St. Martin's Place (Frampton); *Cenotaph* (Lutyens), Whitehall; *Charles I,* Trafalgar Square; *Charles II,* inside the Royal Exchange; *Churchill,* Parliament Square; *Cleopatra's Needle* (68½ ft. high *c.* 1,500 B.C. erected on the Thames Embankment in 1877–8)—the Sphinxes are Victorian; *Clive,* Whitehall; *Captain Cook* (Brock), The Mall; *Crimean,* Broad Sanctuary; *Oliver Cromwell* (Thornycroft), outside Westminster Hall; *Duke of Cambridge,* Whitehall; *Duke of York* (124 ft.), Carlton House Terrace; *Edward VII* (Mackennal), Waterloo Place; *Elizabeth I* (1586, oldest outdoor statue in London) (from Ludgate), Fleet Street; *Eros* (Shaftesbury Memorial) (Gilbert), Piccadilly Circus; *Marechal Foch,* Grosvenor Gardens; *Charles James Fox,* Bloomsbury Square; *George III,* Cockspur Street; *George IV* (Chantrey), riding without stirrups, Trafalgar Square; *George V,* Old Palace Yard; *George VI,* Carlton Gardens; *Gladstone,* facing Australia House, Strand; *Guards'* (Crimea), Waterloo Place; (Great War), Horse Guards' Parade; *Haig* (Hardiman), Whitehall; *Irving* (Brock), N. side of National Portrait Gallery; *James II,* Trafalgar Square; *Samuel Johnson,* opposite St. Clement Danes; *Kitchener,* Horse Guards' Parade; *Abraham Lincoln,* Parliament Square; *Milton,* St. Giles, Cripplegate; *Monument, The* (*see above*); *Mountbatten,* Foreign Office Green; *Nelson* (170 ft. 1½ in.), Trafalgar Square, with Lanseer's lions (cast from guns recovered from the wreck of the *Royal George*); *Florence Nightingale,* Waterloo Place; *Palmerston,* Parliament Square; *Peel,* Parliament Square; *Pitt,* Hanover Square (Chantrey); *Portal,* Embankment Gardens; *Prince Consort,* Holborn Circus; *Raleigh,* Whitehall; *Richard Coeur de Lion* (Marochetti), Old Palace Yard; *Roberts,* Horse Guards' Parade; *Franklin D. Roosevelt,* Grosvenor Square (Reid Dick); *Royal Artillery* (South Africa), The Mall; (Great War), Hyde Park Corner; *Captain Scott,* Waterloo Place (Lady Scott); *Shackleton,* Kensington Gore; *Shakespeare,* Leicester Square; *Smuts* (Epstein), Parliament Square; *Sullivan,* Victoria Embankment; *Trenchard,* Victoria Embankment; *Victoria Memorial,* in front of Buckingham Palace; *George Washington* (Houdon copy), Trafalgar Square; *Wellington,* Hyde Park Corner; *Wellington* (Chantrey) riding without stirrups, Royal Exchange; *John Wesley,* City Road; *William III,* St. James's Square; *Wolseley,* Horse Guards' Parade.

Osterley Park, Isleworth.—House and park of 140 acres given to the National Trust by the Earl of Jersey in 1949 and administered by the Victoria and Albert Museum. The Elizabethan house, built in 1577 for Sir Thomas Gresham, was largely remodelled by Robert Adam, and the staterooms are among the best examples of Adam decoration. Open daily, except Mondays, 11 a.m.–5 p.m. Closed Monday (except Bank Holidays), Christmas Eve, Christmas Day, Boxing Day, New Year's Day, Good Friday and May Day. Admission £1·50, children 75p.

Percival David Foundation of Chinese Art, 53 Gordon Square, W.C.1.—Set up in 1951 to promote the study and teaching of the art and culture of China and the surrounding regions, and provide facilities necessary to that end. The Foundation contains the collection of Chinese ceramics formed by Sir Percival David and his important library of books on Chinese art. To these was added a gift from the Hon. Mountstuart Elphinstone of part of his collection of Chinese monochrome porcelains. The galleries were opened to the public in 1952. The Lady David Gallery was opened in 1983. The Foundation is administered on behalf of the University of London by the School of Oriental and African Studies. *Hours of opening:* Galleries, Mon. 2 to 5 p.m.; Tues. to Fri. 10.30 a.m. to 5 p.m.; Sat. 10.30 a.m. to 1 p.m.; Closed Sats. in August, Bank Holidays and preceding Sats. Library available to ticket holders only; applications in writing to the Curator, Miss R. Scott.

Port of London.—The Port of London comprises the tidal portion of the River Thames from Teddington to the seaward limit (Tongue light vessel), a distance of 95 miles and one operational dock system and land for redevelopment, covering an area of 3,718 acres, of which 512 acres are water. The governing body is the Port of London Authority, whose Head Office is at Leslie Ford House, Tilbury Docks, Tilbury, Essex. Particulars of the docks are as follows:—*India & Millwall Docks,* E.14—remaining area vested in Docklands Development Corporation. *Royal Albert & King George V Docks,* E.16.—Area 512 acres. *Tilbury Docks, Essex.*—Area 1,037 acres, incuding 155 acres water. These docks are 26 miles below London Bridge and are used principally by vessels plying on the Australian, North American, Indian, other Eastern routes, West Africa and the Continent. Tilbury Passenger Landing Stage provides accommodation for liners at all states of the tide and adjoins Tilbury Riverside Station. A development and extension scheme at Tilbury added nearly 2 miles of deepwater quays, in addition to a £7 million Grain Terminal. With the recently completed Northfleet Hope Development, Tilbury is capable of handling forest products, containers and roll-on/roll-off traffic.

The St. Katherine Docks were sold to the G.L.C. in 1969 and the London Docks were closed on May 31, 1969 and sold to Tower Hamlets Council in 1976. Surrey Commercial Docks were closed in 1970 and were sold to the G.L.C. and Southwark Council in 1976 and 1977.

Prince Henry's Room, 17 Fleet Street, E.C.4.— Early 17th century timber-framed house containing fine room on first floor with panelling and moulded plaster ceiling. Includes an exhibition on Samuel Pepys and the London in which he lived. Open Mon. to Fri. 1.45 p.m. to 5 p.m.; Sat to 4.30 p.m. Admission free. Closed Christmas Day, Good Friday and Bank Holidays. Available for morning or evening lettings on application to The Town Clerk, Guildhall, E.C.2.

Richmond, Surrey. Contains the red brick gateway of *Richmond Palace* (Henry VII, 1485–1509) and buildings of the Jacobean, Queen Anne, and early Georgian periods, including *White Lodge* in Richmond Park, the former home of Queen Mary's mother (the Duke of Windsor was born there, June 23, 1894), and now the home of the Royal Ballet School. The *Star and Garter* Home for Disabled Soldiers, Sailors, and Airmen (the Women's Memorial of the Great War) was opened by Queen Mary in 1924. *Richmond Park* (2,469 acres) contains herds of fallow and red deer.

Roman London.—Although visible remains from this period are few, excavations carried out in the City on sites due for redevelopment often reveal Roman features. Sections of the City Wall are the most striking remains to be seen of Roman *Londinium,* although even these are largely medieval due to the Roman wall being rebuilt during the medieval period. Sections may be seen near the White Tower in the Tower of London; at Tower Hill; at Coopers' Row; at All Hallows, London Wall, its vestry being built on the remains of a semi-circular Roman bastion; at St. Alphage, London Wall, showing a striking succession of building repairs from Roman until the late medieval period, and at St. Giles Cripplegate. Excavations in the Cripplegate area have revealed that a Roman fort was built there in about A.D.100–120. It was later incorporated into the city wall when this was built about A.D.200.

The administrative centre of the Roman city was the great forum and basilica, more than 165 metres square, sections of which have been encountered during excavations in the area of Leadenhall, Gracechurch Street and Lombard Street. Excavations during the past few years have revealed Roman activity along the river. Traces of a massive riverside wall, built in the late Roman period, have been found and a succession of Roman timber quays have been excavated along Lower and Upper Thames Street helping to prove that Roman London was a thriving commercial centre.

Other major buildings found are the Provincial Governor's Palace in Cannon Street; remains of a bath-building, preserved in Lower Thames Street; and the Temple of Mithras in Walbrook. The fine sculptures from this temple are displayed in the Museum of London, where many other relics from the Roman City may be seen. There is also an Ordnance Survey map of Roman London.

Royal Albert Hall, Kensington Gore, SW7 2AP. The elliptical hall, one of the largest in the world, was completed in 1871, and since 1941 has been the venue each summer for the Promenade Concerts founded in 1895 by Sir Henry Wood. Also used for public meetings, concerts, sports and other entertainments. *Gen. Manager,* D. C. McNicol.

Royal Exchange, EC3V 3LS. (founded by Sir Thomas Gresham, 1566, opened as "The Bourse" and proclaimed "The Royal Exchange" by Queen Elizabeth I, 1571, rebuilt 1667–69 and 1842–44). The building is occupied by the Guardian Royal Exchange Assurance Group and by the London International Financial Futures Exchange. It is administered by the Gresham Committee (*Clerk,* Mercers' Hall, Ironmonger Lane, E.C.2.).

Royal Geographical Society, Kensington Gore, S.W.7.—Map room open to public, *free.*

Royal Opera House, Covent Garden, W.C.2.— Home of The Royal Ballet (1931) and The Royal Opera (1946) companies, the Royal Opera House is the third theatre to be built on the site, opening May 15, 1858: the first was opened Dec. 7, 1732. The season of the resident companies runs mid Sept.–Aug. *General Director,* Sir John Tooley.

Runnimede.—A meadow of about 100 acres, on S. bank of Thames (part of the Crown Lands), between Windsor and Staines. From June 15–23, 1215, the hostile Barons encamped on this meadow during negotiations with King John, who rode over each day from Windsor. The 48 "Articles of the Barons" were accepted by the King on June 15, and were subsequently embodied in a charter, since known as *Magna Carta,* of which several copies were sealed on June 19. About half a mile N.E. of the meadow is *Magna Carta Island* (claimed as the actual site of the sealing), presented to the National Trust in 1930.

A memorial at *Cooper's Hill,* near Runnimede, to members of the Commonwealth air forces who lost their lives in the Second World War while serving from bases in the United Kingdom and north-western Europe and have no known grave, was unveiled by the Queen on October 17, 1953. Her Majesty on May 14, 1965, unveiled a memorial to the late President of the United States, John F. Kennedy, on ground nearby.

St. James's Palace, in Pall Mall, S.W.1.—(Not open to the public.) Built by Henry VIII; the Gatehouse and Presence Chamber remain, later alterations by Wren and Kent. The Chapel Royal is open to the public for services on Sundays at 8.30 a.m. and 11.15 a.m. between beginning October and Good Friday (*see also* Marlborough House for summer services in The Queen's Chapel). Representatives of Foreign Powers are still accredited "to the Court of St. James's". Clarence House (1825) in the palace precinct is the home of H.M. the Queen Mother.

St. John's Gate, Clerkenwell, E.C.1.—Now the Chancery of the Order of St. John of Jerusalem, and formerly the entrance of the Priory of that Order, of which the gate house (early 16th century) and crypt of Church (12th century) alone survive. They may be inspected on application to the Curator.

Sir John Soane's Museum, 13 Lincoln's Inn Fields, W.C.2. The house and galleries, built 1812–24, are the work of the founder, Sir John Soane (1753–1837) and contain his collections, arranged as he left them, in pursuance of an Act procured by him in 1833. Exhibits include the Sarcophagus of Seti 1 (*c.* 1290 B.C.), Classical vases and marbles, Hogarth's *Rake's Progress* and *Election* series, paintings by Canaletto, Reynolds, Turner, Lawrence, etc., and sculpture by Chantrey, Flaxman, etc. Soane's library of 8,000 vols, and collection of 40,000 architectural drawings are available for study by appointment. Open Tues.–Sat. inclusive, 10 a.m. to 5 p.m. Closed Bank Holidays. *Curator,* P. Thornton, F.S.A. *Assistant Curator,* Mrs M. Richardson.

Somerset House, Strand, W.C.2, and Victoria Embankment, W.C.2.—The beautiful river façade (600 ft. long) was built in 1776–86 from the designs of Sir W. Chambers; the eastern extension, which houses part of King's College, was built by Smirke in 1829. Somerset House was the property of Lord Protector Somerset, at whose attainder in 1552 the palace passed to the Crown, and it was a royal residence until 1692.

South Bank, S.E.1.—The arts complex on the south bank of the River Thames includes the South Bank Concert Halls, owned and managed by the G.L.C. and consisting of the 2,900-seat *Royal Festival Hall* (opened in 1951 for the Festival of Britain), a major venue for concert and ballet seasons, with the adjacent 1,100-seat *Queen Elizabeth Hall* and 370-seat *Purcell Room,* accommodating smaller-scale performances.

The *National Film Theatre* (opened 1958), administered by the British Film Institute, has two auditoria showing films, television and video of outstanding historical, artistic or technical merit. The London Film Festival is held here every November.

The *National Theatre* opened in 1976 and stages classical, modern, new and neglected plays in its three auditoria; the 1,160-seat Olivier theatre (apron stage), the 890-seat Lyttleton theatre (proscenium stage) and the experimental Cottesloe theatre, which holds up to 400.

Stock Exchange, E.C.2.—The market floor of the new Stock Exchange building in London opened for trading in June, 1973. A tower, 331 feet high, and the new Market replace the complex of buildings started in 1801 on the same site. The new building is the headquarters of The Stock Exchange, following the amalgamation of all the Stock Exchanges in Great Britain and Ireland on March 25, 1973.

The Stock Exchange provides a market for the purchase and sale of over 7,000 securities officially listed, and valued at over £1,089,000 million and also securities listed on other Stock Exchanges throughout the World. At present the members of The Stock Exchange, who consist of brokers (agents for clients) and Jobbers (dealers in specific securities) number about 4,300. The Visitors Gallery is open between 9.45 a.m. and 3.15 p.m. Monday to Friday. Admission free and without ticket; film show. Advance bookings are advisable; last complete programme begins at 2.30 p.m.

Syon House, Brentford.—The summer home of the Duke of Northumberland. The House is built on the remains of the Nunnery of Syon, founded by order of Henry V in 1415. At the Dissolution of the Monasteries the estate reverted to the Crown. In 1594 it was granted to the 9th Earl of Northumberland, who altered and improved the property. In the eight years, 1762–1770, the interior was transformed and furnished by Robert Adam. Open Easter to Sept. 29 (Sun. to Thurs.), 12–5·00 p.m. Sun. only in Oct.

Thames Embankments.—The Victoria Embankment, on the N. side (from Westminster to Blackfriars), was constructed by Sir J. W. Bazalgette for the Metropolitan Board of Works, 1864–70 (the seats, of which the supports of some are a kneeling camel, laden with spicery, and of others a winged sphinx, were presented by the Grocers' Company, and by Rt. Hon. W. H. Smith, M.P., in 1874); the Albert Embankment, on the S. side (from Westminster Bridge to Vauxhall), 1866–69; the Chelsea Embankment, 1871–74. The total cost exceeded £2,000,000. Sir J. W. Bazalgette (1819–91) also inaugurated the London main drainage system, 1858–65. A medallion has been placed on a pier of the Victoria Embankment to commemorate the engineer of the Thames waterside improvements ("Flumini vincula posuit"). The headquarters of the G.L.C. include an embankment on the Surrey side.

Thames Flood Barrier.—Officially opened in May 1984, though first used in Feb. 1983, the Barrier consists of ten rising sector gates which span 570 yards from bank to bank of the Thames at Woolwich Reach. When not in use the gates lie horizontally, allowing shipping to navigate the river normally; when the Barrier is closed, the gates turn through 90 degrees to stand vertically more than 50 feet above the river bed. The Barrier took eight years to complete and can be raised within about 30 minutes.

Thames Tunnels.—The *Rotherhithe Tunnel,* constructed by the L.C.C. and opened in 1908, connects Commercial Road, E.14, with Lower Road, Rotherhithe; the total length is 1 mile 332 yards, of which 474 yards are under the river. The cost of the tunnel and its approaches was £1,506,914. The first *Blackwall Tunnel* (pedestrians and vehicles) was constructed by the L.C.C. and opened in 1897, connecting East India Dock Road, Poplar, with Blackwall Lane, East Greenwich. The cost of the tunnel with its approaches was about £1,323,663. A second tunnel (for southbound vehicles only) was opened in August, 1967, at a cost of about £9,750,000 and the old tunnel was improved at a cost of about £1,350,000 and made one-way northbound. Both tunnels are for vehicles only. The relative lengths of the tunnels measured from East India Dock Road to the Gate House on the south side are 6,215 ft. (old tunnel) and 6,152 feet. *Greenwich Tunnel* (pedestrians only), constructed by the L.C.C. and opened in 1902, connects the Isle of Dogs, Poplar, with Greenwich. The length of the subway is 406 yards, and the cost was about £180,000. The *Woolwich Tunnel* (pedestrians only), constructed by the L.C.C. and opened in 1912, connects North and South Woolwich below the passenger and vehicular ferry from North Woolwich Station, E.16, to High Street, Woolwich, S.E.18. The length of the subway is 552 yards, and its cost was about £86,000. The *Thames Tunnel* (1,300 feet) was opened in 1843 to connect Wapping (N.) with Rotherhithe (S.). In 1866 it was closed to the public, and purchased by the East London Railway Company. The *Tower Subway* for pedestrians was opened in 1870, and has long been closed.

Tower Bridge Walkway and Museum, SE1 2UP.—Owned by the Bridge House Trust and open daily Apr. to Oct. 10–6·30 p.m. and Nov. to Mar. 10–4·45 p.m. Admission: Adults £2, children and O.A.P.s £1. Attractions include exhibitions, videos, the observation platform and walkway, engine rooms, working models and souvenir gift shop.

Tower Hill, E.C.1 and E.C.3, was formerly the place of execution for condemned prisoners from the Tower, the site of the scaffold being marked in the gardens of Trinity Square.

Tower of London, E.C.3.—Admission to a general view of the Tower, the White Tower (Armouries), the History, Oriental, Ordnance and 18–19th Century Galleries, and the Wall Walk Phases I and II. Admission (1985): Oct.–Mar., £2 (children £1); April–Sept. £3 (children £1·50); to the Jewel House, 80p, children 40p. (The Jewel House is usually closed for cleaning in Feb. Precise dates available from the Receiver of Fees Office at the Tower.) On Sundays throughout the year (except August) the public is admitted to Holy Communion, 9.15 a.m. and Morning Service, 11 a.m. Open on weekdays, Mar. 1 to Oct. 31, 9.30–5; Nov. 1 to Feb. 28, 9.30–4; Sundays, 2 p.m. to 5 p.m., Mar. 1–Oct. 31 only; Tower closed Christmas Eve, Christmas Day, Boxing Day, Good Friday and New Year's Day. *Constable*, Field Marshal Sir Roland Gibbs, G.C.B., C.B.E., D.S.O., M.C.; *Lieutenant*, Lieut. Gen. Sir Hugh Cunnigham, K.B.E.; *Resident Governor and Keeper of the Jewel House*, Maj.-Gen. A. P. W. MacLellan, M.B.E.; *Master of the Armouries*, A. V. B. Norman; *Chaplain at the Chapel Royal of St. Peter ad Vincula*, Rev. J. F. M. Llewellyn.

The White Tower is the oldest and central building in Her Majesty's Royal Palace and Fortress of the Tower of London. It was built at the order of William I and constructed by Gundulph, Bishop of Rochester, in the years 1078–98. The Inner Wall, with thirteen towers, was constructed by Henry III in the 12th century. The Moat was extended and completed by Richard I and the Wharf first mentioned in 1228. The Outer Wall was completed in the reign of Edward I and now incorporates 6 towers and 2 bastions. The last Monarch to reside in the Tower of London was James I. The Crown Jewels came to the Tower in the reign of Henry III. All coinage used in Great Britain was minted in the Outer Ward of the Tower of London until 1810 when the Royal Mint was formed. The Tower of London has had a military garrison since 1078. The Chapel Royal of St. John the Evangelist, within the White Tower (1080–1088) is the oldest Norman church in London. The chapel of St. Peter ad Vincula was built in the early 16th century.

Waltham Abbey (or **Waltham Holy Cross**), Essex.—The Abbey ruins, Harold's Bridge (14th century), the Nave of the former cruciform Abbey Church and the traditional burial place of King Harold II (1066), and a Lady Chapel of Edward II, with crypt below, which houses a visitors centre with permanent exhibition. New evidence of the position and style of several buildings, which once stood on the site of the Augustinian monastery, were revealed by the prolonged drought in the summer of 1933 and by subsequent excavations. At Waltham Cross, 1 mile from the Abbey, is one of the crosses (partly

restored) erected by Edward I to mark a resting place of the corpse of Queen Eleanor on its way to Westminster Abbey. (Ten crosses were erected, but only those at Geddington, Northampton and Waltham remain; "Charing" Cross originally stood near the spot now occupied by the statue of Charles I at Whitehall.)

Wellington Museum, Apsley House, 149 Piccadilly, at Hyde Park Corner, W.1.—Admission 60p, children 30p. Open weekdays, 10 to 6; Sundays, 2.30 to 6. Closed Mondays and Fridays, Christmas Eve, Christmas Day, Boxing Day and New Year's Day. Apsley House was designed by Robert Adam for Lord Bathurst and built 1771–8. It was bought in 1817 by the Duke of Wellington, who in 1828–29 employed Benjamin Wyatt to enlarge it, face it with Bath stone and add the Corinthian portico. The museum contains many fine paintings, services of porcelain and silver plate and personal relics of the 1st Duke of Wellington (1769–1852) and was given to the Nation by the 7th Duke. It was first opened to the public in 1952, under the administration of the Victoria and Albert Museum.

Westminster Hall, S.W.1.—The only part of the old Palace of Westminster to survive the fire of 1834, Westminster Hall is adjacent to and incorporated in the Houses of Parliament. Westminster Hall was built by William Rufus from 1097–99 and altered by Richard II, 1394–1401. It is about 240 ft. long, 69 ft. wide and 90 ft. high; the hammer beam roof of carved oak dates from 1396–98. The Hall was the scene of the trial of Charles I. Westminster Hall is included on the route followed by those who have arranged a visit to the Houses of Parliament (*q.v.*) with their M.P.

Whitechapel Art Gallery, High Street, E.1.— Opened in 1901; administered by a charitable trust. There is no permanent collection; temporary exhibitions, mainly of modern art, are presented, and community and educational projects are run. Open Tues.–Suns. 11–5.30 p.m.

Wimbledon Lawn Tennis Museum, SW19 5AE.—Exhibits include fashion, trophies, replicas and memorabilia representing the history of lawn tennis and a theatre shows films of great matches. Open Tues.–Sat. 11–5, Sun. 2–5. Admission: Adults £1·50, Children and O.A.P.s 75p.

Windsor Castle (begun by William the Conqueror, A.D. 1066–87).—22 miles from London, by Western and Southern Regions. The Castle Precincts are open daily, free of charge, from 10 a.m. to 4.15 p.m. late October to late March; 5.15 p.m. late March and April and September to late October; and 7.15 p.m. May to August. When the Queen is not in official residence, the *State Apartments* of Windsor Castle are open to the public on every weekday and on Sunday afternoons during the summer months. When the State Apartments are open, the charges for admission are for Adults, £1·40 and for Children and O.A.P.s 60p. By the Queen's command, the net proceeds go to charities. The hours of admission to the State Apartments are: Jan. to late Mar., late Oct. to Dec., 10.30–3; May to late Oct., 10.30–5; Sundays, May to late Oct. 1.30–5; Closed, mid-March, April and mid-June. *Queen Mary's Doll's House, the Exhibition of Dolls, the Exhibition of Drawings by Holbein, Leonardo da Vinci and other artists and the Royal Mews Exhibition* can be seen on the same days and hours as the State Apartments; admission, adults 60p, children and O.A.P.s 20p. When the State Apartments are closed, Queen Mary's Doll's House, the Exhibition of Drawings and the Royal Mews Exhibition remain open to the public. The *Albert Memorial Chapel* is open throughout the year from 10–1; 2–3.45; closed on Sundays; Admission free. A fee is charged to visit *St. George's Chapel.* The *Curfew Tower* may be seen under the guidance of the Keeper to whom application must be made at the entrance.

The *Royal Mausoleum*, Frogmore Gardens, Home Park, is open annually on two days in early May in conjunction with the opening of Frogmore Gardens in aid of the National Garden Scheme, 10 a.m.–7 p.m. Also open on the Wednesday nearest to May 24 (Queen Victoria's birthday) from 11 a.m. to 4 p.m. Admission free.

Zoological Gardens, Regent's Park, N.W.1.— (Opened in 1828). Open daily (except Dec. 25) March– Oct. 9–6 or dusk (7 p.m. Suns. and Bank Hols.), opens 10 a.m. in winter. Admission, £3·20, children under 16, £1·60, under 5 free. Special rates for parties and O.A.P.s. Aquarium and Children's Zoo free.

[London Tourist Board.—26 Grosvenor Gardens, S.W.1. (*Tel.*, 01–730 3450.)]

PARKS, SPACES AND GARDENS

The principal Parks and Open Spaces in the Metropolitan area are maintained as under:—

By the Crown

BUSHY PARK (1,099 acres).—Adjoining Hampton Court, contains avenue of horse-chestnuts enclosed in a four-fold avenue of limes planted by William III. "Chestnut Sunday" (when the trees are in full bloom with their "candles") is usually about May 1 to 15.

GREEN PARK (49 acres), W.1.—Between Piccadilly and St. James's Park with *Constitution Hill*, leading to Hyde Park Corner.

GREENWICH PARK (196½ acres), S.E.10.

HAMPTON COURT GARDENS (54 acres).

HAMPTON COURT GREEN (17 acres).

HAMPTON COURT PARK (622 acres).

HYDE PARK (341 acres).—From Park Lane, W.1, to Kensington Gardens, W.2 containing the Serpentine. Fine gateway at Hyde Park Corner, with Apsley House, the Achilles Statue, Rotten Row and the Ladies' Mile. To the north-east is the *Marble Arch*, originally erected by George IV at the entrance to Buckingham Palace and re-erected in present position in 1851.

KENSINGTON GARDENS (275 acres), W.2.—From western boundary of Hyde Park to Kensington Palace, containing the Albert Memorial.

REGENT'S PARK and PRIMROSE HILL (464 acres), N.W.1.—From Marylebone Road to Primrose Hill surrounded by the Outer Circle and divided by the *Broad Walk* leading to the Zoological Gardens.

RICHMOND PARK (2,469 acres).

ST. JAMES'S PARK (93 acres), S.W.1.—From Whitehall to Buckingham Palace. Ornamental lake of 12 acres. The original suspension bridge built in 1857 was replaced in 1957. The *Mall* leads from the Admiralty Arch to the Queen Victoria Memorial and Buckingham Palace. *Birdcage Walk* from Storey's Gate, past Wellington Barracks, to Buckingham Palace.

By the Corporation of London

BURNHAM BEECHES and FLEET WOOD, Bucks. (510 acres).—Purchased by the Corporation for the benefit of the public in 1880, Fleet Wood (65 acres) being presented in 1921.

COULSDON COMMON, Surrey (127 acres).

EPPING FOREST (6,000 acres).—Purchased by the Corporation for £250,000 and thrown open to the public in 1882. The present forest is 12 miles long by 1 to 2 miles wide, about one-tenth of its original area.

FARTHINGDOWN, Surrey (121 acres).

HIGHGATE WOOD (70 acres).

KENLEY COMMON, Surrey (85 acres).

QUEEN'S PARK, Kilburn (30 acres).

RIDDLESDOWN, Surrey (90 acres).

SPRING PARK, West Wickham (51 acres).

WEST HAM PARK (77 acres).

WEST WICKHAM COMMON, Kent (25 acres).

With smaller open spaces within the City of London, including FINSBURY CIRCUS GARDENS.

By the Greater London Council

ABBEY WOOD PARK (19 acres), S.E.2.

ARCHBISHOP'S PARK (10 acres), S.E.1.

AVERY HILL (96 acres), S.E.9, with winter garden and nursery.

BATTERSEA PARK (200 acres), S.W.11, with zoo and lake.

BLACKHEATH (272 acres), S.E.10.—*Morden College*, founded in 1695 as a home for "decayed Turkey merchants", is near the S.E. corner. The building was designed by Wren and its Chapel doors have carvings attributed to Grinling Gibbons. Concerts and poetry recitals are held at *Rangers House*, an early 18th century mansion, which houses the Suffolk collection of English portraits from the Elizabethan to the Georgian period.

BOSTALL HEATH AND WOODS (159 acres), S.E.2.

BURGESS PARK (90 acres), S.E.5.

CASTLEWOOD, see JACKWOOD.

CRYSTAL PALACE PARK (106 acres), S.E.19, with zoo, and open air concerts in summer.

CUTTY SARK GARDENS (4 acres), S.E.10.

DULWICH PARK (72 acres), S.E.21.

ELTHAM PARK (including Falconwood Field and Shepherdsleas Wood, 122 acres), S.E.9.

FINSBURY PARK (115 acres), N.4.

GEFFRYE'S GARDEN (2 acres), E.2.

GOLDERS HILL (36 acres), N.W.3, adjoining West Heath, Hampstead.

HACKNEY MARSH (336 acres), E.9. 106 football pitches.

HAINAULT FOREST (958 acres), Hainault, Essex.

HAMPSTEAD HEATH and Extension (283 acres), N.W.3.

HAVERING COUNTRY PARK (168 acres).

HERNE HILL STADIUM (9 acres), S.E.24. Cycle racing track.

HOLLAND PARK (55 acres), W.8. Open air theatre and concerts; floodlit gardens; King George VI Memorial Youth Hostel; Restaurant.

HORNIMAN GARDENS (26 acres), S.E.23. Adjoining Horniman Museum.

HOUNSLOW HEATH (204 acres), Staines Road, Hounslow.

KENWOOD (200 acres), N.W.3, the northern part of Hampstead Heath. Part purchased in 1922 by public subscription. Open air symphony concerts each summer. The Iveagh Bequest, in an 18th-century mansion (open to the public), includes valuable art treasures. Recitals and poetry readings in the Orangery.

LESNES ABBEY WOODS (215 acres), Erith, S.E.2.—Ruins of an Augustinian abbey.

LIMEHOUSE CHURCHYARD (2 acres), E.1.

MARBLE HILL (66 acres).—Twickenham, Middlesex.—A beautiful park, running down to the riverside, on the left bank of the Thames; includes a mansion (open to the public). Open air theatre.

MILE END PARK, E.3. (60 acres). Includes the East London Stadium.

OXLEAS WOODLANDS (253 acres), S.E.18. Includes Castlewood and Severndroog Castle, Eltham Common, Jackwood, King George's Field, Oxleas Meadow and Oxleas Wood.

PARLIAMENT HILL (271 acres), N.W.3.—Part of Hampstead Heath. Lido and swimming bath. Important cross-country events are held here.

SOUTH BANK (10 acres, including Jubilee Gardens), Belvedere Road, S.E.1.

STANMORE COUNTRY PARK (78 acres), Stanmore, Middx.

THAMESMEAD OPEN SPACES (213 acres), S.E.2.

TOWER HAMLETS CEMETERY (28 acres), E.3. Conversion to public open spaces.

TRENT PARK (413 acres), Cockfosters, Enfield. Country park with nature trail, riding school, golf course, picnic sites, fishing, etc.

VICTORIA PARK (218 acres), E.9.

WORMWOOD SCRUBS (191 acres), Hammersmith, W.12. West London Stadium.

LATIN NAMES OF ENGLISH TOWNS AND CITIES

Bath	*Aquae Sulis*	Lincoln	*Lindum*
Canterbury	*Durovernum*	London	*Londinium*
Carlisle	*Luguvalium*	Manchester	*Mancunium*
Chelmsford	*Caesaromagus*	Newcastle	*Pons Aelius*
Chester	*Deva*	Pevensey	*Anderida*
Cirencester	*Corinium*	Rochester	*Durobrivae*
Colchester	*Camulodunum*	St. Albans	*Verulamium*
Doncaster	*Danum*	Salisbury	*Sorbiodunum*
Dorchester	*Durinum, Durno-*	(Old Sarum)	
	varia	Silchester	*Calleva Atrebatum*
Dover	*Dubris*	Winchester	*Venta Belgarum*
Exeter	*Isca Dumnoniorum*	Worcester	*Wigornia*
Gloucester	*Glevum*	Wroxeter	*Viroconium*
Lancaster	*Lunecastrum*	Yarmouth	*Magna Gernemutha*
Leicester	*Ratae Coritanorum*	York	*Eboracum*

The Principality of Wales

Position and extent.—Wales (Cymru) occupies the extreme west of the central southern portion of the island of Great Britain, with a total area of 8,019 sq. miles; it is bounded on the N. by the Irish Sea, on the S. by the Bristol Channel, on the E. by the English counties of Cheshire, Shropshire, Hereford and Worcester, and Gloucester, and on the W. by St. George's Channel. Across the Menai Straits is the Welsh island of *Anglesey* or Ynys Mōn (276 sq. miles), communication with which is facilitated by the Menai Suspension Bridge (1,000 ft. long), built by Telford in 1826 and by the tubular railway bridge (1,100 ft. long) built by Stephenson in 1850. Holyhead harbour, on Holy Isle (N.W. of Anglesey), provides accommodation for ferry services to Dublin (70 miles).

Population.—The population at the Census of 1981 was 2,791,851 (males 1,352,639; females 1,439,212). The average density of population in 1981 was 343 per square mile.

Relief.—Wales is a country of extensive tracts of high plateau and shorter stretches of mountain ranges deeply dissected by river valleys. Lower-lying ground is largely confined to the coastal belt and the lower parts of the valleys. The highest mountains are those of Snowdonia in the north-west (*Snowdon*, 3,559 ft.), Berwyn (*Aran Fawddwy*, 2,971 ft.), Cader Idris (*Pen y Gadair*, 2,928 ft.), Dyfed (*Plynlimon*, 2,467 ft.), and the Black Mountain, Brecon Beacons and Black Forest ranges in the south-east (*Carmarthen Van*, 2,630 ft., *Pen y Fan*, 2,906 ft., *Waun Fâch*, 2,660 ft.).

Hydrography.—The principal river of those rising in Wales is the *Severn* (*see* England), which flows from the slopes of Plynlimon to the English border. The *Wye* (130 miles) also rises in the slopes of Plynlimon. The *Usk* (56 miles) flows into the Bristol Channel, through Gwent. The *Dee* (70 miles) rises in Bala Lake and flows through the Vale of Llangollen, where an aqueduct (built by Telford in 1805) carries the Pontcysyllte branch of the Shropshire Union Canal across the valley. The estuary of the Dee is the navigable portion, 14 miles in length and about 5 miles in breadth, and the tide rushes in with dangerous speed over the "Sands of Dee". The *Towy* (68 miles), *Teifi* (50 miles), *Taff* (40 miles), *Dovey* (30 miles), *Taf* (25 miles), and *Conway* (24 miles), the last named broad and navigable, are wholly Welsh rivers.

The largest natural lake in Wales is *Bala* (Llyn Tegid) in Gwynedd, 4 miles long and about 1 mile wide; *Lake Vyrnwy* is an artificial reservoir, about the size of Bala, and forms the water supply of Liverpool, and Birmingham is supplied from a chain of reservoirs in the Elan and Clærwen valleys.

The Welsh Language.—According to the 1981 Census results, the percentage of persons of three years and over able to speak Welsh were:

Clwyd	18·7	Powys	20·2
Dyfed	46·3	S. Glamorgan	5·8
Gwent	2·5	W. Glamorgan	16·4
Gwynedd	61·2		
Mid Glamorgan	8·4	**Wales**	18·9

The 1981 figure represents a slight decline from 20·8 per cent in 1971 (1961, 26 per cent; 1951, 28·9 per cent).

Flag.—A red dragon on a green and white field (per fess argent and vert a dragon passant gules). The flag was augmented in 1953 by a royal badge on a shield encircled with a riband bearing the words *Ddraig Goch Ddyry Cychwyn* and imperially crowned. Only the unaugmented flag is flown on Government offices in Wales and, where appropriate, in London. Both flags continue to be used elsewhere.

EARLY HISTORY

Celts and Romans.—The earliest inhabitants of whom there is any record appear to have been subdued or exterminated by the *Goidels* (a people of Celtic race) in the Bronze Age, and a further invasion of Celtic *Brythons* and *Belgae* followed in the ensuing Iron Age. The *Roman* conquest of South Britain and Wales was for some time successfully opposed by *Caratacus* (Caractacus or Caradog), Chieftain of the Catuvellauni and son of *Cunobelinus* (Cymbeline) King of the Trinobantes. In A.D. 78 the conquest of Wales was completed under Julius Frontinus, and communications were opened up by the construction of military roads from Chester to Caerleon-on-Usk and Caerwent, and from Chester to Conway (and thence to Camarthen and Neath). *Christianity* was introduced (during the Roman occupation) in the 4th century.

The Anglo-Saxon Attacks.—The Anglo-Saxon invaders of South Britain drove the Celtic Goidels and Brythons into the mountain fastness of Wales, and into Strathclyde (Cumberland and S.W. Scotland) and Cornwall, giving them the name of *Waelisc*, or Welsh (= Foreign). The West Saxons' victory of Deorham (577) isolated Wales from Cornwall and the battle of Chester (613) cut off communication with Strathclyde. In the 8th century the boundaries of the Welsh were further restricted by the annexations of Offa, King of Mercia, and counter-attacks were largely prevented by the construction of an artificial boundary from the Dee to the Wye (Offa's Dike). In the 9th century Rhodri Mawr united the country against further incursions of the Saxons by land and against the raids of Norse and Danish pirates by sea, but at his death his three provinces of *Gwynedd* (N.), *Powys* (Mid.) and *Deheubarth* (S.) were divided among his three sons—Anarawd, Mervyn and Cadell—the son of the last named being Hywel Dda, who codified the laws of the country, while Llewelyn ap Seisyll (husband of the heiress of Gwynedd) again united the provinces and reigned as Prince from 1018 to 1023.

The Norman Conquest.—After the Norman conquest of England, William I created Palatine counties along the Welsh frontier, and Robert FitzHamon, the Norman Earl of Gloucester, raided South Wales and erected fortresses from the Wye to Milford Haven. Henry I introduced Flemish settlers into South Wales, but after his death the Welsh rose under the leadership of Griffith ap Rhys and routed the Norman-Flemish forces at the fords of the Teifi (Cardigan) in 1136. From the early years of the 13th century the house of Gwynedd, in the north, gained an ascendancy over the whole of Wales, and Llywelyn ap Iorwerth was in constant strife with England for recognition as an independent sovereign. Llywelyn ap Gruffydd (grandson of Llywelyn ap Iorwerth), the last native prince, was killed in 1282 during hostilities between the Welsh and English, allowing Edward I of England to establish his authority over the country. On Feb. 7, 1301, Edward of Caernarvon, son of Edward I, was created *Prince of Wales*, a title which has subsequently been borne by the eldest son of the sovereign. Strong Welsh national feeling continued, expressed in the early 15th century in the rising led by Owain Glyndŵr, but the situation was altered by the accession to the English throne in 1485 of Henry VI of the Welsh House of Tudor. Wales was politically assimilated to England under the Act of Union of 1535, which extended English laws to the

Principality and gave it parliamentary representation for the first time.

Eisteddfod.—The Welsh are a distinct nationality, with a language and literature of their own, and the national bardic festival (Eisteddfod), instituted by Prince Rhys ap Griffith in 1176, is annually maintained. These *Eisteddfodau* (sessions) form part of the *Gorsedd* (assembly), which is believed to date from the time of Prydian, a ruling prince in an age many centuries before the Christian era.

AREA AND POPULATION OF THE WELSH COUNTIES

County	Administrative Headquarters	Area (*hectares*)	Population	Rateable Value	Actual Rateable Value per head
					p.
Clwyd............	Shire Hall, Mold	242,650	396,300	41,195,314	103·95
Dyfed	*Carmarthen	576,577	377,100	32,537,800	96·52
Gwent	*Cwmbran	137,599	438,500	47,007,406	107·20
Gwynedd	County Offices, Caernarfon	386,708	232,700	26,234,152	112·74
Mid Glamorgan ...	*Cathays Park, Cardiff	101,867	536,400	40,739,825	75·08
Powys............	*Llandrindod Wells	507,741	110,600	10,088,438	91·22
South Glamorgan .	County Headquarters, Newport Road, Cardiff	41,629	391,400	52,926,361	135·22
West Glamorgan ..	*Swansea	81,657	366,600	38,593,741	105·27

* County Hall.

COUNTY OFFICIALS AND CHAIRMEN OF COUNTY COUNCILS

County	Chief Executive	County Treasurer	Chairmen of C.C.
Clwyd............	M. H. Phillips	R. C. Greening	A. E. Jones
Dyfed	D. H. Davies	A. C. Williams	A. C. Francis
Gwent	M. J. Perry	R. Emmott	J. J. Pembridge
Gwynedd	I. B. Rees	J. L. Williams	O. M. Roberts
Mid Glamorgan ...	D. H. Thomas*	R. K. Lacey	A. M. Ellis
Powys............	M. J. Greenwood	M. J. Greenwood	J. T. H. Davies
South Glamorgan .	W. P. Davey	R. G. Tettenborn	K. Hutchings
West Glamorgan ..	M. E. J. Rush	S. G. Dunster	G. Thomas

* County Clerk.

PRINCIPAL WELSH CITIES

CARDIFF

CARDIFF (South Glamorgan), at the mouth of the rivers Taff, Rhymney and Ely, is the capital City of Wales and one of Britain's major administrative, commercial and office centres. It has many industries, including steel works, car component manufacturing, cigars and a flourishing port with a substantial and varied trade. There are many fine buildings in the civic centre started early this century which includes the City Hall, the National Museum of Wales, University Buildings, Law Courts, Welsh Office, County Hall, Police Headquarters and the Temple of Peace and Health. Also in the city are Llandaff Cathedral, the Welsh National Folk Museum at St. Fagans, Cardiff Castle, the New Theatre, the Sherman Theatre and the Cardiff College of Music and Drama. New buildings include St. David's Hall, a 2,000-seat concert and conference hall.

SWANSEA

SWANSEA (in Welsh, Abertawe) is a City and a seaport of West Glamorgan with its own municipal airport. The beautiful Gower Peninsula was brought within the City boundary under local government reform on April 1, 1974. The trade of the port includes coal, patent fuel, ores, and the import and export of oil. The municipal area is 60,511 acres.

The principal buildings are the Norman Castle (rebuilt in 1330), the Royal Institution of South Wales, founded in 1835 (containing Museum and Library), the University College at Singleton and the Guildhall, containing the Brangwyn panels. New buildings include the Industrial and Maritime Museum, the new Maritime Quarter and Marina and the leisure centre. Swansea was chartered by the Earl of Warwick, *circa* 1158–1184, and further charters were granted by King John, Henry III., Edward II., Edward III. and James II., 2 from Cromwell and 1 Lord Marcher.

LORD LIEUTENANTS AND HIGH SHERIFFS OF WELSH COUNTIES

County	Lord Lieutenant	High Sheriff (1985–86)
Clwyd	Sir William Gladstone, bt.	Mrs. N. L. Edwards, o.b.e., t.d.
Dyfed	D. C. Mansel Lewis	Dr. J. H. Cule
Gwent	R. Hanbury-Tenison	M. J. M. Clarke
Gwynedd	The Most Hon. The Marquess of Anglesey	Dr. D. E. Meredith, o.b.e.
Mid Glamorgan	Sir Cennydd Traherne, k.g., t.d.	O. A. M. Williams
Powys	Col. J. L. Corbett-Winder, o.b.e., m.c.	C. R. Woosnam
South Glamorgan	} (*See* Mid Glamorgan)	W. E. Evans, c.b.e.
West Glamorgan		E. G. Thomas

MUNICIPAL DIRECTORY OF WALES

District Councils

Those accorded City Status are shown in Small Capitals; those with
Borough Status are distinguished by having § prefixed.

District	Population	Rateable Value 1985 £	Chief Executive (* Chief Officer)	Chairman 1985–86 (a) Mayor (b) Lord Mayor
§Aberconwy, Gwynedd	51,300	5,593,525	J. E. Davies	(a) R. A. Evans
§Afan, West Glamorgan	55,000	8,600,805	C. A. Millward	(a) Mrs. V. Mescall
Alyn and Deeside, Clwyd	72,800	8,259,863	W. E. Rogers	J. S. Banks
§Arfon, Gwynedd	54,900	6,321,661	D. L. Jones	(a) Miss M. Richards M.B.E.
§Blaenau Gwent, Gwent	79,200	5,854,676	R. Leadbeter	(a) R. Edmonds
§Brecknock, Powys	41,200	3,500,953	E. F. Jones	(a) H. L. Evans
Cardiff, South Glamorgan	281,200	39,748,904	H. T. Crippin	(b) Capt. N. Lloyd-Edwards
Carmarthen, Dyfed	51,500	4,200,743	V. M. Williams	S. D. John
Ceredigion, Dyfed	62,000	5,164,281	D. Morgan	T. I. Jones
§Colwyn, Clwyd	50,300	5,466,980	O. Morris	(a) J. Hughes
§Cynon Valley, Mid Glamorgan	67,197	4,536,349	G. W. Hosgood	(a) Miss M. George
§Delyn, Clwyd	65,700	5,972,000	J. R. Packer	(a) G. D. Evans
§Dinefwr, Dyfed	36,413	2,298,053	E. W. Harries	(a) E. R. Thomas
Dwyfor, Gwynedd	26,100	2,645,627	E. Davies	Canon W. Jones
Glyndwr, Clwyd	40,500	3,546,249	D. Bowen	G. Davies
§Islwyn, Gwent	64,769	4,627,365	B. Bird	(a) W. D. G. Cole, M.B.E.
§Llanelli, Dyfed	75,100	6,490,713	A. B. Thomas	(a) G. J. Jones
§Lliw Valley, West Glamorgan	60,500	4,684,444	J. C. Howells	(a) W. H. Evans
Meirionnydd, Gwynedd	31,300	4,108,297	G. W. Hughes	R. G. Middleton
§Merthyr Tydfil, Mid Glamorgan	61,000	4,677,958	S. Jones	(a) P. Saunders
Monmouth, Gwent	75,400	7,681,215	G. Cummings	G. Jones
Montgomery, Powys	47,661	4,323,754	N. J. Bardsley	E. G. Davies
§Neath, West Glamorgan	65,700	6,186,980	G. H. Griffiths*	(a) C. James
§Newport, Gwent	131,700	19,684,305	G. N. Cook	(a) T. C. Warren
§Ogwr, Mid Glamorgan	130,100	10,698,665	J. G. Cole	(a) W. R. Trigg, B.E.M.
Preseli, Dyfed	70,200	7,081,323	I. W. R. David	E. R. Harries
Radnor, Powys	21,600	2,281,085	K. M. Francis	G. M. Worts
§Rhondda, Mid Glamorgan	81,000	3,935,100	G. Evans	(a) G. P. James
§Rhuddlan, Clwyd	53,300	6,115,940	F. J. K. Davies	(a) Miss C. Ellis
Rhymney Valley, Mid Glamorgan	107,000	7,568,613	P. A. Bennett	K. Forehead
South Pembrokeshire, Dyfed	38,800	7,243,626	D. R. Jones	W. J. Davies
Swansea, West Glamorgan	186,400	18,671,123	A. N. F. Rees	(b) T. G. Burtonshaw
§Taff-Ely, Mid Glamorgan	94,500	9,316,067	D. Gethin	(a) A. F. Watts
§Torfaen, Gwent	90,214	9,138,953	M. B. Mehta	(a) H. J. Rosser
§Vale of Glamorgan, South Glamorgan	111,900	13,803,713	J. R. Gau	(a) J. R. Griffiths
§Wrexham Maelor, Clwyd	113,900	11,624,622	S. F. Tongue	(a) R. W. Squire
§Ynys Môn (Isle of Anglesey), Gwynedd	69,300	7,537,930	E. L. Gibson	(a) J. V. Owen

THE KINGDOM OF SCOTLAND

Position and Extent.—The Kingdom of Scotland occupies the northern portion of the main island of Great Britain and includes the Inner and Outer Hebrides, and the Orkney, Shetland, and many other islands. The Kingdom lies between 60° 51′ 30″ and 54° 38′ N. latitude and between 1° 45′ 32″ and 6° 14′ W. longitude, its southern neighbour being the Kingdom of England, with the Atlantic Ocean on the N. and W., and the North Sea on the E. The greatest length of the mainland (Cape Wrath to the Mull of Galloway) is 274 miles, and the greatest breadth (Buchan Ness to Applecross) is 154 miles. The customary measurement of the Island of Great Britain is from the site of John o' Groats house, near Duncansby Head, Caithness (at the N.E. extremity of the island) to Land's End, Cornwall (at the S.W. extremity), a total distance of 603 miles in a straight line and (approximately) 900 by road.

The total area of the Kingdom is 30,414 square miles (land 29,795; inland water 619). The population (1981 Census) was 5,130,735 (males 2,466,437; females 2,664,298). The average density of the population in 1981 was 168 persons per square mile.

Relief.—There are three natural orographic divisions of Scotland. The Southern Uplands have their highest points in Merrick (2,766 feet), Rhinns of Kells (2,669 feet), and Cairnsmuir of Carsphairn (2,614 feet), in the west; and the Tweedsmuir Hills in the east (*Hartfell* 2,651 ft., *Dollar Law* 2,682 ft., *Broad Law* 2,756 ft.). The Central Lowlands, formed by the valleys of the Clyde, Forth and Tay, divide the Southern Uplands from the heather-clad Northern Highlands, which extend almost from the extreme north of the mainland to the central lowlands, and are divided into a northern and southern system by the *Great Glen*. The Grampian Mountains, which entirely cover the southern Highland area, include in the west *Ben Nevis* (4,406 ft.), the highest point in the British Isles, and in the east the Cairngorm Mountains (*Cairn Gorm* 4,084 ft., *Braeriach* 4,248 ft., *Ben Macdui* 4,296 ft.). The north-western Highland area contains in the mountains of Wester and Eastern Ross *Carn Eige* (3,880 ft.) and *Sgurr na Lapaich* (3,775 ft.).

Created, like the Central Lowlands, by a major geological fault, the *Great Glen* (60 miles long) runs between Inverness and Fort William, and contains Loch Ness, Loch Oich and Loch Lochy. These are linked to each other and to the north-east and south-west coasts of Scotland by the Caledonian Canal, providing a navigable passage between the Moray Firth and the Inner Hebrides.

Hydrography.—The western coast of Scotland is fragmented by peninsulas and islands, and indented by fjords (sea-lochs), the longest of which is *Loch Fyne* (42 miles long) in Argyllshire. Although the east coast tends to be less fractured and lower, there are several great drowned inlets (firths), e.g. Firth of Forth, Firth of Tay, Moray Firth, as well as the Firth of Clyde in the west.

The lochs are the principal hydrographic feature of the Kingdom, both on the mainland and in many of the islands. The largest in the Kingdom and in Great Britain is *Loch Lomond* (27 square miles in area), in the Grampian valleys; the longest and deepest is *Loch Ness* (24 miles long and 800 feet deep), in the Great Glen; and Lochs Shin (20 miles) and Maree in the northern Highlands.

The longest river in Scotland is the *Tay* (117 miles), noted for its salmon. It flows into the North Sea, with Dundee on the estuary, which is spanned by the Tay Bridge (10,289 ft.) opened in 1887 and the Tay Road Bridge (7,365 ft.) opened in 1966. Other noted salmon rivers are the *Dee* (90 miles) which flows into

the North Sea at Aberdeen, and the *Spey* (110 miles), the swiftest flowing river in the British Isles, which flows into Moray Firth. The *Tweed*, which gave its name to the woollen cloth produced along its banks, marks in the lower stretches of its 96-mile course the border between Scotland and England.

The most important river commercially is the *Clyde* (106 miles), formed by the junction of the Daer and Portrail water, which flows through the city and port of Glasgow to the Firth of Clyde. During its course it passes over the picturesque *Falls of Clyde*, Bonnington Linn (30 ft.), Corra Linn (84 ft.), Dundaff Linn (10 ft.) and Stonebyres Linn (80 ft.), above and below Lanark. The *Forth* (66 miles), upon which stands Edinburgh, the capital, is spanned by the *Forth (Railway) Bridge* (1890), which is 5,330 feet long, and the *Forth (Road) Bridge* (1964), which has a total length of 6,156 ft. (over water) and a single span of 3,000 ft.

The highest waterfall in Scotland, and the British Isles, is *Eas a'Chùal Aluinn* with a total height of 658 ft., which falls from Glas Bheinn in Sutherland. The *Falls of Glomach*, on a head-stream of the Elchaig in Wester Ross, have a drop of 370 ft.

Gaelic Language.—According to the 1981 Census, 82,620 people, mainly in the Highlands and western coastal regions, were able to speak, read or write the Scottish form of Gaelic.

THE SCOTTISH ISLANDS

The Hebrides did not become part of the Kingdom of Scotland until 1266, when they were ceded to Alexander III by Magnus of Norway. Orkney and Shetland fell to the Scottish Crown as a pledge for the unpaid dowry of Margaret of Denmark, wife of James III, in 1468, the Danish claims to suzerainty being relinquished in 1590 when James VI married Anne of Denmark.

Orkney.—The Orkney Islands (total area 375½ square miles) lie about six miles north of the mainland, separated from it by the Pentland Firth. Of the 90 islands and islets (holms and skerries) in the group, about one-third are inhabited. The total population at the 1981 Census was 19,040; the 1981 populations of the islands shown here include those of smaller islands forming part of the same civil parish.

Mainland	14,299	Shapinsay	345
Eday	154	South Ronaldsay	1,188
Hoy and Graemsay	80	Stronsay	462
Papa Westray	94	Walls and Flotta	761
Rousay and Egilsay	264	Westray	741
Sanday and North Ronaldsay	652		

The islands are rich in Pictish and Scandinavian remains, the most notable being the Stone Age village of Skara Brae, the burial chamber of Maeshowe, the many brochs (Pictish towers) and St. Magnus Cathedral. Scapa Flow, between the Mainland and Hoy, was the war station of the British Grand Fleet from 1914–19 and the scene of the scuttling of the surrendered German High Seas Fleet (June 21, 1919).

Most of the islands are low-lying and fertile, and farming (principally beef cattle) is the main industry. Flotta, to the south of Scapa Flow, is now the site of the oil terminal for the Piper, Claymore and Tartan fields in the North Sea.

Capital.—Kirkwall (population 6,881) on Mainland.

Shetland.—The Shetland Islands (total area, 551 square miles; population (1981 Census) 27,271) lie about 50 miles north of the Orkneys, with Fair Isle about half way between the two groups. Out Stack, off Muckle Flugga, one mile north of Unst, is the most northern part of the British Isles (60° 51′ 30″ N. lat.). There are over 100 islands, of which 16 are inhabited.

Mainland	22,184	Muckle Roe	101
Bressay	335	Out Skerries	79
East and West Burra,		Papa Stour	29
and Trondra	930	Unst	1,206
Fair Isle	69	Whalsay	1,026
Fetlar	102	Yell	1,168
Foula	39		

Shetland's many archaelogical sites include Jarlshof, Mousa and Clickhimin, and its long connection with Scandinavia has resulted in a strong Norse influence on its place names and dialect.

Industries include fishing, knitwear and farming. In addition to the fishing fleet there are fish processing factories, while the traditional handknitting of Fair Isle and Unst is supplemented now with machine knitted garments,. Farming is mainly crofting, with sheep being raised on the moorland and hills of the islands. Latterly the islands have become an important centre of the North Sea oil industry, with pipelines from the Brent and Ninian fields running to the terminal at Sullom Voe, the largest of its kind in Europe. Lerwick is the main centre for supply services for offshore oil exploration and development.

Capital.—Lerwick (population 7,901) on Mainland.

The Hebrides.—Until the closing years of the 13th century "The Hebrides" included other Scottish islands in the Firth of Clyde, the peninsula of Kintyre (Argyllshire), the Isle of Man, and the (Irish) Isle of Rathlin. The origin of the name is stated to be the Greek *Eboudai*, latinized as *Hebudes* by Pliny, and corrupted to its present form. The Norwegian name *Sudreyjar* (Southern Islands) was latinized as *Sodorenses*, a name that survives in the Anglican bishopric of "Sodor and Man."

There are over 500 islands and islets, of which about 100 are inhabited, though mountainous terrain and extensive peat bogs mean that only a fraction of the total area is under cultivation. Stone, Bronze and Iron Age settlement has left many remains, including those at Callanish on Lewis, and Norse colonization has influenced language, customs and place-names. Occupations include farming (mostly crofting and stock-raising), fishing and the manufacture of tweeds and other woollens. Tourism is also an important factor in the economy.

The Inner Hebrides lie off the west coast of Scotland and relatively close to the mainland. The largest and best-known is *Skye* (area 643 sq. miles; pop. 8,139; chief town, Portree), which contains the Cuillin Hills (*Sgurr Alasdair* 3,257 feet), the Red Hills (*Beinn na Caillich* 2,403 feet) as well as *Bla Bheinn* (3,046 feet) and *The Storr* (2,358 feet). Skye is also famous as the refuge of Prince Charles Edward (The Young Pretender) in 1746. Other islands in the Highland Region include *Raasay* (pop. 182) *Rum, Eigg* and *Muck*. Islands in the Strathclyde Region include *Arran* (pop. 4,726) containing *Goat Fell* (2,868 feet); *Coll* and *Tiree* (pop. 933); *Colonsay and Oronsay* (pop. 137); *Islay* (area 235 sq. miles; pop. 3,997); *Jura* (area 160 sq. miles; pop. 239) with a range of hills culminating in the Paps of Jura (*Beinn-an-Oir*, 2,576 feet, and *Beinn Chaolais*, 2,477 feet); *Mull* (area 367 sq. miles; pop. 2,605; chief town Tobermory) containing *Ben More* (3,171 feet).

The Outer Hebrides, separated from the mainland by the Minch, now form the Western Isles Islands Council area (area 1,119 sq. miles; pop. (1981 Census) 31,842). The main islands are *Lewis with Harris* (area 770 sq. miles, pop. 23,390), whose chief town, Stornoway (pop. 13,409), is the administrative headquarters of the Islands Council; *North Uist* (pop. 1,454); *South Uist* (pop. 2,223); *Benbecula* (pop. 1,988) and *Barra*

(pop. 1,232). Other inhabited islands include *Bernera* (292), *Berneray* (134), *Eriskay* (219), *Grimsay* (206), *Scalpay* (461) and *Vatersay* (108).

EARLY HISTORY

Prehistoric Man.—The *Picts*, believed to be of non-Aryan origin, seem to have inhabited the whole of North Britain and to have spread over the north of Ireland. Remains are most frequent in Caithness and Sutherland and the Orkney Islands. Celtic *Goidels, Brythons* and *Belgae* arrived from Belgic Gaul during the latter part of the Bronze Age and in the early Iron Age, and except in the extreme north of the mainland and in the islands, the civilization and speech of the people were definitely Celtic at the time of the Roman invasion of Britain.

The Roman Invasion.—In A.D. 80 Julius Agricola extended the Roman conquests in Britain by advancing into *Caledonia*, but after a victory at *Mons Graupius* he was recalled. About 60 years later the Roman frontier was carried to the isthmus between the Forth and Clyde and marked by the *Wall of Pius*, but before the close of the second century the northern limit of Roman Britain had receded to *Hadrian's Wall*.

The Scots.—*Christianity* was introduced into Southern Caledonia about 380 by missionaries from Romanized Britain, who penetrated to the northern districts and islands. After the withdrawal (or absorption) of the Roman garrison of Britain there were many years of tribal warfare between the Picts and Scots (the Gaelic tribe then dominant in Ireland), the Brythonic Waelisc (Welsh) of Strathclyde (Southwest Scotland and Cumberland), and the Anglo-Saxons of the Lothians. The Waelisc were isolated from their kinsmen in Wales by the victory of the West Saxons at Chester (613), and towards the close of the 9th century the Scots under *Kenneth Macalpine* became the dominant power in Caledonia. In the reign of Malcolm I (943–954) Strathclyde was brought into subjection, the English lowland kingdom (Lothian) being conquered by Malcolm II (1005–1034). From the late 11th century until the middle of the 16th there were constant wars between Scotland and England, the outstanding figures in the struggle being *William Wallace*, who defeated the English at Stirling Bridge (1297) and *Robert Bruce*, who won the victory of Bannockburn (1314). James IV and many of his nobles fell at the disastrous battle of *Flodden* (1513).

In 1603 James VI of Scotland succeeded Queen Elizabeth I on the throne of England (his mother, Mary Queen of Scots, was the great-granddaughter of Henry VII), his successors reigning as Sovereigns of Great Britain. After the abdication (by flight) in 1689 of James VII and II, the crown devolved upon William III (grandson of Charles I) and Mary (daughter of James VII and II) and then upon Anne (second daughter of James VII and II). Anne's children died young, and the throne devolved upon George I (great-grandson of James VI and I). In 1689 Graham of Claverhouse "roused the Highlands" on behalf of James VII and II, but died after a military success at Killiecrankie. In 1715, armed risings led to the indecisive battle of Sheriffmuir, but the Jacobite movement died down until 1745, when Prince Charles Edward defeated the Royalist troops at Prestonpans and advanced to Derby in England (1746). From Derby, the adherents of "James VIII and III" (the title claimed for his father by Prince Charles Edward) fell back on the defensive, and the movement was finally crushed by the Royalist troops under the Duke of Cumberland at *Culloden* (April 16, 1746).

AREA AND POPULATION OF SCOTTISH REGIONS

Region	Administrative Headquarters	Area (acres)	Population	Rateable value	Actual Rateable Value per head
					p.
Borders	Newtown St. Boswells	1,154,366	101,278	19,390,553	191·45
Central	Stirling	1,015†	272,792	75,000,000	274·93
Dumfries and Galloway ..	Dumfries	1,574,074	146,159	75,613,520	517·31
Fife	Glenrothes, Fife	322,960	344,488	218,907,854	635·46
Grampian	Aberdeen	2,150,731	497,272	340,866,536	685·47
Highland	Inverness	10,091†	197,208	108,380,800	549·57
Lothian	Edinburgh	433,600	744,558	216,175,000	290·34
Orkney	Kirkwall	217,600	19,314	22,676,000	1,174·07
Shetland	Lerwick	551†	23,351	65,963,330	2,824·86
Strathclyde.............	Glasgow	5,348†	2,373,422	1,324,354,324	557·99
Tayside	Dundee	2,897†	394,415	226,447,722	574·00
Western Isles	Stornoway, Lewis	1,119†	31,456	9,500,000	300·00

† Sq. miles

CHIEF EXECUTIVES, DIRECTORS OF FINANCE AND CHAIRMEN OF REGIONAL AND ISLANDS COUNCILS

Region	Chief Executive	Director of Finance	Convener
Borders	K. J. Clark	P. Jeary	T. Hunter
Central	E. Geddes	J. Broadfoot	J. Anderson, C.B.E.
Dumfries and Galloway	N. W. D. McIntosh	J. C. Stewart	J. V. M. Jameson
Fife	J. M. Dunlop, C.B.E.	D. Mitchell	R. Gough
Grampian	J. D. Macnaughton	T. E. Carter O.B.E.	J. Sorrie
Highland	R. H. Stevenson	J. W. Bremner	I. S. Campbell, O.B.E.
Lothian	R. G. E. Peggie	D. B. Chynoweth	B. A. Meek, O.B.E.
Orkney	R. H. Gilbert	R. H. Gilbert	E. R. Eunson
Shetland	M. Gerrard	M. Green	A. I. Tulloch
Strathclyde...............	R. Calderwood	K. R. Paterson	J. Burns
Tayside	J. A. Wallace	I. B. McIver	W. K. Fitzgerald, C.B.E.
Western Isles	R. MacIver	D. G. Macleod	A. Matheson

PRECEDENCE IN SCOTLAND

The Sovereign.

The Prince Philip, Duke of Edinburgh.

The Lord High Commissioner to the General Assembly (while that Assembly *is sitting*).

The Duke of Rothesay (eldest son of the Sovereign). H.R.H. Prince Andrew. H.R.H. Prince Edward.

Nephews of the Sovereign.

Lords Lieutenant of Counties, Lord Provosts of Counties of Cities, and Sheriffs Principal (successively—within their own localities and during holding of office).

Lord Chancellor of Great Britain.

Moderator of the General Assembly of the Church of Scotland.

The Prime Minister.

Keepers of the Great Seal and of the Privy Seal (successively—if Peers).

Hereditary Lord High Constable of Scotland. Hereditary Master of the Household.

Dukes (successively) of England, Scotland, Great Britain and United Kingdom (including Ireland since date of Union).

Eldest sons of Dukes of the Blood Royal.

Marquesses, in same order as Dukes.

Dukes' eldest sons.

Earls, in order as Dukes.

Younger sons of Dukes of Blood Royal.

Marquesses' eldest sons.

Dukes' younger sons.

Keepers of the Great Seal and of the Privy Seal (successively—if not Peers).

Lord Justice General.

Lord Clerk Register.

Lord Advocate.

Lord Justice Clerk.

Viscounts, in order as Dukes.

Earls' eldest sons.

Marquesses' younger sons.

Lord-Barons, in order as Dukes.

Viscounts' eldest sons.

Earls' younger sons.

Lord-Barons' eldest sons.

Knights of the Garter.

Privy Councillors not included in above ranks.

Senators of Coll. of Justice (Lords of Session).

Viscounts' younger sons.

Lord-Barons' younger sons.

Sons of Life Peers.

Baronets.

Knights of the Thistle.

Knights of other Orders as in England.

Solicitor-General for Scotland.

Lord Lyon King of Arms.

Sheriffs Principal (except as shown in column 1).

Knights Bachelor.

Sheriffs Substitute.

Companions of Orders as in England.

Commanders of Royal Victorian and British Empire Orders.

Eldest sons of younger sons of Peers.

Companions of Distinguished Service Order.

Members (Class 4) Royal Victorian Order.

Officers of British Empire Order.

Baronets' eldest sons.

Knights' eldest sons successively (from Garter to Bachelor).

Members of Class 5 of Royal Victorian Order.

Members of British Empire Order.

Baronets' younger sons.

Knights' younger sons.

Queen's Counsel.

Barons-feudal.

Esquires.

Gentlemen.

SCOTTISH DISTRICT COUNCILS

District	Administrative Headquarters	Population	Rateable Value £	Chief Executive	Chairman (a) Convener (b) Provost (c) Lord Provost
Aberdeen City (5)	Aberdeen	214,082	180,478,248	J. M. Wilson	(c) H. E. Rae
Angus (9)............	Forfar	93,906	47,388,040	W. S. McCulloch	(b) A. Welsh
Annandale and Eskdale (3)........	Annan	35,701	18,171,277	J. A. Whitecross	(a) R. G. Greenhow
Argyll and Bute (8) ...	Lochgilphead	63,684	31,794,367	M. A. J. Gossip	D. C. Currie
Badenoch and Strathspey (6)......	Kingussie	9,836	6,200,000	H. G. McCulloch	A. J. McCook
Banff and Buchan (5) .	Banff	83,216	48,814,000	R. W. Jackson†	(a) N. Cowie
Bearsden and Milngavie (8)	Bearsden	39,981	23,469,000	I. C. Laurie	(b) R. W. Robinson
Berwickshire (1)	Duns	18,408	8,928,000	R. A. Christie	Capt. J. Evans
Caithness (6).........	Wick	27,563	10,839,603	A. Beattie	(a) J. M. Young
Clackmannan (2)	Alloa	47,875	11,444,700	I. F. Smith	(a) J. Millar
Clydebank (8)	Clydebank	51,498	23,099,000	(vacant)	(b) D. Granger
Clydesdale (8)	Lanark	57,361	24,774,899	P. W. Daniels	(a) Miss M. T. Hodgson
Cumbernauld and Kilsyth (8)........	Cumbernauld	63,040	30,706,000	J. Hutton	(b) J. Pollock
Cumnock and Doon Valley (8)	Cumnock	44,300	15,917,000	D. T. Hemmings	(a) D. Shankland
Cunninghame (8).....	Irvine	137,291	75,867,000	J. M. Miller	(a) Mrs. T. Beattie
Dumbarton (8)	Dumbarton	78,780	46,721,858	L. MacKinnon	(b) R. McNamara
Dundee City (9)	Dundee	180,748	109,608,868	J. F. Hoey	(c) T. Mitchell
Dunfermline (4)	Dunfermline	129,000	79,821,742	G. Brown	(b) R. Mill
East Kilbride (8)......	East Kilbride	82,000	40,713,600	W. G. McNay, O.B.E.	(b) G. McKillop
East Lothian (7)	Haddington	81,354	45,548,036	D. B. Miller	T. Wilson
Eastwood (8)	Giffnock	55,069	30,762,000	M. D. Henry	(b) Mrs. J. M. Edmondson
Edinburgh City (7) ...	Edinburgh	439,721	348,155,000	M. M. Duncan	(c) Rt. Hon. J. H. McKay
Ettrick/Lauderdale (1)	Galashiels	33,291	16,246,563	J. D. Bell	(b) A. L. Tulley
Falkirk (2)..........	Falkirk	144,500	98,373,756	J. P. H. Paton	(b) J. Docherty
Glasgow City (8)	Glasgow	744,016	473,339,797	S. F. Hamilton	(c) Rt. Hon. R. Gray
Gordon (5)..........	Inverurie	68,768	30,191,229	A. C. Kennedy	(a) J. B. Presly, M.B.E.
Hamilton (8)	Hamilton	107,600	51,260,000	F. T. Malcolm	(b) S. Casserly
Inverclyde (8)	Greenock	99,117	54,417,000	I. C. Wilson	(b) Sir Simpson Stevenson
Inverness (6).........	Inverness	58,341	39,561,000	B. Wilson	(b) A. G. Sellar
Kilmarnock and Loudoun (8)	Kilmarnock	81,459	39,222,849	R. W. Jenner	(b) T. Ferguson
Kincardine and Deeside (5).........	Stonehaven	45,663	23,183,000	T. Hyder	D. J. Mackenzie, M.B.E.
Kirkcaldy (4)	Kirkcaldy	149,491	95,728,949	J. M. Smith†	(a) R. King
Kyle and Carrick (8) ..	Ayr	113,324	65,006,000	I. R. D. Smillie	(b) G. Macdonald
Lochaber (6)	Fort William	19,561	10,926,900	D. A. B. Blair	C. Neilson
Midlothian (7)	Dalkeith	81,951	43,136,000	D. W. Duguid	(a) W. Steele
Monklands (8)	Coatbridge	109,392	50,195,558	J. S. Ness	(b) E. Cairns
Moray (5)............	Elgin	85,543	48,720,993	J. P. C. Bell	E. Aldridge
Motherwell (8)	Motherwell	149,700	78,957,435	F. C. Marks	(b) J. McGhee
Nairn (6)	Nairn	10,117	4,387,838	A. D. Kerr	(b) Lt. Col. H. McLean, M.B.E.
Nithsdale (3)	Dumfries	57,041	31,542,673	W. W. Japp	(b) K. Cameron
North-East Fife (4) ...	Cupar	65,851	37,680,335	(vacant)	D. A. Barrie
Perth and Kinross (9) .	Perth	121,727	69,483,783	J. E. D. Cormie	(b) J. M. Mathieson, O.B.E.
Renfrew (8)	Paisley	206,971	113,046,023	W. McIntosh	(b) W. McCready
Ross and Cromarty (6)	Dingwall	47,478	27,903,540	(vacant)	(a) G. D. Finlayson
Roxburgh (1).........	Hawick	35,210	16,482,000	°K. W. Cramond	J. R. Irvine
Skye and Lochalsh (6).	Portree	10,963	3,997,765	D. H. Noble	J. F. Munro
Stewartry (3)	Kirkcudbright	23,001	10,880,200	W. L. Dick-Smith, O.B.E.	(a) J. Nelson, T.D.
Stirling (2)	Stirling	80,600	49,316,000	R. Black	(a) J. Wyles
Strathkelvin (8)	Kirkintilloch	89,601	39,978,723	C. Mallon	(b) R. M. Coyle
Sutherland (6)	Golspie	13,142	4,329,500	D. W. Martin	Mrs. L. Mackenzie
Tweeddale (1)	Peebles	14,373	7,495,939	G. H. T. Garvie	J. P. Campbell
West Lothian (7)	Bathgate	141,532	31,501,000	D. Morrison	(a) D. McCauley
Wigtown (3)	Stranraer	30,150	14,109,811	A. Geddes	(a) D. R. Robinson

° Principal Officer.   † Director of Administration.

REGIONS.—(1) Borders; (2) Central; (3) Dumfries and Galloway; (4) Fife; (5) Grampian; (6) Highland; (7) Lothian; (8) Strathclyde; (9) Tayside.

LORD LIEUTENANTS IN SCOTLAND

REGION	TITLE	NAME
Borders	Berwickshire	Lt. Col. W. B. Swan, C.B.E., T.D.
	Roxburgh, Ettrick and Lauderdale	The Duke of Buccleuch and Queensberry, K.T., V.R.D
	Tweeddale	Lt. Col. A. M. Sprot of Haystoun, M.C.
Central	Clackmannan	The Earl of Mar and Kellie
	Stirling and Falkirk	Lt. Col. J. Stirling of Garden
Dumfries & Galloway	Dumfries	Lt. Col. A. J. Jardine Paterson, O.B.E., T.D.
	The Stewartry of Kirkcudbright	The Lord Sinclair, M.V.O.
	Wigtown	Maj. H. J. Brewis
Fife	Fife	Sir John Edward Gilmour, Bt., D.S.O., T.D.
Grampian	Aberdeenshire	Sir Maitland Mackie, C.B.E.
	Banffshire	Col. T. R. Gordon-Duff of Drummuir, M.C.
	Kincardineshire	The Viscount of Arbuthnott, D.S.C.
	Morayshire	Capt. I. M. Tennant
Highland	Caithness	The Viscount Thurso
	Inverness	Col. Sir Donald Hamish Cameron of Lochiel, K.T., C.V.O., T.D.
	Nairn	The Earl of Leven and Melville
	Ross and Cromarty	Vice-Adm. Sir John Hayes, K.C.B., O.B.E.
	Sutherland	Col. A. MacD. Gilmour, O.B.E., M.C.
Lothian	East Lothian	The Earl of Wemyss and March, K.T.
	Midlothian	Sir John Dutton Clerk of Penicuik, Bt., C.B.E., V.R.D.
	West Lothian	The Earl of Morton
Strathclyde	Argyll and Bute	The Lord Maclean, K.T., P.C., G.C.V.O., K.B.E.
	Ayr and Arran	Col. B. M. Knox, M.C., T.D.
	Dunbartonshire	Brig. A. S. Pearson, C.B., D.S.O., O.B.E., M.C., T.D.
	Lanarkshire	Col. The Lord Clydesmuir, K.T., C.B., M.B.E., T.D.
	Renfrewshire	Maj. J. D. M. Crichton Maitland
Tayside	Angus	The Earl of Dalhousie, K.T., G.C.V.O., G.B.E., M.C.
	Perth and Kinross	Maj. D. H. Butter, M.C.
Orkney	Orkney	Col. R. A. A. S. Macrae, M.B.E.
Shetland	Shetland	M. M. Shearer
Western Isles	Western Isles	The Earl Granville, M.C.

NOTE.—The Lord Provosts of the four city districts of Aberdeen, Dundee, Edinburgh and Glasgow are Lord Lieutenants for those districts *ex officio*.

PRINCIPAL SCOTTISH CITIES

EDINBURGH

EDINBURGH, the Capital of Scotland, has a municipal area of 100·6 sq. miles. The city is built on a group of hills and contains in Princes Street one of the most beautiful thoroughfares in the world. The principal buildings are the Castle, which includes St. Margaret's Chapel, the oldest building in Edinburgh, and near it, the Scottish National War Memorial; the Palace of Holyroodhouse; Parliament House, the present seat of the judicature; two universities (Edinburgh and Heriot-Watt); St. Giles' Cathedral (restored 1879–83); St. Mary's (Scottish Episcopal) Cathedral (Sir Gilbert Scott); the General Register House (Robert Adam): the National and the Signet Libraries; the National Gallery; the Royal Scottish Academy; and the National Portrait Gallery. The city is governed by the City of Edinburgh District Council which includes the area of South Queensferry, Kirkliston, Currie, Ratho and Balerno.

GLASGOW

GLASGOW, a Royal Burgh, City, largest District in the Strathclyde Region, and the principal commercial and industrial centre in Scotland, has a municipal area of 49,743 acres. The city occupies the north and south banks of the Clyde, one of the chief commercial estuaries in the world. The principal industries include engineering, aero and marine engines, chemicals, printing, etc. The city has also developed recently as a tourism and conference centre. The chief buildings are the 13th century Gothic Cathedral, the University (Sir Gilbert Scott), the City Chambers, Pollok House, the Transport Museum, Kelvingrove Art Galleries, the Burrell Collection museum and the Mitchell Library. The city is home of the Scottish National Orchestra, Scottish Opera, Scottish Ballet, etc.

ABERDEEN

ABERDEEN, 126 miles N.E. of Edinburgh, received its charter as a Royal Burgh from William the Lion in 1179. Scotland's third largest city, it covers an area of 73·25 square miles. Aberdeen is the principal commercial and administrative centre in the N. of Scotland, the second largest Scottish fishing port and the main European centre for offshore oil exploration. It is also an ancient university town and distinguished research centre. Other industries include engineering, shipbuilding, food processing, textiles, paper manufacturing and chemicals. Places of interest: King's College, St. Machar's Cathedral, Brig o' Balgownie, the Kirk of St. Nicholas, Mercat Cross, Marischal College, Provost Skene's House, Art Gallery, James Dun's House (children's museum) and Provost Ross's House (maritime museum).

DUNDEE

DUNDEE, a Royal Burgh, City, is the administrative centre of Tayside Region. Situated on the north bank of the Tay estuary, it extends over 96 square miles. The city's first class port and dock installations are important to the offshore oil industry and the airport also provides servicing facilities. Principal industries include textiles, watches and clocks, computers and other electronic industries, printing, tyre manufacture, food processing, carpets, heavy electrical and marine engineering and clothing manufacture. Six sites, totalling 210 acres, have Enterprise Zone status. These include the Technology Park, airport and port, as well as city centre commercial sites and general industrial sites. The University of Dundee was established in 1967. The unique City Churches—three churches under one roof, together with the 15th century St. Mary's Tower—are the most prominent architectural feature.

CHIEFS OF CLANS AND NAMES IN SCOTLAND

THE ROYAL HOUSE: H.M. The Queen

AGNEW: Sir Crispin Hamlyn Agnew of Lochnaw, Bt., 6 Palmerston Road, Edinburgh.

ARBUTHNOTT: Viscount of Arbuthnott, D.S.C., Arbuthnott House, Laurencekirk, Kincardineshire.

BARCLAY: Peter C. Barclay of that Ilk, Gatemans, Stratford St. Mary, Colchester, Essex.

BORTHWICK: Maj. J. H. S. Borthwick of Borthwick, T.D., Crookston, Midlothian.

BOYD: Lord Kilmarnock, Casa de Mondragon, Ronda (Malaga), Spain.

BOYLE: Rr. Adm. The Rt. Hon. The Earl of Glasgow, C.B., D.S.C., Kelburn, Fairlie, Ayrshire.

BRODIE: Ninian Brodie of Brodie, Brodie Castle, Forres.

BRUCE: Earl of Elgin and Kincardine, Broomhall, Dunfermline, Fife.

BUCHAN: David S. Buchan of Auchmacoy, Auchmacoy, Ellon, Aberdeenshire.

BURNETT: J. C. A. Burnett of Leys, Crathes Castle, Kincardineshire.

CAMERON: Col. Sir Donald Hamish Cameron of Lochiel, K.T., C.V.O., T.D., Achnacarry, Spean Bridge, Inverness.

CAMPBELL: Duke of Argyll, Inveraray, Argyll.

CARMICHAEL: Richard John Carmichael of Carmichael, Carmichael, Thankerton, Biggar, Lanarkshire.

CARNEGIE: Earl of Southesk, K.C.V.O., Kinnaird Castle, Brechin.

CATHCART: Maj. Gen. The Rt. Hon. The Earl Cathcart, C.B., D.S.O., M.C., 2 Pembroke Gardens, W.8.

CHARTERIS: Earl of Wemyss and March, K.T., Gosford House, Longniddry, East Lothian.

CLAN CHATTAN: M. K. Mackintosh of Clan Chattan, Maxwell Park, Gwelo, Zimbabwe.

CHISHOLM: Alastair Chisholm of Chisholm (*The Chisholm*), Silver Willows, Bury St. Edmunds.

COCHRANE: Earl of Dundonald, Lochnell Castle, Ledaig, Argyllshire.

COLQUHOUN: Sir Ivar Colquhoun of Luss, Bt., Rossdhu, Luss, Dunbartonshire.

CRANSTOUN: Lt. Col. Alastair Cranstoun of that Ilk, M.C., Corehouse, Lanarkshire.

CRICHTON: Charles Crichton of that Ilk, Monzie, Perth.

DARROCH: Captain Duncan Darroch of Gourock. The Red House, Branksome Park Rd., Camberley.

DRUMMOND: Earl of Perth, P.C., Stobhall, Perth.

DUNBAR: Sir Jean Ivor Dunbar of Mochrum, Bt., 45/55 39th Street, Long Island City, New York.

DUNDAS: David D. Dundas of Dundas, 8 Derna Road, Kenwyn 7700, South Africa.

ELIOTT: Sir Arthur Eliott of Stobs, Bt., Redheugh, Newcastleton, Roxburghshire.

ERSKINE: Earl of Mar and Kellie, Claremont House, Alloa.

FARQUHARSON: Capt. A. A. C. Farquharson of Invercauld, M.C., Invercauld, Braemar.

FERGUSSON: Sir Charles Fergusson of Kilkerran, Bt., Kilkerran, Maybole, Ayrshire.

FORBES: Lord Forbes, K.B.E., Balforbes, Alford, Aberdeenshire.

FORSYTH: Alistair Forsyth of that Ilk, Ethie Castle, by Arbroath, Angus.

FRASER: Lady Saltoun, Cairnbulg Castle, Fraserburgh, Aberdeenshire.

FRASER (OF LOVAT)*: Lord Lovat, D.S.O., M.C., T.D., Balblair House, Beauly, Inverness-shire.

GAYRE: Lt. Col. Robert Gayre of Gayre and Nigg, 1–3 Gloucester Lane, Edinburgh.

GORDON: Marquess of Huntly, Aboyne Castle, Aberdeenshire.

GRAHAM: Duke of Montrose, Auchmar, Drymen, Stirlingshire.

GRANT: Lord Strathspey, 111 Elms Ride, West Wittering, Sussex.

HAIG: Earl Haig, O.B.E., Bemersyde, Melrose, Roxburgh.

HANNAY: Ramsey W. R. Hannay of Kirkdale and of that Ilk, Cardoness House, Gatehouse-of-Fleet, Kirkcudbright.

HAY: Earl of Erroll, Wolverton Farm, Wolverton, Basingstoke, Hants.

HUNTER: Neil A. Hunter of Hunterston, Tour d'Escas, Carretera d'Escas, La Massana, Andorra.

IRVINE OF DRUM: C. F. Irvine of Drum, 29 Forest Road, Hoylake, Wirral, Merseyside.

JARDINE: Col. Sir William Jardine of Applegirth, Bt., O.B.E., T.D., Denbie, Lockerbie, Dumfriesshire.

JOHNSTONE: Patrick Johnstone of Annandale and of that Ilk, Raehills, Dumfriesshire.

KEITH: The Earl of Kintore, Glenton House, Rickarton, Stonehaven, Aberdeenshire.

KENNEDY: Marquess of Ailsa, O.B.E., Cassillis House, Maybole, Ayrshire.

KERR: Marquess of Lothian, Monteviot, Ancrum, Roxburgh.

KINCAID: A. C. Kincaid of Kincaid, Murarashi, Kenya.

LAMONT: Peter N. Lamont of that Ilk, St. Patrick's College, Manley, N.S.W. 2095, Australia.

LENNOX: Dennis P. H. Lennox of that Ilk, Pools Farm, Dowton on the Rock, Ludlow, Shropshire.

LESLIE: Earl of Rothes, Tanglewood, West Tytherley, Salisbury, Wilts.

LINDSAY: Earl of Crawford and Balcarres, P.C., Balcarres, Colinsburgh, Fife.

LOCKHART: Angus Hew Lockhart of the Lee, Newholme, Dunsyre, Lanark.

McBAIN: J. H. McBain of McBain, 7025, North Finger Rock Place, Tucson, Arizona, U.S.A.

MALCOLM (MACCALLUM): Robin N. L. Malcolm of Poltalloch, Duntrune Castle, Lochgilphead, Argyll.

MACDONALD: Lord Macdonald (*The Macdonald of Macdonald*), Ostaig House, Skye.

MACDONALD OF CLANRANALD*: Ranald A. Macdonald of Clanranald, 55 Compton Road, N.1.

MACDONALD OF SLEAT (CLAN HUSTEAIN)*: Sir Ian Bosville-Macdonald of Sleat, Bt., Thorpe Hall, Rudston, Driffield, Yorks.

MACDONELL OF GLENGARRY*: Air Cdre. Aeneas R. MacDonell of Glengarry, C.B., D.F.C., Elonbank, Castle Street, Fortrose, Ross-shire.

MACDOUGALL: Madame Coline MacDougall of MacDougall, Dunollie, Argyll.

MACGREGOR: Sir Gregor MacGregor of MacGregor, Bt., Bannatyne, Newtyle, Angus.

MACKAY: Lord Reay, 11 Wilton Crescent, S.W.1.

MACKENZIE: Earl of Cromartie, M.C., T.D., Castle Leod, Strathpeffer, Ross-shire.

MACKINNON: Madam Anne Mackinnon of Mackinnon, 16 Purleigh Road, Bridgewater, Somerset.

MACKINTOSH: The Mackintosh of Mackintosh, O.B.E., Moy Hall, Inverness.

MACLACHLAN: Madame Marjorie MacLachlan of MacLachlan, Castle Lachlan, Argyll.

MACLAREN: Donald MacLaren of MacLaren and Achleskine, British Military Government, Berlin (B.F.P.O. 45).

MACLEAN: Lord Maclean, P.C., K.T., G.C.V.O., K.B.E., Duart Castle, Mull.

MACLENNAN: Ronald G. MacLennan of MacLennan, Clachan, Lochbroom, Ullapool, Ross-shire.

MACLEOD: J. MacLeod of MacLeod, Dunvegan Castle, Skye.

MACMILLAN: Gen. Sir Gordon MacMillan of MacMillan, K.C.B., K.C.V.O., C.B.E., D.S.O., M.C., Finlaystone, Langbank, Renfrewshire.

MACNAB: J. C. Macnab of Macnab (*The Macnab*), Finlarig, Killin, Perthshire.

MACNAGHTEN: Sir Patrick Macnaghten of Macnaghten and Dundarave, Bt., Dundarave, Bushmills, Co. Antrim.

MACNEIL OF BARRA: Ian R. Macneil of Barra (*The Macneil of Barra*), Kismull Castle, Barra.

MACPHERSON: Sir William Macpherson of Cluny, T.D., Q.C., Newtown Castle, Blairgowrie, Perthshire.

MACTHOMAS: Andrew P. C. MacThomas of Finegand, c/o The Clan MacThomas Society, 29 Bennan Gardens, Broughty Ferry, Dundee.

MAITLAND: Earl of Lauderdale, The Tower, Castle Gogar, Costorphine, Edinburgh.

MAR: Countess of Mar, 10 Cranberry Drive, Stourport-on-Severn, Worcs.

MARJORIBANKS: William Marjoribanks of that Ilk, Kirklands of Forglen, Turriff, Aberdeenshire.

MATHESON: Sir Torquhil Matheson of Matheson, Bt., Sanderwick Court, Frome, Somerset.

MENZIES: David R. Menzies of Menzies, 20 Nardina Crescent, Dalkeith, Western Australia.

MOFFAT: Francis Moffat of that Ilk, Redacres, Moffat, Dumfriesshire.

MONCREIFFE: (vacant)

MONTGOMERIE: Earl of Eglinton and Winton, The Dutch House, West Green, Hartley Wintney, Hants.

MORRISON: Dr. Iain M. Morrison of Ruchdi, Todhurst Farm, Lake Lane, Barnham, Sussex.

MUNRO: Patrick G. Munro of Foulis, T.D., Foulis Castle, Ross.

MURRAY: Duke of Atholl, Blair Castle, Blair Atholl, Perthshire.

NICOLSON: Lord Carnock, 90 Whitehall Court, London S.W.1.

NICOLSON OF SCORRYBREAC*: Ian Nicolson of Scorrybreac, P.O. Box 420, Ballina, N.S.W. 2478.

OGILVY: Earl of Airlie, Cortachy Castle, Kirriemuir, Angus.

RAMSAY: Earl of Dalhousie, K.T., G.C.V.O., G.B.E., M.C., Brechin Castle, Angus.

RATTRAY: James S. Rattray of Rattray, Craighall, Rattray, Perthshire.

ROBERTSON: Alexander Gilbert Haldane Robertson of Struan (*Struan-Robertson*), The Breach Farm, Goudhurst Road, Cranbrook, Kent.

ROLLO: Rt. Hon. Lord Rollo, Pitcairns, Dunning, Perthshire.

ROSE: Miss Elizabeth Rose of Kilravock, Kilravock Castle, Croy, Inverness-shire.

ROSS: David C. Ross of that Ilk, The Old Schoolhouse, Fettercairn, Kincardineshire.

RUTHVEN: Earl of Gowrie, Castlemartin, Kilcullen, Co. Kildare, Eire.

SCOTT: Duke of Buccleuch and Queensberry, K.T., V.R.D., Bowhill, Selkirk.

SCRYMGEOUR: The Earl of Dundee, Birkhill, Cupar, Fife.

SEMPILL: Lady Sempill, Druminnor Castle, Rhynie, Aberdeenshire.

SHAW: John Shaw of Tordarroch, Newhall, Balblair, By Conon Bridge, Ross-shire.

SINCLAIR: Earl of Caithness, Rangers Lodge, Charlbury, Oxon.

STIRLING: Sir Charles Norman Stirling of Cader, K.C.M.G., K.C.V.O., 17 Park Row, Farnham, Surrey.

SUTHERLAND: Countess of Sutherland, House of Tongue, Brora, Sutherland.

SWINTON: W. F. H. Swinton of that Ilk, 23301 8th Avenue S.S., Calgary, Alberta, Canada.

URQUHART: Kenneth T. Urquhart of that Ilk, 4713 Orleans Blvd., Jefferson, Louisiana, U.S.A.

WALLACE: Lt.-Col. M. R. Wallace of that Ilk, Hilton of Gask, Auchterarder, Perthshire.

WEDDERBURN OF THAT ILK: The Master of Dundee, Birkhill, Cupar, Fife.

WEMYSS: David Wemyss of that Ilk, Wemyss Castle, Fife.

Only chiefs of *whole* Names or Clans are included (except certain special instances (marked *), who though not chiefs of a "whole name", were, or are, for some reason, (*e.g.* the Macdonald forfeiture), independent. Under decision (*Campbell-Gray*, 1950) that a bearer of a "double or triple-barrelled" surname cannot be held chief of a part of such, several others cannot be included in the list at present.

NEW TOWNS IN GREAT BRITAIN

Commission for the New Towns. Glen House, Stag Place, S.W.1.—The Commission was established on October 1, 1961, under the New Towns Act, 1959, to take over new towns in England and Wales from development corporations whose purposes have been achieved or substantially achieved. The assets and liabilities of Crawley and Hemel Hempstead Development Corporations were transferred to the Commission in 1962 and those of the Hatfield and Welwyn Garden City Development Corporations in 1966. In April, 1978, the Commission transferred to the local authorities under the New Towns (Amendment) Act 1976 the housing and related assets of its four towns. The Commission assumed responsibility for the residual industrial and commercial assets in Corby, Harlow and Stevenage in 1980 and in Bracknell in 1982. In April 1985 the industrial and commercial properties of Northampton, Skelmersdale and Redditch were handed over to the Commission. Central Lancashire follows in December 1985 and Basildon in April 1986.

Chairman, Sir Neil Shields, M.C.
Deputy Chairman, A. Jones.
Members, R. B. Caws, C.B.E.; J. N. C. James; M. A. Hastilow; W. J. Mackenzie, O.B.E.; P. M. Vine, C.B.E.; Sir Gordon Roberts, C.B.E., The Lord Bellwin.
Chief Executive, D. M. Woodhall.
Director of Estates and Technical Services, H. J. M. Thomas.
Director of Finance, Administrative and Legal Services, J. N. Kay, M.M.

BRACKNELL, Berks.—Area, 3,303 acres. Population, 50,800.

CORBY, Northants.—*Executive Officer,* J. G. Lloyd. *Offices,* Chisholm House, 9 Queen's Square, Corby, Northants NN17 1PA. Area, 4,423 acres. Population, 48,500.

CRAWLEY, Sussex.—Area 6,047 acres. Population, 72,900.

HARLOW, Essex.—Area, 6,395 acres. Population, 78,000.

HATFIELD, Herts.—Area, 2,340 acres. Population, 25,200.

HEMEL HEMPSTEAD, Herts.—Area, 5,910 acres. Population, 77,100.

NORTHAMPTON.—*Executive Officer,* W. A. Gray. *Offices,* 2/3 Market Square, Northampton NN1 2EN. Area, 20,000 acres. Population, 170,000.

REDDITCH, Worcs.—*Executive Officer,* I. McKay. *Offices,* Highfield House, Headless Cross Drive, Redditch B97 5EU. Area, 7,180 acres. Population, 70,000.

SKELMERSDALE, Lancs.—*Executive Officer,* J. Leigh. *Offices,* Pennylands, Skelmersdale WN8 8AR. Area, 4,124 acres. Population, 41,600.

STEVENAGE, Herts.—Area, 6,256 acres. Population, 75,700.

WELWYN GARDEN CITY, Herts.—Area, 4,317 acres. Population, 40,500.

DEVELOPMENT CORPORATIONS
England and Wales

AYCLIFFE AND PETERLEE, Co. Durham.—Amalgamated 1985 (Aycliffe formed 1947; Peterlee formed 1948). *Chairman,* Sir Michael Straker, C.B.E. *Chief Executive,* E. Henderson. *Offices,* Acorn House, Newton Aycliffe, Co. Durham DL5 6AW. Area, Aycliffe 3,161 acres; Peterlee 2,977 acres. Population, Aycliffe 25,500; Peterlee 24,000. Estimated eventual population, Aycliffe 32,000; Peterlee 25,500.

BASILDON, Essex.—Formed 1949. *Chairman,* Dame Elizabeth Coker, D.B.E. *General Manager,* D. Gallo-

way. *Offices,* Gifford House, Basildon, Essex SS13 2EX. Area, 7,818 acres. Population, 103,000. Estimated eventual population, 130,000.

CENTRAL LANCASHIRE NEW TOWN, Lancs.—Formed 1970. *Chairman,* Sir Frank Pearson, Bt., M.B.E. *General Manager,* R. W. Phelps. *Offices,* Cuerden Hall, Bamber Bridge, Preston PR5 6AX. Area, 30,000 acres. Population, 255,000. Estimated eventual population, 260,000.

CWMBRAN, Gwent.—Formed 1949. *Chairman,* Lt. Col. G. D. Inkin, O.B.E. *Managing Director,* R. W. Howlett. *Offices,* Gwent House, Town Centre, Cwmbran, Gwent NP44 1XZ. Area, 3,500 acres. Population, 46,100. Estimated eventual population, 50,000.

MILTON KEYNES, Bucks.—Formed 1967. *Chairman,* Sir Henry Chilver. *General Manager,* F. C. Henshaw. *Offices,* Saxon Court, 502 Avebury Boulevard, Milton Keynes MK9 3HS. Area, 22,000 acres. Population, 122,500. Estimated eventual population, 200,000.

PETERBOROUGH.—Formed 1967. *Chairman,* J. Rowe, C.B.E. *General Manager,* K. Hutton. *Offices,* Touthill Close, City Road, Peterborough PE1 1UJ. Area, 15,940 acres. Population, 128,125. Estimated eventual population, 150,000.

TELFORD, Shropshire.—Formed 1963. *Chairman,* The Lord Northfield. *General Manager,* J. Boyce. *Offices,* Priorslee Hall, Telford, Shropshire. Area, 19,300 acres. Population, 109,200. Estimated eventual population, 150,000

WARRINGTON AND RUNCORN, Cheshire.—Amalgamated 1981 (Warrington formed 1968; Runcorn formed 1964). *Chairman,* D. Forster. *General Manager,* D. J. Binns. *Offices,* New Town House, Buttermarket St., Warrington, Cheshire. Area, Warrington 18,612 acres; Runcorn 7,234 acres. Population, Warrington 142,000; Runcorn 67,000. Estimated eventual population, Warrington 170,000; Runcorn 90,000.

WASHINGTON, Tyne and Wear.—Formed 1964. *Chairman,* Prof. W. G. McClelland. *Managing Director,* R. G. Tilmouth. *Offices,* Usworth Hall, Washington NE37 3HS. Area, 5,610 acres. Population, 56,000. Estimated eventual population, 63,000.

DEVELOPMENT BOARD FOR RURAL WALES.—Formed 1977. *Chairman,* F. L. Morgan, M.B.E.. *Offices,* Ladywell House, Newtown, Powys.

Scotland

CUMBERNAULD, Strathclyde.—Formed 1956. *Chairman,* F. M. Cook, O.B.E. *Chief Executive,* D. W. Anderson, C.B.E. *Headquarters,* Cumbernauld House, Cumbernauld G67 3JH. Area, 7,788 acres. Population, 49,700. Estimated eventual population, 70,000.

EAST KILBRIDE, Strathclyde.—Formed 1947. *Chairman,* J. A. Denholm. *Managing Director,* G. B. Young, C.B.E. *Offices,* Atholl House, East Kilbride G74 1LU. Area, 10,250 acres. Population, 70,200. Estimated eventual population, 80,000.

GLENROTHES, Fife.—Formed 1948. *Chairman,* Sir George Sharp, O.B.E. *Chief Executive,* W. M. Cracknell. *Offices,* Balbirnie House, Glenrothes, Fife KY7 6NR. Area, 5,730 acres. Population, 38,000. Estimated eventual population, 48,000.

IRVINE, Ayrshire.—Formed, 1966. *Chairman,* vacant. *Managing Director,* Brig. R. A. Rickets. *Offices,* Perceton House, Irvine, Ayrshire KA11 2AL. Area, 12,410 acres. Population, 56,500. Estimated eventual population, 95,000.

LIVINGSTON, West Lothian.—Formed, 1962. *Chairman,* R. S. Watt. *Chief Executive,* J. Wilson. *Offices,* Sidlaw House, Almondvale, Livingston. Area, 6,868 acres. Population, 39,500. Estimated eventual population, 70,000.

Northern Ireland

(For geographical, historical and judicial notes on Ireland, see Index)

The usually resident population of Northern Ireland, as revised, at the 1981 Census was 1,556,039 (males, 761,882; females, 794,157) compared with a total population of 1,536,065 at the Census of 1971. (N.B. This revised figure takes account of the population effect of non-enumerated households, estimated at 74,000 persons.) In 1981 the number of persons in the various religious denominations (expressed as percentages of the total usually resident population) were: Roman Catholic, 28·0; Presbyterian, 22·9; Church of Ireland, 19·0; Methodist, 4·0; others 7·6; not stated, 18·5. Northern Ireland has a total area of 5,516 sq. miles (land, 5,267 sq. miles; inland water and tideways, 249 sq. miles) with a density of population of 282 persons per sq. mile in 1981.

Constitution and Government. A separate parliament and executive Government was established for Northern Ireland in 1921 by the Government of Ireland Act. The Northern Ireland Constitution Act, 1973, abolished the post of Governor and Parliament of Northern Ireland and provided for the transfer of certain legislative functions to a Northern Ireland Assembly and Executive. Devolved Government came into operation with effect from January 1, 1974 but when the Executive collapsed the Northern Ireland Assembly was prorogued on May 29, 1974. The Northern Ireland Constitution Act, 1974, which became law in July 1974, made provision for temporary arrangements for the government of Northern Ireland by the Secretary of State for Northern Ireland and also provided for the holding of elections and a Constitutional Convention. Direct Rule continues in being under the terms of the Northern Ireland Act 1974.

In April 1982, the Government published a White Paper entitled "Northern Ireland: A Framework for Devolution", in which it signified its intention to hold elections for a Northern Ireland Assembly, which would initially perform a consultative and deliberative role, but in due course would also be able to assume administrative and legislative responsibility for transferred functions if a sufficient level of agreement on how these powers should be exercised could be reached by the parties represented in it. The Government subsequently presented to Parliament a Northern Ireland Bill aimed at giving effect to these proposals, and elections to a 78 member Ulster Assembly were held on October 20th, 1982. The first meeting of the Assembly took place on November 11, 1982, although Nationalist members have not taken their seats. In November 1983 Ulster Unionist Party members withdrew but have since returned and the Assembly and its Departmental Committees (one for each N.I. Department) continue to function.

The Assembly, pending agreement on the devolution of powers, has consultative and scrutinising functions. In May 1984 the Assembly set up a Committee on devolution to consider and report on how the Assembly might be strengthened and progress made towards legislative and selective devolution.

FLAG.—The national flag is that of the United Kingdom.

Members of the Northern Ireland Assembly

Abbreviations: All. = Alliance Party; D.U.P. = Democratic Unionist Party; Ind.U. = Independent Unionist; O.U.P. = Official Unionist Party; S.D.L.P. = Social Democratic and Labour Party; S.F. = Sinn Fein; U.P.U.P = Ulster Popular Unionist Party.

G. Adams (S.F.) *Belfast West*; W. A. F. Agnew (O.U.P.) *South Antrim*; J. A. Allen (O.U.P.) *Londonderry*; J. H. Allister (D.U.P.) *North Antrim*; Rev. W. J. Beattie (D.U.P.) *South Antrim*; J. R. Beggs (O.U.P.) *North Antrim*; W. B. Bell (O.U.P.) *South Antrim*; W. G. Bleakes (O.U.P.) *North Down*; W. Brown (O.U.P.) *South Down*; D. J. M. Burchill (O.U.P.) *Belfast East*; D. N. Calvert (D.U.P.) *Armagh*; G. L. Campbell (D.U.P.) *Londonderry*; O. G. Carron (S.F.) *Fermanagh, South Tyrone*; J. Carson (O.U.P.) *Belfast North*; S. A. Close (All.) *South Antrim*; D. S. Cook (All.) *Belfast South*; C. J. Cousley (D.U.P.) *North Antrim*; J. A. Currie (S.D.L.P.) *Fermanagh, South Tyrone*; J. W. Cushnahan (All.) *North Down*; I. Davis (D.U.P.) *South Antrim*; W. A. B. Douglas (O.U.P.) *Londonderry*; Col. Rt. Hon. Lord Dunleath (All.) *North Down*; Mrs. D. Dunlop (O.U.P.) *Belfast East*; S. N. Farren (S.D.L.P.) *North Antrim*; F. Feely (S.D.L.P.) *South Down*; R. Ferguson (O.U.P.) *Fermanagh, South Tyrone*; C. J. Forsythe (O.U.P.) *South Antrim*; Rev. T. J. I. Foster (D.U.P.) *Fermanagh, South Tyrone*; J. A. Gaston (O.U.P.) *North Antrim*; H. J. S. Gibson (D.U.P.) *North Down*; W. Glendinning (All.) *Belfast West*; G. Graham (O.U.P.) *South Down*; P. D. Haughey (S.D.L.P.) *Mid-Ulster*; Dr. J. G. Hendron (S.D.L.P.) *Belfast West*; J. Hume (S.D.L.P.) *Londonderry*; A. J. Kane (D.U.P.) *Mid-Ulster*; J. A. Kilfedder (U.P.U.P.) *North Down*; T. J. Kirkpatrick (O.U.P.) *Belfast South*; H. A. Logue (S.D.L.P.) *Londonderry*; J. McAllister (S.F.) *Armagh*; R. L. McCartney (O.U.P.) *North Down*; W. J. McClure (D.U.P.) *Londonderry*; R. S. McCrea (D.U.P.) *Belfast South*; Rev. R. T. W. McCrea (D.U.P.) *Mid-Ulster*; J. H. McCusker (O.U.P.) *Armagh*; J. McDonald (S.D.L.P.) *South Antrim*; K. W. Maginnis (O.U.P.) *Fermanagh, South Tyrone*; E. K. McGrady (S.D.L.P.) *South Down*; J. M. McGuinness (S.F.) *Londonderry*; P. Maguire (All.) *Belfast North*; J. McKee (D.U.P.) *North Antrim*; A. J. Morrow (All.) *Belfast East*; Mrs. M. K. McSorley (S.D.L.P.) *Mid-Ulster*; G. H. Mawhinney (All.) *South Antrim*; F. Millar (Ind.U.) *Belfast North*; F. Millar (O.U.P.) *Belfast South*; Rt. Hon. J. H. Molyneaux (O.U.P.) *South Antrim*; D. G. Morrison (S.F.) *Mid-Ulster*; Sir Oliver Napier (All.) *Belfast East*; J. L. Neeson (All.) *North Antrim*; H. News (S.D.L.P.) *Armagh*; J. F. Nicholson (O.U.P.) *Armagh*; P. O'Donoghue (S.D.L.P.) *South Down*; P. J. O'Hare (S.D.L.P.) *Belfast North*; Rev. Dr. I. R. K. Paisley (D.U.P.) *North Antrim*; T. Passmore (O.U.P.) *Belfast East*; J. W. Pentland (D.U.P.) *North Down*; P. D. Robinson (D.U.P.) *Belfast East*; G. Seawright (D.U.P.) *Belfast North*; Mrs. M. Simpson (O.U.P.) *Armagh*; J. A. Speers (O.U.P.) *Armagh*; Rev. W. M. Smyth (O.U.P.) *Belfast South*; Rt. Hon. J. D. Taylor (O.U.P.) *North Down*; R. Thompson (D.U.P.) *South Antrim*; W. J. Thompson (O.U.P.) *Mid-Ulster*; D. Vitty (D.U.P.) *Belfast East*; J. H. Wells (D.U.P.) *South Down*.

Seats: O.U.P. 26; D.U.P. 21; S.D.L.P. 13; All. 10; S.F. 5; Ind.U. 1; U.P.U.P. 1.

THE PRIVY COUNCIL

Sir John Andrews, K.B.E. (1957); R. J. Bailie (1971); D. W. Bleakley (1971); R. H. Bradford (1969); Capt. Viscount Brookeborough (1971); W. Craig (1963); J. Dobson (1969); W. K. Fitzsimmons (1965); The Lord Glentoran (1953); Sir Edward Jones (1965); Mr. Justice Kelly (1969); H. V. Kirk (1962); Capt. W. J. Long (1966); Lord Lowry (*Lord Chief Justice*) (1971); R. W. B. McConnell (1964); W. B. McIvor (1971); W. J. Morgan (1961); The Lord Moyola (1966); Sir Ivan Neill (1950); The Lord O'Neill of the Maine (1956); Sir Robert Porter, Q.C. (1969); Lord Rathcavan (1969); R. Simpson (1969); J. D. Taylor (1970); H. W. West (1960).

GOVERNMENT OFFICES

Department of Finance and Personnel

Permanent Secretary, Dr. W. G. H. Quigley.
Under Secretaries, P. Carvill; J. B. C. Lyttle; W. J. Hodges; J. L. Semple; R. B. Spence.
Assistant Secretaries, D. W. Alexander; J. M. Dowdall. *Resources Group*, Dr. J. J. M. Harbison; Dr. D. G. Slattery; P. J. Small; R. G. Smartt. *Efficiency Services*, Dr. D. J. Allott; W. G. Purdy. *Personnel Group*, R. J. Anderson; J. R. Ingram; A. B. MacKay; J. Maguire. *Central Secretariat*, T. Pearson.
Senior Principals, G. E. H. Beamish; J. E. Henderson; R. J. Jordan; R. E. Templeton; J. F. Walker; T. Whiteside.
Solicitor, W. E. M. Reid.
Commissioner of Valuation, D. W. M. Deyermond.
First Legislative Draftsman, T. R. Erskine.

Department of Education

Permanent Secretary, J. H. Parkes, C.B.
Under Secretaries, A. J. Green; E. G. Martin.
Senior Chief Inspector, I. H. N. Wallace.
Asst. Secretaries, A. M. Dodds; N. R. Jennings; R. T. Holmes; K. H. Clark; R. D. Hill; P. S. Holmes; J. S. Smith; T. Johnston.
Chief Inspectors, N. Morrison; J. B. S. O'Kelly.

Department of the Environment

Permanent Secretary, D. Barry.
Under Secretaries, J. M. Beckett (*Personnel, Information Systems Unit, Solicitors Branch, Central Management, Local Government, Conservation, Historic Monuments and Buildings, Environmental Protection*); W. E. C. Ford (*Works Service, Public Records Office, Ordnance Survey, Land Registry, Registry of Deeds, Finance, Rates*); F. McCann (*Housing*); G. F. Loughran (*Planning, Comprehensive Development, Lands Service, Development Officer Services*); J. A. G. Whitlaw (*Roads, Water, Transport*).
Director, Town and Country Planning Service, J. B. Davidson.
Director, Water Service, E. O'Hara.
Director, Roads Service, I. W. Joiner.
Director, Works Services, J. Brennan.
Assistant Secretaries, W. Black; W. N. Campbell; H. E. Carson; J. Cowan; F. A. Dillon; N. Hamilton; J. J. McClenahan; R. H. MacKenzie; A. Miller; F. R. Rodgers; E. A. Simpson; J. Kirk; J. McCormick; J. M. Irvine; D. C. White; J. F. Russell.
Chief Local Government Auditor, S. J. Bailie.
Chief Engineer (Roads Service), Dr. W. M. C. Stevenson.
Chief Planning Officer, E. Hayes.
Chief Engineer (Water Service), S. T. Bratty.
Chief Quantity Surveyor, T. O'Hara.
Chief Survey Officer, M. J. D. Brand.
Chief Civil Engineer, C. E. Ronaldson.
Chief Architect, V. L. Corbett.
Chief M. & E. Engineer, E. Clarke.
Chief Structural Engineer, K. Turkington.

Department of Health & Social Services

Permanent Secretary, Dr. M. N. Hayes.
Under Secretaries, F. A. Elliott; G. Buchanan; R. F. Mills; R. S. Sterling; Miss Z. Davies.
Assistant Secretaries, A. N. Burns; C. McN. Davie; J. G. Hunter; J. R. Kearne; R. J. Minnis; E. H. Elliott; J. Scott; J. A. Wylie; R. McMurray; A. S. Treacy; D. H. McNally; Miss J. Mills; P. Simpson; Dr. R. W. McQuiston.
Chief Medical Officer, Dr. R. J. Weir.
Deputy Chief Medical Officers, Dr. D. J. Sloan; Dr. W. D. Thornton.
Chief Social Work Adviser, P. J. Armstrong.

Department of Economic Development

Permanent Secretary, D. Fell.
Under Secretaries, J. Crozier; W. N. Drummond; E. Mayne.
Chief Engineer and Scientist, Dr. T. B. Copestake.
Asst. Secretaries, W. T. McCrory; R. J. O'Hara; Miss M. L. Johnston; J. D. M. Thompson; J. J. Monaghan; D. C. Gowdy; D. J. Alexander; Miss J. Dixon; I. W. McMurtry; D. J. Watkins; C. Stutt; D. Gibson; R. Wilson; J. C. Wolstencroft.
Director of Industrial Science Division, J. T. McCullins.
Economic Adviser, Prof. W. Black.

Industrial Development Board

Chief Executive, H. S. Tate.
Deputy Chief Executives, A. S. Hopkins; J. B. McAllister.
Directors of Industrial Development, A. I. Devitt; R. A. Burden; P. T. Bill; J. H. Caldwell; P. S. McDowell; F. Hewitt; D. C. Gowdy; W. B. Robinson.

Department of Agriculture

Permanent Secretary, Dr. W. H. Jack.
Under Secretaries, J. C. Chalmers; J. Murray.
Chief Scientific Officer, Dr. C. E. Wright.
Chief Agriculture Officer, T. A. Larmour.
Chief Veterinary Officer, E. W. Sullivan.
Chief Forest Officer, J. C. Phillips.
Assistant Secretaries, W. H. Parker; D. M. Carnson; R. E. Aiken; S. R. Armstrong; N. E. Morrison; I. C. Henderson; K. E. Brady.

Head of Northern Ireland Civil Service and Central Secretariat

Head of Northern Ireland Civil Service, K. P. Bloomfield, C.B.
Under Secretary, P. Carvill.
Assistant Secretary, T. Pearson.
Director of Information, D. Gilliland, C.B.E.

Exchequer and Audit Department

Comptroller and Auditor-General, L. V. D. Calvert, C.B..
Secretary, J. G. W. McComish.
Directors of Audit, D. A. Kerr; K. G. McCormick; B. H. Poulter; S. B. D. McConnell.

Northern Ireland Trade Centre
11 Berkeley Street, W.1.

Principal, R. Bennett.

BELFAST

BELFAST, a City, the seat of Government of Northern Ireland, situated at the mouth of the River Lagan at its entrance to Belfast Lough, has a municipal area of 16,017 acres, exclusive of tidal water (2,034) and a population (mid-1983) of 322,600. The city received its first charter of incorporation in 1613 and has since grown, owing to its easy access by sea to Scottish coal and iron, to be a great industrial centre. The chief industries are ship-building and the manufacture of aircraft, aerostructure, heavy and light engineering, textiles, ropes and tobacco. Belfast is an important seaport with extensive docks.

The principal buildings are of a relatively recent date and include the Parliament Buildings at Stormont, the City Hall, the Law Courts, the Public Library and the Museum and Art Gallery. The Queen's University (previously Queen's College) was chartered in 1908.

Belfast was created a city in 1888 and the title of Lord Mayor was conferred in 1892.

LONDONDERRY

LONDONDERRY, a City situated on the River Foyle, has a population (mid-1983) of 96,100 and was reputedly founded in 546 by St. Columba. Londonderry (formerly *Derry*) has important associations with the City of London. The Irish Society, under its royal charter of 1613, fortified the city and was for long closely associated with its administration.

Famous for the great siege of 1688–89, when for 105 days the town held out against the forces of James II until relieved by sea, Londonderry was an important naval base throughout the Second World War. Interesting buildings are the Protestant Cathedral of St. Columb's (1633) and the Guildhall reconstructed in 1912 and containing a number of beautiful stained glass windows, many of which were presented by the livery companies of London. The famous Walls are still intact and form a circuit of almost a mile around the old city. The traditional activity in Londonderry is shirtmaking. Other industries include mechanical engineering, automobile components including rubber tyres, cord and synthetic fibre. New industries include the manufacture of bicycles. A large part of Ulster's agricultural export trade passes through the port.

FINANCE

Taxation in Northern Ireland is largely imposed and collected by the United Kingdom Government. After deducting the cost of collections and of Northern Ireland's contributions to the European Economic Community the balance, known as the Attributed Share of Taxation, is paid over to the Northern Ireland Consolidated Fund. Northern Ireland's revenue is insufficient to meet its expenditure and is supplemented by a grant in aid.

	1984–85* £	1985–86** £
Public income	3,085,435,685	3,279,703,131
Public expenditure	3,085,353,692	3,279,603,131

* Outturn   ** Estimate

EXTERNAL TRADE*

	Tonnes (000)		
	1982	1983	1984
Total imports ...	10,748	10,179	9,774
Total exports ...	3,256	2,524	2,439

* Including cross-Channel trade with Great Britain.

PRODUCTION

Industries.—The total value of the industrial production (manufacturing, gas, electricity and water) in Northern Ireland by firms employing 20 or more persons in 1981 was approximately £3,652 million and the number of persons employed about 116,000. The products of the engineering, shipbuilding and aircraft industries which employed 35,000 persons, were valued at £591 million. The textile industries, employing about 13,000 persons, produced products valued at approximately £227 million. The food and drink industry, employing about 20,000 persons, produced goods valued at £1,529 million. The value of clothing manufactured in 1981 was about £131 million.

Minerals.—1,359 persons were employed in mining and quarrying operations in Northern Ireland in 1983 and the minerals raised (15,684,358 tonnes) were valued at £22,039,272.

COMMUNICATIONS

Seaports.—The total number of ships using the principal ports in 1984 was 10,076. Regular ferry and container services operate to ports on the Western coast of Great Britain and the Continent of Europe from Belfast, Larne and Warrenpoint.

Road and Rail Transport.—The Northern Ireland Transport Holding Company is responsible for the supervision of the subsidiary companies, Ulsterbus and Citybus (which operate the public road passenger services), Northern Ireland Railways, and Northern Ireland Airports, which is responsible for running the main airport at Aldergrove, near Belfast. A few privately operated bus services are provided in rural areas under licence. Road freight services are also provided by a large number of hauliers operating competitively under licence.

Air Transport.—Passenger and freight services operate between Belfast International Airport and airports throughout Great Britain. It caters for some 1,600,000 passengers and about 34,000 tonnes of air freight per annum, making it the seventh busiest airport in the United Kingdom. Stage II stage of a major development programme costing £25 million was completed in 1983; it has doubled the size of the terminal and improved other operational facilities to cater for a continuing growth of traffic. Stage III works are now under way and will provide increased apron capacity and two passenger airbridges. Scheduled air services are available from Belfast (Harbour) Airport to five destinations.

There are three other licensed aerodromes in Northern Ireland and, apart from some scheduled services in the summer, these are used principally by flying clubs, by private owners and by expanding air taxi businesses flying to destinations in Ireland, Great Britain and continental Europe.

COUNTIES OF NORTHERN IRELAND

Counties and County Boroughs	Area* sq. miles	Lord Lieutenant	High Sheriff, 1985
(1) Antrim	1,093	Capt. R. A. F. Dobbs	J. P. Cooke
Belfast County Borough	25	Sir Robin Kinahan	H. Ditty
(2) Armagh	484	Capt. F. M. A. Torrens-Spence, D.S.O., D.S.C., A.F.C., R.N. (retd.)	E. B. Wilson
(3) Down	945	Col. W. N. Brann, O.B.E., E.R.D.	Maj. E. R. Sandford, M.B.E.
(4) Fermanagh	647	Viola, Duchess of Westminster	T. S. Fisher
(5) Londonderry†	798	Col. M. W. McCorkell, O.B.E., T.D.	R. M. Harvey, O.B.E.
Londonderry City	3·4	T. F. Cooke	A. O. Kennedy
(6) Tyrone	1,211	Lt.-Col. J. H. Hamilton Stubber	M. T. Archdale

* Excluding inland waters and tideways.   † Excluding the City of Londonderry.

MUNICIPAL DIRECTORY OF NORTHERN IRELAND

District and *Borough Councils	Population	Net Annual Value	Council Clerk	Mayor (†) or Chairman 1985
		£		
*Antrim, Co. Antrim	45,800	5,770,331	S. J. Magee	†J. H. Allen
*Ards, Co. Down	60,400	6,632,566	W. C. Scott	†Mrs G. E. K. McIntyre
Armagh, Co. Armagh ...	51,000	4,178,201	N. C. H. Megaw	S. Foster
*Ballymena, Co. Antrim .	55,400	6,939,082	J. S. McIlroy	†A. Spence
*Ballymoney, Co. Antrim	23,500	2,124,250	W. J. Williamson	†C. Steele
Banbridge, Co. Down ...	30,800	2,949,729	R. J. Weatherall	S. J. Cowan
Belfast, Co. Antrim and Co. Down.............	318,600	48,132,698	C. Ward	Rt. Hon. J. Carson (*Lord Mayor*)
*Carrickfergus, Co. Antrim..............	28,800	3,992,674	R. Boyd	†C. Johnston
*Castlereagh, Co. Down ..	59,400	6,866,231	A. D. Nichol	†J. Glass
*Coleraine, Co. Londonderry..........	47,300	6,609,415	W. E. Andrews	†W. H. King
Cookstown, Co. Tyrone .	29,400	2,503,338	W. A. Bownes	A. Kane
*Craigavon, Co Armagh .	74,400	8,934,150	W. J. Mayes	†G. Savage
Derry, (5).............	97,200	9,848,555	C. M. Geary	†J. McNicholl
Down, Co. Down	54,500	4,962,674	S. Byrne	E. G. O'Neill
Dungannon, Co. Tyrone	45,800	3,684,071	R. Paisley	W. R. Brown
Fermanagh, Co. Fermanagh...........	51,400	4,216,566	G. Burns	P. Corrigan
*Larne, Co. Antrim......	29,600	3,526,385	G. McKinley	†T. D. Robinson
Limavady, Co. Londonderry..........	28,500	2,371,415	J. K. Stevenson	S. Gault
*Lisburn, Co. Antrim and Co. Down.............	89,100	10,808,940	H. A. Duff	†T. W. Lilburn
Magherafelt, Co. Londonderry	34,300	2,756,695	W. R. S. McMaster	P. Sweeney
Moyle, Co. Antrim	14,600	1,243,166	J. O'Kane	M. McSparren
Newry and Mourne, Co. Down	84,600	6,466,501	P. J. O'Hagan	P. Toner
*Newtownabbey, Co. Antrim..............	72,400	9,904,054	R. W. Blennerhassett	†R. L. Caul
*North Down, Co. Down .	67,600	8,048,668	J. McKimm	†Mrs. H. E. Bradford
Omagh, Co. Tyrone	47,000	3,436,890	D. R. D. Mitchell	S. J. Kerr
Strabane, Co. Tyrone ...	37,100	2,505,245	J. N. McMorran	J. J. O'Kane
Northern Ireland	1,578,500	179,412,490		

Note.—Since the reorganisation of Local Government, rates in Northern Ireland are collected by the Department of Finance and consist of two rates, a regional rate made by the Department of Finance and a district rate made by individual District Councils.

THE ISLE OF MAN (Ellan Vannin)

An island in the Irish Sea, in lat. 54° 3′–54° 25′ N. and long. 4° 18′–4° 47′ W., nearly equidistant from England, Scotland, and Ireland. Although the early inhabitants were of Celtic origin, the Isle of Man was part of the Norwegian Kingdom of the Hebrides until 1266, when this was ceded to Scotland. Subsequently granted to the Stanleys (Earls of Derby) in the 15th century and later to the Dukes of Atholl, it was brought under the direct administration of the Crown in 1765. The island forms the bishopric of Sodor and Man.

The total land area is 141,263 acres (221 sq. miles), of which 78,853 acres are under cultivation. The report on the 1981 Census showed a resident population of 64,679 (males, 30,901; females, 33,778). In 1984 births numbered 666 and deaths 968. 284 persons were returned at the Census of 1971 as able to speak the Manx language, compared with 4,657 in 1901, 355 in 1951 and 165 in 1961.

Capital, ΨDouglas. Population (1981), 19,944; ΨCastletown (3,141) is the ancient capital; the other towns are ΨPeel (3,688), and ΨRamsey (5,818).

Flag.—Three legs in white and gold armed conjoined on a red ground.

Government

The Isle of Man is a self-governing Crown dependency, the Lieutenant-Governor being the Queen's personal representative in the Island. The legislature, called the Tynwald, has two branches—the Legislative Council and the House of Keys. The Council consists of the Bishop of Sodor and Man, the Attorney-General and 8 members chosen by the House of Keys, one of whom is appointed President of the Council. The House of Keys, one of the most ancient legislative assemblies in the world, consists of 24 members, elected by the adult male and female population. Bills after having passed both Houses are signed by the members, and then sent for the Royal Assent. After receiving the Royal Assent, a Bill does not become law unless promulgated within the ensuing twelve months, and on the first "Tynwald Day" (July 5) following it is announced in the English and Manx languages on the Tynwald Hill. On the promulgation taking place a certificate thereof is signed by the Lieutenant-Governor, the President of the Legislative Council and the Speaker of the House of Keys.

ECONOMY

Most of the income generated in the Island is earned in the services sector with financial and business services being considerably larger than the traditional industry of tourism. Manufacturing industry is also a major generator of income whilst the Island's other traditional industries of agriculture and fishing now play a minor role in the economy.

Under the terms of the Island's special relationship with the European Community the Island has free access to E.C. markets.

The establishment of a "Freeport" in the Island is seen as a potential area for growth.

The Island's unemployment rate is approximately 10 per cent and price inflation is around 7 per cent per annum.

FINANCE

The Island's Budget for 1985–86 provided for expenditure of £90,600,000. The principal sources of Government revenue are taxes on income and expenditure. Income tax is payable at a flat rate of 20 per cent. of both personal and company income after the deduction of various allowances. By agreement with the United Kingdom Government, the Island keeps most of its rates of indirect taxation (Value Added Tax and duties) the same as those in the United Kingdom, but this agreement may be terminated by either party. The Island has a reciprocal arrangement with the United Kingdom regarding social security benefits and pensions and the basic rates of contribution are the same in the Isle of Man and United Kingdom. Taxes are also charged on property (rates), but these are comparatively low.

The major Government expenditure items are health, social security and education, which account for 60 per cent of the Government budget. The Island makes a voluntary annual contribution to the United Kingdom for defence and other external services.

Although the Island has a special relationship with the European Community it neither contributes money to nor receives funds from the E.C. Budget.

Lieutenant-Governor, His Excellency Maj. Gen. Laurence A. W. New, C.B.E.
A.D.C. to the Lieutenant-Governor, M. M. Wood.
President of the Legislative Council, J. C. Nivison, C.B.E.
Speaker, House of Keys, Sir Charles Kerruish, O.B.E.
His Honour the First Deemster and Clerk of the Rolls, A. C. Luft.
Clerk of Tynwald and Secretary to the House of Keys, R. B. M. Quayle.
Attorney-General, T. W. Cain.
Government Secretary, P. J. Hulme.
Government Treasurer, W. Dawson.

THE CHANNEL ISLANDS

Situated off the north-west coast of France (at distances of from ten to thirty miles), are the only portions of the *Dukedom of Normandy* now belonging to the Crown, to which they have been attached ever since the Conquest. They consist of Jersey (28,717 acres), Guernsey (15,654 acres), and the dependencies of Guernsey—Alderney (1,962 acres), Brechou (74), Great Sark (1,035) Little Sark (239), Herm (320), Jethou (44) and Lihou (38)—a total of 48,083 acres, or 75 square miles. In 1981 the population of Jersey was 76,050; and of Guernsey, 54,380; Alderney, 2,000 and Sark, 604.

GOVERNMENT

The islands are Crown dependencies with their own legislative assemblies (the States in Jersey, Guernsey and Alderney, and the Court of Chief Pleas in Sark), and systems of local administration and of law, and their own courts. Acts passed by the States require the sanction of The Queen-in-Council. The British Government is responsible for defence and international relations.

In both Bailiwicks the Lieutenant-Governor and Commander-in-Chief, who is appointed by the Crown, is the personal representative of the Queen and the channel of communication between the Crown (via the Privy Council) and the insular government. The Bailiffs of Jersey and Guernsey, also appointed by the Crown, are President of the States and of the Royal Courts of their respective islands. The government of each Bailiwick is conducted by committees appointed by the States. Justice is administered by the Royal Courts of Jersey and Guernsey, each consisting of the Bailiff and 12 elected Jurats.

Each Bailiwick constitutes a deanery within the diocese of Winchester (*see* Index).

ECONOMY

A mild climate and good soil have led to the development of intensive systems of agriculture and horticulture, which form a significant part of the economy of the Channel Islands. Equally important are invisible earnings, principally from the tourist trade and from banking and finance, the low rate of income tax (20p. in the £ in Jersey and Guernsey; no tax of any kind in Sark) and the absence of super-tax and death duties making the Channel Islands a popular tax-haven. Principal exports are agricultural produce and flowers; imports are chiefly machinery, manufactured goods, food, fuel and chemicals. Trade with the U.K. is regarded as internal trade.

British currency is legal tender in the Channel Islands but each Bailiwick issues its own coins, and some notes, of the same values as those of the U.K. They also issue their own postage stamps; U.K. stamps are not valid.

LANGUAGE

The official languages are English and French, but French is gradually being supplanted by English, which is the language in daily use. In country districts of Jersey and Guernsey and throughout Sark a Norman-French *patois* is also in use, though to a declining extent.

CHIEF TOWNS, ΨSt. Helier on the south coast of Jersey; ΨSt. Peter Port, on the east coast of Guernsey, and St. Anne's on Alderney.

JERSEY

Lieutenant-Governor and Commander-in-Chief of Jersey, His Excellency Admiral Sir William Pillar, G.B.E., K.C.B. (1985).
Secretary and A.D.C., Comdr. D. M. L. Braybrooke, L.V.O., R.N.
Bailiff of Jersey, P. L. Crill, C.B.E.
Deputy Bailiff, V. A. Tomes
Attorney-General and Receiver-General, P. M. Bailhache
Solicitor-General,
Greffier of the States, E. J. M. Potter.
States Treasurer, L. May.

Year to Dec. 31:	1983	1984
Revenue	£143,680,497	£153,394,872
Revenue Expenditure	115,902,191	127,532,927
Capital Expenditure	14,825,425	13,513,409
Public Debt	−71,254	−531,242

FLAG.—A white field charged with a red saltire, and coat of arms.

GUERNSEY AND DEPENDENCIES

Lieutenant-Governor and Commander-in-Chief of the Bailiwick of Guernsey and its Dependencies, His Excellency Lt. Gen. Sir Alexander Boswell, K.C.B., C.B.E. (1985).

Secretary and A.D.C., Capt. D. P. L. Hodgetts.
Bailiff of Guernsey, Sir Charles Frossard.
Deputy Bailiff, G. M. Dorey.
H. M. Procureur and Receiver-General, de Vic G. Carey.
H. M. Comptroller, A. C. K. Day.
States Supervisor, F. N. Le Cheminant.

Year to Dec. 31:	1983	1984
Revenue	£63,795,738	£71,387,194
Expenditure	58,120,436	62,308,590
Net Funded Debt	686,111	579,136

FLAG.—White, bearing a red cross of St. George, with an argent a cross gules superimposed on the cross.

Alderney

President of the States, J. Kay-Mouat.
Clerk of the States, W. R. Jones.
Clerk of the Court, P. Beer.

Sark

Le Seigneur of Sark, J. M. Beaumont.
The Seneschal, L. P. de Carteret.
The Greffier, J. P. Hamon.
Brechou, Lihou and Jethou are leased by the Crown. Herm is leased by the States of Guernsey.

THE ISLES OF SCILLY

There are about 140 islands and skerries in the Scillies group (total area, 6 square miles) situated 28 miles south-west of Land's End, of which only five are inhabited; Bryher, St. Agnes, St. Martin's, St. Mary's and Tresco. The population is 1,951. The entire group has been designated an Area of Outstanding Natural Beauty, and given National Nature Reserve status by the Nature Conservancy Council because of its unique flora and fauna. Tourism is the basis of the economy of the Isles. The island group is a recognised rural development area.

The islands are administered by the Council of the Isles of Scilly, a 21-member non-political body, which combines the powers and duties of a County Council and a District Council under the Local Government Act 1972 and the Isles of Scilly Orders 1978. Legisla-

tion is specifically applied to the Isles of Scilly by Special Order. The Council is responsible for education, fire services, highways, planning and social services, and Cornwall County Council provides other services on an agency basis: the police service is administered by the Devon and Cornwall Police Authority, of which the Council is a member. The Isles are part of the St. Ives electoral division.

Administrative Headquarters, Town Hall, St. Mary's, Isles of Scilly, TR21 0LW.
Chairman of the Council, H. R. Duncan.
Clerk and Chief Executive, I. Glover.
Chief Financial Officer, L. W. Michell.
Chief Technical Officer, B. M. Lowen.

THE CINQUE PORTS

As their name implies the Cinque Ports were originally five in number, Hastings, New Romney, Hythe, Dover and Sandwich. They were in existence before the Norman Conquest and were the Anglo-Saxon successors to the Roman system of coast defence organized from the Wash to Spithead to resist Saxon onslaughts. William the Conqueror reconstituted them and granted peculiar jurisdiction, most of which was abolished in 1855. Only jurisdiction in Admiralty still survives.

At some time after the Conquest the "antient towns" of Winchelsea and Rye were added with equal privileges. The other members of the Confederation, known as Limbs, are:—Lydd, Faversham, Folkestone, Deal, Tenterden, Margate and Ramsgate.

The Barons of the Cinque Ports have the ancient privilege of attending the Coronation Ceremony and are allotted special places in Westminster Abbey.

Lord Warden, H.M. Queen Elizabeth the Queen Mother.
Judge, Court of Admiralty, Gerald Darling, R.D., Q.C.
Registrar, I. G. Gill, P.O. Box 9, Margate, Kent.

Lord Wardens since 1904

Marquess Curzon	1904
The Prince of Wales	1905
Earl Brassey	1908
Earl Beauchamp	1913
Marquess of Reading	1934
Marquess of Willingdon	1936
Sir Winston Churchill	1941
Sir Robert Menzies	1965
H.M. Queen Elizabeth the Queen Mother	1978

THE COMMONWEALTH

The Commonwealth is a free association of the 49 sovereign independent states listed below together with their associated states and dependencies.

ANTIGUA AND BARBUDA
AUSTRALIA
BAHAMAS
BANGLADESH
BARBADOS
BELIZE
BOTSWANA
BRUNEI
CANADA
CYPRUS
DOMINICA
FIJI
GAMBIA (THE)
GHANA
GREAT BRITAIN
GRENADA
GUYANA
INDIA
JAMAICA
KENYA
KIRIBATI
LESOTHO
MALAWI
MALAYSIA
MALTA

MALDIVES
MAURITIUS
NAURU
NEW ZEALAND
NIGERIA
PAPUA NEW GUINEA
SAINT KITTS-NEVIS
SAINT LUCIA
SAINT VINCENT AND THE
  GRENADINES
SEYCHELLES
SIERRA LEONE
SINGAPORE
SOLOMON ISLANDS
SRI LANKA
SWAZILAND
TANZANIA
TONGA
TRINIDAD AND TOBAGO
TUVALU
UGANDA
VANUATU
WESTERN SAMOA
ZAMBIA
ZIMBABWE

Area and Population.—The total area of the independent Commonwealth is estimated at 10,684,847 square miles. Details of the areas and populations of the Member States and dependencies appear in the following pages. The total population of the Commonwealth is estimated to be about one quarter of the world total.

History and Government.—The status and relationship of member nations was first defined by the Inter-Imperial Relations Committee of the 1926 Imperial Conference, under the chairmanship of Lord Balfour, in what came to be known as the "Balfour Declaration": "They are autonomous communities . . . equal in status, in no way subordinate one to another in any aspect of their domestic or external affairs, though united by a common allegiance to the Crown and freely associated as members of the British Commonwealth of Nations." This formula was given legal substance by the Statute of Westminster 1931.

The concept of a group of countries owing allegiance to a single Crown changed in 1949 when India decided to become a republic, and her continued membership of the Commonwealth was agreed by the other members on the basis of her "acceptance of the King as the symbol of the free association of the independent member nations and as such the Head of the Commonwealth". Member nations agreed at the time of the accession of Queen Elizabeth II to recognize Her Majesty as the new Head of the Commonwealth. The position is not vested in the British Crown.

Most members of the Commonwealth are parliamentary democracies.

Queen Elizabeth II is Head of State of 18 member countries of the Commonwealth: Antigua and Barbuda, Australia, the Bahamas, Barbados, Belize, Britain, Canada, Fiji, Grenada, Jamaica, Mauritius, New Zealand, Papua New Guinea, St. Kitts-Nevis, Saint Lucia, Saint Vincent and the Grenadines, Solomon Islands and Tuvalu. In each of these countries (except Britain) The Queen is personally represented by a Governor-General, who holds in all essential respects the same position in relation to the administration of public affairs in the realm as is held by Her Majesty in Britain (with the exception of

certain constitutional functions which are performed by The Queen personally). The Governor-General is appointed by The Queen on the advice of the Government of the country concerned.

Twenty-five member countries are republics: Bangladesh, Botswana, Cyprus, Dominica, The Gambia, Ghana, Guyana, India, Kenya, Kiribati, Malawi, The Maldives, Malta, Nauru, Nigeria, Seychelles, Sierra Leone, Singapore, Sri Lanka, Tanzania, Trinidad & Tobago, Uganda, Vanuatu, Zambia and Zimbabwe. In Malaysia, the Head of State is elected from among the nine hereditary Malay rulers and holds office for five years. Brunei, Lesotho, Tonga, and Swaziland have their own monarchs. Western Samoa has a Head of State whose functions are analogous to those of a constitutional monarch.

Membership of the Commonwealth is subject only to the approval of existing members. Two countries, Nauru and Tuvalu, are special members, with the right to participate in all functional Commonwealth meetings and activities, but not to attend Meetings of Commonwealth Heads of Government.

Consultation.—Commonwealth Heads of Government meet every two years to discuss international developments and to consider cooperation among members. These meetings, the successors to the pre-war Imperial Conferences, have grown in importance as they are the only regular forum of leaders from both developed and developing countries, constituting a broad sample of the world community. Decisions are reached by consensus, and the views of the meeting are set out in a communiqué.

In addition, there are annual meetings of Finance Ministers, and frequent meetings of Ministers and officials in the fields of trade, education, health, law, science, agriculture, labour and employment, and youth affairs.

Defence.—The Commonwealth is not a military alliance and members make their own defence arrangements in the light of their particular requirements. Some are parties to multi-lateral treaties, for example A.N.Z.U.S. and N.A.T.O. Various members of the Commonwealth cooperate with each other in combined exercises, joint research organizations and exchanges of personnel and training facilities.

Law.—English common law forms the basis of the legal system in many Commonwealth countries, although in most cases it has been radically adapted by statute to suit the individual needs and aspirations of a country, and there are countries where other systems have been adopted—for example, the law of Quebec Province and of Mauritius is founded on that of France, and Roman Dutch law forms the basis in Sri Lanka and Lesotho. Of the non-realms in the Commonwealth, Dominica, The Gambia, Malaysia, Singapore, and Trinidad and Tobago retain the right of appeal to the Judicial Committee of the Privy Council in the United Kingdom, which also hears appeals from a number of realms (Antigua and Barbuda, the Australian States, the Bahamas, Barbados, Belize, Fiji, Jamaica, Mauritius, New Zealand, St. Kitts-Nevis, St. Lucia, St. Vincent and the Grenadines, Tuvalu) and the dependent territories.

Citizenship and Nationality.—Each member of the Commonwealth defines the citizenship and nationality of its own people and determines the status of other Commonwealth nationals within its own boundaries. Members of the Commonwealth differentiate, in greater or lesser degree, as regards the grant of privileges, between citizens of the Commonwealth and aliens. The Republic of Ireland, which in 1949 ceased to be a member of the Commonwealth, is not regarded by the other Commonwealth nations as a foreign country nor her citizens as foreigners.

Finance and Development.—Complete financial autonomy is enjoyed by all members of the Commonwealth. In some countries, customs tariffs are lower for merchandise of Commonwealth origin than for imports from foreign countries. Developing countries, including those in the Commonwealth, obtain preference for exports of industrial goods and some agricultural exports from the developed countries under the Generalised Scheme of Preferences (G.S.P.). Many smaller Commonwealth countries are also party to the Lomé Convention which accords preferential access to the European Community. Many former Commonwealth preferences have been replaced by these arrangements.

British aid for the development needs of the Commonwealth countries and dependent territories are dealt with under the provisions of the Overseas Aid Act 1966, administered by the Overseas Development Administration. This Act succeeds the former Colonial Development and Welfare Acts. Those countries which are party to the Lomé Convention also receive aid under that Convention from the European Community.

Commonwealth Secretariat.—This was established by decision of Commonwealth Heads of Government in 1965, and is the main agency for multilateral communication between Commonwealth Governments on issues relating to the Commonwealth as a whole. It promotes consultation and disseminates information on matters of common concern, organizes meetings and conferences, coordinates Commonwealth activities and provides technical assistance for economic and social development through the Commonwealth Fund for Technical Cooperation. *Secretary-General*, Shridath S. Ramphal, Kt., C.M.G., Q.C., Marlborough House, Pall Mall, SW1Y 5HX [01-839 3411].

Dependent Territories and Associated States.—Britain, Australia and New Zealand have a number of dependent territories. New Zealand also has two associated states: Cook Islands (since 1965) and Niue (since 1974).

Member States of the Commonwealth
(with dates of independence)

1867* Canada
1901* Australia
1907* New Zealand
1947 India (Republic, 1950)
1948 Sri Lanka (Republic, 1972)
1957 Ghana (Republic, 1960)
     Federation of Malaya (Federation of Malaysia since 1963—indigenous monarchy)
1960 Cyprus (Republic on independence; joined Commonwealth 1961)
     Nigeria (Republic, 1963)

1961 Sierra Leone (Republic, 1971)
     Tanganyika (Republic, 1962; united 1964 with Zanzibar as TANZANIA)
1962 Western Samoa (Republic on independence; joined Commonwealth 1970)
     Jamaica
     Trinidad and Tobago (Republic, 1976)
     Uganda (Republic, 1967)
1963 Kenya (Republic, 1964)
     Singapore (as State in Federation of Malaysia; seceded as Republic, 1965)
1964 Malawi (Republic, 1966)
     Malta (Republic, 1974)
     Zambia (Republic on independence)
1965 The Gambia (Republic, 1970)
     Maldives (Republic, 1968; joined Commonwealth as a Special Member 1982; full member 1985)
1966 Guyana (Republic, 1970)
     Botswana (Republic on independence)
     Lesotho (indigenous monarchy)
     Barbados
1968 Mauritius
     Nauru (Republic on independence—Special Member)
     Swaziland (indigenous monarchy)
1970 Tonga (indigenous monarchy)
     Fiji
1971 Bangladesh (Republic on independence; joined Commonwealth 1972)
1973 Bahamas
1974 Grenada
1975 Papua New Guinea
1976 Seychelles (Republic on independence)
1978 Solomon Islands
     Tuvalu (Special Member)
     Dominica (Republic on independence)
1979 Saint Lucia
     Kiribati (Republic on independence)
     Saint Vincent and the Grenadines (Joined as a Special Member; became a full member 1985)
1980 Zimbabwe (Republic on independence)
     Vanuatu (Republic on independence)
1981 Belize
     Antigua and Barbuda
1983 Saint Kitts-Nevis
1984 Brunei (indigenous monarchy)

* These are the effective dates of independence, given legal effect by the Statute of Westminster, 1931.

(The above member states are Realms of Queen Elizabeth II unless otherwise stated.)

Associated States

The Cook Islands and Niue are self-governing states in association with New Zealand, which likewise remains responsible for their external affairs and defence.

Countries which have left the Commonwealth

1949 Republic of Ireland
1961 South Africa
1972 Pakistan

AREA AND POPULATION

Provinces or Territories and Capitals (with official contractions)	Area (English Sq. Miles). Land and Water	Population	
		Census, 1976	Census, 1981
Alberta, *Alta.* (Edmonton).....................	255,285	1,838,037	2,237,724
British Columbia, *B.C.* (Victoria)	366,255	2,466,608	2,744,467
Manitoba, *Man.* (Winnipeg)	251,000	1,021,506	1,026,241
New Brunswick, *N.B.* (Fredericton)...........	28,354	677,250	696,403
Newfoundland and Labrador, *Nfld.* (St. John's).	156,185	574,600	567,681
Nova Scotia, *N.S.* (Halifax)	21,425	828,571	847,442
Ontario, *Ont.* (Toronto)	412,582	8,264,465	8,625,107
Prince Edward Island, *P.E.I.* (Charlottetown) ..	2,184	118,229	122,506
Quebec, *Que.* (Quebec)	594,860	6,234,445	6,438,403
Saskatchewan, *Sask.* (Regina)	251,700	921,323	968,313
Yukon Territory, *Y.T.* (Whitehorse)	207,076	21,836	23,153
Northwest Territories, *N.W.T.* (Yellowknife) ..	1,304,903	42,609	45,741
Total...............	3,851,809	22,992,604	24,343,181

Land Area, 3,560,238 square miles; Water Area, 291,571 square miles.
Of the total immigration of 89,157 in 1983, 7,381 were from the United States, 5,737 from the United Kingdom and Ireland, and 7,216 from the Caribbean.

Increase of the People

Census Year	Population			Decennial Increase	Immigrants during Census Year
	Males	Females	Total		
1971...........	10,795,370	10,772,940	21,568,310	3,330,063	121,900
1976...........	11,449,520	11,543,080	22,992,605	2,977,725	149,429
1981...........	12,068,290	12,274,890	24,343,180	1,350,575	128,421

Estimated population, 1985, 25,318,000.

Indian population (1961) 208,286; (1971), 295,215; (1981), 367,810.
Eskimo population (1961), 11,835; (1971), 17,550; (1981), 25,390.

Mother Tongues of the Population

In the 1981 Census a distinction was made for the first time between the many aboriginal languages used in Canada, and a greater number of languages were identified as separate mother tongues than in the 1976 Census. N.B. Processing procedures in 1981 were not strictly comparable to those used in 1976.

	1976	1981		1976	1981
English	14,122,770	14,918,445	Indo-Chinese Languages	..	41,615
			Vietnamese	..	30,105
French	5,887,205	6,249,095	Indo-Pakistani Languages	58,415	116,990
European Languages			Punjabi	..	53,680
Croatian, Serbian, etc.	77,575	87,870	Japanese	15,525	20,130
Czech and Slovak	34,955	42,825	Korean	..	17,100
Finnish	28,470	33,380	Philippino and		
German	476,715	522,855	Tagalog	..	44,865
Greek	91,530	122,960	Semitic Languages	37,100	58,900
Italian	484,050	528,775	Arabic	..	50,115
Magyar (Hungarian)	69,300	83,720	African Languages	..	3,270
Netherlandic Languages	122,555	156,640	North American Languages		
Dutch and Frisian	114,760	146,830	Native Indian Languages	117,105	127,450
Polish	99,845	127,960	Algonkian Langs.	..	102,905
Portuguese	126,535	165,510	Cree	..	67,495
Russian	23,485	31,490	Ojibway	..	19,770
Scandinavian Languages	59,410	67,725	Athapaskan Langs	..	11,665
Spanish	44,135	70,160	Inuktituk	15,900	18,840
Ukrainian	282,060	292,265	Indian, not otherwise specified	..	20,285
Yiddish	23,435	32,760	Not Stated	445,020	..
Asian Languages					
Armenian	10,335	17,140			
Chinese	132,560	224,030	Total	22,992,605	24,343,180

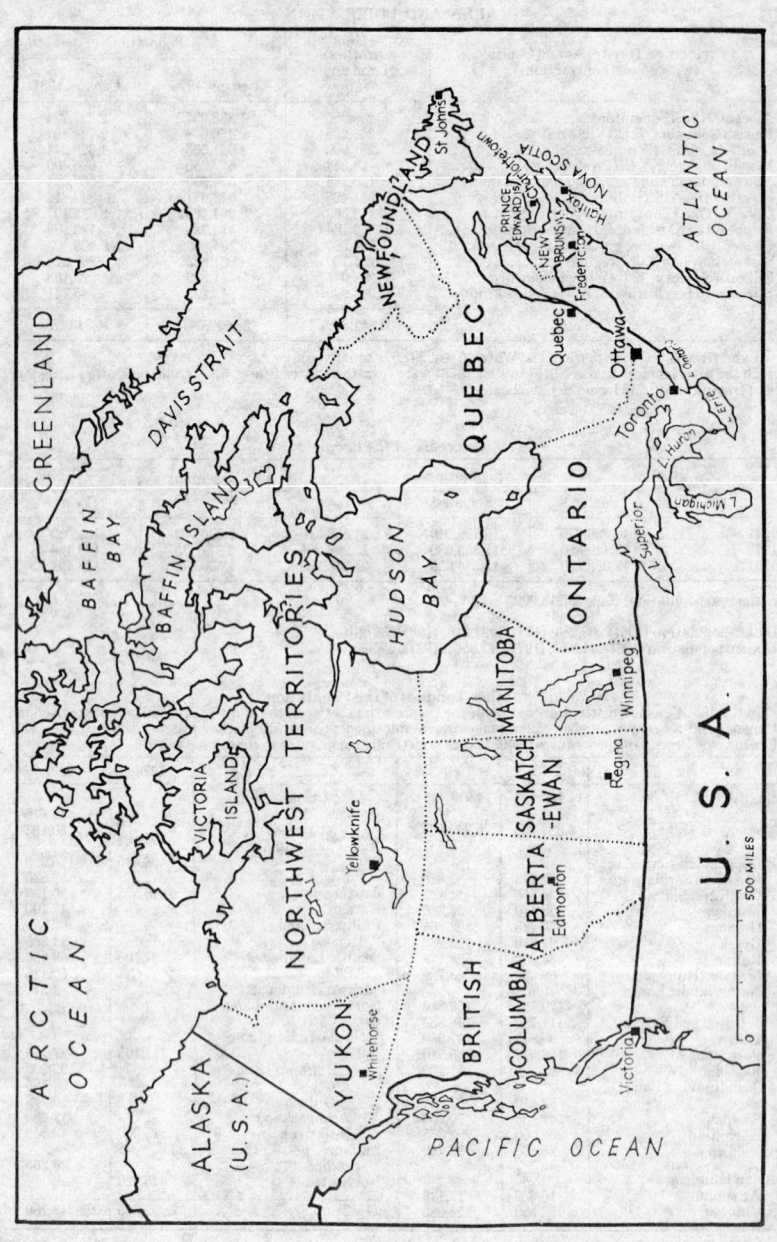

PHYSIOGRAPHY

Canada was originally discovered by Cabot in 1497, but its history dates only from 1534, when the French took possession of the country. The first permanent settlement at Port Royal (now Annapolis), Nova Scotia, was founded in 1605, and Quebec was founded in 1608. In 1759 Quebec was captured by the British forces under General Wolfe, and in 1763 the whole territory of Canada became a possession of Great Britain by the Treaty of Paris of that year. Nova Scotia was ceded in 1713 by the Treaty of Utrecht, the Provinces of New Brunswick and Prince Edward Island being subsequently formed out of it. British Columbia was formed into a Crown colony in 1858, having previously been a part of the Hudson Bay Territory, and was united to Vancouver Island in 1866.

Canada occupies the whole of the northern part of the North American Continent (with the exception of Alaska), from 49° North latitude to the North Pole, and from the Pacific to the Atlantic Ocean. In Eastern Canada, the southernmost point is Middle Island in Lake Erie, at 41° 41′.

Relief.—The relief of Canada is dominated by the mountain ranges running north and south on the west side of the Continent, by the pre-Cambrian shield on the east, with, in between, the northern extension of the North American Plain. From the physiographic point of view Canada has six main divisions. These are: (1) Appalachian-Acadian Region, (2) the Canadian Shield, (3) the St. Lawrence-Great Lakes Lowland, (4) the Interior Plains, (5) the Cordilleran Region and (6) the Arctic Archipelago. The first region occupies all that part of Canada lying southeast of the St. Lawrence. In general, the relief is an alternation of highlands and lowlands and is hilly rather than mountainous. The lowlands area seldom rises over 600 feet above sea level. The great Canadian Shield comprises more than half the area. The interior as a whole is an undulating, low plateau (general level 1,000 to 1,500 feet), with the more rugged relief lying along the border between Northern Quebec and Labrador. Throughout the whole area water or muskeg-filled depressions separate irregular hills and ridges, 150 to 200 feet in elevation. Newfoundland, an outlying portion of the shield, consists of glaciated, low rolling terrain broken here and there by mountains.

The flat relief of the St. Lawrence-Great Lakes lowland varies from 500 feet in the east to 1,700 feet south of Georgian Bay. The whole area in the western part slopes gently to the Great Lakes. The most striking relief is provided by the eastward facing scarp of the Niagara escarpment (elevation 250 to 300 feet). The interior plains, comprising the Pacific Provinces, slope eastward and northward a few feet per mile. The descent from west to east is made from 5,000 feet to less than 1,000 feet in three distinct levels, with each new level being marked by an eastward facing *conteau* or scarp. Horizontal strata and peneplanation make for slight relief of the level to rolling type. Five fairly well-developed topographic divisions mark out the Cordilleran region of western Canada. These are: (1) coastal ranges, largely above 5,000 feet with deep fiords and glaciated valleys, (2) the interior plateau, around 3,500 feet and comparatively level, (3) the Selkirk ranges, largely above 5,000 feet, (4) the Rocky Mountains with their chain of 10,000 to 12,000 feet peaks, and (5) the Peace River or Tramontane region with its rolling diversified country.

The Arctic Archipelago, with its plateau-like character has an elevation between 500 and 1,000 feet, though in Baffin Land and Ellesmere Island the mountain ranges rise to 8,500 and 9,500 feet. Two tremendous waterway systems, the St. Lawrence and the Mackenzie, providing thousands of miles of water highway, occupy a broad area of lowland with their dominant axis following the edge of the shield.

Climate.—The climate of the eastern and central portions presents greater extremes than in corresponding latitudes in Europe, but in the southwestern portion of the Prairie Region and the southern portions of the Pacific slope the climate is milder. Spring, summer, and autumn are of about seven to eight months' duration, and the winter four to five months.

GOVERNMENT

The Constitution of Canada had its source in the British North America Act of 1867 which formed a Dominion, under the name of Canada, of the four provinces: Ontario, Quebec, New Brunswick and Nova Scotia; to this Federation the other Provinces have subsequently been admitted. Under this Act Canada came into being on July 1, 1867 (Dominion Day), and under the Statute of Westminster, which received the royal assent on Dec. 11, 1931, Canada and the Provinces were exempted (in common with other self-governing Dominions of the Commonwealth of Nations) from the operation of the Colonial Laws Validity Act, the Statute of Westminster having removed all limitations with regard to the legislative autonomy of the Dominions, except that the British North America Act could be amended in important respects only by Acts of the British Parliament.

Provinces admitted since 1867 are: Manitoba (1870), British Columbia (1871), Prince Edward Island (1873), Alberta and Saskatchewan (1905) and Newfoundland (1949).

Agreement was reached in Nov. 1981 between the Federal and Provincial Governments (except Quebec) to patriate the Constitution so that it was amendable only in Canada. The inclusion in the Constitution of a Charter of Rights was also agreed. At the request of the Canadian Parliament, legislation was passed at Westminster and the Constitution formally patriated on 17th April 1982.

The Executive power is vested in a Governor-General appointed by the Sovereign on the advice of the Canadian Ministry, and aided by a Privy Council.

FLAG.—Red maple leaf with 11 points on white square, flanked by vertical red bars one half the width of the square.

Governor General's Household

Governor-General and Commander-in Chief, Her Excellency the Rt. Hon. Jeanne Sauvé, C.C., C.M.M., C.D.

Secretary to the Governor-General, E. U. Butler, C.V.O.

Deputy Secretary, T. Smyth.

Comptroller of Household, D. C. McKinnon, C.V.O., C.D.

Assistant Secretary and Director, Chancellery of Canadian Orders and Decorations, R. de C. Nantel, M.V.O., C.D.

Programme and Policy Secretary, Miss F. Katz.

Cultural Attaché, J.-N. Tremblay.

Assistant Secretary to the Governor-General and Travel Officer, Maj. C. A. Sangster, C.D.

Press Secretary, Mlle. M. Bender.

Aides-de-Camp, Capt. P. Richard; Capt. A. Levesque; Lt. (N) P. Maddison.

Attaché, Mlle. L. Benoit.

The Cabinet

Prime Minister, Rt. Hon. M. Brian Mulroney.

Veterans' Affairs, Hon. George H. Hees.

Leader of the Government in the Senate, Hon. Duff Roblin.

External Affairs, Rt. Hon. C. Joseph Clark.

Employment and Immigration, Hon. Flora I. MacDonald.

Deputy Prime Minister and Minister of National Defence, Hon. Erik H. Nielsen.

Justice and Attorney General, Hon. John C. Crosbie.

Public Works, Hon. Roch LaSalle.

Transport, Hon. Donald F. Mazankowski.

Solicitor General, Hon. Perrin Beatty.

National Health and Welfare, Hon. Arthur J. Epp.

Fisheries and Oceans, Hon. John A. Fraser.

Regional Industrial Expansion, Hon. Sinclair M. Stevens.

Agriculture, Hon. John Wise.

President of the Privy Council (Government House Leader), Hon. Ramon J. Hnatyshyn.

Indian Affairs and Northern Development, Hon. David E. Crombie.

President of the Treasury Board, Hon. Robert R. de Cotret.

National Revenue, Hon. Elmer M. MacKay.

Finance, Hon. Michael H. Wilson.

Supply and Services, Hon. Stewart McInnes.

Labour, Hon. William H. McKnight.

Secretary of State, Hon. Benoit Bouchard.

Energy, Mines and Resources, Hon. Patricia Carney.

Environment, Hon. Thomas M. McMillan.

Consumer and Corporate Affairs, Hon. Michel Côté.

International Trade, Hon. James F. Kelleher.

Communications, Hon. Marcel Masse.

External Relations, Hon. Monique Vézina.

Associate Defence Minister, Hon. Harvie Andre.

Ministers of State, Hon. Otto J. Jelinek (*Fitness and Amateur Sport, and Multiculturalism*); Hon. Thomas E. Siddon (*Science and Technology*); Hon. Charles J. Mayer (*Canadian Wheat Board*); Hon. Walter F. McLean (*Immigration*); Hon. Jack B. Murta (*Tourism*); Hon. André Bissonnette (*Small Businesses*); Hon. Suzanne Blais-Grenier (*Transport*); Hon. Andrée Champagne (*Youth*); Hon. Robert E. Layton (*Mines*); Hon. Barbara J. McDougall (*Finance*); Hon. Gerald S. Merrithew (*Forestry*).

The Prime Minister receives remuneration of $139,300; other ministers, each $96,200.

CANADIAN HIGH COMMISSION
Macdonald House, 1 Grosvenor Square, W.1.
[01–629–9492]

High Commissioner, His Excellency Roy R. McMurtry (1985).

Deputy High Commissioner, P. Lapointe.

Ministers, C. M. Forsyth-Smith (*Commercial*); M. Phillips (*Public Affairs*).

Minister-Counsellors, D. Stockwell (*Administration*); G. H. Stewart (*Immigration*).

BRITISH HIGH COMMISSION
80 Elgin Street, Ottawa

High Commissioner, His Excellency Sir Derek Day, K.C.M.G.

Deputy High Commissioner, R. H. Baker.

Counsellor, Miss C. S. Rycroft (*Economic and Commercial*).

Defence and Air Adviser, Air Cdre. D. Whittaker, M.B.E.

Naval Adviser, Capt. J. Laybourne.

Military Adviser, Col. W. M. R. Addison.

1st Secretaries, M. H. Connor (*Head of Chancery*); A. N. Foggo; K. W. Kelley, O.B.E. (*Economic*); A. J. Mitchell; D. J. Pugh, M.B.E. (*Administration*).

Cultural Affairs and British Council Representative, C. M. Chadwick, O.B.E.

THE LEGISLATURE

Parliament consists of a Senate and a House of Commons. The *Senate* consists of 104 members, nominated by the Governor-General (age limit 75). They are distributed between the various provinces thus: 24 each for *Ontario* and *Quebec*, 10 each for *Nova Scotia* and *New Brunswick*, 6 each for *Newfoundland, British Columbia, Manitoba, Alberta*, and *Saskatchewan* and 4 for *Prince Edward Island*, 1 for *North West Territories* and 1 for *Yukon*; each Senator must be at least thirty years old, a resident in the province for which he is appointed, a natural-born or naturalized subject of the Queen, and the owner of a property qualification amounting to $4,000. The Speaker of the Senate is chosen by the Government of the day.

The *House of Commons* has 282 members and is elected every five years at longest. Representation by provinces is at present as follows: Newfoundland 7, Prince Edward Island 4, Nova Scotia 11, New Brunswick 10, Quebec 75, Ontario 95, Manitoba 14, Saskatchewan 14, Alberta 21, British Columbia 28, Yukon 1, Northwest Territories 2.

In every case—including the Prime Minister's—a sessional indemnity of $54,600 *per annum* is paid to members of the House of Commons. In addition, Ministers and members of the House of Commons receive an expense allowance. Certain Members of Parliament for large northern constituencies have larger expense allowances.

THE SENATE

The state of the parties in the Senate in mid-1985 was *Liberal* 72, *Conservative* 25, *Independent* 4, *Independent Liberal* 1 (2 vacant).

Speaker of the Senate, Hon. Guy Chapbonneau, Q.C. $93,000

Clerk of the Senate & Clerk of the Parliaments, C. A. Lussier.

THE HOUSE OF COMMONS

The state of parties in the House of Commons in mid-1985 was *Conservative* 211, *Liberals* 40, *N.D.P.* 30, *Independent* 1 (5 vacant).

Speaker of the House of Commons, Hon. John W. Bosley $108,500
Deputy Speaker, Marcel Danis $94,700
Clerk of the House of Commons, Dr. C. B. Koester.

THE JUDICATURE

The Judicature is administered by judges following the Civil Law in Quebec Province and Common Law in other Provinces. Each Province has its Court of Appeal. All Superior, County and District Court Judges are appointed by the Governor-General, the others by the Lieutenant-Governors of the Provinces.

The highest federal court is the Supreme Court of Canada, composed of a Chief Justice and eight puisne judges, which exercises general appellate jurisdiction throughout Canada in civil and criminal cases, and which usually holds three sessions each year. There is one other federally constituted Court, the Federal Court of Canada, which has jurisdiction on appeals from its Trial Division, from Federal Tribunals and reviews of decisions and references by Federal Boards and Commissions. The Trial Division has jurisdiction in claims by or against the Crown, its officers or servants or Federal bodies. It also deals with inter-Provincial and Federal-Provincial disputes.

SUPREME COURT OF CANADA

Chief Justice of Canada, Rt. Hon. Brian Dickson, P.C. $117,800

Puisne Judges, Hon. J. Beetz; Hon. W. Z. Estey; Hon. W. R. McIntyre; Hon. J. Chouinard; Hon. A. Lamer; Hon. Bertha Wilson; Hon. G. Le Dain; Hon. G. V. LaForest

each $108,400

FEDERAL COURT OF CANADA

Chief Justice, Hon. A. L. Thurlow $103,800
Associate Chief Justice, Hon. J. A. Jerome. $103,800
Appeal Division Judges, Hon. W. F. Ryan; Hon. L. Pratte; Hon. D. V. Heald; Hon. J. J. Urie; Hon. J. K. Hugessen; Hon. P. M. Mahoney, P.C.; Hon. L. Marceau; Hon. M. MacGuigan, P.C.; Hon. A. J. Stone

each $95,800

Trial Division Judges, Hon. Allison Walsh; Hon. J. E. Dubé; Hon. F. U. Collier; Hon. G. A. Addy; Hon. P. U. C. Rouleau; Hon. J. C. McNair; Hon. F. C. Muldoon; Hon. Barbara J. Reed; Hon. B. L. Strayer; Hon. Y. Pinard; Hon. L. M. Joyal; Hon. P. Denault; Hon. B. Cullen . . . . each $95,800

VITAL STATISTICS

BIRTHS, DEATHS AND MARRIAGES, 1983

Province	Births	Deaths	Marriages
Alberta	45,555	12,588	21,172
British Columbia .	42,919	19,827	23,692
Manitoba	16,602	8,521	8,261
New Brunswick . .	10,518	5,206	5,260
Newfoundland . . .	8,929	3,498	3,778
Nova Scotia	12,401	7,042	6,505
Ontario	126,826	64,507	70,893
P.E.I.	1,907	1,050	937
Quebec	88,154	44,275	36,144
Saskatchewan . . .	17,847	7,611	7,504
Yukon	540	113	243
N. W. Territories	1,491	241	286
Total	373,689	174,484	184,675

Canada's birth rate per 1,000 population (1983) 15·0; Death Rate 7·0; Marriage Rate 7·4. Divorces 68,567.

FINANCE

Federal Government gross general revenue and expenditure was ($ millions):—

	1984–85	1985–86
Total Revenue	82,286	85,845
Total Expenditure	111,567	115,422

DEBT ($ millions)

	1983–84	1984–85
Gross Public Debt	196,300	230,500
Net Public Debt	157,000	188,200

Banking.—There were 71 chartered banks on March 31, 1985, with assets of $421,881 m. Deposits were $378,697 m. of which $112,635 m. were personal savings.

NATIONAL DEFENCE

The Minister of National Defence has the control and management of the Canadian Armed Forces and all matters relating to National Defence establishments and works for the defence of Canada.

The Canadian Forces are organized on a functional basis to reflect the major commitments assigned by the government and are formed into National Defence Headquarters and five major Commands reporting to the Chief of the Defence Staff. The roles of the five Commands are: *Mobile Command*—Provision of ground forces for the protection of Canadian territory, combat forces in Canada for support of overseas commitments, and forces for support of United Nations or other peace-keeping operations. *Maritime Command*—Provision of sea forces on the Atlantic and Pacific coasts for the defence of Canada, anti-submarine defence in support of NATO. Support to Canadian Military operations and the conduct of search and rescue operations within the Atlantic and Pacific search and rescue areas. Maritime Command also has operational control of Maritime aircraft. *Air Command*—Provision of operationally ready air forces to national, continental and international commitments. *Canadian Forces Communication Command*—Manages, operates and maintains strategic communications for the Canadian Forces. *Canadian Forces Europe*—Canadian Forces allocated to support NATO in Europe consisting of land and air elements.

National Defence expenditures for the fiscal year 1984–85 was estimated at $8,753 million. Canadian Armed Forces strength at Dec. 1984, 82,740 authorized force.

EDUCATION AND LANGUAGE

Education is under the control of the Provincial Governments, the cost of the publicly controlled schools being met by local taxation, aided by provincial grants. In 1984–85 there were 15,624 publicly controlled elementary and secondary schools with 4,956,280 pupils. Of these, 1,122 were private schools with 234,840 pupils; 364 Indian schools with 43,060 pupils and 21 special schools for the blind and deaf with 3,010 pupils.

In 1984–85 there were 66 degree-granting universities with a full-time enrolment of 471,370, as well as 329,800 students in 197 other post-secondary, non-university institutions.

Canada has two official languages, English and French. At the 1981 census 61·3 per cent. of the total population gave English as their mother language and 25·7 per cent. French.

CANADIAN PRODUCTION

Agriculture.—About 7 per cent. of the total land area of Canada is classified as farm land and approximately half of this is under cultivation, the remainder being woodland or suitable only for grazing purposes. More than three-quarters of the land now cultivated is found in the prairie region of Western Canada. Farm cash receipts from the sale of farm products in 1984 were $20,230,580,000. Livestock, poultry and eggs contributed $9,743,972,000; field crops $9,747,089,000.

Grain crop production ('000 tonnes)

	1983	1984
Wheat	26,914·1	21,199·4
Oats	2,773·1	2,669·9
Barley	10,616·0	10,251·9
Rye	827·5	663·8
Flaxseed	465·0	676·0
Rapeseed	2,681·0	3,245·9
	44,276·7	38,706·9

Livestock.—In Jan. 1985 the livestock included 10,964,900 cattle, 523,100 sheep, 10,851,900 hogs and 23,600,065 chickens (layers).

Fur Production.—Canada in 1983–84 produced pelts valued at $90,983,396. Wild life pelts made up 46 per cent of the total, with a value of $41,810,479.

Fisheries.—The marketed value of catches in 1984 was $1,820,300,000.

Forestry.—About 44 per cent. of the total land areas is in forests. The shipment value of forest products in 1983 was: newsprint $4,155,686,000; paper (other than newsprint) $1,809,158,022; lumber $4,597,771,000; wood pulp $3,519,185,000.

Minerals.—Canada is the world's largest producer of zinc and the second largest of nickel, asbestos and potash. The country is also rich in many other minerals, including gold, silver, aluminium, iron, copper, uranium, cobalt, elemental sulphur and lead. There are considerable petroleum and natural gas resources in Alberta, off the Atlantic coast and in the Canadian Arctic islands, although the development and profitability of this industry has been adversely affected by the fall in world oil prices since 1981–82.

	1983	1984 p
	('000 tonnes)	
Copper	653·0	712·4
Nickel	125·0	174·2
Lead	272·0	259·4
Molybdenum	10·2	10·9
Zinc	987·7	1,022·0
Iron Ore	32,959·0	41,065·0
Asbestos	858·0	836·0
Gypsum	7,507·0	8,725·0
Cement	7,871·0	8,619·0
Lime	2,232·0	2,280·0
Salt	8,602·0	10,294·0
Potash	6,294·0	6,972·0

p = preliminary

Production of gold was 81,316,000 grams in 1984 (73,512,000 in 1983) and of silver was 1,171,000 kg. (1,197,000 kg. in 1983). Uranium production in 1984 was 9,693,000 kilograms (6,823,000 kg. in 1983).

TRADE

Merchandise imports into Canada in 1984 were valued at $95,842,401,000 and merchandise exports (including re-exports) at $112,495,449,000. The main exports in 1984 were motor vehicles and parts, newsprint paper, wheat, crude petroleum, lumber, natural gas, woodpulp, industrial machinery, petroleum and coal products, and television and telecommunication equipment. Trade with the U.S.A. accounts for about 70 per cent of total trade in merchandise, although efforts are being made to develop alternative markets. Value of trade with Canada's largest trading partners in 1984 was as follows ($'000):

Country	Imports	Domestic Exports
United States	68,537,369	82,796,262
Japan	5,710,833	5,628,644
United Kingdom	2,318,583	2,443,424
West Germany	2,173,581	1,220,681
USSR	28,735	2,122,285
France	1,219,488	700,746
South Korea	1,152,369	712,656
Mexico	1,437,696	350,727
Italy	1,116,125	577,939
Taiwan	1,223,805	400,560
Netherlands	545,421	1,063,338
China	333,502	1,272,140
Venezuela	1,207,226	247,857

COMMUNICATIONS

Railways.—The total track of railways in operation on Dec. 31, 1983, was 99,444 km.

	1983
Capital	$13,147,475,447
Operating Revenues	7,027,369,000
Operating Expenses	6,437,560,000

In 1983 revenue freight was 225,380,292,729 tonne-kilometres.

Shipping.—The registered shipping on Dec. 31, 1983 including inland vessels, was 35,622 vessels with gross tonnage 5,360,433. The volume of international shipping handled at Canadian ports in 1983 was 129,490,483 metric tonnes loaded and 46,914,996 metric tonnes unloaded.

Canals.—The bulk of canal shipping in Canada is handled through the two sections of the St. Lawrence Seaway, which provide access to the Great Lakes for ocean-going ships. In 1983, transits on the Montreal-Lake Ontario section numbered 3,870 for a total of 45,060,981 cargo tonnes; transits in the Welland Canal section numbered 4,707 for a total of 49,024,104 cargo tonnes. Principal commodities carried were iron ore, wheat, corn, barley, soybeans, fuel oil, manufactured iron and steel, coal and coke.

Civil Aviation.—The number of passengers carried in 1984 (all carriers) was 44,827,289. 1,120,731 ton-miles of freight were carried in 1984.

Motor Vehicles.—Total motor vehicle registrations numbered 14,590,903 in 1983.

Post.—There were 8,177 postal facilities operating in Canada on March 31, 1985. Post office revenue in the fiscal year 1984–85 was $2,500 m. (estimated); total expenditure $2,895 m. (estimated).

FEDERAL CAPITAL

OTTAWA, the Federal Capital, 111 miles west of Montreal and 247 miles north-east of Toronto, is a city on the south bank of the Ottawa river. The city was chosen as the Capital of the Province of Canada in 1857 and was later selected as the site of the Dominion capital. Ottawa contains the Parliamentary Buildings, the Public Archives, Royal Mint, several national museums, National Art Gallery and the Dominion Observatory.

A National Arts Centre, near the Parliament buildings, includes an opera house with seating for 2,300, a theatre (800 seats), an experimental studio (300 seats) and a hall (100 seats).

Manufacturing is also carried on, high technology (communications, defence), printing and publishing being of greatest importance. Ottawa is connected with Lake Ontario by the Rideau Canal. The City population was 303,114 at the Census of 1981; Metropolitan Ottawa 756,000 (June 1984 estimate).

YUKON TERRITORY

The Yukon Act, 1970, as amended, provides for the administration of the Territory by a Commissioner acting under instructions from time to time given by the Governor in Council or the Minister of Indian Affairs and Northern Development. Legislative powers, analogous to those of a provincial government, are exercised by a Legislative Assembly of 16 members elected from electoral districts in the Territory. The Executive Council of the Assembly consists of the government leader as chairman and four elected members. The area of the Territory is 207,076 square miles with a population (1984 estimate) of 22,100. Mining is the chief industry, though trapping remains important and there is considerable timber production. Mining production, including copper, silver, lead and gold, was valued at $59,574,000 in 1984.

Seat of Government, Whitehorse. Pop. (1981) 14,814.
Commissioner, D. L. D. Bell.

NORTHWEST TERRITORIES

The Northwest Territories Act, 1979, as amended, provides for a Legislative Assembly of 24 elected members, of which the Executive Committee under the chairmanship of the Commissioner is the senior decision-making body of the government in the province.

The Northwest Territories are subdivided into the districts of Mackenzie, Keewatin and Franklin.

The area of the Northwest Territories is 1,304,903 square miles with a population (1984 estimate) of 49,500. The chief industry is mining, with a total value of $737,798,000 in 1984. Zinc and lead contributed 56 per cent. of the total; gold and silver 28 per cent., and since 1982 there have been major developments in natural gas and petroleum extraction on- and off-shore.

Seat of Government, Yellowknife. Pop. (1981) 9,483.
Commissioner, John Parker.

PROVINCES OF CANADA

ALBERTA

Area and Population.—The Province of Alberta has an area of 255,285 square miles, including about 6,485 square miles of water, with a population (Jan. 1985 estimate) of 2,358,100.

Government.—The Government is vested in a Lieutenant-Governor and Legislative Assembly composed of 79 members, elected for five years, representing 79 electoral districts in the Province. At a provincial election held in Nov. 1982, the Progressive Conservative party took 75 seats, the New Democratic Party 2 seats, and Independents 2 seats.

Lieut.-Governor, Her Honour Helen Hunley.

EXECUTIVE

Premier, President of Executive Council; Hon.
 Peter Lougheed Q.C. $76,954
Economic Development, Hon. Hugh Planche.
Provincial Treasurer, Hon. Lou Hyndman.
Energy, Hon. John Zoazirny.
Attorney General and Government House Leader, Hon. Neil Crawford.
Hospitals and Medical Care, Hon. David Russell.
Municipal Affairs, Hon. Julian Koziak.
Agriculture, Hon. LeRoy Fjordbotten.
Federal and Intergovernmental Affairs, Hon. Jim Horsman.
Labour, Hon. Leslie Young.
Education, Hon. David King.
Advanced Education, Hon. Dick Johnston.
Consumer and Corporate Affairs, Hon. Connie Osterman.
Social Services and Community Health, Hon. Dr. Neill Webber.
Solicitor General, The Hon. Graham Harle.
Public Works, Supply and Services, Hon. Tom Chambers.
Environment, Hon. Fred Bradley.
Transportation, Hon. Marvin Moore.
Utilities and Telecommunications, Hon. Bob Bogle.
Tourism and Small Business, Hon. Allen Adair.
Recreation and Parks, Hon. Peter Trynchy.
International Trade, Hon. Horst Schmid.
Associate Minister, Public Lands and Wildlife, Hon. Don Sparrow.
Native Affairs, Hon. Milt Pahl.
Culture, Hon. Mary LeMessurier.
Workers' Health, Safety and Compensation, Hon. Bill Diachuk.
Personnel Administration, Hon. Greg Stevens.
Housing, Hon. Lawrence Shaben.
Manpower, Hon. Ernest Isley.
Without Portfolio, Hon. Bill Payne.
Speaker of the Legislative Assembly, Hon. G.
 Amerongen 68,504

London Office, Alberta House, 1, Mount Street, W.1.

THE JUDICATURE

Court of Appeal of Alberta, Hon. J. H. Laycraft (*Chief Justice*).

Judges, Hons. N. D. McDermid; S. S. Lieberman; D. C. Prowse, A. F. Moir; W. J. Haddad; J. W. McClung; A. M. Harradence; R. P. Kerans; R. H. Belzil; W. A. Stevenson; H. L. Irving.
Court of Queen's Bench of Alberta, Hon. W. K. Moore (*Chief Justice*); Hon. T. H. Miller (*Associate Chief Justice*).

ECONOMY

The Gross Domestic Product at factor cost in 1983 was ($ millions):—

Agriculture, fishing and trapping	1,921
Forestry	59
Mining	12,905
Manufacturing	3,353
Construction	3,315
Transportation	3,582
Utilities	1,739
Trade	4,289
Finance	11,605
Services	7,646
Public Administration	3,066
Total G.D.P. at factor cost	53,479

Mineral Production 1984
(preliminary estimates)

	$ m.
Crude Oil	14,927·0
Natural Gas	6,981·4
Natural Gas By-Products	2,717·2
Coal	479·5
Sulphur (elemental)	556·9
Sand & Gravel	127·6
Cement	116·5
Other	57·6
Total	25,963·7

Manufacturing.—The value of manufacturing shipments (1984 preliminary) was $13,855,893. Number of industrial establishments 2,490. (1982 preliminary), total employees 79,701 (1982). The leading industries are slaughtering and meat processing, petroleum refining, chemicals and chemical products, non-metallic mineral products, primary metal and metal fabricating products.

GOVERNMENT FINANCE
Budgetary Estimates $'000

	1983–84	1984–85
Revenue	8,840,000	9,386,000
Expenditure	9,685,452	9,644,337
Deficit	845,452	258,337

NOTE: The Budgetary revenue figure does not include funds allocated to the Alberta Heritage Savings Trust Fund.

CAPITAL—Edmonton—city population (1983) 560,085, metropolitan area, 683,000. Other centres are Calgary (619,814), Fort McMurray (35,352), Lethbridge (58,586), Medicine Hat (41,493), Red Deer (51,070), St. Albert (35,529).

BRITISH COLUMBIA

Area and Population.—British Columbia has a total area estimated at 366,255 square miles, with a population of 2,865,100 (June 1984).

Government.—The Government consists of a Lieutenant-Governor and an Executive Council together with a Legislative Assembly of 57 members.

Lieut.-Governor, Hon. Robert Gordon Rogers.

EXECUTIVE COUNCIL

Premier and President of the Council, Hon. William Richards Bennett.

Human Resources, Hon. Grace Mary McCarthy.

Attorney-General, Hon. Brian R. D. Smith, Q.C.

Minister of Finance, Hon. Hugh Austin Curtis.

Minister of Agriculture and Food, Hon. Harvey W. Schroeder.

Education, Hon. John H. Heinrich.

Provincial Secretary and Minister of Government Services, Hon. James R. Chabot.

Lands, Parks and Housing and Environment, Hon. Anthony J. Brummet.

Labour, Hon. Terry Segarty.

Health, Hon. James Arthur Nielsen.

Transportation and Highways, Hon. Alexander Vaughan Fraser.

Municipal Affairs, Hon. William S. Ritchie.

Consumer and Corporate Affairs, Hon. James J. Hewitt.

Forests, Hon. Thomas Manville Waterland.

Energy, Mines and Petroleum Resources, Hon. C. Stephen Rogers.

Industry and Small Business Development, Hon. Robert H. McClelland.

Universities, Sciences and Communications, Hon. Patrick Lucey McGeer.

International Trade and Investment, Hon. Donald McGray Phillips.

Intergovernmental Relations, Hon. Garde Basil Gardom.

Tourism, Hon. Claude H. Richmond.

(The Premier receives a total salary of $76,527; Members of the Executive Council receive a total salary of $71,330).

Speaker, Legislative Assembly, Hon. K. Walter Davidson $64,809

Agent-General in London, A. Hart, Q.C., British Columbia House, 1 Regent Street, S.W.1.

THE JUDICATURE

Court of Appeal—Chief Justice of British Colombia, Hon. N. T. Nemetz.

Justices of Appeal, Hons. J. D. Taggart; P. D. Seaton; A. B. B. Carrothers; E. E. Hinkson; W. A. Craig; J. S. Aikins; J. D. Lambert; J. A. Macdonald; R. P. Anderson; H. E. Hutcheon; A. B. Macfarlane; W. A. Esson.

Supreme Court—Chief Justice, Hon. A. McEachern.

Puisne Judges, Hons. J. G. Gould; H. C. McKay; K. E. Meredith; A. A. Mackoff; S. M. Toy; J. C. Bouck; L. G. McKenzie; G. L. Murray; H. P. Legg; W. J. Trainor; P. M. Proudfoot; H. A. Callaghan; A. G. MacKinnon; M. R. Taylor; C. C. Locke; W. J. Wallace; P. D. Dohm; R. M. P. Paris; D. B. Hinds; A. A. W. Macdonell; J. E. Spencer; B. M. McLachlin; W. H. Davies; C. R. Lander; B. D. MacDonald; K. M. Lysyk; L. S. G. Finch; J. Wood; R. J. Gibbs; M. F. Southin; G. S. Cumming.

FINANCE (1985–86)

Estimated Revenue $8,166,000,000
Estimated Expenditure 9,056,000,000
Direct Debt 5,309,200,000

ECONOMY

Production and Industry.—Manufacturing activity is based largely on the processing of the output of the logging, mineral, fishing and agriculture industries. The principal manufacturing centres are Vancouver, New Westminster, Victoria, North Vancouver, Kelowna and Prince George. Forestry and forest-based industries form the most important economic activity, accounting for approximately 40 per cent of total production. British Columbia is the leading province of Canada in the quantity and value of its timber and sawmill products. Mining, the second most important non-service economic activity, is based on copper, zinc, lead, iron concentrates, molybdenum, coal, natural gas, crude petroleum, asbestos, gold and silver. Molybdenum production is approximately 99 per cent of the Canadian total.

The production levels for important industries were estimated for 1984 as follows:—

Lumber .... 30,884,000 cu. metres.
Paper .... 2,085,000 tonnes
Pulp .... 5,190,800 tonnes
Coal .... 20,719,200 tonnes
Natural Gas .... 8,275,900 cu. metres

Mineral production for 1984 was valued at $3,285·2 million.

The most important agricultural products are livestock, eggs and poultry, fruits and dairy products. Salmon accounts for approximately 60 per cent of the value of fisheries. Other species include halibut, herring, sole, cod, flounder, perch, tuna and shellfish. In 1984 farm cash receipts were valued at $971·3 million.

The economy is dependent upon markets outside the province for the disposal of most of the products of her industry. An estimated 55–60 per cent of production is exported to foreign markets. Manufacturing shipments in 1984 were valued at $17,647·4 million.

Transport.—The province has deep water harbours which are well serviced by railways and modern highways. Vancouver is the base for regular scheduled air routes to other parts of Canada, the United States, Europe, Mexico, South America, Hawaii, Fiji, Australia, Japan, Hong Kong and the Middle East.

CAPITAL, ΨVICTORIA, Metropolitan population (1984) 242,000. ΨVANCOUVER metropolitan population (1984) 1,331,000, is the western terminus of the Canadian Pacific Railway and the Canadian National Railways (the C.N.R. also has a terminus at Prince Rupert) and the southern terminus of the British Columbia Railway, and possesses one of the finest natural harbours in the world, servicing a variety of vessels, including large bulk cargo carriers. Other principal cities are Prince George, Kamloops, Kelowna and Nanaimo.

MANITOBA

Area and Population.—Manitoba, originally the Red River settlement, is the central province of Canada. The Province has a considerable area of prairie land but is also a land of wide diversity combining 400 miles of sea-coast, large lakes and rivers covering an area of 30,225 square miles and pre-cambrian rock which covers about three-fifths of the Province. The total area is 250,946 square miles with a population (1984 estimate) of 1,057,400.

Government.—The Government is administered by a Lieutenant-Governor, assisted by an Executive Council of Ministers, who are members of the Legislative Assembly of 57 members. Each member of the Legislative Assembly receives an annual sessional indemnity totalling $33,750 for the year ending July 1, 1985.

The New Democratic Party formed the government of Manitoba in November 1981. The standing in the House at May 1, 1984 was: New Democratic Party 32, Progressive Conservative 23, Independent 2.

Lieut.-Governor, Her Honour Pearl McGonigal (1981).

EXECUTIVE

Premier, President of the Council and Minister of Federal-Provincial Relations, Hon. Howard R. Pawley, Q.C.

Health and Urban Affairs, Hon. Laurent L. Desjardins.

Natural Resources, Hon. Samuel Uskiw.

Employment Services and Economic Security, Hon. Leonard S. Evans.

Agriculture, Hon. Billie Uruski.

Co-operative Development, Hon. Jay M. Cowan.

Energy and Mines, Hon. Wilson D. P. Parasiuk.

Finance and Crown Investments, Hon. Victor Schroeder, Q.C.

Education, Hon. Maureen L. Hemphill.

Culture, Heritage and Recreation; Industry, Trade and Technology, Hon. Eugene M. Kostyra.

Attorney-General, Consumer and Corporate Affairs, Hon. Roland Penner, Q.C..

Deputy Premier, Community Services, Hon. Muriel A. Smith.

Labour, Hon. Alvin H. Mackling Q.C.

Business Development and Tourism, Hon. J. T. Storie.

Highways and Transportation and Government Services, Hon. John G. Plohman.

Housing, Hon. John Bucklaschuk.

Municipal Affairs, Government House Leader, Hon. Andre Anstett.

Environment and Workplace Safety and Health, Hon. Gérard Lécuyer.

Northern Affairs, Hon. Harry M. Harapiak.

THE JUDICATURE

Court of Appeal:—

Chief Justice of Manitoba, Hon. A. M. Monnin	$101,800
Puisne Judges, Hons. R. J. Matas; G. C. Hall; J. F. O'Sullivan; C. R. Huband; A. R. Philp	93,800
Queen's Bench, Chief Justice, Q.B.D. Hon. A. S. Dewar	101,800
Associate Chief Justice (Family Division), Hon. A. C. Hamilton	$101,800

ECONOMY

Finance.—The revenue of the provincial government, 1985–86, is estimated at $3,123 million and the expenditure $3,619 million.

Agriculture.—The total land area in Manitoba is 135,342,565 acres, of which 18,819,359 acres are in occupied farms. The gross value of agriculture production in 1984 was estimated at $2,232 million.

Manufactures.—Manufacturing enterprises employed about 58,000 persons on average in 1984. The chief manufacturing centres are Winnipeg, Brandon, Selkirk and Portage la Prairie. The largest manufacturing industry is the food and beverage industry, followed by the machinery and metal fabricating industries.

CAPITAL.—Winnipeg, population 584,842. Other cities are Brandon (36,242), Thompson (14,288), Portage la Prairie (13,086) and Flin Flon (7,894).

NEW BRUNSWICK

Area and Population.—New Brunswick is situated between 45°–48° N. lat. and 63° 47′–69° W. long. and comprises an area of 28,354 square miles with a population (Jan. 1985 estimate) of 717,200. It was first colonized by British subjects in 1761, and in 1783 by inhabitants of New England, who had been dispossessed of their property in consequence of their loyalty to the British Crown. New Brunswick entered Confederation in 1867.

Government.—Government is administered by a Lieutenant-Governor, an Executive Council, and a Legislative Assembly of 58 members elected by the people. The last General Election was held October 12, 1982. The composition of the Legislature at June 1985 was 38 Progressive Conservative, 18 Liberal and 2 New Democratic Party members.

Lieutenant-Governor, His Honour Dr. George F. G. Stanley.

EXECUTIVE

Premier, Hon. Richard B. Hatfield.

Justice, Hon. F. Dubé, Q.C.

Transportation, Hon. W. G. Bishop.

Agriculture and Rural Development, and Natural Resources, Hon. Malcolm MacLeod.

Commerce and Development, Hon. Paul Dawson.

Health, Hon. Charles Gallagher.

Education, Hon. Clarence Cormier.

Community Colleges, Hon. Mabel Deware.

Labour and Human Resources, Hon. Joseph Mombourquette.

Finance, Hon. John Baxter.

Municipal Affairs, Hon. Yvon Poitras.

Fisheries, Hon. Jean Gauvin.

Tourism, Hon. Omer Leger.

Chairman, Board of Management, Hon. Harold Fanjoy.

Social Services, Hon. Nancy Clark Tweed.

Youth, Hon. Leslie Hull.

Supply and Services, Hon. Edwin Allen.

Environment, Hon. William Harmer.

Historical and Cultural Resources, Hon Jean-Pierre Ouellet.

Chairman, Social Program Reform, (vacant).

Chairman, Public Service Delivery Reform, Hon. Jean-Maurice Simard.

Speaker of the House, Hon. James Tucker.

THE JUDICATURE

Court of Appeal

Chief Justice, Hon. S. G. Stratton.

Judges of Appeal, Hons. H. E. Ryan; J. C. Angers; W. Hoyt; R. C. Rice.

Queen's Bench Division

Chief Justice, Hon. G. A. Richard.

ECONOMY

Finance.—The estimated revenue for the year ending March 31, 1984, was $2,213,420,941 and ordinary expenditure, $2,344,948,500.

Manufactures.—New Brunswick's largest manufacturing group, in terms of shipments, is the food and beverage industry followed by the paper and allied industries, and transport equipment industries. Together these industries accounted in 1984 for over 55 per cent. of the total value of manufacturing shipments of $4,273,535,000. Saint John has a major ice-free port and is the principal manufacturing centre of the province.

Agriculture.—Total land area 27,633 sq. miles; farms numbered 4,063 and averaged 266 acres each in 1981. Dairy products and potatoes are the leading agricultural products. Both industries together accounted for 45·6 per cent of total farm cash receipts in 1984. Farm cash receipts in 1984 totalled $225,159,000.

Fisheries.—Fishing is an important industry, employing about 6,500 fishermen, and there are several development programmes in progress. The chief commercial fish are lobsters, herring, tuna, crab and cod. Landings reached 88,165 metric tons valued at $71,258,000 in 1984.

Minerals.—Extensive zinc, lead and copper deposits are now being mined in the north-eastern part of the Province with New Brunswick being the second largest producer of zinc in Canada. A lead smelter, fertilizer plant and port facilities have been constructed at Belledune. Canada's only primary antimony producer is located at Lake George. There is exploration and development near Sussex and Salt Springs, where potash and salt deposits have been found. A potash terminal has been built at the port of St. John. Coal is mined at Grand Lake and exploration for other deposits is being undertaken. Total mineral production was valued at $590,368,000 in 1984.

Tourism is of increasing value to the economy.

Principal Cities.—CAPITAL ΨFredericton: population (1981), 64,439. ΨSaint John (114,048); Moncton (98,354); Bathurst (24,267); Edmundston (21,901); Campbellton (15,508).

NEWFOUNDLAND AND LABRADOR

Area and Population.—The Island of Newfoundland is situated between 46° 37′–51° 37′ N. latitude and 52° 44′–59° 30′ W. longitude, on the north-east side of the Gulf of St. Lawrence, and is separated from the North American Continent by the Straits of Belle Isle on the N.W. and by Cabot Strait on the S.W. The island is about 317 miles long and 316 miles broad and is triangular in shape, with Cape Bauld (N.), Cape Race (S.E.) and Cape Ray (S.W.) at the angles. It comprises an area of 43,359 sq. miles with a population (1981 Census) (inclusive of Labrador) of 567,681.

Labrador forms the most easterly part of the North American continent, and extends from Point St. Charles, at the northeast entrance to the Straits of Belle Isle, on the south, to Cape Chidley, at the eastern entrance to Hudson's Straits on the north. It has an area estimated at 112,826 sq. miles, with a population (1981 census) of 31,318.

Government.—On March 31, 1949 Newfoundland became the 10th Province of the Dominion of Canada. The Government is administered by a Lieutenant-Governor, aided by an Executive Council and a Legislative Assembly of 52 members. A General Election was held on April 12, 1985. The standings in the current House of Assembly are: 36 Progressive Conservatives, 15 Liberals, and 1 New Democrat.

Lieutenant-Governor, Hon. W. Anthony Paddon, C.M., M.D. (July 10, 1981).

EXECUTIVE

Premier, Hon. A. Brian Peckford.
President of the Council, and Minister responsible for Labrador Hydro and the Petroleum Directorate, Hon. William Marshall, Q.C.
Finance, Hon. Dr. John Collins.
Intergovernmental Affairs, Hon. G. Ottenheimer, Q.C.
President of Treasury Board, Hon. H. N. Windsor.
Mines and Energy, Hon. J. W. Dinn.
Career Development and Advanced Studies, Hon. C. J. Power.
Public Works and Services, Hon. H. Young.
Justice, and Attorney General, Hon. Lynn Verge.
Transportation, Hon. Ronald Dawe.
Forest Resources and Land, Hon. L. A. Simms.
Municipal Affairs, Hon. N. E. Doyle.
Fisheries, Hon. T. G. Rideout.
Health, Hon. Dr. H. M. Twomey.
Rural, Agricultural and Northern Development, Hon. R. J. Aylward.
Social Services, Hon. R. C. Brett.

Consumer Affairs and Communications, Hon. J. M. Russell.
Development, Hon. H. M. Barrett.
Environment, Hon. J. C. Butt.
Education, Hon. W. L. Hearn.
Culture, Recreation and Youth, Hon. W. B. Matthews.
Labour, Hon. T. A. Blanchard.

Speaker of the House of Assembly, Dr. P. McNicholas.
Clerk of the Executive Council, H. M. Clarke.

ECONOMY

Finance.—The estimated gross capital and current account revenues for 1985–86 were $2,136,913,000 and the gross current and capital account expenditures $2,452,884,000.

Production and Industry.—The main primary industries are fishing, forestry and mining. In 1983 shipments of fish products were valued at $455·9 million. In 1984 newsprint shipments from the three pulp and paper mills were valued at $295·1 million. In 1984 the mining operations plus the structural materials producers had combined shipments estimated at $993·5 million of which $867·6 million was from the 3 iron ore mines in Labrador. Manufacturing shipments with the exclusion of fish and paper products totalled approximately $508·0 million in 1984. The hydro-electric plant on the Churchill river is the largest underground plant in the world, with a capacity of 5,225,000 kw.

Petroleum and Natural Gas.—Over 110 wells have been drilled off Newfoundland since 1965. Discovery of oil was made in 1979 on the Grand Banks. The Hibernia field's producing capability is estimated to be in excess of 20,000 barrels of oil per day. In 1984, 12 new wells were drilled and offshore exploration expenditure was over $500 million

Transport.—The province is connected to mainland Canada by a ferry service from North Sydney, Nova Scotia to Port aux Basques and Argentia. The main line of the railway extends from St. John's on the east coast to Port aux Basques on the west coast. Transport between various points on the island is by highway but the south coast and Labrador still rely on the coastal boat service.

CAPITAL, St. John's (population 1981 Census, Greater St. John's 154,820) is North America's oldest city, and thus of historical interest and is the seat of the provincial legislature, the site of most provincial and federal government offices and the principal port for the island of Newfoundland. Newfoundland's second city of Corner Brook (population 1981 Census, 24,339) is situated on the west coast, its principal industry being its pulp and paper mill.

Labrador

Labrador, the most northerly area of the Province of Newfoundland, forms the most easterly part of the North American continent, and extends from Blanc Sablon, at the north-east entrance to the Straits of Belle Isle, on the south, to Cape Chidley, at the eastern entrance to Hudson's Straits on the north. Labrador is noted for its cod fisheries and also possesses valuable salmon, herring, trout and seal fisheries. Newfoundland (Labrador) produces more iron ore than any other province in Canada.

NOVA SCOTIA

Area and Population.—Nova Scotia is a peninsula between 43° 25′–47° N. lat. and 59° 40′–66° 25′ W. long., and is connected with New Brunswick by a low fertile isthmus about 17·5 miles wide. It comprises an area of 21,425 square miles including 1,023 square miles of lakes and rivers and 6,479 miles of shoreline. No place is more than 35 miles from the Atlantic Ocean. Population (1985) 878,300.

Government.—The Government consists of a Lieutenant-Governor and a 52-member elected Legislative Assembly, from which the Executive Council (Cabinet) is selected. The Lieutenant-Governor represents the Queen and is appointed by the Governor-in-Council.

Lieutenant-Governor, Hon. Alan R. Abraham $44,100

EXECUTIVE COUNCIL

Premier, Hon. John M. Buchanan, Q.C.
Health, Hon. G. Sheehy.
Attorney General, Hon. R. Giffen, Q.C.
Mines and Energy, Hon. J. Matheson, Q.C.
Agriculture and Marketing, Hon. R. S. Bacon.
Lands and Forests, Hon. K. Streatch.
Tourism, Hon. R. F. Hudson, Q.C.
Municipal Affairs, Hon. T. J. McInnes.
Transportation, Hon. J. MacIsaac.
Management Board, Hon. R. S. Russell.
Education, Hon. T. Donahoe, Q.C.
Fisheries, Hon. J. Leefe.
Finance, Hon. G. Kerr.
Social Services, Hon. E. Morris.
Government Services, Hon. J. Lawrence.
Environment, Hon. G. Moody.
Consumer Affairs, Hon. L. Stirling.
Culture, Recreation and Fitness, Hon. W. J. MacLean.
Housing, Hon. M. Laffin.
Resource Development Board, Hon. M. Pickings.
Labour and Manpower, Hon. D. Nantes.

Cabinet Ministers receive $31,670 a year (the Premier receives $40,860), *plus* member's sessional indemnity $20,280 and expense allowance $10,140.
Agent-General in London, Donald M. Smith, 14 Pall Mall, S.W.1.

THE JUDICATURE

Supreme Court—Appeal Division
Chief Justice, Hon. G. L. S. Hart $117,800
Judges, Hons. T. H. Coffin; A. G. Cooper;
A. L. Macdonald; L. L. Pace; M. C. Jones;
V. A. Morrison; K. M. Matthews. 108,400

Trial Division
Chief Justice, Hon. Constance R. Glube 117,800
Judges, Hons. A. M. MacIntosh; W. J. Grant;
J. D. Hallett; K. P. Richard; C. Denne
Burchell; L. Clarke; R. M. Rogers; H.
Nathanson; M. Nunn; R. B. MacDonald;
F. B. W. Kelly 108,400

ECONOMY

Finance.—The revenue for the fiscal year ending March 31, 1984, was $2,323,879 and expenditure was $2,558,846. The net direct debt was $2,285,171.

Manufacturing.—Manufacturing constitutes the most important goods producing sector of the economy. Shipments were worth $4,747 million in 1984 with a total added value estimated to be more than $1,500 million. Manufacturing plants provide employment for 43,000 or 13 per cent of the labour force. Capital expenditure in the manufacturing sector has increased from $192 million in 1984 to $208 million in 1985.

Utilities.—Electric power in Nova Scotia is supplied by the Nova Scotia Power Corporation, a Crown corporation. The Corporation's generating stations, which are predominantly coal fired have a nameplate capacity of 2,218,285 kilowatts. The Corporation's generating system is made up of seven thermal plants, three gas turbines and 31 hydro stations scattered throughout the province.

The number of telephones in Nova Scotia was 570,722 in December, 1984, or approximately 65 per 100 population.

Petroleum Activity.—By mid-1985 a total of 107 wells had been completed off-shore since drilling began in 1967, the drilling being done by five major operations. For the first time since 1982, new lands on the Scotian Shelf were issued for oil and gas exploration. Development has continued on the Ventura field, which is expected to be on stream by the end of 1990.

There were no wells drilled onshore in 1984–85, but there is expected to be further exploration in 1986.

Mining.—The total value of mineral production in 1984 was estimated at $333,145,943. Dollar value of production for specific minerals was:—

Coal	$166,272,697
Sand, gravel and crushed rock	47,745,805
Gypsum and anhydrite	42,172,116
Salt	32,384,648
Limestone	6,168,235
Barite	1,366,642

Agriculture.—Farm cash receipts were $261,200,000 in 1984. About 3 per cent of the total area, or 440,000 acres, is classified as farm land. Dairy and poultry products form the largest sectors.

Fishing.—The value of fish landed in 1984 was $267,674,000. Products have been diversified and enlarged into a variety of processed foods that are increasing in number. Primary fishing and fish processing employed 19,843 persons in 1984 (12,543 fishermen and 7,300 plant workers).

Forest Products.—The gross value of primary and secondary forestry was $400,000,000 in 1984. Forest lands total 10,800,000 acres or 84 per cent of the land area. About 75 per cent of forest land is privately owned. Forest based industries employ about 8,000.

Tourism.—Between May 15 and October 31, 1984, about 1·1 million visitors spent about $218 million in the province.

CAPITAL ΨHalifax, including the neighbouring city of Dartmouth, has a population of 176,871. In addition to a container-handling terminal in South Halifax a new terminal at the north end of Halifax Harbour was opened in 1981. A 90-acre autoport has been built at Port Halifax to handle both the export and import of motor vehicles. A shipyard, with dry-dock, can build and repair the largest ocean-going liners. The harbour, ice-free the year round, is the main Atlantic winter port of Canada. Other cities and towns include ΨSydney (29,444), ΨGlace Bay (21,466), Amherst (9,684) and New Glasgow (10,464).

Cape Breton Island

This has been part of Nova Scotia since 1819. It is the centre of the steel manufacturing and coal mining industries, and is also noted for its large lakes and beautiful coastal scenery, making it a tourist attraction in Canada.

ONTARIO

Area and Population.—The Province of Ontario contains a total area of 412,582 sq. miles, with a population (1981) of 8,625,107.

Government.—The Government is vested in a Lieutenant-Governor and a Legislative Assembly of 125 members elected for five years. After the last election on May 2, 1985, there were 52 Progressive Conservatives, 48 Liberals, 25 New Democrats.

The Conservative party formed the Government after the election, but was defeated on a confidence motion in June 1985 and replaced by a Liberal government enjoying New Democrat support.

Lieutenant-Governor, Hon. John Black Aird, Q.C. (1980).

EXECUTIVE COUNCIL

Premier and Minister of Intergovernmental Affairs, Hon. David Peterson.

Treasurer and Minister of Economics, Revenue and Government House Leader, Hon. Robert Nixon.

Education, Hon. Sean Conway.

Environment, Hon. James Bradley.

Chairman of Management Board, and of Cabinet, Minister of Government Services, Hon. Elinor Caplan.

Northern Affairs and Mines, Hon. Rene Fontaine.

Attorney-General, Minister responsible for Women's Issues and Native Affairs, Hon. Ian Scott.

Agriculture and Food, Hon. Jack Riddell.

Tourism and Recreation, Hon. John Eakins.

Natural Resources and Energy, Hon. Vince Kerrio.

Industry, Trade and Technology, Hon. Hugh O'Neil.

Community and Social Services, Hon. John Sweeney.

Health, Hon. Murray Elston.

Labour, Hon. William Wrye.

Municipal Affairs, and Francophone Affairs, Hon. Bernard Grandmaitre.

Housing, Hon. Alvin Curling.

Transportation and Communications, Hon. Ed Fulton.

Solicitor General, Minister of Correctional Services, Hon. Kenneth Keyes.

Consumer and Commercial Relations, Hon. Monte Kwinter.

Citizenship and Culture, Hon. Lily Munro.

Colleges and Universities, Hon. Greg Sorbara.

Ministers Without Portfolio, Hon. Ron Van Horne; Hon. Tony Ruprecht.

Secretary of the Cabinet, Dr. E. E. Stewart.

Speaker, Legislative Assembly, Hon. J. M. Turner.

Agent-General in London, W. R. DeGeer, 13 Charles II Street, S.W.1.

JUDICATURE

Chief Justice of Ontario, Hon. W. G. C. Howland.

Chief Justice of the High Court, Hon. G. T. Evans.

ECONOMY

Agriculture.—Ontario has the highest total of agricultural production in Canada with a gross value of $5,029,900,000 and a total net farm income of $843,100,000 in 1982.

Forestry.—Productive forested lands cover 377,000 sq. km. or 35·3 per cent of the land area of the Province. Paper and allied industries are by far the most important sector of Ontario's forest industry: production in 1981 was worth $1,915,400,000 and accounted for 27·1 per cent by value and 25·5 per cent by quantity of Canada's production.

Minerals.—Ontario's natural resources include 15 basic minerals, such as copper, iron ore, zinc, silver, gold and platinum. The province has half the world's supply of nickel and the largest amount of uranium in the Western World. Total value of the mineral production in 1983 was estimated at $3,532,700,000.

Energy.—Total electrical energy generated in Ontario in 1983 was 117,971 million kWh (31 per cent hydro, 32·4 per cent nuclear and 30·4 per cent other conventional fossil fuels).

Manufacture.—Ontario is the chief manufacturing province in Canada, producing 50 per cent of all manufactured goods. It represents over 43 per cent of total Canadian exports of fully manufactured products. During 1982 Ontario's exports totalled $36,842 million, an increase in value of $2,800 million over 1981. A $3,791 million growth in the value of end products—the sector which contains the bulk of Ontario's manufactured exports—was also achieved.

CAPITAL.—ΨToronto (metropolitan population, 2,137,395) has a wide range of manufacturing and service industries and is a centre of education, business and finance. Other major urban areas are: Ottawa, the national capital (295,163); ΨHamilton

(306,434), with iron and steel industry, metal fabrication, machinery, electrical and chemical industries; London (254,280), a business and manufacturing centre; ΨWindsor (192,083); Kitchener (139,734) and Sudbury (91,829).

PRINCE EDWARD ISLAND

Area and Population.—Prince Edward Island lies in the southern part of the Gulf of St. Lawrence, between 46°–47° N. lat. and 62°–64° 30′ W. long. It is about 140 miles in length, and from 4 to 40 miles in breadth; its area is 2,184 square miles and its population (1984) 125,300.

Government.—The Government is vested in a Lieutenant-Governor and an Executive Council, and Legislative Assembly of 32 members elected for a term of up to 5 years, 16 as Councillors and 16 as Assemblymen. Party representation at July 1, 1985, was : *Conservative* 20; *Liberal* 12.

Lieutenant-Governor, His Honour J. A. Doiron (1980) $44,100
(and expense allowance)

EXECUTIVE

Premier and President of the Executive Council, Hon. J. M. Lee, P.C.

Finance and Tourism, Hon. L. G. MacPhail.

Justice, Attorney-General and Community and Cultural Affairs, Hon. G. R. McMahon, Q.C.

Agriculture, Hon. P. G. Chappell.

Energy and Forestry, Hon. F. L. Driscoll.

Health and Social Services, Hon. A. P. Fogarty.

Fisheries and Labour, Hon. R. B. Pratt.

Education, Hon. L. Bagnall.

Transportation and Public Works, Hon. G. Lank.

Speaker of the Legislative Assembly Hon. Marion Reid.

Members of the Legislative Assembly receive a salary of $15,600 per annum *plus* $7,200 expense allowance; In addition the Premier receives $41,650 per annum; a Minister, $29,400 per annum; and the Speaker, $9,000 per annum, as at July 1, 1985.

SUPREME COURT

Chief Justice, (vacant).................... $101,800

Associate Justices, Hon. F. A. Large; Hon. G. Mitchell; Hon. C. R. McQuaid; Hon. K. R. MacDonald; Hon. A. B. Campbell; Hon. G. J. Mullally .... each $93,800

Finance.—The ordinary revenue in 1984–85 was $432,222,600 and the expenditure was $440,300,700.

Education.—A university and a college of applied arts and technology were established in 1969, estimated full- and part-time enrolment for 1984–85 being 2,409 (University of Prince Edward Island), and 837 for the college of applied arts and technology (Holland College).

CAPITAL, ΨCharlottetown (pop. July 1981 census, 15,282), on the shore of Hillsborough Bay, which forms a good harbour.

QUEBEC

Area and Population.—The Province of Quebec contains an area estimated at 594,860 square miles (1,540,668 sq. km.) with a population (June, 1983), of 6,510,100.

Government.—The Government of the Province is vested in a Lieutenant-Governor, a Council of ministers and a National Assembly of 122 members elected for five years. At June, 1985, there were 61 *Parti Quebecois,* 53 Liberals, 7 Independents and 1 vacant seat.

Lieut.-Governor, The Hon. Gilles Lamontagne.

EXECUTIVE

Premier, René Lévesque.
Vice-Premier and Government Leader in Parliament, Marc-André Bédard.
Finance, Yves Duhaime.
Administration, and President of the Treasury Board, Michel Clair.
Higher Education, Science and Technology, Yves Bérubé.
Justice and Intergovernmental Affairs, Pierre Marc Johnson.
Overseas Trade and International Relations, Bernard Landry.
Agriculture, Fisheries and Food, Jean Garon.
Education, François Gendron.
Manpower and Incomes, and Women's Affairs, Mme. Pauline Marois.
Health and Social Services, Guy Cheviette.
Municipal Affairs, Alain Marcoux.
Transport, Guy Tardif.
Cultural Affairs, Clément Richard.
Ethnic Culture and Immigration, Gérald Godin.
Communications, Jean-François Bertrand.
Industry and Commerce, Roderigue Biron.
Labour, Raynald Fréchette.
Employment, Robert Dean.
Environment, Adrien Ouellette.
Tourism, Marcel Léger.
Energy and Resources, Jean-Guy Rodrigue.
Housing and Consumer Affairs, Jacques Rochefort.
Leisure, Hunting and Fishing, Jacques Brassard.
Revenue, Maurice Martel.
Forests, Jean-Pierre Jolivet.
Regional Development and Management, Henri LeMay.
Citizens' Affairs, Elie Fallu.
Family Affairs, Yves Beaumier.
(M. Lévesque intends to stand down as party leader and Prime Minister as soon as a successor is chosen. His party will elect a new leader in late Sept. 1985.)

Agent-General in London, Patrick Hyndmann, 59 Pall Mall, SW1Y 5JH.

JUDICATURE

Court of Appeal, Chief Justice of Quebec, Hon. Marcel Crète.
Superior Court, Chief Justice of Quebec (Montreal), Hon. Alan B. Gold.

ECONOMY

Finance.—The revenue for the year 1983–84 was $21,410,969,000; expenditure amounted to 24,523,514,000. The net debt (March 31, 1984) was $14,225,644,000.

Production and Industry.—The principal manufacturing centres are Montreal, Montreal East, Quebec, Trois-Rivières, Sherbrooke, Shawinigan Drummondville and Lachine. Forest lands cover 684,480 sq. km., of which 490,693 sq. km. are productive. Forest products in 1982 included: wood pulp, 6,282,713 metric tons; paper and paperboard, 5,490,888 metric tons.

Total estimated value of shipments in the manufacturing industries in 1984 was $57,112,186,000. Value of 1984 shipments in the chief industries:—

Food and beverages	$9,715,843,000
Paper and allied industries	6,069,237,000
Petroleum and coal products	5,951,756,000
Primary metal industries	4,240,470,000
Transportation equipment industries	4,211,701,000

Agriculture and Fisheries.—In 1984 total farm receipts were:

Crops	$469,078,000
Livestock and livestock products	2,291,967,000
Other farm receipts	312,148,000

In 1984 74,701,340 metric tons of fish, to the value of $56,024,502 were landed.

Mineral Production.—Minerals to the value of $2,022,165,182 were mined in 1983 ($2,015,715,315 in 1982). This included copper, $135,279,559; zinc, $52,058,045; and asbestos, $321,212,311.

CAPITAL, ΨQuebec. Population (estimated June 1983), 163,800 historic city visited annually by thousands of tourists; and one of the great seaport towns of Canada; and ΨMontreal (1,005,000), the commercial metropolis. Other important cities are Laval (273,000); Verdun (60,100) and Sherbrooke (73,000), Montreal-Nord (96,500) and La Salle (77,700).

SASKATCHEWAN

Area and Population.—The Province of Saskatchewan lies between Manitoba on the east and Alberta on the west and has an area of 251,700 square miles (of which the land area is 220,182 sq. miles), with a population (estimated, 1984) of 1,016,400. Saskatchewan extends along the Canada–U.S.A. boundary for 393 miles and northwards for 761 miles. Its northern width is 276 miles.

Government.—The Government is vested in the Lieutenant-Governor, with a Legislative Assembly of 64 members. There is an Executive Council of 24 members. The Legislative Assembly is elected for 5 years and the state of the parties in June 1985 was: Progressive Conservative 54; New Democratic Party 8; Independent, 1; Vacant, 1.

Lieut.-Governor, His Honour F. W. Johnson (1983)
$41,600

EXECUTIVE COUNCIL

Premier and President of the Council, Hon. G. Devine.
Deputy Premier, Minister of Economic Development and Provincial Secretary, Hon. E. Berntson.
Attorney-General, Minister for Justice, Hon. G. Lane.
Consumer and Commercial Affairs, Hon. Joan Duncan.
Co-operation and Co-operative Development, Hon. J. Sandberg.
Energy and Mines, Hon. P. Schoenhals.
Education, Hon. Patricia Smith.
Environment, Hon. N. Hardy.
Finance, Hon. R. Andrew.
Health, Hon. G. Taylor.
Highways and Transportation, Hon. J. Garner.
Revenue and Financial Services, Hon. P. Rousseau.
Labour, Hon. L. McLaren.
Advanced Education and Manpower, Science and Technology, Hon. G. Currie.
North Saskatchewan, Supply and Services, Hon. G. McLeod.
Rural Development, Hon. L. Domotor.
Social Services, Hon. G. Dirks.
Agriculture, Hon. L. Hepworth.
Urban Affairs, Hon. T. Embury.
Parks and Renewable Resources, Hon. C. Maxwell.
Culture and Recreation, R. Folk.
Tourism and Small Business, Hon J. Klein.
Minister without Portfolio, Hon. S. Dutchak, Hon. G. Muirhead.
Premier, $72,342; Ministers, each $63,013.

Agent-General in London.—R. A. Larter, 21 Pall Mall, S.W.1.

Finance.—Combined* revenue for year ending March 1986 is $3,175,434,500 and combined* expenditure $3,466,692,590 (*Consolidated Fund and Heritage combined).

CAPITAL.—Regina. Population (estimated 1984), 172,340. Other cities: Saskatoon (170,748), Moose Jaw (35,118); Prince Albert (32,957) and Yorkton (15,895).

The Commonwealth of Australia

AREA AND POPULATION

States and Capitals	Area (English Sq. Miles)	Estimated Resident Population		
		June 30, 1976 (a)	June 30, 1981 (a)	June 30, 1983
States				
New South Wales (Sydney)	309,433	4,959,600	5,234,900	5,360,367
Queensland (Brisbane)	667,000	2,092,400	2,345,200	2,471,623
South Australia (Adelaide)	380,070	1,274,100	1,318,800	1,341,522
Tasmania (Hobart)	26,383	412,300	427,200	432,615
Victoria (Melbourne)	87,884	3,810,400	3,946,900	4,037,598
Western Australia (Perth)	975,920	1,178,300	1,300,100	1,364,455
Territories				
Australian Capital Territory (Canberra)	939	207,700	227,600	236,590
Northern Territory (Darwin)	520,280	98,200	122,600	133,876
Total	2,967,909	14,033,100	14,923,300	15,378,646

Population of Aboriginal or Torres Strait Islander Origin (a)
(from Census of 1981)

	Aboriginal	Torres Strait Islanders	Total
States			
New South Wales	33,414	1,953	35,367
Queensland	33,966	10,732	44,698
South Australia	9,476	349	9,825
Tasmania	2,334	354	2,688
Victoria	5,283	774	6,057
Western Australia	30,749	602	31,351
Territories			
Australian Capital Territory	763	60	823
Northern Territory	28,680	408	29,088
Total	144,665	15,232	159,897

Inter-Censal Increases, 1961–1981

Year of Census	Population at Census			Inter-Censal Increase	Net Immigration during Period	
	Males	Females	Total			
1961	5,333,185	5,215,082	10,548,267	(b) 1,521,656	1954–1961	584,754
1966	5,841,588	5,757,910	11,599,498	1,051,231	1961–1966	395,485
1971 (a)	6,567,936	6,499,329	13,067,265	(c) 1,156,140	1966–1971	521,139
1976 (a)	7,032,034	7,001,049	14,033,083	965,818	1971–1976	281,074
1981 (a)	7,448,267	7,474,993	14,923,260	890,177	1976–1981	370,865

(a) Based on Census counts, place of usual residence, adjusted for under-enumeration, and including an estimate of Australian residents temporarily overseas on Census night.
(b) Excludes full-blood Aboriginals.
(c) Based on 1971 Census figure as enumerated.

Increase of Population

Year	Births	Deaths	Net Overseas Migration (a)	Net Increase (b)	Marriages
1978	224,181	108,425	47,397	149,297	102,958
1979	223,129	106,568	68,611	171,651	104,396
1980	225,527	108,695	100,940	204,889	109,240
1981	235,842	109,003	121,785	242,083	113,905
1982	239,895	114,771	102,228	227,352	117,275
1983	242,570	110,084	42,210	175,093	114,860

(a) Net permanent and long-term overseas migration gain with an adjustment for the net effect of category jumping.
(b) Prior to June 30, 1981, differences between the net increase shown and the sum of natural increase and net overseas migration were due to the distribution of intercensal discrepancy.

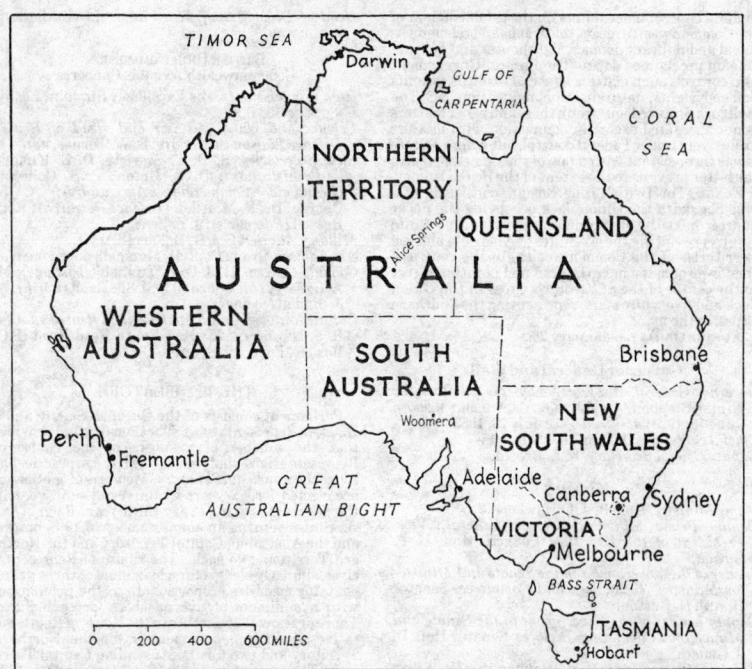

PHYSICAL FEATURES

Australia, including Tasmania, comprises a land area of 7,682,300 square kilometres lying between latitudes 10°41'S (Cape York) and 43°39'S (South East Cape, Tasmania) and longitudes 113°09'E (Steep Point) and 153°39'E (Cape Byron). The latitudinal distance between Cape York and South East Cape is about 3,680 kilometres and the longitudinal distance between Steep Point and Cape Byron is about 4,000 kilometres. (The latitudinal distance between Cape York and the most southerly point on the mainland South Point, Wilson's Promontory, is about 3,180 kilometres.)

Australia has three major landforms: the western plateau, the interior lowlands and the eastern uplands. The western half of the continent consists mainly of a great plateau. The interior lowland includes the Channel country of southwest Queensland (drainage to Lake Eyre) and the Murray-Darling river system to the south. The eastern uplands consist of a broad belt of varied width extending from north Queensland to Tasmania and composed largely of tablelands, ranges and ridges with only limited mountain areas above 1,000 metres.

Australia's large area and latitudinal range have resulted in climatic conditions ranging from the alpine to the tropical. Two thirds of the continent is arid or semi-arid although good rainfalls (over 800 mm annually) occur in the northern monsoonal belt under the influence of the Australian Asian Monsoon and along the eastern and southern highland regions under the influence of the great atmospheric depressions of the Southern Ocean. The effectiveness of the rainfall is greatly reduced by marked alternations of wet and dry seasons, unreliability from year to year, high temperatures and high potential evaporation.

Fifty per cent of the area of Australia has a medium rainfall of less than 300 mm per year and 80 per cent has less than 600 mm. Extreme minimum temperatures are not as low as those recorded in other continents because of the absence of extensive mountain masses and because of the expanse of ocean to the south. However, extreme maxima are comparatively high, reaching 50 C. over the inland, mainly due to the great east-west extent of the continent in the vicinity of the Tropic of Capricorn.

Only one third of the Australian land mass drains directly to the ocean, mainly on the coastal side of the Main Divide and inland with the Murray-Darling system. With the exception of the Murray-Darling system, most rivers draining to the ocean are comparatively short and account for the majority of the country's average annual discharge.

GOVERNMENT

The Commonwealth of Australia was constituted by an Act of the Imperial Parliament dated July 9, 1900, and was inaugurated Jan. 1, 1901. The Government is that of a Federal Commonwealth within the British Commonwealth of Nations, the executive power being vested in the Sovereign (through the Governor-General), assisted by a Federal Ministry of twenty-seven Ministers of State. Under the Constitution the Federal Government has acquired and may acquire certain defined powers as surrendered by the States, residuary legislative power remaining with the States. Trade and customs passed under

Federal control immediately on the establishment of the Commonwealth; posts, telegraphs and telephones, naval and military defence, lighthouses and quarantine on proclaimed dates. The Federal Government also controls such matters as social services, patents and copyrights, naturalization, navigation, &c. The right of a State to legislate on these and other matters is not abrogated except in connection with matters exclusively under Federal control, but where a State law is inconsistent with a law of the Commonwealth the latter prevails to the extent of the inconsistency.

FLAG.—The British Blue Ensign, consisting of a blue flag, with the Union Jack occupying the upper quarter next the staff, differenced by a large white star (representing the six States of Australia and the Territories of the Commonwealth) in the centre of the lower quarter next the staff and pointing direct to the centre of the St. George's Cross in the Union Jack and five white stars, representing the Southern Cross, in the fly.

AUSTRALIA DAY.—January 26.

Governor-General and Staff

Governor-General, His Excellency the Rt. Hon. Sir Ninian Stephen, A.K., G.C.M.G., G.C.V.O., K.B.E., *born* June 15, 1923; *assumed office* July 29, 1982.
Official Secretary, D. I. Smith, C.V.O.
Deputy Official Secretary, K. L. Brown.

Ministry

Prime Minister, Hon. R. J. L. Hawke, A.C.
Deputy Prime Minister; Attorney-General; Vice-President of the Executive Council, Hon. L. F. Bowen.
Leader of the Government in the Senate and Minister for Industry, Technology and Commerce, Senator Hon. J. N. Button.
Deputy Leader of the Government in the Senate and Minister for Community Services, Senator Hon. D. J. Grimes.
Employment and Industrial Relations, Hon. R. Willis.
Treasurer, Hon. P. J. Keating.
Special Minister of State and Leader of the House, Hon. M. J. Young.
Finance, Senator Hon. P. A. Walsh.
Foreign Affairs, Hon. W. G. Hayden.
Education, Senator Hon. Susan M. Ryan.
Resources and Energy, Senator Hon. G. J. Evans, Q.C.
Trade, Hon. J. S. Dawkins.
Primary Industry, Hon. J. C. Kerin.
Housing and Construction, Hon. S. J. West.
Defence, Hon. K. C. Beazley.
Immigration and Ethnic Affairs, Hon. C. Hurford.
Social Security, Hon. B. Howe.
(The above form the Cabinet.)
Transport and Aviation, Hon. P. Morris.
Sport, Recreation and Tourism, Hon. J. Brown.
Health, Hon. N. Blewett.
Science, Hon. B. O. Jones.
Territories, Hon. G. Scholes.
Communications, Hon. M. Duffy.
Arts, Heritage and Environment, Hon. B. Cohen.
Aboriginal Affairs, Hon. A. C. Holding.
Veterans' Affairs, Senator Hon A. T. Gietzelt.
Local Government and Administrative Service, Hon. T. Uren.

AUSTRALIAN HIGH COMMISSION
Australia House, Strand, London, WC2B 4LA.
[01–438–8000]

High Commissioner, His Excellency Alfred R. Parsons.
Deputy High Commissioner, A. L. Vincent.
Official Secretary, D. C. Rutter.
Ministers, J. A. Benson; P. J. Sparkes (*Commercial*); A. S. Cole (*Treasury*); A. J. McFarlane.

Head of Defence Staff, Rear Adm. K. Vonthethoff, A.O., R.A.N.

BRITISH HIGH COMMISSION
Commonwealth Avenue, Canberra

High Commissioner, His Excellency Sir John Leahy, K.C.M.G. (1984).
Defence and Naval Adviser and Head of British Defence Liaison Staff, Cdre. B. W. Turner, R.N.
First Secretaries, R. D. C. Scarlett; D. E. Kipping (*Administration*); D. R. Upton; P. S. Collecott (*Economic, Commercial, Agriculture*); A. N. George; Dr. R. M. Allen (*Defence Research*); R. C. Russell (*Passports*); J. E. Bent.
Military Adviser, Col. G. D. Farrell, M.B.E.
Air Adviser, Group Capt. H. Marshall, O.B.E., D.F.C.
Consuls-General, H. J. O. R. Tunnell (*Brisbane*); M. A. Cafferty (*Melbourne*); H. J. Sharland (*Perth*); A. J. Sindall (*Sydney*).
Cultural Adviser and British Council Representative, R. S. Newberry, 203 New South Head Road (P.O. Box 88), Edgecliff, Sydney.

THE LEGISLATURE

Parliament consists of the Queen, a Senate and a House of Representatives. The Constitution provides that the number of members of the House of Representatives shall be, as nearly as practicable, twice the number of Senators. Members of the Senate are elected for six years by universal suffrage, half the members retiring every third year. Each of the six States returns an equal number of 10 Senators, and the Australian Capital Territory and the Northern Territory two each. The House of Representatives, similarly elected for a maximum of three years, contains members proportionate to the population, with a minimum of five members for each State. There are now 125 members in the House of Representatives, including one member for the Northern Territory and two for the Australian Capital Territory. The state of parties in the Senate in Dec. 1984 was *Labour* 34, *Liberal* 28, *Democratic Party* 7, *National Party* 5, *N.D.P* 1, *Independent* 1. The state of parties in the House of Representatives in Dec, 1984 was *Labour* 82, *Liberal* 45, *National Party* 21. Members of both Houses received $A41,802 per annum, plus allowances, with air and rail travel at Government expense while on parliamentary business.

President of the Senate, Senator Hon. D. McClelland.
Speaker, House of Representatives, Hon. H. A. Jenkins.

THE JUDICATURE

HIGH COURT OF AUSTRALIA

Chief Justice, Rt. Hon. Sir Harry Gibbs, G.C.M.G., K.B.E.
Justices, Hon. Sir Anthony Mason, K.B.E.; Hon. L. K. Murphy; Hon. Sir Ronald Wilson, K.B.E., C.M.G.; Hon. Sir Gerard Brennan, K.B.E.; Hon. Sir William Deane, K.B.E.; Hon. Sir Daryl Dawson, K.B.E., C.B.
Registrar, F. W. D. Jones.

FEDERAL COURT OF AUSTRALIA

Chief Judge, Hon. Sir Nigel Bowen, K.B.E.
Judges, Hons. Sir Reginald Smithers; R. W. Fox; C. A. Sweeney, C.B.E.; Sir William Forster; Sir Albert Woodward, O.B.E.; R. J. A. Franki; J. H. Muirhead; P. G. Evatt, D.S.C.; R. M. Northrop; J. A. Keely; J. L. Toohey; F. R. Fisher; J. F. Gallop; J. D. Davies; J. S. Lockhart; I. F. Sheppard; J. J. A. Kelly; T. R. Morling; K. J. Jenkinson; A. R. Neaves; B. A. Beaumont; M. R. Wilcox; J. E. J. Spender; P. R. A. Gray; M. G. Everett; C. W. Pincus; J. C. S. Burchett; J. A. Miles.
Registrar, J. T. Howard, E.D.

SUPREME COURT OF THE AUSTRALIAN
CAPITAL TERRITORY

Judges, Hons. J. A. Miles (*Chief Justice*); J. J. A. Kelly; J. F. Gallop (*Resident Judges*); Sir Reginald Smithers; Sir Albert Woodward, O.B.E.; R. J. A. Franki; P. G. Evatt, D.S.C.; R. M. Northrop; J. D. Davies; J. S. Lockhart; I. F. Sheppard; T. R. Morling; K. J. Jenkinson; B. A. Beaumont; M. R. Wilcox; J. E. J. Spender; C. W. Pincus (*Additional Judges*).

Registrar, P. Dingwall (*acting*).

SUPREME COURT OF THE NORTHERN TERRITORY

Chief Justice, Hon. J. H. Muirhead (*acting*).

Judges, Hons. J. H. Muirhead; J. A. Nader; Sir William Kearney; K. F. O'Leary; M. D. Maurice; P. J. Rice (*Resident Judges*); J. L. Toohey; J. F. Gallop; Sir William Forster.

Master, N. Patel.

DEFENCE

A single Department of Defence was created on November 30, 1973, following the abolition of the Departments of the Navy, Army and Air, though the separate identities of the three services have been retained. The defence research and development elements of the former Department of Supply, along with other research groups on the three services, were incorporated in 1978 into the Defence, Science and Technology Organization. The Chief of Defence Force Staff is responsible for command of the Defence Force through the three Service Chiefs of Staff and is also the principal military adviser to the Minister.

The Secretary to the Department of Defence is responsible to the Minister for Defence for advice on policy, resources and organization.

Total defence expenditure was estimated at $A5,446,312,000 in 1983–84.

The personnel strengths of the Permanent Defence Force and the Reserve Forces at June 30, 1983 were:—

	P.D.F.	Reserves*
Navy	17,198	1,204
Army	33,072	33,227
Air Force	22,512	1,178
Total	72,782	35,609

(*Reserve components with training obligations.)

Navy.—The Royal Australian Navy (R.A.N.) is equipped with destroyers, destroyer escorts, submarines, guided missile frigates, mines counter-measure vessels, patrol boats, survey ships, fleet support ships, heavy landing craft, oceanographic ships, one training ship, one heavy lift ship and one oiler. The Fleet Air Arm is equipped with Tracker, Macchi, Jindivik and HS748 fixed-wing aircraft, and with Sea King, Wessex, Iroquois and Bell 206 helicopters.

Army.—The three Australian Army commands are: Field Force Command (H.Q. Sydney), responsible for the operation of the Army's fighting formations; Logistic Command (H.Q. Melbourne) responsible for the broad military functions of transport, supply and repair; Training Command (H.Q. Sydney) responsible for the operation of all Army schools and training establishments.

Air Force.—The Royal Australian Air Force (R.A.A.F) consists of the strike/reconnaissance force, tactical fighter force, air transport force, tactical air support force and the maritime force. The support component consists of maintenance, supply, air training, ground training and administrative units and the R.A.A.F. Reserve. The R.A.A.F. is equipped with F-111 and RF-111C strike aircraft and Mirage fighters. Transport aircraft are the Hercules, Caribou, Mystere, HS-748, Boeing 707 and BAC-111, and

maritime squadrons operate Orion aircraft, helicopter squadrons, Iroquois and Chinook helicopters and initial aircrew training is in the CT4A Airtrainer, Macchi and HS-748T2. Two squadrons of Mirage fighters, backed by a maintenance squadron and supporting personnel, are based at Butterworth in Malaysia.

COMMONWEALTH GOVERNMENT FINANCE

Outlays and revenue of the Commonwealth Government were ($Amillion):

	1983–84p
Current outlays	52,399
Capital outlays	6,760
Revenue	49,678
Financing transactions	9,481

p. preliminary

Commonwealth Government outlay (current and capital) by category was ($Amillion):

	1983–84p.
General public services	3,647·7
Defence	5,097·3
Public order and safety	374·1
Education	4,186·8
Health	4,412·3
Social security and welfare	16,408·7
Housing and amenities	1,062·5
Recreation and culture	618·2
Fuel and energy	162·4
Agriculture, forestry, fishing and hunting	863·2
Mining, manufacturing and construction	480·3
Transport and communications	3,482·7
Other economic affairs	1,400·2
Other purposes	16,950·0
TOTAL	59,146·3

p. preliminary

STATE AND LOCAL GOVERNMENT FINANCE 1981–82

State	Outlay $Amillion	Receipts $Amillion	Financing items $Amillion
N.S.W.	9,699·8	8,054·1	1,645·7
Victoria	8,192·7	6,465·3	1,727·4
Queensland	4,914·6	4,059·0	855·6
S. Australia	2,519·3	2,197·8	321·5
W. Australia	2,741·2	2,387·5	353·7
Tasmania	1,071·1	892·4	178·7
N.T.	731·8	568·5	145·3
Total Six States and N.T.	29,852·5	24,624·7	5,227·8

BANKING

In April 1985 the major trading banks had total liabilities of $A58,360 million including total deposits of $A39,816 million; and total assets of $A62,680 million, including $A7,649 million of liquid assets and Commonwealth Government securities.

PRODUCTION AND INDUSTRY

In 1982–83, 63·0 per cent of the Australian land area consisted of agricultural establishments, with the remainder being urban areas, State forests, mining leases and unoccupied land. Crop-growing areas constituted up to 4·0 per cent of the total agricultural establishments, emphasizing the relative importance of the livestock industries in Australia (sheep in the warm, temperate, semi-arid lands and beef cattle in the tropics).

The wide range of climatic and soil conditions over the agricultural regions of Australia has resulted in a diversity of crops being grown throughout the country. Generally, cereal crops (excluding rice and sorghum) are grown in all States over wide areas, while other crops are confined to specific locations in a few States. However, scanty or erratic rainfall, limited potential for irrigation and unsuitable soils or topography have restricted intensive agriculture.

The estimated gross values of agricultural commodities ($A'000):—

	1982–83	1983–84*
Crops	5,010,300	8,438,900
Livestock slaughterings ...	3,452,200	3,434,100
Livestock products	3,245,800	3,576,800
Total agriculture	11,708,300	15,449,800
* Provisional.		

AGRICULTURAL PRODUCTION

The principal products (tonnes) were:—

	1983	1984(p)
Cereal crops		
Barley	1,939,000	4,937,000
Oats	848,000	2,270,000
Wheat	8,876,000	22,064,000
Rice	548,000	635,000
Crops for hay		
Barley	32,000	45,000
Oats	645,000	961,000
Wheat	202,000	215,000
Sugar-cane*	24,817,000	24,263,000
Fruit		
Oranges	410,000	381,000
Apples	301,000	n/a
Pears	119,000	n/a
Bananas..............	140,481,000	163,474,000
Pineapples...........	111,281,000	121,266,000
Passion fruit..........	3,313,000	3,672,000
Strawberries.........	3,409,000	3,792,000
Wool (greasy basis)	701,700	728,100
* Cut for crushing.	(p) preliminary.	

In 1983–84 (preliminary figures), gross value of all crops was $A8,438·9 million; of livestock slaughterings and other disposals, $A3,434·1 million; and of wool production, $A2,030·5 million.

Livestock Numbers at March 31 (in thousands)

	1981	1982	1983	1984(p)
Sheep	134,407	137,976	133,237	138,625
Cattle	25,168	24,553	22,478	21,846
Pigs........	2,430	2,373	2,490	2,478
Poultry		46,004	49,393	49,214

Mines and Minerals.—Significant mineral resources comprise bauxite, coal, copper, crude petroleum, gems, gold, ilmenite, iron ore, lead, limestone, manganese, nickel, rutile, salt, silver, tin, tungsten, uranium, zinc and zircon. Recently, geological exploration has significantly increased the mineral resources of the nation.

Australia now has fourteen oilfields in production: Alton, Bennett, Conloi, Kincora, Moonie and Trinidad in Queensland; Barracouta, Cobia, Halibut, Kingfish, Mackerel and Tuna in Victoria in the offshore Gippsland Basin and from Dongara and Barrow Island in Western Australia.

Stabilised crude oil production from the Australian fields in the year 1980 amounted to 23·24 million cubic metres or some 69 per cent of the country's total requirement. Commercial production of natural gas in 1980 amounted to 26,980,000 cubic metres per day.

In 1982–83, value added by the mining industry was estimated at $A8,147 million. Mine production of black coal was 107, 768,000 tonnes, crude oil (incl. condensate) was 22,069 megalitres and natural gas

11,654 gigalitres. Refinery production of principal metals was:—

Aluminium	403,917 tonnes
Copper	172,456 ,,
Lead	212,176 ,,
Zinc	288,250 ,,
Gold	25,784 k.g.

Manufactures.—In 1982–83 there were in Australia 27,705 industrial establishments, employing 1,053,202 persons; wages paid amounted to $A17,409m; purchases, transfers in and selected expenses $A51,256m; value added by manufacture $A31,074m; and turnover $A82,326m.

Trade Unions.—On December 31, 1983, there were 319 separate trade unions in Australia with a total membership of 2,985,200.

TRADE

Total external trade (including Bullion and Specie.)

	1981–82	1982–83
Imports	$A23,005m	$A21,806m
Exports	19,575m	22,062m

IMPORTS FROM ALL COUNTRIES, 1982–83
(by commodity classifications)

	$A'000
Food and live animals...................	835,598
Fish and fish products	216,369
Vegetables and fruit	170,122
Coffee, tea, cocoa, spices, and products .	218,147
Beverages and tobacco	183,807
Crude materials, inedible (except fuels) ..	648,420
Cork and wood	164,163
Crude fertilizers, crude minerals(except coal, petroleum, precious stones)	197,099
Mineral fuels, lubricants, etc	3,098,416
Petroleum, petroleum products, etc ...	3,092,463
Animal and vegetable oils, fats and waxes	81,508
Chemical and related products, n.e.s.	*1,776,058
Organic chemicals....................	*468,301
Artificial resins, plastics materials, cellulose esters and ethers	*364,228
Manufactured goods....................	*3,445,932
Textile yarn, fabric, made-up articles, n.e.s., etc......................	*1,011,440
Machinery and transport equipment	*8,022,088
Road vehicles	1,807,382
Miscellaneous manufactured articles	*2,733,785
Imports not classified elsewhere	*390,132
Non-merchandise trade	590,434
TOTAL IMPORTS	21,806,179

EXPORTS 1982–83
(by commodity classifications)

	$A'000
Food and live animals...................	5,393,892
Meat and meat preparations	1,677,927
Cereal grains and preparations	1,855,712
Beverages and tobacco	66,671
Crude materials, inedible (except fuels) ..	*6,266,187
Textile fibres and their wastes	1,926,338
Metalliferous ores and metal scrap	*3,753,393
Mineral fuels, lubricants, etc	4,575,782
Coal, coke and briquettes.............	3,079,742
Animal and vegetable oils, fats and waxes	87,057
Chemical and related products, n.e.s.	*457,908
Artificial resins, plastic materials, cellulose esters and ethers	112,896
Manufactured goods	2,292,409
Non-ferrous metals	1,251,419
Machinery and transport equipment	1,132,867
Road vehicles	229,656
Miscellaneous manufactured articles	475,594
Exports not classified elsewhere	*645,713
Non-merchandise trade	667,547
TOTAL EXPORTS	22,061,623

* Statistics may be affected by confidentiality.

MAIN TRADING PARTNERS 1982–83

Imports from:—	Value ($A'000)	Percentage of total trade
Japan	4,506,447	20·7
U.S.A.	4,766,435	21·9
E.E.C.	4,380,356	n/a
Germany, Fed. Rep	1,298,625	6·0
U.K.	1,466,957	6·7
A.S.E.A.N.	1,549,275	n/a
Singapore	599,843	2·8
New Zealand	694,293	3·2

Exports to:—	Value ($A'000)	Percentage of total trade
Japan	5,964,716	27·0
U.S.A.	2,240,286	10·2
E.E.C.	3,120,745	n/a
Germany, Fed. Rep.	548,610	2·5
U.K.	1,178,684	5·3
A.S.E.A.N.	1,960,992	n/a
Singapore	732,144	3·3
New Zealand	1,155,472	5·2

FOOD EXPORTS TO U.K. 1983–84

	$A'000
Meat and meat preparations	26,683
Cereal and cereal preparations	6,004
Dairy products and birds' eggs	7,707
Vegetable and fruit	23,280
Sugar, sugar preparations and honey	4,501

COMMUNICATIONS

Railways.—There are six government owned railways systems, operated by the State Rail Authority of N.S.W., Victorian Railways, Queensland Government Railways, Western Australian Government Railways, the State Transport Authority of Southern Australia, and the Australian National Railways Commission. The A.N.R.C. incorporates the former Commonwealth Railways system, and the Tasmanian and non-metropolitan South Australian railways (urban rail services in Southern Australia remain the responsibility of the State Transport Authority). At June 30, 1983 there was a total of 39,065 route-kilometres open.

Gross earnings 1982–83 were:

	$A'000
New South Wales	694,819
Victoria	247,945
Queensland	549,859
South Australia	41,908
Western Australia	223,925
A.N.R.C.	193,854
Total	1,952,310

Figures for all government rail services in the year to June 30, 1983:

Passenger journeys	412,847,000
Freight carried (tonnes)	124,093,000
Total gross earnings	$A1,952,310,000
Coaching	362,265,000
Freight	1,414,764,000
Total working expenses	3,100,387,000
Deficit at June 30, 1983	−1,180,754,000

Shipping.—Total arrivals and departures (one arrival and one departure per voyage, irrespective of the number of ports visited) of vessels engaged in overseas trade at the various Australian ports in 1982–83 were: arrivals 5,519 (233,978,422 deadweight tonnes); departures 5,686 (230,010,573 deadweight tonnes).

The total number of vessel calls made in 1982–83 were: arrivals 9,998 (315,465,880 dead-weight tonnes); departures 9,914 (316,847,814 dead-weight tonnes).

The total overseas shipping (excluding local shipping) which called at the ports of capital cities during 1982–83 was:

	Arrivals		Departures	
	Calls	Dead Wt. Tonnes	Calls	Dead Wt. Tonnes
Adelaide	461	7,613,955	454	7,556,090
Brisbane	909	16,513,235	884	16,036,966
Darwin	80	991,434	85	1,062,069
Fremantle	1,038	25,154,568	1,046	25,412,789
Hobart	172	3,116,876	158	2,907,867
Melbourne	1,259	22,759,539	1,188	21,686,696
Sydney	1,187	23,798,233	1,200	24,432,091

Posts and Telegraphs.—In the year ended June 30, 1983, there were 4,843 post offices dealing with 2,506,565,000 letters, 398,421,000 packets and newspapers, 6,948,000 registered articles and 32,054,000 parcels. 4,050,740 internal telegrams and 1,300,000 international telegrams were despatched. At June 30, 1983, there were 5,353 telephone exchanges with 5,591,667 services and 8,266,662 instruments.

Broadcasting and Television.—On June 30, 1983, the Australian Broadcasting Corporation operated 136 stations, including 6 short-wave stations in Australia. Privately owned commercial broadcasting stations totalled 137. On June 30, 1983, 272 television stations were in operation.

Motor Vehicles.—At June 30, 1983, there were 8,574,200 motor vehicles registered in Australia. These comprised 6,462,700 cars and station wagons, 401,900 motor cycles, and 1,709,500 commercial vehicles.

Civil Aviation.—At June 30, 1983, there were 443 licensed public aerodromes in the various States and Territories. Aircraft on the Australian Register at June 30, 1983, numbered 6,773.

FEDERAL CAPITAL

CANBERRA is the capital of Australia. It is situated in the Australian Capital Territory which has an area of 939 sq. miles (2,395 sq. km.) and was acquired from New South Wales in 1911. Canberra, which is the seat of the federal government, had a population at June 30, 1982, of 230,800. Apart from Parliament House, the city also contains other National institutions, such as the Australian War Memorial, National Library, Royal Australian Mint and the Australian National University. Most Government departments have their headquarters in Canberra. An artificial lake is a central feature of this planned city, based on Walter Burley Griffin's design.

THE NORTHERN TERRITORY

The Northern Territory has a total area of 1,346,200 square km. and lies between 129°–138° east longitude and 11°–26° south latitude. The estimated population in the Northern Territory at the 1981 Census was 126,300, of which about a quarter are Aboriginals.

The administration was taken over by the Commonwealth on January 1, 1911, from the government of the State of South Australia.

The Northern Territory (Self-Government) Act 1978 established the Northern Territory as a body politic as from 1 July 1978, with Ministers having control over and responsibility for Territory finances and the administration of the functions of government as specified by the Federal Government by regulations made pursuant to the Act. Proposed laws passed by the Legislative Assembly in relation to a transferred function require the assent of the Administrator. Proposed laws in all other cases may be assented to by the Administrator or reserved by the

Administrator for the Governor-General's pleasure. The Governor-General may disallow any laws assented to by the Administrator within six months of the Administrator's assent.

The Northern Territory has federal representation electing one member to the House of Representatives and two members to the Senate.

Administrator, His Hon. Commodore E. E. Johnston, O.B.E.

THE MINISTRY

Chief Minister, Minister for Industrial Development and Tourism, Hon. P. A. E. Everingham.

Deputy Chief Minister and Minister for Health, Youth, Sport, Recreation and Ethnic Affairs, Hon. N. Dondas.

Treasurer, Minister of Lands, Hon. M. B. Perron.

Mines and Energy, and Primary Production, Hon. I. L. Tuxworth.

Leader of the House, Attorney-General, Minister for Transport and Works, Hon. J. M. Robertson.

Education, Hon. T. Harris.

Housing and Conservation, Hon. C. N. Padgham-Purich.

Community Development, Hon. D. W. Manzie.

Various Aboriginal Land Trusts hold title to land previously called Reserves, totalling about one-fifth of the Northern Territory.

The Aboriginal Land Rights (N.T.) Act of 1976 provides for the investigation and determination of Aboriginal traditional claims to vacant Crown land or land already owned by or on behalf of Aboriginals. Successful land claims to date have increased Aboriginal ownership to 27 per cent of the Northern Territory whilst a further 18 per cent is the subject of claims.

A number of major Aboriginal communities previously administered by Church Mission Societies and the Federal Government are now controlled by the Aboriginal people themselves, through local Aboriginal Councils. A recent phenomenon is the voluntary movement of some Aboriginals to their traditional homeland areas where they feel that their culture will be better preserved.

ECONOMY

Northern Territory's primary production is concentrated in two industries—extensive beef cattle production and fishing. However, following the introduction of a number of government measures designed to expand and diversify primary production, the Territory's agricultural and horticultural industries are also beginning to contribute an increasing amount to Territory rural output.

The beef cattle industry continues to be the major user of pastoral lands with a herd of 1·5 million head or approximately 7 per cent of Australia's national herd. Income from cattle and beef production in 1982–83 was:—

Live cattle—sold interstate	$55,000,000
—exported overseas	4,500,000
N.T. export abattoirs	56,000,000
N.T. domestic abattoirs	6,000,000

The buffalo population, estimated at 190,000 head is confined to the Darwin and Gulf districts. In 1982–83, the estimated gross value of production was $A5 million, derived from live exports, slaughtering for home and overseas markets and meat processing.

Egg production was 1,537,000 in 1981–82; the estimated gross value of production was in excess of $2·5 million.

The area planted to grain and seed crops expanded from just over 2,000 hectares in 1981–82 to approximately 4,000 hectares in the 1982–83 season, and the

Territory is approaching self-sufficiency in maize and sorghum. Grain production in 1982–83 was 6,150 tonnes. Promising results are also being obtained with the development of fruit and vegetable crops. The climatic conditions that prevail during the Top End's dry season permit a range of out-of-season crops to be produced at a time when supplies in southern Australia are limited.

Horticultural production

	1982–83
Area (hectares)	230
Yield (tonnes)	4,600
Estimated wholesale value	$A2,300,000

The annual gross value of production of the Northern Territory's fishing industry has averaged about $20 million over the last few years. The industry is based on barramundi and prawn production, with attempts now being made to establish shark fishing locally. To preserve the basic resource and ensure long term profitability, further expansion will depend primarily on the success of developing new, predominantly low-unit value fisheries.

Mining has played a major part in the development of the Northern Territory and is now its major industry with production in 1982 as follows:—

		Value ($A)
Uranium concentrate...	4,488*	325,000,000
Manganese ore	1,700,000*	n/a
Copper	7,150*	3,600,000
Gold	2,700,000g	32,000,000
Silver	527,000g	95,000

*Tonnes

The total value of production in 1982 was $A625 million.

Tourism is of importance to the Territory's economy. It is a major growth industry and generates over $220 million annually.

COMMUNICATIONS

The Northern Territory has three main ports—Darwin, managed by the Northern Territory Port Authority; and the private mining ports of Gove, operated by Nabalco Pty. Ltd., and Groote Eylandt, operated by Groote Eylandt Mining Co. Pty. Ltd.

The new standard gauge rail link between Southern Australia and Alice Springs was officially opened in October, 1980. The link between Alice Springs and Darwin is provided by a fully co-ordinated rail-road service.

The main population centres are linked by the Stuart Highway, which connects Alice Springs to Darwin via Tennant Creek and Katherine. The Barkly Highway (444 km.) east from Tennant Creek, and the Victoria Highway (468 km.) west from Katherine, connect to the National Highway networks of Queensland and Western Australia. Of special interest to the Northern Territory is the operation of "road trains". These are basically massive trucks hauling two or three trailers, having a net capacity of about 100 tonnes and measuring up to 45 metres in length.

The two national domestic carriers, Trans-Australia Airlines (T.A.A.) and Ansett Airlines of Australia, both operate daily services to and from all Australian capital cities and main Northern Territory centres. In addition to the two national domestic carriers, intra-Territory services are provided by Airlines of Northern Australia (A.N.A.), plus a number of smaller commuter operators. There are also a number of charter and general aviation operators providing feeder type services. Qantas currently operates one international flight out of Darwin each week and Garuda provides two services weekly to Bali and Jakarta. Royal Brunei provide a weekly service linking Darwin and Bandar Seri Beyawan, with connections to Hong Kong, etc.

AUSTRALIAN EXTERNAL TERRITORIES

ASHMORE AND CARTIER ISLANDS

Ashmore Islands (known as Middle, East and West Islands) and Cartier Island are situated in the Indian Ocean some 850 km. and 790 km. west of Darwin respectively. The Islands lie at the outer edge of the continental shelf. They are small and low and are composed of coral and sand. Vegetation consists mainly of grass. Turtles are plentiful at certain times of the year and beche-de-mer is abundant. The Islands are uninhabited.

Great Britain took formal possession of the Ashmores in 1878 and Cartier was annexed in 1909. By Imperial Order in Council of July 23, 1931, the Islands were placed under the authority of the Commonwealth of Australia, and were accepted in 1933 under the name of the Territory of Ashmore and Cartier Islands. The Territory was annexed to and deemed to form part of the Northern Territory of Australia with relevant laws of the Northern Territory applying to the Territory of Ashmore and Cartier Islands. From July 1, 1978, responsibility for the administration of Ashmore and Cartier Islands became a direct responsibility of the Commonwealth of Australia.

In accordance with an agreement between the governments of Indonesia and Australia, Indonesian fishermen who have traditionally plied the area may fish within the Territory and land to collect water at certain locations.

THE AUSTRALIAN ANTARCTIC TERRITORY

The *Australian Antarctic Territory* was established by an Order in Council, dated February 7, 1933, which placed under the government of the Commonwealth of Australia all the islands and territories, other than Adélie Land, which are situated south of the latitude 60° S. and lying between 160° E. longitude and 45° E. longitude. The Order came into force on August 24, 1936, after the passage of the Australian Antarctic Territory Acceptance Act, 1933. The boundaries of Terre Adélie were definitely fixed by a French Decree of April 1, 1938, as the islands and territories south of 60° S. latitude lying between 136° E. longitude and 142° E. longitude. The Australian Antarctic Territory Act, 1954 declared that the laws in force in the Australian Capital Territory are, so far as they are applicable, in force in the Australian Antarctic Territory. The Territory is administered by the Antarctic Division of the Department of Science, which, since its inception in 1947, has organized yearly expeditions to Antarctica, known as Australian National Antarctic Research Expeditions (ANARE).

On February 13, 1954, ANARE opened a station in Mac-Robertson Land at latitude 67° 36′ S. and longitude 62° 53′ E. The station was named Mawson in honour of Sir Douglas Mawson and was the first permanent Australian station to be set up on the Antarctic continent. Scientific research conducted at Mawson includes upper atmosphere physics, cosmic ray physics, meteorology, earth sciences, biology and medical science. Mawson is also a centre for coastal and inland exploration.

A second Australian scientific research station was opened on the coast of Princess Elizabeth Land on January 13, 1957, at latitude 68° 35′ S. and longitude 77° 58′ E., and was named in honour of Captain John King Davis. Scientific programmes carried out at Davis include meteorology, biology, upper atmosphere physics, with field investigations in biology.

In February, 1959, the Australian Government accepted from the U.S. Government custody of Wilkes Station on the Budd Coast, Wilkes Land at about 66° 15′ S. and longitude 110° 31′ E. The station was closed in February 1969, and activities were transferred to

Casey station. Casey station was named in honour of Lord Casey, a former Governor-General of Australia. The station, at 66° 17′ S., 110° 32′ E., is of advanced design and scientific programmes carried out there include geophysics, meteorology with field programmes in glaciology, geology, etc.

Since 1948 ANARE has also operated a station on Macquarie Island, a dependency of Tasmania, situated at 54° 30′ S. and 158° 57′ E., about 900 miles north of the Antarctic Continent.

For other Commonwealth dependencies in the Antarctic *see* New Zealand; British Antarctic Territory.

CHRISTMAS ISLAND

Until the end of 1957 a part of the then Colony of Singapore, Christmas Island was administered as a separate colony until October 1, 1958, when it became Australian territory. It is situated in the Indian Ocean about 224 miles S. of Java Head. Area 52 sq. miles. Population (estimated, June 30, 1985) is 2,800, consisting of employees of the Phosphate Mining Company, the Christmas Island Services Corporation, the Administration, and their families. There is no indigenous population.

The island is densely wooded and contains extensive deposits of phosphates, the recovery of which is the major economic activity. An Australian Government company, the Phosphate Mining Company of Christmas Island, carries out the mining activities. New Zealand has the right to purchase up to half of the Island's phosphate rock output. A statutory authority, the Christmas Island Services Corporation, was set up in Oct. 1984 to take responsibility for many municipal functions from the mining company. The island is administered by the Australian Government through the Department of Territories in Canberra.

Administrator, T. F. Paterson.

COCOS (KEELING) ISLANDS

The Cocos (Keeling) Islands were declared a British possession in 1857. In 1878 they were placed under the control of the Governor of Ceylon and were later annexed to the Straits Settlements and incorporated with the colony of Singapore. On Nov. 23, 1955, their administration was transferred to Australia. On April 6, 1984, the Cocos community, in an Act of Self-Determination observed by a U.N. mission, chose to integrate with Australia.

The Islands are two separate atolls (North Keeling Island and, 24 km. to the south, the main atoll) comprising some 27 small coral islands with a total area of about 5½ square miles, situated in the Indian Ocean in latitude 12° 5′ South and longitude 96° 53′ East. The main islands of the southern atoll are West Island (the largest, about 6 miles from north to south) on which are the administrative centre, the aerodrome, and the Australian-based employees of government departments; Home Island, where the Cocos Malay community lives; Direction Island, Horsburgh and South Island.

The main economic activity is the production of copra: total exports 1983–84 were 160 metric tons. The climate is equable and pleasant, being usually under the influence of the south-east trade winds for about three-quarters of the year. A weekly air charter service operates between Perth, the Cocos (Keeling) Islands and Christmas Island. Population (June 30, 1984), 584. The islands are administered by the Australian Government through the Department of Territories and Local Government in Canberra, although all proposed Ordinances, Regulations and By-laws for the Islands must be submitted to the Islands Council (est. 1979) for its consideration.

Administrator, Dr. K. Chan.

CORAL SEA ISLANDS TERRITORY

The territory lies between the Great Barrier Reef and longitude 156° 06′ E., and between latitudes 12° and 24° S. It comprises scattered reefs and islands, often little more than sandbanks, spread over a sea area of 780,000 sq. km. The islands are formed mainly of coral and sand; some have a cover of grassy or scrub-type vegetations. There is a manned metereological station in the Willis Group but the remaining islands and cays are uninhabited. Large populations of sea birds nest and breed in the area, and two national nature reserves were designated in the territory in 1982.

The Australian Government bases its claim to the islands on numerous acts of sovereignty since early this century and enacted the Coral Sea Islands Act 1969 which declares the islands a Territory of the Commonwealth of Australia.

HEARD ISLAND AND McDONALD ISLANDS

The islands, about 4,100 km. south-west of Fremantle, comprise all the islands and rocks lying between 52° 30′ and 53° 30′ S. latitude and 72° and 74° 30′ E. longitude. Sovereignty over the islands was transferred by the U.K. to the Commonwealth of Australia in 1947. The Heard Island and McDonald Islands Act 1953 provides for the government of the islands as one Territory and under this Act the law operating there is that of the Australian Capital Territory. The Islands are administered by the Antarctic Division of the Department of Science.

NORFOLK ISLAND

The island is situated in latitude 29° 02′ S. and longitude 167° 57′ E., being about 1,042 miles from Sydney and 400 miles north of New Zealand. It is about five miles in length by three in breadth, with an area of 8,528 acres and circumference of 20 miles. The climate is mild, with a mean temperature of 20° C. Resident population at the 1981 Census was 1,849. The island served as a penal colony from 1788 to 1814 and 1825 to 1855. In 1856, 194 descendants of the *Bounty* mutineers were brought here from Pitcairn Island, which led to Norfolk Island becoming a separate settlement under the jurisdiction of the Governor of N.S.W. In 1897 Norfolk Island became a dependency of N.S.W., and in 1914 a territory of Australia.

In 1979 Norfolk Island gained a degree of self-government, enabling the island to run its affairs to the greatest practical extent. Wide powers are exercised by a nine-member Legislative Assembly. It is intended that the island will achieve full internal self-government as a Territory under the authority of the Commonwealth. The island is currently administered by the Australian Government through the Department of Territories in Canberra.

The island is a popular tourist resort, and a large proportion of the population depends on tourism and its ancillaries for employment. Regular air services operate from Australia and New Zealand.

Seat of Government and Administration Offices, Kingston.

Administrator, Commodore J. A. Matthew, C.V.O., M.B.E.

STATES OF THE COMMONWEALTH OF AUSTRALIA

NEW SOUTH WALES

The State of New South Wales is situated entirely between the 28th and 38th parallels of S. lat. and 141st and 154th meridians of E. long., and comprises an area of 309,433 square miles (exclusive of 939 sq. miles of Australian Capital Territory which lies within its borders).

POPULATION.—Preliminary estimated resident population at Dec. 31, 1984 was 5,436,900.

Births, deaths and marriages of usually resident population were:

	1982	1983
Births.......	83,908	83,307
Deaths	42,527	40,547
Marriages ...	41,955	39,995

Annual rate per 1,000 of estimated resident population in 1983:—Births, 15·5; Deaths, 7·6; Marriages, 7·5. Deaths under 1 year per 1,000 live births, 9·9.

Religions

The members of the Church of England in New South Wales, according to the Census of 1981, numbered 1,569,374. Roman Catholic (including "Catholic") 1,424,499, Presbyterian 252,725, Uniting 179,271, Orthodox 171,427, Methodist 148,992, Baptist 64,663, Lutheran 31,696, other Christian 239,895, Hebrew 25,176 and Muslim 38,527. The religion of 934,305 persons was either not stated in the census schedules or was stated as "none".

PHYSIOGRAPHY

Natural features divide the State into four strips of territory extending from north to south, viz., the Coastal Divisions; the Tablelands, which form the Great Dividing Range between the coastal districts and the plains; the Western Slopes of the Dividing Range; and the Western Plains. The highest points

are Mounts Kosciusko, 7,314 feet, and Townsend, 7,251 feet. The western portion of the State is watered by the rivers of the Murray-Darling system and immense reservoirs have been constructed for irrigation purposes, as well as many artesian bores. The Darling, 1,712 miles, and the Murrumbidgee, 981 miles, are both tributaries of the Murray, part of which forms the boundary between the States of New South Wales and Victoria.

Climate.—New South Wales is situated entirely in the Temperate Zone. The climate is generally mild and mostly free from extremes of heat and cold. At Sydney the average mean shade temperature is 18° C. The mean (shade) temperature ranges for the various divisions of the State are as follows: coastal, 15° C in the south to 20°C in the north; northern and central tableland, 12° C to 16° C; southern tableland, 7° C to 14° C; and for the rest of the State (western slope, central plains, Riverina and western), 15° C in the south to 20° C in the north.

GOVERNMENT

New South Wales was first colonized as a British possession in 1788, and after progressive settlement a partly elective legislature was established in 1843. In 1855 Responsible Government was granted, the present Constitution being founded on the Constitution Act of 1902. New South Wales federated with the other States of Australia in 1901. The executive authority of the State is vested in a Governor (appointed by the Crown), assisted by a Council of Ministers.

GOVERNOR

Governor of New South Wales, His Excellency Air Marshal Sir James Rowland, K.B.E., D.F.C., A.F.C., *assumed office* Jan. 20, 1981.

Lieutenant-Governor, Hon. Sir Laurence Whistler Street, K.C.M.G.

THE MINISTRY
(at Feb. 6, 1985)

Premier and Minister for Arts, and for Ethnic Affairs, Hon. N. K. Wran, q.c.

Deputy Premier, Minister for Health, Hon. R. J. Mulock.

Youth and Community Services, and Housing, Hon. F. J. Walker, q.c.

Public Works and Ports; Roads, Hon. L. J. Brereton.

Industrial Relations, Hon. P. D. Hills.

Police and Emergency Services, Hon. P. T. Anderson.

Treasurer, Hon. K. G. Booth.

Attorney-General, Hon. T. W. Sheahan.

Transport and Vice-President of the Council, Hon. B. J. Unsworth.

Agriculture and Fisheries, Hon. J. R. Hallam.

Education, Hon. R. M. Cavalier.

Mineral Resources and Energy, Hon. P. F. Cox.

Local Government, Hon. K. J. Stewart.

Industry and Decentralisation; Small Business and Technology, Hon. E. L. Bedford.

Sport and Recreation; Tourism, Hon. M. A. Cleary.

Consumer Affairs; Aboriginal Affairs, Hon. G. Paciullo.

Natural Resources, Hon. J. A. Crosio.

Employment; Finance, Hon. R. J. Debus.

Corrective Services, Hon. J. E. Akister.

Planning and Environment, Hon. R. J. Carr.

The annual salaries of Ministers are: Premier, $A83,406; Deputy Premier, $A75,089; Leader of the Government members in the Legislative Council, $A75,935; (Deputy $A72,328); other Ministers $A70,899 each. Ministers also receive expense allowances and electoral allowances, and a special expense allowance is paid to Ministers who represent or reside in outlying electorates.

AGENT-GENERAL IN LONDON

Agent-General in London, R. F. W. Watson, c.m.g., N.S.W. House, 66 Strand, W.C.2.

THE LEGISLATURE

The *Legislative Council* consists of 45 members, elected by popular vote and the *Legislative Assembly* consists of 99 members elected for a maximum period of 4 years. Party representation in the Council at June 30, 1985 was; Labour 24, Liberal 11, National 6, Australian Democrat 1, and Independent 3. Party representation in the Assembly at June 30, 1985 was: Labour 58, Liberal 22, National 15 and Independent 4. The annual salary of members of the Legislative Council and Legislative Asssembly who are not Ministers is $A40,587. Members also receive expense and electoral allowances, and a special expense allowance is paid to members who reside in, or represent outlying electorates.

President of the Legislative Council, Hon. J. R. Johnson.

Speaker, Legislative Assembly, Hon. L. B. Kelly.

THE JUDICATURE

The judicial system includes a Supreme Court, Industrial Commission, District Court, Land and Environment Court, Compensation Court.

Chief Justice, Supreme Court, Hon. Sir Laurence Street (+ *allce.* $A5,904) $A99,496

President, Court of Appeal, Hon. Mr. Justice Kirby, c.m.g. (+ *allce.* $A4,761) $A93,797

GOVERNMENT FINANCES

Consolidated Fund, for year ended June 30th, was:—

	1983	1984
	$A'000	$A'000
Receipts	6,737,334	7,407,465
Expenditure	6,777,456	7,441,370
Public Debt	5,327,886	5,566,541

Banking, etc.—There were (March 1985) 8 trading banks with deposits of $A19,297 million. Savings bank deposits amounted to $A10,139 million, representing $A1,865 per head of the population.

EDUCATION

Education.—Education is compulsory between the ages of 6 and 15 years. It is non-sectarian and free at all government schools. The enrolment in July 1984 in 2,237 government schools was 770,733. In addition to the government schools there were, in 1984, 829 non-government schools, with an enrolment of 257,928 students (preliminary figures). The six universities had an enrolment of 65,523 students in 1984. In addition, there were 47,917 students enrolled in advanced education courses (predominantly in colleges of advanced education) in 1984. Students enrolled in technical and further education colleges in 1984 numbered 388,336. State Government recurrent expenditure on education was $A2,722,763 in the year 1983–84.

PRODUCTION AND INDUSTRY

Local value of production in 1983–84 was:—

Agricultural commodities	$A3,991,360,670
Crops	2,175,890,604
Livestock products	999,843,650
Slaughterings	815,626,416
Value added 1983–84	
Mining and Quarrying	$A1,639,980,000
Manufacturing	12,724,000,000

Crops.—Production in 1983–84 was (tonnes):

Wheat-grain	8,960,784
Wheat-hay	84,290
Barley	941,131
Oats	1,120,377
Rice	610,551
Cotton	292,444
Oilseed	98,578
Potatoes	129,564
Sugar-cane, crushed	1,468,392

886,785 kilograms of dried leaf tobacco and 67,953,200 kilograms of bananas were obtained; almost every kind of fruit and vegetable is grown.

Livestock and Livestock Products.—A large area is suitable for sheep-raising, the principal breed of sheep being the merino, which was introduced in 1797. On March 31, 1984, there were 5,035,549 cattle, 50,997,324 sheep and lambs, and 799,211 pigs. In 1983–84, 230,611,556 kg. of wool (in the grease) were produced, 2,832,000 kg. of butter, 14,140,000 kg. of cheese, and 21,083,000 kg. of bacon and ham.

Mining Industry.—The principal minerals are coal, lead, zinc, tin, rutile, copper and zircon. The total value of minerals won in 1983–84 was $A2,344,792,000, of which the value of output of the coal mining industry was $A1,733,358,000 and of the silver-lead-zinc industry, $A267,753,000 and the construction materials industry, including stone, gravel and sand, was $A229,466,000. The average number of persons employed in the mining industry during 1983–84 was 27,094. In 1983–84, 66,823,000 tonnes of coal were produced.

Manufacturing Industry.—At June 30, 1984, there were 10,332 manufacturing establishments (employing four of more persons). The average number of persons employed during 1983–84 was 364,700. Large iron and steel works with subsidiary factories are in operation at Newcastle and Port Kembla in proximity to the coalfields. Products of the regions include iron and steel, pipes, boilers, steel wire and wire netting, copper wire, copper and brass cables and tin-plate. Production in 1983–84 was 5,109,490 tonnes.

OVERSEAS TRADE

	1984
Overseas Imports f.o.b.	$10,027,679,000
Overseas Exports f.o.b.	5,228,321,000

The chief exports in 1983–84 were coal and coke, wool, meat, petroleum products and wheat. Chief imports were, office machines, petroleum and petroleum products, transport equipment, telecommunications and recording equipment, and printed matter.

TRANSPORT AND COMMUNICATIONS

Shipping.—2,550 vessels entered the major ports of N.S.W. from overseas during the year ended June 30, 1984, the gross tonnage being 50,809,118. The shipping entries at Sydney were 1,651 vessels of 25,672,073 gross tonnage.

Roads and Bridges.—Expenditures by the State Government and the local authorities on road systems and regulation in 1982–83 was $A913,100,000.

Motor Vehicles.—At Dec. 31, 1984, there were 2,924,867 registered motor vehicles (cars, 1,830,235).

Railways.—The railways of New South Wales are controlled by the State. At June 30, 1984, the route kilometres of the State railways open for traffic was 9,884, revenue in the year 1983–84 being $A1,407,015,000.

Aviation.—Sydney is the principal overseas terminal in Australia. Overseas and local traffic at Sydney airport in 1983 were: passengers 7,642,661; freight 162,303 tonnes; aircraft, 90,270.

Postal and Telecommunication Services.—The postal and telecommunication services are administered by the Australian Government. At June 30, 1984, there were 1,571 post offices in New South Wales.

Radio and Television.—At June 30, 1984, there were 22 national radio stations and 43 commercial radio stations operating under licence. There were also 23 licensed non-profit radio stations providing special interest services not catered for by the national and commercial services. At June 30, 1984, there were 29 television stations (15 national, 14 commercial) in operation.

TOWNS

ΨSYDNEY, the chief city and State capital and the largest city in Australia, stands on the shores of Port Jackson. Sydney Harbour extends inland for 21 km.: the total area of water is about 55 sq. km.

The preliminary estimated resident population at June 30, 1984 of the Sydney Statistical Division was 3,335,250. The Newcastle and Wollongong Statistical Districts contain populations of 418,450 and 235,750 respectively.

The populations of principal municipalities located outside the boundaries of these statistical areas are: Albury 39,150, Dubbo 30,500, Greater Taree 34,750, Hastings 39,750, Lismore 37,050, Orange 32,200, Shoalhaven 56,500, Tamworth 33,350, Wagga Wagga 49,500.

LORD HOWE ISLAND

Lord Howe Island, which is part of New South Wales, is situated 702 kilometres north-east of Sydney. Lat. 31° 33′ 4″ S., Long. 159° 4′ 26″ E. Area 17 sq. km. Pop. June 30, 1984, 300. The island is of volcanic origin with Mount Gower reaching an altitude of 866 m. The affairs of the Island are administered by the Lord Howe Island Board.

QUEENSLAND

This State, situated in lat. 10° 40′–29° S. and long. 138°–153° 30′ E., comprises the whole north-eastern portion of the Australian continent.

Queensland possesses an area of 1,727,000 square km. (*i.e.*, equal to more than 5½ times the area of the British Isles).

POPULATION.—At June 30, 1984, the estimated resident population numbered 2,505,300.

Births, Deaths and Marriages were:

	1983	1984
Births	42,085	40,444
Deaths	17,056	17,399
Marriages	18,645	19,039

Annual rate per 1,000 of mean population in 1984; Births, 16·9; Deaths, 6·9; Marriages 7·6. Deaths under 1 year, 9·1 per 1,000 live births.

Religions

At the Census of 1981, there were 601,537 Anglican, 554,912 Roman Catholics (including Catholics undefined), 146,898 Uniting Church, 132,525 Presbyterians, 86,750 Methodists, 50,401 Lutherans, 34,323 Baptists, and 166,611 other Christians.

PHYSIOGRAPHY

The Great Dividing Range on the eastern coast of the continent produces a similar formation to that of New South Wales, the eastern side having a narrow slope to the coast and the western a long and gradual slope to the central plains, where the Selwyn and Kirby Ranges divide the land into a northern and southern watershed. The Brisbane, Burnett, Fitzroy and Burdekin rise in the eastern ranges and flow into the Pacific, the Flinders, Mitchell, and Leichhardt into the Gulf of Carpentaria, and the Barcoo and Warrego rise in the central ranges and flow southwards.

GOVERNMENT

Queensland was constituted a separate colony with responsible government in 1859, having previously formed part of New South Wales. The executive authority is vested in a Governor (appointed by the Crown), aided by an Executive Council of 18 members.

GOVERNOR

Governor of Queensland, His Excellency Commodore Sir James Maxwell Ramsay, K.C.M.G., K.C.V.O., C.B.E., D.S.C $A60,000

EXECUTIVE COUNCIL.
(H.E. the Governor presides.)

Premier and Treasurer, Hon. Sir Johannes Bjelke-Petersen, K.C.M.G. $A86,015
Deputy Premier and Minister assisting the Treasurer, Hon. W. A. M. Gunn $A73,842
Local Government, Main Roads and Racing, Hon. R. J. Hinze.
Works and Housing, Hon. C. A. Wharton.
Mines and Energy, Hon. I. J. Gibbs.
Industry, Small Business and Technology, Hon. M. J. Ahern.
Transport, Hon. D. F. Lane.
Lands and Forestry, and Police, Hon. W. H. Glasson.
Health, Hon. B. D. Austin.
Education, Hon. L. W. Powell.
Water Resources and Maritime Services, Hon. J. P. Goleby.
Primary Industries, Hon. N. J. Turner.
Employment and Industrial Affairs, Hon. V. P. Lester.
Environment, Valuation and Administrative Services, Hon. M. J. Tenni.
Justice and Attorney-General, Hon. N. J. Harper.
Welfare Services, Youth and Ethnic Affairs, Hon. G. H. Muntz.
Tourism, National Parks, Sport and the Arts, Hon. P. R. McKechnie.
Northern Development and Aboriginal and Island Affairs, Hon. R. C. Katte.
Ministers, each $A67,816.

AGENT-GENERAL IN LONDON

Agent-General for Queensland, J. F. S. Brown, M.C., 392–393 Strand, W.C.2.

THE LEGISLATURE

Parliament consists of a *Legislative Assembly* of 82 members, elected by all persons aged 18 years and over. Members of the Assembly receive \$A41,466 per annum plus an electorate allowance. The Assembly, as elected on October 22, 1983, was composed of: National Party, 41; Liberal Party, 8; Australian Labour Party, 32; Independent, 1.

Speaker, Hon. J. H. Warner	\$A56,761
Chairman of Committees, E. C. Row	\$A47,488

THE JUDICATURE

There is a Supreme Court; District Courts; an Industrial Court; a Land Court and a Medical Assessment Tribunal; a Local Government Court; the Industrial Conciliation and Arbitration Commission; Inferior Courts at all the principal towns, presided over by Stipendiary Magistrates; a Small Claims Tribunal; and a Licensing Court.

Chief Justice, Supreme Court, Hon. D. G. Andrews	\$A99,925
Senior Puisne Judge, Hon. J. C. Kelly	88,250

EDUCATION

Education is compulsory between the ages of 6 and 15 years and is provided free in Government schools. At July 1984 the State administered 1,043 primary, 81 primary/secondary, and 149 secondary schools with 243,606 primary students, and 130,531 secondary students. Special education, which is included in the above figures, was provided to 5,372 children at 59 special schools and 62 primary schools with special classes. The State employed 22,361 teachers at July 1984. Non-government enrolments at July 1983 were 58,264 primary students and 49,727 secondary students taught by 5,654 teachers at 225 primary, 60 primary/secondary and 78 secondary schools.

Post-secondary education involves technical and further education (TAFE), advanced education, and university education. During 1983, 143,440 students were enrolled in TAFE courses, including 64,239 enrolled in adult education courses. At 30 April 1983, there were 12,497 full-time, 7,718 part-time, and 5,889 external students enrolled in advanced education courses. The three universities had enrolments of 12,946 full-time students, 7,784 part-time, and 2,137 external students at April 30, 1983.

PRODUCTION AND INDUSTRY

Agriculture and Livestock.—The gross value of agricultural commodity production in 1983–84 was \$A3,111,825,000 (including crops \$A1,743,833,000, livestock disposals \$A993,982,000, livestock products \$A374,010,000).

The most important crops in 1983–84 were (tonnes):

Sugar (raw)	3,011,590
Wheat	1,922,417
Maize	174,815
Sorghum	1,387,370
Barley	541,750

The livestock on March 31, 1984 included 9,154,447 cattle, 371,669 being dairy cattle, 13,032,828 sheep and 555,771 pigs.

Forestry.—Total Australian grown timber processed in 1983–84 amounted to 1,187,102 cubic metres (gross volume measure).

Minerals.—There are rich deposits of both metallic and non-metallic minerals. Coal is mined extensively in Central Queensland and on a lesser scale in North Queensland and Ipswich districts.

Output in 1983–84

	\$A
Bauxite	144,968,000
Coal	1,668,596,000
Copper concentrate	184,310,000
Crude oil and natural gas	79,579,000
Gold (various forms)	24,870,000
Lead concentrate	181,120,000
Mineral sands	28,782,000
Nickel ore	7,892,000
Scheelite and wolfram concentrate	9,747,000
Tin and tin-wolfram concentrate	24,212,000
Zinc concentrate	73,517,000
Other	204,703,000
Total	2,632,296,000

Manufacturing.—In 1982–83 there were 3,440 establishments with four or more workers, employing 114,646 persons, and producing goods and services worth \$A10,716 million. The value added was \$A3,445 million. Much of the production was the processing of primary products, *e.g.* foodstuffs, timber and minerals. Included in other factory production were the products from engineering, transport equipment, basic and fabricated metal, chemical and fertilizer works, cement, paper and textile mills and oil refineries.

FINANCE

Government finance (\$A'000) was:—

	1983	1984
Revenue	3,690,187	4,212,842
Expenditure	3,690,956	4,211,919
Gross Debt	2,197,901	2,290,951

Banking.—Advances made by Trading Banks (including the Commonwealth Trading Bank of Australia) at June 30, 1984, totalled \$A4,878,827,000. The deposits at the same date amounted to \$A6,067,835,000. Depositors' balances in Queensland savings banks at June 30, 1984, \$A4,708,591,000, averaged \$A1,893 for each inhabitant. There were 3,570,748 operative accounts.

OVERSEAS TRADE

	1983–84
Imports	\$A2,086,861,000
Exports	5,473,451,000

The chief overseas exports are coal, non-ferrous metals, meat, sugar, wool, and cereal grains.

COMMUNICATIONS

Road and Rail.—The State is served by 10,231 kilometres of railways. During 1983–84, 37,602,000 passengers and 53,113,000 tonnes of goods and livestock were carried. At June 30, 1983, there were 142,195 kilometres of formed roads in the State, and at June 30, 1984, 1,533,500 motor vehicles were on the register.

Aviation.—Regular services operate between Brisbane, the main Queensland coastal and inland towns and the southern capitals. Brisbane, Townsville and Cairns are also ports of call on several international services.

Radio and Television.—On June 30, 1984, 27 national and 29 commercial sound broadcasting and 32 national and 11 commercial television stations were operating in Queensland. There were five public broadcasting stations.

TOWNS

CAPITAL, ΨBRISBANE, is situated on the Brisbane River, which is navigable by large vessels to the city, over 23 kilometres from Moreton Bay. The estimated resident population of the Brisbane Statistical Division at June 30, 1984 was 1,145,410. This area includes the cities of Brisbane (734,150), Ipswich (73,480), Logan (105,630) and Redcliffe (44,950).

Other cities and towns with population over 30,000 at June 30, 1984, are: ΨTownsville, 82,140; Gold Coast, 116,540; Toowoomba, 74,280; ΨRockhampton, 54,630; ΨCairns, 38,600; ΨBundaberg, 32,780.

Transmission of mails from London to Brisbane, by air, 3 days; by sea 5 to 6 weeks.

SOUTH AUSTRALIA

The State of South Australia is situated between 26° and 38° S. lat. and 129° and 141° E. long., the total area being 380,070 sq. miles.

POPULATION.—At June 30, 1984, the resident population was estimated to be 1,353,000.

Births, deaths and marriages were:

	1983	1984
Births	19,865	20,244
Deaths	9,882	10,367
Marriages	10,550	10,643

Religions

Religion is free and receives no State aid. At the Census, 1981, the persons belonging to the principal religious denominations were as follows: Anglican, 260,919; Methodists, 85,935; Congregationalists, 2,834; Baptists, 22,287; Lutherans, 63,860; Roman Catholics, 255,332; Presbyterians, 21,725; Churches of Christ, 18,657; Greek Orthodox, 36,423; Uniting Church, 108,857; and Pentecostal, 11,232.

PHYSIOGRAPHY

The most important physical features of South Australia are broad plains, divided longitudinally by four great secondary features, which form barriers to east-west movement, and which have thus largely determined the direction of roads and railways, the sites of towns and villages and the manner of distribution of the population. These four barriers are Spencer Gulf, Gulf St. Vincent, the Mt. Lofty-Flinders Ranges and the River Murray.

The north-western portion of the State is mostly desert, while north of latitude 32° S. the country is unpromising by comparison with the fertile land which surrounds the hill country of the east. The Murray, which flows for some 400 miles through the south-eastern corner, is the only river of importance.

The lack of rivers and fresh-water lakes in the settled areas has necessitated the building of a number of reservoirs, which are supplemented by pipelines from the River Murray.

Climate.—The mean annual temperature at Adelaide is 17·1°C, the winter temperature (June-August) averaging 11·9°C, and the summer (Nov.-Mar.) 22·3°C. During the summer months the maximum temperature at times exceeds 40°C, but is associated with a relatively low humidity. The average annual rainfall at Adelaide, derived from over 140 years' record is 21 inches. This total is rather higher than the approximate average annual rainfall over the whole of the agricultural areas.

GOVERNMENT

South Australia was proclaimed a British Province in 1836, and in 1851 a partially elective legislature was established. The present Constitution rests upon a Law of Oct. 24, 1856, the executive authority being vested in a Governor appointed by the Crown, aided by a Council of 13 Ministers.

GOVERNOR

Governor of South Australia, His Excellency Lt. Gen. Sir Donald B. Dunstan, K.B.E., G.C.B. (1982).

Lieut.-Governor, Hon. Sir Condor Laucke, K.C.M.G. (1982).

THE MINISTRY

Premier, Treasurer, Minister of State Development, and for the Arts, Hon. J. C. Bannon.

Attorney-General; Minister of Consumer Affairs, Corporate Affairs, and Ethnic Affairs, Hon. C. J. Sumner.

Environment and Planning, of Lands and Repatriation, Hon. D. J. Hopgood.

Transport and Marine, Hon. R. K. Abbott.

Health, Hon. J. R. Cornwall.

Education and Technology, Hon. L. M. F. Arnold.

Tourism and Local Government, Hon. G. F. Keneally.

Mines and Energy, Hon. R. G. Payne.

Community Welfare and Aboriginal Affairs, Hon. G. J. Crafter.

Water Resources, and Recreation and Sport, Hon. J. W. Slater.

Housing and Construction; Public Works, Hon. T. H. Hemmings.

Agriculture, Fisheries and Forests; Correctional Services, Hon. F. T. Blevins.

Hon. Miss Barbara Wiese.

AGENT-GENERAL IN LONDON

Agent-General for South Australia, J. L. Rundle, South Australia House, 50 Strand, W.C.2.

THE LEGISLATURE

Parliament consists of a *Legislative Council* of 22 members elected for 6 years, one-half retiring every 3 years; and a *House of Assembly* of 47 members, elected for a maximum duration of 3 years. Election is by ballot, with universal adult suffrage for both the Legislative Council and the House of Assembly.

The representation in the House of Assembly is 22 Liberals, 23 Labour, 1 National Party and 1 Independent.

President of the Legislative Council, Hon.
A. M. Whyte $A60,655

Speaker of the House of Assembly, Hon. T.
M. McRae $A60,655

THE JUDICATURE

Law and Justice.—The Supreme Court is presided over by the Chief Justice and 14 Puisne Judges.

EDUCATION

Education at the primary and secondary level is available at Government schools controlled by the Education Department and at non-government schools, most of which are denominational. In 1984 there were 708 Government schools with 201,220 students, and 174 independent schools with 49,349 students. The Department of Technical and Further Education is responsible for post-secondary education, conducted by 9 community colleges and 16 colleges of technical and further education. The Industrial and Commercial Training Commission administers apprentice training.

The two universities had, in 1984, a total enrolment of 13,764 full-time students. There are also three Colleges of Advanced Education.

FINANCE

Revenue and expenditure of the Consolidated Revenue Account and debt of Southern Australia (year ended June 30) was:—

	1983	1984
Revenue	$A2,217,693,000	2,578,280,000
Expenditure	2,274,767,000	2,579,891,000
Debt	2,035,762,000	2,010,259,000

Banking.—There are 7 trading banks in Adelaide, including the Commonwealth Trading Bank and the State Bank of South Australia, having total average deposits of $A1,976,873,000 in June 1984. The six savings banks had deposits of $A3,327,054,000 at June 30, 1984.

PRODUCTION AND INDUSTRY

The gross value of primary production in 1983–84 was:—

Crops	$A1,120,376,000
Livestock products	390,315,000
Slaughterings	275,168,000
Fisheries	58,865,000

Agriculture.—Wheat harvest 1983–84 2,843,000 tonnes; barley, 1,816,872 tonnes. Oranges, lemons, apples, apricots, peaches, and all stone fruits and olives are successfully grown, and a quantity of this fruit is dried. In 1983–84, 233,307,000 litres of wine and 5,115 tonnes of sultanas, currants and raisins were produced. Considerable quantities of fruits (fresh and dried), wine and brandy, are annually sent to overseas countries, and to other Australian States. Some areas of the State, particularly near Adelaide, are also very suitable for growing all kinds of root crops and vegetables.

Livestock (March 31, 1985).—There were 17,208,900 sheep, 881,900 cattle, 379,000 pigs. Wool production (1983–84), 101,513,000 kg.

Minerals.—Iron, pyrite, gypsum, salt, coal, limestone, clay, oil and gas, &c., are found. The total mineral output was valued at $A641,900,000 in 1983–84, including oil and gas valued at $A462,900,000.

OVERSEAS TRADE

	1983–84
Imports	$A1,318,693,000
Exports	1,635,825,000

The principal exports are wool, wheat, barley, meat, lead and lead alloys, silver, zinc, iron and steel, petroleum products, rock lobster and prawns.

TRANSPORT AND COMMUNICATIONS

There were (June, 1984) 153 kilometres of railway operated by State Transport Authority, 980 kilometres of tram and bus routes and 102,886 kilometres of roads, including roads and tracks outside local government areas. There are a number of excellent harbours, of which Port Adelaide is the most important. The number of vessels (exceeding 200 net tons) entering South Australia from overseas during 1983–84 was 866 with 2,317,627 import tonnes and leaving with 5,629,026 export tonnes. There are 590 post offices in the State.

Civil Aviation.—There are 34 Government and licensed airports; the largest of these, Adelaide airport, recorded 1,688,557 passenger movements during 1983–84.

Motor Vehicles.—The registration on 30 June, 1984, totalled 790,155.

Radio and Television (Jan. 1984)—Broadcasting stations 26; Television stations 32 (including translator and satellite fed stations).

TOWNS

ΨADELAIDE, the chief city and capital, estimated resident population on June 30, 1984, 978,940, inclusive of suburbs. Other centres (with 1984 populations) are: ΨWhyalla (30,870); ΨMt. Gambier (19,160); ΨPort Pirie (15,850); ΨPort Augusta (16,310); and ΨPort Lincoln (12,250).

Transit.—Transmission of mails from London to Adelaide, approximately 35 days by sea and 5 days by air.

TASMANIA

Tasmania is an island state of Australia situated in the Southern ocean off the south-eastern extremity of the mainland. It is separated from the Australian mainland by Bass Strait and incorporates King Island and the Furneaux group of islands which are in the Strait. It lies between 40° 38′–43° 39′ S. lat. and 144° 36′–148° 23′ E. long., and contains an area of 26,383 square miles.

POPULATION.—The estimated resident population at Dec. 31, 1984 was 439,500.

Births, deaths and marriages were:

	1983
Births	7,028
Deaths	3,311
Marriages	3,644

Vital Statistics.—The birth rate in 1983 was 16·3, death rate 7·6, marriage rate 8·4 per 1,000. Infant mortality (1983) 10·5 per 1,000 births.

Religions

In 1981 there were 151,207 members of the Anglican Church of Australia, 78,143 Roman Catholics, 17,668 Uniting Church of Australia, 19,906 Methodists, 11,575 Presbyterians, 1,790 Congregationalists and 7,965 Baptists.

PHYSIOGRAPHY

The surface of the country is generally hilly and timbered, with mountains from 1,500 to 5,300 ft. in height, and expanses of level, open plains. There are numerous rivers, the South Esk, Gordon, Derwent and Huon being the largest. The climate is fine and salubrious, and well suited to European constitutions; the hot winds of Australia do not often reach the island. At Hobart the mean maximum temperature ranges from about 12°C in winter to 21°C in summer, the mean minimum from 5°C to 11°C. The western side of the island is very wet, the eastern side being much drier.

GOVERNMENT

The island was first settled by a British party from New South Wales in 1803, becoming a separate colony in 1825. In 1851 a partly elective legislature was inaugurated, and in 1856 responsible government was established. In 1901 Tasmania became a State of the Australian Commonwealth. The State executive authority is vested in a Governor (appointed by the Crown), but is exercised by Cabinet Ministers responsible to the Legislature, of which they are members.

GOVERNOR

Governor of Tasmania, His Excellency Sir James Plimsoll, A.C., C.B.E.; *assumed office* Oct. 1982.
Lieutenant Governor, Hon. Sir Guy Green, K.B.E.

THE MINISTRY

Premier, Treasurer and Minister for State Development, Energy and Forests, Hon. R. T. Gray.
Deputy Premier, Attorney-General and Minister for Industrial Relations, Tourism, Racing and Gaming, Hon. G. A. Pearsall.
Environment, Licensing, Construction and Administrative Services, Hon. G. B. Davis.
Small Businesses, Housing, Consumer Affairs, and Inland Fisheries, Hon. B. A. Lyons.
Local Government, Main Roads, Primary Industry, and Water Resources, Hon. I. M. Braid.
Health, Ethnic Affairs, Community Welfare and the Elderly, Hon. T. J. Cleary.
Education, Lands and National Parks, Hon. R. J. Beswick.
Transport, Mines, Police and Emergency Services and Sea Fisheries, Hon. F. R. Groom.

THE LEGISLATURE

Parliament consists of two Houses, a *Legislative Council* of 19 members, elected for six years (3 retiring annually, in rotation, except in every sixth year, when four retire) and a *House of Assembly* of 35 members, elected by proportional representation for four years in five 7-member constituencies, the electors for both Houses being all Tasmanians of 18 years and over who have resided continuously in the State for at least 6 months. Elections for the Assembly are held every four years.

The election of May 1983 resulted in the election of the Liberal Government. The state of the parties in the Legislative Council following the election was Independent 18, Labour 1. The state of parties in the House of Assembly in Sept. 1984 was: Liberals 19, Labour 14, Independent 2.

President of the Legislative Council, Hon. A. J. Broadby.

Speaker of the House of Assembly, Hon. M. H. Bushby.

THE JUDICATURE

The Supreme Court of Tasmania, with civil, criminal ecclesiastical, admiralty and matrimonial jurisdiction, was established by Royal Charter on October 13, 1823.

Local Courts are held before Commissioners who are legal practitioners, Courts of General Sessions, constituted by a chairman who is a Justice of the Peace and at least one other Justice, are established in the municipalities, and Courts of Petty Sessions are constituted by Magistrates sitting alone, or any two or more justices. A single justice may hear and determine certain matters.

Chief Justice, Supreme Court, Hon. Sir Guy Green.

EDUCATION

Government schools are of three main types: primary, secondary and matriculation schools. On July 1, 1983, there were 68,387 scholars enrolled in 257 Government schools. There were also 70 independent schools with an enrolment of 15,940. The University of Tasmania at Hobart, established 1890, had 3,101 full-time students and 2,128 part-time (including external) students in 1983. A College of Advanced Education offering degree and diploma courses was established in 1972. Enrolments in 1982 were 929 full-time students and 1,251 part-time students.

FINANCE

Revenue and expenditure of the Consolidated Revenue Fund and debt of Tasmania at current rates of exchange (June 30) was:—

	1981–82	1982–83
Revenue	\$A683,231,327	\$A764,989,770
Expenditure	717,628,276	772,753,011
Debt	1,071,605,763	1,114,396,841

Banking.—The weekly average of depositors' balances at trading banks in April 1984 was \$A629,179,000; the savings bank balances at the end of April 1984, were \$A1,071,117,000.

PRODUCTION AND INDUSTRY

Gross value of agricultural production in 1982–83 was \$A339m. The estimated value added for agricultural enterprises in 1980–81 was \$A107·3m. Total value added in manufacturing in 1981–82 was \$A713·4m.; value added in mining was \$A170m. in 1981–82.

Agriculture and Livestock.—The principal crops are apples, potatoes, green peas, oil poppies, hops, barley, beans and onions.

The livestock included (March 31, 1983) 562,000 cattle, 4,451,000 sheep and 51,000 pigs. The wool production (1982–83) was 19,804 tonnes.

Electrical Energy.—Tasmania, the smallest Australian state, ranks fourth as a producer of electrical energy—most of it derived from water power, with a total installed generator capacity of 1,862,144 kW. By reason of its low-cost electrical energy, Tasmania has large plants producing ferro-manganese and newsprint. A large aluminium plant is situated at Bell Bay and Tasmania is the source of the bulk of Australian requirements of zinc and fine papers. The Hydro-Electric Commission has completed a network of 27 stations including a dual machine oil fired station at Bell Bay. Work is continuing on three hydro-electric developments in the remote western region of the State, which will increase the installed generator capacity to 2·17 million kW.

Forestry.—The quantity of timber (excluding firewood) of various species cut in 1982–83 was 3,853,100 cubic metres, including 3,182,000 cubic metres for woodchip and wood-pulp.

Minerals.—The chief ores mined are those containing copper, tin, iron, silver, zinc and lead.

Manufactures.—The chief manufactures for export are: refined metals, pelletized iron ore, preserved fruit and vegetables, butter, cheese, textiles, paper, confectionery, wood chips and sawn timber. In 1982–83, 528 manufacturing establishments employed 24,088 persons, including working proprietors. Salaries and wages paid totalled \$A387·7m.

OVERSEAS TRADE

	1982–83
Imports	\$A179,814,000
Exports	773,044,000

The principal overseas exports are ores and concentrates, refined metals, woodchips, greasy wool, meat, abalone, fresh fruit, cheese and hides and skins.

COMMUNICATIONS

Road and Rail.—Tasmania is served by a 1,067 mm gauge Federal Government railway system of 864 route kms. An additional 134 route kms of the same gauge is privately operated. Regular passenger services no longer operate. At June 30, 1983 there were 22,211 kilometres of road normally open to traffic. Of this total 8,441 kilometres were sealed. Motor vehicles on the register at Dec. 31, 1983 were: cars and station wagons, 193,300; commercial vehicles, 53,400 and motor cycles, 6,100.

Aviation.—Regular services operate between Tasmania and the other Australian States. During 1982 more than 982,000 passengers were carried on these services. The main cities and town in the State are served by regular internal services.

TOWNS

CAPITAL, ΨHOBART, founded 1804. Population (June 30, 1981), 128,603.

Other towns (with population at June 30, 1981) are ΨLaunceston (64,555), ΨDevonport (21,424), Burnie-Somerset (20,368), Ulverstone (9,413), New Norfolk (6,243) and Kingston-Blackmans Bay (8,556).

VICTORIA

The State of Victoria comprises the south-east corner of Australia, at the part where its mainland territory projects farthest into the southern latitudes; it lies between 34°–39° S. latitude and 141°–150° E. longitude. Its extreme length from east to west is about 493 miles, its greatest breadth is about 290 miles, and its extent of coast-line is about 1,043 geographical miles, including the length around Port Phillip Bay, Western Port and Corner Inlet, the entire area being 87,876 square miles.

Population.—The estimated resident population at June 30, 1984 was 4,075,900.

Births, deaths and marriages were:

	1982	1983
Births	59,983	60,123
Deaths	30,611	29,320
Marriages	28,851	28,974

Preliminary annual rate per 1,000 of estimated resident population in 1983: Births, 14·9; Deaths, 7·26; Marriages, 7·18. Deaths under 1 year per 1,000 live births, 9·3.

Religions

At the Census in 1981, members of the Catholic Church numbered 1,064,514, Church of England 777,551, Uniting (union of Presbyterian, Congregationalist and Methodist) 213,257, Presbyterian 175,291, Orthodox 171,131, Methodist 90,444 and Baptist 40,790. The number of persons who did not state their religion was 451,550.

PHYSIOGRAPHY

The *Australian Alps* and the *Great Dividing Range* pass through the centre of the State, and divide it into a northern and southern watershed, the latter sloping down to the ocean and containing, especially in the south-east, well-wooded valleys. The length of the Murray River, which forms part of the northern boundary of Victoria, is about 1,196 miles along the Victorian bank. Melbourne, the capital city, stands upon the Yarra-Yarra, which rises in the southern slopes of the Dividing Range.

Climate.—The climate of Victoria is characterized by warm to hot summers and rather cold winters. The highest temperature ever recorded in the State is 50·8°C, the lowest being −12·8°C. Normally, rainfalls at most places throughout the year, with a maximum in winter or spring. In Melbourne, the mean annual temperature is 14·8°C.

GOVERNMENT

Victoria was originally known as the Port Phillip District of New South Wales and was created a separate colony in 1851, with a partially elective legislature. In 1855 Responsible Government was conferred. The executive authority is vested in a Governor, appointed by the Crown, aided by an Executive Council of Ministers.

Governor of the State of Victoria, His Excellency Rear Adm. Sir Brian Stewart Murray, K.C.M.G., A.O., *assumed office* March 1, 1982.

Lieutenant-Governor, Hon. Sir John McIntosh Young, K.C.M.G. (1974).

THE MINISTRY

Premier, Hon. J. Cain.

Deputy Premier, and Minister of Industry, Technology and Resources, Hon. R. C. Fordham.

Agriculture and Rural Affairs, Planning and Environment, Hon. E. Walker.

Health, Hon. D. R. White.

Education, Hon. I. R. Cathie.

Employment and Industrial Affairs, Hon. S. M. Crabb.

Consumer Affairs, and Ethnic Affairs, Hon. P. C. Spyker.

Community Services, Hon. C. J. Hogg.

Treasurer, Hon. R. A. Jolly.

Attorney-General, Hon. J. H. Kennan.

Conservation, Forests and Lands, Hon. J. E. Kirner.

Arts, and Police and Emergency Services, Hon. C. R. T. Mathews.

Water Resources, and Property and Services, Hon. A. McCutcheon.

Transport, Hon. T. W. Roper.

Local Government, Hon. J. L. Simmonds.

Consumer Affairs and Ethnic Affairs, Hon. P. C. Spyker.

Sport and Recreation, Hon. N. B. Trezise.

Public Works, Hon. R. W. Walsh.

Housing, Hon. F. N. Wilkes.

Parliamentary Secretary of the Cabinet, Dr. K. A. Coghill.

AGENT-GENERAL IN LONDON

Agent-General for Victoria, Hon. I. M. Haig, Victoria House, Melbourne Place, Strand, WC2B 4LG.

THE LEGISLATURE

Parliament consists of a *Legislative Council* of 44 members, elected for the 22 Provinces for 8 years, one-half retiring every 4 years; and a *Legislative Assembly* of 88 members, elected for a maximum duration of 4 years. Voting is compulsory.

President of the Legislative Council, Hon.

F. S. Grimwade	$A72,279
Speaker of the Legislative Assembly, Hon. C. T. Edmunds	72,279

THE JUDICATURE

There is a Supreme Court with a Chief Justice and 21 Puisne Judges, a County Court and Magistrates' Courts.

Chief Justice, Supreme Court, Hon. Sir John Young, K.C.M.G.	$A89,698
Chief Judge, County Court, Hon. G. R. D. Waldron	$A79,112
Solicitor-General, H. C. Berkeley, Q.C.	$A79,737

EDUCATION

Primary education is compulsory, secular and free between the ages of 6 and 15. At July 1, 1983, there were 1,634 Government Primary Schools attended by 327,681 pupils, 19 Primary–Secondary Schools with 3,678 pupils, and 288 Secondary Schools (excluding Secondary Technical Schools) with an enrolment of 173,022. There were also 108 Government Secondary Technical Schools with 70,112 pupils and 75 Special Schools with 5,408 pupils. In addition there are technical and further education institutions and Colleges of Advanced Education.

At July 1, 1983, 234,171 pupils attended 659 non-Government schools, 492 of which were Roman Catholic.

There are four State-aided Universities.

FINANCE

Revenue and expenditure from the Consolidated Fund, and the debt of Victoria were:—

	1982–83	1983–84
Revenue	$A7,209,260,502	$A7,780,985,185
Expenditure	7,209,260,502	7,752,858,373
Debt	4,045,327,910	4,204,126,406

Banking, etc.—State Savings Bank deposits at June 30, 1984, amounted to $A5,941,904,000; in addition, deposits in the Commonwealth Savings Bank (in the State of Victoria) amounted to $A2,590,680,000, and in other savings banks $A4,383,747,000.

PRODUCTION AND INDUSTRY

The gross value of primary production (excluding mining and quarrying) in 1983–84 was $A3,407,831,000, crops $A1,660,337,000, livestock $A1,747,494,000. The local value of production of primary industries, excluding mining, was $A3,003,469,000. Wool, wheat, flour, butter, livestock, fruits, milk and cream, meats, poultry and eggs are staple products.

Livestock.—There were on establishments with agricultural activity on 31st March, 1984, 24,633,000 sheep, 3,487,000 cattle, and 404,000 pigs. The quantity of wool produced in 1983–84 was valued at $A381,861,000.

Minerals.—Minerals raised include oil and natural gas, brown coal, limestone, clays and stone for construction material. Production of brown coal in 1983–84 amounted to 33,057,000 tonnes.

Crude Oil and Natural Gas.—In 1965 natural gas was first discovered in commercial quantities in the offshore waters of the Gippsland Basin in eastern Victoria and in 1966–67, three more valuable oilfields were located in the same general area. These fields are still the largest yet found in Australia. Following the development of the four fields, commercial gas and crude oil came on stream in October, 1969. Production from the Gippsland fields during the financial year 1983–84 was: stabilized crude oil, 24,050,898 cubic metres; treated natural gas, 5,796,861,900 cubic metres; commercial propane, 1,629,415 cubic metres, and commercial ethane, 174,717,465 cubic metres.

Secondary Industry.—In 1982–83 there were 12,145 manufacturing establishments in which 263,503 males and 107,200 females were employed. Value added in the course of manufacture by all manufacturing establishments with four or more persons employed was $A10,649 million.

OVERSEAS TRADE

The export trade (excluding inter-state trade) consists largely of agricultural and mining products, machinery and transport equipment. The principal overseas imports of the State are apparel and textiles, electrical and other machines and machinery, motor vehicles and tractors, metals and metal manufactures, iron and steel, chemicals, petroleum and petroleum products, artificial resins and plastic materials.

	1983–84
Imports	$A8,186,719,000
Exports	5,132,526,000

TRANSPORT

Victoria State Railways—At June 30, 1985, there were 5,815 kms of railway open for traffic. The revenue and expenditure for the year ended June 30, 1983, were $A248,129,000 and $A680,409,404 respectively. Total distance travelled was 30,165,571 kms and passenger journeys numbered 84,323,000. Goods and livestock carried amounted to 8,569,628 tonnes.

Shipping.—During the year ended June 30, 1983, 1,705 overseas vessels with dead-weight tonnage of 34,719,930 arrived at Victorian ports and 1,637 overseas vessels with dead-weight tonnage of 33,931,467 departed.

Motor Vehicle Registration.—The number of vehicles on the register at June 30, 1984, was: cars and stationwagons, 1,859,700; utilities and panel vans, 193,800; trucks and omnibuses, 206,900, and motor cycles, 81,700.

TOWNS

ΨMELBOURNE, the capital city, had a resident population at June 30, 1983, estimated at 2,888,400. Other urban centres are ΨGeelong, 145,220; Ballarat, 76,190; Bendigo, 62,890; Shepparton-Mooroopna, 38,210; ΨWarrnambool, 22,930; Wodonga, 22,370.

WESTERN AUSTRALIA

Includes all that portion of the continent west of 129° E. long., the most westerly point being in 113° 9′ E. long. and from 13° 44′ to 35° 8′ S. lat. Its extreme length is 1,480 miles, and 1,000 miles from east to west; total area 975,920 sq. miles.

POPULATION.—At June 1984, the estimated resident population was 1,382,468.

Births, deaths and marriages were:

	1982	1983
Births	22,236	23,046
Deaths	8,187	8,359
Marriages	10,455	10,519

Religions

Census of 1981—Church of England 375,848, Roman Catholics 316,337, Methodists 51,225, Uniting Church 32,592, and Presbyterians 32,033.

PHYSIOGRAPHY

Large areas of the State, for some hundreds of miles inland, are hilly and even mountainous, although the altitude, so far as ascertained, rises nowhere above that of Mount Meharry (4,097 ft.) in the north-west division or that of Bluff Knoll (3,640 ft.) in the Stirling Range in the south-west. The coastal regions are undulating, with an interior slope to the unsettled central portion of Australia. The Darling and Hamersley ranges of the west have a seaward slope to the Indian Ocean, into which flow many streams, notably the Preston, Collie, Murray, Swan, Murchison, Gascoyne, Ashburton, Fortescue and De Grey. In the north the Fitzroy flows from the King Leopold ranges into the Indian Ocean, and the Drysdale and Ord into the Timor Sea. The greater portion of the State may be described as an immense tableland, with an average elevation of 1,000 to 1,500 ft. above sea-level, the surface of which varies from stretches of clay soils to the sand dunes of the far interior. The climate is one of the most temperate in the world. Of the total area two-thirds is suitable for pastoral purposes.

GOVERNMENT

Western Australia was first settled by the British in 1829, and in 1870 it was granted a partially elective legislature. In 1890 Responsible Government was granted, and the Administration vested in a Governor, a Legislative Council, and a Legislative Assembly. The present consititution rests upon the Constitution Act, 1889, the Constitution Acts Amendment Act, 1899, and amending Acts. The Executive is vested in a Governor appointed by the Crown and aided by a Council of responsible Ministers.

The Legislative Assembly (elected February, 1983) is composed of Australian Labour Party 32, Liberal Party 22, National Party 2, Independent, 1.

Governor of Western Australia, His Excellency Prof. Gordon Reid.

Lieut.-Governor and Administrator, Hon. Sir Francis Burt, K.C.M.G.

THE MINISTRY

Premier and Cabinet Treasurer, Minister Co-ordinating Economic and Social Development, and for Women's Interests, Hon. B. T. Burke, M.L.A. $A95,830

Deputy Premier, Minister for Industrial Development, Small Business, Technology, Communications, and Defence Liaison, Hon. M. J. Bryce, M.L.A. $A85,220

Minister for Tourism, Racing and Gaming, and Leader of the Government in the Legislative Council, Hon. D. K. Dans, M.L.C. $A82,220

Attorney-General, Minister for Budget Management and Prisons, Hon. J. M. Berinson, M.L.C.

Water Resources, Parliamentary and Electoral Reform, and Leader of the House, Hon. A. R. Tonkin, M.L.A.

Police and Emergency Services, and Local Government, Hon. J. P. Carr, M.L.A.

Environment, Forests, Multi-cultural and Ethnic Affairs, and the Arts, Hon. R. Davies, M.L.A.

Agriculture, Fisheries, and Wildlife, Hon. H. D. Evans, M.L.A.

Education, and Planning, Hon. R. J. Pearce, M.L.A.

Health, Hon. B. J. Hodge, M.L.A.

Works, and Lands and Surveys, Hon. K. F. McIver, M.L.A.

Minerals and Energy, and Minister assisting the Minister co-ordinating Economic and Social Development, Hon. D. C. Parker, M.L.A.

Transport, Regional Development and the North West, Hon. J. F. Grill, M.L.A.

Housing, Youth Affairs, the Aged, Community Services, Sport and Recreation and Minister with special responsibility for Aboriginal Affairs, Hon. K. J. Wilson, M.L.A.

Employment and Training, Industrial Relations and Consumer Affairs, Hon. P. M. Dowding, M.L.C.

Ministers, each $A76,546–$A91,819, according to location of electorate.

Agent-General in London, R. Douglas, Western Australia House, 115 Strand, W.C.2.

The Legislature

Parliament consists of a *Legislative Council* and a *Legislative Assembly*, elected by adult suffrage subject to qualifications of residence and registration. The qualifying age for electors for both the Legislative Council and Legislative Assembly is 18 years. There are 34 members in the Legislative Council, two from each Province, for a period of 6 years, one member from each Province retiring triennially. The Legislative Assembly is composed of 57 members, who are elected for a term of 3 years.

President of the Legislative Council, Hon.
C. E. Griffiths $A71,135

Speaker of the Legislative Assembly, Hon.
J. J. Harman 70,280

The Judicature

Chief Justice, Hon. Sir Francis Burt, K.C.M.G. (+ allce. $A5,000) $A99,859

Senior Puisne Judge, Hon. A. R. A. Wallace (+ allce. $A4,500) 91,869

Puisne Judges, Hons. P. F. Brinsden; C. H. Smith; G. A. Kennedy; H. W. Olney; W. P. Pidgeon; B. W. Rowland (+ allce. $A4,000) .... each 89,342

Education

In 1984 there were 715 government and 221 non-government primary and secondary schools with 209,048 and 55,761 pupils respectively. The total recurrent and capital expenditure expended on education (by State authorities) during the year ended June 30, 1983, was $A768,300,000, including grants totalling $A76,900,000 to the University of Western Australia (9,810 enrolments in 1984), and to

Murdoch University (3,551 enrolments in 1984). These amounts included Commonwealth monies.

Production and Industry

The gross value of agricultural production in 1983–84 was: crops $A1,107,538,000; livestock slaughterings, etc., $A347,325,000; livestock products $A485,980,000; fishing and gross value of fisheries was $A141,425,000.

Crops and Livestock.—The production of wheat for grain in 1983–84 was 4,315,543 tonnes. On March 31, 1984, the livestock included 1,729,533 cattle, 29,518,296 sheep, and 300,455 pigs. Wool production in 1983–84 was 141,359 tonnes in the grease.

Manufacturing Industries.—There were 3,951 manufacturing establishments operating in the State at June 30, 1983. The total number of persons employed (including working proprietors) by these establishments at the end of June, 1983 was 67,877.

Forestry.—The forests contain some of the finest hardwoods in the world. The total quantity of sawn timber produced during 1982–83 was 257,376 cubic metres.

Minerals.—The State has large deposits of a wide range of minerals, many of which are being mined or are under development for production. The ex-mine value of all minerals produced during 1982–83 was $A2,553,430,000.

Communications.—On June 30, 1984, there were 5,623 kms. of State government railway open for general and passenger traffic; and 731 kms. (Kalgoorlie-W.A. border) of the Trans-Australian railway. In the year ended June 30, 1983, 2,445 vessels entered Western Australian ports direct from, and 2,430 were cleared direct to overseas. The number of registered motor vehicles at June 30, 1984, was 830,019 (592,495 motor cars and station wagons, 201,754 light and heavy commercials, and 35,770 motor cycles and motor scooters).

Finance

	1982–83	1983–84
	$A	$A
Revenue	2,324,874,369	2,660,758,263
Expenditure	2,339,070,164	2,659,761,394
Public Debt (June 30)	1,547,497,840	1,614,779,554

Overseas Trade

	1983–84
Imports	$A1,935,552,364
Exports	4,949,762,589

Principal overseas exports in 1983–84 included iron ore and concentrates, wheat, wool, live sheep and lambs, petroleum and petroleum, products, beef and veal, gold bullion, rock lobster tails.

Towns

Capital.—ΨPerth. Estimated resident population (estimate for June 30, 1984) of Perth Statistical Division, including the port of Fremantle, 982,570.

Perth stands on the right bank of the Swan River estuary, 12 miles from Fremantle.

New Zealand
AREA AND POPULATION

Islands	Area (English) Sq. Miles	Population Census Mar. 24, 1981†	Population Estimated Mar. 31, 1984
(a) *Exclusive of Island Territory:*			
North Island	44,281	2,322,989	2,414,400
South Island	58,093	852,748	851,100
Stewart Island	670	600*	500*
Chatham Islands	372	751*	780*
Minor Islands:			
Inhabited—			
Kermadec Islands	13	5*	5**
Campbell Island	44	10*	10**
Uninhabited—			
Three Kings	3	..	..
Snares	1	..	..
Solander	½	..	..
Antipodes	24	..	..
Bounty	⅓	..	..
Auckland	234	..	..
Total exclusive of Island Territory	103,736	3,175,737	3,265,500
(b) *Island Territory:*			
Tokelau Islands	..	1,572‖	1,595§
(c) Niue island¶‡	..	3,226§	3,002**
Cook Islands¶††	..	18,000‡	17,400**
Ross Dependency	175,000	..	..

* Included in North Island and South Island totals.
† Excluding members of the Armed Forces overseas—979 in 1981.
¶ The Cook Islands have had complete internal self-government since Aug. 4, 1965, as has Niue since Oct. 19, 1974, but Cook Islanders and Niueans remain New Zealand citizens.
‖ Nov. 2, 1981. § Oct. 1, 1983. ‡ Dec. 31, 1980. ** March 31, 1983. †† Sept. 30, 1980.
Maori Population included in the totals for New Zealand proper—1976 Census, 257,770; 1981 Census, 279,252; 1983 estimate, 286,500.

Vital Statistics

Year	Births	Deaths	Natural Increase	Deaths of Infants under one year	Infant Mortality per 1,000 live births	Marriages
1979	52,279	25,340	26,939	653	12·49	22,326
1980	50,542	26,676	23,866	650	12·86	22,981
1981	50,794	25,150	25,644	592	11·65	23,660
1982	49,938	25,532	24,406	587	11·75	25,537
1983	50,474	25,991	24,483	633	12·54	24,678
1984	51,636	25,378	26,258	597	11·56	25,272

Inter-Censal Increases

Year	Results of Census Males	Results of Census Females	Results of Census Total	Numerical Increase	Net Inflow or Outflow from Total Migration
1966	1,343,743	1,333,176	2,676,919	261,935	+ 12,950
1971	1,430,856	1,431,775	2,862,631	185,712	+ 8,481
1976	1,562,042	1,567,341	3,129,383	266,752	+ 6,567
1981	1,578,927	1,596,810	3,175,737	46,354	− 15,328

Excluding 1,936 members of the Armed Forces overseas at the time of the 1966 census, 1,482 at the 1971 census, 1,333 at the 1976 census and 979 at the 1981 census.

Races and Religions

Races	1976	1981	Religions	1976	1981
				Per cent	Per cent
Europeans	2,672,919	2,696,568	Church of England	29·2	25·7
Maoris	269,954	279,084	Presbyterians	18·1	16·7
Chinese	14,236	18,480	Roman Catholics	15·3	14·3
Polynesians (other than			Methodists	5·5	4·7
N.Z. Maoris)	60,971	88,827	Baptists	1·6	1·6
Other races	85,185	60,348			

PHYSIOGRAPHY

New Zealand consists of a number of islands of varying size in the South Pacific Ocean, and has also administrative responsibility for a large tract in the Antarctic Ocean. The two larger and most important islands, the North and South Islands of New Zealand, are separated by only a relatively narrow strait. The remaining islands are very much smaller and, in general, are widely dispersed over a considerable expanse of ocean. The boundaries, inclusive of the most outlying islands and dependencies, range from 33° to 53° South latitude, and from 162° East longitude to 173° West longitude.

Geographical Features.—The two principal islands have a total length of 1,040 miles, and a combined area of 102,344 square miles. A large proportion of the surface is mountainous in character. The principal range is that of the Southern Alps, extending over the entire length of the South Island and having its culminating point in Mount Cook (12,349 ft.). The North Island mountains include several volcanoes, two of which are active, others being dormant or extinct. Mt. Ruapehu (9,175 ft.) and Mt. Ngauruhoe (7,515 ft.) are the most important. Of the numerous glaciers in the South Island, the Tasman (18 miles long by 1¼ wide), the Franz Josef and the Fox are the best known. The North Island is noted for its hot springs and geysers. For the most part the rivers are too short and rapid for use in navigation. The more important include the Waikato (270 miles in length); Wanganui (180), and Clutha (210). Lakes (Taupo, 234

sq. miles in area; Wakatipu, 113; and Te Anau, 133) are abundant, many of them of great beauty.

Climate.—New Zealand has a moist-temperate marine climate, but with abundant sunshine. A very important feature is the small annual range of temperature which permits of some growth of vegetation, including pasture, all the year round. Very little snow falls on the low levels even in the South Island. The mean temperature ranges from 15° C. in the North to about 9° C. in the South. Rainfall over the more settled areas in the North Island ranges from 35 to 70 inches and in the South Island from 25 to 45 inches. The total range is from approximately 13 to over 250 inches. The number of rainy days is generally in the neighbourhood of 160 to 180 in the North Island and between 110 and 140 in the South, except in the southern portion of the west coast. The amount of sunshine is generally over 2,000 hours per annum and ranges between 1,600 to 2,500 hours.

GOVERNMENT

The discoverers and first colonists of New Zealand were Polynesian people, ancestors of the Maoris of today. Whether there was a single colonization, several, or many, is not known. By the 13th or 14th century early exploration was over and there were well established Maori settlements.

The first European to discover New Zealand was a Dutch navigator, Abel Tasman, who sighted the coast on December 13, 1642 but did not land. It was the British explorer James Cook who circumnavigated New Zealand and landed in 1769. Traders, whalers and sealers made up the majority of Europeans in New Zealand during the 18th century and until the late 1830s, when the proportion of permanent European settlers became significant.

Largely as a result of increased British emigration, the country was annexed by the British Government in 1840. The British Governor, William Hobson, RN, proclaimed sovereignty over the North Island by virtue of the Treaty of Waitangi, signed by him and many Maori chiefs, and over the South Island and Stewart Island by right of discovery.

On May 3, 1841, New Zealand was, by letters patent, created a separate colony distinct from New South Wales. Organized colonization on a large scale commenced in 1840 with the New Zealand company's settlement at Wellington. On Sept. 26, 1907, the designation was changed to *The Dominion of New Zealand*. The Constitution rests upon the Imperial Act of 1852, and on the New Zealand Constitution (Amendment) Act of Dec. 10, 1947. The Statute of Westminster was formally adopted by New Zealand in 1947. The executive authority is entrusted to a Governor-General appointed by the Crown and aided by an Executive Council, within a Legislature consisting of one chamber, the House of Representatives.

FLAG: Blue ground, with Union Jack in top left quarter, four five-pointed red stars with white borders on the fly. On June 20, 1968, a naval ensign bearing the Southern Cross was adopted, replacing the British white ensign.

Governor-General and Staff

Governor-General and Commander-in-Chief of New Zealand, His Excellency Sir Paul Alfred Reeves, *apptd* 1985.

Official Secretary, J. Brown.

THE EXECUTIVE COUNCIL

His Excellency the GOVERNOR-GENERAL

Prime Minister; Minister of Foreign Affairs, and in charge of Security Intelligence Service, Hon. David Lange.

Deputy P.M.; Leader of the House; Minister of Justice; Attorney-General, Hon. Geoffrey Palmer.

Overseas Trade and Marketing; Tourism, Recreation, Publicity and Sport, Hon. Michael Moore.

Finance; Inland Revenue, Hon. Roger Douglas.

Transport; Pacific Island Affairs, Hon. Richard Prebble.

Maori Affairs; Lands and Forests; Valuation, Hon. Koro Wetere.

Trade and Industry, Hon. David Caygill.

Education; Environment, Hon. Russell Marshall.

Minister of State; Minister of Defence, Hon. Frank O'Flynn.

Health; Local Government, Hon. Michael Bassett.

Police; Social Welfare; Women's Rights, Hon. Ann Hercus.

Energy; Science and Technology; Audit Department; Statistics, Hon. B. Tizard.

Agriculture and Fisheries; Rural Bank and Finance Corporation, Hon. Colin Moyle.

Labour; State Services, Hon. S. Rodger.

Broadcasting; Postmaster-General, Hon. Jonathan Hunt.

Works and Development, Hon. Fraser Colman.

Regional Development; Employment; Immigration, Hon. Kerry Burke.

Customs; Consumer Affairs, Hon. Margaret Shields.

Internal Affairs; Civil Defence; Arts, Hon. Peter Tapsell.

Housing, Hon. P. Goff.

The Prime Minister receives $79,717 per annum with an allowance of $14,000 for expenses of his office and the Ministerial residence. The salary of each Minister holding a portfolio is $55,115 with expense allowance of $5,750 and that of each Minister without portfolio $44,572, with $4,500 expense allowance.

NEW ZEALAND HIGH COMMISSION

New Zealand House, Haymarket, SW1Y 4TQ
[01-930 8422]

High Commissioner, His Excellency Bryce Harland (1985).

Acting High Commissioner, B. M. Brown.

Deputy High Commissioner, N. D. Walter.

Minister (Commercial), R. J. Turnbull.

Head, Defence Liaison Staff, Air Cdre. P. Neville, O.B.E., R.N.Z.A.F.

BRITISH HIGH COMMISSION

Reserve Bank of New Zealand Building,
2 The Terrace (P.O. Box 1812), Wellington, 1

High Commissioner, His Excellency Terence Daniel O'Leary, C.M.G., *apptd,* 1984.

Deputy High Commissioner, Head of Chancery and Counsellor (Political and Economic), J. H. Fawcett.

Defence Adviser, Capt. R. D. Ferguson, R.N.

1st Secretaries, R. Crawshaw (*Agriculture and Food*); S. Prince (*Commercial*); P. Cooper (*Chancery, Information*).

2nd Secretary, R. H. House (*Consular and Administration*).

Attaché, M. R. Rogers (*Consular*).

British Council Representative, D. R. Howell, O.B.E.

BRITISH CHAMBER OF COMMERCE FOR AUSTRALIA AND NEW ZEALAND, P.O. Box 141, Manuka, A.C.T. 2603, Australia; U.K. OFFICE, Suite 615, 6th Floor The Linen Hall, 162/8 Regent Street, W1R 5TB.

THE LEGISLATURE

Parliament consists of a House of Representatives consisting of 95 members elected for 3 years. There are four Maori electorates. Women have been entitled to vote since 1893, and to be elected Members of the House of Representatives since the passing of the Women's Parliamentary Rights Act, 1919. Following the General Election of July 14, 1984, the state of the parties in Parliament was Labour 56, National Party 37 and Social Credit 2.

Members of the House receive $NZ32,271 *per annum,* with an allowance of $NZ2,500 *per annum* for expenses, plus an electorate allowance. The Leader of the Opposition receives $NZ55,115 *per annum* and $NZ5,750 *per annum* for expenses, plus house and travelling allowances.

Speaker of the House of Representatives,
Dr. G. A. Wall (*plus expense allowance and residential quarters in Parliament House*) $NZ51,161

THE JUDICATURE

The judicial system comprises a High Court and a Court of Appeal; also District Courts having both civil and criminal jurisdiction.

Chief Justice, Rt. Hon. Sir Ronald Davison, G.B.E., C.M.G. $NZ87,623

Court of Appeal, Rt. Hon. Sir Arthur Owen Woodhouse, K.B.E., D.S.C. (*President*) 83,863

Judges, Rt. Hons. Sir Robin Cooke; I. L. Richardson; D. W. McMullin; E. J. Somers 81,043

High Court Puisne Judges, Hons. J. P. Quilliam; N. F. Chilwell; M. E. Casey; J. A. Ongley; J. F. Jeffries; R. I. Barker; M. H. Vautier; J. B. Sinclair; G. E. Bisson; A. D. Holland; T. M. Thorp; L. M. Greig; J. P. Cook, O.B.E., E.D.; E. M. Prichard; R. C. Savage; M. Hardie-Boys; J. H. Wallace; J. T. Eichelbaum; P. G. Hillyer; R. G. Gallen; Mr. Tompkins; Mr. Henry; Mr. Heron; Mr. O'Regan; Mr. Williamson ....

High Court Administrative Divn., Rt. Hon. Sir Ronald Davison (*Chief Justice*); Hons. D. W. McMullin; N. F. Chilwell; M. E. Casey; J. F. Jeffries; G. E. Bisson.

Judge, Court of Arbitration, Judge J. R. P. Horn ....

POLICE

On March 31, 1984 the strength of the New Zealand Police Force was 5,088 of all ranks, equivalent to 1 for every 644 of the population. Total police expenditure for the year 1983–84 was $NZ191,224,000.

DEFENCE

A unified Ministry of Defence which retained the three single services was set up in 1964. The Minister of Defence is responsible for national defence, and, with the other members of the Defence Council, commands and administers the three services:

The *Royal New Zealand Navy* consists of 2,745 officers and ratings as at March 31, 1984, as well as the Volunteer Reserve in four divisions. The strength is four frigates, one survey ship and one research vessel, as well as patrol and inshore survey craft.

The *New Zealand Army* consists of the Regular Force, the Territorial Force and the Army Reserve. The strength of the Regular Force at March 31, 1984 was 5,563, and of the Territorial Force and Army Reserve, 8,042. The Army is structured to provide a Regular Force battalion group which is available for rapid deployment on military operations or civil assistance tasks, as well as a framework of integrated Regular Force/Territorial Force Units as a basis for expansion when required. One infantry battalion is based in Singapore.

The *Royal New Zealand Air Force* had a Regular Force strength of 4,296 at March 31, 1984, with 1,033 Territorial and Reserve Forces. Operational units include fighter ground attack, maritime, medium and short-range transport, and helicopter squadrons, and flying training units. A helicopter support unit is based in Singapore, and there is a helicopter detachment serving with the Multinational Force and Observers in the Sinai.

FINANCE

Into the Consolidated Account (New Zealand's main public account) are paid the proceeds of income tax, sales tax, customs and excise duties and other taxes, also interest, profits from trading undertakings, and departmental receipts (departmental expenditure is included gross). Revenue from taxation is also paid into the National Roads Fund principally from a tax on motor spirits and registration and licence fees for motor vehicles.

Revenue and expenditure for year ended March 31 ($NZ'000):

	1984	1985
Revenue	14,172,929	16,162,371
Expenditure	14,172,929*	16,162,371*

Revenue from taxation was ($NZ'000):

	1984	1985
Total	10,431,205	11,913,628
Consolidated Account	10,188,920	11,579,485
National Roads Fund	242,285	334,143

*Includes ($NZ,000):

	1984	1985
Education	1,690,488	1,746,868
Social Welfare	4,005,658	4,386,995
Health	1,807,891	1,914,293
Development of Industry	2,134,762	1,984,750
Defence	672,978	756,408
Debt services	2,229,180	2,781,411
Law and order	328,440	358,297

DEBT

The gross *Public Debt* amounted on March 31, 1984, to $NZ21,878,665,000 of which $NZ4,254,699,000 was domiciled in Europe, $NZ2,432,533,000 in U.S.A. and $NZ1,476,558,000 in Japan; $NZ4,680,000 represented World Bank loans.

BANKING

There are four trading banks, two of which are predominantly New Zealand banks. At Dec. 24, 1984, assets of all trading banks in respect of New Zealand business amounted to $NZ11,202,300,000, liabilities, $NZ9,987,600,000; New Zealand's official overseas reserves at Dec. 1984, amounted to $NZ3,698,400,000. Trading banks' advances in 1984 averaged $NZ6,901,800,000 weekly, and deposits with the trading banks averaged $NZ9,047,500

Post-office, trustee and private savings banks had, at March 31, 1984, over 7,580,000 accounts having $NZ6,182,600,000 to their credit.

The Reserve Bank of New Zealand notes are the legal tender. Value of notes in circulation on March 31, 1984 amounted to $NZ604,242,000.

EDUCATION

Schools are free and attendance is compulsory between the ages of 6 and 15. There are opportunities for apt pupils to proceed to university. At July 1984 there were 454,555 pupils attending public primary schools, and 10,798 pupils attending registered private primary schools. The secondary education of boys and girls in the cities and large towns is carried on in 315 state secondary schools, and 47 private secondary schools. The total number of pupils receiving full-time secondary education in July 1983 was 230,748 and in addition there were 144,984 students attending technical classes including 29,899 receiving part-time tuition from the Technical Correspondence School. Almost all the students attending technical classes are part-time. There are six universities; the Lincoln university college of agriculture is associated with the University of Canterbury. The university system is co-ordinated by the University Grants Committee. The Universities had a total of 58,242 students in 1984.

The total expenditure on education out of public funds in 1983–84 is estimated at $NZ1,690,488,000.

PRODUCTION AND INDUSTRY

Gross Agricultural Production (Gross Output)

	Year ended March	
	1982–83*	1983–84*
	$NZ(million)	
Sheep	499	512
Wool	755	933
Cattle	717	724
Pigs	86	89
Dairy products	1,183	1,193
Crops and seeds	267	280
Fruit, nuts, oilseeds	213	224
Vegetables	225	278
Poultry products	146	152
Agricultural services	293	319
Other horticulture	145	149
Other products n.e.c.	83	96
Value of change in livestock	−81	201
Sales of live animals	558	775
Gross Output	5,092	5,923

*Provisional

Agricultural and Pastoral Production

	1983	1984
*Wheat, metric tons	..	314,600
*Wool, metric tons	371,000	n/a
†Butter, metric tons	254,040	291,900
†Cheese, metric tons	114,390	109,260
‡Stock Slaughtered—		
Lambs, No.	35,995,000	34,711,000
Sheep, No.	9,234,000	8,895,000
Cattle, No.	2,156,000	1,771,000
Calves, No.	962,000	826,000
Pigs, No.	720,000	768,000

* Year ended June 30.
† Year ended May 31.
‡ Year ended Sept. 30. Provisional.

Forestry.—The output of sawn timber for 1984 was 2,096,000 cubic metres, of which 1,959,000 cubic metres represented exotic varieties, mainly radiata pine.

Livestock.—Livestock on farms at June 30, 1984, included 3,246,000 dairy cattle (of which 2,165,000 were dairy cows in milk during season), 4,531,000 beef cattle (of which 1,440,000 were beef breeding cows), and 436,000 pigs. Sheep numbered 69,739,000.

Minerals.—Non-metallic minerals such as coal, clay, limestone and dolomite are both economically and industrially more important than metallic ones. Coal output in 1983 was 2,473,531 tonnes. Of the metals, the most important is ironsand, which is mined for export. In 1983, 2,486,010 tonnes of concentrate were exported. Natural gas deposits in Taranaki are being used for electricity generation and as a premium fuel, piped to an increasing number of North Island centres. Gas and oil exploration continue, and expenditure on exploration for other minerals reached $NZ7,020,000 in 1983.

TRADE

	1982–83	1983–84
Imports (v.f.d.) ..	$NZ6,928,200,000	$NZ8,197,900,000
Exports (f.o.b.) ..	7,935,400,000	8,623,900,000

Trade with U.K.

	1983	1984
Imports from U.K..	$NZ637,800,000	$NZ725,100,000
Exports to U.K. ...	990,100,000	886,800,000

New Zealand produce exported to the U.K. in the 12 months ending June, 1983, included butter, valued at $NZ316,600,000; beef ($NZ2,500,000); wool ($NZ123,600,000); lamb ($NZ228,900,000).

COMMUNICATIONS

Railways.—The national railway system is owned and operated by the New Zealand Railways Corporation. In March, 1984, there were 4,273 kilometres of Government railway in operation.

	1983–84
Passengers carried	14,533,000
Goods railed (tonnes)	10,629,000
Total revenue	$NZ642,362,000
Total expenditure	$NZ618,455,000

Motor Vehicles.—In the year ended June 30, 1984 there were 2,437,077 licensed motor vehicles. These included 1,437,077 cars and 152,609 motor and power cycles. This gives a ratio of 2·2 persons to each passenger car.

Shipping.—During 1984 the vessels entered from overseas ports numbered 3,191 (net tonnage 13,775,000) and those cleared for overseas 3,171 (net tonnage 13,675,000).

Civil Aviation.—Figures are for scheduled services in the year to end Dec. 1984 (provisional):

	Domestic Flights	International Flights
Kilometres flown	34,860	—
Passengers carried ..	2,946	1,830
Freight carried (tonnes)	45,400	87,367
Mail carried (tonnes)	—	3,468

CAPITAL.—ΨWellington, in the North Island (estimated population March 31, 1984, Wellington statistical division, 342,400).

Other large centres; ΨAuckland, 882,000; ΨChristchurch, 322,700; ΨDunedin, 111,400; Palmerston North, 94,800; Hamilton, 167,700; ΨNapier-Hastings, 115,800.

NATIONAL DAY (Waitangi Day).—Feb. 6.

THE TERRITORIES OF NEW ZEALAND

In addition to North, South, Stewart and Chatham Islands:—

The Three Kings (discovered by Tasman on the Feast of the Epiphany), in 34° 9′ S. lat. and 172° 8′ 8″ E. long. (uninhabited). *Auckland Islands*, about 290 miles south of Bluff Harbour, in 50° 32′ S. lat. and 166° 13′ E. long. *Antipodes Group*, 40° 41′ 15″ S. lat. and 178° 43′ E. long. *Bounty Islands*, 47° 4′ 43″ S. lat., 170° 0′ 30″ E. long. *Snares Islands and Solander*. All these islands are uninhabited.

The Kermadec Group (population normally 9 or 10) between 29° 10′ to 31° 30′ S. lat., and 177° 45′ to 179° W. long., includes Raoul or Sunday, Macaulay, Curtis Islands, L'Esperance, and some islets. All the inhabitants are government employees at a meteorological station. *Campbell Island* (used as a weather station).

TOKELAU (OR UNION ISLANDS)

A group of atolls (Fakaofo, Nukunono and Atafu) (estimated population 1,595 at Oct. 1, 1983), proclaimed part of New Zealand as from Jan. 1, 1948.

THE ROSS DEPENDENCY

The *Ross Dependency*, placed under the jurisdiction of New Zealand by Order in Council dated July 30, 1923, and defined as all the islands and territories between 160° E. and 150° W. longitude which are situated south of the 60° S. parallel. The Ross Dependency includes Edward VII Land and portions of Victoria Land. For some years there have been permanent bases in the area, staffed by survey and scientific personnel.

ASSOCIATED STATES

COOK ISLANDS

Included in the boundaries of New Zealand since June, 1901, the group consists of the islands of Rarotonga, Aitutaki, Mangaia, Atiu, Mauke, Mitiaro, Manuae, Takutea, Palmerston, Penrhyn or Tongareva, Manihiki, Rakahanga, Suwarrow, Pukapuka or Danger and Nassau. The total population of the group was estimated at 17,400 (March 1983). The chief exports of the Cook Islands are fruit juice, clothing, copra, bananas, citrus fruit and pulp, and pearl shell. The trade is chiefly with New Zealand, Australia, Japan, the U.K. and the U.S.A. The New Zealand Government continues to give financial aid to the Cook Islands.

The High Commissioner of the Cook Islands is employed in a dual role, since he represents both the Queen and the New Zealand Government. Since Aug. 4, 1965, the Islands have enjoyed complete internal self-government, executive power being in the hands of a Cabinet consisting of the Premier and five other ministers. The new Constitution Act was passed by the New Zealand Parliament in November 1964, but did not come into force until it had been endorsed by the 22-member Legislative Assembly of the Cook Islands, elected in April 1965.

The New Zealand citizenship of the Cook Islanders is embodied in the Constitution, and assurances have been given that the changed status of the Islands will in no way affect the consideration of subsidies or the right of free entry into New Zealand for exports from the group.

NIUE

Geographically part of Cook Islands, but administered separately. Had a population (1983) of 3,002.

A New Zealand Representative is stationed at Niue, which since October 1974 has been self-governing in free association with New Zealand, which is responsible for external affairs and defence, and continues to give financial aid. Executive power is in the hands of a Premier and a Cabinet of 3 drawn from the Assembly of 20 members.

ANTIGUA AND BARBUDA

AREA, POPULATION, ETC.—Antigua and Barbuda comprises the islands of Antigua (108 square miles; population, 78,000), Barbuda (62 square miles; population, 1,500) 25 miles north of Antigua, and Redonda (¼ square mile; uninhabited) 25 miles south-west of Antigua. Antigua is part of the Leeward Islands in the Eastern Caribbean and lies 17° 3′ N. and 61° 48′ W. It is distinguished from the rest of the Leeward group by its absence of high hills and forest, and a drier climate than most of the W. Indies. Barbuda, formerly a possession of the Codrington family, is very flat with a large lagoon and well wooded in the north east. Antigua was first settled by the English in 1632, and was granted to Lord Willoughby by Charles II.

CAPITAL.—ΨSt. John's. Population, 22,000. The town of Barbuda is Codrington.

FLAG.—Inverted triangle (centred on a red field) divided horizontally into three bands of black over blue over white; rising sun device in gold on black band.

GOVERNMENT

Antigua became internally self-governing in 1967 and fully independent on Nov. 1, 1981, as a constitutional monarchy with H.M. The Queen as Head of State, represented by the Governor-General. There is a Senate of 17 appointed members and a House of Representatives elected every 5 years. The Attorney-General may be appointed.

Governor-General, Sir Wilfred Ebenezer Jacobs, K.C.V.O., O.B.E., Q.C.

Cabinet

Prime Minister and Minister of Finance, Rt. Hon. Vere C. Bird, Sr.
Deputy P.M. and Minister for Foreign Affairs, Economic Development, Tourism and Energy, Hon. Lester Bird.
Public Utilities, Aviation and Information, Hon. V. C. Bird, Jnr.
Finance, Hon. John E. St. Luce.
Education, Culture and Youth Affairs, Hon. Reuben H. Harris.
Labour, Housing and Co-operatives, Hon. Adolphus Freeland.
Health, Hon. Christopher M. O'Hard.
Agriculture, Fisheries and Lands, Hon. Robin Yearwood.
Attorney general (apptd), Hon. Keith Ford.
Public Works, Hon. Hilroy Humphreys.
Ministers within a Ministry:
  Foreign Affairs, Economic Development, Tourism and Energy, Hon. Molwyn Joseph.
  Health, Hon. Eustace Cochrane.
  Education, Culture and Youth Affairs, Hon. D. Christian.
  Public Utilities, Aviation and Communications, Hon. Henderson St. Clair Simon.

HIGH COMMISSION FOR
ANTIGUA AND BARBUDA
15 Thayer Street, W.1.
[01–486 7073]

High Commissioner for Eastern Caribbean States, His Excellency Ronald Sanders (1984).

BRITISH HIGH COMMISSION
38 St. Mary's Street (P.O. 483), St. John's

High Commissioner, (resides at Bridgetown, Barbados).
Resident Representative, J M. Crane (*Second Secretary*).

ECONOMY

Tourism is the main feature of the economy, with several hotels (and a number under construction) to take advantage of the many white sand beaches which made Antigua one of the first Caribbean islands to attract tourists.

For many years sugar was the dominant crop but is now produced primarily for local consumption. Areas of agricultural development include livestock, sea island cotton, corn (for cornmeal production) and improved vegetable and fruit production. An oil refinery on the island was reopened in 1982.

FINANCE

	1981	1982
Revenue	EC$77,244,549	EC$99,193,039
Expenditure (recurrent)	85,859,391	106,371,017

Trade with U.K.

	1983	1984
Imports from U.K.	£10,465,000	£22,670,000
Exports to U.K.	1,718,000	820,000

THE BAHAMAS
(The Commonwealth of the Bahamas)

AREA, POPULATION, ETC.—The Bahama Islands are an archipelago lying in the Atlantic Ocean between 20° 55′–25° 22′ N. Lat; 72° 35′–79° 35′ W. Long. They extend from the coast of Florida on the north-west almost to Haiti on the south-east. The group consists of 700 islands, of which 30 are inhabited and 2,400 cays comprising an area of more than 5,382 square miles. The population, at the census of 1980 was 237,090. The principal islands include: Abaco, Acklins, Andros, Berry Islands, Bimini, Cat Cay, Cat Island, Crooked Island, Eleuthera, Exumas, Grand Bahama, Harbour Island, Inagua, Long Cay, Long Island, Mayaguana, New Providence (on which is located the capital, Nassau), Ragged Island, Rum Cay, San Salvador and Spanish Wells. San Salvador was the first landfall in the New World of Christopher Columbus on October 12, 1492.

The Bahamas were settled by British subjects when the islands were deserted. The ownership of the Bahamas was taken over in 1782 by the Spanish, but the Treaty of Versailles in 1783 restored them to the British.

CAPITAL.—ΨNassau. Population (1980 census), 135,437. Nassau is distant from Liverpool 4,000 miles.

FLAG.—Horizontal stripes of aquamarine, gold and aquamarine, with a black equilateral triangle on the hoist.

GOVERNMENT

The Bahamas gained independence on July 10, 1973. The Head of State is H.M. Queen Elizabeth II, represented in the islands by a Governor-General. There is a Senate of 16 members and an elected House of Assembly of 43 members.

Governor-General, His Excellency Sir Gerald Cash, G.C.M.G., K.C.V.O., O.B.E.

Cabinet

Prime Minister and Minister of Finance, Rt. Hon. Sir Lynden Pindling, K.C.M.G.
Foreign Affairs, and Tourism; Government Leader in House of Assembly, Hon. Clement T. Maynard.
Labour, and Youth, Sports and Community Affairs, Hon. Livingstone N. Coakley.
National Security, Hon. A. Loftus Roker.
Works and Utilities, Housing and National Insurance, Hon. Darrell E. Rolle.

Attorney General and Minister of Education, Senator Hon. Paul L. Adderley.
Economic Affairs, and Agriculture, Fisheries and Cooperatives, Hon. Alfred T. Maycock.
Transport, and Local Government, Hon. Philip M. Bethel.
Health, Hon. Dr. Norman Gay
President of Court of Appeal, Sir Joseph Luckhoo.

Chief Justice, Hon. Philip. Telford-Georges.

BAHAMAS HIGH COMMISSION
39 Pall Mall, SW1Y 5JG
[01–930 6967]

High Commissioner, His Excellency Richard C. Demeritte (1984).

BRITISH HIGH COMMISSION
Bitco Building, East St.
P.O. Box N7516, Nassau.

High Commissioner, His Excellency Peter William Heap (1983).
Deputy High Commissioner, M. Holmes, M.B.E. (*Head of Chancery*).

ECONOMY

Tourism is the economic mainstay of the Bahamas, employing about two-thirds of the labour force. It provides about two-thirds of Government revenue and about half the country's foreign exchange earnings. The second main industry is international banking and trust business, the Bahamas' absence of any direct taxation and internal stability enabling the country to become one of the world's leading financial centres.

Agricultural production is mainly of fresh vegetables, fruit, meat and dairy products for the domestic market, and crawfish, mostly for export. There are large reserves of aragonite, and reserves of limestone and salt, all of which are being commercially exploited. Freeport is the country's leading industrial centre, with a cement and pharmaceutical plant, an oil refinery, and port and bunkering facilities. There is also a rum distillery on New Providence.

EDUCATION

Education is compulsory between the ages of 5 and 14. More than 62,000 students are enrolled in Ministry of Education and Independent schools in New Providence and the Family Islands.

COMMUNICATIONS

The main ports are Nassau (New Providence), Freeport (Grand Bahamas), Matthew Town (Inagua). International air services are operated from Nassau and Freeport, and there are also airports at West End (Grand Bahama) and Rock Sound (Eleuthera). About 50 smaller airports and landing strips facilitate services between the islands, the services being provided by Bahamasair, the national carrier. There are roads on the larger islands, and roads are under construction on the smaller islands. There are no railways. Wireless and telephone services are in operation to all parts of the world. There are 132 radio-telephone channels among the islands.

FINANCE AND TRADE

	1983	1984p.
Public revenue	B$339,860,000	B$325,745,000
Expenditure	310,601,000	338,013,000

Trade with U.K.

	1983	1984
Imports from U.K.	£17,815,000	£15,023,000
Exports to U.K.	24,013,000	38,478,000

The imports are chiefly foodstuffs, manufactured articles, building material, vehicles and machinery. The chief exports are petroleum and petroleum products, hormones, salt, rum, crawfish and aragonite.

BANGLADESH
(The People's Republic of Bangladesh)

AREA, POPULATION, CLIMATE, ETC.—The People's Republic of Bangladesh consists of the territory which was formerly East Pakistan (the old province of East Bengal and the Sylhet district of Assam), covering an area of 55,126 sq. miles in the region of the Gangetic delta, and has a population (1983 estimate) of 94,700,000.

The country is crossed by a network of navigable rivers, including the eastern arms of the Ganges, the Jamuna (Brahmaputra) and the Meghna, flowing into the Bay of Bengal. The climate is tropical and monsoon; hot and extremely humid during the summer, and mild and dry during the short winter. The rainfall is heavy, varying from 50 inches to 135 inches in different districts and the bulk of it falls during monsoon season from June to September. The mean temperature during the winter (November to February) is about 20°C. (68°F.) and during the hot season 30°C. (86°F.).

Prior to becoming East Pakistan, the territory had been part of British India. It acceded to Pakistan in October, 1947, which became a Republic on March 23, 1956.

By a proclamation of March 26, 1971, Bangladesh purported to secede from the central government, and a government-in-exile was set up in April in Calcutta. The short war between India and Pakistan, in both the East and the West, and India's overwhelming defeat of the Pakistani Army in the East, brought about a *de facto* secession of the East wing. The Indo-Pakistan war was concluded on December 16, 1971, and Mr. Zulfiqar Ali Bhutto became President of Pakistan on December 20. Sheikh Mujib was sworn in as Prime Minister of Bangladesh on January 12, 1972. Recognition of the new state was accorded swiftly by many countries. Bangladesh was admitted to the Commonwealth on April 18, and to the United Nations in 1974. Pakistan and Bangladesh accorded one another mutual recognition in Feb. 1974 and established diplomatic relations in Jan. 1976.

CAPITAL.—Dhaka. Population (1983 estimate), 4,023,000.

FLAG.—Red circle on a bottle-green ground.

GOVERNMENT

From 1975 a non-political administration ran the country under martial law, initially under President Mr. Justice A. M. Sayem, then from April 1977 under Major General Ziaur Rahman. A Presidential election was held on June 3, 1978, and President Zia was elected by a considerable majority. Parliamentary elections were held in February 1979 and martial law was lifted in April 1979. The 1974 Proclamation of Emergency, which suspended certain sections of the constitution concerned with fundamental rights, was revoked in November 1979. Zia was assassinated in May 1981 in an unsuccessful coup, but the military, led by Lt.-Gen. Ershad, took over in March 1982 and and martial law was again imposed.

President and Chief Martial Law Administrator, Lt.-Gen. H. M. Ershad.

Deputy Chief Martial Law Administrators, Rr. Adm. Sultan Ahmad (*Chief of Naval Staff: Minister of Communications, Port, Shipping and IWT*); Air Vice Marshal Sultan Mahmud (*Chief of Air Staff: Minister of Industries*).

Law and Justice, and Religious Affairs, Mr. Justice A. K. M. Nurul Islam.

Home Affairs, Maj. Gen. Abdul Mannan Siddiqui.

Health and Population Control, Maj. Gen. M. Shamsul Haque.

Food Divn., Ministry of Food, Maj. Gen. Mahabbat Jan Chowdhury.

Agriculture, Maj. Gen. Mohammad Abdul Munim.

Local Government, Rural Development and Co-operatives, Maj. Gen. Mahmudul Hasan.

Irrigation, Water Development and Flood Control, Air Vice Marshal (Retd.) K. M. Aminul Islam.

Commerce, Qazi Zafar Ahmed.

Works, Dr. M. A. Matin.

Land Administration and Land Reforms, M. Korban Ali.

Jute and Textiles, M. A. Sattar.

Planning, Dr. A. Majeed Khan.

Civil Aviation and Tourism Divn., Ministry of Defence, A. R. Yusuf.

Labour and Manpower, Anisul Islam Mahmud.

Information, Sirajul Hossain Khan.

Relief and Rehabilitation Divn., Ministry of Food, Dr. T. I. M. Fazle Rabbi Chowdury.

Social Welfare and Women's Affairs, Rabiya Bhuiya.

Youth and Sports, Zakir Khan Chowdhury.

Energy and Mineral Resources, Anwar Hossain.

Foreign Affairs, Humayun Rasheed Chowdhury.

Ministers of State, Shawfikul Ghaani Shapan (*Communications*); Sunil Gupta (*Energy and Mineral Resources*); Zafar Imam (*Agriculture*).

Deputy Minister, Youth and Sports, Sheikh Shahidul Islam.

BANGLADESH HIGH COMMISSION
28 Queen's Gate, SW7 5JA
[01–584 0081]

High Commissioner, His Excellency Fakhruddin Ahmed (1982).

Deputy High Commissioner, Mohiuddin Ahmed.

BRITISH HIGH COMMISSION
Abu Bakr House, P.O. Box 6079, Gulshan
Dhaka–12

High Commissioner, His Excellency Terence George Streeton, C.M.G, M.B.E. (1983).

Deputy High Commissioner, A. Burgess, C.V.O.

British Council Representative, Dr. R. E. Wright, O.B.E., 5 Fuller Road, (P.O. Box 161), Ramna, Dhaka 2.

EDUCATION

Primary education is free but not universal. Most primary schools are under government management. The majority of secondary schools and colleges are privately managed, but many receive government grants. There are six Universities. In 1981 literacy was estimated at 23·8 per cent of the whole of Bangladesh and 26 per cent of the male population.

TRANSPORT AND COMMUNICATIONS

Principal seaports are Chittagong, and Chalna. The Bangladesh Shipping Corporation has been set up by the Government to operate the Bangladesh merchant fleet. The principal airports are Dhaka-Zia and Chittagong. The international airline, Bangladesh Biman, serves Europe, the Middle East, South and South-East Asia, and an internal network.

There are about 6,880 miles of roads in Bangladesh; 4,724 miles are metalled. There are 2,798 miles of railway track.

Radio Bangladesh is the main national broadcasting service. A television service was introduced in 1965 and colour transmissions began in 1981.

ECONOMY

Bangladesh is a principal producer of raw jute. Other agricultural products are rice, tea, oil seeds, pulses, and sugar cane. The chief industries are jute, cotton, tea, leather, pharmaceuticals, fertilizer, sugar, fishing (prawns), natural gas and garment manufacture.

Aid

Bangladesh is a major recipient of bilateral and multilateral development aid. The total annual development plan for 1985–86 is budgeted at U.S. $1,366 million, of which U.S. $1,146 million will be financed from external sources as follows:

Project aid	U.S. $714 million
Commodity aid	392 million
Food aid	38 million

Trade with U.K.

	1983	1984
Imports from U.K.	£51,000,000	£51,591,000
Exports to U.K.	25,200,000	46,506,000

BARBADOS

AREA, POPULATION, ETC.—Barbados, the most easterly of the Caribbean islands, is situated in latitude 13° 14′ N. and longitude 59° 37′ W. The island has a total area of 166 square miles, the land rising in a series of tablelands marked by terraces to the highest point, Mt. Hillaby (1,116 ft.). It is nearly 21 miles long by 14 miles broad. Some 46 acres are covered by forest. The climate is equable with annual average temperature 26·6°C. (79·8°F.) and rainfall varying from a yearly average of 75 inches in the high central district to 50 inches in some of the low-lying coastal areas.

POPULATION.—The population of Barbados (1984 estimate) was 252,000. There are eleven administrative areas (parishes): St. Michael; Christ Church; St. Andrews; St. George; St. James; St. John; St. Joseph; St. Lucy; St. Peter; St. Philip, and St. Thomas.

CAPITAL.—ΨBridgetown (population, estimated April, 1980, 7,466) in the parish of St. Michael. There are three other towns, Oistins in Christ Church, Holetown in St. James and Speightstown in St. Peter.

FLAG.—Three vertical stripes, dark blue, gold and dark blue, with trident devises on gold stripe.

NATIONAL DAY.—Nov. 30 (Independence Day).

GOVERNMENT

The first inhabitants of Barbados were Arawak Indians but the island was uninhabited when first settled by the British in 1627. It was a Crown Colony from 1652 until it became an independent state within the Commonwealth on November 30, 1966. The Legislature consists of the Governor-General, a Senate and a House of Assembly. The Senate comprises 21 Senators appointed by the Governor-General, of whom 12 are appointed on the advice of the Prime Minister, 2 on the advice of the Leader of the Opposition and 7 by the Governor-General at his discretion to represent religious, economic or social interests in the Island or such other interests as the Governor-General considers ought to be represented. The House of Assembly comprises 27 members elected every five years by adult suffrage. In 1963 the voting age was reduced to 18. The last General Election took place on June 18, 1981 and, as a result, seats in the House of Assembly were distributed as follows: Barbados Labour Party 17; Democratic Labour Party 10. A General Election is due before the end of 1986.

Governor-General, Sir Hugh Springer, K.C.M.G., C.B.E., *apptd* 1984.

Cabinet

Prime Minister, Minister of Finance and Planning, Hon. Bernard St. John, Q.C.
Information and Leader of the House, Hon. L. S. Craig.
Commerce, Industry and Consumer Affairs, Hon. L. R. Tull, Q.C.
Housing and Lands, Hon. L. Braithwaite.
Education and Culture, Hon. Miss B. A. Miller.
Labour and Community Development, Hon. D. O. Bradshaw.
Foreign Affairs and International Trade, Senator Hon. N. A. Barrow.
Health and Social Security, Senator Hon. O'Brien Trotman.
Agriculture and Natural Resources, Dr. Hon. R. L. Cheltenham.
Transport and Works, Hon. V. Johnson.
Minister of State, (Planning) and Leader of the Senate, Senator Hon. C. A. Griffith.
Tourism and the Environment, Hon. A. Truss.
Legal Affairs, and Attorney-General, Hon. D. A. C. Simmons, Q.C.

President of the Senate, Senator Hon. Sir Arnott Cato, K.C.M.G.
Speaker, House of Assembly, Hon. W. C. B. Hinds.

BARBADOS HIGH COMMISSION
6 Upper Belgrave Street, SW1X 8AZ
[01–235 8686]

High Commissioner, His Excellency Dr. The Hon. H. McDonald Forde (1984).

BRITISH HIGH COMMISSION
147–9 Roebuck Street (P.O. Box 676C)
Bridgetown

High Commissioner, His Excellency Giles Lionel Bullard, C.M.G. (1983).

JUDICATURE

There is a Supreme Court of Judicature consisting of a High Court and a Court of Appeal. In certain cases a further appeal lies to the Judicial Committee of H.M. Privy Council. The Chief Justice and Puisne Judges are appointed by the Governor-General on the recommendation of the Prime Minister and after consultation with the Leader of the Opposition.
Chief Justice, Rt. Hon. Sir William Douglas, K.C.M.G.

EDUCATION

Primary and secondary education is free in Gov-érnment schools. There are 111 primary schools, 21 Government secondary schools and 15 approved Government secondary schools.

COMMUNICATIONS

Barbados has some 965 miles of roads, of which about 917 miles are asphalted. The Grantley Adams International airport is situated at Seawell, 12 miles from Bridgetown, and frequent scheduled services connect Barbados with the major world air routes. Bridgetown, the only port of entry, has a deep-water harbour with berths for 8 ships, but oil is pumped ashore at Spring Gardens and at an Esso installation on the West Coast. Barbados has a colour television service, three radio broadcasting services, and a wired broadcasting service.

FINANCE

	1984–85*
Current revenue	BDS$561,800,000
Current expenditure	575,900,000
Capital expenditure	128,600,000
* estimated.	

ECONOMY

The economy of the island is based on tourism, sugar and light manufacturing. In 1984, 7,760,000 tourists visited Barbados and 3,720,000 cruise ship passengers. Chief exports are sugar and its by-products (12·3 per cent of exports in 1984), and electrical components (53·4 per cent) and clothing (11·1 per cent).

	1983 BDS$	1984 BDS$
Total imports	1,258·0 m	1,326·0 m
Total exports	717·4 m	787·4 m

Trade with U.K.

	1984
Imports from U.K.	BDS$100,800,000
Exports to U.K.	54,400,000

BELIZE

AREA, POPULATION, ETC.—Belize lies on the east coast of Central America, bounded on the north and north-west by Mexico, and on the west and south by Guatemala. The total area (including offshore islands) is about 8,867 sq. miles, with a length and breadth of 174 miles and 68 miles respectively. The climate is sub-tropical, with a mean annual temperature of 79°F, but is tempered by sea breezes. There are two dry seasons, the main one from March to May and the other (the Maugre Season) from August to September. The country is occasionally affected by hurricanes.

The coastal areas are mostly flat and swampy but the country rises gradually towards the interior. The northern and western districts are hilly, and in the south the Maya Mountains and the Cockscombs form the backbone of the country, reaching a height of 3,800 feet at Victoria Peak. There are 17 principal rivers, of which the Belize River is the most important, but few are navigable for any distance.

The population is 148,300 (1981 estimate), of which the main racial groups are Creoles, Mestizos (Maya-Spanish) and Caribs, plus a number of East Indian and Spanish descent. The races are now heavily inter-mixed. The majority of the population is Christian, about 60 per cent Catholic and most of the remainder Protestant.

The early history of Belize is little known, although the numerous ruins in the area indicate that it was heavily populated by the Maya Indians. The first British settlement was established in 1638 but was subject to repeated attacks by the Spanish, who claimed sovereignty over the area, until the decline of Spanish power in the Americas in the 19th century. In 1862 the area was recognised by Britain as a Colony and called British Honduras. On June 1, 1973 the colony was officially renamed Belize, and was granted independence on September 21, 1981. The long-standing territorial dispute with Guatemala, which had delayed independence earlier, remains unresolved despite efforts to reach a settlement.

CAPITAL.—Belmopan (estimated population, 1980, 2,935). The largest city and the former capital is Ψ Belize City (population, 1980 census, 39,771), which was badly damaged by a hurricane in October 1961. Other towns are ΨCorozal (6,899), San Ignacio (5,616), Dangriga (6,661), Orange Walk (8,439), Punta Gorda (2,396).

FLAG.—Blue ground with red band along top and bottom edges, and in centre a white disc containing the coat of arms surrounded by a green garland.

GOVERNMENT

The Queen is Head of State, represented in Belize by a Governor-General, who is a citizen of the country, appointed in consultation with the Prime Minister of Belize. There is a National Assembly, comprising a House of Representatives (28 members elected for 5 years) and a Senate (8 members appointed by the Governor-General). Executive power is vested in the Cabinet, which is responsible to the National Assembly.

Governor-General, Her Excellency Dame Minita Elvira Gordon, G.C.M.G.

The Cabinet

Prime Minister and Minister of Finance and Defence, Hon. Manuel Esquivel.
Deputy Prime Minister and Minister of Home Affairs, Hon. Curl Thompson.
Works, Hon. Charles Wagner.
Natural Resources, Hon. Dean Lindo.
Local Government, Social Services and Community Development, Hon. Philip Goldson.
Foreign Affairs and Economic Development, Hon. Dean Barrow.
Energy and Communications, Hon. Israel Alpuche.
Tourism, Transport, Education and Youth, Hon. Derek Aikman.
Attorney General and Minister of Housing, Hon. Hubert Elrington.
Commerce, Industry, Fishing and Cooperatives, Hon. Edwardo Juan.
Health, Labour and Sports, Hon. Elodio Aragon.

ECONOMY

About 42 per cent of the population is engaged in agriculture. Corn (maize), rice, red kidney beans, root crops and fruit are the main food crops, although main agricultural exports are sugar, bananas and citrus products. The country is more or less self-sufficient in fresh beef, pork and poultry, but processed meat and dairy products are imported. About 25 per cent of timber production (mostly mahogany) is exported, and there is a large U.S. market for lobster, conch and scale fish. Tourism is also a valuable source of income.

FINANCE

	1983–84	1984–85
Revenue	BZ $83·7 m	$79·2 m
Expenditure	76·2 m	85·3 m
Surplus (Deficit)	7·5 m	(6·1 m)

The Belize dollar (BZ $) is tied to the U.S. dollar: BZ $2 = U.S. $1.

TRADE

	1983	1984
Total imports	BZ $223·6 m	258·4 m
Total exports	155·5 m	188·5 m

Trade with U.K.

	1983	1984
Imports from U.K.	£11,565,000	£11,501,000
Exports to U.K.	8,726,000	15,911,000

EDUCATION

Education is compulsory from 6 to 14 years of age. In 1980 free primary education was provided by 21 state schools and 180 grant-aided schools (usually run by the churches), with a total enrolment of 35,000. Secondary education was provided by 5 state and 17 grant-aided schools with an enrolment of over 6,000. There are 5 post-secondary institutions, but no universities although the Government offers scholarships for students to go abroad. There is an extra-mural faculty of the University of the West Indies, with a resident tutor.

COMMUNICATIONS

There is a Government-operated radio service but no official television service in the country. An automatic telephone service covers the whole country; internal services are handled by the Belize Telecommunication Authority and external services by Cable and Wireless Ltd. through the earth satellite system (opened 1978).

The principal airport is at Belize City and various airlines operate international flights to U.S. and other Central American states. The main port is also Belize City, where construction of deep water quays was recently completed. There are 1,865 miles of road, including four main highways, but there is no railway system.

BELIZE HIGH COMMISSION
15 Thayer Street,
WIM 5DL
[01–486 8381]
High Commissioner, (new appointment to be announced).

BRITISH HIGH COMMISSION
P.O. Box 91, Belmopan.
High Commissioner, His Excellency John M. Crosby, L.V.O.
Deputy High Commissioner, S. S. Calder.

BOTSWANA
(The Republic of Botswana)

AREA, POPULATION, ETC.—Botswana (formerly the British Protectorate of Bechuanaland) lies between latitudes 18° and 26° S. and longitudes 20° and 28° W. and is bounded by the Cape and Transvaal Provinces of South Africa on the south and east, by Zimbabwe, the Zambesi and Chobe (Linyanti) Rivers on the north and north-east and by South West Africa on the west. Botswana extends some 500 miles by 550 miles, with a total area of 220,000 square miles. The climate of the country is generally sub-tropical, but varies considerably with latitude and altitude. A plateau at a height of about 4,000 feet divides Botswana into two main topographical regions. To the east of the plateau streams flow into the Marico, Notwani and Limpopo Rivers; to the west lies a flat region comprising the Kgalagadi Desert, the Okavango Swamps and the Northern State Lands area. The Kgalagadi Desert is a level tract closely covered with thorn bush and grass, extending 300 miles to the west and bounded by the Makgadikgadi salt pans and the Boteti River in the north. Its rainfall varies from 20 inches in the east to 9 inches in the south-west. The Okavango Swamps, 6,500 square miles in area, lie in the remote north-western corner of Botswana, and, apart from the Limpopo and Chobe Rivers, are the only source of permanent surface water in the country. North of the Boteti River and the Makgadikgadi depression the Kgalagadi Desert gives way to forest and dense bush of the Northern State Lands. Large areas of the country support only herds of game. Elephant numbers have been estimated at 15–30,000.

POPULATION.—Botswana has an estimated population (1981) of about 937,000. The eight principal Botswana tribes are Bakgatla, Bakwena, Bangwaketse, Bamalete, Bamangwato, Barolong, Batawana and Batlokwa. The principal languages in use in Botswana are Setswana and English.

CAPITAL.—Gaborone, estimated population 79,400. Other business centres are Francistown (38,000), Lobatse (22,000), and Selebi-Phikwe (32,500).

FLAG.—Horizontal bands of blue, white, blue, with a black stripe on the white band.

GOVERNMENT

On September 30, 1966, Bechuanaland became a Republic within the Commonwealth under the name Botswana. The President of Botswana is Head of State and appoints as Vice-President a member of the National Assembly who is his principal assistant and leader of Government business in the National Assembly. The Assembly consists of the President, 34 members elected on a basis of universal adult suffrage, 4 specially elected members, the Attorney-General (non-voting) and the Speaker. There is also a House of Chiefs.

President, His Excellency Dr. Q. K. J. Masire.

Cabinet

Vice President, Minister of Finance and Development Planning, Hon. P. S. Mmusi.
External Affairs, Hon. Dr. G. K. T. Chiepe, M.B.E.
Presidential Affairs and Public Administration, Hon. P. H. K. Kedikilwe.
Assistant Minister, Finance and Development Planning, Hon. D. N. Magang.
Health, Hon. P. K. Balopi.
Agriculture, Hon. D. K. Kwelagobe.
Local Government and Lands, Hon. J. H. T. Mothibamele.
Works and Communications, Hon. C. Blackbeard.
Commerce and Industry, Hon. M. P. K. Nwako.
Education, Hon. K. P. Morake.
Mineral Resources and Water Affairs, Hon. A. M. Mogwe, M.B.E.
Home Affairs, Hon. E. M. K. Kgabo.
Assistant Ministers, Local Government and Lands, Hon. I. O. Chilume; Hon. M. R. Tshipinare.
Assistant Minister, Agriculture, Hon. G. M. Oteng.

BOTSWANA HIGH COMMISSION
6 Stratford Place, WIN 9AE
[01–499 0031]

High Commissioner, His Excellency S. A. Mpuchane (1982).

BRITISH HIGH COMMISSION
Private Bag 0023, Gaborone

High Commissioner, His Excellency Wilfred Jones, C.M.G. (1981)
British Council Representative, D. Munro.

ECONOMY

Botswana is predominantly a pastoral country. The national herd is normally around 3 million cattle and 1 million sheep and goats but drought conditions

during the past 4 years have reduced the number of cattle to around 2·6 million.

Cattle rearing accounts for about 80 per cent of agricultural output and livestock products, particularly beef, are a major source of foreign exchange earnings. The Government has a number of programmes to improve land use and cattle and crop production, and schemes to provide financial assistance for farmers.

Mineral extraction and processing is now the major source of income for the country following the opening of large mines for diamonds and copper-nickel. Large deposits of coal have been discovered and are being mined on a small scale; further development, including coal exports, is unlikely until the market for coal improves. Much of the country has yet to be fully prospected. Manufacturing industry is growing and will continue to do so as communications improve but it is still a small sector of the economy.

EDUCATION

There are now over 500 primary schools (enrolment 220,400), and 62 secondary schools (enrolment 30,770). The Government embarked on a massive expansion of secondary education in January 1984. There are now 5 teacher training establishments (total enrolment over 1,500) including one for secondary teachers (enrolment 165), one Polytechnic with 720 students and the University of Botswana with 1,635 undergraduates. Further expansion of the technical education system is planned via a network of vocational training centres linked to the Polytechnic.

COMMUNICATIONS

The railway from Cape Town to Zimbabwe passes through eastern Botswana. The main roads in the country are the north–south road, which closely follows the railway, and the road running east–west that links Francistown and Maun. A new road from Nata to Kazungula provides a direct link to Zambia from Botswana. Air services are provided on a scheduled basis between the main towns, linking with services from South Africa, Swaziland, Zambia and Zimbabwe.

FINANCE

	1982–83	1983–84
Actual Revenue (Recurrent and development)	P394 m	P563 m
Actual Expenditure	414 m	460 m

Currency: In August 1976 Botswana introduced its own currency, the *pula*, to replace the South African *rand* formerly in use. It is linked to a basket of currencies. P1 = $US0·574 (June, 1985).

TRADE

Principal exports are diamonds, copper-nickel matte, and beef and beef products.

	1983	1984
Imports	P806 m	P870 m
Exports	702 m	870 m

Trade with U.K.

	1983	1984
Imports from U.K......	£3,250,000	£9,015,000
Exports to U.K.	21,713,000	14,913,000

BRUNEI
(Negara Brunei Darussalam)

Brunei is situated on the north-west coast of the island of Borneo, total area about 2,226 sq. miles, population (1982), approximately 214,000 of whom 68 per cent are of Malay or other indigenous race and 25 per cent Chinese. The country has a humid tropical climate.

CAPITAL.—Bandar Seri Begawan (population, 58,000).

FLAG.—Yellow, with diagonal bands of white over narrow black band (from top by staff), with red device on diagonal bands.

GOVERNMENT

In 1959, the Sultan of Brunei promulgated the first written Constitution, which provides for a Privy Council, a Council of Ministers and a Legislative Council. On January 1, 1984 Brunei resumed full independence. A ministerial system of government was established at independence, the seven Ministers being appointed by the Sultan and responsible to him. The Sultan presides over the Privy Council and the Council of Ministers. The Legislative Council was disbanded in Feb. 1984.

Sultan, H.M. Sir Muda Hassanal Bolkiah Mu'izzadin Waddaulah, G.C.M.G., *acceded* 1967, *crowned* Aug. 1, 1968.

BRUNEI HIGH COMMISSION
49 Cromwell Road, SW7 2ED
[01–581 0521]

High Commissioner, His Excellency Penigran Setia Raja Pengiran Haji Jaya (1984).

BRITISH HIGH COMMISSION
Hong Kong and Shanghai Bank
Building (3rd floor), Bandar
Seri Begawan.

High Commissioner, His Excellency Robert Francis Cornish, M.V.O. (1983).

FINANCE

	1984 (forecast)
Revenue	B$6,500 million
Expenditure*	2,600 million

*Including development expenditure.

Currency.—The unit of currency is the *Brunei dollar* of 100 *cents,* which is fully interchangeable with the currency of Singapore.

Trade with U.K.

	1984
Imports from U.K.	£122,651,000
Exports to U.K.	21,966,000

CYPRUS

AREA, CLIMATE AND POPULATION.—Cyprus with an area of 3,572 square miles, is the third largest island in the Mediterranean Sea, exceeded in size by Sicily and Sardinia. Its greatest length is 140 miles and greatest breadth 60 miles, situated at latitude 35°N. and longitude 33° 30'E. It is about 40 miles distant from the nearest point of Asia Minor, 60 miles from Syria and 240 miles from Port Said. The main topographical features of Cyprus are: (a) A narrow limestone range of mountains extending in an unbroken chain for nearly 100 miles along the north coast, at an average height of 2,000 feet; (b) A broad central plain, running for some 60 miles from west to east; (c) An extensive igneous massif rising to over 6,000 feet in the west of the island; and (d) Narrow coastal plains between the mountains and the sea. The rivers are little more than mountain torrents. There is no permanent stream of any volume.

Cyprus has a somewhat intense Mediterranean climate with a hot dry summer and a variable warm winter, while the intermediate seasons are short and transitional. The winter is generally sunny with frequent cold spells between the beginning of December and end of February. The rainy season lasts from October to April with average total rainfall of about 20 inches. July and August are the warmest months.

In 1982 the population (U.N. estimate) was 650,000. There are two major communities, Greek Cypriots (78 per cent) and Turkish Cypriots (18·2 per cent); and minorities of Armenians, Maronites and others.

CAPITAL.—Nicosia, near the centre of the island, with a population of 233,500 (1974 estimate); the other principal towns are ΨLimassol, ΨFamagusta, Ψ Larnaca, Paphos and Kyrenia. Nicosia is distant from London 2,028 miles by air.

FLAG.—Gold map of Cyprus on a white ground, surmounting crossed olive branches (green).

GOVERNMENT

Cyprus passed under British administration from 1878. Cyprus was formally annexed to Great Britain on Nov. 5, 1914, on the outbreak of war with Turkey. From 1925 to 1960 it was a Crown Colony administered by a Governor, assisted by an Executive Council and also for a time by a partly-elected Legislative Council. Following the launching in April 1955 of an armed campaign by EOKA in support of ENOSIS (union with Greece), a state of emergency was declared in November, 1955, which lasted for four years. Following a meeting at Zürich between the Prime Ministers of Greece and Turkey, a conference was held in London and an agreement was signed on February 19, 1959, between the United Kingdom, Greece, Turkey and the Greek and Turkish Cypriots which provided that Cyprus would be an independent Republic.

CONSTITUTION

Under the Cyprus Act, 1960, the island became an independent sovereign republic on August 16, 1960. The constitution provided for a Greek Cypriot President and a Turkish Cypriot Vice-President elected for a five-year term by the Greek and Turkish communities respectively. The House of Representatives, elected for five years by universal suffrage of each community separately, was to consist of 35 Greek and 15 Turkish members. The 1960 Constitution proved unworkable in practice and led to intercommunal troubles. The U.N. Peace Keeping Force in Cyprus (UNFICYP) was set up in March 1964: its mandate was last renewed on June 15, 1984.

On July 15, 1974, mainland Greek officers of the Greek Cypriot National Guard launched a *coup d'état* against President Makarios and installed a former E.O.K.A. member, Nikos Sampson, in his place. Turkey reserved to itself the right to maintain constitutional order and the independence and territorial integrity of the island, invaded Northern Cyprus and occupied over a third of the island. In 1975 a "Turkish Federated State of Cyprus" under Mr. Rauf Denktash was declared in this area, and in November 1983 a "Declaration of Statehood" was issued which purported to establish the "Turkish Republic of Northern Cyprus". The declaration has been condemned by the U.N. Security Council and only Turkey has recognized the new "state". In May 1985 a referendum in the north of Cyprus approved a constitution for the "Turkish Federated State": in

June 1985 Mr. Denktash was elected President of the "state" and a General Election was held.

Since 1974 attempts to reach a settlement have focused on the procedure of intercommunal talks under the auspices of the U.N. The latest talks broke down in Jan. 1985 without agreement.

A general election was held for the Greek House of Representatives on May 24, 1981, resulting in the parties gaining the following number of seats: AKEL (Communist) 12; Democratic Rally 12; Democratic Party (Centre) 8; EDEK (Socialist) 3. (In a 1982 by-election, one Democratic Rally M.P. was replaced by one from the Democratic Party.)

President, Spyros Kyprianou, *elected* Feb. 28, 1978, *re-elected*, Feb. 13, 1983.

COUNCIL OF MINISTERS

Foreign Affairs, George Iacovou.
Interior, Constantinos Michaelides.
Finance, Christos Mavrellis.
Education, Andreas Christofides.
Justice and Minister to the President, Demetrios Liveras.
Defence, Elias Eliades.
Communications & Works, Rois Nicolaides.
Health, Christos Pelekanos.
Commerce and Industry, Michalakis Michaelides.
Labour and National Insurance, Andreas Moushioutas.
Agriculture and Natural Resources, Andreas Papasolomontos.

CYPRUS HIGH COMMISSION
93 Park Street, W1Y 4ET
[01-499 8272]

High Commissioner, His Excellency Tasos Panayides (1979).

BRITISH HIGH COMMISSION
Alexander Pallis Street (P.O. Box 1978)
Nicosia

High Commissioner, His Excellency William John Antony Wilberforce, C.M.G. (1981).
British Council Representative, J. Mulholland, O.B.E., P.O. Box 1995, 3 Museum Street, Nicosia.

ECONOMY

Following a period of rapid growth in the years 1975–79 the economy has settled to a more modest and sustainable growth rate averaging about 3·5 per cent over the past two years. Continued growth at about 4 per cent is the aim of the 1982–86 development plan which will also promote Cyprus as a centre for Middle East trade.

Agriculture still occupies a prime position in the Cyprus economy but little further growth is expected. Main products are citrus fruits, grapes and vine products, potatoes and other vegetables. Manufacturing, construction, distribution and other service industries are other major employers. Tourism is the main growth industry with 621,000 long-stay tourists producing C£170 million in foreign exchange earnings in 1983. Plans to establish an "industrial free zone" to attract new foreign investment for exportable commodities are in hand. Some 2,700 foreign firms and individuals have registered as "offshore companies" in Cyprus which supports Cyprus' claim to be a centre for Middle East trade.

Britain is still the country's most important trading partner, taking some 16·5 per cent of its exports in 1983 and supplying 13·5 per cent of its imports. Cyprus is seeking to diversify its export markets and now sells almost half its exports to the Middle East. The trading account continues in

deficit and is offset by invisible earnings, mainly from tourism, foreign aid and development loans, capital inflows and income derived from the Sovereign Base Areas and United Nations personnel.

FINANCE

	1982
Total Revenue	C£245 million
Ordinary Expenditure	C£302 million

TRADE

	1982	1983
Imports	C£577·6 m	C£641·9 m
Exports (including re-exports)	263·8 m	260·5 m

Trade with U.K.

	1983	1984
Imports from U.K....	£127,800,000	£146,773,000
Exports to U.K.	87,400,000	94,381,000

BRITISH SOVEREIGN AREAS

The United Kingdom retained full sovereignty and jurisdiction over two areas of 99 square miles in all—Akrotiri-Episkopi-Paramali and Dhekelia-Pergamos-Ayios Nicolaos-Xylophagou—and use of roads and other facilities. The British Administrator of these areas is appointed by the Queen and is responsible to the Secretary of State for Defence.

Administrator of the British Sovereign Areas, Air Vice Marshal Kenneth Hayr.

DOMINICA
(The Commonwealth of Dominica)

AREA, POPULATION, ETC.—Dominica, the loftiest of the Lesser Antilles, lies in the Windward Group, between 15° 20′ and 15° 45′ N. lat. and 61° 13′ and 61° 30′ W. long., 95 miles S. of Antigua. It is about 29 miles long and 15 broad comprising an area of 290 sq. miles. The island is of volcanic origin and very mountainous and picturesque, abounding in streams fairly well stocked with fish, and the soil is very fertile. The temperature varies, according to the altitude, from 55° to 85°F. The climate is healthy, and during the winter months is very pleasant. Population (1981 census, 74,069).

CAPITAL.—ΨRoseau, on the south-west coast, population, 8,346. The other principal town is Portsmouth, population, 2,220.

FLAG.—Green ground with a cross overall of yellow, white and black stripes, and in the centre a red disc charged with a Sisserou parrot in natural colours within a ring of 11 green stars.

GOVERNMENT

The island was discovered by Columbus in 1493, when it was a stronghold of the Caribs, who remained virtually the sole inhabitants until the French established settlements in the 18th century. It was captured by the British in 1759 but passed back and forth between France and Britain until 1805, after which British possession was not challenged. From 1871–1939 Dominica was part of the Leeward Islands Colony, then from 1940 the island was a unit of the Windward Islands group. Internal self-government from 1967 was followed on Nov. 3, 1978 by independence as a republic with the name The Commonwealth of Dominica. Executive authority is vested in the President, who is elected by the House of Assembly for not more than two terms of five years. Parliament consists of the President and the House of Assembly (representatives elected by universal adult suffrage) and nine Senators, who may be appointed by the President or elected. Parliament has a life of five years.

President, His Excellency Clarence A. Seignoret, O.B.E.

Prime Minister and Minister for Finance and Foreign Affairs, Hon. Mary Eugenia Charles.

DOMINICA HIGH COMMISSION
1, Collingham Gardens, SW5 0HW
[01–370 5194/5]

High Commissioner, His Excellency Arden Shillingford, M.B.E. (1978).

BRITISH HIGH COMMISSION

High Commissioner, (resides at Bridgetown, Barbados).

FINANCE

	1983–84*
Recurrent Revenue	EC$70,456,830
Recurrent Expenditure	70,170,010
Capital Revenue	76,326,690
Capital Expenditure	82,831,120

* Estimated

ECONOMY

Agriculture is the principal occupation, with tropical and citrus fruits the main crops. Products for export are bananas, lime juice, lime oil, bay oil, copra and rum. Forestry and fisheries are being encouraged. The only commercially exploitable mineral is pumice, used chiefly for building purposes. Manufacturing consists largely of the processing of agricultural products.

TRADE

	1984
Imports	EC$156,103,731
Exports	69,225,646

Trade with U.K.

	1984
Imports from U.K.	£8,359,000
Exports to U.K.	14,961,000

FIJI

AREA, POPULATION, ETC.—Fiji is made up of about 332 islands and over 500 islets (including numerous atolls and reefs) in the South Pacific Ocean, about 1,100 miles north of New Zealand. About 100 islands are permanently inhabited. The gross area of the group, which extends 300 miles from east to west, and 300 north to south, between 15° 45′—21° 10′ S. lat. and 176° E.—178° W. long. is 7,072 square miles. The International Date Line has been diverted to the east of the island group. The largest islands are Viti Levu and Vanua Levu. The main groups of islands are Lomaiviti, Lau and Yasawas. Most of the larger islands are mountainous with sharp peaks and crags, but also have conspicuous areas of flat land and many of the rivers have built extensive deltas. The climate is tropical, without extremes of heat and temperatures rarely exceed 32° C. and seldom fall below 15° C.

The population (Dec. 1983) was 677,481, of which about 44 per cent are indigenous Fijians and about 50 per cent Indians.

CAPITAL.—ΨSuva, in the island of Viti Levu. Population (mid-1983) 71,000.

FLAG.—Light blue ground with Union flag in top left quarter and the shild of Fiji in the fly.

GOVERNMENT

Fiji was a British colony from 1874 until October 10, 1970, when it became an independent state and a member of the Commonwealth. Under the Constitution there is a Governor-General appointed by the Queen. The House of Representatives has 52 members—22 Fijians, 22 Indians and 8 General Elector representatives. For the Fijians and Indians, 12 are elected by voters registered on the Communal Roll and 10 by voters on the National Roll. Three General Elector representatives are elected by voters on the Communal Roll and five by voters on the National Roll. General members are in the main representatives of the European, part-European and Chinese communities.

There is a Senate of 22 members, 8 nominated by the Great Council of Chiefs, 7 by the Prime Minister, 6 by the Leader of the Opposition and one by the Council of Rotuma, an island dependency 400 miles from Suva, discovered in 1879 and annexed in 1881.

Governor-General, His Excellency Ratu Sir Penaia Ganilau, G.C.M.G., K.C.V.O., K.B.E., D.S.O., E.D.

Cabinet

Prime Minister, Minister for Information, Rt. Hon. Ratu Sir Kamisese Mara, G.C.M.G., K.B.E.

Deputy P.M. and Minister for Fijian Affairs, Hon. Ratu David Toganivalu.

Deputy P.M. and Minister of Finance, Hon. Mosese Qionibaravi.

Employment and Industrial Relations, Hon. Mohammed Ramzan, M.B.E.

Communications, Transport and Works, Hon. Semesa Sikivou.

Home Affairs, Hon. Militoni Leweniqila.

Lands, Energy and Mineral Resources, Hon. Jone Naisara.

Attorney-General, Minister for Justice, Hon. Qoriniasi Bale.

Primary Industries, Hon. Charles Walker.

Housing and Urban Affairs, Hon. Edward Beddoes.

Foreign Affairs, Tourism and Civil Aviation, Hon. Jonati Mavoa, C.M.G.

Health and Social Welfare, Hon. Dr. Apenisa Kurisaqila.

Education, Hon. Dr. Ahmed Ali.

Speaker, House of Representatives, Hon. Tomasi Vakatora.

President of the Senate, Hon. Senator W. M. Barrett.

FIJI HIGH COMMISSION
34 Hyde Park Gate, SW7 5BN
[01-584 3661/2]

High Commissioner, His Excellency Sailosi Wai Kepa (1985).

BRITISH HIGH COMMISSION
Victoria House, 47 Gladstone Road,
P.O. Box 1355, Suva

High Commissioner, His Excellency Roger Arnold Rowlandson Barltrop, C.V.O. (1982).

JUDICIARY

The Constitution guarantees the independence of the judiciary. Judges are appointed by the Governor-General.

Chief Justice of Fiji, Hon. Sir Timoci Tuivaga.

	1982	1983
Public Income	$276,843,000	$296,405,000
Public Expenditure ...	273,223,000	304,100,000

Currency.—Currency is the *Fiji dollar.*

ECONOMY

The economy is primarily agrarian, with about 600,000 acres under cultivation. The principal cash crop is sugar cane, which is the main export, followed by coconuts, ginger and copra. A variety of other fruit, vegetables and root crops are also grown, and self-sufficiency in rice is a major aim. Forestry, fishing and beef production are being encouraged in order to diversify the economy. The processing of agricultural, marine and timber products are the main industries, along with gold mining.

Tourism is also a major factor in the economy, second only to sugar as a money-earner. There were 235,227 visitors in 1984.

TRADE

	1983	1984
Total Imports	$493,185,000	$487,105,000
Total Exports (including Re-exports)	245,014,000	279,418,000

Trade with U.K.

	1983	1984
Imports from U.K........	£12,184,000	£11,281,000
Exports to U.K.	46,943,000	70,209,000

The chief imports are foodstuffs, machinery, mineral fuels, chemicals, beverages, tobacco and manufactured articles. Chief exports are sugar, coconut oil, gold, lumber, molasses, ginger and canned fish.

COMMUNICATIONS

Fiji is one of the main aerial crossroads in the Pacific. Air Pacific Ltd. is based at Nausori Airport near Suva and operates scheduled domestic services within the Fiji Islands and from Suva provides services to New Zealand, Australia, Tonga, Western Samoa, Vanuatu, the Solomon Islands, Kiribati, Tuvalu, New Caledonia and American Samoa. Fiji Air Services Ltd. operates charter flights within the Fiji group of islands and South Pacific and provides scheduled services within the Fiji group.

Fiji has three ports of entry, at Suva, Lautoka and Levuka.

THE GAMBIA

AREA, POPULATION, ETC.—The Gambia takes its name from the Gambia River, which it straddles for over 200 miles inland from the west coast of Africa. It is a narrow strip, surrounded by the Republic of Senegal, except at the coast, lying between 13° 10′–13° 45′ N. and 13° 90′–16° 50′ W. The area is 4,004 sq. miles of which one fifth is the river. Ocean-going vessels can go up-river for 150 miles and river craft up to 300 miles from the mouth. The Gambia River basin was part of the region dominated in the 10th–16th centuries by the strong Songhai and Mali kingdoms centred on the upper Niger. The population comprises mainly Wolof, Mandinka and Fula peoples who originally migrated there from the north and east. Population (1983 Census) is approximately 700,000.

The first recorded Europeans to reach the Gambia River were the Portuguese in 1447. In 1588 Queen Elizabeth I gave the first charter to English merchants to trade along the river. Merchants from France, Courland (now part of Latvia) and the Netherlands also established trading posts there. The English presence was strongly challenged by the French, who were dominant further north up the coast, but in 1783 the Treaty of Versailles acknowledged English rights. In 1816, after the Napoleonic Wars, and in order to enforce abolition of the slave trade, the British stationed a garrison on a low sandy island called Banjul at the river mouth. Renamed Bathurst, this became the capital of a small British-administered colony, initially under the Governor of Sierra Leone. Negotiations with France continued sporadically until 1889 when it was agreed that the British rights along the upper river should extend 10 km on either bank. British administration was extended from the Colony to this Protectorate. The Gambia became independent within the Commonwealth on February 18, 1965, and a Republic on April 24, 1970.

The Gambia's relationship with Senegal has always been an important factor in political and economic policy. Moves towards a closer association were accelerated after an abortive coup in The Gambia in July 1981 was put down with the help of Senegalese troops. In February 1982 the Senegambia Confederation was formally instituted based on certain joint institutions and integration of policies, but each country remains sovereign and independent.

Except during the rainy season from June to October, when it sometimes becomes uncomfortably humid, Banjul's climate is very pleasant. Rainfall is 32–40 inches a year.

CAPITAL.—ΨBanjul. Population (1983 Census) of island of Banjul was 44,536; and of adjacent Kombo St. Mary district 102,858. Total population of Banjul/Kombo St. Mary, 147,394.

FLAG.—Horizontal stripes of red, blue and green, separated by narrow white stripes.

GOVERNMENT

The constitution is democratic and Parliamentary, with an executive President elected for five years. The House of Representatives has 35 elected members, 5 elected Chiefs Representatives and up to 8 nominated members plus the Attorney-General (*ex-officio*). The Vice President and other Ministers are appointed by the President. Parliament must be dissolved after five years. The last general elections were held in May 1982. The present state of the parties for elected members is PPP (People's Progressive Party) 29; NCP (National Convention Party) 3; Independents 3.

President and Cabinet

President, His Excellency Alhaji Sir Dawda Kairaba Jawara, G.C.M.G.
Vice-President, Hon. Bakary B. Darbo.
External Affairs, Hon. L. K. Jabang.
Finance and Trade, Hon. S. S. Sisay.
Attorney-General, Hon. H. Jallow.
Health, Labour and Social Welfare, Hon. M. C. Jallow.
Agriculture, Hon. S. Sabally.
Information and Tourism, Hon. L. J. Sonko.
Economic Planning and Industrial Development, Hon. A. A. N'Jie.
Water Resources and the Environment, Hon. O. A. Jallow.
Works and Communications, Hon. L. B. M'Boge.
Education, Youth, Sports and Culture, Hon. Mrs. L. N. N'Jie.
Local Government and Lands, Hon. A. Janneh.
Interior, Hon. A. W. Badji.

Chief Justice, Hon. E. O. Ayoola.
Speaker, Alhaji Hon. M. B. N'Jie.

GAMBIA HIGH COMMISSION
57 Kensington Court, W8 5DG
[01-937 6316/7/8]

High Commissioner, His Excellency Samuel J. O. Sarr, M.B.E. (1983).

BRITISH HIGH COMMISSION
48 Atlantic Road, Fajara (P.O. Box 507), Banjul

High Commissioner, His Excellency John Donald Garner, L.V.O., *apptd.* 1984.

COMMUNICATIONS

There is an international airport at Yundum, 17 miles from Banjul, with scheduled services flying to other West African states and to the U.K. Banjul is the main port. Internal communication is by road and river. There is no railway system. There are two broadcasting stations and a U.H.F. telephone service linking Banjul with the principal towns in the provinces. There is no television service.

EDUCATION

There are 23 secondary high schools and technical colleges with a total enrolment of 13,000 students. Two High Schools provide 'A' level education. Gambia College provides post-secondary courses in education, agriculture, public health and nursing. There are seven vocational training institutions with a total enrolment of 800. Higher education and advanced training courses are taken outside The Gambia, currently by over 200 students.

PRODUCTION

Eighty-five per cent of the population depend for their livelihood on agriculture (40 per cent of Gross Domestic Product). The chief product, groundnuts, is also the most important export item, forming over 90 per cent of all domestic exports. Other crops are rice, millet, sorghum, maize and cotton. Fishing and livestock industries are being developed. Thirty per cent of the country's basic food requirements are imported. There are no significant deposits of minerals. Manufactures are limited to groundnut processing, minor metal fabrications, paints, furniture, soap and bottling. Tourism is developing quickly, with 65,000 visitors in 1984–85. The entrepôt trade through The Gambia, re-exporting imported goods to neighbouring countries, is an important element in the national economy.

FINANCE

	1983–84*	1984–85†
Recurrent Revenue ...	D157,362,000	D172,600,000
Recurrent Expenditure	151,827,000	180,900,000

*Approved estimates   †proposed

Over 80 per cent of capital expenditure comes from external aid grants and loans. The Five Year Development Plan 1981–86 envisages an annual GDP growth rate of 5·1 per cent or 2·5 per cent per capita (at 1980–81 prices).

The Government financial year begins on July 1.

Currency.—Decimal currency was introduced in the Gambia on July 1, 1971. The unit is the *dalasi* of 100 *butut*.

TRADE

	1983–1984
Total imports	D314,300,000
Total exports	160,500,000

Trade with U.K.

	1983	1984
Imports from U.K.	£10,565,000	£10,233,000
Exports to U.K.	3,800,000	3,407,000

GHANA

AREA AND POPULATION.—Ghana (formerly known as the Gold Coast) is situated on the Gulf of Guinea, between 3° 07′ W. long. and 1° 14′ E. long. (about 334 miles), and extends 441 miles north from Cape Three Points (4° 45′ N.) to 11° 11′ N. It is bounded on the north by Burkina Faso, on the west by the Ivory Coast, on the east by Togo, and on the south by the Atlantic Ocean. Although a tropical country, Ghana is cooler than many countries within similar latitudes.

Ghana has a total area of 92,100 sq. miles. The population at the Census of 1984 was 12,205,574. Almost all Ghanaians are Sudanese Negroes, although Hamitic strains are common in Northern Ghana. The official language is English. The principal indigenous language group is Akan, of which Twi and Fanti are the most commonly used. Ga, Ewe and languages of the Mole–Dagbani group are common in certain regions.

CAPITAL.—ΨACCRA. Population of the Greater Accra Region (including Tema) was (1984 Census) 1,420,066. Other towns are Kumasi, Tamale, Sekondi-Takoradi, Cape Coast, Sunyani, Ho, Koforidua, Tarkwa and Winneba. Accra is 3,920 miles by sea from Liverpool, transit 12 to 30 days.

FLAG.—Equal horizontal bands of red over yellow over green; five-point black star on gold stripe.

INDEPENDENCE DAY.—March 6.

GOVERNMENT

There is no recorded history of the Gold Coast region before the coming of Europeans in the fifteenth century. The constituent parts of the State came under British administration at various times, the original Gold Coast Colony (the coastal and Southern areas) being first constituted in 1874; Ashanti in 1901; and the Northern Territories Protectorate in 1901. The territory of Trans-Volta-Togoland, part of the former German colony of Togo, was mandated to Britain by the League of Nations after the First World War, and remained under British administration as a United Nations Trusteeship after the Second World War. After a plebiscite in May, 1956, under the auspices of the United Nations, the territory was integrated with the Gold Coast Colony.

The former Gold Coast Colony and associated territories became the independent state of Ghana and a member of the British Commonwealth on March 6, 1957 and adopted a Republican constitution on July 1, 1960. A *coup* in June 1979 led to the formation of an Armed Forces Revolutionary Council chaired by Flt.-Lt. Jerry Rawlings. Civilian rule was restored in Sept. 1979 but overthrown on Dec. 31, 1981, when another *coup* brought back into power Flt.-Lt. Rawlings.

Provisional National Defence Council

Chairman, Flt.-Lt. J. J. Rawlings.

Members, Justice D. F. Annan; Alhaji Iddrisu Mahama; Mrs. A. Enin; Ebow Tawaih; Mrs. S. Alhassan.

P.N.D.C. Coordinating Secretary, P. V. Obeng.

GHANA HIGH COMMISSION
13 Belgrave Square, SW1H 8PR
[01-235 4142/5]

High Commissioner, His Excellency Kenneth Kweku Sinaman Dadzie (1982).

BRITISH HIGH COMMISSION
P.O. Box 296, High Street, Accra

High Commissioner, His Excellency Kevin Francis Xavier Burns, C.M.G. (1983).

British Council Representative, D. Clare, Liberia Road (P.O. Box 771), Accra, and an Office in *Kumasi.*

PRODUCTION, ETC.

Agriculture.—Agriculture forms the basis of Ghana's economy, employing 70 per cent. of the working population. Crops of the *Forest Zone* include cocoa, which is the largest single source of revenue, rice and a variety of other foodstuff crops grown on mixed-crop farms. Fruits such as avocado pears, oranges and pineapples are grown. Cassava is the most important crop of the *Coastal Savannas Zone,* of the lower Volta area. Production of pulses such as groundnuts is widespread. Near the Togo border oil palms, yams, maize, cassava, fruit and vegetables are produced. Livestock is raised in the uncultivated areas. The *Northern Savanna Zone* is Ghana's principal cattle rearing area and other livestock production there is important for home consumption. Corn and millet crops are produced in the far north and maize, yams, rice and groundnut crops in more southerly parts of the Zone.

Attempts are being made to diversify agricultural production, with cash crops being extensively cultivated for export and to provide raw materials for local industry.

Fisheries.—Fishing is important in coastal areas and in the Volta itself. However production cannot meet demand and there are considerable imports of fish products. About 80 per cent of home supply is obtained from sea fisheries, but production from the Volta Lake and other inland fisheries is increasing.

Mineral Production.—The area within a 60 mile radius of Dunkwa produces 90 per cent of Ghana's mineral exports. Manganese production from Nsuta ranks among the world's highest and gold, industrial diamonds and bauxite are also produced. Some 30,000 persons are employed by the mining companies.

Manufactures.—Examples of the small-scale traditional industries are tailoring, goldsmithing and carpentry. Priority has been given in recent years to the establishment of a number of "Pioneer Industries" including timber products, vehicle and refrigerator assembly, cigarettes, boatbuilding, food processing, cotton textiles, clothing, footwear, printing and other light industries. A modern industrial complex is growing in the Accra-Tema area.

Volta River Project.—The Volta River is formed at the confluence of the Black and White Voltas, both of which rise in the neighbouring republic of Burkina Faso. With its tributaries the Volta drains an area of 150,000 sq. miles of which 61,000 sq. miles lie in Ghana. From 1966 the Volta Dam at Akosombo has generated hydro-electric power for the processing of bauxite and fed a power transmission network for the Accra-Kumasi-Takoradi area. Electricity is now also sent to Togo and Benin. The lake raised by the Volta Dam has a maximum area of 3,275 sq. miles, a length of 250 miles and a shore line of 4,500 miles.

COMMUNICATIONS

Accra Airport is an international airport and Ghana Airways Corporation is the national airline. There are also internal airports at Takoradi, Kumasi and Tamale.

There are 20,000 miles of motorable roads, of which 2,335 miles are bitumenized. There are 600 miles of railway, linking Accra and the principal ports of Takoradi and Tema with their hinterlands, and with each other.

Takoradi Harbour consists of seven quay berths—one is leased specially for manganese exports. Tema Harbour has 10 berths for larger ocean going vessels and the largest dry dock on the West African coast. An oil berth has also been built to serve the Ghaip refinery which has been constructed at Tema.

Trade with U.K.

	1983	1984
Imports from U.K.	£82,234,000	£82,897,000
Exports to U.K.	58,192,000	61,561,000

Principal exports are cocoa, timber and gold. Principal imports are road vehicles, manufacturing equipment, petroleum and raw materials.

The currency of Ghana is the *cedi* (¢) of 100 *pesawas.*

GRENADA

AREA, POPULATION.—Grenada is situated between the parallels of 12° 13'–11° 58' N. lat. and 61° 20'–61° 35' W. long., and is about 80 miles north of Trinidad, 68 miles S.S.W. of St. Vincent, and about 120 miles S.W. of Barbados. The island is about 21 miles in length and 12 miles in breadth, with an area of 120 square miles. Also included in the territory of Grenada are some of the Grenadines islets, the largest of which is Carriacou, 13 square miles in area. The population was estimated at Dec. 1982 as 110,410. The country is mountainous and very picturesque, and the climate is healthy.

CHIEF TOWN.—ΨSt. George's (population 7,500) lies on the southwest coast, and possesses a good harbour.

GOVERNMENT

Grenada was discovered by Columbus in 1498, and named Conception. It was originally colonized by the French, and was ceded to Great Britain by the Treaty of Versailles in 1783. It became an Associated State in 1967 and an independent nation on Feb. 7, 1974.

The government of Sir Eric Gairy was overthrown on March 13, 1979 by the New Jewel Movement and a People's Revolutionary Government was set up, headed by Mr. Maurice Bishop, one of the leaders of the revolution. Disagreements within the P.R.G. led, in Oct. 1983, to violence and the death of Mr. Bishop, whose government was replaced by a Revolutionary Military Council. These events prompted the intervention of Caribbean and U.S. forces. The Governor-General installed an advisory council in Nov. 1983 to act as an interim government until a General Election was held, on Dec. 3, 1984. The New National Party won 14 of the 15 seats in the House of Representatives and, following the dissolution of the advisory council, its leader was sworn in as Prime Minister. A phased withdrawal of U.S. forces began in April 1985.

Governor-General, Sir Paul Scoon, G.C.M.G., O.B.E. *apptd.* 1978.

Cabinet

Prime Minister and Minister of Home Affairs, Security, Information, Finance, Trade, Planning, Industrial Development and Carriacou and Petit Martinique Affairs, Herbert A. Blaize.

Deputy P.M. and Minister of External and Legal Affairs, Benjamin Jones.

Agriculture, Lands, Forestry, Fisheries and Tourism, George I. Brizan.

Health, Housing, Community Development and Women's Affairs, Daniel Williams.

Education, Culture, Sport and Youth Affairs, George McGuire.
Communications, Works, Public Utilities, Energy and Civil Aviation, Dr. Keith Mitchell.
Labour, Co-operatives, Social Security and Local Government, Dr. Francis Alexis.

GRENADA HIGH COMMISSION
1 Collingham Gardens, SW5 0HW
[01–373 7808/9 and 7800]

High Commissioner, His Excellency Oswald M. Gibbs, C.M.G. (1984).

BRITISH HIGH COMMISSION
14 Church Street, St. George's.

High Commissioner, (resides at Bridgetown, Barbados).
Resident Representative, J. P. Kelly, M.B.E. (*Second Secretary*).

ECONOMY

The economy is principally agrarian, with cocoa, nutmegs and bananas the major crops. Fruit and vegetables are grown and livestock raised for domestic consumption. The fishing industry is being developed. Manufacturing is mostly confined to processing agricultural products.

Total value of imports in 1982 was EC$152 million. Principal domestic exports for 1982 were cocoa (EC$12·5m), nutmeg (EC$8·2m), mace (EC$2·5m) and bananas (EC$8·9m).

GUYANA

AREA, POPULATION, ETC.—Guyana, the former colony of British Guiana, which includes the Counties of Demerara, Essequibo and Berbice, is situated on the north-east coast of South America, bordering on Venezuela, Brazil and Suriname. It has a total area of 83,000 square miles with a seaboard of about 270 miles. The population at May 1980, was estimated at 793,000, but subsequent years have seen heavy emigration. There are three distinct areas. (1) A narrow alluvial coastal belt 10 to 40 miles deep, eastern part of which is intensively cultivated and contains some 90 per cent of the population. Much of this is below the level of the sea and is drained and irrigated by an intricate system of canals constructed by the Dutch. (2) A mountainous area of dense rain forest behind the coastland, still partly unexplored, which reaches its highest point at *Mount Roraima* (9,000 ft.) on the junction of the Guyana–Brazil–Venezuela borders. (3) The open savannah country of the Rupununi in the south-west where cattle ranching is practised and oil deposits have been discovered.

The entire country is intersected by numerous large rivers, though these are of limited navigational use because of rapids and waterfalls, the most notable of which are the *Kaieteur Fall* on the Potaro River with a sheer drop of 741 ft., the *Horse Shoe Falls* on the Essequibo and the *Marina Fall* on the Ipobe River.

Climate.—The two dry seasons normally last from the middle of February to the end of April, and from the middle of August to the end of November. The climate on the coast is pleasant and healthy for the greater part of the year. In the Aug.–Oct. period it is hot. The mean temperature is 80·3°F., the usual extremes being 70°F. and 90°F. In the interior the mean temperature is higher—82·6°F., its extremes ranging from 66°F. to 103°F. The yearly rainfall is subject to marked variation, its mean on the coast

lands averaging about 90 inches with an average of 58 inches on the savannahs.

CAPITAL.—ΨGeorgetown. Estimated population, including environs, 185,000. Other towns are: Linden (population 29,000); ΨNew Amsterdam (population 23,000); Corriverton (population 17,000).

FLAG.—Red triangle with black border, pointing from hoist to fly, on a yellow triangle with white border, all on a green field.

GOVERNMENT

Guyana became independent on May 26, 1966, with a Governor-General appointed by the Queen. It became a Cooperative Republic on Feb. 23, 1970. Under the Independence Constitution the Prime Minister and Cabinet were responsible to a National Assembly elected by secret ballot every 5 years. The last election under this Constitution was in 1973 and the term of that Assembly was later extended to October 1980.

A new Constitution was passed into law in February 1980 and promulgated in October 1980. It provides for an Executive President, a National Assembly of 65 members, and also for a National Congress of Local Democratic Organs responsible for local government. The Supreme Congress of the People consists of all members of these two assemblies.

The electoral system is a Proportional Representation or "single list" system, each voter casting his vote for a party list of candidates. The voting age is 18.

Executive President.—Desmond Hoyte, *took office* Aug. 1985.

Cabinet

Executive President and Minister of National Security, L. F. S. Burnham.
Prime Minister and First Vice-President, Hamilton Green.
Deputy Prime Minister, Vice-President and Attorney General, Dr. M. Shahabudeen.
Deputy Prime Minister and Vice-President, Mrs. Viola Burnham.
Deputy Prime Minister and Vice-President (National Development), R. Chandisingh.
Deputy Prime Minister, H. Parris.

SENIOR MINISTERS

Home Affairs, J. R. Thomas.
Mobilization, R. H. O. Corbin.
Energy and Mines, Haroon Rashid.
Foreign Affairs, R. E. Jackson.
Education and Social Development, M. Parris.
Economic Planning and Finance, C. Greenidge.
Health, R. Van West Charles.
Forestry, Sullahuddin.

GUYANA HIGH COMMISSION
3 Palace Court, Bayswater Road, W2 4LP
[01-229 7684]

High Commissioner, His Excellency Cedric Joseph (1982).

BRITISH HIGH COMMISSION
44 Main Street (P.O. Box 10849), Georgetown

High Commissioner, His Excellency John Dudley Massingham, *apptd.* 1985.

JUDICATURE

The Supreme Court of Judicature consists of a Court of Appeal and a High Court. There are also Courts of Summary Jurisdiction. The Court of Appeal consists of the Chancellor as President, the

Chief Justice and such number of Justices of Appeal as may be prescribed by Parliament.

The High Court consists of the Chief Justice, as President, and nine Puisne Judges. It is a court with unlimited jurisdiction in civil matters and exercises exclusive jurisdiction in probate, divorce and admiralty, and certain other matters.

Chancellor, K. S. Massiah.

Chief Justice, K. M. George.

PRODUCTION, ETC.

The economy is based almost entirely on the main export items of sugar, rice, bauxite and alumina. Diamonds and gold are also mined, timber and rum are produced and there is some cattle ranching. The fishing industry is being expanded. Industry is fairly small-scale.

COMMUNICATIONS

Georgetown and New Amsterdam are the principal ports, though bauxite ships also sail to Linden, on the R. Demerara, and Everton, on the R. Berbice. There are no public railways and the few roads are confined mainly to the coastal areas. Air transport is the easiest form of communication between the coast and the interior. There are two state-owned radio broadcasting stations; there is no television service.

EDUCATION

In September 1976 Government assumed total control of the education system and made education free from nursery to university level. At Aug. 1981 there were 374 nursery schools with 27,955 pupils, 425 primary schools with 130,832 pupils. There were 75,325 students in secondary schools. Government trains teachers for primary and secondary schools at its own institutions.

Approximately 1,800 students were enrolled at the University of Guyana in degree programmes and certificate and diploma courses.

There are five technical and vocational institutions, and 36 Home Economics and Industrial Arts Centres in various parts of the country; many primary and secondary schools have departments attached to them. There are also a number of technical and vocational institutions not under the aegis of the Ministry of Education.

Trade with U.K.

	1983	1984
Imports from U.K.	£13,685,000	£14,845,000
Exports to U.K.	42,810,000	57,884,000

INDIA

AREA AND POPULATION.—The Republic of India has an area of 1,261,816 square miles, composed of three well-defined regions: the mountain range of the Himalayas; the Indo-Gangetic plain; and the Southern Peninsula. The main mountain ranges are the Himalayas in the north (over 29,000 feet) and the Western and Eastern Ghats (over 8,000 feet). Major rivers include the Ganges, Indus, Krishna, Godavari and Mahanadi.

There are four seasons: the cold season (Dec.–March); the hot season (April–May); the rainy season (June–Sept.); and the season of the retreating S.W. monsoon (Oct.–Nov.). Temperatures vary over the whole country, between averages of about 50° F and 92° F, reaching over 100° F in some parts during the hot season. There are similar variations in rainfall,

from only a few inches a year falling in the western Thar Desert to over 400 inches in Meghalaya.

India is the second most populous country in the world. The population at the 1981 census was 685,184,692, of which slightly more than 20 per cent was urban. The majority of the population are Hindu (453 million = 82 per cent), the rest being Muslim (61 million = 11 per cent), Christian (14 million = 2·5 per cent), Sikh (10 million = 1·8 per cent), Buddhist (4 million = 0·7 per cent) and Jain (2·5 million = 0·5 per cent). The official languages are Hindi in the Devanagari script and English, though 14 regional languages also are recognized for adoption as official State languages.

HISTORY.—The Indus civilization was fully developed by c. 2,500 B.C. but collapsed c. 1,750 B.C., subsequently being replaced by an Aryan civilization spread from the west. The first Arabic invasions of the north west began in the seventh century and Moslem, Hindu and Buddhist states developed until the establishment of the Mogul dynasty in 1526. The British East India Company established settlements throughout the 17th century; clashes with the French and native princes led to the British government taking control of the Company in 1784. The separate dominions of India and Pakistan became independent within the Commonwealth in 1947 and India became a Republic in 1950.

FLAG.—The National Flag is a horizontal tricolour with bands of deep saffron, white and dark green in equal proportions. In the centre of the white band appears an Asoka wheel in navy blue.

CAPITAL.—Delhi (population in 1981 was 6,220,000). Populations of other principal cities (1981 figures) were ΨCalcutta, 9,166,000; ΨBombay,, 8,202,000; Ψ Madras, 4,277,000; Bangalore, 2,914,000; Hyderabad, 2,566,000; Ahmedabad, 2,124,000; Kanpur, 1,685,000; Pune, 1,685,000; Lucknow, 1,007,000.

NATIONAL DAY.—January 26 (Republic Day).

STATES AND TERRITORIES OF THE UNION

There are 22 States and nine Union Territories. Each State is governed by a Governor appointed by the President who holds office for five years, and a Council of Ministers. All States have a Legislative Assembly, and some have also a Legislative Council, elected directly by adult suffrage for a maximum period of five years. The judges of the High Court of a State are appointed by the President.

The Union Territories are administered, except where otherwise provided by Parliament, by the President acting through an Administrator or other authority appointed by him.

GOVERNMENT

The Constitution of India came into force in 1950. Executive power is vested in the President, who is elected for a five year term by an electoral college consisting of the elected members of the Union and State Legislatures. He appoints the Prime Minister and, on the latter's advice, the Ministers, and can dismiss them. The Council of Ministers is collectively responsible to the *Lok Sabha* (Lower House). The Vice President is *ex-officio* chairman of the *Rajya Sabha* (Upper House).

Legislative power rests with the President, the *Rajya Sabha* (which has up to 250 members) and the *Lok Sabha* (which has up to 544 members). Twelve members of the *Rajya Sabha* are nominated by the President, the rest are indirectly elected representatives of the State and Union Territories. They hold office for six years. The 525 members of the *Lok Sabha* representing the States are directly elected by universal adult franchise, and 17 representatives of

	Area (sq. km.)	Population (1981 Census)	State Capital
STATES			
Andhra Pradesh	275,100p	53,549,673	Hyderabad
Assam	78,400	19,896,843†	Dispur
Bihar	173,900p	69,914,734	Patna
Gujurat	196,000p	34,085,799	Gandhinagar
Haryana	44,200p	12,922,618	Chandigarh
Himachal Pradesh	55,700	4,280,818	Shimla
Jammu and Kashmir*	222,200p	5,987,389	Srinagar/Jammu
Karnataka	191,800	37,135,714	Bangalore
Kerala	38,900p	25,453,680	Trivandrum
Madhya Pradesh	443,500p	52,178,844	Bhopal
Maharashtra	307,700p	62,784,171	Bombay
Manipur	22,300	1,420,953	Imphal
Meghalaya	22,400p	1,335,819	Shillong
Nagaland	16,600	774,930	Kohima
Orissa	155,700	26,370,271	Bhubaneswar
Punjab	50,400	16,788,915	Chandigarh
Rajasthan	342,200	34,261,862	Jaipur
Sikkim	7,100	316,385	Gangtok
Tamil Nadu	130,100p	48,408,077	Madras
Tripura	10,500	2,053,058	Agartala
Uttar Pradesh	294,400p	110,862,013	Lucknow
West Bengal	88,800p	54,580,647	Calcutta
UNION TERRITORIES			
Andaman and Nicobar Islands	8,200	188,741	
Arunachal Pradesh	83,700p	631,839	
Chandigarh	100	451,610	
Dadra and Nagar Haveli	500	103,676	
Delhi	1,500	6,220,406	
Goa, Daman and Diu	3,800	1,086,730	
Lakshadweep	30	40,249	
Mizoram	21,100	493,757	
Pondicherry	500	604,471	

p provisional figure   † projected figure

* Jammu and Kashmir is an area disputed between India, Pakistan and China, all three controlling a part of the territory. The area figure includes those parts occupied by Pakistan and China, which are claimed by India, but the population figure excludes the population of these areas, where the census was not taken. The state's capital is at Srinagar in winter and Jamma in summer.

the Union Territories are chosen, for a maximum term of five years. Subject to the provisons of the Constitution, the Union Parliament can make laws for the whole of India and the State legislatures for their respective units.

The Supreme Court consists of the Chief Justice and not more than 17 other judges, appointed by the President. It is the highest court in respect of all constitutional matters and the final Court of Appeal.

President of the Republic of India, Giani Zail Singh, *elected* July 12, 1982.
Vice-President, Ramaswami Venkataraman.

Cabinet

Prime Minister (also head of Ministries of Environment & Forests; External Affairs; Personnel and Training; Administrative Reforms; Planning; Science & Technology; Tourism & Civil Aviation; Atomic Energy; Culture; Electronics; Ocean Development; Space; Youth Affairs & Sports), Rajiv Gandhi.
Defence, P. V. Narasimha Rao.
Home, S. B. Chavan.
Finance (also Commerce), Vishwanath Pratap Singh.
Works & Housing, Abdul Ghafoor.
Law & Justice, A. K. Sen.
Irrigation & Power, B. Shankaranand.

Railways, Bansi Lal.
Agriculture & Rural Development, Buta Singh.
Parliamentary Affairs, H. K. L. Bhagat.
Education, K. C. Pant.
Health & Family Welfare, Mohsina Kidwai.
Food & Civil Supplies, Rao Birendra Singh.
Steel, Mines & Coal, Vasant Sathe.
Chemicals & Fertilisers (also Industry & Company Affairs), Veerendra Patil.

INDIAN HIGH COMMISSION
India House, Aldwych, WC2B 4NA
[01–836 8484]

High Commissioner, Dr. P. C. Alexander (1985).
Deputy High Commissioner, S. R. C. Arora.

BRITISH HIGH COMMISSION
Chanakyapuri, New Delhi, 21, 1100–21.

High Commissioner, His Excellency Sir Robert Wade-Gery, K.C.M.G., K.C.V.O. (1982).
British Council Representative in India, J. G. Hanson, C.B.E., AIFACS Building, Rafi Marg, New Delhi 110 001. Offices also at *Bombay, Madras* and *Calcutta.* There are British Council libraries at these four centres and British libraries at *Ahmedabad, Bangalore, Bhopal, Hyderabad, Lucknow, Patna, Pune, Ranchi* and *Trivandrum.*

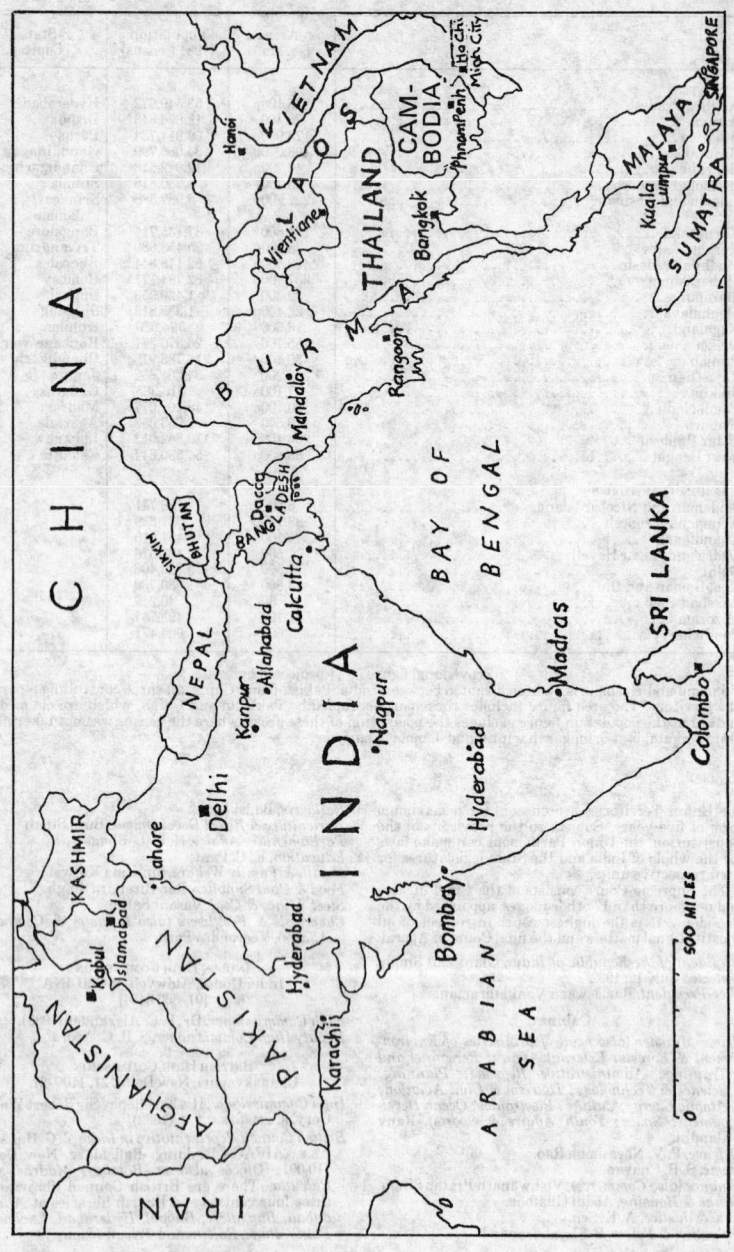

DEFENCE

The supreme command of the armed forces is vested in the President. Administrative and operational control resides in the Army, Navy and Air Headquarters under the supervision of the Ministry of Defence.

The *Army* has five Commands, Southern, Eastern, Northern, Western and Central.

The *Indian Navy* consists of an aircraft-carrier, a number of frigate squadrons, including some of the latest type of anti-submarine and anti-aircraft frigates, a squadron of anti-submarine patrol vessels, minesweeping squadrons, conventional type submarines and a submarine depot ship. A Naval aviation wing and a hydrographic office have also been set up. India has started building her own naval craft.

The *Indian Air Force* is organized in seven major formations, the Western, Eastern, Central, Southern and South Western Air Commands, and the Training and Maintenance Commands. Aircraft in use include SU-7, Hunter, Gnat, MiG 21 and MiG 23, Canberra bomber, Jaguar and Mirage-2000, helicopter and training planes.

PRODUCTION

Agriculture

Agriculture is the chief industry, supporting about 70 per cent of the population, and providing nearly 40 per cent of the Gross Domestic Product. The area under cultivation has been increased by irrigation schemes, but most holdings are less than five acres. Production has grown by three per cent each year since 1951, remaining slightly ahead of the two per cent increase necessary to keep pace with the rising population. Food crops occupy three-quarters of the total cropped area and production of food grains amounted to 150 million tonnes in 1983–84. The main food crops are rice, cereals (principally wheat), pulses, sugar cane, jute, cotton and tea. Other products include oil seeds, spices, groundnuts, tobacco, rubber and coffee. Livestock is raised, principally for dairy purposes or for the hides: cattle (181 million), goats (71 million), sheep (41 million) and pigs (9·9 million).

Industry

India's major industries are based on the exploitation and processing of her mineral resources, principally coal, oil and iron. The coal industry, nationalized in the early 1970s, reached an output in 1983–84 of 138·3 million tonnes. Production of crude oil, from the main fields in Assam and from offshore drilling was about 26 million tonnes in 1983–84. Steel production is mainly in the hands of the public sector, with five public and one private sector integrated steel plants producing 7·9 million tonnes of ingot steel in 1983–84. The engineering industry, heavy and light, is also primarily in the hands of the public sector. The manufacture of chemicals, fertilizers, petrochemicals, automobiles and commercial vehicles has been expanded.

Other principal manufactures are those derived from agricultural products, textiles, jute goods, sugar, leather, which along with tea, fish, and iron ore and concentrates, are India's major exports.

FINANCE

The budget estimates for 1984–85, placed expenditure (on revenue account) at *Rs.*263,410 million. Revenue (excluding States' shares) was estimated at *Rs.*240,160 million.

Trade with U.K.

	1983	1984
Imports from U.K.	£804,779,000	£780,997,000
Exports to U.K.	366,928,000	571,470,000

COMMUNICATIONS

Civil Aviation.—Four international airports—Palam (Delhi), Sahar (Bombay), Dum Dum (Calcutta), Meenambakkam (Madras)—are managed by the International Airports Authority. The other 87 aerodromes are controlled and operated by the Civil Aviation Department of the Government. The national airlines are Indian Airlines (internal) and Air India (international).

Railways.—The railways are grouped into nine administrative zones, Southern, Central, Western, Northern, North-Eastern, North-East Frontier, Eastern, South-Eastern and South-Central.

Gross Traffic Receipts (1983–84), crores of rupees, 5,146. Working expenses, 4,521. Net railway revenues, 671.

Ψ *Ports.*—The chief seaports are Bombay (Mumbai), Calcutta, Haldia, Madras, Mormugao, Cochin, Visakhapatnam, Kandla, Paradip, Mangalore and Tuticorin. There are 139 minor working ports with varying capacity.

Shipping.—On April 30, 1984, 295 ships totalling 3,110,000 gross tons were on the Indian Register.

JAMAICA

AREA, POPULATION, ETC.—Jamaica is situated in the Caribbean Sea south of the eastern extremity of Cuba and lies between latitudes 17° 43′ and 18° 32′ North, and longitude 76° 11′ and 78° 21′ West. Jamaica is 4,243·6 square miles in area and is divided into three counties (Surrey, Middlesex and Cornwall) and 14 parishes. The greatest length from east to west (Morant Point to Negril Point) is 146 miles and the extreme breadth 51 miles.

The topography consists mainly of coastal plains, divided by the Blue Mountain Range in the east, and the hills and limestone plateaus which occupy the central and western areas of the interior. The central chain of high peaks of the Blue Mountains is over 6,000 feet above sea level, and the Blue Mountain Peak, the highest of these, reaches an elevation of 7,402 feet. The rivers flow down from the central mountainous area. Most of the rivers are narrow and fast flowing, and some have rapids. None is navigable except the Black River, and that only for small craft.

At Dec. 31, 1982 Jamaica's population was estimated to be 2,265,400. The island was discovered by Columbus on May 4, 1494, and occupied by the Spanish from 1509 until 1655 when a British expedition, sent out by Oliver Cromwell, under Admiral Penn and General Venables, attacked the island, which capitulated after a token resistance. In 1670 it was formally ceded to England by the Treaty of Madrid.

CAPITAL.—The seat of government is Kingston, the largest town and seaport (estimated population of the Corporate area of Kingston and St. Andrew in 1979, 662,501). Other towns are Montego Bay, Spanish Town, Mandeville and May Pen.

FLAG.—Gold diagonal cross forming triangles of green at top and bottom, triangles of black at hoist and in fly.

NATIONAL DAY.—First Monday in August (Independence Day).

GOVERNMENT

Jamaica became an independent state within the Commonwealth on Aug. 6, 1962. The Legislature consists of a Senate of 21 nominated members and a House of Representatives consisting of 60 members elected by universal adult suffrage. The Senate has no power to delay money bills for longer than one month or other bills for longer than seven months against the wishes of the House of Representatives. The Constitution provides for a Leader of the Opposition.

At the General Election of Dec. 15, 1983, the Jamaica Labour Party won all 60 seats after the People's National Party decided not to contest the election.

Governor-General, His Excellency Sir Florizel Glasspole, G.C.M.G., G.C.V.O.

Cabinet

Prime Minister and Minister of Finance and Planning, Rt. Hon. E. Seaga, P.C., M.P.
Deputy Prime Minister, Minister of Foreign Affairs and Foreign Trade, Rt. Hon. H. Shearer.
Construction and Electoral Affairs, Hon. B. Golding.
Agriculture, Hon. Dr. P. Broderick.
National Security and Justice, and Attorney General, Hon. W. Spaulding.
Local Government, Hon. N. B. Lewis.
Labour, Hon. J. A. G. Smith.
Public Utilities and Transport, Hon. P. Charles.
Education, Hon. Dr. Mavis Gilmour.
Industry and Commerce, Hon. D. Vaz.
Public Service, Hon. E. M. Anderson.
Youth and Community Development, Hon. E. C. Barlett.
Mining, Energy and Tourism, Senator Hon. H. Hart.
Social Security, Hon. Dr. N. E. Gallimore.
Without Portfolio, Senator Hon. O. G. Harding.
Ministers of State, Hon. Enid Bennett (*Local Government*); Hon. H. Brown (*Tourism*); Rt. Hon. R. Marsh (*Construction*); Hon. K. Sangster (*Youth and Community Development*); Hon. K. Samuda (*Industry and Commerce*).

JAMAICAN HIGH COMMISSION
50 St. James's Street, SW1A 1JS
[01–499 8600]

High Commissioner, His Excellency H. S. Walker.

BRITISH HIGH COMMISSION
P.O. Box 575, Trafalgar Road, Kingston 10.

High Commissioner, His Excellency Harold Martin Smith Reid, C.M.G. (1984).

JUDICATURE

Chief Justice and Keeper of Records, Hon. E. Zacca.
Judges of the Court of Appeal, Hon. I. D. Rowe (*President*); Hons. H. D. Carberry; J. S. Kerr; B. H. Carey; R. O. C. White; C. A. B. Ross; J. Campbell.

COMMUNICATIONS

There are several excellent harbours, Kingston being the principal port. The island has 2,944 miles of main roads and over 7,000 miles of subsidiary roads. There are about 204 miles of railway open. Telegraph stations and post offices are established in every town and in very many villages.

There are two international airports capable of handling the largest civil jet aircraft, the Norman Manley International Airport on the south coast serving Kingston, and Sangster Airport on the north coast serving the major tourist areas. In addition there are licensed aerodromes at Port Antonio, Ocho

Rios, Mandeville and Negril. There are 16 privately owned, seven public and two military airstrips.

Air Jamaica, the national airline, operates international services; Trans-Jamaica Airlines operates scheduled internal services.

PRODUCTION

Agriculture.—Most of the staple products of tropical climates are grown; sugar, bananas, pimento, coffee and citrus fruit. Some of the sugar is used to produce rum and molasses. Chief products exported in 1984 were sugar (*US*$45·8 million), bananas (*US*$2·6 million), citrus fruit and citrus products (*US*$6·0 million).

Industry.—Jamaica is the fourth largest producer of bauxite in the world; output for 1984 was 8,937,000 tonnes of which 1,749,000 tonnes were processed into alumina before being exported. The bauxite deposits are worked, and processed into alumina, by one Canadian and four U.S. companies in partnership with the Government. In 1984 exports of bauxite and alumina were valued at *US*$220·2 million. Cement is manufactured locally, the output being 257,000 long tons in 1984. The Esso Oil Refinery processed 6,954,000 barrels of crude oil during 1984.

The Jamaica Industrial Development Corporation is responsible for implementing the Government's industrial development programme. This Corporation administers incentive legislation which was enacted to stimulate the establishment of industries locally. In addition to undertaking promotional activities both locally and abroad, the Corporation maintains offices in the U.S. and the U.K. In the last decade, manufacturing has grown from the processing of a few agricultural products into the production of a whole range of commodities dependent on both local and foreign raw materials. Jamaica is a popular tourist resort, attracting visitors mainly from the U.S.A. In 1984 the total number of visitor arrivals was 843,774, and expenditure was estimated at *US*$406·6 million.

FINANCE

	1983–84	1984–85*
Revenue	J$3,226,824,846	J$2,623,100,000
Expenditure	3,254,716,213	3,298,700,000

*Preliminary

National Debt (Dec. 1984) J$19,340,250,000

TRADE

	1983	1984
Total imports	J$2,841·0m.	J$4,379·7m.
Total exports	1,382·4m.	2,874·8m.

Trade with U.K.

	1983	1984
Imports from U.K.	£116,188,000	£48,088,000
Exports to U.K.	94,036,000	77,895,000

KENYA

AREA, POPULATION, ETC.—Kenya is bisected by the equator and extends approximately from latitude 4° N. to latitude 4° S. and from longitude 34° E. to 41° E. From the coast of the Indian Ocean in the east, the borders of Kenya are with Somalia in the east and Ethiopia and Sudan in the north and north-west. To the west lie Uganda and Lake Victoria. On the south is Tanzania. The total area is 224,960 square miles (including 5,171 square miles of water). The country is divided into 7 Provinces (Nyanza, Rift

Valley, Central Coast, Western, Eastern and North-Eastern). The population is estimated to be about 17 million, and increasing by 3·8 per cent annually. The main tribal groups are the Kikuyu, Luhya, Luo, Kamba, Kalenjin and Masai. The official languages are Swahili, which is generally understood throughout Kenya, and English : numerous indigenous languages are also spoken.

CAPITAL.—Nairobi, population about 1,000,000.

Nairobi : transit from London about 25 days by sea ; by air, 10 hrs.

FLAG.—Three equal horizontal bands of black over red over green ; red and white spears and shield device in centre.

NATIONAL DAY.—December 12.

GOVERNMENT

Kenya became an independent state and a member of the British Commonwealth on December 12, 1963, after six months of internal self-government. Kenya became a Republic on Dec. 12, 1964. In 1982 the Government introduced amendments to the constitution and election law, making the country a one-party (K.A.N.U.) state. There is a uni-cameral National Assembly of 171 members.

President, Daniel T. arap Moi, *took office,* Oct. 14, 1978.
Vice-President and Minister of Home Affairs, Hon. Mwai Kibaki.
Planning and National Development, Hon. Dr. Robert J. Ouko.
Finance, Hon. Prof. George Saitoti.
Water Development, Hon. Paul Ngei.
Cooperative Development, Hon. Henry K. Kosgey.
Agriculture and Livestock Development, Hon. Odongo Omamo.
Education, Science and Technology, Hon. J. Ng'eno.
Local Government, Hon. Moses Mudavadi.
Information and Broadcasting, Hon. Noah Ngala.
Foreign Affairs, Hon. Elijah W. Mwangale.
Lands and Settlement, Hon. Eliud Mwamunga.
Energy and Regional Development, Hon. K. Nicholas K. Biwott.
Works, Housing and Physical Planning, Hon. Maina Wanjigi.
Commerce and Industry, Hon. Peter H. Okondo.
Culture and Social Services, Hon. Kenneth Matiba.
Tourism and Wildlife, Hon. J. A. Omanga.
Transport and Communications, Hon. Arthur K. Magugu.
Environment and Natural Resources, Hon. Jeremiah Nyageh.
Labour, Hon. P. Oloo Aringo.
Health, Hon. Peter Nyakiamo.
Office of the President, Hon. Justus ole Tipis; Hon. Jackson H. Angaine; Hon. Hussein M. Mohammed.
Attorney-General, Hon. Matthew G. Muli.

KENYA HIGH COMMISSION IN LONDON
45 Portland Place, W1N 4AS
[01–636 2371/5]

High Commissioner, His Excellency Benjamin K. Kipkulei (1984).

BRITISH HIGH COMMISSION
Bruce House, Standard Street, P.O. Box 30465
Nairobi

High Commissioner, His Excellency Sir Leonard Allinson, K.C.V.O., C.M.G. (1982).
British Council Representative, D. Aspinell, O.B.E., (P.O. Box 40751) ICEA Building, Kenyatta Avenue, Nairobi. There are offices at *Kisumu* and *Mombasa.*

PRODUCTION

Agriculture provides about 52 per cent of total export earnings (excluding processed oil products). The great variation in altitude and ecology provide conditions under which a wide range of crops can be grown. These include wheat, barley, pyrethrum, coffee, tea, sisal, coconuts, cashew nuts, cotton, maize and a wide variety of tropical and temperate fruits and vegetables. The total area of well-farmed land on which concentrated mixed farming can be practised is small and the remainder is arid or semi-arid country but population pressure and the need to increase agricultural production for export has led to attempts to develop such areas.

Prospecting and mining are carried on in some parts of the country, the principal minerals produced being soda ash, salt and limestone.

Hydro-electric power has been developed, particularly on the Upper Tana River. Kenya is now almost self-sufficient in electric power generation but the connection with Owen Falls in Uganda is still in being.

There has been considerable industrial development over the last 15 years and Kenya has a wide variety of industries processing agricultural produce and manufacturing an increasing range of products from local and imported raw materials. New industries have recently come into being such as steel, textile mills, dehydrated vegetable processing and motor tyre manufacture as well as many smaller schemes which have added to the country's already considerable consumer goods. There is an oil refinery in Mombasa supplying both Kenya and Uganda, and a fuel pipeline now connects Mombasa and Nairobi. Industrial areas have been developed in all the principal towns and light industrial estates are being developed for African entrepreneurs.

COMMUNICATIONS

The Kenya Railways Corporation has 1,300 miles of railway open to traffic. There are also 31,000 miles of road, of which 2,700 are bitumen surfaced. Transborder links with Tanzania were re-opened in 1985 with rail services for freight and steamer services for passengers and freight.

The principal port is Mombasa, operated by the Kenya Ports Authority.

International air services operate from airports at Nairobi and Mombasa.

TRADE

Principal exports are coffee and tea, which account for 33 per cent of total export earnings. Also exported are fruit, vegetables, and crude animal and vegetable material. Petroleum products account for about 37 per cent of imports; other imports are manufactured goods, particularly machinery, transport equipment, metals, pharmaceuticals and chemicals.

Trade with U.K.

	1983	1984
Imports from U.K.	£111,249,000	£176,061,000
Exports to U.K.	128,464,000	203,243,000

KIRIBATI

AREA, POPULATION, ETC.—Kiribati, the former Gilbert Islands, became an independent Republic in 1979. Kiribati comprises 33 islands—the Gilberts Group (17) including Banaba, formerly Ocean Island, the Phoenix Islands (8) and the Line Islands (8)—situated in the South West Central Pacific around the point at which the International Date Line cuts the Equator. The total land area of 264 square miles is spread over some 2 million square miles of ocean. Few of the atolls are more than half a mile in width or more than 12 feet high. The vegetation consists mainly of coconut palms, breadfruit trees and pandanus. The population (1985 Census) was approx. 63,800. The population is predominantly Christian.

CAPITAL.—Tarawa (Population estimated at 24,400).

FLAG.—Red, with blue and white wavy lines in base, and in the centre a gold rising sun and a flying frigate bird.

GOVERNMENT

The President is Head of State as well as Head of Government and is elected nationally. There is an elected House of Assembly (36 members); executive authority is vested in the Cabinet.

President and Minister of Foreign Affairs, Hon. Ieremia Tabai, G.C.M.G..

Vice-President and Minister of Home Affairs and Decentralization, Hon. T. Teannaki.

Finance, Hon. Boanereke Boanereke.

The Line and Phoenix Groups, Hon. Uera Rabaua.

Trade, Industry and Labour, Hon. Teewe Arobati.

Health and Family Planning, Hon. Binata Tetaeka.

Natural Resource Development, Hon. Babera Kirata, O.B.E.

Education, Hon. Baitika Toum.

Communications, Hon. Taomati Iuta.

Works and Energy, Hon. Tiwau Awira.

Chief Justice, Hon. J. R. Jones, C.B.E.

Attorney-General, Hon. Michael N. Takabwebwe.

ECONOMY

Most people still practise a semi-subsistence economy, the main staples of their diet being coconuts and fish, supplemented by some imported staples.

The unit of currency is the Australian dollar. Estimated recurrent revenue for 1984 is $15,368,000, of which $A1,774,000 is provided by the United Kingdom as budgetary assistance under the Independence Financial Settlement. This assistance is necessary following the expiry of the phosphate industry, which previously accounted for approximately 50 per cent. of recurrent revenue. The principal imports are foodstuffs, consumer goods and building materials. The principal exports are copra, which earned around $A7,000,000, and fish, income from which was around $A2,230,000 in 1984. Estimated value of total exports in 1984 was $A13,006,000.

COMMUNICATIONS

Air communication exists between most of the islands, and is operated by Air Tungaru, a statutory corporation. There is a weekly service, in association with the airline of the Marshall Islands, between Tarawa, Tuvalu and Nadi (Fiji), and Air Nauru flies weekly between Tarawa and Nauru. Inter-island shipping is operated by a statutory corporation, the Shipping Corporation of Kiribati.

SOCIAL WELFARE

The Government maintains a teacher training college and a secondary school. Four junior secondary schools are maintained by missions. Throughout the Republic there are about a hundred primary schools. The total enrolment of children of school age is about 14,000. The Marine Training School at Tarawa trains seamen for service with overseas shipping lines. There is a general hospital at Tarawa. The other inhabited islands have dispensaries.

BRITISH HIGH COMMISSION
P.O. Box 61, Bairiki Tarawa
High Commissioner, His Excellency Charles Thompson (1983).

LESOTHO

Lesotho is a landlocked mountainous state entirely surrounded by the Republic of South Africa. Of the total area of 11,716 sq. miles a belt between 20 and 40 miles in width lying across the western and southern boundaries and comprising about one-third of the total is classed as Lowlands, being between 5,000 and 6,000 ft. above sea level. The remaining two-thirds are classed as Foothills and Highlands, rising to 11,425 ft. The population was estimated at 1,204,000 in 1981.

CAPITAL.—Maseru, population, (1979 estimate) 277,307.

FLAG.—Blue with conical white Basotho hat in centre, red and green vertical stripes (next staff).

GOVERNMENT

Lesotho became a constitutional monarchy within the Commonwealth on October 4, 1966. The independence constitution was suspended in January 1970, when the country was governed by a Council of Ministers, until the establishment of a nominated National Assembly in April 1974.

The country is divided into ten administrative districts. In each district there is a District Coordinator who co-ordinates all Government activity in the area, working in co-operation with hereditary chiefs.

Head of State, His Majesty King Moshoeshoe II.

Council of Ministers

Prime Minister and Minister of Defence and Internal Security, Rt. Hon. Dr. Leabua Jonathan.

Planning, Employment and Economic Affairs, Hon. E. R. Sekhoyana.

Interior, Hon. N. S. 'Maseribane.

Foreign Affairs, Hon. V. Monts'i Makhele.

Finance, Hon. K. T. J. Rakhetla.

Water, Energy and Mining, Hon. P. M. Majara.

Commerce and Industry, Hon. M. Molapo.

Works, Hon. L. Joanathan.

Transport and Communications, Hon. Dr. K. T. Maphathe.

Health and Social Welfare, Hon. P. L. Lehleonya.

Education, Sport, Culture and Youth, Hon. J. R. L. Kotsokoane.

Rural Development and Co-operatives, Hon. D. P. G. Makoe.

Agriculture, Hon. P. N. Peete.

Law and Justice, Hon. N. Nkuatsana.

Information and Broadcasting, Hon. D. Sixishe.

Ministers of State, Hon. P. J. Khasoane, Hon. I. J. Mokone.

JUDICIARY

The Lesotho Courts of Law consist of: the Court of Appeal, the High Court, Magistrates' Courts, Judicial Commissioners' Court, Central and local Courts. Magistrates' and higher courts administer the laws of Lesotho which are framed on the basis of the Roman–Dutch law. They also adjudicate appeals from the Judicial Commissioner's and Subordinate Courts.

Chief Justice, Hon. T. S. Cotran, C.B.E.

LESOTHO HIGH COMMISSION
10 Collingham Road, SW5 0NR
[01–373 8581]

High Commissioner, (new appointment to be announced).

BRITISH HIGH COMMISSION
P.O. Box 521, Maseru

High Commissioner, His Excellency Peter Edward
Rosling, M.V.O. (1984).
British Council Representative, B. P. Chenery, Hobson's Square, P.O. Box 429, Maseru.

EDUCATION

Most schools are mission-controlled, the Government providing grants for salaries and buildings.
There are over 1,000 primary and over 100 secondary
schools; few areas lack a school and there is a high
literacy rate of about 70 per cent. Increasing emphasis
is being laid on agricultural and vocational education. The National University of Lesotho at Roma
was established in 1975.

COMMUNICATIONS

A tarred road of 110 miles links Maseru to several
of the main lowland towns, and this is being extended
in the south of the country. The mountainous areas
are linked by 1,300 miles of gravelled and earth roads
and tracks. Roads link border towns in South Africa
with the main towns in Lesotho. Maseru is connected
by rail with the main Bloemfontein–Natal line of the
South African Railways. Scheduled international
air services are operated daily between Maseru and
Johannesburg and other scheduled international
flights are to Manzini and Maputo. There are around
30 airstrips. Internal scheduled services are operated
by the Lesotho Airways Corporation.
The telephone network is fully automated in all
urban centres. Radio telephone communication is
used extensively in the remote rural areas.

PRODUCTION

The economy of Lesotho is based on agriculture
and animal husbandry, and the adverse balance of
trade (mainly consumer and capital goods) is offset
by the earnings of the large numbers of the population
who work in South Africa. Apart from some diamonds, Lesotho has few natural resources and only
small-scale industrial development. The Lesotho
National Development Corporation was set up to
promote the development of industry, mining, trade
and tourism. Using Lesotho's potential as a source of
water is presently under consideration, and the
commercial development of diamonds is intended.
Drilling is being carried out for oil. Tourism is being
developed and is rapidly playing a major role in the
economic progress of the country: a National Park
has been established at Sehlabathebe in the Maluti
mountains. A number of light manufacturing and
processing industries have recently been established.

FINANCE AND TRADE

The main sources of revenue are customs and
excise duty. Estimates of expenditure and revenue
(1982) are recurrent revenue *M*127,000,000; recurrent
expenditure *M*107,900,000; capital revenue
*M*77,000,000; capital expenditure *M*104,000,000.
On Jan. 19, 1980 the *Maloti* was introduced as
Lesotho's currency, on the basis of parity with the
S. Africa *rand*.

Trade with U.K.

	1983	1984
Imports from U.K.	£2,080,000	£1,633,000
Exports to U.K.	216,000	78,000

MALAWI

AREA, POPULATION, ETC.—Malawi comprises Lake
Malawi (formerly Lake Nyasa) and its western shore,
with the high table-land separating it from the basin
of the Luangwa River, the watershed forming the
western frontier with Zambia; south of the lake,
Malawi reaches almost to the Zambesi and is surrounded by Mozambique, the frontier lying on the
west on the watershed of the Zambesi and Shire
Rivers, and to the east on the Ruo, a tributary of the
Shire, and Lakes Chiuta and Chirwa. This boundary
reaches the eastern shore of Lake Malawi and extends
up to the mid-point of the lake for about half its
length where it returns to the eastern and northern
shores to form a frontier with Tanzania.   Malawi
has a total area of 45,747 sq. miles. The population,
according to the Census held in September 1977, is
5,547,460; a U.N. estimate put the figure at 6,270,000
in 1982. The official languages are Chichewa and
English.

CAPITAL.—Lilongwe (population (1977) 102,924).
The city of Blantyre in the Southern Region,
incorporating Blantyre and Limbe (population (1977)
222,153), is the major commercial and industrial
centre. Other main centres are: Mzuzu, Thyolo,
Mulanje, Mangochi, Salima, Dedza and Zomba, the
former capital.

FLAG.—Horizontal stripes of black, red and green,
with rising sun in the centre of the black stripe.

GOVERNMENT

Malawi became a republic on July 6, 1966, having
assumed internal self-government on February 1,
1963, and achieved independence on July 6, 1964, and
is a member of the Commonwealth. There is a Cabinet
consisting of the life President and other Ministers.
The Parliament consists of 101 members, each elected
by universal suffrage. Under the 1981 Amendment
to the Constitution, the life President has the power
to nominate as many Members of Parliament as he
wishes. Being a one-party State (the Malawi Congress Party), all elected members are required to be
members of the Party. The Parliament, which usually
meets three times a year, is presided over by a
Speaker.

*President, Minister of External Affairs, Agriculture
and Justice, Works and Supplies*, Dr. H. Kamuzu
Banda, *elected* 1966, *sworn in as* President for Life,
July 6, 1971.

Cabinet

Minister Without Portfolio, Hon. Robson W. Chirwa.
Minister at Large, Hon. Sidney B. Somanje.
Finance, Hon. Edward C. I. Bwanali.
Labour, Hon. E. C. Katola Phiri.
Local Government, Hon. B. L. R. Kapichira Banda.
Transport and Communications, Hon. Wadson B.
Deleza.
Education and Culture, Hon. Louis Chimango.
Youth, Hon. Poltone C. Mtenje.
Health, Hon. Dalton S. Katopola.
Trade, Industry and Tourism, Hon. S. Chimwemwe
Hara.
Community Services, Hon. Stanford Demba.

JUDICIARY

Chief Justice, J. J. Skinner.
Puisne Judge, N. S. Jere.

MALAWI HIGH COMMISSION
33 Grosvenor Street, W1X 0DE
[01–491 4172/7]

High Commissioner, His Excellency C. M. Mkona
(1981).

BRITISH HIGH COMMISSION
Lingadzi House (P.O. Box 30042),
Lilongwe 3

High Commissioner, His Excellency Arthur Henry
Brind, C.M.G. (1983).
Deputy High Commissioner, M. E. J. Gore.
British Council Representative, C. G. Housden, (P.O.
Box 30222), Lilongwe. There is also a library at
Blantyre.

EDUCATION

Primary education is the responsibility of local
authorities in both urban and rural areas, although
policy, curricula and inspection are the responsibility
of the Ministry of Education and Culture. The
Ministry is also responsible for secondary schools,
technical education and primary teacher training.
Religious bodies, with Government assistance, still
play an important part in these fields. The University
of Malawi was opened in 1965 and has three
constituent colleges.

COMMUNICATIONS

A single-track railway runs from Mchinji on the
Zambian border, through Lilongwe and Salima on
Lake Malawi (itself served by two passenger and a
number of cargo boats) through Blantyre to the
southern frontier into Mozambique, and connecting
with the Mozambique port of Beira. In 1970 a 70-mile
line was opened to Nayuchi, linking the Malawi rail
system with the Mozambique network to the port of
Nacala. There are about 10,772 km. of roads in
Malawi of which about 18 per cent are bituminised.

There is an international airport 26 km. from
Lilongwe, which handles regional and inter-continental flights.

FINANCE

(excluding Development Account)

	1982–83	1983–84
Revenue	*K*218m	*K*259m
Expenditure	252m*	297m

*less appropriations in aid.

The unit of currency is the *kwacha*.

ECONOMY

The economy is largely agricultural, with maize
the main subsistence crop. Tobacco, sugar, tea,
groundnuts and cotton are the main cash crops and
principal exports. There are two sugar mills and total
production in 1983 was 175,291 tonnes. A number of
light manufacturing industries have been established
recently.

TRADE

	1982	1983
Imports	*K*322m	*K*364m
Exports	270m	265m

Trade with U.K.

	1983	1984
Imports from U.K.	£18,893,000	£22,995,000
Exports to U.K.	42,060,000	65,312,000

MALAYSIA

AREA, POPULATION, ETC.—Malaysia, comprising
the 11 states of Peninsular Malaya plus Sabah and
Sarawak, forms a crescent well over 1,000 miles long
between latitudes 1° and 7° N. and longitudes 100°
and 119° E. It occupies two distinct regions—the
Malay Peninsula which extends from the isthmus of
Kra to the Singapore Strait and the north-west
coastal area of the island of Borneo. Each is separated
from the other by 400 miles of the South China Sea.
The total area of Malaysia, including the Federal
Territory of Kuala Lumpur (94 sq. miles), is estimated
to be 130,000 sq. miles, containing a population of
13,435,588 (1980 census). The principal racial groups
are the Malays, the Chinese and those of Indian and
Sri Lankan origin, as well as the indigenous races of
Sarawak and Sabah. Bahasa Malaysia (Malay) is the
sole official language, but English, various dialects of
Chinese, and Tamil are also widely spoken. There
are a few indigenous languages widely spoken in
Sabah and Sarawak.

RELIGION.—Islam is the official religion of Malaysia,
each Ruler being the head of religion in his State,
though the Heads of State of Sabah and Sarawak are
not heads of the Muslim religion in their States. The
Yang di-Pertuan Agung is the head of religion in
Malacca and Penang. The Constitution guarantees
religious freedom.

CLIMATE.—The year is commonly divided into the
Southwest and Northwest monsoon seasons. Rainfall
averages about 100 inches throughout the year,
though the annual fall varies from place to place.
The average daily temperature throughout Malaysia
varies from 70° F. to 90° F., though in higher areas
temperatures are lower and vary widely.

CAPITAL.—Kuala Lumpur was proclaimed Federal
Territory on February 1, 1974. Its population is (1980)
997,100.

NATIONAL DAY.—August 31 (*Hari Kebangsaan*).

FLAG.—Equal horizontal stripes of red (7) and
white (7); 14 point yellow star and crescent in blue
canton.

STATES OF THE FEDERATION

The 13 States of the Federation of Malaysia (State
capitals in brackets) and their populations at the 1980
Census are:

Johore (Johore Bahru)	1,638,200
Kedah (Alor Setar)	1,116,100
Kelantan (Kota Baru)	893,800
ψMelaka (Melaka)	464,800
Negri Sembilan (Seremban)	573,600
Pahang (Kuantan)	798,800
ψPenang (Georgetown)	954,600
Perak (Ipoh)	1,805,200
Perlis (Kangar)	148,300
ψSabah (Kota Kinabalu)	1,011,000
ψSarawak (Kuching)	1,307,600
Selangor (Shah Alam)	1,515,500
Trengganu (Kuala Trengganu)	540,600
ψSeaport	

GOVERNMENT

The Federation of Malaya became an independent
country within the Commonwealth on August 31,
1957, as a result of an agreement between H.M. the

Queen and the Rulers of the Malay States. On Sept. 16, 1963, the Federation was enlarged by the accession of the states of Singapore, Sabah *(formerly* British North Borneo) and Sarawak, and the name of MALAYSIA was adopted from that date. On Aug. 9, 1965, Singapore seceded from the Federation.

The Constitution was designed to ensure the existence of a strong Federal Government and also a measure of autonomy for the State Governments. It provides for a constitutional Supreme Head of the Federation (H.M. the *Yang di-Pertuan Agung*) to be elected for a term of five years by the Rulers from among their number, and for a Deputy Supreme Head (H.R.H. *Timbalan Yang di-Pertuan Agung*) to be similarly elected. The Malay Rulers are either chosen or succeed to their position in accordance with the custom of the particular state. In other states of Malaysia choice of the Head of State is at the discretion of the *Yang di-Pertuan Agung* after consultation with the Chief Minister of the State.

The Federal Parliament consists of two houses, the Senate and the House of Representatives. The Senate (*Dewan Negara*) consists of 58 members, under a President (*Yang di-Pertua Dewan Negara*), 26 elected by the Legislative Assemblies of the States (2 from each) and 32 appointed by the *Yang di-Pertuan Agung.* The House of Representatives (*Dewan Rakyat*), consists of 154 members (Peninsular Malaysia, 114; Sarawak, 24; and Sabah, 16). Members are elected on the principle of universal adult suffrage with a common electoral roll.

The Constitution provides that each State shall have its own Constitution not inconsistent with the Federal Constitution, with the Ruler or Governor acting on the advice of an Executive Council appointed on the advice of the Chief Minister and a single chamber Legislative Assembly. The State Secretary, the State Legal Adviser and the State Financial Officer sit in the Executive Council as *ex-officio* members. The Legislative Assemblies are fully elected on the same basis as the Federal Parliament.

Supreme Head of State, H.M. Sultan Mahmood Iskandar Al-Haj ibni Al-Marhun Sultan Ismail (Sultan of Johore), *assumed office for a term of 5 years,* April 1984, *sworn in* Nov. 15, 1984.
Deputy Supreme Head of State, H.R.H. Raja Tun Azlan Shah (Sultan of Perak).

MINISTRY

Prime Minister and Minister of Defence, Datuk Seri Dr. Mahathir bin Mohamed.
Deputy Prime Minister and Minister of Home Affairs, Dato Musa bin Hitam.
Justice, Datuk James Ongkili.
Minister without Portfolio, Datuk Khalil Yaacob.
Transport, Tan Sri Chong Hon Nyan.
Science, Technology and Environment, Datuk Stephen Yong.
Foreign Affairs, Tunku Ahmad Rithaudeen.
Welfare Services, Datuk Abu Hassan Omar.
Trade and Industry, Tunku Razaleigh Hamzah.
Finance, Daim Zaimuddin.
Health, Datuk Chin Hon Ngiam.
Land and Regional Development, Datuk Adib Adam.
Information, Datuk Rais Yatim.
Labour and Manpower, Datuk Mak Hon Kam.
Primary Industries, Dato Paul Leong Khee Seong.
Agriculture, Annuar Ibrahim.
Energy, Telecommunications and Posts, Datuk Leo Moggie Anak Irok.
Housing and Local Government, Dato Dr. Neo Yee Pan.
Works and Utilities, Dato S. Samy Vellu.
Culture, Youth and Sport, Datuk Sulaiman Daud.
Public Enterprises, Datin Paduka Rafidah Aziz.

Education, Dr. Sulaiman bin Haji Daud.
Federal Territory, Dato Shahrir bin Abdul Samad.
National and Rural Development, Datuk Sanusi bin Junid.
NOTE.—The words "Tunku/Tengku", "Tun", "Tan Sri", and "Datuk" are titles. The word "Tunku/Tengku" is equivalent to "Prince". "Tun" denotes membership of a high Order of Malaysian Chivalry and "Tan Sri" and "Datuk" ("Datuk Seri" in Perak and "Datu" in Sabah) are each the equivalent of a knighthood. The wife of a "Tun" is styled "Toh Puan", that of a "Tan Sri" is styled "Puan Sri" and of a "Datuk" "Datin". The honorific "Tuan" or "Encik" is equivalent to "Mr." and the honorific "Puan" is equivalent to "Mrs.". The words "Al-Haj" or "Haji" indicate that the person so named has made the pilgrimage to Mecca.

MALAYSIAN HIGH COMMISSION
45 Belgrave Square, SW1X 8QT
[01–235 8033]

High Commissioner, His Excellency M. H. Kassim (1983).

BRITISH HIGH COMMISSION
Wisma Damansara, Jalan Semantan
(P.O. Box 11030), Kuala Lumpur 23–03

High Commissioner, David Howe Gillmore, C.M.G. (1983).

British Council Representative, E. T. J. Phillips, Jalan Bukit Aman, Kuala Lumpur 10–01; offices at *Kota Kinabalu* (Sabah) and *Kuching* (Sarawak), and a library in Penang.

JUDICATURE

The Judicial System consists of a Supreme Court and two High Courts, one in Peninsular Malaysia and one for Sabah and Sarawak (sitting alternately in Kota Kinabalu and Kuching).

The Supreme Court comprises a President, the two Chief Justices of the High Courts and other judges. It possesses appellate, original and advisory jurisdiction.

Each of the High Courts consists of a Chief Justice and not less than 4 other judges. The Federal Constitution allows for a maximum of twelve such judges for Malaya and eight for Borneo. In Peninsular Malaysia the Subordinate Courts consist of the Sessions Courts and the Magistrates' Courts. In Sabah/Sarawak the Magistrates' Courts constitute the Subordinate Courts.

DEFENCE

The Malaysian Armed Forces consist of the Army, Navy and Air Force, together with volunteer forces for each arm. The defence of the country is largely borne by the army in its role of providing defence against external threat and counter-insurgency operations and also to assist the police in the performance of public order duties. The *Royal Malaysian Navy (RMN)* has the responsibility of defending the 3,000 miles of the country's coastline and maintaining constant patrol of 500 miles of the high seas that separate Sabah and Sarawak from the mainland. The *Royal Malaysian Air Force (RMAF)* is capable of providing close strategic and tactical support to the army and police in the defence and internal security of the country.

FINANCE

	M$million	
	1983	1984
Revenue	18,608	20,820
Expenditure	28,043	29,412

PRODUCTION AND TRADE

The agricultural sector continues to be the main-stay of the Malaysian economy. However, diversification of crops and rapid growth in the manufacturing sector has made Malaysia less vulnerable to fluctuations in the price of its primary crop, natural rubber.

Malaysia is the largest exporter of natural rubber, tin, palm oil and tropical hardwoods. Other major export commodities are manufactured and processed products, petroleum, oil, and other minerals, palm kernel oil, tea and pepper.

Exports of the four major primary commodities: rubber, tin, palm oil and tropical hardwoods accounted for 33·9 per cent of the total exports in 1983. Export of petroleum, crude and partly refined oil accounted for 24 per cent of total exports, and manufactured goods for 29·1 per cent. Estimated figures for 1984 indicate that exports of the four major primary commodities account for 33·1 per cent of total exports, petroleum, crude and partly-refined oil for 22·1 per cent, and manufactured goods for 30·4 per cent.

Another commodity which is produced throughout Malaysia is rice, the staple food, and efforts are being made to achieve self-sufficiency.

Imports consist mainly of machinery and transport equipment, manufactured goods, foods, mineral fuels, chemicals and inedible crude materials for her growing population and to accelerate the pace of her economic growth and development.

Malaysia's main trading partners are the other member states of A.S.E.A.N., Japan, Singapore, U.S.A., E.E.C. countries, Australia, Korea and India.

	M$million	
	1983	1984
Imports	30,721	33,612
Exports	32,828	38,275
*Estimated		

THE MALDIVES

AREA, POPULATION, ETC.—The Maldives are a chain of coral atolls, some 400 miles to the south-west of Sri Lanka, stretching from just south of the equator for about 600 miles to the north. There are about 20 coral atolls comprising over 1,200 islands, 202 of which are inhabited. No point in the entire chain of islands is more than 8 feet above sea-level. The population of the islands (1982) is 160,200. The people are Sunni Moslems and the Maldivian language is akin to Elu or old Sinhalese.

CAPITAL.—Malé (population, 1982, 37,000). There is an international airport at Malé.

FLAG.—Green field bearing a white crescent, with wide red border.

GOVERNMENT

Until 1952 the islands were a Sultanate under the protection of the British Crown. Internal self-government was achieved in 1948 and full independence in 1965. In 1982 the Republic of the Maldives became a special member of the Commonwealth.

The Maldives form a Republic which is elective. There is a Parliament (the *Citizens' Majlis*) with representatives elected from all the atolls. The life of the Majlis is 5 years. The Government consists of a Cabinet, which is responsible to the Majlis.

President, His Excellency Maumoon Abdul Gay-oom, *elected* 1978, *re-elected* Sept. 30, 1983 (also *Minister of Defence and National Security*).

Cabinet

Foreign Affairs, Hon. Fathulla Jameel.
Justice, Hon. Abdulla Hameed (*acting*).
Home Affairs and Social Services, Hon. Umar Zahir.
Education, Hon. Mohamed Zahir Hussain.
Health, Hon. Abdulla Jameel.
Fisheries, Hon. Abdul Sataar Moosa Didi.
Transport and Shipping, Hon. Ahmed Mujathaba.
Atolls Administration, Hon. Abdulla Hameed.
Trade and Industries, Hon. Ilyas Ibrahim.

BRITISH HIGH COMMISSION

High Commissioner, (*resident* at Colombo).

PRODUCTION

The vegetation of the islands is coconut palms with some scrub. Hardly any cultivation of crops is possible and nearly all food to supplement the basic fish diet has to be imported. The principal industry is fishing and considerable quantities of fish are exported to Japan. Dried fish is exported to Sri Lanka, where it is a delicacy. The tourist industry is expanding very rapidly. Maldives Shipping Ltd. has a fleet of some 30 merchant ships.

MALTA

AREA, POPULATION, ETC.—Malta lies in the Mediterranean Sea, 58 miles from Sicily and about 180 miles from the African coast, about 17 miles in length and 9 in breadth, and having an area of 94·9 square miles. Malta includes also the adjoining island of Gozo (area 25·9 sq. miles); *Comino* and minor islets. The estimated population at March 1981 was 341,000. Malta's climate, although not tropical, is hot in summer.

Malta was in turn held by the Phœnicians, Greeks, Carthaginians, Romans and Arabs. In 1090 it was conquered by Count Roger of Normandy. In 1530 it was handed over to the Knights of St. John, who made of it a stronghold of Christianity. In 1565 it sustained the famous siege, when the last great effort of the Turks was successfully withstood by Grandmaster La Valette. The Knights expended large sums in fortifying the island and carrying out many magnificent works, until they were expelled by Napoleon in 1798. The Maltese rose against the French garrison soon afterwards, and the island was subsequently blockaded by the British fleet. The Maltese people freely requested the protection of the British Crown in 1802 on condition that their rights and privileges would be preserved and respected. The islands were finally annexed to the British Crown by the Treaty of Paris in 1814.

Malta was again closely besieged in the last war. From June, 1940, to the end of the war, 432 members of the garrison and 1,540 civilians were killed by enemy aircraft, and about 35,000 houses were destroyed or damaged. The island was awarded the George Cross in 1942.

CAPITAL.—ΨValletta. Population (estimated 1981), 14,096. Valletta Grand Harbour is one of the finest in the world; it is very deep, and large vessels can anchor alongside the shore. It is an important port of call and ship repairing centre for vessels, being half-way between Gibraltar and Port Said.

FLAG.—Two equal vertical stripes, white at the hoists and red at the fly. A representation of the George Cross is carried edged in red in the top corner of the white stripe.

NATIONAL DAY—March 31.

GOVERNMENT

On Sept. 21, 1964, under the Malta Independence Order, 1964, Malta became an independent state within the Commonwealth; on December 13, 1974, Malta became a republic within the Commonwealth. In the 1981 general election the Malta Labour Party was returned to office. State of the parties; Malta Labour Party, 34 seats; Nationalist Party, 31 seats. The Nationalist Party received 51 per cent of the votes cast but failed to obtain a majority of seats and boycotted Parliament after the election, but eventually took their seats in March 1983.

Maltese and English are the official languages of administration and Maltese is ordinarily the official language in all the courts of law and the language of general use in the islands.

President.—Her Excellency Miss Agatha Barbara, *elected,* Feb. 16, 1982.

Cabinet

Prime Minister and Minister of the Interior, and Education, Hon. Karmenu Mifsud Bonnici.
Senior Deputy P.M. and Minister of Justice and Parliamentary Affairs, Hon. Joseph Cassar.
Deputy P.M. and Minister of Finance and Customs, Hon. Wistin Abela.
Works and Housing, Hon. Lorry Sant.
Labour and Social Services, Hon. F. Micallef.
Foreign Affairs, Hon. A. Sceberras Trigona.
Economic Planning and Commerce, Hon. Lino Spiteri.
Industry, Hon. Karmenu Vella.
Tourism, Hon. Joseph Grima.
Parastatal and People's Industries, Hon. Philip Muscat.
Health, Hon. Vincent Moran.
Fisheries and Agriculture, Hon. J. Debono Grech.

MALTESE HIGH COMMISSION
16 Kensington Square, W.8
[01–938 1712]

High Commissioner, His Excellency Francis F. Cassar (1985).

BRITISH HIGH COMMISSION
7 St. Anne Street, Floriana, Malta

High Commissioner, His Excellency Stanley Frederick St. Clare Duncan, C.M.G., *apptd,* 1985.

EDUCATION

In June 1984 there were 83 Government Primary Schools with 26,130 pupils and 38 Secondary Schools and new Lyceums, with a total of 13,813 pupils.

The Government also runs 4 Technical Institutes and 15 Trade Schools (with an enrolment of 4,169 students). Schools of Art, Music, Secretarial Studies, Catering, Nursing and Dramatic Art are sponsored by the Government. Tertiary education is available at the University of Malta, which has 1,468 students.

A number of private schools offer more or less the same facilities that exist in Government schools. All education is free.

In religion, the Maltese are Roman Catholics. The Maltese language is of Semitic origin and held by some to be derived from the Carthaginian and Phoenician tongues.

AGRICULTURE

Agriculture plays a significant role in the economy. There are 4,332 full time farmers and about 11,026 part time farmers. The yearly crop production is about 99,727 tonnes consisting mainly of tomatoes, potatoes, onions, cabbages and cauliflowers, and some 2,922 tonnes of fruit. Grape is the largest fruit crop. Flowers and cuttings are produced for export markets.

INDUSTRY

The island's leading industry is the state-owned Malta Drydocks, employing about 5,000 people. The main port of Grand Harbour handled traffic (excluding mineral oils) of 1,696,584 tonnes in 1982.

At the end of 1983 manufacturing firms employed some 29,440 people. The wide range of produce includes food processing, textiles and clothing, plastics and chemical products, electronic equipment and components. The gross output of the manufacturing industry in 1983 was £M223·5 million, of which £M141·6 million were export sales.

Tourism has assumed primary importance, with over 490,000 tourists visiting the island in 1983, and there are plans to develop Marsamxett Harbour as a yachting centre. Gross income from this industry stood at £M65 million.

FINANCE

	1984	1985
Revenue	£M228,100,000	£M230,189,000
Expenditure	227,213,000	230,189,000

The Central Bank of Malta has the sole right of issuing legal tender currency notes and coins. The Maltese pound is divided into 100 *cents* and 1,000 *mils.*

TRADE

The principal imports for home consumption are foodstuffs—mainly wheat, meat and bullocks, milk and fruit—fodder, beverages and tobacco, fuels, chemicals, textiles and machinery (industrial, agricultural and transport). The chief domestic exports are flowers and cuttings, processed food, electronics, textiles, and other manufactures.

	1983	1984
Imports	£M316,600,000	£M330,000,000
Exports	156,700,000	181,000,000

Trade with U.K.

	1983	1984
Imports from U.K........	£71,895,000	£89,468,000
Exports from U.K........	40,852,000	45,076,000

MAURITIUS

AREA, POPULATION, ETC.—Mauritius is an island group lying in the Indian Ocean, 550 miles east of Madagascar, between 57° 17′–57° 46′ E. long. and lat. 19° 58′–20° 33′ S., and comprising with its dependencies an area of 805 square miles. The population (1983 census) was 1,000,432 (including 33,569 for Rodrigues and the other islands), made up of Asiatic races (Hindus 52·6 per cent, Muslims 16·5 per cent), and persons of European (mainly French extraction), mixed and African descent (28·3 per cent).

English is the official language but French may be used in the Legislative Assembly and lower law courts. However, Creole is the mostly commonly used language.

CLIMATE.—Mauritius enjoys a sub-tropical maritime climate, with a wide range of rainfall and temperature resulting from the mountainous nature of the island. Humidity is rather high throughout the year and rainfall is sufficient to maintain a green cover of vegetation, except for a brief period in the driest districts.

CAPITAL.—ΨPort Louis, population (1983), 133,702; other centres are Beau Bassin-Rose Hill (89,037); Curepipe (62,524); Vacoas-Phoenix (53,152) and Quatre Bornes (60,446).

FLAG.—Red, blue, yellow and green horizontal stripes.

GOVERNMENT

Mauritius was discovered in 1511 by the Portuguese; the Dutch visited it in 1598, and named it Mauritius, after Prince Maurice of Nassau. From 1638 to 1710 it was held as a small Dutch colony and in 1715 the French took possession but did not settle it until 1721. Mauritius was taken by a British Force in 1810. A British garrison remained on the island until June 1960. The French language and French law were preserved under British rule.

A Crown Colony for 158 years, Mauritius became an independent state within the Commonwealth on March 12, 1968. The Constitution defined by Order in Council in 1964 was slightly altered in 1966 on the recommendation of the Banwell Commission, the effect being to increase the membership of the Legislative Assembly to 70, 62 elected by block voting in multi-member constituencies (including 2 members for Rodrigues) and 8 specially-elected members. Of the latter, 4 seats go to the "best loser" of whichever communities in the island are under-represented in the Assembly after the General Election and the four remaining seats are allocated on the basis of both party and community. The Constitution provides for the appointment of a Governor-General who acts on the advice of the Council of Ministers, collectively responsible to the Legislative Assembly.

In the August 1983 General Election, the Mouvement Socialiste Mauricien, allied with the Labour Party and the Parti Mauricien Social Democrate, defeated the Mouvement Mauricien Militant and formed the Government, with a majority of 43 seats.

Governor-General, Dr. The Rt. Hon. Sir Seewosagur Ramgoolan, G.C.M.G.

Council of Ministers

Premier and Minister of Defence, Internal Security, External Communications, Information and Reform Institutions, Hon. Aneerood Jugnauth.

Deputy Prime Minister and Minister of Justice, Hon. Sir Gaetan Duval.

Women's Rights and Family Affairs, Hon. Mrs. Sheilabia Bappoo.

Works, Dr. The Hon. Rohit Niemo Beedassy.

Commerce, Shipping, Prices and Consumer Protection, Hon. Abdool Kader Ahmed Bhayat.

Economic Planning and Development, Dr. Hon. Beergoonath Ghurburran.

Employment and Social Security and National Solidarity, Dr. The Hon. Diwakur Bundhun.

Industry and Cooperatives, Hon. Ramsamy Chedumbarum Pillay.

Agriculture, Fisheries and Natural Resources, Hon. Nunkeswarsingh Deerpalsingh.

Labour and Industrial Relations, Hon. Joseph Herve Duval.

Rodrigues and The Outer Islands, Hon. France Felicite.

External Affairs, Tourism and Emigration, Hon. Anil Kumarsingh Gayan.

Health, Hon. Kailash Purryag.

Youth and Sports, Hon. Michael James Kevin Glover.

Housing, Lands and the Environment, Hon Dwarkanath Gungah.

Finance, Hon. Seetanah Lutchmeenaraidoo.

Local Government, Hon. Karl Offman.

Education and the Arts and Cultural Affairs and Leisure, Hon. Armoorgum Parsuraman.

Energy and Internal Communications, Hon. Mahyendrah Utchanah.

MAURITIUS HIGH COMMISSION
32–33 Elvaston Place, S.W.7
[01–581 0294]

High Commissioner, His Excellency Gian Nath (1983).

BRITISH HIGH COMMISSION
King George V Avenue, Floreal.

High Commissioner, His Excellency James Nicholas Allan, C.B.E. (1981).

EDUCATION

Primary education is free and in 1984 was provided for 129,744 children at 271 primary schools. Although education is not compulsory it is estimated that about 90 per cent of children of primary age attend school. At post-primary level there are a total of 72,730 students attending secondary schools: fees and teachers' salaries in the private secondary schools are paid by government. 122 students attend the Industrial Trade Training Centre. The College of Education trains primary school teachers. The Institute of Education is responsible for training secondary school teachers and for curriculum development. The University of Mauritius consists of Schools of Agriculture, of Administration and of Industrial Technology. Estimated expenditure on education in 1983–84 was *Rs*.561,600,000.

COMMUNICATIONS

Port Louis, on the N.W. coast, handles the bulk of the island's external trade. A bulk sugar terminal capable of handling the total crop began operating in 1980. The international airport is located at Plaisance in the southeast of the island about 5 miles from Mahébourg. There are 5 daily newspapers and 2 weeklies, mostly in French, and 2 Chinese daily papers and one weekly paper. The Mauritius Broadcasting Corporation has a monopoly of radio broadcasting in the country: television was introduced in 1965. There is a satellite communications ground station near Port Louis.

PRODUCTION

Sugar is the main industry of the island, employing over 50,000 people. About 55 per cent of the total crop is produced on a plantation scale, while smaller owners (cultivating less than 10 acres) cultivate about 24 per cent of the land under cane. Tea and tobacco are also grown commercially but on a smaller scale than sugar.

	1983	1984
	tonnes	
Sugar	604,730	575,617
Tea (manufactured)	6,142	8,018
Tobacco (leaves)	785	950

The bulk of the island's requirements in manufactured products still has to be imported, though there is a diverse and growing local manufacturing sector. The most important industry is the processing of sugar. In 1984 production of molasses, mainly for export, was 150,000 tonnes. Other products include alcohol, rum, denatured spirits, perfumed spirits and vinegar.

FINANCE

The main sources of Government revenue are private and company income tax, customs and excise duties, mainly on imports, but also on sugar exports.

	1981–82	1982–83	1983–84
Public revenue	Rs.3,503 m	Rs.3,771 m	Rs.3,123 m
Public expenditure	4,166 m	4,719 m	3,743 m

Currency—*Rs.* = Rupee.

TRADE

Most foodstuffs and raw materials have to be imported from abroad. Apart from local consumption (about 36,500 metric tons per annum), the sugar produced is exported, mainly to Britain, U.S.A. and Canada.

	1983	1984
Total imports	Rs.5,175 m	Rs.6,486 m
Total exports	4,311 m	5,180 m

Trade with U.K.

	1983	1984
Imports from U.K.	Rs.489 m	Rs. 514 m
Exports to U.K.	2,182 m	2,616 m

RODRIGUES AND DEPENDENCIES OF MAURITIUS

Rodrigues, formerly a dependency but now part of Mauritius, is about 350 miles east of Mauritius. Area, 40 square miles. Population (1984) 34,600. Cattle, salt fish, sheep, goats, pigs and onions are the principal exports. The island is administered by an Administrative Secretary.

Administrative Secretary, Maxime Labour.

The islands of Agalega and St. Brandon are dependencies of Mauritius. Other small islands, formerly Mauritian dependencies, including Six Islands, Peros Banhos, Salomon, Diego Garcia and Trois Frères, have since 1965 constituted the British Indian Ocean Territory.

REPUBLIC OF NAURU

The Republic of Nauru is an island of 8·2 sq. miles in size, situated in 166° 55′ E. longitude and 0° 32′ S. of the Equator. It has a population (Census May 1983) of 8,042 (Nauruans 4,964; other Pacific Islanders 2,134; Asians 682; Caucasians 262). About 43 per cent of Nauruans are adherents of the Nauruan Protestant Church and there is a Roman Catholic Mission on the island.

FLAG.—Twelve-point star (representing the 12 original Nauruan tribes) below a gold bar (representing the Equator), all on a blue ground.

GOVERNMENT

From 1888 until the First World War Nauru was administered by Germany, in 1920 becoming a British mandated territory under the League of Nations administered by Australia. A Trusteeship superceding the Mandate was approved in 1947 by the U.N. and Nauru continued to be administered by Australia until it became an Independent State on February 1, 1968. It was announced in November, 1968, that a limited form of membership of the Commonwealth had been devised for Nauru at the request of its Government. Parliament has eighteen members including the Cabinet and Speaker. Voting is compulsory for all Nauruans over 20 years of age, except in certain specified instances. Elections are held every three years. The Cabinet is chosen by the President and comprises not fewer than five nor more than six members including the President.

President and Minister for External Affairs, Internal Affairs, Island Development and Industry, Civil Aviation Authority and the Public Service, His Excellency Hammer DeRoburt, G.C.M.G., O.B.E.

Cabinet

Finance, Hon. K. Aroi.
Health and Education, Hon. L. Stephen.
Works and Community Services, Hon. R. B. B. Detudamo.
Justice, Hon. B. Dowiyogo.

JUDICIARY

A Supreme Court of Nauru is presided over by the Chief Justice. The District Court, which is subordinate to the Supreme Court, is presided over by a Resident Magistrate. Both the Supreme Court and the District Court are Courts of Record. The Supreme Court exercises both original and appellate jurisdiction.

EDUCATION AND WELFARE

Nauru has a hospital service and other medical and dental services. There is also a maternity and child welfare service. Education is available in 9 primary and 2 secondary schools on the island with a total enrolment of about 1,600 pupils receiving primary education and 500 secondary education.

PRODUCTION, ETC.

The only fertile areas are the narrow coastal belt and local requirements of fruit and vegetables are mostly met by imports. The economy is heavily dependent on the extraction of phosphate, of which the island has one of the world's richest deposits. About 1·5 million tonnes of phosphate are mined each year, providing employment for over 1,000 people. The industry has been run since 1970 by the Nauru Phosphate Corporation. Considerable investments have been made abroad with the royalties on phosphate exports to provide for a time when production declines.

The Nauru Pacific Line owns six ships: the Government-owned Air Nauru operates scheduled air services in the Pacific region and to Australia, New Zealand, Japan, Singapore and the Philippines.

Trade with U.K.

	1983	1984
Imports from U.K.	£1,715,000	£1,332,000
Exports to U.K.	1,421,000	916,000

BRITISH HIGH COMMISSION (*see* Suva, Fiji).

NIGERIA

AREA, POPULATION, ETC.—The Republic of Nigeria is situated on the west coast of Africa. It is bounded on the south by the Gulf of Guinea, on the west by the Republic of Benin, on the north by Niger and on the east by Cameroon. It has an area of 356,669 sq. miles with a population (1963 Census) of 55,654,000. U.N. estimates of the present population suggest a figure of 82,390,000. The population is almost entirely African. The main ethnic groups are Hausa/Fulani, Yoruba and Ibo, and the principal languages are English, Hausa, Yoruba and Ibo. Over half the population are Muslim, these being concentrated in the north and west. In the southern areas in particular there are many Christians.

A belt of mangrove swamp forest 10–60 miles in width lies along the entire coastline. North of this there is a zone 50–100 miles wide of tropical rain forest and oil-palms. North of this the country rises and the vegetation changes to open woodland and savannah. In the extreme north the country is semi-desert. There are few mountains, but in Northern Nigeria the central plateau rises to an average level of 4,000 feet. The Niger, Benue, and Cross are the main rivers.

The climate varies with the types of country described above, but Nigeria lies entirely within the tropics and temperatures are high. Temperatures of over 100°F. in the north are common while coast temperatures are seldom over 90°F. The humidity at the coast, however, is much higher than in the north. The rainy season is from about April to October; rainfall varies from under 25 inches a year in the extreme north to 172 inches on the coast line. During the dry season the *harmattan* wind blows from the desert; it is cool and laden with fine particles of dust.

CAPITAL.—ΨLagos, estimated population, 3,000,000. Other important towns are Ibadan, Kaduna, Kano, Benin City, Enugu and ΨPort Harcourt. Work on a new capital under construction at Abuja was suspended when the military took power.

FLAG.—Three equal vertical bands, green, white and green.

NATIONAL DAY.—October 1 (Republic Day).

GOVERNMENT

The Federation of Nigeria attained independence as a member of the Commonwealth on Oct. 1, 1960 and became a republic in 1963. On Jan. 15, 1966 the military took power, suspended the Constitution and dissolved the legislature. In 1979 civil rule was restored under a new constitution similar to that of the United States after elections at National and State level. After similar elections in 1983 the new administration was removed by the military on Dec. 31, this regime itself being overthrown in Aug. 1985. An Armed Forces Ruling Council was sworn in on Aug. 30.

Originally regional in structure the Federation was divided into 12 states in 1967 and into the present 19 states in 1976.

Head of State, Commander-in-Chief of the Armed Forces, Chairman of the Armed Forces Ruling Council, Maj. Gen. Ibrahim Babangida.

Cabinet

Agriculture, Maj. Gen. Akinrinade (*retd*).
Communications, Lt. Col. A. Y. Ayuba.
Defence, Maj. Gen. Domkat Bali.
Education, Prof. Jibril Aminu.
Employment, Rear Adm. Patrick Koshoni.
External Affairs, Dr. Bolaji Akinyemi.
Federal Capital Territory, Maj. Gen. Mamman Vatsa.
Finance, Dr. Kalu I. Kalu.
Health, Prof. Koye Ransome-Kuti.
Industries, Alhaji Lawan Mala.
Information, Lt. Col. Ukpo.
Internal Affairs, Lt. Col. Shagaya.
Justice, Prince Bola Ajibola.
Mines, Power and Steel, Alhaji Riwan Lukwan.
National Planning, S. P. Okongwu.
Petroleum Resources, Dr. Tam David-West.
Social Development, Youth and Culture, Lt. Col. Ahmed Abdullahi.
Science and Technology, Emmanuel Emovon.
Trade, Maj. Gen. Nasko.
Transport, Brig. Jeremiah Useni.
Works and Housing, Cdre. Hamza Abdullahi.
Special Duties, Air Vice Marshal A. I. Shekarri.

NIGERIAN HIGH COMMISSION
Nigeria House, 9 Northumberland Avenue,
WC2N 5BX
[01–839 1244]

High Commissioner, I. Karfi (*acting*).

BRITISH HIGH COMMISSION
Eleke Crescent, Victoria Island, Lagos

High Commissioner, His Excellency Arthur Hope Wyatt (*acting*).

British Council Representative, D. Waterhouse, Plot 1650, Olosa Street, Opposite Eko Hotel, Victoria Island (P.O. Box 3702), Lagos. Branch offices at Kano, Kaduna and Enugu.

EDUCATION

A programme was introduced in September 1976 intended to achieve universal primary education. Numbers of pupils in 1982–83 are: 15·4 million in primary schools, 3·5 million in secondary schools, 53,766 in polytechnics and 88,636 in universities. There are 24 universities.

COMMUNICATIONS

The Nigerian railway system, which is controlled by the Nigerian Railway Corporation, is the most extensive in West Africa. There are 2,178 route miles of lines. The principal international airlines operating from Lagos, Kano and Port Harcourt bring Nigeria within about six hours of the Western European capitals. There are also services to other parts of Africa and to the United States. A network of internal air services connects the main centres. The principal seaports are served by a number of shipping lines, including the Nigerian National Line. A nationwide television and radio network is being developed, with each State eventually having its own television and radio station. There is a network of meteorological reporting stations.

PRODUCTION AND INDUSTRY

Nigeria was a predominantly agricultural country until the early 1970s with agriculture contributing over 60 per cent of export revenue and 45 per cent of Gross National Product. Tin and calumbite mining on the Jos plateau, textiles and coal mining were also important. The major exports were ground nuts, palm products, tin, cocoa, rubber and timber. Recently oil has provided over 90 per cent of exports revenue and agricultural exports have greatly declined. Nigeria now imports wheat, rice and other food. Though agriculture still employs half the labour force it contributes only 20 per cent of G.N.P., exceeded by trading and oil. The construction sector is twice as large as the manufacturing sector and industries dependent on imported raw materials such as vehicle assembly have faltered recently. Three oil refineries are in operation at Port Harcourt, Warri and Kaduna. A steel plant has been opened near Warri and a larger one is being completed at Ajaokuta. Other projects include natural gas liquifaction, petro-chemicals, fertilizers and several power stations plus the Abuja Federal Capital. Several large irrigation schemes have been completed and more are planned.

TRADE

Oil revenues have been falling since 1981 and are now restricted by an OPEC production quota and lower prices to half their peak level. In March 1982 imports curbs and payments restrictions were introduced but exchange reserves have fallen and debts have increased while shortages of both consumer and production goods and inflation have became worse.

	1982
Total imports (including invisibles)	US$22,381,000 m
Total exports	17,055,000 m

The unit of currency is the *Naira*.

Trade with U.K.

	1983	1984
Imports from U.K....	£798,276,000	£768,479,000
Exports to U.K.	387,975,000	375,796,000

PAPUA NEW GUINEA

AREA, POPULATION, ETC.—Papua New Guinea extends from the equator to Cape Baganowa in the Louisiade Archipelago at 11° S. latitude and from the border with Irian Jaya to 160° E. longitude. The total area of Papua New Guinea is 178,260 square miles, of which approximately 152,420 form the mainland, on the island of New Guinea. The country has many island groups, principally the Bismarck Archipelago, a portion of the Solomon Islands, the Trobriands, the D'Entrecasteaux Islands and the Louisade Archipelago. The main islands of the Bismark Archipelago are New Britain, New Ireland and Manus. Bougainville is the largest of the Solomon Islands within Papua New Guinea.

Papua New Guinea lies within the tropics and has a typically monsoonal climate. Temperature and humidity are uniformly high throughout the year. The average rainfall is about 80 inches per year but there are wide variations—from 47 inches at Port Moresby to over 200 inches in mountainous western areas.

The estimated population in 1983 was 3,160,000. The inhabitants of the country comprise a great diversity of physical types and a large number of linguistic groups. The population increases by approximately 2·7 per cent annually.

CAPITAL.—Port Moresby. Estimated population (1985), 139,300. Other major towns are Lae, Rabaul, Madang, Wewak, Goroka and Mount Hagen.

FLAG.—A rectangle divided diagonally from the top of the hoist to the bottom of the fly, the upper segment scarlet and containing a soaring yellow bird of paradise. The lower segment is black charged with five white five-pointed stars representing the Southern Cross.

GOVERNMENT

New Guinea was sighted by Portuguese and Spanish navigators in the early sixteenth century, but remained largely isolated from the rest of the world. In 1884, a British Protectorate was proclaimed over the southern coast of New Guinea (Papua) and the adjacent islands. British New Guinea, as the Protectorate was called, was annexed outright in 1888. In 1906 the Territory of British New Guinea was placed under the authority of the Commonwealth of Australia. Also in 1884 Germany had formally taken possession of certain northern areas, which later came to be known as the Trust Territory of New Guinea. In 1914 the German areas were occupied by Australian troops and remained under military administration until 1921, when the League of Nations conferred on Australia a mandate for their government.

New Guinea was administered under the Mandate and Papua under the Papua Act until the invasion

by the Japanese in 1942 when the civil administration was suspended until the surrender of the Japanese in 1945.

The first House of Assembly for the whole country met in 1964 and included an elected majority and ten nominated official members. After 1970 there was a gradual assumption of powers by the Papua New Guinea Government, culminating in formal self-government in December 1973. Final reserve powers held by Australia over defence and foreign relations were relinquished to Papua New Guinea in March 1975, and Papua New Guinea achieved full independence on September 16, 1975.

Elections are held every five years. The Parliament comprises 109 elected Members, 20 from Regional electorates, the remainder from Open electorates. There are 19 provinces, which have their own provincial governments with certain legislative and administrative powers.

Governor-General, Sir Kingsford Dibela, G.C.M.G.

National Executive Council
(CABINET)

Prime Minister, Michael Somare, C.H.
Deputy P.M. and Minister for Public Services, Father John Momis.
Transport, Matthew Bendumb.
Foreign Affairs and Trade, John Giheno.
Provincial Affairs, Tony Farapo.
Labour and Employment, Tony Ila.
Education, Sam Tulo.
Works and Supply, Jack Genia.
Corrective Institutions, Arnold Masipal.
Health, Pundia Kange.
Finance (and Minister of State assisting Prime Minister), Philip Bouraga.
Lands, John Nilkare.
Forests, Lukas Waka.
Police, Dennis Young.
Housing, Kala Swokin.
Justice, Tom Pais.
Defence, Stephen Tago.
Post and Telecommunications, Roy Evara.
Youth, Religion, Women and Recreation, Tony Bais.
Administrative Services, Henu Hesingut.
National Planning, Bebes Korowaro.
Home Affairs, Kindi Lawi.
Industrial Development, Karl Stack.
Minerals and Energy, Francis Pusal.
Primary Industry, Rabbie Namaliu, C.M.G.
Civil Aviation, William Wi.
Environment, Soso Tomu.

PAPUA NEW GUINEA HIGH COMMISSION
3rd Floor, 14 Waterloo Place, SW1R 4AR
[01–930 0922/6]

High Commissioner, His Excellency Ilinome F. Tarua, O.B.E. (1983).

BRITISH HIGH COMMISSION
P.O. Box 739, Port Moresby

High Commissioner, His Excellency Arthur John Collins, O.B.E. (1982).

COMMUNICATIONS

Road communications are very limited, the most important road being that linking Lae with the populous Highlands.

Air Niugini (the national airline) and Qantas operate regular air services between Port Moresby and Australia. Air Niugini also operates services to Manila (Philippines), Honiara (Solomon Islands), Jayapura (Indonesia), Honolulu and Singapore. Internal air services are operated by Air Niugini, Douglas Airways, and Talair.

Several shipping companies operate cargo services between Papua New Guinea and Australia, Europe, the Far East and U.S.A. There are very limited cargo and passenger services between Papua New Guinea main ports, outports, plantations and missions.

Papua New Guinea is linked by international cable to Australia, Guam, Hong Kong, Kota Kinabalu, the Far East and U.S.A. Telecommunications are widely available.

ECONOMY

Until the 1970s the Papua New Guinea economy was based almost entirely on agriculture. At the beginning of the 20th century copra plantations formed the basis of the cash economy. Further crops which have been introduced over the years are cocoa, tea, coffee, palm oil, rubber, groundnuts, spices and timber. A variety of commercial agricultural developments now co-exist with the traditional informal rural economy. Government expenditure is still reliant on Australian budgetary support, to the extent of just under 30 per cent in 1983.

In 1972, Bougainville Copper Pty Ltd (BCL) began mining in the North Solomons Province, producing copper, silver and gold. There are extensive mineral deposits throughout Papua New Guinea, including nickel, chromite, bauxite and possibly commercial deposits of oil and gas. The most important new development is the exploitation of large copper and gold deposits on the Ok Tedi, in the Western Province.

In 1984 the Papua New Guinea economy was influenced by good prices for agricultural commodities, offset by low prices for copper and gold. New developments to promote export crops and increase employment, typically involving foreign investment, are planned for the future.

Industry includes processing of primary products, and brewing, bottling and packaging, paint, plywood, and metal manufacturing and the construction industries.

Although the formal economy is still dominated by non-Papua New Guineans, the participation of Papua New Guineans is increasing.

Trade with U.K.

	1983	1984
Imports from U.K.	£18,236,000	£14,643,000
Exports to U.K.	28,142,000	68,245,000

The unit of currency is the *Kina.*

ST. CHRISTOPHER-NEVIS

The State of St. Christopher-Nevis is located at the northern end of the Eastern Caribbean. It comprises the islands of St. Christopher (St. Kitts) (65 sq. miles, population about 35,000) and Nevis (36 sq. miles, 9,300).

St. Christopher, lat. 17° 18′ N. and long. 62° 48′ W. was the first island in the British West Indies to be colonized (1623). The central area of the island is forest-clad and mountainous, rising to the 3,792 ft. Mount Liamuiga.

CAPITAL—ΨBasseterre.

Nevis, lat. 17° 10′ N. and long. 62° 35′ W. is separated from the southern tip of St. Christopher by a strait two miles wide and is dominated by the central Nevis Peak, 3,232 ft. *Chief town*—ΨCharlestown (pop. 1,200), is a port of entry.

FLAG—Three diagonal bands, green, black and red; each colour separated by a stripe of yellow. Two white stars on the black band.

GOVERNMENT

The Territory of St. Kitts-Nevis became a State in Association with Britain on Feb. 27, 1967. The State of St. Kitts-Nevis became an independent nation on Sept. 19, 1983, with a new constitution under which Great Britain relinquished its responsibility for defence and external affairs. Under the new Constitution, H.M. The Queen is Head of State, represented in the islands by the Governor-General. There is a central Cabinet Government with a Ministerial system, the Head of which is the Prime Minister of St. Kitts-Nevis, and a National Assembly located on St. Kitts. On Nevis there is a Nevis Island Administration, the Head being styled Premier of Nevis, and a Nevis Island Assembly.

Governor-General, His Excellency Sir Clement Athelston Arrindell, G.C.M.G. (1981).

Cabinet

Prime Minister and Minister of Finance, Home Affairs and Foreign Affairs,, Rt. Hon. Dr. K. A. Simmonds.
Deputy P.M. and Minister of Labour and Tourism, Rt. Hon. M. O. Powell.
Natural Resources and Environment, Hon. S. Daniel.
Education, Health and Community Affairs, Hon. S. E. Morris.
Communications, Works and Public Utilities, Hon. I. A. W. Stevens.
Agriculture, Lands, Housing and Development, Hon. H. C. Heyliger.
Women's Affairs, Hon. Constance Mitcham.
Trade and Industry, Hon. F. Jones.
In Ministry of Finance, Hon. R. Caines.
Without Portfolio, Hon. U. S. Swanston.
Attorney-General, Hon. S. W. T. Seaton.
Cabinet Secretary, C. Farier.

ECONOMY

The economy of the islands has been based on sugar for over three centuries. Tourism and light industry are now being developed. The economy of Nevis centres on small peasant farmers, but a sea-island cotton industry is being developed for export.

COMMUNICATIONS

Basseterre is a port of registry and has deep water harbour facilities. Golden Rock airport, on St. Kitts, can take most large jet aircraft; Newcastle airstrip on Nevis can take small aircraft and has night landing facilities.

The sea ferry route from Basseterre to Charlestown is 11 miles.

ST. LUCIA

St. Lucia, the second largest of the Windward group, situated in 13° 54′ N. lat. and 60° 50′ W. long., at a distance of about 21 miles N. of St. Vincent, and 24 miles S. of Martinique, is 27 miles in length, with an extreme breadth of 14 miles. It comprises an area of 238 square miles with an estimated population (1984) of 134,000. It possesses perhaps the most interesting history of all the smaller islands. Fights raged hotly around it, and it constantly changed hands between the English and the French. It is mountainous, its highest point being Mt. Gimie (3,145 feet) and for the most part it is covered with forest and tropical vegetation.

CAPITAL—ΨCastries (estimated population 1984, 50,798) is recognized as being one of the finest ports in the West Indies on account of its reputation as a safe anchorage in the hurricane season.

FLAG.—Blue, bearing in centre a device of yellow over black over white triangles having a common base.

GOVERNMENT

St. Lucia became independent within the Commonwealth on Feb. 22, 1979. The Head of State is H.M. The Queen, represented in the island by a St. Lucian Governor-General, and there is a bicameral legislature. The Senate has 11 members, 6 appointed by the ruling party, 3 by the Opposition and 2 by the Governor-General. The House of Assembly, which has a life of five years, has 17 elected Members and a Speaker, who may be elected from outside the House.

Governor-General, His Excellency Sir Allen Lewis, G.C.M.G., Q.C.

Cabinet

Prime Minister, Minister of Finance, Foreign Affairs, Development, Home Affairs and Information, Rt. Hon. J. G. M. Compton.
Deputy P.M. and Minister of Trade, Industry and Tourism, Hon. G. Mallet.
Health, Hon. Allan Bousquet.
Communications, Works and Labour, Hon. Clendon Mason.
Youth, Community Development, Social Affairs, Sport, Information and Broadcasting, Hon. Romanus Lansiquot.
Attorney General and Minister for Legal Affairs, Hon. Leonard Riviere.
Agriculture, Lands, Fisheries and Co-operatives, Hon. Ira d'Auvergne.

ST. LUCIA HIGH COMMISSION
10 Kensington Court, W8 5DL.
[01–937 9522]

High Commissioner, His Excellency Dr. Claudius C. Thomas, C.M.G.

OFFICE OF THE BRITISH HIGH COMMISSION
Columbus Square, P.O. Box 227, Castries.

High Commissioner, (resides at Bridgetown, Barbados).
Resident Representative, D. L. Littlefield.

ECONOMY

The economy is mainly agrarian, with manufacturing based on the processing of agricultural products. Principal crops are bananas, coconuts, cocoa, mangoes, avocado pears, breadfruit, spices, root crops such as cassava and yams, and citrus fruit. Attempts are being made to diversify the economy, in particular through greater industrialization; tourism is also of increasing importance.

The principal exports are bananas, coconut products (copra, edible oils, soap), cardboard boxes, beer, and textile manufactures. The chief imports are flour, meat, machinery, building materials, motor vehicles, cotton piece goods, petroleum and fertilizers.

Trade with U.K.

	1983	1984
Imports from U.K.	£6,276,000	£8,236,000
Exports to U.K.	21,960,000	28,563,000

ST. VINCENT AND THE GRENADINES

The territory of the State of St. Vincent includes certain of the Grenadines, a chain of small islands stretching 40 miles across the Caribbean Sea between Grenada and St. Vincent, some of the larger of which are Bequia, Canouan, Mayreau, Mustique, Union Island, Petit St. Vincent and Prune Island. The whole territory extends 150 square miles (96,000 acres).

The main island, St. Vincent, is situated between 13° 6′ and 14° 35′ N. latitude and 61° 6′ and 61° 20′ W. longitude, approximately 21 miles south west of St. Lucia and 100 miles west of Barbados. The island is 18 miles long and 11 miles wide at its extremities comprising an area of 133 square miles and a population (1982 estimate) of 127,883 of whom about 118,660 inhabit the main island. St. Vincent was discovered by Christopher Columbus in 1498. It was granted by Charles I to the Earl of Carlisle in 1627 and after subsequent grants and a series of occupations alternately by the French and English, it was finally restored to Britain in 1783.

CAPITAL.—ΨKingstown, population approximately 33,694.

GOVERNMENT

St. Vincent and the Grenadines achieved full independence within the Commonwealth on Oct. 27, 1979.

St. Vincent has a constitution under which there is a Governor-General who is Her Majesty's Representative. Except where otherwise provided, the Governor-General is required to act in accordance with the advice of the Prime Minister.

The House of Assembly consists of 13 elected members and 6 Senators appointed by the Governor-General. It is presided over by a Speaker elected by the House from within or without it.

Governor-General, His Excellency Sir Sydney Douglas Gun-Munro, G.C.M.G., M.B.E.

Cabinet

Prime Minister, Minister of Finance and Foreign Affairs, Hon. James Mitchell.
Trade, Industry and Agriculture, Hon. M. P. De-Freitas.
Housing, Labour and Community Development, Hon. D. E. Jack.
Tourism, Information, Culture and Women's Affairs, Hon. J. C. Home.
Education, Hon. A. C. Cruickshank.
Health, Hon. E. G. Griffith.
Communications and Works, Hon. B. B. Williams.
Legal Affairs, and Attorney General, Hon. E. Robertson.
Ministers of State, Hon. H. B. Young (*Trade, Industry and Agriculture*); Hon. J. C. Scott (*Housing, Labour and Community Development*).
Parliamentary Secretaries, Hon. L. Jones (*Communications and Works*); Hon. R. S. Nanton (*Office of the Prime Minister*).

ST. VINCENT AND THE GRENADINES HIGH COMMISSION
10 Kensington Court, W8 5DL
[01-937 9522]

High Commissioner, His Excellency Dr. Claudius C. Thomas, C.M.G.

OFFICE OF THE BRITISH HIGH COMMISSION
Granby Street (P.O. Box 132), Kingstown.

High Commissioner, (resides at Bridgetown, Barbados).
Resident Representative, W. J. Syratt.

ECONOMY

This is based mainly on agriculture but the tourist and manufacturing industries have been expanding. The main products are bananas, arrowroot, coconuts, sugar, cocoa, spices and various kinds of food crops.

The main imports are foodstuffs (meat, rice, beverages), textiles, lumber, cement and other building materials, fertilizers, motor vehicles and fuel.

EDUCATION

Primary and secondary education in Government schools is free but not compulsory. In 1982 there were 24,569 enrolments in state primary schools and 5,123 enrolments in state secondary schools.

Trade with U.K.

	1983	1984
Imports from U.K........	£4,357,000	£5,811,000
Exports to U.K.	12,496,000	14,167,000

SEYCHELLES

The Republic of Seychelles, in the Indian Ocean, consists of 115 islands with a total land area of 171·4 square miles, spread over 400,000 square miles of ocean. There is a relatively compact granitic group, 32 islands in all, with high hills and mountains (highest point about 2,990 ft.), of which Mahé is the largest and most populated (90 per cent of the population live on Mahé): and the outlying coralline group, for the most part, only a little above sea-level. Although only 4° S. of the Equator, the climate is pleasant though tropical. The population was estimated (end 1984) to be 65,032.

CAPITAL.—ΨVictoria (population, 1982, 24,733), on the N.E. side of Mahé.

FLAG.—Orange over green, divided by wavy white band.

GOVERNMENT

Proclaimed as French territory in 1756, the Mahé group began to be settled as a dependency of Mauritius from 1770, was captured by a British ship in 1794, changed hands several times between 1803 and 1814, when it was finally assigned to Great Britain. By Letters Patent of September, 1903, these islands, together with the coralline group, were formed into a separate Colony. On June 29, 1976, the Islands became an independent republic within the Commonwealth. A *coup d'état* took place on June 5, 1977.

A new constitution making Seychelles a one-party state came into force in June 1979. The executive power lies with the President, who is elected by universal suffrage for a five year term. Legislative power lies with the President and the People's Assembly (which has 23 elected members and two nominated by the President), an independent judiciary commission and an integrity commission.

President, France Albert René, *assumed office* June 5, 1977; *elected* June 26, 1979; *re-elected* June 18, 1984.

Council of Ministers

Administration, Finance, Industry, Transport, Foreign Affairs and Economic Planning, The President.
National Development, Jacques Hodoul.
Health, Esmé Jumeau.
Youth and Defence, Col. Ogilvy Berlouis.
Labour and Social Security, Joseph Belmont.
Education and Information, James Michel.

SEYCHELLES HIGH COMMISSION
50 Conduit Street, W1A 4PE
[01–439 0405]

High Commissioner, Her Excellency Mrs. Danielle de St. Jorre (1983).
Counsellor and Acting High Commissioner, R. F. Delpech.

BRITISH HIGH COMMISSION
Victoria House, P.O. Box 161,
Victoria, Mahé.
High Commissioner, His Excellency Colin G. Mays (1983).

ECONOMY

The economy is based on agriculture, fishing and, increasingly, on tourism. The Government has recently been encouraging farmers to diversify from the traditional plantation crops into the growing of food crops and rearing of livestock. However, copra and cinnamon bark remain the principal agricultural exports. Fishing and forestry are also considered to have considerable potential and are being developed.

Tourism has proved a major industry since the opening of an international airport on Mahé. Other industries include the extraction of guano, brewing and tobacco, plastics, soap and detergent factories are in operation. There is also a range of small-scale manufacturing industries.

TRADE

	1983	1984
Imports	Rs.594,082,000	Rs.616,682,000
Exports	25,250,000	21,398,000
Re-exports......	111,997,000	160,085,000

The principal imports are foodstuffs, beverages, tobacco, mineral fuels, manufactured items, building materials, machinery and transport equipment. The chief exports are copra, fish (fresh and frozen), cinnamon bark and guano. Re-exports cover a large proportion of exports from Seychelles and include such items as petroleum products, fuel and services for both aviation and shipping needs.

Trade with U.K.

	1983	1984
Imports from U.K........	£7,502,000	£7,540,000
Exports to U.K.	615,000	586,000

SIERRA LEONE

AREA, POPULATION, ETC.—Sierra Leone, with a total land area of 27,925 square miles, is on the west coast of Africa, between Guinea and Liberia. There was a population at the Census of 1974 of 3,123,000; a U.N. estimate put the population in 1982 at 3,670,000. The origins of the country date back to the late 18th century when a project was begun to settle destitute Africans from England on Freetown peninsula. In 1808 the settlement was declared a Crown Colony and became the main base in West Africa for enforcing the 1807 Act outlawing the slave trade. The Colony was also used as a settlement for Africans from North America and the West Indies, and great numbers of Africans rescued from slave ships, also settled there. Their descendants, known as Creoles, still live on Freetown peninsula. The southern half of Sierra Leone is inhabited by peoples whose languages fall into the Mende group; the northern half by the Temne, and smaller groups such as the Limba, Loko, Koranko and Susu.

CAPITAL.—Freetown (population at 1974 census, 274,000).

FLAG.—Three horizontal stripes of leaf green, white and cobalt blue.

NATIONAL DAY.—April 19 (Republic Day).

GOVERNMENT

Sierra Leone became a fully independent state within the Commonwealth on April 27, 1961. On April 19, 1971 a Republican Constitution was adopted and Dr. Siaka Stevens became the first Executive

President. In June 1978 Sierra Leone became a one-Party State, following approval by Parliament and a Referendum. The first General Election under the one party system was held on May 1, 1982. The Parliament now comprises 85 elected members and 12 Paramount Chiefs, plus seven nominated members, two of whom are the Army Commander and the Commissioner of Police.

President Stevens announced that he intended to retire when a replacement had been elected and a period of transition completed. The national convention of the All People's Congress met in Aug. 1985 to choose a party leader who will then be the sole candidate for the Presidency. The President-designate is Maj. Gen. Joseph Saidu Momoh, subject to approval by referendum in Oct. 1985.

President, His Excellency Dr. Siaka P. Stevens, G.C.M.G.

First Vice-President, Hon. S. I. Koroma.
Second Vice-President, Hon. F. M. Minah.

SIERRA LEONE HIGH COMMISSION
33 Portland Place, W1N 3AG
[01–636 6483/6]

High Commissioner, His Excellency Victor E. Sumner (1980).

BRITISH HIGH COMMISSION
Standard Bank of Sierra Leone Building
Lightfoot Boston Street, Freetown

High Commissioner, His Excellency Richard Dennis Clift, C.M.G.

British Council Representative, G. Reid, P.O. Box 124, Tower Hill, Freetown.

COMMUNICATIONS

Since the phasing out of the railway system in 1974 the road network has been developed considerably and there are now 5,000 miles of roads in the country, over 2,000 miles being surfaced. A bridge has been constructed over the Mano River linking Sierra Leone and Liberia.

The Freetown international airport is situated at Lungi, across the Sierra Leone River from Freetown. The main port is Freetown, which has one of the largest natural harbours in the world, and where there is a deep water quay providing about six berths for medium sized ships. There are smaller ports at Pepel and Bonthe.

Radio and television are operated by the Department of Broadcasting of the Sierra Leone Government. There are two shortwave transmitting and receiving stations in Freetown. A 250 KW radio transmitter has been installed which covers the whole country. Broadcasts are made in several of the more important indigenous languages in addition to English. There is also a weekly broadcast in French.

EDUCATION

In 1984 there were 1,280 primary schools in Sierra Leone and 160 secondary schools. Technical education is provided in the two Government Technical Institutes, situated in Freetown and Kenema, in two Trade Centres and in the technical training establishments of the mining companies. Teacher training is carried out at the university, six colleges in the Provinces and in the Milton Margai Training College near Freetown. The University of Sierra Leone (1967), consists of Fourah Bay College (1827) and Njala University College (1964).

PRODUCTION AND TRADE

On the Freetown Peninsula, farming is largely confined to the production of cassava and garden crops, such as maize and vegetables, for local consumption. In the hinterland, the principal agricultural product is rice, which is the staple food of the country, and cash crops such as cocoa, coffee, palm kernels, and ginger.

The economy depends largely on mineral exports mainly diamonds, bauxite and rutile. Iron ore production recommenced in 1982. Diamonds provide about 60 per cent of export earnings. Total exports in 1983–84 were estimated at Le102·1 million.

Trade with U.K.

	1983	1984
Imports from U.K.	£13,735,000	£19,532,384
Exports to U.K.	17,710,000	25,970,706

FINANCE

In 1964, Sierra Leone adopted decimal currency. The basic unit is the *Leone*.

The revenue for 1984-85 is estimated at Le317·1 million and total expenditure at Le507·1 million resulting in a projected deficit of Le190 million).

SINGAPORE

AREA, POPULATION, ETC.—The Republic of Singapore consists of the island of Singapore and 54 smaller islands, covering a total area of 230 square miles. Singapore Island is 26 miles long and 14 miles in breadth and is situated just north of the Equator off the southern extremity of the Malay Peninsula, from which it is separated by the Straits of Johore. A causeway, carrying a road and railway, crosses the three-quarters of a mile to the mainland. The highest point of the island is 581 feet above sea level. The climate is hot and humid and there are no clearly defined seasons. Rainfall averages 240 cm. a year and temperature ranges from 24°–32° C (76°–89° F).

At the 1980 census the population was 2,362,700. (Chinese, 1,819,600; Malays, 359,700; Indians, 162,800; others (Europeans, Eurasians, etc.), 48,700). In 1984 it was estimated at 2,544,400 (Chinese, 1,945,200; Malays, 377,700; Indians, 163,700; Others (Europeans,Eurasians, etc.) 57,800). At least 8 Chinese dialects are used and Malay, Mandarin, Tamil and English are the official languages.

FLAG.—Horizontal bands of red over white; crescent with five five-point stars on red band near staff.
NATIONAL DAY.—August 9.

GOVERNMENT

Singapore, where Sir Stamford Raffles had first established a trading post under the East India Company in 1819, was incorporated with Penang and Malacca to form the Straits Settlements in 1826. The Straits Settlements became a Crown Colony in 1867. Singapore fell into Japanese hands in 1942 and civil government was not restored until 1946, when it became a separate colony. Internal self-government and the title "State of Singapore" were introduced in 1959. Singapore became a state of Malaysia when the Federation was enlarged in September, 1963, but left Malaysia and became an independent sovereign state within the Commonwealth on August 9, 1965. Singapore adopted a Republican constitution from that date, the Yang di-Pertuan Negara being re-styled President. There is a Cabinet collectively responsible to a fully-elected Parliament of 75 members.

HEAD OF STATE

President, Wee Kim Wee, *elected* Aug. 30, 1985.

Cabinet

Prime Minister, Lee Kuan Yew, G.C.M.G., C.H.
Senior Minister, M. S. Rajaratnam.
First Deputy P.M. and Minister of Defence, Goh Chok Tong.
Second Deputy P.M., Ong Teng Cheong.
Foreign Affairs and Community Development, S. Dhanabalan.
Home Affairs, Prof. S. Jayakumar.
National Development, Teh Cheang Wan.
Environment, Dr. Ahmed Mattar.
Finance and Health, Dr. Richard Hu Tsu Tau.
Law, E. W. Barker.
Trade and Industry, and Education, Tony Tan Keng Yam.
Communications and Information, Dr. Yeo Ning Hong.

Speaker of Parliament, Dr. Yeoh Ghim Seng.

SINGAPORE HIGH COMMISSION
2 Wilton Crescent, SW1X 8RW
[01–235 8315/7]

High Commissioner, His Excellency Dr. Ho Guan Lim (1984).

BRITISH HIGH COMMISSION
Tanglin Road, Singapore 1024

High Commissioner, His Excellency Sir William Hamilton Whyte, K.C.M.G., apptd. 1985.
British Council Representative, Dr. J. L. Munby, O.B.E., Rubber House, Collyer Quay, Singapore 0104.

COMMUNICATIONS

Singapore is one of the largest seaports in the world, with deep water wharves and ship repairing facilities. Ships also anchor in the roads, unloading into lighters. In 1984, 63,849,000 freight tonnes of seaborne cargo was discharged and 40,344,400 freight tonnes loaded. The international airport is at Changi, in the east of the island. There are 25·75 km. of metric gauge railway connected to the Malaysian rail system by the causeway across the Straits of Johore, and 2,569 kilometres of roads. There are both wireless and wired broadcasting services carrying commercial advertizing. There are 3 television channels. Radio Singapore and Television Singapore amalgamated to form the Singapore Broadcasting Authority Corporation in February 1980.

ECONOMY

Historically Singapore's economy was largely based on the sale and distribution of raw materials from surrounding countries and on entrepot trade in finished products. In the last decade, however, new manufacturing industries have been introduced, including ship building and repairing, iron and steel, textiles, footwear, wood products, micro-electronics, scientific instruments, detergents, confectionery, pharmaceuticals, petroleum products, sanitary-ware, building materials, domestic electrical appliances, plastic articles, transport equipment, etc. Singapore has also become a financial centre with 123 commercial banks and 51 merchant banks established in the Republic, and an oil-refining centre.

Projects now being undertaken include the construction of a Mass Rapid Transit Rail system; expansion of the airport; the improvement of public utilities (electricity supply, sewage system) and telecommunications, including a submarine telephone cable system; building projects, especially of schools; and computerization in schools and government departments.

Finance

	1984–85	1985–86
Revenue	S$9,969,349,000	S$10,620,653,000
Expenditure	16,560,640,970	18,831,300,230

Trade

	1983	1984
Total imports	S$59,504·2m	S$61,133·6m
Total exports	46,154·9m	51,340·0m

Trade with U.K.

	1983	1984
Imports from U.K.	£469,155,000	£556,443,000
Exports to U.K.	404,122,000	488,421,000

SOLOMON ISLANDS

Forming a scattered archipelago of mountainous islands and low-lying coral atolls, Solomon Islands stretches about 900 miles in a south-easterly direction from Bougainville, in Papua New Guinea, to the Santa Cruz islands. The archipelago covers an area of about 249,000 square nautical miles while the land area is approximately 11,500 square miles. Solomon Islands lies between the east longitudes 155° 30' and 170° 30' and between south latitudes 5° 10' and 12° 45'. The six biggest islands are: Choiseul, New Georgia, Santa Isabel, Guadalcanal, Malaita and Makira. They are characterised by precipitous, thickly-forested mountain ranges intersected by deep, narrow valleys, and vary between 90 to 120 miles in length and between 20 to 30 miles in width.

Distribution of population at the Census of 1976 was: Melanesian 183,665; Polynesian 7,821; Micronesian 2,783; European 1,359; Chinese 452; Others 773. Total 196,823. A mid-1982 estimate put the total population at 244,000.

CAPITAL, Honiara (population (1979), 18,346).

FLAG.—Blue over green divided by a diagonal yellow band, with five white stars in the top left quarter.

GOVERNMENT

Governor-General, Sir Baddeley Devesi, G.C.M.G, G.C.V.O. (1978).
Prime Minister, Rt. Hon. Sir Peter Kenilorea, K.B.E.
Deputy P.M. and Minister for Home Affairs and Provincial Government, Hon. Ezekiel Alebua.
Foreign Affairs, Hon. Paul Tovua.
Finance, Hon. George Kejoa.
Economic Planning, Hon. Tony Harihiru.
Police and Justice, Hon. Swanson Konofilia.
Trade, Commerce and Industry, Hon. Robert Bera.
Posts and Telecommunications, Hon. John Maetia.
Health and Medical Services, Hon. Alfred Maetia.
Public Service, Hon. Seth Lekalalu.
Transport, Works and Utilities, Hon. John Tepaika.
Agriculture and Lands, Hon. Sethuel Kelly.
Education and Training, Hon. Danny Philip.
Immigration and Labour, Hon. Jason Dorovolomo.
Natural Resources, Hon. Daniel Sande.

JUDICIARY

The High Court of Solomon Islands, constituted by the Solomon Islands Independence Order, consists of a Chief Justice and not fewer than two nor more than three Puisne Judges. The Court of Appeal Act was enacted on May 8, 1978.

FINANCE AND TRADE

Revenue (1983), SI$59,400,000.
The main imports are foodstuffs, consumer goods, machinery and transport materials. Principal exports are timber, fish, copra, and palm oil. Other exports include cocoa and marine shells.

Trade with U.K.

	1983	1984
Imports from U.K.	£1,463,000	£1,513,000
Exports to U.K.	5,486,000	6,836,000

COMMUNICATIONS

An internal air service, Solair, serves 28 airstrips throughout the country, four of which are designated international airports. Solair operates international flights to Vanuatu and to Bourgainville (Papua New Guinea), and combined services with Air Pacific making two air connections weekly to Brisbane via Honiara. Air Nauru makes two flights a week, and Air Niugini also provides flights between Honiara/Port Moresby twice a week.

There are about 52 miles of secondary and minor roads in the urban areas of Honiara, Auki and Gizo. About 18 miles of road in and around Honiara and one mile in Auki and Gizo are bitumen sealed, the remainder being coral or gravel surfaced. In the rural areas there are some 800 miles of road, including those in private plantations, forestry areas and roads built and maintained by councils. All main islands have transceivers to maintain communications with Honiara and there is a telephone link between Honiara and Auki, Gizo and Tulagi.

Soltel, a company jointly owned by Cable and Wireless Limited and Solomon Islands Government operates the international telephone circuits from a ground station in Honiara via the Intelsat Pacific Ocean communication satellite.

BRITISH HIGH COMMISSION
Soltel House, Mendana Avenue,
Honiara.
High Commissioner, His Excellency George N. Stansfield, C.B.E. (1982).

SRI LANKA

(The Democratic Socialist Republic of Sri Lanka)

AREA, POPULATION, ETC.—Sri Lanka (formerly Ceylon) is an island in the Indian Ocean, off the southern tip of the peninsula of India and separated from it by a narrow strip of shallow water, the Palk Strait. Situated between 5° 55′–9° 50′ N. latitude and 79° 42′–81° 52′ E. longitude, it has an area of 25,332 square miles, including 33 square miles of inland water. Its greatest length is from north to south, 270 miles; and its greatest width 140 miles, no point in Sri Lanka being more than 80 miles from the sea.

The population at the 1981 census was 14,800,001. Of these 74 per cent were Sinhalese, 12·6 per cent Sri Lankan Tamils, 5·6 per cent Indian Tamils, 7·1 per cent Sri Lankan Moor and 0·7 per cent Burghers, Malays and others. The religion of the great majority of inhabitants is Buddhism, introduced from India, according to ancient Sinhalese chronicles, in 247 B.C. Next to Buddhism (69·3 per cent), Hinduism has a large following (15·5 per cent); 7·6 per cent of the population are Muslims and 7·5 per cent Christians. The national languages are Sinhalese, Tamil and English.

PHYSIOGRAPHY.—From a central massif of mountains the land slopes down to the sea on all sides in a series of three peneplains. The highest peaks are Pidurutalagala (8,281 ft.), Kirigalpota (7,857 ft.), Totapola Kanda (7,741 ft.), Adam's Peak (7,360 ft), a place of pilgrimage for Buddhists, Hindus and Moslems, and Great Western (7,269 ft.).

The Mahaweli-Ganga, 208 miles long, is the largest river of Sri Lanka, rising on the western side of the central hilly ridge, and flowing north east into Trincomalee Bay. None of the rivers is navigable by ocean-going vessels. Dunhinda (Badulla), Diyaluma (Koslanda), Elgin (Hatton Plateau) and Perawella are among the outstanding waterfalls. Forests, jungle and scrub cover the greater part of the island, often being intermingled. In areas over 2,000 feet above sea level grasslands (*patanas* or *talawas*) are found.

CLIMATE.—The climate of Sri Lanka is warm throughout the year, with a high relative humidity. Temperatures average 80° F. in the lowlands, and 60° F. at elevations over 6,000 ft. Day humidity is over 70 per cent and night humidity over 85 per cent. Temperature ranges vary little between wet and dry seasons. In the hills the climate is more temperate. Rainfall is generally heavy, with marked regional variations; the heaviest falls (200–250 inches) are recorded on the south-west slopes of the central hills. The two main monsoon seasons are mid-May to September (south-west) and November to March (north-east).

CAPITAL.—Ψ Colombo, population (1981, 585,776). Other principal towns are Ψ Jaffna (118,215), Kandy (101,281), Ψ Galle (77,183), Ψ Negombo (51,376) and Ψ Trincomalee (44,913).

FLAG.—On a dark red field, within a golden border, a golden lion passant holding a sword in its right paw, and a representation of a *bo*-leaf, issuing from each corner; and to its right, two vertical stripes of saffron and green also placed within a golden border, to represent the minorities of the country.

INDEPENDENCE DAY.—Feb. 4.

GOVERNMENT

Early in the sixteenth century the Portuguese landed in Ceylon and founded settlements, eventually conquering much of the country. Portuguese rule in Ceylon lasted 150 years during which the Roman Catholic religion was established among the Sinhalese inhabitants and to some extent Portuguese modes of living adopted. In 1658, following a twenty-year period of decline, Portuguese rule gave place to that of the Dutch East India Company which was to exploit Ceylon with varying fortunes until 1796.

The Maritime Provinces of Ceylon were ceded by the Dutch to the British on February 16, 1798, becoming a British Crown Colony in 1802 under the terms of the Treaty of Amiens. With the annexation of the Kingdom of Kandy in 1815, all Ceylon came under British rule.

On February 4, 1948, Ceylon became a self-governing state and a member of the British Commonwealth of Nations. A republican Constitution was adopted on May 22, 1972, providing for a unicameral legislature, the National State Assembly, which has a six year term, and the country was renamed the Republic of Sri Lanka (meaning 'Resplendent Island'). On Sept. 5, 1978 a new Constitution introduced the title the Democratic Socialist Republic of Sri Lanka and a system of proportional representation. Legislative power is exercised by Parliament, the executive power being exercised by the President.

A referendum in Dec. 1982 extended the life of the 1977 Parliament by six years from Aug. 1983.

President, Minister of Defence, Plan Implementation, Energy and Power, Higher Education, Janata Estates Development and State Plantations, His Excellency Junius Jayewardene, *acceded*, Feb. 4, 1978, *elected* Oct. 20, 1982.
Prime Minister, Minister of Local Government, Housing and Construction, Highways and of the Emergency Civil Administration, and Leader of the House of Parliament, Hon. R. Premadasa.

SRI LANKA HIGH COMMISSION
13 Hyde Park Gardens, W2 2LX
[01–262 1841]

High Commissioner, His Excellency Chandra Mone-rawela (1984).

BRITISH HIGH COMMISSION
Galle Road, Kollupitiya (P.O. Box 1433),
Colombo 3

High Commissioner, His Excellency John Anthony Benedict Stewart, C.M.G., O.B.E., *apptd.*, 1984.
British Council Representative, R. A. K. Baker, 47 Alfred House Gardens, Colombo 3. Office also in *Kandy*.

THE JUDICATURE

The Judicial System provides for a Supreme Court, a Court of Appeal, a High Court and other Courts of First Instance.

PRODUCTION

Agriculture.—The staple products of the island are tea, rubber, copra, spices and gems. There is increasing emphasis on local production of food, especially rice, and plans for the large-scale production of sugar cane, cotton and citrus fruits.

Industry.—Factories are established for the manufacture or processing of ceramic ware, vegetable oils and by-products, paper, tobacco, tanning and leather goods, plywood, cement, chemicals, sugar, flour, salt, textiles, ilmenite, tiles, tyres, fertilizers, clothing, jewellery and hardware and there is a petroleum refinery.

Trade with U.K.

	1983	1984
Imports from U.K.	£70,136,000	£61,179,000
Exports to U.K.	39,784,000	77,163,000

COMMUNICATIONS

There are over 15,660 miles of motorable roads in Sri Lanka and a government-run railway system with 984 miles of lines.

There is a satellite earth station at Padukka, in south-west Sri Lanka, which provides telecommunication links *via* satellite with any part of the globe.

The principal airports are at Katunayake, 19 miles north of Colombo, and Ratmalana, nine miles south of the capital. Air Lanka operates on 76 flights weekly to the Gulf States, the Maldives, Western Europe and throughout the Far East.

SWAZILAND

(Kingdom of Swaziland)

AREA, POPULATION, ETC.—Surrounded by South Africa on its northern, western and southern borders and by Mozambique to the east, this small land-locked country is geographically and climatically divided into three principal areas. The broken mountainous Highveld along the western border with an average altitude of 4,000 feet has been densely afforested mainly with conifers and eucalyptus; the Middleveld, averaging about 2,000 feet, is a mixed farming area including cotton and pineapples; and the Lowveld in the east which was mainly scrubland until the introduction of large sugar cane plantations west of the Lubombo mountain range and the Mozambique border. Four rivers, the Komati, Usutu, Mbuluzi and Ngwavuma, flow from west to east, cutting their way through the Lubombo mountains to the Indian Ocean. The exploitation of these rivers is particularly important to the agricultural development of the Middle and Lowveld, where irrigation schemes have promoted the introduction of sugar cane and have effectively altered the landscape of the Bushveld (Lowveld). The total area of Swaziland is 6,782 sq. miles and the population is estimated at some 600,000.

CAPITAL.—Mbabane (population, estimated 30,000), the headquarters of the Government, is situated at an average altitude of 3,800 ft. Other main townships are: Manzini (population, estimated, 30,000), Big Bend, Mhlambanyati, Mhlume, Nhlangano, Pigg's Peak and Simunye.

FLAG.—Five horizontal bands, crimson, bearing shield and spears device, bordered by narrow yellow bands; blue bands at top and foot.

GOVERNMENT

The Kingdom of Swaziland came into being on April 25, 1967, under a new internal self-government constitution and became an independent kingdom, headed by H.M. Sobhuza II, in membership of the Commonwealth on September 6, 1968. On April 12, 1973, the King, in response to a motion passed by both Houses of Parliament, repealed the Parliamentary Constitution of 1968 and assumed supreme legislative, executive and judicial power, to be exercised in collaboration with a Council constituted by his Cabinet Ministers. A new electoral law was introduced in 1978, under which each of the 40 traditional Tinkhundla elect two members to the electoral college who elect 40 members to the House of Assembly. The King nominates 10 members to the House of Assembly, making 50 in all, who then elect 10 members (not of their own number) to the Senate. To these are added 10 senators nominated by the King, bringing the full membership of the Senate to 20. Under the Establishment of the Parliament of Swaziland Order, 1978, the Head of State, advised by the Supreme Council of State (the Liqoqo), continues to reserve a large measure of executive, legislative and judicial authority.

Head of State, H.M. The Queen Regent, mother of the designated heir to the throne, Crown Prince Makhosetive.
Prime Minister, Rt. Hon. Prince Bhekimpi Dlamini, M.P.

SWAZILAND HIGH COMMISSION
58 Pont Street, SW1X 0AE
[01–581 4976/8]

High Commissioner, His Excellency G. M. Mamba (1978).

BRITISH HIGH COMMISSION
Allister Miller Street, Mbabane

High Commissioner, His Excellency Martin Reith (1983).

EDUCATION

In 1982, there were 125,303 pupils enrolled at 470 primary schools and 26,576 at 86 secondary schools.

COMMUNICATIONS

Swaziland's railway is about 150 miles long and runs from Ngwenya in the west to the Mozambique border near Goba in the east, and thence to the Mozambique port of Maputo. A southern link from Phuzumoya in central Swaziland joins up with the South African railway network to Richards Bay. A rail link from Mpaka in central Swaziland to the north-west border is under construction and will provide a link to Komatipoort when completed.

Most passenger and goods traffic is carried by privately-owned motor transport services. There are daily scheduled air services by Royal Swazi National Airways to Johannesburg and scheduled routes to Durban, Harare, Lusaka, Nairobi and Dar-es-Salaam. International telecommunications and television services are provided through a satellite earth station opened in 1983. There is also a national telephone network through a series of microwave links.

FINANCE

Government revenue for 1985–86 is estimated at £218,317,000, of which £136,576,000 (or 62·6 per cent) is anticipated revenue from the South African Common Customs Union with South Africa, Botswana and Lesotho. Total Government-financed recurrent and capital expenditure in 1985–86 is estimated at £217,291,000.

Swaziland is a member of the Rand Monetary Union and its unit of currency *Emalangeni* (singular *Lilangeni*) has a par value with the South African Rand.

Trade with U.K.

	1983	1984
Imports from U.K.	£3,536,000	£2,430,000
Exports to U.K.	23,966,000	41,786,000

TANZANIA

(United Republic of Tanzania)

AREA, POPULATION, ETC.—Tanganyika, the mainland part of the United Republic of Tanzania (Tanganyika and Zanzibar), occupies the east-central portion of the African continent, between 1°–11° 45′ S. lat. and 29° 20′–40° 38′ E. long. It is bounded on the N. by Kenya and Uganda; on the S.W. by Lake Malawi, Malawi and Zambia; on the S. by Mozambique; on the W. it is bounded by Rwanda, Burundi and Zaire; on the E. the boundary is the Indian Ocean. Tanganyika has a coastline of about 500 miles and an area of 362,820 sq. miles (including 20,650 sq. miles of water). The greater part of the country is occupied by the Central African plateau from which rise, among others, Mt. Kilimanjaro, the highest point on the continent of Africa (19,340 ft.) and Mt. Meru (14,974 ft.). The Serengeti National Park, which covers an area of 6,000 sq. miles in the Arusha, Mwanza and Mara Regions, is famous for its variety and number of species of game.

The African population consists mostly of tribes of mixed Bantu race. The total population of Tanzania at the Census held in August, 1978 was 17,551,925; Africans form a very large majority, while the Europeans, the Asians, and other non-Africans form a small minority. Swahili is the national and official language. English is the second official language, both for educational and government purposes.

Zanzibar.—Formerly ruled by the Sultan of Zanzibar, and a British Protectorate until Dec. 10, 1963. Zanzibar consists of the islands of Zanzibar, Pemba and Latham. It has a total area of approximately 1,000 sq. miles. The population of Zanzibar at the 1978 census was 475,655.

CAPITAL.—ΨDar es Salaam (population about 757,346 (mid-1978)). Other towns (1978 population) are ΨTanga (103,409); Mwanza (110,611); Arusha (55,281); Moshi (52,223); Morogoro (61,890); Dodoma (45,703); Tabora (67,392) and ΨMtwara (48,510). Zanzibar (population, 110,669) is the chief town and seaport of the island.

FLAG.—Green (above) and blue; divided by diagonal black stripe bordered by gold, running from bottom (next staff) to top (in fly).

NATIONAL DAY.—April 26 (Union Day).

GOVERNMENT

Tanganyika became an independent state and a member of the British Commonwealth on December 9, 1961, and a Republic, within the Commonwealth, on December 9, 1962, with an executive President, elected by universal suffrage as the Head of State and Head of the Government. On Dec. 10, 1963, Zanzibar became an independent state within the Commonwealth and on April 26, 1964, Tanganyika united with Zanzibar to form the United Republic of Tanzania.

Tanzania became a one-party state on July 10, 1965 but with the Tanganyika African National Union (TANU) and the Afro-Shirazi Party (ASP) remaining the ruling parties in Tanganyika and Zanzibar respectively. On Feb. 5, 1977 these two parties merged to form the Chama Cha Mapinduzi (CCM) (Revolutionary Party).

A new constitution was introduced on April 26, 1977 and revised in Oct. 1984. From 1985 there will be a President and two Vice-Presidents, one the President of Zanzibar and the other the Prime Minister. In future the President may only serve two five year terms and if he comes from Zanzibar the Prime Minister will be the First Vice-President and must come from Tanganyika. If the President comes from Tanganyika the President of Zanzibar will be the First Vice President. In a Presidential election a single Presidential candidate nominated by the C.C.M. has to obtain an affirmative majority of the votes cast, failing which a fresh candidate must be nominated. The new National Assembly will contain 243 members of whom 118 are elected from mainland constituencies and 50 from Zanzibar, 25 are ex-officio, 15 nominated and 35 indirectly elected. The Speaker may either be elected from among the members or be an additional member. Constituency members are elected by popular vote at a general election held at a maximum of five-yearly intervals in which the C.C.M. nominates two candidates to contest each seat. A new constitution was also approved in 1984 for Zanzibar providing for an elected President and House of Representatives. Although Zanzibar has its own government and Chief Minister, Tanganyika is governed by the government of the Union. Overall policy is decided by the C.C.M. whose chairman, Julius Nyerere, was elected in 1982 by the Party National Conference for a 5 year term.

President Nyere is expected to retire in Oct. 1985. The sole candidate in the Presidential election to be held in Oct. 1985 is Ali Hassan Mwinyi. Elections to the National Assembly are also due in autumn 1985.

President of the United Republic, Hon. Mwalimu Julius K. Nyerere, *b.* 1922; *elected* Nov. 1962; *took office* Dec. 9, 1962; *re-elected* Sept., 1965, Nov., 1970, Oct., 1975 and Oct. 1980.

Vice-President of the United Republic and President of Zanzibar, Hon. Ali Hassan Mwinyi.

Cabinet

Prime Minister, Hon. Salim Ahmed Salim.
Foreign Affairs, Hon. Benjamin Mkapa.
Agriculture and Livestock Development, Hon. John Machunda.
Finance, Hon. Cleopa Msuya.
Industry and Trade, Hon. Basil Mramba.
Defence and National Service, Hon. Brig. M. Kimario.
Communications and Works, Hon. John Malecela.
National Education, Hon. Jackson Makweta.
Lands, National Resources and Tourism, Hon. Paul Bomani.
Home Affairs, Hon. Salmin Amour.
Health, Hon. Dr. A. D. Chiduo.
Water, Energy and Minerals, Hon. Al-Noor Kassum.
Justice and Attorney-General, Hon. Joseph Warioba.

Labour and Manpower Development, Hon. Daudi Mwakawago.
Planning and Economic Affairs, Hon. Prof. Kighoma Malima.

TANZANIA HIGH COMMISSION
43 Hertford Street, W1Y 7TF
[01–499 8951]

High Commissioner, His Excellency Anthony B. Nyakyi (1982).

BRITISH HIGH COMMISSION
Hifadhi House, Samora Avenue (P.O. Box 9200), Dar es Salaam.

High Commissioner, (new appointment awaited).
British Council Representative, J. Mayatt, Samora Avenue, (P.O. Box 9100), Dar es Salaam.

EDUCATION

Education, almost entirely under state control, is characterised by official insistence that education must serve the aims of overall Government policy and planning. All Tanzanian secondary schools are expected to include practical subjects in the basic course. All who receive secondary (or equivalent) education are called up for a period of National Service. The school system is administered in Swahili and the intention is for the national language to become the medium at all levels. For higher education most Tanzanian students go to the University of Dar es Salaam, other East African universities, or to Universities and Colleges outside East Africa, mainly in Britain.

COMMUNICATIONS

The main port is Dar es Salaam, and there are other ports on the coast at Tanga, Mtwara, Zanzibar and Wete, in addition to Mwanza, Musoma and Bukoba on Lake Victoria and Kigoma on Lake Tanganyika. Coastal shipping services connect the mainland to Zanzibar, and lake services are operated on Lake Tanganyika and Lake Malawi with neighbouring countries.

The principal international airports are Dar es Salaam and Kilimanjaro. Other airports include Zanzibar, Arusha, Mwanza and Tanga.

There are two railway systems; one connecting Dar es Salaam to Zambia; and the second having two main lines running from Dar es Salaam, one to northern Tanzania and Kenya and the other to Lake Tanganyika and Victoria.

PRODUCTION AND TRADE

The economy is based mainly on the production and export of primary produce and the growing of foodstuffs for local consumption. The islands of Zanzibar, Pemba and Latham produce a large part of the world's supply of cloves and clove oil; and coconuts, coconut oil and copra are also produced. The chief export crops are coffee, cotton, sisal, cloves, tea, tobacco, cashew nuts and diamonds. The most important minerals are diamonds. Hides and skins are another valuable export. Industry is at present largely concerned with the processing of raw material for either export or local consumption. There is also a healthy growth of secondary manufacturing industries, including factories for the manufacture of leather and rubber footwear, knitwear, razor blades, cigarettes and textiles, and a wheat flour mill.

Trade with U.K.

	1983	1984
Imports from U.K.	£62,100,000	£60,449,000
Exports to U.K.	46,500,000	43,179,000

TONGA
(Kingdom of Tonga)

Tonga, or the Friendly Islands, comprises a group of islands situated in the Southern Pacific some 450 miles to the E.S.E. of Fiji, with an area of 288 sq. miles, and population (end 1981 estimate) of 98,000. The largest island, Tongatapu, was discovered by Tasman in 1643. Most of the islands are of coral formation, but some are volcanic (Tofua, Kao and Niuafoou or "Tin Can" Island). The limits of the group are between 15° and 23° 30′ S., and 173° and 177° W.

CAPITAL.—Nuku'alofa (21,000).

FLAG.—Truncated red cross on rectangular white ground (next staff) on a red field.

GOVERNMENT

The Kingdom of Tonga is an independent constitutional monarchy within the Commonwealth. Prior to June 4, 1970 it had been a British-protected state for 70 years. The constitution provides for a Government consisting of the Sovereign, a privy council and cabinet, a legislative assembly and a judiciary. The legislative assembly has 28 members, with a Speaker, and includes the Ministers of the Crown, the two Governors of Island groups, and the representatives of the Nobles and of the people (nine of each), who are elected triennially.

Head of State, H.M. King Taufa'ahau Tupou IV, G.C.M.G., G.C.V.O., K.B.E., *acceded* Dec. 16, 1965.
Heir, H.R.H. Crown Prince Tupouto'a.

Cabinet

Prime Minister and Minister of Agriculture, H.R.H. Prince Fatafehi Tu'ipelehake, K.B.E.
Deputy Prime Minister, Minister of Lands, Hon. Baron Tuita, C.B.E.
Health, Hon. Dr. S. Tapa.
Finance, Hon. C. Cocker.
Education, Works and N.D.O.R.R., Hon. Dr. S. L. Kavaliku.
Police, Hon. 'Akau'ola.
Labour, Commerce and Industries, Baron Vaea.
Foreign Affairs and Defence, H.R.H. Crown Prince Tupouto'a.
Governor of Vava'u, Hon. Dr. Ma'afu Tupou.
Governor of Ha'apai, Hon. Fakafanua.

ECONOMY

The economy is primarily agricultural; the main crops are coconuts, bananas, vanilla, yams, toro, cassava, groundnuts and other fruits. Fish is an important staple food though recent shortfalls have led to canned fish being imported. Industry is based on the processing of agricultural produce, and the manufacture of foodstuffs, clothing and sports equipment.

Finance	1985–86*
Revenue	T$22,788,160
Expenditure	22,760,030
*estimate	

The principal exports are copra, other coconut products, tropical root crops and bananas.

Trade

	1984
Total imports	T$46,614,000
Total exports	9,995,000

Trade with U.K.

	1983	1984
Imports from U.K.	£648,000	£842,000
Exports to U.K.	25,000	328,000

The unit of currency is the *Pa'anga* (T$), which is close to parity with the Australian dollar.

TONGA HIGH COMMISSION
New Zealand House, Haymarket, SW1Y 4TE
[01–839 3287/8]

High Commissioner, His Excellency Sonatane Tu'a Taumoepeau-Tupou (1983).

BRITISH HIGH COMMISSION
P.O. Box 56, Nuku'alofa

High Commissioner, His Excellency Gerald F. Rance, O.B.E.

TRINIDAD AND TOBAGO
(The Republic of Trinidad and Tobago)

AREA, POPULATION, ETC.—*Trinidad*, the most southerly of the West Indian Islands, lies close to the north coast of S. America, the nearest point being Venezuela, 7 miles distant. The island is situated between 10° 3'–10° 50' N. lat. and 60° 55'–61° 56' W. long., and is about 50 miles in length by 37 miles in width, with an area of 1,864 sq. miles. The island was discovered by Columbus in 1498, was colonized in 1532 by the Spaniards, capitulated to the British under Abercromby in 1797, and was ceded to Britain under the Treaty of Amiens (March 25, 1802). Two mountain systems, the Northern and Southern Ranges, stretch across almost its entire width and a third, the Central Range, lies diagonally across its middle portion; otherwise the island is mostly flat. The highest peaks are in the Northern Range (Cerro del Aripo 3,085 ft., El Tucuche 3,072 ft.). The climate is tropical with temperatures averaging 82° F. (27·8° C) by day and 74° F. (23·3° C) by night, and a rainfall averaging 82·7 inches a year. There is a well-marked dry season from January to May and wet season from June to December. The main tourist season is from December to April.

Tobago lies between 11° 9' and 11° 21' N. lat. and between 60° 30' and 60° 50' W. long., 19 miles north-east of Trinidad. It was ceded to the British Crown in 1814 and amalgamated with Trinidad in 1888. The island is 26 miles long, and 7½ wide, and has an area of 116 sq. miles. It is one of the healthiest of the West Indies and a popular tourist resort.

In 1980 the population of Trinidad and Tobago was estimated at 1,055,800 (Trinidad, 1,016,300; Tobago, 39,530).

Other Islands.—Corozal Point and Icacos Point, the N.W. and S.W. extremities of Trinidad, enclose the Gulf of Paria. West of Corozal Point lie several islands, of which Chacachacare, Huevos, Monos and Gaspar Grande are the most important.

CAPITAL.—Port-of-Spain (population approximately 59,800 in 1983) is the administrative centre of the islands. About 33 miles south of the capital is San Fernando (population approximately 36,800 in 1983), a town of growing importance which is emerging as the industrial centre of Trinidad, and which is in close proximity to a number of large industrial plants. The main town of Tobago is ΨScarborough.

FLAG.—Black diagonal stripe bordered with white stripes, running from top by staff, all on a red field.

NATIONAL DAYS.—August 31 (Independence Day); September 24 (Republic Day).

GOVERNMENT

The Territory of Trinidad and Tobago became an independent state and a member of the British Commonwealth on August 31, 1962, and a republic in 1976. The President is elected for 5 years by all members of the Senate and the House of Representatives. The House of Representatives has 36 members, elected by universal adult suffrage, and the Senate has 31, of whom 16 are appointed on the advice of the Prime Minister, 6 on the advice of the Leader of the Opposition and 9 on the advice of the President. Legislation was passed in Sept. 1980 which afforded Tobago a degree of self-administration.

President, His Excellency Sir Ellis Emmanuel Innocent Clarke, G.C.M.G.

Cabinet

Prime Minister and Minister of Finance and Planning, Hon. G. Chambers.
Agriculture, Lands and Food Production, Hon. K. Mohammed.
External Affairs, Hon. E. E. Mahabir.
National Security, Hon. O. R. Padmore.
Labour, Co-operatives and Social Security, Hon. J. S. Donaldson.
Health and Environment, Senator Hon. J. Eckstein.
Attorney-General and Legal Affairs, Senator Hon. S. R. Martineau.
Education, Hon. Mrs. M. Gordon.
Works, Maintenance and Drainage, Hon. H. Francis.
Public Utilities and National Transportation, Hon. Dr. C. Joseph.
Housing and Resettlement, Hon. D. Cartey.
Energy and Natural Resources, Hon. P. Manning.
Local Government and Community Development, Senator Dr. N. Connell.
Industry, Commerce and Consumer Affairs, Hon. H. Mottley.
State Enterprises, Hon. R. J. Williams.
Sport, Culture and Youth Affairs, Senator Hon. Dr. B. Ince.
Other Ministers, Senator Hon. C. Alert (*Ministry of Legal Affairs*); Senator Hon. A. Jacelon (*Ministry of Finance and Planning*); Hon. Mrs. M. Donawa-McDavidson (*Ministry of Community Development and Local Government*); Hon. Mrs. N. Lewis-Phillip (*Ministry of Health and Environment*); Hon. Mrs. E. Clarke-Allen (*Ministry of Housing and Resettlement*).
President of the Senate, Dr. the Hon. W. Ali.
Speaker of the House of Representatives, Hon. M. Ramacharan.

TRINIDAD AND TOBAGO HIGH COMMISSION
42 Belgrave Square, SW1X 8NT
[01–245 9351]

High Commissioner, (new appointment awaited).

BRITISH HIGH COMMISSION
Furness House, 90 Independence Square
(P.O. Box 778) Port of Spain

High Commissioner, His Excellency Martin Seymour Berthoud, C.M.G.

EDUCATION

The education system provides for free education at all state-owned and government-assisted denominational schools and certain faculties at the University of the West Indies. In addition there are various private teaching establishments. Selection to secondary schools is by common entrance examination at 11 years. There are three technical institutes, two teachers' training colleges, and one of the three branches of the University of the West Indies is located in Trinidad, at the St. Augustine campus.

COMMUNICATIONS

There are some 6,435·4 km. of all-weather roads in Trinidad and Tobago. The only general cargo port is Port-of-Spain but there are specialized port facilities elsewhere for landing crude oil, loading refinery products and sugar, and for storing and transmitting bauxite and cement. Regular shipping services call here and many inter-island craft use the port. Another, rapidly growing, port is at Port Lisas where new industries powered by local natural gas are located.

International scheduled airlines, including the national airline, Trinidad and Tobago Airways (BWIA) Corporation, use Piarco International Airport outside Port-of-Spain. The airline also flies between Piarco and Crown Point Airport in Tobago.

Four commercial broadcasting stations and one commercial television station operate in Trinidad and Tobago. There is an internal telephone system and external telephone and telegraph connections.

PRODUCTION

Oil, which is extracted both offshore and onshore, is the main source of the islands' revenue. Production of domestic crude in 1983 was approximately 9·3 million cu. metres, a decline by some 9 per cent from the previous year. The two major oil refineries have a combined capacity of 11,835 cu. metres per day, and refine both local and imported crude. Trinidad has large reserves of natural gas, estimated at 18,000,000 million cu. feet, which has been utilized in the development of manufacturing industries, which are energy intensive. An integrated steel plant and an anhydrous ammonia plant have been constructed at Point Lisas; a methanol plant started production in 1984.

Fertilizers, tyres, clothing, soap, furniture and foodstuffs are manufactured locally while motor vehicles, radios, TV sets, and electro-domestic equipment are assembled from parts, mainly from Japan.

Finance

	1983	1984
Revenue	TT$6,563·5m	TT$6,649·4m
Expenditure	8,790·5m	8,874·2m
Gross public debt	2,575·1m	3,489·4m

TRADE

	1982	1983
Imports	TT$8,873,·1m	TT$6,196·7m
Exports	7,372·4m	5,646·3m

The petroleum sector accounted for 83·5 per cent of total exports; other main export commodities were chemicals and machinery.

Trade with U.K.

	1983	1984
Imports from U.K.	£148,811,000	£113,312,000
Exports to U.K.	52,748,000	164,715,000

TUVALU

Tuvalu, formerly the Ellice islands, formed part of the Gilbert and Ellice Islands Colony until October 1, 1975, when separate constitutions came into force. Separation from the Gilbert Islands was implemented on January 1, 1976.

Tuvalu comprises nine coral atolls situated in the South West Pacific around the point at which the International Date Line cuts the Equator. The total land area is only about 10 square miles. Few of the atolls are more than 12 feet above sea level or more than half a mile in width. The vegetation consists mainly of coconut palms. The resident population in 1983 was 8,364, but it is estimated that about 1,500 Tuvaluans work overseas, mostly in Nauru, or as seamen. The entire population is Christian and is predominantly Protestant. The principal languages are Tuvaluan and English.

CAPITAL.—Funafuti. Estimated population 2,120. The capital has a grass strip airfield from which a service operates regularly to Fiji and Kiribati, and is also the only port.

FLAG.—Blue ground with Union Jack in top left quarter and nine five-pointed gold stars in the fly.

GOVERNMENT

On October 1, 1978, Tuvalu became fully independent as a sovereign state within the Commonwealth. The Constitution provides for a Prime Minister and four other Ministers who must be members of the 12-member elected Parliament. The Prime Minister presides at meetings of the Cabinet, which consists of the five Ministers, and is attended by the Attorney General. Local Government services are provided by elected Island Councils.

Governor-General, His Excellency Sir Fiatau Penitala Teo, G.C.M.G., G.C.V.O., M.B.E., I.S.O.

Cabinet

Prime Minister, Rt. Hon. Dr. Tomasi Puapua.
Deputy Prime Minister and Minister for Finance, Hon. Henry Naisali, C.M.G., M.B.E.
Commerce and Natural Resources, Hon. Lale Seluka.
Works and Communications, Hon. Metia Tealofi.
Social Services, Hon. Falaile Pilitai.
Attorney-General, Hon. Beith Atkinson

ECONOMY

Most people still practise a subsistence economy, the main staples of their diet being coconuts and fish. The main imports are foodstuffs, consumer goods and building materials. The only export is copra (508,000 kilos in 1984), but philatelic sales provide a major source of revenue and handicraft sales are increasing. The unit of currency is the Australian dollar.

Trade

	1984
Imports	A$3,954,000
Exports	307,917

Trade with U.K.

	1983	1984
Imports from U.K.	£55,000	£82,000
Exports to U.K.	35,000	11,000

EDUCATION AND WELFARE

There are eight primary schools in Tuvalu and a church secondary school run jointly with the Government. The total of enrolled children of school age in 1985 was 1,300. A Maritime Training School started in 1979.

There is a 30-bed hospital at Funafuti. All islands are served by a dispensary and a primary school.

UGANDA

(Republic of Uganda)

AREA, POPULATION, ETC.—Situated in Eastern Africa, Uganda is flanked by Zaire, the Sudan, Kenya and on the south by Tanzania and Rwanda. Large parts of Lakes Victoria, Edward and Albert (Mobuto) are within its boundaries, as are Lakes Kyoga,

Kwania, George and Bisina (formerly Salisbury) and the course of the River Nile from its outlet from Lake Victoria to the Sudan frontier post at Nimule. Uganda has an area of 91,000 sq. miles (water and swamp 16,400 sq. miles) and population (estimated, 1980) of 12,600,000. The official language of Uganda is English. The main local vernaculars are of Bantu, Luo and Hamitic origins. Ki-Swahili is generally understood in trading centres.

Despite its tropical location, the climate is tempered by its situation some 3,000 ft. above sea level, and well over that altitude in the highlands of the Western and Eastern Regions. In South Uganda, temperatures seldom rise above 85° F. (29° C.) or fall below 60° F. (15° C.). The rainfall averages about 50 inches a year. Uganda has three National Parks with a wide variety of wildlife and flora, and a fourth (Lake Mburo) has been designated.

CAPITAL.—Kampala (population of Greater Kampala, 400,000).

FLAG.—Six horizontal stripes of black, yellow and red (repeated) with a crested crane emblem on a white orb in the centre.

NATIONAL DAY.—October 9 (Independence Day).

GOVERNMENT

Uganda became an independent state and a member of the Commonwealth on October 9, 1962, after some 70 years of British rule. A Republic was instituted on September 8, 1967, under an executive President, assisted by a Cabinet of Ministers.

Early in 1971, while the President was abroad, the Uganda Army, with the co-operation of the police forces, assumed control of the country. All political activity in Uganda was suspended and Maj.-Gen. Idi Amin, the Army Commander, proclaimed himself Head of State, later suspending those sections of the constitution dealing with executive and legislative powers, and subsequently ruling by decree. In 1979, following on risings and military intervention by Tanzania, President Amin was overthrown. Dr Yusof Lule became President in April, but in June was succeeded by Mr. Godfrey Binaisa. Mr. Binaisa was in turn replaced by the Military Commission of the Uganda National Liberation Front, which governed the country until elections were held in December 1980, which led to Dr. Milton Obote becoming President. A military coup on July 27, 1985 ousted Dr. Obote and installed a military council which is intended to rule the country for a year until elections can be held.

Head of State, Lt. Gen. T. Okello, *sworn in* July 29, 1985.

Prime Minister, Abraham Waligo.

UGANDA HIGH COMMISSION

Uganda House, 58–59 Trafalgar Square, WC2N 5DX
[01–839 5783]

High Commissioner, His Excellency Shafiq Arain (1981).

BRITISH HIGH COMMISSION

10/12 Obote Avenue, P.O. Box 7070, Kampala

High Commissioner, His Excellency Colin McLean, C.M.G. M.B.E. (1983).

British Council Representative, K. F. Burd.

EDUCATION

Education is a joint undertaking by the Government, local authorities and, to some extent, voluntary agencies. In 1981 Uganda had 4,276 primary schools with an enrolment of 1,421,615 children. Secondary schools numbered 199 with 78,727 students enrolled; and 4,979 students in various technical training institutions.

The National University is Makerere University, Kampala, founded as a trade school in 1921 and becoming an independent University in 1970.

COMMUNICATIONS

There is an international airport at Entebbe, with direct flights to destinations in Africa, Asia and Europe. There are 8 other airfields in Uganda. Having no sea coast, Uganda is heavily dependent upon rail and road links to Mombasa for her trade. There are 2,226 kilometres of bituminized and 25,310 kilometres of gravel roads. The state of the roads at present is very poor. A railway network joins the capital to the western, eastern and northern centres. National Corporations have been established to provide rail and air services.

TRADE, ETC.

The principal export earner is coffee (over 90 per cent of all exports), but attempts are being made to increase production of cotton and tea for export. Hydro-electricity is produced from the Owen Falls power station which has a capacity of 150 MW and about 30 MW is exported to Kenya. The principal food crops are plantains, bananas, cassava, sweet potatoes, potatoes and sorghum.

Trade with U.K.

	1983	1984
Imports from U.K.	£21,092,000	£29,294,000
Exports to U.K.	29,645,000	46,750,000

VANUATU

(Republic of Vanuatu)

AREA, POPULATION, ETC.—Vanuatu, the former Anglo-French Condominium of the New Hebrides, is situated in the South Pacific Ocean, between 13° and 21° S. and 166° and 170° E. It includes 13 large and some 70 small islands, of coral and volcanic origin, including the Banks and Torres Islands in the North, and has a total land area of about 6,050 square miles. The principal islands are Vanua Lava and Gaua (Banks), Espiritu Santo, Maewo, Pentecost, Aoba, Malekula, Ambrym, Epi, Efate, Erromango, Tanna and Aneityum. Most islands are mountainous and there are active volcanoes on several. The climate is oceanic tropical, moderated by the south-east trade winds which blow between May and October. At other times winds are variable and cyclones may occur. Temperatures range between 62° F. and 83° F, with annual rainfall averaging 90 in. in the south and 155 in. in the north.

The 1979 Census showed a population of 112,596; about 95 per cent are Melanesian, the rest being small numbers of Micronesians, Polynesians and Europeans. The national language is Bislama (Pidgin), but English and French are also official languages.

SEAT OF ADMINISTRATION—ΨVila, Efate, population (1979), 14,801. The only other town is Luganville (population, 1979, 4,944), on Santo.

FLAG.—Red over green with a black triangle in the hoist, the three parts being divided by fimbriations of black and yellow, and in the centre of the black triangle a boar's tusk overlaid by two crossed fern leaves.

GOVERNMENT

The Condominium of the New Hebrides became an independent republic within the Commonwealth under the name of Vanuatu on July 30, 1980.

President, His Excellency Ati George Sokomanu, M.B.E., *elected* 1980, *re-elected* 1984.

Council of Ministers

Prime Minister and Minister of Justice, Hon. Father Walter Lini, C.B.E.
Deputy P.M. and Minister for Home Affairs, Hon. S. J. Regenvanu.
Finance, Commerce, Industry and Tourism, Hon. K. Kalsakau.
Lands, Energy and Water Supply, Hon. D. Kalpokas.
Foreign Affairs and External Trade, Hon. S. Molisa.
Education, Youth and Sports, Hon. O. Tahi.
Transport, Communications and Public Works, Hon. A. Sande.
Health, Hon. W. Korisa.
Agriculture, Fisheries and Forestry, Hon. J. Hopa.

Chief Justice, Hon. Mr. Justice F. G. Cooke.
Attorney-General, S. Hakwa.

BRITISH HIGH COMMISSION
Melitco House, Rue Pasteur, Vila.
High Commissioner, His Excellency Malcolm Lars Creek, M.V.O., *apptd.* 1985.

ECONOMY

Most of the population is employed on plantations or in subsistence agriculture. Subsistence crops include yams, toro, manioc, sweet potato and breadfruit; principal cash crops are copra, cocoa and coffee. Large numbers of cattle are kept on the plantations and an export trade in meat is being developed. On the island of Santo a plant freezes tuna and bonito for export.

Principal exports are copra, meat (frozen, tinned and chilled), fish and cocoa.

Tourism is an increasingly important revenue earner, and the absence of direct taxation has led to some growth in the finance and associated industries.

The unit of currency is the *Vatu*.

Trade with U.K.

	1983	1984
Imports from U.K.	£811,000	£479,000
Exports to U.K.	28,000	80,000

WESTERN SAMOA

Western Samoa consists of the islands of Savai'i (662 sq. miles) and of Upolu, which, with seven other islands, has an area of 435 sq. miles. All islands are mountainous. Upolu, the most fertile, contains the harbours of ΨApia and ΨSaluafata and Savai'i the harbour of ΨAsau. The population at the 1981 census was 158,130, the largest numbers being on Upolu (114,980) and Savai'i (43,150). The Samoans are a Polynesian people, though the population also includes other Pacific Islanders, Euronesians, Chinese and Europeans. The main languages spoken are Samoan and English. The islanders are Christians of different denominations.

CAPITAL.—ΨApia, on Upolu (population 33,100). Robert Louis Stevenson died and was buried at Apia in 1894.

FLAG.—Five white stars (depicting the Southern Cross) on a quarter royal blue at top next staff, and three quarters red.

GOVERNMENT

Formerly administered by New Zealand (latterly with internal self-government), Western Samoa became, on January 1, 1962, the first fully-independent Polynesian State.The State was treated as a member country of the Commonwealth until its formal admission on August 28, 1970.

The 1962 Constitution provides for a Head of State to be elected by the Legislative Assembly for a five year term. However, it was decided that initially two of the four Paramount chiefs should jointly hold the office of Head of State for life. When one of the chiefs died in April 1963, Malietoa Tanumafili II became the holder of the office of Head of State for life. The Head of State's functions are analogous to those of a constitutional monarch. Executive government is carried out by a Cabinet of Ministers.

Head of State, H. H. Malietoa Tanumafili II, G.C.M.G., C.B.E. (April 15, 1963).
Deputy Head of State, Hon. Mataafa Faasuamaleaui Puela.

Cabinet

Prime Minister and Minister of Foreign Affairs, Hon. Tofilau Eti Alesana.
Finance and Civil Aviation, Hon. Tuilaepa Sailele.
Lands, Hon. Polataivao Fosi.
Health and Shipping, Hon. Nonumalu Faiga.
Economic Development, Hon. Pule Lameko.
Education, Hon. Patu Afaese.
Agriculture, Hon. Toi Aukuso.
Works, Hon. Jack Netzler.
Justice, Hon. Tafua Kalolo.
Secretary to Government and Secretary of Foreign Affairs, Maiava Iulai Toma.

ECONOMY

Agriculture is the basis of Western Samoa's economy, the principal cash crops (and exports) being coconuts (copra), cocoa and bananas. Other agricultural exports include coffee, timber, tropical fruits and seeds. Efforts are being made to develop fishing on a commercial scale. Manufacturing is very small in scope and concerned largely with processing agricultural products, but is being encouraged by the Government. Tourism is increasing rapidly.

The unit of currency is the *tala* (WS $).

Trade with U.K.

	1983	1984
Imports from U.K.	£468,000	£1,183,000
Exports to U.K.	156,000	421,000

BRITISH HIGH COMMISSION (*see* New Zealand)

ZAMBIA

(Republic of Zambia)

AREA, POPULATION, ETC.—The Republic of Zambia lies on the plateau of Central Africa between the longitudes 22° E. and 33° 33′ E. and between the latitudes 8° 15′ S. and 18° S. It has an area of 290,587 square miles within boundaries 3,515 miles in length and a population (mid-year estimate, 1982) of 6,050,000, including about 50,000 non-Africans.

With the exception of the valleys of the Zambesi, the Luapula, the Kafue and the Luangwa Rivers, and the Luano valley, elevations vary from 3,000 to 5,000 feet above sea level, but in the north-east the plateau rises to occasional altitudes of over 6,000 feet. In many localities the evenness of the plateau is broken by hills, sometimes occurring as chains which develop into areas of broken country.

Although Zambia lies within the tropics, and fairly centrally in the African land mass, its elevation relieves it from extremely high temperatures and humidity. The lower reaches of the Zambesi, Luangwa and Kaufe rivers in deeper valleys do experience high humidity and extremes of heat.

CAPITAL.—Lusaka, situated in the Central Province. Population (estimated, 1980), 641,000. Other centres are Livingstone, Kabwe, Chipata, Mazabuka, Mbala, Kasama, Solwezi, Mongu, Mansa, Ndola,

Luanshya, Mufulira, Chingola, Chililabombwe, Kalulushi and Kitwe, the last six towns being the main centres on the Copperbelt.

FLAG.—Green with three small vertical stripes, red, black and orange (next fly); eagle device on green above stripes.

GOVERNMENT

At the dissolution of the Federation of Rhodesia and Nyasaland, on December 31, 1963, Northern Rhodesia (as Zambia was then known) achieved internal self-government under a new constitution. Zambia became an independent republic within the Commonwealth on October 24, 1964—75 years after coming under British rule and nine months after achieving internal self-government.

In July 1973, a new Constitution was introduced, making the United National Independence Party (U.N.I.P.) the only party.

President, Dr. Kenneth David Kaunda, *assumed office* Oct. 24, 1964; *re-elected,* Dec. 1973, Dec. 1978 and Oct. 1983.

Cabinet

Prime Minister, Kebby Musokatwane.
Secretary of State, Defence and Security, A. K. Shapi.
Defence, Lt. Gen. M. Masheke.
Foreign Affairs, Prof. Lameck Goma.
Finance, and National Commission for Development Planning, Luke Mwananshiku.
Legal Affairs (Attorney-General), Gibson Chigaga.
Higher Education, Rajah Kunda.
Health, Clement Mwananshiku.
Commerce and Industry, I. Subulwa
Home Affairs, Frederick Chomba.
Mines, J. Kalaluka.
Agriculture and Water Development, Gen. Kingsley Chinkuli.
Power, Transport and Communications, Fitzpatrick Chuula.
Works and Supply, Haswell Mwale.
Labour and Social Services, Frederick Hapunda.
Tourism, Roger Sakuhuka.
Information and Broadcasting Services, Cosmos Chibanda.
Youth and Sports, Ben Kakoma.
Lands and Natural Resources, Fabiano Chelah.
National Guidance, Arnold Simuchimba.
Co-operatives, Justin Mukando.
Decentralization, Dr. Henry Meebelo.
General Education and Culture, B. Kabwe.

Sec.-Gen., U.N.I.P., A. G. Zulu.

ZAMBIA HIGH COMMISSION
2 Palace Gate, W8 5LS
[01–589 6655]

High Commissioner, His Excellency Peter D. Zuze (1981).

BRITISH HIGH COMMISSION
Independence Avenue (P.O. Box 50050), Lusaka

High Commissioner, His Excellency William Kelvin Kennedy White, C.M.G. (1984).
British Council Representative, R. B. Timms, Heroes Place, (P.O. Box 34571), Lusaka.

JUDICATURE

There is a Chief Justice appointed by the President, all other judges being appointed on the recommendation of the Judicial Service Commission consisting of the Chief Justice, the chairman of the Public Service Commission, a senior Justice of Appeal and one Presidential nominee.

PRODUCTION

Principal products are maize, sugar, groundnuts, cotton, livestock, vegetables and tobacco.

Mineral production was valued at K1,250,730,000 in 1983, of which copper production (of 576,100 tonnes) accounted for K1,076,617,000.

FINANCE AND TRADE

The unit of currency is the *Kwacha.*

Gross Domestic Product (current prices) was K4,205·6m in 1983 and K4,733·3m in 1984. G.D.P. per capita (current prices) was K674 in 1983 and K737·3 in 1984.

	1983
Imports	K893,174,000
Exports	1,047,545,000

Trade with U.K.

	1984
Imports from U.K.	£66,746,000
Exports to U.K.	48,069,000

ZIMBABWE
(Republic of Zimbabwe)

AREA, POPULATION, ETC.—Zimbabwe, the former Southern Rhodesia (named after Cecil Rhodes) comprising eight provinces (Manicaland, Masvingo, Matabeleland North, Matabeleland South, Midlands, Mashonaland West, Central and East), lies south of the Zambesi river. The political neighbours are Zambia and Mozambique on the N.: South Africa and Botswana on the S. and W., and Mozambique on the E. It has a total area of 150,820 square miles and a population (estimated 1984) of 7,966,000 (Africans over 7 million; Europeans, Asians and coloured, estimated at about 180,000). The population is increasing at around 3·5 per cent. annually.

CAPITAL.—Harare (Salisbury) situated on the Mashonaland plateau, estimated population (August 1982) 656,000. Bulawayo—the largest town in Matabeleland, estimated population (August 1982) 413,800. Other centres are Mutare, Gweru, Kadoma, Kwe Kwe, Masvingo and Hwange.

Harare is 5,600 miles from London (air route), transit 12 hours; by sea via Cape Town, 17 days (approx.).

FLAG.—Seven horizontal stripes (green, gold, red, black, red, gold, green) with white triangle at the hoist containing the Zimbabwe bird superimposed on red five-point star.

GOVERNMENT

Southern Rhodesia was granted responsible government in 1923. An illegal declaration of independence on November 11, 1965 was finally terminated on December 12, 1979. Following elections in February 1980 the country obtained independence on April 18, 1980 as the Republic of Zimbabwe, a member of the British Commonwealth. The Parliament consists of a House of Assembly of 100 members and a Senate of 40 Senators and has a maximum life of five years. The President is elected by the Members of Parliament and holds office for a period of six years.

The first post-independence election was held in June and July 1985. Total seats won by black parties were Zanu (PF), 63; Zapu, 15 and Zanu, 1.

President, Rev. The Hon. Canaan Banana, *elected* April 11, 1980.

Ministry

Prime Minister and Minister of Defence, Robert G. Mugabe.
Deputy Prime Minister, Simon V. Muzenda.
Home Affairs, Enos Nkala.
Transport, Herbert Ushewokunze.
Education, Dzingai Mutumbuka.
Health, Sydney Sekeramayi.
Information, Posts and Telecommunications, Nathan Shamuyarira.
Foreign Affairs, Witness Mangwende.
Finance, Economic Planning and Development, Bernard Chidzero.
Trade and Commerce, Oliver Munyaradzi.
Industry and Technology, Senator Callistus Ndlovu.
Lands, Agriculture and Rural Settlement, Movan Mahachi.
Mines, Richard Hove.
Local Government, Rural and Urban Development, Enos Chikoware.
Justice, Legal and Parliamentary Affairs, Eddison Zvobgo.
Labour, Manpower Planning and Social Welfare, Frederick Shava.
Energy and Water Resources and Development, Kumbirai Kangai.
Natural Resources and Tourism, Victoria Chitepo.
National Supplies, Simbi Mubako.
Public Construction and National Housing, Simbarashe Mumbengegwi.
Youth, Sport and Culture, David Karimanzira.
Ministers of State, Maurice Nyagumbo (*Political Affairs and Coordination of Cooperatives*); Ernest Kadungure (*Defence*); Emmerson Munangagwa (*Security*); Teurai Ropa Nhongo (*Community Development and Women's Affairs*); Chris Andersen (*Public Service*).

ZIMBABWE HIGH COMMISSION
Zimbabwe House, 429 Strand, WC2R 0SA
[01-836 7755]

High Commissioner, His Excellency Dr. H. M. Murerwa (1984).

BRITISH HIGH COMMISSION
Stanley House, Stanley Avenue,
(PO Box 4490), Harare

High Commissioner, His Excellency Michael Ramsey Melhuish, C.M.G., apptd 1985.
British Council Representative, C. W. Perchard, O.B.E, 23 Stanley Avenue, (P.O. Box 664), Harare.

EDUCATION

Since independence, a policy of free primary education and accelerated expansion at secondary level has resulted in rapidly expanding enrolment. In 1985 there were 2,229,396 primary school and 497,766 secondary school pupils in both Government and Government aid schools. Over 80 per cent of schools are known as registered aided schools; they receive salary and tuition grants. Other schools are government-owned and run.

ECONOMY

Agriculture is the chief source of income for the population, and the source of a quarter of the country's earnings. Major crops are maize, wheat, cotton, tobacco and sugar, with significant diversification into livestock; Zimbabwe's beef herds and daily herds have been badly affected by three years of drought.

Although mining accounts for only 5 per cent of the Gross National Product and employs only 6 per cent of the labour force, it plays an important role in the economy as almost 80 per cent of output is exported, direct mineral exports accounting for 20 per cent of all exports in 1983, at a value of Z$219·8 million. The most important minerals are gold and asbestos (accounting for nearly 55 per cent of production by value in 1983), silver, copper, nickel, coal, chrome ore, tin, iron ore and cobalt.

Manufacturing industries contributed nearly 25 per cent of the Gross National Product in 1983, employing about 17 per cent of the labour force. Principal products in the light industry sector are foodstuffs, drink and tobacco, textiles, clothing and footwear, wood and furniture, paper, printing and publishing. Heavy industry includes chemical and petroleum products, non-metallic mineral products, metal and metal products, and transport equipment. Growth in the manufacturing sector, however, continues to be inhibited by the current shortage of foreign exchange for raw materials.

FINANCE AND TRADE

	1982-83	1983–84
Revenue	$1,789,000	$2,000,604,000
Expenditure	2,012,000	2,432,769,000

Trade with U.K.

	1983	1984
Imports from U.K.	£64,746,000	£68,636,000
Exports to U.K.	68,449,000	74,090,000

Dependent Territories, etc.

ANGUILLA

Anguilla is a flat coralline island, about 16 miles in length, 3¼ miles in breadth at its widest point and its area is about 35 sq. miles. It lies approximately 18° N. latitude and 63° W longitude, to the north of the Leeward Islands group.

The island is covered with low scrub and fringed with some of the finest white coral-sand beaches in the Caribbean. The climate is pleasant and healthy with temperatures in the range of 75-85°F. throughout the year. The population is about 7,000.
CAPITAL.—The Valley (population 500).

GOVERNMENT

Anguilla has been a British colony since 1650. For most of its history it has been linked administratively with St. Kitts, but three months after the Associated State of Saint Christopher (St. Kitts)-Nevis-Anguilla came into being in 1967 the Anguillans repudiated government from St. Kitts. A Commissioner was installed in 1969 and in 1976 Anguilla was given a new status and separate constitution. Final separation from St. Kitts-Nevis was effected on Dec. 19, 1980 and Anguilla reverted to a British Dependency. A new Constitution was introduced in 1982, providing for a Governor, an Executive Council comprising the Governor, four elected Ministers and two *ex-officio* members (Attorney General and Permanent Secretary, Finance), and an 11-member legislative House of Assembly presided over by a Speaker.

Governor, His Excellency Alastair Turner Baillie (1983).

Executive Council

President, The Governor.
Chief Minister and Minister of Home Affairs, Finance, Tourism and Economic Development, Hon. Emile Gumbs.
Education, Community Development and Youth, Hon. Mrs. Albena Lake-Hodge.
Lands, Agriculture and Fisheries, Health and Prisons, Hon. Eric Reid.
Communications, Public Utilities and Works, Hon. Nashville Webster.
Attorney-General, A. Hoole.
Permanent Secretary (Finance), Hon. Franklin Connor, O.B.E.

ECONOMY

Low rainfall limits agricultural output and export earnings are mainly from sales of lobsters and salt. Tourism is being developed. The unit of currency is the East Caribbean dollar (*EC*$)

FINANCE

	1985
Estimated revenue	*EC*$13,600,000
Estimated expenditure...........	13,300,000

ASCENSION
See St. Helena

BERMUDA

The Bermudas, or Somers Islands, are a cluster of about 100 small islands (about 20 only of which are inhabited) situated in the west of the Atlantic Ocean, in 32° 18′ N. lat. and 64° 46′ W. long., the nearest point of the mainland being Cape Hatteras in North Carolina, about 570 miles distant. The colony derives its name from Juan Bermudez, a Spaniard, who sighted it before 1515, but no settlement was made until 1609, when Sir George Somers, who was shipwrecked here on his way to Virginia, colonized the islands.

The total area is approximately 20·59 sq. miles which includes 2·3 sq. miles leased to the U.S.A. The civil population was 57,237 at the 1980 Census.
CAPITAL.—Hamilton (population, 1980, 1,617).

GOVERNMENT

Internal self-government was introduced on June 8, 1968. There is a Senate of 11 Members and an elected House of Assembly of 40 Members. The Governor retains responsibility for external affairs, defence, internal security and the police, although administrative matters for the Police Service have been delegated to the Minister of Home Affairs.

Governor and Commander-in-Chief, His Excellency The Viscount Dunrossil, C.M.G. (1983).
Deputy Governor, M. Herdman.

Cabinet

Premier, Hon. J. W. Swan.
Deputy Premier and Minister of Finance, Dr. Hon. C. James.

Tourism, Hon. J. Irving Pearman.
Education, Dr. Hon. G. Thomas.
Works and Housing, Hon. Q. L. Edness.
Health and Social Services, Hon. A. F. Cartwright DeCouto.
Transport, Hon. S. Stallard.
Environment, Hon. T. E. Davis.
Labour and Home Affairs, Hon. Sir John Sharpe.
Community, Cultural Affairs and Technology, Sen. Hon. G. Simons.
Youth, Sport and Recreation, Hon. M. A. Burgess.
Legislative Affairs, Sen. Hon. C. T. M. Collis.

President of the Senate, Hon. H. Richardson, C.B.E.
Speaker of the House of Assembly, Hon. F. J. Barritt.

Chief Justice, Hon. Sir James R. Astwood, C.B.E.
Puisne Judges, Hon. G. Collett, C.B.E., Q.C.; Hon. J. Melville.

ECONOMY

Locally manufactured concentrates and pharmaceuticals are now the colony's leading exports. Little food is produced except vegetables and fish, other foodstuffs being imported.

The Islands' economic structure is based on tourism, which continues to be the major industry and source of revenue. In 1984 a total of 528,871 visitors arrived in Bermuda. Cruise ships dock at Hamilton and are expected to dock in St. George's again in 1986.

Free elementary education was introduced in 1949. Free secondary education was introduced in 1965 for those children in the aided and maintained schools who were below the upper limit of the statutory school age of 16 (from 1969 onwards).

There are 5 radio and one television station, one daily and 2 weekly newspapers and overseas telephone and telegraph services are maintained.

FINANCE

	1984–85	1985–86
Public revenue	$186,553,800	$214,800,000
Public expenditure	169,299,755	190,362,000

Currency.—The unit of currency is the Bermudan dollar (*Bd* $).

Trade with U.K.

	1983	1984
Imports from U.K......	£24,924,000	£22,843,000
Exports to U.K.	4,019,000	3,037,000

THE BRITISH ANTARCTIC TERRITORY

The British Antarctic Territory was designated in 1962 and consists of the areas south of 60°S. latitude which were previously included in the Falkland Islands Dependencies. The territory lies between longitudes 20° and 80°W., south of latitude 60°S. and includes the South Orkney Islands, the South Shetland Islands, the mountainous Antarctic Peninsula (highest point *Mount Jackson*, 13,620ft, in Palmer Land) and all adjacent islands, and the land mass extending to the South Pole. The territory has no indigenous inhabitants and the British population consists of the scientists and technicians who man the British Antarctic Survey stations. The number averages about 60 to 70 in winter, but increases considerably in the summer months with the arrival of field workers; Argentina, Brazil, Chile, China, Poland, U.S.A., U.S.S.R. and Uruguay also have scientific stations in the territory.

The first two British Antarctic Survey stations were established in the South Shetland Islands in

1944, and by 1956 the number of stations had risen to twelve. Due to the completion of field work in some areas and increased mobility, the number has now been reduced to five. These are Signy (Signy Island, S. Orkney Islands), Faraday (Argentine Islands, Graham Coast), Rothera (Adelaide Island), Halley (Caird Coast) and, in summer only, Fossil Bluff (George VI Sound). Fifteen other stations have been established but are at present unoccupied.

The territory is administered by a High Commissioner, resident in the Falkland Islands.

High Commissioner, Gordon Wesley Jewkes, C.M.G. *apptd.* (1985).

(*see index also for* The Antarctic)

THE BRITISH INDIAN OCEAN TERRITORY

The British Indian Ocean Territory was established by an Order in Council in 1965 and included islands formerly administered by Mauritius and the Seychelles. After the independence of both, the territory was redefined in 1976 as comprising only the islands of the Chagos Archipelago.

The Chagos Archipelago consists of six main groups of islands situated on the Great Chagos Bank and covering some 21,000 square miles. The largest and most southerly of the Chagos Islands is *Diego Garcia,* a sand cay with a land area of about 17 square miles approximately 1,100 miles east of Mahe, used as a joint naval support base by Britain and U.S.A.

The other main island groups of the archipelago, *Peros Banhos* (29 islands with a total land area of 4 square miles) and *Salomon* (11 islands with a total land area of 2 square miles) are uninhabited. The islands have a typical tropical maritime climate, with average temperatures between 77°F and 84°F in Diego Garcia, and rainfall in the whole archipelago of 90–100 inches a year.

Commissioner, W. N. Wenban-Smith.
Administrator, D. H. Doble.

THE BRITISH VIRGIN ISLANDS

The Virgin Islands are a group of islands at the eastern extremity of the Greater Antilles, divided between Great Britain and the U.S.A. Those of the group which are British number 36, of which 11 are uninhabited, and have a total area of about 59 square miles. The principal are Tortola, the largest (situated in 18° 27′ N. lat. and 64° 40′ W. long., area, 21 sq. miles), Virgin Gorda (8½ sq. miles), Anegada (15 sq. miles) and Jost Van Dyke (3½ sq. miles). The 1980 Census of Population showed a total population of 12,034 (Tortola (9,322); Virgin Gorda (1,443); Anegada (169); Jost Van Dyke (136); and other islands (82). Apart from Anegada, which is a flat coral island, the British Virgin Islands are hilly, being an extension of the Puerto Rico and the U.S. Virgin Islands archipelago. The highest point is Sage Mountain on Tortola which rises to a height of 1,780 feet. Tourism is the main industry, but there is some cattle raising and fishing. Other products are vegetables, fruit, charcoal and rum.

The islands lie within the Trade Winds belt and possess a pleasant and healthy sub-tropical climate. The average temperature varies from 71°–82° F. in winter and 78°–88° F. in summer. The summer heat is tempered by sea breezes and the temperature usually falls by about 10°F. at night. Average rainfall is 53 inches. Hurricanes are very rare—the last occurrence being in 1928.

CAPITAL.—ΨRoad Town, on the south-east of Tortola. Population, 2,479.

GOVERNMENT

Under the 1977 Constitution, the Governor, appointed by the Crown, remains responsible for defence and internal security, external affairs and the civil service but in other matters acts in accordance with the advice of the Executive Council. The Executive Council consists of the Governor as Chairman, one *ex officio* member (the Attorney-General), the Chief Minister and three other ministers. The Legislative Council consists of a Speaker chosen from outside the Council, one *ex officio* member (the Attorney-General), and nine elected members returned from nine one-member electoral districts.

Governor, His Excellency David R. Barwick, C.B.E., Q.C.
Deputy Governor, E. Georges.
Financial Secretary, K. Bain, O.B.E.

The Executive Council

Chairman, The Governor.
Chief Minister and Minister of Finance, Hon. C. B. Romney.
Deputy Chief Minister and Minister for Health, Education and Welfare, Hon. W. Wheatley, M.B.E.
Communications and Works, Hon. E. W. Brewley.
Natural Resources and Labour, Hon. C. Maduro.
Attorney-General, Hon. L. S. Hunte.

Puisne Judge (resident), Hon. Miss M. Joseph.

FINANCE

	1981	1982
		(*estimated*)
Revenue	$U.S. 14,462,599	$U.S. 14,750,000
Expenditure	14,211,871	13,035,615

ECONOMY

Tourism is the main industry but other industries include a rum distillery, three stone-crushing plants and factories manufacturing concrete blocks and paint. The major export items are fresh fish, gravel, sand, fruits and vegetables: exports are largely confined to the U.S. Virgin Islands. Chief imports are building materials, machinery, cars and beverages.

Trade with U.K.

	1983	1984
Imports from U.K........	£3,455,000	£2,543,000
Exports to U.K.	172,000	1,427,000

COMMUNICATIONS

The principal airport is on Beef Island, linked by bridge to Tortola, and an extended runway of 3,600 feet enables larger aircraft to call. There is a second airfield on Virgin Gorda and a third on Anegada. There are direct shipping services to the United Kingdom and the United States and fast passenger services connect the main islands by ferry.

THE CAYMAN ISLANDS

The Cayman Islands, between 79° 44′ and 81° 26′ W. and 19° 15′ and 19° 46′ N., consist of three islands, Grand Cayman, Cayman Brac, and Little Cayman, with a total area of 100 square miles. Population (1983), 18,750.

CAPITAL.—ΨGeorge Town, in Grand Cayman, population (1981) 8,200.

GOVERNMENT

The constitution provides for a Governor, Legislative Assembly and an Executive Council. The Legislative Assembly consists of the Governor, three official members and 12 elected members. The Governor presides over the Executive Council, which consists of three official members appointed by the Governor, and four elected members, chosen by the elected members of the Assembly from among their own number. The normal life of the Assembly is four years.

Governor, His Excellency George Peter Lloyd, C.V.O., C.M.G.

Executive Council

President, The Governor.
Chief Secretary, Hon. D. H. Foster, C.V.O., C.B.E.
Financial Secretary, Hon. T. C. Jefferson.
Attorney-General, Hon. M. J. Bradley.
Member for Health, Education and Social Services, Hon. B. O. E. Banks.
Member for Communications, Works and District Administration, Hon. Capt. C. Kirkconnell.
Member for Tourism, Aviation and Trade, Hon. W. N. Bodden, M.B.E.
Member for Development, Lands and Natural Resources, Hon. V. Johnson, C.B.E.

LONDON OFFICE

Cayman Islands Government Office,
17B Curzon Street, W1Y 7FE.
Government Representative, T. Russell, C.M.G., C.B.E.

FINANCE

	1983	1984
Revenue	CI$49,692,616	CI$60,880,502
Expenditure	39,355,604	62,134,034
Public Debt	9,090,000	14,383,433

TRADE

	1981	1982 (estimated)
Total imports	CI$109,000,000	CI$110,000,000
Total exports	3,000,000	2,000,000

Trade with U.K.

	1983	1984
Imports from U.K.	£4,046,000	£4,905,000
Exports to U.K.	610,000	12,911,000

FALKLAND ISLANDS

The Falkland Islands, the only considerable group in the South Atlantic, lie about 300 miles east of the Straits of Magellan, between 52° 15'–53° S. lat. and 57° 40'–62° W. long. They consist of East Falkland (area 2,610 sq. miles), West Falkland (2,090 sq. miles) and upwards of 100 small islands in the aggregate. Mount Usborne (E. Falkland), the loftiest peak, rises 2,312 feet above the level of the sea.

The climate is cool. At Stanley the mean monthly temperature varies between 49° F. in January and 35·5° F. in July. The air temperature has never been known to exceed 77° F. or to fall below 12° F.; it is notably windy. The islands are chiefly moorland.

The Falklands were sighted first by Davis in 1592, and by Hawkins in 1594: the first known landing was by Strong in 1690. A settlement was made by France in 1764; this was subsequently sold to Spain, but the latter country recognized Great Britain's title to a part at least of the group in 1771. The settlement was destroyed by the Americans in 1831. In 1833 occupa-

tion was resumed by the British for the protection of the seal-fisheries, and the islands were permanently colonized as the most southerly organized colony of the British Empire. Argentina has long claimed sovereignty over the Islands (known to them as las Islas Malvinas), and in pursuance of this claim invaded the Islands on April 2, 1982 and also occupied South Georgia. A Task Force despatched from Great Britain recaptured South Georgia on April 25, and after landing at San Carlos Bay on May 21, recaptured the Islands from the Argentines, who surrendered on June 14, 1982. A large British naval and military presence remains in the area, although it is expected that this will be reduced following the opening of Mount Pleasant airport in May 1985.

The population of 1,813 (at Census of Dec. 5, 1980) is almost totally British, and is principally engaged in sheep-farming to which practically all the land in the colony is devoted, 663,367 sheep being carried in 1979–80. Wool, hides and skins are exported. Main imports are foodstuffs, manufactured goods, timber and machinery.

CHIEF TOWN.—ΨStanley, population 1,050 (1980). The size of the British garrison is about 4,000. Stanley is distant from England about 8,103 miles.

GOVERNMENT

The Governor is advised by an Executive Council, over which he presides, composed of the Chief Executive, the Financial Secretary, and three elected members, elected by and from the elected members of the Legislative Council. The Legislative Council is composed of two *ex officio* members, namely, the Chief Executive and the Financial Secretary, and eight representatives elected by the people, with the Governor as President.

A new constitution was introduced in 1985 and elections to the Legislative Council were due to take place on Oct. 3, 1985.

Governor, Gordon Wesley Jewkes, C.M.G., *apptd.* 1985.
Commander, British Forces, Falkland Islands, Air Vice Marshal R. J. Kemball, C.B.E.
Chief Executive, D. G. P. Taylor.
Financial Secretary, H. T. Rowlands, O.B.E.
Attorney General, M. C. L. Gaiger.

FINANCE AND TRADE

	1982–83	1983–84†
Public Revenue	£3,538,708	£3,295,590
Expenditure	3,456,164	3,531,475
†Estimated.		

Trade with U.K.

	1983	1984
Imports from U.K.	£7,269,000	£9,516,000
Exports to U.K.	4,022,000	5,202,000

Dependencies

SOUTH GEORGIA, An island 800 miles east-south-east of the Falkland group, with an area of 1,450 sq. miles. The population comprises an army unit at King Edward Point, and staff of the British Antarctic Survey at Bird Island, in the north-west of S. Georgia.

THE SOUTH SANDWICH ISLANDS lie some 470 miles S.E. of South Georgia. The group is a chain of uninhabited, actively volcanic islands about 150 miles long, with a wholly Antarctic climate.

GIBRALTAR

Gibraltar is a rocky promontory, 2¼ miles in length, three-quarters of a mile in breadth and 1,396 feet high at its greatest elevation, near the southern extremity of Spain, with which it is connected by a low isthmus. It is about 14 miles distant from the opposite coast of Africa. In a total area of 2¼ sq. miles, the population at the census of Nov. 1981 was 28,719.

Gibraltar is a naval base of strategic importance to Great Britain. It was captured in 1704, during the war of the Spanish Succession, by a combined Dutch and English force, under Sir George Rooke, and was ceded to Great Britain by the Treaty of Utrecht, 1713. Several attempts have been made to retake it, the most celebrated being the great siege in 1779–83, when General Eliott, afterwards Lord Heathfield, held it for 3 years and 7 months against a combined French and Spanish force. The town stands at the foot of the promontory on the W. side.

GOVERNMENT

The Constitution of Gibraltar, approved in 1969, made formal provision for certain domestic matters to devolve on Ministers appointed from among elected members of the House of Assembly then set up to replace the former Legislative Council. The House of Assembly consists of an independent Speaker, 15 elected members, the Attorney-General and Financial and Development Secretary.

Governor and Commander-in-Chief, His Excellency Air Chief Marshall Sir Peter Terry, G.C.B., A.F.C.
Flag Officer, Gibraltar, and Admiral Supr., H.M. Naval Base, Gibraltar, Rear Admiral P. G. V. Dingemans, D.S.O.
Deputy Governor, J. K. E. Broadley £26,909
Financial and Development Secretary, B. Traynor £24,317
Attorney-General, E. Thistlethwaite £24,317
Chief Justice, Sir Dermot Davis, O.B.E. £26,909
Chief Minister, Sir Joshua Hassan, C.B.E., L.V.O., Q.C.
Speaker, A. J. Vasquez, C.B.E.

ECONOMY

Gibraltar enjoys the advantages of an extensive shipping trade and is a popular shopping centre. The chief sources of revenue are the port dues, the rent of the Crown estate in the town, and duties on consumer items. The free port tradition of Gibraltar is still reflected in the low rates of import duty. The gradual change from a fortress city to a holiday centre has led to a flourishing tourist trade.

A total of 2,092 merchant ships (19,250,831 gross registered tons aggregate) entered the port during 1984. Of these 1,118 were deep-sea ships (18,734,654 gross registered tons aggregate). In addition 5,376 yachts (97,920 gross registered tons) called at the port. There are 26·75 miles of roads.

Education is compulsory and free for children between the ages of 4 and 15 whose parents are ordinarily resident in Gibraltar. Scholarships are available for higher education in Britain. The total enrolment in Government schools was 5,263 in Dec. 1984. Government expenditure on education in 1983 was £4,340,648.

Finance and Trade

	1982–83	1983–84
Revenue	£47,900,000	£51,200,000
Expenditure	47,400,000	55,900,000

	1982–83	1983–84
Total imports	£61,651,000	£66,098,000
Total exports	24,468,000	25,072,000

Trade with U.K.

	1983	1984
Imports from U.K.	£26,495,000	£31,978,000
Exports to U.K.	4,266,000	5,333,000

Distance from London 1,209 miles; G.B. Airways and British Airways operate regular direct air services to the U.K. Transit times average 2½ hours.

HONG KONG

Hong Kong, consisting of a number of islands and of a portion of the mainland (Kowloon and the New Territories), on the south-eastern coast of China, is situated at the eastern side of the mouth of the Pearl River, between 22° 9′ and 22° 37′ N. lat. and 113° 52′–114° 30′ E. long. The total area of the territory (including recent reclamation) is 404 sq. miles (1,067·65 sq. km.) with a population which at the end of 1984 was 5,397,500.

The island of *Hong Kong* is about 11 miles long and from 2 to 5 miles broad, with a total area of 29 square miles; at the eastern entrance to the harbour it is separated from the mainland by a narrow strait. The island was first occupied by Great Britain in January, 1841, and formally ceded by the Treaty of Nanking in 1842; *Kowloon* was subsequently acquired by the Peking Convention of 1860; and the *New Territories,* consisting of a peninsula in the southern part of the Guangdong province, together with adjacent islands, by a 99-year lease signed June 9, 1898.

The island is broken in shape and mountainous, the highest point being Victoria Peak, which is 1,805 feet high. The New Territories contain several peaks higher than this, the highest being Tai Mo Shan, 3,140 ft.

Climate.—Hong Kong enjoys unusually varied weather for a tropical area. The mean monthly temperature ranges from 15° C. to 29° C., though summer temperatures can exceed 33° C and winter temperatures drop below 10° C. The average annual rainfall is 2,246 mm., of which nearly 80 per cent falls between May and September. Tropical cyclones passing at various distances from Hong Kong occur between July and September, causing high winds and heavy rain.

CAPITAL.—Victoria, situated on the island of Hong Kong, is about 81 miles S.E. of Canton and 40 miles E. of the Portuguese province of Macau at the other side of the Pearl River. It lies along the northern shore of the island and faces the mainland; the harbour (23 sq. miles water area) lies between the city and the mainland.

GOVERNMENT

Hong Kong is administered as a Crown Colony with a Governor, aided by an Executive Council, consisting of 4 *ex-officio* and 11 nominated members, and a Legislative Council, which consists of 10 official and 46 unofficial members, 24 elected and 22 nominated by the Governor.

There is also an Urban Council which provides services relating to public health and sanitation, culture and recreation in the urban area. A Regional Council will also be set up in 1986 to provide similar services in the New Territories. Both Councils are financially autonomous.

In a Joint Declaration initialled on Dec. 19, 1984 and ratified on May 27, 1985, Great Britain and China agreed to restore sovereignty over Hong Kong to China on July 1, 1997. Thereafter, a Special Administrative Region (S.A.R.) will be established under the direct authority of the Chinese central government. However, the social and economic systems in the S.A.R. will remain unchanged for 50 years.

Governor, His Excellency Sir Edward Youde, G.C.M.G., M.B.E., *appointed* 1982.

Chief Secretary, Hon. Sir David Akers-Jones, K.B.E., C.M.G.

Commander, British Forces, Major General Hon. A. Boam, C.B.E.

Financial Secretary, Hon. Sir John Bremridge, K.B.E.

Attorney-General, Hon. M. D. Thomas, C.M.G., Q.C.

Secretary for Trade and Industry, Hon. E. P. Ho, C.B.E.

Secretary for District Administration, Hon. D. Liao, C.B.E.

Secretary for Economic Services, Hon. P. Jacobs, O.B.E.

Secretary for Security, Hon. D. G. Jeaffreson, C.B.E.

Secretary for Lands and Works, Hon. N. Chan, C.B.E.

Secretary for Education and Manpower, Hon. J. N. Henderson, O.B.E.

Secretary for Health and Welfare, Hon. J. W. Chambers.

Secretary for Administrative Services and Information, Hon. P. Tsao, C.P.M.

Secretary for Housing, Hon. D. R. Ford, L.V.O., O.B.E.

Secretary for Transport, Hon. I. F. C. MacPherson, O.B.E.

Secretary for Monetary Affairs, D. W. A. Blye, C.M.G., O.B.E.

Secretary for the Civil Service, J. M. Rowlands, C.B.E.

Secretary for Municipal Services, G. Barnes.

Secretary (General Duties), P. B. Williams, c.b.e.

Chief Justice, Hon. Sir Denys Roberts, K.B.E.

British Council Representative, O. R. Siddle, O.B.E. Easey Commercial Building, 225 Hennessy Road, Hong Kong.

LONDON OFFICE

Hong Kong Government Office
6 Grafton Street, W1X 3LB
[01-499 9821]

Commissioner, Colvyn Haye, C.B.E.

COMMUNICATIONS

Hong Kong, one of the world's finest natural harbours, possesses excellent wharves. The Kwai Chung container terminal is among the top three in the world. It has six berths which can accommodate six "third-generation" container ships simultaneously. An ocean terminal pier with an overall length of 1,250 ft. can accommodate large liners and cargo vessels. Other vessels up to 305 metres length and 14·6 metres draught can be berthed. Buoy moorings in the harbour are available to vessels of up to 11·2 metres draught. Excellent dockyard facilities are available and include five floating drydocks, the largest of which has a lifting capacity of over 100,000 tonnes. In 1984 some 11,800 ocean-going vessels and 71,200 river-trade vessels called at Hong Kong and loaded and discharged more than 47 million tonnes of cargo.

Hong Kong International Airport, Kai Tak, situated on the north shore of Kowloon Bay, is an important link on the main air routes of the Far East. It is regularly used by over 30 international airlines, providing some 1,000 frequent scheduled passenger and cargo services each week between Hong Kong and the United Kingdom, the People's Republic of China, North and South America, Europe, East and South Africa, the Middle East, Australasia, the South Pacific region, and Asian countries. In addition, some 7 airlines operate about 16 non-scheduled services a week.

British Airways operate 7 passenger services per week from and to London. Cathay Pacific Airways, the Hong Kong based airline, operate 433 passenger and cargo services from Hong Kong weekly to points in the Far East, Australia and the Middle East and, since 1980, the U.K. British Caledonian Airways also flies the London–Hong Kong route.

During 1984, 57,016 aircraft on international flights arrived and departed, carrying 9·5 million passengers and 417,000 metric tonnes of freight.

EDUCATION

In 1984 there were 2,400 schools with 1,377,708 pupils. Free education for children up to the age of 15 was made compulsory in 1979. Post-secondary education is provided by two universities, two polytechnics, the Hong Kong Baptist College and two approved post-secondary colleges. The University of Hong Kong has nine faculties. The Chinese University of Hong Kong comprises three foundation colleges and has five faculties and one school. The Hong Kong Polytechnic and City Polytechnic of Hong Kong have about 7,400 and 500 full-time students respectively. There are also five technical institutes and four teacher-training colleges.

FINANCE

	1983–84	1984–85*
	HK$	HK$
Public revenue	30,399,700,000	36,194,000,000
Public expenditure	33,393,100,000	37,332,600,000

TRADE

Hong Kong is an industrial territory with an economy based on exports rather than the domestic market. Domestic industry, producing mainly light manufactures, has grown rapidly in recent years and now provides the bulk of goods for the export trade; but the secondary role as an *entrepôt*, has also been sustained. In 1984 the value of the re-export trade was 38 per cent of total exports.

Hong Kong produces a wide range of articles, although the economy is very dependent upon clothing (34 per cent of export earnings and 33 per cent of industrial jobs) and the electronics industry (second largest export earner).

Diversification of manufacture continues to be a major feature of recent industrial development, as are industrial partnerships with overseas companies in a wide and varied field of manufactures. Modern manufacturing processes have also been introduced to local industry. The marked improvement in both quality and output of items for which precision engineering is required, has continued.

Attempts are being made to promote the high technology and financial services sectors in the interests of broadening the base of the economy.

The visible trade deficit was reduced from HK$15,000 million in 1983 to below HK$2,000 million in 1984. This, together with a favourable balance on the invisible account-remittances from overseas Chinese, investments, exchange, shipping and insurance profits, and the spending of tourists, etc. gave an overall surplus on the visible and invisible trade account In 1983 Hong Kong's principal customers for its domestic products, in order of value of trade, were U.S.A., China, the United Kingdom, the Federal Republic of Germany, Japan, Canada, Australia, Singapore, the Netherlands and France. China was its principal supplier, followed by Japan, U.S.A., Taiwan, Singapore, the United Kingdom and South Korea.

	1983	1984
	H.K.$	H.K.$
Total Exports	160,699m	221,441m
Total Imports	175,442m	223,370m

Trade with U.K.

	1983	1984
Imports from U.K. ...	£726,711,000	£897,419,000
Exports to U.K.	1,178,343,000	1,266,965,000

MONTSERRAT

Situated in 16° 45′ N. lat. and 61° 15′ W. long., 27 miles S.W. of Antigua, the island is about 11 miles long and 7 wide, with an area of 39 square miles and a population (1984), of 11,793. Discovered by Columbus in 1493, it was settled by Irishmen in 1632, conquered and held by the French for some time, and finally assigned to Great Britain in 1783. It contains two active volcanoes and several hot springs. About two-thirds of the island is mountainous, the rest capable of cultivation.

CHIEF TOWN.—ΨPlymouth (1,623).

GOVERNMENT

A Ministerial system was introduced in Montserrat in 1960. The Executive Council is presided over by the Governor and is composed of 4 elected members (the Chief and 3 other Ministers) and two *ex-officio* members (the Attorney-General and the Financial Secretary). The 4 Ministers are appointed from the members of the political party holding the majority in the Legislative Council. The Legislative Council consists of the Speaker, two *ex officio* members (the Attorney General and the Financial Secretary), two nominated unofficial members and 7 elected members.

Governor, His Excellency Arthur Christopher Watson, C.M.G., *apptd.* 1984.

Executive Council

President, The Governor.
Attorney-General, Hon. O. Adams.
Financial Secretary, Hon. J. E. Ryan.
Chief Minister and Minister of Finance, Hon. J. A. Osborne.
Education, Health and Community Services, Hon. Mrs. M. M. Dyer.
Agriculture, Trade, Lands and Housing, Hon. N. Tuitt.
Communications and Works, Hon. J. B. Chalmers.

Speaker of the Legislative Council, Hon. H. A. Fergus, O.B.E.

ECONOMY

The chief exports are flour bags, sea island cotton products, tomatoes, hot peppers and other fruits and vegetables. Real estate development and tourism have done much to aid the island's economy. Revenue (1984) EC$22,427,805; Expenditure EC$22,364,013.

Trade with U.K.

	1983	1984
Imports from U.K.	£2,159,000	£1,999,000
Exports to U.K.	164,000	115,000

PITCAIRN ISLANDS

Pitcairn, a small volcanic island of less than two square miles in area, is the chief of a group of Islands situated about midway between New Zealand and Panama in the South Pacific Ocean at longitude 130° 06′ W. and latitude 25° 04′ S.

The island rises in cliffs to a height of 1,100 feet and access from the sea is possible only at Bounty Bay, a small rocky cove, and then only by whaleboats. Mean monthly temperatures vary between 66° F. in August and 75° F. in February and the average annual rainfall is 80 inches. Moderate easterly and north-easterly winds predominate but short easterly and south-easterly gales occasionally occur from April to September. With an equable climate, the island is very fertile and produces both tropical and sub-tropical trees and crops.

The small community, numbering 61 (1984), are descendants of the Bounty mutineers and their Tahitian companions who did not wish to remain on Norfolk Island when the entire community was transferred there in 1856, and returned to Pitcairn three years later.

Pitcairn became a British Settlement under the British Settlement Act, 1887, and was administered by the Governor of Fiji from 1952 until 1970, when the administration was transferred to the British High Commission in New Zealand and the British High Commissioner was appointed Governor. The local Government Ordinance of 1964 provides for a Council of ten members of whom four are elected.

Governor of Pitcairn, Henderson, Ducie and Oeno Islands, His Excellency T. O'Leary, C.M.G. (*British High Commissioner to New Zealand*).
Island Magistrate and Chairman of Island Council, B. Young.
Education Officer and Government Adviser, L. Salt.

The Islanders live by subsistence gardening and fishing, and their limited monetary needs are satisfied by the manufacture of wood carvings and other handicrafts which are sold to passing ships and to a few overseas customers. Other than small fees charged for gun and driving licences there are no taxes and Government revenue is derived almost solely from the sale of postage stamps. Communication with the outside world is maintained by cargo vessels travelling between New Zealand and Panama which call at irregular intervals; and by means of telephone telegraphic links with New Zealand.

The New Zealand Education Department provides assistance in recruiting a teacher for the sole-charge school. Education is compulsory between the ages of five and fifteen. Secondary education in New Zealand is encouraged by the Administration which provides scholarships and bursaries for the purpose. Medical care is provided by a registered nurse when a doctor is not present. Since 1887 the islanders have all been adherents of the Seventh Day Adventist Church.

The other three islands of the group (Henderson lying 105 miles E.N.E. of Pitcairn, Oeno lying 75 miles N.W. and Ducie lying 293 miles E.) are all uninhabited. Henderson Island is occasionally visited by the Pitcairn Islanders to obtain supplies of "miro" wood which is used for their carvings. Oeno is visited for excursions of about a week's duration every two years or so.

ST. HELENA

Probably the best known of all the solitary islands in the world, St. Helena is situated in the South Atlantic Ocean, 955 miles S. of the Equator, 702 S.E. of Ascension, 1,140 from the nearest point of the African Continent, 1,800 from the coast of S. America, 1,694 from Cape Town and 4,477 from Southampton (transit 5 days and 16 days respectively), in 15° 55′ S. lat. and 5° 42′ W. longitude. It is 10¼ miles long, 6¼ broad, and encloses an area of 47 square miles, with a population of 5,895 (end 1984).

St. Helena is of volcanic origin, and consists of numerous rugged mountains, the highest rising to 2,700 feet, interspersed with picturesque ravines. Although within the tropics, the south-east "trades" keep the temperature mild and equable. St. Helena was discovered by the Portuguese navigator, Juan da Nova Castella, in 1502 (probably on St. Helena's Day) and remained unknown to other European nations until 1588. It was used as a port of call for vessels of all nations trading to the East until it was annexed by the Dutch in 1633. It was never occupied by them, however, and the English East India Company seized it in 1659. In 1834 it was ceded to the

Crown. During the period 1815 to 1821 the island was lent to the British Government as a place of exile for the Emperor Napoleon Bonaparte who died in St. Helena on May 5, 1821. It was formerly an important station on the route to India, but its prosperity decreased after the construction of the Suez Canal. Since the collapse of the New Zealand flax industry in 1965, there have been no significant exports, but a second five year development plan, launched in 1979, seeks primarily to increase the island's productivity in its limited land and sea resources. ΨSt. James's Bay, on the north-west of the Island, possesses a good anchorage. There is no airport or airstrip.

CAPITAL.—ΨJamestown. Population (1978), 1,516.

GOVERNMENT

The government of St. Helena is administered by a Governor, with the aid of a Legislative Council, consisting of the Governor, two *ex-officio* members (Government Secretary and Treasurer) and twelve elected members. Six committees of the Legislative Council are reponsible for general oversight of the activities of Government Departments and have in addition a wide range of statutory and administrative functions. The Governor is also assisted by an Executive Council of the two *ex-officio* members and the Chairmen of the Council committees.

Governor, His Excellency Francis E. Baker (1984).
Government Secretary, E. C. Brooks, O.B.E.
Treasurer and Development Secretary, P. C. Knights, M.B.E.
Senior Medical Officer, Dr. P. G. H. Summers, F.R.C.S.
Agricultural and Forestry Officer, M. D. Holland.
Education Officer, B. A. George.

FINANCE AND TRADE

	1983	1984
Public revenue	£6,925,717	£8,296,154
Expenditure	6,932,151	7,721,940
Total imports	2,555,000	3,219,960
Imports from U.K.	1,368,675	1,820,782

Figures include development aid, shipping subsidy and grant-in-aid.

ASCENSION

The small island of Ascension lies in the South Atlantic (7° 56′ S., 14° 22′ W.) some 700 miles north-west of the island of St. Helena. It is a rocky peak of purely volcanic origin, the highest point (Green Mountain) some 2,817 ft. is covered with lush vegetation, which with each rainy season is slowly creeping down to the lower areas. B.B.C. (Ascension Island Services) operate a farm of some 10 acres on the mountain, permitting the production of vegetables and livestock. The island is famous for turtles, which land on the beaches from January to May to lay their eggs. It is also a breeding area for the sooty tern, or wideawake, large numbers of which settle on the south-western coastal section every eighth month to hatch their eggs. Other wild life on the island includes feral donkeys and cats, rabbits and francolin partridge. All wild life except rabbits and cats is protected by law. The ocean surrounding the island abounds with shark, barracuda, tuna, bonito and many other fish.

Ascension is said to have been discovered by Juan da Nova Castella, on Ascension Day, 1501, and two years later was visited by Alphonse d'Albuquerque, who gave the island its present name. It was uninhabited until the arrival of Napoleon in St. Helena in 1815 when a small British naval garrison was stationed on the island. It remained under the supervision of the Board of Admiralty until 1922,

when it was made a dependency of St. Helena by Royal Letters Patent.

The British Foreign Secretary appoints the Administrator. There is a small Police Force and Post Office. The British organizations provide and operate various common services for the island (school, hospital, public works etc).

Ascension Island is a main relay point of the coaxial submarine cable system laid between South Africa, Portugal and the United Kingdom, which is operated by the South Atlantic Cable Company. Cable & Wireless Ltd operates the international telephone and cable services, maintains an internal telephone service, and also operates an Earth Station on behalf of N.A.S.A. The B.B.C. opened its Atlantic relay station broadcasting to Africa and South America in 1967.

The resident population in March 1985 totalled 1,708, of whom 1,122 were from St. Helena, 409 from the U.K., 64 from the U.S.A. and 13 from the Republic of South Africa. The residents consist of the employees and families of the British organizations, of the contractors for the U.S. Air Force and N.A.S.A. (Pan American Airways, Radio Corporation of America and Bendix Field Engineering Corporation) and of the St. Helena Government.

British forces returned to the island in April 1982 in support of operations in the Falkland Islands. At present there are about 300 R.A.F. personnel on the island supporting the air link to the Falklands.

Administrator, M. T. Blick.

TRISTAN DA CUNHA

Tristan da Cunha is the chief of a group of islands of volcanic origin lying in lat. 37° 6′ S. and long. 12° 2′ W., discovered in 1506 by a Portuguese admiral (Tristão da Cunha), after whom they are named. They have a total area of 45 square miles. The main island, with a peak rising to 6,760 ft., is about 1,500 miles W. of the Cape of Good Hope, 3,600 miles N.E. of Cape Horn, and about 1,320 miles S.S.W. of St. Helena. It was the resort of British and American sealers from the middle of the 18th century, and in 1760 a British naval officer visited the group and gave his name to Nightingale Island. On August 14, 1816, the group was annexed to the British Crown and a garrison was placed on Tristan da Cunha, but this force was withdrawn in 1817, William Glass, a corporal of artillery (*died* 1853), remaining at his own request, with his wife and two children. This party, with five others, formed a settlement. In 1827 five coloured women from St. Helena, and afterwards others from Cape Colony, joined the party.

The islands form a dependency of St. Helena, being administered by the Foreign and Commonwealth Office through a resident Administrator, with headquarters at the settlement of Edinburgh. Under a new constitution introduced in 1969, he is advised by an elected Island Council of 8 members of whom one must be a woman, and three appointed members, with universal suffrage at 18. The population numbered 296 persons in 1985, plus 5 expatriate Government officers and their families, and a resident chaplain.

In October, 1961, a volcano, believed to have been extinct for thousands of years, erupted and lava was thrown up in some cases to a height of 75 feet. In view of the danger of further volcanic activity, the inhabitants were evacuated and reached the United Kingdom on Nov. 23, 1961, where they remained for nearly two years. An advance party returned to Tristan da Cunha in the spring of 1963, and the main body of the islanders has now returned to the island.

A boat harbour was completed in 1967. The first freezing factory was re-established in 1966. There are no taxes on Tristan, income being derived from royalties paid by the fishing company and from the sale of stamps. The new Camogli Hospital was opened early in 1971 and a new school was opened in 1975.

Administrator, R. Perry.

INACCESSIBLE ISLAND is a lofty mass of rock with sides 2 miles in length; the island is the resort of penguins and sea-fowl. Cultivation was started in 1937, but has been abandoned.

THE NIGHTINGALE ISLANDS are three in number, of which the largest is 1 mile long and ⅓ mile wide, and rises in two peaks, 960 and 1,105 ft. above sea-level respectively. The smaller islands, Stoltenhoff and Middle Isle, are little more than huge rocks. Seals, innumerable penguins, and vast numbers of sea-fowl visit these islands.

GOUGH ISLAND (or Diego Alvarez), in 40° 20′ S. and 9° 44′ W., lies about 250 miles S.S.E. of Tristan da Cunha. The island is about 8 miles long and 4 miles broad, with a total area of 40 square miles, and has been a British possession since 1816. The island is the resort of penguins and sea-elephants and has valuable guano deposits. There is no permanent population, but there is a meteorological station maintained on the island by the South African Government and manned by South Africans.

TURKS AND CAICOS ISLANDS

The Turks and Caicos Islands are situated between 21° and 22° N. latitude and 71° and 72° W. longitude, about 100 miles north of the Dominican Republic and 50 miles south-east of the Bahamas of which they are geographically an extension. There are over 30 islands of which eight are inhabited covering an estimated area of 193 square miles. The principal is Grand Turk. The population in 1980 was 7,436 (Grand Turk 3,146).

The Islands lie in the Trade Wind but with an excellent climate. The average temperature varies from 75°–80°F. in the winter and 85°–90°F. in the summer and humidity is generally low. Average rainfall is 21 inches per annum. Hurricanes are rare, the last occurring in 1960.

GOVERNMENT

A new Constitution was introduced in 1976, providing for an Executive Council and Legislative Council. The Executive Council is presided over by the Governor and comprises the Chief Minister and three elected Ministers, together with the Chief Secretary, the Attorney General and the Financial Secretary *ex officio*.

Governor, His Excellency C. J. Turner, O.B.E.
Chief Minister, Hon. N. J. S. Francis.

The principal airports are on the islands of Grand Turk, South Caicos and Providenciales. There are direct shipping services to the U.S.A. (Miami). There is an air service between Miami and Grand Turk, and between South Caicos and the Bahamas. An internal air service provides a twice daily service between the principal islands. A comprehensive telephone and telex service is provided by Cable and Wireless (W.I.) Ltd.

The most important industries are fishing, tourism and offshore finance.

FINANCE

	1984–85	1985–86*
Revenue	U.S.$12·456m	U.S.$12·808m
Expenditure	8·132m	10·560m
Budgetary Aid	1·951m	1·742m
*estimated.		

Trade with U.K.

	1983	1984
Imports	£902,000	£1,533,000
Exports	18,000	12,000

VIRGIN ISLANDS,
see BRITISH

UNIVERSITIES OF THE COMMONWEALTH
(outside the United Kingdom)

With date of foundation, number of full-time students and name of Executive Head
(*Vice-Chancellor, President* or *Principal*)

Australia

ADELAIDE (1874). (Full-time students, 6,181).—*Vice-Chancellor*, Prof. D. R. Stranks, A.O., PH.D.

AUSTRALIAN NATIONAL (1946), Canberra. (4,019).—*Vice-Chancellor*, Prof. P. H. Karmel, A.C., C.B.E., PH.D., LL.D, D.Litt., D. Univ.

DEAKIN (1974), Geelong. (1,692).—*Vice-Chancellor*, M. Skilbeck, PH.D.

FLINDERS, SOUTH AUSTRALIA (1966), Adelaide. (2,790).—*Vice-Chancellor*, Prof. K. J. Hancock, PH.D.

GRIFFITH (1971), Brisbane. (1,944).—*Vice-Chancellor*, Prof. L. R. Webb, PH.D.

JAMES COOK, NORTH QUEENSLAND (1970), Townsville. (2,051).—*Vice-Chancellor*, vacant.

LA TROBE (1964), Melbourne. (5,638).—*Vice-Chancellor*, Prof. J. F. Scott.

MACQUARIE (1964), Sydney. (4,570).—*Vice-Chancellor*, Prof. E. C. Webb, PH.D., D.SC.

MELBOURNE (1853). (11,350).—*Vice-Chancellor*, Prof. D. E. Caro, O.B.E., PH.D., LL.D.

MONASH (1958), Melbourne. (9,754).—*Vice-Chancellor*, Prof. R. L. Martin, PH.D., SC.D.

MURDOCH (1973), Perth. (1,697).—*Vice-Chancellor*, Prof. P. J. Boyce, PH.D.

NEWCASTLE (1965). (3,019).—*Vice-Chancellor*, Prof. D. W. George, A.O., PH.D.

NEW ENGLAND (1954), Armidale. (2,482).—*Vice-Chancellor*, Prof. L. W. Nichol, PH.D., D.SC.

NEW SOUTH WALES (1949), Sydney. (12,715).—*Vice-Chancellor*, Prof. L. M. Birt, C.B.E., PH.D., D.Phil., D.Litt.

QUEENSLAND (1909), Brisbane. (10,251).—*Vice-Chancellor*, Prof. B. G. Wilson, PH.D.

SYDNEY (1850). (14,098).—*Vice-Chancellor*, Prof. J. M. Ward.

TASMANIA (1890), Hobart. (3,243).—*Vice-Chancellor*, Prof. A. Lazenby, PH.D.

WESTERN AUSTRALIA (1911), Perth. (6,773).—*Vice-Chancellor*, Prof. R. H. T. Smith, PH.D.

WOLLONGONG (1975). (3,364).—*Vice-Chancellor*, K. McKinnon, D.Ed.

Bangladesh

BANGLADESH AGRICULTURAL (1961), Mymensingh. (Full-time students, 2,789).—*Vice-Chancellor*, Prof. A. K. M. Aminul Haque, PH.D.

BANGLADESH U. OF ENGINEERING AND TECHNOLOGY (1961), Dacca. (3,207).—*Vice-Chancellor*, Prof. A. M. Patwari, PH.D.

CHITTAGONG (1966). (36,984).—*Vice-Chancellor*, Prof. M. Ali.

DHAKA (1921). (84,112).—*Vice-Chancellor*, Prof. M. S. Huq, PH.D.

JAHANGIRNAGAR (1970), Dacca. (1,749).—*Vice-Chancellor*, Prof. A. F. M. Kamuluddin, PH.D.

RAJSHAHI (1953). (136,948).—*Vice-Chancellor*, Prof. M. A. Raqib, PH.D.

Botswana

BOTSWANA (1976), Gaborone. (Full-time students, 1,195).—*Vice-Chancellor*, Prof. T. Tlou, PH.D.

Canada

ACADIA (1838), Wolfville. (Full-time students, 3,288).—*President*, J. R. C. Perkin, D.Phil.

ALBERTA (1906), Edmonton. (23,617).—*President*, M. Horowitz, Ed.D., LL.D.

ATHABASCA (1970), Athabasca. (196).—*President*, T. Morrison, PH.D.

BISHOP'S (1843), Lennoxville. (1,171).—*Principal*, C. I. H. Nicholl, PH.D.

BRANDON (1967). (1,573).—*President*, J. Mallea, PH.D.

BRITISH COLUMBIA (1908), Vancouver. (21,803).—*President*, D. W. Strangway, PH.D.

BROCK (1964), St. Catharines. (4,248).—*President and Vice-Chancellor*, A. J. Earp, LL.D.

CALGARY (1966). (15,173).—*President*, N. E. Wagner, PH.D.

U. COLL. OF CAPE BRETON (1982), Sydney (1,740).—*President*, W. M. Reid, PH.D.

CARLETON (1942), Ottawa. (10,348).—*President*, W. E. Beckel, PH.D.

CONCORDIA (1929), Montreal. (12,505).—*Principal*, P. J. Kenniff, PH.D.

DALHOUSIE (1818), Halifax. (7,813).—*President*, W. A. MacKay, Q.C., LL.D.

UNIV. OF KING'S COLL. (1789), Halifax. (524).—*President*, J. F. Godfrey, D.Phil.

DOMINICAN COLL. OF PHILOSOPHY AND THEOLOGY (1967), Ottawa. (100).—*President*, Rev. Father G.-D. Mailhiot.

GUELPH (1964). (11,301).—*Vice-Chancellor*, B. C. Matthews, PH.D., D.U.

LAKEHEAD (1965), Thunder Bay. (3,713).—*Vice-Chancellor*, R. G. Rosehart, PH.D.

LAURENTIAN, SUDBURY (1960). (3,280).—*President*, J. S. Daniel, DèsSc.

LAVAL (1852), Quebec. (20,123).—*Rector*, J.-G. Paquet, D.SC.

LETHBRIDGE (1967). (2,633).—*President*, J. H. Woods, PH.D.

McGILL (1821), Montreal. (17,465).—*Principal*, D. L. Johnston, LL.D.

McMASTER (1887), Hamilton. (11,276).—*President*, A. A. Lee, PH.D.

MANITOBA (1877), Winnipeg. (15,272).—*President*, A. Naimark, M.D.

ST. JOHN'S COLL. (1866), Winnipeg.—*Warden*, Rev. M. R. McLean, D.Phil.

ST. PAUL'S COLL. (1926), Winnipeg.—*Rector*, D. J. Lawless, PH.D.

MEMORIAL, NEWFOUNDLAND (1949), St. John's. (7,904).—*Vice-Chancellor*, L. Harris, PH.D.

MONCTON (1963), Moncton, Edmundston and Shippagan. (3,793).—*Rector*, L.-P. Blanchard, D.SC.

MONTREAL (1876). (22,478).—*Rector*, G. G. Cloutier, O.C. PH.D.

MOUNT ALLISON (1858), Sackville. (1,729).—*President*, G. R. MacLean, PH.D.

MOUNT ST. VINCENT (1925), Halifax. (1,917).—*President*, E. Margaret Fulton, O.C., PH.D., D.Ed., LL.D

NEW BRUNSWICK (1785), Fredericton and St. John. (7,749).—*President*, J. Downey, PH.D.

ST. THOMAS (1934), Fredericton.—*President*, Fr. G. W. Martin.

NOVA SCOTIA AGRICULTURAL COLL. (1905), Truro. (550).—*Principal*, H. F. MacRae, PH.D.

NOVA SCOTIA COLL. OF ART AND DESIGN (1887), Halifax. (490).—*President*, G. N. Kennedy.

OTTAWA (1848). (13,033).—*Rector*, A. D'Iorio, PH.D

ST. PAUL (1848), Ottawa (427).—*President*, Rev. P. Hurtubise.

PRINCE EDWARD ISLAND (1969), Charlottetown (1,720).—*President*, C. W. J. Eliot, PH.D.

QUEBEC (1968), Chicoutimi, Hull, Montreal, Rimouski, Trois-Rivières, and other centres (24,821).—*President*, G. Boulet.

QUEEN'S, KINGSTON (1841). (11,263).—*Principal*, D. C. Smith, PH.D.

REDEEMER REFORMED CHRISTIAN COLL. (1980), Ancaster. (205).—*President*, H. R. De Bolster.
REGINA (1974). (5,286).—*President*, L. I. Barber, O.C., PH.D.
  CAMPION COLL. (1918), Regina.—*President*, Rev. J. B. Gavin, PH.D.
  LUTHER COLL. (1913), Regina.—*President*, M. A. Anderson, LL.D.
ROYAL MILITARY COLL. OF CANADA (1876), Kingston. (844).—*Principal*, B. J. Plant, PH.D.
ROYAL ROADS MILITARY COLLEGE (1942), Victoria. (258). *Principal*, J. S. Mothersill, PH.D.
RYERSON POLYTECHNICAL INSTITUTE (1963), Toronto. (7,529).—*President*, B. Segal, PH.D.
STE.-ANNE (1892), Church Point, N.S. (176).—*President*, R. Runte, PH.D.
ST. FRANCIS XAVIER (1853), Antigonish. (2,499).—*President*, Rev. G. A. MacKinnon, PH.D.
ST. MARY'S (1841), Halifax. (3,211).—*President*, K. L. Ozmon, PH.D.
SASKATCHEWAN (1907), Saskatoon (12,982).—*President*, L. F. Kristjanson, PH.D., LL.D.
  ST. THOMAS MORE COLL. (1936), Saskatoon.—*Principal*, Rev. J. T. Hanrahan.
SHERBROOKE (1954). (8,394).—*Rector*, A. Cabana, PH.D.
SIMON FRASER (1963), Burnaby. (7,490).—*President*, W. G. Saywell, PH.D.
TECHNICAL U. OF NOVA SCOTIA (1909), Halifax. (1,097).—*President*, J. C. Callaghan, LL.D.
TORONTO (1827). (35,081).—*President*, G. E. Connell, PH.D
  UNIV. OF ST. MICHAEL'S COLL. (1852), Toronto. (2,821).—*President*, Rev. J. K. McConica, D.Phil.
  UNIV. OF TRINITY COLL. (1851), Toronto. (1,091).—*Vice-Chancellor*, F. K. Hare, O.C., PH.D., LL.D., D.SC., D.Litt., D.S.Litt.
  VICTORIA (1836), Toronto. (2,533).—*President*, G. S. French, C.D., PH.D.
  ONTARIO INSTITUTE FOR STUDIES IN EDUCATION (1965), Toronto. (614).—*Director*, B. J. Shapiro, ED.D.
TRENT (1963), Peterborough. (2,996).—*President*, D. F. Theall, PH.D.
TRINITY WESTERN (1962), Langley. (729).—*President*, R. N. Snider, PH.D.
VICTORIA (1963), British Columbia. (7,008).—*President*, H. E. Petch, PH.D., D.SC., LL.D.
WATERLOO (1959). (15,946).—*Vice-Chancellor*, D. T. Wright, PH.D., D.Eng., LL.D., D.SC., D.H.L
  ST. JEROME'S COLL., Waterloo.—*President*, N. L. Choate.
WESTERN ONTARIO (1878), London. (20,139).—*President*, K. G. Pedersen, PH.D.
  BRESCIA COLL. (1919), London.—*Principal*, Sister Dolores Kuntz, PH.D.
  HURON COLL. (1863), London.—*Principal*, J. A. Trentman, PH.D.
  KING'S COLL. (1912), London.—*Principal*, J. D. Morgan, PH.D.
WILFRED LAURIER (1973), Waterloo. (4,532).—*President*, J. A. Weir, PH.D.
WINDSOR (1857). (8,396).—*Vice-Chancellor*, R. W. Ianni, PH.D.
WINNIPEG (1967). (3,360).—*President*, R. H. Farquhar, PH.D.
YORK (1959), Toronto. (19,671).—*President*, H. W. Arthurs.

Ghana

CAPE COAST (1962). (Full-time students 1,667).—*Vice-Chancellor*, Prof. K. B. Dickson, PH.D.
GHANA (1961), Legon. (3,112).—*Vice-Chancellor*, Prof. G. F. A. Sawyerr, J.S.D.
UNIV. OF SCIENCE AND TECHNOLOGY (1961), Kumasi. (3,085).—*Vice-Chancellor*, F. O. Kwami, DR. ing.

Guyana

GUYANA (1963), Georgetown. (Full-time students, 992).—*Vice-Chancellor*, G. L. Walcott, PH.D.

Hong Kong

CHINESE UNIV. OF HONG KONG (1963). (Full-time students, 5,459).—*Vice-Chancellor*, Prof. Ma Lin, HON.C.B.E., PH.D., D.SC.
HONG KONG (1911). (5,925).—*Vice-Chancellor*, R. L. Huang, C.B.E., D.Phil., D.SC.

India

AGRA (1927). (Full-time students, 44,487).—*Vice-Chancellor*, A. P. Mathur, PH.D.
AGRICULTURAL SCIENCES (1964), Bangalore. (3,318).—*Vice-Chancellor*, N. G. Perur, PH.D.
ALIGARH MUSLIM (1920). (10,438).—*Vice-Chancellor*, S. H. Ali.
ALLAHABAD (1887). (30,936).—*Vice-Chancellor*, Dr. R. P. Misra.
ALL-INDIA INSTITUTE OF MEDICAL SCIENCES (1956), New Delhi. (1,014).—*Director*, Mrs. S. Bhargava, M.D.
AMRAVATI (1983). (24,826).—*Vice-Chancellor*, K. G. Deshmukh, PH.D.
ANDHRA (1926), Waltair. (69,042).—*Vice-Chancellor*, Prof. K. Ramakyishna Rao.
ANDHRA PRADESH OPEN (1982), Hyderabad. (24,969).—*Vice-Chancellor*, C. Narayana Reddy, PH.D.
ANNA (1978), Madras. (3,721).—*Vice-Chancellor*, V. C. Kulandaiswamy, PH.D., D.Litt.
ANNAMALAI (1928), Annamalainagar. (5,553).—*Vice-Chancellor*, Prof. S. V. Chittibabu.
ASSAM AGRICULTURAL (1969), Jorhat. (947).—*Vice-Chancellor*, Prof. D. Chaliha.
AVADH (1975), Faizabad. (35,505).—*Vice-Chancellor*, A. P. Mehrotra, D.Phil.
AWADHESH PRATAP SINGH VISHWAVIDYALAYA (1968), Rewa. (54,770).—*Vice-Chancellor*, H. L. Nigam, D.Phil., PH.D.
BANARAS HINDU (1915). (14,452).—*Vice-Chancellor*, Dr. R. P. Rastogi.
BANASTHALI VIDYAPITH (1983). (867).—*Director*, Miss Sushila Vyas.
BANGALORE (1964). (74,894).—*Vice-Chancellor*, Dr. D. Shankar Narayan.
BARODA (1949). (14,229).—*Vice-Chancellor*, M. N. Desai, PH.D., D.SC.
BERHAMPUR (1967). (21,878).—*Vice-Chancellor*, Dr. R. C. Das.
BHAGALPUR (1960). (57,290).—*Vice-Chancellor*, M. Q. Towheed, PH.D.
BHARATHIAR (1982), Coimbatore. (29,079).—*Vice-Chancellor*, R. Subbayyan, PH.D.
BHARATHIDASAN (1982), Tiruchirapalli. (30,000).—*Vice-Chancellor*, Dr. A. Gnanam.
BHAVNAGAR (1978). (4,627).—*Vice-Chancellor*, Prof. R. V. Pandya.
BHOPAL (1970). (27,132).—*Vice-Chancellor*, R. C. Shukla, PH.D.
BIDHAN CHANDRA KRISHI VISWAVIDYALAYA (1974), Kalyani. (1,260).—*Vice-Chancellor*, J. C. Sengupta.
BIHAR (1952), Muzaffarpur. (69,686).—*Vice-Chancellor*, L. K. Mishra.
BIRLA INSTITUTE OF TECHNOLOGY AND SCIENCE (1964), Pilani. (2,210).—*Director*, C. R. Mitra, ENG.SC.D.
BIRSA AGRICULTURAL (1980), Ranchi. (638).—*Vice-Chancellor*, Dr. H. R. Mishra.
BOMBAY (1857). (121,784).—*Vice-Chancellor*, M. S. Gore, PH.D.
BUNDELKHAND (1975), Jhansi. (42,484).—*Vice-Chancellor*, P. K. Shukla.
BURDWAN (1960). (62,255).—*Vice-Chancellor*, S. P. Banerjee, PH.D.

CALCUTTA (1857). (130,390).— *Vice-Chancellor*, Prof. S. Bhattacharya.

CALICUT (1968). (110,135).— *Vice-Chancellor*, T. N. Jayachandran.

CENTRAL INSTITUTE OF ENGLISH AND FOREIGN LANGUAGES (1958), Hyderabad. (344).— *Acting Director*, S. K. Verma, PH.D.

CHANDRA SHEKHAR AZAD U. OF AGRICULTURE AND TECHNOLOGY (1975), Kanpur. (967).— *Vice-Chancellor*, Dr. M. B. L. Bharadwaj.

COCHIN (1971), Tripunithura. (683).— *Vice-Chancellor*, K. Gopalan, Dr.ing.

DAKSHINA BHARAT HINDI PRACHAR SABHA (1918), Hyderabad. (160).— *Hon. Vice-Chancellor*, P. V. Narasimha Rao.

DAYALBAGH EDUCATIONAL INST. (1981), Agra. (1,153).— *Director*, Mrs G. P. Sherry, PH.D.

DELHI (1922). (71,434).— *Vice-Chancellor*, Prof. M. Raza.

DEVI AHILYA VISHWAVIDYALAYA (1964), Indore. (25,600).— *Vice-Chancellor*, Dr. S. M. Dasgupta.

DIBRUGARH (1965). (51,934).— *Vice-Chancellor*, S. D. Gogoi, PH.D.

DOCTOR HARISINGH GOUR VISHWAVIDYALAYA (1964), Sagar. (28,560).— *Vice-Chancellor*, M. B. Malhotra.

GANDHIGRAM RURAL INSTITUTE (1956), Madurai. (576).— *Vice-Chancellor*, M. Aram, PH.D.

GANDHIJI (1983), Kottayam. (54,426).— *Vice-Chancellor*, Dr A. T. Devasia.

GARHWAL (1973), Srinagar. (26,969).— *Vice-Chancellor*, B. Darshan

GAUHATI (1948). (113,380).— *Vice-Chancellor*, Prof. J. M. Choudhury, PH.D.

GORAKHPUR (1956). (143,296).— *Vice-Chancellor*, Prof. B. M. Shukla.

GOVIND BALLABH PANT U. OF AGRICULTURE AND TECHNOLOGY (1960), Pantnagar. (2,483).— *Vice-Chancellor*, K. Narain.

GUJARAT (1949), Ahmedabad. (107,992).— *Vice-Chancellor*, Prof. K. S. Shastri.

GUJARAT AGRICULTURAL (1969), Ahmedabad. (829).— *Vice-Chancellor*, Dr. V. Kurien.

GUJARAT AYURVED (1966), Jamnagar. (1,881).— *Actg. Vice-Chancellor*, Prof. V. M. Y Lela.

GUJARAT VIDYAPITH (1920), Ahmedabad. (348).— *Vice-Chancellor*, Prof. R. Parikh.

GULBARGA (1980).— *Vice-Chancellor*, Dr. H. M. Nayak.

GURU GHASIDAS (1983), Bilaspur. (35,161).— *Vice-Chancellor*, S. C. Behar.

GURUKULA KANGRI VISHWAVIDYALAYA (1900), Saharahpur. (517).— *Vice-Chancellor*, Dr. G. B. K. Hooja.

GURU NANAK DEV (1969), Amritsar. (59,408).— *Vice-Chancellor*, Dr. S. S. Bal.

HARYANA AGRICULTURAL (1970), Hissar. (2,505).— *Vice-Chancellor*, L. D. Kataria.

HIMACHAL PRADESH (1970), Simla. (24,686).— *Vice-Chancellor*, L. P. Sinha.

HYDERABAD (1974). (690).— *Vice-Chancellor*, Prof. B. S. Ramakrisha, PH.D.

INDIAN AGRICULTURAL RESEARCH INSTITUTE (1905), New Delhi. (627).— *Director*, A. M. Michael, PH.D.

INDIAN INSTITUTE OF SCIENCE (1909), Bangalore. (1,140).— *Director*, Prof. C. N. R. Rao, PH.D, D.SC.

INDIAN INST. OF TECHNOLOGY, BOMBAY (1958). (2,321).— *Director*, Prof. B. Nag, PH.D.

INDIAN INST. OF TECHNOLOGY, DELHI (1961). (2,419).— *Director*, Prof. N. M. Swani, PH.D.

INDIAN INST. OF TECHNOLOGY, KANPUR (1960). (1,930).— *Director*, Prof. S. Sampath.

INDIAN INST. OF TECHNOLOGY, KHARAGPUR (1951). (2,625).— *Director*, Prof. G. S. Sanyal.

INDIAN INST. OF TECHNOLOGY, MADRAS (1959). (2,313).— *Director*, Prof. L. S. Srinath, PH.D

INDIAN SCHOOL OF MINES (1926), Dhanbad. (668).— *Director*, Prof. G. S. Marwaha.

INDIAN STATISTICAL INST. (1932), Calcutta. (386).— *Director*, Prof. A. Maitra, PH.D.

INDIAN VETERINARY RESEARCH INST., Izatnagar.— *Director*, Dr. P. N. Bhat.

INDIRA KALA SANGIT VISHAVIDYALAYA (1956), Khairagarh. (146).— *Vice-Chancellor*, Miss P. Sharma.

JADAVPUR (1955), Calcutta. (4,533).— *Vice-Chancellor*, M. M. Chakrabarty, PH.D.

JAMIA MILLIA ISLAMIA (1962), New Delhi. (3,543).— *Vice-Chancellor*, Prof. A. Ashraf.

JAMMU (1969). (11,771).— *Vice-Chancellor*, M. R. Puri.

JAWAHARLAL NEHRU KRISHI VISHWA VIDYALAYA (1964), Jabalpur. (2,877).— *Vice-Chancellor*, Prof. S. V. Arya.

JAWAHARLAL NEHRU TECHNOLOGICAL (1972), Hyderabad. (2,904).— *Vice-Chancellor*, G. Lakshminarayana, PH.D.

JAWAHARLAL NEHRU U. (1969), New Delhi. (1,541).— *Vice-Chancellor*, Prof. P. N. Srivastava, D.phil.

JIWAJI (1964), Gwalior. (42,324).— *Vice-Chancellor*, K. K. Tiwari, PH.D.

JODHPUR (1962). (8,583).— *Vice-Chancellor*, S. N. Mehrotra, D.phil.

KAKATIYA (1976), Warangal. (11,340).— *Vice-Chancellor*, Prof. T. Vasudev, PH.D

KALYANI (1960). (2,189).— *Vice-Chancellor*, S. Mookerjee, PH.D.

KAMESHWARA SINGH DARBHANGA SANSKRIT VISHWAVIDYALAYA (1961), Darbhanga.— *Vice-Chancellor*, J. Mishra, PH.D.

KANPUR (1965). (126,132).— *Vice-Chancellor*, D. D. Tewari, D.phil.

KARNATAK (1949), Dharwar. (50,618).— *Vice-Chancellor*, S. G. Desai, M.D.

KASHI VIYAPITH (1921), Varanasi. (4,617).— *Vice-Chancellor*, D. N. Chaturdevi, PH.D.

KASHMIR (1969), Srinagar. (11,997).— *Vice-Chancellor*, Prof. S. M. Alam, PH.D.

KERALA (1937), Trivandrum. (101,462).— *Vice-Chancellor*, P. S. H. Mohamed.

KERALA AGRICULTURAL (1971), Trichur. (1,545).— *Vice-Chancellor*, T. M. Menon.

KONKAN KRISHI VIDYAPEETH (1972), Ratnagiri. (761).— *Vice-Chancellor*, P. V. Salvi, PH.D.

KUMAUN (1973), Nainital. (21,465).— *Vice-Chancellor*, Prof. A. D. Pant.

KURUKSHETRA (1956). (62,856).— *Vice-Chancellor*, K. K. Sharma.

L. N. MITHILA (1972), Darbhanga. (110,355).— *Vice-Chancellor*, C. D. Singh, PH.D.

LUCKNOW (1921). (11,207).— *Vice-Chancellor*, Prof. R. S. Mishra, PH.D., D.SC.

MADRAS (1857). (77,195).— *Vice-Chancellor*, B. B. Sundaresan. PH.D.

MADURAI-KAMARAJ (1966). (117,681).— *Vice-Chancellor*, Prof. J. Ramachandran.

MAGADH (1962), Gaya. (61,157).— *Vice-Chancellor*, F. Ahmad.

MAHARSHI DAYANAND (1976), Rohtak. (67,199).— *Vice-Chancellor*, R. Gopal, PH.D.

MAHATMA PHULE AGRICULTURAL (1967), Ahmednagar. (1,776).— *Vice-Chancellor*, D. K. Salunkhe, PH.D.

MANGALORE (1980). (33,070).— *Vice-Chancellor*, Dr. K. M. Safeeulla.

MANIPUR (1980), Imphal. (26,416).— *Vice-Chancellor*, Prof. K. J. Mahale, PH.D.

MARATHWADA (1958), Aurangabad. (41,588).— *Vice-Chancellor*, B. A. Kulkarni.

MARATHWADA AGRICULTURAL (1972), Parbhani. (1,475).— *Vice-Chancellor*, Dr. N. G. P. Rao.

MEERUT (1966). (59,347).— *Vice-Chancellor*, S. D. Loiwal, D.phil.

MOHAN LAL SUKHADIA (1962), Udaipur. (14,066).— *Vice-Chancellor*, N. Sisodia.

MYSORE (1916). (53,577).—*Vice-Chancellor*, Dr. U. P. Rudrappa.

NAGARJUNA (1976), Nagarjunanagar. (24,201).—*Vice-Chancellor*, Dr. K. R. R. Mohan Rao.

NAGPUR (1923). (52,237).—*Vice-Chancellor*, M. A. Chansarkar, PH.D.

NARENDRA DEV. U. OF AGRICULTURE AND TECHNOLOGY (1974), Faizabad. (231).—*Vice-Chancellor*, Dr. K. Singh.

NORTH BENGAL (1962), Darjeeling. (19,410).—*Vice-Chancellor*, Prof. D. B. Dutta.

NORTH-EASTERN HILL (1973), Shillong. (24,533).—*Vice-Chancellor*, B. D. Sharma, PH.D.

ORISSA U. OF AGRICULTURE AND TECHNOLOGY (1962), Bhubaneswar. (1,803).—*Vice-Chancellor*, K. Ramamurthy.

OSMANIA (1918), Hyderabad. (79,750).—*Actg. Vice-Chancellor*, K. Umpathy.

PANJAB(1947),Chandigarh. (74,975).—*Vice-Chancellor*, Dr. R. P. Bambah.

PATNA (1917). (18,695).—*Vice-Chancellor*, G. P. Sinha, PH.D.

POONA (1948). (102,114).—*Vice-Chancellor*, Prof. V. G. Bhide, PH.D

PUNJAB AGRICULTURAL (1962), Ludhiana. (2,928).—*Vice-Chancellor*, S. Singh, PH.D.

PUNJABI (1961), Patiala. (34,276).—*Vice-Chancellor*, S. S. Johl, PH.D.

PUNJABRAO KRISHI VIDYAPEETH (1969), Akola. (2,872).—*Vice-Chancellor*, K. R. Thakare, PH.D.

RABINDRA BHARATI (1962), Calcutta. (4,982).—*Vice-Chancellor*, Prof. R. Mukherji.

RAJASTHAN (1947), Jaipur. (127,206).—*Vice-Chancellor*, Prof. T. K. N. Unithan, PH.D., D.Litt.

RANCHI (1960). (52,946).—*Vice-Chancellor*, Dr. B. Prasad.

RANI DURGAVATI VISHWAVIDYALAYA (1957), Jabalpur. (38,159).—*Vice-Chancellor*, Dr. A. Avasthi.

RAVISHANKAR (1963), Raipur. (39,662).—*Vice-Chancellor*, S. M. Agarwal, PH.D.

ROHILKHAND (1975), Bareilly. (31,209).—*Vice-Chancellor*, Prof. J. N. Rai.

ROORKEE (1949). (2,559).—*Vice-Chancellor*, B. Singh, PH.D.

SAMBALPUR (1967). (50,140).—*Vice-Chancellor*, Prof. P. K. Pati, PH.D.

SAMPURNANAND SANSKRIT VISHWAVIDYALAYA (1958), Varanasi. (96,889).—*Vice-Chancellor*, Dr. R. K. Sharma.

SARDAR PATEL (1955), Vallabh Vidyanagar. (11,010).—*Vice-Chancellor*, K. N. Shah.

SAURASHTRA(1966),Rajkot. (32,848).—*Vice-Chancellor*, R. B. Shukla.

SCHOOL OF PLANNING AND ARCHITECTURE (1955), New Delhi. (285).—*Director*, Prof. B. D. Souza.

SHIVAJI(1962), Kolhapur. (57,585).—*Vice-Chancellor*, K. Bhogishayana.

SHREEMATI N. D. THACKERSEY WOMEN'S (1951), Bombay. (16,010).—*Vice-Chancellor*, Mrs. Jyoti H. Trivedi, M.D.

SOUTH GUJARAT (1966), Surat. (25,514).—*Vice-Chancellor*, Prof. M. S. Trivedi.

SREE CHITRA TIRUNAL INST. FOR MEDICAL SCIENCES AND TECHNOLOGY (1973), Trivandrum. (32).—*Director*, Dr. M. S. Valiathan.

SRI KRISHNADEVARAYA (1981), Anantapur. (1,352).—*Vice-Chancellor*, Prof. M. Abel, PH.D.

SRI PADMAVATI MAHILA VISWAVIDYALAYAM (1983), Tirupati. (291).—*Vice-Chancellor*, Mrs. Varaja Iyengar, PH.D.

SRI SATHYA SAI INSTITUTE OF HIGHER LEARNING (1981), Anantapur. (386).—*Vice-Chancellor*, Prof. V. K. Gokak, D.Litt.

SRI VENKATESWARA (1954), Tirupati. (49,749).—*Vice-Chancellor*, Prof. G. N. Reddy, PH.D.

TAMIL (1981), Thanjavur. (43).—*Vice-Chancellor*, V. I. Subramoniam, PH.D., D.Litt.

TAMIL NADU AGRICULTURAL (1971), Coimbatore, (3,056).—*Vice-Chancellor*, Dr. V. Rajagopalan.

TATA INSTITUTE OF SOCIAL SCIENCES (1936), Bombay. (195).—*Director*, Miss A. S. Desai, PH.D.

UTKAL (1943), Bhubaneswar. (101,860).—*Vice-Chancellor*, B. K. Mishra.

VIDYASAGAR, Midnapore.—*Vice-Chancellor*, Prof. B. C. Mukherjee.

VIKRAM (1957), Ujjain. (36,308).—*Vice-Chancellor*, D. R. Sharma, PH.D.

VISVA-BHARATI (1951), Santiniketan. (3,270).—*Vice-Chancellor*, Dr. N. S. Bose.

Kenya

MOI (1984), Eldoret.—*Vice-Chancellor*, Prof. D. Odhiambo, PH.D.

NAIROBI (1970). (Full-time students, 6,015).—*Vice-Chancellor*, Prof. J. M. Mungai, PH.D.

KENYATTA UNIV. COLL. (1972), Nairobi. (2,100).—*Principal*, Prof. J. K. Maitha, PH.D.

Lesotho

NATIONAL U. OF LESOTHO (1975), Roma. (Full-time students, 1,118).—*Vice-Chancellor*, B. A. Tlelase.

Malawi

MALAWI (1964), Zomba and other centres. (Full-time students, 1,960).—*Vice-Chancellor*, D. Kimble, O.B.E., PH.D.

Malaysia

UNIV. OF AGRICULTURE, MALAYSIA (1971), Serdang. (Full-time students, 7,321).—*Vice-Chancellor*, Prof. Datuk Nayan bin Ariffin, PH.D.

MALAYA (1962), Kuala Lumpur. (9,475).—*Vice-Chancellor*, Royal Prof. Ungku A. Aziz, D.ECON., D.Litt.H., ED.D.

NATIONAL UNIV. OF MALAYSIA (1970), Kuala Lumpur. (7,824).—*Vice-Chancellor*, Prof. Dato Abdul Hamid Abdul Rahman.

NORTHERN MALAYSIA (1984), Alor Star. (350).—*Vice-Chancellor*, Tan Sri Dato Prof. Awang Had Salleh, PH.D.

SCIENCE U., MALAYSIA (1969). (5,125).—*Vice-Chancellor*, Yang Berbahagia Datuk Musa bin Mohamad.

U. OF TECHNOLOGY (1972), Kuala Lumpur. (6,595).—*Vice-Chancellor*, Y. B. Tan Sri Dato Hj. Ainuddin bin Abdul Wahid.

Malta

MALTA (1980), Msida. (Full-time students, 1,468).—*Rector*, Prof. G. P. Xuereb, D.Phil., M.D.

Mauritius

NATIONAL U., MAURITIUS (1965), Réduit. (Full-time students, 111).—*Vice-Chancellor*, Prof. J. Manrakhan.

New Zealand

AUCKLAND (1882). (Full-time students, 9,047).—*Vice-Chancellor*, C. J. Maiden, D.Phil.

CANTERBURY (1873), Christchurch. (5,427).—*Vice-Chancellor*, Prof. A. D. Brownlie.

LINCOLN COLL. (1878). (1,652).—*Principal*, Emeritus Prof. B. J. Ross.

MASSEY (1964), Palmerston North. (4,882).—*Vice-Chancellor*, Emeritus Prof. T. N. M. Waters, PH.D., D.SC.

OTAGO (1869), Dunedin. (5,694).—*Vice-Chancellor*, R. O. H. Irvine, M.D.

VICTORIA, WELLINGTON (1897). (4,897).—*Vice-Chancellor*, L. C. Holborow.

WAIKATO (1964), Hamilton. (2,429).—*Vice-Chancellor*, W. G. Malcolm, PH.D.

Nigeria

AHMADU BELLO (1962), Zaria. (Full-time students, 18,088).—*Vice-Chancellor*, Prof. A. Abdullahi, PH.D.

ANAMBRA STATE U. OF TECHNOLOGY (1980), Enugu and Awka. (1,379).—*President*, Prof. C. A. Onwumechili, PH.D., D.SC.

BAYERO (1975), Kano. (4,142).—*Vice-Chancellor*, Prof. I. H. Umar, PH.D.

BENDEL STATE (1981), Ekpoma. (1,637).—*Vice-Chancellor*, Prof. P. A. Kuale, PH.D.

BENIN (1970). (8,806).—*Vice-Chancellor*, Prof. D. A. Baikie, ED.D.

CALABAR (1975). (4,816).—*Vice-Chancellor*, Prof. A. N. Mohammed, PH.D.

CROSS RIVER STATE (1983), Uyo. (2,738).—*Vice-Chancellor*, Prof. D. E. U. Ekong, Dr. Rer. Nat.

FEDERAL U. OF TECHNOLOGY, AKURE (1981). (419).—*Vice-Chancellor*, Prof. T. I. Francis.

FEDERAL U. OF TECHNOLOGY, MINNA. (160).—*Vice-Chancellor*, Prof. J. O. Ndagi.

FEDERAL U. OF TECHNOLOGY, OWERRI (1980). (460).—*Vice-Chancellor*, Prof. U. D. Gomwalk, PH.D.

IBADAN (1948). (11,140).—*Vice-Chancellor*, Prof. L. A. Banjo.

IFE (1961), Ile-Ife. (12,116).—*Vice-Chancellor*, Prof. W. Abimbola, PH.D.

ILORIN (1975). (4,665).—*Vice-Chancellor*, S. A. Toye, PH.D.

IMO STATE (1981), Etiti and other centres. (1,225).—*Vice-Chancellor*, Prof. M. J. C. Echeruo, PH.D.

JOS (1975). (5,434).—*Vice-Chancellor*, Prof. O. C. Onazi.

LAGOS (1962). (15,104).—*Vice-Chancellor*, Prof. A. O. Adesola.

LAGOS STATE (1983), Ojo. (343).—*Vice-Chancellor*, Prof. F. Olumide.

MAIDUGURI (1975). (5,419).—*Vice-Chancellor*, Prof. J. M. Aminu, PH.D.

NIGERIA (1960), Nsukka and Enugu. (11,493).—*Vice-Chancellor*, Prof. F. N. Ndili, PH.D.

OGUN STATE (1982), Ago-Iwoye. (1,500).—*Vice-Chancellor*, Prof. J. O. Shodipo.

ONDO STATE (1982), Ado-Ekiti. (1,287).—*Vice-Chancellor*, Prof. I. O. Oladapo, PH.D

PORT HARCOURT (1975). (2,653).—*Vice-Chancellor*, Prof. S. J. S. Cookey, PH.D.

RIVERS STATE U. OF SCIENCE AND TECHNOLOGY (1980), Port Hartcourt and other centres. (3,306).—*Vice-Chancellor*, Prof. E. O. I. Banigo, PH.D.

SOKOTO (1975). (3,100).—*Vice-Chancellor*, Prof. M. Adamu, PH.D.

Papua New Guinea

PAPUA NEW GUINEA (1965), Port Moresby. (Full-time students, 1,585).—*Vice-Chancellor*, E. T. Brash, D.Phil.

PAPUA NEW GUINEA UNIV. OF TECHNOLOGY (1973), Lae. (957).—*Vice-Chancellor*, M. Moramoro.

Sierra Leone

SIERRA LEONE (1966), with colleges at Freetown and Njala. (Full-time students, 2,315).—*Vice-Chancellor*, Prof. M. E. Koso-Thomas.

Singapore

NATIONAL U. OF SINGAPORE (1980). (Full-time students, 12,955).—*Vice-Chancellor*, Lim Pin M.D.

NANYANG TECHNOLOGICAL INST. (1981), Singapore. (1,267).—*President*, Cham Tao Soon, PH.D.

South Pacific

SOUTH PACIFIC (1967), Suva and Alafua. (Full-time students, 1,639).—*Vice-Chancellor*, G. K. Caston.

Sri Lanka

BUDDHIST AND PALI (1982), Colombo. (Full-time students, 68).—*Vice-Chancellor*, Ven. K. Anuruddha Thera, PH.D.

COLOMBO (1979). (3,406).—*Vice-Chancellor*, Prof. S. Wijesundera, D.Phil.

JAFFNA (1979). (2,554).—*Vice-Chancellor*, Prof. S. Vithiananthan, PH.D.

KELANIYA (1979). (2,559).—*Vice-Chancellor*, Prof. I. Balasooriya.

MORATUWA (1979), Katubedda. (943).—*Vice-Chancellor*, Prof. M. W. J. G. Mendis.

OPEN U. OF SRI LANKA (1980), Nugegoda, (12,243 part-time).—*Vice-Chancellor*, Prof. P. D. Gunatilake, PH.D.

PERADENIYA (1979). (6,192).—*Vice-Chancellor*, Prof. R. G. Panabokke.

BATTICALOA U. COLL. (1981). (63).—*Director*, Prof. K. D. Arudpragasam, PH.D

RUHUNA (1979), Matara. (1,118).—*Vice-Chancellor*, Prof. G. P. Samarawickrama, PH.D.

SRI JAYEWARDENEPURA (1979), Gangodawila. (3,233).—*Vice-Chancellor*, K. Kodithuwakku.

Swaziland

SWAZILAND (1976), Kwaluseni. (Full-time students, 1,067).—*Acting Vice-Chancellor*, Prof. A. H. Ward, O.B.E., PH.D.

Tanzania

DAR ES SALAAM (1970). (Full-time students, 3,550).—*Vice-Chancellor*, N. A. Kuhanga.

SOKOINE U. OF AGRICULTURE (1984), Morogoro. (544).—*Vice-Chancellor*, Prof. G. R. Mmari, PH.D.

Uganda

MAKERERE (1970), Kampala. (Full-time students, 5,042).—*Vice-Chancellor*, Prof. A. Wandira.

West Indies

UNIV. OF THE WEST INDIES (1962), Jamaica, with campuses in Trinidad and Barbados. (Full-time students, 7,293).—*Vice-Chancellor*, A. Z. Preston, LL.D.

Zambia

ZAMBIA (1965), Lusaka and Ndola. (Full-time students, 3,628).—*Vice-Chancellor*, J. M. Mwanza, PH.D.

Zimbabwe

ZIMBABWE (1955), Salisbury. (Full-time students, 3,215).—*Principal*, Prof. W. J. Kamba, LL.B.

THE ANTARCTIC

THE ANTARCTIC is generally defined as the area lying within the Antarctic Convergence—the zone where cold northward-flowing Antarctic sea water sinks below warmer southward-flowing water. This zone is at about lat. 50° S. in the Atlantic Ocean and lat. 55°–62° S. in the Pacific Ocean. The continent itself lies almost entirely within the Antarctic Circle, an area of about 5·5 million square miles, 99 per cent of which is permanently ice-covered. The average thickness of the ice is 7,100 ft. but in places exceeds 14,500 ft., submerging entire mountain ranges; some mountains protrude—the highest being Vinson Massif, 16,066 ft. The ice amounts to some 7·2 million cubic miles and represents more than 90 per cent of the world's fresh water.

Along one-third of the Antarctic coastline, land-ice flowing outwards forms extensive ice shelves, fragments of which break off to form tabular icebergs, leaving ice cliffs up to 150 ft. high. Much of the sea freezes in winter, forming fast ice which breaks up in summer and drifts north as pack ice. The presence of ice and continuous darkness in winter restrict access to the coastline by sea to the summer months.

The most conspicuous physical features of the continent are its high inland plateau (much of it over 10,000 ft.), the Transantarctic Mountains (which together with the large embayments of the Weddell Sea and Ross Sea mark the approximate boundary between Greater and Lesser Antarctica), and the mountainous Antarctic Peninsula and off-lying islands (which extend northwards towards South America). The continental shelf averages about 20 miles in width (half the global mean, and in places it is non-existent) and reaches exceptional depths (1,300–2,600 ft., which is 3–6 times the global mean).

Climate.—On land, summer temperatures range from just below freezing around the coast to −30° F. (about −34° C.) on the plateau, and in winter −5° F. (−20° C.) on the coast to −85° F. (−65° C.) inland. Over a large area the maxima do not exceed +5° F. (−15° C.).

Precipitation is scanty over the plateau but amounts to 10–30 in. (water equivalent) along the coast and some scientific stations are permanently buried by snow. Some rain falls over the more northerly areas in summer. Gravity winds on the plateau slopes and cyclonic storms further north can both exceed 100 m.p.h. and gusts have been known to reach 150 m.p.h. Visibility can be reduced to zero in blizzards.

Flora and Fauna.—Although a small number of flowering plants, ferns and clubmosses occur on the sub-Antarctic islands, only two (a grass and a pearlwort) extend south of 60° S. Antarctic vegetation is dominated by lichens and mosses, with a few liverworts, algae, and fungi. Most of these occur around the coast or on islands, but lichens and some mosses also occur inland.

The only land animals are tiny insects and mites with nematodes, rotifers, and tardigrades in the mosses, but large numbers of seals, penguins, and other sea-birds go ashore to breed in the summer. The emperor penguin is the only species which breeds ashore throughout the winter. In contrast, the Antarctic seas abound with life—a wide variety of invertebrates (including krill) and fish providing food for the seals, penguins, and other birds and a residual population of whales.

Exploration and Antarctic Treaty.—In the 180 years from Captain James Cook's circumnavigation of the Antarctic in 1772–75 to the mid-1950's, about half of all expeditions to the Antarctic were British and a number of these made major contributions to geographical and scientific knowledge of the area. Notable, were the expeditions of Sir James Clark Ross, Captain Robert Scott, and Sir Ernest Shackleton.

Apart from four years during World War II, British Antarctic research has been continuous since 1925, and most of it is now organized and carried out by the British Antarctic Survey (a component of the Natural Environment Research Council).

The world-wide International Geophysical Year, 1957–58, gave great impetus to Antarctic research. Prior to the mid-1950's, only 17 stations were operated in the Antarctic by four nations and vast areas of the continent were still unknown. By 1957, 44 stations had been established by 12 nations. The co-operative scientific effort proved so fruitful that the 12 nations involved pledged themselves to continue to promote scientific and technical co-operation unhampered by politics (territorial claims being left in abeyance) and agreed that the continent should be used for peaceful purposes only. These aims were embodied in the Antarctic Treaty (covering the area south of lat. 60° S., excluding the high seas but including the ice shelves), which came into force in 1961. It has since been signed by a further 20 acceding nations, four of which are active in the Antarctic and have therefore been accorded consultative status.

Potential resources.—Increasing pressure on the world's food and mineral supplies has stimulated the search for new sources even in the extremely hostile polar environment. Minerals have been found in great variety but not in commercially exploitable concentrations in accessible localities. (For example, coal seams occur in the Theron Mountains and Horlick Mountains.)

There are indications that off-shore hydrocarbons could be present but mostly below great depths of stormy, ice-infested seas. However, the Antarctic Treaty nations and their scientific advisors are already considering the environmental implications of possible mineral exploration and exploitation.

Currently, the chief interest is in marine protein, including the shrimp-like krill already fished commercially by Japan, Poland and U.S.S.R. Basic research to ensure rational management of stocks of this key organism is being continued by international groups, but it is estimated that they could sustain a yield equal to the present total annual world fish catch.

Scientific research.—At present, five British stations are maintained in the British Antarctic Territory and at South Georgia. Two are biological stations, two geophysical observatories, and one is the centre for airborne earth sciences. One other smaller station is open in the summer only.

There are a further 32 permanently occupied stations operated by 13 other nations including one maintained at the South Pole by the U.S.A.

The staff of these stations and summer field-workers are the only people present on the continent and off-lying islands. There are no indigenous inhabitants.

(British Antarctic Survey, *see* entry on p. 424).

THE NOBEL PRIZES

The Nobel Prizes are awarded each year from the income of a trust fund established by the Swedish scientist Alfred Nobel, the inventor of dynamite, who died on December 10, 1896, leaving a fortune of £1,750,000. They are awarded to those who have contributed most to the common good in the domain of (a) Physics; (b) Chemistry; (c) Physiology and Medicine; (d) Literature; (e) Peace. The first awards were made in 1901 on the fifth anniversary of Nobel's death. The awarding authorities are the Royal Swedish Academy of Sciences: (a) Physics—(b) Chemistry; the Royal Caroline Institute, Stockholm—(c) Physiology and Medicine; the Karolinska Institute —(d) Literature; a committee of five persons elected by the Norwegian Storting—(e) Peace. The Trust is administered by the Board of Directors of the Nobel Foundation, Stockholm. The Board consists of five members and three deputy members. The Swedish Government appoints a chairman and a deputy chairman, the remaining members being appointed by the awarding authorities.

The nationality of prizewinners is indicated as follows: (a) United Kingdom; (b) U.S.A.; (c) France; (d) Sweden; (e) Belgium; (f) U.S.S.R.; (g) Germany; (h) Netherlands; (i) Switzerland; (k) Denmark; (l) Norway; (m) Spain; (n) Poland; (o) Austria; (p) Italy; (q) India; (r) Hungary; (s) Finland; (t) Canada; (u) Chile; (v) Argentina; (w) Japan; (x) Portugal; (y) Irish Free State; (z) Republic of Ireland; (aa) South Africa; (bb) Iceland; (cc) China; (dd) Czechoslovakia; (ee) Australia; (ff) Yugoslavia; (gg) Greece; (hh) Israel; (ii) Guatemala; (kk) Egypt; (ll) Pakistan; (mm) West Indies; (nn) Bulgaria; (oo) Colombia; (pp) Mexico. The distribution by nationalities is shown at foot of table.

For prize winners for the years 1901–1977, *see* earlier editions of WHITAKER'S ALMANACK.

Year	(a) PHYSICS	(b) CHEMISTRY	(c) PHYSIOLOGY AND MEDICINE	(d) LITERATURE	(e) PEACE
1978	Prof. P. L. Kapitsa (f) A. A. Penzias (b) R. W. Wilson (b)	P. Mitchell (a)	Prof. W. Arber (i) D. Nathans (b) H. Smith (b)	I. B. Singer (b)	A. Sadat (kk) M. Begin (hh)
1979	Prof. S. L. Glashow (b) Prof. A. Salam (ll) Prof. S. Weinberg (b)	Prof. H. C. Brown (b) Prof. G. Wittig (g)	Prof. A. M. Cormack (b) G. N. Hounsfield (a)	O. Alepoudellis (gg)	Mother Teresa (ff)
1980	Prof. J. Cronin (b) Prof. V. Fitch (b)	Prof. P. Berg (b) Prof. W. Gilbert (b) Prof. F. Sanger (a)	G. Snell (b) J. Dausset (c) B. Benacerraf (b)	Prof. C. Milosz (n)	A. P. Esquivel (v)
1981	Prof. K. Siegbahn (d) Prof. N. Bloembergen (b) Prof. A. Schawlow (b)	Prof. K. Fukui (w) Prof. R. Hoffmann (n)	Prof. R. Sperry (b) Prof. D. Hubel (b) Prof. T. Wiesel (d)	E. Canetti (nn)	Office of the U.N. High Commission for Refugees
1982	Prof. K. G. Wilson (b)	Dr. A. Klug (a)	Prof. S. K. Bergstrom (d) Prof. B. I. Samuelson (d) Dr. J. R. Vane (a)	G. Garcia Marquez (oo)	A. Garcia Robles (pp) Mrs. A. Myrdal (d)
1983	Prof. S. Chandrasekhar (b) Prof. W. Fowler (b)	Prof. H. Taube (b)	Dr. B. McClintock (b)	W. Golding (a)	L. Walesa (n)
1984	Prof. Carlo Rubbia (p) Dr. Simon van der Meer (h)	Prof. Robert Bruce Merrifield (b)	Dr. Niels K. Jerne (k) Dr. Georges J. F. Köhler (g) Dr. Cesar Milstein (a)	Jaroslav Seifert (dd)	Bishop Desmond Tutu (aa)

The awards have been distributed as follows: PHYSICS.—*U.S.A.*, 47; *U.K.*, 20; *Germany*, 14; *France*, 9; *U.S.S.R.*, 7; *Netherlands*, 6; *Sweden*, 4; *Austria*, 3; *Denmark*, 3; *Japan*, 3; *Italy*, 3; *China*, 2; *India*, 1; *Ireland*, 1; *Pakistan*, 1.

CHEMISTRY.—*U.S.A.*, 27; *Germany*, 24; *U.K.*, 22; *France*, 6; *Sweden*, 4; *Switzerland*, 4; *Netherlands*, 2; *Australia*, 1; *Austria*, 1; *Czechoslovakia*, 1; *Finland*, 1; *Hungary*, 1; *Italy*, 1; *Norway*, 1; *U.S.S.R.*, 1; *Argentina*, 1; *Canada*, 1; *Belgium*, 1; *Japan*, 1; *Poland*, 1.

PHYSIOLOGY AND MEDICINE.—*U.S.A.*, 56; *U.K.*, 20; *Germany*, 11; *France*, 7; *Sweden*, 6; *Denmark*, 5; *Switzerland*, 5; *Austria*, 5; *Belgium*, 4; *Netherlands*, 3; *Australia*, 2; *Canada*, 2; *Hungary*, 2; *Italy*, 2; *U.S.S.R.*, 2; *Argentina*, 1; *Portugal*, 1; *South Africa*, 1; *Spain*, 1.

LITERATURE.—*France*, 11; *U.S.A.*, 8; *Germany*, 7; *U.K.*, 7; *Sweden*, 6; *Italy*, 5; *U.S.S.R.*, 4; *Spain*, 4; *Denmark*, 3; *Norway*, 3; *Poland*, 3; *Chile*, 2; *Greece*, 2; *Ireland*, 2; *Switzerland*, 2; *Australia*, 1; *Belgium*, 1; *Finland*, 1; *Guatemala*, 1; *Iceland*, 1; *India*, 1; *Israel*, 1; *Japan*, 1; *Yugoslavia*, 1; *Bulgaria*, 1; *Colombia*, 1; *Czechoslovakia*, 1.

PEACE.—*U.S.A.*, 16; *Institutions*, 12; *France*, 9; *U.K.*, 8; *Sweden*, 5; *Germany*, 4; *Belgium*, 3; *Switzerland*, 3; *South Africa*, 2; *Austria*, 2; *Norway*, 2; *Argentina*, 2; *Canada*, 1; *Denmark*, 1; *Ireland*, 1; *Italy*, 1; *Japan*, 1; *Netherlands*, 1; *U.S.S.R.*, 1; *Egypt*, 1; *Israel*, 1; *Yugoslavia*, 1; *Mexico*, 1; *Poland*, 1.

In 1969 a Nobel Prize for Economic Sciences was instituted, to be awarded by the Royal Swedish Academy of Sciences. Prize-winners have been: 1969, J. Tintergen (h) and R. Frisch (l); 1970, P. A. Samuelson (b); 1971, S. Kuznets (b); 1972, Sir John Hicks (a) and K. J. Arrow (b); 1973, W. Leontief (b); 1974, F. von Hayek (a) and G. Myrdal (d); 1975, Prof. L. V. Kantorovich (f) and Prof. T. C. Koopmans (b); 1976, Prof. M. Friedman (b); 1977, Prof. J. E. Meade (a) and Prof. B. Ohlin (d); 1978, Prof. H. A. Simon (b); 1979, Prof. T. W. Shultz (b) and Prof. Sir Arthur Lewis (mm); 1980, Prof. L. Klein (b); 1981, Prof. J. Tobin (b); 1982, Prof. G. Stigler (b); 1983, Prof. G. Debreu (b); 1984, Sir Richard Stone (a).

FOREIGN COUNTRIES

The following Articles have been revised under the direction of the various Governments or of the British Representatives at Foreign Capitals and by the Foreign and Commonwealth Office in London, to whom the Editor desires to express his warmest thanks. The Editor is also greatly indebted to the Embassies and Consulates-General in London for various corrections and additions.

AFGHANISTAN

(Afghānistān)

President, Babrak Karmal.

COUNCIL OF MINISTERS

Chairman of the Council, Sultan Ali Kishtmand.
President of State Planning Committee, Sarwar Maugal.
Deputy Chairmen (without portfolio), Maj. Gen. Mohammad Rafi; Abdul Majid Sarbuland; Prof. Guldad.
Foreign Affairs, Shah M. Dost.
Interior, Maj. Gen. Sayed M. Gulabzoi.
Defence, Lt. Gen. Nazar Mohammed.
Communications, Lt. Col. M. Aslam Watanjar.
Finance, Muhammad Kabir.
Tribes and Nationalities, Suleiman Laeq.
Transport, Lt. Col. Sher Jan Mazdooryar
Power, Dr. Raz M. Pakteen.
Mines and Industries, Najibullah Masir.
Public Works, Nazar Mohammad.
Agriculture and Land Reform, Abdul Ghaffar Lakanwal.
Commerce, Mohammad Khan Jalalar.
Public Health, Dr. M. Nabi Kamyar.
Justice, Mohan Bashir Baghliani.
Education, Abdul Samad Qayumi.
Higher Education, Burhanuddin Ghiasi.
Irrigation, Ahmad Shah Sorkhabi.
Without Portfolio, Dr. Faqir M. Yaqubi.

AFGHAN EMBASSY IN LONDON
31 Prince's Gate, SW7 1QQ.
[01–589 8891/2]

Chargé d'Affaires, Mohammad Homayon Mokammil.

Afghanistan lies to the N. and W. of Pakistan. Its ancient name was Aryana, by which title it is referred to by Strabo, the Greek geographer who lived in the 1st century B.C. The estimated area is 250,000 sq. miles, and the population (U.N. estimate, 1982) 16,790,000, although it is estimated that two to three million have become refugees in Pakistan and Iran since the Soviet invasion. The population is very mixed. The most numerous race is the Pathan which predominates in the South and West, the main divisions being the Durranis, from whom the Royal Family came, and the Ghilzais. Then come the Tadjiks, an Iranian people mainly cultivators and small traders. There are also Uzbeks and Turkomen in the North, Hazaras in the centre, Baluchis in the South-West and the Nuristanis who live near the Chitral border. All are Sunni Moslems, except the Hazaras and Kizilbashes, who belong to the Shia sect.

Afghanistan is bounded on the W. by Iran (boundary fixed 1857 and 1904), on the S. by Baluchistan (now Pakistan) (boundary fixed 1896–7), on the N. by the U.S.S.R. (boundary fixed 1886–7 and 1893–5), and on the E. by the N.W. Frontier Province (now Pakistan) (boundary fixed 1895) and China. The northern boundary runs from Zulfikar on the Iran frontier to Kushk, the Russian railway terminus,

and thence N.E. to the Oxus (or Amu Darya, "Mother of Rivers") which forms the boundary from Khamiab to Lake Victoria, whence the line to the Chinese frontier was fixed by the Pamir agreement of 1895. The Russo-Afghan frontier was demarcated by the Tashkent Boundary Commission in 1948. An Afghan-Chinese border treaty was signed in 1963 and the border demarcation in 1964. The Pakistan-Afghan frontier was settled by the Durand agreement of 1893.

By treaty of Nov. 22, 1921 (renewed in 1930), Great Britain and Afghanistan agreed to respect one another's internal and external independence; to recognize boundaries then existent, subject to a slight re-adjustment near the Khyber; and to establish Legations and consular offices. As successor state to the British Government, Pakistan has agreed that her relations with Afghanistan shall be based on the 1921 treaty.

Mountains, chief among which are the Hindu Kush, cover three-quarters of the country, the elevation being generally over 4,000 feet. There are three great river basins, the Oxus, Helmand, and Kabul. The climate is dry, with extreme temperatures.

Government.—The constitutional monarchy, introduced by the 1964 Constitution, was overthrown by a *coup d'etat* on July 17, 1973. The country was ruled by Presidential decree until February 1977 when a constitution was approved by a Loya Jirgah (Grand Assembly). Mohammad Daoud was elected President of the Republic but was overthrown on April 27, 1978, by the Armed Forces and power handed to the People's Democratic Party of Afghanistan (PDPA). In December 1979 Soviet troops invaded Afghanistan and installed Babrak Karmal as Secretary-General of the PDPA, President of the Revolutionary Council and Head of State.

Afghanistan is divided into 26 provinces each under a local Party Secretary.

Judiciary.—Hitherto Afghanistan has been ruled on the basis of Shariat or Islamic law. However, the Constitution introduced in 1965 provided for the creation of a legal code, and for a new structure of courts, consisting of a lower court in each *woleswali* (sub province), and a court of appeal in each province, with a Supreme Court in Kabul. The complete separation of executive and judiciary in this constitution was abolished by Presidential Decree in July, 1973. In late 1976 and early 1977 new Penal and Civil Codes were published.

Defence.—The Army, which numbered about 80,000 before the Soviet invasion, has been greatly depleted by desertions. Men between the ages of 18 and 40 are liable to three years' military service. A military academy and military colleges are located in Kabul; some regular officers are trained in the U.S.S.R. A small Air Force is maintained. All military and air force equipment is now of Russian pattern.

Production.—Agriculture and sheep raising are the principal industries. There are generally two crops a year, one of wheat (the staple food), barley, or lentils, the other of rice, millet, maize, and *dal.* Sugar beet and cotton are grown. Afghanistan is rich in fruits. Sheep, including the Karakuli, and transport animals are bred. Silk, woollen and hair cloths and carpets are manufactured. Salt, silver, copper, coal, iron, lead, rubies, lapis lazuli, gold, chrome, barite, uranium, and talc are found.

Main roads run from Kabul to Kandahar, Herat, Maimana *via* Mazari-Sharif and Faizabad *via* Khanabad. The road from Kabul to the North was shortened by the completion in 1964 of the Salang pass. Roads cross the border with Pakistan at Chaman and *via* the Khyber Pass, and there are roads from Herat to the Russian and Iranian borders. A network of minor roads fit for motor traffic in fine weather links up all important towns and districts.

In 1982 the Afghan and Soviet shores of the River Oxus were linked by a road and rail bridge which joins the Afghan port of Hairatan and the Soviet port of Termez. A network of internal air services operates between the main towns.

Language and Literature.—The principal languages of the country are Dari (a form of Persian) and Pushtu, although a number of minority languages are also spoken in various provinces. All schoolchildren learn both Persian and Pushtu. Education is free and nominally compulsory, elementary schools having been established in most centres; there are secondary schools in large urban areas and two universities, one in Kabul (established 1932) and one in Jalalabad (established early 1970's).

The annual revenue consists largely of payments in kind. There are taxes on land, sales of animals, a grazing tax, customs duties, stamps, fines, receipts from State lands, monopolies, and factories and mining royalties; in addition certain businesses and individuals have become eligible for income-tax.

Trade with U.K.

	1983	1984
Imports from U.K.	£10,310,000	£11,892,000
Exports to U.K.	19,837,000	20,776,000

Exports are mainly Persian lambskins (Karakul), dried fruits, nuts, cotton, raw wool, carpets, spice and natural gas, while the imports are chiefly oil, cotton yarn and piece goods, tea, sugar, machinery and transport equipment.

CAPITAL, Kabul (about 2,000,000). The chief commercial centres are Kabul and Kandahar (185,000). Other provincial capitals are Herat (145,000), Mazar-i-Sharif (105,000), Jalalabad (55,000).

FLAG.—Black, red and green horizontal stripes with a device in top left-hand corner.

BRITISH EMBASSY
Karte Parwan, Kabul

Chargé d'Affaires a.i., C. D. S. Drace-Francis.

Kabul is distant 5,000 miles from London.

ALBANIA

Chairman of the Praesidium of the People's Assembly (i.e. Head of State), Ramiz Alia, *assumed office*, Nov. 22, 1982.
Chairman, Council of Ministers, Adil Çarçani.

Albanian Party of Labour

Politbureau of the Central Committee, R. Alia; M. Asllani; A. Carcani; H. Celiku; H. Isai; R. Marko; P. Miska; M. Myftiu; L. Cuko; S. Stefani (*full members*); L. Gegprifti; Q. Mihali; B. Bekteshi; F. Çami; P. Murra (*candidate members*).
Secretariat of the Central Committee, R. Alia (*First Secretary*); V. Cerava; L. Cuko; H. Isai; S. Stefani.

Situated on the Adriatic Sea, Albania is bounded on the north and east by Yugoslavia and on the south by Greece. The area of the Republic is estimated at 10,700 sq. miles, with a population (1981) of 2,752,300.

Albania was under Turkish suzerainty from 1468 until 1912, when independence was declared. After a period of unrest, a republic was declared in 1925, and in 1928 a monarchy. The King went into exile in 1939 when the country was occupied by the Italians: Albania was liberated in Nov. 1944. Elections in Dec. 1945 resulted in a Communist-controlled Assembly: the King was deposed *in absentia* and a republic

declared in Jan. 1946. United Kingdom diplomatic relations with Albania ceased due to the invasion in 1939 and although U.K. recognised the provisional government of Enver Hoxha in 1945, relations were broken off in 1946 after a mine sunk a British warship in Albanian waters. They have so far not been restored.

Much of the country is mountainous and nearly a half is covered by forest. There are fertile areas along the Adriatic coast and the Koritza Basin and there have been land reclamation and irrigation programmes. The main crops are wheat, maize, sugar-beet, potatoes and fruit.

All industry is nationalised. The principal industries are agricultural product processing, textiles, oil products and cement. Output is small at present but the chemical and engineering industries are being built up and the country's considerable mineral resources are being increasingly exploited.

Exports include crude oil, minerals (bitumen, chrome, nickel, copper), tobacco, fruit and vegetables.

Trade with U.K.

	1983	1984
Imports from U.K.	£2,983,000	£4,481,000
Exports to U.K.	240,000	1,097,000

CAPITAL, Tirana (pop. 200,000).

FLAG.—Black-two-headed eagle surmounted by yellow outline star, all on a red field.

ALGERIA

President of State, Secretary-General of the Party, Bendjedid Chadli, *elected*, Feb. 1979, *re-elected*, Jan. 1984.

Ministers

Prime Minister, Abdelhamid Brahimi.
Secretary-General of the Government, Mohamed Tayebi.
Foreign Affairs, Ahmed Taleb Ibrahimi.
Interior, Mohamed Yala.
Finance, Boualem Benhamouda.
Trade, Abdelaziz Khellef.
Heavy Industry, Salim Saadi.
Light Industry, Zitouni Messaoudi.
Hydraulics, Environment and Forestry, Mohamed Rouighi.
Energy and Petrochemicals, Belkacem Nabi.
Information, Bachir Rouis.
Primary Education, Mohamed Cherif Kherroubi.
Higher Education, Rafik Abdelhak Brerhi.
Vocational Training, Mohamed Nabi.
Transport, Salah Goudjil.
Labour, Mouloud Oumeziane.
Agriculture and Fisheries, Abdellah Khalef dit Kasdi Merbah.
Justice, Boualem Baki.
Culture and Tourism, Abdelmadjid Meziane.
Youth and Sports, Kamal Bouchama.
Planning and Organization of National Territory, Ali Oubouzar.
Public Health, Djamel Eddine Houhou.
Posts and Telecommunications, Boualem Bessaih.
Public Works, Ahmed Benfreha.
Housing and Construction, Abderrahmane Belayat.
Religious Affairs, Abderrahman Chibane.
Social Affairs, Mme. Z'hor Ounissi.
Ex-Combatants, Dejlloul Bakhti Nemiche.

ALGERIAN EMBASSY IN LONDON
54 Holland Park, W11 3RS
[01–221 7800]

Ambassador Extraordinary and Plenipotentiary, His Excellency Ahmed Laidi (1984).

Algeria lies between 8° 45′ W. to 12° E. longitude 27° 6′ N. to a southern limit about 19° N. Area, 855,200 sq. miles (estimated). The population in 1983 was estimated at 20,200,000.

Government.—Algiers surrendered to a French force on July 5, 1830, and Algeria was annexed to France in Feb. 1842. From 1881 the three northern departments of Algiers, Oran and Constantine formed an integral part of France. The Southern Territories of the Sahara, formerly a separate colony, became an integral part of Algeria on the attainment of independence. An armed rebellion led by the Moslem *Front de Liberation Nationale (F.L.N.)* against French rule broke out on Nov. 1, 1954. French control of Algeria came to an end when President de Gaulle declared Algeria independent on July 3, 1962; by October, 1963, all agricultural land held by foreigners had been expropriated and by 1965 more than 80 per cent. of the French population had left Algeria.

Ben Bella was elected President of the Republic in Sept., 1963, but was deposed and a Council of the Revolution presided over by Col. Boumediène assumed power on June 19,1965.

A new constitution was established by referendum on Nov. 19, 1976, and on Dec. 10, 1976 President Boumediène was elected for a six-year term of office. Elections for a national popular assembly were held in Feb. 1977. Following President Boumediène's death in December 1978, M. Bendjedid Chadli was elected President in February 1979.

Development in Algeria is regulated by a series of national development plans. The 1970–73 Plan placed emphasis on industrial development, and the 1974–77 Plan on infrastructure development and social services. The 1980–84 Plan concentrates on housing, water supply and agriculture.

Algeria's main industry is the hydrocarbons industry. Oil and natural gas are pumped from the Sahara to terminals on the coast before being exported; the gas is first liquefied at liquefaction plants at Skikda and Arzew.

Other major industries being developed include a steel industry, motor vehicles, building materials, paper making, chemical products and metal manufactures. All major industrial enterprises are now under State control.

Trade with U.K.

	1983	1984
Imports from U.K.	£233,426,000	£272,438,000
Exports to U.K.	157,645,000	274,155,000

Algeria's main exports are crude oil and liquefied natural gas. Principal imports from the United Kingdom are capital plant and equipment for industrial use.

Algeria has a rapidly expanding network of roads and railways. Considerable sums are also being spent on the development of the State airline, the national shipping company and telecommunications.

CAPITAL.—ΨAlgiers, population 3,250,000 (approx). It is one of the principal ports of the Mediterranean as well as an important industrial centre. Other towns include ΨOran; Constantine; ΨAnnaba; Blida; Setif; Sidi-Bel-Abbès; Tlemcen; Mostaganem; Ψ Skikda; ΨBejaia and Tizi Ouzou.

FLAG.—Red crescent and star on vertically divided green and white background.

NATIONAL DAY.—November 1.

BRITISH EMBASSY
Résidence Cassiopée, 7 Chemin de Glycines, Algiers.

Ambassador Extraordinary and Plenipotentiary, His Excellency Alan Gordon Munro, C.M.G.
Counsellor, Head of Chancery and Consul General, M. Gowlland.

Cultural Attaché, British Council Representative, W. M. Jefferson, 6 Avenue Souidani Boudjemaa, Algiers. There is a British Council library in *Algiers*.

ANDORRA

A small, neutral principality (formed by a treaty in 1278), situated on the southern slopes of the Pyrenees between Spain and France, with an approximate area of 190 square miles and population of about 41,600, less than one-fifth of whom are native Andorrans. It is surrounded by mountains of 6,500 to 10,000 feet. Andorra is divided into seven Parishes, each of which has four Councillors elected by vote to the Valleys of Andorra Council of Twenty-eight. The Council appoints the head of the executive government, who designates the members of his government. Constitutionally, the sovereignty of Andorra is vested in two "Co-Princes", the President of the French Republic and the Spanish Bishop of Urgel. These two "co-princes" can veto certain decisions of the Council of the Valleys but cannot impose their own decisions without the consent of the Council. They are represented by Permanent Delegates of whom one is the French Prefect of the Pyrenees Orientales Department at Perpignan and the other is the Spanish Vicar-General of the Diocese of Urgel. They are in turn represented in Andorra la Vella by two resident "Viguiers" known as the Viguier Français and the Viguier Episcopal, who have a joint responsibility for law and order and overall administration policy, together with judicial powers as members of the Supreme Court.

The language of the country is Catalan, but French and Spanish (Castilian) are also spoken. Spanish *pesetas* and French *francs* are the accepted currency and the Budget is expressed in *pesetas*. The estimated national revenue (1982) was US$375 million, with a per capita income of $9,394. The climate is naturally cold for six months, but mild in spring and summer. Potatoes are produced in the highlands and tobacco in the valleys. The mountain slopes have been developed for skiing, and it is estimated that 10,000,000 tourists visit the Valleys during the year. The economy is largely based on tourism, commerce, tobacco, construction and forestry; a third of the country is classified as forest in which pine, fir, oak, birch and box-tree predominate.

A good road into the Valleys from Spain is open all year round, and that from France is closed only occasionally in winter. An airport at Seo d'Urgell just outside Andorra provides daily air connections with Barcelona. There are two radio stations in Andorra, one privately-owned and one operated by a French Government corporation. Both pay dues to the Council of the Valleys.

Trade with U.K.

	1983	1984
Imports from U.K.	£6,533,000	£9,228,000
Exports to U.K.	381,000	19,000

CAPITAL: Andorra la Vella (population 16,000).
FLAG.—Three vertical bands, blue, yellow, red; Andorran coat of arms frequently imposed on central (yellow) band but not essential.
H.M. Consul-General, Miss P. M. Hutchinson, C.M.G., C.B.E. (*Resident at Barcelona*).

ANGOLA

President, Jose Eduardo Dos Santos.

COUNCIL OF MINISTERS

Interior, Lt. Col. Manuel Rodrigues Quito.
State Security, Col. Julião Paulo Dino Matroce.
Defence, Col. Pedro Tonha Pedale.
Foreign Affairs, Afonso van Dunem.
Planning, Lopo Ferreira do Nascimento.
Internal Trade, Adriano Pereira dos Santos.
External Trade, Ismael Gaspar Martins.
Justice, Diogenes Assis Boavida.
Petroleum and Energy, Lt. Col. Pedro Van Dunen Loi.
  Industry, Henrique de Carvalho Santos Onambwe.
Provincial Co-ordination, (n/a).
Health, Antonio Ferreira Neto.
Labour and Social Security, Horacio Pereira Braz da Silva.
Construction, Jorge Henrique Varela de Melo Dias.
Fisheries, Emilio Guerra.
Agriculture, Maj. Domingos Evaristo Quimba.
Transport and Communications, Manuel Bernardo de Sousa.
Education, Augusto Teixeira Tutu.
Finance Augusto Teixeira de Matos.
Housing, Lourenço Ferreira.

Angola, which has an area of 488,000 square miles, lies on the western coast of Africa; its population in 1983 was estimated at 7,100,000 although in the wake of fighting between the rival liberation movements the white population, formerly of several hundred thousand, has been greatly reduced, by a mass exodus.
After a Portuguese presence of at least four centuries, and an anti-colonial war since 1961, Angola became independent on Nov. 11, 1975 in the midst of civil war. Soviet-Cuban military assistance to the Popular Movement for the Liberation of Angola (M.P.L.A.) enabled it to defeat its rivals early in 1976. However, the M.P.L.A. government remains under pressure from the U.N.I.T.A. guerrilla movement (led by Dr. Jonas Savimbi) which now controls up to one-third of the country and operates freely in another third.
The M.P.L.A., a Marxist-Leninist party, is the sole legal party. The Constitution provides for an executive President, who appoints a Council of Ministers to assist him, and a 203-member National People's Assembly.
Angola has valuable oil and diamond deposits and exports of these two commodities account for 70–80 per cent of total exports.
Principal agricultural crops are cassava, maize, bananas, coffee, palm oil and kernals, cotton and sisal. Coffee, sisal, maize and palm oil are exported: exports

also include mahogany and other hardwoods from the tropical rain forests in the north of the country. Economic activity fell after independence although progress has been made in the provision of electricity supplies, health services and primary education.

Trade with U.K.

	1983	1984
Imports from U.K.	£22,847,000	£35,581,000
Exports to U.K.	45,732,000	158,636,000

CAPITAL.—ΨLuanda (Est. over 1 million in 1984).
FLAG.—Red and black with a yellow star, machete and cog-wheel.

BRITISH EMBASSY
Rua Diogo Cao 4 (Caixa Postal 1244), Luanda.

Ambassador Extraordinary and Plentipotentiary, His Excellency Patrick Stanislaus Fairweather, *apptd.* 1985.

ARGENTINE REPUBLIC
(República Argentina)

President, Dr. Raúl Alfonsín, *took office* Dec. 10, 1983.
Vice President, Dr. Víctor Martínez.

CABINET

Interior, Dr. Antonio Troccoli.
Foreign Affairs, Sr. Dante Caputo.
Labour, Sr. Hugo Barrionuevo.
Economy, Sr. Juan Sourouille.
Education and Justice, Dr. Carlos Alconada Aramburú.
Defence, Sr. Roque Carranza.
Health and Social Welfare, Dr. Aldo Neri.
Public Works, Sr. Roberto Tomasini.

EMBASSY IN LONDON

The Embassy closed after the Argentine invasion of the Falkland Islands. Argentine interests in Great Britain are currently handled by the Brazilian Embassy.

Argentina is a wedge-shaped country, occupying the greater portion of the southern part of the South American Continent, and extending from Bolivia to Cape Horn, a total distance of nearly 2,300 miles; its greatest breadth is about 930 miles. It is bounded on the north by Bolivia, on the north-east by Paraguay, Brazil and Uruguay, on the south-east and south by the Atlantic, and on the west by Chile, from which Republic it is separated by the Cordillera de los Andes. On the west the mountainous Cordilleras, with their plateaux, extend from the northern to the southern boundaries: on the east are the great plains. Those in the north are thickly wooded and are known as *El Gran Chaco*, and further south lie the treeless pampas extending from Cordoba in the north to the Río Negro; and south of the Río Negro are the vast plains of Patagonia. The Paraná River flows through the north-eastern states into the Atlantic, and is navigable throughout its course in Argentina; the Pilcomayo, Bermejo, and Salado del Norte are also navigable for some distance from their confluence with the Paraná. In the Province of Buenos Aires the Salado del Sud flows south-east for some 300 miles into Samborombon Bay (Atlantic). In the south many rivers (notably the Colorado, Rio Negro, Chubut and Santa Cruz) traverse the country from the Andes to the Atlantic. The climate ranges from sub-tropical to cold temperate.
The Republic consists of 22 provinces, one territory (Tierra del Fuego) and one federal district (Buenos

Aires), comprising in all an area of 1,079,965 square miles, with a population (Census of 1980) of 27,862,771, an increase of 19·3 per cent. since 1970.

Government.—The estuary of La Plata was discovered in 1515 by Juan Díaz de Solís, but it was not until 1534 that Pedro de Mendoza founded Buenos Aires. This city was abandoned and later re-founded by Don Juan de Garay in 1580. In 1810 (May 25) Spanish rule was defied, and in 1816 (July 9), after a long campaign of liberation conducted by General José de San Martín, the independence of Argentina was declared by the Congress of Tucumán.

In 1945 Juan Domingo Perón became President until overthrown in 1955. There followed eighteen years of political and economic instability, and eventually in 1973, Perón was recalled from exile. Elected President he died within a year and was succeeded by his widow, Vice President María Estela Martínez de Perón. However, warring factions in the Perónist movement and increasing terrorist activity led to a bloodless *coup* by the armed forces on March 24, 1976. A Junta, consisting of the three commanders of the Armed Forces, was established with one of their number as President. Following the Falkland Islands defeat in 1982 the President, Gen. Galtieri, resigned and the Army appointed Gen. Bignone as President. The Navy and Air Force withdrew from the Junta but this was reconstituted shortly afterwards. Elections for a civilian government to replace the military one were held on October 30, 1983 and the Radical Party's candidate, Raúl Alfonsín, was elected President.

Agriculture.—Of a total land area of approximately 700 million acres, farms occupy about 425 million. About 60 per cent. of the farmland is pasture, 10 per cent. annual crops, 5 per cent. permanent crops and the remaining 25 per cent. forest and wasteland. A large proportion of the land is still held in large estates devoted to cattle raising but the number of small farms is increasing. The principal crops are wheat, maize, oats, barley, rye, linseed, sunflower

seed, alfalfa, sugar, fruit and cotton. Argentina is pre-eminent in the production of beef, mutton and wool, and pastoral and agricultural products provide about 85 per cent. of Argentina's exports.

Mineral Production.—Oil is found in various parts of the Republic and the production of oil is of first importance to her industries and, to some extent, to her economic and financial development. Total petroleum output for 1980 was 28,400,000 cubic metres. There is a refinery in San Lorenzo (Santa Fé province). Natural gas is also produced in a number of provinces.

Coal, lead, zinc, tungsten, iron ore, sulphur, mica and salt are the other chief minerals being exploited. There are small worked deposits of beryllium, manganese, bismuth, uranium, antimony, copper, kaolin, arsenate, gold, silver and tin. Coal production in 1980 was 4,156,000 tons; this is produced at the Rio Turbio mine in the province of Santa Cruz. The output of other materials is not large but greater attention is now being paid to the development of these natural resources, especially copper for which the Government and private companies are carrying out exploration.

Industries.—Meat-packing is one of the principal industries; flour-milling, sugar-refining, and the wine industry are also important. In recent years great strides have been made by the textile, plastic and machine tool industries and engineering, especially in the production of motor vehicles and steel manufactures.

Communications.—There are 25,386 miles of railways, which are State property. Plans are in hand for complete re-organization of the railways in order to improve their operating efficiency and reduce a very large financial deficit. The combined national and provincial road network totals approximately 137,000 miles of which 23,180 miles are surfaced. There are air services between Argentina and all the neighbouring republics, Europe, Asia, Canada, the U.S.A. and South Africa. Total tonnage entering Argentine ports in 1979 was 13,879,391.

Defence.—The Army consists of four corps organized into 12 brigades, including mountain, jungle, airborne and armoured troops. It numbers about 5,000 officers, 15,000 N.C.O.s and 65–70,000 conscripts who serve 1 year.

The Navy consists of 1 aircraft carrier, 9 destroyers, 4 frigates/corvettes, 3 submarines, 4 minesweepers, 1 minehunter and ancillary craft. Strength is about 3,000 officers and 30,000 ratings, including 11,000 conscripts.

The Air Force consists of 9 brigades and a training force, with a strength of 1,600 officers, 15,000 other ranks and 20,000 civilians.

Education—Primary and Secondary. The government is formulating a new education policy. At the moment, education is compulsory for the 7 grades of primary school (6 to 13). Secondary schools (14 to 17+) are available in and around Buenos Aires and in most of the important towns in the interior of the country. Most secondary schools are administered by the Central Ministry of Education in Buenos Aires, while primary schools are administered by the Central Ministry or by Provincial Ministries of Education. Private schools, of which there are many, are also loosely controlled by the Central Ministry. Teacher-Training now takes place at post school level, courses lasting from 2 to 5 years. Many new universities have been created in recent years. The total is now over 50 with 24 national, 25 private and a small number of provincial universities.

Language and Literature.—Spanish is the language of the Republic and the literature of Spain is accepted as an inheritance by the people. There is little indigenous literature before the break from Spain, but all branches have flourished since the latter half of the nineteenth century. About 450 daily newspapers are published in Argentina, including 7 major ones in the city of Buenos Aires. The English language newspaper is the *Buenos Aires Herald* (daily). There are several other foreign language newspapers.

Trade with U.K.

	1983	1984
Imports from U.K.	£4,472,000	£5,232,000
Exports to U.K.	194,000	65,000

CAPITAL.—ΨBuenos Aires, Pop. (Dec. 1980), Metropolitan area 2,908,000; with suburbs, 9,677,200. Other large towns are: ΨRosario de Santa Fé (798,292), Córdoba (798,663), ΨLa Plata (408,300), ΨMar del Plata (317,444), San Miguel de Tucuman (326,000), Santa Fé (312,427) and Mendoza (118,568).

FLAG.—Horizontal bands of blue, white, blue; gold sun in centre of white band.

NATIONAL DAY.—July 9.

BRITISH EMBASSY

The British Embassy was closed after the Argentine invasion of the Falkland Islands. British interests are currently handled by a section at the Swiss Embassy, Dr. Luis Agote 2412, Buenos Aires.

BRITISH CHAMBER OF COMMERCE, Av. Corrientes 457, 10 piso, 1043 Buenos Aires.

AUSTRIA

President of the Republic of Austria, Dr. Rudolf Kirchschläger, *born* 1915; *elected* June 23, 1974, *re-elected* May 18, 1980.

CABINET

Chancellor, Dr. Fred Sinowatz.
Vice-Chancellor and Minister of Commerce and Industry, Dr. Norbert Steger.*
Interior, Karl Blecha.
Justice, Dr. Harald Ofner.*
Finance, Dr. Franz Vranitzky.
Nationalised Industries and Transport, Ferdinand Lacina.
Foreign Affairs, Dr. Leopold Gratz.
Agriculture and Forestry, Günter Haiden.
Defence, Dr. Friedhelm Frischenschlager.*
Construction and Technology, Dr. Heinrich Uebleis.
Science and Research, Dr. Heinz Fischer.
Health and Environment, Dr. Kurt Steyrer.
Social Services, Alfred Dallinger.
Education, Arts and Sports, Dr. Herbert Moritz.
Family Affairs, Youth and Consumer Protection, Gertrude Frölich-Sandner.
* Members of the Freedom Party (Liberals). Other Ministers belong to the Socialist Party.

AUSTRIAN EMBASSY IN LONDON
18 Belgrave Mews West, SW1X 8HU
[01–235 3731]

Ambassador Extraordinary and Plenipotentiary, His Excellency Dr. Reginald Thomas (1982).

Austria is a country of Central Europe bounded on the north by Czechoslovakia, on the south by Italy and Yugoslavia, on the east by Hungary, on the north-west by Germany and on the west by Switzerland and Liechtenstein. Its area is 32,376 square miles and its population (1984 estimate), 7,551,800.

Government.—The Republic of Austria comprises nine provinces (Vienna, Lower Austria, Upper Austria, Salzburg, Tyrol, Vorarlberg, Carinthia, Styria and Burgenland) and was established in 1918 on the break-up of the Austro-Hungarian Empire. In March 13, 1938, as a result of the *Anschluss,* Austria (*Oesterreich*) was incorporated into the German

Reich under the name *Ostmark.* After the liberation of Vienna in 1945, the Austrian Republic was reconstituted within the frontiers of 1937 and a freely-elected Government took office on December 20, 1945. The country was divided at this time into four zones occupied respectively by the U.K., U.S.A., U.S.S.R. and France, while Vienna was jointly occupied by the four Powers. On May 15, 1955, the Austrian State Treaty was signed in Vienna by the Foreign Ministers of the four Powers and of Austria. This Treaty recognized the re-establishment of Austria as a sovereign, independent and democratic state, having the same frontiers as on January 1, 1938.

There is a National Assembly of 183 Deputies. After the elections of April 1983, the Socialists formed a coalition with the Freedom Party.

The state of the parties in the Nationalrat (Lower House) in April 1983, was:

Socialist Party (Social Democrat)	90
People's Party (Conservative)	81
Freedom Party (Liberal)	12

In the Bundesrat (Upper House) in Nov. 1983 the People's Party held 33 seats and the Socialist Party, 30.

Religion and Education.—The predominant religion is Roman Catholic. Education is free and compulsory between the ages of 6 and 15 and there are good facilities for secondary, technical and professional education. There are 12 state-maintained Universities and six colleges of art.

Language and Literature.—The language of Austria is German, but the rights of the Slovene- and Croat-speaking minorities in Carinthia, Styria and Burgenland are protected. The press is free.

Communications.—Internal communications in Austria are partly restricted because of the mountainous nature of the country, and road and rail routes must, of necessity, follow the river valleys. The railways in Austria are state-owned and in 1983 had 5,753 km. of track, over half of which is electrified. There were, in 1983, 34,068 km. of roads, including a network of *autobahn* between major cities which also links up with the West German and Italian networks. Of the 1,733 km. of waterways, 355 km. are navigable and there is considerable trade through the Danube ports by both local and foreign shipping. There are six commercial airports.

Tourism.—In 1984, 15,110,200 tourists visited Austria. Foreign exchange receipts from tourism were 97,446 million Schillings—a major contribution to the balance of payments.

PRODUCTION AND INDUSTRY

The origin of Gross Domestic Product in 1984 was as follows (in per cent.):

Agriculture and forestry	4·9
Mining and material goods production	30·5
Energy and water supply	3·1
Construction	6·4
Commerce, hotels, restaurants	16·4
Transport and communications	6·2
Asset management	12·4
Other services and producers	17·2
Import duties and other items	2·9

The value of G.D.P. in 1984 (at current prices) was AS1,284,800 million: G.D.P. per capita (at current prices) was AS170,130.

Agriculture.—The arable land produces wheat, rye, barley, oats, maize, potatoes, sugar beet, turnips, and miscellaneous crops. Many varieties of fruit trees flourish and the vineyards produce excellent wine. The pastures support horses, cattle and pigs. Timber forms a valuable source of Austria's indigenous wealth, about 44·2 per cent. of the total land area consisting of forest areas. Coniferous species predominate (81 per cent. of afforested area).

Energy.—Energy production in 1984 was:—

Crude oil

—production	1,205,000 tonnes	
—imports	5,907,000	,,
(from U.S.S.R.	1,278,441	,,)
(from Saudi Arabia	751,552	,,)

Natural gas

—production	1,272m. cu. metres	
—imports	4,077m. cu. metres	
(from U.S.S.R.	4,009m. cu. metres)	

Electric power

—output	42,382m. kWh.
—imports	5,401m. kWh.
—exports	6,725m. kWh.

A 700 mw nuclear power station had already been constructed when in November 1978 the Austrian people decided by a very small margin in a national referendum not to allow the introduction of nuclear power stations in Austria.

Mining.—Production was (tonnes):—

	1982	1983
Lignite	3,297,488	3,041,260
Iron/manganese ore	3,330,000	3,540,000
Raw magnesite	1,031,404	1,005,768
Lead/zinc ore	841,027	883,134
Crystal salt	433,557	359,118
Graphite	24,451	40,418

In addition 2,159,931 cu. metres of brine was produced in 1982, and 1,665,789 cu. metres in 1983.

Industry.—Heavy industry production in 1983 included pig iron 3,320,260 tonnes, raw steel 4,410,907 tonnes and rolled steel 3,555,106 tonnes. In addition, petroleum, non-ferrous metals and chemicals are processed in quantity and construction materials, industrial machinery, vehicles, paper and textiles are produced.

FINANCE

	1983*	1984*
	Schillings, million	
Federal Budget:		
Expenditure	407,786	435,135
Revenue	316,667	344,899
Gross Budget Deficit	91,119	90,236
* estimated.		

Federal Budget expenditure (preliminary figures) (AS million):—

	1983	1984
Agriculture, forestry	11,150	11,568·9
Defence	15,750	15,880·3
Education and tuition	35,520	37,492·7
International security, justice	13,210	13,680·0
Public services	7,010	7,890·0
Roads	16,640	16,816·9
Science and research	12,320	13,225·0
Social welfare	103,020	104,437·5
Transportation	80,700	84,592·4
Expenditure on debts	51,906	67,914·0
Other purposes	60,560	61,619·3

TRADE

Main exports are processed goods (iron and steel, textiles, paper and cardboard products), machinery and transport equipment, other finished goods (including clothing) and foodstuffs. Main imports are machinery and transport equipment, processed goods, chemical products, foodstuffs, fuel and energy.

	1983	1984
	Schillings, million	
Imports	348,339	392,879
Exports	277,120	314,560

Over 80 per cent. of all trade is with other European countries, E.E.C. countries accounting for about 60 per cent., Eastern Europe for about 11 per cent. and E.F.T.A. members for 9 per cent.

Trade with U.K.

	1983	1984
Imports from U.K.	£273,702,000	£320,901,000
Exports to U.K.	438,446,000	592,620,000

Currency.—The unit of currency is the *Schilling* (AS) of 100 *Groschen*. For rate of exchange *see* p. 81.

CAPITAL, Vienna, on the Danube, population 1,531,346. Other towns are Graz (243,166), Linz (199,910), Innsbruck (117,287), Salzburg (139,426), and Klagenfurt (87,321).

FLAG.—Horizontal stripes of red, white, red, with eagle crest on white stripe.

NATIONAL DAY.—October 26.

BRITISH EMBASSY
Reisnerstrasse 40, 1030 Vienna

Ambassador Extraordinary and Plenipotentiary, His Excellency Michael O'Donel Bjarne Alexander (1981).

Counsellor, Consul General and Head of Chancery, A. H. Morgan.

1st Secretaries, J. R. Bruce-Lockhart; R. G. Bowen; D. J. Harding (*Commercial*); A. E. Clarke (*H.M. Consul*); J. McDougall (*Administration*).

Defence Attaché, Lt.-Col. M. Legg.

There is a British Consular Office at *Vienna,* and Honorary Consulates at *Innsbruck, Graz and Salzburg.*

British Council Representative, R. Adlam, O.B.E., Schenkenstrasse 4, A-1010 Vienna.

BAHRAIN

Amir, H.H. Shaikh Isa bin Sulman Al Khalifa, G.C.M.G., *born* 1932; *acceded* Dec. 16, 1961.

Crown Prince and C.-in-C., Bahrain Defence Force, H.E. Shaikh Hamad bin Isa Al Khalifa, K.C.M.G.

CABINET

Prime Minister, H.E. Shaikh Khalifa bin Sulman Al-Khalifa.

Minister of Defence, The Crown Prince.

Foreign Affairs, Shaikh Mohammed bin Mubarak Al-Khalifa.

Justice and Islamic Affairs, Shaikh Abdullah bin Khalid Al-Khalifa.

Development and Industry, and Cabinet Affairs, Yusuf Ahmad Shirawi.

Education, Dr. Ali Fakhroo.

Health, Jawad Salim Al-Arayyed.

Transportation, Ibrahim Mohammed Humaidan.

Interior, Shaikh Mohammed bin Khalifa Al-Khalifa.

Information, Tariq Abdulrahman Al Moayed.

Labour and Social Affairs, Shaikh Khalifa bin Sulman bin Mohammed Al-Khalifa.

Works, Power and Water, Majid Jawad Al-Jishi.

Housing, Shaikh Khalid bin Abdullah Al-Khalifa.

Finance and National Economy, Ibrahim Abdulkarim Mohammed.

Commerce and Agriculture, Habib Ahmed Kassim.

Minister of State, Legal Affairs, Dr. Hussain Al-Baharna.

BAHRAIN EMBASSY IN LONDON
98 Gloucester Road, SW7 4AU
[01–370 5132]

Ambassador Extraordinary and Plenipotentiary, His Excellency Salman Abdul Wahab Al Sabbagh (1984).

Area and population.—Bahrain consists of a group of low-lying islands situated about half-way down the Gulf, some 20 miles off the east coast of Arabia. The largest of these, Bahrain island itself, is about 30 miles long and 10 miles wide at its broadest. The capital, Manama, is situated on the north shore of this island. The next largest, Muharraq, with the town and Bahrain International Airport, is connected to Manama by a causeway 1½ miles long.

The population (1981 Census) is 350,798, of whom 112,378 are foreign. About 35 per cent. of the Bahrainis are Sunni Moslems, the remaining 65 per cent. being Shias; the ruling family and many of the most prominent merchants are Sunnis.

Climate.—The climate is humid all the year round, with rainfall of about 3 in., concentrated in the mild winter months, December to March; in summer, May to October, temperatures can exceed 110° F.

Government.—Bahrain has been a fully independent state since 1971. Government takes the form of a constitutional monarchy, in which traditional consultative procedures continue to play an important role.

Economy.—The largest sources of revenue are oil production and refining. The Bahrain field, discovered in 1932, is wholly owned by the Bahrain National Oil Co. Production now stands at about 41,800 bpd. The Sitra refinery derives about 70 per cent. of its crude oil by submarine pipeline from Saudi Arabia. Bahrain also has a half share with Saudi Arabia in the profits of the offshore Abu Sa'afa field. A reservoir of unassociated gas has recently been developed on Bahrain island.

Heavy industry is currently limited to the Aluminium Bahrain (ALBA) smelter, and the Arab Iron and Steel Company's iron ore pelletising plant, which has an annual capacity of 4 million tonnes. ALBA, with an annual capacity of 170,000 tonnes of ingots, billets and slabs, uses alumina from Australia and the local natural gas. The Bahrain Government owns 59·9 per cent. of the shares. A dry dock built for a consortium of the OPEC countries and capable of taking tankers of up to 500,000 dwt was opened in 1977. In 1985 a large petrochemical plant to produce ammonia and methanol is due to start production.

The pearling industry, once the basis of the economy, has virtually ceased to exist. There is however a variety of light industries.

The state has developed as a financial centre. Apart from commercial banks, led by the National Bank of Bahrain, the Standard Chartered Bank, the British Bank of the Middle East and the Bank of Bahrain and Kuwait, many international banks have been licensed as "offshore banking units"; there are also money brokers and merchant banks.

The currency is the Bahraini Dinar (BD) divided into 1,000 fils.

Trade with U.K.

	1983	1984
Imports from U.K.	£150,264,000	£138,614,000
Exports to U.K.	37,488,000	28,212,000

Communications.—The port of Mina Sulman has sixteen alongside berths for ships up to 36' draft.

Bahrain International airport is the main air traffic centre of the Gulf; it is the headquarters of Gulf Air, and a stopping point on routes between Europe and Australia and the Far East for other airlines. A causeway linking Bahrain to Saudi Arabia is due to open in Dec. 1985.

A world-wide telephone and telex service, by satellite and cable, is operated by Bahrain Telecommunications Company.

FLAG.—Red, with vertical serrated white bar next to staff.

CAPITAL.—Manama; population (1981 Census), 121,986.

BRITISH EMBASSY
21 Government Avenue,
Manama 306, P.O. Box 114

Ambassador Extraordinary and Plenipotentiary, His Excellency Francis S. E. Trew, C.M.G. (1984).
1st Secretaries, P. R. Holmes (*Commercial and Head of Chancery*); W. H. Stevens.
2nd Secretaries, R. P. Smith (*Consul*); R. J. Cork (*Commercial*).
British Council Representative, D. R. Thomas, 21 Government Avenue (P.O. Box 452), Manama 306.

BELGIUM
(Royaume de Belgique)

King of the Belgians, H.M. King Baudouin, K.G., *born* Sept. 7, 1930; *succeeded* July 17, 1951, on the abdication of his father, King Leopold III, after having acted as Head of the State since August 11, 1950; *married* Dec. 15, 1960, Doña Fabiola de Mora y Aragón.
Heir Presumptive, H.R.H. Prince Albert, *born* June 6, 1934, *brother* of the King; *married* July 2, 1959, Donna Paola Ruffo di Calabria, and has *issue* Prince Philippe Léopold Louis Marie, *b.* April 15, 1960; Princess Astrid Josephine-Charlotte Fabrizia Elisabeth Paola Marie, *b.* June 5, 1962; Prince Laurent, *b.* Oct. 20, 1963.

CABINET

Prime Minister, Dr. Wilfred Martens (*CVP*).
Deputy Prime Minister and Minister of Finance and for the Middle Classes, Frans Grootjans (*PVV*).
Deputy Prime Minister and Minister for Justice, Institutional Reform and Foreign Trade, Jean Gol (*PRL*).
Deputy Prime Minister and Minister for the Interior and for the Civil Service, Charles-Ferdinand Nothomb (*PSC*).
Public Works, Louis Oliver (*PRL*).
Foreign Affairs, Léo Tindemans (*CVP*).
National Defence, Freddy Vreven (*PVV*).
Flemish Education, Daniel Coens (*CVP*).
French Language Education, André Bertouille (*PRL*).
Economic Affairs, Mark Eyskens (*CVP*).
Labour and Employment, Michel Hansenne (*PSC*).
Communications, Posts and Telecommunications, Herman de Croo (*PVV*).
Budget, Scientific Policy and Planning, Philippe Maystadt (*PSC*).
Brussels Regional Affairs, Paul Hatry (*PRL*).
Social Affairs and Institutional Reform, Jean-Luc Dehaene (*CVP*).
CVP—Social Christian Party (Flemish wing); PSC—Social Christian Party (Francophone wing); PVV—Liberals (Flemish); PRL—Liberals (Francophone).

Parliament has been dissolved and the above Cabinet remains as a caretaker government, ruling by decree on essential financial and foreign affairs matters, until a General Election is held on Oct. 13, 1985.

BELGIAN EMBASSY IN LONDON
103 Eaton Square, SW1W 9AB
[01–235 5422]

Ambassador Extraordinary and Plenipotentiary, His Excellency Jean-Paul van Bellinghen (1984).
Minister Plenipotentiary, M. C. Raulier.
Minister Counsellor, M. B. Lauwaert (*Economic*).
Military, Naval and Air Attaché, Capt. N. H. Stradiot.

A Kingdom of Western Europe, with a total area of 11,781 square miles and a population, (1981) of 9,863,374 (Greater Brussels, 1,000,221; Flanders, 5,634,152; Wallonia, 3,229,001, of whom 64,713 are German-speaking). The majority of Belgians are Roman Catholics. The Kingdom of Belgium is bounded on the N. by the Kingdom of the Netherlands, on the S. by France, on the E. by Germany and Luxemburg, and on the W. by the North Sea.

Belgium has a frontier of 898 miles, and a seaboard of 41 miles. The Meuse and its tributary, the Sambre, divide it into two distinct regions, that in the west being generally level and fertile, while the table-land of the Ardennes, in the east, has for the most part a poor soil. The "polders" near the coast, which are protected by dykes against floods, cover an area of 193 sq. miles. The highest hill, Signal de Botranges, rises to a height of 2,276 feet, but the mean elevation of the whole country does not exceed 526 feet. The principal rivers are the Scheldt and the Meuse. Brussels has a mean temperature of 49° F. (summer 65°, winter 37°).

Government.—The kingdom formed part of the "Low Countries" (Netherlands) from 1815 until Oct. 14, 1830, when a National Congress proclaimed its independence, and on June 4, 1831, Prince Leopold of Coburg was chosen hereditary king. The separation from the Netherlands and the neutrality and inviolability of Belgium were guaranteed by a Conference of the European Powers, and by the *Treaty of London* (April 19, 1839), the famous "Scrap of Paper," signed by Austria, France, Great Britain, Prussia, The Netherlands, and Russia. On Aug. 4, 1914, the Germans invaded Belgium, in violation of the terms of the treaty. The Kingdom was again invaded by Germany on May 10, 1940. The whole Kingdom eventually fell and was occupied by Nazi troops until liberated by the Allies in September 1944.

According to the Constitution of 1831 the form of government is a constitutional representative and hereditary monarchy with a bicameral legislature, consisting of the King, the Senate and the Chamber of Representatives. The parliamentary term is four years.

The last general election was held on November 8, 1981. The results were as follows (seats):

Chamber of Deputies: CVP, 43; PSC, 18; PVV, 28; PRL, 24; SP (Socialist), 26; PS (Socialist), 35; VU (Flemish Nationalist), 20; FDF (Brussels Francophones)/RW (Walloon Regionalists), 8; UDRT (Antitax), 3; Ecologists, 4; PCB/KPB (Communist), 2; VLAAMS BLOK, 1.

Senate: CVP, 22; PSC, 8; PVV, 14; PRL, 11; PS, 18; SP, 13; VU, 10; FDF/RW, 4; UDRT, 1; Ecologists, 4; PCB/KPB, 1. Besides these directly elected representatives the Senate also includes 50 members who are elected by the Provincial Councils and 25 who are co-opted in the proportions of the directly elected seats. H.R.H. Prince Albert is a "sénateur de droit".

Regional Governments.—The 1980 regionalization law made provision for the establishment of three Regional Parliaments (Assemblies) with executive councils which were set up in November 1981 and became effective in January 1982. The executives are autonomous from the central government, and their members are elected by the members of the Assemblies to whom they are responsible. They prepare Bills within the limits of their regional/community competences, and once these Bills have been passed by the regional assembly and published in the *Moniteur Belge*, they have the force of law.

The Flemish Regional Assembly (182 members) and Executive (a President and 8 Regional Ministers) covers the provinces of Antwerp, East and West Flanders, Limbourg and the Flemish *arrondissements* (Hall, Vilvoorde, Leuven) in the province of Brabant, and is also responsible for the Flemish population of Brussels. The Walloon Regional Assembly (106 members) and Executive (a President and 5 Regional Ministers) covers the provinces of Hainaut, Liege, Luxembourg and Naumur, and the *arrondissement* of Nivelles in the province of Brabant. The French Community Assembly (137 members) and Executive (a President and 2 Community Ministers) has no fixed territory but is responsible for the francophone population of Brussels and, in concert with the Walloon Regional Assembly, deals with certain Walloon regional affairs. The German-speaking community (about 60,000) also has an Assembly, which gained autonomy in 1984. It is based in Eupen.

Although the regionalization laws defined the City of Brussels as a region, there is no autonomous regional parliament for the City and its affairs are handled by a Brussels Executive within the national government.

An Arbitration Court was set up in 1984 to resolve conflicts between laws made by the various legislative bodies.

Language and Literature.—Belgium is divided between those who speak Dutch (the Flemings) and those who speak French (the Walloons). Dutch is spoken in the provinces of West Flanders, East Flanders, Antwerp, Limburg, and the northern half of Brabant, and French in the provinces of Hainault, Namur, Luxemburg, Liège and the southern half of Brabant. Dutch is recognized as the official language in the northern areas and French in the southern (Walloon) area and there are guarantees for the respective linguistic minorities. Brussels is officially bi-lingual. There is a small German-speaking area (Eupen and Malmedy) along the German border, east of Liège.

The literature of France and the Netherlands is supplemented by an indigenous Belgian literary activity, in both French and Dutch. Maurice Maeterlinck (1862–1949) was awarded the Nobel Prize for Literature in 1911. Emile Verhaeren (1855–1916) was a poet of international standing. Of contemporary Belgian writers, perhaps the most celebrated is Georges Simenon (*born* at Liège in 1903). There are 39 daily newspapers in Belgium (23 in French, 15 in Dutch and 1 in German).

Education.—The nursery schools provide free education for the 2½ to 6 age group. There are over 8,000 primary schools (6 to 12 years) of which approximately 5,000 are administered by the State, province or commune and the remainder are free institutions (predominantly Roman Catholic). There are more than 1,100 secondary schools offering a

general academic education slightly over half of which are free institutions (predominantly Roman Catholic but subsidized by the State) and the remainder official institutions. The official school leaving age is 14.

Production.—Belgium is essentially a manufacturing country. With no natural resources except coal, annual production of which was 6,430,000 tonnes in 1984, industry is based largely on the processing for re-export of imported raw materials. Gross National Product per capita in 1982 was U.S.\$8,670. Principal industries are steel and metal products, chemicals and petrochemicals, textiles, glass, and foodstuffs.

FINANCE

Budget	1983	1984
	B. Fr. (millions)	
Revenue	1,218·2	1,315·3
Expenditure	1,540·9	1,625·4

The unit of currency is the Belgian *franc*. (*See also* p. 81). External trade figures relate to Luxemburg as well as Belgium since the two countries formed an Economic Union in 1921.

TRADE

	1983	1984
	B. Fr. (millions)	
Total Imports	2,817,019	3,192,500
Total Exports	2,650,762	2,987,500

Trade with U.K. (Belgium and Luxemburg)

	1983	1984
Imports from U.K.	£2,572,673,000	£3,051,722,000
Exports to U.K.	3,133,905,000	3,691,794,000

Communications.—In 1983, there were 3,920 kilometres of normal gauge railways operated by the Belgian National Railways, of which 1,763 kilometres were electrified. The Belgian National Light Railways (SNCV) also operated 27,671 kilometres of regular bus routes. In 1984 there were 2,930,000 telephone subscribers in Belgium.

Ship canals include *Ghent-Terneuzen* (18 miles, of which half is in Belgium and half in the Netherlands) which permits the passage to Ghent of ships up to 60,000 tons; the Canal of *Willebroek Rupel-Brussels* (20 miles, by which ships drawing 18 ft reach Brussels from the sea; opened in 1922); and *Bruges* (from Zeebrugge on the North Sea to Bruges, 6½ miles). The *Albert Canal* (79 miles), links Liège with Antwerp; it was completed in 1939 and accommodates barges up to 1,350 tons. The modernization of the port of Antwerp is well advanced. Inland waterway approaches to Antwerp are also to be improved. The river Meuse from the Dutch to the French frontiers, the river Sambre between Namur and Monceau, the river Scheldt from Antwerp-Ghent and the Brussels-Charleroi Canal are being widened or deepened to take barges up to 1,350 tons. Most of the maritime trade of Belgium is carried in foreign shipping.

In 1981 there were 13,093 km. of trunk roads of which about 1,315 km. are motorways.

The Belgian National Airline *Sabena* operates regular services between Brussels and London, and many continental centres, as well as overseas services to Northern and Central America, Africa, Middle East, Far East, etc. Many foreign airlines call at Brussels.

Cities and Towns.—The Capital, BRUSSELS, has a population (1981) of 1,000,221 (with suburbs). Other towns are ΨAntwerp, the chief port (923,547); Ψ Ghent (486,081); Liège (609,066); Charleroi (441,017); ΨBruges (252,430); ΨOstend (270,888); Malines (291,459). Brussels is 224 miles from London; transit, by rail and sea, 8 hrs.; by air, 50 mins.

NATIONAL FLAG.—Three vertical bands, black, yellow, red.

NATIONAL DAY.—July 21 (Accession of King Leopold I, 1831).

BRITISH EMBASSY.
Britannia House, 28 rue Joseph II,
1040 Brussels.

Ambassador Extraordinary and Plenipotentiary, His Excellency Peter Charles Petrie, C.M.G., *apptd.* 1985.
Counsellors, A. L. S. Coltman (*Head of Chancery*); M. B. Collins, O.B.E. (*Commercial*).
Defence and Military Attaché, Col. C. F. Eaton, O.B.E.
Naval and Air Attaché, Wing Cdr. J. N. Landeryou, R.A.F.

There are British Consular Offices at *Brussels, Antwerp, Ghent* and *Liège.*

British Council Representative to Belgium and Luxemburg, J. P. Harniman, O.B.E., Avenue Galilée-Galileilaan 5 (Boite 10), 1030, Brussels (Council Library at *Brussels*).
BRITISH CHAMBER OF COMMERCE FOR BELGIUM AND LUXEMBURG (INC.), 30 Rue Joseph II, 1040 Brussels.

BENIN
(People's Republic of Benin)

President of the Military Revolutionary Government and Head of State, Brig.-Gen. Ahmed Mathieu Kerekou; *assumed office,* Oct. 26, 1972, *re-elected,* July 31, 1984.

NATIONAL EXECUTIVE COUNCIL
(as at Aug. 1984)

President of the Council and Minister of Defence, Brig.-Gen. Ahmed Mathieu Kerekou.
Minister-Delegate to the Presidency (Interior, Security, Territorial Administration), Maj. Edouard Zodehougan.
Minister-Delegate to the Presidency (Planning, Statistics), Kifouli Salami.
Rural Development and Co-operative Action, Maj. Adolphe Biaou.
Equipment and Transport, Giriguissou Gado.
Finance and Economy, Hospice Antonio.
Commerce, Crafts and Tourism, Soule Dankoro.
Nursery and Primary Education, Capt. Philippe Akpo.
Secondary and Higher Education, Lt.-Col Michel Alladayé.
Culture, Youth and Sports, Traoré Ali Moussa.
Labour and Social Affairs, André Archade.
Public Health, Vincent Guezodje.
Information and Communications, Ali Houdou.
Foreign Affairs and Co-operation, Frédéric Affo.
Justice, and Inspection of Public and Semi-Public Enterprises, Didier Dassi.

A republic situated in West Africa, between 2° and 3° W. and 6° and 12° N., Benin (formerly known as Dahomey) has a short coast line of 78 miles on the Gulf of Guinea but extends northwards inland for 437 miles. It is flanked on the west by Togo, on the north by Burkina Faso and Niger and on the east by Nigeria. It has an area of about 47,000 square miles and a population of 3,338,240 at the 1979 Census. Although poor in resources, Benin is one of the most thickly populated areas in West Africa, with a high level of education. It is divided into four main regions running horizontally: a narrow sandy coastal strip, a succession of inter-communicating lagoons, a clay belt and a sandy plateau in the north.

The first treaty with France was signed by one of the kings of Abomey in 1851 but the country was not placed under French administration until 1892. Benin became an independent republic within the French Community on Dec. 4, 1958; full independence outside the Community was proclaimed on August 1, 1960. In October, 1963, a popular revolution led to the fall of the government and the Army held power until a civilian government was formed. The government's life was very short, however, and in the subsequent 8–9 years successive governments were overthrown by the military after only a short term in office until a *coup d'état* of October 26, 1972 brought to power a Military Revolutionary Government, headed by Lt.-Col. Kerekou. Although now a one-party state, a general election was held in Nov. 1979, and a new Constitution and National Assembly were established.

Benin is a member of the *Conseil de l'Entente*, the *Organisation Commune Africaine et Malgache* (OCAM), the Organization of African Unity (O.A.U.) and the Economic Community of West African States (ECOWAS). The official language is French.

Finance.—The currency of Benin is the *Franc CFA* of 100 *centimes.*

Trade.—The principal exports are cotton, palm products, ground nuts, shea-nuts, and coffee. Small deposits of gold, iron and chrome have been found; oil production started in 1983.

Trade with U.K.

	1983	1984
Imports from U.K.	£10,577,000	£6,828,722
Exports to U.K.	2,887,000	2,100,695

CAPITAL.—Porto Novo (104,000). Political capital and principal commercial town and port, ΨCotonou (178,000).

FLAG.—Green, with five pointed red star in the top left corner.

NATIONAL DAY.—November 30.

British Embassy (see Lagos, Nigeria).

BHUTAN

King of Bhutan, H.M. Jigme Singye Wangchuck, born Nov. 11, 1955; *succeeded his father*, July, 1972; *crowned*, June 2, 1974.

COUNCIL OF MINISTERS

H.M. Representative in the Ministry of Finance, H.R.H. Ashi S. C. Wangchuk.

H.M. Representative in the Ministry of Development, H.R.H. Ashi D. W. Wangchuk.

Trade, Industry and Forests, H.R.H. Namgyel Wangchuk.

Home Affairs and Speaker of the National Assembly, Lyonpo Tamji Jagar.

Foreign Affairs, Lyonpo Dawa Tshering.

Communications and Tourism, Lyonpo Sangye Penjor.

Deputy Minister of Defence, Col. Lam Dorji.

Bhutan is a small Himalayan Kingdom situated between Tibet (to the north) and India (to the west, south and east). The total area is about 18,000 sq. miles, with a mountainous northern region which is infertile and sparsely populated, a central zone of upland valleys where most of the population and cultivated land is found, and in the south the densely forested foothills of the Himalayas, which are mainly inhabited by Nepalese settlers and indigenous tribes-people.

The population of Bhutan is estimated (mid-1984) at 1,400,000, about three-quarters of whom are Buddhists. The remainder (mostly the Nepali Bhutanese) are Hindu. The official language, for administrative and religious purposes, is Dzongkha, a variant of Tibetan, which functions as a *lingua franca*

amongst a variety of languages and dialects. It is government policy to make the study of Dzongkha compulsory in schools, although English is the medium of instruction and has become widely used within the administration.

In 1949, a treaty was concluded with the Government of India under which the Kingdom of Bhutan agreed to be guided by the Government of India in regard to its external relations, but it still retains independence, issues its own passports, has its own diplomatic representatives and is a member of the U.N. and other international and regional organisations.

It also receives from the Government of India an annual payment of *Rs.*500,000 as compensation for portions of its territory annexed by the British Government in India in 1864. India provides 50 per cent of the budget for Bhutan's 5-year plan (1982–7).

Government.—Bhutan has a 150-member National Assembly which meets twice a year. The 8-member Royal Advisory Council, nominated by the King and the National Assembly, acts as a consultative body when the National Assembly is not in session. The King is also assisted by a Council of Ministers.

Economy.—The economy is based on agriculture and animal husbandry, which engage over 90 per cent of the workforce in what is largely a self-sufficient rural society. The principal food crops are rice, wheat, maize and barley. Vegetables and fruit are also produced. Bhutan is the world's largest producer of cardamon, which forms its principal export to countries other than India. Mineral resources include dolomite and small amounts of coal, which are exported to India. A modest industrial base is being developed. A distillery and cement, chemicals and food processing plants are in production : a forestry industries complex is being expanded. Tourism and postage stamps are increasingly important sources of foreign exchange. Over 90 per cent of foreign trade is with India. Principal exports are agricultural products, timber, cement and coal; main imports are textiles, cereals and consumer goods. With Indian assistance a network of roads has been constructed and Bhutan's airline, Druk Air, has become operational, flying between Paro and Calcutta.

Trade with U.K.

	1983	1984
Imports from U.K.	£99,000	£86,000
Exports to U.K.	—	—

CURRENCY.—*Ngultrum* (parity with Indian rupee).

CAPITAL.—Thimphu.

FLAG.—Saffron yellow and orange-red divided diagonally, with dragon device in centre.

BOLIVIA
(República de Bolivia)

President of the Republic, Sr. Victor Paz Estenssoro, *inaugurated*, Aug. 6, 1985.

CABINET

Foreign Affairs, Gastón Araoz Levy.
Interior, Fernando Bartelemy.
Finance, Roberto Gisbert.
Planning, Guillermo Bedregal.
Education, Enrique Ipina.
Transport and Communications, Nestor Dalenz.
Industry and Commerce, Douglas Ascarrunz.
Health, Hugo Rodriguez.
Mines and Metallurgy, Sinforoso Cabrera.
Agriculture, Mauricio Mamani.
Energy and Hydrocarbons, Orlando Donoso.

Housing, Carlos Alcides Aliaga.
Secretary to the Presidency, Guillermo Riveros Tejada.
Information, Reynaldo Peters.
Integration, Fernando Cáceres.
Aeronautics, Gen. Antonio Tovar.
Defence, Luis Fernando Valle.
Labour Walter Costas Badani.

BOLIVIAN EMBASSY IN LONDON
106 Eaton Square, SW1W 9AD
[01–235 2257/4248]

Minister Counsellor, C. Quintanilla.
1st Secretary, Srta. Marta Bosacoma Bonel.
There is a Bolivian Consular Office in *Liverpool.*

The land-locked Republic of Bolivia extends between lat. 10° and 23° S. and long. 57° 30′ and 69° 45′ W. It has an area estimated at 415,000 square miles with a population of 6,000,000. (*For* MAP, *see* Index.) The Republic derives its name from its liberator, Simon Bolivar (1783–1830).

The chief topographical feature is the great central plateau (65,000 square miles) over 500 miles in length, at an average altitude of 12,500 feet above sea level, between the two great chains of the Andes, which traverse the country from south to north, and contain, in Illampu, Illimani, and Sajama, three of the highest peaks of the western hemisphere. The total length of the navigable streams is about 12,000 miles, the principal rivers being the Itenez, Beni, Mamore and Madre de Dios.

Language and Literature.—The official language of the country is Spanish, but many of the Indian inhabitants (about two-thirds of the population) speak Quechua or Aymará, the two linguistic groups being more or less equal in numbers.

The Roman Catholic religion was disestablished in 1961 but relations between it and the State are good. Elementary education is compulsory and free and there are secondary schools in urban centres. Provision is also made for higher education; in addition to St. Francisco Xavier's University at Sucre, founded in 1624, there are six other universities, the largest being the University of San Andres at La Paz. Bolivian literature has not yet produced authors of world-wide renown. There are nine principal daily newspapers in Bolivia.

Production.—Mining, natural gas, petroleum and agriculture are the principal industries. The ancient silver mines of Potosí are now worked chiefly for tin, but gold, partly dug and partly washed, is obtained on the Eastern Cordillera of the Andes; the tin output is one of the largest in the world, and together with other minerals (copper, antimony, lead, zinc, asbestos, wolfram, bismuth salt and sulphur), provides over half of Bolivia's exports.

In 1982 Bolivia produced 1·4 million cubic metres of oil, sufficient for internal consumption. Gas (currently providing about a quarter of Bolivia's export income) is piped to Argentina and there are plans to build a pipeline to Sao Paulo, Brazil, by 1985. Bolivia's agricultural produce consists chiefly of rice, barley, oats, wheat, sugar-cane, maize, cotton, indigo, rubber, cacao, potatoes, cinchona bark, medicinal herbs, brazil nuts etc.

Transport and Communications.—There are 2,200 miles of railways in operation including the lines from Corumbá to Santa Cruz (312 miles). There are about 10,950 miles of telegraphs, and microwave telephone communications between La Paz, Santa Cruz, Cochabamba, Oruro and Sucre. Most other towns of any size have radio/telephone communication with the main cities. There is direct railway communication to the sea at Antofagasta (32 hours),

Arica (10 hours), and Mollendo (2 days), and also to Buenos Aires (3½ days). Communication with Peru is effected by rail to Guaqui and thence by steamer across Lake Titicaca to the railhead at Puno.

Commercial aviation in Bolivia is conducted by the national airline, Lloyd Aereo Boliviano and Transporte Aereo Militar between the major towns, and Lloyd Aereo Boliviano and a number of foreign airlines provide international flights to the U.S.A., South and Central America and Europe.

Bolivia is without a sea-coast, having been deprived of the ports of Tocopilla, Cobija, Mejillones and Antofagasta by the "Pacific War" of 1879–1884.

FINANCE

The economy has deteriorated since 1977, with disappointing petroleum reserves and a large external debt. The position worsened in 1981 when world tin prices remained low. The peso was devalued to 2,000 to 1 U.S. dollar in April 1984. The inflation rate in 1984 was about 560 per cent. Total exports (c.i.f.) in 1982 were U.S. $898 million.

Trade with U.K.

	1983	1984
Imports from U.K.	£4,711,000	£17,170,000
Exports to U.K.	14,834,000	20,052,000

Mineral exports represent about 83 per cent of these totals. A large part of Bolivia's minerals were shipped to U.K. for smelting and re-export, but Bolivia is now developing her own smelters and will in future be exporting metals. The chief imports are wheat and flour, iron and steel products, machinery, vehicles and textiles.

Seat of Government.—La Paz. Population (census 1976) 654,700. Other large centres are Cochabamba (194,000), Oruro (124,000), Santa Cruz (237,000), Potosí (77,000), Sucre, the legal capital and seat of the judiciary (63,000) and Tarija (38,500).

FLAG.—Three horizontal bands; red, yellow, green.
NATIONAL DAY.—August 6 (Independence Day).

BRITISH EMBASSY
Avenida Arce 2732–2754,
(Casilla 694) La Paz.

Ambassador Extraordinary and Plenipotentiary, His Excellency Alan White, C.M.G., *apptd.* 1985.
1st Secretary, P. Sullivan (*Commercial and Head of Chancery*).

BRITISH CONSULAR OFFICES

There is a British Consular Office at *La Paz.*

BRAZIL
(The Federative Republic of Brazil)

President, José Sarney, *inaugurated,* April 22, 1985.

CABINET

Chief Minister Civil Staff, José Hugo Castello Branco.
Chief Minister Military Staff, Gen. Rubens Bayma Denys.
Justice, Fernando Lyra.
Navy, Adm. Henrique Sabóya.
External Relations, Olavo Setúbal.
Army, Gen. Leônidas Pires Gonçalves.
Finance, Dilson Funaro.
Transport, Affonso Camargo.
Agriculture, Pedro Simon.
Education, Marco Maciel.
Labour, Almir Pazzianotto.
Air Force, Brig. Octávio Moreira Lima.

Health, Carlos Sant'Anna.
Industry and Commerce, Robert Gusmão.
Mines and Energy, Aureliano Chaves.
Planning Dr. João Sayad.
Interior, Ronaldo Costa Couto.
Communications, Antonio Carlos Magalhães.
Social Security, Waldir Pires.
National Information Service, Gen. Ivan de Souza Mendes.
Armed Forces General Staff, Adm. José Maria do Amaral Oliveira.
Reform and Development, Nelson Ribeiro.
Debureaucratization, Paulo Lustosa.
Science and Technology, Renato Archer.
Culture, Prof. Aluisio Pimenta.
Urban Planning and Environment, Flavio Peixoto.
Administration, Aluizio Alves.

(Tancredo Neves was elected as President on Jan. 15, 1985 but was unable to take power on March 15, as intended, as he was incapacitated by ill-health. Vice-President Sarney was inaugurated as Acting President on March 15 and subsequently became President when Sr. Neves died on April 21, 1985.)

BRAZILIAN EMBASSY IN LONDON
32 Green Street, W1Y 3FD
[01–499 0877]

Ambassador Extraordinary and Plenipotentiary, His Excellency Mario Gibson-Barboza (1982).

There are also a Brazilian Consulate-General at *Liverpool* and honorary consular offices at *Cardiff* and *Glasgow.*

POSITION AND EXTENT

Brazil, discovered in 1500 by Pedro Alvares Cabral, Portuguese navigator, is bounded on the north by the Atlantic Ocean, the Guianas, Colombia and Venezuela; on the west by Peru, Bolivia, Paraguay, and Argentina; on the south by Uruguay; and on the east by the Atlantic Ocean. Brazil extends between lat. 5° 16′ N. and 33° 45′ S. and long. 34° 45′ and 73° 59′22″ W., being 2,685 miles from north to south, and 2,690 from west to east, with a coast-line on the Atlantic of 4,604 miles. The Republic comprises an area of 3,289,440 square miles, with a population (1980 census) of 119,098,922.

The northern States of Amazonas and Pará are mainly wide, low-lying, forest-clad plains. The central states of Mato Grosso are principally plateau land and the eastern and southern States are traversed by successive mountain ranges interspersed with fertile valleys. The principal ranges are *Serra do Mar,* the *Serra da Mantiqueira* and the *Serra do Espinhaco* along the east coast. The River *Amazon* with a total length of some 4,000 miles has tributaries which are themselves great rivers, and flows from the Peruvian Andes to the Atlantic. Its principal northern tributaries are the *Rio Branco, Rio Negro,* and *Japurá;* its southern tributaries are the *Juruá, Purus, Madeira* and *Tapajós,* while the *Xingú* meets it within 200 miles of its outflow into the Atlantic. The *Tocantins* and *Araguaia* flow northwards from Mato Grosso and Goiás to the Gulf of Pará. The *Parnaiba* flows from Piaui into the Atlantic. The *São Francisco* rises in the South of Minas Gerais and flows to the eastern coast. The *Paraguai,* rising in the south-west of Mato Grosso, flows through Paraguay to its confluence with the *Paraná,* which rises in the mountains of that name and divides Brazil from Paraguay.

Government.—Brazil was colonized by Portugal in the early part of the sixteenth century, and in 1822 became an independent empire under Dom Pedro, son of the refugee King Joao VI. of Portugal. On Nov. 15,

1889, Dom Pedro II., second of the line, was dethroned and a republic was proclaimed.

The Federative Republic of Brazil is made up of the Federal District, 23 States and 3 Territories (the most under-developed frontier regions). The constitution of January 1967 draws on the same conceptual basis as that of the United States, and envisages an equal distribution of power between the executive, the legislature and the judiciary. Under the existing constitutional provisions the President, who heads the executive, is indirectly elected. However, legislation was introduced in 1985 which provides for direct presidential elections in two rounds (the successful candidate will have to obtain a clear majority in the second round); this system will come into use when Pres. Sarney leaves office. The Government also intends that the Congress which will be elected at the elections of Nov. 15, 1985, will undertake a revision of the constitution.

The Congress consists of a Senate (3 Senators per State elected for an 8-year term) and a Chamber of Deputies which is re-elected every 4 years. (The number of Deputies per State depends upon the State's population). Each State has a Governor, and a Legislative Assembly with a 4-year term.

Production.—There are large and valuable mineral deposits including among others, iron ore (hematite), manganese, bauxite, beryllium, chrome, nickel, tungsten, cassiterite, lead, gold, monazite (containing rare earths and thorium) and zirconium. Diamonds and precious and semi-precious stones are also found. The mineral wealth is being exploited to an increasing extent. The iron ore deposits of Minas Gerais are exceeded by those of the Amazon region, principally in the Carajás areas where deposits are estimated at 35,000 million tonnes. Mining operations began in Feb. 1985.

Electric power production in 1984 was 157,128 Gwh. In the same year, the total output of steel was 18,385,000 tonnes. Production of oil was 173,010,000 barrels. Of these 100,346,000 barrels were produced from offshore fields.

Agriculture production in 1984 was:

Black Beans	2,815,981	tonnes
Cassava	23,815,329	„
Castor Beans	409,406	„
Cocoa	415,698	„
Coffee	1,772,000	„
Cotton	2,897,065	„
Maize	21,763,084	„
Oranges	65,173,193	„
Peanuts	303,175	„
Potatoes	1,682,618	„
Rice	9,103,747	„
Sisal	243,102	„
Soya	17,930,751	„
Tobacco	389,109	„
Wheat	1,829,758	„

Defence.—The peace-time strength of the Army is 182,750 of which 15,280 are officers and warrant officers and 35,500 are N.C.O.s and 132,000 conscripts. The Navy consists of 1 aircraft carrier, 7 submarines, 10 destroyers, 6 frigates, 9 patrol vessels, 5 river patrol ships, 1 river monitor, 1 river transport, 6 coastal mine sweepers, 7 survey ships, and 29 other vessels. The strength of the Navy is 49,000. The Air Force, with a strength of 43,000, has 696 aircraft, of which 192 are fast-jet.

Education.—Primary education is compulsory and is the responsibility of State governments and municipalities. At this level approximately 10 per cent. attend private schools. Secondary education is largely the responsibility of State and municipal governments, although a small number of very old foundations (the Pedro II Schools) remain under direct federal control. Over 50 per cent. of all pupils

at this level attend private schools. Higher education is available in Federal, State, municipal and private universities and faculties.

Language and Literature.—Portuguese is the language of the country, but Italian, Spanish, German, Japanese and Arabic are spoken by immigrant minorities, and newspapers of considerable circulation are produced in those languages. English and French are currently spoken by educated Brazilians.

Until the second quarter of the nineteenth century Brazilian literature was dominated by Portugal. French influence is traceable for the next half century, since when a national school has come into existence and there are many modern authors of high standing. Public libraries have been established in urban centres and there is a flourishing national press with widely circulated daily and weekly newspapers.

Communications.—In 1982 there were 1,394,165 km. of highways. The route-length of railways in 1980 was 35,100 km. Internal air services are highly developed. There are 21,944 miles of navigable inland waterways. During 1982, 9,574 vessels entered Rio de Janeiro and Santos, the two leading ports.

FINANCE

	1984
	Cruzeiros
Revenue	33,788 m.
Expenditure	33,766 m.

At Dec. 1984 Brazil's foreign debt stood at U.S.$99,882·0 million. Reserves in mid-1985 were $8,400 million.

TRADE

	1983	1984
Total imports	U.S.$15,408 m.	U.S.$13,916 m.
Total exports	21,899 m.	27,005 m.

Trade with U.K.

	1983	1984
Imports from U.K.	£157,758,000	£238,717,000
Exports to U.K.	560,277,000	637,702,000

Principal imports are fuel and lubricants, machinery, chemicals, wheat, metals and metal manufactures. Principal exports are coffee, iron ore, soya, meat, steel and orange juice. In 1983 the Brazilian automobile industry produced 836,314 vehicles. Of these, 168,674 vehicles (worth U.S. $1,327,000,000) were exported.

CAPITAL.—Brasilia (inaugurated on April 21, 1960). Population (Census 1980), 1,176,748. Other important centres are São Paulo (8,490,763); the former capital ψRio de Janeiro (5,094,396); ψBelo Horizonte (1,774,712); ψRecife (1,204,794); ψSalvador (1,017,591); ψPorto Alegre (1,125,091); ψFortaleza (1,308,859); and Belem (934,330).

FLAG.—Green, with yellow lozenge in centre; blue sphere with white band and stars in centre of lozenge.

NATIONAL DAY.—September 7 (Independence Day).

BRITISH EMBASSY
Setor de Embaixadus Sul, Quadra 801, Conjunto K, Lote 8, 70.408 Brasilia, D.F.

Ambassador Extraordinary and Plenipotentiary, His Excellency John Burns Ure, C.M.G., M.V.O. (1984).
There are British Consulates-General at Rio de Janeiro and São Paulo.

BRITISH COUNCIL.—*Representative*, E. J. Rayner, P.O. Box 14-2336, 70,740 Brasilia D.F. *Regional Directors in Rio de Janeiro, Recife* and *São Paulo*.

BRITISH AND COMMONWEALTH CHAMBER OF COMMERCE IN SÃO PAULO, Rua Barão de Itapetininga 275, 7th Floor, 01042, São Paulo (*Postal Address*, P.O. Box 1621, 01000 Sao Paulo) and Rua Real Grandeza 99, 22281 Rio de Janeiro.

Rio de Janeiro, 5,750 miles distant from London: transit, 15 days.

BULGARIA
(Bulgariya)
COUNCIL OF STATE

Chairman of the Council of State, Todor Zhivkov, *elected*, July 7, 1971; *re-elected*, June 1981 (*Head of State*).
First Deputy Chairman, Petur Tanchev.
Deputy Chairmen, Peko Takov; Georgi Dzhagarov; Mitko Grigorov; Yaroslav Radev.
Secretary, Nikola Manolov.
Chairman of the Committee for State and People's Control, (vacant).

COUNCIL OF MINISTERS

Chairman and Prime Minister, Grisha Filipov.
First Deputy Prime Minister, Chudomir Aleksandrov.
Deputy Prime Ministers, Andrei Lukanov; Grigor Stoichkov; Georgi Yordanov; Stanish Bonev (*Chairman, State Planning Committee*); Georgi Karamanev; Todor Bozhinov (*Minister of Supply*).
Finance, Belcho Belchev.
Interior, Col. Gen. Dimitur Stoyanov.
Defence, Gen. Dobri Dzhurov.
Foreign Affairs, Petur Mladenov.
Education, Prof. Aleksandur Fol.
Chemical Industry, Georgi Pankov.
Mechanical Engineering and Electronics, Ognyan Doynov.
Construction and Territorial Settlement Organisation, Grigor Stoichkov.
Production and Trade in Consumer Goods, Georgi Karamanev.
Foreign Trade, Khristo Khristov.
Forests and Forest Industry, Yanko Markov.
Communications, Pando Vanchev.
Health, Prof. Radoy Popivanov.
Justice, Svetla Daskalova.
Energy, Nikola Todoriev.

Metallurgy, Toncho Chakurov.
Transport, Vasil Tsanov.
Ambassador to the U.S.S.R., Dimitur Zhulev.
Chairmen of Committees, Stanish Bonev (*State Planning*); Aleksandur Petkov (*National Agro-Industrial Union*); Georgi Yordanov (*Culture*).

THE COMMUNIST PARTY

Politbureau of the Central Committee, T. Zhivkov; S. Todorov; P. Kubadinski; G. Filipov; O. Doynov; D. Dzhurov; P. Mladenov; T. Bozhinov; M. Balev; C. Aleksandrov; Y. Yotov (*full members*); A. Lukanov; G. Yordanov; P. Dyulgerov; G. Atanasov; G. Stoichkov; S. Bonev; D. Stoyanov (*candidate members*).
Secretariat of the Central Committee, Todor Zhivkov (*Secretary-General*); O. Doynov; G. Atanasov; D. Stanishev; S. Mikhaylov; M. Balev; V. Tsanov; K. Zarev; E. Khristov.

BULGARIAN EMBASSY AND CONSULATE IN LONDON
186–188 Queen's Gate Gardens, SW7 5HL
[01–584 9400/9433]

Ambassador Extraordinary and Plenipotentiary, His Excellency Kiril Shterev (1980).

The Republic of Bulgaria is bounded on the north by Rumania, on the west by Yugoslavia, on the east by the Black Sea, and on the south by Greece and Turkey. The total area is approximately 43,000 square miles, with a population in December, 1982 of 8,929,000. The largest religion of the Bulgarians is the Bulgarian Orthodox Church. The Gregorian (Western) Calendar is in use.

A Principality of Bulgaria was created by the *Treaty of Berlin* (July 13, 1878) and in 1885 Eastern Roumelia was added to the newly-created principality. In 1908 the country was declared to be an independent kingdom. In 1912–13 a successful war of the *Balkan League* against Turkey increased the size of the kingdom, but in August, 1913, a short campaign against the remaining members of the League reduced the acquired area, and led to the surrender of Southern Dobrudja to Romania. On Oct. 12, 1915, Bulgaria entered the War on the side of the Central Powers by declaring war on Serbia. She thus became involved in the defeats of 1918, and on Sept. 29, 1918, made an unconditional surrender to the Allied Powers. On Nov. 29, 1919, she signed the *Treaty of Neuilly*, which ceded to the Allies her Thracian territories (later handed over to Greece) and some territory on the western frontier to Yugoslavia.

Nazi troops entered the country on March 3, 1941, and occupied Black Sea ports, but Bulgaria was not at war with the Soviet Union. On August 26, 1944, the government declared Bulgaria to be "neutral in the Russo-German war" and sought terms of peace from Great Britain and the United States. The Soviet Union refused to recognize the so-called "neutrality" and called upon Bulgaria to declare war against Germany, and no satisfactory reply being received on Sept. 5, 1944, the U.S.S.R. declared war on Bulgaria. Bulgaria then asked for an armistice and on Sept. 7 declared war on Germany, hostilities with U.S.S.R. ending on Sept. 10. The armistice with the Allies was signed in Moscow, Oct. 28, 1944. The Peace Treaty with Bulgaria was signed on Feb. 22, 1947, and came into force on Sept. 15, 1947. It recognized the return of Southern Dobrudja to Bulgaria.

On Sept. 9, 1944 a *coup d'état* gave power to the Fatherland Front, a coalition of Communists, Agrarians, Social Democrats and officers and intellectuals. In August, 1945, the main body of Agrarians and Social Democrats left the Government. On Sept. 8, 1946, a referendum was held, which led to the

abolition of the Monarchy and the setting up of a Republic. On Oct. 27, a general election to a Grand National Assembly (with power to make a constitution) was held; the Opposition won 101 seats out of 465.

A new Constitution was adopted in 1971 according to which the legislature is a single chamber National Assembly or *Subranie* elected by adult suffrage for a maximum term of 5 years and consisting of 400 deputies representing constituencies of equal size. This Constitution also established the Council of State, being the supreme permanent body of the National Assembly with both legislative and executive functions. The opposition Agrarian Party was suppressed in 1947, but its remnant was later revived as the Agrarian Union which now constitutionally shares power with the Communist Party.

Production.—Until 1939 Bulgaria was a predominantly agricultural country, but has since pursued an elaborate programme of industrialization. About 90 per cent of the country's agriculture has been turned over to co-operatives, and a smaller proportion mechanized. The principal crops are wheat, maize, beet, tomatoes, tobacco, oleaginous seeds, fruit, vegetables and cotton. The livestock includes cattle, sheep, goats, pigs, horses, asses, mules and water buffaloes.

There is now a substantial engineering industry which accounts for about two-thirds of Bulgaria's exports; and considerable production of ferrous and non-ferrous metals. In 1982 production of electricity was 40,438 million kilowatt-hours, of steel 2,586,000 tons and of coal 32,182,000 tons (of which about one-quarter was soft coal).

There are mineral deposits of varying importance. Bulgaria's heavy industry includes the Kremikovtsi Steel Plant near Sofia and the Lenin steel mill at Pernik, the chemical complex at Devnia, the petro-chemical plant at Bourgas and various other chemical and metallurgical works situated around the country. The Soviet-designed nuclear power station at Kozlodui has four reactors, each with a capability of producing 800 million kilowatt/hours.

Defence.—Under the Peace Treaty signed between Bulgaria and the Allies, the Bulgarian Army is limited to 55,000 men, but it is believed at present to be at least 152,000 strong.

Education.—Free basic education is compulsory for children from 7 to 15 years inclusive. The Bulgarian educational system was reorganized on Soviet lines in September, 1950, providing kindergartens and educational establishments for primary and secondary education including vocational, technical and other specialized schools for secondary age pupils. There are three Universities (at Sofia, Plovdiv and

Veliko Turnovo) and 21 higher educational establishments.

Language and Literature.—Bulgarian is a Southern Slavonic tongue, closely allied to Serbo-Croat and Russian with local admixtures of modern Greek, Albanian and Turkish words. There is a modern literature chiefly educational and popular. The alphabet is Cyrillic. In 1983 there were 8 daily newspapers in Sofia.

Finance.—Planned budget revenue for 1984 is 17,754,200,000 *leva*, expenditure 17,739,200,000 *leva*. Currency in Bulgaria is the *lev*.

TRADE

The principal imports are industrial and agricultural machinery, industrial raw materials, machine tools, chemicals, dyestuffs, pharmaceuticals, rubber, paper. The principal exports are non-ferrous metals, electric trucks and motors, pumps, ships, accumulators and machine tools, cereals, tobacco, fruit, vegetables, oil seeds, fats, textiles, eggs, chemicals and oils including attar of roses. In 1983, 77·1 per cent of Bulgaria's foreign trade was within the C.M.E.A., including 57 per cent with the Soviet Union.

Trade with U.K.

	1983	1984
Imports from U.K.	£44,630,000	£55,917,000
Exports to U.K.	12,340,000	17,345,000

CAPITAL.—Sofia, Pop. (1982), 1,082,315, at the foot of the Vitosha Range, the capital and commercial centre is on the main railway line to Istanbul, 338 miles from the Black Sea port of ΨVarna (295,038) and 125 miles from Lom (28,500), on the Danube; ΨBourgas (178,239) is also a Black Sea Port, those on the Danube being ΨRousse (178,920), ΨVidin (60,877). Other important trading and industrial centres are Plovdiv (367,195), Pleven (135,899), Stara Zagora (141,722), Pernik (94,854), Sliven (100,637), Yambol (86,216), Khaskovo (87,639) and Tolbukhin (98,857).

FLAG.—3 horizontal bands, white, green, red; national emblem on white stripe near hoist.

NATIONAL DAY.—Sept. 9 (Day of Freedom).

BRITISH EMBASSY
Boulevard Marshal Tolbukhin, 65–67, Sofia.

Ambassador Extraordinary and Plenipotentiary, His Excellency John Michael Owen Snodgrass, C.M.G. (1983).

1st Secretaries, E. A. Burner (*Consul and Head of Chancery*); J. Daly (*Commercial*).

BURKINA
(Burkina Faso)

Head of State, Minister of the Interior and of Security, Capt. Thomas Sankara, *assumed office*, Aug. 1983.

Burkina is an inland savannah state in West Africa, situated between 9° and 15°N. and 2°E. and 5°W. with an area of about 100,000 square miles and a population estimated in 1983 at 6,666,000. It has common boundaries with Mali on the west, Niger and Benin on the east and Togo, Ghana and the Ivory Coast on the south. The largest tribe is the Mossi whose king, the Moro Naba, still wields a certain moral influence.

Burkina was annexed by France in 1896 and between 1932 and 1947 was administered as part of the Colony of the Ivory Coast. It decided on December 11, 1958, to remain an autonomous republic within the French Community; full independence outside the Community was proclaimed on August 5, 1960. The official language is French.

The 1960 constitution provided for a presidential form of government with a single chamber National Assembly, but in January, 1966, the Army assumed power. A new constitution allowing for a partial return to civilian rule but with the Army still in effective control was adopted in 1970, but in 1974 this was suspended. Full legislative and presidential elections were held again in 1978. In a military *coup* in Nov. 1980, Col. Zerbo assumed power. He was overthrown in Nov. 1982 by Maj. Ouedraogo, who was himself overthrown in Aug. 1983 by radical Army officers led by Capt. Sankara.

On 4 Aug. 1984, Upper Volta changed its name to Burkina (legally the full name is Burkina Faso, Faso meaning Popular and Democratic Republic of).

Finance and Trade.—The currency of the Republic is the *Franc CFA* (*Francs CFA* 50 = 1 *French Franc*). The 1985 Budget totalled *Francs CFA* 76,700 million.

The principal industry is the rearing of cattle and sheep and the chief exports are livestock, groundnuts, shea-nuts and cotton. Small deposits of gold, manganese, copper, bauxite and graphite have been found. Trade in 1983 was valued at Imports, *CFA* 100,000 m. Exports, *CFA* 48,800 m.

Trade with U.K.

	1983	1984
Imports from U.K.	£3,048,000	£2,065,000
Exports to U.K.	1,514,000	3,695,000

CAPITAL.—Ouagadougou (200,000). Other principal towns; Bobo-Dioulasso (90,000) and Kouddougou (35,000).

NATIONAL DAY.—August 4.

BRITISH REPRESENTATION

British Ambassador (*resident in Abidjan*, Ivory Coast).

BURMA
(The Socialist Republic of the Union of Burma)
Government of the Union

President, Gen. San Yu, *elected* Nov. 9, 1981.

COUNCIL OF MINISTERS

Prime Minister, Maung Maung Kha.
Deputy Prime Minister and Planning and Finance, Thura Tun Tin.
Deputy Prime Minister and Defence, Gen. Thura Kyaw Htin.
Home and Religious Affairs, Maj.-Gen. Min Gaung.
Agriculture and Forests, Ye Gaung.
Industry I, Tint Swe.
Education, Kyaw Nyein.
Energy and Industry II, Maung Cho.
Trade, Khin Maung Gyi.
Co-operatives, Livestock and Fisheries, Sein Tun.
Labour and Social Welfare, Ohn Kyaw.
Foreign Affairs, Chit Hlaing.
Culture and Information, U Aung Kyaw Myint.
Construction, Hla Tun.
Transport and Communications, Thura Saw Pru.
Health, Tun Wai.
Mines, Brig.-Gen. Than Tin.

BURMESE EMBASSY AND CONSULATE
19A Charles St., Berkeley Square, W1X 8ER
[01–499 8841]

Ambassador Extraordinary and Plenipotentiary, His Excellency Din Dun (1985).

Area and Population.—Burma forms the western portion of the Indo-Chinese district of the continent of Asia, lying between 9° 58′ and 28° N. latitude and 92° 11′ and 101° 9′ E. longitude, with an extreme length of approximately 1,200 miles and an extreme width of 575 miles. It has a sea coast on the Bay of Bengal to the south and west and a frontier with Bangladesh along the Naaf River (defined in 1964) and India to the north-west (defined in 1967). In the north and east the frontier with China was determined by a treaty with the People's Republic in October, 1960, and has since been demarcated; there is a short frontier with Laos in the east, while the long finger of Tenasserim stretches southward along the west coast of the Malay Peninsula, forming a frontier with Thailand to the east. (*For* MAP, *see* Index). The total area of the Union is about 262,000 square miles, with a population of 35,313,905 (1983 Census).

Physical Features.—Burma falls into four natural divisions. Arakan (with the Chin Hills region), the Irrawaddy basin, Tenasserim, including the Salween basin and extending southwards to the Burma-Thailand peninsula, and the elevated plateau on the east. Mountains enclose Burma on three sides, the highest point being Hka-kabo Razi (19,296 ft.) in the northern Kachin hills. Mt. Popa, 4,981 ft., in the Myingyan district is an extinct volcano and a well-known landmark in Central Burma. The principal river systems are the Kaladan-Lemro in Arakan, the Irrawaddy-Chindwin and the Sittang in Central Burma, and the Salween which flows through the Shan Plateau.

Races, Language and Religions.—The indigenous inhabitants who entered Burma from the north and east are of similar racial types and speak languages of the Tibeto-Burman, Mon-Khmer and Thai groups. The three important non-indigenous elements are Indians, Chinese and those from the former East Pakistan. Numbers of resident foreigners have shown a sharp decline in recent years. Burmese is the official language, but minority languages include Shan, Karen, Chin, Kayah and the various Kachin dialects. English is still spoken in educated circles in Rangoon and elsewhere. Buddhism is the religion of 85 per cent of the people, with 5 per cent Animists, 4 per cent Moslems, 4 per cent Hindus and less than 3 per cent Christians.

Government.—Burma became an independent republic outside the British Commonwealth on January 4, 1948, and remained a parliamentary democracy for 14 years.   On March 2, 1962 the army took power, and suspended the parliamentary Constitution. A Revolutionary Council of senior officers under General Ne Win took measures to create a Socialist State.

In January 1974 a new Constitution was adopted under which the highest authority is the People's Assembly (476 representatives) which meets twice a year. When the Assembly is not in session the Council of State (29 members) is vested with wide powers. The senior executive body is the Council of Ministers. The Chairman of the Council of State is also President of the Socialist Republic of the Union of Burma. The Burmese Socialist Programme Party is the only legal political party.

Political Divisions.—Burma is comprised of seven States (Chin, Kachin, Karen, Kayah, Mon, Rakhine, Shan) and seven Divisions (Irrawaddy, Magwe, Mandalay, Pegu, Rangoon, Sagaing, Tenasserim).

Education.—The literacy rate is high compared with other Asian countries, there is no caste system and women engage freely in social intercourse and play an important part in agriculture and retail trade.

Most Burmese children attend primary school, and about four million are currently enrolled; in middle and high schools, 11 million. There are two universities, at Rangoon and Mandalay, and in 1982–83 the numbers graduating were 6,610. A number of autonomous institutes of university standard award their own degrees. Under the two universities are three affiliated Degree Colleges and the Workers' College, Rangoon. There are also 14 two-year colleges affiliated to the universities, spread throughout the country. After completion of the two-year courses at these colleges students can join the third-year classes of the universities.

There are three Teachers' Training Institutes for middle and primary schools, and 13 Teachers' Training Schools for primary only. Seven Government Technical Institutes offer post-secondary technical training courses and 14 Technical High Schools train semi-skilled tradesmen. Six Agricultural Institutes offer training courses in agriculture and veterinary science; nine Agricultural High Schools train semi-skilled agriculturists. There are 34 Vocational Schools for weaving, handicrafts, etc.

Finance.—The chief sources of revenue are profits on state trading, income-tax, customs duties, commercial taxes and excise duties; the chief heads of expenditure are general administration, defence, education, police and development. The budget estimates for 1984–85 were: Revenue, K86,625,070,000; Expenditure, K40,884,733,000. The monetary unit is the *Kyat* of 100 *Pyas*.

Production, Industry and Commerce.—Three-quarters of the population depend on agriculture; the chief products are rice, oilseeds (sesamum and groundnut), maize, millet, cotton, beans, wheat, grain, tea, sugarcane, Virginia and Burmese tobacco, jute and rubber. Rice has traditionally been the mainstay of Burma's economy and the quantity of rice and by-products available for export was 722,000 tons in 1982–83. The principal export after rice is teak, of which 136,200 cubic tons was exported in 1982–83.

Burma is rich in minerals, including petroleum, lead, silver, tungsten, zinc, tin, wolfram and gemstones. Of these, petroleum products are the most important. Oil is now being produced from oilfields in Myanaung, Prome and Shwepyitha and at Chauk, Yenangyaung, Mann, and Letpando. Production of crude oil in 1982–83 totalled 9,789,000 U.S. barrels. There is a refinery at the main oilfield, Chauk, another at Syriam near Rangoon and a third is being built at Mann. There has been a slight decline in Burma's oil production in recent years and the country is no longer self-sufficient. Onshore exploration continues. In 1982–83 there was also some offshore oil exploration on a small scale. Major reserves of natural gas have been discovered in the Martaban Gulf, which Burma is hoping to develop.

All industrial activity of any size is in the public sector. Under development plans, projects completed or under construction with overseas financial and technical assistance include the production of cement, bricks and tiles, sheet glass, steel sections, jute bags and twine, cotton yarns, cotton and cotton mixture cloth, pharmaceuticals, sugar, paper, plywood, urea fertilizers, soda ash, tractors and tyres; also a hydro-electric scheme and various irrigation works. Japan continues to be the major individual donor of soft loans and grant aid in the industrial and agricultural sectors. West Germany has also been an important contributor of soft loans.

Loans amounting to US $125 million have been extended by the World Bank. As a member of the Colombo Plan since 1952 Burma continues to receive technical assistance from a number of countries and international agencies.

Trade with U.K.

	1983	1984
Imports from U.K.	£21,927,000	£16,488,000
Exports to U.K.	4,726,000	6,420,000

Communications.—The Irrawaddy and its chief tributary, the Chindwin, form important waterways,

the main stream being navigable beyond Bhamo (900 miles from its mouth) and carrying much traffic.

The chief seaports are Rangoon, Moulmein, Akyab and Bassein. Transit from London to Rangoon: by sea, 35 days; by air (via Bangkok), 16 hours.

The Burma Railways network covers 2,764 route miles, extending to Myitkyina, on the Upper Irrawaddy. There were 2,452 miles of Union highways and 11,767 miles of other main roads in 1982–83. The airport at Mingaladon, about 13 miles north of Rangoon, only handles limited international air traffic.

CAPITAL.—The chief city of Lower Burma, and the seat of the government of the Union is Rangoon, on the left bank of the Rangoon river, about 21 miles from the sea. The city contains the Shwe Dagon pagoda, much venerated by Burmese Buddhists. Population (1983): Rangoon District, 3,973,872; city population, 2,458,712.

Mandalay is the chief city of Upper Burma, population (1983): Mandalay district, 4,580,923; city, 532,985; Moulmein of 219,991 and Bassein of 144,092. Pagan, on the Irrawaddy, S.W. of Mandalay, contains many sacred buildings.

FLAG.—The Union flag is red, with a canton of dark blue, inside which are a cogwheel and two rice ears surrounded by 14 white stars.

NATIONAL DAY.—January 4.

BRITISH EMBASSY
80 Strand Road (Box No. 638), Rangoon

Ambassador Extraordinary and Plenipotentiary, His Excellency Nicholas Maxted Fenn, C.M.G. (1982).
1st Secretaries, D. L. Smallman (*Head of Chancery and Consul*); D. Rees (*Commercial*).
Cultural Attaché and British Council Representative, R. P. Hale.

BURUNDI
(Republic of Burundi)

President, Col. Jean-Baptiste Bagaza, *assumed office* Nov. 1, 1976, *elected* Dec. 1979, *re-elected*, Aug. 31, 1984.

COUNCIL OF MINISTERS

Defence, The President.
Parliamentary Relations, Lt.-Col. Stanislas Mandi.
Planning, Mathias Sinameye.
Justice, Vincent Ndikumasabo.
Interior, Lt.-Col. Charles Kazatsa.
Foreign Relations and Co-operation, Laurent Nzeyimana.
Finance, Pierre Ngenzi.
Rural Development, Jean Kabura.
Agriculture, Alexis Ntibakiganya.
Trade and Industry, Albert Muganga.
Transport, Posts and Communications, Rémy Nkengurutse.
Public Works, Energy and Mines, Isidore Nyaboya.
Public Health, Fidèle Nzabimana.
Education, Isidore Hakizimana.
Women's Affairs, Ms. Euphrasie Kandeke.
Social Affairs and Work, Mrs. Caritas Mategeko.
Labour and Professional Training, Cyrile Barancira.
Youth, Sports and Culture, Baltazar Habonimana.
Information, Benoît Muyebe.
Civil Service, Damien Barakamfitye.

Formerly a Belgian trusteeship under the United Nations, Burundi was proclaimed an independent State on July 1, 1962. Situated on the east side of Lake Tanganyika, the State has an area of 10,747 sq. miles and a population (estimated, 1984) of 4,480,000. The majority of the population are of the Bahutu ethnic group, but power rests in the hands of the minority Batutsi ethnic group.

Burundi became independent as a constitutional monarchy but this was overthrown on November 28, 1966 and the country became a republic. On Nov. 1, 1976, the government of President Micombero was overthrown and a Supreme Revolutionary Council led by Col. Jean-Baptiste Bagaza took power. In 1980 the S.R.C. was replaced by a political bureau and central committee as part of a process of political normalization, which continued with elections to the National Assembly, a 65-member legislature. The most recent elections were in Oct. 1982.

The chief crop is coffee, representing about 80 per cent of Burundi's export earnings. Cotton is the second most important crop. Minerals, tea, hides and skins exports are also important.

Trade with U.K.

	1983	1984
Imports from U.K.	£3,200,000	£1,710,000
Exports to U.K.	3,500,000	1,924,000

The currency is the Burundi *Franc*.

CAPITAL.—Bujumbura (*formerly* Usumbura), with about 150,000 inhabitants. Kitega (18,000 inhabitants) is the only other sizeable town. Official languages are Kirundi, a Bantu language, and French. Kiswahili is also used.

FLAG.—White diagonal cross on green and red quarters, with a circular white panel in the centre.

NATIONAL DAY.—July 1.

British Ambassador (see Kinshasa, Zaire).

CAMBODIA

COALITION GOVERNMENT OF
DEMOCRATIC KAMPUCHEA

President, Prince Norodom Sihanouk.
Vice-President responsible for Foreign Affairs, Khieu Samphan.
Prime Minister, Son Sann.

PEOPLE'S REPUBLIC OF KAMPUCHEA

Head of State, Heng Samrin.
Chairman of Council of Ministers and Foreign Minister, Hun Sen.

Area and Population.—Situated between Thailand and the south of Vietnam and extending from the border with Laos on the north to the Gulf of Thailand, Cambodia covers an area of some 70,000 square miles. It has a population (1981) of approximately 6 million. The climate is tropical monsoon with a rainy season from May to October. (*For* MAP, *see* Index.)

Fifty per cent. of the total land area is forest or jungle, abounding in wild life of all kinds, including big game. Around the Tonlé Sap lake in the centre of the country and along the Mekong river, which traverses the country, there is ample fertile land for the support of the population in times of peace.

History.—Once a powerful kingdom, which, as the Khmer Empire, flourished between the tenth and fourteenth centuries, Cambodia became a French protectorate in 1863 and was granted independence within the French Union as an Associate State in 1949. Full independence was proclaimed on November 9, 1953, and the process was completed when, in January, 1955, the Kingdom of Cambodia became financially and economically independent not only of France but also of Laos and Vietnam. For the next fifteen years the political life of the country was dominated by Prince Norodom Sihanouk, first as King, then as Head of Government after he had abdicated in favour of his father and finally (following his father's death in 1960) as Head of State.

On March 18, 1970, during his absence from the country, Prince Sihanouk was deposed as Head of State by a vote of the National Assembly. A Republic was declared on October 9, 1970, and the name of the country changed to the Khmer Republic.

In April 1970 widespread fighting developed between communist Vietnamese and Khmer forces which gradually developed into a general civil war and in April 1975 Phnom-Penh fell to the North Vietnamese-backed Khmer Rouge. Prince Sihanouk returned to Cambodia on September 9, as nominal Head of State. However, a new Constitution was promulgated in Jan. 1976 and elections to a People's Representative Assembly were held in March. Prince Sihanouk resigned as Head of State in April, and when the Assembly met on April 11 Khieu Samphan was elected President of the State Presidium. A Government led by Pol Pot, the leader of the Communist party, was appointed.

On Dec. 25, 1978 Vietnamese troops invaded Cambodia in support of an uprising by the Cambodian National United Front. The Cambodian capital, Phnom-Penh, fell on Jan. 7, 1979. The following day the Cambodian National United Front for National Salvation established a People's Revolutionary Council, recognized by Vietnam, U.S.S.R. and by other, chiefly Soviet-aligned, countries. The regime, which remains almost totally dependent on the Vietnamese, is opposed by the Khmer Rouge forces and non-communist nationalist groups which in June 1982 formed the Coalition Government of Democratic Kampuchea. The C.G.D.K. replaces the purely Khmer Rouge government; and it occupies Cambodia's seat at the U.N.

Economy.—Cambodia has an economy based on agriculture, fishing and forestry, the bulk of its people being rice-growing farmers. In addition to rice, which is the staple crop, the major products are rubber, livestock, maize, timber, pepper, palm sugar, fresh and dried fish, kapok, beans, soya and tobacco. Rice and rubber used to be the main exports though production was brought to a standstill by the hostilities. Following the Khmer Rouge victory, the populations of Phnom-Penh and other towns were forcibly evacuated to the country to work on the land, and re-establish the plantations producing such crops as cotton, rubber and bananas. Following the Vietnamese invasion of 1978 the towns were repopulated and commerce revived; currency was reintroduced. Factories, in particular textile mills, iron smelting works and cement works were put back in production.

Trade with U.K.

	1983	1984
Imports from U.K.	£826,000	£635,000
Exports to U.K.	184,000	72,000

Communications.—The country had over 5,000 kilometres of roads, of which nearly half are hard-surfaced and passable in the rainy season. There are two railways, one from Phnom-Penh to the Thai border; the other from Phnom-Penh to Kampot and Kompong Som, but operations and repairs are hindered by the continuing fighting. Phnom-Penh is on a river capable of receiving ships of up to 2,500 tons all the year round. The deep water port at Kompong Som on the Gulf of Thailand can receive ships up to 10,000 tons. The port is linked to Phnom-Penh by a modern highway.

Religion and Education.—The state religion was Buddhism of the "Little Vehicle". The new constitution guaranteed religious freedom, but in practice Buddhism was suppressed by the Khmer Rouge. There has been some revival recently. There were also small Muslim and Christian communities, but many members of them died or fled the country during Khmer Rouge rule. The national language is Khmer. In the years preceding the civil war considerable efforts were devoted to the development of education and new schools, colleges and technical institutes had been established. Until April 1975 there was a Buddhist University in Phnom-Penh, and several residential teachers' training colleges were in operation. However, most of the country's educated elite died under the Khmer Rouge regime, which closed all institutions of higher education.

CAPITAL.—Phnom-Penh.

FLAG.—(C.G.D.K.) Red, with a yellow three-towered temple in the middle. (P.R.K.) Red with a yellow five-towered temple in the middle.

CAMEROON
(Republic of Cameroon)

President, Head of State, Government and Commander in Chief of the Armed Forces, Paul Biya, *acceded* Nov. 6, 1982 on resignation of Pres. Ahidjo, *elected* Jan. 14, 1984, *sworn in* Jan. 21, 1984.

MINISTRY

Youth and Sports, Mbombo Njoya.
Foreign Affairs, William Eteki Mboumoua.
Territorial Administration, Jean-Marcel Mengueme.
Finance, Etienne Ntsama.
Public Service, René Ze Nguele.
Higher Education and Scientific Research, Bol Alima Gibering.
Animal Husbandry, Fisheries and Animal Industries, Hamadjoda Adjoudji.
Social Affairs, Mrs. Rose Zang Nguele.
Posts and Telecommunications, Félix Tonye Mbog.
Town Planning and Housing, Babale Abdoulaye.
Transport, Benjamin Itoe.
Information and Culture, François Sengat Kuo.
Equipment, Thomas Dakayi Kamga.
Agriculture, Sadou Hayatou.
Computer Services and Public Contracts, Daniel Kamgueu.
Mines and Power, Michael Tabong Kima.
National Education, Robert Mbella Mbappe.
Women's Affairs, Mrs. Yaou Boubakari.
Commerce and Industry, Edouard Nomo Ongolo.
Labour and Social Insurance, Dr. Joseph Fofe.
Public Health, Prof. Victor Anomah Ngu.
Ministers of State, Gilbert Anze Tsoungu (*Armed Forces*); André Ngongang Ouandji (*Justice*); Youssoufa Daouda (*Planning and Territorial Development*).
Ministers Delegate, Dr. Joseph Zambo (*Relations with Assemblies*); Mahamat Paba Sale (*Foreign Affairs*); Joseph C. Awunti (*General State Inspectorate and Administrative Reforms*).
Ministers at the Presidency of the Republic with special functions, Dr. Joseph Zambo; Georges Ngango; Joseph C. Doumba.
Ministers, Presidency of the Republic, D. Abouem á Tchoyi (*Sec.-Gen, Presidency*); J. Nkuete, M. Labarang, C. Nsanhlai (*Asst. Secs.-Gen, Presidency*); P. Mataga (*Dir., Civil Cabinet*).

CAMEROON EMBASSY
84 Holland Park, W11 3SB
[01–727 0771]

Ambassador Extraordinary and Plenipotentiary, His Excellency Ferdinand Leopold Oyono (1984).

The Republic of Cameroon lies on the Gulf of Guinea between Nigeria to the west, Chad and the Central African Republic to the east and Congo and Gabon and Equatorial Guinea to the south. It has an area of 475,400 sq. km. and a population of 8,320,000 (1980 estimate).

The whole territory was administered by Germany from 1884 to 1916. From 1916 to 1959, the former East Cameroon was administered by France as a League of Nations (later U.N.) trusteeship. On Jan. 1, 1960 it became independent as the Republic of Cameroon. The Republic was joined on October 1, 1961, by the former British administered trust territory of the Southern Cameroons, after a plebiscite held under United Nations auspices. Cameroon became a Federal Republic with separate East and West Cameroon state governments. Subsequently, after plebiscite held in May, 1972, Cameroon became a United Republic.

Cameroon is the only country in Africa where French and English are both official languages enjoying equal status, and the government's declared long-term objective is to achieve complete "bilingualism" and "biculturalism".

The main economic emphasis is on agricultural development, both through encouraging small-scale peasant agriculture, and through the development of large-scale agro-industrial complexes, with the aim of making the country agriculturally self-sufficient and a major food exporter.

Principal products are cocoa, coffee, bananas, cotton, timber, ground-nuts, aluminium, rubber and palm products. There is an aluminium smelting plant at Edéa with an annual capacity of 50,000 tons. Oil is now also one of Cameroon's principal products with an estimated production of 6·4m. tonnes during 1983.

TRADE

	1982
Total imports	*FCFA*392,600 m.
Total exports	326,900 m.

Trade with U.K.

	1983	1984
Imports from U.K.	£25,445,000	£23,254,000
Exports to U.K.	52,481,000	132,539,000

CAPITAL.—Yaoundé (1984 estimate, 522,000). Ψ Douala (1984 estimate, 763,000) is the commercial centre.

FLAG.—Vertical stripes of green, red and yellow with single five-pointed yellow star in centre of red stripe.

BRITISH EMBASSY
Avenue Winston Churchill, B.P. 547
Yaoundé

Ambassador Extraordinary and Plenipotentiary, His Excellency James Glaze (1984).
1st Secretaries, Miss K. Oliver (*Head of Chancery and Consul*); R. Godfrey (*Aid*).
2nd Secretary, D. M. Gray (*Commercial/Information*).
British Council Representative, C. H. Mogford, Les Galéries, Rue J. F. Kennedy, (B.P. 818), Yaoundé.

CAPE VERDE ISLANDS
(Republic of Cape Verde)

President, Aristides Pereira *born* 1924, *assumed office,* July 5, 1975.
Prime Minister, Pedro Pires.

The Cape Verde Islands, off the west coast of Africa, consist of two groups of islands, *Windward* (Santo Antão, São Vicente, Santa Luzia, São Nicolau, Boa Vista and Sal) and *Leeward* (Maio, São Tiago, Fogo and Brava) with a total area of 1,516 sq. miles. The population at the 1980 Census was 296,093, the majority of whom are Roman Catholic.

The Islands, colonized in c. 1460, achieved independence from Portugal on July 5, 1975, under the nationalist party of Guinea Bissau and Cape Verde. A federation of the islands with Guinea Bissau was planned (till 1879 Guinea-Bissau and the Islands were a single administrative unit) but this was dropped following the 1980 coup in Guinea Bissau.

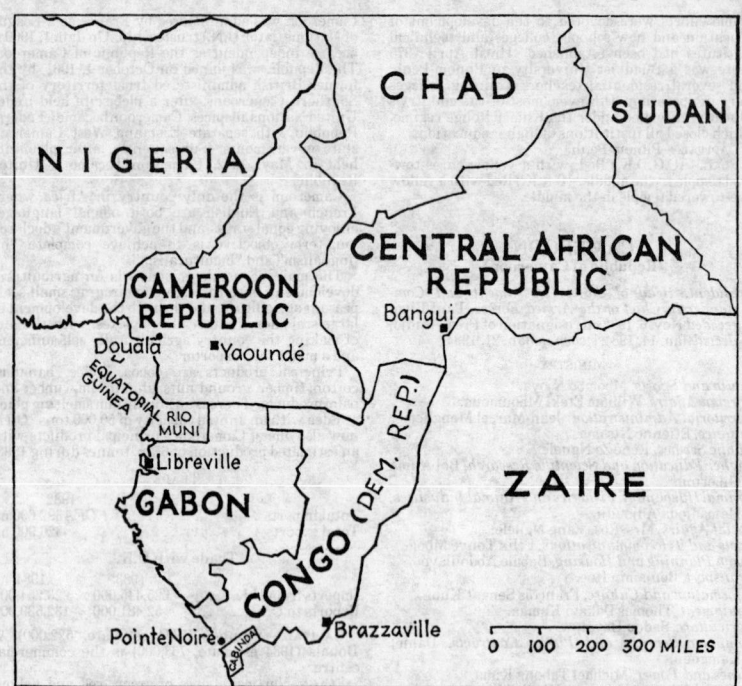

The Republic is a one-party (the P.A.I.C.V.) state with a President elected by the National Assembly. He has a mandate of 5 years, as do Assembly deputies, who are elected by universal adult suffrage.

The islands have had little rain since 1969, and agriculture is mostly confined to irrigated inland valleys, the chief products being bananas and coffee (for export), maize, sugarcane and nuts. Fish and shellfish are important exports. Salt is obtained on Sal, Boa Vista and Maio; volcanic rock is also mined for export. The main ports are Praia and Mindelo, and there is an international airport on Sal.

Trade with U.K.

	1983	1984
Imports from U.K.	£1,246,000	£1,162,000
Exports to U.K.	122,000	211,000

CAPITAL, Ψ Praia (1970, 6,000).

FLAG.—Horizontal band of yellow over green, with a vertical red band in the hoist charged with a black star over a garland of maize sheaves, two corn cobs and a clam shell.

British Ambassador (resident at Dakar, Senegal.)

CENTRAL AFRICAN REPUBLIC

Head of State, Gen. André Kolingba, *assumed power* Sept. 1, 1981.

MILITARY COMMITTEE FOR NATIONAL RECOVERY

Chairman, Defence and War Veterans, Gen. André Kolingba.

Ministers of State, Col. Alphonse Gombadi (*Rural Development*); Lt. Col. Jean-Louis Gervil Yambala (*Economy and Finance*).

Ministers:

Foreign Affairs and International Cooperation, Second Lt. C. M. N'Gai Voueto.
Public Works and Urban Affairs, Maj.-Gen. Abel Nado.
Interior, Lt. Col. Christophe Grelombe.
National Education, Maj. Gabriel Ngaindiro.
Public Health, Maj. Gen. X. S. Yangongo.
Justice, Maj. Gaspard Kalene.
Posts and Telecommunications, Capt. Samuel Ngaiouma.
Civil Service, Labour and Social Security, Maj. S. Pollagba.
Trade and Industry, Capt. Luc Nganafei.
Transport and Civil Aviation, Capt. Raymond Ndougou.
Secretaries of State, Col. G.-L. Djengbot (*Energy*); Capt. R. Adelaye (*Hydraulic Resources*); Lt. M. Salle (*General Secretariat*).

The Republic lies just north of the Equator between the Cameroon Republic, the Republic of Chad, the southern part of Sudan and Zaire. The Republic has an area of about 234,000 sq. miles and a population (1983 estimate) of 2,470,000.

On December 1, 1958, the French colony of Ubanghi Shari elected to remain within the French Community and adopted the title of the Central African Republic. It became fully independent on August 17, 1960. The first President of the Central African

Republic, M. David Dacko, held office from 1960 until Jan. 1, 1966, when he was replaced by the then Col. Bokassa after a *coup d'état*. On Dec. 4, 1976, President Bokassa proclaimed himself Emperor and a new constitution (Parliamentary Monarchy) was introduced, the country being known as the Central African Empire. On Sept. 20, 1979, Emperor Bokassa was deposed by M. David Dacko in a bloodless *coup* and the country reverted to a Republic. President Dacko surrendered power on 1st September 1981 to army commander Gen. Andre Kolingba in a bloodless *coup*.

Economy.—A programme of economic reconstruction is under way, concentrating on agricultural production and private investment. Cotton, diamonds, coffee and timber are the major exports;

Trade with U.K.

	1983	1984
Imports from U.K.	£536,000	£722,000
Exports to U.K.	902,000	357,000

CAPITAL.—Bangui, near the border with Zaire (350,000).

FLAG.—Four horizontal stripes, blue, white, green, yellow, crossed by central vertical red stripe with a yellow five-pointed star in top left-hand corner.

CHAD REPUBLIC

Head of State and President of the Council of Ministers, Hissein Habré, *took office* June 1982.

Situated in north-central Africa, the Chad Republic extends from 23° N. latitude to 7° N. latitude and is flanked by the Republics of Niger and Cameroon on the west, by Libya in the north, by the Sudan on the east and by the Central African Republic on the south. (*For* MAP, *see* Index.) It has an area of 488,000 sq. miles and a population now estimated at 4,000,000.

Chad became a member state of the French Community on Nov. 28, 1958, and was proclaimed fully independent on August 11, 1960. On April 14, 1962, a new Constitution was adopted involving a presidential-type regime. This was suspended on April 13, 1975 when President Tombalbaye was killed in a military coup. The country was run by a Supreme Military Council, under General Felix Malloum until his overthrow in February 1979. A Transitional Government of National Unity, headed by Goukouni Oueddei, was replaced in June 1982 by one headed by Hissein Habre. Forces commanded by Oueddei, and supported by Libyan troops, occupy the north of Chad.

About 90 per cent of the workforce is occupied in agriculture, fishing and forestry. There is an oilfield in Kanem and salt is mined around Lake Chad, but the most important activities are cotton growing (mostly in the south) and animal husbandry (in central areas). Raw cotton and meat are the main exports.

Trade with U.K.

	1983	1984
Imports from U.K	£2,244,000	£3,531,000
Exports to U.K.	8,000	626,000

CAPITAL.—Ndjaména (formerly known as Fort Lamy) south of Lake Chad (150,000).

FLAG.—Vertical stripes, blue, yellow and red.

British Ambassador (*Non-Resident*), His Excellency Michael Daly.

CHILE
(República de Chile)

Head of State, Army Commander-in-Chief and President of the Republic, General Augusto Pinochet (Ugarte), *born*, November 25, 1915.

Junta Members, Admiral José Toribio Merino (Castro), C.-in-C. Navy; General Fernando Matthei (Aubel), C.-in-C. Air Force; General César Mendoza (Durán), Director-General of Carabineros; General César Raul Benavides Escobar (Army).

CABINET

Foreign Affairs, Jaime del Valle Alliende.
Interior, Ricardo García.
Defence, Vice Adm. Patricio Carvajal.
Education, Horacio Aranguiz.
Mines, Samuel Lira.
Finance, Hernán Büchi.
Justice, Hugo Rosende.
Public Works, Brig.-Gen. Bruno Siebert.
Transport, Gen. Enrique Escobar.
Agriculture, Jorge Prado Aranguiz.
National Patrimony, Gen. René Peri Fagerstrom.
Labour and Social Security, Alfonso Márquez de la Plata.
Health, Winston Chinchon.
Housing, Miguel Angel Poduje.
Economic Affairs, Modesto Collados.
Planning, Gen. Sergio Valenzuela.
Energy, Gen. Hernan Brady.
Secretary General of the Government, Francisco Javier Cuadra.

CHILEAN EMBASSY AND CONSULATE IN LONDON
12 Devonshire Street, W1N 2DS
[01–580 6392/4]

Ambassador Extraordinary and Plenipotentiary, His Excellency Mario Silva.

A State of South America lying between the Andes and the shores of the South Pacific, Chile extends coastwise from just north of Arica to Cape Horn south, between lat. 17° 15′ and 55° 59′ S. and long. 66° 30′ and 75° 48′ W. Extreme length of the country is about 2,800 miles, with an average breadth, north of 41°, of 100 miles. The great chain of the Andes runs along its eastern limit, with a general elevation of 5,000 to 15,000 feet above the level of the sea; but numerous summits attain a greater height. The chain, however, lowers considerably towards its southern extremity. The Andes form a boundary with Argentina, and at the head of the pass where the international road from Chile to Argentina crosses the frontier, has been erected a statue of *Christ the Redeemer*, 26 feet high, made of bronze from old cannon, to commemorate the peaceful settlement of a boundary dispute in 1902. There are no rivers of great size, and none of them is of much service as a navigable highway. In the north the country is arid. The total area of the Republic is estimated at 290,000 square miles, with a population (estimated, 1979) of 11,000,000. (*For* MAP, *see* p. 794.)

Among the island possessions of Chile are the *Juan Fernandez* group (3 islands) about 360 miles distant from Valparaiso. One of these islands is the reputed scene of Alexander Selkirk's (Robinson Crusoe) shipwreck. *Easter Island* (27° 8′ S. and 109° 28′ W.), about 2,000 miles distant in the South Pacific Ocean, contains stone platforms and hundreds of stone figures, the origin of which has not yet been determined. The area of the island is about 45 sq. miles.

Chile is divided into 12 regions and the Metropolitan Area. Two of these regions, Arica and Antofagasta, were annexed from Peru and Bolivia respectively after the War of the Pacific (1879–84). The province of Tacna was also annexed but under a treaty signed in 1929 was returned to Peru which at the same time received payment of £1,200,000 for Arica. The disputed boundary with Argentina in the Beagle Channel was settled by a treaty ratified in May 1985. The Chilean population has four main sources: (*a*) indigenous Araucanian Indians, Fuegians, and Changos; (*b*) Spanish settlers and their descendants; (*c*) mixed Spanish Indians; and (*d*) European immigrants. Only the few remaining indigenous Indians and some originally Bolivian Indians in the north are racially separate. Following extensive intermarriage there is no effective distinction among the remainder.

Government.—Chile was discovered by Spanish adventurers in the 16th century and remained under Spanish rule until 1810, when a revolutionary war, culminating in the *Battle of Maipu* (April 5, 1818), achieved the independence of the nation.

At a general election held on Sept. 4, 1970, the Marxist candidate Dr. Allende was elected President by a narrow margin. After severe industrial unrest and widespread violent incidents, Allende was overthrown on September 11, 1973, in a *coup* carried out by leaders of the Armed Forces and National Police. President Allende was said to have committed suicide.

After a national plebiscite, the Constitution of 1925 was replaced early in 1981 and Gen. Pinochet was sworn in as President, to serve until 1989, Economically, the regime is pursuing a free-market economy and the level of inflation has been reduced, from 1,000 per cent in 1973 to about 23 per cent in 1983.

Production.—Cereals, legumes, sugar beet, vegetables, fruit, tobacco, hemp and vines are grown extensively (especially in the central zone) and livestock accounts for nearly 40 per cent of agricultural production. Sheep farming predominates in the extreme south (Province of Magallanes). There are large timber tracts in the central and southern zones of Chile, some types of which are exported, along with wood derivatives such as cellulose.

The mineral wealth is considerable, the country being particularly rich in copper-ore, iron-ore and nitrate. Chile also produces iodine, manganese ore, coal, mercury, molybdenum, zinc, lead and a small quantity of gold. Uranium is also said to have been discovered in small quantities. The rainless north is the scene of the only commercial production of nitrate of soda (Chile saltpetre) from natural resources in the world. The country has also large deposits of high grade sulphur, but mostly around high extinct volcanoes in the Andes Cordillera, difficult of access. Oil was struck in Magallanes (Tierra del Fuego) in December, 1945, and oil and natural gas are produced in the Magallanes area from on- and off-shore wells. This domestic production, which covers approximately 50 per cent of total oil requirement, plus imported crude oil is refined at Concon and San Vicente in the central part of the country. There is a steel plant at Huachipato, near Concepción.

Production figures for 1984 were:

Copper (tonnes)	1,290,000
Potassium and sodium nitrate (tonnes)	712,600
Coal (tonnes)	1,310,450
Steel ingots (tonnes)	662,800
Crude oil (cu. metres)	2,336,800
Natural gas (cu. metres)	4,897,600

Industry is based on the processing of mineral, forestry and agricultural products, and the manufacture of consumer goods.

Communications.—Chilean ships have a virtual monopoly in the coastwide trade, though, with the improvement of the roads, an increasing share of internal transportation is moving by road and rail. The Chilean mercantile marine numbers about 63 vessels (of over 100 tons gross) with a total deadweight tonnage of 737,789 (1983).

There are 6,575 miles of railway track. A metre-gauge line (the *Longitudinál*) runs from La Calera, just north of Santiago, to Iquique. The wide gauge railway runs from Valparaiso through La Calera, 60 miles inland, and after passing through Santiago ends at Puerto Montt.

With the completion of a section of 435 miles from Corumba, Brazil, to Santa Cruz, Bolivia, the Trans-Continental Line will link the Chilean Pacific port of Arica with Rio de Janeiro on the Atlantic. Another line from Antofagasta to Salta (Argentine) was opened in 1948. Further south, the Trans-Andine Railway connects Valparaiso on the Pacific with Buenos Aires, crossing the Andes at 11,500 ft. However services have now been suspended due to financial difficulties.

Chile is served by about 20 international airlines. The domestic traffic is carried by the State-owned Linea Aerea Nacional and the privately-owned LADECO, which also operate internationally, and smaller regional carriers. Chile has an extensive system of airports.

Chile's road system is about 65,000 kilometres in length, but only an estimated 7,000 kilometres are first-class paved highways.

Defence.—Military service is compulsory, but not all those who are liable are required. Recruitment for the Navy is voluntary. The Navy consists of 3 cruisers, 12 destroyers, frigates and escorts, some patrol vessels and FPBs and 3 submarines. There is a support force of transports, tankers, 1 submarine depôt ship and ancillary small craft. The strength of the Navy is 1,000 officers and 14,000 men, plus a Marine Force of 60 officers and 2,000 men. The Army's total strength is 50,000, which includes 3,000 officers and 25,000 conscripts (2 years). In addition there is a police force of "Carabineros" of 30,000 officers and men. The Air Force has 800 officers and 8,700 other ranks, with a strength of 200 aircraft.

Education.—Elementary education is free, and has been compulsory since 1920. There are 8 Universities (3 in Santiago, 2 in Valparaiso, 1 in Antofagasta, 1 in Concepción and 1 in Valdivia). The religion is Roman Catholic.

Language and Literature.—Spanish is the language of the country, with admixtures of local words of Indian origin. Recent efforts have reduced illiteracy and have thus afforded access to the literature of Spain, to supplement the vigorous national output. The Nobel Prize for Literature was awarded in 1945 to Señorita Gabriela Mistral, for Chilean verse and prose, and in 1971 to the poet Pablo Neruda. There are over 100 newspapers and a large number of periodicals.

FINANCE

	1983*
Total revenue	US$3,164 m.
Total expenditure	3,485 m.

* estimated.

Foreign debt at December 31, 1984 was provisionally quoted at U.S. $20,000 million.

EXTERNAL TRADE
($U.S. ,000)

	1983	1984
Total imports	2,969,000	3,481,000
Total exports	3,836,500	3,657,000

Trade with U.K.

	1983	1984
Imports from U.K.	£43,520,000	£74,997,000
Exports to U.K.	107,644,000	108,420,000

The principal exports are metallic and non-metallic minerals (copper represented 43 per cent. of total export earnings in 1984), wood derivatives, some metal products, fish products, vegetables, fruit and wool. The principal imports are wheat, sugar and other food products, industrial raw materials, machinery, equipment and spares, oil fuels, lubricants and transportation equipment.

CAPITAL, Santiago, 4,000,000 (Greater Santiago), Other large towns are:—ΨValparaiso (500,000), Concepción (170,000), Temuco (110,000), ΨAntofagasta (110,000), Chillán (79,461), ΨTalcahuano (75,643), Talca (75,354); ΨValdivia (70,000), ΨIquique (50,000), ΨPunta Arenas (50,000). Punta Arenas on the Straits of Magellan, is the southernmost city in the world.

FLAG.—2 horizontal bands, white, red; in top sixth a white star on blue square, next staff.

NATIONAL DAY.—September 18 (National Anniversary).

BRITISH EMBASSY
Avenida La Concepción 177, Santiago 9
(Casilla 72D)

Ambassador Extraordinary and Plenipotentiary, John K. Hickman, C.M.G.
Counsellor, Head of Chancery and Consul-General, Miss M. G. Fort.
Defence Attaché, Capt. M. S. Ashley, R.N.
Cultural Attaché, D. J. Harvey.

BRITISH CONSULAR OFFICES
There are British Consular Offices at *Santiago, Arica, Valparaiso* and *Punta Arenas.*

BRITISH COUNCIL
Representative, D. J. Harvey, Eliodoro Yañez 832, Santiago (Casilla 154-D). The Council supplies books to the libraries of the *Instituto Chileno-Britanico* in *Santiago, Viña del Mar/Valparaiso* and *Concepción.*

BRITISH-CHILEAN CHAMBER OF COMMERCE
Augustinas 972 O.F. 1011, Santiago
(*Postal Address,* Casilla 536, Santiago).

Valparaiso is distant from London 9,000 miles via Panama, and 11,000 via the Strait; transit 28 to 45 days; by air, 22 hrs.

CHINA
(Zhonghua Renmin Gongheguo—
The People's Republic of China.)

President of the People's Republic of China, Li Xiannian, *elected* June 1983.
Vice President, Ulanhu.
Chairman of the Standing Committee of the Sixth National People's Congress, Peng Zhen.
Chairman of the Central Military Commission, Deng Xiaoping.

STATE COUNCIL
Premier, Zhao Ziyang.
Vice-Premiers, Wan Li; Yao Yilin; Li Peng; Tian Jiyun.
State Councillors, Chen Muhua; Gu Mu; Ji Pengfei; Kang Shien; Song Ping; Wang Bingqian; Wu Xueqian; Zhang Aiping.

Ministers:
Agriculture, Animal Husbandry and Fisheries, He Kang.
Aviation Industry, Mo Wenxiang.
Chemical Industry, Qin Zhongda.
Civil Affairs, Cui Naifu.
Coal Industry, Yu Hongen.
Commerce, Lui Yi.
Communications, Qian Yongchang.

Culture, Zhu Muzhi.
Economic Relations and Foreign Trade, Zheng Tuobin.
Electronics Industry, Li Tieying.
Finance, Wang Bingqian.
Foreign Affairs, Wu Xueqian.
Forestry, Yang Zhong.
Geology and Minerals, Sun Daguang.
Justice, Zou Yu.
Labour and Personnel, Zhao Shouyi.
Light Industry, Yang Bo.
Machine Building Industry, Zhou Jiannan.
Metallurgical Industry, Li Dongye.
National Defence, Zhang Aiping.
Nuclear Industry, Jiang Xinxiong.
Ordnance Industry, Zou Jiahua.
Petroleum Industry, Wang Tao.
Posts and Telecommunications, Yang Taifang.
Public Health, Cui Yueli.
Public Security, Ruan Chongwu.
Radio and Television, Al Zhisheng.
Railways, Ding Guangeng.
Science, Technology and Industry for National Defence, Ding Henggao.
Space Industry, Li Xue.
State Security, Jia Chunwang.
Textile Industry, Wu Wenying.
Urban and Rural Construction and Environmental Protection, Rui Xingwen.
Water Conservancy and Power, Qian Zhengying.

MINISTERS IN CHARGE OF STATE COMMISSIONS
Economic, Lu Dong.
Education, Li Peng.
Family Planning, Wang Wei.
Nationalities Affairs, Yang Jingren.
Physical Culture and Sports, Li Menghua.
Planning, Song Ping.
Restructuring the Economic System, Zhao Ziyang.
Scientific and Technological, Song Jian.
Auditor General, Lu Peijian.
Secretary-General, Tian Jiyun.

President of the People's Bank of China, Chen Muhua.

THE CHINESE COMMUNIST PARTY
General Secretary, Hu Yaobang.
The Politburo Standing Committee, Hu Yaobang; Ye Jianying; Deng Xiaoping; Zhao Ziyang; Li Xiannian; Chen Yun.
The Politburo of the Central Committee, Wan Li; Xi Zhongxun; Wang Zhen; Fang Yi; Deng Xiaoping; Li Xiannian; Yang Shangkun; Yang Dezhi; Yu Qiuli; Chen Yun; Zhao Ziyang; Hu Qiaomu; Hu Yaobang; Ni Zhifu; Peng Zhen; Tian Jiyun; Yao Yilin; Li Peng; Wu Xueqian; Hu Qili; Qiao Shi (*full members*); Qin Jiwei; Chen Muhua (*alternate members*).
The Secretariat of the Central Committee, Wan Li; Deng Liqun; Yu Qiuli; Chen Pixian; Hu Qili; Hu Yaobang; Qiao Shi; Tian Jiyun; Li Peng; Hao Jianxiu; Wang Zhaoguo (*full members*); Qiao Shi (*alternate member*).
The Advisory Commission, Deng Xiaoping (*Chairman*); Bo Yibo; Xu Shiyou (*Vice Chairmen*).
The Discipline Inspection Commission, First Secretary, Chen Yun; Second Secretary, Huang Kecheng; Standing Secretary, Wang Heshou.
Membership, 40,000,000.

EMBASSY IN LONDON
31 Portland Place, W1N 3AG
[01–636 5726]

Ambassador Extraordinary and Plenipotentiary, Hu Dingyi (1985).

AREA AND POPULATION.—The area of China is

about 3,700,000 square miles. A nationwide census (the third) was held in July 1982, which recorded a total population of 1,008,175,288. China is anxious to control the growth of the population and has introduced stringent policies intended to result in a population of 1·2 billion by the year 2,000. About 6 per cent of the population belong to around 60 ethnic minorities. Among the largest are the Zhuang of Guangxi, the Uygurs of Xinjiang, the Tibetans and the Mongols.

THE PROVINCES OF CHINA

1982 census results were:

Anhui	49,665,724
Fujian	25,931,106
Gansu	19,569,261
Guangdong	59,299,220
Guangxi Zhuang Autonomous Region	36,420,960
Guizhou	28,552,997
Hebei	53,005,875
Heilongjiang	32,665,546
Henan	74,422,739
Hubei	47,804,150
Hunan	54,008,851
Jiangsu	60,521,114
Jiangxi	33,184,827
Liaoning	35,721,693
Nei Monggol Autonomous Region	19,274,279
Ningxia Hui Autonomous Region	3,895,578
Peking	9,230,687
Qinghai	3,895,706
Shaanxi	28,904,423
Shandong	74,419,054
Shanghai	11,859,748
Shanxi	25,291,389
Sichuan	99,713,310
(Taiwan	18,270,749)
Tianjin	7,764,141
Tibet Autonomous Region	1,892,392
Xinjiang Uygur Autonomous Region	13,081,681
Yunnan	32,553,817
Zhejiang	38,884,603
Armed Forces	4,238,210

Xinjiang is the largest region or province in area (about one sixth of the whole area of China) and Sichuan the most populous.

Government.—On October 10, 1911, the party of reform forced the Imperial dynasty to a "voluntary" abdication, and a Republic was proclaimed at Wuchang.

On September 30, 1949, the Chinese People's Political Consultative Conference (C.P.P.C.C) met in Peking and appointed the National People's Government Council under the Chairmanship of Mao Tse-tung. On October 1, Mao proclaimed the inauguration of the Chinese People's Republic.

The *régime* was recognized by all the Communist *bloc* countries in quick succession, and soon after by the Asian countries of the Commonwealth, the United Kingdom and by a number of other countries. Others, led by the United States, continued to recognize the Chiang Kai-shek *régime* on Taiwan as the rightful Government of China. In 1971 the People's Republic won acceptance into the United Nations on the expulsion of Taiwan. Since then many more countries have accorded recognition, including, among the most recent, the United States and Japan. To date, 129 countries have established diplomatic relations with China.

A new Constitution was adopted in December 1982, under which the National People's Congress is the highest organ of state power. It is elected for a term of five years and is supposed to hold one session a year. It is empowered to amend the Constitution, make laws, select the President and Vice-President and other leading officials of the state, approve the national economic plan, the state budget and the final state accounts, and to decide on questions of war and peace. The State Council is the highest organ of the state administration. It is composed of the Premier, the Vice Premiers, the State Councillors, heads of Ministries and Commissions, the Auditor General and the Secretary General. Command over the armed forces is vested in the newly established Central Military Commission, of which Deng Xiaoping is the Chairman.

Deputies to congresses at the primary level are "directly elected" by the voters "through a secret ballot after democratic consultation". This is now being extended to county level. These Congresses elect the Deputies to the Congress at the next higher level. Deputies to the National People's Congress are elected by the People's Congresses of the provinces, autonomous regions and municipalities directly under the Central Government, and by the armed forces.

Local government is conducted through People's Governments at provincial, municipal and county levels. Autonomous regions, prefectures and counties exist for national minorities and are described as self-governing. The system prevailing is that found elsewhere, i.e. People's Congresses and People's Governments. Peking, Shanghai and Tientsin continue to come directly under the central government.

Following the deaths of Mao Tse-tung and Chou En-lai in 1976 the disgraced Vice-Premier Deng Xiaoping was recalled. At the 11th Congress in 1977 Deng was elected Vice-Chairman and has since become the dominant force within the Party by eliminating leftist influence, rehabilitating fallen leaders and adjusting Maoist policies to meet the needs of a developing economy. Deng's policies were reaffirmed at the 12th Congress in 1982. The Congress also elected a new Party leadership dominated by Deng and his supporters. The post of Chairman of the Party was abolished. Hu Yaobang, as General Secretary, remained the Party leader.

Armed Forces.—All three military arms in China are parts of the People's Liberation Army (P.L.A.) The size of this body has not been formally given, but it is estimated that China has approximately 3·5 million men under arms, with a further 12 million (or perhaps many more) reserves who take part in militia activities. In June 1985 a planned reduction of over 1 million in the course of a year was officially announced. In 1955 compulsory military service was introduced for all men between the ages of 18 and 40. This service was on a selective basis. The present length of service for those conscripted is three years in the Army, four years in the Air Force and five years in the Navy. With effect from June 1, 1965, the rank structure was abolished, together with all marks of distinction of branch of service. Both are expected to be reinstated.

China exploded her first experimental nuclear device on Oct. 16, 1964 and made further tests in 1965 and in May, Oct. and Dec., 1966. Her first hydrogen bomb was tested in June, 1967. Further tests of nuclear devices and hydrogen bombs have since been announced, the latest being in Nov. 1976. China embarked on a programme of earth-satellite launchings in April 1970, the latest being made in January 1978. A long-range I.C.B.M. was tested in 1980, and a submarine-launched ballistic missile in 1982.

Religion.—The indigenous religions of China are Confucianism (which includes ancestor worship), Taoism (originally a philosophy rather than a religion) and, since its introduction in the first century of the Christian era, Buddhism. There are also Chinese Moslems (officially estimated at about 12 million) and Christians (unofficially estimated at about 50 million). Religious freedoms, severely curtailed during the Cultural Revolution, are reviving slightly under more liberal policies.

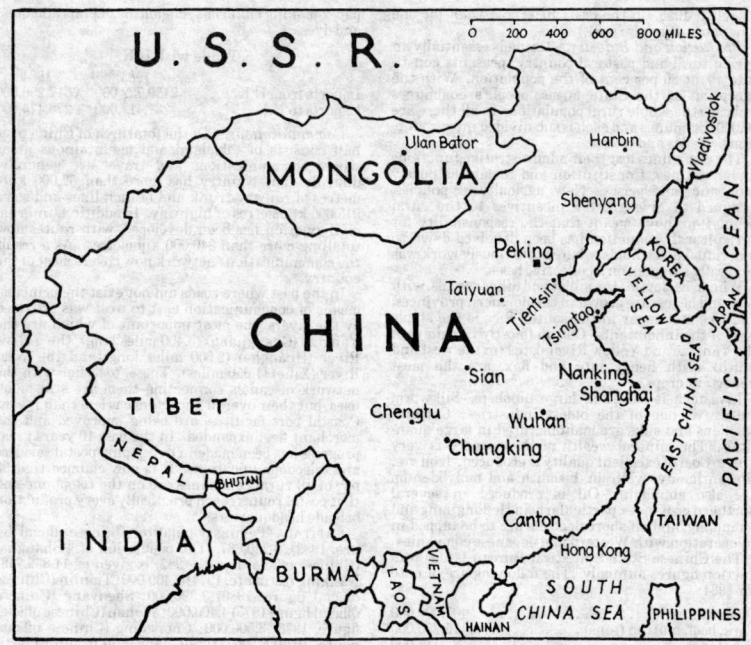

Education.—The Cultural Revolution caused considerable disruption to the educational system and since 1976 attempts have been made to raise academic standards. Primary education now lasts five years, and has a claimed enrolment of 139,720,000 pupils. Secondary education lasts five years (three years in Junior Middle School and two years in Senior Middle School). There were 46,844,000 Middle School pupils in 1982. The proportion of illiterates and semi-illiterates in 1982 was 23·5 per cent, but efforts are being made to expand secondary education, particularly in the rural areas. Particular attention is being paid to higher education where there are over 600 universities, colleges and institutes with an enrolment of 1,159,000 students. In May 1985 the Central Committee of the Party announced the abolition of free higher education except for teacher training, and the aim of providing all children with junior secondary education within 10 years.

Language and Literature.—The Chinese language has many dialects, notably Cantonese, Hakka, Amoy, Foochow, Changsha, Nanchang, Wu (Shanghai) and the northern dialect. The Common Speech or *Putonghua* (often referred to as "Mandarin") which is being taught throughout the country is based on the northern dialect. The Communists have promoted it as the national language and made intensive efforts to propagate it throughout the country. Since the most important aspect of this policy is the use of the spoken language in writing, the old literary style and ideographic form of writing has fallen into disuse.

In 1956, after some 4 years of study, the Government decided to introduce 230 simplified characters with a view to making reading and writing easier. The list was enlarged and there are now over 2,000 simplified characters in use. In Jan. 1956, all Chinese newspapers and most books began to appear with the characters printed horizontally from left to right, instead of vertically reading from right to left, as previously.

In Feb. 1958 The National People's Congress adopted a system of Romanization, known as pinyin, using 25 of the letters of the Latin alphabet (not v). This has been used within the country largely for assisting school children and others to learn the pronunciation of characters in *Putonghua*, and is now used for Chinese names in foreign-language publications.

Chinese literature is one of the richest in the world. Paper has been employed for writing and printing for nearly 2,000 years. The Confucian classics which formed the basis of the traditional Chinese culture date from the Warring States period (4th–3rd centuries B.C.) as do the earliest texts of the rival tradition, Taoism. Histories, philosophical and scientific works, poetry, literary and art criticism, novels and romances survive from most periods. Many have been translated into English. In the past all this considerable literature was available only to a very small class of *literati*, but with the spread of literacy in the 20th century, a process which has received enormous impetus since the Communists took over in 1950, the old traditional literature has been largely superseded by modern works of a popular kind and by the classics of Marxism and modern developments from them.

The most important among the newspapers and magazines are the People's Daily and the twice-monthly Red Flag, the communist party organs.

Currency.—The *yuan* was revalued with effect from

March 1, 1955, on the basis 10,000 old *yuan* for one new *yuan*. (*See also* p. 81.)

Production and Industry.—China is essentially an agricultural and pastoral country: peasants constitute about 80 per cent of the population. With the exception of the State farms, people's communes embrace the whole rural population. In all there are 50,000 communes and each is sub-divided into production brigades and teams.

The communes lost their administrative functions under the new Constitution and remain as purely economic enterprises. New agricultural policies, designed to give greater incentives to the rural population, have meant that the responsibility for agricultural production has been devolved down to individual households, whereas previously work was generally assigned on a collective basis.

Wheat, barley, maize, millet and other cereals, with peas and beans, are grown in the northern provinces, and rice and sugar in the south. Rice is the staple food of the inhabitants. Cotton (mostly in valleys of the Yangtze and Yellow Rivers), tea (in the west and south), with hemp, jute and flax, are the most important crops.

Livestock is raised in large numbers. Silkworm culture is one of the oldest industries. Cottons, woollens and silks are manufactured in large quantities. The mineral wealth of the country is very great. Coal of excellent quality is produced. Iron ore, tin, antimony, wolfram, bismuth and molybdenum are also abundant. Oil is produced in several northern provinces, particularly in Heilongjiang and Shandong, and off-shore deposits are to be tapped in co-operation with Western and Japanese companies.

The Chinese State Statistical Bureau issues production figures annually. The following are of note for 1984:

Grain (tons)	407,000,000
Pork, beef, mutton (tons)	15,250,000
Tea (tons)	411,000
Cotton (tons)	6,077,000
Timber (cu. metres)	55,000,000
Crude oil (tons)	114,000
Pig iron (tons)	40,000,000
Steel (tons)	43,000,000
Chemical fertilizers (tons)	14,800,000
Electric power (KWs)	374,000,000
Machine tools	131,400
Motor vehicles	315,000

The State Statistical Bureau valued the national income for 1984 at Yuan 548,500 million, an increase of 12 per cent over 1983. The total value of industrial and agricultural output was Yuan 1,062,700 million, of which industrial output counted for Yuan 701,500 million. Per capita income in 1980 was estimated at U.S. $270.

All Chinese policies are now directed to realising the "Four Modernisations"—agriculture, industry, national defence and science and technology. Specific targets were announced in 1978 for such items as grain, steel, coal and capital construction by 1985, but these are now judged to be too high and to have caused imbalances in development. China is at present engaged in a reordering of economic priorities in favour of agriculture, light industry, textiles, fuel and power, and transport and communications. This involves severe cuts in capital investment, closure of uneconomic plants, cancellation of large foreign trade contracts and careful control of imports of foreign technology. A new 10-year plan is being formulated.

The principal articles of export are animals and animal products; oil; textiles; ores, metals and tea. The principal imports are raw cotton, cotton yarn and thread; motor vehicles; machinery; chemical fertilizer plants; wheat; aircraft; books, paper and paper-making materials; chemicals; metals and ores; and dyes.

Trade with U.K.

	1983	1984
Imports from U.K.	£159,722,000	£317,256,000
Exports to U.K.	231,417,000	278,474,000

Communications.—Of the total area of China over half consists of tableland and mountainous areas where communications and travel are generally difficult. The country has more than 52,000 kilometres of railway trunk and branch lines and some 915,000 kilometres of highway. In addition, internal civil aviation has been developed, with routes now totalling more than 340,000 kilometres. As a result the communications network now covers most of the country.

In the past where roads did not exist the principal means of communication east to west was provided by the rivers, the most important of which are the Yangtze (Changjiang) (3,400 miles long), the Yellow River (Huanghe) (2,600 miles long) and the West River (Xihe) (1,650 miles). These, together with the network of canals connecting them are still much used, but their overall importance is less than it was. Coastal port facilities are being improved and the merchant fleet expanded. In the past 10 years great progress has been made in developing postal services and telecommunications. It is now claimed that 95 p.c. of all rural communes are on the telephone and that postal routes reach practically every production brigade headquarters.

CAPITAL.—Peking, population (Chinese official figure, 1982), 9,230,687. The population of ΨShanghai (Chinese official figure, 1982) is given as 11,859,748; Nanking (estimate, 1974) 2,400,000; Tianjin (Chinese official figure, 1980) 7,390,000; Shenyang (Chinese official figure 1975) 4,400,000; Wuhan (Chinese official figure, 1976) 3,500,000; Chongqing (Chinese official figure, 1979) 6,200,000; ΨGuangzhou (Canton) (estimate, 1973) 5,000,000; Harbin (estimate, 1974) 2,100,000; Luda (Lushun and Dalien) (estimate, 1973) 4,200,000.

FLAG.—Red, with large gold five-point star and four small gold stars in crescent, all in upper quarter next staff.

NATIONAL DAY.—October 1 (Founding of People's Republic).

BRITISH EMBASSY
11 Guang Hua Lu,
Jian Guo Men Wai, Peking.

Ambassador, His Excellency Sir Richard Evans, K.C.M.G. (1984)
Counsellors, P. Thomson (*Head of Chancery*); H. L. Davies (*Commercial*); A. D. Johnson (*Cultural, and British Council Representative*).
Defence Attaché, Col. B. Aldridge.
1st Secretaries, F. J. Savage; C. W. Parton; A. G. J. Insall; R. F. Wye; S. J. Towlson; D. G. Blunt; D. Utley; T. A. Craig-Cameron.
There is also a Consulate in *Shanghai*.

TIBET

Tibet is a plateau seldom lower than 10,000 feet, forms the northern frontier of India (boundary imperfectly demarcated), from Kashmir to Burma, but is separated therefrom by the Himalayas. The area is estimated at 463,000 square miles with a population of 1,892,392 in 1982.

From 1911 to 1950, Tibet was virtually an independent country but its status was never officially so recognized. In October 1950, Chinese Communist forces invaded Eastern Tibet. On May 23, 1951, an agreement was reached whereby the Chinese army was allowed entry into Tibet. A Communist military and administrative headquarters was set up. In 1954 the Government of India recognized that Tibet was an integral part of China, in return for the right to maintain trade and consular representation there.

A series of revolts against Chinese rule over several years culminated on March 17, 1959, in a rising in Lhasa. Heavy fighting continued for several days before the rebellion was suppressed by Chinese troops and military rule imposed. The Dalai Lama fled to India where he and his followers were granted political asylum. On March 28, 1959, the Chinese Premier issued an order dissolving the Tibetan Government. In its place the 16-member Preparatory Committee for the Tibetan Autonomous Region, originally set up in 1955 with the Dalai Lama as Chairman, was to administer Tibet under the State Council. The Preparatory Committee was to have the Panchen Lama as Acting Chairman and also to include 4 Chinese Officials. Elections were held to choose local People's Congresses in Tibet, thus indicating that the government organization there no longer differed significantly from that of any ordinary province in China.

In December, 1964, the Dalai Lama was declared to be a traitor, and both he and the Panchen Lama were dismissed. The position of Acting Chairman of the Preparatory Committee was assumed by Ngapoi Ngawang Jigmi, who had long been the most prominent secular figure in Tibet. This move marked the end of the period of co-operation by the Chinese Government with the traditional religious authorities, and the eclipse of the latter. The Preparatory Committee completed its work with the setting up of Tibet as an Autonomous Region of China on Sept. 9, 1965. The Panchen Lama is now rehabilitated as an official of the C.P.P.C.C., and the Chinese have invited the Dalai Lama to return from exile.

TAIWAN
(Formosa)

President, Chiang Ching-kuo, *elected*, March, 1978, *re-elected*, March 21, 1984.
Vice-President, Lee Teng-hui, *elected*, March 22, 1984.
Premier, Yu Kuo-hwa (May 20, 1984).

An island of some 13,800 sq. miles in the China Sea, Taiwan lies 90 miles east of the Chinese mainland in latitude 21° 45′N.—25° 38′N. The population (18,203,000 in March, 1982), is almost entirely Chinese in origin and includes about 2,000,000 mainlanders who came to the island with Chiang Kai-shek in 1947–49. The territories administered by the Chinese Nationalists include the Pescadores Islands (50 sq. miles), some 35 miles west of Taiwan, as well as Quemoy (68 sq. miles) and Matsu (11 sq. miles) which are only a few miles from the mainland. Settled for centuries by the Chinese, the island was administered by Japan from 1895 to 1945. General Chiang Kai-shek withdrew to Taiwan in 1949, towards the end of the war against the Communist *régime*, accompanied by 500,000 Nationalist troops, after which the territory continued under his presidency until his death on April 5, 1975. A mutual defence treaty between the United States and Taiwan Governments was signed in 1954 but this has been terminated as the United States recognized the People's Republic of China on January 1, 1979.

The eastern part of the main island is mountainous and forest covered. Mt. Morrison (Yu Shan) (13,035 ft.) and Mt. Sylvia (Tz'ukaoshan) (12,972 ft.)

are the highest peaks. The western plains are watered by many rivers and the soil is very fertile, producing sugar, rice, sweet potatoes, tea, bananas, pineapples and tobacco. Coal, sulphur, iron, petroleum, copper and gold are mined. There are important fisheries. The principal seaports Ψ Keelung and Ψ Kaohsiung are situated in the northern and southern sections of the island.

Trade with U.K.

	1983	1984
Imports from U.K.	£128,467,000	£150,648,000
Exports to U.K.	458,307,000	585,246,000

CAPITAL.—Taipei (population 1979, 2,196,237). Other towns are Ψ Kaohsiung (1,172,777); Tainan (572,590); Taichung (585,205); and Ψ Keelung (345,392).

FLAG.—Red, with blue quarter at top next staff, bearing a twelve-point white sun.

COLOMBIA
(República de Colombia)

President, Dr. Belisario Betancur Cuartas, *assumed office*, August 7, 1982.

CABINET

Interior, Jaime Castro Castro.
Foreign Affairs, Augusto Ramirez Ocampo.
Justice, Enrique Parejo González.
Finance and Public, Roberto Junguito Bonett.
Defence, Gen. Miguel Vega Uribe.
Agriculture, Gustavo Castro Guerrero.
Economic Development, Iván Duque Escobar.
Mines and Energy, Alvaro Leyva Durán.
Education, Doris Eder De Zambrano.
Labour, Oscar Salazar Chávez.
Health, Amaury Garcia Burgos.
Communications, Nohemí Sanin Posada.
Public Works, Hernán Beltz Peralta

COLOMBIAN EMBASSY IN LONDON
3 Hans Crescent, SW1X 0LR
[01–589 9177]

Ambassador Extraordinary and Plenipotentiary, His Excellency Dr. Bernardo Ramirez (1985).
Minister Counsellor, Dr. Ricardo Samper.
There are *Consulates-General* in *London* and *Liverpool*.

The Republic of Colombia lies in the extreme northwest of South America, having a coastline on both the Caribbean Sea and Pacific Ocean. It is situated between 4° 13′ S. to 12° 30′ N. lat. and 68° to 79° W. long., with an approximate area of 456,535 square miles, and a population (estimated 1982) of 27,900,000.

The country is divided into a narrow coastal strip in the west and extensive plains in the east by the Cordillera de los Andes. The Eastern Cordillera consists of a series of vast tablelands. This temperate region is the most densely peopled portion of the Republic. The highest mountain in Colombia is Cristobal Colon (18,946 feet) in the Sierra Nevada de Santa Marta on the Caribbean coast.

The principal rivers are the Magdalena, Guaviare, Cauca, Atrato, Caquetá, Putumayo and Patia. The Patia flows through the famous *Minima Gorge* of the Western Cordilleras, and one of its tributaries (the Carchi, or Upper Guiatara) is spanned by the Rumichaca Arch, or *Inca's Bridge*, of natural stone.

Government.—The Colombian coast was visited in 1502 by Christopher Columbus, and in 1536 a Spanish expedition under Jiménez de Quesada penetrated to the interior and established on the site of the present capital a government which continued under Spanish rule until the revolt of the Spanish–American colonies of 1811–1824. In 1819 Simón Bolívar (1783–1831) established the Republic of Colombia, consisting of the territories now known as Colombia, Panama, Venezuela and Ecuador. In 1829–1830 Venezuela and Ecuador withdrew from the association of provinces, and in 1831 the remaining territories were formed into the Republic of New Granada. In 1858 the name was changed to the Granadine Confederation and in 1861 to the United States of Colombia. In 1866 the present title was adopted. In 1903 Panama seceded from Colombia, and became a separate Republic.

During the early nineteen-fifties Colombia suffered a period of virtual civil war between the supporters of the traditional political parties, the Conservatives and the Liberals. From 1957–1974 the country was governed under the "National Front" agreement with the presidency alternating between the two parties every four years and ministerial posts being shared equally by the parties. The alternation of the presidency was ended in 1974 and parity in appointments in 1978. Thereafter, the constitution lays down that Government portfolios and Administrative appointments shall be divided among the two majority parties in Congress in an "adequate and equitable" manner.

Defence.—The Army peace effective strength is 57,000; war effective, approx. 400,000. The Navy has four new corvettes, four destroyers, three frigates, two submarines, and other small craft. The Air Force, with 6,000 personnel, has old jet trainers and two squadrons equipped with Mirage fighters.

Production.—Much of Colombia's natural resources in coal, natural gas and hydro-electricity remain largely unexploited but the government has designated development as a priority. Coal reserves are estimated at 40,000 million tonnes. To date annual coal production has averaged about 5·5 million tons but this will rise when production from the El Cerrejon coalfield commences in 1985. This is intended primarily for export. Proven reserves of natural gas are 142,000 million cu. metres, with production running at 300,000 cu. ft./day. Crude oil reserves could be as high as 10,000 million barrels/day but production at present is 150,000 barrels/day and Colombia is a net importer of oil, although moving back towards self-sufficiency. Off-shore exploration for oil and natural gas is being encouraged.

The hydrocarbon sector accounts for over half of the mining output with precious metals (gold, platinum and silver) and iron ore accounting for the remainder. Iron ore production in 1982 was 450,000 tons. Other mineral deposits include nickel (a processing plant started operating in 1982), bauxite, copper, gypsum, limestone, phosphates, sulphur and uranium. Colombia is also the world's largest producer of emeralds and has deposits of other precious and semi-precious stones.

Because of the range of climate, a wide variety of crops can be grown, and the country is close to self-suffiency in food. The principal agriculture products are coffee (Colombia is second only to Brazil as the world's largest coffee producer) and other major cash crops are sugar, bananas, cut flowers and cotton. Cattle are raised in large numbers, and meat and cured skins and hides are also exported.

Industry.—The Government has encouraged diversification to reduce dependence on coffee as the major export and this has led to the growth of new export-orientated industries, particularly textiles, paper products and leather goods. Stimulus to the economy has been provided by large loans from the World Bank and IADB for project development, particularly in the power sector (in which hydroelectric projects have predominated) and for telecommunications.

Communications.—The massive ranges of the Andes make surface transport difficult and air transport is used extensively. There are daily passenger and cargo air services between Bogotá and all the principal towns, as well as daily services to the U.S.A., frequent services to other countries in South America, and to Europe. The "Atlantic Railway" links the departmental lines running down to the river, and completes the connection between Bogotá and Santa Marta. The Pacific Railway connects Bogotá with the port of Buenaventura. There are about 2,200 miles of rail in use at present. The total road network (1978) consists of 53,200 km. of roads of all types, of which 21,800 km. are classified as main trunk and transversal roads. Construction of roads, bridges, railways and airports in outlying regions is accorded a high priority.

The national telephone and telegraph system consists primarily of wireless links between the more important centres. Large appropriations have been made for modernization of the country's telecommunication system. There are radio stations in the main cities, and a television station in Bogotá with relays to most parts of the country.

Language and Literature.—Spanish is the language of the country and education has been free since 1870. Great efforts have been made in reducing illiteracy and estimates (1980) put the literacy rate at 77·6 per cent of those over 10 years of age can read and write. In addition to the National University with headquarters at Bogotá there are 26 other universities. There is a flourishing press in urban areas and a national literature supplements the rich inheritance from the time of Spanish rule.

Roman Catholicism is the established religion.

TRADE

Colombia's principal export is coffee which provides 50 per cent of total export earnings; other agricultural products (principally bananas and cut flowers) account for 15 per cent, and manufactured goods (chiefly clothing and textiles) for 15 per cent.

	1981	1982
	$U.S.	$U.S.
Total imports (c.i.f.)	3,863m.	6,094·7m.
Total exports (f.o.b.)	2,926m.	3,347·8m.

Trade with U.K.

	1983	1984
Imports from U.K.	£51,023,000	£43,485,000
Exports to U.K.	56,458,000	80,387,000

CAPITAL, Bogotá, population (estimated, 1978) 5,000,000. Bogotá is an inland city in the Eastern Cordilleras, at an elevation of 8,600 to 9,000 ft. above sea level. Other centres are Medellín (2,000,000); Cali (1,400,000); Barranquilla (1,000,000); Ψ Cartagena (475,000); Bucaramanga (430,000); Buenaventura (123,000) is the country's major port.

FLAG.—Broad yellow band in upper half, surmounting equal bands of blue and red.

NATIONAL DAY.—July 20 (National Independence Day).

BRITISH EMBASSY

Calle 98, 9–03, 4th Floor, Bogotá (Apartado Aereo 4508, Bogotá)

Ambassador Extraordinary and Plenipotentiary, His Excellency John A. Robson, C.M.G. (1982).
There are British Consular Offices at *Bogotá, Barranquilla* and *Cali.*
British Council Representative, Dr. B. J. Lavercombe, Calle 87, No. 12–79, Bogotá 1.

COLOMBO-BRITISH CHAMBER OF COMMERCE, Apartado Aereo 0 54 728, Calle 48 No. 19-10, Bogotá D.E.

THE COMOROS
(Federal and Islamic Republic of the Comoros)

President, Ahmed Abdallah, *took office* May 1978; *elected,* Oct. 22, 1978; *re-elected,* Sept. 30, 1984.

The Comoro archipelago includes the islands of Great Comoro, Anjouan, Mayotte and Moheli and certain islets in the Indian Ocean with an area of 800 sq. miles and a population (estimated 1983) of 378,000, most of whom are Muslim. The islanders voted for independence from France in December 1974 and three islands became independent on July 6, 1975. (The island of Mayotte was against independence and has remained under French administration.) On October 1, 1978 the three islands voted in a referendum to adopt a new Constitution which provides for a President, directly elected for a six year term. The Council of Government, consisting of a Prime Minister and up to nine other Ministers, is appointed by the President. There is a 39-member Federal Assembly elected for 5 years. Each island is administered by a Governor, assisted by up to four Commissioners whom he appoints, and has an elected Legislative Council.

The most important products now are vanilla, copra, cloves and essential oils, which are the principal exports; cacao, sisal and coffee are also cultivated. Great Comoro is well forested and produces some timber.

Trade with U.K.

	1983	1984
Imports from U.K.	£597,000	£316,000
Exports to U.K.	278,000	236,000

CAPITAL.—Moroni, on Great Comoro.

FLAG.—Green ground with a crescent and four stars all in white in the half by the hoist.

CONGO
(People's Republic of the Congo)

President, Col. Denis Sassou-Nguesso, *appointed* 1979, *re-elected,* July 30, 1984 (also holds *Defence and Security Portfolio*).

COUNCIL OF MINISTERS

Prime Minister, Ange Edouard Poungui.
Finance and Budget, J. Lekoundzou.
Administration and Local Government, Col. R. D. Ngollo.
Agriculture and Livestock, Col. F.-X. Katali.
Foreign Affairs and Co-operation, A. N. Oba.
Transport and Civil Aviation, H. Monthault.
Labour, Civil Service and Social Security, B. C. Matsiona.
Public Works, Construction and Housing, Lt. Col. B. M. Ngolo.
Culture and Arts, J.-B. T. Loutard.
Youth and Sports, G. O. Apounou.
Planning, P. Moussa.
Secondary and Higher Education, D. Abibi.
Industry, A. Noumazalaye.
Mines and Petroleum, R. Adada.
Energy and Water Power, J. E. Gamporo.
Scientific Research, P. D. B. Boumba.
President's Office, A. E. Yoka.
Forestry, H. Djombo.
Justice, Dieudonné Kimbembe.
Tourism, Leisure and Environment, P. Ngaka.
Small and Medium Enterprises, A. Poati.
Fisheries, O. Douniam.

Basic Education and Literacy, Mme. B. Bayonne.
Trade and Consumption, A. Gambouele.
Health and Social Affairs, C. Bouramoue.
Information, Posts and Telecommunications, C. G. Bembet.
Rural Supply and Co-operative Action, A. Gisset.

The Republic lies on the Equator between Gabon on the west and Zaire on the east, the River Congo and its tributary the Ubanghi forming most of the eastern boundary of the state. The Congo has a short Atlantic coastline. Area of the Republic of Congo is 129,960 sq. miles, with a population of approximately 1,700,000. Formerly the French colony of Middle Congo, it became a member state of the French Community on November 28, 1958, and was proclaimed fully independent on August 17, 1960.

In 1968, conduct of affairs was assumed by a National Council of Army officers. The Parti Congolais du Travail (*PCT*) was created by the Congress of December 29–31, 1969 and the People's Republic of the Congo was established. Under the present Constitution, approved by referendum in 1979, executive power is vested in the President, who is elected by the Congress of the P.C.T. (the only legal party). The Council of Ministers is appointed and led by the President.

Congo has its own oil deposits, producing about 6 million tonnes annually. It also produces lead, zinc and gold. The principal agricultural products are timber, cassava, sugar cane and yams. Imports are mainly of machinery.

Trade with U.K.

	1983	1984
Imports from U.K.	£9,560,000	£6,207,000
Exports to U.K.	4,335,000	1,958,000

Currency.—The currency is the CFA Franc.

CAPITAL.—Brazzaville (500,000); Ψ Pointe Noire (350,000).

FLAG.—Red, with hammer and sickle in wreath of leaves in top corner.

NATIONAL DAY.—August 15.

BRITISH EMBASSY

B.P. 1038, Brazzaville
British Ambassador resides at Kinshasa, Zaire.
Chargé d'Affaires (resident), T. C. Almond.

COSTA RICA
(República de Costa Rica)

President, Luis Alberto Monge Alvarez, *took office,* May 8, 1982.

MINISTERS

For the Presidency, Danilo Jiménez Veiga.
Foreign Affairs and Religion, C. J. Gutiérrez Gutiérrez.
Government, Enrique Obregón.
Security, Benjamin Piza.
Finance, P. Morera Batres.
Agriculture and Livestock, Carlos Manuel Rojas.
Economy and Trade, Odalier Villalobos.
Public Works and Transport, José Calvo.
Education, E. Rodriquez Vega.
Health, Dr. J. Jaramillo Antillón.
Labour and Social Welfare, G. Sandoval Aguilar.
Culture, Youth and Sport, H. González Guitierréz.
Justice, H. A. Muñoz.
Industry, Energy and Mines, C. Chaves Zamora.
Planning, J. M. Villasuso.
Exports and Investments, J. M. Dengo Obregón.

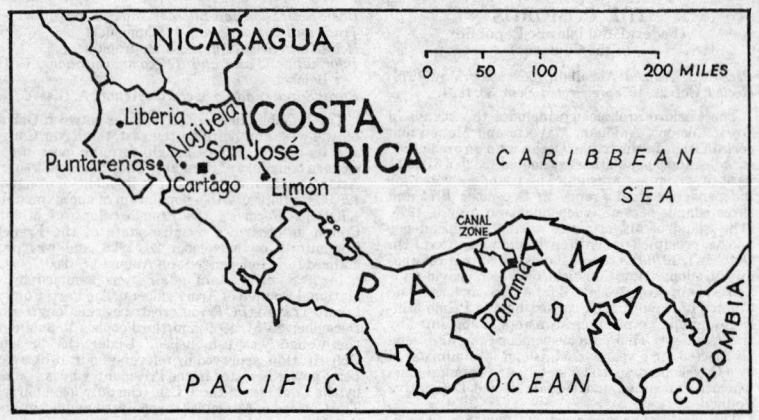

COSTA RICAN EMBASSY
93 Star Street, W2
[01–723 1772/9630]

Ambassador Extraordinary and Plenipotentiary, His Excellency Jorge Borbon Zeller (1982).

The Republic of Costa Rica in Central America extends across the isthmus between 8° 17′ and 11° 10′ N. lat. and from 82° 30′ to 85° 45′ W. long., contains an area of 19,653 sq. miles, and a population (1981 estimate) of 2,276,676. The population is basically of European stock, in which Costa Rica differs from most Latin American countries. The Republic lies between Nicaragua and Panama and between the Caribbean Sea and the Pacific Ocean. The coastal lowlands by the Caribbean Sea and Pacific have a tropical climate but the interior plateau, with a mean elevation of 4,000 feet, enjoys a temperate climate.

For nearly three centuries (1530–1821) Costa Rica formed part of the Spanish-American dominions, the seat of government being at Cartago. In 1821 the country obtained its independence, although from 1824 to 1839 it was one of the United States of Central America.

On Dec. 1, 1948, the Army was abolished, the President declaring it unnecessary, as the country loved peace.

Economy.—Agriculture is the chief industry and the principal products are coffee, bananas, sugar and cattle (for meat), all of which are important exports. Other crops are cocoa, rice, maize, potatoes and hemp. Industrial activity is principally in the manufacturing sector and manufactured goods are the largest category of exports. The main goods are foodstuffs, textiles and clothing, plastic goods, pharmaceuticals, fertilizers and electrical equipment.

Communications.—The chief ports are Limón, on the Atlantic coast, through which passes most of the coffee exported, and Puntarenas and Golfito on the Pacific coast. A new Pacific port, Caldera, currently under construction with Japanese aid, is likely to divert traffic from Puntarenas within a few years. In 1981, 1,013 ships entered Costa Rican ports handling imports and exports of approximately 2,393,374 tons of goods. The railway system is nationalized. About 500 miles of railroad are open. LACSA is the national airline, operating flights throughout Central and South America, the Caribbean and U.S.A., besides internal flights to local airports by SANSA.

Language, etc.—Spanish is the language of the country. Education is compulsory and free. The literacy rate is the highest in Latin America.

FINANCE

	1981
	Colones
Revenue	12,355·2m.
Expenditure	12,423·2m.

Currency is the *colon* of 100 *centimos*.

TRADE

The chief exports were manufactured goods and other products, coffee, bananas, cocoa and sugar. The chief imports were machinery, including transport equipment, manufactures, chemicals, fuel and mineral oils and foodstuffs.

	1980	1981
	$U.S. millions	
Total imports	1,529	1,211
Total exports	1,018	962

Trade with U.K.

	1983	1984
Imports from U.K.	£11,041,000	£9,138,000
Exports to U.K.	22,299,000	21,248,000

CAPITAL.—San José pop. 808,919; Alajuela (377,062); Cartago (237,267); Heredia (154,943); ΨPuntarenas (259,081); ΨLimón (137,329); Guanacaste (209,024). (Populations shown are of provinces, cantons and districts).

FLAG.—Five horizontal bands, blue, white, red, white, blue (the red band twice the width of the others with emblem near staff).

NATIONAL DAY.—September 15.

BRITISH EMBASSY
Apartado 815, Edificio Centro Colon 1007, San José.

Ambassador Extraordinary and Plenipotentiary and Consul-General, His Excellency Peter Wayne Summerscale (1982).

San José is 5,687 miles from London; sea transit direct 18 days; via New York, 20 days; Air Mails (via New York) 4 to 8 days from London. Ocean Mail, 8 to 16 weeks.

CUBA
(Republica de Cuba)

President of Council of State and Head of Government,
Dr. Fidel Castro Ruz, *appointed* Nov. 2, 1976.

COUNCIL OF STATE

President, Dr. Fidel Castro Ruz.
First Vice-President, Raúl Castro Ruz.
Vice-Presidents, Juan Almeida Bosque; Ramiro Valdés Menéndez; Guillermo Garcia Frías; Dr. Carlos Rafael Rodríguez; Blas Roca Calderío.
Secretary, José M. Miyar Barruecos.

COUNCIL OF MINISTERS

President, Dr. Fidel Castro Ruz.
First Vice-President, Raúl Castro Ruz.
Vice-Presidents, Dr. Carlos Rafael Rodríguez; Ramiro Valdés Menéndez; Guillermo García Frías; Pedro Miret Prieto; Diocles Torralba González; José Ramón Fernández Alvarez; Humberto Pérez González; José A. López Moreno; Osmany Cienfuegos Gorriarán; Antonio Esquivel Yedra.
Secretary, Osmany Cienfuegos Gorriarán.
Presidents of State Committees: José A. López Moreno (*Central Planning Board*); Héctor Rodriguez Llompart (*Economic Collaboration*); Rodrigo J. García Leon (*Finance*); Joaquin Benavides Rodríguez (*Labour and Social Security*); Arturo Guzmán Pascual (*Prices*); Ramón Darias Rodés (*Standardization*); Fidel Vascó González (*Statistics*); Irma Sánchez Valdés (*Technical Material Supplies*); Raúl León Torras (*National Bank of Cuba*); Dra. Rosa E. Simbon Negrin (*Academy of Science*).
Ministers, Adolfo Díaz Suarez (*Agriculture*); Guillermo Garcia Frias (*Communications*); Marcos Portal León (*Basic Industries*); José A. López Moreno (*Construction Materials Industry*); Dr. Armando Hart Dávalos (*Culture*); José R. Fernandez Alvarez (*Education*); Ricardo Cabrisas Ruiz (*Foreign Trade*); Jorge A. Fernandez Cuervo Vinent (*Fishing Industry*); Alejandro Roca Iglesias (*Food Industry*); Isidoro Malmierca Peoli (*Foreign Affairs*); Fernando Vecino Alegret (*Higher Education*); Ramiro Valdés Menéndez (*Interior*); Col. Manuel Vila Sosa (*Internal Trade*); Dr. Juan Escalona Reguera (*Justice*); Roberto Ogando Zas (*Light Industry*); Dr. Sergio del Valle Jiménez (*Public Health*); Gen. Raúl Castro Ruz (*Revolutionary Armed Forces*); Antonio Rodríguez Maurell (*Sugar Industry*); Marcos Lage Coello (*Sidero-Mechanic Industry*); Conrado Martinez (*Sports*); Diocles Torralbas Gonzalez (*Transport*); José A. Naranjo Morales, Levi Farah Balmaseda, (*without Portfolio*).

CUBAN EMBASSY IN LONDON
167 High Holborn, W.C.1
[01–240 2488]

Ambassador Extraordinary and Plenipotentiary, new appointment awaited.

Cuba, the largest island in the Caribbean, lies between 74° and 85° W. long., and 19° and 23° N. lat., with a total area of 44,178 sq. miles. The country has now been divided into 14 provinces. The estimated total population in 1984 was 10,042,800.

The island of Cuba was visited by Christopher Columbus during his first voyage, on Oct. 27, 1492, and was then believed to be part of the Western mainland of India. Early in the 16th century the island was conquered by the Spaniards, to be used later as a base of operations for the conquest of Mexico and Central America, and for almost four centuries Cuba remained under a Spanish Captain-General. [The island was under British rule for one year, 1762–1763, when it was returned to Spain in exchange for Florida.] Separatist agitation culminated in the closing years of the 19th century in a fierce and blood-thirsty war. In 1898 the government of the United States intervened and on April 20, 1898, demanded the evacuation of Cuba by the Spanish forces. A short Spanish–American war led to the abandonment of the island, which was occupied by U.S. troops. Cuba was under U.S. military rule from Jan. 1, 1899 until May 20, 1902, when an autonomous government was inaugurated with an elected President, and a legislature of two houses. The island was, however, again the prey of revolution from Aug. to Sept., 1906, when the U.S. Government resumed control. On Jan. 28, 1909, a republican government was again inaugurated.

A revolution led by Dr. Fidel Castro overthrew the Government of General Batista on January 1, 1959. In October, 1965, the Communist Party of Cuba was formed to succeed the United Party of the Socialist Revolution. It is the only authorized political party. The new Socialist Constitution came into force on February 24, 1976 and indirect elections to the National Assembly of People's Power were subsequently held.

The Government has carried out programmes of land and urban reform and of nationalization; by March, 1968, virtually all industrial and commercial enterprises were nationalized. About 80 per cent of the cultivated land is in state farms or State-controlled co-operatives. Private smallholders, who own the remainder, have to sell all their produce to the state.

Although efforts are being made to diversify the economy, sugar is still its mainstay and Cuba's principal source of foreign exchange. It still accounts for some 75 per cent in value of total Cuban exports. In 1983–84 the harvest was 8,200,000 tons. Cuba's other main exports are nickel, seafood, citrus fruits, tobacco and rum.

Despite increased trade with Western Europe and Japan, the Communist countries, particularly the Soviet Union, form Cuba's main trading partners, covering about 86 per cent of imports and exports. In addition, the U.S.S.R. offers substantial aid through a system of subsidies which has recently been estimated to amount to $3,500 million.

There are 14,000 kms. of railway track, of which 5,000 kms. are in public service. In 1980 there were 10,000 kms. of road, 4,700 of which were unpaved. At present scheduled international air services run to North, Central and South American countries and Europe.

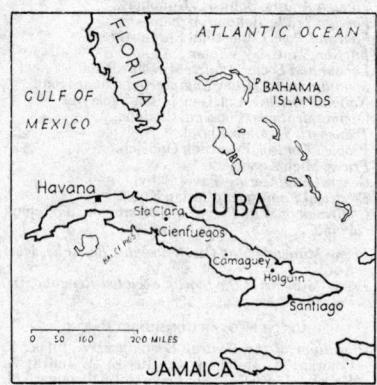

Language and Literature.—Spanish is the language of the island. English, formerly widely understood, is now spoken less. Education is compulsory and free. In 1964 illiteracy was officially declared to be completely eliminated. The press and broadcasting and television are under the control of the Government.

	1983	1984
	Pesos, million	
Imports	6,224	7,207·2
Exports	5,531	5,462·1

Trade with U.K.

	1983	1984
Imports from U.K.	£45,736,602	£64,377,000
Exports to U.K.	14,010,254	13,020,000

CAPITAL.—ΨHavana (pop., est. 1981), 1,924,886; other towns are ΨSantiago (403,604), Santa Clara (189,092), Camagüey (261,831), Holgüin (239,641), and ΨCienfuegos (114,650).

FLAG.—Five horizontal bands, blue and white (blue at top and bottom) with red triangle, close to staff, charged with 5-point star.

NATIONAL DAY.—January 1 (Day of Liberation).

BRITISH EMBASSY

Edificio Bolívar, Cárcel 101–103
e Morro y Prado, Apartado 1069, Havana.

Ambassador Extraordinary and Plenipotentiary, His Excellency P. Robin Fearn, C.M.G. (1984).
Counsellor, Mrs. M. Bryan (*Head of Chancery*).
1st *Secretary,* G. Livesey (*Commercial and H.M. Consul*).

CZECHOSLOVAKIA
(Československá Socialistická Republika)

President, Gustáv Husák, *born* Jan. 10, 1913; *elected* May 29, 1975, *re-elected,* May, 1980, 1985.

Federal Government

Prime Minister, Lubomír Štrougal.
Deputy Prime Ministers, Peter Colotka; Josef Korčák; Karol Laco; Matej Lúčan; Rudolf Rohlíček; Svatopluk Potáč; Ladislav Gerle; Jaromír Obzina.

Ministers

Agriculture and Food, Miroslav Toman.
Finance, Leopold Ler.
Foreign Affairs, Bohuslav Chňoupek.
Foreign Trade, Bohumil Urban.
Fuel and Power, Vlastimil Ehrenberger.
Interior, Vratislav Vajnar.
Labour and Social Affairs, Miroslav Boďa.
Metallurgy and Heavy Engineering, Eduard Saul.
National Defence, Col. Gen. Milan Václavík.
Communications, Vlastimil Chalupa.
Transport, Vladimir Blažek.
People's Control, František Ondřich.
Prices, Michal Sabolčík.
General Engineering, Pavol Bahyl.
Electrical Engineering, Milan Kubat.
Chairman of State Planning Commission, Svatopluk Potáč.

Prime Minister of the Czech Socialist Republic, Josef Korčák.
Prime Minister of the Slovak Socialist Republic, Dr. Peter Colotka.

CZECHOSLOVAK COMMUNIST PARTY

Presidium of the Central Committee, V. Bilak; P. Colotka; K. Hoffman; G. Husák; A. Indra; A. Kapek; J. Korčák; J. Lenárt; L. Štrougal; M. Jakeš; J. Kempný (*full members*); M. Hruškovič; J. Fojtík; J. Haman (*candidate members*).
Secretariat of the Central Committee, Gustáv Husák (*General Secretary*); M. Jakeš; M. Beňo; J. Haman; V. Bilak; J. Fojtík; J. Havlín; J. Poledník; F. Pitra (*secretaries*); M. Kabrhelová (*member*).

CZECHOSLOVAK EMBASSY

25 Kensington Palace Gardens, W8 4QY
[01–229 1255]

Ambassador Extraordinary and Plenipotentiary, His Excellency Dr. Miroslav Houštecký (1983).
Commercial Counsellor, Václav Jarolim.
Military and Air Attaché, Col. Jaromír Široký.
Commercial Attachés, J. Slánský; J. Navara.
Assistant Military and Air Attaché, B. Kramář.
Press Secretary, Josef Konečný.

Area and Population.—Czechoslovakia, formerly part of the Austro-Hungarian Empire, declared its independence on Oct. 28, 1918 (Czechoslovak Independence Day), the territory affected having an area of 53,700 square miles, reduced, by the cession of Ruthenia to U.S.S.R. in 1945, to 49,400 square miles. The population of Czechoslovakia was 15,280,148 in 1980.

Government.—The Communist Party came to power in Czechoslovakia in February, 1948, and Communist control of the country is now unqualified. On July 11, 1960, a new constitution was proclaimed, replacing that of 1948 and the official title of the State was accordingly changed to "The Czechoslovak Socialist Republic".

In January, 1968, pressures for reform of the system led to the proposal of new legislation, which envisaged the democratisation of the country's political life, greater guarantees of fundamental liberties and the establishment of a federal system.

The implications for the internal development of the other communist regimes in Eastern Europe and the Soviet Union, as well as for the system of alliances among these countries, alarmed the Soviet Union. On the night of August 20, Czechoslovakia was invaded by Soviet, Polish, East German, Hungarian and Bulgarian troops, the capital and all major towns being occupied. The Czechoslovak leadership was forced to modify its policies and to legalise the presence of Soviet troops on Czechoslovak territory. With the exception of the Federal system of government, the reforms of 1968 were abandoned when Gustáv Husák became leader of the Communist party in April 1969.

Czechoslovakia now consists of the Czech Socialist Republic and the Slovak Socialist Republic, each of which has its own government responsible to its legislative body—the National Council. Areas such as the constitution, defence, foreign affairs, state material reserves and currency are the responsibility of the Federal Administration. The Federal Government is responsible to the Federal Assembly, which is composed of two Chambers, the Chamber of the People, whose deputies are elected throughout the Federation, and the Chamber of the Nations, consisting of an equal number of Czech and Slovak Deputies. The federal system was not extended to the organization of the Communist Party.

The Economic System.—Under the present political system industry is state-owned, and nearly all agricultural land is cultivated by state or co-operative farms. Economic planning is centralized, and state economic plans have the force of law. Early in 1980 an experiment in limited devolution of responsibility having been considered reasonably successful, was expanded into a "Set of Measures for the Reform of Planned Management" which affects most of the economy. Its main purpose is to introduce some devolution of production and profits control in order

ncourage higher productivity and a better quality
put. It was updated in 1984 but its impact remains
ted.

zechoslovakia is not rich in minerals, although
ificant quantities of coal, brown coal and lignite
mined. Principal agricultural products are sugar-
t, potatoes and cereal crops; the timber industry
lso very important. The country has long been
hly industrialized, and machinery, industrial
sumer goods and raw materials are major exports.
7th Five Year Plan (1981–85) aims to raise
ional income by 2·8 per cent, industrial production
·7 per cent and agricultural production by 2·6 per
t.

anguage and Literature.—Czech and Slovak are
official languages, each having its own literature.
Reformation gave a wide-spread impulse to Czech
rature, the writings of Jan Hus (martyred in 1415
religious and social reformer) familiarizing the
ple with Wyclif's teaching. This impulse endured
he close of the 17th century when Jan Amos
nensky or Comenius (1592–1670) was expelled
n the country. Under Austrian rule and with the
sistent pursuit of Germanization, there was a
od of stagnation until the national revival in the
half of the 19th century. Authors of interna-
al reputation include K. M. Capek-Chod (1860–
7), Viktor Dyk (1877–1931), Jaroslav Hašek (1883–
3), Karel Capek (1890–1938), Vladimír Vančura
1–1942), and Ivan Olbracht (1882–1952). Franti-
Hrubín (b. 1910), Bohumil Hrabal (b. 1914), Václav
el (b. 1936), Ladislav Mňačko (b. 1919), Ladislav
omesky (b. 1904), Arnošt Lustig (b. 1926), Jiří
cha (b. 1915), and others.

ducation.—Education is compulsory and free for
hildren from the ages of 6 to 16. The number of
ls in basic nine-year schools is 1,992,000 (1983).
re are 175,198 students in the secondary grammar
ools and the number given for technical schools
ll kinds is 290,038. There are five universities in
choslovakia of which the most famous is Charles
versity in Prague (founded 1348), the others being
ated at Bratislava, Brno, Olomouc and Košice.
ddition there are a considerable number of other
itutions of university standing, technical col-
s, agricultural colleges, etc.

inance.—The Czechoslovak currency is the
choslovak *Koruna* (*Kčs* = Czechoslovak crown) of
heller.

Trade with U.K.

	1983	1984
Imports from U.K.	£69,456,000	£78,075,000
Exports to U.K.	101,302,000	117,188,000

CAPITAL.—Prague (Praha), on the Vltava (Mol-
dau), the former capital of Bohemia with a population
(1979) of 1,191,125. Other towns are Brno (Brünn),
capital of Moravia (372,793), Bratislava (Pressburg),
capital of Slovakia (374,860), Ostrava (325,473), Košiče
(200,943) and Plzen (Pilsen) (169,466).

FLAG.—Two equal horizontal stripes, white (above)
and red; a blue triangle next to staff.

NATIONAL DAY.—May 9.

BRITISH EMBASSY
Thunovská 14, 11800 Prague 1.

Ambassador Extraordinary and Plenipotentiary, His
Excellency Stephen Jeremy Barrett, C.M.G.
Counsellor, A. B. P. Smart (*Head of Chancery*).
Defence and Military Attaché, Col. R. G. Lee.
Air Attaché, Wing-Cdr. M. Sparkes.
Cultural Attaché, J. F. Green, O.B.E.

DENMARK
(Kongeriget Danmark)

Queen, Margrethe II, eldest daughter of King Fred-
erik IX, *born* April 16, 1940, *succeeded* Jan. 14, 1972,
married June 10, 1967, Count Henri de Monpezat
(Prince Henrik of Denmark) and *has issue* Crown
Prince Frederik *born* May 26, 1968; and Prince
Joachim, *born* June 7, 1969.

CABINET

Prime Minister, Poul Schlüter.
Finance Minister, Palle Simonsen.
Foreign Affairs, Uffe Ellemann-Jensen.
Environment and Nordic Affairs, Christian Christen-
sen.
Ecclesiastical Affairs, Mette Madsen.
Greenland, Tom Høyem.
Culture, Mimi Stilling Jacobsen.
Social Affairs, Elisebeth Kock-Petersen.
Interior, Britta Schall-Holberg.
Justice, Erik Ninn-Hansen.
Agriculture, Niels Anker Kofoed.
Fisheries, Henning Grove.

Education, Bertel Haarder.
Economic Affairs, Anders Andersen.
Taxation, Dr. Isi Foighel.
Defence, Hans Engell.
Labour, Grethe Fenger-Møller.
Industry, Ib Stetter.
Housing, Niels Bollmann.
Public Works, Arne Melchior.
Energy, Knud Enggaard.

ROYAL DANISH EMBASSY IN LONDON
55 Sloane Street, SW1X 9SR
[01–235 1255]

Ambassador Extraordinary and Plenipotentiary, His Excellency Tyge Dahlgaard (1981).
Minister Plenipotentiary, K. A. Eliasen.
Minister Counsellors, I. J. Kelland (*Economic and Consular*); H. J. Rossen (*Commercial*); J. Anker Nielsen (*Press and Culture*).
Counsellor, Per Poulsen-Hansen.
Defence Attaché, Brig. Gen. B. P. Faaberg.

Area and Population.—A Kingdom of Northern Europe, consisting of the islands of Zeeland, Funen, Lolland, etc., the peninsula of Jutland, and the outlying island of Bornholm in the Baltic, the Faroes and Greenland. Denmark is situated between 54° 34'–57° 45' N. lat., 8° 5'–15° E. 12' long., with an area of 17,000 square miles, and a population estimated (1982) of 5,116,464.

Government.—Under the Constitution of the Kingdom of Denmark Act of June 5, 1953, the legislature consists of one chamber, the *Folketing,* of not more than 179 members, including 2 for the Faröes and 2 for Greenland. The voting age is 18.

The Social Democrat Government of Mr. Jørgensen, formed in January 1982, resigned from office in early September 1982 after failing to obtain approval of Budget proposals and a four-party non-Socialist coalition government was formed, which continued unchanged after an election on January 10, 1984.

Education is free and compulsory. Special schools are numerous, commercial, technical and agricultural predominating. There are Universities at Copenhagen (founded in 1479), Aarhus (1933), Odense (1966), Roskilde (1972) and Aalborg (1974). A further University at Esbjerg is planned.

Language and Literature.—The Danish language is akin to Swedish and Norwegian. Danish literature, ancient and modern, embraces all forms of expression, familiar names being Hans Christian Andersen (1805–1875), Sören Kierkegaard (1813–1855) and Georg Brandes (1842–1927), with Henrik Pontoppidan (1857–1943) and Karl Gjellerup (1857–1919), who shared the Nobel Prize for Literature in 1917, and Johannes V. Jensen (1873–1950), who received the same award in 1944. Among recent authors of note are Klaus Rifbjerg (*b.* 1931) and Leif Panduro (1923–1977). Some 48 newspapers are published in Denmark; 10 daily papers are published in Copenhagen.

Production and Industry.—Of the labour force, in 1981, 7·6 per cent was engaged in agriculture, fishing, forestry, etc.; 25·7 per cent. in manufacturing, building and construction; 14·6 per cent. in commerce and 52·1 per cent. in administration, transport, financial services, the liberal professions, etc. The chief agricultural products are pigs, cattle, dairy products, poultry and eggs, seeds, cereals and sugar beet; manufactures are mostly based on imported raw material but there are also considerable imports of finished goods.

Communications.—Mercantile marine (ships above 100 gross tonnage) at end of 1982, totalled 834 ships, with a gross tonnage of 4,686,000. In 1982 there was 2,461 km. of railway.

FINANCE (BUDGET ESTIMATES)

	1984	1985
Revenue	*Kr.* 268,600m.	*Kr.* 295,000m.
Expenditure	299,000m.	315,000m.

Denmark's balance of payments on current account showed a deficit for 1984 of *Kr.*17,000 million (1983 *Kr.* 11,000 million).

MERCHANDISE TRADE

The principal imports are petroleum and its products, machinery, raw materials, vehicles and textile products. The chief exports are agricultural and dairy products and machinery.

	1983	1984
	Kr. million	
Total Imports	148,896	171,846
Total Exports	146,800	165,194

Trade with U.K.

	1983	1984
Imports from U.K.	£1,159,184,000	£1,197,381,000
Exports to U.K.	1,512,620,000	1,660,447,000

CAPITAL.—ΨCopenhagen, pop. (1982), 575,217 Greater Copenhagen, 1,196,314. Other centres are ΨAarhus, 248,294; ΨOdense 170,522; ΨAalborg 154,514; ΨEsbjerg, 80,287; ΨRanders, 61,848; Helsingør 56,262; ΨKolding, 56,381; ΨHorsens, 54,724 Roskilde, 48,692; ΨVejle, 49,637; ΨFredericia, 46,096

FLAG.—Red, with white cross.

NATIONAL DAY.—June 5 (Constitution Day).

Copenhagen, distant from London 728 miles transit 26 hours by rail and sea.

BRITISH EMBASSY
36–40 Kastelsvej, DK-2100 Copenhagen.

Ambassador Extraordinary and Plenipotentiary, His Excellency James Mellon, C.M.G. (1983).
Counsellors, R. N. Dales (*Head of Chancery*); D. P Small, M.B.E. (*Commercial*); H. O. Spankie.
Defence Attaché, Cmdr. J. J. M. Curtis, R.N.
Chaplain, Rev. K. Povey.

There are Consulates at *Aabenraa, Aalborg, Aarhus, Esbjerg, Fredericia, Odense* and at *Tórshavn* (Faröe Islands).

British Council Representative and Cultural Attaché, Dr. W. N. Brown, o.b.e., Møntergade 1, Copenhagen.

Outlying Parts of the Kingdom

THE FARÖES, or Sheep Islands (540 sq. m.; pop. (1976) 41,211), capital, Tórshavn, are governed by a *Lagting* of 26 members, a *Landsstyre* of 4 members which deals with special Faröes affairs, and send 2 representatives to the *Folketing* at Copenhagen. On Sept. 14, 1946, the *Lagting*, with the consent of the Danish Government, for its own guidance held a plebiscite on the Faröes. About one-third of the electors did not, however, take part in the voting: of the rest a little more than half the votes cast were in favour of separation from Denmark and the establishment of a republic. At subsequent general election for the *Lagting* a great majority voted in favour of remaining part of the Kingdom of Denmark with a certain measure of home rule and in 1948 the Faröes received this. The Faröes are not part of the E.E.C.
Prime Minister, Atli Dam.

GREENLAND (ice-free portion about 132,000 sq. m., total area about 840,000 sq. m., population (1976) 49,666) is divided into 3 provinces (West, North and East). Greenland (capital, Nuuk (Godthåb)) has a *Landsraad* of 17 members and sends 2 representatives to the *Folketing* at Copenhagen. Greenland attained a status of internal autonomy on May 1, 1979. The trade of Greenland is mainly under the management of the Royal Greenland Trade Department. Following a plebiscite Greenland has negotiated its withdrawal from the E.E.C., but without discontinuing relations with Denmark, and left in Feb. 1, 1985. Mineral and oil prospecting revealed deposits of lead, zinc, iron ore, oil, gas and uranium. Commercial exploitation of these resources has already begun. The United States of America has acquired certain rights to maintain air bases in Greenland.
Premier, Jonathan Motzfeldt.

DJIBOUTI
(Republic of Djibouti)

President, Hassan Gouled Aptidon.
Vice-Presidents, Omar Kamil Warsama; Youssef Ali Chirdoun.

Formerly known as French Somaliland and then the French Territory of the Afars and the Issas, the country became independent on June 26, 1977. It is situated on the north-east coast of Africa (i.e. the Horn of Africa) and has an estimated population of over 330,000. The climate is harsh and much of the country is semi-arid desert. The French continue to maintain army, navy and air force bases. Djibouti has an excellent port, international airport and a railway line runs to Addis Ababa.
CAPITAL.—Ψ Djibouti (est. pop. 150,000).
FLAG.—Blue over green with white triangle in the hoist containing a red star.

BRITISH CONSULATE
British Bank of the Middle East, P.O. Box 2112, Djibouti.
Honorary Consul, C. H. Reddington.

DOMINICAN REPUBLIC
(República Dominicana)

President, Salvador Jorge Blanco, *took office,* 16 Aug. 1982.

CABINET

Secretary for the Presidency, Hatuey de Camps.
Administrative Secretary for the Presidency, Rafael Flores Estrella.
Technical Secretary of the Presidency, Orlando Haza del Castillo.
Armed Forces, Lt. Gen. Manuel Cuervo Gómez.
Foreign Relations, Dr. José Augusto Vega Imbert.
Interior and Police, Gen. (*ret.*) Oscar Padilla Medrano.
Education and Fine Arts, Ivelisse Prats de Perez.
Agriculture, Domingo Marte de la Cruz.
Public Works and Communications, Pedro Delgado Malagón.
Public Health and Social Welfare, Dr. Amiro Pérez Mera.
Sports and Physical Education, Dr. Luis Schecker.
Labour, Pedro Franco Badía.
Industry and Commerce, José Antonio Najri.
Finance, José Santos Taveras.

HONORARY CONSULATE
6 Queen's Mansions, Brook Green, W6 7EB
[01–602 1885]

Honorary Consul, Mrs. J. De Wardeer.
There are also Consular Offices at *Liverpool, Birmingham, Manchester, Grimsby, Southampton, Cardiff, Glasgow* and *Plymouth.*

The Dominican Republic, formerly the Spanish portion of the island of Hispaniola, is the oldest settlement of European origin in America. The western part of the island forms the Republic of Haiti. (*For Map, see* p. 846.) The island lies between Cuba on the west and Puerto Rico on the east and the Republic covers an area of about 19,322 square miles, with a population (1981 Census) of 5,647,977. The climate is tropical in the low lands and semi-tropical to temperate in the higher altitudes.

Spanish is the language of the Republic.

Government.—Santo Domingo was discovered by Christopher Columbus in December, 1492, and remained a Spanish Colony until 1821. In 1822 it was subjugated by the neighbouring Haitians who remained in control until 1844 when the Dominican Republic was proclaimed. The country was occupied by American marines from 1916 until the adoption of a new Constitution in 1924. From 1930 until May 30, 1961 (when he was assassinated) Generalissimo Rafael Trujillo ruled the country.

Professor Juan Bosch, elected President in December 1962, held office until September, 1963, when he was deposed by a military junta. A revolt in favour of ex-President Bosch in April, 1965, developed into civil war lasting until September the same year when a provisional President was elected. On June 1, 1966, Dr. Joaquin Balaguer was elected President and in Nov. 1966 a new Constitution was introduced.

Executive power is vested in the President, who is elected by direct vote and serves for four years. The President forms his cabinet without reference to the Congress.

Legislative power is exercised by the Congress, which has a term of four years concurrent with the Presidency. The Upper Chamber is the Senate of 27 senators, one for each province and one for Santo Domingo. The lower is the Chamber of Deputies which has 120 members, one for each 50,000 inhabitants in each province, with the provision that no province has less than two members. Judicial power is exercised by the Supreme Court of Justice.

Communications.—According to local classification there are 2,932 miles of first class and 1,392 miles of second class and inter-communal roads in the Republic. There is a direct road from Santo Domingo to Port-au-Prince, the capital of Haiti, but that part of it in the border area has fallen into disuse. The frontier has been closed since Sept., 1967, except for that section crossed by the main road linking the two capitals. A telephone system connects practically all the principal towns of the republic and there is a telegraph service with all parts of the world. There are more than 90 commercial broadcasting stations and six television stations.

The Republic is served by two national and six foreign airlines, and an international airport 18 miles to the east of the capital is in operation. Another has been built near Puerto Plata on the north coast.

Economy.—Sugar, coffee, cocoa, and tobacco are the most important crops. Other products are peanuts, maize, rice, bananas, molasses, salt, cement, ferro-nickel, gold, silver, cattle, sisal products, honey and chocolate. There is a growing number of light industries producing beer, tinned foodstuffs, glass products, textiles, soap, cigarettes, construction materials, plastic articles, shoes, papers, paint, rum, matches, peanut oil and other products.

FINANCE

	1983	1984 (est.)
Budget		
Revenue	RD$1,017,191,620	RD$1,345,751,270

TRADE

The chief imports are machinery, food stuffs, iron and steel, cotton textiles and yarns, mineral oils (including petrol), cars and other motor vehicles, chemical and pharmaceutical products, electrical equipment and accessories, construction material, paper and paper products, and rubber and rubber products. The chief exports are sugar, coffee, cocoa, tobacco, chocolate, molasses, bauxite, ferro-nickel and gold. Tobacco and tobacco manufactures are the principal exports to the U.K.

	1982	1983
Imports	RD$1,255,817,161	RD$1,279,019,958
Exports	791,364,784	811,054,942

Trade with U.K.

	1983	1984
Imports from U.K.	£11,594,000	£12,535,000
Exports to U.K.	6,662,000	5,620,000

CAPITAL.—Ⱳ Santo Domingo, population of the Capital District (1981 census), 1,550,739. Other centres, with populations (1981 census); Santiago de los Caballeros (550,372); La Vega (385,043); San Francisco De Macoris (235,544); San Juan (239,957); San Cristóbal (446,132).

FLAG.—Red and blue, with white cross bearing an emblem at centre.

NATIONAL DAY.—February 27 (Independence Day, 1844).

BRITISH AMBASSADOR, resident at Caracas, Venezuela.

ECUADOR
(Republica del Ecuador)

President Léon Febres Cordero, *took office* Aug. 10, 1984.

CABINET

Interior, Luis Robles Plaza.
Foreign Affairs, Dr. Edgar Teran Teran.
Education, Camillo Gallegos.
Defence, Gen. Luis Pineiros.
Finance, Francisco Swett.

Agriculture and Livestock, Marcel Laniadu Wind.
Natural Resources, Javier Espinosa Teran.
Industry, Commerce and Integration, Xavier Neira.
Public Information, Patricio Quevedo Teran.
Public Works, Alfredo Burneo.
Health, Virgilio Macias.
Social Welfare, Jorge Egas Peña.
Sec. Gen. of the Administration, Joffre Torbay.

EMBASSY AND CONSULATE
Flat 3B, 3 Hans Crescent, SW1X 0LS
[01–584 1367/2648]

Ambassador Extraordinary and Plenipotentiary, His Excellency Dr. Mauricio Gándara (1984).

Area and Population.—Ecuador is an equatorial State of South America, the mainland extending from lat. 1° 38' N. to 4° 50' S., and between 75° 20' and 81° W. long., comprising an area reduced by boundary settlements with Peru (Jan. 29, 1942) to about 226,000 sq. miles. (*For* MAP, *see* Index.)

The Republic of Ecuador is divided into 20 provinces. It has a population (census, 1981) of approximately 8 million, mostly descendants of the Spaniards, aboriginal Indians, and Mestizoes. The territory of the Republic extends across the Western Andes, the highest peaks in Ecuador being Chimborazo (20,408 ft.) and Ilinza (17,405 ft.) in the Western Cordillera; and Cotopaxi (19,612 ft.) and Cayambe (19,160 ft.) in the Eastern Cordillera. Ecuador is watered by the Upper Amazon, and by the rivers Guayas, Mira, Santiago, Chone, and Esmeraldas on the Pacific coast. There are extensive forests, and the cinchona bark tree is common.

Government.—The former *Kingdom of Quito* was conquered by the Incas of Peru in the latter part of the 15th century. Early in the 16th century Pizarro's conquests led to the inclusion of the present territory of Ecuador in the Spanish Vice-royalty of Peru. The independence of the country was achieved in a revolutionary war which culminated in the battle of Mount Pichincha (May 24, 1822).

After seven years of military rule, Ecuador returned to democracy in 1979. The present constitution, introduced in 1978, provides for an elected President and Vice-President who serve for a five year term. (Neither may stand for re-election.) There is a Chamber of Representatives with 71 members elected every five years, 12 of whom are elected on a national basis and the rest by the provinces. The Chamber meets for two months every year (Aug.–Oct.) but can be convoked at any time for extraordinary sessions. Four Legislative Commissions meet through the year.

Voting is compulsory for all literate and (since 1980) voluntary for all illiterate citizens over the age of 18. Thirteen political groupings are recognized.

Agriculture and Industry.—Agriculture is the most important sector of the economy, supporting nearly 50 per cent of the population (particularly the poorest) and contributing 14·5 per cent of the Gross Domestic Product and 19·5 per cent of exports. The main products for export are fish (mainly shrimps, tuna and sardines), which had become the largest agricultural export by early 1982; bananas, which provide a third of agricultural exports; cocoa and coffee. Other important crops are sugar, corn, soya, rice, cotton, African palm (for oil), vegetables, fruit and timber, the temperate crops being produced mostly in the highlands.

The economy was transformed by the discovery in 1972 of major oil fields in the Oriente area, and oil accounted for two thirds of 1981 export earnings. The economy grew rapidly in the 1970s but is now faced with reduced growth, due mainly to the fall in the price of oil. The oil deposits in the Oriente are estimated at between 10–15,000 million barrels, and further exploration and development is taking place. The oil is evacuated by a trans-Andean pipeline to the port of Balao (near Esmeraldes).

Communications.—There are 23,256 km. of permanent roads and 5,044 km. of roads which are only open during the dry season. There are about 750 miles of railway, including the railway from Quito to Guayaquil. Ten commercial airlines operate international flights, linking Ecuador with major foreign cities and there are internal services between all important towns.

Defence.—The standing Army has a strength of about 38,000. There is an Air Force of some 120 aircraft of various kinds and 4,800 personnel. The small Navy is 4,500 strong.

Language, etc.—Spanish is the principal language of the country but Quechua is also a recognized language and is spoken by the majority of the Indian population. As a result of an intensive national education programme more than 75 per cent of the population are now literate. Elementary education is free and compulsory. There are 9 Universities, at Quito (2), Guayaquil (3), Cuenca, Machala, Loja and Portoviejo, Polytechnic Schools at Quito and Guayaquil and 8 technical colleges in other provincial capitals. 3 daily newspapers are published at Quito and 4 at Guayaquil.

Finance.—The estimated government budget at Jan. 1982 was 64,770 million *sucres* (53,600 million *sucres* in 1981). The balance of payments deficit stands at U.S.$3·2 billion, and foreign exchange reserves at U.S.$500 million.

TRADE

Import licences are required for all merchandise and these are issued by the Central Bank of Ecuador.

	1982
Imports	U.S.$1,988,300,000
Exports	2,140,000,000

Trade with U.K.

	1983	1984
Imports from U.K.	£35,008,000	£34,323,000
Exports to U.K.	11,022,000	12,951,000

Manufactured goods and machinery are the main imports.

CAPITAL.—Quito. Population (1981 estimate), 800,000; Ψ Guayaquil (1,000,000) is the chief port; Cuenca (110,000).

FLAG.—Three horizontal bands, yellow, blue and red (the yellow band twice the width of the others); emblem in centre.

NATIONAL DAY.—August 10 (*Dia de la Independencia*).

BRITISH EMBASSY
Calle Gonzalez Suarez, 111 (Casilla 314),
Quito.

Ambassador Extraordinary and Plenipotentiary, His Excellency Michael William Atkinson, C.M.G., M.B.E., *apptd* 1985.

There is a British Consular Office at Guayaquil.

British Council Representative, J. T. Wright, Av. Amazonas 1615 y Orellana (Casilla 8829), Quito.

The GALÁPAGOS (Giant Tortoise) ISLANDS forming the province of the Archipelago de Colón, were annexed by Ecuador in 1832. The archipelago lies in the Pacific, about 500 miles from Saint Elena peninsula, the most westerly point of the mainland. There are 12 large and several hundred smaller islands with a total area of about 3,000 sq. miles and an estimated population (1981) of 5,000. The capital is San Cristobal, on Chatham Island. Although the archipelago lies on the equator, the temperature of the surround-

ing water is well below equatorial average owing to the *Antarctic Humboldt Current*. The province consists for the most part of National Park Territory, where unique marine birds, iguanas, and the giant tortoises are conserved. There is some local subsistence farming; the main industry, apart from tourism, is tuna and lobster fishing.

EGYPT
(Arab Republic of Egypt)

President, Muhammad Hosni Mubarak, *elected*, Oct. 14, 1981.

CABINET

Prime Minister, Ali Lofti.
Deputy P.M., Defence and Military Production, F.M. Mohammed Abdel-Halim Abu Ghazala.
Deputy P.M., Foreign Affairs, Esmat Abdel Meguid.
Deputy P.M., Agriculture and Food Security, Dr. Yousif Wali.
Deputy P.M., Planning, Dr. Kamal Ahmed El-Ganzouri.
Cabinet Affairs, and Minister of State for Administrative Development, Atef Muhammad Ebeid.
Construction, and Minister of State for Land Reclamation, Hasaballah Muhammad el Kafraui.
Culture, Ahmad Haikal.
Education, Mansur Hussain.
Electricity and Energy, Mohamed Maher Abaza.
Economy and Foreign Trade, Dr. Sultan Abu Ali.
Emigration Affairs, Albert Barsoum Salama.
Finance, Dr. Mahmoud Salah Hamed.
Health, Helmi Hadidi.
Higher Education, Fathi Muhammad Ali.
Housing and Infrastructures, Abdul Rahman Labib.
Industry, Muhammad Mahmud Farag Abdel Wahab.
Information, Mohammad Safwat el-Sherif.
Interior, Gen. Ahmed Rochdi.
Irrigation, Issam Radi Abdel Hamid.
Investment Affairs and International Co-operation, Dr. Wagih Shindi.
Justice, Ahmed Mamdouh Atai.
Local Administration, Hassan Soleiman Abu Bacha.
Manpower and Vocational Training, Saad Mohammad Ahmed.
National Education, Abdel Salam Abdel Kader Abdel Ghaffar.
Oil and Mining Resources, Abdel Hadi Kandil.
People's Assembly and Shoura Council Affairs, Mohamed Abdul Hamid Radwan.
Social Insurance, and Minister of State for Social Affairs, Dr. Amal Osman.
Supply and Internal Trade, Mohamed Nagi-Shatla.
Tourism and Civil Aviation, Fuad Sultan.
Transportation, Communications and Shipping, Soliman Metwalli Soliman.
Wakfs, El Sheik Ibrahim el Desouki.
Minister of State, Immigration and Egyptians living abroad, Naguib William Sefeen.

EGYPTIAN EMBASSY
26 South Street, W1Y 8EL
[01–499 2401]

Ambassador Extraordinary and Plenipotentiary, His Excellency Yousef Sharara (1984).

AREA AND POPULATION.—The total area of Egypt is estimated at 1,002,000 square kilometres (386,900 square miles), only three per cent of which is cultivated land, with a population now officially estimated (1983) at 47,000,000.

There are three distinct elements in the native population. The largest, or "Egyptian" element, is a Hamito-Semite race, known in the rural districts as *Fellahin* (*fellâh*—ploughman, or tiller of the soil). A

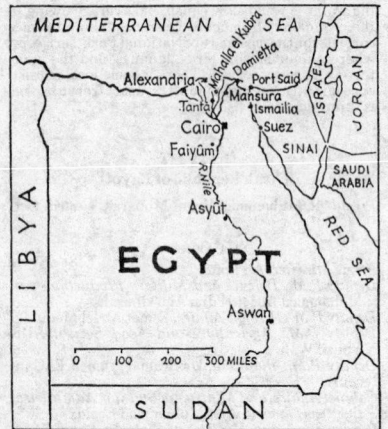

second element is the *Bedouin*, or nomadic Arabs of the Western and Arabian deserts, of whom about one-seventh are real nomads, and the remainder semi-sedentary tent-dwellers on the outskirts of the cultivated end of the Nile Valley and the Fayûm. The third element is the *Nubian* of the Nile Valley between Aswân and Wadi-Halfa of mixed Arab and Negro blood. Over 90 per cent of the population are Moslems of the Sunni denomination, and most of the rest Coptic Christians.

The territory of Egypt comprises (1) *Egypt Proper*, forming the N.E. corner of the African continent, divisible into (a) the valley and delta of the Nile, (b) the Western Desert, and (c) the Arabian or Eastern Desert; (2) *The Peninsula of Sinai*, forming part of the continent of Asia; and (3) a number of *Islands* in the Gulf of Suez and Red Sea, of which the principal are Jubal, Shadwan, Gafatin and Zeberged (or St. John's Island). This territory lies between 22° and 32° N. lat. and 24° and 37° E. long. The northern boundary is the Mediterranean, and in the south Egypt is conterminous with the Sudan. The western boundary runs from a point on the coast 10 kilometres N.W. of Sollüm to the latitude of Siwa and thence due S. along the 25th meridian. The E. boundary follows a line drawn from Rafa on the Mediterranean (34° 15' E. long.) to the head of the Gulf of 'Aqaba.

Physical Features.—The country is mainly flat but there are mountainous areas in the south-west, along the Red Sea coast and in the south of the Sinai peninsula, rising in some places to peaks of over 6,000 ft. The highest mountain in Egypt is Mt. Catherina (8,668 ft). Most of the land is desert but the Nile valley and delta are covered by silt 20–30 feet deep, and areas of desert are increasingly being reclaimed by irrigation and fertilization.

The *Nile* has a total length of 4,145 miles. In the 960 miles of its course through Egypt it receives not a single tributary stream. The river formerly had a regular yearly rise and fall of about 13 feet at Cairo, but since the completion of the Aswan High Dam in 1965, there has been no flood downstream of the dam and the water level remains almost constant throughout the year. The area of fertile land, a 5–15 mile wide strip in the Nile valley and some 6,000 square miles of the Nile delta, has been increased by the

opening of the Aswan Dam. This has allowed the reclamation of about 1,300,000 acres, and a further 700,000 acres have been converted from basin to perennial irrigation. Westward from the Nile Valley stretches the *Western desert*, containing some depressions, whose springs irrigate small areas known as *Oases*, of which the principal, from S.E. to N.W., are known as Kharga, Dakhla, Farafra, Baharia and Siwa.

In the Eastern Desert between the Nile and the mountains along the Red Sea coast, are plateaux of sandstones and limestones, dissected by *wadis* (dry water-courses), often of great length and depth, with some wild vegetation and occasional wells and springs.

History.—The unification of the Kingdoms of Lower and Upper Egypt under the Pharaohs in c. 3,100 B.C. marked the establishment of the Egyptian state, with Memphis as its capital. Egypt was ruled for nearly 2,800 years by a succession of Pharaonic dynasties (31 in all), which built the pyramids at Gizeh. The oldest of these is that of Zoser, built c. 2,700 B.C., and the highest the Great Pyramid of Cheops, at 451 feet; nearby is the Sphinx, 189 feet long. A period of Hellenic rule began in 332 B.C., after the conquest of Egypt by Alexander the Great, followed by a period of rule by Rome (30 B.C. to A.D. 324) and then by the Byzantine Empire. In A.D. 640 Egypt was subjugated by Arab Muslim invaders, becoming a province of the Eastern Caliphate. In 1517 the country was incorporated in the Ottoman Empire under which it remained until early in the 19th century.

A British Protectorate over Egypt declared on Dec. 18, 1914, lasted until Feb. 28, 1922, when Sultan Ahmed Fuad was proclaimed King of Egypt. In July, 1952, following a military *coup d'état*, King Farouk abdicated in favour of his infant son, who became King Ahmed Fuad II. In June, 1953, however, Gen. Neguib's military council deposed the young king, and Egypt became a Republic.

In 1956, as a result of Egypt's trade agreements with Communist countries, Britain and U.S.A. withdrew offers of financial aid and in retaliation Pres. Nasser seized the assets of the Suez Canal Company. An Egyptian invasion of the Canal Zone while repulsing an Israeli attack provoked military action by Britain and France in support of their Suez Canal Company interests. A ceasefire and Anglo-French withdrawal were negotiated by the U.N.

The Israeli invasion of 1956 overran the Sinai peninsula but six months later Israel withdrew and a U.N. peace-keeping force was established in the area. However, mounting tension culminated in a second invasion of Sinai (the Six Day War of June 1967) and occupation of the peninsula by Israel. Egypt's attempt to recapture the territory (the Yom Kippur War of October 1973) was unsuccessful but Sinai was returned to Egypt in April 1982, under the treaty of 1979 which resulted from the Camp David talks between Pres. Sadat and Mr. Begin and formally terminated a 31-year old state of war between the two countries. Pres. Hosni Mubarak came to power on Oct. 6, 1981 after the assassination of Pres. Sadat by Moslem fundamentalists.

Government.—The Constitution of 1971 provides for an executive President who appoints Ministers to the Cabinet. The President determines policy which the Cabinet implements and Ministers are responsible to him. The Legislature consists of the People's Assembly (448 members); the Shura Council, or Consultative Assembly (210 members) has an advisory role. The Constitution guarantees also the independence of the Judiciary. Religious courts were abolished in 1956 and their functions transferred to the national court system. Freedom of the press is guaranteed under the Constitution.

Agriculture.—Despite increasing industrialisation, agriculture remains the most important economic activity, employing over 45 per cent of the labour force and producing nearly half of the country's exports. Agricultural output has been increased as a result of land reclamation programmes and the introduction of more efficient methods, *e.g.* the change from basin to perennial irrigation which yields 2–3 crops per year instead of one, the pivotal sprinkling irrigation system which uses water more efficiently, and the increasing mechanization and use of fertilizers. Egypt is still a net importer of foodstuffs, especially grain, and a food security programme has been set up with the aim of achieving self-sufficiency through the use of more advanced technology. Estimates suggest that an additional 3 million acres of land could be reclaimed by the end of the century.

The main cash crop is cotton, of which Egypt is one of the world's main producers. Production in 1981 was 498,000 tons. Other important summer crops are (1981 figures) maize 3,308,000 tons, rice 2,238,000 tons, millet 653,000 tons and sugar cane 8,616,000 tons. Important winter crops are wheat 1,938,000 tons, beans 208,000 tons and onions 654,000 tons. Citrus fruit and other fruits and vegetables are also grown.

Energy.—With its considerable reserves of petroleum and natural gas in Sinai, the Nile Delta and the Western Desert, and the hydro-electric power produced by the Aswan and High Dams, Egypt is self-sufficient in energy. Electricity has been provided to almost all of the country and there are plans to extend the natural gas network to all major cities.

Industry.—The production of petroleum provides Egypt with its major export and supports a growing refining industry. Steel production is another important heavy industry. The major manufacturing industries are in food processing, motor cars and electrical goods, chemical products and yarns and textiles.

FINANCE

	1984–85	1985–86
Estimated revenue	L.E.12,877m.	L.E. 15,000m.
Total expenditure ...	18,277m.	20,000m.

The fiscal year commences July 1.

The monetary unit of Egypt is the Egyptian *pound* (L.E.) of 100 *piastres.*

TRADE

The main imports are wheat and flour, wood and trucks. The main exports are crude petroleum, cotton, cotton yarn, oranges, rice and cotton textiles.

	1981 (millions)
Imports	L.E.6,187
Exports	2,263

Trade with U.K.

	1983	1984
Imports from U.K.	£370,489,000	£427,688,000
Exports to U.K.	79,826,000	164,946,000

Communications.—The road and rail networks link the Nile Valley and Delta with the main development areas to east and west of the river.

The Suez Canal was re-opened in 1975 and a two-stage development project begun to widen and deepen the canal to allow the passage of larger shipping and to permit two-way traffic. Port Said and Suez have been reconstructed and the port of Alexandria is being improved.

CAPITAL.—Cairo (population, estimated in 1985 at 11,500,000), stands on the E. bank of the Nile, about 14 miles from the head of the Delta. Its oldest part is the fortress of Babylon in old Cairo, with its Roman bastions and Coptic churches. The earliest Arab building is the Mosque of 'Amr, dating from A.D. 643, and the most conspicuous is the Citadel, built by Saladin towards the end of the 12th century and containing in its walls the Mosque of Mohamed Ali built in the 19th century.

ΨALEXANDRIA (estimated population in 1983 of 4,000,000), founded 332 B.C. by Alexander the Great, was for over 1,000 years the capital of Egypt and a centre of Hellenic culture which vied with Athens herself. Its great *pharos* (lighthouse), 480 feet high, with a lantern burning resinous wood, was one of the "Seven Wonders of the World". Other towns are: Ismailia (400,000); ΨPort Said (285,000); Mansura (120,000); Asyût (300,000); Faiyûm (180,000); Tanta (150,000); Mahalla el Kubra (130,000); ΨSuez; Ψ Damietta (100,000).

Cairo is 2,520 miles from London: transit *via* Ancona or Venice, 5 days; *via* Marseilles, 6 days.

FLAG.—Horizontal bands of red, white and black, with an eagle in the centre of the white band.

NATIONAL DAY.—July 23 (Anniversary of Revolution in 1952).

BRITISH EMBASSY
Ahmed Ragheb Street, Garden City, Cairo

Ambassador Extraordinary and Plenipotentiary, His Excellency Sir Alan Urwick, K.C.V.O., C.M.G.
British Council Representative, B. Vale, O.B.E., 192 Sharia el Nil, Agouza, Cairo. There is also a library in Alexandria.

EQUATORIAL GUINEA

President, Col. Teodoro Obiang Nguema Mbasogo, *took office*, Aug. 1979.

Equatorial Guinea (formerly Spanish Guinea) consists of the island of Bioco (formerly Macias Nguema), in the Bight of Biafra about 20 miles from the west coast of Africa, Pagalu Island (formerly Annobon) in the Gulf of Guinea, the Corisco Islands (Corisco, Elobey Grande and Elobey Chico) and Rio Muni, a mainland area between Cameroon and Gabon. It has a total area of about 28,000 sq. km. and a population (1983 estimate) of 300,000.

Government.—Formerly colonies of Spain, the territories now forming the Republic of Equatorial Guinea were constituted as two provinces of Metropolitan Spain, in 1960, became autonomous in 1964 and fully independent in 1968. Serious disorders in Rio Muni early in 1969 caused many of the Spanish community to leave. Following Nigerian allegations of continuing mistreatment, most of the Nigerian labour force, on whom cocoa production largely depended, were repatriated in late 1975 and early 1976.

In Aug. 1979, President Macias was deposed by a revolutionary military council headed by his nephew Col. T. Obiang Nguema. The first parliamentary elections since 1968 were held on Aug. 28, 1983, under a new constitution approved by a referendum in Aug. 1982. Forty-one representatives were elected to the National Assembly for a five-year term.

Economy.—The chief products are cocoa, coffee and wood (which is exported almost entirely from Rio Muni). Production has declined and except for cocoa, there is little commercial agriculture and the economy is now heavily dependent on outside aid, principally from Spain. Equatorial Guinea entered the 'Franc zone' in 1985.

Trade with U.K.

	1983	1984
Imports from U.K.	£10,000	£553,000
Exports to U.K.	13,000	559,000

CAPITAL.—ΨMalabo (formerly known as Santa Isabel) on the island of Bioco (population 25,000). ΨBata is the principal town and port of Rio Muni.

FLAG.—Three horizontal bands, green over white over red; blue triangle next staff; coat of arms in centre of white band.

British Ambassador, (resides at Yaoundé).

ETHIOPIA

Head of State, Chairman of the Derg and of the Council of Ministers, Lt.-Col. Mengistu Haile Mariam.

Secretary General of the Derg and Deputy Chairman of the Council of Ministers, Capt. Fikre-Selassie Wogderes.

EMBASSY IN LONDON
17 Prince's Gate, SW17 1PZ
[01-589 7212]

Ambassador Extraordinary and Plenipotentiary, His Excellency Ato Teferra.

Position and Extent.—Ethiopia is in North-Eastern Africa, bounded on the north-west by the Sudan; on the south by Kenya; on the east by Djibouti and the Republic of Somalia: and on the north-east by the Red Sea. The area is estimated at 400,000 square miles, with a population (1984) of 42,000,000. (Other unofficial estimates put the population even higher.) About one-third are of the dominant race of Semitic origin (Amharas and Tigreans) and the remainder mainly Gallas (about 40 per cent of the population), Somalis and Afar.

Ethiopia has a large central plateau (average height, 6,000–7,000 ft.) which rises to nearly 15,000 ft. at Ras Dashan in the north. The plateau drops to the Nile basin in the west and the Red Sea in the east. To the north (Eritrea) and east (Ogaden) the land is mostly desert. The chief river is the Blue Nile, issuing from Lake Tana; the Atbara and many other tributaries of the Nile also rise in the Ethiopian highlands.

Those of Semitic origin (Amharas and Tigreans), and many of the Gallas, are Christians of the

Ethiopian Orthodox Church, which was formerly led by the head of the Coptic Church, the Patriarch at Alexandria. Since 1959, however, the Ethiopian Church has been autocephalous and the new Patriarch, Abuna Tekle Haimanot, was enthroned in 1976. The Afar people, who inhabit lowland Eritrea, Wollo, Harargne and Bale provinces, and the Somalis, in the south-east, are Moslem. The Falashas, to be found principally in Gandar and Tigre provinces, practise Judaism. Between autumn 1984 and February 1985 a secret airlift ("Operation Moses") took 7,000 of the estimated 25,000 Falashas to Israel, via Sudan.

History.—The basic Hamitic culture was heavily influenced by Semitic immigration from Arabia in the centuries about the time of Christ. Christianity was introduced in the 4th century. The empire expanded sporadically, attaining a zenith in the 6th century under the Axum rulers, but subsequently checked by Islamic expansion from the east. Modern Ethiopia dates from 1855 when Theodore succeeded in establishing supremacy over the various tribes. The last Emperor was Haile Selassie who reigned from 1930, though in exile from 1936–1941 during the Italian occupation. After considerable military and civil unrest the armed forces assumed power in Sept. 1972 and deposed the Emperor. Pending the promulgation of a new Constitution the country is ruled by a Provisional Military Administration Council (the *Derg*). A Worker's Party on the Soviet model was formed in Sept. 1984, with Lt. Col. Mengistu as Secretary-General.

Eritrea was administered by Great Britain from the end of the Second World War until September 15, 1952, when it was federated with Ethiopia. It was incorporated as a province of Ethiopia in 1962. An armed campaign for independence started in 1962 and has intensified since the early 1970's.

Due to the lack of spring rains both the harvests of 1983 and 1984 failed. A famine relief programme launched in October 1984 drew world-wide attention to the problem, and airlifts of food began almost immediately. In two of the worst hit areas, the provinces of Tigre and Eritrea, the situation was exacerbated by the difficulty of supplying food and other aid to areas experiencing guerrilla activity.

In July 1977, Somalia, claiming the Ogaden region of Ethiopia in support of Western Somalia Liberation Front guerrillas, invaded the country. Ethiopia, with Soviet arms, and the aid of Cuban troops, was able to defeat the Somalis. The Somali regular army withdrew in March 1978, but guerrilla activity by the Western Somalia Liberation Front continues.

The Tigrean province, which lies south of Eritrea, has also sought to secede from Ethiopia: the activities of the Tigrean People's Liberation Front have escalated since the early 1980s, and the T.P.L.F. claims to control and administer large areas of the province.

Production and Industry.—The principal pursuit is agriculture, which accounts for approximately 50 per cent. of G.D.P., 90 per cent. of exports and 85 per cent. of total employment. Land was nationalized in 1975 and tenants given rights of use to the land they had tilled: large private holdings became state farms. The major food crops are teff, maize, barley, sorghum, wheat, pulses and oil seeds. Coffee, the principal export crop generates over 60 per cent. of the country's export earnings. The country's livestock herd is the largest in Africa.

Manufacturing industry accounts for 10 per cent. of G.D.P. and is heavily dependent on agriculture. Ethiopia's known, but as yet largely unexploited, natural resources include gold, platinum, copper and potash. Traces of oil and natural gas have been found.

Communications.—With the aid of loans from the IBRD and the International Development Agency, a network of roads has been built linking the major cities with each other, and with the Sudanese and Kenyan borders and the Red Sea coast. There is a railway link from Addis Ababa to Djibouti, though this is vulnerable to guerrilla activity. The narrow gauge line in Eritrea has been closed by conflict. The Ethiopian Air Lines maintain regular services from Addis Ababa to many provincial towns. External services are operated throughout Africa and to Europe and the Middle and Far East.

Defence.—Under the Ministry of Defence the armed forces comprise the Army, the Air Force and the Navy. The Army consists of 300,000 soldiers divided into 24 divisions. Nearly 200,000 of these soldiers are militia.

The Air Force comprises a transport squadron, a bomber squadron, three fighter squadrons, a training squadron, a jet conversion squadron, and an elementary training unit. There are 120 fighter planes, mostly of Russian manufacture, and a few F.5.s. The Air Force Headquarters is situated at Debre Zeit.

The Navy has a headquarters in Addis Ababa with a main base at Massawa and a smaller one at Assab.

National Military Service was established on May 4, 1983 and came into effect in May 1984.

Education.—Elementary education is provided without religious discrimination by Government schools in the main centres of population; there are also Mission schools, and cadet-schools for the Army, Air Force, and Police. Government secondary schools are found mainly in Addis Ababa, but also in most of the provincial capitals. The National University (founded 1961) co-ordinates the institutions of higher education (University College, Engineering, Building and Theological Colleges in Addis Ababa, Agricultural College at Alemaya, near Harar, and Public Health Centre in Gondar, etc.). It is intended to develop the provincial colleges to university level and status. Amharic is the official language of instruction, with English as the first foreign language and main language of instruction from secondary level upwards. Arabic is taught in Koran Schools; and Ge'ez (the ancient Ethiopic) in Christian Church Schools, which abound. Adult education is met to some extent by institutes which provide evening classes in Addis Ababa.

FINANCE

	1984
Revenue	US$1,062·8m.
Expenditure	1,449·3m.

The Ethiopian unit of currency is the *birr* of 100 *cents.*

Trade.—The chief imports by value are machinery and transport equipment, manufactured goods and chemicals (from U.K.); the principal exports by value being coffee, oilseeds, hides and skins, and pulses.

TRADE

	1984
Total Imports	US$917·8m.
Total Exports	402·8m.

Trade with U.K.

	1983	1984
Imports from U.K.	£34,092,000	£63,434,000
Exports to U.K.	12,071,000	13,733,000

CAPITAL.— Addis Ababa (population, estimated 1,300,000), also capital of the province of Shoa; Asmara (population 250,000) is the capital of the Province of Eritrea. Dire Dawa is the most important commercial centre after Addis Ababa and Asmara, Ψ Massawa and ΨAssab (recently enlarged) are the two main ports. There are ancient architectural remains at Aksum, Gondar, Lalibela and elsewhere.

ETHIOPIAN FLAG.—Three horizontal bands; green, yellow, red.

NATIONAL DAY.—September 12 (People's Revolution Day).

BRITISH EMBASSY
Fikre Mariam Abatechan Street (P.O. Box 858),
Addis Ababa

Ambassador Extraordinary and Plenipotentiary, His Excellency Brian L. Barder (1982).

There is a British Consular Office at *Addis Ababa.*

British Council Representative, N. O. Hudson, O.B.E., Artistic Building, Adwa Avenue (P.O. Box 1043), Addis Ababa. There is also a library in Asmara.

FINLAND
(Suomi)

President, Dr. Mauno Koivisto, *born*, 1923, *elected*, Jan 26, 1982.

CABINET

Prime Minister, Kalevi Sorsa (*SDP*).
Foreign Affairs, Paavo Väkyrynen (*CP*).
Foreign Trade, Jermu Laine (*SDP*).
Justice, Christoffer Taxell (*SPPF*).
Interior, Kaisa Raatikainen (*SDP*).
Environment, Matti Ahde (*SDP*).
Defence, Veikko Pihlajamäki (*CP*).
Finance, Ahti Pekkala (*CP*).
Finance II, Pekka Vennamo (*FRP*).
Education, Kaarina Suonio (*SDP*).
Education II, Gustav Björkstrand (*SPPF*).
Agriculture and Forestry, Toivo Yläjärvi (*CP*).
Transport and Communications, Matti Luttinen (*SDP*).
Trade and Industry, Seppo Lindblom (*SDP*).
Social Affairs and Health, Eeva Kuuskoski-Vikatmaa (*CP*).
Social Affairs and Health II, Matti Puhakka (*SDP*).
Labour, Urpo Leppänen (*FRP*).
(*CP*=Centre Party, *SDP*=Social Democratic Party, *SPPF*=Swedish People's Party of Finland, *FRP*=Finnish Rural Party).

FINNISH EMBASSY AND CONSULATE
38 Chesham Place, SW1X 8HW
[01–235 9531]

Ambassador Extraordinary and Plenipotentiary, His Excellency Ilkka Pastinen (1983).
Minister Counsellor, Veijo Sampovaara.
Counsellor, Leif Richard Fagernäs.
1st Secretary, I. Ström.
Press Counsellor, Lasse Lehtinen.
Defence Attaché, Cdr. C. T. R. Gentz.

Area and Population.—A country situated on the Gulfs of Finland and Bothnia, with a total area of 130,165 square miles, of which 70 per cent. is forest, 10 per cent. cultivated, 9 per cent. lakes and 11 per cent. waste and other land. The population (December, 1982) was 4,844,000, of whom 90·3 per cent. are Lutheran, 1·1 per cent. Greek Orthodox and 8·4 per cent. others.

The Aland Archipelago (Ahvenanmaa), a group of small islands at the entrance to the Gulf of Bothnia, covers about 572 square miles, with a population (December, 1980) of 21,682 (95·2 per cent. Swedish-speaking). The islands have a semi-autonomous status.

Government.—Under the Constitution there is a single Chamber (*Eduskunta*) composed of 200 members, elected by universal suffrage. The legislative power is vested in the Chamber and the President.

The highest executive power is held by the President who is elected for a period of 6 years.

The present government came into office on May 6, 1983. The four parties in the coalition are the Social Democratic Party, the Centre Party, the Swedish People's Party of Finland, and the Finnish Rural Party.

Defence.—By the terms of the Peace Treaty (Feb. 10, 1947) with U.K. and U.S.S.R., the Army is limited to a force not exceeding 34,400. The Navy is limited to a total of 10,000 tons displacement with personnel not exceeding 4,500. The Air Force, including naval air arm, is limited to 60 machines with a personnel not exceeding 3,000. Bombers or aircraft with bomb-carrying facilities are expressly forbidden. The Defence Forces contain a cadre of regular officers and N.C.O.'s, but their bulk is provided by conscripts who serve for 8–11 months. Total strength of trained and equipped reserves is over 700,000, 16,500 of which have served in the U.N. peacekeeping force.

Education.—Primary education (co-educational comprehensive school) is compulsory for children from 7 to 16 years, and free of charge. In the autumn of 1981, there were 551,906 in comprehensive schools (332,887 at basic stage and 219,019 at upper stage), 103,369 in senior secondary schools and 135,000 in vocational institutions of senior level. There are 22 universities or other schools of academic level, and enrolment was (1981) 84,716.

Language and Literature.—There are two official languages in Finland. 93·5 per cent of the population speak Finnish as their first language, 6·3 Swedish (1979). The remaining 0·2 per cent. speak other languages (mainly Lapps who number about 2,500 and live in the Far North). Both Finnish and Swedish are used for administration and education; newspapers, books, plays and films appear in both languages. There is a vigorous modern literature. F. E. Sillanpää, who died in 1964, was awarded the Nobel prize for Literature. Best known among the living authors are Väinö Linna, Veijo Meri and Paavo Haavikko. There are 62 daily newspapers in Finland which appear on 4 or more days per week (55 Finnish language, and 7 Swedish).

Production and Industry.—Finland is a highly industrialized country producing a wide range of capital and consumer goods. Timber and the products of the forest-based industries remain the backbone of the economy, accounting for 40 per cent. of her export earnings, but the importance of the metal-working, shipbuilding and engineering industries has been growing. This sector in 1981 accounted for 31 per cent. of Finland's exports. The textile industry is well developed and Finland's glass, ceramics and furniture industries enjoy international reputations. Other important industries are rubber, plastics, chemicals and pharmaceuticals, footwear, foodstuffs and electronic equipment.

Communications.—There are 6,976 kilometres of railroad, a railway connection with Sweden and U.S.S.R., passenger boat connection with Sweden, West Germany, Poland and U.S.S.R. Vessels on the London to Leningrad route call at Helsinki. There are also passenger/cargo services between Britain and Helsinki, Kotka and other Finnish ports. External civil air services are maintained by most European airlines. The merchant fleet at the end of March 1982 totalled 486 vessels (2,441,784 tons gross); 150 passenger vessels (257,677 tons gross), 46 tankers (1,283,583), 192 dry cargo vessels (915,299) and 98 other vessels (15,225).

FINANCE

	1983	1984
	Finnmarks	*Finnmarks*
Revenue (*Budget*) ...	64,938,000	75,395,000
Expenditure (*Budget*)	76,590,000	86,095,000

Currency.—The unit of currency is the *markka* of 10 penniä.

TRADE

The principal imports are raw materials, machinery and manufactured goods. The exports are principally the output of the paper and other forest industries, engineering, metal industry (*e.g.* paper-working machinery and ships) and chemicals.

	1983	1984
	Finnmarks	*Finnmarks*
Total Imports	71,519,000	74,684,000
Total Exports	69,751,000	80,922,000

Trade with U.K.

	1983	1984
Imports from U.K. ...	£539,721,000	£684,477,000
Exports to U.K.	966,017,000	1,248,561,000

CAPITAL.—ΨHelsinki (Helsingfors). Population (Jan. 1981), 482,800; other towns are Tampere (Tammerfors), 166,300; ΨTurku (Åbo), 163,700; Espoo, 137,500; Vantaa, 132,100; Lahti, 94,700; ΨOulu (Uleåborg), 93,800; ΨPori (Björneborg), 79,400; Kuopio, 74,600; Jyväskylä, 64,200.

NATIONAL DAY.—December 6 (Day of Independence).

FLAG.—White with blue cross.

BRITISH EMBASSY
Uudenmaankatu 16–20
00120 Helsinki 12

Ambassador Extraordinary and Plenipotentiary, His Excellency Alan Brooke Turner, C.M.G. (1983).

Counsellor (*Commercial*), B. Rose.

1st Secretaries, P. G. Harborne; Miss M. Ramsay.

Defence, Naval, Military and Air Attaché, Lt.-Col. W. J. Collings, M.B.E., R.A.

There are British Consular offices at *Helsinki, Tampere, Turku, Pori, Kotka, Oulu, Vaasa* and *Kuopio.*

British Council Representative, B. Nightingale, Etelä esplanadi 22A, 00130 Helsinki 13.

FRANCE
(La République Française)

President of the French Republic, Francois Mitterrand, *elected* May 10, 1981.

CABINET

Prime Minister, Laurent Fabius.
Foreign Affairs, Roland Dumas.
Interior and Decentralisation, Pierre Joxe.
Justice, M. Robert Badinter.
Economy, Finance and the Budget, Pierre Bérégovey.
Commerce and Tourism, M. Michel Crepeau.
Defence, Paul Quilès.
Education, Jean-Pierre Chevènement.
Social Affairs and Government Spokesman, Mme. Georgina Dufoix.
Agriculture, Henri Nallet.
Industrial Redeployment and External Trade, Mme. Edith Cresson.
Town Planning, Housing and Transport, Jean Auroux.
Planning and Regional Development, Gaston Defferre.
Labour, Employment and Vocational Training, Michel Delebarre.
Environment, Mme. Huguette Bouchardeau.
Research and Technology, Hubert Curien.
Culture, Jack Lang.
New Caledonian Affairs, Edgard Pisani.

FRENCH EMBASSY IN LONDON
58 Knightsbridge, SW1X 7JT
[01–235 8080].

Ambassador Extraordinary and Plenipotentiary, His Excellency Monsieur Jacques Viot (1984).

Area and Population.—The largest state in Central Europe, extending from 42° 20′ to 51° 5′ N. lat., and from 7° 85′ E. to 4° 45′ W. long. Its area is estimated at 213,000 sq. miles (544,000 sq. km.), divided into 95 departments, including the island of Corsica, in the Mediterranean, off the west coast of Italy. The population of France in 1984 was 54,832,000.

POPULATION OF THE REGIONS 1984
(Names of Departments in brackets)

Alsace (Bas-Rhin, Haut-Rhin)	1,583,000
Aquitaine (Dordogne, Gironde, Landes, Lot-et-Garonne, Pyrénées-Atlantiques)	2,688,300
Auvergne (Allier, Cantal, Haute-Loire, Puy-de-Dôme)	1,335,200
Basse-Normandie (Calvados, Manche, Orne)	1,361,200
Bourgogne (Côte-d'Or, Nièvre, Saône-et-Loire, Yonne)	1,601,400
Bretagne (Côtes-du-Nord, Finistère, Ille-et-Vilaine, Morbihan)	2,737,900
Centre (Cher, Eure-et-Loir, Indre, Indre-et-Loire, Loir-et-Cher, Loiret)	2,293,800
Champagne-Ardenne (Ardennes, Aube, Marne, Haute-Marne)	1,348,900
Corse (Corse-du-Sud, Haute-Corse)	244,600
Franche-Comté (Doubs, Haute-Saône, Jura, Territoire-de-Belfort)	1,090,400
Haute-Normandie (Eure, Seine-Maritime)	1,671,900
Ile-de-France (Essone, Haute-de-Seine, Seine-et-Marne, Seine-St. Denis, Val-de Marne, Val-d'Oise, Ville de Paris, Yvelines)	10,147,400
Languedoc-Roussillon (Aude, Gard, Hérault, Lozère, Pyrénées-Orientales)	1,963,200
Limousin (Corrèze, Creuse, Haute-Vienne)	737,700
Lorraine (Meurthe-et-Moselle, Meuse, Moselle, Vosges)	2,318,500
Midi-Pyrénées (Ariège, Aveyron, Haute-Garonne, Gers, Lot, Hautes-Pyrénées, Tarn, Tarn-et-Garonne)	2,340,200
Nord (Nord, Pas-de-Calais)	3,941,300
Pays-de-la Loire (Loire-Atlantique, Maine-et-Loire, Mayenne, Sarthe, Vendee)	2,972,800
Picardie (Aisne, Oise, Somme)	1,758,900
Poitou-Charentes (Charente, Charente-Maritime, Deux-Sèvres, Vienne)	1,575,700
Provence-Alpes-Côte d'Azur (Alpes-de-Haute Provence, Alpes-Maritime, Bouches-du-Rhône, Var, Vaucluse)	4,028,900
Rhône-Alpes (Ain, Ardèche, Drôme, Isère, Loire, Rhône, Savoie, Haute-Savoie)	5,090,800

Archæology, etc.—There are dolmens and menhirs in Brittany, prehistoric remains and cave drawings in Dordogne and Ariège, and throughout France various megalithic monuments erected by primitive tribes, predecessors of Iberian invaders from Spain (now represented by the Basques), Ligurians from northern Italy and Celts or Gauls from the valley of the Danube. Julius Cæsar found Gaul "divided into three parts" and described three political groups—Aquitanians south of the Garonne, Celts between the Garonne and the Seine and Marne, and Belgae from the Seine to the Rhine. Roman remains are plentiful throughout France in the form of aqueducts, arenas, triumphal arches, &c., and the celebrated Norman and Gothic Cathedrals, including Notre Dame in Paris, and those of Chartres, Reims, Amiens (where Peter the Hermit preached the First Crusade for the recovery of the Holy Sepulchre), Bourges, Beauvais, Rouen, etc., have survived invasions and bombardments, with only partial damage, and many of the renaissance and the XVIIth and XVIIIth century châteaux survived the French Revolution.

Language and Literature.—French is the universal language of France and of a large proportion of the people of Belgium, Luxemburg, Switzerland, North and West Africa, and the Province of Quebec, Canada. The work of the *French Academy,* founded by Richelieu in 1635, has established *le bon usage,* equivalent to "The Queen's English" in Great Britain. French authors have been awarded the Nobel Prize for Literature on 11 occasions—R.F.A. Sully-Prudhomme (1901), F. Mistral (1904), Romain Rolland (1915), Anatole France (1921), Henri Bergson (1927), Roger M. du Gard (1937), André Gide (1947), François Mauriac (1952), Albert Camus (1957), St. John Perse (Alexis Léger) (1960) and Jean Paul Sartre (1964).

GOVERNMENT

Parliament consists of the National Assembly and the Senate. The normal session of Parliament is confined to 5½ months each year and it may also meet in extraordinary session for 12 days at the request of the Prime Minister or a majority of the Assembly.

The Prime Minister is appointed by the President, as is the Cabinet on the Prime Minister's recommendation. They are responsible to Parliament, but as the executive is constitutionally separate from the legislature Ministers may not sit in Parliament.

A Constitutional Council is responsible for supervising all elections and referenda and must be consulted on all constitutional matters and before the President of the Republic assumes emergency powers.

DEFENCE

The personnel of the Defence Forces in September 1983 totalled 246,000. National nuclear forces include medium-range ballistic missiles, submarine-launched ballistic missiles and *Mirage* IV medium bombers.

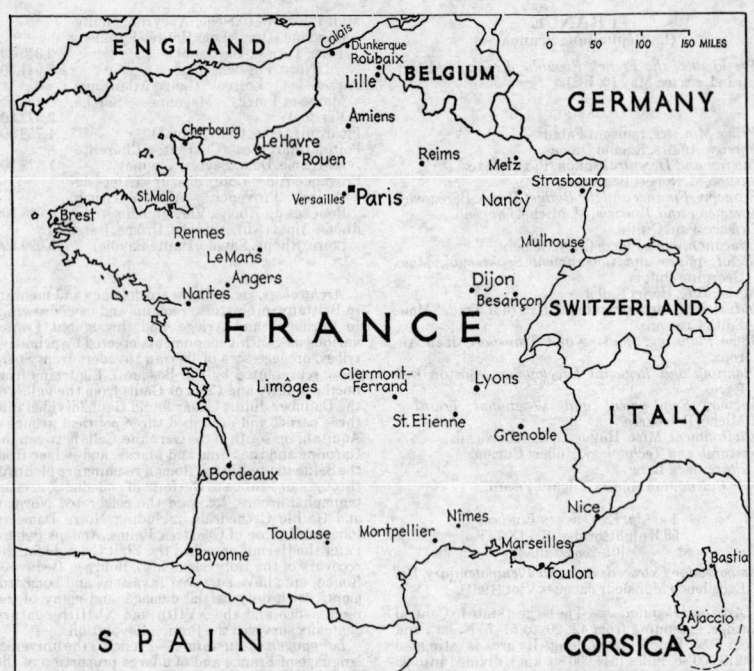

The Army has a variety of new French-made equipment in service, including medium tanks, field and anti-aircraft SP guns, trucks and radio equipment. Defence Budget for 1983, 141,500 million francs.

EDUCATION

The educational system is highly centralized and is administered by the Ministry of National Education. Local Administration comprises 25 Territorial Academies, with inspecting staff for all grades, and Departmental Councils presided over by the *Préfet*, and charged especially with primary education.

Primary and secondary education are compulsory, free and secular, the school age being from 6 to 16. Schools may be single-sex or co-educational. Primary education is given in nursery schools, primary schools and *collèges d'enseignement général* (4-year secondary modern course); Secondary education in *collèges d'enseignement technique, collèges d'enseignement secondaire* and *lycées* (7-year course leading to one of the five *baccalauréats*). Special schools are numerous.

There are numerous *Grandes Ecoles* in France which award diplomas in many subjects not taught at university, especially applied science and engineering. Most of them are State institutions but have a competitive system of entry, unlike the universities. There are universities in twenty-four towns in France, two or three in some major provincial towns and thirteen in Paris and the immediate surrounding district.

In 1982–83 enrolment in primary schools was 4,390,092; in secondary schools 5,135,371, and in post-secondary education 1,096,601 (of which university students accounted for 925,370).

COMMUNICATIONS

Roads.—The length of roads in use at the end of 1983 was 805,000 km. of which 5,500 km. were motorways.

Railways.—The system of railroads in France is very extensive. The length of lines open for traffic at the end of 1983 was 34,600 km., of which 10,700 km. were electrified.

Shipping.—The French mercantile marine consisted in Jan. 1982, of 393 ships of over 100 tons gross, of which 28 were passenger vessels (169,878 tons gross), 100 tankers (7,088,720 tons gross) and 265 cargo vessels (3,060,031 tons gross). The principal rivers of France are the Seine, Loire, Garonne, and Rhône, the navigable waterways in general use in 1983 were 6,500 km.

ECONOMY

Budget.—Government expenditure by function, as provided for in the 1984 general Budget, was:

	F million
Agriculture	1,887
Commerce and the Working Class	71
Culture	2,719
Economy, Finance and Budget	10,828
Education	5,611
Environment	581
Foreign Affairs	1,630
Industry and Research	25,897

Interior	4,256
Justice	525
Leisure, Youth and Sports	442
Overseas Departments and Territories	579
Social Services, Labour, Health and Employment	1,785
Tourism	81
Town Planning and Housing	23,214
Transport	10,121
Other expenditure	5,349
Total general Budget	**95,576**

Currency.—The unit of currency is the *franc* of 100 *centimes*. At April 1982 French gold and currency reserves stood at *F*282,343 million.

PRODUCTION

Gross domestic product in 1983 was *F*3,597,000 million, and G.D.P. per capita *F*72,700.

Agriculture.—Approximately 316,000 sq. km. of land is used for agricultural purposes (173 sq. km. ploughland and 126 sq. km. pasture) and 144 sq. km. is forested. Production in 1983 included wheat 24,800,000 tonnes, and sugar-beet was 26,500,000 tonnes. Value of production in 1983 was crops *F*119,400 million and livestock *F*113,100 million.

The vine is extensively cultivated, regions famous for their wines including Bordeaux, Burgundy and Champagne. Production of wine in 1982 was 79,659,000 hectolitres. Cognac, liqueurs and cider are also important products.

Energy.—France produces its own oil, the greater part coming from fields in the Landes area, but is a net importer of crude oil, for processing by its important oil-refining industry. Natural gas is produced in the foothills of the Pyrenees. Electricity production was 297,100 million KWh in 1983, of which 71,800 million KWh. was hydro-electric and 144,600 million KWh. nuclear power.

Industry.—France's heavy industries include oil-refining and the production of iron and steel, and aluminium. In 1983 production of pig-iron was 13,800,000 tonnes, steel 17,600,000 tonnes, cement 24,400,000 tonnes, plastic and rubber 3,540,000 tonnes, wood pulp 1,870,000 tonnes, sugar 5,440,000 tonnes. Other important industries produce chemicals, tyres, aluminium, textiles, and processed food. Engineering products include motor vehicles, and television and radio sets.

TRADE

The principal imports are raw materials for the heavy and manufacturing industries (*e.g.* oil, minerals, chemicals), machinery and precision instruments, agricultural products and vehicles. Raw materials, semi-manufactured and manufactured goods are also France's principal exports. Other member countries of the E.E.C. are France's main trading partners.

TOTAL TRADE

	1983
	Francs
Imports	799,800 m.
Exports	694,700 m.

Trade with U.K.

	1983	1984
Imports from U.K.	£5,651,521,000	£7,082,389,000
Exports to U.K.	5,043,118,000	5,885,715,000

CAPITAL OF FRANCE. Paris, on the Seine. Population (estimated, 1982), 2,188,918 (town); 8,707,000 (incl. suburbs).

The largest conurbations (populations, 1982) are ΨMarseilles (1,111,000); Lyons (1,221,000); Toulouse (541,000); ΨLille (936,000) and Bordeaux (640,000).

The chief towns of Corsica are ΨAjaccio (55,279) and ΨBastia (45,081).

Paris is distant from London 267 miles; transit by air, 1 *hr.*

FLAG.—The "tricolour", three vertical bands, blue, white, red (blue next to flagstaff).

NATIONAL DAY.—July 14.

BRITISH EMBASSY
35 rue du Faubourg St. Honoré, 75383 Paris

Ambassador Extraordinary and Plenipotentiary, His Excellency Sir John Fretwell (1982).
Minister, P. J. Weston.
Defence and Military Attaché, Brig. A. C. Vivian, C.B.E.
Chancellor and Head of Chancery, A. C. D. S. MacRae.
Counsellor and Consul-General, P. J. Roberts.

BRITISH CONSULAR OFFICES
There are British Consulates-General in Metropolitan France at *Paris, Bordeaux, Lille, Lyons, Marseilles.*

BRITISH COUNCIL
Representative in Paris, P. J. Prescott, 9 rue de Constantine, 75007 Paris.
There are British Council libraries at *Paris, Bordeaux, Lille, Lyons* and *Marseilles.*

FRANCO-BRITISH CHAMBER OF COMMERCE
26 avenue Victor Hugo, 75116 Paris

President, N. Maxwell Lawford.
Vice-Presidents, R. E. King; J. Tuby.

OVERSEAS DEPARTMENTS

Legislation passed in Dec. 1982 by the French Parliament granted greater powers of self-government to four of the five overseas departments—French Guiana, Guadeloupe, Martinique and Réunion. These former colonies had enjoyed departmental status since 1947 and the status of regions of France since 1974. Elections to their new directly-elected Assemblies were held in each department in Feb. 1983 and the Assemblies will operate in parallel with the existing, indirectly constituted Regional Councils.

French Guyana.—Situated on the north-eastern coast of South America, French Guyana is flanked by Surinam on the west and by Brazil on the south and east. Area, 35,135 sq. miles. Population (1982), 73,022. Capital, ΨCayenne (38,135). Under the administration of French Guyana is a group of islands (St. Joseph, Ile Royal and Ile du Diable), known as Iles du Salut. On Devil's Isle, Captain Dreyfus was imprisoned from 1894 to 1899.

Guadeloupe.—A number of islands in the Leeward Islands group of the West Indies, consisting of the two main islands of Guadeloupe (or Basse-Terre) and Grande-Terre, with the adjacent islands of Marie-Galante, La Désirade and Îles des Saintes, and the islands of St. Martin and St. Barthélemy over 150 miles to the north-west. Area, 657 sq. miles. Population (1982), 328,400. Capital ΨBasse Terre (15,778) in Guadeloupe. Other towns are ΨPointe à Pitre (23,889) on Grande-Terre and ΨGrand Bourg (6,611) in Marie Galante.

Martinique.—An island situated in the Windward Islands group of the West Indies, between Dominica in the north and St. Lucia in the south. Area, 427 sq. miles. Population (1982), 328,566. Capital ΨFort de France (100,576). Other towns are ΨTrinité (11,214) and ΨMarin (6,104).

Mayotte.—Area, 144 sq. miles. Population (1980 estimate), 50,400. Capital, Dzaoudzi (4,147). Part of the Comoros Islands group, Mayotte remained a French dependency when the other 3 islands became independent as the Comoros Republic in 1975. Since 1976 the island has been a *collectivité particulière*, an intermediate status between Overseas Department and Overseas Territory.

Réunion.—Réunion, which became a French possession in 1638, lies in the Indian Ocean, about 569 miles east of Madagascar and 110 miles S.W. of Mauritius. Area, 969 sq. miles. Population (1982), 515,814. Capital, St. Denis (109,072).

Also lying in the Indian Ocean adjacent to Madagascar are the smaller, uninhabited islands of Bassas da India, Europa, Iles Glorieuses, Juan de Nova and Tromelin, which are administered from Réunion.

St. Pierre and Miquelon—Area, 93 sq. miles. Population (1982), 6,041. Two small groups of Islands off the coast of Newfoundland. Became an Overseas Department in 1976 but this status is under review.

OVERSEAS TERRITORIES

French Polynesia.—Five archipelagos in the south Pacific, comprising the Society Islands (Windward Islands group includes Tahiti, Moorea, Makatea, Mehetia, Tetiaoro, Tubai Manu, etc: Leeward Islands group includes Huahine, Raiatea, Tahaa, Bora-Bora, Maupiti, etc.), the Tuamotu Islands (Rangiroa, Hao, Turéia, etc.), the Gambier Islands (Mangareva, etc.), the Tubuai Islands (Rimatara, Rurutu, Tubuai, Raivavae, Rapa, etc.) and the Marquesas Islands (Nuku-Hiva, Hiva-Oa, Fatu-Hiva, Tahuata, Ua Huka, etc.). Area, 1,522 sq. miles. Population (1983 estimate) 168,000. Capital, ΨPapeete (15,220) in Tahiti. Economy based on tourism and exports of copra, coffee, vanilla, citrus fruits and cultured pearls.

New Caledonia.—A large island in the Western Pacific, 700 miles E. of Queensland. Dependencies are the Isles of Pines, the Loyalty Islands (Mahé, Lifou, Urea, etc.), the Bélep Archipelago, the Chesterfield Islands, the Huon Islands and Walpole. New Caledonia was discovered in 1774 and annexed by France in 1854; from 1871 to 1896 it was a convict settlement. Area, 7,374 sq. miles. Population (estimate, 1983), 145,000. Capital ΨNoumea (12,000). It is one of the world's largest producers of nickel.

Southern and Antarctic Territories.—Created in 1955 from the former Réunion dependencies, the territory comprises the islands of New Amsterdam (25 sq. miles) and St. Paul (2·7 sq. miles), the Kerguelen Islands (2,700 sq. miles) and Crozet Islands (116 sq. miles) archipelagos and Adélie Land (116,800 sq. miles) in the Antarctic continent. The only population are members of staff of the scientific stations.

Wallis and Futuna Islands.—Two groups of islands (the Wallis Archipelago and the Îles du Hooru) in the central Pacific, N.E. of Fiji. Area, 106 sq. miles. Population (1983) 12,400. Capital, Mata-Utu on Urea, the main island of the Wallis group.

THE FRENCH COMMUNITY

The Constitution of the fifth French Republic promulgated on Oct. 6, 1958, envisaged the establishment of a French Community of States closely linked with common institutions. A number of the former French States in Africa have seceded from the Community but for all practical purposes continue to enjoy the same close links with France as those that remain formally members of the French Community. The Community Institutions in fact never operated as envisaged. Nevertheless, with the exception of Guinea, which opted out of the Community in the 1958 referendum, all the former French African colonies are closely linked to France by a series of financial, technical and economic agreements.

FRANCOPHONE COUNTRIES

In the following countries French is either the official or national language or the language of instruction; where there is another national language the name of it is shown after the name of the country:—Algeria (*Arabic*); Belgium (*Flemish*); Benin; Burkina Faso; Burundi (*Kirundi*); Cambodia (*Khmer*); Cameroon (*English*); parts of Canada (in Quebec, parts of Ontario and New Brunswick) (*English*); Central African Republic (*Sangho*); Chad; Congo; France; Gabon; Guinea; Haiti (*Creole*); Ivory Coast; Laos (*Laotian*); Lebanon (*Arabic*); Luxembourg (*German and Letzeburgesch*); Madagascar (*Malagasy*); Mali; Morocco (*Arabic*); Mauritania (*Arabic*); Niger; Rwanda (*Kinyarwanda*); Senegal; Switzerland (1,000,000 French speaking); Togo; Tunisia (*Arabic*); Vietnam (*Vietnamese*); Zaire. French is also spoken in the Overseas Departments (*see* above).

GABON
(Gabonese Republic)

President, El Hadj Omar Bongo, *assumed office*, Dec. 1967, *re-elected*, Feb. 1973 and Dec. 1979.

EMBASSY IN LONDON
48 Kensington Court, W.8
[01–937 5285/9]

Ambassador Extraordinary and Plenipotentiary, His Excellency Monsieur Léon N'Dong (1980).

Gabon lies on the Atlantic coast of Africa at the Equator and is flanked on the north by Equatorial Guinea and Cameroon and on the east and south by the People's Republic of Congo. It has an area of 101,400 sq. miles (267,667 sq. km.) and a population (estimated 1982) of 1,200,000. (*For* MAP, *see* Index). Gabon elected on Nov. 28, 1958, to remain an autonomous republic within the French Community and was proclaimed fully independent on August 17, 1960.

The Constitution provides for an Executive President directly elected for a seven-year term, who appoints the Council of Ministers. There is a unicameral National Assembly comprising 84 members directly elected for a five-year term and nine members nominated by the President. The sole legal party is the *Parti democratique gabonais*.

Gabon's economy is heavily dependent on oil, and, to a much lesser extent, other mineral resources. Oil production in 1984 was estimated at 8·8 million tons. Manganese and uranium are also mined and Gabon has considerable timber reserves (particularly Okoumé) although production in this industry has declined in recent years.

Since the mid-1970s Gabon's economic growth, due to oil production, has been considerable. Although there was a slackening-off in 1981–83, the GDP growth rate in real terms for 1984 is expected to be almost 10 per cent over the previous year. Gabon is a full member of OPEC.

Trade with U.K.

	1983	1984
Imports from U.K.	£18,798,000	£20,548,000
Exports to U.K.	66,135,000	70,775,000

CAPITAL.—ΨLibreville (251,000).
FLAG.—Horizontal bands, green, yellow and blue.
NATIONAL DAY.—August 17.

BRITISH EMBASSY
B.P. 476, Libreville

Ambassador Extraordinary and Plenipotentiary, His Excellency Ronald H. T. Bates, *apptd.* 1985.
First Secretary, J. Cummins, M.B.E.

GERMANY
* Deutsches Reich (German Realm)

The term "deutsch" (German) probably began to be used in the 8th century and initially described the language spoken in the eastern part of the Frankish realm which reached its apogee in Charlemagne's reign, subsequently being divided into an eastern and western realm whose political and linguistic borders coincided. Then the term was transferred from the language to its speakers, and ultimately to the region they lived in. The first German realm was the Holy Roman Empire, established in A.D. 962 when Otto I of Saxony was crowned Emperor. The Empire endured until 1806, but from as early as the 12th century the achievement of a national state was prevented by territorial fragmentation into small principalities and dukedoms, the gradually increasing autonomy of their rulers weakening the central power.

The Holy Roman Empire was replaced by a loose association of the individual sovereign states known as the German Confederation, which survived until 1866 when it was dissolved and replaced by the Prussian-dominated North German Federation. Prussia, directed by its Prime Minister (later Chancellor) Otto von Bismarck, had translated its earlier economic predominance amongst the German states into political hegemony by the annexation of the duchies of Schleswig and Holstein from Denmark in 1864 and a decisive defeat of Austria in 1866 (the Seven Weeks War) which ended Austrian influence over German politics. After the Franco-Prussian War of 1870–71 resulted in the defeat of France and the cession to Prussia of Alsace and Lorraine, the south German principalities united with the northern federation to form a second German Empire, the King of Prussia being proclaimed Emperor at Versailles on Jan. 18, 1871.

Germany's defeat in the 1914–18 War led to the abdication of the Emperor and the princes, and the country became a Republic. The 1919 Treaty of Versailles returned Alsace and Lorraine to France, large areas in the east of the country were lost to the newly created state of Poland, and all German colonies placed under the administration of other countries. The world economic crisis of 1929 led to the collapse of the Weimar Republic and the subsequent rise to power of the National Socialist movement of Adolf Hitler, who became Chancellor in 1933.

THE WAR OF 1939–1945.—After concluding a Treaty of Non-Aggression with Soviet Russia (Aug. 24, 1939), Germany invaded Poland (Sept. 1, 1939), thus precipitating war with France and Great Britain, which had (March 31) given a pledge to support Poland against aggression.

Hitler committed suicide on April 30, 1945. On May 8, 1945, the unconditional surrender of all German forces was accepted by representatives of the Western Allied and German Supreme Commanders.

THE POST WAR PERIOD.—After the surrender the Allied Powers exercised supreme authority in Germany on lines laid down in the Potsdam agreement (August 1945) between the U.K., U.S.A. and U.S.S.R. Power was exercised by the Commanders-in-Chief, each in his own zone of occupation and jointly in matters affecting Germany as a whole through a Control Council. Berlin was governed jointly by the four occupying powers. The agreement also provided for the total disarmament and demilitarisation of Germany, the destruction of the National Socialist Party, the decentralisation of the economy and the construction of a democratic constitution. No cen-

tral German government was permitted but central German administration was established in the fields of finance, industry, foreign trade, transport and communications as support organs for the Control Council. The Potsdam agreement was to have been confirmed or revised by a peace treaty but no treaty has been drawn up. Some provisions of the Potsdam agreement were carried out but differences in interpretation among the Allies made it impossible to implement in full and the system of quadripartite control broke down when the Russians withdrew from the Control Council in March 1948.

FEDERAL REPUBLIC OF GERMANY

President, Dr. Richard von Weizsäcker, *elected* May 22, 1984, *sworn in*, July 1, 1984, *for five years*.

CABINET

Federal Chancellor, Dr. Helmut Kohl (*CDU*).
Foreign Minister and Vice-Chancellor, Hans Dietrich Genscher (*FDP*).
Interior, Dr. Friedrich Zimmerman (*CSU*).
Justice, Hans Engelhard (*FDP*).
Finance, Dr. Gerhard Stoltenberg (*CDU*).
Economics, Martin Bangemann (*FDP*).
Food, Agriculture and Forestry, Ignaz Kiechle (*CSU*).
Intra-German Relations, Heinrich Windelen (*CDU*).
Labour and Social Affairs, Dr. Norbert Blüm (*CDU*).
Defence, Dr. Manfred Wörner (*CDU*).
Youth, Family Affairs and Health, Dr. Heiner Geissler (*CDU*).
Transport, Dr. Werner Dollinger (*CSU*).
Posts and Telecommunications, Dr. Christian Schwarz-Schilling (*CDU*).
Regional Planning, Building and Urban Development, Dr. Oscar Schneider (*CSU*).
Research and Technology, Dr. Heinz Riesenhuber (*CDU*).
Education and Science, Frau. Dr. Dorothee Wilms (*CDU*).
Economic Co-operation, Dr. Jürgen Warnke (*CSU*).
Federal Minister at the Chancellery, Wolfgang Schäuble (*CDU*)
  CDU = Christian Democratic Union; *CSU* = Christian Social Union; FDP = Free Democratic Party.

EMBASSY IN LONDON
23 Belgrave Square, SW1X 8PZ
[01–235 5033]

Ambassador Extraordinary and Plenipotentiary, His Excellency Baron Rüdiger von Wechmar (1984).
Minister Plenipotentiary, Baron Hans von Stein.
Minister-Counsellor, Dr. Eike Bracklo.
1st *Counsellors*, Oskar Rudolph (*Head of Economic Dept.*); G. H. von Neubronner (*Cultural*); Dr. W. Hoffman (*Scientific Affairs*); Dr. H. Meyer zu Drewer (*Agriculture*); Herr P. J. George (*Defence Research*).

NOTE.—Except where otherwise indicated statistical data on the Federal Republic of Germany include Berlin (West).

Area and Population.—The area of the Federal Republic is approximately 96,015 sq. miles (248,687 sq. km.). Total population of the Federal Republic in Dec. 1984 was 61,049,000. Distribution of the population among the *Länder* in 1983 was:

Baden-Wurttemberg	9,243,000
Bavaria	10,970,000
Berlin (West)	1,855,000
Bremen	677,000
Hamburg	1,610,000

---

* Nazi historians referred to the National Socialist régime as *Drittes Reich*.

Hesse	5,565,000
Lower Saxony	7,249,000
North Rhine Westphalia	16,837,000
Rhineland Palatinate	3,633,000
Saarland	1,053,000
Schleswig-Holstein	2,617,000

Vital Statistics.—There were 9·5 live births per 1,000 inhabitants in the Federal Republic in 1984.

Government.—The Federal Republic grew out of the fusion of the three western zones. The economic union of the U.K. and U.S. zones was later joined by the French zone and in 1948–49 Parliamentary Council, elected by the Diets of the three zones, drafted a provisional democratic federal constitution for Germany. This Basic Law came into force in the three western zones on May 23, 1949. When the Federal Government took office the Allied Military Governors were replaced by High Commissioners. In 1952 a contractual agreement was signed between the Federal Republic and the western Allies, whereby the Republic, in return for certain promises regarding a defence contribution, a foreign debt settlement, and the continuation of allied policies concerning decartelization, democratization, restitution, etc., regained virtual sovereignty in May, 1955, after ratification by all the parties concerned. The High Commissioners then became Ambassadors.

The Basic Law provides for a President, elected for a five-year term, a Lower House (*Bundestag*), with a four-year term of office, elected by direct universal suffrage, and an Upper House (*Bundesrat*) composed of 45 delegates of the *Länder*, without a fixed term of office.

The results of the elections held for the lower House (*Bundestag*) on March 6, 1983, were as follows:

Party	Numbers
Social Democrats	193
Christian Democratic Union	191
Christian Social Union	53
Free Democrats	34
Grüne (Green)	27

with an additional 22 representatives of Berlin elected by the Berlin Chamber of Deputies (CDU 11; SPD 9; FDP 1; Alternative Liste 1).

The Prime Ministers of the *Länder* governments in June, 1985, were:

Ministers-President

Baden-Württemberg.—Lothar Späth.
Bavaria.—Franz Josef Strauss.
Berlin.—Eberhard Diepgen (*Governing Mayor*).
Bremen.—Hans Koschnick (*Mayor*).
Hamburg.—Dr. Klaus v. Dohnanyi (*Mayor*).
Hesse.—Holger Börner.

Lower Saxony.—Dr. Ernst Albrecht.
North Rhine-Westphalia.—Johannes Rau.
Rhineland-Palatinate.—Dr. Bernhard Vogel.
Saarland.—Oskar Lafontaine.
Schleswig-Holstein.—Uwe Barschel.

Law and Justice.—Judicial authority is exercised by the Federal Constitutional Court, the Supreme Federal Court, and the courts of the *Länder*. Judges are independent and subject only to the law. The death sentence has been abolished.

ECONOMY

Despite the difficulties arising from the division of Germany, which cut off from the Federal Republic the main food producing areas of Eastern Germany and some of the principal centres of light industry, Germany has regained her position as the main industrial power on the Continent, and is the most economically powerful member of the European Community. The Gross National Product at current prices in 1984 was estimated at *DM*.1,750,000 million, an increase of 4·6 per cent over 1983. In real terms GNP grew by 2·6 per cent, after a 1·3 per cent growth in 1983.

Agriculture.—In 1983 total area of farmland was 12,079,000 hectares, of which 7,233,000 hectares were arable land. Forest areas cover 7,328,000 hectares.

Crop yields were (tonnes):	1982	1983
Rye	1,639,400	1,599,300
Wheat	8,631,600	8,998,000
Maslin	63,300	47,200
Barley	9,459,700	8,943,800
Oats	3,113,000	2,067,700
Potatoes	7,049,100	5,669,100
Sugar beet	22,732,000	16,295,000
Colza and rape	534,700	599,400
Fruit	4,217,198	2,426,924

Milk production in 1983 was 26,913,200 tonnes. Total yield of fisheries was 273,617 tonnes, valued at *DM*.323,708,000.

Industrial Production.—The Federal Republic has a predominantly industrial economy. Principal industries are coal mining, iron and steel production, machine construction, the electrical industry, the manufacture of steel and metal products, chemicals and textiles, and the processing of foodstuffs. The index of industrial net production adjusted for irregularities of the calendar (1980 = 100) is as follows:

	1983	1984
Mining	90·6	90·0
Manufacturing industry	96·3	99·6
(i) Basic materials	93·9	97·9
(ii) Capital goods	98·8	102·3
(iii) Consumer goods	91·6	94·1
(iv) Foodstuffs	99·4	101·1
Power (electricity and gas)	101·1	105·5
Construction	86·5	89·5
Total industry	95·5	98·7

Annual production figures were:

	1983	1984
	Tonnes '000	
Hard coal	82,202	79,426
Brown coal	124,281	126,739
Crude petroleum	4,116	4,055
Pig iron	25,659	28,915
Raw steel	35,345	38,991
Rolled steel	26,067	27,948
Fuel oils	36,991	36,870
Petrol, special and testing benzines	19,380	19,813

Chemical fibres	906	934
Cement	30,366	28,633
	Number	
Passenger cars	3,568,000	3,476,000
Televisions	4,706,000	3,906,000
A.D.P. equipment	DM9,180m.	—

Labour.—Labour figures, in annual averages, were:

	1983	1984
Employment	25,228,000	25,173,000
Unemployed	2,258,000	2,266,000
Foreign Workers	1,694,000	n/a

Employment in the industrial sector was:

	1983	1984
Coal mining	227,376	217,530
Iron and steel production	238,253	221,994
Mechanical engineering	1,786,000	1,760,829
Chemicals	548,834	550,321
Textiles and clothing	435,431	426,613

FINANCE

Receipts.—As from January 1, 1979, the distribution of taxes in the Fed. Rep. of Germany between Federation, Länder, communities and local authorities has been regulated by the Basic Law (Constitution).

Expenditure.—Figures of budgetary expenditure are:

	1984	1985
	DM million	
Total expenditure	251,800	259,300
Agriculture	5,200	6,600
Defence	47,800	49,000
Social Welfare	73,700	72,900
Transport	24,700	25,200

Currency.—The currency of the Federal Republic is the *Deutsche Mark* of 100 *Pfennig*. (*See also* p. 81.)

TRADE

	1983	1984
	DM million	
Total imports	390,192·0	434,256·9
Total exports	432,281·1	488,223·0

Of imports, 12·6 per cent were foodstuffs and 13·4 per cent industrial raw materials in 1984. Main trading partners in 1984 were (figures shown as percentage of total trade):

	Imports	Exports
E.E.C.	47·9	47·7
E.F.T.A.	13·1	15·5
U.S.A./Canada	8·1	10·5

Trade with U.K.

	1982	1983
Imports from U.K	£6,063,989,000	£7,458,042,000
Exports to U.K.	9,667,444,000	11,090,227,000

The U.K. is currently the largest supplier to the Federal Republic of petroleum and petroleum products (1984: £1,872,235,000).

Communications.—In December, 1982 the state-owned railways of the Federal Republic (*Deutsche Bundesbahn*) measured 28,369 kilometres of which 11,190 kilometres were electrified, and the privately owned railways 3,145 kilometres, a total of 31,514 kilometres. Railway rolling stock included, in 1982,

6,161 locomotives and 335,603 goods waggons; in 1982 the railways handled 320,900,000 tonnes of goods. Classified roads measured 172,490 kilometres at end 1981, of which motorways were 7,784 kilometres. Ocean-going shipping under the German flag in Dec., 1982, amounted to 6,809,000 tons gross. Inland waterways handled 225,200,000 tonnes of goods in 1982. Civil aircraft in service at the same date totalled 227 aircraft.

Social Welfare.—There is compulsory insurance against sickness, accident, old age and unemployment. Children's allowances are payable in respect of the second and subsequent children. Pension schemes for widows and orphans of public servants are in operation. Public assistance is given to persons unable to earn their living, or with insufficient income to maintain a decent standard of living.

Education.—School attendance is compulsory for all children and juveniles between the ages of 6 and 18 and comprises 9 years full-time compulsory education at primary and main schools (*Grund und Hauptschulen*) and 3 years of compulsory vocational education on a part-time basis. In autumn, 1982, there were in the Federal Republic 18,468 primary and main schools (*Grund- und Hauptschulen*) with 4,500,991 pupils. Secondary modern schools (*Realschulen*) numbered 2,639 with 1,278,092 pupils. There were 2,774 other general secondary schools (*Gymnasien* including *Gesamtschulen*) with 2,276,769 pupils.

There were also 2,820 special schools (*Sonderschulen*) for retarded, physically and mentally handicapped and socially maladjusted children in the Federal Republic with 319,254 pupils.

The secondary school leaving examination (*Abitur*) entitles the holder to a place of study at a university or another institution of higher education.

Juveniles below the age of 18 who are not attending a general secondary or a full-time vocational school are obliged to take a three-year course (part-time) at a vocational school. In November, 1982, there were 2,709 full and part-time vocational schools (*Berufsschulen*) and 477 vocational extension schools (*Berufsaufbauschulen*) with 1,920,088 pupils, 2,893 full-time vocational schools (*Berufsfachschulen*) with 398,418 pupils, 1,018 schools for secondary technical studies (*Fachoberschulen/Fachgymnasien*) with 159,213 students.

Results for the winter term 1983–84 show a total of 1,273,168 students at institutions of higher education, of whom 873,172 were attending universities. The largest universities were in Munich, Berlin, Hamburg, Bonn and Cologne.

Language and Literature.—Modern (or New High) German has developed from the time of the Reformation to the present day, with differences of dialect in Austria and Alsace and in the German-speaking cantons of Switzerland. The literary language is usually regarded as having become fixed by Luther and Zwingli at the Reformation, since which time many great names occur in all branches, notably philosophy, from Leibnitz (1646–1716) to Kant (1724–1804), Fichte (1762–1814), Schelling (1775–1854) and Hegel (1770–1831); the drama from Goethe (1749–1832) and Schiller (1759–1805) to Gerhart Hauptmann (1862–1946); and in poetry, Heine (1797–1856). German authors have received the Nobel Prize for Literature on seven occasions—Theodor Mommsen (1902), R. Eucken (1908), P. Heyse (1909), Gerhart Hauptmann (1912), Thomas Mann (1929), N. Sachs (1966) and Heinrich Böll (1972). In 1983 there were 359 daily papers.

Religion.—In 1970 there were 29,696,571 Protestants in the Republic, 27,060,826 Roman Catholics, 31,684 Jews and 3,861,518 others.

CAPITAL, Bonn, in North Rhine Westphalia, 15 miles distant from Cologne. Population 292,900 (end June 1983).

The population of the principal cities and towns in the Federal Republic at end June 1983, was:

Berlin (West)	1,860,500	Dortmund	595,200
ΨHamburg...	1,617,800	Düsseldorf....	579,800
Munich	1,284,300	Stuttgart	571,100
Cologne	953,300	Duisburg	541,800
Essen	635,200	ΨBremen	545,100
Frankfurt am		Hannover	524,300
Main.......	614,700	Nuremberg ...	476,400

FLAG.—Horizontal bars of black, red and gold.

BRITISH EMBASSY
Friedrich-Ebert Allee 77, 5300 Bonn

Ambassador Extraordinary and Plenipotentiary, His Excellency Sir Julian Bullard, K.C.M.G. (1984).

Ministers, N. C. R. Williams, C.M.G.; Miss C. E. Pestell, C.M.G.

Counsellors, D. K. Haskell (*Head of Chancery*); B. Smith, O.B.E. (*Commercial*); A. F. Hatfull (*Labour*); H. H. Chambers (*Defence Supply*); Dr. G. W. Chantry (*Scientific*); A. J. Beamish (*Economic*); J. D. Perris (*Administration*); R. P. Flower; G. Garrett.

1st Secretaries, Miss R. M. Marsden; W. R. Charlesworth; C. H. Salvesen; A. B. Gundersen; J. W. Forbes-Meyler; N. J. Macsween; R. Gwilliams; M. A. Arthur; Dr. S. R. A. Brown; J. Siddle; R. Sands; P. Elliott; D. E. Lyscom; Mrs. A. M. Leslie; P. W. Sprunt; D. J. Skinner.

Defence and Military Attaché, Brig. D. Quayle.

Asst. Military Attaché, G. C. Gray.

Naval Attaché, Capt. M. Bickley, R.N.

Asst. Naval Attaché, Lt.-Cdr. R. Stanton.

Air Attaché, Air Cdre. C. Reineck.

Head of Visa Section (*Düsseldorf*), Miss P. B. Harrison.

Chaplain, Rev. A. M. Cole.

There are British Consulates-General at *Berlin, Hamburg, Düsseldorf, Frankfurt* and *Munich*.

BRITISH COUNCIL
Representative, R. Arbuthnott, Hahnenstrasse 6, 5000 Cologne 1. Offices at *Berlin, Hamburg* and *Munich* and British Council libraries at all four centres.

BRITISH CHAMBER OF COMMERCE
Heumarkt 14, D-5000 Cologne 1.

Director, J. Parr.

BERLIN
G.O.C. British Sector, Maj.-General B. C. Gordon Lennox, M.B.E.

Minister and Deputy Commandant, D. J. Wyatt, C.B.E.

Counsellor, R. H. Smith (*Political Adviser and Head of Chancery*).

GERMAN DEMOCRATIC REPUBLIC

COUNCIL OF STATE

Chairman, Erich Honecker.

Deputy Chairmen, Dr. Manfred Gerlach; Ernst Mecklenburg; Gerald Götting; Prof. Heinrich Homann; Horst Sindermann; Willi Stoph; Egon Krenz; Günter Mittag.

Members, K. Anclam; W. Felfe; Prof. K. Hager; Frau B. Hanke; F. Kind; Prof. L. Kolditz; Frau M. Müller; A. Pisnik; B. Quandt; W. Seifert; Dr. K. Sorgenicht; P. Strauss; Frau I. Thiele; H. Tisch; Prof. J. Töpfer; P. Verner; Frau R. Walther.

COUNCIL OF MINISTERS

Chairman, Willi Stoph.

Chairmen, Werner Krolikowski; Alfred Neumann
(*First Deputy Chairmen*); M. Flegel; H-J. Heusin-
ger; G. Kleiber; W. Rauchfuss; Dr. H. Reichelt; G.
Schürer; R. Schulze; Dr. G. Weiss; Dr. H. Weiz.
Total membership of the Council is 45, including
also 29 Ministers and 4 Secretaries of State.

SOCIALIST UNITY PARTY OF GERMANY

Politbureau of the Central Committee, H. Axen; H.
Dohlus; W. Felfe; Prof. H. Häber; Prof. K. Hager;
J. Herrmann; Gen. H. Hoffmann; E. Honecker; W.
Jarowinsky; G. Kleiber; E. Krenz; W. Kroli-
kowski; E. Mielke; G. Mittag; E. Mückenberger;
K. Naumann; A. Neumann; G. Schabowski; H.
Sindermann; W. Stoph; H. Tisch (*full members*);
Frau I. Lange; Frau M. Müller; G. Schürer; W.
Walde (*candidate members*).

Secretariat of the Central Committee, E. Honecker
(*General Secretary*); H. Axen; H. Dohlus; W. Felfe;
Prof. H. Häber; Prof. K. Hager; J. Herrmann; W.
Jarowinsky; E. Krenz; I. Lange; G. Mittag; K.
Naumann (*secretaries*).

EMBASSY OF THE G.D.R.
34 Belgrave Square, S.W.1
[01-235 9941]

Ambassador Extraordinary and Plenipotentiary, His
Excellency Dr. Gerhard Lindner (1984).

Counsellor, Dr. G. Liebig.

1st Secretaries, E. Schwager; H. Zabel; G. Menzel; Dr.
O. Schneidratus.

Area and Population.—The German Democratic
Republic comprises the five former German *Länder*
of Brandenburg, Mecklenburg, Saxony, Saxony-
Anhalt and Thuringia (an area of 41,768 sq. miles).
The seat of Government is East Berlin (156 sq. miles).
The population of the Republic, including East Berlin
(end of 1980) is 16,740,000. In 1952 the former *Länder*
were replaced by fourteen *Bezirke* (regions): Potsdam, Cottbus and Frankfurt (*formerly* Brandenburg);
Rostock, Schwerin and Neubrandenburg (*formerly*
Mecklenburg); Karl-Marx-Stadt, Dresden and Leipzig (*formerly* Saxony); Halle and Magdeburg (*formerly* Saxony-Anhalt); Erfurt, Gera and Suhl
(*formerly* Thuringia.)

Government.—The present Constitution, which
defines the GDR as a Socialist state, came into force
on April 9, 1968 after endorsement by a referendum.
It replaced the first Constitution of October 7, 1949.
The supreme organ of State power is the *Volkskammer,* which has power to elect and dismiss the Council
of State, the Council of Ministers, the Chairman of
the National Defence Council, the Supreme Court
and the Procurator-General. The Council of State
retains the presidential powers which it has exercised
since the abolition of the office of President on
September 12, 1960, together with responsibility for
the organization of defence with the help of the
National Defence Council. The Council of Ministers
is responsible to the *Volkskammer* for the conduct of
State policy. The present *Volkskammer* is that elected
in June 1981.

As with other communist countries, effective
power lies with the ruling Marxist-Leninist Party,
in this case the Socialist Unity Party of Germany
(SED). The other parties and mass organizations are
members of the SED-controlled National Front.

ECONOMY

The G.D.R. economy, including the control of
industry and foreign trade, is centrally planned and
administered. The State Planning Commission,
which is subordinate to the Council of Ministers, is
responsible for drawing up the 5- and 1-Year Plans.
The 5-Year Plans determine the future development
and structure of the economy; the 1-Year Plans have
to achieve these aims. The implementation of these
plans is the responsibility of the State Production
Enterprises under the supervision of the economic
and industrial Ministries. The economy is very
closely integrated with those of other member
countries of C.M.E.A. and particularly with the
U.S.S.R.

The Budget for 1985 was: revenue, *M*231,084
million; expenditure, *M*230,944 million. The unit of
currency is the *Mark of the G.D.R.* (M) of 100 *pfennig.*

Agriculture.—Land is cultivated mostly on state or
collective farms, though some is cultivated independently. Crop yields in 1984 were: potatoes 9,300,000
tonnes; sugar-beet 8,300,000 tonnes; corn (green and
silage) 10,500,000 tonnes; grain 11,500,000 tonnes, and
oilseeds 270,000 tonnes.

Industry.—Almost all industry is nationally or co-
operatively owned; the percentage of privately
owned enterprises was about 2 in 1978. G.D.R. is the
leading world producer of lignite, production in 1982
was 276,000,000 tonnes, and the iron and steel
industry is also important. Other highly developed
industries include basic chemicals and petro-chemicals, machine tools and industrial plant, ship-building
and transport equipment, electronic and engineering
equipment, precision tools and optical instruments.

Trade with U.K.

	1983	1984
Imports from U.K.	£60,997,000	£92,270,000
Exports to U.K.	167,625,000	198,130,000

Principal cities and towns (population, 1980): East
Berlin (1,166,641); Leipzig (1,412,037); Dresden (District) (1,801,869); Karl-Marx-Stadt (Chemnitz)
(1,913,492); Magdeburg (1,260,892); Halle/Saale
(1,819,034); Rostock (890,613); Erfurt (1,237,117);
Zwickau (120,605); Potsdam (1,118,519).

FLAG.—Horizontal bands of black, red, gold; hammer, compasses and corn device at centre.

BRITISH EMBASSY
108 Berlin, Unter den Linden 32/34

Ambassador Extraordinary and Plenipotentiary, His
Excellency Timothy John Everard, C.M.G. (1984).

Counsellor, A. Ford.

1st Secretaries, D. B. Merry (*Head of Chancery*); F. T.
Cameron; J. E. Brook (*Commercial*).

2nd Secretaries, D. A. Muat (*Administration and
Consul*); D. L. Mather.

Cultural Attaché, G. E. B. Coe (*British Council
Representative*).

GREECE
(Hellas)

President of the Hellenic Republic, Christos Sartze-
takis, *born* 1927, *elected* March 29, 1985.

CABINET

Prime Minister and Minister of National Defence,
Andreas Papandreou.

Vice-Prime Minister, Ioannis Haralambopoulos.

Minister to the Prime Minister, Apostolos Tsohatzo-
poulos.

Interior and Public Order, Agamemnon Koutsogior-
gas.

Foreign Affairs, Carolos Papoulias.

National Economy, Constantine Simitis.

Health, Welfare and Social Security, George Yenni-
matas.

Justice, George-Alexander Mangakis.

Education and Religion, Apostolos Kaklamanis.

Culture, Miss Melina Mercouri.
Finance, Dimitrios Tsovolas.
Northern Greece, Ioannis Papadopoulos.
The Aegean, Kosmas Sfyriou.
Agriculture, Ioannis Pottakis.
Environment, Regional Planning and Public Works, Evangelos Kouloumbis.
Labour, Evangelos Yiannopoulos.
Industry, Energy and Technology, Eleftherios Veryvakis.
Commerce, Nikolaos Akritidis.
Transport and Communications, George Papadimitriou.
Merchant Marine, Efstathios Alexandris.

GREEK EMBASSY IN LONDON
1a Holland Park, W11 3TP
[01–727 8040]

Ambassador Extraordinary and Plenipotentiary, His Excellency Nikos Kyriazides (1982).
Defence Attaché, Capt. H. N. George Togas.
Counsellors, Chr. Tsalikis; A. Anninos (*Consular Affairs*); T. Karavias (*Commercial*); C. Kondoyiannis (*Agricultural*); E. Clis (*Political*); T. Chytiris (*Press*).
Tourist Adviser, C. Analytis.

There are Honorary Consulates at *Belfast, Birmingham, Edinburgh, Falmouth, Glasgow, Leeds, Manchester* and *Southampton.*

A maritime State in the south-east of Europe, bounded on the N. by Albania, Yugoslavia and Bulgaria, on the S. and W. by the Ionian and Mediterranean seas, and on the E. by Turkey, with an estimated area of 51,182 sq. miles. A census held throughout the country on April 5, 1981, recorded a population of 9,740,417.

The area of the mainland is 41,328 sq. miles, and of the islands 9,854 sq. miles. The main divisions are: *Macedonia* (which includes Mt. Athos and the island of Thasos), *Thrace* (including the island of Samothrace), *Epirus, Thessaly, Continental Greece* (which includes the island of Euboea and the Sporades or "scattered islands" of which the largest is Skyros), the *Peloponnese* (or *Morea*), the *Dodecanese* or *Southern Sporades* (12 islands occupied by Italy in 1911 during the Italo-Turkish War and ceded to Greece by Italy in 1947) consisting of Rhodes, Astypalaia, Karpathos, Kassos, Nisyros, Kalymnos, Leros, Patmos, Kos, Symi, Khalki and Tilos, the *Cyclades* (a circular group numbering about 200, with a total area of 923 sq. miles; the chief islands are Syros, Andros, Tinos, Naxos, Paros, Santorini, Milos and Serifos), the *Ionian Islands* (Corfu, Paxos, Levkas, Ithaca, Cephalonia, Zante and Cerigo), the *Aegean Islands* (Chios, Lesbos, Limnos and Samos). In *Crete* there was for over 1,500 years (3000 to 1400 B.C.) a flourishing civilization which spread its influence far and wide throughout the Aegean, and the ruins of the palace of Minos at Knossos afford evidence of astonishing comfort and luxury. Greek civilization emerged about 1300 B.C. and the poems of Homer, the blind poet of Chios, which were probably current about 800 B.C., record the 10-year struggle between the Achaeans of Greece and the Phrygians of Troy (1194–1184 B.C.).

Language and Literature.—The spoken language of modern Greece is descended by a process of natural development from the "Common Greek" of Alexander's empire. *Katharevousa*, a conservative literary dialect evolved by Adamantios Corais (Diamant Coray), who lived and died in Paris (1748–1833) and used for official and technical matters, is to be phased out over the next few years. Novels and poetry are mostly composed in *dimotiki*, a progressive literary dialect which owes much to John Psycharis (1854–1929). The poets Solomos, Palamas, Cavafis, Sikeli-

anos, Seferis and Elytis have won a European reputation.

Religion.—Over 97 per cent of the people are adherents of the Greek Orthodox Church, which is the State religion, all others being tolerated and free from interference. The Church of Greece recognizes the spiritual primacy of the Œcumenical Patriarch of Constantinople, but is otherwise a self-governing body administered by the Holy Synod under the Presidency of the Archbishop of Athens and All Greece. It has no jurisdiction over the Church of Crete, which has a degree of autonomy under the Œcumenical Patriarch, nor over the Monastic Community of Mount Athos and the Church in the Dodecanese, both of which come directly under the Œcumenical Patriarch.

Government.—A military *coup* on April 21, 1967, suspended parliamentary government and, following an unsuccessful royal counter *coup* on December 13, 1967, King Constantine went into voluntary exile in Rome. On June 1, 1973 the monarchy was abolished and a republic established under the Presidency of Mr. George Papadopoulos.

The overthrow of Archbishop Makarios, President of Cyprus, on July 15, 1974, by a military coup led by Greek officers of the Cypriot National Guard caused an international crisis, in the wake of which the heads of the Greek armed forces decided, on July 23, to relinquish power. Mr. Konstantinos Karamanlis, Prime Minister between 1955 and 1963, returned from his self-imposed exile in Paris to form a provisional Government, and the first elections for ten years were held on November 17, 1974.

The constitutional position of the King, who was still in exile, remained unsettled until December 8, when by a referendum, the Greek people rejected "crowned democracy" by 69·2 per cent to 30·8 per cent and Greece became a republic. A new constitution came into force on June 11, 1975.

The Socialist Movement under Andreas Papandreou came into office following the General Election of Oct. 1981, and remained in power after winning the 1985 General Election.

Defence.—The strength of the Army is 130,000 backed up by some 50,000 in the National Guard. The Navy consists of 19,500 men and is equipped with a fleet of destroyers, submarines, fast patrol boats and amphibious warfare vessels, mostly of U.S., French, Dutch and German origin. The Air Force consists of 25,000 men and is equipped with aircraft disposed in

12 combat squadrons supported by the necessary transport, training, helicopter and reconnaissance squadrons. National service is 2 years on average.

Communications.—The 2,650 kilometres of Greek railways are State-owned with the exception of the Athens–Piraeus Electric Railway. Greek roads total somewhat over 35,500 kilometres, of which about 25 per cent are classified as national highways and just under 30,000 km. are classified as provincial roads. The road connection with Albania was reopened in 1985.

On Dec. 31, 1983, the Greek Mercantile fleet numbered 3,422 ships with a total tonnage of 37,707,377 tons gross. On the same day Greek-owned ships registered under foreign flags numbered 1,194 with a total tonnage of 18,431,381 tons gross. (N.B. These figures exclude Greek-owned vessels under 100 tons gross). Athens has direct airline links with Australasia, North America, most countries in Europe, Africa and the Middle East.

Education is free and compulsory from the age of 6 to 15 and is maintained by State grants. There are six Universities, Athens, Salonika, Patras, Thrace, Joannina and Crete. There are several other institutes of higher learning, mostly in Athens.

Production.—Though there has in recent years been a substantial measure of industrialization, agriculture still employs about a quarter of the working population. The most important agricultural products are tobacco, wheat, cotton, sugar and rice. The most important of the fruit trees are the olive, peach, vine, orange, lemon, fig, almond and currant-vine, and now exports of Greek fresh fruit and vegetables have established themselves as an important contributor to the economy and have considerable growth potential. Currants, grown mainly around Patras, remain one of Greece's main exports, the United Kingdom being the principal purchaser.

The principal minerals mined in Greece are nickel, bauxite, iron ore, iron pyrites, manganese magnesite, chrome, lead, zinc and emery, and prospecting for petroleum is being carried on. Oil refineries are in operation near Athens and at Salonika, where there is also a petro-chemical plant. The chief industries are textiles (cotton, woollen and synthetics), chemicals, cement, glass, metallurgy, shipbuilding, domestic electrical equipment and footwear. In recent years new factories have been opened for the production of aluminium, nickel, iron and steel products, tyres, chemicals fertilizers and sugar (from locally-grown beet). Food processing and ancillary industries have also grown up throughout the country. The development of the country's electric power resources, irrigation and land reclamation schemes and the exploitation of Greece's lignite resources for fuel and industrial purposes are also being carried out. Tourism has developed rapidly, but is now slowing down.

Currency.—The Greek *drachma* has a floating exchange rate.

TRADE

	1983	1984
Total imports	*Drs*801,153m.	1,083,940·5m.
Total exports	392,652m.	542,665·7m.

Trade with U.K.

	1983	1984
Imports from U.K.	£280,204,000	£354,332,000
Exports to U.K.	164,917,000	279,367,000

CAPITAL.—Athens. Population (including ΨPiraeus and suburbs), 3,027,331 (1981 Census). Other large towns are ΨSalonika (706,180); ΨPatras (154,596), ΨVolos (107,407); Larissa (102,426); and ΨKavalla (56,705); in Crete—ΨHeraklion or

Candia (102,398), ΨCanea (47,451), and ΨRethymnon (18,190); in the Ionian Islands—ΨCorfu (36,901); in the Dodecanese—ΨRhodes (41,425); in the Cyclades—ΨSyros Hermoupolis (13,877); in Lesbos—Ψ Mytilene (24,991); in Chios—ΨChios (24,070).

FLAG.—Blue and white stripes with a white cross on a blue field in the canton.

NATIONAL DAY.—March 25 (Independence Day).

BRITISH EMBASSY
1 Ploutarchou Street, 106 75 Athens.

Ambassador Extraordinary and Plenipotentiary, His Excellency Jeremy Cashel Thomas, C.M.G., *apptd.* 1985.

Counsellors, C. Hulse, O.B.E. (*Political and Consul-General*); J. Thomas (*Economic and Commercial*).
Defence and Military Attaché, Brigadier J. H. Milburn, O.B.E.
Naval and Air Attaché, Capt. C. N. MacGregor.
Embassy Chaplain, Rev. S. J. B. Peake.
Hon. Attaché, H. W. Catling, O.B.E., D.Phil. (*Director, British School of Archæology*).

BRITISH CONSULAR OFFICES

There are British Consular Offices at *Athens, Corfu, Samos, Rhodes, Salonika, Heraklion* (Crete), *Kavalla* and *Patras.*

BRITISH COUNCIL
17 Plateia Philikis Etairias (P.O. Box 3488),
102 10 Athens.

Representative, P. B. Naylor.
There is also an office at *Salonika* and British Council libraries at both centres.

BRITISH-HELLENIC CHAMBER OF COMMERCE
4 Valaoritou Street, GR-10671 Athens.

GUATEMALA
(República de Guatemala)

Head of State, Gen. Oscar Humberto Mejía Victores, *assumed office*, Aug. 9, 1983.

Guatemala, in Central America, is situated in N. lat. from 13° 45' to 17° 49', and in W. long. from 88° 12' 49" to 92°13' 43", and has an area of 42,042 square miles, and a population (1983 estimate) of 7,932,000 (*for* MAP, *see* p. 847).

The Republic is divided into 22 departments, and is traversed from W. to E. by an elevated mountain chain, containing several volcanic summits rising to 13,000 feet above the sea; earthquakes are frequent, and an earthquake in Feb. 1976 killed about 25,000 people, and caused considerable damage to property and the infrastructure. The country is well watered by numerous rivers; the climate is hot and malarial near the coast, temperate in the higher regions. The rainfall in the capital is 57 in. per annum. The chief seaports are San José de Guatemala and Champerico on the Pacific and Santo Tomás de Castilla and Puerto Barrios on the Atlantic side.

Language and Literature.—Spanish is the language of the country, and since the establishment of the University in the capital, education has received a marked impulse and the high figure of illiteracy is being reduced. The National library contains about 80,000 volumes in the Spanish tongue.

Government.—The constitutionally elected president, Gen. Miguel Ydigoras Fuentes, was overthrown on March 31, 1963, by the Army, which handed executive and legislative powers to the Minister of Defence, Col. Enrique Peralta Azurdia. Important changes were included in a new constitution promulgated on Sept. 15, 1965, and elections for a new Congress and for President and Vice-President took place on March 6, 1966. The constitution was suspended "for as long as the situation demands" following a military coup in March 1982. An amnesty for guerrillas was unsuccessful and the Army is now fully occupied dealing with the proliferating subversive groups throughout the country.

Elections for a Constituent Assembly were held on July 1, 1984, as promised by Gen. Mejía Víctores when he overthrew Gen. Ríos Montt in 1983. The Assembly drew up a new Constitution, promulgated in June 1985, and a new electoral law, paving the way for the general election planned for Nov. 3, 1985. The election of a civilian president is expected to take place on Oct. 24, 1985, and a return to civilian power is envisaged in Jan. 1986.

Finance.—The estimates of ordinary revenue and expenditure balanced at *Quetzales* 1,314 million in 1983.

TRADE

	1983
Imports (c.i.f.)	U.S.$1,054·4m.
Exports (f.o.b.)	1,220·3m.

Trade with U.K.

	1983	1984
Imports from U.K.	£7,440,000	£10,660,000
Exports to U.K.	9,764,000	9,565,000

The principal export is coffee, other articles being manufactured goods, sugar, bananas, cotton, beef and essential oils. The chief imports are petroleum, vehicles, machinery and foodstuffs.

CAPITAL.—Guatemala City. Population: 1,180,000. Quezaltenango has a pop. of over 100,000. Other towns are ΨPuerto Barrios (23,000), Mazatenango (21,000), and Antigua (30,000).

FLAG.—Three vertical bands, blue, white, blue; coat of arms on white stripe.

(Guatemala and the U.K. have no formal diplomatic relations.)

GUINEA
(Republic of Guinea)

President, Col. Lansana Conté, *took power,* April 3, 1984 *(also holds Defence Portfolio)*

CABINET

Ministers of State:
Administrative Reform and Civil Service, Capt. Mamadou Baldet.
National Education, Abou Camara.
Foreign Affairs and International Cooperation, Capt. Faciné Touré.
Planning and Natural Resources, Capt. Jean Traoré.
Ministers:
Agriculture, Maj. Alhoussény Fofana.
Economy and Finance, Maj. Sory Doumbia.
Territorial Administration, Capt. Kerfala Camara.
Labour and Social Welfare, Dr. Mariama Dielo Barry.
Communications and Tourism, Capt. Mohamed Traoré.
Industrial Development, Richard Haba.
Commerce, Capt. Sherif Diallo.
Justice, Maj. Lama Kolipé.
Public Health, Dr. Mamadou Bah Kaba.
Religious Affairs, El-Haj Thierno Ibrahima Bah al-Labé.
Youth, Arts and Sports, Zaïnoul Sanoussi Abidiné.
Permanent Secretary to the C.M.R.N., Samba Kala Traoré.

Formerly part of French West Africa, Guinea has a coastline on the Atlantic Ocean between Guinea-Bissau and Sierra Leone and in the interior is adjacent to Senegal, Mali, Ivory Coast, Liberia and Sierra Leone. Area, 96,865 sq. miles. The population (1980 estimate) is 6,412,000, mostly the Fullah, Malinké and Soussou tribes.

Government.—Guinea was separated from Senegal in 1891 and administered by France as a separate colony until 1958. In a referendum held in Sept. 1958, Guinea rejected the new French Constitution and on Oct. 2, 1958, became an independent republic governed by a Constituent Assembly. M. Sékou Touré, Prime Minister in the Territorial Assembly, assumed office as head of the new Government.

Under a provisional constitution, adopted on Nov. 12, 1958, powers of government are exercised by a president assisted by the Cabinet. The President, eligible for a term of 7 years and for re-election, is head of state and of the armed forces. M. Sékou Touré was elected President of the Republic in January, 1961. Pres. Sékou Touré died in March 1984: a few days later there was a military *coup.* Guinea is now ruled by a military government, which is directed by a Military Committee for National Recovery (C.M.R.N.). The country's foreign policy is one of non-alignment.

Guinea withdrew from the Franc Zone on March 1, 1960, and established her own currency. Guinea is in receipt of economic aid and technical assistance from a number of countries, including the United States, Canada, West Germany, Yugoslavia, the Soviet Union and China.

Production, etc.—The principal products of Guinea are bauxite, alumina, iron-ore, palm kernels, millet, rice, coffee, bananas, pineapples and rubber. At Sangaredi in the mountainous hinterland, where the rivers Senegal, Gambia and Niger have their sources, large deposits of bauxite (the raw material of aluminium) are mined. Deposits of iron ore, gold, diamonds and uranium have also been discovered. Principal imports are cotton goods, manufactured goods, tobacco, petroleum products, sugar, rice, flour and salt; exports, bauxite, alumina, iron-ore, diamonds, coffee, hides, bananas, palm kernels and pineapples.

Trade with U.K.

	1983	1984
Imports from U.K.	£7,190,000	£6,469,000
Exports to U.K.	668,000	1,171,000

CAPITAL.—ΨConakry (655,000). Other towns are Kankan, which is connected with Conakry by a railway, Kindia, N'Zérékoré, Mamou, Siguiri and Labé.

FLAG.—Three vertical stripes of red, yellow and green.

NATIONAL DAY.—October 2 (Anniversary of Proclamation of Independence).

BRITISH EMBASSY

British Ambassador (resident at Dakar, Senegal).

GUINEA-BISSAU

President of the Council of State (Head of State), Gen. João Bernardo Vieira, *took power,* Nov. 1980.

COUNCIL OF MINISTERS

Minister of State for Justice and Local Authorities, Col. Paulo A. Nunes Correia.
Minister of State for the Armed Forces, Col. Iafai Camara.
Minister at the Presidency for Economics Affairs, Dr. Vasco Cabral.
Rural Development and Fisheries, Carlos Correia.
Education, Culture and Sport, Dr. Fidelis Cabral d'Almada.
Social Affairs, Maj. Manuel dos Santos.

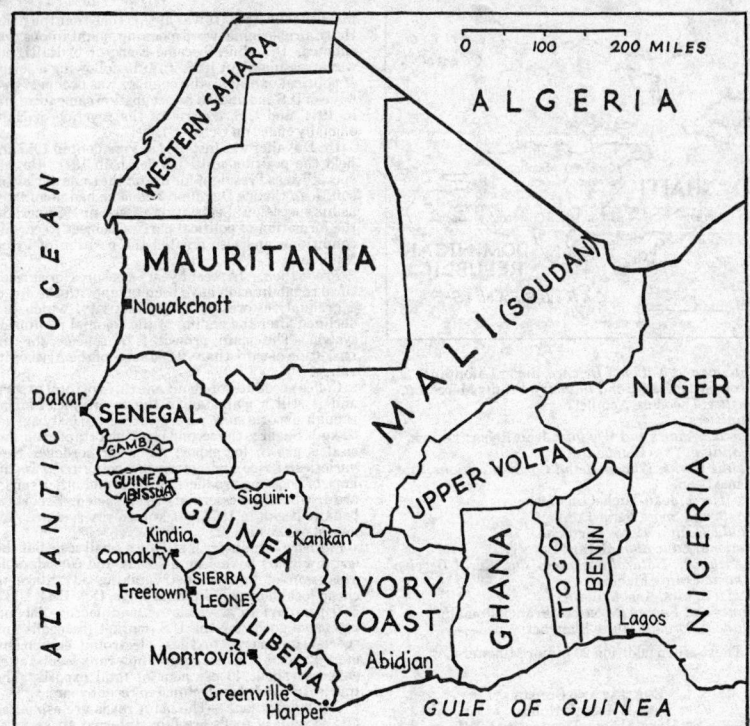

National Security and Public Order, Maj. José
Pereira.
Natural Resources and Industry, Filinto de Barros.
Foreign Affairs, Julio Semedo.
Finance, Dr. Vítor Freire Monteiro.
Health, Adelino Nunes Correia.
Trade and Tourism, Mario Cabral.
*Economic Co-ordination, Planning and International
Co-operation*, Bartolomeu Simões Pereira.
Governor of the National Bank, Pedro Godinho
Gomes.
Information and Telecommunications, Musa Djassi.

Guinea-Bissau, formerly Portuguese Guinea, lies
in Western Africa, between Senegal and Guinea; it
has an area of 14,000 sq. miles and had a population
(1982 U.N. estimate) of 920,000. The main ethnic
groups are the Balante, Malinké, Fulani, Mandjako
and Pepel.
Guinea-Bissau achieved independence on Sept. 10,
1974. Sr. Luis Cabral was ousted in a *coup* led by Maj.
(now Gen.) Vieira in November, 1980. Following the
coup the Assembly was suspended, and a Revolutionary Council was established. Under a new constitution adopted in April 1984 the Revolutionary Council
became a 15-member Council of State, and a parliament was set up.
Currency.—The *escudo* was replaced by the *peso* in
March 1976.

Economy.—The country produces rice, coconuts,
ground-nuts and palm oil products. Cattle are raised,
and there are bauxite deposits in the south.

Trade with U.K.

	1983	1984
Imports from U.K.	£477,000	£499,000
Exports to U.K.	94,000	—

CAPITAL.—ΨBissau, also the chief port.
FLAG.—Horizontal bands of yellow over green with
vertical red band in the hoist charged with a black
star.

BRITISH EMBASSY
British Ambassador, (*resident at* Dakar, Senegal).

HAITI
(République d'Haïti)

President, Jean Claude Duvalier, *born* 1951, *installed
as President for Life*, April 21, 1971.

CABINET

Ministers of State:
Presidency, Information and Public Relations, Jean
Marie Chanoine.

Interior and National Defence, Roger Lafontant.
Economy, Finance and Industry, Frantz Merceron.
Justice, Theodore Achille.
Ministers:
Foreign Affairs and Worship, Jean-Robert Estime.
Planning, Yves Blanchard.
Public Works, Transport and Communications, Maxime Leon.
Commerce, Jean-Michel Ligonde.
Youth and Sport, Serge Conille.
Public Health, Victor Larroche.
National Education, Gerard Dorcely.
Agriculture, Natural Resources, and Rural Development, Frantz Flambert.
Social Affairs, Arnold Blain.
Mines and Energy Resources, Franck Romain.
Without Portfolio, Jules Blanchet.

There are in addition 20 junior Ministers.

EMBASSY AND CONSULATE
33 Abbot's House,
St. Mary Abbot's Terrace, W14 8NU.

Ambassador Extraordinary and Plenipotentiary, His Excellency Theo Duval.

The Republic of Haiti occupies the western third of the island of Hispaniola, which, next to Cuba, is the largest island in the West Indies.

The area of the Republic, including off-shore islands, is 10,700 sq. miles (of which about three-quarters is mountainous), with a population of 6,000,000, 85 per cent of whom live in rural areas. The people are mainly negroes but there are numbers of mulattoes and others with some admixture of European blood.

Climate.—The climate is tropical with comparatively little difference in the temperatures between the summer (March–Oct.) and the winter (Nov.–Feb.). The temperature at Port-au-Prince rarely exceeds 95° F., but the humidity is high, especially in the autumn.

Language.—French is the language of the government and the press, but it is only spoken by the educated minority. The usual language of the people is Creole.

Haiti was a French colony under the name of Saint-Domingue from 1697. The slave population, estimated at 500,000, revolted in 1791 under the leadership of Toussaint L'Ouverture, who was born a slave and made himself Governor-General of the colony. He capitulated to the French in 1802 and died in captivity in 1803. Resistance was continued by Jean Jacques Dessalines, also a former negro slave, who, on January 1, 1804, declared the former French colony to be an independent state. It was at this time that the name Haiti, an aboriginal word meaning mountainous, was adopted. Dessalines became Emperor of Haiti, but was assassinated in 1806. In 1915, following a period of political upheaval, the country was occupied by a force of U.S. marines. The occupation came to an end in 1934, and U.S. control of the revenue of Haiti officially ended on October 1, 1947.

Dr. Duvalier was installed as President in 1957 and held the position until his death in 1971. He was succeeded as President for life on the same day by his son, Jean Claude Duvalier, whom he had nominated as his successor. Legislation passed in 1985 permits the formation of political parties, subject to certain conditions, and also created the position of Prime Minister.

Production.—In recent years measures for agricultural rehabilitation have been taken with the aim of a gradual restoration of productivity, which had declined after the ending of the colonial plantation system. The main project is a scheme for the irrigation of more than 70,000 acres of the Artibonite valley.

Coffee accounts for about one third of total exports and is still a mainstay of the country's economy though exports now rarely exceed 300,000 bags (of 60 kg.). Sugar is the second most important crop, and sisal is grown for export as or for cordage. New varieties of rice and cotton are being tried in the hope of boosting production. Rum and other spirits are distilled, and essential oils extracted. Exports of bauxite began in 1957, but known reserves are now almost exhausted.

Industry.—Industry is still on a small scale but the last few years have seen a steady and considerable expansion of light industry taking advantage of cheap local labour (minimum wage, Oct. 1984, U.S.$ 3·00 per day) to assemble or manufacture labour-intensive goods for the U.S. market (baseballs and sports equipment, textiles, electronic equipment, etc.). Exports of manufactures now rank second after coffee at about 40 per cent of total exports. The tourist industry has declined in recent years.

Communications.—The main roads are asphalted and secondary roads are fair. Internal air services are maintained between the capital and the principal provincial towns. International air-services connect Port-au-Prince with the U.S.A. and other Caribbean and South American cities. The principal towns and villages are connected by telephone and/or telegraph. The telephone company is state owned (51 per cent.) and the service both in Port-au-Prince and Inter-urban has been greatly improved. External telegraph, telephone and postal services are normal. There are several commercial radio stations and two television stations at Port-au-Prince.

Regular passenger liner services to New York have ceased, but cruise ships call occasionally. Freight sailings are frequent for the U.S.A., Canada, Europe, Latin America (except Cuba) and the main Caribbean ports.

Education.—Education is free but estimates of illiteracy are as high as 85 per cent. There are four French daily newspapers. The total circulation is very small.

Currency.—The unit of currency is the *gourde*, which has a fixed value of 5 *gourdes* = U.S.$1. U.S. currency is also legal tender.

Trade.—Value of imports 1984 U.S.$ 474·1 million; exports 1984 U.S.$ 219·4 million.

Trade with U.K.

	1983	1984
Imports from U.K.	£4,171,000	£3,736,000
Exports to U.K.	1,646,000	1,402,000

The principal exports are listed above; the principal

imports are foodstuffs, textiles, machinery, mineral oils, vehicles and raw materials for industry.

CAPITAL.—Ψ Port-au-Prince. Population estimated at about 1 million. Other centres are: Ψ Cap Haitien (54,691); Ψ Gonaives (36,736); Ψ Les Cayes (27,222); Jérémie (25,117); Ψ St. Marc (20,504); Ψ Jacmel (16,449); Ψ Port de Paix (21,733).

FLAG.—Two vertical bands, black (next staff) and red; arms in centre on a white background.

NATIONAL DAY.—January 1.

British Ambassador, (resident at Kingston, Jamaica).

HONDURAS
(Republica de Honduras)

President of the Republic, Dr. Roberto Suazo Cordova, *assumed office,* 27 Jan. 1982.

CABINET

Interior and Justice, Arnulfo Pineda López.
Foreign Affairs, Edgardo Paz Barniça.
Defence, Col. Amilcar Castillo Suazo.
Education, Elmer Lizandro Carranza (*acting*).
Finance, Manuel Fontecha.
Economy, Miguel Orellana Maldonado.
Communications, Public Works and Transport, Miguel Lardizabal Becerra (*acting*).
Health, Dr. Rubén García Martinez.
Labour and Social Security, Amado H. Nuñez.

Natural Resources, Miguel Angel Bonilla.
Culture and Tourism, Prof. Victor Cáceres Lara.
Economic Planning, Daniel Meza Palma.
Director of National Agrarian Institute, Jaime Raúl Murillo.
Minister for the Presidency, Ubudoro Arriaga Iraheta.

HONDURAS EMBASSY IN LONDON
47 Manchester Street, W1M 5PB
[01–486 3380]

Ambassador Extraordinary and Plenipotentiary, His Excellency Sr. Max Velásquez-Diaz (1984).

Honduras, in Central America, lies between lat. 13° and 16° 30′ N. and long. 83° and 89° 41′ W. with a seaboard of about 375 miles on the Caribbean Sea and an outlet, consisting of a small strip of coast 63 miles in length on the Pacific. Its frontiers are contiguous with those of Guatemala, Nicaragua and El Salvador.

The Republic contains a total area of approximately 43,278 sq. miles (112,088 km.) and is very mountainous, being traversed by the Cordilleras, with peaks rising to 1500 and 2400 metres above sea level. Most of the soil is poor and acid, except for the coastal plains of the north and some areas of the interior. Rainfall is seasonal, May to October being wet and November to April dry. The climate varies with the altitude, being tropical throughout the year in the coastal belts and temperate in the uplands. Three-quarters of the territory is covered by pine forests which contribute to much of the country's wealth in natural resources. The population (1982 estimate) of 3,600,000 is of mixed Spanish and Indian blood. There is a foreign negro (West Indian) element in Northern Honduras.

The language of the country is Spanish. Primary and secondary education is free, primary education being compulsory, and the Government have launched a campaign to eradicate illiteracy.

Government.—Originally discovered and settled by the Spaniards at the beginning of the sixteenth century Honduras formed part of the Spanish American Dominions for nearly three centuries until 1821 when independence was proclaimed. Under military government from 1972–81, the present Liberal government was elected in Nov. 1981 and took office in Jan. 1982.

The Republic is divided into 18 departments, the newest of which, Gracias a Dios, formed in Feb. 1957, is now the home of thousands of Miskito Indian refugees from Nicaragua.

Production.—Agriculture is mainly confined to the large and fertile valleys on the wide Caribbean plain, and the extensive valleys found in the Comayagua and Olancho regions of the interior. Reaching inland from the Caribbean towards the eastern border with Nicaragua a vast tropical forest area called the Mosquitia constitues an untapped reserve of precious timber. Lead, zinc and silver are mined and exported.

The chief exports are coffee, bananas and timber, the most important woods being pine, mahogany and cedar. Cattle raising and the exporting of frozen meat is an important industry, and exports of shrimps and lobsters are increasing. Other products are tobacco, beans, maize, rice, cotton, palm oil, sugar cane, cement and tropical fruits. There are large tracts of uncultivated land.

Communications.—There are about 1,004 km. of railway in operation, chiefly to serve the banana plantations and the Caribbean ports. There are 15,006 km. of roads, of which 1,809 are paved, excluding some 250 kms of new major highways recently inaugurated. Improvements are being made and new roads built. There are 33 smaller airstrips and three international airports, Tegucigalpa, San Pedro Sula and La Ceiba.

ΨThe chief ports are Puerto Cortes, Tela and La Ceiba on the North Coast, through which passes the bulk of the trade with the United States and Europe, and Amapala, situated on Tiger Island in the Gulf of Fonseca, on the Pacific side. A new deep-water port, Henecan, has been opened at San Lorenzo, on the mainland, in the Gulf of Fonseca.

The unit of currency is the *Lempira* (also known as *peso*) of 100 *centavos*.

TRADE

	1982	1983
Imports ....*Lempiras*	1,436 m.	1,511·7 m.
Exports .... „	1,308 m.	1,360·6 m.

Trade with U.K.

	1983	1984
Imports from U.K....	£9,539,000	£7,382,000
Exports to U.K.	7,082,000	12,360,000

CAPITAL.—Tegucigalpa. Pop. 533,600 (1982 est.); other towns are San Pedro Sula (397,900), ΨLa Ceiba (68,900), ΨPuerto Cortes (62,300), Choluteca (89,000) and ΨTela (61,200).

FLAG.—Three horizontal bands, blue, white, blue (with five blue stars on white band).

NATIONAL DAY.—September 15.

BRITISH EMBASSY
Apartado Postal 290, Tegucigalpa.

Ambassador Extraordinary and Plenipotentiary, His Excellency Bryan Oliver White, *apptd.* 1984.

Tegucigalpa is 5,930 miles from London; transit, *via* New York, 14 days; *via* Panama 20 days. By air *via* Miami 1 day.

HUNGARY
(Magyarország)

President of the Presidential Council of the Republic, Pál Losonczi, *elected* April, 1967.

COUNCIL OF MINISTERS

Prime Minister, György Lázár.
Deputy Prime Ministers, Judit Csehák; Lajos Czinege; József Marjai; Lajos Faluvégi; László Maróthy.
Foreign Affairs, Peter Varkonyi.
Interior, János Kamara.
Defence, István Oláh.
Finance, Dr. István Hetényi.
Justice, Dr. Imre Markója.
Industry, László Kapolyi.
Foreign Trade, Péter Veress.
Internal Trade, Zoltán Juhar.
Agriculture and Food, Jenö Váncsa.
Health, László Medve.
Culture and Education, Dr. Béla Köpeczi.
Building and Town Planning, László Somogyi.
Transport and Postal Affairs, Lajos Urbán.
President, National Planning Office, Lajos Faluvégi.
President, Technical Development Committee, Pál Tétényi.

THE COMMUNIST PARTY

Politbureau of the Central Committee, G. Aczél; S. Gáspar; K. Grósz; C. Hámori; F. Havasi; J. Kádár; G. Lázár; P. Losonczi; L. Maróthy; K. Németh; M. Ovári; I. Sárlos; I. Szarbó.
Secretariat of the Central Committee, János Kádár (*Gen. Sec.*); K. Németh (*Deputy Gen. Sec.*); J. Berecz; F. Havasi; I. Horváth; L. Pál; M. Ovári; M. Szúrös.

HUNGARIAN EMBASSY AND CONSULATE
35 Eaton Place, S.W.1.
[01–235 4048, 7191; *Consulate:* 01–235 2664]

Ambassador Extraordinary and Plenipotentiary, His Excellency Dr. Mátyás Domokos (1984).
Counsellors, Dr. J. Kalanovics; I. Bene (*Commercial*).
Military and Air Attaché, Col. F. Esztergomi.
1st Secretary, A. Mócsán (*Consular*).

Area and Population.—The area of Hungary may be stated as approximately 36,000 sq. miles with a population (1980) of 10,710,000.

Government.—Hungary was reconstituted a kingdom in 1920 after having been declared a republic on Nov. 17, 1918. She joined the Anti-Comintern Pact

on Feb. 24, 1939, and entered the 1939–45 War on the side of Germany in 1941. On Jan. 20, 1945, a Hungarian provisional government of liberation, which had been set up during the preceding December, signed an armistice under the terms of which the frontiers of Hungary were withdrawn to the limits existing in 1937.

After the liberation, a coalition of the Smallholder, National Peasant, Social Democrat and Communist parties carried out major land reform and mines, heavy industry, banks and schools were nationalized. By 1949 the Communists had succeeded in gaining a monopoly of power. A campaign was opened to collectivize agriculture and by 1952 practically the entire economy had been "socialized". The Party formulates policy and the function of the Government is mainly executive.

The period from July 1956 to the outbreak of the national revolution on Oct. 23 was marked by growing ferment in intellectual circles and increased discord within the Party. The withdrawal of Soviet troops from the country and free elections were among the demands put forward. Fighting broke out on the night of Oct. 23 between demonstrators, who had been joined by large numbers of factory workers, and the State Security Police (A.V.H.). Soviet forces intervened in strength early the next morning. By Oct. 30 Soviet troops had withdrawn from Budapest and on Nov. 3 an all-party coalition government under Imre Nagy was formed. This government was overthrown and the revolution suppressed as the result of a renewed attack by Soviet forces on Budapest in the early hours of Nov. 4. Simultaneously the formation of a new Hungarian Revolutionary Worker Peasant Government under the leadership of Mr. Kádár was announced.

Economy.—Since 1968 the Hungarian economy has been run according to a system which allows more decentralized decision-making than in some other Eastern European countries, although central control in vital areas such as the allocation of fuels and raw materials has remained. Industrialization has made considerable progress in the last decade and now produces 68 per cent of national income. Industry is mainly based on imported raw materials but Hungary has her own coal (mostly brown), bauxite, considerable deposits of natural gas (some not yet under full exploitation), some iron ore and oil. Output figures in 1983 (1,000 tons), coal, 25,213; bauxite, 2,917; steel 3,616; crude oil, 2,004; cement, 4,243. Natural gas production totalled 6,510 million cubic metres.

Agriculture still occupies an important place in the Hungarian economy. Ten and a half per cent. of the entire land area is owned by State farms and a further 63·8 per cent is within co-operative farms. Production in 1983 was:

Wheat	5,968,000
Rye	136,000
Barley	1,007,000
Maize	6,255,000
Rice	46,000
Oats	118,000
Sugar beet	3,782,000
Green and silage maize	1,630,000

In 1983, national income grew by only 0·5 per cent. Consumption and, particularly, investment continued to be squeezed by the adjustment measures necessitated by Hungary's hard currency debts. Retail prices rose by just under 8 per cent, whilst real incomes stagnated.

Religion and Education.—About two-thirds of the population are Roman Catholics, and the remainder mostly Calvinist. There are five types of schools under the Ministry of Education—kindergartens 3–6, general schools 6–14 (compulsory), vocational

schools (15–18), secondary schools (15–18), universities and adult training schools (over 18).

Language and Literature.—Magyar, or Hungarian, is one of the Finno-Ugrian languages. Hungarian literature began to flourish in the second half of the sixteenth century. Among the greatest writers of the nineteenth and twentieth centuries are Mihály Vörösmarty (1800–1855), Sándor Petöfi (1823–1849), János Arany (1817–1882), Imre Madach (1823–1864), Kálmán Mikszáth (1847–1910), Endre Ady (1877–1918), Attila József (1905–1937), Mihály Babits (1883–1941) and Dezsö Kosztolányi (1885–1936).

Finance.—The budget estimates for the year 1985 were: Revenue, *Forints* 607,800 million; Expenditure, *Forints* 610,300 million. The unit of currency is the *forint* of 100 *fillér.*

TRADE

	1984	
	Non-convertible trade (*roubles*)	Convertible trade U.S.$
Imports	7,031·7 m.	4,322·3 m.
Exports	6,810·8 m.	4,929·8 m.

(1 *rouble* = 26 forints: 1 U.S.$ = 48·05 forints)

Trade with U.K.

	1983	1984
Imports from U.K. ...	£91,845,000	£100,502,000
Exports to U.K.	53,834,000	75,905,000

CAPITAL.—Budapest, on the Danube; population (1979), 2,093,000. Other large towns are: Miskolc (212,000); Debrecen (200,000); Szeged (178,000) and Pecs (171,000).

FLAG.—Red, white, green (horizontally).

NATIONAL DAY.—April 4 (Anniversary of Liberation, 1945).

BRITISH EMBASSY
Harmincad Utca 6, Budapest V

Ambassador Extraordinary and Plenipotentiary, His Excellency Peter William Unwin, C.M.G. (1983).
Counsellor, D. H. Colvin (*Head of Chancery*).
Defence and Military Attaché, Lt.-Col. A. Cowie.
Air Attaché, Wg. Cdr. J. Davis.
Cultural Attaché and British Council Representative, W. K. Dobson.
1st Secretaries, P. January (*Commercial*); R. J. A. Golland (*Information*).
Vice-Consul, M. Carbine.

Budapest is distant 1,126 miles from London, transit by rail 30 hours; by air 2 hrs. 20 mins.

ICELAND
(Island)

President, Vigdís Finnbogadóttir, *born* 1930, *elected* June 29, 1980, *re-elected,* July 1984.

CABINET

Prime Minister, Steingrímur Hermannsson (*Pr.*).
Foreign Affairs, Geir Hallgrímsson (*I.*).
Finance, Albert Gudmundsson (*I.*).
Industries and Energy, Sverrir Hermannsson (*I.*).
Fisheries, Halldór Asgrimsson (*Pr.*).
Agriculture, Justice and Ecclesiastical, Jón Helgason (*Pr.*).
Education and Culture, Ragnhildur Helgadóttir (*I.*).
Commerce, Matthías A. Mathiesen (*I.*).
Health, Social Security and Communications, Matthías Bjarnason (*I.*).
Social Affairs (*Housing, Local Government and Labour*), Alexander Stefánsson (*I.*).

(*I.*—Independence Party; *Pr.*—Progressive Party.)

ICELAND

EMBASSY IN LONDON
1 Eaton Terrace, SW1W 8EY
[01–730 5131]

Ambassador Extraordinary and Plenipotentiary, His Excellency Einar Benediktsson (1982).
Counsellors, S. Björnsson; S. Gunnlaugsson (*Commercial*).

Iceland is a large volcanic island in the North Atlantic Ocean, extending from 63° 23′ to 66° 33′ N. lat., and from 13° 22′ to 24° 35′ W. long., with an estimated area of 40,500 square miles, or about one-sixth greater than that of Ireland. The population was 240,122 on Dec. 1, 1984.

Iceland was uninhabited before the ninth century, when settlers came from Norway. For several centuries a form of republican government prevailed, with an annual assembly of leading men called the *Althing,* but in 1241 Iceland became subject to Norway, and later to Denmark. During the colonial period, Iceland maintained its cultural integrity but a deterioration in the climate, together with frequent volcanic eruptions and outbreaks of disease led to a serious fall in the standard of living and to a decline in the population to little more than 40,000. In the nineteenth century a struggle for independence began which led first to home rule for Iceland under the Danish Crown (1918), and later to complete independence under a republican form of rule in 1944.

Government.—The parliamentary (*Althing*) elections in April 1983 gave the Independence Party 23 seats, Progressives 14, People's Alliance 10 and Social Democrats 6, Union of Social Democrats 4 and Feminists 3. In May 1983 Steingrimur Hermansson, chairman of the Progressive Party, formed a coalition government with the Independence Party, the other parties forming the opposition.

Language and Literature.—The ancient Norraena (or Northern tongue) presents close affinities to Anglo-Saxon and as spoken and written in Iceland to-day differs little from that introduced into the island in the ninth century. There is a rich literature with two distinct periods of development, from the mid-11th to the late 13th century and from the early 19th century to the present.

Production.—Iceland has considerable resources of hydro-electric and geothermal energy. It is estimated that exploited water power (3,900 Gigawatt hours/a) represents only about 9 per cent of that economically exploitable, whereas only 5 per cent of the estimated 80,000 Gigawatt hours/a of available geothermal power has so far been harnessed. Energy-intensive heavy industry includes an aluminium smelter, a nitrogen fertilizer factory, a diatomite plant and a ferro-silicone plant.

The principal exports are frozen fish fillets, salt fish, stock fish, fresh fish on ice, frozen scampi, fishmeal and oil, skins and aluminium; the imports consist of almost all the necessities of life, the chief items being petroleum products, transport equipment, textiles, foodstuffs, animal feeds, timber, and alumina.

At January 1, 1985, the mercantile marine consisted of 538 vessels of under 100 gross tons and 401 ships of 100 gross tons and over; a total of 939 vessels (194,360 gross tons), of which 834 (112,847 gross tons) are decked fishing vessels. There are regular shipping services between Reykjavik and Felixstowe, Ipswich, Humber and Mersey ports, and the Continent.

A regular air service is maintained between Glasgow and London and Reykjavik. There are also air services from the island to Scandinavia, U.S.A., Germany, France and Luxemburg.

Road communications are adequate in summer but greatly restricted by snow in winter. Only roads in town centres and a few key highways are metalled the rest being of gravel, sand and lava dust. The climate and terrain make first-class surfaces for highways out of the question.

FINANCE

	1983	1984
	Krónur (millions)	
Revenue	15,100	20,744
Expenditure	16,598	19,964

TRADE

	1983	1984
	Krónur (millions)	
Exports	18,623	23,557
Imports	20,596	26,744

Trade with U.K.

	1983	1984
Imports from U.K.	£47,800,000	£64,242,000
Exports to U.K.	53,200,000	86,104,000

CAPITAL: ΨReykjavík. Population (Dec. 1, 1984), 88,505.

Other centres in approximate order of importance are Akureyri, Kópavogur, Hafnarfjördur, Keflavík, Westmann Islands, Akranes, Isafjördur and Siglufjördur.

FLAG.—Blue, with white-bordered red cross.

NATIONAL DAY.—June 17.

BRITISH EMBASSY
Laufásvegur 49, Reykjavik

Ambassador Extraordinary and Plenipotentiary and Consul-General, His Excellency Richard Thomas (1983).
2nd Secretary and Consul, M. J. Lonsdale.
Vice Consul and Attaché (Commercial), J. N. L. Burgess.

BRITISH CONSULAR OFFICES

There are Consular Offices at *Reykjavík* and *Akureyri.*

INDONESIA
(Republic of Indonesia)

President, General Suharto, *born* June 9, 1921. *Acting President,* March 12, 1967; *confirmed as President,* Mar. 28, 1968, *re-elected for a term of 5 years,* March, 1973, March 1978 and March 1983.
Vice-President, Umar Wirahadi Kusumah, *elected* March 1983.

Minister-Co-ordinators, Gen. Surono (*Political and Security Affairs*); Prof. Ali Wardhana (*Economic, Financial and Industrial Affairs and Development Control*); Lt. Gen. A. Ratu Prawiranegara (*People's Welfare*).

Ministers of State, Maj. Gen. Sudharmono (*State Secretary, and Non-departmental Government agencies*); Dr. J. B. Sumarlin (*National Planning and Development*); Dr. B. J. Habibie (*Research and Technology*); Prof. E. Salim (*Demography and Environment*); K. Batubara (*Public Housing*); Dr. A. Gafur (*Youth and Sports*); Dr. S. Afif (*Reform of State Apparatus*); Mrs. L. Sutanto (*Women's Affairs*).

Ministers, Gen. S. Rustam (*Home Affairs*); Prof. M. Kusumaatmadja (*Foreign Affairs*); Gen. Poniman (*Defence and Security*); I. Saleh (*Justice*); Mr. Harmoko (*Information*); Dr. R. Prawiro (*Finance*); R. Saleh (*Trade*); B. Arifin (*Co-operative Affairs*); A. Affandi (*Agriculture*); Mr. Sujarwo (*Forestry*); Mr. Hartato (*Industry*); Prof. Subroto (*Mining and Energy*); S. Sosrodarsoto (*Public Works*); Air Marshal R. Nurjadin (*Communications*); Gen. A. Tahir (*Tourism, Posts and Telecommunications*); Adm. Sudomo (*Manpower*); Mr. Martono (*Transmigration*); Prof. N. Notosusanto (*Education and Culture*); Dr. S. Surjaningrat (*Health*); M. Sjadzali (*Religious Affairs*); Mrs. N. Sudarsono (*Social Affairs*).

INDONESIAN EMBASSY AND CONSULATE
38 Grosvenor Square, W1X 9AD
[01–499 7661]

Ambassador Extraordinary and Plenipotentiary, His Excellency Sjahabuddin Arifin (1981).
Minister, Mr. Pratjojo (*Deputy Chief of Mission*).

Situated between latitudes 6° North and 11° South and between longitudes 95° and 141° East, Indonesia comprises the islands of *Java, Madura,* and *Sumatra,* the *Riouw-Lingga Archipelago* (which with Karimon, Anambas, Natuna Islands, Tambelan, and part of Sumatra, forms the province of Riau), the islands of *Bangka* and *Billiton,* part of the island of *Borneo* (Kalimantan), *Sulawesi* (*formerly* Celebes) *Island,* the *Molucca Islands* (Ternate, Tidore, Halmahera, Buru, Seram, Banda, Timor-Laut, Larat, Bachiam,

Obi, Kei, Aru, Babar, Leti and Wetar), the island of *Bali* and the islands of *Lombok, Sumbawa, Sumba, Flores, Timor* and others comprising the provinces of East and West *Nusa Tenggara* and the western half of the island of New Guinea (*Irian Jaya*), with a total area of 735,000 sq. miles, and a population (U.N. estimate 1982) of about 153,000,000.

From the early part of the 17th century much of the Indonesian Archipelago was under Netherlands rule. Following the World War 1939–45, during which the Archipelago was occupied by the Japanese, a strong nationalistic movement manifested itself and after sporadic fighting the formal transfer of sovereignty by the Netherlands of all the former Dutch East Indies except W. New Guinea took place on December 27, 1949.

Western New Guinea became part of Indonesia in 1963 under the name West Irian (now Irian Jaya), this interpretation being confirmed in an "Act of Free Choice" in July, 1969, of which the United Nations took note in November 1969. Following a unilateral declaration of independence by the Fretilin, Indonesia took over the former Portuguese colony of East Timor, which in July 1976 was declared the 27th province of Indonesia.

Following a three-week period of unrest and violent student demonstrations the Minister of the Army, General Suharto, took over effective political power in March, 1966.

General Suharto was made Acting President with full powers, on March 11, 1967, and on March 28, 1968, appointed full President for a period of five years.

In the general election of May 1982, Golkar obtained 246 seats, the Moslem Party 94, and the Democratic Party of Indonesia 24. The Fourth Development Cabinet was appointed in March 1983.

Production.—Nearly 70 per cent. of the population of Indonesia is engaged in agriculture and related production. Copra, kapok, nutmeg, pepper and cloves are produced, mainly by smallholders; palm oil, sugar, fibres and cinchona are produced by large estates. Rubber, tea, coffee and tobacco are also produced by both in large quantities. Rice is a traditional staple food for the people of Indonesia and the islands of Java, Sulawesi and Sumatra are important producers. Production has risen rapidly in recent years to over 22 million tons and the country is now nearly self sufficient.

Oil and LNG are the most important assets, the export of which in 1981–82 earned about U.S. $18,800 million (about 80 per cent. of Indonesia's exports), but more recent developments have underscored the vulnerability of the economy to depressed international markets and weak oil prices. Timber is the second largest foreign exchange earner after oil.

Indonesia is rich in minerals, particularly tin, of which the country is the world's third biggest producer; petroleum, coal, nickel and bauxite are the other principal products; there are also considerable deposits of gold, silver, manganese phosphates and sulphur. Aid to Indonesia is channelled through the Inter-Governmental Group on Indonesia (IGGI), which pledged U.S. $2,459,000 in 1984–5.

Indonesia's Fourth Development Programme started in 1984 and its main objectives are the elimination of poverty, agricultural and urban problems, and the continued growth of installed power generation.

Finance.—The drop in oil prices led in March 1983 to the rupiah being devalued by 27 per cent, and a rescheduling of major projects was undertaken. More recently an increase in foreign reserves has meant that several of these projects could be re-instated.

Currency.—The unit of currency is the *rupiah* of 100 *sen.*

Trade with U.K.

	1983	1984
Direct Imports from U.K.	£193,642,000	£186,732,000
Exports to U.K.	169,454,000	181,490,000

Principal exports to the United Kingdom are rubber, timber, non-ferrous metals, tea, coffee, spices, and crude oil for refinement. Imports from the United Kingdom are mainly of machinery, transport equipment and electrical equipment.

Transport.—In Java a main line connects Jakarta with Surabaya in the East of Java and there are several branches. In Sumatra the important towns of Medan, Padang and Palembang are the centres of short railway systems.

Sea communications in the archipelago are maintained by the State-run shipping companies Djakarta-Lloyd (ocean-going) and Pelni (coastal and inter-island) and other small concerns. Transport by small craft on the rivers of the larger islands plays an important part in trade. Air services in Indonesia are operated by Garuda Indonesian Airways and other local airlines, and Jakarta is served by various international services. There are approximately 50,000 miles of roads.

CAPITAL.—ΨJakarta (population 6,503,449). Other important centres are: (Java) ΨSurabaya (7,027,913), ΨSemarang (1,026,671), Bandung (1,462,637); (Sumatra) Palembang (787,187), Medan (1,378,955); (Sulawesi), ΨUjung Pandang (*formerly Makassar*) (709,038); (Kalimantan) Banjarmasin (381,286), ΨPontianak (304,778), ΨBalikpapan (280,675); (Moluccas) Ambon (208,898); (Bali) Denpasar, Singaraja (for whole island 2,174,105); (Nusa Tenggara) Kupang (329,371); (Irian Jaya) Jayapura (107,164).

NATIONAL DAY.—August 17 (Anniversary of Proclamation of Independence).

FLAG.—Equal bands of red over white.

BRITISH EMBASSY
Jalan M. H. Thamrin 75, Jakarta

Ambassador Extraordinary and Plenipotentiary, His Excellency Alan Ewen Donald, C.M.G. (1984).

BRITISH CONSULAR OFFICES

There are British Consular Offices at *Jakarta* and *Medan.*

BRITISH COUNCIL

Representative, Dr. J. C. Blackwell, S Widjojo Centre, 57 Jalan Jendral Sudirman, Jakarta. There are also libraries at *Bandung* and *Medan.*

INDONESIA BRITAIN ASSOCIATION

c/o Mr. R. A. M. Ramsay, Sarinah Building, 13th Floor, J1. M. H. Thamrin 11, Jakarta.

IRAN
(The Islamic Republic of Iran)

Leader of the Islamic Revolution, Ayatollah Ruholla Khomeini, *born* 1902; *assumed power*, Feb., 1979.
President, Hojatoleslam Seyed Ali Khamene'i, *elected* Oct. 2, 1981, *re-elected* Aug. 16, 1985.
Prime Minister, Mir Hossein Moussavi.
Foreign Affairs, Dr. Ali Akbar Velayati.
Education, Seyed Kazem Akrami.
Commerce, Hassan Abedi Jaafari.
Health, Dr. Ali Reza Marandi.
Justice, Dr. Hassan Ebrahim Habibi.
Defence, (vacant).
Oil, Mohammed Gharazi.
Energy, Dr. Hassan Ghaffuri-Fard.
Agriculture, Dr. Abbas Ali Zali.
Economics and Finance, Dr. Hussein Namazi.
Interior, Ali Akbar Nateq Nouri.
Labour, Abol Hassan Sarhadi-Zadeh.
Housing, Serajeddin Kazeruni.
Mining and Metals, Hossein Nili Ahmadabadi.
Industry, Gholamreza Shafei.
Heavy Industry, Behzad Nabavi.
Islamic Guidance, Seyed Mohammed Khatami.
Culture and Higher Education, Dr. Iraj Fazel.
Intelligence, Mohammad Mohammadi Reyshahri.
Roads and Transport, (vacant).
Construction Crusade, Bijan Namdar Zanganeh.
Islamic Revolutionary Guard, Mohsen Rafiqdust.

IRANIAN EMBASSY IN LONDON
27 Prince's Gate, SW7 1PX

Area and Population.—Iran has an area of 628,000 sq. miles, with a population of 42,000,000. It is mostly an arid table-land, encircled, except in the east, by mountains, the highest in the north rising to 18,934 ft. The central and eastern portion is a vast salt desert.

The Iranians are mostly Shi'ah Moslems but among them are Zoroastrians, Bahais, Sunni Moslems and Armenian and Assyrian Christians. Emigration has much reduced the once substantial Jewish community.

Language and Literature.—Persian, or Farsi, the language of Iran, and of some other areas formerly under Persian rule, is an Indo-European tongue with many Arabic elements added; the alphabet is mainly Arabic, with writing from right to left. Among the great names in Persian literature are those of Abu'l Kásim Mansúr, of Firdausi (A.D. 939–1020), Omar Khayyám, the astonomer-poet (died A.D. 1122), Muslihu'd-Din, known as Sa'di (born A.D. 1184) and Shems-ed-Din Muhammad, or Hafiz (died A.D. 1389).

Government.—Iran was ruled from the end of the 18th century by Shahs of the Qajar Dynasty. A nationalist movement became active in Dec., 1905, and in Aug., 1906, the Shah, Muzaffer-ud-Din, admitting the need for reforms, granted a Constitution. After the war of 1914–18, the subsequent troubles and the signature of the Soviet-Iranian Treaty of 1921, a vigorous Prime Minister, Reza Khan re-established general order. On Oct. 31, 1925, the last representative of the Qajar Dynasty, Sultan Ahmed Shah was deposed in his absence by the National Assembly, which handed over the government to the Prime Minister, Reza Khan, who was elected Shah on Dec.

13, 1925, by the Constituent Assembly, and took the title Reza Shah Pahlavi. On September 16, 1941, Reza Shah abdicated in favour of the Crown Prince, who ascended the throne under the title of Mohammed Reza Shah Pahlavi.

Following widespread and persistent opposition to his regime, the Shah departed from Iran in January, 1979. Ayatollah Khomeini, the main spiritual leader of the Shi'ah Moslems, returned to Iran from exile on February 1. Following a national referendum, Iran was declared an Islamic Republic by Ayatollah Khomeini on April 1, 1979. A new constitution, providing for a President, Prime Minister and Consultative Assembly, and also for overall leadership by Khomeini, was approved by referendum in December 1979. Opposition to the fundamentalist policies of the government and religious leaders led initially to assassination and bombings, but the government's subsequent severe measures suppressed violent opposition. In Dec. 1982 an Assembly of Experts was elected to decide the eventual succession to Ayatollah Khomeini.

Iran has been at war with Iraq since the Iraqi invasion of Iran in Sept. 1980. Following their defeat at Khorramshahr Iraqi forces withdrew from most Iranian territory in June 1982. The Iranians launched a major offensive against Basra in July 1982 and several subsequent minor offensives in which they have gained small areas of territory. After Iraq declared a Maritime Exclusion Zone in August 1982, shipping entering the Iranian port of Bandar Khomeini at the head of the Gulf came under Iraqi attack; since the summer of 1984 both sides have carried out attacks on neutral shipping further south in the Gulf.

Defence.—The Army has a strength of about 150,000 men, in 4 armoured divisions, 4 infantry divisions and one airborne division. The Air Force has a strength of about 35,000, with some 70 combat aircraft. The Navy has a strength of about 20,000 and consists of 3 destroyers, 4 frigates, 4 corvettes, 5 minesweepers, and patrol boats, support ships, landing craft and hovercraft. The Islamic Revolutionary Guards Corps numbers about 500,000 men, of whom approximately half are at the front. Total armed forces personnel including paramilitary forces number over one million.

Education.—Since 1943 primary education has been compulsory and free, but there is large scale absenteeism, particularly outside the towns. There are in Iran 22 universities (8 in Tehran, 14 in the provinces). They were closed in July 1981 for "Islamization" but have now reopened. The educational system has been reformed following the revolution.

Finance.—The budget for the Iranian year beginning March 22, 1985, was revenue *Rials.* 3,638,000 million; expenditure *Rials.* 4,032,000 million. The unit of currency is the *Rial* (for rate of exchange, *see* p. 82).

Agriculture.—While petroleum is the principal product and by far the greatest export, Iran is otherwise largely an agricultural and pastoral country. After the 1979 revolution the Provisional Government announced its intention of giving greater emphasis to the development of agriculture with a view to reducing Iran's dependence on food imports. Although half of Iran's area is either mountain or desert, more than half the country's population live in rural areas, depending on the 10 million hectares under crop, sheep, goats and cattle for their livelihood. Wheat is the principal crop; other important crops are barley, rice, cotton, sugar beet, fruit, nuts and vegetables. Wool is also a major product. There are extensive forests in the north and west, the conservation of which is an urgent problem.

Industry.—Under the Shah, great emphasis was given to the development of industry. Apart from oil, the principal industrial products are carpets, textiles, sugar, cement and other construction materials, ginned cotton, vegetable oil and other food products, leather and shoes, metal manufactures, pharmaceuticals, automobiles, fertilizers and plastics. Industrial output was severely curtailed by the 1979 revolution, as a result of which many industrialists left the country. In July 1979 the Provisional Government nationalized a wide range of major industrial concerns, having nationalized the banks and the insurance companies the previous month. Foreign trade is controlled by the State, although recently more encouragement has been given to private sector companies.

Energy.—The oilfields, which lie in South Western Iran, were nationalised in 1951. From 1957 until the 1979 revolution a consortium of eight oil companies (one British, one French, one Dutch, and five U.S.) was responsible for the production, refining and sale of oil. In July 1979 the National Iranian Oil Company assumed full control of the oil industry. In addition to that extracted from the onshore wells, oil is also produced from a number of off-shore oilfields. Oil production by June 1979 had reached an average of 3·5 million b.p.d., but is now approximately 2·2 million b.p.d., of which some 1·5 million b.p.d. is exported. Iran is a member of O.P.E.C.

Communications.—Tehran is at the centre of a network of highways linking the capital with other major towns, the ports and the frontiers with Turkey, U.S.S.R., Afghanistan and Pakistan, and with the Caspian Sea. The Trans-Iranian Railway runs from Bandar Turcoman, on the Caspian Sea, via Tehran to Bandar Khomeini, on the Persian Gulf. Other lines link Tehran with Tabriz and with Mashad. There are also railways from Tabriz to Julfa and from Zahedan to Quetta, and branch lines from Ahwaz to Khorramshahr and from Khorramshahr to Tanuma (Iraq). An extension from Qom to Yazd via Kashan is now in operation, as is one from Bandar Turcoman to Gorgan. An extension from Yazd to Kerman is partially complete. The Iranian rail system is linked to the Turkish system via Van. There is an international airport at Tehran (Mehrabad), and airports at all the major provincial centres. The national airline, Iranair, is government-owned and operates international and domestic routes.

TRADE

Imports to Iran declined dramatically at the beginning of 1979 as a result of the economic disruption caused by the revolution. Iran's aggressive oil sales policy during 1982 enabled foreign exchange reserves to recover from the 1981 low level and made possible increased imports.

Imports into Iran consist mainly of industrial and agricultural machinery, motor vehicles and motor vehicle components for assembly, iron and steel (including manufactures), electrical machinery and goods, meat, various other foods, and certain textile fabrics and yarns. The principal exports, apart from oil, are cotton, carpets, dried fruit, nuts, hides and skins, mineral ores, wool, gums, caviare, cumin seed and spices. West Germany, Japan and the U.K. are Iran's leading suppliers.

	1983
Imports	US$18,277 m.
Exports	19,476 m.

Trade with U.K.

	1983	1984
Imports from U.K. . .	£629,980,000	£703,097,000
Exports to U.K.	100,545,000	368,572,000

CAPITAL: Tehran, population 10,000,000. Other large towns are Tabriz (700,000), Isfahan (1,000,000) Meshed (500,000), Shiraz (300,000), Resht (150,000), Kerman (100,000), Hamadan (130,000), Yazd (70,000), Kermanshah (152,000), Ahwaz (175,000).

FLAG.—Equal horizontal bands of green, white and red; with an emblem of the Islamic Republic.

BRITISH INTERESTS SECTION
Tehran

Minister, M. K. O. Simpson-Orlebar, C.M.G.
Counsellor, P. F. M. Wogan.
(The Embassy was closed on September 9, 1980, and British interests are handled by the Swedish Embassy.)

IRAQ

REVOLUTIONARY COMMAND COUNCIL

Chairman, President of the Republic, and Supreme Commander of the Armed Forces, Saddam Hussain, assumed office July 16, 1979.
Members, Izzat Ibrahim (*RCC Vice-Chairman*); Taha Muhiddin Ma'aruf (*Vice-President of the Republic*); Taha Yasin Ramadhan (*First Deputy Prime Minister*); Na'im Haddad; Tariq 'Aziz (*Deputy Prime Minister and Foreign Minister*); General Adnan Khairallah (*Deputy Prime Minister and Minister of Defence*); Sa'doun Shakir (*Interior*); Hassan Ali (*Trade*); Khalid Abdul Mun'im Rasheed (*acting Secretary-General*).
In addition to those members of the R.C.C. holding departmental portfolios listed above, there are 17 other Ministers and 4 Ministers of State.

EMBASSY OF THE REPUBLIC OF IRAQ
21 Queen's Gate, SW7 5JG
[01–584 7141/6]

Ambassador Extraordinary and Plenipotentiary, new appointment awaited.

Area, etc.—Traversed by the Rivers Euphrates and Tigris, Iraq extends from Turkey on N. and N.E. to the Gulf on the S. and S.E. and from Iran on E. to Syria and Arabian Desert on W., the approximate position lying between 37¼° to 48¼° E. long., and from 37¼° to 30° N. lat. (*see* MAP, p. 853). The area of Iraq is officially estimated at 172,000 sq. miles of which 37 per cent. is desert land. About 35 to 40 per cent. of

the remainder is potentially cultivable either by rainfall or by irrigation.

The *Euphrates* (which has a total length of 1,700 miles from its source to its outflow in the Persian Gulf) is formed by two arms, of which the Murad Su (415 miles) rises in eastern Erzurum, and flows westwards to a junction with the Kara Su, or Frat Su (275 miles); the other arm rises in the north-west of Erzurum in the Dumlu Dagh. The *Tigris* has a total length of 1,150 miles from its source to its junction with the Euphrates at Qurna, 70 miles from the Gulf, and rises in two arms south of the Taurus mountains, in Kurdistan, uniting at Til, where the boundaries of the districts of Diarbekir, Van and Bitlis conjoin.

Population.—At the Census of October 1977 Iraq had a total population of 12,171,480. The population was estimated recently at 14 million.

Language.—The language is mainly Arabic and English is widely used in commerce, science and the arts.

Antiquities.—In 1944 excavations at Tell Hassuna, near Shura (on the Tigris in North Iraq) unearthed abundant traces of culture dating back to 5000 B.C. Excavations in 1948 at Tel Abu Shahrain, south of "Ur of the Chaldees," confirm Eridu's claim to be the most ancient city of the Sumerian world. Hillah, the ancient city on the left bank of the Shatt el Hillah, a branch of the Euphrates, about 70 miles south of Baghdad, is near the site of Babylon and of the "house of the lofty-head" or "gate of the god" (Tower of Babel). Mosul Governorate covers a great part of the ancient kingdom of *Assyria*, the ruins of Nineveh, the Assyrian capital, being visible on the banks of the Tigris, opposite Mosul. Qurna, at the junction of the Tigris and Euphrates, is the traditional site of the *Garden of Eden*.

Government.—Under the Treaty of Lausanne (1923), Turkey renounced sovereignty over Mesopotamia. A provisional Arab Government was set up in Nov., 1920, and in Aug., 1921, the Emir Faisal was elected King of Iraq. The country was a monarchy until July, 1958, when King Faisal II was assassinated. From 1958 Iraq has been under Presidential rule. The ruling Party is the Arab Ba'ath Socialist Party, which came to power on July 17, 1968.

Iraq has been engaged in hostilities with Iran since September 1980, originally over control of the Shatt-al-Arab waterway. In July 1982 Iranian forces moved across the border into Iraq, and since that time a series of inconclusive battles have been fought along the borders. Iraq declared a Maritime Exclusion Zone in Aug. 1982 and thereafter regularly attacked shipping entering the Iranian port of Bandar Khomeini at the head of the Gulf. The war extended further down the Gulf in the summer of 1984, with both sides attacking neutral shipping, including tankers and in 1985 Iraq launched several attacks on Iran's oil installations on Kharg Island.

Communications and Trade.—New roads are being rapidly built, and communications between Baghdad and the provincial capitals are being improved and secured. Facilities at the port of Basrah have been improved but the port has not been used since the outbreak of hostilities with Iran in Sept. 1980. Continuous dredging of the Shatt-al-Arab has also been suspended by hostilities and the channel has seriously silted. The port of Um Qasr near the Kuwaiti border has been developed for freight and sulphur handling and a container terminal is ready for operation but not in use due to the port's proximity to the war zone. Road routes from Turkey and the Mediterranean are well used, and carry through traffic to Kuwait and the south. The border between Syria and Iraq was closed in late 1977, reopened in November, 1978 and closed again in April 1982.

There is an international airport at Baghdad. Iraqi

Airways and British Airways provide flights between Baghdad and London, and other international airlines operate to Europe. Iraqi Republican Railways provide regular passenger and goods services between Basra, Baghdad and Mosul, and links up through Syria and Turkey with the Mediterranean and the Bosphorus, though no through traffic has used the line since the Syrian government cut the rail link in April 1982. There is also a metre gauge line connecting Baghdad with Khanaqin, Kirkuk and Arbil.

Agriculture and Industry.—Apart from the valuable revenues to be derived from oil, agricultural development makes a valuable contribution to the wealth of the country and two harvests can usually be gathered in the year. Production fluctuates from year to year according to rainfall. The Government's concern with agricultural development is shown in the large financial allocations made to the sector. Salinity and soil erosion, caused by a high water table, inadequate irrigation and drainage and traditional farming methods, are the major problems now being addressed by development planners.

Increasing industrialization is taking place, mainly in the public sector. Priority is being given to petrochemicals, food industries, construction industries and engineering. Existing industries include cement, building materials, steel fabrications, food processing and the manufacture of consumer goods, as well as the development of mineral resources.

Iraq's major industry is oil production. It was nationalized on June 1, 1972 and accounts for approximately 98 per cent. of the total government revenue and 45 per cent. of the Gross National Product. Production was some 3·5 million barrels per day in 1979 but the effects of war damage on the Basra terminals and the closure of the trans-Syria pipeline have reduced production to an estimated 1 million barrels per day. Total revenues from oil are believed to be about $10,000 million.

FINANCE

	1981*
Total revenue	ID19,434,856,809
Total expenditure	19,250,261,450

* Estimates.

TRADE

(Excluding oil)

	1982
Total Imports	$17,758,000
Total Exports	142,000,000

Trade with U.K.

	1983	1984
Imports from U.K.	£399,900,000	£343,120,000
Exports to U.K.	30,600,000	69,047,000

The principal imports are iron and steel, cement and other building materials, mechanical and electrical machinery, motor vehicles, textiles and clothing, essential foodstuffs, grain, tinned foods and raw industrial materials. The chief exports are crude petroleum, dates, raw wool, raw hides and skins and raw cotton.

CAPITAL.—Baghdad. Population of the governorate (Census 1977) 3,205,645. Other towns of importance are Ψ Basrah, Mosul and Kirkuk.

FLAG.—Horizontal stripes of red, white and black, with three green stars on the white stripe.

BRITISH EMBASSY

Sharia Salah Ud-Din,
Karkh, Baghdad

Ambassador Extraordinary and Plenipotentiary, His Excellency Terence Joseph Clark, C.M.G., C.V.O., *apptd.* 1985.

Counsellor, I. R. Callan (*Consul General*).

1st Secretary, D. A. Wright, O.B.E. (*Commercial*).
Defence Attaché, Col. R. G. Eccles.
Air and Naval Attaché, Wg.-Cdr. J. F. H. Marriott.
There are no British Consular Offices outside Baghdad.

British Council Representative, G. E. P. Ness, O.B.E., Waziriya, 301, Street 3, (P.O. Box 298), Baghdad.

IRELAND

Position and Extent.—Ireland lies in the Atlantic Ocean, to the West of Great Britain, and is separated from Scotland by the North Channel and from Wales by the Irish Sea and St. George's Channel. The land area of the island is 32,408 sq. miles and its geographical position between 51° 26′ and 55° 21′ N. latitude and from 5° 25′ to 10° 30′ W. longitude. The greatest length of the island, from N.E. to S.W. (Torr Head to Mizen Head), is 302 miles, and the greatest breadth, from E. to W. (Dundrum Bay to Annagh Head), is 174 miles. On the N. Coast of *Achill Island* (Co. Mayo) are the highest cliffs in the British Isles, 2,000 feet sheer above the sea. Ireland is occupied for the greater part of its area by the *Central Plain*, with an elevation 50 to 350 ft. above mean sea level, with isolated mountain ranges near the coastline. The principal mountains, with their highest points, are the *Sperrin Mountains* (Sawel 2,240 ft.) of County Tyrone; the *Mountains of Mourne* (Slieve Donard 2,796 ft.) of County Down, and the *Wicklow Mountains* (Lugnaquilla 3,039 ft.); the *Derryveagh Mountains* (Errigal 2,466 ft.) of County Donegal; the *Connemara Mountains* (Twelve Pins 2,695 ft.) of County Galway; *Macgillicuddy's Reeks* (Carrantuohill 3,414 ft., the highest point in Ireland); and the *Galtee Mountains* (3,018 ft.) of County Tipperary, and the *Knockmealdown* (2,609 ft.) and *Comeragh Mountains* (2,470 ft.) of County Waterford. The principal river of Ireland (and the longest in the British Isles) is the *Shannon* (240 miles), rising in County Cavan and draining the central plain; the Shannon flows through a chain of loughs to the city of Limerick, and thence to an estuary on the western Atlantic seaboard. The *Slaney* flows into Wexford Harbour, the *Liffey* to Dublin Bay, the *Boyne* to Drogheda, the *Lee* to Cork Harbour, the *Blackwater* to Youghal Harbour, and the *Suir, Barrow* and *Nore,* to Waterford Harbour. As in Scotland, the principal hydrographic feature is the *Loughs,* of which Lough *Neagh* (150 sq. miles) in the north-east is the largest in Ireland and the British Isles, others being the Shannon Chain of *Allen, Boderg, Forbes, Ree* and *Derg,* and the Erne Chain of *Gowna, Oughter, Lower Erne,* and *Erne; Melvin, Gill, Gara* and *Conn* in the north-west; and *Corrib* and *Mask* (joined by a hidden channel) in the west. In County Kerry, to the east of Macgillicuddy's Reeks, are the famous *lakes of Killarney.*

Primitive Man.—Although little is known concerning the earliest inhabitants of Ireland, there are many traces of neolithic man throughout the island; a grave containing a polished stone axehead assigned to 2,500 B.C. was found at Linkardstown, Co. Carlow, in 1944, and the use of bronze implements appears to have become known about the middle of the 17th century B.C. In the later Bronze Age a Celtic race of *Goidels* appears to have invaded the island, and in the early Iron Age *Brythons* from South Britain are believed to have effected settlements in the southeast, while *Picts* from North Britain established similar settlements in the north. Towards the close of the Roman occupation of Britain, the dominant tribe in the island was that of the *Scoti,* who afterwards established themselves in Scotland.

History.—According to Irish legends, the island of Ierne was settled by a Milesian race, who came from Scythia by way of Spain, and established the *Kingdom of Tara*, about 500 B.C. The supremacy of the *Ardri* (high king) of Tara was acknowledged by eight lesser kingdoms (Munster, Connaught, Ailech, Oriel, Ulidia, Meath, Leinster and Ossory) ruled by descendants of the eight sons of Miled. The basalt columns on the coast of Antrim, eight miles from Portrush, known as the *Giant's Causeway*, are connected with the legendary history of Ireland as the remnants of a bridge built in the time of Finn M'Coul (Fingal) to connect Antrim with Scotland (Staffa).

Hibernia was visited by Roman merchants but never by Roman legions, and little is known of the history of the country until the invasions of *Northmen* (Norwegians and Danes) towards the close of the 8th century A.D. The Norwegians were distinguished as Findgaill (White Strangers) and the Danes as Dubgaill (Black Strangers), names which survive in "Fingall," "MacDougall" and "MacDowell," while the name of the island itself is held to be derived from the Scandinavian *Ira-land* (land of the Irish), the names of the Provinces being survivals of Norse dialect forms (Ulaids-tir, Laiginstir, Mumans-tir and Kunnak-tir). The outstanding events in the encounters with the Northmen are the *Battle of Tara* (980), at which the Hy Neill king Maelsechlainn II defeated the Scandinavians of Dublin and the Hebrides under the king Amlaib Cuarán; and the *Battle of Clontarf* (1014) by which the Scandinavian power was completely broken. After Clontarf the supreme power was disputed by the O'Briens of Munster, the O'Neills of Ulster, and the O'Connors of Connaught, with varying fortunes. In 1152 Dermod MacMurrough (Diarmit MacMurchada), the deposed king of Leinster, sought assistance in his struggle with Rauidhri O'Connor (the high king of Ireland), and visited Henry II, the Norman king of England. Henry authorized him to obtain armed support in England for the recovery of his kingdom, and Dermod enlisted the services of Richard de Clare, the Norman Earl of Pembroke, afterwards known as *Strongbow*, who landed at Waterford (Aug. 23, 1170) with 200 knights and 1,000 other troops for the reconquest of Leinster, where he eventually settled, after marriage with Dermod's daughter. In 1172 (Oct. 18) Henry II himself landed in Ireland. He received homage from the Irish kings and established his capital at Dublin. The invaders subsequently conquered most of the island and a feudal government was created. In the 14th and 15th centuries, the Irish recovered most of their lands, while many Anglo-Irish lords became virtually independent, royal authority being confined to the "Pale," a small district round Dublin. Though, under Henry VII, Sir Edward Poynings, as Lord Deputy, had passed at the *Parliament of Drogheda* (1494) the act later known as *Poynings' Law*, subordinating the Irish Legislature to the Crown, the Earls of Kildare retained effective power until, in 1534, Henry VIII began the reconquest of Ireland. Parliament in 1541 recognized him as King of Ireland and by 1603 English authority was supreme.

Christianity.—Christianity did not become general until the advent of St. Patrick. *St. Patrick* was born in Britain about 389, and was taken to Ireland as a slave about sixteen years later escaping to Gaul at the age of 22. In 432 he was consecrated Bishop of Auxerre and landed in Wicklow to establish and organize the Christian religion throughout the island.

REPUBLIC OF IRELAND

Uachtarán-na-hÉireann (*President*), Patrick J. Hillery, *born* 1923, *assumed office*, Dec. 3, 1976, *sworn in for 2nd term*, Dec. 3, 1983.

MEMBERS OF THE GOVERNMENT

Taoiseach, Garret Fitzgerald.
Tánaiste and Minister for Energy, Dick Spring.
Finance, Alan Dukes.
Foreign Affairs, Peter Barry.
Defence, Patrick Cooney.
Industry, Trade, Commerce and Tourism, John Bruton.
Justice, Michael Noonan.
Environment, Liam Kavanagh.
Public Service, John Boland.
Education, Gemma Hussey.
Agriculture, Austin Deasy.
Gaeltacht, and Fisheries and Forestry, Paddy O'Toole.
Health and Social Welfare, Barry Desmond.
Communications, Jim Mitchell.
Labour, Ruairi Quinn.

The present Government was formed by a coalition of the Fine Gael and Labour parties following a general election on Nov. 24, 1982.

EMBASSY IN LONDON
17 Grosvenor Place, SW1X 7HR
[01-235 2171]

Ambassador Extraordinary and Plenipotentiary, His Excellency Noel Dorr (1983).

Area and Population.—The Republic has a land area of 26,600 sq. miles, divided into the four Provinces of *Leinster* (Carlow, Dublin, Kildare, Kilkenny, Laoighis, Longford, Louth, Meath, Offaly, Westmeath, Wexford and Wicklow); *Munster* (Clare, Cork, Kerry, Limerick, Tipperary and Waterford); *Connacht* (Galway, Leitrim, Mayo, Roscommon and Sligo); and part of *Ulster* (Cavan, Donegal and Monaghan).

Total population of the Republic at the Census held on April 5, 1981, was 3,443,405, a density of 50 persons per sq. kilometre. Provisional figures showed 64,237 births, 18,355 marriages and 32,154 deaths in the year 1984.

GOVERNMENT

The Constitution.—The constitution, approved by a plebiscite on July 1, 1937, came into operation on December 29, 1937. The Constitution declares the national territory to be the whole island of Ireland, its islands and the territorial seas. Pending the reintegration of the national territory, and without prejudice to the right of the Parliament and the Government established by the Constitution to exercise jurisdiction over the whole of the national territory, the laws enacted by that Parliament shall have the like area and extent of application as those of the Irish Free State, which did not include the six counties of Northern Ireland.

The Irish language, being the national language, is the first official language. The English language is recognized as a second official language.

The President (*Uachtarán na hEireann*) is elected by direct vote of the people for a period of seven years. A former or retiring President is eligible for a second term. The President summons and dissolves Dáil Éireann on the advice of the *Taoiseach* (Head of the Government). He signs and promulgates laws. The supreme command of the Defence forces is vested in him, its exercise being regulated by law. He has the power of pardon. The President, in the exercise and performance of certain of his constitutional powers and functions, is aided and advised by a Council of State.

The National Parliament (*Oireachtas*) consists of the President and two Houses: a House of Representatives (*Dáil Éireann*) and a Senate (*Seanad Éireann*).

Dáil Eireann is composed of 166 members elected by adult suffrage on a basis of proportional representation by means of the single transferable vote. All citizens, and such other persons in the state as may be determined by law, who have reached the age of 18 years and are not disqualified by law have the right to vote. Each Dáil may continue for a period not exceeding five years from the date of election.

Seanad Éireann is composed of 60 members, of whom 11 are nominated by the Taoiseach and 49 are elected; six by institutions of higher education, and 43 from panels of candidates, established on a vocational basis.

Members of Dáil Éireann are paid an allowance of IR£17,978 per annum (and members of Seanad Éireann IR£9,998). They are allowed travelling facilities between Dublin and their constituencies and are, subject to certain restrictions, granted free telephone and postal facilities from Leinster House and allowances for overnight stays in Dublin.

The executive authority is exercised by the Government subject to the Constitution. The Government is responsible to Dáil Éireann, meets and acts as a collective authority, and is collectively responsible for the Departments of State administered by the Ministers.

The Taoiseach is appointed by the President on the nomination of Dáil Éireann. The other members of the government are appointed by the President on the nomination of the Taoiseach with the previous approval of Dáil Éireann. The Taoiseach appoints a member of the Government to be the *Tánaiste* who acts for all purposes in the place of the Taoiseach in the event of the death, permanent incapacitation, or temporary absence of the Taoiseach. The Taoiseach, the Tánaiste and the Minister for Finance must be members of Dáil Éireann. The other members of the Goverment must be members of Dáil Éireann or Seanad Éireann, but not more than two may be members of Seanad Éireann.

The result of the general election on Nov. 24, 1982 was as follows: *Fianna Fáil*, 75; *Fine Gael*, 70; *Labour*, 16; *Independent*, 3; *Workers' Party*, 2. Total membership including the *Ceann Comhairle* (Chairman), 166.

JUDICIAL SYSTEM

The Judicial system comprises Courts of First Instance and a Court of Final Appeal called the Supreme Court (*Cúirt Uachtarach*). The Courts of First Instance include a High Court (*Ard-Chúirt*) and Courts of local and limited jurisdiction, with a right of appeal as determined by law. The High Court alone has original jurisdiction to consider the question of the validity of any law having regard to the provisions of the Constitution. The Supreme Court has appellate jurisdiction from all decisions of the High Court, with such exceptions and subject to such regulations as may be prescribed by law.

Chief Justice, Hon. Thomas A. Finlay .... IR£48,587
President of the High Court, Hon. Liam Hamilton .... IR£42,144
Judges, Supreme Court, Hon. Brian Walsh; Hon. Seamus Henchy; Hon. Francis Griffin; Hon. Anthony Hederman; Hon. Niall J. McCarthy .... IR£39,729
Judges, High Court, Hon. Donal Barrington; Hon. John M. Gannon; Hon. James McMahon; Hon. Herbert R. McWilliam; Hon. Rory O'Hanlon; Hon. Declan Costello; Hon. James A. D'Arcy; Hon. Ronan Keane; Hon. Ms. Mella Carroll; Hon. Henry D. Barron; Hon. Francis D. Murphy; Hon. Kevin Lynch; Hon. Seamus Egan; Hon. Robert Barr; Hon.

Gerard Lardner; Hon. Thomas J. Neylon (*ex officio*) .... IR£35,702
Attorney-General, John Rodgers.

RELIGION
(Census of 1981) (Provisional)

Catholic	3,203,574
Church of Ireland	95,339
Presbyterians	14,252
Methodists	5,813
Others	124,427
Total	3,443,405

DEFENCE

Establishments provide at present for a Permanent Defence Force of approximately 17,956 all ranks, including the Air Corps and the Naval Service. Recruitment is on a voluntary basis. Minimum term of enlistment is three years in the Permanent Defence Force followed by six years in the Reserve Defence Force. The Defence Vote for the year ending Dec. 31, 1985, provides for approximately 22,214 all ranks of the Reserve Defence Force. Recruitment is also on a voluntary basis; minimum term of enlistment is three years. The Defence Estimate for the year ending Dec. 31, 1985 provides for an expenditure of IR£240,633,000.

FINANCE

	1985 *(Estimated)*
Revenue	IR£6,400·0 m.
Expenditure	7,634·0 m.

The estimated revenue for 1985 includes:

	IR£m
Customs Duties	105·0
Excise Duties	1,317·2
Capital Taxes	33·5
Stamp Duties	116·4
Income Tax	2,131·2
Income Levy	77·0
Corporation Tax	218·5
Value-Added Tax	1,483·9
Agricultural Levies (E.E.C.)	15·0
Motor Vehicle Duties	120·5
Youth Employment Levy	85·8
Total (including other non-tax items) ...	6,400·0

The principal items of current expenditure in the 1985 Budget:

	IR£m.
Debt Service	1,991
Industry and labour	252
Agriculture	306
Fisheries	13
Forestry	17
Tourism	27
Roads	28
Sanitary services	46
Transport	2
Health	952
Education	850
Welfare	1,386
Housing	209
Subsidies	312
Defence	272
Garda	235
Prisons	38
Legal, etc.	32
Other	666
Total	7,634

The Gross Debt at end 1984 was IR£18,475,739,445 and capital assets were IR£4,664,232,045.

Primary education is directed by the State, with the exception of approximately 75 private primary schools with an enrolment of about 11,969 in 1983–84.

There were 3,385 State-aided primary schools with an enrolment of 563,507.

In 1983-84 there were 511 recognized secondary schools with 209,026 pupils under private management (mainly religious orders), and 250 vocational schools with 76,916 pupils. All these schools and colleges are controlled by 38 statutory local Vocational Education Committees. There were 15 State comprehensive schools in 1983–84 with a total enrolment of 8,684 students, and 42 community schools with an enrolment of 26,068 students. There were also other miscellaneous second-level schools and the total full-time enrolment at second-level for 1983–84 was 324,409.

Third-level education is catered for by five University Colleges, two National Institutes for Higher Education, and also by third-level courses offered by the Technical Colleges and Regional Technical Colleges and other miscellaneous third-level institutions. There were 49,814 full-time third-level students in 1983–84, of whom 25,249 were attending university courses.

The estimated State expenditure on education in the calendar year 1985, excluding administration and inspection, is Primary IR£357,795,000; Post-Primary IR£400,476,000. The vote for Universities and third-level Colleges amounted to IR£101,825,000, while, in addition, grants of IR£9,987,000 were provided in respect of the Faculties of General Agriculture, Veterinary Medicine and Dairy Science.

MINERALS AND FISHERIES

Minerals.—320 persons were employed in the coal mines in 1984 and 70,400 tons of coal was produced.

Sea Fisheries.—8,572 persons were employed in the fisheries in 1983. Total value of all fish landed in 1983 was IR£51,900,000.

COMMUNICATIONS

Railways.—In the year ended Dec. 31, 1983, there were 1,235 miles of railway; 13,027,000 passengers and 3,319,000 tons of merchandise were conveyed; the receipts were IR£52,349,000 and expenditure IR£127,581,000. These figures are in respect of railway working by *Coras Iompair Eireann.*

Road Motor Services.—In 1983 road motor vehicles carried 207,881,377 passengers, the gross receipts being IR£93,411,649.

Shipping.—In 1983 the number of ships with cargo and in ballast in the foreign trade which arrived at Irish ports was 12,860 (23,452,463 net registered tons); of these 3,288 (7,190,246 net registered tons) were of Irish nationality.

CIVIL AVIATION

Shannon Airport, 15 miles W. of Limerick, is on the main transatlantic air route. In 1984 the airport handled 1,087,804 passengers.

Dublin Airport, 6 miles N. of Dublin, serves the cross-channel and European services operated by the Irish national airline *Aer Lingus* and other airlines. In 1984 the airport handled 2,599,064 passengers.

Cork Airport, 5 miles S. of Cork serves the cross Channel and European services operated by *Aer Lingus* and other airlines. In 1984 the airport handled 334,495 passengers.

Trade with U.K.

	1983 £ Sterling	1984 £ Sterling
Imports from U.K.	3,055,275,000	3,393,499,000
Exports to U.K.	2,290,067,000	2,635,039,000

OVERSEAS TRADE

	1983 IR£	1984 IR£
Imports	7,366,775,383	8,912,906,850
Exports	6,943,836,265	8,897,606,936
Trade balance	422,939,118	15,299,914

PRINCIPAL ARTICLES

Principal imports in 1984 were:

	IR£
Live animals	110,556,146
Food, drink and tobacco............	907,322,820
Petrol and petroleum products......	977,140,421
Chemicals	1,031,929,663
Machinery	2,332,617,897
Transport equipment	445,875,360
Metal and manufactures	542,328,058
Textiles and clothing	717,475,370
Paper, paperboard and manufactures	247,262,997
Professional, scientific etc. goods....	196,731,737

Principal exports in 1984 were:

	IR£
Live animals	256,691,067
Meat and meat preparations	535,660,535
Other food, drink and tobacco	1,479,822,169
Machinery and transport equipment	2,550,162,567
Clothing, headgear and footwear ...	191,618,617
Textiles	375,496,982
Metal ores and scrap	229,820,773
Metal and manufactures	248,471,144
Non-metallic mineral manufactures .	148,795,725
Chemicals	1,236,319,566
Professional, scientific etc., goods ...	395,223,022

CAPITAL.—Dublin (*Baile Atha Cliath*) is a City and County Borough on the River Liffey at the head of Dublin Bay. In April, 1981, its population (1981 Census) was 525,882.

Other cities and towns, with their populations at the Census of 1981 are Ψ Cork (136,344); Ψ Limerick (60,736); Ψ Dun Laoghaire (54,496); Ψ Waterford (38,473); Ψ Galway (37,835); Ψ Dundalk (25,663).

FLAG.—Equal vertical stripes of green, white and orange.

NATIONAL DAY.—March 17 (St. Patrick's Day).

BRITISH EMBASSY
33 Merrion Road, Dublin 4

Ambassador Extraordinary and Plenipotentiary, His Excellency Sir Alan Goodison, K.C.M.G., C.V.O. (1983).

Counsellor and Head of Chancery, R. F. Stimson.

First Secretaries, Miss D. M. Mills; D. L. S. Coombe (*Commercial*); J. C. Radcliffe; J. D. F. Holt; P. M. Innes.

ISRAEL
(Yisrael)

President of Israel, Chaim Herzog, *born* 1918, *elected* Mar. 22, 1983, *inaugurated*, May 5, 1983.

CABINET

* *Prime Minister*, Shimon Peres (*Lab.*).

* *Vice-Premier and Foreign Minister*, Yitzhak Shamir (*L.H.*).

EMBASSY IN LONDON
2 Palace Green, Kensington, W8 4QB
[01–937 8050]

Ambassador Extraordinary and Plenipotentiary, His Excellency Yehuda Avner (1983).

Area and Population.—Israel lies on the western edge of the continent of Asia at the eastern extremity of the Mediterranean Sea, between lat. 29° 30′–33° 15′ N. and longitude 34° 15′–35° 40′ E. Its political neighbours are Lebanon on the North, Syria on the North and East, Jordon on the East and the Egyptian province of Sinai on the South-West.

The area is estimated at 7,992 square miles, although this increased through occupation following the Six Day War in June 1967. The population was estimated in 1983 at 4,148,500. During the upheavals of 1948–49 a large number of Arabs left the country as refugees and settled in neighbouring countries.

Hebrew and Arabic are the official languages of Israel. Arabs are entitled to transact all official business with Government Departments in Arabic, and provision is made in the *Knesset* for the simultaneous translation of all speeches into Arabic.

Physical Features.—Israel comprises four main regions: (*a*) the hill country of Galilee and Judea and Samaria, rising in places to heights of nearly 4,000 feet; (*b*) the coastal plain from the Gaza strip to North of Acre, including the plain of Esdraelon running from Haifa Bay to the south-east, and cutting in two the hill region; (c) the Negev, a semi-desert triangular-shaped region, extending from a base south of Beersheba, to an apex at the head of the Gulf of 'Aqaba; and (d) parts of the Jordan valley, including the Hula Region, Tiberias and the south-western extremity of the Dead Sea. The principal river is the Jordan, which rises from three main sources in Israel, the Lebanon and Syria, and flows through the Hula valley and the canals which have replaced Lake Hula, drained in 1958. Between Hulata and Tiberias (Sea of Galilee) the river falls 926 ft. in 11 miles and becomes a turbulent stream. Lake Tiberias is 696 ft. below sea-level and liable to sudden storms. Between it and the Dead Sea the Jordan falls 591 ft. The other principal rivers are the Yarkon and Kishon. The largest lake is the *Dead Sea* (shared between Israel and Jordan); area 393 sq. miles, 1,286 feet below sea-level, 51·5 miles long, with a maximum width of 11 miles and a maximum depth of 1,309 ft.; it receives the waters of the Jordan and of six other streams, and has no outlet, the surplus being carried off by evaporation. The water contains an extraordinarily high concentration of mineral substances. The highest mountain peak is Mount Meron, 3,962 feet above sea-level, near Safad, Upper Galilee.

Climate.—The climate is variable, similar to that of Lower Egypt, but modified by altitude and distance from the sea. The summer is hot but tempered in most parts by daily winds from the Mediterranean. The winter is the rainy season lasting from November to April, the period of maximum rainfall being January and February.

Antiquities.—The following are among the principal historic sites in Israel: *Jerusalem*: the Church of the Holy Sepulchre: the Al Aqsa Mosque and Dome of the Rock, standing on the remains of the Temple Mount of Herod the Great, of which the Western (wailing) Wall is a fragment; the Church of the Dormition and the Cœnaculum on Mount Zion; Ein Karem: Church of the Visitation, Church of St. John the Baptist. *Galilee*: The Sea; Church and Mount of the Beatitudes, ruins of Capernaum and other sites connected with the life of Christ. *Mount Tabor*: Church of the Transfiguration. *Nazareth*: Church of the Annunciation and other Christian shrines associated with the childhood of Christ. There are also numerous sites dating from biblical and mediæval days, such as Ascalon, Cæsarea, Atlit, Massada, Megiddo and Hazor. Other antiquities in the West Bank of Jordan and the Golan Heights at present occupied by Israel can now be visited from Israel. In accordance with the terms of the peace treaty signed between Egypt and Israel on March 26, 1979, Israel withdrew in April 1982 to the pre-1967 boundary, returning the Sinai area to Egyptian sovereignty.

Government.—There are a Cabinet and a single-chamber Parliament (*Knesset*) of 120 members. A general election is held at least once every four years. The last General Election was held on July 23, 1984; the result was inconclusive. After about six weeks of negotiations between political parties a Government of National Unity was formed.

Immigration.—The Declaration of Independence of May 14, 1948, laid down that "the State of Israel will be open to the immigration of Jews from all countries of their dispersion." The Law of Return, passed by the *Knesset* on July 5, 1950, provides that an immigrant visa shall be granted to every Jew who expresses his desire to settle in Israel. From the establishment of the State until April 1978, about 1·7 million immigrants had entered Israel from over 100 different countries.

Education.—Elementary education for all children from 5 to 15 years is free, though secondary education is not compulsory. The law also provides for working

youth, age 15–18 who for some reason have not completed their primary education, to be exempted from work in order to do so.

In 1983–84 enrolment in all educational establishments was 1,330,026: kindergartens 273,180; elementary education, 731,635; secondary education, 187,670; post-secondary, 91,413.

Finance.—Government expenditure in 1984 was *IS*2,390,799 million at market prices. GNP at market prices was *IS*6,485,810 million.

The unit of currency, is the Shekel (of 100 agorot). Exchange rate, *see* p. 82.

COMMUNICATIONS

Railways and Roads.—Israel State Railways started operating in August 1949. Towns now served are Haifa, Tel Aviv, Jerusalem, Lod, Nahariya, Beersheba, Dimona, Ashdod and intermediate stations. In 1983 the total railway network amounted to 866 km. There were 12,482 km. of paved road and in 1984 760,213 licensed vehicles.

Shipping.—Israel's merchant marine had reached a total of 3,077,000 tons deadweight by December, 1983.

The chief ports are Haifa, a modern harbour, with a depth of 30 ft. alongside the main quay; the harbour on the Red Sea at Eilat, inaugurated in September 1965, has a capacity of 10,000 tons a day; Acre has an anchorage for small vessels; the deep-water port at Ashdod, 20 miles south of Tel Aviv, which started operations at the end of 1965, handled 7,111,000 tons of cargo in 1984. In the same year Israel's three main ports handled 13,693,000 tons of cargo.

Civil Aviation.—In 1984, 3,118,800 passengers passed through Ben Gurion airport, of which 318,351 arrived by charter flight.

PRODUCTION AND INDUSTRY

Agriculture.—The country is generally fertile and climatic conditions vary so widely that a large variety of crops can be grown, ranging from temperate crops, such as wheat and cherries, to subtropical crops such as sorghum, millet and mangoes. The famous "Jaffa" orange is produced in large quantities mostly in the coastal plain for export: high-profit export crops such as strawberries and cut flowers are increasingly important. The citrus yield during the 1983–84 season was 1,522,407 tons. Specialized glasshouse crops for export, such as flowers, tomatoes and strawberries, are becoming increasingly popular and exports of flowers in 1983 earned U.S.$73,161,000. Olives are cultivated, mainly for the production of oil used for edible purposes and for the manufacture of soap. The main winter crops are wheat and barley and various kinds of pulses, while in summer sorghum, millet, maize, sesame and summer pulses are grown. Large areas of seasonal vegetables are planted. Beef, cattle and poultry farming have been developed and the production of mixed vegetables and dairy produce has greatly increased. Tobacco and medium staple cotton are now grown. Fishing has also been extended, and production (mostly from fish ponds) was 16,078 tons in 1983–84. All kinds of summer fruits such as figs, grapes, plums and apples are produced in increasing quantities for local consumption. Water supply for irrigation is the principal limiting factor to greater production. The area under cultivation is 4,370,000 dunams, of which 2,200,000 is under irrigation. The Israel land measure is the *dunam*, equivalent to 1,000 square metres (approximately a quarter of an acre).

Industry.—In value polished diamonds account for about one quarter of Israel's total exports. Amongst the most important of her exporting industries are textiles, foodstuffs, chemicals (mainly fertilisers and pharmaceuticals). Her metal-working and science-based industries are highly sophisticated and technologically advanced. These include the aircraft and military industries. Other important manufacturing industries include plastics, rubber, cement, glass, paper and oil refining.

TRADE

The principal imports are foodstuffs, crude oil, machinery and vehicles, iron, steel and manufactures thereof, and chemicals. The principal exports are citrus fruits and by-products, polished diamonds, plywood, cement, tyres, minerals, finished and semi-finished textiles.

	1983	1984
Imports	U.S.\$8,445·8 m	U.S.\$8,139·5 m
Exports	4,893·8 m	5,597·9 m

Trade with U.K.

	1983	1984
Imports from U.K....	£354,860,000	£393,025,000
Exports to U.K.	314,148,000	392,757,000

CAPITAL.—Most of the Government departments are in Jerusalem (population, 1983, 472,900). A resolution proclaiming Jerusalem as the capital of Israel was adopted by the Israel parliament on Jan. 23, 1950. It is not, however, recognized as the capital by the United Nations. Other principal towns are ΨTel Aviv and district (1,830,900); ΨHaifa and district (575,300) and Beersheba and district (275,000).

FLAG.—White, with two horizontal blue stripes. the Shield of David in the centre.

NATIONAL DAY (1982)—April 28.

JERUSALEM

Until 1967 Jerusalem was divided between Israel and Jordan, two of the 36 recognized Christian Holy Places (in the New City) being under Jewish administration, the remainder under Arab administration in the Old City. At the conclusion of hostilities between Israel and the surrounding Arab countries in 1967 the entire city was under Israeli control.

BRITISH EMBASSY
192 Hayarkon Street, Tel Aviv.

Ambassador Extraordinary and Plenipotentiary, His Excellency C. W. Squire, C.M.G., M.V.O. (1984).

Counsellor, W. K. Prendergast (*Head of Chancery, Consul-General and Counsellor, Commercial*).

Defence Attaché, Col. P. Mitchell, M.B.E.

British Council Representative, I. Watts, 140 Hayarkon Street, (P.O. Box 3302), Tel Aviv. There is a library in *Tel Aviv* and in *Jerusalem.*

ISRAEL-BRITISH CHAMBER OF COMMERCE, 104 Hayarkon Street, P.O. Box 3540, 61034 Tel Aviv.

ITALY
(Repubblica Italiana)

President of the Italian Republic, Francesco Cossiga, *born* 1928, *sworn in,* July 3, 1985.

COUNCIL OF MINISTERS

Prime Minister, Bettino Craxi (*S*).
Deputy P.M., Arnaldo Forlani (*CD*).
Regions, Carlo Vizzini (*SD*).
Public Administration, Remo Gaspari (*CD*).
Relations with Parliament, Oscar Mammi (*Rep*).
Civil Defence, Giuseppe Zamberletti (*CD*).
Aid and E.E.C. Policy, Loris Fortuna (*S*).
Scientific Research, Luigi Granelli (*CD*).
Southern Development, Salverino de Vito (*CD*).
Foreign Affairs, Giulio Andreotti (*CD*).
Interior, Oscar Scalfaro (*CD*).
Justice, Fermo Mino Martinazzoli (*CD*).

Budget, Pier-Luigi Romita (*SD*).
Finance, Bruno Visentini (*Rep*).
Treasury, Giovanni Goria (*CD*).
Defence, Giovanni Spadolini (*Rep*).
Education, Franca Falcucci (*CD*).
Public Works, Franco Nicolazzi (*SD*).
Agriculture, Filippo Maria Pandolfi (*CD*).
Transport, Claudio Signorile (*S*).
Posts, Antonio Gava (*CD*).
Industry, Renato Altissimo (*Lib*).
Labour, Gianni de Michelis (*S*).
Foreign Trade, Nicola Capria (*S*).
Merchant Navy, Gianuario Carta (*CD*).
State Participation, Clelio Darida (*CD*).
Health, Costante Degan (*CD*).
Tourism, Lelio Lagorio (*S*).
Cultural Heritage, Antonino Gullotti (*CD*).
Ecology, Valerio Zanone (*Lib*).

S = Socialist; *CD* = Christian Democrat; *SD* = Social Democrat; *Rep* = Republican; *Lib* = Liberal.

ITALIAN EMBASSY IN LONDON
14 Three Kings Yard, Davies Street, W1Y 2EH
[01-629 8200]

Ambassador Extraordinary and Plenipotentiary, His Excellency Signor Andrea Cagiati (1980).

Minister-Counsellor, Sig. Umberto Vattani.

First Counsellors, Sig. Giancarlo Aragona; Sig. Mario Fugazzola; Sig. Uberto Pestalozza; Sig. Gianfranco Varvesi; Sig. Teodoro Fuxa.

Italian Consulate General, 38 Eaton Place, S.W.1. (01-235 9371).

Consul General, Sig. T. Fuxa.

Italy is a Republic in the south of Europe, consisting of a peninsula, the large islands of Sicily and Sardinia, the island of Elba and about 70 other small islands. Italy is bounded on the N. by Switzerland and Austria, on the S. by the Mediterranean, on the E. by the Adriatic and Yugoslavia, and on the W. by France and the Ligurian and Tyrrhenian Seas. The total area is about 324,000 sq. kilometres (131,000 sq. miles).

The peninsula is for the most part mountains, but between the Apennines, which form its spine, and the East coastline are two large fertile plains; of Emilia/Romagna in the north and of Apulia in the south. The Alps form the northern limit of Italy, dividing it from France, Switzerland, Austria and Yugoslavia. *Mont Blanc* (15,771 feet), the highest peak, is in the French Pennine Alps, but partly within the Italian borders are Monte Rosa (15,217 feet), Matterhorn (14,780 feet) and several peaks from 12,000 to 14,000 feet.

The chief rivers are the Po (405 miles), which flows through Piedmont, Lombardy and the Veneto, and the Adige (Trentino and Veneto) in the north, the Arno (Florentine Plain) and the Tiber (flowing through Rome to Ostia). The *Rubicon,* a small stream flowing into the Adriatic near Rimini formed the boundary between Italy and Cisalpine Gaul: "crossing the Rubicon" (as Cæsar did in 49 B.C., thus "invading" Italy in arms) is used to indicate definite committal to some course of action.

Population.—In Oct. 1984, Italy's population was 57,080,498. The annual rate of population increase between 1981 and 1984 was 0·3 per cent.

Government.—Italian unity was accomplished under the House of Savoy, after a struggle from 1848 to 1870, in which Mazzini (1805–72), Garibaldi (1807–82) and Cavour (1810–61) were the principal figures. It was completed when Lombardy was ceded to Austria in 1859 and Venice in 1866, and through the evacuation of Rome by the French in 1870. In 1871 the King of Italy entered Rome, and that city was declared to be the capital.

Benito Mussolini, known as *Il Duce* (The Leader) was continuously in office as Prime Minister from

Oct. 30, 1922, until July 25, 1943, when the Fascist *régime* was abolished. He was captured by Italian partisans while attempting to escape across the Swiss frontier and was put to death on April 28, 1945.

In fulfilment of a promise given in April, 1944, that he would retire when the Allies entered Rome a decree was signed on June 5, 1944, by the late King Victor Emmanuel III under which Prince Umberto, the King's son, became "Lieutenant-General of the Realm." The King remained head of the House of Savoy and retained the title King of Italy until his abdication on May 9, 1946, when he was succeeded by the Crown Prince.

A general election was held on June 2, 1946, together with a referendum on the future of the monarchy. The result showed a majority in favour of replacing the monarchy with a Republic. The Royal Family left the country on June 13, and on June 28, 1946, a Provisional President was elected.

Constitution.—The constitution of the Republic of Italy, approved by the Constituent Assembly on December 22, 1947, provides for the election of the President by an electoral college which consists of the two Houses of Parliament (the Chamber of Deputies and the Senate) sitting in joint session together with three delegates from each region (one in the case of the Valle d'Aosta). The President, who must be over 50 years of age, holds office for 7 years. He has numerous carefully defined powers, the main one of which is the right to dissolve one or both Houses of Parliament, after consultation with the Speakers.

Defence.—The Armed Forces are largely manned by conscripts, who serve for 12 months. The Army has approx. 258,000 men, of whom 40,000 are regular officers and N.C.O.s. In addition, the elite paramilitary *Carabinieri* force, which is part of the Army, has over 94,000 men, most of whom are regulars. The Army, which has three Corps concentrated in the North, is equipped with Leopard 1 and M60 tanks and M113 armoured personnel carriers. There is also a parachute brigade, 5 alpine brigades, a missile brigade, and a Light Aviation Arm with over 300 helicopters. The Navy consists of one helicopter carrier, 2 cruisers, 28 escorts including 4 destroyers, 9 submarines, 33 anti-mine vessels, coastal craft, 5 groups of helicopters and support vessels. Manpower strength is approx. 42,000. The Air Force has 70,000 men and 300 combat aircraft. It is largely a tactical airforce, equipped with Tornado, F104 and G91 aircraft, but also has transport, anti-submarine and helicopter search and rescue units. There is a large Reserve Force of ex-conscripts under the age of 35.

REGIONS OF ITALY

Rome and Central Italy.—Rome was founded, according to legend, by Romulus in the year now known as 753 B.C. It was the focal point of Latin civilization and dominion under the Republic and afterwards under the Roman Empire, and became the capital of Italy when the Kingdom was established in 1871. The capital is concerned mainly with tourism and government, but its importance as a business centre is steadily increasing, and it is reportedly the third largest industrial centre in the country.

Lombardy and Milan.—In the Lombardy region are to be found some 15·7 per cent of Italy's commercial and banking services and some 21·9 per cent of her manufacturing industry. The whole range of Italian industry is represented, most important being the steel, machine tool and motor car factories.

Turin and Piedmont.—Turin between 1861 and 1865 was Italy's first capital as the home of the Piedmontese Royal Family. Now it is the headquarters of Europe's largest manufacturer of motor cars, produces 75 per cent. of Italy's motor vehicles and over 80 per cent. of its roller bearings. Turin is also Italy's second largest steel producing city. Piedmont is the centre of the Italian textile industry based mainly on Biella.

Genoa and the Ligurian Riviera.—Genoa has been one of Europe's major ports since the Middle Ages, and handles one-third of Italy's foreign trade. About 80 per cent. of the goods handled are imports.

Venice and the North-East.—Venice is primarily a tourist attraction of unique beauty. It was founded in the middle of the 5th century by refugees from the mainland fleeing attacks, and by the 16th century it was one of the strongest and richest states of Europe, dominating Eastern Mediterranean trade. It lost its independence in 1797 when Napoleon handed it over to Austria. Industry (paper and stationery, mechanical equipment, consumer goods, electrical appliances, woollens) is now developing in the Venice area, particularly on the autostrada linking Venice with her historical and now developing rivals, Verona, Vicenza, Padua and in the areas around Treviso and Pordenone. Near Trieste, is the modern Monfalcone shipyard.

Tuscany, Emilia and Romagna.—Florence, the capital of Tuscany, was one of the greatest cities in Europe from the 11th to the 16th centuries, and the cradle of the Renaissance. Under the Medici family in the 15th century flourished many of the greatest names in Italian art, including Filippo Lippi, Botticelli, Donatello and Brunelleschi and in the 16th century great Florentine artists like Michelangelo and Leonardo da Vinci. These regions were the agricultural centre of Italy but the post-war period has seen the development of large industrial centres at Bologna, Florence, Modena, Pistoia and Ravenna. Most of the new firms are small or medium-sized. The footwear industry is based on Florence, textiles in Prato, reproduction furniture at Cascina and Poggibonsi, ceramics at Sassuolo, and glass and pottery at Empoli and Montelupo. Bologna is an important centre for the food industry.

Naples and the Toe of Italy.—Naples, formerly the capital and administrative centre of the Kingdom of Naples and Sicily, remains the dominant city in the area, but it is beset with great problems of unemployment and the need for modernization. Around it, however, helped by Government incentives, industry is slowly developing, northwards to Caserta, southwards to Salerno and eastwards to Benevento.

Puglia.—Bari has always been a commercial centre and now industrial development is also taking place in the areas of Taranto, Brindisi and Foggia. At Taranto there are a highly-mechanized steel-works and a modern oil refinery. The Bari industrial zone has factories producing electronic and pneumatic valves, specialized vehicle bodies and tyres, etc. The main industry of Brindisi is a petro-chemical plant. At Foggia there is a textile factory.

Sicily.—The main source of income is agriculture, particularly citrus fruits, almonds and tomatoes, but this faces severe competition. Oil in small quantities has been found off the southern shore of the island and drilling continues, while onshore there are growing oil-refining, natural gas and petrochemical industries. Small and medium sized industries, benefiting from the Government's incentives, are developing, and tourism is bringing an increasing amount of revenue to the island.

Sardinia.—Sardinia is an autonomous region, with its capital at Cagliari. Six main industrial development areas have been officially designated. The major industries are aluminium production (there is a smelting plant at Porto Vesme), petrochemicals, lead and zinc mining; and the tourist industry is flourishing.

The Economy

Italian gross domestic product in 1984 was *L*612,112,000 million. The economy has recovered from the setbacks of the early seventies, reversing the balance of payments and halving inflation, but this was accompanied by stagnation and increasing unemployment. The rate of inflation for 1983–84 was 10·8 per cent.

Currency.—The unit of currency is the *lira*. (*see* also p. 81).

Industry.—The general index of industrial production (1980 = 100) stood at +3·1 per cent in 1983–84. The State-owned sector of Italian industry is important, dominated by the holding companies IRI (mechanical, steel, airlines), ENI (petro-chemicals) and ENEL (electricity).

Mineral Production.—Italy is generally poor in mineral resources but since the war deposits of natural methane gas and small deposits of oil have been discovered and rapidly exploited. Production of lignite has also increased. Other minerals produced in significant quantities include iron ores and pyrites, mercury (over one-quarter of the world production), lead, zinc and aluminium. Marble is a traditional product of the Massa Carrara district.

Agriculture.—Agriculture accounted for 5·2 per cent. of gross domestic product in 1984. The agricultural labour force was 2,426,000.

Tourist Traffic.—In 1984 an estimated 18·5 million foreign tourists visited Italy, and in 1984 foreigners spent an estimated *L*15,000,000 million. The net balance on tourism was about *L*11,000,000 million.

Communications.—The main railway system is State-run by the *Ferrovia dello Stato*. A network of motorways (*autostrade*) covers the country, built and operated mainly by the IRI State-holding company and ANAS the State highway authority. The autostrada network covered 5,176 kms. in 1974. *Alitalia*, the principal international and domestic airline, is also State-controlled by the IRI group. Other smaller companies, including ATI (an *Alitalia* subsidiary) and Air Mediterranea operate on domestic routes. The Italian mercantile marine totalled 9,116,782 tons in December, 1984.

Foreign Trade

The balance of trade in 1984 showed a deficit of 19,163 billion lire, 1,498 billion lire above the 1983 total.

The main markets for Italian exports in 1984 were the E.E.C. countries, which accounted for almost half of the total, and the U.S.A. Imports came principally from West Germany, France, U.S.A., the Netherlands, the U.S.S.R. and the U.K. The E.E.C. provided about 42 per cent. of imports.

Trade with U.K.

	1983	1984
Imports from U.K.	£2,292,788,000	£2,902,666,000
Exports to U.K.	3,188,219,000	3,814,163,000

Language and Literature.—Italian is a Romance language derived from Latin. It is spoken in its purest form in Tuscany, but there are numerous dialects, showing variously French, German, Spanish and Arabic influences. Sard, the dialect of Sardinia, is accorded by some authorities the status of a distinct Romance language. Italian literature (in addition to Latin literature, which is the common inheritance of Western Europe) is one of the richest in Europe, particularly in its golden age (Dante, 1265–1321; Petrarch, 1304–1374; Boccaccio, 1313–1375) and in the renaissance (Ariosto, 1474–1533; Machiavelli, 1469–1527; Tasso, 1544–1595). Modern Italian literature has many noted names in prose and verse, notably Manzoni (1785–1873), Carducci (1835–1907) and Gabriele d'Annunzio (1864–1938). The Nobel Prize for Literature has been awarded to Italian authors on four occasions—G. Carducci (1906), Signora G. Deledda (1926), Luigi Pirandello (1934) and Salvatore Quasimodo (1959). In 1985, there were 48 daily newspapers published in Italy, of which 6 were published in Rome and 7 in Milan.

Education.—Education is free and compulsory between the ages of 6 and 14; this comprises five years at primary school and three in the "middle school", of which there are about 8,000. Pupils who obtain the middle school certificate may seek admission to any "senior secondary school", which may be a lyceum with a classical or scientific or artistic bias, or an institute directed at technology (of which there are eight different types), trade or industry (including vocational schools), or teacher-training. Courses at the lyceums and technical institutes usually last for five years and success in the final examination qualifies for admission to university. There are 35 State and 14 private universities, some of ancient foundation; those at Bologna, Modena, Parma and Padua were started in the 12th century. University education is not free, but entrants with higher qualifications are charged reduced fees according to a sliding scale. In general, schools, lyceums and universities are financed by local taxation and central government grants.

CAPITAL.—Rome. Population of the commune (1984) 2,826,733.

1984 estimates of the population of the communes of the principal cities and towns are Milan, 1,535,722; ΨNaples, 1,206,955; Turin, 1,049,997; ΨGenoa, 738,099; Bologna, 442,307; Florence, 435,698; Sicily, Palermo, 716,149; *Sardinia,* ΨCagliari, 224,007.

ISLANDS.—*Pantelleria Island* (part of Trapani Province) in the Sicilian Narrows, has an area of 31 sq. miles and a population of 9,601. The *Pelagian Islands* (Lampedusa, Linosa and Lampione) are part of the Province of Agrigento and have an area of 8 sq. miles, pop. 4,811. The Tuscan Archipelago (including Elba), area 293 sq. km., pop. 31,861; Pontine Archipelago (including Ponza, area 10 sq. km., pop. 2,515); Flegrean Islands (including Ischia, area 60 sq. km., pop. 51,883); Capri; Eolian Islands (including Lipari, area 116 sq. km., pop. 18,636); Tremiti Islands (area 3 sq. km., pop. 426).

FLAG.—Vertical stripes of green, white and red.
NATIONAL DAY.—June 2.

BRITISH EMBASSY
Via XX Settembre 80a, 00187 Rome

Ambassador Extraordinary and Plenipotentiary, His Excellency The Lord Bridges, K.C.M.G. (1983).
Minister, G. E. Fitzherbert, C.M.G..
Minister, R. F. R. Deare (*FAO*).
Defence and Military Attaché, Brig. M. J. Hague.
Naval Attaché, Capt. R. F. Channon, R.N.
Air Attaché, Group-Capt. I. Madelin, R.A.F.
Counsellors, T. L. Richardson (*Head of Chancery*); G. Tantum.

1st Secretaries, C. A. Capella (*Labour*); J. Easton (*Administration*); Miss C. M. T. Elmes (*Economic*); Mrs. E. T. Gregory (*Consul*); P. J. Morrice, J. H. Culver (*Commercial*); D. B. A. Evans (*Agriculture*); G. A. Pirie (*Information*); S. M. J. Lamport.
Chaplain, Rev. B. Wardrobe.
There are British Consular Offices at *Milan, Rome, Naples, Genoa, Florence, Venice, Trieste* and *Cagliari* and a trade representative at *Turin.*

British Council Representative, D. J. Sharp, Palazzo del Drago, Via delle Quattro Fontane 20, 00184, Rome.
There are *British Council Offices* at Milan and Naples, each with a library.

BRITISH CHAMBER OF COMMERCE, Corso Buenos Aires 77, 20124 Milan.

IVORY COAST
(République de Côte d'Ivoire)

President, Félix Houphouët-Boigny, *elected* for five years in 1960; *re-elected* 1965, 1970, 1975 and 1980.

CABINET

Ministers of State, A. Denise; M. Ekra; C. Alliali (*Justice*); M. S. Gnoleba (*Planning and Industry*); E. K. Boguinard (*Public Service*).
Ministers, J. K. Banny (*Defence*); L. Coulibaly (*Justice*); S. Ake (*Foreign Affairs*); L. K. Koffi (*Interior*); A. Koné (*Economy and Finance*); D. B. Kanon (*Agriculture, Water and Forest Resources*); A. Barry-Battesti (*Public Works, Construction, Posts and Telecommunications*); Dr. B. Keita (*National Education and Scientific Research*); B. Dadié (*Cultural Affairs*); A. Thiam (*Information*); A. V. Bi Tra (*Labour*); L. D. Fologo (*Youth and Sport*); P. G. Dibo (*Mining*); Gen. O. N'daw (*Internal Security*); L. Fadiga (*Navy*); G. Laubhouet (*Rural Development*); B. Ehui (*Industry*); A. D. Madi (*Public Health and Population*); N. K. Angba (*Commerce*); J.-J. Bechio (*Civil Service*); D. Sadia (*Tourism*); E. Brou (*National Assembly relations*); Y. Ouattara (*Social Affairs*); A. B. Tanoh (*Environment*).

IVORY COAST EMBASSY IN LONDON
2 Upper Belgrave Street, SW1X 8BJ
[01-235 6991]

Ambassador Extraordinary and Plenipotentiary, new appointment awaited.
1st Counsellor, N' Goran Kouame.

The Ivory Coast is situated on the Gulf of Guinea between 5° and 10° N. and 3° and 8° W. and is flanked on the West by Guinea and Liberia, on the North by Mali and Burkina and on the East by Ghana. It has an area of about 127,000 square miles—tropical rain forest in the southern half and savannah in the northern—and a population of 9,924,000 (1983 estimate) divided into a large number of ethnic and tribal groups.

Although French contact was made in the first half of the 19th century, the Ivory Coast became a Colony only in 1893 and was finally pacified in 1912. It decided on December 5, 1958 to remain an autonomous republic within the French Community; full independence outside the Community was proclaimed on August 7, 1960. Special agreements with France, covering financial and cultural matters, technical assistance, defence, etc., were signed in Paris on April 24, 1961. The official language is French.

The Ivory Coast has a presidential system of government modelled on that of the United States and the French Fifth Republic. The single Chamber National Assembly of 147 members was elected in 1980. The defence of the Constitution which was promulgated on Nov. 3, 1960, is vested in a Supreme Court.

Finance.—The unit of currency of the Ivory Coast is the *Franc CFA* . In 1985, the Ivory Coast Budget allocated *CFA* 418,100 m. for current expenditure and *CFA* 87,600 m. for investment and equipment.

Trade.—The principal exports are coffee, cocoa, timber, palm oil, pineapples, bananas, and cotton. Diamonds are exported. There are a few deposits of minerals including manganese and iron. Trade in 1983 was valued at: Imports, *Francs CFA* 704,240 m.; Exports, *Francs CFA* 796,700 m.

Trade with U.K.

	1983	1984
Imports from U.K. .	£25,591,000	£25,347,000
Exports to U.K.	79,255,000	93,875,000

CAPITAL, ΨAbidjan (population, 2,000,000) which is also the main port. In March 1983 the National Assembly ratified a decision to transfer the political and administrative capital from Abidjan to Yamoussoukro, but the date of the transfer is not yet known.

FLAG.—3 vertical stripes, orange, white and green.

NATIONAL DAY.—December 7.

BRITISH EMBASSY
Immeuble Les Harmonies, 01 B.P. 2581, Abidjan 01.

Ambassador Extraordinary and Plenipotentiary, His Excellency John Michael Willson (1983).

BRITISH CHAMBER OF COMMERCE, c/o Price Waterhouse & Co., Boite Postale 2921, Abidjan 01.

JAPAN
(Nihon Koku—Land of the Rising Sun)

Emperor of Japan, His Majesty Hirohito, *born* April 29, 1901; *succeeded* Dec. 25, 1926; *married* (1924) Princess Nagako (*born* March 6, 1903), daughter of the late Prince Kuniyoshi Kuni, and has issue two sons and four daughters.

Heir-Apparent, His Imperial Highness Prince Akihito, *Crown Prince, born* Dec. 23, 1933; *married* April 10, 1959, Miss Michiko Shoda and has issue Prince Naruhito Hironomiya, *born* Feb. 23, 1960, Prince Fumihito, *born* Nov. 30, 1965 and Princess Sayako, *born* April 18, 1969.

THE CABINET

Prime Minister, Yasuhiro Nakasone.
Justice, Hitoshi Shimazaki.
Foreign Affairs, Shintaro Abe.
Finance, Noboru Takeshita.
Education, Hikaru Matsunaga.
Health and Welfare, Hiroyuki Masuoka.
Agriculture, Forestry and Fisheries, Moriyoshi Sato.
International Trade and Industry, Keijiro Murata.
Transport, Tokuo Yamashita.
Posts and Telecommunications, Megumu Sato.
Labour, Toshio Yamaguchi.
Construction, Yoshiaki Kibe.
Home Affairs, Toru Furuya.
Management and Coordination, Masaharu Gotoda.
Hokkaido Development Agency and National Land Agency, Kakuzo Kawamoto.
Defence, Koichi Kato.
Economic Planning, Ippei Kaneko.
Science and Technology, Reiichi Takeuchi.
Environment, Shigeru Ishimoto.
Okinawa Development Agency, Takao Fujimoto.
Chief Cabinet Secretary, Takao Fujinami.

JAPANESE EMBASSY AND CONSULATE
46 Grosvenor Street, W1X 0BA
Information Centre: 9 Grosvenor Square, W1X 9LB
[01–493 6030]

Ambassador Extraordinary and Plenipotentiary, His Excellency Toshio Yamazaki (1985).

Minister Plenipotentiary, Eiji Seki.

Ministers, Mitsukazu Ishikawa (*Financial*); Shunichi Uchimura (*Commercial*); Katshuisa Ushida.

Counsellors, Atsushi Tokinoya; Masao Kawase; Hiroshi Shigeta; Keishiro Fukushima.

Defence Attaché, Capt. Kiyomichi Terashita.

Area and Population.—Japan consists of 4 large and many small islands situated in the North Pacific Ocean between longitude 128° 6′ East and 145° 49′ East and between latitude 26° 59′ and 45° 31′ N., with a total area of 142,812 square miles and a population (1983) of 119,430,000. In 1983 the birth rate was 12·7 per 1,000, and the death rate 6·2 per 1,000.

Japan Proper consists of *Honshū* (or Mainland), 230,448 sq. km. (88,839 sq. m.), *Shikoku*, 18,757 sq. km. (7,231 sq. m.), *Kyūshū*, 42,079 sq. km. (16,170 sq. m.), *Hokkaido*, 78,508 sq. km. (30,265 sq. m.).

Physiography.—The coastline exceeds 17,000 miles and is deeply indented, so that few places are far from the sea. The interior is very mountainous, and crossing the mainland from the Sea of Japan to the Pacific is a group of volcanoes, mainly extinct or dormant. Mount Fuji, the loftiest and most sacred mountain of Japan, about 60 miles from Tokyo, is 12,370 ft. high and has been dormant since 1707, but there are other volcanoes which are active, including Mount Aso in Kyūshū. There are frequent earthquakes, mainly along the Pacific coast near the Bay of Tokyo. Japan proper extends from sub-tropical in the south to cool temperate in the north. Heavy snowfalls are frequent on the western slopes of Hokkaidō and Honshū, but the Pacific coasts are warmed by the Japan current. There is a plentiful rainfall and the rivers are short and swift-flowing offering abundant opportunities for the supply of hydro-electric power.

Government.—According to Japanese tradition, Jimmu, the First Emperor of Japan, ascended the

throne on Feb. 11, 660 B.C. Under the *Meiji* constitution of Feb. 11, 1889, the monarchy was hereditary in the male heirs of the Imperial house.

After the unconditional surrender to the Allied Nations (Aug. 14, 1945), Japan was occupied by Allied forces under General MacArthur (Sept. 15, 1945). A Japanese peace treaty conference opened at San Francisco on Sept. 4, 1951, and on Sept. 8, 48 nations signed the treaty, which became effective on April 28, 1952. Japan then resumed her status as an independent power.

A new constitution came into force on May 3, 1947. Legislative authority rests with *The Diet*, which is bicameral, consisting of a *House of Representatives* and a *House of Councillors*, both Houses being composed of elected members. Executive authority is vested in the Cabinet which is responsible to the Legislature.

The conservatives have governed Japan almost without interruption since World War II. Since 1955, when it was formed, the Liberal Democratic Party has maintained an absolute majority in the House of Representatives, though it lost a number of seats in the December 1983 election and subsequently formed a coalition government with the 8 members of the New Liberal Club. The strength of the parties in the House of Representatives in July 1985 were Liberal Democratic Party, 262 (including New Liberal Club, 8); Japan Socialist Party, 112; Komeito, 59; Democratic Socialist Party, 38; Japan Communist Party, 27; Shaminren, 3; Independents, 5; vacant, 5.

The House of Councillors whose powers are subordinate to the House of Representatives, re-elects half of its members every three years. In July, 1985, the strength of the Parties was: Liberal Democratic Party, 139; Japan Socialist Party, 42; Komeito, 27; Japan Communist Party, 14; Democratic Socialist Party, 13; Sangiin no kai, 3; Shinsei Club, 3; Niin Club, 3; Independents, 4; vacant, 5.

Agriculture and Livestock.—Owing to the mountainous nature of the country not more than one-sixth of its area is available for cultivation. The forest land includes Cryptomeria japonica, Pinus massoniana, Zeikowaskeaki, and Paulownia imperialis, in addition to camphor trees, mulberry, vegetable wax tree and a lacquer tree which furnishes the celebrated lacquer of Japan. The soil is only moderately fertile, but intensive cultivation secures good crops. Tobacco, tea, potato, rice, wheat and other cereals are all cultivated: rice is the staple food of the people, about 10,270,000 metric tons being produced in 1982. Fruit is abundant, including the mandarin, persimmon, loquat and peach; European fruits such as apples, strawberries, pears, grapes and figs are also produced.

Minerals.—The country has mineral resources, including gold and silver, and copper, lead, zinc, iron chromite, white arsenic, coal, sulphur, petroleum, salt and uranium, but iron ore, coal and crude oil are among the principal post-war imports to supply deficiencies at home.

Industry.—Japan is the most highly industrialized nation in the Far East, with the whole range of modern light and heavy industries, including automobiles, electronics, metals, machinery, chemicals, textiles (cotton, silk, wool and synthetics), cement, pottery, glass, rubber, lumber, paper, oil refining and shipbuilding. The labour force of Japan in 1983 (average) was 58,890,000, of which 1,560,000 were unemployed. Of the total labour force, some 52,020,000 were engaged in non-agricultural industries, 5,310,000 in agriculture, forestry and fisheries.

Communications.—There were 26,587 kilometres of Government and private railroad (steam and electric) in March, 1982. The merchant fleet (ocean-going ships over 3,000 tons gross) consisted of 1,079 vessels totalling 34,220,000 tons gross in March, 1982.

Links between the principal islands are provided by bridges and tunnels. Currently under construction are road and rail suspension bridges between Shikoku and Honshu, and a rail tunnel between Honshū and Hokkaido.

Armed Forces.—After the unconditional surrender of August, 1945, the Imperial Army and Navy were disarmed and disbanded.

Although the Constitution of Japan prohibits the maintenance of armed forces, internal security forces came into being in 1950, and 1952. In July, 1954, the mission of the forces was extended to include the defence of Japan against direct and indirect aggression.

The defence budget allocated for the fiscal year 1985–86 amounted to *Yen* 3,137 million, equivalent to 6·0 per cent of the General Account budget. The authorized uniformed strength was: Ground Self-Defence Force (GSDF) 180,000 (Reserve 43,000); Maritime Self-Defence Force (MSDF) 43,897 (Reserve 600); Air Self-Defence Force (ASDF) 46,204. Actual strengths of all three services are slightly below their authorised figure.

The GSDF is organized into five regional Armies, totalling thirteen Divisions, one of which is an Armoured Division. Major equipment includes tanks, APC's, towed and SP guns and rocket launchers, Hawk AA missiles, and 400 aircraft. Equipment is now largely manufactured in Japan.

The MSDF has 164 warships and auxiliaries including four DDH, four TARTAR-equipped GMDs, 42 destroyers, 14 submarines and 99 others, 205 fixed-wing aircraft and 97 helicopters.

The ASDF has 800 aircraft including 380 trainers; 41 transports and 56 support aircraft including helicoptors). There are 6 groups of Nike SAM missiles.

Religion.—All religions are tolerated. The principal religions of Japan are Mahayana Buddhism and Shinto. About 1 per cent of Japanese are Christians. The Roman Catholic Church has 2 archbishops and 16 bishops. The Nippon Seikokai (Holy Catholic Church of Japan) has 11 Japanese bishops (1978) and is an autonomous branch of the Anglican communion. There is also a United Protestant Church.

Education.—Under the Education Law of 1948 education at elementary (6 year course) and lower secondary (3 year course) schools is free, compulsory and co-educational. The (3 year) upper secondary schools are attended by 93 per cent of the age group. They have courses in general, agricultural, commercial, technical, mercantile marine, radio-communication and home-economics education, etc. 37·4 per cent of upper secondary school leavers went on to higher education in 1981. There are 2 or 3 year junior colleges and 4 year universities. Some of the 4 year universities have graduate schools. In May 1981 there were 974 universities and junior colleges, 128 state maintained, 86 local authority maintained and 760 privately maintained. The most prominent universities are the seven State Universities of Tokyo, Kyoto, Tohoku (Sendai), Hokkaido (Sapporo), Kyushu (Fukuoka), Osaka and Nagoya, and the two private universities, Keio and Waseda.

Language and Literature.—Japanese is said to be one of the Uro-Altaic group of languages and remained a spoken tongue until the fifth–seventh centuries A.D., when Chinese characters came into use. Japanese who have received school education (99·8 per cent of the population) can read and write the Chinese characters in current use (about 1,800 characters) and also the syllabary characters called Kana. English is the best known foreign language. It is taught in all middle and high schools and universities. There are 125 daily newspapers in Japan.

FINANCE

The Budget for the financial year 1984–85, ending on March 31, was initially estimated at *Yen* 52,499,600 million for revenue and expenditure on the general account, an increase of *Yen* 2,000 million from the previous year.

For rate of exchange *see also* p. 81.

PRODUCTION AND TRADE

Being deficient in natural resources, Japan has had to develop a complex foreign trade. Principal imports in 1984 consisted of mineral oils (44·4 per cent), raw materials (14·3 per cent) e.g. metal ores and scrap, 4·8 per cent, timber, 2·9 per cent, foodstuffs (11·7 per cent) (e.g. wheat and sugar), machinery (8·8 per cent), chemicals (6·1 per cent) and textiles (2·8 per cent).

Principal exports consist of steel (8·1 per cent), ships (4·3 per cent), automobiles (17·5 per cent), electric machinery and appliances (17·2 per cent), non-electric machinery (16·4 per cent), chemicals (4·5 per cent) and textile goods (4·0 per cent).

FOREIGN TRADE

	1983 ($1,000)	1984 ($1,000)
Total imports	126,393,051	136,503,049
Total exports	146,902,471	170,113,888

Trade with U.K.

	1983	1984
Imports from U.K.	£797,848,000	£925,311,000
Exports to U.K.	3,555,450,000	3,768,019,000

CAPITAL—TOKYO. Population, 11,806,729. The other chief cities had the following populations: ΨOsaka (2,629,135); ΨNagoya (2,103,460); ΨYokohama (2,925,877); Kyoto, the ancient capital (1,486,873), ΨKobé (1,401,928); Kita-Kyushu (1,060,470); ΨSapporo (1,515,582); ΨKawasaki (1,076,673); ΨFukuoka (1,144,802).

FLAG.—White, charged with sun (red).

Yokohama, by sea *via* Suez Canal, 11,072 miles (30 days); *via* Panama, 12,544 miles (27 days); Tokyo, by air (British Airways polar route), 8,382 miles distant from London: transit, 17 hrs.

BRITISH EMBASSY

No. 1 Ichiban-cho, Chiyoda-ku, Tokyo 102

Ambassador Extraordinary and Plenipotentiary, His Excellency Sir Sydney Giffard, K.C.M.G. (1984).
Minister, B. Hitch, C.M.G., C.V.O.
Counsellors, D. J. Wright (*Economic*); J. W. Hodge (*Commercial*); M. R. Lewis (*Financial*); J. A. Barnett, C.B.E., (*Cultural*); A. N. R. Millington (*Head of Chancery*); Dr. C. C. Bradley (*Science and Technology*).
1st Secretaries, S. D. M. Jack, P. A. Heald, M.B.E., D. J. Fitton (*Economic*); D. L. Brown *Administration*); P. S. Dimond, D. Cockerham (*Commercial*); Dr. W. J. Gillan (*Science and Technology*); C. E. A. Ripley (*Consul*); A. F. Pinnell (*Information*); A. J. G. Moore (*Cultural*); C. E. J. Wilton; Dr. G. Thom; P. J. B. Roberts; J. R. H. Walker.
Defence and Military Attaché, Col. M. R. Grove.
Naval Attaché, Capt. R. H. S. Thompson, R.N.
Air Attaché, Gp. Capt. D. I. Oakden, R.A.F.
There is a British Consulate-General at *Osaka* and an Honorary Consulate at *Kita Kyushu*.

British Council Representative, J. A. Barnett, C.B.E., 1 Jimbo-cho, 2-chome, Kanda, Chiyoda-Ku, Tokyo 101. There is also an office and library in Kyoto.

BRITISH CHAMBER OF COMMERCE

World Import Mart Branch 7th Floor, 1–3 Higashi-Ikebukuro 3-chome, Toshima-ku, Tokyo 170 (*Postal Address*, P.O. Box 2145, World Import Mart Branch, Toshima-ku, Tokyo 170).

JORDAN
(The Hashemite Kingdom of The Jordan)

King of the Jordan, Hussein, G.C.V.O., *born* November 14, 1935, *succeeded* on the deposition of his father, King Talal, Aug. 11, 1952, *assumed constitutional powers*, May 2, 1953, on coming of age.

Crown Prince, Prince Hassan, third son of King Talal of Jordan, *born* 1948, *appointed* Crown Prince, April 1, 1965.

CABINET

Prime Minister and Minister for Defence, Zaid Rifa'i.
Deputy P.M. and Minister of Education, Abdul Wahab Majali.
Minister of State, Prime Ministry Affairs, Dr. Hazim Nusaibeh.
Foreign Affairs, Taher Masri.
Communications, Muhieddin Al-Husseini.
Supply, Trade and Industry, Dr. Raja'i Mu'asher.
Higher Education, Dr. Nasreddin Al-Asad.
Information, Culture, Tourism and Antiquities, Mohammed Khatib.
Finance, Dr. Hanna Odeh.
Municipal and Rural Affairs and the Environment, Marwan Al-Hammoud.
Awqaf and Islamic Affairs, Sheikh Aboul Aziz Al-Khayyat.
Agriculture, Ahmed Dakhoan.
Labour and Social Development, Khaled Al Haj Hassan.
Occupied Territory Affairs, Dr. Tahir Kan'an.
Health, Dr. Zaid Hamzi.
Public Works, Mahmoud Hawamdeh.
Transport, Farhi Obeid.
Planning, Dr. Abdullah Nsour.
Energy and Natural Resources, Dr. Hisham Khatib.
Youth, Hisham Sharari.
Minister of State, Parliamentary Affairs, Dr. Sami Joudeh.
Interior, Hasan Al-Kayid.
Justice, Riyadh Shaka'a.

JORDANIAN EMBASSY

6 Upper Phillimore Gardens, W8 7HB
[01-937 3685/7]

Ambassador Extraordinary and Plenipotentiary, His Excellency Nabih Al-Nimr (1985).
Counsellor, Nayef al-Kadi.
Defence Attaché, Brig. Shafic Yacoub Ajeilat.
Service Office: 16 Upper Phillimore Gardens, W.8. (01–937–9611).

Area and Population.—The Kingdom, which covers 37,700 sq. miles, is bounded on the north by Syria, on the west by Israel, on the south by Saudi Arabia and on the east by Iraq. Since the hostilities of June, 1967, that part of the country lying to the west of the Jordan River has been under Israeli occupation. The majority of the population are Sunni Moslems and Islam is the religion of the State, freedom of belief is, however, guaranteed by the Constitution. Total population on the East Bank of the Jordan was estimated (1983) to be 2,495,000. (*For* MAP. *see* p. 859).

History.—After the defeat of Turkey in the First World War the Amirate of Transjordan was established in the area east of the River Jordan as a state under British mandate. The mandate was terminated after the Second World War and the Amirate, still ruled by its founder, the Amir Abdullah, became the Hashemite Kingdom of Jordan. Following the 1948 war between Israel and the Arab States, that part of Palestine remaining in Arab hands (but excluding Gaza) was incorporated into the Hashemite Kingdom. King Abdullah was assassinated in 1951; his son Talal ruled briefly but abdicated in favour of the present King, Hussein, in 1952. All of Jordan west of the River has been under Israeli occupation since 1967. As a result of the wars of 1948 and 1967 there are about 991,000 refugees and displaced persons living in East Jordan, about 200,000 of whom live in refugee and displaced persons camps established by the U.N. Relief and Works Agency (UNRWA). In addition there are some 300,000 entirely self-supporting Palestinian members of the East Jordanian community.

Government.—The present constitution of the Kingdom came into force in 1952. It provides for a senate of 30 members (all appointed by the King) and an elected House of Representatives of 60 persons. Half of the constituencies of the latter are on the West Bank and since the Israeli occupation of this area in 1967 it has not been possible to hold elections there. For a time membership of the House continued on the basis of pre-1967 membership but was eventually suspended in 1974. The Lower House was recalled in January 1984. By-elections were held in March 1984 to fill East Bank seats which had become vacant as a result of the death of deputies elected in 1967, and the House appointed new West Bank members to bring itself up to full strength. The King himself appoints the members of the Council of Ministers. Crown Prince Hassan normally acts as Regent when King Hussein is away from Jordan. Following the Arab summit meeting at Rabat in October 1974, and the U.N. General Assembly in November, at which the Palestinian Liberation Organization achieved recognition as the sole legitimate representative of the Palestinian people, King Hussein took measures to amend the 1952 constitution to take account of the resultant change in the status of the West Bank in relation to the administration of Jordan east of the river.

Production and Industry.—West Jordan is fertile, though many areas have suffered from soil erosion. In East Jordan the main agricultural areas are the east part of the Jordan Valley, the hills overlooking the Valley and the flatter country to the south of Amman and around Madaba and Irbid. The rest of the country is desert and semi-desert. The principal crops are wheat, barley, vegetables, olives and fruit (mainly grapes and citrus fruits). Agricultural production in the Jordan Valley has increased considerably in recent years due to the extension of the East Ghor Canal and the King Talal Dam. The only important industrial products are raw phosphates (production 1984: 6,213,000 tons) and potash, most of which is exported. There are schemes under construction for the production of potash and phosphate fertilizers. The Trans-Arabian oil pipeline (Tapline) runs through North Jordan on its way from the eastern province of Saudi Arabia to the Lebanese coast of Sidon. A branch pipeline feeds a refinery at Zerqa (production 1984: 2,500,000 tons) which meets most of Jordan's requirements for refined petroleum products.

Tourism has recovered fast since the Israeli occupation of the West Bank in 1967. International-class hotels have been built to cater for businessmen, and for tourists visiting the archæological sites of East Jordan and the resort of Aqaba.

Communications.—The trunk road system is good. Amman is linked to Damascus, Baghdad and Jedda by tarred roads which are of considerable importance in the overland trade of the Middle East. The former Hejaz Railway enters Jordan east of Ramtha and runs through Zerqa and Amman to Ma'an with a

spur to the top of the Ras al-Naqb escarpment. The formerly abandoned section from Ma'an to Medina in Saudi Arabia is being studied and redesigned by consultants. A total of 2,329 vessels called at Aqaba in 1984 and 11,158,000 tons of cargo were handled. Much of Jordan's trade moves overland to and from the ports in Syria and Lebanon. The Royal Jordanian Airline (ALIA) operates from Amman Airport to other cities in the Middle East and Gulf area, to most major European cities, to New York, and to Bangkok in the Far East. There is also a service to the airport at Aqaba.

FINANCE

	1983	1984
	JD (Thousands)	
Revenue	681,277	705,256
Expenditure	709,722	746,151
Surplus/Deficit	− 28,445	− 40,895

Trade with U.K.

Britain has been a leading source of supply of imported goods to Jordan for some time.

	1983	1984
Imports from U.K.	£262,503,000	£192,508,000
Exports to U.K.	28,688,000	18,114,000

CAPITAL.—Amman. Population, 744,000 (1983).

FLAG.—Black, white and green horizontal stripes, surcharged with white seven-point star on red triangle.

NATIONAL DAY.—May 25 (Independence Day).

BRITISH EMBASSY
Third Circle, Jebel Amman (P.O. Box 87),
Amman

Ambassador Extraordinary and Plenipotentiary, His Excellency Arthur John Coles (1984).
Counsellors, P. A. Raftery, C.V.O., M.B.E. (*Consul-General*); D. R. Spedding, C.V.O., O.B.E.
Defence Attaché, Col. D. C. Whitten.
Air Attaché, Wing-Cdr. N. M. J. Fraser.
1st Secretaries, D. J. Hawkes, M.B.E. (*Commercial*); A. J. Coulson, L.V.O. (*Information*).
2nd Secretaries, M. Hicks (*Administration*); L. B. Evans (*Development*); Miss J. James (*Consul*); Miss S. C. Rowland Jones; E. S. Alleyn.

BRITISH COUNCIL
Representative, D. A. M. Latta, Amman Centre, Rainbow Street, (P.O. Box 634), Jebel Amman, Amman.

KOREA

Korea is situated between 124° 11″ and 130° 57′ E. long., and between 33° 7′ and 43° 1″ N. lat. It has an area of 85,256 sq. miles with an estimated population of approx. 62 million, of whom about 42 million live south of the present dividing line. The southern and western coasts are fringed with innumerable islands, of which the largest, forming a province of its own, is Cheju.

History.—The last native dynasty (Yi) ruled from 1392 until 1910, in which year Japan formally annexed Korea. The country remained an integral part of the Japanese Empire until the defeat of Japan in 1945, when it was occupied by troops of the U.S.A. and the U.S.S.R., the 38th parallel being fixed as the boundary between the two zones of occupation. The U.S. Government endeavoured to reach agreement with the Soviet Government for the creation of a Korean Government for the whole country and the withdrawal of all Russian and American troops. These efforts met with no success, and in September, 1947,

CHINA

SEA OF JAPAN

KOREA

YELLOW SEA

Inchon ■ Seoul

Taegu

Pusan

0   100   200 MILES

and the Commander of the North Korean army and the Chinese People's "volunteers" on July 27, 1953. By this Agreement (which was not signed by the representatives of the Republic of Korea) the line of division between North and South Korea remained in the neighbourhood of the 38th parallel. The Geneva Conference discussed Korea in 1954, but failed to agree on measures for re-unifying the country. Talks between North and South Korea on the reunification of the country have taken place intermittently.

Language and Literature.—Despite the great cultural influence of the Chinese, Koreans have developed and preserved their own cultural heritage. The Korean language is of the Ural-Altaic Group. Its script, Hangul, was invented in the 15th century; prior to this Chinese characters alone were used. Also invented around this time was the first metal movable printing type. The first works translated into Hangul were Buddhist, Confucian and other classics and it was only in the late 19th century that the European influence first began to be felt.

Republic of Korea

President, Chun Doo Hwan (August, 1980).

CABINET

Prime Minister, Lho Shin Yong.
Deputy P.M. and Minister of the Economic Planning Board, Shin Byong Hyan.
Foreign Affairs, Lee Won Kyung.
Home Affairs, Chung Suk Mo.
Finance, Kim Mahn Je.
Justice, Kim Suk Hwi.
Defence, Gen. Yoon Sung Min.
Education, Sohn Jae Suk.
Sports, Lee Young Ho.
Agriculture and Fisheries, Hwang In Sung.
Commerce and Industry, Kum Chin Ho.
Energy and Resources, Choi Dong Kyu.
Construction, Kim Sung Bae.
Health and Welfare, Rhee Hai Won.
Labour Affairs, Cho Chull Kwon.
Transport, Sun Soo Ik.
Communications, Lee Ja Hon.
Culture and Information, Lee Won Hong.
Government Affairs, Park Sae Jik.
Science and Technology, Kim Seong Jin.
National Unification, Lee Sei Kee.
First State Minister for Political Affairs, Chung Jae Chull.

KOREAN EMBASSY
4 Palace Gate, W8 5NF
[01-581 0247]

Ambassador Extraordinary and Plenipotentiary, His Excellency Dr. Young Choo Kim (1984).
Minister, Wam Chan Kah.

The Republic of Korea has been officially recognized by the Governments of the United States, France, Great Britain, and most other countries except the U.S.S.R. and its satellites.

President Syngman Rhee was overthrown by a popular rising in 1960. After a year of unstable government a new regime was set up on May 16, 1961 by an army officers' *coup* led by Major General Park Chung Hee. On March 22, 1962 he took over as acting President. He was elected President in December 1963 and again in 1967, 1971, 1972 and 1978, but was assassinated on October 26, 1979. The country was placed under partial martial law. The then Prime Minister Choi Kyu Hah was elected President that December but resigned in August 1980 to be succeeded by Gen. Chun Doo Hwan. The constitution was

he U.S. Government laid the whole question of the future of Korea before the General Assembly of the United Nations. The Assembly in November, 1947, resolved that elections should be held in Korea for a National Assembly under the supervision of a temporary Commission formed for that purpose by the United Nations and that the National Assembly then elected should set up a Government. The Soviet Government refused to allow the Commission to visit the Russian Occupied Zone and in consequence it was only able to discharge its function in that part of Korea which lies to the south of the 38th parallel.

A general election was held on May 10, 1948, and the first National Assembly met in Seoul on May 31. The Assembly passed a constitution on July 12, and on July 20 elected Dr. Syngman Rhee as the first President of the Republic of Korea. On August 15, 1948, the Republic was formerly inaugurated and American Military Government came to an end.

Meanwhile in the Russian-occupied zone north of the 38th parallel the Democratic People's Republic had been set up with its capital at Pyongyang; a supreme People's Soviet was elected in September 1948, and a Soviet-style Constitution adopted.

The Korean War.—The country remained effectively divided into two along the line of 38th parallel until the aggression of June 25, 1950, when the North Korean forces invaded South Korea. An emergency meeting of the U.N. Security Council adopted a resolution calling for an immediate cease fire and the withdrawal of North Korean forces. This was ignored and the communist advance continued. In response to Security Council recommendations that United Nations members should furnish assistance to repel the attack, 16 nations including the U.S.A. and the U.K. came to the aid of the Republic of Korea. However the communist advance could not be contained until eventually a front was established round Pusan. Later, following a successful U.S. marine landing at Inchon, the communist forces were driven beyond the 38th parallel. At this point the Chinese "volunteers" joined the campaign and although the U.N. forces were initially driven back beyond Seoul they regrouped and threw the communist forces back to approximately the old dividing line. The fighting was ended by an Armistice agreement signed by the U.N. Commander-in-Chief revised and new elections held. President Chun was re-elected and his Democratic Justice Party gained a majority in the National Assembly after elections in March 1981. It retained its majority in the Feb. 1985 elections but now faces stronger opposition.

Constitution.—The President, who is Head of State, Chief of the Executive and Commander-in-Chief of the Armed Forces, is indirectly elected for a single term of seven years by an electoral college of over 5,000 members, who are directly elected. He appoints the Prime Minister with the consent of the National Assembly, and members of the State Council on the recommendation of the Prime Minister. The President is also empowered to take wide-ranging measures in an emergency, including the declaration of martial law, but must obtain the agreement of the National Assembly.

The National Assembly is directly elected for a four-year term, one third by proportional representation, two thirds from constituencies.

Armed Forces.—The Republic of Korea has an army of about 520,000, a small navy mostly for coastal patrol and protection duties, an air force with over 500 combat aircraft and a marine corps which is incorporated in the navy. About six per cent of the nation's G.N.P. is currently spent on defence.

Education and Religion.—Primary education is compulsory for six years from the age of seven. Secondary and higher education is extensive. The national illiteracy rate is among the lowest in Asia. There is freedom of religion. Buddhism has the most followers (13 million) followed by Protestantism (5 million) and Confucianism (4¼ million). Catholics number about one million.

Agriculture and Fisheries.—The soil is fertile but the arable land is limited by the mountainous nature of the country. Staple agricultural products are rice, barley and other cereals, beans, tobacco and hemp. Fruit growing and sericulture are also practised. Ginseng, a medicinal root much used by both the Chinese and Koreans, forms a useful source of revenue. The Korean fishing industry is a major contributor to both food supply and exports.

Minerals.—The Republic of Korea is deficient in mineral resources, except for deposits of coal on the East Coast and tungsten. There are some prospects of discovering oil in the sea between Korea and Japan.

Finance.—The budget for 1985 totals about £11,000 million.

Trade and Industry.—Since the beginning of 1962 a series of successful five-year plans resulted in real economic growth averaging around 10 per cent a year. The 6th economic development plan (1987–91) envisages a growth rate of 7·5 per cent. Annual per capita G.N.P. is U.S.$2,094.

Since the 1960s the Republic of Korea has industrialised rapidly on the basis of greatly expanded exports. Important exports include cars, electrical and electronic equipment, footwear, ships, railway rolling stock and iron and steel products.

TRADE

	1982	1983
Imports	U.S.$23,473 m.	U.S.$25,634 m.
Exports	20,879 m.	23,825 m.

Currency.—The unit of currency is the *won.*

Trade with U.K.

	1983	1984
Imports from U.K.	£168,942,000	£219,406,000
Exports to U.K.	440,354,000	443,819,000

Communications and Transport.—Modern highways mean that the whole country is now within one day's drive of Seoul. In 1980 there were 15,599 km. of paved road. Seoul has a subway system and there are national railway and airline systems. Korean Air Lines operates regular flights to Europe, the United States, the Middle East and South East Asia. Pusan and Inchon are the major ports with Pusan serving the industrial areas of the southeast. Inchon, 28 miles from Seoul, serves the capital, but development and operation at Inchon are hampered by a tidal variation of 9–10 metres.

CAPITAL.—Seoul, population (1980), 8,367,000. Other main centres are Ψ Pusan (pop. 3,160,000), Taegu (pop. 1,607,000) and Ψ Inchon (pop. 1,084,000).

FLAG.—White, with red over blue device in centre, three black parallel bars, some broken, in each quarter.

NATIONAL DAY.—August 15 (Independence Day).

BRITISH EMBASSY
No. 4, Chung-Dong, Chung-Ku, Seoul

Ambassador Extraordinary and Plenipotentiary, His Excellency John Nicholas Teague Spreckley, C.M.G. (1983).
Counsellor, P. H. D. Wetton (*Commercial*).
Defence and Military Attaché, Brig. B. S. Burditt.
1*st Secretaries,* W. B. McCleary (*Head of Chancery and Consul*); S. J. Hiscock (*Commercial/Information*).
Cultural Attaché and British Council Representative, S. S. Newton.
There is an Honorary British Consul at Pusan.

BRITISH CHAMBER OF COMMERCE, c/o Chartered Bank, 1st and 2nd Floors, Samsung Building, 50, 1-Ka Ulchi Road, Chung-Ku, Seoul.

Democratic People's Republic of Korea

Political Committee of the Central Committee, Kim Il-sung; Kim Chong-il; O Chin-u (*full members and members of the presidium*); Pak Song-chol; Yim Chun-chu; So Chol; Kim Yong-nam; Chon Mun-sop; Kim Hwan; Yon Hyong-muk; O Kuk-yol; Kang Song-san; Paek Hak-nim; Choe Yong-nim; So Yun-sok; Ho Tam; Yi Chong-ok (*full members*). Choe Kwang; Cho Se-ung; Kong Chin-tae; Chong Chun-ki; Chong Kyong-hui; Yi Kun-mo; Hyon Mu-kwang; Kim Kang-hwan; Kye Ung-tae; Kang Hui-won; Chon Pyong-ho; Kim Tu-nam; An Sung-hak; Hong Song-yong; Kim Pok-sik; Kim Chung-nin (*alternate members*).
Secretariat of the Central Committee, Kim Il-sung (*General Secretary*); Kim Chong-il; Yon Hyong-muk; Hwang Chang-yop; Hyon Mu-Kwang; Ho Chong-suk; So Kwan-hui; Chae Hui-chong; An Sung-hak; Ho Tam; Kim Yong-sun; Pak Nam-ki; Kim Chung-nin.

The population of North Korea is around 19,500,000. North Korea is rich in minerals and industry has been developed, but the economy has stagnated in recent years because of poor planning and a shortage of foreign exchange. The armed forces are believed to number about 750,000 men.

Trade with U.K.

	1983	1984
Imports from U.K.	£2,527,000	£2,935,000
Exports to U.K.	362,000	458,000

CAPITAL.—Pyongyang (population, approx. 1,500,000).

FLAG.—Broad red horizontal band bordered by white lines bearing a five-point red star on a white disc in centre; blue horizontal bands at top and bottom.

KUWAIT
(The State of Kuwait)

Amir, H. H. Shaikh Jaber Al Ahmad Al Sabah, *born* 1928; acceded Jan. 1, 1978.

Crown Prince and Prime Minister, H. H. Shaikh Sa'ad Al Abdallah Al Sabah.

Deputy Prime Minister and Minister for Foreign Affairs, H. E. Shaikh Sabah al Ahmad al Jabir al Sabah.

Defence, H. E. Shaikh Salim al Sabah al Salim al Sabah.

Interior, H. E. Shaikh Nawwaf al Ahmed al Sabah.

Oil and Industry, H. E. Shaikh Ali Khalifa al Athbi al Sabah.

KUWAIT EMBASSY IN LONDON
45–46 Queen's Gate, S.W.7.
[01–589 4533]

Ambassador Extraordinary and Plenipotentiary, His Excellency Ghazi M. A. Al-Rayes (1980).

Area and Population.—Kuwait extends along the shore of the Persian Gulf from Iraq to Saudi Arabia, with an area of 17,818 sq. km. (6,877 sq. miles). Kuwait has a dry, desert climate with a summer season extending from April to September. The mean temperature varies between 84° and 113° F. in summer, and 46° and 64° F. in winter. Humidity rarely exceeds 60 per cent except in July and August. The population is 1,786,616 (mid-1984), of which about 42 per cent are Kuwaiti citizens, the remainder being large numbers of other Arab peoples, Persians, Indians and Pakistanis. The total European and American population is about 12,500. The gross population growth rate is 6·4 per cent, a growth rate of 3·5 per cent for Kuwaiti citizens.

The official language is Arabic, and English is widely spoken as a second language. Islam is the official religion, though religious freedom is constitutionally guaranteed.

Government.—Although Kuwait had been independent for some years, the "exclusive agreement" of 1899 between the Shaikh of Kuwait and the British Government was formally abrogated by an exchange of letters dated June 19, 1961. This exchange was immediately followed by Iraqi claims to sovereignty over Kuwait, but on Oct. 4, 1963, Iraq recognized Kuwait's independence although the Kuwait-Iraqi border has not yet been determined formally. Under the Constitution legislative power is vested in the Amir and the 50-member National Assembly, and executive power in the Amir and the Cabinet. The sixth National Assembly was elected for a four year term in March 1985.

Education, etc.—As a result of the very considerable oil revenues, the Kuwait Government embarked on a large scale development scheme and plans for social services. Education and medical treatment are free. New hospitals and schools continue to be built. Kuwait University was opened in 1966, and in 1985 had 16,000 students. In 1983 there were over 433,000 pupils at government and private schools.

Public Utilities.—Kuwait has a domestic water supply from water distillation plants which operate on natural gas from the oil fields. These plants can produce over 118,000,000 gallons of fresh water daily. Total water storage capacity, in reservoirs and water towers, amounts to over 1,201 million gallons. A natural source of fresh water, discovered at Raudhatain in the north of the State, has been developed to produce up to 3,000,000 gallons per day for at least 20 years and a pipeline has been built to carry the water to Kuwait town.

Electricity is produced by four power stations in Kuwait. Production in 1983 was 12,499 million Kwh.

Communications.—Ships of British, Dutch, Kuwaiti and other lines make regular calls at Kuwait. Several international and Middle Eastern airlines operate regular air services, and other companies make non-scheduled flights to Kuwait under charter. There is a network of dual-carriageway roads and more are under construction. Telecommunications, and postal services are conducted by the Kuwait Government, which has built an earth satellite station.

Finance.— Revenue for the financial year 1983–84 was budgeted at *KD*3,038 million. Oil revenues constitute 91·8 per cent. of total revenue. Estimated total expenditure for the same year was *KD*3,376·3 million. The financial year begins on July 1. There are a large number of investment banks in some of which the Government holds equity. The banking system is controlled by the Central Bank of Kuwait.

Production.—The G.N.P. of Kuwait in 1983 was estimated at *KD*7,593 million.

Despite the desert terrain, 8·4 per cent of land is under cultivation, fruit and vegetables being the main crops. Shrimp fishing is becoming important.

The Government of Kuwait began to participate in the ownership of the British- and American-owned Kuwait Oil Company in 1974 and an agreement was signed in November 1975 which brought 100 per cent government ownership. After a reorganisation of the national oil industry in 1980, all the business was taken over by the Kuwait Petroleum Corporation.

The centre of Kuwait oil production is at Burgan, south of Kuwait City. Oil is also lifted in the Kuwait/Saudi Arabia Partitioned Zone (Wafra) south of the State. Oil is exported through a specially constructed port at Mina al Ahmadi. Production of crude oil in 1984 was approximately 1,115 million barrels per day. About 3,000 people are employed, including Kuwaitis, British, Americans, Indians, Pakistanis and citizens of other Arab countries.

Trade.—Oil exports constitute about 88 per cent. of Kuwait's total exports. Non-oil exports include chemical fertilizers, ammonia and other chemicals, metal pipes, shrimps and building materials; re-exports accounted for 73 per cent. of non-oil exports in 1982. Major trading partners are Asian countries, followed by E.E.C. countries and Arab states.

	1982*
Imports	*KD*2,098·0m
Exports	3,261·7m

* estimated

Trade with U.K.

	1983	1984
Imports from U.K.	£333,273,000	£301,520,000
Exports to U.K.	67,281,000	141,606,000

CAPITAL.—Ψ Kuwait (population, excluding suburbs, 400,000).

FLAG.—Three horizontal stripes of green, white and red, with black trapezoid next to staff.

NATIONAL DAY.—February 25.

BRITISH EMBASSY
P.O. Box Safat 2,
Arabian Gulf Street, Kuwait

Ambassador Extraordinary and Plenipotentiary, His Excellency Sir Peter Moon, K.C.V.O., C.M.G., *apptd.* 1985.

Counsellor, A. S. M. Marshall, O.B.E.

1st Secretaries, R. Bland, O.B.E.; C. J. Hurran; A. Heath (*Financial and Economic, and Head of Chancery*); B. R. R. Rainbow (*Consul*); P. Newall (*Commercial*).

British Council Office Representative, D. Brown, P.O. Box 345, Safat, Kuwait. There is a library in *Kuwait*.

LAOS
(People's Democratic Republic of Laos)

President, Souphanouvong, *assumed office,* Dec. 2, 1975.
Prime Minister, Kaysone Phomvihane.

EMBASSY IN LONDON
7 Heath Drive, Hampstead, NW3.
[01–794 0011/2]

Ambassador Extraordinary and Plenipotentiary (vacant).
Chargé d' Affaires, Ouan Phommachack.

Position and Extent.—The People's Democratic Republic of Laos is in the northerly part of Indo-China, lying between China and Vietnam, on the north and east, and Burma and Thailand on the west. Laos has a common boundary with Cambodia to the south. The area of the country is approximately 90,000 sq. miles, with a population (U.N. estimate, 1982) of about 3,900,000.

History.—The Kingdom of Lane Xang, the Land of a Million Elephants, was founded in the 14th century, but broke up at the beginning of the 15th century into the separate kingdoms of Luang Prabang and Vientiane and the Principality of Champassac, which together came under French protection in 1893. In 1945 the Japanese executed a *coup de force* and suppressed the French administration. Under a Constitution of 1947 Laos became a constitutional monarchy under King Sisvang Vong of the House of Luang Prabang, and an independent sovereign state in 1949.

The next twenty-five years in Laos were marked by power struggles and civil war. International conferences were held in Geneva in 1954 and 1961–2 to produce a settlement based on neutrality and independence, but the resulting coalition governments were short-lived. After 1967 North Vietnamese forces steadily increased their military activities in Laos. Although there were regular seasonal fluctuations in the fighting, which resulted in many areas of the country changing hands several times, Government forces gradually lost ground. By February 21, 1973, when a ceasefire agreement was signed in Vientiane between the *Pathet Lao* (communists) and the Government in Vientiane, Communist forces had occupied or dominated most of the strategic areas of Laos, including the Plain of Jars in the north, and the Bolovens Plateau in the south.

After the fall of Saigon in April 1975, internal resistance to the Pathet Lao crumbled; Communist troops occupied the whole country and, though still paying lip-service to the 1973 Agreement and maintaining a façade of coalition, the *Pathet Lao* took over the government and began to implement an authoritarian régime with policies of austerity and economic self-sufficiency. On December 2, 1975, following the abdication of the King, Laos was declared a People's Democratic Republic and the *Pathet Lao* assumed full charge of the country.

Economy.—There is no significant industrial base in Laos, an estimated 85 per cent. of the work force being engaged in agriculture, largely concerned with rice cultivation. Rice production in 1982 amounted to 1·2 million tonnes, thus rendering the country theoretically self-sufficient in this staple food. In 1983, however, the authorities stated that due to late rains there was an overall shortfall of about 100,000 tons.

The main exports are electricity, timber and coffee. Total exports in 1982 were valued at $39·8 m. Imports during 1982 amounted to $124·2 m. Clearing agreements have been signed with certain socialist countries and the trade gap is largely financed by foreign

aid, of which some 60 per cent. is provided by socialist countries.

Laos' economic performance so far has been poor and shows no signs of early recovery, the free market rate for the dollar is much higher than the official rate and prices of consumer items continue to increase.

Currency.—In January 1980 a "new" *Kip* replaced the former currency. In July 1983 the non-commercial rate of exchange was rectified by the State Bank.

Trade with U.K.

	1983	1984
Imports from U.K.	£626,000	£721,000
Exports to U.K.	56,000	238,000

CAPITAL.—Vientiane, population (estimated 1978) 90,000.

FLAG.—Blue background with a central white circle, framed by 2 horizontal red stripes.

NATIONAL DAY.—December 2.

BRITISH AMBASSADOR, *resides at* Bangkok, Thailand.

LEBANON

President of the Republic of Lebanon, Amin Gemayel, *elected,* Sept. 21, 1982.
Prime Minister, Rashid Karami.

LEBANESE EMBASSY IN LONDON
21 Kensington Palace Gardens, W8 4QM
[01–229 7265/8485]

Ambassador Extraordinary and Plenipotentiary, His Excellency Gen. Ahmed El-Hajj (1983).
1st Secretary, Sleiman Chafic Rassi.
Counsellor, Hussein Moussawi.
Consular Section, 15 Palace Gardens Mews, W.8 (01–727 6696)

Area and Population.—Lebanon forms a strip about 120 miles in length and varying in width from 30 to 35 miles, along the Mediterranean littoral, and extending from the Israel frontier on the south to the Nahr al Kebir (15 miles north of Tripoli) on the north; its eastern boundary runs down the Anti-Lebanon range and then down the Great Central depression, the *Beqaa*, from which flow the rivers Orontes and Litani. It is divided into 5 districts, North Lebanon, Mount Lebanon, Beirut, South Lebanon and Beqaa. The seaward slopes of the mountains have a Mediterranean climate and vegetation. The inland range of Anti-Lebanon has the characteristics of steppe country. There is a mixed Arabic-speaking population of Christians, Moslems and Druses. The total area of Lebanon is about 4,300 sq. miles, population (U.N. estimate, 1982), 2,740,000. (*For* MAP, *See* Index.)

Government.—Lebanon became an independent State on Sept. 1, 1920, administered under French Mandate until Nov. 22, 1943. Powers were transferred to the Lebanese Government from Jan. 1, 1944, and French troops were withdrawn in 1946.

In April 1975, serious fighting broke out in Beirut between members of the predominantly Christian Phalangist Party and Palestinian guerrillas based in Lebanon. The fighting continued and increased throughout 1975 and 1976. In the autumn of 1976 the Arab Deterrent Forces composed mainly of Syrian troops, imposed an effective ceasefire and brought nineteen months of civil war to an end throughout Lebanon. Major bouts of fighting took place in October 1978 and April/May 1981, interspersed with regular clashes on a smaller scale. There was renewed fighting in the summer of 1982 when Israeli forces invaded the country, penetrating as far as Beirut. Following negotiations, Palestine Liberation Organisation guerrillas left Beirut for various Arab countries. Frequent minor clashes in the following twelve months escalated into serious fighting in Aug.–Sept. 1983. The north-east of the country is currently occupied by Syrian and Palestian forces. Although Israeli troops withdrew from southern Lebanon in 1985, a buffer zone controlled by Israeli-backed Christian militias has been established along the Israeli-Lebanon border.

After reconciliation talks in Lausanne, Switzerland, in March 1984, moves were made towards the disengagement of rival militias in Beirut. In April 1984, Mr. Rashid Karami formed a 10-man Cabinet which included the leaders of the principal factions.

Production.—Fruits are the most important products and include citrus fruit, apples, grapes, bananas and olives. There is a considerable amount of light industry, mostly for the production of consumer goods, but most factories have been adversely affected by the instability of the past 10 years. There is little remaining of the famous cedars of Lebanon.

Communications.—A railway runs from Beirut to Damascus, connecting at Rayak with a branch line which runs from Tripoli through Homs, Hama and Aleppo to the Turkish frontier, from Nusaybin to the Iraq frontier at Tel Kotchek. A railway also runs up the coast from Nakowia to Tripoli. The railways are not functioning as a result of the 1975–6 civil war. There is an international airport at Beirut, served by several airlines, although operations can be disrupted by fighting in the city.

Archæology, etc.—Lebanon has some important historical remains, notably Baalbek (Heliopolis) which contains the ruins of first to third century Roman temples and Jubail (Biblos), one of the oldest continuously inhabited towns in the world, and ancient Tyre.

Language and Literature.—Arabic is the official language, and French and English are also widely used.

Education.—There are five universities in Beirut, the American and the French (R.C.) Universities established in the last century, and the Lebanese National University, the Beirut University College and the Arab University which are recent foundations in the early stages of development. There are several institutions for vocational training, some of which have been rendered inoperative by the civil war, and there is a good provision throughout the country of primary and secondary schools, among which are a great number of private schools.

Finance.—Revenue and Expenditure, 1980 (Estimated) £L5,211,200,000, including a deficit of £L1,500m. The monetary unit is the Lebanese £(L). (*See also* p. 82.)

Trade.—Principal imports are gold and precious metals, machinery and electrical equipment, textiles and yarns, vegetable products, iron and steel goods, motor vehicles, mineral products, chemicals and chemical products, pharmaceuticals, prepared foods, beverages, tobacco products, live animals and animal products.

Principal exports include gold and precious metals, fruits and vegetables, textiles, building materials, furniture, plastic goods, foodstuffs, tobacco and wine.

There is also a considerable and very important transit trade through Beirut, including gold, crude oil and a wide range of machinery and consumer goods. Lebanon is the terminal for two oil pipe lines, one formerly belonging to the Iraq Petroleum Company, debouching at Tripoli, the other belonging to the Trans Arabian Pipeline Company, at Sidon. The latter supplies most of Lebanon's requirements as the former has not functioned for some years.

Trade with U.K.

	1983	1984
Imports from U.K.	£81,435,000	£76,223,000
Exports to U.K.	11,521,000	6,869,000

CAPITAL.— Ψ Beirut (population, 702,000). Other towns are Ψ Tripoli (175,000), Zahlé (46,800), Ψ Sidon (24,740), Ψ Tyre (14,000).

FLAG.—Horizontal bands of red, white and red with a green cedar of Lebanon in the centre of the white band.

NATIONAL DAY.—November 22.

BRITISH EMBASSY
Avenue de Paris, Ras Beirut, Beirut

Ambassador Extraordinary and Plenipotentiary, His Excellency Sir David Miers, K.B.E., C.M.G.

British Council Representative, N. O. Hudson, O.B.E., Beit Fawzi Azar, Sharia Sidani, Ras Beirut.

LIBERIA
(Republic of Liberia)

Head of State, Commander-in-Chief Samuel K. Doe.

Rural Development, Maj. Yudu S. Gray.
Agriculture, Gblorzuo S. Toweh.
Commerce, Industry and Transportation, Mrs. McLeod Turkett-Darpoh.
Education, Maj. G. S. Boley.
Finance, G. Alvin Jones.
Foreign Affairs, Dr. Ernest Eastman.
Health and Social Affairs, Mrs. M. S. Belleh.
Information, Cultural Affairs and Tourism, Carlton Karpeh.
Justice, J. K. Z. B. Scott.
Labour, Manpower and Development, Frank Senkpeni.
Lands, Mines and Energy, Dr. F. Kromah.
Internal Affairs, Col. E. K. Sackor.
National Defence, Maj. Gen. Gray D. Allison.
Planning and Economic Affairs, Maj. Emmanuel O. Gardiner.
Postal Affairs, Dr. John Kolleh.
Public Works, Maj. James Burphy.
State for Presidential Affairs, Dr. Bernard Blamo.
Dir.-Gen. of the Cabinet, Dr. Peter Naigow.

LIBERIAN EMBASSY IN LONDON
21 Prince's Gate, SW7 1QB
[01–589 9405]

Ambassador Extraordinary and Plenipotentiary, His Excellency Willie A. Givens (1985).

An independent republic of Western Africa, occupying that part of the coast between Sierra Leone and the Ivory Coast, which is between the rivers Mano in the N.W. and Cavalla in the S.E., a distance of about 350 miles, with an area of about 43,000 square miles, and extending to the interior to latitude 8° 50', a distance of 150 miles from the seaboard. It was founded by the American Colonization Society in 1822, and has been recognized since 1847 as an independent State. The population at the Census of 1974 was 1,481,524: a 1982 U.N. estimate put the figure at 2,110,000.

William V. S. Tubman, President of Liberia since 1944, died on July 23, 1971, and was succeeded by Dr. Tolbert. The Constitution was suspended following a military *coup* on April 12, 1980 led by M/Sgt. Samuel K. Doe, who then became Head of State. Executive power is now vested in the Head of State assisted by an appointed Cabinet of 18. A new Constitution was endorsed by a referendum on July 3, 1984 and on July 22 the People's Redemptive Council was dissolved and replaced by an interim National Assembly, comprising the Council and 35 civilian members, which will oversee the country's return to civilian rule. Presidential and legislative elections are scheduled for Oct. 1985, after which an elected civilian government will replace military rule.

The Army of Liberia consists of one division of 2 brigades of militia, three regular infantry battalions, one engineer battalion and a small coastguard.

The artificial harbour and free port of Monrovia was opened on July 26, 1948. There are 9 ports of entry, including 3 river ports. International and African airlines call at Robertsfield, 35 miles from Monrovia. Spriggs Payne airfield, on the outskirts of Monrovia, is used by Air Liberia for internal flights.

Liberia is receiving assistance from a number of countries, including the United Kingdom, and from the E.E.C. and various international agencies. This aid is mainly directed towards the implementation of Liberia's National Socio-Economic Development Plan.

FINANCE

	1981–82	1982–83
Revenue	$223,000,000	$237,300,000
Expenditure	303,000,000	317,800,000

$ = U.S. Dollar

TRADE

The principal exports are iron ore, crude rubber, timber, uncut diamonds, palm kernels, cocoa and coffee. The chief imports are manufactured goods of all kinds, transport and iron-ore mining equipment and foodstuffs.

	1981	1982
Imports	$477,420,000	428,400,000
Exports	531,420,000	477,400,000

Trade with U.K.

	1983	1984
Imports from U.K.	£13,877,000	£30,980,000
Exports to U.K.	7,181,000	6,975,000

The language of the Republic is English. American weights and measures are used.

CAPITAL, ΨMonrovia. Est. Pop. 300,000. Other ports are ΨBuchanan, ΨGreenville (Sinoe) and ΨHarper (Cape Palmas).

FLAG.—Alternate horizontal stripes (5 white, 6 red), with 5-pointed white star on blue field in upper corner next to flagstaff.

NATIONAL DAY.—July 26.

BRITISH EMBASSY
Mamba Point (P.O. Box 120), Monrovia

Ambassador Extraordinary and Plenipotentiary and Consul-General, His Excellency Alec Ibbott, *apptd.* 1985.

2nd Secretary and Consul, R. G. Jones.
Pro-Consul, G. D. Hart.

LIBYA
(Socialist People's Libyan Arab Jamahiriya)

Leader of the Revolution, Col. Muammar Qadhafi.
Secretary of the General People's Committee, Muhammad az-Zarruq Rajab.

LIBYAN DIPLOMATIC MISSION IN LONDON

Following the break of diplomatic relations with Libya in April 1984, the Royal Embassy of Saudi Arabia has handled Libyan interests in Britain.

Libya, on the Mediterranean coast of Africa, is bounded on the East by Egypt and the Sudan, on the South by the Republics of Chad and Niger, and on the West by Algeria and Tunisia. It consists of the three former provinces of Tripolitania, Cyrenaica and the Fezzan, with a combined area of approximately 810,000 square miles (1,760,000 sq. kms) and a population (1983 estimate) of 3,300,000. The people of Libya are principally Arab with some Berbers in the West and aboriginal tribes in the Fezzan. Islam is the official religion of Libya, but other religions are tolerated. The official language is Arabic.

Vast sand and rock deserts, almost completely barren, occupy the greater part of Libya. The Southern part of the country lies within the Sahara Desert. There are no rivers, and, as rainfall is precarious, a good harvest is infrequent. The ancient ruins in Cyrenaica, at Cyrene, Ptolemais (Tolmeta) and Apollonia, are outstanding, as are those at Leptis Magna near Homs, 70 miles from Tripoli and at Sabratha, 40 miles west of Tripoli. An Italian expedition has found in the S.W. of the Fezzan a series of rock-paintings more than 5,000 years old.

Production and Industry.—Agriculture is confined mainly to the coastal areas of Tripolitania and Cyrenaica, where barley, wheat, olives, almonds, citrus fruits and dates are produced, and to the areas of the oases, many of which are well supplied with springs supporting small fertile areas. Among the important oases are Jaghbub, Ghadames, Jofra, Sebha, Murzuq, Brak, Ghat, Jalo and the Kufra group in the South-East. The main industry is oil and gas production. There are pipelines from Zelten to the terminal at Mersa Brega, from Dahra to Ras-es-Sider, from Amal to Ras Lanuf and from the Intisar field to Zuetina. In 1984 average production of crude oil was about 1 million barrels per day. A major petrochemical complex is under construction at Ras Lanuf where a refinery and ethylene plant began operations in early 1985. The construction of an iron and steel plant at Misurata is well under way, with completion expected in 1986. However, economic constraints have slowed some projects, particularly since Libya decided in 1983 to go ahead with a major irrigation scheme, the "Great Man-Made River".

Exports from Libya are dominated by crude oil, but some wool, cattle, sheep and horses, olive oil, and hides and skins are also exported. Principal imports are foodstuffs, including sugar, tea and coffee and most constructional materials and consumer goods. In recent years the private sector has been virtually eliminated and Libya is now a state trading country with imports controlled by state monopolies.

Communications in Libya are good. Besides the coastal road running from the Tunisian frontier through Tripoli to Benghazi, Tobruk and the Egyptian border, which serves the main population centres, main roads now link the provincial centres, and the oil-producing areas of the south with the coastal towns. There are airports at Tripoli and Benghazi (Benina), Tobruk, Mersa Brega, Sebha, Ghadames and Kufra regularly used by commercial airlines, and military airfields near Tobruk, near Tripoli and at Al Watiya, south of Zuara.

Government.—Libya was occupied by Italy in 1911–12 in the course of the Italo-Turkish War, and under the Treaty of Ouchy (Oct. 1912) the sovereignty of the province was transferred by Turkey to Italy. In 1939 the four Provinces of Libya (Tripoli, Misurata, Benghazi and Derna) were incorporated in the national territory of Italy as *Libia Italiana.* After the Second World War Tripolitania and Cyrenaica were placed provisionally under British and the Fezzan under French administration, and in conformity with a resolution of the U.N. General Assembly on Nov. 21, 1949, Libya became on Dec. 24, 1951, the first independent state to be created by the United Nations. The monarchy was overthrown by a revolution on Sept. 1, 1969, and the country was declared a republic. It was ruled by the Revolutionary Command Council (RCC) under the leadership of Colonel Muammar Qadhafi.

In March 1977 a new form of direct democracy, the "Jamahiriya" (state of the masses) was promulgated and the official name of the country was changed to Socialist People's Libyan Arab Jamahiriya. At local level authority is now vested in about 2,200 Basic and 25 Municipal People's Congresses which appoint Popular Committees to execute policy. Officials of these Congresses and Committees, together with representatives from unions and other organisations, form the General People's Congress, a body of some 1,000 delegates which normally meets for about a week early each year. This is the highest policy-making body in the country. The General People's Congress appoints its own General Secretariat and the General People's Committee, whose members head the 19 government departments which execute policy at national level. The Secretary of the General People's Committee has functions similar to those of a Prime Minister.

Since a reorganization in March 1979 neither Col. Qadhafi nor his former RCC colleagues have held formal posts in the administration. Qadhafi continues to hold the ceremonial title "Leader of the Revolution".

Currency.—The unit of currency is the Libyan *dinar* of 1,000 *dirham.* (*See also* p. 81.)

Libya has technical assistance agreements with a number of countries, and also employs large numbers of foreign labourers and experts.

Trade with U.K.

	1983	1984
Imports from U.K.	£274,169,000	£246,467,000
Exports to U.K.	224,050,000	155,276,000

CAPITAL.—Tripoli, pop. 1981, about 1,000,000.
The principal towns are: ΨBenghazi (500,000); Ψ Misurata (194,047).

FLAG.—Libya uses a plain emerald green flag.
NATIONAL DAY.—Sept. 1.

BRITISH EMBASSY

Diplomatic relations between the U.K. and Libya were broken in April 1984. British interests are currently handled by a section at the Italian Embassy, 1 Sharia Oran, Tripoli.

LIECHTENSTEIN
(Fürstentum Liechtenstein)

Prince, Franz Josef II., *b.* Aug. 16, 1906; *suc.* July 26, 1938; *married* March 7, 1943, Countess Gina von Wilczek.

Heir, Crown Prince Hans Adam, *b.* Feb. 14, 1945; *married* July 30, 1967, Countess Marie Kinsky.

From Aug. 26, 1984, Prince Adam took over official duties and executive authority; Prince Franz Josef remains titular Head of State.

MINISTRY

Prime Minister, Hans Brunhart (*Foreign Affairs; Interior; Education; Finance; Culture; Construction*).

Deputy Prime Minister, Hilmar Ospelt (*Justice; Economy; Communications; Youth and Sport*).

Government Counsellors, Dr. Walter Oehry (*Agriculture and Forestry*); Dr. Egmond Frommelt (*Social Services*); Anton Gerner (*Health*).

Liechtenstein is represented in diplomatic and consular matters in the United Kingdom by the Swiss Embassy, *q.v.*

At the General Election on Feb. 7, 1982, the Patriotic Union Party won 8 seats and Progressive Citizens Party 7.

A Principality on the Upper Rhine, between Vorarlberg (Austria) and Switzerland, with an area of 62 square miles and a population in 1984 of 26,680. The industries are mainly textiles and manufactures. The chief products are cotton yarn, cotton material, metal goods, knitting machinery, ceramics, artificial teeth, precision measuring instruments, vacuum pumps, coated lenses, leather goods, bed down, conveyor belts, boilers, preserves, damask cloth, socks and stockings, and furniture.

FINANCE

	1983	1984
Revenue	F260,377,610	F275,871,839
Expenditure	252,146,084	267,987,672

(*F* = Swiss *francs*)

The language of the Principality is German.
CAPITAL, Vaduz. Pop. (1984), 4,872.

FLAG.—Equal horizontal bands of blue over red; gold crown on blue band near staff.

British Consul General, Gordon Aldridge Duggan (*office* at Dufourstrasse 56, 8008 Zürich).

LUXEMBURG
(Grand-Duché de Luxembourg)

Grand Duke, H.R.H. Jean, *born* Jan. 5, 1921, *married,* April 9, 1953, Princess Joséphine-Charlotte of Belgium, and has issue, 3 sons and 2 daughters; *succeeded* (on the abdication of his mother) Nov. 12, 1964.

Heir Apparent, Prince Henri, *born* April 16, 1955, *married* February 14, 1981, Maria Teresa Mestre, and *has issue,* Prince Guillaume, *born* 11 Nov. 1981, and Prince Felix, *born* June 3, 1984.

CABINET

Christian Socialists:
Minister of State, President of the Government, Minister of Finance, National Development, Posts, Telecommunications and Information Technology, M. Jacques Santer.
Interior, the Family, Housing, Social Solidarity, M. Jean Spautz.
Education and Tourism, M. Fernand Boden.
Labour and Minister-Delegate for Finance, M. Jean-Claude Juncker.

Defence, Agriculture, Sport and the Civil Service, M. Marc Fischbach.
Agriculture and Viticulture, M. Rene Steichen.

Social Democrats:
Vice-President of the Government, Minister of the Economy, Foreign Affairs, Foreign Trade and Co-operation, Middle Classes and Treasury, M. Jacques Poos.
Public Health and Social Security, M. Benny Berg.
Justice, Cultural Affairs and the Environment, M. Robert Krieps.
Energy, Transport and Public Works, M. Marcel Schlechter.
State Secretary for Foreign Affairs, Foreign Trade and Co-operation and the Middle Classes, M. Robert Goebbels.
State Secretary for the Economy, M. Johnny Lahure.

EMBASSY AND CONSULATE
27 Wilton Crescent, SW1X 8SD
[01–235 6961]

Ambassador Extraordinary and Plenipotentiary, His Excellency Roger Hastert, C.M.G. (1978).

A Grand Duchy in Western Europe, bounded by Germany, Belgium, and France. Established as an independent State under the sovereignty of the King of the Netherlands as Grand Duke by the Congress of Vienna in 1815, it formed part of the Germanic Confederation, 1815–66, and was included in the German "Zollverein". In 1867 the Treaty of London declared it a neutral territory. On the death of the King of the Netherlands in 1890 it passed to the Duke of Nassau. The territory was invaded and overrun by the Germans at the beginning of the war in 1914, but was liberated in 1918. By the *Treaty of Versailles*, 1919, Germany renounced her former agreements with Luxemburg in respect of the customs union, etc., and in 1921 an economic union was made with Belgium. The Grand Duchy was again invaded and occupied by Germany on May 10, 1940. The constitution of the Grand Duchy was modified on April 28, 1948, and the stipulation of permanent neutrality was then abandoned. Luxemburg is now a fully effective member of the Western association of powers and a signatory of the Brussels and North Atlantic Treaties, and also a member of the European Communities. Luxemburg is a member of the Belgium-Netherlands-Luxemburg Customs Union (Benelux, 1960).

The Court of the European Communities has its seat in Luxemburg, as does the Secretariat of the European Parliament, the European Investment Bank, the European Audit Court and the European Monetary Co-operation fund.

The area is 999 square miles; the population (Jan. 1983) 365,500, nearly all Roman Catholics. There is a Chamber of 64 Deputies, elected by universal suffrage for 5 years. Legislation is submitted to the Council of State. The Grand Duchy was rich in iron-ore and possesses an important iron and steel industry with an annual productive capacity over 5,200,000 tons. Government revenue for 1982 was estimated at *L.F.* 5,300 million, expenditure *L.F.* 5,300 million. The Luxemburg *franc* has at present the same value as the Belgian *franc* and the latter is legal tender in the Grand Duchy. There are 170 miles of railway.

Trade with U.K. (Luxembourg and Belgium)

	1982	1983
Imports from U.K.	£21,000,000	£34,525,000
Exports to U.K.	49,586,000	64,238,000

CAPITAL.—Luxemburg, pop. (1983), 78,900, is a dismantled fortress. The country is well wooded, with many deer and wild boar. The language is Letzeburgesch but French is the official language; most speak German and many English.

FLAG.—Three horizontal bands, red, white and blue. NATIONAL DAY.—June 23.

BRITISH EMBASSY
28 Boulevard Royal, L-2449, Luxemburg

Ambassador Extraordinary and Plenipotentiary, His Excellency Richard Oliver Miles, C.M.G., *apptd.* 1985.

MADAGASCAR
(The Democratic Republic of Madagascar)

President, Didier Ratsiraka, *took office* 1975, *re-elected* Nov. 7, 1982 for a seven-year term.

COUNCIL OF MINISTERS

Prime Minister, Lt. Col. Désiré Rakotoarijaona.
Finance and Economy, Pascal Rakotomavo.
Agricultural Production, Yves Léone Ramélison.
Animal Production, Water and Forests, Joseph Randrianasolo.
Trade, Georges Solofoson.
Industry, Energy and Mines, Tantely René.
Population and Social Affairs, Rémi Tiandraza.
Revolutionary Art and Culture, Giselle Rabesahala.
Posts and Telecommunications, Rakotovoa Andriantiana.
Justice, Gilbert Sambson.
Transport, Supplies and Tourism, Joseph Bedo.
Civil Service and Labour, Georges Ruphin.
National Defence, Col. Guy Sibon.
Health, Dr. Jean-Jacques Séraphin.
Interior, Ampy Porthos.
Primary and Secondary Education, Charles Zeny.
Higher Education, Ignace Rakoto.
Scientific Research, Antoine Zafera.
Information, Bruno Rakotomavo.
Foreign Affairs, Jean Bemananjara.
Public Works, Lt. Col. Victor Ramahatra.

Madagascar lies 240 miles off the east coast of Africa and is the fourth largest island in the world. It has an area of 228,000 sq. miles and a population of about 9,230,000. The people are of mixed Polynesian, Arab and Negro origin. The languages spoken are Malagasy and French. There are sizeable French, Chinese and Indian communities.

Government.—It became a French protectorate in 1895, and a French colony in 1896 when the former queen was exiled. Republican status was adopted on October 14, 1958, and independence was proclaimed on June 26, 1960.

The post-independence civilian government was replaced by a military government in Jan. 1975 and the following month martial law was declared. A Supreme Council of the Revolution of 18 members under Capitaine de Frégate (now Admiral) Didier Ratsiraka was established on June 15, 1975.

In December 1975 a new constitution was approved in a referendum, which vested executive power in the President. He appoints a Council of Ministers to assist him, with the guidance of the Revolutionary Supreme Council. There is a 137-member National People's Assembly elected for a 5-year term by universal suffrage.

Revised agreements with France, signed on June 4, 1973, provided for the withdrawal of the French forces stationed in the country after independence. The French naval base at Diégo Suarez was turned into a civilian ship repair yard. Madagascar also withdrew from the Franc Zone and announced a claim to the Islands of Juan de Nova, Glorieuses, Isle de l'Europe, Bassa da India and Tromelin which had remained integral parts of the French Republic after independence.

The island's economy is still largely based on agriculture, which accounts for three-quarters of its exports. Development plans have placed emphasis on increasing agricultural and livestock production, the improvement of communications, the exploitation of mineral deposits and the creation of small industries.

TRADE

	1983
Imports	$U.S.522,000,000
Exports	432,000,000

The unit of currency is the Malagasy *franc* (FMG).

Trade with U.K.

	1983	1984
Imports from U.K.	£4,907,000	£6,936,000
Exports to U.K.	3,731,000	4,529,000

CAPITAL.—Antananarivo (population about 800,000). Other main towns are the chief port Toamasina (55,000); Mahajanga (50,000); Fianarantsoa (47,000); Antsiranana (41,000).

FLAG.—Equal horizontal bands of red (above) and green, with vertical white band by staff.

NATIONAL DAY.—June 26 (Independence Day).

BRITISH EMBASSY
(BP 167, Antananarivo)

Ambassador Extraordinary and Plenipotentiary, His Excellency David Malcolm McBain, L.V.O. (1984).
2nd Secretary, R. W. Hyde, M.B.E.
Vice-Consul (Commercial), J. A. Marcelin.

MALI
(Republic of Mali)

Secretary-General of the U.D.P.M. and President of the Government, Gen. Moussa Traore, *born* 1937, *assumed office* Nov. 20, 1968, *elected* June 19, 1979, re-elected June 9, 1985.

The Republic of Mali, an inland state in north-west Africa has an area of 465,000 square miles and a population (1982 estimate) of 7,340,000.

Formerly the French colony of Soudan, the territory elected on Nov. 24, 1958, to remain as an autonomous republic within the French Community. It associated with Senegal in the Federation of Mali which was granted full independence on June 20, 1960. The Federation was effectively dissolved on

August 22 by the secession of Senegal. The title of the Republic of Mali was adopted on Sept. 22, 1960. The Republic rejoined the CFA franc zone on June 1, 1984 when measures were taken to convert the *Franc Malien* at the rate of 2*FM*:1 *Franc CFA*.

Government.—The *régime* of Modibo Keita was overthrown on Nov. 19, 1968, by a group of Army officers who formed a National Liberation Committee and appointed a Prime Minister. Moussa Traore assumed the functions of Head of State. A new civil constitution to come into being in 1979 was approved in a national referendum on June 21, 1974. The new government formed on May 4, 1978 contained a majority of civilians. On June 19, 1979, elections were held for an 82-member National Assembly. Presidential elections held on the same day confirmed Traore as President.

Mali's principal exports are groundnuts (raw and processed), cotton fibres, meat and dried fish. The principal rivers are the Niger and the Senegal.

Trade with UK.

	1983	1984
Imports from UK.	£15,856,000	£5,471,000
Exports to U.K.	3,833,000	5,646,000

G.N.P. per capita in 1980 was estimated at U.S.$190.

CAPITAL.—Bamako (600,000). Other towns are Gao, Kayes, Mopti, Sikasso, Segou and Timbuktu (all regional capitals).

FLAG.—Vertical stripes of green (by staff), yellow and red. NATIONAL DAY.—September 22.

BRITISH EMBASSY
British Ambassador (resident at Dakar, Senegal).

MAURITANIA
(Islamic Republic of Mauritania)

President, Col. Moaouia Ould Sidi Mohamed Taya, took power Dec. 12, 1984 (*also holds portfolios of Prime Minister and Defence*).
Foreign Affairs and Co-operation, Maj. Ahmed Ould Minnih.
Interior, Lt. Col. Djibril Ould Abdallah.
Justice and Islamic Affairs, Mafoud Ould Murabit.
Finance and Commerce, Lt. Col. Ann Amadou Babaly.
Planning and Territorial Development, Mohamed Salem Ould Lekhal.
Fisheries and Maritime Economy, Taki Ould Sidi.
Mines and Economy, Maj. Mohamed Mahmoud Ould Deh.
Equipment and Transport, Ba Mahmoud.
National Education, Hassiny Ould Didi.
Civil Service, Cadre Training, Youth and Sports, Camara Ali Gueladio.
Energy and Water, Mohamed Fadel Ould Da.
Rural Development, Messmoud Ould Belkhair.
Health and Social Welfare, Djibo Tafsirou.
Information, Posts and Telecommunications, Culture, Ahmed Ould Ghnahallah.
Sec.-Gen. to the Government, Selmouth Ould Mohamed Wane.

Mauritania lies on the north-west coast of Africa immediately to the north of Senegal. It is bounded on the east by the Republic of Mali. To the north it is bounded by Morocco and the Western Sahara. Mauritania and Morocco took possession of that territory in February 1976 when Spain formally relinquished all right to it and in April 1976 agreed on a new frontier dividing the territory between them. In August 1979, Mauritania relinquished all claim to the southern sector of the Western Sahara after a three-year war against the Polisario front guerrilla army. Area 419,000 sq. miles. The population was estimated at 1,730,000 in 1982. (For MAP, *see* above.) The Republic of Mauritania elected on November 28, 1958, to remain within the French Community as an autonomous republic. It became fully independent on Nov. 28, 1960. In 1972 Mauritania broke with the franc zone and established its own unit of currency, the *Ougiya*, equal in value to 5 *francs CFA*.

Mauritania's main source of potential wealth lies in rich deposits of iron ore around Zouérate, in the north of the country. Exports began in 1963, via a railway laid for the purpose from the mine to the port of Nouadhibou. The deposits are being exploited under the aegis of the *Société Nationale Industrielle Miniere* following the nationalization in 1974 of the internationally based company MIFERMA. There are copper deposits at Akjoujt which are being exploited by SOMIMA, a company nationalized on Feb. 25, 1975; the mine was closed in 1978, but reopened in 1981.

Trade with U.K.

	1983	1984
Imports from U.K.	£1,719,000	£2,656,000
Exports to U.K.	6,044,000	10,343,000

G.N.P. per capita in 1980 was estimated at U.S.$320.

FLAG.—Yellow star and crescent on green ground.
NATIONAL DAY.—November 28.
CAPITAL.—Nouakchott (500,000).
British Ambassador, (Resident at *Dakar, Senegal*).

MEXICO
(Estados Unidos Mexicanos)

President (1982–88), Lic. Miguel de la Madrid Hurtado, *elected*, 4 July 1982, *took office*, 1 Dec. 1982.

THE CABINET

Interior, Sr. Manuel Bartlett Diaz.
Foreign Affairs, Sr. Bernardo Sepúlveda Amor.
Finance and Public Credit, Sr. Jesús Silva Herzog Flores.
Defence, Gen. Juan José Arévalo Gardoqui.
Navy, Adm. Miguel Angel Gómez Ortega.
Budget and Planning, Sr. Carlos Salinas de Gortari.
Energy, Mines and Parastatal Industries, Sr. Francisco Labastida Ochoa.
Trade and Industrial Development, Sr. Héctor Hernández Cervantes.
Agriculture and Water Resources, Sr. Eduardo Pesqueira Olea.
Communications and Transport, Sr. Daniel Diaz Diaz.
Education, Sr. José Miguel González Avelas.
Urban Development and Ecology, Sr. Guillermo Carillo Arena.
Health, Dr. Guillermo Soberón Acevedo.
Labour and Social Security, Sr. Arsenio Farell Cubillas.
Agrarian Reform, Sr. Luis Martinez Villacaña.
Tourism, Sr. Antonio Enríquez Savignac.
Fisheries, Sr. Pedro Ojeda Paullada.
Attorney-General, Sr. Sergio García Ramírez.
Attorney-General of Federal District, Sra. Victoria Adato de Ibarra.
Comptroller-General, Sr. Francisco Rojas.

MEXICAN EMBASSY IN LONDON
8 Halkin St., SW1X 7DW
[01–235 6393]

Ambassador Extraordinary and Plenipotentiary, His Excellency Francisco Cuevas-Cancino (1983).

Area and Population.—Mexico occupies the southern part of the continent of North America, with an extensive seaboard to both the Atlantic and Pacific Oceans, extending from 14° 33′ to 32° 43′ N. lat. and 86° 46′ to 117° 08′ W. long., and comprising one of the

most varied zones in the world. It contains 31 states and the federal district of Mexico, making in all 32 political divisions, covering an area of 761,604 square miles. At the 1980 Mexican General Census, the total population was 67,383,000, but a present day estimate is 76·8 million.

The two great ranges of North America, the Sierra Nevada and Rocky Mountains, are prolonged from the north to a convergence towards the narrowing isthmus of Tehuantepec, their course being parallel with the west and east coasts. The surface of the interior consists of an elevated plateau between the two ranges, with steep slopes both to the Pacific and Atlantic (Gulf of Mexico). In the west is the peninsula of Lower California, with a mountainous surface, separated from the mainland by the Gulf of California. The Sierra Nevada, known in Mexico as the *Sierra Madre*, terminates in a transverse series of volcanic peaks, from Colima on the west to Citlaltepetl ("El Pico de Orizaba") on the east. The low-lying lands of the coasts form the *Tierra Caliente*, or tropical regions (below 3,000 ft.), the higher levels form the *Tierra Templada*, or temperate region (from 3,000 to 6,000 ft.), and the summit of the plateau with its peaks is known as *Tierra Fria*, or cold region (above 6,000 ft.). The only considerable rivers are the *Rio Grande del Norte* which forms part of the northern boundary, and is navigable for about 70 miles from its mouth in the Gulf of Mexico, and the *Rio Grande de Santiago*, the *Rio Balsas* and *Rio Papaloapan*. The remaining streams are governed by the formation of the land, and run in mountain torrents between deep-cut cañons or "barrancas". The largest fresh-water lakes are *Chapala* (70 miles long and 20 miles wide), and *Pátzcuaro*. In the north-west are saline lakes amid bare and dry regions. The climate varies according to the altitude, the rainy season lasting from June to October.

History and Archæology.—The present Mexico and Guatemala were once the centre of a remarkable indigenous civilization, which had unknown beginnings in the centuries before Christ, flowered in the periods from A.D. 500 to 1100 and A.D. 1300 to 1500 and collapsed before the little army of Spanish adventurers under Hernán Cortés in the years following 1519. Pre-Columbian Mexico was divided between different but connected Indian cultures, each of which has left distinctive archæological remains: the best-known of these are Chichén Itzá, Uxmal, Bonampak and Palenque, in Yucatán and Chiapas (Maya); Teotihuacon, renowned for the Pyramid of the Sun (216 feet high) in the Valley of Mexico (Teotihuacáno); Monte Albán and Mitla, near Oaxaca (Zapotec); El Tajín in the State of Veracruz (Totonac); and Tula in the

State of Hidalgo (Toltec). The last and most famous Indian culture of all, the Aztec, based on Tenochitlán suffered more than the others from the Spaniards and only very few Aztec monuments remain.

A few years after the Conquest, the Spaniards built Mexico City on the ruins of Tenochitlán, and appointed a Viceroy to rule their new dominions, which they called New Spain. The country was largely converted to Christianity, and a distinctive colonial civilization, representing a marriage of Indian and Spanish traditions, developed and flourished, notably in architecture and sculpture. In 1810 a revolt began against Spanish rule. This was finally successful in 1821, when a precarious independence was proclaimed. Friction with the United States in Texas led to the war of 1845–48, at the end of which Mexico was forced to cede the northern provinces of Texas, California and New Mexico. In 1862 Mexican insolvency led to invasion by French forces which installed Archduke Maximilian of Austria as Emperor. The empire collapsed with the execution of the Emperor in 1867 and the austere reformer, Juárez, restored the republic. Juárez's death was followed by the dictatorship of Porfirio Diaz, which saw an enormous increase of foreign, particularly British and United States, investment in the country. In 1910 began the Mexican Revolution which reformed the social structure and the land system, curbed the power of foreign companies and ushered in the independent industrial Mexico of today.

Government.—Under the Constitution of Feb. 5, 1917 (as subsequently amended), Congress consists of a Senate of 64 members, elected for six years, and of a Chamber of Deputies, at present numbering 400, elected for three years. Presidents, who wield full executive powers, are elected for six years; they cannot be re-elected.

There are nine political parties registered in Mexico, of which by far the largest and most influential is the *Partido Revolucionario Institucional* (P.R.I.) which has for many years constituted the governing party. The Mexican Communists allied with several like-minded smaller parties to form the Mexican United Socialist Party (P.S.U.M.) in 1982.

Communications.—Veracruz, Tampico and Coatzacoalcos are the chief ports of the Atlantic, and Guaymas, Mazatlán, Puerto Lázaro Cárdenas, Acapulco, Salina Cruz and Puerto Madero on the Pacific. Work is proceeding on the reorganization and re-equipment of the whole system; help in this has been forthcoming from the World Bank, the Export-Import Bank and private sources in the United States. The railways were completely nationalized in 1970.

Mexico City may be reached by at least three highways (with 14 entry points) from the United States, and work is complete on roads southward from Mexico City to Yucatán as well as on two principal highways to the Guatemalan border (with three entry points).

International telegraph services to the United States frontier are provided by the government-owned Mexican Telegraph Company and then through the United States to Canada and Europe.

Teléfonos de México, a state-controlled company, controls about 98 per cent of all telephone services. Satélite Latinoamericano, S.A. (SATELAT) is a joint government/private sector venture disseminating television programmes to Latin America through Intelstat IV satellite facilities leased by the Mexican Government.

There is a good national and international network of air services. There are 1,113 airports and landing fields in Mexico, of which eighteen are equipped to handle long-distance flights. There are 166 airline companies, including two of the major national airlines—*Mexicana de Aviación* and *Aeroméxico.* Passenger traffic is growing by about 14 per cent

yearly, while cargo is increasing by a similar percentage.

Production.—The principal agricultural crops are maize, beans, rice, wheat, sugar cane, coffee, cotton, tomatoes, chili, tobacco, chick-peas, groundnuts, sesame, alfalfa, vanilla, cocoa and many kinds of fruit, both tropical and temperate. The maguey, or Mexican cactus, yields several fermented drinks, mezcal and tequila (distilled) and pulque (undistilled). Another species of the same plant supplies sisal-hemp (henequen). The forests abound in mahogany, rosewood, ebony and chicle trees.

The principal industries (apart from agriculture) are mining and petroleum, but during recent years there has been very considerable expansion of both light and heavy industries. The steel industry has expanded steadily and produced 7,508,700 tons of steel in 1984. The mineral wealth is great, and principal minerals are gold, silver, copper, lead, zinc, quicksilver, iron and sulphur. Substantial reserves of uranium have been found. In the non-metals sector, Mexico continues to produce 25 per cent of the world's supply of fluorspar.

The total proven petroleum reserves were 72 billion barrels in 1983. Crude oil production is currently about 2,600,000 barrels. Daily production of natural gas is approximately 3 billion cubic feet. Oil reserves have increased substantially due to very important new discoveries in the Gulf of Campeche. A new refinery at Tula, State of Hidalgo is the nation's largest; and new refineries in Monterrey, State of Nuevo Leon, and Salina Cruz, State of Oaxaca, are under construction.

Textile production is led by the artificial fibres sector, which comprised 66 per cent. of the industry's output in 1983. A dramatic recession in the textile industry followed the 1982 economic crisis but 1984 saw the start of a recovery.

Defence.—Supreme command is vested in the President, exercised through the Ministries of Defence (for Army and Air Force) and Marine.

The country is divided into 35 zones in which the regular army (120,000) and part-time conscripts (250,000) are trained. The Army in 1984 had three HQ Brigades, three Artillery Regiments, 25 Cavalry Regiments, Transport, Engineering and Signals Regiments, and 67 Infantry Battalions. To combat illiteracy in the Army, literacy programmes have been established in regular and conscript groups.

The Navy has a strength of about 23,000 officers and men including the Naval Air Force and Marines. It is equipped with four destroyers, six frigates, six OPVs, 19 corvettes, 17 minesweepers, 31 coastal craft patrol; 12 inshore and river patrol boats, 13 transports and tugs, and one sail training ship. Many vessels are non-operational. The Marine Infantry has 10 battalions (4,300 officers and men). The Naval Air Force consists of four squadrons and 49 aircraft.

The Air Force has an approximate strength of 5,500 officers and men and 298 aircraft, including tactical/training aircraft, reconnaissance aircraft/helicopters and transport aircraft. There is a Parachute Brigade consisting of three Parachute battalions (approx. 2,000 men).

Language and Literature.—Spanish is the official language of Mexico and is spoken by about 95 per cent of the population. In addition to Spanish, there are five basic groups of Indian languages spoken in Mexico. The 1970 Census showed that of the 3,111,415 inhabitants speaking an Indian language, 25·7 per cent spoke Náhuatl; 14·6 per cent Maya; 9·1 per cent Zapotec; 7·1 per cent Otomí; 7·5 per cent Mixtec and 36 per cent one or other of the 59 dialects derived from these basic languages.

Education.—Education is divided into primary, secondary, preparatory and university. Primary education is free, secular and nominally compulsory.

Trade with U.K.

	1983	1984
Imports from U.K......	£95,673,513	£150,126,000
Exports to U.K.	160,977,775	175,487,000

Imports consist largely of machinery and equipment for industry, mining and agriculture, engines, vehicle components and chemicals. Principal exports are oil, silver, gold, molybdenum, honey, tropical fruits and nuts, polyesters and yarns, and office equipment.

CAPITAL.—Mexico City, metropolitan area 16,000,000 (est. pop.). Other cities (est. pop. 1980) are: Guadalajara (4,371,998); Monterrey (2,513,044); León (3,006,110); Puebla (3,347,685); Mexicali (1,177,886); Chihuahua (2,005,477); San Luis Potosí (1,673,893); and Mérida (1,063,733).

FLAG.—Three vertical bands in green, white, red, with the Mexican emblem (an eagle on a cactus devouring a snake) in the centre.

NATIONAL DAY.—September 16 (Proclamation of Independence).

BRITISH EMBASSY
Calle Río Lerma 71, Colonia Cuauhtémoc,
06500 Mexico City, D.F.

Ambassador Extraordinary and Plenipotentiary, His Excellency Sir Cynlais Morgan James, K.C.M.G. (1983).

There are British Consular Offices at *Mexico City, Acapulco, Mérida, Monterrey, Tampico* and *Cuidad Juarez.*

British Council Representative.—R. Watkins, Maestro Antonio Caso 127, Col. San Rafael (P.O. Box 30-588), Mexico 4, D.F.

BRITISH CHAMBER OF COMMERCE, British Trade Centre, Rio Tiber 103–60, Mexico 5 D.F.—*Manager*, T. King.

Transit from London to Mexico City:—By air, 13 hours; By sea, U.K.–New York, 5 to 10 days; New York–Mexico City, by rail, 3 days; by air, 4 hours. There is a direct freight service from Liverpool to ports on both the Mexican Gulf and the Pacific Coast.

MONACO
(Principauté de Monaco)

Sovereign Prince, H.S.H. Rainier III-Louis-Henri-Maxence Bertrand, *born* May 31, 1923, *succeeded his grandfather* (H.S.H. Prince Louis II), May 9, 1949; *married* April 19, 1956, Miss Grace Patricia Kelly (died Sept. 14, 1982) and *has issue* Prince Albert Alexandre Louis Pierre, *born* March 14, 1958, Princess Caroline Louise Marguerite, *born* January 23, 1957; and Princess Stephanie Marie Elisabeth, *born* Feb. 1, 1965.

President of the Crown Council, M. Jean-Charles Marquet.

President of the National Council, M. Jean-Charles Rey.

Minister of State, Jean Herly, *appointed* 1979.

CONSULATE-GENERAL IN LONDON
4 Audley Square, W1Y 5DR
[01–629 0734]

Consul-General, I. S. Ivanovic.
Consul, A. J. Hucker, 5–6 Raymond Buildings, Gray's Inn, WC1R 5BZ [01–242 8404].

A small Principality on the Mediterranean, with land frontiers joining France at every point, and consisting of the old town of Monaco, La Condamine, Fontvielle and Monte Carlo, where is the famous casino. The Principality comprises a narrow strip of country about 2 miles long (area approx. 467 acres),

with approximately 28,000 inhabitants (1983) and a yearly average of over 1,000,000 visitors.

The principality, ruled by the Grimaldi family since the late 13th century, was abolished during the French Revolution and re-established in 1815 under the protection of the Kingdom of Sardinia. In 1861 Monaco came under French protection. The 1962 Constitution, which can be modified only with the approval of the National Council, maintains the traditional hereditary monarchy and guarantees freedom of association, trade union freedom and the right to strike. Legislative power is held jointly by the Prince and a uni-cameral, 18 member National Council elected by universal suffrage. Executive power is exercised by the Prince and a four-member Council of Government, headed by a Minister of State. The judicial code is based on that of France.

The whole available ground is built over, so that there is no cultivation, though there are some notable public and private gardens. Monaco has a small harbour (30 ft. alongside quay) and the import duties are the same as in France.

CAPITAL.—Monaco-ville (1,443).

FLAG.—Two equal horizontal stripes, red over white.

H.M. Consul-General, D. A. S. Gladstone (*Resident at Marseilles*).

MONGOLIA
(Mongolian People's Republic—
Bugd Nairamdakh Mongol Ard Uls)

President: J. Batmunkh.
Prime Minister: D. Sodnom.

Mongolian People's Revolutionary
(= *Communist*) Party

Politbureau of the Central Committee, J. Batmunkh; D. Molomjamts; T. Ragchaa; B. Altangerel; D. Gombojav; B. Dejid; T. Namsrai; D. Sodnom (*full members*); N. Jagvaral; S. Luvsangombo (*candidate members*).

Secretariat of the Central Committee, J. Batmunkh (*1st*); D. Molomjamts; D. Gombojav; P. Damdin; M. Dash; Ts. Namsrai; T. Balkhaajav.

MONGOLIAN EMBASSY
7 Kensington Court, W8 5DL
[01–937 0150]

Ambassador Extraordinary and Plenipotentiary, His Excellency Jambalyn Banzar (1984).
Attaché, T. O. Munkhsaikhan.

Area and Population.—The Mongolian People's Republic (Mongolia) is a large and sparsely populated country to the north of China. Its area is over 600,000 square miles. Its population (Dec. 1984) is about 1,866,300. However, this total constitutes only part of the Mongolians of Asia, a number of whom are to be found in China and in the neighbouring regions of the Soviet Union (especially the Mongolian Buryat Autonomous Region). This country, which is almost nowhere below 1,000 metres above sea level, forms part of the Central Asiatic Plateau and rises towards the west in the high mountains of the Mongolian Altai and Khanggai Ranges. The Khentai Mountain Range, situated to the north-east of the capital Ulan Bator, is less high. The Gobi region covers much of the southern half of the country. It contains some sand deserts, but between these less hospitable areas there is semi-desert which provides pasture for great numbers of sheep, goats, camels and horses (the latter is still the characteristic means of transport for the rural population) and some cattle. In the steppe areas to the north pasturage is better and livestock more abundant. Even further north, in the better watered provinces, grain, fodder and vegetable crops are increasingly grown. There are several long rivers and many lakes, but good water is scarce since much of the lake water is salty. The climate is hard, with a short mild summer giving way to a long winter when temperatures can drop as low as minus 50° Centigrade.

History.—Mongolia, under Genghis Khan the conqueror of China and much of Asia, was for many years a buffer state between Tsarist Russia and China, although it was under general Chinese suzerainty. The outbreak of the Chinese Revolution in 1911 led to a declaration of autonomy under Chinese suzerainty which was confirmed by the Sino-Russian Treaty of Kiakhta (1915), but cancelled by a unilateral Chinese declaration in 1919. Later the country became a battleground of the Russian Civil War, and Soviet and Mongolian troops occupied Ulan Bator in 1921: this was followed by another declaration of independence. However, in 1924 the Soviet Union in a Treaty with China again recognized the latter's sovereignty over Mongolia; but this was never properly exercised because of China's preoccupation with internal affairs, and later by the anti-Japanese war. The Mongolian People's Republic was formally established in 1924. Under the Yalta Agreement, Chiang Kai-shek agreed to a plebiscite, held in 1945, in which the Mongolians declared their desire for independence and this was formally recognized by Nationalist China. The country entered the United Nations in 1961. The heroes of Mongolian history during the earlier part of the century were Sukhebator, who died in 1923, and the Communist Choibalsan (died 1952), who did much to turn the country into the Communist state it is today, and carried out a systematic destruction of the power of the Lamas and the old princely houses which had previously been the dominant force in both the economy and the government.

Production, etc.—The total of Mongolia's livestock was 23 million in 1984. Traditionally the Mongolian is a herdsman, tending his flock of sheep, goats and horses, cows and camels and leading a totally nomadic life. With the coming of the Communist régime (under the Mongolian People's Revolutionary Party) and especially since 1952, great efforts have been made to settle the population, but a large proportion still live nomadically or semi-nomadically in the traditional *ger* (circular tent). The pastoral population was collectivized at the end of the 1950s into huge *negdels* (co-operatives) and State farms which have hastened the process of settlement, but within these the herdsmen and their families still move with their *gers* from pasture to pasture as the seasons change. The country, and three city districts (Ulan Bator, Darkhan and Erdenet), is today divided into 18 *aimaks* (provinces) and beneath these into 258 *somons* (districts), and these form the basis of the State organization of the country, parallel with which runs the apparatus of the Revolutionary Party.

Membership of the Communist bloc has brought Mongolia considerable quantities of aid from other Socialist countries, especially Czech, Polish and East German aid to supplement the massive assistance from the Soviet Union. Soviet and Bloc aid is hastening the process of industrialization; for although the economy remains predominantly based on the herds of animals, and the principal exports of the country are still animal by-products (especially wool, hides and furs) and cattle, factories serving the needs of the country have been started up and the coal and electricity industries are being developed to provide an industrial base. A joint Mongolian/Soviet enterprise for copper and molybdenum mining was opened in 1978, at Erdenet in northern Mongolia. It is now in full production and processes 16 million tonnes of ore annually. A major geological survey is

being carried out by the CMEA countries, in order to prepare for the extraction of the considerable mineral deposits known to exist in Mongolia. Coal production in 1980 was 4·5 million tons and was expected to rise to 6·8 million tons by 1985.

Ulan Bator, which contains almost a quarter of the country's population, is the main seat of industry. The second largest industrial centre is at Darkhan, north of the capital, near the Soviet frontier. Its industries include lime, cement and building materials, a flour mill and a power station. Choibalsan, in the east, is also being developed industrially. Agriculture, formerly little practised, is now being extended. Average cereal production for 1976–80 was 347,000 tons, but by 1983 had risen to 800,000 tonnes. Communication is still difficult in the country as there are very few tarmac roads. The trans-Mongolian railway, following the line of the old north-south trade route, was opened in 1955 and links Mongolia with both China and Russia. Mongolia's fundamental difficulty is its very small population and labour force.

Foreign trade is dominated by the Soviet Union, with the eastern European countries taking most of what is left. Trade with western countries and Japan is developing slowly.

Trade with U.K.

	1983	1984
Imports from U.K........	£242,000	£100,000
Exports to U.K.	1,350,000	4,561,000

CAPITAL.—Ulan Bator. (Pop. 480,000.)

FLAG.—Vertical tri-colour red, blue, red and in the hoist the traditional Soyombo symbol in gold.

NATIONAL DAY.—July 11 (Anniversary of the Mongolian People's Republic).

BRITISH EMBASSY
30 Enkh Taivny Gudamzh (P.O. Box 703)
Ulan Bator 13

Ambassador Extraordinary and Plenipotentiary, His Excellency Allan Geoffrey Roy Butler (1984).
2nd Secretary, N. A. S. Jones.
Attachés, W. Hampson; A. C. Campbell.

MOROCCO
(Kingdom of Morocco)

King, H.M. King Hassan II (Moulay Hassan Ben Mohammed), *born* July 9, 1929; *acceded* February 26, 1961, *on the death of his father,* King Mohammad V. *Heir,* Crown Prince Sidi Mohamed, *b.* August 21, 1963.

CABINET

Prime Minister, Mohamed Karim Lamrani.
Ministers of State, Hadj M'hamid Bahnini; Moulay Ahmed Alaoui.
Justice, Moulay Mustapha Belarbi Alaoui.
Interior, Driss Basri.
Foreign Affairs, Co-operation and Information, Abdellatif Filali.
Religious Endowments and Islamic Affairs, Abdelkebir Alaoui M'Daghri.
Equipment, Training of Cadres and Professional Training, Mohamed Kabbaj.
National Education, Dr. Azzedine Laraki.
Finance, Abdellatif Jouahri.
Tourism, Moussa Saadi.
Traditional Industry and Social Affairs, Mohamed Labied.
Transport, Mohamed Bouamoud.
Energy and Mines, Mohamed Fettah.
Health, Tayeb Bencheikh.
Youth and Sport, Abdellatif Semlali.

Fisheries and Merchant Shipping, Bensalem Smili.
Secretary General of the Government, Abbès Kaissi.
Culture, Mohamed Benaissa.
Environment, Abderrahmane Boufettass.
Posts and Telecommunications, Mohamed Laensar.
Agriculture and Agricultural Reform, Othman Demnati.
Trade and Industry, Tahar Masmoudi
Employment, Hassan Abbadi.
Prime Minister's Office, Azeddine Guessous (*Relations with E.C.*); Moulay Zine Zahidi (*Economic Affairs*); Khali Hanna Ould Errachid (*Development of the Sahara Provinces*); Rachidi Ghazouani (*the Plan*); Tahar Afifi (*Relations with Parliament*); Abderrahim Ben Abdeljalil (*Administrative Affairs*).

EMBASSY OF THE KINGDOM OF MOROCCO AND
CONSULATE
49 Queen's Gate Gardens, SW7 5NE
[01–581 5001]

Ambassador Extraordinary and Plenipotentiary, His Excellency Mohamed-Mehdi Benabdeljalil (1982).
Military, Naval and Air Attaché, Col. Mustapha Jabrane.

Area and Population.—Morocco is situated in the north-western corner of the African continent between latitude 27° 40′–36° N. and longitude 1°–13° W. with an area estimated at approximately 180,000 sq. miles, and a population (1982) of 20,419,555. It is traversed in the north by the Rif Mountains and in a general S.W. to N.E. direction, by the Middle Atlas, the High Atlas, the Anti-Atlas and the Sarrho ranges. The northern flanks of the Middle and High Atlas Mountains are well wooded but their southern slopes, exposed to the dry desert winds, are generally arid and desolate, as are the whole of the Anti-Atlas and Sarrho ranges. The north-westerly point of Morocco is the peninsula of Tangier which is separated from the continent of Europe by the narrow strait of Gibraltar. The Jebel Mousa dominates the promontory and, with the rocky eminence of Gibraltar, was known to the ancients as the *Pillars of Hercules,* the western gateway of the Mediterranean.
Western Sahara.—Formerly the Spanish Sahara, the territory was split between Morocco and Mauritania in 1976 after Spain withdrew in Dec. 1975. In 1979 Mauritania renounced its claim to its share of the territory, which was added by Morocco to its area. Morocco's annexation is being opposed by Polisario guerrillas, who want the territory to become an independent state.
Climate.—The climate of Morocco is generally good and healthy, especially on the Atlantic coast, (where

a high degree of humidity is, however, prevalent) the country being partially sheltered by the Atlas mountains from the hot winds of the Sahara. The rainy season may last from November to April. The plains of the interior are intensely hot in summer. Average summer and winter temperatures for Rabat are 81° F. and 45° F.; for Marrakesh 101° F. and 40° F. respectively.
Government.—Morocco became an independent sovereign state in 1956, following joint declarations made with France on March 2, 1956, and with Spain on April 7, 1956. The Sultan of Morocco, Sidi Mohammad ben Youssef, adopted the title of King Mohammad V.
Following serious disturbances in Casablanca in March, 1965, attempts were made by King Hassan, in consultation with all political parties, to form a government of national union. These efforts were unsuccessful and on June 7, 1965, the King proclaimed a "state of exception" and suspended Parliament. Assuming himself the office of Prime Minister, he announced the formation of a new government and indicated that constitutional changes were to follow. A revised Constitution was approved by a national referendum on July 24, 1970 and brought into effect soon after. It was superseded by another constitution, also approved by a national referendum, on March 1, 1972. This provides that not only political parties, but trade unions, chambers of commerce and professional bodies will participate in the organization of the State and representation of the people; specifies that the King is the supreme representative of the people; makes changes in the composition of the Regency Council and the Sovereign's rights and establishes a unicameral legislature. The Chamber has 306 members, 204 elected by direct universal suffrage (including 5 representing overseas workers) and 102 members elected by electoral colleges representing local government, industry, agriculture and working class groups. There were elections in Sept.–Oct 1984 and the new Parliament began its 6 year term on Oct. 12. A new government was named in April 1985 which included members of three political parties, though over half the portfolios went to non-political appointees.
Defence.—The Moroccan army, formed in 1956, is about 170,000 strong. A Moroccan air force was formed in 1959 and a navy in 1960. The armed forces possess quantities of French, Soviet and American equipment, including aircraft.
Production and Trade.—Morocco's main sources of wealth are agricultural and mineral. The present Five Year Plan (1981–85) for economic development places particular emphasis on social improvement. Other priority sectors are industrial development, agriculture and tourism. The world recession and high energy prices, coupled with a fall in the price of phosphates and poor harvests due to low rainfall pose problems for the economy.
Agriculture employs more than 40 per cent. of the working population and accounts for about 36 per cent. of Morocco's exports. The main agricultural products are cereals, citrus fruits, olives, grapes, tomatoes and vegetables. Dates and figs are also grown and exported. Cork and wood-pulp are the most important commercial forest products. Esparto grass is also produced. There is a fishing industry and substantial quantities of canned fish, mainly sardines, are exported. In 1980 3,160,500 sheep, 823,300 goats and 686,000 cattle were slaughtered in controlled abattoirs. Horses, camels, donkeys and pigs are also raised.
Morocco's mineral exports are phosphates, fluorite, barite, manganese, iron ore, lead, zinc, cobalt, copper and antimony. Production of phosphates totalled 18,562,000 tonnes in 1981, of which 15,635,500 tonnes were exported. Production of crude oil in 1981

amounted to 17,500 tonnes. There are oil refineries at Mohammedia and Sidi Kacem handling about 4 million tonnes of crude oil per year.

Morocco's main import requirements are petroleum products, motor vehicles, building materials, agricultural and other machinery, chemical products, sugar, green tea and other foodstuffs.

The trade of Morocco is chiefly with France, the U.S.A., W. Germany, Italy, the United Kingdom and Spain.

	1983
Imports	*DH*25,591 million
Exports	14,724 million

Trade with U.K.
	1983	1984
Imports from U.K.	£99,727,000	£79,850,000
Exports to U.K.	75,602,000	79,738,000

Currency.—The unit of currency is the *dirham.* Exchange rate (*see* p. 82).

The 1984 General Budget (as amended, April 26, 1984) amounted to *DH*44,000 million.

Communications.—The railway runs south from Tangier to Sidi Kacem. From this junction, one line runs eastwards through Fez to Oujda, and another continues southwards, through Rabat and Casablanca, to Marrakesh. A line running due south from Oujda skirts the Morocco-Algeria frontier and reaches Bouarfa. Moroccan railroads cover 1,250 miles and traction is electric or diesel. An extensive network of well-surfaced roads covers all the main towns in the kingdom.

Tangier is distant from London about 1,200 miles or a matter of 2 hours by air, 4 days by sea. Royal-Air-Maroc operates a service between Casablanca and London. There are air services between Tangier, Agadir (seasonal), Marrakesh and London, and also between Tangier and Gibraltar connecting with London. Royal Air Inter operates internal services. There are also regular services by many airlines with many parts of the world.

Language.—Arabic is the official language. Berber is the vernacular mainly in the mountain regions. French and Spanish are also spoken mainly in the towns. The foreign population is estimated at 61,935 (1982). The national daily press consists of 6 Arabic and 5 French newspapers.

Education.—There are government primary, secondary and technical schools. At Fez there is a theological university of great repute in the Moslem world. There is a secular university at Rabat. Schools for special denominations, Jewish and Catholic, are permitted and may receive government grants.

CAPITAL.—ΨRabat (population 518,616). Regional capitals, with municipal population figures as at 1982, are: ΨCasablanca (2,139,204); Marrakesh (439,728); Fez (448,823); Oujda (260,082); Meknes (319,783); Agadir (110,479). The towns of Fez, Marrakesh and Meknes were capitals at various times in Morocco's history.

FLAG.—Red, with green pentagram (the Seal of Solomon).

NATIONAL DAY.—March 3 (Anniversary of the Throne).

BRITISH EMBASSY
17 Boulevard de la Tour Hassan (B.P. 45), Rabat

Ambassador Extraordinary and Plenipotentiary, His Excellency Ronald Archer Campbell Byatt, C.M.G., *apptd.* 1985.

1st Secretary, R. Kinchen (*Head of Chancery/Commercial, and Consul*).

Defence Attaché, Lt.-Col. G. Latham.
Vice Consul (Tangier), W. A. T. Pulleyblank, M.B.E.

There is a British Consular/Commercial Office at *Casablanca.*

British Council Representative, J. W. Edmundson, (P.O. Box 427), 22 Avenue Moulay Youssef, Rabat.

BRITISH CHAMBER OF COMMERCE, 291 Boulevard Mohamed V, Casablanca.

MOZAMBIQUE
(Moçambique)

President, Samora Moïses Machel, *took office,* 1975, *re-elected* April 1983.

Area and Population.—The People's Republic of Mozambique lies on the east coast of Africa, and is bounded by Swaziland in the south, South Africa in the south and west, Zimbabwe in the west, Zambia and Malawi in the north-west and Tanzania in the north. It has an area of 297,657 square miles, with a population estimated at 12,600,000 (1983). The official language is Portuguese.

Government.—Mozambique, discovered by Vasco de Gama in 1498, and colonized by Portugal, achieved complete independence from Portugal on June 25, 1975. The date had been agreed in September 1974 by Portugal and *Frelimo* (*Frente de Libertação de Moçambique*), the Marxist liberation movement.

Constitution.—The country is governed by a Council of Ministers and by the Permanent Political Committee of the *Frelimo* Party; membership of these two bodies virtually overlaps. No other political parties are permitted. The principal legislative body, the People's Assembly, consists of 216 members nominated by *Frelimo.*

The basis of the economy is subsistence agriculture, but there is an industrial sector based mainly in Beira and Maputo. After giving priority to the development of collective farms and state enterprises in all sectors, the government is now encouraging the private sector and foreign investment, particularly in agriculture and consumer goods production. Main exports are sugar, cashew nuts, copra, cotton, tea and sisal. There are substantial coal deposits in Tete province. Mozambique has a range of aid and cooperation agreements with a number of countries in Eastern Europe and in the West. An agreement of non-aggression and good neighbourliness with South Africa was signed on March 16, 1984 (the Nkomati Accord).

Trade with U.K.
	1983	1984
Imports from U.K.	£28,618,000	£15,671,000
Exports to U.K.	9,176,000	8,589,000

CAPITAL.—Ψ Maputo (pop. 850,000). Other main ports are Beira and Nacala.

FLAG.—From top left corner, diagonal bands of green, red, black and yellow separated by white stripes, and in top left quadrant a cog-wheel enclosing a book over which is superimposed a crossed rifle and hoe, and on the right a red star.

BRITISH EMBASSY
C.P. 55, Av. V. I. Lenine, 310, Maputo.

Ambassador Extraordinary and Plenipotentiary, His Excellency E. V. Vines, C.M.G., O.B.E.

1st Secretary, John W. Guy (*Head of Chancery and Consul*).

2nd Secretaries, A. Featherstone; R. F. Terry.

NEPAL

Sovereign, H.M. King Birendra Bir Bikram Shah Dev, *born* 1945; *succeeded* January 31, 1972; *crowned* Feb. 24, 1975; *married*, Feb. 1970, H.M. Queen Aishwara Rajya Laxmi Devi Shah. *Heir*, H.R.H. Crown Prince Dipendra Bir Bikram Shah Dev, *born*, June 27, 1971.

COUNCIL OF MINISTERS

Prime Minister and Minister for Palace Affairs and Defence, Lokendra Bahadur Chand.
Home Affairs and Local Administration, Jog Meher Shrestha.
Panchayat and Local Development, Forests and Soil Conservation, Narayan Dutta Bhatta.
Water Resources and Supply, Pashupati Shumsher Rana.
Commerce and Local Supply, Parshu Narayan Chaudhary.
Health, Rudra Prasad Giri.
Agriculture and Land Reform, Hem Bahadur Malla.
Foreign Affairs and Education, Randhir Subba.
Public Works and Transport, Shri Prasad Budathoki.
Finance, Prakesh Chandra Lohani.
Communications and Industry, Padma Sunder Lawati.

ROYAL NEPALESE EMBASSY IN LONDON
12A, Kensington Palace Gardens, W8 4QU
[01-229 1594/6231]

Ambassador Extraordinary and Plenipotentiary, His Excellency Ishwari Raj Pandey (1983).
1st Secretary, Prabal S. J. B. Rana, c.v.o.
Military Attaché, Lt.-Col. C. B. Gurung.
Attaché, Baikuntha Prasad Aryal.

Area and Population.—Nepal lies between India and the Tibet Autonomous Region of China on the slopes of the Himalayas, and includes Mount Everest (29,028 feet). It has a total area of 54,362 square miles and a population estimated at about 16 million. The country comprises three distinct horizontal formations. In the south, joining the Indian plains, is the Terai, a fair proportion of which was covered with jungle. It has recently been more widely cultivated but wild life is preserved in parts. The region represents 10 per cent of the total land area and nearly 40 per cent of the population live there. The central belt of the country is hilly, but with many fertile valleys, leading up to the snowline at about 14,000 feet. The hills account for 60 per cent of the area of the country and about 50 per cent of the population. The remainder of the country consists of high mountains which are sparsely inhabited. The country is drained by three great river systems rising within and beyond the Himalayan mountain ranges and eventually flowing into the Ganges in India.
The inhabitants are of mixed stock, with Mongolian characteristics prevailing in the North and Indian in the south. The official religion is Hinduism but there is also a strong Buddhist adherence. Gautama Buddha was born in Nepal.
History and Government.—The country was originally divided into numerous hill clans and petty principalities, but Nepal emerged as a nation in the middle of the 18th Century when its component parts were unified by the warrior Raja of Gorkha, Prithvi Narayan Shah, who founded the present Nepalese dynasty. In 1846 power was seized by Jung Bahadur Rana after a massacre of nobles, and he was the first of a line of hereditary Rana Prime Ministers who ruled Nepal for 104 years. During this time the role of the Monarchs was mainly ceremonial.
In 1950–51 a revolutionary movement achieved its aim of breaking the hereditary power of the Ranas and restoring the Monarchy to its former position.

After 10 years, during which various parties and individuals tried their hand at government, the late King Mahendra proscribed all political parties and assumed direct powers on December 16, 1960, with the object of leading a united country to democracy. In 1962 he introduced a new Constitution embodying a tiered, partyless system of panchayat (council) democracy, under which there were elected councils at village level which in turn elect members to district council and thence to zonal councils; a referendum in May 1980 decided in favour of retaining the panchayat system, with some reforms; namely, election to the Rastriaya Panchayat (National Parliament) by universal adult franchise (over 21 years old); selection of the Prime Minister by the Rastriaya Panchayat and responsibility of his government to that body. The King retains certain reserve powers. In a general election in May 1981, 112 members were elected from the 75 districts of Nepal. The King appoints 28 other members, making a total of 140.
Economy.—Nepal exports jute, rice and other grains, hides, oil seeds, ghi, cattle, timber, etc., and imports cotton goods and yarns, sugar, salt, spices, petrol, metals, etc. Foreign aid supports 60 per cent of the development budget of the Kingdom and tourism is the single largest commercial earner of foreign exchange (U.S.$35 million in 1982–83).
Revenue for the fiscal year 1983–84 is estimated at *N Rps.* 4,306m; foreign aid *N Rps.* 4,000m; and internal borrowing *N Rps.* 1,216m.

Trade with U.K.

	1983	1984
Imports from U.K.	£5,011,000	£6,453,000
Exports to U.K.	6,155,000	5,564,000

A State Bank was inaugurated on April 26, 1956, to issue bank notes, regulate the Nepalese currency, fix foreign exchange rates and help in the preparation of a national budget. There are three commercial banks with branches throughout Nepal.
Communications.—Kathmandu is connected with India by a road, the mountain section of which was built by India under the Colombo Plan, and to Tibet by a road to Kodari on the border which was built by the Chinese and opened on May 26, 1967. The Indian-aided Sunauli-Pokhara road (128 miles) was inaugurated in April 1972, and a road between Pokhara and Kathmandu, constructed by the Chinese, was opened in 1973. A link road between Mugling and Naryanghat, completed by the Chinese in 1981, has further improved communications between Kathmandu and the Terai. The East–West Highway (Mahendra Raj Marg) to run the length of the country, is almost complete. Work is in progress from Butwal westwards. Sections of the highway have been built, with aid from India, Great Britain, U.S.S.R., America and the Asian Development Bank. British assistance has included the building of an external communications satellite, improving telex and telephone services, and the completion in 1984 of the mountainous Dharan-Dhankuta highway.
There are daily flights from Kathmandu to New Delhi, and frequent flights to Calcutta and Patna. There are also daily flights to Bangkok, a twice weekly direct flight to Dacca, flights from Kathmandu to Rangoon, Colombo, Hong Kong and Karachi.
CAPITAL.—Kathmandu, population (1981) 235,000. Other towns of importance are Biratnagar (94,000), Lalitpur (81,000) and Bhaktapur (50,500) and Pokhara (48,500).
FLAG.—Double pennant of crimson with blue border on peaks; white moon with rays in centre of top peak; white quarter sun, recumbent in centre of bottom peak.
NATIONAL DAY.—February 18.

BRITISH EMBASSY
(Lainchaur Kathmandu, P.O. Box 106)

Ambassador Extraordinary and Plenipotentiary, His Excellency Anthony G. Hurrell, C.M.G. (1983).
First Secretary, P. H. Roberts, O.B.E. (*Head of Chancery and Consul*).
Defence and Military Attaché, Lt.-Col. M. G. Allen.
Vice-Consul, G. E. Perkins.

British Council Representative, A. J. Pattison, (P.O. Box 640), Kanti Path, Kathmandu.

NETHERLANDS (or HOLLAND)
(Koninkrijk der Nederlanden)

Queen of the Netherlands, Her Majesty Queen Beatrix Wilhelmina Armgard, G.C.V.O., *born* Jan. 31, 1938; *married* March 10, 1966, H.R.H. Prince Claus George Willem Otto Frederik Geert of the Netherlands, Jonkheer van Amsberg; *and has issue*, Prince Willem Alexander, *b.* April 27, 1967; Prince Johan Friso, *b.* Sept, 25, 1968; Prince Constantijn Christof, *b.* Oct. 11, 1969; *succeeded*, April 30, 1980, upon the abdication of her mother Queen Juliana.

CABINET

Prime Minister and Minister of General Affairs, Ruud Lubbers (*C.D.A.*).
Deputy P.M. and Minister for Economic Affairs, Gijs van Aardenne (*V.V.D.*).
Social Affairs and Employment, and Antilles Affairs, Dr. Jan de Konig (*C.D.A.*).
Defence, Jacob de Ruiter (*C.D.A.*).
Finance, Dr. Herman Ruding (*C.D.A.*).
Transport and Waterways, Mrs. Neetie Smit-Kroes (*V.V.D.*).
Education and Science, Dr. Wim Deetman (C.D.A.).
Welfare, Public Health and Culture, Elco Brinkman (*C.D.A.*).
Development Co-operation, Mrs. Eegje Schoo (*V.V.D.*).
Agriculture and Fisheries, Gerrit Braks (*C.D.A.*).
Housing, Planning and Environment, Pieter Winsemius (*V.V.D.*).
Justice, Frits Korthals Altes, (*V.V.D.*).
Home Affairs, Koos Rietkerk, (*V.V.D.*).
Foreign Affairs, Hans van den Broek (*C.D.A.*).
(*C.D.A.* = Christian Democrats; *V.V.D.* = Liberals.)

ROYAL NETHERLANDS EMBASSY IN LONDON
38 Hyde Park Gate, SW7 5DP
[01–584 5040]

Ambassador Extraordinary and Plenipotentiary, His Excellency Jonkheer J. L. R. Huydecoper (1982).
Minister Plenipotentiary, L. W. Veenendaal.
Minister Plenipotentiary, J. W. Semeijns de Vries van Doesburgh.
Counsellors, A. J. van der Stadt; D. Vries; A. D. H. Simonsz; J. P. Kleiweg de Zwaan, C.V.O.; J. T. de Jonge.
1st Secretaries, Jonkheer M. D. Reuchlin; R. G. Brinks; C. W. Andreae; W. A. J. Alkemade.
Defence, Naval and Air Attaché, Capt. W. H. van Riet.
Military Attaché, Col. J. Smit.

Area and Population.—The Kingdom of the Netherlands is a maritime country of Western Europe, situated on the North Sea, in lat. 50° 46′–53° 34′ N. and long. 3° 22′–7° 14′ E., consisting of 11 provinces plus Eastern and Southern Flevoland (reclaimed parts of the Ysselmeer) and containing a total area of 13,500 sq. miles (34,830 sq. km). The population in Jan. 1984 was estimated at 14,394,589. The live birth

rate in Jan., 1983 was 11·8 per 1,000 of the population, and the death-rate was 8·2.

The land is generally flat and low, intersected by numerous canals and connecting rivers—in fact, a network of water courses. The principal rivers are the Rhine, Maas, Yssel and Scheldt.

Language and Literature.—Dutch is a West-Germanic language of Saxon origin, closely akin to Old English and Low German. It is spoken in the Netherlands and the northern part of Belgium. It is also used in the Netherlands Antilles. Afrikaans, one of the two South African languages, has Dutch as its origin, but differs from it in grammar and pronunciation. There are six national papers, four of which are morning papers, and there are many regional daily papers.

Government.—In 1815 the Netherlands became a constitutional Kingdom under King William I, a Prince of Orange-Nassau, a descendant of the house which had taken a leading part in the destiny of the nation since the 16th century. The States-General comprise the *Eerste Kamer* (First Chamber) of 75 members, elected for 4 years by the Provincial Council; and the *Tweede Kamer* (Second Chamber) of 150 members, elected for 4 years by men and women voters of 18 years and upwards. Members of the *Tweede Kamer* are paid.

Production.—The chief agricultural products are potatoes, wheat, rye, barley, corn, sugar beet, cattle, pigs, milk and milk products, cheese, butter, poultry, eggs, beans, peas, flax seed, vegetables, fruit, flower bulbs, plants and cut flowers and there is an important fishing industry. Among the principal industries are engineering, both mechanical and electrical, electronics, nuclear energy, petro-chemicals and plastics, shipbuilding, steel, textiles of all types, leather goods, electrical appliances, metal ware, furniture, paper, cigars, sugar, liqueurs, beer, clothing, rubber products, etc.

In 1984 the production of crude oil was 3,102 million kgs and refined oil products 62,059 million kgs; steel (1983) 4,477 million kgs, and gas (1983) 76,536 million cubic metres.

Defence.—The armed forces are almost entirely committed to NATO. All ground and air units are assigned to the NATO Central Region, and naval forces to the Atlantic and Channel commands. Total armed forces number 108,000, which includes 50,000 conscripts and 1,450 women. In addition there are over 180,000 reservists. There is compulsory military service of 14–17 months.

Education.—Primary and secondary education is given in both denominational and State schools, the denominational schools being eligible for State assistance on equal terms with the State schools. Attendance at primary school is compulsory. The principal Universities are at Leiden, Utrecht, Groningen, Amsterdam (2), Nijmegen (R.C.) and Rotterdam, and there are technical Universities at Delft (polytechnic); Eindhoven (polytechnic), Enschede (polytechnic) Wageningen (agriculture). Illiteracy is practically non-existent.

Communications.—The total extent of navigable rivers including canals, was 3,536 km. at Jan. 1, 1982, and of metalled roads 92,525 km. In 1982 the total length of the railway system amounted to 2,956 km., of which 1,799 km. were electrified. The mercantile marine in January 1981 consisted of 550 ships of total 3,417,000 gross registered tons. The total length of air routes covered by K.L.M. (Royal Dutch Airlines) in 1982 was 367,000 km.

FINANCE

	1985
Budget Revenue	D.fl. 134,900 m.
Budget Expenditure	171,700 m.

TRADE

The Dutch are traditionally a trading nation. *Entrepôt* trade, banking and shipping are of particular importance in their economy. The geographical position of the Netherlands, at the mouths of the Rhine, Meuse and Scheldt, brings a large volume of transit trade to and from the interior of Europe to Dutch ports.

Principal trading partners are the Federal Republic of Germany and Belgium/Luxemburg. U.K. supplied 8·7 per cent of Netherlands imports in 1984 and took 10 per cent of Netherlands exports.

Excluding the building industry, the index of industrial production in the Netherlands (1980 = 100) was 101 in 1984 and the index of industrial production per worker (1980 = 100) was 122 in 1984.

	1984
Imports	D.fl.198,922 m.
Exports	210,691 m.

Trade with U.K.

	1983	1984
Imports from U.K.	£5,440,701,000	£6,127,991,000
Exports to U.K.	£5,097,763,000	6,147,298,000

SEAT OF GOVERNMENT, The Hague (Den Haag or, in full, 's-Gravenhage). Pop. 449,364.

CAPITAL.—ΨAmsterdam, 687,397. Other principal cities; ΨRotterdam, 558,832; Utrecht, 230,347; Eindhoven, 192,715; Haarlem, 152,529; Groningen, 166,942; Tilburg, 153,893.

FLAG.—Three horizontal bands of red, white and blue.

BRITISH EMBASSY
Lange Voorhout, 10, The Hague, 2514 ED

Ambassador Extraordinary and Plenipotentiary, His Excellency John William Denys Margetson, C.M.G. (1984).

Counsellors, M. F. Chapman, C.V.O.; C. Wilson (*Commercial*).
Defence and Naval Attaché, Capt. B. J. Clarke, R.N.
Military and Air Attaché, Lt. Col. M. J. Woodcock.
Head of Chancery, A. R. Paul.
H. M. Consul-General, T. W. Sharp.

British Council Representative, W. E. Moss, O.B.E., Keizersgracht 343, Amsterdam (Library).

NETHERLANDS-BRITISH CHAMBER OF COMMERCE, The Dutch House, 307–308 High Holborn, WC1V 7LS; U.K. OFFICE, Holland Trade House, Bezuidenhoutseweg 181, 2594 AH The Hague.

OVERSEAS TERRITORY

The Netherlands Antilles comprise certain islands in the West Indies (Curaçao, Bonaire, Aruba, part of St. Martin, St. Eustatius, and Saba). The area of the Netherlands Antilles is 394·1 sq. miles with a population of 253,234. Under the Realm Statute which took effect on December 29, 1954, the Netherlands Antilles became an autonomous part of the Kingdom of the Netherlands, and are governed as a federation by the Governor and the federal parliament, the Staten. A conference in 1983 agreed that Aruba would achieve a status comparable to associate statehood on Jan. 1, 1986, and that during the transitional period to independence (approx. 10 years), would be part of a "Union of the Netherlands Antilles and Aruba" with a veto over legislation in the Staten.

Although there are some manufacturing industries, the economy is based almost entirely upon the refining of oil. The soil is too poor to permit large-scale agriculture and most products for consumption, and industrial raw materials must be imported.

Governor, Dr. R. A. Römer (1983).
Prime Minister, Mrs. Maria Liberia Peters (Sept. 20, 1984).

Trade with U.K.

Netherlands Antilles	1983	1984
Imports from U.K.	£84,489,000	£20,225,000
Exports to U.K.	97,486,000	221,012,000

The capital of Curaçao is ΨWillemstad (pop. over 100,000), of Aruba, ΨOranjestad; of Bonaire, Ψ Kralendijk; of St. Martin, Philipsburg; of Statius (St. Eustatius), Oranjestad; and of Saba, Bottom.

NICARAGUA

President, Sr. Daniel Ortega Saavedra, *inaugurated*, Jan. 10, 1985.
Vice-President, Sr. Sergio Ramírez Mercado.

NICARAGUAN EMBASSY IN LONDON
8 Gloucester Road, SW7 4PP
[01–584 4365]

Ambassador Extraordinary and Plenipotentiary, His Excellency Señor Francisco José d'Escoto (1981).

Nicaragua is the largest State of Central America, with a long seaboard on both the Atlantic and Pacific Oceans, situated between 10° 45′–15° N. lat. and 83° 40′–87° 38′ W. long., containing an area of 57,145 English square miles (*see index for* MAP). It has a population of 3,200,000 (1984), of whom about three-quarters are of mixed blood. Another 15 per cent are white, mostly of pure Spanish descent and the remaining 10 per cent are Indians or negroes. The latter group includes the Mosquitos, who live on the Atlantic coast and were formerly under British protection.

Government.—The eastern coast of Nicaragua was touched by Columbus in 1502, and in 1518 was overrun by Spanish forces under Davila, and formed part of the Spanish Captaincy-General of Guatemala until 1821, when its independence was secured. In 1927, Augusto Cesar Sandino began a guerrilla war against the occupation of Nicaragua by U.S. Marines, which continued until they were expelled in 1933. Sandino was assassinated by Anastasio Somoza, Director of the National Guard, and in 1936 Somoza assumed the Presidency. He was succeeded in power by his sons Luis and Anastasio Somoza, until 1979 when the family and the National Guard were overthrown by guerrillas of the Sandinista National Liberation Front. A Junta of National Reconstruction subsequently took power.

Elections for President, Vice-President and a National Assembly were held on Nov. 4, 1984, and on Jan. 10, 1985 replaced the Junta and the Council of State. Distribution of seats in the National Assembly was: Sandinista National Liberation Front 61; Democratic Conservative Party 14; Independent Liberal Party 9; People's Christian Social Party 6; Communist Party 2; Socialist Party 2; Marxist–Leninist Popular Action Movement 2.

Agriculture and Industry.—The country is mainly agricultural. The major crops are cotton, coffee (30 per cent of total export earnings), sugar cane, tobacco, sesame and bananas. Beans, rice, maize and ipecacuanha, livestock and timber production are also important. However, fishing, forestry, grain and cattle production have been hit by the civil war in the main growing areas. Nicaragua possesses deposits of gold and silver.

Communications.—There are 252 miles of railway, all on the Pacific side and approximately 5,500 miles of telegraph. There are 51 radio stations and two television stations in Managua. An automatic telephone system has been installed in the capital and extended to all major cities. A ground station for satellite communication was inaugurated in 1973. Transport except on the Pacific slope, is still attended with difficulty but many new roads have either been opened or are under construction. The Inter-American Highway runs from the Honduras frontier in the north to the Costa Rican border in the south; the interoceanic highway runs from the Corinto on the Pacific coast viá Managua to Rama, where there is a natural waterway to Bluefields on the Atlantic. The country's main airport is at Managua. The chief port is Corinto on the Pacific.

Language and Literature.—The official language of the country is Spanish and the majority profess Catholicism, although the English language and the Moravian Church are widespread on the Atlantic coast. There are 3 daily newspapers published at Managua, apart from the official Gazette (*La Gaceta*). A national literacy campaign in 1980 has reduced illiteracy to 12 per cent. There are universities at León and Managua.

Trade with U.K.

	1983	1984
Imports from U.K.	£2,367,000	£4,755,000
Exports to U.K.	1,180,000	2,176,000

Considerable quantities of foodstuffs are imported as well as cotton goods, jute, iron and steel, machinery and petroleum products. The chief exports are cotton, coffee, beef, gold, sugar, cottonseed, bananas and soluble coffee.

CAPITAL.—Managua, population 615,000. The centre was almost totally destroyed in the earthquake of December 1972. León, 158,577; Granada, 72,640; Masaya, 78,308; Chinandega, 144,291.

British Ambassador, (resident at San José, Costa Rica).

NIGER
(République du Niger)

President, Maj. Gen. Seyni Kountché, *assumed power*, April 15, 1974 (*also holds Defence and Interior portfolios*).
Prime Minister, Hamid Algabid.

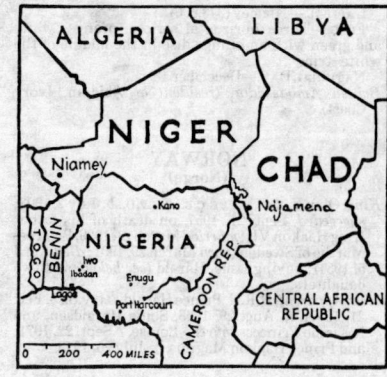

Situated in West Central Africa, between 12° and 24° N. and 0° and 16° E., Niger has common boundaries with Algeria and Libya in the north, Chad, Nigeria, Benin, Mali and Burkina Faso.

It has an area of about 458,075 square miles with a population (estimate, 1984) of 6,170,000. Apart from a small region along the Niger Valley in the south-west near the capital the country is entirely savannah or desert. The main ethnic groups are the Hausa (54 per cent.) in the south, the Songhai and Djerma in the south-west, the Fulani, the Beriberi–Manga, and the nomadic Tuareg in the north. The official language is French.

The first French expedition arrived in 1891 and the country was fully occupied by 1914. It decided on December 18, 1958, to remain an autonomous republic within the French Community; full independence outside the Community was proclaimed on August 3, 1960. Special agreements with France, covering financial and cultural matters, technical assistance, defence, etc., were signed in Paris on April 24, 1961. These are now being revised.

The constitution of Niger, adopted on November 8, 1960, provided for a presidential system of government, modelled on that of the United States and the French Fifth Republic, and a single Chamber National Assembly. In April 1974 Lt.-Col. Seyni Kountché seized power, suspended the Constitution, dissolved the National Assembly, and suppressed all political organizations. He then set up a Supreme Military Council with himself as President.

Finance.—The currency of Niger is the *Franc CFA.* The 1984–85 Budget allocated *CFA* 69,000 million for investment and *CFA* 79,900 million for current expenditure.

Trade.—The cultivation of ground-nuts and the production of livestock are the main industries and provide two of the main exports. A company formed by the Government, the French Atomic Energy Authority and private interests is exploiting uranium deposits at Arlit, and this is the main export. Value of exports in 1984 was: uranium, *CFA* 100,560 m.; livestock, *CFA* 20,200 m.; and other exports *CFA* 14,700 m.

Trade with U.K.

	1983	1984
Imports from U.K.	£9,660,000	£10,682,000
Exports to U.K.	6,854,000	391,000

CAPITAL.—Niamey (343,600).

FLAG.—Three horizontal stripes, orange, white and green with an orange disc in the middle of the white stripe.

NATIONAL DAY.—December 18.

British Ambassador, (*resident at* Abidjan, Ivory Coast).

NORWAY
(Norge)

King, Olav V, K.G., K.T., G.C.B., G.C.V.O., *b.* July 2, 1903; *succeeded*, Sept. 21, 1957, on death of his father King Haakon VII; *married* March 21, 1929, Princess Märthe of Sweden (*born* March 29, 1901; *died* April 5, 1954); having issue, Harald (*see below*) and two daughters.

Heir-Apparent, H.R.H. Prince Harald, G.C.V.O., *b.* Feb. 21, 1937; *m.* Aug. 29, 1968, Sonja Haraldsen, and has issue Princess Märthe Louise, *b.* Sept. 22, 1971; and Prince Haakon Magnus, *b.* July 20, 1973.

CABINET

Prime Minister, Kåre Willoch.
Foreign Affairs, Svenn Stray.
Finance, Rolf Presthus.
Oil and Energy, Kåre Kristiansen.
Defence, Anders C. Sjaastad.
Justice, Mona Røkke.
Industry, Jan P. Syse.
Consumer Affairs and Government Administration, Astrid Gjertsen.
Fisheries, Thor Listau.
Local Government and Labour, Arne Rettedal.
Transport and Communications, Johann J. Jakobsen.
Environment, Rakel Surlien.
Church and Education, Kjell Magne Bondevik.
Higher Education and Culture, Lars Roar Langslet.
Agriculture, Finn T. Isaksen.
Social Affairs, Leif Arne Heløe.
Commerce, Asbjørn Haugstvedt.
Development Aid, Reidun Brusletten.
(The three-party coalition of the Conservative, Centre and Christian People's parties formed the above cabinet at the time of the General Election on Sept. 9, 1985. The coalition won the election but at the time of going to press it was not known whether any changes would be made in the cabinet.)

ROYAL NORWEGIAN EMBASSY IN LONDON
Offices: 25 Belgrave Square, SW1X 8QD
[01–235 7151]

Ambassador Extraordinary and Plenipotentiary, His Excellency Rolf Busch (1982).
Minister-Counsellor, Kai Lie.
Counsellors, Jan Flatla (*Press and Cultural*); S. Remøy (*Fisheries*); B. Syvertsen, M.V.O. (*Economic*); Jan Enger (*Commercial*).
1st Secretaries, Eva Bugge (*Political*); Tore Karlsvik (*Consul*).
2nd Secretaries, Harald Neple (*Economic*); Oystein Steiro (*Press, Information and Cultural*).

Area and Population.—Norway ("The Northern Way"), a kingdom in the northern and western portion of the Scandinavian peninsula, was founded in 872. It is 1,752 km. in length, its greatest width about 430 km. The length of the coastline is 2,650 km., and the frontier between Norway and the neighbouring countries is 2,531 km. (Sweden 1,619 km., Finland 716 km. and U.S.S.R. 196 km.). It is divided into 19 counties (*fylker*) and comprises an area of 386,308 sq. km. of which Svalbard is 62,049 and Jan Mayen 372 sq. km., with a population (estimated, Jan. 1984) of 4,145,845.

The Norwegian coastline is extensive, deeply indented with numerous fiords, and fringed with an immense number of rocky islands. The surface is mountainous, consisting of elevated and barren tablelands, separated by deep and narrow valleys. At the North Cape the sun does not appear to set from the second week in May to the last week in July, causing the phenomenon known as the *Midnight Sun*; conversely, there is no apparent sunrise from about Nov. 18 to Jan. 23. During the long winter nights are seen the multiple coloured *Northern Lights* or *Aurora Borealis*, which have a maximum intensity in a line crossing North America from Alaska to Labrador and Northern Europe to the Arctic coast and Siberia.

Language and Literature.—Old Norse literature is among the most ancient and richest in Europe. Norwegian in both its present forms is closely related to other Scandinavian languages. Independence from Denmark (1814) and resurgent nationalism led to the development of "new Norwegian" based on dialects, which now has equal official standing with "bokmål", in which Danish influence is more obvious. This was formed in the time of the Reformation, and Ludvig Holberg (1684–1754) is regarded as the father of Norwegian literature, though the modern period begins with the patriotic and romantic writings of Henrik Wergeland (1808–1845). Some of the famous names are Henrik Ibsen (1828–1906), Bjørnstjerne Bjørnson (1832–1910), Nobel Prize winner in 1903, and the novelists Jonas Lie (1833–1908), Alexander Kielland (1849–1906), Knut Hamsun (1859–1952) and Sigrid Undset (1882–1949), the latter two both Nobel Prizewinners, and the latter a champion of Norwegian womanhood. In 1984 there were 163 daily newspapers.

Government.—From 1397 to 1814 Norway was united with Denmark, and from Nov. 4, 1814, with Sweden, under a personal union which was dissolved on June 7, 1905, when Norway regained complete

independence. Under the constitution of May 17, 1814, the *Storting* (Parliament) itself elects one-quarter of its members to constitute the *Lagting* (Upper Chamber), the other three-quarters forming the *Odelsting* (Lower Chamber). Legislative questions alone are dealt with by both parts in separate sittings.

Production.—The cultivated area is about 8,636 sq. km. (2·3 per cent of total surface area); forests cover nearly 25 per cent; the rest consists of highland pastures or uninhabitable mountains.

The *Gulf Stream* pours from 140 to 170 million cubic feet of warm water per second into the sea around Norway and causes the temperature to be higher than the average for the latitude. It brings shoals of herring and cod into the fishing grounds and causes a warm current of air over the west coast, making it possible to cultivate potatoes and barley in latitudes which in other countries are perpetually frozen. In normal years the quantity of fish caught by Norwegian fishing vessels is greater than that of any other European country except U.S.S.R. In 1984 the total catch amounted to 2,555,800 metric tonnes.

The chief industries are manufactures, agriculture and forestry, fisheries, mining, production of metals and ferro-alloys and shipping. Also in recent years industries providing both manufactured products and services for the development of North Sea oil and gas resources have assumed growing importance. In 1984, the total workforce was 1,920,000 of which 363,000 persons were employed in Norwegian industry. Manufactures are aided by great resources of hydro-electric power. Actual production in 1984 amounted to 106,660 million kwh.

Defence.—Norway is a member of the North Atlantic Treaty Organization, and the Headquarters of Allied Forces, Northern Europe, is situated near Oslo. The period of compulsory national service is 15 months (without refresher training) in the Navy and Air Force, and 12 months (with refresher training) in the Army. In March 1978 Norway committed an infantry battalion with additional support to the U.N. Interim Force in the Lebanon.

Education from 7 to 16 is free and compulsory in the "basic schools" maintained by the municipalities with State grants-in-aid. The majority of the pupils receive post-compulsory schooling at "upper secondary" schools, colleges of education (19) regional colleges akin to polytechnics (12), universities (4) and other university-level specialist institutions.

Communications.—The total length of railways open at the end of 1984 was 4,242 km., excluding private lines. There are 84,562 km. of public roads in Norway (including urban streets). At the end of 1984, 2,445,147 road motor vehicles were registered.

Scheduled internal air services are operated by Scandinavian Airlines System (SAS) on behalf of Det Norske Luftfartselskap (DNL), by Braathens South American and Far East Airtransport (SAFE), and by Wideróes Flyveselskap A.S.

The Mercantile Marine, 1983, consisted of 1,567 vessels of 15,914,000 gross tons (vessels above 100 gross tons, excluding fishing boats, floating whaling factories, tugs, salvage vessels, icebreakers and similar types of vessel). The fleet ranks seventh among the merchant navies of the world.

FINANCE, 1984

Total Revenue	*K*192,896 m
Total Expenditure	171,369 m

TRADE

	1983	1984
	million *Kroner*	
Total imports	152,581	172,057
Total exports	185,187	215,439

Trade with U.K.

	1983	1984
Imports from U.K.	£828,612,000	£968,404,000
Exports to U.K.	2,820,760,000	3,852,657,000

The chief imports are raw materials, motor vehicles, chemicals, motor spirit, fuel and other oils; coal, ships and machinery; together with manufactures of silk, cotton and wool. The exports consist chiefly of crude oil and gas, manufactured goods, fish and products of fish (as canned fish, whale oils), pulp, paper, iron ore and pyrites, nitrate of lime, stone, calcium carbide, aluminium, ferro-alloys, zinc, nickel, cyanamide, etc.

CAPITAL.—ΨOslo (incl. Aker). Pop. (Jan. 1983), 448,747. Other towns are ΨTrondheim, 134,652; ΨBergen, 207,232; ΨStavanger, 92,012; ΨKristiansand, 61,834; ΨDrammen, 50,605; ΨTromsø, 47,322.

FLAG.—Red, with white-bordered blue cross.

NATIONAL DAY.—May 17 (Constitution Day).

AIR TRANSIT FROM U.K.—London–Bergen or Oslo, 1 *hr.* 50 *mins.* London–Stavanger, 1 *hr.* 40 *mins.*

BRITISH EMBASSY
Thomas Heftyesgate, 8 Oslo 2.

Ambassador Extraordinary and Plenipotentiary, His Excellency Sir William Bentley, K.C.M.G.

Counsellors, D. B. C. Logan (*Head of Chancery*); A. C. Hunt, (*Economic*).

BRITISH CONSULAR OFFICES

There is a British Consular Office at *Oslo* and Honorary Consulates at *Bergen, Tromsø, Alesund, Kristiansund N., Narvik, Stavanger, Trondheim, Kristiansand S.* and *Haugesund.*

BRITISH COUNCIL

Representative, P. A. Thompson, Fridtjof Nansens Plass 5, Oslo 1.

SVALBARD
(Spitsbergen and Bear Island)

By Treaty (Feb. 9, 1920) the sovereignty of Norway over the Spitsbergen ("Pointed Mountain") Archipelago was recognized by the Great Powers and other interested nations, and on Aug. 14, 1925, Norway assumed sovereignty. In September, 1941, Allied forces (British, Canadian and Norwegian) landed on the main island. After destruction of the accumulated stocks of coal and dismantling of mining machinery and the wireless installation, the Norwegian inhabitants (about 600) were evacuated to a British port and the Russians (about 1,500) to the U.S.S.R. After the war the Norwegian mining plants were rebuilt. 288,000 metric tons of coal were extracted from Norwegian mines in Svalbard in 1980.

The Svalbard Archipelago lies between 74°–81° N. lat. and between 10°–35° E. long., with an estimated area of 24,295 square miles. The archipelago consists of a main island, known as Spitsbergen (15,200 sq. miles); North East Land, closely adjoining and separated by Hinlopen Strait; the Wiche Islands, separated from the mainland by Olga Strait; Barents and Edge Islands, separated from the mainland by Stor Fjord (or Wybe Jansz Water); Prince Charles Foreland, to the W.; Hope Island, to the S.E.; Bear Island (68 square miles) 127 miles to the S.; with many similar islands in the neighbourhood of the main group. In addition to those engaged in coal-mining, the archipelago is also visited by hunters for seal, foxes and polar bears.

South Cape is 355 miles from the Norwegian Coast. Ice Fjord is 520 miles from Tromsø, 650 miles from Murmansk, and 1,300 miles from Aberdeen. Transit from Tromsø to Green Harbour 2 to 3 days; from Aberdeen 5 to 6 days.

JAN MAYEN, an island in the Arctic Ocean (70° 49′–71° 9′ N. lat. and 7° 53′–9° 5′ W. long.) was joined to Norway by law of Feb. 27, 1930.

Norwegian Antarctic

BOUVET ISLAND (54° 26′ S. lat. and 3° 24′ E. long.) was declared a dependency of Norway by law of Feb. 27, 1930.

PETER THE FIRST ISLAND (68° 48′ S. lat. and 90° 35′ W. long.), was declared a dependency of Norway by resolution of Government, May 1, 1931.

PRINCESS RAGNHILD LAND (from 70° 30′ to 68° 40′ S. lat. and 24° 15′ to 33° 30′ E. long.) has been claimed as Norwegian since Feb. 17, 1931.

QUEEN MAUD LAND.—On Jan. 14, 1939, the Norwegian Government declared the area between 20° W. and 45° E., adjacent to Australian Antarctica, to be Norwegian territory.

OMAN
(The Sultanate of Oman)

Sultan, Qaboos Bin-Said, *succeeded* on deposition of Sultan Said bin Taimur, July 23, 1970.
(The Sultan acts as his own Prime Minister, Minister of Foreign Affairs, Defence and Finance.)

COUNCIL OF MINISTERS

Agriculture and Fisheries, H.E. Abdul Hafidh bin Salim bin Rajab.
Commerce and Industry, H.E. Col. Salim bin Abdullah al Ghazali.
Communications, H.E. Sayyid Salim bin Nasser Al Bu Saidi.
Deputy P.M., Security and Defence, H.H. Sayyid Fahr bin Taimur Al Said.
Office of the Personal Representative of H.M. The Sultan, H.H. Sayyid Thuwaini bin Shihab Al Said.
Education and Youth Affairs, H.E. Yahya bin Mahfuth al Manthari.
Electricity and Water, H.E. Khalfan bin Nasr al Wahaibai.
Environment, H.H. Sayyid Shabib bin Taimur Al Said.
Deputy P.M., Financial and Economic Affairs, H.E. Qais bin Abdul Munim al Zawawi.
Minister of State for Foreign Affairs, H.E. Yusuf bin Alawi bin Abdullah.
Health, H.E. Dr. Mubarak bin Salih al Khaduri.
Housing, H.E. Ahmad bin Abdullah al Ghazali.
Information, H.E. Abdul Aziz bin Muhammad al Rowas.
Interior, H.E. Sayyid Badr bin Saud bin Harib.
Justice, Awqaf and Islamic Affairs, H.E. Sayyid Hilal bin Hamad Al Bu Saidi.
Office of the Deputy Prime Minister for Legal Affairs, H.H. Sayyid Fahd bin Mahmoud Al Said.
National Heritage and Culture, H.H. Sayyid Faisal bin Ali Al Said.
Petroleum and Minerals, H.E. Said bin Ahmad bin Said al Shanfari.
Posts, Telegraphs and Telephones, H.E. Ahmid bin Suwaidan al Balushi.
Regional Municipalities, H.E. Brig. Sayyid al Mutassim bin Hamoud Al Bu Saidi.
Royal Diwan Affairs, H.E. Sayyid Hamad bin Hamoud.
Social Affairs and Labour, H.E. Shaikh Mustahail bin Ahmad al Mashani.
Chairman, Consultative Council of the State, H.E. Hamoud bin Abdullah al Harithi.
Office of the Minister of State and Wali of Dhofar, H.E. Sayyid Hilal bin Saud bin Harib.
President, Diwan of Royal Court Affairs, H.E. Col. Said bin Salim al Wahaibi.

First ADC to H.M. The Sultan and President of the Palace Office, H.E. Maj. Gen. Ali bin Majid al Mamari.
Acting Secretary to the Council of Ministers, H.E. Sayyid Hamoud bin Faisal Al Bu Saidi.

OMAN EMBASSY IN LONDON
44a/b Montpelier Square, SW7 1JJ
[01–584 6782/3/4]

Ambassador, His Excellency Hussain bin Mohamed bin Ali (1984).

The independent Sultanate of Oman lies at the eastern corner of the Arabian Peninsula. Its seaboard is nearly 1,000 miles long and extends from near Tibat on the west coast of the Musandam Peninsula round to Ras Darbat Ali, with the exception of the stretch between Dibba and Kalba on the east coast which belongs to Sharjah and Fujairah of the United Arab Emirates. Ras Darbat Ali marks the boundary between the Sultanate and the People's Democratic Republic of Yemen. The Sultanate extends inland to the borders of the Rub al Khali, or "Empty Quarter" of the Arabian Desert.

The area of Oman has been estimated at 120,000 sq. miles and the population at 850,000 (1982). The inhabitants of the North are for the most part Arab but along the coast there is a strong infusion of negro blood, while in the Capital Area which stretches from Muscat to Seeb there are large communities of Hindus, Khojas and Baluch, in addition to Zanzibaris of Omani origin. In Dhofar there is also an infusion of negro blood around Salalah, but in the mountains the inhabitants are either of pure Arab descent or belong to tribes of pre-Arab origin, the Qarra and Mahra, who speak their own dialects of semitic origin.

Physically and historically modern Oman can be split into two main parts, the North and the South, divided by a large tract of desert. *Northern Oman* has three main sections. The *Batinah*, the coastal plain, varies in width from 30 miles in the neighbourhood of Suwaiq to almost nothing at Muscat where the mountains descend abruptly to the sea. The plain is fertile, with date gardens extending over its full length of 150 miles. The *Hajjar*, a mountain spine running from north east to south west, reaching nearly 10,000 feet in height on Jebal Akhdar. For the most part the mountains are barren, but numerous valleys penetrate the central massif of Jabal Akhdar and in these there is considerable cultivation irrigated by wells or a system of underground canals called *falajs* which tap the water table. The two plateaus leading from the western slopes of the mountains, the *Dhahirah*, in the north and the *Sharqia* in the south east also have centres of settlements and cultivation. They fall from an average height of 1,000 feet into the sands of the Empty Quarter. The north is separated from the south by nearly 400 miles of inhospitable country crossed by one trunk road, the only land link. *Dhofar*, the southern province, is the only part of the Arabian Peninsula to be touched by the south west monsoon. Temperatures are more moderate than in the north and sugar cane and coconuts are grown on the coastal plain, while cattle are bred on the mountains.

Government.—A Consultative Council for the State was established by Sultanic decree on October 18, 1981. The Council is a nominated body consisting of 55 members (36 representing the public and 19 representing the government). The Council's jurisdiction is confined to economic affairs and social development.

Finance.—The main unit is the *Rial Omani* of 1,000 baiza.

Commerce and Trade.—Trade is mainly with the United Kingdom, Japan, the Netherlands, U.S., West

Germany, France and India. Total imports for the year 1984 were *OR*949,217,037. Chief imports were machinery, cars, building materials, refined petroleum and food and telecommunications equipment.

Trade with U.K.

	1983	1984
Imports from U.K.	£448,900,000	£390,275,000
Exports to U.K.	91,400,000	82,655,000

Production.—Petroleum Development (Oman) Ltd. (owned 60 per cent by Oman Government and 34 per cent by Shell) began exporting oil in 1967. Concessions (off and on shore) are held by several major international companies. The current level of oil production is over 470,000 barrels per day.

Development.—For many years the Sultanate was a poor country with a total annual income of less than £1,000,000. The advent of oil revenues since 1967 and the change of régime in 1970 led to the initiation of a wide-ranging development programme, especially concerned with health, education and communications. New hospitals have been completed in the main provincial centres and there are now 14 hospitals with 2,041 beds, and 455 schools, with 143,000 pupils, were in operation in 1983. A gas turbine power station operates at Rusail, where there is also a 200 plot industrial estate. There is a desalination plant near Muscat and flour, animal feed, cement and copper production facilities.

Communications.—Since 1972 ships have been using Port Qaboos at Matrah, where eight deep water berths have been constructed as part of the new harbour facilities.

The telegraph office, an automatic telephone service in Muscat and Matrah and an international telephone service are operated by the General Telecommunications Service. There are now good tarmac roads linking most main population centres of the country with the coast and with the towns of the United Arab Emirates. Major projects including a by-pass and fly-overs to ease traffic congestion in the capital should be completed by the end of 1985, when there will be 3,800 km. of asphalted road in the Sultanate.

CAPITAL.—Ψ Muscat, population (estimated), 30,000. The commercial centre has grown around Mutrah, 3 miles away and the main port, and Ruwi. The main towns on the northern coast are Sur, Khaburah and Sohar, all ports. The main town of Dhofar is Salalah, and Raysut and Murbat are the ports.

FLAG.—Red, green and white with crossed daggers in red sector.

BRITISH EMBASSY
P.O. Box 300, Muscat

Ambassador Extraordinary and Plenipotentiary, His Excellency Duncan Slater, C.M.G. (1982).
First Secretary, R. J. Dalton (*Head of Chancery and Consul*).
Defence Attaché, Col. B. M. Lees, L.V.O., O.B.E.
Naval and Air Attaché, Wg. Cdr. M. E. Williamson, O.B.E., R.A.F.
1*st Secretaries,* M. Cozens; R. French.
British Council Representative, E. K. Jones, P.O. Box 7090, Mutrah, Oman.

PAKISTAN

President, Gen. Mohammad Zia-ul-Haq, *assumed power,* July 1977; *elected,* Dec. 19, 1984.

CABINET

Prime Minister, Mohammad Khan Junejo (*also responsible for Cabinet Division, Establishment,*

Political, Science and Technology, Population, Defence).
Commerce, Petroleum and Natural Resources, Saleem Saifullah Khan.
Communications, Prince Mohyuddin Baluch.
Finance and Planning, Dr. Mahbubul Haq.
Foreign Affairs, Sahabzada Yaqub Khan.
Housing and Works, Syed Yousaf Raza Gilani.
Industries, Zafar Ali Shah.
Information and Broadcasting, Hamid Nasir Chattha.
Justice and Parliamentary Affairs, Iqbal Ahmad Khan.
Labour, Manpower and Overseas Pakistanis, Hanif Tayyab.
Local Government and Rural Development, Ghulam Muhammad Ahmad Maneka.
Production, Mohammad Khakan Abbasi.
Railways, Nawabzada Abdul Ghafoor Hoti.
Water and Power, Mir Zafarullah Khan Jamali.
Kashmir Affairs and Northern Areas and States, Frontier Region, Syed Qasim Shah.
Interior, Mohammad Aslam Khan Khattak.
Food, Agriculture and Co-operatives, Kazi Abdul Majid Abid.
Health, Special Education and Social Welfare, Malik Noor Hayat Noon.
Culture, Sports and Tourism, Lt. Gen.(retd.) Jamal Said Mian.
Education, Mian Mohammad Yasin Khan Watto.
Chairman, Senate, Ghulum Ishaq Khan.
Speaker, National Assembly, Syed Fakhar Imam.

PAKISTAN EMBASSY
35 Lowndes Square, SW1X 9JN
[01–235 2044]

Ambassador Extraordinary and Plenipotentiary, His Excellency Ali Arshad (1981).
Ministers, Mansoor Alam; Zafar Habib; Qutubuddin Aziz (*Information*).
Defence Attaché, Brig. Ayaz Ahmad.

Area and Population.—The Islamic Republic of Pakistan consists of country situated to the north-west of the Indian sub-continent, bordered by Iran, Afghanistan, the disputed territory of Kashmir and India. It covers a total area of 310,403 sq. miles. The Government of Pakistan census in 1981 showed a population figure of 83,780,000. Of these, about 95 per cent are Moslems, about 1 per cent Hindus, 3·5 per cent Christians, and 0·5 per cent Buddhists.

Running through Pakistan are five great rivers, the Indus, Jhelum, Chenab, Ravi and Sutlej. The upper reaches of these rivers are in Kashmir, and their sources in the Himalayas.

Government.—Pakistan was constituted as a Dominion under the Indian Independence Act, 1947, which received Royal Assent on July 18, 1947. In terms of the Act the Dominion of Pakistan consisted of former territories of British India. The States of Bahawalpur and Khairpur (in Punjab and Sind), with a Muslim population of almost 80 per cent and with Muslim rulers, acceded to Pakistan in October, 1947. The following States also acceded to Pakistan: the Baluchistan States of Kalat, Mekran, Las Bela and Kharan, and the North-West Frontier States of Amb, Chitral, Dir and Swat. (The States of Junagadh and Manavadar which had acceded to Pakistan were occupied by India on November 8, 1947.) Boundaries of the Provinces of East Bengal and of Punjab (West Punjab) were defined by a Boundary Commission. Thus, until 1972, when East Pakistan seceded Pakistan consisted of two geographical units, West and East Pakistan, which were separated by about 1,100 miles of Indian territory.

Pakistan became a Republic on March 23, 1956,

when a Parliamentary Constitution came into force. On October 7, 1958, however, this Constitution was abrogated and Pakistan came under martial law.

The first general elections ever held in Pakistan on a basis of "one man, one vote", were held in Dec. 1970 and Jan. 1971. The Awami League in East Pakistan, led by Shiekh Mujibur Rahman, and the Pakistan People's Party in West Pakistan, led by Zulfikar Ali Bhutto, won large majorities. Following the elections there was total disagreement between the two main parties on the question of a new Constitution for Pakistan, Sheikh Mujib insisting on complete autonomy for East Pakistan. The proposed opening of the National Assembly at Dacca on March 25, 1971, was postponed and civil war broke out. East Pakistan seceded by unilateral declaration the following day. Fighting continued until Dec. 1971 when a ceasefire was arranged, and "The Democratic Government of Bangladesh" was formally proclaimed on April 17, 1972.

Following general elections in March 1977 and allegations of vote-rigging the Armed Forces under Gen. Zia-ul-Haq assumed power on July 5, 1977 and imposed martial law throughout the country. The military government scheduled new general elections for October 1977, but these were postponed. Gen. Zia declared himself President on Sept. 16, 1978. In Dec. 1984 Gen Zia got a five-year mandate as a civilian President through a national referendum, but remains Chief Martial Law Administrator. There was a general election to a National Assembly on Feb. 25, 1985. The President has stated martial law will give way to civil rule by Dec. 31,1985.

Education.—Formal education in Pakistan is organized into five stages. These are five years of primary education (5–9 years), three years of middle or lower secondary (general or vocational), two years of upper secondary, two years of higher secondary (intermediate) and two to five years of higher education in colleges and universities. Education is free to upper secondary level. It is anticipated that primary education will become universal for boys by mid-1985 and for girls by mid-1988.

At primary level enrolment has increased to 6·5 million in 1981–82, and the number of schools from 54,000 to 58,400. At the middle level enrolment has increased to 1·5 million in 1982–83, and the number of schools from 5,000 to 6,100. At the upper secondary level it was hoped to increase enrolment to 722,000 in 1982–83. At university level, enrolment rose to 57,000 and at college level to 366,000 in 1982.

Provincial Governments are responsible for the total financial support of the government institutions and for grants to non-government institutions. But policy making is authorized by the national Government, which makes annual grants.

Production.—Pakistan's economy is chiefly based on agriculture. The principal crops are cotton, rice, wheat, sugar cane, maize and tobacco. There are large deposits of rock salt. Pakistan has one of the longest irrigation systems in the world. The total area irrigated is 33 million acres. There are substantial natural gas mains near the Baluchistan Sind border. Distribution now extends to most urban areas.

Pakistan also produces hides and skins, leather, wool, fertilizers, paints and varnishes, soda ash, paper, cement, fish, carpets, sports goods, surgical appliances and engineering goods, including switchgear, transformers, cables and wires.

Trade.—Pakistan imported manufactured goods and raw materials to the value of *Rupees* 76,706 million in 1983–84 and exported mainly agricultural products valued at *Rupees* 34,441 million. Principal imports are listed as: petroleum products, machinery, fertilizers, transport equipment, edible oils, chemicals and ferrous metals. Principal exports are raw cotton, cotton yarn and cloth, carpets, rice, petroleum products, synthetic textiles, leather, and fish.

Trade with U.K.

	1983	1984
Imports from U.K.	£191,647,000	£282,536,000
Exports to U.K.	80,277,000	93,136,000

Finance.—The unit of currency is the *Rupee* of 100 *Paisa* (1 *crore = 10 million Rupees*). For rate of exchange, see p. 81.

The 1984–85 Budget anticipated gross Revenue receipts of *Rs*.59,185 million and expenditure (excluding development expenditure) of some *Rs*.70,736 million.

Communications.—The main seaport is Karachi. The main airport at Karachi occupies an important position on international trunk routes and is equipped with modern facilities and equipment. Pakistan International Airlines (P.I.A.) operates air services between the principal cities within the country as well as abroad.

Post and telegraph facilities are available to every country in the world.

CAPITAL.—Islamabad, pop. 250,000. ΨKarachi (pop. 5,500,000) is the largest city and seaport; Lahore has a population of 2,950,000.

FLAG.—Dark green ground, with white vertical stripes at the mast, the green portion bearing a white crescent in the centre and a five-pointed heraldic star.

NATIONAL DAYS.—March 23 (Pakistan Day), August 14 (Independence Day).

BRITISH EMBASSY
Diplomatic Enclave, Ramna 5,
P.O. Box 1122, Islamabad.

Ambassador Extraordinary and Plenipotentiary, His Excellency Richard A. Fyjis-Walker, C.M.G., C.V.O. (1984).

There is a British Consulate-General at *Karachi*.

British Council Representative, R. F. Budd, P.O. Box 1135, Islamabad. There are regional offices at Karachi and Lahore, and a library in Peshawar.

PANAMA
(República de Panama)

President of the Republic, Eric Arturo del Valle, *took office*, Sept. 1985.

MINISTERS OF STATE

Government and Justice, Sr. Rodolfo Chiari.
Foreign Affairs, Sr. Oyden Ortega.
Treasury and Finance, Dr. Ricaurte Vasquez.
Agricultural Development, Sr. Ramón Sieiro.
Public Works, Sr. Nestor Tomas.
Commerce and Industry, Sr. Carlos Julio Quijano.
Labour and Social Welfare, Sr. Arturo Melo.
Health, Dr. Alberto Clavo.
Housing, Sra. Zia Elena Lee.
Planning and Economic Policy, Dr. Hector Alexander.
Education, Sra. Susana Richa de Torrijos.
Presidency, Sr. Gustavo Gonzalez.

(The above Cabinet may change as a result of Pres. Barletta's resignation and replacement by Vice-Pres. del Valle.)

PANAMANIAN EMBASSY IN LONDON
Eagle House, 109–110 Jermyn Street, S.W.1
[01–930 1591]

Ambassador Extraordinary and Plenipotentiary, His Excellency Lic. Guillermo Vega (1984).
Minister-Counsellor, Prof. Dionisio Johnson.

CONSULATE
24 Tudor Street, EC4Y 0JD
[01–353 4792/3].

There are also Consular Offices of the Republic at *Glasgow* and *Liverpool.*

Panama lies on the isthmus of that name which connects N. and S. America (*for* MAP, *see* INDEX). The area of the Republic is 31,890 sq. m., the population (1982 est.) 2,040,000. After a revolt (Nov. 3, 1903) it declared its independence from Colombia and established a separate Government.

After 1968 control of Panama was increasingly taken over by Gen. Omar Torrijos, Commander of the National Guard, following a military *coup.* On October 11, 1972, at an assembly of representatives from the 505 electoral districts, the President and Vice-President were installed for a six-year term, and General Torrijos was designated as "Leader of the Revolution" with wide overriding powers. In October 1978 he withdrew from government, and Dr. Aristides Royo was elected President by the Assembly of Representatives. In a Presidential election in May 1984, Sr. Nicolas Barletta was elected president and took office in Nov. 1984. However, he resigned in Sept. 1985 after disagreements with military leaders and was succeeded by his Vice-President.

The Panama Canal Zone.—With effect from Oct. 1, 1979 the Canal Zone (647 sq. miles) was disestablished, with all areas of land and water within the Zone reverting to Panama. By the 1977 treaty with the U.S.A., the U.S.A. is allowed the use of operating bases for the Panama Canal, together with several military bases, but the Republic of Panama is sovereign in all such areas. Control of the Canal will revert to Panama in the year 2000.

The soil is moderately fertile, but nearly one-half of the land is uncultivated. The chief crops are bananas, sugar, coconuts, cacao, coffee and cereals. The shrimping industry plays an important rôle in the Panamanian economy. A railway 47 miles in length joins the Atlantic and Pacific oceans.

Education is compulsory and free from 7 to 15 years.

Language and Literature.—The official language is Spanish. There are five Spanish language and one English language newspaper published daily in the capital.

Currency.—The monetary unit is the *Balboa* (= $1 U.S.); no Panamanian paper currency is issued, and U.S. dollar bills of all values are in circulation in the Republic.

TRADE

	1980 (provisional)
Imports	U.S.$1,396 million
Exports	406 million

Trade with U.K.

	1983	1984
Imports from U.K.	£42,276,000	£74,322,000
Exports to U.K.	5,341,000	9,681,000

† Including Colon Free Zone.

The imports are mostly manufactured goods, machinery, lubricants, chemicals and foodstuffs; exports are bananas, petroleum products, shrimps, sugar, meat and fishmeal.

CAPITAL,ΨPanama City. Population (1970 Census), 418,000.

FLAG.—Four quarters; white with blue star (top, next staff), red (in fly), blue (below, next staff) and white with red star.

NATIONAL DAY.—November 3.

Dependencies of Panama.—Taboga Island (area 12 sq. miles) is a popular tourist resort of some 12 miles from the Pacific entrance to the Panama Canal.

Tourist facilities are also being developed in the Las Perlas Archipelago in the Gulf of Panama. There is a penal settlement at Guardia on the island of Coiba (area 19 sq. miles) in the Gulf of Chiriqui.

BRITISH EMBASSY
(120 Via España, Panama)

Ambassador Extraordinary and Plenipotentiary, His Excellency Terence Harry Steggle (1983).
1st Secretary and Consul, D. V. Thornley.

There is a British consular office at *Panama City.*

PARAGUAY
(República del Paraguay)

President, General Alfredo Stroessner, *inaugurated* Aug. 15, 1954, *re-elected* 1958, 1963, 1968, 1973, 1978 and 1983.
Foreign Affairs, Dr. Carlos Augustus Saldívar.
Finance, General César Barrientos (*ret.*).
Interior, Dr. Sabino A. Montanero.
Defence, General Gaspar Germán Martínez.
Justice and Labour, Dr. José Eugenio Jacquet.
Education and Worship, Dr. Carlos Ortíz Ramirez.
Public Works and Communications, General de División Juan A. Cáceres.
Agriculture and Livestock, Ing. Hernando Bertoni.
Industry and Commerce, Dr. Delfin Ugarte Centurión.
Public Health and Social Welfare, Dr. Adán Godoy Jiménez.
President of Central Bank, Dr. César Romero Acosta.

PARAGUAYAN EMBASSY AND CONSULATE IN LONDON
Braemer Lodge, Cornwall Gardens, SW7 4AQ
[01–937 1253; *Consulate*: 01-937 6629]

Ambassador Extraordinary and Plenipotentiary, His Excellency Antonio Zuccolillo (1981).
Counsellor and Consul General, Rubén Alvarenga-Cabañas.
Consulate Official, Mrs. Teresa M. de Castillo.

Area and Population.—Paraguay is an inland subtropical state of South America, situated between Argentina, Bolivia and Brazil.

The area is computed at 157,000 square miles, with a population (1983 Census) of 3,477,000.

Paraguay is a country of grassy plains and dense forest, the soil being marshy in many parts and liable to floods; while the hills are covered for the most part with immense forests. The streams flowing into the Alto Paraná descend precipitously into that river. In the angle formed by the Paraná-Paraguay confluence are extensive marshes, one of which, known as "Neembucú," or "endless," is drained by *Lake Ypoa,* a large lagoon, south-east of the capital. The *Chaco,* lying between the rivers Paraguay and Pilcomayo and bounded on the north by Bolivia, formed the subject of a long-standing dispute with that country and led to war between Paraguay and Bolivia from 1932 to 1935. The Chaco is a flat plain, rising uniformly towards its western boundary to a height of 1,140 feet; it suffers much from floods and still more from drought, but the building of dams and reservoirs has converted part of it into good pasture for cattle raising.

Government.—In 1535 Paraguay was settled as a Spanish possession. In 1811 it declared its independence of Spain.

The 1967 constitution provides for a two-chamber parliament consisting of a 30-member Senate and a 60-member Chamber of Deputies. Two-thirds of the seats in each chamber are allocated to the majority party and the remaining one-third shared among the minority parties in proportion to the votes cast. Voting is compulsory for all citizens over 18.

The President is elected for 5 years and may be re-elected for a further term. He appoints the Cabinet, which exercises all the functions of government. During parliamentary recess it can govern by decree through the Council of State, the members of which are representative of the Government, the armed forces and various other bodies.

Production.—About three-quarters of the population are engaged in agriculture and cattle raising. Cotton, soya beans, tobacco, edible and essential oils, sugar, coffee and timber are the main exports. The forests contain many varieties of timber which find a good market abroad. Paraguay's hydroelectric power station at Acaray produced in 1983, 847,748 k.w. of which a surplus is exported to Argentina and Brazil.

At Itaipú the largest hydroelectric dam in the world, a joint project by Paraguay and Brazil, was inaugurated in 1982. It is expected to be completed in 1990 when it will have a capacity of over 12 million k.w. Work is also under way on a hydroelectric project with Argentina at Yacyretá which it is hoped will be in operation by the end of the decade.

Communications.—A railway, 985 miles in length, connects Asunción with Buenos Aires. The journey takes 55 hours. Train ferries enable the run to be accomplished without break of bulk. River steamers also connect Buenos Aires and Asunción (3 to 5 days). This service is liable to cancellation without warning when the river is low or in flood. There are direct shipping services to Asunción from England, Western Europe and the U.S.A. Eight airlines operate services from Asunción.

There are 1,176 km. of asphalted roads in Paraguay, connecting Asunción with São Paulo (26 hrs.) *via* the Bridge of Friendship and Foz de Yguazú and with Buenos Aires (24 hrs.) *via* Puerto Pilcomayo, and about 4,050 miles of earth roads in fairly good condition, but liable to be closed or to become impassable in wet weather. A 1000 km. road, of which 300 km. are paved, links Asunción with the Bolivian border. There are services to Buenos Aires, São Paulo and Paranagua, a port on the Brazilian coast.

Defence.—There is a permanent military force of about 25,000 all ranks, most of whom are conscripts doing their military service; and about 6,500 armed police (again mostly conscripts). Three gunboats and a number of small armed launches patrol inland waters.

Language and Literature.—Spanish is the official language of the country but outside the larger towns *Guarani*, the language of the largest single unit of original Indian inhabitants, is widely spoken. Four daily, one weekly and one bi-weekly newspapers are published in Asunción. There are 48 AM, 15 FM and three TV stations in the country.

Education.—Education is free and compulsory. In 1982 there were 3,071 government primary schools and 542 private schools with 539,889 pupils and 20,746 teachers. There are 632 secondary schools with 135,829 pupils and 2,448 teachers. The National University in Asunción had in 1984 20,343 students. The Catholic University had 10,971 students.

BUDGET 1985
(*in million guaranies*)

Central Government	Decentralized Bodies
Expenditure ....118·8	277·2

Currency.—The unit is the *guarani* of 100 *céntimos*. (*See also* p. 82.)

Trade.—The imports are chiefly articles of food and drink, consumer goods, textiles, vehicles and machinery. Main exports: Soja, cotton, tobacco, meat, timber, seeds, maize, fruit and vegetable oils.

Trade with U.K.

	1983	1984
Imports from U.K.	£15,263,000	£16,884,000
Exports to U.K.	3,129,000	2,961,000

CAPITAL, ΨAsunción, about 1,000 miles up the River Paraguay from Buenos Aires. Pop. (census, 1983), 708,000; other centres being Ciudad Presidente Stroessner, 92,000; ΨEncarnación, 28,800; Concepción, 24,000.

FLAG.—Three horizontal bands, red, white, blue with the National seal on the obverse white band and the Treasury seal on the reverse white band.

NATIONAL DAY.—May 14.

BRITISH EMBASSY
Calle President Franco 706,
(PO Box 404)

Ambassador Extraordinary and Plenipotentiary and Consul-General, His Excellency Bernard Coleman (1984).

1st Secretary, B. Robertson.

Asunción is approximately 4,000 miles distant from London by air. Transit by sea 25 days. By air approximately 21 hours flying time *via* Rio de Janeiro.

PERU
(República del Peru)

President, Sr. Alan García Pérez, *assumed office*, July 28, 1985.

PERUVIAN EMBASSY AND CONSULATE
52 Sloane Street, SW1X 9SP
[01–235 1917/2545]

Ambassador Extraordinary and Plenipotentiary, new appointment awaited.

Minister, J. Eduardo Ponce-Vivanco.

Naval and Military Attaché, Vice-Adm. Javier Llerena.

Air Attaché, Maj. Gen. Alfredo Lima.

Area and Population.—Peru is a maritime Republic of South America, situated between 0° 00′ 48″ and 18° 21′ 00″ S. latitude and between 68° 39′ 27″ and 81° 20′ 13″ W. longitude. The area of the Republic including 4,440 square kilometres of the Peruvian section of Lake Titicaca and 32 square kilometres of the coastal islands, is about 531,000 square miles with a population estimated (1982) at 18,790,000.

Physical Features.—The country is traversed throughout its length by the Andes, running parallel to the Pacific coast, the highest points in Peru being *Huascaran* (22,211 feet), *Huandoy* (20,855 feet), *Ausangate* (20,235 feet), *Misti* volcano (18,364 feet), *Hualcan* (20,000 feet), *Chachani* (19,037 feet), *Antajasha* (18,020 feet), *Pichupichu* (17,724 feet), and *Mount Meiggs* (17,583 feet).

There are three main regions, the Costa, west of the Andes, the *Sierra* or mountain ranges of the Andes, which include the *Punas* or mountainous wastes below the region of perpetual snow and the *Montaña*, or *Selva*, which is the vast area of jungle stretching from the eastern foothills of the Andes to the eastern frontiers of Peru. The coastal area, lying upon and near the Pacific, is not tropical, though close to the Equator, being cooled by the Humboldt Current. It contains the capital, Lima, and most of the white population.

In the mountains, where most of the Indians live, are to be found minerals in great richness and variety, and cattle, sheep, llamas and alpacas are bred there.

Language and Literature.—Spanish, the language of the original Spanish stock from which the governing and professional classes are mainly recruited, was formerly the only official language of the country. However, in May 1975, the Quechua language was declared the second official tongue. Quechua and Aymará are widely spoken by more than half the population of the country. Before the arrival of Pizarro, the Incas had attained a high state of culture, some traces of which survived three centuries of Spanish rule. Modern Peruvian literature includes a national drama in the Spanish tongue and many Peruvian writers have attained international fame.

Government.—Peru was conquered in the early 16th century by Francisco Pizarro (born 1478, died 1541). He subjugated the Incas (the ruling caste of the Quechua Indians), who had started their rise to power some 500 years earlier, and for nearly three centuries Peru remained under Spanish rule. A revolutionary war of 1821–1824 established its independence, declared on July 28, 1821. The constitution rests upon the fundamental law of Oct. 18, 1856, and is that of a democratic Republic. A new constitution was drawn up and approved in July 1979.

Production.—The chief products of the coastal belt are cotton, sugar and petroleum. There are large tracts of land suitable for cultivation and stock raising on the eastern slopes of the Andes, and in the mountain valleys maize, potatoes and wheat are grown. The jungle area is a source of timber and petroleum. Other major crops are fruit, vegetables, rice, barley, grapes and coffee. Mineral exports include lead, zinc, copper, iron ore and silver. Peru is normally the world's largest exporter of fishmeal. The value of fishmeal exports dropped for some years but is now recovering.

Communications.—In recent years the coastal and sierra zones have been opened up by means of roads and air routes and there is air communication, as well as communication by protracted land routes, with the tropical and little known eastern zones, which lie east of the Andes towards the borders of Brazil. The completion in 1944 of the trunk road of the *Andean Highway* from the Pacific port of Callao, *via* Lima to Pucallpa, the river port on the Ucayali, forms a link between the Pacific, the Amazon and the Atlantic.

The first railway was opened in 1850 and the 2,400 miles of track are now administered by the Government. There is also steam navigation on the Ucayali and Huallaga, and in the south on Lake Titicaca. Air

services are maintained throughout Peru, and many international services call at Lima.

Defence.—The Army is recruited by voluntary enlistment, supplemented by conscription (2 years), and numbers about 45,000 of all ranks. Armoured units are equipped with American, Russian and French vehicles. Engineer units are employed on the construction of roadways in Peru using American equipment. The main Naval base is in Callao and supports all ships of the Fleet. There are training establishments in Callao and La Punta. The Naval Air Arm consists of U.S. and French helicopters; U.S. anti-submarine aircraft and DC3's. The Air Force is equipped with British, U.S. and French aircraft and U.S. and French helicopters. There are military airfields at Talara, Piura, Chiclayo, Lima, Pisco, Joya, Iquitos and Arequipa plus a seaplane base at Iquitos. There are also a Civil Guard and a Republican Guard whose members number respectively 30,000 and 5,000.

Education.—Education is compulsory and free for both sexes between the ages of 6 and 15.

Finance.—The unit of currency is the *Sol* of 100 *centavos.* For rate of exchange, *see* p. 82.

Trade.—Import trade of Peru in 1980 totalled U.S.$3,134 million and exports U.S.$3,904 million.

Trade with U.K.

	1983	1984
Imports from U.K.	£32,947,000	£33,841,000
Exports to U.K.	118,414,000	119,423,000

The principal imports are machinery, foodstuffs, metal and manufactured metal goods, chemicals and pharmaceutical products. The chief exports are minerals and metals, fishmeal, sugar, cotton and coffee.

CAPITAL.—Metropolitan Lima (including ΨCallao), population 3,595,000. Arequipa (561,338) Ψ Iquitos (540,560), ΨChiclayo (533,266).

FLAG.—Three vertical bands, red, white, red; coat of arms on white band.

NATIONAL DAY.—July 28 (Anniversary of Independence).

BRITISH EMBASSY

Edificio El Pacifico-Washington (Piso 12), Plaza Washington, Avenida Arequipa, Lima.

Ambassador Extraordinary and Plenipotentiary, His Excellency John William Richmond Shakespeare, C.M.G., M.V.O. (1983).

1st *Secretaries,* J. W. Thorp (*Head of Chancery and Consul*); M. L. Creek, L.V.O., O.B.E. (*Commercial*).

Defence, Naval, Military and Air Attaché, Capt. D. H. Ross, R.N.

There are British Consular Offices at *Lima* and *Callao.*

British Council Representative, T. F. Hibbett, Apartado 11114, Edif. Pacifico-Washington, Ave Arequipa, Lima.

THE PHILIPPINES
(Repúblika ng Pilipinas)

President, Ferdinand Marcos, *b.* 1917, *elected* Nov. 10, 1965, *assumed office* Dec. 30, 1965, *re-elected,* June 16, 1981.

MINISTERS

Prime Minister and Minister of Finance, Cesar E. A. Virata.

Deputy P.M. and Minister of Local Government, José Rono.

Foreign Affairs, Pacifico Castro (*acting*).

Justice and Solicitor General, Estelito Mendoza.

Agriculture and Food, Salvador Escudero.

Public Works and Highways, Jesus Hipolito.
Education, Culture and Sports, Jaime Laya.
Labour and Employment, Blas F. Ople.
Defence, Juan Ponce Enrile.
Health, Jesus Azurin.
Industry and Trade, Roberto Ongpin.
Agrarian Reform, Conrado Estrella.
Tourism, Jose D. Aspiras.
Natural Resources, Rodolfo del Rosario.
Energy, Geronimo Velasco.
Human Settlements and Community Development, Imelda R. Marcos.
Transportation and Communications, Jose P. Dans.
Social Services, Sylvia Montes.
National Economic and Development Authority, Vicente Valdepenas, jr.
Office of Media Affairs, Gregorio Cendana.
Office of Budget and Management, Manuel Alba.
Office of Muslim Affairs and Cultural Communities, Simeon Datumanong.
National Food Authority, Jesus Tanchangco.
Philippine Coconut Authority, Rolando de la Cuesta.
National Science and Technology Authority, Emil Javier.
Presidential Executive Assistant, Juan Tuvera.
Presidential Advisers, Leonardo Perez (*Political Affairs*); Alejandro Melchor.

PHILIPPINE EMBASSY
9a Palace Green, W8 4QE
[01–937 1600/9]

Ambassador Extraordinary and Plenipotentiary, His Excellency José V. Cruz (1982).
Minister-Counsellor and Consul General, Alfredo Almendrala.
Armed Forces Attaché, Col. Reynaldo Wycoco.
Commercial Counsellor, Peregrino Sales.

Area and Population.—The Philippines are situated between 21° 20′–4° 30′ N. Lat. and 116° 55′–126° 36′ E. long., and are distant about 500 miles from the south-east coast of the continent of Asia.

The total land area of the country is 114,834 square miles, of which total 106,914 square miles are contained in the eleven largest islands, the 7,079 other islands having a combined area of 7,929 square miles.

The principal islands are:—

Name	sq. miles	Name	sq. miles
Luzon	40,422	Mindoro	3,759
Mindanao	36,538	Leyte	2,786
Samar	5,050	Cebu	1,703
Negros	4,906	Bohol	1,492
Palawan	4,550	Masbate	1,262
Panay	4,446		

Other groups in the Republic are the Sulu islands (Capital, Jolo), Babuyanes and Batanes; the Catanduanes; and Culion Islands.

The population of the Philippines was estimated (mid 1985) at 54,400,000.

The inhabitants, known as Filipinos, are basically all of Malay stock, with a considerable admixture of Spanish and Chinese blood in many localities, and about 90 per cent of them are Christians, predominantly Roman Catholics. Most of the remainder are Moslems, in the south, and animists and pagans, mainly in the north. There is a Chinese minority estimated at 500,000, and other much smaller foreign communities, notably Spanish, American and Indian.

History.—The Portuguese navigator Magellan came to the Philippines in 1521 and was slain by the natives of Mactan, a small island near Cebu. In 1565 Spain undertook the conquest of the country which was named "Filipinas", after the son of the King of Spain, and in 1571 the city of Manila was founded by the conquistador Legaspi, who subdued the inhabitants of almost all the islands, their conversion being undertaken by the Augustinian friars in Legaspi's train. In 1762 Manila was occupied by a British force, but in 1764 it was restored to Spain. In the Spanish-American War of 1898, Manila was captured by American troops with the help of Filipinos and the Islands were ceded to the United States by the *Treaty of Paris* of Dec. 10, 1898. Despite a rebellion against the U.S. government between 1899 and 1902, the Americans remained in control of the country until 1946.

The Republic of the Philippines came into existence on July 4, 1946 with a presidential form of government based on the American system.

Martial law was imposed on September 21, 1972. This was lifted, except in two southern provinces, on January 17, 1981. On January 17, 1973, a revised constitution, providing for a parliamentary form of government with a unicameral legislative, was proclaimed, and elections were held on April 7, 1978 for the new Interim National Assembly, which is intended to prepare the way for a permanent body. This met for the first time on June 12, 1978 when the President was sworn in as Prime Minister. Constitutional amendments were approved in April 1981 providing for a French-style system of parliamentary government with a strong executive Presidency. President Marcos subsequently fought and won a Presidential election.

There is unrest in some of the Islands due to insurgency. Muslim insurgents, the Moro National Liberation Front, operate in western Mindanao and the Sula archipelago, though they are far less active now than in the early 1970s. Most of the current activity is due to the Communist New People's Army, which is strongest in eastern Mindanao, Negros, Samar, Bicol, the mountains of northern Luzon, and Bataan.

Language and Literature.—The official languages are Pilipino and English. Pilipino, the national language, is based on Tagalog, one of the Malay-Polynesian languages and the language of the part of Luzon surrounding Metro Manila. According to the 1970 census Pilipino is spoken by 55·2 per cent of the population, but local languages and dialects are strong, and in 1975 Cebuano speakers outnumbered first-language Tagalog speakers. English, which is the language of government and of instruction in secondary and university education, is spoken by at least 44 per cent of the population. Spanish, which ceased to be an official language in 1973, is now spoken by only 3·6 per cent. 89 per cent of the population are literate.

Education.—Secondary and higher education is extensive and there are 37 private universities recognized by the Government, including the Dominican University of Santo Tomas (founded in 1611); there are also 213 State-supported colleges and universities, including the University of the Philippines, founded 1908. Students at private and state colleges and universities in 1980–81 numbered 1,276,016.

Roads and Railways.—The highway system covered 153,528 kilometres in 1981 and there was a total of 1,006,130 registered road vehicles. The Philippine National Railway operate 740 km. of track on Luzon Island.

Shipping.—There are 94 ports of entry in the Philippines and 142,483 vessels of various types totalling 48,422,000 tons, are engaged in inter-island traffic.

Civil Aviation.—There 86 national airports and 131 privately operated airports. Philippine Air Lines have regular flights throughout the Far East, to the U.S.A. and Europe, in addition to inter-island services.

TRADE

	1983	1984
Total imports	$7,469,164,000	$6,069,612,000
Total exports	5,005,291,000	5,390,646,000

Trade with U.K.

	1983	1984
Imports from U.K.	£102,949,000	£91,751,000
Exports to U.K.	160,701,000	199,659,000

The Philippines is a predominantly agricultural country, the chief products being rice, coconuts, maize, sugar-cane, abaca (manila hemp), fruits, tobacco and lumber. There is, however, an increasing number of manufacturing industries and it is the policy of the Government to diversify its economy.

Principal exports are sugar, coconut oil, copper concentrate, logs and lumber and copra.

CAPITAL.—ΨManila, in the island of Luzon: population (1980): City area, 1,630,485; Manila with suburbs (incl. Quezon City, Pasay City, Caloocan City, Makati, Parañaque, San Juan Mandaluyong and Navota), 5,925,884. The next largest cities are ΨCebu (490,281), ΨDavao (610,375), ΨIloilo (244,027), ΨZamboanga (343,722), and Bacolod (262,415).

FLAG.—Equal horizontal bands of blue (above) and red; gold sun with three stars on a white triangle next staff.

NATIONAL DAY.—June 12 (Independence Day).

BRITISH EMBASSY
(P.O. Box 1970 MCC), Manila

Ambassador Extraordinary and Plenipotentiary, His Excellency Robin John Taylor McLaren, C.M.G., *apptd.* 1985.
Counsellor, A. S. Payne, O.B.E.
1st Secretary, N. A. Thorne (*Head of Chancery*).
2nd Secretaries, C. T. Imrie; J. R. Albright (*Commercial*); P. J. Karmy (*Consul*).
Cultural Attaché, H. Salmon (*British Council Representative*).

POLAND
(Polska Rzeczpospolita Ludowa)

COUNCIL OF STATE

Chairman (i.e. Head of State), Henryk Jabłoński.
Deputy Chairmen, T. Mlynczak; K. Secomski; B. Struzek; J. Zietek.

COUNCIL OF MINISTERS

Prime Minister, Gen. Wojciech Jaruzelski.
Deputy Prime Minister and Chairman, Planning Commission, Manfred Gorywoda.

Deputy Prime Ministers, Janusz Obodowski; Zenon Komender; Edward Kowalczyk; Zbigniew Messner; Roman Malinowski; Mieczyslaw Rakowski; Zbigniew Szalajda.
Chairman, Supreme Chamber of Control, Tadeusz Hupalowski.
Member of Presidium and Plenipotentiary for Economic Reform, Wladyslaw Baka.
Interior, Lt.-Gen. Czeslaw Kiszczak.
Foreign Affairs, Stefan Olszowski.
Defence, Gen. Florian Siwicki.
Finance, Stanislaw Nieckarz.
Foreign Trade, Tadeusz Nestorowicz.
Administration, Wlodzimierz Oliwa.
Justice, Lech Domeradzki.
Higher Education, Science and Technology, Prof. Benon Miskiewicz.
Health and Social Welfare, Tadeusz Szelachowski.
Labour, Stanislaw Gebala.
Culture, Kazimierz Zygulski.
Building and Building Materials Industry, Stanislaw Kukuryka.
Metallurgical and Engineering Industries, Janusz Maciejewicz.
Agriculture and Food, Stanislaw Zieba.
Forestry, Waldemar Kozlowski.
Internal Trade, Mrs. Anna Kedzierska.
Transport, Jan Kaminski.
Raw Materials, Jerzy Wozniak.
Education, Boleslaw Faron.
Chemical and Light Industries, Edward Grzywa.
Communications, Wladyslaw Majewski.
Mining and Energy, Czeslaw Piotrowski.
Religious Affairs, Adam Lopatka.
Price Affairs, Zdislaw Krasinski.
Maritime Economy, Jerzy Korzonek.
Environmental Protection and Water Economy, Stefan Jarzebski.
Without Portfolio, Wladyslaw Jablonski; Andrzej Ornat.

POLISH UNITED WORKERS' PARTY

First Secretary, Gen. Wojciech Jaruzelski.
Politburo, Gen. W. Jaruzelski; K. Barcikowski; T. Czechowicz; J. Czyrek; Z. Grzyb; S. Kalkus; H. Kubiak; Z. Messner; S. Olszowski; S. Opalko; T. Porebski; J. Romanik; A. Siwak; M. Wozniak.
Secretariat, Gen. W. Jaruzelski; K. Barcikowski; H. Bednarski; J. Czyrek; J. Glowczyk; Z. Michalek; W. Mokrzyszczak; T. Porebski; W. Swirgon.

POLISH EMBASSY IN LONDON
47 Portland Place, W1N 3AG
[01–580 4324]

Ambassador Extraordinary and Plenipotentiary, His
Excellency Stefan Staniszewski (1981).

Area and Population.—Poland adjoins East Germany in the west, the boundary being formed by the
rivers Oder and Neisse, Czechoslavakia in the south,
and the U.S.S.R. in the east. (The present frontiers
were established at the end of the Second World
War.) To the north is the Baltic Sea. The country
has an area of 120,628 sq. miles and a population (1982
census) of 36,400,000. Roman Catholicism is the
religion of 95 per cent. of the inhabitants.

Government.—The Polish Commonwealth had
ceased to exist in 1795 after three successive parti-
tions in 1772, 1793 and 1795, in which Prussia, Russia
and Austria shared. The Republic of Poland (reconstituted within the limits of the old Polish Commonwealth) was proclaimed at Warsaw in November,
1918, and its independence guaranteed by the signa-
tories of the Treaty of Versailles.

German forces invaded Poland on Sept. 1, 1939; on
Sept. 17, Russian forces invaded eastern Poland, and
on September 21, 1939, Poland was declared by
Germany and Russia to have ceased to exist. A line
of demarcation was established between the areas
occupied by German and Russian forces. At the end
of the war a Coalition Government was formed in
which the Polish Workers' Party played a large part.
In December, 1948, the Polish Workers' Party and
the Polish Socialist Party fused in the new Polish
United Workers' Party. This is a Communist Party
which closely controls every branch of State activity.
A new Constitution modelled on the Soviet Constitution of 1936 was adopted on July 22, 1952, and was
modified in February 1976. It changed the title of the
country to the Polish People's Republic (*Polska
Rzeczpospolita Ludowa*). It made no provision for a
President of the Republic, whose functions were to
be jointly exercised by a Council of State. Private
ownership of land and freedom of religion were
recognized. Church and State were to be separate.

Despite the guarantee of religious freedom in the
Constitution, a campaign of encroachment in 1953
culminated in the arrest of the Primate of the Roman
Catholic Church, and dissatisfaction with the *régime*
and conditions of life have led periodically to unrest.
The expression of severe popular discontent in
December 1970 led to the ousting of Gomulka, and
substantial Government and Party changes followed.
In July 1980 steep rises in food prices but static wages
led to widespread strikes. The strikes continued
throughout August, causing a major government
reshuffle and obliging the government to agree to
allow independent trade unions, the right to strike,
the easing of censorship and other political and
economic demands. The independent trade union
movement, Solidarity, led by Lech Walesa, became a
powerful force but many of its leaders, including
Walesa, were detained and union activity suspended
when martial law was declared on Dec. 13, 1981.
Initially there was some passive resistance to martial
law, which was suspended on Dec. 31, 1982. Solidarity
has been banned.

Education.—Elementary education (ages 7–15) is
compulsory and free. Secondary education is optional
and free. There are universities at Kraków, Warsaw,
Poznan, Lódź, Wroclaw, Lublin and Toruń and a
considerable number of other towns.

Language and Literature.—Polish is a western
Slavonic tongue (*see* U.S.S.R.), the Latin alphabet
being used. Polish literature developed rapidly after
the foundation of the University of Cracow (a
printing press was established there in 1474 and there
Copernicus died in 1543). A national school of poetry

and drama survived the dismemberment and the
former era of romanticism, whose chief Polish expo-
nent was Adam Mickiewicz, was followed by realistic
and historical fiction, including the works of Henryk
Sienkiewicz (1846–1916), Nobel Prize-winner for
Literature in 1905, Boleslaw Prus (1847–1912), and
Stanislaw Reymont (1868–1925), Nobel Prize-winner
in 1924.

Production and Industry.—On January 3, 1946, a
decree was issued to provide for the nationalization
of mines, petroleum resources, water, gas and electricity services, banks, textile factories and large
retail stores. At present over 99 per cent of Polish
industry is stated to be "socialized", but 68 per cent
of agricultural land is privately farmed.

Trade with U.K.

	1983	1984
Imports from U.K.	£151,721,000	£169,962,000
Exports to U.K.	177,067,000	266,961,000

CAPITAL.—Warsaw, on the Vistula, pop. (1979)
1,572,000. Other large towns are Lódź (832,000);
Kraków (705,000); Wroclaw (608,000); Poznan
(544,000); Gdansk (448,000); Szczecin (388,000);
Katowice (353,000); Lublin (298,000).

FLAG.—Equal horizontal stripes of white (above)
and red.

NATIONAL DAY.—July 22.

BRITISH EMBASSY
No. 1 Aleja Róz, Warsaw

Ambassador Extraordinary and Plenipotentiary, His
Excellency John Albert Leigh Morgan, C.M.G.
(1983).

Counsellor, A. E. Furness (*Head of Chancery*).
Defence and Air Attaché, Gp.-Capt. A. A. Ramus.
Naval and Military Attaché, Lt.-Col. P. de S. Barrow.
British Council Representative, J. J. Barnett, O.B.E.,
Al. Jerozolimskie 59, 00–697 Warsaw.

PORTUGAL
(República Portuguesa)

President of the Republic, General António Ramalho
Eanes, *elected*, June 27, 1976, *re-elected*, 1980.

Prime Minister, Dr. Mário Soares.*
Vice P.M. and Minister for Defence, Dr. Rui Machete.†
State and Parliamentary Affairs, Dr. António Al-
meida Santos.*
Finance, Dr. Ernâni Lopes.
Internal Administration, Eduardo Pereira.*
Foreign Affairs, Dr. Jaime Gama.*
Sea, Dr. José Almeida e Serra.*
Health, António Maldonado Gonelha.*
Justice, Dr. Mario Raposo.†
Culture, Dr. António Coimbra Martins.*
Social Infrastructure, Dr. Carlos Melancia.*
Industry, Prof. José Veiga Simão.*
Labour and Social Affairs, Dr. Amândio Anes de
Azevedo.†
Education and Universities, Dr. João de Deus Pin-
heir.†
Quality of Life and Environment, Dr. Joaquim Fer-
nando Nogueira.*
Trade and Tourism, Dr. Joaquim Ferreira do
Amaral.†
Agriculture, Álvaro Barreto.†

* P.S.P., † *P.S.D.* Dr. Lopes is an Independent.

(This Cabinet may change following the General
Election called for Oct. 6, 1985.)

EMBASSY IN LONDON
11 Belgrave Square, SW1X 8PP
[01–235 5331]

Ambassador Extraordinary and Plenipotentiary, His Excellency João Hall Themido (1984).

Minister-Counsellor, Sr. José Maria de A. S. de Lemos Macedo.

Counsellor, Sr. Paulo G. Castilho.

Area and Population.—Continental Portugal occupies the western part of the Iberian Peninsula, covering an area of 34,000 square miles. It lies between 36° 58′–42° 12″ N. lat. and 6° 11′ 48″–9° 29′ 45″ W. long., being 362 miles in length from N. to S., and averaging about 117 in breadth from E. to W. The population (including the Azores and Madeira) was estimated at 10,030,700 in 1982.

Language and Literature.—Portuguese is a Romance language with admixtures of Arabic and other idioms. It is the language of Portugal and Brazil, and is the *lingua franca* of Angola, Mozambique and Guinea-Bissau.

Portuguese language and literature reached the culminating point of their development in the *Lusiadas* (dealing with the voyage of Vasco da Gama) and other works of Camoens (Camões) (1524–1580).

Government.—From the eleventh century until 1910 the government of Portugal was a monarchy, and for many centuries included the Vice-Royalty of Brazil, which declared its independence in 1822. In 1910 an armed rising in Lisbon drove King Manuel II and the Royal family into exile, and the National Assembly of Aug. 21, 1911, sanctioned a Republican form of government. A period of great political instability ensued until eventually the military stepped in. The Constitution of 1933 gave formal expression to the corporative "Estado Novo" (New State) which was personified by Dr. Salazar, Prime Minister from 1932–68. Dr. Caetano succeeded Salazar as Prime Minister in 1968 but his failure to liberalize the régime or to conclude the wars in the African colonies resulted in his government's overthrow by a military coup on April 25, 1974. The next two years were characterized by great political turmoil with no fewer than 6 provisional governments between April 1974 and July 1976 but with the failure of an attempted coup by the extreme left in November 1975 the situation began to become more stable.

Constitutional reforms introduced in Aug. 1982 have reduced the President's scope for day-to-day intervention in government but the decision to dissolve the Assembly is still largely the President's. The revisions also ended the military's capacity for political interference, and created two new organs of state, the Constitutional Tribunal and the Council of State, to advise the President.

In the April 1983 General Election, the Portuguese Socialist Party (*P.S.P.*) won 101 seats, the Social Democratic Party (*P.S.D.*) 75 seats, the Communist Party (*P.C.P.*) 44 seats and the Democratic Social Centre Party (*C.D.S.*) 30 seats. A coalition of the *P.S.P.* and *P.S.D.* formed the government, but the coalition broke down in June 1985 with the withdrawal of the P.S.D. As it proved impossible to form a new government, the President dissolved the Assembly on July 12 and called a General Election for Oct. 6, the existing cabinet remaining in office as a caretaker government.

Defence.—Most physically fit males are liable for military service but conscription is becoming increasingly selective as the armed forces were greatly reduced following the end of the colonial wars, and reorganized and re-equipped for a conventional national defence role. The present strength of the Army is about 39,000. One brigade is earmarked for N.A.T.O. service. The Navy consists of about 13,000 officers and men, including 2,600 marines, manning about 60 craft of various types, many of which are obsolete. The present serving strength of the Air Force is about 12,000, (including paratroops) and about 80 aircraft of various types.

Education is free and compulsory for six years from the age of 7. Secondary education is mainly conducted in State lyceums, commercial and industrial schools, but there are also private schools. There are also military, naval, technical and other special schools. There are old established Universities at Coimbra (founded in 1290), Oporto and Lisbon. New Universities have been established at Lisbon, Braga, Aveiro and in the Azores; a University at Faro is expected to open in 1986–87.

Newspapers and Broadcasting.—There are now 8 main daily newspapers in Lisbon and 3 in Oporto, and 4 main weekly newspapers. There are 2 TV channels (broadcasting in colour) and 5 radio stations (4 state controlled) broadcasting nationwide.

Civil aviation is controlled by the Administração Nacional Aeronaútica. There is an international airport at Portela, about 5 miles from Lisbon, and the airport of Pedras Rubras near Oporto is also used for some international services. There are direct flights between London and Faro in the Algarve.

Agriculture.—The chief agricultural products are cork, cereals, rice, vegetables, olives, figs, citrus fruits, almonds, timber, port wine and table wines. There are extensive forests of pine, cork, eucalyptus and chestnut covering about 20 per cent of the total area of the country.

Minerals.—The principal mineral products are pyrites, wolfram, tin, iron ores, copper and sodium and calcium minerals.

Industry.—The country is so far only moderately industrialized, but is fairly rapidly extending its industries. The principal manufactures, some of which are still protected by high tariffs, are textiles, clothing and footwear, machinery (including electric machinery and transport equipment), foodstuffs (tomato concentrates and canned fish), chemicals, fertilizers, wood, cork, furniture, cement, glassware and pottery. There is a modern steelworks, and two modern and very large shipbuilding and repair yards at Lisbon and Setúbal working mainly for foreign ship-owners. There are several hydro-electric power stations and a new thermal power station.

Finance.—Portugal is a member of the European Monetary Agreement, the World Bank, the International Monetary Fund and the International Finance Corporation. The country has substantial, but declining, gold and foreign exchange reserves.

Currency.—*Escudos* (of 100 *Centavos*). A *Conto* consists of 1,000 *Escudos*.

Trade.—Portugal will join the E.E.C. with effect from January 1, 1986.

The principal imports are cereals, meat, raw and semi-manufactured iron and steel, industrial machinery, chemicals, crude oil, motor vehicles and raw materials for textiles.

The principal exports are textiles, footwear, timber, cork, electrical and other machinery, and chemicals.

	1983	1984
Total imports	*E*885,704 m.	*E*1,134,242 m.
Total exports	504,713 m.	757,049 m.

Trade with U.K.

	1983	1984
Imports from U.K.	£396,988,000	£385,799,000
Exports to U.K.	475,902,000	644,520,000

The British share of the Portuguese market was 7 per cent in 1984 and the U.K. was the largest market for Portuguese exports (15·4 per cent).

CAPITAL.—ΨLisbon. Population (estimated, 1974) 1,707,500. ΨOporto 1,389,800; ΨSetubal 526,000.

FLAG.—Vertical band of green (next staff) and square of red, bearing arms of the Republic, framed.

NATIONAL DAY.—June 10.

BRITISH EMBASSY
35–37 Rua de S. Domingos à Lapa,
1296 Lisbon

Ambassador Extraordinary and Plenipotentiary, His Excellency Sir Hugh Campbell Byatt, K.C.M.G.

There are British Consulates in *Oporto*, *Portimão*, *Funchal* (Madeira) and *Ponta Delgada* (Azores).

British Council Representative, J. Mallon, O.B.E., The British Institute, Rua de Luis Fernandes 3,1294 Lisbon.

BRITISH PORTUGUESE CHAMBER OF COMMERCE, Rua da Estrela 8, 1200 Lisbon and Rua Sa de Bandeira 784–20E, Frente, 4000 Oporto.

MADEIRA AND THE AZORES

Madeira and The Azores are two administratively autonomous regions of Portugal, having locally elected Assemblies and Governments.

Madeira is a group of islands in the Atlantic Ocean about 520 miles south-west of Lisbon, and consist of Madeira, Porto, Santo and 3 uninhabited islands (Desertas). The total area is 314 square miles with a population of 265,600 (1978). ΨFunchal in Madeira, the largest island (270 square miles), is the capital, with a population of 54,068; Machico (10,905).

The Azores are a group of 9 islands (Flores, Corvo, Terceira, São Jorge, Pico, Faial, Graciosa, São Miguel and Santa Maria) in the Atlantic Ocean, with a total area of 922 square miles and a population of 254,200 (1981). ΨPonta Delgada, on São Miguel, is the capital of the group; population is 21,347. Other ports are Ψ Angra, in Terceira, (16,476) and ΨHorta (2,509).

MACAO

Macao, situated at the mouth of the Pearl River, comprises a peninsula and the islands of Coloane and Taipa, having an area of six square miles with a population (Census, 1981) of 261,680. Portuguese trade with China began early in the 16th century and Macao became a Portuguese colony in 1557: in a Sino-Portuguese treaty of Dec. 1887 China recognised Portugal's sovereignty over, and government of, Macao. In 1974 Portugal changed Macao's status from that of an Overseas Province to "a territory under Portuguese administration". Following the Sino-British Joint Declaration on Hong Kong in 1984, Sino-Portuguese negotiations on the transfer of administration are expected to begin in 1986. Macao is subject to Portuguese constitutional law but otherwise enjoys administrative, economic and financial autonomy. The Governor is appointed by the Portuguese President and since 1976 there has been a 17 member legislative assembly, which has a three year term. The assembly comprises 12 elected deputies appointed by the Governor. A new electoral system which came into effect February 28th 1984, gave equal voting rights to all residents, thus enfranchising the Chinese population.

Macao's major industry is textile manufacturing which accounts for 62 per cent. of all exports. Port Macao is served by British, Portuguese and Dutch shipping lines and has regular services to Hong Kong, some 35 miles away.

Governor, Rear Admiral Vasco Almeida e Costa.

Trade with U.K.

	1984
Imports from U.K.	£1,034,000
Exports to U.K.	40,508,000

QATAR

Amir of Qatar, H.H. Sheikh Khalifa Bin Hamad Al-Thani, G.C.M.G.; *assumed power* February 22, 1972 (*also Prime Minister*).

COUNCIL OF MINISTERS

Heir Apparent, Minister of Defence and Commander-in Chief, H.H. Sheikh Hamad Bin Khalifa Al-Thani, K.C.M.G.

Minister of Education, H.E. Shaikh Mohammad Bin Hamad Al-Thani.

Foreign, H.E. Shaikh Suhaim bin Hamad Al-Thani.

Finance and Petroleum Affairs, H.E. Shaikh Abdul Aziz Bin Khalifa Al-Thani.

Municipal Affairs, (vacant).

Economy and Commerce, H.E. Shaikh Naser Bin Khaled Al-Thani.

Justice (vacant).

Electricity and Water, H.E. Shaikh Jasem Bin Moh'd Al-Thani.

Interior, H.E. Shaikh Khalid Bin Hamad Al-Thani.

Industry and Agriculture, H.E. Shaikh Faisal Bin Thani Al-Thani.

Health, H.E. Sayed Khalid Bin Mohammed Al-Mana.

Public Works, H.E. Sayed Khaled Bin Abdullah Al-Attiyah.

Labour and Social Welfare Affairs, H.E. Sayed Ali Bin Ahmed Al-Ansari.

Communications and Transport, H.E. Sayed Abdullah Bin Naser Al-Suwaidi.

Information, H.E. Sayed Issa Ghanim Al-Kawari.

Minister of State for Foreign Affairs, H.E. Shaikh Ahmed bin Saif Al-Thani.

EMBASSY IN LONDON
27 Chesham Place, SW1X 8HG
[01–235 0851]

Ambassador Extraordinary and Plenipotentiary, His Excellency Sherida Sa'ad Jubran Al-Ka'abi.

Minister Plenipotentiary, Abdulrahman A. Al-Wohaibi.

The state of Qatar covers the peninsula of Qatar from approximately the northern shore of Khor al Odaid to the eastern shore of Khor al Salwa. The area is about 4,000 sq. miles, with a population estimated in 1982 at about 250,000. The great majority of the population is concentrated in the urban district of the capital Doha. Only a small minority still pursue the traditional life of the semi-nomadic tribesmen and fisherfolk.

Until 1971, Qatar was one of the nine independent Emirates in the Arabian Gulf in special treaty relations with the U.K. In that year, with the withdrawal of H.M. Forces from the area, these special treaty relations were terminated. On April 2, 1970 a Provisional Constitution for Qatar was proclaimed, providing for the establishment of a Council of Ministers and for the formation of a Consultative Council to assist the Council of Ministers in running the affairs of the State. The first Cabinet was formed of 10 members on May 29, 1970. Qatar is a member of the Arab League as well as of the United Nations.

Production.—Although Qatar is a desert country, there are gardens and smallholdings near Doha and to the north and encouragement is being given to the development of agriculture.

The Qatar General Petroleum Corporation is the state-owned company controlling Qatar's interests in oil, gas and petrochemicals. The corporation is responsible for Qatar's oil production onshore and offshore. The production level for Qatar agreed in O.P.E.C. is currently 280,000 b.p.d. Explorations continue for further oil and also in connection with the large reserves of natural gas in the North Field, which has yet to be tapped. A new 50,000 b.p.d. oil refinery was commissioned in 1984 to increase domestic refinery capacity.

Current industries include a steel mill, a fertiliser plant, a cement factory, a petrochemical complex and two natural gas liquids plants. With the exception of the cement works, which is at Umm Bab, all these industries are at Umm Said, about 30 miles south of Doha. Qatar is also expanding its infrastructure including electrical generation and water distillation, roads, houses, and Government buildings, although reduced demand for crude oil in international markets has led to a downturn in the economy and a slower rate of development than hitherto.

Communications.—Doha is an expanding town with an airport built to international standards. Regular air services connect Qatar with Bahrain and the United Arab Emirates, Kuwait, Muscat, Saudi Arabia, Jordan, Syria, Lebanon, Egypt, the Indian sub-continent and Europe. The Qatar Broadcasting Service transmits on medium, shortwave, and V.H.F. Regular television transmissions in colour began in 1974 and a second channel opened in 1982.

Trade with U.K.

	1983	1984
Imports from U.K....	£216,385,000	£133,803,000
Exports to U.K.	10,956,000	28,212,000

CAPITAL.—Doha. Population (estimated) 200,000. Other towns include Khor, Dukhan, Wakra and Umm Said.

FLAG.—White and maroon, white portion nearer the mast; vertical indented line comprising 17 angles divides the colours.

BRITISH EMBASSY

P.O. Box 3, Doha

Ambassador Extraordinary and Plenipotentiary, His Excellency Julian Fortay Walker, C.M.G., M.B.E. (1984).

1st Secretary, K. N. Johnson (*Commercial*).
2nd Secretary, J. W. Bradley (*Consul and Administration*).
3rd Secretary, S. H. Innes.
Attaché, P. R. Sizeland (*Commercial*).
Vice Consul, D. J. B. Torrance.
British Council Representative, W. S. Beniston, Ras Abu Aboud Road (P.O. Box 2992), Doha.

ROMANIA
(Republica Socialistă România)

President of the Republic, Nicolae Ceauşescu, *first elected*, 1967; *latest re-election*, March 28, 1985.
State Council, N. Ceauşescu (*President*); Manea Mănescu; Gheorghe Rădulescu; Petru Enache; Maria Ghitulica; Árpád Páll (*Vice-Presidents*).

COUNCIL OF MINISTERS

Prime Minister, Constantin Dascalescu.
1st Deputy Prime Ministers, Elena Ceauşescu; Ion Dinca; Gheorghe Oprea.
Deputy Prime Ministers, Ioan Avram; Alexandrina Gainuse; Gheorghe Petrescu; Ludovic Fazekas; Ion Nicolae; Ion Totu; Nicolae Constantin.
Secretary, Lucian Dragut.
Agriculture and Food Industry, Gheorghe David.
Chemical Industry, Gheorghe Dinu.
Education and Instruction, Ion Teoreanu.
Electric Power, Nicolae Busui.
Finance, Petre Gigea.
Foreign Affairs, Stefan Andrei.
Foreign Trade, Vasile Pungan.
Forestry Administration, Ion Cioara.
Geology, Ioan Folea.

Health, Victor Ciobanu.
Industrial Construction, Ion Petre.
Internal Affairs, George Homostean.
Internal Trade, Ana Muresan.
Justice, Gheorghe Chivulescu.
Labour, Maxim Berghianu.
Light Industry, Ion Patan.
Heavy Equipment Industry, Mihai Moraru.
Machine-Building Industry, Marin Nedelcu.
Electrical Engineering Industry, Alexandru Necula.
Metallurgical Industry, Niculai Agachi.
Mines, Marin Stefanache.
National Defence, Col. Gen. Constantin Olteanu.
Oil, Ilie Cisu.
Technical and Material Supply, Petre Preoteasa.
Tourism and Sports, Ion Stanescu.
Transportation and Communications, Vasile Bulucea.
Timber and Building Materials, Richard Winter.
Youth, Nicu Ceausescu.
Minister, Chairmen of Central Bodies, Teodor Coman (*Committee of People's Councils' Affairs*); Aneta Spornic (*State Prices Committee*); Cornel Mihulecea (*State Committee for Nuclear Power*); Stefan Birlea (*State Planning Committee*); Lina Ciobanu (*Central Council of General Confederation of Trade Unions*); Ion Bucur (*1st Vice-Chairman, Council of Economic and Social Organisations*); Suzana Gadea (*Council for Socialist Culture and Education*); Elena Ceausescu (*National Council of Science and Technology*); Ioan Ursu (*1st Vice-Chairman, National Council of Science and Technology*); Ion Badea (*National Council for Water Resources*); Ana Muresan (*National Council of Women*); Vasile Marin (*National Union of Producer Co-operative Farms*).
Minister, Secretaries of State, T. Postelnicu (*Internal Affairs, and Chief of State Security Dept.*); A. Duma (*Foreign Affairs*); I. Ceausescu (*1st Vice-Chair, State Planning Committee*); I. Constantinescu (*State Planning Committee*); D. Bejan (*Technical and Material Supply*); A. Rosu, G. Cazan (*Foreign Trade*); I. Licu (*Machine Building Industry*); A. Stoica (*Chemical Industry*); M. Capisizu, C. Eremia; F. Nagy (*Agriculture and Food Industry*); M. Florescu, E. Dobrescu (*National Council for Science and Technology*); I. Albuletu (*Chief of Food Products Contracting, Purchasing and Storing Dept.*).

THE COMMUNIST PARTY

Political Executive Committee, N. Ceauşescu; I. Banc; E. Bobu; V. Cazacu; E. Ceauşescu; L. Ciobanu; I. Coman; N. Constantin; C. Dascalescu; I. Dinca; M.

Dobrescu; L. Fazekąs; A. Gainuşe; P. Lupu; M. Mănescu; P. Niculescu; C. Olteanu; G. Oprea; G. Pana; I. Pătan; D. Popescu; G. Rădulescu; I. Verdeţ (full members); S. Andrei; S. Birlea; N. Ceausescu; L. Constantin; G. David; M. Enache; P. Enache; S. Gadea; M. Gere; M. Ghitulica; N. Giosan; N. Mihalache; I. Moga; A. Mureşan; E. Nae; M. Nedelcu; C. Pacoste; T. Postelnicu; I. Radu; I. Stoian; I. Szasz; I. Totu; I. Ursu; R. Winter (candidate members).

Permanent Bureau of the Political Executive Committee, N. Ceauşescu; E. Bobu; E. Ceauşescu; C. Dascalescu; M. Mănescu; G. Oprea; G. Rădulescu; I. Verdet.

Secretariat of the Central Committee, N. Ceauşescu (Secretary General); I. Banc; I. Coman; P. Enache; E. Bobu; G. Stoica; L. Ciobanu; S. Curticeanu; C. Radu; I. Radu; I. Stoian; I. Verdet.

ROMANIAN EMBASSY IN LONDON
4 Palace Green, W8 4QD
[01-937 9666]

Ambassador Extraordinary and Plenipotentiary, His Excellency Vasile Gliga (1980).

Area and Population.—Romania is a republic of South-Eastern Europe, formerly the classical *Dacia* and *Scythia Pontica*, having its origin in the union of the Danubian principalities of *Wallachia* and *Moldavia* under the *Treaty of Paris* (April, 1856). The area of Romania is 237,500 sq. km. and the population in July, 1982 was 22,480,000.

Government.—The principalities remained separate entities under Turkish suzerainty until 1859, when Prince Alexandru Ion Cuza was elected Prince of both, still under the suzerainty of Turkey. Prince Cuza abdicated in 1866 and was succeeded by Prince Charles of Hohenzollern-Sigmaringen, in whose successors the crown was vested. By the *Treaty of Berlin* (July 13, 1878) the Principality was recognized as an independent State, and part of the *Dobrudja* (which had been occupied by the Romanians) was incorporated. On March 27, 1881, it was recognized as a Kingdom.

The outcome of the War of 1914–18 added Bessarabia, the Bukovina, Transylvania, The Banat and Crisana-Maramures, these additions of territory being confirmed in the Treaty of St. Germain, 1919, and the Treaty of Petit Trianon, 1920.

On June 27, 1940, in compliance with an ultimatum from U.S.S.R., Bessarabia and Northern Bukovina were ceded to the Soviet Government, and in August, 1940, Romania ceded to Bulgaria the portion of Southern Dobrudja taken from Bulgaria in 1913.

Romania became "The Romanian People's Republic" in December, 1947, on the abdication of King Michael. A new Constitution, modelled on the Soviet Constitution of 1936, was adopted unanimously on September 24, 1952, by the Grand National Assembly. The Assembly was later dissolved and elections were held for a new Grand National Assembly on November 30, 1952; in each constituency there was only one candidate for election, representing the People's Democratic Front, now the Socialist and Democratic Unity Front (S.D.U.F.) A new Constitution was approved by the Grand National Assembly in 1965 when the name of the state was changed to The Socialist Republic of Romania. The Constitution states (Art. 3) that the leading political force of the whole society is the Romanian Communist Party. The Constitution was modified in March, 1974.

Agriculture.—Wallachia, Moldavia and Transylvania are among the most fertile areas in Europe, and agriculture and sheep and cattle raising are the principal industries of Romania, although the intense winter cold and summer heat, and fierce summer drought sometimes have adverse effects on crops. These are principally cereal crops, legumes and other vegetables, flax and hemp. Vines and fruits are also grown. The forests of the mountainous regions are extensive, and the timber industry is important.

Socialization of agriculture was completed when collectivization was achieved in the spring of 1962.

Natural Resources and Industry.—Before the war petroleum and agriculture were the backbone of the Romanian economy but rapid industrialisation since 1948 has meant that they no longer hold the same dominant position. There are plentiful supplies of natural gas, together with various mineral deposits including coal, iron ore, bauxite, lead, zinc, copper and uranium in quantities which allow a substantial part of the requirements of industry to be met from local resources. Production of crude oil was put at about 11,600,000 tonnes in 1983.

The economy has faced increasing problems since the late 1970s, the result of over investment in energy-intensive heavy industry and neglect of agriculture, which has led to food shortages. The effects of these policies were aggravated by the international recession and by high interest rates, and Romania was severely in debt by the early 1980s. The government has sought to alleviate the situation by reducing borrowing and cutting imports. The economy is centrally organized on the basis of Five-Year Plans which cover all branches of national activity including investment and production.

Language and Literature.—Romanian is a Romance language with many archaic forms and with admixtures of Slavonic, Turkish, Magyar and French words. The folk-songs and folklore, transmitted orally through many centuries and collected in the 19th century, form one of the most interesting of such collections. The publication of all books and reviews is controlled and authorized by the Council for Socialist Culture and Education, which has the status of a Ministry. The leading religion is that of the Romanian Orthodox Church; the Roman Catholics and some Protestant denominations are of importance numerically. The Jewish community has declined through emigration.

Education is free and nominally compulsory. There are Universities at Bucharest, Iasi, Cluj, Timisoara, Craiova and Brasov, polytechnics at Bucharest, Timisoara, Cluj, Brasov, Galati and Iasi, two commercial academies at Bucharest and Brasov, and agricultural colleges at Bucharest, Iasi, Cluj, Craiova and Timisoara.

Communications.—In 1979 there were 11,113 km. of railway open for traffic. The mercantile marine had a gross tonnage of 13,220,000 tons in 1979. The principal ports are Constanta (on the Black Sea), Sulina (on the Danube Estuary), Galati, Braila, Giurgiu and Turnu Severin. The Danube and the Black Sea are linked by a canal completed in 1984. Romania is a member of the Danube Commission whose seat is at Budapest.

FINANCE

	1983
Revenue	Lei 259,359·0m.
Expenditure	236,796·2m.

The unit of currency is the *Lei* of 100 *Bani* (see also p. 82).

TRADE

	1983
Imports	Lei130,370m.
Exports	173,324m.

Imports are chiefly semi-manufactured goods, raw materials, machinery and metals; export consists principally of maize, wheat, barley, oats, petroleum, timber, cattle, machines and industrial equipment. External trade with Communist countries dropped from 80 per cent. in 1960 to 45 per cent. in 1978.

Trade with U.K.

	1983	1984
Imports from U.K.	£82,160,000	£71,641,000
Exports to U.K.	58,865,000	226,091,000

CAPITAL, Bucharest, on the Dimbovita, population 1,960,097. Other large towns are: Constanța (279,308); Iasi (262,493); Timișoara (281,320); Cluj-Napoca (274,095); Brașov (299,172); Ploiești (207,009); Craiova (220,893); ΨGalați (252,884); ΨBrăila (208,983); Arad (172,669); Oradea (178,407); Sibiu (156,854); Pitești (133,179); Tirgú Mures (129,284).

FLAG.—Three vertical bands, blue, yellow, red, with the emblem of the Republic in the centre band.

NATIONAL DAY.—August 23 (Liberation Day, 1944).

BRITISH EMBASSY
24 Strada Jules Michelet, Bucharest

Ambassador Extraordinary and Plenipotentiary, His Excellency Philip McKearney (1983).
Counsellor, Miss M. MacGlashan (*Head of Chancery*).
Defence, Naval and Military Attaché, Lt.-Col. S. P. Walters.
Cultural Attaché and British Council Representative, K. McGuinness.

RWANDA
(Republic of Rwanda)

President, Maj. Gen. Juvénal Habyarimana, *assumed office*, July 5, 1973, *elected*, Dec. 24, 1978, *re-elected*, Dec. 19, 1983.

Rwanda, formerly part of the Belgian-administered trusteeship of Ruanda-Urundi, has an area of 10,169 sq. miles and a population (1982 estimate) of 5,110,000, mainly of the Bahutu tribe, with Batutsi and Batwa minorities.

A referendum held in September, 1961, showed the majority of the population were opposed to the retention of the monarchy which was accordingly abolished on Oct. 2, 1961. Rwanda became an independent Republic on July 1, 1962, with Gregoire Kayibanda as Head of State and Head of the Government. He was deposed in 1973, and replaced by a military government under Maj.-Gen. Juvénal Habyarimana.

Coffee (the chief cash crop), tea and sugar are grown. Tin, hides, bark of quinine and extract of pyrethrum flowers are also exported.

A University was opened at Butare in 1963.

The currency is the *Rwanda franc*. In 1980 total imports were valued at *Rw.Fr.*22,568 m.; total exports, *Rw.Fr.*7,025 m.

Trade with U.K.

	1983	1984
Imports from U.K.	£2,326,000	£2,385,000
Exports to U.K.	2,919,000	7,842,000

CAPITAL.—Kigali (7,000).

FLAG.—Three vertical bands, red, yellow and green with letter R on yellow band.

NATIONAL DAY.—July 5.

British Ambassador (resident at *Kinshasa*, Zaire).

EL SALVADOR
(República de El Salvador)

President, José Napoleon Duarte, *elected* March 25, 1984, *assumed office*, June 1, 1984.

CABINET

Vice-President and Foreign Minister, Rodolfo Castillo Claramount.
Minister of the Presidency, Dr. Jorge E. Tenorio.
Culture and Communications, Julio A. Rey Prendes.
Planning and Co-ordination of Economic and Social Development, Dr. Fidel Chávez Mena.
Justice, Dr. Julio A. Samayoa.
Finance, Ricardo J. López.
Trade, Julio Rivas Gallont.
Economy, Dr. Ricardo Gonzalez Comacho.
Education, Prof. Alberto Buendía Flores.
Defence and Public Security, Gen. Carlos E. Vides Casanova.
Labour and Social Security, Dr. Miguel A. Gallegos.
Agriculture, Carlos A. Duarte Funes.
Public Works, Roberto Mueza.

SALVADOREAN EMBASSY AND CONSULATE
9 Welbeck House, 62 Welbeck Street, W.1
[01-486 8182/3]

Chargé d'Affaires, Sr. Roberto T. Rivas Gardiner.

Area and Population.—The Republic of El Salvador extends along the Pacific coast of Central America for 160 miles with a general breadth of about 50 miles, and contains an area of 8,200 square miles with a population (1983 estimate) of 4,950,000. It is divided into 14 Departments.

The surface of the country is very mountainous, many of the peaks being extinct volcanoes. The highest are the Santa Ana volcano (7,700 ft.) and the San Vicente volcano (7,200 ft.). Much of the interior has an average altitude of 2,000 feet. The lowlands along the coast are generally hot, but towards the interior the altitude tempers the severity of the heat. There is a wet season from May to October, and a dry season from November to April. Earthquakes have been frequent in the history of El Salvador, the most recent being that of May 3, 1965, when considerable damage was done to San Salvador.

The principle river is the Rio Lempa. There is a large volcanic lake (Ilopango) a few miles to the east of the capital, while farther away and to the west lies the smaller lake of Coatepeque, which appears to have been formed in a vast crater flanked by the Santa Ana volcano.

Government.—El Salvador was conquered in 1526 by Pedro de Alvarado, and formed part of the Spanish vice-royalty of Guatemala until 1821.

After two years of government by a Junta headed by José Napoleon Duarte, elections for a Constituent Assembly were held in March 1982. The Assembly has completed its principal task of adopting a new Constitution. Presidential elections, although boycotted by the guerrilla movement, were held in March 1984 and in the run-off between the two largest parties, Sr. Duarte, the Christian Democrat leader, won with a 54 per cent. majority over the ARENA candidate, Roberto d'Aubuisson. Assembly and municipal elections took place in March 1985.

Despite the new government, guerrilla warfare continues.

Agriculture.—The principal cash crops are coffee, which is grown principally on the slopes of the volcanoes, cotton, which is cultivated on the coastal plains, and sugarcane. (However, cotton and sugar production have decreased as a result of the civil war.) Also cultivated are maize, sesame, indigo, rice, balsam, etc. In the lower altitudes towards the east, sisal is produced and used in the manufacture of coffee and cereal bags. Land reforms, announced in March 1980, are being undertaken. The Salvadorean Coffee Company, sugar exports and the banking system are nationalised.

Industry.—Existing factories make textiles, constructional steel, furniture, cement and household items. El Salvador is a member of the Central American Common Market. The first trade zone was inaugurated in November 1974 and the National Assembly approved a new Export Development Law.

Education.—The illiteracy rate is about 30·5 per cent (1980). Primary education is nominally compulsory, but the number of schools and teachers available is too small to enable education to be given to all children of school age. In recent Budgets, however, a high percentage of the national revenue has been devoted to education and great efforts are being made to eliminate the existing shortage of schools and teachers.

Language and Literature.—The language of the country is Spanish. Indigenous literature has not yet produced work of international repute. There are 4 daily newspapers published at the capital, and 4 in the provinces.

Communications.—The Executive Autonomous Port Commission (CEPA) which administers the previously foreign-owned port of Cutuco, at La Union and the principal port of Acajutla, and the railways under the new railroad organization, FENADESAL. There is continuous railway communication between San Salvador and Guatemala City and Puerto Barrios on the Caribbean coast. The roads are paved and in good condition but bridges are frequently dynamited. There are good motor roads between Port Acajutla and the capital (60 miles), and between the capital and Guatemala City. The Pan-American Highway from the Guatemalan frontier follows this route and continues to the Honduran frontier. The El Salvador international airport can receive jet aircraft and many international airlines fly to San Salvador.

There are post and telegraph offices throughout the country. There are 40 broadcasting stations and six television stations.

BUDGET

	1981	1982
	Colones '000	
Revenue	1,068,316	1,091,532
Expenditure	1,581,292	1,649,423

TRADE

	1982	1983
	Colones '000	
Imports	2,207,161	2,230,000
Exports	1,760,038	1,838,500

Trade with U.K.

	1983	1984
Imports from U.K.	£7,653,000	£7,589,000
Exports to U.K.	425,000	2,551,000

There is strict foreign exchange control (*see also* p. 82).

Coffee to the value of ₡1,020,000 was exported in 1983. Exports of cotton were valued at ₡1,400,000. Other exports are sugar (₡1,000,000), shrimps, sisal (in the form of bags used for exporting coffee, sugar, etc.), balsam, meat, towels, hides and skins. The chief imports are chemicals, fertilizers, pharmaceutical goods, petroleum, manufactured goods, industrial and electronic machinery and equipment.

CAPITAL.—San Salvador. Population, (est. 1980) 425,119. Other towns are Santa Ana (204,570), San Miguel (157,838), Ψ La Union (Cutuco), Ψ La Libertad and Ψ Acajutia.

FLAG.—Three horizontal bands light blue, white, light blue; coat of arms on white band.

NATIONAL DAY.—September 15.

BRITISH EMBASSY
P.O. Box 1591, San Salvador

British Ambassador, (resident at Tegucigalpa, Honduras).
Chargé d'Affaires a.i., David Ridgway (*First Secretary*).

SAN MARINO
(Repubblica di San Marino)

Regents, Two "Capitani Reggenti".

CONSULATE GENERAL IN LONDON
86 Park Lane, W1A 3AA
[01–499 6363]
Consul-General, The Lord Forte.

A small Republic in the hills near Rimini, on the Adriatic, founded, it is stated, by a pious stonecutter of Dalmatia in the 4th century. The Republic always resisted the Papal claims, and those of neighbouring dukedoms, during the 15th–18th centuries, and its integrity and sovereignty is recognized and respected by Italy. The Republic is governed by a State Congress of 10 members, under the Presidency of two Heads of State, who are elected at six-monthly intervals. The Great and General Council, a legislative body of 60 members, is elected by a universal suffrage for a term of 5 years. A Council of Twelve forms in certain cases a Supreme Court of Justice. The area is approximately 23 square miles, the population (April 30, 1985) is 22,361. The city of San Marino, on the slope of Monte Titano, has three towers, a fine church and Government palace, a theatre and museums. The principal products are wine, cereals, and cattle, and the main industries are tourism, ceramics, lime, concrete, cotton yarns, colour and paints. A Treaty of Extradition between the Governments of Great Britain and the Republic of San Marino has been in force since 1899.

FLAG.—Two horizontal bands, white, blue (with coat of arms of the Republic in centre).

BRITISH CONSULATE-GENERAL

Consul-General, I. J. Rawlinson (resides at Florence).

SÃO TOMÉ AND PRÍNCIPE

President, Dr. Manuel Pinto da Costa (*also holds Foreign Affairs and Planning portfolios*).

COUNCIL OF MINISTERS

Defence and National Security, Maj. Oscar A. Sacramento e Sousa.
Agriculture and Animal Husbandry, Tomé Dias da Costa.
Co-operation, Carlos Alberto Tini.
Industry, Works and Housing, José Frete Lau Chong.
Commerce and Fisheries, Celestino Rocha da Costa.
Health and Sports, Frederico José Henriques Sequeira.
Education and Culture, Mrs. Ligia Silva Graça do Espírito Santo Costa.
Justice, Francisco Fortunato Peres
Employment and Social Security, Armindo Vaz de Almeida.
Information, Secretary to the Council of Ministers, Manuel Vaz Afonso Fernandez.

The islands of São Tomé and Príncipe are situated in the gulf of Guinea, off the west coast of Africa. They have an area of 372 square miles, and a population (1981 est.) of 115,000.

Following Portugal's decision to grant independence, a transitional government was installed on Dec. 21, 1974, and the islands became an independent democratic republic on July 12, 1975.

Cacao is the main product.

Trade with U.K.

	1983	1984
Imports from U.K.	£597,000	£962,000
Exports to U.K.	218,000	450,000

CAPITAL.—Ψ São Tomé (3,187).

FLAG.—Horizontal stripes of green, yellow, green, the yellow of double width and bearing two black stars; and a red triangle in the hoist.

British Ambassador (resident in *Luanda*, Angola).

SAUDI ARABIA
(Al Mamlaka al Arabiya as-Sa'udiyya)

King of Saudi Arabia, H.M. King Fahd bin Abdul Aziz, born, 1921, *ascended the throne* June 1, 1982.

Crown Prince, H.R.H. Amir Abdullah bin Abdul Aziz.

COUNCIL OF MINISTERS

Prime Minister, H.M. King Fahd bin Abdul Aziz.

First Deputy Prime Minister and Commander of the National Guard, H.R.H. Prince Abdullah bin Abdul Aziz.

Second Deputy Prime Minister and Defence, H.R.H. Prince Sultan bin Abdul Aziz.

Public Works and Housing, H.R.H. Prince Mit'ab bin Abdul Aziz.

Interior, H.R.H. Prince Naif bin Abdul Aziz.

Foreign Affairs, H.R.H. Prince Saud al-Faisal bin Abdul Aziz.

Finance and National Economy, Shaikh Muhammad Aba al-Khail.

Agriculture and Water, Dr. Abdul Rahman bin Abdul Aziz bin Hassan Al al-Shaikh.

Municipal and Rural Affairs, Shaikh Ibrahim bin Abdullah al-Angari.

Higher Education, Shaikh Hassan bin Abdullah Al al-Shaikh.

Commerce, Dr Sulaiman Al-Abdul Aziz al-Solaim.

Communications, Shaikh Husain Mansouri.

Petroleum and Mineral Resources, Shaikh Ahmad Zaki Yamani.

Justice, Mohammed bin Ibrahim Al al-Shaikh.

Labour and Social Affairs, Dr. Mohamed Ali al-Faiz.

Information, Ali Sha'er.

Health, Faisal bin Abdul Aziz al Hejailan.

Pilgrimage and Endowments, Shaikh Abdul Wahhab Ahmed Abdul Wasi.

Education, Dr. Abdul Aziz Al-Abdullah al-Khuwaiter.

Planning, Shaikh Hisham Mohiyiddin Nazer.

Posts, Telegraphs and Telephones, Dr. Alawi Darwish Kayyal.

Industry and Electricity, Abdul Aziz al-Zamil.

Ministers of State, Shaikh Muhammad Ibrahim Mas'oud; Dr. Muhammad al-Amran; Dr. Muhammad Abdul Latif al-Melhem; Shaikh Nasir ash-Shitri.

ROYAL SAUDI ARABIAN EMBASSY
30 Belgrave Square, SW1X 8QB
[01–235 0831]

Ambassador Extraordinary and Plenipotentiary, His Excellency Sheikh Nasser Almanqour, G.C.V.O. (1980).

Minister Plenipotentiary, Naji S. Mufti.

The Kingdom of Saudi Arabia is a personal union of two countries, the Sultan of Nejd becoming also King of the Hijaz. Great Britain recognized Abdulaziz Ibn Saud as an independent ruler, King of the Hijaz and of Nejd and its Dependencies, by the Treaty of Jedda (May 20, 1927). The name was changed to the Kingdom of Saudi Arabia in Sept 1932.

The total area of the Kingdom is about 927,000 sq. miles, with a population (1976 est.) of 9,160,000, of whom perhaps 4 million are non-Saudis. Islam is the established and only permitted religion.

In the 18th century Nejd was an independent state governed from Diriya (now in ruins, 25 km. from Riyadh) and the stronghold of the Wahhabis, a puritanical Islamic sect. It subsequently fell under the Turkish yoke, but in 1913 Abdulaziz Ibn Saud threw off Turkish rule and captured the Turkish province of al Hasa. In 1920 he captured the Asir, and in 1921, by force of arms, he added to his dominions the Jebel Shammar territory of the Rashid family. In 1925 he completed the conquest of the Hejaz.

Saudi Arabia comprises almost the whole of the Arabia peninsula, with the exception of the small states in the extreme south (N. and S. Yemen), south-east (Oman and the U.A.E.) and east (Qatar). In the north-west it borders Jordan and in the north-east Iraq and Kuwait, while to the west lies the Red Sea and to the east the Gulf. The Nejd ("Plateau"), now the Central Province, extends over the centre of the peninsula, including the Nafud and Dahna deserts. The Hijaz ("the Boundary") now the Western Province, extends along the Red Sea coast to Asir and contains the holy towns of Mecca and Medina. The former, about 60 km. east of Jedda, is the birthplace of the Prophet Muhammad, and contains the Great Mosque, within which is the Kaaba or sacred shrine of the Muslim religion. This is the focus of the annual Hajj ("Pilgrimage") performed by 1·6 million in 1984. The latter, Medina al Munawwarah ("The City of Light") was 300 km. north of Mecca, is celebrated as the first city to embrace Islam and as the Prophet Muhammad's burial place (he died there on Rabia 12, 11 AH, corresponding to June 7, 632 AD).

Asir ("Inaccessible") is named for its mountainous terrain, and, with the coastal plain of the Tihama, lies along the southern Red Sea coast from Hijaz to the border with Yemen. It is the only region to enjoy substantial rainfall. Water supplies are, however, supplemented by dams and irrigation. The east and south-east of the country are lower-lying and largely desert. Outside the manufacturing centres which have grown up around some of the towns, most of the population are engaged in agriculture. The productivity of traditional dryland farming is increasingly supplemented by irrigation.

Industry.—Oil was found in commercial quantities in Dhahran, near Dammam, in 1938. Total production of crude oil peaked at 9·9 m.b.d. in 1980, and in 1984 was 4,444,000 b.p.d. About 97 per cent of the total is extracted by the Arabian–American Oil Company. Aramco's 66-year lease will terminate in 1999 but the company was nationalized in 1980. Aramco operates a deepwater oil terminal at Ras Tanura.

The Government actively encourages the establishment of manufacturing industries in the country. The policy includes the provision of industrial estates and loans covering 50 per cent of capital investment. By the end of 1984 about 3,000 private industrial licences had been granted, and 1,751 were in production. These establishments were concentrated in the fields of construction materials, metal fabrication, simple machinery and electrical equipment, food and beverages, chemicals and plastics. The Government is trying to encourage future investment in industrial gases, intermediate petrochemicals, light engineering, machinery and all kinds of spare parts.

The Government has also established two industrial poles at Jubail and Yanbu, financed by the state agency Saudi Basic Industries Corp., to be the focus of heavy industrial development. Linked by gas and oil pipelines, both are to have petrochemical complexes producing, initially, ethylene and methanol,

six of the seven plants now on-stream are joint ventures with American and Japanese companies. In addition an integrated steel complex and a urea fertilizer factory are in production in Jubail with West German and Taiwanese partners. Complete new cities are being built at each pole: Jubail will eventually house 300,000 and Yanbu 150,000. The state agency Petromin operates three domestic refineries and two lubricant plants and the last of three joint-venture export refineries will come on-stream in 1986. Total refining capacity will then be 1,225,000 b.p.d.

Communications.—The railway from the port of Dammam to the oilfields at Abqaiq and through Hofuf to Riyadh was opened in 1951, and a direct Dammam-Riyadh line opened in 1985. An extension to Jedda via Medina and the reopening of the Hejaz railway are planned. Metalled roads connect all the cities and main towns: the network consisted of 27,900 km. in 1984. The principal port of the Gulf is Dammam which has 37 piers and an annual capacity of 9·1 million tons. Jedda is the centre of commercial traffic on the Red Sea and has 43 piers, giving an annual capacity of 17 million tons. The Government-owned Saudi Arabian Airlines (Saudia) operate scheduled services to 19 domestic airports. There are international class airports at Dhahran, Jedda and Riyadh; new international airports have opened at the latter two, and work has begun on a new Dhahran airport. Saudia have an extensive overseas operation, and a large number of international airlines operate into the country. Telecommunications are being rapidly expanded. By mid-1984 16,570 telex and 857,800 telephone lines were installed; telephone and telex exchanges will be able to handle 2·25 million lines by 1990. The Government is a major participant in the Arab Satellite Communications Organisation.

Education.—With the exception of a few schools for expatriate children, all schools are Government supervised and segregated for boys and girls. In 1984 there were a total of 1·9 million schoolchildren in 7,269 primary and 3,085 intermediate and secondary schools. There are Universities in Jedda, Mecca, Riyadh (branches in Abha and Qassim) and Dammam (branch at Hofuf). There is a University of Petroleum and Minerals at Dhahran, and there are Islamic Universities in Medina and Riyadh. In addition there is great emphasis on vocational training, provided at 24 literacy and artisan skill training centres and 21 more advanced industrial, commercial and agricultural education institutes in 1984. Education in government-owned institutes is free at all levels.

Finance and Trade.—Oil remains the main source of receipts in the balance of payments. As a result, Government revenues have been markedly affected by oil prices and volume of production, and fell away from a peak of SR368,000 million in 1981–82 to SR167,000 million in 1984–85. The 1985 budget provided for balanced revenue and expenditure of SR200,000 million, of which 55 per cent of outlay was allocated to development projects. There is no public debt. There are no restrictions on foreign exchange transactions. The currency is strong, backed by gold and foreign exchange reserves, and maintained on a close parity to the U.S. dollar.

With the exceptions of alcohol, pork products and firearms there are no restrictions on imports. The leading suppliers of imports are U.S.A., Japan, West Germany, the U.K., Italy and France and the chief customers for exports are Japan, France, U.S.A. and Singapore.

	1982
Total imports	SR139,335 m.
Total exports	271,090 m.

Trade with U.K.

	1983	1984
Imports from U.K.	£1,478,587,354	£1,387,163,000
Exports to U.K.	897,701,728	545,149,000

CAPITAL.—Riyadh, population about 1 million. Other major centres are Jedda (pop. approx. 1 million), Dramman, Buraydah, Hufuf and Tabuk.

FLAG.—Green oblong, white Arabic device in centre: "There is no God but God, Muhammad is the Prophet of God," and a white scimitar beneath the lettering.

BRITISH EMBASSY
Riyadh.

Ambassador Extraordinary and Plenipotentiary, His Excellency Sir Patrick Wright, K.C.M.G. (1984).
Counsellors, A. F. Green; J. Q. Greenstock (*Commercial*); G. L. St. L. Rollestan.
Defence Attaché, Col. J. R. A. Daniel.
Air Attaché, Wing-Cdr. Springett.
Naval Attaché, Cdr. I. A. Vosper.
1st Secretaries, R. J. Newell (*Commercial*); R. D. Lamb (*Commercial*); M. J. Copson (*Defence Sales*); J. H. Smyth (*Administration*).

Consul General, Jedda, G. P. Lockton.
British Council Representative, M. R. W. Dexter, O.B.E., Mura'aba, P.O. Box 2701, Riyadh 11461. There is also an office in Jeddah.

SENEGAL
(République du Sénégal)

President and Head of Government, Abdou Diouf, installed, Jan. 1, 1981, elected for 5-year term, Feb. 27, 1983.

SENEGAL EMBASSY IN LONDON
11 Phillimore Gardens, W8 7QG
[01–937 0925/6, 3139]

Ambassador Extraordinary and Plenipotentiary, His Excellency Gen. Idrissa Fall, M.B.E. (1984).

Senegal lies on the west coast of Africa between Mauritania in the north, Mali in the east, and Guinea-Bissau and Guinea in the south. The Gambia lies entirely within Senegal, except for its sea-coast. (*For* MAP, *see* index.) It has an area of 77,814 sq. miles and a population (1980 estimate) of 5,661,000.

Formerly a French colony, Senegal elected on Nov. 25, 1958, to remain within the French Community as an autonomous republic. In March, 1963 (after an attempted *coup d'état* by the then Prime Minister in the previous December) a new constitution was approved giving executive powers to the President, on the lines of the present French constitution. The process of political liberalisation continued; there are now 16 political parties officially recognised. Eight parties contested the General Election in Feb. 1983. The P.S. took 111 seats, the P.D.S. 8, and the R.N.D. 1.

In Feb. 1982, after an attempted coup in The Gambia in July 1981 had been put down with the aid of Sengalese troops, the Senegambia Confederation was established, based on certain joint institutions and the integration of defence, security and some other matters. Each country remains sovereign and independent. The President of Senegal is President of the Confederation and the President of The Gambia is Confederal Vice-President.

Senegal's principal exports are groundnuts (raw and processed) and phosphates. Tourism is also of growing importance as a revenue earner. G.N.P. per capita in 1980 was about U.S.$450.

Trade with U.K.

	1983	1984
Imports from U.K.	£13,212,000	£15,772,000
Exports to U.K.	22,333,000	23,789,000

CAPITAL—ΨDakar (1,000,000).

FLAG.—Three vertical bands, green, yellow and red; a green star on the yellow band.

NATIONAL DAY.—April 4.

BRITISH EMBASSY
B.P. 6025, Dakar.

Ambassador Extraordinary and Plenipotentiary, His Excellency Peter Laurence O'Keeffe, C.M.G., C.V.O. (1982).
1st Secretary, S. F. Howarth (*Head of Chancery*).
2nd Secretary, M. N. Napier (*Consul*).
3rd Secretaries, R. D. Fitchett; S. Buckley (*Administration/Vice-Consul*).
Cultural Attaché (*British Council Representative*), J. M. Tod.

SOMALIA
(Somali Democratic Republic)

President and Sec. Gen. of Council, Maj.-Gen. Mohamed Siad Barre, *assumed office* Oct. 21, 1969.
First Vice-President and Minister of Defence, Lt. Gen. M. A. Samantar.
Second Vice-President and Minister of Planning, Maj. Gen. H. K. Afrah.
Industry and Commerce, Maj. Gen. A. M. Fadil.
Interior, Brig. Gen. A. S. Abdalla.
Finance, Dr. M. S. Osman.
Mineral Resources, Col. A. M. Farah.
Information, Col. M. O. Jess.
Public Works, A. S. Hassan.
Livestock, Col. M. R. Ghod.
Labour and Sports, Col. M. A. Jama.
Minister of State, Presidential Affairs, A. A. Adow.
Chairman, Central Committee, Somali Revolutionary Socialist Party, A. A. Botan.
Chairman, People's Assembly, Brig. Gen. M. I. Ahmed.

SOMALI EMBASSY
60 Portland Place, W1N 3DG
[01-580 7148]

Ambassador Extraordinary and Plenipotentiary, His Excellency Salah Mohamed Ali (1985).

The Somali Democratic Republic occupies part of the north-east horn of Africa, with a coast-line on the Indian Ocean extending from the boundary with Kenya (2° South latitude) to Cape Guardafui (12° N.);

and on the Gulf of Aden to the boundary with Djibouti. Somalia is bounded on the west by Djibouti, Ethiopia and Kenya and covers an area of approximately 246,000 sq. miles. The population, of which a large proportion is nomadic, is estimated (Jan. 1983) at 5,000,000.

Government.—The Somali Democratic Republic, consisting of the former British Somaliland Protectorate and the former Italian trust territory of Somalia, was established on July 1, 1960. British rule in Somaliland lasted from 1887 until 1960 except for a short period in 1940–41 when the Protectorate was occupied by Italian forces. Somalia, formerly an Italian colony, was occupied by British forces in 1941. In 1950 it was placed under Italian administration by a resolution of the U.N.; this trusteeship lasted until independence. Following the assassination of President Shermake on October 15, 1969, the armed forces, assisted by the police, took over the Government without resistance and a Revolutionary Council under Siad Barre assumed control of the country. A new constitution was introduced following a referendum in 1979. This provides for an elected People's Assembly of 171 seats. The Assembly met for the first time in January 1980. There is an outstanding territorial dispute with Ethiopia and incursions by Ethiopian-backed Somali rebels occurred in disputed areas in July 1982.

Livestock raising is the main occupation in Somalia and there is a modest export trade in livestock on the hoof, skins and hides. Italy and the Gulf States import the bulk of the banana crop, the second biggest export.

Trade with U.K.

	1983	1984
Imports from U.K.	£18,987,000	£14,165,000
Exports to U.K.	681,000	1,582,000

CAPITAL.—ΨMogadishu, population (estimated 1982), 600,000. Other towns are Hargeisa (150,000), Kisimayu (30,000), ΨBerbera (60,000) and Burao (15,000).

FLAG.—Five-pointed white star on blue ground.

NATIONAL DAY.—July 1.

BRITISH EMBASSY
(PO Box No. 1036) Mogadishu

Ambassador Extraordinary and Plenipotentiary, His Excellency William Hugh Fullerton (1983).
1st Secretary and Consul, P. H. Gay (*Head of Chancery*).

SOUTH AFRICA
(Republiek van Suid-Afrika)

State President, Pieter Willem Botha, *sworn in*, Sept. 14, 1984.

CABINET

Defence, Gen. Magnus Malan.
Manpower, P. T. du Plessis.
Co-operation and Development and (*Black*) *Education*, Dr. G. van N. Viljoen.
Agricultural Economics and Water Affairs, J. J. G. Wentzel.
Industries and Commerce, Dr. David J. de Villiers.
Finance, B. J. du Plessis.
Transport, H. Schoeman.
National Education, and Chairman, Ministers Council for White Own Affairs, F. W. De. Klerk.
Interior, S. Botha.
Justice, H. J. Coetzee.
Environment and Tourism, J. Wiley.
Communications and Public Works, Dr. L. A. P. Munnik.

Foreign Affairs, R. F. Botha.
Mineral and Energy Affairs, D. W. Steyn.
Law and Order, L. le Grange.
Health and Welfare, Dr. W. Van Niekerk.
Constitutional Development and Planning, J. C. Heunis.
Administration and Advisory Services to the Office of the State President, E. Louw.
Chairman, Ministers Council for Coloured Own Affairs, A. Hendrickse.
Chairman, Ministers Council for Indian Own Affairs, A. Rajbansi.

EMBASSY AND CONSULATE
South Africa House, Trafalgar Square, WC2N 5DP
[01–930 4488]

Ambassador Extraordinary and Plenipotentiary, His Excellency Dr. Denis John Worrall (1984).
Minister, L. H. Evans.
Armed Forces Attaché, Col. M. J. van Niekerk.
Minister (Commercial), E. A. Erasmus.
Director of Information, J. J. Venter.

There is a consulate-general at Golden Cross House, 8 Duncannon Street, W.C.2. [01–839 2211]

Area and Population.—The Republic, comprising the Provinces of the Cape of Good Hope, Natal, the Transvaal and the Orange Free State, occupies the southernmost part of the African continent from the courses of the Limpopo, Molopo and Orange Rivers (34° 50′ 22″ South latitude) to the Cape of Good Hope, with the exception of Lesotho, Botswana and Swaziland, and part of Mozambique. It has a total area of 472,494 sq. miles (1,223,712 sq. km.) and a total population (U.N. estimate, 1984) of 31,010,000 (of which approx. 18 per cent are white).

The southernmost province contains many parallel ranges, which rise in steps towards the interior. The south-western peninsula contains the famous *Table Mountain* (3,582 feet), while the *Great Swartberg* and *Langeberg* run in parallel lines from west to east of the Cape Province. Between these two ranges and the *Roggeveld* and *Nuweveld* ranges to the north is the Great Karoo Plateau, which is bounded on the east by the *Sneeuberg*, containing the highest summit in the province (Kompasberg, 7,800 feet). In the east are ranges which join the *Drakensberg* (11,000 feet) between Natal and the Orange Free State.

The Orange Free State presents a succession of undulating grassy plains, with good pasture-land, at a general elevation of some 3,800 feet, with occasional hills or kopjes. The Transvaal is also mainly an elevated plateau with parallel ridges in the *Magaliesberg* and *Waterberg* ranges of no great height. The veld or plains of this northernmost province is

divisible into the High Veld of the south, the Bushveld of the centre, and the Low Veld of the north and east, the first and second forming the grazing and agricultural region of the Transvaal and the last a fertile sub-tropical area. The eastern province of Natal has pastoral lowlands and rich agriculture land between the slopes of the Drakensberg and the coast, the interior rising in terraces as in the southern provinces. The *Orange*, with its tributary the *Vaal*, is the principal river of the south, rising in the Drakensberg and flowing into the Atlantic between Namibia and the Cape Province. The *Limpopo*, or Crocodile River, in the north, rises in the Transvaal and flows into the Indian Ocean through Mozambique. Most of the remaining rivers are furious torrents after rain, with partially dry beds at other seasons.

Government.—The self-governing colonies of the Cape of Good Hope, Natal, the Transvaal and the Orange River Colony became united on May 31, 1910, under the South Africa Act, 1909, in a legislative union under the name of the Union of South Africa, the four colonies becoming Provinces of the Union. The Union of South Africa continued as a member of the British Commonwealth until 1961. After a referendum held among white voters on October 5, 1960, the Union of South Africa became a republic on May 31, 1961, and withdrew from the Commonwealth.

A new Constitution came into effect on Sept. 30, 1984, which provided for an executive President and a three-chamber Parliament; the House of Assembly (178 members) representing Whites, the House of Representatives (85 members) representing Coloureds, and the House of Delegates (45 members) representing Indians. The black population has no representation. There is joint parliamentary responsibility for "general" affairs (foreign policy, defence, finance, law and order, justice, transport, manpower, commerce and industry, agriculture), and each chamber has separate responsibility for the "own" affairs of the population group it represents (housing, social welfare, health, education, local government and some aspects of agriculture). Disputes between the chambers may be referred by the President to the President's Council (60 members—20 White, 10 Coloured, 5 Indian elected by their respective chambers, 15 nominated by the President, 10 nominated by Opposition parties).

The President is chosen by an 88-member electoral college (in the proportion 4 White : 2 Coloured : 1 Indian) of the majority parties of the three chambers. The President appoints the Cabinet, which he chairs, from all three communities, and also appoints each community's ministerial council for "own" affairs.

Elections to the House of Representatives and House of Delegates took place in Aug. 1984. The turnout for the Coloured assembly election was estimated at 29·6 per cent of registered voters (18 per cent of those eligible) and for the Indian assembly election at 20·3 per cent of registered voters (16·6 per cent of those eligible).

The promulgation of the new Constitution on Sept. 3, 1984 coincided with rioting in the black townships and the continuing unrest led to the declaration on July 20, 1985 of a State of Emergency in 36 districts of the eastern Cape and Johannesburg areas.

The Black Homelands.—The homelands are areas set aside for occupation by blacks. Six areas—Gazankulu, Lebowa, KwaNdebele, KaNgwane, Qwaqwa and KwaZulu—are designated self-governing "national states". A further four areas—Bophuthatswana, Ciskei, Transkei and Venda—are regarded as independent republics by the South African government but they are not recognised as such by the United Nations.

Education.—The Provinces have been relieved of all vocational education (technical and industrial), and the Department of National Education under the

Minister is concerned with universities, technical colleges, schools of industries, reformatories and State technical, housecraft and commercial high schools, State-aided vocational schools and State and State-aided special schools for the physically handicapped.

Communications.—The State-owned and controlled South African Transport Services operates the national railway system, the principal harbours, most long-distance passenger and freight road transport services, the South African Airways airline and a network of pipelines for petroleum products.

There are international airports at Johannesburg (Jan Smuts), Durban (Louis Botha) and Cape Town (D. F. Malan), with another under construction at La Mercy, Natal. South African Airways operates international services to Europe, North and South America, Australia, the Far East and the Middle East, as well as to neighbouring countries, and it is the principal operator of domestic flights.

The largest sea-port is Durban, Natal. Other major ports are Cape Town, Port Elizabeth, East London, Saldanha Bay and Mossel Bay in Cape Province and Richards Bay, Natal.

Production.—Mining is of the greatest importance to the South African economy, contributing 14·3 per cent to G.D.P. in 1982 (of which gold mining accounted for 10 per cent). Principal minerals produced are: gold, coal, iron ore, diamonds, copper, manganese, lime and limestone and asbestos.

Agriculture, forestry and fishing accounts for 6·2 per cent of G.D.P. Over 50 per cent of land is pasture so livestock farming is widespread with meat and wool important products. Principal crops are: maize, sugar-cane, fruits and vegetables, wheat, sorghum, sunflower seed and groundnuts. Cotton is widely grown because of its suitability to the climate, and viticulture is also widespread.

Industries, concentrated most heavily around Johannesburg, Pretoria and the major ports, process foodstuffs, metals and non-metallic mineral products, and also produce beverages and tobacco, motor vehicles, chemicals and chemical products, machinery, textiles and clothing, and paper and paper products.

Trade.—Principal exports are: gold, base metals and metal products, diamonds, food (especially fruit), chemicals, machinery and transport equipment, and wool. Principal imports are: machinery, chemicals, motor vehicles, metals and metal products, food, inedible raw materials and textiles. Preliminary trade figures for 1982 were:

Imports	*R*18,377·9 million
Exports	19,129·4 million

Trade with U.K.

	1983	1984
Imports from U.K.	£1,039,039,000	£1,205,143,000
Exports to U.K.	764,909,000	725,631,000

Currency.—The unit of currency is the *Rand* of 100 cents. For exchange rate, *see* p. 81.

Finance.—Estimated revenue for 1983–84 was *R*19,094 million, and estimated expenditure was *R*21,176 million.

CAPITAL.—The administrative seat of the Government is Pretoria, Transvaal; population (1980 estimate), 528,407; the seat of the Legislature is ΨCape Town, population (1970) 1,107,764. Other large towns (1980 figures) are Johannesburg, Transvaal (1,536,457); Ψ Durban, Natal, the largest seaport (505,963); Ψ Port Elizabeth, Cape (492,140); Bloemfontein, capital of Orange Free State (230,688); Ψ East London, Cape (160,582); and Pietermaritzburg, capital of Natal (178,972).

FLAG.—Three horizontal stripes of equal width; from top to bottom, orange, white, blue; in the centre of the white stripe, the old Orange Free State flag hanging vertical, towards the pole the Union Jack horizontal, away from the pole the old Transvaal Vierkleur, all spread full.

NATIONAL DAY.—May 31.

BRITISH EMBASSY
6 Hill Street, Pretoria
91 Parliament Street, Cape Town (Jan.–June)

Ambassador Extraordinary and Plenipotentiary, His Excellency Patrick Hamilton Moberley, C.M.G. (1984).
Minister, D. Tonkin.
Defence Attaché, Gp. Capt. D. W. Hanson, O.B.E.
Counsellors, G. R. Archer (*Head of Chancery*); J. H. Owen, O.B.E.
1st Secretaries, A. J. Gooch; D. J. White; A. E. Lewis; G. W. W. Charlton, M.B.E. (*Administration*).
Cultural Attaché and British Council Representative, R. E. Underwood, 170 Pine Street, Arcadia, Pretoria.

There are British Consular Offices at *Cape Town, Johannesburg* and *Durban*; and Honorary Consuls at *Port Elizabeth* and *East London*.

NAMIBIA

Namibia (South West Africa) stretches from the southern border of Angola (lat. 17° 23′ S.) to part of the northern (Orange River) and north-western borders of the Cape Province of the Republic of South Africa; and from the Atlantic Ocean in the west to Botswana in the east.

The territory has an area of 318,261 sq. miles, including the area of Walvis Bay (434 sq. miles) which is claimed by South Africa. The population was estimated at 1,039,400 in 1982 and the main population groups are: Ovambo (516,600), Whites (75,000), Damara (76,800), Kavango (98,000), Herero (77,600), Nama (49,700), Coloured (43,500), Caprivians (39,500), Bushmen (29,500), Rehoboth Baster (25,800), Tswana (6,800).

Government.—A German protectorate from 1880 to 1915, South West Africa was administered until the end of 1920 by the Union of South Africa. In terms of the Treaty of Versailles the Territory was entrusted to South Africa with full powers of administration and legislation over the Territory. After the dissolution of the League of Nations and in the absence of a trusteeship agreement, South Africa informed the United Nations that she would continue to administer South West Africa in the spirit of the Mandate. Since the establishment of the United Nations, South West Africa has been the subject of dispute.

On June 21, 1971, the International Court of Justice at The Hague delivered an advisory opinion as requested by the U.N. Security Council on the legal consequences for States of the continued presence of South Africa in "Namibia" (South West Africa). The Court decided by 13 votes to 2, that (*inter alia*) "the continued presence of South Africa being illegal, South Africa is under obligation to withdraw its administration from Namibia immediately and thus put an end to its occupation of the Territory". The South African Government rejected this opinion, but accepted the principle that the territory should attain independence. In September 1975 constitutional talks (known as the Turnhalle Conference) were begun in Windhoek between delegates from the 11 ethnic groups of the territory in order to determine the future of South West Africa. But their representative nature was contested by, *inter alia*, SWAPO, a liberation movement with substantial international support and when, in April 1977, it became clear that independence based on the Turnhalle would not solve the problem, the Five Western members of the U.N. Security Council at that time drew up a plan, later incorporated into Security Council Resolution 435, for a peaceful settlement. The plan involves free and fair elections under U.N. supervision leading to independence. The plan has been accepted by all the parties to the Namibia question and attempts to implement the plan are continuing.

Meanwhile, the South African Government appointed an Administrator-General in 1977 to establish a central administration there for those functions previously administered from Pretoria. In December 1978, the South Africans organized an election for a constituent assembly which SWAPO and most of the internal political parties boycotted. The resultant assembly was transformed into a National Assembly with legislative powers in May 1979, and a Council of Ministers was established in 1980 but both were abolished in Jan. 1983 and the territory again came under direct rule. However, in May 1985 legislative powers and executive authority were restored under a "transitional government" intended to hold office while South Africa and the U.N. negotiate Namibia's independence.

Production.—Mining, agriculture and fisheries are important. Animal husbandry accounts for 99 per cent of the total gross output of commercial agriculture. The average rainfall over 70 per cent of the Territory is below 400 mm. per annum.

Trade with U.K.

	1983	1984
Imports from U.K.	£3,425,000	£5,200,000
Exports to U.K.	62,437,000	64,015,000

CAPTIAL.—Windhoek (population, 1970 census, 61,260). The only port of any size is Ψ Walvis Bay.

SPAIN
(España)

Head of the Spanish State, King Juan Carlos I de Borbón y Borbón, *born* Jan. 5, 1938, *acceded to the throne*, Nov. 22, 1975, *married* May 14, 1962, Princess Sophie of Greece *and has issue*, Infante Felipe Juan Pablo Alfonso Todos Los Santos (Prince of Asturias) *born* Jan. 30, 1968; Infanta Elena Maria Isabel Dominica, *born* Dec. 20, 1963; and Infanta Christina Frederica Victoria, *born* June 13, 1965.

CABINET

Prime Minister (President of the Government), Felipe González Márquez.
Deputy P.M. (Vice-President), Alfonso Guerra González.
Foreign Affairs, Francisco-José Fernández Ordoñez.
Territorial Administration, Félix Pons Irazazábal.
Defence, Narcis Serra Serra.
Minister of the Presidency, Javier Moscoso del Prado y Muñoz.
Education and Science, José María Maravall Herrero.
Labour and Social Security, José Joaquín Almunia Amann.
Health and Consumption, Ernesto Lluch Martín.
Economy and Finance, Carlos Solchaga Catalán.
Public Works and Urbanisation, Javier Sáenz de Cosculluela.
Agriculture, Fisheries and Food, Carlos Romero Herrera.
Industry and Energy, Joan Majó Cruzate.
Justice, Fernando Ledesma Bartret.
Culture, Javier Solana Madariaga.

Interior, José Barrionuevo Peña.
Transport, Tourism and Communications, Abel Caballero Alvarez.

SPANISH EMBASSY IN LONDON
24 Belgrave Square, SW1X 8QA
[01-235 5555]

Ambassador Extraordinary and Plenipotentiary, His Excellency José Joaquin Puig de la Bellacasa (1983).
Minister-Counsellor, Sr. D. J. I. Benavides.

Area and Population.—Situated in the south-west of Europe, between 36°–43° 45′ N. lat. and 4° 25′ E.–9° 20′ W. long., Spain is bounded on the south and east by the Mediterranean, on the west by the Atlantic and Portugal, and on the north by the Bay of Biscay and France, from which it is separated by the Pyrenees. Continental Spain occupies about eleven-thirteenths of the Iberian peninsula, the remaining portion forming the Republic of Portugal. Its coastline extends 1,317 miles—712 formed by the Mediterranean and 605 by the Atlantic—and it comprises a total area of 196,700 square miles, with a population (1982) of 37,833,863.

Physical Features.—The interior of the Iberian Peninsula consists of an elevated tableland surrounded and traversed by mountain ranges—the Pyrenees, the Cantabrian Mountains, the Sierra Guadarrama, Sierra Morena, Sierra Nevada, Montes de Toledo, &c. The principal rivers are the Duero, the Tajo, the Guadiana, the Guadalquivir, the Ebro and the Miño.

Government.—Spain was a monarchy until April 1931, when King Alfonso XIII left the country and a Republic was proclaimed and a Provisional Government, drawn from the various Republican and Socialist parties, was formed. On July 18, 1936, a counter-revolution broke out in many military garrisons in Spanish Morocco and spread rapidly throughout Spain. The principal leader was General Francisco Franco Bahamonde, formerly Governor of the Canary Islands. The struggle, in its later phases, threatened to embroil other European countries, those of Nazi-Fascist tendency lending aid to General Franco (leader of the Military-Fascist fusion, or *Falange*) while those of Communist views supported the Azaña (*Popular Front*) government. In October, 1938, many of the supporting troops were withdrawn, and on March 29, 1939, the Civil War was declared to have ended, the Popular Front Governments in Madrid and Barcelona surrendering to the *Nationalists* (as General Franco's followers were then

named). On June 5, 1939, the Grand Council of the *Falange Española Tradicionalista y de las Juntas Ofensivas Nacional-Sindicalistas*, met at Burgos to legislate for the reorganization of the country under the Presidency of General Franco, who had assumed the title of *Caudillo* (*Leader*) *of Spain and Chief of the State*. In the Civil War of 1936–39 over 1,000,000 lives were lost.

On July 22, 1969, General Franco nominated Prince Juan Carlos (Alfonso) of Bourbon (grandson of the late King Alfonso XIII) to succeed him as head of state at his death or retirement. The nomination was approved in the *Cortes* by a large majority. Following the death of General Franco, on November 20, 1975, Juan Carlos acceded to the throne on Nov. 22, 1975.

Under the Constitution drawn up in 1977–78 there is a bi-cameral *Cortes* comprising a 350-member Congress of Deputies elected for 4 years by universal adult suffrage, and a Senate consisting of directly elected representatives of the provinces, islands, autonomous regions and Ceuta and Melilla.

At the General Election on Oct. 28, 1982, the P.S.O.E. under Sr. Felipe Gonzalez won 202 seats, the A.P. 106, the U.C.D. 13, and the P.C.E. 4 seats. In the Regional and the Municipal elections of May 1983 the P.S.O.E. won the majority of the votes. In elections held in the Basque country in February and in Cataluña in April 1984 local nationalist parties (P.N.V. and C.i.U.) retained their majorities and formed autonomous governments.

Regions.—Since the promulgation of the 1978 Constitution, 17 autonomous regions have been established, with their own parliaments and governments. These are Andalucia, Aragon, Asturias, Balaerics, the Basque country, Canaries, Castilla-La Mancha, Castilla-Leon, Cantabria, Cataluña, Extremadura, Galicia, Madrid, Murcia, Navarre, La Rioja and Valencia.

Defence.—Army: There are in Spain 1 armoured, 2 motorized, and 2 mountain divisions; 1 armoured cavalry brigade, 2 artillery brigades, 1 air-transportable brigade, 1 parachute brigade, 10 infantry brigades, 1 mountain brigade and 2 artillery brigades (including surface to air missile battalions). The *Guardia Civil* also forms part of the Army though it operates as a gendarmerie in the rural areas under the control of the Ministry of the Interior.

The active Spanish *Navy* consists of 1 aircraft carrier, 11 destroyers, 15 frigates and corvettes, 12 minesweepers, 6 major amphibious vessels, 7 submarines, 12 fast patrol craft, 6 hydrographic vessels, 1 tanker, and many smaller patrol craft and auxiliaries. The Navy also has 50 helicopters and 11 Harrier aircraft.

The *Air Force* is divided geographically into 3 Regions covering Spain plus an Air Zone for the Canaries. There are also separate functional Air Defence, Tactical and Transport Commands. The Air Force consists of 4 attack squadrons, 6 air defence squadrons, 1 maritime squadron, 9 transport squadrons, 3 search and rescue squadrons, 9 training squadrons and 1 firefighting squadron.

Spain became a member of N.A.T.O. in May 1982. The present government has frozen progress towards military integration pending a referendum on N.A.T.O. membership scheduled for 1986. It has also initiated reorganization of the military structure.

Education.—Under the Education Law 1985 free education for all children aged 6 to 15 is guaranteed. Under the new law, private schools (30 per cent of primary and 80 per cent of secondary schools) will have to fulfill certain criteria to receive government maintenance grants.

There are 29 state universities, the oldest of which, Salamanca, was founded in 1230. Other ancient foundations are Valencia (1245), Oviedo (1317), Valladolid (1346), Barcelona (1450), Zaragoza (1474),

Santiago (1501), Seville (1502), Granada (1526), and Madrid (1590). Private universities are Deusto in Bilbao, and Navarra in Pamplona. Student numbers in the universities have risen to over 700,000.

Language and Literature.—Castilian is the language of more than three-quarters of the population of Spain. Basque, reported to have been the original language of Iberia, is spoken in the rural districts of Vizcaya, Guipuzcoa and Alava. Catalan is spoken in Provençal Spain, and Galician, spoken in the northwestern provinces, is akin to Portuguese; the governments of these regions actively encourage use of their local languages.

The literature of Spain is one of the oldest and richest in the world, the *Poem of the Cid*, the earliest and best of the heroic songs of Spain, having been written about A.D. 1140. The outstanding writings of its golden age are those of Miguel de Cervantes Saavedra (1547–1616), Lope Felix de Vega Carpio (1562–1635) and Pedro Calderón de la Barca (1600–1681). The Nobel Prize for Literature has four times been awarded to Spanish authors—J. Echegaray (1904), J. Benavente (1922), Juan Ramón Jimenez (1956) and Vicente Aleixandre (1977).

Currency.—The *peseta* = 100 *céntimos*. (*See also* p. 81).

Production and Industry.—The country is generally fertile, and well adapted to agriculture and the cultivation of heat-loving fruits—olives, oranges, lemons, almonds, pomegranates, bananas, apricots, tomatoes, peppers, cucumbers and grapes. The agricultural products include wheat, barley, oats, rice, hemp and flax. The orange crop is exported mainly to Germany, France and the United Kingdom. The vine is cultivated widely; in the south-west, Jerez, the well-known sherry and tent wines are produced. The fishing industry is important.

Spain's mineral resources of coal, iron, wolfram, copper, zinc, lead and iron ores are variously exploited. Many of the richer and more easily worked deposits have been exhausted, but the authorities are actively engaged in stimulating the exploitation of hitherto unworked or lower grade deposits. Output of coal in 1984 was 40 million tonnes; output of iron ore (1983) was 3·5 million tonnes and of steel (1984) 13·5 million tonnes.

The principal goods produced are cars, steel, ships, manufactured goods, textiles, chemical products, footwear and other leather goods, ceramics, sewing machines and bicycles. In 1984 tourism contributed (net) an estimated 1,240,000 m. *pesetas* to the balance of payments.

TRADE

	1983	1984
	million pesetas	
Imports	4,176,470·4	4,628,991·1
Exports	2,838,601·1	3,734,487·1

The balance of payments on current account showed an estimated deficit of $288 m. in 1984 and reserves stood at $16,029 million at the end of the year.

Trade with U.K.
(inc. Canary Islands)

	1983	1984
Imports from U.K.	£1,235,232,000	£1,322,382,000
Exports to U.K.	1,190,334,000	1,667,861,000

The principal imports are cotton, tobacco, cellulose, timber, coffee and cocoa, fertilizers, dyes, machinery, motor vehicles and agricultural tractors, wool and petroleum products. The principal exports include iron ore, cork, salt, vegetables, fruits, wines, olive oil, potash, mercury, pyrites, tinned fruit and fish, tomatoes, passenger cars and footwear.

CAPITAL, Madrid. Population (1982) 3,188,297. Other large cities are ΨBarcelona (1,754,900), Valencia (751,734), ΨSeville (653,833), Zaragoza (590,750), ΨMálaga (503,251), Bilbao (433,030); Murcia (288,631).

FLAG.—Three horizontal bands, red, yellow and red, with coat of arms on yellow band.

NATIONAL DAY.—October 12.

AIR TRANSIT FROM U.K.—London–Barcelona (713 miles), 2 *hrs.* 25 *mins.*; Madrid (775 miles), 2 *hrs.* 5 *mins.*; Valencia, 2 *hrs.* 10 *mins.*

BRITISH EMBASSY
Calle Fernando el Santo, 16, Madrid 4

Ambassador Extraordinary and Plenipotentiary, His Excellency Lord Nicholas Gordon Lennox, C.M.G., M.V.O. (1984).

Minister, R. B. R. Hervey, C.M.G.

Counsellor, J. Flynn.

Defence and Military Attaché, Brig. J. K. Chater.

Head of Chancery, R. H. T. Gozney.

Second Secretary, Mrs. C. Pegg-Tsivanidis.

British Council Representative, S. R. Smith, Almagro 5, Madrid 4. There is also an office and a library in Barcelona and Valencia, and an office and English language resource centre in Granada.

BRITISH CHAMBER OF COMMERCE, Marques de Valdeiglesias 3, Madrid 4 also Paseo de Gracia 11, Barcelona 7 and Alameda de Mazarredo 5, Bilbao 1.

The BALEARIC ISLES form an archipelago off the east coast of Spain. There are four large islands (Majorca, Minorca, Ibiza and Formentera), and seven smaller (Aire, Aucanada, Botafoch, Cabrera, Dragonera, Pinto and El Rey). The islands were occupied by the Romans after the destruction of Carthage and provided contingents of the celebrated Balearic slingers. The total area is 1,935 square miles, with a population of 655,910. The archipelago forms a province of Spain, the capital being ΨPalma in Majorca, pop. 290,372; ΨMahon (Minorca), pop. 21,860.

The CANARY ISLANDS are an archipelago in the Atlantic, off the African coast, consisting of 7 islands and 6 uninhabited islets. The total area is 2,807 square miles, with a population of 1,367,646. The Canary Islands form two Provinces of Spain.—*Las Palmas* (Gran Canaria, Lanzarote (38,500), Fuerteventura (19,500) and the islets of Alegranza, Roque del Este, Roque del Oeste, Graciosa, Montaña Clara and Lobos), with seat of administration at ΨLas Palmas (pop. 360,098) in Gran Canaria, where major oil companies have installations for re-fueling shipping; and *Santa Cruz de Tenerife* (Tenerife, La Palma (76,000), Gomera (31,829), and Hierro (10,000)), with seat of administration at ΨSanta Cruz in Tenerife, pop. 185,900.

ISLA DE FAISANES is an uninhabited Franco-Spanish condominium, at the mouth of the Bidassoa in La Higuera bay.

ΨCEUTA is a fortified post on the Moroccan coast, opposite Gibraltar. The total area is 5 square miles, with a population (1981) of 65,264.

ΨMELILLA is a town on a rocky promontory of the Rif coast, connected with the mainland by a narrow isthmus. Melilla has been in Spanish possession since 1492. Population (1981) 53,593. Ceuta and Melilla are parts of Metropolitan Spain.

OVERSEAS TERRITORIES

Spanish settlements on the Moroccan seaboard are:—

Peñon de Alhucemas, the bay of that name includes six islands: population 366.

Peñon de la Gomera (or *Peñon de Velez*) is a fortified rocky islet about 40 miles west of Alhucemas Bay; population 450.

The Chaffarinas (or Zaffarines) are a group of three islands near the Algerian frontier, about 2 miles north of Cape del Agua; population 610.

The former provinces of Spanish Guinea, Fernando Póo and Rio Muni achieved independence on October 12, 1968, under the title of Equatorial Guinea.

The protectorate of Spanish Morocco was incorporated in Morocco on the latter's independence in 1956. Ifni, the former enclave in Morocco, was incorporated by treaty, on June 30, 1969, and the Spanish Sahara came under joint Moroccan and Mauritanian control in November 1975.

SUDAN
(Democratic Republic of the Sudan)

Chairman of the Transitional Military Council, Gen. Abdel Rahman Sowar El Dahab, *assumed office*, April 6,1985.

Prime Minister, Dr. El Gizouli Dafalla

Deputy Prime Minister, Samuel Aru Bol.

SUDANESE EMBASSY IN LONDON
3 Cleveland Row, SW1A 1DD
[01-839 8080]

Ambassador Extraordinary and Plenipotentiary, His Excellency Sayed Ibrahim Mohamed Ali (1985).

Area and Population.—The Sudan extends from the southern boundary of Egypt, 22° N. lat., to the northern boundary of Uganda, 3° 36′ N. lat., and reaches from the Republic of Chad about 21° 49′ E. (at 12° 45′ N.) to the north-west boundary of Ethiopia in 38° 35′ E. (at 18° N.). On the east lie the Red Sea and Ethiopia; on the south lie Kenya, Uganda and Zaire; and on the west the Central Arican Republic, Chad, and Libya. The greatest length from north to south is approximately 1,300 miles, and east to west 950 miles.

The *White Nile* enters from Uganda at Nimule as the *Bahr el Jebel*, and leaves the Sudan at Wadi Halfa. The *Blue Nile* flows from Lake Tana on the Ethiopian Plateau. Its course in the Sudan is nearly 500 miles long, before it joins the White Nile at Khartoum. The next confluence of importance is at Atbara where the main Nile is joined by the River Atbara. Between Khartoum and Wadi Halfa lie five of the six *Cataracts.*

The estimated area is about 967,500 sq. miles with a population of 19,500,000, partly Arabs, partly Negros, and partly of mixed Arab-Negro blood, with a small foreign element, including some 8,000 Europeans. The Arabs are mostly Moslems. The Nilotics of the Bahr el Ghazal and Upper Nile Valleys are generally animists, but some have been converted to Christianity and others are Moslems.

Government.—The Anglo-Egyptian Condominium over the Sudan which had been established in 1899 ended when the Sudan House of Representatives, on Dec. 19, 1955, voted unanimously a declaration that the Sudan was a fully independent sovereign state. A Republic was proclaimed on Jan. 1, 1956, and was recognized by Great Britain and Egypt, a Supreme Commission being sworn in to take over sovereignty. The Sudan was under military rule from Nov., 1958, until 1964 when a new civilian Cabinet was appointed. Government of the country was taken over on May 25, 1969, by a ten-man revolutionary council headed by Col. Gaafar Mohamed El Nimeri. In February 1972 an agreement was signed at Addis Ababa which brought to an end nearly 17 years of insurrection and civil war in the six southern provinces, and which recognized southern regional autonomy within a unified Sudanese State. Insurrection broke out again in 1983. In April 1985 the Army command assumed power after popular demonstrations, deposed Nimeiri and appointed a civilian Cabinet. The transitional government has undertaken to organise a general election and relinquish power in April 1986.

services connect Khartoum with Juba in Equatoria Province which in turn is connected by a bus service with Nimule on the Uganda border. (Services to Wau and Juba have been interrupted by the insurrection.) ΨPort Sudan is a well-equipped modern seaport. Sudan Airways fly regular services from Khartoum to many parts of the Sudan and to other African states, Europe and the Middle East.

FINANCE

	1981–82	1982–83*
Revenue	£S 1,042 m	£S 1,342·6 m
Expenditure	1,715 m	1,910·1 m

*Proposed budget.
£S = Sudanese *Pound* of 100 *Piastres*.

TRADE

	1983–84
Total Imports	£S1,608,100,000
Total Exports	893,500,000

Trade with U.K.

	1983	1984
Imports from U.K.	£133,432,000	£95,627,000
Exports to U.K.	18,693,000	16,858,000

The principal exports are cotton and cotton seed, ground-nuts and gum arabic. The chief imports are cotton piece goods, base metals, vehicles and transport equipment, machinery, petroleum products, sugar, tea, coffee, chemicals and pharmaceuticals.

CAPITAL, Khartoum. The town contains many mosques, a Catholic cathedral and an Anglican cathedral, and the University with extensive government buildings. The combined population of Khartoum, Khartoum North and Omdurman is just over 2,000,000.

FLAG.—Three horizontal stripes of red, white and black with a green triangle next to the hoist.

NATIONAL DAY.—January 1 (Independence Day).

BRITISH EMBASSY
Khartoum

Ambassador Extraordinary and Plenipotentiary, His Excellency Sir Alexander Stirling, K.B.E., C.M.G. (1984).
Counsellor, B. S. T. Eastwood (*Head of Chancery*).
Defence and Military Attaché, Col. H. Diamond.
British Council Representative, R. A. Jarvis, O.B.E., 31 Zubeir Pasha Street, P.O. Box 1253, Khartoum. There are British Council libraries at *El Obeid,* and *Omdurman.*

Education.—School education is free for most children, but not compulsory, beginning with six years primary education, followed by three years secondary education at general secondary schools, the more academic higher secondary schools or vocational schools. The medium of instruction is Arabic. English is taught as the principal foreign language in all schools.

Khartoum University has 10 faculties. There is a branch of Cairo University in Khartoum, an Islamic University at Omdurman and a University at Juba.

In addition to the four universities there are various technical post-secondary institutes as well as professional and vocational training establishments.

Production.—The principal grain crops are *dura* (great millet) and wheat, the staple food of the people in the Sudan. Sesame and ground-nuts are other important food crops, which also yield an exportable surplus and a promising start has been made with castor seed. The principal export crop is cotton. Main production is of long-staple (mainly Egyptian type) cotton of which the Sudan is a major producer, but increasing quantities of short and medium staple (American) type cotton are being grown. Production in 1984–85 is expected to total 1,030,000 bales. The Sudan also produces the bulk of the world's supply of gum arabic. Sugar is an increasingly important crop. The Sudan has almost become self-sufficient in sugar and aims to produce an exportable surplus by 1986. Livestock is the mainstay of the nomadic Arab tribes of the desert and the negro tribes of the swamp and wooded grassland country in the South. Production has, however, been affected by drought and famine.

A new dam at Khashm el Girba began to store water in May, 1964, and will eventually provide irrigation to about 500,000 acres, most of which has been used to resettle the population of the Wadi Halfa area which has been flooded by the reservoir of the Egyptian High Dam. Another dam at Roseires on the Blue Nile provides increased irrigation on a further 3,000,000 acres as well as providing hydro-electric power.

Communications.—The railway system has a route length of about 3,200 miles, linking Khartoum with Wadi Halfa, Karima, Port Sudan, Wad Medani, Sennar, El Damazin, Kosti, El Obeid and Nyala. A line branches out southwards to Wau from the Sennar/Nyala western line. Regular Nile steamer

---

· SURINAM

Head of the National Military Council, Lt. Col. Desi Bouterse.

CABINET

Prime Minister and Minister of Foreign Affairs, Wim Udenhout.
Interior and Justice, Franklin Leeflang.
Transport, Trade and Industry, Imro Fong Poen.
Natural Resources and Energy, Erik Tjon Kie Sim.
Army and Police, Wilfred Maynaard.
Labour, Housing and Social Affairs, Edmund Dankerlui.
Education and Science, Allen Lie Fo Choen.
Finance and Economic Affairs, Norman Kleine.
Health, S. Ritfield.
Agriculture, Livestock and Fisheries, Rajkumar Ranjit Singh.
Public Works, Telecommunications and Construction, Jainul Abdoel.

Surinam is situated on the north coast of South America and is bounded by French Guiana in the east, Brazil in the south and Guyana in the west. It has an area of 63,250 square miles, with a population (1982 estimate) of 410,000.

Formerly known as Dutch Guiana, Surinam remained part of the Netherlands West Indies until November 25, 1975, when it achieved complete independence. Surinam had received autonomy in domestic affairs under the Realm Statute which took effect on December 29, 1954. The civilian government was ousted by the military in Feb. 1982, who appointed the predominantly civilian Cabinet. A National Assembly of 31 members was appointed on Jan. 1, 1985 to draft a new constitution.

Surinam has large timber resources. Rice and sugar cane are the main crops. Bauxite is mined, and is the principal export.

TRADE

	1979
	Surinam Guilders
Imports	647,500,000
Exports	777,000,000

Trade with U.K.

	1983	1984
Imports from U.K.	£8,914,000	£9,593,000
Exports to U.K.	11,584,000	18,316,000

CAPITAL.—ΨParamaribo (population, 1971, 110,000).

British Ambassador (resides at *Georgetown*, Guyana). There is a *British Consulate* at Paramaribo. *Honorary Consul*, J. J. Healy.

SWEDEN
(Sverige)

King of Sweden, Carl XVI Gustaf, *born* April 30, 1946, *succeeded* September 15, 1973, *married* June 19, 1976 Fraulein Silvia Renate Sommerlath *and has issue*, Crown Princess Victoria Ingrid Alice Désirée, Duchess of Västergötland, *born* July 14, 1977; Prince Carl Philip Edmund Bertil, Duke of Värmland, *born* May 13, 1979; Princess Madeleine Thérèse Amelie Josephine, Duchess of Hälsingland and Gästrikland, *born* June 10, 1982.

COUNCIL OF MINISTERS

Prime Minister, Olof Palme.
Deputy P.M., Ingvar Carlsson.
Justice, Sten Wickbom.
Foreign Affairs, Lennart Bodström.
Agriculture, Svante Lundkvist.
Finance, Kjell-Olof Feldt.
Public Health and Medical Services, Gertrud Sigurdsen.
Housing, Hans Gustafsson.
Labour, Anna-Greta Leijon.
Education, Lena Hjelm-Wallén.
Industry, Thage Peterson.
Health and Social Affairs, Sten Andersson.
Culture, Bengt Göransson.
Equality and Immigration, Anita Gradin.
Energy, Birgitta Dahl.
State Industries, Roine Carlsson.
Public Sector, Bo Holmberg.
Foreign Trade, Mats Hellström.
Defence, Anders Thunborg.

(The above Cabinet may change as a result of the General Election which takes place on Sept. 15, 1985.)

SWEDISH EMBASSY IN LONDON
11 Montagu Place, W1H 2AL
[01-724 2101]

Ambassador Extraordinary and Plenipotentiary, His Excellency Leif Leifland, G.C.V.O. (1982).
Minister Plenipotentiary, H. Granqvist.
Counsellors, A. A. E. Alsterdal (*Press*); P. G. Larsson (*Consular*); K. Wahlbäck; P. Lindström.
Defence and Naval Attaché, Capt. R. Klintebö.
Air and Military Attaché, Group Capt. J. Westberg.
Trade Commissioner, S. Widenfelt (73 Welbeck Street, W1M 8AN.).

Area and Population.—Sweden occupies the eastern area of the Scandinavian peninsula in N.W. Europe and comprises 24 local government districts, "*Län*", with a total area of 173,436 sq. miles, and population Dec. 31, 1983 of 8,330,573. In 1983 the birth rate was 11·0 per 1,000 inhabitants, the death rate 10·9 per 1,000 inhabitants and infant mortality rate was 7·0 per 1,000 live births.

Government.—Under the Act of Succession of June 6, 1809 (with amendments) the throne is hereditary in the House of Bernadotte. (A 1979 amendment vested the succession in the monarch's eldest child, irrespective of sex.) Jean-Baptiste Jules Bernadotte, Prince of Ponte Corvo, a Marshal of France, was invited to accept the title of Crown Prince, with succession to the throne. He succeeded Charles XIII in 1818. There is a unicameral Diet (*Riksdag*) of 349 members elected for 3 years. The Council of Ministers (*Statsråd*) is responsible to the *Riksdag*.

Production and Industry.—The country's industrial prosperity is based on an abundance of natural resources in the form of forests, mineral deposits and water power. The forests are extensive, covering about half the total land surface, and sustain flourishing timber, pulp and paper milling industries. The mineral resources include iron ore, lead, zinc, sulphur, granite, marble, precious and heavy metals (the latter not exploited) and extensive deposits of low grade uranium ore. Industries based on mining, principally iron and steel, aluminium and copper are

important but it is the general engineering industry that provides the basis of Sweden's exports. Growth areas are largely in the specialised machinery and systems and chemical industries. The relative importance of agriculture has declined and in 1983 only 5·4 per cent of the population was engaged in farming.

Apart from water power Sweden has no significant indigenous resources of conventional hydrocarbon fuels and relies to a high degree upon imported oil. Much of Sweden's electricity is generated by nuclear power but as a result of a referendum in 1980 the nuclear programme is to be discontinued by 2010. Small supplies of natural gas are imported from Denmark into southern Sweden.

Communications.—The total length of Swedish railroads is 12,323 km. The number of passenger cars in use on December 31, 1983 was 3,006,761.

The Mercantile Marine amounted on December 31, 1983 to 3,258,000 gross tonnage. The Board of Civil Aviation under the control of the Ministry of Communications handles civil aviation matters. Regular domestic air traffic is maintained by the Scandinavian Airlines System and by A. B. Linjeflyg. Regular European and inter-continental air traffic is maintained by the Scandinavian Airlines System.

Defence.—Based on the policy of non-alignment in peace leading to neutrality in war Sweden maintains a Total Defence intended to make any attack on her costly. Total Defence includes peacetime organizations for civil, economic and psychological defence as well as compulsory national service for all acceptable males. Some 50,000 National Servicemen are called up for 7–15 months training each year and all are recalled every fourth year for refresher training. On mobilization the Army strength totals 4 armoured brigades, 1 mechanised brigade and 23 infantry and winter warfare brigades. The Navy has 12 submarines, 36 fast attack craft, a number of minor craft and auxiliaries and 5 coast artillery units. The Air Force has modern supersonic aircraft of Swedish manufacture forming a standing force of 216 air defence, 85 attack and 55 reconnaissance with support aircraft and a modern air defence radar system. Facilities exist for rapid dispersal from main bases in war.

Religion.—The State religion is Lutheran Protestant, to which over 95 per cent of the people officially adhere.

Language and Literature.—Swedish belongs, with Danish and Norwegian, to the North Germanic language group. Swedish literature dates back to King Magnus Eriksson, who codified the old Swedish provincial laws in 1350. With his translation of the Bible, Olaus Petri (1493–1552) formed the basis for the modern Swedish language. Literature flourished during the reign of Gustavus III, who founded the Swedish Academy in 1786. Swedish literature is studded with names such as Almquist (1795–1866), Strindberg (1849–1912) and Lagerlöf (1858–1940), Nobel Prize Winner in 1909. Contemporary authors include Lagerquist (1891–1974), Nobel Laureate in 1951, Martinson (1904–1978) and Johnson (1900–1976), Nobel Laureates jointly in 1974. The Swedish scientist Alfred Nobel (1833–1896) founded the Nobel Prizes for Literature, Science and Peace.

Education.—Tuition within the State system, which is maintained by the State and by local taxation, is free. It provides 9 years' compulsory schooling from the age of 7 to 16 in the comprehensive elementary schools; further education of 2, 3 or 4 years in the upper secondary schools; a unified higher education system administered in 6 regional areas containing one of the universities—Uppsala (founded 1477); Lund (1668); Stockholm (1878); Gothenburg (1887); Umeå (1963) and Linköping (1967). At present there are 33 institutions of higher education including three technical universities in Stockholm, Goth-

enburg and Luleå, and the Karolinska Institute in Stockholm, which specializes in medicine and dentistry.

FINANCE

	1982/83	1983/84
	Kronor million	*Kronor* million
Revenue	180,700	208,100
Expenditure	256,400	298,000

The currency is the Swedish *Krona* of 100 *Ore*. (*See also* p. 81.)

TRADE

	1983	1984
	Kronor million	*Kronor* million
Imports	200,235	217,876
Exports	210,311	242,485

Trade with U.K.

	1983	1984
Imports from U.K.	£2,397,464,000	£2,888,625,000
Exports to U.K.	2,051,931,000	2,416,383,000

Sweden's main imports from Britain are crude oil and petroleum products, machinery and parts, road vehicles and components, clothing and textiles and steel. Britain's main imports from Sweden are paper and board, road vehicles, machinery, wood, steel and pulp.

CAPITAL.—ΨStockholm. Population (1983): City 650,952; Greater Stockholm, 1,409,048; ΨGothenburg (Göteborg) (424,186); ΨMalmö (229,380); Uppsala (150,579)

FLAG.—Yellow cross on a blue ground.

NATIONAL DAY.—June 6 (Day of the Swedish Flag).

BRITISH EMBASSY
Skarpögatan 6–8, 115 27 Stockholm

Ambassador Extraordinary and Plenipotentiary, His Excellency Sir Richard Parsons, K.C.M.G., *apptd.*, 1984.
British Council Representative, J. R. Day.

BRITISH CONSULAR OFFICES

There is a British Consular Office at *Stockholm*.
BRITISH-SWEDISH CHAMBER OF COMMERCE: Nybrokajen 7, 11148 Stockholm.

SWITZERLAND
(Schweizerische Eidgenossenschaft—
Confédération Suisse—Confederazione
Svizzera.)

CABINET

President of the Swiss Confederation (1985) *and Head of Public Economy*, Kurt Furgler.
Vice-President (1985) *and Head of Interior*, Alphons Egli.
Military, Jean-Pascal Delamuraz.
Justice and Police, Mrs. Elizabeth Kopp.
Foreign Affairs, Pierre Aubert.
Finance, Otto Stich.
Transport, Energy and Communications, Leon Schlumpf.

SWISS EMBASSY IN LONDON
16–18 Montagu Place, W1H 2BQ
[01–723 0701]

Ambassador Extraordinary and Plenipotentiary, His Excellency F. C. Pictet (1984).
Counsellor, H. Buchmann (*Commodities and Agriculture*).
Ministers, Willy Hold; Milan J. A. Lusser (*Economic and Financial*).

Defence, Military, Naval and Air Attaché, Col. W. Hertach.
Consul and Head of Administration, C. Duboulet.

There is a Swiss Consulate-General in *Manchester*.

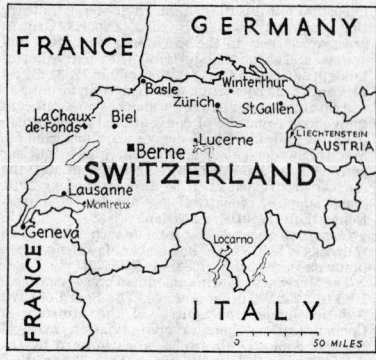

Area and Population.—The Helvetia of the Romans, a Federal Republic of Central Europe, situated between 45° 50′–47° 48′ N. lat. and 5° 58′–10° 3′ E. long. It is composed of 23 Cantons, 3 subdivided, making 26 in all, and comprises a total area of 15,950 square miles with a population (estimated December, 1983) of 6,482,000. In 1983 there were 73,659 live births, 60,756 deaths and 37,645 marriages. Of the total population in 1980, 44·3 per cent of the population was Protestant, 47·6 per cent Roman Catholic and 0·3 per cent Jewish.

Physical Features.—Switzerland is the most mountainous country in all Europe. The Alps, covered with perennial snow and from 5,000 to 15,217 feet in height, occupy its southern and eastern frontiers, and the chief part of its interior; and the Jura mountains rise in the north-west. The Alps occupy 61 per cent, and the Jura mountains 12 per cent, of the country. The *Alps* are a crescent-shaped mountain system situated in France, Italy, Switzerland, Bavaria and Austria, covering an area of 80,000 square miles from the Mediterranean to the Danube (600 miles). The highest peak, Mont Blanc, Pennine Alps (15,782 feet) is partly in France and Italy; Monte Rosa (15,217 feet) and Matterhorn (14,780 feet) are partly in Switzerland and partly in Italy. The highest wholly Swiss peaks are Dufourspitze (15,203 ft.), Finsteraarhorn (14,026), Aletschhorn (13,711), Jungfrau (13,671), Mönch (13,456), Eiger (13,040), Schreckhorn (13,385), and Wetterhorn (12,150) in the Bernese Alps, and Dom (14,918), Weisshorn (14,803) and Breithorn (13,685).

The Swiss lakes are famous for their beauty and include Lakes Maggiore, Zürich, Lucerne, Neuchâtel, Geneva, Constance, Thun, Zug, Lugano, Brienz and the Walensee. There are also many artificial lakes.

Government.—The legislative power is vested in a Parliament, consisting of two Chambers, a National Council (*Nationalrat*) of 200 members, and a States Council (*Ständerat*) of 46 members; both Chambers united are called the Federal Assembly, and the members of the National Council are elected for four years, an election taking place in October. The executive power is in the hands of a Federal Council (*Bundesrat*) of seven members, elected for four years by the Federal Assembly and presided over by the President of the Confederation. Each year the Federal Assembly elects from the Federal Council the President and the Vice-President. Not more than one of the same canton may be elected member of the Federal Council; on the other hand, there is a tradition that Italian and French-speaking areas should between them be represented on the Federal Council by at least two members.

Defence.—All Swiss males must undertake military service in the Army or the Air Force, which is part of the Army. Swiss Army equipment includes some British items, such as Centurion tanks, Bloodhound missiles, Vampire and Hunter aircraft and the Medium Girder Bridge. The Rapier guided missile system is being delivered.

Production and Industry.—Agriculture is followed chiefly in the valleys, where cereals, flax, hemp, and tobacco are produced, and nearly all temperate zone fruits and vegetables as well as grapes are grown. Dairying and stock-raising are the principal industries, about 3,000,000 acres being under grass for hay and 2,000,000 acres pasturage. The forests cover about one-quarter of the whole surface. The chief manufacturing industries comprise engineering and electrical engineering, metal-working, chemicals and pharmaceuticals, textiles, watchmaking, woodwork-ing, foodstuffs and footwear. Banking, insurance and tourism are major industries.

Communications.—There are 4,997 km of railway tracks (Swiss Federal Railways, 2,946 km; Swiss privately owned railways 2,951 km). At the end of 1983 the number of telephone subscribers amounted to 3,095,057 and the network was fully automatic throughout the country. At the same time there were 2,379,461 licensed radio receivers and 2,094,787 television receivers.

At the end of 1982 the total length of motorways was 1,288 km. The number of motor vehicles licensed in 1983 was 2,887,117.

A merchant marine, established in 1940, consisted at the end of 1983 of 33 vessels with a total gross tonnage of 355,413 tonnes. In addition 456 vessels with a total tonnage of 634,696 were engaged in Rhine shipping. In 1982, goods handled at Basle Rhine ports amounted to 9,423,093 tonnes. In 1982 151 lake vessels transported 9,146,000 passengers and 2,640 tonnes of freight. Swiss airlines have a network covering 314,762 km and in 1983 carried 7,281,328 passengers. Swissair, the State airline, which owned 51 aircraft in 1983, flies to and from the Swiss airports at Zürich, Geneva and Basle.

Education.—Control by cantonal and communal authorities. No central organization. Illiteracy practically unknown. (i) *Primary*: Free and compulsory. School age varies, generally 7 to 14. (ii) *Secondary*: Age 12–15 for boys and girls. Schools numerous and well-attended, and there are many private institutions. (iii) *Special schools* make a feature of commercial and technical instruction. (iv) *Universities*: Basle (founded 1460), Berne (1834), Fribourg (1889), Geneva (1873), Lausanne (1890), Zürich (1832), and Neuchâtel (1909), and the technical Universities of Lausanne and Zürich and commercial University of St. Gall.

Language and Literature.—There are three official languages: French, German and Italian. In addition Romansch is recognized as a national, but not an official language. German is the dominating language in 19 of the 26 cantons; French in Fribourg, Jura, Geneva, Neuchâtel, Valais and Vaud; Italian in Ticino, and Romansch in parts of the Grisons.

Many modern authors, alike in the German school and in the Suisse Romande, have achieved international fame. Karl Spitteler (1845–1924) and Hermann Hesse (1877–1962) were awarded the Nobel Prize for Literature, the former in 1919, the latter in 1946.

FINANCE

	Budget 1983
	Swiss Francs
Revenue	18,700,000,000
Expenditure	19,700,000,000

TRADE

	1983
	Sw. Frs.
Total Imports	61,064,200,000
Total Exports	53,723,500,000

Trade with U.K.
(including Liechtenstein)

	1983	1984
Imports from U.K.	£1,385,894,000	£1,549,469,000
Exports to U.K.	2,154,085,000	2,490,593,000

The principal imports are machinery, electrical and electronic equipment, textiles, motor vehicles, non-ferrous metals, chemical elements, clothing, food, medicinal and pharmaceutical products. The principal exports are machinery, chemical elements, nonferrous metals, watches, electrical and electronic equipment, textiles, dyeing, tanning and colouring equipment. Switzerland is a member of E.F.T.A.

CAPITAL.—Berne. Population (1982) 145,700. Other large towns are Zürich (367,900), Basle (181,800), Geneva (161,000), Lausanne (128,000), Winterthur (86,758), St. Gallen (75,300), Lucerne (63,278), Bienne (54,100).

FLAG.—Red, with white cross.

NATIONAL DAY.—August 1.

AIR TRANSIT FROM U.K.—London-Basle (446 miles), 1 *hr.* 30 *mins.*; Geneva (468 miles), 1 *hr.* 30 *mins.*; Zürich (491 miles), 1 *hr.* 35 *mins*; Berne, 1 *hr.* 40 *mins.*

RAIL TRANSIT FROM U.K.——London-Berne, 16 *hrs.*

BRITISH EMBASSY
Thunstrasse 50, 3000 Berne 15

Ambassador Extraordinary and Plenipotentiary, His Excellency John Rowland Rich, *apptd.* 1985.
Counsellor, R. B. Crowson.
1st Secretary, G. C. Duncan.
2nd Secretary, B. England.
Defence, Naval and Military Attaché, Lt.-Col. T. H. G. Duke.
Air Attaché, Wing. Cdr. T. N. King.
Attaché, P. C. Albrecht (*Commercial*).

BRITISH CONSULAR OFFICES

There is a Consular Section at H.M. Embassy, Berne; *Consulates-General* at *Zürich* and *Geneva* and Consular offices at *Lugano* and *Montreux*. The Directorate of British Export Promotion in Switzerland is in the Consulate-General Office in *Zürich*.

BRITISH-SWISS CHAMBER OF COMMERCE, Dufourstrasse 51, 8008 Zürich.
SWISS-BRITISH SOCIETIES:
Berne.—*President*, Dr. H. Beriger.
Zürich.—*President*, Dr. R. J. Schneebeli.
Basle.—*President*, G. Simons.

SYRIA
(Syrian Arab Republic)

President, Lt.-Gen. Hafez el Assad, *b.* 1930, *assumed office* March 14, 1971, *re-elected*, Feb. 1978, March 13, 1985.
Vice-Presidents, Abdul Halim Khaddam, Rifaat Al Assad, Zuhair Mashariqa.
Prime Minister, Abdul-Raouf Al-Kasam.
Deputy Prime Minister and Minister for Defence, Gen. Mustafa Tlass.

Deputy Prime Minister for Public Services, Mahmoud Qaddur.
Deputy Prime Minister for Economic Affairs, Dr. Salim Yassin.

SYRIAN EMBASSY IN LONDON
8 Belgrave Square, SW1X 8PH
[01–245 9012]

Ambassador Extraordinary and Plenipotentiary, His Excellency Dr. Loutof Allah Haydar (1982).

Area and Population.—Syria is in the Levant, covering a portion of the former Ottoman Empire, with an estimated area of 70,800 sq. miles and a population (1981 estimate) of 10,400,000, most of whom are Arabic-speaking and Muslim. (*For* Map, *see* index.) The Orontes flows northwards from the Lebanon range across the northern boundary to Antakya (Antioch, Turkey). The Euphrates crosses the northern boundary near Jerablus and flows through north-eastern Syria to the boundary of Iraq.

Archæology, etc.—The region is rich in historical remains. Damascus (*Dimishq ash-Sham*) is said to be the oldest continuously inhabited city in the world (although Aleppo disputes this claim), having an existence as a city for over 4,000 years. It is situated on the river Barada, in an oasis at the eastern foot of the Anti-Lebanon, and at the edge of the wide sandy desert which stretches to the Euphrates. The city contains the Omayed Mosque, the Tomb of Saladin, and the "Street Called Straight" (Acts ix. 11), while to the North-East is the Roman outpost of Dmeir and further east is Palmyra.

On the Mediterranean coast at Amrit are ruins of the Phœnician town of Marath, where the well has been found and is being excavated and also ruins of Crusaders' fortresses at Markab, Sahyoun, and Krak des Chevaliers. At Tartous (also on the coast) the cathedral of Our Lady of Syria, built by the Knights Templars in the 12th and 13th centuries has been restored as a museum. One of the oldest alphabets in the world has been discovered at Ugarit (Ras Shamra), a Phoenician village near the port of Latakia.

Hittite cities dating from 2,000 to 1,500 B.C., have recently been explored on the west bank of the Euphrates at Jerablus and Kadesh.

Government.—Syria, which had been under French mandate since the 1914–18 war, became an independent Republic during the 1939–45 war. The first independently elected Parliament met on August 17, 1943, but foreign troops were in part occupation until April, 1946. Syria remained an independent Republic until February, 1958, when it became part of the United Arab Republic. It seceded from the United Arab Republic on Sept. 28, 1961.

A new Constitution was promulgated in March 1973; this declared that Syria is a "democratic, popular socialist State", and that the Ba'ath Party, which has been the ruling party since 1963, is "the leading party in the State and society". Elections to the 195-seat Peoples' Council in August 1977 resulted in a large majority for the Ba'ath Party, which has since been maintained.

Production and Industry.—Agriculture is the principal source of production; wheat and barley are the main cereal crops, but the cotton crop is the highest in value. Tobacco is grown in the maritime plain in Sahel, the Sahyoun and the Djebleh district of Lattakia. Large new areas are coming under irrigation and cultivation in the north-east of the country as a result of the Thawra dam. Skins and hides, leather goods, wool and silk, textiles, cement, vegetable oil, glass, soap, sugar, plastics and copper and brass utensils are produced. There are an increasing number of light assembly plants as Syria's industrialisation programme develops. Oil has been found at Karachuk and other parts in the north-eastern corner of the country and exploitation and further excavations have recently discovered considerable high quality reserves in the region of Deir ez Zor. Syria produces about 8·2 million tons of oil per year at present. A pipeline has been built to the Mediterranean port of Banias, *viâ* Homs. Two oil refineries are in production at Homs and Banias. Revenue is derived from the pipeline from the oilfields of Saudi Arabia to Sidon in Lebanon (Tapline). Another pipeline from the Iraq oilfields was closed in April 1982. Syria also has deposits of phosphate and rock salt, and produces asphalt.

Language and Literature.—Arabic is the principal language, but Kurdish, Turkish and Armenian are spoken among significant minorities and a few villages still speak Aramaic, the language spoken by Christ and the Apostles. There are 3 daily newspapers and several periodicals in Arabic published in Damascus, and also a daily newspaper in English. English has taken over from French as the main foreign language, especially among the young.

Education.—Education in Syria is under State control and, although a few of the schools are privately owned, they all follow a common system and syllabus. Elementary education is free at State Schools, and is compulsory from the age of seven. Secondary education is not compulsory and is free only at the State Schools. Because of the shortage of places, entry to these State Schools is competitive. Damascus University, founded in 1924, has nine faculties and a Higher Teachers' Training College. The number of students has risen to over 60,000. There are also about 20,000 students at Aleppo University (founded 1961), over 10,000 at Tishrin University, Latakia (founded 1975) and 6,000 at Ba'ath University, Homs. Approximately 10 per cent of all students receive scholarships, and at the present time Palestinian refugees are admitted free. The rest pay fees.

Communications.—Although railway lines run from Damascus to both Beirut and Amman, train services go only as far as the border towns. A track has been opened connecting Homs with Damascus but is not yet open to passengers. A track links Homs, Hamah, Aleppo and Qamishliye to the Iraq frontier. Branch lines connect the ports of Tartous and Latakia to the system and another line runs from Aleppo down Euphrates valley to Deir ez Zor and thence north to Qamishliye, with a branch going to the Euphrates Dam. All the principal towns in the country are connected by roads which vary from modern dual carriageways to narrow country lanes. An internal air service operates between all major towns. The main International Airport is at Damascus and there are also flights to Eastern Europe, Turkey, Greece and Armenia from Aleppo.

Currency.—The monetary unit is the Syrian pound (£*Syr.*). Exchange rate, *see* p. 82.

Trade.—The principal imports are foodstuffs (fruit, vegetables, cereals, meat and dairy products, tea, coffee and sugar), mineral and petroleum products, yarn and textiles, iron and steel manufactures, machinery, chemicals, pharmaceuticals, fertilizers and timber. Raw cotton, oil, cereals, fruit, phosphates, livestock and dairy products, other foodstuffs, textiles and raw wool.

Trade with U.K.

	1983	1984
Imports from U.K.	£72,320,000	£91,909,000
Exports to U.K.	18,859,000	59,245,000

CHIEF TOWNS.—Damascus (population (estimated) 2,250,000) is the capital of Syria. Other important towns are Aleppo, Homs and Hama, and the principal port is Latakia.

FLAG.—Red over white over black horizontal bands, with two green stars on central white band. NATIONAL DAY.—April 17.

BRITISH EMBASSY
Quartier Malki, 11 rue Mohammad Kurd Ali,
Imm. Kotob, Damascus.

Ambassador Extraordinary and Plenipotentiary, His Excellency William Roger Tomkys, C.M.G. (1984).

British Council Representative, Dr. J. M. Compton, British Cultural Centre, 60 Atta al Ayoubi Street, Damascus.

THAILAND

King, His Majesty Bhumibol Adulyadej, *born* 1927; *succeeded his brother*, June 9, 1946; *married* Princess Sirikit Kityakara, April 28, 1950; *crowned* May 5, 1950; *and has issue*, Princess Ubolratana, *born*, April 6, 1951; Crown Prince Vajiralongkorn, *born*, July 28, 1952; Crown Princess Sirindhorn, *born*, April 2, 1955; Princess Chulabhorn *born*, July 4, 1957.

CABINET

Prime Minister and Minister for Defence , Gen. Prem Tinsulanonda.

Deputy Prime Ministers, Gen. Prachuab Soontrangkoon; Boontheng Thongswasdi; Bhichai Rattakul; Adm. Sonthee Boonyachai.

Ministers attached to the Prime Minister's Office, Kramol Tongdhamachart; Police Lt. Charn Manoodham; Meechai Ruchupan; Flt. Lt. Suli Mahasantana; Sawat Khumprakob; Chaisiri Ruangkanchanaseth; Banyat Bantadtan.

Foreign Affairs, Air Chief Marshal Siddhi Savetsila.
Communications, Samak Sundaravej.
Commerce, Kosol Krairiksh.
Interior, Gen. Sitthi Chirarochana.
Justice, Pipop Asitirat.
Science, Technology and Energy, Damrong Lathapipat.
Education, Chuan Leekpai.
Public Health, Marut Bunnag.
Industry, Ob Vasuratna.
Agriculture, Narong Wongwan.
Finance, Sommai Hoontrakool.
University Affairs, Preeda Patanathabutr.

ROYAL THAI EMBASSY IN LONDON
30 Queen's Gate, SW7 5JB
[01–589 0173]

Ambassador Extraordinary and Plenipotentiary, His Excellency Dr. Owart Suthiwart-Narueput, C.M.G. (1984).

Area and Population.—The Kingdom of Thailand, formerly known as Siam, has an area of 198,247 sq. miles with a population (estimated 1984) of 50,583,105. It has a common boundary with Malaysia in the south, is bounded on the west by Burma and on the north-east and east by Laos and Cambodia. (For MAP, *see* INDEX.) Although there is no common boundary between Thailand and China, the Chinese province of Yunnan is separated from the Thai northern border only by a narrow stretch of Burmese and Laotian territory.

The capital, Bangkok, is situated in the south of the central plain area. To the north-east there is a plateau area and to the north-west mountains. The south of Thailand consists of a narrow mountainous peninsula. The principal rivers are the Chao Phraya in the central plains, and the Mekong on the northern and north-eastern borders.

Government.—Thailand became a Constitutional Monarchy in 1932. The Constitution promulgated in

December 1978 provides for a National Assembly consisting of a Senate appointed by the King and a House of Representatives elected by universal adult suffrage.

Language, Religion and Education.—Thai is basically a monosyllabic, tonal language, a branch of the Indo-Chinese linguistic family, but its vocabulary especially has been strongly influenced by Sanskrit and Pali. It is written in an alphabetic script derived from ancient Indian scripts. The principal religion is Buddhism. In 1984 95·49 per cent of the population were Buddhists, 3·83 per cent Moslems, 0·5 per cent Christians and 0·1 per cent other religions.

Education.—Primary education is compulsory and free and secondary education in Government Schools is free. In 1983 there were 35,846 schools and training colleges, with a total of 10,058,295 pupils and 539,680 teachers. Private universities and colleges are playing an increasing role in higher education. In 1984 the Government agreed to upgrade four private colleges to universities. Out of 29 universities and other similar higher institutes of learning, 11 are private and attended by some 25,000 students. In 1984 their total enrolment was 668,810 students. The two open universities, Ramkamhaeng and Sukhothaithammathirat, had an enrolment of 409,686 and 73,000 students respectively.

Production and Industry.—The agricultural sector provides just under half the national income and employs about 70 per cent of the working population. Rice remains the most important crop, accounting for 60 per cent of the area planted. After rice the main crops are cassava, maize, sugar cane, rubber, groundnuts, sorghum, kenaf, cotton, kapok and coconuts. In recent years the production of livestock and poultry, especially pigs and chickens for export, has gained importance. There is a large fishing industry with more than 20,000 vessels registered. Fish farming is popular in many inland areas. A ban on hardwood export has resulted in the decline of the forestry industry.

The discovery of onshore oil and offshore gas in the late 1970s ushered in a new economic era. Crude production which began in 1983 stood at around 20,000 barrels per day in mid-1985, or about 10 per cent of the country's need. At the same time gas and condensate output stood at over 350 million cubic feet per day. It was estimated that by the end of 1985 indigenous oil and gas supplies should account for about half of Thailand's petroleum demand. Another energy resource becoming more important is lignite which is found mainly in the north and is being used increasingly for electricity production.

Mineral resources are mainly tin, tungsten, lead, antimony and iron. Among these, tin is the most important, with exports totalling 18,455 tons in 1984. In addition, about 60,000 tons of zinc ingots a year are expected to be produced by a zinc refinery which was opened in early 1984.

Industry is divided into two main categories: service and manufacturing. Since 1982 tourism has replaced rice as the country's top foreign exchange earner. An estimated 2·3 million tourists spent about £700 million in 1984. Other top performers in the service industry are commercial banks. The banking system is large and contributes much to the economy, especially employment. There are over 1,800 bank branches in the country employing some 72,000 workers.

Since 1962 the Government has actively promoted industrial investments by means of tax relief and other incentives to local and foreign investors. Most of the industries established under this scheme in early years were import-substituting. However, there has been an increasing shift to export-oriented industries, taking advantages of low-wage labour and available domestic resources. The predicted surplus

of natural gas has led the Government to designate an area on the east coast as the future centre of the petrochemical industry. Manufacturing now accounts for about 20 per cent of the national income.

Government continues to monopolise some industries and most of the essential services. However, the idea of privatisation and deregulation is finding favour. There were 66 state enterprises in 1984, the largest being the Electricity Generating Authority of Thailand (EGAT) and the Petroleum Authority of Thailand (PTT).

Communications.—The importance of rivers and canals as the traditional mode of transportation has been replaced by highways and roads. The existing road and highway network, totalling 34,701 kilometres in 1984, reaches all parts of the country. Most of the smaller towns and bigger villages are now served by paved roads.

Navigable waterways have a length of about 1,100 km. in the dry season and 1,600 km. in the wet season. About 3,825 km of State-owned railways were open to traffic in 1984. Main lines run from Bangkok to Aranya Prathet on the Cambodian border (160 miles E.); via Korat to Ubon (about 352 miles E.) and to Nong Khai (415 miles N.E.), the ferry terminal on the River Mekong opposite Vientiane, capital of Laos; to Chiang Mai (411 miles N); and to Hat Yai (600 miles S), whence lines go down the eastern and western sides of the Malay peninsula, via Sungei Galok and Penang respectively, to Singapore. A new line to Sattahip on the east coast is being constructed.

Bangkok is an important international air centre and has direct flights to most of the world's major cities. The airports at Chiang Mai and Hat Yai also receive international flights. Most major provincial towns have airports. Thai International, founded in 1960, operates international routes. Domestic routes are operated by Thai Airways. Both are state-owned.

Thailand has an extensive network of telecommunications services, and the telephone service though still poor is being improved. Most major cities and towns are linked by direct long-distance calls.

There are two important ports in the country. Bangkok, which is a river port, can serve vessels up to 27 ft. draught. The deep-sea port at Sattahip caters for larger vessels. Many existing ports in the south are being upgraded to allow more direct cargo shipments. All are owned and operated by a state enterprise.

TRADE

Thailand's main exports are rice, garments and textiles, tapioca products, rubber, maize, and sugar. Increasingly frozen and canned food, integrated circuits, gemstones and jewellery, footwear and toys are becoming important export items. Main imports are petroleum and petroleum products, machinery, transport equipment, iron and steel, electrical machinery, chemicals and cotton.

	1983	1984
	millions of *Baht*	
Total imports	222,888·6	241,679
Total exports	146,238·9	173,571

Trade with U.K.

	1983	1984
Imports from U.K.	£131,833,000	£149,742,000
Exports to U.K.	87,823,000	112,353,000

The Baht currency was devalued by 14·8 per cent in November 1984. At the same time as this devaluation was announced, the Government ordered the unpegging of the Baht from the dollar and the floating of its against a basket of currencies of seven major trading partners. The floating is 'managed' and is done on a daily basis by the central bank. In mid-

1985 it was valued at 26·82 Baht per one U.S. dollar (see also p. 82).

CAPITAL.—ΨBangkok (population 5,174,682 (1984)); at the mouth of the River Chao Phraya. Other centres are Chiang Mai, Phitsanuloke, Chon Buri, Korat, Khon Kaen, Surat Thani, Hat Yai and Phuket but none approaches Bangkok in size or importance.

FLAG.—Five horizontal bands, red, white, dark blue, white, red (the blue band twice the width of the others).

NATIONAL DAY.—December 5 (King's Birthday).

BRITISH EMBASSY
Wireless Road, Bangkok

Ambassador Extraordinary and Plenipotentiary, His Excellency Hubert Anthony Justin Staples, C.M.G. (1981).
British Council Representative, Miss A. Lambert, O.B.E., 428 Rama 1 Road, Siam Square, Bangkok 10500.

BRITISH CHAMBER OF COMMERCE,
302 Silom Road, Bangkok

TOGO
(Republic of Togo)

President and Minister of Defence, Gen. Gnassingbé Eyadéma, *born* 1937, *assumed office*, April 14, 1967; *re-elected for seven-year term*, Dec. 30, 1979.
Minister for Foreign Affairs and Co-operation, Atsu-Koffi Amega.

EMBASSY IN LONDON
30 Sloane Street, S.W.1.
[01–235 0147/9]

Chargé d'Affaires, Fusuasu Kossi Metsoko.

The Republic is situated in West Africa between 0°–2° W. and 6°–11° N., with a coastline only 35 miles long on the Gulf of Guinea, and extends northward inland for 350 miles. It is flanked on the west by Ghana, on the north by Burkina Faso and in the east by Benin. It has an area of 21,000 sq. miles and a population (estimate, 1979) of 2,470,000, including people of several African races. The official language is French.

The first President of Togo, Sylvanus Olympio, assassinated on January 13, 1963, was succeeded by Nicolas Grunitzky, who was himself overthrown by an army *coup d'état* on January 13, 1967. On April 14, 1967, the Commander-in-Chief of the Togolese army, Lt. Colonel (later promoted General) Eyadéma named himself President.

Finance.—The currency of Togo is the *Franc C.F.A.*

Production and Trade.—Although the economy of Togo remains largely agricultural, exports of phosphates have superseded agricultural products as the main source of export earnings. Other exports include palm kernels, copra and manioc. The production of phosphates entirely for export was taken over completely by the government in February 1974.

Trade with U.K.

	1983	1984
Imports from U.K.......	£12,212,000	£12,166,000
Exports to U.K.	2,161,000	3,224,000

CAPITAL.—ΨLomé, population (1979), 247,000.

FLAG.—Five alternating green and yellow horizontal stripes; a quarter in red at top next staff bearing a white star.

NATIONAL DAY.—April 27 (Independence Day).

BRITISH EMBASSY
British Ambassador, (resides at *Accra, Ghana*).

TUNISIA
(Tunisian Republic)

President, Habib Bourguiba, *elected* July 25, 1957; *re-elected* 1959, 1964, 1969 and 1974. Proclaimed President for life March 1975.
Prime Minister and Minister of the Interior, Mohamed Mzali.
Special Advisor to the President, Habib Bourguiba jnr.
Justice, Ridha Ben Ali.
Foreign Affairs, Beji Caid Essebsi.
National Defence, Slaheddine Baly.
Planning, Ismail Khelil.
Finance, Salah M'Barka.
National Economy, Rachid Sfar.

TUNISIAN EMBASSY IN LONDON
29 Prince's Gate, SW7 1QG
[01–584 8117]

Ambassador, His Excellency Sadek Bouzayen (1981).

Area and Population.—Tunisia lies between Algeria and Libya and extends southwards to the Sahara Desert, with a total area of 63,380 sq. miles and an estimated population in 1984 of 6,966,173.

Government.—A French Protectorate from 1881 to 1956, Tunisia became an independent sovereign State with the signing on March 20, 1956, of an agreement whereby France recognized Tunisia's independence and right to conduct her own foreign policy and to form a Tunisian Army.

Following a first general election held on March 25, 1956, a Constituent Assembly met for the first time on April 8. On July 25, 1957, the Constituent Assembly deposed the Bey, abolished the monarchy and elected M. Bourguiba first President of the Republic. On June 1, 1959, the Constitution was promulgated and on December 7, 1959, the National Assembly held its first session. In March 1975 the National Assembly proclaimed M. Bourguiba as President for life.

The country is divided into 22 regions (*gouvernorats*) each administered by a Governor.

Production, Trade, etc.—The valleys of the northern region support large flocks and herds, and contain rich agricultural areas, in which wheat, barley, and oats are grown. The vine and olive are extensively cultivated.

The chief exports are crude oil, phosphates, olive oil, finished textiles, and wine. The chief imports are machinery and equipment, foodstuffs, petroleum products, and textiles. Some oil has been discovered and production reached an annual rate of 5·4 million tons in 1984. Gas has also been discovered off the east coast but exploitation is not viable at present. Tourists numbered 1,579,607 in 1984.

	1983	1984
Total Imports ...	TD2,109,700,000	TD2,260,000
Total Exports ...	1,263,900,000	1,395,000

France remains the main trading partner, supplying 25·1 per cent of the country's imports and purchasing 19·7 per cent of Tunisia's exports.

Trade with U.K.

	1983	1984
Imports from U.K.......	£44,659,000	£44,077,000
Exports to U.K.	18,126,000	21,086,000

Currency.—The unit of currency is the *dinar* of 1,000 *millimes*.

Tunisia became an associate member of E.E.C. early in 1969, and signed a new agreement with the E.E.C. in 1976. In 1977 the introduction of import quota measures by the E.E.C. on some textile goods resulted in a reduction of growth in this important sector of the Tunisian market. The quotas for some textile products was renegotiated and increased in 1982.

CAPITAL.—Ψ Tunis, connected by canal with La Goulette on the coast, has a population (1984) of 1,394,749. The ruins of ancient Carthage lie a few miles from the city. Other towns of importance are: Ψ Sfax (577,992); Ψ Sousse (322,491); Ψ Bizerta (394,670); Kairouan; Gabes; Menzel Bourguiba.

FLAG.—Red crescent and star in a white orb, all on a red ground.

NATIONAL DAY.—June 1.

BRITISH EMBASSY
Place de la Victoire, Tunis

Ambassador Extraordinary and Plenipotentiary and Consul-General, His Excellency William James Adams, C.M.G. (1984).
1*st Secretary,* B. E. Stewart (*Head of Chancery and Consul*).
Commercial Attaché, J. F. Larner.
British Council Representative, Dr. P. J. A. Clark. There is a British Council Library in *Tunis.*

TURKEY

President, Gen. Kenan Evren, *assumed power,* Sept. 12, 1980; *elected for 7-year term,* Nov. 1982.

GOVERNMENT

Prime Minister, Turgut Özal.
Deputy Prime Minister, Kaya Erdem.
Ministers of State, Kazim Oksay; Mesut Yilmaz; Mustafa Tinaz Titiz; Abdullah Tenekeci; Cemal Büyükbas; Ahmet Karaevli.
Justice, M. Necat Eldem.
National Defence, Zeki Yavuztürk.
Interior, Yildirim Akbulut.
Foreign Affairs, Vahit Halefoğlu.*
Finance and Customs, A. Kurtcebe Alptemoçin.
National Education, Youth and Sport, M. Vehbi Dinçerler.
Public Works and Construction, I. Safa Giray.
Health and Social Welfare, Mehmet Aydin.
Communications, Veysel Atasoy.
Agriculture, Forestry and Rural Affairs, Hüsnü Doğan.*
Labour and Social Security, Mustafa Kalemli.
Industry and Commerce, Cahit Aral.
Energy and Natural Resources, Sudi Neşet Turel.
Culture and Tourism, Mukerrem Taşcioğlu.
Presidential Council, Pres. Kenan Evren; Gen. Nurettin Ersin; Gen. Tahsin Sahinkaya; Adm. Nejat Tumer; Gen. Sedat Celasun.
(* not an M.P.)

TURKISH EMBASSY IN LONDON
Chancery: 43 Belgrave Square, SW1X 8PA
[01–235 5252]

Ambassador Extraordinary and Plenipotentiary, His Excellency Rahmi Gümrükçüoglu (1981).

Area and Population.—People of Turkic stock are to be found scattered throughout a wide belt extending from China through the Soviet Union, Afghanistan and Iran to the present day Turkish State, and into Bulgaria.

Turkey itself extends from Edirne (Adrianople) to Transcaucasia and Iran, and from the Black Sea to the Mediterranean, Syria and Iraq. Total population at the Census of October, 1980 was 45,217,556.

Turkey in Europe consists of Eastern Thrace, including the cities of Istanbul and Edirne, and is separated from Asia by the Bosphorus at Istanbul and by the Dardanelles—about 40 miles in length with a width varying from 1 to 4 miles—the political

neighbours being Greece and Bulgaria on the west. Population (est. 1980), 4,500,000.

Turkey in Asia comprises the whole of Asia Minor or Anatolia and extends from the Aegean Sea to the western boundaries of Georgia, Soviet Armenia and Iran, and from the Black Sea to the Mediterranean and the northern boundaries of Syria and Iraq. Population (est. 1980), 40,500,000.

Government.—On October 29, 1923, the National Assembly declared Turkey a Republic and elected Gazi Mustafa Kemal (later known as Kemal Ataturk) President. In 1945 a multi-party system was introduced but in 1960 the government was overthrown by the Turkish Armed Forces which ruled through the Committee of National Union, a body of military officers. A new constitution was adopted in July 1961 and in Oct., after a general election, a civilian government took office. Civilian governments remained in power until Sept. 1980 when mounting problems with the economy and terrorism led the military to assume legislative powers. A civilian technocratic government was appointed later that month.

A new Constitution, extending the powers of the President, was approved by a referendum on Nov. 7, 1982. It provided for the separation of powers between the legislature, executive and judiciary, and the holding of free elections to the unicameral Grand National Assembly, which has 400 members elected every five years. Following the General Election on Nov. 6, 1983 the military leadership handed over power to a newly elected civilian government.

Party representation in the Assembly after the General Election was: Motherland Party, 211 seats; Populist Party, 117; Nationalist Democracy Party, 67; Independents 4. (One seat was not filled at the election).

Turkey is divided for administrative purposes into 67 *il* with subdivisions into *kaza* and *nahiye.* Each *il* has a governor (*vali*) and elective council.

Religion and Education.—On April 10, 1928, the Grand National Assembly passed a law in virtue of which Islam ceased to be the State religion of the Republic. However, 98·99 per cent of the population are Moslems. The main religious minorities, which are concentrated in Istanbul and on the Syrian frontier, are: Greek Orthodox, 10,000; Armenians, 42,000; Syriani Christians, 42,000; Others, 6,000. (Total Christians, 100,000); Jewish, 44,000. Education is free, secular and compulsory at primary level. There are elementary, secondary and vocational schools.

There are 27 universities in Turkey, including four in Istanbul, four in Ankara, two in Izmir, and one each in Erzurum and Trabzon.

The expenditure allocated to education in the 4th Five Year Plan (1979–83) was TL76,000,000,000, compared with TL14,000,000,000 in the 3rd Five Year Plan (1973–77), but past experience has shown that targets in this field are not always met.

Language and Literature.—Until 1926, Turkish was written in Arabic script, but in that year the Roman alphabet was substituted for use in official correspondence and in 1928 for universal use, with Arabic numerals as used throughout Europe. Ancient Turkish literature aped the Arabic manner, but the revolution of 1908 led to the introduction of a native literature free from foreign influences and adapted to the understanding of the people. The leading Turkish newspapers are centred in Istanbul and Ankara, although most provincial towns have their own daily papers. There are foreign language papers in French, Greek, Armenian and English and numerous magazines and weeklies on various subjects, but few trade commercial publications.

Agricultural Production.—In 1981 agricultural production accounted for some 21 per cent of the

gross domestic product at constant factor prices. About 60 per cent of the working population are in the rural sector, but agriculture is still primitive in many areas and agricultural productivity is low. Estimated production figures for the principal crops in 1981 were ('000 tons):

Wheat	17,000	Tobacco	200
Barley	5,900	Sugar Beet	11,000
Maize	1,100	Potatoes	3,000
Rye	500	Grapes	3,600
Oilseeds	1,507	Citrus Fruits	1,200
Pulses	825	Figs	200
Cotton	500	Hazelnuts	350

With the important exception of wheat, which is mostly grown on the arid Central Anatolian Plateau, most of the crops are grown on the fertile littoral. Tobacco, sultana and fig cultivation is centred around Izmir, where substantial quantities of cotton are also grown. The main cotton area is in the Cukurova Plain around Adana. The forests which lie between the littoral plain and the Anatolian Plateau, contain beech, pine, oak, elm, chestnut, lime, plane, alder, box, poplar and maple. During recent years the Government has attempted, so far not altogether successfully, to combat the depredations of peasant and goat which threaten to destroy the existing forests within the next 25 years.

Industry.—After agriculture, Turkey's second most important industry is based on her considerable mineral wealth which is, however, as yet comparatively unexploited. The main export minerals are chromite and boron. Production in 1981 was (tons):

Coal	7,223,000
Lignite	17,400,000
Iron ore	2,856,000
Chrome ore	507,000
Copper	45,000
Boron minerals	1,333,000

Industrial production figures for 1981 ('000 tons): cement, 15,008; sugar, 1,270; pig iron, 1,830; steel ingots, 1,830; paper, 368; petroleum products, 12,606; crude oil, 2,100; artificial fertilizer, 6,609; electric energy (billion of kilowatt hours), 25; cotton fabrics (thousand metres), 228.

The progress made in the manufacture of sugar, cotton, woollen and silk textiles, and cement, has been such that the bulk of the country's requirements can now be produced locally, while other industries contributing substantially to local needs include vehicle assembly, paper, glass and glassware, iron and steel, leather and leather goods, sulphur refining, canning and rubber goods, soaps and cosmetics, pharmaceutical products, prepared foodstuffs and a host of minor industries.

In common with other developing countries, Turkey's economy was adversely affected by the steep rises in oil prices from 1973 onwards. This led to a succession of economic crises and high inflation culminating in Jan. 1980 in the introduction of an economic stability programme. Exports have since risen dramatically, inflation has largely been brought under control, and modest growth has resumed although the internal economy is still depressed with high unemployment.

COMMUNICATIONS

Railways.—The complete network became the property of the State Railways Administration in 1948. The total length of lines in operation is 8,193 kilometres.

Roads.—At the end of 1980 there were 31,976 km. of national roads (24,972 of which were macadamized). The total state and provincial road system is some 60,761 km. in length. The estimated number of vehicles in 1980 was 1,135,000.

Shipping.—In August 1980 there were 343 merchants ships over 300 gross tons, 79 passenger ships and 73 tankers, giving a total draft weight of 1,545,062 tons.

Civil Aviation.—The State airlines (T.H.Y.) operate all internal services and have services to Europe and the Middle East. Most of the leading European airlines, including British Airways, operate services to Istanbul and some also to Ankara.

FINANCE

(In 1982 the financial year is being aligned with the calendar year: these figures are for Mar. 1–Dec. 31)

	1982 TL'000,000
Estimated Expenditure	1,755,200
Estimated Revenue	1,680,000

Currency.—The Turkish *Lira* (*TL*) is divided into 100 *Kurus*. For rate of exchange *see also* p. 82.

TRADE

	1980	1981
Total imports	$7,909,000,000	$8,911,000,000
Total exports	2,910,000,000	4,703,000,000

The 1981 foreign trade deficit figure was U.S., $4,208,000,000.

All imports are subject to licence and the issue of licences is limited to goods considered necessary for the country's economy. Lists of permitted imports are published annually at the beginning of January. The main imports are machinery, crude oil and petroleum products, iron and steel, vehicles, medicines and dyes, chemicals, fertilizers and electrical appliances. Agricultural commodities (cotton, tobacco, fruits, nuts, livestock) represent 47 per cent of total exports. Other exports are minerals, textiles, glass and cement.

Trade with U.K.

	1983	1984
Imports from U.K........	£244,024,000	£331,350,000
Exports to U.K.	184,976,000	204,131,000

CAPITAL.—Ankara (Angora), an inland town of Asia Minor, about 275 miles E.S.E. of Istanbul, with a population (1980) of 3,196,460. Ankara (or Ancyra) was the capital of the Roman Province of *Galatia Prima*, and a marble temple (now in ruins), dedicated to Augustus, contains the *Monumentum* (*Marmor*) *Ancyranum*, inscribed with a record of the reign of Augustus Cæsar. ΨIstanbul (4,870,747), the former capital, was the Roman city of Byzantium. It was selected by Constantine the Great as the capital of the Roman Empire about A.D. 328 and renamed Constantinople. Istanbul contains the celebrated church of St. Sophia, which, after becoming a mosque, was made a museum in 1934; it also contains Topkapi, former Palace of the Ottoman Sultans, which is also a museum. Other cities are ΨIzmir (1,968,614); Adana (1,467,346); Bursa (1,161,553); Gaziantep (387,093); and Eskişehir (543,733).

FLAG.—Red, with white crescent and star.

NATIONAL DAY.—October 29 (Republic Day).

BRITISH EMBASSY
(Ankara)

Ambassador Extraordinary and Plenipotentiary, His Excellency Sir Robert Russell, K.C.M.G.,(1982).

Counsellor, A. P. F. Bache; Dr. F. H. Taylor (*Cultural Affairs*)

1st Secretaries, K. R. Tebbitt (*Head of Chancery*); N. J. Morley; R. M. D. Barrett (*Consul*); R. D. Wilkinson (*Economic and Commercial*); Ms. C. M. Street (*Cultural Affairs*); M. R. Willson (*Cultural and Science Affairs*); D. J. Ray (*Administration*).

Defence and Military Attaché, Brig. C. W. G. Bullocke, O.B.E.

Naval and Air Attaché, Wing Cdr. A. J. Raley, M.B.E.

BRITISH CONSULAR OFFICES

There is a British Consulate-General at *Istanbul*, a Vice-Consulate at *Izmir* and an Hon. British Consulate at *Iskenderun*.

BRITISH COUNCIL.—50–52 Güniz Sokak, Kavaklidere, Ankara. *Representative*, Dr. F. H. Taylor.—There is also a centre and library at *Istanbul* and a library at *Ankara*.

BRITISH CHAMBER OF COMMERCE OF TURKEY INC., Mesrutiyet Caddessi No. 34, Tepebasi Beyoğlu, Istanbul (Postal Address, P.O. Box 190 Karaköy, Istanbul).

UNITED ARAB EMIRATES

President, Shaikh Zaid bin Sultan al Nahayyan (*Abu Dhabi*).

Vice-President and Prime Minister, Shaikh Rashid bin Said al Maktum.

Deputy Prime Ministers, Shaikh Maktum bin Rashid al Maktum; Shaikh Hamdan bin Muhammad al Nahayyan.

Interior, Shaikh Mubarak bin Muhammad al Nahayyan.

Finance and Industry, Shaikh Hamdan bin Rashid al Maktum.

Defence, Shaikh Muhammad bin Rashid al Maktum.

Minister of State for Foreign Affairs, Sayyid Rashid Abdullah al Nu'aimi.

Petroleum and Mineral Resources, Dr. Mana Said al Otaiba.

Economy and Commerce, Sayyid Saif al Jarwan.

Information and Culture, Shaikh Ahmad bin Hamid bin Butti.

Communications, Sayyid Muhammad Said al Mulla.

Public Works and Housing, Sayyid Muhammad Khalifa al Kindi.

Education, Sayyid Faraj Fadel al Mazroni.

Planning, (vacant).

Justice, Sayyid Abdullah Humaid al Mazroni.

Islamic Affairs and Awqaf, Shaikh Mohammad bin Hassan al Khazraji.

Agriculture and Fisheries, Sayyid Said al Ragabani.

Water and Electricity, Sayyid Humaid Nasser al Owais.

Labour and Social Affairs, Sayyid Khalfan al Roumi.

Health, Sayyid Hamad Abdul Rahman al Madfa.

EMBASSY IN LONDON
30 Prince's Gate, SW7 1PT
[01–581 1281]

Ambassador Extraordinary and Plenipotentiary, His Excellency Sayed Mohammed Mahdi Al-Tajir.

Area and Population.—The approximate area of the U.A.E. is 33,000 square miles and the population in 1984 was estimated at about 1·3 million.

The United Arab Emirates (formerly the Trucial States) is composed of seven Emirates (Abu Dhabi, Ajman, Dubai, Fujeirah, Ras al Khaimah, Sharjah and Umm al Qaiwain) which came together as an independent state on December 2, 1971, when they ended their individual special treaty relationships with the British Government (Ras al Khaimah joined the other six on February 10, 1972).

The British Government, by virtue of a treaty made in 1892, had been responsible for the external affairs of the states through the British Political Resident in the Persian Gulf and the British Political Agents in each state, but on independence the Union Government assumed full responsibility for all internal and external affairs apart from some internal matters that remained the prerogative of the individual Emirates. Six of the Emirates lie on the shore of the Gulf between the Musandam peninsula in the East and the Qatar peninsula in the West while the seventh, Fujeirah, lies on the gulf of Oman.

Security in the area is maintained by the U.A.E. Armed Forces. The Ministry of Defence is located in Dubai with a General Headquarters in Abu Dhabi. Most of the separate police forces have also been merged.

Revenue is chiefly derived from oil, re-exports and customs dues on imports. A substantial amount is spent on overseas aid, where commitments in 1980 totalled £154·8 million, doubling those of 1979.

Trade with U.K.

	1983	1984
Imports from U.K.	£567,765,000	£541,858,000
Exports to U.K.	309,806,000	87,227,000

FLAG.—Horizontal stripes of green over white over black with vertical red stripe in the hoist.

Abu Dhabi

Abu Dhabi is the largest Emirate of the U.A.E. in area, stretching from Khor al Odaid in the west to the borders with Dubai in the Jebel Ali area. It includes six villages in the Buraimi oasis, the other three being part of the Sultanate of Oman, and a number of settlements in the Liwa Oasis system. Following negotiations with Saudi Arabia, some adjustment of the border has now been made in the Khor al Odaid region, but the agreement has not yet been ratified. The population of the Emirate is now about 509,000

The Abu Dhabi Government controls oil, gas and petrochemical operations in the Emirate through the Abu Dhabi National Oil Company (ADNOC) which has majority shareholdings in the several oil operating and gas treatment companies. ADNOC also has majority shareholdings in oil industry-related companies covering drilling, refining, distribution, chemical manufacture and investment. Offshore production began in 1962, the most important fields being Umm Shaif and Lower Zakum, near Das Island, site of a large associated gas liquefaction plant. The Upper Zakum field came on stream in late 1982, and four other offshore fields are being developed, one near Abu Dhabi city and three near Delma. Production of oil onshore began in 1963 from the Murban field. A large onshore associated gas liquefaction project based at Ruwais started production in 1981. Other large natural gas finds in recent years will consolidate Abu Dhabi's position as a holder of some of the largest reserves of natural gas in the world. Abu Dhabi's crude oil production in 1983 was 255 million barrels.

With its oil wealth the Emirate has seen a decade of growth (which is currently slowing down), not only at Abu Dhabi, now a modern city of about 400,000 people, but also at Al Ain in the Buraimi Oasis and at the new petro-chemical city at Ruwais. An international airport opened in 1982 at Abu Dhabi and another is under construction at Al Ain. There are airfields at Das Island and Jebel Dhanna. The port and harbour on Abu Dhabi island are now almost completed and there are port facilities at Ruwais.

Dubai

Dubai is the second largest Emirate both in size and in population, which is now about 350,000. The town of Dubai is the main port for the import of goods into the U.A.E. and has a wide re-export trade to the other Gulf States. Dubai's prosperity was established by this trade long before the discovery of oil. Oil was discovered in 1966 and production began in September 1969. The main operator of Dubai's offshore oilfields is Dubai Petroleum Company, a subsidiary of CONOCO. In 1982 an ARCO-Britoil joint venture discovered an extensive gas and condensate field onshore.

Oil income has been used to finance Dubai's infrastructure and major construction projects include an international airport, a dry dock complex and an international trade and exhibition centre. There is also a 66 berth port at Jebel Ali, forming the heart of an industrial complex which includes an aluminium smelter with an associated de-salination plant and a gas processing plant. The port and its immediate area is a free trade zone which is expected to attract more industry.

Sharjah

Sharjah, with a present population of approx. 120,000, has declined from its position 50 years ago as principal town in the area. It became the third oil producing Emirate in the summer of 1974, following the discovery of oil offshore. The field declined over the years and by 1982 was yielding less than 6,000 b.p.d. However, new oil and gas discoveries were made in 1982 in the northern emirates and production now stands at about 50,000 b.p.d. Sharjah is well connected by metalled roads to all the other Northern Emirates. It experienced a construction boom in the mid-1970's including an ambitious layout of roads and flyovers within the town. A new container port has been constructed on the Gulf of Oman at Khor Fakkan. The international airport was officially opened in 1979.

Ras al Khaimah

Ras al Khaimah has a population of 80,000 of whom more than half live in the town. An ancient sea-port, near to which archaeological remains have been found, Ras al Khaimah is developing as the most agricultural of the Emirates, producing vegetables, dates, fruit and tobacco. In 1982 Ras al Khaimah announced the discovery of oil and gas offshore and this field is currently being developed. An industrial area has been developed to the north of the Emirate, which includes 2 cement works. Ras al-Khaimah has an international airport and has also expanded its port.

Fujeirah

Fujeirah, with a population of 40,000, is the poorest and most remote of the seven Emirates lying on the Gulf of Oman coast, and only connected by a metal road to the rest of the country since the end of 1975. Largely agricultural, its population is spread between the slopes of the inland Hajar mountain range and the town of Fujeirah itself, together with a number of smaller settlements on the comparatively fertile plain on the coast. Although exploration work continues, there have been no hydrocarbon discoveries in the Emirate. However, there are some chrome and other mineral deposits. Fujeirah has a new general cargo port.

Ajman and Umm al Qaiwain

Ajman and Umm al Qaiwain are the smallest Emirates, having populations of approx. 36,000 and 30,000 respectively. Both lie on the Gulf coast although Ajman has two inland enclaves at Manama and Masfut. Exploration work continues in both Emirates for oil and gas but so far only Umm Al Qaiwain has experienced any success, with the offshore discovery of natural gas, but the field has yet to be commercially developed. The discovery of onshore gas in nearby Sharjah has increased hopes of similar discoveries in both Ajman and Umm Al Qaiwain.

BRITISH EMBASSY
P.O. Box 248, Abu Dhabi

Ambassador Extraordinary and Plenipotentiary, His Excellency Harold Berners Walker, C.M.G. (1981).
British Council Representative, W. H. Jefferson, P.O. Box 248, Abu Dhabi.

(Dubai)
Counsellor and Consul General, J. C. Kay.
British Council Representative, J. D. Ewart, P.O. Box 65, Dubai.

UNITED STATES OF AMERICA

PHYSIOGRAPHY

The conterminous States of the Republic occupy nearly all that portion of the North American Continent between the Atlantic and Pacific Oceans, in latitude 25° 07′–49° 23′ North and longitude 66° 57′–124° 44′ West, its northern boundary being Canada and the southern boundary Mexico. The separate State of Alaska reaches a latitude of 71° 23′ N., at Point Barrow (2,502 miles from the U.S. geographic centre).

The general coastline of the 50 States has a length of about 2,069 miles on the Atlantic, 7,623 miles on the Pacific, 1,060 miles on the Arctic, and 1,631 miles on the Gulf of Mexico.

The principal river is the mighty Mississippi-Missouri-Red, traversing the whole country from north to south, and having a course of 3,710 miles to its mouth in the Gulf of Mexico, with many large affluents, the chief of which are the Yellowstone, Platte, Arkansas, and Ohio, Rivers. The rivers flowing into the Atlantic and Pacific Oceans are comparatively small; among the former may be noticed the Hudson, Delaware, Susquehanna, Potomac, James, Roanoke and Savannah; of the latter, the Columbia-Snake, Sacramento, and Colorado. The Nueces, Brazos, Trinity, Pearl, Mobile-Tombigbee-Alabama, Apalachicola-Chattahoochee, Suwannee and Colorado of Texas fall into the Gulf of Mexico, also the Rio Grande, a long river partly forming the boundary with Mexico. The areas of the water-basins have been estimated as follows:—Rivers flowing to the Pacific, 647,300 square miles; to the Atlantic, 488,877; and to the Gulf of Mexico, 1,683,325 square miles, of which 1,234,600 are drained by the Mississippi-Missouri-Red. The chain of the Rocky Mountains separates the western portion of the country from the remainder, communications being carried on over certain elevated passes, several of which are now traversed by railroads and major highways; west of these, bordering the Pacific coast, the Cascade Mountains and Sierra Nevada form the outer edge of a high tableland, consisting in part of stony and sandy desert and partly of grazing land and forested mountains, and including the Great Salt Lake, which extends to the Rocky Mountains. In the Eastern States (which form the more settled and most thickly inhabited portion of the country) large forests of valuable timber, as beech, birch, maple, oak, pine, spruce, elm, ash, walnut; and in the south, live oak, water-oak, magnolia, palmetto, pine, tulip-tree, cypress, etc., still exist, the remnants of the forests which formerly extended over all the Atlantic slope, but into which great inroads have been made by the advance of civilization. The mineral kingdom produces ore of iron, copper, lead, zinc, and aluminium, the non-metallic minerals include large quantities of coal, petroleum, stone, phosphate rock, and salt. The highest point is Mount McKinley (Alaska), 20,320 ft. above sea level and the lowest point of dry land is in Death Valley (Inyo, California), 282 ft. below sea-level.

AREA AND POPULATION

	Area, 1980 (sq. miles)		Population	
	Total	Land	Census 1970	Census 1980
The United States (a)	3,618,770	3,539,289	203,302,031*	226,545,805
Puerto Rico	3,515	3,459	2,712,033	3,196,520
Outlying areas under U.S. jurisdiction	1,176	1,176	314,657*	368,856
Territories	459	459	179,519**	235,927
Guam	209	209	84,996	105,979
Virgin Islands of U.S.	132	132	62,468	96,569
American Samoa	77	77	27,159	32,297
Midway Islands	2	2	2,220	453
Wake Island	3	3	1,647	302
Canton Island and Enderbury Island	27	27	—	—
Johnston Atoll (b)	0·5	0·5	1,007	327
Other (c)	9	9	—	—
Pacific Islands Trust Territory (excluding N. Mariana Is.)........	533	533	81,300	116,149
N. Mariana Islands	184	184	9,640	16,780
Population abroad (d)			1,737,836†	995,546
Armed Forces....................			1,057,776	515,408
Total	3,543,924	3,623,461	208,066,557	231,106,727

(a) The 50 States and the Federal *District of Columbia* (*see* pp. 927–8).

(b) Formerly listed as Johnston and Sand Island. Sand Island uninhabited at time of enumeration.

(c) Navassa, Baker, Howland and Jarvis Islands, Kingman Reef, and Palmyra Atoll.

(d) Excludes U.S. citizens temporarily abroad on private business.

* Includes population of Swan Islands (22) and Panama Canal Zone (44,198). Jurisdiction over the Swan Islands was transferrred to Honduras in 1972. Due to the 1978 Treaty, the Census is no longer conducted in the Canal Zone.

** Includes population of Swan Islands (22).

† Includes U.S. citizens abroad for long periods who were not connected with the U.S. government (236,336) and crews of U.S. merchant vessels (15,910).

THE UNITED STATES

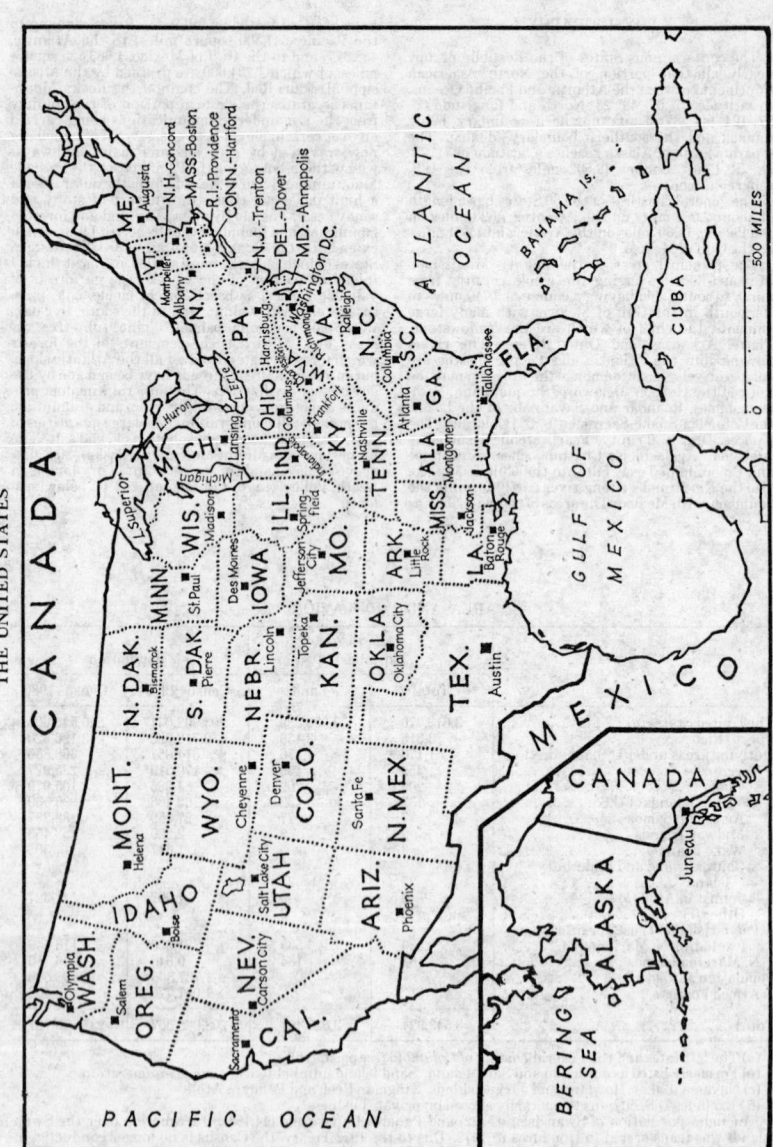

Resident Population by Race 1980
(in thousands)

White	188,372	Filipino	774·7	Vietnamese	261·7	Puerto Rican	2,014
Black	26,495	Japanese	701	Spanish origin**	14,609	Other Spanish	3,051
American		Asian Indian	361·5	Cuban	803	All other races	6,999·2
Indian*	1,420·4	Korean	354·6	Mexican	8,740	TOTAL	226,546
Chinese	806						

*Includes Eskimo and Aleut.
** Persons of Spanish origin may be of any race.

REGISTERED BIRTHS AND DEATHS

	Live Births		Deaths	
Cal- endar Year	Number	Rate per 1,000	Number	Rate per 1,000
1980	3,612,258	15·9	1,989,841	8·8
1981	3,629,238	15·8	1,977,981	8·6
1982	3,680,537	15·9	1,974,797	8·5
1983*	3,614,000	15·5	2,010,000	8·6
1984*	3,697,000	15·7	2,047,000	8·7

Births based on 100 per cent sample in most states and 50 per cent. sample in remaining states.
Note.—Figures tabulated are for the United States. Deaths exclude foetal deaths. Rates are based on the population as estimated on July 1 (April 1 in 1980).
* Provisional.

MARRIAGE AND DIVORCE

Laws of marriage and of divorce are within the exclusive jurisdiction of each State. Each State legislature enacts its own laws prescribing rules and qualifications pertaining to marriage and its dissolution.

Year	Marriages	Per 1,000 Pop.§	Estimated Divorces	Per 1,000 Pop.§
1980	2,390,252	10·6	1,189,000	5·2
1981	2,422,145	10·6	1,213,000	5·3
1982	*2,495,000	*10·8	1,170,000	5·0
1983*	2,444,000	10·5	1,179,000	5·0
1984*	2,487,000	10·5	1,155,000	4·9

§ Population as estimated on July 1.
* Provisional.

Immigrants, by Place of Birth, 1951–84
(1951–76, year ends June 30: from 1977, year ends Sept. 30)

Place of Birth	1951–60	1961–70	1971–80	1984
Europe	1,492,200	1,238,600	801,300	64,076
Asia	157,100	445,300	1,633,800	256,273
North America	769,100	1,351,100	1,645,000	166,701
Canada	274,900	286,700	114,800	10,791
Mexico	319,300	443,300	637,200	57,557
West Indies	122,800	519,500	759,800	74,265
Central America	44,600	97,700	132,400	24,088
South America	72,200	228,300	284,400	37,460
Africa	16,600	39,300	91,500	15,540
Australia	3,700	9,900	14,300	1,308
New Zealand	1,300	3,700	5,300	595
Other countries	3,300	5,500	17,700	1,950
TOTAL	2,515,500	3,321,700	4,493,300	543,903

From 1820 to 1984, 51,950,348 immigrants were admitted to the United States: in 1981, 166,317 people were naturalized.

THE UNITED STATES

State (with date and *order* of admission)	Land Area Sq. M.	Population, April 1, 1980 (census)	Capital	Governor (term of office in years, and expiry year)
Alabama (Ala.) (1819) (*22*)	50,767	3,893,888	Montgomery	George Wallace (*D*) (4—1987)
Alaska (1959) (*49*)	570,833	401,851	Juneau	William Sheffield (*D*) (4—1986)
Arizona (Ariz.) (1912) (*48*)	113,508	2,718,215	Phoenix	Bruce E. Babbit (*D*) (4—1987)
Arkansas (Ark.) (1836) (*25*)	52,078	2,286,435	Little Rock	Bill Clinton (*D*) (2—1987)
California (Calif.) (1850) (*31*)	156,299	23,667,902	Sacramento	George Deukmejian (*R*) (4—1987)
Colorado (Colo.) (1876) (*38*)	103,595	2,889,964	Denver	Richard D. Lamm (*D*) (4—1987)
Connecticut (Conn.)§(1788) (*5*)	4,872	3,107,576	Hartford	William O'Neill (*D*) (4—1987)
Delaware (Del.) § (1787) (*1*)	1,932	594,338	Dover	Michael Castle (*R*) (4—1989)
Florida (Fla.) (1845) (*27*)	54,153	9,746,324	Tallahassee	Robert Graham (*D*). (4—1987)
Georgia (Ga.) § (1788) (*4*)	58,056	5,463,105	Atlanta	Joe F. Harris (*D*) (4—1987)
Hawaii (1959) (*50*)	6,425	964,691	Honolulu	George R. Ariyoshi (*D*) (4—1986)
Idaho (1890) (*43*)	82,412	943,935	Boise	John V. Evans (*D*) (4—1987)
Illinois (Ill.) (1818) (*21*)	55,645	11,426,518	Springfield	James R. Thompson (*R*) (4—1987)
Indiana (Ind.) (1816) (*19*)	35,932	5,490,224	Indianapolis	Robert Orr (*R*) (4—1989)
Iowa (1846) (*29*)	55,965	2,913,808	Des Moines	Terry Branstad (*R*) (4—1987)

State (with date and *order* of admission)	Land Area Sq. M.	Population, April 1, 1980 (census)	Capital	Governor (term of office in years, and expiry year)
Kansas (Kan.) (1861) (34)	81,778	2,363,679	Topeka	John Carlin (D) (4—1987)
Kentucky (Ky.) (1792) (15)	39,669	3,660,777	Frankfort	Martha L. Collins (D) (4—1987)
Louisiana (La.) (1812) (18)	44,521	4,205,990	Baton Rouge	Edwin W. Edwards (D) (4—1988)
Maine (Me.) (1820) (23)	30,995	1,124,660	Augusta	Joseph E. Brennan (D) (4—1987)
Maryland (Md.)§ (1788) (7)	9,837	4,216,975	Annapolis	Harry Hughes (D) (4—1987)
Massachusetts (Mass.)§ (1788) (6)	7,824	5,737,037	Boston	Michael Dukakis (D) (4—1987)
Michigan (Mich.) (1837) (26)	56,954	9,262,078	Lansing	James Blanchard (D) (4—1987)
Minnesota (Minn.) (1858) (32)	79,548	4,075,970	St. Paul	Rudy Perpich (D) (4—1987)
Mississippi (Miss.) (1817) (20)	47,233	2,250,638	Jackson	William A. Allain (D) (4—1988)
Missouri (Mo.) (1821) (24)	68,945	4,916,686	Jefferson City	John Ashcroft (R) (4—1989)
Montana (Mont.) (1889) (41)	145,388	786,690	Helena	Ted Schwinden (D) (4—1989)
Nebraska (Neb.) (1867) (37)	76,644	1,569,825	Lincoln	Bob Kerrey (D) (4—1987)
Nevada (Nev.) (1864) (36)	109,894	800,493	Carson City	Richard Bryan (D) (4—1987)
New Hampshire (N.H.)§ (1788) (9)	8,993	920,610	Concord	John Sununu (R) (2—1987)
New Jersey (N.J.)§ (1787) (3)	7,468	7,364,823	Trenton	Thomas H. Kean (R) (4—1986)
New Mexico (N.M.) (1912) (47)	121,335	1,302,894	Santa Fé	Toney Anaya (D) (4—1987)
New York (N.Y.)§ (1788) (11)	47,377	17,558,072	Albany	Mario Cuomo (D) (4—1987)
North Carolina (N.C.)§ (1789) (12)	48,843	5,881,766	Raleigh	Jim Martin (R) (4—1989)
North Dakota (N.D.) (1889) (39)	69,300	652,717	Bismarck	George Sinner (D) (4—1989)
Ohio (1803) (17)	41,004	10,797,630	Columbus	Richard Celeste (D) (4—1987)
Oklahoma (Okla.) (1907) (46)	68,655	3,025,290	Oklahoma City	George Nigh (D) (4—1987)
Oregon (Ore.) (1859) (33)	96,184	2,633,105	Salem	Victor Atiyeh (R) (4—1987)
Pennsylvania (Pa.)§ (1787) (2)	44,888	11,863,895	Harrisburg	Richard Thornburgh (R) (4—1987)
Rhode Island (R.I.)§ (1790) (13)	1,055	947,154	Providence	Edward Di Prete (R) (2—1987)
South Carolina (S.C.)§ (1788) (8)	30,203	3,121,820	Columbia	Richard Riley (D) (4—1987)
South Dakota (S.D.) (1889) (40)	75,952	690,768	Pierre	William Janklow (R) (4—1987)
Tennessee (Tenn.) (1796) (16)	41,155	4,591,120	Nashville	Lamar Alexander (R) (4—1987)
Texas (1845) (28)	262,017	14,229,191	Austin	Mark White (D) (4—1987)
Utah (1896) (45)	82,073	1,461,037	Salt Lake City	Norman Bangerter (R) (4—1989)
Vermont (Vt.) (1791) (14)	9,273	511,456	Montpelier	Madeleine Kunin (D) (2—1987)
Virginia (Va.)§ (1788) (10)	39,704	5,346,818	Richmond	Charles S. Robb (D) (4—1986)
Washington (Wash.) (1889) (42)	66,511	4,132,156	Olympia	Booth Gardner (D) (4—1989)
West Virginia (W. Va.) (1863) (35)	24,119	1,949,644	Charleston	Arch Moore (R) (4—1989)
Wisconsin (Wis.) (1848) (30)	54,426	4,705,767	Madison	Anthony Earl (D) (4—1987)
Wyoming (Wyo.) (1890) (44)	96,989	469,557	Cheyenne	Ed Herschler (D) (4—1987)
Dist. of Columbia (D.C.) (1791)	63	638,333	..	†
OUTLYING TERRITORIES AND POSSESSIONS				
Puerto Rico (1899)	3,421	3,196,520	San Juan	Rafael Hernández Colón (4—1989)
Guam (1899)	209	105,979	Agaña	Ricardo J. Bordallo (D) (4—1987)
Samoa (1900)	77	32,297	Pago Pago	A. P. Lutali (1986)
Virgin Islands (1917)	132	96,569	Charlotte Amalie	Juan Luis (I) (4—1987)

D.—Democratic Party.   *R.—Republican Party.*   *I.—Independent.*   § The 13 Original States.
† The capital territory is governed by Congress through a Commissioner and City Council (*see* p. 930).

Largest Cities 1982 (estimated populations)

Ψ New York, NY	7,086,096	San Jose, California	659,181
Ψ Los Angeles, California	3,022,247	Memphis, Tennessee	645,760
Ψ Chicago, Illinois	2,997,155	Washington, D.C.	633,425
Ψ Houston, Texas	1,725,617	Ψ Milwaukee, Wisconsin	631,509
Ψ Philadelphia, Pennsylvania	1,665,382	Columbus, Ohio	570,588
Ψ Detroit, Michigan	1,138,717	Ψ New Orleans, Louisiana	564,561
Dallas, Texas	943,848	Ψ Boston, Massachusetts	560,847
Ψ San Diego, California	915,956	Ψ Cleveland, Ohio	558,869
Phoenix, Arizona	824,230	Jacksonville, Florida	556,370
San Antonio, Texas	819,021	Denver, Colorado	505,563
Ψ Baltimore, Maryland	774,113	Ψ Seattle, Washington	490,077
Indianapolis, Indiana	707,655	Nashville-Davidson, Tennessee	455,252
Ψ San Francisco, California	691,637	Ψ Seaport	

THE PRESIDENTS OF THE UNITED STATES OF AMERICA

Name (*with Native State*)	Party	Born	Inaug.	Died	Age
1. GEORGE WASHINGTON, *Va*	Fed.	1732, Feb. 22	1789	1799, Dec. 14	67
2. John Adams, *Mass.*	,,	1735, Oct. 30	1797	1826, July 4	90
3. Thomas Jefferson, *Va.*	Rep.	1743, April 13	1801	1826, July 4	83
4. James Madison, *Va.*	,,	1751, Mar. 16	1809	1836, June 28	85
5. James Monroe, *Va.*	,,	1758, April 28	1817	1831, July 4	73
6. John Quincy Adams, *Mass.*	,,	1767, July 11	1825	1848, Feb. 23	80
7. Andrew Jackson, *S.C.*	Dem.	1767, Mar. 15	1829	1845, June, 8	78
8. Martin Van Buren, *N.Y.*	,,	1782, Dec. 5	1837	1862, July 24	79
9. William Henry Harrison†, *Va.*	Whig.	1773, Feb. 9	1841	1841, April 4	68
10. John Tyler (a), *Va.*	,,	1790, Mar. 29	1841	1862, Jan. 17	71

Name (*with Native State*)	Party	Born	Inaug.	Died	Age
11. James Knox Polk, *N.C.*	Dem.	1795, Nov. 2	1845	1849, June 15	53
12. Zachary Taylor† *Va.*	Whig.	1784, Nov. 24	1849	1850, July 9	65
13. Millard Fillmore (*a*), *N.Y.*	„	1800, Jan. 7	1850	1874, Mar. 8	74
14. Franklin Pierce, *N.H.*	Dem.	1804, Nov. 23	1853	1869, Oct. 8	64
15. James Buchanan, *Pa.*	„	1791, April 23	1857	1868, June 1	77
16. Abraham Lincoln†§, *Ky.*	Rep.	1809, Feb. 12	1861	1865, April 15	56
17. Andrew Johnson (*a*), *N.C.*	„	1808, Dec. 29	1865	1875, July 31	66
18. Ulysses Simpson Grant, *Ohio*	„	1822, April 27	1869	1885, July 23	63
19. Rutherford Birchard Hayes, *Ohio*	„	1822, Oct. 4	1877	1893, Jan. 17	70
20. James Abram Garfield†§, *Ohio*	„	1831, Nov. 19	1881	1881, Sept. 19	49
21. Chester Alan Arthur (*a*), *Vt.*	„	1830, Oct. 5	1881	1886, Nov. 18	56
22. Grover Cleveland, *N.J.*	Dem.	1837, Mar. 18	1885	1908, June 24	71
23. Benjamin Harrison, *Ohio*	Rep.	1833, Aug. 20	1889	1901, Mar. 13	67
Grover Cleveland, *N.J.*	Dem.	1837, Mar. 18	1893	1908, June 24	71
24. William McKinley†§, *Ohio*	Rep.	1843, Jan. 29	1897	1901, Sept. 14	58
25. Theodore Roosevelt (*a*), *N.Y.*	„	1858, Oct. 27	1901	1919, Jan. 6	60
26. William Howard Taft, *Ohio*	„	1857, Sept. 15	1909	1930, Mar. 8	72
27. Woodrow Wilson, *Va.*	Dem.	1856, Dec. 28	1913	1924, Feb. 3	67
28. Warren Gamaliel Harding†, *Ohio*	Rep.	1865, Nov. 2	1921	1923, Aug. 2	57
29. Calvin Coolidge (*a*), *Vt.*	„	1872, July 4	1923	1933, Jan. 5	60
30. Herbert Clark Hoover, *Iowa.*	„	1874, Aug. 10	1929	1964, Oct. 20	90
31. Franklin Delano Roosevelt†‡, *N.Y.*	Dem.	1882, Jan. 30	1933	1945, April 12	63
32. Harry S. Truman (*a*), *Missouri*	„	1884, May 8	1945	1972, Dec. 26	88
33. Dwight David Eisenhower, *Texas*	Rep.	1890, Oct. 14	1953	1969, Mar. 28	78
34. John Fitzgerald Kennedy, *Mass.*†§	Dem.	1917, May 29	1961	1963, Nov. 22	46
35. Lyndon Baines Johnson (*a*), *Texas*	„	1908, Aug. 27	1963	1973, Jan. 22	64
36. Richard Milhous Nixon, *California*	Rep.	1913, Jan. 9	1969	..	..
37. Gerald Rudolph Ford (*a*), *Nebraska*	„	1913, July 14	1974	..	..
38. James Earl Carter, *Georgia*	Dem.	1924, Oct. 1	1977	..	..
39. Ronald Wilson Reagan, *Illinois*	Rep.	1911, Feb. 6	1981	..	..

† Died in office.   § Assassinated.   (*a*) Elected as Vice-President.

‡ Re-elected Nov. 5, 1940, the first case of a third term; re-elected for a fourth term Nov. 7. 1944.

GOVERNMENT

The United States of America is a Federal Republic consisting of 50 States and 1 Federal District (of which 13 are Original States, 7 were admitted without previous organization as Territories, and 30 were admitted after such organization), and of organized Territories. Hawaii formally entered the Union as the 50th State on Aug. 21, 1959, from which date the flag of the United States has 13 stripes and 50 stars in 9 horizontal rows of six and five alternatively. July 4 (Independence Day) is observed as the National Day.

THE CONSTITUTION.—By the Constitution of Sept. 17, 1787 (to which ten amendments were added on Dec. 15, 1791 and eleventh to twenty-sixth, Jan. 8, 1798, Sept. 25, 1804, Dec. 18, 1865, July 28, 1868, March 30, 1870, Feb. 25, 1913, May 31, 1913, Jan. 16, 1920, Aug. 26, 1920, Feb. 6, 1933, Dec. 5, 1933, Feb. 26, 1951, March 29, 1961, Jan. 23, 1964, Feb. 10, 1967 and June 30, 1971), the government of the United States is entrusted to three separate authorities—the Executive, the Legislative, and the Judicial.

THE EXECUTIVE

THE *Executive* power is vested in a President, who is elected every four years. The mode of electing the President is as follows:—Each State elects (on the *first Tuesday after the first Monday in November* of the year preceding the year in which the Presidential term expires), a number of electors, equal to the whole number of Senators and Representatives to which the State may be entitled in the Congress; but no Senator or Representative, or anyone holding office under Government, shall be appointed an elector. The electors for each State meet in their respective States on the *first Monday after the second Wednesday in December* following, and there vote for a President

by ballot. The ballots are then sent to Washington, and opened on the *sixth day of January* by the President of Senate in presence of Congress, and the candidate who has received a majority of the whole number of electoral votes cast is declared President for the ensuing term. If no one has a majority, then from the highest on the list (not exceeding three) the House of Representatives elects a President, the votes being taken by States, the representation from each State having one vote. There is also a Vice-President, who, on the death of the President, becomes President for the remainder of the term. Under the XXth Amendment to the Constitution the terms of the President and Vice-President end at noon on the 20th day of January of the years in which such terms would have ended if the Amendment had not been ratified, and the terms of their successors then begin. In case of the removal or death of both President and Vice-President, a statute provides for the succession. Under the XXIInd Amendment to the Constitution, the tenure of the Presidency is limited to two terms.

Executive duties:—(1) He is Commander-in-Chief of the Army and of the Navy (and of the Militias when they are in Federal service), and he commissions all officers therein. (2) With the consent of the Senate, he appoints the Cabinet officers and all the chief (and many minor) officials. (3) He exercises a general supervision over the whole Federal Administration and sees that the Federal Laws are duly carried out. Should disorder arise in any state which the authorities thereof are unable to suppress, the aid of the President is invoked. (4) He conducts the foreign policy of the Republic, and has power, "by and with the Advice and Consent of the Senate, to make Treaties, provided two thirds of the senators present concur." The declaration of war rests with Congress. (5) He makes recommendation of a general nature to Congress, and when laws are passed by Congress he may return them to Congress with a veto. But if a measure so vetoed is again passed by both Houses of Congress by two-thirds majority in each House, it becomes law, notwithstanding the objection of the President. The President must be at least 35 years of age and a native citizen of the United States. He receives a taxable salary of $200,000 with a taxable expense allowance of $50,000 and a non-taxable travelling allowance not exceeding $100,000.

President of the United States, RONALD WILSON REAGAN, *born* Feb. 6, 1911, *sworn in* January 20, 1981; *for a second term* January 20, 1985. Republican.

Vice-President, George Herbert Walker Bush, *born* June 12, 1924, *sworn in* Jan. 20, 1981; *for a second term* Jan. 20, 1985.

THE CABINET

Secretary of State, George Shultz.
Secretary of the Treasury, James A. Baker III.
Secretary of Defence, Caspar W. Weinberger.
Attorney-General, Edwin Meese III.
Secretary of the Interior, Donald P. Hodel.
Secretary of Agriculture, John R. Block.
Secretary of Commerce, Malcolm Baldrige.
Secretary of Labour, William E. Brock.
Secretary of Health and Human Services, Mrs. Margaret M. Heckler.
Secretary of Housing and Urban Development, Samuel R. Pierce, Jr.
Secretary of Transportation, Mrs. Elizabeth Dole.
Secretary of Energy, John S. Herrington.
Secretary of Education, William J. Bennett.

UNITED STATES EMBASSY
Grosvenor Square W1A 1AE
[01-499 9000]

Ambassador Extraordinary and Plenipotentiary, His Excellency Charles H. Price II (1983).
Minister, Hon. Raymond G. H. Seitz.
Minister for Economic and Commercial Affairs, Michael Calingaert.
Counsellors, Edward Kreuser (*Consular Affairs*); Lawrence D. Russell (*Administrative Affairs*); Gerald M. Marks (*Commercial Affairs*); Robert A. Stella (*Scientific Affairs*); Robert J. Korengold (*Public Affairs*); Turner L. Oyloe (*Agricultural Affairs*); Ernest Nagy; Richard L. McCormack (*Political Affairs*); William J. Graver (*Programme Coordinator*).
Defence Attaché, Col. Kent E. Harbaugh.
Army Attaché, Col. George M. Houser.
Naval Attaché, Cpt. Walter W. Salmon Jr.

CAPITAL OF THE UNITED STATES

In 1790 Congress ratified the cession of 100 sq. miles by the States of Maryland and Virginia as a site for a Federal City to be the national capital of the United States. In 1791 it was decided to name the capital *Washington* and in 1793 the foundation-stone of the Capitol building was laid. In 1800 the seat of Government was removed to Washington, which was chartered as a city in 1802. In 1846 the Virginia portion was retroceded and the present area of the *District of Columbia* (with which the City of Washington is considered co-extensive) is 63 square miles, with a population of 638,333.

The District of Columbia is governed by an elected mayor and City Council.

The *City of Washington* is situated on the west central edge of Maryland, opposite the State of Virginia, on the left bank of the Potomac at its confluence with the Anacostia.

THE CONGRESS

The Legislative power is vested in two Houses, the Senate and the House of Representatives, the President having a *veto* power, which may be overcome by a two-thirds vote of each House. The Senate is composed of two Senators from each State, elected by the people thereof for the term of six years, and each Senator has one vote. Representatives are chosen in each State, by popular vote, for two years. The average number of persons represented by each Congressman is 1 for 500,000. The *Senate* consists of 100 members. The salary of a Senator is $75,100 per annum. The *House of Representatives* consists of 435 Representatives, a resident commissioner from Puerto Rico and a delegate from American Samoa, the District of Columbia, Guam and the Virgin Islands. The salary of a Representative is $75,100 per annum. By the XIXth Amendment, sex is no disqualification for the franchise. The Bureau of the Census estimated on July 1, 1984 there were 173,469,000 persons of voting age, excluding members of the armed forces overseas.

THE NINETY-NINTH CONGRESS

President of the Senate, George Bush (*Vice President of the United States*).
Speaker of the House of Representatives, Thomas P. O'Neill, Jr., *Massachusetts*.
Secretary of the Senate, Jo-Anne L. Coe, *Virginia*.
Clerk of the House of Representatives, Benjamin J. Guthrie, *Virginia*.
Members of the 99th Congress were elected on Nov. 6, 1984.

The 99th Congress is constituted as follows:
Senate.—Democrats 47; Republicans, 53; Total, 100.
House of Representatives.—Democrats, 252; Republicans, 182, and 1 vacancy. Total, 435.

THE JUDICATURE

The *Federal Judiciary* consists of three sets of Federal Courts: (1) The *Supreme Court* at Washington, D.C., consisting of a Chief Justice and eight Associate Justices, with original jurisdiction in cases affecting Ambassadors, etc., or where a State is a party to the suit, and with appellate jurisdiction from inferior Federal Courts and from the judgments of the highest Courts of the States. (2) The *United States Courts of Appeals*, dealing with appeals from District Courts and from certain federal administrative agencies, and consisting of all the Circuit Judges within the circuit. (3) The 94 *United States District Courts* served by 516 District Court Judges.

THE SUPREME COURT
(U.S. Supreme Court Building, Washington, D.C.)

Chief Justice, Warren E. Burger *Va.*, *born* Sept. 17, 1907, *appointed* June 23, 1969.

ASSOCIATE JUSTICES

Name	Born	Apptd
William J. Brennan, Jr., *N.J.*	1906	1956
Byron R. White, *Colo.*	1917	1962
Thurgood Marshall, *N.Y.*	1908	1967
Harry Blackmun, *Minn.*	1908	1970
Lewis F. Powell, Jr., *Va.*	1907	1971
William R. Rehnquist, *Ariz.*	1924	1971
John Paul Stevens, *Ill.*	1920	1975
Sandra Day O'Connor, *Ariz.*	1930	1981

Clerk of the Supreme Court, Alexander L. Stevas.

CRIMINAL STATISTICS, U.S.

Crime	No. of offences	
	1983	1984
Murder and Non-negligent Manslaughter	19,308	18,692
Rape	78,918	84,233
Robbery	506,567	485,008
Aggravated Assault	653,294	685,349
Burglary	3,129,851	2,984,434
Larceny—Theft	6,712,759	6,591,874
Thefts of Motor Vehicles	1,007,933	1,032,165
Total	12,108,630	11,881,755

DEFENCE
Department of Defence

Secretary of Defence (in the Cabinet), Caspar W. Weinberger.

Secretary of the Army, John O. Marsh, Jr.

Secretary of the Navy, John Lehman.

Secretary of the Air Force, Verne Orr.

Chairman, Joint Chief of Staff, Adm. William Crowe.

The Department of Defence includes the Secretary of Defence as its head, the Deputy Secretary of Defence, the Defence staff offices, the Joint Chiefs of Staff and the Joint Staff, the three military departments and the military services within those departments, the unified and specified commands, and other Department of Defence agencies as the Secretary of Defence establishes to meet specific requirements. The Defence staff offices and the joint Chiefs of Staff, although separately organized, function in full coordination and cooperation. They include the offices of the Director of Defence Research and Engineering, the Assistant Secretaries of Defence, the General Counsel of the Department of Defence and such other staff offices as the Secretary of Defence may establish. The Joint Chiefs of Staff, as a group, are directly responsible to the Secretary of Defence for the functions assigned to them. Each member of the Joint Chiefs of Staff, other than the Chairman, is responsible for keeping the Secretary of his military department fully informed on matters considered or acted upon by the Joint Chiefs of Staff.

Each military department is separately organized under its own Secretary and functions under the direction, authority and control of the Secretary of Defence.

The Department of Defence maintains and employs armed forces: (1) to support and defend the Constitution of the United States against all enemies, foreign and domestic; (2) to insure, by timely and effective military action, the security of the United States, its possessions, and areas vital to its interests; (3) to uphold and advance the national policies and interest of the United States; and (4) to safeguard the internal security of the United States. All functions in the Department of Defence and its component agencies are performed under the direction, authority and control of the Secretary of Defence.

Commanders of unified and specified commands are responsible to the President and the Secretary of Defence for the accomplishment of military missions assigned to them.

Unified Defence Commands
COMMANDERS-IN-CHIEF

U.S. European Command, Brussels.—Gen. Bernard W. Rogers (*U.S. Army*) (concurrently *N.A.T.O. Supreme Allied Commander*).

U.S. Southern Command, Quarry Heights, Panama Canal Zone.—Gen. John R. Galvin (*U.S. Army*).

Atlantic, Norfolk, Virginia.—Adm. Wesley L. McDonald (*U.S. Navy*) (concurrently *N.A.T.O. Supreme Allied Commander, Atlantic*).

Pacific, Hawaii.—Adm. William J. Crowe (*U.S. Navy*).

H.Q., Aerospace Defence Command, Gen. R. T. Herres.

Strategic Air Command, Omaha.—Gen. Bennie L. Davis (*U.S.A.F.*).

Military Air Lift Command, Gen. Thomas M. Ryan, Jr. (*U.S.A.F.*).

U.S. Readiness Command, Gen. Wallace H. Nutting (*U.S. Army*).

* *U.S. Central Command*, Gen. Robert C. Kingston (*U.S. Army*).

Military Sea Lift Command, Commodore Richard Donnelly (*U.S. Navy*).

* A Specified Command.

Army.—The U.S. Army had a strength on March 31, 1985, of 778,639. Stationed in Germany were four divisions.

Chief of the Staff of the Army, Gen. John A. Wickham, Jr.

Navy.—The strength of the Navy (including Marine Corps) on April 30, 1985 was 765,863 active duty personnel.

The U.S. Navy had in service in 1984, 523 active fleet ships (Strategic Forces, 41; Battle Forces, 425; Support Forces, 45; Mobilization Forces, 12).

Chief of Naval Operations, Adm. James D. Watkins.

Marine Corps.—Established 1775. Strength on April 30, 1985 was 198,643 active duty personnel.

Commandant, Gen. Paul X. Kelley.

Air.—The United States Air Force was established as a separate organization on September 18, 1947. On Sept. 30, 1984, there were 592,649 officers and airmen on active duty, with 256,400 civilian employees. Air Force Reserve and Air National Guard numbered 220,519.

The Air Force has up to 30 per cent of the strategic bomber and tanker forces maintaining constant alert as well as 1,000 inter-continental ballistic missiles in silos. In addition, the Air Force maintains the capability to carry out limited war and special warfare operations, with more than 5,500 strategic, tactical and support aircraft. In March, 1961, the Air Force was assigned primary responsibility for the Department of Defence space development programmes and projects. In September 1982, Space Command was established to manage and operate all military space assets and programmes. On May 29, 1985, the United States had a total of 1,509 spacecraft in earth or deep space orbits. These included military, other government agency and commercial equipment.

Chief of Staff of the U.S. Air Force, Gen. Charles A. Gabriel.

FINANCE

SOCIAL WELFARE EXPENDITURE

Total expenditure by programme was:

	\$ million		
	1981	1982	1983
Social insurance	267,395	303,033	330,551
Education	128,145	133,874	141,506
Public aid	82,424	80,852	85,830
Health and medical	30,720	33,793	36,918
Veterans' programmes	23,441	24,708	25,826
Other social welfare	11,983	11,654	11,990
Housing	6,734	7,954	9,090
TOTAL	550,842	595,868	641,711

Expenditure per capita was (\$):

	1981	1982	1983
Social insurance	1,144·48	1,284·52	1,387·79
Education	550·75	569·73	596·44
Public aid	354·38	344·21	361·91
Health and medical	133·95	145·91	157·66
Veterans' programmes	99·95	104·32	108·08
Other social welfare	51·52	49·62	50·56
TOTAL	2,362·11	2,530·13	2,698·72

THE UNITED STATES BUDGET
(fiscal year; in millions of dollars)

	1984 (actual)	1985 (estimated)
Receipts by Source		
Individual income taxes	296,206	329,677
Corporation income taxes	56,893	66,403
Social insurance taxes and contributions	241,651	268,367
Excise taxes	37,361	36,995
Estate and gift taxes	6,010	5,603
Customs duties	11,370	11,809
Miscellaneous	16,905	18,004
Total	666,457	736,859
Outlays by Function		
National defence	227,413	253,830
International affairs	15,876	19,583
General science, space, and technology	8,317	8,740
Energy	7,086	8,164
Natural resources and environment	12,591	13,024
Agriculture	13,613	20,165
Commerce and housing credit	6,917	5,987
Transportation	23,669	26,994
Community and regional development	7,673	8,553
Education, training, employment, and social services	27,579	30,434
Health	30,417	33,879
Social security and medicare	235,764	257,363
Income security	112,668	127,240
Veterans' benefits and services	25,614	26,850
Adminnistration of justice	5,660	6,686
General government	5,053	5,782
General purpose fiscal assistance	6,770	6,552
Interest	111,058	130,426
Undistributed offsetting receipts	−31,957	−32,296
Total	851,781	959,085

PUBLIC DEBT

At the end of 1984, the total gross *Federal Debt* of the United States stood at $1,576,700 million, an increase on the 1982 figure of $1,147,000 million.

COST OF LIVING IN U.S.A.

The Consumer Price Index (for city wage-earner and clerical workers—single persons and families—in 50 cities representative of all cities in the United States) showed an annual average during the calendar year 1984 of 223·4 (1972 = 100), a rise of 3·8 per cent over the 1983 figure.

GROSS NATIONAL PRODUCT

Gross National Product by industry in 1984 was ($ million):—

All industries, total	3,662,800
Agriculture, forestry, fisheries	91,100
Mining	118,500
Construction	148,000
Manufacturing	775,700
Transportation	129,800
Communications	102,800
Electric, gas, sanitary services	109,600
Trade	601,800
Finance, insurance, real estate	598,100
Services	529,400
Government enterprises	421,900
Statistical discrepancy	−7,400
Rest of the world	43,600

G.N.P., national and personal income in 1983 were ($ million):—

Gross national product	3,304,800
Net national product	2,927,700

National income	2,646,700
Compensation of employees	1,984,900
Proprietors' income	121,700
Rental income of persons	58,300
Corporate profits	225,200
Net interest	256,600
Personal income	2,744,200
Personal tax and non-tax payments	404,200
Disposable personal income	2,340,100
Personal outlays	2,222,000
Personal saving	118,100

Personal consumption expenditure in 1983 was $2,155,900 million, of which durable goods accounted for $280,000 million, non-durable goods $802,000 million and services $1,074,000 million. Gross private domestic investment in 1983 was $472,000 million.

UNITED STATES STOCK OF CURRENCY AND COIN

U.S. stock of currency and coin at Sept. 30, 1984 was:—

	$ million
Gold*	11,097·2
Dollars†	2,024·7
Subsidiary Coin	10,408·3
Minor Coin	3,208·5
Silver Certificates§	202·5
U.S. Notes	322·5
Federal Reserve Notes	189,882·3
Total‡	217,216·6

*Held by U.S. Treasury only.

† Figures consist of $481·8 m in standard silver and the balance in cupro-nickel clad dollars.

‡ Totals include value of early issue notes in process of withdrawal, not separately shown. Value, September 1984, $70·6 m.

§In process of withdrawal. Not redeemable in silver.

AGRICULTURE AND LIVESTOCK

The total number of farms in 1984 was 2,332,600, with a total area of land in farms of 1,019,503,000 acres, and an average acreage per farm of 437 acres. The total number of people employed on farms in 1984 was 3,750,000, of whom, 2,315,000 were family members and 1,435,000 hired workers.

Principal crops are corn for grain, soybeans, wheat hay, cotton, tobacco, grain sorghums, rice, potatoes, oats and sugar-beets.

Livestock on farms on Jan. 1, 1984 (*Dec. 1, 1983) (preliminary figures) was:—

	Head
All cattle	113,700,000
Milk cows	11,109,000
Sheep and lambs	11,486,500
Hogs and pigs*	56,694,000
Chickens*	364,880,000
Turkeys*	3,155,000

Gross income from farming in 1983 was $151,400 million, of which cash receipts from marketing were $138,700 million and Government payments $9,300 million. Cash income from all crops in 1983 was $69,516 million and from livestock and livestock products $69,203 million.

NONFUEL MINERALS

The value of nonfuel raw mineral production in the United States in 1984 totalled an estimated $22,700 million compared with $21,100 million in 1983.

Trading Figures

	1982	1983
Imports	$24,400 m	$24,000 m
Exports	$13,200 m	$12,300 m

Production Figures
(*'000 metric tons*)

	1983	1984
Aluminium*	3,696	4,518
Iron Ore†	37,562	51,000
Phosphate rock	42,573	49,197
Zinc	275	253
Refined Copper	1,584	1,509
Lead	1,018	978

* *measured in short tons*
† *measured in long tons*

ENERGY

Energy Summary

(*Quadrillion (10^{15}) Btu*)

	1982	1983	1984
Production	63·892	61·196	65·535
Consumption	70·842	70·497	73·723
Imports	12·093	12·024	12·712
Exports	4·636	3·719	3·818

Breakdown of Production and Consumption
(*Quadrillion (10^{15}) Btu*)

	1983	1984
Production		
Crude Oil	18·392	18·590
Coal	17·252	19·696
Natural Gas (dry)	16·530	17·748
Natural Gas Plant Liquids	2·184	2·367
Hydroelectric	3·502	3·387
Nuclear	3·203	3·573
Other*	0·133	0·174
Total	61·196	65·535

Consumption		
Petroleum	30·054	31·004
Natural Gas (dry)	17·352	18·027
Coal	15·900	17·172
Hydroelectric	3·871	3·784
Nuclear	3·203	3·573
Other*	0·133	0·174
Total	70·497	73·723

* Includes geothermal power and electricity produced from wood and waste.

During 1984 oil and gas drilling rigs in operation averaged 2,428 and the number of well completions totalled 88,880. Seismic exploration work in progress involved a total of 494 crews, 49 in offshore areas and 445 on shore. Domestic crude oil production in 1984 averaged 8,757,000 barrels per day and total petroleum imports averaged 5,381,000 barrels per day, of which 2,023,000 barrels per day came from members of O.P.E.C. Production of dry natural gas in 1984 was 17,214 billion cubic feet (Bcf) and imports were 861 Bcf, supplying 17,485 Bcf required for domestic consumption. Stocks of gas available for withdrawal were estimated at 2,038 Bcf. Production of coal in 1984 was 890,143,000† short tons and imports were 1,286,000† short tons. Domestic consumption required 791,296,000† short tons, and 81,483,000† short tons were exported. In 1984 U.S. nuclear power generators produced 327,634 million net kilowatt-hours of electricity, accounting for 13·6 per cent of domestic electricity generation. Operable reactors at end Dec. 1984 totalled 86, with a maximum dependable capacity of 69·522 million net kilowatts.

† Preliminary figures.

LABOUR

Organized Labour.—The combined membership of the American Federation of Labour and Congress of Industrial Organizations in 1984 was 17,340,000. Members of labour organizations not affiliated to the AFL–CIO are estimated to number over 7 million.

Approximately 18·8 per cent. of the employed wage and salary workers in the United States are members of labour organizations.

Work Stoppages.—There were 62 stoppages involving 1,000 or more workers in 1984. They resulted in 8,499,000 man-days of idleness, representing 0·04 per cent. of estimated working time of all non-agricultural workers.

Employment and Unemployment.—The civilian labour force (working population) was 115,373,000 in May 1985. This includes self-employed wage and salary-earners, and unpaid family workers, employed and unemployed. Unemployment was estimated at 8,413,000 in May 1985 (7·3 per cent.) (it was 7·5 per cent. in May 1984).

Wages.—In March 1985, gross average weekly earnings in industry ranged from $660·48 per week in malt beverage industry (43·0 hours and $15·36 average hourly earnings) to $112·05 in eating and drinking places (25·7 hours and $4·36 average hourly earnings). The average for all manufacturing was $381·78 compared with $370·78 in March 1984.

On Jan. 1, 1978, the minimum wage set by federal law became $2·65 an hour for most non-agricultural employees subject to the Fair Labour Standards Act. The rate rose to $2·90 an hour on Jan. 1, 1979, $3·10 on Jan. 1, 1980 and $3·35 on Jan. 1, 1981. The law requires at least time and a half of an employee's regular rate of pay for all hours over 40 a week for most covered workers.

The Fair Labour Standards Act covers all employees of certain enterprises having workers engaged in interstate commerce, producing goods for interstate commerce, or handling, selling, or otherwise working on goods or materials that have been moved in or produced for such commerce by any person.

There are certain exemptions from these requirements in specific occupations and industries.

In addition to cash wages, most workers receive some type of "fringe" benefits—the most common forms being paid vacations, and public holidays, various types of retirement plans, insurance and health benefits financed by the employer or by employer and employees jointly.

EXTERNAL TRADE OF THE UNITED STATES

	1983	1984
	\$ million	
General Imports:		
c.i.f. value	269,878·2	341,176·8
customs value	258,047·8	325,725·7
Exports and re-exports:		
f.a.s. value†	200,485·8	217,865·2
Trade balance:		
f.a.s. exports: c.i.f.		
imports	−69,392·4	−123,311·6
f.a.s. exports: customs		
imports	−57,562·0	−107,860·5

† Excluding military aid.

EXPORTS BY PRINCIPAL COMMODITIES OF DOMESTIC ORIGIN, 1984

Commodity	Value
	\$ (million)
Food and Live Animals	24,462·6
Grain and cereal preparations	16,075·8
Beverages and Tobacco	2,849·4
Crude materials (inedible) except fuel .	20,248·9
Raw cotton	2,441·4
Metal ores, concentrates, scrap	2,665·6
Mineral fuels, lubricants, etc.	9,310·5
Coal (bituminous)	4,090·4
Petroleum and products	4,469·7
Oils and Fats (animal and vegetable) ..	1,922·2
Chemicals and products	22,336·3
Machinery and Transport Equipment .	89,972·7
Electronic computers, parts, etc.	7,127·8
Electrical machinery, appliances,	
etc.	13,855·2
Motor vehicles and parts	17,547·9
Other Manufactured Goods	15,698·7
Unclassified Commodities	10,115·8

U.S. IMPORTS BY PRINCIPAL COMMODITIES, 1984

Commodity	Value
	\$ (million)
Food and Live Animals	17,972·8
Fish and fish preparations	3,671·4
Vegetables and fruit	3,891·2
Coffee–crude....................	3,063·9
Beverages and Tobacco	3,653·4
Crude materials (inedible), except fuels	11,081·7
Mineral fuels, lubricants, etc.	60,979·8
Crude petroleum	36,528·8
Petroleum products	19,377·2
Oils and Fats (animal and vegetable) ..	696·0
Chemicals and products	13,697·4
Machinery and Transport Equipment .	119,191·7
Telecommunications, sound recording apparatus	15,934·0
Electrical machinery, parts........	18,290·5
Motor vehicles	36,593·0
Other Manufactured Goods	42,480·7
Unclassified Commodities	9,827·6

U.S. FOREIGN TRADE BY ECONOMIC CLASS 1984

	\$ million	
Class	Imports	Exports*
Crude Materials...	49,264	16,985
Crude Foodstuffs ..	8,809	8,330
Manufactured		
Foods	12,289	12,810
Semi-manufactures	48,233	40,627
Finished		
Manufactures...	207,130	133,305
Total..........	325,726	212,057

*Excluding the total military grant-aid of \$195,918 million.

U.S. FOREIGN TRADE BY PRINCIPAL AREAS AND COUNTRIES, 1984

Area/Country	Exports and Re-exports to	General Imports from
	\$ million	
Africa...................	8,826·6	14,996·0
Asia	64,532·6	128,048·0
Japan	23,575·0	60,371·4
Saudi Arabia	5,564·4	4,008·9
Taiwan	5,003·4	16,088·2
Korea, Rep. of.........	5,982·7	10,027·4
Hong Kong	3,062·4	8,898·8
Oceania	5,744·5	3,885·2
Australia..............	4,792·7	2,898·9
Europe	62,740·3	77,851·7
Germany, West	9,083·6	17,810·1
U.K.	12,209·7	15,044·3
Other E.E.C.	25,682·2	27,412·1
Other O.E.C.D.	10,510·6	14,074·6
Communist bloc	4,187·8	2,352·0
N. & Central America....	53,722·2	92,774·4
Canada	46,524·3	66,911·1
Mexico	22,819·5	18,266·9
S. America	10,827·4	22,242·2

COMMUNICATIONS

RAILWAYS

Data on Class I line-haul railroads (*dollars in thousands*)

	1982	1983*
Operating Revenues		
Freight	25,627,000	25,829,000
Passenger	573,000	112,000
Total.......	27,504,000	26,726,000
Total operating expenses	26,490,000	24,965,000
Net working capital	1,372,000	1,312,000
Average number of employees	436,397	348,000

* Preliminary figures.

ROADS

In 1983 there were 3·88 million miles of public roads and streets in the United States, of which 3·22 million miles were in rural areas and 662,000 miles were in urban areas. Surfaced roads and streets account for 3·42 million miles, or 89·0 per cent, of the total; 455,000 miles, or 11·0 per cent, were unimproved or graded and drained.

An estimated total of $43,960 million was spent in 1983 for roads and streets in the United States. Capital outlay accounts for 46·8 per cent of the total expenditure; 31·9 per cent was spent for maintenance, and 7·5 per cent for administration; 9·7 per cent for highway police and safety; and 4·3 per cent for interest on highway bonds.

Motor Vehicles and Taxation.—The number of motor vehicles registered in 1983 in the United States was 163,861,169, an increase of 2·8 per cent over the 1982 total of 159,449,166. In 1983 the State governments received $18,833,004,000 in State Highway-User Tax Receipts, including road and crossing tolls, and $8,502,000,000 in Federal Highway-User Tax Receipts.

Accidents.—In 1983 there were 42,596 deaths caused by motor vehicle accidents. The death rate per 100,000,000 vehicle-miles of travel was 2·58 in 1983 compared with 2·75 in 1982.

SHIPPING

The ocean-going Merchant Marine of the U.S. on June 1, 1985, consisted of 734 vessels of 1,000 gross tons and over, of which 484 were privately owned and 250 were government-owned ships. Of the 484 privately owned vessels, 389 were active including 2 combination passenger and cargo ships, 44 freighters, 18 bulk carriers, 174 tankers, 19 tug-barge units, 8 liquefied natural gas carriers and 124 intermodal

ships. There were 228 ships in the National Defence Reserve Fleet of inactive government-owned vessels, of which 9 were to be sold for scrap.

AIR TRANSPORT

United States domestic and international scheduled airlines in 1984 carried 344,460,600 passengers over 304,987,288,000 revenue passenger miles. Cargo revenue ton-miles totalled 8,200,000,000, an increase of 8·0 per cent over 1983. Air cargo ton-miles were distributed as follows: freight 6,500,000,000 (up 7·7 per cent); express 64,400,000 (up 2·8 per cent); and air mail 1,600,000,000 (up 9·3 per cent).

Total operating revenues of all U.S. scheduled airlines were $43,800,000,000 in 1984, an increase of 13·5 per cent from 1983.

Total operating expenses rose to $41,700,000,000 in 1984, a 9·0 per cent increase over 1983. Scheduled operations showed a net operating profit of $2,100,000,000 in 1984, compared with a net operating profit of $361,700,000 in 1983.

Three principal classes of commercial air carriers have been established in the United States based on annual operating revenues. They are: Majors, with annual operating revenues of over $1,000 million; Nationals, with annual operating revenues of $75–1,000 million; and Regionals, with annual operating revenues of up to $75,999,000.

U.S. SCHEDULED AIRLINE INDUSTRY STATISTICS, 1984 (Thousands)

	Majors	Nationals	Regionals	System
Revenue Passenger Carried	250,150	80,337	13,974	344,461
Revenue Passengers Miles	252,295,400	43,820,182	8,871,706	304,987,288
Air Mail Ton Miles	1,402,063	199,028	15,841	1,616,932
Express Ton Miles	60,255	2,024	131	62,410
Freight Ton Miles	3,905,550	2,445,897	145,714	6,497,161
Revenue Ton Miles	30,597,429	7,028,968	1,048,857	38,675,254
Revenue Plane Miles	2,391,806	579,533	159,890	3,131,229

EDUCATION
State School Systems

All the 50 States and the District of Columbia have compulsory school attendance laws. In general, children are obliged to attend school from 7 to 16 years of age. Officers of local administrative units, usually known as truant or attendance officers, are charged with enforcing the compulsory attendance laws.

In the autumn of 1984, 44,625,000 children were enrolled in regular elementary and secondary day schools in the United States, of whom 5·7 million or 12·8 per cent attended private schools.

The following percentages of the school-age population were estimated to be enrolled in school in the autumn of 1983; of 5- and 6-year-olds, 95 per cent; of 7- to 13-year-olds, 99 per cent; of 14- to 17-year-olds, 95 per cent; and of 18- to 24-year-olds, 30 per cent.

During the 1984–85 school year, the average daily attendance in regular public elementary and secondary day schools was 36,481,000. In the 1984–85 academic year 2,393,000 students graduated from regular public high schools, 263,000 graduated from private high school. In addition 25,000 graduated from evening schools and adult education programmes, and 500,000 received high school equivalency certificates. Classroom teachers numbered 2,117,000, with an average salary of $23,546.

Revenue for public elementary and secondary school purposes comes from the Federal, State, and local governments, sales of bonds, real property and equipment, loans and proceeds from insurance

adjustments. Estimated revenue receipts from Government sources during 1984–85 amounted to $137,600,000,000; 6·2 per cent from the Federal Government, 49 per cent from State governments, and 44·8 per cent from local governments. Estimated current expenditure in the 1984–85 school year was $127,400 million; for sites, buildings, furniture and equipment expenditures, $7,300 million; for interest in school debt $2,600 million.

Institutions of Higher Education

In the autumn of 1984, total enrolment in universities, colleges, professional schools, and two-year schools numbered 12,345,000.

Degrees conferred during the academic year 1984–85 were:—

Degree
Bachelor's	960,000
First-Profession	73,700
Master's	295,000
Doctorates	33,200

During 1981–82 the major fields for bachelor's degrees were business and management (215,817), education (101,063) and social sciences (99,898). First-profession degrees in law (35,991) and medicine (15,814) predominated. Master's degrees were heavily concentrated in education (93,104) and business and management (61,428). The most popular fields of study for doctorates were education (7,676) and social sciences (3,065).

During the 1983–84 academic year, the 3,284 colleges and universities employed about 551,000 (full-time equivalent) instructional faculty. Total expenditures for colleges and universities during the 1984–85 academic year were $95,500,000,000.

Particulars of some of the Universities (with opening autumn enrolment figures, 1983) are: *Harvard* (20,433 students, including 7,764 women), founded at Cambridge, Mass. on Oct. 28, 1636, and named after John Harvard of Emmanuel College, Cambridge, England, who bequeathed to it his library and a sum of money in 1638; *Yale* (10,386 students, including 4,478 women), founded at New Haven, Connecticut, in 1701; *Bowdoin*, Brunswick, Me. (founded 1794; 1,371 students including 600 women); *Brown*, Providence, R.I. (founded 1764; 6,974 students, including 3,714 women); *Columbia*, New York, N.Y. (founded 1754; 21,027 students, including 9,497 women); *Cornell* (founded at Ithaca, N.Y., 1865; 19,475 students, including 8,334 women); *Dartmouth*, Hanover, N.H. (founded 1769, 4,715 students, including 1,915 women); *Georgetown*, Washington, D.C. (founded 1789; 11,939 students, including 5,348 women); *North Carolina*, Chapel Hill, N.C. (founded in 1789; 21,812 students, including 12,087 women); *Pennsylvania*, Philadelphia, Pa. (founded 1740; 22,277 students, including 9,900 women); *Princeton*, N.J. (founded 1746; 6,175 students and 2,169 women); and *William and Mary*, Williamsburg, Va. (founded 1693; 6,607 students, including 3,404 women).

WEIGHTS AND MEASURES

The weights and measures in common use in the United States are of British origin, and date back to the American Revolution when practically all the standards were intended to be equivalent to those used in England at that period. Divergencies in these weights and measures were, however, quite common, due no doubt to the fact that the system of weights and measures in England was not itself well established, and hence the copies brought to the United States were often adjusted to different standards. Because of these discrepancies, the system of weights and measures in the United States (U.S. inch-pound system) is not identical with the British system.

The U.S. ton (short) = 2,000 pounds (British Imperial ton = 2,240 pounds, or 1 U.S. long ton). The U.S. gallon = 231 cubic inches (277.42 cubic inches in U.K.) or 128 fluid ounces (160 fluid ounces in U.K.). In the British system the units of dry measure are the same as those of liquid measure. In the United States these two are not the same, the gallon and its subdivisions being used in the measurement of liquids, while the bushel, with its subdivisions, is used in the measurement of certain dry commodities. The U.S. gallon is divided into 4 liquid quarts and the U.S. bushel into 32 dry quarts.

The International System of Units—officially abbreviated SI—is a modernized version of the metric system. It was established by international agreement to provide a logical and interconnected framework for all measurements in science, industry and commerce.

In 1971, a study recommended a concerted, co-ordinated, but voluntary national effort to make the SI the predominant form of measurement in the United States. In December 1975, legislation was passed which established the United States Metric Board to coordinate voluntary conversion to the metric system. Since 1982 this function has been assumed by the Office of Metric Programmes of the U.S. Department of Commerce.

TERRITORIES, ETC. OF THE UNITED STATES

The territories and the principal islands and island groups under the sovereignty of the United States of America comprise the Commonwealth of Puerto Rico, the Commonwealth of the Northern Mariana Islands, and the following territories: Guam; American Samoa; U.S. Virgin Islands; Jarvis Island, Palmyra Island and Kingman Reef; Johnston Atoll; Midway Islands; Wake Islands.

Jarvis Island, Palmyra Island and Kingman Reef are uninhabited islands in the Line Island group. Johnston Atoll (formerly Johnston and Sand Islands) comprises two small islands, less than 1 sq. mile in area, to the south-west of Hawaii which are administered by the U.S. Air Force. The two Midway Islands (area, 2 sq. miles; population (1970), 2,200), at the western end of the Hawaiin chain, are administered by the U.S. Navy. The Wake Islands have an area of about 3 sq. miles and a population (1979) of 300. They lie about 2,300 miles west of Hawaii and are administered by the U.S. Air Force.

Under the terms of a Treaty of Friendship between the United States and Kiribati, signed in 1979 and subsequently ratified by the U.S. Senate, the United States renounced its claim to Canton and Enderbury Islands.

There are certain small guano islands, rocks, or keys which, in pursuance of action taken under the Act of Congress, August 18, 1856, subsequently embodied in Sections 5570–5578 of the Revised Statutes are considered as appertaining to the United States. Responsibility for territorial affairs generally is centred in the Office of the Assistant Secretary, Territorial and International Affairs, Dept. of the Interior, Washington, D.C. Puerto Rico was removed from the Department of the Interior's administrative jurisdiction with the acquisition of Commonwealth status in 1952.

The Trust Territory of the Pacific Islands is under the jurisdiction of the United States pursuant to a trusteeship agreement between the U.S. Government and the Security Council of the United Nations. It consists of the Mariana (except Guam), Caroline and Marshall Islands: the Northern Mariana Islands voted in 1975 to become a Commonwealth of the U.S. but this status will not come fully into effect until the trusteeship agreement is terminated.

As a result of the Panama Canal Treaty of 1977 the Canal Zone was placed under Panamanian jurisdiction. The Panama Canal Commission, an arm of the U.S. Government, will continue to operate the canal until the year 2000.

THE COMMONWEALTH OF PUERTO RICO

Puerto Rico (Rich Port) is an island of the Greater Antilles group in the West Indies, and lies between 17° 50′–18° 30′ N. lat. and 65° 30′–67° 15′ W. long., with a total area of 3,459 square miles and a population (1980) of 3,196,520. The majority of the inhabitants are of Spanish descent and Spanish and English are the official languages. The island is about 111 miles from west to east, and 36 miles from north to south. The capital is 1,600 miles distant from New York, and 1,000 miles from Miami.

Puerto Rico was discovered in 1493 by Christopher Columbus and explored by Ponce de Léon in 1508. It continued a Spanish possession until Oct. 18, 1898, when the United States took formal possession as a result of the Spanish-American War. It was ceded by Spain to the United States by the Treaty ratified on April 11, 1899.

The Constitution approved by the Congress and the President of the United States, which came into rce on July 25, 1952, establishes the Commonwealth f Puerto Rico with full powers of local government. egislative functions are vested in the Legislative ssembly, which consists of 2 elected houses; the enate of 27 members (2 from each of 8 senatorial stricts and 11 at large) and the House of Representatives of 51 members (1 from each of 40 representative stricts and 11 at large). Membership of each house lay be increased slightly to accommodate minority epresentatives. The term of the Legislative Assembly is 4 years. The selection of the Secretary of State lust be approved also by the House of Representatives.

The Governor is popularly elected for a term of 4 ears. A Supreme Court of 7 members is appointed y the Governor, with the advice and consent of the enate. The Governor appoints all Judges. Residents f Puerto Rico are U.S. citizens. Puerto Rico is epresented in Congress by a Resident Commissioner, lected for a term of 4 years, who has a seat in the louse of Representatives, but not a vote, although e has a right to vote on those committees of which e is a member.

Preliminary 1983 figures for the Commonwealth overnment's budget were Receipts, $4,948 million of which $1,180 million were transfers from the ederal Government) and Expenditures, $4,111 million (including payments of $135 million to the ederal Government). Manufacturing added $5,765 illion to net Commonwealth income in 1983 (preliminary figures), trade $1,743 million, finance, insurance nd real estate $1,841 million and agriculture $435 illion. Principal crops are sugar cane, coffee, egetables, fruits and tobacco. Most valuable areas f manufacturing are chemicals and allied products, etal products and machinery. Public and private chools are established throughout—enrolment in 981 was 910,300. Enrolment in the public and private niversities for 1981 was 131,900.

CAPITAL.—ΨSan Juan, population of the municiality, 518,700; Other major towns are: ΨPonce 88,500); Bayamón (205,800); ΨMayagüez (99,800); nd ΨArecibo (83,300).

overnor, Rafael Hernández Colón.
ecretary of State, Carlos S. Quirós.
esident Commissioner, Baltasar Corrada del Rio.
hief Justice, José Trias Monge.

TRADE

	1982	1983
otal Imports	$8,167 m.	$8,708 m.
otal Exports	8,888 m.	8,970 m.

Trade with U.K.

	1983	1984
mports from U.K.	£35,936,000	£72,695,000
xports to U.K.	58,804,000	76,854,000

GUAM

Guam, the largest of the Ladrone or Mariana slands in the North Pacific Ocean, lies in 13° 26′ N. t. and 144° 39′ E. long., at a distance of about 1,506 iles east of Manila. The area of the island is stimated at 209 square miles, with a population 980) of 105,979.

The Guamanians are of Chamorro stock mingled vith Filipino and Spanish blood. The Chamorro nguage belongs to the Malayo-Polynesian family, ut has had considerable admixture of Spanish. nglish is the language used throughout the island, though Chamorro is also used in Guamanian homes.

Guam was occupied by Japanese in Dec. 1941 but vas recaptured and occupied throughout by U.S. rces before the end of August, 1944. Under the rganic Act of Guam of August 1, 1950 (Public Law

630 of the 81st Congress), Guam has statutory powers of self-government, and Guamanians are United States citizens. A 21-member unicameral legislature is elected biennially. The Governor and Lieutenant Governor are popularly elected. A non-voting Delegate is elected to serve in the U.S. House of Representatives. There is also a District Court of Guam, with original jurisdiction in cases under federal law.

CAPITAL.—Agaña. Port of entry, ΨApra.

Governor, Ricardo J. Bordallo, *elected* Nov. 1982.
Lt. Governor, Edward D. Reyes, *elected* Nov. 1982.

AMERICAN SAMOA

American Samoa consists of the island of Tutuila, Aunu'u, Ofu, Olosega, Ta'u, Rose and Swains Islands, with a total area of 76·5 square miles and a population of 32,297 in 1980.

Tutuila, the largest of the group, has an area of 52 square miles and contains a magnificent harbour at ΨPago Pago. The remaining islands have an area of about 24 square miles. Tuna and copra are the chief exports.

American Samoans are U.S. nationals, but some have acquired citizenship through service in the United States armed forces or other naturalization procedure.

The 1960 Constitution grants American Samoa a measure of self-government, with certain powers reserved to the U.S. Secretary of the Interior. There is a bicameral legislature with popularly elected Representatives and Governors, and a popularly-elected Governor. A non-voting Delegate is elected to serve in the U.S. House of Representatives.

The constitution of American Samoa designates the village of Fagatogo as the seat of government.

Governor, A. P. Lutali.
Lt.-Governor, Eni Hunkin.

VIRGIN ISLANDS

Purchased by the United States from Denmark for the sum of $25 million, and proclaimed, January 25, 1917. The total area of the islands is 132 sq. miles, with a population (1980) of 96,569. There are three main islands, *St. Thomas* (28 sq. miles), *St. Croix* (84 sq. miles), *St. John* (20 sq. miles) and about 50 small islets or cays, mostly uninhabited.

The government of the Virgin Islands is organized under the provisions of the Revised Organic Act of the Virgin Islands, enacted by the Congress of the United States on July 22, 1954. Legislative power is vested in the Legislature of the Virgin Islands, a unicameral body composed of 15 senators popularly elected for two-year terms. Virgin Islanders are citizens of the United States. From the elections of November, 1970, the Governor has been popularly elected. A non-voting Delegate is elected to serve in the U.S. House of Representatives. The Virgin Islands are now a favourite tourist area in the Caribbean. The climate of the islands is delightful at all times, and particularly so during the winter months.

CAPITAL.—ΨCharlotte Amalie on St. Thomas.

Governor, Juan F. Luis.
Lt.-Governor, Julio Bradley.

TRUST TERRITORY OF THE PACIFIC ISLANDS

The Trust Territory of the Pacific Islands consists of the Mariana (excluding Guam), Caroline and

ΨSeaport.

Marshall Islands which extend from latitude 1° to 20° N. and from longitude 130° to 172° E. They cover an ocean area of 3,000,000 square miles but have a total land area of only 687 square miles. There are 96 separate islands and island groups in the Trust Territory. The population in 1980 was 116,662 (excluding the Northern Mariana Islands). The inhabitants of the Trust Territory are broadly classed as Micronesians. The native cultures vary considerably among island groups and even more among islands and atolls in the same geographic area. Nine different languages are spoken in the territory. Copra is the principal export.

The Trust Territory is administered by the United States pursuant to a Trusteeship Agreement with the Security Council of the United Nations of July 18, 1947, administration being under the general jurisdiction of the Secretary of the Interior.

The Trust Territory has been divided into three separate and distinct governments (*see* below for Northern Mariana Islands). In May, 1979, duly constituted governments were inaugurated in the Marshall Islands and the Federated States of Micronesia (comprising Yap, Truk, Pohnpei (Ponape), and Kosrae), and in January, 1981 a constitutional government was established in Palau. A future political relationship between these governments and the United States, known as Free Association, is currently being negotiated. This relationship, detailed in the Compact of Free Association, must be approved by the people of the Trust Territory, the U.S. Congress and the United Nations. The Trusteeship Agreement will be terminated by the United Nations.

CAPITAL.—Saipan, Mariana Islands.

High Commissioner, Janet J. McCoy.
President of Palau, Sen. Lazarus Salii.
President of the Federated States of Micronesia, Tosiwo Nakayama.
President of the Marshall Islands, Amata Kabua.

NORTHERN MARIANA ISLANDS

The land area of the Northern Mariana Islands is 184 sq. miles with a population (1980) of 16,780.

A law enacted by Congress on March 24, 1976 provides a Covenant to establish a Commonwealth of the Northern Mariana Islands. The provisions of the Covenant will become fully effective upon termination of the Trusteeship Agreement. In the transition period, however, many aspects of the U.S. Constitution and many Federal laws have been extended to the Northern Mariana Islands. There is popularly elected bicameral legislature and popularly elected Governor.

Governor, Pedro P. Tenorio.
Lt.-Governor, Pedro A. Tenario.

THE PANAMA CANAL

With effect from October 1, 1979 the Canal Zone was disestablished, with all areas of land and water within the former Canal Zone reverting to Panama. By treaty, the United States is allowed the use of operating areas for the Panama Canal, together with several military bases, although the Republic of Panama is sovereign in all such areas.

The canal is fifty statute miles long (44·08 nautical miles), and the channel is from 500 to 1,000 feet wide at the bottom. It contains 12 locks in twin flights; 3 steps at Gatun on the Atlantic side, 1 step at Pedro Miguel and 2 at Miraflores on the Pacific side. Each lock chamber is 1,000 feet long and 110 feet wide.

Transit from sea to sea takes on average 8 to 10 hours. The least width is in Gaillard Cut, and the greatest in Gatun Lake.

OCEAN GOING COMMERCIAL TRAFFIC

Fiscal Year	No. of Transits	Canal, Net Tons	Cargo Tons
1980	13,507	182,063,175	167,214,955
1981	13,884	188,656,491	171,221,762
1982	14,009	202,884,207	185,452,332
1983	11,707	169,503,918	145,590,759
1984	11,384	163,469,927	140,800,425

BRITISH EMBASSY
3100 Massachusetts Avenue, N.W.
Washington, D.C. 20008

Ambassador Extraordinary and Plenipotentiary, His Excellency Sir (John) Oliver Wright, G.C.M.G., G.C.V.O., D.S.C. (1982).
Ministers, T. Lankester (*Economic*); J. S. Shrimplin (*Defence Equipment*); B. L. Crowe, C.M.G. (*Commercial*).
Head of British Defence Staff and Defence Attaché, Air Vice-Marshal R. Dick.
Naval Attaché, Rear Adm. N. R. D. King.
Military Attaché, Brig. T. K. Thompson.
Air Attaché, Air Cdre. L. Swart.
Counsellors and Attachés, J. O. Kerr (*Head of Chancery*); D. V. Morris (*Admin. and H.M. Consul-General*); H. G. Walsh (*Economic*); T. G. Harris (*Commercial*); R. G. M. Manning (*Overseas Development*); (vacant) (*Hong Kong Commercial Affairs*); R. P. Maynard (*Civil Aviation and Shipping*); P. A. Escritt (*Civil Aviation Air Traffic Systems*); P. Meiklem (*Civil Aviation, Safety*); Dr. A. R. Cox (*Science and Technology*); B. Hampton (*Energy*); Dr. J. Gaunt (*Atomic Energy*); R. J. Harding (*Defence Supply*); J. France (*Technical Works Group*); P. Foley (*Crown Suppliers Area Officer*); R. J. Priestley (*Defence Supply*); V. G. Munns (*Labour*); Dr. J. Russell (*Defence Equipment*); H. G. Williams (*Defence Equipment*); Dr. D. F. Downing (*Defence Equipment*); H. G. T. P. Rissone (*Defence Equipment*); R. A. Burns (*Information*); A. F. Green; N. C. C. Girardot; A. W. Parsons; A. W. Saunders; M. E. Pellew; A. C. M. De Vere; M. P. Barrett; P. I. Bourdillon.
1st Secretaries, T. P. Holloway (*Private Secretary to H.M. Ambassador*); Mrs. V. E. M. Hartles, M.B.E. (*Administration*); J. J. M. Exeter (*Economic*); R. Shaw; R. D. Gordon; D. J. Plumbly (*Commercial*); Dr. S. E. Brown (*Agricultural and Commercial*); Mrs. E. Mok (*Hong Kong Commercial Affairs*); A. J. Hunt (*Civil Aviation and Shipping*); Dr. M. G. Norton (*Science*); Dr. R. S. Baxter (*Technology*); C. V. Anson, M.V.O. (*Information*); C. G. Patterson (*Accountant*); A. F. Goulty; S. Band; A. Robinson; S. J. Gomersall; R. O. L. Fraser Darling; C. M. R. Woodley; N. E. Sheinwald; D. E. Tarling; N. K. Alston; J. N. Davies.
Cultural Attaché and British Council Representative, H. R. Crooke, O.B.E.
Assistant Cultural Attaché, S. J. Cox.

There are British Consulates in Atlanta, Boston, Chicago, Cleveland, Dallas, Houston, Los Angeles, New York, San Francisco and Seattle.

BRITISH-AMERICAN CHAMBER OF COMMERCE, 275 Madison Avenue, New York 10016; U.K. OFFICE, Suite 201, High Holborn, WCIV 6RR.

Union of Soviet Socialist Republics
Soyuz Sovetskikh Sotsialisticheskikh Respublik

THE COMMUNIST PARTY OF THE SOVIET UNION
(K.P.S.S. = Kommunisticheskaya Partiya Sovetskogo Soyuza)

Constitutionally, the highest executive organ of the C.P.S.U. is its *Central Committee*, as elected by the *Party Congress*. The Central Committee elected at the XXVIth Party Congress in March, 1981 consisted of 319 full members and 151 candidate members with a consultative voice; another 75 were elected members of the *Central Revision Commission*. The real power in the Party is vested, however, in the *Politbureau*, the *Secretariat* and the permanent Departments of the Central Committee.

Politbureau, G. A. Aliev; V. M. Chebrikov; M. S. Gorbachev; V. V. Grishin; A. A. Gromyko; D. A. Kunaev; E. K. Ligachev; N. I. Ryzhkov; V. V. Shcherbitsky; E. A. Shevardnadze; M. S. Solomentsev; N. A. Tikhonov; V. I. Vorotnikov (*full members*); P. N. Demichev; V. I. Dolgikh; V. V. Kuznetsov; B. N. Ponomarev; S. L. Sokolev (*candidate members*).

Secretariat, Mikhail Sergevich Gorbachev (*General Secretary since* March 11, 1985); V. I. Dolgikh; B. N. Eltsin; I. V. Kapitonov; E. K. Ligachev; V. P. Nikonov; B. N. Ponomarev; K. V. Rusakov; L. N. Zaikov; M. V. Zimyanin.

Committee of Party Control, M. S. Solomentsev (*Chairman*).

Komsomol (*Young Communist League*). V. M. Mishin (1st *Secretary*).

GOVERNMENT OF THE U.S.S.R.

The Presidium of the Supreme Soviet of the U.S.S.R.

Chairman (= *President of the U.S.S.R.*), Andrei A. Gromyko, *since* July 2, 1985.
Secretary,T. N. Menteshashvili.
The Supreme Soviet (= Parliament) consists of two chambers.
Chairman (= *Speaker*) *of the Council of the Union*, L. N. Tolkunov.
Chairman (= *Speaker*) *of the Council of Nationalities*, A. E. Voss.

The Council of Ministers of the U.S.S.R.

Chairman (= *Prime Minister*), Nikolai Ryzhkov *since* Sept. 27, 1985.
First Vice-Chairmen, G. A. Aliev; I. V. Arkhipov.
Vice-Chairmen, A. K. Antonov; N. K. Baybakov; V. E. Dymshits; G. I. Marchuk; N. V. Martynov; Z. N. Nuriyev; Ya. P. Ryabov; B. E. Shcherbina; L. V. Smirnov; N. V. Talyzin.

Ministries.—There are three groups of departmental ministries, with a total of 86 ministers—33 All Union Ministries, *i.e.* federal ministries, 31 Union Republican Ministries (co-ordinating ministries of individual republics) and 22 State Committees whose Chairmen rank as Ministers. The Prime Ministers of the 15 constituent republics belong to the Council *ex officio*.

FEDERAL MINISTERS
(as at July 2, 1985)

Automobile Industry, V. N. Polyakov.
Aviation Industry, I. S. Silaev.
Chemical Industry, V. V. Listov.
Chemical and Oil Machine Building, K. I. Brekhov.
Civil Aviation, B. P. Bugaev.
Communications Equipment Industry, E. K. Pervyshin.

Construction, Road and Municipal Machine Building, V. I. Chudin.
Construction in Far East and Transbaikal, A. A. Babenko.
Defence, Marshal S. L. Sokolov.
Defence Industry, P. V. Finogenov.
Electronics Industry, A. I. Shokin.
Electrical Engineering Industry, G. P. Voronovsky.
Foreign Affairs, E. A. Shevardnadze.
Foreign Trade, N. S. Patolichev.
Gas Industry, V. S. Chernomyrdin.
General Machine Building, O. D. Baklanov.
Heavy, and Transport, Machine Building, S. A. Afanasiev.
Instrument-Making, Automation and Control Systems, M. S. Shkabardnya.
Internal Affairs, V. V. Fedorchuk.
Machine Building, V. V. Bakhirev.
Machine Building, Light, Food and Domestic Appliances, L. B. Vasiliev.
Machine Building, Livestock Farming and Animal Foods Production, K. N. Belyak.
Machine-Tool Building and Tool Industry, B. V. Balmont.
Medical Industry, A. K. Melnichenko.
Medium Machine Building, E. P. Slavsky.
Merchant Marine, T. B. Guzhenko.
Oil Industry, V. A. Dinkov.
Petroleum and Gas Industry Enterprises Construction, V. G. Chirskov.
Power Machine Building, V. M. Velichko.
Production of Mineral Fertilizers, A. G. Petrishchev.
Radio Industry, P. S. Pleshakov.
Railways, N. S. Konarev.
Ship Building Industry, I. S. Belousov.
Tractor and Agricultural Machine Building, A. A. Ezhevsky.
Transport Construction, V. A. Brezhnev.

ALL-UNION STATE COMMITTEES

Foreign Economic Relations, M. A. Sergeichik.
Hydrometeorology and Monitoring of the Environment, Yu. A. Izrael.
Inventions and Discoveries, I. S. Nayashkov.
Material Reserves, A. V. Kovalenko.
Science and Technology, G. I. Marchuk.
Standards, G. D. Kolmogorov.
Supervision of Atomic Energy Industry Safety, E. V. Kulov.

EMBASSY OF THE U.S.S.R. IN LONDON
13 Kensington Palace Gardens, W8 4QX
[01–229 3628]

Ambassador Extraordinary and Plenipotentiary, His Excellency Victor I. Popov (1980).

AREA AND POPULATION

The total area of the U.S.S.R. is 8,620,822 sq. miles; the total population: (1 Jan. 1984) 273,843,000.

Area and population (January, 1984) of the constituent Republics of the U.S.S.R. with their capitals:—

Republic (Capital)	Sq. miles	Population
I. R.S.F.S.R.		
(Moscow)	6,593,391	142,117,000
II. Ukraine (Kiev)	252,046	50,667,000
III. Belorussia (Minsk) .	80,300	9,878,000
IV. Uzbekistan		
(Tashkent)	157,181*	17,498,000
V. Kazakhstan		
(Alma-Ata)	1,064,980*	15,648,000
VI. Georgia (Tbilisi) . . .	26,911	5,167,000
VII. Azerbaidjan (Baku).	33,436	6,506,000
VIII. Lithuania (Vilnius)	26,173	3,539,000
IX. Moldavia (Kishinev)	13,912	4,080,000
X. Latvia (Riga)	24,695	2,587,000
XI. Kirghizia (Frunze) .	76,642	3,886,000

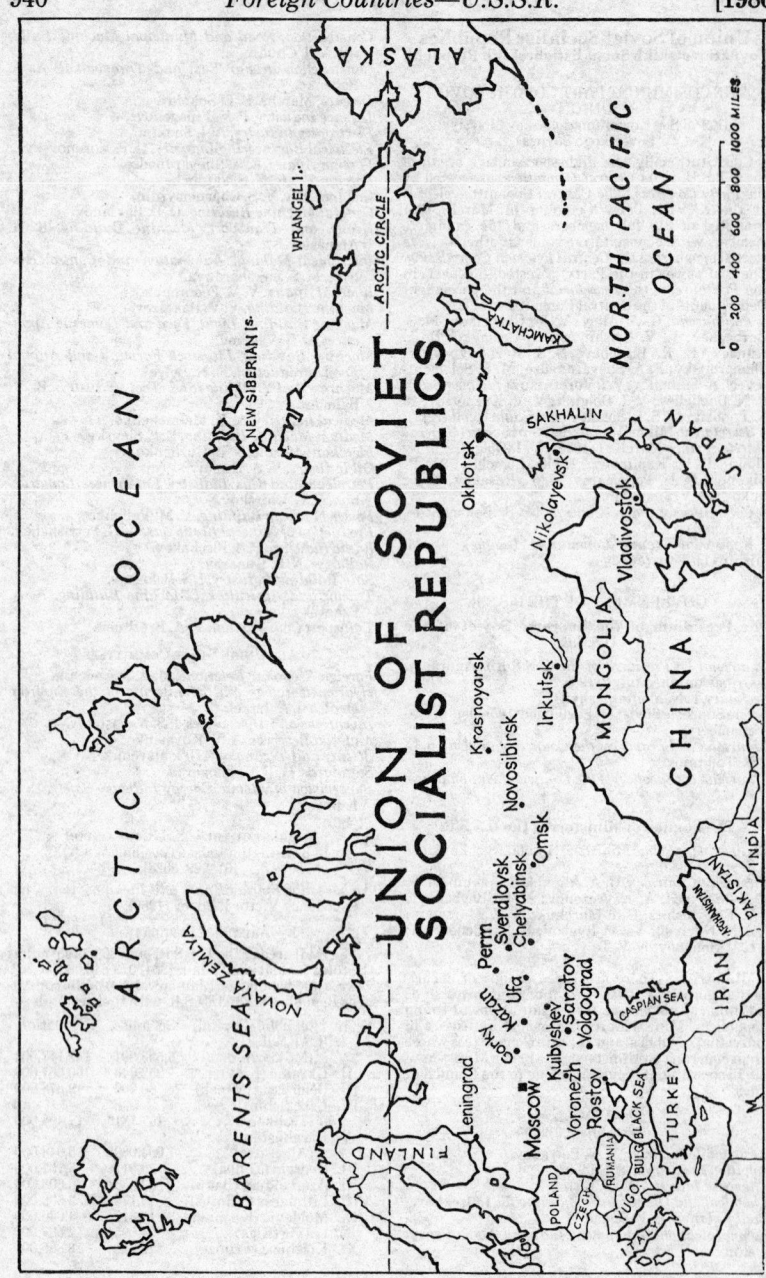

XII.	Tadjikistan		
	(Dushanbe)	54,019	4,365,000
XIII.	Armenia (Erevan) ..	11,306	3,267,000
XIV.	Turkmenistan		
	(Ashkhabad).....	188,417	3,118,000
XV.	Estonia (Tallinn) ...	17,417	1,518,000

* (Adjusted to include transfer of 3 border regions—888 sq. miles and 162,000 inhabitants—by Uzbek S.S.R., Kazakh S.S.R. and U.S.S.R. decrees of May–June 1971.)

In 1984 64·8 per cent of the population lived in urban areas.

The proportion of women to men is 53·1 to 46·9. In 1983 the birth-rate was 20·1 and the mortality rate, 10·3.

Before the outbreak of the Second World War (1941–45 in U.S.S.R.), the U.S.S.R. consisted of 11 Republics. In August 1940, the major part of *Bessarabia* ceded by Romania in June was joined to the Moldavian A.S.S.R. to form a Moldavian S.S.R. The same month, the three independent Baltic States, *Estonia, Latvia* and *Lithuania,* were forcibly incorporated into the Soviet Union. In October, 1944, *Tannu-Tuva,* until the Second World War a nominally independent state lying to the N.W. of Outer Mongolia, became the Autonomous province of *Tuva* and, in 1961, the Autonomous Republic of Tuva, within the R.S.F.S.R.

In July, 1956, the Karelo-Finnish Republic (formed in 1940 from the Karelian A.S.S.R. and land ceded by Finland) reverted to the status of an Autonomous (*Karelian*) Republic within the R.S.F.S.R.

Main Nationalities
(1979 Census)

The most numerous national groups of U.S.S.R. are: Russian, 137 m. and Ukrainian, 42 m. There are between 6 and 12 million Kazakhs, Tatars, Belorussians, and Uzbeks respectively. Azerbaidjani, Armenians and Georgians number between 3·5 and 5·5 million each group. There are some 1·9 to 2·9 million Lithuanians, Kirghizians, Turkmens, Germans, Moldavians and Tadjiks. In each of the following nationality groups the population numbers between 1·02 and 1·8 millions: Chuvashes, Latvians, Poles, Mordovians, Bashkirs, Estonians, Dagestanis and Jews.

The 1979 census revealed a marked difference between the growth rates of individual nationalities: while the Slav nations showed an annual increase of under one per cent, certain Central Asian and Caucasian (mostly Moslem) nations recorded an annual net growth of 2·5 to 3·5 per cent.

Chronological System.—On February 14, 1918, the Soviet Government adopted the Gregorian (Western) Calendar. In 1981 Summer Time was introduced between April 1 and October 1, but there are some geographical anomalies in its application. The country is divided into 11 time zones (Moscow time is 3 hours ahead of G.M.T.).

Language, Literature and Arts

Language and Literature.—Russian is a branch of the Slavonic family of languages which is divided into the following groups: *Eastern,* including Russian, Ukrainian and White Russian; *Western,* including Polish, Czech, Slovak and Sorbish (or Lusatian Wendish); and *Southern,* including Serbo-Croat, Slovene, Macedonian and Bulgarian. The Western group and part of the Southern group are written in the Latin alphabet, the others in the Cyrillic, said to have been instituted by SS. Cyril and Methodius in the ninth century, and largely based on the Greek alphabet. Before the Westernization of Russia under Peter the Great (1682–1725), Russian literature consisted mainly of folk ballads (*byliny*),

epic songs, chronicles and works of moral theology. The eighteenth and particularly the nineteenth centuries saw a brilliant development of Russian poetry and fiction. Romantic poetry reached its zenith with Alexander Pushkin (1799–1837) and Mikhail Lermontov (1814–1841). The 20th century produced great poets like Alexander Blok (1880–1921), the 1958 Nobel Prize laureate Boris Pasternak (1890–1960), Vladimir Mayakovsky (1893–1930) and Anna Akhmatova (1888–1966). Realistic fiction is associated with the names of Nikolai Gogol (1809–1852), Ivan Turgenev (1818–1883), Fedor Dostoyevsky (1821–1881) and Leo Tolstoy (1828–1910), and later with Anton Chekhov (1860–1904), Maxim Gorky (1868–1936), Ivan Bunin (1870–1953) and Alexander Solzhenitsyn (b. 1918).

Great names in music include Glinka (1804–1857), Borodin (1833–87), Mussorgsky (1839–1881), Rimsky-Korsakov (1844–1908), Rubinstein (1829–1894), Tchaikovsky (1840–1893), Rakhmaninov (1873–1943), Skriabin (1872–1915), Prokofiev (1891–1953), Stravinsky (1882–1971) and Shostakovich (1906–1975). Performers include Igor Oistrakh, M. Rostropovich, S. Richter and the famous conductor G. Rozhdestvensky.

The Constitution

On October 7, 1977 a new Constitution was adopted to replace the 1936 ("Stalin") Constitution.

The Constitution is divided into a preamble and 9 Sections. The preamble describes the Soviet Union as a "developed Socialist society", which is said to be a logical stage on the road to communism. The highest aim of the Soviet state is said to be the building of a classless communist society.

Section I covers the *bases of the social-political and economic system.* The economic system is based on "socialist ownership of the means of production", which comprises either state ownership or ownership by collective farms and other cooperative organizations or trade unions and other public organizations (Article 9). The economy is managed on the basis of state plans (Article 15).

This section also contains chapters on *social development and culture, foreign policy,* and the *defence of the socialist Fatherland.* The foreign policy of the U.S.S.R. is said to be "directed to ensuring favourable international conditions for the building of communism in the U.S.S.R." (Article 28).

Section II is devoted to the *state and the individual.* This includes a long chapter on the basic rights, freedoms and duties of citizens of the U.S.S.R., all of which are subject to the proviso that "exercise by citizens of rights and freedoms must not injure the interests of society and state, and the rights of other citizens" (Article 39). The rights are listed in Articles 40–50. Freedom to profess or not profess any religion and to conduct atheistic (but not religious) propaganda, and the separation of the Church from the State and the school from the Church are provided for by Article 52. Section II also includes a list of obligations which is more comprehensive than that of the 1936 Constitution (Articles 59–68).

Section III on the *national-state structure of the U.S.S.R.* describes it as a "unitary federal multinational state, formed as a result of the free self-determination of nations and the voluntary union of equal Soviet Socialist Republics (Article 69). "Each Union Republic shall retain the right freely to secede from the U.S.S.R." (Article 71).

Section IV on the *Soviets of people's deputies and the procedure for electing them* provides for the Supreme Soviet of the U.S.S.R. and the Supreme Soviets of Union and Republics to be elected for a term of 5 years and for local Soviets to be elected for 2½ years (Article 89). The minimum voting age and minimum age for deputies in all Soviets is 18 (Article 95).

Under Section V, *the higher organs of State power and administration of the U.S.S.R.*, the Supreme Soviet of the U.S.S.R. is the highest organ of State power (Article 106). It consists of two chambers, a Council of the Union and Council of Nationalities, which are to be equal in rights and consist of the same number of deputies (Articles 107 and 108). Sessions of the Supreme Soviet are convoked twice a year (Article 110); between sessions the Supreme Soviet is represented by its Presidium, which consists of a Chairman (President), a First Deputy Chairman, 15 Deputy Chairmen, one from each Union Republic, a Secretary and 21 Members (Articles 117 and 118).

The highest executive organ of the State is the Council of Ministers of the U.S.S.R. (Article 127), consisting of the Chairman, his Deputies, U.S.S.R. Ministers and Chairmen of State Committees, Chairmen of the Councils of Ministers of Union Republics *ex officio* and others (Article 128). The Council of Ministers is accountable to the Supreme Soviet (Article 129). A smaller body, the Presidium of the Council of Ministers, comprising the Chairman and his Deputies, acts as the permanent organ of the Council of Ministers (Article 131).

Section VI covers the *bases of the structure of organs of state power and administration in Union Republics*. Section VII deals with *justice, arbitration and supervision by the Procuracy*. Section VIII deals with the *arms, flag, anthem and capital* of the U.S.S.R. Section IX is on the *procedure for bringing the Constitution into effect and amending it*.

FINANCE

A new "heavy" Rouble was introduced on January 1, 1961. Prices and wages were changed accordingly at the rate of 10 old Roubles=1 new Rouble. The official exchange rate bears little relation to the actual purchasing power of the currency.

DEFENCE

Defence expenditure in the U.S.S.R. for 1985 is put officially at 19,060,000 million roubles (or 4·7 per cent of total budget). It is believed, however, that this does not represent the total spent on defence in the U.S.S.R. Much of this is concealed in estimates for other ministries. The general trend is a continuing emphasis on nuclear weapons while improving the levels and capabilities of conventional arms.

The basic military service is two years in the Army and Air Force and two to three years in the Navy and Border Guards.

The total size of the Soviet regular forces is now estimated to be about 5,050,000, excluding some 400,000 Border Guard, internal security, railway and construction troops (mainly uniformed civilians), but including some 1,500,000 command and general support troops not otherwise listed.

Operational ICBMs, i.e. Inter-Continental Ballistic Missiles, now total about 1,400. SLBMs number 1,019. The number of MRBMs and IRBMs deployed is some 606. The operational personnel of the Strategic Rocket Forces totals about 325,000 (not including Air Defence Troops—500,000).

The Air Forces comprise about 11,600 operational aircraft (including about 8,640 combat aircraft). The total strength of the Air Forces, excluding the Naval Air Force (68,000) and the bomber forces of the Aviation Armies (100,000), is about 475,000 men. The total personnel of the separate Air Defence Command, now merged with the Air Defence Troops of the Ground Forces, is estimated at 630,000 men.

The total size of the Soviet Army is estimated at 1,800,000 men. It is thought to be organized in 191 divisions, distributed as follows: 30 divisions in Central and Eastern Europe, 65 in European U.S.S.R., 28 in Southern Theatre (includes 4 in Afghanistan), 52 in Far Eastern Theatre, and 16 in the Central Strategic Reserve.

The total strength of the Soviet Navy and Naval Air Force is 460,000 men. In total tonnage, it is the second largest navy in the world, and its main strength lies in the submarine fleet. There are now 276 cruise missile and attack submarines, 119 nuclear-powered and 157 diesel-powered submarines, with a further 95 attack submarines in reserve.

The Soviet Navy now has 290 major surface combat vessels, including four aircraft carriers, 37 cruisers and 73 destroyers and more than 180 frigates. The landbased Naval Air Force comprises about 755 combat aircraft, 390 of which are bombers, and some 300 helicopters.

The para-military forces number some 560,000, including 300,000 border troops and 260,000 internal security troops. There are also DOSAAF members (claimed active membership, 80 million) who participate in such activities as athletics, flight training, shooting, parachuting and pre-military training.

Minister of Defence, S. L. Sokolov (with rank of Marshal of the Soviet Union).
Chief of General Staff, Marshal S. F. Akhromeyev.
Chief, Political Administration, Soviet Army and Navy, Army Gen. A. A. Yepishev.

On May 14, 1955, a Treaty of Friendship, Mutual Assistance and Co-operation was signed in Warsaw between the Soviet Union and its European associates (Bulgaria, East Germany, Hungary, Poland, Romania, and Czechoslovakia) (and Albania which left the Pact in Sept. 1968) to serve as a counterpoise to NATO. A united military command was set up in Moscow, *C.-in-C.*, Marshal V. G. Kulikov; *Chief of Staff*, Army General A. I. Gribkov. The Treaty (Warsaw Pact), due to have expired in June 1985, was extended by Protocol in its existing form for a further 20 years, with provision for a further 10 year extension thereafter, at a meeting of Pact leaders in Warsaw on April 26, 1985. The Pact came into force on May 31, 1985.

INDUSTRY AND AGRICULTURE

One of the most remarkable aspects of the Soviet economy has been the transformation of an essentially agricultural country into the second-strongest industrial power in the world. The 1983 output amounted to 153 million tonnes of steel, 107 million tonnes of rolled metal, 716 million tonnes of coal, 616 million tonnes of crude oil, 128 million tonnes of cement, 1,416,000 million kW/h of electricity and 1,315,000 cars.

Agricultural development has been slower, mainly owing to lack of incentives among peasants organized in *kolkhozy* (collective farms). Repeated droughts, such as in 1980-81, were a contributing factor to a permanent shortage of grain; the 1982 harvest is estimated at 170–180 million tonnes, and the 1983 harvest was officially stated to have exceeded 190 million tonnes. Stock breeding has also suffered from the general mismanagement of farming, and from shortages of fodder in recent years. The livestock at Jan. 1, 1983 included 43,800,000 cows, 78,500,000 pigs and 151,500,000 sheep and goats. Besides *kolkhozy* (collective farms) and *sovkhozy* (state farms) a significant contribution to agricultural production is made by the private plots cultivated by individual peasants. The cultivation of these plots is encouraged by the Soviet authorities. The level of productivity remains very low. *Forests* cover nearly 40 per cent of the whole area of the Union and form a considerable source of wealth.

Trade with U.K.

	1983	1984
Imports from U.K.	£445,008,000	£735,173,000
Exports to U.K.	728,491,000	854,307,000

COMMUNICATIONS

European Russia is relatively well served by railways, Leningrad and Moscow being the two main focal points of rail routes. The centre and south have a good system of north-south and east-west lines, but the eastern part (the Volga lands), traversed as it is by trunk lines between Europe and Asia which enter Siberia *via* Sverdlovsk, Chelyabinsk, Magnitogorsk and Ufa, lacks north-south routes. In Asia, there are still large areas of the U.S.S.R., notably in the Far North and Siberia, with few or no railways. Railways built since 1928 include the Turkestan-Siberian line (*Turksib*) which has made possible a large-scale industrial exploitation of Kazakhstan, a number of lines within the system of the *Trans-Siberian Railway* (Magnitogorsk-Kartaly-Troitsk, Sverdlovsk-Kurgan, Novosibirsk-Proyektnaya, etc.), which are of great importance for the industrial development in the east, the Petropavlovsk-Karaganda-Balkhash line which has made possible the development of the Karaganda coal basin and of the Balkhash copper mines, and the Moscow-Donbass trunk line. In the northern part of European Russia, the North Pechora Railway has been completed, while in the Far East a recently completed second Trans-Siberian line (the Baikal-Amur Railway) is partially in use; it follows a more northerly alignment than the earlier Trans-Siberian and terminates in the Pacific port of Sovetskaya Gavan.

Sea Ports and Inland Waterways.—The most important ports (Odessa, Nikolayev, Batumi, Taganrog, Rostov, Kerch, Sevastopol and Novorossiisk) lie around the Black Sea and the Sea of Azov. The northern ports (Leningrad, Murmansk and Archangel) are, with the exception of Murmansk, icebound during winter. Several ports have been built along the Arctic Sea route between Murmansk and Vladivostok and are in regular use every summer. The great Far Eastern port of Vladivostok, the Pacific naval base of the U.S.S.R., is kept open by icebreakers all the year round. Inland waterways, both natural and artificial, are of great importance in the country, although all of them are icebound in winter (from 2½ months in the south to 6 months in the north). The great rivers of European Russia flow outwards from the centre, linking all parts of the plain with the chief ports, an immense system of navigable waterways which carried about 606,000,000 tons of freight in 1983. They are supplemented by a system of canals which provide a through traffic between the White, Baltic, Black and Caspian Seas. The most notable of them are the *White Sea-Baltic Canal*, the *Moscow-Volga Canal* and the *Volga-Don Canal* linking the Baltic and the White Seas in the north to the Caspian, the Black Sea and the Sea of Azov in the south.

FLAG.—Red, with five-pointed star above hammer and sickle.

NATIONAL DAY.—November 7 (Commemorating the October Bolshevist Revolution of 1917).

BRITISH EMBASSY

(Naberezhnaya Morisa Toreza 14, Moscow)

Ambassador Extraordinary and Plenipotentiary, His Excellency Sir Bryan Cartledge, K.C.M.G., *apptd.* 1985.

Minister, D. J. E. Ratford, C.M.G., C.V.O.

There is a Consular Section attached to the Embassy.

I.—R.S.F.S.R.

(The Russian Soviet Federal Socialist Republic)

Chairman of the Presidium of the Supreme Soviet, V. P. Orlov.

Chairman of the Council of Ministers, V. I. Vorotnikov.

The R.S.F.S.R. has no central Communist Party organization of its own.

The R.S.F.S.R., the largest and the most important of the Republics, occupies the major half of the European part of the U.S.S.R. and the major northern portion of its Asiatic part and makes up 77 per cent of the total territory of the U.S.S.R. with 53 per cent of the total population. (About 83 per cent of the population are Russians.) It consists of 16 Autonomous Republics (the Bashkir, Buryat, Checheno-Ingush, Chuvash, Daghestan, Kabardin-Balkar, Kalmyk, Karelian, Komi, Mari, Mordovian, North-Osetian, Tatar, Tuva, Udmurt and Yakut, A.S.S.R.s); 6 regions (Altai, Khabarovsk, Krasnodar, Krasnoyarsk, Maritime and Stavropol) containing in their turn 5 autonomous provinces; 49 provinces (Amur, Archangel, Astrakhan, Belgorod, Bryansk, Chelyabinsk, Chita, Gorky, Irkutsk, Ivanovo, Kalinin, Kaliningrad, Kaluga, Kamchatka, Kemerovo, Kirov, Kostroma, Kuibyshev, Kurgan, Kursk, Leningrad, Lipetsk, Magadan, Moscow, Murmansk, Novgorod, Novosibirsk, Omsk, Orel, Orenburg, Penza, Perm, Pskov, Rostov, Ryazan, Sakhalin, Saratov, Smolensk, Sverdlovsk, Tambov, Tomsk, Tula, Tyumen, Ulyanovsk, Vladimir, Volgograd, Vologda, Voronezh and Yaroslavl).

There are three principal geographic areas: a low-lying flat Western part stretching eastwards up to the Yenisei and divided in two by the Ural ridge; an eastern part, between the Yenisei and the Pacific, consisting of a number of tablelands and ridges, and a southern mountainous part. Climatically, the R.S.F.S.R. extends from arctic and tundra belts to the sub-tropical in the south. It has a very long coast-line, including the longest Arctic coast-line in the world (about 17,000 miles). The most important rivers are the Volga, the Northern Dvina and the Pechora, the Neva, the Don and the Kuban in the European part, and in the Asiatic part, the Ob, the Irtysh, the Yenisei, the Lena and the Amur, and, further north, Khatanga, Olenek, Yana, Indigirka, Kolyma and Anadyr. Lakes are abundant, particularly in the north-west. The huge Baikal Lake in Eastern Siberia is the deepest lake in the world. There are also two large artificial water reservoirs within the Greater Volga canal system, the Moscow and Rybinsk "Seas".

Minerals.—The Republic has some of the richest mineral deposits in the world. Coal is mined in the Kuznetsk area, in the Urals, south of Moscow, in the Donets basin (its Eastern part lies in the R.S.F.S.R.) and in the Pechora area in the North. Oil is produced in the Northern Caucasus, in the area between the Volga and the Ural and in Western Siberia, which also has large deposits of natural gas. Coal and gas deposits in Siberia and the Far East (especially Yakutia) are currently being developed, now that some deposits in the western parts of the U.S.S.R. are approaching exhaustion. The Ural mountains contain a unique assortment of minerals—high-quality iron ore, manganese, copper, aluminium, gold, platinum, precious stones, salt, asbestos, pyrites, coal, oil, etc. Iron ore is also mined near Kursk, Tula, Lipetsk, in several areas in Siberia and in the Kola Peninsula. Non-ferrous metals are found in the Altai, in Eastern Siberia, in the Northern Caucasus, in the Kuznetsk-Basin, in the Far East and in the Far North. Nine-tenths of all U.S.S.R. forests are located in the R.S.F.S.R.

Production and Industry.—The vastness of the territory of the Republic and the great variety in climatic conditions cause great differences in the structure of agriculture from north to south and from west to east. In the far north reindeer breeding, hunting and fishing are predominant. Further south, timber industry is combined with grain growing. In the southern half of the forest zone and in the adjacent forest-steppe zone, the acreage under grain crops is far larger and the structure of agriculture more complex. An extensive programme of land improvement mainly involving this zone aims to double its total agricultural output by 1990. In the eastern part of this zone, between the Volga and the Urals, cericulture is predominant (particularly summer wheat), with cattle breeding next. Beyond the Urals is another important grain-growing and stock-breeding area in the southern part of the Western-Siberian plain. The southern steppe zone is the main wheat granary of the U.S.S.R., containing also large acreages under barley, maize and sunflower. In the extreme south cotton is now cultivated. Vine, tobacco and other southern crops are grown on the Black Sea shore of the Caucasus.

Industrially, the R.S.F.S.R. occupies the first place among the Soviet Republics. Moscow and Leningrad are still the two largest industrial centres in the country, but new industrial areas are being developed in the Urals, the Kuznetsk basin, and more recently in Siberia and the Far East. Most of the oil produced in the U.S.S.R. now comes from the R.S.F.S.R., half annual output comes from Tyumen Oblast in Western Siberia. All industries are represented in the R.S.F.S.R., including iron and steel and engineering.

CAPITAL.—Moscow. Population 8,537,000 (Jan. 1, 1984). Moscow, founded about A.D. 1147 by Yuri Dolgoruki, became first the centre of the rising Moscow principality and in the 15th century, the capital of the whole of Russia (Muscovy). In 1325, it became the seat of the Metropolitan of Russia. In 1703 Peter the Great transferred the capital to the newly built St. Petersburg, but on March 14, 1918, Moscow was again designated as the capital. ΨLeningrad (before the First World War "St. Petersburg" and from 1914–1924 "Petrograd") has a population of 4,827,000 (Jan. 1, 1984).

Other towns with populations exceeding 1,000,000 are:—

Gorky (Nizhny-Novogorod)	1,392,000
Novosibirsk (Novonikolayevsk)	1,384,000
Sverdlovsk (Yekaterinburg)	1,286,000
Kuibyshev (Samara)	1,250,000
Omsk	1,094,000
Chelyabinsk	1,086,000
Perm (Molotov)	1,048,000
Ufa	1,048,000
Kazan	1,039,000

II.—UKRAINE

First Secretary of the Party Central Committee, V. V. Shcherbitsky.
Chairman of the Presidium of the Supreme Soviet, V. S. Shevchenko.
Chairman of the Council of Ministers, A. P. Lyashko.

This Republic, second largest in population, lying in the south-western part of the European half of the U.S.S.R., was formed in December, 1917. It consists of 25 provinces—Cherkassy, Chernigov, Chernovtsy, Crimea, Dnepropetrovsk, Donetsk, Ivano-Frankovsk, Kharkov, Kherson, Khmelnitsky, Kiev, Kirovograd, Lvov, Nikolayev, Odessa, Poltava, Rovno, Sumy, Ternopol, Transcarpathia, Vinnitsa, Volhynia, Voroshilovgrad, Zaporozhye and Zhitomir.

Physical Features.—The larger part of the Ukraine forms a plain with small elevations. The Carpathian mountains lie in the south-western part of the Republic. The climate is moderate, with relatively mild winters (particularly in the south-west) and hot summers. The main rivers are the Dnieper with its tributaries, the Southern Bug and the Northern Donets (a tributary of the Don).

Production and Industry.—The main centre of Soviet coal mining and iron and steel industry is situated in the southern part of the Ukraine. In 1980, the Ukraine provided 36 per cent of the total Soviet steel, 51 per cent of iron ore and 27 per cent of coal. The engineering and chemical industries are also of importance. The central forest-steppe region (mainly on the right bank of the Dnieper) is the greatest sugar-producing area in the U.S.S.R. The Ukraine also leads in grain-growing and stock-raising.

There are large deposits of coal and salt in the Donets Basin, of iron ore in Krivoy Rog and near Kerch in the Crimea, of manganese in Nikopol, and of quicksilver in Nikitovka.

CAPITAL (since 1934), Kiev, one of the oldest cities in the U.S.S.R., founded in the 6th–7th century A.D., was the capital of the Russian State from 865 to 1240. Population (Jan. 1, 1984), 2,409,000. Other towns are:—

Kharkov	1,536,000
Dnepropetrovsk (Yekaterinoslav)	1,114,000
Ψ Odessa	1,113,000
Donetsk (Stalino; Yuzovka, *i.e.* Hughesovka)	1,064,000

III.—BELORUSSIA
(White Russia)

First Secretary of the Party Central Committee, N. N. Slyunkov.
Chairman of the Presidium of the Supreme Soviet, I. E. Polyakov.
Chairman of the Council of Ministers, V. I. Brovikov.

The Belorussian S.S.R., lying in the western part of the European area of the U.S.S.R., was formed early in 1919. It now consists of six provinces (Brest, Gomel, Grodno, Minsk, Mogilev and Vitebsk). Belorussians make up four-fifths of the population, with Russians and Poles coming next. It is largely a plain with many lakes, swamps and marshy land. Before the revolution of 1917 the area was one of the most backward parts of European Russia. Since then, agriculture has been greatly developed, thanks to draining of swamps. Most of the Republic's industry is also of recent growth. Woodworking is of great importance, but engineering has also been greatly extended with several major plants built in Gomel and Minsk.

The main rivers are the upper reaches of the Dnieper, of the Niemen and of the Western Dvina.

CAPITAL, Minsk. Population 1,442,000 (Jan. 1, 1984).

IV.—UZBEKISTAN

First Secretary of the Party Central Committee, I. B. Usmankhodzhaev.
Chairman of the Presidium of the Supreme Soviet, A. V. Salimov.
Chairman of the Council of Ministers, G. Kh. Kadyrov.

The Uzbek S.S.R. was formed in 1924 and consists of the Kara-Kalpak A.S.S.R. and of 12 provinces (Andizhan, Bokhara, Dzhizak, Ferghana, Kashka-darya, Khorezm, Namangan, Navoi, Samarkand, Surkhan-darya, Syr-darya and Tashkent). It lies between the high Tienshan Mountains and the Pamir highlands in the east and south-east and sandy lowlands in the west and north-west. The major part of the territory is a plain with huge waterless deserts and several large oases, which form the main centres of population and economic life. The largest is the Ferghana valley, watered by the Syr-Darya. Other oases include Tashkent, Samarkand, Bokhara and Khorezm. The climate is continental and dry. Minerals include gold, natural gas, oil, copper, lead, zinc and coal.

The Uzbeks, a Turkic people, make up 68·7 per cent of the population, the Russians (10·8 per cent), Tatars (4·2 per cent) and Kazakhs (4 per cent) come next.

There are major agricultural and textile machinery plants and several chemical combines. Uzbekistan is the main cotton-growing area of the U.S.S.R. producing more than 60 per cent of all Soviet cotton. Irrigation has always been of decisive importance in this area, and the Soviet Government has done much in this field, including the construction of the Great Ferghana Canal (230 miles).

CAPITAL, Tashkent. Population 1,986,000 (Jan. 1, 1984). Samarkand (population (1984), 515,000) contains the Gur-Emir (Tamerlane's Mausoleum), completed A.D. 1400 by Ulugbek, Tamerlane's astronomer-grandson, and a 15th-century observatory.

V.—KAZAKHSTAN

First Secretary of the Party Central Committee, D. A. Kunayev.
Chairman of the Presidium of Supreme Soviet, B. A. Ashimov.
Chairman of the Council of Ministers, N. A. Nazarbaev.

The Kazakh S.S.R., the second-largest Union-Republic, stretching from the lower reaches of the Volga and the Caspian in the west to the Altai and Tienshan in the east, and bordering on China, was formed in 1920 as an autonomous republic (under the name of the Kirghiz A.S.S.R.) within the R.S.F.S.R., and was constituted a Union Republic in 1936. It consists of 19 Provinces: Aktyubinsk, Alma-Ata, Chimkent, Dzhambul, Dzhezkazgan, East-Kazakhstan, Guryev, Karaganda, Kokchetav, Kustanay, Kzyl-Orda, Mangyshlak, North-Kazakhstan, Pavlodar, Semipalatinsk, Taldy-Kurgan, Tselinograd, Turgay and Uralsk.

Kazakhstan is a country of arid steppes and semi-deserts, flat in the west, hilly in the east and mountainous in the south-east (Southern Altai and Tienshan). The climate is continental and very dry. The main rivers are the (Upper) Irtysh, the Ural, the Syr-Darya and the Ili. Kazakhstan is very rich in minerals: copper in Kounrad and Dzhezkazgan, lead and zinc in the Altai and Karatau mountains, iron ore in Radryg and Lisakovsk, coal in Ekibastuz and Karaganda and oil and natural gas in the Mangyshlak peninsula. Major centres of metal industry exist in the Altai Mountains, in Chimkent, north of the Balkhash Lake and in Central Kazakhstan. Stock-raising is highly developed, particularly in the central and south-western parts of the Republic. Grain is grown in the north and north-east and cotton in the south and south-east.

The Kazakhs (a Turkic people) are in a minority in the Republic named after them; they constitute only 36 per cent of its population, Russian settlers make up 41 per cent and Ukrainians 6 per cent.

CAPITAL, Alma-Ata (formerly Verny). Population 1,046,000 (Jan. 1, 1984). Karaganda, a major mining centre, has a population of 608,000 (Jan. 1, 1984).

VI.—GEORGIA

First Secretary of the Party Central Committee, n/a
Chairman of the Presidium of the Supreme Soviet, P. G. Gilashvili.

Chairman of the Council of Ministers, D. L. Kartvelishvili.

The Georgian, S.S.R., occupying the north-western part of Transcaucasia, lies on the shore of the Black Sea and borders in the south-east on Turkey. It was formed in 1921; in 1922 it joined the Transcaucasian Federation which, in its turn, adhered to the U.S.S.R. in the same year. After the liquidation of the Transcaucasian S.F.S.R. in 1936 Georgia became a Union Republic. It contains two Autonomous Republics (Abkhazia and Adjaria) and the South-Osetian Autonomous Province. Georgia is a country of mountains, with the Greater Caucasus in the north and the Lesser Caucasus in the south. A relatively low-lying land between these two ridges is divided into two parts by the Surz Ridge: Western Georgia with a mild and damp climate and Eastern Georgia with a more continental and dry climate. The Black Sea shore and the Rioni lowland are subtropical in their climatic character. The most important mineral deposits are manganese (Chiatura), coal (Tkibuli and Tkvarcheli) and oil (Kakhetia). Georgia is a leading producer of manganese in the U.S.S.R. There are also many oil refineries. viniculture, tea and tobacco-growing are the three main agricultural industries. The Black Sea harbours many famous holiday resorts. Georgians make up 68·8 per cent of the population, the remainder being largely composed of Armenians, Russians, Azerbaidjanis and Osetians.

CAPITAL, Tbilisi (Tiflis), population 1,140,000 (Jan. 1, 1984).

VII.—AZERBAIDJAN

First Secretary of the Party Central Committee, K. M. Bagirov.
Chairman of the Presidium of the Supreme Soviet, K. A. Khalilov.
Chairman of the Council of Ministers, G. N. Seidov.

The Azerbaidjan S.S.R. occupies the eastern part of Transcaucasia, on the shore of the Caspian Sea, and borders on Iran. It was formed in 1920. Between 1922 and 1936 it formed part of the Transcaucasian Federation. In 1936 it became a Union Republic. It contains the Nakhichevan Autonomous Republic and the Nagorno-Karabakh Autonomous Province.

The north-eastern part of the Republic is taken up by the south-eastern end of the main Caucasus ridge, its south-western part by the smaller Caucasus hills, and its south-eastern corner by the spurs of the Talysh Ridge. Its central part is a depression irrigated by the Kura and by the lower reaches of its tributary Araks. Sheltered by the mountains from the humid west winds blowing from the Black Sea, Azerbaidjan has a continental climate. The land requires artificial irrigation. Industry is dominated by oil and natural gas extraction and related chemical and engineering industries centred on Baku and Sumgait. A large power station on the Araks was completed in 1969, in conjunction with Iran. Azerbaidjan is also important as a cotton growing area. The Azerbaidjani (Turkic) make up more than three-quarters of the population of the Republic, Armenians, about 8 per cent, and Russians, 8 per cent.

CAPITAL, Ψ Baku. Population 1,661,000 (Jan. 1, 1984).

VIII.—LITHUANIA

First Secretary of the Party Central Committee, P. P. Grishkyavichus.
Chairman of the Presidium of the Supreme Soviet, A. S. Barkauskas.
Chairman of the Council of Ministers, R.-B. I. Songaila.

Lithuania, formerly a Province of the Russian Empire, was declared an independent Republic at Vilna in 1918 and was incorporated into the U.S.S.R. in August, 1940. The Republic forms a plain with a large number of lakes and swamps. The forests occupy 19 per cent of the whole area. The main river is the Niemen with its tributaries.

The chief industries are agriculture and forestry, the chief products being rye, oats, wheat, barley, flax, sugar-beet and potatoes.

The Lithuanians make up four-fifths of the population, Russians and Poles, 7–9 per cent each.

CAPITAL, Vilnius (Vilna). Population 535,000 (Jan. 1, 1984).

IX.—MOLDAVIA

First Secretary of the Party Central Committee, S. K. Grossu.
Chairman of the Presidium of the Supreme Soviet, I. P. Kalin.
Chairman of the Council of Ministers, I. G. Ustiyan.

Moldavia, occupying the south-western corner of the U.S.S.R., borders in the west on Romania with the Pruth forming the frontier. In 1918, Romania seized the Russian Province of Bessarabia, but in 1940 the U.S.S.R. forced Romania to give back Bessarabia, the major part of which was merged with the Moldavian A.S.S.R. (formed in 1924) to create the Moldavian S.S.R.

The northern part of the Republic consists of flat steppe lands, now all under plough. Some forests skirt the Dniester. Further south, around Kishinev, there are woody hills and further south again, low-lying steppe lands. The climate is moderate. The main river is the Dniester, navigable along the whole course.

The main industry is agriculture (viniculture, fruit-growing and market-gardening). Industry is insignificant in both parts of Moldavia, but the Republic has the densest population in the U.S.S.R. Moldavians make up 64 per cent of the population, with Ukrainians, and Russians next.

CAPITAL, Kishinev (Chisinau). Population, 605,000 (Jan. 1, 1984).

X.—LATVIA

First Secretary of the Party Central Committee, B. K. Pugo.
Chairman of the Presidium of the Supreme Soviet, Ya. Ya. Vagris.
Chairman of the Council of Ministers, Yu. Ya. Ruben.

The Latvian S.S.R., lying on the shores of the Baltic and of the Gulf of Riga, was formerly a Baltic Province of the Russian Empire. It was proclaimed an independent state in 1918 and was forcibly incorporated into the U.S.S.R. in August 1940.

The surface of the country is generally flat, interspersed by occasional chains of hills. The climate is moderately continental. The main rivers are the lower reaches of the Western Dvina and its tributaries. Forests occupy 20 per cent of the total territory.

The Latvians make up 53·7 per cent of the Republic's population, Russians 32·8 per cent.

Latvian industry was always highly developed, with shipbuilding, engineering, chemical industry, textile industry, wood-working and dairying being the chief occupations. Both Riga and Liepaja (Libava, Libau) are important sea-ports.

CAPITAL, Ψ Riga. Population, 875,000 (Jan. 1, 1984).

XI.—KIRGHIZIA

First Secretary of the Party Central Committee, T. U. Usubaliyev.

Chairman of the Presidium of the Supreme Soviet, T. Kh. Koshoev.
Chairman of the Council of Ministers, A. D. Duisheev.

The Kirghiz S.S.R. occupies the north-eastern part of Soviet Central Asia and borders in the south-east on China. In 1924, a Kara-Kirghiz Autonomous Province was formed within the R.S.F.S.R. In 1926 it became a Kirghiz Autonomous Republic, and in 1936 a Union Republic. It contains three provinces, Issyk-Kul, Naryn and Osh. The Kirghiz Republic is a mountainous country, the major part being covered by the ridge of the Central Tienshan, while mountains of the Pamir-Altai system occupy its southern part. There are a number of spacious mountain valleys, the Alai, Susamyr, the Issyk-Kul lake and others. The majority of the population is concentrated in plains, lying at the foot of mountains—Chu, Talass, part of the Ferghana Valley where agriculture prospers. Crops include sugar beet and cotton, and sheep are important in the mountains. Industry is being developed and some mining is done. The Kirghiz constitute 47·9 per cent of the population, the Russians 25·9 per cent. The Uzbeks (in Eastern Ferghana) amount to 12·1 per cent.

CAPITAL, Frunze (formerly Pishpek). Population, 590,000 (Jan. 1, 1984).

XII.—TADJIKSTAN

First Secretary of the Party Central Committee, R. N. Nabiev.
Chairman of the Presidium of the Supreme Soviet, G. Pallaev.
Chairman of the Council of Ministers, K. M. Makhkamov.

The Tadjik S.S.R. lies in the extreme south-east of Soviet Central Asia and borders in the south on Afghanistan and in the east on China. It was originally formed in 1924 as an Autonomous Republic within the Uzbek S.S.R. and became a Union Republic in 1929. It includes the Gorno-Badakhshan Autonomous Province and the Kulyab and Leninabad Provinces.

The country is mountainous: in the east lie the Pamir highlands with the highest point in the U.S.S.R., Pik Kommunizma (24,500 feet), in the centre the high ridges of the Pamir-Altai system. Plains are formed by wide stretches of the Syr-Darya valley in the north and of the Amu-Darya in the south.

Like the other Central-Asiatic Republics, Tadjikistan is a cotton-growing country. Its climatic conditions favour the cultivation of Egyptian cotton. Irrigation is of great importance. Of the population 58·8 per cent are Tadjiks (linguistically and culturally akin to the Persians), 23 per cent Uzbeks, the rest Russians and others.

CAPITAL, Dushanbe (formerly Stalinabad; Dyushambe). Population, 539,000 (Jan. 1, 1984).

XIII.—ARMENIA

First Secretary of the Party Central Committee, K. S. Demirchyan.
Chairman of the Presidium of the Supreme Soviet, B. E. Sarkisov.
Chairman of the Council of Ministers, F. T. Sarkisyan.

The Armenian S.S.R. occupies the south-western part of Transcaucasia: it was formed in 1920. In 1922 it joined the Transcaucasian Federation, and on its liquidation in 1936 became a Union Republic. In the south it borders on Turkey. It is a mountainous country consisting of several vast table lands surrounded by ridges. The population and the economic life are concentrated in the low-lying part of Armenia, the Aras valley and the Erevan hollow; the climate is continental, dry and cold, but the Araks valley has a long, hot and dry summer. Irrigation is essential for agriculture. In Turkey, at the junction of the former Turkish, Persian and Russian boundaries, is *Mount Ararat* (17,160 ft.), the traditional resting place of "Noah's Ark." Industrial and fruit crops are grown in the low-lying districts, grain in the hills. Armenia is traditionally noted for her wine. There are large copper ore and molybdenum deposits and other minerals. The Armenian Church centred in Etchmiadzin is the oldest established Christian Church, Christianity having been recognized as the State religion in A.D. 300.

Nearly 90 per cent of the population is Armenian.

CAPITAL, Erevan. Population, 1,114,000 (Jan. 1, 1984).

XIV.—TURKMENISTAN

First Secretary of the Party Committee, M. N. Gapurov.
Chairman of the Presidium of the Supreme Soviet, B. Yazkuliev.
Chairman of the Council of Ministers, S. A. Niyazov.

Turkmenia occupies the extreme south of Soviet Central Asia, between the Caspian and the Amu-Darya, and borders in the south on Iran and Afghanistan. It was formed in 1924 and contains five Provinces: Ashkhabad, Chardjou, Krasnovodsk, Mary and Tashauz. The country is a low-lying plain, fringed by hills in the south. Ninety per cent of the plain is taken up by the arid Kara-Kum desert. Of all Central-Asiatic Republics, Turkmenia is the lowest and driest. The cultivation of cotton, stock-raising and mineral extraction are the principal industries. The republic produces about 16 per cent of the Soviet Union's natural gas, as well as astrakhan furs and carpets. Most of the land under plough is artificially irrigated. The oil and silk industries are of old standing. There are also some fisheries in the Caspian.

Turkmens make up 68·4 per cent of the population, Russians 12·6 per cent, and Uzbeks 8·5 per cent.

CAPITAL, Ashkhabad (formerly Askhabad, Poltoratsk). Population, 346,000 (Jan. 1, 1984).

XV.—ESTONIA

First Secretary of the Party Central Committee, K. G. Vaino.
Chairman of the Presidium of the Supreme Soviet, A. F. Ryuitel.
Chairman of the Council of Ministers, B. E. Saul.

Estonia, formerly a Baltic province of the Russian Empire, was proclaimed an independent Republic in 1918. In 1940, it was forcibly incorporated into the U.S.S.R. It lies on the shores of the Baltic and of the Finnish Gulf in the north and of the Gulf of Riga in the south-west. Some 800 islands, among them Dagö and Ösel, form part of Estonian territory.

The country forms a low-lying plain with many lakes, among them the Chud (or Pskov) Lake, on the border with the R.S.F.S.R. Forests take up about one-fifth of the territory. Agriculture and dairy-farming are the chief industries, rye, oats, barley, flax and potatoes being the chief crops, and butter, bacon and eggs the chief products of dairy farming. There are important manufactures, including textiles, engineering, shipbuilding, woodworking, etc.

The population consists of Estonians (64·7 per cent) and Russians (27·9 per cent).

CAPITAL, Ψ Tallinn (formerly Reval). Population, 458,000 (Jan. 1, 1984).

URUGUAY
(República Oriental del Uruguay)

President, Dr. Julio María Sanguinetti, *took office*, March 1, 1985.
Vice President, Sr. Enrique Tarigo.

CABINET

Interior, Dr. Carlos Manini Ríos.
Foreign Affairs, Cr. Enrique Iglesias.
Economy and Finance, Cr. Ricardo Zerbino.
Transport and Public Works, Sr. Jorge Sanguinetti.
Public Health, Dr. Raúl M. Ugarte.
Labour and Social Security, Sr. Hugo Fernández Faingold.
Agriculture and Fisheries, Sr. Roberto Vázquez Platero.
Education and Culture, Dra. Adela Reta.
National Defence, Dr. Juan Vicente Chiarino.
Industry and Energy, Dr. Carlos José Pirán.
Planning and Budget Office, Cr. Ariel Davrieux.

URUGUAYAN EMBASSY AND CONSULATE
48 Lennox Gardens, SW1X 0DL
[01–589 8835; *Consulate* 01–589 8735]

Ambassador Extraordinary and Plenipotentiary, His Excellency Dr. Luis M. de Posadas (1983).
Minister, Dr. José Luis Bruno.
1st Secretary, Dr. Alberto Fajardo.
Financial Attaché, Sr. Miguel Pereira.

Area and Population.—The smallest Republic in South America, on the east coast of the Rio de la Plata situated in lat. 30°–35° S. and long. 53° 15'–57° 42' W., with an area of 72,172 square miles, and an estimated population (1984) of 3,012,146, almost entirely white and predominantly of Spanish and Italian descent. Many Uruguayans are Roman Catholics. There is complete freedom of religion and no church is established by the State.

Physical Features.—The country consists mainly (and particularly in the south and west) of undulating grassy plains. The principal chains of hills are the Cuchilla del Haedo, which cross the Brazilian boundary and extend southwards to the Cuchilla Grande of the south and east. In no case do the peaks exceed 2,000 feet.

The principal river is the *Rio Negro* (with its tributary the Yi), flowing from north-east to south-west into the *Rio Uruguay*. The boundary river *Uruguay* is navigable from its estuary to Salto, about 200 miles north, and the Negro is also navigable for a considerable distance. Smaller rivers are the Cuareim, Yaguaron, Santa Lucia, Queguay and the Cebollati. On the south-east coast are several lagoons, and the north-east boundary crosses (the Brazilian) Lake Merin.

The climate is reasonably healthy. The summer is warm, but the heat is often tempered by the breezes of the Atlantic. The winter is, on the whole, mild, but cold spells, characterized by winds from the South Polar regions, are experienced in June, July and August. Rainfall is regular throughout the year, but there are occasional droughts. Floods also occur.

Government.—Uruguay—or the *Banda Oriental*, as this territory lying on the eastern bank of the Uruguay River was then called—resisted all attempted invasions of the Portuguese and Spaniards until the beginning of the 17th century, and 100 years later the Portuguese settlements were captured by the Spaniards. From 1726 to 1814 the country formed part of Spanish South America and underwent many vicissitudes during the Wars of Independence. In 1814 the armies of the Argentine Confederation captured the capital and annexed the province, and it was afterwards annexed by Portugal and became a province of Brazil. In 1825, the country threw off the

Brazilian yoke. This action led to war between Argentina and Brazil which was settled by the mediation of the United Kingdom, Uruguay being declared an independent state in 1828. In 1830 a Republic was inaugurated.

According to the Constitution the President appoints a council of 10 ministers and a Secretary (Planning and Budget Office), and the Vice-President presides over Congress. The legislature consists of a Chamber of 99 deputies and a Senate of 30 members (plus the Vice-President), elected for five years by a system of proportional representation. Voting is obligatory and extends to all citizens of good repute and certain long standing residents who are not citizens, from the age of 18. General elections held in Nov. 1984 marked the return to democracy after 11 years of presidential rule with military support. The new government took office on March 1, 1985 and the provisions of the 1967 Constitution now prevail.

The Republic is divided into 19 Departments each with a chief of police and a Departmental Council.

Production and Industry.—Wheat, barley, maize, linseed, sunflower seed and rice are cultivated. The wealth of the country is obtained from its pasturage, which supports large herds of cattle and sheep, the wool of which is of excellent quality. There are just under 11 million cattle and just under 21½ million sheep. In addition to meat packing, other foodstuffs, (citrus, wine, beer), fishing and textile industries are of importance.

The development of local industry continues and, in addition to the greatly augmented textile industry, marked expansion in local production is notable in respect of tyres, sheet-glass, three-ply wood, cement, leather-curing, beet-sugar, plastics, household consumer goods, edible oils and the refining of petroleum and petroleum products.

Mineral Deposits.—There are some ferrous minerals, not extracted at present. Non-ferrous exploited minerals include clinker, dolomite, marble and granite.

Communications.—There are about 9,899 km. of national highways, and about 12,083 km. of telegraph, with 48,375 miles of telephones.

There are about 2,987 km. of standard gauge railway in use in Uruguay. A State Autonomous Entity was formed to administer the railway systems purchased by the Government from four British companies in 1948.

An airline, PLUNA, which is owned by the State, runs daily services to southern Brazil, Paraguay and Argentina, and two flights a week to Madrid. The principal capitals of the interior and a limited freight service are connected to Montevideo by TAMU, another State owned airline, using principally military aircraft and personnel. International passenger and freight services are maintained by American, South American and European airlines. The international airport of Carrasco lies 12 miles outside Montevideo.

Education and Social Services.—Uruguay is one of the most advanced of the South American states, with old-age pensions, maternity and child welfare centres, accident insurance, etc. Primary education is compulsory and free, and technical and trade schools and evening courses for adult education are state controlled. There are about 322,053 pupils in the 2,362 state schools. The University at Montevideo (founded in 1849) has about 18,000 students enrolled in its ten faculties.

Language and Literature.—Spanish is the language of the Republic. Modern literature has provided some authors with international reputations and the literature of Spain is accessible in all public libraries. Five daily newspapers are published in Montevideo with an estimated total circulation of 150,000. Most of them are distributed throughout the country.

FINANCE

	1983	1984
	N$ million	
Revenue	29,486·4	39,796·7
Expenditure	36,897·4	55,473·3

The external debt at Dec. 1984 was U.S.$4,600 million. Central Bank reserves (March 31, 1985) were US$448·9 million.

Currency.—The monetary unit is the *peso* (N$). For sterling exchange see p. 82.

TRADE

	1983	1984
	U.S.$	
Total exports	1,044,500,000	924,588,000
Total imports	787,507,000	735,564,000

The major exports are meat and by-products, wool and by-products, hides and bristle and agricultural products. The principal imports are raw materials, construction materials, oils and lubricants, automotive vehicles, kits and machinery.

Trade with U.K.

	1983	1984
Imports from U.K.	£10,763,000	£13,980,000
Exports to U.K.	33,361,000	33,292,000

The principal export items to the U.K. are wool and beef, the main imports are chemicals, kits, machinery, raw materials and metals.

CAPITAL.—ΨMontevideo. Population (1984) 1,355,312. Other centres (with 1967 estimates) are ΨSalto (60,000), ΨPaysandu (60,000), ΨMercedes (34,000), Minas (34,000), Melo (30,000), and Rivera (40,000).

FLAG.—Four blue and five white horizontal stripes surcharged with sun on a white ground in the top corner, next flagstaff.

NATIONAL DAY.—August 25 (Declaration of Independence, 1825).

Time of transit from London to Montevideo, by air, 20–22 hours.

BRITISH EMBASSY
Calle Marco Bruto 1073 Montevideo

Ambassador Extraordinary and Plenipotentiary, His Excellency Charles William Wallace, C.M.G., C.V.O.
1st Secretaries, G. Finlayson; J. C. Lamb.
2nd Secretary, J. Waterton.
Defence Attaché, Col. R. Garnett, M.B.E.

BRITISH CONSULAR OFFICES

There is a British Consular Office at *Montevideo*.

ANGLO-URUGUAYAN CULTURAL INSTITUTE, San José 1426, Montevideo. There are branch Institutes throughout Uruguay.
BRITISH-URUGUAYAN CHAMBER OF COMMERCE, Avenida Labertador Brig. Gen., Lavalleja 1641, P2- OF 201, Montevideo.

THE VATICAN CITY STATE
(Stato della Città del Vaticano)

Sovereign Pontiff, His Holiness Pope John Paul II (Karol Wojtyla), *born* at Wadowice (Krakow, Poland), May 18, 1920, *elected* Pope (in succession to Pope John Paul I), Oct. 16, 1978.
Secretary of State, Cardinal Agostino Casaroli, *appointed* April, 1979.

Apostolic Pro Nuncio, new appointment awaited.
Counsellor, Mons. Rino Passigato.

The office of the ecclesiastical head of the Roman Catholic Church (Holy See) is vested in the Pope, the Sovereign Pontiff. For many centuries the Sovereign Pontiff exercised temporal power, but by 1870 the Papal States had become part of unified Italy. The temporal power of the Pope was in suspense until the treaty of Feb. 11, 1929, which recognized the full and independent sovereignty of the Holy See in the City of the Vatican. Accompanying the treaty were conventions regulating the condition of religion and the Catholic Church in Italy and finally settling the claims of the Holy See against Italy for the loss of temporal power. The area of the Vatican City is 108 acres and its population in 1978 was 731.

FLAG.—Square flag; equal vertical bands of yellow (next staff), and white; crossed keys and triple crown device on white band.

BRITISH EMBASSY TO THE HOLY SEE
91 Via Condotti, 00187 Rome

Ambassador Extraordinary and Plenipotentiary, His Excellency David Neil Lane, C.M.G., *apptd.* 1985.
1st Secretary, M. J. Long.

VENEZUELA
(La Republica de Venezuela)

President, Dr. Jaime Lusinchi, *elected* Dec. 4, 1983, *assumed office* Feb. 2, 1984.

COUNCIL OF MINISTERS

Interior, Dr. Octovio Lepage.
Foreign Affairs, Dr. Simon Alberto Consalvi.
Treasury, Dr. Manuel Azpúrua Arreaza.
Defence, Vice Adm. Andres Brito Martinez.
Development, Dr. Héctor Hurtado.
Education, Luis Carbonell.
Health and Social Welfare, Otto Hernandez Pieretti.
Agriculture and Livestock, Dr. Felipe Gómez Alvarez.
Labour, Dr. Simón Antoni Paván.
Transport and Communications, Dr. Juan Pedro Del Moral.
Justice, Sr. José Manzo González.
Mines and Energy, Dr. Arturo Hernández Grisanti.
Environment and Natural Resources, Juan Francisco Otaola.
Urban Development, Dr. Rafael Martín Guédez.
Youth, Dra. Milena Sardi de Selle.
Secretariat of the Presidency, Dr. Carmello Lauria.
Ministers of State, Leopoldo Carnevalli (*Co-ordination and Planning*); Carlos Rafael Silva (*Pres., Venezuelan Investment Fund*); Ignacio Iribarren Borges (*Culture*); Tulio Arens (*Science and Technology*); Manuel Pérez Guerrero (*International Economic Affairs*); Leopoldo Sucre Figarella (*Pres., Venezuelan Corporation of Guyana*); Miguel A. Contraez Laguado (*Governor of Federal District*).

VENEZUELAN EMBASSY IN LONDON
1 Cromwell Road, S.W.7
[01–584 4206]

Ambassador Extraordinary and Plenipotentiary, His Excellency Dr. Jose Luis Salcedo-Bastardo (1984).
Minister Counsellor, Sr. Hector Tarchetti.
Counsellors, Dr. Kaldone G. Nweihed; Srta. Milena Santana.

There is also a Consulate-General at *Liverpool.*

Area and Population.—A South American Republic, situated approximately between 0° 45′ S. lat. and 12° 12′ N. lat. and 59° 45′–73° 09′ W. long. It consists of one Federal District, 20 states and 2 territories. Venezuela has a total area of 352,143 sq. miles and a population (1983) of 17,257,000.

Venezuela lies on the north of the South American continent, and is bounded on the north by the Caribbean Sea, west by the Republic of Colombia, east by Guyana, and south by Brazil. Included in the area of the Republic are 72 islands off the coast, with a total area of about 14,650 square miles, the largest being *Margarita,* which is politically associated with Tortuga, Cubagua and Coche to form the State of *Nueva Esparta.* Margarita has an area of about 400 square miles.

Physical Features.—The Eastern Andes from the south-west cross the border and reach to the Caribbean Coast, where they are prolonged by the Maritime Andes of Venezuela to the Gulf of Paria on the north-east. The main range is known as the Sierra Nevada de Merida, and contains the highest peaks in the country in Pico Bolivar (16,411 feet) and Picacho de la Sierra (15,420 feet). Near the Brazilian border the Sierras Parima and Pacaraima, and on the eastern border the Sierras de Rincote and de Usupamo, enclose the republic with parallel northward spurs, between which are valleys of the Orinoco tributaries. The slopes of the mountains and foothills are covered with dense forests, but the basin of the Orinoco is mainly *llanos,* or level stretches of open prairie, with occasional woods.

The principal river is the *Orinoco,* with innumerable affluents, the main river exceeding 1,600 miles in length from its rise in the southern highlands of the republic to its outflow in the deltaic region of the north-east. The Orinoco is navigable for large steamers from its mouth for 700 miles, and by smaller vessels as far as the Maipures Cataract, some 200 miles farther up-stream. Dredging operations have opened the Orinoco to ocean-going ships, of up to 40 ft. draft, as far as Ciudad Guayana (about 150 miles up-stream). Among the many tributaries of the main stream are the Venturi, Apure (with its tributary the Portuguesa), Arauca, Meta, and Guaviare from the west, the Meta and Guaviare being principally Colombian rivers. The upper waters of the Orinoco are united with those of the Rio Negro (a Brazilian tributary of the Amazon) by a natural river or canal, known as the *Casiquiare.*

The coastal regions of Venezuela are much indented and contain many lagoons and lakes, of which *Maracaibo*, with an area of 8,296 square miles, is the largest lake in South America. Other lakes are Zulia (290 square miles), south-west of Maracaibo, and Valencia (216 square miles) about 1,400 ft. above sea-level in the Maritime Andes. The *llanos* also contain lakes and swamps caused by the river floods, but they are dry in summer seasons.

The climate is tropical and, except where modified by altitude or tempered by sea breezes, is unhealthy, particularly in the coastal regions and in the neighbourhood of lowland streams and lagoons. The hot, wet season lasts from April to October, the dry, cooler season from November to March.

Language and Literature.—Spanish is the language of the country. There are 61 daily newspapers in Venezuela, of which ten are published in Caracas, and about 60 to 70 weekly news magazines. There are also a large number of fortnightly, monthly and quarterly publications.

Education is free and compulsory between the ages of 7 and 13. There are ten universities in Venezuela, five in Caracas and the others in Maracaibo, Mérida, Valencia, Cumaná and Barquisimeto.

Production and Industry.—Products of the tropical forest region include: orchids, wild rubber, timber, mangrove bark, balata gum and tonka beans: of agricultural areas, cocoa beans, coffee, cotton, rice, maize, sugar, sesame, groundnuts, potatoes, tomatoes, other vegetables, sisal and tobacco. There is an extensive beef and dairy farming industry. Despite substantial improvements in agriculture, Venezuela is heavily reliant upon food imports, which constitute about 60 per cent of total consumption.

The principal industry is that of petroleum, which in 1981 contributed 95 per cent of Venezuela's foreign exchange income. Daily production in the oilfields (nationalized 1976) has steadily declined since 1973 in line with Venezuela's conservation policies, reaching 2·1 million barrels a day (average) in 1981 (1973—3·366 mbd). There are refineries at Punta Cardon, Amuay, Caripitó, San Lorenzo, Puerto La Cruz, Tucupeido, El Chaure and El Palito. Development of the Orinoco heavy oil belt is now moving ahead with the inauguration of the Lagovén continuous steam injection pilot plant at El Jobo in southern Monagas. It has been estimated conservatively that there might exist recoverable resources of 70,000 million barrels in the Orinoco region, but the initial aim of the Lagovén project is the production of 125,000 and 500,000 bpd of up-graded crude by 1988 and 2000 respectively.

Aluminium is the second highest source of foreign exchange after petroleum. The Venezuelan state now holds the majority stake in both the principal producing companies, Venalum and Alcasa, and is moving towards a consolidation of the aluminium industry, with both companies sharing their resources and adopting general policies of marketing and procurement of supplies. Output in 1980 was 222,100 tons, with 151,250 tons exported.

Rich iron ore deposits in Eastern Venezuela have been developed. Secondary processes for pelletizing and briqueting ore for export have been installed. The government-owned steel mill at Matanzas in the Guayana uses local iron ore and obtains its electric power from hydro-electric installations on the Caroni River. It produces seamless steel tubes, billets, wire and profiles. The production of more steel products is planned over the next few years. A mill at Ciudad Guayana for the production of centrifugally-cast iron pipe came into operation at the end of 1970, with an annual capacity of 30,000 tons. It is planned to increase steel production to 15,000,000 tons a year by 1985.

Other industries include petrochemicals, gold, diamonds and asbestos; textiles, clothing and footwear; plastics; manufacture or preparation of foodstuffs, alcoholic and non-alcoholic beverages; manufacture of paper, cement, glass, tyres, cigarettes, soap, animal feeding concentrates, simple steel products, tins, jewellery, rope, furniture, sacks, paint and motor-vehicle assembly; preparation of pharmaceutical goods; pearl fishing, sanitary ware, electric home appliances, pumps, toys, agricultural machinery, bicycles, electronic components, cosmetics and many others.

Communications.—There are about 62,449 km. of roads, 22,975 km. of them paved. The State has now acquired all but a very few of the railway lines, whose total length is only some 372 kilometres. Road and river communications have made railways of negligibile importance in Venezuela except for carrying iron ore in the south-east. However, the government is restoring the Puerto Cabello-Barquisimeto line and expanding it to Turén in the agricultural heartland of Venezuela. A new line connecting Caracas with La Guaira and the Litoral is planned, and in 1983 the Caracas Metro came into operation. British, U.S. and European airlines provide Venezuela with a wide range of services. There are three Venezuelan airlines (two of them state-owned) which between them have a comprehensive network of internal lines and also connect Caracas with the United States, Central and South America, the Caribbean and Europe. Foreign vessels are not permitted to engage in the coast trade. The telegraph, radio-telegraph and radio-telephone services are state-owned. There are two government-controlled, 150 commercial and one cultural, FM, broadcasting stations. There are four television stations in Venezuela, all in Caracas. Two are government controlled.

TRADE

	1983
Total imports	US$6,115 m
Total exports	16,180 m

Trade with U.K.

	1983	1984
Imports from U.K.	£87,937,000	£102,400,000
Exports to U.K.	183,731,000	253,770,000

CAPITAL.—Caracas (3,000 ft.). Population, 1979, 3,507,800. Other principal towns are ΨMaracaibo (870,000), Barquisimeto (495,000), Valencia (495,000), Maracay (322,000), San Cristobal (164,000), Cumaná (135,000) and Ciudad Guayana (250,000).

FLAG.—Three horizontal bands, yellow, blue, red (with seven white stars on blue band and coat of arms next staff on yellow band).

NATIONAL DAY.—July 5.

BRITISH EMBASSY
Apartado 1246, Caracas 1010-A.

Ambassador Extraordinary and Plenipotentiary, His Excellency Michael John Newington, C.M.G., *apptd.* 1985.

Counsellor, W. Quantrill *(Head of Chancery)*.
Defence Attaché, Capt. J. B. Lean, R.N.

BRITISH CONSULAR OFFICES

There are British Consular Offices at *Caracas, Maracaibo, Puerto La Cruz* and *Valencia*.

British Council Representative, J. W. Daniel, Aparto 1246, Caracas 1010.

BRITISH-VENEZUELAN CHAMBER OF COMMERCE, Apartado 5713 Edificio Blandin, Piso I Oficina I-C, Plaza Chacaito, Caracas.

VIETNAM
(Socialist Republic of Vietnam)

President, Truong Chinh.

Prime Minister, Pham Van Dong.

Deputy Premiers, Pham Hung; Vo Nguyen Giap; Do Muoi, To Huu, Vu Dinh Lieu, Tran Phuong, Dong Si Nguyen, Tran Quynh, Vo Van Kiet (*Chairman of State Planning Commission*).

EMBASSY IN LONDON
12–14 Victoria Road, W8 5RD
[01–937 1912–8564]

Ambassador Extraordinary and Plenipotentiary, His Excellency Dang Nghiem Bai (1982).

3rd Secretary, Le Van Bang.

Attaches, Pham Binh Man; Pham Binh Minh; Bui Minh Dung; Miss. Nguyen Thi Nguyet Nga.

Vietnam, with an area of 129,000 square miles, and an estimated population (1984) of 60,000,000, is bordered on the north by China and the west by Laos and Cambodia (For MAP, *see* INDEX).

Government.—Following the end of the war in Vietnam in 1975, and the establishment of a Provisional Revolutionary Government to administer South Vietnam, a National Assembly representing the whole of Vietnam was elected on April 25, 1976. The Assembly met in Hanoi on June 24, and on July 2 approved the reunification of North and South Vietnam under the name of the Socialist Republic of Vietnam. The national flag, anthem and capital of North Vietnam were unanimously adopted for the Socialist Republic, and Saigon was renamed Ho Chi Minh City.

A new constitution was adopted in December 1980. The elected National Assembly elects a Council of

Ministers and a Council of State which combines the functions of President and Standing Committee of the National Assembly.

Economy.—During the last five years, Vietnam's economy has faced considerable problems. These include harvest failures as a result of climatic disasters, reductions in foreign aid, border hostilities and the continued allocation of resources to military expenditure. Efforts to integrate the economies of the North and South have not been very successful.

A modest recovery was noted in 1981. Food production reached 15 m tons. Production of light industrial goods rose by 7 per cent over 1980 but other sectors stagnated. In 1983 real GDP is estimated to have risen by about 6 per cent, compared with about 8 per cent in 1982. In the same year exports were estimated at U.S.$538 m and imports at U.S.$1,240 m, leaving a substantial trade gap. The 1981–85 Five Year Plan was finalised in late 1982 and provided for more modest targets than previous Plans.

Trade with U.K.

	1983	1984
Imports from U.K.	£951,000	£1,787,000
Exports to U.K.	603,000	1,154,000

CAPITAL.—Hanoi (population (1984), City, 925,000; Province, 2,800,000).

FLAG.—Red, with yellow five-point star in centre.

NATIONAL DAY.—September 2.

BRITISH EMBASSY
16 Pho Ly Thuong Kiet, Hanoi

Ambassador Extraordinary and Plenipotentiary, His Excellency Richard Gilbert Tallboys, C.M.G., O.B.E., *apptd.* 1985.
Head of Chancery and H.M. Consul, M. J. H. Wood.

YEMEN (North)
(Yemen Arab Republic)

President and Commander of the Armed Forces, Col. Ali Abdullah Saleh, *elected* July 19, 1978, *re-elected* May 23, 1983.
Prime Minister, Maj. Abdul Aziz al Ghani.
Deputy Prime Minister for Internal Affairs, Lt.-Col. Mujahid Abu Shuwarib.
Deputy Prime Minister and Foreign Minister, Dr. Abdel Karim Ali al-Iryani.

YEMEN EMBASSY
41 South Street, W1Y 5PD
[01–629 9905]

Ambassador Extraordinary and Plenipotentiary, His Excellency Ahmed Daifellah Alazeib (1981).

Yemen, the *Arabia Felix* of the ancients, occupies the S.W. corner of Arabia between the kingdom of Saudi Arabia and the People's Democratic Republic of Yemen, with an estimated area of 75,000 square miles and a population of about 8,556,974 including about 1,396,123 emigrant workers in the Arabian peninsula and elsewhere, including the U.K. The highlands and central plateau of Yemen, and the highest portions of the maritime range, form the most fertile part of Arabia, with an abundant but irregular rainfall.

The ruins of Marib, the ancient Sabæan capital, and its dam are in the Yemen.

Government.—A General Popular Conference was established in Aug. 1982, consisting of 700 elected members and 300 appointed members. It agreed a new National Charter and elected a Permanent Council of 75 members (50 elected, 25 appointed), with a General Council and four sub-committees (eco-

nomic; political; administrative and public works; cultural and reform).

The General Popular Conference meets every two years and is re-elected every four. The Permanent Council meets regularly for two months, followed by a two-month break. The General Council and sub-committees meet regularly.

Trade.—The main exports are cotton, coffee, hides and skins.

Trade with U.K.

	1983	1984
Imports from U.K.	£56,313,000	£58,761,000
Exports to U.K.	1,857,000	2,536,000

CAPITAL.—Sana'a (pop. 277,817). Other main cities are Taiz (119,572) and Hodeida (126,386).

FLAG.—Horizontal bands of red, white and black, with 5-point green star in centre of white band.

BRITISH EMBASSY
P.O. Box 1287, Sana'a

Ambassador Extraordinary and Plenipotentiary, His Excellency David Everard Tatham (1984).
1st Secretaries, J. Dando (*Head of Chancery and Aid*); J. D. Orr (*Commercial*); D. J. Baker.
British Council Representative, P. J. Chenery, Beit Al-Mottahar, Harat Handhal (P.O. Box 2157), Sana'a.

YEMEN (South)
(People's Democratic Republic of Yemen)

President, Ali Nasser Mohammed, *assumed power* April 1980.
Prime Minister, Haider Abu Bakr al Attas.
Deputy Prime Ministers, Ali Abdel Razzaq Badib; Dr. Yasin Said Numan (*Fisheries Resources*).

EMBASSY
57 Cromwell Road, SW7 2ED
[01–584 6607/9]

Ambassador Extraordinary and Plenipotentiary, His Exellency Saleh Abdulla Muthana (1983).

Area and Population.—The Democratic Republic of Yemen lies at the southern end of the Arabian peninsula, having a frontier with the Yemen Arab Republic, Saudi Arabia and the Sultanate of Oman, and a coastline extending 700 miles from the Red Sea eastwards along the Gulf of Aden. The area is largely composed of mountains and desert. Rainfall is generally scarce and unpredictable. The population outside Aden is concentrated in the fertile districts. In the more extensive desert and near-desert areas nomadic communities depend on their livestock for a livelihood.

Included in the State are the offshore islands of Perim (in the Bab al-Mandeb Straits) and Socotra. Sovereignty over the island of Kamaran (area 70 sq. miles) in the Red Sea is under dispute following its occupation by forces of the Yemen Arab Republic during border conflicts in October, 1972. The area of the People's Democratic Republic is 112,000 sq. miles, with a population (1981 estimate) of 2,030,000.

Government.—The People's Republic of South Yemen was set up on Nov. 30, 1967 when the British government ceded power to the National Liberation Front, thus bringing to an end 129 years of British rule in Aden and some years of protectorate status in the hinterland. Its name was changed to People's Democratic Republic of Yemen on Nov. 30, 1970. Territory of the Republic is that of the former Federation of South Arabia and the Aden Protectorates, consisting of the State of Aden and some 17 sultanates and emirates. It is now divided into six

Governorates. Under a constitution promulgated on Nov. 30, 1970, a Supreme People's Council of 101 members was appointed in May, 1971. Elections to a new council (112 strong) took place from 16–18 December 1978. At its first plenary session, on Dec. 27, the SPC appointed an 11-member Presidium to replace the five-man Presidential Council. The Chairman of the Presidium is head of state.

The Government receives substantial development from the World Bank, Kuwait and Abu Dhabi (Arab Development Funds). Other aid is provided by China, the E.E.C., U.S.S.R. (including military aid) and other Socialist Bloc countries.

Production.—Agriculture is the main occupation of the inhabitants outside Aden town. This is largely of a subsistence nature, sorghum, sesame and millets being the chief crops, with wheat and barley widely grown at the higher elevations. Disastrous floods in 1983 caused major damage to the principal agricultural areas.

Yemen is not an oil producing country but significant traces of hydrocarbons were found during exploration activities offshore in 1982. The Aden Refinery Company has a refining capacity of 8 m. tons per annum but for a number of years throughput has not exceeded a rate equivalent to 5 m. tons annually.

Under the Five Year Development Plan 1974–79 much importance was attached to the development of agricultural and fisheries projects. Under the second Five Year Plan (1981–85) emphasis has shifted to industrial development, which has been allocated 29 per cent of the total investment budget (YD508m); agricultural development has been allocated 12 per cent. Light industries are being established which will replace imports and use locally produced raw materials.

Communications.—Following the closure of the Suez Canal in 1967 the once prosperous trading economy of Aden fell into a steady decline, which has not been reversed by the re-opening of the Canal. In the main harbour, cargo handling for larger vessels is by lighter, but wharves at Maalla can accommodate alongside vessels up to 300 feet in length and 18 feet in draught.

There are no railways in the Republic. Yemen has 760 miles of good roads and construction of a further 300 miles is in hand. A system of undeveloped but motorable roads links the towns and villages outside Aden. There is an international airport at Aden (Khormaksar) into which a limited number of international airlines operate.

Finance and Currency.—During 1977 revenue was estimated at about £51,000,000 and expenditure £68,000,000. Currency is the South Yemen *dinar* (YD).

Trade with U.K.

	1983	1984
Imports from U.K.	£36,673,000	£45,221,000
Exports to U.K.	10,627,000	18,238,000

CAPITAL.—Aden (population, 270,000). Other towns are Shaikh Othman, Mukalla and Maalla.

FLAG.—A tricolour, red, white and black horizontal bands, with a triangle of light blue at the hoist pointing towards the fly and charged with a five pointed red star.

NATIONAL DAYS.—Independence Day, Nov. 30; Revolution Day, Oct. 14.

BRITISH EMBASSY
Khormaksar, Aden.

Ambassador Extraordinary and Plenipotentiary, His Excellency Peter Keegan Williams (1982).

YUGOSLAVIA
(Socijalistička Federativna Republika Jugoslavije)

President of the Presidency (1985–86), Radovan Vlajković (*Vojvodina*).
Vice-President of the Presidency (1985–86), Sinan Hasani (*Kosovo*).
Members of the Presidency, Lazar Mojsov (*Macedonia*); Branko Mikulić (*Bosnia/Hercegovina*); Stane Dolanc (*Slovenia*); Nikola Ljubičić (*Serbia*); Josip Vrhovec (*Croatia*); Veselin Djuranović (*Montenegro*); Vidoje Žarković (*L.C.Y.*).

FEDERAL EXECUTIVE COUNCIL

President, Milka Planinc.
Vice-Presidents, Borislav Srebrić; Mijat Šuković; Janez Zemljaric.
Foreign Affairs, Raif Dizdarević.
National Defence, Branko Mamula.
Internal Affairs, Dobroslav Ćulafić.
Finance, Vlado Klemenčić.
Foreign Trade, Dr. Milenko Bojanić.
Trade and General Economic Affairs, Siniša Korica.
Justice and Organization of Federal Administration, Borislav Krajina.
Information, Aleksandar Petković (*acting*).
  Federal Committee Presidents:—
Energy and Industry, Rade Pavlović.
Agriculture, Milorad Stanojević.
Transport and Communications, Mustafa Pljakić.
Labour, Health and Social Security, Djordje Jakovljević.
Questions concerning War Veterans and Disabled Veterans, Jovko Jovkovski.
Legislature, Janko Česnik.
  Other F.E.C. members, Ljubomir Baban; Boro Denkov; Jernej Jan; Živorad Kovačević; Nedeljko Mandić; Spasoje Medenica; Mito Pejovski; Jon Srbovan; Ante Sučić; Rikard Stajner; Dimitrije Tasić.

President of the SFRY Assembly, Ilijaz Kurteši.
President of the Socialist Alliance of the Working People, Aleksandar Grličkov.

LEAGUE OF COMMUNISTS OF YUGOSLAVIA

Presidency of the Central Committee
President of the Presidency, Vidoje Žarković (*elected for one year in June* 1985).
Secretary, Dimce Belovski (*elected for two years in June* 1984).
Members, M. Andrić; J. Bilić; D. Dragosavać; K. Hadzivasilev; G. Jovičic; M. Kučan; A. Marinc; D. Marković; P. Matić; M. Orlandić; M. Pancevski; H. Pozderać; M. Radović; M. Ribičić; K. Široka; I. Stambolić; N. Stojanovic; D. Stojšić; A. Šukrija; M. Spiljak; D. Vidić.

YUGOSLAV EMBASSY IN LONDON
5–7 Lexham Gardens W8 5JJ
[01–370 6105/9]

Ambassador Extraordinary and Plenipotentiary, His Excellency Mitko Čalovski (1985).
Minister Counsellors, Milutin Stojanović; Predrag Mitic (*Economic*).
Counsellors, Mario Mikolic (*Press and Culture*); Ivan Plese (*Consular*).
Defence Attaché, Capt. Uros Trbojevic.

Area and Population.—Yugoslavia is a Federation comprising the Socialist Republics of Serbia, Croatia, Slovenia, Montenegro, Bosnia and Herzegovina, and Macedonia. Serbia includes the Socialist Autono-

mous Provinces of Vojvodina and Kosovo. The area of Yugoslavia is estimated at 255,804 square kilometres (98,725 square miles). The population was estimated (1983) at 22,800,000; the latest Census (April 1981) broke down the population into 8,140,000 Serbs, 4,430,000 Croats, 1,750,000 Slovenes, 1,730,000 Albanians, 1,341,000 Macedonians and 1,220,000 "Yugoslavs", as well as a variety of other minorities.

Government.—On Nov. 29, 1945, the Constituent Assembly of Yugoslavia at a joint session of the Skupština and the House of Nationalities, proclaimed Yugoslavia a Republic.

The official name of the country, "The Socialist Federal Republic of Yugoslavia", was adopted by the 1963 Constitution.

Several amendments to the Constitution were made in 1971. The most important formed a new ruling body called the Presidency, which has 8 members, one from each Republic and Autonomous Province. Since the death of President Tito in May 1980, its members take it in turns according to a fixed order of succession to become President of the Presidency of the Republic for a period of 12 months each. A new Constitution was proclaimed in 1974 followed by the reconstitution of the Federal Assembly into two chambers consisting of the Federal Chamber (220 delegates) and the Republican/Provincial Chamber (88 delegates). A new Federal Executive Council (i.e. government) was also formed. The current Council was elected in May 1982 with a 4 year mandate. The first election of the S.F.R.Y. Presidency since Pres. Tito's death took place in May 1984; each new member has a five-year mandate.

There is only one political party in Yugoslavia, the "League of Communists of Yugoslavia" (within which each Republic and Province has its own separate L.C.Y. organization) but there is a formal separation of State and Party; no-one may hold a post in the Federal or Republican/Provincial governments and a paid L.C.Y. post simultaneously. Political and economic decisions on many issues are devolved from Federal to Republican/Provincial level. Yugoslavia has a "self-management" form of industrial organization under which the workforce have the constitutional right to own and control their own enterprises.

Defence.—The Army, Navy and Air Force on a peace footing consist of 250,000 officers and men.

Religion and Education.—The three main religions are the Orthodox, Catholic and Islamic, and freedom to practice is constitutionally guaranteed. Religion is separated from the State and no religious instruction is allowed in state schools, although it is permitted in churches.

Education.—Eight years' elementary education is compulsory and all education is free. There are 18 universities.

Language and Literature.—The language mainly used throughout Yugoslavia and in the Federal Government is Serbo-Croat but Slovenian and Macedonian (also South-Slav tongues) and Albanian, Bulgarian, Rumanian, Italian, Slovak, Ruthenian, Hungarian and Turkish are also spoken in certain areas. There is, however, no official language since all are constitutionally equal, except in the Armed Forces where Serbo Croat is obligatory. In Serbia, Macedonia and Montenegro the Cyrillic script is used and in the rest of the country the Latin. There are 4 Serbian daily newspapers in Belgrade, 2 Slovene dailies in Ljubljana, 2 Croat dailies in Zagreb, and many other dailies published in other towns. There are also many local newspapers and radio programmes in the different "minority" languages.

Production and Industry.—The share of industry in Gross Domestic Product (average annual rate in real terms of 6·5 per cent in 1981) is now 40 per cent, while agriculture is 14 per cent. In industry the high level of investment of recent years is being cut back and present efforts are directed towards development of high priority areas such as mining, energy resources and transport and communications. Agricultural policy is directed towards substantially increased production, to make the the country self-sufficient and to provide significant exports of foodstuffs. Some 80 per cent of land is still privately owned.

The main crops are wheat, maize, sugar beet, sunflower and soya. Yields in 1983 were (tons): wheat, 5·5 m; maize, 10·7 m; sugar beet, 5·6 m. According to Yugoslav official estimates, the livestock population in 1983 was approximately as follows: cattle, 5,351,000; sheep, 7,452,000; pigs, 8,370,000; poultry, 69,680,000.

Minerals are an important source of wealth particularly in the central and south eastern regions. Production in 1983 included the following (tons):—

Coal	57,900,000
Coke	3,440,000
Iron ore	5,090,000
Pig iron	2,870,000
Steel	4,165,000
Crude oil	4,130,000

Smaller quantities of copper, zinc and mercury are produced.

Communications.—In 1982 there were 9,389 kms of standard and narrow gauge railway and approximately 115,200 kms of classified roads. In 1982 there were 2,542,000 telephones in use in the country. The principal Ψports on the long Adriatic seaboard of Yugoslavia are Rijeka, Bakar, Šibenik, Split, Zadar, Kardeljeva (formerly Ploče), Dubrovnik, Bar, Kotor (Cattaro) and Koper. The Danube forms a great commercial highway and the tributary rivers Sava and Tisa provide other shipping routes.

FINANCE

	1982 million *Dinars*	1983 million *Dinars*
Revenue	1,068,000	1,140,000
Expenditure	1,068,000	1,140,000

The rate of exchange is variable. On June 6, 1980 the *dinar* was devalued against all convertible currencies and there have been several devaluations since then. (*See also* p. 82.)

Trade with U.K.

	1983	1984
Imports from U.K.......	£148,646,000	£163,871,000
Exports to U.K.	83,951,000	108,479,000

CAPITAL.—Belgrade, population (1981) 1,455,000. Other towns are Zagreb (763,000); Skopje (503,000); Ljubljana (253,000); Sarajevo (447,000); Novi Sad (169,000); Priština (1971) (153,000); Ψ Split (152,000); Ψ Rijeka (133,000); Titograd (95,000).

FLAG.—Five-point red star outlined by narrow yellow stripe, on a ground of three horizontal bars, blue, white and red.

NATIONAL DAY.—November 29.

BRITISH EMBASSY
General Ždanova 46, Belgrade.

Ambassador Extraordinary and Plenipotentiary, His Excellency Andrew Marley Wood, *apptd.* 1985.

Counsellor, P. Yarnold.

Defence and Military Attaché, Col. E. J. Everett-Heath.

Naval and Air Attaché, Wg. Cdr. A. J. Harris, M.B.E.

1st Secretaries, M. J. S. Allen (*Economic*); F. B. Holroyd (*Admin. and Consular*); G. M. Johnston (*Commercial*).

Attachés, D. Snape; E. Newton.

2nd Secretary, M. J. L. Kirk (*Chancery and Information*).

BRITISH CONSULAR OFFICES

There are British Consular Offices at *Belgrade, Zagreb* and *Split.*

British Council Representative, D. Gunton, Generala Ždanova 34, (P.O. Box 248), 11001 Belgrade. British Council Reading Room, Knez Mihajlova 45, Belgrade. There are also a centre and library at Zagreb.

ZAIRE
(The Republic of Zaire)

President of the Republic and National Security, Marshal Mobuto Sésé Séko, *born* Oct. 30, 1930; *assumed office* November 25, 1965; *elected* Nov. 5, 1970; *re-elected for third term,* July 28, 1984.

Premier, Kengo wa Dondo.

Internal Affairs, Mozagba Ngbuka.

Foreign Affairs, Mokola wa Mpombo.

Finance, Djamboleka Loma Okitangana.

Economy and Industry, Tshibambe Kabambe.

Agriculture, Bokana w'Ondangela.

Mines and Energy, Umba Kyamitala.

External Trade, Lengema Dulia Yubassa.

ZAIRE EMBASSY
26 Chesham Place, SW1X 8HG
[01–235 6137]

Ambassador Extraordinary and Plenipotentiary, His Excellency C. Mukamba (Kadiata Nzemba) (1984).

The State of the Congo, founded in 1885, became a Belgian Colony on Nov. 15, 1908, and was administered by Belgium until 1960, when it became the Democratic Republic of the Congo. In October 1971 the name changed to the Republic of Zaire. Situated between long. 12°–31° E. and lat. 5° N.–13° S., the Republic of Zaire comprises an area of 905,582 sq. miles, with a population (1982 estimate) of 29,950,000.

Climate.—Apart from the coastal district in the West which is fairly dry, the rainfall averages between 60 and 80 inches. The average temperature is about 80° F., but in the South the winter temperature can fall nearly to freezing point. There has been some increase in sleeping-sickness since

independence. Malaria, formerly under control in Kinshasa and Matadi, has also begun to increase.

Extensive forest covers the central districts.

Government.—On June 30, 1960, the Belgian Congo became an independent unitary state under the Presidency of M. Kasavubu with a provisional constitution drawn up by the metropolitan Belgian Parliament. On July 11, M. Moise Tshombe announced the independence of the State of Katanga although he failed to obtain international recognition. Katanga did not come under the Government at Leopoldville until January 14, 1963.

The constitutional and political situation remained unsettled, the United Nations having mixed forces in the country until 1964. By the middle of 1965, the Congolese Government formed by M. Tshombe in July, 1964, had succeeded in gaining control of all the towns from the rebels and depriving them of military aid from outside the Congo. Gen. Joseph-Désiré Mobutu, Commander-in-Chief of the Congolese National Army, announced on November 25, 1965 that he had assumed the Presidency.

A Presidential régime was instituted by the 1967 Constitution, subsequently amended in 1974 and totally revised in Feb. 1978. The Mouvement Populaire de la Révolution is the sole political party. The President changed his name to Mobutu Sésé Séko Kuku Ngbendu Wa Za Banga in 1972, but is usually known by the first three of these names only.

Provinces.—There are 8 regions, each under a Governor and provincial administration (names of capitals in brackets) Bas-Zaire (*Matadi*); Bandundu (*Bandundu*); Equateur (*Mbandaka*); Haut-Zaire (*Kisangani*); Kivu (*Bukavu*); Shaba, *formerly* Katanga (*Lubumbashi*); East Kasai (*Mbuji-Mayi*); West Kasai (*Kananga*).

Language, Religion and Education.—The people are mainly of Bantu-Negro stock, divided into semi-autonomous tribes, each speaking a Bantu tongue. Swahili, a Bantu dialect with an admixture of Arabic, is the nearest approach to a common language in the East and South, while Lingala is the language of a large area along the river and in the north, and Kikongo of the region between Kinshasa and the sea. French is the language of administration. It is estimated there are 9,500,000 African Christians in the Republic (Roman Catholic 5,800,000, Protestant 1,600,000). The local Kimbanguist religion has over two million adherents. The National University of Zaire has campuses in Kinshasa, Kisangani and Lubumbashi, with approximately 28,000 students (1978–79).

Production.—The cultivation of oil palms is widespread, palm oil being the most important agricultural cash product though it is no longer exported. Coffee, rubber, cocoa and timber are the most important agricultural exports. The production of cotton, pyrethrum and copal fell sharply on independence but is now increasing. The country is rich in minerals, particularly Shaba (*ex*-Katanga) province. Copper is widely exploited, and industrial diamonds and cobalt are also produced. Oil deposits are exploited off the Zaire estuary and reef-gold is mined in the north-east of the country.

There is a wide variety of small secondary industries, the main products being: cotton fabrics, blankets, sacks, footwear, beer, cigarettes, cement, paint, sugar, furniture, metal goods and tyres, and local assembly of motor vehicles. There are very large reserves of hydro-electric power and the huge Inga dam on the river Zaire is now supplying electricity to Matadi, Kinshasa and Shaba.

The chief exports are copper, crude oil, coffee, diamonds, rubber, cobalt, gold, cassiterite, zinc and other metals.

Communications. There are approximately 20,500 km of roads (earth-surfaced) of national importance, and 6,000 km of railways. The country has two international and 40 principal airports.

Currency.—The unit of currency is the *Zaire*.

Trade with U.K.

	1983	1984
Imports from U.K.	£21,128,512	£36,254,000
Exports to U.K.	11,192,157	7,720,000

CAPITAL.—Kinshasa (*formerly* Leopoldville), population (estimated, 1980) 2,500,000. Principal towns, Lubumbashi (*formerly* Elisabethville) (403,623); Kisangani (*formerly* Stanleyville) (310,705); Likasi (146,394); Kananga (601,239); Ψ Matadi (143,598); and Mbandaka (134,495).

FLAG.—Dark brown hand and torch with red flame in yellow roundel on green background.

NATIONAL DAY.—November 24.

BRITISH EMBASSY
B.P. 8049, Kinshasa.

Ambassador Extraordinary and Plenipotentiary, His Excellency Patrick Howard Charles Caines Eyers, C.M.G., L.V.O., *apptd.* 1985.
1*st Secretary*, M. R. Crompton.
2*nd Secretary*, J. McGoran (*Commercial and Vice-Consul*).
3*rd Secretary*, J. D. Bevan.

U.K. TRADE OVERSEAS (£'000)

	1983		1984	
	Imports	Exports	Imports	Exports
Benelux*	8,231,668	8,013,374	9,839,092	9,179,713
Denmark	1,512,620	1,159,184	1,660,447	1,197,381
Faroe Islands	15,932	2,332	17,649	5,140
France	5,043,118	5,651,521	5,885,715	7,082,389
W. Germany	9,667,444	6,063,989	11,090,227	7,458,042
Greece	164,917	280,204	279,367	354,332
Rep. of Ireland	2,290,067	3,055,275	2,635,039	3,393,499
Italy	3,188,219	2,292,788	3,814,163	2,902,666
E.E.C.—Total	30,098,053	26,516,335	35,204,049	31,568,022
Afghanistan	19,837	10,310	20,776	11,892
Albania	240	2,983	1,097	4,481
Algeria	157,645	233,426	274,155	272,438
Andorra	381	6,533	19	9,228
Angola	45,732	22,847	158,636	35,581
Anguilla	—	—	14	896
Antigua	1,718	10,465	820	22,670
Argentina	194	4,472	65	5,232
Australia	552,642	940,279	612,087	1,186,521
Austria	438,446	273,702	529,620	320,901
Bahamas	24,013	17,815	38,478	220,356
Bahrain	37,488	150,264	28,240	138,614
Bangladesh	25,189	50,979	46,506	51,591
Barbados	11,899	31,938	22,509	30,654
Belize	11,565	8,726	15,911	11,501
Benin	2,887	10,577	2,101	6,829
Bermuda	4,019	24,924	3,037	22,843
Bhutan	—	99	—	86
Bolivia	14,834	4,711	20,052	17,170
Botswana	21,713	3,250	14,913	9,015
Brazil	560,277	157,758	637,702	238,717
Brit. Indian Ocean Terr.	7	714	52	206
Brunei	27,154	106,477	21,966	122,651
Bulgaria	12,355	44,577	17,345	55,917
Burkina Faso	1,514	3,048	3,695	2,065
Burma	4,726	21,927	6,420	16,488
Burundi	3,485	3,155	1,924	1,710
Cameroon	52,481	26,445	132,539	23,254
Canada	1,552,187	968,269	1,617,476	1,183,231
Cape Verde	122	1,246	211	1,162
Cayman Is.	610	4,046	12,911	4,905
Central African Rep.	902	536	357	722
Chad	8	2,244	626	3,531
Chile	107,644	43,520	108,420	74,997
China	231,417	159,722	278,474	317,256
Colombia	56,458	51,023	80,387	43,485
The Comoros	278	597	236,	316
Congo	4,335	9,560	1,958	6,207
Cook Is.	144	197	9	165
Costa Rica	22,299	11,041	21,248	9,138
Cuba	14,010	45,737	13,020	64,377
Cyprus	87,436	127,837	94,381	146,773
Czechoslovakia	101,302	69,456	117,188	78,075
Djibouti	184	7,712	59	8,896
Dominica	12,251	7,653	14,961	8,359
Dominican Rep.	6,662	11,594	5,620	12,535
Ecuador	11,022	35,008	12,951	34,323
Egypt	79,826	370,489	164,946	427,688
El Salvador	425	7,653	2,551	7,589
Equatorial Guinea	13	10	559	553
Ethiopia	12,071	34,092	13,733	63,434
Falkland Is.	4,022	7,269	5,202	9,516
Fiji	46,943	12,184	70,209	11,281
Finland	996,017	539,721	1,248,561	684,477
French Guyana	853	897	795	3,106
French Polynesia	93	2,601	2	3,276
Gabon	66,135	18,798	70,775	20,548
Gambia	3,781	13,261	3,407	10,233
German Dem. Rep.	167,625	50,997	198,130	92,270

* Belgium, Luxembourg and the Netherlands

	1983		1984	
	Imports	Exports	Imports	Exports
Ghana	58,192	82,234	61,561	82,897
Gibraltar	4,266	26,495	5,333	31,978
Greenland	3,114	140	3,983	99
Grenada	5,387	7,293	5,703	8,319
Guadeloupe	587	2,124	317	2,750
Guatemala	9,764	7,440	9,565	10,660
Guinea	668	7,190	1,171	6,469
Guinea-Bissau	94	477	—	499
Guyana	42,810	13,685	57,884	14,845
Haiti	1,646	4,171	1,402	3,736
Honduras	7,082	9,539	12,360	7,382
Hong Kong	1,178,343	726,711	1,266,965	8.7,419
Hungary	53,834	91,845	75,905	100,502
Iceland	66,505	65,176	86,104	64,242
India	366,928	804,779	571,470	780,997
Indonesia	169,454	193,642	181,490	186,732
Iran	100,545	629,980	368,572	703,097
Iraq	30,334	400,259	69,047	343,120
Israel	314,148	354,860	392,757	393,025
Ivory Coast	79,255	25,591	93,875	25,347
Jamaica	94,036	116,188	77,895	48,088
Japan	3,355,450	797,848	3,768,019	925,311
Jordan	28,680	262,503	18,114	192,508
Kampuchea	184	826	72	635
Kenya	128,464	111,249	203,243	176,061
Kiribati	42	371	20	401
Korea, North	362	2,527	458	2,935
Korea, South	440,354	168,942	443,819	219,406
Kuwait	67,281	333,273	141,606	301,520
Laos	56	626	238	721
Lebanon	11,521	81,435	6,869	76,223
Lesotho	216	2,080	78	1,633
Liberia	7,181	13,877	6,975	30,980
Libya	224,050	274,169	155,276	246,467
Macao	24,220	1,039	40,508	1,034
Madagascar	3,731	4,907	4,529	6,936
Malawi	42,060	18,183	65,327	22,995
Malaysia	222,673	248,239	320,325	283,269
Maldives	44	840	529	747
Mali	3,833	15,856	5,646	5,471
Malta	40,852	71,895	45,076	89,468
Martinique	35	3,029	229	2,980
Mauritania	6,044	1,719	10,343	2,656
Mauritius	128,437	22,499	160,042	24,358
Mayotte	26	771	67	343
Mexico	160,978	95,674	175,487	150,126
Mongolia	1,350	242	4,561	100
Montserrat	164	2,159	115	1,999
Morocco	75,602	99,727	79,738	79,850
Mozambique	9,176	28,618	8,589	15,671
Namibia	62,437	3,425	64,015	5,200
Nauru	1,421	1,715	916	1,332
Nepal	6,115	5,011	5,564	6,453
Netherlands Antilles	97,486	84,489	221,012	20,235
New Caledonia	73	1,965	55	1,856
New Zealand	486,305	286,054	483,747	367,512
Nicaragua	1,810	2,367	2,176	4,755
Niger	6,854	9,660	391	10,682
Nigeria	387,975	798,276	375,796	768,479
Niue & Tokelau	50	198	12	103
Norway	2,820,760	828,612	3,852,657	968,404
Oceania, Australian	69	1,011	94	788
Oceania, U.S.	418	3,418	27	7,370
Oman	91,216	448,900	82,655	390,275
Pakistan	80,277	191,647	93,136	282,536
Panama	5,341	42,276	9,681	74,322
Papua New Guinea	28,142	18,236	68,245	14,643
Paraguay	3,129	15,263	2,961	16,884
Peru	118,414	32,947	119,423	33,841
Philippines	160,701	102,949	199,659	91,751
Pitcairn	14	760	—	855
Poland	177,067	151,727	266,961	169,962
Polar Regions	4,864	901	209	623

	1983		1984	
	Imports	Exports	Imports	Exports
Portugal	475,902	396,988	644,520	385,799
Puerto Rico	58,804	35,936	76,854	72,695
Qatar	10,063	216,385	28,212	133,803
La Réunion	73	3,684	407	3,327
Romania	58,865	82,160	226,091	71,641
Rwanda	2,919	2,326	7,842	2,385
St. Helena	457	10,343	979	6,294
St. Kitts-Nevis	1,798	4,498	3,096	5,133
St. Lucia	21,960	6,276	28,563	8,236
St. Pierre & Miquelon	578	250	743	523
St. Vincent	12,496	4,357	14,167	5,811
Sao Tomé & Principé	218	597	450	962
Saudi Arabia	897,702	1,478,587	545,149	1,387,16ɜ
Senegal	22,333	13,212	23,789	15,772
Seychelles	615	7,502	586	7,540
Sierra Leone	17,710	13,735	25,971	19,532
Singapore	404,122	469,155	488,421	556,443
Solomon Is.	5,486	1,463	6,838	1,513
Somalia	681	18,987	1,582	14,165
South Africa	764,909	1,109,039	725,631	1,205,143
Spain	1,110,029	1,128,439	1,604,405	1,234,584
Canary Is.	56,305	98,603	63,456	84,550
Ceuta & Melilla	24	8,190	—	3,248
Sri Lanka	39,784	70,136	77,163	61,179
Sudan	18,693	133,432	16,858	95,627
Surinam	11,584	8,914	18,316	9,593
Swaziland	23,966	3,536	41,786	2,430
Sweden	2,051,931	2,397,464	2,416,383	2,888,625
Switzerland	2,154,085	1,385,894	2,490,593	1,549,469
Syria	18,859	72,320	59,245	91,909
Taiwan	458,307	128,467	585,246	150,648
Tanzania	46,525	62,056	43,179	60,449
Thailand	87,823	131,833	112,353	149,742
Tonga	25	648	328	842
Togo	2,161	12,212	3,224	12,166
Trinidad & Tobago	52,748	148,811	164,715	113,312
Tunisia	18,126	44,659	21,086	47,077
Turkey	184,976	244	204,131	331,360
Turks & Caicos Is.	18	902	12	1,533
Tuvalu	35	55	11	82
Uganda	29,645	21,092	46,750	29,294
U.A.E.	309,806	567,765	87,227	541,858
U.S.A.	7,442,671	8,836,979	9,356,029	10,149,479
U.S.S.R.	728,491	445,008	854,307	735,173
Uruguay	33,361	10,763	33,292	13,980
Vanuatu	28	811	80	479
Vatican City	289	615	194	241
Venezuela	183,731	87,937	253,770	102,400
Vietnam	603	951	1,154	1,787
Virgin Is., British	172	3,455	1,427	2,543
Virgin Is., U.S.	9,706	4,981	56,871	3,657
Wallis & Futuna	—	5	—	14
Western Samoa	156	468	421	1,183
Yemen, North	1,857	56,315	2,536	58,761
Yemen, South	10,627	36,673	18,238	45,221
Yugoslavia	83,951	148,646	108,479	163,871
Zaire	11,192	21,129	7,720	36,254
Zambia	50,242	55,501	48,069	66,746
Zimbabwe	68,446	64,734	74,090	68,636

LAND AND WATER SPEED RECORDS

PROGRESSIVE LAND SPEED RECORD

Due to disagreements between various governing bodies in the early days of racing and speed attempts a number of apparently authentic performances were never officially acknowledged. From 1911, the AIACR (Association Internationale des Automobile Clubs Reçonnus), the fore-runner of the FIA (Fédération Internationale de l'Automobile), required that for record purposes only the average of two runs, in opposite directions over the course, would be accepted. The AAA (American Automobile Association) accepted one-way records until 1920. Where unofficial performances have been considered authentic, albeit unofficial, they have been included chronologically in the list but within brackets.

km/h	mph	Car	Driver	Venue	Year
63·16	39·24	Jeantaud	Comte Gaston de Chasseloup-Laubat	Achères, France	1898
66·66	41·42	Jenatzy	Camille Jenatzy	Achères, France	1899
70·31	43·69	Jeantaud	Comte Gaston de Chasseloup-Laubat	Achères, France	1899
80·34	49·62	Jenatzy	Camille Jenatzy	Achères, France	1899
92·78	57·65	Jeantaud	Comte Gaston de Chasseloup-Laubat	Achères, France	1899
105·88	65·79	Jenatzy	Camille Jenatzy	Achères, France	1899
(105·88	65·79)	Mercedes-Simplex	William Vanderbilt jr	Achères, France	1899)
120·80	75·06	Serpollet	Leon Serpollet	Nice, France	1902
(120·80	75·06	Mors	Baron de Caters	Bruges, Belgium	1902)
122·44	76·08	Mors	William Vanderbilt jr	Ablis, France	1902
123·28	76·60	Mors	Henri Fournier	Dourdan, France	1902
124·13	77·13	Mors	M Augieres	Dourdan, France	1902
(133·32	82·84	Mors	Charles Rolls	Clipstone, UK	1903)
134·33	83·47	Gobron-Brillié	Arthur Duray	Ostend, Belgium	1903
(135·33	84·09	Mors	Baron de Forest	Dublin, Ireland	1903)
(136·36	84·73	Mors	Charles Rolls	Clipstone, UK	1903)
136·36	84·73	Gobron-Brillié	Arthur Duray	Dourdan, France	1903
147·03	91·37	Ford Arrow	Henry Ford	Lake St Clair, USA	1904
148·52	92·30	Mercedes	William Vanderbilt jr	Daytona, USA	1904
152·54	94·78	Gobron-Brillié	Louis Rigolly	Nice, France	1904
156·25	97·25	Mercedes	Baron de Caters	Ostend, Belgium	1904
166·65	103·55	Gobron-Brillié	Louis Rigolly	Ostend, Belgium	1904
168·21	104·52	Darracq	Paul Baras	Ostend, Belgium	1904
168·42	104·65	Napier	A Macdonald	Daytona, USA	1905
(176·62	109·75	Mercedes	Herbert Bowden	Daytona, USA	1905)
174·46	109·65	Darracq	Victor Héméry	Arles, France	1905
195·65	121·57	Stanley Steamer	Fred Marriott	Daytona, USA	1906
202·69	125·95	Benz	Victor Héméry	Brooklands, UK	1909
211·98	131·72	Benz	Barney Oldfield	Daytona, USA	1910
(228·09	141·73	Benz	Bob Burman	Daytona, USA	1911)
199·72*	124·10	Benz	L. Hornsted	Brooklands, UK	1914
(241·20	149·87	Packard	Ralph de Palma	Daytona, USA	1919)
(251·11	156·03	Duesenberg	Tommy Milton	Daytona, USA	1920)
215·25	133·75	Sunbeam	Lee Guinness	Brooklands, UK	1922
230·64	143·31	Delage	Rene Thomas	Arpajon, France	1924
234·98	146·01	Fiat	Ernest Eldridge	Arpajon, France	1924
235·22	146·16	Sunbeam	Malcolm Campbell	Pendine, UK	1924
242·80	150·87	Sunbeam	Malcolm Campbell	Pendine, UK	1925
245·15	152·33	Sunbeam	Henry Segrave	Southport, UK	1926
272·46	169·30	Thomas Special	Parry Thomas	Pendine, UK	1926
275·23	171·02	Thomas Special	Parry Thomas	Pendine, UK	1926
281·45	174·88	Napier-Campbell	Malcolm Campbell	Pendine, UK	1927
327·97	203·79	Sunbeam	Henry Segrave	Daytona, USA	1927
330·06	206·96	Napier-Campbell	Malcolm Campbell	Daytona, USA	1928
334·02	207·55	White-Triplex	Ray Keech	Daytona, USA	1928
372·48	231·44	Irving-Napier	Henry Segrave	Daytona, USA	1929
396·04	246·09	Napier-Campbell	Malcolm Campbell	Daytona, USA	1931
408·73	253·97	Napier-Campbell	Sir Malcolm Campbell	Daytona, USA	1932
438·48	272·46	Campbell Special	Sir Malcolm Campbell	Daytona, USA	1933
445·49	276·82	Campbell Special	Sir Malcolm Campbell	Daytona, USA	1935
484·62	301·13	Campbell Special	Sir Malcolm Campbell	Bonneville, USA	1935
502·12	312·00	Thunderbolt	George Eyston	Bonneville, USA	1937
556·01	345·49	Thunderbolt	George Eyston	Bonneville, USA	1938
563·59	350·20	Railton	John Cobb	Bonneville, USA	1938
575·34	357·50	Thunderbolt	George Eyston	Bonneville, USA	1938
595·04	369·74	Railton	John Cobb	Bonneville, USA	1939
634·39	394·20	Railton-Mobil	John Cobb	Bonneville, USA	1947
(654·3	406·6	Challenger	Micky Thompson	Bonneville, USA	1960)
(655·72	407·45	Spirit of America	Craig Breedlove	Bonneville, USA	1963)
648·73**	403·10	Bluebird-Proteus	Donald Campbell	Lake Eyre, Australia	1964
664·98	413·20	Wingfoot Express	Tom Green	Bonneville, USA	1964

km/h	mph	Car	Driver	Venue	Year
698·49	434·02	Green Monster	Art Arfons	Bonneville, USA	1964
754·33	468·72	Spirit of America	Craig Breedlove	Bonneville, USA	1964
846·97	526·28	Spirit of America	Craig Breedlove	Bonneville, USA	1964
863·75	536·71	Green Monster	Art Arfons	Bonneville, USA	1964
893·96	555·48	Spirit of America-Sonic I	Craig Breedlove	Bonneville, USA	1965
927·87	576·55	Green Monster	Art Arfons	Bonneville, USA	1965
966·67	600·60	Spirit of America-Sonic I	Craig Breedlove	Bonneville, USA	1965
1014·51	630·38	The Blue Flame	Gary Gabelich	Bonneville, USA	1970
1019·46***	633·46	Thrust	Richard Noble	Black Rock Desert, USA	1983

* The first official two-way run record.

** The last time that a wheel-driven car has held the record. The current best by such a car is 658·67 km/h (409·27 mph) by Robert Summers in "Goldenrod" at Bonneville in 1965. However in 1964 at Lake Eyre, Donald Campbell in Bluebird attained a speed of 690·90 km/h (429·31 mph).

*** In 1979 at Rogers Dry Lake, USA, Stan Barrett in "The Budweiser Special" reached a speed of 1190·37 km/h (739·66 mph) over a short distance.

PROGRESSIVE WATER SPEED RECORD

(as homologated by the Union Internationale Motonautique)

km/h	mph	Boat	Pilot	Venue	Year
149·40	92·83	Miss America VII	George Wood	Detroit	1928
149·86	93·12	Miss America VII	Gar Wood	Indian Creek, Miami	1929
158·94	98·76	Miss England II	Sir Henry Segrave	Lake Windermere	1930
164·56	102·25	Miss America IX	Gar Wood	Indian Creek, Miami	1931
166·55	103·49	Miss England II	Kaye Don	Parana River	1931
177·38	110·22	Miss England II	Kaye Don	Lake Garda	1931
179·78	111·71	Miss America IX	Gar Wood	Indian Creek, Miami	1932
188·98	117·43	Miss England III	Kaye Don	Loch Lomond	1932
192·81	119·81	Miss England III	Kaye Don	Loch Lomond	1932
201·02	124·91	Miss America X	Gar Wood	Revier Canal	1932
203·31	126·33	Bluebird K3	Sir Malcolm Campbell	Lake Maggiore	1937
208·4	129·5	Bluebird K3	Sir Malcolm Campbell	Lake Maggiore	1937
210·73	130·94	Bluebird K3	Sir Malcolm Campbell	Lake Hallwyl	1938
228·10	141·74	Bluebird K4	Sir Malcolm Campbell	Coniston Water	1939
258·01	160·32	Slo-Mo-Shun IV	Stan Sayres	Lake Washington	1950
287·26	178·49	Slo-Mo-Shun IV	Stan Sayres	Lake Washington	1952
325·60	202·32	Bluebird K7	Donald Campbell	Ullswater	1955
347·9	216·2	Bluebird K7	Donald Campbell	Lake Mead	1955
363·12	225·63	Bluebird K7	Donald Campbell	Coniston Water	1956
384·75	239·07	Bluebird K7	Donald Campbell	Coniston Water	1957
400·12	248·62	Bluebird K7	Donald Campbell	Coniston Water	1958
418·99	260·35	Bluebird K7	Donald Campbell	Coniston Water	1959
444·71*	276·33	Bluebird K7	Donald Campbell	Lake Dumbleyung	1964
459·00	285·21	Hustler	Lee Taylor jr	Lake Guntersville	1967
464·45**	288·60	Spirit of Australia	Ken Warby	Blowering Dam	1977
514·39	319·627	Spirit of Australia	Ken Warby	Blowering Dam	1978

* Prior to his fatal crash on Coniston Water in 1967, Donald Campbell reached a speed of 528 km/h (328 mph).
** Warby reached an estimated speed of 555·9 km/h (345·4 mph) on one run.

THE UNITED NATIONS

The foundations of the Charter of the United Nations were laid at the Conference of Foreign Ministers in Moscow in 1943, and upon those foundations a structure was built at the meetings at Dumbarton Oaks, Washington, D.C., Aug. 21–Oct. 7, 1944. The design was discussed and criticized at San Francisco from April 25 to June 26, 1945, on which date representatives of 50 Allied Nations appended their signatures to the Charter.

The United Nations formally came into existence on October 24, 1945. It was later decided that its seat should be in the United States. Permanent headquarters have been erected at Manhattan, New York. October 24 has been designated "United Nations Day".

The following 159 states are members of the United Nations:—

Afghanistan, Albania, Algeria, Angola, Antigua and Barbuda, Argentina,* Australia,* Austria, Bahamas, Bahrain, Bangladesh, Barbados, Belgium, Belize,* Benin, Bhutan, Bolivia,* Botswana, Brazil,* Brunei Darusalam, Bulgaria, Burkina Faso, Burma, Burundi, Byelorussian Soviet Socialist Republic,* Cambodia, Cameroon, Canada,* Cape Verde, Central African Rep., Chad, Chile,* China,* Colombia,* Comoros, Congo (Pop. Repub.), Costa Rica,* Cuba,* Cyprus, Czechoslovakia,* Denmark,* Djibouti, Dominica, Dominican Republic,* Ecuador,* Egypt,* El Salvador,* Equatorial Guinea, Ethiopia,* Fiji, Finland, France,* Gabon, Gambia, Germany (East), Germany (West), Ghana, Greece,* Grenada, Guatemala,* Guinea, Guinea-Bissau, Guyana, Haiti,* Honduras,* Hungary, Iceland, India,* Indonesia, Iran,* Iraq,* Republic of Ireland, Israel, Italy, Ivory Coast, Jamaica, Japan, Jordan, Kenya, Kuwait, Laos, Lebanon,* Lesotho, Liberia,* Libya, Luxemburg,* Madagascar, Malawi, Malaysia, Maldive Islands, Mali, Malta, Mauritania, Mauritius, Mexico,* Mongolia, Morocco, Mozambique, Nepal, Netherlands,* New Zealand,* Nicaragua,* Niger, Nigeria, Norway,* Oman, Pakistan, Panama,* Papua New Guinea, Paraguay,* Peru,* Philippines,* Poland,* Portugal, Qatar, Romania, Rwanda, St. Christopher and Nevis, St. Lucia, St. Vincent and the Grenadines, Sao Tome and Principe, Saudi Arabia,* Senegal, Seychelles, Sierra Leone, Singapore, Solomon Islands, Somalia, South Africa,* Spain, Sri Lanka, Sudan, Surinam, Swaziland, Sweden, Syria,* Tanzania, Thailand, Togo, Trinidad and Tobago, Tunisia, Turkey,* Uganda, Ukrainian Soviet Socialist Republic,* Union of Soviet Socialist Republics,* United Arab Emirates, United Kingdom,* United States of America,* Uruguay, Vanuatu,* Venezuela,* Vietnam, Western Samoa, Yemen (Arab Repub.), Yemen (P.D.R.), Yugoslavia,* Zaire, Zambia, Zimbabwe.

*Original member (*i.e.* from 1945). (From October 25, 1971, "China" was taken to mean the People's Republic of China.)

The principal organs of the United Nations are:—
(1) The General Assembly; (2) The Security Council; (3) The Economic and Social Council; (4) The Trusteeship Council; (5) The International Court of Justice; (6) The Secretariat.

1. The General Assembly

The General Assembly consists of all the Members of the United Nations. Each Member is entitled to be represented at its meetings by five representatives, but has only one vote. The General Assembly meets once a year in regular session beginning on the third Tuesday in September. A new President is elected by the General Assembly at the start of every annual session. Special Sessions may also be held.

The work of the General Assembly is divided among seven Main Committees, on each of which every Member has the right to be represented:—(1) Disarmament and related security questions; (2) Economic and Financial; (3) Social, Humanitarian and Cultural; (4) Decolonization (including Non-Self Governing Territories); (5) Administrative and Budgetary; (6) Legal. There is also a Special Political Committee, to relieve the burden on the first Committee.

The Main Committees consider items referred to them by the General Assembly and recommend draft resolutions for submission to the Assembly's plenary meetings.

The Assembly has two procedural committees—a General Committee and a Credentials Committee; and three standing committees—an Advisory Committee on Administrative and Budgetary Questions, a Committee on Contributions and a Disarmament Commission.

The General Assembly appoints such *ad hoc* committees as may be required from time to time for special purposes. The Assembly is also assisted in its work by subsidiary bodies such as the Board of Auditors, the Committee on Conferences, the International Law Commission, etc. In 1964 the General Assembly set up the United Nations Conference on Trade and Development (UNCTAD) as a permanent body.

The United Nations Industrial Development Organization was set up on Jan. 1, 1967, to promote industrialization and co-ordinate United Nations activities in this field.

President of the United Nations General Assembly, Paul Lusaka (*Zambia*) (1984).

2. The Security Council

The Security Council consists of fifteen Members, each of which has one representative and one vote. There are five *permanent* Members (China, France, U.K., U.S.A., U.S.S.R) and ten non-permanent Members elected for a two-year term.

The Security Council bears the primary responsibility for the maintenance of peace and security. Decisions on procedural questions are made by an affirmative vote of nine Members. On all other matters the affirmative vote of nine Members must include the concurring votes of the *permanent Members*, and it is this clause which makes the *Veto* possible.

The General Assembly, any member of the United Nations, or the Secretary-General, can bring to the Council's attention any matter considered to threaten international peace and security. A non-member State can bring a dispute before the Council provided it accepts in advance the U.N. Charter obligations for peaceful settlement.

The Security Council also establishes *ad hoc* committees and commissions which may be required from time to time for special purposes.

3. The Economic and Social Council

This body is responsible under the General Assembly for carrying out the functions of the United Nations with regard to international economic, social, cultural, educational, health and related matters.

It has established the following Commissions: Statistical, Human Rights, Social Development, Status of Women, Narcotic Drugs, Population, Regional Economic Commissions for Europe, Asia and the Pacific, Western Asia, Latin America and Africa. The Council also makes recommendations for the co ordination of the policies and activities of 15 specialized agencies and other organizations in the U.N. system.

4. Trusteeship Council

The Trusteeship Council now consists of five members: the U.S.A. (administering authority of Micronesia, the only remaining trust Territory of the original 11), and the other four permanent members of the Security Council, China, France, U.K. and U.S.S.R.

The Trusteeship Council considers reports from administering authorities; examines petitions in consultation with the administering authority; makes periodic inspection visits; and checks conditions with an annual questionnaire on the political, economic, social, and educational advancement of the inhabitants of trust territories.

5. International Court of Justice

The International Court of Justice is the principal judicial organ of the United Nations. The Statute of the court is an integral part of the Charter and all Members of the United Nations are *ipso facto* parties to it. The Court is composed of 15 judges, no two of whom may be nationals of the same State, and is based at The Hague.

If any party to a case fails to adhere to the judgment of the Court, the other party may have recourse to the Security Council.

President, Taslim Olawale Elias (*Nigeria*).

THE SECRETARIAT

Secretary-General, Javier Perez de Cuellar (*Peru*).
Director-General, Development and International Economic Co-operation, Jean Ripert (*France*).

U.N. Office and Information Centre, Ship House, 20 Buckingham Gate, S.W.1.

OTHER ORGANS

The U.N. Centre for Human Settlements (Habitat), Nairobi; U.N. Children's Fund (UNICEF), New York; U.N. Conference on Trade and Development (UNCTAD), Geneva; U.N. Development Programme (UNDP), New York; U.N. Disaster Relief Office (UNDRO), Geneva; U.N. Environment Programme (UNEP), Nairobi; U.N. Fund for Population Activities (UNFPA), New York; U.N. High Commissioner for Refugees (UNHCR), Geneva; U.N. Industrial Development Organisation (UNIDO), Vienna (N.B. UNIDO is to be upgraded to the status of a specialized agency); U.N. Institute for Training and Research (UNITAR), New York; International Research and Training Institute for the Advancement of Women (INSTRAW); U.N. Relief and Works Agency for Palestine Refugees in the Near East (UNRWA), Vienna; U.N. University (UNU), Tokyo; World Food Council (WFC), Rome; World Food Programme (WFP), Rome.

These programmes are supported by voluntary contributions from governments, non-governmental organizations and individuals. The U.N. programmes receiving the largest total contributions in 1983 were: the U.N. Development Programme (U.N.D.P.—$714m); the U.N. Children's Fund (U.N.I.C.E.F.—$297m), and the U.N. Fund for Population Activities (U.N.F.P.A.—$310m). The World Food Programme (W.F.P.), jointly administered by the U.N. and F.A.O., provided aid worth $900m in 1983.

BUDGET OF THE UNITED NATIONS

The budget is now approved for periods of two years, and the appropriation for the biennium 1984–85 is U.S.$1,587,159,800 (*gross*). The scale of assessments for 1984–85 includes: Australia, 1·57 per cent.; Canada, 3·08 per cent.; China, 0·88 per cent.; France, 6·51 per cent.; India, 0·36 per cent.; Japan, 10·32 per cent.; New Zealand, 0·26 per cent.; U.K., 4·67 per cent.; U.S.S.R., 10·54 per cent.; U.S.A., 25 per cent.

U.K. MISSION TO THE UNITED NATIONS
845 Third Avenue, New York

Permanent Representative to the United Nations and Representative on the Security Council, Sir John Thomson, G.C.M.G. (1982).
Deputy Permanent Representative, P. M. Maxey, C.M.G.
Counsellors, Hon. D. A. Gore-Booth (*Head of Chancery*); F. D. Berman (*Legal Adviser*); E. J. Field (*Economic and Social Affairs*); A. J. Breeze; M. W. Marshal, O.B.E. (*Administration*).

U.K. MISSION TO THE U.N. AND OTHER INTERNATIONAL ORGANIZATIONS IN GENEVA
37–39 rue de Vermont, 1211 Geneva 20

Permanent U.K. Representative, John Anthony Sankey, C.M.G., apptd. 1985.
Counsellor, Head of Chancery and Deputy Permanent Representative, D. J. Moss.

SPECIALIZED AGENCIES

Fifteen other independent international organizations, each with its own membership, budget and headquarters, carry out their responsibilities in coordination with the U.N. under agreements made with the Economic and Social Council. These agencies set standards and provide technical assistance in economic, social and cultural and technical fields.
Food and Agriculture Organization of the United Nations (FAO)
International Bank for Reconstruction and Development (IBRD)
International Civil Aviation Organization (ICAO)
International Development Association (IDA)
International Finance Corporation (IFC)
International Fund for Agricultural Development (IFAD)
International Labour Organization (ILO)
International Maritime Organization (IMO)
International Monetary Fund (IMF)
International Telecommunication Union (ITU)
United Nations Educational, Scientific and Cultural Organization (UNESCO)
Universal Postal Union (UPU)
World Health Organization (WHO)
World Intellectual Property Organization (WIPO)
World Meteorological Organization (WMO)

International Labour Organization (ILO)
Geneva (London Branch Office, 96–98 Marsham Street, S.W.1.). Established with the League of Nations in 1919 under the Treaty of Versailles, the ILO became in 1946 the first specialized agency associated with the United Nations. In May, 1984 the Organization had 151 member States. The aim of the ILO is to promote lasting peace through social justice, and to this end it works for better economic and social conditions everywhere. It was awarded the Nobel Peace Prize in 1969.

The ILO establishes international labour standards, which set guidelines for improving working conditions and protecting basic human rights; runs a world-wide programme of technical assistance to developing countries; conducts research and disseminates information on the human aspects of economic activity, with a view to improving social and economic well-being. Through its World Employment Programme, the ILO is attacking unemployment and its associated ills by aiding national and international efforts to provide productive work for the world's fast-growing population. It is also developing an international programme for the improvement of working conditions and the working environment.

The ILO is financed by contributions from its member states. A proportion of its budget is devoted to its technical assistance programme, but this is financed mainly by funds from UNDP and other sources. The total technical co-operation budget for 1984 amounted to about $83,488,000.

The International Labour Conference, composed of national delegations of two government delegates, one worker delegate and one employer delegate, meets at least once a year. It formulates international labour standards and broad policies of the Organization, provides a forum for discussion of world labour and social problems, and approves the ILO's work programme and budget, which is financed by member States.

A 56-member Governing Body, composed of 28 government members, 14 worker members and 14 employer members, acts as the Organization's executive council. Ten governments hold seats on the Governing Body because of their industrial importance.

The International Labour Office, the secretariat of the Organization, collects and distributes information, assists governments on request in drafting legislation on the basis of international labour standards, directs technical co-operation activities, and issues publications.

Director-General, Francis Blanchard (*France*).

Food and Agriculture Organization of the United Nations (FAO), Via delle Terme di Caracalla, 00100 Rome.

—Established on October 16, 1945, to raise levels of nutrition and standards of living, to secure improvements in the efficiency of the production and distribution of all food and agricultural products and to better the condition of rural populations, thus contributing to the expansion of world economy and ensuring man's freedom from hunger. Among its many activities the Organization promotes the global exchange of information in the fields of agriculture, forestry and fisheries, facilitates international agreement in these fields and provides technical assistance in such subjects as nutrition and food management, soil erosion control, re-afforestation, the establishment of paper industries, irrigation engineering, control of infestation of stored foods, production of fertilizers, control of crop pests and diseases, and improvement of fishing vessels, fish distribution and marketing. Jointly with the United Nations it administers the World Food Programme, which in 1984 committed nearly $1,160,000,000 in cash and commodities to low-income countries. The 1983 session of the FAO governing Conference approved a budget of $421,000,000 for the two years 1983–84. In addition FAO is carrying out field programmes involving annual expenditure of about $270,000,000 under the U.N. Development Programme and other aid programmes including trust funds. Through its co-operative programme with the World Bank it is helping to increase international investment in agriculture and allied fields.

The policy of the Organization is directed by a two-yearly Conference of the 156 member countries. A council (49 members) acts for the Conference between its sessions.

Director-General, Edouard Saouma (*Lebanon*).
Permanent U.K. Representative, R. F. R. Deare.

United Nations Educational, Scientific and Cultural Organization (UNESCO), 7 Place de Fontenoy, Paris 75700.

—Under its constitution, the Organization makes its contribution to peace and security by promoting collaboration among its Member States in the fields of education, science, culture and communication. It aims at furthering a universal respect for justice, for the rule of law and for human rights, without distinction of race, sex, language or religion, in accordance with the Charter of the United Nations.

The Organization is composed of three organs: (i) the *General Conference*, consisting of representatives of Member States, which meets biennially to decide the programme and budget; (ii) the *Executive Board*, composed of 50 members elected by the General Conference to supervise the execution of the approved programme and (iii) the *Secretariat*, which is responsible for Unesco's day-to-day functioning and the execution of the programme. In most Member States National Commissions serve as a link with Unesco and help to carry out the programme. Member States in June 1985, 160 and three Associate Members (British Eastern Caribbean group, Netherlands Antilles and the British Virgin Islands).

Director-General, Amadou-Mahtar M'Bow (*Senegal*).
Permanent U.K. Representative, Paris, J. K. Gordon.
U.K. National Commission for UNESCO, Ministry of Overseas Development, Stag Place, S.W.1.

World Health Organization (WHO), 1211 Geneva 27.

Established on April 7, 1948, the aim of the World Health Organization is the attainment by all peoples of the highest possible level of health. It co-operates with its member governments in their efforts to develop health manpower, streamline health services, control communicable diseases, promote family health—including mother and child care, family planning, nutrition and health education—and strengthen environmental health. It promotes biomedical and health services research through some 500 collaborating research centres in different parts of the world. Its other services include the International Pharmacopoeia, drug evaluation and monitoring, biological standardization, epidemiological surveillance and scientific publications. Approved budget for 1986 and 1987, $543,300,000. Membership (May 1985), 166.

Organs are a *World Health Assembly* meeting annually to frame policy, an *Executive Board* (31 members), meeting at least twice a year, and a *Secretariat*.

Director-General, H. T. Mahler (*Denmark*).

International Bank for Reconstruction and Development (IBRD), Washington, D.C. 20433; European office, 66 Ave. d'Iéna, 75116, Paris, France; Tokyo office, Kokusai Building 1–1, Narunouchi 3-Chome, Chiyoda-ku, Tokyo 100.

—Established on Dec. 27, 1945, to help raise standards of living in developing countries by the provision of financial resources through loans made for productive purposes to a government, or guaranteed by the government concerned. Loans are directed towards developing countries at more advanced stages of economic and social growth.

The Bank, which is owned by the governments of 148 countries and whose capital is subscribed by its member countries, finances its lending operations primarily from its own borrowing in the world capital markets, and derives a substantial contribution to its resources from its retained earnings and the repayment of loans. The interest rate on its loans is calculated in relation to its cost of borrowing; loans generally have a grace period of five years and are repayable over 20 years or less. The loans made by the Bank since its inception to June 30, 1984, totalled

$101,565,400,000 to 106 countries. Subscribed capital, $56,010,584,000.

The *Board of Governors* consists of one Governor and one alternate appointed by each of the member countries. Twenty-one *Executive Directors* exercise all powers of the Bank except those reserved to the Board of Governors. The *President*, selected by the Executive Directors, conducts the business of the Bank, with the assistance of an international staff.
President, A. W. Clausen (*U.S.A.*).
U.K. Executive Director, N. L. Wicks, C.B.E.

International Development Association (IDA), Washington, D.C. 20433; European office, 66 Ave. d'Iéna, 75116 Paris, France; Tokyo office, Kokusai Building 1-1, Narunouchi 3-Chome, Chiyoda-ku, Tokyo 100.—The IDA is an affiliate of the IBRD (the two together comprising the *World Bank*) and was established in September 1960 to provide assistance for the same purposes as the IBRD but primarily in the poorer developing countries and on terms that bear less heavily on their balance of payments than IBRD loans. Assistance is concentrated on the very poor countries, i.e. those with an annual per capita GNP of less than $806 (in 1982 dollars); more than 50 countries are eligible.

Membership is open to all members of IBRD and 133 have joined to date. Funds, called credits to distinguish them from IBRD loans, come mostly in the form of subscriptions, general replenishments and special contributions from IDA's richer members, and transfers from the net earnings of the IBRD. The term of IDA credits, which are made to governments only, are ten-year grace periods, 50-year maturities, and no interest. By June 30, 1984, IDA had extended development credits totalling $33,654,000,000 in 86 countries.

Although legally and financially distinct from the IBRD, IDA is administered by the same staff, and the Board of Governors and Executive Directors are the same as those holding equivalent positions in the IBRD.

International Finance Corporation (IFC), 1818 H Street, Washington, D.C. 20433; European representative, New Zealand House, Haymarket, S.W.1.— The IFC was established in 1956 as an affiliate of the World Bank to assist less developed member countries by promoting the growth in the private sector of their economies and helping to mobilize domestic and foreign capital for this purpose. Membership of the IBRD is a prerequisite for membership in the IFC, which has 127 members. Legally and financially the IFC and IBRD are separate entities; and the Corporation has its own operating and legal staff, but draws upon the Bank for administrative and other services. IFC's share capital was $544,784,000 at June 30, 1985, and it is also empowered to borrow up to approximately $3,200,000,000 from the World Bank for use in its lending programme. At the end of June 1985, IFC had made approvals totalling more than $6,216,000 in 84 countries.
President, A. W. Clausen (*U.S.A.*).

International Monetary Fund (IMF), 700 19th Street, N.W. Washington, D.C.—Established on Dec. 27, 1945, the Fund exists to promote international monetary co-operation and the expansion of international trade; to promote exchange stability, maintain orderly exchange arrangements and avoid competitive exchange depreciations; and to assist in the establishment of a multilateral system of payments in respect of current transactions between members and in the elimination of foreign exchange restrictions which hamper world trade. 148 countries were in membership of the Fund in June, 1985.

The Fund's financial assistance takes the form of a foreign exchange transaction. The member pays to the Fund an amount of its own money equivalent to the amount of foreign currency it wishes to purchase. The member is expected to "repurchase" its own currency from the Fund, usually within three to five years, with a payment of SDR or dollars or usable currency acceptable to the Fund. These arrangements are subject to certain charges which rise in proportion to the amount of foreign exchange involved.

Currencies drawn from the Fund may be used in a flexible way to relieve the member's payments difficulty, and usually the member is expected to undertake policy changes, where needed, to correct the payment imbalance.

Each member of the Fund is assigned a quota which determines its voting power and the amount of resources that it may draw from the Fund. The subscription of each member is equal to its quota, and is payable in the member's own currency and SDRs.
Managing Director, Jacques de Larosière (*France*).
U.K. Executive Director, (vacant).

International Civil Aviation Organization (ICAO), 1,000 Sherbrooke Street, Suite 400, W., Montreal, Quebec, Canada.—The ICAO was established on April 4, 1947, to study problems of international civil aviation to establish international standards and regulations for civil aviation in areas such as airworthiness, personnel licensing, aeronautical charts, rules of the air, etc., ICAO encourages the use of safety measures, uniform regulations or operation, and simpler procedures at international airports. It promotes the use of new technical methods and equipment. With the co-operation of members, it has evolved a pattern for meteorological services, traffic control, telecommunications, search and rescue organization, and other facilities required for safe international flight. It has secured much simplification of government customs, immigration, and public health regulations as they apply to international air transport. 156 states are now members of ICAO.

An *Assembly* of delegates from member states meets at least once every three years. A *Council* of 33 members is elected by the Assembly, taking into account the countries of chief importance in air transport and the need for representation of the main geographical areas of the world. The Council is the executive body, working through subsidiary committees.
President of Council, Dr. Assad Kotaite (*Lebanon*).
Secretary-General, Yves Lambert (*France*).

Universal Postal Union (UPU), Weltpostrasse 4, 3000 Berne 15.—Established on October 9, 1874, by the postal Convention of Berne and in operation from July 1, 1875, UPU exists to form a single postal territory of all the countries, members of the Union, for the reciprocal exchange of correspondence in order to secure the organization and improvement of the various postal services and to promote in this sphere the development of international collaboration. Every member agrees to transmit the mail of all other members by the best means used for its own mail. The Union includes almost all the countries of the world. Budget, 1985, S.Fr. 22,961,300. A *Universal Postal Congress* meets at five-yearly intervals. The last was held in Hamburg in June-July 1984, and the next is scheduled to take place in Washington in the autumn of 1989.
Director-General, A.C. Botto de Barros (*Brazil*).

International Telecommunication Union (ITU), Place des Nations, Geneva.—Founded at Paris in 1865 as the International Telegraph Union. ITU became a U.N. Specialized Agency in 1947 and as from

Jan. 1, 1975, is governed by the Convention adopted by the Torremolinos Conference held in 1973, amended at Nairobi in 1982. ITU exists to set up international regulations for telegraph, telephone and radio services to further their development and extend their utilization by the public, at the lowest possible rates; to promote international co-operation for the improvement and rational use of telecommunications of all kinds; the development of technical facilities and their most efficient operation. ITU allocates the radio frequency spectrum and registers radio frequency assignments. It studies, recommends, collects and publishes information on telecommunication matters, including space radio communications. The Budget for 1985 is 122,000,000 *Swiss francs.*

Secretary-General, R. E. Butler (*Australia*).

World Meteorological Organization (WMO), Geneva.—Came into existence in 1951. The present membership is 154 States and 5 Territories. WMO exists to facilitate world-wide co-operation in establishing networks of stations making observations related to meteorology and hydrology, and to promote the establishment and maintenance of centres providing meteorological and related services; to promote the establishment of systems for the rapid exchange of weather information; to promote standardization of meteorological observations and to ensure their uniform publication; to further the application of meteorology to aviation, shipping, water problems, agriculture, and other human activities; to promote activities in operational hydrology and to further close co-operation between meteorological and hydrological services; to encourage research and training in meteorology and to co-ordinate their international aspects. Budget (1984–87), \$U.S.77,516,400. A *World Meteorological Congress* meets at least once every four years. An *Executive Council* (36 members), meeting at least annually, carries out the resolutions of the Congress, initiates studies and makes recommendations on matters requiring international action. Other organs are six *Regional Meteorological Associations* (Africa, Asia, S. America, N. and Central America, Europe and South-West Pacific), eight technical commissions and a Secretariat.

Secretary-General, G. O. P. Obasi (*Nigeria*).

International Maritime Organization (IMO), Albert Embankment, S.E.1. A United Nations Specialized Agency established on March 17, 1958, to provide means for co-operation and exchange of information among governments on technical matters related to international shipping, especially with regard to safety at sea and preventing marine pollution caused by ships. IMO is responsible for calling maritime conferences and drafting maritime agreements. It has produced numerous technical codes relating to the carriage of various types of cargo such as chemicals, ores, and dangerous goods and to the construction and equipment of ships, e.g., gas and chemical carriers. In June, 1984, 125 nations were in membership. Budget, 1984–85, \$25,772,000. (The Organization changed its name from the Inter-Governmental Maritime Consultative Organization (IMCO) on May 22, 1982.)

Secretary-General, C. P. Srivastava (*India*).

World Intellectual Property Organization (WIPO), 34 chemin des Colombettes, 1211 Geneva 20, Switzerland.—Established by a 1967 convention to succeed the United International Bureau for the Protection of Intellectual Property. Became a specialised agency of the United Nations in 1974. WIPO promotes the protection of intellectual property

throughout the world through co-operation among states and, where appropriate, in collaboration with other international organisations; and ensures administrative co-operation among states in the development of various international agreements on such matters as trademarks, industrial design, the classification of goods and services, the protection of appellations of origin, of literary and artistic works, of performers, producers of phonograms and broadcasting organizations.

The *Conference* and the *General Assembly* control the *International Bureau* (or secretariat). The Bureau provides the necessary documentation and other services for meetings and carries out projects for the promotion of increased international co-operation among member states.

Director-General: Arpad Bogsch (*United States*)

International Fund for Agricultural Development (IFAD), 107 Via del Serafico, 00142 Rome, Italy.—The establishment of the Fund was proposed by the 1974 World Food Conference and it began operations in December 1977. The Fund's purpose is to mobilize additional funds for agricultural and rural development in developing countries through projects and programmes directly benefiting the poorest rural population.

The Fund's operations are directed by the *Governing Council,* consisting of the entire membership. It has an 18-member Executive Board. Its governing structure provides for equal voting rights among the three groups of member countries, namely, the developed, the oil-exporting developing countries and other developing countries.

President (chief executive of IFAD and Chairman of the Executive Board): Idriss Jazairy (*Algeria*).

RELATED ORGANISATIONS

International Atomic Energy Agency, Vienna International Centre, P.O. Box 100, A-1400, Vienna. Set up on July 29, 1957, to accelerate and enlarge the contribution of atomic energy to peace, health and prosperity throughout the world and to ensure that assistance provided by it or under its supervision is not used to further any military purpose. Agreements have been reached concerning the Agency's working relationship with the United Nations and some of the specialized agencies. In June, 1985, 113 states were members.

A General Conference of all members meets in regular annual session and in such special session as may be necessary. A Board of Governors (35 members) carries out the functions of the Agency and meets usually four times a year. The Regular Budget for 1984 amounted to \$106,805,000.

Director-General, Hans Blix (*Sweden*).
Permanent U.K. Representative, D. I. Morphet.

General Agreement on Tariffs and Trade (GATT), Centre William Rappard, Rue de Lausanne 154, CH-1211 Geneva 21. A multilateral treaty, in operation since 1948, to which 90 countries are parties, and one acceded provisionally; a further 31 countries apply GATT *de facto.* Its rules thus govern over four-fifths of world trade. Objectives of GATT are to expand international trade and promote economic development. GATT provides a permanent forum for discussion and solution of particular international trade problems, and for multilateral negotiations to reduce tariffs and other obstacles to the expansion of international trade. Special attention is given to trade problems of developing countries. In November 1979, participating countries concluded the Tokyo Round of multilateral trade negotiations (launched in Tokyo in September 1973) with agreements covering tariff reductions, non-tariff measures, an improved framework for the conduct of international trade, bovine meat, dairy products, tropical products, civil aircraft, and a revised GATT anti-dumping code. More recently, the GATT's work has been covering areas such as agriculture, textiles, quantitative restrictions and services. An International Trade Centre, set up by GATT in 1964 to aid developing countries in export promotion, is now operated jointly by GATT and UNCTAD.

Director-General, A. Dunkel (*Switzerland*).

EUROPEAN COMMUNITY

The twelve member states: Belgium, Denmark, France, Federal Republic of Germany, Greece, Ireland, Italy, Luxemburg, The Netherlands, Portugal, Spain, the United Kingdom.

The beginnings of the European Community date from May 9, 1950, when Robert Schuman, France's Foreign Minister, proposed that France and Germany should pool their coal and steel industries under an independent ("supranational") High Authority, in a Community open to the membership of any other European country wishing to join. Not only West Germany, but also Italy, Belgium, the Netherlands, and Luxemburg accepted this invitation.

The Coal and Steel Community (E.C.S.C.), European Economic Community and Euratom share a single institutional framework: a Commission, Council of Ministers, Parliament and Court of Justice. The core of the Community policymaking process is the "dialogue" between the Commission, which initiates and implements policy, and the Council of Ministers, which takes major policy decisions. The beginnings of democratic control are exercised by the European Parliament, while the Court of Justice ensures the rule of law and is the final arbiter in all matters arising from the Community Treaties.

Since the start of the European Economic Community and Euratom in 1958, the Parliament and Court of Justice have been common to all three Communities. Up to July, 1967, each Community had its own executive body (the E.E.C. and Euratom Commissions, and the E.C.S.C. High Authority) and its own Council of Ministers.

In April, 1965, the Six signed a treaty providing for the merger of the three executive bodies in a single Commission and the three Councils in a single Council, with a view to the eventual merger of the three Communities themselves. The merger treaty came into force on July 1, 1967; the single Commission and single Council then took office. They enjoy the same powers under the three Community Treaties as did their predecessors.

On December 1 and 2, 1969, the Heads of State or Government of the Six met at the Hague and decided on the completion, strengthening, and, provided that other European countries wished to accept the Treaties of Rome, enlargement of the Community. They instructed the Commission to draw up a plan for economic and monetary union, and the Foreign Ministers to report by the end of July on possible moves towards political unification. They also resolved to intensify the co-ordination of research and development programmes.

In accordance with the Hague decisions the Council of Ministers agreed in April, 1970, that as from 1975 the Community would have its own revenue, independent of national contributions. The Foreign Ministers agreed (May, 1970) to hold formal political consultations twice a year.

In June, 1970, the Six invited Britain, the Irish Republic, Denmark and Norway to open negotiations on June 30 at Luxemburg on their applications to join the Community. Negotiations continued in 1971 and were concluded with the United Kingdom Government for all major questions by the end of June; on July 8, H.M. Government issued a White Paper on the results. On Jan. 22, 1972, the four applicant countries signed the Treaty of Accession in Brussels. Norway conducted a referendum on its Common Market entry and as a result withdrew its application. The enlarged Community of the Nine came into existence on Jan. 1, 1973.

With the advent of a Labour Government in the U.K. in 1974, there followed a period of renegotiation of the terms of Britain's entry into the Community, culminating in a referendum on June 5, 1975, as to whether or not the country should remain a member of the E.E.C. The result of the referendum showed two to one in favour of staying in. British Labour Party representatives who had hitherto boycotted the European Parliament then took up their 18 allotted seats.

In January 1976 the European Parliament approved a Report urging direct elections to the Parliament in 1978. On July 12–13, 1976, the Heads of Government or State, meeting in European Council, decided to approve a 410 member Parliament with Britain, France, West Germany and Italy allocated 81 seats each; the Netherlands 25, Belgium 24, Denmark 16, Ireland 15 and Luxemburg 6. Because some countries (including Britain) had not passed the relevant legislation in time, the date of European Elections was postponed until June 1979. When Greece joined the E.E.C. in January 1981, she was allocated 24 seats in the Parliament, bringing the total number to 434.

The "European Council", an addition to the institutionalized meetings provided under the Treaties, evolved from the "summit" conference of December 1974, when the Heads of Government decided to meet at least three times a year in order to discuss Community problems and matters requiring political co-operation.

OFFICE OF THE UNITED KINGDOM PERMANENT
REPRESENTATIVE TO THE EUROPEAN COMMUNITIES
Rond-point Robert Schuman 6, 1040 Brussels

Ambassador and U.K. Permanent Representative,
David Hugh Alexander Hannay, C.M.G., *apptd.* 1985.

The Commission

On July 1, 1970, the Commission was reduced from 14 members to nine, two each from Germany, France and Italy, and one each from Belgium, the Netherlands and Luxemburg. Following the 1973 enlargement, the number rose to 13, with two seats each from Britain, France, Germany, and Italy and one each for the other members. The admission of Greece in 1981, with 1 seat, brought the total to 14 Commissioners.

The members of the Commission are appointed by agreement among the ten member governments for a four-year renewable term; the president and vice-presidents are appointed from among the members for a two-year term, also renewable.

The members of the Commission are pledged to independence of the governments and of national or other particular interests. They accept joint responsibility for their decisions, which are taken by majority vote.

In addition to being the initiator of Community action and having specific powers, the Commission acts as a mediator between the member governments in Community affairs and is the guardian of the Community Treaties.

Commission of the European Communities
200 Rue de la Loi, 1049 Brussels

President, Jacques Delors (France) (from 1985).
Vice-Presidents, Frans Andriessen (Netherlands), Henning Christophersen (Denmark), Lord Cockfield (U.K.), Karl-Heinz Narjes (West Germany), Lorenzo Natali (Italy). *Members,* Claude Cheysson (France), Stanley Clinton Davis (U.K.), Willy de Clercq (Belgium), Nicolas Mosar (Luxemburg), Alois Pfeiffer (West Germany), Carlo Ripa di Meana (Italy), Peter Sutherland (Ireland), Grigoris Varfis (Greece).

The Commission maintains information offices in London (8 Storey's Gate, SWIP 3AT), Edinburgh (7 Alva Street EH2 4PH), Cardiff (4 Cathedral Road), Belfast (Windsor House, 9/15 Bedford Street), Dublin (39 Molesworth Street), Washington (2100 M. Street, N.W. (Suite 707), Washington, D.C. 20037, New York (1 Dag Hammarskjöld Plaza, 245 East 47th Street, New York, N.Y. 10017), Ottawa (Inn of the Provinces, Office Tower (Suite 1110), 350 Sparks Street, Ontario, KIR 7S8), and other cities.

The new 14-member Commission was appointed by the Governments of the Ten and was announced on January 29, 1985.

The Council of Ministers
170 Rue de la Loi, 1048 Brussels

This consists of ministers from the governments of each of the ten member states, the ministers concerned depending on the subject under discussion. A single Council exists for the three European Communities. It is the main decision-taking body within the Community legislative process. The Council acts, in almost all cases, on the basis of proposals submitted by the Commission, which is present at Council sessions to participate in the shaping of the measures taken. Before examining Commission proposals the Council normally obtains the opinions of the European Parliament and the Economic and Social Committee on them.

As prescribed by the E.E.C. treaty, under which the great majority of the Council's business falls, decisions are taken by majority vote, qualified majority vote (a system in which the members' votes are weighted) or by unanimity. The Council acts under the E.E.C. treaty by issuing (*a*) "regulations" which are binding in their entirety and directly applicable in all member states; (*b*) "directives" which are binding as to the result to be achieved but leave open to national governments the method of attaining this result; (*c*) "decisions" which bind those addressed; (*d*) "recommendations" and (*e*) "opinions", which have no binding force. The Euratom treaty has the same system of voting and taking action; the E.C.S.C. system differs in certain respects.

The Presidency of the Council is held in rotation for periods of six months. The sessions of the Council are prepared by a Committee of Permanent Representatives of the member states. The Council and its committees are serviced by a general secretariat.

European Parliament

Secretariat: Centre Européen, Kirchberg, Luxemburg.
U.K. Information Office, 2 Queen Anne's Gate, SW1H 9AA.

The first direct elections to the European Parliament were held in mid-1979. Of 434 seats, the United Kingdom, France, Germany and Italy have 81 each, the Netherlands 25, Belgium 24, Greece 24, Denmark 16, Ireland 15 and Luxemburg 6. The Parliament meets in Strasbourg and its Committees in Brussels. The former Parliament consisted of 198 members nominated by their national Parliaments—the United Kingdom, France, Germany and Italy had 36 seats each, Belgium and the Netherlands 14 each, Denmark and Ireland 10 each and Luxemburg 6. Set up in 1952 under the European Coal and Steel Community Treaty of 1951, the Parliament's authority was extended by the 1957 Convention on Common Institutions to cover the European Economic Community and Euratom. It must be consulted on all major issues and has the right to dismiss the Commission by a vote of censure. Apart from general powers of supervision and consultation, it questions the Commission and the Council of Ministers and has a measure of control over the Community's annual budget including its final adoption. It can reject the budget as a whole and can amend items of non-obligatory expenditure (i.e. expenditure not specified in the original treaties or derived legislation—amounting to some 27 per cent. of the total budget). The Members of the Parliament serve on specialized committees and sit in political groups—Socialists, Christian Democrats, Liberals and Democrats, European Democrats, European Progressive Democrats and Communists. There are also a number of Independents in the Parliament.

President, Pierre Pflimlin (France).

European Court of Justice
L–2920 Luxemburg

The European Court superseded the Court of Justice of E.C.S.C. and is common to the three European Communities. It exists to safeguard the law in the interpretation and application of the Community treaties, to decide on the legality of decisions of the Council of Ministers or the Commission and to determine violations of the Treaties. Cases may be brought to it by the member States, the Community institutions, firms or individuals. Its decisions are directly binding in the member countries. The eleven judges and five advocates-general of the Court are appointed for renewable six-year terms by the member Governments in concert. During 1983 the court gave 181 judgements.

Judges, Hon. Lord Mackenzie Stuart (*President*); G. Bosco (*President of 1st Chamber*); O. Due (*President of 2nd Chamber*); C. Kakouris (*President of 3rd Chamber*); P. Pescatore; T. Koopmans; U. Ever-, ling; K. Bahlmann; Y. Galmot; R. Joliet; T. F. O'Higgins.

Advocates-General, P. Verloren van Themaat (*1st Advocate-General*); C. O. Lenz; M. Darmon; G. F. Mancini; Sir Gordon Slynn.

Registrar, P. E. Heim.

The European Investment Bank
100 Boulevard Konrad Adenauer,
L-2950 Luxemburg

The European Investment Bank (E.I.B.) was set up in 1958 under the terms of the Treaty of Rome with the essential function of contributing to the balanced development of the Common Market.

It grants long-term loans to enterprises, public authorities and financial institutions, to finance projects which assist the development of less advanced regions and the conversion or modernization of older, exhausted industries. Another important role of the E.I.B. is that of helping to finance projects which serve the interests of the Community as a whole or more than one member country such as intra-Community communications and development and diversifications of the E.E.C.'s energy sources.

E.I.B. activities have also been extended outside member countries under the terms of different association or cooperation agreements which more than 70 countries have signed with the Community.

The Bank's total financing operations in 1984 amounted to 6,903·2 million E.C.U.,* of which 6,194·2 million (including 1181·8 million from the resources of the New Community Instrument for Borrowing and Lending—'Ortoli Facility') were for investments in the E.E.C. and 708·3 million for outside the Community. Between 1973 and 1984 the E.I.B. had made available a total of 5,788·0 million E.C.U. for investment in the U.K., about 18 per cent of its total operations in the Community during this period (31,700·0 million E.C.U.).

---

* The financial statements of the European Investment Bank are drawn up in E.C.U. which at July 1, 1985 equalled ± £0·57, U.S.$0·73.

The members of the European Investment Bank are the ten member countries of the Community, who have all subscribed to the Bank's capital, which the Bank's Board of Governors doubled to 28,800 million E.C.U., with effect from January 1, 1986. The funds required by the Bank to carry out its tasks are borrowed on the capital markets of the Community and non-member countries, and on the international market.

As it operates on a non-profit-making basis, the interest rates charged by the E.I.B. are therefore close to the average rates charged on the markets where it obtains its funds.

The Board of Governors of the European Investment Bank consists of Ministers nominated by the member countries, usually the Finance Minister, who lay down general directives on the policy of the Bank and appoint members to the Board of Directors (18 nominated by the member states, 1 by the Commission of the European Communities), which takes decisions on the granting and raising of loans and the fixing of interest rates. A Management Committee, also appointed by the Board of Governors, is responsible for the day-to-day operations of the Bank.

President, Ernst-Günther Bröder.
Vice-Presidents, Alain Prate; C. Richard Ross; Arie Pais; Lucio Izzo; Noel Whelan.
 (The President and Vice-Presidents also preside as Chairman and Vice-Chairmen at meetings of the Board of Directors.)
U.K. Office: 68 Pall Mall, SW1Y 5ES.

EUROPEAN COAL AND STEEL COMMUNITY

This, the first of the European Communities, was established in 1952. Since then, for coal, iron ore and scrap, it has abolished customs duties, quantitative restrictions, the dual pricing system whereby prices charged on exported coal or steel differed from those charged to home consumers, currency restrictions and discrimination in transport rates based on the nationality of customers and the special frontier charges which made international transport of these goods within the Community dearer than transport within national frontiers. It has applied rules for fair competition and a harmonized external tariff for the whole Community.

THE TREATY OF ROME

Discussions were held at Messina, Sicily, in 1955 between the foreign ministers of the six member states of E.C.S.C. (Belgium, France, Germany, Italy, Luxemburg and The Netherlands) on proposals for further advances towards economic integration in Europe, and after intensive study of these proposals, a treaty was signed at Rome on March 25, 1957, setting up the European Economic Community.

The Treaty aimed to lay the foundations of an enduring and closer union between the European peoples by gradually removing the economic effects of their political frontiers. The Treaty provides for the elimination of customs duties and quotas in trade between member states; the establishment of a common customs tariff and a common trade policy towards third countries; the abolition of the obstacles to free movement of persons, services and capital between member states; the inauguration of common policies for agriculture and transport; the establishment of a system ensuring that competition shall not be distorted in the Common Market; the co-ordination of economic policies; the harmonization of social and economic legislation to the extent necessary in order to enable the Common Market to work; the creation of a European Social Fund in order to improve the possibilities of employment for workers and to contribute to the raising of their standard of living; the establishment of an Economic and Social Committee which must be consulted on major proposals, consisting of representatives of employers, workers, consumers and other groups; the establishment of a European Investment Bank intended to aid investment in underdeveloped areas and help to finance modernization; and the association of overseas countries and territories with the Community with a view to increasing trade and to pursuing jointly their effort towards economic and social development.

ENLARGEMENT OF THE COMMUNITY

The question of possible enlargement of the Community played an important part in its development from the autumn of 1961 when Britain, the Irish Republic, Denmark and Norway first sought membership, and Austria, Sweden, Switzerland, Spain and Cyprus sought association with the Community. The negotiations were vetoed by France in January, 1963. In May, 1967, Britain, the Irish Republic and Denmark formally submitted applications for Community membership. In July Norway followed suit and Sweden announced that it would seek to participate in the enlargement of the Community on terms compatible with its neutrality. These applications made very slow progress and appeared to come to a standstill when in December, 1967, France declared that Britain's economy would have to be strengthened before negotiations could begin. But shortly after taking office as President of France, Georges Pompidou stated in July, 1969, that there was no objection in principle to the admission of Britain to the Community. At the Hague "summit" meeting in December, 1969, the Six decided that provided that the completion of the Community was not prejudiced, and provided that the Community was strengthened to provide for enlargement, then the entry of other European countries would be desirable. After deciding on a common negotiating position, the Six invited Britain and the other applicants to begin negotiations for membership.

A single overall transitional period of five years, during which the Three were to adopt Community rules and regulations, started on January 1, 1973, giving time for the gradual integration of the economies of the Three with the Six by the end of 1977.

The first 40 per cent alignment on the Community's Common External Tariff (C.E.T.)—i.e. 40 per cent of the difference between the new members' tariffs and the C.E.T.—was made at the beginning of 1974, and three further alignments of 20 per cent each followed.

Negotiations with Greece were concluded and the Treaty of Accession signed on May 28, 1979. Greece became the tenth member of the Community on January 1, 1981. Portugal and Spain applied to join the Community and will become the eleventh and twelfth members on January 1, 1986.

Following a plebiscite, Greenland negotiated its withdrawal from the E.E.C. (but without discontinuing relations with Denmark) formally left on February 1, 1986.

EUROPEAN ATOMIC ENERGY COMMUNITY (EURATOM)

A second treaty, arising from the Messina discussions between the E.C.S.C. powers on additional means of co-operation, was signed in Rome on March 25, 1957, setting up the European Atomic Energy Community. The task of *Euratom*, defined in detail in the Treaty, is to create within a short period the technical and industrial conditions necessary to utilize nuclear discoveries and especially to produce nuclear energy on a large scale. The United Kingdom, Denmark and Ireland joined Euratom on Jan. 1, 1973, and Greece on Jan. 1, 1981.

EUROPEAN PARLIAMENT SUMMARY, 1984–85

Britain's rebate

The thorny problem of payment of Britain's 1983 rebate from the Common Market budget of £457 million was a continuing major issue for the European Parliament which on Sept. 12, 1984 adjourned further its vote on a decision so that the repayment remained temporarily frozen. In the previous July, in 1983, Euro-M.P.s voted to suspend the payment and declared this should be part of an overall financial agreement which should embrace a supplementary budget for that year. Britain promised support for the emergency supplementary budget but it was made clear that the UK would not provide aid until the 1983 rebate was paid, financing of the 1984 refund was assured, and strict controls over future E.E.C. expenditure were implemented. However, Parliament did not regard this as sufficient and ignored a plea for a prompt unblocking of the rebate. After agreement for an emergency financial arrangement for the E.E.C. in 1984, the President of the Parliament, M. Pierre Pflimlin, said on Oct. 4 that the logic of this agreement on the budget discipline meant that it would require them to release the British repayment. The President disclaimed that Parliament's witholding of the rebate was irresponsible although both he and a member of the Parliament's budget committee, said there were further problems to be resolved about future overall authority of the Parliament on E.E.C. spending. Their view was that the agreement by the Finance Ministers of the Ten in Luxemburg this week, the first week of October, was not adequate on the issue of the control over expenditure by the Parliament. Then on Oct. 9, the Parliament's budget committee voted 27 to 4 to release the British rebate, those opposing the decision being three French Gaullists and an Irish Fianna Fail member. Officials in Strasbourg stated on Oct. 11, that the Commission was to repay Britain £411 million in the next few days, being 90 per cent. of the rebate claimed and which was ultimately approved by the Parliament on Oct. 10. The outstanding 10 per cent. was to be handed over when all details of the specific programmes qualifying for the money had been cleared. On Oct. 25, the Common Market avoided bankruptcy when the Parliament agreed to an emergency budget for 1984, but stressed it would not accept the proposed budget for 1985.

Spending levels

After some skirmishing throughout November, Euro-M.P.s voted overwhelmingly on Nov. 16 for a resolution which effectively gave them a joint authority with the E.E.C. ministers to establish spending levels, and rejected that week's agreement by the ministers to set new disciplines over the budget. Already this week, Parliament had introduced into the budget £1.8 billion more than the Ministers had authorized under which control of E.E.C. expenditure overall would be given to national treasuries. A head-on clash between Parliament and Ministers was imminent and it occurred on Dec. 13 when the Parliament voted 319 to five to reject the 1985 budget proposals, there being 16 abstentions. Consequently, without this spending authority, the E.E.C. Commission was limited to expenditure only on the basis of 1984 levels. The motion to reject the budget was supported by all U.K. Euro-M.P.s. The budget approved by ministers of the 10 Governments totalled about £16 billion but Parliament wanted an expenditure of £17·5 billion. Euro-M.P.s were disappointed that the budget ministers did not arrange the traditional meeting between the two sides to try to mutually agree terms on spending.

Budget deadlock

According to new figures presented to the Parliament on Feb. 13, the U.K. might have to contribute an extra £250 million to rescue the budget this year. Mr. Henning Christopherson, E.E.C. Budget Commissioner, told Euro-M.P.s that the estimated gap between Common Market income and revenue in 1985 had widened since the Parliament rejected the original budget plans last Dec. According to most recent Commission forecasts, normal E.E.C. revenues would fall £1.2 billion short of financing Community spending this year. This compared with the shortfall of £750 million which prompted Euro-M.P.s to reject the budget. Mr. Christopherson said the increase was due to extra spending on the Common Agricultural Policy caused by deferred payments from last year and increased farm production. In March, a summit meeting of the E.E.C. in Brussels broke the budget deadlock.

Budget compromise

There was a rare combination of U.K. Tory and Labour members on May 9 to prevent some members challenging the repayment to Britain of its 1985

E.E.C. budget rebate worth £600 million. The move against repayment would have given the Parliament control over the rebate and blocked the payment agreed by the other nine Community Governments, but the old system of cash lump payments by the Commission's special E.E.C. funding of regional development projects in Britain was replaced with future payments of British refunds through automatic cash cuts in the U.K.'s V.A.T. transfers to the E.E.C. the following year. However, on May 9, the Parliament voted for a series of changes and additions to the £15·9 billion budget proposed to replace the first version rejected in Dec. by Euro-M.P.s who now voted to add an extra £500 million to the revised budget. In the event, a compromise budget was agreed by member Governments and the Parliament by the end of June.

Plastic bullets in N. Ireland

On Oct. 11, Euro-M.P.s voted by 150 to 29 to condemn the use of plastic bullets in Northern Ireland. Members approved a motion calling on the British Government to ban them, although it was opposed by the British Conservative members with U.K. Labour members supporting the condemnation.

Debate on British miners' strike

After pressure from British Labour members, the Parliament decided on Oct. 24 to discuss the miners' strike in the U.K. In the Chamber, Mr. Leslie Huckfield (Lab. Merseyside East) staged a demonstrations to draw attention to the ongoing strike. Mr. Huckfield used a megaphone to make himself heard as the amplification system was switched off when the scenes became noisy and unruly and he refused to obey the Chairman's directions. The sitting was temporarily suspended, and later when passions subsided the decision to debate the issue was taken. The debate on Oct. 25 was initiated by Mr. Huckfield, whose motion calling for the National Union of Mineworkers to "win an outright victory" was defeated by 150 to 114 votes.

On Jan. 15, the Parliament, on the prompting of Labour Euro-M.P.s, set-up an inquiry into alleged police brutality on the miners' picket lines in the U.K.

The Parliament voted on Jan. 17 to investigate allegations of human rights violations against Irish nationals resident in Britain.

On Feb. 14, E.E.C. Governments were asked to join an investigation against the Mafia after a resolution was carried by Euro-M.P.s. The Parliament called on member Governments to set-up special efforts to deal with the growing infiltration of the Mafia. It voted to set-up an E.E.C. inquiry, particularly in Sicily, into the way the Mafia was infiltrating life in the Community.

It was reported on Feb. 25 that at hearings conducted by the Foreign Trade Committee of the Parliament it was estimated that the trade in counterfeit records and tapes alone was costing the Community between £600 and £900 million a year. Euro-M.P.s were told that cheap fakes of quality goods cost the Common Market 6,000 jobs last year and placed the lives of motorists and others at serious risk.

Farm prices

By 149 to 139 votes, the Parliament voted on Mar. 14 to increase Common Market farm prices by 3·5 per cent. this year. However, the resolution had no authority and the final decision on prices was within the ambit of the ministers of agriculture from the member States. The Community Commission had set forth a programme which included a freeze on all farm prices this year and a reduction of 3·6 per cent. in the prices for cereals, and U.K. Euro-M.P.s supported these views although they contended that in many respects they did not go far enought to bring the Common Agricultural Policy regime into line. Mrs. Castle, the British Labour group leader, said it was nothing short of madness to propose any increase in the price of milk as the Commission had recommended. Mr. Frans Andreissen, Commissioner for Agriculture, admitted his proposals would be hard for farmers to accept but he stressed that Community food surpluses were enormous.

President Reagan's speech

British Labour Euro-M.P.s unsuccessfully attempted to prevent a visit by President Reagan to the Parliament in Strasbourg, but their efforts to move to delete the President's VE-Day speech from the agenda were rejected as inadmissible. There was no surprise therefore on May 8 when Left-wing Euro-M.P.s, led by the majority of British Labour members, heckled and acted disruptively as President Reagan delivered his speech. Eventually, Mrs. Barbara Castle, the British Labour leader, led a walk-out and was followed by all but four of the 32 British Labour members and several continental Socialist and Communist Euro-M.P.s.

Mr. Stanley Clinton Davis, the British E.E.C. Commissioner, apologized on May 9 to the Parliament after twice refusing to withdraw his description of a Right-wing group in the European Parliament as on "the Fascist Right." His remark was made in a debate on the United States' policy towards Nicaragua.

The European Court of Justice ruled in Luxemburg on May 22 that Euro-M.P.s had the right to take the Council of Ministers of the E.E.C. to court for failing to fulfil its obligations under the Treaty of Rome.

Golden handshake

Euro-M.P.s blocked proposals on June 14 to pay E.E.C. officials golden handshakes to create Community jobs for the Spanish and Portuguese new members. However the Parliament remitted the early retirement plans to a committee after the Brussels Commission declined to give an estimate of the likely cost to the Common Market budget.

The Parliament gave substantial support on July 9 to an inter-governmental conference of Common Market States with the objective of negotiating changes in the E.E.C. treaties.

OTHER INTERNATIONAL ORGANIZATIONS

ASSOCIATION OF SOUTH EAST ASIAN NATIONS (A.S.E.A.N.)

Central Secretariat: Jakarta, Indonesia

Formed in 1967, the main aims of the Association are the acceleration of economic growth, social progress and cultural development, the promotion of collaboration and mutual assistance in matters of common interest, and the continuing stability of the South East Asian region.

The Heads of Government of the member countries are the highest authority and give directions to A.S.E.A.N. as and when necessary. The main policy-making body is the annual Meeting of Foreign Ministers of the member countries. The members of the Association are Brunei, Indonesia, Malaysia, the Philippines, Singapore and Thailand.

Sec. Gen., Phan Wannamethee (Thailand).

BANK FOR INTERNATIONAL SETTLEMENTS

(1930), Centrebahnplatz 2, 4002 Basle, Switzerland.

The objectives of the Bank are to promote the co-operation of central banks; to provide facilities for international financial operations; and to act as trustee or agent in international financial settlements entrusted to it. The London agent is the Bank of England, and the Governor of the Bank of England is a member of the Board of Directors, in which administrative control is vested.

Chairman of the Board of Directors and President of the Bank for International Settlement, Jean Godeaux (*Belgium*), from Jan. 1, 1985.

CARIBBEAN COMMUNITY AND COMMON MARKET (CARICOM)

P.O. Box 10827, Georgetown, Guyana

CARICOM was established on 1973 with three objectives: economic co-operation through the Caribbean Common Market; the co-ordination of foreign policy among the independent member states; the provision of common services and co-operation in functional matters such as health, education and culture, communications and industrial relations. The principal organs are the Conference of Heads of Government, which determines policy, and the Common Market Council of Ministers, consisting of Ministers of Government (usually Ministers of Trade) designated by each member state, which is responsible for the development and smooth running of the Common Market and for the settlement of any problems arising out of its functioning. The principal administrative arm is the Secretariat, based in Guyana.

The 13 member states are Antigua and Barbuda, The Bahamas, Barbados, Belize, Dominica, Grenada, Guyana, Jamaica, Montserrat, St. Kitts.-Nevis, St. Lucia, St. Vincent and the Grenadines and Trinidad and Tobago.

Sec. Gen., R. Rainford (*Jamaica*).

COUNCIL FOR MUTUAL ECONOMIC ASSISTANCE (C.M.E.A. OR COMECON)

56 Kalinin Avenue, Moscow G–205, U.S.S.R

Established in 1949, the Council's aim is to promote the development of the national economies of the member states and the development of socialist economic integration, through the co-operation of members in the most rational use of resources and the acceleration of economic and technical progress, industrialisation and productivity. The highest body is the Session of the Council, which consists of delegations from all member states, usually led by the heads of government. The Executive Committee consists of representatives of member states at the level of deputy heads of government, and is responsible for the implementation of the tasks set by the Session of the Council and for directing the work of the Committees, Standing Commissions, Secretariat and other bodies.

The member countries are Bulgaria, Cuba, Czechoslovakia, East Germany, Hungary, Mongolia, Poland, Romania, U.S.S.R. and Vietnam. Yugoslavia participates in the work of some C.M.E.A. bodies, and there are co-operation agreements with Finland, Iraq, Mexico and Nicaragua.

THE COUNCIL OF EUROPE

Headquarters: 67006 Strasbourg, France.
Secretary-General, M. Oreja

A European organization founded in 1949 whose aim is to achieve greater unity between its Members to safeguard their European heritage and to facilitate their economic and social progress through discussion and common action in economic, social, cultural, educational, scientific, legal and administrative matters and in the maintenance and furtherance of human rights and fundamental freedoms.

The 21 members are Austria, Belgium, Cyprus, Denmark, France, the Federal Republic of Germany, Greece, Iceland, the Republic of Ireland, Italy, Liechtenstein, Luxemburg, Malta, Netherlands, Norway, Portugal, Spain, Sweden, Switzerland, Turkey and the U.K.

The organs are the Committee of Ministers, consisting of the Foreign Ministers of member countries, who meet twice yearly, and the Parliamentary Assembly of 170 members, elected or chosen by the national parliaments of member countries in proportion to the relative strength of political parties. There is also a Joint Committee of Ministers and Representatives of the Parliamentary Assembly.

The Committee of Ministers is the executive organ of the Council. Certain of its conclusions take the form of international agreements or recommendations to governments. Decisions of the Ministers may also be embodied in partial agreements to which a limited number of member governments are party. All Ministers have appointed Deputies to act on their behalf. The Committee of Deputies meets every month to transact business and to take decisions on behalf of Ministers. Member governments accredit Permanent Representatives to the Council in Strasbourg, who are also the Ministers' Deputies.

The Committee is a forum for political discussions between member governments, supervises the work of the technical expert committees and considers recommendations received from the Parliamentary Assembly. Conferences of Ministers responsible for such areas as education, justice, the environment and public health meet at the invitation of a member government every two or three years and address their proposals for action in their respective fields to the Committee of Ministers.

The Parliamentary Assembly holds three week-long sessions a year. It debates reports on, inter alia, political, economic, agricultural, social, educational, legal and regional planning affairs, and also reports received annually from the O.E.C.D., other European organisations and certain specialised agencies of the United Nations. Its 13 permanent committees meet, normally in private, once or twice between each public plenary session of the Assembly. The Standing Conference of Local and Regional Authorities of Europe each year brings together mayors and municipal councillors in the same numbers as the members of the Parliamentary Assembly.

One of the principal achievements of the Council of Europe is the European Convention of Human Rights (1950) under which was established the European Commission and the European Court of Human Rights. Over 115 other conventions and agreements have now been concluded. They include the European Social Charter, the European Social Security Code, and conventions on extradition, the legal status of migrant workers, the conservation of European wildlife and natural habitats, the protection of individuals with regard to the automatic processing of personal data, transfrontier co-operation and the transfer of sentenced prisoners.

Non-member states take part in certain Council of Europe activities on a regular or ad hoc basis; thus Finland and the Holy See participate in all the educational, cultural and sports activities. The European Youth Foundation funds events in both Eastern and Western European countries and in some outside Europe, while nationals of these countries attend courses and seminars at the European Youth Centre.

Permanent U.K. Representative, His Excellency Christopher Duncan Lush, C.M.G.

EUROPEAN FREE TRADE ASSOCIATION (E.F.T.A.)

Member States: Austria, Iceland, Norway, Portugal, Sweden, Switzerland. Associate Member: Finland.

Following the unsuccessful attempt to create a European Free Trade Area linking the E.E.C. with other members of the O.E.E.C., seven European States came together in 1959 to form the European Free Trade Association. The seven were Austria, Denmark, Norway, Portugal, Sweden, Switzerland and the United Kingdom. The E.F.T.A. Convention became effective on May 3, 1960, and just over a year later, on June 26, 1961, Finland became an associate member. Iceland applied for full membership in November, 1968, and acceded to the Association and to the Finland–E.F.T.A. Agreement on March 1, 1970.

In 1973 all the E.F.T.A. Member States entered into a new relationship with the E.E.C. Two—Denmark and the United Kingdom—withdrew from E.F.T.A. at the end of December 1972 to become members of the E.E.C. on January 1, 1973. Agreements establishing industrial free trade between five of the other E.F.T.A. Member States (Austria, Iceland, Portugal, Sweden and Switzerland) and the E.E.C. came into force on that same date. Similar agreements with Norway and Finland came into force on July 1, 1973, and January 1, 1974, respectively.

The Convention defines the objects of the Association as (1) to promote economic expansion in the area of the Association and in each member state; (2) to ensure that trade between member states takes place in conditions of fair competition; (3) to avoid significant disparity between member states in the condition of supply of raw materials produced within the area; and (4) to contribute to the harmonious development and expansion of world trade and to the progressive removal of barriers to it.

Since December 31, 1966 the member countries of the Association have constituted a virtually complete industrial free trade area. There is no common external tariff for the Association, each member country being free to fix the level of its tariffs against countries outside the area. The Convention includes rules governing the origin of goods manufactured in the area. It also contains provisions relating to the "rules of competition"—government subsidies, restrictive business practices, etc. There are special provisions relating to trade in agricultural and fish products.

The free trade agreements between the E.F.T.A. countries and the E.E.C. provided for the complete removal by July 1, 1977 of the tariffs on almost all industrial products traded between them. This deadline was observed, and free trade was thereby established over almost all of Western Europe. From Jan. 1, 1986, the scheduled date of entry into the E.E.C. of Portugal (a member of E.F.T.A. until that date) and Spain, the free trade agreements will apply also to trade between the countries remaining in E.F.T.A. and Portugal and Spain.

E.F.T.A. has done much work on the removal of non-tariff barriers to trade, especially technical barriers to trade. Seven international schemes and two international conventions to overcome obstacles to trade in specific categories of products were devised in E.F.T.A. but are independent of the Association, and now involve the participation of other countries alongside E.F.T.A. countries.

The Council of E.F.T.A. meets every two weeks at the level of officials—the heads of the permanent national delegations to E.F.T.A.—usually twice a year at the level of ministers. Each state has a single vote and recommendations must normally be unanimous. Decisions of the Council are binding on member countries.

Secretary-General, Per Kleppe (Norway) 9–11 Rue de Varembé, 1211 Geneva 20.

LEAGUE OF ARAB STATES

37 Av. Khereddine Pacha, Tunis, Tunisia

The purpose of the League of Arab States (founded 1945) is to ensure co-operation among member states and protect their independence and sovereignty, to supervise the affairs and interests of Arab countries and to control the execution of agreements concluded among the member states. The League considers itself a regional organization and is an observer at the United Nations.

Member states are Algeria, Bahrain, Djibouti, Iraq, Jordan, Kuwait, Lebanon, Libya, Mauritania, Morocco, Oman, Palestine, Qatar, Saudi Arabia, Somalia, Sudan, Syria, Tunisia, United Arab Emirates, Arab Republic of Yemen and Democratic Republic of Yemen. (The membership of Egypt, a founder state, was suspended in 1979.)

Secretary-General, Chedli Klibi (*Tunisia*).

U.K. OFFICE.—Arab Information Centre, 52 Green Street, WIY 3RH.

NORTH ATLANTIC TREATY ORGANIZATION

Headquarters: Brussels 1110, Belgium.
Secretary General, Lord Carrington
(*United Kingdom*).

The North Atlantic Treaty was signed on April 4, 1949, by the Foreign Ministers of twelve nations. The twelve are Belgium, Canada, Denmark, France, Iceland, Italy, Luxemburg, the Netherlands, Norway, Portugal, the United Kingdom and United States. Greece and Turkey acceded to the Treaty in 1952, the Federal Republic of Germany in 1955, and Spain in 1982. The North Atlantic Council, chaired by the Secretary General, is the highest authority of the Alliance and is composed of permanent representatives of the sixteen member countries. It meets at ministerial levels (Foreign Ministers) at least twice per year. The permanent representatives (Ambassa-

dors) head national delegations of advisers and experts.

Defence matters are dealt with in the Defence Planning Committee (D.P.C.), composed of representatives of the member countries participating in the N.A.T.O. integrated military structure. Within the specialized field of defence, the D.P.C. has the same functions and authority as the Council. Like the Council it meets regularly at ambassador level and twice a year in ministerial sessions, when the nations are represented by their Defence Ministers.

The Council/D.P.C., as a unique forum for confidential and constant inter-governmental consultation and as the main decision-making body within the North Atlantic Alliance, is assisted by an International Staff, divided into five divisions: Political Affairs; Defence Planning and Policy; Defence Support; Infrastructure, Logistics and Council Operations; Scientific Affairs.

U.K. Permanent Representative, His Excellency Sir John Graham, K.C.M.G. (1979).

The senior military authority in N.A.T.O. is the Military Committee composed of the Chief of Defence of each member country except France and Iceland. The Military Committee, which is assisted by an international military staff, functions in permanent session with permanent military representatives and is responsible for making recommendations to the Council and Defence Planning Committee on measures considered necessary for the common defence of the N.A.T.O. area and for supplying guidance on military matters to the major N.A.T.O. Commanders.

Chairman of the Military Committee, Gen. C. de Jager (*Netherlands*).

The strategic area covered by the North Atlantic Treaty is divided among three Commands (European, Atlantic and Channel) and a Regional Planning Group (Canada and the United States).

The Major N.A.T.O Commanders are responsible for the development of defence plans for their respective areas, for the determination of force requirements and for the deployment and exercise of the forces under their command. The Major N.A.T.O. Commanders report to the Military Committee.

The three Major N.A.T.O Commanders are:

Supreme Allied Commander, Europe, Gen. Bernard W. Rogers (*U.S.*).

Supreme Allied Commander, Atlantic, Adm. Wesley L. McDonald (*U.S.*).

Commander-in-Chief, Channel, Ad. Sir Nicholas Hunt (*U.K.*).

ORGANIZATION FOR ECONOMIC CO-OPERATION AND DEVELOPMENT

Headquarters: 2, rue André-Pascal, 75116 Paris.
Secretary-General, J. C. Paye.

Formed on September 30, 1961, the O.E.C.D. replaced the Organization for European Economic Co-operation (O.E.E.C.). The O.E.C.D. is the instrument for international co-operation among industrialized member countries on economic and social policies. Its objectives are to assist its member governments in the formulation and co-ordination of policies designed to achieve high, sustained economic growth while maintaining financial stability, to contribute to world trade on a multilateral basis and to stimulate members' aid to developing countries.

The following countries belong to the O.E.C.D.: Australia, Austria, Belgium, Canada, Denmark, Federal Republic of Germany, Finland, France, Greece, Iceland, Irish Republic, Italy, Japan, Luxemburg, the Netherlands, New Zealand, Norway, Portugal, Spain, Sweden, Switzerland, Turkey, U.K. and U.S.A. (Yugoslavia participates with a special status).

The Council is the supreme body of the Organization. Composed of one representative for each member country, it meets at Permanent Representative level under the Chairmanship of the Secretary General, or at Ministerial level (usually once a year) under the Chairmanship of a Minister elected annually. Decisions and Recommendations are adopted by mutual agreement of all members of the Council. Fourteen members of the Council are chosen annually to form an Executive Committee to assist the Council. However, most of the O.E.C.D.'s work is undertaken in over 200 specialized committees and working parties. Four autonomous or semi-autonomous bodies also belong to the Organization: the Nuclear Energy Agency, the International Energy Agency, the Development Centre, and the Centre for Educational Research and Innovation. These bodies, the committees and the Council are serviced by an international Secretariat headed by the Secretary-General of the Organization.

U.K. Permanent Representative, Nicholas Peter Bayne, C.M.G., 19 rue de Franqueville, Paris 75116.

ORGANIZATION OF AFRICAN UNITY (O.A.U.)

P.O. Box 3243, Addis Ababa, Ethiopia

The Organization of African Unity was established in 1963 and has 32 members. It aims to further African unity and solidarity, to co-ordinate political, economic, social and defence policies, and to eliminate colonialism in Africa.

The chief organs are the Assembly of heads of state or government and the Council of Foreign Ministers. The main administrative body is the Secretariat, based in Addis Ababa.

Sec. Gen., Ide Oumarou (Niger).

ORGANIZATION OF AMERICAN STATES (O.A.S.)

17th Street and Constitution Ave. N.W., Washington D.C. 20006, U.S.A.

Originally founded in 1890 for largely commercial purposes, the O.A.S adopted its present name and charter in 1948. Its aims are to strengthen the peace and security of the continent; to prevent possible causes of difficulties and to ensure the pacific settlement of disputes that may arise among the member states; to provide for common action on the part of those states in the event of aggression; to seek the solution of political, juridical and economic problems that may arise among them; and to promote, by co-operative action, their economic, social and cultural development. The O.A.S. is a regional organization within the United Nations.

Policy is determined by the annual General Assembly. Meetings of Ministers of Foreign Affairs consider urgent problems, and advise in cases of armed attack and threats to peace.

The 32 member states are Antigua and Barbuda, Argentina, Bahamas, Barbados, Bolivia, Brazil, Chile, Colombia, Costa Rica, Cuba, Dominica, Dominican Republic, Ecuador, El Salvador, Grenada, Guatemala, Haiti, Honduras, Jamaica, Mexico, Nicaragua, Panama, Paraguay, Peru, St. Christopher-Nevis, St. Lucia, St. Vincent and the Grenadines, Surinam, Trinidad and Tobago, U.S.A., Uruguay and Venezuela.

Secretary-General, João Clemente Baena Soares.

ORGANIZATION OF THE PETROLEUM EXPORTING COUNTRIES (O.P.E.C.)

Obere Donaustrasse 93, A-1020 Vienna, Austria

The Organization of the Petroleum Exporting Countries was created in 1960 as a permanent intergovernmental organization with the aims of unifying and co-ordinating the pertroleum policies of members and determining the best means of protecting their interests, individually and collectively.

The supreme authority is the Conference of Ministers of Oil, Mines and Energy of member countries which meets at least twice a year and formulates policy. The Board of Governors, nominated by member countries, directs the management of O.P.E.C. and implements Conference resolutions. The Secretariat, based in Vienna, carries out executive functions under the direction of the Board of Governors.

The 13 member countries are Algeria, Ecuador, Gabon, Indonesia, Iran, Iraq, Kuwait, Libya, Nigeria, Qatar, Saudi Arabia, U.A.E. and Venezuela.

THE WORLD COUNCIL OF CHURCHES

150 route de Ferney, CH–1211 Geneva 20, Switzerland

General-Secretary, Dr. Emilio Castro (*Uruguay*).

The World Council of Churches was constituted in 1948 to promote unity between the many different Christian churches. It has a membership of 303 churches of widely varying traditions and cultural backgrounds, representing 400 million Christians in over 100 countries.

The policies of the Council are determined by delegates of the member churches meeting in Assembly, every 10 years, the last Assembly being in Vancouver in 1983. More detailed decisions are taken by a 150-member Central Committee which is elected by the Assembly and meets, with the seven W.C.C. Presidents, annually. The Central Committee in turn appoints a smaller Executive Committee and also nominates commissions and working groups, and guides the various programmes. The implementation of the policies laid down by the churches and the co-ordination of the 14 programmes are the responsibility of the General Secretariat.

British Council of Churches, 2 Eaton Gate, S.W.1.

CURRENCIES OF THE WORLD

Country	Monetary Unit	Denomination in Circulation	
		Notes	Coins
Afghanistan	*Afghani* of 100 *Puls*	*Afghanis* 1,000, 500, 100, 50, 20, 10	*Afghanis* 5, 2, 1; *Puls* 50, 25
Albania	*Lek* of 100 *Qindarka*	*Leks* 100, 50, 25, 10, 5, 3, 1	*Lek* 1: *Quindarka* 50, 20, 10, 5
Algeria...........	*Dinar* of 100 *Centimes*	*Dinars* 200, 100, 50, 20, 10, 5	*Dinars* 5, 1; *Centimes* 50, 20, 10, 5, 2, 1
Angola	*Kwanza* of 100 *Lweis*	*Kwanzas* 1,000, 500, 100, 50, 20	*Kwanzas* 20, 10, 5, 2, 1; *Lweis* 50
Argentina	*Austral* of 100 *Centavos* or 1,000 *Pesos*	*Austral* 1,000, 500, 100, 50, 10, 5, 1	*Centavos* 50, 10, 5, 1
Australia.........	*Dollar* of 100 *Cents*	$A 100, 50, 20, 10, 5, 2, 1	$A200, 10; *Cents* 50, 20, 10, 5, 2, 1
Austria	*Schilling* of 100 *Groschen*	*Schillings* 1,000, 500, 100, 50, 20	*Schillings* 1,000, 500, 100, 50, 25, 20, 10, 5, 1; *Groschen* 50, 10, 5, 2, 1
Bahamas	*Bahamian Dollar* of 100 *Cents*	B.$ 100, 50, 20, 10, 5, 3, 1; *Cents* 50	B.$ 5, 2, 1; *Cents* 50, 25, 15, 5, 1
Bahrain	*Dinar* of 1,000 *Fils*	*Dinars* 20, 10, 5, ½	*Fils* 100, 50, 25, 10, 5
Bangladesh	*Taka* of 100 *Poisha*	*Taka* 500, 100, 50, 20, 10, 5, 1	*Taka* 1; *Poisha* 50, 25, 10, 5, 1
Barbados	*Dollar* of 100 *Cents*	BDS$100, 20, 10, 5, 2, 1	BDS$1; *Cents* 25, 10, 5, 1
Belgium	*Belgian Franc* of 100 *Centimes*	*Frs.* 5,000, 1,000, 500, 100, 50	*Frs.* 500, 250, 100, 20, 10, 5, 1; *Centimes* 50
Belize	*Dollar* of 100 *Cents*	$100, 20, 10, 5, 1	*Cents* 50, 25, 10, 5, 1
Benin	*Franc C.F.A.*	*Frs.* 10,000, 5,000, 1,000, 500, 100, 50	*Frs.* 100, 50, 25, 10, 5, 2, 1
Bermuda	*Dollar* of 100 *Cents*	$100, 50, 20, 10, 5, 1	*Cents* 50, 25, 10, 5, 1
Bolivia	*Peso* of 100 *Centavos*	*Pesos* 100, 50, 20, 10, 5, 1	*Peso* 1; *Centavos* 50, 25, 20, 10, 5
Botswana	*Pula* of 100 *Thebe*	*Pula* 20, 10, 5, 2, 1	*Pula* 1; *Thebe* 50, 25, 10, 5, 2, 1
Brazil	*Cruzeiro* of 100 *Centavos*	*Cruzeiro* 5,000, 1,000, 500, 200, 100, 50, 10, 5, 1	*Cruzeiro* 50, 20, 10, 5, 1; *Centavos* 50, 20, 10
Brunei	*Brunei Dollar* of 100 *Sen*	$1,000, 500, 100, 50, 10, 5, 1	*Sen* 50, 20, 10, 5, 1
Bulgaria	*Lev* of 100 *Stotinki*	*Léva* 20, 10, 5, 2, 1	*Léva* 2, 1; *Stotinki* 50, 20, 10, 5, 2, 1
Burkina Faso	*Franc C.F.A.*	*Frs. C.F.A.* 10,000, 5,000, 1,000, 500, 100, 50	*Frs. C.F.A.* 100, 50, 25, 10, 5, 2, 1
Burma	*Kyat* of 100 *Pyas*	*Kyats* 100, 50, 25, 20, 10, 5, 1	*Kyat* 1; *Pyas* 50, 25, 10, 5, 1
Burundi..........	*Burundi Franc*	*Frs.* 5,000, 1,000, 500, 100, 50, 20, 10	*Frs.* 10, 5, 1
Cameroon (Federal Republic of)	*Franc C.F.A.*	*Frs.* 10,000, 5,000, 1,000, 500, 100	*Frs.* 100, 50, 25, 10, 5, 2, 1
Canada...........	*Dollar* of 100 *Cents*	$1,000, 100, 50, 20, 10, 5, 2, 1	$1; *Cents* 50, 25, 10, 5, 1
Cape Verde Islands	*Escudo* of 100 *Centavos*	*Esc* 1,000$00, 500$00, 100$00	*Esc* 50$00, 20$00, 10$00, 2$50, 1$00, *Centavos* $50, $20
Cayman Islands ...	*Dollar* of 100 *Cents*	$100, 40, 25, 10, 5, 1	*Cents* 25, 10, 5, 1
Central African Republic	*Franc C.F.A.*	*Frs.* 10,000, 5,000, 1,000, 500, 100	*Frs.* 100, 50, 25, 10, 5, 2, 1
Chad	*Franc C.F.A.*	*Frs.* 10,000, 5,000, 1,000, 500, 100	*Frs.* 100, 50, 25, 10, 5, 2, 1
Chile.............	*New Peso* of 100 *Centavos*	*Pesos* 5,000, 1,000, 500, 100, 50	*Pesos* 50, 10, 5, 1
China	*Renminbi* or *Yuan* of 10 *Jiao* or 100 *Fen*	*Yuan* 10, 5, 2, 1; *Jiao* 5, 2, 1	*Fen* 5, 2, 1
Colombia	*Peso* of 100 *Centavos*	*Pesos* 2,000, 1,000, 500, 200, 100, 50, 20, 10, 5, 2, 1	*Pesos* 10, 5, 2, 1; *Centavos* 50, 25, 20, 10
Congo............	*Franc C.F.A.*	*Frs.* 10,000, 5,000, 1,000, 500, 100	*Frs.* 100, 50, 25, 10, 5, 2, 1
Costa Rica	*Colon* of 100 *Céntimos*	*Colones* 1,000, 500, 100, 50, 20, 10, 5	*Colones* 20, 10, 5, 2, 1; *Centimos* 50, 25, 10, 5
Cuba	*Peso* of 100 *Centavos*	*Pesos* $100, 50, 20, 10, 5, 1	*Centavos* 40, 20, 5, 2, 1
Cyprus	*Cyprus Pound* of 100 *Cents*	£10, 5, 1; *Cents* 50	*Cents* 20, 10, 5, 2, 1, ½
Czechoslovakia ...	*Koruna* (Crown) of 100 *Haléru* (Heller)	*Kcs* 500, 100, 50, 20, 10	*Kcs* 5, 2, 1; *Heller* 50, 20, 10, 5, 1
Denmark	*Krone* of 100 *Öre*	*Kroner* 1,000, 500, 100, 50, 20	*Kroner* 10, 5, 1; *Öre* 25, 10, 5
Dominican Republic	*Peso* of 100 *Centavos*	RD$1,000, 500, 100, 50, 20, 10, 5, 1	*Peso* 1; *Centavos* 50, 25, 10, 5, 1
East Caribbean Territory	*East Caribbean Dollar* of 100 *Cents*	$100, 20, 5, 1	*Cents* 50, 25, 10, 5, 2, 1

Country	Monetary Unit	Denomination in Circulation	
		Notes	Coins
Ecuador	*Sucre* of 100 *Centavos*	*Sucres* 1,000, 500, 100, 50, 20, 10, 5	*Sucre* 1; *Centavos* 50, 20, 10
Egypt	*Egyptian Pound* of 100 *Piastres* or 1,000 *Millièmes*	£E100, 20, 10, 5, 1, ½, ¼; *Piastres* 10, 5	*Piastres* 10, 5; *Millièmes* 20, 10, 5, 2, 1
El Salvador	*Colon* of 100 *Centavos*	*Colones* 100, 50, 25, 10, 5, 2, 1	*Centavos* 50, 25, 10, 5, 3, 2, 1
Equatorial Guinea	*Ekuele*	E. 5,000, 1,000, 500, 100, 50, 25	
Ethiopia..........	*Ethiopian Birr* of 100 *Cents*	EB 100, 50, 10, 5, 1	*Cents* 50, 25, 10, 5, 1
Falkland Islands ..	*Pound* of 100 *Pence*	£10, 5, 1; 50p	*Pence* 50, 20, 10, 5, 2, 1, ½ United Kingdom coins are also in circulation except the £1, 50p, 20p
Faröe Islands	*Kronur* of 100 *Ore*	*Kr.* 1,000, 500, 100, 50, 10	As in Denmark
Fiji	*Fiji Dollar* of 100 *Cents*	$20, 10, 5, 2, 1	*Cents* 50, 20, 10, 5, 2, 1
Finland	*Markka* of 100 *Penniä*	*Mk* 500, 100, 50, 10, 5, 1	*Mk* 5, 1; *P* 50, 20, 10, 5, 1
France	*Franc* of 100 *Centimes*	*Francs* 500, 200, 100, 50, 20, 10	*Francs* 10, 5, 2, 1, ½; *Centimes* 20, 10, 5
Gabon............	*Franc C.F.A.*	*Frs.* 10,000, 5,000, 1,000, 500, 100	*Frs.* 100, 50, 25, 10, 5, 2, 1
Gambia (The)	*Dalasi* of 100 *Bututs*	*Dalasis* 25, 10, 5, 1	*Dalasi* 1; *Bututs* 50, 25, 10, 5, 1
Germany (East) ...	*Mark der Deutschen Demokratischen Republik (M.)* of 100 *Pfennig*	M. 100, 50, 20, 10, 5	M. 20, 10, 5, 2, 1; *Pfennig* 50, 20, 10, 5, 1
Germany (Federal Republic of)	*Deutsche Mark* of 100 *Pfennig*	*D.M.* 1,000, 500, 100, 50, 20, 10, 5	*D.M.* 10, 5, 2, 1; *Pfennig* 50, 10, 5, 2, 1
Ghana	*Cedi* of 100 *Pesewa*	*Cedis* 200, 100, 50, 10, 5, 2, 1	*Pesewas* 20, 10, 5, 2½, 1, ½
Gibraltar	*Pound* of 100 *pence*	£20, 10, 5, 1	As in U.K.
Greece	*Drachma* of 100 *Lepta*	*Drachmae* 5,000, 1,000, 500, 100, 50	*Drachmae* 20, 10, 5, 2, 1; *Lepta* 50, 20, 10
Guatemala	*Quetzal* of 100 *Centavos*	*Quetzales* 100, 50, 20, 10, 5, 1; *Centavos* 50	*Centavos* 25, 10, 5, 1
Guinea...........	*Syli* of 100 *Cauris*	*Sy* 100, 50, 25, 10	*Sy* 5, 2, 1, ½
Guinea-Bissau (Republic of)	*Escudos* of 100 *Centavos*	*Esc.* 1,000$00, 500$00, 100$00, 50$00	*Esc.* 20$00, 10$00, 5$00, 2$50, 1$00 *Centavos* $50, $20, $10, $05
Guyana	*Guyana Dollar* of 100 *Cents*	*Dollars* 20, 10, 5, 1	*Cents* 100, 50, 25, 10, 5, 1
Haiti.............	*Gourde* of 100 *Centimes**	*Gourdes* 500, 250, 100, 50, 10, 5, 2, 1	*Gourdes* 1,000, 200, 100, 50, 25, 20, 10, 5; *Centimes* 50, 20, 10, 5
Honduras	*Lempira* of 100 *Centavos*	*Lempiras* 100, 50, 20, 10, 5, 2, 1	*Centavos* 50, 20, 10, 5, 2, 1
Hong Kong	*Hong Kong Dollar* of 100 *Cents*	*Dollars* 1,000, 500, 100, 50, 10; *Cents* 1	*Dollars* 5, 2, 1; *Cents* 50, 20, 10, 5
Hungary	*Forint* of 100 *Fillér*	*Forints* 500, 100, 50, 20, 10	*Forints* 100, 20, 10, 5, 2, 1; *Fillér* 50, 20, 10, 5, 2
Iceland	*Króna* of 100 *Aurar*	*Kr.* 500, 100, 50, 10	*Kr.* 5, 1; *Aurar* 50, 10, 5
India.............	*Rupee* of 100 *Paise*	*Rupees* 100, 50, 20, 10, 5, 2, 1	*Rupees* 2, 1; *Paise* 50, 25, 20, 10, 5
Indonesia	*Rupiah* of 100 *Sen*	*Rupiahs* 10,000, 5,000, 1,000, 500, 100; *Sen* 25, 10, 5, 1	*Rupiahs* 100, 50, 25, 10, 5, 2, 1
Iran	*Rial* of 100 *Dinars*	*Rials* 10,000, 5,000, 1,000, 500, 200, 100	*Rials* 50, 20, 10, 5, 2, 1
Iraq..............	*Iraqi Dinar* of 1000 *Fils*	*Dinars* 25, 10, 5, 1, ½, ¼	*Fils* 100, 50, 25, 10, 5, 1
Ireland (Republic of)	*Pound* of 100 *Pence*	£20, 10, 5, 1	*New Pence* 50, 10, 5, 2, 1, ½
Israel	*Israeli Shekel* of 100 *New Agora*	*IS* 5,000, 1,000, 500, 100, 50, 10, 5, 1	*IS* ½; *New Agora* 10, 5, 1
Italy	*Lira* of 100 *Centesimi*	*Lire* 100,000, 50,000, 20,000, 10,000, 5,000, 2,000, 1,000, 500	*Lire* 1,000, 500, 200, 100, 50, 20, 10, 5, 2, 1
Ivory Coast (Republic of)	*Franc C.F.A.*	*Frs. C.F.A.* 10,000, 5,000, 1,000, 500, 100, 50	*Frs. C.F.A.* 100, 50, 25, 10, 5, 2, 1
Jamaica	*Jamaican Dollar* of 100 *Cents*	$20, 10, 5, 2, 1	$1, *Cents* 50, 25, 20, 10, 5, 1
Japan	*Yen*	*Yen* 10,000, 5,000, 1,000, 500	*Yen* 500, 100, 50, 10, 5, 1

* U.S.A. Currency also used.

Country	Monetary Unit	Denomination in Circulation	
		Notes	Coins
Jordan (Hashemite Kingdom of)	*Jordanian Dinar* of 1,000 *Fils*	*J. Dinars* 20, 10, 5, 1; *Fils* 500	*Fils* 250, 100, 50, 25, 20, 10, 5, 1
Kenya	*Kenya Shilling* of 100 *Cents*	*Shillings* 100, 50, 20, 10, 5	*Shillings* 1; *Cents* 50, 10, 5
Korea (South)	*Won* of 100 *Jeon*	*Won* 10,000, 5,000, 1,000, 500	*Won* 500, 100, 50, 10, 5, 1
Korea (North)	*Won* of 100 *Chon*	*Won* 100, 50, 10, 5, 1	*Jeon* 50, 10, 5, 1
Kuwait	*Kuwait Dinar* of 1,000 *Fils*	*Dinars* 10, 5, 1, ½, ¼	*Fils* 100, 50, 20, 10, 5, 1
Laos	*Kip* of 100 *Ats*	*Kips* 500, 200, 50, 20, 10	——
Lebanon	*Lebanese Pound* of 100 *Piastres*	*LL.* 250, 100, 50, 25, 10, 5, 1	*LL.* 1; *Piastres* 50, 25, 10, 5, 2½, 1
Liberia	*Liberian* $ of 100 *Cents*	$20, 10, 5, 1 (U.S. notes)	$5, 1; *Cents* 50, 25, 10, 5, 1*
Libya	*Libyan Dinar* of 1,000 *Dirhams*	*LD.* 10, 5, 1, ½, ¼	*Dirham* 100, 50, 20, 10, 5, 1
Luxembourg	*Franc* of 100 *Centimes*†	*Francs* 100, 50, 20	*Francs* 250, 100, 20, 10, 5, 1; *Centimes* 25
Macau	*Pataca* of 100 *Avos*	*Patacas* 500, 100, 50, 10, 5	*Patacas* 5, 1; *Avos* 50, 20, 10
Malagasy Republic	*Franc Malgache (F.M.G.)*	*Frs.* 10,000, 5,000, 1,000, 500, 100, 50	*Frs.* 100, 50, 20, 10, 5, 2, 1
Malawi	*Malawi Kwacha* of 100 *Tambala*	*K.* 20, 10, 5, 1; *Tambala* 50	*Tambala* 20, 10, 5, 2, 1
Malaysia	*Malaysian Dollar (Ringgit)* of 100 *Cents*	*Dollars* 1,000, 500, 100, 20, 10, 5, 1	*Dollar* 1; *Cents* 50, 20, 10, 5, 1
Maldive Islands	*Rufiyaa* of 100 *Laris*	*Rs* 100, 50, 10, 5, 2, 1, ½	——
Mali (Republic of)	*Franc C.F.A.*	*Frs.* 10,000, 5,000, 1,000, 500, 100	*Frs.* 100, 50, 25, 10, 5
Malta	*Maltese Lira* of 100 *cents* or 1,000 *Mils*	*LM*10, 5, 1	*Cents* 50, 25, 10, 5, 2, 1; *Mils* 5, 3, 2
Mauritania	*Ouguiya* of 5 *Khoums*	*UM* 1,000, 500, 200, 100	*UM* 20, 10, 5, 1, ⅕
Mauritius	*Rupee* of 100 *Cents*	*Rs.* 50, 25, 10, 5	*R.* 1; *Cents* 50, 25, 10, 5, 2, 1
Mexico	*Peso* of 100 *Centavos*	*Pesos* 10,000, 5,000, 2,000, 1,000, 500, 100, 50, 20, 10, 5, 1	*Pesos* 10, 5, 1; *Centavos* 50, 20, 10
Monaco	*Franc* of 100 *Centimes*	As in France	*Francs* 50, 10, 5, 1; *Centimes* 50, 20, 10
Mongolian People's Republic	*Tugrik* of 100 *Mongo*	*Tugriks* 100, 50, 25, 10, 5, 3, 1	*Tugrik* 1; *Mongo* 50, 20, 15, 10, 5, 2, 1
Morocco	*Dirham* of 100 *Centimes*	*DH* 100, 50, 10, 5	*DH* 5, 1; *Centimes* 50, 20, 10, 5, 2, 1
Mozambique	*Metical* of 100 *Centavos*	*Meticais* 1,000, 500, 100, 50	*Meticais* 20, 10, 5, 2½, 1, ½
Nepal	*Rupee* of 100 *Paisa*	*Rupees* 1,000, 500, 100, 50, 20, 10, 5, 2, 1	*Rupee* 100, 50, 25, 20, 10, 5, 2, 1; *Paisa* 50, 25, 20, 10, 5, 2, 1
Netherlands (The)	*Florin (Guilder)* of 100 *Cents*	*Florins* 1,000, 100, 50, 25, 10, 5, 2½, 1	*Florins* 10, 2½, 1; *Cents* 25, 10, 5
Netherlands Antilles (The)	*N.A. Guilder* of 100 *Cents*	*Guilders* 250, 100, 50, 25, 10, 5, 2½, 1	*Guilders* 2½, 1, ¼, $\frac{1}{10}$; *Cent* 5, 2½, 1
New Zealand	*New Zealand Dollar* of 100 *Cents*	N.Z.$ 100, 50, 20, 10, 5, 2, 1	*Cents* 50, 20, 10, 5, 2, 1
Nicaragua	*Córdoba* of 100 *Centavos*	*Córdobas* 1,000, 500, 100, 50, 20, 10, 5, 2, 1	*Cordobas* 5, 1; *Centavos* 50, 25, 10, 5
Niger (Republic of)	*Franc C.F.A.*	*Frs. C.F.A.* 10,000, 5,000, 1,000, 500, 100, 50	*Frs. C.F.A.* 100, 50, 25, 10, 5, 2, 1
Nigeria	*Naira* of 100 *Kobo*	N.20, 10, 5, 1	*k.*25, 10, 5, 1, ½
Norway	*Krone* of 100 *Öre*	*Kroner* 1,000, 500, 100, 50, 10	*Kroner* 5, 1; *Öre* 50, 25, 10, 5
Oman	*Rial Omani* of 1,000 *Baiza*	*Rial Omani* 50, 20, 10, 5, 1, ½, ¼; *Baiza* 100	*Baiza* 500, 250, 100, 50, 25, 10, 5, 2
Pakistan	*Rupee* of 100 *Paisa*	*Rupees* 100, 50, 10, 5, 2, 1	*Rupee* 1, ½, ¼; *Paisa* 50, 25, 10, 5, 2, 1
Panama	*Balboa* of 100 *Cents* (= *U.S.$*)	As in U.S.A.	*Balboa* 500, 150, 100, 5, 1, ½, ¼, $\frac{1}{10}$, $\frac{1}{20}$; *Cent* 1.*
Papua New Guinea	*Kina* = 100 *Toea*	*K* 20, 10, 5, 2	*K* 1; *T* 50, 20, 10, 5, 2, 1
Paraguay	*Guarani* of 100 *Céntimos*	*Guaraníes* 10,000, 5,000, 1,000, 500, 100, 50, 10, 5, 1	——
Peru	*Gold Sol* of 100 *Centavos*	*Soles* 10,000, 5,000, 1,000, 500	*Soles* 100, 50, 10, 5, 1
Philippines	*Philippine Peso* of 100 *Centavos*	*Pesos* 100, 50, 20, 10, 5, 2	*Peso* 1; *Centavos* 50, 25, 10, 5, 1
Poland	*Zloty* of 100 *Groszy*	*Zlotys* 5,000, 2,000, 1,000, 500, 200, 100, 50, 20, 10	*Zlotys* 2,000, 1,000, 500, 200, 100, 50, 20, 10, 5, 2, 1; *Groszy* 50, 20, 10, 5, 2

* U.S. coins also circulate. † Belgian currency is also legal tender.

Country	Monetary Unit	Denomination in Circulation	
		Notes	Coins
Portugal	*Escudo* of 100 *Centavos*	*Escudos* 5,000$00, 1,000$00, 500$00, 100$00, 50$00	*Escudos* 25$00, 5$00, 2$50, 1$00, $50
Portuguese Timor .	*Escudo* of 100 *Centavos*	*Esc.* 1,000$00, 500$00, 100$00, 50$00, 20$00	*Esc.* 10$00, 5$00, 2$50, 1$00; *Centavos* $50, $20, $10
Qatar	*Qatar Riyal* of 100 *Dirhams*	*Qatar Riyals* 500, 100, 50, 10, 5, 1	*Dirhams* 50, 25, 10, 5, 1
Romania	*Leu* of 100 *Bani*	*Lei* 100, 50, 25, 10, 5, 3, 1	*Lei* 5, 3, 1; *Bani* 25, 15, 10, 5, 3, 1
Rwanda	*Rwanda Franc*	*Frs.* 5,000, 1,000, 500, 100	*Frs.* 50, 20, 10, 5, 1
St. Helena	St. Helena *Pound* of 100 *Pence*	£10, 5, 1, 50p	As in U.K.
Samoa (Western) ..	*Tala* of 100 *Sene*	*Tala* 20, 10, 5, 2, 1	*Sene* 50, 20, 10, 5, 2, 1
Sao Tomé and Princípe	*Dobra* of 100 *Centimos*	*Dobras* 1,000, 500, 100, 50	*Dobras* 20, 10, 5, 2, 1; *Centimos* 50
Saudi Arabia	*Riyal* of 20 *Qursh* or 100 *Halalas*	*Riyals* 500, 100, 50, 10, 5, 1	*Halala* 100, 50, 25, 10, 5, 1
Senegal	*Franc C.F.A.*	*Frs.* 10,000, 5,000, 1,000, 500, 100, 50	*Frs.* 100, 50, 25, 10, 5, 2, 1
Seychelles	*Rupee* of 100 *Cents*	*S.R.* 100, 50, 25, 10	*Rupees* 1,500, 1,000, 100, 50, 25, 20, 10, 5, 1; *Cents* 25, 10, 5
Sierra Leone	*Leone* of 100 *Cents*	*Le.* 20, 10, 5, 2, 1; *Cents* 50	*Cents* 50, 20, 10, 5, 1, ½
Singapore	*S. Dollar* of 100 *Cents*	*S*$10,000, 1,000, 500, 100, 50, 25, 20, 10, 5, 1	*S*$1; *Cents* 50, 20, 10, 5, 1
Solomon Islands ...	*Solomon Islands Dollar* of 100 *Cents*	*SI*$20, 10, 5, 2	*SI*$1; *Cents* 20, 10, 5, 2, 1
Somali Democratic Republic	*Somali Shilling* of 100 *Cents*	*S. Shillings* 100, 20, 10, 5	*Shillings* 1, ½; *Cents* 10, 5, 1
South Africa	*Rand* of 100 *Cents*	*R* 20, 10, 5, 2, 1	*R* 1; *Cents* 50, 20, 10, 5, 2, 1, ½
Spain	*Peseta* of 100 *Céntimos*	*Pesetas* 5,000, 2,000, 1,000, 500, 200, 100	*Pesetas* 100, 50, 25, 5, 1; *Céntimos* 50
Sri Lanka	*Rupee* of 100 *Cents*	*Rupees* 1,000, 500, 100, 50, 20, 10, 5, 2	*Re.* 1; *Cents* 50, 25, 10, 5, 2, 1
Sudan	*Sudanese Pound* of 100 *Piastres* or 1,000 *Milliemes*	£S 20, 10, 5, 1; *Piastres* 50, 25	*Piastres* 50, 10, 5, 2; *Milliemes* 10, 5, 2, 1
Surinam	*Guilder* of 100 *Cents*	*Guilders* 500, 100, 25, 10, 5, 2½, 1	*Guilder* 1; *Cents* 25, 10, 5, 1
Swaziland	*Lilangeni* (plural *Emalangeni*) of 100 *cents*	*E* 20, 10, 5, 2, 1	*E* 2, 1; *Cents* 50, 20, 10, 5, 2, 1
Sweden	*Krona* of 100 *Öre*	*Kronor* 10,000, 1,000, 100, 50, 10	*Kronor* 200, 100, 50, 10, 5, 2, 1; *Öre* 50, 25, 10, 5
Switzerland	*Franc* of 100 *Centimes*	*Francs* 1,000, 500, 100, 50, 20, 10	*Francs* 5, 2, 1; *Centimes* 50, 20, 10, 5, 1
Syria.............	*Syrian Pound* of 100 *Piastres*	*S. Pounds* 500, 100, 50, 25, 10, 5, 1	*Pound* 1, ½; *Piastres* 50, 25, 10, 5, 2½
Taiwan	*New Taiwan Dollar* of 100 *Cents*	*NT*$ 1,000, 500, 100, 50, 10, 5, 1	*NT*$10, 5, 1; *Cents* 50, 10
Tanzania	*T. Shilling* of 100 *Cents*	*Shillings* 100, 20, 10	*Shilling* 5, 1; *Cents* 50, 20, 10, 5
Thailand	*Baht* of 100 *Stangs*	*Bahts* 500, 100, 20, 10, 5, 1; *Stangs* 50	*Baht* 5, 1; *Stangs* 50, 25, 10, 5, 1
Togo (Republic of) .	*Franc C.F.A.*	*Frs. C.F.A.* 10,000, 5,000, 1,000, 500, 100, 50	*Frs. C.F.A.* 100, 50, 25, 10, 5, 2, 1
Tonga............	*Pa'anga* (*T*$) of 100 *Seniti*	*Pa'anga* 10, 5, 2, 1, ½	*Pa'anga* 2, 1; *Seniti* 50, 20, 10, 5, 2, 1
Trinidad and Tobago	*Trinidad and Tobago Dollar* of 100 *Cents*	*Dollars* 100, 20, 10, 5, 1	*Dollar* 1; *Cents* 50, 25, 10, 5, 1
Tunisia	*Tunisian Dinar* of 1,000 *Millimes*	*Dinars* 10, 5, 1, ½	*Dinars* 5, 1, ½; *Millimes* 100, 50, 20, 10, 5, 2, 1
Turkey...........	*Turkish Lira* of 100 *Kurus*	*TL* 10,000, 5,000, 1,000, 500, 100, 50, 20, 10	*TL* 100, 50, 20, 10, 5, 2, 1; *Kurus* 50, 25, 10, 5, 1
Uganda	*U. Shilling* of 100 *Cents*	*Shillings* 100, 50, 20, 10	*Shillings* 5, 2, 1; *Cents* 50, 20, 10, 5
United Arab Emirates	*Dirham* of 100 *Fils*	*Dirhams* 1,000, 100, 50, 10, 5, 1	*Dirham* 1; *Fils* 50, 25, 10, 5, 1
United Kingdom ..	*Pound* of 100 *pence*	£50, £20, £10, £5, £1	£1; *Pence* 50, 20, 10, 5, 2, 1, ½; 5s. (25p)
U.S.A............	*Dollar* of 100 *Cents*	$100, 50, 20, 10, 5, 2, 1	$1; *Cents* 50, 25, 10, 5, 1
Uruguay	*New Peso* of 100 *Centésimos*	*New Pesos* 10,000, 5,000, 1,000, 500, 100, 50	*New Pesos* 10, 5, 2, 1; *Cents* 50, 20, 10

Country	Monetary Unit	Denomination in Circulation	
		Notes	Coins
U.S.S.R.	*Rouble* of 100 *Copecks*	*Roubles* 100, 50, 25, 10, 5, 3, 1	*Rouble* 1; *Copecks* 50, 20, 15, 10, 5, 3, 2, 1
Venezuela	*Bolívar*	*Bolívares* 500, 100, 50, 20, 10, 5	*Bolívares* 100, 20, 10, 5, 2, 1, ½, ¼, 1/10, 1/20
Vietnam	*Dông* of 10 *Hào* or 100 *Xu*	*Dông* 10, 5, 2, 1; *Hào* 5, 2, 1; *Xu* 5	*Xu* 5, 2, 1
Yemen (Arab Republic)	*Riyal* of 100 *Fils*	*Riyals* 100, 50, 20, 10, 5, 1	*Fils* 50, 25, 10, 5, 1
Yemen (People's Democratic Republic)	*Southern Yemen Dinar* (*YD*) of 1,000 *Fils*	*YD* 10, 5, 1; *Fils* 500, 250	*Fils* 50, 25, 5, 2½, 1
Yugoslavia	*Dinar* of 100 *Paras*	*Dinars* 1,000, 500, 100, 50, 20, 10, 5	*Dinar* 10, 5, 2, 1; *Paras* 50, 20, 10, 5
Zaire (Congolese Republic)	*Zaire* of 100 *Makuta* or 10,000 *Sengi*	*Zaires* 50, 10, 5, 1; *Makuta* 50	*Makuta* 20, 10, 5, 1; *Sengi* 10
Zambia	*Kwacha* of 100 *Ngwee*	*Kwacha* 20, 10, 5, 2, 1	*Ngwee* 50, 20, 10, 5, 2, 1
Zimbabwe	*Dollar* of 100 *Cents*	*Z$* 20, 10, 5, 2, 1	*Z$1, Cents* 50, 20, 10, 5, 1

WEATHER INFORMATION AND FORECASTS

Recorded weather forecasts for the areas listed below are available by telephoning the numbers shown:

Herts, Beds and		Blackburn 8091	Doncaster 8091
Inland Essex	Bedford 8091	Blackpool 8091	Dorset and Hants. Coast
Bishops Stortford 8091		Southport 8091	(including I.O.W.)
Cambridge 8091		West	Bournemouth 8091
London 01–246 8099		Yorkshire Bradford 8091	Portsmouth 8091
Luton 8091		Huddersfield 8091	Southampton 8091
Northern Ireland	Belfast 8091	Leeds 8091	Gloucestershire, Hereford
West Midlands and	021–246 8091	Greater London 01–246 8091	and Worcester
Warwickshire	Coventry 8091	Tunbridge Wells 8091	Cheltenham 8091
Avon and	Bristol 8091	Guildford 8091	Gloucester 8091
Somerset	Swindon 8091	East Anglia Cambridge 8092	Hereford 8091
Glamorgan, Gwent		Norwich 8091	Sussex and
and South Dyfed		Ipswich 8091	S. Kent Coast 01–246 8097
Cardiff 8091		Lowestoft 8091	Brighton 8091
Newport 8091		North East England	Hastings 8091
Swansea 8091		(incl. N. Yorks)	Canterbury 8092
Devon and Cornwall	Exeter 8091	Peterborough 8091	Oxon, Berks and
Plymouth 8091		Middlesbrough 8091	Bucks 01–246 8090
Torquay 8091		Newcastle upon Tyne 8091	High Wycombe 8091
Dundee, Tayside		Lincs &	Oxford 8091
and Fife	Dundee 8091	Humberside Grimsby 8091	Reading 8091
Edinburgh, S. Fife		Lincoln 8091	North Downs and
and Borders	031–246 8091	Anglesey and	the Weald 01–246 8092
Glasgow area	041–246 8091	N. Wales Coast 051–246 8093	Staffs and Shropshire
Grampian	Aberdeen 8091	061–246 8093	Stoke-on-Trent 8091
N. Kent and	01–246 8096	Chester 8091	Shrewsbury 8091
S. Essex Coast	Canterbury 8091	Colwyn Bay 8091	Lake District Carlisle 8092
Medway 8091		East Midlands Nottingham 8091	Kendal 8092
Chelmsford 8091		Leicester 8091	Leeds 8092
Colchester 8091		Derby 8091	Wiltshire, N. Dorset
Southend 8091		Northampton 8091	and Hampshire Swindon 8091
N.W. England	051–246 8091	S. Yorkshire and	Andover 8091
061–246 8091		Peak District Sheffield 8091	

RETROSPECT OF SPORT 1984–85

ATHLETICS
WORLD RECORDS

(All the world records given below have been accepted by the International Amateur Athletic Federation except those marked with an asterisk* which are awaiting homologation.)

Fully automatic timing to 1/100th second is mandatory up to and including 400 metres. For distances up to and including 10,000 metres records will be accepted to 1/100th second if timed automatically, and to 1/10th if hand timing is used.

MEN'S EVENTS
Running

Distances	hr.	min.	Time sec.	Name	Nation	Year
100 metres			9·93	C. Smith	U.S.A.	1983
200 metres (turn)			19·72	P. Mennea	Italy	1979
400 metres			43·86	L. Evans	U.S.A.	1968
800 metres		1	41·73	S. Coe	G.B.	1981
1,000 metres		2	12·18	S. Coe	G.B.	1981
1,500 metres		3	29·45*	S. Aouita	Morocco	1985
1 mile		3	46·31*	S. Cram	G.B.	1985
2,000 metres		4	51·39*	S. Cram	G.B.	1985
3,000 metres		7	32·1	H. Rono	Kenya	1978
5,000 metres		13	00·40*	S. Aouita	Morocco	1985
10,000 metres		27	13·81	F. Mamede	Portugal	1984
20,000 metres		57	24·2	J. Hermens	Netherlands	1976
20,944 metres (13 miles 24 yards 2 feet)	1	00	00·0	J. Hermens	Netherlands	1976
25,000 metres	1	13	55·8	T. Seko	Japan	1981
30,000 metres	1	29	18·8	T. Seko	Japan	1981
110 metres hurdles			12·93	R. Nehemiah	U.S.A.	1981
400 metres hurdles			47·02	E. Moses	U.S.A.	1983
3,000 metres steeplechase		8	05·4	H. Rono	Kenya	1978

Relay Racing

Distance	min.	Time sec.	Nation	Year
4 × 100 metres		37·83	U.S.A.	1984
4 × 200 metres	1	20·26	Univ. of S. Calif.	1978
4 × 400 metres	2	56·16	U.S.A.	1977
4 × 800 metres	7	03·89	G.B.	1982
4 × 1,500 metres	14	38·8	F.R.G.	1977

Jumping and Throwing

	ft.	in.	metres	Name	Nation	Year
High Jump	7	10½	2·41*	I. Paklin	U.S.S.R.	1985
Pole Vault	19	8¼	6·00*	S. Bubka	U.S.S.R.	1985
Long Jump	29	2½	8·90	R. Beamon	U.S.A.	1968
Triple Jump	58	11½	17·97*	W. Banks	U.S.A.	1985
Shot	72	10½	22·22	U. Beyer	G.D.R.	1983
Discus	235	9	71·86	Y. Dumchev	U.S.S.R.	1983
Hammer	283	3	86·34	Y. Sedykh	U.S.S.R.	1984
Javelin	343	9	104·80	U. Hohn	G.D.R.	1984
Decathlon			8,847 pts.°	D. Thompson	G.B.	1984

Walking (Track)

Distance	hr.	min.	Time sec.	Name	Nation	Year
20,000 metres	1	18	40	E. Canto	Mexico	1984
28,358 metres (17 miles 1029 yards)	2	00	00·0	R. Kowalsky	G.D.R.	1982
30,000 metres	2	06	07·3*	M. Damilano	Italy	1985
50,000 metres	3	41	39·00	R. Gonzalez	Mexico	1979

° Scored with new scoring tables.

WOMEN'S EVENTS
Running

Distance	Time min. sec.		Name	Nation	Year
100 metres		10·76	E. Ashford	U.S.A.	1984
200 metres		21·71	M. Koch	G.D.R.	1979
400 metres		47·99	J. Kratochvilova	Czechoslovakia	1983
800 metres	1	53·28	J. Kratochvilova	Czechoslovakia	1983
1,500 metres	3	52·47	T. Kazankina	U.S.S.R.	1980
1 mile	4	16·71*	M. Slaney	U.S.A.	1985
3,000 metres	8	28·83	Z. Budd	G.B.	1985
5,000 metres	14	48·07*	Z. Budd	G.B.	1985
10,000 metres	30	59·42*	I. Kristiansen	Norway	1985
100 metres hurdles (2 ft. 9 in.)		12·36	G. Rabsztyn	Poland	1980
400 metres hurdles		53·58	M. Ponomaryeva	U.S.S.R.	1984

Relays

Distance	Time min. sec.		Nation	Year
4 × 100 metres		41·53	G.D.R.	1983
4 × 200 metres	1	28·15	G.D.R.	1980
4 × 400 metres	3	15·92	G.D.R.	1984
4 × 800 metres	7	50·17	U.S.S.R.	1984

Women's Jumping and Throwing

	ft.	in.	metres	Name	Nation	Year
High Jump	6	9½	2·07	L. Andonova	Bulgaria	1984
Long Jump	24	4½	7·43	A. Cusmir	Romania	1983
Shot Putt	73	8	22·45	I. Slupianek	G.D.R.	1980
Discus	244	7	74·56	Z. Silhava	Czechoslovakia	1984
Javelin	247	4	75·40*	P. Felke	G.D.R.	1985
Heptathlon†		6,867 pts.		S. Paetz	G.D.R.	1984

†Seven events comprising 100 m hurdles, shot, high jump, 200 m, long jump, Javelin, 800 m.

UNITED KINGDOM (NATIONAL) RECORDS
(Records made anywhere by athletes eligible to represent Great Britain and Northern Ireland)

Men

100 *metres*—10·11 sec. (A. Wells 1980).
200 *metres*—20·21 sec. (A. Wells, 1980).
400 *metres*—44·82 (D. Redmond, 1985).
800 *metres*—1 min. 41·73 (S. Coe, 1981).
1,000 *metres*—2 min. 12·18 sec. (S. Coe, 1981).
1,500 *metres*—3 min. 29·67 sec. (S. Cram, 1985).
1 *mile*—3 min. 46·31 sec. (S. Cram, 1985).
2,000 *metres*—4 min. 51·39 sec. (S. Cram, 1985).
3,000 *metres*—7 min. 32·79 sec. (D. Moorcroft, 1982).
5,000 *metres*—13 min. 00·41 sec. (D. Moorcroft, 1982).
10,000 *metres*—27 min. 30·3 sec. (B. Foster, 1978).
20,000 *metres*—58 min. 39·0 sec. (R. Hill, 1968).
12 *miles* 1,268 *yards*—1 hr. (R. Hill, 1968).
25,000 *metres*—1 hr. 15 min. 22·6 sec. (R. Hill, 1965).
30,000 *metres*—1 hr. 31 min. 30·4 sec. (J. Alder, 1970).
3,000 *metres Steeplechase*—8 min. 13·50 sec. (C. Reitz, 1985).
110 *metres Hurdles*—13·43 sec. (M. Holtom, 1982).
400 *metres Hurdles*—48·12 sec. (D. P. Hemery, 1968).
4 × 100 *metres Relay*—38·62 (G.B. Team, 1980)
4 × 200 *metres*—1 min. 24·1 sec. (G.B. Team, 1971).
4 × 400 *metres*—2 min. 59·13 sec. (G.B. Team, 1984).
4 × 800 *metres*—7 min. 03·89 sec. (G.B. Team, 1982).
4 × 1,500 *metres*—14 min. 56·8 sec. (G.B. Team, 1979).
High Jump—2·26 m.,7ft. 5 in. (G. Parsons, 1984).
Pole Vault—5·65 m., 18 ft. 6¼ in. (K. Stock, 1981).
Long Jump—8·23 m., 27 ft. 0 in. (L. Davies, 1968).
Triple Jump—17·57 m., 57 ft. 7¼ in. (K. Connor, 1982).
Shot—21·68 m., 71 ft. 1½ in. (G. Capes, 1980).
Discus—64·32 m., 211 ft. 0 in. (W. Tancred, 1974).
Hammer—77·54 m., 254 ft. 5 in. (M. Girvan, 1984).
Javelin—91·40 m., 299 ft. 10 in. (R. Bradstock, 1985).
Decathlon—8,847 pts.° (D. Thompson, 1984).
° Scored with new scoring tables.

Walking (Track)

20,000 *metres*—1 hr. 26 min. 22 sec. (S. Barry, 1981).
2 *Hours*—16 miles 315 yds. (R. Wallwork, 1971).
30,000 *metres*—2 hr. 19 min. 18 sec. (C. Maddocks, 1984).
50,000 *metres*—4 hr. 05 min. 48 sec. (C. Maddocks, 1984).

Women

100 *metres*—11·10 sec. (K. Cook, 1981).
200 *metres*—22·10 sec. (K. Cook, 1984).
400 *metres*—49·43 sec. (K. Cook, 1984).
800 *metres*—1 min. 57·42 sec. (K. McDermott, 1985).
1,500 *metres*—3 min. 59·96 sec. (Z. Budd, 1985).
1 *mile*—4 min. 17·57 sec. (Z. Budd, 1985).
3,000 *metres*—8 min. 35·32 sec. (Z. Budd, 1985).
5,000 *metres*—14 min. 48·07 sec. (Z. Budd, 1985)
10,000 *metres*—32 min. 57·17 sec. (K. Binns, 1980).
100 *metres Hurdles*—12·87 sec. (S. Strong, 1983).
400 *metres Hurdles*—56·04 sec. (S. Morley, 1983).
4 × 100 *metres Relay*—42·43 sec. (G.B. Team, 1980).
4 × 200 *metres Relay*—1 min. 31·57 sec. (G.B. Team, 1977).
4 × 400 *metres Relay*—3 min. 25·51 sec. (G.B. Team, 1984).
4 × 800 *metres Relay*—8 min. 23·8 sec. (G.B. Team, 1971).
High Jump—1·95 m., 6 ft. 4¼ in. (D. Elliott, 1982).
Long Jump—6·90 m., 22 ft. 7¼ in. (B. Kinch, 1983).
Shot—18·99 m., 62 ft. 3¼ in. (M. Ritchie, 1983).
Discus—67·48 m., 221 ft. 5 in. (M. Ritchie, 1981).
Javelin—73·58 m., 241 ft. 5 in. (T. Sanderson, 1983).
Heptathlon—6,353 pts. (J. Livermore, 1983).

Oxford v. Cambridge

Cross Country, held December 10, 1984, at Wimbledon Common. Oxford beat Cambridge by 31 points to 52. Individual winner—M. Barton (C). Women, Cambridge beat Oxford by 11½ points to 30. Individual winner—A. O'Neill (C).

Athletics, held at Oxford on May 18, 1985. Oxford beat Cambridge by 114 points to 96. Women, Cambridge beat Oxford, 80 points to 77.

A.A.A. and W.A.A.A. Indoor Championships

Held at Cosford, January 25–26, 1985

Men's Events

Metres		min.	sec.
60—R. Desruelles (Belgium)			6·65
200—M. Lattany (U.S.A.)			21·36
400—T. Bennett (Southampton & Eastleigh)			46·83
800—I. Billy (Wirral)		1	49·85
1,500—R. Harrison (Liverpool)		3	42·95
3,000—D. Lewis (Rossendale)		7	58·41
Steeplechase—C. Walker (Gateshead)		5	35·92
60 *Hurdles*—J. Ridgeon (Cambridge & Coleridge)			7·71
			metres
High Jump—A. Metellus (Canada)			2·23
Pole Vault—V. Bubka (U.S.S.R.)			5·60
Long Jump—Liu Yuhuang (China)			7·67
Triple Jump—Zou Zhenxian (China)			16·50
Shot—W. Cole (Thurrock)			17·32

Women's Events

Metres		min.	sec.
60—H. Oakes (Haringey)			7·24
200—C. Smart (Cardiff)			24·44
400—L. Macdonald (Pitreavie)			54·74
800—K. McDermott (Bristol)		2	02·70
1,500—Z. Budd (Aldershot)		4	11·20
60 *Hurdles*—J. Simpson (Birchfield)			8·25
			metres
High Jump—O. Turchak (U.S.S.R.)			1·88
Long Jump—Liao Wenfen (China)			6·26
Shot—J. Oakes (Croydon)			17·85

Held at Cosford, January 12, 1985

Metres		min.	sec.
3,000—S. Crehan (Sutton & St. Helens)		9	27·63

United Kingdom v. Federal Republic of Germany

Held at Cosford, February 9, 1985

Men's Events

Metres		min.	sec.
60(A)—L. Asquith (U.K.)			6·70
(B)—H. Fritsche (G.)			6·76
200—A. Mafe (U.K.)			21·46
400—T. Bennett (U.K.)			46·93
800—A. Harries (G.)		1	48·75
1,500—R. Harrison (U.K.)		3	43·88
3,000—D. Lewis (U.K.)		7	59·84
60 *Hurdles* (A)—J. Ridgeon (U.K.)			7·75
(B)—J. Ridgeon (U.K.)			7·73
4 × 400 *Relay*—United Kingdom		3	11·47
			metres
High Jump—G. Nagel (G.)			2·16
Pole Vault—P. Volmer (G.)			5·10
Long Jump—D. Brown (U.K.)			7·67
Triple Jump—R. Jaros (G.)			16·77
Shot—K. Stolz (G.)			18·88

U.K. beat F.R.G. by 71½ pts. to 65½.

Women's Events

Metres		min.	sec.
60(A)—P. Baker (U.K.)			7·37
(B)—P. Baker (U.K.)			7·35
200—A. Bertsch (G.)			24·37
400—E. Decker (G.)			54·18
800—K. McDemott (U.K.)		2	02·20
1,500—L. MacDougall (U.K.)		4	14·51
3,000—Z. Budd (U.K.)		8	56·13
60 *Hurdles* (A)—S. Braun (G.)			8·34
(B)—S. Braun (G.)			8·30
4 × 200 *Relay*—United Kingdom		1	34·28
			metres
High Jump—H. Redetzky (G.)			1·91
Long Jump—U. Keller (G.)			6·19
Shot—J. Oakes (U.K.)			18·03

U.K. beat F.R.G. by 63 pts. to 53.

National Cross-Country Championships (Women)

Held at Birkenhead, February 16, 1985

Senior Race		min.	sec.
1. A. Tooby (Cardiff)		18	25
2. R. Smeeth (Aldershot)		18	30
3. P. Fudge (Hounslow)		19	02
Team result			
1. Crawley			109 pts.
2. Aldershot, Farnham & District			110 pts.
3. Borough of Hounslow			138 pts.
Intermediate Race			
1. C. Keller (Sale)		14	28
2. W. Wright (Derby)		14	34
3. A. Reason (Havering)		14	35
Team result			
1. Sale			137 pts.
2. Aldershot, Farnham & District			178 pts.
3. Victoria Park			185 pts.
Junior Race		min.	sec.
1. A. Holmes (Liverpool)		12	48
2. N. Watts (Swindon)		12	50
3. S. Parker (Warrington)		12	56
Team result			
1. Leicester			62 pts.
2. Warrington			110 pts.
3. Liverpool			121 pts.

United Kingdom v. Italy v. Yugoslavia

Held at Genoa, February 16, 1985

Men's Events

Metres		min.	sec.
60—A. Ullo (I.)			6·72
200—C. Simonato (I.)			21·08
400—R. Black (U.K.)			47·24
800—R. Harrison (U.K.)		1	47·81
1,500—S. Mei (I.)		3	44·90
3,000—W. Merlo (I.)		7	58·29
60 *Hurdles*—N. Walker (U.K.)			7·79
4 × 400 *Relay*—U.K.		3	10·83
			metres
High Jump—G. Palomba (I.)			2·22
Pole Vault—G. Stecchi (I.)			5·20
Long Jump—D. Brown (U.K.)			7·70
Triple Jump—R. Mazzucato (I.)			16·20
Shot—A. Andrei (I.)			21·24

Italy beat U.K. by 87 pts. to 63.
U.K. beat Yugoslavia by 92 points to 47.

Women's Events

Metres		min.	sec.
60—H. Oakes (U.K.)			7·26
200—J. Baptiste (U.K.)			23·78
400—E. Rossi (I.)			54·19

Metres	min.	sec.
800—J. Finch (U.K.)	2	06·46
1,500—A. Possamai (I.)	4	14·30
60 *Hurdles*—L-A. Skeete (U.K.)		8·39
4 × 400 *Relay*—U.K.	3	40·96

	metres
High Jump—D. Davies (U.K.)	1·84
Long Jump—A. Capriotti (I.)	6·09
Shot—J. Oakes (U.K.)	17·95

U.K. beat Italy by 65 pts. to 41.
U.K. beat Yugoslavia by 76 pts. to 28.

National Cross-Country Championships (Men)

Held at Milton Keynes, March 2, 1985

Senior Race	min.	sec.
1. D. Lewis (Rossendale)	44	30
2. D. Clarke (Hercules– Wimbledon)	44	36
3. D. Murphy (Liverpool)	44	50
Team result		
1. Aldershot, Farnham & District	251 pts.	
2. Birchfield	296 pts.	
3. Tipton	399 pts.	

Junior Race	min.	sec.
1. P. Roden (East Cheshire)	29	49
2. R. Findlow (Airedale & Spen Valley)	30	10
3. K. Palmer (Highgate)	30	17
Team result		
1. Birmingham University	166 pts.	
2. Hallamshire	181 pts.	
3. Westbury	196 pts.	

Youth Race	min.	sec.
1. D. Mead (Thetford)	22	21
2. C. Teague (Liverpool)	22	37
3. S. Fury (GEC Avionics)	22	38
Team result		
1. Wolverhampton & Bilston	186 pts.	
2. Sale	195 pts.	
3. East Cheshire	218 pts.	

European Indoor Championships

Held at Athens, March 2–3, 1985

Men's Events

Metres	min.	sec.
60—M. McFarlane (U.K.)		6·61
200—S. Tilli (Italy)		20·77
400—T. Bennett (U.K.)		45·56
800—R. Harrison (U.K.)	1	49·09
1,500—J-L. Gonzalez (Spain)	3	39·26
3,000—R. Verbeek (Belgium)	8	10·84
60 *Hurdles*—G. Bakos (Hungary)		7·60

	metres
High Jump—P. Sjoberg (Sweden)	2·35
Pole Vault—S. Bubka (U.S.S.R.)	5·70
Long Jump—G. Paloczki (Hungary)	8·15
Triple Jump—G. Markov (Bulgaria)	17·29
Shot—R. Machura (Czechoslovakia)	21·74

Women's Events

Metres	min.	sec.
60—N. Cooman (Holland)		7·10
200—M. Koch (G.D.R.)		22·82
400—S. Busch (G.D.R.)		51·35
800—E. Kovacs (Romania)	2	00·51
1,500—D. Melinte (Romania)	4	02·54
3,000—A. Possamai (Italy)	8	55·25
60 *Hurdles*—C. Oschkenat (G.D.R.)		7·90

	metres
High Jump—S. Kostadinova (Bulgaria)	1·97
Long Jump—G. Christiakova (U.S.S.R.)	7·02
Shot—H. Fibingerova (Czechoslovakia)	20·84

R.W.A. 10 miles Road Walk

Held at York, March 23, 1985

	min.	sec.
1. I. McCombie (Cambridge H)	66	32
2. P. Vesty (Leicester)	68	04
3. R. Mills (Ilford)	71	37
Team:—Leicester	39 pts.	

National 20 km. Walk

Held at Thamesmead, May 11, 1985

	hr.	min.	sec.
1. I. McCombie (Cambridge H)	1	22	37
2. P. Vesty (Leicester)	1	26	22
3. M. Easton (Surrey)	1	28	15
Team result: Leicester		21 pts.	

Women's R.W.A. 5,000 metres Road Walk

Held at Thamesmead, May 11, 1985

	min.	sec.
1. J. McCaffrey (Canada)	23	12
2. V. Birch (Brighton)	23	27
3. H. Elleker (Sheffield)	24	06
Team result: Sheffield	26 pts	

National 35 km. Road Walk

Held at Leicester, June 15, 1985

	hr.	min.	sec.
1. D. Jackson (York)	2	41	03
2. L. Morton (Sheffield)	2	42	47
3. M. Day (Belgrave/N.Z.)	2	43	35
Team result: Sheffield		22 pts.	

I.A.A.F. World Cross-Country Championships

Held at Lisbon, Portugal, March 24, 1985

Men	min.	sec.
1. C. Lopes (Portugal)	33	33
2. P. Kipkoech (Kenya)	33	37
3. W. Bulti (Ethiopia)	33	38
Team result		
1. Ethiopia (3,4,6,28,33,56)	130 pts.	
2. Kenya (2,14,17,22,41,45)	141 pts.	
3. U.S.A. (10,12,16,19,40,57)	154 pts.	

Women	min.	sec.
1. Z. Budd (England)	15	01
2. C. Branta (U.S.A.)	15	24
3. I. Kristiansen (Norway)	15	27
Team result		
1. U.S.A. (2,9,15,16)	42 pts.	
2. U.S.S.R. (7,19,20,31)	77 pts.	
3. Romania (4,10,34,48)	96 pts.	

Juniors	min.	sec.
1. K. Kipkemboi (Kenya)	22	18
2. H. Negash (Ethiopia)	22	37
3. M. Woldsilasse (Ethiopia)	22	37
Team result		
1. Ethiopia (2,3,4,7)	16 pts.	
2. Kenya (1,5,6,14)	26 pts.	
3. Spain (9,16,17,22)	64 pts.	

A.A.A./London Marathon

Held in London, April 21, 1985

Men	hr.	min.	sec.
1. S. Jones (Newport)	2	08	16
2. C. Spedding (Gateshead)	2	08	33
3. A. Hutton (Edinburgh)	2	09	16

Women	hr.	min.	sec.
1. I. Kristiansen (Norway)	2	21	06
2. S. Rowell (Dartford)	2	28	06
3. S-A. Hales (Sheffield)	2	28	38

United Kingdom v France v Czechoslovakia

Held at Gateshead, June 29, 1985

Men's Events

Metres		min.	sec.
100—L. Christie (U.K.)			10·42
200—D. Sangouma (F.)			20·78
400—P. Brown (U.K.)			45·97
800—T. Mckean (U.K.)		1	47·25
1,500—C. McGeorge (Guest–U.K.)		3	50·50
3,000—P. Davies-Hale (U.K.)		7	52·70
5,000—M. McLeod (Guest–U.K.)		13	45·46
3,000 *Steeplechase*—J. Mahmoud (F.)		8	26·25
110 *Hurdles*—S. Caristan (F.)			13·61
400 *Hurdles*—O. Gui (F.)			50·51
4 × 100 *Relay*—France			39·34
4 × 400 *Relay*—U.K.		3	04·23
			metres
High Jump—J. Zvara (Cz.)			2·32
Pole Vault—P. Collet (F.)			5·70
Long Jump—C. Moriniere (F.)			7·87
Triple Jump—S. Helan (F.)			16·66
Shot—R. Navara (Cz.)			19·50
Discus—I. Bugar (Cz.)			66·60
Hammer—F. Vrbka (Cz.)			78·88
Javelin—D. Ottley (U.K.)			90·16

France 155½ pts., U.K. 148½ pts., Czechoslavakia 118 pts.

Women's Events

Metres		min.	sec.
100—T. Kocembova (Cz.)			11·55
200—J. Kratochvilova (Cz.)			22·73
400—J. Kratochvilova (Cz.)			51·88
800—K. McDermott (U.K.)		1	59·44
1,500—C. Boxer (U.K.)		4	07·32
3,000—Z. Budd (U.K.)		8	44·54
100 *Hurdles*—L. Elloy (F.)			13·12
400 *Hurdles*—C. Beaugeant (F.)			57·41
4 × 100 *Relay*—Czechoslovakia			44·15
4 × 400 *Relay*—Czechoslovakia		3	30·74
			metres
High Jump—M. Ewanje-Epee (F.)			1·85
Long Jump—N. Fourcade (F.)			6·75
Shot—Z. Silhava (Cz.)			18·69
Discus—Z. Silhava (Cz.)			67·90
Javelin—F. Whitbread (U.K.)			68·84

Czechoslavakia 118 pts., U.K. 110 pts., France 84 pts.

United Kingdom v German Democratic Republic v Japan (Men only)

Held at Birmingham, July 6–7, 1985

Men's Events

Metres		min.	sec.
100—L. Asquith (U.K.)			10·20
200—F. Emmelmann (G.D.R.)			20·72
400—T. Schonlebe (G.D.R.)			45·88
800—T. McKean (U.K.)		1	47·11
1,500—A. Busse (G.D.R.)		3	42·71
3,000—S. Ovett (U.K.)		7	49·83
5,000—W. Schildhauer (G.D.R.)		13	47·45
3,000 *Steeplechase*—P. Davies-Hale (U.K.)		8	36·32
110 *Hurdles*—W. Greaves (U.K.)			13·67
400 *Hurdles*—M. Robertson (U.K.)			50·28
4 × 100 *Relay*—U.K.			39·09
4 × 400 *Relay*—G.D.R.		3	01·02
			metres
High Jump—A. Sam (G.D.R.)			2·27
Pole Vault—C. Pietz (G.D.R.)			5·30
Long Jump—U. Lange (G.D.R.)			7·87
Triple Jump—V. Mai (G.D.R.)			16·56
Shot—U. Beyer (G.D.R.)			20·41

Discus—H. Hossfeld (G.D.R.)			60·00
Hammer—M. Moder (G.D.R.)			76·62
Javelin—U. Hohn (G.D.R.)			92·86

G.D.R. 110 pts., U.K. 99 pts.; U.K. 127½ pts., Japan 74½ pts.

Women's Events

Metres		min.	sec.
100—M. Gohr (G.D.R.)			10·92
200—M. Koch (G.D.R.)			22·41
400—P. Muller (G.D.R.)			51·17
800—H. Korner (G.D.R.)		2	01·32
1,500—K. McDermott (U.K.)		4	07·35
3,000—I. Bibernell (G.D.R.)		9	01·12
100 *Hurdles*—C. Oschkenat (G.D.R.)			12·83
400 *Hurdles*—E. Fiedler (G.D.R.)			56·40
4 × 100 *Relay*—U.K.			44·50
4 × 400 *Relay*—G.D.R.		3	22·87
			metres
High Jump—S. Helm (G.D.R.)			1·91
Long Jump—H. Radtke (G.D.R.)			6·96
Shot—I. Muller (G.D.R.)			20·27
Discus—I. Meszynski (G.D.R.)			66·72
Javelin—P. Felke (G.D.R.)			72·82

G.D.R. 101 pts., U.K. 54 pts.

A.A.A. Championships

Held at Crystal Place, July 13–14, 1985

Metres		min.	sec.
100—E. Obeng (Ghana)			10·44
200—A. Mafe (London Irish)			20·99
400—D. Clark (Australia)			45·45
800—J-L. Barbosa (Brazil)		1	45·48
1,500—M. O'Sullivan (Ireland)		3	40·27
5,000—D. Lewis (Rossendale)		13	42·82
10,000—K. Ryan (U.S.A.)		28	50·70
3,000 *Steeplechase*—B. Diemer (U.S.A.)		8	31·51
3,000 *Walk*—I. McCombie (Cambridge H)		11	41·73
110 *Hurdles*—H. Andrade (U.S.A.)			13·83
400 *Hurdles*—A. Hamada (Bahrain)			49·82
			metres
High Jump—M. Ottey (Canada)			2·28
Pole Vault—K. Tarpenning (U.S.A.)			5·40
Long Jump—D. Jackson (U.S.A.)			7·89
Triple Jump—W. Banks (U.S.A.)			17·22
Shot—W. Cole (Thurrock)			17·88
Discus—J. Martinez (Cuba)			65·72
Hammer—D. Smith (Hull)			77·30
Javelin—D. Ottley (Telford)			88·32

Held at Hendon, June 29, 1985

10,000 *Walk*—M. Day (Belgrave)		43	35·3

Held at Birmingham, July 20–21, 1985

Decathlon—G. Richards (North London)			7,456 pts.

National 50 km. Walk

Held at Corby, July 18, 1985

	hr.	min.	sec.
1. L. Morton (Sheffield)	4	19	09
2. B. Graham (York)	4	24	52
3. C. Berwick (Leicester)	4	27	29
Team result: Leicester			35 pts.

Women's R.W.A. 10 km. Walk

Held at Corby, July 18, 1985

		min.	sec.
1. S. Ashforth (Sheffield)		53	08
2. B. Allen (Brighton)		53	44
3. L. Simpson (Mitcham)		53	58

W.A.A.A. Championships

Held at Birmingham, July 26–27, 1985

Metres	min.	sec.
100—H. Oakes (Haringey)		11·37
200—K. Cook (Wolverhampton)		23·39
400—M. Chapman (Australia)		51·51
800—C. Boxer (Aldershot)	2	00·60
1,500—J-A. Laughton (Derby)	4	15·08
3,000—Z. Budd (Aldershot)	8	50·50
5,000—M. Joyce (Ireland)	16	16·58
100 *Hurdles*—G. Nunn (Australia)		13·27
400 *Hurdles*—Y. Wray (Stretford)		57·86
5,000 *Walk*—V. Birch (Brighton)	23	53·47

		metres
High Jump—D. Davies (Leicester)		1·89
Long Jump—J. Oladapo (Bromley)		6·56
Shot—J. Oakes (Croydon)		17·57
Discus—J. Avis (Barnet)		50·82
Javelin—T. Sanderson (Wolverhampton)		66·38

Held at Bournemouth, July 20, 1985

	min.	sec.
10,000—S. Crehan (Sutton)	33	53·3
Heptathlon—A. Turnbull (Australia)	5,289 pts.	

Held at Hendon, June 29, 1985

	min.	sec.
10,000 *Walk*—H. Elleker (Sheffield)	51	22·3

European Cup Final

Held at Moscow, August 17/18, 1985

Men's Events

Metres	min.	sec.
100—M. Woronin (Poland)		10·14
200—F. Emmelmann (G.D.R.)		20·23
400—T. Schonlebe (G.D.R.)		44·96
800—T. McKean (U.K.)	1	49·11
1,500—S. Cram (U.K.)	3	43·71
5,000—A. Cova (Italy)	14	05·45
10,000—A. Cova (Italy)	28	51·46
3,000 *Steeplechase*—P. Ilg (F.R.G.)	8	16·14

110 *Hurdles*—S. Ussov (Soviet Union)		13·56
400 *Hurdles*—H. Schmid (F.R.G.)		47·85
4 × 100 *Relay*—Soviet Union		38·28
4 × 400 *Relay*—F.R.G.	3	00·33

		metres
High Jump—J. Zvara (Czechoslovakia)		2·29
Pole Vault—S. Bubka (Soviet Union)		5·80
Long Jump—S. Layevsky (Soviet Union)		8·19
Triple Jump—J. Herbert (U.K.)		17·39
Shot—S. Smirnov (Soviet Union)		22·05
Discus—I. Bugar (Czechoslovakia)		66·80
Hammer—Y. Tamm (Soviet Union)		82·90
Javelin—U. Hohn (G.D.R.)		92·88

Soviet Union 125 pts., G.D.R. 113 pts., F.R.G. 91 pts., U.K. 89 pts., Poland 85 pts., Czechoslovakia 79 pts., Italy 71 pts., France 67 pts.

Women's Events

Metres	min.	sec.
100—M. Göhr (G.D.R.)		10·95
200—M. Koch (G.D.R.)		22·02
400—O. Vladykina (Soviet Union)		48·60
800—J. Kratochvilova (Czechoslovakia)	1	55·91
1,500—R. Agletdinova (Soviet Union)	3	58·40
3,000—Z. Budd (U.K.)	8	35·32
10,000—O. Bondarenko (Soviet Union)	31	47·38
100 *Hurdles*—G. Zagorcheva (Bulgaria)		12·77
400 *Hurdles*—S. Busch (G.D.R.)		54·13
4 × 100 *Relay*—G.D.R.		41·65
4 × 400 *Relay*—Soviet Union	3	18·58

		metres
High Jump—S. Kastadinova (Bulgaria)		2·06
Long Jump—G. Christiakova (Soviet Union)		7·28
Shot—N. Lisovskaya (Soviet Union)		21·10
Discus—G. Savinkova (Soviet Union)		70·24
Javelin—P. Felke (G.D.R.)		73·20

Soviet Union 118 pts., G.D.R. 111 pts., U.K. 67 pts., Bulgaria 65 pts., Czechoslovakia 62 pts., Poland 60 pts., F.R.G. 57 pts., Italy 35 pts.

THE TURF

Horseracing in Great Britain is under the control of The Jockey Club.

The *Jockey Club* (incorporating the National Hunt Committee, 42 Portman Square, London, W1H 0EN). Stewards are: The Lord Fairhaven (*Senior Steward*); Gen. Sir Cecil Blacker (*Deputy Senior Steward*); L. Freedman; The Marquess of Hartington; Capt. M. Gosling; Sir William Dugdale.

Leading Owners and Trainers, 1984

Winning Owners		Winning Trainers	
R. E. Sangster	£395,901	H. Cecil	£551,939
K. Abdullah	380,831	J. Dunlop	516,607
Sheikh Mohammed	369,556	G. Harwood	472,378
L. Miglitti	227,680	M. Stoute	434,840
Hamdan Al-Maktoum	225,325	W. Hern	406,676
J. C. Smith	193,582	B. Hills	356,083
I. Allen	179,747	L. Cumani	346,717
Sir Robin McAlpine	177,038	D. O'Brien (Ire)	227,680
E. B. Moller	175,004	G. Wragg	223,153
H. H. Aga Khan	174,651	P. Cole	215,914

Leading Breeders, 1984

	Value
E. P. Taylor	£348,693
Swettenham Stud	219,783
Capt. A. D. D. Rogers	215,834
H. H. Aga Khan	201,133
Mrs. C. Drake	165,733
E. B. Moller and White Lodge Stud	157,095
Red House Stud	141,344
Majors Racing International Stud	140,344
Warren Hill Stud and Mimika Financiers	120,437
R. J. McAlpine	109,278

Winning Jockeys, 1984

	1st	2nd	3rd	Unpl.	Total Mts.
S. Cauthen	130	107	108	436	781
P. Eddery	107	93	72	362	634
L. Piggott	100	79	72	240	491
W. Swinburn	99	72	67	334	572
W. Carson	97	106	99	374	676
T. Ives	90	107	75	412	684
G. Duffield	86	94	70	472	722
B. Rouse	67	55	85	468	675
G. Starkey	63	55	52	238	408
T. Quinn	62	49	41	225	377

Winning Sires, 1984

	Horses	Races won	Value
Northern Dancer (1961), by Nearctic	9	11	£429,232
Sharpen Up (1969), by Atan	25	39	235,401
Habitat (1966), by Sir Gaylord	19	36	218,995
High Top (1969), by Derring-Do	12	21	214,192
Ballad Rock (1974), by Bold Lad (Ire)	4	8	201,739
Be My Guest (USA) (1974), by Northern Dancer	18	28	168,907
Youth (1973), by Ack Ack	3	5	160,844
The Minstrel (1974), by Northern Dancer	10	12	159,429
Run The Gauntlet (1968), by Tom Rolfe	3	9	152,640
Home Guard (1969), by Forli	10	14	148,327

THE DERBY, 1974–1985

For particulars of the Derby from 1780–1973 see 1921–74 editions.

The *Distance* of the Derby course at Epsom is 1½ miles. Lord Egremont won Derby in 1782, 1804, 5, 7, 26 (also, 5 Oaks); Duke of Grafton, 1802, 9, 10, 15 (also, 9 Oaks); Mr. Bowes, 1835, 43, 52, 3; Sir J. Hawley, Teddington (1851), Beadsman (1858), Musjid (1859), and Blue Gown (1868), the 1st Duke of Westminster, Bend Or (1880), Shotover (1882), Ormonde (1886), and Flying Fox (1899). Lady James Douglas was the first lady to win the Derby—War Substitute at Newmarket (1918); at Epsom, Mrs. G. B. Miller (1937). First winner was Sir Charles Bunbury's Diomed in 1780. From 1940 to 1945 a substitute Derby was run at Newmarket. By winning his 5th Derby, the late Aga Khan equalled Lord Egremont's record. He also won 2 Oaks.

Year	Owner and Name of Winner	Betting	Jockey	Trainer	No. of Run'rs
1974	Mrs. N. Phillips' Snow Knight	50–1	B. Taylor	P. M. Nelson	25
1975	Dr. C. Vittadini's Grundy	5–1	P. Eddery	P. Walwyn	18
1976	Mr. N. B. Hunt's Empery (Fr.)	10–1	L. Piggott	M. Zilber	23
1977	Mr. R. Sangster's The Minstrel (Ir.)	5–1	L. Piggott	M. V. O'Brien	22
1978	Lord Halifax's Shirley Heights	8–1	G. Starkey	J. Dunlop	25
1979	Sir Michael Sobell's Troy	6–1	W. Carson	W. R. Hern	23
1980	Mrs. A. Plesch's Henbit	7–1	W. Carson	W. R. Hern	24
1981	H. H. Aga Khan's Shergar	10–11 F.	W. R. Swinburn	M. R. Stoute	18
1982	Mr. R. Sangster's Golden Fleece (Ir.)	3–1 F.	P. Eddery	M. V. O'Brien	18
1983	Mr. E. Moller's Teenoso	9–2 F.	L. Piggott	G. Wragg	21
1984	Mr. L. Miglitti's Secreto	14–1	C. Roche	D. O'Brien	17
1985	Lord H. de Walden's Slip Anchor	9–4 F.	S. Cauthen	H. Cecil	14

Record times, 2 min. 34 secs. by Hyperion in 1933; Windsor Lad in 1934; 2 min. 33·8 sec. Mahmoud in 1936.

TWO THOUSAND GUINEAS. First Run, 1809. Rowley Mile. Newmarket. 9st.

Year	Owner and Name of Winner	Betting	Jockey	Trainer	No. of Run'rs
1981	Mrs. A. Muinos's To-Agori-Mou	5 to 2 F.	G. Starkey	G. Harwood	19
1982	Mr. G. Oldham's Zino	8 to 1	F. Head	F. Boutin	26
1983	Mr. R. Sangster's Lomond	9 to 1	P. Eddery	M. V. O'Brien	16
1984	Mr. R. Sangster's El Gran Senor	15 to 8 F.	P. Eddery	M. V. O'Brien	9
1985	Maktoum Al Maktoum's Shadeed	4 to 5 F.	L. Piggott	M. Stoute	14

ONE THOUSAND GUINEAS. 1814. Rowley Mile. Newmarket. Fillies. 9st.

Year	Owner and Name and Winner	Betting	Jockey	Trainer	No. of Run'rs
1981	Mr. H. Joel's Fairy Footsteps	6 to 4 F.	L. Piggott	H. Cecil	14
1982	Sir Philip Oppenheimer's On The House	33 to 1	J. Reid	H. Wragg	15
1983	Maktoum Al Maktoum's Ma Biche	5 to 2 F.	F. Head	Miss C. Head	18
1984	Capt. M. Lemos's Pebbles	8 to 1	P. Robinson	C. Brittain	15
1985	Sheikh Mohammed's Oh So Sharp	2 to 1 F.	S. Cauthen	H. Cecil	17

OAKS. 1779. Epsom. 1½ Mile. Fillies. 9 st.

Year	Owner and Name of Winner	Betting	Jockey	Trainer	No. of Run'rs
1981	Mrs. B. Firestone's Blue Wind	3 to 1 JF.	L. Piggott	D. Weld	12
1982	R. Barnett's Time Charter	12 to 1	W. Newnes	H. Candy	13
1983	Sir Michael Sobell's Sun Princess	6 to 1	W. Carson	W. R. Hern	15
1984	Sir Robin McAlpine's Circus Plume	4 to 1	L. Piggott	J. Dunlop	15
1985	Sheikh Mohammed's Oh So Sharp	6 to 4 F.	S. Cauthen	H. Cecil	12

ST. LEGER. 1776(8). Doncaster. 1¾ mile, 127 yards.

Year	Owner and Name of Winner	Betting	Jockey	Trainer	No. of Run'rs
1981	Sir John Astor's Cut Above	28 to 1	J. Mercer	W. R. Hern	7
1982	Maktoum Al Maktoum's Touching Wood	7 to 1	P. Cook	T. Jones	15
1983	Sir Michael Sobell's Sun Princess	11 to 8F.	W. Carson	W. R. Hern	10
1984	Mr. I. Allan's Commanche Run	7 to 4 F.	L. Piggott	L. Cumani	11
1985	Sheikh Mohammed's Oh So Sharp	8 to 11 F.	S. Cauthen	H. Cecil	6

	Lincoln Handicap Doncaster—1 mile.	**Free Handicap** Newmarket—3yrs.—7f.	**Jockey Club Stakes** Newmarket—1½ miles.	**Coronation Cup** Epsom—1½ miles.
1982	King's Glory 4y 8st 3lb	Match Winner 9st 4lb	Ardross 6y 8st 12lb	Easter Sun 5y 9st
1983	Mighty Fly 4y 8st 4lb	Boom Town Charlie 8st 11lb	Electric 4y 8st 10lb	Be My Native 4y 9st
1984	Saving Mercy 4y 8st 9lb	Cutting Wind 8st 8lb	Gay Lemur 4y 8st 7lb	Time Charter 5y 8st 11lb
1985	Cataldi 4y 9st 10lb	Over the Ocean 8st 11lb	Kirmann 4y 8st 7lb	Rainbow Quest 4y 9st

	Goodwood Cup 2 m. 5f.	**Gold Cup** Ascot—2½ miles.	**Coventry Stakes** Ascot—2 yrs—6 furlongs.	**Irish Sweeps Derby** Curragh—3 yrs—1½ miles.
1982	Heighlin 6y 9st	Ardross 6y 9st	Horage 8st 11lb	Assert
1983	Little Wolf 5y 9st 7lb	Little Wolf 5y 9st	Chief Singer 8st 11lb	Shareef Dancer
1984	Gildoran 4y 9st 7lb	Gildoran 4y 9st	Primo Dominie 8st 11lb	El Gran Senor
1985	Valuable Witness 5y 9st	Gildoran 5y 9st	Sure Blade 8st 11lb	Law Society

	Chester Cup Chester—2¼m. 97 yd.	**Gimcrack Stakes** York—2yrs.—6 Furlongs.	**Eclipse Stakes** Sandown Park—1¼m.	**King George VI and Queen Elizabeth Stakes** Ascot—1½ miles.
1982	Dawn Johnny 5y 8st 8lb	Horage 9st	Kalaglow 4y 9st 7lb	Kalaglow 4y 9st 7lb
1983	(Abandoned)	Precocious 9st	Solford 3y 8st 8lb	Time Charter 4y 9st 4lb
1984	Contester 4y 8st 2lb	Doulab 9st	Sadler's Wells 3y 8st 8lb	Teenoso 4y 9st 7lb
1985	Morgan's Choice 8y 7st 11lb	Stalker 9st	Pebbles 4y 9st 4lb	Petoski 3y 8st 8lb

	Prix de L'Arc de Triomphe Longchamp—1½ m.	**Cheltenham Gold Cup** abt. 3¼ m.	**Cambridgeshire** Newmarket—9f.	**Middle Park Stakes** Newmarket—2yrs.—6f.
1982	Akiyda 3y 8st 8lb	Silver Buck 10y 12st	Century City 3y 9st 6lb	Diesis 9st
1983	All Along 4y 9st 1lb	Bregawn 12st	Sagamore 4y 7st 8lb	Creag-an-Sgor 9st
1984	Sagace 4y 9st 4lb	Burrough Hill Lad 8y 12st	Leysh 3y 8st 7lb	Bassenthwaite 9st
1985	Rainbow Quest 4y 9st 4lb	Forgive 'N Forget 8y 12st	Tremblant 4y 9st 8lb	Stalker 9st

	Cesarewitch Newmarket—2¼m.	**Washington Int'national** Laurel Park—1½ m.	**Champion Stakes** Newmarket—1¼ m.	**Grand National** Liverpool—4½ m.
1982	Mountain Lodge 3y 7st 10lb	April Run	Time Charter 3y 8st 7lb	Grittar 9y 11st 5lb
1983	Bajan Sunshine 4y 8st 8lb	All Along	Cormorant Wood 3y 8st 7lb	Corbiere 8y 11st 4lb
1984	Tom Sharp 4y 7st 5lb	Seattle Song	Palace Music	Hallo Dandy 10y 10st 2lb
1985	Kayudee 5y 7st 11lb		Pebbles 4y 9st	Last Suspect 11y 10st 5lb

CRICKET

Marylebone Cricket Club (1787), Lord's, NW8 8QN. *Pres.,* J. G. W. Davies, o.b.e.; *Sec.,* J. A. Bailey; *Asst. Sec. Admin.,* Lt.-Col. L. G. James; *Asst. Sec. Cricket,* Lt.-Col. J. R. Stephenson, o.b.e.; *Asst. Sec. Chief Accountant,* Wg. Cdr. V. J. W. M. Lawrence; *Curator,* S. E. A. Green.

TEST MATCHES
Pakistan v. India, 1984

First Test.—(Lahore, Oct. 17–22). Drawn. Pakistan 428 for 9 dec.; India 156 and 371 for 6.

Second Test.—(Faisalabad, Oct. 24–29). Drawn. India 500; Pakistan 674 for 6.
(*Series abandoned*)

Australia v. West Indies, 1984–85

First Test.—(Perth, Nov. 9–12). West Indies won by an innings and 112 runs. West Indies 416; Australia 76 and 228.

Second Test.—(Brisbane, Nov. 23–26). West Indies won by eight wickets. Australia 175 and 271; West Indies 424 and 26 for 2.

Third Test.—(Adelaide, Dec. 7–11). West Indies won by 191 runs. West Indies 356 and 292 for 7 dec.; Australia 284 and 173.

Fourth Test.—(Melbourne, Dec. 22–27). Drawn. West Indies 479 and 186 for 5 dec.; Australia 296 and 198 for 8.

Fifth Test.—(Sydney, Dec. 30–Jan. 2). Australia won by an innings and 55 runs. Australia 471 for 9 dec.; West Indies 163 and 253.

Pakistan v. New Zealand, 1984

First Test.—(Lahore, Nov. 16–20). Pakistan won by six wickets. New Zealand 157 and 241; Pakistan 221 and 181 for 4.

Second Test.—(Hyderabad, Nov. 25–29). Pakistan won by seven wickets. New Zealand 267 and 189; Pakistan 230 and 230 for 3.

Third Test.—(Karachi, Dec. 10–15). Drawn. Pakistan 328 and 308 for 5; New Zealand 426.

India v. England, 1984–85

First Test.—(Bombay, Nov. 28–Dec. 3). India won by eight wickets. England 195 and 317; India 465 for 8 dec. and 51 for 2.

Second Test.—(New Delhi, Dec. 12–17). England won by eight wickets. India 307 and 235; England 418 and 127 for 2.

Third Test.—(Calcutta, Jan. 1–5). Drawn. India 437 for 7 dec. and 29 for 1; England 276.

Fourth Test.—(Madras, Jan. 13–18). England won by nine wickets. India 272 and 412; England 652 for 7 dec. and 35 for 1.

Fifth Test.—(Kanpur, Jan. 31–Feb. 5). Drawn. India 553 for 8 dec. and 97 for 1 dec.; England 417 and 91 for no wkt.

New Zealand v. Pakistan, 1985

First Test.—(Wellington, Jan. 18–22). Drawn. New Zealand 492 and 103 for 4; Pakistan 322.

Second Test.—(Auckland, Jan. 25–28). New Zealand won by an innings and 99 runs. New Zealand 451 for 9 dec.; Pakistan 169 and 183.

Third Test.—(Dunedin, Feb. 9–14). New Zealand won by two wickets. Pakistan 274 and 223; New Zealand 220 and 278 for 8.

West Indies v. New Zealand, 1985

First Test.—(Port of Spain, Mar. 29–Apr. 3). Drawn. West Indies 307 and 261 for 8 dec.; New Zealand 262 and 187 for 6.

Second Test.—(Georgetown, Apr. 6–11). Drawn. West Indies 511 for 6 dec. and 268 for 6 dec.; New Zealand 440.

Third Test.—(Bridgetown, Apr. 26–May 1). West Indies won by ten wickets. New Zealand 94 and 248; West Indies 336 and 10 for no wkt.

Fourth Test.—(Kingston, May 4–8). West Indies won by ten wickets. West Indies 363 and 59 for no wkt.; New Zealand 138 and 283.

England v. Australia, 1985

First Test.—(Headingley, June 13–18). England won by five wickets. Australia 331 and 324; England 533 and 123 for 5.

Second Test.—(Lord's, June 27–July 2). Australia won by four wickets. England 290 and 261; Australia 425 and 127 for 6.

Third Test.—(Trent Bridge, July 11–16). Drawn. England 456 and 196 for 2; Australia 539.

Fourth Test.—(Old Trafford, Aug. 1–6). Drawn. Australia 257 and 340 for 5; England 482 for 9 dec.

Fifth Test.—(Edgbaston, Aug. 15–20). England won by an innings and 118 runs. Australia 335 and 142; England 595 for 5 dec.

Sixth Test.—(The Oval, Aug. 29–Sept. 2). England won by an innings and 94 runs. England 464; Australia 241 and 129.
(*See next page for averages*)

England v. Australia, 1985 (Averages)

ENGLAND BATTING

Batsmen	Innings	Times not out	Runs	Highest Score	Average
M. W. Gatting	9	3	527	160	87.83
D. I. Gower	9	0	732	215	81.33
R. T. Robinson	9	1	490	175	61.25
G. A. Gooch.......	9	0	487	196	54.11
A. J. Lamb........	8	1	256	67	36.57
J. E. Emburey	6	2	130	33	32.50
I. T. Botham	8	0	250	85	31.25
P. R. Downton	7	1	114	54	19.00
P. H. Edmonds	5	0	47	21	9.40
P. J. W. Allott.....	5	1	27	12	6.75

Also batted: L. B. Taylor 1*; R. M. Ellison 3; P. Willey 36, 3*; N. G. Cowans 22*; N. A. Foster 3, 0; J. P. Agnew 2*; A. Sidebottom 2.
*Not out

BOWLING

Bowlers	Overs	Maidens	Runs	Wickets	Average
R. M. Ellison	75.5	20	185	17	10.88
I. T. Botham	251.4	36	855	31	27.58
J. E. Emburey	248.4	75	544	19	28.63
P. H. Edmonds	225.5	59	549	15	36.60
L. B. Taylor	63.3	11	178	4	44.50
P. J. W. Allott.....	111	22	297	5	59.40

Also bowled: G. A. Gooch, 41.2-10-102-2; N. G. Cowans, 33-6-128-2; A. Sidebottom, 18.4-3-65-1; N. A. Foster, 23-1-83-1; A. J. Lamb, 1-0-10-0; M. W. Gatting, 5.4-0-16-0; J. P. Agnew, 23-2-99-0.

AUSTRALIAN BATTING

Batsmen	Innings	Times not out	Runs	Highest Score	Average
A. R. Border	11	2	597	196	66.33
G. M. Ritchie	11	1	422	146	42.20
A. M. J. Hilditch ..	11	0	424	119	38.54
W. B. Phillips	11	1	350	91	35.00
K. C. Wessels	11	0	368	83	33.45
G. M. Wood	9	0	260	172	28.88
S. P. O'Donnell	8	1	184	48	26.28
D. C. Boon	7	0	124	61	17.71
G. F. Lawson......	9	1	119	53	14.87
C. J. McDermott ...	9	1	103	35	12.87
R. G. Holland	5	1	15	5*	3.75
J. R. Thomson	4	4	38	28*	—

Also batted: M. J. Bennett, 12, 11; G. R. J. Matthews, 4, 17; D. M. Wellham, 13, 5; D. R. Gilbert, 1, 0*.
*Not out

BOWLING

Bowlers	Overs	Maidens	Runs	Wickets	Average
C. J. McDermott ...	234.2	21	901	30	30.03
G. F. Lawson......	246	34	830	22	37.72
R. G. Holland	172	41	465	6	77.50
S. P. O'Donnell	146.4	31	487	6	81.16
J. R. Thomson	56	4	275	3	91.66

Also bowled: D. R. Gilbert, 21-2-96-1; M. J. Bennett, 32-8-111-1; G. M. Ritchie, 1-0-10-0; K. C. Wessels, 6-2-18-0; G. R. J. Matthews, 9-2-21-0; A. R. Border, 11-1-37-0.

Other Results, 1985

NatWest Trophy.—Essex beat Nottinghamshire by one run. Essex 280 for 2; Nottinghamshire 279 for 5.

Benson and Hedges Cup Final.—Leicestershire beat Essex by five wickets. Essex 213 for 8; Leicestershire 215 for 5.

John Player Sunday League Champions.—Essex.

Universities.—Match drawn. Oxford 364 for 6 dec.; Cambridge 134 and 141 for 3.

Eton v. Harrow.—Eton won by three runs. Eton 141; Harrow 138.

County Champions since 1948

1948	Glamorgan		
1949	{ Middlesex	1967	Yorkshire
	{ Yorkshire	1968	Yorkshire
1950	{ Lancashire	1969	Glamorgan
	{ Surrey	1970	Kent
1951	Warwickshire	1971	Surrey
1952	Surrey	1972	Warwickshire
1953	Surrey	1973	Hampshire
1954	Surrey	1974	Worcestershire
1955	Surrey	1975	Leicestershire
1956	Surrey	1976	Middlesex
1957	Surrey	1977	{ Kent
1958	Surrey		{ Middlesex
1959	Yorkshire	1978	Kent
1960	Yorkshire	1979	Essex
1961	Hampshire	1980	Middlesex
1962	Yorkshire	1981	Nottinghamshire
1963	Yorkshire	1982	Middlesex
1964	Worcestershire	1983	Essex
1965	Worcestershire	1984	Essex
1966	Yorkshire	1985	Middlesex

County Championship Table, 1985

Order for 1984 in brackets	Played	Won	Lost	Drawn	Bonus Btg.	Bonus Blng.	Points
Middlesex (3)	24	8	4	12	61	85	274
Hampshire (15)	24	7	2	15	66	78	256
Gloucestershire (17)....	24	7	3	14	51	78	241
Essex (1)	24	7	2	15	42	70	224
Worcestershire (10)	24	5	6	13	65	68	221
Surrey (8)	24	5	5	14	62	76	218
Sussex (6)	24	6	1	17	52	57	205
Nottinghamshire (2)....	24	4	2	18	66	69	199
Kent (5)...............	24	4	5	15	51	71	186
Northamptonshire (12) .	24	5	4	15	52	51	183
Yorkshire (14)	24	3	4	17	58	59	165
Glamorgan (13)	24	4	4	16	50	50	163
Derbyshire (11)	24	3	9	12	46	69	163
Lancashire (16)	24	3	7	14	44	67	159
Warwickshire (9)	24	2	8	14	47	74	153
Leicestershire (4)	24	2	3	19	48	65	145
Somerset (7)	24	1	7	16	70	45	131

(Worcestershire and Glamorgan records include eight points for drawn matches in which scores finished level.)

BATTING AND BOWLING AVERAGES

English Batting Averages, 1985 (Qualification, 8 Innings)						English Bowling Averages, 1985 (Qualification, 10 Wickets)					
Batsmen	Number of Innings	Times not out	Total Runs	Highest Innings	Average	Bowlers	Overs	Maidens	Runs	Wickets	Average
I. V. A. Richards	24	0	1836	322	76·50	R. Ellison	432·1	113	1118	65	17·20
G. Boycott	34	12	1657	184	75·31	R. Hadlee	473·5	136	1026	59	17·38
G. Gooch	33	2	2208	202	71·22	M. Marshall	688·1	193	1680	95	17·68
I. Botham	27	5	1530	152	69·54	G. Sainsbury	178	59	481	27	17·81
Imran Khan	21	8	890	117*	68·46	C. Walsh	560·3	132	1706	85	20·07
Younis Ahmed	30	8	1421	177	64·59	Imran Khan	422·1	114	1040	51	20·39
Javed Miandad	29	6	1441	200*	62·65	T. Tremlett	665·5	181	1620	75	21·60
R. T. Robinson	31	4	1619	175	59·96	Kapil Dev	304·5	83	805	37	21·75
C. Smith	39	4	2000	143*	57·14	M. Holding	354·5	67	1124	50	22·48
J. Wright	16	2	797	177*	56·92	P. Allott	560·2	167	1328	58	22·89
M. Gatting	34	5	1650	160	56·89	L. Taylor	566·5	141	1376	60	22·93
P. Bainbridge	38	9	1644	151*	56·68	N. Cowans	474·2	85	1676	73	22·95
C. Rice	33	8	1394	171*	55·76	A. Gray	524	99	1816	79	22·98
D. Gower	29	2	1477	215	54·70	K. Curran	469·5	104	1419	61	23·26
W. Slack	43	8	1900	201*	54·28	J. Garner	295·4	76	739	31	23·83
D. Randall	47	7	2151	117	53·77	D. Lawrence	544·5	66	2093	85	24·62
M. Lynch	39	7	1714	145	53·56	N. Radford	779·4	130	2493	101	24·68
C. Radley	38	12	1375	200	52·88	D. Graveney	410·1	133	1013	41	24·70
G. Hick............	25	1	1265	230	52·70	R. Doughty	223·5	36	867	34	25·50
D. Thorne	20	3	849	124	49·94	P. Edmonds	850·1	243	1942	76	25·55
R. Ontong	30	7	1121	130	48·73	J. Inchmore	338·5	72	844	33	25·57
G. Barlow	32	4	1343	141	47·96	K. Cooper	604·3	187	1566	61	25·67
G. Mendis	43	6	1756	143*	47·45	J. Lever	720·3	188	1995	77	25·90
D Bairstow	35	10	1181	122*	47·24	P. De Freitas	234·2	43	703	27	26·03
G. Clinton	32	6	1225	123	47·11	R. Maru	704·5	197	1923	73	26·34
N. Taylor	25	7	843	120*	46·83	P. Newport	362·2	57	1214	46	26·39
W. Athey	38	7	1442	170	46·51	M. Gatting	93·5	17	293	11	26·63
D. Smith	28	4	1113	112	46·37	G. Gooch	284·2	66	773	29	26·65
P. Willey	32	4	1292	147	46·14	G. Monkhouse	383·4	78	1068	40	26·70
P. Roebuck	33	5	1255	132*	44·82	W. Daniel	575·1	90	2111	79	26·72
J. Richards	27	12	665	75*	44·33	G. Small	592·3	113	1850	69	26·81
P. Neale	42	10	1411	152*	44·09	D. Underwood	807	290	1802	67	26·89
P. Whitticase	8	2	263	79	43·83	J. Lloyds	180·1	42	575	21	27·38
S. Henderson	12	5	306	111	43·71	R. Finney	449·3	81	1453	53	27·41
T. Jesty	36	8	1216	141*	43·42	J. Agnew	445·4	89	1512	55	27·49
Kapil Dev	22	2	864	100	43·20	N. Foster	436·3	87	1434	52	27·57
R. Smith	44	8	1533	140*	42·58	R. Ontong	585·5	145	1777	64	27·76
A. Green	43	4	1646	133	42·20	B. Patterson	364·3	59	1144	41	27·90
M. Moxon	37	2	1447	168	41·34	N. Cowley	247·5	60	699	25	27·96
C. G. Greenidge ...	32	2	1236	204	41·20	A. Ferreira	673·3	130	2167	77	28·14
A. Lamb	26	4	903	122*	41·04	P. Willey	399·3	115	1017	36	28·25
J. Love	29	6	937	106	40·73	R. Illingworth	406·5	116	1046	37	28·27
A. Storie	12	2	407	106	40·70	G. le Roux	402·2	72	1132	40	28·30
C. Broad..........	47	3	1786	171	40·59	E. Baptiste	562	116	1661	58	28·63
K. Barnett	41	2	1568	134*	40·20	B. Griffiths	324	76	918	32	28·68
D. Amiss	44	5	1555	140	39·87	D. Pringle	604·1	146	1556	53	29·35
N. Fairbrother	39	4	1395	164*	39·85	J. Emburey	797·1	230	1737	59	29·44
D. Ward	10	3	279	143	39·85	J. Barclay	300·4	55	913	31	29·45
M. Nicholas........	41	5	1419	146	39·41	P. Carrick	712·3	179	1923	65	29·58
P. Downton	29	7	856	104	38·90	D. Reeve	475·5	107	1424	48	29·66
T. Lloyd	34	2	1230	160	38·43	P. Bainbridge	200	46	570	19	30·00
K. James	11	4	268	124	38·28	P. Jarvis	371·5	54	1330	44	30·22
A. Needham	37	5	1223	198	38·21	K. Barnett	173·4	33	514	17	30·23
G. Cook	38	4	1295	126	38·08	N. Williams	490·2	69	1784	58	30·75
N. Popplewell	30	2	1064	172	38·00	P. Clift...........	606·3	169	1446	47	30·76
G. Humpage	42	6	1360	159	37·77	O. Mortensen	340	75	1026	33	31·09
M. Benson	43	3	1501	162	37·52	C. Rice	284	82	779	25	31·16
R. Bailey	39	7	1194	107*	37·31	I. Botham	406·2	67	1376	44	31·27
R. Butcher	36	6	1118	120	37·26	N. Mallender	521·4	98	1533	49	31·28
W. Larkins	42	0	1549	163	36·88	P. Newman	400	79	1315	42	31·30
R. Harper	28	7	763	127	36·33	I. Folley	456·3	110	1286	41	31·36
J. C. Balderstone ..	40	5	1271	134	36·31	M. Watkinson	420·1	94	1228	39	31·48
I. Gould	25	8	616	101	36·23	J. Thomas	340·3	54	1232	39	31·58
G. Toogood	15	1	507	149	36·21	D. Capel	384·3	63	1299	42	31·68
B. Hardie	45	7	1374	162	36·15	P. Waterman	115	25	382	12	31·83
T. Cotterell	12	4	289	69*	36·12	N. Taylor	149	22	579	18	32·16
Asif Din	11	2	325	89	36·11	K. Jarvis	530·4	115	1674	51	32·82

* Denotes not out.

RUGBY FOOTBALL

International Union Table, 1985

Country	Played	Won	Drawn	Lost	Points Scored		Points
					For	Against	
Ireland	4	3	1	0	67	49	7
France	4	2	2	0	49	30	6
Wales	4	2	0	2	61	71	4
England	4	1	1	2	44	53	3
Scotland	4	0	0	4	46	64	0

Calcutta Cup
England *v.* Scotland

1971 Scotland 16–15
1972 Scotland 23–9
1973 England 20–13
1974 Scotland 16–14
1975 England 7–6
1976 Scotland 22–12
1977 England 26–6
1978 England 15–0
1979 Draw 7–7
1980 England 30–18
1981 England 23–17
1982 Draw 9–9
1983 Scotland 22–12
1984 Scotland 18–6
1985 England 10–7

County Championship

Surrey.
Gloucestershire.
Lancashire.
Gloucestershire.
Gloucestershire.
Gloucestershire.
Lancashire.
North Midlands.
Middlesex.
Lancashire.
Northumberland.
Lancashire.
Gloucestershire.
Gloucestershire.
Middlesex.

International Matches, 1984–85

1984
Nov. 3 Twickenham: England 3 Australia 19
Nov. 10 Dublin: Ireland 9 Australia 16
Nov. 24 Cardiff: Wales 9 Australia 28
Dec. 8 Edinburgh: Scotland 12 Australia 37
1985
Jan. 5 Twickenham: England 22 Romania 15
Feb. 2 Twickenham: England 9 France 9
Edinburgh: Scotland 15 Ireland 18
Feb. 16 Paris: France 11 Scotland 3
Mar. 2 Dublin: Ireland 15 France 15
Edinburgh: Scotland 21 Wales 25
Mar. 16 Twickenham: England 10 Scotland 7
Cardiff: Wales 9 Ireland 21
Mar. 30 Dublin: Ireland 13 England 10
Paris: France 14 Wales 3
Apr. 20 Cardiff: Wales 24 England 15
June 1 Christchurch: N. Zealand 18 England 13
June 8 Wellington: N. Zealand 42 England 15

County Championship Final

Middlesex beat Notts., Lincs. and Derbys. 12–9

Other Chief Matches, 1984–85

Universities. 1984. Cambridge beat Oxford by 32–6 at Twickenham on Dec. 11.

Services Championship.—Army beat Royal Navy 11–6; R.A.F. beat Army 15–12; R.A.F. beat Royal Navy 29–23.

John Player Special Cup Final.—Bath beat London Welsh 24–15 at Twickenham on April 27.

Hospitals' Cup Final.—St. Mary's beat Charing Cross–Westminster 16–11.

Middlesex Sevens.—Wasps.

Rugby Football League (Est. 1895)

Test Matches

1985
Mar. 3 Headingley: Gt. Britain 50 France 4
17 Perpignan: Gt. Britain 16 France 24

Under 21—Internationals

1984
Nov. 25 Castleford: Gt. Britain 24 France 8
Dec. 16 Albi: Gt. Britain 8 France 2

Rugby League Challenge Cup.—Final. Wigan beat Hull 28–24 pts. at Wembley on May 4, 1985.

Premiership Trophy Final.—St. Helens beat Hull K.R. 36–14 pts. at Elland Road on May 11, 1985.

Slalom Lager Champions.—Hull K.R.

Second Division Champions.—Swinton.

Yorkshire Cup.—Hull beat Hull K.R. 29–12 pts.

Lancashire Cup.—St. Helens beat Wigan 26–18 pts.

John Player Special Trophy.—Final. Hull K.R beat Hull 12–0 pts.

HOCKEY, 1984–85

MEN'S HOCKEY

County Championship Final.—Worcestershire beat Middlesex 3–2.

National Club Championship Final.—Southgate beat Blackheath 2–1.

National Indoor Club Championship Final.—St. Albans and Teddington drew 3–3 (St. Albans won on penalties).

Universities.—Cambridge beat Oxford 2–0.

WOMEN'S HOCKEY, 1985

Leading Matches

England beat Wales 1–0; England lost to Ireland 0–1; England beat Scotland 3–0. *European Indoor Championship:* England won bronze medal.

CHESS, 1985

British Championship.—J. S. Speelman.

Ladies.—R. Hamid.

Under-21.—M. Condie.

Under-18.—S. Elliott.

ASSOCIATION FOOTBALL

ENGLAND *v.* FOOTBALL
SCOTLAND ASSOCIATION CUP

		g. g.			g. g.
1971	England	3—1	Arsenal *b.* Liverpool	2—1
1972	England	1—0	Leeds U. *b.* Arsenal	1—0
1973	England	1—0	Sunderland *b.* Leeds U.	1—0
1974	Scotland	2—0	Liverpool *b.* Newcastle	3—0
1975	England	5—1	West Ham U. *b.* Fulham	2—0
1976	Scotland	2—1	Southampton *b.* Man. U.	1—0
1977	Scotland	2—1	Man.U. *b.* Liverpool	2—1
1978	England	1—0	Ipswich T. *b.* Arsenal	1—0
1979	England	3—1	Arsenal *b.* Man. U.	3—2
1980	England	2—0	West Ham U. *b.* Arsenal	1—0
1981	Scotland	1—0	Tottenham H. *b.* Man. C.	3—2
1982	England	1—0	Tottenham H. *b.* Q.P.R.	1—0
1983	England	2—0	Man. U. *b.* Brighton	4—0
1984	Draw	1—1	Everton *b.* Watford	2—0
1985	Scotland	1—0	Man. U. *b.* Everton	1—0

LEAGUE COMPETITION, 1984–85

Div. I.—Everton, 90 pts. Runners-up: Liverpool, 77 pts. Relegated: Norwich C., 49 pts.; Sunderland, 40 pts.; Stoke C., 17 pts.

Div. II.—Promoted: Oxford U., 84 pts.; Birmingham C., 82 pts.; Manchester C., 74 pts. Relegated: Notts. Co., 37 pts.; Cardiff, 35 pts.; Wolverhampton W., 33 pts.

Div. III.—Promoted: Bradford C., 94 pts.; Millwall, 90 pts.; Hull C., 87 pts. Relegated: Burnley, 46 pts.; Orient, 46 pts.; Preston, 46 pts.; Cambridge, 21 pts.

Div. IV.—Promoted: Chesterfield, 91 pts.; Blackpool, 86 pts.; Darlington, 85 pts.; Bury, 84 pts.

SCOTTISH LEAGUE.—*Premier Div.*—Aberdeen, 59 pts. *Div. I.*—Motherwell, 50 pts. *Div. II.*—Montrose, 53 pts.

OTHER INTERNATIONALS

1984					
Sept. 12	Wembley:	England	1	East Germany	0
1985					
Mar. 26	Wembley:	England	2	Republic of Ireland	1
May 25	Hampden Park:	Scotland	1	England	0
June 6	Mexico City:	England	1	Italy	2
June 9	Mexico City:	Mexico	1	England	0
June 12	Mexico City:	England	3	West Germany	0
June 16	Los Angeles:	U.S.A.	0	England	5

WORLD CUP

1984					
Oct. 17	Wembley:	England	5	Finland	0
Nov. 14	Istanbul:	Turkey	0	England	8
1985					
Feb. 27	Belfast:	N. Ireland	0	England	1
May 1	Bucharest:	Romania	0	England	0
May 22	Helsinki:	Finland	1	England	1

EUROPEAN UNDER-21 CHAMPIONSHIP

1984					
Oct. 16	Southampton:	England	2	Finland	0
Nov. 13	Bursa:	Turkey	0	England	0
1985					
April 30	Brasov:	Romania	0	England	0
May 21	Mikkeli:	Finland	3	England	1

OTHER UNDER-21 INTERNATIONALS

1984					
Nov. 13	Nottingham:	England	2	N. Zealand	0
	(*B International*)				
1985					
Feb. 27	Tel Aviv:	Israel	1	England	2
Mar. 25	Portsmouth:	England	3	Republic of Ireland	2

CUP FINALS, 1984–85

F.A. CUP.—*S.F.:* April 13 (Villa Park), Everton beat Luton T., 2–1; April 17 (Maine Road), Manchester Utd., beat Liverpool 2–1 (after 2–2 draw). *Final:* May 18 (Wembley Stadium), Manchester Utd. beat Everton 1–0.

MILK CUP.—*Final:* March 24 (Wembley Stadium), Norwich beat Sunderland 1–0.

FREIGHT ROVER TROPHY.—*Final:* Wigan beat Brentford 3–1.

F.A. VASE.—*Final:* Halesowen Town beat Fleetwood Town 3–1.

F.A. TROPHY.—*Final:* Wealdstone beat Boston U. 2–1.

F.A. YOUTH CUP.—*Winners:* Newcastle.

ARTHUR DUNN CUP.—*Final:* Lancing beat Foresters 5–0.

SCOTTISH F.A. CUP.—*Centenary Final:* May 18 (Hampden Park), Celtic beat Dundee Utd. 2–1.

SCOTTISH LEAGUE CUP.—*Final:* Rangers beat Dundee Utd. 1–0.

EUROPEAN CUP.—*Final:* Juventus beat Liverpool 1–0 in Brussels.

EUROPEAN CUP-WINNERS' CUP.—*Final:* Everton beat Rapid Vienna 3–1 in Rotterdam.

U.E.F.A. CUP.—*Final:* Real Madrid beat Videoton 3–1 (on aggregate).

Universities.—Cambridge beat Oxford 4–2.

PAST WORLD CUP WINNERS

1930 (*Played in Uruguay*)	Uruguay
1934 (*Italy*)	Italy
1938 (*France*)	Italy
1950 (*Brazil*)	Uruguay
1954 (*Switzerland*)	West Germany
1958 (*Sweden*)	Brazil
1962 (*Chile*)	Brazil
1966 (*England*)	England
1970 (*Mexico*)	Brazil
1974 (*West Germany*)	West Germany
1978 (*Argentina*)	Argentina
1982 (*Spain*)	Italy

GOLF, 1984–85

CHAMPIONSHIPS

OPEN (Instituted 1860)	
1967 R. de Vicenzo (Argentina), 278.	1970 M. F. Bonallack.
1968 G. Player (S. Africa), 289.	1971 S. N. Melnyk (U.S.A.).
	1972 T. Homer.
1969 A. Jacklin (G.B.). 280.	1973 R. Siderowf (U.S.A.).
1970 J. Nicklaus (U.S.A.) beat D. Sanders (U.S.A.) after tie, 283.	1974 T. Homer.
	1975 M. Giles (U.S.A.).
	1976 R. Siderowf (U.S.A.).
1971 L. Trevino (U.S.A.), 278.	1977 P. McEvoy.
1972 L. Trevino (U.S.A.), 278.	1978 P. McEvoy.
	1979 J. Sigel (U.S.A.).
1973 T. Weiskopf (U.S.A.), 276.	1980 D. Evans.
1974 G. Player (S. Africa), 282.	1981 P. Ploujoux (France).
1975 T. Watson (U.S.A.) beat J. Newton (Australia) after tie, 279.	1982 M. Thompson.
	1983 P. Parkin.
	1984 J.-M. Olazabal (Spain).
1976 J. Miller (U.S.A.), 279.	1985 G. McGimpsey.
1977 T. Watson (U.S.A.), 268.	LADIES (1893)
1978 J. Nicklaus (U.S.A.), 281.	1967 Miss D. E. Chadwick.
1979 S. Ballesteros (Spain), 283.	1968 Mlle. B. Varangot (France).
1980 T. Watson (U.S.A.), 271.	1969 Mlle. C. Lacoste (France).
1981 W. Rogers (U.S.A.), 276.	1970 Miss D. L. Oxley.
	1971 Miss M. Walker.
1982 T. Watson (U.S.A.), 284.	1972 Miss M. Walker.
	1973 Miss A. Irvin.
1983 T. Watson (U.S.A.), 275.	1974 Miss C. Semple (U.S.A.).
1984 S. Ballesteros (Spain), 276.	1975 Mrs. N. Syms (U.S.A.).
1985 S. Lyle (G.B.), 282.	1976 Miss C. Panton.
	1977 Mrs. A. Uzielli.
AMATEUR (1885)	1978 Miss E. Kennedy (Australia).
1967 B. Dickson (U.S.A.).	1979 Miss M. Madill.
1968 M. F. Bonallack.	1980 Mrs. A. Sander (U.S.A.).
1969 M. F. Bonallack.	1981 Mrs. B. Robertson.
	1982 Miss K. Douglas.
	1983 Mrs. J. Thornhill.
	1984 Miss J. Rosenthal (U.S.A.).
	1985 Miss L. Behan.

WALKER CUP
(Pine Valley, Aug. 1985)

U.S.A. beat Great Britain and Ireland by 13 to 11.

RYDER CUP
(The Belfry, Sept. 1985)

Europe beat U.S.A. 16½–11½.

OTHER GOLF EVENTS, 1984–85

Spanish Open.—B. Langer (W. Germany).

Australian Open.—T. Watson (U.S.A.).

Halford Hewitt Cup (Final).—Harrow beat Shrewsbury 4–1.

World Men's Amateur Team Championship.—Japan.

Cannes Open.—D. Frost (S. Africa).

GSI Open.—M. James.

English Amateur Championship.—R. Winchester.

Brabazon Trophy.—Shared by P. Baker and R. Roper.

Whyte and Mackay P.G.A. Championship.—P. Way.

Madrid Open.—M. Pinero (Spain).

Golf Illustrated Gold Vase.—M. Davis.

Portuguese Open.—T. Jonhstone (Zimbabwe).

World Cup.—Spain.

Berkhamsted Trophy.—F. George.

Glasgow Open.—H. Clark.

British Women's Strokeplay Championship.—Mrs. B. Robertson.

U.S. Masters.—B. Langer (W. Germany).

U.S. Open.—A. North.

U.S., P.G.A. Championship.—H. Green.

U.S. Tournament Players' Championship.—C. Peete.

World Series.—R. Maltbie (U.S.A.).

Four Stars Tournament.—K. Brown.

European Amateur Team Championship.—Scotland.

Seniors' Championship.—N. Coles.

Dunhill Masters.— L. Trevino (U.S.A.).

Home International Championship.—England.

Universities.—Oxford beat Cambridge by 11½–3½.

Tunisian Open.—S. Bennett.

Car Care Plan International.—D. Russell.

British Youths' Championship.—J.-M. Olazabal (Spain).

President's Putter.—E. R. Dexter.

Lytham Trophy.—M. Walls.

South African Open.—G. Levenson.

French Open.—S. Ballesteros (Spain).

British Girls' Championship.—S. Shapcott.

Benson and Hedges International.—S. Lyle.

Lawrence Batley Tournament.—G. Marsh (Australia).

Jersey Open.—H. Clark.

European Open.—B. Langer (W. Germany).

Carris Trophy.—P. Baker.

Italian Open.—M. Pinero (Spain).

Sunningdale Open Foursomes.—S. Torrance and J. O'Leary.

German Open.—B. Langer.

European Masters.—C. Stadler (U.S.A.).

Dutch Open.—G. Marsh (Australia).

Irish Open.—S. Ballesteros (Spain).

Scandinavian Open.—I. Baker-Finch (Australia).

Monte Carlo Open.—S. Torrance.

Canadian Open.—C. Strange (U.S.A.).

British Boys' Championship.—J. Cook.

LAWN TENNIS

1937 U.S.A. beat Great Britain... 4–1	1957 Australia beat U.S.A. 3–2	1971 U.S.A. beat Romania 3–2
1938 U.S.A. beat Australia 3–2	1958 U.S.A. beat Australia 3–2	1972 U.S.A. beat Romania 3–2
1939 Australia beat U.S.A. 3–2	1959 Australia beat U.S.A. 3–2	1973 Australia beat U.S.A. 5–0
1946 U.S.A. beat Australia 5–0	1960 Australia beat Italy 4–1	1974 S. Africa won by default.
1947 U.S.A. beat Australia 3–1	1961 Australia beat Italy 5–0	1975 Sweden beat Czechoslovakia 3–2
1948 U.S.A. beat Australia 5–0	1962 Australia beat Mexico 5–0	1976 Italy beat Chile 4–1
1949 U.S.A. beat Australia 4–1	1963 U.S.A. beat Australia 3–2	1977 Australia beat Italy 3–1
1950 Australia beat U.S.A. 4–1	1964 Australia beat U.S.A. 3–2	1978 U.S.A. beat Great Britain .. 4–1
1951 Australia beat U.S.A. 3–1	1965 Australia beat Spain 4–1	1979 U.S.A. beat Italy 5–0
1952 Australia beat U.S.A. 4–1	1966 Australia beat India 4–1	1980 Czechoslovakia beat Italy .. 4–1
1953 Australia beat U.S.A. 3–2	1967 Australia beat Spain 4–1	1981 U.S.A. beat Argentina 3–1
1954 U.S.A. beat Australia 3–0	1968 U.S.A. beat Australia 4–1	1982 U.S.A. beat France 4–1
1955 Australia beat U.S.A. 5–0	1969 U.S.A. beat Romania 5–0	1983 Australia beat Sweden 3–2
1956 Australia beat U.S.A. 3–2	1970 U.S.A. beat W. Germany.... 5–0	1984 Sweden beat U.S.A......... 4–1

THE CHAMPIONSHIPS (WIMBLEDON)
1985

Men's Singles.—B. Becker (W. Germany) beat K. Curren (U.S.A.), 6–3, 6–7, 7–6, 6–4.

Women's Singles.—Miss. M. Navratilova (U.S.A.) beat Mrs. C. Lloyd (U.S.A.), 4–6, 6–3, 6–2.

Men's Doubles.— H. Gunthardt (Switzerland) and B. Taroczy (Hungary) beat P. Cash and J. Fitzgerald (Australia) , 6–4, 6–3, 4–6, 6–3.

Women's Doubles.—Miss K. Jordan (U.S.A.) and Mrs. P. Smylie (Australia) beat Miss M. Navratilova and Miss P. Shriver (U.S.A.), 5–7, 6–3, 6–4.

Mixed Doubles.—P. McNamee (Australia) and Miss M. Navratilova (U.S.A.) beat J. Fitzgerald and Mrs. P. Smylie (Australia), 7–5, 4–6, 6–2.

WIGHTMAN CUP, 1984
(Royal Albert Hall, Nov.)

U.S.A. beat G.B. by 5 matches to 2.

Australian Championships:
  Men's Singles.—M. Wilander (Sweden).
  Women's Singles.—Mrs. C. Lloyd (U.S.A.).
  Men's Doubles.—M. Edmondson (Australia) and S. Stewart (U.S.A.).
  Women's Doubles.—Miss M. Navratilova and Miss P. Shriver (U.S.A.).

U.S.A. Championships:
  Men's Singles.—I. Lendl (Czechoslovakia).
  Women's Singles.—Miss H. Mandlikova (Czechoslovakia).
  Men's Doubles.—K. Flach and R. Seguso (U.S.A.) .
  Women's Doubles.—C. Kohde-Kilsch (W. Germany and H. Sukova (Czechoslovakia).
  Mixed Doubles.—Miss M. Navratilova (U.S.A.) and H. Gunthardt (Switzerland).

French Championships.
  Men's Singles.—M. Wilander (Sweden).
  Women's Singles.—Mrs. C. Lloyd (U.S.A.).
  Men's Doubles.—M. Edmondson and K. Warwick (Australia).
  Women's Doubles.—Miss M. Navratilova and Miss P. Shriver (U.S.A.).
  Mixed Doubles.—H. Gunthardt (Switzerland) and Miss M. Navratilova (U.S.A.).

Youll Cup.—Repton.
Clark Cup.—Repton.

Prudential County Cup—Men: Essex; *Women:* Surrey.

REAL TENNIS, 1984–85

Amateur Singles Championship.—A. Lovell beat H. Angus, 3–2.

British Open Singles Championship.—C. Ronaldson beat W. Davies (Australia), 3–2.

British Open Doubles Championship.—W. Davies (Australia) and L. Deuchar beat C. Ronaldson and M. Dean, 3–1.

Henry Leaf Cup.—Radley beat Winchester, 2–1.

Universities.—Cambridge beat Oxford, 4–2.

BADMINTON, 1984
ALL-ENGLAND CHAMPIONSHIPS (WEMBLEY)

Men's Singles.—Z. Jianhua (China) beat M. Frost (Denmark), 2–1.

Ladies' Singles.—H. Aiping (China) beat L. Lingwei (China), 2–0.

Men's Doubles.—Kim Moon Soo and Park Joo Bong (S. Korea) beat M. Christiansen and M. Kjeldsen (Denmark), 2–1.

Ladies' Doubles.—L. Lingwei and H. Aiping (China) beat Guan Weizhen and Wu Jianqiu (China), 2–0.

Mixed Doubles.—W. Gilliland (Scotland) and Mrs. N. Perry (England) beat T. Kihlstrom (Sweden) and Miss G. Clark (England), 2–0.

WEIGHTLIFTING
WORLD WEIGHTLIFTING RECORDS (TOTALS)
(as at Sept. 15, 1985)

Class	Kg		
52 kg	262·5	N. Terziski (Bulgaria)	1984
56 kg	300	N. Shalamanov (Bulgaria)	1984
60 kg	327·5	N. Shalamanov (Bulgaria)	1984
67·5 kg	352·5	A.Behm (G.D.R.)	1984
75 kg	377·5	Z. Stoichkov (Bulgaria)	1984
82·5 kg	405	Y. Vardanyan (U.S.S.R.)	1984
90 kg	422·5	V. Solodov (U.S.S.R.)	1984
100 kg	440	Y. Zakharevich (U.S.S.R.)	1983
110 kg	442·5	L. Taranenko (U.S.S.R.)	1984
Over 110 kg	465	A. Gunyashev (U.S.S.R.)	1984

SQUASH RACKETS, 1984–85

World Open Championship.—J. Khan (Pakistan) beat Q. Zaman (Pakistan), 3–0.
British Open Championship.—J. Khan (Pakistan) beat C. Dittmar (Australia), 3–0.
British Women's Open Championship.—Miss S. Devoy (N.Z.) beat M. Le Moignan (England), 3–1.
British Closed Championship.—G. Williams beat B. Beeson, 3–0.
British Women's Closed Championship.—M. Le Moignan beat Miss A. Cumings, 3–0.
British Under-23 Open.—D. Lloyd (England) beat F. Johnson (Sweden), 3–0.
Home International Championships.—*Men:* England; *Women:* England.
Inter-County.—Yorkshire.
Drysdale Cup.—D. Harris (England) beat G. Waite (Canada), 3–0.

FENCING, 1984–85

British Championships:
  Foil.—W. Gosbee (Salle Paul).
  Sabre.—M. Slade (Salle Boston).
  Epée.—R. Johnson (Salle Boston).
  Ladies' Foil.—Miss L. Martin (Salle Paul).
Sporting Record Cup.—Salle Paul "B".
Granville Cup.—Salle Goodall.
Magrini Cup.—Salle Boston.
Savage Shield.—Salle Boston.
Martin Edmunds Cup.—Salle Paul.
Eden Cup.—Ahlgren (Sweden).
Challenge Martini International Epée.—P. Boisse (France).

RACKETS, 1984–85

Celestion Amateur Singles Championship.—W. Boone beat J. Prenn, 3–2.
Celestion Amateur Doubles Championship.—C. Hue Williams and J. Prenn beat W. Boone and R. Crawley, 4–0.
Celestion Open Singles Championship.—J. Prenn beat W. Boone, 4–1.
Swallow Under-24 Trophy.—J. Male beat N. Smith, 3–0.
Noel Bruce Cup.—Eton (W. Boone and T. Pugh) beat Harrow (J. Prenn and C. Hue Williams), 4–2.
Foster Cup.—R. Owen-Browne (Tonbridge) beat D. Dick (Harrow), 3–1.
Public Schools Doubles Championship.—Tonbridge beat Eton, 4–0.
Universities.—Oxford.

ETON FIVES, 1985

Ballantines Championship (Kinnaird Cup).—B. C. Matthews and J. W. Reynolds beat A. E. Gibson and D. B. Wainwright, 3–1.
Nat West County Championship.—Middlesex beat Warwickshire, 2½–½.
Holmwoods School Championships.—Highgate beat Wolverhampton G.S., 3–0.
Alan Barber Cup.—Old Cholmeleians.
League Championship (Douglas Keeble Cup).—Old Berkhamstedians.

RUGBY FIVES, 1984–85

Amateur Singles Championship.—G. W. Enstone beat I. P. Fuller.

Amateur Doubles Championship.—D. J. Hebden and I. P. Fuller beat G. W. Enstone and A. R. Wynn.
Invitation World Championships.—*Singles:* G. W. Enstone beat D. J. Hebden; *Doubles:* G. W. Enstone and S. Ashton beat D. J. Hebden and I. P. Fuller.
National Schools' Championships.—*Singles:* A. Hajialexandrou (St. Dunstan's) beat P. Bishop (St. Dunstan's).
  Doubles: St. Paul's I beat St. Paul's II.

POLO, 1985

Queen's Cup.—Centaurs beat Tramontana, 8–7.
Cowdray Park Gold Cup.—Maple Leafs beat Les Diables Bleus, 11–10.
Royal Windsor Cup.—Saracens beat Brent Walker, 6–2.
Coronation Cup.—Mexico beat England, 8–6.
Silver Jubilee Cup.—England II beat Brazil, 6–5.
Universities.—Cambridge beat Oxford, 5–4.
Warwickshire Cup.—Centaurs beat Los Locos, 9–5.

TABLE TENNIS, 1985

ENGLISH CLOSED CHAMPIONSHIPS
(Bletchley)

Men's Singles: D. Douglas beat A. Cooke, 3–1.
Women's Singles: L. Bellinger beat J. Bellinger, 3–0.
Men's Doubles: D. Douglas and C. Prean beat C. Wilson and J. Souter, 3–1.
Women's Doubles: J. Bellinger and L. Bellinger beat K. Witt and S. Sandley, 2–1.
Mixed Doubles: G. Sandley and A. Gordon beat J. Kennedy and K. Witt, 2–1.

CYCLING, 1985

Tour de France.—B. Hinault (France).
Milk Race.—E. Van Lancker (Belgium).
British Professional Road Race Championship.—I. Banbury.
Sealink International.—J. McLaughlin.
British Amateur Road Race Championship.—P. Watson.

BOWLS, 1985

English Bowling Association Championships (Worthing).
Fours.—*S.F.:* Aldersbrook (Essex) beat Holderness (Yorks.) 26–15; Christchurch (Cambs.) beat Paddington (Middlesex) 19–17. *F.:* Aldersbrook beat Christchurch 27–15.
Triples.—*S.F.:* Clevedon (Somerset) beat Hove & Kingsway (Sussex) 21–8; Wigton (Cumbria) beat Middlesbrough (Yorks.) 21–13. *F.:* Clevedon beat Wigton 21–11.
Pairs.—*S.F.:* Hylton Colliery (Durham) beat Winget (Glos.) 22–19; Hacksby Road (Yorks.) beat North Shields West End (Northumberland) 19–13. *F.:* Hacksby Road beat Hylton Colliery 16–15.
Singles: *S.F.:* R. Keating (Plymouth Civil Service, Devon) beat M. Davies (Hinckley, Leics.) 21–13; R. Gass (Wigton, Cumbria) beat W. Firby (St. Andrews, Somerset) 21–15. *F.:* R. Keating beat R. Gass 21–8.
Inter-County Championship (Middleton Cup).—Northumberland beat Lincolnshire 117–108.

ANGLING

Year	Venue	No. of teams	Individual Winner	Weight	Team Winners	Points	Division
				lb. oz.			
1983	U. Trent	79	D. Howell (Atherstone)	42 8½	Notts. Fed.	741	1
	Yorkshire Ouse & R. Ure	74	A. Whitehead (Winsford)	12 15¼	Redditch	689	2
	Oxford Canal	73	W. Pearce (Lamb A.C.)	9 10	Northern Awards B.C.	724	3
	R. Witham	90	A. V. Curd (Rye & Dist.)	22 3½	Kirkstead A.C.	980	4
				k. g.			
1984	R. Nene	77	C. Gregg (Worcester)	19 370	Coleshill	672	1
	Grand Union Canal	78	C. Hibbs (Leigh & D.)	4 570	Southport	873	2
	R. Trent	73	M. Day (Travellers)	19 730	Catch Match A.C.	680	3
	R. Ancholme	96	R. Ayre (Pendle)	15 740	Weybridge	990	4

SWIMMING

NATIONAL SWIMMING CHAMPIONSHIPS
1985

Men:
50 metres Free Style.—M. Reynolds.
400 metres Free Style.—P. Easter.
100 metres Butterfly.—P. Easter.
200 metres Individual Medley.—S. Willmott.
200 metres Free Style.—M. Reynolds.
200 metres Back Stroke.—M. Matthews.
1,500 metres Free Style.—D. Stacey.
200 metres Butterfly.—N. Hodgson.
200 metres Breast Stroke.—A. Moorhouse.
100 metres Back Stroke.—M. Matthews.
400 metres Individual Medley.—G. Robins.
100 metres Free Style.—M. Mellor.
100 metres Breast Stroke.—A. Moorhouse.
400 metres Team Free Style.—Barnet Copthall.
400 metres Team Medley.—City of Leeds.

Women:
50 metres Free Style.—A. Jones.
100 metres Breast Stroke.—S. Bowman.
200 metres Breast Stroke.—G. Stanley.
800 metres Free Style.—K. Mellor.
100 metres Back Stroke.—K. Read.
200 metres Free Style.—K. Mellor.
200 metres Butterfly.—S. Purvis.
400 metres Individual Medley.—K. Read.
100 metres Free Style.—A. Jones.
200 metres Individual Medley.—Z. Long.
400 metres Free Style.—K. Mellor.
100 metres Butterfly.—C. Cooper and S. Purvis (deadheat).
200 metres Back Stroke.—K. Read.
400 metres Team Medley.—Wigan Wasps.
400 metres Team Free Style.—Stockport Metro.

WORLD SWIMMING RECORDS
(As at 15 Sept. 1985)

Men:
100 metres Free Style.—M. Blondi (U.S.A.), 48·95 s.
200 metres Free Style.—M. Gross (F.R.G.), 1 m. 47·44 s.
400 metres Free Style.—M. Gross (F.R.G.), 3 m. 47·80 s.
800 metres Free Style.—V. Salnikov (U.S.S.R.), 7 m. 52·33 s.

1,500 metres Free Style.—V. Salnikov (U.S.S.R.), 14 m. 54·76 s.
100 metres Breast Stroke.—S. Lundquist (U.S.A.), 1 m. 01·65 s.
200 metres Breast Stroke.—V. Davis (Canada), 2 m. 13·34 s.
100 metres Butterfly.—M. Gross (F.R.G.), 53·08 s.
200 metres Butterfly.—M. Gross (F.R.G.), 1 m. 56·65 s.
100 metres Back Stroke.—R. Carey (U.S.A.), 55·19 s.
200 metres Back Stroke.—I. Polyanski (U.S.S.R.), 1 m. 58·14 s.
200 metres Medley.—A. Baumann (Canada), 2 m. 01·42 s.
400 metres Medley.—A. Baumann (Canada), 4 m. 17·41 s.
4 × 100 metres Free Style Relay.—U.S.A., 3 m. 17·08 s.
4 × 200 metres Free Style Relay.—U.S.A., 7 m. 15·89 s.
4 × 100 metres Medley Relay.—U.S.A., 3 m. 38·28 s.

Women:
100 metres Free Style.—B. Krause (G.D.R.), 54·79 s.
200 metres Free Style.—K. Otto (G.D.R.), 1 m. 57·75 s.
400 metres Free Style.—T. Wickham (Australia), 4 m. 06·28 s.
800 metres Free Style.—T. Wickham (Australia), 8 m. 24·62 s.
1,500 metres Free Style.—K. Linehan (U.S.A), 16 m. 04·49 s.
100 metres Breast Stroke.—S. Gerasch (G.D.R.), 1 m. 08·29 s.
200 metres Breast Stroke.—S. Hörner (G.D.R.), 2 m. 28·33 s.
100 metres Butterfly.—M. Meagher (U.S.A.), 57·93 s.
200 metres Butterfly.—M. Meagher (U.S.A), 2 m. 05·96 s.
100 metres Back Stroke.—I. Kleber (G.D.R.), 1 m. 00·59 s.
200 metres Back Stroke.—C. Sirch (G.D.R.), 2 m. 09·91 s.
200 metres Medley.—U. Geweniger (G.D.R.), 2 m. 11·73 s.
400 metres Medley.—P. Schneider (G.D.R.), 4 m. 36·10 s.
4 × 100 metres Freestyle Relay.—G.D.R., 3 m. 42·41 s.
4 × 200 metres Freestyle Relay.—G.D.R., 8 m. 02·27 s.
4 × 100 metres Medley Relay.—G.D.R., 4 m. 03·69 s.

HENLEY ROYAL REGATTA, 1985

Grand Challenge Cup.—Harvard Univ. (U.S.A.) beat Princeton Univ. (U.S.A.) by 3¾ lengths, 6 m. 27 s.
Ladies Challenge Plate.—Leander Club "A" beat Garda Siochana (Ireland) by canvas, 6 m. 26 s.
Princess Elizabeth Cup.—Hampton School beat St. Paul's School, Concord (U.S.A.) by ⅓ length, 6 m. 45 s.
Thames Cup.—Ridley College (Canada) beat Univ. College (Dublin) by 1¾ lengths, 6 m. 34 s.
Stewards' Cup.—Univ. of London Tyrian beat Bagsvaerd (Denmark) by 3 lengths, 7 m. 8 s.
Prince Philip Cup.—Tideway Scullers School beat Thames Tradesmen & Univ. of London Tyrian by 3 lengths, 7 m. 11 s.
Queen Mother Cup.—Bewdley R.C. and Thames Tradesmen beat Tideway Scullers School easily, 7 m. 55 s.
Visitors' Cup.—Imperial College London beat Univ. of London easily, 7 m. 15 s.
Wyfold Cup.—Molesey "A" beat Nautilus Lightweight "A" by 1 length, 7 m. 3 s.
Britannia Challenge Cup.—Maidenhead beat Lea by 2½ lengths, 7 m. 22 s.
Silver Goblets.—E. Pearson and C. Riches (Molesey) beat F. Moore and P. Brown (Neptune, Ireland) by 5 lengths, 7 m. 49 s.
Double Sculls.—B. Eltang and L. Kruse (Kolding & Danske Studenten, Denmark) beat B. Lewis and G. Springer (Dirty Dozen R.C., U.S.A.) by 3¼ lengths, 7 m. 14 s.
Diamond Sculls.—S. Redgrave (Marlow) beat B. Lewis (Dirty Dozen R.C., U.S.A.) by 4 lengths, 8 m. 28 s.
Special Schools Race.—Shrewsbury School beat King's School, Canterbury by 2¼ lengths, 4 m. 36 s.

THE UNIVERSITY BOAT RACE

(Putney-Mortlake, 4 m. 1 f. 180 yds.)

Year	Winner	m. s.	Won by
1978	Oxford	19	Camb. sank
1979	Oxford	20 33	3½ lengths
1980	Oxford	19 20	A canvas
1981	Oxford	18 11	8 lengths
1982	Oxford	18 21	3¼ lengths
1983	Oxford	19 7	4½ lengths
1984	Oxford	16 45*	3¾ lengths
1985	Oxford	17 11	4¾ lengths

Cambridge have won 68 times, Oxford 62 and there has been 1 dead-heat.
*Record.

OTHER ROWING EVENTS

Oxford Summer Eights.—Christ Church.
Oxford Torpids.—Oriel.
Cambridge Lents.—Downing.
Cambridge Mays.—Pembroke.
Doggett's Coat and Badge (*Estab.* 1715, 271st race, *London Bridge-Chelsea,* 4½ miles).—R. Spencer.
Wingfield Sculls.—S. Redgrave.
Head of the River.—A.R.A. National Squad.

ICE SKATING, 1984–85

WORLD CHAMPIONSHIPS
(Tokyo)

Men's Figure.—A. Fadeev (U.S.S.R.).
Ladies' Figure.—Miss K. Witt (E. Germany).
Pairs.—O. Vasiliev and E. Valova (U.S.S.R.).
Ice Dancing.—A. Bukin and N. Bestemianova (U.S.S.R.).

EUROPEAN CHAMPIONSHIPS
(Gothenburg)

Men's Figure.—J. Sabovcik (Czechoslovakia).
Ladies' Figure.—Miss K. Witt (East Germany).
Pairs.—O. Vasiliev and E. Valova (U.S.S.R.).
Ice Dancing.—A. Bukin and N. Bestemianova (U.S.S.R.).

BRITISH CHAMPIONSHIPS

Men's Figure.—S. Pickavance.
Ladies' Figure.—Miss S. Jackson.
Pairs.—Miss L. and M. Cushley.
Dancing.—N. Slater and K. Barber.

SHOOTING–BISLEY, 116th N.R.A., 1985

Queen's Prize.—1, J. P. S. Bloomfield, 290 pts.; 2, M. J. Brister, 289 pts.; 3, J. Corbett, 288 pts.
Prince of Wales Prize.—J. E. M. Bellringer.
St. George's Challenge Vase.—1, R. L. Mundy, 148 pts.; 2, H. M. Wong Shui, 148 pts; 3, S. D. Gray, 147 pts.
Grand Aggregate.—1, J. D. Warburton, 586 pts.; 2, A. E. Clarke, 581 pts.; 3, J. P. S. Bloomfield, 580 pts.
Elcho Challenge Shield.—1, England, 1,603; 2, Scotland, 1,576; 3, Ireland, 1,511.
National Match.—1, England, 1,938; 2, Scotland, 1,927; 3, Wales, 1,900; 4, Ireland, 1,877.
Kolapore.—1, Australia, 1,174; 2, Great Britain, 1,170; 3, Canada, 1,164.
International Service Rifle Match.—1, Great Britain, 2,472; 2, Canadian Forces, 2,222; 3, Australian Army, 2,211.
Chancellor's Challenge Plate.—1, Cambridge Univ., 1,138; 2, Oxford Univ., 1,050.
Inter-Services Long Range.—1, Royal Air Force, 561; 2, Regular Army, 555; 3, U.K. Cadets, 540.
Inter-Services Short Range.—1, Territorial Army, 1,111; 2, Regular Army, 1,103; 3, Canadian Cadets, 1,099.
United Service.—1, Regular Army, 1,343; 2, Royal Navy, 1,317; 3, The Royal Marines, 1,310.
Ashburton Shield.—1, Bradfield, 525; 2, Oundle, 523; 3, Elizabeth, 518.

CLAY PIGEON SHOOTING, 1985

International Cup (*Down-the-Line*).—1, England, 7,197/7,500; 2, Ireland, 7,151; 3, Wales, 7,139; 4, Scotland, 7,127.
British Open Down-the-Line Championship.—K. Bond (England), 299/300.
Down-the-Line High Gun Trophy.—D. Dowery (Ireland), 591/600.
Mackintosh Trophy.—Canada, 7,344/7,500.
British Open Skeet Championship.—D. C. Summerbee, 100/100.
British Open Sporting Championship.—P. Thorrold, 94/100.
Coronation Cup.—A. B. Hebditch, 388/400.
Grand Prix of Great Britain (*Olympic Trap*).—G. Leary (Canada), 193/200.
Grand Prix of Great Britain (*International Skeet*).—B. Newton, 193/200.
Grand Prix of Great Britain (*International Sporting*).—P. Thorrold, 133/150 (after shoot-off).
World Championship (*International Sporting*).—B. J. Simpson (G.B. 176/200; *Juniors:* P. Foster (G.B.), 158/200; *Ladies:* G. Batut (France), 133/200; *Team:* Great Britain, 651.
Game Fair Championship.—G. Stirzaker, 29/30.

BOXING, 1985
A.B.A. Championships (Winners)

Light-Flyweight.—M. Epton; *Flyweight.*—P. Clinton; *Bantam.*—S. Murphy; *Feather.*—M. Havard; *Light.*—E. McAuley; *Light-Welter.*—I. Mustafa; *Welter.*—E. McDonald; *Light-Middle.*—R. Douglas; *Middle.*—D. Cronin; *Light-Heavy.*—J. Beckles; *Heavy.*—H. Hylton; *Super Heavy.*—G. Williamson.

PROFESSIONAL BOXING
World (W.B.C.) Champions

Heavy.—P. Thomas (U.S.A.); *Cruiser.*—A. Ratliff (U.S.A.); *Light-Heavy.*—M. Spinks (U.S.A.); *Middle.*—M. Hagler (U.S.A.); *Light-Middle.*—T. Hearns (U.S.A.); *Welter.*—M. McCrory (U.S.A.); *Light-Welter.*—L. Smith (U.S.A.); *Light.*—H. Camacho (Puerto Rico); *Super-Feather.*—J. C. Chavez (Mexico); *Feather.*—A. Nelson (Ghana); *Super-Bantam.*—J. Meza (U.S.A.); *Bantam.*—D. Zaragoza (Mexico); *Super-Fly.*—J. Watonabe (Japan); *Fly.*—S. Chitalada (Thailand); *Light-Fly.*—J. Chang (Korea).

World (W.B.A.) Champions

Heavy.—T.Tubbs (U.S.A.); *Cruiser.*—D. Braxton (U.S.A.); *Light-Heavy.*—M. Spinks (U.S.A.); *Middle.*—M. Hagler (U.S.A.); *Light-Middle.*—M. McCallum (Jamaica); *Welter.*—D. Curry (U.S.A.); *Light-Welter.*—U. Sacco (Argentina); *Light.*—L. Bramble (U.S.A.); *Super-Feather.*—W. Gomez (Puerto Rico); *Feather.*—B. McGuigan (G.B.); *Super-Bantam.*—V. Callejas (Puerto Rico); *Bantam.*—R. Sandoval (U.S.A.); *Super-Fly.*—K. Galaxi (Thailand); *Fly.*—vacant; *Light-Fly.*—J. Oliva (U.S.A.).

British Champions

Heavy.—vacant; *Cruiser.*—vacant; *Light-Heavy.*—D. Andries; *Middle.*—H. Graham; *Light-Middle.*—P. Rodney; *Welter.*—K. Petrou; *Light-Welter.*—T. Marsh; *Light.*—T. Willis; *Super-Feather.*—vacant; *Feather.*—B. McGuigan; *Bantam.*—R. Gilbody; *Fly.*—D. McKenzie.

Commonwealth Champions

Heavy.—T. Berbick (Canada); *Cruiser.*—C. Mutti (Zambia);; *Light-Heavy.*—L. Stewart (Trinidad); *Middle.*—T. Sibson (G.B.); *Light-Middle.*—N. Wilshire (G.B.); *Welter.*—S. Mittee (G.B.); *Light-Welter.*—B. Famous (Nigeria); *Light.*—B. Michael (Australia); *Super-Feather.*—J. Sichula (Zambia); *Feather.*—A. Nelson (Ghana); *Bantam.*—P. Ferreri (Australia); *Fly.*—vacant.

European Champions

Heavy.—A. Eklund (Sweden); *Light-Heavy.*—A. Blanchard (Holland); *Middle.*—A. Kalule (Denmark); *Light-Middle.*—G. Steinherr (W. Germany); *Welter.*—L. Honeyghan (G.B.); *Light-Welter.*—P. Oliva (Italy); *Light.*—R. Weller (Germany); *Super-Feather.*—P. Cowdell (G.B.); *Feather.*—B. McGuigan (G.B.); *Bantam.*—C. de Leva (Italy); *Fly.*—F. Cherchi (Italy).

SNOOKER AND BILLIARDS, 1984–85

World Professional Snooker Championship.—D. Taylor beat S. Davis by 18–17.

Benson and Hedges Masters Snooker Tournament.—C. Thorburn beat D. Mountjoy by 9–6.

U.K. Professional Snooker Championship.—S. Davis beat A. Higgins by 16–8.

World Doubles Snooker Championship.—A. Higgins and J. White beat C. Thorburn and W. Thorne by by 10–2.

English Professional Snooker Championship.—S. Davis beat T. Knowles by 9–2.

World Professional Billiards Championship.—R. Edmonds beat N. Dagley, 3–1.

British Open Snooker Championship.—S. Francisco (S. Africa) beat K. Stevens (Canada) by 12–9.

World Amateur Billiards Championship.—Geet Sethi (India) beat R. Marshall (Australia) by 3,809 to 2,453.

OXFORD AND CAMBRIDGE
Principal Events and Winners, 1984–85

Event (with date of first meeting)	Summary of Results			Results 1984–85
	Ox.	Camb.	Drawn	
Cricket (1827)	46	53	42	Draw
Boat Race (1829)	62	68	1	Oxford
Athletics (1864)......	55	49	7	Oxford
Football—				
Association (1873–4)	38	43	21	Camb
Rugby (1871–2)	43	47	13	Camb.
Golf (1878)	38	51	5	Oxford.
Hockey (1890)	28	39	15	Camb.

Other University Events and Winners, 1984–85

Rackets	Oxford
Polo	Cambridge
Real Tennis	Cambridge
Boxing	Cambridge
Yachting	Cambridge

MOTOR CYCLING, 1985

Senior Manx Grand Prix.—B. Yeardsley (Suzuki).

Senior T.T., Isle of Man.—1, J. Dunlop (Honda); 2, R. Marshall (Honda); 3, M. Johns (Suzuki).

Junior T.T., Isle of Man.—1, J. Dunlop (Honda): 2, S. Cull (Honda); 3, E. Roberts (Kimoco).

British 500 c.c. Grand Prix (Silverstone).—F. Spencer (Honda).

Transatlantic Trophy.—Great Britain.

MOTOR SPORT, 1985

European Grand Prix, 1984.—(*Nurburgring, W. Germany*).—1, A. Prost (McLaren); 2, M. Alboreto (Ferrari); 3, N. Piquet (Brabham).

Portuguese Grand Prix, 1984.—1, A. Prost (McLaren); 2, N. Lauda (McLaren); 3, A. Senna (Toleman).

Monaco Grand Prix.—1, A. Prost (McLaren); 2, M. Alboreto (Ferrari); 3, E. de Angelis (Lotus-Renault).

French Grand Prix.—1, N. Piquet (Brabham); 2, K. Rosberg (Williams); 3, A. Prost (McLaren).

San Marino Grand Prix.—1, E. de Angelis (Lotus-Renault); 2, T. Boutsen (Arrows–BMW); 3, P. Tambay (Renault).

British Grand Prix.—(*Silverstone*).—1, A. Prost (McLaren); 2, M. Alboreto (Ferrari); 3, J. Laffite (Ligier).

Brazilian Grand Prix.—1, A. Prost (McLaren); 2, M. Alboreto (Ferrari); 3, E. de Angelis (Lotus-Renault).

Italian Grand Prix.—1, A. Prost (McLaren); 2, N. Piquet (Brabham); 3, A. Senna (Lotus-Renault).

Portuguese Grand Prix.—1, A. Senna (Lotus-Renault); 2, M. Alboreto (Ferrari); 3, P. Tambay (Renault).

Austrian Grand Prix.—1, A. Prost (McLaren); 2, A. Senna (Lotus-Renault); 3, M. Alboreto (Ferrari).

German Grand Prix.—1, M. Alboreto (Ferrari); 2, A. Prost (McLaren); 3, J. Laffite (Ligier).

Canadian Grand Prix.—1, M. Alboreto (Ferrari); 2, S. Johansson (Ferrari); 3, A. Prost (McLaren).

Dutch Grand Prix.—1, N. Lauda (McLaren); 2, A. Prost (McLaren); 3, A. Senna (Lotus-Renault).

Detroit Grand Prix.—1, K. Rosberg (Williams); 2, S. Johansson (Ferrari); 3, M. Alboreto (Ferrari).

Le Mans (24-hour).—K. Ludwig, P. Barilla and L. Krages (Porsche).

Lombard R.A.C. Rally, 1984.—A. Vatanen (Peugeot).

SPORTS REPRESENTATIVE BODIES

ANGLING.—National Anglers' Council, 11 Cowgate, Peterborough PE1 1LZ. *Exec. Dir.*, P. H. Tombleson, O.B.E.

ASSOCIATION FOOTBALL.—The Football Association. *Gen. Sec.*, E. A. Croker, 16 Lancaster Gate, W2 3LW.

ATHLETICS.—Amateur Athletic Association. *Gen. Sec.*, M. A. Farrell, Francis House, Francis Street, SW1P 1DL.

— British Amateur Athletic Board. *Gen. Sec.*, N. Cooper, Francis House, Francis Street, SW1P 1DL.

— Women's Amateur Athletic Association. *Hon. Sec.*, Miss M. Hartman, C.B.E., Francis House, Francis Street, SW1P 1DE.

BADMINTON.—Badminton Association of England. *Chief Exec.*, Air Vice-Marshal G. C. Lamb, C.B., C.B.E., A.F.C., National Badminton Centre, Loughton Lodge, Bradwell Road, Milton Keynes MK8 9LA.

BASKET BALL.—English Basket Ball Association. *Dir.*, K. K. Mitchell, O.B.E., Dept. of Physical Education, The University, Leeds.

BILLIARDS.—Billiards and Snooker Control Council. *Sec.*, R. Stobbs, Coronet House, Queen Street, Leeds LS1 2TN.

BOBSLEIGH.—British Bobsleigh Association, 118 Eaton Square, S.W.1. *Sec.*, Camilla Fane.

BOWLS.—English Bowling Association. *Sec.*, J. F. Elms, 2a Iddesleigh Road, Bournemouth BH3 7JR.

BOXING.—Amateur Boxing Association of England, Francis House, Francis Street, SW1P 1DE.—*Sec.*, L. Mills, M.B.E.

— British Boxing Board of Control, 70 Vauxhall Bridge Road, SW1V 2RP.—*Gen. Sec.*, R. L. Clarke, O.B.E.

CANOEING.—British Canoe Union, Flexel House, 45-47 High Street, Addlestone, Weybridge, Surrey KT15 1JV.—*Dir.*, R. W. Emes, M.B.E.

CLAY PIGEON SHOOTING.—Clay Pigeon Shooting Association. *Dir.*, K. J. Murray, 107 Epping New Road, Buckhurst Hill, Essex IG9 5TQ.

CRICKET.—International Cricket Conference, Lord's Ground, NW8 8QN. *Chmn.*, J. G. W. Davies, O.B.E., *Sec.*, J. A. Bailey. Cricket Council, Lord's Ground, NW8 8QN. *Sec.*, D. B. Carr.

CYCLING.—British Cycling Federation, 16 Upper Woburn Place, WC1H 0QE.—*Sec.*, L. A. Unwin.

ETON FIVES.—Eton Fives Association.—*Hon. Sec.*, R. M. Knight, Saintbury Close, Saintbury, near Broadway, Glos.

FENCING.—Amateur Fencing Association, 83 Perham Road, W. Kensington, W14 9SP.

GLIDING.—British Gliding Association, Kimberley House, Vaughan Way, Leicester. *Sec.*, B. Rolfe.

GOLF.—Royal and Ancient Golf Club, St. Andrews, Fife KY16 9JD. *Sec.*, M. F. Bonallack, O.B.E.

— English Golf Union. *Sec.*, K. Wright, 1-3 Upper King Street, Leicester LE1 6XF

— Ladies' Golf Union, 12, The Links, St. Andrews, Fife KY16 9JB.—*Gen. Administrator*, Miss A. McIntosh.

GYMNASTICS.—British Amateur Gymnastics Association, 2 Buckingham Avenue East, Slough, Berks SL1 3EA. *Sec.*, T. D. Rowe.

HOCKEY.—Hockey Association, 16 Upper Woburn Place, WC1H 0QD.

— All England Women's Hockey Association, 3rd Flr, Argyle House, 29-31 Euston Road, NW1 2SD. *Sec.*, Miss T. Morris.

JUDO.—British Judo Association, 16 Upper Woburn Place, WC1H 0QH. *Gen. Sec.*, Miss G. M. Kenneally.

LACROSSE.—English Lacrosse Union. *Hon. Sec.*, R. Balls, 70 High Road, Rayleigh, Essex SS6 7AD.

— All England Women's Lacrosse Association, 16 Upper Woburn Place, WC1H 0QJ. *Organising Secretary*, Mrs. J. Cantell.

LAWN TENNIS.—Lawn Tennis Association. *Sec.*, J. C. U. James, Barons Court, W14 9EG.

— International Tennis Federation, Church Road, Wimbledon, S.W.19.

MOTOR CYCLING.—Auto-Cycle Union, Millbuck House, Corporation Street, Rugby, Warwicks. CV21 2DN. *Chief Exec.*, A. Tranter.

NETBALL.—All England Netball Association, Francis House, Francis Street, SW1P 1DE. *Director.*, Mrs. J. Holt.

ORIENTEERING.—British Orienteering Federation, "Riversdale", Dale Road North, Darley Dale, Matlock, Derbyshire DE4 2JB. *Gen. Sec.*, R. Mason.

POLO.—The Hurlingham Polo Association, Ambersham Farm, Ambersham, Midhurst, W. Sussex GU29 0BX. *Hon. Sec.*, Lt.-Col. A. F. Harper, D.S.O.

RACING.—The Jockey Club (incorporating National Hunt Committee), 42 Portman Square, W1H 0EN *Sec.*, C. N. Foster.

RIFLE SHOOTING.—National Rifle Association. *Sec.*, Brig. P. G. A. Prescott, M.C., Bisley Camp, Brookwood, Woking, Surrey GU24 0PB.

— National Small-bore Rifle Association. *Sec.*, Gp. Capt. D. King, M.B.E., Lord Roberts House, Bisley Camp, Brookwood, Woking, Surrey GU24 0NP.

ROWING.—Amateur Rowing Association. *Exec. Sec.*, D. C. Lunn-Rockliffe, 6 Lower Mall, W6 9DJ.

RUGBY FIVES.—Rugby Fives Association. *Hon. Sec.*, P. J. Reeder, 127 Newlands Park, SE26 5PP.

RUGBY FOOTBALL.—The Rugby Football Union, Whitton Road, Twickenham, Middx. TW2 7RQ. *Sec.*, Air Commodore R. H. G. Weighill, C.B.E., D.F.C.

— The Rugby Football League. *Sec.-Gen.*, D. S. Oxley, 180 Chapeltown Road, Leeds LS7 4HT.

SKATING.—National Skating Association of Great Britain. *Gen. Administrator*, E. Waughray, 117 Charterhouse Street, E.C.1.

SKI-ING.—British Ski Federation. *Sec.*, Brig. A. A. Fielder, 118 Eaton Square, SW1W 9AF.

SQUASH RACKETS.—Squash Rackets Association. *Chief Executive*, R. I. Morris, Francis House, Francis Street, SW1P 1DE.

— Women's Squash Rackets Association. *Sec.*, Miss C. Myers, 345 Upper Richmond Road West, SW14 8QN.

SWIMMING.—Amateur Swimming Association, Harold Fern House, Derby Square, Loughborough, Leics. LE11 0AL. *Sec.*, H. W. Hassall.

TABLE TENNIS.—English Table Tennis Association. *Gen. Sec.*, A. W. Shipley, 21 Claremont, Hastings TN34 1HF.

UNDERWATER SWIMMING.—British Sub-Aqua Club, 16 Upper Woburn Place, WC1H 0QW. *General Manager*, D. D. Robertson.

WALKING.—Race Walking Association. *Gen. Sec.*, R. Wells, 4 Brecon Close, Luton, Beds.

WATER SKI-ING.—British Water Ski Federation, 390 City Road, EC1V 2QA. *Sec.*, Ms. G. Hill.

WEIGHT-LIFTING.—British Amateur Weight Lifters Association. *Hon. Sec.*, W. Holland, O.B.E., 3 Iffley Turn, Oxford OX4 4DU.

WRESTLING.—English Olympic Wrestling Association. *Sec.*, H. I. Jacob, O.B.E., 2 Huxley Drive, Bramhall, Stockport, Cheshire SK7 2PH.

YACHTING.—Royal Yachting Association, Victoria Way, Woking, Surrey GU21 1EQ. *Sec.-Gen.*, J. Durie.

SPORTS COUNCIL.—16 Upper Woburn Place, WC1H 0QP. *Dir. Gen.*, J. D. Wheatley.

DRAMA SUMMARY, 1984–85

The improvement in the fortunes of London theatre, which became apparent in 1983–84, continued, with attendances expected to total 10 million in 1984–85. There was a boom in overseas visitors, by whom a theatre visit is considered almost obligatory, with a notable influx of American tourists in particular, helped by the weakness of the pound against the dollar earlier in the year. Ticket sales in 1984 were 10 per cent up on 1983, which was 6 per cent up on the previous year.

The main problems occurred in the subsidised theatre, with reductions in Arts Council grants, in real terms, causing most concern. The great expense of putting on West End shows continued to rise, the most obvious effect of which was an understandable reluctance to invest money in shows which broke new ground artistically. There was therefore a preponderance of revivals, especially musicals.

The musical *Blondel*, which had been the first production at the newly restored Old Vic, transferred to the Aldwych, but although it covered its weekly costs, it closed without recouping its initial investment of £400,000. A new musical entitled *Sherwood* was scheduled to open at the Dominion Theatre in July, costing £300,000 to stage. Stephanie Lawrence left the successful *Starlight Express* cast to take the part of Maid Marion, but at the last moment, the financial backing fell through and the show was abandoned.

At the Mermaid, the musical *Blockheads*, created by the team which was responsible for the show *Snoopy – the Musical*, folded in three short weeks. Based on the stars of the silent cinema, Laurel and Hardy, their well-timed routines were faithfully and effectively recreated, but their private lives were less well treated in a somewhat disorganised plot.

One musical which managed to survive its first few weeks was *Mutiny!*, an expensively staged production based on the familiar story of the mutiny on the *Bounty*. The opening of the show was delayed by technical problems, but it had been extensively publicised and promoted on the strength of its instigator, the actor and singer David Essex. It was claimed that advance box office takings exceeded £1 million, a figure subsequently disputed, but nevertheless probably sufficient to save the show from the fate that would have befallen it on Broadway – instant demise, following one of the worst critical hammerings of any production since O'Toole's *Macbeth*. If reviews were to be believed, the songs were unmemorable and banal, the plot muddled and Essex totally miscast as Fletcher Christian. The only redeeming element was the *Bounty* herself, a miracle of theatrical design and engineering created by William Dudley, which dominated the stage and the action whenever it was called upon to liven up the longueurs in the plot, which were all too frequent. Frank Finlay played Captain Bligh. *Mutiny!* had replaced *Pump Boys and Dinettes* at the Piccadilly, an anodyne concoction of songs and good, clean fun set in a U.S. highway service station restaurant, and celebrating the lives of its waitresses and petrol-pump attendants. This exuberant musical began life off-Broadway, and seemed an unlikely London success, but the casting of Paul Jones, Kiki Dee and Carlene Carter ensured professionalism and the cast's enthusiasm was infectious.

Richard Harris's *Stepping Out* at the Duke of York's was an English *Chorus Line*; directed by Julia McKenzie, it followed the fortunes of a ladies' tap-dancing class in a church hall in north London, and although somewhat contrived, was both witty and entertaining. A more serious English musical was *The Hired Man*, based on Melvyn Bragg's novel about his grandfather's life as a farmworker and miner in

Cumbria at the turn of the century. Although well-intentioned, and with fine music by Howard Goodall, the unexceptional plot, and the romanticised view of the working class (which compared unhappily with the real-life dramas of the mine-workers' dispute), meant that this was one production from Andrew Lloyd-Webber which closed early.

Sandy Wilson's *The Boy Friend* was revived at the Albery, while *Me and My Girl*, a dated musical best known for 'The Lambeth Walk', was staged successfully at the Adelphi, due to some judicious and imaginative updating of the material. The National Theatre production of *Guys and Dolls* was restaged at the Prince of Wales. At the Phoenix, Alan Bleasdale's musical on Elvis Presley was well recieved, with Martin Shaw effective as the singer at the end of his life, and Simon Bowman winning widespread praise for his portrayal of the early years. At Wyndham's, the ubiquitous Adrian Mole was brought to life on stage, after previous appearances on radio and in print (later in the year, he was seen on television). *The Secret Diary of Adrian Mole Aged 13¾* featured Simon Schatzberger in the titla role; the adaptation was largely successful, although the songs added little to the performance.

For the first time in 40 years, the Lyceum staged live theatre: having closed with Gielgud's *Hamlet*, this famous venue, renowned for its association with Sir Henry Irving and Sarah Bernhardt among others, had subsequently been used as a dance hall. However, in May it staged the National Theatre's successful *Mysteries*, for a limited season, and this prompted a vociferous campaign for its permanent restoration as a live theatre.

Recent problems in the Conservative Government appeared to have inspired G. F. Newman's heavy-handed attack on that party in *An Honourable Trade*, at the Royal Court. A similar theme was handled with infinitely more skill and subtlety in Harley Granville-Barker's *Waste*, which was effectively revived at the Barbican Pit. *Waste* had in fact fallen foul of the Lord Chamberlain when it was written in 1907, and the Barbican version was based on an amalgam of the first version and the revised play produced in 1936. It concerned a rising politician involved in a major Bill to disestablish the Church of England, whose career was wrecked by personal scandal.

Howard Brenton's *Bloody Poetry* at Hampstead examined the relationship between Shelley and Byron in Geneva, while the Almeida staged the Bristol Old Vic production of Shelley's rarely-seen and somewhat pedestrian melodrama *The Cenci*, written in 1819 and first performed on the professional stage in 1886. Charlton Heston made his first appearance on the London stage in *The Caine Mutiny Court-Martial*, based on Herman Wouk's Pulitzer Prize-winning novel. Heston was effective as Lt.-Commander Queeg, with good support from Ben Cross. The Royal Court staged Ron Hutchinson's powerful drama *Rat in the Skull*, a tense, well-written play about the confrontation between an Irish terrorist and an R.U.C. inspector, set in Paddington Green police station. The Royal Court also revived Edward Bond's *The Pope's Wedding* and *Saved*, the latter still able to shock audiences 20 years after its first performance, with its notorious scene of the baby killed in its pram by youths. In contrast, Bond's *War Plays* trilogy at the Barbican Pit dulled the senses, being wordy, depressing, and too long at 8 hours.

William Douglas-Home's new play, *After the Ball is Over*, appeared at the Old Vic. Concerning the goings on in a country house on the night the government imposed a ban on fox-hunting, the material did not do justice to the cast, which included Anthony Quayle and Patrick Cargill. The Old Vic also staged a dramatisation of Charles Dicken's *Great Expectations*, condensed to 3¼ hours; the production was competent, but the novel gained nothing in translation to the stage, and the adaptation lacked the spark that made the R.S.C.'s *Nicholas Nickleby* so successful.

William Mastrosimone's *Extremities* featured Helen Mirren in a powerful drama about a woman who, having been attacked by a man in her home, overpowers him and exacts a violent revenge. The dramatic opening was somewhat dissipated later, when moral issues were raised which were not satisfactorily resolved; and there was a sense that the audience was being manipulated at times, but this production at the Duchess at least raised contemporary and controversial matters, and treated them in a serious dramatic manner. Mastrosimone's *The Woolgatherer* was also produced during the year, at the Lyric Studio.

Arnold Wesker's *Annie Wobbler*, a series of East End sketches written in 'homage to a childhood memory', had been started by the playwright in 1949. Having seen Nichola McAuliffe on stage, he completed the work specifically for her, and she gave a remarkable solo performance in the three monologues for three characters, spanning 45 years. Another interesting work was Anthony Minghella's *Two Planks and a Passion*, performed at Greenwich. Set in York during the reign of Richard II, it concerned the King and court's visit to the city during the annual passion plays, and the contrast between the visitors and the workmen's guilds, and the play was both witty and thought-provoking.

George Axelrod's *The Seven Year Itch* had not been seen on the London stage since 1958, and is best remembered for the screen version starring Marilyn Monroe. Revived at the Albery, as a vehicle for Patrick Mower and Adrienne Posta, this curiosity about adultery showed its age. Graham Swannell's *A State of Affairs* at the Lyric Studio was a more contemporary view of marriage, and it transferred successfully to the Duchess.

Comic Cuts

Bamber Gascoigne's *Big in Brazil* was first performed in Greenwich 12 years ago as *The Feydeau Farce Festival of 1909*. Substantially revised, it resurfaced at the Old Vic, but this account of a touring company from Huddersfield performing in the Amazonian jungle was felt to be too strained, and was consigned to oblivion for a further dozen years. Andy de la Tour's *Viva!* at the Theatre Royal, Stratford East, about a South American revolution, was better constructed and more amusing, but Ray Cooney's *Two Into One* at the Shaftesbury, a send-up of political intrigue and scandal, had the advantage of a tightly-constructed plot and a well-drilled cast, with Donald Sinden in his element. Sinden achieved similar success later in the year with his performance as the Scarlet Pimpernel in Chichester, another performance that 'went over the top'. The production of Joe Orton's *Loot*, seen at the Ambassadors earlier in the year, reappeared at the Lyric, Shaftesbury Avenue later in 1984. Sadly, Leonard Rossiter, who had excelled as Inspector Truscott, died during the run, and was succeeded in the role by Dinsdale Landen. Richard O'Brien created the immensely successful *Rocky Horror Show*, but his *Top People*, a comedy of bad manners, survived only two weeks at the Ambassadors. This attempt to satirise the stalwarts of the gossip columns was a resounding flop. Larry Shue's *The Nerd* benefited from a bravura performance by the rubber-faced Rowan Atkinson as the totally insensitive sponger who ruined people's lives. It was followed at the Aldwych by a revival of Tom Stoppard's *Jumpers*, originally performed by the National Theatre Company in 1972. The author had revised the text, and Paul Eddington and Felicity Kendal took the parts created by Michael Hordern and Diana Rigg.

NATIONAL THEATRE

The National Theatre began the season optimistically. In October 1984, it was announced that the company would be divided into five separate groups, of 20 to 25 actors each, under an expanded team of directors. Sir Peter Hall, Bill Bryden and Peter Wood would each be responsible for one group, Richard Eyre would be assisted by David Hare in another and the fifth would be under the direction of Ian McKellen and Edward Petherbridge. Each group would produce at least three plays in a twelve-month period, and there would be no crossing over of actors between groups. In addition, Michael Bogdanov would direct a 'breakaway' section, specialising in both large and small tours and educational projects, and Peter Gill would be responsible for the National Theatre studio in the Old Vic annexe.

However, the situation was altered when it became apparent that the National Theatre was to receive an increase of only 1.9 per cent in its Arts Council grant—a total of £6,705,200—having claimed an extra £1.5 million. The increase, which was well below the level of inflation, caused the director, Sir Peter Hall, to announce that the future of the Cottesloe was in jeopardy, as were the plans for the five acting companies. He considered that the National was a victim of its own success, and would have received a larger grant if it had made bigger losses in previous years. Since 1979 the R.S.C. had received an increase in its grant of 131 per cent, while the National's grant had risen by 44 per cent. On February 7, 1985, it was announced that the Cottesloe Theatre would close, one in seven staff would be made redundant, and the National would consider moving out of its South Bank home. Foyer productions would end unless sponsored, and touring would cease unless grant-aided by the Arts Council. On February 20, the G.L.C. offered an emergency grant of £370,000 to keep the Cottesloe open, subject to its arts budget surviving rate-capping by the Government. However, although grateful for the offer, the National stated that uncertainty about its funding meant that the Cottesloe would definitely close on April 20. The Cottesloe did close as planned, but by April the situation had improved sufficiently for it to be announced that it would reopen in September for 6 months. Furthermore, its successful production of the *Mysteries* would be performed at the Lyceum Theatre for a limited season, assisted by an extra grant from the G.L.C. of £25,000.

It was fortunate that the National Theatre was still able to produce work of the highest quality, in spite of its financial worries. The Cottesloe *Mysteries* were widely acclaimed. Adapted by Tony Harrison from the mystery plays from the York and Wakefield cycles, with elements from the Coventry and Chester plays, the full sequence was seen for the first time in January, with *Doomsday* now added to *The Nativity* and *The Passion* eight years after the National first began presenting the works. The Cottesloe also produced *Fool for Love* by the prolific American playwright Sam Shepard, in its British première; this also transferred to the West End.

At the Lyttelton, Tom Stoppard's fruitful collaboration with director Peter Wood continued with *Rough Crossing*, freely adapted from Ferenc Molnar's Hungarian comedy *Play at the Castle*, which P. G. Wodehouse had previously adapted in 1928 as *The Play's the Thing*. With its setting now moved from a castle to an ocean liner, and music by André Previn, the piece was amusing and well performed, if lightweight. Goldsmith's *She Stoops to Conquer* received competent if not sparkling treatment, and other productions included Athol Fugard's *The Road to Mecca*, inspired by the life of the Afrikaaner sculptress Helen Martins, and Jean-Jacques Bernard's *Martine*, considered revolutionary when first produced in the 1920s. Eleanor Bron took on the challenging title role in Webster's tragedy *The Duchess of Malfi*.

Ian McKellen was prominent in the leading role in *Coriolanus* at the Olivier, and received excellent support from Irene Worth as Volumnia and Greg Hicks as Tullus Aufidius in an imaginative, politicised reading of the play. Gogol's *The Government Inspector* feated Rik Mayall as the clerk Ivan Khlestakov, mistaken for the inspector in this deservedly still popular satire on corruption. Although the set tended to dominate the players, Mayall gave a bravura performance which was much praised. Howard Brenton and David Hare's *Pravda* was a heavy-handed satire on the newspaper world; subtitled 'a Fleet Street Comedy', the play was redeemed solely by Anthony Hopkins' brilliant portrayal of South African newspaper proprietor Lambert Le Roux. *A Chorus of Disapproval* was Alan Ayckbourn's 31st play, and a welcome return to his best form. It concerned a widower who joined the Pendon Amateur Light Operatic Society for companionship, but acted as a catalyst on those around him, rising from minor parts to the leading role in their production of John Gay's *The Beggar's Opera*, without conscious effort.

ROYAL SHAKESPEARE COMPANY

The Royal Shakespeare Company, faced like the National with a grant increase of 2 per cent, well below the rate of inflation, announced that the number of Shakespeare productions at Stratford would be cut from six to four, and an export drive would be mounted to raise money. *Nicholas Nickleby* would be revived for the U.S.A. and commercial aspects of the company's work would be emphasised, for example with television productions of major successes such as *Cyrano de Bergerac*. 'An aggressive self-help policy will be adopted which not only lays emphasis on the commercial potential of already successful productions but also embraces an artistic policy which reconfirms the R.S.C.'s long-standing commitment to new writing'.

The 1983–84 season of Shakespeare at Stratford was completed with Barry Kyle's production of *Love's Labour's Lost*. 1984–85 productions opened with *The Merry Wives of Windsor*, set in the second Elizabethan age, the 1950s, and directed by Bill Alexander, followed by *As You Like It*, with Juliet Stevenson notable as Rosalind in Adrian Noble's production, and an imaginative stage-setting in the ducal palace designed by Bob Crowley. Juliet Stevenson featured with Anton Lesser in Howard Davies's production of *Troilus and Cressida*. Productions at The Other Place included Robert Holman's *Today* and Nicholas Wright's *The Desert Air*.

At the Barbican, the outstanding success was Antony Sher's demonic *Richard III*, with Kenneth Branagh also receiving plaudits for his interpretation of *Henry V*. John Napier's set in Howard Davies's production of Brecht's *Mother Courage* was impressive. In the Pit, Stephen Poliakoff's new play *Breaking the Silence*, based on his grandfather's experiences in revolutionary Russia, was absorbing and well acted, and later transferred to the Mermaid. Trevor Griffiths's *The Party* featured Ian McDiarmid in the role of the Communist orator John Tagg,

which Olivier had played in 1973 in his last stage role.

Awards

In the 30th Standard Drama Awards, the prize for best play was won by Michael Frayn for *Benefactors*. Best actor was Ian McKellen in *Coriolanus*, and best actress Maggie Smith in *The Way of the World*. Best musical was *42nd Street*, and best comedy Richard Harris's *Stepping Out*. Christopher Morahan was adjudged best director for *Wild Honey*, and most promising playwright was Sharman Macdonald for *When I Was a Girl I Used to Scream and Shout*.

In the Laurence Olivier Theatre Awards (formerly, the Society of West End Theatre Awards), musical of the year was *42nd Street*; best play was Michael Frayn's *Benefactors*; best director, Christopher Morahan for *Wild Honey*, and best actor in a revival, Ian McKellen in *Wild Honey*. In the British Theatre Association Awards, best actress was Glenda Jackson in *Strange Interlude*; best actors, Brian Cox for *Rat in the Skull* and Antony Sher for *Richard III*; best directors, Peter Gill for *Venice Preserv'd* and Christopher Morahan for *Wild Honey*; best new play was Harold Pinter's *One for the Road*.

PRODUCTIONS

London productions between September 1, 1984 and August 31, 1985, included the following:

ADELPHI: Strand, W.C.2. (1985) Feb. 12. *Me and My Girl*, music by Noel Gay, book and lyrics by L. Arthur Rose and Douglas Furber, revised by Stephen Fay, with Robert Lindsay, Frank Thornton, Emma Thompson, Roy Macready and Susannah Fellowes, directed by Mike Ockrent, designed by Martin Johns, choreographed by Gillian Gregory (Leicester Haymarket production).

ALBERY: St. Martin's Lane, W.C.2. (1984) Sept. 20. *The Boy Friend* by Sandy Wilson, with Anna Quayle, Derek Waring, Peter Bayliss and Paddie O'Neil. (1985) Feb. 21. *The Seven Year Itch* by George Axelrod, with Patrick Mower, Adrienne Posta, Royce Mills and Isabelle Amyes, dir. by James Roose-Evans, des. by Inigo Monk.

ALDWYCH: W.C.2. (1984) Oct. 3. *The Nerd* by Larry Shue, with Rowan Atkinson, Tony Steadman, Bridget Turner, Harry Ditsen, Michael J. Jackson and Mary Maddox, dir. by Mike Ockrent, des. by Roger Glossop. (1985) April 1. *Jumpers* by Tom Stoppard, with Paul Eddington, Felicity Kendal, Simon Cadell and Andrew Sachs, dir. by Peter Wood.

ALMEIDA: Almeida St., N.1. (1985) March 22. *The Possessed* by Dostoevsky, dir. by Yuri Lyubimov. May 7. *Medea* by Euripides (trans. Rex Warner), with Linda Bassett, Frank Baker, Vincent Ebrahim and Michael Mears, dir. by Nancy Meckler (Leicester Haymarket prod.). July 15. *The Cenci* by Percy Bysshe Shelley, with Leonie Mellinger, William Hoyland and Alan Bennion, dir. by Debbie Shewell (Bristol Old Vic prod.).

AMBASSADORS: West St., Cambridge Circus, W.C.2. (1984) Oct 11. *Top People*, written and dir, by Richard O'Brien, with Peter Blythe and Jane Howe. (1985) June 12. *Figaro*, adapted by Nick Broadhurst and Tony Britten, with Terence Hillyer, Prue Clarke, Lesley Duff and Janet Dibley, dir. by Nick Broadhurst.

APOLLO: Shaftesbury Ave., W.1. (1985) May 1. *Look to the Rainbow* by Robert Cushman, with Jack

Gilford, Isabelle Lucas, Mandy More and Barbara Rosenblat. Aug. 6. *Fighting Chance* by N. J. Crisp, with Simon Williams, Elizabeth Quinn, Brian Marshall, Victor Maddern and Lewis Jones, dir. by Roger Clissold.

ASTORIA: Charing Cross Rd., W.C.2. (1984) Oct. 31. *The Hired Man*, book by Melvyn Bragg, music and lyrics by Howard Goodall, with Paul Clarkson, Julie Hills, Clare Burt, Stephen Earle and Billy Hartman, dir. by David Gilmore.

BARBICAN: E.C.2. (1984) Sept. 12. Shakespeare's *Henry VIII*, with Richard Griffiths, Gemma Jones, Stephen Moore, David Schofield, Paul Greenwood and Lesley Duff, dir. by Howard Davies (with David Edgar), des. by Hayden Griffin. Nov. 7. *Mother Courage* by Bertolt Brecht (trans. by Sue Davies, adapted by Hanif Kureishi), with Judi Dench, Barbara Alexander, Miles Anderson, Stephen Moore, Trevor Peacock and Zoe Wanamaker, dir. by Howard Davies, des. by John Napier. (1985) April 16. Shakespeare's *Hamlet*, with Roger Rees, Virginia McKenna, Frances Barber, Kenneth Branagh, John Stride and Christopher Benjamin, dir. by Ron Daniels, des. by Maria Bjornson. April 30. Shakespeare's *Richard III*, with Antony Sher, Penelope Beaumont, Malcolm Storry, John Carlisle, Peter Postlethwaite, Patricia Routledge and Roger Allam, dir. by Bill Alexander, des. by William Dudley. May 16. Shakespeare's *Henry V*, with Kenneth Branagh, Ian McDiarmid, Cecile Paoli, Sion Probert and Nicolas Woodeson, dir. by Adrian Noble, des. by Bob Crowley. July 2. *Red Noses* by Peter Barnes, with Antony Sher, Polly James, Richard Easton, Christopher Benjamin, Nicholas Farrell, Jim Hooper and Bernard Horsfall, dir. by Terry Hands, des. by Farrah. Aug. 7. Shakespeare's *Love's Labour's Lost*, with Roger Rees, Kenneth Branagh, Emily Richard, Josette Simon, Brian Parr, Richard Easton, Christopher Benjamin and John Carlisle, dir. by Barry Kyle, des. by Bob Crowley.

BARBICAN PIT: (1984) Sept 12. *A New Way to Pay Old Debts* by Philip Massinger, with Emrys James, Julie Peasgood, Anthony O'Donnell, John Cater, Jane Booker, Paul Spence and Miles Anderson, dir. by Adrian Noble, des. by Bob Crowley. Nov. 6. *Breaking the Silence* by Stephen Poliakoff, with Gemma Jones, John Kane, Daniel Massey and Juliet Stevenson, dir. by Ron Daniels, des. by Alison Chitty. (1985) Jan. 15. *Waste* by Harley Granville-Barker, with Maria Aitken, Judi Dench, Sylvia Coleridge, Eileen Page, Tony Church, Daniel Massey, Charles Kay and Bruce Alexander, dir. by John Barton, des. by Chris Morley. April 15. *The Party* by Trevor Griffiths, with Ian McDiarmid, Roger Allam, Malcolm Storry and Nicholas Woodeson, dir. by Howard Davies with David Edgar. April 29. *Golden Girls* by Louise Page, with Polly James, Katharine Rogers, Sarah Berger, Martin Jacobs, Josette Simon, Alphonsia Emmanuel, Jimmy Yuill and Cathy Tyson, dir. by Barry Kyle. May 15. *Today* by Robert Holman, with Roger Allam and Polly James, dir. by Bill Alexander. July 3. *Dreamplay* by August Strindberg, with Roger Allam, Penny Downie, George Raistrick, Simon Templeman and Liz Moscrop, dir. by John Barton. July 25. *The War Plays* (*Red, Black and Ignorant, The Tin Can People* and *Great Peace*) by Edward Bond, with Maggie Steed, Ian McDiarmid and Gary Oldman, dir. by Nick Hamm. Aug. 7. *The Desert Air* by Nicholas Wright, with Peter Eyre, Geoffrey Hutchings, Nicholas Woodeson, Cecile Paoli and Nicholas Farrell, dir. by Adrian Noble.

DONMAR WAREHOUSE: Earlham St., Covent Garden, W.C.2. (1984) Sept. 24. *Up 'n' Under* by John Goldberg, with Richard Ridings, Peter Geeves, Andrew Dunn and Jane Clifford (Hull Truck Company prod.). Oct. 15. *Gymslip Vicar*, written and performed by Peter McCarthy, Tony Haase, Rebecca Stevens and Robin Driscoll (Cliff Hanger Company prod.). Nov. 20. *Happy Days* by Samuel Beckett, with Darlene Johnson and Richard Wilding, dir. by Clare Davidson (Shared Experience prod.). (1985) Jan. 7. *Vanity Fair* by Thackeray. Jan. 14. Shakespeare's *Pericles*. Jan. 21. *Andromache* by Racine (Cheek by Jowl Company prod.) with Amanda Harris, Andrew Collins, Sadie Shimmin and Duncan Bell, dir. by Declan Donnellan. Jan. 28. *Bouncers* by John Godberg, with Peter Jeeves and Richard Ridings (Hull Truck Company prod.). Feb. 26. *The Playboy of the Western World* by J. M. Synge, with Maeliosa Stafford, Brid Brennan and Marie Mullen, dir. by Garry Hynes (Druid Theatre Company, Galway, prod.).

DUCHESS: Catherine St., W.C.2. (1984) Nov. 26. *Extremities* by William Mastrosimone, with Helen Mirren, Kevin McNally, Marty Cruickshank and Johanna Kirby, dir. by Robert Allan Ackerman. (1985) March 7. *Other Places* by Harold Pinter, with Colin Blakely, Dorothy Tutin, Roger Davidson, Rosie Kerslake and Susan Engel, dir. by Kenneth Ives, des. by Eileen Diss. July 10. *A State of Affairs* by Graham Swannell, with Gary Bond, Nichola McAuliffe and Amanda Boxer (Lyric Studio, Hammersmith prod.).

DUKE OF YORK'S: St. Martin's Lane, W.C.2. (1984) Sept. 24. *Stepping Out* by Richard Harris, with Barbara Ferris, Marcia Warren, Diane Langton, Ben Aris, Barbara Young, Gabrielle Lloyd and Sheri Shepstone, dir. by Julia McKenzie.

FORTUNE: Russell St., W.C.2. (1984) Oct. 2. *Falstaff* by Robert Nye, with David Buck, dir. by John Tydeman, des. by Kate Burnett and Kevin McCloud. Nov. 7. *Annie Wobbler* by Arnold Wesker, with Nichola McAuliffe, dir. by Arnold Wesker, des. by Pamela Howard. (1985) Feb. 25. *The Mill on the Floss* by George Eliot, with Margaret Wolfit, dir. by Richard Digby Day. March 26. *Up 'n' Under* by John Goldberg (Hull Truck Company prod.).

GREENWICH: Croom's Hill, S.E.10. (1984) Sept. 19. *It's My Party* by John Flanagan and Andrew McCulloch, with David Roper, Caroline Hutchison, Diane Bull, Elaine Lordan, Tom Chadbon, Tom Georgeson and Brian Stephens, dir. by Antonia Bird. Oct. 31. *Two Planks and a Passion* by Anthony Minghella, with Madge Hindle, Gillian Barge, Cathryn Harrison, Michael Maloney and Christopher Fulford, dir. by Danny Boyle, des. by Deirdre Clancy. Dec. 19. *Cider with Rosie* by Laurie Lee, adapted and dir. by James Roose-Evans, with Christopher Timothy, Simon Butteriss and Sarah Crowden. (1985) Feb. 6. *My Brother's Keeper* by Nigel Williams, with John McEnery, Reginald Marsh, John Price, Doreen Andrew and John Biggerstaff, dir. by Alan Dossor, des. by Dermot Hayes. March 27. *Intermezzo* by Arthur Schnitzler (trans. by Robert David MacDonald), with Sheila Gish and Jonathan Kent, dir. by Christopher Fettes, des. by Yolanda Sonnabend. May 15. *The Glass Menagerie* by Tennessee Williams, with Constance Cummings, Gerard Murphy, Toria Fuller and Michael J. Shannon, dir. by Alan Strachan. Aug. 22. *Buddy Holly at the Regal* by Phil Woods, with Pikey Butler, David Thewlis and Colin Starkey, dir. by Ian Watt-Smith.

HAMPSTEAD: Swiss Cottage, N.W.3. (1984) Sept. 7. *Fall* by James Saunders, with Gwen Watford, Julie Covington, Cecily Hobbs and Sylvestra Le Touzel, dir. by Robin Lefevre. Nov. 5. *Bloody Poetry* by Howard Brenton, with William Gaminara, James Aubrey, Valentine Pelka, Fiona Shaw, Jane Gurnett and Sue Burton, dir. by Roland Rees (Leicester Haymarket prod.). Dec. 18. *Kissing God* devised by Phil Young, with Kate Lock, David Bamber, Feroza Syal and Anton Lesser. (1985) Jan. 24. *The Power of the Dog* by Howard Barker, with Sean Baker, Amelda Brown, Stephanie Fayerman, Philip McGough and Hugh Fraser, dir. by Kenny Ireland. March 4. *'Night, Mother'* by Marsha Norman, with Marjorie Yates and Susan Wooldridge, dir. by Michael Attenborough. April 16. *Gertrude Stein and a Companion* by Win Wells, with Miriam Margolyes and Natasha Morgan, dir. by Sonia Fraser. July 1. *Grafters* by Billy Hamon, with Richard Butler, John Benfield, David Hayman and Tim Roth, dir. by Jane Howell. Aug. 12. *The Daughter-in-Law* by D. H. Lawrence, with Cheryl Campbell, James Hazeldine, Lorcan Cranitch, Sandra Voe and Mary Wimbush, dir. by John Dove.

LYCEUM: Strand, W.C.2. (1985) May 15. *The Mysteries* (National Theatre prod.).

LYRIC: Hammersmith, W.6. (1984) Sept. 13. *The Devil and the Good Lord* by Jean-Paul Sartre (trans. by Frank Hauser), with Gerard Murphy, Simon Ward, Sean Baker and Maia Simon, dir. by John Dexter, des. by Jocelyn Herbert. Oct. 23. *Tramway Road* by Ronald Harwood, with Freddie Jones, Annette Crosbie, William Vanderpuye and Richard E. Grant, dir. by David Jones, des. by Timothy O'Brien. Dec. 12. *The Wiz*, book by William F. Brown, score by Charles Smalls, with Clarke Peters, Earlene Bentley and Clem Jones, dir. by Peter James. (1985) Feb. 13. *Little Eyolf* by Henrik Ibsen (trans. by Michael Meyer), with Diana Rigg, Ronald Pickup, Cheryl Campbell and Anne Dyson, dir. by Clare Davidson. April 16. *The Seagull* by Chekhov, with John Lynch, Natasha Richardson, Phoebe Nicholls, Alfred Burke, John Hurt and Samantha Eggar, dir. by Charles Sturridge. June 6. *The London Cuckolds* by Edward Ravenscroft, adapted and des. by John Byrne, with Sylvestra Le Touzel, Michael Maloney and Diana Hardcastle, dir. by Stuart Burge. July 8. *Bengal Lancer* by Willian Ayot, with Tim Pigott-Smith, dir. by Michael Joyce, des. by Bob Crowley.

LYRIC STUDIO: Hammersmith, W.6. (1985) Feb. 20. *A State of Affairs* by Graham Swannell, with Gary Bond, Amanda Redman and Julie Legrand, dir. by Peter James. May 23. *In the Belly of the Beast* by Jack Henry Abbott, with William L. Petersen, Tim Halligan and Peter Aylward, dir. by Robert Falls (Wisdom Bridge Theatre, Chicago prod.). June 11. *The Woolgatherer* by William Mastrosimone, with Kate Lock and George Irving, dir. by Terry Johnson.

LYRIC: Shaftesbury Ave., W.1. (1984) Sept. 19. *Loot* by Joe Orton, with Leonard Rossiter, Gemma Craven, Neil Pearson, David John, John Channell Mills and Patrick O'Connell, dir. by Jonathan Lynn. (1985) Feb. 4. *Fool for Love* by Sam Shepard (National Theatre prod.). May 24. *Waste* by Harley Granville-Barker (Barbican Pit prod.).

MERMAID: Puddle Dock, Blackfriars, E.C.4. (1984) Oct. 17. *Blockheads*, book by Michael Landwehr, Kay Cole and Arthur Whitelaw, lyrics by Hal Hackady, music by Alexander Peskanov, with Mark Hadfield and Kenneth H. Waller, dir. by Arthur Whitelaw, chor. by Kay Cole, des. by Tim Goodchild. Nov. 19. *Of Mice and Men* by John Steinbeck, with Clive Mantle, Lon Hirsch, Susan Penhaligon and Francis Drake, dir. by Geoff Bullen (Nuffield Theatre, Southampton prod.). May 28. *Breaking the Silence* by Stephen Poliakoff, with Alan Howard, Jenny Agutter and Gemma Jones (Barbican Pit prod.).

NATIONAL THEATRE: South Bank, S.E.1. COTTESLOE: (1984) Oct. 4. *Fool for Love* by Sam Shepard, with Ian Charleson, Julie Walters, David Troughton and Tom Watson, dir. by Peter Gill, des. by Alison Chitty. (1985) Jan. 19. *The Mysteries*, edited and arranged by Tony Harrison, with Brian Glover, Karl Johnson, Edna Doré, Dave Hill, Jack Shepherd and Robert Stephens, dir. by Bill Bryden, des. by William Dudley.

LYTTELTON: (1984) Oct. 30. *Rough Country* by Tom Stoppard, with Michael Kitchen, John Standing, Sheila Gish, Niall Buggy, Robin Bailey and Andrew C. Wadsworth, dir. by Peter Wood, des. by Carl Toms, music by André Previn. Nov. 8. *She Stoops to Conquer* by Oliver Goldsmith, with Dora Bryan, Hwyel Bennett, Tom Baker, Tony Haygarth, Gregory Floy and Julia Watson, dir. by Giles Block, des. by Alison Chitty. (1985) Feb. 27. *The Road to Mecca* by Athol Fugard, with Yvonne Bryceland, Charlotte Cornwell and Bob Peck, dir. by Athol Fugard, des. by Douglas Heap. April 20. *Martine* by Jean-Jacques Bernard (trans. by John Fowles), with Wendy Morgan, Andrew C. Wadsworth, Jessica Turner, Jean Anderson and Barrie Rutter, dir. by Peter Hall, des. by Alison Chitty. July 4. *The Duchess of Malfi* by John Webster, with Eleanor Bron, Ian McKellen, Edward Petherbridge, Jonathan Hyde, Sheila Hancock and Roy Kinnear, dir. by Philip Prowse.

OLIVIER: (1984) Nov. 14. *The Ancient Mariner* by Samuel Taylor Coleridge, adapted and dir. by Michael Bogdanov, with Michael Bryant, des. by Marty Flood. Dec. 15. Shakespeare's *Coriolanus*, with Ian McKellen, Irene Worth, Basil Henson, Wendy Morgan, Frederick Treves, Greg Hicks and David Ryall, dir. by Peter Hall, des. by John Bury. (1985) Jan. 31. *The Government Inspector* by Nikolai Gogol (adapted by Adrian Mitchell), with Rik Mayall, Jim Broadbent, Ron Pember and Peter Blythe, dir. by Richard Eyre, des. by John Gunter. May 2. *Pravda* by Howard Brenton and David Hare, with Anthony Hopkins, Bill Nighy, Peter Blythe, Tim McInnerny, Kate Buffery, Fred Pearson, Ron Pember and Basil Henson, dir. by David Hare, des. by Hayden Griffin. Aug. 2. *A Chorus of Disapproval*, written and dir. by Alan Ayckbourn, with Bob Peck, Gemma Craven, Michael Gambon, Imelda Staunton, David Ryall and James Hayes.

OLD VIC: The Cut, S.E.1. (1984) Sept. 19. *Big in Brazil* by Bamber Gascoigne, with Timothy West, Prunella Scales, Rodney Bewes, Derek Smith and Jimmy Mulville, dir. by Mel Smith. Nov. 14. *Phedra* by Racine (trans. by Robert David MacDonald), with Glenda Jackson, Robert Eddison, Georgina Hale, Gerard Murphy, Joyce Redman and Tim Woodward, dir. and des. by Philip Prowse. (1985) Jan. 2. *Great Expectations* by Charles Dickens, adapted and dir. by Peter Coe, with Roy Dotrice, Sheila Burrell, Leon Greene, Tony Jay, Charles Lewsen, Lynn Clayton, Collin Johnson and Ian McCurrach, des. by Peter Rice (Churchill Theatre, Bromley and Birmingham Rep. prod.). March 27. *After the Ball is Over* by William Douglas-Home, with Patrick Cargill, Anthony Quayle, Maxine Audley and John Sharpe, dir. by Maria Aitken, des. by Kenneth Mellor. Feb. 6. *The Lonely Road* by Arthur Schnitzler (adapted by Ronald Adam and Christopher Fettes), with Alan Dobie, Anthony Hopkins, Samantha Eggar, Colin Firth and Rupert Frazer, dir. by Christopher Fettes, des. by Maria Bjornson. May 22. *The Corn is Green* by Emlyn Williams, with Deborah Kerr, George Winter, Imelda Staunton, Bridget Turner, Allan Cuthbertson and Elizabeth Counsell, dir. by Frith Banbury. July 3. *Seven Brides for Seven Brothers*, music by Gene de Paul, lyrics by Johnny Mercer, with Steve Devereaux and Roni Page, dir. by Michael Winter, des. by Bill Pinner, choreog. by Stephanie Carter.

OPEN AIR: Regent's Park, W.1. (1985) June 3. Shakespeare's *Twelfth Night*, with Michael Denison, Ruth Madoc, John Moffatt, Alyson Spiro, Paul Raffield, Paul Bradley and Sarah Finch, dir. by Richard Digby Day, des. by Tim Reed. June 18. Shakespeare's *A Midsummer Night's Dream*, with Patrick Ryecart, Jenny Quayle, John McAndrew, Vincenzo Nicoli, dir. by Tim Robertson, des. by Simon Higlett, costumes by Jim Goodchild. July 30. *Ring Round the Moon* by Jean Anouilh (adapted by Christopher Fry), with Patrick Ryecart, Ruth Madoc, Sarah Finch, James Cairncross, Helen Lindsay and Michael Denison, dir. by David Conville, des. by Simon Higlett, costumes by Tim Goodchild.

PHOENIX: Charing Cross Rd., W.C.2. (1984) Nov. 15. *Trumpets and Raspberries* by Dario Fo (trans. by Roger McAvoy and Anna-Maria Guigni), with Griff Rhys Jones, Gwen Taylor and Francesca Brill, dir. by Roger Smith, des. by Fran Thompson. (1985) May 29. *Strippers* by Peter Terson, with Bill Maynard, Judi Lamb, Jackie Lye and Lynda Bellingham, dir. by John Blackmore. Aug. 13. *Are You Lonesome Tonight?* by Alan Bleasdale, with Martin Shaw and Simon Bowman, dir. by Robin Lefevre, des. by Voytek.

PICCADILLY: Denman St., W.1. (1984) Sept. 21. *Pump Boys and Dinettes* by John Foley, Mark Hardwick, Cass Morgan, Debra Monk, John Schimmel and Jim Wann, with Paul Jones, Carlene Carter, Kiki Dee, Brian Protheroe, Gary Holton and Julian Littman, dir. by David Taylor. (1985) July 18. *Mutiny!*, book by Richard Crane, music by David Essex, with David Essex, Frank Finlay, Sinitta Renet and Frank Olegario, dir. by Michael Bogdanov, des. by William Dudley.

PRINCE OF WALES: Coventry St., W.1. (1985) June 19. *Guys and Dolls* with Lulu, Norman Rossington, Clarke Peters, Betsy Brantley and David Healy, dir. by Antonia Bird (National Theatre prod.).

QUEEN'S: Shaftesbury Ave., W.1. (1985) Feb. 28. *The Caine Mutiny Court Martial* by Herman Wouk, with Charlton Heston, Ben Cross, John Corey and William Wright, dir. by Charlton Heston, des. by Saul Radomsky. July 31. *The Seagull* by Anton Chekhov, with Vanessa Redgrave, Jonathan Pryce and Julia Swift (Lyric, Hammersmith prod.).

RIVERSIDE STUDIO: Hammersmith, W.6. (1984) Oct. 12. *Tea in a China Cup* written and dir. by Christina Reid, with Caroline Embling, Theresa Boden, Margaret D'Arcy and Mary Duddy. (1985) April 10. *The Trojan Women* by Euripides, with the Suzuki Company of Toga, dir. by Tadashi Suzuki. May 30. *The Dance of Death* by August Strindberg (trans. by Ted Whitehead), with Alan Bates, Frances de la Tour. Michael Byrne and Anne Louise Lambert, dir. by Keith Hack.

ROYAL COURT: Sloane Sq., S.W.1. (1984) Sept. 4. *Rat in the Skull* by Ron Hutchinson, with Brian Cox, Colum Convey, Philip Jackson and Gary Oldman, dir. by Max Stafford-Clark. Oct. 16. *An Honourable Trade* by G. F. Newman, with Felicity Dean, Shirley Dixon, David Gant, David Howey, Donald Sumpter, Philip Voss and Richard Wilson, dir. by Mike Bradwell. Nov. 27. *The Pope's Wedding* by Edward Bond, with Gary Oldman, Tony Rohr, Lesley Manville and Joanna Whalley, dir. by Max Stafford-Clark, des. by Peter Hartwell. Dec. 20. *Saved* by Edward Bond, with Peter Hugo-Daly, Joanna Whalley, June

Watson and Tony Rohr, dir. by Danny Boyle. (1985) March 20. *Tom and Viv* by Michael Hastings, with Julie Covington, Edward Herrman, Margaret Tyzack and David Haig, dir. by Max Stafford-Clark. June 4. *The Overgrown Path* by Robert Holman, with Peter Vaughan, Doreen Mantle, Deborah Findlay and Stuart Wilson, dir. by Les Waters, des. by Sue Plummer. Aug. 27. *Aunt Dan and Lemon* by Wallace Shawn, with Linda Hunt, John Heard, Larry Pine and Kathryn Pogson, dir. by Max Stafford-Clark.

SADLER'S WELLS: Rosebery Ave., E.C.1. (1985) June 11. *Children of a Lesser God* by Mark Medoff, with Jean St. Clair and Ron Aldridge, dir. by Gordon Davidson.

SHAFTESBURY: Shaftesbury Ave., W.C.2. (1984) Oct. 24. *Two Into One* written and dir. by Ray Cooney, with Michael Williams, Barbara Murray, Donald Sinden, Derek Royle, Linda Hayden and Lionel Jefferies.

SHAW: Euston Rd., N.W.1. (1984) Oct. 9. *Six Men of Dorset* by Miles Malleson and Harry Brooks, adapted by John McGrath, with Paul Moriarty and William Hoyland (7:84 England Company prod.).

STRAND: Aldwych, W.C.2. (1985) March 5. *Why Me?* by Stanley Price, with Liz Smith, Richard Briers, Diane Fletcher and Polly Hemingway, dir. by Robert Chetwyn.

THEATRE ROYAL: Haymarket, S.W.1. (1984) Nov. 13. *The Way of the World* by William Congreve, with Maggie Smith, Joan Plowright, Michael Jayston, Sheila Allen, James Grout, John Moffatt and James Villiers, dir. by William Gaskill, des. by Hayden Griffin (Chichester Festival prod.). (1985) April 24. *Old Times* by Harold Pinter, with Liv Ullman, Nicola Pagett and Michael Gambon, dir. by David Jones, des. by Timothy O'Brien. July 9. *Sweet Bird of Youth* by Tennessee Williams, with Lauren Bacall, Michael Beck, James Grout, Geraldine Alexander, Simon Rouse and Frances Cuka, dir. by Harold Pinter, des. by Eileen Diss.

THEATRE ROYAL: Stratford East, E.15. (1984) Sept. 17. *Old Story Time* by Trevor Rhone, with Rudolph Walker, Mona Hammond, Larrington Walker and Okon Jones. Oct. 29. *Lazydays, Limited* by Tony Marchant, with Stephen Tiller, Will Knightley, Edna Doré, Donald Morley and Marion Bailey, dir. by Adrian Shergold. (1985) Feb. 4. *Better Times* by Barrie Keeffe, with Robert Keegan and Larry Dann, dir. by Philip Hedley. March 11. Shakespeare's *The Taming of the Shrew*, des. and dir. by Ultz. April 17. *Viva!* by Andy de la Tour, with Tom Wilkinson, Joanne Pearce, Alfred Molina and Julian Curry, dir. by Roger Smith, des. by Saul Radomsky.

VICTORIA PALACE: S.W.1. (1985) March. *Barnum* with Michael Crawford.

WESTMINSTER: Palace St., S.W.1. (1985) *Man of Two Worlds* by Daniel Pearce, with Ian Cullen, dir. by Bernard Hopkins.

WYNDHAM'S: Charing Cross Rd., W.C.2. (1984) Dec. 12. *The Secret Diary of Adrian Mole*, by Sue Townsend, music and lyrics by Ken Howard and Alan Blaikley, with Simon Schatzberger, Mandy Travis, Nigel Bennett, Antony Howes, Sheila Collings and Katharine Schlesinger, dir. by Graham Watkins, des. by Anthony Dean.

YOUNG VIC: 66 The Cut, S.E.1. (1984) Oct. 11. Shakespeare's *Macbeth*, with Malcolm Tierney, Brian Bovell, Shope Shodeinde, T-Bone Wilson and Jeffrey

Kissoon, dir. by David Thacker. (1985) Feb, 5. Shakespeare's *Hamlet*, with Matthew Marsh, Jonathan Burn, Natasha Richardson, Andrew Secombe, Michael Cronin and Heather Canning, dir. by David Thacker.

Productions outside London included the following:

STRATFORD MEMORIAL THEATRE (Royal Shakespeare Company): (1984) Sept. 6. *Hamlet* with Roger Rees, Frank Middlemass, Frances Barber, Nicholas Farrell, Virginia McKenna, Brian Blessed, Sebastian Shaw and Kenneth Branagh, dir. by Ron Daniels, des. by Maria Bjornson. Oct. 10. *Love's Labour's Lost* with Edward Petherbridge, Kenneth Branagh, Roger Rees, Emily Richard, Harold Innocent, Josette Simon, Frances Barber, Amanda Root and Frank Middlemass, dir. by Barry Kyle, des. by Bob Crowley. (1985) April 3. *The Merry Wives of Windsor* with Sheila Steafel, Peter Jeffrey, Janet Dale, Lindsay Duncan, Graham Turner, Trevor Martin, David Bradley and Nicky Henson, dir. by Bill Alexander, des. by William Dudley. April 23. *As You Like It* with Juliet Stevenson, Nicky Henson, Joseph O'Conor, Hilton McRae, Alan Rickman, Mary Jo Randle, Fiona Shaw, Leslie Manville and Bruce Alexander, dir. by Adrian Noble, des. by Bob Crowley. June 25. *Troilus and Cressida* with Anton Lesser, Juliet Stevenson, Alan Rickman, Clive Morrison, Peter Jeffrey, Hilton McRae and Alun Armstrong, dir. by Howard Davies, des. by Ralph Koltai.

STRATFORD OTHER PLACE: (1984) Oct. 31. *Today* by Robert Holman, with Roger Allam, George Raistrick, Amanda Root, David Whittaker and Polly James, dir.

by Bill Alexander. Nov. 27. *The Desert Air* by Nicholas Wright, with Geoffrey Hutchings, Peter Eyre and Polly James, dir. by Adrian Noble, des. by Chris Dyer. (1985) April 5. *Philistines* by Maxim Gorky (revised by Dusty Hughes), with David Burke, Sean Baker, Anna Calder-Marshall and Fiona Shaw, dir. by John Caird.

CHICHESTER FESTIVAL THEATRE: (1985) May 1. *Cavalcade* by Noël Coward, with Joanna McCallum, Lewis Fiander, Julian Wadham, Janet Behan, Sophia Winter and Robert Demeger, dir. by David Gilmore, des. by Roger Glossop. May 15. Shakespeare's *Antony and Cleopatra*, with Diana Rigg, Denis Quilley, Norman Rodway and Philip Frank, dir. by Robin Phillips, des. by Daphne Dare. July 10. *The Philanthropist* by Christopher Hampton, with Edward Fox, John Wells, Jeremy Sinden, Julian Wadham, Laura Davenport and Celia Imrie, dir. by Patrick Garland. July 31. *The Scarlet Pimpernel* by Baroness Orczy (adapted by Beverley Cross), with Donald Sinden, Rowland Davies, Desmond Barrit, Joanna McCallum and Charles Kay, dir. by Nicholas Hytner, des. by Mark Thompson.

MANCHESTER ROYAL EXCHANGE: (1985) March. *Long Day's Journey Into Night* by Eugene O'Neill, with Dilys Hamlett, James Maxwell, Jonathan Hackett and Michael Mueller, dir. by Braham Murray, des. by Johanna Bryant. April. *Three Sisters* by Chekhov (trans. by Michael Frayn), with Janet McTeer, Emma Piper, David Ashton, Nicholas Blaine, Christopher Bramwell, Sven-Bertil Taube and Espen Skjonberg, dir. by Casper Wrede, des. by Di Seymour.

TELEVISION IN 1984–85

BBC

Mr. Stuart Young, Chairman of the BBC, concluded his foreword to the 1985 Annual Report and Handbook with the words: "We are confident the Government will conclude that our case for a realistic licence fee settlement is convincing and justified". His confidence was misplaced, but Mr. Young could hardly have foreseen how traumatic the year ahead would be. The BBC was about to enter probably the worst year in its history, with its activities under constant scrutiny, from the Peat, Marwick & Mitchell report on its efficiency, to the Peacock Inquiry into its future financing. Every aspect of the BBC was under investigation, and the Corporation was in the unenviable position of making the news as much as reporting it—and even misreporting it: at one stage the Chairman was compelled to apologise that an item on the *Nine O'clock News*, which claimed that the accountants Peat, Marwick & Mitchell had cleared the BBC of overmanning and backed its claim for a £65 licence fee, was "not as accurate as it should have been". When the BBC fired its opening salvoes in its campaign for the licence fee to be increased, it cannot have anticipated the bombardment in return, and that the whole issue of public service broadcasting would become the subject of debate.

Problems later in the year, with Government intervention over a programme on terrorism in Northern Ireland, and the news that the security service vetted current affairs staff, ensured that the BBC remained in the news, and inevitably overshadowed much of the good work that it continued to produce during a period of soul-searching and reassessment. It had been a film report on the Ethiopian famine disaster on BBC which finally alerted the country, and the world, to the enormity of that tragedy, and provoked a massive relief effort to Africa. Much of this was lost sight of in a year that may be seen to have been crucial for the future of broadcasting in the UK.

The year began fairly quietly. Not long before the BBC was due to begin negotiating an increase in the licence fee with the Government, an advertising agency suggested, in September 1984, that the licence could be pegged at the current rate of £46 if the BBC accepted some advertising. This piece of "kite-flying" from the advertising world was seen as a matter of self-interest, as if the BBC were to take advertisements, the independent television companies' monopoly would be broken and the ensuing competition would reduce the rates charged for air-time. The BBC responded that advertisements would lead to a lowering of standards (just as, 30 years previously, the introduction of commercial television was opposed on the same grounds).

In November, it was widely reported that a routine computer check of the BBC's finances showed that in the current financial year it was overspending its television budget by £7 million, at the same time as it had requested a substantial increase in the £46 licence fee. The exact figure sought was not immediately made public, but was thought to be in the region of £67. It was reported that the BBC ordered savage cutbacks in news reporting, current affairs, and new drama, and increases in repeated programmes, although this was subsequently denied. Later, the Chairman, Stuart Young, was interviewed in *The Times* about the licence review. He strongly opposed advertising, and indicated that a fee of between £60 and £70 was sought. The Home Secretary was awaiting the outcome of a review by Peat, Marwick & Mitchell, before deciding on the figure; traditionally, the discussions between the Home Office and the BBC were not conducted in public. However, on the defensive because of press criticism of the large increase which it was known the BBC was seeking, the Corporation began to go on to the offensive, and to open up the debate. The licence fee had risen to £46 in December 1981, when a figure of £53 had been requested. This brought in an annual revenue of £760 million. The BBC claimed that a figure of £60 would lose it all its development plans, including increased daytime television, a new Broadcasting House, and ten proposed local radio stations; a figure of less than £60 would mean cuts in its main broadcasting output, and force the closure of Radio 3 and possibly Radio 2 as well; and it also proposed a £10 car radio licence. The licence fee, however, was widely seen as an inefficient way of funding the BBC because of widespread evasion. In November, it was estimated that 1·5 million households avoided paying it, resulting in a loss of £60 million in revenue.

In December, as the BBC began a campaign in defence of the proposed increase, which had been revealed as £19 on a colour television licence, making the new figure £65, the Prime Minister let it be known that she was in favour of limited advertising on BBV TV and radio. The increase was condemned in Parliament, and in January 1985, Labour MP Joe Ashton sponsored a Bill under the ten-minute rule in the House of Commons, calling for the BBC to take advertising. It was defeated by 159 votes to 118, but showed that the subject was now being taken seriously. Furthermore, serious division was revealed on the Labour benches, and there was some notable Conservative support. *The Times* then took up the subject: in a series of three leading articles, entitled "Whither the BBC?", it examined the paradox of public service broadcasting in Britain, the dichotomy between service and entertainment of the public. It questioned whether there was enough advertising revenue to sustain both ITV and the BBC—there was no bottomless pit. What had not long previously seemed wholly unthinkable was now a matter of serious and informed discussion, and the BBC was subject to the most sustained scrutiny it had experienced since the 1977 Annan Report. The BBC was felt to be overstretching its resources, by competing in such areas as breakfast television, and with its local radio network. The licence fee was seen as an increasing burden on the population, and the BBC's campaign in its support was aimed at convincing the Government and the public that its services were a bargain, without addressing the larger issues, of the whole question of the nature of broadcasting and the desirability of licence fee funding for it.

In January, the Home Office denied that the BBC had been informed that the new licence fee would be no more than £58, and reiterated that no decision would be taken until the Peat, Marwick & Mitchell report on its efficiency had been received. The BBC received the first draft at the begining of January. It released 30 pages of the report on March 5 (a further 200 pages were deemed confidential) and the Chairman claimed that it gave them "a clean bill of health", which Peat Marwick & Mitchell denied. The report was, they said, "a mixed judgment on the BBC. The very fact that the BBC is implementing 30 recommendations from it can't mean that it is a clean bill of health." Peat, Marwick & Mitchell also criticised television coverage of its report, stating that the licence fee and staffing levels were outside their terms of reference; they had been asked to consider ways "of achieving economies through increased efficiency, while maintaining the range and quality of existing services". The report said that the BBC was in fact less cost-effective in producing drama series than the independent producers who supplied Channel 4, the new twice-weekly "soap opera" *East Enders* being twice as expensive as Channel 4's *Brookside*. The report praised the BBC's efficiency on the whole, and its "commitment to quality" and "awareness of the need to seek constantly to improve efficiency and effectiveness". However, management was criticised, and organisational changes proposed. The report had cost £250,000 and taken six months to produce.

Peacock

On March 27, 1985, after months of speculation and debate, the Home Secretary (Mr. Brittan) announced to the House of Commons that the licence fee would be increased to £58 for colour television and to £18 for black and white. He referred to the BBC's request for an increase to £65, which had "stimulated renewed discussion about the possibility and desirability of some or all of the BBC's services being financed through advertising or by other means than the licence fee". Mr. Brittan continued: "The issues raised are complex. In my view, they required more detailed, careful and above all comprehensive analysis than they have so far received before any conclusion can be reached." He accordingly appointed a committee to review these matters, under the chairmanship of Prof. Alan Peacock. The committee's full terms of reference were: "To assess the effects of the introduction of advertising or sponsorship on the BBC's home services, either as an alternative or a supplement to the income now received through the licence fee, including (a) the financial and other consequences for the BBC, for independent television and independent local radio, for the prospective services of cable, independent national radio and direct broadcasting by satellite, for the press and the advertising industry and for the Exchequer; and (b) the impact on the range and quality of existing broadcasting services; to identify a range of options for the introduction, in varying amounts and on different conditions of advertising or sponsorship on some or all of the BBC's home services, with an assessment of the advantages and disadvantages of each option; to consider any proposals for securing income from the consumer other than through the licence fee."

It was hoped that the committee would complete its work by summer 1986, after which its conclusions would have to be carefully considered. The Home Secretary therefore decided that the present licence fee settlement should be for a period of two years, with the intention that any possible changes in the system of financing broadcasting should be considered in the light of the committee's report before the licence fee falls to be further renewed. However, if decisions could not be made in the light of the report within two years, or it was decided that there should be no change to the system, the settlement would run for a third year with the licence fee continuing at the new rates announced. The Home Secretary said that his task was, as always, "to balance the interests of the licence fee payer with the need to ensure that the Corporation's home services are adequately funded." He believed that the BBC "could and must achieve greater productivity than it has done in the past or has so far planned for the future". In the light of the report from Peat, Marwick & Mitchell, Mr. Brittan believed "there is scope for the BBC to achieve greater efficiency through improved management procedures and strengthened management attitudes". He appreciated that the review he had announced would lead to "a period of uncertainty, not only for the BBC but for the other media, in particular independent broadcasting. But our broadcasting system has inevitably had to develop over the years, and there is nothing new in the fact that it has to face the possibility of change now. What will not change is the Government's commitment to broadcasting services which achieve the highest standards,

in quality, popularity and diversity of consumer choice."

Mr. Gerald Kaufman, chief Opposition spokesman on home affairs, replied on behalf of the Labour Party that "whatever the outcome of the inquiry, there are no circumstances in which a Labour Government would permit advertising either on BBC television or radio".

The Peacock Committee held its first meeting on May 29, and released a consultation document, which stated that it would be investigating whether the introduction of television advertising on BBC would lower standards, and whether advertising on television had reached saturation point. The Committee accepted written submissions throughout the year from interested parties, the release of which to the press ensured that the debate was conducted in the public eye. The BBC found an ally in its case for the preservation of the status quo in the Independent Broadcasting Authority, whose Chairman, Lord Thomson of Monifieth, said in the IBA's Annual Report and Accounts for 1984–85: "The principle of competition for quality of programming but separate sources of finance from licence fee and advertising has for long been seen as an essential element in the success of British public service broadcasting. It is not easy to see how it could be changed in any significant way while maintaining existing standards."

The BBC's problems were not confined to the licence debate; in fact, it seemed that the Corporation could do little right. Still smarting from the criticism it received the previous year for scheduling an imported programme of limited merit against Granada's majestic *Jewel in the Crown*, it referred in the Annual report to "a growing impatience with the restrains holding back the brightest creative talents within the BBC from the levels of excellence of which they believed themselves capable: an impatience aggravated by public critical comparisons made, not over the whole output, but with a single particularly brilliant but very expensive production in the independent sector. The Board took this problem very seriously . . .".

In March, it was announced that six plays commissioned at a cost of £2 million could not be fitted into the BBC 1 schedules, but might be shown later on BBC 2. This postponement of high-quality plays such as Sartre's *Vicious Circle*, and *Antigone*, featuring distinguished casts, caused the BBC's commitment to drama to be questioned, and gave the impression that the independent companies, and in particular Channel 4, now led the way with what might be described as programmes of culture.

In April, BBC current affairs programmes were hit by a walk-out by journalists, in protest at the decision not to renew the contracts of nine well-known reporters. The same month, the BBC incurred the highest-ever costs in an English court, in an action lasting 87 days, totalling £1 million, and was forced to pay £75,000 in damages to a Harley Street slimming expert over allegations in *That's Life* in June 1983. Widespread offence was caused to the Roman Catholic community when the BBC cancelled the screening of the Pope's Easter Sunday message for the first time in 30 years; after the Board's intervention, it was stated that the coverage would be reinstated the following year. The popular consumer-investigation programme *Checkpoint* on Radio 4 was dropped in May, ostensibly because its presenter Roger Cook was leaving to join Central Television, but prompting fears that the BBC's commitment to investigative reporting had been severely dampened by the libel action. The BBC was also accused of making a grave error of judgment with its decision to continue the screening of the European Cup Final after the appalling tragedy at the Heysel Stadium in Brussels.

Michael Grade, Controller of BBC 1, inherited the programmes of his predecessor with his autumn 1984 schedules, and his influence was not to be evident until January 1985 on the screen. However, he did announce that programmes such as *Miss Great Britain*, which he found "close to offensive", *International Superstars* and *The World's Strongest Man* would be dropped, as they were contests which had become anachronisms. His main hopes rested with the new "soap opera" *East Enders* and the three-times weekly *Wogan* chat show, introduced in February.

Oil Wells that End Well?

The BBC appeared to have been outflanked when Thames TV, acting unilaterally, outbid the BBC for the imported American series *Dallas*. The BBC had been paying £29,000 per episode, and Thames offered £55,000. However, the move backfired. Thames had failed to inform the other independent companies of its bid, and its managing director, Bryan Cowgill, was called in by the IBA to explain his actions. Granada and Yorkshire stated that they would not show the programme, and Thames's move was seen as particularly inopportune while ITV companies were resisting Government moves to raise their Exchequer levy and to increase their subsidy for Channel 4. That Thames could so outbid the BBC was perhaps an indication of profligacy, but which secretly delighted the BBC, which was pleading financial stringency. However, the BBC then proceeded to lose most of the public sympathy it had gained in the affair, the machinations of which began to resemble some of the programme's own bizarre plots about oil barons in Texas, by halting the screening of the remaining episodes in its possession and threatening to run them later in the year in direct competition with those acquired by Thames. Whatever the rights of the matter, the viewer was the loser, but the dispute rumbled on; the American company Worldvision, would not release Thames from its contract, as it felt the BBC had been purchasing the series too cheaply, but Mr. Cowgill had seriously embarrassed the ITV network. Furthermore, he failed to win the backing of his board, which made his position untenable, and he resigned on July 12.

The BBC denied that *Dallas* was dropped out of pique, but somewhat disingenuously used the new series of *Wogan* to announce that it would after all be screening the remaining episodes. That Worldvision had a case for claiming the BBC was paying too little seemed to be justified, however. Later, the BBC paid £¼ million for an American series, *Kane and Abel*, based on Jeffrey Archer's novel. ITV did not bid, claiming that the BBC had pushed the price too high. The BBC had also announced that it was suspending production of the popular *Dr. Who* series because of a shortage of funds for drama; this raised uproar from fans of the programme, who offered to raise money themselves to finance it, including an offer of £1·5 million from America. Another error of judgment occurred when the BBC copied an exclusive interview which TV-AM had broadcast with Princess Michael of Kent following the allegations that her father had been a member of the SS. TV-AM obtained an injunction, restraining the BBC from further unauthorised use of its material, and seeking £100,000 in damages.

At the Edge . . .

These rows seemed relatively minor compared with the storm that broke over a BBC programme in the *Real Lives* series, entitled "At the Edge of the Union",

which interviewed the alleged former IRA chief of staff, and a Unionist who advocated violence against the IRA. The programme was scheduled for transmission in early August. The Prime Minister, when addressing the American Bar Association's conference in London, had urged that terrorism should be starved of the "oxygen of publicity". When asked an apparently hypothetical question about her attitude to the broadcasting of an interview with a terrorist, she condemned it absolutely, without realising that the BBC intended to screen such a programme. The resulting publicity caused the Home Secretary to intervene: he wrote to the Chairman of the BBC, requesting that the programme be not screened. The BBC Board of Governors held an emergency meeting, after which they stated that "Having seen the programme, we believe it would be unwise for it to be transmitted in its present form". They felt that if they had not withdrawn the programme, the Home Secretary would have exercised his powers and banned it.

The decision to ban the programme provoked a 24-hour strike by BBC journalists on the day the programme should have been screened. ITN and TV-AM journalists voted to strike in sympathy. The dispute in the BBC itself continued, with the BBC board of management under the control of the Director-General, Alasdair Milne, criticised by staff for giving in to pressure from the Government, and abdicating editorial control to the Board of Governors. Various face-saving exercises were attempted: it was claimed that the programme makers had failed to adhere to detailed guidelines laid down for programmes involving terrorist organisations in Northern Ireland, and that internal chains of consultation and set referral procedures were not strictly followed. The BBC board of management hoped to save face and reassert their authority by broadcasting an edited version of the programme, but the Board of Governors reaffirmed their decision to ban it, criticised the breach of the guidelines, whilst rejecting the Government's attempt at censorship. The Home Secretary's intervention was the cause of much concern and comment. He had claimed that he had been expressing the right of any citizen to express concern over the nature of a programme he had not seen; since his Cabinet responsibilities covered both broadcasting and the administration of law and order in Northern Ireland, this was considered disingenuous. The BBC Board objected "most strongly to certain of the contents of the Home Secretary's letter of July 29. It is most disturbed that the decision (to ban the programme) has been seen as a yielding to government pressure. . . The decision not to transmit the programme at the present time was because the board considered the programme to be flawed in its present state, and, even if amended, unsuitable for viewing in the prevailing atmosphere".

Stronger words were used by Lord Annan, whose Committee on the Future of Broadcasting (he wrote to *The Times*). "gave considerable thought to the conflict which will always exist between the freedom of broadcasters and their public accountability, particularly in Northern Ireland . . . For the Home Secretary is the villain of the piece. Like a charging rhinoceros he trampled on the delicate relationship which should be maintained between the Government and the broadcasters."

Particularly unfortunate was the fact that BBC external service foreign language broadcasts were halted, which led to the BBC being derided in Eastern bloc countries as a Government mouthpiece. Whatever the rights and wrongs of the situation, the BBC suffered immense damage over what was, by all accounts from those who had seen it, a competent and sincere programme which attempted to examine the extreme views on both sides of the sectarian divide, but was accorded a notoriety out of all proportion to its content.

It seemed that the BBC had dominated the press for so long that it had exhausted all possibilities for producing further news; and yet, in August, it was revealed that senior BBC current affairs staff were subject to vetting by MI5, a procedure introduced in 1937 at the Corporation's request, and that an MI5 officer was attached to the BBC personnel department to facilitate the process. Yet again, the BBC's supposed independence from the Government was seen to be compromised.

In July, the BBC outlined the cuts it would have to make to exist on a £58 licence fee, which meant a shortfall of £350 million on its original budget over three years. The scope of local radio would be reduced, casual staff would be introduced in production departments, and such services as catering, cleaning and security would be put out to private contractors. Furthermore, the BBC announced an extra £33 million of cuts, and promised an expansion in television output. The planned all-day service was still envisaged, and a fund was established to finance in-house "blockbuster" drama. Output from independent producers would rise from 20 hours a year to 150 hours by 1988. That the BBC was able to produce such a radically revised budget without the threatened major cuts added credence to the widespread belief that its earlier campaign for a £65 licence was misguided and ill-judged.

With all the crises of confidence it suffered during the year, it is reassuring to note that the BBC was still capable of producing programmes of the highest class. Although, as the IBA Annual Report pointed out, Central Television's *Seeds of Despair* had first shown the British public the scale of the famine problems in Ethiopia, the film report in October 1984 by Mohamed Amin of Visnews and Michael Buerk of the BBC first pricked the collective conscience of the public. The film was shown on a lunchtime programme, and the same evening led the news bulletins of 425 of the world's broadcasting stations, initiating a world-wide famine relief effort which culminated in the joint UK/USA Live Aid concert which was screened by the BBC in July.

On a more mundane level, but as evidence of the worth of public service broadcasting, was the BBC's excellent coverage of the bombing outrage at the Conservative Party conference in Brighton, which brought home to the public the enormity of the crime, and its potential implications.

Mr. Alasdair Milne, Director-General of the BBC, in an article in *The Times* in February, wrote that "The basic premise of public service broadcasting ... is this: if you address yourself to the nation as a whole, you must *appeal* to the nation as a whole—in all its diversity ... What public service broadcasting must constantly seek to do it to provide enough satisfaction in the belief that allegiance to taste and interest is never certain, is constantly changing, and that therefore you must offer the widest variety of programming."

It was therefore logical that the BBC should feel compelled to produce once more a twice-weekly "soap opera", a field it had not entered seriously for some years. With Granada's competent but tired-looking *Coronation Street* still dominating the ratings after nearly 25 years, and Central's amateurish and inept *Crossroads* not far behind, the BBC was justified in re-entering the market. Its *East Enders* was set in the fictional Albert Square, London E.20, in fact an expensively created, but authentic looking set on the newly acquired Elstree studios. Conceived by Julia Smith, the series was crisply plotted, well acted and showed a refreshing willingness to take contemporary issues head on. It made *Coronation Street* look distinctly cosy and tired, and began to nudge it from its top perch in the ratings. In execution and concept, it matched Channel 4's excellent *Brookside*, which was set on a real housing estate on Merseyside, and went from strength to strength, both in scripting and performance.

A notable television event was the screening on BBC 2 of Peter Watkins's film about the effects of a nuclear war, *The War Game* some 20 years after it was made and banned. Its cause was helped by the screening of *Threads* in September 1984, a dramatised documentary about the effects of a nuclear explosion over Sheffield. *Threads* was a harrowing and skilful polemic, unrelieved in its awful view of the future, which made the continued supression of *The War Game* all the more inexcusable. Thus, when *Threads* was repeated in the summer of 1985, the opportunity was taken to remove one of the enduring black marks on the BBC's record. Although dated, *The War Game* was still relevant in the nuclear debate. Another triumph for BBC scheduling was the screening of a film made by Bavarian TV, with some financial assistance from the BBC. *Das Boot* was a brilliant film about life in a U-boat during the Second World War. Adapted and directed by Wolfgang Petersen from Lothar-Gunther Buchheim's book, it lasted five hours, and recreated the claustrophobic life in a submarine in 1941 with skill and sympathy. Particularly notable was Juergen Prochonow as the U-boat captain. *Das Boot* contrasted well with BBC 1's own fascinating look at the world of the submariner in *Submarine*, another in its series of documentaries on enclosed or elitist worlds.

Also of note was the BBC's adaptation of Graham Greene's short novel *Doctor Fischer of Geneva*. The production cost £1·25 million, and featured James Mason in his last role, with Alan Bates, Cyril Cusack and Greta Scacchi. The ending was altered, with the author's approval, but although the production was faultless, some weaknesses in the story were exposed. However, a more serious problem was that union agreements meant that the film was denied a cinema screening, which would have recouped the investment. The BBC also proved that it had not lost the knack of producing high quality drama productions with its adaptation of Charles Dickens's *Bleak House* by Arthur Hopcraft. Featuring Denholm Elliott and Bernard Hepton, the eight-part series expertly recreated Dickens's searing indictment of the English legal system. Other notable productions on BBC television included *Poppyland*, based on Gilbert Scott's account of his Norfolk sojourns; Carla Lane's bitter-sweet comedy *Mistress*, with Felicity Kendal, Jane Asher and Jack Galloway; *Late Starter* by Brian Clark, featuring Peter Barkworth as a retired professor experiencing middle-aged *angst* when his wife leaves him, and *In the Secret State*, adapted by Brian Phelan from Robert McCrum's novel, directed by Christopher Morahan.

IBA

The year on independent television began unpromisingly, with a dispute on Thames Television over the operation of new technology blacking out screens for three days in October 1984. Eventually Thames management ran an emergency service, until a peace formula was worked out with ACAS. The dispute was not confined to London, because Thames is the national network transmitter for all ITV evening programmes. It was ironic that the hero of Thames while management struggled to produce a service, consisting mainly of repeats, was Bryan Cowgill, who became the villain eight months later over the *Dallas* affair.

In the IBA Annual Report, the Chairman, Lord Thomson of Monifieth, was able to report "a year of consolidation and success on the programme side of

Independent Broadcasting but growing uncertainty about the outlook for public service broadcasting in a rapidly changing environment". As he pointed out, however, "In television the number of viewers watching ITV and Channel 4 reached very high figures, although the monthly increase in advertising revenue was not maintained at the end of the year". By March 1985 the slump in advertising income caused major difficulties; companies were forced to make cutbacks in production of programmes—Tyne Tees cancelled its top networked children's show, *Supergran*, as the new series would have cost £2 million, and Thames sold the Royalty Theatre, which it used for programmes such as *This is Your Life*. Because programmes were winning such high ratings, the advertisements which funded them were seen by more people, and the manufacturers were able to reach their sales targets earlier, so they needed less air time.

The IBA emerged victorious from its battles in the courts with Mrs. Whitehouse over the transmission on Channel 4 of the film *Scum*. The Divisional Court had declared that the IBA had not been in breach of its statutory responsibilities in transmitting the film, but the Director General had committed "a grave error of judgment" in failing to refer the film to members of the Authority for decision, and that members themselves were "in breach of duty in not instructing the Director General upon the nature of and the circumstances in which programmes should be referred to it". The Court of Appeal upheld the IBA's appeal. As Lord Thomson of Monifieth wrote, "The terms of the judgment not only vindicated the Director General's decision permitting the showing of the programme itself but were particularly welcome in placing the responsibility for the operation of the system, within which such decisions are made, on the IBA rather than with the courts. Members and staff will continue to carry out their responsibilities in these matters with care and sensitivity."

Double Vision

In February 1985 the IBA banned a programme in the 20/20 Vision series, entitled *MI5's Official Secrets*, having been advised that "the programme was in breach of the Official Secrets Act and that its transmission would constitute a criminal offence by the Authority". However, the public response to this decision—although muted in comparision with the uproar over the BBC's later troubles with the *Real Lives* programme—made a nonsense of this decision. The programme was shown to MPs and the press, its contents became widely known, and arrangements were made to distribute the programme on video tape. This, instead of making the IBA look ridiculous, in fact enabled it to change its mind with no loss of face. Without implying its earlier decision was wrong, when it had in fact erred on the side of caution, "A week later the Authority again considered the programme in the light of these developments and decided it was in the public interest to permit its transmission together with a second programme examining the issues raised."

However, later in the year the IBA became involved in the somewhat farcical position of banning a programme on Channel 4 about censorship in Brazil. The programme was rescheduled for September, and banned again.

Channel 4

Channel 4 continued to carve a niche for itself, and confirm its reputation for varied and original programmes. In February 1985, its ratings totalled about 8·5 per cent of the viewing population, often gaining it more viewers than BBC 2. In 1985 the annual contributions of the independent television companies towards its running costs were increased by 16·3 per cent to £129 million. Channel 4 had increased its broadcasting hours by 25 per cent in October 1984, beginning transmission at 2.30 instead of 5pm, and an hour earlier at weekends. Horse-racing and party conferences were moved to Channel 4, but the planned move of educational programmes was postponed because some schools were unable to receive the signals. Less certain was the future of the Welsh Channel 4, S4C. A working party was being established in September 1985 to monitor its progress and to recommend on whether it should continue in its present form, be adapted or abolished. In the year 1984/85 the ITV companies funded S4C to the tune of £28 million, but its revenue from advertising was only £1·7 million.

Notable programmes on independent television included Channel 4's nightly reconstruction of the Clive Ponting trial. The court forbade the station to use actors to read from the transcripts, in what many felt was the abuse of the Contempt of Court Act, but the programme continued with journalists reading selections from the trial. Channel 4 also broadcast Rainer Werner Fassbinder's 15-hour adaptation of Alfred Döblin's novel, *Berlin Alexanderplatz*. An imaginative construction of a historical trial was Channel 4's *The Trial of Richard III*, in which the full panoply of the modern court was applied to resolving whether that monarch was guilty of the murder of the Princes in the Tower; he was acquitted.

One of the year's major successes was Granada's *28 Up*, directed by Michael Apted. The programme began in 1964, when fourteen 7-year-old children were interviewed about their lives, and their progress was followed at seven-yearly intervals. The series turned into a fascinating social documentary of contemporary Britain. Granada also produced a 13-part series entitled *Television*, which examined the development of the medium and its effects worldwide. Central TV's *The Last Place on Earth* was an expensive reconstruction of Roland Huntford's controversial book about Robert Scott's race to the South Pole. Scripted by Trevor Griffiths, and brilliantly filmed on location near the Arctic Circle, the programme provoked complaints from Scott's family, but the IBA felt that the public would not be misled about the nature of the series, and it should not intervene. Also notable was Channel 4's taut thriller *The Price*, which concerned kidnapping and terrorism in Ireland, and featured Peter Barkworth; Granada's fine adaptation of John Fowles's *The Ebony Tower*, which was dramatised by John Mortimer, and featured Laurence Olivier; and Granada's new "soap operas", *The Practice* and *Albion Market*, which showed how lifeless their long-running *Coronation Street* had become.

Cable and Satellite

Stuart Young wrote in the 1985 BBC Annual report, "It has been a year when the need for decision about new technology and the pattern of broadcasting in the future has been insistent and dominant. In television, satellites will provide the opportunity to offer additional channels to the nation overnight; whilst cable favours the development of specialised and local services." However, the same report sounded a warning note about "the very high cost of establishing a market for DBS in the early years". In September, 1984, the BBC, ITV and independent companies involved in the proposed direct broadcasting by satellite project warned the Government that it would take ten years or more to be profitable; unless two million subscribers could be attracted in the first four years, losses in that period could exceed

£300 million, and it might take 15 years to pay its way.

The Satellite Broadcasting Board was established in October 1984, its first six members being Stuart Young, Chairman of the BBC, and BBC governors Sir John Johnston and Malcolm McAlpine, and IBA Chairman Lord Thomson of Monifieth, and IBA Board members Prof. Alexander Cullen and Michael Caine. The SBB would meet to formulate technical and ethical standards for satellite broadcasting, and to negotiate with potential participants.

Sky Channel exceeded its 1984 target, reaching 2·8 million homes equipped with cable in Europe, and 100,000 in Britain. However, Windsor TV, one of the eleven companies originally awarded a franchise, deferred any investment in cable laying, due to the phasing out of capital allowances in the Finance Act. Visionhire announced that it was pulling out of cable, and the Rediffusion cable network was sold to Pergamon Press. In January 1985, Mr. Jon Davey was appointed director general of the Cable Authority, and said that he thought the future for cable television might be in the provision of business services, with few entertainment channels.

The satellite debate continued, with the Government favouring Unisat, the British consortium of British Aerospace, Marconi and British Telecom, but the estimated cost of £560 million for a three-channel system, with a life expectancy of only seven years, was considered prohibitive. In June, the DBS scheme finally collapsed, the companies having agreed that it was not viable, and there was insufficient evidence of demand for its services. The Government was expected to readvertise the contract, removing the clause which insisted that a British satellite should be used, and in August asked the IBA how the project might be revived and who could operate it. However, with ITV companies interested in joining a Super Channel beamed over Europe, and a French satellite scheduled to be launched in 1986 which might carry such a service, the future of direct broadcasting by satellite in Britain was far from certain.

B.A.F.T.A. Awards

In the 1985 British Academy of Film and Television Arts Awards, the best drama series was *The Jewel in the Crown* (Granada); best comedy series was BBC 2's *The Young Ones*; best single drama, *Threads* (BBC); the writer's award went to Leon Griffiths for *Minder* (Thames); the best light entertainment programme was *Another Audience with Dame Edna Everage* (Ch 4/LWT); the best factual series was *River Journey* (BBC); best actuality coverage, Michael Buerk and Mohamed Amin for the film report on Ethiopia; best programme or series without a category was *Did You See* (BBC); best foreign television programme was *Das Boot* (Bavarian TV); the Robert Flaherty Documentary Award was presented to Granada for *28 Up*; best television actress was Peggy Ashcroft and best television actor Tim Pigott-Smith for *The Jewel in the Crown*; best light entertainment performance was Judi Dench in *A Fine Romance*.

The Jewel in the Crown also received prizes in the 12th Annual International Emmy Awards and the 1984 Broadcasting Press Guilds Awards.

BRITISH FORCES BROADCASTING SERVICE
(A division of the Services Sound & Vision Corporation)
Bridge House, 63/65 North Wharf Road, W2 1LA

The service came into existence during the middle of the Second World War to provide radio programmes of entertainment and information, and a link with home. No exact date can be given for the inception of the service because it began in many different places almost simultaneously during 1943.

In 1960 B.F.B.S. was reorganized: a Director was appointed and a Head Office was created in London to co-ordinate the activities of the service and to provide programme material specifically aimed at H.M. Forces, and their dependents overseas, and featuring leading personalities in all walks of life which the stations cannot produce themselves. These programmes are recorded in London and flown to B.F.B.S. stations abroad, as well as to H.M. Ships in many parts of the world, and for the benefit of personnel serving in places such as Belize and Dharan.

Over the years output has increased considerably and the stations in Germany, Cyprus and Gibraltar are now on the air round the clock. In Cyprus and Gibraltar a second channel for minority tastes is also available on medium wave. In Hong Kong and Brunei, B.F.B.S. stations provide services in Gurkhali and in English.

B.F.B.S. Television—a service combining programmes from B.B.C. and I.T.V., with some specially produced, started at Celle, near Hanover on September 18, 1975. When the full transmitter chain is completed, it will serve all the main concentrations of personnel and their families in West Germany.

The Combined Services Entertainment section of B.F.B.S. arranges stage and cabaret shows, as well as solo artistes, to tour Northern Ireland and Commands overseas.

The staff of B.F.B.S. are all civilian, professional broadcasters and engineers. The Service is sponsored by the Army on behalf of the other two Services, and is financed from Ministry of Defence funds.

On April 1, 1983, B.F.B.S. was merged with the Services Kinema Corporation to form the Services Sound & Vision Corporation (S.S.V.C.). B.F.B.S. now forms the broadcasting division of S.S.V.C., still transmitting under its original title.

B.F.B.S. supplies two programme staff and one engineer in support of Falkland Islands Broadcasting Station.

Managing Director, S.S.V.C., J. Grist.

BROADCASTING

BRITISH BROADCASTING CORPORATION
(*see also* entry on page 377)

Radio

BBC Radio broadcasts four national services to the United Kingdom, Isle of Man and the Channel Islands plus a fifth tier consisting of national regional services in Wales, Scotland and Northern Ireland and local radio services in England and the Channel Islands. In Wales there are two regional services based on the Welsh and English languages respectively.

The four national services are:

Radio 1: ("Pop" and "rock" network)—Monday to Sunday 6 a.m. to 12 midnight. Frequencies: MF 1053 kHz/285m and 1089 kHz/275m, plus two local fillers giving population coverage 96% (day) and 57% (night); VHF 88–91 MHz (shared with Radio 2), coverage 97%.

Radio 2: (Light music, entertainment and sport)—24 hours a day. Frequencies: MF 693 kHz/433m and 909 kHz/330m plus three local fillers giving population coverage 98% (day) and 65% (night); VHF 88–91 MHz (shared with Radio 1), coverage 97%.

Radio 3: (Serious music, drama and documentaries)—Monday to Friday 6.55 a.m. to 11.15 p.m.; Saturday and Sunday 7.55 a.m. to 11.15 p.m. Frequencies: VHF 90·2–92·5 MHz, population coverage 97%. MF (Main centres of population only), 1215 kHz/247m, plus four local fillers on 1197 kHz/251m, coverage 87% (day) and 38% (night).

Radio 4: (News, documentaries, drama and entertainment)—Monday to Friday 6 a.m. to 12 midnight, Saturday and Sunday 6.30 a.m. to 12 midnight. Frequencies: LF 200 kHz/1500m plus eight local fillers on MF giving population coverage 98% (day) and 91% (night): VHF (England, C.I. and I.O.M. plus part of South Wales, S.W. Scotland) 92–95 MHz, coverage 98%.

The national regional services are:

Radio Scotland: Frequencies: MF 810 kHz/370m plus two local fillers, coverage 95% (day) and 87% (night); VHF 92–95 MHz, coverage 94%.

Radio Ulster: Frequencies: MF 1341 kHz/224m plus one local filler, coverage 96% (day) and 80% (night); VHF 92–95 MHz, coverage 97%.

Radio Wales: Frequency: MF 882 kHz/340m plus two local fillers giving coverage 95% (day) and 63% (night).

Radio Cymru (Welsh-language): Frequencies: VHF 92–95 MHz, coverage 91%.

Local Radio: There are 30 local stations serving England and the Channel Islands (*see* below).

Television

The BBC's experiments in television broadcasting started in 1929 and in 1936 the BBC began the world's first public service of high-definition television from Alexandra Palace.

The BBC broadcasts two national television services, BBC 1 (BBC Wales in Wales) and BBC 2. These are broadcast in colour on 625-lines and UHF from a network of transmitting stations planned and built jointly with the Independent Broadcasting Authority. All stations (with a few exceptions) carry four channels including the two IBA channels.

The original service of BBC Television (latterly BBC 1) was broadcast on 405 lines in the VHF band and was finally closed down at the end of 1984. The 625-line UHF service was introduced in 1964 (BBC 2) with BBC 1 added in 1969. Colour was introduced in

July 1967. Transmissions from 49 main stations and more than 650 relays are available to more than 99% of the population.

External Services

The External Services broadcast over 700 hours of programmes a week in 37 languages including English on the BBC World Service. Eighty five transmitters are used, 50 of them in the U.K. and 35 at relay stations overseas. In addition the External Services supply many recorded programmes to other radio stations.

World Service, on the air in English for 24 hours a day, directed to all parts of the world, and with additional streams of programmes specially designated for audiences in Africa and South Asia at appropriate peak listening times.

African Service, which broadcasts in Swahili, Somali and Hausa.

Arabic Service, on the air for 9 hours a day to Middle East and North Africa.

Eastern Service, which broadcasts in Bengali, Burmese, Hindi, Nepali, Pashto, Persian, Tamil and Urdu.

Far Eastern Service, in Chinese (Cantonese and Standard Chinese), Indonesian, Japanese, Malay, Thai and Vietnamese.

Latin American Service, in Spanish and Portuguese.

French Service, directed to Europe and Africa.

German Service, directed to West and East Germany and Austria.

Central European Service, in Czech and Slovak, Hungarian, Polish and Finnish.

East European Service, in Bulgarian, Romanian, Russian, Serbo-Croat and Slovene.

South European Service, in Greek, Portuguese to Europe and Africa, and Turkish.

Topical Tapes provides a variety of programmes on tape for overseas radio stations and produces the twice-weekly Calling the Falklands programme.

BBC English by Radio and Television teaches English to learners outside Britain through radio, television and a wide range of published courses.

Transcription Service produces and sells to overseas radio stations recorded programmes drawn from the whole range of BBC Radio.

Monitoring Service provides regional summaries and a teleprinted news service from the output of overseas radio stations.

BBC Local Radio Stations

BEDFORDSHIRE, P.O. Box 476, Hastings Street, Luton LU1 5BA. (Tel: 0582 459111). *Wavelengths:* 258/476m, 1161/630 kHz, 96·9/103·7 vhf.

BRISTOL, 3 Tyndalls Park Road, Bristol BS8 1PP. (Tel: 0272 741111). *Wavelengths:* 194/227m, 1548/1323 kHz, 95·5/104·4 vhf.

CAMBRIDGESHIRE, Broadcasting House, Hills Road, Cambridge CB2 1LD. (Tel: 0223 315970). *Wavelengths:* 207/292m, 1449/1026 kHz, 96·0/103·9 vhf.

CLEVELAND, PO Box 1548, Broadcasting House, Middlesbrough, Cleveland TS1 5DG. (Tel: 0642 225211). *Wavelengths:* 194m, 1548 kHz, 96·6/95·8 vhf.

CORNWALL, Phœnix Wharf, Truro, Cornwall TR1 1UA. (Tel: 0872 75421). *Wavelengths:* 476/457m, 630/657 kHz, 95·2/96·4/97·3 vhf.

CUMBRIA, Hilltop Heights, London Road, Carlisle, Cumbria CA1 2NA. (Tel : 0228 31661). *Wavelengths* : 397/206/358m, 756/1458/837 kHz, 95·6/96·1 vhf.

DERBY, 56 St. Helen's Street, Derby DE1 3HY. (Tel : 0332 361111). *Wavelengths* : 269m, 1116 kHz, 96·5/94·2 vhf.

DEVON, St. David's Hill, Exeter, Devon EX4 4DB. (Tel : 0392 215651). *Wavelengths* : 351/303/206/375m, 855/990/1458/801 kHz, 97·5/97·0/96·2/103·9 vhf.

HUMBERSIDE, 63 Jameson Street, Hull HU1 3NU. (Tel : 0482 23232). *Wavelengths* : 202m, 1485 kHz, 96·9 vhf.

KENT, 30 High Street, Chatham, Kent. (Tel : 0634 46284). *Wavelengths* : 290/388/187m, 1035/774/1602 kHz, 96·7/102·8 vhf.

LANCASHIRE, King Street, Blackburn, Lancs. BB2 2EA. (Tel : 0254 62411). *Wavelengths* : 351/193m, 855/1557 kHz, 96·4/103·3 vhf.

LEEDS, Broadcasting House, Woodhouse Lane, Leeds LS2 9PN. (Tel : 0532 442131). *Wavelengths* : 388m, 774 kHz, 92·4/195·3 vhf.

LEICESTER, Epic House, Charles Street, Leicester LE1 3SH. (Tel : 0533 27113). *Wavelengths* : 358m, 837 kHz, 95·1 vhf.

LINCOLNSHIRE, Radion Buildings, Newport, Lincoln LN1 3DF. (Tel : 0522 40011). *Wavelengths* : 219m, 1368 kHz, 94·9 vhf.

LONDON, PO Box 4LG, 35a Marylebone High Street, London W1A 4LG. (Tel : 01-486 7611). *Wavelengths* : 206m, 1458 kHz, 94·9 vhf.

MANCHESTER, PO Box 90, New Broadcasting House, Oxford Road, Manchester M60 1SJ. (Tel : 061-228 3434). *Wavelengths* : 206m, 1458 kHz, 95·1 vhf.

MERSEYSIDE, 55 Paradise Street, Liverpool L1 3BP. (Tel : 051-708 5500). *Wavelengths* : 202m, 1485 kHz, 95·8 vhf.

NEWCASTLE, Crestina House, Archbold Terrace, Newcastle upon Tyne NE2 1DZ. (Tel : 091 281 4243). *Wavelengths* : 206m, 1458 kHz, 95·4/96·3 vhf.

NORFOLK, Norfolk Tower, Surrey Street, Norwich NR1 3PA. (Tel : 0603 617411). *Wavelengths* : 351/344m, 855/873 kHz, 95·1/96·7 vhf.

NORTHAMPTON, PO Box 1107, Northampton NN1 2BE. (Tel : 0604 20621). *Wavelengths* : 271m, 1107 kHz, 96·6/103·3 vhf.

NOTTINGHAM, York House, Mansfield Road, Nottingham NG1 3JB. (Tel : 0602 415161). *Wavelengths* : 197/189m, 1521/1584 kHz, 95·4 vhf.

OXFORD, 242/254 Banbury Road, Oxford OX2 7DW. (Tel : 0865 53411). *Wavelengths* : 202m, 1485 kHz, 95·2 vhf.

SHEFFIELD, Ashdell Grove, 60 Westbourne Road, Sheffield SI0 2QU. (Tel : 0742 686185). *Wavelengths* : 290m, 1035 kHz, 97·4/88·6 vhf.

SHROPSHIRE, 2–4 Boscobel Drive, Shrewsbury, Shropshire SY1 3TT. (Tel : 0743 248484). *Wavelengths* : 189/397m, 1584/756 kHz, 95·0/96·0 vhf.

SOLENT, South Western House, Canute Road, Southampton SO9 4PJ. (Tel : 0703 31311). *Wavelengths* : 300m, 999 kHz, 96·1 vhf, 221m, 1359 kHz (in Bournemouth).

STOKE ON TRENT, Conway House, Cheapside, Hanley, Stoke-on-Trent, Staffs. ST1 1JJ. (Tel : 0782 24827). *Wavelengths* : 200m, 1503 kHz, 94·6 vhf.

SUSSEX, Marlborough Place, Brighton, Sussex BN1 1TU (Tel : 0273 680231). *Wavelengths* : 202/258/219m, 1485/1161/1368 kHz, 95·3/103·1/102·7 vhf.

WM (WEST MIDLANDS), PO Box 206, Birmingham B5 7SD. (Tel : 021-472 5141). *Wavelengths* : 206/362m, 1458/828 kHz, 95·6 vhf.

YORK, 20 Bootham Row, York YO3 7BR. (Tel : 0904 641351). *Wavelengths* : 450/238m, 666/1260 kHz, 90·2/97·2 vhf.

Two Stations outside the UK :—

GUERNSEY, Commerce House, Les Banques, St. Peter Port, Guernsey. (Tel : 0481 28977). *Wavelengths* : 293m, 1116 kHz, 93·2 vhf.

JERSEY, Broadcasting House, Rouge Bouillon, St. Helier, Jersey. (Tel : 0534 70000). *Wavelengths* : 292m, 1026 kHz, 88·8 vhf.

INDEPENDENT BROADCASTING AUTHORITY
(*see also* entry on pages 405–6)

Independent Television Programme Companies, etc.

ANGLIA TELEVISION (*East of England*), Anglia House, Norwich (Tel : 0603 615151).

BORDER TELEVISION (*The Borders*), Television Centre, Carlisle. (Tel : 0228 25101).

CENTRAL INDEPENDENT TELEVISION (*East and West Midlands*), Central House, Broad Street, Birmingham. (Tel : 021-643 9898).

CHANNEL TELEVISION (*Channel Islands*), The Television Centre, St. Helier, Jersey. (Tel : 0534 73999).

GRAMPIAN TELEVISION (*North Scotland*), Queen's Cross, Aberdeen. (Tel : 0224 646464).

GRANADA TELEVISION (*North-West England*), Granada TV Centre, Manchester. (Tel : 061-832 7211).

HTV (*Wales and West of England*), HTV Wales, Television Centre, Cardiff CF5 6XJ. (Tel : 0222 590590).

LONDON WEEKEND TELEVISION (*London* [*weekends*]), South Bank Television Centre, Kent House, Upper Ground, London SE1. (Tel : 01-261 3434).

SCOTTISH TELEVISION (*Central Scotland*), Cowcaddens, Glasgow. (Tel : 041-332 9999).

THAMES TELEVISION (*London* [*weekdays*]), Thames Television House, 306–316 Euston Road, London NW1. (Tel : 01-387 9494).

TSW (TELEVISION SOUTH WEST) (*South-West England*), Derry's Cross, Plymouth. (Tel : 0752 663322).

TVS (TELEVISION SOUTH) (*South and South-East England*), Television Centre, Southampton. (Tel : 0703 34211).

TYNE TEES TELEVISION (*North-East England*), The Television Centre, City Road, Newcastle upon Tyne. (Tel : 0632 610181).

ULSTER TELEVISION (*Northern Ireland*), Havelock House, Ormeau Road, Belfast. (Tel : 0232 225122).

YORKSHIRE TELEVISION (*Yorkshire*), The Television Centre, Leeds. (Tel : 0532 438283).

TV-AM, Hawley Crescent, London N.W.1. (Tel : 01-267 4300).

CHANNEL FOUR TELEVISION COMPANY LTD, 60 Charlotte Street, London W.1. (Tel : 01-631 4444).

INDEPENDENT TELEVISION COMPANIES ASSOCIATION LTD., Knighton House, 56 Mortimer Street, London W.1. (Tel : 01-636 6866).

INDEPENDENT TELEVISION NEWS LTD, ITN House, 48 Wells Street, London W.1. (Tel : 01-637 2424).

ORACLE TELETEXT LTD., Craven House, 25–32 Marshall Street, London W.1. (Tel : 01-434 3121).

[NOTE: It has only been possible to give one address for each of the Programme Companies].

Independent Local Radio Stations

LBC (London Broadcasting Company Limited), Communications House, Gough Square, London EC4. (Tel : 01-353 1010). *Wavelengths* : 261m, 1152 kHz, 97·3 vhf.

CAPITAL RADIO LIMITED, Euston Tower, London NW1. (Tel : 01-388 1288). *Wavelengths* : 194m, 1548 kHz, 95·8 vhf.

RADIO CLYDE LIMITED, Clydebank Business Park, Clydebank, Glasgow. (Tel : 041-941 1111). *Wavelengths* : 261m, 1152 kHz, 95·1 vhf.

BRMB RADIO, (Birmingham Broadcasting Limited), PO Box 555, Radio House, Aston Road North,

Aston, Birmingham. (Tel: 021-359 4481/9). *Wavelengths*: 261m, 1152 kHz, 94·8 vhf.

PICCADILLY RADIO LIMITED, 127/131 The Piazza, Piccadilly Plaza, Manchester. (Tel: 061-236 9913). *Wavelengths*: 261m, 1152 kHz, 97·0 vhf.

METRO RADIO (North East Broadcasting Company Limited), Radio House, Long Rigg, Swalwell, Newcastle upon Tyne. (Tel: 0632 883131). *Wavelengths*: 261m, 1152 kHz, 97·0 vhf.

SWANSEA SOUND LIMITED, Victoria Road, Gowerton, Swansea. (Tel: 0792 893751). *Wavelengths*: 257m, 1170 kHz, 95·1 vhf.

RADIO HALLAM LIMITED, PO Box 194, Hartshead, Sheffield. (Tel: 0742 71188). *Wavelengths*: 194m, 1548 kHz, 95·9 vhf (Rotherham), 95·2 vhf (Sheffield).

RADIO CITY (Sound of Merseyside Limited), PO Box 194, 8–10 Stanley Street, Liverpool. (Tel: 051-227 5100). *Wavelengths*: 194m, 1548 kHz, 96·7 vhf.

RADIO FORTH LIMITED, Forth House, Forth Street, Edinburgh. (Tel: 031-556 9255). *Wavelengths*: 194m, 1548 kHz, 96·8 vhf.

PLYMOUTH SOUND LIMITED, Earl's Acre, Alma Road, Plymouth. (Tel: 0752 27272). *Wavelengths*: 261m, 1152 kHz, 96·0 vhf.

RADIO TEES (Sound Broadcasting (Teesside) Limited), 74 Dovecot Street, Stockton-on-Tees, Cleveland. (Tel: 0642 615111). *Wavelengths*: 257m, 1170 kHz, 95·0 vhf.

RADIO TRENT LIMITED, 29–31 Castle Gate, Nottingham. (Tel: 0602 581731). *Wavelengths*: 301m, 999 kHz, 96·2 vhf.

PENNINE RADIO (Bradford Community Radio Limited), PO Box 235, Pennine House, Forster Square, Bradford. (Tel: 0274 731521). *Wavelengths*: 235/196m, 1278/1530 kHz, 96·0 vhf.

RADIO VICTORY LIMITED, PO Box 257, 247 Fratton Road, Portsmouth. (Tel: 0705 827799). *Wavelengths*: 257m, 1170 kHz, 95·0 vhf.

RADIO ORWELL LIMITED, Electric House, Lloyds Avenue, Ipswich. (Tel: 0473 216971). *Wavelengths*: 257m, 1170 kHz, 97·1 vhf.

RADIO 210 THAMES VALLEY (Thames Valley Broadcasting Limited), PO Box 210, Reading, Berkshire. (Tel: 0734 413131). *Wavelengths*: 210m, 1431 kHz, 97·0 vhf.

DOWNTOWN RADIO (Community Radio Services Limited), PO Box 293, Kiltonga Industrial Estate, Newtownards, Northern Ireland. (Tel: 0247 815555). *Wavelengths*: 293m, 1026 kHz, 96·0 vhf.

BEACON RADIO (Beacon Broadcasting Limited), PO Box 303, 267 Tettenhall Road, Wolverhampton. (Tel: 0902 757211). *Wavelengths*: 303m, 990 kHz, 97·2 vhf.

CARDIFF BROADCASTING COMPANY LIMITED, Radio House, West Canal Wharf, Cardiff. (Tel: 0222 384041). *Wavelengths*: 221m, 1359 kHz, 96·0 vhf.

MERCIA SOUND (Midland Community Radio Limited), Hertford Place, Coventry. (Tel: 0203 28451). *Wavelengths*: 220m, 1359 kHz, 95·9 vhf.

HEREWARD RADIO LIMITED, PO Box 225. 114 Bridge Street, Peterborough. (Tel: 0733 46225). *Wavelengths*: 225m, 1332 kHz, 95·7 vhf.

TWO COUNTIES RADIO LIMITED, 5–7 Southcote Road, Bournemouth. (Tel: 0202 294881). *Wavelengths*: 362m, 828 kHz, 97·2 vhf.

RADIO TAY (Tay Sound Broadcasting Limited), PO Box 123, Dundee. (Tel: 0382 29551). *Wavelengths*: Dundee 258m, 1161 kHz, 95·8 vhf; Perth 189m, 1584 kHz, 96·4 vhf.

SEVERN SOUND (Gloucestershire Broadcasting Company Limited), PO Box 388, Old Talbot House, 67 Southgate Street, Gloucester. (Tel: 0452 423791). *Wavelengths*: 388m, 774 kHz, 95·0 vhf.

DEVONAIR RADIO LIMITED, The Studio Centre, 35–37 St. David's Hill, Exeter. (Tel: 0392 30703). *Wavelengths*: Exeter 450m, 666 kHz, 95·8 vhf; Torbay 314m, 954 kHz, 95·1 vhf.

NORTHSOUND (North of Scotland Radio Limited), 45 Kings Gate, Aberdeen. (Tel: 0224 632234). *Wavelengths*: 290m, 1035 kHz, 96·9 vhf.

RADIO AIRE (West Yorkshire Broadcasting P.L.C.), PO Box 362, 51 Burley Road, Leeds. (Tel: 0532 452299). *Wavelengths*: 362m, 828 kHz, 94·6 vhf.

ESSEX RADIO P.L.C., Radio House, Clifftown Road, Southend-on-Sea, Essex. (Tel: 0702 333711). *Wavelengths*: Southend 210m, 1431 kHz, 95·3 vhf; Chelmsford 220m, 1359 kHz, 96·4 vhf.

CHILTERN RADIO P.L.C., Chiltern Radio, Dunstable, Bedfordshire. (Tel: 0582 666001). *Wavelengths*: Luton 362m, 828 kHz, 97·6 vhf; Bedford 378m, 792 kHz, 95·5 vhf.

WEST SOUND (Radio Ayrshire Limited), Radio House, 54 Holmston Road, Ayr. (Tel: 0292 283662). *Wavelengths*: Ayr 290m, 1035 kHz, 96·2 vhf; Girvan 97·1 vhf.

RADIO WEST (Radio Avonside Limited), PO Box 963, Watershed, Canons Road, Bristol. (Tel: 0272 279900). *Wavelengths*: 238m, 1260 kHz, 96·3 vhf.

MORAY FIRTH RADIO LIMITED, PO Box 271, Inverness. (Tel: 0463 224433). *Wavelengths*: 271m, 1107 kHz, 95·9 vhf.

RADIO WYVERN P.L.C., 5/6 Barbourne Terrace, Worcester. (Tel: 0905 612212). *Wavelengths*: Hereford 314m, 954 kHz, 95·8 vhf; Worcester 196m, 1530 kHz, 96·2 vhf.

RED ROSE RADIO P.L.C., PO Box 301, St. Paul's Square, Preston, Lancashire. (Tel: 0772 556301). *Wavelengths*: 301m, 999 kHz, 97·3 vhf.

WILTSHIRE RADIO P.L.C., Old Lime Kiln, High Street, Wootton Bassett, Swindon, Wiltshire. (Tel: 0793 853222). *Wavelengths*: Swindon 258m, 1161 kHz, 96·4 vhf; West Wiltshire 321m, 936 kHz, 97·4 vhf.

SAXON RADIO LIMITED IN ASSOCIATION WITH RADIO ORWELL LIMITED, Long Brackland, Bury St. Edmunds, Suffolk. (Tel: 0284 701511). *Wavelengths*: 240m, 1251 kHz, 96·3 vhf.

COUNTY SOUND P.L.C., The Friary, Guildford. (Tel: 0483 505566). *Wavelengths*: 203m, 1476 kHz, 96·6 vhf.

SOUTHERN SOUND P.L.C., Radio House, Franklin Road, Portslade. (Tel: 0273 422288). *Wavelengths*: 225m, 1332 kHz, 103·4 MHz.

MARCHER SOUND/SAIN-Y-GORORAU, The Studios, Mold Road, Gwersyllt, Wrexham, Clwyd. (Tel: 0978 752202). *Wavelengths*: 238m, 1260 kHz, 95·4 vhf.

SIGNAL RADIO, 67–73 Stoke Road, Stoke-on-Trent, Staffordshire. (Tel: 0782 417111). *Wavelengths*: 257m, 1170 kHz, 104·3 vhf.

VIKING RADIO LTD., Commercial Road, Hull. (Tel: 0482 25141). *Wavelengths*: 258m, 1161 kHz, 102·7 vhf.

INVICTA RADIO P.L.C. (incorporating Northdown Radio), 15 Station Road East, Canterbury, Kent. (Tel: 0227 58761). *Wavelengths*: 242m, 1242 kHz, 103·8 vhf.

RADIO MERCURY, Broadfield House, Brighton Road, Crawley, W. Sussex. (Tel: 0293 519161). *Wavelengths*: 197m, 1521 kHz, 103·6 vhf.

INVICTA RADIO P.L.C. (incorporating Network East Kent), 15 Station Road East, Canterbury, Kent. (Tel: 0227 58761). *Wavelengths*: 497m, 603 kHz, Dover 97·0 vhf, Thanet 95·9 vhf, Canterbury 95·1 vhf, Ashford 96·3 MHz.

RADIO BROADLAND, PO Box 260, Norwich. (Tel: 0603 660926). *Wavelengths*: 260m, 1152 kHz, 97·6 MHz.

HEREWARD RADIO P.L.C., PO Box 193, 73 Abington Street, Northampton. (Tel: 0733 46225). *Wavelengths*: 193m, 1557 kHz, vhf to be announced.

FILM AND CINEMA, 1984–85

1985 was designated British Film Year; £12 million was allocated to be spent on cinema refurbishment by Thorn EMI, Rank and Cannon, and £3 million (of which the Government contributed £500,000) was to be spent on promotion, including an exhibition at the Festival Hall, and a roadshow, which would be visiting 40 British and overseas cities. The campaign was launched at the Cannes Film Festival.

The Government's White Paper on Film Policy had proposed an end to the Eady Levy, and the National Film Finance Corporation, the latter to be succeeded by a privately-owned Film Bank, funded by the industry. Moving the second reading of the Films Bill, in November 1984, Mr. Norman Lamont, Minister of State for Industry, said that the Eady Levy had become a penalty for cinema owners, and the time had come to sweep away "the archaic legislative framework of the film industry which would be better off without the tiresome bureaucratic restraints of registering every film and licensing every distributor and exhibitor". He announced that the Government would provide £1·5 million a year to the successor to the NFFC for the purpose of co-financing film production, and £500,000 a year would be set aside for project development work. "The proposal to grant £7·5 million over five years was", he said, "the Government's response to the industry's representations that the NFFC performed an essential role in encouraging new and relatively untried talent. ... However, by being rooted in the private sector the new company will bring a keener commercial edge to its operations". The Government was also proposing to transfer to the new company the NFFC's portfolio of rights and interests in some 800 films made since the late 1930s, worth an estimated £600,000 a year.

The Minister had also announced that leading companies in the film industry had promised additional finance. It was reported in January 1985 that the British Screen Finance Consortium (composed of Channel 4, the British Videogram Association, Rank and Thorn EMI) would contribute £1·1 million a year to the new company. In the committee stage of the Bill, however, Opposition M.P.s and some Conservative members combined to force an amendment to the effect that television companies should pay a levy for showing films, to help the British film industry; it was estimated that this could cost them between £10–20 million a year.

Academy Awards

British hopes were high once again at the Oscar ceremonies in Hollywood. However, the nominations for *A Passage to India* and *The Killing Fields* were not converted into major awards, and the American film *Amadeus*, based on Peter Shaffer's stage play, won the main prizes. The results at the 57th Academy Awards in March 1985 were as follows: best film, *Amadeus*; best director, Milos Forman (*Amadeus*); best actor, F. Murray Abraham (*Amadeus*); best screenplay adaptation, Peter Shaffer (*Amadeus*); *Amadeus* also won awards for best costume design, art direction, sound and make-up; best actress, Sally Field (*Places in the Heart*); best supporting actor, Haing S. Ngor (*The Killing Fields*); best supporting actress, Peggy Ashcroft (*A Passage to India*); best original screenplay, Robert Benton (*Places in the Heart*); best animated short film, *Charade* (Jon Minnis); best foreign language film, *Dangerous Moves* (Switzerland); best documentary short subject, *The Stone Carvers*; best documentary feature, *The Times of Harvey Milk* (Robert Epstein); best cinematography, Chris Menges (*The Killing Fields*); best visual effects, *Indiana Jones and the Temple of Doom*; and best film editing, Jim Clark (*The Killing Fields*).

At the British Academy of Film and Television Arts Awards, the prize for best film went to David Puttnam for *The Killing Fields*. Best director was Wim Wenders for *Paris, Texas*; best actor, Haing S. Ngor (*The Killing Fields*); best actress, Maggie Smith (*A Private Function*); best supporting actor, Denholm Elliott (*A Private Function*); best supporting actress, Liz Smith (*A Private Function*); most outstanding newcomer in film, Haing S. Ngor (*The Killing Fields*); best original screenplay, Woody Allen (*Broadway Danny Rose*); best adapted screenplay, Bruce Robinson (*The Killing Fields*); best short film, *The Dress* (Eva Sereny); and best foreign language film, *Carmen* (Emiliano Piedra and Carlos Saura).

Film Festivals

Derek Malcolm, film critic of *The Guardian*, was guest director for the 28th London Film Festival, which showed 140 films from 40 countries between November 15 and December 2, 1984. Without the prestige of other film festivals, from which it draws a lot, but not all, of its material, it was nevertheless (in the words of its director) "a celebration of cinema in all its forms, from the frankly commercial to the overtly experimental ... the only proviso has been that each film is good of its kind". One of the highlights was the British première of Edgar Reitz's *Heimat*, which lasted 15 hours and 40 minutes, an epic account of the life of a Rhineland family spanning four generations and 70 years. Four years in the making, the film had achieved massive success throughout Europe, and in particular at the Venice Festival. It raised "soap opera" to the level of art, and is due to be screened by BBC television. *Heimat* had been shown out of competition at the 41st Venice Festival in September 1984, but had been awarded the International Critics Prize. The Golden Lion was awarded to *Year of the Quiet Sun*, a Polish film directed by Krzysztof Zanussi, and the Special Jury Prize to *Les Favoris de la Lune* (France), directed by Otar Yoselliani. Pascale Ogier won the prize for best actress in Eric Rohmer's *Full Moon in Paris* (tragically, she died in November of the same year).

At the Berlin Film Festival in February 1985, the Golden Bear was won jointly by *Wetherby*, co-financed by Channel 4, and the East German film *Die Frau und der Fremde*. *Flowers of Reverie* from Hungary received the Silver Bear.

At the 38th Cannes Film Festival in May 1985, the Palme d'Or was won by Emir Kusturica of Yugoslavia, for *Daddy's on a Business Trip*, the Grand Prix Jury by Istvan Szabo of Hungary for *Colonel Redhl*, and the Special Jury Prize by Alan Parker for *Birdy*. Best actor was William Hurt for the Brazilian film, *Kiss of the Spider Woman*, and best actress, Cher, for Peter Bogdanovich's *Mask*. *Mask* was the subject of some controversy at Cannes, as the director claimed that cuts totalling some eight minutes, and the change of music, ruined his film.

Productions

The major British film of the year was undoubtedly David Puttnam's *The Killing Fields*. Directed by Roland Joffé, his first cinema film, and costing about £10 million, the film told the true story of *New York Times* war correspondent Sydney Schanberg in Cambodia, and his friendship with his Cambodian assistant, who saved his life, but remained behind when the Khmer Rouge conquered the country. Written by Bruce Robinson, the film featured Sam Waterston and Dr. Haing S. Ngor in the leading roles. The film was brilliantly filmed by Chris Menges, and was a tense powerful drama, about friendship and survival against horrifying odds. Haing S. Ngor had suffered in real life much as Dith Pran, whose life he portrayed, and his performance was justly rewarded in both Britain and the U.S.A.

Richard Burton's last screen role was in *1984*, written and directed by Michael Radford from George Orwell's novel. The film was made quickly so that it would be completed within the year of its title, although it has not been invalidated as a work of art by the passing of that year. Orwell's widow had been horrified by the 1955 film version, which had imposed a happy ending on the story, and had been reluctant for any further films to be made. However, before her death she had assigned the film rights to an American lawyer, with a proviso that if the book were

to be filmed again, no high technology or special effects were to be used. This suited the purposes of Radford and his producer, Simon Perry, who saw the film not as science fiction, but as Orwell intended, "a kind of collapsed futurism, a false future as perceived by the past", with the emphasis on "the internal complexities of the human mind". The film was a major achievement, but presented a thoroughly depressing view of totalitarianism. Burton gave a fine performance, playing down his distinctive voice, and was convincing as O'Brien, with John Hurt excellent as usual as Winston Smith. It was unfortunate that the producers altered the music after the film had been released, provoking a strong attack by Radford at the Standard Film Awards. He said, having received the award for best film, that "the film ... currently showing in London is not the film I made", and the score had been "foisted" on him, an ironic situation in the light of what Orwell had written about the truth being rewritten after the event.

David Lean's *A Passage to India* received eleven Oscar nominations. His first film for 15 years, it was not wholly true to E. M. Forster's novel, but was visually splendid, an epic production. Dame Peggy Ashcroft's performance was rightly rewarded with an Oscar, and there were notable performances also from Victor Banerjee, Judy Davis, Nigel Havers and James Fox, although the casting of Sir Alec Guinness in an Indian part provoked some surprise.

Neil Jordan's second feature film, following the widely-acclaimed *Angel*, was *The Company of Wolves*, based on stories by Angela Carter. A reworking of the Red Riding Hood story, the film portrayed the sexual awakening of a young girl, and the darker message behind traditional fables. The excellent studio sets by Anton Furst helped create the impression of dreams in a Gothic landscape. The film featured Sarah Patterson, Terence Stamp, Angela Lansbury, Kathryn Pogson, David Warner and Stephen Rea.

Helen Mirren won the best actress award at Cannes in 1984 for her part in *Cal*. Written by Bernard MacLaverty, and directed by Pat O'Connor, it was a sensitive love story set against the background of the troubles in Northern Ireland, with John Lynch also excellent in the title role.

Bill Forsyth's *Comfort and Joy* was a disappointing story about the rivalry between Glasgow ice-cream firms; the insubstantial plot and the undisciplined nature of the film were nevertheless imbued with the director's affectionate view of human nature. It featured Bill Paterson, Roverto Bernardi and Claire Grogan.

Alan Bennett's first screenplay, *A Private Function*, was an outstanding success. Directed by Malcolm Mowbray, the film was a black comedy set in a Yorkshire town in 1947, and concerned the kidnapping of a pig that had been fattened illegally for a banquet to commemorate the wedding of Princess Elizabeth. There were splendid performances from Maggie Smith, Michael Palin, Liz Smith, Bill Paterson, Denholm Elliott and Richard Griffiths.

Joseph Losey's last film was *Steaming*, based on the successful stage play by Nell Dunn. Adapted by Patricia Losey, this story about a group of women in a Turkish baths threatened with closure was well acted by Vanessa Redgrave, Sarah Miles, Patti Love, Diana Dors, Brenda Bruce and Felicity Dean.

Dance with a Stranger was the story of Ruth Ellis, the last woman to be hanged in Britain. Written by Shelagh Delaney and directed by Mike Newell, the film atmospherically evoked the 1950s, with good performances from Miranda Richardson as Ruth Ellis, and Rupert Everett and Ian Holm as her lovers.

David Hare wrote and directed *Wetherby*, an imaginative and thought-provoking film, with Vanessa Redgrave as a teacher at a Yorkshire school who is devastated by the suicide of a young man who, uninvited, had attended a dinner at her home. The film traced the effects of this event on herself and the small community of her friends, through flashback, until the explanation was revealed. The film also featured Suzanna Hamilton, Ian Holm, Judi Dench, Tim McInnerny and Joely Richardson.

Also of note was *The Hit* directed by Stephen Frears, a well-acted thriller featuring Terence Stamp, John Hurt, Tim Roth and Laura del Sol. *The Shooting Party*, based on Isabel Colegate's novel, was scripted by Julia Bond, directed by Alan Bridges, and featured James Mason (who replaced Paul Scofield who was injured in an accident on the first day's filming), Edward Fox, Cheryl Campbell, Dorothy Tutin and John Gielgud. Terry Gilliam wrote and directed *Brazil*, an imaginative but bizarre cross between *1984* and *Monty Python's Flying Circus*, with Jonathan Pryce, Ian Holm and Michael Palin, and a cameo role from Robert de Niro.

American Films

Milos Forman's *Amadeus* transferred Peter Shaffer's acclaimed play about the rivalry between child-prodigy Mozart and court musician Salieri to the screen; filmed in Prague, and with the music splendidly played by the Academy of St. Martin-in-the-Fields, the performance of F. Murray Abraham as Salieri was rewarded with an Oscar, and Tom Hulce's Mozart was also nominated. The film also featured Simon Callow, Roy Dotrice, and Elizabeth Berridge.

Robert Benton wrote and directed *Places in the Heart*, one of a clutch of rural dramas about middle America. Sally Field won the Oscar for her role as the widow fighting to hold on to her land against all odds. Other films on the same theme were Richard Pearce's *Country*, with Jessica Lange and Sam Shepard, and Mark Rydell's *The River*, with Sissy Spacek and Mel Gibson.

Norman Jewison's *A Soldier's Story* was adapted by Charles Fuller from his stage play. Set in an army camp in Louisiana in 1944, it was a penetrating analysis of racial attitudes. Adolph Caesar was the black army sergeant murdered on the camp, with Howard J. Rollins as the Harvard-educated black officer sent to investigate. Peter Weir's *Witness* featured Harrison Ford and Kelly McGillis in an excellent murder thriller set around the Amish sect, who reject modern values and inventions.

Francis Ford Coppola's *The Cotton Club* cost some $47 million to make; the production was troubled from the start, and the uncertainty showed on screen in this account of the famous Harlem jazz club. The film featured Richard Gere, Bob Hoskins, Gregory Hines and Maurice Hines.

Peter Bogdanovich's *Mask* told the story of a young man suffering from a condition which caused a disfiguring excess of bone growth on his skull. The film contained fine performances by Eric Stoltz as the boy and Cher as his mother, fighting to have him treated as a human being, but appealed more to American tastes with its sentimental approach and manipulation of audience responses.

Frank Herbert's popular science fiction novel *Dune* was filmed by David Lynch, and the special effects were spectacular in the vastly expensive production, but the plot was incomprehensible to all but students of the book. The cast included Sian Phillips, Sting, Freddie Jones and Kyle Maclachlan.

Two of the most popular films of the year were *Ghostbusters*, directed by Ivan Reitman, and *Gremlins*, produced by Steven Spielberg and directed by Joe Dante. The former featured Sigourney Weaver, with Bill Murray, Dan Aykroyd, and Harold Ramis as three redundant professors who decide to hunt down ghosts. *Gremlins* was a darker version of *ET*, with cuddly toys turning nasty; the film was clever, but self-indulgent with its use of "in" cinema jokes.

Joel and Ethan Coen's *Blood Simple* was a brilliantly accomplished *film noir*, made on a low budget, but with great skill, and fine performances from M. Emmet Walsh and Frances McDormand. *2010* directed by Peter Hyams updated Arthur C. Clarke's classic science fiction film *2001*, while Nick Castle's *The Last Starfighter*, showed that imaginative science fiction films could be made without huge budgets.

Sergio Leone's *Once Upon a Time In America* was a splendid gangster saga from the master of the spaghetti Western. Featuring Robert de Niro, James Woods and Elizabeth McGovern, it cost $30 million, and lasted nearly four hours. It told the story of immigrant Jews in America who turned to crime, and was widely adjudged a masterpiece. The film was recut for U.S. distribution, but the director's original version was shown in Europe.

Robert Redford returned to the screen in *The Natural*, an excellent morality play based on the novel by Bernard Malmud. Redford played a baseball player who returned to the game after a 16-year absence; it was one of his finest film performances.

Alex Cox's *Repo Man* was an original, quirky and anarchic comedy, with Harry Dean Stanton and Emilio Estevez. Roger Donaldson's *The Bounty* was the third film version of the famous mutiny, featuring Anthony Hopkins as a more sympathetic Bligh than usual, and Mel Gibson as Fletcher Christian. Sylvester Stallone's *Rambo* was a preposterous but extremely popular follow-up to his *First Blood*, with an unpleasant underlying message about America avenging the Vietnam defeat.

Also notable were Woody Allen's *The Purple Rose of Cairo*, a clever and funny film set in the 1930s, which imagined a character leaving the screen during a film to join the audience, and causing chaos. It featured Mia Farrow, Danny Aliello and Jeff Daniels. Alan Parker's *Birdy* featured Nicholas Cage and Matthew Modine in a moving and poetic film about freedom through flight.

Notable foreign productions included *The Wall*, by exiled Turkish director Yilmaz Güney (who died in 1985); set in a children's prison in Ankara, it was a brutal and powerful production. *Strikebound* was directed by Richard Lowenstein, and was a true Australian story about a mining lock-out and sit-in, while *Careful, He Might Hear You*, directed by Carl Schultz was based on the novel by Sumner Locke Elliott. *Phar Lap—The Story of a Horse*, directed by Simon Wincer, was based on the famous race horse of the 1930s, which went to America to continue its career and died in mysterious circumstances. The Canadian film *Grey Fox* was directed by Philip Borsos, and was based on the true story of a gentleman robber struggling to make his way after 35 years in San Quentin prison; Richard Farnsworth was excellent in the leading role.

THE ACADEMY AWARDS, 1981–84

1981 Best Picture: *Chariots of Fire*.
   Best Director: Warren Beatty, *Reds*.
   Best Actor: Henry Fonda, *On Golden Pond*.
   Best Actress: Katharine Hepburn, *On Golden Pond*.
1982 Best Picture: *Gandhi*.
   Best Director: Sir Richard Attenborough, *Gandhi*.
   Best Actor: Ben Kingsley, *Gandhi*.
   Best Actress: Meryl Streep, *Sophie's Choice*.

1983 Best Picture: *Terms of Endearment*.
   Best Director: James L. Brooks, *Terms of Endearment*.
   Best Actor: Robert Duvall, *Tender Mercies*.
   Best Actress: Shirley Maclaine, *Terms of Endearment*.
1984 Best Picture: *Amadeus*.
   Best Director: Milos Forman, *Amadeus*.
   Best Actor: F. Murray Abraham, *Amadeus*.
   Best Actress: Sally Field, *Places in the Heart*.

OPERA AND DANCE, 1984–85

The choice of works performed during the 1984–85 season was influenced considerably by the desire of companies to commemorate the 80th birthdays of Sir Frederick Ashton and Sir Michael Tippett, and the tercentenary of the birth of Handel.

Sir Frederick Ashton

Sir Frederick Ashton started his career as a dancer, studying with Massine and Rambert, and it was whilst working with Marie Rambert's company that he choreographed his first work, *A Tragedy of Fashion* (1926). In the following nine years he made nearly a score of works for the company, including his first major work, *Façade* (1931). In 1935 Ashton went to the Vic-Wells Ballet (later the Royal Ballet) as principal choreographer, and his 35 years in this post, seven of them as Director, had a profound influence on the style and repertoire of the Royal Ballet. In recognition of this seminal role the Royal Ballet opened their season on Oct. 18, 1984, in the presence of H.R.H. Princess Margaret, with a Gala tribute to Sir Frederick Ashton. Past and present members of the company performed *Birthday Offering, Monotones II, The Sleeping Beauty* awakening pas de deux, *Sylvia* pas de deux, *Façade* tango and *Daphnis and Chloë* final scene. These works were included in the autumn programmes, to be joined later in the season by *A Wedding Bouquet, Divertissements, Enigma Variations, A Month in the Country, Varii Capricci* (Ashton's most recent work) and the full-length ballets *Cinderella* and *La Fille mal gardée*. Anticipating the Royal Ballet by a month, the Sadler's Wells Royal Ballet, on Sir Frederick's 80th birthday (Sept. 17, 1984), introduced into their autumn schedule an Ashton triple bill, *Les Rendezvous, The Dream* and *Façade*, and subsequently revived *Les Patineurs*.

The most remarkable tribute, however, was the revival by London Festival Ballet of Ashton's *Romeo and Juliet*. Originally created for the Royal Danish Ballet in 1955, the ballet had not been performed by that company for about 20 years and had never before been seen in London. The idea of reviving the ballet, which many feared had been lost, was that of Peter Schaufuss, the new Director of London Festival Ballet, whose parents appeared as Juliet and Mercutio in the original production. With the help of notes, film, members of the original cast and Sir Frederick, the ballet was reconstructed and a new production given a royal première on July 23, 1985 (*see* below for production details).

Sir Michael Tippett

Recognition came less easily to Sir Michael Tippett, whose 80th birthday fell on Jan. 2, 1985. Although his work began to appear in the mid-thirties it was rarely performed professionally and Tippett's break-through was not until 1944, with the oratorio *A Child of Our Time*. The concern expressed in this work with the reconciliation of the light and dark sides of human nature is a theme which runs through all of Tippett's operas—*The Midsummer Marriage* (1955), *King Priam* (1962), *The Knot Garden* (1970) and *The Ice Break* (1977). The first two of these are the more popular works in the modern repertoire of professional companies and were the ones chosen by them to mark Sir Michael's birthday. A new production by Kent Opera of *King Priam* was premièred in Sept. 1984, while the original production of the opera was revived at Covent Garden in April 1985, and a new production of *The Midsummer Marriage* was given by English National Opera, with Opera North planning one for their autumn 1985 season. (For details of new productions, *see* below).

Handel Tercentenary

However, the most important anniversary with regard to the history of music in England was that of George Frederick Handel's birth on Feb. 23, 1685. When Handel arrived in London in 1710/11 he found Italian *opera seria* all the rage and, having spent the previous few years working in Italy, was well able to cater to the prevailing fashion. *Rinaldo* (1711) was a success and by 1725 Handel had gained the ascendency over his rivals, in the process bringing to maturity a style which over the next twenty years showed as great a degree of invention and originality as was possible within the rigid conventions of the *opera seria* form. Handel's operas were, however, little performed after his death and it was only a revival of interest in Germany after the First World War which led to their rediscovery. This fate was not shared by the oratorios, which continued to be performed and became an integral part of English music tradition.

Although already popular on the Continent, in the early eighteenth century there did not exist in England anything that could be called an oratorio before the form was introduced by Handel, although his earliest, *Esther*, was an adaptation of an earlier masque and its original performances, given privately by the Children of the Chapel Royal, had scenery, costumes and dramatic action. It was episcopal objections to the Children of the Chapel Royal performing at a theatre (deeply mistrusted as dens of vice) which led to the abandonment of the theatrical trappings for the first public performances in 1732. The concert oratorio also subsequently proved a useful means of circumventing the law forbidding theatrical performances on

Wednesdays and Fridays during Lent; hence a predominance of religious subjects.

Handel wrote his last operas in the mid-1740s and thereafter turned exclusively to oratorios. Unsurprisingly, given his previous career, Handel's oratorios are intensely dramatic. Freed from the constraints of *opera seria* with its *da capo* arias, etc., Handel was able to achieve a greater dramatic range, a more organic structure and richer accompaniment to the arias. Religious scruples had earlier dictated against theatre performances but with the revival of interest in Handel's operas many of the dramatic oratorios have also been staged, and one of these, *Samson* (1743), was included in the Royal Opera's celebration of the tercentenary. The operas were represented by *Tamerlano* (or *Tamburlaine*) (1724), *Serse* (or *Xerxes*) (1738) and *Orlando* (1733) in new productions by the major companies (*see* below for production details), with revivals of *Agrippina* (1709, Venice), *Giulio Cesare* (or *Julius Caesar*) (1724) and *Semele* (1744) planned for autumn 1985. Handel's works also received performances by amateur and smaller companies, notably *Rodrigo* (*c*. 1707/8, Florence) by Handel Opera, *Teseo* (1713) by the English Bach Festival Trust and *Alcina* (1735) by Opera Stage in the summer of 1985.

Comings and Goings

The opening of the season saw a new Director at the London Festival Ballet. The 35-year-old Peter Schaufuss began dancing with the Royal Danish Ballet but left his native land for a mainly peripatetic career with spells at the London Festival Ballet and the National Ballet of Canada. His appointment comes at a time when the company had seemed to have lost a sense of its identity and purpose, its repertory coming increasingly to resemble that of the Royal Ballet and Sadler's Wells Royal Ballet, whereas the original conception of the Festival Ballet was as an alternative to these companies. It is to this role that Schaufuss is eager to return, believing that Festival Ballet must develop a company style and repertory identity in order to build up its own following. To this end he plans to introduce more contemporary works from home and abroad, and to commission works for the company from a wider range of British and foreign choreographers. This policy got underway immediately with the introduction of the American jazz ballet *Night Creature*, plus *L'Arlésienne* and *Song of a Wayfarer*. A start was also made on improving the quality of the dancing with the recruitment of Armand and Paganini to strengthen the male ranks, to which Schaufuss himself is a notable addition, and the co-ordination of teaching styles within the company. (The ultimate aim is that Festival Ballet should have its own school to train prospective

recruits rather than being able to choose only from those graduates of the Royal Ballet School who are not taken into the Royal Ballet.)

The new Director's firm sense of purpose and view of the company's role had already begun to make their mark when Schaufuss crowned the achievements of his first season with the English première of Ashton's *Romeo and Juliet*. Ashton's version had become legendary but the choreographer was reluctant to revive a ballet which, being small-scale, delicate and romantic, he feared might suffer by comparison with later versions. In overcoming this reluctance and obtaining Sir Frederick's wholehearted collaboration, Schaufuss not only pulled off a remarkable *coup* and fulfilled a long-held personal ambition, but also preserved a ballet considered to be amongst Ashton's finest creations (*see* also above, and dance production details).

The season closed with the retirement of Lord Harewood as Managing Director of English National Opera. He had held this position with the company since 1972 but his involvement with opera had begun many years earlier. Lord Harewood was co-founder with Harold Rosenthal of the magazine *Opera* in 1950 and the following year began a long association with the Royal Opera, where he served twice on the Board of Directors (1951–53 and 1969–72) and between 1953 and 1960 was Controller of Opera Planning. When he joined Sadler's Wells Opera (renamed English National Opera in 1974), Lord Harewood expressed a commitment to performing opera in English and the desire to create a permanent company with a style of its own giving performances "putting forward a coherent view of opera" through ensemble playing. The application of this principle to the standard works consolidated a solid core of repertory from which the company was able to turn to less familiar areas. The personal preferences of Lord Harewood were reflected in the expansion of the French romantic and the Slavonic repertoire, the thirteen years of his incumbency seeing productions of Gounod (*Romeo and Juliet* and *Mireille*, with *Faust* included in the 1985–86 season), Massenet (*Manon*, *Werther*), Charpentier (*Louise*) and Debussy (*Pelleas and Mélisande*); while the Slavonic works have included all major Janáček except *Jenufa*, Smetana's *Dalibor* as well as *The Bartered Bride*, *Rusalka* (Dvořák) and Prokofiev's *The Gambler* in addition to the epic *War and Peace*. The company's tradition of presenting less familiar work of the standard composers was also continued with productions such as Verdi's *The Two Foscari* and *The Sicilian Vespers*, and in the Norwest Holst sponsored series which has included to date *Rienzi* (Wagner) and *Mazeppa* (Tchaikovsky) with *Moses* (Rossini) scheduled for the forthcoming season.

Lord Harewood was also committed to the

performance of contemporary work and in addition to such English twentieth century classics as the works of Britten and Tippett, six foreign twentieth century works have been given their English premières by English National Opera since 1972—*The Devils of Loudoun* (Penderecki), *Bomarzo* (Ginastra), *Julietta* (Martinů), *The Bassarids* (Henze), *Le Grand Macabre* (Ligeti) and *Akhnaten* (Glass). Nor have new works been neglected, English National Opera staging the world premières of *The Story of Vasco* (Crosse), *The Royal Hunt of the Sun* (Hamilton), *Toussaint* (Blake) and *Anna Karenina* (Hamilton).

An adventurous choice of works and a willingness to risk controversy (a "Freudian" interpretation of *Rusalka*: the 1950s American Mafiosa setting of Jonathan Miller's *Rigoletto*) have created a repertoire of unrivalled scope and interest. And the conception of the dramatic portrayal being as important as the vocal, and the emphasis on the integration of all aspects of the production, have reinvigorated opera, setting new standards of performance and making English National Opera possibly the most exciting company in the country. These achievements owe much to Lord Harewood's stewardship through a period when the company was adapting initially to its larger home at the Coliseum, and in latter years to the problems of maintaining standards and breadth of repertoire in the face of financial constraints. Past and present members of the company gathered on June 23, 1985, to pay tribute to these achievements in a Gala Celebration for Lord Harewood, before he left to devote more time to estate matters in Yorkshire and to take up the presidency of the British Board of Film Classification, leaving, in the words of Peter Jonas, his successor, "a hard act to follow."

OPERA PRODUCTIONS

In the summaries of company activities shown below the dates in brackets indicate the year in which the current production entered the repertoire of that company.

THE ROYAL OPERA (1946)
Royal Opera House, Covent Garden, W.C.2.

Productions from the repertoire were *Tosca* (1964), *Don Pasquale* (1973), *Carmen* (1973), *Boris Godunov* (1983), *Don Giovanni* (1981), *Die Fledermaus* (1977), *Die Zauberflöte* (1979), *La Traviata* (1967), *I Capuleti e i Montecchi* (1984), *Don Carlos* (1958), *Lucia di Lammermoor* (1959), *King Priam* (1962), *Andrea Chénier* (1984), *Samson et Delila* (1981), *La Bohème* (1974), *Così fan tutte* (1968), *Macbeth* (1981).

New productions were:
Sept. 1, 1984. **Turandot** (Puccini). *Conductor*, Colin Davis; *producer*, Andrei Serban; *designer*, Sally Jacobs; *choreographer*, Kate Flatt.

Turandot, Gwyneth Jones; *Liù*, Helen Donath; *Calaf*, Placido Domingo; *Altoum*, Robert Tear; *Pang*, Kim Begley; *Pong*, Laurence Dale; *Pang*, William Workman; *Timur*, Gwynne Howell; *Mandarin*, Gordon Sandison.

Sept. 25, 1984. **Tannhäuser** (Wagner). *Conductor*, Colin Davis; *producer*, Elijah Moshinsky; *set designer*, Timothy O'Brien; *costume designer*, Luciana Arrighi; *choreographer*, Kenneth MacMillan.

Tannhäuser, Klaus König; *Venus*, Eva Randová; *Elisabeth*, Gwyneth Jones; *Walther von der Vogelweide*, Horst Laubenthal; *Hermann*, Fritz Hubner; *Wolfram von Eschenbach*, Thomas Allen; *Heinrich der Schreiber*, Kim Begley; *Reinmar von Zweter*, Roderick Earle; *Biterolf*, John Gibbs; *Shepherd Boy*, Nicholas Sillitoe.

Dec. 4, 1984. **Der Rosenkavalier** (R. Strauss). *Conductor*, Georg Solti; *producer*, John Schlesinger; *set designer*, Willian Dudley; *costume designer*, Maria Björnson; *movement*, Eleanor Fazan.

Octavian, Agnes Baltsa; *Marschallin*, Kirite Kanawa; *Baron Ochs*, Aage Haugland; *Major Domo Act I*, Kim Begley; *Notary*, John Gibbs; *Valzacchi*, Robert Tear; *Annina*, Cynthia Buchan; *Italian Tenor*, Dennis O'Neill; *von Faninal*, Jonathan Summers; *Marianne*, Phyllis Cannan; *Sophie*, Barbara Bonney; *Major Domo to Faninal*, John Dobson; *Landlord*, Paul Crook; *Police Inspector*, Roderick Earle.

Feb. 20, 1985. **Samson** (Handel). *Conductor*, Julius Rudel; *producer*, Elijah Moshinsky; *designer*, Timothy O'Brien; *choreography*, Eleanor Fazan.

Samson, Jon Vickers; *Delila*, Carol Vaness; *Micah*, Sarah Walker; *Manoah*, Robert Lloyd; *Harapha*, John Tomlinson; *Israelite/Philistine Woman*, Marie McLaughlin; *Philistine Man*, Kim Begley; *Three Virgins*, Jeanette Wilson, Linda Humphries, Juliet Oppenheimer; *Messenger*, Paul Wilson.

March 22, 1985. **Il barbiere di Siviglia** (Rossini). *Conductor*, Gabriele Ferro; *producer*, Michael Hampe; *designer*, Ezio Frigerio.

Almaviva, Deon van der Walt; *Rosina*, Alicia Nafe; *Figaro*, Thomas Allen; *Bartolo*, Enzo Dare; *Basilio*, Samuel Ramsey; *Berta*, Elizabeth Bainbridge; *Fiorello*, Matthew Best.

June 17, 1985. **Ariadne auf Naxos** (R. Strauss). *Conductor*, Jeffrey Tate; *producer*, Jean-Louis Martinoty; *set designer*, Hans Schavernoch; *costume designer*, Lore Haas.

Prima Donna/Ariadne, Jessye Norman; *Tenor/Bacchus*, James King; *The Composer*, Ann Murray; *Zerbinetta*, Kathleen Battle; *Harlequin*, Olaf Baer; *Scaramuccio*, Kim Begley; *Truffaldino*, Eric Garrett; *Brighella*, Wilfried Gahmlich; *Music Master*, Norman

Bailey; *Wig-maker*, Brian Donlan; *Dancing Master*, Robin Leggate; *Major Domo*, Paul Hansard; *Naiad*, Cathryn Pope; *Dryad*, Claire Powell; *Echo*, Joan Rodgers.

June 27, 1985. *La donna del lago* (Rossini), a co-production with Houston Grand Opera. *Conductor*, Lawrence Foster; *producer*, Frank Corsaro; *set designer*, Ming Cho Lee; *costume designer*, Jane Greenwood.

Elena, Frederica von Stade; *'Uberto' (Giacomo)*, Chris Merritt; *Malcolm*, Marilyn Horne; *Roderigo*, David Rendall; *Douglas*, Dimitri Kavrakos; *Albina*, Patricia Parker; *Serano*, John Dobson; *Bertram*, Paul Crook.

The Royal Opera also appeared, by invitation, at the 1985 Athens Festival in July, where the Company gave two performances each of *Macbeth* and *King Priam* at the outdoor Herod Atticus Theatre beneath the Parthenon.

ENGLISH NATIONAL OPERA (1931)
London Coliseum, St. Martin's Lane, W.C.2.

Productions from the repertoire were *The Flying Dutchman* (1982), *The Barber of Seville* (1978), *Manon* (1979), *Arabella* (1980), *Patience* (1969), *Rusalka* (1983), *Cosi fan tutte* (1980), *The Makropoulos Case* (1982), *Tosca* (1981), *Rigoletto* (1982), *Anna Karenina* (1981), *Count Ory* (1963), *Fidelio* (1980), *Aida* (1980).

New productions were:
Sept. 8, 1984. *Osud* (Janáček). *Conductor*, Mark Elder; *producer*, David Pountney; *designer*, Stefanos Lazaridis.

Milá, Eilene Hannan; *Zivńy*, Philip Langridge; *Milá's Mother*, Ludmilla Andrew; *Dr. Suda*, Emile Belcourt; *Doubek (as child)*, Stewart Hunt; *Doubek (as student)*, David Aldred; *Jean*, Lawrence Holderness; *Nana*, Nicola Bowie; *Hrazda*, Stuart Kale; *Verva*, Christopher Booth-Jones; *Součkova*, Christine Thompson; *Kosinska*, Hilary Western.

and *Mahagonny Songs* (Weill). *Conductor*, Lionel Friend; *producer*, Keith Hack; *set designer*, Michael Levine; *costume designer*, Sally Gardner.

Presenter, Emile Belcourt; *Johnnie*, Terry Jenkins; *Billy*, Alan Woodrow; *Bobby*, Malcolm Rivers; *Jimmy*, Richard Angas; *Jessie*, Elise Ross; *Bessie*, Sally Burgess.

Sept. 27, 1984. *Madam Butterfly* (Puccini). *Conductor*, John Mauceri; *producer*, Graham Vick; *designer*, Stefanos Lazaridis; *assistant costume designer*, Clare Mitchell.

Madam Butterfly, Janice Cairns; *Pinkerton*, David Rendall; *Suzuki*, Anne-Marie Owens; *Sharpless*, Norman Bailey; *Goro*, Edward Byles; *The Bonze*, Richard Angas; *Yamadori*, John Kitchiner; *Sorrow*, Hiroshi Kuwako; *Kate Pinkerton*, Penelope Walker.

Dec. 20, 1984. *Mazeppa* (Tchaikovsky). *Conductor*, Mark Elder; *producer*, David Alden; *designer*, David Fielding.

Mazeppa, Malcolm Donnelly; *Maria*, Janice Cairns; *Andrei*, Rowland Sidwell; *Liubov*, Felicity Palmer; *Kochubei*, Richard Van Allen; *Iskra*, Alan Woodrow; *Orlik*, Malcolm Rivers; *Drunken Cossack*, Graeme Matheson-Bruce.

Jan. 26, 1985. *Tristan and Isolde* (Wagner), a production on loan from De Nederlandse Operastichting. *Conductor*, Reginald Goodall; *producer*, Götz Friedrich; *set designer*, Heinrich Wendel; *costume designer*, Jan Skalicky.

Isolde, Johanna Meier; *Brangäne*, Linda Finnie; *Tristan*, Alberto Remedios; *Shepherd*, Edward Byles; *Young Sailor*, Alan Woodrow; *Kurwenal*, Geoffrey Chard; *King Marke*, John Tomlinson; *Melot*, Malcolm Rivers; *Helmsman*, Mark Richardson.

Feb. 23, 1985. *Xerxes* (Handel). *Conductor*, Charles Mackerras; *producer*, Nicholas Hytner; *designer*, David Fielding.

Xerxes, Ann Murray; *Romilda*, Valerie Masterson; *Amastris*, Jean Rigby; *Atalanta*, Lesley Garrett; *Arsamenes*, Christopher Robson; *Ariodates*, Rodney Macann; *Elviro*, Christopher Booth-Jones.

April 4, 1985. *The Bartered Bride* (Smetana). *Conductor*, Herbert Prikopa; *producer*, Elijah Moshinsky; *designer*, John Bury; *choreographer*, Eleanor Fazan.

Mařenka, Penelope Thorn; *Esmeralda*, Rosemary Ashe; *Ludmilla*, Patricia Payne; *Háta*, Anne-Marie Owens; *Jenik*, Edmund Barham; *Vašek*, Graham Clark; *Ringmaster*, Terry Jenkins; *Kecal*, Stafford Dean; *Krušina*, Patrick Wheatley; *Tobias Micha*, Malcolm Rivers; *Indian*, Mark Richardson.

May 15, 1985. *The Midsummer Marriage* (Tippett). *Conductor*, Mark Elder; *producer*, David Pountney; *set designer*, Stefanos Lazaridis; *costume designer*, Sally Gardner.

Jenifer, Helen Field; *Mark*, John Treleaven; *Bella*, Lesley Garrett; *Jack*, Maldwyn Davies; *King Fisher*, Anthony Raffell; *Sosostris*, Alfreda Hodgson; *She-Ancient*, Anne-Marie Owens; *He-Ancient*, Dennis Wicks; *Half-Tipsy Man*, Simon Masterson-Smith; *Dancing Man*, Ivor Morris.

June 17, 1985. *Akhnaten* (Glass), the British première. *Conductor*, Paul Daniel; *producer*, David Freeman; *designer*, David Roger.

Akhnaten, Christopher Robson; *Nefertiti*, Sally Burgess; *Queen Tye*, Marie Angel; *Haremhab*, Christopher Booth-Jones; *Aye*, Richard Angas.

WELSH NATIONAL OPERA (1946)
John Street, Cardiff.

Productions from the repertoire were *The Merry Widow* (1984), *The Greek Passion* (1981), *La Bohème* (1984), *Ernani* (1979), *From the House of the Dead* (1982), *Carmen* (1983) and *Tosca* (1980).

New productions were:

Oct. 27, 1984. **Don Giovanni** (Mozart). *Conductor*, Charles Mackerras; *producer*, Ruth Berghaus; *designer*, Marie-Luise Strandt.

Don Giovanni, William Shimell; *Leporello*, Nicholas Folwell; *Donna Elvira*, Elaine Woods; *Donna Anna*, Anne Evans; *Don Ottavio*, Laurence Dale; *Zerlina*, Beverley Mills; *Masetto*, Matthew Best; *Commendatore*, John Tranter.

Feb. 23, 1985. *Siegfried* (Wagner). *Conductor*, Richard Armstrong; *producer*, Göran Järvefelt; *designer*, Carl Friedrich Oberle.

Siegfried, Jeffrey Lawton; *Brünnhilde*, Anne Evans; *Erda*, Anne Collins; *Mime*, John Harris; *The Wanderer*, Phillip Joll; *Fafner*, John Tranter; *Alberich*, Nicholas Folwell; *Woodbird*, Kate Flowers.

March 8, 1985. **Norma** (Bellini). *Conductor*, Julian Smith; *producer*, Andrei Serban; *designer*, Michael Yeargan.

Norma, Suzanne Murphy; *Adalgisa*, Kathryn Harries; *Pollione*, Frederick Donaldson; *Oroveso*, Harry Dworchak; *Flavio*, Timothy German; *Clotilde*, Elizabeth-Anne Price.

May 14, 1985. **Rigoletto** (Verdi). *Conductor*, Richard Armstrong; *producer*, Lucian Pintilie; *designer*, Radu and Miruna Boruzescu.

Rigoletto, Donald Maxwell; *Gilda*, Anne Dawson; *Duke of Mantua*, Dennis O'Neill; *Maddalena*, Wendy Varcoe; *Sparafucile*, Sean Rea; *Marullo*, Mark Holland; *Monterone*, Donald Adams.

All new productions were premièred at the New Theatre, Cardiff. Performances were given also at Birmingham, London (Dominion), Bristol, Swansea, Liverpool, Southampton, Oxford and Llandudno. Performances of The Threepenny Opera were given in January and February, 1985 at small venues throughout Wales.

SCOTTISH OPERA (1962)
Theatre Royal, Hope Street, Glasgow 2.

Productions from the repertoire were *Fidelio* (1970), *Rigoletto* (1979) and *The Bartered Bride* (1978).

New productions were:

Aug. 21, 1984. **Orion** (Cavalli), a co-production with Santa Fe Opera, premièred at the Edinburgh Festival. *Conductor*, Raymond Leppard; *producer*, Peter Wood; *designer*, John Bury.

Orion, Michael Myers; *Diana*, Anne Howells; *Aurora*, Linda Ormiston; *Venus*, Ann Howard; *Amor*, Lillian Watson; *Apollo*, Peter Jeffes; *Jove*, Donald Stephenson; *Filotero*, Barry Moro; *Vulcan*, Willard White; *Titon*,

Keith Latham; *Neptune*, Brian Bannatyne-Scott.

Jan. 9, 1985. **Capriccio** (Strauss). *Conductor*, Norman Del Mar; *producer*, John Cox; *designer*, Jack Notman.

The Countess, Margaret Marshall; *The Count*, Ian Caddy; *Flamand*, Ian Caley; *Oliver*, Alan Oke; *La Roche*, Stafford Dean; *Clairon*, Anne Howells; *Italian Singers*, Maria Moll and Francis Egerton.

Feb. 13, 1985. **Il barbiere di Siviglia** (Rossini). *Conductor*, Alexander Gibson; *producer*, Robert David MacDonald; *designer*, Sue Blane.

Rosina, Zehava Gal; *Almaviva*, Patrick Power; *Figaro*, Russell Smythe; *Dr. Bartolo*, Donald Adams; *Don Basilio*, Geoffrey Moses; *Berta*, Ludmilla Andrews.

April 17, 1985. **Don Giovanni** (Mozart). *Conductor*, Alexander Gibson; *producer*, Graham Vick.

Don Giovanni, Sergei Leiferkus; *Leporello*, Willard White; *Donna Elvira*, Karita Mattila; *Donna Anna*, Kristine Ciesinski; *Don Ottavio*, Anthony Roden; *Zerlina*, Faith Elliott; *Masetto*, John Best.

May 8, 1985. **Orlando** (Handel). *Conductor*, Richard Hickox; *producer*, Christopher Fettes.

Orlando, James Bowman; *Dorinda*, Lillian Watson; *Angelica*, Eiddwen Harrhy; *Medoro*, Timothy Wilson; *Zoroastro*, Stephen Varcoe.

June 5, 1985. **Hedda Gabler** (Harper). *Conductor*, Diego Masson; *producer*, Graham Vick; *designer*, Russell Craig.

Hedda, Kathryn Harries; *Loevborg*, William Neill; *Tesman*, Robert Dean; *Mrs. Elvsted*, Anne Mason; *Judge Brack*, Rodney Macann; *Miss Tesman*, Jane Guy; *Berta*, Eleanor Bennett; *Mlle. Danielle*, Patricia Hay.

With the exception of *Orion*, all new productions were premièred at the Theatre Royal, Glasgow. Performances were also given on tour at Aberdeen, Liverpool, Newcastle, Edinburgh, Leeds and Belfast. Performances of the Rossini double bill *The Silken Ladder* and *The Marriage Contract* (1984) were given at smaller venues throughout Scotland in May–June 1985.

OPERA NORTH (1978)
Grand Theatre, 46 New Briggate, Leeds.

Productions from the repertoire were *Nabucco* (1980), *The Threepenny Opera* (1984), *Il trovatore* (1983) and *Werther* (1982).

New productions were:

Sept. 26, 1984. **Cavalleria Rusticana** (Mascagni). *Conductor*, Clive Timms; *producer*, Steven Pimlott; *designer*, Raimonda Gaetani.

Santuzza, Phyllis Cannan; *Turiddu*, Frederick Donaldson; *Mamma Lucia*, Maureen

Morelle; *Lola*, Margaret McDonald; *Alfio*, Florian Cerny.

and *I Pagliacci* (Leoncavallo). *Conductor*, David Lloyd-Jones;*producer*,Steven Pimlott; *designer*, Raimonda Gaetani.

Nedda, Kate Flowers; *Canio*, Angelo Marenzi; *Beppe*, Peter Bodenham; *Tonio*, Florian Cerny; *Silvio*, Geoffrey Dolton.

Oct. 6, 1984. *Johnny Strikes Up* (Krenek), presented in association with the New Opera Company. *Conductor*, David Lloyd-Jones; *producer*, Anthony Besch; *designer*, John Stoddart; *choreographer*, Terry Gilbert.

Anita, Penelope Mackay; *Max*, Kenneth Woollam; *Johnny*, Jonathan Sprague; *Daniello*, Lyndon Terracini; *Yvonne*, Gillian Sullivan; *Artists' Manager*, Thomas Lawlor; *Hotel Director*,Paul Wade; *Railway Employee*, Brian Cookson; *Policemen*, Philip Mills,Mark Lufton, Bruce Budd.

Dec. 19, 1984. *The Magic Flute* (Mozart). *Conductor*, Peter Hirsch; *producer*, Graham Vick; *designer*, Russell Craig.

Pamina, Jane Leslie Mackenzie; *Tamino*, Laurence Dale; *Queen of the Night*, Evelyn Nicholson; *Pagageno*, Alan Watt; *Sarastro*, Geoffrey Moses; *Speaker*, Henry Newman; *First Lady*, Elizabeth Ritchie; *Second Lady*, Anne Mason; *Third Lady*, Catriona Bell; *Boys*, Kieran Forsyth, Dean Mullen, James Bowden.

Dec. 20, 1984. *The Gondoliers* (Sullivan/Gilbert), presented in association with New Sadler's Wells Opera. *Conductor*, David Lloyd-Jones; *producer*, Christopher Renshaw; *designer*, Tim Goodchild; *choreographer*, Michael Corder.

Casilda, Helen Walker; *Gianetta*, Gillian Sullivan; *Tessa*, Beverley Mills; *Duchess of Plaza Toro*, Nuala Willis; *Marco*, Gordon Christie; *Giuseppe*, Peter Savidge; *Luiz*, Hugh Hetherington; *Duke of Plaza Toro*, Derek Hammond-Stroud; *Don Alhambra del Bolero*, Thomas Lawlor.

March 5, 1985. *La Traviata* (Verdi). *Conductor*, Roderick Brydon; *producer*, François Rochaix; *designer*, Jean-Claude Maret.

Violetta, Helen Field; *Alfredo*, Adrian Martin; *Germont*, Jonathan Summers.

March 7, 1985. *Tamburlaine* (Handel). *Conductor*, Clive Timms; *producer and designer*, Philip Prowse.

Tamburlaine, Felicity Palmer; *Asteria*, Eiddwen Harrhy; *Irene*, Wendy Varcoe; *Andronicus*, Sally Burgess; *Bajazet*, Richard Morton; *Leone*, Peter Savidge.

May 28, 1985. *The Mastersingers of Nuremburg* (Wagner). *Conductor*, David Lloyd-Jones; *producer*, Ladislav Strös; *set designer*, Vladimir Nyvllt; *costume designer*, Josef Jelinec.

Eva, Marie Slorach; *Magdalena*, Della Jones; *Walther*, Denes Striny; *David*, Bona-

ventura Bottone; *Hans Sachs*, Michael Burt; *Beckmesser*, Nicholas Folwell; *Pogner*, John Tranter; *Nightwatchman*, Alan Oke.

In addition to performances in Leeds, the company also toured to Manchester, Nottingham, Hull, Newcastle, London (Sadler's Wells), York and Oxford.

Opera North was invited to perform *Tamburlaine* in East Germany in February 1985 and gave a performance at the Berlin Komische Oper before going to the Tercentenary Handel Festival in Halle, the composer's birthplace, where one of their two performances fell on the day of Handel's birth.

KENT OPERA (1969)
Pembles Cross, Egerton, Ashford, Kent.

Productions from the repertoire were *The Seraglio* (1984) and *The Marriage of Figaro* (1981).

New productions were:

Sept. 27, 1984. *King Priam* (Tippett). *Conductor*, Roger Norrington; *producer*, Nicholas Hytner; *designer*, David Fielding.

Priam, Rodney Macann; *Paris*, Howard Haskin; *Hector*, Omar Ebrahim; *Hecuba*, Janet Price; *Helen*, Anne Mason; *Andromache*, Sarah Walker; *Achilles*, Neil Jenkins; *Hermes*, Christopher Gillett.

March 21, 1985. *The Barber of Seville* (Rossini). *Conductor*, Arnold Östman; *producer*, Jonathan Hales; *designer*, Roger Butlin.

Figaro, Gordon Sandison; *Almaviva*, Francis Egerton; *Rosina*, Eirian James; *Bartolo*, Andrew Shore; *Basilio*, William Mackie.

Both new productions were premièred at the Marlowe Theatre, Canterbury, and performances were also given at Northampton, Poole, Bath, Cambridge, Dartford, Brighton, Southsea, Norwich, Plymouth and Eastbourne.

GLYNDEBOURNE FESTIVAL OPERA (1934)
Glyndebourne, Lewes, East Sussex.

The 1985 Festival ran from May 20 to August 14 and the resident orchestra was the London Philharmonic, with the London Sinfonietta playing for the Knussen double bill. Seven operas were presented, of which three were revivals: *La Cenerentola* (John Cox production, 1983), *Arabella* (John Cox production, 1984) and *Idomeneo* (Trevor Nunn production, 1983).

May 21, 1985. *Carmen* (Bizet). *Conductor*, Bernard Haitink; *director*, Peter Hall; *designer*, John Bury.

Carmen, Maria Ewing; *Don José*, Warren Ellsworth; *Escamillo*, David Holloway; *Zuniga*, Xavier Depraz; *Moralès*, Malcolm Walker; *Micaëla*, Marie McLaughlin; *Fras-

quita, Elizabeth Collier; *Mercedès,* Jean Rigby.

July 5, 1985. *Albert Herring* (Britten). *Conductor,* Bernard Haitink; *director,* Peter Hall; *designer,* John Gunter.

Albert Herring, John Graham-Hall; *Mrs. Herring,* Patricia Kern; *Florence Pike,* Felicity Palmer; *Lady Billows,* Patricia Johnson; *Miss Wordsworth,* Elizabeth Gale; *Mr. Gedge,* Derek Hammond-Stroud; *Mr. Upfold,* Alexander Oliver; *Supt. Budd,* Richard Van Allan; *Sid,* Alan Opie; *Nancy,* Jean Rigby; *Emmie,* Marie Bovino; *Cis,* Bernadette Lord; *Harry,* Richard Peachey.

Aug. 5, 1985. *Higglety Pigglety Pop!* (Knussen). *Conductor,* Oliver Knussen/ Stephen Barlow; *director,* Frank Corsaro; *designer,* Maurice Sendak.

Rhoda/Voice of Baby's Mother, Karen Beardsley/Rosmary Hardy; *Jennie,* Cynthia Buchan; *Potted Plant/Baby/Mother Goose,* Deborah Rees; *Pig/low voice of Ash Tree,* Andrew Gallacher; *Cat/high voice of Ash Tree,* Hugh Hetherington; *Lion,* Stephen Richardson.

and *Where the Wild Things Are* (Knussen). *Conductor,* Oliver Knussen/Stephen Barlow; *director,* Frank Corsaro; *designer,* Maurice Sendak.

Max, Karen Beardsley/Rosemary Hardy; *Mama/Tzippy,* Linda Hirst; *Moishe/Goat,* Hugh Hetherington; *Bruno,* Stephen Richardson; *Emile,* Stephen Rhys-Williams; *Bernard,* Andrew Gallacher.

The Touring Company presented *Carmen, Idomeneo* and *A Midsummer Night's Dream* at Glyndebourne, Oxford and Manchester.

DANCE PRODUCTIONS

THE ROYAL BALLET (1931)
Royal Opera House, Covent Garden, W.C.2.

Full-length ballets from the repertoire performed in the 1984–85 season were *Mayerling* (MacMillan: 1978), *Swan Lake* (Petipa/Ivanov; additional choreography by Ashton and Nureyev: 1979), *Cinderella* (Ashton: 1965), *The Sleeping Beauty* (Sergueyev after Petipa, additional choreography by Ashton: 1977), *Manon* (MacMillan:1974), *La Fille mal gardée* (Ashton: 1960) and *Romeo and Juliet* (Mac-Millan: 1975).

Shorter ballets from the repertoire, performed in triple-bills, were *Birthday Offering* (Ashton), *Monotones II* (Ashton), *Daphnis and Chloë, final scene* (Ashton), *A Wedding Bouquet* (Ashton), *Varii Capricci* (Ashton), *Elite Syncopations* (MacMillan), *Raymonda Act III* (Petipa/Nureyev), *Ballet Imperial* (Balanchine), *L'Invitation au voyage* (Corder), *Façade* (Ashton), *The Firebird* (Fokine), *Return to the Strange Land* (Kylián), *Different Drummer* (MacMillan), *La Bayadère* (Petipa/

Nureyev), *Consort Lessons* (Bintley), *A Month in the Country* (Ashton), *Enigma Variations* (Ashton).

One full-length ballet was performed in a new production:
Dec. 20, 1984. *The Nutcracker.* Choreography, Ivanov, after Petipa, and Wright; *music,* Tchaikovsky; *producer,* Peter Wright; *designer,* Julia Trevelyan Oman. Cast at the première included Lesley Collier, Anthony Dowell, Michael Coleman, Julie Rose and Guy Niblett. The première was a Royal Gala Performance in the presence of H.M. The Queen, H.R.H. The Duke of Edinburgh and H.R.H. Princess Margaret.

New ballets were:
Nov. 17, 1984. *Young Apollo,* a one-act ballet. *Choreography,* by David Bintley; *music,* Benjamin Britten/Gordon Crosse;*designs,* Victor Pasmore.. The cast included Mark Silver (*Young Apollo*), Bryony Brind (*Mnemosyne*), Deirdre Eyden, Pippa Wylde, Gail Taphouse, Karen Paisley and Ravenna Tucker.

March 9, 1985. *Number Three,* a one-act ballet. *Choreography,* Michael Corder; *music,* Prokofiev's *Piano Concerto No. 3; designs,* Helen Frankenthaler. The cast included Lesley Collier, Mark Silver, Karen Paisley, Nicola Roberts, Ravenna Tucker and Bryony Brind.

July 25, 1985. *Half the House,* a one-act ballet. *Choreography,* Jennifer Jackson; *music,* Bartok's *Divertimento for Strings; designs,* William Henderson.

July 26, 1985. *Frankenstein, the Modern Prometheus.* Choreography, Wayne Eagling; *score,* commissioned from Vangelis; *costume designs,* David and Elizabeth Emmanuel.

The Royal Ballet paid a one-week visit to Birmingham (Hippodrome) in April and presented a two-week season in The Big Top in Battersea Park, London in July 1985. April 1985 also saw a tour of Eastern Europe, performing *Manon, Consort Lessons, A Month in the Country* and *Elite Syncopations* in Budapest, Dresden and Berlin, as part of a British Council tour which in May also took the company to Barcelona with the same triple bill plus *The Sleeping Beauty* and *La Fille mal gardée,* and to Lisbon to perform *The Sleeping Beauty.*

SADLER'S WELLS ROYAL BALLET (1931)
Sadler's Wells Theatre, Rosebery Avenue, EC1R 4TN.

Full-length ballets from the repertoire were *Swan Lake* (Petipa and Ivanov, additional choreography by Peter Wright: 1980), *Giselle* (Petipa after Coralli and Perrot: 1968), *La Fille mal gardée* (Ashton: 1960), *Coppélia* (after Petipa and Cecchi: 1979).

Programmes also included the following shorter ballets: *Common Ground* (Jackson), *Petrushka* (Fokine), *Elite Syncopations* (MacMillan), *Les Rendezvous* (Ashton), *The Dream* (Ashton), *Façade* (Ashton), *Raymonda Act III* (Nureyev after Petipa), *Metamorphosis* (Bintley), *5 Tangos* (van Manen), *Las Hermanas* (MacMillan), *Concerto* (MacMillan), *Les Patineurs* (Ashton), *The Lady and the Fool* (Cranko), *Les Sylphides* (Fokine), *Choros* (Bintley).

One full-length ballet was presented in a new production:

Oct. 15, 1984. *The Sleeping Beauty*. Choreography, Petipa and Wright; *producer*, Peter Wright; *designer*, Philip Prowse. The cast at the première included Marion Tait (*Princess Aurora*), Roland Price (*Prince Florimund*), Margaret Barbieri (*Lilac Fairy*), Galina Samsova (*Carabosse*), Sandra Madgwick (*Princess Florine*) and David Yow (*Bluebird*). The first London performance was given on April 30, 1985 at a Royal Gala performance in the presence of H.R.H. Princess Margaret.

New works were:

Oct. 2, 1984. *Vocalise, Opus 34*, a pas de deux. *Choreography*, André Prokovsky; *music*, Rachmaninoff. Performed at the première by Galina Samsova and Alain Dubreuil.

Jan. 3, 1985. *Median*, a one-act ballet. *Choreography*, Jennifer Jackson; *music*, Stephen Montague's *From the White Edge of Phrygia*; *designer*, Ella Huhne. The cast of twelve dancers was led by Marion Tait, Leanne Benjamin, Stephen Wicks and Nicholas Millington.

June 14, 1985. *Flowers of the Forest*; *Two Scottish Ballets. Choreography*, David Bintley; *music*, Malcolm Arnold's *Four Scottish Dances* and Benjamin Britten's *Scottish Ballad*; *designer*, Jan Blake. The cast included Margaret Barbieri, Alain Dubreuil, Marion Tait and Roland Price.

In addition to performances at Sadler's Wells Theatre and The Royal Opera in London, the company also toured to Cambridge, Birmingham, Liverpool, Oxford, Manchester, Leeds, Eastbourne, Southampton and Milton Keynes. An eight-week overseas tour of New Zealand, South Korea and India was undertaken in early Spring 1985, giving performances of *The Sleeping Beauty*, *Giselle*, *5 Tangos*, *La Fille mal gardée* and *Swan Lake*.

LONDON FESTIVAL BALLET (1950)
Festival Ballet House, 39 Jay Mews, S.W.7.

Performances of full-length ballets from the repertoire were *The Nutcracker* (Hynd: 1976), *Onegin* (Cranko: 1984), *Giselle* (Skeaping, after Perrot, Coralli, Petipa: 1971) and *La Sylphide* (Schaufuss, after Bournonville: 1971).

Programmes of shorter ballets included *The Sanguine Fan* (Hynd), *Don Quixote pas de deux* (after Petipa), *The Three-Cornered Hat* (Massine), *Etudes* (Lander) and *Pulcinella* (Tetley).

Two full-length ballets were presented in new productions.

July 2, 1985, at the London Coliseum. *Coppélia*. *Choreography*, Ronald Hynd; *music*, Delibes; *designs*, Desmond Heeley. The cast at the first performance, a Charity Gala Première, was led by Eva Evdokimova (*Swanilda*), Peter Schaufuss (*Franz*) and Niels Bjørn Larsen (*Dr. Coppélius*).

July 23, 1985, at the London Coliseum. *Romeo and Juliet*. *Choreography*, Sir Frederick Ashton; *music*, Prokofiev; *designs*, Peter Rice. The first night was a Royal Première in the presence of H.R.H. Princess Margaret. The cast was led by Peter Schaufuss (*Romeo*), Katherine Healy (*Juliet*), Raffaele Paganini (*Mercutio*), Matz Skoog (*Benvolio*), Nicholas Johnson (*Tybalt*), Patrick Armand (*Paris*), Janet Mulligan (*Livia*), Freya Dominic (*Nurse*), Kirsten Ralov (*Lady Capulet*), Niels Bjørn Larsen (*Lord Capulet*), Frank Schaufuss (*Prince of Verona*) and David Scott (*Friar Lawrence*).

Other new productions were:

Nov. 23, 1984. *Night Creature*. *Choreography*, Alvin Ailey; *music*; "Duke" Ellington; *restaging*, Ulysses Dove; *costumes*, Jane Greenwood. The first performance by the company was in Nottingham: the London première was on July 15, 1985.

Feb. 15, 1985. *L'Arlésienne*. *Choreography*, Roland Petit; *music*, Bizet; *designs*, René Allio. The cast was led by Peter Schaufuss (*Frederi*) and Mireille Bourgeois (*Vivette*). The first performance by the company was in Liverpool: the London première was on July 15, 1985.

March 8, 1985. *Song of a Wayfarer*. *Choreography*, Maurice Béjart; *music*, Mahler's *Lieder eines fahrenden Gesellen*. Performed by Matz Skoog and Patrick Armand at the première, which took place in Eastbourne: the first London performance was on July 19, 1985.

July 19, 1985. *Land*. *Choreography*, Christopher Bruce; *music*, Arne Nordheim's *Warsaw*; *designer*, Walter Nobbe. The cast was led at the première, which took place in London, by Janet Mulligan and Martyn Fleming.

The works were performed in London, at the Coliseum and the Royal Festival Theatre, and on tour at Newcastle, Manchester, Plymouth, Nottingham, Bristol, Birmingham, Liverpool, Norwich, Stratford-upon-Avon, Eastbourne and Oxford. *La Sylphide, The Sanguine Fan, Don Quixote pas de deux,*

Sphinx and *Etudes* were performed in Monaco in April and *La Sylphide*, *Giselle* and a triple bill in Copenhagen in June 1985.

BALLET RAMBERT (1926)
Mercury Theatre Trust Ltd., 94 Chiswick High Road, W4 1SH.

Repertoire works performed during the year were *Wildlife* (Alston), *Intimate Pages* (Bruce), *Entre Dos Aguas* (North), *Voices and Light Footsteps* (Alston), *Colour Moves* (North), *Lonely Town, Lonely Street* (North) and *Rainbow Ripples* (Alston). In Nov. 1984, Ballet Rambert introduced into its repertoire the Robert North ballet *Death and the Maiden*, a London Contemporary Dance Theatre work; and in May 1985 the Glen Tetley ballet *Pierrot Lunaire*, set to music by Schoenberg, with designs by Rouben Ter-Arutunian, was revived.

New works were:
Oct. 5, 1984, at the Marlowe Theatre, Canterbury. **Sergeant Early's Dream.** *Choreographer*, Christopher Bruce; *set* to English, Irish and American folk songs; *set designer*, Walter Nobbe. The London première was on March 13, 1985, at Sadler's Wells Theatre.

Feb. 8, 1985, at the Palace Theatre, Manchester. **An Occasion for Some Revolutionary Gestures.** *Choreography*, Dan Wagoner; *music*, Michael Sahl's *Piano Variations on Yankee Doodle Dandy*; *designer*, John Macfarlane. The London première was on March 18, 1985, at Sadler's Wells Theatre.

March 13, 1985, at Sadler's Wells Theatre, London. **Mythologies.** *Choreographer*, Richard Alston; *score*, Nigel Osbourne's *Mythologies*; *set designer*, Peter Mumford; *costume designer*, Candida Cook. The dancers included Mark Baldwin (*Asdiwal*), Lucy Bethune (*Asdiwal's wife*), Diane Walker (*Evening Star/White Bear*) and Robert North (*Hatsenas*).

April 30, 1985, at the Gaumont Theatre, Southampton. **Dangerous Liaisons.** *Choreographer*, Richard Alston; *music*, Simon Waters; *costume designer*, Richard Smith. The London première was on July 22, 1985, at the Big Top season.

May 9, 1985, at the Theatre Royal, Brighton. **Light and Shade.** *Choreographer*, Robert North; *music*, Stravinsky's *Duo concertant* and *Pastorale*; *designer*, Andrew Storer. The London première was on July 26, 1985, at the Big Top season.

July 26, 1985, at the Big Top, Battersea Park. **Java.** *Choreographer*, Richard Alston; *music* by The Inkspots; *costume designer*, Jenny Henry.

The company's home tours took this repertoire to Canterbury, Oxford, Nottingham, Norwich, Bath, Newcastle, Glasgow, Manchester, Birmingham, Leicester, London (Sadler's Wells), Southampton, Brighton, Bristol, Mold and a season in the Big Top, Battersea Park, London. Also included was a special school's matinée programme, *Let's Face the Music and Dance.* An overseas tour to Poland was undertaken in May 1985, visiting Gdansk, Warsaw and Lodz.

LONDON CONTEMPORARY DANCE THEATRE (1967)
The Place, 16 Flaxman Terrace, WC1H 9AT.

Performances from the repertoire were *Run Like Thunder* (Jobe), *Carnival* (Davies), *New Galileo* (Davies), *Agora* (Cohan), *No Man's Land* (Cohan), *The Dancing Department* (Davies), and *Esplanade* (Taylor). On Sept. 28, 1984, the company also introduced into their repertoire Richard Alston's *Doublework* (*music*, James Fulkerson; *costume design*, Jenny Henry), originally created for his own company, but reworked for L.C.D.T.

New works were:
Sept. 19, 1984, at Derngate Theatre, Northampton. **Skylark** (later renamed **Skyward**). *Choreographer*, Robert Cohan; *music*, *Clouds*, piano quintet by Eleanor Alberga; *designer*, Norberto Chiesa. The London première was on Nov. 20, at Sadler's Wells Theatre.

Sept. 21, 1984, at Derngate Theatre, Northampton. **Rite Electrik.** *Choreographer*, Tom Jobe; *music*, Barrington Pheloung; *set design*, Peter Mumford; *costume design*, Paul Dart. The London première was on Nov. 27, at Sadler's Wells Theatre.

Feb. 7, 1984, at the Apollo Theatre, Oxford. **Bridge the Distance.** *Choreographer*, Siobhan Davies; *music*, Britten's *Third Quartet*; *designer*, David Buckland. The London première was on June 3, at Sadler's Wells Theatre.

In addition to two seasons at Sadler's Wells Theatre the company also toured to Northampton, Exeter, Swansea, Mold, Bristol, Southampton, Oxford, Leeds, Stirling, Aberdeen, Glasgow, Liverpool, Birmingham, Plymouth and Canterbury. The company also staged a Royal Gala, in the presence of H.R.H. Prince Andrew, at the Royal Opera House on July 11, 1985. Two American companies, The Alvin Ailey American Dance Theatre and The New York City Breakers, shared the bill with L.C.D.T.

THE SCOTTISH BALLET (1969)
261 West Princes Street, Glasgow G4 9EE.

Performances from the repertoire were *Cinderella* (Darrell: 1979), *The Nutcracker* (Darrell after Ivanov: 1973) and *Swan Lake* (Darrell after Petipa and Ivanov: 1977). A triple bill of new works was introduced on

March 29, 1985 at the Theatre Royal, Glasgow, comprising **Pococurantis**. *Choreography*, Peter Royston; *music*, Paul Robinson; *designs*, Graham Bower. The cast was led by Linda Packer (*The Lady*), Paul Tyers (*Her Husband*), Vincent Hantam (*The Lover*) and Christopher Gilliard (*Tokolosh*). **Remembered Dances. Choreography**, Christopher Bruce; *music*, Janáček; *designs*, Walter Nobbe. The cast was led by Elaine McDonald and Christopher Long. **HAIL the classical**. *Choreography*, Michael Clark; *music*, Ravel's *Introduction and Allegro* and rock songs by The Fall; *designs*, Charles Atlas. The company was led by Michael Clark.

The above ballets were performed at the Theatre Royal, Glasgow and on tour at Edinburgh, Bath, Hull, Aberdeen, Belfast, Bristol, Liverpool and Inverness. A programme of works suitable for smaller venues went on tour to Glasgow, Edinburgh, Dunfermline and St. Andrews in Feb. 1985; the works performed were *Dance Diversions*, *Shoals of Herring* (Maldoom), *Sylvia* pas de deux (Aitken), *The Water's Edge* (North) and *Three Dances to Japanese Music* (Carter).

The 1985 Nureyev Festival, which took place at the London Coliseum in July and August, featured the Matsuyama Ballet Company of Tokyo on its first appearance in Britain. Two ballets, *Swan Lake* and *Giselle*, were presented during the two-week season, the leading roles in both being taken by Yoko Morishito and Nureyev.

BRASS BAND CHAMPIONS

The British Open Brass Band Championships 1985 (Sept.)

Test Piece—*Salute to Youth* (G. Vinter).

1. Black Dyke Mills (Maj. P. Parkes)—195 pts.
2. British Aerospace (Wingates) (J. Scott)—194 pts.
3. Fodden O.T.S. (H. Snell)—193 pts.
4. Leyland Vehicles (R. Evans)—192 pts.
5. Fairey Engineering Wks. (H. Williams)—190 pts.
6. Grimethorpe Colliery (G. Brand)—189 pts.

The National Brass Band Championship of Great Britain 1985 (Oct.)

Championship.—Black Dyke Mills (Maj. P. Parkes)—195 pts.
Second Section.—Rhodian Brass (F. M. Slater)—190 pts.
Third Section.—Swinton Concert Brass (D. King)—185 pts.
Fourth Section.—Hesketh Bank Silver (H. Bentham)—186 pts.
Youth Section.—West Lothian Schools (N. Boddice)—190 pts.

European Championships 1985 (May) Black Dyke Mills (Maj. P. Parkes)

LITERATURE OF THE YEAR

The Booker

The Booker Prize continued to exert its influence on the publishing world, and the effects were not wholly benign. Autumn schedules are jammed with contenders, and much good writing is overlooked as editors of the review pages in the press are inundated with new novels. Apart from this avoidable distortion in the market imposed by the Booker Prize conditions, a more serious criticism is the lack of consistency in the judging, and uncertainty of what the Prize is intended to achieve. Inevitably, there will be worthy winners, but frequently the judging panel appear overwhelmed by their task, producing an eccentric short list and a perverse choice of winner.

Richard Cobb, former professor of modern history at Oxford, and chairman of the judging panel in 1984, declared in his speech at the prize ceremony that: "It is not for a panel of judges in a novel prize to tell the general public what it ought to be reading; but to choose books that people are likely to want to read. In an operation of this kind one would not go for a Proust or a Joyce—not that I would know about that, never having read either." Unfortunately, of the six finalists, five had writers as their protagonists; the sixth, the popular choice before the judging, which continued to sell throughout the year, did not receive the award. This seemed to contradict the somewhat odd judging criteria, and reinforce the view that the prize is a literary game or lottery beyond the comprehension of mere readers of novels, who might have recognized in the works of Joyce some of the qualities they could have hoped to find in a Booker winner.

Anita Brookner's *Hotel du Lac* received the 1984 Booker Prize, and it was a work of high quality, but on a small scale. It was described by the judges as "a work of perfect artistry" (although this was widely misquoted in the press as "a work of perfect artifice"). Its heroine was Edith Hope, a writer of romantic fiction under the name of Vanessa Wilde, who was staying in a hotel by Lake Geneva in Switzerland out of season, in disgrace for something she had done in London. In an interview, the author described her novel, somewhat enigmatically, as a "vindication of the rights of tortoises". J. G. Ballard's *Empire of the Sun* encompassed wider themes, and was the "ante post" favourite for the prize. Ballard's apocalyptic vision is familiar from his science fiction novels, but this powerful and poetic work was based on his own wartime experiences. The events are seen through the eyes of 11-year-old Jim, who becomes separated from his parents when the Japanese capture Shanghai, and is subsequently interned at the Lunghua Civilian Centre until the end of the war. The title refers not only to the Land of the Rising Sun, but also to the nuclear age which began with the explosion at Hiroshima—"the light that lay over the land, the shadow of another sun ... here would be fought ... the last war to decide the planet's future."

The other finalists were Julian Barnes with *Flaubert's Parrot*, a literary romp, with retired doctor Geoffrey Braithwaite, who parallels himself with Charles Bovary, engaged in searching for the stuffed parrot which Gustave Flaubert borrowed to write *Un Coeur Simple*. Anita Desai's *In Custody* was a comic and well-written account of the Indian literary world, with a scholar in northern India asked to interview a famous but forgotten Urdu poet for a literary magazine. Penelope Lively's *According to Mark* was a literary detective story about the biography of Gilbert Strong, Edwardian man of letters, and the discovery of his secret love affair recorded in previously hidden letters and notebooks. *Small World* by David Lodge was a clever and witty novel set in the world of academic conferences.

Controversy surrounded the exclusions from the Booker short-list as much as the final six. Angela Carter's *Nights at the Circus* was a brilliantly inventive and imaginative work. Its heroine was Fevvers, a Cockney woman with wings, who, at the turn of the century, became a celebrated *aerialiste* in a circus. She relates her bizarre tale to Jack Walser, an American journalist; the story moves from London to Siberia *via* St. Petersburg, with the travelling circus of Colonel Kearney and his clairvoyant pig called Sybil. Martin Amis's *Money* is a stylish, if almost too clever, work, supposedly concerning the efforts of the gross John Self, from the world of advertizing, to set up a Hollywood film. Self is addicted to money, pornography, alcohol, fast food and fighting, and his exploits are funny and compelling in a perverse way as he staggers from London to New York. However, the novel has more to say than the mere celebration of excess: it is subtitled "A suicide note", and the reader is told that by the time the book is laid aside, "John Self will no longer exist". He is in fact one aspect of the author's nature, as is Martina Twain, another of the characters, and Amis himself appears in the book as a writer who becomes involved in Self's film script. "The distance between author and narrator corresponds to the degree to which the author finds the narrator wicked, deluded, pitiful or ridiculous ... The further down the scale he is, the more liberties you can take with him. You can do what the hell you like to him, really. This creates an appetite for punishment. The author is not free of sadistic impulses." John Self is certainly a long way down Amis's scale, but no doubt has been purged with the writing of this novel.

Keith Waterhouse's *Thinks* describes the last day in the mind of Edgar Samuel Bapty, "as sane as anyone on this 8.33 from Portsea to Victoria, except when he's overweight. That's when his blood pressure goes up and he thinks vicious thoughts." Waterhouse creates Bapty's world with humour and skill, until his choleric commuter finally expires, "a reasonably happy man".

The hero of Howard Jacobson's *Peeping Tom* is Barney Fugleman, his life dominated by Thomas Hardy, whose spirit entered his body during hypnosis; his first wife ran a Hardy bookshop in Hampstead, and his second wife a Hardy summer school. Poor Hardy, who had witnessed the hanging of a woman outside Dorchester Prison in 1856, is the butt of much extravagant humour. In *Watson's Apology*, Beryl Bainbridge has taken the true story of a clergyman, scholar and former grammar school headmaster who beat his wife to death in 1871, and attempted, largely successfully, to analyse what drove him to such an act. The title of Muriel Spark's *The Only Problem* refers to the difficulty in accepting that God can be both omnipotent and yet allow human suffering. The main character is Harvey, a rich man trapped in a loveless marriage to Effie; he leaves her when she steals two chocolate bars as an anti-establishment gesture, and escapes to France, where he studies The Book of Job in solitude, while his former wife becomes a terrorist. The novel is both entertaining, and a serious examination of theological and moral ideas.

André Brink examines apartheid in *The Wall of the Plague*; the wall of the title was built by the French in the mountains of Vaucluse in a futile attempt to stop the plague from spreading, and the analogy is drawn through Andrea, a coloured South African expatriate, filming the story of the plague in Provence. The image of the wall is powerful and apt, although the implications sit uneasily in the text with the triangular multi-racial love story. William Boyd's *Stars and Bars* relates the comic misadventures of Henderson Dores, a middle-aged Englishman employed by a firm of art dealers, who goes to America to value an art collection in The Deep South. Robert McCrum's *The Fabulous Englishman* is set in London and Prague in the 1960s, and contrasts the new-found freedom in the West with the oppression in the East.

Dick Francis continues to produce well-crafted thrillers at the rate of one each year, and his 23rd novel, *Proof*, concerns fraud and violence in the drinks trade, with wine and whisky consignments hijacked and resold under false labels. The opening sequence, in which a runaway lorry ploughs into a crowded marquee, is excellently handled. Nevertheless, although the author is to be commended for moving away from the horseracing world which he describes so well, there is a predictability about his heroes—loners, who suffer, and are drawn into violence against their will. In this book, the hero is Tony Beach, a widower running a wine shop. However, Dick Francies continues to write with a fluency and skill that must be the envy of many lesser authors.

A. S. Byatt's *Still Life* is the second volume in the trilogy begun with *The Virgin in the Garden*, and covers the years 1954–59. *Helliconia Winter* concludes Brian Aldiss's brilliantly imaginative and well-constructed science fiction trilogy. Anthony Burgess is a writer of prodigious talent and prolific output: *The Kingdom of the Wicked* is an epic account of the early Christians and Imperial Rome. The book developed from research carried out by the author for a television series, but it is an undisciplined accumulation of information, a catalogue of excesses that become tedious. Joseph Heller's *God Knows* is a more successful recreation of Biblical times, with the Old Testament recounted by King David, still alive but now reflecting on his life. No longer on speaking terms with God, David adopts the style of a Jewish comedian from Brooklyn in this witty *tour-de-force* from the author of *Catch-22*. Without descending into blasphemy, the book has serious points to make about questioning superstition and myth, and some marvellous comedy, not least the notion that Solomon was really the least intelligent of David's children who would actually have cut the baby in half in one of his more famous judgments!

Gore Vidal's *Lincoln* is a convincing and rounded portrait of the dominant figure from America's historical and political past. In a postscript Vidal states, in anticipation of the question "How much of *Lincoln* is true?", that "All of the principal characters really existed, and they said and did pretty much what I have them saying and doing . . . As for Lincoln and the other historical figures, I have reconstructed them from letters, journals, newspapers, diaries . . . For those who may be alarmed at my version of the Gettysburg Address, I used not Lincoln's final tinkered-with draft but what someone who was there wrote down." The result matches his *Burr* and *1876* in its absorption of thorough research to produce a lively and readable recreation of a turbulent era, with the complex politics assimilated into the very fabric of the story without its degenerating into a lesson in history or politics. Naturally, the book ends with Lincoln's assassination, "a form of atonement for the great and terrible thing that he had done by giving so bloody and absolute a rebirth to his nation".

Vintage Greene

A new work by Graham Greene is always welcome, but of especial interest was *The Tenth Man*, since it had been written while he was under "an almost slave contract" to MGM film studios in the 1940s, and had been "ticking away like a time-bomb somewhere in the archives". Greene had completely

forgotten about the work, and when it was brought to his attention thought it amounted to no more than a scenario for a film. The story actually runs to some 30,000 words, which Greene "found . . . very readable—indeed I prefer it in many ways to *The Third Man*". Set in France during and after the Second World War, the story begins with 30 Frenchmen held prisoner by the Germans; they are instructed to select three of their number for execution in retaliation for the death of a German officer. One of the losers in the grim lottery is a wealthy Parisian lawyer, Jean-Louis Chavel, who offers all his worldly goods to anyone who will take his place. A young man, Janvier, does, bequeathing his new-found and short-lived wealth to his mother and sister. After the war, Chavel is drawn inevitably back to his old house, and under an assumed name he works there as an odd-job man, until one day a stranger arrives, claiming to be Chavel. Although little more than an extended short story, the subject, the themes and the author's treatment of them are vintage Greene. It is a tale of cowardice, and redemption: "after all, anybody's liable to play the coward once. Most of us do and forget about it . . . All one's life one has to think: Today it may happen . . . When it happens you know what you've been all your life." Graham Greene relates the background to the belated publication of this long-lost gem in his introduction to the book, which also includes the outline of a story called "Jim Braddon and the War Criminal" and a film sketch entitled "Nobody to Blame".

In Barbara Pym's recently published autobiography there is reference to a previously unknown novel, her second, entitled *Crampton Hodnet*, which was written in 1940 when she was 26. She set the novel aside during the War, and afterwards felt it too old-fashioned and dated and never submitted it for publication. The manuscript was traced to the Bodleian Library, and has now been issued. It relates the story of Francis Cleveland, a lecturer in 17th century English literature at Randolph College, Oxford, who is seen with a student in the Botanical Gardens, and wrongly suspected of adultery. There are signs of immaturity in the writing, but the book is to be welcomed as completing the Pym *oeuvre*, and illustrating her development. By contrast, Richard Adams shows signs of regression rather than development; his *Maia* inhabits the same imagined world as *Shardik*, but says very little, in its 1000-plus pages, of interest to any except devotees of the Beklan Empire.

Ernest Hemingway's last major work has now been published as *The Dangerous Summer*. Hemingway was commissioned by *Life* magazine in 1959 to write this postscript to *Death in the Afternoon*, and it recounts the rivalry between Spain's two leading matadors, Antonio Ordonez and Luis Miguel Dominguin. Some 30,000 words appeared in the magazine in 1960, and the 108,000 words of the manuscript were cut to 80,000 for publication in book form in 1961, but publication was cancelled on his death. The book now published contains some 55,000 words, with Hemingway past his best but still worth reading, especially for *aficionados* of the *corrida*.

Graham Greene also published an account of his friendship with General Omar Torrijas Herrera, ruler of Panama from 1968 to 1981, entitled *Getting to Know the General*. Greene had first visited the central American state in 1976, and the book is based on his diaries. Subtitled "The Story of an Involvement", it seems that Greene did not actually get to know the General very well, and this is a curiously impersonal and lightweight piece.

Houses on the Site is the fourth novel in Stuart Evans' "Windmill Hill" sequence, and is an accomplished but difficult work, about educated and articulate people living in their own community in Sussex.

The House of Spirits by Isabel Allende, niece of the Chilean Marxist president, is a family saga covering four generations, with those magical and fantastic elements that seem obligatory in the South American novel.

Nobel

The 1984 Nobel Prize for Literature was awarded to the dissident Czech poet, Jaroslav Seifert. According to the citation, he was chosen for his poetry "which, endowed with freshness, sensuality, and rich inventiveness, provides a liberating image of the indomitable spirit of man". His best-known volumes are *Clothed in Light* and *On Wireless Waves*. Seifert has no great international reputation, but is well thought of in Czechoslovakia, where his writings were banned for many years, as he represents the pre-invasion era. This award again raises the question of whether the Nobel Prize should be awarded to the most deserving candidate on literary grounds, or whether, like the Peace Prize, political considerations should intrude. If a Czech writer was due the award the first choice of many would have been the exiled novelist Milan Kundera, who has an international reputation; but then many people were surprised that Golding should have been honoured before Graham Greene, who is prominent among a distinguished band (such as Hardy, Conrad, Henry James, D. H. Lawrence, Proust, Kafka, and Borges, to name but a few) who have been passed over. Unfortunately, the financial clout of Nobel assures its publicity out of all proportion to its worth as a yardstick of international literary ability.

Awards

The Whitbread Literary Awards, presented with less brouhaha than Booker, are spread over a wider literary field. The prize for best novel was awarded to Christopher Hope for *Kruger's Alp*, and Peter Ackroyd received the biography award for his life of *T. S. Eliot. A Parish of Rich Women*, by James Buchan, a runner-up for the first Betty Trask Award, was adjudged best first novel, and the best children's novel was *The Queen of the Pharisees' Children* by Barbara Willard. The best short story by a writer aged 16–25 was won by Diane Rowe, for "Tomorrow is Our Permanent Address". The Wolfson Literary Award was shared by Maurice Keen for *Chivalry* and Antonia Fraser for *The Weaker Vessel*. The John Llewellyn Rees Memorial Prize was awarded to Andrew Motion for his collection of poems entitled *Dangerous Play*. The 27th W. H. Smith Annual Literary Award was won by David Hughes for his novel *The Pork Butcher*, another conspicuous absentee from the Booker lists. The 2nd Betty Trask Award, for first novels of a romantic or traditional nature by writers aged under 35, was awarded to Susan Kay for *Legacy*, with the runners-up Elizabeth Ironside for *A Very Private Enterprise* and Gary Armitage for *A Season of Peace*.

The late-lamented John Betjeman was succeeded as Poet Laureate by Ted Hughes, a choice which surprised many who thought the honour was Philip Larkin's for the asking. Hughes is a distinguished modern poet, and may well prove an inspired selection for a position that is largely anachronistic in the present day.

Authors' Rights

What must seem like annual literary prizes to many writers struggling to make ends meet are the payments from the Public Lending Right Fund, now in its second year. 47 authors received the maximum pay-out of £5,000 (1 more than in 1984), but 1,715 of those registered received no payment. The rate per loan was reduced from 1·02p to 0·92p, because of the wider criteria for eligibility and the growing number of authors registering. The average payment was £216 (1984, £261), and the money was shared between 9,395 authors. Particularly commendable in the execution of this worthy if long-overdue measure of justice for writers was the fact that the administration costs were actually reduced (to £338,000 from £412,000 out of the £2 million allocated by the Government) and that the Fund for the forthcoming year is to be increased to £2·75 million.

Solzhenitsyn

"Solzhenitsyn speaks from another tradition and this, for me, is impressive: his voice is not modern but ancient. It is an ancientness tempered in the modern world. His ancientness is that of the old Russian Christianity, but it is a Christianity that has passed through the central experience of our century—the dehumanization of the totalitarian concentration camps—and has emerged intact and strengthened. If history is the testing ground, Solzhenitsyn has passed the test...." In his massive biography, Michael Scammell cites the above words of Octavio Paz, which give some idea of the force that drives Solzhenitsyn, one of the major figures of 20th century literature. A brilliant but difficult man, his influence in the West has waned since his dramatic expulsion from the Soviet Union in 1974, but Michael Scammell shows that Solzhenitsyn's life and his development has mirrored Soviet society and the history of Communism in the 20th century, which can better be understood through him. Scammell had some assistance from the writer in the preparation of the work, which runs to 1,000 pages, but it is neither authorized nor approved as an official biography. At times the mass of detail becomes overwhelming, but the subject is worthy of the treatment, and this must be counted as the definitive work, only to be amended or approved in the light of new information or developments in Solzhenitsyn's life and work. "Solzhenitsyn's is a personality that is writ uncommonly large. It would be idle to deny that he is a man with substantial faults, as well as with some towering virtues. Some have called him a saint, a prophet, a political visionary, a living literary classic. Others think him a megalomaniac, a monster of egotism, and a literary mediocrity." Scammell's aim has been "not to act as advocate or judge, but to illuminate and explain a quintessential Russian and a major figure of our era."

Coffee Spoons

J. Alfred Prufrock "measured out (his) life with coffee spoons": Peter Ackroyd has now taken the measure of the life of one of the most influential 20th century poets in his excellent biography of *T. S. Eliot*. Eliot had not wanted his life to be written, and so the author was forbidden by the Eliot estate to quote from his published work, except for purposes of fair comment in a critical context, or to quote from his unpublished work or correspondence. Ackroyd has made a virtue out of what to many would have been an insuperable obstacle, and has presented a detailed portrait of a very private man which places his life and work in a proper relation to each other. In his prelude he states: "Thomas Stearns Eliot, in his last years, declared that there had been only two periods of his life when he had been happy—during his childhood, and during his second marriage. This will be in large part an account of the years between, the years in which he wrote his poetry. The best of that poetry, he once confessed, had cost him dearly in experience; the connection between the life and the work is here explicitly made, and it will be the purpose of this book to attempt to elucidate the mystery of that connection." As noted above, Ackroyd was the well-deserved winner of the Whitbread Award for this meticulously researched biography, which closes with Eliot's own words on Edwin Muir, to justify what may be seen by some as a breach of Eliot's privacy: "We also understand the poetry better when we know more about the man."

Wells Beloved

The H. G. Wells industry flourishes, following the publication last year of Anthony West's *Heritage* and *Aspects of a Life*. With the death of Dame Rebecca West, it has now been possible to publish the final part of Wells's *Experiment in Autobiography. H. G. Wells in Love* was written in the 1930s as an extension and completion of that work, and to correct "the dangers of posthumous misrepresentation". Whether these amorous confessions will enhance his reputation is doubtful, but they will certainly present a fuller picture of his life; ". . . all these women I have kissed, solicited, embraced and lived with, have never entered intimately and deeply into my emotional life". His relationships with Odette Keun, Amber Reeves, Moura Budberg and Rebecca West are chronicled in detail; of West he wrote, "I do not know if I loved Rebecca West, though I was certainly in love with her towards the latter part of our liaison". When one of the women he had treated badly attempted to commit suicide in his flat, Wells managed to avoid any whiff of scandal by consulting the press barons Beaverbrook and Rothermere, who instructed their editors to ignore any stories about him.

The Mysterious Affair at Harrogate

Agatha Christie's autobiography was published in 1977, the year after her death, but a fuller, objective account, has now been written by Janet Morgan, who has had access to her private papers and cooperation from her family and friends. The central incident in Agatha Christie's life has always been her mysterious disappearance in 1926, after her first husband, Colonel Archie Christie, had informed her that he had fallen in love with another woman. The story dominated the news, and showed that the excesses of the popular press are not a recent phenomenon. She was eventually found in Harrogate, registered under the name of the woman for whom her husband had left her. The whole incident is well handled by Janet Morgan, who presents a thoroughly researched account of a woman whose life was otherwise remarkably devoid of incident.

Also published was John Halperin's *The Life of Jane Austen*, the first major critical biography of her since 1938, and a scholarly and authoritative study of her life and works, containing much perceptive critical analysis.

Mountbatten

"His vanity, though child-like, was monstrous, his ambition unbridled. The truth, in his hands, was swiftly converted from what it was to what it should have been. He sought to rewrite history with cavalier indifference to the facts to magnify his own achievements." Such a verdict in a major biography of a dominant 20th century figure shows only too clearly that *Mountbatten: The Official Biography* is no hagiography, but neither is it a hatchet-job. Philip Ziegler has had unrestricted access to his subject's official papers and produced a model study of his life. His analysis is masterly, not least on the more controversial aspects, such as the ill-fated Dieppe raid, Mountbatten's time as Governor-General of India, and his actions as First Sea Lord during the Suez crisis. Mountbatten is portrayed as "royal, rich, glamorous, eloquent, internationally celebrated, dynamic, arrogantly self-confident. . . curiously vulnerable". A great, but flawed, man, who "flared brilliantly across the face of the 20th century; the meteor is extinguished but the glow lingers in the mind's eye".

Chamberlain

Neville Chamberlain is best remembered for his return from Munich in 1938, and the unfortunate words, "Peace in our time". David Dilks has now written a scholarly assessment of this widely misunderstood politician, and has been greatly assisted by the release of official papers, which he has compared with the private papers to compile a detailed portrait. *Neville Chamberlain: Volume 1, 1869–1929, Pioneering and Reform* helps show what governed Chamberlain's actions, and provides the background that determined why he acted as he did in the 1930s and underestimated Hitler. Chamberlain had entered politics late, having been overshadowed by his domineering father Joseph and his half-brother Austen, who had been made Chancellor of the Exchequer by the time he was 40 years of age. Neville had been sent to the Bahamas when young, to restore the family fortunes by growing sisal; the venture had failed, losing £50,000 and he had endeavoured to redeem himself by his business concerns in Birmingham and service to that city. Chamberlain had not entered national politics until he was nearly 50, and was plucked from obscurity by Lloyd George to be Director of National Service in the First World War. His career was in fact marked by a reluctance for high office, and he was widely disliked—Austen said of him, it was "his coldness which kills". This volume is particularly good on his successful tenure of the Ministry of Health, and on his relations with Lloyd George, Baldwin and Churchill. Dilks portrays him as a "figure of wide culture, many international connections and much reserve in his personal dealings, but with astonishing energy and resourcefulness in administration and boldness in policy". His half-brother's own distinguished career is dealt with in *Austen Chamberlain: Gentleman in Politics?* by David Dutton.

The third volume in John Grigg's definitive biography of Lloyd George has now been published. *Lloyd George: From Peace to War, 1912–1916* contains penetrating analysis of such key events in his life as the Marconi scandal, his affair with his secretary Frances Stevenson, the war crises and the displacement of Asquith.

Mr. Speaker contains the memoirs of George Thomas, now Viscount Tonypandy, whose political career seemed to have reached its peak when he became Secretary of State for Wales. However, his elevation to the Speakership in 1976, the office which he graced till 1983, won him the love and respect of the House of Commons, and of the British public. That he has a sharper side is shown by his remarks about some of his one-time political allies, such as former premier James Callaghan and former leader of the Labour Party Michael Foot, who were stung into responding to his waspish comments, accusing him of breaches of confidence and misusing the position he had held with such widespread acclaim.

In *Hugh Dalton*, Ben Pimlott relates the career of the leading Labour politician, who is now best remembered for his indiscreet remarks to a journalist when, as Chancellor of the Exchequer, he was on his way in to the Chamber of the House of Commons to deliver his 1947 Budget speech; the infamous "leak" led to his resignation.

Barbara Castle was a prominent member of the labour administrations under Harold Wilson, until her summary dismissal by his successor James Callaghan. *The Castle Diaries 1964–1970* are only for those as steeped in and addicted to politics as their perpetrator, for yet another perspective on a Government that seems to have driven almost all of its leading members in to print. More rewarding and entertaining is Julian Critchley's irreverent exposé of parliament, *Westminster Blues*.

Law Books

Lord Denning, former Master of the Rolls, has followed a distinguished career on the Bench with several successful incursions into print. In *Landmarks in the Law*, he discusses such important episodes in British legal history as the Tolpuddle Martyrs, the Libyan Embassy siege, the Cheltenham GCHQ affair and the Profumo scandal (the public inquiry into which he chaired). Lord Denning has a succinct and staccato prose style, and a remarkable ability to penetrate to the essential facts of a matter. He takes as his motto in this book the words of Thomas Fuller (which he himself used to devastating effect against the one-time Attorney-General Sam Silkin): "Be you ever so high, the law is above you."

Another legal landmark is registered with the publication of *Easing the Passing: The Trial of Dr. John Bodkin Adams*, believed to be the first account of an English trial by the judge who presided. Lord Devlin was renowned for his incisive mind, and his analysis of the notorious 1957 murder trial, in which the Eastbourne doctor Adams was accused of the murder of an elderly patient, is a masterpiece and a valuable counterbalance to the other accounts of this *cause célèbre* which have appeared in print. "A quarter of a century is long enough to allow publication without indecorum and not too long to destroy recollection", writes Patrick Devlin: his readers will concur, whilst mourning his premature retirement from the Bench.

Companion of Literature

The long-awaited revised edition of *The Oxford Companion to English Literature* has now been published. Sir Paul Harvey's first edition was issued in 1932, his original purpose being to provide "a useful companion to ordinary everyday readers of English literature", by compiling "a list of English authors, literary works, and literary societies which have historical or present importance". Margaret Drabble has remained faithful to Harvey's original intentions in her volume, which has some 9,000 entries on authors, their works, clubs, coffee houses, literary societies, printers, publishers, private presses, critics, philosophers, scholars and editors. In 1,150 pages, the entries range from *Aaron's Rod* by D. H. Lawrence to *Zuleika Dobson* by Max Beerbohm, and covers the intellectual movements from Acmeism to Vorticism, by way of Structuralism. Harvey's appendices on copyright, calendars and censorship have been updated, and the book is informative and fascinating. The compiler has included authors born in or before 1939, but some of the modern writers have received entries of disproportionate length to their importance; although the emphasis is rightly on primary information rather than critical appreciation, this distortion mars an otherwise splendid work of reference. One notable omission, no doubt on grounds of modesty, is Margaret Drabble herself, an accomplished author, especially since she has included an entry for the infamous William McGonagall, perpetrator of "naive and unscanned doggerel . . . [who] enjoys a reputation as the world's worst poet".

The New Oxford Book of Eighteenth Century Verse, chosen and edited by Roger Lonsdale, is both an excellent anthology and a major work of scholarship. It contains 550 poems from 250 poets, one-quarter of whom had not been reprinted since their first publication, with generous selections from Swift, Pope, Gray, Goldsmith, Blake and Burns. Lonsdale's intention, to give a "more complete picture of an age, which was less stable, decorous, and inhibited than is often assumed", is triumphantly realized.

Jon Stallworthy's *The Oxford Book of War Poetry* is less satisfactory, and its organization, chronologically by date of conflict rather than by date of birth of poet, causes some confusion. It encompasses the Bible—"Then sang Moses and the Children of Israel . . . The Lord is a man of war"—Homer, Virgil, Milton, Marvell, Dryden, Defoe, Shelley, Tennyson, Byron, Hardy, Kipling, Yeats, Sassoon, Owen and Auden, ending with Peter Porter's vision of nuclear war, "Your Attention Please", with the chilling final words, "Now go quickly to your shelters."

Also of note were Martin Seymour-Smith's revised *Macmillan Guide to Modern World Literature*, first issued in 1973; *A Comprehensive Grammar of the English Language* by Professor Randolph Quirk, and *The Craft of Literary Biography*, edited by Jeffrey Meyers.

Also published during the year were: *An Egyptian Journal* by William Golding; *Cousin Randolph: The Life of Randolph Churchill* by Anita Leslie; *Now to My Mother: A Very Personal Memoir of Antonia White* by Susan Chitty; *Paths from a White Horse: A Writer's Memoir* by Peter Vansittart; *SOE* by M. R. D. Foot; *Chaplin—His Life and Art* by David Robinson; *A Traveller in Romance: Uncollected Writings 1901–1964* by W. Somerset Maugham, edited by John Whitehead; *Queen Victoria in Her Letters and Journals*, selected by Christopher Hibbert; and *The Oxford Book of Ages*, chosen by Anthony and Sally Sampson.

ARCHAEOLOGY IN 1984–85

Swanscombe Revisited

The 50th anniversary of the discovery of the first fragment of the Swanscombe Skull in 1935 was marked by the Nature Conservancy Council (the present owners of the site which has been a National Nature Reserve since 1954) with the "Swanscombe Man Event". This included the cutting of two sections through the sediments which were available for public inspection over the weekend of 29 June–1 July, 1985 and the publication of *The Story of Swanscombe Man*.

The Swanscombe Skull Site, in what was once known as the Barnfield Pit, lies on the south bank of the Thames Estuary between Dartford and Gravesend in Kent. It is one of the most important archaeological locations in the U.K. as well as one of the very few to have an international reputation. Geologically, the Barnfield Pit has been recognized during the last century as providing a typical section of the 100 ft. terrace of the Thames. The Pleistocene stratigraphic sequence of gravels, sands, and loams, indicates in climatic terms four cold phases alternating with three temperate ones and is significant for the study especially of the Middle Pleistocene, not only for the British Isles but in a European context as well.

At least thirty different species of mammals have been identified, including elephants, rhinoceros, bears, lions, and monkeys. In addition, some tens of thousands of flint implements have been recovered, some of which provide evidence for the existence on the site of an early Clactonian flint industry, which did, of course, pre-date the Acheulian flint hand-axes associated with the skull fragments. Naturally, because of the discovery of the flint hand-axes the area had attracted investigators for over a century, the first published reference being in 1883. Organized excavations were undertaken in 1912–13, 1937, 1955–60 and in 1968–72.

The first fragment, an occipital bone, of what has come to be known as the Swanscombe Skull, was found on a Saturday afternoon, 29 June, in 1935 by a Clapham dentist who was an amateur archaeologist; the same person recovered the left parietal of the skull on 15 March, 1936, while the right parietal bone was discovered by a professional archaeologist on 30 July, 1955; this last bone fragment fitted to those found almost twenty years earlier.

Together, the skull fragments represent some of the oldest human remains to have been found in Europe and scientific study suggests that they belonged to a young woman who lived about a quarter of a million years ago. However, one of the main problems is to determine precisely where in the evolutionary scale these human remains should be placed, a difficulty compounded by the lack of comparative evidence. Indeed, not only is the Swanscombe Skull the only example of this type known from the British Isles, but there would appear to be only one similar find from Continental Europe—the skull from Steinheim in Germany. There is general agreement that these two individuals belong to the species *Homo sapiens* and were therefore the ancestors of ourselves, so-called "modern man", *Homo sapiens sapiens*. However, specialists also see characteristics which relate these two skulls to those of Neanderthal man, an extinct form of *Homo sapiens* who lived between about 100,000 to 35,000 years ago. Therefore on the present evidence it is appropriate to see the Steinheim and Swanscombe skulls as representing a distinct hominid sub-species, now extinct, which has been designated *homo sapiens steinheimensis*.

"Pete Marsh" or the Lindow Man

The appearance of a human leg and foot on the elevator at a peat mill on the 1 August, 1984 led archaeologists, police, and other specialists to the related remains of a man lying face down, sliced at the waist by a peat cutting machine, at Lindow Moss, near Wilmslow in Cheshire. During the past year enormous public interest has been shown in the excavation of the body and its subsequent investigation at the British Museum. This is the first prehistoric "bog body" to be found in Great Britain, at least in recent times, and the remains are similar to those discovered in Denmark, where nine burials have been dated to the first millennium B.C.

This great interest is justified because, unlike most other archaeologically excavated human remains, Lindow Man—or "Pete Marsh" to give him his colloquial name—has much of his skin and tissue surviving as a result of the circumstances of his deposition in what was probably a shallow pool in the bog. Usually only the skeleton survives, more or less intact, or in cases of extreme acidity no more than a stain in the ground remains to tell the archaeologists that a body was once present.

Although the careful work of the scientific investigation of the remains continues, it is clear that the person in question was once a man of just over twenty-five years of age at the time of his death some 2,500 years ago. He had mousey coloured hair, a red moustache, beard and sideburns, as well as well-manicured fingernails, indicating perhaps an unfamiliarity with heavy manual work.

The importance of this discovery has prompted an interim report entitled *Lindow Man* by I. Stead and R. C. Turner published in *Antiquity*, Volume LIX, for 1985. Of particular significance was the discovery that around the neck was a twisted sinew which had cut in so deeply as to cause the vertebrae to separate, thus suggesting death by garrotting rather than by hanging.

The examination by Dr. Iain West of the Department of Forensic Medicine at Guy's Hospital enabled him to suggest "a sequence of events starting with Lindow Man being felled by a weapon resembling a narrow-bladed axe: he had been struck twice on the top of the head, with sufficient force to drive pieces of bone deep into the cranium. Stunned, but not necessarily killed, he was then garrotted: the sinew was tied tightly round the throat (and the loose ends trimmed close to the knot), a stick was inserted at the side of the neck to twist the sinew, and the neck was broken between the third and fourth cervical vertebrae. Finally, the throat seems to have been slit with a sharp deep cut to the right of the larynx, possibly severing the jugular vein."

Roman Britain

A comprehensive account of current work relevant to the Roman period may be found in *Britannia*, Vol. XV for 1984. Among the reports, it may be noted that excavations have been carried out on the fort at Newcastle in Tyne and Wear which lies within the confines of the existing medieval castle. It was found that the *principia* faced north and consisted of a cross-hall in front of two rooms, one of which was a sunken strong room. At least half of the *principia* lies underneath the present castle keep. Also discovered, was evidence of a building which once had a hypocaust, as well as the remains of two granaries. "It is suggested, on the evidence of rather scant pottery and an inscription of Julia Domna, that this fort was built in the late second or early third century." At Chesters in Northumberland excavations were undertaken in advance of consolidation of the east bridge abutment. The inside of the tower was excavated resulting in evidence of an earlier abutment being found. The large stone blocks which had probably provided the river-bank retaining-wall had been robbed, but stone slabs had been left on the river bed to give foundations for the tower. As a portion of the original floor in the tower survived and as above it there was a hearth, it was possible to obtain an archaeomagnetic date from the latter, which was A.D. 220 ± 10. Moving on to Greater Manchester, it is particularly noteworthy that the investigations of three small sites just south of The Wiend "revealed the first Roman structures to be recorded in Wigan." The evidence includes a gravel street on the north side of which were timber buildings of three periods. It would seem that the dating is from the early second to the early third century A.D. An important discovery in Cheshire was the site of a second fort in Northwich which is to

the west of and probably partly overlapping the one already discovered. The area investigated was the Bowling Green on the north side of the Chester road and a ditch five metres wide with a rampart was discovered as well as the *via sagularis*. There were traces of timber buildings and evidence that the fort had been reduced in size. "A provisional suggestion is that the fort was first built during one of the periods in the second century when Scotland was abandoned."

In Nottinghamshire at Scaftworth, Bawtry, the opportunity was taken to check indications from field work and aerial photographs that the Roman road crossed the River Idle north of Bawtry fort. The excavation did indeed show that there was a timber causeway in good condition, road-metalling, and two lines of pointed stakes which had been driven through the metalling which rested on substantial transverse timbers between longitudinal ones. At Mancetter in Warwickshire, the investigation of various sites "has revealed the outline of a probable vexillation fortress of the pre-Flavian period". At Cherry Tree Farm, four pottery kilns and other features were recovered during excavations in advance of pipe-laying. Three more kilns were found to the north-west and "In both areas mortaria and coarse wares were being made in the second and third centuries." At Wasperton in the same county, excavations on a crop-mark site threatened by gravel extraction, revealed features of Iron Age to Pagan Saxon date, amongst which was a pit which contained a slab of local sandstone on which was inscribed *feliciter*, while "above this a layer of heavily-burnt material embraced two sets of unburnt antlers with parts of the skulls still attached, arranged to form a square." There was also a cemetery which seemed to have been in use from late Roman into Saxon times, and of the 200 inhumations and 21 cremations which have been investigated, some 82 of the former and 20 of the latter were Saxon while at least 17 inhumations were Romano-British. The Romano-British bodies tended to have been buried with their heads pointing to the north, although a few are orientated to the east, while the Saxon inhumations have their heads to the south or west.

At Haddenham in Cambridgeshire, the site of a shrine was excavated on a gravel peninsular which projected into the peat fens. It was found that this feature overlay a Bronze Age barrow and was near an Iron Age penannular ditched enclosure. "The first-phase shrine, of the late first or early second century, overlay ten Bronze Age cremations (over which turf had first been deposited) and was represented by an octagon of shallow gravel footings on the south part of the barrow; there was an eastern porch approached by a ditched path. The temenos was a rectangular enclosure embracing the barrow and formed of a turf bank and shallow ditches later recut and deepened. Within the building lay a complete skeleton of goat or sheep and around the interior were four clusters of sheep/goat mandibles with hooves laid on either side; two jaws were accompanied by coins. Five more sheep/goat skeletons, each associated with a pot, lay beside a square emplacement of gravel within the north-west corner of the temenos, which also yielded votive deposits of cattle mandibles and a boar's skeleton." In Oxfordshire at Watkins' Farm, Northmoor, excavations prior to gravel extraction revealed an Iron Age and Romano-British settlement "previously unknown". In the neighbouring county of Buckinghamshire, the Bancroft Mausoleum and Shrine were investigated, the former building, resembling in plan a Romano-Celtic temple, was found to have had stone foundations and to have been of fourth century date. A small circular stone building to the north-west was of similar date and has been interpreted as a shrine. Between the two buildings lay some eight inhumations on a north-south line with their heads to the west and without any grave goods. Three were males aged between thirty and fifty, while one was a pregnant female aged eighteen to twenty-four, and four were children under four years of age. It is noted that most of the graves were stone lined and in three were found fragments of columns and capitals. At Baldock in Hertfordshire, "a rich Belgic cremation accompanied by a bronze-bound wooden vessel, a pig's skeleton and fragments of chain mail was recovered with satellite burials within a ditched enclosure 37 m. square; it underlay a Romano-British corn-drier."

Over in the West Country at Claydon Pike in Gloucestershire, two shrines were investigated, the first being a rectangular enclosure surrounded by ditches, having much pottery and glass in association, as well as two rolled strips of lead, three stone columns and part of a carved capital. By contrast, the second shrine was circular and had a flagged floor. "Within were over two hundred third and fourth century coins, a complete beaker, a bronze votive leaf and a miniature bronze votive axe." At Kingsholm, Gloucester, in the area covered by the cemetery of the *colonia* some twenty-three adult and child inhumations were found. Their heads were to the west, there were no grave goods and nails indicated the former presence of wooden coffins. Together with a further group of nine coffined inhumations with the same orientation it is suggested that "these may represent a Christian cemetery." At Gambier Parry Lodge, north Kingsholm there was a cemetery of about 125 burials. "There were cremations in urns and both crouched and supine coffined inhumations. Jewellery, coins of Constantine I and pottery of the first to fourth centuries

were associated. A stone tombstone with figure in relief records a veteran of Legion XX." In the southern counties, excavations were completed at Great Cansiron Farm, Hartfield, East Sussex, in the course of which a tile-kiln and drying-shed were investigated while to the east a possible workers' hut was noted. In addition to roller-stamped tiles, there were wasters indicating that pottery was also being made.

Amongst the great many discoveries from London there is one which illuminates the social life of the time. At St. Mary Overy Dock in Southwark a broken amphora was found, which had been dumped in its entirety and contained fish bones, probably mackerel, as well as a few iris and box seeds. There was an inscription on the neck which has been translated as "Lucius (?) Tettius Africanus' finest fish sauce from Antipolis, (product) of Africanus"!

More from Sutton Hoo

The now famous Anglo-Saxon ship burial from Sutton Hoo, the contents of which were so generously presented to the nation by the landowner, Mrs. Pretty, after a jury had decided the precious objects were not treasure trove, has received substantial recent media coverage. Not least this is because of the opening of the re-displayed Early Medieval Room in the British Museum. This has enabled the magnificent items from this burial of Anglo-Saxon Royalty to be shown in association with other material of the relevant period from the British Isles and Europe, after they had been conserved in accordance with the latest techniques.

The site itself has also been receiving renewed attention and this not for the first time, for after the initial 1938–39 excavations, a British Museum team returned to work there between 1965 and 1971. However, the recently established Sutton Hoo Research Project has now completed its first year's work, with the result that the size of the cemetery is known to be double what it was previously thought to be. In addition to the fourteen barrows, under the largest of which was found the famous ship-burial, there were also much less grand inhumations. Some of these have now been found well away from the area of the barrows during the course of the excavations to determine the extent of the original cemetery and also that of the prehistoric habitation on the site. While the latter had already been known, the recent excavations have shown areas of both Neolithic and considerable Bronze Age occupation.

As the burials are not consistent so far as orientation is concerned, the following observations were prompted and are noted in *Current Archaeology* no. 95: "This variety of orientation emphasizes what the excavator calls the eclecticism of Sutton Hoo; they drew inspiration from all over Northern Europe. Thus their jewellery and regalia drew on Germanic, late Antique, Scandinavian and native British traditions. Some burials were in barrows, some in flat graves, some were inhumed and others were cremated. Some of the barrow burials were in ships, others, apparently not. This variety of burial rite might be caused by differences in chronology, social position or belief; whatever the answer, the site has great potential for the interpretation of the society which built it, and this remains the goal of the present campaign."

The Medieval Period

Recent investigations concerning the medieval period are noted in *Medieval Archaeology* Vol. XXVIII for 1984. Among them may be recalled the rescue excavations at Brill in Buckinghamshire, an important centre for ceramic production. These investigations revealed a kiln of "two opposed stoke-pits and a funnel-shaped, brick-built flue, presumably part of an up draught pedestal clamp." In association, there were a number of deep pits either for storage or sand quarries. To the west, there was a trench which had been sealed by the remains of two fired clay bases which may have been used for making bricks needed for the second kiln, which had a rectangular firing chamber. Dating to the late fifteenth century, it is noted that: "The design of the structure is clearly that of a roof-tile kiln, which, very unusually, was subsequently used to fire pottery. In fact, there was approximately three times the quantity of pottery wasters to tile wasters; most of the latter were crested ridge tiles. Large numbers of sagger sherds were found, and these had been used to fire small jugs and Cistercian-type cups. The other predominant forms were large jars, pancheons, jugs and bung-hole pitchers."

Moving north-west to Cheshire, the deserted medieval village site around Tatton Old Hall has been investigated. It was established that the early hall was timber-framed and had been foreshortened perhaps in the early eighteenth century, while an adjacent structure in use in the late fifteenth/early sixteenth centuries was probably a kitchen. It is noted that the earliest occupation of the hall was in the latter part of the fifteenth century and its construction indicates a shift in emphasis away from the village street. The occupation of the village site was found to extend from the late prehistoric and Roman periods up to about 1400 when the pottery sequence stops. In Gloucester, the final season of excavations at St. Oswald's Priory was carried out and resulted in the addition of three phases to the late Saxon development of the Minster built by Aethelflaed of Mercia in about 890. It is possible now to reconstruct the complete plans of the late ninth and tenth century church. Another religious site where excavations have been completed is that of St. Mary's Abbey in Winchester, where a radio-carbon date for industrial refuse, probably concerned with iron-smithing, has been obtained of about 800 A.D. At St. Peter's church, Barton-upon-Humber, excavations in the cemetery revealed another eleven preserved Anglo-Saxon timbered coffins and like ones previously discovered these are all of oak except for one: "a child's coffin in pine is the most perfectly preserved of all and is potentially a Scandinavian import. Some eighteen late Saxon coffins (without preserved timbers) had been filled at the time of burial with riverine mud, completely enveloping the corpse; this is seen as temporary protection against the spread of contagious disease."

On the site of Stratford Langthorne Abbey in the London borough of Newham, excavations disclosed part of the chancel as well as the north transept of the Abbey church. The wall lines of the north-east part of the chancel and the north transept were recorded. There was a lime kiln near the church in the cemetery and a wide selection of building material was recovered including carved and painted stone and floor tiles. From the cemetery, about 150 skeletons, most of which had not been in coffins, were recovered. At Middle Harling in Norfolk, excavations were undertaken in an arable field which lay within the confines of this deserted village and was centered on the site of a dispersed hoard of pennies of the mid-eighth century East Anglian king, Beonna. Part of the graveyard of St. Andrew's Church was within the area investigated and although most of the burials were medieval, "one accompanied by a bronze buckle, hone stone, iron knives and an iron strike-a-light, was late Saxon. There were many finds in the top soil of Middle Saxon to Medieval date and among these was a silver seal matrix enclosing an antique intaglio. It is noted that the Middle Saxon pottery was almost entirely Ipswich-type ware, while the Saxo-Norman pottery was of Thetford-type, St. Neot's and early medieval wares, whereas Headingham ware was the only glazed pottery used in the late twelfth and early thirteenth centuries. At Watchfield in Oxfordshire, work on the Shrivenham bypass led to the discovery of an Anglo-Saxon cemetery. It is reported that under difficult conditions twenty-seven inhumations of fifth to sixth century date were investigated. "The earliest burial excavated may date from the first half of the 5th century A.D., but most are of the later 5th or 6th century. These include the grave of a woman buried with a pair of gilt-bronze saucer brooches, and iron cloak-pin, a pair of bronze tweezers and a string of amber beads, and that of a warrior buried with his sword, spear, shield, knife and a bronze cauldron which may have been made in the Rhineland. Another male burial contained an iron knife and iron shield-boss, an elaborate bronze belt buckle and fittings, and a balance inside the remains of a leather and bronze case which also contained weights and Roman coins." Evidence of late Saxon occupation was found during excavations in Stafford where at Tipping Street there was evidence for the production of Stafford ware in the form of two kilns which were excavated. Large quantities of wasters were examined and some new forms of vessels recovered. It is noted that "The end of the pottery industry was marked by large-scale dumping of rubbish and use of the area for cultivation. By the 12th to 13th centuries, timber houses had been built on the Tipping and Eastgate Street frontages." Coming south to Reigate in Surrey, investigations at 16 Bell Street enabled the medieval origins of a domestic building to be demonstrated. The discovery of a penny of Henry VIII in the upper of three floor layers confirmed its demolition in the sixteenth century. Below the house, a coin, an Angouleme denier, probably of late twelfth century date was found in grey sandy loam at the base of which was a spread of large pottery sherds dating to about 1200, which satisfactorily relates to the evidence of the coin.

The Abbey of St. Mary Graces

The Royal Mint, since 1975 based at Llantrisant in Wales, was once housed in an 1806 building on the site of the former Abbey of St. Mary Graces, otherwise known as Eastminster, at Tower Hill in London, and the latter has been the subject of recent excavations by the Museum of London.

The Abbey has an interesting history, the area being in 1136 a vineyard belonging to Holy Trinity Priory, Aldgate, but was converted to an emergency burial ground when the City churchyards could no longer cope with the level of mortality caused by the Black Death in 1345. This plot with its chapel was purchased by King Edward III, who had sworn in 1350 that if he survived a rough Channel crossing he would found an Abbey dedicated to Our Lady of Grace.

This the King did and the new Abbey of Our Lady of Grace, or St. Mary Graces became, although it could not be known at the time, the last Cistercian house to be founded in Britain and indeed one of the very few established in an urban environment. By 1391, the Abbey church was substantially complete and the Abbey was to become a centre of the Order where the General Chapter of Cistercian Abbots met. It also became particularly wealthy, not least from the rents of its urban properties, and by the time of its surrender in 1538 during the Dissolution of the Monasteries under King Henry VIII, it was the third richest Cistercian house in Britain after Fountains and Furness.

The excavations by the Museum of London on this important monastic site have revealed medieval walls standing to a height of 2·5 metres. In addition, by comparing the newly discovered archaeological remains with the earliest known plan of the site of 1623 it is possible to make a provisional reconstruction of the Cistercian conventual plan. On the basis of this interpretation it was demonstrated that the walls of the Infirmary survived to a height of 1·8 metres above floor level, the Lady Chapel built in about 1490 had walls surviving some 1 to 1·8 metres high, whilst those of the South Transept reached 2·4 metres. These excavations have therefore shown that the Abbey of St. Mary Graces is unique in central London in respect of the extent of the preservation of its medieval fabric.

Battlefield St. Mary Magdalene

In open country about three miles to the north of Shrewsbury in Shropshire stands the isolated Church of Battlefield St. Mary Magdalene. While we have become accustomed to the existence of deserted medieval villages where only the church survives, or, villages which have moved their centres of population leaving the parish churches isolated, Battlefield St. Mary never was associated with a village, because it was erected on the sight of the Battle of Shrewsbury (fought in 1403) as a memorial to those who died in the carnage.

Originally served by a Rector and a College of Chaplains until 1547 when the College was dissolved and the chapel became a parish church, it was in a ruinous condition by the mid-eighteenth century but was subsequently restored. Still preserving its collegiate design, this remarkable Church which provides a direct and specific link with an event of considerable significance in the history of England, has been vested in the Redundant Churches Fund, being described in the latter's *Fifteenth Annual Report.*

NFU MUTUAL AND AVON INSURANCE GROUP HQ BUILDING, STRATFORD-UPON-AVON

Architect: Robert Matthew,
Johnson-Marshall & Partners

In 1978, the National Farmers Union Mutual and the Avon Insurance Group, two established insurance companies who were at that time based in a number of separate buildings in Stratford-upon-Avon, made a joint decision to move to a new purpose-built combined headquarters building on the edge of the town. Not surprisingly, for people used to life in and around a famous and historic town, they decided that they really did not relish the idea of occupying one of the currently fashionable air-conditioned Hi-Tech glazed warehouses that often pass for an office building these days, but that a more substantial and traditional approach was called for, a building designed to last a hundred years rather than thirty, and one that could provide a more "user-friendly" environment, smaller and more intimate offices, good daylighting, windows that can be opened and a minimal use of mechanical air-conditioning, while at the same time presenting itself to the outside world with sufficient presence and dignity to be unmistakeable as an important headquarters building.

The architects' response to these requests has resulted in a remarkable and in its way significant building, a formal, symmetrical and indeed classically inspired composition, traditional both in its selection of materials and in the organization and clarity of its plan, yet at the same time thoroughly modern in its treatment of surfaces and crisp uncluttered detailing. The building is set well back on its site which occupies a narrow band of country separating Stratford from the neighbouring village of Tiddington, and is orientated roughly east–west so that it divides the site into two. The northern half is laid out as a formal approach leading to the main public entrance, the southern half, with the better view over the undulating countryside of the Avon Valley and the sunniest aspect, is treated as an informal garden and landscaped for recreation.

In contrast to many Modern Movement buildings, where the literal fulfilling of functional requirements has been deliberately interpreted as a mandate for asymmetry and spatial complexity, if not confusion, this building displays an almost disarming clarity of form and disposition, starting right from the moment one passes between the pair of low pylons guarding the entrance to the formal approach from Tiddington Road. From this point, reinforced by lines of new trees either side of the driveway, the axis leads directly to the centre line of the north front, where, with reassuring logic, one finds the main entrance, unequivocally expressed with a boldly cantilevered angular glazed entrance canopy flanked by two tall columns. In front of the entrance, the roadway is terminated by a circular arrangement of steps and ramps surrounding a pool and fountain, a cleverly organized device for accommodating a change in levels between the surrounding landscape and the slightly uplifted ground floor that at the same time extends the building's influence out towards the visitor and reinforces the already established expectations of symmetry and balance that are subsequently confirmed throughout the building's internal organization and decorative treatment.

The ramp and stairs lead up through a series of ascending paved levels to a long narrow forecourt, formed where the accommodation of the ground floor of the building is set back to create a colonnade of square stone clad columns flanking a central recessed bay containing the main entrance. This in turn leads into a central top lit galleried entrance hall rising through the full three storey height of the building. This space signals the heart of the building, effectively terminating the formal north–south axis of the approach while establishing the twin secondary parallel axes running east–west around which the accommodation is organized.

The central hall is a lovely cool dignified space, restrained in its use of materials, and exploiting the simple yet effective detailing of its hybrid Modern-Classical style. In a true classical design for instance the balconies would run in to the columns and the surfaces would be modulated with mouldings and string courses. Here the columns are simple and round, their slender proportions rising uninterrupted through their full three storeyheight, and the different elements of the construction are clearly articulated, as for instance by the narrow gaps deliberately introduced to separate the lengths of balcony wall from the columns. This emphasis on structural "honesty" is a hallmark of modern architecture. The primary vertical circulation is organized around the hall with stairs and lifts separated and on opposite sides of the galleried well at each level. Two lifts face each other across a small secondary foyer opening on to one side of the gallery, while the staircase is handled as a series of double flights, each a mirrored version of the other, either side of an opening directly off the opposite side of the gallery. The duplication of flights adds a touch of austere grandeur and the absence of separating doors permits an extra dimension of spatial interplay to enliven the galleried central space.

The building is organized into four storeys of accommodation, with the lower floor sunk into the ground by a metre and the main ground floor consequently raised above the surrounding levels. The main entrance being on the upper ground level reduces the dependence on lifts for vertical circulation and helps to reduce the external impact of the lower floor which largely contains services and plant rooms, storage and archive areas and a computer suite, and offers the opportunity, exploited here, of providing a discreet access for servicing and deliveries at the far ends of the building well away from the main entrance and other amenity areas. The spatial organization of the plan is controlled by the regular structural grid, a series of trabeated spans crossing the open office areas along each perimeter with a clear span of 13·5 m. and the adjacent circulation and services route with a span of 2 m. A third major span, shorter than the outer ones, creates the central spine of the building, within which zone are located either those facilities not requiring daylight or natural ventilation, such as toilet and storage areas, or connecting links of open office space overlooking internal open landscaped courtyards, which permit sunlight to penetrate deep into the office zones and allow natural cross ventilation to be effected through manually openable high level windows.

As the total structural cross section is separated into three major and two minor spans, the two major longitudinal axes are defined by pairs of columns at each bay. These help to modulate the space in open office areas and also function as primary circulation routes running the length of the building on both sides of the courtyards, connected at intervals by the cross wings in a manner that could be represented diagrammatically by the rungs and side rails of a ladder. Where the courtyards occur the corridors usually merge into the large open office areas on either side, but at the cross wings become more enclosed where areas are divided into cellular offices or where toilet blocks fill the internal "dead" areas, until at the centre of the building they all emerge and link together to form the open galleries of the central entrance hall. The planning is direct, simple and easily comprehensible, yet capable of great variation and adaptation as requirements change. The use of structure also successfully humanizes the scale of larger office areas by virtue of its implied rather than physical sub-division into smaller spaces without loss of flexibility.

The staff benefit from a number of generous amenity facilities, which far from being tucked away in some pokey basement room, are here brought right out into the open to play a prominent part in the total spatial composition, linked closely to the major circulation routes and public spaces. The most dramatic of these is the swimming pool, set within a glazed conservatory-like structure which occupies the westernmost of the four courtyard spaces and looks out to the surrounding landscape. Its existence is hinted at from the main entrance hall, where the continuation of the axis passing between the paired staircases at ground floor level generates a dramatic vista out over the pool and on to the distant trees and garden, the brightness beyond silhouetting the sculptured form of a diving swimmer poised in mid air where a balcony overlooks the pool.

In the south-west corner of the building, a coffee lounge on the upper ground level looks down over a grand double height space which functions as a crush area for a lower level bar and leads on to the long restaurant space which overlooks a sheltered and sunny terrace running along the southern side of the building. Long paired staircases leading down from the internal corridor, a further pair projecting out dramatically beyond the glazed façade, and into the garden, and the confident split level treatment of the lower ground floor combine to create a most stylish and enjoyable sequence of spaces and vistas. The structural system, which is expressed throughout the building, is here reinforced and extended with the introduction of non-loadbearing circular fibrous plaster columns set immediately in front of the rectangular structural columns. As with the entrance hall, so here in the amenity areas, the detailing reflects a not altogether convincing resolution between the Classical and the Modern approach to design. The artificial keystones over the seating bays in the restaurant serve only to enliven an awkward piece of ducting, bearing no relation to structural necessity, and are an unfortunate intrusion into a building that is generally most successful in resolving a classical approach to planning and structural organization with a thoroughly modern way of handling materials, surfaces, details and the possibilities of interpenetrating spaces.

If, in the last resort, this building fails to side completely with either its Beaux-Arts or Modern Movement influences, nevertheless it maintains the strong traditions of both in that its final form results from a logical development of both the plan and the structure, resulting in an honesty of expression both inside and out, a clarity of organization and a commendable lack of contrivance. This will prove to be a truly significant building if a recognition of these qualities leads to a renewed understanding that modern architecture for all its technical innovation, can nevertheless honour its roots in the classical tradition.

THE CAMERON TOLL SHOPPING CENTRE, EDINBURGH

Architect: Michael Laird & Partners

In recent years the pattern of shopping has been undergoing a marked change, with the emphasis moving away from the traditional High Street, with its problems of widely separated stores, exposure to the vagaries of the British climate and inevitable lack of convenient parking facilities, towards the more compact and better serviced shopping complex with enclosed pedestrian malls and ample car parking, located either on the outskirts or completely out of town. It is a pattern of shopping gaining widespread and popular acceptance and the design of new shopping centres has reached a level of technical and aesthetic accomplishment in recent years that puts ever increasing economic pressure on the old town centre shops to either adapt and modernize or fall by the wayside.

Continuing the trend is this large new retailing development located on the south-eastern outskirts of Edinburgh. Built at a cost of £30 million, and opened at the end of 1984, it contains over 18,000 square metres of shopping space distributed among some 32 shops, large and small. Typically for such developments, the plan is based on a central enclosed mall and includes two major space users, of which the largest, a supermarket, is large enough to justify the provision of 36 checkout points.

The site was formerly an area of boggy ground crossed by the Braid Burn and used by a tennis club. The burn was diverted through a concrete channel around the site and the tennis club relocated and provided with a new clubhouse and four indoor courts at the expense of the developer, to leave the site clear for the new building. The burn has not completely disappeared, however, and it reappears at the narrower southern end of the site as the focus of a new landscaped walkway to satisfy one of the conditions of the planning permission.

One of the most difficult problems with this building type, particularly on "green field" sites and where the focus of interest is entirely internal, is to reduce the visual impact of such a large and uninspiring mass on the surrounding buildings and landscape. A number of architectural devices are available which help to reduce the apparent bulk, and in this instance the architects have opted to eliminate all hard corners and provide a more modelled form than usual, by faceting the profile on plan and section and by adding to what would otherwise be a simple brick box an angled glazed upper level cladding that fulfills a number of useful functions.

The glazed façade is carried up some two metres above roof level, so that from the ground, and also from nearby houses, it is impossible to see any of the usually chaotic collection of bits and pieces generated by the servicing plant and other equipment mounted on the roof. Not only does this produce a neat and tidy roofline, but it has the added benefit of allowing the equipment to be replaced or altered at any time without ruining or at least materially altering the visual appearance of the building. The upper part of the space enclosed by the glazed cladding also allows for the horizontal distribution of services, together with a maintenance walkway, which is also used to add a spark of colour behind the reflective glass façade, being picked out in bright red.

Except at the main entrances and loading bays, where the angled slope of glazing continues down and out to a lower level to enclose the entrance doors, for the most part the sloping cladding angles back on itself to meet a facing brick wall reaching to a height roughly level with the ground floor ceiling height. Above this level and behind the glass rises a cavity wall constructed from dark coloured blockwork. This greatly assists in increasing the reflectivity of the toughened glass cladding panels, enabling them to mirror the surrounding landscape and the changing moods of the sky, and thereby help to reduce the building's scale and visual impact.

A number of existing trees were retained and a sizeable investment made in new landscaping around the site, helping to soften the impact of the inevitable expanses of car parking and link the site to the neighbouring Inch Park, from which the building can be seen against the distant skyline or Arthur's Seat.

Though well-disguised from the outside, and difficult to comprehend as a simple formal arrangement because of the continuous chamfering of corners, the plan is in principle derived from two superimposed rectangular blocks, one eating into the corner of the other. Main entrances to the shopping centre are located at both ends of the central pedestrian mall, which forms a direct spine running north–south, offset in the middle of one of the two rectangles, with a cross link in the centre leading to the main supermarket, which occupies the whole of the other rectangular block. At the centre of the mall a single staircase leads off at an angle, giving access to a mezzanine level called the Terrace, featuring seven "fast-food" outlets capable of serving up to 300 people at any one time and providing a balcony view over the mall for diners.

The long central mall is spacious, bright and full of sparkle with daylight flooding down from the glazed lantern overhead and reflecting off the mirror strip fascias above the shops and the sloping ceiling surfaces fabricated from continuous chrome finished slats. Along the centre of the mall a number of mature Ficus Benjamina trees have been planted, adding a touch of softness and colour that contrasts well with the predominantly hard and reflective interior surfaces, qualities that are further emphasized by the extensive use of twinkler lights. The individual shop units flanking the mall have been encouraged to be more than usually adventurous in the design of their shop frontages in a deliberate attempt to blur the boundaries between mall and shop and avoid the repetitive conventional flat window approach. Many of the tenants have responded with enthusiasm to this opportunity to create a constantly changing and visually complex series of elevations, highlighted by fluorescent lighting displays and bold graphics.

As a concept for the new "High Street", this type of enclosed complex has undeniable benefits and attractions and these are not only for the car owning shopper, for as the designers and developers of new out of town centres have realized, in striving to compete with their traditional High Street competitors, they are generating the kind of environments which have something to offer for the whole family over the duration of an increasingly lengthy average trip, places which people quite simply enjoy being in, and this is proving to be the key to their undoubted success. This success was further emphasized when the Cameron Toll Centre received the official accolade of being awarded, as outright winner, the European Council of Shopping Centres Award for 1985.

RESEARCH CENTRE FOR SCHLUMBERGER CAMBRIDGE RESEARCH LTD, CAMBRIDGE

Architect: Michael Hopkins Ltd.

The use of tensioned lightweight membranes suspended from large span structures of steel columns and cables is providing an exciting new range of architectural possibilities in the enclosure of space and control of natural light. This striking new application of the principles in a new research and testing facility for the Schlumberger Group in Cambridge provides dramatic evidence of design and technical skills of a high order, and an appropriately innovative environment for a workforce aiming to discover better and more efficient methods of exploiting the earth's remaining reserves of oil.

The imagery of this daring structure has an affinity with that of heavy industry and it was no accident that the architect chose to place the test station, with its drilling test pits and major items of testing equipment right at the heart of the building, and visible enough from many other areas for all the workforce to be aware of work in progress. The design appearance and overall form of the building has everything to do with the structure necessary to contain this space; the supporting skeleton is exposed both externally and internally and is also the major organizing factor in the planning of the remaining office and laboratory facilities grouped together in long low side wings.

The material used to enclose the major central spaces is a Teflon-coated glass fibre fabric, the coating being an inert plastic highly resistant to chemical attack and unaffected by ultraviolet light, which is translucent enough to generate minimum internal light levels at desk height of 250 lux during normal working hours without artificial lighting and with a satisfactorily low level of glare. The fabric is woven like cloth, with a weft and a warp, and because of the ability of the material to withstand forces better in the direction of the weft, this determines how the strips of material are joined together and how the final membrane is supported and tensioned.

In view of the three dimensional complexity of the surfaces created, calculation of the forces generated in the suspension structure is only easily done with the aid of a computer program.

To maintain the tension in the membrane it is important that the force should be exerted evenly along the perimeter of the fabric and to achieve this the edge of the material is wrapped over a 20 mm. galvanized steel strand cable which is in turn clamped continuously to the main structural steel frame. The detailing is similar to that used in sailing boats. To achieve the required surface tension in the membrane, a series of 36 mm. diameter spiral steel strand cables are used to suspend the membrane from the structural steel masts.

The primary support structure comprises pairs of linked tubular masts supporting a triangulated truss in a clear span from side to side, forming three 28 × 18 metre bays, two of which enclose the test station. At the junction point of the masts and trusses, pairs of outriggers extend out, one pair continuing upwards and slightly outwards, a second pair sloping down and away, over the roofs of the low adjoining wings. The ends of all these projecting booms are united in a single though complex truss action by interconnecting solid tie rods that spring from independent anchor masts or are bedded into ground anchors. The whole effect is not unlike that of an enormously complex and glamorous marquee cocooned in a spiders web.

The steel structure of the two long wings that contain the central spaces is also exposed on the outside, though of a much simpler design, and the construction is based on a prefabricated standardized component system used for many types of office and commercial accommodation. It takes the form of a series of simple flat roofed box-like building segments supported clear of the ground by an external trussed structure, and clad in glass or steel insulated panels. These long wings project beyond the end of the central atrium-like spaces to enclose a terrace leading to the main entrance at one end, and the service yard at the other. They house all the scientists' office accommodation which is grouped along the outer perimeter, while the conference rooms, laboratories, workshops and open discussion areas face inwards directly overlooking the test station and the other principal central space, known as the "winter garden", containing the reception area, library and a restaurant.

As with the laboratory and conference areas, so

here the winter garden has a direct view to the all important test station through a full height glazed screen. The immediate juxtaposition of work and leisure related spaces leads to a heightened sense of involvement with all the various activities throughout the building and must reflect a deliberate policy on the part of the company aimed at maximizing the cross flow of information and stimulating new ideas.

The transparent quality of this building, so obvious from the inside during the day, becomes even more so from the outside at night, when the huge tented shapes glow and the lighting in the offices reveals the internal order of the adjoining wings. It is at any time an exhilarating exhibition of structural gymnastics. Schlumberger started to occupy the building from early in 1985, work on this first phase having finished at the end of January 1985, and the design appears to be working successfully thus far. Only the passage of time will confirm whether the considerable social potential of visually interlocking such diverse activities will survive the rigorous physical demands of the test station in full operation.

THE SEDGWICK CENTRE, ALDGATE, LONDON

Architect: Frederick Gibberd Coombes & Partners

Located beside Aldgate East Underground station on the eastern boundary of the City of London, and marooned on its island site opposite Gardiner's Corner by the endless streams of traffic pouring in and out of the famous "square mile" via Commercial Road and Mile End Road, this striking new sports and conference centre certainly does its best to stamp a cool and authoritative presence on its chaotic and impersonal surroundings.

The construction of this multi-purpose leisure complex has come as a very welcome planning gain in association with the continuing development of the Gardiner's Corner site, where The Sedgwick Group of International Insurance Brokers has recently built new headquarters offices opposite their existing building at the western end of the site. The site of the leisure centre was owned in the early nineteenth century by the Cavell family, and the name Gardiner's Corner comes from Gardiners the outfitters, who had a store opposite the site.

Perhaps the most important legacy of the past however lay in the complexity and extent of the Underground services which the new building had to avoid, and these, in conjunction with a planned extension of the existing system of underground pedestrian walkways, to encompass a new subterranean shopping mall with restaurants and links to the adjacent new and proposed office buildings, were to prove major determinants of the form of the new building. Most of the major services follow the line of the old road network, as it was before the island site was created by new road alignments, and these include such serious obstacles as a 4 metre diameter gas main subway, a large watermain, and three sewers, the largest of which is 3 metres in diameter.

The scrap of land which remained between these services and the pedestrian link to Leman Street was roughly triangular, but rather than follow this shape for the building profile, the architect chose instead to design an efficient rectangular box housing the main activity spaces, and to siphon off nearly all of the circulation and servicing elements such as plant rooms, services distribution ducts, lifts and escape stairs into separate circular towers linked to the corners of the main block at each apex of the triangle. The very restricted site area also meant that the components of the required accommodation, which

included a 350-seat auditorium, reception areas, a seminar complex, a four court squash club and a multi-purpose sports hall, has almost literally to be piled on top of each other, and dovetailed together in such a way as to exploit to the full every square (indeed cubic) inch. The planning of the various elements and their three dimensional co-ordination displays much ingenuity, and the architect's imaginative response to these problems transformed a set of potentially crippling restraints into the key to an exciting and efficient three dimensional concept.

Entry to the Centre is effected from two levels, either through the main entrance at ground level or by means of a lift and stairs connected through a lower level foyer opening immediately off the pedestrian subway and aligned with the entrance to the shopping mall opposite. The control and reception desk is housed in a circular enclosure so placed that part of it cantilevers daringly over the lower foyer. From this point visitors can be directed easily to the major functions of the building. The entrance to the sports hall and squash courts is within the north tower, while the west tower contains stairs to the suite of seminar rooms. A lift immediately adjacent to this tower and within the foyer connects the basement level entrance direct to the seminar rooms, thus enabling staff from the office buildings to be able to gain quick access to the conference/seminar facilities without passing through other parts of the building.

A full height glazed screen separates the entrance area from the foyer to the auditorium, which is logically placed at the lowest level in view of the concentration of people that will use this particular part of the building. Stairs at either side of the foyer rise up the sides of the building, giving access at two levels into the auditorium and thence to the theatre bar occupying the full width of the building over the entrance foyer. The ground level foyer is also designed to function as an exhibition area, and has a bar, toilet and cloakroom facilities tucked away under the lowest part of the auditorium.

At the eastern end of the building is the unloading dock, and in the east tower a scenery hoist which can lift scenery up to the stage level. Tucked between the tower and the building is the stage door, which leads through to all the backstage accommodation comprising offices, dressing rooms, lockers, showers, lavatories and storage. Stairs at each end give access to the stage and also to a small orchestra pit which can be opened up by removing sections of the stage. The auditorium seats 350 and has a simple proscenium type stage which can be adapted as required for theatre productions or conferences. A series of control, projection and translation rooms are suspended at the rear of the auditorium, and these back on to the lower of the two levels of seminar facilities, with a reception area and three seminar rooms.

Immediately over the auditorium on the next two floors, is the squash club with changing facilities, office, bar/servery and small kitchen. The reception area to both the squash club and sports hall is on the upper fourth floor, next to the north tower with the two largest seminar rooms placed under the changing facilities. Because of its need for a large clear span, the multi-purpose sports hall is logically placed on top and occupies the whole of the top floor, with a spectators gallery along one side, and an instructor's office housed in the west tower overlooking the hall. A wide variety of indoor sports activities can be accommodated, together with cricket and golf nets and archery.

Externally, the building has been treated with a simple modular panelled cladding system constructed from white aluminium framing containing opaque off-white glass infill panels, which give way to clear glass, where views out are desirable or daylighting of internal spaces such as offices and seminar rooms is required.

The structural grid and the principal floor levels are expressed by means of horizontal and vertical recesses in the façades and grey infill panels, and these endow the building with some of the characteristics of a Rubic cube, and help to reduce its apparent bulk. The circular service towers are clad in specially radiused white aluminium panels, and topped with conical caps. However, the most distinctive feature of the exterior appearance is surely the series of large white lighting globes projecting out beyond the building façade, suspended on metal framework bracketed out at roof parapet level and tied back at the points where the main floor levels are emphasized. These globes encompass the entire building, with one occurring at each expressed vertical joint, and do much to relate the separated forms of the towers and the box within a single unified design concept. It is a bold and successful gesture and one aimed no doubt at drawing the public's attention to the varied facilities to be enjoyed within.

The Centre was officially opened by H.R.H. Princess Alexandra on June 18, 1985 and is already making a valuable contribution to the social life of an area of the City not overendowed with public amenities.

SUPERMARKET FOR J. SAINSBURY PLC, CANTERBURY, KENT

Architect: Ahrends, Burton and Koralek

It is a matter of regret, but a fact nevertheless, that one does not instantly equate the modern supermarket with architectural designs of great quality or innovation. This competition-winning design for a Sainsbury supermarket in the ancient city of Canterbury, which opened to the public on September 11, 1984, is a refreshing exception to the rule, and is the result of the second of the retail chain's two limited architectural competitions which were held in 1982.

The building is situated just a little to the north of the Cathedral Precinct on a "backlands" site, just outside the central area of the old town enclosed by the city walls and its busy ring road. Although not directly fronting on to Northgate, the main road, nor to any great extent on to Kingsmead Road, which defines the northern limit of the site, it could nevertheless be regarded as occupying a sensitive location in the context of the historic city, overshadowed as it is by the dominant mass of the Cathedral, whose towers and pinnacles punctuate the skyline, and with the River Stour passing close by on the western boundary of the site.

Many of the supermarkets which have been constructed in recent years, particularly where they have needed to "fit in" to an existing historic context, have been forced to masquerade as humble dwelling houses, old barns or even maltings in an attempt to render the uncomfortable mass of what is nearly always just a huge low shed into something acceptable in terms of style and scale. Here, the architects have responded to the soaring structural expression of the Cathedral with a thoroughly contemporary design in which the structure is similarly highlighted as the major dramatic and decorative element. Admittedly this is on an edge-of-town site, and the building is not forced to make a partial and well mannered entrance into an existing street full of old buildings, as many have been required to do, but nevertheless the confidence of the judges has been vindicated and the consistently applied skills of the architects have produced a visual delight in circumstances which all too often produce eyesores.

The plan of the building is generated from its three major functions, firstly the receiving area where deliveries are handled, then the processing and preparation area, and finally the largest space, the sales floor. The building form reflects this progression of activities with three separate major structural spans and three blocks of different lengths. The gross floor area is approximately 4,500 square metres and of this the sales area takes up just over 2,300 sq. metres. Each of the three blocks has its own structure and in order to provide a clear span over each to give maximum flexibility for dividing up the space and to cater for changing requirements, the architects designed a suspension system with pairs of structural steel columns, hangers and tie rods, all clearly expressed outside the main building enclosure. The eastern faces of each major span are aligned and the different block lengths therefore generate a stepped profile to the west, along which side are ranged the staff rooms, offices and other ancillary accommodation, again in a stepped profile, with a conventional structure, and at one end an enclosed courtyard providing a modest oasis of peace and calm to be overlooked by the staff in their offices and dining rooms as a break from the noise and bustle of the sales floor.

The structural system comprises pairs of 245 mm. diameter mild steel masts at 3 metre centres, with a triangulated system of paired 60 mm. diameter mild steel tie rods, supporting paired hangers welded to castings pin jointed to a raised plate supporting the steel roof beams at the centre of the roof span. Each span has its own paired sets of masts at each end, and where the blocks adjoin therefore, the masts are doubled up and spaced a distance apart so that the projecting triangulated tie rods neatly intersect to form an "X" pattern. In the narrow zone between adjoining spans the roof is at a lower level and supports servicing elements such as air handling equipment and water tanks. The delivery storage and processing areas are housed behind solid windowless walls of glazed concrete block, but the public shopping side has an elegant square panelled glass and aluminium skin. Both types of wall construction are capped by a sloping metal fascia that sets back to form a recess underneath the edge beams of the roof structure. This emphasizes the thinness of the roof plane, and enables the roof structure itself to read through separately from the vertical enclosure.

From a technical point of view it also provides a neat solution to the complicated movement joints needed at the eaves junction to allow for the many differential movements arising from changes in wind or other loading factors and temperature.

All the exposed steelwork has a crisp white aluminium finish, and this is also true of the bollards, lighting columns and fence posts around the site that repeat in their design the linked double pole motif of the main structure, and thereby help to relate the building to its surroundings and define the extent of the architect's influence.

The one exception to the regular order of structural bays comes at the main entrance to the supermarket at the south-west corner. Here the rectangular bays give way to a radiused structure suspended from a single central mast, with hangers supporting a number of booms in a manner strongly reminiscent of yacht rigging.

All along the south side and around the fan-shaped main entrance is suspended a steel framed and fabric covered canopy. Being suspended from the ends of the projecting outriggers of the pairs of masts, it is clearly related to the structure of the building and yet is sufficiently separated from the external skin to read as a protected route around the building for pedestrians, particularly those arriving from the Northgate end, for whom the entrance to the supermarket is at the far end of the building.

TRAINING AND CONFERENCE CENTRE, HIGH WYCOMBE, BUCKINGHAMSHIRE

Architect: Edward Cullinan Architects

It has often been remarked that the residential training course is the nearest many an ordinary office worker ever gets to participating in that glorious but fading institution—the weekend country house party, for so long the preserve of the rich and landed classes. With fewer and fewer of our more or less stately country houses actually being occupied as dwelling houses by their owners, a pattern has emerged in which the largest become national tourist centres, while many of the more modest estates have been transformed into conference centres or business headquarters. This recent development at High Wycombe is a typical example of the latter, centred around an old house known as Uplands, a modest and architecturally unexceptional Victorian country house, occupying a superb site in a large mature park overlooking the Hughenden Valley in Buckinghamshire.

For many years, a succession of owners had unsuccessfully tinkered about with the building, adding new wings, rear extensions and even crenellated parapets in an attempt to maintain its social status, until recently following its acquisition in the 1970s by the Nationwide Building Society, it was partially restored and considerably extended to quite palatial proportions in order to function as a 64-bedroom residential training and conference centre, primarily for the Society's employees. Construction work began in June 1982 and was completed by May 1984.

The design of the new conference centre was immediately influenced by the insistence of both client and the local planners that the old house be retained, not so much because of any architectural merit but in recognition of its symbolic value in setting an appropriate tone for the new buildings. In the event, only the southernmost part of the old house was retained. The front porch and various other accretions at the rear were removed, and even the crenellated parapets were reconstructed, the former yellow bricks being replaced with red Milton Hall bricks to match those used in the walls of the new buildings. However, although the old house has certainly not predetermined the architectural style of the new extensions, it has certainly exercised a significant influence on the plan and form of the new development, which continues as an extension of the symmetrical layout of the front elevation of the old house, with a series of axes connecting discrete two storey link blocks and terminating in four storey pavilions at each end in a composition of almost Baroque grandeur.

The retained portion of the old house contains eight rooms disposed symmetrically on two floors and now functions happily as it was always intended to do in its country house days as the social heart of the complex, with a bar and lounge to one side of the ground floor, and on the other side of the hall a library and billiards room. Beyond this group of rooms, centred on the axis of the hall which leads through to the new dining hall extension at the rear, and linking this with the new east–west axis of the residential blocks, is a spectacular new main staircase and foyer, the architects own version of the classic focal point of the grand Baroque palace. Two green carpeted flights of stairs, facing each other symmetrically about the north–south axis, flow gracefully up and around two large white drums, housing the reception and information desk in one, the office of the conference centre manager in the other. The curving staircases lead up enticingly to a first floor landing from which one can either continue forward to enter the two large seminar rooms located over

the dining room and kitchen, or return back along the north–south axis between the two white cylinders and across a bridge to the first floor of the old house, containing a further four seminar rooms. The effect is not unlike that of a drawbridge springing from two white buttresses.

Clearly this space is intended to function not just as a circulation area but as the architectural and social focal point of the entire complex. At the lower end, the stair flights widen out and become extended into seats at the outer edges, creating a natural theatre-like space where informal conversations can be held without impeding others walking up and down. In fact many of the details of this space are designed specifically to encourage its use as a meeting place. Even the balustrades of the bridge have been developed as seats, interspersed with small ledges and tables. Over this remarkable stage set is a simple barn-like roof with green stained timber boarding and exposed rafters and a long central roof light projecting upwards at the ridge. Light floods in from the sides as well as through a series of full height sliding glazed doors running the length of the link at first floor level.

The two white cylindrical forms also act as the pivot for the new east–west axis around which all the residential accommodation is arranged. This is developed as a cloister-like covered walk leading out past groups of study bedrooms to the east and west wings, where secondary north–south corridors terminate the composition and provide links to the flanking four storey pavilions. The standard study bedrooms are grouped into two storey blocks, and are organized around groups of four units, two at ground level, two at first floor, around a common staircase leading up from the cloister. Two eight room blocks are strung like beads on the main east–west axis, while the remainder of the standard rooms adjoin the north–south corridors terminating the axis at each end. The four storey pavilions which adjoin these end wings and project forward in line with the old house contain larger non-standard study bedrooms, for VIP use. The new east–west axis, with its link blocks, end wings, cloistered walkways and pavilions, spreads out from the old house at its core to encompass the whole site, and at its western end extends beyond the line of buildings to form the central axis of the main approach from the car park.

This is laid out in the form of an arc, at the centre of which is a newly planted circular maze through which the arriving visitors are required to pass in order to proceed up the slope, across the garage court and thence through a narrow slot in the west wing, where a staircase leads up to the principal cloister. The double-H shape of the plan creates four partially enclosed landscaped areas, rather like outside rooms with building on three sides and the fourth open to the surrounding park and woodland. Each is treated in a different style, and two in particular feature fine mature trees which have been retained.

Perhaps taking their cue from the formal axial symmetry of the plan, the architects have developed an interesting exterior treatment using a vocabulary of structural elements assembled in a number of ways to create what is essentially a Classical composition. The elevations divide clearly into base and superstructure, the base solid without being massive, the upper parts lighter, with glass and stained timber framing. The base is treated like a series of frames, rather than as a monolithic wall, with quoins and string courses of red brickwork infilled with panels of random coursed Portland Stone. This system has the advantage of being able to incorporate windows or clear openings without disturbing the rhythm of the brickwork piers and is used in a number of different ways, for instance where it frames the openings of the cloister colonnades, or where it is piled up in tiers to create the stepped three storey bases for the end pavilions.

The timber superstructure is built up primarily as a series of single or double monopitched roofs, again adapting easily to the varying requirements of the plan. Over the standard bedroom blocks the roofs reflect the plan, the largest pitch over the bedrooms meeting the smaller pitch over the bathrooms with a vertical clerestorey. In the end pavilions, the mono-pitch roofs over the second storey are set back to back and combine with the double pitch over the central bay at the third floor to create the effect on end elevation of a double pediment, an appropriately Classical motif with which to cap the flanking wings of a Baroque elevation. The consistent articulation and precise detailing of the structural elements provides an inherently decorative effect, but this is further highlighted with the introduction of a few bright coloured elements, most noticeably the green "set square" devices which are used to conceal the eaves junction at the exposed gable ends and which, by providing visual anchors at the ends of the pediments, reinforce the neo-Classical character of the new buildings.

It would be possible to argue at length about whether or not a modern brief can be successfully clothed in the apparel of the Classical tradition, and there is no doubt that this resourceful design will be in the forefront of such discussions. What is surely beyond doubt here is that the architects have taken what was an ordinary building, at least by the standards of its own time, and in adapting and extending it, have transformed it into something unique, enjoyable and memorable.

PRISONS

Receptions into prison: by number of previous convictions (England and Wales)

Number of previous convictions	1975	1976	1977	1978	1979	1980	1981	1982	1983
Males: total	30,667	32,914	33,906	34,832	36,412	38,016	43,388	46,779	42,716
None	1,915	2,028	2,135	1,936	1,634	1,731	1,518	1,773	1,848
1–2 sentences	2,309	2,511	2,516	2,500	2,484	2,685	3,002	3,164	2,969
3–5 sentences	4,804	5,079	5,401	5,399	5,652	6,092	7,161	7,312	6,104
6–10 sentences	8,631	8,960	9,177	9,470	9,412	9,665	11,152	11,845	10,048
11 or more sentences	9,221	10,280	10,893	11,011	11,340	11,905	13,343	14,057	13,632
Previous conviction information not recorded	3,787	4,056	3,784	4,516	5,890	5,938	7,212	8,628	8,115
Females: total	1,351	1,614	1,839	2,000	2,109	2,265	2,533	2,692	2,349
None	226	259	231	240	156	155	177	176	271
1–2 sentences	71	120	152	149	148	172	234	261	273
3–5 sentences	118	204	285	279	293	322	423	445	419
6–10 sentences	135	230	279	253	287	331	434	443	401
11 or more sentences	94	125	207	189	196	195	267	322	294
Previous conviction information not recorded	707	676	685	890	1,029	1,090	998	1,045	691

SCIENCE AND DISCOVERY, 1984–85

Age of the Universe.—An accurate estimate of the age of the universe is of paramount importance to the cosmologist who is trying to determine whether the universe will expand for ever, or will start to contract some time in the future and collapse down to a state similar to that existing when the "big bang" triggered off the expansion which we now observe. Several methods of estimating when the "big bang" took place do not give consistent answers and all that can be said at the present time is that it lies within the range of 10 to 20 thousand million years, with more recent work tending to a value towards the lower part of this range.

A new method has been developed by a team at the University of Hamburg using the double image of a quasar produced by a gravitational lens. If a massive cluster of galaxies lies in the line of sight of a very distant quasar, the gravitational field of the cluster acts like a lens, bending the light travelling on either side of the cluster and we observe the quasar as two distinct but identical images. The new technique involves measuring the time difference between the arrival of any light fluctuations from the quasar due to the differing path lengths. The actual distance of the quasar is calculated from the redshift of the spectral lines, this shift being proportional to its distance. The proportionality constant, the so-called Hubble constant, puts numerical values to this ratio and so it is essential to have an accurate value for this constant. The reciprocal of this constant gives an upper limit to the age of the universe. If the difference in time taken by two routes is known, it is possible to obtain an accurate value for the Hubble constant. The Hamburg team noticed that the brightening of one image was followed by an identical brightening about 1½ years later. If the delay was due solely to a path difference, then it was concluded that the maximum age of the universe is about 13 thousand million years.

This figure indicates that the universe is very close to the critical value which separates an open one (one that will expand continually) and the closed one (one that will contract some time in the future). The value suggests that the universe is flat, a condition which is in line with the new theory of the universe called inflation.

An even more accurate clock.—It was not so very long ago when it was considered that the pendulum clock capable of keeping time to better than one second per year was good enough for most purposes. Later, the quartz oscillator clocks improved the accuracy to one second per century, only to be replaced by atomic time based on the frequency of the transition between two hyperfine levels of the ground state of the cesium atom. This has an accuracy equivalent to one second in a thousand centuries. Even this has now been surpassed. The stored-ion laser-cooled clock, now being developed will have an accuracy in the region of one second in 50 million years.

This new technique involves using three tiny electrodes a few millimetres apart to create an electric field that traps a tenuous cloud of ions. The special shape of this field prevents the escape of the ions and they behave in a similar manner to a group of boxers trying to kill the motion of a punchbag by hitting it from all sides. By irradiating the trap with tuned laser light the kinetic energy of the ions can be reduced considerably. In the ultimate situation the trap contains only one ion which has so slow a motion that its "temperature" is 0·01 Kelvin, nearly absolute zero. Under these conditions the frequency of a hyperfine transition in its ground state can be measured without having to allow for the usual Doppler shifts.

Work in this field has been carried out at the National Bureau of Standards in Boulder, Colorado and at Heidelberg University in West Germany. Although there is no need for clocks with such accuracy in everyday life, they will have applications in quite a wide-range of cosmological experiments, such as improving the accuracy of the measurements of gravitational redshifts. It will also make it possible to monitor the Earth's rotation to a very high degree of accuracy, the results of which will be of great value to geologists and meteorologists.

Apollo Asteroid 1983TB.—Much has been written about the asteroid discovered by the I.R.A.S. infra-red satellite and the similarity of its orbit to that of the Geminid meteor stream. Arguments have been put forward for and against the theory that the object is a remnant of a comet. Some scientists believe there is an evolutionary link between comets and asteroids, this belief being based principally on the fact that a group of asteroids have orbits which cross those of the inner planets. During the lifetime of the solar system collisions with the inner planets must have occurred and calculations have shown that there are far too many for them to be remnants of a single cometary breakup. Therefore they must be regularly topped up by new objects and it is thought that a source of this material is the nuclei of short period comets stripped of volatile material.

Recent studies have shown that object 1983TB is not the burned out remnant of a comet despite it having an orbit similar to that of the Geminid stream. It has now been designated as Minor Planet 3200. The identification of it as a minor planet is the result of detailed study during the object's close encounter with the Earth in December 1984. Spectroscopic observations, carried out at the Kitt Peak National Observatory, have provided evidence to support the view that it is a member of the S-class of stony asteroids, but photometric studies by David Tholen of the University of Hawaii indicate that the body is bluer than the Sun and hence cannot be an S-type. The observed light curve suggests a rotational period of just under 4 hours, such a rapid rotation implies that the object is rocky because a spinning icy body would soon break up.

Observations made using the U.K. infra-red Telescope (U.K.I.R.T.) are not consistent with those from an inactive comet nor with any of the more common asteroids. Nevertheless, when the U.K.I.R.T. data is compared with computer modelling of the thermal properties of the asteroid, the results indicate that

3200 is most likely to be a rapidly rotating rocky object rather than that which would be expected from an extinct comet.

Centre of our Galaxy.—The centre of our Galaxy has been the target for considerable study during the last few decades. Unfortunately this region is barred for optical astronomers because of the large amounts of intervening dust which cannot be penetrated at visible wavelengths. Studies of the centres of galaxies similar to our own have provided much information but they are so far away that detailed studies are virtually impossible. Hence the desire to use every available technique to glean as much information as possible from this relatively near region.

Work carried out by astronomers from the University of California at Berkeley has revealed evidence to support the theory that the centre is really a huge black hole with a mass equivalent to 4 million Suns. This mass is concentrated into such a small volume that the gravitational pull does not even allow light to escape. This particular study at infra-red wavelengths and carried out over the last 10 years using the Kuiper air-borne observatory, has revealed the existence of a stream of very hot gas travelling as fast as 400 to 700,000 km. per hour around the centre of the galaxy. These gas streams lie about 5·5 light years from the centre. Outside this region lies cooler gas extending outwards for 32 light years and moving much more slowly—a mere 160,000 km. per hour. Inside the region a cavity had been detected where matter appears to have been swept away. The astronomers believe that the gap was caused when an extremely violent explosion occurred, possibly within the last million years, when a large quantity of gas was sucked into the black hole.

Another group of workers at the California Institute of Technology has identified a strong radio source at the centre of the galaxy whose size is so small that, once again, it implies the presence of a black hole. In this case, the radio emission is thought to have originated from material being sucked into the hole.

Cold Enduring Insect.—Most insects are very sensitive to low temperatures, either being immobilized completely or reducing activity to an absolute minimum, but this does not apply to a newly discovered insect intimately associated with a Himalayan glacier. This new insect, a chironomid midge with the name *Diamesa*, was discovered by zoologist Shiro Kohshima of the University of Kyoto, Japan.

The adult midge has small wings but it cannot fly. It walks about on the snow covered glacier although it appears to be more at home in the cavities between the ice and snow covering. It is quite active even at temperatures as low as −16°C. The larvae live in the pits produced in the glacier's drainage channels, where they live on aquatic blue-green algae and bacteria. The midge seems to be restricted to the Himalayas because although similar deposits occur in the Antarctic there is no evidence of its existence on that continent.

The *Diamesa* is unusual in other respects. Apart from its ability to keep active at temperatures which would immobilize other insects, it lives for a much longer time. Most adult midges live for just a few hours, or at the most a few days, but in this case its life span runs into months. Kohshima found adult females on the glacier at the end of October, the beginning of winter. Apart from containing large amounts of fat, they carried immature eggs. It appears that the midge survives the severe winter to lay its eggs in the spring. It is thought that the egg laying is delayed until then because it would not be possible to know the locality of the drainage channels beforehand.

To survive and keep active at these low temperatures, the constitution of the midge must be most unusual and must have some outstanding enzymes. No doubt, now that one species has been discovered, further research will bring to light more cases. A study of these may provide information enabling man to survive very low temperatures.

Dating Early Hominids.—There has always been controversy over the dating of the Hominid sites in East Africa, but recently a new line of investigation has helped to sort out some of the problems and it now looks as though a reasonably acceptable picture is emerging. A team of American geologists, having access to the facilities of the Deep Sea Drilling Project, have matched the volcanic ash in sediments in the Gulf of Aden with the tuffs at the sites in the Rift Valley where remains of early man have been found—Hadar in Ethiopia and Koobi Fora in Kenya. Hadar was the site of the fossilized skeleton of "Lucy" and many hundreds of fragments of other hominids found in 1970.

These hominid fragments were found interbedded with tuffs and lava flows, the tuffs being especially important because each layer has its own characteristic chemical composition. In 1983, Frank Brown of the University of Utah found that the Tulu Bor tuff at Koobi Fora was similar in composition to that of the Sidi Hakoma tuff underlying the Hadar hominids, implying that they were both formed from the same ashfall. It was then considered possible that some of the ash from this outburst could have blown over to the sea and so deep sea cores were examined for the presence of this ash layer. Eight layers of ash were identified in distinct bands in the ooze formed by calcareous skeletons of single-celled algae called coccolithophores. These so-called nanofossils are important stratigraphic markers because different groups characterize successive intervals of geologic time. The information provided by the oozes puts the age of the Tulu Bor tuff at less than 3·4 million years. The age of this tuff was not known to any reasonable degree of accuracy. The age for the Hadar hominids is therefore deduced as less than 3·3 million years, which is in general agreement with recent land based estimates of between 3·2 and 2·9 million years.

These values are much younger than the 4 to 3 million years proposed by Donald Johanson, who found the site at Koobi Fora. It is thought that much of the controversy that has existed in the past will now be removed.

Death of the Dinosaurs.—Although not accepted by many scientists, there is fairly wide support for the theory that some 65 million years ago the Earth was hit by a large asteroid, or comet, which ejected so much dust into the atmosphere that it blocked out the Sun's light producing conditions which caused the death of the dinosaurs. The strongest evidence in favour of such a theory is the presence of unusually high concentrations of trace elements such as iridium, more abundant in meteorites, found in rocks of identical age to the date of the dinosaur's extinction. A weakness in the theory lies in the fact that the extinctions took place over 2 million years. The iridium-rich clay also appears at levels of slightly different ages.

A modified theory which accounts for these and other objections has been put forward by Victor Clube and Bill Napier, astronomers at the Royal Observatory, Edinburgh. They have related cometary activity with the motion of the Sun round our own galaxy. The Sun moves up and down through the plane of the galaxy every 30 million years and crosses one of the spiral arms every 50 to 200 million years. It is thought that material from which comets are formed is plentiful in the plane of the galaxy and in the spiral arms. This material consists of lumps of ice and rock and some of it is captured by the Sun as it passes through. As this cometary material approaches the Sun, it tends to break up into debris ranging in size from dust to objects about 10 km. in diameter. If these larger pieces were to collide with the Earth, the effect would be catastrophic. Several such events could occur over a few million years and then activity would die away until the Sun passed through the critical regions again.

Although this could explain the events 65 million years ago, the best evidence for the theory comes from the relatively recent past. It is conjectured that about 17,700 years ago a giant comet broke up and produced the very high concentration of cosmic dust recorded in Greenland ice cores of that date. This date is coincident with the peak of the last ice age. As the dust settled, the ice receded. It is thought that remnants of this giant comet are Encke's comet, the Taurid meteor stream and at least 4 to 5 minor planets with diameters up to 200 km., all of which have approximately the same orbits. Because the Greenland ice deposits have a trace element composition identical to that of material associated with the Tunguska event of 1908, it is possible that this event was caused by an icy fragment from the same source. This new theory may be strengthened when data is received from the space-probes sent to study the make-up of Halley's comet.

Deepest Hole in the World.—Since 1970 Soviet geologists have been drilling a well in the Kola Peninsula, some 250 km. north of the Arctic Circle. At a meeting of the International Geological Union, held in Moscow in August 1984, some details of the problems experienced and some results were announced. At that time they had reached a depth of 12,000 metres and were cutting into hitherto unsampled rocks. This depth exceeds the previous deepest well in Oklahoma by just under 3,000 metres. One technical aspect illustrates the difficulties experienced in drilling at such depths. Each time the drill bit wears out, the entire drill string has to be withdrawn and it is estimated that so far about 25,000 km. of pipe have passed through the well mouth. The drill cannot be rotated in the normal manner and so it is mounted on a turbine which is driven by pressurized mud and pumped down the well at 250 atmosphere pressure.

The bottom half of the hole passes through rocks more than 2,700 million years old and which were originally laid down as sediment eroded from granite outcrops. Later the sediments were intruded by more granites and as they were buried and heated they were converted into metamorphic rocks at pressures of 5,000 to 10,000 atmospheres and temperatures in the region of 800°C. The rock contains up to 40 to 50 per cent iron and titanium at a depth of 8,711 metres. The upper half of the hole penetrates through rock formed about 1,100 million years ago.

A highly surprising result was the identification of large amounts of mineralized water at great depths. Gases consisting of helium, hydrogen, methane and carbon dioxide have been found at all levels. At a depth from 4,500 to 9,000 metres, the water was at such high pressures that it had fractured the rock, increasing its porosity by a factor of over three. Hydrothermal deposits of copper, zinc and cobalt sulphides were also found at these depths.

The identification of water and fractured rocks at great depths has thrown new light on the interpretation of the data obtained from seismic reflection methods of probing sedimentary rocks in the search for hydrocarbons. The methods have also been used to map structures deep in the crust and mantle. The layered reflections obtained from these surveys could be explained by highly cracked, fluid bearing rocks at the base of the crust.

Dinosaur Locomotion.—It is possible to determine how fast dinosaurs moved and the way in which they moved by studying their footprints. Recent research carried out in the United Kingdom and France has revealed much interesting data. Dr. McNeil Alexander of Leeds has concentrated on biomechanical analyses of their skeletons to determine the limitations of the manner of their movement. By using models provided by the Natural History Museum in London, he first located the centre of mass of the reptile. By using the ratio of mass to volume of living reptiles and the volume derived from the models, he was able to determine the overall mass and also how much of this mass could be supported by the hind legs with the reptile in various postures. The *Tyrannosaurus* was found to weigh about 7·7 tons and because it was a biped, all of this could be supported on its hind legs. The *Diplodocus* and *Stegosaurus* weighed 11·7 and 2 tons respectively, but being quadrupeds, were only capable of supporting about 80 per cent and 73 per cent of their mass on their back legs. Dr. Alexander therefore concluded that both were capable of rearing up on their hind legs for feeding from high trees. By relating the length of the leg to the length of their stride, it was possible to estimate the speed of travel. It is thought that the *Diplodocus* could have moved steadily at just over 2 m.p.h. but smaller bipeds could possibly have reached about 10 m.p.h. If they had exceeded these speeds, the bone structure was such that they would have very likely broken their legs.

Studies carried out by Paul Bernier of Lyons on fossil footprints in the late Jurassic deposits near Cerin in central France have revealed unusual patterns. They were not of the normal type in which alternating footsteps were made by the right and left feet but were such that the right and left feet appeared in pairs side by side and the next pair of prints would be found some 1·4 to 2·2 metres distant. The prints were 15 to 25 centimetres wide and their shape indicated that they were made by a medium sized carnivorous dinosaur. The spacing suggested that the reptile hopped like a kangaroo and it used its long tail for balancing. The geology of the area suggests that the reptiles lived on dry land but ventured into warm lagoons for food. Whether the hopping was used for stunning fish or whether it was their normal mode of travel has yet to be ascertained.

Driving Mechanism for Plate Tectonics.—The rate of movement of the various plates over the surface of the Earth has been determined to a reasonable degree of accuracy over recent years, but one big problem is the understanding of why and how these plates move. A new insight into the driving mechanism has been gained by studies of the collision between the Indian and Eurasian plates. The collision started about 50 million years ago and has produced the upthrusting we know as the Himalayas. It is estimated that the collision has shortened the continental crust by as much as 2,600 km. and the effect of the collision has been felt as far away as Hawaii and Australia.

The research ships *Gallieni* and *Mario Dufresne* have been studying the magnetic patterns laid down in the rocks in the Indian Ocean, the results indicating that about 45 million years ago, there occurred a major reorganisation of the plates surrounding the Ocean. Prior to the collision, the thinner oceanic crust lying to the north of the Indian plate was quietly being subducted under the Eurasian plate. The important question is what caused the collision. Was the Indian plate pushed or was it pulled by the original oceanic crust?

Prior to the collision, there was an active spreading ridge between India and Australia, indicating a drift apart of these two continents. When the collision took place, the ridge became inactive with the result that India and Australia moved as a single plate. On the far side of Australia, the activity between Australia and Antarctica increased. To the east, the Pacific plate altered its direction of motion, which manifested itself by the change in direction of the straight line of islands (Hawaiian chain) formed as the crust passed over a stationary hot spot beneath the crust. The time of this change in direction has been found to coincide with the time of the Indian collision.

The important outcome of this research is the identification of a pull mechanism and this may help in solving problems arising in other parts of the world.

Early Life on Earth.—It is well established that the Earth was formed some 4 thousand million years ago but there is considerable discussion on how long ago life first appeared on the planet. Until recently the most reliable evidence pointed to about 3½

thousand million years, this figure being based on the identification a few years ago of microfossils in sedimentary rocks found in Western Australia. Reports have now been published of the discovery of fossils of the same age in rocks in eastern Transvaal, South Africa. This region has long been thought of as a promising location for exceptionally old fossils because it contains some of the most ancient and well preserved sedimentary rocks.

Geologists from the Louisiana State University— Maud M. Walsh and Donald R. Lowe—have described the primitive forms of life found in the rocks as resembling filamentous bacteria or cyanobacteria. Their sedimentary location suggests that they were stromatolite-building micro-organisms. The filaments are abundant and have a fairly restricted range of diameters. Each filament has, however, an approximately constant diameter throughout its length. Many of the filaments which are aligned to the bedding plane of the rocks appear ribbon-like, possibly being flattened during sediment compaction.

Stromatolites are well-known from Precambrian rocks older than 600 million years and they still form in some warm shallow waters today. The structures build up through the accumulation of fine grains of sediment between matted colonies of bacteria. Characteristics of the filaments themselves show that they are without doubt biological in origin and that they were formed at the same time as the rocks. The biologists claim that it is difficult to explain these features as anything but the fossil remains of filamentous organisms and that they provide evidence for the existence of mat-forming structures in early Archean shallow water environments.

Early Records of Halley's Comet.—Much interest has been generated in the coming passage of Halley's comet through the inner regions of the solar system. This happens on average every 76 years although the actual value can range from 75 to 80 years. It was definitely recorded in 240 B.C. by the Chinese and there are vague references for earlier dates. There is a possibility that the comet seen by the Chinese in 467 B.C. was Halley's and a 1059 B.C. report cannot be ruled out completely. Of the more recent passages, an interesting one is the 1066 A.D. visit which is recorded on the Bayeaux Tapestry. The only gap in the record since 240 B.C. was the 164 B.C. visit but observations of this have recently come to light.

F. R. Stephenson and K. K. C. Yau of the University of Durham and H. Hunger of the University of Vienna found three clay tablets recording the sighting of the comet in 164 B.C. and 87 B.C. in the British Museum. The records are part of a collection of about 1,200 fragments containing astronomical data which were made by Babylonian astronomers from the time of King Nabonassar (747–734 B.C.). On the tablet describing the 164 B.C. passage, the following description is given: "the comet which previously had appeared in the east in the path of Anu in the area of the Pleiades and Taurus, to the west . . . and passed along in the path of Ea." Although the tablets are badly damaged sufficient information has been deciphered to enable astronomers to fix quite accurately the date of perihelion passage (the point in the orbit where the comet is nearest to the Sun). The actual orbit is perturbed by the gravitational pull of the planets and so with this new information it will be possible to go back further in time to determine the actual dates of previous passages through perihelion. This in turn may enable historians to identify earlier visits of the comet.

Exploration of Venus.—Although Venus is the nearest planet to the Earth, it has proved most difficult to obtain any detailed information about its surface conditions and atmosphere. Much has been learned from radar mapping and spaceprobes, but it is necessary to learn much more before we have a real understanding of the conditions existing on the planet. The latest probes have successfully completed their assignments and the full results are awaited.

On their way to rendezvous with Halley's comet, two Soviet *Vega* probes passed near to Venus in June 1985 and each released a French-made balloon and landing craft. Two days prior to the fly-by of the planet, each spacecraft released a spherical capsule which descended towards the planet, entering the upper reaches of the atmosphere at about 11 km. per second. After they had been slowed down by friction, the capsules split into two hemispheres, one containing the balloon and the other the landing craft.

The balloons were 3·4 metres in diameter and filled with helium. They floated at a height of 54 km. in the sulphuric acid clouds. Suspended on a cable some 12 metres long was an instrument package containing sensors to measure temperature, pressure, absorption and diffusion of the light and lightning flashes. Another sensor recorded the vertical motion of the balloon. Radio observatories round the world monitored the signals, which were analysed by a French team at Toulouse. The horizontal motion of the balloon was determined to an accuracy of 1 km. The balloons drifted for about two days covering some 10,000 km. They were released on the dark side of the planet and the 60 to 70 metres per second winds carried them to the sunlit side where the Sun's heat caused the balloons to explode. During their travel to the sunlit side, Soviet scientists reported that the balloons were subjected to vertical currents which hurled them up and down by 200 to 300 metres. The landing craft descended to regions well away from the sites of earlier landing probes, this time on the dark side. The main function of the probes was to analyse the composition and structure of the rocks. This, together with that collected from earlier probes, will enable Soviet scientists to obtain a more balanced picture of the geology and geochemistry of the planet.

Galactic Cirrus Cloud.—The Infra-red Astronomical Satellite (IRAS) in its relatively short active life produced so much sensational data that in many fields of research our views of the universe have had to be modified drastically. Although not in a sensational category, the discovery of wispy filaments of material high above the plane of our galaxy has resulted in suggestions that they are potential sites for star formation. These areas have been referred to as "infra-red cirrus" because of their strong emission of infra-red radiation. These clouds are one of the more striking features on maps of the infra-red sky recorded by IRAS.

Although there is a reasonable link between the IRAS data and the distribution of atomic hydrogen, it appears that there is also a close correlation with molecular clouds, which consist mainly of molecular hydrogen. Unfortunately, molecular hydrogen is difficult to detect and so astronomers tend to use the strong 2·6 mm. line of carbon monoxide, although this molecule is relatively rare. Research carried out at many institutions using various techniques all comes to the same conclusion that the infra-red cirrus and carbon monoxide clouds coincide in many cases. Recent work by a team from the Space Research Department in Groningen, Netherlands, has now shown that this correlation extends to neutral interstellar hydrogen.

The clouds that form this cirrus lie about 300 light years away and it is thought that in these regions stars are currently being formed. They form in the denser parts and astronomers from the University of Maryland have recently located a newly formed star in one of the clouds. The Groningen team have found that parts of the clouds are at temperatures of a few hundred degrees Kelvin, too high a value if heating is from local interstellar radiation. They suggest that the high temperature is due to temporary heating of very small grains of dust when they absorb a photon of light. The presence of atomic and molecular hydrogen and dust particles supports the idea that the cirrus is the birth place of stars.

Halocarbons and the Ozone Layer.—Much has been written in the past about the world-wide use of halocarbons, in particular chlorofluorocarbons, as aerosol propellants and the effect these could have on the destruction of the ozone layer. Recent work carried out by David B. Harper of Queen's University, Belfast, has shown that the ozone layer is not being threatened at the present time.

As the halocarbons are released they rise into the upper atmosphere where they are attacked by the high concentration of ultra-violet light from the Sun. This causes the carbon-halogen bonds to break, releasing the highly reactive halogens. By a series of quite involved reactions the ozone which is present at these levels is decomposed. If this were to take place on a large scale, the Earth's surface would soon be exposed to high concentrations of deadly ultra-violet light and life would rapidly come to an end. Harper carried out some calculations and has shown that the emission of synthetic halocarbons is by comparison quite small compared with the huge quantities pushed into the atmosphere from natural sources such as fungi. It is thought that about 5 million tons of chloromethane are produced naturally each year compared with the annual synthetic production of 26,000 tons.

Harper obtained his figures by quantifying chloromethane production by the wood-rotting fungus *Phellinus pomaceus*. This fungus is able to methylate chloride ions existing in living cells with an efficiency of over 90 per cent. The process by which this is achieved is of great importance to chemists who at present have to employ dangerous reagents in the synthetic production of chloromethane. The process is also costly so it is expected that much more research will be carried out in this field.

Major Earthquakes.—The most devastating earthquake (magnitude 7·8) during the year ending July 1985, occurred in the vicinity of Chile on 3 March. The epicentre lay just off the coast of Central Chile but it created extensive damage on the mainland. It killed 177 people, injured more than 2,500 and left 212,000 homeless. Hardest hit were the ports of San Antonio and Valparaiso and the coastal city of Viña del Mar. Santiago, the capital, was badly damaged and many villages between the coast and the capital suffered near-total destruction. Damage estimates have been quoted as at least 1,000 million pounds sterling. The main shock followed the foreshock by 10 seconds and was felt over an area covering much of Argentina and parts of Brazil. Tsunamis were generated, some reaching as far away as Japan, some 7,000 km. from the epicentre. Several quite strong aftershocks were recorded causing further damage. In addition, several new tremors occurred during the following month, with epicentres quite near to that of the 3 March event. The most severe of these (mag. 7·2) occurred on 9 April. Although two people died of heart attacks, no further deaths were reported. Many people were injured.

The other area which experienced a series of intense tremors was Papua New Guinea. The first, of magnitude 7·1 on 10 May, caused extensive landslides on both sides of the Nakanai Mountains of West New Britain. Layers of waterlogged limestone and mudstone were fluidized by the main shock and flowed *en masse* into several rivers, causing extensive flooding and damage to bridges. Another strong tremor occurred on 3 July, causing further extensive damage, even at Rabaul, some 70 km. from the epicentre. A 1·3 metre tsunami was observed in Simpson Harbour. Many aftershocks, recorded virtually continuously for 12 hours, followed the main event. The earthquake caused large ground deformations in the Rabaul caldera. In the caldera itself, further deformations were caused by over 1,200 tremors during the months of June and July.

In addition to the above, earthquakes of magnitude 7 or greater were reported from the central Atlantic Ocean on the mid-Atlantic Ridge, in Indonesia and the Philippines.

Mysterious Cloud over the Pacific.—On 9 April 1984, a Japanese airliner, on a flight from Tokyo to Alaska encountered a large mushroom shaped cloud of rising dust about 270 km. from the Japanese coast. Two other airliners also reported seeing the cloud. All the aircraft were flying above cloud and all reported seeing the mushroom develop out of the cloud, rising at a rate of about 800 km. per hour. The cloud then thinned out and disappeared. One of the original explanations given was that the cloud was formed by the explosion of a nuclear submarine, but dust collected by Phantom fighters showed no evidence of radioactivity. Another explanation involved the eruption of an underwater volcano. A weakness in this theory lay in the fact that the most likely source was situated some 1,500 km. away from the location of the cloud. Calculations have subsequently shown that only an eruption immediately beneath the cloud could have produced the observed

phenomena. No such event in that area was recorded by the hydrophones at Wake Island.

The possibility of a nuclear test in the atmosphere has not been ruled out because of the similarities between this event and the one reported over the South Atlantic Ocean in 1979. The American *Vela* satellites are capable of recording and distinguishing between the various types of flash produced by lightning, laser beams, sunlight and nuclear explosions and it has only been revealed recently that the flash in the Atlantic was due to an atomic explosion. However, on this more recent event no flash was reported.

The latest explanation, given by André Chang and James Burnetti of the research group Teledyne Geotech, of Virginia, suggests a natural cause. They believe that a meteoroid entering the atmosphere exploded more or less at the same time that it entered the cloud layer. The heat from the explosion heated up the cloud layer over a diameter of about 10 km. They claim that convection, producing a plume of cloud, would have behaved in the manner witnessed. Not all investigators accept this so it is felt that the last word on this has still to be written.

Neutrino Problem.—It has been known for a long time that the number of neutrinos being recorded on Earth is only about one third of that required by current astrophysical theories and there have been many attempts to explain this discrepancy. The theoretical number has been based on the premise that the temperature of the Sun increases continually right through to the centre, where the temperature is thought to be about 15 million degrees. Work carried out by John Faulkner and Ronald Gilliland at Lick Observatory some 8 years ago and never published because they thought it too bizarre to be taken seriously, has now been sent to the *Astrophysical Journal* for publication.

The observed number of neutrinos implies that the centre of the Sun is at a lower temperature and so the astronomers developed a model to account for this. They said that this was possible if the central region of the Sun, say a core containing about 6 per cent. of the Sun's mass, was at roughly a constant temperature. They based their ideas on the suggestion that there could exist some very heavy neutrinos. Neutrinos are thought to have zero or at least an exceedingly low mass, say just a few electron volts, compared with a mass of about half a million electron volts for an electron. If there existed very heavy neutrinos with masses of about a thousand million electron volts (MeV), this would provide a mechanism for an isothermal core.

Evidence that the universe contains large quantities of dark matter has increased considerably recently, giving much support to the new theory of inflation. Researchers advocating a Grand Unified Theory for all the forces of nature have put forward a case for a whole new family of particles with masses of about a few thousand MeV. Preliminary results from C.E.R.N. in Europe, although still controversial, indicate this possibility. How the Sun could capture these particles is open to question. One idea is that the Sun collects these as it travels through interstellar space and since they react weakly with ordinary matter, they can pass unhindered through the outer layers of the Sun to the proposed isothermal core.

New Class of Supernova.

New Class of Supernova.—Supernovae are the largest and most spectacular explosions known to astronomers and until recently they could be classed into two distinct types depending on the manner in which the light output rises and falls, although on a few occasions difficulties have arisen in classifying some events. However, a recent event has shown that the associated outburst would in no way fit into the accepted picture. In Type I, the explosion occurs when a white dwarf, one component of a binary system, is suddenly inundated by material from its companion causing the dwarf to explode. With Type II, supernovae occur in very massive stars which have evolved to the state where much of the mass of the star has been converted into heavy elements. When the core of the star has been converted to iron, it cannot support the overlying layers and the star collapses in less than a second. The resulting shock wave causes the star to blow up.

Astronomers in California, using the 5-metre telescope on Mount Palomar, discovered the new supernova during studies of nearby galaxies. Designated SN 1985f, the star lies close to the nucleus of the spiral galaxy NGC 4618 and an examination of the spectrum of the outburst showed prominent lines of atomic oxygen. These lines appear very broad, indicating that the oxygen is moving very fast along the line of sight, at about 15,000 km. per second. The dominance of the oxygen lines suggests that the star had already peeled off the outer layers of hydrogen and helium before it exploded. How the star disposed of these outer layers is a complete mystery.

Investigations have also been made into other non-classifiable events which are also oxygen rich. Cassiopiea-A, such a remnant, is thought to have erupted in the 17th century. If it had been a normal supernova, it would have been an exceptionally bright object, but no reports of such an event have come to light. It has been suggested that this new event is of the same category and the absence of the outer layers produces an explosion which is nowhere near as bright as the more traditional types. The monitoring of the light curve of SN 1985f should provide answers to some of the problems.

New Method for Dating the Past.

New Method for Dating the Past.—One of the major problems for archaeologists is that of obtaining a very accurate estimate of the date of a site under investigation. In the past the dating of sediments has been based almost entirely on radio-carbon dating of any organic material present. A new method, using the same property that enables pottery and sediments to be dated using thermoluminescence, combines laser techniques with the detection of ancient sunlight.

The thermoluminescence technique depends on the fact that electrons build up in the defects of the crystal lattice of certain minerals. Exposure to light or heat disperses these electrons so that once a crystal is shielded from the sun's rays by sediments covering it, this electron build up will gradually take place. On exposure to light, the electrons are expelled as photons and the intensity of this light can be measured. Although the mineral feldspar has been used in the past, it has been shown that the method is open to considerable error and has been limited to deposits younger than 120,000 years.

Much more satisfactory results have been obtained by replacing feldspar with quartz. Quartz loses its electrons much more slowly when exposed to sunlight, but if the sample is exposed to an argon-ion laser with a 514·5 nanometre beam, use can be made of the most light sensitive electron traps which would be emptied by just 10 seconds exposure to sunlight. The big problem is to ensure that the samples under investigation have not been exposed to sunlight during collection. Research workers at the Simon Frasar University in British Columbia have studied sand from a well-dated sequence of sand dunes in South Australia, formed over the last million years. They found that the thermoluminescence signal varied smoothly with age. The experiment was then repeated at an archaeological site in British Columbia dating back about 6,000 years and the results compared favourably with those obtained by radio-carbon dating. The next test involved silt lying below a wood layer dated by radio-carbon at 59,000 years. This new technique gave 62,000 years ($+/- 8,000$ years). It is therefore concluded that the method can be used satisfactorily over a time range of 1,000 to 700,000 years.

Oldest Amphibian.

Oldest Amphibian.—One of the big problems facing palaeontologists is the understanding of and dating the transition of life in water to life on land. Many theories have been put forward but none have been wholly satisfactory. The latest find from oil shale near Edinburgh will certainly contribute to the problem and could alter some well-established ideas.

Mrs. S. P. Wood, an amateur turned professional fossil collector, recently collected a variety of fossils from the 340 million year old rocks and amongst these was the first articulated amphibian to be found in the Lower Carboniferous of Europe in this century. The find was the earliest well-preserved amphibian skeleton ever discovered.

The skeleton is 40 cm. long and is preserved in part and counterpart on two blocks of limestone. The skull, vertebral column and limbs are still articulated and the specimen is remarkable for the preservation of the hands and feet. It has a tail, the shape of which is defined by its investing scales. A preliminary investigation showed no signs of a lateral canal or other features which could indicate that the animal had an aquatic mode of life. Six other specimens from the same location have been provisionally classified as belonging to the same species. They include a skull of the same size as that of the complete specimen and a pelvis with paired hind limbs. The other fossils collected from the rocks include poor specimens of amphibians which showed no evidence of a purely aquatic existence. No fossil fish were found.

Before this discovery, only aquatic amphibians were known to exist in the Late Carboniferous. This new finding indicates that the amphibian ancestors of the tetrapods (the collective name for amphibians, reptiles, birds and mammals) lived on land in the Early Carboniferous, much earlier than hitherto thought.

Outer Region of the Solar System.—Just as when the first space probes penetrated the boundary between the Earth's magnetosphere and the region dominated by the solar wind, producing many sensational and unexpected discoveries, so we are now approaching the time when man will probe the regions separating those dominated by the Sun and those of interstellar space. The spacecraft approaching the edge of the solar system have already started providing surprising information.

The boundary where the outward motion of charged particles from the Sun is halted by the pressure of gases in the interstellar space is called the heliopause and at this boundary the gases of the solar wind pile up in a shock-wave as they hit the interstellar gas. The distance of this heliopause was first measured from *Pioneer 10*, the most distant of all man-made objects and currently at just over 35 astronomical units (AU) from the Sun. The data suggested that the heliopause lies about 65 AU from the Sun, but data obtained from *Voyagers I* and *II* indicates that the distance is much less. *Voyager I*, after leaving the vicinity of Saturn, is currently heading upwards out of the plane of the orbits of the planets whilst *Voyager II* is keeping in the plane and passing Uranus in January 1986. Instruments designed to measure radio signals from Jupiter and Saturn went silent after the planets were passed, but on 30 August 1983, *Voyager I* started picking up signals again. Studies of these emissions have shown that it was impossible for them to have originated from either Jupiter or Saturn and that if they did in fact originate from outside the solar system, their properties were unlike any other known radio source.

It is concluded that the most likely source is the generation of signals from the shock-wave at the heliopause. This explanation is strengthened by the fact that the signal strength increases as the probe moves outwards. The present estimate is that the heliopause lies at a distance of 46 AU. The two values are in line with current ideas that the heliopause is pear-shaped, due to the motion of the Sun through interstellar gas. Although now it is only about 20 AU from the Sun, it could be the first to penetrate interstellar space and produce many surprises.

Planetary Systems outside our Solar System.— For many years astronomers have suspected that planetary systems exist outside our own solar system, but the actual evidence for this has always been rather weak. This situation has changed somewhat over the last few years and now more positive evidence has become available. Towards the end of 1984, astronomers identified a flattened disc of material surrounding the star Beta Pictoris. It had properties which indicated that planets were in the process of forming. This discovery was soon followed by an announcement that a planet-like object had been detected orbiting another star. This was the first occasion on which such a body had been identified directly.

The star concerned is known as Van Biesbroeck 8, a faint red dwarf in the constellation of Ophiuchus. In 1963, astronomers at the U.S. Naval Observatory reported that the movement of the star VB 8 fluctuated from a straight line, suggesting the presence of an unknown companion. It may be recalled that in 1915 a similar motion by the bright star Sirius led to the discovery of the important class of stars known as white dwarfs. Infra-red studies of VB8 have revealed the existence of a companion having a suspected mass several times greater than that of Jupiter. This new object has been labelled a "brown dwarf". It is definitely a planet as it is too small to produce nuclear reactions. It orbits the star at a distance of about 1,000 million kilometres. Although the planet and star are roughly the same size, the star is about 100,000 times brighter at visual wavelengths.

The investigation was carried out using speckle interferometric techniques at wavelengths of 1.6 and 2.2 micrometres, a technique which averages out atmospheric fluctuations which degrade stellar images. The success of these observations was made possible because of the relative nearness of the star and the large size of its companion. The discovery has led to the suggestion that planetary companions to stars are quite common and that they may account for much of the so-called missing mass, required in cosmological studies.

Progress towards a Malaria Vaccine.—It is estimated that about 150 million people suffer from malaria at any one time and that about one million children in Africa die of it in any one year. At present the attack on the disease has been along two main fronts—the elimination of the anapheles mosquito which carries the parasites and by attacking the parasite, *Plasmodium falciparum*, with drugs. Neither have been very successful and what is causing great concern is the fact that the parasites are rapidly becoming resistant to the drugs.

Research has been carried out at many establishments and it is now thought possible that soon the way will become clear to produce a vaccine for trials in humans. Robin Anders and colleagues at the Walter and Eliza Hall Institute of Medical Research at Melbourne, Australia have applied a technique previously developed at the University of Columbia, New York, to separate the malarial D.N.A. into seven different sizes, representing seven different chromosomes. These seven sizes are unfortunately not the same when parasites from different parts of the world are compared. This variation could be due to varying resistances to drugs but at the moment there is no positive explanation. The more that is learned about the reasons for the variation in size, the better the chance of developing a vaccine. Dr. Anders' team has already been able to identify on which of the seven chromosomes are located the genes for four different proteins that might be the basis of vaccines.

In other recent investigations, it has been found possible to immunize the body against the first stage of the parasite's life cycle in humans—the sporozoite, the form in which Plasmodium enters the blood stream from the saliva of the mosquito. These make their way to the liver and develop into another form called metazoites. These re-enter the blood stream to produce the symptoms of malaria. A vaccine capable of stimulating the body to produce antibodies which would attack the sporozoites is theoretically possible and research is centred on finding a method to produce large quantities of the part of the parasite which stimulates the body's immune system.

Last year, John Dame and his team from the U.S. Institute of Health managed to identify and clone the gene responsible for making the theoretical protein. Other teams in America have announced that they have successfully carried out this piece of genetic engineering. Although the stage for trials with humans will soon be reached, much more work will be needed before a vaccine is available on a wide scale.

Rare Oxide of Carbon.—The old idea that elements combined in relatively simple ways has long since departed. As our knowledge of sub-atomic chemistry increases, chemists have concentrated on theoretical aspects of molecular structure and have revealed that most unlikely combinations of elements are possible. Chemists at Monash University, in Australia, first of all showed that theoretically it was possible for three atoms of carbon to combine with just one atom of oxygen to form tricarbon monoxide. It would bear the same relation to carbon monoxide (CO) as does carbon suboxide (C_3O_2) to carbon dioxide (CO_2). The use of quantum mechanics to predict molecular bonding involves quite difficult calculations and it is currently only possible to describe accurately relatively small molecules. The physical structure and spectroscopic characteristics were predicted. Of importance was that characteristic frequency of this theoretically new oxide lay in the microwave spectrum and hence it would be possible to use microspectroscopy to identify the molecule if it existed.

The theoretical team combined with experimental chemists from the same University in an attempt to synthesize the compound. Its existence was confirmed using a mass spectrograph and a microwave spectrograph. The molecule is not stable under normal conditions and exists for only about 1 second at pressures of 1 pascal (one ten-thousandth of an atmosphere). It therefore plays no major part in the chemistry of the Earth.

It is important, however, in the study of the chemistry of interstellar clouds. The experimenters suggest that, like another odd molecule (HC_3N), tricarbon monoxide may be a normal constituent in interstellar clouds where pressures as low as 10^{-16} pascals and temperatures as low as 10 Kelvin are the norm. Like all new discoveries, although completely insignificant at the time, it is possible that this new compound may assume some importance in future studies in vacuum chemistry.

Ring around Neptune?—Three of the major planets—Jupiter, Saturn and Uranus—now have well documented rings but until recently there was little positive evidence that Neptune, the fourth and outermost, possessed a similar feature. Work carried out by French and American astronomers seems to indicate that a ring system does in fact exist, although more observations are required before this can be considered as a certainty.

The evidence for a ring arose during observations of a near-occultation by Neptune of the star SAO 186001. A group of French astronomers working under the direction of André Brahic of the University of Paris and operating from the European Southern Observatory in Chile, recorded a 35 per cent. reduction in the intensity of the light from the star lasting for less than 2 seconds. A reduction of light was also reported from the Cerro Tololo Inter-American Observatory, situated some 95 km. farther south, where a team from the University of Arizona was observing. Unfortunately, the computer printout did not display the event very clearly and it was only after the French results had been published that it was realized that they had in fact recorded the same phenomenon. The observations imply that there exists something about 10–20 km. wide situated in Neptune's equatorial plane about 76,000 km. from the centre of the planet. It is highly unlikely that small satellites could be responsible because it would require two such objects to cause occultations at both sites. Evidence against the case for a ring lies in the fact that neither observations reported a second occultation, a requirement if the ring was complete.

Two possibilities have been put forward. One suggests that the ring may resemble the outermost ring of Uranus, which is narrower on one side than the other. The other is that the ring is fragmented and discontinuous. In the past there have been several observations which have suggested the possibility of a ring round the planet but in all cases the observational evidence has not been positive enough. The above adds to the evidence but it is most likely that the problem will not be solved until *Voyager 2* passes the planet in 1989.

Supernova in a Quasar.—There is still much to be learned about the true nature of quasars and how they fit into the overall picture of the universe. Recent observations by Bruce Campbell and colleagues at the Dominion Astrophysical Observatory in Canada, have shown the existence of a supernova in the luminous "fuzz" surrounding the quasar QSO 1059 + 730, which lies near to the Draco-Ursa Major boundary. It is a relatively close quasar, lying between 1 and 2 thousand million light years distant.

The astronomers were studying this particular quasar as part of a programme for examining the colours and luminosity profiles of the fuzz around quasars in general. On 10 May 1983, six red-light images taken with a charge-coupled device (CCD) using the Hawaii 2·2 metre reflector, all showed a 20th magnitude star 2·6 seconds of arc south east of the quasar. In July 1985, a CCD image obtained using the 3·6 metre telescope showed no evidence for the star. Many ideas have been proposed to explain this object, ranging from a flare star to an asteroid, but only one explanation seems to satisfy all the observed data. It is therefore concluded that it was either a Type II supernova near maximum brightness, or a Type I some 20 to 40 days after maximum. (*See also* "New Class of Supernova").

If this was a supernova, it is the first to be detected in a galaxy containing a quasar at its centre. It provides evidence to support the theories that stars exist in the fuzz surrounding quasars. Calculations deduced from the recorded magnitudes provide further evidence that quasars are at cosmological distances and not relatively near to us.

Survival of the Cheetah.—Anyone who has seen the cheetah in the wild will marvel at its graceful movement and its sheer speed when hunting. Nevertheless, it is one of the most endangered of all the cats. This is not due to its inability to obtain food because it does this quite efficiently. The trouble lies in the fact that there is virtually a lack of genetic variation throughout the species. Biochemical analyses of enzymes and other protein have shown that the species has 10 to 100 times less genetic variation than is normally found in mammals, whose rate of reproduction is poor, whether in the wild or in captivity. Cub mortality in the wild is estimated to be in the region of 70 per cent and nearly 30 per cent of the cheetahs born in captivity die before the age of six months. Much of the trouble lies before the cub is born. The semen contains only about 10 per cent of the number of sperm found in the semen of domestic cats and up to 70 per cent of the sperm has been found to be abnormal.

Research carried out by a joint team of biologists from South Africa and the U.S.A. has found further evidence of genetic troubles. They have studied the rejection time taken for skin grafts between unrelated cheetahs (allografts). This gives a measure of the genetic variability in the cheetah immune system. Allografts between domestic cats are rejected suddenly some 7 to 13 days after grafting. The allografts between cheetahs did not show any rapid rejection. A quarter of those tested rejected slowly after 39 to 70 days, but with the remainder the grafts were accepted. This indicates that there was a high degree of shared antigens in the group. All mammals produce antigens responsible for allograft rejection, being genetically determined by a particular chromosomal segment known as the major histo-compatibility complex (M.H.C.). An important function of the M.H.C. is in immunization against infection. The research team have suggested that the lack of genetic variation in the M.H.C. could leave the animals wide open to attack by a virus, as was the case, it is thought, in the outbreak of feline infectious peritonitis which killed 18 out of 42 cheetahs in a wild life park in Oregon.

However, the knowledge gained from studies of other inbred species, such as Père David's deer, may help the cheetahs to survive. A similar situation existed with the northern elephant seal, which also had a very low genetic variation. The problem arose in this case due to overhunting in the last century but it appears to have made a successful recovery on the Californian coast.

Third Optical Pulsar Discovered.—Several hundred pulsars are known to exist and all but two have been identified only by X-ray or radio wavelengths. Pulsars are thought to be neutron stars which spin rapidly, sending out a narrow beam of intense radiation, pulsing at between 640 times a second to once every few seconds. The two cases which have been identified by visual wavelengths lie in our own galaxy. One of them lies in the well-known Crab Nebula. A third optical pulsar has recently been discovered, this one lying outside our galaxy in the Large Magellanic Cloud, visible in the southern hemisphere.

The object was identified as a pulsar from X-ray data sent back by the Einstein Observatory satellite in 1978. The pulsar characteristics were similar to that of the Crab and like the latter surrounded by a supernova remnant. Astronomers were sent to Cerro Tololo Observatory in Chile to study the object at visual wavelengths and they located a 23rd magnitude object pulsing at 20 times a second, the same as the X-ray pulsar, proving that the two objects were the same.

Unfortunately, further studies have shown that the similarities with the Crab pulsar are not as strong as at first thought. Although they emit about the same amount of light, the new object has only about a third of the energy budget. Also, the new object is emitting about 2 per cent. of the total energy from the surrounding nebula, some twenty times more than the Crab pulsar. It is also redder than the Crab pulsar. This new object, designated 0540–69·3, is at a distance of 165,000 light years from the Earth and is virtually a new type of object.

Current theories for the formation and behaviour of pulsars have of necessity to be altered drastically and it is possible that a satisfactory explanation will not emerge until more extra-galactic objects have been discovered. Studies of this new pulsar continue in an attempt to learn more of the way in which the rotational period slows down.

Tornadoes in Britain.—Most people tend to think that tornadoes are restricted to warmer climates and that such events in the British Isles are freak occurrences. This, however, is not borne out by the facts. Britain experiences tornadoes on as many as 31 days in a year and it is possible for more than 100 to occur on a single day in these islands. Because of the immense amount of damage that can be caused, an organization called the Tornado and Storm Research Organization (T.O.R.R.O.) was set up in 1974 to document these events and recently the first conference was held in Oxford to report on its findings.

The meeting, organized by Derek Elsom of Oxford Polytechnic and Terence Meaden, editor of the *Journal of Meteorology*, discussed papers on tornadoes, waterspouts, wind devils and other severe storm phenomena documented in the intervening decade and also those recorded in historical documents over the last thousand years. During the last thirty years, the records show that there were fewer storms during the period from June to September, although some of those that did occur were quite devastating. For example, the tornado which hit the village of Gotham, near Nottingham, on the night of 2 August 1984, caused over £100,000 damage to buildings in just a few seconds.

Tornadoes are very localized events lasting only a few seconds or minutes and are not normally picked up by weather satellites, radar or weather stations. They are the most severe form of whirlwind and can range in intensity right down to the humble wind devil, often seen on hot sunny days scattering new mown hay. All have the common property of an ascending current of warm air, rotating rapidly as a narrow vortex and being sustained by the input of a continuous supply of air at the bottom from all directions.

An important aspect of the conference was to alert civil engineers to the dangers of tornadoes when they are designing bridges and buildings, especially those associated with oil refineries, chemical manufacturing and nuclear power stations. It is essential, say the researchers, that full allowance be made for sudden wind speeds of up to 80 metres per second (180 miles per hour).

White Dwarf in the Making.—The generally accepted picture of the evolution of low mass stars in the later stages of their lives is that, towards the end of the period as a red giant, the distended envelope is shed as a planetary nebula revealing the core of the star which eventually becomes a white dwarf. The theoretical understanding of the way this is carried out is very thin, partly due to the speed at which this stage of the evolution takes place. Our knowledge of this stage has increased considerably by the identification of a star actually going through this process.

Astronomers at the University of Texas and at the University of Cape Town, using a variety of instruments, have been analysing the light curve from a star known as PG 1159–035 for the last six years. This star is a 14·5 magnitude blue star in the constellation of Virgo and a member of a small class of helium-rich compact objects with surface temperatures in excess of 100,000°K.

It has been found that the star pulsates over a range of frequencies, with at least eight different periods ranging from 350 to 842 seconds. These different oscillations interfere with each other producing a complicated light curve. However, the investigators have concentrated on the strongest and most stable component—one having a period of 516 seconds and a brightness variation of about 0·2 magnitudes. Analysis has shown that the period is shortening at a rate of 1 second in 2,600 years. Theoretical studies predict that cooling will lengthen the period of oscillation whereas contraction will shorten it and so it is thought that here is an example of a star actually in the process of shrinking from the giant stage into a white dwarf. Studies of the rate of change are of great importance not only for understanding this stage of stellar evolution but they could also lead to an independent method for determining the age of the galaxy and also a lower limit to the age of the universe.

Wind Devils on Mars.—Most people are familiar with wind or dust devils, the gentlest form of tornado. They are often seen swirling new mown hay and dust in columns as they sweep rapidly across a field. Photographs taken by the *Viking* planetary probes have revealed similar features occurring on the planet Mars. The conditions existing on the surface of Mars are very different from those existing on Earth. The pressure is less than 1 per cent. of that on Earth and because it is roughly 1½ times as far away

from the Sun, the strength of the Sun's rays are less than half that experienced on Earth. Nevertheless, solar heating is sufficient to produce wind devils, some of which reach as high as 6 km. above the Martian surface.

Such phenomena had been predicted as long ago as 1964, but they have only recently been identified on high resolution pictures taken from the most recent spacecraft. Most of the 51,000 photographs do not have sufficient resolution to pick up these features but they seem to be quite plentiful on those photographs taken relatively close to the surface of the planet. The astronomers responsible for identifying the dust devils—Peter Thomas and Peter Gierasch of Cornell University—reported their findings at a meeting of lunar and planetary scientists at Houston in March 1985.

The dust devils have so far only been seen in two regions, areas near to features known as Utopia Planitia and Arcadia Planitia. On one photograph of the Arcadia Planitia region, four dust devils can clearly be seen, the height of the largest being about 5 km.

World's Oldest Dinosaur.—Dinosaurs reigned supreme for a very long time, so their sudden extinction some 65 million years ago has created much interest in recent years. What is also of great importance is the reason for the emergence of these reptiles into a world which had no flowering plants, birds, mammals or butterflies. The recent find in the Petrified Forest National Park in Arizona of fossils of dinosaurs about the size of a small ostrich and more than 225 million years old has been heralded as a major discovery. It is thought that they may give some clues to the way in which dinosaurs evolved from reptiles which waddled about on limbs extending from the sides of their bodies in a similar manner to present day crocodiles.

The bones were first identified by Brian Small, a geology student, and they were taken to the Museum of Palaeontology at the University of California at Berkeley. A team of workers led by Robert Long has already examined bones from the ankle, shin, thigh, pelvis and about a dozen vertebrae and is now eagerly waiting for the rest of the skeleton to arrive. Much of this is, however, encased in siltstone. Two other hind legs exist, indicating that more than one animal is involved. But the bones lead into the rock, so great care is being taken in their recovery.

Long remarked that the ankle bone is unlike that of any other known dinosaur. These are normally oblong in shape but this one is almost square. The reptile was about 2½ metres in length with a long neck and tail. It weighed about 90 kg. It is thought that it could be related to the plateosaur which emerged 10 to 15 million years later, about 215 million years ago. These eventually evolved into the giant brontosaurus. The scientists are quite confident about the age of this new creature because the fossils have been found in well-documented deposits of fossilized leaves, pollen and spores. The animal had legs directly underneath its body and it is thought that it could probably have stood on its hind legs although normally it would have spent most of its time on all fours. So far, no name has been given to it.

ARCHITECTURAL CONSERVATION IN 1985

The world of architectural conservation was greatly saddened in the course of the year by the sudden death, after a visit to India, of the celebrated architectural historian, Alec Clifton-Taylor who, in his books, and latterly in his television series had greatly advanced both scholarly and popular appreciation of historic buildings. His passing was the more painful in coming so soon after that of Sir Nikolaus Pevsner and coinciding with the deaths of Peter Fleetwood-Hesketh, who played a major role in the post-war development of the conservation movement and of Gordon Barnes, the well-known architectural photographer.

However, the sad news was countered by the pleasurable and the elevation of Mrs. Jennifer Jenkins to a Dame, was a widely-acclaimed reward for her years as Chairman of the Historic Buildings Council. On the same occasion, Bernard Feilden, former architect to York Minster and St. Paul's Cathedral, was created a knight.

In similar vein, conservation cases in the year brought applications to demolish and, welcome reprieves.

The latter included a number to destroy buildings protected in the especially important Grade II* category: 20 Bridge Street, Haverfordwest, with a notable 18th century interior (now likely to be repaired); Ranby Hall, Nottinghamshire, of the late 18th century (damaged by fire); Longbottoms Mill, Sowerby Bridge, West Yorkshire, of c.1780 and an early, and huge, example of a brick-built mill, its fate unfortunately sealed by a serious fire; the "Long Stores" at Devizes, Wiltshire (application refused); various buildings at Woodlands, Dorset (now reprieved); Pell Wall Hall, near Market Drayton, Shropshire, the last country house of Sir John Soane and the subject of repeated applications to demolish; the warehouse at the rear of 3/4 Old Market, Wisbech, Cambridgeshire, one of several that lend drama to the riverbanks of the Nene; and New Hall, Ribchester Road, Clayton-le-Dale, Lancashire, a derelict mansion of 1663 where the proposal was to deroof and demolish the west wing.

Buildings in the Grade II category threatened by application to demolish included: the Unitarian Chapel, Percy Street, Preston, with fabric of 1716; the Edgerton Cemetery Chapels, Birkby, West Yorkshire; Dukinfield Chapel, Greater Manchester, one of the first independent chapels in the country and originally constructed in the mid-16th century as a private chapel to a long lost house; the Smardale Gill Viaduct, Crosby Garrett, Cumbria, of 1850 (an application by British Rail that was refused); 34 Fisher Street, Carlisle, an impressive early 19th century Classical townhouse (now to be retained); Goodwyns Place, Dorking, Surrey, a handsome arts and crafts design of 1901 by Thackeray Turner; a charming, if derelict, mid-18th century gazebo at Ham Green Hospital, Easton-in-Gordano, Avon; a timber frame and stone barn of interest at Shore Hall Farm, Penistone, Sheffield; the former United Reformed church at Newton Abbot, Devon, of 1875, with a proud tower and spire (application refused); the Angel Mill, Westbury, Wiltshire, a major monument of industrial archaeology from the early 19th century; the Great Synagogue, Manchester, of 1857; Shawe Hall, Kingsley Holt, Staffordshire; the State Cinema, Grays, Essex, of 1938; the stable block at the now-demolished Eaton Hall, Cheshire, designed in 1834 by Lewis Wyatt; surviving Georgian terraces in Liverpool at Shaw Street and Upper Parliament Street and part of a good 18th century terrace in Worcester.

A tale hangs on the only application to demolish totally a Grade I listed building. This is Hammerwood Park in Sussex, near East Grinstead. It was built c.1790 and is of international importance as one of the very few works in this country by Benjamin Latrobe who, after his emigration to America in 1795, was responsible for the Capitol in Washington. After a long period of dereliction, Hammerwood was bought in 1980 by a young man determined to save the building and to open it to the public. Unfortunately a legal tussle with neighbours led to an unfavourable Court decision limiting public access and precipitated an application to demolish, prompted by frustration. This was swiftly refused and an amicable settlement may yet emerge.

One of the more unusual cases revolved around the diminutive and very early church of St. Teilo at Llandeilo Tal-y-Bont, near Swansea. Visible from the M4, but virtually inaccessible, the church attracted renewed interest when the most important collection of wallpaintings in the Principality were found to be surviving beneath limewash on its internal walls. St. Fagans Folk Museum offered to dismantle the whole church including the paintings and re-erect it on its open site near Llandaff. Permission for this exercise was granted and work began immediately.

The execution of extensions to national monuments is always a difficult area in which to achieve concensus and the proposal to add additional floorspace to the top of the Royal Exchange stirred up the expected hornet's nest. Even more controversial is any large-scale development at the heart of an historic city and certainly when it is the City of London. Rarely can a single planning application have attracted so much publicity as that by Mr. Peter Palumbo to redevelop the site opposite the Royal Exchange, christened somewhat ambiguously "Mansion House Square". Following the two-month public inquiry the long expected decision by the Secretary of State was handed down at the beginning of the summer. Permission for the tower block by Mies van der Rohe and consent to clear the buildings bordered by Queen Victoria Street and Poultry were both refused.

Reprieves spared two outstanding churches in Wolverhampton. The Anglican St. George's, previously the subject of an application to demolish, is now to be retained as part of a Sainsbury scheme for a new hypermarket whilst the Roman Catholic SS. Peter and Paul, similarly threatened by an application to demolish, is now to be repaired by the archdiocese and kept in use as a church. SS. Peter and Paul is an outstanding Neo Classical design and historically significant as the resting place of Archbishop Milner. Other major churches saved by new uses include St. Philip's, Stepney, to be converted into a medical library for the adjacent hospital and SS. Philip and James, North Oxford, known locally as "Phil and Jim", and an important work by G. E. Street, which is to become the headquarters of the "Centre for Mission". Churches too important to be either demolished or converted, including St. Mary's, Sandwich, St. John the Baptist, Bristol and the great tower of c.1240 at West Walton, Norfolk were passed into the hands of the Redundant Churches Fund for care and maintenance.

The National Heritage Memorial Fund continued to prove its indispensability. Extra Government "topping up" of £25m, promised a satisfactory end to the uncertainty over three outstanding houses—Kedleston, Derbyshire, Nostell Priory, Yorkshire and Weston, Staffordshire. Government money is also to be contributed towards the cost of returning Temple Bar to the City, on a site next to St. Paul's. Planning consent for the move was granted in February.

Major planning inquiries in the year covered:

Maristow House, near Plymouth, a Grade II* mansion dating from 1760 and 1909 but damaged by two fires; St. Wilfrid's Church, Brighton, an outstanding inter-war design of H. R. Goodhart Rendel, recommended for vesting in the Redundant Churches Fund by the Advisory Board for Redundant Churches but proposed for demolition nevertheless by the Church Commissioners; Highhead Castle, Ivegill, Cumbria, a Grade II* mansion of the 1740s gutted by fire and Our Lady Immaculate Roman Catholic Church at Everton in Liverpool, originally intended to be the nucleus for the city's Catholic Cathedral. One of the more idiosyncratic inquiries considered two alternative schemes for the residential conversion of one of the great Georgian garden buildings—the Mausoleum at Cobham Hall, Kent. An inquiry was expected late in 1985, or early in 1986, to consider the fate of St. Alban's Church, Teddington, west London, suburban in its setting, but cathedralesque in its scale.

NAUTICAL MEASURES

Distance is measured in nautical (or sea) miles. The nautical mile is traditionally defined as the length of a minute of arc of a great circle of the earth; but as this length varies in different latitudes (owing to the fact that the earth is not a perfect sphere), 6,080 feet, a "rounded off value" of the mean length, has been adopted in British practice as the standard length of the nautical mile. On this basis 33 nautical miles exactly equal 38 statute miles; the statute (land) mile contains 5,280 feet. A *cable*, as a measure used by seamen, is 600 feet (100 fathoms) approximately one-tenth of a nautical mile. *Soundings at sea* are recorded in fathoms (6 feet); 100 fathoms = 1 cable length; 10 cables = 1 nautical mile.

NOTE.—The British standard nautical mile of 6,080 feet is now obsolete. The international nautical mile of 1,852 metres was adopted in the Hydrographic Department in 1970. Also, the cable and the fathom are obsolescent. Distances are tending to be expressed in decimal parts of a sea mile, or in metres, rather than cables. Depths are expressed in metres on all new Admiralty charts.

Speed is measured in *nautical miles per hour*, called *knots*. A knot is a measure of speed and is not used to express distance. A ship moving at the rate of 30 nautical miles per hour is said to be "doing 30 knots" and as the nautical mile is longer than the land or statute mile this represents a land speed of over 34½ miles per hour.

Knots	m.p.h.	Knots	m.p.h.	Knots	m.p.h.
1	1·1515	15	17·2727	29	33·3939
2	2·3030	16	18·4242	30	34·5454
3	3·4545	17	19·5757	31	35·6969
4	4·6060	18	20·7272	32	36·8484
5	5·7575	19	21·8787	33	38·0000
6	6·9090	20	23·0303	34	39·1515
7	8·0606	21	24·1818	35	40·3030
8	9·2121	22	25·3333	36	41·4545
9	10·3636	23	26·4848	37	42·6060
10	11·5151	24	27·6363	38	43·7575
11	12·6666	25	28·7878	39	44·9090
12	13·8180	26	29·9393	40	46·0606
13	14·9696	27	31·0908	41	47·2121
14	16·1212	28	32·2424	42	48·3636

Net tonnage.—The gross tonnage less certain deductions for crew space, engine room, water ballast and other spaces not used for passengers or cargo.
Gross tonnage.—The total volume of all the enclosed spaces of a vessel, the unit of measurement being a ton of 100 cubic feet.

EDUCATION IN THE UNITED KINGDOM

ENGLAND AND WALES

Decline in numbers

In primary education and, increasingly, in secondary education pupil numbers continue to decline. It is estimated that, in England, primary school numbers will drop to 3·3 million in 1985 as compared to 4·4 million in 1973, and secondary school numbers to 2·8 million in 1991 from 3·9 million in 1979.

Expenditure

For 1985–86 the planned expenditure of government on education and science is £13·6 billion in cash terms. For 1986–87 the corresponding figure is £14 billion and for 1987–88 £14·2 billion.

Department of Education and Science

The Department of Education and Science (D.E.S.) is responsible for all aspects of education in England and for government policy towards universities in England, Scotland and Wales. Responsibility in Wales for nursery, primary and secondary education, and for all non-university institutions of higher and further education, the youth and community services, and adult education lies with the Secretary of State for Wales.

The Department's main concern is the formulation of national policies for education. It is responsible for the broad allocation of resources for education, for the rate and distribution of educational building and for the supply, training and superannuation of teachers. It is concerned with basic educational standards. The Department does not run any schools or colleges or engage any teachers.

The D.E.S. is also responsible for government support for civil science.

It acts within a framework of estimates approved by Parliament. The money which the Department itself spends is a small part of the total public expenditure on education, the major part being expenditure by local authorities (*see below*). This expenditure by local authorities is financed from rates and from the rate support grant payable from the national Exchequer.

The Department commissions research, related to policy interests of the D.E.S. and the L.E.A.s, from universities and other bodies such as the National Foundation for Educational Research.

Between 1980 and 1984 the number of staff at the D.E.S. decreased by 4 per cent to 2,435.

H.M. Inspectorate

Her Majesty's Inspectors inspect schools and other educational establishments apart from universities, report to the Secretary of State for Education and Science on the efficiency of the educational system (excluding universities) and offer independent professional advice based on their observation and judgement to the Secretary of State, the Department of Education and Science, the local education authorities, and teachers. There are some 390 H.M.I.s in England and some 50 in Wales. Much of the work of H.M. Inspectorate relates to national surveys of primary and secondary education. In 1984, 256 of H.M. Inspectors' reports were published after school and college inspections.

Local Education Authorities

The educational service is a national service locally administered. Among its main features are:—

(a) its administration is largely decentralized, the responsibility for providing state primary, secondary and further education (but not university education) to meet the needs of their areas being that of the local education authorities (L.E.A.'s). However, subject to guidelines issued by the central education departments in England and Wales and the requirements of examination syllabuses, each educational establishment has great freedom to determine its own curriculum and the content of its courses.

These local authorities appoint education committees consisting of some of their own members (a majority of the committee) and other people with experience in education and knowledge of the local education situation. The L.E.A.'s own and maintain schools and colleges and build new ones, employ teachers and provide equipment. Most of the public money spent on education is disbursed by the local authorities. L.E.A.'s are financed by rate support grants from the Department of the Environment and from the rates; teachers' salaries account for about half of local authority expenditure on education and related services.

Voluntary Agencies

(b) Voluntary agencies play an important part in educational provision often in co-operation with the State. Some indication of its nature and extent is given below.

SCHOOLS AND PUPILS

Schooling is compulsory for all children between 5 and 16 years. Some provision is made for children under 5 and many pupils remain at school after the minimum leaving age. No fees are charged in any publicly maintained school.

There are two main categories of school: (a) those *maintained* by local education authorities, the authorities meeting their expenditure partly from local rates and partly from grants made by the Department of the Environment; (b) *independent* schools.

County and Voluntary Schools

Maintained schools are of two types: (i) *county schools* (16,581 in 1984 in England) which are built, maintained and staffed by local education authorities. Their managers (primary schools) and governors (secondary schools) are appointed by the L.E.A.'s. (ii) *voluntary schools* (7,864 in 1984 in England and attended in 1984 by about 22 per cent of all pupils in maintained schools) which although built by voluntary bodies (mainly religious denominations) are financially maintained by an L.E.A. Voluntary schools are of three kinds: controlled (3,254), aided (4,512), and special agreement (98). In *controlled* schools the L.E.A. nominates two-thirds of the managers or governors (the rest are nominated by the voluntary body), bears all costs and appoints the teachers.

In *aided* schools the managers or governors (two-thirds appointed by the voluntary interest and one-third by the L.E.A.) are responsible for repairs to the outside of the school building and for improvements and alterations to it though the Department of Education and Science may reimburse part of approved capital expenditure. The L.E.A. meets all running costs. The managers or governors control the appointment of teachers. *Special agreement* schools are those where the L.E.A. may, by special agreement, pay between one-half and three-quarters of the cost of building a new, or extending an existing, voluntary school, almost always a secondary school. Two-thirds of the governors are appointed by the voluntary body and the remainder by the L.E.A. Expenditure is normally apportioned between the authority and the voluntary body.

New government policies were set out in March 1985 in an important White Paper, *Better Schools*. It describes in detail how the government aims to raise standards for children of all abilities and to secure the best possible return from the resources invested in the schools. Recent government initiatives are covered and the next steps are described in the process of reform. These steps include: the promotion of national agreement on the purposes and content of the curriculum; the encouragement of schools to do more to prepare young people for work; the completion of the reform of the public examination system at age 16; the introduction of a national system of records of achievement; and the improvement of the training, deployment and management of the more than 400,000 teachers in England and Wales. The White Paper also sets out government decisions to: legislate to reform school governing bodies; introduce a new grant to make in-service teacher training more effective; extend the Secretary of State's powers to regulate the employment of teachers to cover the appraisal of their performance; to introduce the new AS-level examination for sixth-formers (*see below*); to set new guidelines for the minimum size of schools; and tackle truancy.

Public Schools

By the term *public schools* is usually meant the independent schools in the membership of the Head-masters' Conference, the Governing Bodies Association or the Governing Bodies of Girls' Schools Association. Most public schools are for one sex (about half of them for girls only) but some boys' schools admit girls to their sixth forms.

Independent schools charge fees and do not receive grants from public funds. *Preparatory schools* are mainly for boys from about 7 to 13 years who wish to enter public schools. All independent schools are open to inspection by H.M. Inspectors (*see above*) and must register with the Department of Education and Science which lays down certain minimum standards and can make schools remedy any unacceptable features of their building or instruction and exclude any unsuitable teacher or proprietor. In 1984 there were in England 2,333 independent schools. This was 11 fewer than the previous year; pupil numbers dropped by only 0·3 per cent over the year. The arrangements by which independent schools could be "recognized as efficient", *i.e.* could satisfy the D.E.S. that their standards were broadly comparable with those of grant-aided schools, have been discontinued.

The Education Act 1980 empowered the Secretary of State to establish and operate a scheme for assisted places, under which some parents receive income-related help with the cost of tuition fees at selected independent schools. 5,000–6,000 *assisted places* are available each year at more than 200 independent schools in England and Wales for academically able children whose parents cannot afford the full tuition fees. In September 1984 4,078 of the new places offered for 11–13 year olds were taken up and 766 of the sixth-form places. 70 per cent of the grand total of 16,117 pupils who benefited in this fourth year of the scheme came from families with below average incomes and 38 per cent of them qualified for a completely free place. The cost of the scheme in the financial year 1984–85 was expected to be £22·5 million.

The State System

Nursery Education is for children under 5 years who may attend a nursery school or a primary school. The number of pupils under 5 years of age in maintained nursery and primary schools increased from 458,100 in 1983 to 495,000 in 1984. Most of this increase was in full-time pupils in nursery and infant classes in primary schools. The 495,000 in 1984 was 41·6 per cent of the population aged 3 and 4 years and compared with 28·3 per cent in 1975 and 39·1 per cent in 1980.

Primary Stage.—This begins at 5 years and the transfer to secondary school is generally made at 11 years. Primary schools consist mainly of *infants' schools* for children aged 5 to 7, *junior schools* for those aged 7 to 11 and *junior and infant schools* for both age groups. In addition *first schools* in some areas cater for ages from 5 to 8, 9 or 10. (They are the first stage of a three-tier system: first, middle and secondary.)

Middle Schools.—Middle schools (which take children from first schools) cover varying age ranges between 8 and 14 and usually lead on to comprehensive upper schools.

Secondary Stage.—Secondary schools are for children aged 11 to 16 and over. The largest have over 2,000 pupils but 83 per cent of the schools take between 400 and 1,500 pupils. In January, 1984, when there were in England 3,645,586 pupils in maintained secondary schools the main types were: (*a*) *comprehensive* schools (84 per cent of pupils), whose admission arrangements are without reference to ability or aptitude; (*b*) *middle deemed secondary* schools (7 per cent); (*c*) *secondary modern* schools (5 per cent) providing mainly a general education with a practical bias; (*d*) *secondary grammar* schools (3 per cent) providing an academic course from 11 to 16–18 years; and (*e*) *technical* schools (1 per cent) providing an integrated academic and technical course.

Tertiary Colleges provide normal sixth form school courses as well as a range of courses for further education students over the age of 16.

Special Education is provided for children who require it because of physical or mental disability. In January 1984 there were 114,800 full-time and part-time pupils in special schools (of whom about 107,900 were in maintained schools) in England and, in addition, about 3,500 pupils with special educational needs were receiving education in hospital special schools. About 7,000 pupils also attended independent schools catering wholly or mainly for the handicapped and around 18,300 handicapped pupils were attending special classes in county and voluntary schools.

Primary and Secondary Schools

In 1984 there were 28,910 maintained and non-maintained schools in England, 508 fewer than in 1983. The total number of full-time and part-time pupils in them fell by 179,869 over the year to 8,096,233 in 1984. The number of maintained secondary schools (4,444 in 1984) fell slightly for the seventh successive year since the peak in 1977. Over the same period the number of primary schools has also fallen; in 1984 the total of 20,020 was 364 below the total for 1983.

Of the 8,096,233 pupils at school in January 1984 97 per cent were full-time. Of those in maintained schools, 49,500 were in nursery schools, 3,765,900 in primary schools, and 3,645,600 in secondary schools. In addition there were 515,200 in non-maintained schools and 120,100 in special schools (maintained and non-maintained).

The downward trend of maintained primary school enrolments continues with 2 per cent fewer in 1984 than in 1983 but within the total there was an increase in the number of under-fives attending school full-time. Since 1975 the total number of pupils in primary schools has fallen by 1,110,600.

Boys and girls are taught together in almost all maintained primary schools. Most pupils in maintained secondary schools in England and Wales attend mixed schools. At secondary level most recognized independent schools are for boys only or girls only.

Staying on. The number of boys staying on in maintained secondary schools in England beyond the school-leaving age rose from 123,000 in 1975 to 157,800 in 1984 but the increase in the number of girls was greater—from 116,400 to 169,600. Of such boys, 79·2 per cent were on A-level courses and 17 on O-level/ C.S.E. courses. For girls, the percentages were 74·3 and 19·5. In 1984 the percentage of 16-year-olds staying on at school was 27·4 (23·2 in 1975 and 28·9 in 1983) and of 17-year-olds 17·3 (15·1 in 1975 and 17·9 in 1983).

Pupil-teacher ratios fell slightly in 1984 as compared to 1983. The ratio within maintained primary schools improved from 24·2 pupils per qualified teacher in 1975 to 22·3 in 1983 but fell to 22·1 in 1984. For maintained secondary schools the ratio in 1984 was 16·2 compared to 16·5 in 1983, 16·6 the previous year, and 17·2 in 1975.

Class Sizes.—The average size of class in maintained primary and secondary schools continued to fall in 1984. In primary schools the drop was from 25·1 in 1983 to 25·0 in 1984. In secondary schools, the average size of class fell from 21·1 to 20·9.

School Meals. In 1984 at maintained schools in England, 51·3 per cent of pupils present took meals.

Advanced levels.—The number of boys in England taking A-level courses for the G.C.E. (*see below*) at maintained schools fell from 131,000 in 1983 to 125,700 in 1984 and the number of girls from 132,900 to 126,800. For the fourth year in succession, the number of girls taking A-level courses exceeded the number of boys. Half the school leavers who attempted A-levels in 1982–83 achieved three or more passes and a further 22 per cent achieved two passes. 9·3 per cent of the 17-year old age group got three or more A-level passes, 4·2 per cent got two passes, and 3·1 per cent got one pass.

Examinations: current and future.—Secondary school pupils (and others) can at present take the General Certificate of Education (G.C.E.) or the Certificate of Secondary Education (C.S.E.). The G.C.E. was introduced in 1951 (it replaced the School Certificate and Higher School Certificate) and the C.S.E. in 1965. The examinations for the G.C.E., which are conducted by eight examining bodies (most connected with universities) are set at two levels: Ordinary level ("O") and Advanced level ("A"). A-level is usually taken after two years in the sixth form following O-level, which is normally taken at 16 years (earlier only if the head teacher agrees). The G.C.E. is not a "grouped subject" examination and candidates at either level may take one or more subjects as they wish. At A-level, passes are awarded in five grades. A-level candidates may take Special papers which are usually set on the same syllabus as the basic A-level papers but contain more searching questions.

Under the grading system for O-level, attainment in an O-level subject is indicated by a grade A, B, C, D or E of which grade A is the highest and grade E the lowest. Candidates awarded grade A, B or C have reached the standard of the former subject pass at O-level. Grades D and E indicate lower levels of attainment.

Like the G.C.E. the Certificate of Secondary Education (C.S.E.) can be taken in one or more subjects. It is open to boys and girls in any school completing five years of secondary education, and is meant for pupils of about 16 years who are around the average in terms of ability for their age groups. Five grades are awarded. The C.S.E. can be examined in a number of ways, internal and external, and is controlled largely by serving teachers sitting on the 13 regional examining boards.

It was, however, announced by the Secretary of State for Education and Science in 1984 that the G.C.E. O-level and C.S.E. examinations are to be replaced by a new single system of examinations— the *General Certificate of Secondary Education (G.C.S.E.) examinations*. Under a tight timetable it is planned that the last O-level, C.S.E. and joint 16+ examinations will be held in summer and winter

1987, and that the first G.C.S.E. courses will start in the autumn of 1986 with the first examinations being held in summer 1988.

The purpose of the change is to improve the examination courses and to raise the standard of performance of all candidates. To achieve this, there would be: fewer examining groups; syllabuses based on national criteria covering course objectives, content and assessment methods; differentiated assessment (i.e. different papers or questions for different ranges of ability); and grade-related criteria (i.e. grades to be awarded on absolute rather than relative performance). The G.C.S.E. will be a single system of examinations, not a single examination.

The G.C.S.E. certificates will be awarded, it is planned, with a seven-point scale: A to G. Grades A to C will embody standards at least as high as the corresponding O-level grades A to C now do. Distinction certificates will be awarded to candidates achieving good grades in a broad range of subjects. The possibility of merit certificates at a slightly lower level is also under discussion. The G.C.S.E. examination is to be administered by four groups of examining boards in England and one in Wales. All G.C.S.E. syllabuses, assessment and grading procedures will be monitored by the Secondary Examinations Council (*see below*).

The Secretary of State said that the new examinations would: do more than O-levels to stretch the ablest pupils; do more than C.S.E. to motivate other pupils; promote more effectively worthwhile knowledge, understanding and skills; grade candidates by what they know, understand and can do; be clearer to candidates, their parents and employers than the present system; and be more cost effective.

Nearly £7 million is being spent on in-service teacher training for the G.C.S.E.

A-level examinations will continue though there will be changes to the grading system.

In addition to A-level examinations, the Secretary of State announced in 1984 proposals to introduce new *Advanced Supplementary level (AS-level) examinations*. Their purpose will be to broaden the curriculum for A-level students but without diluting academic standards. AS-levels are seen by the D.E.S. as "making a useful, if limited, contribution to the problems associated with overspecialisation." It is expected that courses leading to AS-level will start in September 1987 and that the first examinations will be held in summer 1989.

AS-levels will be for full-time A-level students but others can take them too. An AS-level syllabus will cover not less than half the amount of ground covered by the corresponding A-level syllabus and will in most cases be closely related to it. An AS-level course will last two years and require not less than half the teaching time of the corresponding A-level course. It is envisaged that students hoping to go on to higher education would continue (where they do so now) to take A-level courses in the subjects they want to specialize in. AS-level courses will supplement and broaden these studies.

AS-levels are being developed by the G.C.E. boards in co-operation with the Secondary Examinations Council (*see below*) and examinations will be held at the same time as A-levels.

At the Government's request, the Business and Technician Education Council and the City and Guilds of London Institute established in 1983 a joint board for pre-vocational education. It is devising a curriculum and administrative structure for a new 17+ qualification, the *Certificate of Pre-Vocational Education*, in schools and colleges. This new national qualification is meant for young people who are not vocationally committed and do not wish to follow an A-level course, but would like to continue their education at school or college after compulsory education. The one-year courses, which are planned to begin in September 1985, will lead to more specific and advanced vocational education and to employment, and will have a practical emphasis.

In 1983 two new bodies were set up to replace the Schools Council. They are the *Secondary Examinations Council* (S.E.C.) and the *School Curriculum Development Committee* (S.C.D.C.). The purpose of the S.E.C. is to co-ordinate and try to improve the school examination system and other forms of school-based assessment in England and Wales; and to advise the Government on these policy areas. The S.C.D.C.'s task is to inform itself of school curriculum development work being done by others in England and Wales; to identify any important gaps; to undertake appropriate work in such areas or to stimulate others to do so; and to promote the dissemination of curriculum development. The S.E.C. is wholly funded by Central Government but the S.C.D.C. is jointly funded by the Department of Education and Science and the local authorities.

TEACHERS
(see also p. 532)

Although it is the duty of each Local Education Authority to ensure that there is efficient education to meet the needs of the local population, what is taught in the schools is normally decided on their behalf by the head teachers of schools, and is subject to guidelines issued by the central education departments and to the requirements of examination syllabuses.

Teachers are appointed by local education authorities, school governing bodies or managers. Those in publicly maintained schools must be approved as "qualified" by the Department of Education and Science. To become a qualified teacher it is necessary to have successfully completed an initial course of teacher training. Teacher training is now largely integrated with the rest of higher education with training places concentrated in polytechnics, institutes or colleges of higher education, and universities. Non-graduates usually qualify by way of a three- or four-year course leading to a B.Ed. degree while graduates take a one-year postgraduate certificate of education.

Entry requirements are high with a reduced number of training places available. On entry to a course of initial teacher training leading to qualified teacher status (whether at undergraduate or postgraduate level) students are expected to provide evidence of, inter alia, a level of competence in English and mathematics at least equivalent to passes at a minimum of Grade C at G.C.E. "O" level or Grade 1 in C.S.E.

For entry at undergraduate level candidates must also normally have five passes in the G.C.E. (two of which should be at "A" level) or four passes (three of which should be at "A" level).

With certain exceptions, the profession now has an all-graduate entry. Teachers in further education, however, are not required to have qualified teacher status but roughly half have a teaching qualification and most have industrial, commercial or professional experience.

The Government has set up a Council for the Accreditation of Teacher Education to ensure that in future all initial teacher training courses meet new stringent conditions. It first met in September 1984.

New Intake. In recent years there has been a sharp drop in the number of places for students admitted to teacher-training courses. This was due to the drop in pupil numbers at school (*see above*) and to restrictions on public spending. The intake for initial teacher training in 1981 in England and Wales was around 18,700 and this dropped to 17,000 in 1982, and to 16,220 in 1983, and rose again to 96,710 in 1984. The target intakes for the next few years are as follows. *Primary teacher training*—1985: 8,620; 1986: 9,520; 1987: 9,850; 1988: 10,400; 1989: 10,950. *Secondary teacher training*—1985: 9,032; 1986: 9,250; 1987: 9,450; 1988: 9,650; 1989: 9,850.

Shortage Subjects. In recent years there have been shortages of teachers in a number of secondary subjects, particularly mathematics, the physical sciences and craft, design and technology (C.D.T.). In C.D.T. as an incentive the Department of Education and Science runs a Training Award Scheme under which there are payable maintenance allowances (at a higher level than the normal student grant) for suitably qualified and experienced mature people taking certain shortened courses. For 1984–85, 180 awards were available.

Serving Teachers. In 1985 there were 405,300 full-time and full-time equivalent teachers in maintained nursery, primary and secondary schools in England. Numbers have been dropping. The percentage decrease in relation to the previous year was 1980: −2.7; 1981: −8.9; 1982: −9.2; 1983: −5.4; 1984: −4.1; 1985: −5.93.

The latest breakdown available by the type of school relates to 1984. In that year, of the 452,500 teachers in maintained and non-maintained schools in England, 391,800 were in maintained schools (1,600 in nursing schools, 165,600 in primary schools, and 224,600 in secondary schools), 43,800 in independent schools and 16,900 in special schools.

Unemployed Teachers. 12 per cent of those who in 1983 successfully completed initial training courses in public sector institutions in England and Wales were unemployed in October 1983 and still seeking a teaching post. This compares with 16 per cent in 1982 and 18 per cent in 1981.

HIGHER EDUCATION

"Higher Education" consists of the education provided in universities and in "advanced" courses in polytechnics and certain other educational establishments.

Between 1982 and 1995, the 18-year-old population of Great Britain will fall from about 940,000 to about 640,000 a fall of about one third. But it is not thought likely that total demand for higher education will drop by anything like as much.

In 1984–85 there were 735,000 students enrolled in universities in Great Britain and in polytechnics and colleges of higher education in England.

Of the 325,000 (provisional figure) *university* students, 290,000 were full-time or sandwich and 35,000 were part-time; 34,000 were from overseas. In addition, there were 76,000 students at the Open University and 600 at the University of Buckingham.

Of the 410,000 students in *non-university institutions* of higher education, 238,000 were full-time or sandwich and 172,000 were part-time; 12,000 were from overseas.

In 1984 there were an estimated 213,000 new entrants to full-time or sandwich courses in higher education (53 per cent of them in universities and 47 per cent in other institutions). The university total was 2 per cent up on the previous year and the 'other institutions' figure was about the same.

In May 1985, the government issued a Green (Consultative) Paper on *The Development of Higher Education into the 1990s.* It outlined the government's thinking on such issues as: the relationship of higher education to the economic performance of the country; access to higher education; continuing education; research and postgraduate education; patterns of provision and academic standards; the management of institutions; and the national planning of higher education.

Outside the universities higher education covers any course—full-time, sandwich or part-time—of a standard higher than G.C.E. "A" level. It thus includes research, degree-level courses, higher diploma and higher certificate courses, and courses leading to a wide variety of professional qualifications. In that sense higher education is offered in some 400 institutions outside the universities most of them maintained by L.E.A.s within the overall provision they make for further education.

An important body with few, if any, parallels in other countries is the *Council for National Academic Awards* (C.N.A.A.) which awards degrees to students taking courses approved by it in non-university institutions. Following a recommendation of the Robbins Committee it was established by Royal Charter in 1964 as a self-governing body. More than 100 colleges in Britain conduct courses leading to its degrees: B.A., B.Ed., B.Sc., and the higher degrees of M.A. and M.Sc. (for post-graduate course work) and M.Phil. and Ph.D. (for research which may be undertaken jointly in industry and college).

The *Diploma of Higher Education* (Dip.H.E.) is a two-year diploma intended to serve as either a terminal qualification or as a stepping stone to a degree or other further study; it has a normal entry requirement of two "A" levels. The Dip. H.E. is usually awarded by the Council for National Academic Awards (*see above*). In England and Wales, courses leading to it are offered by some 40 polytechnics and colleges.

A *National Advisory Body for Public Sector Higher Education* advises the Secretary of State on a co-ordinated approach to the academic provision and the allocation of funds in Polytechnics and other local authority and voluntary colleges in respect of courses leading to qualifications higher than A-level. *See also* "Universities" *below*.

FURTHER EDUCATION

The term "Further Education" usually means all post-school education except "higher education"(*see above*).

In November 1983 full-time and sandwich course enrolments at maintained, assisted and grant-aided establishments in England were just over 574,000; this is only marginally higher than 1982 following an 8 per cent rise the year before. Those in advanced courses were 6 per cent greater at 231,000 while those in non-advanced courses dropped by 3 per cent. In addition there were at those establishments 1,407,000 part-time course enrolments. If adult education and youth centres are included the total for all further education establishments was 3,609,000 course enrolments, 5 per cent up on 1982. (Some students enrol on more than one course so the number of students is lower than the number of course enrolments.)

Local Education Authorities are responsible for providing full-time and part-time courses of post-secondary education (other than university education) in their areas.

Regional Advisory Councils. Responsibility for coordinating further education provision in different areas of England and Wales rests with 10 Regional Advisory Councils (*see* pp. 532–33) set up by the local education authorities in each region. The councils bring together representatives of the L.E.A.s, colleges, universities, industry and commerce.

The 4,439 further education establishments in England may be grouped in the following main categories. All three are grant-aided and were in 1983 attended by a total of 3,522,311 students of whom 11 per cent were on advanced courses:—

1. *Polytechnics (see also* pp. 510–11)—Thirty major centres in which a wide range of full-time, sandwich and part-time courses are provided for students at all levels of higher education, and entirely or almost entirely for those of 18 years or more. They have governing bodies with a large measure of autonomy and are mainly teaching institutions though provision is made for certain research where it is essential to the proper fulfilment of teaching functions and the maintenance of close links with industry. A centralized admissions system for polytechnics has been set up. It deals with admissions to full-time and sandwich first degree and Dip.H.E. courses in polytechnics, excluding art and design, and teacher training courses. In England in November 1983 there was a total of 231,939 students enrolled at polytechnics; of these 214,458 were on advanced courses and 17,481 on non-advanced courses; of those on advanced courses 148,086 were full-time or sandwich.

2. *Other Major Establishments* (472 in England).—Including all major establishments (maintained, assisted by L.E.A.s, direct grant from D.E.S. or voluntary), other than polytechnics, providing courses in teacher training, art, agricultural, commercial, technical and other subjects. In England there were 184,725 on advanced courses including 82,565 on full-time or sandwich; and 1,477,628 on non-advanced courses.

3. *Adult Education Centres* (3,938). Establishments maintained by local education authorities and offering a wide range of courses, many of them recreational, mainly for evening students, and often housed in premises used by day for other educational purposes. 1,628,019 students in England; 69 per cent were women.

In November 1983, of the 399,183 enrolments on advanced courses in major establishments of further education in England, 58 per cent were full-time or sandwich and 42 per cent part-time.

In 1983, the *Business and Technician Education Council* (B.T.E.C.) was set up by the Secretary of State for Education and Science to replace the Business Education Council (1974) and the Technician Education Council (1973) and to continue their work of developing a national system of non-degree vocational courses in these fields.

Adult Education (see pp. 516–17).

Trade Union Education.—The Secretaries of State for Education and Science and Employment support financially approved expenditure on trade union education and training. In 1983–84 the joint grant was £1·754 million including £50 for unions not affiliated to the T.U.C.

Value for money. In June 1985, the Audit Commission for Local Authorities in England and Wales issued a report on *Obtaining Better Value from Further Education* based on a detailed examination of how resources were being used in 165 polytechnics and colleges of further education.

The Youth Service provides for the spare-time activities of young people. The Local Education Authorities co-operate with voluntary bodies in their areas and may maintain their own youth clubs. There are various national voluntary youth organizations. There are some 3,000 full-time youth workers in England and Wales who are employed by local education authorities and voluntary youth organizations. In addition there are many thousands of part-time paid and unpaid workers. In 1984–85 the D.E.S. grant to national voluntary youth organizations was £3·06 million. In England and Wales there is a basic two-year training for youth and community workers, and in-service courses, both validated by the Council for Education and Training in Youth and Community Work.

Training Services.—The main responsibility for carrying out industrial and commercial training lies with individual employers, but the Manpower Services Commission (M.S.C.), which is separate from government but responsible to the Secretary of State for Employment, provides, with government support, opportunities for individuals to acquire new skills and helps to improve the effectiveness of training generally.

A major new programme, the *Youth Training Scheme* (Y.T.S.) began in 1983 with the aim of finding places for 460,000 young people in 1983–84. It offered year-long training programmes for employed and unemployed 16-year old school-leavers and some unemployed 17-year old school-leavers. Under that scheme, young people who took part as employees were paid a wage. If they were unemployed they were paid a training allowance. All programmes included direct practical experience; training in a group of skills related to an area of work; at least 13 weeks off-the-job further education or training; and a certificate at the end to show what the young person could do.

More than 700,000 young school-leavers have entered the scheme since it began.

The Y.T.S. is meant not just as an alternative to unemployment but as a permanent training scheme. It is part of an overall policy whose aim is to ensure that all young people under 18 have a better opportunity than in the past either to continue in full-time education or to enter upon a period of planned work-experience combined with work-related training and education.

In April 1985, in a White Paper on *Education and Training for Young People* the government announced its intention to expand the Y.T.S. to provide a *two*-year training scheme leading to recognized vocational qualifications for 16-year-olds. It will start in April 1986. The new scheme will give broad-based training in the first year with a greater emphasis on more specific training in the second. There will be at least 20 weeks off-the-job training over the two years in addition to a planned period of on-the-job training and work experience. There will be two years' training for 16-year-old school leavers and one year for 17-year-old school leavers.

Information about the Y.T.S. can be obtained from local careers offices and job centres or from the area offices of the Manpower Services Commission's Training Division.

An *Advanced Further Education Information Service* is provided in August and September by the local education authorities in cooperation with the polytechnics and other colleges offering full-time degree and higher diploma courses, and the Department of Education and Science. It aims to provide up-to-date information and advice about full-time degree, higher diploma and Dip.H.E. courses in the colleges for those who find themselves, late in the summer, without a place on a course. In 1984 it provided advice for nearly 30,000 young people. A list of local advisory officers is available from local careers offices, education offices, public libraries and from the D.E.S.

UNIVERSITIES

Universities are self-governing institutions, usually established by Royal Charter, which are responsible for all academic matters including appointments, curriculum and student admissions. They depend on the State for most of their income.

There are 46 universities in the United Kingdom (*see* pp. 504–10). Of these, 35 are in England, eight in Scotland, two in Northern Ireland and one (a federal institution) in Wales.

The non-residential "*Open University*" provides courses leading to degrees by a combination of television, radio, correspondence, tutorials, short residential courses and local audio-visual centres. The Open University offers undergraduate (no qualifications needed for entry), post-experience and postgraduate courses. It is grant-aided directly by the Department of Education and Science and does not come within the University Grants Committee system.

The independent University at Buckingham provides a two-year course leading to a bachelor's degree and its tuition fees are £4,960 for 1986. It receives no capital or recurrent income from the government but its students are eligible for mandatory awards from L.E.A.'s. Its academic year consists of 4 terms of 10 weeks each.

Reshaping the university system. Unprecedented cuts to the income and home student numbers of universities in Great Britain have been implemented as part of the government's intention to cut public spending.

Enrolments. 286,474 (provisional figure) full-time students were enrolled at Universities in Great Britain in 1984–85. Of these, 240,491 were undergraduates and 45,983 postgraduates. 259,201 were charged home fees and 27,273 overseas fees. Of those charged home fees, 73,014 were undergraduate new entrants and 27,730 were postgraduate new entrants.

More detailed figures available for 1983–84. They show that the percentage increase or decrease compared to 1978–79 were: total enrolment +1·2 per cent; undergraduates +2·1 per cent; postgraduates −3·5 per cent; undergraduate new entrants −6·6 per cent; postgraduate new entrants +2·7 per cent; those charged home fees +4·5 per cent; those charged overseas student fees −22·2 per cent. Of the 291,722 full-time students enrolled in 1983–84, 23·8 per cent were studying science; 23·2 per cent social, administrative or business studies; 14·5 per cent engineering or technology; 11·7 per cent language, literature or area studies; 10·9 per cent medicine, dentistry or health; 8 per cent arts other than languages; 4 per cent education; 2 per cent agriculture, forestry or veterinary science; and 1·9 per cent architecture and other professional or vocational studies.

In addition, in 1983–84 there were 34,626 part-time students, 3·3 per cent more than the previous year. Undergraduate numbers rose (by 9·3 per cent) and so did postgraduate (by 2·2 per cent).

At the Open University in 1984 there were 66,763 undergraduates, 8,675 associate students and 469 postgraduate-external students.

As well as all the above categories of student, there were in 1982–83 449,452 continuing education students.

Degrees and diplomas awarded. In 1983–84 universities, other than the Open, awarded 73,089 first degrees (3·2 per cent more than in the previous year), 6,392 doctorates (2·6 per cent more), 14,430 other higher degrees (6·6 per cent more), and 9,842 higher diplomas (11·2 per cent less). In 1984 the Open University awarded 5,950 BA degrees, 1,150 BA honours degrees and 141 higher degrees; the percentage increases over 1983 were 7, 1·8 and 69·8 respectively.

Staff paid wholly from general university funds. In 1983–84, there were 27,859 full-time non-clinical teaching and research staff (3,218 professors, 7,053 readers and senior lecturers, and 17,588 lecturers, assistant lecturers etc), 2,261 full-time clinical staff, 8,034 full-time academic-related staff (including 1,342 senior library and 3,973 administrative staff) and some 39,200 other full-time staff (clerical, technical, manual and computer staff). The full-time staff—full-time student ratio in 1983–84 was 1 : 9·7; this compares with 1 : 8·8 in 1978–79.

In 1983–84 the cost of meeting claims for *redundancy compensation* for some 1,000 academic and academic-related staff was £30 million, and for 400 non-academic staff £16 million. This brings the total number of claims settled between 1981–82 and 1983–84 to 3,700 in respect of academic and academic-related staff at a cost of £96 million, and to 2,200 for non-academic staff at a cost of £24 million.

The Secretary of State for Education and Science intends to introduce legislation to limit the nature of *tenure* for future appointments of academic staff so that such appointments can be terminated for reasons of redundancy or financial exigency.

Admission. Students applying for admission to a first degree course at a university do so through the Universities Central Council on Admissions (U.C.C.A.) which was set up by the universities in 1961 on the initiative of the Committee of Vice-Chancellors and Principals. All universities participate in the U.C.C.A. scheme except the Open University and the University of Buckingham, which conduct their own admissions direct. The U.C.C.A. office is in Cheltenham.

The requirements for entry to first degree courses vary somewhat from one university to another, but the universities publish co-operatively an annual Compendium which describes these requirements in detail.

Fees. Students with mandatory awards (*see* pp. 513–14) do not pay tuition fees.

The *University Grants Committee* advises the Secretary of State for Education and Science on university matters. Most of its members are academics or businessmen. The U.G.C. acts as a buffer between the Government from which it receives a block grant of money and the universities to which it allocates this grant.

Although the universities have freedom in academic matters, the government, through the U.G.C., determines the total size of the university student population, its distribution between arts, science, medicine, etc., and the part which the university sector plays in the whole higher education system. In 1985 a committee, under the chairmanship of Lord Croham, was appointed to review the role and functions of the U.G.C.

Finance. In 1983–84 the income of universities in Great Britain was more than £2,000 million. Most of this was recurrent income of which £1,597 was for general purposes and £385 million was in respect of research grants and contracts etc.

SCOTLAND

The educational system of Scotland has developed independently to that of England and has a number of distinctive features. The general supervision of the national system of education, except for the universities, is the responsibility of the Secretary of State for Scotland acting through the Scottish Education Department. The duty of providing education locally rests with the nine regional councils and three island councils. Educational facilities of various kinds are also provided by the governing bodies of grant-aided schools, "central institutions", colleges of education, and national voluntary organizations in the field of informal further education.

Schools in Scotland fall into three main categories, viz. *education authority schools* which are financed and managed by the regional and islands councils; *grant-aided schools*, conducted by voluntary managers who receive grants direct from the department; and *independent schools* which receive no direct grant, but which are subject to inspection and registration.

In 1983–84, there were 3,827 education authority and grant-aided schools and departments, of which 552 were nursery, 2,481 primary, 464 secondary and 330 special. There were also 81 registered independent schools. The total number of pupils in education

authority and grant-aided schools and departments (including special) was 902,778 (460,371 boys, 442,407 girls) of which 36,883 (18,897 boys, 17,986 girls) received nursery education. There were a further 14,997 pupils in independent schools (8,517 boys, 6,460 girls).

Schooling normally starts at the age of 5, and the primary school course lasts for 7 years. Primary schools usually take both boys and girls. Pupils transfer from the primary course to secondary courses about the age of 12.

Over 99 per cent of pupils in education authority secondary schools attend schools with a comprehensive intake. Most of these schools provide a full range of courses appropriate to all levels of ability from first to sixth year.

The Scottish Certificate of Education Examination is conducted by the Scottish Examination Board. Pupils may attempt as many of a wide range of subjects as they are capable of, on either the Ordinary grade which corresponds to the Ordinary level of the General Certificate of Education, or on the Higher grade which is normally taken one year after Ordinary grade. The shorter length of course inevitably means that Higher grades are normally studied to a lesser depth than Advanced levels; on the other hand it is common for pupils to be presented for four or more Higher grades at a single diet of the examination. The Board grants a Certificate of Sixth Year Studies designed to give direction and purpose to sixth-year work by encouraging pupils who have completed their main subjects at Higher grade to study a maximum of three such subjects in depth. Pupils may also use the sixth year to gain improved or additional Higher grades or Ordinary grades.

Further Education.—Facilities for further education are provided by 14 Central Institutions (grant-aided colleges administered by independent Boards of Governors) and by 61 further education colleges managed by education authorities. The Central Institutions provide mainly advanced courses in science and technology, commerce, art, music, domestic science, and other subjects, leading to their own diplomas, to professional qualifications or to degrees validated by C.N.A.A. or universities.

The further education colleges normally provide less advanced courses which are mainly part-time covering vocational and non-vocational subjects, but a few offer courses of degree level. Courses are offered in a wide variety of subjects but to make the most economic use of resources, provision of certain courses is made on a regional or even a national basis.

Teachers.—All teachers in public or grant-aided schools in Scotland are required to be registered with the General Teaching Council for Scotland (which is independent of the Scottish Education Department) and normally to hold a teaching qualification awarded by a Scottish College of Education. There are seven of these colleges, five of which provide both one and four year courses leading to a Teaching Qualification (Primary Education), and a one year course leading to a Teaching Qualification (Secondary Education). Of the remaining two colleges, one is a residential college of physical education for women and the other provides only courses leading to a Teaching Qualification (Primary Education).

The basic scales of teachers' salaries are for primary and secondary levels, with additional payments for qualifications and for posts of special responsibility.

NORTHERN IRELAND

Education in Northern Ireland is administered centrally by the Department of Education and locally by five Education and Library Boards. There are two main categories of school: controlled schools which are managed by the Education and Library Boards with all costs paid from public funds; and voluntary schools which get grants towards capital costs.

Nursery education for under-fives is provided in nursery schools or nursery classes in primary schools. Primary education is for children up to 11–12 years and is free, though children educated in preparatory departments of grammar schools pay fees. Entry, at 11–12 years, to a secondary (intermediate) school or grammar school is selective in most areas but children can subsequently transfer from one to the other. Grammar schools provide an academic type of secondary education leading to O- and A-levels, while secondary (intermediate) schools follow a curriculum suited to aptitudes and abilities leading to C.S.E. and G.C.E. examinations. Northern Ireland has 26 institutions of further education (with 154 out-centres), three general colleges of education, and two universities (the Ulster Polytechnic has merged with the New University of Ulster to form the University of Ulster).

In January 1984 the total number of pupils enrolled in the 1,387 grant-aided schools was 350,420 of whom 4,499 were in nursery schools, 181,395 in primary schools, 161,920 in secondary schools and 2,606 in special schools. Total enrolments are now just over 6 per cent lower than their peak in 1977. Primary school enrolments are almost 10 per cent down on the 1979 total and secondary school enrolments continue to fall from their peak and are expected to go down further during the rest of the decade. Between 1979 and 1984 pupil-teacher ratios improved from 23·8 to 23·4 in primary schools and 15·6 to 15·4 in secondary schools; staying-on rates for 16-year olds increased from 35·5 per cent to 41·8 per cent.

There were 18,704 full-time equivalent teachers (123 down on 1983) of whom 10,499 were in secondary schools and 7,739 in primary.

In 1982–83, there were 8,465 students on advanced courses of whom 41 per cent were part-time. In addition, there were 43,521 students on non-advanced vocational courses of further education of whom 64 per cent were part-time.

Public expenditure on education and related services in 1982–83 was: current—£485·6 million; capital £40·8 million.

DUKE OF EDINBURGH'S AWARD SCHEME

The Duke of Edinburgh's Award Scheme, which operates under a variety of titles in over forty countries around the world, provides an incentive and a challenge to young people to reach certain standards in leisure-time activities with the voluntary help of adults. Entrants must be between their 14th and 23rd birthdays, and can enter through their school, their firm, a youth organization, or on their own. Bronze, Silver and Gold Awards can be gained by those who qualify in the four sections of the Scheme: Service, Expeditions, Skills and Physical Recreation. The qualifying standards are expressed in terms of proficiency, perseverance or sustained effort, participants being assessed on the use they make of their personal abilities and aptitudes, and not in competition with others.

In 1984, there were 67,617 new entrants from the United Kingdom and 40,486 from overseas; a total of 51,334 Awards were gained world-wide. Since the Scheme began in 1956, over two million young people have taken part.

Head Office: 5 Prince of Wales Terrace, W8 5PG.   Director: R. Heron.

PRINCIPAL BOOK PUBLISHERS AND THEIR ADDRESSES

More than 9,000 firms, individuals and societies have published one or more books in recent years. The list which follows is a selective one comprising, in the main, firms whose names are most familiar to the general public. An interleaved list containing some 2,500 names and addresses is issued annually in April by the publishers of "Whitaker".

Abelard-Schumann, Furnival House, 14–18 High Holborn, W.C.1.
Allan (Ian), Coombelands Ho., Addlestone, Weybridge, Surrey.
Allen (J. A.), 1 Lower Grosvenor Pl., S.W.1.
Allen (W. H.), 44 Hill St., W.1.
Allen & Unwin, 40 Museum St., W.C.1.
Angus & Robertson, 16 Golden Square, W.1.
Architectural Press, 9 Queen Anne's Gate, S.W.1.
Argus Books, P.O. Box 35, Hemel Hempstead, Herts.
Arlington Books, 15 King St., S.W.1.
Armada Books, 8 Grafton St., W.1.
Arms & Armour Press, 2 Hampstead High St., N.W.3.
Arnold (Edward), 41 Bedford Sq., W.C.1.
Arnold (E. J.) & Son, Parkside Lane, Leeds.
Arrow Books, 62 Chandos Pl., W.C.2.
Athlone Press, 44 Bedford Row, W.C.1.
Autobooks, Tong Hall, Bradford, Yorks.
B.B.C. Publications, 35 Marylebone High St., W.1.
Baillière, Tindall, 1 St. Anne's Rd., Eastbourne, Sx.
Bantam Bks., 61 Uxbridge Rd., W.5.
Barker (Arthur), 91 Clapham High St., S.W.4.
Barrie & Jenkins, 62 Chandos Pl., W.C.2.
Bartholomew & Son, 12 Duncan St., Edinburgh.
Batsford, 4 Fitzhardinge St., Portman Square, W.1.
Bell & Hyman, 37 Queen Elizabeth St., S.E.1.
Benn (Ernest), 35 Bedford Row, W.C.1.
Bingley (Clive), 7 Ridgmount St., W.C.1.
Black (A. & C.), 35 Bedford Row, W.C.1.
Blackie, Bishopbriggs, Glasgow, and Furnival House, 14–18 High Holborn, W.C.1.
Blackwell (Basil), 108 Cowley Rd., Oxford.
Blackwood Pillans & Wilson, 162 Leith Walk, Edinburgh.
Blandford Press, Link Ho., West St., Poole, Dorset.
Blond (Anthony), 55 Gt. Ormond St., W.C.1.
Bodley Head, 30 Bedford Sq., W.C.1.
Boyars (Marion), 24 Lacy Rd., S.W.15.
British Museum, 46 Bloomsbury St., W.C.1.
Brown, Son & Ferguson, 4 Darnley St., Glasgow.
Burke Pub. Co., 116 Golden Lane, E.C.1.
Butterworth & Co., Borough Green, Sevenoaks, Kent.
Calder (John), 18 Brewer St., W.1.
Cambridge Univ. Press, Shaftesbury Rd., Cambridge.
Cape (Jonathan), 32 Bedford Sq., W.C.1.
Cassell, 1 Vincent Sq., S.W.1.
Centaur Press, Fontwell, Arundel, Sx.
Century Hutchinson, 62 Chandos Pl., W.C.2.
Century Publishing Co., *see* Century Hutchinson
Chambers (W. & R.), 43 Annandale St., Edinburgh.
Chapman & Hall, 11 New Fetter Lane, E.C.4.
Chapman (Geoffrey), 1 Vincent Sq., S.W.1.
Chatto & Windus, 40 William IV St., W.C.2.
Churchill Livingstone, 1–3 Baxter's Place, Leith Walk, Edinburgh.
Collins (William), 8 Grafton St., W.1.
Colour Library, 86 Epsom Rd., Guildford, Sy.
Constable & Co., 10 Orange St., W.C.2.
Consumers' Assn., 14 Buckingham St., W.C.2.
Corgi Books, 61 Uxbridge Road, W.5.
Darton, Longman & Todd, 89 Lillie Rd., S.W.6.
David & Charles, Brunel House, Newton Abbot, Devon.
Davies (Peter), 10 Upper Grosvenor St., W.1.
Deans International, 52 Southwark St., S.E.1.
Dent (J. M.) & Sons, 33 Welbeck St., W.1.
Deutsch (A.), 105 Gt. Russell St., W.C.1.
Dobson Books, Brancepeth Castle, Durham.
Dorling Kindersley, 9 Henrietta St., W.C.2.
Duckworth & Co., 43 Gloucester Crescent, N.W.1.

Elliot Right Way Books, Kingswood Bldg., Kingswood, Tadworth, Surrey.
Encyclopædia Britannica, 4 Winsley St., W.1.
Epworth Press, 1 Central Bldgs., S.W.1
Evans Bros., 2A Portman Mans., Chiltern St., W.1.
Eyre & Spottiswoode, North Way, Andover, Hants.
Faber & Faber, 3 Queen Square, W.C.1.
Focal Press, Borough Green, Sevenoaks, Kent.
Fontana, 8 Grafton St., W.1.
Foulis (G. T.), Sparkford, Yeovil, Som.
Foulsham & Co., Yeovil Rd., Slough, Berks.
Fountain Press, 65 Victoria St., Windsor, Berks.
French (Samuel), 52 Fitzroy St., W.1.
Futura, *see* Macdonald & Co.
Gall & Inglis, 62 Buckstone Terrace, Edinburgh, 10.
Gee & Co., 7 Swallow Pl., W.1.
Geographia, 105 Bath Rd., Cheltenham, Glos.
Gibbons (Stanley), 5 Parkside, Christchurch Rd., Ringwood, Hants.
Gibson (Robert), 17 Fitzroy Place, Glasgow.
Ginn & Co., Prebendal Ho., Parson's Fee, Aylesbury, Bucks.
Glasgow (Mary), 140 Kensington Church St., W.8.
Gollancz (Victor), 14 Henrietta St., W.C.2.
Gower Publishing Co., Croft Rd., Aldershot, Hants.
Grafton Books, 8 Grafton St., W.1.
Graham (Frank), 6 Queen's Terrace, Newcastle.
Granada Publishing, 8 Grafton St., W.1.
Green (W.), 2 St. Giles St., Edinburgh.
Griffin (Charles), 5A Crendon St., High Wycombe, Bucks.
Guinness Superlatives, 2 Cecil Court, London Road, Enfield.
H.M. Stationery Office, 51 Nine Elms Lane, S.W.8.
Hale (Robert), 45 Clerkenwell Green, E.C.1.
Hamilton (Hamish), 57 Long Acre, W.C.2.
Hamlyn, 69 London Rd., Twickenham.
Harlequin, 15 Brook's Mews, W.1.
Harrap, 19 Ludgate Hill, E.C.4.
Hart-Davis, 8 Grafton St., W.1.
Harvester Press, 16 Ship St., Brighton, Sussex.
Haynes (J. H.), Sparkford, Yeovil, Som.
Heinemann (Wm.), 10 Upper Grosvenor St., W.1.
Hodder & Stoughton, 47 Bedford Sq., W.C.1.
Hodge & Co., 34 N. Frederick St., Glasgow.
Hogarth Press, 40 William IV St., W.C.2.
Hollis & Carter, 30 Bedford Sq., W.C.1.
Holmes McDougall, 137 Leith Walk, Edinburgh.
Holt-Saunders, 1 St. Anne's Rd., Eastbourne, Sx.
Hutchinson, 62 Chandos Pl., W.C.2.
Jane's Publishing Co., 238 City Rd., E.C.1.
Jarrold Colour, Barrack Street, Norwich.
Jarrolds, 62 Chandos Pl., W.C.2.
Johnston & Bacon, P. O. Box 1, Stirling.
Jordan & Sons, 15 Pembroke Rd., Bristol.
Joseph (Michael), 44 Bedford Sq., W.C.1.
Kaye & Ward, 10 Upper Grosvenor St., W.1.
Kelly's Directories, East Grinstead House, East Grinstead, Sussex.
Kimber (Wm.), 100 Jermyn St., S.W.1.
Kimpton Medical, 205 Gt. Portland St., W.1.
Ladybird, Beeches Rd., Loughborough.
Lane (Allen), *see* Viking.
Lawrence & Wishart, 39 Museum St., W.C.1.
Lewis (H. K.), 136 Gower St., W.C.1.
Lion Publishing, Icknield Way, Tring, Herts.
Longman Group, Burnt Mill, Harlow, Essex.
Lund Humphries, 26 Litchfield St., W.C.2.
Lutterworth Press, 7 All Saints Passage, Cambridge.
Macdonald & Co., 74 Worship St., E.C.2.
Macdonald & Evans, Estover Rd., Plymouth.

McGraw-Hill, Shoppenhangers Rd., Maidenhead, Berks.
Macmillan Publishers, Little Essex St., W.C.2.
Marshall Cavendish, 58 Old Compton St., W.1.
Marshall, Morgan & Scott, 3 Beggarwood Lane, Basingstoke, Hants.
Mayflower, 8 Grafton St., W.1.
Methodist Publishing, Wellington Rd., S.W.19.
Methuen & Co., 11 New Fetter Lane, E.C.4.
Mills & Boon, 15 Brook's Mews, W.1.
Mitchell Beazley, 14 Manette St., W.1.
Mowbray, St. Thomas Ho., Becket St., Oxford.
Muller, Blond & White, 55 Gt. Ormond St., W.C.1.
Murray (John), 50 Albemarle St., W.1.
National Christian Education Council, Robert Denholm Ho., Nutfield, Redhill, Sy.
Nelson (T.), Mayfield Rd., Walton-on-Thames, Sy.
New English Library, 47 Bedford Sq., W.C.1.
Nisbet & Co., Digswell Pl., Welwyn Garden City, Herts.
Nonesuch Library, 30 Bedford Sq., W.C.1.
Novello & Co., Borough Green, Sevenoaks, Kent.
Octopus Books, 59 Grosvenor St., W.1.
Oliphants, 3 Beggarwood Lane, Basingstoke, Hants.
Oliver & Boyd, 1–3 Baxter's Place, Leith Walk, Edinburgh.
Owen (Peter), 73 Kenway Rd., S.W.5.
Oxford Univ. Press, Walton St., Oxford.
Paladin Bks., 8 Grafton St., W.1.
Pan Books, 18 Cavaye Place, S.W.10.
Panther, 8 Grafton St., W.1.
Paul (Kegan), 14 Leicester Sq., W.C.2.
Paul (Stanley), 62 Chandos Pl., W.C.2.
Pelham Books, 44 Bedford Sq., W.C.1.
Penguin Books, Harmondsworth, Mddx.
Pergamon Press, Headington Hill Hall, Oxford.
Phaidon Press, St. Ebbes St., Oxford.
Pharmaceutical Press, 1 Lambeth High St., S.E.1.
Philip (George), 12 Long Acre, W.C.2.
Piatkus Books, 40 Hanway St., W.1.
Piccadilly Press, 64 Greenfield Gdns., N.W.2.
Pickering & Inglis, 3 Beggarwood Lane, Basingstoke, Hants.
Pitkins, 11 Wyfold Rd., S.W.6.
Pitman Publishing, 128 Long Acre, W.C.2.
Purnell Books, Paulton, Bristol.
Putnam & Co., 30 Bedford Sq., W.C.1.
Quartet Books, 27 Goodge St., W.1.
Queen Anne Press, *see* Macdonald & Co.
Quiller Press, 50 Albemarle St., W.1.
Reader's Digest, 25 Berkeley Sq., W.1.
Reinhardt (Max), 30 Bedford Sq., W.C.1.
Religious & Moral Education Press, Hennock Rd., Exeter.
Rider & Co., 62 Chandos Pl., W.C.2.

Routledge & Kegan Paul, 14 Leicester Sq., W.C.2.
S.C.M. Press, 26 Tottenham Rd., N.1.
S.P.C.K., Holy Trinity Church, Marylebone Rd., N.W.1.
St. Andrew Press, 121 George St., Edinburgh.
Scripture Union, 130 City Rd., E.C.1.
Secker & Warburg, 54 Poland St., W.1.
Severn House, 4 Brook St., W.1.
Sheed & Ward, 2 Creechurch Lane, E.C.3.
Sheldon Press, Holy Trinity Church, Marylebone Rd., N.W.1.
Sidgwick & Jackson, 1 Tavistock Chambers, W.C.1.
Smith (M. Temple), Gower Ho., Croft Rd., Aldershot, Hants.
Smythe (Colin), P.O. Box 6, Gerrards Cross, Bucks.
Souvenir Press, 43 Gt. Russell St., W.C.1.
Sphere Books, 30 Gray's Inn Rd., W.C.1.
Spon (E. & F. N.), 11 New Fetter Lane, E.C.4.
Stanford Maritime, 12–14 Long Acre, W.C.2.
Stephens (Patrick), Denington Estate, Wellingborough, Northants.
Stevens & Sons, 11 New Fetter Lane, E.C.4.
Sunshine Books, 12 Little Newport St., W.C.2.
Sweet & Maxwell, 11 New Fetter Lane, E.C.4.
Talbot Press, Ballymount Rd., Dublin, 12.
Tavistock Publications, 11 New Fetter Lane, E.C.4.
Technical Press, Gower Ho., Croft Rd., Aldershot, Hants.
Thames & Hudson, 30 Bloomsbury St., W.C.1.
Thorsons, Denington Estate, Wellingborough, Northants.
Times Books, 16 Golden Sq., W.1.
Turnstone Books, Denington Estate, Wellingborough, Northants.
University of Wales Press, Gwennyth St., Cardiff.
University Tutorial Press, 842 Yeovil Rd., Slough.
Vallentine Mitchell, 11 Gainsborough Rd., E.11.
Viking, 536 Kings Rd., S.W.10.
Virago Press, 41 William IV St., W.C.2.
Walker Books, 184 Drummond St., N.W.1.
Ward Lock, 82 Gower Street, W.C.1.
Ward Lock Educational Co., 47 Marylebone Lane, W.1.
Warne, 536 Kings Rd., S.W.10.
Webb & Bower, 9 Colleton Cres., Exeter.
Weidenfeld & Nicolson, 91 Clapham High St., S.W.4.
Wheaton (A.), Hennock Rd., Exeter.
"Whitaker," 12 Dyott St., W.C.1.
Wildwood House, Gower Ho., Croft Rd., Aldershot, Hants.
Witherby (H. F. & G.), 32 Aylesbury St., E.C.1.
Wolfe Publishing, 3–5 Conway St., W.1.
World's Work, Kingswood, Tadworth, Surrey.
Wright (John), Techno Ho., Redcliffe Way, Bristol 1.
Zomba Books, 165 Willesden High Rd., N.W.10.

Most of the principal book publishers are members of The Publishers Association (*see* Index).

BOOK PRODUCTION AND BOOK EXPORTS

These figures for book production and exports are issued by the Department of Trade and Industry. The totals for the years 1971 to 1984 are shown below:

Year	Total value of Books produced in U.K.	Total value of Books exported from U.K.	Year	Total value of Books produced in U.K.	Total value of Books exported from U.K.
1971	£179,099,000	£77,856,000	1978	521,425,000	211,782,000
1972	205,266,000	81,207,000	1979	580,380,000	215,333,000
1973	230,106,000	95,855,000	1980	666,928,000	213,691,000
1974	281,508,000	119,359,000	1981	737,974,000	234,451,000
1975	342,408,000	138,621,000	1982	759,142,000	232,781,000
1976	408,301,000	175,778,000	1983	831,901,000	261,111,000
1977	467,036,000	203,904,000	1984 (Provisional)	932,108,000	307,228,000

BOOKS PUBLISHED IN GREAT BRITAIN IN 1984

This table shows the books published in 1984 with the number of new editions, translations and limited editions. Books and pamphlets priced at less than 12½p have been omitted, as are also all Government publications except the more important issued by H.M. Stationery Office.

Classification	Total	Reprints and New Editions	Translations	Limited Editions
Aeronautics	234	35	2	—
Agriculture and Forestry	530	105	10	—
Architecture	457	96	9	2
Art	1,377	208	45	8
Astronomy	138	43	3	—
Bibliography and Library Economy	641	124	1	2
Biography	1,702	438	66	2
Chemistry and Physics	695	111	17	—
Children's Books	4,430	802	163	13
Commerce	1,610	392	6	—
Customs, Costumes, Folklore	193	47	13	—
Domestic Science	931	251	10	1
Education	1,432	283	8	—
Engineering	1,787	364	12	1
Entertainment	744	117	17	2
Fiction	5,537	2,405	202	10
General	1,325	153	4	—
Geography and Archaeology	536	143	2	4
Geology and Meteorology	304	32	18	—
History	1,586	317	59	1
Humour	251	39	—	—
Industry	644	123	2	1
Language	655	122	12	1
Law and Public Administration	1,610	372	6	—
Literature	1,342	201	55	4
Mathematics	1,293	174	21	—
Medical Science	3,381	603	24	2
Military Science	188	40	9	—
Music	471	85	20	1
Natural Sciences	1,229	212	32	1
Occultism	207	53	13	—
Philosophy	538	117	57	—
Photography	242	46	1	1
Plays	326	80	21	2
Poetry	757	92	74	36
Political Science and Economy	3,904	828	81	—
Psychology	698	121	19	—
Religion and Theology	1,881	347	165	2
School Textbooks	1,893	275	14	—
Science, General	113	21	3	—
Sociology	996	149	15	—
Sports and Outdoor Games	658	139	7	1
Stockbreeding	374	77	6	1
Trade	620	121	1	1
Travel and Guidebooks	911	372	18	1
Wireless and Television	184	34	—	—
Totals	51,555	11,309	1,343	101

COPYRIGHT

The Government Department dealing with Copyright is the *Industrial Property and Copyright Dept., Department of Trade,* 25 Southampton Bldgs., WC2A 1AY.

Subject to the provisions of the Copyright Act, 1956, copyright subsists automatically in every original literary, dramatic, musical and artistic work and continues to subsist until the end of the period of fifty years from the end of the calendar year in which the author died and shall then expire. *No registration nor other formalities are required in order to obtain the protection of the Act.* Protection is conferred not only against reproduction but also against the public performance of a work without permission. Copyright may also subsist in sound recordings, cinematograph films (including video recordings) and television, sound broadcasts and cable programmes. Libraries entitled, under a provision still in force of the Copyright Act, 1911, to receive free copies of books published in the United Kingdom are the British Library, the Bodleian Library, Oxford, University Library, Cambridge, the National Library of Wales, the National Library of Scotland and Trinity College, Dublin.

As the U.K. is a party to both the Berne Copyright Convention and the Universal Copyright Convention, a work originating in this country is automatically protected in all the other countries which are members of these Conventions.

Voluntary Registration at Stationers' Hall.—Compulsory registration at Stationers' Hall was terminated by the Copyright Act of 1911, but in 1924 the Stationers' Company established a *new* Register in which Books and Fine Arts can be registered.

ANNUAL REFERENCE BOOKS

Advertiser's Annual.—East Grinstead House, East Grinstead, W. Sussex. £38·00.

Aeromodeller Annual.—14 St. James Rd., Watford. £3·25.

Aircraft Annual.—Terminal House, Shepperton, Middx. £4·95.

Annual Art Sales Index.—Pond Ho., Weybridge, Sy. (Nov.) 2v. £76·00.

Annual Register of World Events.—Fourth Avenue, Harlow, Essex. £40·00.

Antique Shops of Britain, Guide to the.—5 Church St., Woodbridge, Suffolk. £6·95.

Astronomical Ephemeris.—H.M. Stationery Office, Atlantic House, Holborn Viaduct, E.C.1. (Jan.) £13·00.

Automobile Year.—Bar Hill, Cambridge. (Feb.) £19·95.

B.B.C. Annual Report & Handbook.—144 Bermondsey St., S.E.1. £3·00.

Baily's Hunting Directory.—1 Lower Grosvenor Place, S.W.1. (Oct.) £18·00.

Banker's Almanac & Year Book.—East Grinstead House, East Grinstead, W. Sussex. (Feb.) £80·00.

Bar List of the U.K.—11, New Fetter Lane, E.C.4. (May) £10·00.

Benedictine Year Book.—Ampleforth Abbey, York. £0·60.

Benn's Hardware & Do-it-Yourself Buyer's Guide.—Union Ho., Eridge Rd., Tunbridge Wells, Kent. £20·00.

Benn's Press Directory.—Union Ho., Eridge Rd., Tunbridge Wells, Kent. (Feb.) 2v. £50·00; £52·00.

Boat World.—39 East St., Epsom, Surrey. £6·00.

British Art & Antiques Year Book.—72 Broadwick St., W.1. £7·50.

British Books in Print.—12 Dyott St., W.C.1. £85·00.

British Clothing Industry Year Book.—1–5 Bath St., E.C.1. £21·50.

British Industry & Services in the Common Market.—East Grinstead House, East Grinstead, W. Sussex. £15·00.

British Music Year Book.—35 Bedford Row, W.C.1. £9·50.

British Paperbacks in Print.—12 Dyott St., W.C.1 (June) £27·00.

British Textile Register.—East Grinstead House, East Grinstead, W. Sussex. (Mar.) £10·50.

Brown's Nautical Almanack.—4–10 Darnley St., Glasgow, S.1. (Sept.) £17·00.

Building Societies Who's Who.—2–3 Burgon St., E.C.4. (July) £15·00.

Building Societies Year Book.—2–3 Burgon St., E.C.4. £25·00.

Buses Annual.—Terminal Ho., Shepperton, Middx. £4·95.

Caravan & Camp Sites in the United Kingdom.—Diary Ho., Borough Rd., S.E.1. £2·95.

Carpet Annual.—Union Ho., Eridge Rd., Tunbridge Wells, Kent. £32·00.

Catholic Directory.—18 Crosby Road North, Liverpool. £12·00.

Charities Digest.—501–5 Kingsland Rd., E.8. £7·65.

Chemical Industry Directory.—Sovereign Way, Tonbridge, Kent. (Nov.) £46·00.

Chemist & Druggist Directory.—Union Ho., Eridge Rd., Tunbridge Wells, Kent. £41·00.

Christies' Review of the Season.—Littlegate House, Oxford. (Dec.) £25·00.

Church of England Year Book.—Church House, Dean's Yard, Westminster, S.W.1. (Jan.) £12·50.

Church of Scotland Year Book.—121 George St., Edinburgh 2. (Apr.) £6·75.

City of London Directory.—Fairfax Ho., Colchester. £15·50, £13·50.

Commonwealth Universities Year Book.—36 Gordon Square, W.C.1. (Sept.) £56·00.

Computer Users' Year Book.—Evelyn House, 62 Oxford St., W.1. £52·95.

Concrete Year Book.—Swan House, Leatherhead, Surrey £30·00.

Consulting Engineers Who's Who & Year Book.—178–202 Gt. Portland St., W.1. £19·50.

"Containerization International" Year Book.—72 Broadwick St., W.1. (Mar.) £67·00.

Contractors and Public Works, Annual Directory of.—Beauchamp Clark Garden Centre, Willesborough, Ashford, Kent. £9·90.

Coventry Evening Telegraph Year Book and Who's Who.—Coventry Newspapers Ltd., Corporation St., Coventry. (Nov.) £6·95.

Current Law Year Book.—11 New Fetter La., E.C.4. £45·00.

"Daily Mail" Year Book.—Carmelite House, Fleet St., E.C.4. (Dec.) £3·00, £2·00.

Decorating Contractor Annual Directory.—2 Queensway, Redhill, Surrey. £5·50.

Decorative Art & Modern Interiors.—35 Red Lion Sq., W.C.1. £19·95.

Diplomatic Service List.—H.M.S.O., Atlantic House, Holborn Viaduct, E.C.1. (April) £16·95.

Directory of Directors.—East Grinstead House, East Grinstead, W. Sussex. (Apr.) £53·00.

Directory of Official Architecture & Planning.—Fourth Avenue, Harlow, Essex. £25·00.

Directory of Opportunities for Graduates.—76 Dean St., W.1. £11·50.

Do-it-Yourself Annual.—Link House, Dingwall Ave., Croydon. (Jan.) 85p.

Dod's Parliamentary Companion.—Elm Cottage, Chilsham Lane, Herstmonceux, Sx. £31·00.

Education Authorities' Directory and Annual.—Derby House, Bletchingley Rd., Merstham, Surrey. (Jan.) £30·00.

Education Year Book.—Fourth Avenue, Harlow, Essex. £28·15.

Electrical & Electronic Trader Year Book.—40 Bowling Green Lane, E.C.1. £10·00.

Electrical & Electronics Trades Directory.—P.O. Box 26, Station House, Hitchin, Herts. (Feb.) £36·00.

Electrical Contractor's Yearbook.—34 Palace Court, W.2. £2·50.

Electricity Supply Handbook.—40 Bowling Green Lane, E.C.1. (Apr.) £9·00.

"Engineer" Buyers' Guide, 30 Calderwood St., S.E.18. £18·00.

Europa Year Book.—18 Bedford Square, W.C.1. 2 vols. (Apr.) £53·00, £58·00.

European Chemical Buyers' Guide.—40 Bowling Green Lane, E.C.1. £25·00.

European Glass Directory & Buyer's Guide.—2 Queensway, Redhill, Surrey. £25·00.

European Plastics Buyers' Guide.—40 Bowling Green Lane, E.C.1. £25·00.

Export Data: Exporter's Year Book.—Sovereign Way, Tonbridge, Kent. (Dec./Jan.) £20·00.

Fairplay World Shipping Year Book.—52–54 Southwark St., S.E.1. £27·00.

Farm and Garden Equipment Guide.—40 Bowling Green Lane, E.C.1. £5·50.

Finishing Diary.—4 Local Board Rd., Watford. £6·00.

Finishing Handbook and Directory.—127 Stanstead Rd., S.E.23. £28·00.

Fire Protection Directory.—Sovereign Way, Tonbridge, Kent. (Nov.) £15·00.

"Flight" Directory of British Aviation.—40 Bowling Green Lane, E.C.1. £20·00.

Food Industry Directory.—48 Poland St., W1V 4PP. £25·00.

Frozen & Chilled Foods Year Book.—2 Queensway, Redhill, Surrey. £22·00.

Fruit Trades World Directory.—1–5 Bath St., E.C.1. (Jan.) £5·00.

Furnishing Trade, Directory to the.—Union Ho., Eridge Rd., Tunbridge Wells, Kent. (Jan.) £49·00.

Gas Directory.—Union Ho., Eridge Rd., Tunbridge Wells, Kent. (Jan.) £34·00.

Gibbons' Stamps of the World Catalogue.—391 Strand, W.C.2. (Oct.) 2v. each £11·50.

Girls' School Year Book.—35 Bedford Row, W.C.1. (May) £7·50.

Good Food Guide.—14 Buckingham St., W.C.2. £10·95, £8·95.

Good Hotel Guide.—47 Bedford Sq., W.C.1. (Nov.) £8·95.

Government & Municipal Contractors Register.—39 East St., Epsom, Surrey. (Jan.) £15·00.

Guinness Book of Records.—2 Cecil Court, London Rd., Enfield. (Oct.) £6·95.

Hambro Tax Guide.—Fourth Avenue, Harlow, Essex. £9·95.

Hi-fi Year Book.—40 Bowling Green Lane, E.C.1. £3·00.

Hollis Press and P.R. Annual.—Contact House, Lower Hampton Rd., Sunbury-on-Thames. (Oct.) £33·50.

Horse & Hound Hunter Chasers & Point to Pointers.—King's Reach Tower, Stamford St., S.E.1. £5·45.

Hospitals & Health Services Yearbook.—75 Portland Place, W.1. (Nov.) £24·30.

Hotel, Restaurant & Catering Supplies.—39 East St., Epsom, Sy. £25·00.

Hutchins' Priced Schedules.—33 Station Rd., Bexhill-on-Sea. £20·00.

Insurance Directory & Yearbook.—The Butts, Half Acre, Brentford, Middx. £12·50.

International Art & Antiques Yearbook.—72 Broadwick St., W.1. (Jan.) £12·00.

International Film & Television Year Book.—142 Wardour St., W.1. (Jan./Feb.) £18·00.

International Shipping & Shipbuilding Directory.—Sovereign Way, Tonbridge, Kent. £29·00.

International Yearbook & Statesman's Who's Who.—East Grinstead House, East Grinstead, W. Sussex. (Apr.) £55·00.

Iron & Steel Year Book.—Atlantic House, Holborn Viaduct, E.C.1. £11·40.

Jane's All The World's Aircraft.—238 City Rd., E.C.1. (Oct.) £64·00.

Jane's Armour & Artillery.—238 City Rd., E.C.1. (Nov.) £62·50.

Jane's Fighting Ships.—238 City Rd., E.C.1. (Aug.) £62·50.

Jane's Freight Containers.—238 City Rd., E.C.1. (Nov.) £64·00.

Jane's Infantry Weapons.—238 City Rd., E.C.1. (May) £61·00.

Jane's Major Companies of Europe.—238 City Rd., E.C.1. (May) £30·00.

Jane's Surface Skimmer Systems.—238 City Rd., E.C.1. (Dec.) £55·00.

Jane's Weapon Systems.—238 City Rd., E.C.1. (Dec.) £67·50.

Jane's World Railways.—238 City Rd., E.C.1. £62·50.

Jewish Year Book.—25 Furnival St., E.C.4. (Jan.) £9·50.

Kelly's Handbook to the Titled, Landed and Official Classes.—East Grinstead House, East Grinstead, W. Sussex. £18·00.

Kelly's Post Office London Business Directory.—East Grinstead House, East Grinstead, W. Sussex. (Jan.) 2v, £55·00.

Kempe's Engineers Year Book.—30 Calderwood St., S.E.18. £38·00.

Kemp's Directory.—1–5 Bath St., E.C.1. (Sept.) 3 v, £18·00.

Kemp's International Film & T.V. Directory.—1–5 Bath St., E.C.1. (May) £22·50.

Kemp's International Music & Recording Industry Year Book.—1–5 Bath St., E.C.1. £15·00.

Kemp's Property Industry Year Book.—1–5 Bath St., E.C.1. (Feb.) £17·50.

Kime's International Law Directory.—170 Sloane St., S.W.1. (June) £16·50.

Law List, International.—Pitman Ho., Parker St., W.C.2. £21·00.

Laxton's Building Price Book.—East Grinstead House, East Grinstead, W. Sussex. £29·00.

Library Association Yearbook.—7 Ridgmount St., Store St., W.C.1. (May) £14·75.

Lloyd's Nautical Year Book.—Sheepen Pl., Colchester CO3 3LP. (Sept.) £15·50.

London Chamber of Commerce and Industry Directory.—2 Queensway, Redhill, Surrey. (Nov.) £32·00.

Macmillan & Silk Cut Nautical Almanack.—Little Essex St., W.C.2. £11·95.

Magistrates' Court Guide.—Borough Green, Sevenoaks, Kent. £11·75.

Manufacturers & Merchants Directory.—East Grinstead House, East Grinstead, W. Sussex. £55·00.

"Mechanical World" Electrical Year Book.—14 St. James Rd., Watford. £3·95.

"Mechanical World" Year Book.—14 St. James Rd., Watford. £4·50.

Medical Annual.—42–44 Triangle West, Bristol. (Sept.) £19·50.

Medical Directory.—Fourth Avenue, Harlow, Essex. (Apr.) 2v, £56·00.

Medical Register.—44 Hallam St., W.1. (Mar.) £52·00.

Middle East & North Africa.—18 Bedford Sq., W.C.1. (Oct.) £52·00.

"Mining" Annual Review.—P.O. Box 10, Edenbridge, Kent. £12·50.

Mining International Year Book.—Fourth Avenue, Harlow, Essex. (June) £46·00.

Modern Publicity.—35 Red Lion Sq., W.C.1. (Sept.) £19·50.

Motor Industry of Great Britain.—Forbes House, Halkin St., S.W.1. (Oct.) £34·00.

Municipal Yearbook & Public Services Directory, 178 Gt. Portland St., W.1. (Dec.) £42·50.

Music Guide, International.—136 Tooley St., S.E.1. £6·95.

National Trust Year Book.—18 Bedford Sq., W.C.1. £7·00.

Nautical Almanac.—H.M.S.O., Atlantic House, Holborn Viaduct, E.C.1. (Oct.) £9·50.

North Sea & Europe Offshore Yearbook.—Minster Ho., Arthur St., E.C.4. £25·00.

Off Licence News Directory.—5 Southwark St., S.E.1. £6·00.

Offshore Oil & Gas Year Book.—126 Pentonville Rd., N.1. £50·00.

Old Moore's Almanac.—Yeovil Rd., Slough, Bucks. (July) 35p.

Owen's Business Directory and Travel Guide.—22 Mount Pleasant, Alperton, Middx. (Mar.) £52·00.

Packaging Review Directory.—40 Bowling Green Lane, E.C.1. £28·00.

Paper Trade Directory of the World, Phillips'.—Union Ho., Eridge Rd., Tunbridge Wells, Kent. (Jan.) £50·00.

Pears Cyclopedia.—44 Bedford Square, W.C.1. £8·95.

Penrose Annual.—10–16 Elm St., W.C.1. (Apr.) £21·00.

Personnel & Training Databook.—120 Pentonville Rd. N.1. £17·95.

Photography Year Book.—14 St. James Rd., Watford. £12·95.

Polymers, Paint & Colour Year Book.—2 Queensway, Redhill, Surrey. £25·00.

Ports of the World.—Union Ho., Eridge Rd., Tunbridge Wells, Kent. £59·00.

Printing Industries Annual.—11 Bedford Row, W.C.1. £20·00.

Printing Trades Directory.—Union Ho., Eridge Rd., Tunbridge Wells, Kent. £46·00.

Public and Preparatory Schools Year Book.—35 Bedford Row, W.C.1. (May) £10·95, £14·95.

Publishing, Directory of.—35 Red Lion Square, W.C.1. (Oct.) £17·95.

R.A.C. Continental Handbook.—P.O. Box 100, RAC House, Lansdowne Rd., Croydon. (Mar.) £5·00.

R.A.C. Guide & Handbook.—P.O. Box 100, RAC House, Lansdowne Rd., Croydon. (Apr.) £4·50.

R.U.S.I. & Brassey's Defence Year Book.—Headington Hill Hall, Oxford. £29·50, £12·95.

Raceform Up-to-date Form Book: Flat Racing.—2 York Rd., S.W.11. (Dec.) £10·00.

Raceform Up-to-date Form Book: National Hunt.—Thomson Ho., Withy Grove, Manchester. (Aug.) £10·00.

Railway Directory & Year Book.—40 Bowling Green Lane, E.C.1. (Dec.) £24·00.

Reed's Nautical Almanac & Tide Tables.—36–37 Cock Lane, E.C.1. (Oct.) £12·50.

Register of Defunct & Other Companies.—East Grinstead House, East Grinstead, W. Sussex. £5·00.

RIBA Directory of Practices.—Royal Institute of British Architects, 35–37 Moreland St., E.C.1. (Oct.) £9·00.

Royal Society Year Book.—6 Carlton Ho. Terr., S.W.1. (Feb.) £9·00.

Ruff's Guide to the Turf & "Sporting Life" Annual.—Paulton, Bristol BS18 5LQ. (Dec.) £45·00.

Salvation Army Year Book.—117–121 Judd St., W.C.1. (Nov.) £2·75, £5·50.

Scottish Current Law Year Book.—St. Giles St., Edinburgh. £21·00.

Scottish Law Directory.—34–36 North Frederick St., Glasgow. £15·00.

Screen World.—Victoria Works, Edgware Rd., N.W.2. £12·95.

Sell's Aviation Europe.—39 East St., Epsom, Surrey. £30·00.

Sell's British Exporters.—39 East St., Epsom, Surrey. £20·00.

Sell's Building Index.—39 East St., Epsom, Surrey. £20·00.

Sell's Directory of Products and Services.—39 East St., Epsom, Surrey. (July) £30·00.

Sell's Health Service Buyers Guide.—39 East St., Epsom, Surrey. £25·00.

Sheet Metal Industries Year Book.—2 Queensway, Redhill, Surrey. £21·50.

Shipowners, Shipbuilders & Marine Engineers, Directory of.—40 Bowling Green Lane, E.C.1. £38·00.

Specification.—9–13 Queen Anne's Gate, S.W.1. (May) 5v. £45·00.

Spon's Architects' & Builders' Price Book.—11 New Fetter La., E.C.4. (Oct.) £25·00.

Spon's Mechanical & Electrical Services Prices Book.—11 New Fetter La., E.C.4. £24·50.

Statesman's Yearbook.—Little Essex St., W.C.2. (Aug.) £22·50.

Stock Exchange Official Year Book.—Houndmills Estate, Basingstoke, Hants. £80·00.

Stone's Justices' Manual.—Borough Green, Sevenoaks, Kent. 3v. (May) £78·00.

Stores, Shops, Hypermarkets Retail Directory.—48 Poland St., W.1. £58·00.

T.V. & Radio: Guide to Independent Television.—247 Tottenham Court Rd., W.1. £3·90.

Tanker Register.—12 Camomile St., E.C.3. (May) £80·00.

Theatre Directory, British.—P.O. Box 64, Eastbourne, Sx. £13·95.

Timber Trades Directory.—Sovereign Way, Tonbridge, Kent. £25·00.

Trades Register of London.—1–5 Bath St., E.C.1. (Jan.) £4·50.

Travel Trade Directory.—30 Calderwood St., S.E.18. (July) £12·50.

U.K. Kompass Register of British Industry & Commerce.—East Grinstead House, East Grinstead, W. Sussex. £90·00.

Unit Trust Year Book.—Greystoke Pl., Fetter Lane, E.C.4. (Mar.) £13·50.

United Reformed Church Year Book.—86 Tavistock Pl., W.C.1. (Sept.) £5·50.

Veterinary Annual.—42–44 Triangle West, Bristol. (Dec.) £18·00.

"Watchmaker, Jeweller & Silversmith" Directory.— 40 Bowling Green Lane, E.C.1. £5·00.

Water Services Year Book.—2 Queensway, Redhill, Surrey. (Oct.) £25·00.

Which Degree?—53 Frith St., W.1. 5v. £34·75.

Whitaker's Almanack.—12 Dyott St., W.C.1. (Nov.) £19·95, £12·95, £6·50.

Whitaker's Publishers in the United Kingdom and their Addresses.—12 Dyott St., W.C.1. (Mar.) £3·50.

Who Owns Whom?—6–8 Bonhill St., E.C.2. 2v. £79·00.

Who's Who.—35 Bedford Row, W.C.1. (Apr.) £48·00.

Who's Who, International.—18 Bedford Sq., W.C.1. (Sept.) £60·00.

Willing's Press Guide.—East Grinstead House, East Grinstead, W. Sussex. (Feb.) £40·00.

Wine & Spirit Trade International Year Book.—76 Dean St., W.1. £18·50.

Wisden Cricketers' Almanack.—13–14 Eldon Way, Lineside Estate, Littlehampton. £11·95; £9·95.

World Hotel Directory.—Fourth Avenue, Harlow, Essex. £30·00.

World Insurance Year Book.—Fourth Avenue, Harlow, Essex. £46·00.

World of Learning.—18 Bedford Square, W.C.1. (Jan.) 2v. £77·00.

World Shipping Year Book.—Minster House, Arthur St., E.C.4. £27·00.

Writers' & Artists' Year Book.—35 Bedford Row, W.C.1. (Jan.) £5·50.

Year Book of World Affairs.—11 New Fetter Lane, E.C.4. £21·00.

THE PRESS COUNCIL
1 Salisbury Square, EC4Y 8AE
[01–353 1248]

In April, 1947, a Royal Commission was appointed to enquire into the control, management and ownership, etc., of the Press and news agencies and to make recommendations thereon. The Commission, in its report of June, 1949, recommended *inter alia* that a voluntary Press Council be formed.

A constitution ultimately set up provided for the establishment of such a council on July 1, 1953. This constitution was materially amended in 1963 by the introduction of an independent chairman and up to 20 per cent lay membership. In 1973, the Council was increased to 30 (excluding the Chairman) of whom one-third were lay members. Following a recommendation of the third Royal Commission on the Press made in 1977, the size of the Council was increased in 1978 to 36 (excluding the Chairman) of which half are press members and half non-press members. The objects of the Council are (1) to preserve the established freedom of the British Press; (2) to maintain the character of the British Press in accordance with the highest professional and commercial standards; (3) to consider complaints about the conduct of the Press or the conduct of persons and organizations towards the Press; to deal with these complaints in whatever manner might seem practical and appropriate and record resultant action; (4) to keep under review developments likely to restrict the supply of information of public interest and importance; (5) to report publicly on developments that may tend towards greater concentration or monopoly in the Press (including changes in ownership, control and growth of Press undertakings) and to publish statistical information relating thereto; (6) to make representations on appropriate occasions to the Government, organs of the United Nations and Press organizations abroad; and (7) to publish periodical reports recording the Council's work and to review, from time to time, developments in the Press and the factors affecting them.

The constitution of the Council provides for editorial and managerial nominees of The Newspaper Publishers Association Ltd. (3), The Newspaper Society (3), The Periodical Publishers Association Ltd. (2), The Scottish Daily Newspaper Society (1), Scottish Newspaper Proprietors' Association (1), The Guild of British Newspaper Editors (2), The National Union of Journalists (4), The Institute of Journalists (2) plus (18) lay members appointed by the Press Council Appointments Commission. In addition each constituent body nominates one official as a non-voting member.

Chairman, Rt. Hon. Sir Zelman Cowen, G.C.M.G., G.C.V.O., Q.C.
Director, K. Morgan, O.B.E.

PRINCIPAL NEWSPAPERS

DAILY NEWSPAPERS

National

Daily Express, 121–128 Fleet St., EC4P 4JT.

Daily Mail, Carmelite House, EC4 0JA.

Daily Star, Great Ancoats Street, Manchester M60 4HB.

Daily Telegraph, 135 Fleet St., EC4P 4BL.

Financial Times, 10 Cannon St., EC4P 4BY.

The Guardian, 119 Farringdon Rd., EC1R 3ER.

The Mirror, 33 Holborn, EC1P 1DQ.

Morning Advertiser, 57 Effra Rd., SW2 1DA.

Morning Star, 75 Farringdon Rd., EC1M 3JX.

Sporting Life, 9 New Fetter Lane, EC4A 1AR.

The Standard, 121 Fleet St., EC4P 4DD.

The Sun, 30 Bouverie St., EC4Y 8DE.

The Times, Gray's Inn Road, WC1X 8EZ.

ABERDEEN—Press and Journal and Evening Express, Lang Stracht, Mastrick.

BARROW—North-Western Evening Mail, Abbey Road.

BATH—Bath and West Evening Chronicle, 33–34 Westgate Street BA1 1EW.

BELFAST—Belfast Telegraph, 124 Royal Avenue BT1 1EB; Irish News, 113–117 Donegall Street BT1 2GE.

BIRMINGHAM—Birmingham Post, Colmore Circus B4 6AX; Evening Mail, Colmore Circus B4 6AX.

BLACKBURN—Lancs. Evening Telegraph, New Telegraph House, High Street.

BLACKPOOL—W. Lancs. Ev. Gazette, Victoria Street.

BOLTON—Evening News, Mealhouse Lane.

BOURNEMOUTH—Evening Echo, Richmond Hill BH2 6HH.

BRADFORD—Telegraph and Argus, Hall Ings.

BRIGHTON—Evening Argus, North Road.

BRISTOL—Evening Post, Temple Way, Old Market BS99 7HD; Western Daily Press, Temple Way, Old Market BS99 7HD.

BURTON—Burton Daily Mail, 65–68 High Street DE14 1LE.

CAMBRIDGE—Cambridge Evening News, 51 Newmarket Road CB5 8EJ.

CARDIFF—South Wales Echo, Thomson House; Western Mail, Thomson House.

CARLISLE—Cumberland Evening News, Newspaper House, Dalston Road CA2 5UA.

CHELTENHAM—Gloucestershire Echo, 1 Clarence Parade GL50 3NZ.

CLEVELAND—Evening Gazette, Borough Road, Middlesbrough.

COLCHESTER—Evening Gazette, Culver Street West; Lloyd's List, Sheepen Place CO3 3LP.

COVENTRY—Coventry Evening Telegraph, Corporation Street CV1 1FP.

DARLINGTON—Northern Echo, Priestgate; Evening Despatch, Priestgate DL1 1NF.

DERBY—Derby Evening Telegraph, Northcliffe House DE1 2DW.

DONCASTER—Doncaster Evening Post, 10 North Bridge Road.

DUNDEE—Courier and Advertiser, 7 Bank Street DD1 9HU; Evening Telegraph and Post, 7 Bank Street DD1 9HU.

EDINBURGH—Scotsman, 20 North Bridge EH1 1YT; Evening News, 20 North Bridge EH1 1YT.

EXETER—Express and Echo, 160 Sidwell Street EX4 6RS.

GLASGOW—Glasgow Herald, 195 Albion Street G1 1QP; Daily Record, Anderston Quay G3 8DA; Evening Times, 195 Albion Street G1 1QP.

GLOUCESTER—Citizen, St. John's Lane.

GREENOCK—Evening Telegraph, 2 Crawfurd Street PA15 1LH.

GRIMSBY—Evening Telegraph, 80 Cleethorpes Road.

GUERNSEY—Guernsey Evening Press and Star, Braye Road, Vale.

HALIFAX—Halifax Evening Courier, P.O. Box 19, King Cross Street.

HEREFORD—Evening News, Berrow's House, Bath Street WR2 5JX.

HUDDERSFIELD—Huddersfield Daily Examiner, Ramsden Street HD1 2TD.

HULL—Daily Mail, Jameson Street.

IPSWICH—East Anglian Daily Times, 30 Lower Brook Street.

JERSEY—Evening Post, P.O. Box 582, Five Oaks, St. Saviour.

KETTERING—Northants Evening Telegraph, Northfield Avenue NN16 9JN.

LEAMINGTON SPA—Leamington & District Morning News, Tachbrook Road.

LEEDS—Yorkshire Evening Post, Wellington Street LS1 1RF; Yorkshire Post, Wellington Street LS1 1RF.

LEICESTER—Leicester Mercury, St. George Street.

LINCOLN—Lincolnshire Echo, St. Benedict Square LN5 7AT.

LIVERPOOL—Liverpool Daily Post, P.O. Box 48, Old Hall Street L69 3EB; Liverpool Echo, P.O. Box 48, Old Hall Street L69 3EB; Journal of Commerce, Fowler Buildings, 7 Victoria Street L2 5QA.

MAIDSTONE—Kent Evening Post, Messenger House, New Hythe Lane, Larkfield ME20 6SG.

MANCHESTER—Manchester Evening News, 164 Deansgate M60 2RD.

NEWCASTLE—Evening Chronicle, Thomson House, Groat Market NE1 1ED; Journal, Thomson House, Groat Market NE1 1ED.

NEWPORT—South Wales Argus, Cardiff Road, Maesglas NPT 1QW.

NORTHAMPTON—Chronicle and Echo (Northampton), Upper Mounts NN1 3HR.

NORWICH—Eastern Daily Press, Prospect House, Rouen Road NR1 1RE; Eastern Evening News, Prospect House, Rouen Road NR1 1RE.

NOTTINGHAM—Evening Post, P.O. Box 99 NG1 4AB.

NUNEATON—Nuneaton Evening Tribune, Watling House, Whitacre Road.

OLDHAM—Oldham Evening Chronicle, Union Street OL1 1EQ.

OXFORD—Oxford Mail, Osney Mead OX2 0EJ.

PAISLEY—Paisley Daily Express, Express Buildings, 20 New Street.

PETERBOROUGH—Peterborough Evening Telegraph, Oundle Road, Woodston PE2 9QR.

PLYMOUTH—Western Morning News, Leicester Harmsworth House, 65 New George Street; Western Evening Herald, Leicester Harmsworth House, 65 New George Street.

PORTSMOUTH—The News, The News Centre, Hilsea PO2 9SX.

PRESTON—Lancashire Evening Post, 127 Fishergate PR1 2DN.

READING—Evening Post, 8 Tessa Road RG1 8NS.

SCARBOROUGH—Scarborough Evening News, Aberdeen Walk YO11 1BB.

SCUNTHORPE—Scunthorpe Evening Telegraph, Telegraph House, Doncaster Road.

SHEFFIELD—Morning Telegraph, York Street S11PU; Star, York Street S1 1PU.

South Shields—Shields Gazette and Shipping Telegraph, Chapter Row.

Southampton—Southern Evening Echo, Above Bar SO9 7BA.

Stoke-on-Trent—Evening Sentinel, Northcliffe House, Foundry Street, Hanley ST1 5HA.

Sunderland—Echo, Pennywell Industrial Estate SR4 9ER.

Swansea—South Wales Evening Post, Adelaide Street.

Swindon—Evening Advertiser, Newspaper House, 100 Victoria Road.

Telford—Shropshire Star, Ketley TF1 4HU.

Torquay—Herald Express, Barton Hill Road.

Weymouth—Dorset Evening Echo, 57 St. Thomas Street DT4 8EU.

Wolverhampton—Express and Star, 50 Queen Street WV1 3BU.

Worcester—Evening News, Berrow's House, Hylton Road.

York—Yorkshire Evening Press, 15 Coney Street.

SUNDAY NEWSPAPERS

Mail on Sunday—Carmelite House, EC4Y 0JA.

News of the World—30 Bouverie St., EC4Y 8EX.

Observer—8 St. Andrews Hill, EC4V 5JA.

Sunday Express—121–128 Fleet St., EC4P 4JT.

Sunday Mail—Anderston Quay, Glasgow G3 8DA.

Sunday Mercury—Colmore Circus, Birmingham B4 6AZ.

Sunday Mirror—33 Holborn, EC1P 1DQ.

Sunday News—51 Donegall St., Belfast BT1 2GB.

Sunday People—33 Holborn, EC1P 1DQ.

Sunday Post—144 Port Dundas Road, Glasgow G4 0HZ.

Sunday Sun—Groat Market, Newcastle-on-Tyne NE1 1ED.

Sunday Telegraph—135 Fleet St., EC4P 4BL.

Sunday Times—200 Gray's Inn Rd., WC1X 8EZ.

RELIGIOUS PAPERS

[*W.* = Weekly; *M.* = Monthly; *Q.* = Quarterly]

Baptist Times—4 Southampton Row, WC1B 4AB. *W.*

British Weekly and Christian Record—146 Queen Victoria St., EC4V 4EH. *W.*

Catholic Herald—Lambs Passage, Bunhill Row, E.C.1. *W.*

Challenge, the Good News Paper—Revenue Buildings, Chapel Rd., Worthing, West Sussex BN11 1BQ. *M.*

Christian Herald—27 Chapel Road, Worthing, West Sussex BN11 1EG. *W.*

Church of England Newspaper—146 Queen Victoria St., E.C.4. *W.*

Church of Ireland Gazette—48 Bachelor's Walk, Lisburn, co. Antrim. *W.*

Church Times—7 Portugal St., WC2A 2HP. *W.*

English Churchman—P.O. Box 217, SE5 8NP. *Alt. W.*

Friend—Drayton House, Gordon St., WC1H 0BQ. *W.*

Inquirer—1–6 Essex St., WC2R 3HY. *Alt. W.*

Jewish Chronicle—25 Furnival St., EC4A 1JT. *W.*

Jewish Gazette—18 Cheetham Parade, Manchester M8 6DJ. *W.*

Jewish Telegraph—11 Park Hill, Bury Old Road, Prestwich, Manchester M25 8HH. *W.*

Life and Work—121 George St., Edinburgh EH2 4YN. *M.*

Methodist Recorder—122 Golden Lane, EC1Y 0TL. *W.*

Tablet—48 Great Peter St., SW1P 2HB. *W.*

Today—37 Elm Road, New Malden, Surrey KT3 3HB. *M.*

Universe—33–39 Bowling Green Lane, EC1R 0DA. *W.*

War Cry—101 Queen Victoria St., EC4P 4EP. *W.*

PERIODICALS, MAGAZINES AND REVIEWS

[*W.* = Weekly; *M.* = Monthly; *Q.* = Quarterly]

Amateur Gardening—Westover House, West Quay Road, Poole, Dorset BH15 1JG. *W.*

Amateur Photographer—1 Throwley Way, Sutton, Surrey SM1 4QQ. *W.*

Angler's Mail—King's Reach Tower, Stamford St., S.E.1. *W.*

Antiquaries' Journal—Ass. Sec., Society of Antiquaries, Burlington House, Piccadilly, W1V 0HS. *Twice a year.*

Antique Collector—72 Broadwick St., W1V 2BP. *M.*

Apollo—22 Davies Street, W1Y 1LH. *M.*

Art and Artists—445 Brighton Road, South Croydon, Surrey CR2 6EU. *M.*

Autocar—38–42 Hampton Road, Teddington, Middlesex TW11 0JE. *W.*

Birds and Country Magazine—79 Surbiton Hill Park, Surbiton, Surrey. *Twice a year.*

Boxing News—30–34 Langham St., W1N 5LB. *W.*

Brain—Oxford U. Press, Walton Street, Oxford OX2 6DP. *Q.*

Brides and Setting-up Home—Vogue House, Hanover Sq., W1R 0AD. *Alt. M.*

British Birds—Fountains, Park Lane, Blunham, Bedford MK44 3NJ. *M.*

British Book News—The British Council, 65 Davies St., W1Y 2AA. *M.*

Bunty—185 Fleet St., EC4A 2HS. *W.*

Burlington Mag.—10–16 Elm St., WC1X 0BP. *M.*

Buses—Terminal House, Shepperton TW17 8AS. *M.*

Cage and Aviary Birds—1 Throwley Way, Sutton, Surrey SM1 4QQ. *W.*

Caravan—Link House, Dingwall Ave., Croydon, Surrey CR9 2TA. *M.*

Caravanning Monthly—Link House, Dingwall Ave., Croydon, Surrey CR9 2TA.

Classical Quarterly—Oxford U. Press, Walton St., Oxford OX2 6DP. *Twice a Year.*

Classical Review—Oxford U. Press, Walton St., Oxford OX2 6DP. *Twice a Year.*

Coal News—Hobart House, Grosvenor Place, SW1X 7AE. *M.*

Coin and Medal News—Wheel House, 5 Station Road, Liphook, Hants GU30 7DW. *M.*

Coin Monthly—Sovereign House, Brentwood, Essex CM14 4SE.

Connoisseur—72 Broadwick St., W1V 2BP. *M.*

Contemporary Review—61 Carey St., WC2 2JG. *M.*

Country Life—King's Reach Tower, Stamford St., SE1 9LS. *W.*

Countryman—Sheep Street, Burford, Oxford OX8 4LH. *Q.*

Cricketer International—29 Cavendish Road, Redhill, Surrey. *M.*

Criminologist—P.O. Box 18, Bognor Regis, Sussex PO22 7AA. *Q.*

Cycling—1 Throwley Way, Sutton, Surrey SM1 4QQ. *W.*

Dalton's Weekly—Apex Tower, High Street, New Malden, Surrey KT3 4EE. *W.*

Dancing Times—45–47 Clerkenwell Green, EC1R 0BE. *M.*

Dog World—Clergy House, Churchyard, Ashford, Kent TN23 1QW. *W.*

Do It Yourself Magazine—Link House, Dingwall Ave, Croydon CR9 2TA. *M.*

Drama—9 Fitzroy Sq., W1P 6AE. *Q.*

Drive & Trail—Fanum House, Basingstoke, Hants RG21 2EA. *M.*

Economic Journal—Cambridge U. Press, Shaftesbury Road, Cambridge CB2 2RU. *Q.*

Economica—Lond. Sch. of Economics, Houghton St., WC2A 2AE. *Q.*

Economist, The—25 St. James's St., SW1A 1HG. *W.*

Edinburgh Gazette (*Official*)—Exchequer Office, 13A Castle Street, Edinburgh EH2 3AR. *Twice a week.*

Encounter—59 St. Martin's Lane, WC2N 4JS. *Ten times a year.*

English Historical Review—Westgate House, Harlow, Essex CM20 1NE. *Q.*

Exchange and Mart—Link House, West Street, Poole, Dorset BH15 1LL. *W.*

Family Circle—Elm House, 10–16 Elm St., WC1X 0BP. *M.*

Field, The—Carmelite House, EC4Y 0JA. *W.*

Freethinker, The—702 Holloway Rd., N19 3NL. *M.*

Garden News—Bushfield House, Orton Centre, Peterborough PE2 0UW. *W.*

Gardeners' Chronicle—38–42 Hampton Rd., Teddington, Middx. TW11 0JE *W.*

Geographical Magazine—23–27 Tudor Street, EC4. *M.*

Golf Illustrated—Carmelite House, Carmelite St., EC4Y 0JA. *W.*

Golf Monthly—1 Park Circus, Glasgow G3 6AS.

Good Housekeeping—72 Broadwick St., W1V 2BP. *M.*

Good Motoring—352 Lewisham High Street, SE13 6LE. *Alt. M.*

Gramophone—177–179 Kenton Road, Harrow, Mddx. MA3 0MA *M.*

Greece and Rome—Oxford U. Press, Walton St., Oxford OX2 6DP. *Twice a year.*

Guiding—17–19 Buckingham Palace Rd., SW1W 0PT. *M.*

Harper's and Queen—72 Broadwick St., W1V 2BP. *M.*

Health & Strength—30 Craven Street, Strand, WC1N 5NT. *M.*

Health Education Journal—78 New Oxford St., WC1A 1AH. *Q.*

History—59A Kennington Park Road, SE11 4JH. *Three times a year.*

Homes and Gardens—King's Reach Tower, Stamford Street, SE1 9LS. *M.*

Homoeopathy—27A Devonshire St., W1N 1RJ *Alt. M.*

Honey—King's Reach Tower, Stamford Street, SE1 9LS. *M.*

Horse and Hound—King's Reach Tower, Stamford Street, SE1 9LS. *W.*

House and Garden—Vogue House, Hanover Sq., W1R 0AD. *Ten times a year.*

Ideal Home—King's Reach Tower, Stamford Street, SE1 9LS. *M.*

Illustrated London News—Elm House, 10–16 Elm Street, WC1X 0BP. *M.*

In Britain—B.T.A., 4 Bromells Rd., SW4 0BJ. *M.*

International Affairs—Chatham House, St. James's Square, S.W.1. *Q.*

Jazz Journal International—35 Great Russell Street, WC1B 3PP. *M.*

Kennel Gazette—1 Clarges St., Piccadilly, W1Y 8AB. *M.*

Labour Research— 78 Blackfriars Rd., SE1 8HF. *M.*

Lady—39–40 Bedford St., Strand, WC2E 9ER. *W.*

Land and Liberty—177 Vauxhall Bridge Rd., SW1V 1EU. *Alt. M.*

Liberal News—1 Whitehall Place, SW1A 2HE. *W.*

Light (*Psychic*)—16 Queensbury Place, SW7 2EB. *Q.*

Listener, The—35 Marylebone High St., W1M 4AA *W.*

Living—Elm House, Elm St., WC1X 0BP. *M.*

Local Government Chronicle—11–12 Bury St., EC3A 5AP. *W.*

London Gazette (*Official*)—P.O. Box 276, SW8 5DT. *Five times a week.*

London Magazine—30 Thurloe Place, S.W.7. *M.*

London Weekly Diary of Social Events—26 D'Arblay Street, W1V 3FH.

Mayfair—95A Chancery Lane, WC2A 1DZ. *M.*

Melody Maker—1–19 New Oxford Street, WC1A 1NG. *W.*

Meteorological Magazine—P.O. Box 276, SW8 5DT. *M.*

Mind—Walton Street, Oxford OX2 6DP. *Q.*

Model Boats—Wolsey House, Hemel Hempstead, Herts. HP2 4SS *M.*

Model Railway Constructor—Terminal House, Shepperton TW17 8AS. *M.*

Modern Languages—24A Highbury Grove, N5 2EA. *Q.*

Month—114 Mount St., W1Y 6AH. *M.*

Monthly Digest of Statistics (*Official*)—P.O. Box 276, SW8 5DT.

Mother—Commonwealth House, 1–19 New Oxford St., WC1A 1NG. *M.*

Motor Cycle News—38 High St., Kettering NN16 8SS. *W.*

Movie Maker—Wolsey House, Wolsey Road, Hemel Hempstead, Herts. HP2 4SS. *M.*

Municipal Review—36 Old Queen St., Westminster, SW1H 9JE. *Ten times a year.*

Museums Bulletin—34 Bloomsbury Way, WC1A 2SF. *M.*

Music and Letters—Oxford U. Press, Walton St., Oxford OX2 6DP. *Q.*

My Weekly—185 Fleet St., EC4A 2HS.

Nature—4 Little Essex St., WC2R 3LF. *W.*

Nautical Magazine—4-10 Darnley Street, Glasgow G41 2SD. *M.*

Navy International—Hunters Moon, Hogspudding Lane, Newdigate, Dorking, Surrey. *M.*

New Homes News—10 East Road, N1 6AU. *M.*

N.M.E.—5-7 Carnaby St., W1V 1PG. *W.*

New Scientist—1-19 New Oxford St., W.C.1. *W.*

New Society—5 Sherwood St., W1V 7RA. *W.*

New Statesman—14-16 Farringdon Lane, EC1R 3AU. *W.*

19—King's Reach Tower, Stamford Street, SE1 9LS. *M.*

Notes and Queries—Oxford U. Press, Walton St., Oxford OX2 6DP. *Q.*

Nursery World—Gloucester Mansions, Cambridge Circus, WC2H 8HD. *Alt. Th.*

Opera—6 Woodland Rise, N.10. *M.*

Our Dogs—5 Oxford Road, Station Approach, Manchester M60 1SX. *W.*

Oxford—8 Wellington Square, Oxford OX1 2HY. *Twice a year.*

Parade—Gadoline Hse., Whyteleafe, Surrey. *M.*

Parliamentary Debates (Lords) (Hansard)—P.O. Box 276, SW8 5DT. *Daily during Session.*

Parliamentary Debates (Commons) (Hansard)—P.O. Box 276, SW8 5DT. *Daily during Session.*

Penthouse—2 Bramber Rd., W14 9PB. *M.*

People's Friend—Albert Square, Dundee DD1 9QJ. *W.*

Philosophy—Cambridge U. Press, Shaftesbury Road, Cambridge CB2 2RU. *Q.*

Pins and Needles—20 Soho Square, W1V 6DT. *M.*

Playhour—King's Reach Tower, Stamford Street, SE1 9LS. *W.*

Poetry Review—21 Earls Court Square, SW5 9DE. *Q.*

Political Quarterly, The—Elm House, 10-16 Elm Street, WC1X 0BP.

Pony—104 Ash Road, Sutton, Surrey SM3 9LD. *M.*

Popular Gardening—Commonwealth House, 1-19 New Oxford Street WC1A 1NG. *W.*

Poultry World—1 Throwley Way, Sutton, Surrey SM1 4QQ. *W.*

Practical Boat Owner—Westover House, West Quay Rd., Poole, Dorset BH15 1JG. *M.*

Practical Camper—38-42 Hampton Rd., Teddington, Middx. TW11 0JE. *M.*

Practical Caravan—38-42 Hampton Rd., Teddington, Middx. TW11 0JE. *M.*

Practical Gardening—Bushfield House, Orton Centre, Peterborough PE2 0UW. *M.*

Practical Householder—Westover House, West Quay Rd., Poole, Dorset BH15 1JG. *M.*

Progress (*Braille Type*)—338-346 Goswell Rd., EC1V 7JE. *M.*

Punch—23-27 Tudor St., EC4 0HR. *W.*

Racing Calendar—Sanders Road, Wellingborough, Northants NN8 4BX. *W.*

Radio Control Models and Electronics—Wolsey House, Wolsey Road, Hemel Hempstead, Herts. HP2 4SS. *M.*

Radio Times—35 Marylebone High St., W1M 4AA. *W.*

Railway Magazine—Quadrant House, Sutton, Surrey SM2 5AS. *M.*

Railway World—Terminal House, Shepperton TW17 8AS. *M.*

Readers Digest—25 Berkeley Sq., W1X 6AB. *M.*

Riding—King's Reach Tower, Stamford Street, SE1 9LS. *M.*

Scots Independent—51 Cowane St., Stirling. *M.*

Scottish Field—302 St. Vincent St., Glasgow G2. *M.*

Scouting—Baden Powell House, Queen's Gate, SW7 5JS. *M.*

Seafarer—202 Lambeth Rd., SE1 7JW. *Q.*

She—72 Broadwick St., W1V 2BP. *M.*

Shoot!—King's Reach Tower, Stamford Street, SE1 9LS. *W.*

Shooting Times and Country Magazine—10 Sheet St., Windsor SL4 1BG. *W.*

Sociological Review—University of Keele, Staffs. ST5 5BG. *Q.*

Spectator—56 Doughty Street, WC1. *W.*

Strad—8 Lower James St., W1R 4DN. *M.*

Studio International—25 Denmark St., WC2. *Q.*

Tatler—Vogue House, Hanover Square. W1R 0AD. *M.*

Tennis World—2-4 Wendell Rd., W12. *Ten times a year.*

35 mm Photography—1 Golden Square, W1R 3AB. *M.*

This England—Alma House, Rodney Road, Cheltenham, Glos. *Q.*

Time (British Isles)—Time and Life Bldg., New Bond St., W1Y 0AA. *W.*

Times Educational Suppl't.—Gray's Inn Rd., WC1X 8EZ. *W.*

Times Higher Education Suppl't.—Gray's Inn Rd., WC1X 8EZ. *W.*

Times Literary Suppl't.—Gray's Inn Rd., WC1X 8EZ. *W.*

Tribune—308 Grays Inn Rd., WC1X 8DY. *W.*

Trout and Salmon—Bretton Court, Bretton, Peterborough PE3 8DZ. *M.*

True Romances—12-18 Paul St., EC2A 4JS. *M.*

True Story Magazine—12-18 Paul Street, EC2A 4JS. *M.*

TV Times—247 Tottenham Court Rd., W1P 0AU. *W.*

Vacher's Parliamentary Companion—Leeder House, Erskine Road, NW3 3AJ. *Q.*

Vogue—Vogue House, Hanover Square, W1R 0AD. *Sixteen times a year.*

Weather—James Glaisher House, Grenville Place, Bracknell, Berks. RG12 1BX *M.*

Weekend—Carmelite House, EC4Y 0JA. *W.*

Welsh Nation—51 Cathedral Rd., Caerdydd, Cardiff CF1 9HD. *M.*

West Africa—53 Holborn Viaduct, EC1A 2FD. *W.*

Woman—King's Reach Tower, Stamford Street, SE1 9LS. *W.*

Woman and Home—King's Reach Tower, Stamford Street, SE1 9LS. *M.*

Woman's Journal—King's Reach Tower, Stamford Street, SE1 9LS. *M.*

Woman's Own—King's Reach Tower, Stamford Street, SE1 9LS. *W.*

Woman's Realm—King's Reach Tower, Stamford Street, SE1 9LS. *W.*

Woman's Weekly—King's Reach Tower, Stamford Street, SE1 9LS.

World Today—Chatham House, St. James's Sq., SW1. *M.*

Yachting Monthly—King's Reach Tower, Stamford Street, SE1 9LS.

Yachting World—Quadrant House, Sutton, Surrey SM2 5AS. *M.*

Yachts and Yachting—196 Eastern Esplanade, Southend-on-Sea SS1 3AB. *Alt. W.*

Your Model Railway—Wolsey House, Hemel Hempstead, Herts HP2 4SS. *M.*

TRADE, PROFESSIONAL AND BUSINESS JOURNALS

[*W.* = Weekly ; *M.* = Monthly ; *Q.* = Quarterly]

Accountancy—40 Bernard St., WC1N 1LD. *M.*

Accountant—17 Scarbrook Rd., Croydon CR0 1SQ. *W.*

Accountants' Magazine—27 Queen St., Edinburgh EH2 1LA. *M.*

Achievement—145 High St., Sevenoaks, Kent. *Eight times a year.*

Administrator—16 Park Crescent, W1N 4AM. *M.*

Agricultural Machinery Journal—1 Throwley Way, Sutton, Surrey SM1 4QQ. *M.*

Anti-Corrosion—127 Stanstead Rd., SE23 1JE. *M.*

Antique Dealer and Collectors Guide—Kings Reach Tower, Stamford Street, SE1 9LS. *M.*

Architects' Journal—9 Queen Anne's Gate, SW1H 9BY. *W.*

Architectural Review—9 Queen Anne's Gate, SW1H 9BY. *M.*

Artist—102 High St., Tenterden TN30 6HT. *M.*

Bakers' Review—Penn Place, Rickmansworth, Herts WD3 1SN. *M.*

Banker—Greystoke Place, Fetter Lane, EC4A 1ND. *M.*

Banking World—Maxwell House, 74 Worship St., EC2A 2EN. *M.*

Bookseller—12 Dyott St., WC1A 1DF. *W.*

Brewers' Guardian—178–202 Great Portland Street, W1N 6NH. *M.*

British Baker—Maclaren House, 19 Scarbrook Rd., Croydon CR9 1QH. *W.*

British Business—Dept. of Industry, Millbank Tower, SW1P 4QU. *W.*

British Clothing Manufacturer—20 Soho Sq., W1V 6DT. *Q.*

British Dental Journal—64 Wimpole St., W1M 8AL. *Twice a month.*

British Food Journal—Peterson House, Northbank, Droitwich, Worcs. WR9 9BL. *Alt. M.*

British Jeweller—27 Frederick St., Birmingham B1 3HJ. *M.*

British Journal for the Philosophy of Science—Farmers Hall, Aberdeen AB9 2XT. *Q.*

British Journal of Photography—28 Great James Street, WC1N 3HL. *W.*

British Medical Journal—B.M.A. House, Tavistock Square, WC1H 9JR. *W.*

British Printer—76 Oxford St., W1N 9FD. *M.*

British Sugar Beet Review—P.O. Box 26, Oundle Rd., Peterborough PE2 9QU. *Q.*

British Tax Review—11 New Fetter Lane, EC4P 4EE. *Alt. M.*

British Veterinary Journal—1 Vincent Square, SW1P 2PN. *Alt. M.*

Brushes and Brushmaking International—Penn House, Penn Place, Rickmansworth WD3 1SN. *Alt. M.*

Builders' and Timber Merchant—Sovereign Way, Tonbridge, Kent TN9 1RW. *M.*

Building—1–3 Pemberton Row, Red Lion Court, Fleet St., EC4P 4HL. *W.*

Cabinet Maker and Retail Furnisher—Sovereign Way, Tonbridge, Kent TN9 1RW. *W.*

Campaign—22 Lancaster Gate, W2 3LY. *W.*

Carpet and Floorcoverings Review—Sovereign Way, Tonbridge, Kent TN9 1RW. *Alt. W.*

Caterer and Hotelkeeper—Quadrant House, Sutton, Surrey SM2 5AS. *W.*

Catering Management—Quadrant House, Sutton, Surrey SM2 5AS. *M.*

Chemist and Druggist—Sovereign Way, Tonbridge, Kent TN9 1RW. *W.*

Chemistry and Industry—14–15 Belgrave Sq., SW1X 8PS. *Twice a month.*

Chemistry in Britain—Burlington House, W1V 0BN. *M.*

Child Education—Westfield Road, Southam, Warks. CV33 0JH. *M.*

Chiropodist—53 Welbeck St., W1M 7HE. *M.*

Civil Engineering and Public Works Review—Morgan Grampian House, Calderwood St., SE18 6QH. *M.*

Club Mirror—18 Queens Rd., Brighton BN1 3XA. *M.*

Colliery Guardian—Queensway House, Redhill, Surrey RH1 1QS. *M.*

Commerce International—Albany House, Hurst Street, Birmingham B5 4BD. *M.*

Commercial Motor—The Quadrant, Sutton, Surrey SM2 5AS. *W.*

Computer Survey—33–35 Bowling Green Lane, EC1R 0DA. *Alt. M.*

Concrete—11 Grosvenor Crescent, SW1X 7EE. *M.*

Containerisation International—72 Broadwick St., W1V 2BP. *M.*

Contract Journal—1 Throwley Way, Sutton, Surrey SM1 4QQ. *W.*

Control and Instrumentation—Morgan Grampian House, Calderwood St., SE18 6QH. *M.*

Cordage, Canvas and Jute World—177 Hagden Lane, Watford, Herts. WD1 8LW. *Yearly.*

C.S.E. News (Camping and Sports Equipment)—4 Spring St., W2. *M.*

Dairy Farmer—Wharfedale Rd., Ipswich 1PI 4LG. *M.*

Dairy Industries International—33–35 Bowling Green Lane, EC1R 0DA. *M.*

Design—The Design Council, 28 Haymarket, SW1Y 4SU. *M.*

Dock and Harbour Authority—19 Harcourt St., W1H 2AX. *M.*

Drapers Record—20 Soho Sq., W1V 6DT. *W.*

Education—Westgate House, Harlow, Essex CM20 1NE. *W.*

Education Equipment—Sovereign Way, Tonbridge, Kent TN9 1RW. *M.*

Electrical & Electronic Trader—Quadrant House, Sutton, Surrey SM2 5AS. *W.*

Electrical and Radio Trading—Quadrant House, Sutton, Surrey SM2 5AS. *W.*

Electrical Review—Quadrant House, Sutton, Surrey SM2 5AS. *W.*

Electrical Times—Quadrant House, Sutton, Surrey SM2 5AS. *M.*

Electronic Engineering—Morgan Grampian House, Calderwood St., SE18 6QH. *M.*

Electronics Weekly—Quadrant House, Sutton, Surrey SM2 5AS.

Embroidery—161 Kenton Road, Kenton, Harrow HA3 0EU. *Q.*

Engineer—Morgan Grampian House, Calderwood St., SE18 6QH. *W.*

Engineering—28 Haymarket, SW1Y 4SU. *M.*

Engineer's Digest—33–35 Bowling Green Lane, EC1R 0DA. *M.*

Estates Gazette—151 Wardour St., W1V 4BN. *W.*

Export News—The International Export Association, Bourne, Lincs. *Q.*

Fairplay International Shipping Weekly—52–54 Southwark St., SE1 1UJ.

Farmers Weekly—1 Throwley Way, Sutton, Surrey SM1 4QQ.

Fire (British Fire Service)—Queensway House, Redhill, Surrey RH1 1QS. *M.*

Fire Protection—Stanley House, 9 West Street, Epsom, Surrey. *M.*

Fish Friers Review—289 Dewsbury Road, Leeds LS11 5HW. *M.*

Fish Trader—2 Queensway, Redhill, Surrey RH1 1QS. *W.*

Flight International—Quadrant House, Sutton, Surrey SM2 5AS. *W.*

Food Trade Review—29 High Street, Orpington, Kent BR6 6LS. *M.*

Forestry and British Timber—Sovereign Way, Tonbridge, Kent TN9 1RW. *M.*

Foundry Trade Journal—Queensway House, Redhill, Surrey RH1 1QS. *Alt. W.*

Frozen Foods—Queensway House, Redhill, Surrey RH1 1QS. *M.*

Fuel—Westbury House, Bury St., Guildford GU2 5BH. *M.*

Funeral Service Journal—King & Hutchings, Cricketfield Rd., Uxbridge, Middx. *M.*

Fur Weekly News—122 Lea Bridge Rd., E5 9RB.

Gas Marketing—Sovereign Way, Tonbridge, Kent TN9 1RW. *M.*

Gas World—Sovereign Way, Tonbridge, Kent TN9 1RW. *M.*

Gifts International—Sovereign Way, Tonbridge, Kent TN9 1RW. *M.*

Glass—Queensway House, Redhill, Surrey RH1 1QS. *M.*

Grocer—5–7 Southwark St., SE1 1RQ. *W.*

Grower—50 Doughty St., WC1N 2LP. *W.*

Hair and Beauty—Quadrant House, Sutton, Surrey SM2 5AS. *M.*

Hairdressers' Journal International—Quadrant House, The Quadrant, Sutton SM2 5AS. *W.*

Handy Shipping Guide—230–234 Long Lane, SE1 4QE. *W.*

Hardware Trade Journal—Sovereign Way, Tonbridge, Kent TN9 1RW. *W.*

Harper's Sports—Unit 3, Weeldon Place, Bradbourne Vale Rd., Sevenoaks, Kent. *Alt. W.*

Harper's Wine and Spirit Gazette—Unit 3, Weeldon Place, Bradbourne Vale Rd., Sevenoaks, Kent. *W.*

Health Visitor—124 Belgrave Road, SW1V 2BL. *M.*

Heating and Ventilating Engineer—886 High Rd., Finchley N12 9SB. *Ten times a year.*

Hospital and Health Services Review—Westgate House, Harlow, Essex. *M.*

Ice Cream & Frozen Confectionery—90–94 Grays Inn Rd., WC1X 8AH. *M.*

Industrial Society—Peter Runge House, 3 Carlton House Terrace, SW1Y 5DG. *Q.*

Insurance Mail—44 Fleet St., EC4Y 1BS. *M.*

Investors Chronicle (inc. Investor's Review)—Greystoke Place, Fetter Lane, EC4A 1ND. *W.*

Jeweller—177 Hagden Lane, Watford, Herts. *M.*

Journal of Advertising—1 St. Anne's Road, Eastbourne, E. Sussex BN21 3UN. *Q.*

Journal of the Chemical Society—Burlington House, W1V 0BN. *In six parts.*

Journalist—314 Gray's Inn Rd., WC1K 8DB. *M.*

Justice of the Peace—Little London, Chichester. *W.*

Knitting and Haberdashery Review—80A South Street, Romford, Essex RM1 1RX. *Alt. M.*

Lancet—7 Adam Street, WC2N 6AD. *W.*

Law Quarterly Review—11 New Fetter Lane, EC4P 4EE.

Law Reports—3 Stone Buildings, Lincoln's Inn, WC2A 3XN. *M.*

Law Society's Gazette—113 Chancery Lane, WC2A 1PL. *W.*

Leather—Sovereign Way, Tonbridge, Kent TN9 1RW. *M.*

Leathergoods—Sovereign Way, Tonbridge, Kent TN9 1RW. *M.*

Legal Executive—Kempston Manor, Kempston, Bedford MK42 7AB. *Alt. M.*

Library Review—137 Leith Walk, Edinburgh EH6 8NS. *Q.*

Litho Week—38–42 Hampton Rd., Teddington, Middx. TW11 0JE.

Lloyd's Loading List—Sheepen Place, Colchester, Essex CO3 3LP. *W.*

Locomotive Journal—9 Arkwright Rd., NW3 6AB. *M.*

London Corn Circular—52–57 Mark Lane, EC3R 7NE. *W.*

Machinery and Production Engineering—Franks Hall, Horton, Kirby, Kent DA4 9LL. *Twice a month.*

Machinery Market—6 Blyth Road, Bromley, Kent BR1 3RX. *W.*

Management Accounting—63 Portland Place, W1N 4AB. *M.*

Management Decision—69 Toller Lane, Bradford BD8 9BY. *Six times a year.*

Management Today—76 Dean St., W1A 1BU. *M.*

Manufacturing Chemist—Morgan Grampian House, Calderwood St., SE18 6QH. *M.*

Marketing—22 Lancaster Gate, W2 3LY. *W.*

Materials Reclamation Weekly—Maclaren House, 19 Scarbrook Rd., Croydon CR9 1QH.

Meat Trades Journal—93–99 Goswell Rd., EC1V 7QA. *W.*

Medico-Legal Journal—129 Long Lane, Southwark SE1 4PL. *Q.*

Men's Wear—20 Soho Sq., W1V 6DT. *W.*

Metal Bulletin—Park House, Park Terrace, Worcester Park, Surrey KT4 7HY. *Twice a week.*

Metallurgia—Queensway House, Redhill, Surrey RH1 1QS. *M.*

Metals and Minerals International—5 Pond St., Hampstead NW3 2PN. *Alt. M.*

Milk Industry—19 Cornwall Terrace, NW1 4QP. *M.*

Mining Journal—15 Wilson St., Moorgate, EC2M 2TR. *W.*

Mining Magazine—15 Wilson St., Moorgate, EC2M 2TR. *M.*

Model Engineer—Wolsey House, Hemel Hempstead, Herts. HP2 4SS. *Twice a month.*

Modern Law Review—11 New Fetter Lane, EC4P 4EE. *Alt. M.*

Modern Railways—Terminal House, Shepperton TW17 8AS. *M.*

Motor—1 Throwley Way, Sutton, Surrey SM1 4QQ. *W.*

Motor Boat and Yachting—Quadrant House, Sutton, Surrey SM1 5AS. *M.*

Motorcycle Trader—Penn House, Penn Place, Rickmansworth, Herts. WD3 1SN. *M.*

Motor Trader—Quadrant House, Sutton, Surrey SM2 5AS. *W.*

Motor Transport—Quadrant House, Sutton, Surrey SM2 5AS. *M.*

Musical Times—8 Lower James St., W1R 4DN. *M.*

National Builder—82 New Cavendish St., W1M 8AD. *M.*

Natural Gas—Sovereign Way, Tonbridge, Kent TN9 1RW. *Alt. M.*

New Law Journal—Butterworths, Borough Green, Sevenoaks, Kent TN15 8PH. *W.*

Nuclear Engineering International—Quadrant House, Sutton, Surrey SM2 5AS. *M.*

Nurseryman & Garden Centre—Sovereign Way, Tonbridge, Kent TN9 1RW. *W.*

Nursing Mirror—1 Throwley Way, Sutton, Surrey SM1 4QQ. *W.*

Nursing Times—4 Little Essex St., WC2R 3LF. *W.*

Off Licence News—5–7 Southwark St., SE1 1RQ. *W.*

Ophthalmic Optician—233–234 Blackfriars Rd., SE1 8NW. *Alt. W.*

Optician—Quadrant House, Sutton, Surrey SM2 5AS. *W.*

Packaging—Penn Place, Rickmansworth, Herts. WD3 1SN. *M.*

Packaging Review—Quadrant House, Sutton, Surrey SM2 5AS. *M.*

Paint & Resin—Penn House, Penn Place, Rickmansworth WD3 1SN. *Alt. M.*

Painting and Decorating Journal—23 Low Street, Diss, Norfolk. *M.*

Paper—Sovereign Way, Tonbridge, Kent TN9 1RW. *Alt. W.*

Personnel Management—1 Hills Place, W1R 1AG. *M.*

Pharmaceutical Journal—1 Lambeth High Street, SE1 7JN. *W.*

Philatelic Magazine—100 Fleet St., EC4Y 1OE. *Twice a month.*

Photographer, The—1 Gayford Road, W12 9BY. *M.*

Physics Bulletin—Techno House, Redcliffe Way, Bristol BS1 6NX. *Twelve issues a year.*

Physics Education—Techno House, Redcliffe Way, Bristol BS1 6NX. *Seven issues a Year.*

Physics in Technology—Techno House, Redcliffe Way, Bristol BS1 6NX. *Alt. M.*

Plumbing and Heating Equipment News—Peterson House, Northbank, Droitwich, Worcs. WR9 9BL. *M.*

Police Review—14 St. Cross St., EC1N 8FE. *W.*

Policy Holder Insurance News—1 Harlequin Ave., Brentford, Middx. TW8 9EW. *W.*

Post Magazine and Insurance Monitor—38 The Butts, Brentford, Middx. TW8 8BN. *W.*

Power Farming—1 Throwley Way, Sutton, Surrey SM1 4QQ. *M.*

Practical Wireless—Westover House, West Quay Rd., Poole, Dorset B15 1JG. *M.*

Practical Woodworking—Kings Reach Tower, Stamford St., SE1 9LS. *M.*

Practitioner—Morgan-Grampian House, Calderwood St., SE18 6QH. *M.*

Printing World—Sovereign Way, Tonbridge, Kent TN9 1RW. *M.*

Product Finishing—127 Stanstead Rd., SE23 1JE. *M.*

Public Law—11 New Fetter Lane, EC4P 4EE. *Q.*

Public Ledger and Daily Freight Register—Penn House, Penn Place, Rickmansworth, Herts. WD3 1SN *Daily.*

Public Service—1 Mabledon Place, WC1H 9AJ *M.*

Quarry Management—7 Regent St., Nottingham NG1 5BY. *M.*

Quarterly Journal of Experimental Psychology—24–28 Oval Rd., NW1 7DX.

Quarterly Journal of Medicine—Oxford U. Press, Walton St., Oxford OX2 6DP.

Railway Gazette International—Quadrant House, Sutton, Surrey SM2 5AS. *M.*

Rating and Valuation Reporter—2 Paper Bldgs., Temple, EC4. *M.*

Resale Weekly—Unit 4, Sewell St., Plaistow, E13 0PE.

Retail Jeweller—Knightway House, 20 Soho Square, W1V 6DT. *Alt. W.*

Retail Newsagent, Tobacconist & Confectioner—Onslow House, 60/66 Saffron Hill, EC1N 8QX. *W.*

Review: Worldwide Reinsurance—33–35 Bowling Green Lane, EC1R 0DA. *Alt. W.*

Review of English Studies—Oxford U. Press, Walton St., Oxford OX2 6DP. *Q.*

Safety at Sea—Queensway House, Redhill, Surrey RH1 1QS. *M.*

Scottish Farmer—302 St. Vincent St., Glasgow G2 8LG. *W.*

Scottish Grocer—34–6 North Frederick St., Glasgow G1 2BT. *W.*

Service Station—178–202 Gt. Portland St., W1N 6NH. *W.*

Sheet Metal Industries—Queensway House, Redhill, Surrey RH1 1QS. *M.*

Shipping World and Shipbuilder—42–43 Lower Marsh, SE1 7RQ. *M.*

Shoe and Leather News—84–88 Great Eastern St., EC2A 3ED. *W.*

Soap, Perfumery and Cosmetics—33–35 Bowling Green Lane, EC1R 0DA. *M.*

Solicitors' Journal—21–27 Lamb's Conduit Street, WC1N 3NJ. *W.*

Sports Trader—Sovereign Way, Tonbridge, Kent TN9 1RW.*Alt. W.*

Stage and Television Today—47 Bermondsey St., SE1 3XT. *W.*

Structural Engineer—11 Upper Belgrave St., SW1X 8BH. *16 issues a year.*

Surveyor and Public Works Weekly—1 Throwley Way, Sutton, Surrey SM1 4QQ.

Tableware International—Queensway House, Redhill, Surrey RH1 1QS. *M.*

Taxation—17 Scarbrook Rd., Croydon CR0 1SQ. *W.*

Teacher—Hamilton House, Hastings Street, WC1H 9BD. *W.*

Teaching History—59A Kennington Park Rd., SE11 4JH. *Three times a year.*

Television—Tavistock House East, Tavistock Square, WC1H 9HR. *Alt. M.*

Textile Horizons—10 Blackfriars St., Manchester M3 5DR. *M.*

Textile Month—Grove House, Skerton Rd.,Old Trafford, Manchester M16 0WL.

Timber Trades Journal and Wood Processing—Sovereign Way, Tonbridge, Kent TN9 1RW. *W.*

Tobacco—Queensway House, Redhill, Surrey RH1 1QS. *M.*

Tooling and Machining–127 Stanstead Rd., SE23 1JE. *M.*

Town and Country Planning—17 Carlton House Terrace, SW1Y 5AS. *M.*

Town Planning Review—Dept. of Civic Design, Liverpool University. *Q.*

Toy Trader—Penn House, Penn Place, Rickmansworth WD3 1SN. *M.*

Trade Marks Journal—25 Southampton Bldgs., Chancery Lane, WC2A 1AY. *W.*

Traffic Engineering and Control—29 Newman St., W1P 3PE. *M.*

U.K. Press Gazette—244–249 Temple Chambers, Temple Avenue, EC4Y 0DT. *W.*

Ultrasonics—P.O. Box 63, Westbury House, Bury Street, Guildford, Surrey GU2 5BH. *Alt. M.*

Weekly Law Reports—3 Stone Buildings, Lincoln's Inn, WC2A 2LL.

Welding and Metal Fabrication—Quadrant House, Sutton, Surrey SM2 5AS. *Ten times a year.*

Which?—14 Buckingham St., WC2N 6DS. *M.*

Whitaker's Books of the Month and Books to Come—12 Dyott St., WC1A 1DF. *M.*

Whitaker's Classified Monthly Booklist—12 Dyott St., WC1A 1DF.

Whitaker's Cumulative Book List—12 Dyott St., WC1A 1DF. *Q.*

Wire Industry—110–12 Station Road East, Oxted, Surrey RH8 0QA. *M.*

Woodworker—Wolsey House, Hemel Hempstead HP2 4SS. *M.*

Woodworking Crafts—170 High St., Lewes, E. Sussex BN7 1YE. *M.*

World Crops—Yew Tree House, Horne, Horley, Surrey. *Alt. M.*

World's Fair—2 Daltry St., Shaw Rd., Oldham OL1 4BB. *W.*

NORTHERN IRISH NEWSPAPERS

London Offices

Ballymena Observer—30 Fleet St., EC4Y 1AH.

Banbridge Chronicle—30 Fleet St., EC4Y 1AH.

Belfast Telegraph—Greater London House, Hampstead Road, NW1 7SH.

Coleraine Chronicle—30 Fleet St., EC4Y 1AH.

Derry Journal—30 Fleet St., EC4Y 1AH.

Down Recorder—30 Fleet St., EC4Y 1AH.

Impartial Reporter (Enniskillen)—30 Fleet St., EC4Y 1AH.

Irish News—70 Hatton Garden, EC1N 8JT.

Irish Weekly—70 Hatton Garden, EC1N 8JT.

Mid Ulster Mail—30–32 Fleet St., EC4Y 1AH.

Northern Constitution (Coleraine)—30 Fleet St., EC4Y 1AH.

Strabane Weekly News—30 Fleet St., EC4Y 1AH.

Tyrone Constitution—30 Fleet St., EC4Y 1AH.

Ulster Gazette (Armagh)—30 Fleet St., EC4Y 1AH.

Ulster Herald (Omagh)—80 Fleet Street, EC4Y 1PN.

REPORTING AND NEWS AGENCIES IN LONDON

ASSOCIATED PRESS LTD.,
36/38 Whitefriars Street, E.C.4. 01–353 7191.

BRENARD PRESS LTD.,
Heathrow Airport, Hounslow, Middx. 01–759 1235.

CENTRAL PRESS FEATURES,
161 Fleet, Street, E.C.4. 01–353 7131.

EXCHANGE TELEGRAPH CO., LTD.,
Extel House, East Harding Street, E.C.4. 01–353 1080.

HAYTERS SPORTS REPORTING
4–5 Gough Square, E.C.4. 01–353 0971.

NATIONAL PRESS AGENCY LTD.,
Newspaper House, 8–16 Great New Street, E.C.4. 01–353 1030.

PARLIAMENTARY NEWS SERVICES,
19 Kingsdowne Road, Surbiton. 01–339 2049.

PRESS ASSOCIATION LTD.,
85 Fleet Street, E.C.4. 01–353 7440.

REUTERS LTD.,
85 Fleet Street, E.C.4. 01–250 1122.

UNITED PRESS INTERNATIONAL, LTD.,
8 Bouverie St., EC4P 4BE. 01–353 2282.

UNIVERSAL NEWS SERVICES, LTD.,
Gough Square, Fleet St., EC4 4DP. 01–353 5200.

PRINCIPAL LONDON CLUBS

ALPINE (1857), 74 South Audley Street, W1Y 5FF.—
Hon. Sec., S. W. Town.

AMERICAN (1919), 95 Piccadilly, W1V 0BS.—*Sec.*,
D. J. Child.

AMERICAN WOMEN'S (1899), 95 Piccadilly, W1V 0BS.—
Sec., Ms. M. Dougan.

ANGLO-BELGIAN (1955), 60 Knightsbridge, SW1X
7LF.—*Hon. Sec.*, Baron de Gerlache de Gomery,
M.V.O.

ARMY AND NAVY (1837), 36–39 Pall Mall, SW1Y 5JN.—
Sec., Col. D. O. O'Reilly.

ARTS (1863), 40 Dover Street, W1X 3RB.—*Sec.*, M. W.
Luck.

ARTS THEATRE (1927), 7 Great Newport Street,
W.C.2.—*Sec.*, Miss C. Dowling.

THE ATHENAEUM (1824), 107 Pall Mall, SW1Y 5ER.—
Sec., R. Smith.

AUTHOR'S (1892), 40 Dover Street, W1X 3RB.—*Sec.*,
Mrs. H. Ridgway.

BEEFSTEAK (1876), 9a Irving Street, WC2H 7AT.—
Sec., E. Pool, M.C.

BOODLE'S (1762), 28 St. James's Street, S.W.1.—*Sec.*,
R. J. Edmonds.

BROOKS'S (1764), 60 St. James's Street, SW1A 1LN.—
Sec., M. A. Roberts.

BUCK'S (1919), 18 Clifford Street, W.1.—*Sec.*, A.
Cowley.

CALEDONIAN (1891), 9 Halkin Street, SW1X 7DR.—
Sec., Cdr. C. M. Bagguley, R.N.

CANNING (1910), 42 Half Moon Street, W1Y 8DS.—
Sec., R. B. Baker.

CARLTON (1832), 69 St. James's Street, SW1A 1PJ.—
Sec., R. N. Linsley.

CAVALRY AND GUARDS (1893), 127 Piccadilly,
W1V 0PH.—*Sec.*, L. D. de Pinna.

CHALLONER (1949), 59/61 Pont Street, S.W.1—*Sec.*,
J. S. Tosh.

CHELSEA ARTS (1891), 143 Old Church Street,
SW3 6EB.—*Sec.*, Hon. D. Winterbottom.

CITY LIVERY (1914), Sion College, Victoria Embankment, EC4Y 0DN.—*Hon. Sec.*, B. L. Morgan, C.B.E.

CITY OF LONDON (1832), 19 Old Broad Street, EC2N
1DS.—*Sec.*, P. Merritt.

CITY UNIVERSITY (1895), 50 Cornhill, E.C.3.—*Sec.*,
Mrs. B. J. Latta.

EAST INDIA (Devonshire, Sports and Public Schools)
(1849), 16 St. James's Square, SW1Y 4LH.—*Sec.*,
D. E. Unwin.

ECCENTRIC (1890), 9 Ryder Street, SW1Y 6PZ.—*Sec.*,
J. F. W. Hawkins.

FARMERS' (1842), 3 Whitehall Court, SW1A 2EL.—
Sec., Lt. Col. J. L. S. Andrews, O.B.E.

FLYFISHERS' (1884), 24a Old Burlington Street, W.1.—
Sec., Cdr. N. T. Fuller, R.N. (*ret.*).

GARRICK (1831), 15 Garrick Street, WC2E 9AY.—*Sec.*,
M. J. Harvey.

GREEN ROOM (1877), 9 Adam Street, WC2N 6AA.—
Hon. Sec., P. Corneille.

GRESHAM (1843), 15 Abchurch Lane, EC4N 7BB.—
Sec., Mrs. J. S. Downing.

HURLINGHAM (1869), Ranelagh Gardens, SW6 3PR.—
Chief Exec., Maj. Gen. R. E. J. Gerrard-Wright,
C.B., C.B.E.

KEMPTON PARK (1878), Sunbury-on-Thames, Middx.,
TW16 5AQ.—*Sec.*, Miss S. Bainbridge.

KENNEL (1873), 1 Clarges Street, W1Y 8AB.—*Sec.*,
M. H. Sinnatt, C.B.

LANSDOWNE (1934), 9 Fitzmaurice Place, Berkeley
Square, W1X 6JD.—*Sec.*, M. de Lisle Bush.

LONDON ROWING (1856), Embankment, Putney, SW15
1LB.—*Sec.*, N. A. Smith.

LONDON THAMES FENCING (1848), 83 Perham Road,
W.14.—*Sec.*, Miss K. Smith.

M.C.C. (MARYLEBONE CRICKET CLUB) (1787), Lord's
Cricket Ground, NW8 8QN.—*Sec.*, J. A. Bailey.

MINING (1910), 3 London Wall Buildings, E.C.2.—
Sec., Miss P. Warner.

NATIONAL (1845), c/o Carlton Club (*q.v.*).—*Sec.*, I. E.
Nash.

NATIONAL LIBERAL (1882), 1 Whitehall Place,
SW1A 2HE.—*Hon. Sec.*, M. J. Cook.

NAVAL (1946), 38 Hill Street, W1X 8DP.—*Sec.*, Cdr.
C. R. Parkes (*ret.*).

NAVAL AND MILITARY (1862), 94 Piccadilly, W1V
0BP.—*Sec.*, R. B. Raworth, V.R.D.

ORIENTAL (1824), Stratford House, Stratford Place,
W1N 0ES.—*Sec.*, R. N. Rapson, M.V.O.

PORTLAND (1816), 42 Half Moon Street, W1Y 7RD.—
Sec., R. B. Little.

PRATT'S (1841), 14 Park Place, SW1A 1LP.—*Sec.*,
Capt. P. W. E. Parry, M.B.E.

PRESS (1882), International Press Centre, 76 Shoe
Lane, E.C.4.—*Sec.*, J. Newton.

QUEEN'S (1886), Palliser Road, W. Kensington, W14
9EQ.—*Sec.*, J. A. S. Edwardes.

RAILWAY (1899), Keen House, 4 Calshot Street, N1
9DA.—*Hon. Sec.*, N. C. Farebrother.

REFORM (1836), 104–5 Pall Mall, SW1Y 5EW.—*Sec.*,
R. A. M. Forrest.

ROEHAMPTON (1901), Roehampton Lane, SW15 5LR.—
Sec., R. W. Varley.

ROYAL AIR FORCE (1918), 128 Piccadilly, W1V 0PY.—
Sec., Sqn. Ldr. J. Swaffield.

ROYAL AUTOMOBILE (1897), 89–91 Pall Mall, S.W.1.—
Sec., Capt. John C. Judge, R.N.

ROYAL COMMONWEALTH SOCIETY (1868), 18 Northumberland Avenue, WC2N 5BJ.—*Sec. Gen.*, Sir
Michael Scott, K.C.V.O., C.M.G.

ROYAL OCEAN RACING (1925), 20 St. James's Place,
SW1A 1NN.—*Sec.*, E. A. Green.

ROYAL OVER-SEAS LEAGUE (1910), Over-Seas House,
Park Place, St. James's Street, S.W.1.—*Dir. Gen.*,
Capt. J. B. Rumble, R.N.

ROYAL THAMES YACHT (1775), 60 Knightsbridge,
SW1X 7LF.—*Sec.*, Capt. A. R. Ward, C.B.E., R.N.

ST. STEPHEN'S CONSTITUTIONAL (1870), 34 Queen
Anne's Gate, S.W.1.—*Sec.*, L. D. Mawby.

SAVAGE (1857), 9 Fitzmaurice Place, Berkeley Square,
W1X 5DE.—*Hon. Sec.*, D. Coomber, O.B.E..

SAVILE (1868), 69 Brook Street, W1Y 2ER.—*Sec.*, P.
Aldersley.

SKI CLUB OF GREAT BRITAIN (1903), 118 Eaton Square,
SW1W 9AF.—*Sec.*, P. R. Doyne.

THAMES ROWING (1860), Embankment, Putney, SW15
1LB.—*Hon. Sec.*, F. S. Beardmore.

TRAVELLERS' (1819), 106 Pall Mall, SW1Y 5EP.—*Sec.*,
G. S. Chisholm.

TURF (1868), 5 Carlton House Terrace, SW1Y 5AQ.—
Sec., P. A. Chandler.

UNITED NURSING SERVICES (1921), 40 South Street, W.1.—*Sec.*, W. Oakes.

UNITED OXFORD AND CAMBRIDGE UNIVERSITY (1972), 71 Pall Mall, SW1Y 5HD.—*Sec.*, D. J. McDougall.

UNIVERSITY WOMEN'S (1886), 2 Audley Square, W1Y 6DB.—*Sec.*, Mrs. E. Hord.

V.A.D. (1920), 44 Great Cumberland Place, W1H 8BS.—*Sec.*, G. Maylett.

VICTORIA (1863), 150–162 Edgware Road, W.2.—*Sec.*, L. A. Holland.

VICTORY SERVICES (1907), 63–79 Seymour Street, W2 2HL.—*Gen. Manager*, D. G. Stovey.

WHITE'S (1693), 37–38 St. James's Street, SW1A 1JG.—*Sec.*, W. H. West.

WIG AND PEN (1908), 229–230 Strand, WC2R 1BA.— *Sec.*, J. Reynolds.

PRINCIPAL CLUBS OUTSIDE LONDON

Aldershot.—ROYAL ALDERSHOT OFFICERS CLUB (1856), Farnborough Road, Aldershot, Hants.— *Sec.*, Lt. Col. A. F. J. Channon, M.B.E.

Bath.—BATH AND COUNTY CLUB (1865), Queen's Parade, Bath, Avon.—*Sec.*, D. R. L. Brown.

Birmingham.—BIRMINGHAM CLUB (1872), Winston Churchill House, 8 Ethel Street, Birmingham B2 4BG.—*Hon. Sec.*, Lt. Cdr. R. M. Woodgate, R.D., R.N.R.

St. PAUL'S CLUB (1859), 34 St. Paul's Square, Birmingham B3 1QZ.—*Hon. Sec.*, J. S. Scott, T.D.

Bishop Auckland.—THE CLUB (1868), 1 Victoria Avenue, Bishop Auckland, Co. Durham DL14 7JH.—*Hon. Sec.*, A. Chapman.

Bristol.—THE BEAUFORT CLUB (1885), Marsh Street, Bristol BS1 4BG.—*Sec.*, M. Lansdell.

CLIFTON CLUB (1882), 22 The Mall, Bristol BS8 4DS.—*Hon. Sec.*, H. Walder.

Cambridge.—THE AMATEUR DRAMATIC CLUB (1855), A.D.C. Theatre, Park Street, Cambridge.—*Hon. Sec.*, B. Ball.

HAWKS CLUB (1874), Jesus Lane, Cambridge.— *Hon. Sec.*, R. W. Tyler.

UNION CLUB (1815), Bridge Street, Cambridge CB2 1UB.—*Sec.*, B. Thoday.

Canterbury.—KENT AND CANTERBURY CLUB (1868), 17 Old Dover Road, Canterbury CT1 3JB.—*Sec.*, P. L. Wood.

Cardiff.—CARDIFF AND COUNTY CLUB (1866), Westgate Street, Cardiff CF1 1DA.—*Hon. Sec.*, A. G. Robertson, T.D.

Cheltenham.—THE NEW CLUB (1874), Montpellier Parade, Cheltenham, Glos. GL5O 1UD.—*Hon. Sec.*, J. A. Warhurst, O.B.E.

Chester.—THE CITY CLUB (1807), St. Peter's Churchyard, Chester CH1 2AG.—*Sec.*, G. R. Hargreaves.

GROSVENOR CLUB (1866), Vicars Lane, Chester CH1 1QX.—*Hon. Sec.*, Maj. U. C. E. Farr.

Chichester.—WEST SUSSEX COUNTY CLUB (1872), 5 Stirling Road, Chichester, W. Sussex.—*Sec.*, J. S. Winny.

Colchester.—THE CLUB (1874), 3–5 Culver Street West, Colchester, Essex.—*Sec.*, N. Duncan.

Devizes.—DEVIZES AND DISTRICT CLUB (1932), 27 St. John Street, Devizes, Wilts SN10 1BN.—*Sec.*, D. J. J. Cox.

Durham.—COUNTY CLUB (1890), 52 Old Elvet, Durham.—*Sec.*, Mrs. C. Arnot.

Eastbourne.—THE DEVONSHIRE CLUB (1872), Hartington Place, Eastbourne, Sussex BN21 3RN.—*Hon. Sec.*, B. S. M. Kerry.

Exeter.—EXETER AND COUNTY CLUB (1871), 5 Cathedral Close, Exeter, Devon EX1 1EZ.—*Sec.*, S. F. Hodge, M.B.E.

Guildford.—COUNTY CLUB, 158 High Street, Guildford GU1 3HF.—*Hon. Sec.*, R. M. Pritchett.

Harrogate.—THE CLUB (1857), 36 Victoria Avenue, Harrogate, N. Yorks.—*Hon. Sec.*, C. L. Leslie.

Henley-on-Thames.—LEANDER CLUB (1818), Henley, Oxon. RG9 2LP.—*Hon. Sec.*, J. D. Randall.

PHYLLIS COURT CLUB (1906), Marlow Road, Henley.—*Sec.*, R. I. Bulloch.

Hove.—THE HOVE CLUB (1882), 28 Fourth Avenue, Hove, Sussex BN3 2PJ.—*Sec.*, Sqn. Ldr. G. A. Inverarity, D.F.C.

Jersey.—THE VICTORIA CLUB (1853), Beresford Street, St. Helier, Jersey.—*Sec.*, Gp. Capt. J. W. E. Holmes, D.F.C., A.F.C.

Leamington.—TENNIS COURT CLUB (1846), 50 Bedford Street, Leamington, Warwicks. CV32 5DT.—*Hon. Sec.*, O. D. R. Dixon.

Leeds.—THE LEEDS CLUB (1850), 3 Albion Place, Leeds LS1 6JL.—*Manager*, M. J. C. Reynolds.

Leicester.—LEICESTERSHIRE CLUB (1873), 9 Welford Place, Leicester LE1 6ZH.—*Manager*, J. A. Evans.

Liverpool.—THE ATHENAEUM (1797), Church Alley, Liverpool L1 3DD.—*Hon. Sec.*, D. R. Wetherell.

Manchester.—THE MANCHESTER CLUB (1867), 50 Spring Gardens, Manchester M2 1EN.—*Hon. Sec.*, Fiona Riley.

St. JAMES'S CLUB—St. James's House, Charlotte Street, Manchester M1 4DZ.—*Hon. Sec.*, C. A. Hadfield.

Newcastle-upon-Tyne.—NORTHERN CONSTITUTIONAL CLUB (1882), 37 Pilgrim Street, Newcastle-upon-Tyne NE1 6QE.—*Hon. Sec.*, J. L. Browne.

Northampton.—NORTHAMPTON AND COUNTY CLUB (1873), George Row, Northampton NN1 1DF.—*Sec.*, Maj. G. D. Denholm, B.E.M.

Norwich.—NORFOLK CLUB (1770), 17 Upper King Street, Norwich NR3 1RB.—*Sec.*, A. J. M. Williamson.

Oxford.—THE FREWEN CLUB (1869), 98 St. Aldates, Oxford OX1 1BT.—*Hon. Sec.*, W. H. Miller, B.E.M.

OXFORD UNION SOCIETY (1823), Frewin Court, Oxford OX1 3TB.—*Sec.*, D. J. Burden.

VINCENT'S CLUB (1863), King Edward Street, Oxford OX1 4HS.—*Steward*, R. I. Glynn.

Peterborough.—CITY AND COUNTIES CLUB (1867), Priestgate, Peterborough.—*Sec.*, Mrs. S. Rycroft.

Reading.—BERKSHIRE ATHENAEUM CLUB (1972), 53 Blagrave Street, Reading, Berks.—*Hon. Sec.*, W. J. Stuck.

Rye.—DORMY HOUSE CLUB (1896), Rye, Sussex TN31 7LD.—*Hon. Sec.*, A. Dale.

St. Leonards on Sea.—EAST SUSSEX CLUB (1893), 1 Warrior Square, St Leonards on Sea, E. Sussex.— *Hon. Sec.*, E. J. Morris.

Sheffield.—THE CLUB (1843), Church Street, Sheffield S1 1HG.—*Sec.*, Lt. Col. J. R. Pattison.

Shrewsbury.—THE SALOP CLUB (1974), 6 The Square, Shrewsbury ST1 1LA.—*Hon. Sec.*, T. P. Roberts.

Teddington.—ROYAL CANOE CLUB (1866), Trowlock Island, Middx.—*Hon. Sec.*, Mrs. G. V. Barnard.

Torbay.—THE PAIGNTON CLUB (1882), The Esplanade, Torbay, Devon TQ4 6ED.—*Hon. Sec.*, P. Grafton.

Worcester.—UNION AND COUNTY CLUB (1861), 40 Foregate Street, Worcester.—*Sec.*, M. G. Maton.

York.—YORKSHIRE CLUB (1839), 17 Museum Street, York YO1 2DW.—*Hon. Sec.*, Miss I. C. Corner.

CITY CLUB (1976), 4 Museum Street, York.—*Hon. Sec.*, C. H. Copeland.

Scotland

Ayr.—COUNTY CLUB (1872), Savoy Park Hotel, Ayr.—*Hon. Sec.*, W. W. McHarg.

Edinburgh.—CALEDONIAN CLUB (1825), 32 Abercromby Place, Edinburgh EH3 6QE.—*Manager*, P. A. S. Walker.

NEW CLUB (1787), 86 Princes Street, Edinburgh EH2 2BB.—*Sec.*, Cdr. G. J. T. Creedy, L.V.O., R.N.

Glasgow.—ART CLUB (1867), 185 Bath Street, Glasgow G2 4HU.—*Sec.*, L. J. McIntyre.

ROYAL SCOTTISH AUTOMOBILE CLUB (1899), 11 Blythswood Square, Glasgow G2 4AG.—*Sec.*, H. Dewar.

WESTERN CLUB (1825), 32 Royal Exchange Square, Glasgow G1 3AB.—*Sec.*, D. H. Gifford.

Ireland

Belfast.—ULSTER REFORM CLUB (1885), 4 Royal Avenue, Belfast.—*Sec.*, D. G. Johnston.

Dublin.—STEPHEN'S GREEN CLUB (1840), 9 St. Stephen's Green, Dublin 2.—*Sec.*, J. P. Oxley.

Enniskillen.—FERMANAGH COUNTY CLUB (1883), 20 Church Street, Enniskillen, N. Ireland BT74 7EJ.—*Sec.*, Lt. Col. G. E. Liddle, C.B.E.

YACHT CLUBS

Beaumaris.—ROYAL ANGLESEY YACHT CLUB (1802), 6–7 Green Edge, Beaumaris, Gwynedd LL58 8AL.—*Hon. Sec.*, K. G. Brettell.

Bembridge.—THE BEMBRIDGE SAILING CLUB (1886), Embankment Road, Bembridge, I.o.W. PO35 5NR.—*Sec.*, J. Linaker.

Birkenhead.—ROYAL MERSEY YACHT CLUB (1844), Bedford Road East, Rock Ferry, Birkenhead, Merseyside L42 1LS.—*Hon. Sec.*, H. H. Browne.

Bridlington.—ROYAL YORKSHIRE YACHT CLUB (1847), 1 Windsor Crescent, Bridlington, Yorks. YO15 3HX.—*Sec.*, I. Harness.

Burnham-on-Crouch.—ROYAL CORINTHIAN YACHT CLUB (1872), Burnham-on-Crouch, Essex.—*Hon. Sec.*, A. J. Marsh.

Caernarvon.—ROYAL WELSH YACHT CLUB (1847), Porth-Yr-Aur, Caernarvon.—*Hon. Sec.*, J. N. L. Thomas.

Cowes.—ROYAL YACHT SQUADRON (1815), The Castle, Cowes, I.o.W. PO31 7QT.—*Sec.*, Maj. R. P. Rising, R.M. (*ret.*).

ROYAL LONDON YACHT CLUB (1838), The Parade, Cowes, I. o. W. PO31 7QS.—*Sec.*, A. J. Clarke.

Dover.—ROYAL CINQUE PORTS YACHT CLUB (1872), 415 Waterloo Crescent, Dover CT16 1LA.—*Sec.*, R. J. Barrett.

Fishbourne.—ROYAL VICTORIA YACHT CLUB (1844), Fishbourne Lane, Fishbourne, I. o. W.—*Sec.*, B. Bowers.

Fowey.—ROYAL FOWEY YACHT CLUB (1881), Fowey, Cornwall PL23 1BH.—*Hon. Sec.*, Cdr. W. P. T. Croome, R.N. (*ret.*).

Harwich.—ROYAL HARWICH YACHT CLUB (1843), Woolverstone, Ipswich IP9 1AT.—*Sec.*, Col. C. H. Bavin.

Jersey.—ROYAL CHANNEL ISLANDS YACHT CLUB (1862), The Bulwarks, St. Aubin, Jersey.—*Hon. Sec.*, A. K. Jackson.

Kingswear.—ROYAL DART YACHT CLUB (1866), Priory Street, Kingswear, S. Devon TQ6 0AB.—*Hon. Sec.*, P. Youd.

Leigh-on-Sea.—THE YACHT CLUB (1890), H.Q.S. Bembridge, Foreshore, Leigh-on-Sea, Essex.—*Hon. Sec.*, A. Manning.

London.—THE CRUISING ASSOCIATION (1908), Ivory House, St. Katharine Dock, E1 9AT.—*Gen. Sec.*, L. Nunn.

ROYAL CRUISING CLUB (1880), c/o Naval and Military Club.—*Hon. Sec.*, E. Bourne.

Lowestoft.—ROYAL NORFOLK AND SUFFOLK YACHT CLUB (1859), Royal Plain, Lowestoft, Suffolk NR33 0AQ.—*Sec.*, Sqn. Ldr. F. W. Flowers, R.A.F. (*ret.*).

Lymington.—ROYAL LYMINGTON YACHT CLUB (1922), Bath Road, Lymington, Hants.—*Sec.*, Gp. Capt. H. L. Lewis.

Penarth.—PENARTH YACHT CLUB (1880). The Esplanade, Penarth, S. Glamorgan CF6 2AU.—*Hon. Sec.*, W. H. Jones.

Plymouth.—ROYAL WESTERN YACHT CLUB (1827), 9 Grand Parade, West Hoe, Plymouth PL1 3DG.—*Sec.*, Cdr. L. R. R. Foster, R.N. (*ret.*).

ROYAL PLYMOUTH CORINTHIAN YACHT CLUB (1877), Madeira Road, Plymouth PL1 2NY.—*Hon. Sec.*, A. R. Trim.

Poole.—EAST DORSET SAILING CLUB (1875), 352 Sandbanks Road, Poole BH14 8HY.—*Hon. Sec.*, Mrs. B. Okey.

PARKSTONE YACHT CLUB (1895), Pearce Avenue, Parkstone, Poole BH14 8EH.—*Sec.*, Brig. H. J. Goodson, O.B.E.

POOLE HARBOUR YACHT CLUB (1949), 38 Salterns Way, Lilliput, Poole BH14 8JR.—*Club Manager*, R. Kelly-Wiseman.

YACHT CLUB (1865), New Quay Road, Hamworthy, Poole, Dorset.—*Sec.*, Capt. G. E. Thornton, M.N. (*ret.*).

Portsmouth.—ROYAL NAVAL CLUB AND ROYAL ALBERT YACHT CLUB (1867), 17 Pembroke Road, Portsmouth, Hants. PO1 2NT.—*Hon. Sec.*, Cdr. T. C. C. Greaves, O.B.E., RN.

Ramsgate.—ROYAL TEMPLE YACHT CLUB (1857), 6 Westgate Mansions, Ramsgate, Kent CT11 9HY.—*Hon. Sec.*, B. L. Martin.

Southampton.—ROYAL AIR FORCE YACHT CLUB (1932), Riverside House, Hamble, Southampton.—*Sec.*, Mrs. J. Hill.

ROYAL SOUTHAMPTON YACHT CLUB, 10 Northlands Road, Southampton, SO9 4PF.—*Sec.*, Mrs. J. Freer.

ROYAL SOUTHERN YACHT CLUB (1837), Hamble, Southampton.—*Sec.*, Mrs. W. J. F. Clampett.

Southend.—ALEXANDRA YACHT CLUB (1873), Clifton Terrace, Southend, Essex.—*Hon. Sec.*, Mrs. P. Spacey.

Swansea.—BRISTOL CHANNEL YACHT CLUB (1875), 744 Mumbles Road, Mumbles, Swansea SA3 4EL.—*Hon. Sec.*, P. G. Cawker.

Westcliff-on-Sea.—THAMES ESTUARY YACHT CLUB (1895), 3 The Leas, Westcliff-on-Sea, Essex SS0 7ST.—*Hon. Sec.*, G. R. Noble.

Weymouth.—ROYAL DORSET YACHT CLUB (1875), 11 Custom House Quay, Weymouth, Dorset DT4 8BG.—*Acting Sec.*, Mrs. J. Cannon.

Windermere.—ROYAL WINDERMERE YACHT CLUB (1860), Lowside, Bowness-on-Windermere, Cumbria LA23 3DH.—*Hon. Sec.*, C. H. Peters.

Yarmouth.—ROYAL SOLENT YACHT CLUB (1878), Yarmouth, I. o. W. PO41 0NS.—*Sec.*, Maj. F. R. Sillitoe, R.M.

Scotland

Dundee.—ROYAL TAY YACHT CLUB (1885), 34 Dundee Road, Broughty Ferry, Dundee DD5 1LX.—*Hon. Sec.*, T. Black.

Edinburgh.—ROYAL FORTH YACHT CLUB (1868), Granton Harbour, Edinburgh, EH5 1HF.—*Hon. Sec.*, W. E. Brydon.

Glasgow.—ROYAL CLYDE YACHT CLUB (1856), Rhu, Dunbartonshire.—*Sec.*, D. M. Paul, 111 Union Street, Glasgow.

ROYAL WESTERN YACHT CLUB (1875), 48 St. Vincent Street, Glasgow.—*Hon. Sec.*, G. Jeffrey.

Oban.—ROYAL HIGHLAND YACHT CLUB (1881), 'Whins', 8 Grianach Gardens, Oban, Argyll PA34 4LZ.—*Sec.*, M. Bolton.

Rhu.—ROYAL NORTHERN AND CLYDE YACHT CLUB (1978), Rhu, By Helensburgh, Dunbartonshire G84 8NG.—*Hon. Sec.*, J. A. Ritchie.

Northern Ireland

Bangor.—ROYAL ULSTER YACHT CLUB (1866), 101 Clifton Road, Bangor, Co. Down BT20 5HY.—*Hon. Sec.*, N. Sheals.

THE ZODIAC

The Zodiac is an imaginary belt in the heavens within which lie the apparent paths of the Sun, Moon and major planets. It is bounded by two parallels generally taken as lying 8° on either side of the ecliptic or path of the Sun in its annual course. The Zodiac is divided into twelve equal parts of 30° called Signs, which are not used by astronomers, but have some import in astrology, for which the division of the Zodiac was probably made originally. The Signs of the Zodiac take their names from certain of the constellations with which they once coincided. They are assumed to begin at the vernal equinox or intersection of the plane of the ecliptic with that of the equator. This point is still called the First Point of Aries, although the Sign of Aries now lies in the constellation of Pisces, some 30° to the west. This retrograding of the equinox by about 50″ a year is due to precession; the signs no longer coincide with the constellation whose names they bear.

A catalogue has been made (Grimaldi, 1905) of all, so far as is known, sculptured or incised representations on ancient monuments or tablets of the traditional constellation figures, either Zodiacal or otherwise, together with many modern pictures of the Zodiac. The first in the list is a roughly shaped upright, black stone about 2½ feet high and 1¼ feet broad in the Babylonian room of the British Museum on the front of which are lightly incised ten out of the twelve Signs and other constellation figures. This was found near Baghdad and its date is estimated to be about 1187–1175 B.C.

PRINCIPAL BRITISH AND IRISH SOCIETIES AND INSTITUTIONS

THE ROYAL ACADEMY OF ARTS (1768), Burlington House W1V 0DS—*President*, Roger de Grey, R.A., (1984); *Keeper*, Edward Middleditch, M.C., R.A.; *Treas.*, Sir Philip Powell, C.H., O.B.E., R.A.; *Sec.* Piers Rodgers; *Comptroller*, K. J. Tanner, L.V.O.

Royal Academicians

1972 Adams, Norman
1956*Bawden, Edward, C.B.E.
1976 Blackadder, Elizabeth, O.B.E.
1981 Blake, Peter, C.B.E.
1975 Blamey, Norman
1978 Blow, Sandra
1975 Bowey, Olwyn
1981 Bowyer, William
1971 Bratby, John R.
1972 Brown, Ralph
1956 Buhler, Robert
1972 Butler, James
1975 Cadbury-Brown, H. T., O.B.E.
1984 Camp, Jeffery
1970 Casson, Sir Hugh, C.H., K.C.V.O.
1976 Clarke, Geoffrey
1973 Clatworthy, Robert
1972 Coker, Peter
1972 Cooke, Jean E.
1968 Cowern, Raymond T.
1974 Cuming, Frederick
1983 Dannatt, Trevor
1969 de Grey, Roger
1976 Dickson, Jennifer
1955*Dring, William
1968 Dunstan, Bernard
1953*Eurich, Richard, O.B.E.
1985 Fraser, Donald Hamilton
1965 Freeth, H. Andrew
1977 Frink, Dame Elisabeth, D.B.E.
1972*Fry, E. Maxwell, C.B.E.
1975*Goldfinger, Ernö
1972 Gore, Frederick
1977 Green, Anthony
1960*Greenham, Peter, C.B.E.

1981 Harpley, Sydney
1970 Hayes, Colin
1961*Hepple, Norman
1984 Hogarth, Paul
1974 Kneale, Bryan
1963 McFall, David
1956 Machin, Arnold, O.B.E.
1979 Manasseh, Leonard, O.B.E.
1985*Martin, Sir Leslie, M.C.
1973 Middleditch, Edward
1979 Moynihan, Rodrigo, C.B.E.
1979 Paolozzi, Eduardo, C.B.E.
1983*Pasmore, Victor, C.H., C.B.E.
1981 Philipson, Sir Robin
1977 Powell, Sir Philip, C.H., O.B.E.
1973 Roberts-Jones, Ivor, C.B.E.
1984 Rogers, Richard
1969 Rosoman, Leonard, O.B.E.
1983*Rothenstein, Michael
1961*Sanders, Christopher C.
1984 Scott, William, C.B.E.
1969*Soukop, Willi
1954 Spear, Ruskin, C.B.E.
1979 Swanwick, Betty
1979 Tindle, David
1965 Ward, John S., C.B.E.
1965*Weight, Carel, C.B.E.
1974 Williams, Kyffin, O.B.E.

Associates

1978 Aitchison, Craigie
1982 Ayres, Gillian
1980 Christopher, Ann
1982 Crosby, Theo
1979 Dowson, Sir Philip, C.B.E.
1976 Eyton, Anthony
1983 Foster, Norman
1978 Gowing, Sir Lawrence, C.B.E.
1985 Hockney, David
1983 Howard, Ken
1983 Hoyland, John
1981 Jones, Allen
1976 Kenny, Michael
1977 King, Phillip, C.B.E.

1984 Kitaj, R. B.
1982 Lawson, Sonia
1975 Levene, Ben
1980 Partridge, John, C.B.E.
1984 Phillips, Tom
1975 Stephenson, Ian
1983 Stevens, Norman
1985 Stirling, James
1977 Sutton, Philip
1983 Symons, Patrick
1985 Tilson, Joe
1980 Whishaw, Anthony
1983 Wragg, John

* Senior.

Former Presidents of the Royal Academy

Sir J. Reynolds, 1768	Sir F. Dicksee, 1924
Benjamin West, 1792	Sir W. Llewellyn, 1928
James Wyatt, 1805	Sir E. Lutyens, 1938
Benjamin West, 1806	Sir A. J. Munnings, 1944
Sir T. Lawrence, 1820	
Sir M. A. Shee, 1830	Sir G. F. Kelly, 1949
Sir C. Eastlake, 1850	Sir A. E. Richardson, 1954
Sir F. Grant, 1866	
Lord Leighton, 1878	Sir C. Wheeler, 1956
Sir J. Millais, 1896	Sir T. Monnington, 1966
Sir E. Poynter, 1896	
Sir A. Webb, 1919	Sir Hugh Casson, 1976

THE ROYAL CAMBRIAN ACADEMY OF ART (1882), Plas Mawr, High Street, Conwy, Gwynedd LL32 8DE—*Pres.*, R. Fields; *Hon. Sec.*, Audrey Hind; *Curator and Sec.*, L. H. S. Mercer.

THE ROYAL SCOTTISH ACADEMY (1826), Princes Street, Edinburgh EH2 2EL—*Pres.*, H. A. Wheeler, O.B.E., R.S.A.; *Sec.*, R. R. Steedman, R.S.A.; *Treas.*, W. J. L. Baillie, R.S.A.; *Librarian*, A. Campbell, R.S.A.; *Admin. Sec.*, W. T. Meikle.

Hon. Retired Academicians:

1958 Armour, Mrs. M.
1956 Kininmonth, Sir William
1964 Miller, James
1966 Johnston, Ninian
1937 Schotz, Benno
1970 Sutherland, Scott
1967 Lorimer, Hew

Royal Scottish Academicians

1979 Baillie, W. J. L.
1972 Blackadder, Elizabeth
1977 Butler, Vincent
1971 Cameron, Gordon S.
1981 Campbell, Alex
1974 Collins, Peter
1974 Crosbie, William
1970 Cumming, James
1962 Donaldson, David A.
1956 Fleming, Ian
1981 Glover, J. Hardie, O.B.E.
1967 Gordon, Esmé
1972 Houston, John
1979 Knox, John
1973 Littlejohn, W.
1971 McClure, David

1976 Malcolm, Ellen
1972 Michie, David
1963 Morocco, Alberto
1957 Patrick, J. McIntosh
1966 Peploe, Denis
1962 Philipson, Sir Robin
1976 Reeves, Philip
1977 Robertson, R. Ross
1984 Scott, Bill
1985 Snowden, Michael (*elect.*)
1979 Steedman, R. R.
1975 Wheeler, H. Anthony, O.B.E.
1977 Whiston, Peter
1982 Walker, Frances

Associates

Balmer, Barbara
Boys, John
Brotherston, William
Brown, Neil Dallas
Bryce, Gordon
Buchan, Dennis
Bushe, Frederick
Campbell, A. Buchanan
Clifford, J. G.
Cocker, Douglas
Docherty, Michael
Donald, George
Evans, David
Fairgrieve, James

Fraser, Alexander
Harvey, Jake
Howard, Ian
Johnstone, John
Law, Graham C.
McIntosh, Iain R.
Maclean, William J.
MacMillan, Andrew
Main, Kirkland
Merrylees, Andrew
Metzstein, Isi
Mooney, John
Morris, James
Morrison, James

Onwin, Glen
Pelly, Frances
Pottinger, Frank
Rae, Barbara
Reiach, Alan, O.B.E.
Renton, James S., O.B.E.
Richards, John, C.B.E.

Robertson, James D.
Ross, Alastair
Shanks, Duncan F.
Smart, Alastair
Smith, Ian McKenzie
Squire, Geoffrey
Stiven, Fred

Hon. Retired Associates, Miss Elizabeth Dempster.
Non-Resident Associates, Charles Pulsford; Peter Womersley, Leon Morrocco, Joyce Cairns, Barry Gasson.

ROYAL IRISH ACADEMY (1786), 19 Dawson Street, Dublin 2.—*Pres.*, T. K. Whitaker; *Treas.*, T. D. Spearman; *Sec.*, J. O. Scanlan.

ABBEYFIELD SOCIETY, 186–192 Darkes Lane, Potters Bar, Herts EN6 1AB—Supportive housing for lonely elderly people.—*Gen. Sec.*, D. A. L. Charles.

ACCOUNTANTS, INSTITUTE OF CHARTERED, in England and Wales (1880), P.O. Box 433, Moorgate Place EC2P 2BJ—*Sec.*, E. J. D. Warne, C.B.

ACCOUNTANTS, CHARTERED ASSOCIATION OF CERTIFIED (1904), 29 Lincoln's Inn Fields WC2A 3EE—*Sec.*, R. A. Dudman.

ACCOUNTANTS OF SCOTLAND, THE INSTITUTE OF CHARTERED (1854), 27 Queen Street, Edinburgh EH2 1LA—*Pres.*, Prof. W. C. C. Morrison; *Sec.*, E. Tait, M.B.E.

ACCOUNTANTS IN IRELAND, INSTITUTE OF CHARTERED (1888), 87/89 Pembroke Road, Dublin 4.—*Dir.*, R. F. Hussey.

ACCOUNTANTS, SOCIETY OF COMPANY AND COMMERCIAL (1974), 40 Tyndalls Park Road, Bristol BS8 1PL—*Sec.-Gen.*, B. T. Banks.

ACTION RESEARCH FOR THE CRIPPLED CHILD (National Fund for Research into Crippling Diseases) (1952), Vincent House, North Parade, Horsham, West Sussex RH12 2DA—*Dir.*, Col. A. N. Brearley-Smith, O.B.E.

ACTORS' BENEVOLENT FUND (1882), 6 Adam Street WC2N 6AA—*Sec.*, Mrs. R. Stevens.

ACTORS' CHARITABLE TRUST (incorporating DENVILLE HALL), Euston Tower NW1 3DR—Assists children of theatrical parentage who are in need; Home for elderly and infirm actors and actresses.—*Admin. Sec.* Althea Stewart.

ACTORS' CHURCH UNION (1899), St. Paul's Church, Bedford Street WC2E 9ED—*Senior Chaplain*, Rev. M. Hurst-Bannister.

ACTUARIES IN SCOTLAND, THE FACULTY OF (1856), Hall and Library, 23 St. Andrew Square, Edinburgh EH2 1AQ—*Sec.*, W. W. Mair.

ACTUARIES, INSTITUTE OF (1848), Staple Inn Hall, High Holborn WC1V 7QJ—*Sec.-Gen.*, C. D. Mackie.

ADDICTION (TO ALCOHOL AND OTHER DRUGS), SOCIETY FOR THE STUDY OF (1884).—*Sec.*, Prof. M. Lader, 3 Oakfield Gardens, Dulwich Wood Avenue SE21.

ADMINISTRATIVE ACCOUNTANTS, INSTITUTE OF (1916), Burford House, 44 London Road, Sevenoaks, Kent TN13 1AS.—*Dir.-Gen.*, D. W. Bradley, F.C.I.S.

ADMINISTRATIVE MANAGEMENT, INSTITUTE OF (1915), 40 Chatsworth Parade, Petts Wood, Orpington, Kent BR5 1RW—*Sec.*, M. J. Ainsworth.

ADVERTISING BENEVOLENT SOCIETY, NATIONAL (1913), 3 Crawford Place W1H 1JB—*Gen. Sec.*, D. Larkin.

ADVERTISING, INSTITUTE OF PRACTITIONERS IN, 44 Belgrave Square SW1X 8QS—*Dir.*, D. Wheeler.

ADVERTISING STANDARDS AUTHORITY (1962), Brook House, 2–16 Torrington Place WC1E 7HN—*Director General*, P. Thomson.

AERONAUTICAL SOCIETY, ROYAL (1866) (incorporating the Institution of Aeronautical Engineers and the Helicopter Association of Great Britain), 4 Hamilton Place W1V 0BQ—*Pres.* (1984–85), T. H. Kerr, C.B.; *Sec.*, B. P. Laight, O.B.E.

AEROSPACE COMPANIES LTD., SOCIETY OF BRITISH (1916), 29 King Street, St James's SW1Y 6RD—*Dir.*, Sir John Curtiss, K.C.B.; K.B.E.

AFRICAN INSTITUTE, INTERNATIONAL (1926), 38 King Street, W.C.2.—*Hon. Dir.*, Prof. I. M. Lewis.

AFRICAN MEDICAL AND RESEARCH FOUNDATION, London House, 68 Upper Richmond Road SW15 2RP—*Exec. Dir.*, Mrs. E. Young.

AGED PILGRIMS' FRIEND SOCIETY (1807), 175 Tower Bridge Road, S.E.1.—*Sec.*, R. D. Stewart.

AGED POOR SOCIETY (1708) AND ST. JOSEPH'S HOUSE, 42 Brook Green W6 7BW—*Sec.*, Flt. Lt. W. Watson (*ret'd*).

AGEING, CENTRE FOR POLICY ON, Nuffield Lodge Studio, Regent's Park NW1 4RS—*Dir.*, Dr. E. Midwinter.

AGE RESEARCH, FOUNDATION FOR (1978), 49 Queen Victoria Street EC4N 4SA—*Dir.*, J. Allfrey.

AGRICULTURAL BENEVOLENT INSTITUTION, ROYAL, Shaw House, 27 West Way, Oxford OX2 0QH—*Chairman*, W. T. Gauntlett, O.B.E.; *Chief Exec.*, Maj.-Gen. P. L. Spurgeon, C.B.

AGRICULTURAL BENEVOLENT INSTITUTION, ROYAL SCOTTISH (1897), Ingliston, Newbridge, Midlothian EH28 8NB—*Sec.*, Miss M. Ritchie Hay.

AGRICULTURAL BOTANY, NATIONAL INSTITUTE OF (1919), Huntingdon Road, Cambridge.—*Director*, G. M. Milbourn, PH.D.

AGRICULTURAL SOCIETY, EAST OF ENGLAND, East of England Showground, Peterborough PE2 0XE—*Sec. and Chief Exec.*, R. W. Bird, M.B.E..

AGRICULTURAL SOCIETY, ROYAL ULSTER (1826), The King's Hall, Balmoral, Belfast BT9 6GW—*Chief Exec.*, W. H. Yarr.

AGRICULTURE, ASSOCIATION OF (1947), Victoria Chambers, 16/20 Strutton Ground SW1P 2HP—*Gen. Sec.*, Miss J. H. D. Bostock, M.B.E.

AIR LEAGUE, THE (1909), 4 Hamilton Place W1V 0BQ—*Chairman*, Dr. J. E. Henderson; *Sec. Gen.*, Air Comm. C. A. Alldis, C.B.E., D.F.C., A.F.C.

ALEXANDRA ROSE DAY FUND, 1 Castelnau, Barnes SW13 9RP—*Nat. Organiser and Administrator*, Mrs. L. Weston.

ALLOTMENT AND LEISURE GARDENERS LIMITED, NATIONAL SOCIETY OF, 22 High Street, Flitwick, Beds MK45 1DT—*Sec.*, G. Jones.

ALMSHOUSES, NATIONAL ASSOCIATION OF, Billingbear Lodge, Wokingham, Berks RG11 5RU—*Dir.*, D. M. Scott.

ANAESTHETISTS OF GREAT BRITAIN AND IRELAND, ASSOCIATION OF (1932), 9 Bedford Square WC1B 3RA—*Hon. Sec.*, Dr. M. T. Inman.

ANCIENT BUILDINGS, SOCIETY FOR THE PROTECTION OF (1877), 37 Spital Square E1 6DY—*Sec.*, P. Venning.

ANCIENT MONUMENTS SOCIETY (1924).—*Sec.*, M. J. Saunders, St. Andrew-by-the-Wardrobe, Queen Victoria Street EC4V 5DE.

ANGLO-ARAB ASSOCIATION (1961), The Arab British Centre, 21 Collingham Road SW5 0NU.—*Exec. Dir.*, D. R. Collard, O.B.E.

ANGLO-BELGIAN SOCIETY (incorporating the Anglo-Belgian Union (1918) and the Cercle Royal Belge de Londres (1922)).—*Hon. Sec.*, Mrs. S. G. Ault, Tor House, Maybury Hill, Woking, Surrey GU22 7DU.

ANGLO-BRAZILIAN SOCIETY (1943), 2 Belgrave Square SW1X 8PJ—*Sec.*, Mrs. M. J. Fyfe.

ANGLO-DANISH SOCIETY (1924), 7 St. Helen's Place, Bishopsgate EC3A 6BH—*Chairman*, Sir Andrew Stark, K.C.M.G., C.V.O.

ANGLO-NORSE SOCIETY, 25 Belgrave Square, SW1X 8QD—*Chairman*, Sir Peter Scott, K.B.E., C.M.G.

ANGLO-POLISH SOCIETY (1832), London H.Q., c/o S.P.K., 238–246 King Street W6 0RF—*Hon. Sec.*, C. Roberts.

ANGLO-SWEDISH SOCIETY, 5 Mansfield Street, W.1.

ANGLO-THAI SOCIETY (1962).—*Hon. Sec.*, Lt. Col. H. Docherty, O.B.E., 14 Saxonbury Gardens, Long Ditton, Surrey KT6 5HF.

ANIMAL HEALTH TRUST, Lanwades Hall, Kennett, Newmarket, Suffolk CB8 7PN—*Dir.*, W. B. Singleton, C.B.E., F.R.C.V.S.

ANTHROPOLOGICAL INSTITUTE, ROYAL (1843), 56 Queen Anne Street W1M 9LA—*Dir.*, J. Benthall.

ANTHROPOSOPHICAL SOCIETY IN GREAT BRITAIN, Rudolf Steiner House, 35 Park Road NW1 6XT—*Chairman and Gen. Sec.*, N. Thomas.

ANTIQUARIES, SOCIETY OF (1717), Burlington House W1V 0HS—*Pres.*, Prof. J. D. Evans, PH.D., F.B.A.; *Treas.*, R. M. Robbins, C.B.E.; *Dir.*, G. J. Wainwright, PH.D.; *Sec.*, R. W. Lightbown.

ANTIQUARIES OF SCOTLAND, SOCIETY OF (1780), National Museum of Antiquities of Scotland, Queen Street, Edinburgh EH2 1JD—*Sec.*, T. F. Watkins, PH.D.; *Treas.*, R. J. Mercer.

ANTI-SLAVERY SOCIETY FOR THE PROTECTION OF HUMAN RIGHTS (1839), 180 Brixton Road, S.W.9.—*Dir.*, R. P. H. Davies, O.B.E.

ANTI-VIVISECTION: BRITISH UNION FOR THE ABOLITION OF VIVISECTION (INC.) (1898), 16A Crane Grove N7 8LB—*Office Manager*, Margaret Manzoni.

ANTI-VIVISECTION SOCIETY, THE NATIONAL (1875), 51 Harley Street W1N 1DD—*Gen. Sec.*, B. Gunn.

ANTI-VIVISECTION SOCIETY, SCOTTISH, 121 West Regent Street, Glasgow G2 2SD—*Organising Sec.*, J. F. Robins.

APOSTLESHIP OF THE SEA (1920). For active seafarers. *National Headquarters.*—Atlantic House, New Strand, Bootle, Merseyside L20 4TQ—*Dir.*, Very Rev. Mgr. A. Stringfellow.

APOTHECARIES, SOCIETY OF (1617).—Black Friars Lane EC4V 6EJ—*Clerk*, Maj. J. C. O'Leary; *Registrar*, D. H. C. Barrie.

ARBITRATORS, THE CHARTERED INSTITUTE OF, 75 Cannon Street EC4N 5BH—*Dir. and Sec.*, B. W. Vigrass, O.B.E., V.R.D.

ARCHÆOLOGICAL ASSOCIATION, BRITISH (1843), 61 Old Park Ridings, Winchmore Hill N21 2ET—*Hon. Asst. Treas. and Sec.*, Miss I. B. McClure.

ARCHÆOLOGICAL ASSOCIATION, CAMBRIAN (1846).—*Pres.* (1984–85), H. A. Wheeler; *Gen. Sec.*, G. L. Jones, Lleifior, 60 Dan-y-Coed, Aberystwyth, Dyfed SY23 2HD.

ARCHÆOLOGICAL INSTITUTE, ROYAL (1843).—*Hon. Sec.*, J. G. Coad, F.S.A.; *Asst. Sec.*, Miss W. E. Phillips, 304 Addison House, Grove End Road NW8 9EL.

ARCHÆOLOGY, COUNCIL FOR BRITISH (1944), 112 Kennington Road SE11 6RE—*President*, T. G. Hassall, F.S.A.; *Sec.*, Dr. P. W. Dixon, F.S.A.; *Dir.*, Dr. H. F. Cleere, F.S.A., F.B.I.M.

ARCHITECTS, THE ROYAL INSTITUTE OF BRITISH (1834), 66 Portland Place W1N 4AD—*Pres.*, L. A. L. Rolland; *Sec.*, P. K. Harrison, C.B.E.

ARCHITECTS REGISTRATION COUNCIL OF THE UNITED KINGDOM, 73 Hallam Street W1N 6EE—*Chairman*, Prof. D. Hinton; *Registrar*, K. J. Forder.

ARCHITECTS AND SURVEYORS, INCORPORATED ASSOCIATION OF (1925), Jubilee House, Billing Brook Road, Weston Favell, Northampton NN3 4NW—*Pres.*, F. A. Hunt; *Hon. Sec.*, W. J. Clark.

ARCHITECTS AND SURVEYORS, THE FACULTY OF, LTD: (incorporating The Institute of Registered Architects Ltd), 15 St. Mary Street, Chippenham, Wiltshire—*Sec.*, A. D. G. Webb.

ARCHITECTS BENEVOLENT SOCIETY (1850), 66 Portland Place W1N 4AD—*Sec.*, J. Double.

ARCHITECTS IN SCOTLAND, ROYAL INCORPORATION OF (1922), 15 Rutland Square, Edinburgh EH1 2BE—*Sec. and Treasurer*, C. A. McKean, F.R.S.A., F.S.A.

ARCHITECTURAL ASSOCIATION (INC.) (1847), 34–36 Bedford Square, W.C.1.—*Sec.*, E. Le Maistre.

ARCHIVISTS, SOCIETY OF (1947), *Hon. Sec.*, Amanda U. E. Arrowsmith, Suffolk Record Office, County Hall, Ipswich IP4 2JS.

ARLIS (Art Libraries Society) (1969).—*Sec.*, G. Bullock, Humberside College of Higher Education, Inglemire Avenue, Hull HU6 7LU.

ARMY BENEVOLENT FUND (1944), 41 Queen's Gate, S.W.7.—*Controller*, Maj.-Gen. P. J. Bush, O.B.E.

ARMY CADET FORCE ASSOCIATION (1930), Cheltenham Terrace SW3 4RR—*Gen. Sec.*, Brigadier D. M. Pontifex, C.B.E.

ART-COLLECTIONS FUND, NATIONAL (1903), 20 John Islip Street SW1P 4LL—*Dir.*, Sir Peter Wakefield, K.B.E., C.M.G.

ART WORKERS GUILD (1884), 6 Queen Sq., Bloomsbury WC1N 3AR—*Master*, P. Curzon-Price; *Sec.*, D. Pullen.

ARTHRITIS AND RHEUMATISM COUNCIL FOR RESEARCH, 41 Eagle Street WC1R 4AR—*Gen. Sec.*, J. Norton.

ARTHRITIS CARE, 6 Grosvenor Crescent SW1X 7ER—*Sec.*, A. M. Davey.

ARTISTS' GENERAL BENEVOLENT INSTITUTION (1814) AND ARTISTS' ORPHAN FUND (1871), Burlington House, Piccadilly W1V 0DJ—*Sec.*, T. Miles.

ARTISTS UNITED SOCIETY OF (1921), 17 Carlton House Terrace, S.W.1.—*Pres.*, R. Hill.

ASLIB (1924). (The Association for Information Management), Information House, 26–27 Boswell Street WC1N 3JZ—*Sec. and Dir.*, Dr. D. A. Lewis.

ASSISTANT MASTERS AND MISTRESSES ASSOCIATION, 7 Northumberland Street WC2N 5DA—*Secs.*, E. G. Beynon, Miss J. E. L. Baird.

ASTHMA RESEARCH COUNCIL, St. Thomas' Hospital, Lambeth Palace Road SE1 7EH—*Chairman*, D. M. Walters, M.B.E., M.P.

ASTRONOMICAL ASSOCIATION, BRITISH.—*Office*, Burlington House, Piccadilly W1V 0NL. Meetings at 23 Savile Row, W.1.—*President*, Miss H. Couper; *Sec.*, J. Isles; *Asst. Sec.*, E. Watson Jones.

ASTRONOMICAL SOCIETY, ROYAL (Founded 1820), Burlington House W1V 0NL—*Pres.*, Prof. D. Lynden-Bell, F.R.S.; *Secs.*, Prof. R. D. Davies; Dr. B. A. Hobbs; Dr. Carole Jordan.

A.T.S. and W.R.A.C. BENEVOLENT FUNDS (1964), Queen Elizabeth Park, Guildford, Surrey GU2 6QH—*Sec.*, Mrs. E. Laurence-Smith.

AUDIT BUREAU OF CIRCULATIONS LTD., 13 Wimpole Street W1M 7AB—*Dir.*, K. Derbyshire.

AUTHORS, THE SOCIETY OF, 84 Drayton Gardens SW10 9SB—*Gen. Sec.*, M. Le Fanu.

AUTOMOBILE ASSOCIATION (1905), Fanum House, Basingstoke, Hants.—*Chairman*, The Lord Erroll of Hale, P.C.; *Dir. Gen.*, O. F. Lambert, C.B.E.

AVICULTURAL SOCIETY (1894).—*Hon. Sec.*, H. J. Horswell, Windsor Forest Stud, Mill Ride, Ascot, Berks SL5 8LT.

AYRSHIRE CATTLE SOCIETY OF GREAT BRITAIN AND IRELAND (1877), 1 Racecourse Road, Ayr.—*Gen. Sec.*, S. J. Thomson.

BALTIC AIR CHARTER ASSOCIATION, The Baltic Exchange, 24 St. Mary Axe EC3A 8BU—*Chief Exec.*, D. Shepherd.

BALTIC EXCHANGE LTD. (1903), 14–20 St. Mary Axe EC3A 8BU—*Chairman*, R. B. Hunt, F.I.C.S.; *Sec.*, D. J. Walker.

BALTIC EXCHANGE CHARITABLE SOCIETY (1978), 14–20 St. Mary Axe EC3A 8BU—*Sec.*, R. T. Wheelans.

BANKERS, THE INSTITUTE OF (1879), 10 Lombard Street EC3V 9AS—*Sec.-Gen.*, E. Glover.

BANKERS IN SCOTLAND, THE INSTITUTE OF (1875), 20 Rutland Square, Edinburgh EH1 2DE—*Sec.*, B. McKenna.

BAPTIST MISSIONARY SOCIETY (1792), 93–97 Gloucester Place W1H 4AA—*Gen. Sec.*, Rev. R. G. S. Harvey.

BAR ASSOCIATION FOR LOCAL GOVERNMENT AND THE PUBLIC SERVICE.—*Chairman*, T. Standen, 65 Oakdene Avenue, Chislehurst, Kent BR7 6DZ.

(DR.) BARNARDO'S (1866), *Head Offices:* Tanners Lane, Barkingside, Essex IG6 1QG. Over 13,000 handicapped or deprived children, young people and families are helped each year in more than 160 projects throughout the United Kingdom and Republic of Ireland.—*Senior Dir.*, R. Singleton.

BARONETAGE, STANDING COUNCIL OF THE (1898), *Sec.*, H. Bedingfeld, Rouge Croix Pursuivant, The College of Arms, Queen Victoria Street EC4V 4BT.

BARRISTERS' BENEVOLENT ASSOCIATION (1873), 3 Raymond Buildings, Grays Inn WC1R 5BH—*Hon. Treasurers*, P. Curry, Q.C.; C. H. McCall; *Sec.*, Miss K. M. Hopper.

BEIT MEMORIAL FELLOWSHIPS (for Medical Research) (1909).—*Admin. Sec.*, D. Billington, Histopathology Dept., St. Bartholomew's Hospital, E.C.1.

BERNARD SHAW SOCIETY, 125 Markyate Road, Dagenham, Essex.—*Sec.*, E. Ford.

BIBLE CHURCHMEN'S MISSIONARY SOCIETY (1922), 251 Lewisham Way SE4 1XF—*Gen. Sec.*, Rev. J. M. Ball.

BIBLE SOCIETY, BRITISH AND FOREIGN (1804), Stonehill Green, Westlea, Swindon SN5 7DG—*Exec. Dir.*, R. Worthing-Davies.

BIBLIOGRAPHICAL SOCIETY (1892), c/o British Library, Great Russell Street WC1B 3DG—*Hon. Sec.*, Dr. M. M. Foot.

BIBLIOGRAPHICAL SOCIETY, EDINBURGH (1890), c/o National Library of Scotland, Edinburgh EH1 1EW—*Hon. Sec.*, I. C. Cunningham.

BIOCHEMICAL SOCIETY, THE (1911), 7 Warwick Court, High Holborn WC1R 5DP—*Exec. Sec.*, G. D. Jones.

BIOLOGICAL ENGINEERING SOCIETY.—*Hon. Sec.*, c/o Royal College of Surgeons, Lincoln's Inn Fields WC2A 3PN.

BIOLOGY, INSTITUTE OF, 20 Queensberry Place SW7 2DZ—*Pres.*, Prof. J. L. Harvey, C.B.E., F.R.S.; *Gen. Sec.*, P. N. O'Donoghue.

BIRD PRESERVATION, INTERNATIONAL COUNCIL FOR (BRITISH SECTION), c/o Institute of Biology, 20 Queensberry Place SW7 2DZ—*Hon. Sec.*, R. D. Chancellor.

BIRMINGHAM AND MIDLAND INSTITUTE (1854) and PRIESTLEY LIBRARY (1779), Margaret Street, Birmingham B3 3BS—*Admin. and Lib.* J. Hunt.

BLIND, GREATER LONDON FUND FOR THE, 2 Wyndham Place W1H 2AQ—*Pres.*, The Lord Mayor of London; *Gen. Sec.*, Group Capt. J. S. Goodwin, M.B.E.

BLIND, GUIDE DOGS FOR THE, ASSOCIATION, Alexandra House, 9–11 Park Street, Windsor, Berks SL4 1JR—*Dir.-Gen.*, Maj.-Gen. J. P. Groom, C.B., C.B.E.

BLIND, INCORPORATED ASSOCIATION FOR PROMOTING THE GENERAL WELFARE OF THE (1854), 37–55 Ashburton Grove N7 7DW—*Chief Exec.*, G. P. Robinson, F.C.A.

BLIND, LONDON ASSOCIATION FOR THE (1857), 14–16 Verney Road SE16 3DZ. A national charity helping blind and partially-sighted people throughout the country.—*Dir.*, G. J. Entwistle.

BLIND, ROYAL COMMONWEALTH SOCIETY FOR THE (1950), Commonwealth House, Heath Road, Haywards Heath, West Sussex RH16 3AZ—*Dir.*, A. W. Johns, O.B.E.

BLIND, ROYAL NATIONAL INSTITUTE FOR THE (1868), 224 Great Portland Street, W.1.—*Runs education advisory service for parents, nurseries and schools for blind and additionally handicapped children, a further education college for school leavers, training centres, a rehabilitation centre, homes for elderly blind and deaf-blind people, hotels for holidays and a London hostel; helps blind people find commercial and professional jobs; runs Homeworkers scheme in S.E. England; runs braille and tape libraries for students and Talking Book Library; publishes books, magazines and music in braille and Moon and information leaflets in print; sells specially designed or adapted goods; gives financial assistance to blind people in need; funds research into the prevention of blindness; helps blind sportsmen and women; trains sighted mobility instructors.*

BLIND, NATIONAL LIBRARY FOR THE (1882), Cromwell Road, Bredbury, Stockport, Cheshire SK6 2SG—A national charity providing free library service in embossed types for the blind and partially-sighted. Also large-print service. Over 350,000 volumes available.—*Director-General*, A. Leach, F.L.A.

BLIND, THE ROYAL LONDON SOCIETY FOR THE (1838), *Head Office and Workshops*, 105–9 Salusbury Road, Kilburn NW6 6RH; *School*, Dorton House, Seal, nr. Sevenoaks, Kent TN15 0EB; *Home Workers' Scheme.*—*Sec.-Gen.*, R. J. Pocock.

BLIND, ROYAL NATIONAL COLLEGE (1872), College Road, Hereford HR1 1EB—*Principal*, L. Marshall. Further education and training for open employment for visually-handicapped.

BLIND, ROYAL SCHOOL FOR THE (1799), Leatherhead, Surrey.—*Dir.*, Rev. B. A. E. Coote.

BLIND (LONDON) SPORTS CLUB FOR THE (1932).—*Sec.*, Miss E. Wright, 27 Underhill Road, Dulwich, S.E.22.

BLOOD TRANSFUSION. *See* GREATER LONDON RED CROSS BLOOD TRANSFUSION SERVICE.

BLUE CROSS, THE (Incorporating Our Dumb Friends' League) (1897), Animals' Hospital, Hugh Street, Victoria, S.W.1.—*Sec.*, P. Carpmael, M.B.E.

BMMF INTERNATIONAL (formerly Bible and Medical Missionary Fellowship) (1852), 186 Kennington Park Road, S.E.11.—*Gen. Sec.*, A. M. S. Pont.

BODLEIAN, FRIENDS OF THE, Bodleian Library, Oxford OK1 3BG—*Sec.*, G. Groom.

BOOK-KEEPERS, INSTITUTE OF (1916), (see under Administrative Accounting, Institute of).

BOOKSELLERS ASSOCIATION OF GREAT BRITAIN AND IRELAND (1895), 154 Buckingham Palace Road SW1W 9TZ—*Dir.*, T. E. Godfray.

BOOK TRADE BENEVOLENT SOCIETY (1967), Dillon Lodge, The Booksellers Retreat, Kings Langley, Herts WD7 8LT—*Pres.*, T. Joy, L.V.O., F.R.S.A.; *Exec. Sec.*, Mrs. A. R. Brown.

BOTANICAL SOCIETY OF THE BRITISH ISLES (1836), c/o Dept. of Botany, British Museum (Natural History), Cromwell Road SW7 5BD—*Hon. Gen. Sec.*, Mrs. M. Briggs, M.B.E., F.P.S.

BOTANICAL SOCIETY OF EDINBURGH, Royal Botanic Garden, Inverleith Row, Edinburgh 3.—*Hon. Gen. Sec.*, Miss J. Muscott.

BOY SCOUTS ASSOCIATION, *see* SCOUT ASSOCIATION, THE.

BOYS' BRIGADE, THE (INCORPORATED) (1883), Brigade House, Parsons Green SW6 4TH. Membership worldwide: 400,000.—*Sec.*, A. A. J. Hudson, C.B.E.

Boys' Clubs, National Association of, 24 Highbury Grove N5 2EA. Incorporated 1925. Responsible for the development and co-ordination of boys' clubs throughout the country, and has affiliated to it, either directly or through local organizations, 2,000 clubs—*Nat. Dir.*, D. P. C. Harris.

Boys' Clubs, Northern Ireland Association of (1940), Bryson House, 28 Bedford Street, Belfast BT2 7FE—*Gen. Sec.*, C. E. Larmour, M.B.E.

Brewing, Institute of (1886), 33 Clarges Street W1Y 8EE—*Sec.*, Capt. K. A. Leppard, C.B.E., R.N.

Bridewell Royal Hospital (1553), King Edward's School, Witley, Surrey GU8 5SG—*Treas.*, I. Allan; *Clerk to the Governors*, Mrs. A. C. R. Mitchell.

British Academy, The (1901), 20–21 Cornwall Terrace NW1 4QP—*President*, Sir Randolph Quirk, C.B.E.; *Treas.*, Prof. P. Mathias, C.B.E.; *Sec.*, P. W. H. Brown; *Foreign Sec.*, Prof. E. W. Handley, C.B.E.

British and Foreign School Society (1808). Richard Mayo Hall, Eden Street, Kingston on Thames, Surrey KT1 1HZ—*Sec.*, S. M. A. Banister.

British Anti-Common Market Campaign (1976), 52 Fulham High Street SW6 3LQ—*Hon. Sec.*, Sir Robin Williams, Bt.

British Artists, Federation of (1959), 17 Carlton House Terrace, S.W.1.—*Sec. Gen.*, O. Warman.

British Association for the Advancement of Science (1831), Fortress House, 23 Savile Row W1X 1AB—*Pres.*, Sir George Porter, F.R.S.; *Exec. Sec.*, Dr. D. Morley.

British Association for Commercial and Industrial Education, 16 Park Crescent W1N 4AP—*Dir.*, B. V. Murphy; *Sec.*, R. W. Lyne, F.B.I.M., F.I.I.M.

British Association for Early Childhood Education, Montgomery Hall, Kennington Oval SE11 5SW—*Sec.*, Mrs. B. Boon.

British Association of the Hard of Hearing.—*Sec.-Gen.*, Roslyn J. Taylor, 7/11 Armstrong Road W3 7JL.

British Atlantic Committee, 30A St. James's Square, Whitehall SW1Y 4JH—*Dir.*, Maj. Gen. C. J. Popham, C.B.

British Bee-Keepers' Association (1874).—*Gen. Sec.*, M. H. F. Coward, National Agricultural Centre, Stoneleigh, Kenilworth, Warwicks CV8 2LZ.

British Board of Film Classification, 3 Soho Square, W.1.—*Dir.*, J. Ferman.

British Butterfly Conservation Society (1968), Tudor House, Quorn, Nr. Loughborough, Leics LE12 8AD—*Chairman*, C. J. Tatham, M.B.E.

British College of Ophthalmic Opticians (Optometrists), 10 Knaresborough Place SW5 0TG—*Gen. Sec.*, T. H. Collingridge.

British Commonwealth Ex-Services League, 48 Pall Mall SW1Y 5JG—*Sec.-Gen.*, Col. G. Stocker, C.B.E.

British Computer Society (1957), 13 Mansfield Street W1M 0BP—*Sec.-Gen.*, D. W. Harding.

British Cotton Growing Association Ltd. (1904), Ralli House, 60 Old Hall Street, Liverpool L3 9PP—*Managing Director*, R. Derbyshire.

British Cycling Federation (1878), 16 Upper Woburn Place WC1H 0QE—*Sec.*, L. Unwin.

British Dental Association (1880), 64 Wimpole Street W1M 8AL—*Sec.*, E. R. Crerar.

British Diabetic Association (1934), 10 Queen Anne Street W1M 0BD—*Sec.-Gen.*, D. Armytage, C.B.E.

British Driving Society, 27 Dugard Place, Barford, Warwick CV35 8DX—*Sec.*, Mrs. J. M. Dillon.

British Educational Management and Administration Society (1971).—*Sec.*, Miss M. E. Hewitt, Buxton Girls' School, Derbys SK17 6RB.

British Equestrian Federation, British Equestrian Centre, Kenilworth, Warwicks CV8 2LR—*Dir. Gen.*, Maj. M. C. R. Wallace.

British Export-Finance Advisory Council (1981), 1 Grosvenor Place SW1X 7JB—*Chairman*, C. D. Hankes-Drielsma.

British Field Sports Society (1930), 59 Kennington Road, S.E.1.—*Dir.*, J. Hopkinson.

British Film Institute (1933), 127 Charing Cross Road WC2H 0EA—*Dir.*, A. Smith; *Controller, National Film Theatre*, L. Hardcastle, O.B.E.

British Foundrymen, The Institute of (1904), Bridge House, 121 Smallbrook Queensway, Birmingham B5 4JP—*Sec.*, G. A. Schofield.

British Gliding Association (1930), affiliated to Royal Aero Club. Kimberley House, Vaughan Way, Leicester.—*Gen. Sec.*, B. Rolfe.

British Goat Society (1879), *Sec.*, Mrs. S. May, Lion House, Rougham, Bury St. Edmunds, Suffolk IP30 9LJ.

British Heart Foundation (1963), 102 Gloucester Place W1H 4DH—*Dir. Gen.*, Brig. M. C. T. Pelham.

British Hedgehog Preservation Society, The (1982), *Sec.*, Maj. A. H. Coles, T.D., Knowbury House, Knowbury, Ludlow, Shropshire SY8 3JT.

British Homoeopathic Association, The (1902), 27A Devonshire Street W1N 1RJ—*Gen. Sec.*, Mrs. M. Munday.

British Horse Society (*incorporating* The Pony Club), British Equestrian Centre, Kenilworth, Warwicks CV8 2LR—*Dir.*, Col. N. F. Grove-White.

British Institute in Eastern Africa, 1 Kensington Gore SW7 2AR—*London Sec.*, Mrs. B. White.

British Institute of Archæology at Ankara, c/o British Academy, 20–21 Cornwall Terrace NW1 4QP—*Hon. Sec.*, Dr. T. F. Watkins, F.S.A., F.S.A.(Scot).

British Institute of International and Comparative Law, Charles Clore House, 17 Russell Square, W.C.1.—*Dir.*, The Lady Fox.

British Institute of Interior Design (1899), 1C Devonshire Avenue, Beeston, Nottingham NG9 1BS—*Sec.*, N. Parker.

British Institute of Persian Studies (1961), *Sec.*, Mrs. M. E. Gueritz, M.B.E., 13 Cambrian Road, Richmond, Surrey TW10 6JQ.

British Institute of Radiology, 36 Portland Place, W.1.—*Gen. Sec.*, Mrs. S. Johnstone.

British Insurance Brokers Association, BIBA House, 14 Bevis Marks EC3A 2NT—*Dir. Gen.*, J. C. T. Hackett, F.B.I.M.

British Interplanetary Society (1933), 27–29 South Lambeth Road SW8 1SZ—*Exec. Sec.*, L. J. Carter.

British Invisible Exports Council (1983), 14 Austin Friars EC2N 2HE—*Dir. Gen.*, W. M. Clarke, C.B.E.

British Israel World Federation (1919), Mount Avalon, Bove Town, Glastonbury, Somerset BA6 8JG—*Sec.*, R. B. H. Hall.

British Legion, Royal. *Headquarters*, 48 Pall Mall SW1Y 5JY—*Gen. Sec.*, Maj. R. Tomlins, O.B.E.

British Medical Association (1832), B.M.A. House, Tavistock Square, W.C.1.—*President*, Sir Douglas Black, F.R.C.P.; *Sec.*, J. D. J. Havard, M.D.

British Migraine Association, 178A, High Road, Byfleet, Weybridge, Surrey KT14 7ED—*Hon. Sec.*, Mrs. J. Liddell.

British Music Hall Society (1963), 1 King Henry Street, N.16.—*Chairman*, J. Seaton.

British Music Information Centre, 10 Stratford Place W1N 9AE—*Manager*, R. W. Wright.

British Naturalists' Association (1905).—*Hon. Mem. Sec.*, Mrs. Y. H. Griffiths, 23 Oak Hill Close, Woodford Green, Essex.

British Nutrition Foundation (1967), 15 Belgrave Square SW1X 8PS—*Dir. Gen.*, Prof. D. M. Conning.

British Polio Fellowship (1939), Bell Close, West End Road, Ruislip, Middx HA4 6LP—*Gen. Sec.*, L. P. Jackson.

BRITISH POULTRY BREEDERS AND HATCHERIES ASSOCIATION LTD., 52–54 High Holborn, W.C.1.—*Gen. Sec.*, I. S. Knight.

BRITISH PROPERTY FEDERATION, 35 Catherine Place, S.W.1.—*Sec.*, S. H. Bristow.

BRITISH RECORDS ASSOCIATION (1932), Master's Court, The Charterhouse, Charterhouse Square EC1M 6AU—*Pres.*, Rt. Hon. Sir John Donaldson, Master of the Rolls; *Hon. Sec.*, T. R. Padfield.

BRITISH RED CROSS SOCIETY (1870).—*National Headquarters*, 9 Grosvenor Crescent SW1X 7EJ—*Dir. Gen.*, D. J. Piggott.

BRITISH SAILORS' SOCIETY (1818), 406/410 Eastern Avenue, Ilford, Essex IG2 6NG—*Gen. Sec.*, G. Chambers.

BRITISH SCHOOL AT ATHENS.—*Chairman of the Managing Committee*, Prof. R. M. Cook, F.B.A.; *Dir.*, H. W. Catling, O.B.E., D.Phil, F.S.A.; *Sec.*, Mrs. S. E. Waywell, PH.D., 31–34 Gordon Square, W.C.1.

BRITISH SCHOOL AT ROME (1901).—*Chairman of Executive Committee*, A. G. Shepherd Fidler, C.B.E.; *Director*, Dr. G. Barker; *Hon. Gen. Sec.*, C. A. H. James, 1 Lowther Gardens, Exhibition Road SW7 2AA.

BRITISH SCHOOL OF ARCHÆOLOGY IN JERUSALEM (1919), The British Academy, 20 Cornwall Terrace, N.W.1.—*Pres.*, The Rev. Prof. H. Chadwick, D.D., F.B.A.; *Dir.*, Dr. R. Harper, F.S.A.

BRITISH SEAMEN'S BOYS HOME, Grenville House, Brixham, Devon TQ5 9AF—*Supt.*, Capt. E. M. Marks, R.D., R.N.R.

BRITISH THEATRE ASSOCIATION (1919) (incorporating the British Theatre Play Library), 9 Fitzroy Square W1P 6AE—*Dir.*, Jane Hackworth-Young.

BRITISH TRAVEL AGENTS, THE ASSOCIATION OF (1950), 55–57 Newman Street W1P 4AH—*Chief Exec.*, M. Elton.

BRITISH VETERINARY ASSOCIATION (1881), 7 Mansfield Street W1M 0AT—*Sec.*, P. B. Turner, M.A.

BRUSH MANUFACTURERS' ASSOCIATION, BRITISH, 6A East Street, Epsom, Surrey KT17 1HH—*Sec.*, J. A. Snellgrove.

BUDDHIST SOCIETY, THE (1924), 58 Eccleston Square, S.W.1.—*Gen. Sec.*, J. Snelling.

BUILDING, CHARTERED INSTITUTE OF (1834), Englemere, Kings Ride, Ascot, Berks SL5 8BJ—*Chief Exec.*, D. A. Neale, O.B.E., M.C.

BUILDING SERVICES ENGINEERS, CHARTERED INSTITUTION OF (1897), Delta House, 222 Balham High Road SW12 9BS—*Sec.*, A. V. Ramsay.

BUILDING SOCIETIES ASSOCIATION, 3 Savile Row W1X 1AF—*Sec.-Gen.*, R. S. Weir.

BUILDING SOCIETIES INSTITUTE, THE CHARTERED, Fanhams Hall, Ware, Hertfordshire SG12 7PZ—*Sec.*, R. D. Crerar.

BULWER LYTTON CIRCLE, 125 Markyate Road, Dagenham, Essex.—*Sec.*, E. Ford.

BUSINESS AND PROFESSIONAL WOMEN, UNITED KINGDOM FEDERATION OF (1938), 23 Ansdell Street W8 5BN—*Sec.*, C. E. Smith.

BUSINESS ARCHIVES COUNCIL, 185 Tower Bridge Road SE1 2UF—*Chairman*, S. H. G. Twining, O.B.E.; *Sec. Gen.*, A. M. Turton.

BUTCHERS' CHARITABLE INSTITUTION (1828).—*Sec.*, J. A. Fordyce, 61 West Smithfield EC1A 9EA.

CALOUSTE GULBENKIAN FOUNDATION, LISBON, United Kingdom Branch (1956), 98 Portland Place W1N 4ET—*Dir.*, L. C. Taylor.

CAMBRIDGE PRESERVATION SOCIETY (1929).—*Chairman*, Sir Desmond Lee; *Sec.*, M. R. Francis, Wandlebury Ring, Gog Magog Hills, Babraham, Cambridge CB2 4AE.

CAMERA CLUB (1885), 8 Great Newport Street WC2H 7JA—*Sec.*, J. Legate.

CAMERON FUND LTD., (1971), Tavistock House North, Tavistock Square WC1H 9JP—*Sec.*, Miss H. C. Pullen.

CAMPAIGN FOR NUCLEAR DISARMAMENT (1958), 11 Goodwin Street, N.4.—*Gen. Sec.*, Mgr. Bruce Kent.

CANADA UNITED KINGDOM CHAMBER OF COMMERCE, 3 Regent Street SW1Y 4NZ—*Exec. Dir.*, W. E. Ferguson.

CANCER RESEARCH CAMPAIGN, 2 Carlton House Terrace SW1Y 5AR—For research into the disease of cancer in all its forms.—*Sec. Gen.*, D. de Peyer.

CANCER RELIEF, NATIONAL SOCIETY FOR (1911), Michael Sobell House, 30 Dorset Square, N.W.1.—*Gen. Sec.*, S. H. Creswell.

CANCER RESEARCH FUND, IMPERIAL (1902), P.O. Box 123, Lincoln's Inn Fields WC2A 3PX. Research into causes, prevention, treatment and cure of all forms of cancer; in own laboratories and extramural units.—*Sec.*, Maj-Gen. A. Dennis, C.B., O.B.E.

CANCER RESEARCH, THE INSTITUTE OF: Royal Cancer Hospital, 17a Onslow Gardens SW7 3AL—*Sec.*, J. Defries.

CAREER TEACHERS, ASSOCIATION OF, Hillsboro., Castledine Street, Loughborough, Leics.—*Gen. Sec.*, Miss R. Yaffé.

CARNEGIE DUNFERMLINE TRUST (1903). (Social and cultural purposes in Dunfermline) Income £200,000.—*Sec.*, F. Mann, Abbey Park House, Dunfermline KY12 7PB.

CARNEGIE HERO FUND TRUST (1908). Income £90,000. Makes grants and allowances to people injured or the dependants of people killed in saving human life within the British Isles and territorial waters.—*Sec.*, F. Mann, Abbey Park House, Dunfermline KY12 7PB.

CARNEGIE UNITED KINGDOM TRUST (1913). Comely Park House, Dunfermline, Fife KY12 7EJ—*Object*, The improvement of the well-being of the masses of the people of Great Britain and Ireland by means which are "charitable" in law and are to be selected by the Trustees. The Trust is particularly concerned with innovatory schemes in community services, amateur participation in the arts, particularly for the disabled, and heritage interpretation developments; grants are not made to individuals, or in response to general appeals, or for research and travel. Management—By trustees. *Sec.*, G. Lord.

CATHEDRALS ADVISORY COMMISSION FOR ENGLAND, 83 London Wall EC2M 5NA—*Sec.*, P. A. T. Burman, F.S.A., F.R.S.A.

CATHOLIC MARRIAGE ADVISORY COUNCIL (National Headquarters), 15 Lansdowne Road W11 3AJ; *Chief Exec.*, B. L. Cawley.

CATHOLIC RECORD SOCIETY (1904).—*Hon. Sec.*, Ms. R. Rendel, c/o 114 Mount Street, W.1.

CATHOLIC TRUTH SOCIETY (1868), P.O. Box 422, 38–40 Eccleston Square SW1V 1PD—*Gen. Sec.*, D. Murphy.

CATHOLIC UNION OF GREAT BRITAIN.—*Pres.*, The Duke of Norfolk, C.B., C.B.E., M.C., K.G.; *Hon. Sec.*, Mrs. J. Stuyt, M.B.E., 1 Bolton Gardens Mews SW10 9LW.

CATTLE BREEDER'S CLUB, LTD., BRITISH, Lavenders, Isfield, nr. Uckfield, Sussex TN22 5TX—*Sec.*, C. R. Stains.

CECIL HOUSES (Inc.) (Housing Association, Charity), 2 Priory Road, Kew, Richmond, Surrey TW9 3DG—*Gen. Man. and Sec.*, A. G. Wilmot.

CERAMIC SOCIETY, BRITISH (1900), Shelton House, Stoke Road, Shelton, Stoke-on-Trent, Staffs.—*Pres.*, A. J. Owen.

CERAMICS INSTITUTE OF (1955), Shelton House, Stoke Road, Stoke-on-Trent, Staffs ST6 2NS—*Pres.*, Prof. R. J. Brook.

CHADWICK TRUST (1895) (for the promotion of health and prevention of disease).—Chadwick Professor of Civil Engineering, University College London, Gower Street WC1E 6BT.

CHAMBERS OF COMMERCE.—*See* COMMERCE.

CHANTREY BEQUEST (1875).—*Sec. to the Trustees*, P. Rodgers, Royal Academy of Arts, Burlington House, Piccadilly, W.1.

CHARTERED SECRETARIES AND ADMINISTRATORS, IN-STITUTE OF (1891), 16 Park Crescent, W.1.—*Sec.*, B. Barker, M.B.E.

CHEMICAL ENGINEERS, INSTITUTION OF (1922), George E. Davis Building, 165–171 Railway Terrace, Rugby, Warks CV21 3HQ—*Gen. Sec.*, T. J. Evans.

CHEMICAL INDUSTRY, SOCIETY OF, 14/15 Belgrave Square, S.W.1.—*Pres.*, K. H. Walley, C.B.I.M.; *Gen. Sec.*, P. P. King, F.R.S.C.

CHEMISTRY, THE ROYAL SOCIETY OF, Burlington House, Piccadilly W1V 0BN—*Pres.*, Prof. R. O. C. Norman, F.R.S.; *Sec.-Gen.*, R. D. Guthrie, PH.D.

(LEONARD) CHESHIRE FOUNDATION (1955), 26–29 Maunsel Street SW1P 2QN. Foundation presides over 75 homes and 20 family support services in U.K. and affiliated to a further 150 world-wide.—*Dir.*, A. L. Bennett.

CHESS FEDERATION, BRITISH, 9a Grand Parade, St. Leonards-on-Sea, East Sussex TN38 0DD—*Gen. Sec.*, P. Buswell.

CHEST, HEART AND STROKE ASSOCIATION (1899), Tavistock House North, Tavistock Square WC1H 9JE—*Dir. Gen.*, Sir David Atkinson, K.B.E., F.R.C.P.E., F.F.C.M., F.F.O.M.

CHILDREN'S AID & ADOPTION, MISSION OF HOPE FOR, 14 South Park Hill Road, Croydon, Surrey CR2 7YB—*Gen. Sec.*, Rev. R. H. Johnson.

CHILDREN'S COUNTRY HOLIDAYS FUND, 1 York Street, W.1.—*Gen. Sec.*, Mrs. J. M. Meekins, M.B.E.

CHINA ASSOCIATION (1889), Regis House, 43–46 King William Street EC4R 9BE—*Exec. Dir.*, Brig. B. G. Hickey, O.B.E., M.C.

CHIROPODISTS, THE SOCIETY OF, 53 Welbeck Street W1M 7HE—*Sec.*, G. C. Jenkins.

CHOIRS SCHOOLS ASSOCIATION (1921).—*Hon. Sec.*, R. A. Ford, King's School, Rochester, Kent ME1 1TD.

CHRISTIAN ACTION—*Dir.*, Canon E. James, St. Peter's House, 308, Kennington Lane SE11 5HY.

CHRISTIAN AID (1945), P.O. Box 1, S.W.9.—*Dir.*, Rev. Dr. C. Elliott.

CHRISTIAN EDUCATION MOVEMENT (1965), 2 Chester House, Pages Lane N10 1PR. *Gen. Sec.*, Rev. J. M. Sutcliffe.

CHRISTIAN EVIDENCE SOCIETY (1870).—*Hon. Sec.*, Mrs. G. M. Ryeland, 23 Rickman Hill, Coulsdon, Surrey CR3 3DS.

CHRISTIAN KNOWLEDGE, SOCIETY FOR PROMOTING (1698), Holy Trinity Church, Marylebone Road NW1 4DU—*Gen. Sec.*, P. N. G. Gilbert.

CHRISTIANS AND JEWS, COUNCIL OF (1942), 1 Dennington Park Road, West End Lane NW6 1AX—*Exec. Dir.*, Rev. M. Braybrooke.

CHURCH ARMY, Independents Road, Blackheath SE3 9LG. *Chief Sec.*, Rev. M. Rees.

CHURCH BUILDING SOCIETY, INCORPORATED (1818), Fulham Palace SW6 6EA—*Sec.*, Maj. R. I. Radford, M.B.E.

CHURCH EDUCATION CORPORATION, Bedgebury School, Goudhurst, Kent TN17 2SH.—*Sec.*, R. P. Gilbert.

CHURCH HOUSE, THE CORPORATION OF (1888), Dean's Yard SW1P 3NZ—*Sec.*, Capt. P. W. E. Parry, M.B.E.

CHURCH LADS' AND CHURCH GIRLS' BRIGADE, *National Headquarters*, Claude Hardy House, 15 Etchingham Park Road N3 2DU—*Gen. Sec.*, Rev. C. Grice, M.B.E.

CHURCH MISSIONARY SOCIETY (1799), 157 Waterloo Road SE1 8UU. Income, 1984, £3,316,998.—*Secs.*, Rev. Canon S. Barrington-Ward (*General*); Miss E. A. E. Pointon (*Britain*); C. B. Fernihough (*Financial*).

CHURCH OF ENGLAND CHILDREN'S SOCIETY (1881) (The Children's Society), Old Town Hall, Kennington Road SE11 4QD—*Dir.*, Miss C. W. Stone.

CHURCH OF ENGLAND PENSIONS BOARD (1926), 53 Tufton Street SW1P 3QP—*Sec.*, R. G. Radford.

CHURCH OF ENGLAND SOLDIERS', SAILORS' AND AIRMEN'S CLUBS (1891), and CHURCH OF ENGLAND SOLDIERS', SAILORS' AND AIRMEN'S HOUSING ASSOCIATION LTD. (1974), 1 Shakespeare Terrace, 126 High Street, Portsmouth PO1 2RH. *Chairman*, Rear-Adm. A. G. Watson, C.B.

CHURCH PASTORAL AID SOCIETY (1836), Falcon Court, 32 Fleet Street, E.C.4.—*Gen. Sec.*, Rev. D. B. Bubbers.

CHURCH UNION (1859), 7 Tufton Street, S.W.1.—*Gen. Sec.*, Rev. P. J. E. Geldard.

CHURCHES, BRITISH COUNCIL OF (1942), 2 Eaton Gate SW1N 9BL—*Gen. Sec.*, Rev. Dr. P. Morgan.

CHURCHES, COUNCIL FOR CARE OF, 83 London Wall EC2M 5NA.—*Sec.*, P. A. T. Burman, F.S.A., F.R.S.A.

CHURCHES, FRIENDLESS, FRIENDS OF (1957), 12 Edwardes Square W8 6HG—*Hon. Dir.*, I. Bulmer-Thomas; *Hon. Sec.*, L. E. Jones.

CHURCHES MAIN COMMITTEE (1941), Fielden House, Little College Street SW1P 3JZ—*Sec.*, B. M. Thimont, C.B.

CITIZENS ADVICE BUREAUX, NATIONAL ASSOCIATION OF (1931), Myddelton House, 115/123 Pentonville Road N1 9LZ—*Chief Exec. Officer*, Elizabeth Filkin.

CITY PAROCHIAL FOUNDATION (Trustees of the London Parochial Charities), 10 Fleet Street EC4Y 1AU—*Clerk*, B. H. Woods, M.B.E.

CIVIL DEFENCE, INSTITUTE OF (1938), P.O. Box 229, 3 Little Montague Court, E.C.1.—*Hon. Gen. Sec.*, E. C. Stanbridge.

CIVIL ENGINEERS, INSTITUTION OF (1818) (*Amalgamated with* Municipal Engineers, Institution of), Great George Street SW1P 3AA—*Pres.*, J. A. Gaffney; *Sec.*, J. C. McKenzie.

CIVIL LIBERTIES, NATIONAL COUNCIL FOR (1934), 21 Tabard Street SE1 4LA—*Sec.*, Sarah Spencer.

CIVIL SERVICE COUNCIL FOR FURTHER EDUCATION.—*Sec.*, J. Muir, Training Division, 11 Belgrave Road SW1V 1RB.

CLASSICAL ASSOCIATION (1903).—*Hon. Treas.*, R. Wallace, Dept. of Classics, University of Keele, Keele, Staffs ST5 5BG.

CLASSICAL TEACHERS, JOINT ASSOCIATION OF (1962), 31–34 Gordon Square WC1H 0PY—*Exec. Sec.*, Dr. R. Garland.

CLERGY ORPHAN CORPORATION (1749), 57B Tufton Street, Westminster SW1P 3QL—*Sec.*, Miss J. Buncher.

CLERKS OF WORKS OF GREAT BRITAIN INCORPORATED, INSTITUTE OF (1882), 41 The Mall, Ealing W5 3TJ—*Sec.*, A. P. Macnamara.

COACHING CLUB (1871), 2 Treville Street, S.W.15.—*Sec.*, D. H. Clarke.

COAL TRADE BENEVOLENT ASSOCIATION (1888), 63 Narrow Street, Limehouse, E.14.—*Sec.*, H. C. F. Squire, O.B.E.

COMBINED CADET FORCE ASSOCIATION (1952), Cheltenham Terrace SW3 4RR—*Sec.*, Brig. D. M. Pontifex, C.B.E.

COMMERCE, ASSOCIATION OF BRITISH CHAMBERS OF (1860).—*Pres.*, Sir David Nicolson; *Dir. Gen.*, R. G. Taylor, Sovereign House, 212A Shaftesbury Avenue, W.C.2.

COMMERCE AND INDUSTRY, LONDON CHAMBER OF (1881), 69 Cannon Street EC4N 5AB—*Pres.*, Sir Andrew Jolliffe, G.B.E.; *Dir.*, A. M. W. Platt.

COMMERCE, ASSOCIATION OF SCOTTISH CHAMBERS OF, 30 George Square, Glasgow G2 1EQ—*Sec.*, E. Marwick.

COMMERCE AND MANUFACTURES, EDINBURGH CHAMBER OF (1786), 3 Randolph Crescent, Edinburgh EH3 7UD—*Chief Exec.*, D. M. Mowat, J.P.

COMMERCE AND MANUFACTURES, GLASGOW CHAMBER OF (1783), 30 George Square, Glasgow G2 1EQ—*Sec.*, E. Marwick.

COMMERCIAL TRAVELLERS' BENEVOLENT INSTITUTION (1849), 49 Lawrie Park Avenue SE26 6HA—*Chief Exec.*, E. B. Auger.

COMMISSIONAIRES, THE CORPS OF (1859), founded by the late Captain Sir Edward Walter; for the employment of ex-Soldiers, Sailors and Airmen and ex-police, fire service and merchant navy servicemen. *Headquarters*, 3 Crane Court, Fleet Street EC4A 2EJ. *Outquarters*, War Memorial Building, Waring St., Belfast 1.; Room 53, Guildhall Buildings, Navigation Street, Birmingham; 87 Park Street, Bristol; 99 Shandwick Place, Edinburgh; 180 W. Regent Street, Glasgow; 10–12 East Parade, Leeds; 61 Lord Street, Liverpool; 2 St. John Street, Deansgate, Manchester; 10 Bigg Market, Newcastle upon Tyne 1. Total strength, 2,700—*Commandant*, Col. R. B. Robertson; *Deputy Commandant*, Col. The Hon. H. E. C. Willoughby.

COMMONWEALTH ASSOCIATION OF PLANNERS (1971), 26 Portland Place W1N 4BE—*Hon. Sec.*, G. Franklin.

COMMONWEALTH PRESS UNION (1909), Studio House, 184 Fleet Street EC4A 2DU—*Dir.*, Lt.-Col. T. Pierce-Goulding, M.B.E., C.D.

COMMONWEALTH SETTLEMENT, CHURCH OF ENGLAND COUNCIL FOR (1925), (see OVERSEAS SETTLEMENT, C. of E. COMMITTEE FOR).

COMMONWEALTH SOCIETY FOR THE DEAF (1959), 105, Gower Street, W.C.1.—*Admin. Sec.*, Miss E. Lubienska.

COMMUNITY MEDICINE, SOCIETY OF (1856), 28 Portland Place W1N 4DE—*Pres.*, Dr. M. W. Beaver.

COMPOSERS' GUILD OF GREAT BRITAIN, THE (1945), 10 Stratford Place W1N 9AE—*Gen. Sec.*, Miss E. Yeoman.

CONSERVATION OF HISTORIC AND ARTISTIC WORKS, INTERNATIONAL INSTITUTE FOR, 6 Buckingham Street WC2N 6BA—*Pres.*, G. Thomson; *Sec. Gen.*, N. S. Brommelle.

CONSERVATION SOCIETY, LTD. (1966), 12A Guildford Street, Chertsey, Surrey KT16 9BQ—*Dir.*, Dr. J. Davoll.

CONSERVATION VOLUNTEERS, BRITISH TRUST FOR (1970), 36 St. Mary's Street, Wallingford, Oxon OX10 0EU—*Dir.*, I. Branton.

CONSERVATIVE AND UNIONIST ASSOCIATIONS, NATIONAL UNION OF (1867), 32 Smith Square SW1P 3HH—*Sec.*, R. Nelder.

CONSERVATIVE CLUBS, LTD., ASSOCIATION OF (1894), 56 Buckingham Gate SW1E 6AW—*Sec.*, L. G. Waterman, O.B.E.

CONSTRUCTION SURVEYORS' INSTITUTE (1952), Wellington House, 203 Lordship Lane, S.E.22.—*Exec. Officer*, B. A. Hunt.

CONSULTING ENGINEERS, ASSOCIATION OF (1913), Alliance House, 12 Caxton Street SW1H 0QL—*Sec.*, Maj.-Gen. P. J. M. Pellereau, F.B.I.M.

CONSULTING SCIENTISTS, ASSOCIATION OF, Owles Hall, Buntingford, Herts SG9 9PL—*Sec.*, Mrs. H. M. W. Gibbons.

CO-OPERATIVE SOCIETIES AND ASSOCIATIONS:—

Co-operative Party, 158 Buckingham Palace Road, S.W.1.—*Sec.*, D. Wise, O.B.E.

Co-operative Union (1869), Holyoake House, Hanover Street, Manchester M60 0AS—*Chief Exec. Officer*, D. L. Wilkinson.

Co-operative Wholesale Society (C.W.S.) (1863), New Century House, Manchester 4.—*Chief Exec. Officer*, D. M. Landau; *Sec.*, G. J. Melmoth.

Co-operative Women's Guild, 342 Hoe Street, Walthamstow E17 9PX—*Nat. Officer.*, Miss D. Paskin.

Fisheries Organization Society, Ltd. (1914), New Fish Quay, Brixham, Devon.—*Sec.*, A. H. Dobbie.

International Co-operative Alliance (1895), 15 route des Morillons, Grand-Saconnex, CH 1218, Geneva.—*Dir.*, R. L. Beasley.

Plunkett Foundation for Co-operative Studies (1919), 31 St. Giles, Oxford OX1 3LF—*Dir.*, E. Parnell.

COPYRIGHT COUNCIL, BRITISH (1953), 29–33 Berners Street W1P 4AA—*Sec.*, G. V. Adams.

CORONERS' SOCIETY OF ENGLAND AND WALES (1846).—*Hon. Sec.*, J. Burton, Coroner's Court, 77 Fulham Palace Road W6 8JA.

CORPORATE TREASURERS, ASSOCIATION OF, 16 Park Crescent, Regents Park W1N 4AM—*Sec.*, Richenda Eaton.

CORPORATE TRUSTEES, ASSOCIATION OF, 2 Withdean Rise, Brighton BN1 6YN.—*Sec.*, L. C. Howes.

CORRESPONDENCE COLLEGES, ASSOCIATION OF BRITISH (1955), 6 Francis Grove SW19 4DT—*Sec.*, Mrs. M. Coren.

COUNCIL FOR SMALL INDUSTRIES IN RURAL AREAS, 141 Castle Street, Salisbury, Wilts SP1 3TP—*Chief Exec.*, A. D. Scott.

COUNSEL AND CARE FOR THE ELDERLY (Elderly Invalids Fund), 131 Middlesex Street E1 7JF—*Sec.*, J. H. Hobart.

COUNTRY LANDOWNERS' ASSOCIATION (1907), 16 Belgrave Square SW1X 8PQ—*Dir. Gen.*, J. M. Douglas, C.B.E.

COUNTY CHIEF EXECUTIVES, ASSOCIATION OF.—*Hon. Sec.*, R. W. Adock, County Hall, Chelmsford, Essex CM1 1LX.

COUNTY COUNCILS, ASSOCIATION OF, Eaton House, 66A Eaton Square SW1W 9BH—*Sec.*, J. Stevenson.

COUNTY EMERGENCY PLANNING OFFICERS' SOCIETY, County Hall, Spetchley Road, Worcester.—*Hon. Sec.*, P. W. Fenn, T.D.

COUNTY SECRETARIES, SOCIETY OF.—*Hon. Sec.*, W. J. Church, County Hall, Hertford SG13 8DE.

COUNTY SURVEYORS' SOCIETY (1884).—*President*, F. D. J. Johnson; *Hon. Sec.*, K. B. Madelin, Shropshire County Council, The Shirehall, Abbey Foregate, Shrewsbury, Shropshire SY2 6ND.

COUNTY TREASURERS, SOCIETY OF (1903), County Hall, Beverley, N. Humberside HU17 9BA—*President*, J. E. Barton-Cambridgeshire; *Hon. Sec.*, J. A. Parkes.

CRAFTS CENTRE, BRITISH (1948), 43 Earlham Street, Covent Garden WC2H 9LD—*Dir.*, Tatjana Marsden.

CRUELTY TO ANIMALS, ROYAL SOCIETY FOR THE PREVENTION OF. See "ROYAL."

CRUELTY TO ANIMALS, CENTRAL COUNCIL OF SOCIETIES IN SCOTLAND FOR PREVENTION OF (1950), 19 Melville Street, Edinburgh EH3 7PL—*Hon. Sec.*, Sir Cameron Rusby, K.C.B., L.V.O.

CRUELTY TO CHILDREN. See "NATIONAL" and "ROYAL SCOTTISH."

CULTURAL EXCHANGE, ASSOCIATION FOR (1958), Babraham, Cambridge CB2 4AP—*Sec.*, P. B. Barnes.

CURATES' AUGMENTATION FUND (1866), 27 Medway Street, S.W.1.—*Hon. Sec.*, J. M. Greany.

CWMNI URDD GOBAITH CYMRU, Swyddfa'r Urdd, Aberystwyth. Dyfed SY23 1EN—*Dir.*, J. E. Williams.

CYCLISTS TOURING CLUB (1878), Cotterell House, 69 Meadrow, Godalming, Surrey GU7 3HS—*Sec.*, A. J. Leng.

CYMMRODORION, THE HONOURABLE SOCIETY OF (1751).—*Hon. Sec.*, Mrs. J. Gruffydd, 30 Eastcastle Street W1N 7PD.

DAIRY ASSOCIATION, UNITED KINGDOM (1950), Giggs Hill Green, Thames Ditton, Surrey.—*Sec.*, Miss J. E. Smith.

DAIRY TECHNOLOGY, SOCIETY OF (1943), 72 Ermine Street, Huntingdon, Cambs PE18 6EZ—*Nat. Sec.*, P. H. F. Lee.

D-DAY AND NORMANDY FELLOWSHIP.—*Hon. Secs.*, Mr. and Mrs. L. R. Reed, 9 South Parade, Southsea, Hants PO5 2JB.

DEAF ASSOCIATION, BRITISH (1890 *formerly* BRITISH DEAF AND DUMB ASSOCIATION), 38 Victoria Place, Carlisle CA1 1HU.—*Gen. Sec.*, A. W. Verney.

DEAF, ROYAL NATIONAL INSTITUTE FOR THE (1911), 105 Gower Street WC1 6AH—*Dir.*, R. Sydenham.

DEAF AND DUMB, ROYAL ASSOCIATION IN AID OF, To promote the general, social and spiritual welfare of deaf and blind/deaf people in Greater London, Essex, Surrey and Kent. 27 Old Oak Road, Acton W3 7HN—*Director Gen.*, Rev. I. Scott-Oldfield.

DEAF AND DUMB WOMEN, BRITISH HOME FOR, 26 Clapton Common, E.5.—*Sec.*, Mrs. A. Knightley.

DEAF CHILDREN, ROYAL SCHOOL FOR (1792), Margate. *Office*, Victoria Road, Margate, Kent CT9 1NB—*Sec.* D. E. Downs.

DEER MANAGEMENT SOCIETIES, THE FEDERATION OF (1975), The Old Well Cottage, Beech Road, Yorkney, Lydney, Glos GL15 4TJ—*Hon. Co-ordinator*, J. H. Absalom.

DEER SOCIETY, BRITISH.—*Dir.*, N. J. Foll, Church Farm, Lower Basildon, Reading, Berks.

DENTAL COUNCIL, GENERAL, 37 Wimpole Street W1M 8DQ—*Registrar*, N. T. Davies, M.B.E.

DENTAL HOSPITALS OF THE UNITED KINGDOM, ASSOCIATION OF (1942).—*Hon. Sec.*, Mrs. P. Harrington, Dental Hospital, St. Chad's Queensway, Birmingham B4 6NN.

DESIGN AND INDUSTRIES ASSOCIATION (1915), 17 Lawn Crescent, Kew Gardens, Surrey TW9 3NR—*Hon. Dir.*, R. Plummer.

DEVON AND CORNWALL RECORD SOCIETY (1904).—c/o Devon and Exeter Institution, 7 The Close, Exeter EX1 1EZ.—*Hon. Sec.*, J. D. Brunton.

DICKENS FELLOWSHIP, Dickens House, 48 Doughty Street, W.C.1.—*Hon. Gen. Sec.*, A. S. Watts.

DIRECTORS, INSTITUTE OF, 116 Pall Mall SW1Y 5ED—*Dir. Gen.*, Sir John Hoskyns.

DISABILITY AND REHABILITATION, THE ROYAL ASSOCIATION FOR, 25 Mortimer Street W1N 8AB—*Dir.*, G. Wilson, C.B.E.

DISPENSING OPTICIANS, ASSOCIATION OF (1925), 22 Nottingham Place W1M 4AT—*Sec. Gen.*, A. P. D. Westhead.

DISTRESSED GENTLEFOLK'S AID ASSOCIATION (1897), (Headquarters and London Nursing Home), Vicarage Gate House, Vicarage Gate, Kensington, W.8.—*Gen. Sec.*, J. A. Marshall, C.B.

DISTRICT COUNCILS, ASSOCIATION OF (1974), 9 Buckingham Gate SW1E 6LE—*Sec.*, G. McCartney.

DISTRICT MEDICAL OFFICERS, ASSOCIATION OF (1982). *Hon. Sec.*, Dr. P. W. Briggs, Ealing Hospital, St. Bernard's Wing, Uxbridge Road, Southall, Middx.

DISTRICT SECRETARIES ASSOCIATION OF, 9 Margaret Road, Bishopworth, Bristol BS13 9DQ.—*Hon. Sec.*, B. J. Quoroll.

DITCHLEY FOUNDATION, Ditchley Park, Enstone, Oxford OX7 4ER—*Dir.*, Sir Reginald Hibbert, G.C.M.G.

DOCKLAND SETTLEMENTS, headquarters and office at Carpenters and Dockland Centre, Gibbins Road, Stratford E15 2HU. Branches at Rotherhithe S.E.16; Stratford, E.15; Hainault, Essex; Isle of Dogs, E.14.

DOMESTIC SERVANTS' BENEVOLENT INSTITUTION (1846), Royal Bank of Scotland P.L.C., 7 Burlington Gardens W1A 3DD—*Sec.*, D. C. F. Small.

DOWSERS, BRITISH SOCIETY OF.—*Sec.*, M. D. Rust, Sycamore Cottage, Tamley Lane, Hastingleigh, Nr. Ashford, Kent TN25 5HW.

DRAINAGE AUTHORITIES, ASSOCIATION OF (1937).—*Sec.*, D. Noble, Ambury Road, Huntingdon, Cambs PE18 6NZ.

DRINKING FOUNTAIN ASSOCIATION (formerly Metropolitan Drinking Fountain and Cattle Trough Association) (1859), 105 Wansunt Road, Bexley, Kent DA5 2DN—*Sec.* D. R. W. Randall.

DRUG DEPENDENCE, INSTITUTE FOR THE STUDY OF, 1/4 Hatton Place EC1N 8ND—*Dir.*, J. Woodcock.

DYERS AND COLOURISTS, SOCIETY OF (1884), Perkin House, P.O. Box 244, 82 Grattan Road, Bradford, W. Yorks BD1 2JB—*Gen. Sec.*, M. Tordoff, PH.D.

EARL HAIG'S (BRITISH LEGION) APPEAL FUND. See "BRITISH LEGION."

EARL HAIG FUND (SCOTLAND). Established for the relief of distress among ex-service personnel and their dependants in Scotland. Applications to *North, South and East Area*, New Haig House, Logie Green Road, Edinburgh.—*Gen. Sec.*, Brig. R. W. Riddle, O.B.E.; or *Glasgow and South-West Area*, 1 Fitzroy Place, Glasgow, G.3.—*Sec.*, Maj. J. B. A. Smyth.

EARLY ENGLISH TEXT SOCIETY (1864).—*Hon. Director*, Prof. J. Burrow; *Exec. Sec.*, Dr. M. Godden, Exeter College, Oxford.

ECCLESIASTICAL HISTORY SOCIETY.—*Sec.*, Dr. Judith Champ, Department of Christian Doctrine and History, King's College, Strand WC2R 2LS.

ECCLESIOLOGICAL SOCIETY.—*Hon. Sec.*, S. C. Humphrey, St. Andrew-by-the-Wardrobe, Queen Victoria Street EC4V 5DE.

ECOLOGY PARTY (1973), 36–38 Clapham Road SW9 0JQ—*Gen. Sec.*, J. Bishop.

EDUCATION IN ART AND DESIGN, NATIONAL SOCIETY FOR (1888), 7a High Street, Corsham, Wilts SN13 0ES—*Gen. Sec.*, J. Steers.

EDUCATION OFFICERS, SOCIETY OF.—*Gen. Sec.*, R. P. Harding, C.B.E., 5 Bentinck Street W1M 5RN.

EDUCATION OFFICERS' SOCIETY, COUNTY.—*Hon. Sec.*, R. D. Clark, Education Dept., The Castle, Winchester, Hants SO23 8UG.

EDUCATIONAL CENTRES ASSOCIATION, Chequer Centre, Chequer Street EC1Y 8PL.—*Sec.*, D. J. Delahunt.

EDUCATIONAL FOUNDATION FOR VISUAL AIDS, Paxton Place, Gipsy Road SE27 9SR—*Chief Exec.*, G. C. Marchant.

EDUCATIONAL INSTITUTE OF DESIGN, CRAFT AND TECHNOLOGY.—*Gen. Sec.*, G. Day, 24 Elm Road, Kingswood, Bristol, Avon BS15 2ST.

EDUCATIONAL INSTITUTE OF SCOTLAND (1847), 46 Moray Place, Edinburgh.—*Gen. Sec.*, J. D. Pollock.

EDUCATIONAL RESEARCH IN ENGLAND AND WALES, NATIONAL FOUNDATION FOR, The Mere, Upton Park, Slough, Berks SL1 2DQ—*Dir.*, Dr. Clare Burstall.

EDUCATIONAL VISITS AND EXCHANGES, CENTRAL BUREAU FOR (1948), Seymour Mews House, Seymour Mews W1H 9PE—*Dir.*, (vacant).

EDWARDIAN STUDIES ASSOCIATION, 125 Markyate Road, Dagenham, Essex.—*Sec.*, E. Ford.

EGYPT EXPLORATION SOCIETY (1882), 3 Doughty Mews WC1N 2PG—*Chairman*, T. G. H. James, F.B.A.; *Sec.*, Patricia A. Spencer.

ELECTORAL REFORM SOCIETY OF GREAT BRITAIN AND IRELAND (founded 1884 as Proportional Representation Soc.), 6 Chancel Street SE1 0UX—*Chief Exec.*, David Austick.

ELECTRICAL ENGINEERS, INSTITUTION OF (1871), Savoy Place, W.C.2.—*Sec.*, H. H. W. Losty, F.I.E.E.

ELECTRICITY CONSUMERS' COUNCIL, Brook House, 2/16 Torrington Place WC1E 7LL—*Dir.*, Jennifer Kirkpatrick.

ELECTRONIC AND RADIO ENGINEERS, INSTITUTION OF (1925), 99 Gower Street WC1E 6AZ—*Sec.*, D. D. Duffett.

ELGAR FOUNDATION, Elgar's Birthplace, Crown East Lane, Lower Broadheath, Worcester WR2 6RH—*Hon. Sec.*, A. J. Bennett.

ELGAR SOCIETY (1951).—*Sec.*, A. H. A. Neill, 17 Earlsfield Road, S.W.18.

ENERGY INDUSTRIES COUNCIL, Newcombe House, 45 Notting Hill Gate W11 3LQ—*Dir. Gen.*, R. A. Custis.

ENERGY, INSTITUTE OF (1927), 18 Devonshire Street, Portland Place, W.1.—*Sec.*, H. M. Lodge.

ENGINEERING COUNCIL, THE, 10 Maltravers Street WC2R 3ER—*Sec.*, J. Carlill, O.B.E.

ENGINEERING DESIGNERS, INSTITUTION OF (1945), Courtleigh, Westbury Leigh, Westbury, Wilts BA13 3TA—*Gen. Sec.*, P. J. Booker.

ENGINEERING, FELLOWSHIP OF (1976), 2 Little Smith Street SW1P 3DL—*Exec. Sec.*, V. J. Osola, C.B.E.

ENGINEERING INDUSTRIES ASSOCIATION, 16 Dartmouth Street SW1H 9BL—*Dir.*, Col. W. T. Williams.

ENGINEERS AND SHIPBUILDERS IN SCOTLAND, INSTITUTION OF (1857), Charing Cross Tower, 10 Elmbank Gardens, Glasgow, G.2.—*Pres.*, Prof. John Rorke, C.B.E.

ENGINEERS AND SHIPBUILDERS, N.E. COAST INSTITUTION OF (1884), 12 Windsor Terrace, Jesmond, Newcastle upon Tyne NE2 4HE.—*Sec.*, J. Davison.

ENGINEERS, INSTITUTION OF BRITISH (1928), Regency House, 3 Marlborough Place, Brighton BN1 1UB—*Sec.*, Mrs. D. Henry.

ENGINEERS, SOCIETY OF (Incorporated) (1854), Parsifal College, 527 Finchley Road NW3 7BG—*Sec.*, E. C. Burton.

ENGLISH ASSOCIATION, THE (1906), 1 Priory Gardens, W.4.—*Sec.*, Dr. Ruth Fairbanks-Joseph.

ENGLISH FOLK DANCE AND SONG SOCIETY (1932), Cecil Sharp House, 2 Regent's Park Road NW1 7AY—*Dir.*, James Lloyd.

ENGLISH PLACE-NAME SOCIETY (1923).—*Hon. Director*, Prof. K. Cameron, PH.D., F.S.A., F.B.A., The University, Nottingham NG7 2RD.

ENGLISH-SPEAKING UNION OF THE COMMONWEALTH (1918), 37 Charles Street, Berkeley Square W1X 8AB—*Chairman*, Sir Donald Tebbit, G.C.M.G.; *Dir. Gen.*, A. L. Williams, O.B.E.

ENTOMOLOGICAL SOCIETY OF LONDON, ROYAL (1833), 41 Queen's Gate SW7 5HU—*Registrar*, G. G. Bentley.

ENTOMOLOGY, COMMONWEALTH INSTITUTE OF (1909), 56 Queen's Gate, S.W.7.—*Director*, N. C. Pant, PH.D.

ENVIRONMENTAL CONSERVATION, COUNCIL FOR (1969), Zoological Gardens, Regent's Park NW1 4RY—*Pres.*, The Duke of Wellington, M.V.O., O.B.E., M.C.; *Chairman*, G. England; *Sec.*, D. Hughes.

ENVIRONMENTAL HEALTH OFFICERS, INSTITUTION OF, Chadwick House, Rushworth Street SE1 0QT—*Sec.*, K. J. Tyler.

EPILEPSY ASSOCIATION, BRITISH, Crowthorne House, Bigshotte, New Wokingham Road, Wokingham, Berks RG11 3AY—*Sec.*, T. J. O'Leary.

EPILEPSY, THE NATIONAL SOCIETY FOR (1892), Chalfont Centre for Epilepsy, Chalfont St. Peter, Gerrards Cross, Bucks SL9 0RJ—*Sec.*, Col. D. W. Eking.

ESPERANTO ASSOCIATION OF BRITAIN (1977), 140 Holland Park Avenue W11 4UF—*Hon. Sec.*, J. Brownlee.

EUGENICS SOCIETY (1907), 69 Eccleston Square SW1V 1PJ—*Gen. Sec.*, Miss S. E. Walters.

EUROPEAN SCHOOL (1978), Culham, Abingdon, Oxon OX14 3DZ—*Head*, D. G. E. Hurd.

EVANGELICAL ALLIANCE (1846), 186 Kennington Park Road SE11 4BT—*Gen. Sec.*, Rev. C. R. Calver.

EVANGELICAL LIBRARY, THE, 78A Chiltern Street W1M 2HB—*Deputy Librarian*, Dr. T. P. Crosby.

EXAMINERS UNDER SOLICITORS (SCOTLAND) ACT (1980), Law Society's Hall, 26 Drumsheugh Gardens, Edinburgh EH3 7YR—*Clerk*, K. W. Pritchard.

EXECUTIVES ASSOCIATION OF GREAT BRITAIN LTD., 7 Central Buildings, 24 Southwark Street SE1 1TY—*Sec.*, C. E. Nicholson.

EXPORT, INSTITUTE OF, World Trade Centre, E.1.—*Sec.*, D. N. Royce.

EX-SERVICES MENTAL WELFARE SOCIETY (for H.M. Forces and Merchant Navy men and women, suffering from psychiatric disabilities), Broadway House, The Broadway, Wimbledon SW19 1RL—*Gen. Sec.*, J. S. Le Blanc Smith, R.N.

FABIAN SOCIETY (1884), 11 Dartmouth Street, S.W.1.—*Gen. Sec.*, I. Martin.

FAIRBRIDGE SOCIETY (1909), 119–126 Bush House (N.E.), Aldwych, W.C.2.—*Dir. and Sec.*, Mrs. C. P. MacGregor.

FAIR ISLE BIRD OBSERVATORY TRUST, 21 Regent Terrace, Edinburgh EH7 5BT—*Hon. Sec.*, R. A. Broad.

FAMILY CONCILIATION COUNCIL, NATIONAL (1982), c/o 155 High Street, Dorking, Surrey.—*Chairman*, B. R. Pearce.

FAMILY HISTORY SOCIETIES, FEDERATION OF (1974)—*Administrator*, Mrs. P. A. Saul, 31 Seven Star Road, Solihull, West Midlands B91 2BZ.

FAMILY PLANNING ASSOCIATION, 27–35 Mortimer Street W1N 7RJ—*Gen. Sec.*, A. Service.

FAMILY WELFARE ASSOCIATION (Founded 1869 as CHARITY ORGANIZATION SOCIETY), 501–5 Kingsland Road E8 4AU—*Dir.*, R. E. Morley.

FAUNA AND FLORA PRESERVATION SOCIETY (1903).—*Office*, c/o Zoological Society of London, Regent's Park NW1 4RY—*Exec. Sec.*, J. A. Burton.

FELLOWSHIP HOUSES TRUST (Flatlets for the elderly) (1937), Clock House, Byfleet, Surrey KT14 7RN—*Sec.*, L. P. Leech, J.P.

FIELD STUDIES COUNCIL (1943), Preston Montford, Montford Bridge, Shrewsbury SY4 1HW—*Dir.*, A. D. Thomas.

FIRE ENGINEERS, INSTITUTION OF, 148 New Walk, Leicester LE1 7QB—*Gen. Sec.*, Mrs. C. E. Mackwood.

FIRE PROTECTION ASSOCIATION, 140 Aldersgate Street EC1A 4HX—*Dir.*, C. D. Woodward.

FIRE SERVICES ASSOCIATION, THE BRITISH, 86 London Road, Leicester.—*Gen. Sec.*, T. A. Plummer.

FIRE SERVICES NATIONAL BENEVOLENT FUND (1943), Marine Court, Fitzalan Road, Littlehampton, W. Sussex BN17 5NF—*Hon. Treasurer*, T. Dagnall.

FLEET AIR ARM OFFICERS ASSOCIATION (1957), 94 Piccadilly W1V 0BP.

FOLKLORE SOCIETY, c/o University College London, Gower Street, W.C.1.—*Hon. Sec.*, A. R. Vickery.

FOOD SCIENCE AND TECHNOLOGY, INSTITUTE OF, 20 Queensberry Place SW7 2DR—*Chief Exec.*, Helen G. Wild.

FOOD FROM BRITAIN, 301–344 Market Towers, New Covent Garden Market SW8 5NQ—*Chairman*, N. Saphir.

FORCES HELP SOCIETY AND LORD ROBERTS WORKSHOPS (1899), 122 Brompton Road SW3 1JE—*Comptroller and Sec.*, Col. A. W. Davis, M.B.E.

FOREIGN BONDHOLDERS, COUNCIL OF (1873), 35 High Street, Bromley, Kent.—*Dir.*, M. Gough.

FOREIGN PRESS ASSOCIATION IN LONDON, 11 Carlton House Terrace, S.W.1.—*Pres.*, R. Hill.

FORENSIC SCIENCES, BRITISH ACADEMY OF (1959).—*Sec.-Gen.*, Dr. P. J. Lincoln, Dept. of Haematology, The London Hospital Medical College, Turner Street E1 2AD.

FORESTERS, INSTITUTE OF CHARTERED (1982), 22 Walker Street, Edinburgh EH3 7HR—*Sec.*, Mrs. M. W. Dick.

FORESTRY ASSOCIATION, COMMONWEALTH (1921), c/o Commonwealth Forestry Institute, South Parks Road, Oxford OX1 3RB.

FORESTRY SOCIETY OF ENGLAND, WALES AND NORTHERN IRELAND, ROYAL (1882), 102 High Street, Tring, Herts HP23 4AH—*Dir.*, E. H. M. Harris.

FORESTRY SOCIETY, ROYAL SCOTTISH (1854), 10–11 Atholl Crescent, Edinburgh EH3 8HE—*Sec. and Treas.*, W. B. C. Walker.

FRANCO-BRITISH SOCIETY, Room 636, Linen Hall, 162–168 Regent Street W1R 5TB—*Sec.*, Mrs. C. Stowell.

FREE CHURCH FEDERAL COUNCIL, 27 Tavistock Square WC1H 9HH—*Moderator*, Rev. Dr. D. English; *Gen. Sec.*, Rev. R. J. Hamper, J.P.

FREEDOM ASSOCIATION (1975), Avon House, 360–366 Oxford Street W1N 0AA—*Executive Officer* J. F. Fletcher.

FREEMASONS, GRAND LODGE OF SCOTLAND (1736), Freemasons' Hall, 96 George Street, Edinburgh EH2 3DH—*Grand Master Mason of Scotland*, J. M. Marcus Humphrey of Dinnet, O.ST.J.; *Grand Sec.*, E. S. Falconer, K.ST.J., J.P.

FREEMASONS, UNITED GRAND LODGE OF ENGLAND, Freemasons' Hall, Great Queen Street WC2B 5AZ—*Grand Master*, H.R.H. the Duke of Kent, G.C.M.G., G.C.V.O., A.D.C.; *Pro Grand Master*, The Lord Cornwallis, O.B.E., D.L.; *Deputy Grand Master*, Hon. E. L. Baillieu; *Asst. Grand Master*, The Lord Farnham; *Grand Wardens*, The Viscount Gough; Sir Peter Lane; *Grand Chaplain*, Rev. Dr. M. Morgan; *Grand Sec.*, Cdr. M. B. S. Higham, R.N.

FREEMEN OF CITY OF LONDON, GUILD OF (1908), P.O. Box 153, 40A Ludgate Hill EC4M 7DE—*Master*, B. L. Morgan, C.B.E., O.ST.T., J.P.; *Clerk*, D. Reid.

FREEMEN OF ENGLAND (1966), Pradoe, Oswestry, Shropshire SY11 4ER—*Pres.*, Col. J. F. Kenyon, O.B.E., M.C.

FREIGHT FORWARDERS LTD., THE INSTITUTE OF, Suffield House, 9 Paradise Road, Richmond, Surrey.

FRESHWATER BIOLOGICAL ASSOCIATION (1929), The Ferry House, Far Sawrey, Ambleside, Cumbria LA22 0LP—*Sec. and Director of Laboratories*, Dr. R. T. Clarke.

FRIENDLY SOCIETIES, NATIONAL CONFERENCE OF—*Sec.*, P. M. Madders, Room 313, Victoria House, Vernon Place WC1B 4DP.

FRIENDS OF CATHEDRAL MUSIC (1956), c/o Addington Palace, Croydon CR9 5AD.—*Hon. Gen. Sec.*, N. T. Barnes.

FRIENDS OF THE CLERGY CORP. (incorporating the Friend of the Clergy Corp. and the Poor Clergy Relief Corp.), 27 Medway Street SW1P 2BD—*Sec.*, J. M. Greany.

FRIENDS OF THE NATIONAL LIBRARIES, The British Library WC1B 3DG—*Chairman*, The Lord Egremont; *Hon. Sec.*, J. F. Fuggles.

FRIENDS OF THE ELDERLY & GENTLEFOLK'S HELP (*formerly* FRIENDS OF THE POOR), 42 Ebury Street SW1W 0LZ—*Gen. Sec.*, Rev. J. Schofield.

FURNITURE HISTORY SOCIETY (1964).—*Hon. Sec.*, Mrs. H. Hayward, c/o Dept. of Furniture and Woodwork, Victoria and Albert Museum SW7 2RL.

GALLIPOLI ASSOCIATION (1915).—*Hon. Sec.*, K. Tranmer, 100 Ramsgill Drive, Ilford, Essex IG2 7TP.

GAME CONSERVANCY, THE, Fordingbridge, Hants SP6 1EF—*Dir.*, R. M. Van Oss.

GARDEN HISTORY SOCIETY (1965), 66 Granville Park SE13 7DX—*Hon. Membership Sec.*, Mrs. A. Richards.

GARDENERS' ASSOCIATION, THE GOOD, Arkley Manor Farm, Rowley Lane, Arkley, Barnet, Herts EN5 3HS—*Hon. Dir.*, C. R. G. Shewell-Cooper, N.C.H.

GARDENERS' ROYAL BENEVOLENT SOCIETY (1839), Bridge House, 139 Kingston Road, Leatherhead, Surrey KT22 7NT—*Sec./Administr.*, C. R. C. Bunce.

GAS CONSUMERS' COUNCIL, NATIONAL, 4th Floor, 162 Regent Street, W.1.—*Dir.*, J. Hosker.

GAS ENGINEERS, INSTITUTION OF (1863), 17 Grosvenor Crescent, S.W.1.—*Sec.*, D. J. Chapman.

GEMMOLOGICAL ASSOCIATION OF GREAT BRITAIN (1931), St. Dunstan's House, Carey Lane EC2V 8AB—*Sec.*, C. Lenan.

GENEALOGICAL RESEARCH SOCIETY, IRISH.—*Sec.*, F. B. Payton, Glenholme, High Oakham Road, Mansfield, Notts NG18 5AJ.

GENEALOGISTS AND RECORD AGENTS, ASSOCIATION OF (1968), 1 Woodside Close, Caterham, Surrey CR3 6AU—*Sec.*, Mrs. J. Tooke.

GENEALOGISTS, SOCIETY OF (1911), 14 Charterhouse Buildings, Goswell Road EC1M 7BA—*Dir.*, A. J. Camp.

GENERAL PRACTITIONERS, ROYAL COLLEGE OF (1952), 14–15 Princes Gate, Hyde Park SW7 1PU—*Gen. Adminstr.*, Mrs. S. Fountain.

GENTLEPEOPLE, GUILD OF AID FOR (1904), 10 St. Christopher's Place W1M 6HY—*Sec.*, Mrs. G. A. Burgess.

GEOGRAPHICAL ASSOCIATION, 343 Fulwood Road, Sheffield S10 3BP.—*Joint Hon. Secs.*, Dr. J. A. Binns; Miss E. M. Fyfe.

GEOGRAPHICAL SOCIETY, ROYAL (1830), 1 Kensington Gore SW7 2AR—*Pres.*, Sir George Bishop, C.B., O.B.E.; *Hon. Secs.*, Prof. E. H. Brown; Prof. A. S. Goudie; *Hon. Foreign Sec.*, Lt.-Col. S. Gilbert; *Hon. Treas.*, A. Tritton; *Director and Sec.*, Dr. J.

Hemming; *Keeper of the Map Room*, Brig. G. R. Gathercole; *Librarian*, D. Wileman.

GEOGRAPHICAL SOCIETY, MANCHESTER (1884), 274 The Corn Exchange Buildings, Manchester M4 3EY—*Sec.*, Miss E. Whalley.

GEOGRAPHICAL SOCIETY, ROYAL SCOTTISH (1884), 10 Randolph Crescent, Edinburgh 3.—*Sec.*, D. G. Moir.

GEOLOGICAL SOCIETY (1807), Burlington House, Piccadilly W1V 0JU—*Pres.*, Prof. C. H. Holland; *Secs.*, Dr. R. G. Park; Dr. A. J. Martin; Dr. L. R. M. Cocks; W. J. French, PH.D.; *Foreign Sec.*, Prof. J. B. Dawson; *Exec. Sec.*, R. M. Bateman.

GEOLOGISTS' ASSOCIATION—*Hon. Gen. Sec.*, Dr. R. B. Stokes, Burlington House, Piccadilly W1V 9AG

GEOLOGISTS, THE INSTITUTION OF (1977), Burlington House, Piccadilly W1V 9HG—*Pres.*, D. C. Ion; *Secs.*, B. N. F. Hunt, Dr. P. C. Wright.

GEORGIAN GROUP (1937), 37 Spital Square E1 6DY—*Sec.*, R. White.

GIFTED CHILDREN, NATIONAL ASSOCIATION FOR (1966), 1 South Audley Street W1Y 5DQ—*Dir.*, J. Welch.

GILBERT AND SULLIVAN SOCIETY.—*Hon. Sec.*, 273 Northfield Avenue W5 4UA

GIRL GUIDES ASSOCIATION.—An organization founded by the first Lord Baden-Powell as a sister movement to the Scouts and incorporated by Royal Charter in 1922. In 1984 the total membership in the United Kingdom was 784,631. *Commonwealth Headquarters*, 17–19 Buckingham Palace Road, SW1W 0PT.

GIRLS' BRIGADE, THE, Brigade House, Parsons Green, SW6 4TH—*Brigade Sec. for Eng. & Wales*, Miss D. M. Cosser.

GIRLS' FRIENDLY SOCIETY AND TOWNSEND FELLOWSHIP (1875), 126 Queens Gate SW7 5LQ—*Gen. Sec.*, Miss H. G. Smith.

GIRLS OF THE REALM GUILD (1900).—Small educational grants towards professional training of women. Applications before April for ensuing academic year to: Mrs. B. Hayward, 2 Watchoak, Blackham, Tunbridge Wells, Kent TN3 9TP.

GIRLS' VENTURE CORPS, Redhill Aerodrome, Kings Mill Lane, South Nutfield, Redhill, Surrey RH1 5JY. A uniformed youth movement for girls between 13 and 20.—*Sec.*, Miss H. Prosper.

GLASS TECHNOLOGY, SOCIETY OF (1916), 20 Hallam Gate Road, Sheffield S10 5BT—*Hon. Sec.*, T. S. Busby.

GRAPHIC ARTISTS, SOCIETY OF (1919), 17 Carlton House Terrace, S.W.1.—*Pres.*, Lorna B. Kell.

GREATER LONDON PLAYING FIELDS ASSOCIATION (1926), 147 Church Street W2 1NA—*Sec.*, Capt. D. N. Forbes, D.S.C., R.N. (ret.).

GREATER LONDON RED CROSS BLOOD TRANSFUSION SERVICE (1921), 4 Collingham Gardens SW5 0HW [01–373 1056]. Hours, 9 a.m. to 10 p.m. every day.

GREEK INSTITUTE (1969) (for the promotion of modern Greek studies), 34 Bush Hill Road N21 2DS—*Dir.*, Dr. Kypros Tofallis.

GROCERS ASSOCIATION, BRITISH INDEPENDENT, 17 Farnborough Street, Farnborough, Hants. GU14 8AG—*Nat. Sec.*, I. A. McKee.

GULBENKIAN FOUNDATION, see CALOUSTE.

HAKLUYT SOCIETY (1846), c/o Map Library, The British Library, Ref. Div., Great Russell Street WC1B 3DG—*Joint Hon. Secs.*, Dr. T. E. Armstrong; Mrs. S. Tyacke.

HANSARD SOCIETY FOR PARLIAMENTARY GOVERNMENT (1944), 16 Gower Street WC1E 6DP—*Sec.*, Mrs. M. T. Goudie.

HARVEIAN SOCIETY OF LONDON.—*Exec. Sec.*, Maj. T. Tudor-Williams, 11 Chandos Street, Cavendish Square W1M 0EB

HEAD TEACHERS, NATIONAL ASSOCIATION OF.—*Gen. Sec.*, D. M. Hart, Holly House, 6 Paddockhall Road, Haywards Heath, West Sussex RH16 1RG.

HEALTH AUTHORITIES IN ENGLAND AND WALES, THE NATIONAL ASSOCIATION (1974), Garth House, 47 Edgbaston Park Road, Birmingham B15 2RS—*Dir.*, P. A. Hunt.

HEALTH EDUCATION COUNCIL, THE (1968), 78 New Oxford Street WC1A 1AH—*Dir.-Gen.*, Dr. D. A. Player.

HEALTH EDUCATION, INSTITUTE OF.—*Hon. Sec.*, Dr. L. Baric, 14 High Elm Road, Hale Barns, Cheshire WA15 0JE.

HEALTH, GUILD OF (1904), Edward Wilson House, 26 Queen Anne Street W1M 9LB—*Sec.*, Ms. T. F. Parker.

HEALTH SERVICES MANAGEMENT, INSTITUTE OF (1902), 75 Portland Place W1N 4AN—*Sec.*, L. B. Akid.

HELLENIC STUDIES, SOCIETY FOR THE PROMOTION OF (1879), 31–34 Gordon Square WC1H 0PP—*Pres.*, Prof. G. B. Kerferd; *Hon. Sec.*, Prof. J. P. Barron, F.S.A.

HENRY GEORGE FOUNDATION, 177 Vauxhall Bridge Road SW1V 1EU—*Sec.*, Mrs. B. P. Sobrielo.

HERALDIC AND GENEALOGICAL STUDIES, INSTITUTE OF (1961), 79–82 Northgate, Canterbury, Kent CT1 1BA—*Dir.*, Dr. G. M. Swinfield.

HERALDRY SOCIETY, THE (1947), 44–45 Museum Street WC1A 1LY—*Sec.*, Mrs. V. Wreford Smith.

HERALDRY SOCIETY OF SCOTLAND (1977).—*Sec.*, W. R. M. Adams, Limegrove, High Street, Gifford, Haddington, East Lothian EH41 4QU.

HERPETOLOGICAL SOCIETY, BRITISH (1947), c/o Zoological Society of London, Regent's Park NW1 4RY—*Pres.*, The Earl of Cranbrook.

HIGHWAYS AND TRANSPORTATION, INSTITUTION OF (1930), 3 Lygon Place, Ebury Street SW1W 0JS—*Sec.*, Miss P. A. Steel.

HILL FARMING RESEARCH ORGANIZATION.—*Hon. Gen. Sec.*, Dr. P. Newbould, Bush Estate, Penicuik, Midlothian EH26 0PY.

HISTORICAL ASSOCIATION (1906), 59A Kennington Park Road SE11 4JH—*Sec.*, Mrs. M. Stiles.

HISTORICAL SOCIETY, ROYAL (1868), University College London, Gower Street WC1E 6BT—*Pres.*, Dr. G. E. Aylmer; *Exec. Sec.*, Mrs. J. Chapman.

HONG KONG ASSOCIATION, THE (1961), Regis House, 43–46 King William Street EC4R 9BE—*Exec. Dir.*, Brig. B. G. Hickey, O.B.E., M.C.

HORATIAN SOCIETY (1933).—*Hon. Sec.*, C. P. Sydenham, 4 Stone Buildings, Lincolns Inn WC2A 3XT.

HOROLOGICAL INSTITUTE, BRITISH (1858), Upton Hall, Upton, Newark, Notts NG23 5TE—*Sec.*, W. M. G. Evans.

HOROLOGICAL SOCIETY, ANTIQUARIAN (1953), New House, High Street, Ticehurst, E. Sussex TN5 7AL—*Sec.*, Cdr. G. Clarke.

HOSPITAL FEDERATION, INTERNATIONAL (1947), 2 St. Andrew's Place NW1 4LB—*Dir. Gen.*, M. C. Hardie.

HOSPITALS CONTRIBUTORY SCHEMES ASSOCIATION, BRITISH (1948), 4th Floor, Refuge Building, Baldwin Street, Bristol BS1 1SE—*Sec.*, C. D. M. Kerr.

HOSPITAL SATURDAY FUND, THE (1873).—*Head Office*, 192–198 Vauxhall Bridge Road, S.W.1. *Sec.*, Miss I. Gleeson.

HOSPITAL SAVING ASSOCIATION, THE, Hambleden House, Andover, Hants SP10 1LQ—*Gen. Sec.*, I. Forbes, M.B.E., D.F.C.

HOTEL CATERING AND INSTITUTIONAL MANAGEMENT ASSOCIATION, 191 Trinity Road SW17 7HN—*Dir.*, Miss E. Gadsby.

HOTELS, RESTAURANTS AND CATERERS ASSOCIATION, BRITISH (1907), 40 Duke Street W1M 6HR—*Chief Exec.*, C. Derby, O.B.E.

HOUSE OF HOSPITALITY LTD., Holy Cross Priory, Cross-in-Hand, Heathfield, Sussex. 28 homes for old people.—*Dir.*, Mother Mary Garson.

HOUSE OF ST. BARNABAS IN SOHO (House of Charity for Homeless Women in London) (1846), 1 Greek Street, Soho Square W1V 6NQ—*Dir.*, Gp. Capt. H. A. Lax.

HOUSING AID SOCIETY, CATHOLIC (1956), 189a Old Brompton Road SW5 0AR—*Dir.*, R. Kahn.

HOUSING AND TOWN PLANNING COUNCIL, NATIONAL (1900), 14–18 Old Street EC1V 9AB—*Dir.*, R. Walker.

HOUSING ASSOCIATION FOR OFFICERS' FAMILIES (1916), Alban Dobson House, Green Lane, Morden, Surrey SM4 5NS—*Gen. Sec.*, R. Davis.

HOVERCRAFT SOCIETY, THE (1971), Forest Lodge West, Fawley Road, Hythe, Southampton, Hants. SO4 6ZZ—*Sec.*, Miss J. M. Walker.

HOWARD LEAGUE, THE (1866), 322 Kennington Park Road SE11 4PP. For education and research into the criminal justice system.—*Dir.*, D. E. S. Jenkins.

HUGUENOT SOCIETY OF LONDON (1885), c/o Barclays Bank Ltd., 1 Pall Mall East SW1Y 5AX—*Hon. Sec.*, Miss I. Scouloudi, M.SC., F.S.A., F.R.Hist.S.

HYDROFOIL SOCIETY, INTERNATIONAL, 51 Welbeck Street W.1.—*Chief Exec.*, Juanita Kalerghi.

HYDROGRAPHIC SOCIETY (1972), North East London Polytechnic Dept. of Land Surveying, Dagenham, Essex RM8 2AS—*Hon. Sec.*, Dr. R. C. Britton.

HYMN SOCIETY OF GREAT BRITAIN AND IRELAND, THE (1936), *Sec.*, Rev. A. Luff, 7 Little Cloister, Westminster Abbey SW1P 3PL.

INDEPENDENT SCHOOLS BURSARS' ASSOCIATION, *Sec.*, D. J. Bird, Woodlands, Closewood Road, Denmead, Hants PO7 6JD.

INDEPENDENT SCHOOLS CAREERS ORGANIZATION, 12a–18a Princess Way, Camberley, Surrey GU15 3SP—*Dir. and Chief Exec.*, R. N. Exton, M.A., J.P.

INDEPENDENT SCHOOLS INFORMATION SERVICE (I.S.I.S.) (1972), 56 Buckingham Gate SW1E 6AG—*Dir.*, D. J. Woodhead.

INDEPENDENT SCHOOLS JOINT COUNCIL, *Gen. Sec.*, A. G. Hearnden, 25 Victoria Street SW1H 0EX.

INDEXERS, SOCIETY OF, 38 Stanhope Road, Reading RG2 7HN—*Hon. Sec.*, D. T. O'Rourke.

INDUSTRIAL ARTISTS AND DESIGNERS, SOCIETY OF (1930), 12 Carlton House Terrace SW1Y 5AH—*Dir.*, M. Sadler-Forster.

INDUSTRIAL CHRISTIAN FELLOWSHIP (1877), 4 Streche Road, Swanage, Dorset BH19 1NF—*Dir.*, J. D. Davis.

INDUSTRIAL MANAGERS, INSTITUTION OF, Industrial Management House, Cardiff Road, Luton, Beds.

INDUSTRIAL MARKETING RESEARCH ASSOCIATION.—*Admin. Sec.*, Mrs. M. Everard, 11 Bird Street, Lichfield, Staffs. WS13 6PW.

INDUSTRIAL PARTICIPATION ASSOCIATION (1884), 85 Tooley Street SE1 2QZ—*Dir.*, D. Wallace Bell.

INDUSTRIAL SOCIETY, THE (1918), 3 Carlton House Terrace SW1Y 5DG—*Dir.*, W. J. P. M. Garnett, C.B.E.; *Sec.*, M. R. Hyde.

INDUSTRY AND PARLIAMENT TRUST, 25 Victoria Street S.W.1. Aims to provide practical ways for parliamentarians and industrialists to bridge the gap between industry and parliament.—*Pres.*, Rt. Hon. B. Weatherill, M.P.; *Dir.*, A. Maisner, C.B., C.B.E., A.F.C.

INFORMATION SCIENTISTS, INSTITUTE OF (1958), 44 Museum Street WC1A 1LY—*Exec. Sec.*, Mrs. S. A. Carter.

INNER WHEEL CLUBS IN GREAT BRITAIN AND IRELAND, ASSOCIATION OF (1934), 51 Warwick Square SW1V 2AT—*Gen. Sec.*, Miss J. Dobson.

INSTITUTE OF MASTERS OF WINE, (1955), Black Swan House, Kennet Wharf Lane EC4V 3BE—*Sec.*, Mrs. B. H. Andrews.

INSURANCE BROKERS REGISTRATION COUNCIL, 15 St. Helen's Place EC3A 6DS—*Registrar and Sec.*, J. E. Fryer, M.B.E.

INSURANCE INSTITUTE, CHARTERED (1897), 20 Aldermanbury EC2V 7HY—*Sec.-Gen.*, P. V. Saxton.

INSURERS, ASSOCIATION OF BRITISH (1985), Aldermary House, Queen Street EC4N 1TT—*Sec. Gen.*, T. H. M. Oppé.

INTERCONTINENTAL CHURCH SOCIETY, 175 Tower Bridge Road SE1 2AQ—*Gen. Sec.*, Rev. Canon D. R. Irving.

INTERNATIONAL FRIENDSHIP LEAGUE (1931), 3 Creswick Road, Acton, W.3.—*Chairman.*, M. J. A. Prowse.

INTERNATIONAL LAW ASSOCIATION (1873), 3 Paper Buildings, Temple EC4Y 7EU—*Chairman*, The Rt. Hon. Lord Wilberforce, P.C., C.M.G., O.B.E.; *Sec.*, R. C. H. Briggs.

INTERNATIONAL POLICE ASSOCIATION (British Section).—*National Headquarters*, 1 Fox Road, West Bridgford, Nottingham NG2 6AJ—*Chief Exec. Officer*, K. H. Robinson.

INTERNATIONAL SHIPPING FEDERATION (1909), 30–32 St. Mary Axe EC3A 8ET—*Pres.*, W. N. Menzies-Wilson; *Sec.*, D. A. Dearsley.

INTERNATIONAL STUDENTS TRUST (1962), 229 Gt. Portland Street, W.1.—*President*, The Duke of Grafton, K.G.; *Dir.*, G. Rates.

INTERNATIONAL TIN RESEARCH INSTITUTE (1932), Fraser Road, Greenford, Middlesex UB6 7AQ—*Dir.*, D. A. Robins, PH.D.

INTERNATIONAL UNION FOR LAND VALUE TAXATION AND FREE TRADE, 177 Vauxhall Bridge Road SW1V 1EU—*Sec.*, Mrs. B. P. Sobrielo.

INTERNATIONAL VOLUNTARY SERVICE (1920), Ceresole House, 53 Regent Road, Leicester LE1 6YL—*Publicity Co-ordinator*, B. Greaves.

INTER-VARSITY CLUBS, ASSOCIATION OF (1946), 3–5 The Piazza, Covent Garden WC2E 8HF—*Sec.*, M. Rooke-Matthews.

INVALID CHILDREN'S AID ASSOCIATION (LONDON), INCORPORATED (1888), 126 Buckingham Palace Road SW1W 9SB—Information service on all aspects of handicap; family social work in parts of London and Surrey; residential special schools.—*Dir.*, J. McKinnon.

INVALIDS-AT-HOME (1966).—*Hon. Sec.*, Mrs. E. Pierce, 23 Farm Avenue NW2. Helps seriously disabled people living at home.

IRAN SOCIETY (1936), 42 Devonshire Street W1N 1LN—*Pres.*, The Viscount Runciman of Doxford, O.B.E., A.F.C.; *Hon. Sec.*, K. Bradford.

IRISH SOCIETY, THE HONOURABLE THE (1613), Irish Chamber, Guildhall Yard, E.C.2.—*Sec.*, B. E. Manning; *Representative (Ireland)*, Cmdr. P. C. D. Campbell, M.V.O., D.L., R.N.

IRON AND STEEL INSTITUTE, see METALS, THE INSTITUTE OF.

JAPAN ASSOCIATION, THE (1950), Regis House, 43–46 King William Street EC4R 9BE—*Exec. Dir.*, Brig. B. G. Hickey, O.B.E., M.C.

JERUSALEM AND THE MIDDLE EAST CHURCH ASSOCIATION (1887), The Old Gatehouse, Castle Hill, Farnham, Surrey GU9 0AE—*Gen. Sec.*, The Rev. R. Roberts, C.B.

JEWISH WELFARE BOARD (1859).—*Exec. Dir.*, M. I. Carlowe, 221 Golders Green Road, N.W.11.

JEWISH HISTORICAL SOCIETY OF ENGLAND—*Hon. Sec.*, C. Drukker, 33 Seymour Place W1H 5AP.

JEWISH YOUTH, ASSOCIATION FOR (1899), A.J.Y. House, 50 Lindley Street E1 3AX.—*Exec. Dir.*, A. Greenbat, J.P.

JEWS, CHURCH'S MINISTRY AMONG THE, 30c Clarence Road, St. Albans, Herts AL1 4JJ—*Sec.*, Rev. W. F. Barker.

JEWS AND CHRISTIANS, LONDON SOCIETY OF (1927), 28 St. John's Wood Road, N.W.8.—*Pres.*, Rev. Prof. G. Parrinder, D.D., Ph.D., D.Litt.; *Joint Chairmen*, Very Rev. Edward F. Carpenter, Ph. D., Rabbi Dr. John D. Rayner, D.D.; The Dean of Westminster; *Sec.*, Mrs. E. Nathan.

JOHN INNES INSTITUTE (1910), Colney Lane, Norwich NR4 7UH—*Director*, Prof. H. W. Woolhouse, Ph.D.

JOURNALISTS, THE INSTITUTE OF, Bedford Chambers, Covent Garden WC2E 8HA—*Gen. Sec.*, R. F. Farmer, O.B.E.

JULES VERNE CIRCLE, 125 Markyate Road, Dagenham, Essex.—*Sec.* E. Ford.

JUSTICE (British Section of the International Commission of Jurists) (1957), 95A Chancery Lane WC2A 1DT—*Dir.*, Leah Levin.

JUSTICES' CLERKS' SOCIETY (1839).—*Hon. Sec.*, B. H. Forster, Magistrates' Court, Cwmbran, Gwent NP44 3YA.

KEEP BRITAIN TIDY GROUP, Bostel House, 37 West Street, Brighton, Sussex BN1 2RE—*Dir. Gen.*, D. J. Lewis.

KING EDWARD'S HOSPITAL FUND FOR LONDON (1897), 14 Palace Court W2 4HT—A charity which uses its annual income to help hospitals improve the effectiveness and efficiency of their service to patients. The Fund divides its income between several major activities; making grants to hospitals and related organizations both within and outside the National Health Service but confined to those in or serving the Greater London area; providing education for health services staffs through the King's Fund College; sponsoring experiment and enquiry and providing information through its various experts and through the King's Fund Centre.—*Chairman of Management Committee*, The Hon. H. Astor; *Treasurer*, R. J. Dent; *Secretary*, R. J. Maxwell.

KING GEORGE'S FUND FOR SAILORS (1917), 1 Chesham Street SW1X 8NF. The central and only fund which supports all seafarers—or their dependants—in need. Distributes over £100,000 in grants annually.—*Gen. Sec.*, K. Sutherland.

KING GEORGE'S JUBILEE TRUST, 8 Buckingham Street WC2N 6BU—Inaugurated in 1935 in commemoration of the Silver Jubilee of King George V. Its objects are the advancement of the physical, mental and spiritual welfare of the younger generation.—*Dir.*, H. Haywood, O.B.E., D.L.

KIPLING SOCIETY, THE (1927), c/o Royal Commonwealth Society, 18 Northumberland Avenue WC2N 5BJ—*Hon. Sec.*, N. Entract.

LADIES IN REDUCED CIRCUMSTANCES, SOCIETY FOR THE ASSISTANCE OF (1886), Lancaster House, 25 Hornyold Road, Malvern, Worcs WR14 1QQ—*Sec.*, Mrs. E. M. Klee.

LANCASTRIANS IN LONDON, ASSOCIATION OF (1892), Burnley House, 129 Kingsway WC2B 6NJ—*Hon. Sec.*, J. D. Dwyer.

LANDSCAPE INSTITUTE (Professional Institute for Landscape Architects, Managers and Scientists), 12 Carlton House Terrace SW1Y 5AH.

LAND-VALUE TAXATION LEAGUE, 177 Vauxhall Bridge Road SW1V 1EU—*Pres.*, V. G. Saldji.

LAW REPORTING FOR ENGLAND AND WALES, INCORPORATED COUNCIL OF (1865), 3 Stone Buildings, Lincoln's Inn WC2A 3XN—*Sec.* R. H. Pettit.

LEAGUE OF THE HELPING HAND, Baileys, Church Street, Charlbury, Oxford OX7 3PR.—*Sec.*, Mrs. D. R. Colvin.

LEAGUE OF WELLDOERS (incorporated) (1893), 119–121 Limekiln Lane, Liverpool L5 8SN—*Warden and Sec.*, K. H. Stanton.

LEATHER AND HIDE TRADES' BENEVOLENT INSTITUTION (1860), 60 Wickham Hill, Hurstpierpoint, Sussex BN6 9NP—*Sec.*, Mrs. G. M. Stapleton, M.B.E.

LEGAL EXECUTIVES, INSTITUTE OF, Kempston Manor, Kempston, Bedford MK42 7AB—*Sec.*, L. A. Evans.

LEPROSY GUILD, ST FRANCIS (1895), 21 The Boltons, S.W.10.—*Hon. Sec.*, Sr. Eileen McKee.

LEPROSY MISSION, THE (England and Wales) (1874), 50 Portland Place W1N 3DG—*Chairman*, Lady Richardson; *Exec. Dir.*, The Rev. R. J. Findlay.

LEUKAEMIA RESEARCH FUND (1962), 43 Great Ormond Street WC1N 3JJ—*Dir.*, G. J. Piller, O.B.E.

LIBRARY ASSOCIATION (1877), 7 Ridgmount Street WC1E 7AE—*Chief Exec.*, G. Cunningham.

LIFEBOATS. See "ROYAL NATIONAL."

LINGUISTS, INSTITUTE OF (1910), 24a Highbury Grove, N.5.—*Gen. Sec.*, A. Bell.

LINNEAN SOCIETY OF LONDON (1788), Burlington House W1V 0LQ—*Pres.*, Prof. W. G. Chaloner; *Treas.*, C. M. Hutt; *Secs.*, Dr. F. A. Bisby (*Botany*); Dr. Doris M. Kermack (*Zoology*); Prof. J. D. Pye (*Editorial*); *Exec. Sec.*, Cdr. J. H. Fiddian-Green.

LIONS CLUBS INTERNATIONAL (British Isles & Ireland) (1949).—*Gen. Sec.*, T. L. Packer, 22 Craddock Street, Swansea, W. Glamorgan SA1 3HE.

LIVERPOOL COTTON ASSOCIATION LTD., 620 Cotton Exchange Building, Edmund Street, Liverpool L3 9LH.—*Dir. Gen. and Sec.*, J. Wilson-Smith.

LLOYD'S, Lime Street EC3M 7HA—*Chairman* (1984), P. N. Miller; *Deputy Chairmen*, W. N. M. Lawrence; D. E. Coleridge; *Deputy Chairman and Chief Exec.*, I. H. Davison.

LLOYD'S PATRIOTIC FUND (1803), Lloyd's, Lime Street EC3M 7HA—*Sec.*, Miss J. H. Eifert.

LLOYD'S REGISTER OF SHIPPING (1760), 71 Fenchurch Street EC3M 7HA—*Chairman*, H. R. MacLeod [Office of *Lloyd's Register Book, Rules for the Classification of Ships, Marine and Industrial Inspection Services.*] *Deputy Chairman and Chairman of the Sub-Committees of Classification*, H. J. C. Browne, O.B.E.; *Chief Ship Surveyor*, J. G. Beaumont; *Chief Engineer Surveyor*, C. Archer; *Secretary*, W. T. Leadbetter.

LOCAL AUTHORITIES, INTERNATIONAL UNION OF (1913), (also COUNCIL OF EUROPEAN MUNICIPALITIES AND REGIONS (1951)), British Section, 12 Old Queen Street SW1H 9HP—*Exec. Sec.*, P. N. Bongers.

LOCAL AUTHORITY CHIEF EXECUTIVES, SOCIETY OF.—*Hon. Sec.*, A. J. Greenwell, County Hall, Northampton, NN1 1DN.

LONDON APPRECIATION SOCIETY (1932), 17 Manson Mews SW7 5AF. Visits to places of historic and modern interest in and around London.—*Hon. Sec.*, Bryant Peers.

LONDON BOROUGHS ASSOCIATION (1964), Westminster City Hall, Victoria Street SW1E 6QP—*Hon. Sec.*, R. G. Brooke.

LONDON CITY MISSION (1835), 175 Tower Bridge Road SE1 2AH—*Gen. Sec.*, Rev. D. M. Whyte.

LONDON CORNISH ASSOCIATION (1898), *Hon. Gen. Sec.*, N. S. Bunney, 119 Warwick Road N11 2SR.

LONDON COURT OF INTERNATIONAL ARBITRATION (1892), 75 Cannon Street EC4N 5BH—*Chairman*, J. F. Phillips, C.B.E. *Registrar*, B. W. Vigrass, O.B.E., V.R.D.

LONDON FLOTILLA (Association of Reserve and Retired Officers of The Royal Navy).—*Hon. Sec.*, Lt. Cdr. P. A. G. Norman R.D., R.N.R., Marden Rise, 81 Marden Hill, Fetcham, Surrey KT22 9HG.

LONDON LIBRARY, THE (1841), 14 St. James's Square SW1Y 4LG—*Librarian*, D. Matthews.

LONDON MAGISTRATES' CLERKS' ASSOCIATION (1889), *Hon. Sec.*, Miss A. F. Damazer, Deputy Chief Clerk, Thames Magistrates' Court, Aylward Street E.1.

"LONDON OVER THE BORDER" CHURCH FUND (1878), New Street, Chelmsford, Essex CM1 1NG—*Sec.*, D. J. Newman.

LONDON PLAYING FIELDS SOCIETY (1890), Headquarters, Boston Manor Playing Field, Boston Gardens, Brentford, Middlesex.—*Sec.*, C. J. M. Clayton.

LONDON SOCIETY, THE, Room G210, The City University, Northampton Square EC1V 0HB—*Hon. Sec.*, Mrs. G. M. Gorer.

LORD MAYOR TRELOAR COLLEGE, for education and care of physically handicapped boys and girls. Administered by the Treloar Trust, Holybourne, Nr. Alton, Hants. GU34 4JX—*Headmaster*, A. M. MacPherson.

LORD'S DAY OBSERVANCE SOCIETY (1831), 5 Victory Avenue, Morden, Surrey SM4 6DL—*Gen. Sec.*, J. G. Roberts.

LORD'S TAVERNERS, THE, 1 Chester Street SW1X 7HP—*Dir.*, Capt. J. A. R. Swainson, O.B.E., R.N.

LOTTERIES COUNCIL, c/o Winkworth and Pemberton, 22 Greencoat Place S.W.1.—*Sec.* R. A. Cummins.

MAGISTRATES' ASSOCIATION (1920), 28 Fitzroy Square, W1P 6DD—*Pres.*, The Lord Chancellor; *Sec.*, G. Norman, J.P.

MAIL USERS' ASSOCIATION, Communications House, 137 Dulwich Road SE24 0NG—*Exec. Dir.*, M. E. Corby.

MALAYSIA, SINGAPORE AND BRUNEI ASSOCIATION (1955), 90 Fenchurch Street EC3M 4BY—*Sec.*, Mrs. J. Taylor.

MALAYSIAN RUBBER PRODUCERS' RESEARCH ASSOCIATION (1938), Tun Abdul Razak Laboratory, Brickendonbury, Herts SG13 8NL—*Co. Sec.*, S. Singh.

MALCOLM SARGENT CANCER FUND FOR CHILDREN.—*Gen. Administrator*, Miss S. Darley, 14 Abingdon Road W8 6AF.

MALONE SOCIETY (for the publication of scholarly editions and facsimiles of early English dramatic texts and records).—*Hon. Sec.*, Dr. Lois Potter, Dept. of English, University of Leicester LE1 7RH.

MANAGEMENT, BRITISH INSTITUTE OF, Management House, Parker Street WC2B 5PT—*Dir.-Gen.*, Dr. J. Constable.

MANAGEMENT AND PROFESSIONAL STAFFS, ASSOCIATION OF, Parkgates, Bury New Road, Prestwich, Manchester M25 8JX—*Exec. Sec.*, Dr. M. Gillibrand.

MANAGEMENT SERVICES, INSTITUTE OF, 1 Cecil Court, London Road, Enfield, Middx. EN2 6DD—*Dir. and Gen. Sec.*, E. A. King.

MANORIAL SOCIETY OF GREAT BRITAIN (1906), 104 Kennington Road SE1 6RE—*Hon. Chairman*, R. A. Smith.

MARIE CURIE MEMORIAL FOUNDATION (for the welfare of cancer patients), 28 Belgrave Square SW1X 8QG—*Sec.*, P. A. Sturgess.

MARINE ARTISTS, ROYAL SOCIETY OF (1939), 17 Carlton House Terrace, S.W.1.—*Pres.*, D. Cobb.

MARINE BIOLOGICAL ASSOCIATION OF THE U.K. (1884), The Laboratory, Citadel Hill, Plymouth, PL1 2PB—*Sec. to Council and Director of Plymouth Laboratory*, E. J. Denton, C.B.E., SC.D., F.R.S.

MARINE ENGINEERS, INSTITUTE OF (1889), 76 Mark Lane EC3R 7JN—*Sec.*, J. Stuart Robinson.

MARINE SOCIETY, THE (1756), 202 Lambeth Road, SE1 7JW—*Dir.*, R. Hope, O.B.E., D.Phil.; *Sec.*, Lt. Cdr. R. M. Frampton, R.N.

MARIO LANZA EDUCATIONAL FOUNDATION (for Singers)—*Hon. Sec.*, Pauline Franklin, Flat 21, Chiswick House, 210 Bell Barn Road, Edgbaston, Birmingham BI5 2AA.

MARKET AUTHORITIES, NATIONAL ASSOCIATION OF BRITISH.—*Sec.*, B. Ormshaw, 19 Derwent Avenue, Milnrow, Rochdale, Lancs. OL16 3UD.

MARKETING, INSTITUTE OF (1911), Moor Hall, Cookham, Maidenhead, Berks. SL6 9QH—*Sec.*, W. E. Hinder.

MARK MASTER MASONS, GRAND LODGE OF (1856), Masons' Hall, 86 St. James's Street SW1—*Grand Master*, H.R.H. Prince Michael of Kent; *Grand Sec.*, W. J. Leake.

MASONIC BENEVOLENT INSTITUTION, ROYAL (1842), 20 Great Queen Street WC2B 5BG—*Sec.*, N. A. Grout.

MASONIC BENEVOLENT INSTITUTIONS IN IRELAND; *Masonic Girls' Benefit Fund* (1792); *Masonic Boys' Benefit Fund* (1867); *Victoria Jubilee Masonic Annuity Fund* (1887).—*Sec.*, R. J. Clinton, 19 Molesworth Street, Dublin 2.

MASONIC DEGREES.—ORDER OF THE TEMPLE, Masons' Hall, 86 St. James's Street, S.W.1.—*Grand Master*, H. D. Still; *Great Seneschal*, Lord Swansea; *Great Vice-Chancellor*, W. J. Leake.

MASONIC TRUST FOR GIRLS AND BOYS (1985), P.O. Box 135, Great Queen Street WC2B 5BD—*Joint Secs.*, A. R. Jole, Col. R. K. Hind.

MASTER BUILDERS, FEDERATION OF, Gordon Fisher House, 33 John Street, W.C.1.—*Nat. Dir.*, W. S. Hilton.

MASTERS OF FOXHOUNDS ASSOCIATION (1881), Parsloes Cottage, Bagendon, Cirencester, Glos.—*Sec.*, A. H. B. Hart.

MATERNAL AND CHILD WELFARE, NATIONAL ASSOCIATION FOR (1911), 1 South Audley Street W1Y 6JS—*Gen. Sec.*, W. Rice.

MATHEMATICAL ASSOCIATION (1871), 259 London Road, Leicester LE2 3BE—*Pres.*, Miss H. B. Shuard; *Hon. Secs.*, Miss M. M. Lawton; J. A. Goodwin.

MATHEMATICS AND ITS APPLICATIONS, INSTITUTE OF (1964), Maitland House, Warrior Square, Southend, Essex SS1 2JY—*Sec. and Registrar*, N. Clarke, O.B.E.

MEASUREMENT AND CONTROL, INSTITUTE OF (1944), 20 Peel Street, W.8.—*Sec.*, A. Sensicle.

MECHANICAL ENGINEERS, INSTITUTION OF, 1 Birdcage Walk, S.W.1.—*Sec.*, A. McKay, C.B.

MEDIC-ALERT FOUNDATION, 11–13 Clifton Terrace N4 3JP—*Hon. Chairman*, D. J. C. Gilchrist. For the protection, in emergencies, of those with a medical disability; to prevent mistakes.

MEDICAL COUNCIL, GENERAL, 44 Hallam Street W1N 6AE. *Registrar*, P. L. Towers.

MEDICAL SOCIETY OF LONDON (1773), 11 Chandos Street, Cavendish Square W1M 0EB—*Pres.* (1985–86), Sir John Harrison, K.B.E.; *Hon. Secs.*, P. S. London, M.B.E.; Dr. G. Rettie; *Registrar*, Maj. T. Tudor-Williams.

MEDICAL WOMEN'S FEDERATION (1917), Tavistock House North, Tavistock Square WC1H 9HX—*Pres.*, Miss C. Doig; *Hon. Sec.*, Dr. Lotte T. Newman.

MEDIEVAL ARCHAEOLOGY, SOCIETY FOR (1957), University College, Gower Street WC1E 6BT—*Hon. Sec.*, Dr. Helen Clarke.

MEN OF THE TREES (1922), Crawley Down, Crawley, Sussex RH10 4HL—*Sec.*, Mrs. E. Sandwell.

MENTAL AFTER CARE ASSOCIATION (1879), for the care and rehabilitation of those recovering from mental illness.—*Dir.*, Mrs. J. Jefferies, M.B.E., 110 Jermyn Street SW1Y 6HB.

MENTAL HEALTH FOUNDATION (1949), 8 Hallam Street W1N 6DH—*Dir.*, R. B. Loudoun, C.B., O.B.E.

MERCHANT NAVY WELFARE BOARD, 19–21 Lancaster Gate, W.2.—*Sec.*, J. I. K. Walker.

METALS, THE INSTITUTE OF (1985) (*Amalgamation of* The Institution of Metallurgists and The Metals Society), 1 Carlton House Terrace SW1Y 5DB—*Sec.*, Sir Geoffrey Ford, K.B.E., C.B.

METEOROLOGICAL SOCIETY, ROYAL (1850), James Glaisher House, Grenville Place, Bracknell, Berks RG12 1BX—*Pres.*, A. Gilchrist; *Hon. Secs.*, D. N. Axford, PH.D.; I. N. James, PH.D.; G. J. Jenkins, PH.D.

METROPOLITAN AND CITY POLICE ORPHANS FUND (1870), 30 Hazlewell Road, Putney SW15 6LH—*Sec.*, J. Murray, M.B.E.

METROPOLITAN AUTHORITIES, ASSOCIATION OF (1974), 36 Old Queen Street SW1H 9JE—*Sec.*, A. Gronow.

METROPOLITAN HOSPITAL-SUNDAY FUND (1872), 40 High Street, Teddington, Middx. TW11 8EW. In 1984, £42,503 was distributed to N.H.S. hospitals in the form of Samaritan Fund grants, special grants and long stay/geriatric patient holiday grants through hospital social workers. £131,476 was distributed to hospitals outside the N.H.S., and £18,000 to other medical charities.—*Sec.*, D. A. B. Lynch.

METROPOLITAN PUBLIC GARDENS ASSOCIATION (1882), 4 Carlos Place W1Y 5AE—*Sec.*, M. Upward.

MIDDLE EAST ASSOCIATION (1961), 33 Bury Street, St. James's SW1Y 6AX—*Dir.-Gen.*, Sir James Craig, G.C.M.G.; *Sec.*, Miss L. V. Marsh-Smith.

MIDWIVES, ROYAL COLLEGE OF (1881), 15 Mansfield Street, W1M 0BE—*Gen. Sec.*, Miss R. M. Ashton.

MIGRAINE TRUST (1965), 45 Great Ormond Street WC1N 3HD—*Dir.*, Cdr. O. Wright.

MILITARY HISTORICAL SOCIETY.—*Hon. Sec.*, J. Gaylor, National Army Museum, Royal Hospital Road, Chelsea SW3 4HT

MIND (National Association for Mental Health), 22 Harley Street W1N 2ED—*Dir.*, C. Heginbotham.

MINERALOGICAL SOCIETY (1876).—*Pres.*, Dr. A. C. Bishop; *Hon. Gen. Sec.*, Dr. M. G. Bown, 41 Queen's Gate SW7 5HR.

MINES OF GREAT BRITAIN, FEDERATION OF SMALL, 30 King Street, Wigan, Lancs.—*Sec.*, J. Wainwright.

MINIATURE PAINTERS, SCULPTORS AND GRAVERS, ROYAL SOCIETY OF (1895), 17 Carlton House Terrace, S.W.1.—*Pres.*, Mrs. Suzanne Lucas.

MINIATURISTS, SOCIETY OF (1895), Castle Gallery, Castle Hill, Ilkley, West Yorks. LS29 9DT—*Dir.*, L. Simpson.

MINING AND METALLURGY, INSTITUTION OF (1892), 44 Portland Place, W.1.—*Sec.* M. J. Jones.

MINING ENGINEERS, THE INSTITUTION OF (1889), 6A South Parade, Doncaster.—*Pres.* (1984–85), R. Rawlinson; *Sec.*, W. J. W. Bourne.

MINING INSTITUTE OF SCOTLAND, c/o National Coal Board, Green Park, Greenend, Edinburgh, EH17 7PZ—*Sec.*, E. R. Rodger.

MISSIONS TO SEAMEN, THE, AND ST. ANDREW'S WATERSIDE CHURCH MISSION FOR SAILORS, St. Michael Paternoster Royal, College Hill EC4R 2RL—*Gen. Sec.*, Rev. W. J. D. Down.

MODERN CHURCHMEN'S UNION (1898), for the Advancement of Liberal Religious Thought—*Pres.*, The Dean of Westminster; *Hon. Gen. Sec.*, P. Croft, 4 Cathedral Close, Guildford, Surrey GU2 5TL.

MODERN LANGUAGE ASSOCIATION (incorporating the Association of Teachers of German), Seymour Mews House, Seymour Mews, Wigmore Street W1H 9PE—*Gen. Sec.*, Miss E. Ingham.

MONUMENTAL BRASS SOCIETY (1887), *Hon. Sec.*, W. Mendelsson, 57 Leeside Crescent NW11 0HA.

MORAVIAN MISSIONS, LONDON ASSOCIATION IN AID OF (1817), Moravian Church House, 5/7 Muswell Hill N10 3TJ—*Sec.*, Rev. F. Linyard.

MOTOR INDUSTRY, THE INSTITUTE OF THE, Fanshaws, Brickendon, Hertford SG13 8PQ—*Sec.*, R. K. Ward.

MOUNTBATTEN MEMORIAL TRUST (1979), 18 Northumberland Avenue WC2N 5BJ—*Dir. and Sec.*, Mrs. C. Barnett, O.B.E.

MOUNTBATTEN TRUST, THE EDWINA 1 Grosvenor Crescent SW1X 7EF—*Sec.*, J. Boyd-Brent.

MULTIPLE SCLEROSIS SOCIETY, 25 Effie Road SW6 1EE—*Gen. Sec.*, J. Walford.

MUSEUMS ASSOCIATION (1889), 34 Bloomsbury Way WC1A 2SF—*Dir. Gen.*, J. A. Fox.

MUSICIANS BENEVOLENT FUND, 16 Ogle Street W1P 7LG—*Sec.*, M. B. M. Williams. *Private Hotel*, Westgate-on-Sea. *Permanent Homes*, Hereford and Bromley.

MUSICIANS, INCORPORATED SOCIETY OF (1882) 10 Stratford Place W1N 9AE—*Gen. Sec.*, D. Padgett-Chandler.

MUSICIANS OF GREAT BRITAIN, ROYAL SOCIETY OF (1738), 10 Stratford Place W1N 9AE—*Sec.*, Mrs. M. E. Gleed, M.B.E.

MUSIC SOCIETIES, NATIONAL FEDERATION OF (1935), Francis House, Francis Street SW1P 1DE—*Gen. Sec.*, J. Crisp.

NATIONAL ADULT SCHOOL ORGANISATION (1899), Norfolk House, Smallbrook Queensway, Birmingham B5 4LJ—*Sec.*, W. Scarle.

NATIONAL AND UNIVERSITY LIBRARIES, STANDING CONFERENCE OF (1950).—*Sec.*, A. J. Loveday, 102 Euston Street NW1 2HA.

NATIONAL ASSOCIATION OF ESTATE AGENTS (1962), Arbon House, 21 Jury Street, Warwick CV34 4EH—*Sec.*, A. B. Clark.

NATIONAL ASSOCIATION OF LOCAL COUNCILS (1947), 108 Great Russell Street WC1B 3LD—*Gen. Sec.*, J. Clark.

NATIONAL BENEVOLENT INSTITUTION (1812), 61 Bayswater Road, W.2.—*Sec.*, Air Cmdre, D. C. Saunders, C.B.E., A.F.C.

NATIONAL BIRTHDAY TRUST FUND (1928), 57 Lower Belgrave Street SW1W 0LR. For Extension of Maternity Services.—*Sec.*, Mrs. M. C. Matthews.

NATIONAL BOOK LEAGUE (1925), Book House, 45 East Hill, Wandsworth SW18 2QZ—*Dir.*, M. Goff, O.B.E.

NATIONAL CATTLE BREEDERS' ASSOCIATION, 106 High Street, Tring, Herts HP23 4AF—*Sec.*, J. Thorley.

NATIONAL CHILDBIRTH TRUST, THE, (1956), 9 Queensborough Terrace, Bayswater W2 3TB—*Nat. Sec.*, Mrs. H. Corbishley.

NATIONAL CHILDREN'S HOME (1869). *Chief Office*, 85 Highbury Park N5 1UD. Cares for 7,000 socially, educationally, or physically handicapped children annually in residential homes, special schools, family centres, foster homes and community projects in Great Britain and overseas.—*Principal*, Rev. G. E. Barritt, O.B.E..

NATIONAL CHRISTIAN EDUCATION COUNCIL (*incorporating* International Bible Reading Association and Denholm House Press), Robert Denholm House, Nutfield, Redhill, Surrey RH1 4HW—*Exec. Officer*, E. A. Thorn.

NATIONAL COUNCIL FOR VOLUNTARY ORGANISATIONS, 26 Bedford Square WC1B 3HU—*Dir.*, W. Griffiths.

NATIONAL COUNCIL OF WOMEN OF GREAT BRITAIN (1895). 34 Lower Sloane Street SW1W 8BP—*Sec.*, Mrs. J. D. Norman.

NATIONAL FEDERATION OF RETIREMENT PENSIONS ASSOCIATIONS, (PENSIONERS' VOICE), 91 Preston New Road, Blackburn, Lancs BB2 6BD—*Gen. Sec.*, G. Dunn.

NATIONAL FEDERATION OF SELF EMPLOYED AND SMALL BUSINESSES LTD. (1974), 32 St. Annes Road West, Lytham St. Annes, Lancs FY8 1NY—*National Chairman*, Dr. B. A. Juby.

NATIONAL FEDERATION OF YOUNG FARMERS' CLUBS, Y.F.C. Centre, National Agricultural Centre, Kenilworth, Warwicks CV8 2LG—*Gen. Sec. and Treasurer*, F. E. Shields, M.B.E.

NATIONAL LIGHT HORSE BREEDING SOCIETY (H.I.S.) (1885), 96 High Street, Edenbridge, Kent TN8 5AR—*Sec.*, G. W. Evans.

NATIONAL MARKET TRADERS' FEDERATION (1899).— *Pres.*, J. Burton; *Gen. Sec.*, D. J. Glasby, Hampton House, Hawshaw Lane, Hoyland, Barnsley.

NATIONAL MARRIAGE GUIDANCE COUNCIL, Herbert Gray College, Little Church Street, Rugby, Warwicks CV21 3AP—*Chief Officer*, N. J. Tyndall.

NATIONAL MONUMENTS RECORD (1941), Royal Commission on Historical Monuments (England), Fortress House, 23 Savile Row W1X 1AB—*Sec.*, P. J. Fowler, PH.D.

NATIONAL OPERATIC AND DRAMATIC ASSOCIATION (1899), 1 Crestfield Street WC1H 8AU—*Gen. Administrator*, B. Clarke.

NATIONAL PEACE COUNCIL (1908), 29 Great James Street WC1N 3ES—*Gen. Sec.*, Sheila Oakes.

NATIONAL PURE WATER ASSOCIATION.—*Sec.*, N. Brugge, Southern Ash, Gilberts Lane, Whixall, Whitchurch, Shropshire SY13 2PR.

NATIONAL SECULAR SOCIETY (1866), 702 Holloway Road N19 3NL—*Gen. Sec.*, T. Mullins.

NATIONAL SOCIETY FOR CLEAN AIR (1899), 136 North Street, Brighton, E. Sussex BN1 1RG—*Sec.-Gen.*, Air Cmdre. J. Langston, C.B.E.

NATIONAL SOCIETY (CHURCH OF ENGLAND) FOR PROMOTING RELIGIOUS EDUCATION (1811), Church House, Dean's Yard, S.W.1.—*Gen. Sec.*, C. Alves.

NATIONAL SOCIETY FOR THE PREVENTION OF CRUELTY TO CHILDREN (1884), *Headquarters*, 67 Saffron Hill EC1N 8RS—*Chairman*, Lady Holland-Martin, D.B.E., D.L.; *Hon. Treas.*, M. Weinberg; *Dir.*, Dr. A. Gilmour, C.B.E.

NATIONAL UNION OF STUDENTS, 461 Holloway Road N7 6LJ—*Nat. Sec.*, J. Doran.

NATIONAL VIEWERS' AND LISTENERS' ASSOCIATION.— *President*, Mrs. M. Whitehouse, C.B.E, Blachernae, Ardleigh, Colchester, Essex CO7 7RH.

NATION'S FUND FOR NURSES, 57 Lower Belgrave Street SW1W 0LR—*Administrator*, P. E. Starr.

NATURE CONSERVATION, ROYAL SOCIETY FOR (1912).— *Gen. Sec.*, Dr. F. H. Perring, The Green, Nettleham, Lincoln.

NAUTICAL RESEARCH, SOCIETY FOR (1911), c/o National Maritime Museum, Greenwich SE10 9NF—*Hon. Sec.*, Lt. Cdr. L. Phillipps, R.N.R.

NAVAL, MILITARY AND AIR FORCE BIBLE SOCIETY (1780), Radstock House, 3 Eccleston Street SW1W 9LZ Copies and portions of the Scriptures circulated to the Forces (1984), 245,608.—*Sec.*, R. Kennedy.

NAVAL ARCHITECTS, ROYAL INSTITUTION OF (1860), 10 Upper Belgrave Street, S.W.1.—*Sec.*, P. W. Ayling.

NAVIGATION, ROYAL INSTITUTE OF, at the Royal Geographical Society, 1 Kensington Gore SW7 2AT. *Dir.*, Rear Adm. R. M. Burgoyne, C.B.

NAVY RECORDS SOCIETY, Public Record Office, Kew, Richmond, Surrey TW9 4DU. Publishes editions of historical documents relating to the Royal Navy.—*Hon. Sec.*, N. A. M. Rodger.

NEWCOMEN SOCIETY (1920), for the Study of the History of Engineering and Technology, Science Museum SW7 2DD—*Exec. Sec.*, I. McNeil.

NEW ENGLISH ART CLUB (1886), 17 Carlton House Terrace, S.W.1.—*Sec.*, W. Bowyer, R.A.

NEWSAGENTS, NATIONAL FEDERATION OF RETAIL, 2 Bridewell Place EC4V 6AR—*Gen. Sec.*, K. E. J. Peters.

NEWSPAPER EDITORS, GUILD OF BRITISH (1946), Whitefriars House, Carmelite Street, E.C.4.—*Pres.*, J. Hardeman (*Berrows Newspapers, Worcester*); *Sec.-Treas.*, C. Gordon Page.

NEWSPAPER PRESS FUND (1864), Dickens House, 35 Wathen Road, Dorking, Surrey RH4 1JY.—*Gen. Sec.*, P. W. Evans.

NEWSPAPER SOCIETY (1836), Whitefriars House, 6 Carmelite Street EC4Y 0BL—*Pres.*, D. R. Thomas (*North Wales Newspapers Ltd., Oswestry*); *Dir.*, D. Nisbet-Smith.

NEWSVENDORS' BENEVOLENT INSTITUTION (1839), P.O. Box 306, Dunmow, Essex CM6 1HY.—*Sec.*, R. A. Jones.

NOISE ABATEMENT SOCIETY, P.O. Box 8, Bromley, Kent BR2 0UH.—*Chairman*, J. Connell.

NON-SMOKERS, NATIONAL SOCIETY OF (1926), Latimer House, 40–48 Hanson Street W1P 7DE—*Hon. Dir. and Sec.*, T. W. Hurst.

NORTHERN IRELAND TOURIST BOARD, River House, 48 High Street, Belfast BT1 2DS—*Chief Exec.*, S. Belford.

NORWOOD CHILD CARE (Jewish Welfare Organization for Jewish children), 221 Golders Green Road NW11 9DL—*Exec. Dir.*, S. Brier.

NUCLEAR ENERGY SOCIETY, BRITISH (1962), 1—7 Great George Street SW1P 3AA.

NUFFIELD FOUNDATION (1943), Nuffield Lodge, Regent's Park NW1 4RS—*Dir.*, J. P. Cornford.

NUFFIELD PROVINCIAL HOSPITALS TRUST (1939), 3 Prince Albert Road, N.W.1.—*Gen. Sec.*, G. McLachlan, C.B.E.

NUMISMATIC SOCIETY, BRITISH.—*Hon. Sec.*, W. Slayter, 63 West Way, Edgware, Middx HA8 9LA.

NUMISMATIC SOCIETY, ROYAL, c/o Dept. of Coins and Medals, The British Museum, Great Russell Street WC1—*Pres.*, Dr. J. P. C. Kent, PH.D., F.S.A.; *Hon. Secs.*, A. Burnett, PH.D., F.S.A.; J. E. Cribb.

NURSES', RETIRED, NATIONAL HOME, Riverside Avenue, Bournemouth BH7 7EE—*Chairman*, Dr. R. E. Chaplin.

NURSES, ROYAL NATIONAL PENSION FUND FOR, 15 Buckingham Street WC2—*General Manager and Actuary*, V. G. West.

NURSING, MIDWIFERY AND HEALTH VISITING, U.K. CENTRAL COUNCIL FOR, 23 Portland Place, W1N 3AF—*Registrar and Chief Exec.*, Miss M. Storey. *England.*—Victory House, 170 Tottenham Court Road W1P 0HA.
Wales.—Floor 13 Pearl Assurance House, Greyfriars Road, Cardiff CF1 3AG.
Scotland.—22 Queen Street, Edinburgh EH2 1JX.
N.I.—RAC House, 79 Chichester Street, Belfast BT1 4JE.

NURSING, ROYAL COLLEGE OF, 20 Cavendish Square W1M 0AB—*Gen. Sec.*, T. Clay.

NUTRITION SOCIETY (1941).—*Hon. Sec.*, Dr. Margaret Ashwell, Chandos House, 2 Queen Anne Street, W.1.

OBSTETRICIANS AND GYNAECOLOGISTS, ROYAL COLLEGE OF (1929), 27 Sussex Place, Regent's Park

NW1 4RG—*Pres.*, Prof. M. C. Macnaughton; *Sec.*, A. G. S. Taylour.

OCCUPATIONAL SAFETY AND HEALTH, INSTITUTION OF, 222 Uppingham Road, Leicester LE5 0QG—*Sec.*, J. R. Barrell.

OFFICERS' ASSOCIATION, THE (1920), 48 Pall Mall SW1Y 5JY. Affords relief to ex-officers of the Royal Navy, Army and R.A.F. and their widows and dependants in distress; assists such persons to find accommodation in homes for the elderly; helps unemployed ex-officers to find employment.—*Gen. Sec.*, Brig. P. D. Johnson.

OFFICERS' FAMILIES FUND (1899), 48 Pall Mall SW1Y 5JY—*Sec.*, Mrs. I. C. Riley.

OFFICERS' PENSIONS SOCIETY, LTD., 15 Buckingham Gate SW1E 6NS—*Gen. Sec.*, Maj. Gen. L. W. A. Gingell, C.B., O.B.E.

OIL PAINTERS, ROYAL INSTITUTE OF (1883), 17 Carlton House Terrace, S.W.1.—*Pres.*, K. Barratt.

OILSEED, OIL AND FEEDINGSTUFFS TRADES BENEVOLENT ASSOCIATION, THE, 14–20 Mary Axe, E.C.3.—*Sec.*, R. T. Wheelans.

ONE PARENT FAMILIES, NATIONAL COUNCIL FOR, 255 Kentish Town Road NW5 2LX—*Dir.*, Dr. Carol Smart.

OPEN-AIR MISSION (1853), 19 John Street WC1N 2DL—*Sec.*, A. J. Greenbank.

OPEN SPACES SOCIETY (COMMONS, OPEN SPACES AND FOOTPATHS PRESERVATION SOCIETY) (1865), 25A Bell Street, Henley-on-Thames, Oxon RG9 2BA—*Hon. Sec.*, Miss K. Ashbrook.

OPTICAL COUNCIL, GENERAL, 41 Harley Street W1N 2DJ—*Registrar*, J. D. Devlin, O.B.E.

ORDERS AND MEDALS RESEARCH SOCIETY.—*Gen. Sec.*, N. G. Gooding, 123 Turnpike Link, Croydon CR0 5NU.

ORIENTAL CERAMIC SOCIETY (1921), 31B Torrington Square WC1E 7LJ—*Sec.*, Vice-Admiral Sir John Gray, K.B.E., C.B.

ORNITHOLOGISTS' CLUB, THE SCOTTISH, 21 Regent Terrace, Edinburgh EH7 5BT.—*Sec.*, J. C. Davies.

ORNITHOLOGISTS' UNION, BRITISH, c/o Zoological Society of London, Regent's Park NW1 4RY—*Sec.*, Dr. D. C. Houston.

ORNITHOLOGY, BRITISH TRUST FOR (1932), Beech Grove, Tring, Herts HP23 5NR—*Administrator*, J. C. G. Wolf.

ORTHOPÆDIC ASSOCIATION, BRITISH (1918), at the Royal College of Surgeons, 35–43 Lincoln's Inn Fields WC2A 3PN—*Hon. Sec.*, L. Klenerman.

OUTWARD BOUND TRUST, Chestnut Field, Regent Place, Rugby CV21 1RJ—*Dir.*, I. L. Fothergill.

OVERSEAS DEVELOPMENT INSTITUTE (1960), 10–11 Percy Street W1P 0JB—*Dir.*, T. Killick.

OVERSEAS SERVICE PENSIONERS' ASSOCIATION (1960), 63 Church Road, Hove, Sussex BN3 2BD—*Sec.*, C. D. Stenton.

OVERSEAS SETTLEMENT, CHURCH OF ENGLAND BOARD FOR SOCIAL RESPONSIBILITY (1925), Church House, Dean's Yard SW1P 3NZ—*Admin.-Sec.*, Miss P. J. Hallett.

OXFAM (1942), 274 Banbury Road, Oxford.—*Dir.*, A. G. Stringer.

OXFORD AND CAMBRIDGE SCHOOLS EXAMINATION BOARD (1873). *Offices*, 10 Trumpington Street, Cambridge and Elsfield Way, Oxford.—*Secs.*, K. Schoenenberger, Oxford; H. F. King, Cambridge.

OXFORD PRESERVATION TRUST (1927), 10 Turn Again Lane, St. Ebbes, Oxford OX1 1QL—*Sec.*, Mrs. H. Turner.

OXFORD SOCIETY (1932), 8 Wellington Square, Oxford OX1 2HY—*Sec.*, Mrs. D. M. Lennie.

PAINTER-ETCHERS AND ENGRAVERS, ROYAL SOCIETY OF (1880), Bankside Gallery, 48 Hopton Street, Blackfriars SE1 9JH—*Pres.*, H. N. Eccleston, O.B.E.; *Sec.*, M. Spender.

PAINTERS IN WATER COLOURS, ROYAL INSTITUTE OF (1831), 17 Carlton House Terrace, S.W.1.—*Pres.*, C. Bone; *Treas.*, Mr. Folkes.

PAINTERS IN WATER COLOURS, ROYAL SOCIETY OF (1804), Bankside Gallery, 48 Hopton Street, Blackfriars SE1 9JH—*Pres.*, M. Sheppard; *Sec.*, M. Spender.

PAINTERS, SCULPTORS AND PRINTMAKERS, NATIONAL SOCIETY OF (1930), 17 Carlton House Terrace, S.W.1.—*Pres.*, K. Barratt.

PALÆONTOGRAPHICAL SOCIETY (1847). *Sec.*, F. G. Dimes, c/o British Geological Survey, Keyworth, Nottingham NG12 5GG—*Sec.*, S. P. Tunnicliff.

PALÆONTOLOGICAL ASSOCIATION (1957).—*Sec.*, Dr. P. W. Skelton, Dept. of Earth Sciences, Open University, Walton Hall, Milton Keynes MK7 6AA.

PALESTINE EXPLORATION FUND (1865), 2 Hinde Mews, Marylebone Lane W1M 5RR—*Chairman*, Brig. A. Walmesley White, C.B.E., M.A., F.R.G.S.

PARKINSON'S DISEASE SOCIETY (1969), 36 Portland Place W1N 3DG—*Exec. Dir.*, C. A. A. Kilmister.

PARLIAMENTARY AND SCIENTIFIC COMMITTEE.—*Sec.*, A. Butler, 22 Red Lion Street WC1R 4PX.

PASTEL SOCIETY (1899), 17 Carlton House Terrace, S.W.1.—*Pres.*, L. Parry.

PASTORAL PSYCHOLOGY, GUILD OF (1936).—*Hon. Sec.*, Mrs. M. Ditchfield, 37 Hogarth Hill NW11 6AY.

PATENT AGENTS, CHARTERED INSTITUTE OF (1882), Staple Inn Buildings WC1V 7PZ—*Sec. and Registrar*, Miss M. E. Poole.

PATENTEES AND INVENTORS, INSTITUTE OF (1919), Staple Inn Buildings South, 335 High Holborn, W.C.1.—*Sec.*, E. J. Gear.

PATHOLOGISTS, ROYAL COLLEGE OF, 2 Carlton House Terrace SW1Y 5AF—*Sec.*, B. A. Prideaux.

PATIENTS ASSOCIATION (1963), Room 33, 18 Charing Cross Road WC2H 0HR—*Chairman*, Dame Elizabeth Ackroyd, D.B.E.

PEARSON'S HOLIDAY FUND, 2a Amity Grove, Raynes Park SW20 0LJ—*Gen. Sec.*, G. Holloway.

PEDESTRIANS' ASSOCIATION, 1–5 Wandsworth Road SW8 2LJ—*Chairman*, C. Myerscough.

P.E.N., INTERNATIONAL (1921), 38 King Street WC2E 8JT. World association of writers.—*International Sec.*, A. Blokh.

PENSION FUNDS, NATIONAL ASSOCIATION OF, LTD (1923).—*Dir. Gen.*, H. L. James, C.B.; *Sec.*, B. W. Lofthouse, 12–18 Grosvenor Gardens SW1W 0DH.

PEOPLE'S DISPENSARY FOR SICK ANIMALS (1917), PDSA House, South Street, Dorking, Surrey RH4 2LB—*Gen. Sec.*, M. R. Curtis, M.B.E.

PERFORMING RIGHT SOCIETY LTD. (1914), 29–33 Berners Street W1P 4AA—*Chief Executive*, M. J. Freegard; *Sec.*, G. M. Neighbour.

PERIODICAL PUBLISHERS ASSOCATION LTD., Imperial House, 15–19 Kingsway WC2B 6UN—*Exec. Dir.*, M. J. Finley.

PESTALOZZI CHILDREN'S VILLAGE TRUST, Sedlescombe, Battle, Sussex TN33 0RR—*Warden*, A. G. Hatter.

PHARMACEUTICAL SOCIETY OF GREAT BRITAIN, 1 Lambeth High Street, S.E.1.—*Sec. and Registrar*, D. F. Lewis, O.B.E.

PHARMACOLOGICAL SOCIETY, BRITISH.—*Hon. Gen. Sec.*, Dr. G. N. Woodruff, Merck Sharp and Dohme Research Labs.; Neuroscience Research Centre, Terlings Park, Eastwick Road, Harlow, Essex CM20 2QE.

PHILOLOGICAL SOCIETY (1842).—*Hon. Sec.*, Prof. R. H. Robins, School of Oriental and African Studies, Malet Street WC1E 7HP—*Hon Sec.*, Prof. R. H. Robins.

PHILOSOPHY, ROYAL INSTITUTE OF, 14 Gordon Square WC1H 0AG—*Director*, Prof. A. Phillips Griffiths.

PHOTOGRAMMETRIC SOCIETY (1952), Dept. of Land Surveying, North-East London Polytechnic, Longbridge Road, Dagenham, Essex RM8 2AS—*Hon. Sec.*, A. S. Walker.

PHOTOGRAPHY, BRITISH INSTITUTE OF PROFESSIONAL (1901), 2 Amwell End, Ware, Herts SG12 9HN— *Sec.*, P. A. Large.

PHYSICAL EDUCATION ASSOCIATION OF GREAT BRITAIN AND N. IRELAND, THE, 162 King's Cross Road WC1X 9DH—*Gen. Sec.*, A. J. Petherick.

PHYSICAL RECREATION, CENTRAL COUNCIL OF (1935), Francis House, Francis Street SW1P 1DE—*Gen. Sec.*, P. Lawson.

PHYSICIANS, ROYAL COLLEGE OF (1518), 11 St. Andrew's Place NW1 4LE—*Pres.*, Sir Raymond Hoffenberg, K.B.E., M.D., F.R.C.P.; *Treas.*, A. M. Dawson, M.D.; *Registrar*, D. A. Pyke, M.D.; *Sec.*, G. M. G. Tibbs.

PHYSICIANS AND SURGEONS, ROYAL COLLEGE OF (Glasgow) (1599), 234–242 St. Vincent Street, Glasgow G2 5RJ—*Pres.*, I. A. McGregor; *Hon. Sec.*, A. D. Beattie.

PHYSICIANS OF EDINBURGH, ROYAL COLLEGE OF (1681), *Hall and Library*, 9 Queen Street, Edinburgh EH2 1JQ—*Sec.*, Dr. T. M. Chalmers.

PHYSICS, INSTITUTE OF (1874), 47 Belgrave Square SW1X 8QX—*Pres.*, Sir Robert Clayton; *Sec.*, L. Cohen, PH.D.

PHYSIOLOGICAL SOCIETY (1876), Dept. of Physiology, The University, Sheffield S10 2TN—*Hon. Sec.*, Prof. A. Angel.

PHYSIOTHERAPY, THE CHARTERED SOCIETY OF (1894), 14 Bedford Row WC1R 4ED—*Sec.*, G. F. Barber.

PIG BREEDERS ASSOCIATION, NATIONAL (1884), 7 Rickmansworth Road, Watford, Herts WD1 7HE— *Chief Exec. and Sec.*, G. E. Welsh.

PILGRIM TRUST, THE (1930), Fielden House, Little College Street SW1P 3SH—*Sec.*, Hon. A. H. Millar.

PILGRIMS OF GREAT BRITAIN, THE (1902), Savoy Hotel WC2—*Pres.*, The Rt. Hon. Lord Carrington, C.H., K.C.M.G., M.C.; *Hon. Sec.*, Lt.-Col. S. W. Chant-Sempill, O.B.E., M.C.

PLANT ENGINEERS, INSTITUTION OF, 138 Buckingham Palace Road SW1W 9SG—*Sec. Gen.*, J. K. Bennett.

PLASTICS AND RUBBER INSTITUTE, THE (1921), 11 Hobart Place SW1W 0HL—*Sec.-Gen.* G. W. Stockdale.

PLAYING CARD SOCIETY, THE INTERNATIONAL (1972), 188 Sheen Lane, East Sheen SW14 8LF—*Sec.*, M. Collett.

PLAYING FIELDS ASSOCIATION, NATIONAL (1925), 25 Ovington Square SW3 1LQ—*Chairman*, A. C. Gilmour; *Director Gen.*, C. W. McFadyean.

P.N.E.U., WORLD-WIDE EDUCATION SERVICE OF THE (1888), Strode House, 44/50 Osnaburgh Street NW1 3NN—*Dir.*, H. Boulter.

POETRY SOCIETY (1909), 21 Earl's Court Square SW5 9DE—*Dir. and Gen. Sec.*, B. G. Mitchell.

POLICY STUDIES INSTITUTE, 100 Park Village East, NW1 3SR—*Dir.*, D. J. Derx, C.B.

POLYTECHNICS, COMMITTEE OF DIRECTORS OF, 309 Regent Street W1R 7PE—*Chairman*, Dr. H. D. Law; *Sec.*, Dr. M. S. Lewis.

POLYTECHNIC TEACHERS, ASSOCIATION OF (1973), Throgmorton House, 27 Elphinstone Road, Southsea, Hants PO5 3HP—*Nat. Sec.*, Dr. A. J. Pointon.

PORTRAIT SCULPTORS, SOCIETY OF (1962), 17 Carlton House Terrace, S.W.1.—*Pres.*, R. Browne, F.R.B.S..

POST OFFICE USERS' NATIONAL COUNCIL (1970), 8 Bulstrode Street, W.1.—*Sec.*, J. F. Heath.

POULTRY CLUB, THE (1877) (incorporating the British Bantam Association).—*Sec.*, Mrs. M. A. Carefoot, Cliveden, Sandy Bank Farm, Chipping, Nr Preston, Lancs PR3 2GA.

PRAYER BOOK SOCIETY, THE (1975), 40 Great Smith Street SW1P 3BU—*Deputy Chairman*, C. A. A. Kilmister.

PRECEPTORS, COLLEGE OF, Coppice Row, Theydon Bois, Epping, Essex CM16 7DN. Membership is admitted to practising educationalists; Fellowships are reserved for those who have made an outstanding contribution to education.—*Chief Admin. Officer*, P. R. Daniels.

PREPARATORY SCHOOLS, INCORPORATED ASSOCIATION OF, 138 Kensington Church Street W8 4BN—*Sec.*, J. M. C. Coates.

PRE-SCHOOL PLAYGROUPS ASSOCIATION.—Alford House, Aveline Street SE11 5DH—*Gen. Sec.*, Miss J. Atkinson.

PRESS ASSOCIATION (1868), 85 Fleet Street EC4P 4BE—*Chairman* (1985–86), T. D. Morris (*Birmingham Post and Mail*); *General Manager*, I. H. N. Yates; *Sec.*, E. G. Rhodes.

PRINCESS LOUISE SCOTTISH HOSPITAL (Erskine Hospital) for disabled ex-servicemen and women (1916), Bishopton, Renfrewshire PA7 5PU—*Commandant*, Col. W. K. Shepherd; *Treasurer*, I. W. Grimmond.

PRINTERS' CHARITABLE CORPORATION (1827), 61 Doughty Street WC1N 2NH. Homes for elderly printers and widows at Basildon and Bletchley, holidays and convalescence, and direct benefits for those of the printing and allied trades who are in need following retirement, and for one parent children throughout schooling.—*Dir. & Sec.*, Cpt. D. J. Bradby, R.N. (*ret.*).

PRINTING HISTORICAL SOCIETY (1964), St. Bride Institute, Bride Lane, E.C.4.—*Hon. Sec.*, C. L. Hicks.

PRINTING, INSTITUTE OF (1961), 8 Lonsdale Gardens, Tunbridge Wells, Kent.—*Sec.*, M. A. Smith.

PRISON VISITORS, NATIONAL ASSOCIATION OF (1922), 466 Hartington Street, Bedford MK41 7RP—*Gen. Sec.*, Mrs. A. G. McKenna.

PRIVATE LIBRARIES ASSOCIATION (1957), Ravelston, South View Road, Pinner, Middlesex HA5 3YD— *Hon. Sec.*, F. Broomhead.

PROCURATORS IN GLASGOW, ROYAL FACULTY OF (1600).—*Treas.*, *Clerk and Fiscal*, J. H. Sinclair, 62 St. Georges Place, Glasgow G2 1BT.

PRODUCTION CONTROL, INSTITUTE OF, National Westminster House, Wood Street, Stratford-upon-Avon, Warwickshire CV37 6JF—*Gen. Sec.*, K. Roberts.

PRODUCTION ENGINEERS, INSTITUTION OF, Rochester House, 66 Little Ealing Lane W5 4XX—*Sec.*, R. J. Miskin.

PROFESSIONAL CLASSES AID COUNCIL, 10 St. Christopher's Place W1M 6HY—*Sec.*, Mrs. G. A. Burgess.

PROFESSIONAL ENGINEERS, U.K. ASSOCIATION OF, Hayes Court, West Common Road, Bromley, Kent BR2 7AU—*Sec.*, C. K. Hickling.

PROFESSIONAL FOOTBALLERS' ASSOCIATION, 124 Corn Exchange Buildings, Manchester M4 3BN.—*Sec.*, G. Taylor.

PROFESSIONS SUPPLEMENTARY TO MEDICINE, COUNCIL FOR, Park House, 184 Kennington Park Road SE11 4BU—*Registrar*, F. Whitehill.

PROPAGATION OF THE GOSPEL, UNITED SOCIETY FOR THE (U.S.P.G.), 15 Tufton Street SW1P 3QQ—*Sec.*, Rev. H. V. Taylor.

PROTECTION OF LIFE FROM FIRE, SOCIETY FOR THE (1836), 140 Aldersgate Street, EC1A 4HX—*Sec.*, E. H. Gledhill.

PROTESTANT ALLIANCE, THE (1845), 112 Colin Gardens NW9 6ER—*Gen. Sec.*, Rev. A. G. Ashdown.

PROVINCIAL NOTARIES SOCIETY (1907), P.O. Box 102, Amersham, Bucks HP7 0QB—*Sec.*, P. D. Leonard.

PSORIASIS ASSOCIATION, THE (1968), 7 Milton Street, Northampton NN2 7JG—*Nat. Sec.*, Mrs. L. A. Henley.

PSYCHIATRISTS, ROYAL COLLEGE OF (1971, *formerly* Royal Medico-Psychological Association founded in 1841), 17 Belgrave Square, SW1X 8PG—*Registrar*, Prof. R. G. Priest.

PSYCHICAL RESEARCH, SOCIETY FOR (1882), 1 Adam and Eve Mews, Kensington W8 6UG—*Pres.*, Prof. D. J. West.

PSYCHOLOGICAL SOCIETY, THE BRITISH (1901), St. Andrews House, 48 Princess Road East, Leicester LE1 7DR—*Pres.*, Prof. R. M. Farr; *Hon. Gen. Sec.*, Dr. P. E. Morris.

PUBLIC ADMINISTRATION, ROYAL INSTITUTE OF (1922), 3 Birdcage Walk SW1H 9JH—*Dir. Gen.*, W. Plowden.

PUBLIC FINANCE AND ACCOUNTANCY, CHARTERED INSTITUTE OF (1885).—*Dir.*, N. P. Hepworth, O.B.E., 3 Robert Street WC2N 6BH.

PUBLIC HEALTH AND HYGIENE, THE ROYAL INSTITUTE OF (1937), 28 Portland Place W1N 4DE—*Sec.*, Rear-Adm. W. A. Waddell, C.B., O.B.E.

PUBLIC HEALTH ENGINEERS, INSTITUTION OF (1895), Grosvenor Gardens House, 35–37 Grosvenor Gardens SW1W 0BS—*Sec.*, D. J. Dacam, O.B.E.

PUBLIC RELATIONS, INSTITUTE OF (1948), Gate House, St. John's Square EC1M 4DH—*Exec. Dir.*, J. B. Lavelle.

PUBLIC TEACHERS OF LAW, SOCIETY OF (1908).—*Pres.*, Prof. L. Neville Brown, University of Birmingham; *Hon. Sec.*, Prof. D. B. Casson, University of Buckingham.

PURCHASING AND SUPPLY, INSTITUTE OF (1967), Easton House, Easton on the Hill, Stamford, Lincs PE9 3NZ—*Dir.-Gen.*, I. G. S. Groundwater.

QUALITY ASSURANCE, INSTITUTE OF, 54 Princes Gate, Exhibition Road SW7 2PG—*Sec.-Gen.*, R. Knowles, C.B.E.

QUARRIER'S HOMES (1871), Bridge of Weir, Renfrewshire.—*Chief Exec.*, Dr. J. R. Minto.

QUARRYING, INSTITUTE OF (1917), 7 Regent Street, Nottingham NG1 5BY—*Sec.*, R. Oates.

QUEEN ELIZABETH'S FOUNDATION FOR THE DISABLED (1967), Leatherhead, Surrey KT22 0BN—*Dir.*, M. B. Clark, PH.D. Incorporating Queen Elizabeth's Training College (1934), Banstead Place Assessment and Further Education Centre for Handicapped School Leavers (1973), Dorincourt Sheltered Workshops (1958) and Lulworth Court Holiday and Convalescent Home (1959).

QUEEN VICTORIA CLERGY FUND (1897), *Central Fund*, Church House, Dean's Yard SW1P 3NZ—*Sec.*, Capt. P. W. E. Parry, M.B.E.

QUEEN VICTORIA SCHOOL, Dunblane, Perthshire FK15 0JY—*Commandant*, Brig. O. R. Tweedy (*ret.*); *Headmaster*, J. D. Hankinson.

QUEEN'S ENGLISH SOCIETY—*Hon. Sec.*, A. I. Thompson, 2 South Side, Pulborough, Sussex RH20 2DH.

QUEEN'S NURSING INSTITUTE (1887), 57 Lower Belgrave Street SW1W 0LR—*Dir.*, P. E. Starr.

QUEKETT MICROSCOPICAL CLUB, c/o British Museum (Natural History), Cromwell Road SW7 5BD—*Hon. Sec. and Administrator*, S. H. Henderson.

RADIO SOCIETY OF GREAT BRITAIN (Incorporated), Alma House, Cranbourne Road, Potters Bar, Herts.—*Gen. Manager*, D. A. Evans.

RADIOLOGISTS, ROYAL COLLEGE OF (1934), 38 Portland Place W1N 3DG—*Sec.*, A. J. Cowles.

RAILWAY AND CANAL HISTORICAL SOCIETY, THE.—*Hon. Sec.*, R. E. Kilsby, Banestree, Jacobs Well Road, Guildford, Surrey GU4 7PA.

RAILWAY BENEVOLENT INSTITUTION (1858), 67 Ashbourne Road, Derby. Railway Children's and Old People's Home at Derby; financial assistance given.—*Exec. Officer*, W. W. K. Humphreys.

RAINER FOUNDATION, 89a Blackheath Hill SE10 8TJ. Direct help for young people at risk or in need: administers the national Intermediate Treatment Fund on behalf of the D.H.S.S.—*Dir.*, R. Kay.

RAMBLERS' ASSOCIATION (1935), 1–5 Wandsworth Road SW8 2LJ—*Sec.*, A. Mattingly.

RATEPAYERS' ASSOCIATIONS, NATIONAL UNION OF, 4 Eysham Court, Station Road, New Barnet, Herts EN5 1PS—*Hon. Gen. Sec.*, Mrs. D. E. Pannell.

RATING AND VALUATION ASSOCIATION (1882), 115 Ebury Street SW1W 9QT—*Sec.*, B. L. Hill.

RED CROSS SOCIETY, BRITISH. See BRITISH.

RED POLL CATTLE SOCIETY AND BRITISH DANE CATTLE SOCIETY OF GREAT BRITAIN AND IRELAND, 6 Church Street, Woodbridge, Suffolk IP12 1DH—*Sec.*, P. Ryder-Davies.

REEDHAM CHILDREN'S TRUST (1844), Purley, Surrey.—*Sec.*, Mrs. E. M. Johnston.

REFRIGERATION, INSTITUTE OF (1899), Kelvin House, 76 Mill Lane, Carshalton, Surrey SM5 2JR—*Sec.*, M. J. Horlick.

REGIONAL STUDIES ASSOCIATION, 29 Great James Street WC1N 3ES—*Exce. Sec.*, Gloria Frankel.

REGULAR FORCES EMPLOYMENT ASSOCIATION (1885), 25 Bloomsbury Square WC1A 2LN. Finds employment for non-commissioned ex-Regulars.—*General Manager*, Maj.-Gen. A. M. L. Hogge, C.B.

REINDEER COUNCIL OF THE UNITED KINGDOM (1949), Newton Road, Harston, Cambridge CB2 5NZ—*Hon. Sec.*, Dr. E. J. Lindgren.

RELIGION AND MEDICINE, INSTITUTE OF (1964).—*Organising Sec.*, C. H. Sinclair, St. Marylebone Parish Church, Marylebone Road NW1 5LT.

RENT OFFICERS, INSTITUTE OF.—*Hon. Sec.*, M. R. Webber, Musgrave House, Musgrave Row, Exeter, EX4 3TW.

RESEARCH DEFENCE SOCIETY, Grosvenor Gardens House, Grosvenor Gardens SW1W 0BS—*Hon. Sec.*, Prof. T. J. Biscoe.

RETAIL, BOOK, STATIONERY AND ALLIED TRADES EMPLOYEES' ASSOCIATION, 8/9 Commercial Road, Swindon, Wilts SN1 5RB—*Gen. Sec.*, D. A. Williamson.

RICHARD III SOCIETY.—*Sec.*, Miss E. M. Nokes, 4 Oakley Street SW3 5NN.

ROAD SAFETY OFFICERS, INSTITUTE OF (1971), 21 Windmill Drive, Northowram, Halifax, W. Yorks HX3 7DF—*Sec.*, Mrs. J. A. Thornton.

ROAD TRANSPORT ENGINEERS, INSTITUTION OF (1945), 1 Cromwell Place SW7 2JF—*Sec. and Chief Exec.*, D. M. Ivison.

ROMAN AND MEDIEVAL LONDON EXCAVATION COUNCIL.—*Hon. Sec.*, R. A. Woods, M.B.E., F.S.A., 31 Goodyers Avenue, Radlett, Herts.

ROMAN STUDIES, SOCIETY FOR PROMOTION OF, 31–34 Gordon Square WC1H 0PP—*Pres.*, Prof. S. S. Frere, C.B.E., F.S.A.; *Secs.*, Mrs. P. Gilbert.

ROTARY INTERNATIONAL IN GREAT BRITAIN AND IRELAND (1914), Sheen Lane House, Sheen Lane SW14 8AF—*Sec.*, J. H. Jackson.

ROUND TABLES OF GREAT BRITAIN AND IRELAND, NATIONAL ASSOCIATION OF (1927), Marchesi House, 15 Park Road, N.W.1.—*Gen. Sec.*, P. W. Tipton.

ROYAL AFRICAN SOCIETY (1901), 18 Northumberland Avenue, W.C.2.—*Sec.*, Mrs. P. North.

ROYAL AGRICULTURAL SOCIETY OF ENGLAND (1838), National Agricultural Centre, Stoneleigh, Kenilworth, Warwicks CV8 2LZ.—*Chief Exec.*, J. D. M. Hearth C.B.E.

ROYAL AGRICULTURAL SOCIETY OF THE COMMONWEALTH (1957).—*Hon. Sec.*, F. R. Francis, L.V.O., M.B.E., Robarts House, Rossmore Road NW1 6NP.

ROYAL AIR FORCE BENEVOLENT FUND (1919), 67 Portland Place W1N 4AR—*Controller*, Air Chief Marshal Sir Alasdair Steedman, G.C.B., C.B.E., D.F.C.

ROYAL AIR FORCES ASSOCIATION, 43 Grove Park Road W4 3RU—*Sec. Gen.*, D. Milne.

ROYAL ALEXANDRA AND ALBERT SCHOOL (1758), *Offices*, Foundation Office, Gatton Park, Reigate, Surrey RH2 0TW—*Sec.*, A. R. Rainbow, M.B.E.

ROYAL ALFRED SEAFARERS' SOCIETY (1865), Weston Acres, Woodmansterne Lane, Banstead, Surrey SM7 3HB—*Gen. Sec.*, J. H. Moore.

ROYAL ARMOURED CORPS BENEVOLENT FUND, *Headquarters*, R.A.C. Centre, Bovington Camp, Wareham, Dorset; *Sec.*, Lt.-Col. C. H. Rayment, M.B.E.

ROYAL ARTILLERY ASSOCIATION, Artillery House, Connaught Barracks, Grand Depot Road SE18 6SL—*Gen. Sec.*, Col. R. H. Haynes, M.B.E.

ROYAL ASIATIC SOCIETY OF GREAT BRITAIN AND IRELAND (1823), 56 Queen Anne Street W1M 9LA—*Dir.*, F. G. Goodwin.

ROYAL ASSOCIATION OF BRITISH DAIRY FARMERS (1876), Robarts House, Rossmore Road NW1 6NP—*Chief Exec.*, F. R. Francis, L.V.O., M.B.E.

ROYAL BRITISH NURSES ASSOCIATION, 94 Upper Tollington Park N4 4NB—*Hon. Sec.*, Mrs. H. M. Vorstermans, M.B.E.

ROYAL CALEDONIAN SCHOOLS (1815), Bushey, Herts WD2 3TS—*The Master*, Capt. R. E. Wilson, C.B.E., D.F.C., R.N.

ROYAL CAMBRIDGE HOME FOR SOLDIERS' WIDOWS, 82–84 Hurst Road, East Molesey, Surrey KT8 9AH—*Superintendent*, Mrs. M. Bland.

ROYAL CELTIC SOCIETY (1820), 49 Queen Street, Edinburgh EH2 3NT—*Sec.*, J. G. S. Cameron, W.S.

ROYAL CHORAL SOCIETY (1871), Royal Albert Hall SW7 2AP—*Gen. Man.*, M. Heyland.

ROYAL COLLEGE OF VETERINARY SURGEONS, 32 Belgrave Square SW1X 8QP—*Pres.*, Prof. I. A. Silver, PH.D.; *Registrar*, A. R. W. Porter, C.B.E.

ROYAL COMMONWEALTH SOCIETY (1868), Northumberland Avenue WC2N 5BJ—(22,000 members). —*Sec.-Gen.*, Sir Michael Scott, K.C.V.O., C.M.G.

ROYAL DESIGNERS FOR INDUSTRY, FACULTY OF (1936) (Royal Society of Arts), John Adam Street WC2N 6EZ—*Master*, K. Grange, C.B.E.; *Sec.*, C. T. Lucas.

ROYAL ENGINEERS ASSOCIATION, *Headquarters*, at R.H.Q. Royal Engineers, Brompton Barracks, Chatham, Kent ME4 4UG—*Controller*, Col. G. S. Harris.

ROYAL ENGINEERS, THE INSTITUTION OF (1875), Brompton Barracks, Chatham, Kent ME4 4UG.—*Sec.*, Col. G. W. A. Napier.

ROYAL HIGHLAND AND AGRICULTURAL SOCIETY OF SCOTLAND (1784), Ingliston, Newbridge, Midlothian EH28 8NF—*Sec.*, J. R. Good.

ROYAL HORTICULTURAL SOCIETY (1804).—*Offices*, 80 Vincent Square, S.W.1. *Garden*, Wisley, Woking, Surrey.—*Sec.*, J. R. Cowell.

ROYAL HOSPITAL AND HOME FOR INCURABLES, PUTNEY (1854), West Hill, Putney SW15 3SW—*Chief Exec.*, Col. B. E. Blunt.

ROYAL HUMANE SOCIETY (1774).—Gives bravery awards for saving and attempting to save human life.—*Offices*, Brettenham House, Lancaster Place WC2E 7EP—*Sec.*, Maj. A. J. Dickinson.

ROYAL INSTITUTE OF INTERNATIONAL AFFAIRS (1920), Chatham House, 10 St. James's Square SW1Y 4LE—*Dir.*, Adm. Sir James Eberle, G.C.B.

ROYAL INSTITUTION OF GREAT BRITAIN (1799), 21 Albemarle Street W1X 4BS—*Pres.*, H.R.H. The Duke of Kent, G.C.M.G., G.C.V.O.; *Dir.*, Prof. Sir George Porter, F.R.S.; *Sec.*, Prof. E. A. Ash, C.B.E., F.R.S.

ROYAL LIFE SAVING SOCIETY, THE (1891), Mountbatten House, Studley, Warwickshire B80 7NN—*Dir.*, K. H. Sach.

ROYAL LITERARY FUND (1790), 144 Temple Chambers, Temple Avenue EC4Y 0DT Grants to necessitous authors of some published work of approved literary merit or to their immediate dependants.—*Pres.*, A. Crook; *Sec.*, A. Mackenzie Smith, O.B.E., M.C.

ROYAL MEDICAL BENEVOLENT FUND (1836), 24 King's Road, Wimbledon SW19 8QN—*Sec.*, P. G. Gordon-Smith.

ROYAL MEDICAL SOCIETY (1737), Students Centre, 5/5 Bristo Square, Edinburgh EH8 9AL—*Sec.*, P. Sigston.

ROYAL METAL TRADES BENEVOLENT SOCIETY (1843), 9 Totteridge Avenue, High Wycombe, Bucks HP13 6XG—*Sec.*, A. Whittle, M.B.E.

ROYAL MICROSCOPICAL SOCIETY, 37–38 St. Clements, Oxford OX4 1AJ—*Administrator*, Lt.-Col. P. G. Fleming.

ROYAL MILITARY POLICE ASSOCIATION (1946), Regimental Headquarters, Corps of Royal Military Police, Roussillon Barracks, Chichester, Sussex PO19 4BN—*Sec.*, Major P. N. Ross (*ret.*).

ROYAL MUSICAL ASSOCIATION (1874), 5 Church Street, Harston, Cambridge CB2 5NP—*Sec.*, Rosemary Dooley.

ROYAL NATIONAL LIFEBOAT INSTITUTION, THE (1824).—*Income* (1984) £20,239,000, expenditure £17,604,000; rescued in 1984, 1,319. 256 lifeboats are maintained on the coasts of Great Britain and Ireland. *Offices*, West Quay Road, Poole, Dorset BH15 1HZ—*Chairman*, The Duke of Atholl.

ROYAL NATIONAL MISSION TO DEEP SEA FISHERMEN (1881), 43 Nottingham Place W1M 4BX—*Sec.*, Mjr. Gen. L. A. W. New, C.B.E.

ROYAL NAVAL AND ROYAL MARINES CHILDREN'S TRUST (1834), H.M.S. *Nelson*, Portsmouth PO1 3HH—*Sec.*, Mrs. M. Bateman.

ROYAL NAVAL ASSOCIATION (1950), 82 Chelsea Manor Street SW3 5QJ—*Gen. Sec.*, Capt. D. W. Beadle, C.B.E., R.N.

ROYAL NAVAL BENEVOLENT SOCIETY (1739), 1 Fleet Street EC4Y 1BD—*Sec.*, Lt. Cdr. A. J. G. Newbery, O.B.E., R.N. (*ret.*).

ROYAL NAVAL BENEVOLENT TRUST (Grand Fleet and Kindred Funds) (1922), 1 High Street, Brompton, Gillingham, Kent ME7 5QZ (Local Committees at Chatham, Devonport, Portsmouth and Rosyth).—*Gen. Sec.*, Lt.-Cdr. D. C. Lawrence, R.N. (*ret.*).

ROYAL NAVY OFFICERS, ASSOCIATION OF (Trafalgar Day, 1925), 70 Porchester Terrace W2 6BL—*Sec.-Treas.*, Lt.-Cdr. J. V. Watson, M.B.E., R.N.

ROYAL OVER-SEAS LEAGUE (1910), Over-Seas House, Park Place, St. James's Street SW1A 1LR—*Chairman*, Sir David Scott, G.C.M.G.; *Dir. Gen.*, Capt. J. Rumble.

ROYAL PATRIOTIC FUND CORPORATION (1854), Golden Cross House, Duncannon Street, WC2 4JR. Administers funds for the benefit of widows, children and other dependants of deceased officers and servicemen of the Armed Forces.—*Sec.*, Brig. D. C. Blomfield-Smith, M.B.E.

ROYAL PHILHARMONIC SOCIETY (1813), 10 Stratford Place, W.1.—*Hon. Sec.*, M. Pope.

ROYAL PHOTOGRAPHIC SOCIETY (1853), R.P.S. National Centre of Photography, The Octagon, Milsom Street, Bath BA1 1DN—*Sec.*, K. R. Warr.

ROYAL PINNER SCHOOL FOUNDATION, 110 Old Brompton Road, S. Kensington SW7 3RB. (Trustee: The Royal Commercial Travellers' School Trust Ltd.) Assists in the education of children of sales representatives where families have suffered some adversity.—*Sec.*, S. Thurtell.

"ROYAL SAILORS' RESTS" (Miss Agnes Weston's) (1876). *Head Office*, 2a South Street, Gosport, Hants PO12 1ES. Centres for naval personnel at Devonport, St. Budeaux, Ilchester, Portland, Gosport, Portsmouth, Faslane and Rosyth.—*Sec.*, A. A. Lockwood.

ROYAL SCHOOL OF NEEDLEWORK (1872), 25 Princes Gate SW7 1QE—*Principal*, Mrs. J. Field.

ROYAL SCOTTISH COUNTRY DANCE SOCIETY (1923), 12 Coates Crescent, Edinburgh EH3 7AF—*Sec.*, Miss M. M. Gibson.

ROYAL SCOTTISH SOCIETY FOR PREVENTION OF CRUELTY TO CHILDREN (1884), Melville House, 41 Polwarth Terrace, Edinburgh EH11 1NU—*Gen. Sec.*, A. M. M. Wood, O.B.E.

ROYAL SEAMEN'S PENSION FUND (Incorporated) (1919), P.O. Box 62, 58 High Street, Sutton, Surrey SM1 1HD—*Sec.*, R. F. Van Houten.

ROYAL SIGNALS INSTITUTION (1950), 56 Regency Street SW1P 4AD—*Editor*, Lt. Col. K. E. P. Andrews, M.B.E.

ROYAL SOCIETY, THE (1660), 6 Carlton House Terrace SW1Y 5AG—*Pres.*, Sir Andrew Huxley, O.M., F.R.S.; *Treas. and Vice-Pres.*, Sir John Mason, C.B., F.R.S.; *Secretaries and Vice-Presidents*, Prof. R. J. Elliott, F.R.S.; Prof. D. C. Smith, F.R.S.; *Foreign Secretary and Vice-Pres.*, Sir Arnold Burgen, F.R.S.; *Executive Sec.*, Dr. P. T. Warren.

ROYAL SOCIETY FOR ASIAN AFFAIRS (1901). 42 Devonshire Street W1N 1LN—*Pres.*, The Lord Denman, M.C., C.B.E.; *Sec.*, Miss M. FitzSimons.

ROYAL SOCIETY FOR THE ENCOURAGEMENT OF ARTS MANUFACTURES AND COMMERCE (Royal Society of Arts) (1754), 8 John Adam Street, Adelphi WC2N 6EZ—*Chairman*, Sir Peter Baldwin, K.C.B.; *Sec.*, C. T. Lucas.

ROYAL SOCIETY FOR THE PREVENTION OF ACCIDENTS, Cannon House, Priory Queensway, Birmingham B4 6BS—*Dir. Gen.*, R. M. Warburton.

ROYAL SOCIETY FOR THE PREVENTION OF CRUELTY TO ANIMALS (1824), Causeway, Horsham, Sussex RH12 1HG—*Exec. Dir.*, F. D. Ward, C.B.E.

ROYAL SOCIETY FOR THE PROTECTION OF BIRDS (1889), The Lodge, Sandy, Beds SG19 2DL—*Dir. Gen.*, I. Prestt.

ROYAL SOCIETY OF BRITISH ARTISTS (1823), 17 Carlton House Terrace, S.W.1.—*Pres.*, P. Garrard; *Vice-President*, D. Carpanini; *Keeper*, C. de Winter.

ROYAL SOCIETY OF BRITISH SCULPTORS (1904), 108 Old Brompton Road, S.W.7.—*Pres.*, M. Rizzello, O.B.E.; *Sec.*, Miss M. O'Connor.

ROYAL SOCIETY OF EDINBURGH (1783), 22–24 George Street, Edinburgh EH2 2PQ—*Pres.*, Sir Alwyn Williams, C.B.E.; *Gen. Sec.*, Prof. R. M. S. Smellie,

PH.D., D.SC.; *Treas.*, Dr. Ian Forbes; *Curator*, Prof. D. M. Henderson.

ROYAL SOCIETY OF HEALTH (1876), to promote the health of the people, 38a St. Georges Drive SW1V 3QN—*Sec.*, G. M. T. Large.

ROYAL SOCIETY OF LITERATURE (1823), 1 Hyde Park Gardens W2 2LT—*Sec.*, Mrs. P. M. Schute.

ROYAL SOCIETY OF MEDICINE (1805), 1 Wimpole Street W1M 8AE—*Pres.*, (1985–86), Sir John Walton, T.D., F.R.C.P.; *Exec. Dir.*, R. N. Thomson.

ROYAL SOCIETY OF PORTRAIT PAINTERS (1891), 17 Carlton House Terrace, S.W.1.—*Pres.*, D. Poole.

ROYAL SOCIETY OF ST. GEORGE (1894), 4 Wilton Mews SW1X 8BD—*Hon. Gen. Sec.*, Mrs. W. M. Bourne.

ROYAL STAR AND GARTER HOME FOR DISABLED SAILORS, SOLDIERS, AND AIRMEN (1916), Richmond-upon-Thames, Surrey TW10 6RR—*Commandant*, Col. R. N. Harris, M.B.E.

ROYAL STATISTICAL SOCIETY (1834), 25 Enford Street W1H 2BH—*Pres.*, Dr. J. A. Melder, F.R.S.; *Sec.*, I. H. Blenkinsop.

ROYAL TANK REGIMENT ASSOCIATION and BENEVOLENT FUND, H.Q. R.A.C. Centre, Bovington Camp, Wareham, Dorset.—*Regimental Sec.*, Lt.-Col. C. H. Rayment, M.B.E.

ROYAL TELEVISION SOCIETY, Tavistock House East, Tavistock Square WC1H 9HR—*Hon. Sec.*, A. Pilgrim.

ROYAL UNITED KINGDOM BENEFICENT ASSOCIATION (1863), 6 Avonmore Road W14 8RL—*Gen. Sec.*, Rear Adm. B. C. Perowne, C.B.

ROYAL UNITED SERVICES INSTITUTE FOR DEFENCE STUDIES, Whitehall SW1A 2ET—*Dir.*, Gp. Capt. D. Bolton, R.A.F. (ret.)

RUBBER GROWERS' ASSOCIATION LTD., 90 Fenchurch Street EC3M 4BY—*Sec.*, Mrs. J. Taylor.

RURAL ENGLAND, COUNCIL FOR THE PROTECTION OF (1926), 4 Hobart Place SW1W 0HY—*Dir.*, R. B. Grove-White.

RURAL SCOTLAND, ASSOCIATION FOR PROTECTION OF (1926), 14a Napier Road, Edinburgh EH10 5AY—*Dir. and Sec.*, R. L. Smith, O.B.E., J.P.

RURAL WALES, COUNCIL FOR THE PROTECTION OF, Ty Gwyn, 31 High Street, Welshpool, Powys SY21 7JP—*Dir.*, S. R. J. Meade.

SAILORS' CHILDREN'S SOCIETY, THE (1821), Newland, Hull HU6 7RJ. Cares for British seamen's children who have lost a parent and for short periods during a mother's illness if father is at sea. Provides welfare facilities for seamen in Humber area, and Homes for aged seafarers at Hull and S. Shields.—*Sec.*, C. G. R. Streatfeild-James.

ST. DEINIOL'S RESIDENTIAL LIBRARY (1902), Hawarden, Deeside, Clwyd CH5 3DF—*Warden and Chief Librarian*, Rev. P. J. Jagger, F.R.Hist.S.

ST. DUNSTAN'S, for men and women blinded on War Service, P.O. Box 4XB, 12–14 Harcourt Street W1A 4XB. In March 1984, the number of blinded men and women in the care of the organization was 1,306.—*Pres.*, Col. Sir Michael Ansell, C.B.E., D.S.O.; *Chairman*, Adm. of the Fleet Sir Henry Leach, G.C.B.; *Sec.*, W. C. Weisblatt.

ST. JOHN AMBULANCE ASSOCIATION AND BRIGADE, 1 Grosvenor Crescent, S.W.1. Voluntary unpaid body providing first-aid cover at public gatherings.—*Chief Commander*, Maj.-Gen. P. R. Leuchars, C.B.E.; *Commissioner-in-Chief*, Maj.-Gen. Sir John Younger, Bt., C.B.E. *Brigade Strengths* (U.K. 1983), Ambulance Personnel, 15,509; Nursing Personnel, 16,029; Ambulance Cadets 11,244; Nursing Cadets, 25,943.—*Chief Sec.*, Brig. P. R. Body.

SALES AND MARKETING MANAGEMENT, INSTITUTE OF.—*Chief Exec.*, J. H. Goodman, Georgian House, 31 Upper George Street, Luton, Beds LU1 2RD.

SALMON AND TROUT ASSOCIATION (1903), Fishmongers' Hall EC4R 9EL—*Dir.*, J. Ferguson.

SALTIRE SOCIETY (1936), Saltire House, 13 Atholl Crescent, Edinburgh EH3 8HA—*Administrator*, Miss K. Austin.

SAMARITANS, THE (to help the suicidal and despairing).—*Gen. Sec.*, Rev. D. Evans, 17 Uxbridge Road, Slough, Berks SL1 1SN.

SAMUEL PEPYS CLUB—*Sec.*, R. H. Adams, T.D., F.S.A., 14 Dale Close, Oxford OX1 1TU.

SANITARY ENGINEERS, INSTITUTION OF. *See* PUBLIC HEALTH ENGINEERS.

SAVE THE CHILDREN FUND, THE (1919), 17 Grove Lane, SE5 8RD—*Dir. Gen.*, N. Hinton.

SCHOOL LIBRARY ASSOCIATION, Victoria House, 29–31 George Street, Oxford OX1 2AY—*Sec.*, Miriam Curtis.

SCHOOL NATURAL SCIENCE SOCIETY, 10 Plantation Road, Faversham, Kent ME13 8QU—*Hon. Gen. Sec.*, J. Williams.

SCHOOLMASTERS, SOCIETY OF (1798) (for the relief of Necessitous Schoolmasters and of their Widows and Orphans), 1 Turk's Head Court, Eton, Berks SL4 6AG—*Sec.*, Mrs. M. S. Freeburn.

SCHOOLMISTRESSES AND GOVERNESSES BENEVOLENT INSTITUTION, Queen Mary House, Manor Park Road, Chislehurst, Kent BR7 5PY. Helps schoolmistresses, matrons and women employed in an administrative capacity in independent schools, as well as governesses, grants, a residential home which also accepts ladies from comparable professions—*Dir. and Sec.*, R. W. Hayward.

SCIENCE AND LEARNING, SOCIETY FOR THE PROTECTION OF, 20–21 Compton Terrace NI 2UN—*Sec.*, Miss E. Fraser.

SCIENCE EDUCATION, ASSOCIATION FOR, College Lane, Hatfield, Herts AL10 9AA—*Gen. Sec.*, B. G. Atwood.

SCOTCH WHISKY ASSOCIATION, 20 Atholl Crescent, Edinburgh EH3 8HF.—*Dir. Gen. and Sec.*, Col. H. F. O. Bewsher, O.B.E.; *Information and Development Office*, 17 Half Moon Street W1Y 7RB.

SCOTTISH CHURCH HISTORY SOCIETY (1922).—*Hon. Sec.*, C. G. F. Brockie, Grange Manse, 51 Portland Road, Kilmarnock KA1 2EQ.

SCOTTISH GENEALOGY SOCIETY (1953).—*Hon. Sec.*, Miss J. P. S. Ferguson, 21 Howard Place, Edinburgh EH3 5JY.

SCOTTISH HISTORY SOCIETY (1886).—*Hon. Sec.*, Dr. A. M. Smith, Dept. of Modern History, University of Dundee DD1 4HN.

SCOTTISH LANDOWNERS' FEDERATION (1906).—*Dir.*, D. J. Hughes Hallett, 18 Abercromby Place, Edinburgh EH3 6TY.

SCOTTISH LAW AGENTS SOCIETY, 33–34 Charlotte Square, Edinburgh EH2 4HF—*Sec.*, G. F. Davidson.

SCOTTISH LIFE OFFICES, ASSOCIATED (1841), 23 St. Andrew Square, Edinburgh EH2 1AQ—*Sec.*, G. C. Train.

SCOTTISH MARINE BIOLOGICAL ASSOCIATION (1914), Dunstaffnage Marine Research Laboratory, P.O. Box 3, Oban, Argyll PA34 4AD—*Dir., and Sec.*, Prof. R. I. Currie, C.B.E., F.R.S.E.

SCOTTISH NATIONAL BLOOD TRANSFUSION ASSOCIATION (1940), 29 Abercromby Place, Edinburgh EH3 6UE—*Sec.*, P. C. Taylor.

SCOTTISH NATIONAL INSTITUTION FOR THE WAR BLINDED. Workshops at Glasgow and Linburn.—*Appeals Director*, Maj. D. F. Callander, M.C., P.O. Box 304, 38 Albany Street, Edinburgh.

SCOTTISH NATIONAL WAR MEMORIAL (1927), The Castle, Edinburgh EH1 2YT—*Sec.*, J. D. M. Watson; *Curator*, T. C. Barker.

SCOTTISH RECORD SOCIETY, Scottish History Dept., Univ. of Glasgow G12 8QQ—*Hon. Sec.*, Dr. J. Kirk.

SCOTTISH SECONDARY TEACHERS' ASSOCIATION, 15 Dundas Street, Edinburgh EH3 6QG—*Gen. Sec.*, A. A. Stanley.

SCOTTISH SOCIETY FOR PREVENTION OF CRUELTY TO ANIMALS (1839), 19 Melville Street, Edinburgh EH3 7PL—*Chief Exec.*, Sir Cameron Rusby, K.C.B., L.V.O.

SCOTTISH SOCIETY FOR THE PROTECTION OF WILD BIRDS (1927), Foremount House, Kilbarchan, Renfrewshire PA10 2EZ—*Hon. Sec. and Treas.*, Dr. J. A. Gibson.

SCOTTISH TOURIST BOARD (1969), 23 Ravelston Terrace, Edinburgh EH4 3EU—*Chief Exec.*, Dr. D. A. Pattison.

SCOTTISH WILDLIFE TRUST (1964), 25 Johnston Terrace, Edinburgh EH1 2NH—*Chief Exec.*, J. R. Baldwin.

SCOTTISH WOMEN'S RURAL INSTITUTES (1917), 42 Heriot Row, Edinburgh EH3 6ES—*Gen. Sec.*, Mrs. J. A. Noble.

SCOUT ASSOCIATION, THE, *Headquarters*, Baden-Powell House, Queen's Gate SW7 5JS—*Chief Scout*, Maj.-Gen. M. J. H. Walsh, C.B., D.S.O.; *Chief Exec.*, Comm. K. H. Stevens, C.B.E. Membership in U.K. (1984), 605,000; World Membership over 16,000,000 in over 150 countries and territories.

SCRIBES AND ILLUMINATORS, THE SOCIETY OF.—*Hon. Sec.*, Mrs. S. Cavendish, c/o 43 Earlham Street WC2H 9LD

SCRIPTURE GIFT MISSION (1888), Radstock House, 3 Eccleston Street SW1W 9LZ Copies and selections of the Scriptures circulated (1984), 14,838,188.—*Sec.*, R. Kennedy.

SCRIPTURE UNION (1867), 130 City Road EC1V 2NJ—*Gen. Dir.*, A. C. N. Martin.

SEA CADET ASSOCIATION, Broadway House, Broadway, Wimbledon SW19 1RL—*Pres.*, Admiral of the Fleet Sir Henry Leach, G.C.B.; *Gen. Sec.*, Cmdr. P. J. Everett, O.B.E., R.N.

SEAMEN'S CHRISTIAN FRIEND SOCIETY (1846), 26 Davyhulme Road East, Stretford, Manchester M32 0DW—*Sec.*, D. J. Laurie.

SECONDARY HEADS ASSOCIATION, 107 St. Paul's Road N1 2NB—*Gen. Sec.*, T. P. Snape. (Association formed from amalgamation of Headmasters Association and Association of Headmistresses).

SELDEN SOCIETY (1887), Faculty of Laws, Queen Mary College, Mile End Road, E.1. To encourage the study and advance the knowledge of the History of English Law.—*Pres.*, Prof. S. F. C. Milsom, F.B.A.; *Sec.*, V. Tunkel.

SHAFTESBURY HOMES AND *Arethusa* (1843), 3 Rectory Grove, S.W.4.—*Gen. Sec.*, Maj. R. P. A. de Berniere-Smart.

SHAFTESBURY SOCIETY, THE (1844), Shaftesbury House, 2a Amity Grove, Raynes Park SW20 0LJ. Engaged in caring for physically and mentally handicapped, the elderly and socially deprived. Maintains residential schools and hostels, further education centres and holiday centres, and mission centres in Greater London.—*Sec.*, G. Holloway.

SHEEP ASSOCIATION, NATIONAL, 106 High Street, Tring, Herts HP23 4AF—*Sec.*, J. Thorley.

SHELLFISH ASSOCIATION OF GREAT BRITAIN, Fishmongers' Hall, London Bridge EC4R 9EL—*Dir.*, Dr. E. Edwards.

SHELTER (National Campaign for the Homeless), 157 Waterloo Road SE1 8XF; *Pres.*, Lord Pitt of Hampstead; *Dir.*, Miss S. McKechnie.

SHERLOCK HOLMES SOCIETY OF LONDON (1951), The Old Crown Inn, Lopen, Somerset TA13 5JX—*Hon. Sec.*, Capt. W. R. Michell, R.N. (*ret.*).

SHIPBROKERS, INSTITUTE OF CHARTERED (1911), 24 St. Mary Axe EC3A 8DE—*Sec.*, J. H. Parker.

SHIPWRECKED FISHERMEN AND MARINERS' ROYAL BENEVOLENT SOCIETY (1839), 1 North Pallant, Chichester, West Sussex PO19 1TL—*Gen. Sec.*, Miss V. G. Austin.

SHIRE HORSE SOCIETY (1878), East of England Showground, Peterborough PE2 0XE.—*Sec.*, R. W. Bird, M.B.E.

SHRIEVALTY ASSOCIATION, c/o A. J. Wilson, The Sheriff's Office, 6 Chapel Street, Preston, Lancs PR1 8AN—*Sec.-Treas.*, E. A. Nickson.

SIMPLIFIED SPELLING SOCIETY (1908).—*Chairman*, C. J. H. Jolly, 12 Pembridge Mews, Notting Hill W11 3EQ.

SIR OSWALD STOLL FOUNDATION, 446 Fulham Road SW6 1DT—*Sec.*, Rev. J. A. Garwell, R.N.

SMALLFARMERS' ASSOCIATION, THE (1979), Freepost EC3B 3EH—*Hon. Sec.*, Mrs. R. B. Weiss.

SOCIAL RESPONSIBILITY AND EDUCATION DEPARTMENT OF THE RELIGIOUS SOCIETY OF FRIENDS, Friends House, Euston Road, N.W.1.

SOCIAL WORKERS, BRITISH ASSOCIATION OF (1970), 16 Kent Street, Birmingham B5 6RD—*Gen. Sec.*, D. Jones.

SOCIALIST PARTY OF GREAT BRITAIN (1904), 52 Clapham High Street SW4 7UN—*Gen. Sec.*, A. G. Atkinson.

SOLDIERS' AND AIRMEN'S SCRIPTURE READERS ASSOCIATION, THE (1838), Havelock House, Barrack Road, Aldershot, Hants GU11 3NP—*Gen. Sec.*, Lt.-Col. K. W. Sear (*ret.*).

SOLDIERS' DAUGHTERS' SCHOOL, ROYAL (1855), 65 Rosslyn Hill, Hampstead, N.W.3.—*Sec.*, Col. J. G. Palmer, O.B.E.

SOLDIERS', SAILORS' AND AIRMEN'S FAMILIES ASSOCIATION (1885), 27 Queen Anne's Gate SW1H 9BZ—*Chairman*, Lt.-Gen. Sir Napier Crookenden, K.C.B., D.S.O., O.B.E.; *Controller*, Mjr. Gen. C. R. Grey, C.B.E.; *Sec.*, Capt. W. Stuart.

SOLDIERS, SAILORS AND AIRMEN'S HELP SOCIETY (Incorporated) (1899), See FORCES HELP SOCIETY.

SOLICITORS' BENEVOLENT ASSOCIATION (1858), Lonsdale Chambers, 27 Chancery Lane WC2A 1NF—*Sec.*, Lt.-Col. D. G. Martin, O.B.E.

SOLICITORS IN THE SUPREME COURTS OF SCOTLAND, SOCIETY OF.—*Sec.*, A. R. Brownlie, 2 Abercromby Place, Edinburgh EH3 6JZ—*Treas.*, D. A. Lamb, 24 York Place, Edinburgh.

S.O.S. SOCIETY, THE (1929), 38 Kensington Park Road W11 3BU. Old people's homes (5), Mental Rehabilitation homes (2), Ex-offenders hostel (1), Young Men's Hostel (1).—*Chief Exec.*, Lt.-Col. P. Rew.

SOUTH AMERICAN MISSIONARY SOCIETY, Allen Gardiner House, Pembury Road, Tunbridge Wells, Kent TN2 3QU—*Gen. Sec.*, Rev. Canon P. D. King.

SOUTH WALES INSTITUTE OF ENGINEERS (1857), Institute Buildings, Park Place, Cardiff CF1 3UG—*Hon. Sec.*, R. E. Lindsay, J.P.

SPASTICS SOCIETY, THE (1952), 12 Park Crescent W1N 4EQ—*Sec.*, Sir John Cox, K.C.B.

SPEAKERS CLUBS, THE ASSOCIATION OF (1971), 16 Rowanbank, Scone PH2 6PU—*Sec.*, K. A. MacLeod Lewison.

SPINA BIFIDA AND HYDROCEPHALUS, ASSOCIATION FOR, 22 Upper Woburn Place WC1H 0EP—*Exec. Dir.*, Miss M. P. Gilbertson.

SPORTS MEDICINE, INSTITUTE OF (1963), c/o Faculty of Engineering & Science, Polytechnic of Central London, 115 New Cavendish Street W1M 8JS—*Hon. Sec.*, P. Sebastian.

SPURGEON'S HOMES (1867), Haddon House, Station Road, Birchington, Kent CT7 9DH—*Sec.*, P. E. Johnson.

STATISTICIANS, INSTITUTE OF (1948), 36 Churchgate Street, Bury St. Edmunds, Suffolk IP33 1RD—*Sec.*, Dr. L. W. Hudson.

STATUTE LAW SOCIETY (1968), 186 City Road EC4V 2NU—*Hon. Sec.*, H. Hudson.

STEWART SOCIETY (1899), 48 Castle Street, Edinburgh EH2 3LX—*Hon. Sec.*, D. F. Stewart, W.S.

STRATEGIC STUDIES, THE INTERNATIONAL INSTITUTE FOR (1958), 23 Tavistock Street WC2E 7NQ—*Sec.*, Dr. R. O'Neill.

STRUCTURAL ENGINEERS, INSTITUTION OF (1908), 11 Upper Belgrave Street, S.W.1.—*Sec.*, D. J. Clark.

STUDENT CHRISTIAN MOVEMENT (1889), Manor House, 40 Moat Lane, Birmingham B5 5RD—*Gen. Sec.*, Rev. T. E. McClure.

SUFFOLK HORSE SOCIETY, 6 Church Street, Woodbridge, Suffolk IP12 1DH—*Sec.*, P. Ryder-Davies.

SURGEONS OF ENGLAND, ROYAL COLLEGE OF (1800), 35–43 Lincoln's Inn Fields WC2A 3PN—*Pres.*, Prof. Sir Geoffrey Slaney, K.B.E.; *Sec.*, R. S. Johnson-Gilbert, O.B.E.

SURGEONS OF EDINBURGH, ROYAL COLLEGE OF (1505), Nicolson Street, Edinburgh EH8 9DW—*Sec.*, P. Edmond, C.B.E., Q.H.S., T.D.

SURGICAL TECHNOLOGISTS, BRITISH INSTITUTE OF, 103 New Oxford Street, W.C.1.—*Sec.*, I. F. Sherwood.

SURVEYORS, ROYAL INSTITUTION OF CHARTERED (incorporating the Institute of Quantity Surveyors) (1868), 12 Great George Street SW1P 3AD—*Sec. Gen.*, M. Pattison.

SUSSEX CATTLE SOCIETY (1887), Station Road, Robertsbridge, E. Sussex TN32 5DG—*Manager*, Mrs. D. Jowitt.

SUTTON HOUSING TRUST (1901), Sutton Court, Tring, Herts HP23 5BB—*Dir.*, I. C. F. Butcher.

SWEDENBORG SOCIETY (1810), 20–21 Bloomsbury Way WC1A 2TH—*Sec.*, Madeline G. Waters.

TALKING BOOKS FOR THE HANDICAPPED (National Listening Library), 12 Lant Street SE1 1QH—*Exec. Dir.*, R. Shead.

TAVISTOCK INSTITUTE OF HUMAN RELATIONS, Tavistock Centre, 120 Belsize Lane NW3 5BA—*Sec.*, P. M. Foster.

TAXATION, INSTITUTE OF (1930), 3 Grosvenor Crescent SW1X 7EL—*Sec.*, J. F. Martin.

TAX PAYERS' SOCIETY, Room 22, Wheatsheaf House, 4 Carmelite Street EC4Y 0JA—*Dir.*, D. J. Bryant.

TEACHERS IN COMMERCE LTD., FACULTY OF, 141 Bedford Road, Sutton Coldfield, West Midlands B75 6DB—*Sec.*, J. Snowdon.

TEACHERS OF HOME ECONOMICS LTD., NATIONAL ASSOCIATION OF, Hamilton House, Mabledon Place WC1H 9BJ—*Gen. Man.*, P. G. Higgins.

TEACHERS OF MATHEMATICS, ASSOCIATION OF, Kings Chambers, Queen Street, Derby DE1 3DA—*Hon. Sec.*, J. D. Warwick.

TEACHERS OF THE DEAF, BRITISH ASSOCIATION OF.—Rycroft Centre, Royal Schools for the Deaf, Stanley Road, Cheadle Hulme, Cheshire SK8 6RF—*Sec.*, R. S. Eldridge.

TEACHERS' UNION, ULSTER (1919), 94 Malone Road, Belfast BT9 5HP—*Gen. Sec.*, D. Allen.

TELECOMMUNICATIONS USERS' ASSOCIATION, 34 Grand Avenue N10 3BP—*Dir.*, M. Elwes.

TEMPERANCE SOCIETIES:—

British National Temperance League (1834), Livesey-Clegg House, 44 Union Street, Sheffield S1 2JP—*Hon. Sec.*, Miss. M. Daniel.

British Women's Temperance Association, S.C.U. (1876), 8 North Bank Street, Edinburgh EH1 2LP—*Hon. Sec.*, Miss J. E. H. Gillon.

Church of England National Council for Social Aid, 38 Ebury Street SW1W 0LU—*Gen. Sec.*, Rev. E. W. F. Agar.

Churches Council on Alcohol and Drugs (1915), 4 Southampton Row WC1B 4AA—*Gen. Sec.*, Mrs. B. Smith.

Division of Social Responsibility of the Methodist Church, No. 1 Central Buildings, Westminster SW1H 9NH—*Gen. Sec.*, Rev. G. M. Burt.

Independent Order of Rechabites, Salford Unity Friendly Society, London District (1870), No. 30, 18 Doughty Street, W.C.1.

International Christian Federation for the Prevention of Alcoholism and Drug Addiction, 27 Tavistock Square, WC1H 9HH—*Gen. Sec.*, Rev. J. K. Lawton.

Order of the Sons of Temperance, 21 Victoria Avenue, Harrogate HG1 5RD—*Sec.*, K. Unsworth.

Royal Naval Temperance Society (auxiliary of Royal Sailors' Rests), 2a South Street, Gosport, Hants PO12 1ES—*Sec.*, A. A. Lockwood.

Social Responsibility Dept., General Assembly of Unitarian and Free Christian Churches, Essex Hall, Essex Street, W.C.2.—*Sec.*, G. Cox.

Social Responsibility Committee of the Mission Board, Scottish Episcopal Church (1919).—*Gen. Sec.*, M. D. Patterson, General Synod of the Scottish Episcopal Church, 21 Grosvenor Crescent, Edinburgh EH12 5EE.

United Kingdom Alliance, Alliance House, 12 Caxton Street, SW1H 0QS—*Gen. Sec.*, Rev. B. Kinman.

Templeton Foundation, 16 Kingfisher Lane, Turners Hill, Crawley, Sussex RH10 4QP.—*U.K. Rep.*, Rev. H. E. Pearse.

Territorial, Auxiliary and Volunteer Reserve Associations, Council of (1908), Centre Block, Duke of York's Headquarters, Chelsea SW3 4SG—*Sec.*, Maj.-Gen. M. Matthews, c.b.

Textile Institute (1910), 10 Blackfriars Street, Manchester.—*Gen. Sec.*, R. G. Denyer.

Theatre Research, Society for (1948).—*Hon. Secs.*, Dr. K. M. Barker, D. Forbes, 77 Kinnerton Street SW1X 8ED.

Theatrical Fund Association, Royal General (1839), 11 Garrick Street WC2E 9AR—*Sec.*, J. Berkeley.

Theatrical Ladies' Guild of Charity (1892), Shaftesbury Theatre, Shaftesbury Avenue WC2H 8DP—*Admin. Sec.*, Mrs. K. Nichols.

Theosophical Society in England (1875), 50 Gloucester Place W1H 3HJ—*Gen. Sec.*, Dr. H. Gray.

Thistle Foundation, The (1945), 27a Walker Street, Edinburgh EH3 7HX—*Dir.*, P. Croft.

Thomas Coram Foundation for Children (1739), 40 Brunswick Square WC1N 1AZ—*Dir. and Sec.*, C. P. Masters.

Thoracic Society, The British.—*Hon. Secs.*, A. E. Tattersfield, f.r.c.p., Centre Block, Southampton General Hospital, Tremone Road, Southampton; I. A. Campbell, m.r.c.p., Llandough Hospital, Cardiff.

Toc H (1915), *Headquarters*, 1 Forest Close, Wendover, Bucks HP22 6BT—*Gen. Sec.*, (vacant).

Town and Country Planning Association, 17 Carlton House Terrace, SW1Y 5AS—*Dir.*, D. Hall.

Town Planning Institute, Royal (1914), 26 Portland Place, W.1.

Townswomen's Guilds, National Union of (1929), 75 Harborne Road, Edgbaston, Birmingham.—*Nat. Sec.*, Mrs. R. Campbell-Tanner.

Toynbee Hall, The Universities' Settlement in East London, 28 Commercial Street, Whitechapel E1 6LS—*Warden*, D. P. Chesworth.

Trade Mark Agents, Institute of (1934), Suite 3, Panther House, 38 Mount Pleasant, WC1X 0AP—*Sec.*, E. R. Wenman.

Trade, National Chamber of (1897), Enterprise House, Henley-on-Thames, Oxon. RG9 1TU—*Dir. Gen.*, L. E. S. Seeney, o.b.e.

Trading Standards Administration, The Institute of—*Admin. Officer*, J. T. Fisher, Metropolitan House, 37 Victoria Avenue, Southend-on-Sea, Essex SS2 6DA.

Transport Administration, Institute of (1944), 32 Palmerston Road, Southampton SO1 1LL—*Nat. Sec.*, P. F. Green.

Transport, Chartered Institute of (1919), 80 Portland Place W1N 4DP—*Dir.-Gen.*, J. C. F. Cameron.

Transport Consultative Committee, Central (1948), 1st Floor, Golden Cross House, Duncannon Street WC2N 4JF—*Sec.*, L. A. Dumelow.

Tropical Medicine and Hygiene, Royal Society of (1907), Manson House, 26 Portland Place W1N 4EY.

Turner Society, BCM Box Turner, WC1N 3XX—*Sec.*, Mrs. P. Assender.

UFAW (Universities Federation for Animal Welfare) (1926), 8 Hamilton Close, South Mimms, Potters Bar, Herts EN6 3QD—*Sec.*, Lt. Col. T. J. Reynolds.

Unit Trust Association (1959), Park House, 16 Finsbury Circus, E.C.2.—*Sec.*, A. C. Smith.

United Nations Association of Great Britain and Northern Ireland (1945), 3 Whitehall Court SW1A 2EL—*Dir.*, M. Harper.

United Reformed Church History Society, 86 Tavistock Place WC1H 9RT—*Hon. Sec.*, Rev. Dr. S. Orchard.

United Society for Christian Literature, The, Robertson House, Leas Road, Guildford, Surrey GU14 4QW—*Gen. Sec.*, Rev. A. Gilmore.

United Synagogue (1870).—*Pres.*, V. Lucas; *Sec.*, J. J. Julius, Woburn House, Upper Woburn Place WC1H 0EZ.

Universities Central Council on Admissions (1961), P.O. Box 28, Cheltenham, Glos. GL50 1HY—*Gen. Sec.*, P. A. Oakley.

University Women, British Federation of (1907), Crosby Hall, Cheyne Walk, S.W.3.—*Sec.*, Mrs. C. Ellis.

Valuers and Auctioneers, Incorporated Society of, 3 Cadogan Gate SW1X 0AS—*Sec.*, M. Astbury.

Vegan Society, The (1944), 33/35 George Street, Oxford OX1 2AY—*Gen. Sec.*, B. Kew.

Vegetarian Society of the United Kingdom Ltd., Parkdale, Dunham Road, Altrincham, Cheshire WA14 4QG—*Chief Exec.*, P. Cox.

Venereal Diseases, Medical Society for the Study of—*Hon. Sec.*, Dr. M. A. Waugh, Dept. of Genito-Urinary Medicine, Leeds General Infirmary, Great George Street, Leeds LS1 3EX.

Vernacular Architecture Group (1953), 18 Portland Place, Leamington Spa, Warwicks CV32 5EU—*Hon. Sec.*, Dr. N. W. Alcock.

Vice-Chancellors and Principals of the Universities of the United Kingdom, Committee of, 29 Tavistock Square, W.C.1.—*Chairman*, M. Shock; *Sec. Gen.*, B. H. Taylor.

Victoria Cross and George Cross Association, The, Room 04, Archway Block South, Old Admiralty Building SW1A 2BE—*Chairman*, Rear-Adm. B. C. G. Place, V.C., c.b., d.s.c.

Victoria Institute (Philosophical Society of Great Britain).—*Pres.*, Dr. D. J. E. Ingram; *Asst. Sec.*, B. H. T. Weller, 29 Queen Street EC4R 1BH.

Victoria League for Commonwealth Friendship (1901), 18 Northumberland Avenue, W.C.2.—*Sec.*, Mrs. S. Barnett, o.b.e.

Victorian Society (1958), 1 Priory Gardens, Bedford Park W4 1TT—*Sec.*, Mrs. J. Freeman.

Victory (Services) Association Ltd. and Club, The, 63–79 Seymour Street W2 2HF—*Chief Exec.*, D. G. Stovey.

Viking Society for Northern Research, University College, Gower Street WC1E 6BT.—*Hon. Secs.*, Mrs. U. Dronke; Prof. M. P. Barnes.

Vitreous Enamellers, Institute of, Ripley, Derby DE5 3EB.—*Sec.*, J. D. Gardom.

VOLUNTARY SERVICE OVERSEAS (1958), 9 Belgrave Square SW1X 8PW—*Dir.*, N. McIntosh.

WAR ON WANT (1952), Three Castles House, 1 London Bridge Street SE1 9SG—*Gen. Sec.*, G. Galloway.

WATER ENGINEERS AND SCIENTISTS, INSTITUTION OF, 31–33 High Holborn WC1V 6AX—*Pres.* (1985–86), R. J. Slater; *Sec.*, B. J. Dangerfield.

WELDING INSTITUTE, THE, Abington Hall, Cambridge CB1 6AL, and 54 Princes Gate SW7 2PG—*Dir.-Gen.*, Dr. A. A. Wells, O.B.E., F.R.S.

WELFARE OFFICERS, INSTITUTE OF (1945), 25 Cross Street, Manchester M2 1WL—*Hon. Gen. Sec.*, E. Rhodes, PH.D.

WELLCOME TRUST (1936), 1 Park Square West, N.W.1.—*Dir.*, P. O. Williams, M.B., F.R.C.P.

WELLS (H. G.) SOCIETY, Dept. of Language and Literature, Polytechnic of North London, Prince of Wales Road NW5 3LB—*Sec.*, C. Rolfe.

WESLEY HISTORICAL SOCIETY (1893).—*Gen. Sec.*, Mrs. E. D. Graham, 34 Spiceland Road, Birmingham B31 1NJ.

WEST AFRICA COMMITTEE (1956), 315 Oxford Street W1R 2BQ—*Secs.*, Group Capt. P. R. Magrath; J. A. R. Macdonald, O.B.E..

WEST INDIA COMMITTEE (1750), 48 Albemarle Street W1X 4AR—*Dir.*, D. A. Jessop.

WEST LONDON MISSION (1887), 19 Thayer Street W1M 5LJ—*Supt.*, Rev. Dr. J. A. Newton.

WHICH? CONSUMERS' ASSOCIATION (1957), 14 Buckingham Street WC2N 6DS—*Dir.*, P. Goldman, C.B.E.

WIDOWS, SOCIETY FOR THE RELIEF OF DISTRESSED (1823) (residing within seven miles of Charing Cross and applying within four months of widowhood), 175 Tower Bridge Road, S.E.1.—*Sec.*, W. N. Barr.

WILDLIFE ARTISTS, SOCIETY OF (1962), 17 Carlton House Terrace, S.W.1.—*Pres.*, K. Shackleton.

WILLIAM MORRIS SOCIETY AND KELMSCOTT FELLOW-SHIP (1918).—*Hon. Sec.*, Dr. R. S. Smith, Kelmscott House, 26 Upper Mall W6 9TA.

WINE AND SPIRIT ASSOCIATION OF GREAT BRITAIN AND NORTHERN IRELAND (INC), Five Kings House, Upper Thames Street EC4V 3BH—*Dir.*, R. H. Insoll, E.R.D.

WOMEN ARTISTS, SOCIETY OF (1855), 17 Carlton House Terrace, S.W.1.—*Pres.*, Mrs. G. Dawson.

WOMEN, NATIONAL ADVISORY CENTRE ON CAREERS FOR (formerly Women's Employment Federation) (1933), Drayton House, 30 Gordon Street WC1H 0AX—*Dir.*, Miss K. M. Menon.

WOMEN PILOTS' ASSOCIATION, BRITISH (1955), 25 Foubert's Place, W.1.

WOMEN, SOCIETY FOR PROMOTING THE TRAINING OF (1859) (Women's Loan Training Fund), The Dean Cottages, Hedgerley, Bucks SL2 3UY.—*Sec.*, Mrs. W. M. Golding.

WOMEN'S ENGINEERING SOCIETY (1920), 25 Foubert's Place W1V 2AL—*Sec.*, Mrs. A. Soteriou.

WOMEN'S HOLIDAY FUND (1895), 125 Wilton Road SW1V 1LE—*Sec.*, Mrs. E. Hendrie.

WOMEN'S INSTITUTES, NATIONAL FEDERATION OF (1915), 39 Eccleston Street SW1W 9NT—*Gen. Sec.*, Mrs. A. Ballard.

WOMEN'S INTERNATIONAL LEAGUE FOR PEACE AND FREEDOM (1915) British Section, 17 Victoria Park Square E2 9PB—*Hon. Sec.*, Alison Britton.

WOMEN'S NATIONAL CANCER CONTROL CAMPAIGN, 1 South Audley Street W1Y 5DQ—*Dir.*, Alice Burns.

WOMEN'S ROYAL NAVAL SERVICE BENEVOLENT TRUST, 1a Chesham Street SW1X 8NL—*Sec.*, Mrs. J. Y. Ellis.

WOMEN'S ROYAL VOLUNTARY SERVICE (WRVS) (1938), 17 Old Park Lane W1Y 4AJ—*National Chairman*, Mrs. B. Shenfield.

WOMEN'S TRANSPORT SERVICE (FANY) (1907), Duke of York's H.Q., Chelsea SW3 4RX—*Corps Commander*, Mrs. S. Y. Parkinson, O.B.E.

WOOD PRESERVING ASSOCIATION, BRITISH, Premier House, 150 Southampton Row WC1B 5AL—*Dir.*, J. Bick.

WORCESTERSHIRE ASSOCIATION (1926).—*Hon. Sec.*, D. M. Alexander, 8 Sansome Walk, Worcester WR1 1LW.

WORKERS' EDUCATIONAL ASSOCIATION, Temple House, 9 Upper Berkeley Street W1H 8BY—*Gen. Sec.*, R. Lochrie.

WORKS AND HIGHWAYS TECHNICIAN ENGINEERS, IN-STITUTION OF, Suite 21, 4th Floor, 125 High Holborn, W.C.1.—*Gen. Sec. and Registrar*, S. H. Crowle.

WORLD CONGRESS OF FAITHS (1936), 28 Powis Gardens, W.11.—*Pres.*, Very Rev. E. F. Carpenter.

WORLD EDUCATION FELLOWSHIP (1921), *International Headquarters*, 33 Kinnaird Avenue W4 3SH—*Gen. Sec.*, Mrs. R. Crommelin.

WORLD ENERGY CONFERENCE (1924), *Central Office*, 34 St. James's Street SW1A 1HD—*Sec.-Gen.*, *International Executive Council*, E. Ruttley.

WORLD MISSION, COUNCIL FOR (1977), Livingstone House, 11 Carteret Street SW1H 9DL—Formerly the Congregational Council for World Mission, the London Missionary Society, the Commonwealth Missionary Society and the Presbyterian Church of England Overseas Mission.—*Gen. Sec.*, B. D. Scopes (*acting*).

WORLD SHIP SOCIETY (1946).—*Sec.*, S. J. F. Miller, 35 Wickham Way, Haywards Heath, W. Sussex RH16 1UJ.

WORLD SOCIETY FOR THE PROTECTION OF ANIMALS, *Headquarters*, 106 Jermyn Street SW1Y 6EE—*Dir. Gen.*, T. H. Scott.

WORLD WILDLIFE FUND—U.K. (1961), Panda House, 11–13 Ockford Road, Godalming, Surrey GU7 1QU—*Dir.*, G. J. Medley.

WRITERS TO H.M. SIGNET, SOCIETY OF, Signet Library, Parliament Square, Edinburgh EH1 1RF—*Deputy Keeper of the Signet*, P. C. Millar, O.B.E.; *Sub-Keeper and Clerk*, A. M. Kerr.

YEOMANRY BENEVOLENT FUND, 206 Brompton Road SW3 2BH—*Sec.*, Mrs. C. W. Chrystie.

YORKSHIRE AGRICULTURAL SOCIETY (1837), Great Yorks Showground, Hookstone Oval, Harrogate HG2 8PW—*Sec.-Gen.*, Lt.-Col. M. G. A. Young.

YORKSHIRE SOCIETY, THE (1812), 18 Broom Lock, Teddington, Middx.—*Sec.*, G. G. Prince, T.D.

YOUNG MEN'S CHRISTIAN ASSOCIATION, *National Council*, 640 Forest Road E17 3DZ—*Nat. Sec.*, C. J. Naylor.

YOUNG WOMEN'S CHRISTIAN ASSOCIATION (1855), Clarendon House, 52 Cornmarket Street, Oxford OX1 3EJ—*Gen. Sec.*, Miss F. E. Sharples.

YOUTH CLUBS, NATIONAL ASSOCIATION OF, 30 Peacock Lane, Leicester LE1 5NY.—*Chief Exec.*, J. M. Butterfield.

YOUTH CLUBS, NORTHERN IRELAND ASSOCIATION OF, Hampton, Glenmachan Park, Belfast BT4 2PJ—*Dir.*, G. Johnston.

YOUTH HOSTELS ASSOCIATION (ENGLAND AND WALES) (1930), *National Office*, Trevelyan House, 8 St. Stephens Hill, St. Albans, Herts AL1 2DY—*Chief Exec.*, A. G. F. Chinneck.

YOUTH HOSTELS ASSOCIATION (SCOTTISH) (1931), *National Office*, 7 Glebe Crescent, Stirling FK9 2JA—*Gen. Sec.*, J. Martin.

YOUTH HOSTELS ASSOCIATION OF NORTHERN IRELAND LTD. (1931), Bradbury Buildings, 56 Bradbury Place, Belfast BT7 1RU—*Hon. Sec.*, E. R. Henderson.

ZOOLOGICAL SOCIETY OF LONDON, Regent's Park NW1 4RY—*Pres.*, R. M. Laws, C.B.E. Attendances (1984), Regent's Park, 1,225,000, and Whipsnade Park, 385,000.

ZOOLOGICAL SOCIETY OF SCOTLAND, ROYAL, Scottish National Zoological Park, Murrayfield, Edinburgh EH12 6TS—*Dir.*, R. J. Wheater.

THE CIVIC TRUST

17 Carlton House Terrace, S.W.1.
[01–930 0914]

Founded in 1957, the Trust is a recognized charity supported by voluntary contributions. It encourages the protection and improvement of the environment. It makes Awards for good development of all kinds. Among some particular concerns have been the initiation of co-operative street improvement schemes; the promotion of new techniques for transplanting semi-mature trees; industrial dereliction and urban wasteland; the problems of damage and disruption caused by heavy lorries. The Trust encourages the formation of local amenity societies and gives advice and support to nearly 1,000 such societies now on its register. It was closely associated with the drafting of the Civic Amenities Act 1967, which created the concept of the Conservation Area, and of the Town and Country Amenities Act 1974. It administers the Architectural Heritage Fund, which provides loan capital to local buildings preservation trusts; and on behalf of the Department of the Environment, the work of the Heritage Education Group. Associate Trusts are linked with it in the North West, the North East, Scotland and Wales. From 1973 to 1981 it administered government grant-aid to conservation projects in non-outstanding conservation areas on behalf of the Historic Buildings Council—*Dir.*, M. Middleton, C.B.E.

LOCAL HISTORY AND ARCHÆOLOGICAL SOCIETIES

England and Wales

Anglesey.—ANGLESEY ANTIQUARIAN SOCIETY. *Hon. Sec.*, S. C. G. Caffell, 7 Hendurnpike, Tregarth, Bangor, Gwynedd.

Bedfordshire.—SOUTH BEDFORDSHIRE ARCHÆOLOGICAL SOCIETY. *Hon. Sec.* D. H. Kennett, 27 Lords Lane, Bradwell, Great Yarmouth, Norfolk NR31 8NY.

Berkshire.—BERKSHIRE ARCHÆOLOGICAL SOCIETY. *Hon. Sec.*, L. J. Over, 43 Laburnham Road, Maidenhead, Berks. SL6 4DE.

NEWBURY DISTRICT FIELD CLUB. *Hon. Sec.*, Mrs. D. E. Hawkes, 22 Westgate Road, Newbury.

Buckinghamshire.—BUCKS ARCHÆOLOGICAL SOCIETY. *Hon. Sec.*, Dr. R. P. Hagerty, County Museum, Church Street, Aylesbury, Bucks. HP20 2QP.

Cambridgeshire.—CAMBRIDGE ANTIQUARIAN SOCIETY. *Sec.*, Dr. E. Leedham-Green, University Library, West Road, Cambridge.

Cheshire.—CHESTER ARCHÆOLOGICAL SOCIETY. *Hon. Sec.*, B. E. Harris, PH.D., 2nd Floor, 24 Nicholas Street, Chester CH1 2NX. *See also* under *Lancashire.*

Cornwall.—ROYAL INSTITUTION OF CORNWALL, County Museum and Art Gallery, Truro. *Hon. Sec.*, A. J. Lyne.

Cumberland and Westmorland.—CUMBERLAND AND WESTMORLAND ANTIQUARIAN AND ARCHÆOLOGICAL SOCIETY. *Hon. Sec.*, R. Hall, 2 High Tenterfell, Kendal, Cumbria LA9 4PG.

Derbyshire.—DERBYSHIRE ARCHÆOLOGICAL SOCIETY, Dept. of Archæology, University of Nottingham, Nottingham NG7 2RD. *Hon. Sec.*, C. J. Drage.

Devonshire.—DEVON ARCHÆOLOGICAL SOCIETY. *Hon. Sec.*, N. Shiel, 4 St. Leonards Road, Exeter, F.S.A.

Dorset.—DORSET NATURAL HISTORY AND ARCHÆOLOGICAL SOCIETY, Dorset County Museum, Dorchester DT1 1XA. *Curator and Sec.*, R. N. R. Peers.

Durham.—DURHAM AND NORTHUMBERLAND ARCHITECTURAL AND ARCHÆOLOGICAL SOCIETY. *Hon. Sec.*, c/o The University, Dept. of Archæology, 46 Saddler Street, Durham.

Dyfed.—CEREDIGION ANTIQUARIAN SOCIETY. *Hon. Sec.*, D. M. Jones, Tal-y-werydd, Aberarth, Aberaeron, Dyfed SA46 0LX.

Essex.—ESSEX ARCHÆOLOGICAL SOCIETY, Hollytrees Museum, High Street, Colchester CO1 1UG. *Sec.*, Mrs. E. Sellars.

Gloucestershire.—BRISTOL AND GLOUCESTERSHIRE ARCHÆOLOGICAL SOCIETY, 9 Pembroke Road, Bristol BS8 3AU. *Hon. Sec.*, Miss E. Ralph, F.S.A.

Hampshire.—HAMPSHIRE FIELD CLUB AND ARCHÆOLOGICAL SOCIETY. *Hon. Sec.*, Dr. M. A. Hicks, King Alfred's College, Winchester, Hants SO22 4NR.

Herefordshire.—WOOLHOPE NATURALISTS' FIELD CLUB. *Hon. Sec.*, c/o The Hereford Library, Broad Street, Hereford.

Hertfordshire.—EAST HERTFORDSHIRE ARCHÆOLOGICAL SOCIETY. *Hon. Sec.*, C. L. Lee, 107 Queens Road, Hertford.

St. Albans and Hertfordshire Architec-
tural and Archæological Society. *Hon. Sec.*, F.
I. Kilvington, 122 Marshalswick Lane, St. Albans
AL1 4XD.

Kent.—Kent Archæological Society. *Gen. Sec.*,
A. C. Harrison, f.s.a., Prings Cottage, Pilgrims
Road, Upper Halling, Rochester ME2 1HR.

Lancashire. Historic Society of Lancashire and
Cheshire. *Hon. Sec.*, Miss J. E. Hollinshead,
Liverpool Institute of H.E., Stand Park Road,
Liverpool LI6 9JD.

London and Middlesex.—City of London
Archæological Society. *Hon. Sec.*, D. R. Lewis,
28 Rothesay Avenue SW20 8JU.

London and Middlesex Archæological Society, Museum of London, London Wall
EC2Y 5HN. *Hon. Sec.*, J. Clark, f.s.a.

Norfolk.—Norfolk and Norwich Archæological
Society. *Hon. Gen. Sec.*, I. Cresswell, f.s.a., The
Old Rectory, Shelton, Norwich NR15 2SD.

Northumberland and Tyne and Wear.—Society of
Antiquaries of Newcastle upon Tyne. *Sec.*, Dr.
C. M. Fraser, c/o Department of Adult Education,
University of Newcastle upon Tyne NE1 7RU.

Sunderland Antiquarian Society. *Hon. Sec.*,
G. Patterson, 8 Humbledon View, Sunderland
SR2 7RX.

Nottinghamshire.—Thoroton Society of Nottinghamshire, Bromley House, Angel Row, Nottingham NG1 6HL. *Hon. Sec.*, J. S. Childs, f.r.s.a.

Oxfordshire. Oxfordshire Architectural and Historical Society. *Hon. Sec.*, Miss J. M. Cook, c/o
Ashmolean Museum, Oxford OX1 2PH.

Powys: Montgomery District; Powysland Club.
Hon. Sec., W. G. J. Hughes, The Library, Brook
Street, Welshpool, Powys SY21 7PH.

Radnor District; Radnorshire Society. *Hon.
Sec.*, A. Batley, c/o Radnor College of F.E., Llandrindod Wells, Powys LD1 5ES.

Shropshire.—Shropshire Archæological Society.
Hon. Sec., Yvette Staelens, c/o Much Wenlock
Museum, High Street, Much Wenlock TF13 6HR.

Somerset.—Somerset Archæological and Natural History Society, Taunton Castle, Taunton
TA1 4AD. *Hon. Sec.*, J. V. Carrington.

Staffordshire.—North Staffordshire Field Club.
Hon. Sec., R. A. Tribbeck, Dept. of Chemistry and
Biology, North Staffordshire Polytechnic, College
Road, Stoke-on-Trent.

City of Stoke-on-Trent Museum Archæo-
logical Society, City Museum and Art Gallery,
Stoke-on-Trent.
Chairman, C. F. Hawke-Smith.

Suffolk.—Suffolk Institute of Archæology and
History. *Hon. Sec.*, E. A. Martin, Oak Tree Farm,
Finborough Road, Hitcham, Ipswich IP7 7LS.

Surrey.—Surrey Archæological Society, Castle
Arch, Guildford GU1 3SX. *Hon. Secs.*, J. L. and M.
Gower.

Sussex.—Sussex Archæological Society, Barbican
House, High Street, Lewes BN7 1YE. *Gen. Administrator*, J. Houghton.

Warwickshire.—Birmingham and Warwickshire
Archæological Society, c/o Birmingham and
Midland Institute, Margaret Street, Birmingham
B3 3BS. *Hon. Sec.*, M. A. Hodder.

Wight.—Isle of Wight Natural History and
Archæological Society, 66 Carisbrooke Road,
Newport. *Hon. Sec.*, Mrs. T. Goodley, Ivy Cottage,
New Barn Lane, Shorwell PO30 3JQ.

Wiltshire.—Wiltshire Archæological and Natural History Society, The Museum, 41 Long Street,
Devizes SN10 1NS. *Sec.*, M. Heath.

Worcestershire.—Worcestershire Archæological
Society. *Hon. Sec.*, Mrs. G. Grice, 91 Hallow Road,
Worcester WR2 6DF.

Yorkshire.—Hunter Archæological Society. *Hon.
Sec.*, S. R. Penny, 37 Chesterwood Drive, Sheffield
10.

Yorkshire Archæological Society. *Hon. Sec.*,
P. B. Davidson, Claremont, 23 Clarendon Road,
Leeds LS2 9NZ.

Halifax Antiquarian Society. *Hon. Sec.*, E.
Webster, 28 Westborough Drive, Highroad Well,
Halifax HX2 7QL.

Thoresby Society, Claremont, 23 Clarendon
Road, Leeds LS2 9NZ. *Hon. Sec.*, D. M. Watson.

Channel Islands

Societe Jersiaise, Archaeological Section, The Jersey Museum, Pier Road, St. Helier. *Hon. Sec.*, Rev.
Canon L. Hibbs.

Scotland

Ayrshire Archæological and Natural History
Society. *Hon. Sec.*, G. E. Sleight, 1 Portmark
Avenue, Ayr KA7 4DD.

Dumfriesshire and Galloway Natural History
and Antiquarian Society. *Hon. Sec.*, R. H.
McEwen, Seaforth, 13 Douglas Terrace, Lockerbie,
Dumfries DG11 2DZ.

Hawick Archæological Society. *Hon. Sec.*, I. A.
Landles, Orrock House, Stirches Road, Hawick,
Borders TD9 7HF.

Inverness Field Club, c/o Innes and MacKay, 19
Union Street, Inverness. *Hon. Sec.*, Mrs. E. H. L.
MacAskill, 9 Dores Road, Inverness IV2 4QX.

CONFEDERATION OF BRITISH INDUSTRY

Centre Point, 103 New Oxford Street, London WC1A 1DU

[01-379 7400]

The Confederation of British Industry was founded in August 1965 and is an independent non-party political body financed entirely by industry and commerce. It exists primarily to ensure that the Government understands the intentions, needs and problems of British business. It is the recognized spokesman for the business viewpoint and is consulted as such by the Government.

The C.B.I. represents, directly and indirectly, more than 300,000 companies. All the nationalized industries are in membership and thereby able to work with the C.B.I. on problems that are the concern of all management.

The governing body of the C.B.I. is the 400-strong Council, which meets monthly in London under the chairmanship of the President. It is assisted by some 24 expert standing committees which advise on the main aspects of policy. There are 13 Regional Councils and offices covering the administrative regions of England, Scotland, Wales and Northern Ireland.

President, Sir James Cleminson (to be succeeded in 1986 by David Nickson).
Director-General, Sir Terence Beckett.
Secretary, D. E. Jackson.

NATIONAL ASSOCIATION OF INDUSTRIES FOR THE BLIND AND DISABLED INC.

Triton House, 43A High Street South,
Dunstable, Beds. LU6 3RZ
[0582–606796]

The National Association of Industries for the Blind and Disabled Inc. was established in 1929 and incorporated in 1936; it is registered as a charity.

The Association acts in the nature of a trade association providing facilities for consultation and co-operation between its 40 members who operate workshops employing blind and disabled people and it represents their interests in discussions with, and representations to, other organisations (e.g. government departments and local authorities) concerned with sheltered employment. It does not own or operate any of the workshops, which are run by local authorities or voluntary organisations acting as their agents.

Chairman (1984–85), J. J. Williams.
Hon. Secretary, G. W. Guy.

EMPLOYERS' AND TRADE BODIES

ADVERTISING ASSOCIATION, Abford House, 15 Wilton Road, SW1V 1NJ.—*Dir. Gen.,* R. Underhill, O.B.E.

AGRICULTURAL EXPORT COUNCIL, BRITISH, 35 Belgrave Square, SW1X 8QN.—*Chief Exec.,* J. Thorneloe.

BAKERS, FEDERATION OF, 20 Bedford Square, WC1B 3HF.—*Dir.,* A. Casdagli, C.B.E.

BANKERS' ASSOCIATION, BRITISH, 10 Lombard Street, EC3V 9EL.—*Sec.-Gen.,* J. B. Atherton.

BREWERS' SOCIETY, 42 Portman Square, W1H 0BB.—*Dir. and Chief Exec.,* Maj. Gen. W. D. Mangham, C.B.

BUILDING EMPLOYERS CONFEDERATION, 82 New Cavendish Street, W1M 8AD.—*Dir. Gen.,* J. A. Newby.

BUILDING MATERIAL PRODUCERS, NATIONAL COUNCIL OF, 10 Great George Street, SW1P 3AE.—*Dir. Gen.,* N. M. Chaldecott.

BUS AND COACH COUNCIL, Sardinia House, 52 Lincoln's Inn Fields, WC2A 3LZ.—*Dir. Gen.,* D. R. Quin.

CHEMICAL INDUSTRIES ASSOCIATION LTD., Alembic House, 93 Albert Embankment, SE1 7TU.—*Dir. Gen.,* M. E. Trowbridge.

CLOTHING INDUSTRY ASSOCIATION LTD., BRITISH, Wellington House, 6/9 Upper St. Martin's Lane, WC2H 9DL.—*Dir.* J. R. Wilson.

DAIRY TRADE FEDERATION, 19 Cornwall Terrace, NW1 4QP.—*Dir. Gen.,* M. Evans.

ENGINEERING EMPLOYERS' FEDERATION, Broadway House, Tothill Street, SW1H 9NQ.—*Dir. Gen.,* Dr. J. McFarlane.

FARMERS' UNION OF ENGLAND AND WALES, THE NATIONAL, Agriculture House, 25–31 Knightsbridge, SW1X 7NJ.—*Dir. Gen.,* D. Evans.

FARMERS' UNION OF SCOTLAND, NATIONAL, 17 Grosvenor Crescent, Edinburgh EH12 5EN.—*Dir.,* D. S. Johnston.

FARMERS' UNION, ULSTER, Dunedin, 475–477 Antrim Road, Belfast BT15 3DA.

FOOD AND DRINK FEDERATION, 6 Catherine Street, WC2B 5JJ.—*Dir. Gen.,* Maj.-Gen. Sir Jeremy Moore, K.C.B., O.B.E., M.C.

FREIGHT TRANSPORT ASSOCIATION LTD., Hermes House, 157 St. John's Road, Tunbridge Wells, Kent TN4 9UZ.—*Dir. Gen.,* G. Turvey.

INSURERS, ASSOCIATION OF BRITISH, Aldermary House, Queen Street, EC4N 1TT.—*Sec. Gen.,* R. C. W. Bardell, O.B.E.

KNITTING INDUSTRIES' FEDERATION LTD., 7 Gregory Boulevard, Nottingham NG7 6NB.—*Dir.,* J. P. Harrison.

LEATHER CONFEDERATION, BRITISH, Leather Trade House, Kings Park Road, Moulton Park, Northampton NN3 1JD.—*Dir.,* Dr. R. L. Sykes.

LEATHER PRODUCERS' ASSOCIATION, Leather Trade House, Kings Park Road, Moulton Park, Northampton NN3 1JD.—*Nat. Sec.,* J. Purvis.

MAN-MADE FIBRES FEDERATION, BRITISH, 24 Buckingham Gate, SW1E 6LB.—*Dir.*, D. Anderson.

MOTOR MANUFACTURERS AND TRADERS LTD., SOCIETY OF, Forbes House, Halkin Street, SW1X 7DS—*Dir.*, A. W. Fraser.

NEWSPAPER PUBLISHERS ASSOCIATION LTD., 6 Bouverie Street, EC4Y 8AY.—*Dir.*, J. E. Lepage.

PAPER AND BOARD INDUSTRY FEDERATION, BRITISH, 3 Plough Place, Fetter Lane, EC4A 1AL.—*Dir. Gen.*, W. J. Bartlett.

PLASTICS FEDERATION, BRITISH, 5 Belgrave Square, SW1X 8PH.—*Dir.*, R. Lewis, O.B.E.

PORT EMPLOYERS, NATIONAL ASSOCIATION OF, Commonwealth House, 1–19 New Oxford Street, WC1A 1DZ.—*Dir.*, N. H. Finney.

PORTS ASSOCIATION, BRITISH, Commonwealth House, 1–19 New Oxford Street, WC1A 1DZ.—*Dir.* N. H. Finney.

PRINTING INDUSTRIES FEDERATION, BRITISH, 11 Bedford Row, WC1R 4DX.—*Dir. Gen.*, S. Bradley.

PUBLISHERS' ASSOCIATION, THE, 19 Bedford Square, WC1B 3HJ.—*Chief Exec.*, C. Bradley.

RADIO CONTRACTORS LTD., ASSOCIATION OF INDEPENDENT, Regina House, 259–269 Marylebone Road, NW1 5RA.—*Dir.*, B. West.

RETAIL CONSORTIUM, THE, Commonwealth House, 1–19 New Oxford Street, WC1A 1PA.—*Dir. Gen.*, T. McNally.

ROAD FEDERATION LTD., BRITISH, Cowdray House, 6 Portugal Street, WC2A 2HG.—*Dir.*, P. Witt.

ROAD HAULAGE ASSOCIATION LTD., Roadway House, 104 New Kings Road, SW6 4LN.—*Dir. Gen.*, F. J. Plaskett, C.B., M.B.E.

RUBBER MANUFACTURERS' ASSOCIATION LTD., BRIT-

ISH, 90–91 Tottenham Court Road, W1P 0BR.—*Dir.*, G. C. Gullan.

SHIP AND BOAT BUILDERS NATIONAL FEDERATION, Boating Industry House, Weybridge, Surrey KT13 9NS.—*Dir. Gen.*, T. A. Webb, O.B.E.

SHIPPING, GENERAL COUNCIL OF BRITISH, 30–32 St. Mary Axe, EC3A 8ET.—*Pres.*, (1985–86), B. P. Shaw; *Dir. Gen.*, P. Le Cheminant, C.B.

SPORT AND ALLIED INDUSTRIES FEDERATION LTD., BRITISH, Prudential House (10th Floor, East Wing), Wellesley Road, Croydon, Surrey CR0 9XY.—*Chief Exec.*, E. Bainbridge.

STATIONERY AND OFFICE PRODUCTS FEDERATION, BRITISH, 6 Wimpole Street, W1M 8AS.—*Dir.*, D. F. Hall.

TELEVISION COMPANIES ASSOCIATION LTD., INDEPENDENT, 56 Mortimer Street, W1N 8AN.—*Gen Sec.*, D. Shaw.

TEXTILE CONFEDERATION, BRITISH, 24 Buckingham Gate, SW1E 6LB.—*Dir.*, I. MacArthur.

TIMBER GROWERS' UNITED KINGDOM, Agriculture House, Knightsbridge, SW1X 7NJ.—*Chief Exec.*, A. R. Williams.

TIMBER MERCHANTS' ASSOCATION, BRITISH, Ridgeway House, 6 Ridgeway Road, Long Ashton, Bristol BS18 9UE.—*Sec.*, H. B. Roberts.

TIMBER TRADE FEDERATION OF THE U.K., Clareville House, 26/27 Oxenden Street, SW1Y 4EL. *Dir. Gen.*, A. A. Lockyer.

U.K. OFFSHORE OPERATORS ASSOCIATION LTD., 3 Hans Crescent, SW1X 0LN.—*Dir.*, G. C. Band.

U.K. PETROLEUM INDUSTRY ASSOCIATION LTD., 9 Kingsway, WC2B 6XH.—*Dir. Gen.*, Dr. I. D. G. Berwick.

CAR PRODUCTION IN MAIN PRODUCING COUNTRIES (thousands)

	1975	1976	1977	1978	1979	1980	1981	1982	1983	1984
United Kingdom	1,268	1,333	1,328	1,223	1,070	924	955	888	1,645	909
France	2,546	2,980	3,092	3,111	3,220	2,939	2,612	2,777	2,961	2,713
W. Germany	2,908	3,547	3,790	3,890	3,933	3,521	3,578	3,761	3,878	3,790
Italy	1,349	1,471	1,440	1,509	1,481	1,445	1,257	1,297	1,396	1,439
Sweden	316	317	235	254	297	235	258	295	345	353
Japan	4,568	5,028	5,431	5,748	6,176	7,038	6,974	6,887	7,152	7,073
U.S.A..............	6,717	8,498	9,214	9,176	8,434	6,376	6,253	5,073	6,781	7,774
Canada.............	1,045	1,137	1,162	1,143	988	847	863	808	969	1,021
Total...............	20,717	24,311	25,692	26,054	25,599	23,325	22,750	21,786	24,527	25,072
UK % of total	6	5	5	5	4	4	4	4	4	4

BRITISH MOTOR VEHICLE PRODUCTION AND EXPORTS

Year	Weeks	Passenger Cars (including taxis)			Commercial Road Vehicles		
		For Export*	Total	Weekly average	For Export*	Total	Weekly average
1978......	...52...	494,579	1,222,949	23,518	168,968	384,518	7,395
1979......	...52...	392,637	1,070,452	20,586	162,570	408,060	7,847
1980......	...52...	349,592	923,744	17,764	156,270	389,170	7,484
1981......	...52...	304,678	954,650	18,359	113,862	229,555	4,416
1982......	...52...	225,865	887,679	17,070	92,510	268,798	5,169
1983......	...53...	237,376	1,044,597	19,709	62,801	244,514	4,613
1984......	...52...	192,213	908,906	17,479	49,808	224,825	4,323

*Export Allocation

TRADES UNION CONGRESS (T.U.C.)

Congress House, 23–28 Great Russell Street, WC1B 3LS
[01–636–4030]

The Trades Union Congress, founded in 1868, is a voluntary association of Trade Unions, the representatives of which meet annually to consider matters of common concern to their members. The Congress has met annually since 1871 and in recent years has met normally on the first Monday in September, its sessions extending through the succeeding four days. Congress is constituted by delegates of the affiliated unions on the basis of one delegate for every 5,000 members, or fraction thereof, on whose behalf affiliated fees are paid. Affiliated unions (in 1985–86) totalled 91 with an aggregate membership of 9,854,956.

The main business of the annual Congress is to consider the report of its General Council dealing with the activities of the Congress year, along with motions from affiliated societies on questions of policy and organization.

The Standing Committees of the General Council are serviced by a full time staff appointed by the General Secretary, who is himself elected by Congress and who remains in office until the age of 65, subject to decision of Congress or the General Council.

Through the General Council and its committees the trade union movement maintains systematic relations with the Government and Government Departments, with the Confederation of British Industry and with a large number of other bodies. It is represented on the National Economic Development Council, the Manpower Services Commission, the Health and Safety Commission, the Council of the Advisory Conciliation and Arbitration Service and a number of other bodies.

Among powers vested in the General Council by consent of the unions in Congress is the responsibility of intervening in disputes and differences between affiliated organizations; if possible this is done through informal conciliation meetings under T.U.C. auspices but where necessary a Disputes Committee is formed consisting of one member of the General Council and two senior officials of unions not involved in the dispute. This investigates the matter concerned and issues its findings.

Unions retain full control of their own affairs and the only sanctions which Congress can apply are suspension or exclusion from membership.

Chairman (1985–86), K. Gill, (*Amalgamated Union of Engineering Workers (Technical, Administrative and Supervisory Section)*).
General Secretary, N. D. Willis.

SCOTTISH TRADES UNION CONGRESS

16 Woodlands Terrace, Glasgow G3 6DF
[041-332 4946]

The Congress was formed in 1897 and acts as a national centre for the trade union movement in Scotland. In 1985 it consisted of 66 unions with a membership of 962,149 and 49 directly affiliated Trades Councils. The majority of the unions organize throughout Britain and affiliate on their membership in Scotland.

The Annual Congress in April elects a 26-member General Council on the basis of 13 industrial sections. Congress has been prominent in pressing for economic expansion and full employment in Scotland and the development of the social services, most of which are separately organized in Scotland.

Chairperson (1985–86), H. Wyper.
General Secretary, J. Milne.

TRADE UNIONS AFFILIATED TO T.U.C.

A list of the Trade Unions affiliated to the Trades Union Congress in September, 1985. The number of members of each Union is shown in parenthesis.

AMALGAMATED ASSOCIATION OF BEAMERS, TWISTERS AND DRAWERS, THE (550), 27 Every Street, Nelson, Lancs. BB9 7NE—*Gen. Sec.*, A. H. Edmondson.

AMALGAMATED SOCIETY OF TEXTILE WORKERS AND KINDRED TRADES (3,360), Foxlowe, Market Place, Leek, Staffs. ST13 6AD—*Gen. Sec.*, A. Hitchmough.

AMALGAMATED SOCIETY OF WIRE DRAWERS AND KINDRED WORKERS, THE (5,222), Prospect House, Alma Street, Sheffield S3 8SA—*Gen. Sec.*, A. M. Ardron.

AMALGAMATED TEXTILE WORKERS' UNION (15,500), 5 Caton Street, Rochdale, Lancs. OL16 1QJ—*Gen. Sec.*, J. Brown.

AMALGAMATED UNION OF ASPHALT WORKERS, THE (2,244), Jenkin House, 173a Queens Road, Peckham, SE15 2NF—*Gen. Sec.*, H. M. Wareham.

AMALGAMATED UNION OF ENGINEERING WORKERS (A.U.E.W.) (ENGINEERING, FOUNDRY & CONSTRUCTION) (1,000,883), 110 Peckham Road, SE15 5EL—*Gen. Sec.*, G. H. Laird.

TECHNICAL, ADMINISTRATIVE AND SUPERVISORY SECTION (TASS) (220,000), Onslow Hall, Little Green, Richmond, Surrey TW9 1QN—*Gen. Sec.*, K. Gill.

ASSOCIATED METALWORKERS' UNION, THE (2,000), 92 Deansgate, Manchester M3 2QG—*Gen. Sec.*, R. Marron.

ASSOCIATED SOCIETY OF LOCOMOTIVE ENGINEERS AND FIREMEN (A.S.L.E.F.) (22,835), 9 Arkwright Road, Hampstead, NW3 6AB—*Sec.*, R. W. Buckton.

ASSOCIATION OF CINEMATOGRAPH, TELEVISION AND ALLIED TECHNICIANS (24,573), 2 Soho Square, W1V 6DD—*Gen. Sec.*, A. Sapper.

ASSOCIATION OF FIRST DIVISION CIVIL SERVANTS (7,703), 17 Northumberland Avenue, WC2N 5AP—*Gen. Sec.*, C. J. Ward.

ASSOCIATION OF PROFESSIONAL, EXECUTIVE, CLERICAL AND COMPUTER STAFF (APEX) (94,846), 22 Worple Road, SW19 4DF—*Gen. Sec.*, R. Grantham.

ASSOCIATION OF SCIENTIFIC, TECHNICAL AND MANAGERIAL STAFFS (A.S.T.M.S.) (400,000), 79 Camden Road, NW1 9ES—*Gen. Sec.*, C. Jenkins.

ASSOCIATION OF UNIVERSITY TEACHERS (31,684), United House, 1 Pembridge Road, W11 3HJ—*Gen. Sec.*, Diana Warwick.

BAKERS', FOOD AND ALLIED WORKERS' UNION (36,286), Stanborough House, Great North Road, Welwyn Garden City, Herts. AL8 7TA—*Gen. Sec.*, J. Marino.

BANKING, INSURANCE AND FINANCE UNION, THE (154,579), 17 Hillside, Wimbledon, SW19 4NL—*Gen. Sec.*, L. Mills.

BRITISH ACTORS' EQUITY ASSOCIATION (32,525), 8 Harley Street, W1N 2AB—*Gen. Sec.*, P. Plouviez.

BRITISH AIR LINE PILOTS ASSOCIATION, THE (3,715), 81 New Road, Harlington, Hayes, Middlesex UB3 5BG—*Gen. Sec.*, M. Young.

BRITISH ASSOCIATION OF COLLIERY MANAGEMENT, THE (14,802), 317 Nottingham Road, Old Basford, Nottingham NG7 7DP—*Gen. Sec.*, A. Wilson.

BROADCASTING AND ENTERTAINMENT TRADES ALLIANCE (45,000), Kings Court, 2–16 Goodge Street, W1P 2AE—*Gen. Secs.*, D. A. Hearn; J. L. Wilson.

CARD SETTING MACHINE TENTERS' SOCIETY (106), 36 Greenton Avenue, Scholes, Cleckheaton, W. Yorks. BD19 6DT—*Sec.*, G. Priestley.

CERAMIC AND ALLIED TRADES UNION, THE (30,297), Hillcrest House, Garth Street, Hanley, Stoke-on-Trent ST1 2AB—*Gen. Sec.*, A. W. Clowes.

CIVIL AND PUBLIC SERVICES ASSOCIATION, THE (149,782), 215 Balham High Road, SW17 7BN—*Sec.*, J. A. Graham.

CIVIL SERVICE UNION (35,037), 5 Praed Street, W2 1NJ—*Sec.*, J. D. Sheldon.

COMMUNICATION MANAGERS' ASSOCIATION (19,200), Hughes House, Ruscombe Road, Twyford, Reading RG10 9JD—*Gen. Sec.*, R. J. Cowley.

CONFEDERATION OF HEALTH SERVICE EMPLOYEES (C.O.H.S.E.) (214,321), Glen House, High Street, Banstead, Surrey SM7 2LH—*Gen. Sec.*, D. Williams.

EDUCATIONAL INSTITUTE OF SCOTLAND, THE (45,559), 46 Moray Place, Edinburgh EH3 6BH—*Gen. Sec.*, J. D. Pollock.

ELECTRICAL, ELECTRONIC, TELECOMMUNICATION AND PLUMBING UNION (E.E.T.P.U.) (394,283), Hayes Court, West Common Road, Bromley BR2 7AU—*Sec.*, E. A. Hammond, O.B.E.

ENGINEERS' AND MANAGERS' ASSOCIATION (40,886), Station House, Fox Lane North, Chertsey, Surrey KT16 9HW—*Gen. Sec.*, J. Lyons.

FILM ARTISTES' ASSOCIATION (2,335), 61 Marloes Road, W8 6LF—*Sec.*, S. Brannigan.

FIRE BRIGADES UNION, THE (43,256), 59 Fulham High Street, SW6 3JN—*Gen. Sec.*, K. Cameron.

FURNITURE, TIMBER AND ALLIED TRADES UNION (54,267), Fairfields, Roe Green, Kingsbury, NW9 0PT—*Sec.*, B. Rubner.

GENERAL, MUNICIPAL, BOILERMAKERS AND ALLIED TRADES UNION (GMW) (846,565), Thorne House, Claygate, Esher, Surrey KT10 0TL—*Gen. Sec.*, J. Edmonds.

GENERAL UNION OF ASSOCIATIONS OF LOOM OVERLOOKERS (1,293), Overlookers Institute, Jude Street, Nelson, Lancs. BB9 7NP—*Pres.*, E. Macro.

GREATER LONDON COUNCIL STAFF ASSOCIATION (16,046), 150 Waterloo Road, SE1 8SB—*Sec.*, A. Capelin.

HEALTH VISITORS' ASSOCIATION (15,608), 36 Eccleston Square, SW1V 1PF—*Gen. Sec.*, Shirley Goodwin.

HOSPITAL CONSULTANTS AND SPECIALISTS ASSOCIATION, THE (2,645), The Old Court House, London Road, Ascot, Berks. SL5 7EN—*Chief Exec.*, R. B. Martin.

INLAND REVENUE STAFF FEDERATION (55,048), Douglas Houghton House, 231 Vauxhall Bridge Road, SW1V 1EH—*Gen. Sec.*, A. M. G. Christopher, C.B.E.

INSTITUTION OF PROFESSIONAL CIVIL SERVANTS, THE (90,242), 75–79 York Road, SE1 7AQ—*Gen. Sec.*, W. McCall.

IRON AND STEEL TRADES CONFEDERATION, THE (79,082), Swinton House, 324 Gray's Inn Road, WC1X 8DD—*Gen. Sec.*, R. L. Evans.

MILITARY AND ORCHESTRAL MUSICAL INSTRUMENT MAKERS' TRADE SOCIETY (100), 47 Mornington Crescent, NW1.—*Gen. Sec.*, J. Barker.

MUSICIANS' UNION (37,637), 60–62 Clapham Road, SW9 0JJ—*Gen. Sec.*, J. Morton.

NATIONAL AND LOCAL GOVERNMENT OFFICERS' ASSOCIATION (N.A.L.G.O.) (766,390), 1 Mabledon Place, WC1H 9AJ—*Gen. Sec.*, J. Daly.

NATIONAL ASSOCIATION OF COLLIERY OVERMEN, DEPUTIES AND SHOTFIRERS (15,848), Simpson House, 48 Netherhall Road, Doncaster, S. Yorks. DN1 2PZ—*Sec.*, P. McNestry.

NATIONAL ASSOCIATION OF CO-OPERATIVE OFFICIALS (4,899), Saxone House, 56 Market Street, Manchester M1 1PW—*Gen. Sec.*, L. W. Ewing.

NATIONAL ASSOCIATION OF LICENSED HOUSE MANAGERS (17,138), 9 Coombe Lane, Raynes Park, SW20 8NE—*Nat. Sec.*, L. Adams.

NATIONAL ASSOCIATION OF PROBATION OFFICERS (5,814), 3–4 Chivalry Road, SW11 1HT—*Sec.*, B. Beaumont.

NATIONAL ASSOCIATION OF SCHOOLMASTERS/UNION OF WOMEN TEACHERS (N.A.S./U.W.T.) (126,435), 22 Upper Brook Street, W1Y 2HD—*Gen. Sec.*, F. A. Smithies.

NATIONAL ASSOCIATION OF TEACHERS IN FURTHER AND HIGHER EDUCATION (73,745), Hamilton House, Mabledon Place, WC1H 9BH—*Gen. Sec.*, J. P. Dawson.

NATIONAL COMMUNICATIONS UNION (166,483), Greystoke House, 150 Brunswick Road, W5 1AW.—*Gen. Sec.*, B. C. Stanley.

NATIONAL GRAPHICAL ASSOCIATION (N.G.A.'82) (126,267), Graphic House, 63/67 Bromham Road, Bedford MK40 2AG—*Sec.*, A. D. Dubbins.

NATIONAL LEAGUE OF THE BLIND AND DISABLED, THE (2,800), 2 Tenterden Road, N17 8BE—*Sec.*, M. A. Barrett.

NATIONAL SOCIETY OF METAL MECHANICS (27,035), 70 Lionel Street, Birmingham B3 1JG—*Sec.*, C. P. McCarthy.

NATIONAL UNION OF DOMESTIC APPLIANCES AND GENERAL OPERATIVES, THE (4,000), First Floor, Imperial Buildings, Corporation Street, Rotherham, S. Yorks. S60 1PB—*Gen. Sec.*, R. D. Preston.

NATIONAL UNION OF HOSIERY AND KNITWEAR WORKERS, THE (51,645), 55 New Walk, Leicester LE1 7EB—*Gen. Sec.*, T. Kirk.

NATIONAL UNION OF INSURANCE WORKERS (18,423), 91/93 Gray's Inn Road, WC1X 8TX—*Sec.*, R. Main.

NATIONAL UNION OF JOURNALISTS (N.U.J.) (33,337), Acorn House, 314/320 Gray's Inn Road, WC1X 8DP—*Gen. Sec.*, H. Conroy.

NATIONAL UNION OF LOCK AND METAL WORKERS (5,118), Bellamy House, Wilkes Street, Willenhall, West Midlands WV13 2BS—*Sec.*, J. Martin, M.B.E.

NATIONAL UNION OF MARINE, AVIATION AND SHIPPING TRANSPORT OFFICERS, THE (25,385), Oceanair House, 750–760 High Road, Leytonstone, E11 3BB—*Gen. Sec.*, E. Nevin.

NATIONAL UNION OF MINEWORKERS (N.U.M.) (200,000), St. James' House, Vicar Lane, Sheffield S1 2EX—*Sec.*, P. E. Heathfield.

NATIONAL UNION OF PUBLIC EMPLOYEES (N.U.P.E.) (673,445), Civic House, 20 Grand Depot Road, SE18 6SF—*Sec.*, R. K. Bickerstaffe.

NATIONAL UNION OF RAILWAYMEN (N.U.R.) (136,315), Unity House, Euston Road, NW1 2BL—*Gen. Sec.*, J. Knapp.

NATIONAL UNION OF SCALEMAKERS (1,123), 4th Floor, Herbert House, 71 Cornwall Street, Birmingham B3 2EE—*Gen. Sec.*, A. F. Smith.

NATIONAL UNION OF SEAMEN (N.U.S.) (25,000), Maritime House, Old Town, Clapham, SW4 0JP—*Gen. Sec.*, J. H. Slater, C.B.E.

NATIONAL UNION OF TAILORS AND GARMENT WORKERS (76,699), 16 Charles Square, N1 6HP—*Gen. Sec.*, A. Smith.

NATIONAL UNION OF TEACHERS (N.U.T.) (214,361), Hamilton House, Mabledon Place, WC1H 9BD—*Gen. Sec.*, F. Jarvis.

NATIONAL UNION OF THE FOOTWEAR, LEATHER AND ALLIED TRADES (41,113), The Grange, 108 Northampton Road, Earls Barton, Northampton NN6 0JH—*Sec.*, G. G. Stewart.

NORTHERN CARPET TRADES' UNION (1,008), 22 Clare Road, Halifax HX1 2HX—*Gen. Sec.*, K. Edmondson.

PATTERN WEAVERS' SOCIETY (60), New Field End, Hill Top, Cumberworth, Huddersfield HD8 8YE—*Gen. Sec.*, D. G. Hawley.

POWER LOOM CARPET WEAVERS' AND TEXTILE WORKERS' UNION (3,000), Callows Lane, Kidderminster, Worcs. DY10 2JG—*Gen. Sec.*, B. C. Moule.

PRISON OFFICERS' ASSOCIATION (23,395), Cronin House, 245 Church Street, Edmonton, N9 9HW—*Gen. Sec.*, D. Evans.

ROSSENDALE UNION OF BOOT, SHOE AND SLIPPER OPERATIVES, The (3,960), Taylor House, 7 Tenterfield Street, Waterfoot, Rossendale, Lancs. BB4 7BA.—*Gen. Sec.*, M. Murray.

SCOTTISH PRISON OFFICERS' ASSOCIATION (2,845), 21 Calder Road, Edinburgh EH1 3PF—*Gen. Sec.*, J. B. Renton, M.B.E.

SCOTTISH UNION OF POWER-LOOM OVERLOOKERS (105), 3 Napier Terrace, Dundee, Tayside.—*Sec.*, J. Reilly.

SCREW, NUT, BOLT AND RIVET TRADE UNION (550), 368 Dudley Road, Birmingham B18 4HH—*Gen. Sec.*, E. C. Bowcott.

SHEFFIELD WOOL SHEAR WORKERS' UNION (27), 50 Bankfield Road, Malin Bridge, Sheffield S6 4RD—*Sec.*, J. H. R. Cutler.

SOCIETY OF CIVIL AND PUBLIC SERVANTS (85,597), 124/130 Southwark Street, SE1 0TU—*Gen. Sec.*, B. A. Gillman.

SOCIETY OF GRAPHICAL AND ALLIED TRADES (SOGAT '82) (210,462), Sogat House, 274/288 London Road, Hadleigh, Essex SS7 2DE—*Gen. Sec.*, Brenda Dean.

SOCIETY OF SHUTTLEMAKERS (49), 31 Moorside Avenue, Intack, Blackburn BB1 2BA.—*Gen. Sec.*, H. Bell.

SOCIETY OF TELECOM EXECUTIVES (27,996), 102/104 Sheen Road, Richmond, Surrey TW9 1UF—*Gen. Sec.*, H. J. Jordon (*acting*).

SPRING TRAPMAKERS' SOCIETY (90), Bellamy House, Wilkes Street, Willenhall, West Midlands WV13 2BS—*Sec.*, J. Martin.

TOBACCO MECHANICS ASSOCIATION (189), 16 Clifton Terrace, Whitley Bay, Tyne-and-Wear NE26 2JD—*Sec.*, J. Middleton.

TOBACCO WORKERS' UNION, The (13,448), 9 Station Parade, High Street, Wanstead, E11 1QF—*Sec.*, C. D. Grieve.

TRANSPORT AND GENERAL WORKERS' UNION (T.G.W.U.) (1,490,555), Transport House, Smith Square, Westminster, SW1P 3JB—*Sec.*, R. Todd.

TRANSPORT SALARIED STAFFS' ASSOCIATION (49,254), Walkden House, 10 Melton Street, NW1 2EJ—*Gen. Sec.*, C. A. Lyons.

UNION OF COMMUNICATION WORKERS, The (195,374), UCW House, Crescent Lane, SW4 9RN—*Gen. Sec.*, A. D. Tuffin.

UNION OF CONSTRUCTION, ALLIED TRADES AND TECHNICIANS (U.C.A.T.T.) (249,961), UCATT House, 177 Abbeville Road, Clapham, SW4 9RL—*Sec.*, A. Williams.

UNION OF SHOP, DISTRIBUTIVE AND ALLIED WORKERS (U.S.D.A.W.) (392,307), Oakley, 188 Wilmslow Road, Fallowfield, Manchester M14 6LJ—*Sec.*, W. H. P. Whatley.

UNITED ROAD TRANSPORT UNION (22,139), 76 High Lane, Manchester M21 1FD—*Gen. Sec.*, J. Moore, M.B.E.

WRITERS' GUILD OF GREAT BRITAIN, The (1,231), 430 Edgware Road, W2 1EH—*Gen. Sec.*, W. J. Jeffrey.

YORKSHIRE ASSOCIATION OF POWER LOOM OVERLOOKERS (514), Textile Hall, Westgate, Bradford BD1 2RG—*Sec.*, G. Slack.

LABOUR STATISTICS

Industrial Stoppages (Thousands)

	Workers involved	Total working days lost						
		All industries and services	Coal, coke, mineral oil and natural gas	Metals, engineering and vehicles	Textiles, clothing and footwear	Construction	Transport and communication	All other industries and services
Estimated number of employees in employment at June 1982		*21,103*	*326*	*2,941*	*587*	*1,050*	*1,383*	*14,817*
1979	4,583	29,474	128	20,390	109	834	1,419	6,594
1980	830	11,964	166	10,155	44	281	253	1,065
1981	1,499	4,266	237	1,731	39	86	359	1,814
1982	2,101	5,313	380	1,457	61	41	1,675	1,699
1983	573	3,754	591	1,420	32	68	295	1,348
1984	1,375	26,564	22,265	2,024	64	93	660	1,458
1985 January	19	2,132	2,008	13	2	20	15	73
February	87	1,991	1,815	42	3	13	8	110
March	68	529	308	47	1	1	9	163
April	63	188	19	40	5	—	46	78
May	28	229	19	56	—	13	3	137
June	10	166	1	29	—	5	1	130

INDUSTRIAL RESEARCH ASSOCIATIONS

The following are members of the C.D.R.A., The Federation of Technology Centres, Palace Chambers, Bridge Street, SW1A 2JY.:—

ASLIB, 26–27 Boswell Street, WC1N 3JZ.—*Dir.*, Dr. D. A. Lewis.

ASSOCIATED BRITISH PORTS, Hayes Road, Southall, Middlx.—*Dir.*, W. H. Jackson.

ATOMIC ENERGY AUTHORITY, U.K., Bldg. 329, A.E.R.E. Harwell, Oxon.—*Dir., Industrial Research*, Dr. R. G. Sowden.

BHRA FLUID ENGINEERING, Cranfield, Beds.—*Dir.*, F. W. Adler, O.B.E.

BRICK DEVELOPMENT ASSOCIATION, Woodside House, Winkfield, Windsor, Berks.—*Dir.-Gen.*, R. Lloyd-Jones.

BRITISH BRUSH MANUFACTURERS' RESEARCH ASSOCIATION, c/o Dept. of Textile Industries, The University, Leeds.—*Dir.*, D. I. Fothergill.

BRITISH CERAMIC RESEARCH ASSOCIATION, Queen's Road, Penkhull, Stoke-on-Trent.—*Dir.*, Dr. D. W. F. James.

BRITISH GLASS INDUSTRY RESEARCH ASSOCIATION, Northumberland Road, Sheffield 10.—*Dir.*, Dr. E. A. Kellett.

BRITISH INTERNAL COMBUSTION ENGINE RESEARCH INSTITUTE, 111–12 Buckingham Avenue, Slough, Bucks.—*Dir.*, I. A. C. Brown.

BRITISH LEATHER MANUFACTURERS' RESEARCH ASSOCIATION, King's Park Road, Moulton Road, Northampton.—*Dir.*, Dr. R. L. Sykes.

BUILDING SERVICES RESEARCH AND INFORMATION ASSOCIATION, Old Bracknell Lane, Bracknell, Berks.—*Dir.*, Dr. D. P. Gregory.

CONSTRUCTION INDUSTRY RESEARCH AND INFORMATION ASSOCIATION, 6 Storey's Gate, S.W.1.—*Dir.*, L. S. Blake, PH.D.

CUTLERY AND ALLIED TRADES RESEARCH ASSOCIATION, Henry Street, Sheffield, 3.—*Dir.*, E. A. Oldfield.

DROP FORGING RESEARCH ASSOCIATION, Shepherd Street, Sheffield 3.—*Dir.*, S. E. Rogers, PH.D.

FIRE INSURERS' RESEARCH AND TESTING ORGANISATION, Melrose Avenue, Borehamwood, Herts.—*Dir.*, R. W. Pickard.

FURNITURE INDUSTRY RESEARCH ASSOCIATION, Maxwell Road, Stevenage, Herts.—*Dir.*, D. M. Heughan.

LAMBEG INDUSTRIAL RESEARCH ASSOCIATION (*Linen*), Research Institute, Lambeg, Lisburn, Co. Antrim, N. Ireland.—*Dir.*, Dr. W. W. Foster.

MACHINE TOOL INDUSTRY RESEARCH ASSOCIATION, Hulley Road, Hurdsfield, Macclesfield, Cheshire.—*Dir.*, L. K. Lord.

NATIONAL COMPUTING CENTRE, Oxford Road, Manchester 1.—*Dir.*, D. R. Fairbairn.

PAINT RESEARCH ASSOCIATION, Paint Research Station, Waldegrave Road, Teddington, Middlesex.—*Dir.*, G. de W. Anderson, PH.D.

PAPER AND BOARD, PRINTING AND PACKAGING INDUSTRIES RESEARCH ASSOCIATION (Pira), Randalls Road, Leatherhead, Surrey.—*Dir.*, N. K. Bridge, PH.D.

PROCESSORS AND GROWERS RESEARCH ORGANISATION, The Research Station, Great North Road, Peterborough.—*Dir.*, G. P. Gent.

PRODUCTION ENGINEERING RESEARCH ASSOCIATION OF GREAT BRITAIN, Melton Mowbray, Leics.—*Dir.-Gen.*, R. A. Armstrong.

RUBBER AND PLASTICS RESEARCH ASSOCIATION OF GREAT BRITAIN, Shawbury, Shrewsbury, Shropshire.—*Dir.*, Dr. J. P. Berry.

SHIPOWNERS REFRIGERATED CARGO RESEARCH ASSOCIATION, 140 Newmarket Road, Cambridge.—*Dir.*, G. R. Scrine.

SHOE AND ALLIED TRADES RESEARCH ASSOCIATION, Satra House, Rockingham Road, Kettering, Northants.—*Dir.*, J. G. Butlin, O.B.E.

SPRING RESEARCH AND MANUFACTURERS' ASSOCIATION, Henry Street, Sheffield 3.—*Dir.*, J. A. Bennett.

STEEL CASTINGS RESEARCH AND TRADE ASSOCIATION, 5 East Bank Road, Sheffield 2.—*Dir.*, Dr. J. A. Reynolds.

TIMBER RESEARCH AND DEVELOPMENT ASSOCIATION, Hughenden Valley, High Wycombe, Bucks.—*Dir.*, J. G. Sunley.

WATER RESEARCH CENTRE, Henley Road, Medmenham, Marlow, Bucks.—*Chief Exec.*, M. J. Rouse.

WINTECH, Pearl House, Greyfriars Road, Cardiff CF1 3XX.—*Dir.*, C. B. Thomas.

WIRA TECHNOLOGY GROUP LTD. (*Wool industries*), Wira House, West Park Ring Road, Leeds 16.—*Dir.*, B. E. King, PH.D.

The following are members of the Association of Independent Contract Research Organisations (A.I.C.R.O.), Bridge Works, Shoreham-by-Sea, W. Sussex BN4 5FG.

BCIRA (*Foundry and associated industries*), Alvechurch, Birmingham.

BHRA FLUID ENGINEERING, Cranfield, Bedford.

BNF METALS (*Non-ferrous metals*), Denchworth Road, Wantage, Oxon.

CAMBRIDGE CONSULTANTS LTD. (*Product development and process improvement*), Science Park, Milton Road, Cambridge CB4 4DW.

ERA TECHNOLOGY (*Electrotechnology*), Cleeve Road, Leatherhead, Surrey.

FULMER RESEARCH INSTITUTE (*The science and technology of materials*), Stoke Poges, Slough, Berks.

HAZLETON LABORATORIES EUROPE LTD. (*Life sciences*), Otley Road, Harrogate, N. Yorks.

INTERNATIONAL RESEARCH AND DEVELOPMENT (*Engineering, materials technology, applied physics and biotechnology*), Fossway, Newcastle-upon-Tyne.

INVERESK RESEARCH INTERNATIONAL LTD. (*Life sciences*), Inveresk Gate, Musselburgh, Midlothian.

LIFE SCIENCE RESEARCH, Eye, Suffolk.

MOTOR INDUSTRY RESEARCH ASSOCIATION, Watling Street, Nuneaton, Warwicks.

RICARDO CONSULTING ENGINEERS, P.L.C. (*Combustion engine technology*), Bridge Works, Shoreham-by-Sea, Sussex.

SHIRLEY INSTITUTE (*Textiles*), Didsbury, Manchester.

SIRA INSTITUTE LTD. (*Instrumentation technology*), South Hill, Chislehurst, Kent.

THE WELDING INSTITUTE, Abington Hall, Abington, Cambs.

AGRICULTURAL RESEARCH INSTITUTES AND UNITS

The following research institutes are under the direct control of the Agricultural and Food Research Council (*see* Index):—

Animal Breeding Research Organisation, West Mains Road, Edinburgh EH9 3JQ.—*Dir.* R. B. Land, PH.D.

Computing Centre, West Common, Harpenden, Herts. AL5 2JE.—*Dir.*, P. Chandler.

Food Research Institute, Langford, nr. Bristol.—*Dir.*, Prof. A. J. Bailey, PH.D.

Food Research Institute, Colney Lane, Norwich.—*Dir.*, R. F. Curtis, C.B.E., PH.D., SC.D.

Food Research Institute, Shinfield, Reading RG2 9AT.—*Dir.*, Prof. M.I. Gurr.

Insect Chemistry and Physiology Group, University of Sussex, Falmer, Brighton BN1 9RQ.—*Head of Group*, G. T. Brooks, PH.D.

Institute of Animal Physiology, Babraham, Cambs. CB2 4AT.—*Dir.*, B. A. Cross, C.B.E., PH.D., SC.D., F.R.S.

Institute for Research on Animal Diseases, Compton, Newbury, Berks. RG16 0NN.—*Dir.*, J. M. Payne, PH.D.

Poultry Research Centre, Roslin, Midlothian EH25 9PS.—*Dir.*, D. W. F. Shannon, PH.D.

A.F.R.C./M.R.C. Neuropathogenesis Unit, Ogston Building, West Mains Road, Edinburgh EH9 3JF.—*Dir.*, Prof. J. Postgate.

Unit of Insect Neurophysiology and Pharmacology, Zoology Dept., University of Cambridge, Downing Street, Cambridge CB2 3EJ.—*Hon. Dir.*, J. E. Treherne, PH.D., SC.D.

Unit of Nitrogen Fixation, University of Sussex, Brighton BN1 9RQ.—*Dir.*, Prof. J. Postgate, F.R.S.

Unit of Statistics, University of Edinburgh, Edinburgh EH9 3JZ.—*Acting Dir.*, Prof. H. D. Patterson, M.SC.

Statistics Group, Dept. of Applied Biology, Pembroke Street, Cambridge CB2 3DX.—*Officer in Charge*, D. E. Walters.

GRANT-AIDED RESEARCH INSTITUTES

In addition to the above there are other institutes which, while retaining their own individuality, are financed wholly or in the main by grants made from Government funds. Most of these Institutes have governing bodies of their own to which they are directly responsible. The maintenance grants for Institutes in England and Wales are met from funds voted by Parliament and administered by the Agricultural and Food Research Council; the Scottish Institutes are borne on the vote of the Department of Agriculture and Fisheries for Scotland.

Animal and Grassland Research Institute, Hurley, nr. Maidenhead, Berks. SL6 5LR.—*Dir.*, Prof. J. H. D. Prescott, PH.D.

Animal Virus Research Institute, Pirbright, Surrey GU24 0NF.—*Dir.*, B. Mahey, PH.D.

East Malling Research Station, Maidstone, Kent ME19 6BJ.—*Dir.*, L. J. Graham-Bryce, D.Phil.

Glasshouse Crops Research Institute, Worthing Road, Littlehampton, West Sussex BN17 6LP.—*Dir.*, D. Rudd-Jones, C.B.E., PH.D.

Hannah Research Institute, Ayr KA6 5HL.—*Dir.*, Prof. M. Peaker, PH.D.

Hill Farming Research Organisation, Bush Estate, Penicuik, Midlothian EH26 0PY.—*Dir.*, J. Eadie.

Hop Research Department, Wye College, Ashford, Kent TN25 5AH.—*Dir.*, R. E. Gunn.

Houghton Poultry Research Station,* Houghton, Huntingdon PE17 2DA.—*Dir.*, Prof. P. M. Biggs, PH.D., F.R.S.

John Innes Institute, Colney Lane, Norwich NR4 7UH.—*Dir.*, Prof. H. W. Woolhouse, PH.D., F.R.S.C.

Long Ashton Research Station, Bristol BS18 9AF.—*Dir.*, Prof. K. J. Treharne, PH.D.

Macaulay Institute for Soil Research, Craigiebuckler, Aberdeen AB9 2QJ.—*Dir.*, Prof. T. West, PH.D., F.R.S.E.

Moredun Research Institute, 408 Gilmerton Road, Edinburgh EH17 7JH.—*Dir.*, I. D. Aitken, PH.D.

National Institute of Agricultural Engineering, Wrest Park, Silsoe, Bedford MK45 4HS.—*Dir.*, J. Matthews.

National Vegetable Research Stn. Wellesbourne, Warwick CV35 9EF.—*Dir.*, Prof. J. K. A. Bleasdale, PH.D.

Plant Breeding Institute, Maris Lane, Trumpington, Cambridge CB2 2LQ.—*Dir.*, Prof. P. R. Day, PH.D.

Rothamsted Experimental Station, Harpenden, Herts. AL5 2JQ.—*Dir.*, Sir Leslie Fowden, PH.D., F.R.S.

Rowett Research Institute, Bucksburn, Aberdeen AB2 9SB.—*Dir.*, W. P. T. James, PH.D.

Scottish Crop Research Institute, Invergowrie, Dundee DD2 5DA.—*Dir.*, C. E. Taylor, C.B.E., PH.D., F.R.S.E.

Scottish Institute of Agricultural Engineering, Bush Estate, Penicuik, Midlothian EH26 0PH.—*Dir.*, D. P. Blight, PH.D.

Welsh Plant Breeding Station, Plas Gogerddan, nr. Aberystwyth SY23 3EB.—*Dir.*, Prof. R. Q. Connell, PH.D.

*Financed jointly by the Agricultural and Food Research Council and the Animal Health Trust.

MASTERS OF THE QUEEN'S/KING'S MUSIC

	Apptd.		Apptd.
Nicholas Lanier	1626	Francois (Franz) Cramer	1834
Louis Grabu	1666	George Frederick Anderson	1848
Nicholas Staggins	1674	Sir William George Cusins	1870
John Eccles	1700	Sir Walter Parratt	1893
Maurice Greene	1735	Sir Edward Elgar	1924
William Boyce	1755 (1757)	Sir Henry Walford Davies	1934
John Stanley	1779	Sir Arnold Edward Trevor Bax	1941
Sir William Parsons	1786	Sir Arthur Bliss	1953
William Shield	1817	Malcolm Williamson	1975
Christian Kramer	1829		

POETS LAUREATE

Samuel Daniel	1599	Rev. Laurence Eusden	1718	Lord Tennyson	1850
Ben Jonson	1619	Colley Cibber	1730	Alfred Austin	1890
Sir William D'Avenant	1637	William Whitehead	1757	Robert Bridges	1913
John Dryden	1670	Rev. Thomas Warton	1785	John Masefield	1930
Thomas Shadwell	1688	Henry James Pye	1790	Cecil Day Lewis	1967
Nahum Tate	1692	Robert Southey	1813	Sir John Betjeman	1972
Nicholas Rowe	1715	William Wordsworth	1843	Edward (Ted) Hughes	1984

PRINCIPAL CHARITABLE BEQUESTS OF THE YEAR

The alphabetical list below represents the principal charitable bequests from estates published since the last edition. In almost all cases the value of the residue available for distribution is not known, since legacies, testamentary expenses and Capital Transfer Tax have to be deducted from the net estate.

The largest estate proved in the year—that of James Sainsbury, a director of the grocery chain of that name—contained probably the largest charitable bequest, since he left the residue of his £18 million estate towards leukaemia research, with the wish that it be named the Kay Kendall Leukaemia Fund, after the former actress who died from the disease. Another large bequest for medical research was left by Arthur Englert, who left all of his £511,260 estate to the Muscular Dystrophy Group. Beatrice Bird left the residue of her £948,733 estate to the British Kidney Patients Association.

A number of hospitals feature in the list, including Royal Victoria Hospital, Bournemouth, and the Great Ormond Street Hospital for Sick Children, London, who shared the residue of the £519,302 estate of Eleanor Peek; the United Birmingham Hospitals, who received 2/3rds of the residue of the £721,530 estate of Gladys Price, a doctor's widow, for research into children's diseases; the Bromley Hospital Group was bequeathed half the residue of the £406,720 estate of Florence Parker; and a Dublin woman, Alfreda O'Gorman, left all her £357,981 English and Irish estate, bar £100, to St. Patrick's Hospital, Dublin.

Paul Luty, the actor and former wrestler, made over all his £124,236 estate to the Cancer Research Campaign, who were also left the residue of the £742,858 estate of Marguerite Haworth. The entire £128,004 estate of Irene Williams was left to the Pat Seed Appeal Fund at the Christie Hospital, Manchester, and Pat Seed, the Fund's founder, who had raised over £3 million for cancer research since contracting the disease in 1977, left the Fund the royalties on her books "One Day at a Time" and "Another Day".

A number of unusually large charitable bequests appear this year headed by a single legacy of £2 million made in the will of Mary Shannon, who left over £7 million in all. Her legacy followed the trusts of a charitable settlement already made in her lifetime. Aetheldreda Hadow, a widow who lived in Jersey, left estate in the U.K. valued at £1·7 million, with nearly all to the R.S.P.C.A., for the department dealing with prosecution of cases of animal cruelty. Her total estate world-wide was believed to be even larger. Sylvia Kyriakides, of Cardiff, left the bulk of her estate between just three charities, while no less than fifteen, including a number in Scarborough, shared the residue of the estate left by Dorothy Allatt. Four Jewish charities shared virtually all the estate of Londoner Richard Harris, while retired Shropshire farmer James George left half the residue of his estate to seven charities, including three Herefordshire hospitals. Derek Williams left the residue of his estate, which included a collection of paintings, to the National Museum of Wales, and former Conservative Minister Baron Geoffrey-Lloyd left £200,000 and his collection of works by Constantin Guys to Leeds Castle Foundation. All the last six people mentioned left estates of over £1 million.

Charities for the elderly also feature prominently with a single bequest of £300,000 to Hertfordshire Old People's Establishment from the £5·7 million estate of Donald Forrester, while retired Northampton farmer David Taylor left the residue of his £778,026 estate to a trust for the elderly created in his lifetime. Three of the more unusual bequests include the entire £147,136 estate of Win-

ifred Edwards, which she left to the Buddhist Society, London, the £200,355 estate of Jack Marsh, left entirely to the Leicester Model Aero Club, for purchase of land, and the residue of the £100,191 estate of a Lincolnshire man James Baxter, which was left towards the reduction of the National Debt.

Mrs. Dorothy Eileen Allatt, of Scarborough, North Yorks. £2,007,706
(The residue equally between Queen Street Methodist Central Hall, Scarborough, the Y.M.C.A., Scarborough, the R.N.L.I., Scarborough Ladies Guild, the Scarborough Flower Fund Homes, St. Catherine's Hospice, Scarborough, the George Edward Smart Homes, Scarborough, the Scarborough Council of Voluntary Services, the R.N.I.B., the R.N.I.D., Institute of Child Health, Methodist Homes for the Aged, Royal British Legion Poppy Appeal, Salvation Army, Age Concern and the R.S.P.B.)

Cora Winifred Ayers, of Nursling, Hants. . . £346,169
(The residue equally between St. Mary's Redcliffe Church, Bristol, Historic Churches Preservation Trust, National Trust, R.N.L.I., Help the Aged, Imperial Cancer Research Fund, Marie Curie Memorial Foundation, Church of England Winchester Diocese and Church of England Monmouth Diocese)

Mrs. Mary Elizabeth Baillie, of Melton Mowbray, Leics. £159,234
(The residue to the R.N.L.I.)

Miss Phyllis Barker, of Northiam, Rye, East Sussex.................................. £357,345
(The residue to the Haberdasher's St. Katherine Foundation)

Mr. James Baxter, of Skellingthorpe, Lincs. £100,191
(The residue to be applied in the reduction of the National Debt)

Mrs. Lilian Elizabeth St. John Beahan, of Broadstone, Dorset £332,970
(The residue equally between the Cancer Research Campaign, R.N.L.I. and N.S.P.C.C.)

Beatrice Mary Bird, of Wylde Green, Sutton Coldfield, West Midlands £948,733
(The residue to the British Kidney Patients Association)

Mary Birtwell, of Vicars Cross, Chester.... £223,379
(The residue to the National Trust)

Miss Amy Adeline Blake, of Hove, East Sussex.................................... £428,978
(The residue to the British Red Cross Society)

Miss Mary Brearley, of Old Colwyn, Clwyd................................. £313,081
(The residue equally between the Church Army, Salvation Army, the Historic Churches Preservation Trust and Cheshire Foundation)

Edith Gladys Maud Brown, of Worlebury, Weston-super-Mare, Avon £405,774
(The residue equally between Christian Aid, League Against Cruel Sports, National Anti-Vivisection Society, World Healing Crusade, the Churches Fellowship for Psychical and Spiritual Studies, Dr. Barnardo's, Church Missionary Society, the Defence and Aid Fund, Shelter and the Salvation Army)

Mr. Henry Robert Bull, of Idbury, Kingham, Oxon................................. £639,037
(All his property for a charitable trust, the income to be used for charitable purposes, including the Royal Agricultural Benevolent Institution, as his trustees select)

Helena Millicent Carr, of East Chinnock, Yeovil, Somerset £259,785
(All her property for Fiveways School, Yeovil)

Mr. Arthur Cyril Cooper, of Ledbury, Herefordshire £268,460
(The residue to St. Edmund Hall, Oxford)

Mrs. Eliza Montgomery Boyd Cullen, of St. Leonards, East Sussex £192,728
(The residue to the Distressed Gentlefolk's Aid Association)

Madeleine Violet De Hulsters, of Ealing, London W.5. .... £154,838
(The residue to the Marie Curie Memorial Foundation)

Bertha Rosamund Dickson, of Grayshott, Hants. £595,032
(The residue equally between the Cancer Research Campaign and Imperial Cancer Research Fund)

Miss Vera Emily Down, of Worthing, West Sussex £568,761
(1/3rd of residue each to the B.M.A. Scholarship Trust Fund and Oxfam, 1/6th of residue to the Voluntary and Christian Service, and 1/12th of residue each to Christian Aid and Save the Children Fund)

Muriel Evelyn Drew, of Norbury, London S.W.16. .... £100,460
(All her property to the Imperial Cancer Research Fund)

Agnes Mary Dunn, of Sowerby, Thirsk, North Yorks. £663,824
(1/4th of residue each for the Church of Our Lady of Mount Carmel, Stock, St. Joseph's Hospice, Hackney, and the Little Sisters of the Poor, Fulwood, Preston)

Winifred Edwards, of Stotfold, Beds. £147,136
(All her property to the Buddhist Society, London)

Mr. Arthur Henry Englert, of Pinner, Middlesex £511,260
(All his property to the Muscular Dystrophy Group)

Mr. William Gordon Finlayson, of Kingsmead Road, London S.W.2. .... £766,506
(The residue equally between the R.S.P.C.A. and Salvation Army)

Mr. Donald Forrester, of Portland Place, London W.1. .... £5,797,352
(£300,000 to the Hertfordshire Old People's Establishment)

Miss Evelyn May Gale, of West Bridgford, Notts. £468,705
(The residue to form a charitable fund to provide accommodation for poor, aged or infirm people born in Nottinghamshire)

Mr. James Picton Evans George, of Orleston, Ludlow, Salop. £1,151,717
(Half the residue equally between the British Red Cross Society, Arthritis and Rheumatism Council, Marie Curie Memorial Foundation, Distressed Gentlefolk's Aid Association, Hereford General Hospital, Hereford County Hospital and the Nuffield Hospital, Hereford)

Wilhelmina Dunn Hadden, of Norwich, Norfolk £527,321
(The residue equally between the Norwich Institution for the Blind, the Grove Cheshire Home, East Carleton, Norwich, Dr. Barnardo's, Children's Society, St. Dunstan's, Imperial Cancer Research Fund and Royal Association in Aid of the Deaf and Dumb)

Mrs. Aetheldreda Mary Luxton Hadow, of St. Helier, Jersey £1,756,550
(The residue to the R.S.P.C.A., for the department dealing with the prosecution of cases of cruelty to animals)

Rev. Charles Wyatt Cater Freeman Harding, of Kingsland, Leominster, Herefordshire ... £215,997
(The residue to the Church Commissioners of the Church of England)

Nesta Harries, of Dorchester, Dorset £329,244
(The residue equally between the Distressed Gentlefolk's Aid Association and the National Trust)

Mr. Richard Maurice Harris, of Cadogan Lane, London S.W.1. .... £1,923,071
(The residue equally between the Jewish Welfare Board, Jewish Home and Hospital, Tottenham, Home for Aged Jews, London S.W.12., the Spanish and Portuguese Jews Home, Wembley, and the Jewish Philanthropic Association)

Mrs. Marguerite Jeanne Haworth, of Bowdon, Greater Manchester £742,858
(The residue to the Cancer Research Campaign)

Margery Hewens, of Hindhead, Surrey £291,174
(The residue to the National Trust)

Miss Myfanwy Hibbert, of Shortlands, Bromley, Kent £312,358
(The residue equally between the Mental After Care Association, the National Association for Mental Health, the Queen Elizabeth Training College for the Disabled, Leatherhead, and Red House School for Maladjusted Children, East Sutton, Maidstone)

Miss Mary Barratt-Hine, of Lyme Regis, Dorset £456,312
(The residue equally between the Salvation Army, R.N.I.B., the National Society for Cancer Relief, Royal Hospital and Home for Incurables, Putney, Guide Dogs for the Blind Association and St. Joseph's Hospice, Hackney)

Mr. Richard Crewdson Leaver Howitt, of Farndon, Notts. £578,343
(The residue to the National Trust)

Mrs. Norah Hughes, of Abersoch, Gwynedd £177,210
(The residue to the Imperial Cancer Research Fund)

Sir Daniel Thomson Jack, of Chalfont St. Peter, Bucks. £154,145
(The residue to the University of Glasgow)

Monica James, of Bromley, Kent £539,788
(£5,000 and 1/10th of the residue to the Over Forty Association for Women Workers, and 1/10th of the residue each to Bromley Council of Social Services, R.U.K.B.A., Age Concern, Bromley, Imperial Cancer Research Fund, Multiple Sclerosis Society, British Heart Foundation, R.N.L.I., Save the Children Fund and St. Christopher's Hospice, Sydenham)

Miss Rosalie Sarah Jonas, of Wembley Park, Middlesex £193,036
(The residue to the Society of Friends Yearly Meeting Fund)

Mrs. Ethel Winifred Astley-Jones, of Tenbury Wells, Worcs. £263,804
(The residue to the National Trust)

Hilda Jones, of Sidmouth, Devon £239,237
(The residue equally between the Society for the Assistance of Ladies in Reduced Circumstances and Belfast Cathedral)

Mrs. Sheila Jordison, of Salcombe, Devon .. £322,364
(The residue for such charities as her trustee thinks fit)

Marianne Millard Kennard, of Leatherhead, Surrey £312,601
(The residue equally between the N.S.P.C.C., Cancer Research Campaign and R.S.P.C.A.)

Mrs. Norah Kathleen Kirby, of Westgate on Sea, Kent £116,350
(The residue to the John Ireland Charitable Trust)

Sylvia Elaine Kyriakides, of Cardiff, South
Glamorgan £1,341,099
(The residue equally between MIND, the Na-
tional Society for Cancer Relief and the Save the
Children Fund)

Dr. Constance Rougier La Trobe, of Blackpool,
Lancs. £210,749
(Half the residue to the P.D.S.A., Birmingham,
and 1/4th of the residue each to the P.D.S.A.,
Blackpool, and R.S.P.C.A., Blackpool)

Estella Lilian Leak, of Bournemouth, Dorset £164,030
(The residue to Guy's Hospital, London)

Mr. Frederick Lilley, of Herne Bay, Kent .. £177,991
(The residue to Stoke Mandeville Hospital)

Geoffrey William, Baron Geoffrey-Lloyd, P.C., of
Chester Square, London, S.W.1. ...... £1,895,119
(£200,000 and his collection of works by Constantin Guys to the Leeds Castle Foundation)

Mr. Philip Graham Luty, of Leeds, West
Yorks. £124,236
(All his property to the Cancer Research Cam-
paign)

Miss Winifred Marris, of Exmouth,
Devon.............................. £544,617
(The residue equally between the Imperial Can-
cer Research Fund, the Arthritis and Rheuma-
tism Council, Muscular Dystrophy Group,
R.N.I.B., R.N.L.I., Distressed Gentlefolk's Aid
Association and the Guide Dogs for the Blind
Association)

Mr. Arthur Marsden, of Bristol, Avon £258,431
(7/10ths of the residue to the Friends of Bristol
Radiotherapy Centre, for cancer research, and
3/10ths of the residue to Bristol University, for a
bursary)

Mr. Jack Marsh, of Leicester £200,355
(All his property to the Leicester Model Aero
Club)

Mrs. Florence Anne Millicent Emma Maxwell, of
Walsingham Mansions, London S.W.6. .. £160,561
(The residue to the R.A.F. Benevolent Fund)

Mrs. Henni Mester, of Woolacombe Road, London
S.E.3. .... £237,495
(The ultimate residue to University College,
Oxford, for rheumatism and arthritis research)

Mr. Leslie Hugh Moorhouse, of Warwick .. £213,556
(The residue for such charitable institutions in
England as his executor shall select)

Rt. Rev. Bishop Stephen Charles Neill, F.B.A., of
Oxford £165,163
(The residue to the British and Foreign Bible
Society)

Mr. Alfons Neuberger, of Norrice Lea, London
N.2. .... £666,111
(The residue equally between the Imperial Can-
cer Research Fund and the Belsize Square
Synagogue, London N.W.3.)

Miss Ada Mary Nuttall, of Burnley,
Lancs. £627,137
(1/4th of her property to St. Peter's Parish
Church, Burnley, 3/16ths of her property to the
World Society for the Protection of Animals,
1/8th of her property to the R.S.P.C.A., Lanca-
shire East, and 1/16th of her property to the
Animal Shelter, Altham)

Miss Alfreda O'Gorman, of Baily Howth, Dublin £357,981
(The residue to St. Patrick's Hospital, Dublin)

Mr. Arthur Oliver, of Binbrook, Lincs. £312,219
(The residue to the National Trust, for use in
Lincolnshire)

Mrs. Helen Macaulay Orr, of Painswick,
Gloucs. £185,062
(The residue to the Musicians Benevolent Fund)

Mr. Denis Joseph O'Shea, of Yardley Wood,
Birmingham £103,208
(All his property to Holy Trinity Roman Catholic
Church, Chipping Norton, Oxon.)

Mr. Peter Oxley, of Beeston, Notts. £194,058
(The residue to Queen's College, Oxford)

Mrs. Florence Louise Parker, of Bromley,
Kent £406,720
(Half the residue to Bromley Group Hospital
Management Committee—1 part each to Bromley and Farnborough Hospitals, and 1/4th of the
residue each to the R.N.I.B. and Guide Dogs for
the Blind Association)

Eleanor Mary Elizabeth Peek, of Southbourne,
Dorset £519,302
(The residue equally between Royal Victoria
Hospital, Bournemouth, and the Hospital for
Sick Children, Great Ormond Street, London)

Mrs. Amelia Elizabeth Porter, of West Kirby,
Merseyside £988,019
(£10,000 and a share of the residue to St. Luke's
Methodist Church, Hoylake, £5,000 and a share
of the residue each to the Methodist Central
Hall, Liverpool, and "the Sisters of Jesus Way",
£2,000 and a share of the residue to the Salvation
Army, and £1,000 and a share of the residue to
the Methodist Ministers Retirement Fund)

Mrs. Gladys Mary Price, of Solihull, West Midlands £721,530
(2/3rds of the residue to the Endowment Fund of
United Birmingham Hospitals, for research into
children's diseases)

Mr. Basil John Prigmore, of New Malden, Surrey £249,455
(The residue to Queens' College, Cambridge)

Mrs. Constance Elizabeth Pymm, of Roker, Sunder-
land, Tyne and Wear £129,371
(The residue to the Methodist Homes for the
Aged)

Commander John Curthoys Richards, R.N., retd., of
Warsash, Hants. £371,503
(The residue equally between the Salvation
Army and Dr. Barnardo's)

Miss Nina Blanche Sadler, of Chiddingfold, Surrey £424,859
(£1,000 and half the residue to the National
Children's Home and £500 and half the residue
to the Lord Mayor Treloar College, Alton)

Mr. James Arthur Sainsbury, C.B.E., of Lowndes
Street, London S.W.1. .... £18,367,303
(The ultimate residue of his estate to his trustees
for such charitable purposes in the field of
leukaemia research as they select, payments to
be known as "the Kay Kendall Leukaemia
Fund")

Mrs. Patricia Victoria Seed, M.B.E., of Garstang,
Lancs. £169,401
(The royalties, income or profits from her books
"One Day at a Time" and "Another Day" to the
Pat Seed Appeal Fund, Christie Hospital, Man-
chester)

Mrs. Mary Orovida Shannon, of Kirk Ella, North
Humberside £7,440,733
(£2,000,000 to follow the trusts of a charitable
settlement or to form a charitable trust)

Mr. Arthur Shepherd, of Loughborough,
Leics. £521,241
(The residue to the Loughborough Endowed
Schools)

Mr. Henry James Sier, of Eastbourne, East Sus-
sex £564,532
(The residue equally between the R.N.L.I.,
R.N.I.B., Imperial Cancer Research Fund, Dr.
Barnardo's, Salvation Army, Royal Association
in Aid of the Deaf and Dumb, Chest and Heart
Association, Royal British Legion, Spastics So-

ciety, Cripplecraft, the London Association for the Blind and Muscular Dystrophy Group)

Rev. Cyril Laurence Smith, of Woking, Surrey £627,484
(Half the residue to the Rochester Diocesan Board of Finance, 3/10ths of the residue to Rochester Cathedral, and 1/5th of the residue to the Friends of Rochester Cathedral)

Mr. Ian MacFarlane Smith, of Thames Ditton, Surrey £227,837
(The residue to the National Foundation for Educational Research in England and Wales)

Miss Matilda Theresa Steer, of Ashtead, Surrey £116,823
(The residue to Guildford Cathedral)

Miss Gladys May Stoddard, of Basnetts Wood, Endon, Staffs. £415,832
(The residue equally between the Mental Health Foundation, National Anti-Vivisection Society, the Association for the Propagation of the Faith)

Mr. Clifford William Stone, of Taunton, Somerset £362,859
(The residue equally between the Muller Homes for Children, Bristol, and Dr. Barnardo's)

Naomi Frances Aleyne Stubbs, of Eastbourne, East Sussex £748,466
(£1,000 and 1/5th of the residue each to the Chichester Diocesan Board of Finance and the Distressed Gentlefolk's Aid Association, some effects and 1/5th of the residue to the National Trust, and 1/5th of the residue each to the Sussex Historic Churches Trust and the Cancer Research Campaign)

Mr. David Norman Taylor, of Northampton £778,026
(The residue to the Norman Taylor Educational and Aid for the Elderly Trust)

Mr. Louis Montague Tribe, of Lancing, West Sussex £163,657
(All his property to the British Heart Foundation)

Alice May Trump, of Exeter, Devon £189,609
(All her property to the National Trust)

Mrs. Evelyn Vernon, of Biddulph, Staffs. .. £140,182
(The residue to the Blind Centre, Fenton, Stoke-on-Trent)

Mr. George Edward Irons Ward, of Paddock Wood, Harpenden, Herts. £615,759
(3/8ths of the residue each to St. John's Church, Harpenden, and St. Michael's Church, Barton le Clay, Beds.)

Mr. John Ward, of Wolverhampton, West Midlands £136,655
(The residue to Wolverhampton Methodist Church, towards the opening of a home for elderly people in Wolverhampton)

Elsie Louisa Bernice Westwood, of St. Albans, Herts. £126,133
(The residue to the Guide Dogs for the Blind Association)

Mr. Derek Mathias Tudor Williams, of Lisvane, Cardiff £1,424,161
(The residue to the National Museum of Wales)

Irene Williams, of Rhos on Sea, Clwyd £128,004
(All her property to the Pat Seed Appeal Fund, Christie Hospital, Manchester)

Miss Edna Litchfield Winter, of Ramsgate, Kent £409,028
(The residue to the Linen and Woollen Drapers Institution and Cottage Homes, London)

Mr. Arthur Bernard Woodbury, of Luton, Beds. £190,806
(The residue to the Salvation Army, mostly to the Luton Corps)

Dorothy Woodin, of Telham, Battle, East Sussex.................................. £559,484
(The residue to St. Michael's Hospice, Hastings)

Mrs. Vera May Wootton, of Nuneaton, Warwickshire £304,041
(The residue equally between the R.N.I.B., for use in the Nuneaton District, the R.S.P.C.A., Nuneaton, the Donkey Sanctuary, Sidmouth, National Kidney Research Fund, Cats Protection League and the Guide Dogs for the Blind Association, Leamington Spa)

Mr. Anthony Egerton Wright, of Hemel Hempstead, Herts................................. £388,273
(The residue to the Micklefield School Educational Trust, Seaford)

Mr. Richard Geoffrey Wedgwood Wrigley, of Heathfield, East Sussex £140,709
(The residue to Holy Cross Priory, Heathfield, for the nursing unit)

Mr. David Christopher Yorke, of Challoner Mansions, London W.14. .... £446,266
(The residue equally between the R.N.L.I. and the R.S.P.C.A.)

LIFE ASSURANCE AND GENERAL INSURANCE

BRITISH INSURANCE COMPANIES IN 1984

The worldwide general business underwriting loss of Insurance Companies on their 1984 business amounted to 15·6% on premiums of £14 billion (1983—11·3% on premiums of £12 billion). After taking into account income from invested general insurance assets, there was a sharp deterioration in the trading result and a net loss of £85 million was incurred. This reflected poor experience in all major classes.

RESULTS IN MAJOR TERRITORIES
United Kingdom

Fire and accident business showed an underwriting loss of 14·0% of premiums against a loss of 7·4% in 1983. Weather losses were heavy, costing £175 million and house contents business was affected by a 17·5% increase in the cost of theft claims at £201 million, a figure that has quadrupled in the last 5 years. The house buildings account suffered from greater claims for subsidence damage which, at an estimated £140 million, were higher than 1976, the previous peak year, even after allowing for inflation.

The estimated cost of fire damage in 1984 was £554 million and was notable for the increase in very large fires, with 5 fires each costing more than £10 million. Weather losses also affected the commercial property account. Whilst higher rates are now being obtained, the need for further rate increases remains.

Motor premium income increased by 8%: much of this was due to higher rates but the increases were insufficient to keep pace with higher claims costs and an underwriting loss of 11·9% of premiums was sustained (1983—6·9%). Claims frequency, increasing by about 7½%, had a particularly severe impact on total claims costs and this was coupled with a rise in the average cost of a private claim of approximately 2½%.

United States

Allowing for changes in the sterling:dollar exchange rate, there was no growth in premium income. The underwriting loss on fire and accident business was 27·2% and on motor, 15·4% of premiums.

The increase in the amount of underwriting losses, in themselves largely due to a long period of underpricing on commercial lines in particular, also reflected the increase in the value of the dollar against the pound over the year. Exceptional weather damage claims also contributed to the extent of the losses. Towards the end of 1984 substantial rate increases began to be obtained, especially in commercial lines, and the process has continued in 1985.

Rest of the World

Results varied by territory but overall the under writing loss deteriorated to 10·9% of total premiums of £3·3 billion, compared with the 1983 loss of 7·7%.

Overseas Earnings

Insurance Companies derived 56% of general premium income from their operations overseas. Insurance activities, comprising companies, Lloyd's and brokers, produced invisible earnings of £1·6 billion in 1983, the latest published figure, compared with £1·2 billion in 1982.

Long Term Insurance

Invested assets relating to long term insurance totalled £114·6 billion, an increase of 18·9% and the income from these assets was £7·3 billion, an increase of 16·2% over 1983.
NOTE: Insurance company figures refer to British Insurance Association members who transact some 95% of the worldwide business of the British insurance company market.

WORLDWIDE GENERAL PREMIUMS 1983 & 1984

	1983	1984	Increase
	£m	£m	%
Fire and Accident (non-motor)	7,227	8,474	17·3
Motor....................................	3,897	4,469	14·7
Marine, Aviation and Transport......................	875	1,134	29·6
TOTAL	11,999	14,077	17·3

WORLDWIDE UNDERWRITING RESULTS 1983 & 1984

	1983			1984		
	Premiums	Profit/ Loss	% of Premiums	Premiums	Profit/ Loss	% of Premiums
	£m	£m	%	£m	£m	%
Fire and Accident (non-motor) ...	6,116	−684	−11·2	7,223	−1,198	−16·6
Motor..........................	3,864	−349	−9·0	4,431	−560	−12·6
Marine, Aviation & Transport....	875	−82	−9·4	1,134	−84	−7·4
Treaty Reinsurance & other 3 year Account business	1,144	−239	−20·9	1,289	−355	−27·5
TOTAL	11,999	−1,354	−11·3	14,077	−2,197	−15·6

WORLDWIDE LONG-TERM PREMIUMS 1983 & 1984

	1983	1984	Increase
	£m	£m	%
Ordinary Long-Term (U.K.)	8,714	10,637	22·1
Ordinary Long-Term (Overseas)	1,720	2,285	32·8
Industrial Long-Term (U.K.)	1,080	1,175	8·8
TOTAL	11,514	14,097	22·4

U.K. UNDERWRITING 1983 & 1984

	1983			1984		
	Premiums	Profit/Loss	% of Premiums	Premiums	Profit/Loss	% of Premiums
	£m	£m	%	£m	£m	%
Fire and Accident (non-motor)	2,955	−217·9	−7·4	3,319	−463·5	−14·0
Motor	1,723	−118·1	−6·9	1,870	−222·4	−11·9
TOTAL	4,678	−336·0	−7·2	5,189	−685·9	−13·2

U.S.A. UNDERWRITING 1983 & 1984

	1983			1984		
	Premiums	Profit/Loss	% of Premiums	Premiums	Profit/Loss	% of Premiums
	£m	£m	%	£m	£m	%
Fire and Accident (non-motor)	1,540	−322·9	−21·0	1,896	−515·2	−27·2
Motor	1,058	−167·7	−15·9	1,306	−201·3	−15·4
TOTAL	2,598	−490·6	−18·9	3,202	−716·5	−22·4

REST OF THE WORLD UNDERWRITING 1983 & 1984

	1983			1984		
	Premiums	Profit/Loss	% of Premiums	Premiums	Profit/Loss	% of Premiums
	£m	£m	%	£m	£m	%
Fire and Accident (non-motor)	1,621	−143·6	−8·9	2,008	−219·4	−10·9
Motor	1,083	−63·3	−5·8	1,255	−136·2	−10·9
TOTAL	2,704	−206·9	−7·7	3,263	−355·6	−10·9

LLOYD'S OF LONDON

Lloyds of London is an incorporated society of private underwriters who provide an international market for almost any type of insurance. Ships, aircraft, oil rigs, cargo of all descriptions, motor cars, civil engineering projects, fire, personal accident and third party liability are a few random examples of the everyday risks placed at Lloyd's which currently bring some £4,000 million of premiums to underwriters each year. Three-quarters of this business comes from outside Great Britain and makes a valuable contribution to the country's balance of payments.

Today, as it was three centuries ago, a policy is subscribed at Lloyd's by private individuals with unlimited liability. Now that Lloyd's members are numbered in their thousands, however, the method of underwriting is the same only in principle. The merchant of the past, signing policies in a coffee house as a sideline to his main business, has long since given way to the specialist underwriter who accepts risks at Lloyd's on behalf of members (often referred to as "names") grouped in a syndicate. There are currently about 400 syndicates of varying sizes, some with over two thousand names and each managed by an underwriting agent approved by the Council of Lloyd's.

Lloyd's membership today is drawn from many sources. Industry, commerce and the professions are strongly represented while many members work at Lloyd's either for brokerage firms or for underwriting agencies.

Underwriting membership of Lloyd's is open to men and women of any nationality provided that they meet the stringent financial requirements of the Society, or Corporation, of Lloyd's. Assets of up to £500,000 have to be shown and a deposit lodged with the Corporation as security for underwriting liabilities. This deposit, which must be in the form of approved securities, is determined at a percentage of the member's annual premium income, ranging from 25% for an "external" member resident in the United Kingdom, to 50% for a name working in the Lloyd's market and showing nominal means.

Lloyd's is incorporated by Act of Parliament (Lloyd's Acts 1871–1982) and governed by a Council of 28 members, 16 of whom are elected from and by underwriting members working at Lloyd's and 8 from and by the external membership. Four Council members are nominated by the Council subject to confirmation by the Governor of the Bank of England.

The Council is a legislative body responsible for deciding on major policy matters, for regulating the

Lloyd's market, for the election of new underwriting members, and for establishing the requirements of membership and the rules governing the financial security to be provided by those doing business at Lloyd's.

The Council's "working" members form the Committee of Lloyd's, an executive body which is responsible for putting the Council's directives into effect, managing the Society's affairs, and administering the Lloyd's market on a day-to-day basis.

The Corporation is a non-profit-making body chiefly financed by its members' subscriptions. It provides the premises, administrative staff and services enabling Lloyd's underwriting syndicates to conduct their business. It does not, however, assume corporate liability for the risks accepted by its members, who remain responsible to the full extent of their personal means for their underwriting affairs.

Lloyd's syndicates have no direct contact with the public. All business is transacted through some 270 firms of insurance brokers accredited by the Corporation of Lloyd's. In addition, non-Lloyd's brokers in the United Kingdom when guaranteed by Lloyd's brokers, are able to deal directly with Lloyd's motor syndicates, a facility which has made the Lloyd's market more accessible to the insuring public.

Lloyd's also provides the most comprehensive shipping intelligence service available in the world. The enormous volume of shipping and other information received from Lloyd's Agents, shipowners, news agencies and other sources throughout the world, is collated and distributed to newspapers, radio and television services, as well as to the maritime and commercial communities in general.

This information is compiled, edited and published by a subsidiary company, Lloyd's of London Press Ltd., and distributed worldwide. "Lloyd's List" is London's oldest daily newspaper and contains news of general commercial interest as well as shipping information. "Lloyd's Shipping Index" also published daily, lists some 20,000 ocean-going vessels in alphabetical order and gives the latest known report of each.

LLOYD'S THREE YEAR BUSINESS SUMMARY

	Premiums	Underwriting Profit	Investment Income and Appreciation
	£'000	£'000	£'000
Short Term Life			
1978	1,286	257	87
1979	1,766	450	194
1980	2,051	585	286
Accident & Health			
1978	77,723	13,786	5,966
1979	103,554	14,084	8,819
1980	121,390	9,082	13,163
Motor Vehicle Damage & Liability			
1978	222,362	16,968	15,256
1979	273,072	26,882	21,710
1980	325,342	38,722	34,075
Ships, Aircraft Damage & Liability & Transit			
1978	897,454	59,497	67,823
1979	1,184,438	18,324	92,839
1980	1,568,384	64,682	147,548
All other Insurance Business			
1978	964,456	20,303	80,153
1979	1,296,638	(22,607)	110,063
1980	1,636,205	(91,323)	179,355

LLOYD'S MEMBERSHIP SYNDICATES AND BROKERS 1977–1983

	1983	1982	1981	1980	1979	1978	1977
Membership	21,601	20,145	19,136	18,552	17,278	14,091	10,730
Including: Overseas	3,013	2,181	1,982	1,841	1,650	1,209	740
Syndicates	417	431	427	437	404	363	330
Lloyd's Brokers	272	266	270	265	268	269	267

LLOYD'S GLOBAL UNDERWRITING ACCOUNTS

Net Premium Income			
	1980 A/C	1981 A/C	1982 A/C
	£'000	£'000	£'000
Life	1,458	1,246	2,284
Accident & Health	89,046	97,958	73,024
Motor Vehicle Damage & Liability	237,060	265,481	246,385
Ships, Aircraft Damage & Liability and Transit	877,202	951,282	748,378
All Other Insurance Business	657,521	745,747	607,496
TOTAL	1,862,287	2,061,714	1,677,567

LIFE ASSURANCE IN 1984

	1984 £m	1983 £m
Total new premiums— annual and single	6,430	5,430
Benefits secured by these premiums—		
New sums assured	87,200	85,100
New annuities per annum, deferred and immediate	2,010	1,720

Total new premiums for life assurances and annuities increased in 1984 by 18%, to £6,430 million. New sums assured rose by 2·5% to £87,200 million and new annuities per annum by 17%, to £2,010 million. The following figures include all forms of life assurance and annuities, including linked-life assurance and occupational pension and life assurance schemes in the United Kingdom.

HOME SERVICE INSURANCE IN 1984

The following figures are based on returns from 19 "home service" insurance offices, which together transact over 99% of industrial (collected premium) life business. While they, unlike all other insurers, transact industrial life business, they also carry on a very substantial volume of ordinary life and general insurance, much of it in policyholders' homes through the field staffs.

	1984 £m	1983 £m
Industrial Life Business		
1. Premium Income	1,175·3	1,079·4
2. Payments to policyholders:		
(a) On death	188·9	174·1
(b) On maturity	400·0	326·0
(c) On surrender	316·6	282·7
(d) Other	26·8	26·8
TOTAL	932·3	809·6

NEW LINKED LIFE ASSURANCE BUSINESS
ANNUAL STATISTICS

	Year ended Dec. 31, 1981 £m	Year ended Dec. 31, 1982 £m	Year ended Dec. 31, 1983 £m	Year ended Dec. 31, 1984 £m
1. *New Annual Premiums:*				
(a) Assurances & Annuities	180	217	302	295
(b) Personal Pensions (See note below)	54	65	73	128
Total new annual premiums:	234	282	375	423
2. *New Single Premiums:*				
(a) Assurances & Annuities	548	740	1,440	1,790
(b) Personal Pensions (See note below)	40	57	71	106
Total new single premiums:	588	797	1,511	1,896

NOTE: Personal pensions are contracts available to the self-employed and those not in pensionable employment.

POLICYHOLDERS PROTECTION BOARD
Aldermary House, Queen Street, London E.C.4

The Policyholders Protection Act 1975 put into effect the scheme whereby private policyholders of companies in liquidation will normally be granted 90 per cent (100 per cent for any policyholder in the case of compulsory insurance) of the benefits due under their policies at the date of winding up. The scheme will be financed mainly by a compulsory levy on insurance companies limited to a maximum of 1 per cent of their annual net premium income. The Board consists of five members, of whom three are drawn from the management of insurance companies and at least one must be qualified to represent the interests of policyholders.

INSURANCE COMPANY INVESTMENTS
Long Term Funds

	1983		1984	
	£m	%	£m	%
British Government authority securities	24,129	25·0	25,976	22·7
Foreign and Commonwealth Government, provincial and municipal stocks	3,675	3·8	5,098	4·4
Debentures, loan stocks, preference and guaranteed stocks and shares	4,491	4·7	5,687	5·0
Ordinary stocks and shares................................	36,451	37·9	46,605	40·7
Mortgages	5,496	5·7	6,407	5·6
Real property and ground rents...........................	17,673	18·3	19,278	16·8
Other investments	4,444	4·6	5,528	4·8
TOTAL INVESTED FUNDS	96,359	100·0	114,579	100·0
INCOME FROM INVESTMENTS	6,278		7,294	

NOTE: The above figures are at market value.

INSURANCE COMPANY INVESTMENTS
Other Funds

	1983		1984	
	£m	%	£m	%
British Government authority securities	3,962	17·3	3,717	14·3
Foreign and Commonwealth Government, provincial and municipal stocks	4,251	18·6	5,442	20·9
Debentures, loan stocks, preference and guaranteed stocks and shares..	3,104	13·6	3,989	15·3
Ordinary stocks and shares................................	6,526	28·5	7,449	28·6
Mortgages	786	3·4	821	3·2
Real property and ground rents...........................	2,140	9·4	2,243	8·6
Other investments	2,105	9·2	2,378	9·1
TOTAL INVESTED FUNDS	22,874	100·0	26,039	100·0
INCOME FROM INVESTMENTS	1,882		2,112	

NOTE: The above figures are at market value.

THE LIFE ASSURANCE COMPANIES

The list on the following pages contains the names of all the more important British life offices, and of Commonwealth offices (marked C) which transact life business in this country.

Class of business. The second column shows whether the company is conducted on the mutual system whereby the whole of the divisible profit is allotted to participating policyholders (M), or whether the company has proprietors by whom part (usually a very small proportion) of such profits received (P). Life offices transacting other business are marked (O) in this column. In such cases the life funds are kept separately, and are not liable for the claims of other departments. The share capital is usually liable for the claims of all branches. Those having an industrial branch are indicated by letter (I).

Figures. These are taken from the latest annual accounts available at date of going to press and in the majority of cases refer to annual reports for the financial year ended December 31, 1984.

Life funds. The amounts of these funds, though of interest, are not in themselves a sufficient indication of the financial stability of a company, which cannot be judged unless liabilities are actually compared with assets.

Premium income. The annual premium income is in all cases stated after deduction of the amount paid to other companies for reassuring parts of the risk.

Consideration for annuities.—These are the amounts received to provide various types of annuities.

Interest.—The rate of interest earned is important for comparison with the rate assumed in valuing liabilities, since the greater the margin between these rates the greater is the surplus available from this source bonus declaration. The rate of interest given is before deduction of Income Tax except where marked (N)—net.

Valuation.—The valuation returns which are required to be made by the companies to the Department of Trade and Industry indicate liability under existing policies, after making allowance for the amounts to be paid and received. It is assumed that deaths will occur in accordance with a mortality table (various tables are used) and that interest will be earned at a certain rate. If a company assumes that it will earn a high rate of interest in the future the net liability will appear less than if it assumes a low rate, while the liability on account of mortality appears greater by some tables than by others. The position of an office is most satisfactory when a stringent basis of valuation is adopted, because the margin between the calculated and experienced liability is larger and the surplus available for bonuses is greater. The lower the rate of interest assumed the more stringent is the valuation. The foregoing remarks, however, do not apply in the case of an office which has adopted a Bonus Reserve Valuation.

Types of policy.—Although there are scores of life offices in Britain each offering their own particular products under a wide variety of labels, there are really only four basic types of contract. These are:

1. "Term" assurance (sometimes called "temporary" assurance). With this type of policy the assurer, in return for a regular premium agrees to pay the sum assured if the person assured should die within the term of years stated by the policy.

Such policies take care of the temporary need for protection of the family while the children are growing up, and the family is therefore most vulnerable. The commonest and most popular forms are to cover the mortgage on the family home or to assume a regular tax-free income for the family over so many years should the breadwinner die. This is much the cheapest form of life assurance because the majority of policies invariably do not result in claims.

2. "Whole-life" assurance is one under which the assurer undertakes to keep the assurance in force provided the premiums are paid for the whole life of the assured. They will then pay the agreed sum whenever death takes place. This costs a good deal more than term, naturally. All policies end in claims.

3. "Endowment" assurance. This contract really is one which uses a fund for saving to a particular target sum by a particular future date and at the same time secures payment of the sum assured should the saver die before that date arrives. In return for the continued payment of a regular premium over a fixed number of years, the assurer agrees to pay the sum assured at the end of that time, or earlier if the assured person should die. The bulk of an endowment assurance premium is savings; consequently the premium of such a contract is a lot higher than that for a whole life assurance.

4. "Annuities". Life assurance can be divided broadly speaking into death or survival benefits. Death benefits are paid to a policyholder's dependants if and when he dies. Survival benefits are paid to the policyholder himself either in the form of a cash sum when he reaches a certain age or in the form of a guaranteed annual income for life, which is known as an annuity. Pensions are annuities of a kind and a very large proportion of the pensions due to people are being and will be paid by funds run by life offices.

INDUSTRIAL COMPANIES

Established	Class	Name of Office	Life Funds	Life Premium Income	Rate of interest % Earned	Interest % assumed at Valuation
			£m	£,000		
1866	PO	Britannic	504·3	92,895	13·04	3·00
1862	M	City of Glasgow	23·2	2,472	11·76	3·00
1867	MIO	Co-operative	955·4	172,300	10·40	3·00
1939	P	Irish Life	102·3	16,089	11·72	4·00
1843	M	Liverpool Victoria	685·5	77,189	11·78	3·50
1869	PO	London and Manchester	190·2	30,067	—	3·00
1864	PO	Pearl....................	960·5	185,116	12·49	3·00 & 3·50
1891	M	Pioneer Mutual	35·3	2,688	7·26	3·00
1848	PO	Prudential....................	2,232·1	364,400	11·80	3·00 & 4·50
1911	MI	Reliance Mutual	16·5	2,392	—	2·50 & 3·25
1850	M	Royal Liver	263·1	47,323	11·93	3·75
1861	MO	Royal London....................	557·0	50,996	11·17	2·50
1908	P	United Friendly†	321·1	83,468	10·80	3·00
1841	MO	Wesleyan and General	151·2	24,113	12·45	3·00

†1983 Figures.

INDUSTRIAL LIFE NEW BUSINESS 1984

Name of Office	No. of policies issued	Net sums assured	Net annual premiums
		£	£
Britannic	420,035	395,808,000	23,064,000
City of Glasgow	16,709	9,040,000	616,001
Co-operative....................	474,930	539,100,000	32,500,000
Irish Life	57,146	96,818,000	3,341,000
Liverpool Victoria	194,500	144,600,000	11,392,000
London and Manchester	186,476	92,398,000	6,404,000
Pearl....................	523,837	404,766,000	34,016,000
Pioneer Mutual*	2,211	2,278,117	94,121
Prudential....................	822,735	1,901,200,000	72,000,000
Reliance Mutual†	17,404	10,725,000	747,000
Royal Liver	133,105	99,148,506	7,603,397
Royal London....................	115,238	152,971,000	9,542,000
United Friendly†	492,902	288,668,000	88,239,000
Wesleyan and General	80,215	58,083,282	4,428,259

†1983 Figures   *1982 Figures.

PRINCIPAL LIFE ASSURANCE COMPANIES

Established	Class	Name of Office	Annual Accounts				
			Life and Annuity Funds	Life Premium Income	Consideration for Annuities	Rate of Interest % Earned	Interest % assumed at Valuation
			£m	£000	£000		
1965	P	Allied Dunbar	2,737·0	251,900	239,900	—	—
1921	P	American Life*	216·0	124,161	9,291	11·49	Various
1849	M	Australian Mutual Prov. (C)	139·3	12,224	136	13·01	Various
1925	PO	Avon	37·5	3,568	827	12·37	Various
1965	P	Barclays Life	416·0	59,000	19,000	5·53	—
1866	PIO	Britannic (Ord.)	250·4	30,096	208	13·04	3·00
1920	PO	British National	26·0	10,000	—	14·00	Various
1847	M	Canada Life	2,883·9	173,788	297,902	11·87	Various
1963	P	Cannon*	162·3	35,777	3,801	8·50	Various
1862	MI	City of Glasgow (Ord.)	19·3	4,706	2	11·76	3·00
1824	M	Clerical, Medical Group	1,628·8	122,600	214,100	7·40	7·00
1873	M	Colonial Mutual (C)†	488·0	82,000		12·00	3·50-7·00
1861	PO	Commercial Union	4,224·6	270,284	225,317	9·78	3·00
1871	M	Confederation Life	2,502·0	141,418	37,000	—	—
1867	MIO	Co-operative (Ord.)	858·0	111,700	11,700	10·30	2·75
1900	M	Crown Financial	205·2	73,400	848	—	—
1899	PO	Crusader	407·9	57,582	14,397	9·80	Various
1904	PO	Eagle Star	2,630·8	234,300	80,000	9·53	Various
1887	MO	Ecclesiastical	39·7	4,646	1,941	8·20	3·50
1901	P	Economic*	15·3	2,409	329	9·50	5·00
1762	M	Equitable Life	1,366·5	263,100		9·90	Various
1832	M	Friends' Provident	1,994·8	346,992	20,969	11·75	2·75
1899	M	FS Assurance	71·9	7,997	4,983	7·24	Various
1837	P	General Accident Life	700·3	66,523	44,051	13·18	3·50
1848	P	Gresham Life	164·8	27,258	37	10·90	3·50 & 4·50
1821	PO	Guardian Royal Exchange	3,309·7	287,600	125,900	7·30	Various
1960	P	Hill Samuel	446·8	66,100	16,500	15·40	Various
1932	P	Ideal	1·3	286	—	15·16	3·00
1896	P	Imperial Life of Canada (C)	1,402·2	213,474		12·16	Various
1935	PI	Insurance Corp. Life	166·0	71,863	5,662	—	—
1939	PI	Irish Life (Ord.)	1,365·1	126,218	198,292	7·95	3·50
1836	PO	Legal and General	3,250·0	433,000	23,000	12·00	Various
1838	P	Life Assoc. of Scotland	406·0	116,981		11·00	Various
1843	MI	Liverpool Victoria (Ord.)	148·0	18,346	—	11·83	3·50
1971	P	Lloyd's Life	204·2	68,227	3,237	7·30	Various
1869	PIO	London and Manchester (Ord.)	495·8	87,524		—	Various
1806	M	London Life	1,019·6	93,000	20,900	8·77 (N)	Various
1887	M	Manufacturers Life (C)*	3,573·0	221,600	270,400	—	Various
1961	P	M & G Assurance	266·9	53,280	—	3·70	6·00
1852	M	MGM Assurance	390·7	31,889	48,289	—	Various
1884	M	Medical, Sickness	55·9	6,848	418	11·58	Various
1970	P	Merchant Investors	194·5	30,226	7,253	12·30	10·00
1890	M	Nalgo Insurance	22·1	1,702	—	6·20	2·50
1910	MO	National Farmers Union	373·9	18,133	12,889	12·32	Various
1869	M	National Mut. Life of Australasia†	174·8	10,515	134	—	—
1830	M	National Mutual	240·6	24,263	23,154	11·37	Various
1835	M	National Provident	1,150·8	187,740	2,276	9·65	Various
1924	PIO	New Ireland†	155·1	32,269	—	—	—
1808	M	Norwich Union	4,838·6	738,500	155,340	11·89	4·00-9·00
1864	PIO	Pearl (Ord.)	1,110·7	132,782	18,641	12·56	Various
1782	PO	Phoenix	1,345·4	179,200	22,900	9·92	3·00 & 3·50
1891	MI	Pioneer Mutual (Ord.)	110·2	27,124	—	10·72	3·00
1877	P	Provident Life Assoc.	159·4	26,589	418	9·13	3·25-7·50
1840	M	Provident Mutual	1,255·9	52,085	107,453	—	Various
1848	PIO	Prudential Group (Ord.)	8,059·6	1,074,900	118,700	10·70	Various
1911	MI	Reliance Mutual (Ord.)	54·7	10,398	1	—	2·75 & 4·25
1845	PO	Royal Life	2,264·4	180,500	120,600	9·95	2·50-3·75
1850	MI	Royal Liver (Ord.)	109·9	13,791	—	11·93	3·75
1861	MIO	Royal London (Ord.)	340·7	44,800	69	9·48	3·00
1887	M	Royal Nat. Pen. Fund for Nurses	130·5	15,449	1,852	12·05	6·25
1963	P	Save & Prosper	605·4	60,646	34,297	—	Various
1965	P	Schroder	245·2	46,225	32,188	5·00	Various
1826	M	Scottish Amicable	2,773·0	619,000	—	—	Various
1831	M	Scottish Equitable	1,100·0	99,700	14,900	8·33	3·50
1881	M	Scottish Life	715·8	116,821	23,686	10·10	3·50
1883	MO	Scottish Mutual†	442·8	44,724	7,869	10·91	Various
1837	M	Scottish Provident	980·0	111,000		10·20	Various
1815	M	Scottish Widows'	3,640·0	137,640	291,411	8·77	Various
1964	P	Stalwart Assurance†	18·1	128	5,488	12·30	10·00
1825	M	Standard Life	6,310·5	866,600		9·69	Various
1710	PO	Sun Alliance	1,628·2	250,271	5,120	—	Various
1810	P	Sun Life Ass. Group	3,267·0	415,604		10·60	Various
1865	M	Sun Life of Canada (C)	7,198·8	336,810	165,126	11·38(N)	Various
1936	P	Teachers'	33·1	11,221	—	10·33	2·25
1969	P	Trident Life	280·4	104,100	—	12·20	Various
1908	P	United Friendly (Ord.)†	95·4	14,557	—	10·80	3·00
1963	P	UK Life Assurance	8·4	2,125	—	10·00	Various
1840	M	UK Provident	1,152·3	154,200	94,400	5·90	Various
1841	MIO	Wesleyan & General (Ord.)	103·8	11,028	878	11·07(N)	Various
1963	P	Windsor Life	50·6	25,088	—	9·00	Various
1960	P	Zurich Life	70·5	27,664	539	10·00	Various

† 1983 figures   * 1982 figures   (C) denotes Commonwealth Office

LIFE ASSURANCE NEW BUSINESS 1984

Name of Office	No. of policies issued	Net sums assured	Net annual premiums	Net single premiums
		£000	£000	£000
Allied Dunbar	167,600	3,010,000	90,300	159,000
American Life*	206,735	3,397,047	38,957	10,983
Australian Mutual Provident (C)	10,440	126,282	2,125	140
Avon	2,909	29,165	597	258
Barclays Life	53,340	386,000	13,900	24,100
Britannic (Ord.)	44,325	212,341	6,397	3,112
British National	6,300	60,000	1,100	8,800
Canada Life	92,867	5,444,633	25,309	268,879
Cannon*	27,928	254,126	4,911	21,743
City of Glasgow (Ord.)	2,706	15,629	247	3,461
Clerical, Medical Group	75,235	2,117,900	32,900	134,000
Colonial Mutual (C)†	60,000	711,000	16,000	10,000
Commercial Union	172,332	5,236,724	37,024	31,313
Confederation Life	67,823	6,098,655	166,246	43,725
Co-operative (Ord.)	119,060	1,087,900	23,000	28
Crown Financial	63,000	1,020,779	18,947	36,552
Crusader	22,000	1,152,000	10,700	17,300
Eagle Star	53,949	3,661,000	51,500	100,900
Ecclesiastical	2,929	57,469	787	2,204
Economic*	4,694	60,521	254	1,423
Equitable Life	53,129	1,223,500	79,100	45,100
Friends' Provident	126,428	3,144,000	51,234	66,718
FS Assurance	7,860	129,459	3,140	4,957
General Accident Life	88,000	2,966,666	24,362	16,912
Gresham Life	23,817	376,774	5,542	3,338
Guardian Royal Exchange	267,000	5,646,300	61,000	143,500
Hill Samuel	65,427	690,000	9,600	45,900
Ideal	427	3,738	37	—
Imperial Life of Canada (C)	42,370	1,984,477	39,908	46,085
Insurance Corp. Life	13,884	320,157	4,823	68,300
Irish Life (Ord.)	86,227	1,826,340	45,126	171,063
Legal & General	214,000	5,113,000	60,000	53,000
Life Association of Scotland	14,847	305,442	7,468	9,026
Liverpool Victoria (Ord.)	21,571	94,246	3,416	—
Lloyd's Life	73,203	352,407	7,510	42,546
London & Manchester (Ord.)	77,142	494,292	15,475	41,594
London Life	42,000	472,400	39,200	34,600
Manufacturers Life (UK) (C)*	27,885	270,000	7,108	20,963
M & G Assurance	31,214	137,802	5,028	31,481
MGM Assurance	43,809	150,076	8,630	45,682
Medical, Sickness	5,514	91,000	1,297	440
Merchant Investors	22,407	268,963	5,248	19,526
Nalgo Insurance	2,247	36,019	197	—
National Farmers Union	11,825	81,389	3,379	3,404
National Mut. Life of Australasia†	12,842	183,855	2,980	351
National Mutual	21,433	304,865	11,548	7,561
National Provident	65,583	443,722	23,915	85,595
New Ireland†	44,309	—	5,000	1,113
Norwich Union	331,780	5,446,106	106,711	277,406
Pearl (Ord.)	88,830	539,310	21,125	36,913
Phoenix		5,420,700	38,742	60,095
Pioneer Mutual (Ord.)	15,646	243,378	4,179	10,976
Provident Life Association	16,367	277,007	5,388	4,521
Provident Mutual	119,705	994,824	36,792	37,150
Prudential Group (Ord.)	459,051	8,492,500	198,600	308,600
Reliance Mutual (Ord.)†	10,404	88,696	2,083	1,175
Royal Life	150,000	2,444,200	50,800	92,600
Royal Liver (Ord.)	14,194	53,279	2,473	8
Royal London (Ord.)	35,769	312,270	8,247	5,550
Royal Nat. Pen. Fund for Nurses	13,989	33,047	2,921	1,852
Save & Prosper	46,987	230,337	12,463	51,148
Schroder	47,960	170,920	15,014	36,225
Scottish Amicable	219,000	3,100,000	97,000	245,000
Scottish Equitable	216,000	585,200	27,300	36,800
Scottish Life	31,465	680,572	18,337	39,343
Scottish Mutual†	33,921	784,500	14,330	7,870
Scottish Provident	111,489	728,000	14,600	33,300
Scottish Widows'	44,909		17,338	48,654
Stalwart Assurance†	3,659	29,340	518	5,523
Standard Life	242,967		116,000	327,600
Sun Alliance		2,299,551	46,915	63,427
Sun Life Assurance Group	116,264	1,444,897	20,649	70,288
Sun Life of Canada (C)	275,705	10,570,432	218,233	
Teachers'	4,016	26,385	491	8,866
Trident Life	35,000	277,000	8,700	44,400
United Friendly (Ord.)†	23,752	220,059	2,830	—
UK Provident	71,645	1,333,800	47,200	94,400
Wesleyan & General (Ord.)	8,460	82,800	1,803	121
Windsor Life	22,425	163,060	2,610	7,981
Zurich Life	18,545	652,800	6,090	414

† 1983 figures   * 1982 figures   (C) denotes Commonwealth Office

DIRECTORY OF INSURANCE COMPANIES

The class of Insurance undertaken is shown in the second column as follows: A—Accident (which includes Motor, Employers' Liability, etc.); F—Fire (including Burglary); L—Life; and M—Marine. A number of offices are now included in a Group—the initials of which appear after the name. The main Groups are as follows—E.S.—Eagle Star; C.U.—Commercial Union; G.R.E.—Guardian Royal Exchange; G.A.—General Accident; N.U.—Norwich Union; R—Royal; S.A.—Sun Alliance & London.

Est'd.	Nature of Business	Name of Company	Address
1961	L	Abbey Life	Holdenhurst Rd., Bournemouth.
1951	AFM	Albion	Plantation House, 31/35 Fenchurch St., E.C.3.
1824	AFM	Alliance ............S.A.	1 Bartholomew Lane, E.C.2.
1965	L	Allied Dunbar	Allied Dunbar Centre, Swindon.
1921	L	American Life	2–8 Altyre Road, Croydon.
1960	AFLM	Ansvar	St. Leonards Rd., Eastbourne.
1808	ALFM	Atlas ............G.R.E.	Royal Exchange, E.C.3.
1849	L	Australian Mutual Provident	A.M.P. Ho., Dingwall Rd., Croydon.
1925	AFL	Avon	Tiddington Road, Stratford-upon-Avon.
1905	AFM	Baptist	4 Southampton Row, W.C.1.
1965	L	Barclays	252 Romford Rd., E.7.
1883	AFM	Beacon ............S.A.	1 Bartholomew Lane, E.C.2.
1894	AFM	Bedford General	Zurich House, Stanhope Rd., Portsmouth.
1925	AFM	Black Sea and Baltic	65 Fenchurch St., E.C.3.
1959	AFLM	Bradford	North Park, Halifax.
1866	AFL	Britannic	Moor Green, Moseley, Birmingham.
1863	M	British & Foreign Marine ....R.	New Hall Place, Liverpool.
1878	Machinery	British Engine, &c ....R.	Longbridge House, Manchester 4.
1854	AFL	British Equitable ........G.R.E.	Royal Exchange, E.C.3.
1904	AFM	British General ..........C.U.	St. Helen's, 1 Undershaft, E.C.3.
1888	AFM	British Law ............S.A.	1 Bartholomew Lane, E.C.2.
1896	L	British Life	Reliance House, Tunbridge Wells, Kent.
1920	AFL	British Nat. Life	Perrymount Rd., Haywards Heath, W. Sussex.
1908	AFM	British Oak ............G.R.E.	Royal Exchange, E.C.3.
1881	A	Builders' Accident	31 & 32 Bedford St., Strand, W.C.2.
1805	AFLM	Caledonian ............G.R.E.	Royal Exchange, E.C.3.
1934	AFM	Cambrian ............G.R.E.	Royal Exchange, E.C.3.
1847	AL	Canada Life	Canada Life House, Potters Bar, Herts.
1963	L	Cannon	1 Olympic Way, Wembley.
1903	AFM	Car & General ..........G.R.E.	Royal Exchange, E.C.3.
1885	AFM	Century	4–5 King William St., E.C.4.
1922	AFMex-motor	Chemists' Mutual	321 Chase Rd., Southgate, N.14.
1862	L	City of Glasgow Friendly	200 Bath Street, Glasgow G.2.
1824	L	Clerical, Medical & Gen.	Narrow Plain, Bristol.
1873	L & Pers. Acc.	Colonial Mutual	24 Ludgate Hill, E.C.4.
1919	AFM	Comrcl. Ins. Co. of Ireland	5 Donegall Square, S., Belfast.
1861	AFLM	Commercial Union	St. Helen's, 1 Undershaft, E.C.3.
1871	L	Confederation	50/52 Chancery Lane, W.C.2.
1891	AF	Congregational	21–22 Apsley Crescent, Bradford 8.
1867	AFLM	Co-operative	Miller St., Manchester.
1905	AFM	Cornhill	32 Cornhill, E.C.3.
1900	L	Crown Financial Management	Crown House, Woking, Surrey.
1899	AFLM	Crusader	Woodhatch, Reigate, Surrey.
1908	AFM	Dominion	92/94 Gracechurch St., E.C.3.
1904	AFLM	Eagle Star	1 Threadneedle St., E.C.2.
1887	AFL	Ecclesiastical	Beaufort House, Brunswick Rd., Gloucester.
1901	AFLM	Economic	125/135 Fenchurch St., E.C.3.
1823	AFM	Edinburgh ............C.U.	St. Helen's, 1 Undershaft, E.C.3.
1880	AFM	Employers' Liability ......C.U.	St. Helen's, 1 Undershaft, E.C.3.
1932	Animal Ins.	Equine and Livestock	610–616 Chiswick High Rd, W.4.
1762	L	Equitable Life	4 Coleman St., E.C.2.
1844	L	Equity & Law	20 Lincoln's Inn Fields, W.C.2.
1802	AF	Essex & Suffolk ........G.R.E.	Royal Exchange, E.C.3.
1894	AFM	Excess	13 Fenchurch Avenue, E.C.3.
1925	AFL	Federation Mutual	29 Linkfield Lane, Redhill, Surrey.
1890	AF	Fine Art & General ......C.U.	St. Helen's, 1 Undershaft, E.C.3.
1832	L	Friends' Prov	Pixham End, Dorking, Surrey.
1899	L	FS Assurance	190 West George St., Glasgow.
1885	AFM	General Accident	General Buildings, Perth, Scotland.
1837	L	General Accident Life	2 Rougier St., York.
1848	L	Gresham Life	2–6 Prince of Wales Rd., Bournemouth.
1910	AFM	Gresham Fire & Accident	11 Queen Victoria St., E.C.4.
1840	AFM	Guarantee Society .......G.A.	36–37 Old Jewry, E.C.2.
1821	ALFM	Guardian............G.R.E.	Royal Exchange, E.C.3.

Est'd.	Nature of Business	Name of Company	Address
1908	AFM	Hibernian	Haddington Road, Dublin, 4.
1960	L	Hill Samuel	NLA Tower, Addiscombe Rd., Croydon.
1966	AF	Household & General ......S.A.	1 Bartholomew Lane, E.C.2.
1932	FL	Ideal	Pitmaston, Birmingham, 13.
1896	L	Imperial Life of Canada	London Road, Guildford, Surrey.
1935	AFM	Insurance Corporation Life	Burlington Road, Dublin 4.
1939	L	Irish Life	Lr. Abbey St., Dublin 2.
1880	A	Iron Trades Employers'	Iron Trades Ho., 21–24 Grosvenor Pl., S.W.1.
1845	AF	Law Fire .................S.A.	1 Bartholomew Lane, E.C.2.
1806	AFM	Law Union & Rock ....R.	1 North John St., Liverpool, 2.
1907	AFM	Legal ....R.	1 North John St., Liverpool, 2.
1836	AFLM	Legal and General	Temple Court, 11 Queen Victoria St., E.C.4.
1970	L	Liberty Life	Kingmaker House, Station Rd., New Barnet.
1890	AFLM	Licenses & General	14 Bonhill Street, E.C.2.
1838	L	Life Assoc. of Scotland	10 George St., Edinburgh.
1836	AFM	L'pool & London & Globe. ....R.	New Hall Place, Liverpool.
1918	AFM	Liverpool Marine & General....	4–5 King William St., E.C.4.
1843	L	Liverpool Victoria Friendly	Victoria House, Southampton Row., W.C.1.
1971	L	Lloyds Life	20 Clifton St., E.C.2
1890	AFM	Local Government Guarantee G.R.E.	Royal Exchange, E.C.3
1836	AFM	Lombard Insurance............	31–35 Fenchurch St., E.C.3.
1720	AFLM	London Assurance ........S.A.	1 Bartholomew Lane, E.C.2.
1869	AFM	London Guar. & Reinsurance...	4 King William St., E.C.4.
1919	AFM	London & Lancashire..........	New Hall Place, Liverpool.
1806	L	London Life	100 Temple St., Bristol.
1869	AFL	London & Manchester	Winslade Park, Exeter, Devon.
1860	AFM	London & Provincial Marine G.A.	Lloyd's Building, Lime St., E.C.3.
1862	AFM	London & Scottish .... C.U.	St. Helen's, 1 Undershaft, E.C.3.
1961	L	M & G Assurance	91/99 New London Rd., Chelmsford
1887	L	Manufacturers Life	St. George's Way, Stevenage.
1836	M	Marine.....................R.	34–36 Lime St., E.C.3.
1852	L	Marine & General	MGM House, Heene Rd., Worthing.
1864	M	Maritime .... N.U.	Surrey St., Norwich.
1884	L Sickness A	Med., Sickness, Ann. and Life. ..	7–10 Chandos St., Cavendish Sq., W.1.
1907	Reinsurance	Mercantile & General..........	Moorfields House, Moorfields, E.C.2.
1970	L	Merchant Investors	High Street, Croydon.
1871	M	Merchants' Marine .... C.U.	St. Helen's, 1 Undershaft, E.C.3.
1872	AF	Methodist	Brazennose House, Brazennose St., Manchester.
1940	AFM	Minster	Minster House, Arthur St., E.C.4.
1906	AFM	Motor Union ...........G.R.E.	Royal Exchange, E.C.3.
1903	AF	Municipal Mutual.............	22 Old Queen St., Westminster, S.W.1.
1890	AFL	Nalgo Insurance Association ...	1 Mabledon Place, W.C.1.
1935	L	National Employers' Life	Milton Court, Dorking, Surrey.
1914	AFM	National Employers' Mutual ...	N.E.M. House, Mitre Sq., E.C.3.
1910	AFL	National Farmers' Union	Tiddington Rd., Stratford-upon-Avon.
1863	Fidelity Guar.	Natl. Guaran. & Suretyship C.U.	St. Helen's, 1 Undershaft, E.C.3.
1894	AF	National Ins. & Guarantee Cor. .	Heron House, 145 City Rd., E.C.1.
1830	L	National Mutual Life	5 Bow Churchyard (off Cheapside), E.C.4.
1869	L	National Mutual of Australasia .	N.M. House, Serpentine Rd., Poole, Dorset
1835	L	National Provident............	48 Gracechurch St., E.C.3.
1854	Plate Glass	National Provincial .....G.R.E.	Royal Exchange, E.C.3.
1864	Machinery	National Vulcan Eng. Ins. Group.................S.A.	Empire House, St. Martin's-le-Grand, E.C.1.
1921	Naval Officers risks, etc.	Navigators & General ..... E.S.	1 Threadneedle St., E.C.2.
1924	L	New Ireland	11/12 Dawson St., Dublin, 2.
1809	AFLM	North British & Mercantile C.U.	St. Helen's, 1 Undershaft, E.C.3.
1862	FM	North Pacific ...........G.R.E.	Royal Exchange, E.C.3.
1836	AFLM	Northern............... C.U.	St. Helen's, 1 Undershaft, E.C.3.
1797	AFM	Norwich Union Fire...........	Surrey Street, Norwich.
1808	L	Norwich Union Life	Surrey Street, Norwich.
1871	AFM	Ocean Accident .... C.U.	St. Helen's, 1 Undershaft, E.C.3.
1859	M	Ocean Marine .... C.U.	4 Fenchurch Ave., E.C.3.
1931	AFM	Orion	70–72 King William St., E.C.4.
1886	AF	Palatine......................	108 Cannon St., E.C.4.
1864	AFLM	Pearl.........................	High Holborn, W.C.1.
1958	Sickness A	Permanent	7–10 Chandos Street, Cavendish Sq., W.1.
1782	AFLM	Phoenix	Phoenix House, King William St., E.C.4.

Est'd.	Nature of Business	Name of Company	Address
1891	L	Pioneer Mutual	16 Crosby Rd. N., Liverpool.
1920	AFM	Planet Assurance .........S.A.	1 Bartholomew Lane, E.C.2.
1969	L	Property Growth	Leon House, High St., Croydon
1877	L	Prov. Life Assocn. of London ...	266 Bishopsgate, E.C.2.
1840	L	Provident Mutual Life	25/31 Moorgate, London E.C.2.
1903	AFM	Provincial	Stramongate, Kendal, Cumbria.
1848	AFLM	Prudential...................	Holborn Bars, E.C.1.
1849	AF	Railway Passengers ...... C.U.	St. Helen's, 1 Undershaft, E.C.3.
1864	AFL	Refuge	Oxford St., Manchester M60.
1911	L	Reliance Mutual	Reliance House, Tunbridge Wells, Kent.
1906	AF	Reliance Fire & Accident	Reliance House, Tunbridge Wells, Kent.
1881	AFM	Reliance Marine .......G.R.E.	Royal Exchange, E.C.3.
1823	Reversions	Reversionary Interest Society. .	4 Coleman St., E.C.2.
1918	AF	Road Transport & General G.A.	77 Upper Richmond Rd., S.W.15.
1845	AFLM	Royal Life	New Hall Place, Liverpool.
1720	AFL	Royal Exchange	Royal Exchange, E.C.3.
1850	L	Royal Liver Friendly	Royal Liver Building, Liverpool 3.
1861	AFL	Royal London	Royal London House, Middleborough, Colchester.
1887	L	Royal Nat. Pensions (Nurses) ...	15 Buckingham St., W.C.2.
1909	AFM	Salvation Army	101 Queen Victoria St., E.C.4.
1963	L	Save and Prosper	1 Finsbury Ave., London E.C.2.
1965	L	Schroder	Enterprise House, Isambard Brunel Rd., Portsmouth.
1826	L	Scottish Amicable	150 St. Vincent St., Glasgow.
1881	FM	Scottish Boiler .... G.A.	250 St. Vincent St., Glasgow.
1831	L	Scottish Equitable	28 St. Andrew Square, Edinburgh.
1919	AFM	Scottish General .... G.A.	100 West Nile St., Glasgow, G.2.
1852	L	Scottish Legal	95 Bothwell St., Glasgow, G.2.
1881	L	Scottish Life	19 St. Andrew Square, Edinburgh, 2.
1876	AF	Scottish Metropolitan .... C.U.	St. Helen's, 1 Undershaft, E.C.3.
1883	AL	Scottish Mutual..............	109 St. Vincent Street, Glasgow, G.2.
1837	L	Scottish Provident	6 St. Andrew Square, Edinburgh.
1824	AFLM	Scottish Union & National N.U.	Surrey St., Norwich.
1815	L	Scottish Widows'	15 Dalkeith Rd., Edinburgh.
1875	AFM	Sea ......................S.A.	1 Bartholomew Lane, E.C.2.
1904	AFL	Sentinel	2 Eyre Street Hill, E.C.1.
1964	L	Stalwart Assurance	Tuition Hse., St. George's Rd., Wimbledon.
1825	L	Standard Life	3 George Street, Edinburgh.
1891	AFM	State....................G.R.E.	Royal Exchange, E.C.3.
1710	AFM	Sun ......................S.A.	1 Bartholomew Lane, E.C.2.
*	AFLM	Sun Alliance & London	1 Bartholomew Lane, E.C.2.
1810	L	Sun Life Assurance Group	107 Cheapside, E.C.2.
1865	L	Sun Life of Canada	2, 3 & 4 Cockspur St., S.W.1.
1936	FL	Teacher's Assurance	12 Christchurch Rd., Bournemouth.
1969	L	Trident	London Road, Gloucester.
1869	L	Tunstall & District	Station Chambers, Tunstall, Stoke on Trent.
1867	M	Ulster Marine .... G.A.	5 Donegall Sq., S., Belfast.
1714	AFM	Union Assurance .... C.U.	St. Helen's, 1 Undershaft, E.C.3.
1835	AFM	Union Ins. Soc. of Canton G.R.E.	Royal Exchange, E.C.3.
1863	M	Union Marine	4–5 King William St., E.C.4.
1915	AFM	United British ..........G.R.E.	Royal Exchange, E.C.3.
1908	AFL	United Friendly..............	42 Southwark Bridge Road, S.E.1.
1963	L	UK Life Assurance	Royal Albert House, Windsor.
1840	L	U.K.Provident	Castle St., Salisbury, Wiltshire.
1825	L	University	4 Coleman St., E.C.2.
1974	L	Vanbrugh	41–43 Maddox St., W.1.
1919	Reinsurance	Victory Reinsurance	Castle Hill Ave., Folkestone, Kent
1875	AFM	Warden ....R.	1 North John St., Liverpool.
1911	AF	Welsh Insurance Corpn. . . C.U.	St. Helen's, 1 Undershaft, E.C.3.
1841	AFL	Wesleyan & General	Colmore Circus, Ringway, Birmingham 4.
1886	AF	West of Scotland .... C.U.	26 George St., Edinburgh 2.
1851	AFM	Western Assurance ....R.	New Hall Place, Liverpool.
1912	AFLM	Western Australian	Swan Court, Mansel Rd., Wimbledon, S.W.19.
1717	AF	Westminster Fire .........S.A.	1 Bartholomew Lane, E.C.2.
1865	AF	White Cross .... C.U.	St. Helen's, 1 Undershaft, E.C.3.
1963	L	Windsor Life	Royal Albert House, Windsor.
1894	AFM	World Marine & General . . C.U.	Dunster House, Mark Lane, E.C.3.
1872	AF	Zurich	Stanhope Road, Portsmouth.

* Sun Alliance & London—Incorporating Funds established 1710, 1720 and 1824.

BRITISH MONETARY UNITS

COIN

GOLD COINS	NICKEL-BRASS (COPPER/
Five Pound £5	NICKEL/ZINC)
Two Pound £2	One Pound £1
Sovereign £1	
Half-Sovereign 10s.	

BRONZE COINS	CUPRO-NICKEL (SILVER)
*2 Pence 2p	Crown 5s. (25p)
*1 Penny 1p	Florin 2s. (10p)
	Shilling 1s. (5p)
	*50 Pence 50p
	*Crown 25p
	*20 Pence 20p
	*10 Pence 10p
	*5 Pence 5p

SILVER

*Crown 25p
Maundy Money‡

Fourpence 4p	Twopence 2p
Threepence 3p	Penny 1p

*For further details of decimal coins, see next page.
‡Gifts of special money distributed by the Sovereign annually on Maundy Thursday to the number of aged poor persons corresponding to the Sovereign's own age.

Gold Coin.—Gold ceased to circulate during the First World War. An Order of April 27, 1966, made it illegal for U.K. residents to continue holding more than 4 gold coins minted after 1837, or to acquire such coins unless they had been licensed as genuine collectors by the Bank of England. This Order was revoked on April 1, 1971, by the Exchange Control (Gold Coins Exemption) Order, 1971, whereby residents of the United Kingdom, Channel Islands and the Isle of Man may freely buy and sell and hold gold coins.

The 1971 Order was revoked on April 15, 1975, by the Exchange Control (Gold Coins Exemption) Order, 1975. Under this Order Section 1 of the Exchange Control Act 1947 (which prohibits dealings in gold or foreign currency except with Treasury permission) was exempted for gold coins minted in or before 1837. The import of gold coins minted after 1837 was prohibited except by authorised dealers in gold with individual import licences from the Department of Trade, and dealing between other U.K. residents was restricted to coins already held in the U.K.

Under an amendment, dated December 16, 1977, the exemptions contained in the 1975 Order were extended to cover gold coins minted in or before 1937.

The 1975 controls over the import of and dealing in gold coins were abolished on June 13, 1979 under the Exchange Control (Gold Coins Exemption) Order 1979, and gold coins, with certain exceptions,* may now be imported and exported without restriction.

On April 1, 1982 the Government introduced VAT (currently 15 per cent) on sales of all gold coin.

Silver.—Prior to 1920 our silver coins were struck from standard silver—an alloy of which 925 parts in 1,000 were silver. In 1920 the proportion of silver was reduced to 500 parts. From January 1, 1947 all "silver" coins, except Maundy money, have been struck from cupro-nickel—an alloy of copper 75 parts and nickel 25 parts. Maundy coins since 1947 have been struck from standard silver.

Bronze, introduced in 1860 to replace copper, is an alloy of copper 97 parts, zinc 2½ parts and tin ½ part. These proportions are subject to slight variation.

*Gold coins which are more than fifty years old and valued at a sum in excess of £8,000 cannot be exported without specific authorization from the Department of Trade.

The "Remedy" is the amount of variation from standard permitted in weight and fineness of coins when first issued from the Mint.

Legal tender of coin.—Gold, dated 1838 onwards, if not below least current weight, is legal tender to any amount. The £1 coin introduced on April 21, 1983 is legal tender to any amount. 50p and 20p coins are legal tender up to £10; 10p and 5p coins are legal tender up to £5 and bronze coins are legal tender for amounts up to 20p. Farthings ceased to be legal tender on December 31, 1960, the halfpenny on August 1, 1969, the halfcrown on January 1, 1970, the threepence and penny on August 31, 1971, the sixpence on June 30, 1980 and the decimal ½ penny on 31st December, 1984.

Since 1982 the word "new" in "new pence" displayed on decimal coins has been dropped.

BANK NOTES

Bank of England notes are currently issued in denominations of £5, £10, £20 and £50 for the amount of the Fiduciary Note Issue, and are legal tender in England and Wales.

The old white notes for £10, £20, £50, £100, £500 and £1,000, which were issued until April 22, 1943, ceased to be legal tender in May 1945.

The old white £5 notes dated up to September 20, 1956, the £5 notes issued between 1957 and 1963, bearing a portrait of Britannia and the first series to bear a portrait of the Queen, issued between 1963 and 1971, ceased to be legal tender on March 14, 1961, June 27, 1967 and September 1, 1973 respectively. The series of £1 notes issued during the years 1928 to 1960 and the 10s. notes of the same type issued from 1928 to 1961—those without the royal portrait—ceased to be legal tender on May 29 and October 30, 1962 respectively. The £1 note first issued in March 1960 (bearing on the back a representation of Britannia) and the £10 note first issued in February 1964 (bearing a lion on the back) both bearing a portrait of the Queen on the front ceased to be legal tender on June 1, 1979. The 10s. note was replaced by the 50p coin in October 1969, and ceased to be legal tender on November 21, 1970. Bank notes which are no longer legal tender are payable when presented at the Head Office of the Bank of England in London.

The first of the current series of Bank notes was a £20 note issued on July 9, 1970. This was followed by the £5 note on November 11, 1971, £10 note on February 20, 1975, £1 note on February 9, 1978 and £50 note on March 20, 1981. The £1 denomination ceased to be issued after December 1, 1984. The predominant identifying feature of each note is the portrayal on the back of a prominent figure from Britain's history namely, £5: The Duke of Wellington; £10: Florence Nightingale; £20: William Shakespeare; and £50: Sir Christopher Wren.

Note circulation is highest at the two peak spending periods of the year—around Christmas and during the summer holiday period. A peak of £13,900 million was reached immediately prior to Christmas 1984, a 7·96 per cent increase on the previous year.

The proportion of the total value of notes in circulation of £1 and £5 notes at end-February 1985 compared with the previous year, fell from 5·1 per cent and 22·3 per cent to 4·4 per cent and 20·2 per cent respectively; whereas £10 notes increased from 42·3 per cent to 43·5 per cent, £20 notes increased from 17·3 per cent to 17·8 per cent and £50 from 7·9 per cent to 9·1 per cent.

On February 28, 1985 the values of notes in circulation were; £1: £527,382,576; £5: £2,426,073,315; £10: £5,232,827,750; £20: £2,136,212,420; £50: £1,089,116,250.

Other Bank Notes.—Bank notes are issued by three

Scottish banks. The Royal Bank of Scotland and the Bank of Scotland issue notes for £1, £5, £10, £20 and £100. The Clydesdale Bank issues notes for £1, £5, $10, £20, £50, £100. Scottish notes are not legal tender, but in Scotland they enjoy a status equal to that of the Bank of England note.

Channel Islands and the Isle of Man.—The states of Jersey and Guernsey issue notes for £1, £5, £10 and £20. The Government of the Isle of Man issues notes for 50p, £1, £5, £10 and £20. These are legal tender only in their respective islands.

Although none of the series of notes specified above is legal tender in the United Kingdom they are generally accepted by the banks irrespective of their place of issue. At one time the banks made a commission charge for handling Scottish and Irish notes but this was abolished some years ago.

The Channel Islands and the Isle of Man also issue their own coinage. The states of Jersey and Guernsey issue coins for ½p, 1p, 2p, 5p, 10p, 20p, 50p and £1. The Isle of Man issues coins for ½p, 1p, 2p, 5p, 10p, 20p, 50p and £1.

Denomination	Metal	Standard Weight (grams)	Standard Diameter (centimetres)
Penny	bronze	3·56400	2·0320
2 pence	bronze	7·12800	2·5910
5 pence	cupro-nickel	5·65518	2·3595
10 pence	cupro-nickel	11·31036	2·8500
20 pence	cupro-nickel	5·0	2·14
25p Crown	silver	28·27590	3·8608
25p Crown	cupro-nickel	28·27590	3·8608
50 pence	cupro-nickel	13·5	3·0
£1	copper/nickel/zinc	9·5	2·25

THE STOCK EXCHANGE IN THE UNITED KINGDOM AND IRELAND

Broker Members of The Stock Exchange buy and sell shares for members of the public. This is done for individual investors, for their advisers such as bank managers, solicitors and accountants, and for investing institutions like insurance companies, pension funds, unit trusts and merchant banks. For this the stockbroker is paid a fixed scale of commission based on the value of the securities purchased. In addition to this service, brokers advise their clients, according to their particular circumstances and needs, on how to invest their money to greatest advantage. In addition, they will undertake to review periodically the portfolios of their clients.

The Stock Exchange provides facilities for raising capital for industry. Any Broker will give advice on how a company can finance its growth by getting a listing. For companies already listed, other methods are possible—such as rights issues and debenture or loan stocks—for obtaining additional funds. Brokers' advice is also available to industrialists on matters such as mergers and acquisitions.

All listed British companies are incorporated under the Companies' Acts, which contain stringent regulations for their management and control. They are limited liability companies, which means that if you are a shareholder in such a company you cannot be called upon to pay any part of its debt or liabilities if it gets into difficulties, unless, in quite exceptional cases, you are a holder of partly-paid shares, in which event your liability is limited to the amount required to make the shares fully paid. The Stock Exchange serves investors, whether inexperienced or expert, big or small, and the authorities of The Stock Exchange insist on compliance with stringent regulations to ensure that the public are fully informed of the constitution and record of every company whose securities are admitted to the market.

In London the foundation stone of the building was laid in 1801, but the building was almost entirely reconstructed in 1854 from the designs of Thomas Allason. The Stock Exchange has now been rebuilt as a large tower block, 331 feet high with a new Trading Floor to the west of the block.

There are other Trading Floors in Liverpool, Birmingham, Glasgow, Belfast and Dublin.

The Stock Exchange provides a market for the purchase and sale of about 7,000 securities valued at over £1,100,000,000,000, and also securities listed on overseas Exchanges. At present, the Members of The Stock Exchange, consisting of Brokers (agents for clients) and Jobbers (dealers as principals in specific securities), number about 4,500.

The Stock Exchange

Chairman, Sir Nicholas Goodison; *Deputy Chairmen*, R. H. Lawson; G. Ross Russell; *Chief Exec.*, J. R. Knight.

Administrative Units

The Stock Exchange, London, EC2N 1HP; Stock Exchange, Margaret Street, Birmingham; Stock Exchange, Norfolk Street, Manchester; Stock Exchange, 69 St. George's Place, Glasgow; Stock Exchange, 28 Anglesea Street, Dublin 2; Stock Exchange, Northern Bank House, 10 High Street, Belfast.

COUNCIL FOR THE SECURITIES INDUSTRY, 20th Floor, The Stock Exchange Building, E.C.2.—*Dir. Gen.*, T. G. Barker.

FRIENDLY SOCIETIES—GREAT BRITAIN

Acts 1974–1984

Friendly societies are voluntary mutual organizations the main purposes of which are the provision of relief or maintenance during sickness, unemployment or retirement, and the provision of life assurance. Many of the older traditional societies complement their business activities by social activity and a general care for individual members in ways normally outside the scope of a purely commercial organization. There are three main categories of friendly societies—societies with separately registered branches, commonly called orders, centralized societies, which conduct business directly with members (having no separately registered branches), and collecting societies. Collecting societies conduct industrial assurance business and are subject to the requirements of the Industrial Assurance Acts in addition to the Friendly Societies Acts. Industrial assurance is life assurance, the premiums in respect of which are payable at intervals of less than two months and are received by means of collectors who make house to house visits for the purpose.

At the end of 1984 there were 25 orders with 3,266 branches, 368 centralized societies, and 41 collecting societies.

Long before the term "Friendly Society" came into use, the seeds of voluntary mutual insurance had been sown in the ancient religious and trade "Guilds". As is evident from the many extant parchment returns detailing their rules and possessions under a decree of Richard II, Guilds had become widespread in Britain by the 14th century. By then, the purely charitable character of the original Guilds had largely changed with the emergence of numerous small institutions adopting primitive mutual insurance methods of a regular flat rate contribution to insure relief when sick or in old age and a payment to the widow in the event of death.

The present register of Friendly Societies includes several societies which have been in existence for upwards of 200 years, the oldest, operating in Scotland, being the "Incorporation of Carters in Leith" established as long ago as 1555.

The first Act for the encouragement and protection of "Friendly Societies" in this country was not passed until 1793, but various amending Acts were put on the Statute Book during the next century as the result of the recommendations of successive Select Committees (including a Royal Commission in 1871). For example, it was not until the 1829 Act that all registered Friendly Societies were required to keep proper records of individual sickness and mortality amongst their members, which data enabled the construction of standard actuarial tables showing the expected (average) duration of sickness at successive ages, and also (with data from the Census) the corresponding mortality rates.

The rules and other documents of societies deposited with local justices passed into the custody of the Registrar following the Act of 1846 and are of considerable interest to social historians. Those relating to some societies no longer on the register have been transferred to the Public Record Office for permanent preservation.

The Friendly Societies Act 1974, which came into force in April, 1975, consolidated the nine Acts which comprised the Friendly Societies Acts 1896 to 1971 and a few other minor enactments relating to societies to which those Acts applied. The Act allows various specific classes other than "Friendly Societies" to be registered thereunder, but tax exemption (irrespective of the extent of interest income) is enjoyed only by registered "Friendly Societies". Removal of life assurance premium relief, and a reduction from £2,000 to £750 in the limit applying to the tax-exempt business announced in the Budget in March, significantly affected Friendly Societies in 1984. Particularly affected were those registered in recent years to maximize the tax advantages, with what is in form a life assurance contract, but in practice a savings facility. Although tax-exempt limits were reduced these societies were allowed to offer a wider range of business.

Doubts arising in 1984 about the enforceability of contracts were put beyond doubt by measures in the Finance Act 1985 and the Friendly Societies Act 1984. The latter also abolished the limits on the size of taxable life and annuity business societies could write.

In addition to Friendly Societies there are three other main classes of society which may be registered under the Friendly Societies Act 1974: benevolent societies, working men's clubs and specially authorized societies. Benevolent societies are established for any charitable or benevolent purpose, to provide the same type of benefits as would be permissible for a friendly society, but in contrast the benefits must be for persons who are not members instead of, or in addition to, members. Working men's clubs provide social and recreational facilities for members. Specially authorized societies are registered for any purpose authorized by the Treasury as a purpose to which some or all of the provisions of the 1974 Act ought to be extended. Examples are societies for the promotion of science, literature and the fine arts, or to enable members to pursue an interest in sports and games. At the end of 1984 there were 91 benevolent societies, 2,469 working men's clubs, and 158 specially authorized societies.

The principal statistics at the end of 1983 are given in the table below.

	Friendly Societies (a)	Collecting Societies	Benevolent Societies	Working Men's Clubs	Special Authorized Societies		Other
					Loan	Others	Other
Number of Societies	3,814	41	93	2,484	12	151	3
Number of Members 000's	3,246	18,480 (b)	329	2,331 (c)	16	122	3
Total Benefits Paid £000's	67,463	103,192	4,212	Not applicable	Not applicable	15	45
Total Funds £000's	851,790	1,177,384	13,830	122,912 (c)	513	11,362	360

(a) Centralized societies, orders and branches of orders
(b) Assurances

(c) 1980 figures

INDUSTRIAL AND PROVIDENT SOCIETIES—GREAT BRITAIN

Acts 1965–1978

The familiar "Co-op" societies are amongst the wide variety which are registered under the Industrial and Provident Societies Act 1965. This consolidating Act, which like the Friendly and the Building Societies Act is administered by the Chief Registrar of Friendly Societies, provides for the registration of societies and lays down the broad framework within which they must operate. Internal relations of societies are governed by their registered rules.

Registration under the Act confers upon a society corporate status by its registered name with perpetual succession and a common seal, and limited liability. A society qualifies for registration if it is carrying on an industry, business or trade, and it satisfies the Registrar that either (a) it is a bona fide co-operative society or (b) in view of the fact that its business is being, or is intended to be, conducted for the benefit of the community there are special reasons why it

should be registered under the Act rather than as a company under the Companies Act.

Registration of a new class of society under the 1965 Act was introduced in Great Britain by the Credit Unions Act 1979 which also lays down supervision requirements. A similar framework of law for credit unions has existed in Northern Ireland since 1969.

During 1984 the number of registered societies increased by 177 to 9,799. The largest single group was the 3,720 social and recreational clubs. The largest group in terms of turnover was that consisting of the retail societies which includes those trading under the familiar "Co-op" sign, with sales (in 1983) of £3,914 million. Sales of wholesale and productive societies amounted to £2,642 million in 1983. The principal statistics at the end of 1983 are given in the table below.

	Retail	Wholesale and Productive	Agricultural	Fishing	Social and Recreational Clubs	General Service	Housing	Credit Unions	Total
Number of Societies	237	205	1,066	106	3,703	849	3,416	80	9,662
Number of Members 000's	8,359	46	400	8	2,954	530	147	16	12,460
Funds of Members 000's	571,324	359,541	187,425	3,408	145,427	1,974,506	3,680,609	2,714	6,924,953
Total Assets £000's	1,243,495	761,276	408,513	9,012	247,829	2,342,925	6,855,965	2,838	11,871,853

BUILDING SOCIETIES—GREAT BRITAIN

Act 1962

The purposes of a building society are defined in section 1 of the Building Societies Act 1962 as being the raising of a fund of money from its members (investors) to advance on the security of first mortgage of freehold or leasehold property to other members (borrowers). Societies can only undertake those activities which are permitted by the 1962 Act, which is administered by the Chief Registrar of Friendly Societies: the rules, annual returns and accounts which societies are required to send to him are open to public inspection, with other relevant documents, at the Registry.

The number of building societies declined from 206 at the end of 1983 to 190 at the end of 1984. There were 13 mergers, one society was dissolved and two had their registrations cancelled. The number of societies has declined by more than half (226) in the last decade from the total of 416 at the end of 1974. At the end of 1960 the number was 726. Over the last decade the total assets of all building societies have increased five-fold from the figure of £20,094 million at the end of 1974 to £102,688 million at the end of 1984. The largest 5 societies (Halifax, Abbey National, Nationwide, Leeds Permanent, and Woolwich) ac-

counted for 56 per cent of the 1984 figure and the largest 20 societies accounted for 88 per cent. In contrast, the smallest 112 societies (about 59 per cent of the total number of societies) accounted for less than 2 per cent of total assets. Building societies experienced a very successful year in 1984. For the first time over one million house purchase loans were made, an increase of almost two-thirds since 1980. Net receipts from investors rose by a quarter over the 1983 level and total assets increased by almost one-fifth. Publication of the government green paper on new building society legislation led societies to look ahead to new powers. Owner-occupation continued to grow in 1984 and it is estimated that some 61 per cent of dwellings were owner-occupied at the end of the year. Private sector house building starts were down on 1983, but completions rose to their highest level since 1973. House prices continued to rise but a little more slowly than in 1983. The mortgage market was generally well supplied with finance during the year despite a decline in bank lending. The principal statistics for the years 1974 to 1984 are set out in the table below:

BUILDING SOCIETIES, GREAT BRITAIN, 1974–1984

Year	1 Number of Societies	2 Number of Share Holders 000's	3 Number of Depositors 000's	4 Number of Borrowers 000's	5 Share Balances £m	6 Deposit Balances £m
1974	416	15,856	641	4,250	18,021	633
1975	382	17,916	677	4,397	22,134	762
1976	364	19,991	712	4,609	25,760	848
1977	339	22,536	760	4,836	31,110	1,224
1978	316	24,999	781	5,108	36,186	1,254
1979	287	27,878	797	5,251	42,023	1,281
1980	273	30,636	915	5,383	48,915	1,742
1981	253	33,388	995	5,490	55,463	2,539
1982	227	36,609	1,094	5,643	64,977	3,447
1983	206	37,713	1,202	5,928	75,180	5,610
1984	190	39,385	1,550	6,317	88,078	8,426

Year	7 Mortgage Balances £m	8 Total Assets £m	Advances during year		11 Average Mortgage Rate %	12 Average Share Rate %
			9 Number 000's	10 Amount £m		
1974	16,030	20,094	546	2,945	11·05	7·53
1975	18,802	24,204	798	4,908	11·08	7·21
1976	22,565	28,202	913	6,183	11·06	7·02
1977	26,427	34,288	946	6,745	11·05	6·98
1978	31,598	39,538	1,184	8,808	9·55	6·46
1979	36,801	45,789	1,040	9,002	11·94	8·45
1980	42,437	53,793	936	9,503	14·92	10·34
1981	48,875	61,815	1,096	12,005	14·01	9·19
1982	56,691	73,033	1,320	14,971	13·32	8·77
1983	67,490	85,868	1,513	19,357	11·05	7·26
1984	81,879	102,688	1,657	23,767	11·83	7·71

There were notable changes in the methods by which building societies determined the interest rates they should pay and charge in 1983. There were indications during the year that some of the larger societies were no longer willing to see other societies continually offering higher than Building Societies Association recommended rates which they could equally afford. This eventually led to the decision in October 1983 to replace the BSA's recommended rate system to one in which advised rates were given to societies.

During the following year the advised rate system became increasingly incompatible with societies' different responses to the competitive environment in which they were operating, and the system was abolished in November 1984. This further weakened the role of the Building Societies Association in the determination of building society interest rates and meant that individual societies had much greater control over their interest rate policy. New types of investment account continued to proliferate and the importance of ordinary shares declining so that at the end of 1984 they comprised only 32 per cent of retail liabilities. A noticeable trend was the introduction by a number of major societies of instant access, no penalty accounts offering a much higher rate of interest than ordinary shares provided that a minimum amount remained invested.

The Building Societies (Authorization) Regulations 1981 came into effect on 1st December 1981, representing a change in emphasis of prudential supervision of building societies. Hitherto, the powers in the Building Societies Act 1962 had essentially been to allow intervention when something was seen to be going wrong. The intention of authorization is that the onus rests with the building society to satisfy the Chief Registrar that it is a safe recipient of investors' money if authorization is to be granted or is to continue. The system came immediately into full effect only for new societies. Other societies, which were not subject to control orders or in the course of winding up, were deemed to be authorized on 1st December, 1981. Their authorization could not be revoked on grounds of inadequate capital or absence of effective direction until 1st June 1983. The Chief Registrar now has to be satisfied that those authorized do in fact meet the requirements and continue to do so.

A society meeting certain basic requirements as to assets and liabilities, liquid funds, reserves and other matters may be designated by the Chief Registrar under section 1 of the House Purchase and Housing Act 1959 for the purposes of trustee status. The requirements are set out in The Building Societies (Designation for Trustee Investment) Regulations 1972, (as amended). The shares and deposits of a society so designated become authorized investments for trustees subject to the provisions of the Trustee Investments Act 1971. Designated societies are identified in the list below by a letter "D" in the first column.

SOCIETIES WITH TOTAL ASSETS EXCEEDING £1 MILLION AT END OF
FINANCIAL YEAR 1984

Year Established	* Name of Society (abbreviated) Head Office	Share Investors	Assets Total £'000
1849D	Abbey National, Abbey House, 27 Baker St., London NW1 6XL	7,966,400	16,988,244
1885	Aid to Thrift, 38 Finsbury Sq., London EC2	823	2,741
1863D	Alliance, Alliance House, Hove Park, Hove, East Sussex	896,525	3,220,298
1848D	Anglia, Moulton Park, Northampton	1,764,583	4,449,412
1870D	Argyle, Argyle Ho., 105 Seven Sisters Rd., Holloway, London N7	5,325	24,222
1853D	Barnsley, Regent St., Barnsley, South Yorks	17,919	67,246
1953D	Bath Investment and Bldg. Soc., 20 Charles St., Bath	10,094	18,457
1879D	Bedford, 65 Midland Rd., Bedford	10,784	28,497
1881D	Bedford Crown, 117 Midland Rd., Bedford	2,969	7,821
1866D	Beverley, 57 Market Place, Beverley, Yorks	5,341	10,468
1914D	Bexhill-on-Sea, 2 Devonshire Sq., Bexhill-on-Sea, Sussex	4,095	8,901
1853D	Bideford, 5 The Quay, Bideford, Devon	5,840	18,077
1889D	Birmingham and Bridgwater, 42/44 Waterloo Street, Birmingham	215,365	511,074
1903D	Blackheath, Cranford Ho., 14 Long Lane, Rowley Regis, Warley, West Midlands	9,906	26,737
1864D	Bolton, 235–237 Baker St., London NW1	6,512	50,780
1851D	Bradford and Bingley, P.O. Box 2, Bingley, West Yorks.	1,431,689	3,266,932
1853D	Bristol Econ., St. John's Court, Broad St., Bristol	2,147	6,329
1850D	Bristol and West, Broad Quay, Bristol	614,378	1,912,043
1856D	Britannia, P.O. Box 20, Newton House, Leek, Staffs.	1,035,485	2,847,043
1907D	Buckinghamshire, High St., Chalfont St. Giles, Bucks.	5,434	16,922
1866D	Bury St. Edmunds, 8 Guildhall St., Bury St. Edmunds	3,506	11,508
1850D	Cambridge, 32 St. Andrew's St., Cambridge	32,993	110,253
1865D	Cardiff, 92 St. Mary St., Cardiff	4,340	21,070
1960D	Catholic, 7 Strutton Ground, London SW1	2,520	8,756
1899	Century, 21–23 Albany St., Edinburgh	1,436	6,193
1862D	Chatham, Room 704, Corn Exchange Bldg, Fenwick St., Liverpool	300	591
1898D	Chatham Reliance, Reliance House, Manor Rd., Chatham, Kent	41,054	83,113
1875D	Chelsea, Chelsea House, 255 Kensington High St., London W8	139,839	471,368
1850D	Cheltenham and Gloucester, 37–43 Clarence St., Cheltenham, Glos.	642,183	2,638,626
1845D	Chesham, 12 Market Sq., Chesham, Bucks.	8,385	22,743
1888D	Chilterns, Norfolk House, Station Rd., Chesham, Bucks.	2,606	6,091
1870D	Cheshire, Castle St., Macclesfield	171,172	352,190
1861D	Cheshunt, 100 Crossbrook St., Waltham Cross, Herts.	48,640	139,452
1859D	Chorley and Dt., 51 St. Thomas's Rd., Chorley, Lancs.	6,124	19,809
1905D	Citizens Regency, Clarence Hse., 30/31 North Street, Brighton, Sussex	41,742	119,438
1946D	City and Metropolitan, 37 Ludgate Hill, London EC4	12,494	43,449
1862D	City of London, 34 London Wall, London EC2	28,168	142,223
1931D	Civil Service, 5 Brighton Road, South Croydon, Surrey	6,487	32,877
1859D	Clay Cross Benefit, 42 Thanet St., Clay Cross, Chesterfield	3,393	7,196
1869D	Colchester, 42–48 North Station Road, Colchester	11,711	43,277
1884D	Coventry, P.O. Box 9, High Street, Coventry	321,561	658,852
1850D	Cumberland, 38 Fisher St., Carlisle	67,544	168,197
1946D	Darlington, Tubwell Row, Market Pl., Darlington, Co. Durham	41,737	104,155
1859D	Derbyshire, Duffield Hall, Duffield, Derby	224,692	525,064
1858D	Dudley, Dudley Hse., Stone St., Dudley, Worcs.	15,005	33,971
1869D	Dunfermline, 48–56 East Port, Dunfermline, Fife.	75,768	243,673
1927D	Ealing and Acton, 55 The Mall, Ealing, London W5	2,328	10,092
1857D	Earl Shilton, 22 The Hollow, Earl Shilton, Leicester	8,746	21,175
1903D	East Surrey, 54 Station Rd., Redhill, Surrey	9,955	38,290
1877D	Eastbourne Mut., Eastbourne Hse., 22 Gildredge Rd., Eastbourne, Sussex	55,480	177,875
1980	Ecology, 43 Main St., Cross Hills, Keighley, West Yorks BD20 8TT	631	863
1847D	Essex Eq., 5 Brooke Road, Grays, Essex	4,480	15,854
1970	Foresters, 13 College Place, London Road, Southampton SO9 1FP	698	1,728
1860D	Frome Selwood P., 3 Market Pl., Frome, Som.	11,413	23,534
1865D	Furness, 51–55 Duke Street, Barrow-in-Furness	54,403	119,511
1911D	Gainsborough, 26 Lord St., Gainsborough, Lincs.	3,095	7,691
1924D	Gateway, P.O. Box 18, Worthing, W. Sussex	438,324	1,366,176
1852D	Greenwich, 279–283 Greenwich High Rd., London SE10	30,506	75,559
1871D	Guardian, Guardian Hse., 120 High Holborn, London WC1	71,290	633,819
1853D	Halifax, P.O. Box 60, Trinity Rd., Halifax, West Yorks.	7,301,044	20,492,353
1866D	Hampshire, Anchor Hse., Kingston Crescent, Portsmouth	14,684	47,253
1854D	Hanley Econ., 42 Cheapside, Hanley, Stoke-on-Trent, Staffs.	32,146	65,385
1953D	Harpenden, 14 Station Rd., Harpenden, Herts.	6,011	16,803
1882D	Harrow, Cunningham Hse., Bessborough Rd., Harrow, Middx.	8,291	35,839
1866	Hartlepool and Dt., 5 Victoria Rd., Hartlepool, County Cleveland	1,629	4,127
1931D	Haslemere, 18 High St., Haslemere, Surrey	1,550	5,089

* P. = Permanent; B. = Benefit. The words "Building Society" are the last words in every society's name.

Year Established	Name of Society (abbreviated) Head Office	Share Investors	Assets Total £'000
1890D	Haywards Heath and Dt., 33 The Broadway, Haywards Heath, West Sussex	18,613	56,080
1863D	Heart of England, 22–26 Jury St., Warwick	136,620	281,584
1884D	Hemel Hempstead, 43 Marlowes, Hemel Hempstead, Herts.	10,449	43,941
1926D	Hendon, 9 Central Circus, Hendon, London NW4	3,757	20,017
1888D	Herne Bay, 39 William St., Herne Bay	5,841	21,496
1888D	Herts. and Essex, 4 Market Sq., Bishop's Stortford, Herts.	4,291	13,373
1874D	Hibernian, 22 High St., Cardiff, Glam.	4,108	11,919
1865D	Hinckley, and Rugby, Upper Bond St., Hinckley, Leics.	41,698	91,090
1855D	Holmesdale B., 43 Church St., Reigate, Surrey	7,095	25,467
1875	Huntley, 10 The Square, Huntley, Aberdeenshire	436	1,227
1853D	Ilkeston P., 16 Queen St., Ilkeston, Derby	3,937	8,220
1849D	Ipswich, 44 Upper Brook St., Ipswich	27,517	61,484
1961	Kidderminster Eq., 17 Church St., Kidderminster	890	2,774
1852D	Lambeth, 118–120 Westminster Bridge Rd., London SE1	64,399	283,535
1853D	Leamington Spa, Imperial House, Holly Walk, Leamington Spa, Warws.	109,728	456,806
1875D	Leeds and Holbeck, 105 Albion St., Leeds	198,713	507,861
1848D	Leeds P., Permanent Hse., The Headrow, Leeds	2,221,168	5,904,027
1863D	Leek United and Midlands, 50 St. Edward St., Leek, Staffs.	47,152	114,240
1875D	Leicester, Oadby, Leicester	1,130,867	2,950,499
1848	London P., 14 Tufton St., London SW1P 3QZ	2,014	3,884
1867D	Loughborough P., 6 High St., Loughborough, Leics.	8,405	27,994
1877	Louth, Mablethorpe and Sutton P.B., 3 Eastgate, Louth, Lincs.	1,283	3,332
1922D	Manchester, 18–20 Bridge St., Manchester	6,306	31,136
1956	Manchester Unity of Odd Fellows, Odd Fellows House, 40 Fountain Street, Manchester M2 2AB	692	792
1870D	Mansfield, Regent Hse., Regent St., Mansfield, Notts.	14,794	45,976
1870D	Market Harborough, Welland Hse., The Sq., Market Harborough, Leics.	25,388	60,950
1860D	Marsden, 6–20 Russell St., Nelson, Lancs.	32,877	96,116
1874D	Melton Mowbray, 39 Nottingham St., Melton Mowbray, Leics.	24,852	72,604
1966D	Mercantile, 75 Howard St., North Shields, Tyne and Wear	19,300	47,276
1882	Merseyside, 41 North John St., Liverpool	652	2,798
1886D	Metrogas, Katherine Hse., Katherine St., Croydon	5,033	12,044
1872D	Middleton, Sadler Street, Middleton, Manchester	36,446	91,972
1859D	Midshires, 35–49 Litchfield Street, Wolverhampton	409,259	800,882
1880D	Mid-Sussex, Mid-Sussex Hse., 66 Church Rd., Burgess Hill, Sussex	6,315	13,754
1883D	Mitcham and Metropolitan, 173 London Rd., Mitcham, Surrey	2,792	5,930
1869D	Monmouthshire, John Frost Sq., Newport, Gwent	13,000	42,243
1866D	Mornington, 158 Kentish Town Rd., London NW5	19,720	87,221
1869D	National and Provincial, Provincial Hse., Bradford	1,359,301	4,449,392
1896D	National Counties, Waterloo Hse., High St., Epsom, Surrey	37,145	197,128
1884D	Nationwide, New Oxford Hse., High Holborn, London WC1	3,301,399	8,738,016
1856D	Newbury, 17–20 Bartholomew St., Newbury, Berks.	27,241	77,132
1863D	Newcastle, Grainger Chambers, Hood Street, Newcastle upon Tyne	94,848	350,767
1876D	North East Globe, 18 Ridley Place, Newcastle upon Tyne	4,157	13,914
1866D	North Kent, North Kent Hse., Windmill St., Gravesend, Kent	23,001	56,115
1877D	North of England, 57 Fawcett St., Sunderland	60,492	113,762
1983D	North Wilts Ridgeway, 18 and 19 Commercial Rd., Swindon, Wilts.	10,578	33,429
1850D	Northern Rock, Northern Rock Hse., P.O. Box No. 2, Gosforth, Newcastle upon Tyne	481,084	1,316,663
1852D	Norwich, St. Andrew's Hse., St. Andrew St., Norwich, Norfolk	64,374	162,905
1850D	Nottingham, 5–13 Upper Parliament St., Nottingham	121,693	227,360
1935D	Nottingham Oddfellows, Imperial Bldg., 29 Bridgeford Rd., West Bridgeford, Nottingham	5,362	10,307
1879D	Paddington, 125 Westbourne Grove, London W2	10,983	35,598
1879D	Peckham Graylaw Hse., 1 Copers Cope Rd, Beckenham, Kent BR3 1MB	10,453	28,614
1877D	Penrith, 7 King St., Penrith, Cumb.	7,119	22,578
1860D	Peterborough, Manor Hse., 57 Lincoln Rd., Peterborough	71,318	193,259
1881D	Portman, 40 Portman Sq., London W1	133,912	409,069
1896D	Portsmouth, 176 London Rd., North End, Portsmouth	58,349	229,415
1860D	Principality, Principality Bldgs., Queen St., Cardiff	176,893	360,571
1941D	Property Owners, 4 Cavendish Place, London W1	56,465	265,820
1846D	Ramsbury, 25 High Street, Ramsbury, Marlborough, Wilts.	72,781	161,833
1888D	Rowley Regis, 223 Halesowen Rd., Crawley Heath, Warley, Worcs	28,170	62,929
1849D	Saffron Walden and Essex, Market Place, Saffron Walden, Essex	28,609	66,517
1937D	St. Pancras, 200 Finchley Rd., London NW3	8,819	41,526
1955	St. Stephens, 70 Chepstow Road, London W2	372	1,293
1846D	Scarborough, Prospect House, 442/444 Scalby Road, Scarborough, Yorks.	40,562	100,423
1848D	Scottish, 2 York Place, Edinburgh	13,018	35,586
1935D	Sheffield, 66 Campo Lane, Sheffield, Yorks.	3,798	11,134
1879D	Shepshed, Bull Ring, Shepshed, Loughborough, Leics.	6,511	12,938
1853D	Skipton, 59 High St., Skipton, Yorks.	147,824	471,191

Year Established	Name of Society (abbreviated)　　　Head Office	Share Investors	Assets Total £'000
1876	South Shields Sun P., 9 Beach Rd., South Shields, Co. Durham	800	2,588
1877D	Stafford Railway, 4 Market Sq., Stafford	7,955	19,554
1902D	Staffordshire, 5 Princes St., Jubilee Hse., P.O. Box 66, 84 Salop St., Wolverhampton	135,544	302,925
1875D	Standard, 64 Church Way, North Shields, Tyne and Wear	2,414	6,812
1970D	Stanley, Cromarty Hse., Front St., Stanley, Co. Durham	5,679	11,887
1850D	Stroud, 7 Russell St., Stroud, Glos.	49,254	93,322
1853D	Sunderland and Shields, 50 Fawcett St., Sunderland, Co. Durham	136,417	268,459
1870D	Sussex County, 40/42 Friars Walk, Lewes, East Sussex	81,313	241,440
1872D	Sussex Mutual, Sussex Hse., 130 Western Rd., Hove, Sussex	32,287	168,518
1923	Swansea, 11 Cradock St., Swansea	3,124	9,512
1868D	Swindon P., 1 Commercial Rd., Swindon, Wilts.	7,773	21,535
1966D	Teachers, Allenview Hse., Wimborne, Dorset	10,194	56,181
1886	Thrift, 3/4 Turnpike Parade, Green Lanes, London N15	3,918	9,007
1901D	Tipton and Coseley, 57–60 High St., Tipton, Staffs.	14,172	30,065
1853D	Town and Country, 215 Strand, London WC2	260,067	810,109
1866D	Tyldesley, 209–215 Elliott St., Tyldesley, Manchester	13,442	27,882
1855D	Tynemouth, 53–55 Howard St., North Shields, Tyne and Wear	5,696	14,242
1863D	Universal, 41 Pilgrim St., Newcastle upon Tyne	21,107	58,756
1924D	Vernon, 26 St. Petersgate, Stockport, Chesh.	14,723	35,531
1847D	Waltham Abbey, 6 Church St., Waltham Abbey, Essex	24,277	41,971
1877D	Walthamstow, 869 Forest Rd., Walthamstow, London E17	35,438	103,848
1949D	Wessex, 115 Old Christchurch Rd., Bournemouth, Hants.	26,794	121,539
1849D	West Bromwich, 374 High St., West Bromwich, Staffs.	264,340	394,545
1882D	West Cumbria, Cumbria Hse., Murray Rd., Workington	5,980	17,747
1862D	Western Counties, Bank End, Bideford, Devon	49,095	126,063
1847D	Woolwich Eq., Equitable Hse., London SE18	2,498,251	5,722,607
1885D	Yorkshire, Yorkshire House, Westgate, Bradford	541,655	1,522,349

PERIODS OF GESTATION AND INCUBATION

The table shows approximate periods of gestation or incubation for some common animals and birds. In some cases the periods may vary and where doubt arises professional advice should be sought.

Species	Shortest Period. Days	Usual Period. Days	Longest Period. Days	Species	Shortest Period. Days	Usual Period. Days	Longest Period. Days
Human	240	273	313	Duck	28	28	32
Mare	305	336	340	Goose	28	30	32
Ass	365	—	374	Pigeon	17	18	19
Cow	273	280	294	Canary	12	14	14
Ewe	140	147–50	160	Guinea Pig	63	—	70
Goat	147	151	155	Mouse	18	—	19
Sow	109	112	125	Rat	21	—	24
Bitch	55	63	70	Elephant		21–22 months	
Cat	53	56	63				
Rabbit	30	32	35	Camel		45 weeks	
Hen	20	21	22	Zebra		56 weeks	
Turkey	25	28	28				

BANKING IN BRITAIN

The main institutions within the British banking system are the Bank of England (the central bank, *see* p. 376), the clearing banks (the major retail banks), the merchant banks, the overseas banks and the discount houses.

The clearing banks are Barclays, Co-operative, Coutts, Lloyds, Midland, National Girobank, National Westminster, Williams & Glyns, the Trustee Savings Bank of England and Wales and the Yorkshire Bank (the latter two banks clearing through the Central Trustee Savings Bank Ltd, and William & Glyns respectively), and in Scotland, the Bank of Scotland, Clydesdale, Royal Bank of Scotland and the Trustee Savings Bank of Scotland.

Under the Banking Act 1979 deposit-taking businesses require authorization from the Bank of England unless they are specifically exempted from the authorization provisions of the Act. Institutions may be authorized either as recognized banks or as licensed deposit-takers and are subject to the Bank of England's supervision. There follows a list of these recognized banks and licensed deposit-taking institutions (as at August 17, 1985):—

Recognized Banks

A P Bank Ltd.
Alexanders Discount p.l.c.
Algemene Bank Nederland N.V.
Allied Arab Bank Ltd.
Allied Bank International
Allied Bank of Pakistan Ltd.
Allied Irish Banks p.l.c.
Allied Irish Investment Bank p.l.c.
American Express Bank Ltd.
American National Bank and Trust Company of Chicago
Amsterdam-Rotterdam Bank N.V.
Anglo-Romanian Bank Ltd.
Henry Ansbacher & Co. Ltd.
Arab Bank Ltd.
Arbuthnot Latham Bank Ltd.
Associated Japanese Bank (International) Ltd.
Atlantic International Bank Ltd.
Australia & New Zealand Banking Group Ltd.

Banca Commerciale Italiana
Banca Nazionale del Lavoro
Banco Central, S.A.
Banco de Bilbao S.A.
Banco de la Nación Argentina
Banco de Santander, S.A.
Banco de Vizcaya S.A.
Banco di Roma S.p.A.
Banco di Sicilia
Banco do Brasil S.A.
Banco do Estado de São Paulo S.A.
Banco Espirito Santo e Comercial de Lisboa
Banco Exterior-U.K. S.A.
Banco Hispano Americano Ltd.
Banco Mercantil de São Paulo S.A.
Banco Nacional de Mexico S.N.C.
Banco Português do Atlântico
Banco Real S.A.
Banco Totta & Açores E.P.
Bancomer, S.N.C.
Bangkok Bank Ltd.
Bank Julius Baer & Co. Ltd.
Bank Bumiputra Malaysia Berhad
Bank für Gemeinwirtschaft A.G.
Bank Hapoalim B.M.
Bank Leumi (U.K.) p.l.c.
Bank Mellat
Bank Melli Iran
Bank of America International Ltd.
Bank of America N.T. & S.A.
Bank of Baroda
The Bank of California N.A.
Bank of Ceylon
Bank of China
Bank of Cyprus (London) Ltd.
Bank of India
The Bank of Ireland
Bank of London & South America Ltd.
Bank of Montreal
The Bank of New York
Bank of New Zealand

The Bank of Nova Scotia
Bank of Scotland
The Bank of Tokyo, Ltd.
Bank of Tokyo International Ltd.
The Bank of Tokyo Trust Company
The Bank of Yokohama Ltd.
Bank Saderat Iran
Bank Sepah
Bankers Trust Company
Banque Belge Ltd.
Banque Belgo-Zairoise S.A.
Banque Bruxelles Lambert S.A.
Banque Française du Commerce Extérieur
Banque Indosuez
Banque Nationale de Paris p.l.c.
Banque Paribas
Barclays Bank p.l.c.
Barclays Merchant Bank Ltd.
Baring Brothers & Co. Ltd.
Bayerische Hypotheken-und-Wechsel-Bank A.G.
Bayerische Landesbank Girozentrale
Bayerische Vereinsbank
Berliner Bank A.G.
The British Bank of the Middle East
The British Linen Bank Ltd.
Brown, Shipley & Co. Ltd.

CIC—Union Européenne, International et Cie
Canadian Imperial Bank of Commerce
Carolina Bank Ltd.
Cassa di Risparmio delle Provincie Lombarde
Cater Allen Ltd.
Centerre Bank N.A.
Central Bank of India
Central Trustee Savings Bank Ltd.
Charterhouse Japhet p.l.c.
Chase Bank (Ireland) Ltd.
The Chase Manhattan Bank, N.A.
Chase Manhattan Ltd.
Chemical Bank
Chemical Bank International Ltd.
The Cho-Hung Bank
The Chuo Trust & Banking Company Ltd.
Citibank N.A.
Citicorp Investment Bank Ltd.
City Merchants Bank Ltd.
Clive Discount Company Ltd.
Clydesdale Bank p.l.c.
Comerica Bank-Detroit
Commercial Bank of Korea Ltd.
The Commercial Bank of the Near East p.l.c.
Commercial Bank of Wales p.l.c.
Commerzbank A.G.
Commonwealth Bank of Australia
Continental Illinois National Bank and Trust Company of Chicago
Co-operative Bank p.l.c.
County Bank Ltd.
Coutts & Co.
Crédit du Nord
Crédit Lyonnais

Credit Lyonnais Bank Nederland N.V.
Crédit Suisse
Credit Suisse First Boston Ltd.
Creditanstalt-Bankverein
Credito Italiano
Crocker National Bank
The Cyprus Popular Bank

The Dai-Ichi Kangyo Bank, Ltd.
The Daiwa Bank, Ltd.
Deutsche Bank A.G.
Discount Bank (Overseas) Ltd.
Dresdner Bank A.G.

Euro-Latinamerican Bank Ltd.
European Arab Bank Ltd.
European Banking Company Ltd.
European Brazilian Bank Ltd.

Fidelity Bank N.A.
First City National Bank of Houston
First Interstate Bank of California
First Interstate Capital Markets Ltd.
The First National Bank of Boston
The First National Bank of Chicago
First National Bank of Maryland
First National Bank of Minneapolis
First Pennsylvania Bank N.A.
First Wisconsin National Bank of Milwaukee
Robert Fleming & Co. Ltd.
French Bank of Southern Africa Ltd.
The Fuji Bank, Ltd.

Gerrard & National p.l.c.
Ghana Commercial Bank
Girozentrale und Bank der österreichischen Sparkassen A.G.
Grindlay Brandts Ltd.
Grindlays Bank p.l.c.
Guinness Mahon & Co. Ltd.
Gulf International Bank B.S.C.

Habib Bank A.G. Zurich
Habib Bank Ltd.
Hambros Bank Ltd.
Hanil Bank
Havana International Bank Ltd.
Hessische Landesbank-Girozentrale
Hill Samuel & Co. Ltd.
C. Hoare & Co.
The Hokkaido Takushoku Bank, Ltd.
The Hongkong Bank Ltd.
The Hongkong and Shanghai Banking Corporation
Hungarian International Bank Ltd.

The Industrial Bank of Japan, Ltd.
InterFirst Bank Dallas, N.A.
International Commercial Bank p.l.c.
International Mexican Bank Ltd.
International Westminster Bank p.l.c.
Irving Trust Company
Istituto Bancario San Paolo di Torino
Italian International Bank p.l.c.

Japan International Bank Ltd.
Johnson Matthey Bankers Ltd.
Leopold Joseph & Sons Ltd.

King & Shaxson p.l.c.
Kleinwort, Benson Ltd.
Korea Exchange Bank
Korea First Bank
The Kyowa Bank, Ltd.

Lazard Brothers & Co., Ltd.
Libra Bank p.l.c.
Lloyds Bank p.l.c.
Lloyds Bank International Ltd.
Lloyds Bank International (France) Ltd.
Lloyds Merchant Bank Ltd.
London & Continental Bankers Ltd.

London Interstate Bank Ltd.
The Long-Term Credit Bank of Japan, Ltd.

Malayan Banking Berhad
Manufacturers Hanover Ltd.
Manufacturers Hanover Trust Company
Marine Midland Bank N.A.
Mellon Bank, N.A.
Mercantile Bank Ltd.
Merrill Lynch International Bank Ltd.
Midland Bank p.l.c.
The Mitsubishi Bank Ltd.
The Mitsubishi Trust and Banking Corporation
The Mitsui Bank Ltd.
The Mitsui Trust & Banking Company Ltd.
Samuel Montagu & Co. Ltd.
Morgan Grenfell & Co. Ltd.
Morgan Guaranty Trust Company of New York
Moscow Narodny Bank Ltd.

NCNB National Bank of North Carolina
National Australia Bank Ltd.
National Bank of Abu Dhabi
National Bank of Canada
National Bank of Detroit
National Bank of Greece S.A.
The National Bank of New Zealand Ltd.
National Bank of Pakistan
National Westminster Bank p.l.c.
Nederlandsche Middenstandsbank N.V.
Nedbank Ltd.
The Nippon Credit Bank, Ltd.
Noble Grossart Ltd.
Nordic Bank p.l.c.
Northern Bank Ltd.
The Northern Trust Company

Orion Royal Bank Ltd.
Oversea-Chinese Banking Corporation Ltd.
Overseas Union Bank Ltd.

PK Christiania Bank (UK) Ltd.
Philippine National Bank
Postipankki (UK) Ltd.
Privatbanken Ltd.
Punjab National Bank

Qatar National Bank S.A.Q.
Gerald Quin, Cope & Co. Ltd.

Rafidain Bank
Rea Brothers p.l.c.
RepublicBank Dallas, N.A.
Reserve Bank of Australia
The Riggs National Bank of Washington, D.C.
N. M. Rothschild & Sons Ltd.
The Royal Bank of Canada
The Royal Bank of Scotland p.l.c.
The Royal Trust Company of Canada

S.F.E. Bank Ltd.
The Saitama Bank, Ltd.
The Sanwa Bank, Ltd.
Saudi International Bank (Al-Bank Al-Saudi Al-Alami Ltd.)
Scandinavian Bank Ltd.
J. Henry Schroder Wagg & Co. Ltd.
Seccombe Marshall & Campion p.l.c.
Security Pacific National Bank
Shanghai Commercial Bank Ltd.
Singer & Friedlander Ltd.
Smith St. Aubyn & Co. Ltd.
Société Générale
Société Générale Merchant Bank p.l.c.
Sonali Bank
Standard Chartered Bank p.l.c.
Standard Chartered Merchant Bank Ltd.
State Bank of India
The Sumitomo Bank, Ltd.
The Sumitomo Trust and Banking Company Ltd.

Swiss Bank Corporation
Syndicate Bank

The Taiyo Kobe Bank Ltd.
Texas Commerce Bank N.A.
The Thai Farmers Bank Ltd.
The Tokai Bank, Ltd.
The Toronto-Dominion Bank
The Toyo Trust & Banking Company Ltd.

UBAF Bank Ltd.
Ulster Bank Ltd.
Ulster Investment Bank Ltd.
Union Bank of Switzerland
The Union Discount Company of London p.l.c.
United Bank Ltd.

The United Bank of Kuwait Ltd.
United Commercial Bank
United Overseas Bank Ltd.

S. G. Warburg & Co. Ltd.
Westdeutsche Landesbank Girozentrale
Westpac Banking Corporation
Williams & Glyn's Bank p.l.c.
Wintrust Securities Ltd.
Württembergische Kommunale Landesbank Girozentrale

The Yasuda Trust and Banking Co., Ltd.
Yorkshire Bank p.l.c.

Zambia National Commercial Bank Ltd.
Zivnostenská Banka National Corporation

Licensed Deposit-taking Institutions

A1 (Investment) Ltd.
Abbey Finance Co. Ltd.
Adam & Company p.l.c.
Afghan National Credit & Finance Ltd.
African Continental Bank Ltd.
Aitken Hume Ltd.
Ak International Ltd.
Al Baraka International Ltd.
Al Saudi Banque S.A.
The Alliance Trust p.l.c.
Allied Banking Corporation
Allied Dunbar & Co. p.l.c.
Allied Irish Finance Co. Ltd.
Altajir Ltd.
Anglo-Yugoslav (LDT) Ltd.
Arab African International Bank
Arab Bank Investment Co. Ltd.
Arab Banking Corporation B.S.C.
Armada Investments Ltd.
Assemblies of God Property Trust
Associated Credits Ltd.
Associates Capital Corporation Ltd.
Auban Finance Ltd.
Avco Trust Ltd.

B.A.I.I. p.l.c.
B.C.F. Finance Ltd.
BMI (Hampshire) Ltd.
Badische Kommunale Landesbank Girozentrale
Banca Nazionale dell'Agricoltura SpA
Banca Serfin S.N.C.
Banco di Santo Spirito
Bank Handlowy w Warszawie S.A.
Bank Mees & Hope N.V.
Bank of Credit and Commerce International S.A.
Bank of Ireland Finance Ltd.
Bank of Ireland Finance (N.I.) Ltd.
The Bank of Nova Scotia Trust Company (United Kingdom) Ltd.
Bank of Oman Ltd.
Bank of Seoul
Bank Tejarat
Bankers Trust International Ltd.
Banque du Liban et d'Outre-Mer
Banque Internationale pour l'Afrique Occidentale S.A.
The Baptist Union Corporation Ltd.
Barbados National Bank
Barclays Bank Trust Company Ltd.
Barclays Bank UK Ltd.
Thomas Barlow & Bro. Ltd.
Barrie Vanger & Co. Ltd.
Beaver Guarantee Ltd.
Beirut Riyad Bank S.A.L.
Beneficial Trust Ltd.
Boston Trust & Savings Ltd.
Bradford Investments
Bridgeover Ltd.

Bridgeway Finance Ltd.
British Credit Trust Ltd.
British Railways Savings Company Ltd.
Buchanan Securities Ltd.
Bucks Land & Building Co. Ltd.
Bunge Finance Ltd.
Burns-Anderson Trust Company Ltd.
Business Mortgages Trust p.l.c.
Byblos Bank S.A.L.

Caisse Nationale de Crédit Agricole
Calculus Finance p.l.c.
Canada Permanent Mortgage Corporation (U.K.) Ltd.
Canara Bank
Castle Phillips Finance Co. Ltd.
Cattles Holdings Finance Ltd.
Cayzer Ltd.
Cedar Holdings Ltd.
Century Factors Ltd.
Chancery Securities p.l.c.
Charter Consolidated Financial Services Ltd.
Chartered Trust p.l.c.
Charterhouse Japhet Credit Ltd.
Chesterfield Street Trust Ltd.
Citibank Trust Ltd.
City Trust Ltd.
Close Brothers Ltd.
Clydesdale Bank Finance Corporation Ltd.
CE Coates & Co. Ltd.
Cobnar Finance Co. Ltd.
Combined Capital Ltd.
Commercial Credit Services Ltd.
Commonwealth Savings Bank of Australia
Consolidated Credits & Discounts Ltd.
Consumer Credit Investments Ltd.
The Continental Trust Ltd.
Co-operative Bank (Commercial) Ltd.
Copenhagen Handelsbank A/S
Coutts Finance Co.
Craneheath Securities Ltd.
Crédit Commercial de France
Credito Italiano International Ltd.
Cue & Co.
Cyprus Credit Bank Ltd.
Cyprus Finance Corporation (London) Ltd.

Dalbeattie Finance Co. Ltd.
Darlington Merchant Credits Ltd.
Dartington & Co. Ltd.
Den Danske Bank af 1871 Aktieselskab
Deutsche Genossenschaftsbank
The Development Bank of Singapore Ltd.
The Dorset, Somerset & Wilts Investment Society Ltd.
Dryfield Finance Ltd.
Duncan Lawrie Ltd.
Dunsterville Allen p.l.c.

E. T. Trust Ltd.
Eagil Trust Co. Ltd.
East Anglian Securities Trust Ltd.
East Midlands Finance Co. Ltd.
Eccles Savings and Loans Ltd.
The English Association Trust Ltd.
Ensign Discount Co. Ltd.
Enskilda Securities-Skandinaviska Enskilda Ltd.
Equatorial Trust Corporation Ltd.
Everett Chettle Associates
Exeter Trust Ltd.

FIBI Financial Trust Ltd.
Fairmont Trust Ltd.
Family Finance Ltd.
Farmers (WCF) Finance Ltd.
Federated Trust Corporation Ltd.
FennoScandia Ltd.
Financial and General Securities Ltd.
James Finlay Corporation Ltd.
Finova Finance Ltd.
First Bank of Nigeria Ltd.
First Commercial Bank
First Co-operative Finance Ltd.
First Indemnity Credit Ltd.
First National Boston Ltd.
First National Securities Ltd.
Fleet National Bank
Ford Financial Trust Ltd.
Ford Motor Credit Co. Ltd.
Foreign & Colonial Management Ltd.
Forward Trust Ltd.
Robert Fraser & Partners Ltd.

Goldman Sachs Ltd.
Goode Durrant Trust p.l.c.
Gota (U.K.) Ltd.
Granville Finance Ltd.
H. T. Greenwood Ltd.
Greetwell Finance Ltd.
Gresham Trust p.l.c.
Greyhound Guaranty Ltd.
Grindlays Humberclyde Ltd.
Grindlays Industrial Finance Ltd.
Grosvenor Acceptances Ltd.
Gulf Guarantee Trust Ltd.

HFC Trust & Savings Ltd.
H. & J. Finance Co. (Midlands) Ltd.
Habibsons Trust and Finance Ltd.
The Hardware Federation Finance Co. Ltd.
Harris Trust and Savings Bank
Harrods Trust Ltd.
Harton Securities Ltd.
The Heritable & General Trust Ltd.
Holdenhurst Securities Ltd.

IBJ International Ltd.
Industrial Finance and Investment Corporation p.l.c.
Industrial Funding Trust Ltd.
The Investment Bank of Ireland Ltd.
Investment Trustees Ltd.
Investors in Industry p.l.c.
Investors in Industry Group p.l.c.
Iran Overseas Investment Corporation Ltd.
ItaB Group Ltd.

Jabac Finances Ltd.
Jordan Finance Consortium p.l.c.

Kansallis-Osake-Pankki
Keesler Federal Credit Union
Knowsley & Co. Ltd.
Kredietbank N.V.

Laurentian Financial Services Ltd.
Liechtenstein (U.K.) Ltd.
Little Lakes Finance Ltd.
Lloyds & Scottish p.l.c.
Lloyds Bank (LABCO) Ltd.

Lloyds Bowmaker Ltd.
Lodhi Finance Ltd.
Lombard Acceptances Ltd.
Lombard & Ulster Ltd.
Lombard North Central p.l.c.
Lombard Street Investment Trust Co. Ltd.
London and Arab Investments Ltd.
London and Pacific Trust Ltd.
London Law Securities Ltd.
London Scottish Finance Corporation p.l.c.
Lordsvale Finance Ltd.

McNeill Pearson Ltd.
Manchester Exchange Trust Ltd.
W. M. Mann & Co. (Investments) Ltd.
Edward Manson & Co. Ltd.
Manufacturers Hanover Export Finance Ltd.
Manufacturers Hanover Finance Ltd.
The Mardun Investment Co. Ltd.
Matheson Trust Co. Ltd.
Medens Trust Ltd.
Meghraj & Sons Ltd.
Mercantile Credit Company Ltd.
Mercury Provident Society Ltd.
The Methodist Chapel Aid Association Ltd.
Middle East Bank Ltd.
Midland Bank Equity Holdings Ltd.
Midland Bank Finance Corporation Ltd.
Midland Bank Trust Company Ltd.
Milford Mutual Facilities Ltd.
Minster Trust Ltd.
Moneycare Ltd.
Moorgate Mercantile Holdings p.l.c.
Mount Credit Corporation Ltd.
Multibanco Comermex S.N.C.
Muslim Commercial Bank Ltd.
Mynshul Trust Ltd.

N.I.I.B. Group Ltd.
National Bank of Egypt
National Bank of Fort Sam Houston
The National Bank of Kuwait S.A.K.
National Bank of Nigeria Ltd.
National Commercial & Glyns Ltd.
National Guardian Finance Corporation Ltd.
New Nigeria Bank Ltd.
Norddeutsche Landesbank Girozentrale
The North of Scotland Finance Co. Ltd.
North West Securities Ltd.
Northern Bank Development Corporation Ltd.
Northern Bank Executor & Trustee Company Ltd.
Norwich General Trust Ltd.

Omega Trust Co. Ltd.
Omnibank A.G.
Oppenheimer Money Management Ltd.
Oriental Credit Ltd.
Osterreichische Länderbank A.G.
Overseas Trust Bank Ltd.

PKFinans International (U.K.) Ltd.
Park Street Securities Ltd.
The People's Trust & Savings Ltd.
Philadelphia National Bank
Pointon York Ltd.
Prestwick Investment Trust p.l.c.
Provincial Trust Ltd.
Punjab & Sind Bank

Ralli Investment Company Ltd.
R. Raphael & Sons p.l.c.
Rathbone Bros. & Co.
Reliance Trust Ltd.
Republic National Bank of New York
Riyad Bank
Roxburghe Guarantee Corporation Ltd.
The Rural and Industries Bank of Western Australia

S.P. Finance Ltd.
St. Margaret's Trust Ltd.

Schroder Leasing Ltd.
Scottish Amicable Money Managers Ltd.
Seattle First National Bank Secure Homes Ltd.
Security Pacific Trust Ltd.
Shawlands Securities Ltd.
The Siam Commercial Bank, Ltd.
Smith & Williamson Securities
South Notts Finance Ltd.
Southsea Mortgage & Investment Co. Ltd.
Spring Gardens Securities p.l.c.
Spry Finance Ltd.
Standard Property Investment p.l.c.
State Bank of New South Wales
State Bank of South Australia
State Bank of Victoria
State Street Bank and Trust Company
Sterling Trust Ltd.
Svenska International Ltd.
Swiss Bank Corporation International Ltd.
Swiss Volksbank

TCB Ltd.
The Teachers & General Investment Co. Ltd.
Thames Trust Ltd.
Thorncliffe Finance Ltd.
Trade Development Bank
Treloan Ltd.

Trucanda Trusts Ltd.
The Trust Bank of Africa Ltd.
Tullett and Riley Money Management Ltd.
Turkish Bank Ltd.
Türkiye Iş Bankasi A.Ş.
Tyndall & Co.

Ulster Bank Trust Company
Union Bank of Finland Ltd.
Union Bank of India
Union Bank of Nigeria Ltd.
United Dominions Trust Ltd.
United Mizrahi Bank Ltd.
Unity Trust Ltd.
Universal Credit Ltd.

Venture Finance Ltd.
Vernons Trust Corporation
Volkskas Ltd.

Wagon Finance Ltd.
Wallace, Smith Trust Co. Ltd.
Welbeck Finance p.l.c.
Western Trust & Savings Ltd.
Whiteaway Laidlaw & Co. Ltd.
Wimbledon & South West Finance Co. Ltd.
N. H. Woolley & Co. Ltd.

H. F. Young & Co. Ltd.

Banking Hours: England and Wales, 9.30–3.30; *City of London town clearers,* 9.30–3.00; (Saturdays; Barclays, 9.30–12.00; Lloyds, 9.30–12.30 or 10.00–3.00; Midland and National Westminister, 9.30–12.30; Trustee Savings Bank, 9.30–4.00). *Scotland.*—Banking hours in Scotland are: Mon.–Wed., 9.30–12.30; 1.30–3.30; Thursday, 9.30–12.30; 1.30–3.30; 4.30–6 p.m.; Fri. 9.30–3.30; Saturday, *closed. Northern Ireland;* Mon.–Fri. 10.00–12.30; 1.30–3.30; 9.30 opening two mornings per week. Open until 5.00 one summer evening per week.

FINANCIAL FIGURES, ETC. FOR THE "BIG FOUR" BANKS, 1984

Bank Group	Profit before taxation £m	Profit (*loss) after taxation £m	Total Asssets £m	Number of U.K. branches
Barclays	655 (557)	313 (337)	73,623 (64,904)	Over 2,900
Lloyds	468 (419)	237 (284)	44,009 (38,432)	2,700
Midland	135 (225)	25* (125)	61,483 (52,613)	2,300
National Westminster	671 (518)	294 (401)	71,517 (60,017)	3,400

1983 figures in parentheses.

NATIONAL GIROBANK

The National Girobank provides a broad range of corporate and personal banking facilities. It operates through more than 20,000 U.K. post offices.

OPERATING STATISTICS	1983–84	1984–85
Number of accounts at year end, thousands	1,600	1,827
Average customer balances for year, £m	810	926
Number of transactions (including social security payments), millions	356	410

CLEARING BANKS, ETC.

Committee of London Clearing Bankers
(1821), 10 Lombard Street, EC3V 9AP

The Committee consists of the Chairmen of Barclays, Coutts, Lloyds, Midland, National Westminster, and Williams & Glyn's and meets regularly to discuss matters of common interest. It is the body through which the Bank of England communicates official policy to the banks and through which the banks may present their views to the Bank of England and the Treasury.
Secretary-General, K. S. Lucas.

Bankers' Automated Clearing Services, Ltd.
3 De Havilland Road, Edgware, Middlesex HA8 5QA

Bankers' Automated Clearing Services, (BACS) is the U.K. automated clearing house, owned and administered by the Association for Payment Clearing Services. BACS is wholly owned by the five largest clearing banks. Its function is to accept transactions recorded on magnetic media, check, merge and sort them and distribute them to the 14 sponsoring banks. Nearly all standing orders are interchanged through BACS, as are direct debits originated by non-banking organizations for payments of rates, insurance premiums, hire purchase payments etc, and automated credit transfers. Credits are also received on magnetic media, mainly for payment of salaries and pensions.

A direct telecommunications service, linking users direct to BACS became available in 1983.
Managing Director, D. J. Pyne.

London Bankers' Clearing House
10 Lombard Street, EC3V 9AP

The Clearing System came into being in London during the second half of the 18th century and the London Bankers' Clearing House has served as a pattern for the Clearing Houses that have been established since throughout the world.

Two Cheque Clearings are operated each business day. The Town Clearing enables cheques of £10,000 and over to be cleared the same day, provided that such cheques are paid into and drawn on one of the hundred Clearing Bank branches, designated as Town Clearing branches, situated within a half-mile radius of the Clearing House. The General Clearing handles cheques which cannot be passed through the Town Clearing. On an average day, 7,000,000 cheques with a total value of £30,000 million are exchanged and paid through these two clearings. Inter-branch clearings are dealt with separately by each Bank.

A Credit Clearing is also operated. The daily average for this clearing, including work passed through the Bankers' Automated Clearing Service, is 2,350,000 items with a total value of £800 million.

At the end of the day each bank works out the net balance resulting from its transactions in that day's Town Clearing, the previous day's General Clearing and Credit Clearing and B.A.C.S. output and such differences as need to be adjusted. This net balance is either credited to or deducted from the bank's own account at the Bank of England.
Chief Inspector, E. W. Stubbs.

British Bankers' Association
10 Lombard Street, EC3V 9EL

The Association provides a means of communication and consultation for the banking industry in this country. Membership is open to institutions accepted as recognized banks by the Bank of England—nearly 300. The Association is a member of the E.C. Banking Federation.
Secretary-General, J. B. Atherton.

Finance Houses Association
18 Upper Grosvenor Street, W1X 9PB

Director-Secretary, J. B. Damer, O.B.E.

THE NATIONAL DEBT

Net central government borrowing each year represents an addition to the National Debt. At the end of March 1984 the National Debt amounted to some £143,000 million of which £3,000 million was in currencies other than sterling. Of the £140,000 million sterling debt, £109,000 million consisted of gilt-edged stock; of this, 32 per cent had a maturity of up to five years, 43 per cent a maturity of over five years and up to 15 years and 25 per cent a maturity of over 15 years or undated. The remaining sterling debt was made up mainly of national savings (£20,000 million), certificates of tax deposits, Treasury bills, and Ways and Means advances (very short-term internal government borrowing).

SAVINGS

PREMIUM BONDS

These bonds are a United Kingdom Government security and were first introduced on November 1, 1956. Instead of earning interest, however, each bond offers to its holder the chance of winning a money prize in a prize draw. Bonds are issued in values ranging from £10 (the minimum purchase) to £10,000, and may be purchased in multiples of £5; each £1 buys one bond unit, which has one chance in each prize draw. Individual holdings are limited to £10,000.

Prizes are paid from a fund formed by the interest, at present 7¼ per cent *per annum*, on each bond eligible for the draw. A bond becomes eligible for the draw three clear calendar months following the month of purchase and goes into every subsequent draw whether or not it has won a prize until the end of the month in which it is repaid.

Bonds belonging to a deceased bondholder will remain eligible for all Prize Draws held in the month of death and in the following 12 calendar months, provided they have not been repaid earlier. They will then become ineligible for all further draws. These terms also apply to bonds purchased before August 1, 1960 (Series "A").

The winning numbers are selected by the electronic random number indicator equipment—usually called "ERNIE". Winning numbers are printed monthly in the *London Gazette*.

It is estimated that by the end of April 1985, bonds to the value of £3,497,900,000 had been sold. Of these £1,726,100,000 had been cashed, leaving £1,771,900,000 still invested. After the draws in September 1985, 24,800,000 prizes, totalling £1,389,400,000 had been distributed since the inception of the Premium Savings Bond Scheme.

INCOME BONDS

National Savings Income Bonds were introduced on August 2, 1982. They are particularly suitable for those who want to receive regular monthly payments of interest while preserving the full cash value of their capital. The Bonds are sold in multiples of £1,000. The minimum holding is £2,000 and the maximum £50,000.

Interest is calculated on a day-to-day basis and paid monthly. The rate may be varied from time to time, but it is kept competitive. Interest is taxable, but is paid without deduction of tax at source. The Bonds have a guaranteed life of ten years, but may be repaid at par before maturity on giving three months' notice. No formal period of notice for repayment is required if the holder dies.

Net investment in National Savings Income Bonds was £3,002,500,000 at the end of June 1985.

ORDINARY AND INVESTMENT ACCOUNTS

National Savings Bank.—On May 31, 1985, there were approximately 15,100,000 active accounts with the sum of £1,736,100,000 due to depositors in Ordinary accounts and approximately 3,100,000 active accounts with the sum of £5,208,000,000 due to depositors in Investment accounts.

Interest is earned at 6 per cent per year on each Ordinary account with a balance of £500 or more maintained throughout 1985 and at 3 per cent per year for all other Ordinary accounts. The minimum deposit is £1; maximum balance £10,000 plus current interest. On May 31, 1985 the average amount held in Ordinary accounts was approximately £115.

The Investment account pays a higher rate of interest (the current rate can be ascertained at any Savings Bank Post Office). The minimum deposit is £5; maximum balance £50,000 plus current interest. On May 31, 1985 the average amount held in Investment accounts was approximately £1,705.

Trustee Savings Banks.—There are 4 Trustee Savings Banks with more than 1,620 branches in the United Kingdom. On November 20, 1984, the Banks operated nearly 13,000,000 active accounts and total customer balances exceeded £9,000,600,000. *T.S.B. Group Central Executive*, P.O. Box 33, 25 Milk Street, EC2V 8LU.

DEPOSIT BONDS

National Savings Deposit Bonds were introduced on October 17, 1983. They offer a premium rate of interest on lump sum savings and are best suited for money not needed in less than a year. The minimum purchase is £100, larger purchases can be made in multiples of £50 and the maximum holding is £50,000 plus current interest.

Interest is taxable, but tax is not deducted at source. The interest rate is variable but is kept competitive. Interest is calculated on a daily basis and credited on the anniversary of purchase. Minimum amount of repayment is £50 and 3 months notice is required. Any amount repaid within a year of purchase earns interest at half the published rate. No interest is lost once a Bond has been held for a full year. Net investment in National Savings Deposit Bonds was £270,400,000 at May 31, 1985.

YEARLY PLAN

The National Savings "Yearly Plan" was introduced on July 2, 1984, following the withdrawal of Third Issue Save As You Earn. It offers a guaranteed tax-free return. Applicants agree to make 12 monthly payments, leading to the issue of a Yearly Plan Certificate. The maximum guaranteed rate of interest is earned if the certificate is held for a full four years. Applications may be made by any individuals aged 7 or over; in the name of children under 7; and by not more than two trustees for a sole beneficiary.

Payments must be made on the same date every month by standing order from a bank or other acceptable account. Only one payment may be made in any one month and must be in multiples of £5. Minimum monthly contribution is £20, maximum £200. Net investment in National Savings Yearly Plan was £49,500,000 at June 30th 1985.

On receipt of an application the applicant is sent an Offer Letter telling him the interest rates he will receive on his agreement if he accepts. The Certificate is sent at the end of the first year. It shows the total value of the payments made and the value of the Certificate if held for four years. The Certificate earns interest compounded annually on the anniversaries of the Certificate Date. Maximum interest is earned if the Certificate is held for the full four years. At the end of each year, providing at least seven payments have been made during that year, the applicant is given the option to take up a subsequent agreement, leading to the issue of a further Certificate.

NATIONAL SAVINGS CERTIFICATES

The amount, including accrued interest, index-linked increase or bonus remaining to the credit of investors in National Savings Certificates on March 31, 1985 was approximately £16,508·2m. In 1984–85, approx. £2,244·3m was subscribed and £1,304m (excluding interest, index-linked increase or bonus) was repaid. Interest, index-linked increase, bonus or other sum payable is free of United Kingdom income tax (including investment income surcharge) and capital gains tax. The 1st–11th issues continue to attract interest.

Issue and Maximum Holding (in units)	Unit Cost £	Value after		Interest Per Unit
		Years	£ p	
Decimal (1970–74) ... (1,500)	1	9	1·74½	During 9th year, 4p per completed 4 months.
		10	1·90	During 10th year, 5p per completed 4 months plus ½p bonus at end of 10th year.
		11	2·08½	During 11th year, 6p per completed 4 months plus ½p bonus at end of 11th year.
		12	2·26½	During 12th year, 6p per completed 4 months.†
Fourteenth .... June 17, 1974 to Dec. 11, 1976 and April 1, 1977–Jan. 27, 1979 (3,000)	1	5	1·43	During 5th year, 3p per completed 4 months.
		6	1·55	During 6th year, 4p per completed 4 months.
		7	1·70½	During 7th year, 5p per completed 4 months plus ½p bonus at end of 7th year.
		8	1·85	During 8th year, 4½p per completed 4 months plus 1p bonus at end of 8th year.†
Index-Linked Retirement Issue (June 2, 1975–Nov. 15, 1980) (120)	10			Unlike conventional issues where interest is accrued periodically the repayment value of Index-Linked Certificates, subject to their being held a year, is related to the movement of the United Kingdom General Index of Retail Prices.** N.B. Certificates of the Retirement Issue were on sale only to men aged 65 years and over and women aged 60 years and over, but may now be transferred to anyone.
Sixteenth .... (Dec. 13, 1976 to Mar. 31, 1977) (300)	5	6	8·51½	After 1st year, 20p is added, during 2nd year, 10p per completed 4 months, during 3rd year, 20p per completed 4 months, during 4th year, 20p per completed 4 months plus 30p bonus at year end, during 5th year, 24p per completed 4 months, during 6th year, 26½p per completed 4 months.†
Eighteenth .... (Jan. 29, 1979–Feb. 2, 1980) (150)	10	5	15·00	After 1 year, 50p is added, during 2nd year, 25p per completed 4 months, during 3rd year, 33p per completed 4 months, during 4th year, 42p per completed 4 months, during 5th year, 50p per completed 4 months.†
Nineteenth .... (Feb. 4, 1980–May 9, 1981) (500)	10	5	16·35	After 1 year 50p is added, during 2nd year 30p per completed 4 months, during 3rd year 35p per completed 4 months, during 4th year 55p per completed 4 months and during 5th year 75p per completed 4 months.†*
2nd Index-Linked Issue (Nov. 17, 1980–June 26, 1985) (1,000)	10			Like Retirement Issue, the repayment value of 2nd Index-Linked Issue Certificates, subject to their being held a year, is related to the movement of the United Kingdom General Index of Retail Prices.** N.B. Certificates of the 2nd Index-Linked Issue were made available to anyone, regardless of age, from September 7, 1981.
Twenty-First .... Issue (May 11, 1981–Nov. 7, 1981) (500)	10	5	15·40	After 1 year, 75p is added, during 2nd year, 28p per completed 4 months, during 3rd year, 33p per completed 4 months, during 4th year 40p per completed 4 months and during 5th year 54p per completed 4 months.*
Twenty-Third ...... (Nov. 9, 1981–March 10, 1982) (200)	25	5	41·20	After 1 year, £2·25 is added, during 2nd year, 87p per completed 4 months, during 3rd year, £1·02 per completed 4 months, during 4th year, £1·23 per completed 4 months and during 5th year £1·53 per completed 4 months.*
Twenty-Fourth ..... (April 19, 1982–Nov. 4, 1982) (200)	25	5	38·32	After 1 year, £1·80 is added, during 2nd year, 53p per completed 3 months, during 3rd year, 63p per completed 3 months, during 4th year, 77p per completed 3 months and during 5th year 95p per completed 3 months.*
Twenty-Fifth .... (Nov. 17, 1982–Aug. 13, 1983) (200)	25	5	35·90	After 1 year, £1·50 is added, during 2nd year, 43p per completed 3 months, during 3rd year, 51p per completed 3 months, during 4th year, 62p per completed 3 months and during 5th year 79p per completed 3 months.*

Issue and Maximum Holding (in units)	Unit Cost £	Value after		Interest Per Unit
		Years	£ p	
Twenty-Sixth .... (Aug. 15, 1983–Mar. 19, 1984) (200)	25	5	37·17	After 1 year, £1·53 is added, during 2nd year, 47p per completed 3 months, during 3rd year, 58p per completed 3 months, during 4th year, 72p per completed 3 months and during 5th year 89p per completed 3 months.*
Twenty-Seventh .... (April 5, 1984–Aug. 7, 1984) (200)	25	5	35·48	After 1 year, £1·32 is added, during 2nd year, 41p per completed 3 months, during 3rd year, 50p per completed 3 months, during 4th year, 62p per completed 3 months and during 5th year 76p per completed 3 months.*
Twenty-Eighth ..... (Aug. 8, 1984–Sept. 11, 1984) (200)	25	5	38·74	After 1 year, £1·63 is added, during 2nd year, 51p per completed 3 months, during 3rd year, 64p per completed 3 months, during 4th year, 80p per completed 3 months and during 5th year £1·01 per completed 3 months.*
Twenty-Ninth ...... (Oct. 15, 1984–Feb. 12, 1985) (200)	25	5	36·74	After 1 year, £1·50 is added, during 2nd year, 46p per completed 3 months, during 3rd year, 56p per completed 3 months, during 4th year, 69p per completed 3 months and during 5th year 85p per completed 3 months.*
Thirtieth .... (Feb. 13, 1985–Sept. 9, 1985) (200)	25	5	38·21	After 1 year, £1·69 is added, during 2nd year, 50p per completed 3 months, during 3rd year, 62p per completed 3 months, during 4th year, 78p per completed 3 months and during 5th year 98p per completed 3 months.*
3rd Index-Linked.... Issue (July 1, 1985–) (200)	25			Like 2nd Issue Index-Linked Certificates, the repayment value of 3rd Issue Index-Linked Certificates, subject to their being held for one year, is related to the movement of the United Kingdom General Index of Retail Prices.** In addition, there is guaranteed extra interest of 2·5 per cent for the 1st year, 2·75 per cent for the 2nd year, 3·25 per cent for the 3rd year, 4·0 per cent for the 4th year and 5·2 per cent for the 5th year. This interest is worth 3·54 per cent compound over a full five years.
Thirty-First .... (Sept. 26, 1985–) (200)	25	5	36·48	After 1 year, £1·44 is added, during 2nd year, 44p per completed 3 months, during 3rd year, 55p per completed 3 months, during 4th year, 68p per completed 3 months and during 5th year, 84p per completed 3 months.*

* As announced by the Treasury.

† From June 1982, savings certificates of the 7th to 14th, 16th, 18th and 19th Issues will be extended on common interest terms as they reach the end of their existing extension periods. The percentage interest rate is determined by the Treasury and any change in this common interest rate will be applicable from the 1st of the month following its announcement.

Under the new system, a certificate earns interest for each complete period of three months beyond the expiry of the previous extension terms. Within each three month period interest is calculated separately for each month at the rate applicable from the beginning of that month. The interest for each month is 1/12 of the annual rate (*i.e.* it does not vary with the number of days in the month) and is capitalised annually on the anniversary of the date of purchase. The current rate of interest under the common extension terms is displayed on special posters at most post offices.

** Index-linked certificates are eligible for an annual supplement of 3 per cent for the year to November 1, 1986. There have been three previous annual supplements of 2·4 per cent for 1982–83 and 1983–84 and 3 per cent for 1984–85. Certificates bought after October 31, 1985, kept for a full year, earn 0·25 per cent of the purchase price for each whole calendar month up to the end of October 1986. At the 5th anniversary there is a bonus of 4 per cent of the purchase price and at the 10th anniversary there is a second bonus of 4 per cent of the full 5th anniversary value. All supplements and bonuses are fully index-linked once earned.

LEGAL NOTES

IMPORTANT

The Purpose of these notes is to outline some of the more common parts of the law as they may affect the average person, and they are, of course, believed to be correct at the time of going to press. The law is constantly developing and changing, however, and it is dangerous for the layman to seek to be his own lawyer—he may not have access to completely up to date books and his case may, because of its special facts, come within an exception to the general rules set out herein.

It is always best to take expert advice, and if you have a Solicitor who has acted for you in the past you should take any legal problems you have to him. If you do not have a Solicitor a friend may be able to recommend one. Failing this your local Citizens' Advice Bureau (whose address can be obtained from the Telephone Directory or from any Post Office or Town Hall) has a list of Solicitors in your area who deal with that particular type of problem which you have. If you are not able to find a Solicitor in any of these ways you should ask for help in doing so from The Law Society, 113 Chancery Lane, London, W.C.2 or The Law Society of Scotland at 26 Drumsheugh Gardens, Edinburgh.

The Legal Aid and Legal Advice and Assistance schemes exist to make the help of the trained lawyer available to everyone whatever their means as of right. The best policy is if in doubt go to a Solicitor without delay—timely advice will set your mind at rest but sitting on your rights can mean that you lose them.

Remember also that it is not necessary for a dispute to have arisen before you go to a Solicitor—the Legal Advice and Assistance Scheme enables him to advise you on your rights say under a tenancy agreement, the estate of a deceased person or in connection with matrimonial and consumer matters, and to write letters or take other steps on your behalf. He can also act for you where there is no question of a dispute at all, e.g. in the making of a will.

Your entitlement to take advantage of the Scheme depends on your means (see below) but a Solicitor or Citizens' Advice Bureau will be able to tell you whether you are covered by it.

BRITISH CITIZENSHIP

Types of citizenship.—There are three types of citizenship known as "British Citizenship", "Citizenship of the British Dependent Territories", and "British Overseas Citizenship".

Acquisition of citizenship on change of law.—The British Nationality Act 1981 which came into force on 1st January 1983 made substantial changes to the law of citizenship (which before that date did not distinguish between the three types of citizenship referred to above). Almost all persons who were then both citizens of the U.K. and Colonies *and* who had a right of abode in the U.K. became British Citizens when the Act came into force. Most U.K. and Colonies Citizens who did not have a right of abode in the U.K. became Citizens of the British Dependent Territories. This type of citizenship was, broadly speaking, conferred on citizens of the U.K. and Colonies by birth naturalization or registration in dependent territories. Dependent territories include Hong Kong, Gibraltar, the Falkland Islands, St Christopher and Nevis and St Helena and its dependencies. Any U.K. and Colonies Citizen who, on 1st Jan. 1983, did not acquire either British or British Dependent Territories' Citizenship became a British Overseas Citizen.

Later acquisition of British Citizenship.—British Citizenship is acquired automatically by those born in the U.K. (including, for this purpose, the Channel Islands and the Isle of Man) who have a parent who is a British Citizen or a parent who is settled in the U.K. Certain other categories of children born in the U.K. also acquire this type of citizenship i.e. foundlings, those whose parents subsequently settle in the U.K., those who live in the U.K. for 10 years from birth and those adopted in the U.K.

A person born outside the U.K. may acquire British Citizenship in the following ways:—

(i) if one of his parents is a British Citizen otherwise than by descent (e.g. parent was born in the U.K.).

(ii) if one of his parents is a British Citizen serving the Crown overseas.

(iii) if the Secretary of State consents to his registration while he is a minor.

(iv) if he is a Citizen of the British Dependent Territories, a British Overseas Citizen, a British Subject or a British Protected Person (these last two are residual categories of people who have not acquired one of the 3 new types of citizenship) and has been lawfully resident in the U.K. for 5 years without any time restriction.

(v) if he is a British Dependent Territories Citizen who is a national of the U.K. for the purposes of the E.E.C. (i.e. a Gibraltarian).

(vi) if he is naturalized. Naturalization may be applied for only by adults and the Secretary of State has a discretion whether to permit it. The basic requirements are five years' residence, good character, sufficient knowledge of the English or Welsh language, and an intention to reside in the U.K. permanently. The requirements are somewhat less restrictive in the case of an applicant who is married to a British Citizen.

(vii) various rights to Citizenship given under the old law are perserved for a period of five years in respect of Commonwealth Citizens settled in the U.K. before 1973, wives of Citizens of the U.K. and Colonies, persons descended from U.K. Citizens and persons who have previously renounced citizenship.

Acquisition of British Dependent Territories and British Overseas Citizenship after the Act.—These citizenships are intended for persons connected with certain Commonwealth countries other than the U.K. In the case of Dependent Territories the rules are very similar to those for acquiring British Citizenship except that the connection is with the Dependent Territory rather than with the U.K. British Overseas Citizenship may be acquired by the minor children and wives of British Overseas Citizens in certain circumstances.

Retention of nationality by persons born in or who are citizens of the Republic of Ireland.—By the Ireland Act 1949, a person who was born before December 6th, 1922, in what is now the Republic of Ireland (Eire) and was a British subject immediately before January 1st, 1949, is not deemed to have ceased to be a British subject unless either (i) he was domiciled in the Irish Free State on December 6th, 1922 or (ii) was on or after April 10th, 1935, and before January 1st, 1949, permanently resident there, or (iii) had before January 1st, 1949, been registered as a citizen of Eire under the laws of that country.

In addition by the British Nationality Act 1948, any citizen of Eire who immediately before January 1st, 1949, was also a British subject can retain that status by submitting at any time a claim to the Home Secretary on any of the following grounds:

(a) he has been in the service of the United Kingdom Government;

(b) he holds a British passport issued in the United Kingdom or in any colony, protectorate, United Kingdom mandated or trust territory;

(c) he has associations by way of descent, residence or otherwise with any such place; or on complying with similar legislation in any of the "Dominions".

The British Nationality Act 1981 provides that persons who have made a claim may continue to be British subjects. Any citizen of Eire who was a British subject before January 1st, 1949, who has not yet made a claim may do so provided:

(a) that he is or has been in Crown Service under the government of the United Kingdom; or

(b) he has associations by way of descent, residence or otherwise with the United Kingdom or any dependent territory.

Renunciation and Resumption.—A person may cease to be a British Citizen by renouncing his citizenship (with the consent of the Secretary of State in wartime). The renunciation will be required to be registered with the Secretary of State and will be revoked if no new citizenship or nationality is acquired within six months. Once renounced, citizenship may be reacquired if the renunciation was necessary to retain or acquire some other citizenship or nationality. Similar rules as to renunciation and reacquisition apply in the case of British Dependent Territories Citizenships and of renunciation (but not reacquisition) in the case of British Overseas Citizenship.

Status of Aliens.—Property may be held by an alien in the same manner as by a natural-born British subject, but he may not hold public office, exercise the franchise or own a British ship or aircraft. The Republic of Ireland Act 1949 declares that the Republic, though not part of H.M. Dominions, is not a foreign country, and any reference in an Act of Parliament to foreigners, aliens, foreign countries, etc., shall be construed accordingly.

CONSUMER LAW

1. THE SUPPLY OF GOODS AND SERVICES

(a) The Sale of Goods Act 1979 provides protection to the purchaser of goods, by implying certain terms into every contract for the Sale of Goods. These implied terms are:

(i) A condition that the seller will pass good title to the buyer (unless the seller agrees to transfer only such title as he or his principal has) and warranties that the goods will be free from undisclosed encumbrances, and that the buyer will enjoy quiet possession of the goods.

(ii) Where there is a sale of goods by description, a condition that the goods will correspond with that description, and where the sale is by sample and description, a condition that the bulk of the goods shall correspond with both sample and description.

(iii) Where the seller sells goods in the course of a business, a condition that the goods will be of merchantable quality, unless before the contract is made, the buyer has examined the goods and ought to have noticed the defect, bearing in mind the purchaser's knowledge of the goods and the extent of the examination, or the seller has specifically drawn the attention of the buyer to the defect. Merchantable quality means fit for the purpose for which goods of the kind are commonly bought, taking into account any description applied to them, the price and other relevant circumstances.

(iv) A condition that where the seller sells goods in the course of a business, the goods are reasonably fit for any purpose made known to the seller by the buyer, unless the buyer does not rely on the seller's skill and judgment, or it would be unreasonable for him to do so.

(v) Where there is a sale of goods by sample, conditions that the bulk of the goods shall correspond with the sample in quality, that the buyer will have a reasonable opportunity of comparing the bulk with the sample, and that the goods are free from any defect rendering them unmerchantable, which would not be apparent from the sample.

For these purposes, the broad difference between a condition and a warranty is that the remedy for a breach of an implied condition may enable the buyer to reject the goods and recover damages if he has suffered loss whereas the remedy for a breach of warranty will only enable the buyer to recover damages.

It is possible for a seller to exclude some of the above terms from a contract, subject to restrictions imposed by the Unfair Contract Terms Act 1977 as given below. These restrictions give more protection ... where the buyer "deals as consumer". In a contract of sale of goods, a buyer "deals as consumer" where there is . . . a sale by a seller in the course of a business, the goods are of a type ordinarily bought for private use or consumption, and are sold to a person who does not buy or hold himself out as buying them in the course of a business. A buyer in a sale by auction or competitive tender never "deals as consumer".

The 1977 Act prohibits the exclusion of the implied terms given in (ii) to (v) above, where the buyer "deals as consumer". In sales where the buyer does not "deal as consumer", terms purporting to exclude these implied terms, may be relied upon only to the extent that it would be reasonable to allow reliance. The Act provides guidelines for determining whether it would be reasonable to allow reliance. The implied terms in (i) above cannot be excluded whether the buyer "deals as consumer" or not.

(b) Similar terms to those implied in contracts of sale of goods are implied into contracts of hire-purchase by the Supply of Goods (Implied Terms) Act, 1973 and the 1977 Act limits the exclusion of these implied terms in a similar manner.

(c) Under the Supply of Goods and Services Act 1982, terms similar to those in the Sale of Goods Act relating to quiet possession, compliance with description, merchantable quality, fitness for purpose and correspondence with sample are implied into other types of contract under which ownership of goods passes (e.g. a contract for "work and materials" such as a supply of new parts during the servicing of a motor car) and also into contracts for the hire of goods. In the case of contracts under which ownership of goods is to pass, there is also an implied condition as to title.

The 1977 Act limits the exclusion of these implied terms in a similar manner to the implied terms in the Sale of Goods Act.

(d) The Supply of Goods and Services Act 1982 also implies into a contract for the supply of services, terms that the supplier will use reasonable care and skill, carry out the service within a reasonable time (unless the time is agreed) and charge a reasonable charge (unless the charge is agreed).

(e) The Trade Descriptions Act 1968 provides that it is a criminal offence for a trader or business-man to apply a false trade description to any goods, or to supply or offer to supply any goods to which a false trade description has been applied. A trade description includes a description as to quantity, size, method, place and date of manufacture, other history, composition, other physical characteristics, fitness for purpose, behaviour or accuracy, testing or approval. It is also an offence to give a false indication as to the price of goods. Prosecutions are brought by Inspectors of Weights and Measures.

(f) The Fair Trading Act 1973 is also designed to protect the consumer. It provides for the appointment of a Director General of Fair Trading, whose duties include keeping under review commercial activities in the U.K. relating to the supply of goods or services to consumers, and to collect information to discover practices that may adversely affect the economic interests of the consumer. He may refer certain consumer trade practices to the Consumer Protection Advisory Committee, or, of his own initiative take proceedings against firms that are trading unfairly. He may also publish information and advice to consumers. Examples of practices which have been prohibited by virtue of references made under this Act, include the use of certain void exclusion clauses in contracts for the sale of goods and hire-purchase, and advertisements by traders appearing to sell as private persons.

Scotland

The Sale of Goods Act, 1979, a consolidating Act, applies with some modification to Scotland. For example, it is not necessary in Scotland to distinguish between the words condition and warranty. The remedies of the buyer in both cases are the same, that is, he can either within a reasonable time reject the goods and treat the contract as repudiated, or retain the goods and treat the failure to perform such material part as a breach which may give rise to a claim for compensation or damages.

2. CONSUMER CREDIT

England and Wales

The Consumer Credit Act 1974 is now fully in force. It provides a new system for the protection of the consumer, of licensing and control of all matters relating to the provision of credit, or the supply of goods on hire or hire-purchase, administered by the Director-General of Fair Trading. The Act takes the place of previous Acts of Parliament relating to moneylenders, pawnbrokers and hire-purchase traders. A licence is required to carry on a consumer credit or consumer hire business, or to deal in credit brokerage, debt adjusting, counselling or collecting, for which group licences are available. Any "fit person" may apply to the Director of Fair Trading for a licence which is normally renewable after 10 years. A licence is not necessary if such types of business are only transacted "occasionally" or if exempt agreements only are involved.

For the Act's provisions to apply the agreement must be "regulated", *i.e.* be to individuals or partnerships only; must not be exempt, *e.g.* certain loans by local authorities or building societies; and the total credit must not exceed £15,000. The terms of a regulated agreement can be varied by the creditor, but only if the agreement gives him the right to do so, and the debtor receives notice in the prescribed form.

To be enforceable the agreement must be properly executed, and the specified information must be given during the antecedent negotiations for the contract. These are conducted by the creditor, credit broker or supplier (these being the creditor's agents) and begin when the parties first begin discussions.

The agreement must state certain information such as the amount of credit, the annual percentage rate of interest and the amount and timing of repayments.

An agreement is cancellable under the Act if oral representations were made in the debtor's presence during antecedent negotiations and the debtor signed the agreement other than at the creditor's (or credit-broker's or negotiator's) place of business. Time for cancellation expires five clear days after the debtor receives a second copy of the agreement. The agreement must inform the debtor of his right to cancel and how to cancel.

Where there are arrangements or connections between the creditor and supplier the former is generally liable for any misrepresentation or breach of contract by the latter, and will thus be liable to indemnify the debtor.

If the debtor is in arrears or is otherwise in breach of the agreement, the creditor may not enforce the agreement, e.g. by repossessing goods, without serving a default notice on the debtor. This notice will give the debtor a chance to remedy the default. Even if the default is not remedied by the debtor, if the agreement is a hire-purchase or conditional sale agreement, the creditor cannot repossess the goods without an order of the court, if the debtor has paid one-third of the total price of the goods.

Where the agreement requires the debtor to make grossly exorbitant payments or is contrary to the ordinary principles of fair dealing the Court can reopen it either at the debtor's request or during enforcement proceedings and (*inter alia*) alter the terms of the contract or set aside any obligations it imposes so as to do justice between the parties. Whether an agreement is such an extortionate credit bargain is decided by reference (*inter alia*) to interest rates prevailing at the date of agreement, the pressure for finance the debtor was under, etc.

If a credit reference agency was used to check the debtor's financial standing the creditor must give the agency's name to the debtor who is entitled to see the agency's file on him on payment of a fee of 25 pence.

Scotland

The Hire Purchase (Scotland) Act 1965 provides a Scots code corresponding to, but not identical with English law. The Supply of Goods (Implied Terms) Act 1973 also applies to Scotland. Parts II and III only of the Unfair Contract Terms Act 1977 apply to Scotland.

The Sale of Goods Act, 1979, applies with some modification to Scotland. The Consumer Credit Act (see above) also extends to Scotland, and goes far in assimilating the Scots law on this topic with English law.

3. RECEIPTS

The law on receipts in Scotland is governed by the Prescription and Limitations (Scotland) Act 1973, which for this purpose came into force on July 25, 1976. Now, receipts need only be kept for a period of five years and if a creditor does not make a relevant claim within that period no action can be raised.

CROWN—PROCEEDINGS AGAINST

Before 1947 proceedings against the Crown were generally possible only by a procedure known as a petition of right, which placed the litigant at a considerable disadvantage and which was not normally available at all in cases of tort (i.e., civil wrongs other than breach of contract). Thus, no proceedings would normally lie against the Government if a subject were injured by the negligent driving of a Government vehicle (although the driver could be sued) or if a Government employee were injured by the defective condition of the Crown premises on which he worked. Now however, by the Crown Proceedings Act 1947, which came into operation on Jan. 1, 1948, the Crown, in its public capacity, is largely placed in the same position as a subject, although some procedural disadvantages remain. Exceptions to the Act include the immunity of the Crown and any member of the armed forces when on duty from liability in tort in respect of death of, or personal injury to, another member of the armed forces on duty (or even if not on duty, on any land, ship or vehicle being used for the purposes of the Armed Forces of the Crown), provided that the death or injury is certified as attributable to service for purposes of pension.

Scotland.—The Act extends to Scotland and has the effect of bringing the practice of the two countries as closely together as the different legal systems will permit. While formerly actions against the Crown, when permissible, were confined to the Court of Session, proceedings may now be brought in the Sheriff Court.

The Act lays down that arrestment of money in the hands of the Crown or of a Government Department is competent in any case where arrestment in the hands of a subject would have been competent, but an exception is made in respect of National Savings Bank deposits. Section 2 (1) of the Law Reform (Miscellaneous Provisions) (Scotland) Act 1966 removes the privilege whereby the wages of Crown servants, other than serving members of the armed forces, are exempt from arrestment in execution.

DEATHS

REGISTRATION, BURIAL AND CREMATION

REGISTRATION
(For Certificates, *see* under FAMILY LAW–CERTIFICATES)

In England and Wales.—When a death takes place, personal information of it must be given to the local Registrar of Births and Deaths, and the register signed in his presence, by one of the following persons: (1) A relative of the deceased present at the death, or in attendance during the last illness. If they fail (2) some other relative of the deceased. In default of any relatives (3) a person present at the death; or, the occupier of the house in which the death happened. If all the above-named fail (4) an inmate of the house. A person (other than a relative) registering the death must be causing the disposal of the body. Relatives present or in attendance are first required to attend to the registration. The registration must be made within five days of the death, or within the same time written notice of the death sent to the Registrar. If the deceased was attended during his last illness by a registered medical practitioner, a

certificate of cause of death must be sent by the doctor to the Registrar. The doctor must give to the informant of the death a written notice of the signing of the certificate, which must be delivered to the Registrar. It is essential that a certificate for disposal should be obtained from the Registrar before the funeral and delivered to the clergyman or other person in charge of the churchyard or cemetery. No fee is chargeable for this certificate. If the death is not registered within five days (or fourteen days if written notice of the occurrence of the death is sent to him) the Registrar may require any one of the above-mentioned persons to attend to register at a stated time and place. Failure to comply involves a penalty of ten pounds. The registration of a death is free of charge. After twelve months no death can be registered without the Registrar General's consent.

Whenever the death of a child is registered, particulars of the name and occupation of the mother are to be entered in the register.

A body must not be disposed of until (1) either the Registrar has given a certificate to the effect that he has registered or received notice of the death, or (2) until the Coroner has made a disposal order (*Births and Deaths Registration Act* 1926, s. 1).

A person disposing of a body must within ninety-six hours deliver to the Registrar a notification as to the date, place, and means of the disposal of the body (*ib.*, S. 3).

"Still-born" child (*see* under Births (Registration) *below*).

Death at Sea.—The master of a British ship must record any death on board and send particulars to the Registrar General of Shipping.

Death Abroad.—Consular Officers are authorized to register deaths of British subjects occurring abroad. Certificates are procurable at the Registrar General's Office, London. If the deceased was of *Scottish* domicile, particulars are sent to the Registrar General for Scotland.

With regard to the registration of deaths of members of the armed forces, and deaths occurring on H.M. ships and aircraft, *see* the Registration of Births, etc. Act 1957.

Deaths (Registration) in Scotland.—The Registration of Births, Deaths and Marriages (Scotland) Act 1965 supersedes provisions in former Acts.

Personal notification within 8 days must be given to the registrar of (*a*) the registration district in which the death took place or (*b*) any registration district in which the deceased was ordinarily resident immediately before his death, and (*c*) when a body is found and the place of death is not known, either the registration district in which the body was found or any other registration district appropriate by virtue of the preceding paragraph. When a person dies (in or out of Scotland) in a ship, aircraft or land vehicle during a journey and the body is conveyed therein to any place in Scotland the death shall, unless the Registrar General otherwise directs, be deemed to have occurred at that place.

The register must be signed in the presence of the registrar by one of the following: (*a*) any relative of the deceased; (*b*) any person present at the death; (*c*) the deceased's executor or other legal representative; (*d*) the occupier, at the time of the death, of the premises where the death took place; (*e*) if these fail, any other person having knowledge of the particulars to be registered. Failure to comply involves a penalty not exceeding £50.

The medical practitioner who attended the deceased during the last illness must sign a certificate of the cause of death within 7 days. If there is no such medical practitioner, any medical practitioner who is able to do so, may sign the certificate. At the time of registering the death the registrar shall, without charge, give the informant a certificate of registration, and the person to whom the certificate is given must hand it to the undertaker previous to cremation. A body may, however, be interred before the death is registered, in which case the undertaker must deliver a certificate of burial to the Registrar within three days.

There is, available from the Department of Health and Social Security, a death grant. Provided the deceased had paid enough Class I contributions and, if male, was not born before July 5, 1883 and if female, was not born before July 5, 1888, then the grant will be paid to his or her personal representatives. It normally amounts to £30 and is meant to help to pay for the deceased's funeral.

BURIAL

The duty of burial is incumbent on the deceased person's executors (if any appointed); it is also a recognized obligation of the husband of a woman, and the parent of a child, also of a householder where the body lies. Funeral expenses of a reasonable amount will be repayable out of deceased's estate in priority to any other claims. Directions as to place and mode of burial are frequently contained in the deceased's will or in some memorandum placed with private papers, or may have been communicated verbally to a relative. Consequently steps should immediately be taken to ascertain the deceased's wishes from the above sources. If the wishes are considered objectionable, they are not necessarily enforceable; legal advice should be taken. A person may legally leave directions for the anatomical examination of his body. As to the place of burial—unless closed by Order in Council—the parish churchyard is the normal burying place for parishioners, or any person dying in the Parish, but nowadays this will apply only in villages and the smaller towns. In populous districts cemeteries and crematoria have been established either by the local council, or a private company, and burials will take place there in accordance with the regulations. For an exclusive right to a burial space in the churchyard a faculty is required from the Ecclesiastical Court. Poor persons may be buried at the public expense by the local authority. As to the necessity for obtaining a registrar's certificate or authority from the Coroner for disposal, *see* above.

CREMATION

Under the Cremation Acts, 1902 and 1952, regulations are made by the Home Secretary dealing fully with the cremation of a body, disposal of ashes, etc., and containing numerous essential safeguards.

If Cremation is desired it is advisable for instructions to be left in writing to that effect. However, in Scotland, even if the deceased wished his body to be cremated or anatomically dissected, relatives can still veto his or her wishes.

To arrange for Cremation the Executor or near relative should instruct the undertaker to that effect and obtain from him the Statutory Forms required as given in the Cremation Regulations issued in 1930 (Statutory Rules and Orders, 1930, No. 1016), as amended by the Cremation Regulations 1965 (No. 1146) and the Cremation (Amendment) Regulations 1985 (No. 153).

INTESTACY

ENGLAND AND WALES

As regards deaths on or after March 15, 1977, the position is governed by the Administration of Estates Act, 1925, as amended by the Intestates' Estates Act, 1952, the Family Provision Act, 1966 and Orders made thereunder. The S.I. 1981/255 increased the benefits of a surviving spouse of an intestate. These notes deal with the present position, so that if the death occurred before March 1, 1981 reference must be made elsewhere. If the intestate leaves a spouse and issue, the spouse takes (i) the "personal chattels"; (ii) £40,000 with interest at 6 per cent. from death until payment; and (iii) a life interest in half of the rest of the estate. This life interest can be capitalized at the option of the spouse. "Personal chattels" are articles of household use or ornament (including motor-cars), not used for business purposes. The rest of the estate goes to the issue. If the intestate leaves a spouse and no issue, but leaves a parent or brother or sister of the whole blood or issue of such brothers and sisters the spouse takes (i) the "personal chattels"; (ii) £85,000 with interest at 6 per cent. from death until payment, and (iii) half of the rest of the estate absolutely. The other half of the rest of the estate goes to the parents, equally if more than one, or, if none, to the brothers and sisters of the whole blood or issue of such brothers and sisters. If the intestate leaves a spouse, but no issue, no parents and no brothers or sisters of the whole blood or their issue, the spouse takes the whole estate absolutely. If resident therein at the intestate's death, the surviving spouse may generally require the personal representatives to appropriate the interest of the intestate in the matrimonial home in or towards satisfaction of any absolute interest of the spouse, including the capitalized value of a life interest. In certain cases, leave of Court is required. On a partial intestacy any benefit (other than personal chattels specifically bequeathed) received by the surviving spouse under the will must be brought into account against the statutory legacy of £40,000 or £85,000, as the case may be. If there is no surviving spouse, the estate is distributed among those who survive the intestate in the following order (those entitled under earlier numbers taking to the exclusion of those entitled under later numbers):—(1) children; (2) father or mother (equally, if both alive); (3) brothers and sisters of the whole blood; (4) brothers and sisters of the half blood; (5) grandparents (equally, if more than one alive); (6) uncles and aunts of the whole blood; (7) uncles and aunts of the half blood; (8) the Crown.

In cases (1), (3), (4), (6) and (7) the persons entitled lose their interests unless they or their issue not only survive the intestate, but also attain eighteen and marry under that age, their shares going to the persons (if any) within the same group who do attain eighteen or marry. Moreover, in the same cases, succession is not *per capita*, but *per stirpes, i.e.*, by stocks or families. Thus, if the intestate leaves one child and two grandchildren, being the children of a child of the intestate, who pre-deceased the intestate, the two grandchildren represent their deceased parent and take between them one-half of the issue's share, the remaining half going to the surviving child. Similarly, nephews and nieces represent a deceased brother, and so on.

When the deceased died partially intestate (*i.e.*, leaving a will which disposed of only part of his property), the above rules apply to the intestate part.

Children must bring into account (hotchpot) any substantial advances received from the intestate during his lifetime before claiming any further share under the intestacy. Special hotchpot provisions apply to partial intestacy.

By the Family Law Reform Act, 1969, the position of an illegitimate child is equated with that of a legitimate child in respect of all deaths occurring on or after January 1, 1970. In respect of deaths after

March 1976 the provisions of the Inheritance (Provision for Family and Dependants) Act 1975 may allow other persons to claim provision out of the estate. See *post* under "Wills".

For personal application for Letters of Administration—*see below*.

SCOTLAND

The Succession (Scotland) Act, 1964, provides that the whole estate of any person dying intestate shall devolve without distinction between heritable and moveable property. By that Act the surviving spouse of an intestate may, as a prior right (in addition to legal rights, *see* below), claim the matrimonial home to a maximum of £50,000, or a choice of one matrimonial home if more than one (or in certain circumstances the value thereof), with its furniture and plenishings not exceeding £10,000 in value, plus the sum of £15,000 if the deceased left issue or, if no issue, the sum of £25,000. These figures apply from 1st August 1981 and may be increased from time to time by order of the Secretary of State.

The Act has been modified by the Law Reform (Miscellaneous Provisions) (Scotland) Act, 1968, which provided that an illegitimate child had exactly the same rights of succession in the estate of his parents as a legitimate child. However, the position still remains that an illegitimate child has no succession rights in the estate of a grandparent even though such would have fallen to his predeceasing parent.

Legal rights, referred to above, are:—

Jus relicti (*æ*): the right of a surviving spouse to one half of the deceased's net moveable estate after satisfaction of prior rights if there are no surviving children, or to one third if there are any surviving children.

Legitim: right of surviving children to one-half of the net moveable estate of deceased parents if no surviving spouse, or one-third of the net moveable estate of deceased parents after satisfaction of prior rights where there is a surviving spouse.

There are no legal rights in heritage.

In general, the lines of succession are: (1) descendants; (2) collaterals; (3) ascendants and their collaterals, and so on in the ascending scale. The Crown is ultimus haeres. The right of representation, *i.e.*, the right of the issue of a person, who would have succeeded if he had survived the intestate, is open to any line of succession where previously it was limited to apply only when there were next of kin or the issue of predeceasing next of kin. The surviving mother of an intestate now has equal rights of succession with the surviving father, where formerly these were restricted. The intestate's maternal relations, who prior to the Act had no rights of succession, are now on an equal footing with his paternal relations. Where the intestate is survived only by parents, and by brothers and sisters (collaterals) half of the estate is taken by the parents and the other half by the brothers and sisters, those of the whole blood being preferred to those of the half blood; where, however, succession opens to collaterals—(which expression can include the brothers and sisters of an ancestor of the intestate)—of the half blood, they shall rank equally amongst themselves, whether related to the intestate (or his ancestor) through their father or their mother.

WILLS

IMPORTANT NOTE.—The following notes and those on Intestacy must be read subject to the provisions of the Inheritance (Provision for Family and Dependants) Act 1975 which can affect the estate of anyone dying domiciled in England and Wales after March 1976. Very broadly a spouse, former spouse who has not remarried, a child of the deceased himself or one treated by him as a child of his family, or any person maintained by him at his death may apply to the Court under the Act. If the Court thinks that the will or the law of intestacy or both do not make reasonable provision for the applicant it may order payment out of the net estate of maintenance or a lump sum. It may also order the transfer of property, vary certain trusts and the powers can affect property disposed of by the deceased in his lifetime intending to defeat the Act. It is up to the applicant to take the initiative, and the application must generally be made within six months of the grant of Probate or Letters of Administration.

In respect of earlier deaths, earlier Acts apply with a narrower class of applicants and less ample powers for the Court.

REASONS FOR MAKING A WILL.—Every person over the age of 18 should make a will. However small the estate the rules of Intestacy (see above) may not reflect a person's wishes as to his property; in any case a will can do more than just deal with property—it can in particular appoint executors, give directions as to the disposal of the body and appoint guardians to take care of children in the event of the parents' death. For the wealthier person an appropriately drawn will can operate to reduce the burden of Capital Transfer Tax.

It is considered desirable for a will to be properly drawn up by a Solicitor, and the making of a will is one of the services which he can provide under the Legal Advice and Assistance Scheme (see above).

In no circumstances should one person prepare a Will for another person where the former is to take any benefit under it—this can easily lead to a suggestion of undue influence which may cause the will to be held bad.

Assuming a lawyer is not employed, a person having resolved to make a will must remember that it is only after a person is dead, and cannot explain his meaning, that his will can be open to dispute. It is the more necessary, therefore, to express what is meant in language of the utmost clearness, avoiding the use of any word or expression that admits of another meaning than the one intended. Avoid the use of "legal terms," such as "heirs" and "issue," when the same thing may be expressed in plain language. If in writing the will a mistake be made, it is better to rewrite the whole. Before a will is executed (*see below*) an alteration *may* be made by striking through the words with a pen, but opposite to such alteration the testator and witnesses should write their names or place their initials. Never scratch out a word with a knife or other instrument, and no alteration *of any kind whatever* must be made after the will is executed. If the testator afterwards wishes to change the disposition of his estate, it is best to make a new will, revoking the old one. The use of *codicils* should be left to the lawyer. *A will should be written in ink and very legibly, on a single sheet of paper.* Although, of course, forms of wills must vary to suit different cases, the following forms may be found useful to those who, in cases of emergency, are called upon to draw up wills, either for themselves or others.

Nothing more complicated should be attempted. The forms should be studied in conjunction with the notes following.

This is the last will and testament of me [*Thomas Smith*] of [*Vine Cottage, Silver Street, Reading, Berks*] which I make this [*thirteenth*] day of [*February, 1986*] and whereby I revoke all previous wills and testamentary dispositions.

1. I hereby appoint [*John Green of —— and Richard Brown of ——*] to be the executor(s) of this my will.

2. I give all my property real and personal to [*my wife Mary* or *my sons Raymond and David equally* or as the case may be].

Signed by the testator in the presence of us both present at the same time who, at his request, in his presence and in the presence of each other have hereunto set our names as witnesses.

Thomas Smith
Signature of Testator;

William Jones (*signed*) of Green Gables, South Street, Reading, tailor.

Henry Morgan (*signed*) of 16, North Street, Reading, butcher.

Should it be desired to give legacies and/or gifts of specific property, instead of giving the whole estate to one or more persons, the form above should be used with the substitution for clause 2 of the following clauses:—

2. I give to —— of —— the sum of £—— and to —— of —— the sum of £—— and to —— of —— all my books (*or as the case may require*).

3. All the residue of my property real and personal I give to —— of ——.

TERMS.—Real property includes freehold land and houses; while personal property includes debts due, arrears of rents, money, leasehold property, house furniture, goods, assurance policies, stocks and shares in companies, and the like. The words "my money," apart from the context, will normally only include actual real money. The expression "goods and chattels" should not be used. In giving *particular* property, ordinary language is sufficient, *e.g.*, "my house, Vine Cottage, Silver Street, Reading, Berks." Such specific gifts fail if not owned by the testator at his death.

RESIDUARY LEGATEES.—It is well in all cases where legacies or specific gifts are made, to leave to some person or persons "the residue of my property," although it may be thought that the whole of the property has been disposed of in legacies, etc., already mentioned in the will. *It should be remembered that a will operates on property owned at the time it is made or acquired after it has been made.*

EXECUTION OF A WILL, AND WITNESSES.—The testator should sign his name at the foot or end of the will, in the presence of two witnesses, who will immediately afterwards sign their names in his and in each other's presence. A person who has been left any gift or share of residue in the will, or whose wife or husband has been left such a gift, should not be an attesting witness. Their attestation would be good, but they would forfeit the gift. It is better that a person named as executor should not be a witness. Husband and wife may both be witnesses, provided neither is a legatee. If a solicitor be appointed executor, it is lawful to direct that his ordinary fees and charges shall be paid; but in this case he (as an interested party) must not be a witness to the will.

It is desirable that the witnesses should be fully described, as they may possibly be wanted at some future time. If the testator should be too ill to sign, even by a mark, another person may sign the testator's name to the will for him, in his presence and by his direction, and in this case it should be shown that the testator knew the contents of the document. The attestation clause should therefore be worded: "Signed by Thomas Brown, by the direction and in the presence of the testator, Thomas Smith, in the joint presence of us, who thereupon signed our names in his presence and in the presence of each other, the will having been first read over to the testator, who appeared fully to understand the same."

Where there is any suspicion that the Testator is not, by reason of age or infirmity, fully in command of his faculties it is desirable to ask his Doctor to act as a witness (see Testamentary capacity below).

A *blind person* may make a will in Braille. If the testator be blind the will should be read aloud to him in the presence of the witnesses, and the fact mentioned in the attestation clause. A blind person cannot witness a will.

If by inadvertence the testator should have signed his will without the witnesses being present, then the attestation should be:—"The testator acknowledged his signature already made as his signature to his last will and testament, in the joint presence," etc. Any omission in the observance of these details may invalidate the will. *The stringency of the law as to signature and witnessing of a will is only relaxed in favour of soldiers, sailors and airmen in certain circumstances.*

EXECUTORS.—It is usual to appoint two executors, although one is sufficient; any number up to and including four may be appointed. The name and address of each executor should be given in full. An executor may be a legatee. Thus a child of full age or wife to whom the whole or a portion of the estate is left may be appointed sole executor, or one or two executors. The addresses of the executors are not essential; but it is desirable here as elsewhere, to avoid ambiguity or vagueness.

LAPSED LEGACIES.—If a legatee dies in the lifetime of the testator, the legacy generally lapses and falls into the residue. Where a residuary legatee predeceases the testator, his share of the residuary estate will not generally pass to the other residuary legatees, but will pass to the persons entitled on the deceased's intestacy. In all such cases it is desirable to make a new will.

An important exception to the general rule of lapse stated above is contained in the Administration of Justice Act 1982, where there is a gift to a child or remoter issue of the testator who dies before the testator leaving issue who survive the testator.

TESTAMENTARY CAPACITY.—A person under the age of 18 cannot make a will (except for soldiers, sailors and airmen and then only in exceptional circumstances).

So far as mental capacity is concerned the Testator must be able to understand and appreciate the nature and effect of making a will, the property of which he can dispose and the claims to which he ought to give effect. If a person is not mentally able to make a will provision exists (under the Mental Health Act, 1983) for the Court to do this for him.

REVOCATION.—A later will revokes an earlier will if it expressly says so, or is completely inconsistent with it. Otherwise the earlier one is only revoked insofar as it is inconsistent with the later one. A will may also be revoked by burning, tearing or otherwise *destroying* the will with the intention of revoking it. Such destruction must either be by the testator or by some other person in his presence and at his direction. *It is not sufficient to obliterate the will with a pen.* Marriage in every case acts as the revocation of a will, except that under the Administration of Justice Act 1982, there is a provision to the effect that if it appears from a will that at the time it was made the testator was expecting to be married to a particular person and that he intended that the will (or a disposition in the will) should not be revoked by the marriage to that person, the will will not be revoked by marriage to that person. The Act also provides that where after a testator has made a will the testator's marriage is terminated by a decree of divorce or nullity, any gift to a spouse shall lapse and any appointment of the spouse as executor shall be omitted from the will unless the will shows a contrary intention.

Personal Application for Probate or Letters of Administration

Application for probate or for letters of administration may be made *in person* at the Personal Application Dept. of the Principal Registry of the Family Division, a district probate registry or sub-registry, or a probate office by the executors or persons entitled to a grant of administration. Applicants should bring (1) the will, if any; (2) a certificate of death; (3) particulars of all property and assets left by the deceased; and (4) a list of debts and funeral expenses.

Intending applicants, before attending at a registry or probate office, should write or telephone to the nearest probate registry or sub-registry for the necessary forms. Postal or telephone applications cannot be dealt with at the local probate offices, which are part-time only.

Certain property can be disposed of on death without a grant of probate or administration, or in pursuance of a nomination made by the deceased, provided the amount involved does not exceed £5,000. *See* the Administration of Estates (Small Payments) Act, 1965.

Where to Find a Proved Will

A will proved since 1858 must have been proved either at the Principal Registry at Somerset House, or a District Registry. In the former case the original will itself is carefully preserved at Somerset House, the copy of which probate has been granted is in the hands of the executors who proved the will, and another copy for Parliament is bound up in a folio volume of wills made by testators of that initial and date; the indices to these volumes fill a room of considerable size at Somerset House, where the indices may be examined and a copy of any will read. In the latter case, the original will proved in the District Registry, is kept there, and may be seen or a *copy* obtained, but a copy is sent to and filed at Somerset House, where also it may be seen. A general index of grants, both probates and administrations, is prepared and printed annually in lexicographical form, and may be seen at either the Principal or a District Registry. This index is usually ready by about October of the following year.

RECENT DEATHS.—A system introduced in 1975 enables a person to discover when a grant of Probate or Letters of Administration is made which may be invaluable to a creditor of the deceased or applicant under the Inheritance (Provision for Family and Dependants) Act 1975—*see above*. A "standing search" may be made by sending a request in the form set out below to the Record Keeper at the Principal Registry of the Family Division with a small fee. The searcher will receive particulars of any grant made in the previous 12 months or the following 6 months, including names and addresses of the executors or administrators and the Registry in which the grant was made.

Form of Search

In the High Court of Justice
Family Division
The Principal Registry (Probate)
I/We apply for the entry of a standing search so that there shall be sent to me/us an office copy of every grant of representation in England & Wales in the estate of:—
Full name of deceased:
Alternative or alias name
Full address
Exact date of death

Which either has issued not more than 12 months before the entry of this application or issues within 6 months hereafter
Sgd.—(full address).

SCOTS LAW OF WILLS

A domiciled Scotsman, unlike a domiciled Englishman, cannot in certain circumstances dispose effectively of the entirety of his estate. If he leave a widow and children, the widow is entitled to a one-third share in the whole of the moveable estate (her *jus relictae*), and the children are entitled to another one-third share equally between them (their *legitim*). If he leave a widow but no children—or children but no widow—the *jus relictae* or *legitim* is increased to a one-half share of the net moveable estate. The remaining portion is known as the *dead's part*. A surviving husband and children have comparable rights (*jus relicti* and *legitim*) in the wife's estate. The *dead's part* is the only portion of which the testator can freely dispose. Legacies and bequests are payable only out of the *dead's part*. All debts are payable out of the whole estate before any division. Pupils, *i.e.* a girl up to the age of twelve or a boy up to the age of fourteen, cannot make wills. Formerly a minor could dispose only of movables but since the passing of the Succession (Scotland) Act, 1964 he has a like capacity to test on heritable property. A will must be in writing and even in pencil. A will may be either (1) *holograph, i.e.* written, dated and subscribed by the testator himself, in which case no witnesses are necessary; a printed form filled up by the testator or a typewritten document is not necessarily a *holograph* but may become so if the testator writes, in hand, at the foot of the form or document the words "*adopted as holograph*" followed by his signature and the date. Words written on erasure or marginal additions or interlineations in *holograph* writings, if proved to be in the handwriting of the maker of the deed, are valid; (2) *attested,* i.e. signed in presence of two witnesses. It is not necessary that these witnesses should sign in presence of one another, or even that they should see the testator signing so long as the testator acknowledges his signature to the witnesses. The Conveyancing and Feudal Reform (Scotland) Act, 1970 whilst altering generally the rules for the subscription of deeds, specifically (s. 44 (2)) makes no change in the rules applying to wills which must still be signed by the testator on every page. If the testator cannot write, or is blind, his will may be authenticated by a law agent, notary public or justice of the peace and two witnesses. It is better that the will be not witnessed by a beneficiary thereunder, although this circumstance will not invalidate the attestation of the will or (as it would in England) the gift. A parish minister may act as a notary for the purpose of subscribing a will in his own parish. Wills may be registered in the Books of the Sheriffdom in which the deceased died domiciled, or in the Books of Council and Session, H.M. General Register House, Edinburgh. The original deed may be inspected on payment of a small fee and a certified official copy may be obtained. A Scottish will is not revoked by the subsequent marriage of the testator. The subsequent birth of a child, no testamentary provision having been made for him, may revoke a will. A will may be revoked by a subsequent will, either expressly or by implication; but in so far as the two can be read together both wills have effect. If a subsequent will is revoked, the earlier will is revived.

"Confirmation", the Scottish equivalent of Probate, is obtained in the Sheriff Court of the Sheriffdom in which the deceased was domiciled at the date of his death or, where he had no fixed domicile or died abroad, in the commissariot of Edinburgh. Executors are either "nominate" or "dative". An Executor nominate is one nominated by the deceased in his will or, where such person has predeceased the testator, by the residuary beneficiary. An Executor dative is one appointed by the Court in the case of intestacy or where the deceased had failed to name an executor in his will and there is no residuary beneficiary. In the former case the deceased's next-of-kin are all entitled to be declared executors dative. An inventory of the deceased's estate and a schedule of debts, together with an affidavit, must first be given up. In estates under £13,000 gross, confirmation is obtained under a simplified procedure at reduced fees.

Presumption of Survivorship.—The Succession (Scotland) Act, 1964, referred to above provides, by s. 31, that where two persons die in circumstances indicating that they died simultaneously or if it is uncertain which was the survivor, the younger will be deemed to have survived the elder unless the elder person left testamentary provision in favour of the younger, whom failing in favour of a third person, the younger person having died intestate (partially or wholly); but if the persons so dying were husband and wife, neither shall be presumed to have survived the other.

EMPLOYMENT
WAGES AND HOLIDAYS

Under the Truck Acts, it is in general forbidden for an employer to pay wages other than in current coin of the realm, and it is illegal for an employer to deduct from the employee's wages sums alleged to be due to the employer. However, the application of these Acts is confined to manual workers, and domestic servants are specifically excluded from their operation. Even in the case of payments to workmen, certain deductions, including rent and the price of food to be consumed on the employers' premises, are not forbidden where the employee's written consent is obtained. Further, under the Payment of Wages Act, 1960, it is permissible for wages to be paid otherwise than in cash at the request of the employee, *e.g.*, by cheque, money order, postal order or into a banking account.

Under the Social Security and Housing Benefits Act 1982, an employee absent from work due to illness or injury is entitled to receive Statutory Sick Pay from the employer for a maximum of eight weeks in any year. No payment is made for the first three days of any period of illness. The employer can recoup the payments from his National Insurance contributions.

The Equal Pay Act 1970, which extends to Scotland, and which came into force on December 29, 1975, prevents discrimination, as regards terms and conditions of employment between men and women employed on like work in the same employment.

PARTICULARS OF TERMS OF EMPLOYMENT

Under the Employment Protection (Consolidation) Act 1978, an employer must give each full-time employee within 13 weeks of the beginning of the employment a written statement containing the following particulars of the contract between them:

(1) the date when the employment began (when continuous employment began if previous work counts as continuous with this job);
(2) the rate of remuneration (or how it is calculated);
(3) the intervals at which wages are paid;
(4) the hours of work;
(5) the employee's entitlement to holidays (including public holidays) and holiday pay;
(6) the title of the employee's job;
(7) terms relating to sickness, injury and sick pay;
(8) details of any pension scheme;
(9) the length of notice which the employee should give and receive in order to terminate the contract.

In addition, the written particulars must specify any disciplinary rules; and also must identify the person to whom the employee can apply if he is dissatisfied with any disciplinary decision or to seek redress of any grievance and what further steps may ensue.

TERMINATION OF EMPLOYMENT

An employee may be dismissed without notice if he is guilty of gross breach of contract, such as disobedience to a lawful order or dishonesty. He is then only entitled to wages accrued due at the date of dismissal.

In other cases, the employee is entitled to reasonable notice which, under the Employment Protection (Consolidation) Act 1978, must not be less than one week if he has been continuously employed for four weeks, but less than two years; after two years it is two weeks' notice increasing by one week's notice for each further full year worked up to a maximum of 12 weeks' notice after 12 years' service.

An employer who wrongfully dismisses an employee (i.e. with less than the length of notice to which he is entitled) is generally liable to pay wages for the period of proper notice.

An employee who has a fixed term contract has no claim against his employer for wrongful dismissal if his contract is not renewed when it expires. He may, however, have a claim for a redundancy payment or compensation for unfair dismissal. If he is wrongfully dismissed before his contract expires, he is generally entitled to remuneration payable over the full period of the contract.

An employee may be entitled to a redundancy payment or to compensation for unfair dismissal if the employment has been terminated by the employer (with or without proper notice) or he has a fixed term contract which expires without being renewed or the employment has been terminated by the employee by reason of the employer's breach of contract.

Under the Employment Protection (Consolidation) Act 1978, an employee who satisfies the foregoing conditions and has been continuously employed for two years and who is dismissed by reason of redundancy may be entitled to a redundancy payment calculated by reference to his age, pay and length of service.

The Employment Protection (Consolidation) Act 1978 also enables an employee who is unfairly dismissed to complain to an Industrial Tribunal (generally within 3 months of dismissal). The onus will then be on the employer to prove that the dismissal was due to capability, conduct, redundancy, illegality or some other substantial reason justifying dismissal. The tribunal must then decide whether the employer acted reasonably in dismissing the employee. If the employer fails to prove that the dismissal was due to one or more of the above five reasons, or the tribunal decides that the employer did not act reasonably in dismissing the employee, the dismissal will be unfair, in which case the tribunal can

   (a) order re-engagement or reinstatement or
   (b) award compensation consisting of a basic and a compensatory award.

For an employee to bring himself within the unfair dismissal provisions, he must have been continuously employed for a period not less than one year (2 years if the employer has not more than 20 employees) unless his employment commenced on or after 1st June 1985, in which case the period is 2 years, regardless of the number of employees.

All complaints of unfair dismissal are referred to a conciliation officer or the Department of Employment and a very high proportion of complaints are disposed of in this way.

FAMILY LAW
ADOPTION OF CHILDREN

In England and Wales this is now mainly governed by the Children Act 1975 and the Adoption Act 1976 though these are not yet fully in force. A court order is necessary to legalise the adoption, which, when completed, has the effect of making the adopted child the child of the adopter as if he or she had been born to the adopter in lawful wedlock, and the original rights and duties of the natural parents are thereby cut. The adopter has full rights as to custody, education etc. and the child is treated as his for the purpose of any devolution of property on an intestacy occurring or under any disposition made after the adoption order. The application may be made to the High Court (Family Division) or to a County Court or Magistrates' Court.

Orders may be made in favour of married couples, single, widowed or divorced persons, but not of one party to a marriage alone unless the other spouse cannot be found, is physically or mentally incapable of making an application, or they are separated in circumstances likely to be permanent. A person aged under 21 cannot adopt.

The child's parents or guardians must consent unconditionally to the making of the order unless the court dispenses with the consent, which it may do if the parent cannot be found or is incapable of giving his consent, is withholding his consent unreasonably, or has neglected or ill-treated the child.

Restrictions are placed on societies which may arrange adoptions.

An adopted person aged over 18 may apply to the Registrar General for information to enable him to obtain a full certificate of his birth, but before being supplied with the information he will be informed that counselling services are available to him.

An adopter and the adopted child are within the prohibited degrees for the purposes of marriage to one another.

All Adoptions in Great Britain are registered in the Registers of Adopted Children kept by the Registrars General in London and Edinburgh respectively. Certificates from these registers including short certificates which contain no reference to adoptions, can be obtained on conditions similar to those relating to birth certificates, (See below.)

Scotland.—The Adoption Act 1958 and the Children Act 1975 are the main statutes governing adoption in Scotland. The Law is consolidated in the Adoption (Scotland) Act 1978 which is now fully in force. The Law relating to fostering is consolidated in the Foster Children(s) Act 1984. A petition for adoption is presented either to the Sheriff Court or the Court of Session. As in England the petitioner(s) must be 21 or over and may be a married couple or one person who, if married, is living apart permanently from his or her spouse. The consent of the child's natural parents/guardians is required unless dispensed with, or the child is already free for adoption.

The Succession (Scotland) Act 1964, gives the adopted child the same rights of succession as a child born to the adopter in wedlock but deprives him of any such rights in the estates of his natural parents. The law is consolidated in the Adoption (Scotland) Act 1978 which is not yet in force.

BIRTHS (REGISTRATION)

When a birth takes place, personal information of it must be given to the Registrar of Births and Deaths for the sub-district in which the birth occurred, and the register signed in his presence, by one of the following persons:—

1. The father or mother of the child. If they fail; 2. the occupier of the house in which the birth happened; 3. a person present at the birth; or, 4. the person having charge of the child. The duty of attending to the registration therefore rests firstly on the parents. The mother is responsible for the registration of the birth of an illegitimate child. The registration is required to be made within 42 days of the birth. Failure to do this, without reasonable cause, involves liability to a penalty of twenty pounds. The registration of a birth is free. In England or Wales, the informant, instead of attending before the registrar of the sub-district where the birth occurred, may make a declaration of the particulars required to be registered in the presence of any registrar. Under the Public Health Act 1936, notice of every birth must be given by the father, or person in attendance on the mother, to the district medical officer of health by post within 36 hours of the birth. *This is in addition to the registration already mentioned.*

A "Stillbirth" must be registered and a certificate signed by the doctor or midwife who was present at the birth or has examined the body of the child must be produced to the registrar. The certificate must, where possible, state the cause of death and the estimated duration of the pregnancy. A stillbirth may only be registered within 3 months of the birth.

The re-registration of the birth of a person legitimated by the subsequent marriage of the parents is provided for in the Births and Deaths Registration Act 1953. When the Children Act 1975 takes effect special provisions will apply to the registration and re-registration of births of abandoned children, and the re-registration of births of illegitimate children showing the father's name; the mother must be party to the latter application and if the child is under 16 must show the father's formal admission or a court's finding of paternity.

Birth at Sea: The master of a British ship must record any birth on board and send particulars to the Registrar General of Shipping.

Birth Abroad: Consular Officers are authorized to register births of British subjects occurring abroad. Certificates are procurable in due course at Registrar General's Office, London.

The registration of births occurring out of the United Kingdom among members of the armed forces, or occurring on board H.M. ships and aircraft, is provided for by the Registration of Births, Deaths and Marriages (Special Provisions) Act 1957, applicable also to Scotland.

SCOTLAND

The Registration of Births, Deaths and Marriages (Scotland) Act 1965, supersedes former Acts. Personal notification within 21 days of any birth, must be given to the registrar of (a) the registration district in which the birth took place, or (b) any registration district in which the mother of the child was ordinarily resident at the time of the birth and (c) in the case of a foundling child, dead or alive, when the place of birth is not known, the registration district in which the child, or the body, was found, within two months from the date on which the child was found. When a child is born (in or out of Scotland) in a ship, aircraft or land vehicle during a journey and the child is conveyed therein to any place in Scotland, the birth shall, unless the Registrar General otherwise directs, be deemed to have occurred at that place.

The register must be signed in the presence of the registrar by the father or mother of the child, and if they fail, by one of the following: (a) any relative of either parent who has knowledge of the birth; (b) the occupier of the premises in which the child was, to the knowledge of that occupier, born; (c) any person present at the birth; (d) any person having charge of the child. Failure without reasonable cause involves a penalty not exceeding £50.

The name of the father of an illegitimate child may be entered in the register of births at the time of registration if jointly requested by the mother and father, and the latter's name may also be recorded at a later date on declaration by both parents. A free abbreviated certificate of birth will be issued to the informant at the time of registration. Provision is made for the re-registration of the birth of a person made legitimate by the subsequent marriage of the parents or whose birth entry is affected by any matter respecting status or paternity, or has been so made as to imply that he is a foundling.

A still-birth must be registered and a certificate, signed by the doctor or certified midwife present at the birth or who has examined the body of the child, must be produced.

CERTIFICATES OF BIRTHS, MARRIAGES, OR DEATHS

England and Wales.—Certificates of Births, Deaths, or Marriages can be obtained at the Office of Population Censuses and Surveys, St. Catherine's House, 10, Kingsway, W.C.2 or from the Superintendent Registrar having the legal custody of the register containing the entry of which a certificate is required. Certificates of marriage can also be obtained from the incumbent of the church in which the marriage took place; or from the Nonconformist minister (or other "authorized person") where the marriage takes place in a registered building (*see, post,* under Marriage).

It is considered desirable when a certificate is required to consult the nearest Register Office who, if told the exact or approximate date and place of registration, will be able to advise on the best way of obtaining it, and any fees payable, which vary according to the type of certificate required and other factors.

English Registers.—Records of births, deaths and marriages registered in England and Wales since 1837 are kept at the Office of Population Censuses and Surveys, St. Catherine's House, 10, Kingsway, W.C.2. *The Society of Genealogists,* 37 Harrington Gardens, S.W.7, possess many records of Baptisms, Marriages and Deaths prior to 1837, including copies, in whole or in part of about 4,000 Parish Registers.

Scottish Registers of Births, Deaths, Marriages and Divorces.—Certificates of births, deaths or marriages registered from 1855 when compulsory registration commenced in Scotland can be obtained personally at the General Register Office, New Register House, Edinburgh, or from the appropriate local Registrar, on payment of the fee of £5·00 for a full extract entry of birth, death, or marriage, and £2·50 for an abbreviated certificate of birth. An abbreviated certificate of registration of deaths is issued free of charge for National Insurance purposes in certain cases. As from May 1, 1984 a central register of divorces was set up to accommodate the new divorce procedure in the Sheriff Courts. The fee for an extract decree of divorce is £5.

There are also available at the General Register Office old parish registers of the date prior to 1855, which were formerly kept under the administration of the Established Church of Scotland. An extract of an entry in these registers may be obtained on payment of the appropriate fee. A fee of £7·50 per day is payable for a general search of all the Scottish registers.

Registration of Presumed Deaths. (Prescription of Particulars) (Scotland) Regulations 1978 as read with Presumption of Death (Scotland) Act 1977 prescribe the particulars to be notified by the Clerk of Court to the Registrar General after a decree or variation order has been granted in an action of declarator of death of a missing person.

DIVORCE, SEPARATION AND ANCILLARY MATTERS

Preliminary—Matrimonial Suits may be conveniently divided into two classes, viz. (1) those in which it is sought to annul the marriage because of some defect; and (2) those in which, the marriage being admitted, it is sought to end the marriage or the duties arising from it. By virtue of the Matrimonial Causes Act 1967, all matrimonial causes are now commenced in one of the divorce county courts designated by the Lord Chancellor or in the Divorce Registry in London. If the suit becomes defended, it must be transferred to the High Court.

(1) *Nullity of Marriage.*—This is now mainly governed as to England and Wales by the Matrimonial Causes Act 1973. A marriage is void *ab initio* if the parties were within the prohibited degrees of affinity, or were not male and female, or if it was bigamous or if one of the parties was under the age of consent, i.e. 16, or in the case of a polygamous marriage entered into outside England and Wales, that either party was at the time of the marriage domiciled in England and Wales. Where the *formalities* of the marriage were defective, the marriage is generally void if *both* parties knew of the defect (*e.g.,* where marriage took place otherwise than in an authorized building). But absence of the consent of parents or guardians (or of the Court or other authority, in lieu thereof) in the case of minors does not invalidate the marriage.

A marriage is voidable (i.e. a decree of nullity may be obtained but until such time the marriage remains valid) on the following grounds—(a) incapacity of either party to consummate; (b) respondent's wilful refusal to consummate; (c) that either party did not validly consent to the marriage, whether in consequence of duress, mistake, unsoundness of mind or otherwise, (d) that either party at the time of marriage was a mentally disordered person; (e) that at the time of marriage the respondent was suffering from communicable venereal disease; (f) that at the time of the marriage the respondent was pregnant by another man. In cases (e) and (f) the petitioner must have been ignorant of the grounds at the date of the marriage and in (c), (d), (e) and (f) proceedings must be instituted within 3 years of the marriage. In all cases the court shall not grant a decree where the petitioner has led the respondent to believe that he would not seek a decree and it would be unjust for it to be granted.

The 1973 Act provides that a decree of nullity in a voidable marriage only annuls the marriage from the date of the decree. The marriage remains valid until the decree, and any children of the marriage are legitimate. Children of a void marriage are illegitimate unless the father was domiciled in England and Wales at the child's birth (or father's death, if earlier) and at the time of conception (or marriage if later) both or either of the parents reasonably believed the marriage was valid.

A spouse's insistence upon the use of contraceptives will not constitute wilful refusal to consummate within (b) above, even though there has been no normal intercourse, but it may in certain circumstances constitute unreasonable behaviour for the purpose of divorce (as to which *see* below). Further it has been allowed as a *defence* to a charge of desertion against the aggrieved party.

(2) *Judicial Separation and Divorce.*—The second class of suit includes a suit for judicial separation (which does not dissolve a marriage) and a suit for divorce (which, if successful, dissolves the marriage altogether and leaves the parties at liberty to marry again). Either spouse may petition for judicial separation. It is not necessary to prove that the marriage has broken down irretrievably and the five facts listed (a) to (e) under divorce (below) are grounds for judicial separation.

Divorce.—The sole ground on which a divorce is obtained by either husband or wife is the irretrievable breakdown of the marriage. However, the court is precluded from holding that a marriage has irretrievably broken down unless it is satisfied of one or more of the following facts: (a) that the respondent has committed adultery since the marriage and the petitioner finds it intolerable to live with the respondent; (b) such behaviour by the respondent that the petitioner cannot reasonably be expected to continue co-habitation; (c) desertion by the respondent for 2 years immediately before the petition; (d) 5 years separation immediately before the petition (but only 2 years where the respondent consents to the decree). Matrimonial Causes Act 1973.

The foregoing is subject to a clause prohibiting any petition for divorce (but not for judicial separation) before the lapse of three years from the date of marriage, except in the case of exceptional hardship (upon petitioner) or of exceptional depravity of respondent (either party will be entitled to petition after one year when the Matrimonial and Family Proceedings Bill comes into force).

Desertion may be defined as a voluntary withdrawal from cohabitation by one spouse without just cause and against the wishes of the other. Where one spouse is guilty of conduct of a serious nature which forces the other to leave, the party at fault is said to be guilty of constructive desertion.

Provisions designed to encourage reconciliation.—The 1973 Act requires the solicitor for the petitioner to certify whether he has or has not discussed the possibility of a reconciliation and whether or not he has given the petitioner the names and addresses of persons qualified to help effect a reconciliation.

A total period of less than six months during which the parties have resumed living together is to be disregarded in determining whether the prescribed period of desertion or separation has been continuous. Similar provision for effecting a reconciliation exists in relation to the other proofs of break-down, but a petitioner cannot claim that it is intolerable to live with the other party if they have lived together for more than six months after discovery of the respondent's adultery.

Obtaining the Decree Nisi. Where the suit is defended, *i.e.* the respondent opposes the dissolution or the fact/ground on which the petitioner seeks it—the petition will be heard by a Judge in open court, the parties giving oral evidence. Where the suit is undefended, the evidence will normally take the form of a sworn written statement made by the petitioner which will be sent to the Court and read over by the Registrar. If he is satisfied that he or she has proved the contents of the petition, he will simply fix a date for a Judge to pronounce the decree nisi, it being unnecessary for either party to attend. Only if the Registrar is not satisfied as above will he order that the petition be heard formally by the Judge.

Children.—Subject to exceptions, the decree nisi cannot be made absolute unless a Judge by order declares that he is satisfied with the proposed arrangements for the welfare of any child of the family who is under 16 or under 18 and receiving education or vocational training. If the petition is heard in open court the Judge will normally do so at that time. Otherwise if there is no dispute as to the children between the parties and the proposed arrangements for residence, education etc. are specific, an appointment will be made for the Judge to interview one or both parents informally and if satisfied he will make an order to that effect. If not the Registrar may inform the parties that it is up to them to seek a hearing before the Judge to resolve the matters in dispute.

Decree Absolute.—Every decree of divorce or nullity is in the first instance a decree nisi, and the marriage subsists until the decree is made absolute, usually six weeks after decree nisi on the petitioner's application. After the decree absolute either party is free to remarry.

Maintenance, etc.—The court has wide powers to order either party to the marriage to make financial provision (*e.g.* periodical payments, a lump sum, the transfer of property) for the other party or any child of the family, having regard to the party's means, the recipient's needs and all the important aspects of the case. These so-called 'ancillary matters' often present more difficulty than the divorce itself especially affecting the home, and may go on long after the marriage is dissolved. There is, however, nothing to stop financial matters being negotiated by the parties through their solicitors before the divorce goes through.

The court may, where the husband has wilfully neglected to provide reasonable maintenance for the wife or children, order the husband to make provision for them, *even though* no matrimonial suit is pending between the parties to the marriage, and while such an order is in force the court may also deal with custody and access to the children.

CUSTODY OF CHILDREN ETC.

The Court may make orders in respect of access to and the custody, maintenance and education of children in connection with a suit for divorce, nullity or judicial separation (above) or with an application to the Magistrates (below) whether the suit succeeds or not. In addition, if there is no other matrimonial suit involved a parent may apply for custody under the Guardianship of Minors Acts 1971, and any person may apply to the High Court for the child to be made a ward of court.

In all cases the welfare of the child is the first and paramount consideration. The categories of child who may be covered by any particular type of proceedings differ according to the nature of those proceedings and to the nature of the particular relief sought, but it should be borne in mind that in connection with divorce, nullity and judicial separation a child which has been *treated* by the spouses as a child of the family may be included as a 'child of the family' as well as the children of the spouses themselves. This also applies to most maintenance cases in the magistrate's court—*see below.*

When the Children Act 1975 comes into effect a new procedure called "Custodianship" will be introduced, basically allowing long term foster parents to apply for custody of the foster child.

Any dispute relating to the above matters should be placed in the hands of a Solicitor without delay (see Legal Aid, etc. below) and in particular it should be borne in mind that where there is financial need (because of, *e.g.* continuing education or disability) maintenance may be ordered for children even beyond the age of majority.

SEPARATION BY AGREEMENT

Husband and wife may enter into an agreement to separate and live apart, but the agreement, to be valid, must be followed by an immediate separation. It is most desirable to consult a solicitor in every such case, who will often advise obtaining a court order by consent to reduce the burden of tax.

MAGISTRATES' CUSTODY AND MAINTENANCE ORDERS

For many years the law relating to domestic proceedings in magistrates' courts was out of line with the divorce law which was reformed in 1969. The Domestic Proceedings and Magistrates' Courts Act 1978 took effect in early 1981 and now contains the relevant law.

A husband or wife can apply to a magistrates' court for a matrimonial order on the grounds that the other spouse (a) has failed to pay reasonable maintenance for the applicant or (b) has failed to make a proper contribution towards the reasonable maintenance of a child of the family or (c) has deserted the applicant or (d) has behaved in such a way that the applicant cannot reasonably be expected to live with the respondent. If the case is proved the court can order (a) periodical payments for the applicant (b) periodical payments for a child of the family (c) a lump sum (not exceeding £500) for the benefit of the applicant and for any child of the family. In deciding what orders (if any) to make the magistrates must consider a number of guidelines which are similar to those governing financial orders on divorce. There are also special provisions relating to consent orders and separation by agreement. The court also has powers to make orders relating to the legal custody of a child of the family and these orders together with orders for child maintenance can be made even though the court makes no order for spouse maintenance. Legal custody can only be granted to one person but the court may order that the other party shall retain certain parental rights and exercise them jointly with the person who is awarded legal custody. Other provisions of the Act relate to access by grandparents, interim orders, and variation, discharge and revival of orders. An order may be enforceable even though the parties are living together, but in some cases it will cease to have effect if they continue to do so for six months. The hearing of matrimonial disputes is separate from ordinary court business, and the public are not admitted.

DOMESTIC VIOLENCE

The Domestic Violence and Matrimonial Proceedings Act 1976, the Domestic Proceedings and Magistrates' Courts Act 1978 (the former not being applicable to Scotland and the latter only to a limited extent; but see note below) and the Matrimonial Homes Act 1983 have made it easier for one spouse who has been subjected to violence by the other to obtain an order to restrain further violence and if need be to have the other excluded from the home. Such orders can be obtained very quickly, and a person disobeying them is liable to be imprisoned for contempt of court. There are some differences of detail between the three Acts; in particular the 1976 Act also applies to unmarried couples. Such orders may also be obtained in the issue of suits for divorce and judicial separation.

SCOTLAND
Divorce

Actions of divorce could formerly only be raised in the Court of Session, having jurisdiction to entertain such actions only if either of the parties to the marriage in question (a) is domiciled in Scotland on the date when the action is begun; or (b) was habitually resident in Scotland throughout the period of one year ending with that date. As from May 1, 1984, however, when the Divorce Jurisdiction, Court Fees and Legal Aid (Scotland) Act 1983 came into force, actions of divorce may also be raised in the Sheriff Courts provided the above conditions (a) and (b) are complied with, and provided either party to the marriage was resident in the Sheriffdom for a period of forty days ending with the date the action was begun, or was resident in the Sheriffdom for a period of not less than forty days ending not more than forty days before the date the action was begun.

The Scots Law of Divorce is now governed by the Divorce (Scotland) Act 1976, which for the purposes of divorce came into force on January 1, 1977. The sole ground of divorce is now irretrievable breakdown of the marriage. This can only be established in one of the following ways:

(a) The defending spouse has committed adultery since the date of the marriage. Here it is not necessary for the pursuing spouse to prove that the fact of adultery made it intolerable to live with the defending spouse.

(b) The defending spouse has behaved in such a way that the pursuing spouse cannot reasonably be expected to cohabit with him or her. It is immaterial whether or not the conduct founded upon is active or passive.

(c) The defending spouse has deserted the pursuing spouse for a continuous period of two years. There must be no question of the pursuing spouse having refused a genuine and reasonable offer to adhere. Nor is irretrievable breakdown established if cohabitation is resumed for a period of more than three months, after the two year period has expired.

(d) There has been no cohabitation at any time during a continuous period of two years immediately preceding the action between the parties to the action, and the defending spouse consents to the divorce being granted.

(e) There has been no cohabitation at any time during a continuous period of five years, as in (d) *supra*, except that on the expiry of the five year period, the consent of the defending spouse is not required.

The facts of desertion and separation are not interrupted by the parties cohabiting for a period or periods not exceeding six months. However such a period or periods of cohabitation would not be included in the calculation of the two-year or five-year periods.

Encouragement of Reconciliation: The burden of promoting a reconciliation between spouses in a divorce action in Scotland falls upon the Court by virtue of the 1976 Act. Where an action of divorce has been raised, it may be postponed by the Court to enable the parties to seek to effect a reconciliation, if the Court feels that there may be a reasonable prospect of such reconciliation. If the parties do cohabit during such postponement, no account shall be taken of such cohabitation if the action later proceeds.

Maintenance, etc.: The 1976 Act also provides that either party to a marriage can apply to the Court at any time prior to decree being granted for (a) an order for interim aliment for him or herself and/or for children of the marriage under 16 years of age of whom he/she has custody (b) an order for interim custody of all or some of the children of the marriage under 16 years of age (c) an order for access to all or some of the children of the marriage under 16 years of age in the custody of the other party (d) an order for a capital sum or a variation of a marriage settlement. The Court in granting or refusing such an order, known as an *interim* award, takes into account the respective means of the parties, and also all the circumstances of the case.

Nullity of Marriage.—A declaration of nullity of marriage may be obtained on the ground of any impediment, viz., consanguinity and affinity, subsistence of a previous marriage, non-age of one of the parties, incapacity or insanity of one of the parties, or by the absence of genuine consent.

Procedure.—Appearance in Court at a Proof in an undefended Divorce Action has been rendered unnecessary since April, 1978. A full Proof is still necessary if the action is defended in any respect. In place of court appearance Affidavits (Statements sworn before a Notary Public) by the pursuer and any witnesses are lodged in the Court together with a Minute by Counsel craving Decree.

A new Simplified Procedure for "do-it-yourself divorce" was introduced in January 1983 for certain divorces. Thus, if the action is based on (d) or (e) above and will not be opposed, there are no children under 16 and no financial claims, then the applicant can write directly to the Court of Session, Divorce Section (SP), Parliament House, Edinburgh or the local Sheriff Court for the appropriate forms to enable him or her to proceed. The fee is £40 unless the applicant receives supplementary benefit, family income supplement or legal advice and assistance in which case there is no fee.

Separation

Under the Divorce (Scotland) Act 1976 *supra,* a decree of Judicial Separation can be obtained by proof of the same facts necessary to obtain decree of divorce—except that for the principle of irretrievable breakdown there is substituted that of grounds justifying separation. This type of action is competent in both the Court of Session and the Sheriff Court.

Custody of Children

In actions for divorce and separation, the Court has a discretion in awarding the custody of the children of the parties. The welfare of the children is the paramount consideration, and the mere fact that a spouse, by reason of his or her behaviour, brought about the breakdown of the marriage does not of itself preclude him or her from being awarded custody. The Children Act 1975 (*supra*) also applies to Scotland.

Domestic Violence

The Matrimonial Homes (Family Protection) (Scotland) Act 1981 introduces a provision where one spouse—whether or not he or she has title to the matrimonial home—can obtain an exclusion order suspending the other spouse's occupancy rights in the matrimonial home. The Court (either Court of Session or Sheriff Court) is empowered to make such an order if satisfied that it is necessary to protect the applicant or any child of the family from any conduct, actual or threatened or reasonably apprehended of the other spouse which would be injurious to the physical or mental health of the applicant or child. In making the order the Court may include a warrant for the summary ejection of the non-applicant spouse from the matrimonial home and for an interdict prohibiting him/her from entering it.

ILLEGITIMACY AND LEGITIMATION
ENGLAND AND WALES

A man may be summoned to petty sessions on the application of the mother of an illegitimate child, or by the Supplementary Benefits Commission where benefit has been paid for the requirements of the child, and the Justices, on his being proved to be the father of the child, may make an order requiring him to pay for its maintenance and education a sum in their discretion. The woman is not bound to give evidence in every case but if she does so it must be *corroborated* in some material particular. The mother has the custody of her illegitimate children. *Prima facie* every child born of a married woman during a marriage is legitimate; and this presumption can only be rebutted by strong evidence. However, under the Family Reform Act 1969, any presumption of law as to the legitimacy (or illegitimacy) of any person may in civil proceedings be rebutted by evidence showing that it is more probable than not that the person is illegitimate (or legitimate) and in any proceedings where paternity is in question, blood tests may be ordered. If however the husband and wife are separated under an Order of the Court, a child conceived by the wife during such separation is presumed not to be the husband's child.

LEGITIMATION.—The Legitimacy Act 1976 consolidates earlier legislation dating back to January 1, 1927. Where the parents of an illegitimate person marry, or have married, whether before or after that date, the marriage, if the father is at the date thereof domiciled in England or Wales, renders that person, if living, legitimate as from Jan. 1, 1927, or from the date of the marriage, whichever last happens. Marriage legitimates a person even though the father or mother was married to a third person at the time when the illegitimate person was born. It is the duty of the parents to supply to the Registrar-General information for re-registration of the birth of a legitimate child.

Declarations of Legitimacy.—A person claiming that he, his parents, or any remoter ancestor has become legitimated, may petition the High Court or the County Court for the necessary declaration.

Rights and Duties of Legitimated Persons.—A legitimated person, his spouse or issue may take property under an intestacy occurring after the date of legitimation, or under any disposition (*e.g.*, a will) coming into operation after such date, as if he had been legitimate.

He must maintain all persons whom he would be bound to maintain had he been born legitimate, and he is entitled to the benefit of any Act of Parliament which confers rights on legitimate persons to recover damages or compensation. The Act specially provides that nothing therein contained is to render any person capable of succeeding to or transmitting a right to any dignity or title.

Property Rights of Illegitimate Children.—By the Family Law Reform Act 1969 the rights of an illegitimate child on an intestacy are now broadly equated with those of a legitimate child. Also, in any disposition made after December 31, 1969, any reference to "children" or other relatives shall, unless the contrary intention appears, be construed as including any person who is illegitimate or who is related through another person who is illegitimate.

SCOTLAND

Illegitimate Children (Scotland) Act 1930.—The mother of an illegitimate child may raise an action of affiliation and aliment against the father, either in the Court of Session or, more usually, in the Sheriff Court. Where in any such action the Court finds that the defender is the father of the child, the Court shall, in awarding inlying expenses, or aliment, have regard to the means of the parties, and the whole circumstances of the case. The Court may, upon application by the mother or by the father of any illegitimate child, or in any action for aliment for an illegitimate child, make such order as it may think fit regarding the custody of such child and the right of access thereto of either parent, having regard to the welfare of the child and to the conduct of the parents and to the wishes as well of the mother as of the father and may on the application of either parent recall or vary such order. The obligation of the mother and of the father of an illegitimate child to provide aliment for such child shall (without prejudice to any obligation attaching at common law) endure until the child attains the age of sixteen.

By Scots Law an illegitimate child is legitimated by and on the date of the subsequent marriage of its parents and there is no objection to there having been an impediment to the marriage of the parents at the time of the child's conception—*see* the Legitimation (Scotland) Act 1968, which came into operation on June 8, 1968, on which date thousands of existing illegitimate children were regarded as legitimated. By the Registration of Births, Deaths and Marriages (Scotland) Act 1965, a child so legitimated, who has already been registered as illegitimate, may be re-registered as legitimate. The consent of the father of an illegitimate child to its adoption is not required.

The Law Reform (Miscellaneous Provisions) (Scotland) Act 1968, gives an illegitimate child full rights of succession (including legitim) in the estate of both parents, while the father and mother share equally in the estate of their illegitimate child. Unless expressly excluded, a reference in a deed executed on or after November 25, 1968, to a relationship, *e.g.*, "issue" or "children" is presumed to include illegitimate children.

MARRIAGE
A.—MARRIAGE ACCORDING TO RITES OF THE CHURCH OF ENGLAND

1. MARRIAGE BY BANNS.—The Marriage Act 1949, prescribes audible publication according to the rubric, on three Sundays preceding the ceremony during morning service or, if there is no morning service on a Sunday on which the banns are to be published, during evening service. Where the parties reside in different parishes, the banns must be published in both. Under the Act, banns may be published and the marriage solemnized in the parish church, *which is the usual place of worship* of the persons to be married or either of them, although neither of such persons dwells in such parish; but this publication of banns is *in addition* to any other publication required by law and does not apply if the church or the residence of either party is in Wales. The Act provides specially for the case where one of the parties resides in Scotland and the other in England, the publication being then in the parish in England in which one

party resides, and, according to the law and custom in Scotland, in the place where the other party resides. After the lapse of three months from the last time of publication, the banns become useless, and the parties must either obtain a licence (*see below*), or submit to the republication of banns.

2. MARRIAGE BY LICENCE.—Marriage licences are of two kinds:—

(i) *A Common Licence*, dispensing with the necessity for banns, granted by the Archbishops and Bishops through their Surrogates, for marriages in any church or chapel duly licensed for marriages. A Common Licence can be obtained in London by application at the Faculty Office (1 The Sanctuary, Westminster, S.W.1) and (for marriages in London) at the Bishop of London's Diocesan Registry (1 The Sanctuary, S.W.1), by one of the parties about to be married. In the country they may be obtained at the offices of the Bishop's Registrars, but licences obtained at the Bishop's Diocesan Registry only enable the parties to be married in the diocese in which they are issued; those procured at the Faculty Office are available for *all* England and Wales. No instructions, either verbal or in writing, can be received, except from one of the parties. Affidavits are prepared from the personal instructions of one of the parties about to be married, and the licence is delivered to the party upon payment of fees amounting to six pounds. *No previous notice is required and the licence is available as soon as it is issued.* Before a licence can be granted one of the parties must make an affidavit that there is no legal impediment to the intended marriage; and also that one of such parties has had his or her usual place of abode for the space of fifteen days immediately preceding the issuing of the licence within the parish or ecclesiastical district of the church in which the marriage is to be solemnized, *or* the church in which the marriage is to be solemnized is the usual place of worship of the parties or one of them. In the country there may generally be found a parochial clergyman (Surrogate) before whom the affidavit may be taken, and whose office it is to deliver the licence personally to the applicant. (In some dioceses it is necessary for the Surrogate to procure the licence from the Bishop's Registry.) The licence continues in force for three months from its date.

(ii) *A Special Licence* granted by the Archbishop of Canterbury, under special circumstances, for marriage at any place with or without previous residence in the district, or at any time, etc.; but the reasons assigned must meet with his Grace's approval. Application must be made to the Faculty Office. Fees for licence, etc., £25.

3. MARRIAGE UNDER SUPERINTENDENT REGISTRAR'S CERTIFICATE.—A marriage may be performed in church on the Superintendent Registrar's Certificate (as to which see below) without banns, provided that the incumbent's consent is obtained. One of the parties must be resident within the ecclesiastical parish of the church in which the marriage is to take place unless the church is the usual place of worship of the parties or one of them.

MARRIAGE FEES.—The Church Commissioners settle tables of fees for all parishes. The usual fees are paid although a stranger-clergyman may be invited to perform the service.

B.—MARRIAGE UNDER SUPERINTENDENT REGISTRAR'S CERTIFICATE

The following marriages may be solemnized on the authority of a Superintendent Registrar's Certificate (either with or without a licence):—

(a) A marriage in a registered building (*e.g.*, a nonconformist church registered for the solemnization of marriages therein).

(b) A marriage in a register office.

(c) A marriage according to the usages of the Society of Friends (commonly called Quakers).

(d) A marriage between two persons professing the Jewish religion according to the usages of the Jews.

(e) A marriage according to the rites of the Church of England (*see* above—in this case the marriage can only be *without* licence).

NOTICE.—Notice of the intended marriage must be given as follows:—

(i) Marriage by certificate (*without* licence)—if both parties reside in the same registration district, they must both have resided there for seven days before the notice can be given. It may then be given by either party. If the parties reside in different registration districts, notice must be given by each to the Superintendent Registrar of the district in which he or she resides, and the preliminary residential qualification of seven days must be fulfilled by each before either notice can be given.

(ii) Marriage by certificate (*with* licence)—one notice only is necessary, whether the parties live in the same or in different registration districts. Either party may give the notice, which must be given to the Superintendent Registrar of any registration district in which one of the parties has resided for the period of fifteen days immediately preceding the giving of notice, but both parties must be resident in England or Wales on the day notice is given.

The notice (in either case) must be in the prescribed form and must contain particulars as to names, marital status, occupation, residence, length of residence, and the building in which the marriage is to take place. The notice must also contain or have added at the foot thereof a solemn declaration that there is no legal impediment to the marriage, and, in the case of minors, that the consent of the person whose consent to the marriage is required by law (*see below*) has been duly given, and that the residential qualifications (mentioned above) have been complied with. A person making a false declaration renders himself or herself liable to prosecution for perjury. The notice is entered in the marriage notice book.

ISSUE OF CERTIFICATE:

(i) *Without licence.*—The notice (or an exact copy thereof) is affixed in some conspicuous place in the Superintendent Registrar's office for 21 days next after the notice was entered in the marriage notice book. After the lapse of this period the Superintendent Registrar may, provided no impediment is shown, issue his certificate for the marriage which can then take place at any time within three months from the date of the entry of the notice.

(ii) *With licence.*—The notice in this case is not affixed in the office of the Superintendent Registrar. After the lapse of one whole day (other than a Sunday, Christmas Day or Good Friday) from the date of entry of the notice, the Superintendent Registrar may, provided

no impediment is shown, issue his certificate and licence for the marriage, which can then take place on any day within three months from the date of entry of the notice.

SOLEMNIZATION OF THE MARRIAGE:

(i) *In a Registered Building.*—The marriage must generally take place at a building within the district of residence of one of the parties, but if the usual place of worship of either is outside the district of his or her residence, it may take place in such usual place of worship. Further, if there is not within the district of residence of one of the parties a registered building within which marriages are solemnized according to the rites and ceremonies which the parties desire to adopt in solemnizing their marriage, it may take place in an appropriate registered building in the nearest district.

The presence of a Registrar of Marriages is not necessary at marriages at registered buildings which have adopted the provisions of section 43 of the Marriage Act 1949. This section provides for the appointment of an "authorized person" (a person, usually the minister or an official of the building, certified by the trustees or governing body as having been duly authorized for the purpose) who must be present and must register the marriage.

The marriage must be solemnized between the hours of 8 a.m. and 6 p.m., with open doors in the presence of two or more witnesses. The parties must at some time during the ceremony make the following declaration—"I do solemnly declare that I know not of any lawful impediment why I, A. B., may not be joined in matrimony to C. D." Also each of the parties must say to the other: "I call upon these persons here present to witness that I, A. B., do take thee, C. D., to be my lawful wedded wife [or husband]," *or*, if the marriage is solemnized in the presence of an authorized person without the presence of a Registrar, each party may say in lieu thereof: "I, A. B., do take thee, C. D., to be my wedded wife [or husband]."

(ii) *In a Register Office.*—The marriage may be solemnized in the office of the Superintendent Registrar to whom notice of the marriage has been given. The marriage must be solemnized between the hours of 8 a.m. and 6 p.m., with open doors in the presence of the Superintendent Registrar or a Registrar of the registration district of that Superintendent Registrar, and in the presence of two witnesses. The parties must make the following declaration: "I do solemnly declare that I know not of any lawful impediment why I, A. B., may not be joined in matrimony to C. D.," and each party must say to the other: "I call upon these persons here present to witness that I, A. B., do take thee, C. D., to be my lawful wedded wife [or husband]." No religious ceremony may take place in the Register Office, though the parties may, on production of their marriage certificate, go through a subsequent religious ceremony in any church or persuasion of which they are members.

(iii) *Other Cases.*—If both parties are members of the Society of Friends (Quakers), or if, not being in membership, they have been authorized by the Society of Friends to solemnize their marriage in accordance with its usages, they may be married in a Friends' meetinghouse. The marriage must be registered by the registering officer of the Society appointed to act for the district in which the meeting house is situated. The presence of a Registrar of Marriages is not necessary.

If both parties are Jews they may marry according to their usages in a synagogue, which has a certified marriage secretary, or private dwelling-house at any hour; the building may be situated within or without the district of residence. The marriage must be registered by the secretary of the synagogue of which the man is a member. The presence of a Registrar of Marriages is not necessary.

C.—MARRIAGE UNDER REGISTRAR GENERAL'S LICENCE

The main purpose of the Marriage (Registrar General's Licence) Act 1970, which came into force on January 1, 1971, is to enable non-Anglicans to be married in unregistered premises where one of the persons to be married is seriously ill, is not expected to recover and cannot be moved to registered premises. A fee of £15 is payable to the Registrar General for the licence, though he has power to remit this in whole or in part to avoid hardship.

D.—DETAINED AND HOUSE-BOUND PERSONS

The Marriage Act 1983 (which does not extend to Scotland) enables marriages of detained persons and house-bound persons to be solemnized at their place of residence . The Act came into operation on May 1, 1984.

MISCELLANEOUS NOTES

Consanguinity and Affinity.—A marriage between persons within the prohibited degrees of consanguinity or affinity is void. Relaxations have, however, been made by various statutes which have now been replaced by the Marriage Act 1949 (see the 1st Schedule to the Act) and the Marriage (Enabling) Act 1960. It is now permitted to contract a marriage with:—

Sister, aunt or niece of a former wife (whether living or not). Former wife of brother, uncle or nephew (whether living or not).

No clergyman can be compelled to solemnize any of the foregoing marriages, but he may allow his church to be used for the purpose by another minister.

Minors.—Persons under 18 years of age are generally required to obtain the consent of certain persons (see Marriage Act 1949, section 3 and 2nd Schedule as amended by the Family Law Reform Act 1969). Where both parents are living, both must consent, where one is dead, the survivor, or, if there is a guardian appointed by the deceased parent, the guardian and the survivor. No consent is required in the case of an infant's second marriage. In certain exceptional cases consent may be dispensed with, *e.g.*, the insanity of a parent. If consent is refused the Court may, on application being made, consent to the marriage; application can be made for this purpose to the High Court, the County Court, or a Court of Summary Jurisdiction. The Act *prohibits* any marriage where either party is under 16 years of age.

E.—MARRIAGE IN ENGLAND OR WALES WHEN ONE PARTY LIVES IN SCOTLAND OR NORTHERN IRELAND

Notice for a marriage by a Superintendent Registrar's certificate in a register office or registered building may be given in the usual way by the party resident in England. As regards Scotland, the party there should give notice of intention to marry to the registrar; as regards Northern Ireland, the party there, after a residence of seven days, must give notice to the District Registrar of Marriages. Notice cannot be given for such marriages to take place by Certificate *with* licence of the Superintendent Registrar.

Marriage of such parties may take place in a church of the Church of England after the publication of banns, or by Ecclesiastical licence.

MARRIAGES IN SCOTLAND

According to the law of Scotland, marriage is a contract which is completed by the mutual consent of parties. The Marriage (Scotland) Act 1977, which came into force on January 1, 1978, states or restates the law in convenient form. References in this section are to that Act.

Impediments to Marriage: These are (a) Nonage, *i.e.*, where either party is under the age of 16. (b) Forbidden degrees of relationship (Section 2). (c) Subsisting previous marriage. (d) Incapacity to understand the nature of the contract. (e) Both parties of the same sex. (f) Non-residence, *i.e.*, if the requirements of prior residence of one or other of the parties in Scotland have not been complied with. The Act also states the grounds on which certain marriages may be declared void but this is amended by the Law Reform (Miscellaneous Provisions) (Scotland) Act 1980 which prevents a marriage being rendered void solely due to the failure to comply with certain formalities, provided the particulars of that marriage are entered in a register of marriages by or at the behest of an appropriate registrar.

Marriages may be regular or irregular, thus:—

REGULAR MARRIAGES

A regular marriage is one which is celebrated by a Minister of Religion or authorised Registrar or other celebrant specified in the Act. The parties must submit to the District Registrar a statutory notice of intention to marry the fee for which is £6·50. The Registrar will then enter the parties' names and particulars in the Marriage Notice Book which must also show the intended date of the marriage. He must then display the notice of intention to marry in a prominent public place until the intended date, and any person claiming an interest may lodge written objections thereto with the Registrar (Section 5). The Registrar, after fourteen days of receipt of the Marriage Notice and on being satisfied that there are no legal impediments to the marriage, will issue to either or both parties a Marriage Schedule. The fourteen day period may be shortened under exceptional circumstances. The Marriage Schedule must be produced to the celebrant of the marriage. The fee for the solemnization ceremony in a Registry Office is £10. After the ceremony the marriage must be registered with the Registrar General for inclusion in the Register of Births, Deaths and Marriages, within three days. Within one month of the ceremony, the fee for an extract marriage certificate is £2; thereafter it is £5.

IRREGULAR MARRIAGES

Since the Marriage (Scotland) Act 1939 the only form of irregular marriage to be recognised by law— viz., marriage by habit and repute, remains competent under the 1977 Act. If the parties live together constantly as husband and wife and are held to be such by the general repute of the neighbourhood and among their friends and relations, then there may arise a presumption from which marriage can be inferred. Before such a marriage can be registered, however, a decree of declarator of marriage must be obtained from the Deputy Principal Clerk of the Court of Session. It is the duty of the Deputy Principal Clerk to register the decree as soon as it is granted.

JURY SERVICE

Every local or parliamentary elector between the ages of eighteen and sixty-five who has resided in the United Kingdom, Channel Islands or Isle of Man for at least five years since he attained the age of thirteen will be qualified to serve on a jury unless he is "ineligible" or "disqualified".

Ineligible persons include those who have at any time been judges, magistrates and certain senior court officials, those who within the previous ten years have been concerned with the law (such as barristers and solicitors and their clerks, court officers, coroners, police, prison and probation officers); priests of any religion and vowed members of religious communities; and certain sufferers from mental illness.

Disqualified persons are those who have at any time been sentenced by a Court in the United Kingdom, Channel Islands or Isle of Man, to a term of imprisonment of five years, or more, or a person who in the last ten years has (a) served any part of a sentence of imprisonment, youth custody or dentention; or (b) been detained in a Borstal institution, or (c) had passed on him or made in respect of him a suspended sentence of imprisonment or order for detention; or (d) had made in respect of him a community service order. A person who at any time in the last five years has been placed on probation is also disqualified.

Some others are excusable as of right. These include members and officers of the Houses of Parliament, full-time serving members of the forces (including Women's forces) and registered and practising members of the medical, dental, nursing, veterinary and pharmaceutical professions and any person who has served on a jury in the two years before he is summoned. In other cases the court may excuse a juror at its discretion (e.g., where the service would be a hardship to the juror).

If a person serves on a jury knowing himself to be disqualified or ineligible he is liable to be fined up to £400 or £100 respectively.

A juror is entitled to subsistence and travelling expenses, compensation for other expenses incurred in consequence of attendance for jury service, loss of earnings and loss of national insurance benefits, but certain maximum figures (which are revised from time to time) are laid down.

A verdict of a jury must normally be unanimous but after two hours consideration (or such longer period as the Court thinks reasonable), a majority verdict is acceptable if ten jurors agree to it (or nine if the size of the jury has been reduced to ten, e.g., by illness during the trial).

Jury trial is now very unusual in civil cases but a person charged with any but the least serious crimes is entitled to be tried by a jury. The defendant may object to any juror if he can show that that juror ought not to be on the jury (e.g., because he is ineligible or is biased against him) and may object to three jurors without giving any reason.

The Coroners' Juries Act 1983 (which does not extend to Scotland) makes new provision in relation to qualification to serve on coroners' juries.

JURY SERVICE IN SCOTLAND

It is the duty of the sheriff principal of each sheriffdom, in respect of each sheriff court district in his sheriffdom, to maintain a book, known as the "general jury book", containing the names and designations of persons within the district who are qualified and liable to serve as jurors. The book, which is compiled from information which every householder is required to provide, is kept open for the inspection by any person, upon payment of a nominal fee, at the sheriff clerk's office for the district. Part II of the Juries Act 1949 (amended by regulations following thereon and by the Law Reform (Miscellaneous Provisions) (Scotland) Act 1980) applies only to Scotland and provides, *inter alia*, for the payment of travelling expenses and subsistence allowances to jurors and for loss of earnings.

The number of a jury in a civil cause in the Court of Session is twelve and in the Sheriff Court seven. In a criminal trial the number is fifteen.

QUALIFICATIONS

Under S.1 of the Law Reform (Miscellaneous Provisions) (Scotland) Act 1980, every man or woman between the ages of 18 and 65 who is for the time being registered as a parliamentary or local government elector and who has been ordinarily resident in the United Kingdom, the Channel Islands or the Isle of Man for any period of at least five years since attaining the age of 13 years, is qualified to serve on a jury.

Ineligible persons include those who at any time within the past ten years have been judges of the supreme courts, sheriffs and certain other senior court officials, those who at any time within the past five years have been concerned with the administration of justice (such as advocates and their clerks, solicitors, court staff, police officers, prison officers, sheriff officers, procurator fiscals, and members of parole boards and children's panels), and certain sufferers from mental illness.

The same rules for disqualified persons operate in Scotland as in England. Those excusable as of right are members and officers of the Houses of Parliament, full time serving members of H.M. naval, army and air forces, registered and practising members of the medical, dental, nursing, veterinary and pharmaceutical professions, ministers of religion and other persons in holy orders, and any person who has attended for jury service in the past five years.

If a person serves on a jury knowing himself to be disqualified or ineligible, he is liable to be fined up to £1,000 or £200 respectively. Jurors failing to attend without good cause are liable to a maximum fine of £200.

LANDLORD AND TENANT

ENGLAND AND WALES

Although basically the relationship between the parties to the lease is governed by the lease itself, the position is complicated by numerous statutory provisions. The few points dealt with may show the desirability of seeking professional assistance in these matters. Important provisions include:—

(1) As to agricultural holdings—the Agricultural Holdings Act 1948 and later statutes. Among other things, these Acts regulate the length of notice necessary to determine an agricultural tenancy, the tenant's right to remove fixtures on the land, his right to compensation for damage done by game, for improvements and for disturbance, and his right to require the consent of the Agricultural Land Tribunal to the operation of a notice to quit.

The Agriculture (Miscellaneous Provisions) Act 1976, contains provisions for succession on the death of a tenant of an agricultural holding. Subject to certain conditions and qualifications, a member of a deceased tenant's family (as defined in the Act) can within three months of the death apply to the Agricultural Land Tribunal for a direction entitling him to a tenancy of the holding. However, the Agricultural Holdings Act 1984 provided for the abolition of statutory succession to agricultural holdings in the case of new tenancies except by agreement.

(2) As to business premises—the Landlord and Tenant Acts 1927 and 1954, and the Law of Property Act 1969, Pt. I. Part II of the 1954 Act gives security of tenure to the tenant of most business premises, and in effect he can only be ousted on one or more of the seven grounds set out in the Act. In some cases, where the landlord can resume possession, the tenant is entitled to compensation.

(3) As to dwelling houses. The complicated mass of legislation is now mainly embodied in the Rent Act 1977, which does not extend to Scotland or Northern Ireland. If the house is within the Act, a tenant has a personal right to reside there, and he may only be ousted on certain grounds.

A number of amendments to the 1977 Act have been made by the Housing Act 1980.

Tenancies with full Rent Act protection are known as regulated tenancies. The maximum rent recoverable under such a tenancy is the rent agreed between the landlord and tenant, unless a fair rent has been registered, in which case that is the maximum rent recoverable. Application for the registration of a fair rent may be made by either the landlord or tenant, to the Local Rent Officer, and appeal against his decision lies to the Rent Assessment Committee.

(4) As to dwelling houses with resident landlords. The Rent Act 1974 gave tenants of dwellings let furnished the same security of tenure as those of unfurnished dwellings unless the landlord lived in part of the house. In the latter case, and in the case of a tenancy of a dwelling granted by a resident landlord after August 13, 1974, the tenancy will usually be outside full Rent Act protection, but may fall within the restricted contract provisions of the Rent Act 1977. In this event, the landlord or the tenant may apply to the Rent Tribunal for a reasonable rent to be registered, and once registered, this is the maximum rent recoverable.

(5) The Protection from Eviction Act 1977 provides that if any person with intent to cause the residential occupier of any premises to give up the occupation thereof does any act calculated to interfere with the peace or comfort of the residential occupier or members of his household, he shall be guilty of an offence. A further provision prevents a landlord enforcing a right to possession against a tenant (who is not protected by any security of tenure legislation) without a court order, and there are special rules in such cases relating to agricultural employees.

(6) A notice to quit *any* dwellinghouse must be given at least four weeks before it is to take effect, and must be in writing and in the prescribed statutory form.

(7) Part I of the Landlord and Tenant Act 1954, applies to most tenancies of houses for over twenty-one years at a ground rent. Where it applies, the contractual tenancy is continued until brought to an end in the manner prescribed by the Act, and in effect the landlord can only get possession on limited grounds.

Further, under the Leasehold Reform Act 1967, tenants of houses under leases for over twenty-one years at a rent less than two-thirds of the rateable value of the house are in most cases given a right to

purchase the freehold or to take an extended lease for a term of fifty years, provided the tenant at the time when he seeks to exercise the right has been occupying the house as his residence for the last three years or for periods amounting to three years in the last ten years.

(8) Full Rent Act protection is available only if a house is let on a tenancy, so that if the occupier of a house has a mere licence to occupy, he does not have Rent Act protection. Further, even if he has a tenancy, he will not be Rent Act protected if the rent payable is less than two-thirds of the rateable value of the house. For these reasons, many occupants of houses owned by farmers and occupied by farm workers did not enjoy full security of tenure. The Rent (Agriculture) Act 1976 contains detailed provisions conferring security of tenure on certain agricultural workers housed by their employers and on their successors on death.

(9) Under the Housing Act, 1961 (which does not extend to Scotland), in a lease of a dwelling-house granted after October 24, 1961, for a term of less than 7 years, there is implied a covenant by the landlord (a) to keep in repair the structure and exterior of the house and (b) to keep in repair and proper working order the installations in the house (i) for the supply of water, gas and electricity, and for sanitation, and (ii) for space heating or heating water.

(10) The Housing Act 1980 gives security of tenure to tenants of local authorities and certain other bodies. Further, and subject to certain conditions, such tenants may have the right to purchase their houses or to take a long lease of their flats. Certain amendments to the 1980 Act have been made by the Housing and Building Control Act, 1984.

SCOTLAND

A Lease is a Contract, the relationship of the parties being governed by the terms thereof. As is also the case in England (see the foregoing Section) legislation has played an important part in regulating that relationship. Thus, what at Common Law was an Agreement binding only the parties to the deed, becomes in virtue of the Leases Act 1449, a contract binding the landlord's successors, as purchasers or creditors, provided the following four conditions are observed: (1) the lease, if for more than one year, must be in writing, (2) there must be a rent, (3) there must be a term of expiry, and (4) the tenant must have entered into possession.

It would be impracticable in a brief section of these Notes to enter upon a general discussion of this branch of the law and, accordingly, the plan adopted in the preceding Section of quoting a few important Statutes is followed here.

The Agricultural Holdings (Scotland) Act 1949 (amended by the Agriculture Act 1958), which is a consolidating Act applicable to Scotland, contains provisions similar to those in the English Act, alluded to in the preceding Section. It cannot here be analysed in detail.

It is of interest to note that the Small Landholders Act, 1911, provided for the setting up of the Land Court which has jurisdiction over a large proportion of agricultural and pastoral land in Scotland.

In Scotland business premises are not controlled by Statute to so great an extent as in England, but the Tenancy of Shops (Scotland) Act, 1949 gives a measure of security to tenants of shops. This Act enables the tenant of a shop who is threatened with eviction to apply to the Sheriff for a renewal of the tenancy. If the landlord has offered to sell the subjects to the tenant at an agreed price the application for a renewal of the tenancy may be dismissed. Reference should be made to Section 1 (3) of the 1949 Act for particulars of other circumstances under which the Sheriff has a discretion to dismiss an application. The Act extends to premises held by the Crown or Government Departments, either as landlord or tenant.

The Housing (Scotland) Act 1969 and the Rent (Scotland) Act 1971, as amended by the Rent Act 1974, define controlled tenancies and regulated tenancies, both furnished and unfurnished, and lay down the system by which a landlord or tenant may obtain from the Rent Officer registration of a fair rent. The Acts also give to the tenants either of furnished or unfurnished lets a substantial degree of security of tenure. There are, however, certain exceptions; thus, they do not apply to tenancies where the interest belongs to the Crown or to a Government Department or to a local authority, a development corporation of a new town or a Housing Corporation. There must be a true tenancy for the Acts to apply. They do not apply to licensees such as lodgers or persons allowed to occupy houses on a grace and favour basis or to service occupiers. The Acts define the circumstances under which a landlord may apply for increased rent as a consequence of having carried out improvements to his property and also lay down the system of phasing of such rent increases. On the death of a statutory successor to a tenancy the tenancy may pass for a second time to a member of the family or a relative who has been in residence in the house for a period of at least six months. The Acts also lay down the duties and functions of Rent Officers and Rent Assessment Committees with regard to unfurnished accommodation and of Rent Tribunals for furnished accommodation.

The Rent(s) Act 1984, consolidates in relation to Scotland, the Rent Act 1965, the Rent(s) Act 1971, the Rent Act 1974 and the provisions relating to rent and tenant's rights of the Housing(s) Act 1972, the Tenant's Rights Etc(s) Act 1980 and other enactments. The Rent (Amendment) Act 1985 contains further provisions.

The Tenants Rights, Etc. (Scotland) Act 1980 as amended by Tenant's Rights Etc(s) Amendment Act 1984, contains a number of important provisions and deals mainly with the rights of public sector tenants to purchase the houses which they occupy. S. 46 converts all remaining controlled tenancies into regulated tenancies and s. 34 creates a particular type of protected tenancy known as a "short tenancy."

It also makes provisions in relation to housing rents and connected tenancies; the Act makes provision for a tenant's right to security of tenure and to a written lease. It also allows for amendment to the Housing Bill by introducing a landlord's right, in certain circumstances, to refuse to sell a house designed or adapted for occupation by the elderly to a tenant who would otherwise have the right to buy.

Commissioners, and civil proceedings in Magistrates' Courts. In any event, an application for legal aid will not be approved if it appears that the applicant would gain only a trivial advantage from the proceedings. Further, proceedings wholly or partly in respect of defamation are excepted from the scheme, as are also relator actions and election petitions. It is generally not available for obtaining the decree in undefended divorce and judicial separation, although the Legal Advice and Assistance Scheme (*post*) will be, and Legal Aid is still available to deal with property, custody disputes etc., arising in the suit.

Where a person is concerned in proceedings only in a representative, fiduciary or official capacity, his personal resources are not to be taken into account in considering eligibility for legal aid. Apart from this, eligibility in civil proceedings depends upon an applicant's "disposable income" and "disposable capital". The figures change frequently; particulars can be obtained from a solicitor, the Law Society or a Citizens' Advice Bureau. Disposable income is calculated by making deductions from gross income in respect of certain matters such as dependants, interest on loans, income tax, rates, rent and other matters for which the applicant must or reasonably may provide. Disposable capital is calculated by excluding from gross capital part of the value of the house in which the applicant resides, of furniture and household possessions; allowances are made in respect of dependants. Except in cases where the spouses are living apart, or have a contrary interest, any resources of a person's wife or husband are to be treated as that person's resources. These figures will be assessed by the Department of Health and Social Security, and will be referred to a General Committee, who will determine whether reasonable grounds exist for the grant of a civil aid certificate. Appeal from refusal of a certificate lies to an Area Committee. A person resident in England or Wales desiring legal aid should apply for a certificate to the appropriate General Committee for the area in which s/he resides; if resident elsewhere application should be made to a General Committee for London. If a certificate is granted, the applicant may select his solicitor, and, if necessary, counsel from a panel. The costs of the assisted person's solicitor and counsel will be paid out of the legal aid fund. When, however, damages or property are recovered or preserved by the assisted person the legal aid fund has a charge over them in respect of these costs less any contribution towards costs recovered from the unsuccessful party. In matrimonial cases, maintenance is exempt, as is the first £2,500 of any property settlement. The court may order that the costs of a successful unassisted party shall be paid out of the legal aid fund.

In an urgent case, say of domestic violence, or to restrain the kidnapping abroad of a child, Legal Aid may be granted without the applicant's means being fully investigated beforehand. If on a full examination later he is found financially ineligible he is liable to pay all the costs incurred on his behalf, if he does not attend for an examination.

LEGAL AID

LEGAL AID IN CIVIL PROCEEDINGS

The Legal Aid Act 1974 (as amended) is designed to make legal aid and advice more readily available for persons of small and moderate means. The main structure of the service is contained in the Act itself and the Regulations made thereunder, administered by the Law Society.

Legal aid is available for proceedings (including matrimonial causes) in the House of Lords, Court of Appeal, High Court, County Courts, Lands Tribunal, Restrictive Practices Court, before the Commons

LEGAL ADVICE AND ASSISTANCE

The Scheme is governed by the Legal Aid Act 1974 (as amended).

Under this legal advice and assistance scheme a client may obtain such advice or assistance as is normally provided by a solicitor and if necessary the advice of a barrister may be obtained, but, with the exception of domestic proceedings in a magistrates' court and certain other proceedings (see below) the scheme does not extend to taking any step in any proceedings before any court or tribunal. Where legal aid is available for civil proceedings (see above) or in criminal cases (see below) the scheme covers work done in making application for such legal aid.

A person is eligible for advice or assistance under the scheme provided his disposable capital and his disposable income do not exceed limits in force from time to time or if he receives Supplementary Benefit or Family Income Supplement. For a married man or person with children or other dependants deductions will be made from gross income and capital and allowances are made in respect of income tax, National Insurance contributions, etc. It is intended that the financial limits shall approximate to those applying for legal aid in civil proceedings (see above). Except when they are separated or have conflicting interests the means of husband and wife will be aggregated for the purpose of determining financial eligibility. As in the case of Legal Aid, depending on his means, a person may be called upon to pay a contribution towards the costs of work done for him. Particulars may again be obtained from a solicitor, the Law Society or a Citizens' Advice Bureau.

Solicitor's costs and expenses, which should not together exceed £50 (V.A.T. exclusive), or £75 in the case of divorce etc. (not applicable to Scotland, where the £50 limit still applies) without leave of the Area Legal Aid Committee, will be paid out of the client's contribution and any monies recovered in respect of costs or damages from another party (although this may be waived by leave of the Area Committee in cases of hardship) and the balance will be paid by the Legal Aid Fund.

The Act also extends the scheme to cover the costs of a solicitor who is present within the precincts of a magistrates' court or county court and is requested by the court to advise or represent a person who is in need of help.

In April 1980 the Scheme was enlarged to cover the cost of representation in domestic proceedings in a magistrates' court. It has since been extended to cover the representation of patients in case proceedings in a magistrates' court, of patients before Mental Health Review Tribunals, and certain parents of children who are the subject of care proceedings. Subject to financial eligibility limits, application is made to the area or local committee for "approval of assistance by way of representation" which will replace legal aid for such proceedings. However the £50 costs limit referred to above will not apply. An applicant who is outside the financial limits but eligible for *legal aid* will still have to apply for a legal aid certificate as before.

LEGAL AID IN CRIMINAL CASES

The Legal Aid Act 1974 Part II and Legal Aid Act 1982 provide for legal aid in criminal proceedings. A criminal court (*e.g.* magistrates' court, Crown Court) has power to order legal aid to be granted where it appears desirable to do so in the interests of justice. The court shall make an order in certain cases, *e.g.*, where a person is committed for trial on a charge of murder. However, the court may not make an order unless it appears to the court that the person's disposable income and capital are such that he requires assistance in meeting the costs of the particular proceedings in question. Application should be made to the appropriate court where proceedings are to take place.

An applicant shall be required to make a contribution towards the costs of the action if his disposable income and capital exceed certain prescribed limits. Persons in receipt of Supplementary Benefit are automatically exempt. In order to ascertain the amount of this contribution he will have to produce

written evidence of his means. Investigation of means will be carried out by the court. Any person who falls into arrears with the payment of contribution is liable to have the order revoked.

Any practising barrister or solicitor may act for a legally aided person in criminal proceedings unless excluded by reason of misconduct. In general where legal aid is given it will normally include representation by both counsel and solicitor. However, in connection with magistrates' courts, representation will be by solicitor alone unless it is a serious offence.

Where any doubt arises about the grant of a legal aid order that doubt is to be resolved in favour of the applicant. The court also has power to amend or revoke a legal aid order. Legal aid may also be granted in connection with appellate proceedings, *e.g.*, on appeal to the Criminal Division of the Court of Appeal under the Criminal Appeal Act 1968.

SCOTLAND
CIVIL PROCEEDINGS

The Legal Aid (Scotland) Act 1967 and the Legal Advice and Assistance Act 1972 form the basis of a scheme to provide legal advice in most civil actions in the House of Lords on appeals from the Court of Session, in the Court of Session, the Lands Valuation Appeal Court, the Scottish Land Court, the Employment Appeal Tribunal, the Sheriff Court, the Restrictive Practices Court and Lands Tribunal for Scotland.

As to those to whom legal aid is available, the same considerations as to income and capital apply in Scotland as in England. (*See* the preceding paragraph.) The decision of the Supplementary Benefits Commission is final as to financial eligibility. A person believing himself to be eligible may instruct any solicitor of his own choice who is on the official lists, or he may apply for a solicitor to one of the various Legal Aid Committees which are set up to administer the scheme. In a case where litigation is not immediately necessary, the client can seek advice under the Legal Advice and Assistance Act 1972 which is similar to the legal advice and assistance provisions of the Legal Aid Act 1974 (see above). In an instance where litigation is expected, application for a certificate granting legal aid is thereafter made to the appropriate Committee by the applicant's solicitor. He is required to prepare for the signature of the applicant a memorandum setting forth the grounds of the proposed action, and submit the same along with supporting documentation and relevant application forms to the Committee. Investigation into the applicant's financial means is carried out by the Supplementary Benefits Commission after the Committee has considered the memorandum and accompanying papers and, on a suitable contribution, if any, by the applicant being approved, a Certificate is granted enabling the applicant to proceed with his action. The Legal Aid (Scotland) Act 1967 provides for the payment (to a limited extent) out of the legal aid funds of expenses incurred by successful opponents of legally aided litigants.

LEGAL ADVICE

Legal advice, as distinct from legal aid in proceedings, is available to anyone in Scotland on terms similar to those stated in a preceding paragraph dealing with legal advice in England—the Scottish scheme being administered under the Legal Advice and Assistance Act 1972.

CRIMINAL PROCEEDINGS

Legal Aid in criminal cases is administered under the Legal Aid (Scotland) (Criminal Proceedings) Scheme and Regulations, 1975.

Subject to the financial eligibility of the applicant and the merits of his case, Legal Aid is available for proceedings in the High Court of Justiciary, the Sheriff Court and the District Court, as well as for appeals from those courts. Separate lists of practitioners prepared to act on behalf of assisted persons are kept, as regards counsel, by the Faculty of Advocates, and, as regards solicitors, by the Supreme Court and Local Legal Aid Committees of the Law Society of Scotland. Generally, an applicant may nominate to act on his behalf any solicitor whose name appears on the lists. The Scheme also provides for a rota of Duty Solicitors to act for persons taken into custody on homicide charges and persons who are in custody awaiting the first hearing of their case before the Sheriff or District Court.

Applications for Legal Aid must normally be made on the prescribed form to the clerk of the court in question and an applicant is required to provide therein particulars of the merits of his case and his financial circumstances. Where less than 7 days before his trial an accused lodges an application it shall be refused unless, on special cause shown, the court decides the application to be timeously made. In certain cases, i.e. where a person is in custody on a charge of serious crime, an oral application to the clerk of court will be sufficient. Applications are dealt with by the courts themselves and the results communicated to the relevant Committee of the Law Society. An award may be made subject to a contribution to the Legal Aid Fund. Where an applicant has a right to legal representation at the expense of a third party—e.g. a Trade Union—he will be refused Legal Aid, although a person with a high income may be awarded Legal Aid if the Court is satisfied that he would be unable without grave financial hardship to meet the costs of his defence.

A solicitor acting for an assisted person in a murder trial or appeal may instruct without the prior sanction of the Law Society both senior and junior counsel. In all other cases before the High Court only junior counsel may be instructed without prior sanction.

TOWN AND COUNTRY PLANNING

The Town and Country Planning Act 1971 (consolidating earlier Acts) contains very far-reaching provisions affecting the liberty of an owner of land to develop and use it as he will. A person has generally to get planning permission before carrying out any development on his land from the Local Planning Authority.

What is Development:—

(a) Carrying out of building, engineering, mining or other operations.

(b) Making a material change in use.

It is expressly provided that if one dwelling-house is converted into two or more dwelling-houses, this involves a material change in use.

Examples of what is not deemed Development:—

(a) Maintaining, improving or altering the interior of a building (except works for making good war damage), provided there is no material change to the exterior, with the exception that since December 5, 1968, any expansion, or works begun for the expansion, of a building below ground level constitutes development.

(b) Change of use of property within the curtilage of a dwelling-house for a purpose incidental to the use of the dwelling-house as such. (It will, however, be development if building operations are carried out.)

Application can be made to the Local Planning Authority to determine whether or not an operation or change of use constitutes development.

*Planning Permission.—*Application for such permission is not always necessary, as the Secretary of State may make Development Orders giving general permission for a specified type of development. Thus a General Development Order of 1977 as amended in 1981, specifies a number of types of development for which no permission is usually required, *e.g.*, enlargement of a dwelling-house (including erection of a garage), so long as the cubic content of the original dwelling (external measurement) is not exceeded by more than 70 cubic metres or 15 per cent, whichever is greater, subject to a maximum of 115 cubic metres.

Appeal against refusal of permission lies to the Secretary of State and from his decision, in limited circumstances, to the High Court. If the result of the appeal is unsatisfactory, an applicant may in certain circumstances require the Council to purchase the land.

SCOTLAND

The Town and Country Planning (Scotland) Act 1972 consolidates the statute law relating to town and country planning in Scotland.

The Act contains provisions for an appeal to the Secretary of State against the refusal of planning permission. The decision of the Secretary of State is final.

Sections 87 and 92 of the Local Government, Planning and Land Act 1980 contain important provisions on planning applications and, unlike certain parts of this Act, extend to Scotland.

VOTERS' QUALIFICATIONS

The franchise is governed by the Representation of the People Act 1983. Those entitled to vote as electors at a parliamentary election in any constituency are all persons resident thereon the qualifying date who, at that date and on the date of the poll are Commonwealth citizens or citizens of the Republic of Ireland and not subject to any legal incapacity to vote and who on the date of the poll are at least 18 years of age. However, a person is not entitled to vote at a parliamentary election in any constituency in Northern Ireland unless he was resident in Northern Ireland during the whole of the period of three months ending on the qualifying date for that election. Also, no person can use his vote unless he is on the Register of electors kept for the constituency. A person who is of voting age on the date of the poll at a parliamentary or local government election is entitled to vote, whether or not he is of voting age on the qualifying date. Accordingly, a qualified person will be entitled to be registered in a register of parliamentary electors or a register of local government electors if he will attain voting age within twelve months from the date on which the register is required to be published.

The Register is prepared by the Registration Officer in each constituency in Great Britain. It is the registration officer's duty to have a house to house or other official inquiry made as to the persons entitled to be registered and to publish preliminary electors lists showing the persons appearing to him to be entitled to be registered. Any person whose name is omitted may claim registration, and any person on the list may object to the inclusion therein of other persons' names: the registration officer determines the claims and objections.

Voters at a parliamentary or local government

election must generally vote in person at the allotted polling station, except for those entitled to vote by post or at any polling station, and those for whom proxies have been appointed. Certain people can apply to be treated as absent voters at a parliamentary election and thus able to vote by post—among these are registered service voters, those unable by reason of blindness or other physical incapacity to go in person to the polling station, and those unable to go in person from their qualifying address to the polling station without making a journey by air or sea.

Unless entitled to vote by post, a person registered as a service voter may vote by proxy at a parliamentary or local government election. A proxy may also be appointed by a registered elector who is unable to go in person to the polling station by reason of the general nature of his occupation and who is likely to be at sea or out of the United Kingdom on the date of the poll, provided he applies to be treated as an absent voter. The appointment of a person to vote as proxy at parliamentary elections has effect also for the purposes of local government elections.

THE PROBATION SERVICE

The Probation Service is employed in each county by an independent committee of justices and it provides a professional social work agency in the courts, with responsibility for a wide range of duties which include: (a) a social enquiry service for the criminal courts; (b) provision of a range of non-custodial measures involving the supervision of offenders in the community; (c) supervisory aftercare for offenders released from custody, together with social work in penal establishments and help for the families of those serving sentences; (d) an enquiry, conciliation and supervision service in the divorce and domestic courts; (e) support for and promotion of preventive and containment measures in the community designed to reduce the level of crime and domestic breakdown. It is a direct grant service funded 80 per cent from the Home Office and 20 per cent from the relevant County Council.

Its national representative bodies are: (i) The Central Council of Probation Committees, 38 Belgrave Square, London SW1X 8NT—Tel: 01–245–9364 (*Secretary*, R. S. Bailey); (ii) The Association of Chief Officers of Probation, 20–30 Lawefield Lane, Wakefield WF2 8SP—Tel: 0924 364141 (*Hon. Secretary*, W. R. Weston); (iii) The National Association of Probation Officers, 3/4 Chivalry Road, Battersea, London SW11 1HT—Tel: 01–223–4887 (*Gen. Secretary*, W. Beaumont).

INCOME TAX 1985–86

INTRODUCTION

Income tax is charged on the total income of individuals for a year of assessment commencing on April 6 and ending on the following April 5. The rates of tax and the calculation of liability will frequently differ as between one year of assessment and another. The following information is confined to the year of assessment 1985–86, ending on April 5, 1986.

Liability is determined by establishing the taxable income for a year of assessment. The income may be reduced by an individual's personal allowances and other reliefs. The first slice of taxable income remaining is assessable to income tax at the basic rate of 30 per cent. The rates of tax progressively increase and eventually reach 60 per cent on the slice of income exceeding £40,200. The full rates of income tax chargeable are as follows:

£	%
1–16,200	30
16,201–19,200	40
19,201–24,400	45
24,401–32,300	50
32,301–40,200	55
over 40,200	60

In some earlier years, where investment income exceeded stated limits the excess incurred liability at the additional rate of 15 per cent (the investment income surcharge). This rate has no application for 1985–86. It follows that both earned and investment income now receive identical treatment when calculating liability to income tax.

The tables on the following pages show the income tax payable for 1985–86 by an individual on the amount of income specified, after deducting the personal allowance and age allowance. The taxpayer may, however, be entitled to further reliefs and allowances which reduce the tax payable below the amount shown in the tables.

The special rules for taxing income derived by a husband and wife are examined later.

Trustees administering settled property are chargeable to income tax at the basic rate of 30 per cent. Where the trustees retain discretionary powers, or income is accumulated, there will also be liability to the additional rate of 15 per cent. Companies residing in the United Kingdom are not liable to income tax but suffer corporation tax on income, profits and gains.

The charge to income tax broadly arises on all taxable income accruing from sources in the United Kingdom. Individuals who are resident in this territory may also become liable on income arising overseas. An individual is resident in the United Kingdom if he or she normally resides here. Persons not normally residing in the United Kingdom may become resident if they visit this territory for periods which average three months or more throughout a period of years. The existence of a place of abode in the United Kingdom may be sufficient to indicate residence if visits of any duration are made during the year of assessment.

Income arising overseas will often incur liability to foreign taxation. If that income is also chargeable to United Kingdom income tax, excessive liability may well arise. The United Kingdom has concluded Double Taxation Agreements with many overseas territories which ensure that the same slice of income is not doubly assessed. In the absence of such an agreement, foreign tax suffered can usually be relieved when calculating liability to United Kingdom income tax.

INCOME TAXABLE

Income tax is assessed and collected under several Schedules. Each Schedule determines the extent of liability and establishes the amount to be included in taxable income. In some instances the actual income arising in a year of assessment will be charged to income tax for that year. A different basis of assessment may arise for income taxable under Cases I to V of Schedule D. Frequently, income assessable under these Cases will be that arising in a previous year or period but there are special rules where a new source is acquired or an existing source discontinued. The contents of the various Schedules are shown below:

Schedule A.—Tax is charged on annual profits from the ownership or occupation of land in the United Kingdom. This will include rents, ground rents and other income arising from land. Expenditure incurred by the landlord on maintenance, repairs, insurance and management can be subtracted from the annual profits. This Schedule does not include profits from farming, market gardening or woodlands, nor does it extend to mineral rents and royalties. Premiums arising on the grant of a lease for a period not exceeding fifty years are assessed to income tax. However, the amount of the taxable premium may be reduced by 2 per cent for each year, after the first year, of the leasing period. Income from furnished lettings is assessable under Case VI of Schedule D, unless an option is exercised for own income to be assessed under Schedule A. Where income arises from furnished holiday lettings additional expenditure may be included in calculating income chargeable to tax. Income of this nature is treated as earned income.

Schedule B.—Assessment is confined to woodlands in the United Kingdom managed on a commercial basis and with a view to the realisation of profits. The assessment will be based on one-third of the annual value. The occupier of woodlands retains the option of being assessed under Case I of Schedule D on profits arising from management.

Schedule C.—This Schedule is confined to interest or dividends on Government or public authority funds and certain payments made out of the public revenues of overseas countries.

Schedule D.—This Schedule is divided into six Cases as follows:

Cases I and II.—Profits arising from trades, professions and vocations, including farming and market gardening. Capital expenditure incurred on assets used for business purposes will often produce an entitlement to capital allowances which reduce the profits chargeable. These profits may also be reduced following the submission of claims for loss relief and other matters.

Case III.—Interest on Government Stocks not taxed at source (e.g. War Loan and British Savings Bonds), interest on National Savings Bank deposits and discounts. Interest up to £70 on ordinary National Savings Bank deposits is exempt from income tax. The exemption applies to both husband and wife separately. Interest on National Savings Bank Special Investment Accounts is not exempt.

Cases IV and V.—Interest from overseas securities, rents, dividends and all other income accruing outside the United Kingdom. Assessment is based on the full amount arising, whether remitted to the United Kingdom or retained overseas, but individu-

(1) Single Persons

Income	Persons under 65		Persons 65 or over	
	Income Tax	Average Rate	Income Tax	Average Rate
£	£	per cent	£	per cent
2,500	88	3·5	—	—
3,000	238	8·0	93	3·1
4,000	538	13·5	393	9·8
5,000	838	16·8	693	13·9
6,000	1,138	19·0	993	16·6
7,000	1,438	20·6	1,293	18·5
8,000	1,738	21·7	1,593	19·9
9,000	2,038	22·7	1,933	21·5
10,000	2,338	23·4	2,338	23·4
12,000	2,938	24·5	2,938	24·5
14,000	3,538	25·3	3,538	25·3
16,000	4,138	25·9	4,138	25·9
18,000	4,738	26·3	4,738	26·3
20,000	5,498	27·5	5,498	27·5
25,000	7,678	30·7	7,678	30·7
30,000	10,097	33·7	10,097	33·7
50,000	21,252	42·5	21,252	42·5
100,000	51,252	51·3	51,252	51·3

als who are either not domiciled in the United Kingdom or who are ordinarily resident overseas may apply the remittance basis. Overseas pensions are taxable but the amount arising may be reduced by 10 per cent for assessment purposes.

Case VI.—Sundry profits and annual receipts not assessed under any other Case or Schedule. These may include insurance commissions, post-cessation receipts and numerous other receipts specifically charged under Case VI.

Schedule E.—All emoluments from an office or employment are assessable under this Schedule. There are three Cases as follows:

Case I.—This applies to all emoluments of an individual resident and ordinarily resident in the United Kingdom.

Case II.—Of application where the individual is not resident or not ordinarily resident and extends to emoluments for duties undertaken in the United Kingdom.

Case III.—Applies in rare situations to other emoluments remitted to the United Kingdom.

Special rules apply to emoluments received by non-domiciled employees employed by non-resident employers. In general, where the duties are performed in the United Kingdom such earnings will be assessable subject to a percentage deduction. This deduction, which is gradually being withdrawn, applies at different rates which are governed by personal circumstances.

Although foreign earnings may be assessable under Case I where the employee is resident and ordinarily resident in the United Kingdom, a deduction of 100 per cent may be available for 1985–86. This deduction can be obtained where duties are performed overseas for a continuous period reaching or exceeding 365 days.

The emoluments assessable under Schedule E include all salaries, wages, director's fees and other money sums. In addition, there is a wide range of benefits which must also be added to taxable emoluments. These include the provision of living accommodation on advantageous terms and advantages arising from the use of vouchers.

Further taxable benefits accrue to directors and employees receiving emoluments of £8,500 or more in the year of assessment. These benefits include the reimbursement of expenses, the availability of motor cars for private motoring, the provision of petrol or other fuel for private motoring, the provision of interest free loans, and other benefits provided at the employer's expense.

In arriving at the amount to be assessed under Schedule E all expenses incurred wholly, exclusively and necessarily in the performance of the duties may be deducted. This includes fees and subscriptions paid to certain professional bodies and learned societies.

Compensation for loss of office and other sums received on the termination of an office or employment are assessable to tax. However, the first £25,000 may be excluded and only the balance remains chargeable, subject to some reduction in the amount of tax payable.

Schedule F.—This Schedule is concerned with company dividends and distributions. A United Kingdom resident company paying a dividend or distribution must account to the Inland Revenue for advance corporation tax on the amount paid. A shareholder residing in the United Kingdom receives the dividend or distribution, together with a tax credit equal to the amount of advance corporation tax. The dividend or distribution is regarded as having suffered income tax, equal to the tax credit, at the basic rate, and where the shareholder is not liable, or fully liable, at this rate a repayment can be obtained. Payments at rates in excess of the basic rate will incur further liability. Some payments made by an unquoted trading company to redeem or purchase its own shares will not be treated as distributions.

Building society interest and bank interest. A special composite rate tax scheme applies to payments of building society interest and most payments of bank interest made to individuals. Interest of this nature incurs no liability to basic rate income tax in the hands of the depositor, nor can tax be recovered by a depositor not liable to income tax. The actual interest received must be "grossed up" at three-sevenths to establish the amount of total income received by a depositor liable at rates in excess of the basic rate.

(2) MARRIED COUPLES

Income	Couples under 65		Couples 65 or over	
	Income Tax	Average Rate	Income Tax	Average Rate
£	£	per cent	£	per cent
3,500	13	0·4	—	—
4,000	163	4·1	—	—
5,000	463	9·3	223	4·5
6,000	763	12·7	523	8·7
7,000	1,063	15·2	823	11·8
8,000	1,363	17·0	1,123	14·0
9,000	1,663	18·5	1,463	16·3
10,000	1,963	19·6	1,963	19·6
12,000	2,563	21·4	2,563	21·4
14,000	3,163	22·6	3,163	22·6
16,000	3,763	23·5	3,763	23·5
18,000	4,363	24·2	4,363	24·2
20,000	4,998	25·0	4,998	25·0
25,000	7,115	28·5	7,115	28·5
30,000	9,472	31·6	9,472	31·6
50,000	20,502	41·0	20,502	41·0
100,000	50,502	50·5	50,502	50·5

INCOME NOT TAXABLE

This includes interest on National Savings Certificates, most scholarship income, bounty payments to members of the armed services and annuities payable to the holders of certain awards.

SOCIAL SECURITY BENEFITS

Many Social Security benefits are not liable to income tax. These include the maternity allowance, long term sickness benefit, child benefit, war widow's pension, death grant, mobility allowance and numerous others. Among the limited range of benefits which are taxable is the retirement pension, widow's allowance, widowed mother's allowance, and most unemployment benefit and supplementary benefit paid to the unemployed. Short-term sickness benefit payable by an employer is also chargeable to tax.

PAY AS YOU EARN

The Pay As You Earn system is not an independent form of taxation but has been designed to collect income tax by deduction from most emoluments. When paying emoluments to employees an employer is usually required to deduct income tax and account for that tax to the Inland Revenue. In many cases this deduction procedure will fully exhaust the individual's liability to income tax, unless there is other income.

PERSONAL ALLOWANCES

The following personal allowances are available to individuals and may be subtracted when calculating income chargeable to income tax:

Personal Allowance.—A single person is entitled to a personal allowance of £2,205. This is increased to £3,455 for a married man whose wife is living with or maintained by him. For the year of marriage the increased allowance will only be available if marriage occurs before May 6. The increased allowance is then reduced by one-twelfth of £1,250 (£3,455 less £2,205) for each complete month preceding the marriage date.

The increased married man's allowance may be withdrawn where a wife's earning election is made (see "Husband and Wife" below).

Age Allowance.—A single person who has attained the age of 65 years and is in receipt of income not exceeding £8,800 receives an age allowance of £2,690. This is increased to £4,255 where a married man, or his wife living with him, has reached 65. If the income exceeds £8,800 the allowance is reduced by two-thirds of the amount of the excess. This reduction continues until the age allowance is reduced to the amount of the normal personal allowance. Age allowance is in substitution for, and not in addition to, the personal allowance.

Wife's Earned Income Allowance.—An allowance equal to the wife's earned income, but limited to a maximum of £2,205, may be obtained. This allowance is not granted in the year of marriage or where a wife's earnings election is made (see "Husband and Wife" below).

Additional Personal Allowance.—An allowance of £1,250 is available to a single person who has a qualifying child resident with him or her in the year of assessment. The allowance can also be obtained by a married man whose wife is totally incapacitated by physical or mental infirmity throughout the year and a child is similarly resident.

A "qualifying child" for 1985–86 must be born during the year, be under the age of 16 years at the commencement of the year, or over the age of 16 years at the commencement of the year and either receiving full-time instruction at a university, college, school or other educational establishment or undergoing training for a trade, profession or vocation throughout a minimum period of two years. It is also necessary that the child is the claimant's own or, if not such a child, was either born during 1985–86 or under the age of 18 years at the commencement of the year and maintained by the claimant at his or her own expense during the whole of the succeeding twelve month period.

Housekeeper Allowance.—An allowance of £100 is available to a widow or widower having a relative residing to act as a housekeeper. This allowance is also available where a housekeeper is employed for a similar purpose.

Son's or Daughter's Services Allowance.—A person who, by reason of his or his wife's old age or infirmity, has to retain the services of a son or daughter is entitled to an allowance of £55.

Dependent Relative Allowance.—The maximum deduction for each dependent relative is normally £100 but an increased allowance of £145 may be claimed where the claimant is a woman (other than a married woman living with her husband). The allowance is reduced by £1 for every £1 by which the relative's own taxable income exceeds the basic Social Security Retirement Pension. The relative must be incapacitated by old age or infirmity from maintaining himself or herself, except in the case of the claimant's, or the claimant's wife's, mother who may be widowed, living apart from her husband or divorced. Additionally, the relative must be maintained by the claimant. If more than one person provides support to the dependent relative the allowance must be apportioned between them.

Blind Person's Allowance.—An allowance of £360 is available to a single person if at any time during the year ending on April 5, 1986, that person was registered as blind on a register maintained by a local authority. The allowance will also be available to a married man if either he or his wife living with him is similarly registered. An increased allowance of £720 will be available if both husband and wife are registered blind persons.

Widow's Bereavement Allowance.—For the year of assessment in which a husband dies his surviving widow may obtain a widow's bereavement allowance of £1,250. It is a necessary requirement that the parties were living together immediately before death. A similar allowance will be available in the year following death, unless the widow remarried in the year of death. The special widow's bereavement allowance is available only for the year of death and the following year. It cannot be obtained in subsequent years.

Life Assurance Relief.—Life assurance deduction relief is limited to premiums paid on policies made before March 14, 1984. No relief is available for policies issued after this date. Where the terms of a policy made before March 14, 1984 are subsequently varied or extended to produce increased benefits, future premiums paid may no longer qualify for relief.

In those cases where relief can be obtained for premiums paid on life assurance and other policies, this is not given through the tax system. To qualify for relief premiums must be paid on an approved policy providing life assurance or deferred annuities. Relief is confined to policies made by the payer and covering his own life or that of his or her spouse. Only policyholders residing in the United Kingdom can usually obtain relief and payments must be made to a United Kingdom company or friendly society or to a United Kingdom branch of an overseas company.

When paying premiums under a qualifying policy made before March 14, 1984 the payer will deduct and retain income tax at the rate of 15 per cent. The ability to retain deductions made in this manner is not affected by the payer's liability to income tax on taxable income. No restriction to the deduction procedure arises if aggregate premiums paid during a year of assessment do not exceed £1,500. Should premiums exceed this amount, relief will be confined to £1,500 or one-sixth of total income, whichever is the greater. Where sums deducted exceed the maximum limit, the excess must be accounted for to the Inland Revenue.

OTHER DEDUCTIONS

In addition to personal allowances, which may reduce taxable income, other eligible deductions may be available to an individual. These include payments of interest.

In some instances interest paid by a business proprietor may be relieved when calculating profits chargeable to income tax under Case I or Case II of Schedule D. Many private individuals cannot obtain relief in this manner and must satisfy stringent requirements before relief will be forthcoming. In general terms, before interest can qualify for relief it must be annual, as opposed to short, interest or paid to a bank, stockbroker or discount house. Relief will not be available to the extent that interest exceeds a reasonable commercial rate and no relief will be forthcoming for interest on an overdraft.

For 1985–86 relief will be available on the following payments:

(i) Interest on a loan to purchase, develop or improve an interest in land owned by the individual and used as his only or main residence or similarly used by a dependent relative or a former or separated spouse, "Land" includes larger houseboats and caravans used for a similar purpose. If the loan or aggregate of several loans, exceeds £30,000 relief is restricted to interest on that amount. Relief may also be forthcoming for interest on a loan used to acquire some other property, perhaps to be used as the only or main residence on retirement, by an individual who is compelled to occupy property by reason of his or her work.

(ii) Interest on a loan to purchase or improve an interest in land which is let or available for letting at a commercial rent. This interest is only capable of being deducted from rental income.

(iii) Interest on a loan made to acquire an interest in a close company or in a partnership.

(iv) Interest on a loan to a member of a partnership to acquire machinery or plant for use in the partnership business.

(v) Interest on a loan to an employed person to acquire machinery or plant for the purposes of his employment.

(vi) Interest on a loan made for the purpose of contributing capital to an industrial co-operative.

(vii) Interest on a loan applied for investment in an employee-controlled company.

(viii) Interest on a loan made to elderly persons for the purchase of an annuity where the loan is secured on land. If the loan exceeds £30,000 relief is limited to interest on this amount.

(ix) Interest on a loan to personal representatives for the payment of capital transfer tax.

Relief for many payments of mortgage interest is obtained through a special system known as MIRAS (mortgage interest relief at source). This applies to interest paid to a building society, bank, insurance company and certain other persons. When making payments of this nature the payer will deduct and retain income tax at the basic rate. This will provide the payer with full relief at the basic rate and no other relief will be necessary, unless the payer is liable at rates in excess of the basic rate. Qualifying payments of interest outside the MIRAS system continue to produce relief by deduction for income chargeable to income tax.

Many individuals pay contributions to approved pension schemes. The amount of their contributions may be deducted when establishing emoluments assessable under Schedule E.

Self-employed individuals and those who are not in pensionable employment may pay premiums on qualifying retirement annuity policies. The amount of these premiums may usually be relieved in calculating taxable income but limitations are placed on the maximum amount available for relief.

Subject to a maximum of £40,000 in any one year the cost of subscribing for shares in an unquoted company may qualify as a deduction from taxable income under the Business Expansion Scheme. This applies to subscriptions in 1983–84 and each of the following three years. Many requirements must be satisfied before this relief can be obtained.

HUSBAND AND WIFE

It is a general rule that the income of a married woman living with her husband must be aggregated with his income for the purpose of charging income tax. Aggregation does not, however, apply for the year of assessment in which the parties marry. For that year the husband will receive the personal allowance appropriate to a married man, although the amount of this allowance may require some restriction if marriage takes place after May 5. The wife will be taxed for the year of marriage as if she were a single person and no wife's earned income allowance can be obtained by the husband.

For subsequent years of assessment the incomes of husband and wife will be aggregated and if the husband does not satisfy the total tax liability the Inland Revenue may require the wife to pay the tax appropriate to her income.

Husband and wife may, however, claim to be separately assessed. This claim does not affect the total amount of income tax payable but allocates the liability between the parties. A quite different election may be made for separate assessment of wife's earnings. The effect of such an election is that the husband will be assessed on his income and on the wife's investment income and will receive the personal allowance appropriate to a single man. The wife will be separately assessed on her earned income and receive allowances as a single person. The wife's earnings election may be of advantage where the saving in higher rates of tax on the wife's income is greater than the increased tax resulting from the loss of the married personal allowance.

CAPITAL GAINS TAX

INTRODUCTION

A person is chargeable to capital gains tax on chargeable gains which accrue to him or her during a year of assessment ending on April 5. The application of the tax has been amended substantially in recent years and the following information is confined to the year of assessment 1985–86, ending on April 5 1986.

Liability extends to persons who are either resident or ordinarily resident for the year but special rules apply where a person permanently leaves the United Kingdom or comes to this territory for the purpose of acquiring residence. Non-residents are not liable to capital gains tax unless, exceptionally, they carry on a business in the United Kingdom through a branch or agency.

Chargeable gains accruing to companies are assessable to corporation tax and not to capital gains tax.

Capital gains tax is chargeable on the total of chargeable gains which accrue to a person in a year of assessment, after subtracting allowable losses arising in the same year. Unused allowable losses brought forward from some earlier year may be offset against current chargeable gains but in the case of individuals this must not reduce the net chargeable gains for 1985–86 below £5,900.

RATE OF TAX

Where the net chargeable gains accruing to an individual during 1985–86 do not exceed £5,900 there will be no liability to capital gains tax. If the net gains exceed £5,900 the excess is chargeable at the flat rate of 30 per cent.

Capital gains tax for 1985–86 normally falls due for payment on or before December 1, 1986. If the return or other information recording chargeable gains is delayed, interest may become chargeable at the rate of 11 per cent per annum.

HUSBAND AND WIFE

In the year of marriage chargeable gains accruing to husband and wife are separately assessed. Each party may independently obtain the £5,900 exemption for 1985–86 and there is no aggregation. For subsequent years, however, chargeable gains arising to a married woman living with her husband are assessed and charged on the husband, unless an election for separate assessment is made. This election will not reduce the aggregate tax payable but merely apportions liability between the spouses on an equitable basis.

DISPOSAL OF ASSETS

Before liability to capital gains tax can arise a disposal, or deemed disposal, of an asset must take place. This occurs not only where assets are sold or exchanged but applies on the making of a gift. There is also a disposal of assets where any capital sum is derived from assets, for example, where compensation is received for loss or damage to an asset.

The date on which a disposal must be treated as having taken place will determine the year of assessment in which the chargeable gain or allowable loss falls. In those cases where a disposal is made under an unconditional contract, the time of disposal will be that when the contract was entered into and not the subsequent date of conveyance or transfer. A disposal under a conditional contract or option is treated as taking place when the contract becomes unconditional or the option is exercised. Disposals by way of gift are undertaken when the gift becomes effective.

VALUATION OF ASSETS

The amount actually received as consideration for the disposal of an asset will be the sum from which very limited outgoings must be deducted for the purpose of establishing the gain or loss. In some cases, however, the consideration passing will not accurately reflect the value of the asset and some other basis must be used. This applies, in particular, where an asset is transferred by way of gift or otherwise than by a bargain made at arm's length. Such transactions are deemed to take place for a consideration representing market value, which will determine both the disposal proceeds accruing to the transferor and the cost of acquisition to the transferee.

Market value represents the price which an asset might reasonably be expected to fetch on a sale in the open market. In the case of unquoted shares or securities it is to be assumed that the hypothetical purchaser in the open market would have available all the information which a prudent prospective purchaser of shares or securities might reasonably require if he were propsoing to purchase them from a willing vendor by private treaty and at arm's length. This is an important consideration as the amount of information deemed to be available to a hypothetical purchaser may materially affect the price "reasonably" offered in an open market situation. The market value of unquoted shares or securities will usually be established following negotiations with the Shares Valuation Division of the Capital Taxes Office.

Special rules apply to determine the market value of shares quoted on the Stock Exchange.

DEDUCTION FOR OUTGOINGS

Once the actual or notional disposal proceeds have been determined it only remains to subtract eligible outgoings for the purpose of computing the gain or loss. There is the general rule that any outgoings deducted, or which are available to be deducted, when calculating income tax liability must be ignored. Subject to this, deductions will usually be limited to—

(a) the cost of acquiring the asset, together with incidental costs wholly and exclusively incurred in connection with the acquisition;

(b) expenditure incurred wholly and exclusively on the asset in enhancing its value, being expenditure reflected in the state or nature of the asset at the time of the disposal, and any other expenditure wholly and exclusively incurred in establishing, preserving or defending title to, or a right over, the asset; and

(c) the incidental costs of making the disposal.

Where the disposal concerns a leasehold interest having less than 50 years to run, any expenditure falling under (a) and (b) must be written off throughout the duration of the lease. This recognises that a lease is a wasting asset which, at the termination of the leasing period, will retain no value.

INDEXATION ALLOWANCE

An indexation allowance will be available when calculating the chargeable gain or allowable loss. For disposals made after April 5, 1985 this allowance is based on percentage increases in the retail prices index between the month of March 1982, or if later the month in which expenditure is incurred, and the month of disposal. The increase is applied to the claims of expenditure in (a) and (b) above to determine the indexation allowance. However, if the asset was acquired before March 31, 1982 a claim may be made to base the indexation allowance on world market at this date.

The amount of the indexation allowance will be subtracted from the gain, or added to the loss, to calculate the chargeable gain or allowable loss arising on disposal.

Different rules apply when calculating the indexation allowance for disposals made before April 6, 1985.

EXEMPTIONS

There is a general exemption from liability to capital gains tax where the net gains of an individual for 1985–86 do not exceed £5,900.

The disposal of many assets will not give rise to chargeable gains or allowable losses and these include—

(a) private motor cars;

(b) Government securities retained for a minimum period of twelve months. Total exemption becomes available for disposals after July 1, 1986.

(c) Loan stock and other securities (but not shares) quoted on a United Kingdom stock exchange or dealt in on the Unlisted Securities market and retained for a minimum period of twelve months; (with total exemption for disposals after July 1, 1986)

(d) National Savings Certificates, Premium Bonds, Defence Bonds and National Development Bonds;

(e) currency of any description acquired for personal expenditure outside the United Kingdom;

(f) decorations awarded for valour;

(g) betting wins and pools, lottery or games prizes;

(h) compensation or damages for any wrong or injury suffered by an individual in his person or in his profession or vocation;

(i) life assurance and deferred annuity contracts where the person making the disposal is the original beneficial owner;

(j) dwelling-houses and land enjoyed with the residence which is an individual's only or main residence;

(k) tangible movable property, the consideration for the disposal of which does not exceed £3,000;

(l) certain tangible movable property which is a wasting asset having a life not exceeding 50 years;

(m) assets transferred to charities and other bodies;

(n) works of art, historic buildings and similar assets;

(o) assets used to provide maintenance funds for historic buildings;

(p) assets transferred to trustees for the benefit of employees.

DWELLING-HOUSES

Exemption from capital gains tax will usually be available for any gain which accrues to an individual from the disposal of, or of an interest in, a dwelling-house or part of a dwelling-house which has been his only or main residence. The exemption extends to land which has been occupied and enjoyed with the residence as its garden or grounds. Some restriction may be necessary where the land exceeds one acre.

The gain will not be chargeable to capital gains tax if the dwelling-house, or part, has been the individual's only or main residence throughout the period of ownership, or throughout the entire period except for all or any part of the last two years. A proportionate part of the gain will be exempt if the dwelling-house has been the individual's only or main residence for part only of the period of ownership.

Where part of the dwelling-house has been used exclusively for business purposes, part of the gain arising on disposal will not be exempt. It will be comparatively unusual for any part to be used exclusively for such a purpose, except perhaps in the case of doctors' or dentists' surgeries.

In those cases where part of a qualifying dwelling-house has been used to provide rented accommodation this non-personal use may frequently be ignored when calculating exemption from capital gains tax, unless relatively substantial sums are involved.

Dwellings occupied by dependent relatives, separated or divorced former spouses, and also by beneficiaries under trusts, may also qualify for the exemption.

ROLL-OVER RELIEF

Persons carrying on business will often undertake the disposal of an asset and use the proceeds to finance the acquisition of a replacement asset. Where this situation arises a claim for roll-over relief may be made. The broad effect of such a claim is that all or part of the gain arising on the disposal of the old assset may be disregarded. The gain or part is then subtracted from the cost of acquiring the replacement asset. As this cost is reduced, any gain arising from the future disposal of the replacement asset will be correspondingly increased, unless of course a further roll-over situation then develops.

It remains a requirement that both the old and the replacement asset must be used for the purpose of the taxpayer's business. Relief will only be available if the acquisition of the replacement asset takes place within a period commencing twelve months before, and ending three years after, the disposal of the old asset, although the Board of Inland Revenue retain a discretion to extend this period where the circumstances were such that it was impossible for the taxpayer to acquire the replacement asset before the expiration of the normal time limit.

Whilst many business assets qualify for roll-over relief there are exceptions.

GIFTS

Although the gift of an asset is deemed to be a disposal made for a consideration representing market value, a claim can frequently be made to avoid capital gains tax liability. This claim applies to the gift of all assets by one individual to a second individual, by an individual to trustees, by trustees to an individual, or between trustees, residing in the United Kingdom. The effect of the claim is similar to that arising following a claim for roll-over relief and the cost to the transferee will be reduced. Adjustments will be necessary where a transaction undertaken, otherwise than by way of bargain made at arm's length, involves some inadequate consideration.

A limited claim may also be made on the disposal of assets by an individual to some other person, perhaps a company. This claim is confined to the disposal of business assets, including shares in certain companies.

RETIREMENT RELIEF

Retirement relief is available to an individual who disposes by way of sale or gift of the whole or part of a business. It does not necessarily follow that the isolated disposal of assets will represent the disposal of the whole or part of a business. The main condition for granting this relief is that throughout a period of at least one year the business has been owned either by the individual or by a trading company in which the individual retained a sufficient shareholding interest. The relief extends also to cases where an individual disposes by way of sale or gift of shares or securities of a company. It must be demonstrated that the company was a trading company, the individual retained a sufficient shareholding interest, and he was engaged as a full-time working director.

An individual who has attained the age of 60 years at the time of a disposal may obtain maximum retirement relief of £100,000. The amount of this relief must be reduced if the conditions have not been satisfied throughout a ten year period. With a single exception no relevant relief can be obtained if the disposal occurs before the individuals 60th birthday. This exception arises where an individual is compelled to retire and only on the grounds of ill-health. The normal retirement relief may then be obtained, any unclaimed relief must be subtracted from the net gains arising on disposal, leaving the balance chargeable to capital gains tax in the normal manner.

Retirement relief applied differently for disposals made before April 6, 1985.

ASSETS HELD ON APRIL 6, 1965

Capital gains tax is chargeable on gains which accrue from disposals undertaken after April 6, 1965. Special rules must therefore be applied to calculate gains and losses arising from the disposal of assets acquired before this date.

This is often achieved by computing the overall gain and apportioning that gain rateably throughout the period of ownership. Only that part of the gain attributable to the period commencing on April 6, 1965, and ending at the time of disposal will be chargeable to capital gains tax.

This time apportionment procedure may be withdrawn in certain circumstances. It cannot apply to the disposal of quoted shares or securities, unit trust holdings or land retaining development value which are deemed to be acquired for a consideration representing market value on April 6, 1965. Where time apportionment is otherwise available, an election can be made to treat the asset as having been acquired at market value on April 6, 1965. A comparison between this notional cost of acquisition and the eventual disposal proceeds will usually disclose the chargeable gain, subject to an adjustment for the indexation allowance. Restrictions may have to be applied where the calculation produces a loss.

DEATH

No capital gains tax is chargeable on the value of assets retained at the time of death. However, the personal representatives administering the deceased's estate are deemed to acquire assets for a consideration representing market value on death. This ensures that any increase in value occurring before the date of death will not be chargeable to capital gains tax. If a legatee or other person acquires an asset under a will or intestacy no chargeable gain will accrue to the personal representatives, and the person taking the asset will also be treated as having acquired it at the time of death for its then market value.

CAPITAL TRANSFER TAX

INTRODUCTION

Liability to capital transfer tax may arise on lifetime gifts and other dispositions and also on the value of assets retained at the time of death. The tax became effective in 1974 but numerous changes have been made subsequently both to the rates charged and in the calculation of liability.

An individual's domicile at the time of any gift or on death is an important matter. Domicile will generally be determined by applying normal rules but special considerations may be necessary where an individual was domiciled in the United Kingdom during 1974, or on a subsequent occasion, and eventually acquires a different domicile overseas. Where a person was domiciled in the United Kingdom at the time of a disposition, or on death, the location of assets is immaterial and full liability to capital transfer tax arises. Individuals domiciled outside the United Kingdom are, however, chargeable to capital transfer tax only on transactions affecting assets located in the United Kingdom.

The assets of husband and wife are not merged for capital transfer tax purposes. Each spouse is treated as a separate individual entitled to receive the benefit of his or her exemptions, reliefs and rates of tax. Where both husband and wife retain similar assets special "related property" provisions may require the merger of those assets for valuation purposes.

LIFETIME DISPOSITIONS

Lifetime dispositions are vulnerable to capital transfer tax liability. Liability is measured by the "value transferred", which represents the difference between the value of an individual's estate immediately before and immediately following the transfer. It will sometimes be found that the value transferred considerably exceeds the value received by a donee or transferee. This may arise where an individual transfers part of a shareholding interest in an unquoted company. The fall in value reflected by the transfer may well substantially exceed the actual value of shares transferred.

Unless the donee satisfies any capital transfer tax becoming payable, the value transferred must be increased by the amount of that tax. This "grossing up" procedure may considerably increase liability to capital transfer tax.

A disposition is not a transfer of value if it can be shown that there was no intention to confer gratuitous benefit. This requires that the transaction was concluded on terms similar to those expected from persons dealing at arm's length.

DEATH

Immediately before the time of death an individual is deemed to make a transfer of value. This transfer will comprise the value of assets forming part of the deceased's estate after subtracting most liabilities. The "grossing up" procedure does not apply to the value of assets at the time of death.

SETTLED PROPERTY

Complex rules apply to establish capital transfer tax liability on settled property. Where a person is beneficially entitled to an interest in possession, that person will be deemed to "own" the property in which the interest subsists. It follows that, where the interest comes to an end during the beneficiary's lifetime and some other person becomes entitled to the property, the beneficiary is treated as having made a transfer of value. No liability will arise, however, where the property vests into the absolute ownership of the previous beneficiary. The death of a person entitled to an interest in possession will require the value of the underlying property to be added to the value of the deceased's estate.

In the case of other settled property where there is no interest in possession (e.g. discretionary trusts), liability to tax will arise on each ten-year anniversary. There will also be liability if property ceases to be held on discretionary trusts before the first ten-year anniversary date is reached or between anniversaries. The rate of tax suffered will be governed by several considerations including previous dispositions made by the settlor, transactions concluded by the trustees, and the period throughout which property has been held in trust.

Accumulation and maintenance settlements which require assets to be distributed not later than a beneficiary's twenty-fifth birthday may be exempt from any liability to capital transfer tax.

EXEMPT TRANSFERS

A wide range of exempt transfers are excluded from any liability to capital transfer tax. These apply to lifetime dispositions and, subject to restrictions, are of application to assets retained at the time of death. The exempt transfers are listed below:

Transfers between Spouses.—Transfers between husband and wife are usually exempt. However, if the transferor is, but the transferee spouse is not, domiciled in the United Kingdom transfers will be exempt only to the extent that the total does not exceed £55,000. Unlike the requirement used for income tax and capital gains tax purposes, it is immaterial whether husband and wife are "living together".

Annual Exemption.—The first £3,000 of gifts and other dispositions made in a year ending on April 5 is exempt. If the exemption is not used, or not wholly used, in any year the balance may be carried forward to the following year only. This exemption has no application on death.

Small Gifts.—Outright gifts of £250 or less to any person in one year ending on April 5 are exempt. The exemption is not available on death.

Normal Expenditure.—A transfer made during lifetime and comprising normal expenditure is exempt. To obtain this exemption it must be shown that—

(a) the transfer was made as part of the normal expenditure of the transferor;

(b) taking one year with another, the transfer was made out of income; and

(c) after allowing for all transfers of value forming part of normal expenditure, the transferor was left with sufficient income to maintain his or her usual standard of living.

Gifts in consideration of marriage.—These are exempt if they satisfy certain requirements. The amount allowed will be governed by the relationship between the donor and a party to the marriage. The allowable amounts comprise—

(a) gifts by a parent—£5,000

(b) gifts by a grandparent—£2,500

(c) gifts by a party to the marriage—£2,500

(d) gifts by other persons—£1,000

Gifts to Charities.—Gifts to charities are exempt from liability. Before March 15, 1983 gifts made on death, or within a period of one year preceding death were limited to £250,000 for exemption purposes but this restriction no longer applies.

Gifts to Political Parties.—Gifts to political parties which satisfy certain requirements are generally exempt. However, a limit of £100,000 is placed on gifts made on or within a period of one year before the date of death.

Gifts for National Purposes.—Gifts made to an extensive list of bodies are exempt from liability. These include, among others—

(a) The National Gallery;

(b) The British Museum;

(c) The National Trust for Places of Historic Interest or Natural Beauty;

(d) The National Art Collections Fund;

(e) The Nature Conservancy Council;

(f) The Historic Buildings and Monuments Commission for England;

(g) Any local authority;

(h) Any university or university college in the United Kingdom.

A number of other gifts made for the public benefit are also exempt.

VALUATIONS

The valuation of assets is an important matter as this will establish the value transferred for lifetime dispositions and also the value of a person's estate at the time of death. The value of property will represent the price which might reasonably be expected from a sale in the open market. This price cannot be reduced on the ground that the whole property is placed on the market simultaneously and may therefore depress values.

In some cases it may be necessary to incorporate the value of "related property". This will include property comprised in the estate of the transferor's spouse and certain property previously transferred to charities. The purpose of the related property valuation rules is not to add the value of that property to the estate of the transferor. Related property must be merged to establish the aggregate value of the respective interests and this value is then apportioned, usually on a pro rata basis, to the separate interests.

The value of shares and securities quoted on a stock exchange will be determined by extracting figures from the daily list of official prices.

Where quoted shares and securities are sold within a period of twelve months following the date of death a claim may be made to substitute the proceeds for the value on death. This claim will only be beneficial if the gross proceeds realized are lower than market value on death. A similar claim may be available for interests in land sold within a period of three years following death.

RELIEF FOR ASSETS

Special relief is made available for certain assets, notably woodlands, agricultural property and business property. The effect of this relief, which may require the submission of an election, is summarized below:

Woodlands.—Where woodlands pass on death the value will usually be included in the deceased's estate. However, an election may be made in respect of land in the United Kingdom on which trees or underwood are growing to delete the value of those assets. Relief is confined to the value of trees or underwood and does not extend to the land on which they are growing. Liability to tax will arise if and when the trees or underwood are sold on a future occasion.

Agricultural property.—Relief is available for the agricultural value of agricultural property. Such property must be occupied and used for agricultural purposes and relief is confined to the agricultural value. Where that value is increased by development potential no relief can be obtained on the excess value.

For transfers made or deaths occurring before March 10, 1981, relief was broadly confined to working farmers. The effect of this relief was to reduce the value transferred by 50 per cent.

Transfers made, or deaths occurring, on or after this date may obtain alternative percentage deductions from the value transferred. A higher deduction of 50 per cent will be available if the transferor had vacant possession or could obtain that possession within a period of twelve months following the transfer. The increased deduction of 50 per cent may also be obtained for certain agricultural property held on March 9, 1981. In other cases, notably including land let to tenants, a reduced deduction of 30 per cent (or 20 per cent for transfers made before March 15, 1983) is available.

It remains a requirement that the agricultural property was either occupied by the transferor for the purposes of agriculture throughout a two year period ending on the date of the transfer or was owned by him throughout a period of seven years ending on that date and occupied for agricultural purposes.

Business Property.—Where value transferred is attributable to relevant business property, that value may be reduced by a percentage. The reduction in value applies to—

(a) property consisting of a business or an interest in a business;

(b) shares or securities of a company which, either by themselves or together with other shares or securities owned by the transferor, gave the transferor control of the company immediately before the transfer. Control for this purpose may include that created by related property.

(c) shares in a company which do not fall within (b) and are not quoted on a recognized stock exchange;

(d) any land, building, machinery or plant which, immediately before the transfer, was used wholly or mainly for the purposes of a business carried on by a company of which the transferor had control;

(e) any land, building, machinery or plant which, immediately before the transfer, was used wholly or mainly for the purposes of a business carried on by a partnership of which the transferor was a partner; and

(f) any land, building, machinery or plant which, immediately before the transfer, was used wholly or mainly for the purposes of a business carried on by the transferor, and was then settled property in which he retained an interest in possession.

For property falling within (a) or (b) the deduction is 50 per cent. A reduced deduction of 30 per cent applies to property in (d) or (e). The deduction for property in (c) was originally 20 per cent but for transfers after March 14, 1983 this increased to the present level of 30 per cent.

It is a general requirement that the property must have been retained for a period of two years before the transfer or death and restrictions may be necessary if the property has not been used wholly for business purposes. The same slice of property cannot obtain both the business property relief and the relief available for agricultural property.

RATES OF TAX

Once the amount of chargeable transfers has been established it will be necessary to determine the amount of capital transfer tax payable. Each chargeable transfer made during lifetime is added to earlier transfers to establish a cumulative total. On death the value of the estate must be added to lifetime transfers also to arrive at a cumulative total. However, this cumulative total will only include chargeable transfers made within a period of ten years before the current lifetime disposition or death.

The cumulative total which includes the current transfer or the value on death must be compared with a table to establish the rate or rates of capital transfer tax payable. There are two separate tables—

(a) one applying to lifetime dispositions, other than those made within a period of three years before the date of death; and

(b) one applying to the value of the estate at the time of death and also to lifetime dispositions made within the previous three year period.

The rates of capital transfer tax have been amended on several occasions. The first table reproduced below shows the rates of capital transfer tax for deaths occurring on or after April 6, 1985. It also applies to lifetime dispositions made within a period of three years preceding the date of death and falling after that date. The second table is of application to other lifetime dispositions made on or after April 6, 1985.

It will be noted that the rates in the second table are exactly one half of those in the first.

First Table
For values on death and transfers within 3 years before death

Deaths or transfers on or after April 6, 1985	
Portion of value	Rate of tax
£ £	%
0– 67,000	Nil
67,001– 89,000	30
89,001–122,000	35
122,001–155,000	40
155,001–194,000	45
194,001–243,000	50
243,001–299,000	55
299,001 and above	60

Second Table
For lifetime gifts (other than in 3 years before death)

Gifts on and after April 6, 1985	
Portion of value	Rate of tax
£ £	%
0– 67,000	Nil
67,001– 89,000	15
89,001–122,000	17½
122,001–155,000	20
155,001–194,000	22½
194,001–243,000	25
243,001–299,000	27½
299,001 and above	30

PAYMENT OF TAX

Capital transfer tax usually falls due for payment six months after the end of the month in which the chargeable transaction takes place. Where a transfer, other than that made on death, takes place after April 5 and before the following October 1, tax falls due on the following April 30, although there are some exceptions to this general rule.

Capital transfer tax attributable to the transfer of certain land, controlling shareholding interests, unquoted shares, businesses and interests in businesses, together with agricultural property, may usually be satisfied by instalments. No liability to interest arises where tax is paid on the due date. In other cases, delay in the payment of tax may involve liability to interest.

CORPORATION TAX

INTRODUCTION

Profits, gains and income accruing to companies resident in the United Kingdom incur liability to corporation tax. Non-resident companies are immune from this tax unless they carry on a trade in the United Kingdom through a permanent establishment, branch or office. Companies residing outside the United Kingdom may be liable to income tax at the basic rate on other income arising in the United Kingdom, perhaps from letting property. The following comments are confined to companies resident in the United Kingdom and have little application to those residing overseas.

Liability to corporation tax is governed by the profits, gains or income for an accounting period. This is the period for which financial accounts are made up, and in the case of companies preparing accounts to the same accounting date annually will comprise successive periods of twelve months.

RATE OF TAX

The amount of profits or income for an accounting period must be determined on normal taxation principles. The special rules which apply to individuals where a source of income is acquired or discontinued do not apply and consideration is confined to the actual profits or income for an accounting period.

The rate of corporation tax is fixed for a financial year ending on March 31. Where the accounting period of a company overlaps this date and there is a change in the rate of corporation tax, profits and income must be apportioned.

For several years the full rate of corporation tax was 52 per cent but this is being progressively reduced as follows:

Financial year	Per cent
12 months ending March 31, 1984	50
12 months ending March 31, 1985	45
12 months ending March 31, 1986	40
12 months ending March 31, 1987	35

The progressive reduction in the rate of corporation tax is being made to compensate companies for the loss of stock relief and the progressive withdrawal of certain allowances for capital expenditure which increase the amount of profits and income chargeable to that tax.

SMALL COMPANIES RATE

Where the profits of a company do not exceed stated limits corporation tax becomes payable at the small companies rate. It is the amount of profits and not the size of the company which governs the application of this rate.

The level of profits which a company may derive without losing the benefit of the small companies rate has been frequently changed. However, for financial years commencing on and after April 1, 1983, the following small companies rate applies where profits do not exceed £100,000:

Financial year	Per cent
12 months ending March 31, 1984	38
12 months ending March 31, 1985, 1986 and 1987	30

If profits do exceed £100,000 but fall below £500,000 marginal small companies rate relief applies. The broad effect of marginal relief is that the first £100,000 of profits is taxed at the small companies rate of 38 or 30 per cent. Profits falling in the margin exceeding £100,000 then incur liability at the following marginal rates:

Financial year	Per cent
12 months ending March 31, 1984	55
12 months ending March 31, 1985	48·75
12 months ending March 31, 1986	42·5
12 months ending March 31, 1987	36·25

If the accounting period of a company overlaps March 31, profits must be apportioned to establish the appropriate rate for each part of those profits.

The lower limit of £100,000 and the upper limit of £500,000 applies for a period of twelve months in duration and must be proportionately reduced for shorter periods. Some restriction in the small companies rate and the marginal rate may be necessary if there are two or more "associated companies", namely companies under common control.

CAPITAL GAINS

Chargeable gains arising to a company are calculated in a manner similar to that used for individuals. However, companies cannot obtain the annual exemption of £5,900, nor are they assessed to capital gains tax. In place of this tax companies suffer liability to corporation tax on chargeable gains. Only a fraction of the chargeable gains arising are taxable at the full corporation tax rate. The fraction selected ensures that companies effectively suffer corporation tax at the rate of 30 per cent on the full chargeable gain.

DISTRIBUTIONS

Dividends and other qualifying distributions made by a United Kingdom resident company are not satisfied after deduction of income tax. However, when making a distribution a company is required to account to the Inland Revenue for an amount of advance corporation tax. For distributions made in the year ending April 5, 1986, the amount of advance corporation tax will represent three-sevenths of the distribution. Thus a cash dividend of £70 paid to a shareholder will also require satisfaction of advance corporation tax amounting to £30.

Advance corporation tax accounted for in this manner for distributions made in an accounting period may usually be set against a company's corporation tax liability for the same period. Some restrictions are imposed on the amount which can be offset but any surplus can be carried forward, or carried backwards, and set against corporation tax due for other accounting periods.

A United Kingdom resident shareholder receiving a qualifying distribution also obtains a tax credit, which for the year ending April 5, 1986, is equal to three-sevenths of the distribution made. Therefore the total income of the individual comprises the aggregate of the distribution and the tax credit. If the individual is not liable, or not fully liable, to income tax at the basic rate, all or part of the tax credit can be refunded by the Inland Revenue. Individuals with substantial income incur liability to income tax at the higher rates exceeding 30 per cent on the aggregate of the distribution and the tax credit.

PAYMENT OF TAX

Corporation tax, less any relief for advance corporation tax, usually falls due for payment nine months following the end of the accounting period to which the tax relates. Companies who were carrying on business before 1966 may have a later due and payable date.

INTEREST

On making many payments of interest a company is required to deduct income tax at the basic rate and account for the tax deducted to the Inland Revenue. The gross amount of interest paid will usually comprise a charge on income to be offset against profits on which corporation tax becomes payable.

GROUPS OF COMPANIES

Each company within a group is separately charged to corporation tax on profits, gains and income. However, where one group member realizes a loss, other than a capital loss, a claim may be made to offset the deficiency against profits of some other member of the same group.

Claims are also available to avoid the payment of advance corporation tax on distributions, or the deduction of income tax on the payment of interest, for transactions between members of a group of companies. The transfer of capital assets from one member of a group to a fellow member will incur no liability to tax on chargeable gains.

VALUE ADDED TAX

INTRODUCTION

Unlike income tax, capital gains tax, capital transfer tax and corporation tax, which are collected and administered by the Inland Revenue, value added tax is the responsibility of Customs and Excise. Value added tax is charged on the value of supplies made in the United Kingdom by a registered trader and extends both to the supply of goods and to the supply of services. Liability also arises on the value of goods imported into the United Kingdom.

REGISTRATION

All traders, including professional men and women, together with companies, making taxable supplies of a value exceeding stated limits are required to register for value added tax purposes. Taxable supplies represent the supply of goods and services potentially chargeable with value added tax. The limits which govern mandatory registration are amended annually but from March 20, 1985, an unregistered trader must register—

(a) at any time, if there are reasonable grounds for believing that the value of taxable supplies in the year then beginning will exceed £19,500, or

(b) at the end of any quarter, namely March 31, June 30, September 30 or December 31, if the total value of taxable supplies has exceeded either £6,500 in the last quarter or £19,500 in the last four quarters. Registration will not be mandatory if it can be shown that the value of taxable supplies in the last quarter and the next three quarters is not expected to exceed £19,500.

Where the limits governing mandatory registration have been exceeded it is necessary for the trader to notify Customs and Excise. Failure to provide prompt notification may have unfortunate results as the person concerned will be required to account for value added tax from the proper registration date. In some situations a trader whose taxable supplies do not reach the mandatory registration limits may apply for voluntary registration.

A registered trader may submit an application for de-registration if the value of taxable supplies subsequently falls. From June 1, 1985, an application for de-registration can be made if the value of taxable supplies for the year beginning on the application date is not expected to exceed £18,500. De-registration can also be achieved if the value of taxable supplies in each of the two previous years did not exceed £19,500 and is unlikely to exceed this threshold in the following twelve-month period.

INPUT TAX

A registered trader will both suffer tax (input tax) when obtaining goods or services for the purposes of his business and also become liable to account for tax (output tax) on the value of goods and services which he supplies. Relief can usually be obtained for input tax suffered, either by setting that tax against output tax due or by repayment. Most items of input tax can be relieved in this manner but there are exceptions including the prohibition of relief for the cost of business entertaining. Where a registered trader makes both exempt supplies and also taxable supplies to his customers or clients there may be some restriction in the amount of input tax which can be recovered.

OUTPUT TAX

When making a taxable supply of goods or services a registered trader must account for output tax, if any, on the value of the supply. Usually the price charged by the registered trader will be increased by adding value added tax but failure to make the required addition will not remove liability to account for output tax.

EXEMPT SUPPLIES

No value added tax is chargeable on the supply of goods or services which are treated as exempt supplies. These include the provision of burial and cremation facilities, insurance, finance and education. The granting of a lease to occupy land will usually comprise an exempt supply, but there are numerous exceptions.

Exempt supplies do not enter into the value of taxable supplies which govern liability to mandatory registration. Such supplies made by a registered trader may however limit the amount of input tax which can be relieved.

RATES OF TAX

Two rates of value added tax have applied since June 18, 1979, namely:

(a) a zero, or nil, rate; and

(b) a standard rate of 15 per cent.

Although no tax is due on a zero-rated supply, this does comprise a taxable supply which must be included on the calculation governing liability to register.

ZERO-RATING

A large number of supplies are zero-rated, including the following, among others—

(a) the supply of many items of food and drink for human consumption. This does not include ice creams, chocolates, sweets, potato crisps and alcoholic drinks. Nor does it extend to supplies made in the course of catering, for example, at a wedding reception or other social function, or to items supplied for consumption in a restaurant or cafe. At earlier times, many take-away items of food and drink supplied for consumption outside the supplier's premises were zero-rated. Although this continues to apply to the supply of "cold" items, for example, sandwiches, the supply of "hot" food, for example, fish and chips, ceased to remain zero-rated after April 30, 1984;

(b) animal feeding stuffs;

(c) sewerage and water;

(d) books, brochures, pamphlets, leaflets, newspapers, maps and charts;

(e) talking books for the blind and handicapped and wireless sets for the blind;

(f) newspaper advertising for supplies made before May 1, 1985. Supplies made on or after this date are no longer zero-rated;

(g) electricity, gas and coal;

(h) supplies made in the construction of a building. Zero-rating previously applied to the installation of double glazing, the alteration of a building, the installation of fitted cupboards and the construction of a garage or other building in the grounds of a dwelling-house. However, for supplies made after May 31, 1984, this list of items was substantially reduced and zero-rating is limited to the alteration of a listed building, the construction of a garage in conjunction with the construction of a new dwelling and the installation of working surfaces in the kitchen of a new building;

(i) the transportation of persons in a vehicle, ship or aircraft designed to carry not less than twelve persons;

(j) supplies of drugs, medicines and other aids for the handicapped;

(k) supplies of clothing and footwear for young persons;

(l) exports.

This list is not exhaustive but indicates the wide range of supplies which may be zero-rated.

COLLECTION OF TAX

Registered traders submit value added tax returns for accounting periods. Each accounting period is for three months in duration but arrangements can be made to submit returns on a monthly basis. The return will show both the output tax due for supplies made by the trader in the accounting period and also the input tax for which relief is claimed. If the output tax exceeds input tax the balance must be remitted with the value added tax return. Where input tax suffered exceeds the output tax due the registered trader may claim recovery of the excess from Customs and Excise.

This basis for collecting tax explains the structure of value added tax. Where supplies are made between registered traders the supplier will account for an amount of tax which will usually be identical to the tax recovered by the person to whom the supply is made. However, where the supply is made to a person who is not a registered trader there can be no recovery of input tax and it is on this person that the final burden of value added tax eventually falls.

Tax on imports into the United Kingdom must be satisfied at the time of importation or perhaps later where special arrangements have been agreed.

BAD DEBTS

Many retailers operate special retail schemes for calculating the amount of value added tax due. These schemes are, broadly, based on the volume of consideration received in an accounting period. Should a customer fail to pay for goods or services supplied, there will be no consideration on which value added tax falls to be calculated. In other cases, where the special retailers' schemes do not apply, output tax falls due on the value of the supply and liability is not affected by failure to receive consideration. This implies that there will be no relief for the value added tax element in bad debts. However, relief for this element may be obtained where the debtor becomes insolvent.

OTHER SPECIAL SCHEMES

In addition to the schemes for retailers, there are several special schemes applied to calculate the amount of value added tax due and which also limit the ability to recover input tax. These schemes apply to the supply of second-hand motor cars, motor cycles, caravans, boats, electronic organs, aircraft and firearms, together with works of art, antiques and collectors' pieces.

OTHER TAXES AND STAMP DUTIES

The Commissioners as a general rule allow deeds, etc., to be stamped after execution:—

WITHOUT PENALTY, ON PAYMENT OF DUTY ONLY.
Deeds and instruments not otherwise excepted, within 30 days of *first* execution.
NOTE.—Where wholly executed *abroad,* the period begins to run from the date of arrival here.

PENALTIES ENFORCEABLE ON STAMPING IN ADDITION TO DUTY:—
Instruments presented after the proper time (subject to special provisions in some cases and subject to the commissioner's power to mitigate) a penalty equal to the duty . £10

AGREEMENT for Lease, *see* LEASES.

AGREEMENT FOR SALE OF PROPERTY—charged with *ad val.* duty as if an actual conveyance on sale with certain exceptions, *e.g.* agreements for the sale of land, stocks and shares, goods, wares or merchandise, or a ship (*see* s. 59 (1), Stamp Act 1891). If *ad val.* duty is paid on an agreement in accordance with this provision, the subsequent conveyance or transfer is not chargeable with any *ad val.* duty and the Commissioners will upon application either place a denoting stamp on such conveyance or transfer or will transfer the *ad val.* duty thereto. Further, if such an agreement is rescinded, not performed, etc., the Commissioners will return the *ad val.* duty paid.

AGREEMENT under seal subject to exemptions . 50p

ASSIGNMENT:
By way of sale—*see* Conveyance.
By way of gift—*see* Voluntary Disposition.

ASSURANCE—*see* Insurance Policies.

BEARER INSTRUMENT:
Inland bearer instrument, *i.e.* share warrant, stock certificate to bearer or any other instrument to bearer by which stock can be transferred, issued by a company or body formed or established in U.K. Duty of an amount equal to three times the transfer duty (usually £3% of the market value).

Overseas bearer instrument, *i.e.,* such an instrument issued in G.B. by a company formed out of the U.K. Duty equal to twice the transfer duty (usually £2% of the market value). Even if issued out of G.B. the instrument must be stamped before transfer in G.B. The issue or transfer of a bearer instrument relating to stock expressed in the currency of a territory outside the Scheduled territories is exempt from duty.

BILL OF SALE, Absolute, *see* CONVEYANCE ON SALE.

CAPITAL DUTY.—Where a *chargeable transaction* of a *capital company* takes place after July 31, 1973, duty of £1 is payable on every £100 or fraction of £100 of the actual value of the assets contributed by the members (as opposed to the previous duty of 50p per £100 of the nominal capital), provided the place of effective management of the company is in G.B. or its registered office is in G.B. but the place of its effective management is outside the E.E.C. (Finance Act 1973).

A statement containing prescribed particulars must be delivered to the Commissioners within one month of the transaction unless there is an obligation under the Companies Act 1948 (*e.g.*, on the formation of a limited liability company) or the Limited Partnerships Act 1907 (*e.g.*, on the registration of a limited partnership) to send a statement to the registrar of companies as a result of the transaction.

Capital company includes a company incorporated with limited liability under U.K. law, a limited partnership under the Limited Partnerships Act 1907, a company incorporated according to the law of any other member of the E.E.C. and any other corporation or body of persons whose members have the right freely to dispose of their shares and whose liability for debts is limited.

Chargeable transactions includes the formation of a capital company, an increase in its capital by the contribution of assets of any kind, the transfer to G.B. of its place of effective management from a country outside the E.E.C. if its registered office is in such a country, and the transfer to G.B. of its registered office from a country outside the E.E.C. if its place of effective management is in such a country.

CAPITAL TRANSFER TAX

A tax on the transmission of wealth, made by way of gift during a person's lifetime and on death, was introduced by the Finance Act 1975. It applies retrospectively to March 27, 1974, unless the donor died before March 13, 1975 (when Estate Duty or modified Estate Duty will apply).

Tax is charged at progressive rates on the cumulative totals of chargeable gifts made during a person's lifetime, with a final cumulation of the value of a person's estate on his death. The rates of tax for lifetime transfers are those shown in Table 1. For transfers on death, or within 3 years of death, the rates applicable are those in Table 2.

Table 1

Value transferred		Rate of tax
Lower limit £	Upper limit £	Per cent
0	67,000	*Nil*
67,000	89,000	15
89,000	122,000	17½
122,000	155,000	20
155,000	194,000	22½
194,000	243,000	25
243,000	299,000	27½
299,000	—	30

Table 2

Value transferred		Rate of tax
Lower limit £	Upper limit £	Per cent
0	67,000	*Nil*
67,000	89,000	30
89,000	122,000	35
122,000	155,000	40
155,000	194,000	45
194,000	243,000	50
243,000	299,000	55
299,000	—	60

In calculating the value transferred on lifetime gifts, the amount of tax paid by the donor on the gift must be taken into account. The value transferred on death is the value of the person's estate at the moment before his death.

Certain exemptions and reliefs are given, including:

(a) *For lifetime transfers only:*

  (i) The first £3,000 of gifts made in each tax year (April 6 to the following April 5) are exempt. Only the balance over £3,000 is taxable. There is provision for the carry forward of this relief for one year only, in so far as it has not been used in the previous year.

  (ii) Gifts not exceeding £250 to any one donee in the tax year are exempt. This cannot be used to exempt the first £250 of a larger gift.

  (iii) Gifts which are normal expenditure out of income are exempt, provided the donor is left with sufficient income to maintain his standard of living.

  (iv) Gifts in consideration of marriage are exempt up to £5,000 if made by a parent; £2,500 if made by a grandparent or some other lineal ancestor, or by one party to another; and £1,000 in any other case.

  (v) Gifts of certain types of property, including works of art, are exempt if made to a body not established or conducted for profit.

(b) *For lifetime transfers and on death:*

  (i) Transfers between spouses are exempt to the extent that the gift increases the value of the donee spouse's estate.

  (ii) Lifetime gifts to Charities and certain Political Parties are exempt without limit. If made on death or within one year of death, gifts to charities are exempt (political parties £100,000).

  (iii) Gifts to listed heritage bodies including National Gallery, British Museum, and Government Departments, are exempt.

  (iv) Agricultural relief:
Provided certain conditions are satisfied, on a transfer of Agricultural land, the agricultural value is reduced by 50% if the transferor has occupied the land for the purposes of Agriculture for two years up to the time of the transfer, or by 20% if he has owned the land for the last seven years and it has been occupied by someone for the purposes of Agriculture throughout that period.

  (v) There is also relief for business property in certain circumstances.

(c) *For transfers on death only:*
Conditional exemptions exist for works of art, timber and for death on active service. There is an exemption in respect of woodlands available on death.

Tax must be paid within 6 months of the end of the month in which the chargeable event occurs unless the event is a lifetime transfer, made between April 5 and October 1 in any year, when tax is due at the end of the next following April. In certain circumstances, tax may be payable by instalments.

Interest on unpaid tax runs from the date the tax is due.

CONTRACT, *see* AGREEMENT.

CONTRACT OR GRANT FOR PAYMENT OF A SUPERANNUATION ANNUITY: for every £10 or fractional part of £10 . . . .   5p

CONVEYANCE OR TRANSFER ON SALE (in the case of a Voluntary Disposition, *see* below) of any property (*except* stock or marketable securities), where the Conveyance or Transfer contains a certificate of value certifying that the transaction does not form part of a larger transaction or a series of transactions in respect of which the aggregate amount or value of the consideration exceeds £30,000. . *nil*

Exceeds £30,000 (for every £100 or fraction of £100) **£1**

If the Conveyance or Transfer on Sale does not contain the appropriate statement duty at the full rate of £1 for every £100 or fraction of £100 will be payable whatever the amount of the consideration.

However, if the consideration does not exceed £500, and the instrument does not contain a certificate of value, there are graduated duties ranging from 50p to £5.

Conveyances to charities are exempt from duty under this head provided the instrument is stamped with a denoting stamp.

CONVEYANCE OR TRANSFER of any other kind . . . . fixed duty **50p**

Included under this head are Transfers for nominal consideration within any of the following categories:

(a) Transfers vesting the property in trustees on the appointment of a new trustee of a pre-existing trust, or on the retirement of a trustee.

(b) Transfers, where no beneficial interest in the property passes, (i) to a mere nominee of the transferor; (ii) from a mere nominee of the transferee; (iii) from one nominee to another nominee of the same beneficial owner.

(c) Transfer to a residuary legatee of stock, etc., forming part of the residue divisible under a will.

(d) Transfers to a beneficiary under a will of a specific legacy of stock, etc.

(e) Transfers of stock, etc., forming part of an intestate's estate to the person entitled to it.

(f) Transfers to a beneficiary under settlement on a distribution of the trust funds of stock, etc., forming the share or part of the share of those funds to which the beneficiary is entitled in accordance with the terms of the settlement.

(g) Transfers on the occasion of a marriage to trustees of stocks, etc., to be held on the terms of a settlement made in consideration of marriage.

(h) Transfers by the liquidator of a company of stocks, etc., forming part of the assets of the company to the persons who were shareholders, in satisfaction of their rights on a winding-up.

The evidence necessary to establish that a transfer is liable to the fixed duty of 50p should take the form of a certificate setting forth the facts of the transaction. In cases falling within (b) such a certificate should be signed by (1) both transferor and transferee or (2) a member of a Stock Exchange or a solicitor acting for one or other of the parties or (3) an accredited representative of a bank; in the last case when the bank or its official nominee is a party to the transfer, the certificate, instead of setting out the facts, may be to the effect that "the transfer is excepted from Section 74 of the Finance (1909–10) Act 1910." A certificate in other cases should be signed by a solicitor or other person (*e.g.*, a bank acting as trustee or executor) having a full knowledge of the facts.

Registering Officers will in any case in which a Marketing Officer's certificate has not been given require such evidence in order to satisfy themselves that a transfer stamped with the 50p fixed duty is duly stamped.

COVENANT—For original creation and sale of any annuity, *see* CONVEYANCE.

DECLARATION OF TRUST, not being a Will or Settlement 50p

DEMISE, *see* LEASE

DUPLICATE OR COUNTERPART
Same duty as original, but not to exceed . . . 50p

GIFT (*see* VOLUNTARY DISPOSITION).

GUARANTEE:
If under seal 50p

INSURANCE POLICIES:
Life:—
Exc. £50 and not exc. £1,000, for every £100 or part of £100 . . . . 5p
Exc. £1,000, for every £1,000 or any fractional part of £1,000 . . . . 50p
Made after 1 August 1966 for period not exceeding 2 years 5p

LEASES:—Lease or tack for any definite term less than a year of any furnished dwelling-house or apartments where the rent for such term exceeds £500, £1; of any lands, tenements, etc., in consideration of any rent, according to the following table:—

Annual rent not exceeding	*Term not exceeding			Term exceeding 100 years
	7 years	35 years	100 years	
£	£ p	£ p	£ p	£ p
5	*Nil*	0·10	0·60	1·20
10	*Nil*	0·20	1·20	2·40
15	*Nil*	0·30	1·80	3·60
20	*Nil*	0·40	2·40	4·80
25	*Nil*	0·50	3·00	6·00
50	*Nil*	1·00	6·00	12·00
75	*Nil*	1·50	9·00	18·00
100	*Nil*	2·00	12·00	24·00
150	*Nil*	3·00	18·00	36·00
200	*Nil*	4·00	24·00	48·00
250	*Nil*	5·00	30·00	60·00
300	*Nil*	6·00	36·00	72·00
350	*Nil*	7·00	42·00	84·00
400	*Nil*	8·00	48·00	96·00
450	*Nil*	9·00	54·00	108·00
500	*Nil*	10·00	60·00	120·00
Exceeding £500 for every £50 or fraction of £50	0·50	1·00	6·00	12·00

*If the term is indefinite the same duty is payable as if the term did not exceed 7 years.

Agreement for lease, same as actual lease.

Where a consideration other than rent is payable and duty is charged on that consideration at conveyance rates, the same rule applies where the consideration does not exceed £30,000 as under Conveyance or Transfer on Sale (except stock or marketable securities), provided that any rent payable does not exceed £300 a year.

Leases to charities are exempt from duty under this head provided the instrument is stamped with a denoting stamp.

MORTGAGES are exempt.

RECEIPTS FOR SALARIES, Wages and Superannuation, and other like allowances are exempt.

TRANSFER OF STOCK AND SHARES by way of gift or sale—for each £50 or part of £50 . . . .   £1

UNIT TRUST INSTRUMENT—Any trust instrument of a unit trust scheme—For every £100, and also for any fractional part of £100, of the amount or value of the property subject to the trusts created or recorded by the instrument 25p

VOLUNTARY DISPOSITION *inter vivos:*— 50p

THE COST OF LIVING

The first cost-of-living index to be calculated in Great Britain was the one which took July, 1914, as 100 and was based on the pattern of expenditure of working class families in 1904. Since 1947 the Index of Retail Prices has superseded the cost-of-living index, although the older term is still often popularly applied to it. This index is designed to reflect the month-by-month changes in the average level of retail prices of goods and services purchased by the "majority" of households in the United Kingdom, including practically all wage-earners and most small and medium salary-earners. For spending coming within the scope of the index, a representative list of items is selected and the prices actually charged for these items are collected at regular intervals. In working out the index figure, the price changes are "weighted"—that is, given different degrees of importance—in accordance with the pattern of consumption of the average family.

A more widely used guide when considering changes in the average level of prices of all consumer goods and services, particularly over a number of years, is the consumer price index, now renamed the consumers' expenditure deflator. This index, which has been calculated back to 1938, covers the expenditure of all consumers as defined for national income

purposes, and compares the price of goods and services actually purchased in a given year with the prices of the same goods and services in a base year.

During 1973 the Central Statistical Office constructed an annual index of prices of consumer goods and services over the period 1914 to 1972. This index has been constructed by linking together the pre-war cost of living index for the period 1914–1938, the consumers' expenditure deflator for the period 1938 and 1946–62* and the General Index of Retail Prices for the period 1962–1972.

In August 1979, the tax and price index (TPI) was introduced in order to provide a statistic which incorporates the effects of direct and indirect taxation, as well as prices, on taxpayers. The TPI is not directly concerned with the purchasing power of money, however, but with the purchasing power of pre-tax income. The General Index of Retail Prices thus retains its function of measuring the changes in the prices of goods and services purchased by households (from their post-tax income), and therefore as an indicator of the purchasing power of money.

In 1974 the General Index of Retail Prices was rebased taking January 1974 = 100. Using this index the following table has been constructed:

	General Index of Retail Prices (all items) Jan. 1974 = 100	Comparable Purchasing Power of £1 in 1984
	Annual averages	
1914.	11·1	31·69
1915.	13·7	25·67
1920.	27·7	12·70
1925.	19·6	17·94
1930.	17·6	19·98
1935.	15·9	22·12
1940.	24·4	14·41
1945.	29·3	12·00
1950.	35·6	9·88
1955.	44·1	7·97
1960.	49·6	7·09
1965.	58·4	6·02
1970.	73·1	4·81
1971.	80·0	4·40
1972.	85·7	4·10
1973.	93·5	3·76
1974.	108·5	3·24
1975.	134·8	2·61
1976.	157·1	2·24
1977.	182·0	1·93
1978.	197·1	1·78
1979.	223·5	1·57
1980.	263·7	1·33
1981.	295·0	1·19
1982.	320·4	1·10
1983.	335·1	1·05
1984.	351·8	1·00

By employing this table an annual purchasing power of the pound index may be derived by taking the inverse of the price index. So, for example, if the purchasing power of the pound is taken to be 100p in 1972, then its comparable purchasing power in 1984 would be:

$$100 \times \frac{85·7}{351·8} = 25·5p$$

It should be noted that these figures can only be approximate.

* There are no official figures for 1939–45.

NATIONAL HEALTH SERVICE
(and Local Authority Personal Social Services)

The National Health Service came into being on July 5, 1948, as a result of the *National Health Service Act* 1946. The Act placed a duty on the Secretary of State for Social Services to promote the establishment in England and Wales of a comprehensive Health Service designed to secure improvement in the mental and physical health of the people and the prevention, diagnosis and treatment of illness. The Secretary of State for Wales administers the National Health Service in Wales. There are separate Acts for Scotland and Northern Ireland, where the Health Services are run on very similar lines. The Secretaries of State are responsible to Parliament for seeing that Health Services of all kinds of the highest possible quality are available to all who need them.

The National Health Service covers a comprehensive range of hospital, specialist, family practitioner (medical, dental, ophthalmic and pharmaceutical), artificial limb and appliance, ambulance, and community health services. Everyone normally resident in this country is entitled to use any of these services, there are no contribution conditions and the charges made (except those for amenity beds) are reduced or waived in cases of hardship. In addition the Secretary of State for Social Services is responsible under the Local Authority Social Services Act 1970 for the provision by local authorities of social services for the elderly, the mentally handicapped, the physically disabled and also for families and children. The 1980 Health Services Act led to major changes in the structure of the Health Service. Under arrangements which became operational in April 1982, District Health Authorities (DHAs)—of which there are 192 in England and nine in Wales—are responsible for the operational management of health services and for planning within regional and national strategic guidelines. Each DHA is required to arrange its services into units of management at hospital and community services level, and as many decisions as possible are delegated to unit level. Arrangements for the Family Practitioner Service continued to be administered by Family Practitioner Committees (FPCs)—90 in England and eight in Wales. FPCs also contribute to the planning of health services.

The 14 Regional Health Authorities (RHAs) in England are responsible for regional planning, the allocation of resources to District Authorities, and the promotion of national policies and priorities. Performance review meetings are held annually between each hospital unit and its DHA, each DHA and its RHA, and between each RHA and Department of Health and Social Security Ministers, thereby strengthening Authorities' accountability to Parliament, whilst respecting the essentially locally-based nature of decision making. Professional advisory machinery incorporated within the structure ensures that Health Authorities and their staffs make decisions in the full knowledge of expert opinion.

The cost of the reorganized NHS is still financed mainly from taxation and met from moneys voted by Parliament. In Great Britain this amounts to more than £12 billion a year. The Department of Health and Social Security makes capital and revenue allocations to the RHAs and from these the RHAs meet the cost of their own services and make allocations to DHAs as well as funding Community Health Councils.

THE HEALTH SERVICES

Family Doctor Service

In England and Wales the Family Doctor Service (or General Medical Services) is organized by 98 Family Practitioner Committees which also organize the General Dental, Pharmaceutical and Ophthalmic Services for their areas. There is a Family Practitioner Committee for one or more District Health Authorities. Under the Health and Social Security Act 1984, FPCs became employing authorities in their own right on April 1, 1985, and all the members and the chairmen (31 in all) are appointed by the Secretary of State. Twenty-three of the appointments are made from the nominations received from local doctors (8), dentists (3), pharmacists (2), opticians (2), DHAS (4) and local authorities (4). The remainder (7) are appointed after such consultations as the Secretary of State considers appropriate. The change is to bring DHAs and FPCs into a closer working partnership and to improve the efficiency and accountability of FPCs.

Any doctor may take part in the Family Doctor Scheme, provided the area in which he wishes to practise has not already an adequate number of doctors, and about 25,000 general practitioners in England and Wales do so. They may at the same time have private fee-paying patients. Family doctors are paid for their Health Service work in accordance with a scheme of remuneration which includes *inter alia* a basic practice allowance, capitation fees, reimbursement of certain practice expenses and payments for "out of hours" work.

Everyone aged 16 or over can choose his doctor (parents or guardians choose for children under 16) and the doctor is also free to accept a person or not as he chooses. A person may change his doctor if he wishes, either at once if he has changed his address or obtained permission from the doctor on whose list he is, or by informing the Family Practitioner Committee (in which case 14 days must elapse before the other doctor can accept him). When people are away from home they can still use the Family Doctor Service if they ask to be treated as "temporary residents", and in an emergency, if a person's own doctor is not available, any doctor in the service will give treatment and advice.

Patients are treated either in the Doctor's surgery or, when necessary, at home. Doctors may prescribe for their patients all drugs and medicines which are medically necessary for their treatment and also a certain number of surgical appliances (the more elaborate being provided through the hospitals).

Dental Service

Dentists, like doctors, may take part in the Service and may also have private patients. About 13,000 of the dentists available for general practice in England provide National Health Service general dental services. They are responsible to the Family Practitioner Committees in whose areas they provide services.

Patients are free to go to any dentist taking part in the Service and willing to accept them, and cannot register with any particular dentist. Dentists receive payment for items of treatment for individual patients, instead of the capitation fee received by doctors. There is no need for the patient to obtain a recommendation before seeking dental treatment. All treatment and dentures considered by the dentist to be necessary for dental fitness are available under the NHS. But for certain more expensive items such as metal dentures, bridges and gold fillings, it is necessary for the dentist to obtain the prior approval of the Dental Estimates Board.

A dentist may, with the approval of the Dental Estimates Board, charge his patients a prescribed sum for such types of treatment as crowns, inlays or metal dentures where these are not clinically necessary, if the patient wishes to have them. Where a denture supplied under the Service has to be replaced because of loss or damage the whole or part of the cost may be charged to the patient if he has been careless. Under the current system of charges a patient pays the full cost of each item of treatment (excluding dentures), with a maximum charge for one course of treatment. The most recent revision of charges was introduced on April 1, 1985. They are as follows:—

1. The patient pays the full cost of each item of treatment (except dentures, bridges, crowns, inlays, pinlays and gold fillings) up to a maximum charge of £14·50 for one course of treatment.

2. For a denture or a bridge—

	Synthetic resin	Metal or Porcelain
(a) 1, 2 or 3 teeth	£26	£50
(b) 4–8 teeth	£28	£52
(c) More than 8 teeth	£30	£55
Maximum for more than one denture (or bridge)	£47	£98

3. For crowns, inlays, pinlays and gold fillings—
   (a) per tooth restored — £33 or £63 depending on the percentage of gold used (these charges include any other restorations in the same tooth, apart from root fillings)
   (b) maximum if more than one tooth restored £115

The most anyone can pay for all the treatment they need (including crowns, bridges and dentures) is £115.

No charge is made for clinical examination of a patient's mouth, arrest of bleeding, repairs to dentures, the cost of travelling if the dentist has to visit the patient at home or re-opening of the surgery in an emergency. Expectant mothers or women who have had a child during the preceding twelve months, children under 18 (except that you have to pay for dentures and bridges if you are over 16 and not in full-time education), or up to 19, but still in full-time attendance at school, do not pay charges. Full remission of charges is automatically available to people in receipt of supplementary benefit or F.I.S., and those entitled to free prescriptions and milk and vitamins on income grounds. Full or partial remission may also be available to those with incomes somewhat above supplementary benefits if they claim.

Pharmaceutical Service

Patients may obtain medicines, appliances and oral contraceptives prescribed under the NHS from any pharmacy whose owner has entered into arrangements with the Family Practitioner Committee to provide this service. Almost all pharmacy owners have done so and display notices that they dispense under the NHS: the number of these pharmacies in England and Wales at the end of 1984 was about 10,000. There are also some appliance suppliers who only provide special appliances. In country areas where access to a pharmacy may be difficult patients may be able to obtain medicines etc. from their doctor.

Except for contraceptives (for which there is no charge), a charge of £2·00 is payable for each item supplied unless the patient is exempt and the declaration on the back of the prescription form is completed. Exemptions cover children under 16, men aged 65 and over and women aged 60 and over, pregnant women and mothers who have had a baby within the last 12 months, people suffering from certain medical conditions, people who receive F.I.S. or supplementary benefit, people on low income and war pensioners (for their accepted disablements). In addition prepayment certificates may be purchased by those patients not entitled to exemption who require frequent prescriptions. Further information about the exemption and prepayment arrangements is given in leaflet P.11.

General Ophthalmic Services

General Ophthalmic Services, which are administered by Family Practitioner Committees, form part of the ophthalmic services available under the National Health Service and provide for the testing of sight and, for children and people on a low income, the supply of NHS glasses. Diagnosis and specialist treatment of eye conditions is available through the Hospital Eye Service as well as the provision of glasses of a special type. Testing of sight may be carried out by any ophthalmic medical practitioner or ophthalmic optician. The optician must hand the prescription to the patient who can take this to any supplier of glasses of his choice to have dispensed.

From 1 April 1985 only children, those on a low income and people who require high powered lenses are eligible to have NHS glasses. All others must obtain their glasses privately. An NHS sight test remains free. Children up to the age of 16 or young people under 19 in full-time education may be supplied free of charge with standard lenses in children's standard frames. Additionally, school-children aged 10 years or over and young people under 19 in full-time education may be supplied with standard lenses without charge if any other type of NHS frame is used. The charge for the frame must then be paid. People on a low income may receive help with all or part of the cost of NHS glasses. People in receipt of supplementary benefit, F.I.S., free milk or vitamins, or free prescriptions because of low income are automatically entitled to have free NHS glasses.

Primary Health Care Services

Primary health care services include the general medical, dental, ophthalmic and pharmaceutical services, health centres and clinics, family planning outside the hospital service and preventive activities in the community including vaccination, immunisation and fluoridation. The district nursing and health visiting services, much ante- and post-natal care; and chiropody are also an integral part of the primary health care service.

Community Child Health Services

Pre-school services, usually at child health clinics, provide regular surveillance of children's physical, mental and emotional health and development, and advice to parents on their children's health and welfare. The School Health Service provides for the medical and dental examination of school-children, and advises the local education authority, the school, the parents and the pupil of any health factors which may require special consideration during the pupil's school life.

Hospitals and Other Services

The Secretary of State for Social Services has a duty to provide, to such extent as he/she considers necessary to meet all reasonable requirements, hospital and other accommodation; medical, dental, nursing and ambulance services; other facilities for the care of expectant and nursing mothers and young children, facilities for the prevention of illness, and the care and after-care of persons suffering from illness and such other services as are required for the diagnosis and treatment of illness. Rehabilitation services (occupational therapy, physiotherapy and speech therapy) may also be provided for those who need it and surgical and medical appliances are supplied in appropriate cases.

Specialists and consultants who take part in the Service can engage in private practice, including the treatment of their private patients in NHS hospitals.

In a number of hospitals accommodation is available for the treatment of private in-patients who undertake to pay full hospital maintenance costs and (usually) separate medical fees to a specialist as well. The amount of the medical fees is a matter for agreement between doctor and patient.

Hospital charges for private resident patients are determined annually, on a national basis for classes of hospitals, by the Secretary of State in accordance with the National Health Service Act 1977. These charges are revised annually from April 1 each year to reflect the average cost, which it is estimated will be incurred during the current financial year in the treatment of in-patients in each class of hospital. They also include a contribution towards capital costs.

For in-patients paying specialists' fees separately, the hospital daily charges from April 1, 1985, for accommodation and services in each class of hospital are as follows:

Class A. Long stay hospitals

Single Room	Other Accommodation
£66·00	£60·00

Class B. Psychiatric hospitals

Single Room	Other Accommodation
£52·00	£47·00

Class C1. Mainly acute and other hospitals in non-teaching districts

Single Room	Other Accommodation
£106·00	£96·00

Class C2. Acute and other hospitals in non-teaching districts

Single Room	Other Accommodation
£120·00	£109·00

Class D. London teaching hospitals

Single Room	Other Accommodation
£166·00	£151·00

Class E. Provincial teaching hospitals

Single Room	Other Accommodation
£137·00	£124·00

Class F. London Postgraduate teaching hospitals managed by Special Health Authorities; (other than hospitals in *Class G*)

Single Room	Other Accommodation
£183·00	£167·00

Class G. Hospitals for sick children and the National Heart and Chest hospitals

Single Room	Other Accommodation
£253·00	£230·00

For those patients who have not made separate arrangements with a specialist for private treatment the charges range from £62 in a long stay hospital to £266 in certain London Postgraduate teaching hospitals.

The following daily charges apply to services provided for overseas visitors who are in-patients.

	Single Room £	Other Accommodation £
Class A (Long-Stay Hospitals)	68·00	62·00
Class B (Psychiatric Hospitals)	54·00	49·00
Class C1 (Mainly acute and other hospitals in non-teaching districts)	110·00	100·00
Class C2 (Acute and other hospitals in non-teaching districts)	125·00	114·00
Class D (Hospitals in London teaching districts (other than hospitals in *Classes A* and *B*))	174·00	159·00
Class E (Hospitals in provincial teaching districts (other than hospitals in *Classes A* and *B*))	144·00	131·00
Class F (London Postgraduate Teaching Hospitals managed by Boards of Governors or Special Health Authorities except the hospitals managed by Hammersmith Special Health Authority)	193·00	176·00
Class G (Hospitals managed by Hammersmith Special Health Authority)	266·00	243·00

Certain hospitals have accommodation in single rooms or small wards which, if not required for patients who need privacy for medical reasons, may be made available to patients who desire it as an amenity. Amenity bed charges are at present £12 per day in single rooms and £6 per day in small wards. In such cases the patients are treated in every other respect as National Health patients.

There is no charge for drugs supplied to National Health hospital in-patients but out-patients pay £1 per item unless they are exempt.

With certain exceptions, hospital out-patients have to pay fixed charges for dentures, glasses and certain appliances. The charge for glasses will be related to the type of lens prescribed; and for dentures will be up to a maximum charge of £60·00.

Local Authority Personal Social Services

Local authorities are responsible for the organization, management and administration of the personal social services and each authority has a Director of Social Services and a Social Services Committee responsible for the social services functions placed upon them by the Local Authority Social Services Act 1970.

NATIONAL INSURANCE AND RELATED CASH BENEFITS

The State insurance and assistance schemes, comprising schemes of national insurance and industrial injuries insurance, national assistance, and non-contributory old age pensions came into force from July 5, 1948. The Ministry of Social Security Act, 1966, replaced national assistance and non-contributory old age pensions with a scheme of non-contributory benefits, termed supplementary allowances and pensions. These, and subsequent measures relating to social security provision in Great Britain, were consolidated by the Social Security Act, 1975 (now the principal Act); the Social Security (Consequential Provisions) Act, 1975; and the Industrial Injuries and Diseases (Old Cases) Act, 1975: corresponding measures were passed for Northern Ireland. The Social Security Pensions Act, 1975, introduced a new State pensions scheme, which came into force on April 6, 1978, and the graduated pension scheme 1961–1975 has been wound up, existing rights being preserved. The Pensioners' Payments and Social Security Act, 1979, provided for a £10 bonus for pensioners in 1979 and also for the payment of a bonus in succeeding years at levels then to be determined. The Child Benefit Act, 1975, replaced family allowances (introduced 1946) with child benefit and one parent benefit.

The Government published on June 3, 1985 a Green Paper setting out its proposals for reform of certain aspects of social security. A White Paper is expected in late 1985.

NATIONAL INSURANCE SCHEME

The National Insurance scheme operates under the Social Security Acts, 1975 to 1980, and orders and regulations made thereunder. The scheme is financed by contributions payable by earners, employers and others (such as non-employed persons, paying voluntary contributions), together with the Treasury supplement. It provides the funds required for paying benefits payable under the Social Security Acts out of the National Insurance Fund and not out of other public money; for the making of payments towards the cost of the National Health Service and into the Redundancy and Maternity Pay Funds; and for paying benefit under the Industrial Injuries and Diseases (Old Cases) Act, 1975.

From April 6, 1985, the yearly Treasury supplement to the National Insurance Fund is equal to 9 per cent of all contributions (calculated so as to include those that would have been received if there had been no contracting out or statutory sick pay) after deducting the allocations to the National Health Service and the Redundancy and Maternity Pay Funds.

CONTRIBUTIONS

Contributions are of four classes:

Class 1 contributions are earnings-related, based on a percentage of the employee's earnings.

(a) *primary Class 1* contributions are payable by employed earners and office-holders over age 16 with gross earnings at or above the lower earnings limit of £35·50 per week. For those with gross earnings at or above this level, contributions are payable on *all* earnings up to an upper limit of £265 per week. "Gross earnings" include overtime pay, commission, bonus, etc., without deduction of any superannuation contributions.

Women who marry for the first time no longer have a right to elect not to pay the full contribution rate. Married women and widows who before May 12, 1977, elected not to pay contributions at the full rate retain the right to pay a reduced rate over the same earnings range, which covers industrial injuries benefits and a contribution to the National Health Service. They lose this right if, after April 5, 1978, there are two consecutive tax years in which they have no earnings on which primary Class 1 contributions are payable and in which they have not been at any time self-employed earners. No primary contributions are due on earnings paid for a period on or after the employee's pension age, even when retirement is deferred.

(b) *secondary Class 1* contributions are payable by employers of employed earners, and by the appropriate authorities in the case of office-holders. From Oct. 6, 1985, the upper earnings limit for employers' contributions is abolished and secondary contributions are payable on *all* the employee's earnings if they reach or exceed £35·50 per week.

Primary contributions are deducted from earnings by the employer, and are paid, together with the employer's contributions, to the Inland Revenue along with income tax collected under the PAYE system, so dispensing with contribution cards for employed earners. On Oct. 6, 1985 several lower percentage rates of contribution for lower paid employees and their employers were introduced.

Class 2 contributions are flat-rate, paid weekly by self-employed earners over age 16. Those with earnings below £1,925 a year for the tax year 1985–86 can apply for exception from liability to pay Class 2 contributions. People who while self-employed are excepted from liability to pay contributions on the grounds of small earnings may pay either Class 2 or Class 3 contributions voluntarily. Self-employed earners (whether or not they pay Class 2 contributions) may also be liable to pay Class 4 contributions based on profits or gains within certain limits. There are special rules for those who are concurrently employed and self-employed. Married women and widows can no longer choose not to pay Class 2 contributions. Those who elected not to pay Class 2 contributions before May 12, 1977, retain the right until there is a period of two consecutive tax years after April 5, 1978 in which they were not at any time either self-employed earners or had earnings on which primary Class 1 contributions were payable.

Class 2 contributions may be paid by direct debit through a bank or National Giro account or by stamping a contribution card.

Class 3 contributions are voluntary flat-rate contributions payable by persons over school-leaving age who would otherwise be unable to qualify for retirement pension and certain other benefits because they have an insufficient record of Class 1 or Class 2 contributions. Married women and widows who on or before May 11, 1977, elected not to pay Class 1 (full rate) or Class 2 contributions cannot pay Class 3 contributions while they retain this right.

Payment may be made by stamping a contribution card or by direct debit through a bank Giro account.

Class 4 contributions are payable by self-employed earners, whether or not they pay Class 2 contributions, on annual profits or gains from a trade, profession or vocation chargeable to income tax under Schedule D, where these fall between £4,150 and £13,780 a year. The maximum Class 4 contribution, payable on profits or gains of £13,780 or more, is £606·69.

Class 4 contributions are generally assessed and collected by the Inland Revenue along with Schedule D income tax. Self-employed persons under 16, or who at the beginning of a tax year are over pension age even where retirement is deferred, are not liable to pay Class 4 contributions. There are special rules for people who have more than one job, or who pay Class 1 contributions on earnings which are chargeable to income tax under Schedule D.

Regulations state the cases in which earners may be excepted from liability to pay contributions, and the conditions upon which contributions are credited to persons who are excepted. Leaflet NI 208 is obtainable from local Social Security offices.

The Secretary of State for Social Services is empowered by the Social Security Acts to alter certain rates of contributions by order approved by both Houses of Parliament, and is required by the same enactments to make annual reviews of the general level of earnings in order to determine whether such an order should be made.

For the period Oct. 6, 1985 to April 5, 1986 the earnings brackets determining Class 1 contributions are:

	Weekly earnings £
a	0 — 35·49
b	35·50 — 54·99
c	55·00 — 89·99
d	90·00 — 129·99
e	130·00 — 265·00
f	over 265·00

Contribution rates for the period Oct. 6, 1985 to April 5, 1986 are:

Class 1 contributions—not contracted out

Earnings bracket	Percentage of reckonable income		
	Employee's rate		Employer's rate
	standard	reduced	
a	0	0	0
b	5	3·85	5
c	7	3·85	7
d	9	3·85	9
e	9	3·85	10·45
f	9	3·85	10·45

Class 1 contributions—contracted out (see also p. 1200)

Employee's rates

Earnings bracket	On first £35·50		On earnings from £35·50–£265·00	
	standard	reduced	standard	reduced
a	0	0	0	0
b	5	3·85	2·85	3·85
c	7	3·85	4·85	3·85
d, e, f.	9	3·85	6·85	3·85

Employer's rates

Earnings bracket	On first £35·50	On earnings from £35·50–£265·00	On any earnings over £265·00
a	0	0	0
b	5	0·9	0
c	7	2·9	0
d	9	4·9	0
e	10·45	6·35	0
f	10·45	6·35	10·45

	Weekly flat rate
Class 2 contributions	£3·50
Class 3 contributions	£3·40

	Percentage of profits or gains
Class 4 contributions	6·3

THE STATE EARNINGS RELATED PENSION SCHEME

The Social Security Pensions Act, 1975, which came into force in April, 1978, aims to reduce reliance upon means-tested supplementary benefit in old age, in widowhood and in chronic ill-health by providing better pensions; to ensure that occupational pension schemes which are contracted out of part of the State scheme fulfil the conditions of a good scheme; that pensions are adequately protected against inflation; and that in both the State and occupational schemes men and women are treated equally. Retirement, widow's and invalidity pensions under the new scheme started in April 1979. Since April 6, 1979, flat-rate retirement and other State pensions have been augmented for employed earners by additional pensions related to earnings, but it will be twenty years before these additional pensions become payable at the full rate.

Under the scheme retirement, invalidity and widow's pensions for employees are related to the earnings on which national insurance contributions have been paid. For employees of either sex with a complete insurance record the scheme provides a category A retirement pension in two parts, a basic and an additional component. The basic pension corresponds to the old personal flat-rate national insurance pension. The additional component is 1¼ per cent of average earnings between the lower weekly earnings limit for Class 1 contribution liability and the upper earnings limit for each year of such earnings under the scheme, and will thus build up to 25 per cent in twenty years. When the number of years exceeds twenty, pensions will be based on contributors' twenty best years of earnings between age 16 and pension age (65 for men, 60 for women). Actual earnings are to be revalued in terms of the earnings level current in the last complete tax year before pension age (or death or incapacity). Both components of pensions in payment will be uprated annually in line with the movement of prices. Graduated retirement pensions in payment, and rights to such pensions earned by people who are still working, will be brought into the annual review of benefits.

Self-employed persons pay contributions towards the basic pension. The non-employed and employees with earnings below the lower limit may contribute voluntarily for basic pension. Although no primary Class 1 contributions or Class 2 or Class 4 contributions are payable by persons who work beyond pension age (65 for men, 60 for women), the employer's liability for secondary Class 1 contributions continues if earnings are at or above the lower earnings limit. Class 4 contributions are still payable up to the end of the tax year during which pension age is reached.

Widows will get the whole or part of additional pensions earned by their husbands with their widowed mother's allowances or widow's pensions; and can add to the retirement pensions earned by their own contributions any additional pensions earned by their husbands up to the maximum payable on one person's contributions. Men whose wives die when they are both over pension age can add together their own and their wives' pension rights in the same way as widows. Among the steps taken to give women equal treatment in benefit provision the State scheme permits years of home responsibilities to count towards satisfying the contribution conditions for retirement pension, widowed mother's allowance and widow's pension (and the "half-test" by which a married woman who married before age 55 could not qualify for a Category A retirement pension unless she had contributed on earnings at the basic level in at least half the years between marriage and pension age has been abolished with effect from Dec. 22, 1984). The range of short-term social security benefits and industrial injury benefits under the Social Security Act, 1975, continues with only minor changes.

Contracted Out Schemes.—Members of occupational pension schemes which meet the standards laid down by the Pensions Act can be contracted out of a part of the State retirement and widow's benefits. A contracted-out scheme will be required to provide a minimum level of pension calculated on a basis similar to that for the additional component of retirement pension under the State scheme, with a widow's pension at half this rate. The benefits payable from the State scheme will be correspondingly reduced. The State scheme will help in meeting the cost of giving pensions under contracted-out schemes the same protection against inflation as if they had not been contracted out. The Act contains provisions designed to give women the same rights as men to belong to an occupational pension scheme. The Occupational Pension Board, an independent statutory body established under the Social Security Act, 1973, is responsible for deciding whether an occupational scheme should be accepted as a contracted-out scheme, and for ensuring that a contracted-out scheme has adequate financial resources. The Secretary of State for Social Services has made regulations for employers to inform employees and their organisations and to have consultations before deciding whether or not to contract out. Leaflets relating to the pensions and for the guidance of employers with occupational pension schemes are obtainable from local Social Security offices.

In contracted-out schemes, both the employee and the employer pay the full ordinary rate of contribution on the first £35·50 of earnings but earnings above that amount attract a lower rate of contribution from the employee, and from the employer where the employee's earnings are under £265·00: where the employee's earnings exceed this amount, the full ordinary rate of contribution is due (*see also* p. 1199).

BENEFITS

The benefits payable under the Social Security Acts are as follows:

(1) Contributory Benefits:
  Unemployment benefit.
  Sickness benefit.
  Invalidity pension and allowance.
  Maternity allowance.
  Widow's benefit, comprising widow's allowance, widowed mother's allowance and widow's pension.
  Child's special allowance.
  Retirement pensions, categories A and B.
  Death grant.

(2) Non-contributory Benefits:
  Child benefit.
  One parent benefit.
  Maternity grant.
  Guardian's allowance.
  Attendance allowance.
  Severe disablement allowance.
  Mobility allowance.
  Invalid care allowance.
  Retirement pensions, categories C and D.
  Supplementary benefits.
  Family income supplement.

(3) Benefits for Industrial Injuries and Diseases.

Leaflets relating to the various benefits are obtainable from local Social Security offices.

The Social Security Acts empower the Secretary of State to increase certain rates of benefit by order approved by both Houses of Parliament, and require him to increase certain rates by such an order if an annual review shows that they have not retained their value in relation to the general level of prices obtaining in Great Britain.

The latest order providing for increases in benefit rates took effect from the week commencing Nov. 25, 1986.

CONTRIBUTORY BENEFITS

Entitlement to the contributory benefits (except invalidity benefit) depends on contribution conditions being satisfied either by the claimant or by some other person (depending on the kind of benefit). The class or classes of contribution which for this purpose are relevant to each benefit are as follows:

Short-term benefits

Unemployment benefit	Class 1
Sickness benefit	Class 1 or 2
Maternity allowance	Class 1 or 2
Widow's allowance	Class 1, 2 or 3

Other benefits

Widowed mother's allowance
Widow's pension
Child's special allowance
Category A retirement pension }Class 1, 2 or 3
Category B retirement pension
Death grant

The system of contribution conditions relates to yearly levels of earnings on which contributions have been paid. The contribution conditions for different benefits are set out in summary form in leaflets available at local Social Security offices.

Unemployment Benefit

Benefit is payable in a period of interruption of employment for up to 312 days (a year, excluding Sundays). Spells of unemployment and sickness not separated by more than 8 weeks count as one period of interruption of employment. A person who has exhausted benefit requalifies when he has again worked as an employed earner for at least 16 hours a week for 13 weeks. These weeks need not be consecutive nor fall within the same year.

Disqualifications.—There are disqualifications from receiving benefit, *e.g.* for a period not exceeding six weeks if a person has lost his employment through his misconduct, or has voluntarily left his employment without just cause, or has, without good cause, refused an offer of suitable employment or training.

Sickness Benefit

Sickness benefit is payable for up to 28 weeks of sickness in a period of interruption of employment and is then replaced by invalidity benefit (*see* below).

Disqualifications.—There are disqualifications from receiving sickness or invalidity benefit for a period not exceeding six weeks if a person has become incapable of work through his own misconduct or if he fails without good cause to attend for or submit himself to prescribed medical or other examination or treatment, or observe prescribed rules of behaviour.

Since April 1983 Statutory Sick Pay (S.S.P.) has been paid by employers to most of their employees for the first 8 weeks of sickness in any tax year. Employers are compensated for these payments through deductions in their National Insurance contributions. Those who do not qualify for S.S.P., or who have used up their 8 weeks, may apply for State sickness benefit.

From April 6, 1986, S.S.P. will be paid for a maximum of 28 weeks in any period of sickness. S.S.P. will then completely replace sickness benefit for most employees.

Invalidity Benefit

Normally, after 28 weeks of sickness, sickness benefit is replaced by an invalidity pension. In addition an invalidity allowance is payable if incapacity for work begins more than five years before pension age. The allowance varies according to the age on falling sick, and if still in payment at pension age will continue at a higher rate as an addition to retirement pension. From Sept. 16, 1985 invalidity allowance is reduced or withdrawn completely if there is entitlement to an additional earnings-related pension and/or a guaranteed minimum pension.

Maternity Allowance

A woman who has been employed or self-employed and paying contributions at the full rate receives a maternity allowance, normally for 18 weeks beginning eleven weeks before the expected week of confinement, provided that she has no paid work during that period. The rate of allowance is increased where the woman has an adult dependent.

Widow's Benefits

Only the late husband's contributions of any class count for widow's benefit in any of its three forms.

Widow's Allowance.—A woman who at her husband's death is under 60 (or over 60, if he had not retired), receives a cash allowance during the first 26 weeks of widowhood, with increases for each child, in addition to child benefit.

Widowed Mother's Allowance.—When the 26 weeks of widow's allowance have elapsed, a widow who is left with one or more dependent children receives a weekly cash allowance with increases for each child, in addition to child benefit. A widowed mother's personal allowance is payable to widows who, when their widow's or widowed mother's allowance ends, have living with them a son or daughter under 19, who has left school.

Widow's Pension.—A widow receives this pension when widow's allowance ends, if she was over 50 at the time of her husband's death; or when her widowed mother's allowance or widowed mother's personal allowance ends, if she is then over 50 (40 if widowed before February 4, 1957).

Flat-rate widow's pensions on a graduated scale were introduced in April 1971 for women who are widowed between the ages of 40 and 50, or who cease to be entitled to a widowed mother's allowance between those ages.

Widow's benefit of any form ceases upon remarriage.

Child's Special Allowance

A woman whose marriage has been dissolved or annulled, and who has not re-married and is not living with a man as his wife, is paid a special allowance on the ex-husband's death based on his contribution record. The normal condition is that she has a child living with her to whose maintenance he was contributing, or had been liable to contribute, at least 25p a week in cash or its equivalent. The allowance is in addition to child benefit.

Retirement Pension
Categories A and B

A *Category A pension* is payable for life to men or women on their own contributions if (a) they are over pension age (65 for a man and 60 for a woman), and (b) they have retired from regular employment. Men aged 70 or over and women aged 65 or over are not required to satisfy condition (b).

Where a person does not retire at 65 (60 for a woman) or later cancels retirement, and does not draw a Category A pension, the weekly rate of pension is increased, when he or she finally retires or reaches the age of 70 (65 for a woman), in respect of weeks when pension is foregone during the five years after reaching minimum pension age. Details of the increase in the rate of pension due to deferred retirement are given in leaflet NP32, available at D.H.S.S. offices. A married man can also earn extra pension for his wife.

A *Category B pension* is normally payable for life to a woman on her husband's contributions when he has retired, or is over 70, and has qualified for his own Category A pension, and she has reached 60 and retired from regular work or has reached 65. It is also payable on widowhood after 60 whether or not the late husband had retired and qualified for his own pension. The weekly pension is payable at the rate of the increase for a wife while the husband is alive, and at the single person's rate on widowhood after 60. Where a woman is widowed before she reaches 60, a Category B pension is paid to her on reaching 60 at the same weekly rate as her widow's pension if she retires. If a woman qualifies for a pension of each category she receives whichever pension is the larger. Details of the increase in the rate of pension due to deferred retirement are given in leaflet NP32A, available at D.H.S.S. offices.

A man aged 65 to 70, or a woman aged 60 to 65, who has qualified for pension will have it reduced if he or she earns more than a certain amount. Where an adult dependant is living with the claimant, an Adult Dependents Allowance will only be payable if the dependent's earning do not exceed the standard rate of unemployment benefit for a single person under pensionable age (*see* p. 1202). For the purpose of the dependency rule only, earnings will include payments by way of occupational pension. The earnings of a separated spouse affect the increase of retirement pension if they exceed £23·00 a week.

Unemployment, sickness or invalidity benefit is payable to men between 65 and 70 and women between 60 and 65 who have not retired from regular work and who would have been entitled to a retirement pension if they had retired at pension age. This applies in the case of sickness and invalidity benefit if incapacity for work is the result of an industrial accident or prescribed disease. These rates of benefit for people over pension age are shown in leaflet N.I. 196. A retirement pension will be increased by the amount of any invalidity allowance the pensioner was getting within the period of 8 weeks and one day before reaching minimum pension age. An age addition of 25p per week is payable if a retirement pensioner is aged 80 or over. (For attendance allowance and invalidity care allowance, *see* Noncontributory Benefits).

Graduated Pension

The graduated pension scheme under which national insurance contributions and retirement pensions were graduated within specified limits, according to earnings, was discontinued in April, 1975, under the Social Security Act, 1975. Any graduated pension which an employed person over 18 and under 70 (65 for a woman) had earned by paying graduated contributions between April 6, 1961, when the scheme started and April 5, 1975, will be paid when the contributor retires, or at 70 (65 for a woman), in addition to any retirement pension for which he or she qualifies.

Graduated pension is at the rate of 5·00p a week for each "unit" of graduated contributions paid by the employee (half a unit or more counts as a whole unit). A unit of contributions is £7·50 for men, and £9·00 for women, of graduated contributions paid.

A wife can get a graduated pension in return for her own graduated contributions, but not for her husband's. A widow gets a graduated addition to her retirement pension equal to half of any graduated additions earned by her late husband, plus any additions earned by her own graduated contributions. If a person defers retirement beyond 65 (60 for a woman), half the graduated pension he or she has forgone by deferring retirement for any period before April 6, 1979, will be treated as extra graduated contributions paid, and will count towards further graduated pension on retirement or at 70 (65 for a woman). From April 6, 1979, graduated pension will normally be increased by one-seventh of one per cent for each week of deferred retirement.

Death Grant

A death grant is payable on the death of a qualifying contributor or of his wife, child or widow or, if the contributor is a woman, of her husband, child or widower, and also in respect of the deaths of certain handicapped persons on the insurance of close relatives. No grant is payable for deaths of persons already over pension age on July 5, 1948.

The grant is paid to the deceased person's executors or administrators, if any; otherwise it is paid to the person who meets the funeral expenses or to the next of kin.

Rates of Benefits
(from week commencing Nov. 25, 1985)

Benefit	Weekly rate £
Unemployment Benefit—standard rate	
Person under pension age	30·45
Increase for wife/other adult dependent	18·80
Person under pension age*	38·30
Increase for wife/other adult dependent	23·00
Sickness Benefit—standard rate	
Person under pension age	29·15
Increase for wife/other adult dependent	18·00
Person over pension age*	36·65
Increase for wife/other adult dependent	22·00
Invalidity Pension	
Person (under or over pension age)	38·30
Increase for wife or adult dependent	23·00
Invalidity Allowance* (maximum amounts payable)	
higher rate	8·05
middle rate	5·10
lower rate	2·55
Maternity Allowance	29·15
Widow's Allowance*	53·60
Widowed Mother's Allowance* and Widow's Pension*	38·30
Child's Special Allowance	8·05
Retirement pension*—*categories A and B*	
Single person	38·30
Increase for wife or adult dependent	23·00
Earnings limit for retirement pensioners	75·00
Death Grant	
Adult	30·00
Man aged 55–65 or woman aged 50–60 on July 5, 1948	15·00
Child aged 6–17	22·50
aged 3–5	15·00
under 3	9·00

* These benefits attract an increase for each dependent child (in addition to child benefit) of £8·05.

NON-CONTRIBUTORY BENEFITS
Child Benefit

Child benefit is payable for all children in a family within the age limits, including the first or only child. There is an additional payment for the first or only child in certain one-parent families.

Guardian's Allowance

Where the parents of a child are dead, the person who has the child in his family receives a guardian's allowance in addition to child benefit. The allowance in exceptional circumstances, is payable on the death of only one parent.

Invalid Care Allowance

Invalid care allowance is payable to persons of working age, other than married women supported by their husbands, who are not gainfully employed because they are regularly and substantially engaged in caring for a severely disabled person who is receiving attendance allowance or constant attendance allowance with either a war or services pension, industrial disablement workman's compensation, or an allowance under the Pneumoconiosis, Byssinasis and Miscellaneous Diseases Benefit Scheme.

Maternity Grant

A cash grant of £25 for each confinement. Extra grants are payable, in certain circumstances, if more than one child is born. There are no contribution conditions for the grant, which is payable to all mothers who can satisfy a simple "presence in Great Britain" test.

Mobility Allowance

The allowance is, subject to certain conditions, payable to persons who are suffering from such physical disablement that they are unable to walk or virtually unable to walk, and their handicap is likely to last for at least a year. It can be claimed by persons over the age of 5 and under 65 (for this purpose a claim may be made up to 12 months from that birthday) and may be retained to age 75.

Severe Disablement Allowance

Persons of working age who have been continuously incapable of work for a period of at least 28 weeks but who do not qualify for a contributory invalidity pension may be entitled to severe disablement allowance. People who first become incapable of work after their 20th birthday must be at least 80 per cent disabled.

Attendance Allowance

Attendance allowance is payable to the severely disabled, as determined by the Attendance Allowance Board. The full rate is paid to those in need of a great deal of attention or supervision both by day and by night. The allowance is paid at the lower rate to those whose need for attention or supervision arises either by day or by night.

Non-contributory Retirement Pension
Categories C and D

A *Category C pension* is provided, subject to a residence test, for persons who were over pensionable age on July 5, 1948, and for women whose husbands are so entitled if they are over pension age and have retired from regular work, with increases for adult and child dependents. A *Category D pension* is provided for others when they reach 80 if they are not already getting a retirement pension of any category or if they are getting that pension at less than these rates. An age addition of 25p per week is payable if persons entitled to retirement pension or their dependants are aged 80 or over.

Rates of Benefits
(from week commencing Nov. 25, 1985)

Benefit	Weekly rate £
Child Benefit (per child).............	7.00
One Parent Benefit	
First or only child of certain lone parents.......................	4.55
Guardian's Allowance...............	8.05
Severe Disablement Allowance*......	23.00
Increase for wife/other adult dependent.....................	13.75
Mobility Allowance	21.40
Invalid Care Allowance*.............	23.00
Increase for wife/other adult dependent.....................	13.75
Attendance Allowance	
higher rate	30.60
lower rate	20.45
Retirement Pension—Categories C* and D.	
Single person	23.00
Increase for wife/other adult dependent.....................	13.75
(not payable with Category D pension)	

*These benefits attract an increase for each dependent child (in addition to child benefit) of £8.50.

SUPPLEMENTARY BENEFITS

The Supplementary Benefits scheme is operated under the provisions of the Supplementary Benefits Act, 1976, as amended by the Social Security Act, 1980. Leaflets explaining in detail the calculation of income and capital resources and of each category of requirements (normal requirements, additional requirements and certain housing costs) are available from social security offices. Claimants will be sent a written notice showing how their benefit has been worked out, as is done for family income supplement.

The supplementary pension may be claimed by persons of pension age (65 for men, 60 for women) and the supplementary allowance normally by persons aged 16 or over but under pension age, who are not in full-time work. Benefit can be paid on top of retirement pension or other benefits or of earnings from part-time work. The benefit payable is the amount, assessed under the provisions of the Act and regulations made thereunder, by which the claimant's resources fall short of his requirements. Supplementary benefit is paid at two rates: the ordinary and the long-term scale rates. The long-term rates apply to all beneficiaries who are aged over 60, and also younger beneficiaries who are not required to be available for work, after they have been in receipt of supplementary allowance or another qualifying benefit continuously for at least one year. Otherwise, supplementary benefit is paid at the ordinary rate.

There is an addition of £1.25 to the standard scale rates for blind people. Claimants and dependents aged 80 or over qualify for an addition of 25p to long-term rates. Additional payments are made for certain housing costs.

FAMILY INCOME SUPPLEMENT

The supplement is payable to families, including one parent families, with at least one dependent child under 16 (or over 16 if still at school), whose total family income is below the "prescribed amount" if the man or woman is employed or self-employed, and normally so engaged, in remunerative full-time work (*i.e.*, 30 or more hours per week, 24 in the case of single parents). "Total income" includes the gross earnings of the claimant and his wife, but excludes child benefit or children's income, except for children's maintenance. The supplement is one-half of the amount by which the family's total income falls below the "prescribed amount", subject to a maximum payment; odd amounts are rounded up to the next 10p above, and the minimum amount payable is 20p a week. Usually the supplement is awarded for 52 weeks and is not affected if the claimant's circumstances change during that time. Claim forms (FIS 1) can be obtained at a Social Security Office or a Post Office.

Rates of Benefits
(from week commencing Nov. 25, 1985)

	Weekly rate £
SUPPLEMENTARY ALLOWANCES/PENSION	
Ordinary scale rate	
Couple	47.85
Single householder	29.50
Non-householder aged 18 and over ..	23.60
aged 16–17........	18.20
Any other person aged 11–15	15.10
under 11	10.10
Long-term scale rate	
Couple	60.00
Single householder	37.00
Non-householder aged 18 and over ..	30.00
aged 16–17........	23.00
Any other person aged 11–15	15.10
under 11	10.10
Boarders' personal expenses	
Ordinary scale rates	
Couple	19.40
Single person	9.70
Dependent child 18–19	9.70
16–17	5.85
11–15	5.00
under 11	3.25
Long-term scale rates	
Couple	21.70
Single person	10.85
Residents in private and voluntary residential care and nursing homes.	8.95

Board and lodging limits (depending on* area† type of home)

Ordinary board and lodging*	45.00–70.00
Hostels	70.00
Residential care homes	120.00–180.00
Nursing homes†	150.00–230.00
Heating additions	
Lower rate	2.20
Higher rate	5.45
Central heating additions	
Lower rate	2.20
Higher rate	4.40
(claims or entitlement to central heating addition must predate Aug. 5, 1985).	
Estate rate heating additions	
Lower rate	4.40
Higher rate	8.80
Housing Benefit Needs Allowances	
Single person	47.70
Single handicapped person	53.20
Couple/single parent..............	70.20

Couple, one handicapped/single handicapped parent	75·70
Couple, both handicapped	78·25
Dependent child addition	14·50
Pensioner addition	0·85

FAMILY INCOME SUPPLEMENT
Prescribed amount of income

Family with one child—under 11	97·50
aged 11–15	98·50
aged 16 and over	99·50
Family with more than one child	
For each additional child—under 11 .	11·50
aged 11–15	12·50
aged 16 and over	13·50
Maximum amount payable	
Family with one child—under 11	25·00
aged 11–16	25·50
aged 16 and over	26·00
Family with more than one child	
For each additional child—under 11 .	2·50
aged 11–15	3·00
aged 16 and over	3·50

DETERMINATION OF CLAIMS AND QUESTIONS

With a few exceptions, claims and questions relating to Social Security benefits are decided by statutory authorities who act independently of D.H.S.S. and Department of Employment. The first of the statutory authorities, the Adjudication Officer, determines entitlement to benefit. A claimant who is dissatisfied with that decision has the right of appeal to a Social Security Appeal Tribunal. There is a further right of appeal to a Social Security Commissioner against the Tribunal's decision and in most cases leave to appeal must first be obtained. In supplementary benefit and family income supplement cases appeals must be on a point of law. Provision is also made for the determination of certain questions by the Secretary of State for Social Services.

Disablement questions are decided by medical boards or an adjudicating medical practitioner or Medical Appeal Tribunals. Appeal to the Commissioner is with leave and on a point of law only.

Leaflet NI 246 which is available from D.H.S.S. offices, explains how to appeal to a Social Security Appeal Tribunal.

INDUSTRIAL INJURIES AND DISEASES BENEFITS

The Industrial Injuries scheme, administered under the Social Security Act 1975 and subsequent Acts and Regulations, provides a range of benefits designed to compensate for disablement resulting from an industrial accident (i.e. an accident arising out of and in the course of an employed earner's employment) or from a prescribed disease due to the nature of a person's employment. Rates of benefit are reviewed periodically.

Supplementary allowances payable in certain circumstances in cases arising before the Industrial Injuries scheme started are governed by the Industrial Injuries and Diseases (Old Cases) Act, 1975, as amended and regulations made under the Act. Statutory schemes have also been made providing for the payment of allowances supplementing workmen's compensation in certain circumstances, and for the payment of benefits in certain cases where neither workmen's compensation nor Industrial Injuries benefits are payable.

The scheme extends insurance to prescribed industrial diseases and prescribed personal injuries not caused by accident, which are due to the nature of an employed earner's employment and developed on or after July 5, 1948.

Determination of Claims and Questions.—Provision is made for the determination of certain questions by the Secretary of State for Social Services, and of "disablement questions" by a medical board (or a single doctor) or, on appeal, by a medical appeal tribunal. An appeal on a point of law against a medical appeal tribunal decision is determined by the Social Security Commissioner. Claims for benefit and certain questions arising in connection with a claim for or award of benefit (*e.g.* whether the accident arose out of and in the course of the employment) are determined by an adjudication officer appointed by the Secretary of State, or a Social Security Appeal Tribunal, or, on further appeal, by the Commissioners.

Benefits

Disablement Benefit is normally payable 15 weeks (90 days) after the date of accident or onset of disease if the employed earner suffers from loss of physical or mental faculty such that the resulting disablement is assessed at not less than one per cent. The amount of disablement benefit varies according to the degree of disablement (in the form of a percentage) assessed by a medical board or medical appeal tribunal. In cases of disablement of less than 20 per cent, except in pneumoconiosis, byssinosis or diffuse mesotheliama cases, benefit normally takes the form of a gratuity paid according to a prescribed scale, but not exceeding £4,150. Where the degree of disablement is 20 per cent or more, or if it is due to pneumoconiosis, byssinosis or diffuse mesotheliama, the benefit is a weekly pension payable either for a limited period or for life.

The basic rates are applicable to adults and to juveniles entitled to an increase for a child or adult dependent; other juveniles receive lower rates.

Basic rates of pension are not related to the pensioner's loss of earning power, and are payable whether he is in work or not. Upon prescribed conditions, however, pension is supplemented for unemployability and in cases of special hardship. There is provision also for increases of pension during approved hospital treatment or if the pensioner requires constant attendance or if his disablement is exceptionally severe. If the beneficiary is entitled to an unemployability supplement there are increases for each child in addition to child benefit, and, subject to the earnings rule, for an adult dependent. Subject to certain exceptions, a pensioner who is not in receipt of unemployability supplement can draw S.S.P., sickness or invalidity benefit as appropriate, in addition to disablement pension, during spells of incapacity for work.

Death Benefit in the form of a pension, a gratuity or a weekly allowance for a limited period, available for widows and other dependents in fatal cases, depends in amount upon their relationship to the deceased and their circumstances at the time of death and not upon the deceased's earnings. A widow who was living with her husband at the time of his death receives a higher rate of pension for the first 26 weeks, and thereafter a lower rate of pension according to circumstances.

Regulations impose certain obligations on claimants and beneficiaries and on employers, including, in the case of claimants for disablement benefit, that of submitting to medical examination.

Rates of Benefits
(from Nov. 27, 1985)

	Weekly rate £
Disablement Benefit/Pension	
Degree of disablement—100 per cent.	62·50
90	56·25
80	50·00
70	43·75
60	37·50
50	31·25
40	25·00
30	18·75
20	12·50
Unemployability supplement*	38·30
Addition for adult dependent (subject to earnings rule)	23·00
Special Hardship allowance (maximum)	25·00
Constant Attendance allowance (normal maximum rate)	25·00
Exceptionally severe disablement allowance	25·00
Industrial death benefit widow's pension*	
First 26 weeks	53·60
Higher permanent rate	38·85
Lower permanent rate	11·49

* These benefits attract an increase for each dependent child (in addition to child benefit) of £8·05.

FINANCE

The National Insurance Fund receives all social security contributions (less only the National Health Service and Redundancy Fund and Maternity Pay Fund allocations and the National Insurance Surcharge for taxation purposes) together with the Consolidated Fund supplement; and it bears the cost of all contributory benefits provided by the Social Security Acts and the cost of administration.

Approximate receipts and payments of the National Insurance Fund for the year ended March 31, 1984, were as follows:

Receipts	£'000
Balance, April 1, 1983	4,023,461
Contributions under the Social Security Acts (net of S.S.P.)	17,777,062
Consolidated Fund Supplement	2,807,000
Income from Investments	489,658
Other receipts	15,792
	25,112,973

Payments	£'000	£'000
Benefit:—		
Unemployment benefit.	1,496,648	
Sickness benefit	254,363	
Invalidity benefit	1,871,952	
Maternity benefit	141,000	
Widow's benefit	771,000	
Guardian's allowance and child's special allowance	2,000	
Retirement pension	14,613,112	
Death grant	16,749	
Industrial injuries benefits	7,322	
Disablement benefits	369,107	
Death benefit	53,870	
Other benefits	n/a	
Pensioners lump sum payments	103,000	
Payments in lieu of benefit forgone	10,415	
		19,715,938
Transfers to Northern Ireland		77,000
Administration		715,879
Other payments		316
Balance, March 31, 1984		4,603,840
		25,112,973

WAR PENSIONS

War pensions are awarded under The Naval, Military and Air Force, Etc. (Disablement and Death) Service Pensions Order 1983, which was a consolidation of the previous Royal Warrants, Orders in Council and Orders by Her Majesty.

The D.H.S.S. award war pensions in respect of the periods Aug. 4, 1914 to Sept. 30, 1921 and subsequent to Sept. 3, 1939 (including present members of the armed forces). The D.H.S.S. also have special schemes for the Merchant Navy, Naval Auxiliary personnel, civil defence, civilians, Home Guard, Polish armed forces under British command and Polish resettlement forces.

War pensions for the period Oct. 1, 1921 to Sept. 2, 1939 are dealt with by the Ministry of Defence who are also responsible for the Armed Forces Pension Scheme.

ELIGIBILITY

War disablement pension is awarded for the disabling effects of any injury, wound or disease which is attributable to, or aggravated by, conditions of service in the armed forces. It cannot be paid until the serviceman has left the armed forces.

War widows pension is awarded where death occurs as a result of service. Where a war disablement pensioner was receiving constant attendance allowance at the time of his death, or would have been receiving it if he were not in hospital, his widow has automatic entitlement to a war widow's pension, regardless of the cause of death.

Claims.—Where a claim is made no later than 7 years after the termination of service, the claimant does not have to prove that the disablement or death on which the claim is based is related to service and receives the benefit of any reasonable doubt. Where a claim is made more than 7 years after the termination of service the claimant has to show that disablement or death is related to service. However, the claim succeeds if reliable evidence is produced which raises a reasonable doubt whether disablement or death is related to service. There is no time limit for making a claim for war pension.

Payment.—Rank additions are normally paid with war pensions where the rank held was above that of private (or equivalent).

When a war disablement pensioner is sick, unemployed or retired, the appropriate social security benefits are paid in addition to the war pension. Any sickness, invalidity or unemployment benefit or retirement pension for which a war widow qualifies on her own contributions, and any graduated retirement benefit, can be paid in addition to her war pension or temporary allowance. A war pensioner or war widow who claims supplementary benefit has the first £4 of pension disregarded. A similar provision operates for housing benefit but the local authority may, at its discretion, disregard any or all of the balance. A special tax free Christmas bonus of £10.00 is payable to war disablement pensioners who are in receipt of unemployability supplement, constant attendance allowance, have retired, or are aged over 70 (65 for women); and to all war widows.

A reduced weekly rate is payable to war widows below the rank of Lieutenant-Colonel who are under the age of 40, without children and capable of maintaining themselves. This is increased to the standard rate at age 40.

D.H.S.S. is responsible for the payment of war pensions, and provision of necessary treatment for accepted disablement, to pensioners who reside overseas. They receive the same pension rates as war pensioners in this country and benefit from the same annual upratings.

BASIC DISABLEMENT PENSION

Disablement is assessed by comparison of the disabled person's condition with that of a normal, healthy person of the same age and sex, without taking into account the disabled person's earnings or occupation, and is expressed on a percentage scale up to 100 per cent. Disablement above 20 per cent is assessed in steps of 10 per cent. For assessment of less than 20 per cent a lump sum is payable. Maximum assessment does not necessarily imply total incapacity.

A 100 per cent disabled pensioner may receive an allowance of 60p a week for his dependent. Where disablement is less than 100 per cent the allowance is proportionate to the degree of disablement. The allowance is no longer paid under the social security scheme, but it still being paid to war pensioners.

SUPPLEMENTARY ALLOWANCES

A number of supplementary allowances may be awarded to a war pensioner which are intended to meet the various needs which may result from disablement or death and take account of its particular effect on the pensioner. Decisions on supplementary allowances are made on a discretionary basis on behalf of the Secretary of State and there is no provision for a statutory right of appeal against them. However, war pensioners may have any aspect of their pension position discussed by their local War Pensions Committees, which may be able to arrange help or make representations to the war pensions branch of the D.H.S.S.

Unemployability supplement, with additional allowances for dependants, may be paid to a war pensioner who is so seriously disabled as to be unemployable. In addition, an invalidity allowance may be payable if the incapacity for work began more than 5 years before normal retirement age.

Allowance for lowered standard of occupation may be awarded to a partially disabled pensioner whose pensioned disablement permanently prevents him from following his pre-service occupation and from doing another job of equivalent financial standard. The allowance, together with the basic war disablement pension, must not exceed pension at the 100 per cent rate.

Constant attendance allowance may be awarded to a war pensioner who is so severely handicapped by the nature of his pensioned disablement, assessed at not less than 80 per cent, that he must depend to a greater or lesser extent upon the attendance of some other person. There are four rates of the allowance and these vary according to the amount of time attendance is needed.

Exceptionally severe disablement allowance is paid to pensioners who are receiving constant attendance allowance on a permanent basis at either of the two highest rates.

Severe disablement occupational allowance is paid to those pensioners who qualify for constant attendance allowance at either of the two highest rates and who, despite their handicap, are normally in employment. This allowance is not payable if the pensioner is in receipt of unemployability supplement.

Comforts allowance is payable at one of two rates. The higher rate is paid to those pensioners who are receiving both constant attendance allowance and unemployability supplement. When only one of these allowances is in payment the lower rate of comforts allowance is normally paid, but the higher rate can be paid under certain conditions where only constant attendance allowance is in payment.

Clothing allowance may be awarded where the pensioned disablement causes exceptional wear and tear of clothing. It is payable at two rates, depending on the degree of wear and tear caused.

Mobility supplement is intended to help those war pensioners who have problems in walking caused wholly or mainly by their pensioned disablement.

Treatment allowance may be paid to a pensioner receiving medical treatment in hospital or at home if the treatment is for the pensioned disablement, is necessary because of the continuing effects of service, and is of a kind which prevents the pensioner from working for more than seven days. The allowance replaces the disablement pension and is paid at the 100 per cent rate.

Age allowance may be awarded to those war pensioners aged 65 or over whose war disablement is assessed at 40 per cent or more. It is payable at four rates, depending on the degree of disablement.

Widows age allowance is paid at three different rates according to age (65–69, 70–79 and over 80).

Widow's child's allowance may be paid in addition to child benefit.

Rent allowance may be paid to a widow who receives a war widows pension and maintains a home for a child eligible for an allowance.

Education allowance may be payable to a war disablement pensioner or war widow in respect of a dependent child if the D.H.S.S. is satisfied that the education is suitable for the child and that the family circumstances are such as to require an allowance.

Temporary allowance for widows may be payable in the form of a special allowance for the first 26 weeks of widowhood for widows of war pensioners receiving constant attendance allowance or unemployability supplement. After 26 weeks the widow will get any war widows pension or national insurance widows benefit to which she is entitled.

PENSION APPEALS TRIBUNALS

There are independent Pensions Appeal Tribunals which hear appeals against the decisions of the D.H.S.S. on entitlement, and assessment of disablement, in respect of 1939 War and subsequent service cases. There now no rights of appeal in the 1914 War disablement cases, the great majority of which were given final assessment in the 1920s with a 12 months right of appeal at the time. An appeal by a 1914 war widow must be made within twelve months of the date on which the rejection of the claim is notified.

WAR PENSIONERS WELFARE SERVICE

The D.H.S.S. operates a war pensioners welfare service to advise and assist war pensioners on any matters affecting their welfare. Welfare officers are attached to War Pensions Welfare Offices located in the major towns, and work closely with central and local Government agencies as well as the various ex-service organisations. The service is available on call to any war pensioner who needs it. In addition the service takes the initiative in arranging regular visits in certain cases.

Rates of Benefits
(from week commencing Nov. 25, 1985)

Weekly rates
£

Disablement pension	
(for Private or equivalent rank)	
Degree of disablement—	
100 per cent	62.50
90 per cent	56.25
80 per cent	50.00
70 per cent	43.75
60 per cent	37.50
50 per cent	31.25
40 per cent	25.00
30 per cent	18.75
20 per cent	12.50
Unemployability supplement	
Personal allowance	40.65
Increase for wife/other adult dependent	23.00
Increase for child	8.05
Allowance for lowered standard of occupation (maximum)	25.00
Constant attendance allowance	
Exceptional rate	50.00
Intermediate rate	37.50
Normal maximum	25.00
Half and quarter day	12.50
Exceptionally severe disablement allowance	25.00
Severe disablement occupational allowance	12.50
Comforts allowance	
Higher rate	10.80
Lower rate	5.40
Clothing allowance (per annum)	
Higher rate	85.00
Lower rate	54.00
Mobility supplement	23.80
Age allowance	
Disablement assessment—	
40–50 per cent	4.35
50–70 per cent	6.80
70–90 per cent	9.75
over 90 per cent	13.60
Widow's pension	
(widow of Private or equivalent rank)	
Standard rate	49.80
Childless widow under 40	11.49
Widow's age allowance	
Age—65–69	5.35
70–79	10.70
80 and over	13.40
Rent allowance	18.95

BOOKER-McCONNELL PRIZEWINNERS

The finalists for the 1985 prize are:
The Battle of Pollocks Crossing—J. L. Carr (Viking), *The Bone People*—Keri Hulme (Hodder & Stoughton), *The Good Apprentice*—Iris Murdoch (Chatto & Windus), *The Good Terrorist*—Doris Lessing (Cape), *Illywhacker*—Peter Carey (Faber), *Last Letters from Hav*—Jan Morris (Viking).

THE WARNOCK REPORT

The birth of the first child resulting from the technique of *in vitro* fertilisation in July 1978 was a considerable achievement which opened up new horizons in the alleviation of infertility and in the science of embryology. However, it led also to anxieties that events were moving too fast for their implications to be assimilated. Against this background of public concern, a Committee of Inquiry into Human Fertilisation and Embryology was established in July 1982, with the following terms of reference: "To consider recent and potential developments in medicine and science related to human fertilisation and embryology; to consider what policies and safeguards should be applied, including consideration of the social, ethical and legal implications of these developments; and to make recommendations."

Within the terms of reference were given two words that had to be clarified. The first of these was *embryology*. The Committee regarded the embryonic stage to be the six weeks immediately following fertilisation which usually corresponds with the first eight weeks of gestation counted from the first day of the woman's last menstrual period. The second word in need of clarification was *potential*. The pace of scientific discovery is unpredictable. Indeed, a number of major developments took place during the lifetime of the Inquiry, and the changes which take place in society itself are also difficult to predict. The impact of scientific discoveries on the society of the future is therefore doubly hard to predict. The Committee took the pragmatic view that it could react only to what it knew, or could realistically foresee.

The members of the Committee were: Dame Mary Warnock, D.B.E., M.A., B.Phil. (Chairman); Q. S. Anisuddin, M.A.; T. S. G. Baker, Q.C.; Dame Josephine Barnes, D.B.E., F.R.C.P., F.R.C.S., F.R.C.O.G.; Mrs. M. M. Carriline, M.A.; Dr. D. Davies, M.A., PhD.; Prof. A. O. Dyson, M.A., B.D., M.A.Theol., D.Phil.; Mrs. N. L. Edwards, O.B.E., S.R.N., S.C.M.; Dr. W. Greengross, M.B., B.S., D.Obst., R.C.O.G.; Prof. W. G. Irwin, M.B., B.chir., B.A.O., M.D., F.R.C.G.P., D.Obst., R.C.O.G.; Prof. J. Marshall, D.SC., M.D., F.R.C.P., F.R.C.P. (Edin), D.P.M.; Prof. M. C. Macnaughton, M.D., F.R.C.P. (Glas), F.R.C.O.G., F.R.S.E.; Dr. A. McLaren, M.A., D.Phil., F.R.S.; D. J. McNeil, w.s.; Prof. K. Rawnsley, C.B.E., M.B., ChB., F.R.C.Psych., F.R.C.P., D.P.M.; Mrs. M. J. Walker, M.A., A.P.S.W.

The Committee sat for nearly 2 years and issued its report in July 1984. The list of recommendations was as follows.

The licensing body and its functions

A new statutory licensing authority should be established to regulate both research and those infertility services which we have recommended should be subject to control (indicated below).

There should be substantial lay representation on the statutory authority to regulate research and infertility services and the chairman must be a lay person.

All practitioners offering the services we have recommended should only be provided under licence, and all premises used as part of any such provision, including the provision of fresh semen and banks for the storage of frozen human eggs, semen and embryos should be licensed by the licensing body.

Artificial insemination by donor (A.I.D.) should be available, on a properly organised basis and subject to the licensing arrangements, to those infertile couples for whom it might be appropriate. The provision of A.I.D. services without a licence for the purpose should be an offence.

The service of *in vitrio* fertilisation (I.V.F.) should continue to be available, subject to the same type of licensing and inspection as we have recommended with regard to the regulation of A.I.D.

Egg donation be accepted as a recognised technique in the treatment of infertility subject to the same type of licensing and controls as we have recommended for the regulation of A.I.D. and I.V.F.

The form of embryo donation involving donated semen and egg which are brought together *in vitro* should be accepted as a treatment for infertility, subject to the same type of licensing and controls as we have recommended with regard to the regulation of A.I.D., I.V.F. and egg donation.

The technique of embryo donation by lavage should not be used at the present time.

The use of frozen eggs in therapeutic procedures should not be undertaken until research has shown that no unacceptable risk is involved. This will be a matter for review by the licensing body.

The clinical use of frozen embryos may continue to be developed under review by the licensing body.

Research conducted on human *in vitro* embryos and the handling of such embryos should be permitted only under licence.

No live human embryo derived from *in vitro* fertilisation, whether frozen or unfrozen, may be kept alive, if not transferred to a woman beyond fourteen days after fertilisation, nor may it be used as a research subject beyond fourteen days after fertilisation. This fourteen day period does not include any time during which the embryo may have been frozen.

Consent be obtained as to the method of use or disposal of spare embryos.

As a matter of good practice no research should be carried out on a spare embryo without the informed consent of the couple from whom the embryo was generated, whenever this is possible.

When trans-species fertilisation is used as part of a recognised programme for alleviating infertility or in the assessment or diagnosis of sub-fertility it should be subject to licence and that a condition of granting such a licence should be that the development of any resultant hybrid should be terminated at the two cell stage.

The licensing body should be asked to consider the need for follow-up studies of children born as a result of the new techniques, including consideration of the need for a centrally maintained register of such births.

The sale or purchase of human gametes or embryos should be permitted only under licence from, and subject to, conditions prescribed by the licensing body.

Principles of provision

As a matter of good practice any third party donating gametes for infertility treatment should be unknown to the couple before, during and after the treatment, and equally the third party should not know the identity of the couple being helped.

Counselling should be available to all infertile couples and third parties at any stage of the treatment, both as an integral part of N.H.S. provision and in the private sector.

In the case of more specialised forms of infertility treatment the consent in writing of both partners should be obtained, wherever possible, before treatment is begun, as a matter of good practice. Any written consent should be obtained on an appropriate consent form.

The formal consent in writing by both partners should, as a matter of good practice, always be obtained before A.I.D. treatment begins. A consent form should be used and thoroughly explained to both partners.

For the present, there should be a limit of ten children who can be fathered by one donor.

In cases where consultants decline to provide treatment they should always give the patient a full explanation of the reasons.

The N.H.S. numbers of all donors be checked by the clinics where they make their donations against a new centrally maintained list of N.H.S. numbers of existing donors, which is to be held separately from the N.H.S. donor register.

There should be a gradual move towards a system where semen donors should be given only their expenses.

In relation to egg donation the principles of good practice we have already considered in relation to other techniques should apply, including the anonymity of the donor, limitation of the number of children born from the eggs of any one donor to ten, openness with the child about his genetic origins, the availability of counselling for all parties and informed consent.

It should be accepted practice to offer donated gametes and embryos to those at risk of transmitting hereditary disorders.

All types of "do-it-yourself" sex selection kits should be brought within the ambit of control provided by the Medicines Act with the aim of ensuring that such products are safe, efficacious and of an acceptable standard for use.

The use of frozen semen in artificial insemination should continue.

There should be automatic five-yearly reviews of semen and egg deposits.

There should be a maximum of ten years for the storage of embryos after which time the right to use or disposal should pass to the storage authority.

When one of a couple dies the right to use or dispose of any embryo stored by that couple should pass to the survivor. If both die that right should pass to the storage authority.

Where there is no agreement between the couple the right to determine the use or disposal of an embryo should pass to the storage authority as though the ten year period had expired.

Service provision

Funding should be made available for the collection of adequate statistics on infertility and infertility services.

Each health authority should review its facilities for the investigation and treatment of infertility and consider the establishment, separate from routine gynaecology, of a specialist infertility clinic with close working relationships with specialist units, including genetic counselling services, at regional and supra-regional level.

Where it is not possible to have a separate clinic, infertility patients should be seen separately from other types of gynaecological patient, wherever possible.

A working group at national level made up of central health departments, health authorities and those working in infertility, should be established to draw up detailed guidance on the organisation of services.

Consideration should be given to the inclusion of plans for infertility services as part of the next round of health authority strategic plans.

I.V.F. should continue to be available within the N.H.S.

One of the first tasks of the working group recommended above should be to consider how best an I.V.F. service can be organised within the N.H.S.

Legal limits on research

The embryo of the human species should be afforded some protection in law.

Any unauthorised use of an *in vitro* embryo would in itself constitute a criminal offence.

Legislation should provide that research may be carried out on any embryo resulting from *in vitro* fertilisation, whatever its provenance, up to the end of the fourteenth day after fertilisation, but subject to all other restrictions as may be imposed by the licensing body.

It shall be a criminal offence to handle or to use as a research subject any live human embryo derived from *in vitro* fertilisation beyond that limit (i.e. fourteen days after fertilisation).

No embryo which has been used for research should be transferred to a woman.

Any unlicensed use of trans-species fertilisation involving human gametes should be a criminal offence.

The placing of a human embryo in the uterus of another species for gestation should be a criminal offence.

The proposed licensing body should promulgate guidance on what types of research, apart from those precluded by law, would be unlikely to be considered ethically acceptable in any circumstances and therefore would not be licensed.

Unauthorised sale or purchase of human gametes or embryos should be made a criminal offence.

Legal changes

The A.I.D. child should in law be treated as the legitimate child of its mother and her husband, where they have both consented to the treatment.

A change in the law so that the semen donor will have no parental rights or duties in relation to the child is recommended.

Following the English Law Commission, it should be presumed that the husband has consented to A.I.D., unless the contrary is proved.

The law should be changed so as to permit the husband to be registered as the father where he has consented to treatment.

Legislation should provide that when a child is born to a woman following donation of another's egg the woman giving birth should, for all purposes, be regarded in law as the mother of that child, and that the egg donor should have no rights or obligations in respect of the child.

The legislation proposed regarding A.I.D. children should cover children born following embryo donation.

Legislation should be introduced to render criminal the creation or the operation in the United Kingdom of agencies whose purposes include the recruitment of women for surrogate pregnancy or making arrangements for individuals or couples who wish to utilise the services of a carrying mother; such legislation should be wide enough to include both profit and non-profit making organisations.

Legislation should be sufficiently wide to render criminally liable the actions of professionals and others who knowingly assist in the establishment of a surrogate pregnancy.

It should be provided by statute that all surrogacy agreements are illegal contracts and therefore unenforceable in the courts.

Legislation should provide that where a person dies during the storage period or cannot be traced at a review date the right of use or disposal of his or her frozen gametes should pass to the storage authority.

Legislation should be introduced to provide that any child born by artificial insemination by husband (A.I.H.) who was not *in utero* at the date of the death of its father shall be disregarded for the purposes of succession to and inheritance from the latter.

Legislation should be enacted to ensure there is no right of ownership in a human embryo.

For the purposes of establishing primogeniture the date and time of birth and not the date of fertilisation shall be the determining factor.

Legislation should be introduced to provide that any child born following I.V.F., using an embryo that had been frozen and stored, who was not *in utero* at the date of the death of the father shall be disregarded for the purposes of succession to and inheritance from the latter.

Expressions of Dissent

Dissent from some of the views of the Inquiry were expressed by some members with regard to surrogacy, and the use of human embryos in research. Dr. Davies and Dr. Greengross expressed the view that there are rare occasions when surrogacy could be beneficial to couples as a last resort, and that on those occasions gynaecologists should not be denied the option of suggesting surrogacy to their patients. However, they believe that, in the best interests of the child that may ensue, stringent care and control

is necessary, and recommend that the licensing authority proposed by the Committee should include surrogacy within its terms of reference, and that any non-profit making agency that wished to assist in making surrogacy arrangements would have to be licensed by the authority.

Mrs. Carriline, Prof. Marshall and Mrs. Walker, whilst agreeing with their colleagues that the embryo of the human species has a special status, differed from them as to what this implies. They felt that the protection to be afforded to the human embryo by law should not depend upon the decision as to when it becomes a person, considering it wrong to create something with the potential for becoming a human person and then deliberately to destroy it.

They recommended that nothing should be done that would reduce the chance of successful implantation of the embryo, that experimentation on the human embryo should not be permitted, and the human embryo should be afforded special protection in law against unauthorised handling.

Mr. Baker, Prof. Dyson, Mrs. Edwards and Dr. Greengross dissented from the view that research should be permitted on embryos brought into existence specifically for that purpose or coming into existence as a result of other research.

THE HONG KONG AGREEMENT

Background to the Agreement

During the nineteenth century Britain concluded three Treaties with the then Chinese Government relating to Hong Kong: the Treaty of Nanking, signed in 1842 and ratified in 1843 under which Hong Kong Island was ceded in perpetuity; the Convention of Peking in 1860 under which the southern part of the Kowloon Peninsula and Stonecutters Island were ceded in perpetuity; and the Convention of 1898 under which the New Territories (comprising 92 per cent of the total land area of the territory) were leased to Britain for 99 years from 1 July 1898. It was the fact that the New Territories are subject to a lease with a fixed expiry date which lay behind the decision by H.M. Government to seek to enter negotiations with the Government of the People's Republic of China on Hong Kong's future.

The Chinese Government has consistently taken the view that the whole of Hong Kong is Chinese territory. Its position for many years was that the question of Hong Kong came into the category of unequal treaties left over from history; that it should be settled peacefully through negotiations when conditions were ripe; and that pending a settlement the status quo should be maintained.

In the late 1970s there was increasing awareness of the need to remove the uncertainty which the 1997 deadline generated. Against this background H.M. Government decided that the Prime Minister's visit to China in September 1982 would provide an opportunity to open discussions with the Chinese Government on the future of Hong Kong. Substantive discussions took place during the visit and an agreement was reached to enter talks through diplomatic channels following the visit. Two years of negotiations between the two Governments, undertaken with the common aim of maintaining the stability and prosperity of Hong Kong, resulted in an Agreement, consisting of a Joint Declaration and three Annexes. The draft text of the agreement was initialled by representatives of the British and Chinese Governments on Sept. 26, 1984; signed by the Rt. Hon. Margaret Thatcher and Deng Xiaoping

in Peking on Dec. 19, 1984, and ratified on May 27, 1985.

JOINT DECLARATION OF THE GOVERNMENT OF THE UNITED KINGDOM OF GREAT BRITAIN AND NORTHERN IRELAND AND THE GOVERNMENT OF THE PEOPLE'S REPUBLIC OF CHINA ON THE QUESTION OF HONG KONG

The Government of the United Kingdom of Great Britain and Northern Ireland and the Government of the People's Republic of China have reviewed with satisfaction the friendly relations existing between the two Governments and peoples in recent years and agreed that a proper negotiated settlement of the question of Hong Kong, which is left over from the past, is conducive to the maintenance of the prosperity and stability of Hong Kong and to the further strengthening and development of the relations between the two countries on a new basis. To this end, they have, after talks between the delegations of the two Governments, agreed to declare as follows:

1. The Government of the People's Republic of China declares that to recover the Hong Kong area (including Hong Kong Island, Kowloon and the New Territories, hereinafter referred to as Hong Kong) is the common aspiration of the entire Chinese people, and that it is decided to resume the exercise of sovereignty over Hong Kong with effect from 1 July 1997.

2. The Government of the United Kingdom declares that it will restore Hong Kong to the People's Republic of China with effect from 1 July 1997.

3. The Government of the People's Republic of China declares that the basic policies of the People's Republic of China regarding Hong Kong are as follows:

(1) Upholding national unity and territorial integrity and taking account of the history of Hong Kong and its realities, the People's Republic of China has decided to establish, in accordance with the provisions of Article 31 of the Constitution of the People's Republic of China, a Hong Kong Special Administrative Region upon resuming the exercise of sovereignty over Hong Kong.

(2) The Hong Kong Special Administrative Region will be directly under the authority of the Central People's Government of the People's Republic of China. The Hong Kong Special Administrative Region will enjoy a high degree of autonomy, except in foreign and defence affairs which are the responsibilities of the Central People's Government.

(3) The Hong Kong Special Administrative Region will be vested with executive, legislative, and independent judicial power, including that of final adjudication. The laws currently in force in Hong Kong will remain basically unchanged.

(4) The Government of the Hong Kong Special Administrative Region will be composed of local inhabitants. The chief executive will be appointed by the Central People's Government on the basis of the results of elections or consultations to be held locally. Principal officials will be nominated by the chief executive of the Hong Kong Special Administrative Region for appointment by the Central People's Government. Chinese and foreign nationals previously working in the public and police services in the government departments of Hong Kong may remain in employment. British and other foreign nationals may also be employed to serve as advisers or hold certain public posts in government departments of the Hong Kong Special Administrative Region.

(5) The current social and economic systems in Hong Kong will remain unchanged, and so will the life-style. Rights and freedoms, including those of the person, of speech, of the press, of assembly, of association, of travel, of movement, of correspondence, of strike, of choice of occupation, of academic research and of religious belief will be ensured by law in the Hong Kong Special Administrative Region. Private property, ownership of enterprises, legitimate right of inheritance and foreign investment will be protected by law.

(6) The Hong Kong Special Administrative Region will retain the status of a free port and a separate customs territory.

(7) The Hong Kong Special Administrative Region will retain the status of an international financial centre, and its markets for foreign exchange, gold, securities and futures will continue. There will be free flow of capital. The Hong Kong dollar will continue to circulate and remain freely convertible.

(8) The Hong Kong Special Administrative Region will have independent finances. The Central People's Government will not levy taxes on the Hong Kong Special Administrative Region.

(9) The Hong Kong Special Administrative Region may establish mutually beneficial economic relations with the United Kingdom and other countries, whose economic interests in Hong Kong will be given due regard.

(10) Using the name of "Hong Kong, China", the Hong Kong Special Administrative Region may on its own maintain and develop economic and cultural relations and conclude relevant agreements with states, regions and relevant international organisations.

The Government of the Hong Kong Special Administrative Region may on its own issue travel documents for entry into and exit from Hong Kong.

(11) The maintenance of public order in the Hong Kong Special Administrative Region will be the responsibility of the Government of the Hong Kong Special Administrative Region.

(12) The above-stated basic policies of the People's Republic of China regarding Hong Kong and the elaboration of them in Annex I to this Joint Declaration will be stipulated, in a Basic Law of the Hong Kong Special Administrative Region of the People's Republic of China, by the National People's Congress of the People's Republic of China, and they will remain unchanged for 50 years.

4. The Government of the United Kingdom and the Government of the People's Republic of China declare that, during the transitional period between the date of the entry into force of this Joint Declaration and 30 June 1997, the Government of the United Kingdom will be responsible for the administration of Hong Kong with the object of maintaining and preserving its economic prosperity and social stability; and that the Government of the People's Republic of China will give its cooperation in this connection.

5. The Government of the United Kingdom and the Government of the People's Republic of China declare that, in order to ensure a smooth transfer of government in 1997, and with a view to the effective implementation of this Joint Declaration, a Sino-British Joint Liaison Group will be set up when this Joint Declaration enters into force; and that it will be established and will function in accordance with the provisions of Annex II to this Joint Declaration.

6. The Government of the United Kingdom and the Government of the People's Republic of China declare that land leases in Hong Kong and other related matters will be dealt with in accordance with the provisions of Annex III to this Joint Declaration.

7. The Government of the United Kingdom and the Government of the People's Republic of China agree to implement the preceding declarations and the Annexes to this Joint Declaration.

8. This Joint Declaration is subject to ratification and shall enter into force on the date of the exchange of instruments of ratification, which shall take place in Beijing before 30 June 1985. This Joint Declaration and its Annexes shall be equally binding.

Memoranda

The occasion of the signing of the Agreement also saw an exchange of Memoranda, dealing with the question of citizenship, issue of passports, etc. The U.K. Memorandum declared that, subject to the completion of the necessary amendments to the relevant United Kingdom legislation: (a) all persons who on 30 June 1997 are, by virtue of a connection with Hong Kong, British Dependent Territories citizens (BDTCs) under the law in force in the United Kingdom will cease to be BDTCs with effect from 1 July 1997, but will be eligible to retain an appropriate status which, without conferring the right of abode in the U.K., will entitle them to continue to use passports issued by the U.K. Government. This status will be acquired by such persons only if they hold or are included in such a British passport issued before 1 July 1997, except that eligible persons born on or after 1 January 1997 but before 1 July 1997 may obtain or be included in such a passport up to 31 December 1997: (b) no person will acquire BDTC status on or after 1 July 1997 by virtue of a connection with Hong Kong. No person born on or after 1 July 1997 will acquire the status referred to as being appropriate in (a): (c) U.K. consular officials in the Hong Kong Special Administrative Region and elsewhere may renew and replace passports of persons mentioned in (a) and may also issue them to persons, born before 1 July 1997 of such persons, who had previously been included in the passport of their parent: (d) those who have obtained or been included in passports issued by the U.K. Government under (a) and (c) will be entitled to receive, upon request, British consular services and protection when in third countries.

In the Chinese Memoradum the Government of the People's Republic of China declared that, under the

Nationality Law of the People's Republic of China, all Hong Kong Chinese compatriots, whether they are holders of the "British Dependent Territories citizens' Passport" or not, are Chinese nationals. The competent authorities of the Government of the People's Republic of China will, with effect from 1 July 1997, permit Chinese nationals in Hong Kong who were previously called "British Dependent Territories citizens" to use travel documents issued by the Government of the U.K. for the purpose of travelling to other states and regions. These Chinese nationals will not be entitled to British consular protection in the Hong Kong Special Administrative Region and other parts of the People's Republic of China on account of their holding the above-mentioned British travel documents.

WHITE PAPERS

AN INDEPENDENT PROSECUTION SERVICE FOR ENGLAND AND WALES

At the opening of the post-election Parliamentary session in June 1983, the Queen's Speech announced the Government's intention to bring forward proposals for the establishment in England and Wales of a prosecution service independent of the police. With a view to consultation and discussion in advance of legislation, a White Paper, "An Independent Prosecution Service for England and Wales", was published which set out proposals on the functions and structure of such a service. These proposals take account of the report of an interdepartmental Working Party on Prosecution Arrangements on what would be the best model for the organisation of an independent prosecution service.

The setting up of an independent prosecution service was recommended by the Royal Commission on Criminal Procedure in their report published in January 1981 (*see also*, Whitaker's Almanack 1982, pp. 999–1001). The Royal Commission concluded that the present arrangements were unsatisfactory in a number of respects. In particular the present system, in the view of the Royal Commission, is lacking in openness and accountability and does not make for consistency in policy and practice. Moreover, the lack of overall coherence in the present arrangements, and the division of responsibility for funding and determining expenditure, in the Royal Commission's view, do not permit the pursuit of maximum cost-effectiveness and efficiency. The Government has already accepted the Royal Commission's recommendations in principle, and intends to introduce a system which will remove the unsatisfactory features of the present piecemeal arrangements.

The Government sees the force of objections to a system which would involve an element of accountability to a local supervisory body and favours the establishment of a national prosecution service headed by the Director of Public Prosecutions and under the superintendence of the Attorney General. This service would bring together the work of the Director's Department and police prosecuting solicitors' departments.

Under these proposals there would be local prosecutors who would have responsibility for the conduct of criminal proceedings in all cases now prosecuted by or on behalf of the police. These prosecutors, together with the headquarters staff of the Director of Public Prosecutions, would all be officers of a single national prosecution service, controlled and directed by the Director of Public Prosecutions. They would not be subject to direction or influence by the police or any local body in deciding whether charges should proceed or be dropped or how a case should be conducted. The investigation of criminal offences, including the initial decision whether to make a charge, would remain with the police.

The Government believes that the establishment of an independent prosecution service on this basis would promote consistency and fairness; would reduce the proportion of cases pursued despite lack of sufficient evidence; would improve the preparation and presentation of cases in court; would provide an attractive career structure, and would lead to greater efficiency and better accountability for the use of resources.

The Director of Public Prosecutions would be the head of the new service, and his present Department would form its central headquarters. The responsibilities which the Director would discharge, under the superintendence of the Attorney General, would include:—

(a) the preparation and promulgation of guidance to be given by the Attorney General;

(b) decisions on prosecution in particular cases of importance or difficulty;

(c) appointments, promotions, transfers, training and other personnel matters for the service;

(d) the central management of the finance, manpower and other resources allocated to the service.

The headquarters staff of the Director of Public Prosecutions would be strengthened for the purpose of discharging these functions. An important objective would be to ensure that the Director personally was not involved in day-to-day administrative and supervisory functions to the prejudice of his primary responsibility for policy and important cases. Both in taking prosecution decisions, and in matters of personnel and financial management, responsibility would be delegated to local prosecutors to the fullest extent consistent with sound administration.

The Attorney General would, of course, be answerable in Parliament for decisions or actions that he or the Director takes on prosecution matters, and also for the principles that are applied by the prosecution service in the handling of particular cases. Although the Director of Public Prosecutions would be able to give the local prosecutor instructions on how any case is to be handled, the great majority of prosecution decisions (including many now reserved to the Director) would be taken locally, and it would be the responsibility of the appropriate local prosecutor to apply the general guidance given by the Attorney General to the facts of an individual case. The Government agrees with the view expressed by members of the House of Commons Select Committee on Home Affairs that Parliamentary scrutiny should be addressed to issues of general policy rather than particular proceedings. Accordingly, the Government envisages that the Attorney General will not be expected to answer in Parliament for the intrinsic merits of particular decisions taken by local prosecutors unless he or the Director has in fact intervened in the case in question.

In relation to private prosecutions and those initiated by agencies of government other than the police, requirements for the consent of the Attorney General or Director of Public Prosecutions and the

Attorney General's power to enter a *nolle prosequi* (where applicable) will continue to apply.

The Royal Commission recommended that there should be a Crown prosecutor in each police area, accountable to a local supervisory authority. The Commission proposed that for this purpose each existing police authority should be developed into a police and prosecutions authority to which both the chief constable and the Crown prosecutor would be answerable. However, further consultation has confirmed doubts expressed in the House of Commons about whether this aspect of the Royal Commission's proposals would be workable, or consistent with the service's independence.

The Government does not believe that it would be appropriate for local authorities to have control over the conduct of prosecutions under the general criminal law. But to divorce control over policy from control over resources would not be conducive to sensible and efficient management of the new service. The Government therefore proposes that there should be a single line of accountability for the management of resources as well as for decisions on cases to the Director of Public Prosecutions.

The Government is satisfied that these proposals would enable a stronger element of consistency, of policy and practice, to be introduced into the prosecution process of England and Wales than the present system permits. They would improve efficiency by injecting a coherent structure into the present variety of arrangements, and would make for a continuing improvement in the procedure for checking that prosecutions are justified and practicable in individual cases. Finally, they are designed to introduce a clear line of public accountability for policy, accompanied by an essential degree of control over cost and efficiency.

Working Party Report

The report of the Working Party on Prosecution Arrangements put forward three possible options for the organisation of the service; an integrated national system; a decentralised national system; and a local system. The report favoured the first of these, and its recommendations regarding the operation of an integrated national system were as follows:

"The principal distinguishing feature of an integrated national system is that the prosecution service would form a single Department of central government for which a Minister would be responsible to Parliament. Those engaged in the day-to-day handling of prosecutions would, of course, be located near the courts they serve and the police forces who submit cases to them, so that the system would retain much of its present local character. Work might be arranged so that local offices would cover a single police force area; but the staff in these offices ... would be responsible as civil servants, through a line management structure to the Department's headquarters. At present there are about 1,600 staff employed in prosecuting solicitors' departments, most of whom might be expected to transfer to a new service. The Department would also have ultimate control over their recruitment, training, postings and promotions. In addition, the headquarters would exercise direct control over prosecution policy, with the local prosecutor ultimately accountable to it for decisions in individual cases as well as for compliance with that policy.

Under an integrated national system it would seem natural for the Director of Public Prosecutions to become head of the prosecution service. His responsibilities would include:—
  (a) responsibility for appointments, staffing, training and other personnel matters;
  (b) monitoring of performance by local offices (in respect of which some assistance might be found in the performance indicators used by the Crown Office in Scotland which performs a similar function on behalf of the Lord Advocate);
  (c) giving consent to the prosecution of certain offences otherwise than by the national prosecution service;
  (d) considering certain categories of cases required to be referred to him; and
  (e) the formulation and promulgation, under the superintendence of the Attorney General, of policy on prosecution.

Because the role of the national prosecution service would, certainly initially, be confined to the handling of police prosecutions the Director would need to retain in relation to other prosecutions his powers to intervene in, and take over, cases and, if he saw fit, offer no evidence. The Attorney General would, similarly, retain his power to enter a *nolle prosequi* (and, in appropriate cases where it was required, to give his consent to prosecution).

The Director would continue to work, as now, "under the superintendence of" the Attorney General. The Attorney General would be formally answerable to Parliament for the decisions and actions of the prosecution service, as he is now for those of the Director. He would also be responsible to Parliament for the general efficiency of the prosecution service and the standards of performance achieved. The additional work which would fall on the Law Officers' Department as a result of the supervisory functions of the Attorney General would probably require some strengthening of that Department.

The fact of the Attorney General's formal responsibility to Parliament for every decision taken at any level in the prosecution service would create some risk of concentration at the service's headquarters and the Law Officers' Department of an insupportable burden of cases referred either for decision or for scrutiny in consequence of a complaint. If an integrated national system is chosen, it will be essential to introduce safeguards against this centripetal tendency. There is no reason why the large number of cases now dealt with satisfactorily at local level *should* be referred any higher. The safeguards we have in mind are as follows:—
  (a) We suggest that it would be desirable for the Attorney General to continue what has long been the general practice in relation to the Director's decisions on individual cases—that of answering questions raised in Parliament by simply stating whether he is satisfied that the correct principles were applied.
  (b) While we do not consider it feasible to make the Attorney General responsible for prosecution policy without making local prosecutors accountable to him for its application in particular cases, we welcome the view expressed to our representatives by some Members of the House of Commons Select Committee on Home Affairs that Parliamentary scrutiny of the prosecution service should be addressed to issues of general policy rather than the handling of particular proceedings.
  (c) It is the Government's general policy that responsibility for decisions should be delegated to the fullest extent that is consistent with sound administration. We would expect to see the principle of maximum delegation applied within an independent prosecution service as much as in any other area of government activity.
  (d) Quite a large proportion of cases which now, under the Prosecution of Offences Regulations or otherwise, have to be referred to the Director

of Public Prosecutions could, within the framework of a single integrated system, be dealt with at local level in accordance with policy laid down by headquarters.

In our view if safeguards on these lines are consistently observed, there is no reason why the number of cases referred to the headquarters of the service need exceed that with which the Director's Department now has to deal.

The principle of maximum delegation ... is equally applicable in matters of financial and personnel management ... there would be required someone to act as Principal Finance and Establishment Officer for the new service, probably at about Under Secretary level. ...

We have considered whether there should be a regional tier of offices under an integrated national system. The main justification for regional offices is that they avoid the referral of large numbers of cases to the centre while preserving consistency and accountability (ultimately through the Minister to Parliament) for decisions. But ... original evidence from Rayner scrutinies, the chain of command review and departmental studies all suggest that on purely management grounds a regional tier can be dispensed with where the number of local offices does not exceed up to forty-five, depending on function. Furthermore, while some personnel and financial functions could be devolved to any regional offices that might be set up, this would not necessarily be a more cost-effective arrangement. The balance of advantage would thus not seem to lie with regionalisation. That is not, however, to rule out the possibility of posting out of London staff from headquarters whose work is concentrated in a particular area of the country, but we would distinguish such dispersal from the insertion of a regional tier in the management hierarchy of the system ...

The main *advantage* of the integrated national system seems to us to be that it would provide clear lines of accountability in relation to both policy and resources. On policy, there would be accountability to the responsible Minister who would be answerable to Parliament. On resources, financial accountability would lie through the Director of Public Prosecutions (who would presumably be Accounting Officer) answerable to the Public Accounts Committee in the normal way. There is much to be said for the clarity and simplicity of the straightforward lines of decision-making which in an integrated service would run from the local prosecutor ultimately to the central Department. This could well offer the best prospect of achieving nationally the degree of consistency in policy that should be a feature of any independent service; and it would facilitate also securing the maximum cost-effectiveness.

An integrated national system would also seem to provide fullest scope for improving the performance of prosecutors through training and career development. The position of the local prosecutor as a servant of the Crown would strengthen his detachment from improper local influence and emphasise the end of the solicitor-client relationship with the police.

The *disadvantages* of an integrated national system arise chiefly from the scale on which it would have to be constructed to cover the whole of England and Wales. The only other country with a unitary constitution which to our knowledge has established a fully integrated prosecution service on a comparable scale is Japan; and because of the scale of service that would be required in England and Wales many commentators are concerned about the risk of overloading the central headquarters. Such fears could be realised if an integrated national service did not contain appropriate safeguards against unnecessary centralisation of decision-making."

FINANCIAL SERVICES IN THE U.K.

Britain is one of the world's great financial centres, and the financial services industry contributes a growing share to the nation's wealth and to its earnings abroad. Its activities include the raising and distribution of funds to government, industry and commerce; trading in stocks and shares, in financial and commodity futures and options; the management of investment portfolios; the management and marketing of investment trusts, unit trusts, and life assurance policies. These activities are conducted by banks, finance and investment houses, insurance companies, stockbrokers and jobbers, brokers and dealers in futures, insurance intermediaries, investment managers and advisers; and in The Stock Exchange, the over-the-counter markets, and the financial and commodity futures markets.

The Government, feeling that existing investor protection laws are outdated and incomplete, introduced a White Paper, "Financial services in the United Kingdom: a new framework for investor protection", setting out the Government's proposals for a new system of regulation for the financial services industry in the United Kingdom. The Government expect to introduce legislation based on these proposals for England and Wales, Scotland and Northern Ireland in the 1985–86 Parliamentary Session.

To achieve consistent treatment of different forms of investment, the Government propose a new regulatory framework, which will cover for the first time the entire field of dealing in financial and commodity futures and options. It will be based on new and wide definitions of "investment" and "investment businesses". It will be an offence for any "investment business" to be carried on without authorisation, and only those judged "fit and proper" to carry on investment business will be so authorised. More information relevant to investors will be made available about a wider range of investments. The Government propose to relax the rules on distribution of information to help small companies raise money more easily. The Government will also strengthen the criminal law against fraud and enforce that law vigorously.

To achieve their aims the Government intend to build upon what is best in self-regulation. The proposed new legislation will give the Secretary of State for Trade and Industry the power to authorise investment businesses and enable him to delegate it to one or more regulatory bodies, composed of both those who provide and those who use financial services. The Secretary of State will delegate these powers of authorisation and regulation only if he is satisfied on the composition and constitution of the bodies. In particular, he will need to be satisfied that rules and practices neither are nor become anti-competitive. The Secretary of State will appoint an independent tribunal to be the final determinant of any dispute about authorisation decisions or about penalties for breaches of the rules.

The Government's proposals for new legislation on financial services in the United Kingdom may be summarised as follows:

The Regulatory System

The regulatory system will include: (*i.*) a definition of *investments*, which will include financial and commodity futures and options contracts, securities covered by the Prevention of Frauds (Investments) Act and certain other products. The Department of Trade and Industry will continue to be responsible for authorisation and prudential supervision of insurance companies; the marketing of life assurance contracts will be treated as far as possible on the same footing as other similar investments. The definition will exclude property which passes under the direct physical control of the investor if purchased; (*ii.*) a definition of *investment business* which will include, e.g. any business which effects transactions in investments with or for others, manages investments or gives advice about them. There will be various exclusions, including companies issuing their own shares, newspapers and investment clubs; (*iii.*) provisions making it an offence to carry on investment business as defined without authorisation; (*iv.*) provisions giving the Secretary of State authority (which he will be empowered to delegate to a regulatory body which appears to him to satisfy criteria laid down by the legislation) to grant, vary, make subject to conditions, suspend or revoke such authorisation and to lay down requirements for the conduct of business by those authorised. These requirements will include the application of a "fit and proper" test to all investment businesses: sole traders, partnerships and corporate entities. Rules for the conduct of business will be based on principles set out in the legislation, including a principle of fair dealing, duties of disclosure and of skill, care and diligence, the protection of clients' assets, suitability of investment recommendations, compensation for investors and disclosure of terms of business to customers.

Criteria for delegation by the Secretary of State

The main criteria for delegation will be that: (*i.*) the body's proposed rules and practices are such as to ensure that those authorised by it are and remain "fit and proper" to carry on investment business; (*ii.*) its proposed conduct of business rules will afford adequate protection to investors and are consistent with basic principles set out in the legislation; and (*iii.*) all these rules would not impose restrictions on competition greater than are justified for the adequate protection of investors.

Institutional Structure

The Government favour practitioner-based regulation within a statutory framework. The arrangements recommended by the Governor of the Bank of England after consultation with leaders of City institutions, and by representatives of the life assurance and unit trust industries, envisaged two practitioner-based regulatory bodies, a "securities and investments board", and a "marketing of investments board" covering in particular life assurance and unit trusts. However, the legislation will in no way prevent delegation to a single practitioner-based regulatory body.

There will be provision for the Boards to recognise self-regulatory organisations such as The Stock Exchange, the National Association of Security Dealers and Investment Managers, the Association of Futures Brokers and Dealers and the Insurance Brokers Registration Council as providing the authorisation required for an investment business.

Accountability to Government and Parliament

The Government propose that the Chairman and members of the Board or Boards of the regulatory bodies will be appointed by the Secretary of State or with his agreement, and Board members will include users and other lay members as well as practitioners. The Secretary of State will be entitled to withdraw regulatory authority if he considers that at any time a Board ceases to conform to the criteria set out in the legislation.

A Board's rules and practices will be subject to initial and continuing scrutiny for anti-competitive elements; after obtaining the advice of the Director General of Fair Trading, the Secretary of State will have power to require the amendment or withdrawal of rules of the Boards which are judged to be detrimental to competition and not justified in the interests of investor protection, or if they are contrary to the international obligations of the United Kingdom.

The Boards will report annually to the Secretary of State who will lay their reports before Parliament.

There will be provision for a new and independent tribunal, whose members will be appointed by the Secretary of State, to be the final determinant of any dispute about authorisation decisions or about penalties for breach of the rules.

Unit Trusts

The present controls will be relaxed to allow a greater variety of unit trusts to be made available to the general public and more speculative arrangements to be offered (and promoted) to authorised businesses, and by them to those investors who have appropriate financial resources and experience.

Investment Advice and the Marketing

Investment advisers, including those who advise on life assurance or units in unit trusts, will be subject to the conduct of business principles. They will be under a duty to disclose "relevant information" including any material interest they have in a recommendation, e.g. commissions or other reward which they might receive from other parties. This will enable investors to make more informed decisions.

Under the Prevention of Fraud (Investments) Act, it is already a criminal offence to make misleading, false, deceptive or reckless statements or forecasts about investments. The new legislation will extend this provision to cover acts or courses of conduct likely to defraud or deceive investors or potential investors.

Pensions

There will be a requirement to disclose comprehensive information about the way pension scheme assets are invested. Any investment manager or adviser involved in the administration of pension schemes as a business (that is other than simply as an employee) will require authorisation. On the regulation of personal pensions the intention is that these should be subject at least to the same safeguards as other forms of investment.

Advertisements and Circulars

Only authorised investment businesses will have a statutory right to issue advertisements or circulars likely to lead to the sale or purchase of investments.

"Advertisements and circulars" will be defined to include all media. "Cold-calling" will not be banned for the sale of investment products where a cooling off period can be provided.

Public Issues and Take-Overs

The legislation will provide that all public offers of securities, primary or secondary, including offers made on take-over bids, will be subject to the same statutory regime. All offers to the public will have to comply with requirements regarding their contents, unless specifically excepted. The minimum contents of prospectuses will be set out in regulations made by the Secretary of State.

If the securities market felt that it would be helpful, the Government would be willing to consider providing statutory backing for the City Panel on Take-overs and Mergers.

Insider Dealing

The legislation will extend the insider dealing provisions of the Companies Act, 1980, to cover all securities, including options and futures contracts based on them, and also to make enforcement more effective.

Enforcement

The regulatory Board (or Boards) and its recognised self-regulatory organisations will be responsible for enforcing their respective rules. The Department of Trade and Industry and the prosecution authorities will be responsible for enforcing the criminal law. There will be provision for civil law remedies for loss due to breach of the criminal law or of rules of business conduct. Finally, to facilitate the enforcement of these civil law rights, the Government propose powers for the Secretary of State (which he could delegate) to seek injunctions and "disgorgement orders" against businesses in breach of the criminal law, the rules of the Boards or those of recognised self-regulatory organisations.

A TABLE OF THE NUMBER OF DAYS FROM ANY DAY IN ONE MONTH TO THE SAME IN ANY OTHER MONTH IN ORDINARY YEARS

	Jan.	Feb.	Mar.	April	May	June	July	Aug.	Sept.	Oct.	Nov.	Dec.
January	365	31	59	90	120	151	181	212	243	273	304	334
February	334	365	28	59	89	120	150	181	212	242	273	303
March	306	337	365	31	61	92	122	153	184	214	245	275
April	275	306	334	365	30	61	91	122	153	183	214	244
May	245	276	304	335	365	31	61	92	123	153	184	214
June	214	245	273	304	334	365	30	61	92	122	153	183
July	184	215	243	274	304	335	365	31	62	92	123	153
August	153	184	212	243	273	304	334	365	31	61	92	122
September	122	153	181	212	242	273	303	334	365	30	61	91
October	92	123	151	182	212	243	273	304	335	365	31	61
November	61	92	120	151	181	212	242	273	304	334	365	30
December	31	62	90	121	151	182	212	243	274	304	335	365

PRIME MINISTERS AND SPEAKERS

PRIME MINISTERS SINCE 1782

Marquess of Rockingham, *Whig,* March 27, 1782.
Earl of Shelburne, *Whig,* July 13, 1782.
Duke of Portland, *Coalition,* April 4, 1783.
William Pitt, *Tory,* Dec. 7, 1783.
Henry Addington, *Tory,* March 21, 1801.
William Pitt, *Tory,* May 16, 1804.
Lord Grenville, *Whig,* Feb. 10, 1806.
Duke of Portland, *Tory,* March 31, 1807.
Spencer Perceval, *Tory,* Dec. 6, 1809.
Earl of Liverpool, *Tory,* June 16, 1812.
George Canning, *Tory,* April 30, 1827.
Viscount Goderich, *Tory,* Sept. 8, 1827.
Duke of Wellington, *Tory,* Jan. 26, 1828.
Earl Grey, *Whig,* Nov. 24, 1830.
Viscount Melbourne, *Whig,* July 13, 1834.
Sir Robert Peel, *Tory,* Dec. 26, 1834.
Viscount Melbourne, *Whig,* March 18, 1835.
Sir Robert Peel, *Tory,* Sept. 6, 1841.
Lord John Russell, *Whig,* July 6, 1846.
Earl of Derby, *Tory,* Feb. 28, 1852.
Earl of Aberdeen, *Peelite,* Dec. 28, 1852.
Viscount Palmerston, *Liberal,* Feb. 10, 1855.
Earl of Derby, *Conservative,* Feb. 25, 1858.
Viscount Palmerston, *Liberal,* June 18, 1859.
Earl Russell, *Liberal,* Nov. 6, 1865.
Earl of Derby, *Conservative,* July 6, 1866.
Benjamin Disraeli, *Conservative,* Feb. 27, 1868.
W. E. Gladstone, *Liberal,* Dec. 9, 1868.
Benjamin Disraeli, *Conservative,* Feb. 21, 1874.
W. E. Gladstone, *Liberal,* April 28, 1880.
Marquess of Salisbury, *Conservative,* June 24, 1885.
W. E. Gladstone, *Liberal,* Feb. 6, 1886.
Marquess of Salisbury, *Conservative,* Aug. 3, 1886.
W. E. Gladstone, *Liberal,* Aug. 18, 1892.
Earl of Rosebery, *Liberal,* March 3, 1894.
Marquess of Salisbury, *Conservative,* July 2, 1895.
A. J. Balfour, *Conservative,* July 12, 1902.
Sir H. Campbell-Bannerman, *Liberal,* Dec. 5, 1905.
H. H. Asquith, *Liberal,* April 8, 1908.
H. H. Asquith, *Coalition,* May 26, 1915.
D. Lloyd-George, *Coalition,* Dec. 7, 1916.
A. Bonar Law, *Conservative,* Oct. 23, 1922.
S. Baldwin, *Conservative,* May 22, 1923.
J. R. MacDonald, *Labour,* Jan. 22, 1924.
S. Baldwin, *Conservative,* Nov. 4, 1924.
J. R. MacDonald, *Labour,* June 8, 1929.
J. R. MacDonald, *Coalition,* Aug. 25, 1931.
S. Baldwin, *Coalition,* June 7, 1935.
N. Chamberlain, *Coalition,* May 28, 1937.
W. S. Churchill, *Coalition,* May 11, 1940.
W. S. Churchill, *Conservative,* May 23, 1945.
C. R. Attlee, *Labour,* July 26, 1945.
Sir W. S. Churchill, *Conservative,* Oct. 26, 1951.
Sir A. Eden, *Conservative,* April 6, 1955.
H. Macmillan, *Conservative,* Jan. 13, 1957.
Sir A. Douglas-Home, *Conservative,* Oct. 19, 1963.
J. H. Wilson, *Labour,* Oct. 16, 1964.
E. R. G. Heath, *Conservative,* June 19, 1970.

J. H. Wilson, *Labour,* March 4, 1974.
L. J. Callaghan, *Labour,* April 5, 1976.
Mrs. M. H. Thatcher, *Conservative,* May 4, 1979.

SPEAKERS OF THE COMMONS SINCE 1660

PARLIAMENT OF ENGLAND

1660 Sir Harbottle Grimston.
1661 Sir Edward Turner.
1673 Sir Job Charlton.
1673 Sir Edward Seymour.
1678 Sir Robert Sawyer.
1679 Sir William Gregory.
1680 Sir William Williams.
1685 Sir John Trevor.
1688 Henry Powle.
1694 Paul Foley.
1698 Sir Thomas Lyttelton.
1700 Robert Harley (*Earl of Oxford and Mortimer*).
1702 John Smith.

PARLIAMENT OF GREAT BRITAIN

1708 Sir Richard Onslow (*Lord Onslow*).
1710 William Bromley.
1713 Sir Thomas Hanmer.
1715 Spencer Compton (*Earl of Wilmington*).
1727 Arthur Onslow.
1761 Sir John Cust.
1770 Sir Fletcher Norton.
1780 Charles Cornwall.
1788 Hon. William Grenvill (*Lord Grenville*).
1789 Henry Addington (*Viscount Sidmouth*).

PARLIAMENT OF UNITED KINGDOM

1801 Sir John Mitford (*Lord Redesdale*).
1802 Charles Abbot (*Lord Colchester*).
1817 Charles M. Sutton (*Viscount Canterbury*).
1835 James Abercromby (*Lord Dunfermline*).
1839 Charles Shaw-Lefevre (*Viscount Eversley*).
1857 J. Evelyn Denison (*Viscount Ossington*).
1872 Sir Henry Brand (*Viscount Hampden*).
1884 Arthur Wellesley Peel (*Viscount Peel*).
1895 William Court Gully (*Viscount Selby*).
1905 James W. Lowther (*Viscount Ullswater*).
1921 John Henry Whitley.
1928 Hon. Edward Algernon FitzRoy.
1943 Col. D. Clifton Brown (*Viscount Ruffside*).
1951 William Shepherd Morrison (*Viscount Dunrossil*).
1959 Sir Harry Hylton-Foster.
1965 Horace Maybray King, PH.D. (*Lord Maybray-King*).
1971 (John) Selwyn (Brooke) Lloyd (*Lord Selwyn-Lloyd*).
1976 (Thomas) George Thomas (*Viscount Tonypandy*).
1983 (Bruce) Bernard Weatherill.

POSTAL AND TELECOMMUNICATIONS INFORMATION

GENERAL POSTAL REGULATIONS

Export Restrictions.—Under Department of Trade and Industry regulations the exportation of some goods by post is prohibited except under Department of Trade licence. Enquiries in the matter should be addressed to the Export Data Branch, Overseas Trade Divisions, Department of Trade and Industry, 1 Victoria Street, London, SW1H 0ET. Tel. 01–215 7877.

Prohibited Articles.—Among prohibitions are offensive or dangerous things, packets likely to impede the P.O. sorters, and certain kinds of advertisement.

Certificate of Posting.—Issued free on request at the time of posting.

Recorded Delivery (inland). Charge: 21p.—This service provides for a record of posting and delivery and is available for inland letters. Advice of delivery, a further 20p at time of posting, 50p after time of posting. No compensation is payable in respect of money or jewellery sent by this service.

Unpaid Mail.—All unpaid or underpaid letters are treated as second class mail. The recipient will be charged the amount of underpayment plus 10p per item. The same rates apply to unpaid or underpaid parcels.

Undelivered Mail.—Undelivered mail is returned to the sender without charge provided the return address is indicated either on the outside of the envelope or inside. If the sender's address is not available, items not containing property are destroyed; however, if the packet contains something of intrinsic value, it is retained for up to three months pending reclaim before being disposed of. Perishable items within this category are dealt with as requisite. Exceptionally, items in the minimum weight step on which a rebate of postage has been allowed are destroyed unopened unless there is a return address shown on the outside of the cover. In addition, undeliverable second class mail in the minimum weight step, which, upon opening, is found to consist only of newspapers, magazines or commercial advertising material is also destroyed. *British packets undelivered abroad*: instructions for disposal are required if parcel is undeliverable and must be given at the time of posting. A parcel which cannot be delivered will be returned to sender at his expense.

International Reply Coupons, for the purpose of prepaying replies to letters, are exchangeable abroad for stamps representing the minimum surface mail letter rate from the country concerned to the U.K. Cost: 35p each.

Poste Restante (solely for the convenience of travellers, and for three months only in any one town).—A packet may be addressed as a rule to any Post Office except Town Sub-Offices, and should have the words "Poste Restante" or "to be called for" in the address. If addressed to initials, fictitious names, or Christian name only, it is treated as undeliverable. Applicants must furnish sufficient particulars to ensure delivery to the proper person. Redirection from a Poste Restante is undertaken for up to three months. Letters at a seaport for an expected ship are kept 2 months; otherwise letters are kept for 2 weeks—or for 1 month if originating from abroad—at the end of which time they are treated as undeliverable, unless bearing a request for return at or before the end of the period.

Redirection.—(1) By agent of addressee: *Packets other than parcels, business reply and Freepost items* may be reposted free not later than the day after

delivery (not counting Sundays and public holidays) if unopened and not tampered with, and if original addressee's name is unobscured. *Parcels* may be redirected free of charge within the same time limits, only if the original and the substituted address are both within the same local parcel delivery area (or within the London Postal Area). *Registered packets*, which must be taken to a Post Office, are *re-registered* free only up to the day after delivery. (2) By the Post Office: Requests for redirection of *letters*, etc., should be on printed forms, obtainable from any post office, and must be signed by the person to whom the letters are to be addressed. The fees for redirection are as follows:—redirection for an initial period of up to one calendar month, £2·25; redirection for a period of up to three calendar months, commencing before the first anniversary of redirection, £5·50; redirection for a period of up to twelve calendar months, commencing before the first anniversary of redirection, £13·00; redirection for a period of up to 12 calendar months where redirection has already been in operation for 12 months or more, £45·00. A fee is payable for each different surname on the application form. Additional postage is generally due on redirected parcels (*see* above). Separate forms must be filled in for the forwarding of *telegrams*.

Registration, Inland (First Class letters only).—All packets intended for registration *must be handed to an officer of the Post Office, and a certificate of posting obtained*. The fees for registration (exclusive of first class postage) are: £1·10 covering compensation up to £600; £1·25, £1,250; £1·40, £1,750 (maximum). (No legal right to compensation exists in respect of registered letters sent to and from Irish Republic or the Channel Islands.) Compensation Fee (C.F.) parcels, fees: 27p up to £60 compensation; 37p up to £125; 55p up to £225; 70p up to £350. Advice of delivery, a further 20p at time of posting, 50p after time of posting.

Compensation in respect of money of any kind (coin, notes, orders, cheques, stamps, etc.) is only given if the money is sent by *registered letter* post in one of the special envelopes sold officially. Compensation cannot be paid for loss or damage in the case of any packet containing anything not legally transmissible by post; and for fragile articles only if they have been adequately packed. No compensation is paid for deterioration due to delay of perishable articles or for damage to exceptionally fragile articles, liquids or semi-liquids sent by letter or parcel post to or from Irish Republic, whether registered or not.

Compensation, Inland.—The ordinary mail services are not designed as compensation services, however, compensation up to a maximum limit of £18·00 may be paid where it can be shown that a letter or parcel was damaged or lost in the post. The onus of making up properly any packet sent by post and of packing adequately any article or articles enclosed therein lies on the sender, and the Post Office does not accept any responsibility for loss arising from faulty or inadequate packing. No compensation may be claimed for consequential injury or damage arising in respect of anything sent by post unless the item is registered and covered by Consequential Loss Insurance. This special insurance is arranged with certain Lloyds underwriters. Ask for details at the Post Office. The service is available only to U.K. addresses. *Recorded delivery packets:* maximum compensation £18 provided no contents inadmissible. Fee 21p.

Registration, Overseas (except for parcels and printed paper items posted in bulk), is in force to all countries with the exception of British Indian Ocean

Territory or Republic of Maldives. No compensation is payable for the loss of or damage to valuable articles or other items sent in an unregistered letter. Fee £1·10. If claimed within a year compensation is paid to the sender for entire loss of registered packets while in the custody of a country in the Universal Postal Union, subject to certain conditions. Compensation is also payable for the partial or complete loss of or damage to the contents of registered items in the service with certain countries (*see* Post Office Guide for list).

Insurance, Overseas, may be effected on packets to many countries at the following rates:—£1·10 for up to £100 cover; 20p for each additional £100 up to £2·90 for £1,000. *For H.M. Ships abroad and also members of H.M. Army and Air Force overseas using closed Forces addresses* (*e.g.*, British Forces Post Office followed by a number) only parcels are insurable, up to £100. Fee £1·10. Packets containing valuable papers, (banknotes, etc.), documents (press, etc.) and, in some cases, valuable articles such as jewellery, can be insured as letters, or as parcels if the country of destination does not accept dutiable goods in the letter post.

The Post Office Guide should be consulted for details of the conditions of Insurance.

Compensation up to a maximum of £13·00 for parcels up to 5 kg. in weight, £20·00 for parcels up to 10 kg., £25·00 for parcels up to 15 kg. and £30·00 for parcels up to 20 kg may be given for loss or damage in the U.K. to *uninsured* parcels to or from most overseas countries, if certificate of posting is produced.

No compensation will be paid for any loss or damage due to the act of the Queen's Enemies.

Cash on Delivery Service, Inland (*not* to or from Irish Republic, nor to H.M. Ships).—A sum (Trade Charge) up to £350 can, under certain conditions, be collected from addresses and remitted to sender of a parcel containing an invoice. Invoice values over £50 are only collected at Post Office premises. Fee (extra to normal postage and registration charges): 65p.

Cash on Delivery, Overseas.—Applicable to parcels only, but not all countries, nor to H.M. Naval and Military Forces and R.A.F. serving overseas. A fee, starting at £2.20 per parcel, must be prepaid in addition to the postage for outward parcels. For inward parcels the delivery fee is 70p. The Trade Charge (amount to be collected) may not exceed £1,000, but to most non-European countries the limit is lower. Addressee has also to pay on delivery, besides Customs, if any, a further fee (£1 in U.K.) but not prepayable. If Trade Charge cannot be collected, special rules for undeliverable C.O.D. parcels apply.

Datapost.—A guaranteed service for the delivery of important documents and packages. Datapost Sameday provides same day collection and delivery in many areas. Datapost Overnight offers next day delivery nationwide. Items may be collected or handed in at post offices. Contractual arrangements may be made for regular consignments. There are also equally reliable and secure Datapost links with a number of overseas countries. For further details contact your local Head Post Office.

Swiftair.—Express delivery of air mail letters and packets anywhere in the world. Items normally arrive at least one day in advance of normal air mail. Items should be handed in at a post office counter. Cost: normal postage plus £1·50.

Intelpost.—A public facsimile transmission service linking many towns and cities in the U.K. and also with international connections. Documents up to A4 size can be transmitted and received within minutes and the service can be used with hand delivery and collection services. Cost: from £3.

Royal Mail Special Delivery.—Offers special messenger treatment where necessary to ensure next day delivery of first class letters and packets. Special fee of £1·50 refunded if next working day delivery is not achieved provided items are posted before latest recommended posting times.

Airway Letters.—On certain internal air routes operated by the British Airways (European Division), First Class letters may be handed in at certain Airport offices for conveyance by the next available direct air service to be transferred to the post at the distant airport or town terminal or to be called for at the airport or town terminal. Fee (besides postage) £3·45 plus VAT, maximum weight 1 lb. This service is not available to the Irish Republic, Isle of Man or to any country overseas. Full information can be obtained from any office of British Airways (European Division).

Express Delivery.—This service from the office of delivery by special messenger is available to or from certain countries. In some countries the service is restricted to certain towns. Fee payable in addition to postage, £1·50.

Business Reply and Freepost (Inland, excluding Irish Republic).—These services enable a person or firm to receive replies to advertisements, letters from clients, etc. without prepayment of postage, the addressee paying the postage together with a handling charge of 0·5p per item delivered. A licence costing £20 p.a. must be obtained to use either service and these are available from Head Postmasters who will also provide any further information required.

Postage Forward Parcel Service.—This service enables a person or firm to receive parcels from clients without prepayment of postage, the addressee pays a fee of 8p on each parcel in addition to postage. A special label is used for this service. A licence costing £22 p.a., to use the service must first be obtained from the local Head Postmaster.

Articles for the Blind (Inland, including Irish Republic).—Books, papers, literature and specified articles specially adapted for the use of the blind are admissible subject to certain conditions. A packet should bear on the outside the indication "Articles for the Blind" and the name and address of the sender. Packets must be capable of easy examination in the post. Postage free up to a maximum weight of 7 kg.

Blind Literature, Overseas (in other respects treated as Printed Papers).—Papers, periodicals and books, if printed in special type (also plates for embossing blind literature, and voice recordings and special paper intended solely for the use of the blind) subject to certain conditions of posting, marked outside "Literature for the Blind (Cécogrammes)", with name and address of sender. Packets must be capable of easy examination in the post. They may be sent post free up to 7 kg by surface route to all parts and free by air mail up to 1 kg to Europe; the air mail charge to other countries is 1p per 50 g up to 7 kg.

Small Packets Post (OVERSEAS).—For the transmission of goods (including trade samples) in the same mails as Printed Papers up to 1 kg. Registration is allowed; not insurance. Available to all countries, but to some countries there is a limit of 500 g. A customs declaration is required.

Newspaper Post (INLAND).—For newspapers "registered at the P.O.".

Copies of registered newspapers may be posted by the publishers or their agents in wrappers open at both ends, in unsealed envelopes approved by the Post Office for the purpose or without covers and tied with string which can be removed without cutting. Wrappers and envelopes must be prominently marked

NEWSPAPER POST in the top left-hand corner and be easily removable for the purpose of examination. No writing or additional printing is permitted, other than the words "with compliments", name and address of sender, request for return if undeliverable and a reference to a page.

Newspapers posted by the public or supplements to registered newspapers despatched apart from their ordinary publications are transmitted under the conditions governing the First or Second Class Letter Services.

STAMPS, ENVELOPES, POSTCARDS, &c.

POSTAGE STAMPS are sold in values of ½p, 1p, 2p, 3p, 4p, 5p, 10p, 13p, 16p, 17p, 18p, 20p, 22p, 24p, 26p, 28p, 31p, 34p, 50p, 75p, £1, £1·33, £2, and £5.

Books containing stamps to the value of 50p are only available at vending machines. Books are sold containing 10 at 13p (£1·30); 6 at 17p (£1·02); 4 at 13p (£1·54) and 10 at 17p (£1·70). Rolls of 13p and 17p stamps are sold: mixed value rolls are only available on special order from post offices.

REGISTERED LETTER ENVELOPES printed with a £1·27 stamp (£1·10 for registration and 17p for postage) are in three sizes: G, 156 mm × 95 mm, £1·35 each; H, 203 mm × 120 mm, £1·38 each; K, 292 mm × 152 mm, £1·46 each.

FORCES AEROGRAMMES, 13p.

ENVELOPES printed with 13p stamp: (220 mm × 110 mm) 17p each. With 17p stamp: (220 mm × 110 mm) 21p each.

POSTNOTES: Notepaper and envelope all in one, with first class postage paid up to 60g, 22p each (pack of 5, 99p).

Aerogrammes to all destinations, 26p.

Printed postage stamps cut out of envelopes, postcards, lettercards, air letter forms or newspaper-wrappers may be used as adhesive stamps in payment of postage or telegrams provided they are not imperfect, mutilated or defaced in any way.

POSTAL ORDERS

Postal Orders (British pattern) are issued and paid at nearly all post offices in the United Kingdom during the ordinary hours of business on weekdays. They are also issued and/or paid in many countries overseas. These countries are listed in the Post Office Guide which may be seen at any post office transacting postal order business. Transmission of postal orders to any other country is prohibited except to members of H.M. Forces. British postal orders are paid and issued in the Channel Islands and the Isle of Man and paid in the Irish Republic. They are printed, with a counterfoil, for denominations of 25p and then every multiple of 5p up to and including 50p, then 60p, 70p, 75p, 80p, 90p, £1, followed by £1 steps to £10. Adhesive unmarked British Postage Stamps not exceeding two in number, if affixed in the space provided, may increase the value of an order by not more than 9p. Fees: 20p on each order up to £1, then 20p. The name of the payee must be inserted. If not presented within six months of the last day of the month of issue orders must be sent to the local Head Postmaster or, in London, to the District Postmaster, to ascertain whether the order may still be paid.

TELEMESSAGE

The inland telegram service was replaced on Oct. 1, 1982 by the telemessage service. Telemessages can be sent by telephone or telex to anywhere in the UK for 'hard copy' delivery the next working day, including Saturdays. To achieve this, a Telemessage

must be telephoned/telexed before 10 p.m. Monday to Saturday (7 p.m. Sundays and Bank Holidays). Dial 100 (190 in London) and ask for the Telemessage Service or see the telex directory for dialling codes. The telephone or telex calls are free.

A Telemessage costs £3·50 for the first 50 words and £1·75 for each subsequent group of 50 words— the name and address are free. A sender's copy costs 80p. A wide selection of colourful cards is available for special occasions at 65p per card. All prices are subject to VAT. Telemessage has a number of services for businesses. Call Freefone 2741 for details.

Telemessage is also available to the U.S.A. For next working day delivery in America a Telemessage must be filed by 10 p.m. U.K. time Monday to Saturday (7 p.m. Sundays and Bank Holidays). U.S. addresses must include the ZIP code. Charges are £5·75 for the first 50 words and £2·50 for each subsequent group of 50 words—the name and address are free. All charges are subject to VAT.

INTERNATIONAL TELEGRAMS

Ordinary telegrams are available to all countries. Dial 100 (193 in London) for full details and tariffs.

MARITIME COMMUNICATIONS

British Telecom International Maritime and Aeronautical Radio provides a comprehensive range of maritime communication services and facilities to all suitably equipped ships and boats, ranging from radiotelegram to data over satellite.

RADIOTELEGRAMS

Radiotelegrams should be addressed Portishead Radio unless the sender nominates another coast station. The address should contain (1) the name or rank of the addressee, (2) the name of the ship and (3) the name of the coast station in the British Isles if the sender knows that the ship is within range of that station.

Radiotelegrams to H.M. Ships should contain in the address (1) the name of the addressee and his rank or rating, (2) the word "Warship" (or "Submarine"), (3) the name of the ship (or identifying letters and number) and (4) the word "Admiraltyradio".

Radiotelegrams may also be sent to R.A.F. vessels. Such radiotelegrams should be addressed in the same way as for commercial vessels and in addition should include the words "R.A.F. Vessel" before the name of the ship.

RADIOTELEPHONE SERVICE

Radiotelephone services are available between telephone subscribers (but not from coin-box telephones or call offices unless the caller is a holder of a British Telecom telephone credit card) in Great Britain, Northern Ireland, the Channel Islands and the Isle of Man and suitably equipped ships. The service is generally available at all hours of the day and night, but the periods of communication with a particular ship vary with the ship's position and are dependent on radio conditions.

Calls are normally made through the coast stations, listed below, and callers should ask the local exchange telephone operator for SHIPS' TELEPHONE SERVICE adding, if known, the telephone number and name of the coast station through which the call should be made. If the name of the coast station is not known, the caller will be connected to Portishead Radio. When connected to the coast station operator, the caller should ask for SHIPS' RADIO TELE-PHONE CALL giving the name of the ship and the name (or designation) of the person required.

Anglesey Radio	0407 83 0541
Bacton Radio (restricted short range VHF services)	0521 73447
Buchan Radio (restricted short range VHF services)	0569 62917
Cardigan Bay Radio (restricted short range VHF services)	0407 830541
Celtic Radio (restricted short range VHF services)	0271 63453
Clyde Radio (restricted short range VHF services)	0776 81 311
Collafirth Radio (restricted short range VHF services)	0955 2271
Cromarty Radio (restricted short range VHF services)	0955 2271
Cullercoats Radio	091 253 1318
Forth Radio (restricted short range VHF services)	0569 62917
Grimsby Radio (restricted short range VHF services)	0521 73447
Hastings Radio (restricted short range VHF services)	0843 220592
Hebrides Radio (restricted short range VHF services)	0569 62917
Humber Radio	0521 73447
Ilfracombe Radio	0271 63453
Islay Radio (restricted short range VHF services)	0776 81 311
Land's End Radio	0736 87 363
Lewis Radio (restricted short range VHF services)	0569 62917
Morecambe Bay Radio (restricted short range VHF services)	0407 830541
Niton Radio	0983 730495
North Foreland Radio	0843 220592
Orfordness Radio (restricted short range VHF services)	0843 220592
Orkney Radio (restricted short range VHF services)	0955 2271
Pendennis Radio (restricted short range VHF services)	0736 87 363
Portishead Radio	0278 781111
Portpatrick Radio	0776 81 311
Scillies Radio (restricted short range VHF services)	0736 87 363
Severn Radio (restricted short range VHF services)	0271 63453
Shetland Radio (restricted short range VHF services)	0955 2271
Skye Radio (restricted short range VHF services)	0569 62917
Start Point Radio (restricted short range VHF services)	0736 87 363
Stonehaven Radio	0569 62917
Thames Radio (restricted short range VHF services)	0843 220592
Whitby Radio (restricted short range VHF services)	091 253 1318
Wick Radio	0955 2271

The service is also available for calls to and from H.M. Ships, subject to the approval of the Duty Commander M.O.D. Navy, through whom all calls to H.M. Ships should be booked. H.M. Ships do not normally keep watch for private radiotelephone calls from the shore, no attempt should be made to book a call to one of H.M. Ships unless prior arrangements have been made with the person concerned on the ship. The caller must be able to give the name of the coast station through which the call is to be made, or the approximate position of the ship at the time the call is required.

The holder of a British Telecom telephone credit card issued in Great Britain, Northern Ireland, the Channel Islands or the Isle of Man may use it to make radio-telephone calls to ships at sea from any telephone in this country (including coin-box telephones and call offices).

Radioteleprinter Service.—Telex subscribers may be connected for two-way teleprinter communication with suitably equipped ships at sea via the following:

Cullercoats Radio	53345	BTGCC	G
Hebrides Radio............	73159	BTGND	G
Land's End Radio	45250	BTGLD	G
North Foreland Radio	96137	BTGNF	G
Portishead Radio..........	46116	BTGKA	G
Stonehaven Radio.........	73159	BTGND	G
Wick Radio	75553	BTGKR	G

INLAND TELEPHONES

The quarterly rental for an exclusive business exchange line is £19·95 and £12·40 for a residential exclusive exchange line. For shared service, in which two subscribers share one line but have practically the same facilities as those provided by individual lines, each customer pays £4·20 per annum less than for exclusive line service. A condition of telephone service is that all new and removing residential customers since January, 1948, are liable to share their lines if called upon to do so. Subscriber trunk dialling (STD) facilities are provided to most destinations at all exchanges. Local and dialled national calls from these exchanges are charged in 5p units when made from ordinary lines, in 10p units when dialled from pay on answer coin-box lines and 10p minimum charge from Press-Button payphones with 2p incremental units. All charges are subject to Value Added Tax (VAT). VAT on call charges from ordinary lines is charged as a percentage of the total on quarterly bills and VAT on calls from pay on answer coin-box lines is included in the unit fee. The length of time per unit depends on the distance of the call and time of day, from eight minutes for a local call to fifteen seconds for distances over 56 kilometres.

Operator connected national calls from ordinary lines have a three minute minimum charge (and thereafter by the minute) which varies with distance and time of day, but those from coinbox lines are charged in 3 minute periods at the coinbox tariff. For calls that have to be passed through the operator because the caller cannot dial or because a dialled call had failed, the charge is equivalent to the dialled rate, subject normally to the three minute minimum. Generally higher charges apply to other operator connected calls including special services calls and those to the Irish Republic and the Channel Isles. All national calls are cheaper if made after 6 p.m. or at weekends. Personal calls (to specified person) 88p extra from ordinary lines and £1·10 from coinbox lines, if the person cannot be found nothing further is charged. For fuller information *see* Preface to Telephone Directory, Dialling Instruction Booklet (where appropriate) and Post Office Guide.

TELEX SERVICE

There are now 201 countries that can be reached by Telex from the UK; 190 of them by Direct Dial.

For most customers Direct Dialled calls to all international destinations are charged in six second units costing between 2·3p and 11·5p depending upon the country called. Calls via the operator are charged in one minute steps with a three minute minimum, plus a surcharge of £1·60 per call.

Calls made via British Telecom's Telex Plus store and forward facility attract normal Telex charges plus a surcharge of 10p for inland delivered messages and 20p for international delivered messages. For information regarding Telex contact your local Area telephone office Telex Sales Department.

INTERNATIONAL DATA TRANSMISSION SERVICES

(i) PUBLIC SWITCHED TELEPHONE NETWORK

BTI International Business Services offer data transmission over the public switched telephone network using International Direct Dialling (IDD). Calls are charged at the same rate as for telephone calls. Modems used must be approved for connection to the public network.

BTI does not impose limitations as regards transmission speeds or standards but recommends that where possible terminal equipment used conforms to the recommendations of the CCITT (Consultative Committee on Telephones and Telegraphs).

BTI has reached agreement with 70 countries for such use of the telephone network.

(ii) PRIVATE CIRCUITS

International private circuits are available for data transmission and are provided in accordance with the Recommendations of the International Telephone & Telegraph Consultative Committee (CCITT). Using suitable modems, higher transmission rates than those offered by the Datel services are usually obtainable over voice bandwidth circuits.

In addition, high speed data transmission, e.g. 72K Bit/s may be achieved over wide-band leases (telephone circuits grouped together to give 48KHz bandwidth). A reduced tariff for 1200–9600 bit/s service and a 56K bit/s service is available to some countries.

(iii) INTERNATIONAL PACKET SWITCHING SERVICE (IPSS)

Packet switching is the switching and transmission of data in discrete quantities called packets, each packet or block of data carrying its own routing and control information. Packet switching technology permits intercommunication between different terminal types and transmission rates and is sufficiently flexible to support a diversity of data communications applications on dedicated data networks providing high reliability and low error rates.

IPSS provides service with over 60 networks in more than 40 countries in Australasia, Europe, North and South America, the Caribbean and the Middle and Far East.

International Kilostream offers digital international private leased circuits to certain countries at a range of transmission rates from 2·4 Kbit/s to 56 Kbit/s on a full time basis. The 56 Kbit/s transmission rate can also be offered to the U.S.A. on a time assigned basis. The circuits can be multiplexed by the customer to allow a number of applications on one circuit.

Satstream is British Telecom International's small-dish satellite service, combining satellites, small-dish earth terminals and digital transmission. It provides links, at present, to Western Europe and North America.

BTI International Telephones offer an automatic freephone service available across international boundaries. International 0800 allows U.K. based companies to be called by their overseas contacts and customers, free of charge, without operator involvement. The service is available at present from the U.S.A., France and the Netherlands. A number may be rented on a monthly basis; calls are charged at rates higher than IDD rates.

PRESTEL

Prestel, British Telecommunications' public videotex service, links adapted television screens to computers through ordinary telephone lines so information and two-way services can be delivered directly into offices and homes. Over 98 per cent of the U.K. telephone population can now use Prestel at local call rates, and over 60,000 terminals are attached to the network. Information on Prestel (from over 1,200 different sources) can be updated by the minute and is available 24 hours a day.

In addition, by using "Gateways" private computers can be linked to Prestel sets via Prestel computers. This facility makes possible services such as home banking, home shopping and for travel agents confirmed reservations of airline tickets.

Because the system is two-way, all customers can send messages, make bookings or request information at the touch of a button. There are well over 330,000 frames (or "pages") of information available. Some of the specialist services Prestel offers are Homelink, CitiService, Messaging, Private Prestel and Prestel Microcomputing.

INTERNATIONAL TELEPHONES

The charges are the same for calls originating in any part of Great Britain, Northern Ireland and the Isle of Man. All U.K. customers have had access to International Direct Dialling from this country since 28 July, 1982 and can now dial direct to numbers on most exchanges in over 160 countries worldwide. The number of places abroad to which calls may be dialled direct is also increasing. Callers should consult their dialling codes booklets or International Telephone Guide for information on how to make calls.

Directly dialled calls are charged in units of time costing 4·7p. For charge bands A, B, C, D and F cheap rates apply from 8 p.m. to 8 a.m. nightly, at any time on Saturdays and Sundays and all day on selected Bank Holidays. For charge band E, the economy rate applies from 12 p.m. to 7 a.m. and 2.30 p.m. to 7.30 p.m. every day and all day at Bank Holidays and weekends adjoining Bank Holidays. For charge band C, the peak rate applies on weekdays from 3 p.m. to 5 p.m. Standard rate applies on all charge bands at all other times. Cheap rates are not available for calls in charge band G. Where I.D.D. access to a country is not yet available callers should dial the International Exchange, specifying the country required.

BRITISH TELECOM

81 Newgate Street EC1A 7AJ
[01-356 5000]

British Telecom, formerly part of the Post Office, was established as a separate public corporation on 1 October, 1981. Consequent upon the Telecommunications Act 1984, it became a public limited company on 6 August, 1984. *Chairman*, Sir George Jefferson, C.B.E.

FINANCIAL RESULTS

	1983/4 £m.	1984/5 £m.
Turnover	6,876	7,653
Main services income	6,308	6,990

Sales and other operating income	568	663
Total expenditure including interest	5,886	6,173
Profit on ordinary activities	990	1,480
†Tax on profit	—	535
*Preference dividend	—	41
Profit attributable to shareholders	—	904
*Ordinary dividend	—	234
Retained profit	—	670

† Result of tax law changes under the 1984 Finance Act.

* Result of privatisation.

BASIC RATE OF INLAND LETTER POST

1840	1d	1975	7p
1918	1½d	Sept. 1975	8½p
1940	2½d	June 1977	9p
1957	3d	Aug. 1979	10p
1965	4d	Feb. 1980	12p
1968*	5d	Jan. 1981	14p
1971	3p	Feb. 1982	15½p
1973	3½p	April 1983	16p
1974	4½p	Sept. 1984	17p

(*Two-tier postal system introduced—subsequent figures are for 1st class letter post)

POST OFFICE FINANCIAL RESULTS, etc

	1983–84 (£m.)			1984–85 (£m.)		
	Posts	National Giro-bank	£m. Total 1983–84	Posts	National Giro-bank	£m. Total 1984–85
INCOME						
Main Services	2268·8	144·5	2363·6	2500·9	168·1	2669·0
Other Services	648·8	82·6	640·1	782·7	96·7	879·4
Less inter-service charges	(141·0)			(153·6)		(153·6)
Total	2776·6	227·1	3003·7	3130·0	264·8	3394·8
EXPENDITURE						
Staff costs	1789·1	52·9	1842·0	1998·7	61·7	2060·4
Depreciation	35·9	3·6	39·5	42·6	—	42·6
Other operating charges	836·1	158·7	994·8	966·2	184·3	1150·5
Extraordinary charges	—	—	—	—	—	—
Interest payable (receivable)	(1·4)	2·0	0·6	(11·2)	2·1	(9·1)
Tax	5·6	2·3	7·9	28·6	3·6	32·2
Dividend	—	2·0	2·0	—	2·0	2·0
Total	2665·3	221·5	2886·8	3024·9	253·7	3278·6
PROFIT RETAINED/(LOSS)	111·3	5·6	116·9	105·1	11·1	116·2

DUTY AND TAX-FREE ALLOWANCES

You are entitled to the allowances in either of the columns below (but not both) for any category of goods, as represented by the boxes (see Notes on allowances). Passengers under 17 are not, however, entitled to tobacco and drinks allowances.

Column 1
Goods obtained duty and tax free in the EEC, or duty and tax free on a ship or aircraft, or goods obtained outside the EC.

Column 2
Goods obtained duty and tax paid in the EC.

Tobacco goods
200 cigarettes
or
100 cigarillos ⎫
or ⎬ double if you live
50 cigars ⎭ outside Europe
or
250 grammes of tobacco

Tobacco goods
300 cigarettes
or
150 cigarillos
or
75 cigars
or
400 grammes of tobacco

Alcoholic drinks
2 litres of still table wine
plus
1 litre over 22% vol. (e.g. spirits and strong liqueurs)
or
2 litres not over 22% vol. (e.g. low strength liqueurs, fortified wine or sparkling wine)
or
A further 2 litres of still table wine

Alcoholic drinks
4 litres of still table wine
plus
1½ litres over 22% vol. (e.g. spirits and strong liqueurs)
or
3 litres not over 22% vol. (e.g. low strength liqueurs, fortified wine, or sparkling wine)
or
A further 3 litres of still table wine

Perfume
50 grammes (60 cc or 2 fl oz)

Perfume
75 grammes (90 cc or 3 fl oz)

Toilet water
250 cc (9 fl oz)

Toilet water
375 cc (13 fl oz)

Other goods
£28 worth

Other goods
£207* worth

* Subject to Parliamentary approval.

N.B. A maximum of 50 litres of beer and 25 lighters may be imported duty-free, subject to the limitations of the 'Other goods' monetary allowance.

If you are visiting the United Kingdom for less than six months, you are also entitled to bring in, free of duty and tax, all personal effects (except tobacco goods, alcoholic drinks and perfume) which you intend to take with you when you leave.

NOTES ON ALLOWANCES

(1) The countries of the EEC (Common Market) are Belgium, Denmark, France, West Germany, Greece, the Irish Republic, Italy, Luxemburg, the Netherlands, the United Kingdom (but not the Channel Islands) and from Jan. 1986 Spain and Portugal.
(2) The allowances apply only to goods carried and cleared by you at the time of your arrival.
(3) The allowances do not apply to goods brought in for sale or for other commercial purposes.
(4) Reduced allowances apply to certain persons crossing the Irish land boundary and to seamen and aircrew members.
(5) Whisky, gin, rum, brandy, vodka and most liqueurs normally exceed 22% vol. (38.8° proof) but advocaat, cassis, fraise, suze and aperitifs may be less. Fortified wines include port, sherry, vermouth and madeira. Sparkling wines include champagne, perelada, spumante and semi-sparkling wines. Still table wines include claret, Sauterne, Graves and Chianti. Burgundy, Chablis, hock and Moselle may be either sparkling or still, depending on manufacture.
(6) You may not mix goods obtained duty and tax free or outside the EC with goods of the same category (as represented by the boxes) obtained duty and tax paid in the EC to obtain the higher allowance. E.g. you will not get the higher allowance for Tobacco goods if *any* of the items in that category were obtained duty and tax free or outside the EC.
(7) Where there are alternative quantities within a category of goods they may be apportioned. For example, 150 cigarettes (half allowance) plus 75 cigarillos (half allowance).
(8) One litre is approximately 1¾ pints or 35 fl oz.
(9) A cigarillo is a cigar with a maximum weight of 3 grammes.

PROHIBITED AND RESTRICTED GOODS

The customs officer will be able to provide full information. This is a list of commoner and more frequently met items:

Controlled drugs, such as opium, heroin, morphine, cocaine, cannabis, amphetamines, lysergide (LSD) and barbiturates.
Firearms (including gas pistols and similar weapons), ammunition and explosives (including fireworks).
Flick knives.
Counterfeit currency.
Horror comics. Indecent and obscene books, magazines, films and other articles.
Radio transmitters (walkie-talkies, Citizen's Band radios etc.) not approved for use in the U.K.

Meat and poultry, and most of their products (whether or not cooked), including ham, bacon, sausage, pâté, eggs and milk.

Plants, parts thereof and plant produce, including trees and shrubs, potatoes and certain other vegetables, fruit, bulbs and seeds.

Animals and birds, whether alive or dead (e.g. stuffed); certain articles derived from rare species including furskins, ivory, reptile leather and goods made from them.

NOTE: Cats, dogs and other mammals must not be landed unless a British import licence (rabies) has previously been issued: nor certain fish and fish eggs, whether live or dead, or bees.

EXPORT CONTROL

The following are some of the goods subject to export control and should be declared to the customs officer.

There are formalities to be completed in respect of these goods prior to your arrival at the port of exportation and further information is available through any local office of Customs and Excise (address in the telephone directory).

● Controlled drugs.
● Firearms and ammunition.
● Photographic material over 60 years old and valued at £400 or more.
● Portraits (including sculptures) of British Historical Personages which are over 50 years old and valued at £4,000 or more.
● Antiques, collectors' items, etc. (including paintings and other works of art) over 50 years old and valued at £16,000 or more.
● Certain archaeological material.
● Most live animals and birds, and items made from animals occurring wild in the U.K.

BRITISH PASSPORT REGULATIONS

Applications for United Kingdom passports must be made on the forms obtainable at any of the Passport Offices (addresses given below) or at any Main Post Office (except in Northern Ireland).

London.—Clive House, 70–78 Petty France, SW1H 9HD.

Liverpool.—India Buildings, Water Street, Liverpool L2 0QZ.

Newport, Gwent.—Olympia House, Upper Dock Street NPT 1XA.

Peterborough.—Passport Office, 55 Westfield Road, Peterborough PE3 6TG.

Glasgow.—1st Floor, Empire House, 131 West Nile Street, Glasgow G1 2RY.

Belfast.—Passport Office, Hampton House, 47–53 High Street, Belfast BT1 2QS.

Hours. The above offices are open Mon.-Fri. 9 a.m. to 4.30 p.m. The Passport Office, London, is also open for cases of special emergency (*e.g.* death or serious illness) arising outside normal office hours between 4.30 p.m. and 6.00 p.m. and on Saturdays between 10 a.m. and noon.

Completed forms of application should be sent to one of the six Passport Offices, with photographs, supporting documents and the fee of £15 (£22·50 if particulars of spouse included), in the form of a Cheque or Postal Order which should be crossed and made payable to the Passport Office.

A Passport cannot be issued or extended on behalf of *a person already abroad*; such person should apply, in a foreign country, to the nearest British Mission or Consulate, or, within the British Commonwealth outside the United Kingdom of Great Britain and N. Ireland, to the nearest British Passport issuing authority.

United Kingdom Passports are granted to:—
(i) British Citizens.
(ii) British Dependent Territories Citizens.
(iii) British Overseas Citizens.
(iv) British Subjects.
(v) British Protected Persons.

A passport granted to a child under 16 will normally be valid for an initial period of five years, after which it may be extended for a further five years with no extra charge. A passport granted to a person over 16 will normally be valid for 10 years and will not be renewable. Thereafter, or if at any time the Passport contains no further space for visas, a new Passport must be obtained.

A Passport including particulars of the *holder's spouse* is not available for his/her use when he/she is travelling alone. A spouse's particulars may *only* be added at the time of issue of a passport.

Children who have reached the age of sixteen years require separate Passports. Their applications must be signed by one of their parents.

Passport applications must be countersigned by a Member of Parliament, Justice of the Peace, Minister of Religion, Doctor, Lawyer, Bank Officer, Police Officer or any person of similar standing who has been personally acquainted with the applicant for at least two years. The applicant's birth certificate and other evidence in support of the statements made in the application must be produced.

In the case of children under the age of 16 requiring a separate passport, an application should be made by one of the parents on form (B).

If the applicant for a Passport be a British national by naturalization or registration, the Certificate of Naturalization or registration must be produced with the application.

British Passports are generally available for travel *to all countries.* The possession of a Passport does not, however, exempt the holder from compliance with any *Immigration Regulations* in force in British or foreign countries, or from the necessity of obtaining a *visa* where required.

Photographs

Duplicate unmounted photographs of applicant (and wife/husband, if to be included in the Passport) must be sent. These photographs should be printed on normal thin photographic paper. They should measure not more than 2¼ in. by 2 in. (63 mm. by 50 mm.), or less than 2 in. by 1½ in. (50 mm. by 38 mm.), and should be taken full face without a hat.

Extension of Passports

Applications for the extension of United Kingdom passports must be made on Form D.

94-Page Passports

On May 1, 1973, a new type of passport became available. Intended to meet the needs of frequent travellers who fill standard passports well before the ten-year validity has expired, it contains 94 pages, is valid for ten years and costs £30 (£45 if particulars of spouse included).

British Visitors' Passports

A simplified form of travel document is available for British Citizens, British Dependent Territories Citizens or British Overseas Citizens wishing to pay short visits (not exceeding three months) to certain foreign countries, *viz.*

ANDORRA; AUSTRIA; BELGIUM; BERMUDA; CAN-

ADA; DENMARK; FINLAND; FRANCE (incl. CORSICA); GREECE (& the GREEK ISLANDS); W. GERMANY (incl. West Berlin by air only); GIBRALTAR; ICELAND; ITALY; LIECHTENSTEIN; LUXEMBOURG; MALTA; MONACO; NETHERLANDS; NORWAY; PORTUGAL (incl. MADEIRA & AZORES); SAN MARINO; SPAIN (incl. BALEARIC & CANARY ISLANDS); SWEDEN; SWITZERLAND; TUNISIA; TURKEY.

A fee of £7·50 (£11·25 if particulars of spouse included) is charged for the issue of a British Visitors' Passport, which is valid for 12 months, cannot be amended and is not renewable; on expiry application should be made for a new passport if required. Particulars of an applicant's spouse and/or children under 16 years can be included at *the time of issue only* at no extra cost. A child of 8 years of age and over is eligible to hold a British Visitors' Passport. Applications for, or including, a person under 18 years of age (unless married or serving in H.M. Forces) must be countersigned by the legal guardian.

British Visitors' Passports are obtainable by application on Form VP (from any Main Post Office except in Northern Ireland). Applicants in England, Scotland and Wales should take the completed form in person to any Main Post Office which will normally issue the passport without further delay; applicants in Northern Ireland to the Passport Office, Belfast from whom application forms may be obtained. *British Visitors' Passports are not obtainable from Passport Offices other than Belfast.* Two recent passport photographs will be required of the applicant and of his/her spouse, if to be included; photographs of children are not required. Size of photographs must be 2 in. × 1½ in. (50 mm. by 38 mm.) They should be unmounted and must be printed on normal thin photographic paper. No visas are required on British Visitors' Passports.

Applicants must also produce for the purpose of identification a N.H.S. Medical Card, birth certificate or retirement pension book.

VISAS

Visa regulations are liable to change and enquiries should be made at the Consulate or Embassy concerned (addresses and telephone numbers are given in the Commonwealth and Foreign Countries sections).

For entry into the following countries a visa or permit may be required: Afghanistan; Albania; Algeria; Angola; Antigua; Argentina; Austria; Bahrain; Benin; Bermuda; Bolivia; Brazil; Brunei; Bulgaria; Burkina Faso (Upper Volta); Burma; Burundi; Cameroon Republic; Cape Verde; Central African Republic; Chad; Chile; China; Colombia; Congo; Costa Rica; Cuba; Czechoslovakia; Dominica; Dominican Republic; Ecuador; Egypt; El Salvador; Equatorial Guinea; Ethiopia; Finland; Gabon; German Democratic Republic; Germany, Federal Republic of; Gibraltar; Grenada; Guatemala; Guinea; Guinea Bissau; Haiti; Honduras; Hong Kong; Hungary; Indonesia; Iran; Iraq; Israel; Ivory Coast; Japan; Jordan; Korea; Kuwait; Laos; Lebanon; Liberia; Libya; Madagascar; Mali; Mauritania; Mexico; Mongolia; Morocco; Mozambique; Nepal; Nicaragua; Niger; Oman; Pakistan; Panama; Paraguay; Peru; Philippines; Poland; Qatar; Romania; Rwanda; St. Lucia; St. Vincent and the Grenadines; Saudi Arabia; Senegal; Somali Democratic Republic; South Africa; Sudan; Sweden; Switzerland; Syria; Thailand; Togo; Tunisia; Turkey; United Arab Emirates; Uruguay; U.S.A.; U.S.S.R.; Venezuela; Vietnam; Yemen Arab Republic; Yemen, People's Democratic Republic of; Yugoslavia; Zaire.

WORK AND BUSINESS OVERSEAS

A passport issued after December 31, 1982 showing the holder's national status as British citizen will secure for the holder the right to take employment or to establish himself in business or other self-employed activity in another member state of the European Community (except Greece). A passport bearing the endorsement "holder has the right of abode in the United Kingdom" where the holder so qualifies will also secure the same right. Employment permits are required in most other countries, even for casual labour. The nearest representative of the country concerned should be consulted. Local Employment Offices have a booklet entitled "Working abroad".

Those planning to travel abroad on export business are advised to contact the Overseas Trade Divisions of the Department of Trade and Industry, 1 Victoria Street, London S.W.1 or the Export Section of Regional Offices in London S.W.1, Birmingham, Bristol, Leeds, Manchester, Newcastle upon Tyne and Nottingham. For Wales: Welsh Office Industry Department, New Crown Building, Cathays Park, Cardiff; for Scotland: Export Office for Scotland, Scottish Economic Planning Department, Alhambra House, 45 Waterloo Street, Glasgow; for Northern Ireland: Industrial Development Board for Northern Ireland, I.D.B. House, 64 Chichester Street, Belfast. These offices will send advance notification of the visit to the Commercial Section of the relevant Consulate or Embassy, and can offer advice and information about the markets to be visited.

VACCINATION

In very general terms vaccination for protection against cholera, typhoid and polio are recommended for all countries outside Europe, except North America, Australia and New Zealand. Protection, in the form of tablets, is advised for malaria similarly.

Vaccination against yellow fever is essential for entry into Benin, Burkina Faso (Upper Volta), Cameroon, Central African Republic, Congo, French Guiana, Gambia, Ivory Coast, Mali, Mauritania, Niger, Nigeria, Sao Tome and Principe, Senegal, and Uganda, and is recommended for most other African and South American countries. Fuller details are set out in D.H.S.S. leaflet SA 35 "Protect your health abroad". For up-to-date information about vaccination requirements, contact one of the following health departments: *England*—International Relations Division, D.H.S.S., Alexander Fleming House, Elephant and Castle, London SE1 6BY (01-407 5522 ext. 6749), Communicable Disease Surveillance Centre, 61 Colindale Avenue, London NW9 5EQ (01-200 4400); *Wales*—Welsh Office, Cathays Park, Cardiff CF1 3NQ (0222-825111 ext. 3395); *Scotland*—Scottish Home and Health Department, St. Andrew's House, Edinburgh EH1 3DE (031-5568501 ext. 2438); *Northern Ireland*—D.H.S.S., Dundonald House, Upper Newtownards Road, Belfast BT4 3SF (0232-63939 ext. 2593).

Your doctor should be consulted six to eight weeks before departure, and will advise you and arrange vaccinations. If children will be travelling outside Europe, North America, Australia and New Zealand the doctor should be informed, especially if they have not completed their full course of childhood immunization.

Details of free or reduced cost medical treatment when visiting other European countries, Hong Kong or New Zealand are set out in leaflet SA 30 "Medical costs abroad", available from travel agents, local social security offices or the D.H.S.S. Leaflets Unit, P.O. Box 21, Stanmore, Middx.

VEHICLE LICENCES, ETC.

From October 1, 1974, registration and first licensing of vehicles has been done through local offices (known as Local Vehicle Licensing Offices) of the Department of Transport's Driver and Vehicle Licensing Centre in Swansea. The records of existing vehicles are held at Swansea. Local facilities for relicensing are available as follows:—

   (i) with a licence reminder (form V11) in person at any Post Office which deals with vehicle licensing or post it to the Head Post Office, shown on the form.
   (ii) with a vehicle licence application (form V10) either in person at any "licensing" Post Office if you have the Registration Document or post it to the Head Postmaster at one of the Head Post Offices listed on the back of the V10. If you do not have the Registration Document only, apply to a Local Vehicle Licensing Office, not to D.V.L.C.

Details of the present duties chargeable on motor vehicles are available at Post Offices and Local Vehicle Licensing Offices. The Vehicles (Excise) Act, 1971 provides *inter alia* that any vehicle kept on a public road but not used on roads is chargeable to excise duty as if it were in use.

Rates of duty for motor car and motor cycle licences are shown below. For Hackney Carriages the rates of duty are: Hackney Carriage with seating capacity not exceeding 20 persons, £50·00; additional for each person above 20 (excluding the driver) for which the vehicle has seating capacity, £1·00.

Type of Vehicle	Exceeding	Not Exceeding	12 Months	6 Months
			£	£
MOTOR CARS				
Those first registered before January 1, 1947	—	—	60·00	33·00
Other than above	—	—	100·00	55·00
MOTOR CYCLES				
With or without sidecar	—	150 c.c.	10·00	—
With or without sidecar	150 c.c.	250 c.c.	20·00	—
With or without sidecar	250 c.c.	—	40·00	22·00
If first licensed before 1 Jan. 1933 and weighs not more than 101·6 kgs.	250 c.c.	—	20·00	—
THREE WHEELERS				
Other than pedestrian-controlled	—	150 c.c.	10·00	—
Other than pedestrian-controlled	150 c.c.	—	40·00	22·00
PEDESTRIAN-CONTROLLED VEHICLES (Other than mowing machines)				
Three wheeled	—	150 c.c.	10·00	—
Three wheeled	150 c.c.	—	20·00	—
More than three wheels	—	—	20·00	—

Driving Licences—Fees

	On or after 1.10.82		On or after 1.10.82
FULL LICENCE		(iii) Issued after 1.1.76 not being an Exchange licence and no additional entitlement claimed ...	Free
First full licence	£10·00*		
Renewal of full licence if last full licence was:		**PROVISIONAL LICENCE**	
(i) Issued before 1.1.76	£10·00*	First provisional licence	£10·00*
(ii) Issued after 1.1.76 and additional entitlement claimed ...	£3.00	DUPLICATE LICENCE	£3·00
		EXCHANGE LICENCE	£3·00

* Once you have paid £10 for *either* a provisional *or* a full licence all renewals are free except where additional entitlement is required.

Driving Test–Fees

For cars	£14·40
For motor cycles, part I	£17·95*
part II	£14·40

*When conducted by the Department of Transport. Appointed motor cycle training organisations, who conduct the majority of part I tests within the framework of their own training courses, are free to set their own fee.

Driving tests for invalid carriages are free.

M.o.T. Testing

Cars, motor cycles, motor caravans, light goods and dual-purpose vehicles which are more than three years old must be covered by an effective vehicle test certificate (often called the M.o.T. certificate). Copies of the legislation governing M.o.T. testing can be obtained from any H.M.S.O. bookshop or bookshops which stock H.M.S.O. publications. The legislation comprises The Road Traffic Act 1972 (Sections 44 and 45), The Motor Vehicles (Test) Regulations 1981, The Motor Vehicles (Extension) Order 1981, and The Motor Vehicles (Production of Test Certificate) Regulations 1969.

HALLMARKS ON GOLD, SILVER AND PLATINUM WARES
London (Goldsmiths' Hall) Date Letters
From 1498

	Black letter, small	1498–9 to 1517–8		Roman letter, small	1739–40 to 1755–6
	Lombardic	1518–9 ,, 1537–8		Old English, capitals ..	1756–7 to 1775–6
	Roman and other capitals	1538–9 ,, 1557–8		Roman letter, small ...	1776–7 ,, 1795–6
	Black letter, small	1558–9 ,, 1577–8		Roman letter, capitals .	1796–7 ,, 1815–6
	Roman letter, capitals	1578–9 ,, 1597–8		Roman letter, small ...	1816–7 ,, 1835–6
	Lombardic, external cusps	1598–9 ,, 1617–8		Old English, capitals ..	1836–7 ,, 1855–6
	Italic letter, small	1618–9 ,, 1637–8		Old English, small	1856–7 ,, 1875–6
	Court hand	1638–9 ,, 1657–8		Roman letter, capitals [A to M *square* shield N to Z as shown]	1876–7 ,, 1895–6
	Black letter, capitals ..	1658–9 ,, 1677–8		Roman letter, small ...	1896–7 ,, 1915–6
	Black letter, small	1678–9 ,, 1696–7		Black letter, small	1916–7 ,, 1935–6
	Court hand	1697 ,, 1715–6		Roman letter, capitals .	1936–7 ,, 1955–6
	Roman letter, capitals	1716–7 ,, 1735–6		Italic letter, small	1956–7 ,, 1974
	Roman letter, small ...	1736–7 ,, 1738–9		Italic letter, capitals ..	1975 ,, ...

Hallmarks are the symbols stamped on gold, silver, or platinum articles to indicate that they have been chemically tested and that they conform to one of the legal standards. With certain exceptions, all gold, silver, or platinum articles are required by law to be hallmarked before they are offered for sale. Hallmarking was instituted in 1300 under a statute of Edward I.

Normally a complete modern hallmark consists of four symbols—the maker's mark or sponsor's mark, assay office mark, standard mark and date letter.

Additional marks have been authorized from time to time.

Maker's Mark.—Instituted in 1363, the maker's mark was originally a device such as a bird or *fleur-de-lys* and now consists invariably of the initials of the Christian and surnames of the maker or sponsor, or of the firm.

Assay Office Mark.—The existing assay offices and their distinguishing marks are:—

LONDON (Goldsmiths' Hall).

A leopard's head (uncrowned from 1300 to 1478–9, when it became crowned until 1821, since when it has been uncrowned). From 1697 to 1974 a lion's head erased was used on silver of the higher (Britannia) standard.

BIRMINGHAM (Newhall Street) . . . . An anchor
SHEFFIELD (137 Portobello Street) . . . . A rose
EDINBURGH (Goldsmiths' Hall, 15 Queen Street)
A castle

Offices formerly existed in other towns, *e.g.* Chester, Glasgow, Newcastle, Exeter, York and Norwich, each having its own distinguishing mark.

Standard Mark.—Instituted in 1544. The current legal standards and their marks are as follows:—

PLATINUM

SILVER.—Sterling silver (92·5 per cent. silver) is marked by English assay offices with a *lion passant* and by the Edinburgh Assay Office with a *lion rampant*. A full-length figure of *Britannia* was impressed on silver of a higher standard (95·84 per cent. silver) between 1697 and 1720 and this mark is still used occasionally by all British assay offices.

GOLD.—Since 1975 gold articles are marked with a crown followed by the millesimal figure for the standard, i.e. 916 for 22 carat, 750 for 18 carat, 585 for 14 carat and 375 for 9 carat.

Date Letter.—Instituted in 1478. The date letter denotes the year in which an article was assayed and hallmarked. Each alphabetical cycle has a distinctive style of lettering or shape of shield. The date letters were different at the various assay offices and the particular office must be established from the assay office mark before reference is made to tables of date letters. Specimen shields and letters used by the London Office on silver articles in each period from 1498 to date are shown on the previous page. The same letters are found on gold articles but the surrounding shield may differ.

OTHER MARKS

Duty Mark.—In 1784 an additional mark of the reigning sovereign's head was introduced to signify that the excise duty had been paid. The mark became obsolete on the abolition of the duty in 1890.

Commemorative Marks.—There are three other marks to commemorate special events, the Silver Jubilee of King George V and Queen Mary in 1935, the Coronation of Queen Elizabeth II in 1953 and her Silver Jubilee in 1977.

Foreign Wares.—Since 1842 foreign wares imported into Great Britain have been required to be hallmarked before sale. The marks consist of the importer's mark, a special assay office mark (*see below*), the figures denoting fineness and the annual date letter. The current assay office marks for foreign wares are as follows:—

LONDON.—The sign of the Constellation Leo.
BIRMINGHAM.—Equilateral triangle.
SHEFFIELD.—The sign of the Constellation Libra.
EDINBURGH.—St. Andrew's Cross.

Special marks at authorised Assay Offices of the signatory countries of the International Convention—United Kingdom, Austria, Finland, Ireland, Portugal, Norway, Sweden and Switzerland—are legally recognised in the United Kingdom as approved hallmarks. These marks consist of a Sponsor's Mark, a Common Control Mark, a Fineness Mark (arabic numerals showing the standard in parts per thousand) and an Assay Office Mark. There is no date letter.

CLOSE SEASONS AND TIMES

Hunting and Ground Game.—There is no statutory close-time for fox-hunting or rabbit-shooting, nor for hares: but by an Act passed in 1892 the *sale* of hares or leverets in Great Britain is prohibited from March 1 to July 31 inclusive under a penalty of a pound. The First of November is the recognized date for the opening of the *fox-hunting* season, which continues till the following April.

Deer.—The table below shows the statutory close seasons for deer (all dates inclusive).

Species	Sex	England and Wales	Scotland
RED	M.	1 May–31 July	21 Oct.–30 June
	F.	1 Mar.–31 Oct.	16 Feb.–20 Oct.
FALLOW	M.	1 May–31 July	1 May–31 July
	F.	1 Mar.–31 Oct.	16 Feb.–20 Oct.
SIKA	M.	1 May–31 July	21 Oct.–30 June
	F.	1 Mar.–31 Oct.	16 Feb.–20 Oct.
ROE	M.	1 Nov.–31 Mar.	21 Oct.–31 Mar.
	F.	1 Mar.–31 Oct.	1 Apr.–20 Oct.
RED/SIKA HYBRIDS	M.		21 Oct.–30 June
	F.		16 Feb.–20 Oct.

Wild Birds.—The *Wildlife and Countryside Act, 1981,* lays down a close season for wild birds (other than Game Birds) from February 1 to August 31 inclusive, each year. Exceptions to these dates are made for—

Capercaillie and (except Scotland) *Woodcock,* Feb. 1—Sept. 30.

Snipe, Feb. 1—Aug. 11.

Wild Duck and *Wild Goose* (below high water mark), Feb. 21—Aug. 31.

Birds which may be killed or taken outside the close season (except on Sundays and on Christmas Day in Scotland, and on Sundays in prescribed areas of England and Wales) are the above and coot, certain wild duck (gadwall, goldeneye, mallard, pintail, pochard, shoveler, teal, tufted duck, wigeon), certain wild geese (Canada, greylag, pink-footed, white-fronted (in England and Wales only)), moorhen, golden plover and woodcock.

Certain wild birds may be killed or taken at any time by authorized persons—crow, collared dove, gull (great and lesser black-backed or herring), jackdaw, jay, magpie, pigeon (feral or wood), rook, sparrow and starling.

Game Birds.—In each case the dates are inclusive:—

Black Game—Dec. 11 to Aug. 19 (Aug. 31 in Somerset, Devon, and New Forest).

*Grouse—Dec. 11 to Aug. 11.

*Partridge—Feb. 2 to Aug. 31.

Pheasant—Feb. 2 to Sept. 30.
Ptarmigan—(Scotland only) Dec. 11 to Aug. 11.

It is also unlawful (in *England* and *Wales*) to kill the game marked * on a Sunday or Christmas Day.

All other British birds are fully protected by law throughout the year.

Angling.—Close seasons (dates inclusive) are: *Coarse fishing.*—Yorkshire, last day in Feb. to May 31; South West, none; rest of country, March 15 to June 15. *Game fishing.*—Trout, Oct. 1 to last day of Feb.*; Salmon, Nov. 1 to Jan. 31*.

* The above dates are statutory close times. Particularly with salmon, migratory trout and trout, close seasons vary in accordance with water authority local by-laws. In all cases, it is best to check with the water authority concerned.

PROTECTED SPECIES:—The following are protected animals under the provision of the *Wildlife and Countryside Act*, 1981:—

Bat (all species of the horseshoe and the typical bat), rainbow leaf beetle, burbot, butterfly (chequered skipper, heath fritillary, large blue, swallowtail),

cricket (field, mole), dolphin (bottle-nosed, common), Norfolk aeshna dragonfly, wart-biter grasshopper, sand lizard, moth (barberry carpet, black-veined, Essex emerald, New Forest burnet, reddish buff), great-crested newt, common otter, harbour porpoise, snail (Carthusian, glutinous, sandbowl), smooth snake, spider (fen raft, ladybird), red squirrel, natterjack toad.

It is illegal to buy or sell the following:—adder, common frog, viviparous lizard, newt (palmate, smooth), slow-worm, grass snake, common toad.

THE COUNTRY CODE:—The following are the points of The Country Code, issued by the Countryside Commission:

(a) Enjoy the countryside and respect its life and work; (b) Guard against all risks of fire; (c) Fasten all gates; (d) Keep your dogs under close control; (e) Keep to public paths across farmland; (f) Use gates and stiles to cross fences, hedges and walls; (g) Leave livestock, crops and machinery alone; (h) Take your litter home; (i) Help to keep all water clean; (j) Protect wildlife, plants and trees; (k) Take special care on country roads; (l) Make no unnecessary noise.

EXPECTATION OF LIFE

Age	England and Wales Life Table, 1981–83		Scotland Life Table, 1981–83		Northern Ireland Life Table, 1981–83	
	Males	Females	Males	Females	Males	Females
0	71·3	77·2	69·3	75·5	70·0	76·0
5	67·3	73·0	65·3	71·3	66·2	72·0
10	62·4	68·1	60·4	66·4	61·3	67·1
15	57·5	63·2	55·5	61·4	56·4	62·1
20	52·7	58·3	50·7	56·5	51·7	57·2
25	47·9	53·4	46·0	51·6	47·0	52·3
30	43·1	48·5	41·2	46·7	42·2	47·5
35	38·3	43·6	36·5	41·9	37·5	42·6
40	33·5	38·8	31·8	37·1	32·8	37·8
45	28·9	34·1	27·2	32·5	28·2	33·1
50	24·4	29·5	23·0	28·0	23·8	28·5
55	20·3	25·1	19·0	23·7	19·7	24·2
60	16·5	21·0	15·5	19·8	16·1	20·1
65	13·1	17·1	12·4	16·1	12·9	16·3
70	10·2	13·5	9·6	12·8	10·1	12·7
75	7·8	10·3	7·4	9·8	7·7	9·6
80	5·8	7·5	5·6	7·3	5·9	7·1
85	4·4	5·4	4·3	5·3	4·5	5·2

WEIGHTS AND MEASURES

The Weights and Measures Act of 1963 enacts the legal measures for Great Britain, basing them upon "United Kingdom primary standards" in the custody of the Standards Department of the Dept. of Trade. The primary standards are the yard, pound, metre and kilogramme. The GALLON, the capacity standard, wet or dry, is based upon the Pound. The Act of 1963 defines the GALLON as the space occupied by 10 pounds weight of distilled water of density 0·998 859 gramme per millilitre weighed in air of density 0·001 217 gramme per millilitre against weights of density 8·136 grammes per millilitre. The METRE and the LITRE have the meanings assigned by order of the Dept. of Trade to reproduce in English the international definition of these measures in force at the time of making of the orders.

New definitions for an *international yard* and *pound* were adopted on Jan. 1, 1959, by the standards laboratories of the United Kingdom, Canada, Australia, New Zealand, South Africa and the United States: *international yard* = 0·914 4 metre.   *international pound* = 0·453 592 37 kilogramme.

The following list shows the definitions of measures set out in the Weights and Measures Act, 1963 and some useful conversions.

Measurement of Length

Imperial Units

Mile = 1,760 yards.	1 mil = 1/1000 inch.
Furlong = 220 yards.	12 inches (*in.*) = 1 foot (*ft.*).
Chain = 22 yards.	3 feet = 1 yard (*yd.*).
YARD = 0·914 4 metre.	6 feet = 1 fathom.
Foot′ = ⅓ yard.	22 yards = 1 chain = 100 links.
Inch″ = 1/36 yard.	10 chains = 1 furlong.
	8 furlongs = 1 mile = 1,760 yards.

Metric Units

Kilometre = 1,000 metres.	10 millimetres (*mm.*) = 1 centimetre (*cm.*) = 0·393 701 inch.
METRE (*see above*) = 1·094 yards.	10 centimetres = 1 decimetre (*dm.*) = 3·937 011 inches.
Decimetre = 1/10 metre.	10 decimetres = 1 METRE (*m.*) = 1·093 614 yards.
Centimetre = 1/100 metre.	10 metres = 1 dekametre (*dam.*) = 10·936 143 yards.
Millimetre = 1/1000 metre.	10 dekametres = 1 hectometre (*hm.*) = 109·361 43 yards.
	10 hectometres = 1 kilometre (*km.*) = 0·621 371 mile.

A kilometre is approximately *five-eighths* of a mile, so that 8 kilometres may be regarded as 5 miles.

Measurement of Area

Imperial Units

Square mile = 640 acres.	144 sq. inches = 1 sq. foot.
Acre = 4,840 square yards.	9 sq. feet = 1 sq. yard.
Rood = 1,210 square yards.	4 roods = 1 acre.
SQUARE YARD = a superficial area equal to that of a square each side of which measures one yard.	10 square chains = 1 acre = 4,840 sq. yards.
	640 acres = 1 square mile.
Square foot = 1/9 square yard.	
Square inch = 1/144 square foot.	

Metric Units

Hectare = 100 ares.	1 sq. centimetre = 0·155 sq. inch.
Dekare = 10 ares.	1 sq. METRE = 10·763 9 sq. feet = 1·195 99 sq. yds.
Are = 100 square metres.	1 are (*a.*) = 0·098 8 rood.
SQUARE METRE = a superficial area equal to that of a square each side of which measures one metre.	1 hectare (10,000 sq. metres) (*ha.*) = 2·471 05 acres.
	1 sq. kilometre = 0·386 102 sq. mile.
Square decimetre = 1/100 square metre.	
Square centimetre = 1/100 square decimetre.	
Square millimetre = 1/100 square centimetre.	

Measurement of Volume

Imperial Units

CUBIC YARD = a volume equal to that of a cube each edge of which measures one yard.	1,728 cubic inches = 1 cubic foot.
	27 cubic feet = 1 cubic yard.
Cubic foot = 1/27 cubic yard.	
Cubic inch = 1/1728 cubic foot.	

Metric Units

CUBIC METRE = a volume equal to that of a cube each edge of which measures one metre.	1 cubic metre (*cbm.* or *m³.*) = 35·314 7 cu. ft. = 1·307 95 cu. yds.
Cubic decimetre = 1/1000 cubic metre.	(1 stere (= 1 cu. metre) is used as a unit of measurement of timber.)
Cubic centimetre = 1/1000 cubic decimetre.	1 cubic cm. (water) = 1 gram; 1,000 cubic cm. (water) or 1 litre = 1 kilogram; 1 cubic metre (1,000 litres, 1,000 kilograms) = 1 metric ton.

Measurement of Capacity

Imperial Units

GALLON (*see above*).	4 gills = 1 pint.
Quart = ¼ gallon.	2 pints = 1 quart.
Pint = ½ quart.	4 quarts = 1 GALLON.
Gill = ¼ pint.	1 gallon = 160 fluid ounces.
Fluid ounce = 1/20 pint.	= 277·274 cubic inches.

	2 gallons = 1 peck.	1 hectolitre = 2·749 69 bushels.
Bushel = 8 gallons.	4 pecks = 1 bushel.	1 hectolitre per hectare = 1·11 bushels per acre.
Peck = 2 gallons.	8 bushels = 1 quarter.	1 quintal = 3·674 3 bushels.
	A chaldron is 36 bushels = 4½ quarters.	1 quintal per hectare = 1·49 bushels per acre.

Fluid drachm = ⅛ fluid ounce.
Minim = 1/60 fluid drachm.

See Apothecaries' Weight (*below*).

Metric Units
Hectolitre = 100 litres.
  LITRE = The volume occupied by the mass of 1 kilogramme of pure water at its temperature of maximum density and under a pressure of one standard atmosphere (14·696 lb. per sq. inch).
Decilitre = 1/10 litre.
Centilitre = 1/100 litre.
Millilitre = 1/1000 litre.

1 centilitre (*cl.*) = 0·070 4 gill.
1 LITRE (1/1,000 cubic metre) (*lit.*) = 1·759 8 pints = 0·88 Imp. quart = 80·22 Imp. gallon = 61·025 5 cu. inch = 0·035 315 7 cu. ft.
1 hectolitre (*hl.*) = 21·997 5 Imp. gallons = 26·417 1 U.S. gallons = 2·749 Imp. bushels = 2·837 7 U.S. bushels.

Measurement of Mass or Weight

Imperial Units
Ton = 2,240 pounds.
Hundredweight = 112 pounds.
Cental = 100 pounds.
Quarter = 28 pounds.
Stone = 14 pounds.
POUND = 0·453 592 37 kilogram.
Ounce = 1/16 pound.
Dram = 1/16 ounce.
Grain = 1/7,000 pound.

7,000 grains (*gr.*) = 1 pound (*lb.*).
16 drams (*dr.*) = 1 ounce (*oz.*).
16 ounces = 1 POUND (*lb.*).
14 pounds = 1 stone.
28 pounds = 1 quarter (of a *cwt.*).
4 quarters (112 *lb.*) = 1 hundredweight (*cwt.*).
20 hundredweight (2,240 *lb.*) = 1 ton.

    20 pennyweights (*dwt.*) = 1 Troy ounce.
    For gold and silver the ounce, divided decimally, and *not* into grains, is the sole unit of weight. The Troy ounce is the same as the Apothecaries' ounce = 480 Avoirdupois grains (31·1035 *Grammes*) in weight. A Troy POUND (= 5,760 grains) is legalized in the United States.

Ounce Troy = 480 grains
Pennyweight = 24 grains

Ounce apothecaries' = 480 grains.
Drachm = ⅛ ounce apothecaries.
Scruple = ⅓ drachm.

See Apothecaries' Weight (*below*)

Metric Units
Metric ton = 1,000 kilograms.
Quintal = 100 kilograms.

1 milligram (*mg.*) = 0·015 432 grains.
1 centigram (*cg.*) = 0·154 32 grains.
1 decigram (*dg.*) = 1·543 2 grains.
1 gramme (*grm.*) = 15·432 4 grains.
1 dekagram (*dag.*) = 5·643 8 drams.
1 hectogram (*hg.*) = 3·527 4 oz.
1 KILOGRAM (*kg.*) = 32·150 7 oz. Troy = 35·273 4 oz. Avoirdupois = 2·204 62 lb. Avoirdupois.
1 myriagram = 22·046 2 lb. Avoirdupois.
1 quintal (*q.*) = 100 kg. = 220·5 lb. Avoirdupois = 1·968 4 cwt.
1 tonne (*t.*) = 0·984 207 U.K. or long ton = 1·102 31 U.S. or short ton

Measurement of Electricity

Units of measurement of electricity, the AMPERE (unit of electrical current), the OHM (unit of electrical resistance), the VOLT (unit of difference of electrical potential) and the WATT (unit of electrical power) have the meanings assigned to them respectively by order of the Dept. of Trade, to reproduce in English the international definitions in force at the date of the making of the order.
    Kilowatt = 1,000 watts.   Megawatt = 1,000,000 watts.

Apothecaries' Weight
Measures of Weight.
20 grains = 1 scruple (℈1).
3 scruples = 1 drachm (ʒ1).
8 drachms = 1 ounce.

Measures of Capacity.
60 minims (*min.*) = 1 fluid drachm.
8 fluid drachms = 1 fluid ounce.
5 fluid ounces = 1 gill.
4 gills = 1 pint.
8 pints = 1 GALLON.

The Apothecaries' grain is the Avoirdupois grain, and the Apothecaries' ounce is the Troy ounce, of 480 grains. The Apothecaries' *drachm* is not the same as the Avoirdupois *dram*, and is spelled differently. A fluid ounce of distilled water at a temperature of 62° Fahrenheit is equal in weight to the Avoirdupois ounce (437·5 grains). A fluid *drachm* (54·6875 grains) is equal in weight to TWO Avoirdupois *drams*.

Angular or Circular Measure

60 seconds (″) = 1 minute (′).
60 minutes = 1 degree (°).

90 degrees = 1 right angle or quadrant.
Diameter of circle × 3·141 6 = circumference.
Diameter squared × ·7854 = area of circle.
Diameter squared × 3·141 6 = surface of sphere.
Diameter cubed × ·523 = solidity of sphere.
One degree of circumference × 57·3 = radius.*
Diameter of cylinder × 3·141 6; product by length or height, gives the surface.
Diameter squared × ·7854; product by length or height, gives solid content.
  * Or, one radian (the angle subtended at the centre of a circle by an arc of the circumference equal in length to the radius) = 57·3 degrees, nearly.
  Note.—A circle of 7 yards diameter has, in practice, a circumference of 22 yards = 1 chain.

Water Measures

Cubic inch .... = 252·458 grains.
Gallon (277·274 cu. in.) .... = 10 lb. (distilled).
Cubic foot .... = 62·321 lb.
35·943 cubic ft. (224 gals.) .. = 1 ton.
Water for Ships: Tun, 210 gals., Butt 110, Puncheon 72, Barrel 36, Kilderkin 18 gals.

THERMOMETER COMPARISONS

Comparison between Scales of Fahrenheit, Réaumur and Centigrade

Cent.	Fah't.	Rmr.	Cent.	Fah't.	Rmr.
°	°	°	°	°	°
100B.	212B.	80B.	25	77	20
99	210·2	79·2	24	75·2	19·2
98	208·4	78·4	23	73·4	18·4
97	206·6	77·6	22	71·6	17·6
96	204·8	76·8	21	69·8	16·8
95	203	76	20	68	16
94	201·2	75·2	19	66·2	15·2
93	199·4	74·4	18	64·4	14·4
92	197·6	73·6	17	62·6	13·6
91	195·8	72·8	16	60·8	12·8
90	194	72	15	59	12
89	192·2	71·2	14	57·2	11·2
88	190·4	70·4	13	55·4	10·4
87	188·6	69·6	12	53·6	9·6
86	186·8	68·8	11	51·8	8·8
85	185	68	10	50	8
84	183·2	67·2	9	48·2	7·2
83	181·4	66·4	8	46·4	6·4
82	179·6	65·6	7	44·6	5·6
81	177·8	64·8	6	42·8	4·8
80	176	64	5	41	4
79	174·2	63	4	39·2	3·2
78	172·4	62·4	3	37·4	2·4
77	170·6	61·6	2	35·6	1·6
76	168·8	60·8	1	33·8	0·8
75	167	60	*zero*	32	*zero*
74	165·2	59·2	1	30·2	0·8
73	163·4	58·4	2	28·4	1·6
72	161·6	57·6	3	26·6	2·4
71	159·8	56·8	4	24·8	3·2
70	158	56	5	23	4
69	156·2	55·2	6	21·2	4·8
68	154·4	54·4	7	19·4	5·6
67	152·6	53·6	8	17·6	6·4
66	150·8	52·8	9	15·8	7·2
65	149	52	10	14	8
64	147·2	51·2	11	12·2	8·8
63	145·4	50·4	12	10·4	9·6
62	143·6	49·6	13	8·6	10·4
61	141·8	48·8	14	6·8	11·2
60	140	48	15	5	12
59	138·2	47·2	16	3·2	12·8
58	136·4	46·4	17	1·4	13·6
57	134·6	45·6	18	0·4	14·4
56	132·8	44·8	19	2·2	15·2
55	131	44	20	4	16
54	129·2	43·2	21	5·8	16·8
53	127·4	42·4	22	7·6	17·6
52	125·6	41·6	23	9·3	18·4
51	123·8	40·8	24	11·2	19·2
50	122	40	25	13	20
49	120·2	39·2	26	14·8	20·8
48	118·4	38·4	27	16·6	21·6
47	116·6	37·6	28	18·4	22·4
46	114·8	36·8	29	20·2	23·2
45	113	36	30	22	24
44	111·2	35·2	31	23·8	24·8
43	109·4	34·4	32	25·6	25·6
42	107·6	33·6	33	27·4	26·4
41	105·8	32·8	34	29·2	27·2
40	104	32	35	31	28
39	102·2	31·2	36	32·8	28·8
38	100·4	30·4	37	34·6	29·6
37	98·6	29·6	38	36·4	30·4
36	96·8	28·8	39	38·2	31·2
35	95	28	40	40	32
34	93·2	27·2	41	41·8	32·8
33	91·4	26·4	42	43·6	33·6
32	89·6	25·6	43	45·4	34·4
31	87·8	24·8	44	47·2	35·2
30	86	24	45	49	36
29	84·2	23·2	46	50·8	36·8
28	82·4	22·4	47	52·6	37·6
27	80·6	21·6	48	54·4	38·4
26	78·8	20·8	49	56·2	39·2

Note.—The *normal* temperature of the *human body* is 98·4°F., or 37° (36·9°) C., or 29·5° R. *Freezing* point = 32°F. = 0°C. = 0°R.; *Boiling* point = 212° F. = 100° C. = 80° R.

"*Absolute*" Temperature is Temperature reckoned from "*Absolute Zero*," which is at 273° C. below 0° C., 459·4° below 0° F., and 218·4° below 0° R. and is denoted by the letter "K."

Conversion: Let F = Fahr., „ C = Cent., „ R = Réaum.

$$*F = \frac{9C}{5} + 32 \qquad C = \frac{5(F-32)}{9}$$

$$F = \frac{9R}{4} + 32 \qquad R = \frac{4(F-32)}{9}$$

$$F = C + R + 32$$

* Below 32° F. *subtract* 32.

An *Inch of Rain* on the surface of an acre (43,560 sq. feet) = 3,630 cubic feet = 100·992 tons.

Cisterns: A cistern 4 feet by 2½ and 3 deep will hold brimful 186·963 gallons, weighing 16 cwt. 2 qrs. 21·6 lbs. in addition to its own weight.

Million, Billion, etc.

Value in the United Kingdom

Million .... thousand × thousand (10^6)
Billion .... million × million (10^{12})
Trillion .... million × billion (10^{18})
Quadrillion .... million × trillion (10^{24})

Value in U.S.A.

Million .... thousand × thousand (10^6)
Billion .... thousand × million (10^9)
Trillion .... million × million (10^{12})
Quadrillion .... million × billion U.S. (10^{15})

United Kingdom (and other European) usage above follows the decision of the 9th Gen. Conference on Weights and Measures, 1948.

PAPER AND BOOK MEASURES

Writing Paper	*Printing Paper*
480 sheets = 1 ream	516 sheets = 1 ream
24 sheets = 1 quire	2 reams = 1 bundle
20 quires = 1 ream	5 bundles = 1 bale

Sizes of Writing and Drawing Papers

Emperor	=	72 × 48	inches
Antiquarian	=	53 × 31	„
Double Elephant	=	40 × 26¾	„
Grand Eagle	=	42 × 28¾	„
Atlas	=	34 × 26	„
Colombier	=	34½ × 23½	„
Imperial	=	30 × 22	„
Elephant	=	28 × 23	„
Cartridge	=	26 × 21	„
Super Royal	=	27 × 19	„
Royal	=	24 × 19	„
Medium	=	22 × 17½	„
Large Post	=	21 × 16½	„
Copy or Draft	=	20 × 16	„
Demy	=	20 × 15½	„
Post	=	19 × 15¼	„
Pinched Post	=	18½ × 14¾	„
Foolscap	=	17 × 13½	„
Sheet and ⅓ Foolscap	=	22 × 13½	„
Sheet and ½ Foolscap	=	24½ × 13½	„
Double Foolscap	=	26½ × 16½	„
Double Post	=	30½ × 19	„
Double Large Post	=	33 × 21	„
Double Demy	=	31 × 20	„
Brief	=	16½ × 13¼	„
Pott	=	15 × 12½	„

Sizes of Printing Papers

Foolscap	=	17 × 13½	inches
Double Foolscap	=	27 × 17	„
Crown	=	20 × 15	„
Double Crown	=	30 × 20	„
Quad Crown	=	40 × 30	„
Double Quad Crown	=	60 × 40	„
Post	=	19¼ × 15½	„
Double Post	=	31½ × 19½	„
Double Large Post	=	33 × 21	„
Sheet and ½ Post	=	23½ × 19½	„
Demy	=	22½ × 17½	„
Double Demy	=	35 × 22½	„
Quad Demy	=	45 × 35	„
Music Demy	=	20 × 15½	„
Medium	=	23 × 18	„
Royal	=	25 × 20	„
Super Royal	=	27½ × 20½	„
Elephant	=	28 × 23	„
Imperial	=	30 × 22	„

Sizes of Brown Papers

Casing	=	46 × 36	inches
Double Imperial	=	45 × 29	,,
Elephant	=	34 × 24	,,
Double Four Pound	=	31 × 21	,,
Imperial Cap	=	29 × 22	,,
Haven Cap	=	26 × 21	,,
Bag Cap	=	24 × $19\frac{1}{2}$	,,
Kent Cap	=	21 × 18	,,

Sizes of Bound Books

Demy 16mo	=	$5\frac{5}{8}$ × $4\frac{3}{8}$	inches
Demy 18mo	=	$5\frac{3}{4}$ × $3\frac{3}{4}$	,,
Foolscap Octavo (8vo)	=	$6\frac{3}{4}$ × $4\frac{1}{4}$	,,
Crown 8vo	=	$7\frac{1}{2}$ × 5	,,
Large Crown 8vo	=	8 × $5\frac{1}{4}$	,,
Demy 8vo	=	$8\frac{3}{4}$ × $5\frac{5}{8}$	,,
Medium 8vo	=	$9\frac{1}{2}$ × 6	,,
Royal 8vo	=	10 × $6\frac{1}{4}$	,,
Super Royal 8vo	=	$10\frac{1}{4}$ × $6\frac{7}{8}$	,,
Imperial 8vo	=	11 × $7\frac{1}{2}$	,,
Foolscap Quarto (4to)	=	$8\frac{1}{2}$ × $6\frac{3}{4}$	,,
Crown 4to	=	10 × $7\frac{1}{2}$	,,
Demy 4to	=	$11\frac{1}{4}$ × $8\frac{3}{4}$	,,
Royal 4to	=	$12\frac{1}{2}$ × 10	,,
Imperial 4to	=	15 × 11	,,
Crown Folio	=	15 × 10	,,
Demy Folio	=	$17\frac{1}{2}$ × $11\frac{1}{4}$	,,
Royal Folio	=	20 × $12\frac{1}{2}$	,,
Music	=	14 × $10\frac{1}{4}$	,,

NOTE.—*Folio* means a sheet folded in half, *quarto* folded into four, and so on; thus, a crown 8vo page is one-eighth the size of a crown sheet. Books are usually bound up in sheets of 16 or 32 pages. *Octavo* books are generally printed 64 pages at a time (32 pages on each side of a sheet of quad); a crown octavo book of 320 pages will therefore require 5 sheets of quad crown, or 10 reams per 1,000 copies, the odd 16 sheets in each ream being allowed as waste. Newspapers (and some books in editions of 50,000 or over) are printed on rotary presses, for which the paper is supplied in continuous reels.

INTERNATIONAL PAPER SIZES

Simplification of the large number of stock paper sizes in use in the United Kingdom has been proceeding since publication of British Standard 730 in 1937. Recommendations made by the International Organization for Standardization were accepted by the United Kingdom in 1959 and it is considered that general adoption of the international or A size will bring great economies to users of paper.

The basis of the international series of paper sizes is a rectangle having an area of one square metre, the sides of which are in the proportion of 1: √2. In other words, taking one side as X and the other as Y, the basic size provides the equation—X: Y = 1: √2; and X × Y = 1. It may be noted that the proportions 1: √2 have a geometrical relationship, the side and diagonal of any square being in this proportion. As the basic size is one square metre in area, this means that X = 841 millimetres and Y = 1,189 millimetres. The effect of this arrangement is that if the short side is doubled or the longer side is halved, *i.e.*, if the area of the sheet is doubled or halved, the shorter side and the longer side of the new sheet are still in the same proportion 1: √2. This feature is particularly useful where photographic enlargement or reduction is used, as the proportions remain the same.

Description of the A series is by capital A followed by a figure. The basic size has the description A0 and the higher the figure following the letter, the greater is the number of sub-divisions and therefore the smaller the sheet. Half A0 is A1 and half A1 is A2. Where larger dimensions are required the A is *preceded* by a figure. Thus 2A means twice the size A0; 4A is four times the size of A0.

It is an essential feature of these series that the dimensions are of the trimmed or finished size.

'A' Series of Trimmed Sizes

Designation	SIZE	
	mm	inches
A0	841 × 1189	33·11 × 46·81
A1	594 × 841	23·39 × 33·11
A2	420 × 594	16·54 × 23·39
A3	297 × 420	11·69 × 16·54
A4	210 × 297	8·27 × 11·69
A5	148 × 210	5·83 × 8·27
A6	105 × 148	4·13 × 5·83
A7	74 × 105	2·91 × 4·13
A8	52 × 74	2·05 × 2·91
A9	37 × 52	1·46 × 2·05
A10	26 × 37	1·02 × 1·46

Subsidiary Series.—A series of B sizes has been devised for use in exceptional circumstances when sizes intermediate between any two adjacent sizes of the A series are needed.

'B' Series of Trimmed Sizes

Designation	SIZE	
	mm	inches
B0	1000 × 1414	39·37 × 55·67
B1	707 × 1000	27·83 × 39·37
B2	500 × 707	19·68 × 27·83
B3	353 × 500	13·90 × 19·68
B4	250 × 353	9·84 × 13·90
B5	176 × 250	6·93 × 9·84
B6	125 × 176	4·92 × 6·93
B7	88 × 125	3·46 × 4·92
B8	62 × 88	2·44 × 3·46
B9	44 × 62	1·73 × 2·44
B10	31 × 44	1·22 × 1·73

In addition there is a series of C sizes which is used much less. A is for magazines and books, B for posters, wall charts and other large items, C for envelopes particularly where it is necessary for an envelope (in C series) to fit into another envelope. The size recommended for business correspondence is A4.

Long Sizes.—Long sizes are obtainable by dividing any appropriate sizes from the two series above into three, four or eight equal parts parallel with the shorter side in such a manner that the proportions mentioned in paragraph 2 (above) are not maintained, the ratio between the longer and the shorter sides being greater than √ 2:1. In practice long sizes should be produced from the A series only.

CONVERSION TABLES FOR WEIGHTS AND MEASURES

NOTE.—The central figures in heavy type represent either of the two columns beside them, as the case may be. *Examples:*—1 centimetre = 0·394 inch and 1 inch = 2·540 centimetres. 1 metre = 1·094 yards and 1 yard = 0·914 metre. 1 kilometre = 0·621 mile and 1 mile = 1·609 kilometres.

Length			Area			Volume			Weight (Mass.)					
Centimetres		Inches	Square Centimetres		Square Inches	Cubic Centimetres		Cubic Inches	Long Tons		Short Tons	Metric Tonnes		Short Tons
2·540	1	0·394	6·452	1	0·155	16·387	1	0·061	0·893	1	1·120	0·907	1	1·102
5·080	2	0·787	12·903	2	0·310	32·774	2	0·122	1·786	2	2·240	1·814	2	2·205
7·620	3	1·181	19·355	3	0·465	49·161	3	0·183	2·679	3	3·360	2·722	3	3·305
10·160	4	1·575	25·806	4	0·620	65·548	4	0·244	3·571	4	4·480	3·629	4	4·409
12·700	5	1·969	32·258	5	0·775	81·936	5	0·305	4·464	5	5·600	4·536	5	5·512
15·240	6	2·362	38·710	6	0·930	98·323	6	0·366	5·357	6	6·720	5·443	6	6·614
17·780	7	2·756	45·161	7	1·085	114·710	7	0·427	6·250	7	7·840	6·350	7	7·716
20·320	8	3·150	51·613	8	1·240	131·097	8	0·488	7·143	8	8·960	7·257	8	8·818
22·860	9	3·543	58·064	9	1·395	147·484	9	0·549	8·036	9	10·080	8·165	9	9·921
25·400	10	3·937	64·516	10	1·550	163·871	10	0·610	8·929	10	11·200	9·072	10	11·023
50·800	20	7·874	129·032	20	3·100	327·742	20	1·220	17·857	20	22·400	18·144	20	22·046
76·200	30	11·811	193·548	30	4·650	491·613	30	1·831	26·786	30	33·600	27·216	30	33·069
101·600	40	15·748	258·064	40	6·200	655·484	40	2·441	35·714	40	44·800	36·287	40	44·092
127·000	50	19·685	322·580	50	7·750	819·355	50	3·051	44·643	50	56·000	45·359	50	55·116
152·400	60	23·622	387·096	60	9·300	983·226	60	3·661	53·571	60	67·200	54·431	60	66·139
177·800	70	27·559	451·612	70	10·850	1147·097	70	4·272	62·500	70	78·400	63·503	70	77·162
203·200	80	31·496	516·128	80	12·400	1310·968	80	4·882	71·429	80	89·600	72·575	80	88·185
228·600	90	35·433	580·644	90	13·950	1474·839	90	5·492	80·357	90	100·800	81·647	90	99·208
254·000	100	39·370	645·160	100	15·500	1638·710	100	6·102	89·286	100	112·000	90·719	100	110·231

Metres		Yards	Square Metres		Square Yards	Cubic Metres		Cubic Yards	Metric Tonnes		Long Tons	Kilograms		Av. Pounds
0·914	1	1·094	0·836	1	1·196	0·765	1	1·308	1·016	1	0·984	0·454	1	2·205
1·829	2	2·187	1·672	2	2·392	1·529	2	2·616	2·032	2	1·968	0·907	2	4·409
2·743	3	3·281	2·508	3	3·588	2·294	3	3·924	3·048	3	2·953	1·361	3	6·614
3·658	4	4·374	3·345	4	4·784	3·058	4	5·232	4·064	4	3·937	1·814	4	8·819
4·572	5	5·468	4·181	5	5·980	3·823	5	6·540	5·080	5	4·921	2·268	5	11·023
5·486	6	6·562	5·017	6	7·176	4·587	6	7·848	6·096	6	5·905	2·722	6	13·228
6·401	7	7·655	5·853	7	8·372	5·352	7	9·156	7·112	7	6·889	3·175	7	15·432
7·315	8	8·749	6·689	8	9·568	6·116	8	10·464	8·128	8	7·874	3·629	8	17·637
8·230	9	9·843	7·525	9	10·764	6·881	9	11·772	9·144	9	8·858	4·082	9	19·842
9·144	10	10·936	8·361	10	11·960	7·646	10	13·080	10·161	10	9·842	4·536	10	22·046
18·288	20	21·872	16·723	20	23·920	15·291	20	26·159	20·321	20	19·684	9·072	20	44·092
27·432	30	32·808	25·084	30	35·880	22·937	30	39·239	30·481	30	29·526	13·608	30	66·139
36·576	40	43·745	33·445	40	47·840	30·582	40	52·318	40·642	40	39·368	18·144	40	88·185
45·720	50	54·681	41·806	50	59·799	38·228	50	65·398	50·802	50	49·210	22·680	50	110·231
54·864	60	65·617	50·168	60	71·759	45·873	60	78·477	60·963	60	59·052	27·216	60	132·277
64·008	70	76·553	58·529	70	83·719	53·519	70	91·557	71·123	70	68·894	31·752	70	154·324
73·152	80	87·489	66·890	80	95·679	61·164	80	104·636	81·284	80	78·737	36·287	80	176·370
82·296	90	98·425	75·251	90	107·639	68·810	90	117·716	91·444	90	88·579	40·823	90	198·416
91·440	100	109·361	83·613	100	119·599	76·455	100	130·795	101·605	100	98·421	45·359	100	220·464

Kilometres		Miles	Square Kilometres		Square Miles	Litres		Gallons	Bushels U.S.		Bushels U.K.	Hectares		Acres
1·609	1	0·621	2·590	1	0·386	4·546	1	0·220	1·032	1	0·969	0·405	1	2·471
3·219	2	1·243	5·180	2	0·772	9·092	2	0·440	2·064	2	1·938	0·809	2	4·942
4·828	3	1·864	7·770	3	1·158	13·638	3	0·660	3·096	3	2·907	1·214	3	7·413
6·437	4	2·485	10·360	4	1·544	18·184	4	0·880	4·128	4	3·876	1·619	4	9·884
8·047	5	3·107	12·950	5	1·931	22·730	5	1·100	5·160	5	4·845	2·023	5	12·355
9·656	6	3·728	15·540	6	2·317	27·276	6	1·320	6·192	6	5·814	2·428	6	14·826
11·265	7	4·350	18·130	7	2·703	31·822	7	1·540	7·224	7	6·783	2·833	7	17·297
12·875	8	4·971	20·720	8	3·089	36·368	8	1·760	8·256	8	7·752	3·237	8	19·769
14·484	9	5·592	23·310	9	3·475	40·914	9	1·980	9·288	9	8·721	3·642	9	22·240
16·093	10	6·214	25·900	10	3·861	45·460	10	2·200	10·321	10	9·689	4·047	10	24·711
32·187	20	12·427	51·800	20	7·722	90·919	20	4·400	20·641	20	19·379	8·094	20	49·421
48·280	30	18·641	77·700	30	11·583	136·379	30	6·599	30·962	30	29·068	12·140	30	74·132
64·374	40	24·855	103·600	40	15·444	181·839	40	8·799	41·282	40	38·758	16·187	40	98·842
80·467	50	31·069	129·499	50	19·305	227·298	50	10·999	51·603	50	48·447	20·234	50	123·555
96·561	60	37·282	153·399	60	23·166	272·758	60	13·199	61·923	60	58·137	24·281	60	148·263
112·654	70	43·496	181·299	70	27·027	318·218	70	15·398	72·244	70	67·826	28·328	70	172·974
128·748	80	49·710	207·199	80	30·888	363·677	80	17·598	82·564	80	77·516	32·375	80	197·684
144·841	90	55·923	233·099	90	34·749	409·137	90	19·798	92·885	90	87·205	36·422	90	222·395
160·934	100	62·137	258·999	100	38·610	454·596	100	21·998	103·205	100	96·695	40·469	100	247·105

DIARY OF EVENTS IN 1986

This diary is based on information (available at the time of going to press) supplied by the British Tourist Authority. The horse-racing fixtures are the copyright of The Jockey Club.

SHOWS, PAGEANTS AND EXHIBITIONS

Jan. 2–12	London International Boat Show	Earls Court, London
Feb. 7–9	Cruft's Dog Show	Earls Court, London
Mar. 4–31	*Daily Mail* Ideal Home Exhibition	Earls Court, London
April 9–11	The London Book Fair	Barbican Centre, London
May 8–11	Royal Windsor Horse Show	Home Park, Windsor
*May 20–23	Chelsea Flower Show	Royal Hospital, Chelsea, London
June 14	Trooping the Colour	Horse Guards Parade, London
June 30–July 3	Royal International Agricultural Show	Stoneleigh, Warwicks.
July 9–26	Royal Tournament	Earls Court, London
Aug. 14	Battle of Flowers	Jersey
Aug. 8–30	Edinburgh Military Tattoo	Edinburgh Castle
Sept. 6	Royal Highland Gathering	Braemar, Grampian
*Sept. 12–20	Southampton International Boat Show	Mayflower Park, Southampton
Nov. 8	Lord Mayor's Procession and Show	City of London
Dec. 1–4	Royal Smithfield Show and Agricultural Machinery Exhibition	Earls Court, London

MUSIC AND DRAMA FESTIVALS

May 23–June 8	Bath Festival	Bath, Avon
May 27–Aug. 18	Glyndebourne Festival Opera Season	Glyndebourne, nr. Lewes
June 6–22	Aldeburgh Festival	Aldeburgh, Suffolk
Aug. 2–9	Royal National Eisteddfod of Wales	Fishguard, Dyfed
Aug. 10–30	Edinburgh International Festival	Edinburgh
Aug. 16–23	Three Choirs Festival	Gloucester

HORSE RACING

March 13	Cheltenham Gold Cup	Cheltenham
March 22	Lincoln Handicap	Doncaster
April 5	Grand National	Liverpool
May 1	One Thousand Guineas	Newmarket
May 3	Two Thousand Guineas	Newmarket
June 4	The Derby	Epsom
June 5	Coronation Cup	Epsom
June 7	The Oaks	Epsom
June 17–20	Royal Ascot	Ascot
July 26	King George VI and Queen Elizabeth Diamond Stakes	Ascot
Sept. 13	St. Leger	Doncaster
Oct. 4	Cambridgeshire	Newmarket
Oct. 18	Cesarewitch	Newmarket

OTHER SPORTS

Jan. 18	Rugby Union: England v. Wales	Twickenham, London
Feb. 15	Rugby Union: Scotland v. England	Murrayfield
April 17–20	Badminton Horse Trials	Badminton, Avon
May 10	Football: F.A. Cup Final	Wembley Stadium, London
June 2–7	Golf: British Amateur Championship	Royal Lytham & St. Annes
June 23–July 6	Lawn Tennis Championships	Wimbledon, London
July 3–6	Henley Royal Regatta	Henley-on-Thames
July 17–20	Golf: Open Championship	Turnberry, Strathclyde
July 24–Aug. 2	XIII Commonwealth Games	Edinburgh
Oct. 6–11	Horse of the Year Show	Wembley Arena, London

*Provisional dates only.